ENCYCLOPÆDIA
BRITANNICA

MACROPÆDIA

The New Encyclopædia Britannica

in 30 Volumes

MACROPÆDIA
Volume 4

Knowledge in Depth

FOUNDED 1768
15 TH EDITION

Encyclopædia Britannica, Inc.
William Benton, Publisher, 1943–1973
Helen Hemingway Benton, Publisher, 1973–1974

Chicago
Auckland/Geneva/London/Manila/Paris/Rome
Seoul/Sydney/Tokyo/Toronto

Ceylon, History of

The island of Ceylon has a continuous record of settled and civilized life for over two millennia. The content and direction of this civilization has been shaped by that of the Indian subcontinent. The island's two major ethnic groups, the Sinhalese and the Tamils, and its two dominant religious cultures, Buddhist and Hindu, made their way onto the island from India. The various expressions of literate culture parallel those of India, and overall the culture and civilization of Ceylon are of the Indic pattern.

Yet it is also clear that in many respects the island's civilization has achieved an individuality and identity that distinguishes it from its neighbour. Cultural traits brought from India have undergone independent growth and change. The Sinhalese language, which grew out of Indo-Aryan dialects, exists only in Ceylon and has a distinctive and distinguished literary tradition. Likewise, Buddhism, which has had a continuing existence on the island, disappeared from India after a Hindu revival and persists only in the Himalayan kingdoms. Sinhalese Buddhist art shows similar individuality.

A common experience of European colonial rule and its modernizing influences brought Ceylon closer to India and, with the attainment of independence in the mid-20th century, both countries developed similar social institutions and ideologies.

The historic connection between Ceylon and India was the result mainly of geographic proximity. Geologically an extension of peninsular India, Ceylon's separation from the Indian mainland dates from comparatively recent times. Historically, the island has also been influenced by its location along the east-west sea route. Even before the discovery of the oceanic route from Europe to India in the 15th century, Ceylon was a meeting point for Eastern and Western trade. The island was known to Greek and Roman cartographers and sailors and later to Persian, Armenian, and Arab navigators. With the coming of the Europeans, Ceylon's strategic importance increased and Western maritime powers fought to control its shores.

The island's first human settlers were probably tribes of the proto-Australoid ethnic group, akin to the pre-Dravidian hill tribes of southern India. Remnants of these people were absorbed by the Indo-Aryans who immigrated from India around the 5th century BC and developed into the Sinhalese. The Tamils were probably later immigrants from Dravidian India, their migrations being spread out over a period dating from the early centuries AD to about 1200. The Tamil element was strengthened in the 19th century with the immigration of southern Indians to work on the plantations.

Ceylon possesses a continuous historical tradition preserved in written form by Buddhist chroniclers. The core of this tradition—the chronicle called the *Mahāvaṃsa* (Great Lineage) and its continuation the *Cūlavaṃsa* (Little Lineage)—constitutes a literary record of the establishment and growth of Sinhalese political power and of the Buddhist faith on the island. These works were written at various times by Buddhist monks and are based on other written records and on oral tradition. The *Mahāvaṃsa* accounts, supplemented by commentaries on them and by other historical works in Pāli and Sinhalese, provide a sequential narrative and a chronological framework for the history of the island up to the fall of the Kandyan kingdom in 1815. The excavation of

Relationship with India

Early Ceylon

ancient cities and monuments and the deciphering of inscriptions have supplemented and provided a corrective to the evidence from the written records.

Development up to AD 1200

PREHISTORIC

Studies of prehistoric Ceylon have not yet achieved a sequence of datable strata. The Stone Age appears to have begun with the Paleolithic, or Old Stone Age (about 1,750,000 years ago), when chert and quartz were abundant because of climatic changes. The earliest Stone Age implements found were made from those materials with a technique similar to that of the Old Stone Age cultures of India, which had identical environmental conditions. The Middle and Upper Paleolithic ages cannot be clearly distinguished because of the difficulty of correlating finds and putting them in a proper sequence. Stone implements of good workmanship, similar to those in India and Europe, have been discovered.

The transformation from food gathering to food producing and some form of settled life marks the transition to the Neolithic Age, or New Stone Age (probably more than 5,000 years ago). The grinding, rubbing, and polishing of stone tools; the use of the axe; and the use of wood, horn, bone, and other materials characterize this period.

The Mesolithic Age, or Middle Stone Age, which preceded the Neolithic Age, has produced rather more artifacts in the island; microliths have been found spread almost throughout, especially among the grasslands in the hill country and the sandy tracts of the coast.

COLONIZATION AND THE SPREAD OF BUDDHISM

According to the earliest Sinhalese tradition, recorded in the *Mahāvaṃsa*, the first Indian colonists on Ceylon were Prince Vijaya and his 700 followers, who landed on the west coast near Puttalam (5th century BC). They had been banished for misconduct from the kingdom of Sinhapura by Vijaya's father, King Sinhabāhu, who put them all in a ship and drove them away. According to tradition, when Vijaya's band landed on the island, it was inhabited by *yakṣas* (demons), whom they defeated and chased into the interior. Vijaya married a *yakṣa* princess and had two children by her. Later he drove her and the children away and sent to the Madurai court in India for a Paṇḍu princess and for wives for his 700 followers. Vijaya settled down to reign as king after a ceremonial enthronement and marriage and founded a dynasty. He had no heir to the throne, and toward the end of his reign he sent for his younger brother at Sinhapura. The brother, unwilling to leave his native land, sent his youngest son, Paṇḍuvāsudeva, to Ceylon. Paṇḍuvāsudeva landed with 32 followers at Gokaṇṇa (now Trincomalee) on the east coast. He was enthroned at Upatissagama and continued the Vijaya dynasty.

Indo-Aryan settlement. This traditional account contains a kernel of historical fact—the settlement of Ceylon by Indo-Aryan tribes from North India. Controversy exists as to the provenance of the early colonists; the legends contain evidence for both the northeastern and the northwestern parts of the Indo-Gangetic Plain. Vijaya's ancestors hailed from Bengal, but his father established himself subsequently in Gujarāt, from where the adventurers were put out to sea. Before arriving in Ceylon, their ship called at Supāra on the west coast of India. Their landing in Ceylon at Tambapaṇṇi, near Puttalam, would indicate their arrival from western In-

Early settlements

dia. Some early tribal names occurring in Ceylon also suggest connections with northwestern India and the Indus region.

While considerable evidence points to western India as the home of the first immigrants, it seems probable that a subsequent wave arrived from the east around Bengal and Orissa. One band of settlers landed on the east coast port of Gokaṇṇa, a natural port of disembarkation for vessels arriving from the Bay of Bengal. The traditional accounts of the arrival of Paṇḍuvāsudeva may portray a second wave of migration following the first mentioned in the Vijaya legend. Linguistic affinities between the early Sinhalese and the Prākrits of eastern India strengthen the hypothesis of a migration from this area.

The tradition speaks primarily of colonization by conquest, and tribes of conquerors led by a warrior nobility would have been an important factor in Aryan settlement. But this would have formed only one element of the Aryan migrations. Indo-Aryan traders probably reached Ceylon while sailing down the Indian coast; the natural products of Ceylon were lucrative items of trade and may have influenced some of these merchants to found settlements. Then there may have been settlements of Buddhist monks, as indicated in the traditional account of Paṇḍuvāsudeva.

The early settlers appear to have encountered a less civilized people, whom they pushed into the interior; some intermarriage probably took place. They also seem to have established contact with the Dravidians of southern India, who helped them in founding the first settlements. This feature is enshrined in the tradition that Vijaya secured a consort for himself and brides for his followers from the Paṇḍu kingdom of Madurai, if this may be presumed to be the Pāṇḍyan Tamil kingdom of southern India.

Indo-Aryan settlements grew in different parts of the island from about the 5th century BC. The settlers came in numerous clans or tribes; the most powerful were the Sinhalas, who eventually gave their name to the descendants of the various groups. The earliest settlers were those on the west-central coast, who pushed inland along the Malwatu Oya and founded a number of river-bank villages. Their seat of government was Upatissagama, where the first kings of the Vijaya dynasty reigned. The settlers of the east coast moved inland along the Mahavali Gaṅga. Somewhat later there was perhaps an independent band of immigrants who settled in Ruhuṇa in the southeast, on the mouth of the Walawē Gaṅga, with Mahāgama as the chief seat of government.

Tradition attributes the founding of the kingdom of Anurādhapura to Paṇḍukābhaya, the third king of the Vijaya dynasty. With its growth as the strongest Sinhalese kingdom, the city of Anurādhapura and the nearby settlements flourished. Kings built up the city and developed it for urban life; they extended royal control over villages and outlying settlements. The establishment of strong government led to population growth and to extensive colonization of the north-central region. The political system was Brahminic, similar to that of Indo-Aryan kingdoms of the Gangetic Plain.

Intro-duction of Buddhism

Conversion to Buddhism. According to Sinhalese tradition, Buddhism was first brought to Ceylon by a mission sent out under the patronage of the Mauryan emperor Aśoka (c. 269–232 BC) and led by his son, Mahinda. Mahinda and his colleagues were transported by air to the island, in the *Mahāvaṃsa* tradition, and landed on the Mihintalē hill, eight miles from the royal capital. There Mahinda chanced to meet the Sinhalese king Tissa and preached the king a sermon on Buddhism. The king was immediately converted and invited the missionaries to the city. The missionaries were settled in a royal pavilion in the city park of Mahāmegha from where they preached, first to members of the royal family and then to the people. Many embraced the new faith and some took holy orders and joined the Buddhist *saṅgha* (community of monks). The king donated the Mahāmegha park to the *saṅgha*, and the monastery of Mahāvihāra was established and became the prime centre of Bud-

dhism in Ceylon. Mahinda sent for his sister Saṅghamitthā, who arrived with a branch of the Bo tree at Gayā, sacred to Buddhists as the tree under which Buddha attained enlightenment. The sapling was ceremonially planted in the city. Saṅghamitthā founded an order of nuns. A *stūpa* (shrine), the Thūpārāmacetiya, was built by the king for popular worship. Thus, various institutions of Buddhism were founded in the kingdom, and the faith became its established religion.

Though the conversion of King Tissa is of historic importance, the spread of Buddhism among the Sinhalese must have been more gradual, before and after the reign of Tissa. This was the work of many monks, both foreign and local, who went into every village converting people and founding Buddhist institutions among them. By the 2nd century BC the Sinhalese had accepted Buddhism totally, and this faith helped produce a unity and consciousness on which subsequent political and economic strength was founded.

THE CLASSICAL AGE (C. 200 BC–AD 1200)

As Buddhism spread, the Anurādhapura kingdom extended its political control over the rest of Ceylon. This age of political centralization began with Duttagāmaṇī Abhaya (reigned 161–137 BC).

The Anurādhapura period. The Vijaya dynasty of kings continued, with brief interruptions, until AD 65, when Vasabha founded the Lambakaṇṇa dynasty. The Lambakaṇṇas ruled for about four centuries; their most noteworthy king was Mahasena (reigned 276–303), who constructed many major irrigation systems and championed heterodox Buddhist sects.

A Pāṇḍyan invasion from southern India put an end to this dynasty and, briefly, to Sinhalese rule in 432. Dhātusena (459–477) defeated the Pāṇḍyas and re-established Sinhalese rule with a line of Moriya kings. His son Kāśyapa I (reigned 477–495) moved the capital from Anurādhapura to the rock fortress of Sīgiriya. After Kāśyapa's dethronement the capital was returned to Anurādhapura.

From the 7th century there was an increase in the involvement of South Indian powers in Ceylonese politics and in the presence of Tamil mercenaries in and around the capital. Mānavamma, a Sinhalese royal fugitive, was installed on the throne in 684 with the support of the Pallavas of South India.

Mānavamma founded the second Lambakaṇṇa dynasty, which reigned in Anurādhapura for about 400 years. The dynasty produced a number of distinguished kings who consolidated and extended Sinhalese political power. During this period, Sinhalese involvement with southern India was even closer. Sinhalese kings were drawn into the dynastic battles between the Pāṇḍyas, Pallavas, and Cōḷas. Invasions from South India to Ceylon and retaliatory raids were a recurrent phenomenon. The 10th century saw a weakening of political and military power, and the Cōḷas, hostile because of the Sinhalese alliance with Pāṇḍya, attacked and occupied the kingdom in 993 and annexed Rajarata as a province of the Cōḷa empire. The conquest was completed in 1017 when the Cōḷas seized the southern province of Ruhuṇa.

The Polonnaruva period. The Cōḷas occupied Ceylon until 1070, when Vijayabāhu liberated the island and re-established Sinhalese power. He shifted the capital to Polonnaruva, a city that was easier to defend, that controlled the route to Ruhuṇa, and the easterly location of which provided more time to prepare for South Indian attacks. The capital remained there for 150 years. The most colorful king of the Polonnaruva period, and indeed of Sinhalese history, was Parākramabāhu I (reigned 1153–86), under whom the kingdom enjoyed its greatest prosperity. He followed a strong foreign policy, sending a punitive naval expedition to Burma and an army of invasion to the Pāṇḍyan kingdom but achieved no permanent success. After Parākramabāhu, the throne passed to the Kaliṅga dynasty, and the influence of South India increased. Nissankamalla (reigned c. 1186–96), a brother of Parākramabāhu's Kaliṅga queen, was the last effective ruler of this period. The last Polonnaruva king was Māgha (reigned 1215–36), an adventurer from South India who seized power and ruled with severity and disrespect for traditional authority.

Government. Kingship was the unifying political institution in the classical period, a symbol of the aims and achievements of the Sinhalese people. The Ceylonese kingship was essentially Brahminic, with strong Buddhist influences. The king's authority was supreme and was elevated by the adoption of Brahminic symbolism. There was a trend toward sanctifying the person of the monarch, with the adoption of extravagant titles and mythical genealogies, and a tendency to style kings as *devas* (gods) and *bodhisattva*s (Buddhas-to-be). Although the absence of a definite law of succession was a weakness leading to many disputes, it had the advantage of ensuring the succession of the ablest candidate; it also gave rise to a strong element of personal despotism, and many kings put the stamp of their personalities on their periods of rule.

All of the kings were practicing Buddhists and patrons of Buddhist institutions; the support and blessing of the clergy was essential in a peaceful and continuous reign. This connection between kingship and Buddhism, which continued throughout the period, enabled Buddhism to flourish. Kings built, maintained, and endowed many shrines and monasteries, and intervened to establish order and prevent schism within the Buddhist church. Nobles and commoners too were lavish in their support, and thus Buddhist institutions prospered. Many beautiful temples were built with finely carved sculpture; monasteries throve as centres of learning in the Pāli and Sinhalese languages and in Buddhist philosophy.

The king was supported by an inner administrative hierarchy consisting of members of his family and of influential nobles. A council of state of the highest officers served in a purely advisory capacity. The administration was conducted by various departments whose ministers dealt personally with the king. The *yuvarāja*, the king's chosen heir to the throne, was given responsible office. The army was the major prop of royal absolutism, and the *senāpati*, or commander in chief, was the king's closest counsellor and confidant.

The country was divided into three divisions. Rajarata was the most important, administered under the king's personal control and embracing the most populated prosperous parts of the country. Ruhuna, to the south and southeast, was next in importance and was always ruled by a high officer, often the *yuvarāja;* owing to its remoteness, it sheltered rebels and fugitives and was used by kings under attack to take refuge and organize resistance. Dakkhiṇadesa, to the west, was organized as a province in the mid-Anurādhapura period and was also ruled by a high-ranking viceroy. These divisions were subdivided into cantons (*maṇḍala*) and districts (*rattha*), and they had a descending hierarchy of local officials down to the village headman.

Society was divided into castes, each performing a certain occupation, but the divisions were not as deep as in India. The *govi*, or cultivators, made up the highest caste. Many other castes also engaged in farming. Administrative officials were drawn from the *govi* caste, which was stratified into chiefs, titled men, and peasants. Chiefs were important supporters of royal absolutism and helped administer the government. Nonagricultural people, the *hina*, were considered of lower rank and divided into occupational groups. These caste groups were endogamous; each lived in its own section, along particular streets. Castes were stratified in terms of status, with the lowest on the scale—the *caṇḍāla*s—performing the meanest occupation. The nobility owned slaves who worked for them in their fields and also in their homes. Many of the professional castes were self-regulating to a great degree.

Irrigation. The Sinhalese civilization was hydraulic, based on the storage and use of water for the regular cultivation of wet fields. The early Indo-Aryan settlers were cultivators of rice, and they settled along river valleys and other suitable lands. They began with simple schemes for damming rivers and storing water below them. Small village works, which stored water in reservoirs by tapping seasonal streams, spread throughout the country and were characteristic of every village; these were probably undertaken communally by the landowners of the village. With the increase in royal power, the attraction of greater revenue through greater production made kings play an active role in the construction of irrigation schemes. Beginning in the reign of King Vasabha (reigned AD *c.* 65–110), large perennial rivers were blocked with massive earthen dams to create colossal reservoirs. From these, water was led through canals to distant fields and through underground channels into the capital city. From this time the technical knowledge of irrigation became more sophisticated.

Further technical progress was achieved in the reign of King Mahāsena; a number of storage tanks and canals are attributed to him, the most outstanding of which is the Minnēriya tank and its feeder canals. Thenceforth the construction and maintenance of large-scale irrigation works became a regular preoccupation of kings. Reservoirs and canals studded the northern and north-central plains, tapping every source of water. Among the most noteworthy was the magnificent Parākrama Samudra in Polonnaruva, the crowning glory of Parākramabāhu's reign, with a storage area of over 5,000 acres for the irrigation of 18,000 acres.

The large works needed a great deal of coordination and central control; they required the mobilization of labour and technical skill at the construction stage and a bureaucratic machinery to operate them and keep them in repair. Regulations to coordinate cultivation of irrigated plots, to control the flow of water, and to collect water dues from the operators had to be administered effectively. These were major functions of the central administration; and in turn they increased the power of the king, to whom accrued the benefits of the resulting increased productivity.

A grain tax, the water dues, and trade in surplus grain were major sources of the king's revenue. They sustained strong political and military power for more than a millennium and enabled the dispatch of expeditions abroad. They also made possible widespread religious building, which culminated in the great age of Parākramabāhu I. His reign also witnessed the high point of Sinhalese creativity in the plastic arts and the greatest strides in irrigation.

Drift to the southwest, 1200–1505

POLITICAL CHANGES

After the death of Nissaṅkamalla, the Polonnaruva kingdom was weakened by a succession of ineffective rulers. Non-Sinhalese factions such as the Kaliṅgas and Pāṇḍyas gained power in Ceylon as a result of dynastic marriages with South Indian royalty; conflicts between these factions was a common feature. South Indian notables occupied positions of influence under Kaliṅga kings, and their power was buttressed by mercenaries of various races. Māgha's rule was a veritable reign of terror, disregarding traditional authority and established religion. Polonnaruva fell into the hands of non-Sinhalese elements, each vying with the other for power and office.

Central control from Polonnaruva was weakened. Kings of foreign extraction ruling there were unable to exercise political control over outlying provinces. Members of the traditional ruling class gravitated to centres of Sinhalese power located away from the reach of Polonnaruva in strategic terrain relatively inaccessible and defensible from attack; Dakkhiṇadesa, or Māyārata as it was now called, was suitable for this. The first place chosen to re-establish the Sinhalese kingdom was Dambadeniya, about 70 miles southwest of Polonnaruva; Vijayabāhu III (reigned 1232–36) and his three successors ruled from there. They made occasional successful raids into Rajarata to attack the Kaliṅga and Tamil rulers but did not attempt to reoccupy Polonnaruva. Under Parā-

Authority of the kings

Social castes

Rise of non-Sinhalese factions

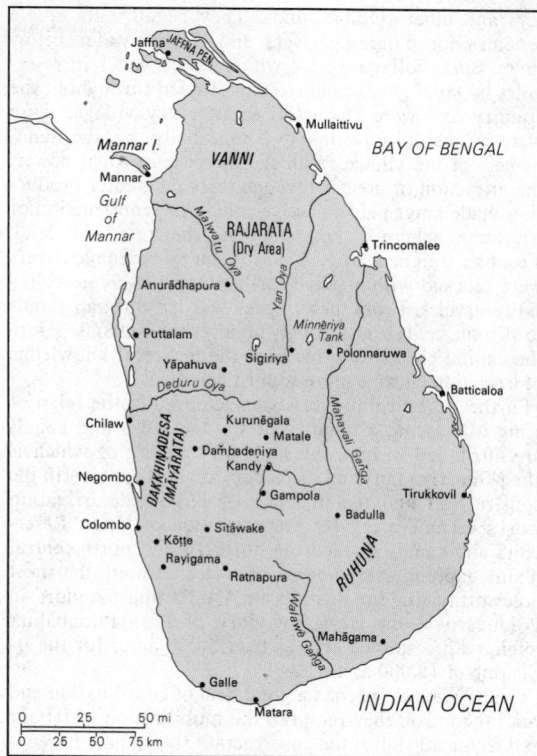

Medieval Ceylon.

From E.F.C. Ludowyk, *A Short History of Ceylon*, © 1962 E.F.C. Ludowyk; published by Praeger Publishers, Inc., New York (1967); reprinted by permission of the publishers

kramabāhu II (reigned 1236–70) the Daṁbadeṇiya kingdom achieved great power; it was able to expel the Kaliṅgas from the island with Pāṇdyan help and to repel an invasion from the Malay Peninsula.

Bhuvanaika Bāhu I (reigned 1272–84) moved the capital northward to Yāpahuva, an isolated rock, which he strengthened with ramparts and trenches. His successors moved the capital southward again to Kurunēgala, and *c.* 1344 to Gampola toward the central highlands. At about the same time, the Alagakōnāra, a powerful Sinhalese family, attained a strong position at Rayigama, near the west coast; the Muslim traveller Ibn Baṭṭūṭah, who visited Ceylon in 1344, referred to one of the Alagakōnāras as a sultan named Alkonar. In 1412 the capital was taken by Parākramabāhu VI (reigned 1412–67) to Kōṭṭe, a few miles from present-day Colombo; for a brief period under this king, the Kōṭṭe kingdom expanded and acquired sovereignty over the island.

Generally, the effective control of the Sinhalese kings of the period 1200–1505 did not extend far beyond their capital cities, though they often made extravagant claims. Taking advantage of the collapse of the Polonnaruva kingdom after Māgha's fall and of the drift of Sinhalese political authority to the southwest, a South Indian dynasty called the Ārya Chakaravartis seized power in the north. By the beginning of the 14th century it had founded a Tamil kingdom, its capital at Nallūr in the Jaffna Peninsula. The kingdom of Jaffnapatnam soon expanded southward, initiating a tradition of conflict with the Sinhalese, though Rajarata—by then a largely depopulated country—existed as a buffer between them. Ibn Baṭṭūṭah left a good description of the Jaffna kingdom and its trade.

A politically divided and weakened island was an enticement to foreign invasions in the 13th, 14th, and 15th centuries. The second Pāṇdyan Empire was constantly interfering in the affairs of Ceylon; its forces often supported rival claimants to power and took back considerable sums in payment and booty including, on one occasion, the Tooth Relic—sacred symbol of Sinhalese sovereignty. The Malay ruler Chandrabhānu invaded the island in 1247 and 1258, for reasons not altogether clear. Forces of the Vijayanagar Empire in South India invaded

Ceylon on a few occasions in the 15th century, and for a brief period the Jaffna kingdom became its tributary. Cheng Ho, the great admiral of the third Ming Emperor of China, led a series of expeditions into the Indian Ocean: in his first expedition (1405–07) Cheng landed in Ceylon but withdrew hastily; he returned in 1411, defeated the ruler Vīra Alakeśvara, and took him and his minister captive to China.

ECONOMIC CHANGES

The drift of Sinhalese political power to the southwest had drastic social and economic consequences. Population gradually shifted in the direction to which the capital was shifting; this led to the neglect of the interconnected systems of water storage. The once-flourishing Rajarata became a devastated ruin of depopulated villages, overgrown jungle, and dried up tank beds, and the centres of Sinhalese population soon became the monsoon-wasted lands of the south, southwest, and the central highlands. Consequent changes in agricultural techniques, land use, ownership patterns, and ways of life followed swiftly.

Consequences of drift to the southwest

Collapse of dry zone civilization. A combination of factors had brought about the collapse of Ceylon's dry zone hydraulic civilization. The pursuit of an active foreign policy under Parākramabāhu I and the many wars it involved was a serious burden on the treasury. The Polonnaruva kings had to maintain a strong standing army and navy. The construction and maintenance of the magnificent Buddhist monuments of the Polonnaruva period must have strained the country's economy. The Polonnaruva state was thus carrying a burden of excessive expenditure that only continuous strong government and high productivity could sustain. The later Polonnaruva kings had neither the ability nor the favourable circumstances to maintain such a high level of revenue and expenditure.

The country's productivity depended on the elaborate system of irrigation, the operation of which was the work of a bureaucracy drawn from the landed gentry, both at the centre and at the village level. When the Kaliṅga dynasty came to power and non-Sinhalese factions rose to high office, the traditional Sinhalese aristocracy was eased out of authority. Mercenary military officers were spread out in the country to control law and order and to assume administrative functions. The Sinhalese noble families withdrew from Rajarata to the courts of Sinhalese leaders who had set themselves up in other parts of the country. Thus the traditional officialdom that had maintained the agricultural and irrigation system disappeared, and traditional methods broke down. The new military administrators had neither the capacity nor the interest to attend to this task. Many of the larger reservoirs breached, and smaller tanks that were fed by excess waters from them also lost their supply. (Some of the destruction was deliberate, caused by rival armies to flood a part of the country.) The amount of water stored for cultivation was reduced, which in turn reduced the area of cultivable land. Jungle spread fast into land left uncultivated. Many tanks dwindled into muddy swamps, breeding mosquitoes. Agriculture became dependent on the uncertain rains, and the people waged a losing battle against the advancing forest. The country could not maintain a population of its previous density. People started following their leaders toward areas of greater rainfall.

Changes in farming techniques

New cultivation techniques. Population centres formed in the hospitable areas of the south, southwest, and the central highlands. The marked difference in climate and topography required new techniques of cultivation. Though rice cultivation continued as an important activity, other grains suitable for highland cultivation were adopted to supplement rice. Paddies had to be terraced and the flow of water had to be regulated to suit the undulating land. Irrigation techniques had to be different and could not be attempted on the scale of the dry-zone schemes. Farming was generally of a subsistence character, and in the absence of sufficient rice, garden or highland cultivation became an important peasant activity, helped by excessive rains. Because of the abundance of land, shifting cultivation was practiced along the slopes of the hills. Coconut, easily grown in the wet lands of the coast and the highlands, became an important food. Cattle breeding, a major occupation in the dry zone, became less prevalent, and milk products were not an important constituent in the people's diet. The nutritive value of the popular diet declined.

Foreign trade. With the decline in agricultural productivity, trade became an important source of state revenue. Spices were the most important exports: cinnamon, indigenous to the southwestern forests, became an export article in the 14th century; pepper and other spices also increased in export value. These articles were royal monopolies; kings entered into contracts with foreign merchants, fixed prices, and derived the revenue. The people of the land were not involved in any aspect of this trade, nor did they benefit directly from it. Colombo and Galle became prominent ports of external trade; smaller ports in the southwest became centres of coastal and Indian trade. Almost all of the traders were foreigners who settled in colonies in and around these ports.

The major international traders were the Arabs. (Arab interest in the luxury products of Ceylon dates from about the 10th century. Arab shipping and trade in the Indian Ocean produced Arab and Indo-Arab colonies in western India and coastal Ceylon.) Now Arabs became interested in cinnamon and spices, which began to fetch good prices in Western markets. In 1283 the Sinhalese king Bhuvanaika Bāhu I sent an embassy to the Mamlūk sultan of Egypt to seek a commercial agreement. Arab merchants had friendly contact with royal port officials of Colombo and Galle and helped collect customs and port dues. There is no evidence of seaborne trade by the Sinhalese themselves in this period, and the Sinhalese merchant groups of an earlier era appear to have declined.

Land control. Some significant changes took place in land relations and land control. The grain tax, which had been the pivot of the land revenue system—payable directly to the state in cash or kind—was on its way out during this period. This is partly explained by a breakdown in the administration: kings could not now maintain a specialized machinery for the assessment and collection of the grain tax and other miscellaneous land taxes. These were replaced by a system of service tenure, under which a large proportion of the land was held on the basis of service to the state. This service could be used in a multitude of ways beneficial to the state: to cultivate royal land, to be assigned to various officials as payment, or for the upkeep of public utilities. Tithe-paying lands and service lands were gradually merged. Each plot had a fixed obligatory service attached to it, and anyone who enjoyed that land had to perform that service. These services were extensively assigned to village and regional notables in order to attract their support. The commutation of tax for service also meant a decrease in the circulation of money; copper coins replaced those of gold and silver. This trend was further attentuated by the subsistence character of farming, which curtailed internal trade.

Cities. Capitals were now selected for their military defensibility, and cities were constructed with this in mind—relatively small, located in difficult terrain, somewhat isolated from populated areas. Communications from one place to another were difficult, and excessive mobility was discouraged for military reasons. Cities were not centres of economic life as in the past; they no longer attracted large groups of artisans, merchants, servants, and others dependent on the ruling groups. They were primarily of military importance, with a small cluster of buildings around the palace.

BUDDHISM AND SOCIETY

The Buddhist church had been a beneficiary of the hydraulic system of the dry zone. Lands, taxes, and water

dues were assigned to temples, which also invested in land, had their own tanks excavated and derived benefits therefrom. Now these sources of revenue had declined. Kings continued their patronage of Buddhism, but their wealth and power had diminished. Nobles and commoners were not rich enough to make substantial benefactions. The great monasteries of Anurādhapura and Polonnaruva were disbanded, and new institutions arose in and around the capitals of Daṁbadeṇiya, Kurunēgala, Gampola, Rayigama, and Kōṭṭe, but they were not of the size or stature of their predecessors in the dry zone.

The absence of strong political authority also affected the unity and coherence of the Buddhist church. In this period there was a greater incidence of indiscipline and schism than before. Kings were called upon frequently to purge the *saṅgha* of undesirable elements, and its purification had to be undertaken now and then. Close contacts were maintained, however, with Burma and Siam, and Buddhist missions were exchanged with these countries.

The influence of Hinduism on Buddhist institutions, theology, and ways of life was more marked during this period. The ruling classes mixed extensively with Tamil royal and noble families, and there was an influx of Brahmins from South India to all parts of the country. *Deva* worship became a marked feature of popular Buddhism. Vedic and post-Vedic gods now assumed importance and were worshipped by kings and commoners in elaborate festivals.

One of the consequences of the drift of the Sinhalese kingdoms to the southwest and the establishment of the Tamil kingdom to the north was the division of the island into two ethnolinguistic areas. Before this, Tamil settlements were interspersed among the Sinhalese throughout the island. Now the northern and eastern areas became predominantly Tamil; their numbers were strengthened by fresh migrations from South India after the collapse of the Pāṇḍyan kingdom in the 14th century. Jaffna, as the capital of the Tamil kingdom, became the seat of Tamil Hindu culture, with a social organization somewhat akin to that of Tamil Nad. The land-owning cultivators, or *vellalas*, were the pivot of the social structure and the holders of political and economic power. A number of lesser castes stood in varying degrees of service relationship to the *vellalas*. Hindu institutions were supported by the kings and the people and were strengthened by the influx of Brahmins. Brahminic temples sprang up in many parts of Jaffna, and rituals and public worship were regularly carried on. The Tamil language struck firm roots in the island and became one of its indigenous languages. Tamil literary culture was fostered by the support of the Jaffna kings and was enriched by the constant contact with South India, yet it developed an individuality of idiom and speech and acquired some linguistic characteristics that distinguished it from its South Indian parent.

Ceylon under foreign rulers, 1505–1947

THE PORTUGUESE IN CEYLON (1505–1658)

By 1500, the Portuguese had begun their penetration of the Indian Ocean. In 1505 a Portuguese fleet commanded by Lourenço de Almeida was blown into Colombo by adverse winds. Almeida received a friendly audience from the king of Kōṭṭe, Vīra Parākrama Bāhu, and was favourably impressed with the commercial and strategic value of the island. The Portuguese soon returned and established a regular and formal contact with Kōṭṭe. In 1518 they were permitted to build a fort at Colombo and were given trading concessions.

In 1521 three sons of Vijayabāhu, the reigning king of Kōṭṭe, put their father to death and partitioned the kingdom among themselves. The oldest of the brothers, Bhuvanaika Bāhu, ruled at Kōṭṭe, and the two others set up independent kingdoms at Sītāwake and Rayigama. Māyādunnē, the king of Sītāwake, was an ambitious and able ruler who sought to expand his frontiers at the expense of his brother at Kōṭṭe. Bhuvanaika Bāhu could not resist the temptation of seeking Portuguese assistance.

The Portuguese were eager to help the king, and the more he was pressed by Māyādunnē, the greater was his reliance on them. Bhuvanaika Bāhu defended his kingdom against Māyādunnē, who in turn allied himself with the Zamorin of Calicut (in India), an inveterate enemy of the Europeans.

Bhuvanaika Bāhu was succeeded by his grandson the Prince Dharamapāla, who was even more dependent on Portuguese support. An agreement (1543) between Bhuvanaika Bāhu and the King of Portugal had guaranteed the protection of the prince on the throne and the defense of the kingdom; in return the Portuguese were to be confirmed in all their privileges and to receive a tribute of cinnamon. The prince was educated by Franciscans; in 1557, when his conversion to Christianity was announced, he became nothing more than a Portuguese protégé. This act undermined the Kōṭṭe dynasty in the eyes of the people. Māyādunnē's wars of aggression were now transformed into a struggle against Portuguese influence and interests in the island, and he annexed a large part of the Kōṭṭe kingdom. After his death, his son Rājasinha continued these wars successfully on land, though like his father he had no way of combating Portuguese seapower.

At the death of Rājasinha in 1593, the Sītāwake kingdom disintegrated for want of a strong successor. The Portuguese captured much of the lands of the Kōṭṭe patrimony and emerged as a strong power in the island. In 1580 Dharmapāla had been persuaded to deed his kingdom to the Portuguese and, when he died in 1597, they took formal possession of it. Meanwhile a Portuguese expedition to Jaffna in 1560 had no lasting success. A second invasion of 1591, undertaken at the instigation of Christian missionaries, succeeded in installing a Portuguese protégé. Continued unrest and succession disputes made the Portuguese undertake a third expedition, and the kingdom of Jaffna was annexed in 1619.

The Portuguese were now in possession of all Ceylon but the central highlands and eastern coast, where an able Sinhalese nobleman, Vimala Dharma Sūrya, had established himself and consolidated his authority. The temptation for the Portuguese to establish hegemony over the entire island was strong and some attempts were made. These led to protracted warfare and to popular hostility against the foreigners. The Portuguese expanded to the lower reaches of the central highlands and annexed the east coast ports of Trincomalee and Batticaloa.

The Portuguese possessions in Ceylon were a part of their *Estado de India;* a captain-general, with his residence at Malwāne, near Colombo, headed the administration and was subordinate to the viceroy at Goa. The most important civil officer was the *vidor da fazenda*, in charge of all revenue matters. An *ouvidor*, or judge, was in charge of all judicial affairs. The administrative structure of the Kōṭṭe kingdom was retained. Ceylon was divided into four *dissavanies*, or provinces, each headed by a *dissava*. Other territorial subdivisions were retained. Portuguese held the highest offices, though local officials came from the Sinhalese nobility loyal to the Portuguese.

The Sinhalese system of service tenure was retained and used extensively to secure the essential produce of the land such as cinnamon and elephants. The caste system was retained intact and all obligations that had been due to the sovereign now accrued to the Portuguese state. The payment in land to officials was retained and extended to Portuguese officials as well.

The Portuguese lacked a proper understanding of the traditional Ceylonese social and economic structure, and excessive demands put upon it led to hardships and popular hostility. Cinnamon and elephants became articles of monopoly; they provided good profits, as did the trade in pepper and areca nuts (betel nuts). Portuguese officials compiled a *tombo*, or land register, to provide a detailed statement of landholding, crops grown, tax obligations, and nature of ownership.

The period of Portuguese rule was marked by intense Roman Catholic missionary activity. Franciscans established centres in the country from 1543 onward. Jesuits

Portuguese administration of Ceylon

were active in the north. Toward the end of the century Dominicans and Augustinians arrived. With the conversion of Dharmapāla, many members of the Sinhalese nobility followed suit. Dharmapāla endowed missionary orders lavishly, often from the properties of Buddhist and Hindu temples. After the Portuguese secured control of Ceylon, they used their extensive powers of patronage and preference in appointments to promote Christianity. Members of the landed aristocracy embraced Christianity and took Portuguese surnames at Baptism. Many coastal communities underwent mass conversion, particularly Jaffna, Mannar, and the fishing communities north of Colombo. Catholic churches with schools attached to them served Catholic communities all over the country. The Portuguese language spread extensively, the upper classes soon gaining proficiency in it.

THE KANDYAN KINGDOM

When Rājasinha I occupied Kandy about 1580, the ruler of that kingdom took refuge with the Portuguese. In 1591 the Portuguese launched an expedition to Kandy to enthrone Dom Philip, an heir of the dispossessed ruler. They were accompanied by an ambitious and distinguished Sinhalese military nobleman, Konnappu Bandāra. Dom Philip was installed as king but died under suspicious circumstances, and Konnappu Bandāra enthroned himself, proclaiming independence from the Portuguese and taking the regnal name of Vimala Dharma Sūrya. The demise of Sītāwake after Rājasinha's death left Kandy the only independent Sinhalese kingdom.

The Portuguese launched another expedition to Kandy in 1594 under Gen. Lopez de Souza, planning to enthrone Dona Catherina, a baptized Sinhalese noblewoman. Popular hostility soon built up toward the continued presence of Portuguese troops. Vimala Dharma Sūrya utilized this to his advantage and, making use of guerrilla warfare tactics, routed the Portuguese army in 1594. He captured Dona Catherina, made her his queen, and legitimized and consolidated his rule. He expanded into the old Sītāwaka kingdom and emerged as leader of resistance to the Portuguese. Subsequently, the Portuguese made a few unsuccessful attempts to subjugate Kandy.

Vimala Dharma realized that without sea power he could not drive the Portuguese out of Ceylon. He saw the arrival of the Dutch as an excellent opportunity to get naval support against his adversaries. The first Dutch envoy, Joris van Spilbergen, met the King in July 1602 and made lavish promises of military assistance. A few months later another Dutch official, Sebald de Weert, arrived with a concrete offer of help and, in view of favourable terms offered by the king, decided to launch a joint attack on the Portuguese. But a misunderstanding between the King and de Weert caused an altercation between the Kandyans and the Dutch, and de Weert and his men were killed.

Arrival of the Dutch

King Senarat succeeded to the Kandyan throne in 1604 and continued to solicit Dutch support. In 1612 a Dutch envoy, Marcelis Boschouwer, concluded a treaty with Senarat. The King granted the Dutch extensive commercial concessions and a harbour for settlement on the east coast in return for a promise of armed assistance against Portuguese attack. The Dutch were unable to offer adequate assistance, and Senarat turned to the Danes. But by the time a Danish expedition arrived in May 1620, Senarat had concluded peace with the Portuguese. The truce was short-lived, and in 1630 the Kandyans, taking the offensive, invaded Portuguese territory and laid siege to Colombo and Galle. Again the absence of sea power proved a handicap, and another peace was concluded in 1634.

In 1635 Senarat was succeeded by his son Rājasinha II. The Dutch were now firmly established in Batavia in Java and were developing their trade in southern Asia. The King sent emissaries to meet the admiral of the Dutch fleet, Adam Westerwolt, who was then blockading Goa. The fleet came to Ceylon and captured Batticaloa from the Portuguese. Westerwolt and Rājasinha concluded a treaty on May 23, 1638, giving the Dutch a monopoly on most of Ceylon's cinnamon and a repayment in merchandise for expenses incurred in assisting the King. In May 1639 the Dutch fleet captured Trincomalee and in February 1640 the Dutch and Kandyans combined to take Negombo. But differences arose between the allies over the occupation of captured forts. The Dutch refused to give Trincomalee and Batticaloa to the King until their expenses were paid in full, and Rājasinha realized that the Dutch really wanted to replace the Portuguese as the rulers of the coast.

He nevertheless continued to work with them to expel the Portuguese. In March 1640 Galle was taken, but the progress of the allies was temporarily halted by a truce declared in Europe between the United Provinces and Spain, which at that time ruled Portugal and its overseas possessions. In 1645, the boundaries between Portuguese and Dutch territory in Ceylon were demarcated. Jan Thijssen was appointed the first Dutch governor.

The Dutch peace with the Portuguese and occupation of captured territory incensed the king and strained relations between him and the Dutch. In May 1645 war broke out between them. Though Rājasinha could not conquer the occupied lands, he made them worthless to the Dutch, who realized the advantage of coming to terms with the King. In 1649 a revised treaty was signed. The Dutch agreed to hand over some of the lands but again delayed because of the immense debt the King was held to owe them.

The truce with the Portuguese expired in 1652 leaving the Dutch free to resume the war. Kandyans launched attacks on Portuguese positions in the interior provinces of Seven Korles, Four Korles, and Sabaragamuwa, pushing them back to their coastal strongholds, despite fierce Portuguese resistance, Rājasinha was anxious to attack Colombo, but he was put off by the Dutch. He tried to secure guarantees from them for the return of this city after its conquest, and the Dutch made lavish promises. In August 1655 the Dutch were strengthened by the arrival of a large fleet under Gerard Hulft, and they laid siege to Colombo by sea and by land. In May 1656 the Portuguese surrendered the city to the Dutch, who shut the Kandyans out of its gates. Requests for the cession of Colombo met with evasive replies. Highly incensed, Rājasinha destroyed the lands around Colombo, removed its inhabitants, and withdrew to his mountain kingdom.

After a brief respite the Dutch resumed the expulsion of the Portuguese from Ceylon. Admiral Ryckloff van Goens arrived with a fleet to continue the attack on Portuguese strongholds in northern Ceylon. The Dutch took Mannar in February 1658 and Jaffna in June. They had replaced the Portuguese as masters of coastal Ceylon.

DUTCH RULE IN CEYLON (1658–1796)

Though the Dutch East India Company first controlled only the coastal lands, the Dutch gradually pushed inland, occupying considerable territory in southern, southwestern, and western Ceylon. In 1665 they expanded to the east coast, and thus controlled most of the cinnamongrowing lands and the points of exit and entry in the island.

Government. The governor, residing in Colombo, was the chief executive; he was assisted by a council of the highest officials. The country was divided into three administrative divisions: Colombo, Galle, and Jaffna. Colombo was ruled by the governor, Galle and Jaffna by commanders. The three divisions were subdivided into dissavanies and districts (korles) in the traditional manner. Each dissavani was ruled by a dissava, invariably a Dutch officer; subordinate offices were held by Sinhalese or Tamils loyal to the Dutch.

Economy. Cinnamon, the most lucrative product derived by the Dutch from Ceylon, was collected at little or no cost and fetched high prices in European and Asian markets. The peeling of cinnamon was the obligatory duty of the chalia caste, which was sent into the woods by Dutch and native officials to obtain the required quantity of the spice. Similarly, another caste was used to supply elephants, also a valuable commodity of trade.

The Dutch continued the Portuguese policy of respecting the traditional land structure and service relationship, but they used it more methodically to further their interests. Officials were remunerated in land, and obligatory services were used for the state. Taxes in kind were collected for the state and used in trade. The Dutch encouraged agricultural production; they tried to increase rice and cash crop cultivation by land grants and tax concessions as well as through state-owned farms cultivated by slave and serf labour.

The Dutch tried to promote trade with neighbouring countries, but under a strictly controlled system. They sought monopolies in the export of cinnamon, elephants, pearls, areca nuts, and other products. This tended to stifle commerce, and thus trade with India declined, leading to a shortage of such essential commodities as rice and textiles. In the early 18th century some relaxation occurred, and private traders from India were admitted into the Ceylon trade. But control of trade commodities and prices was sought through a system of passes and inspection, and major articles such as cinnamon, elephants, and pearls remained a strict monopoly. Smuggling of contraband goods was encouraged by local traders, Kandyan authorities, and even by Dutch officials. The directors in Holland sent strict instructions to maintain the restrictions, despite the pleas of officials in Ceylon for a freer trade, and much effort was spent to curb smuggling.

Law. The Dutch judicial system was well organized. There were three major courts of justice—in Colombo, Galle, and Jaffna; appeals from these courts were heard by the Colombo court. A circuit court, the *Land Raad*, was presided over by the dissava and sat in various districts. Native chiefs were invited to sit on cases involving local custom. The customary law of the land was administered in the courts, unless it clashed violently with Dutch jurisprudence.

Some attempt was made to codify customary law. The *Thesavalamai*, or laws and customs of the Tamils of Jaffna, was codified in 1707. A code of Muslim law was applied with the approval of Muslim headmen. Because of the difficulty in codifying Sinhalese law and custom, Roman-Dutch law was increasingly applied to the Sinhalese of the cities and the sea coast, especially to those who professed Christianity.

Religion. The Netherlands state was ardently Calvinist, and in the early years of Dutch rule an enthusiastic effort was made to spread the reformed faith in Ceylon. Catholicism was declared illegal and its priests were banned from the country; Catholic churches were given to the reformed faith, with Calvinist pastors appointed to them. Many Sinhalese and Tamil Catholics nominally embraced Protestantism. But the knowledge of the religion was rudimentary because there were not enough ministers, and very few of them could speak either indigenous language fluently. A body of Christian literature in Sinhalese and Tamil was published (after the establishment of a printing press in 1737). Churches had schools attached to them for elementary education, and there were two seminaries for higher education. Protestantism, however, did not have any substantial impact on the people.

THE BRITISH IN CEYLON (1796–1900)

The British East India Company's conquest of Ceylon occurred during the wars of the French Revolution. When the Netherlands came under French control, the British began to move into Ceylon from their base in India. The Dutch, after a half-hearted resistance, surrendered the island in 1796. The British had thought the conquest temporary, and they administered the island from Madras, but the war with France revealed Ceylon's strategic value and persuaded the British to make their hold on the island permanent. In 1802 Ceylon was made a Crown Colony and, by the Treaty of Amiens with France, British possession of maritime Ceylon was confirmed.

Dutch
administration of
Ceylon

Control of Kandy. Upon their arrival in 1796, the British established contact with the king of Kandy and contracted to replace the Dutch as protectors of the kingdom. As they began to organize the administration, the British realized that the continuing independence of Kandy posed problems: the frontier with Kandy had to be guarded at much expense, trade with the highlands was hampered by customs posts and political insecurity, land communications between West and East would be quicker if roads could be built through the centre. The advantages of political unification were obvious, but the Kandyans remained deeply suspicious of all foreigners.

Dissensions within the kingdom gave the British an opportunity to interfere in Kandyan affairs. They failed to reduce the kingdom in 1803 but succeeded in 1815 with the help of Kandyan chiefs whose relations with the king had deteriorated and the kingdom had reached an advanced stage of disintegration. They guaranteed Kandyans their privileges and rights and the preservation of customary laws, institutions, and religion. Though Kandy was administered separately, the trend toward reducing the status of its chiefs and of the Buddhist faith was unmistakable; this led to a popular rebellion against British control in 1818. After its suppression the Kandyan provinces were integrated with the rest of the country.

British reforms

Though reluctant to upset traditional Ceylonese institutions, the British quickly set a reform process in motion. They abolished slavery, relieved native officials of judicial authority, paid salaries in cash, and relaxed the system of compulsory service tenure. Agriculture was encouraged, and production of cinnamon, pepper, sugarcane, cotton, and coffee flourished. Internal communications were extended. Restrictions on European ownership of land were lifted. There was intensive Christian missionary enterprise in education.

The early changes under British rule were systematized by a series of reforms enacted in 1833, which laid the foundation for the subsequent political and economic structure of Ceylon. The British adopted a unitary administrative and judicial system for the whole island. They reduced the autocratic powers of the governor and set up Executive and Legislative councils to share in the task of government; unofficial members (not officials of the government) were gradually appointed to the Legislative Council. English became the language of government and the medium of instruction in schools.

Economic changes. The British eliminated restrictions on the economy. They abolished all state monopolies, did away with compulsory labour service, and promoted the liberation of the economy leading to new economic enterprises. Crown land was sold cheaply to cultivators to encourage plantation agriculture, and capital flowed in. Cultivation of coffee was profitable.

Coffee. From 1830 to the 1870s the phenomenal growth of coffee dominated Ceylon's economic development. Acreage under coffee expanded, and roads were constructed to fill the needs of coffee planters. Because of a labour shortage in the plantations, coolie labour under indenture contracts came from southern India in large numbers beginning in the 1840s.

Tea and rubber. In the 1870s coffee was destroyed by a leaf disease. Experiments with tea as a plantation crop in the 1880s were immediately successful, and tea spread along the upper and lower slopes of the hill country. About the same time, rubber plantations were developed both in the highlands and lowlands, and coconut was cultivated as a plantation crop.

Capital investment poured into tea and rubber, which grew as large-scale industries. These products needed a permanent labour force, and steps were taken to settle Indian labour in the plantations. Ancilliary services soon arose. Increasing export trade led to the development of the Colombo Harbour and to railway and road construction. Opportunities were created for the Ceylonese entrepreneur, and employment was plentiful for the English educated.

Capitalist enterprise was restricted, however, to the urban areas and the plantation country. The rest of the country continued with subsistence agriculture, using traditional methods, though the isolation of the village was broken somewhat by roads and railways and the people there were brought into the monetary economy by the increased trade.

CONSTITUTIONALISM AND NATIONALISM, 1900–48

In the 19th century Ceylonese nationalist consciousness expended itself on the social, religious, and educational fronts. Revivalist movements in Buddhism and Hinduism sought to modernize their institutions and to defend themselves against Christian inroads by establishing schools to impart Western education unmixed with Christianity.

Constitutional reforms. Gradually this consciousness spread to the political plane. Regional and communal associations were founded in the educationally advanced parts of the country and began to articulate proposals for constitutional reform. They asked for some Ceylonese participation in the executive, a wider representation in the legislature on a territorial basis, and the adoption of the elective principle in place of nomination. These demands showed a common ideology and approach and revealed a desire to advance within the framework of the colonial constitution.

Because demands were not coordinated or vociferous, the imperial government ignored them. Constitutional reforms passed in 1910 retained the old structure with an appointed executive and a legislature with an appointed majority. There was, however, a limited recognition of the elective principle; an "educated Ceylonese" electorate was established to elect one member to the Legislative Council. Other Ceylonese members were to be nominated on a communal basis.

Growth of nationalist power. During World War I the forces of nationalism in Ceylon gathered momentum. Civil disturbances in 1915 and subsequent political repercussions helped the growth of political consciousness. British arrests of prominent Sinhalese leaders during what was at first a minor communal riot provoked widespread opposition. Leaders of all communities, feeling the need for a common platform to voice a common viewpoint, came together for the first political agitation in the island. In 1919 the Ceylon National Congress was formed, uniting existing Sinhalese and Tamil organizations. The Congress drafted proposals for constitutional reforms, demanding an elected majority in the legislature, control of the budget, and partial control of the executive.

A new constitution was promulgated in 1920 under the governor Sir William Manning and modified in 1924 to satisfy nationalist demands. It provided for an elected majority in the legislature, an increase in the number of territorially elected members, and the election of communal representatives. The country thus attained representative government, but no share was given in the executive, which remained under the governor and the official Executive Council. A finance committee of the legislature was formed, consisting of three unofficial and three official members, which could examine the budget.

The concession of greater power to the nationalists produced the first fissions among them. Sinhalese leaders wanted to do away with communal representation and make territorial representation universal, but minorities desired to retain it to secure power for their communities. Minorities broke away from the Congress to form their own organizations.

A new constitution, framed in 1931, gave Ceylonese leaders opportunities to exercise political power and to gain governmental experience with a view toward eventual self-government. It provided for a State Council with both legislative and executive functions. Besides being a legislative council with an overwhelming majority of territorially elected members, the State Council was divided for executive work into seven committees, each electing its own chairman. These chairmen, or ministers, formed a board of ministers to coordinate their activities and to present an annual budget. The constitution granted uni-

Preparation for self-government

versal franchise, thus for the first time bringing all Ceylonese into the political process. It was in operation for more than 15 years and provided the people and their leaders with valuable experience in democracy.

Dominion status. In response to pressure from Ceylonese nationalist leaders, the British in 1945 appointed the Soulbury Constitutional Commission, which drafted a constitution that gave Ceylon internal self-government, retaining some imperial safeguards in defense and external affairs. In 1947 the Ceylon Independence Act conferred dominion status on the colony.

Ceylon since independence

The constitution of independent Ceylon provided for a bicameral legislature with a popularly elected House of Representatives and a Senate partly nominated and partly elected indirectly. A prime minister and his cabinet, chosen from the largest political group in the legislature, held collective responsibility for executive functions. The governor general, as head of state, represented the British monarch. In matters on which the constitution was silent, the conventions of the United Kingdom were observed.

When the first elections were held in 1947, a number of nationalist and communal parties came together to form the United National Party (UNP); it chose Don Stephen Senanayake as prime minister and advocated orderly and conservative progress. Initially, the coalition government had a substantial majority in Parliament and attracted support as it went. There were, however, some basic weaknesses in the structure. The political consensus that the government represented embraced the upper seven percent of the population—the English-educated, westernized elite groups. To the great mass of Sinhalese-educated or illiterate people, their values appeared irrelevant and incomprehensible. The continued neglect of traditional culture created a gulf that divided the ruling elite from the ruled. Inevitably, leaders and movements arose that articulated the voices of traditionalism and revivalism.

Meanwhile, the country began to face economic difficulties. A rapidly increasing population and free import of consumer goods swiftly ate into the country's foreign exchange. The falling price of Ceylon's rubber and tea and the increase in the price of imported food added to the acute foreign exchange problem. Additionally, the expanded school system produced a large number of educated persons who could not find employment.

These factors of political and economic discontent converged after 1955, and a new Sinhala nationalism was unleashed. It found a champion in S.W.R.D. Bandaranaike. In the 1956 elections the UNP was swept out of office, and Bandaranaike's Sri Lanka Freedom Party (SLFP) was installed in power at the head of a coalition of like-minded parties—the Mahajana Eksath Peramuna (People's United Front). The new government immediately set about changing the political structure. It made Sinhalese the sole official language and took measures for state support of the Buddhist faith and of Sinhala culture. It wedded the new nationalism to a form of socialism, in which the state was given a positive role in economic development and creation of economic equality.

The period of Sinhala nationalism was also a time of political instability. The language policy alienated the Tamils, who, under the Federal Party, carried on a bitter opposition. Educational policies alienated the small but influential Christian community. Cultural and Buddhist reforms alienated different factions within the Sinhalese.

Bandaranaike was assassinated in September 1959, and his widow, Sirimavo Bandaranaike, was persuaded to gather together the fragments of the SLFP. In 1960 she formed a government that continued to implement the policies of Sinhala nationalism. All private schools were nationalized, and state-subsidized private schools were abolished, in response to a demand the Buddhists had made consistently because of the dominance of Christian missions in the country's educational system. The policy of nationalization of economic enterprise was carried further.

By 1965 the tide of Sinhala nationalism had begun to recede. An economic crisis, caused by increasing unem-

Sinhala nationalism

ployment, the rising cost of living, an acute shortage of consumer goods, and the failure of state enterprise in industry and trade, made people look back to the UNP. This party gained the support of minorities, and in 1965 it returned to power under Dudley Shelton Senanayake, who, as the son of Don Stephen Senanayake, had served as prime minister (1952–53) after his father's death and briefly in 1960. Senanayake's government enjoyed a five-year term of office, during which it encouraged private enterprise and made an effort to extend agricultural productivity. These measures, while having moderate success, also tended to create inflation and to increase social inequality. The problem of unemployment of the educated could not be solved. The SLFP formed an alliance with Marxist parties and waged a campaign against the government that called for increased state control of the economy. In 1970 this coalition won a landslide victory, and Mrs. Bandaranaike again became prime minister.

During its period of office (1970–77), the Bandaranaike government enacted a number of reforms that restricted private enterprise and extended nationalization to a number of private industries, a large part of the wholesale and distributive trade, agency houses, and foreign-owned plantations. A number of measures aimed at reducing social inequality were enacted, and an ambitious program of land reform was put under way. These reforms, while satisfying the vast majority of underprivileged, did nothing to touch the basic problems of the island's economy. The Sinhala-educated youth, impatient for radical change, were disillusioned within a year. Their discontent was headed by the Jatika Vimukti Peramuna (National Liberation Front), a group of revolutionary youth who launched an unsuccessful armed rebellion.

In a new constitution proclaimed in 1972, Ceylon became the Republic of Sri Lanka, with a president as the formal head of state but with effective executive power continuing in the hands of a prime minister and cabinet. All existing restraints on the lawmaking powers of the new unicameral legislature were removed. Buddhism was given "the foremost place," and Sinhalese was recognized as the official language.

Constitution of 1972

The continuing economic decline, however, could not be arrested. The acquisition of immense economic power by the state provided the party in power with the opportunity for patronage, nepotism, and corruption. By 1977, unemployment had risen to 1,000,000 in a work force of 7,000,000. The SLFP was left to face the polls on its own in July 1977, and it was defeated by a reorganized UNP under the leadership of J.R. Jayawardene, who became prime minister.

The Jayawardene government arrested the drift toward state control of the economy and took steps to revitalize the private sector and to attract foreign capital. One of its innovations was the creation in 1978 of a free trade zone north of Colombo, where industries would be geared to an export market. The UNP government set about revising radically the constitution of 1972. In a new constitution promulgated in September 1978, the country was renamed the Democratic Socialist Republic of Sri Lanka and a presidential system, somewhat on the French model, was introduced. The president was to be popularly elected for a term of six years and was head of state as well as head of the executive and of government. Sinhalese and Tamil were recognized as national languages, but Sinhalese was to be the official language. Jayawardene in 1978 became the first president under the new constitution.

Constitution of 1978

BIBLIOGRAPHY

Survey works: S. ARASARATNAM, *Ceylon* (1964), an interpretative essay of historical development; S.D. BAILEY, *Ceylon* (1952), stronger on the period of Western impact than on early history; H.W. CODRINGTON, *A Short History of Ceylon*, rev. ed. (1947), valuable factual information, though somewhat outdated; B.H. FARMER, *Ceylon: A Divided Nation* (1963), an attempt to explain the contemporary situation in terms of past history; E.F.C. LUDOWYK, *The Story of Ceylon* (1962), a well-presented historical survey, using much recent research; S.A. PAKEMAN, *Ceylon* (1964), a historical survey with much emphasis on British and independent Ceylon; and K.M. DE SILVA (ed.), *Sri Lanka: A Survey* (1977), a collection of essays on political evolution, economy, and society.

Ceylon to 1500: G.C. MENDIS, *Early History of Ceylon* (1932), first critical treatment of the pre-European period; C.W. NICHOLAS and S. PARANAVITANA, *A Concise History of Ceylon* (1961), the most up-to-date history for this period; *History of Ceylon*, vol. 1, 2 pt. (1959–60), a standard work containing a collection of essays by specialists on different aspects; *The Mahāvaṃsa*, trans. and ed. by W. GEIGER (1912), and *The Cūlavaṃsa*, trans. and ed. by W. GEIGER, pt. 1 and 2 (1929–30), traditional accounts of succeeding royal dynasties that provide an insight into traditional historiography; W. GEIGER, *Culture of Ceylon in Medieval Times* (1960), a remarkable attempt at social history of the Sinhalese from the 5th century BC to the 15th century AD; H.W. CODRINGTON, *Ancient Land Tenure and Revenue in Ceylon* (1938), a description of the traditional system of land tenure and the changes introduced by the European powers; and A. LIYANAGAMAGE, *The Decline of Polannaruwa and the Rise of Dambadeniya, circa 1180–1270 A.D.* (1968), an authoritative study of a hitherto neglected period.

Ceylon after 1500: P.E. PIERIS, *Ceylon: The Portuguese Era*, 2 vol. (1913–14), a detailed survey with emphasis on military and diplomatic history; G.C. MENDIS, *Ceylon Under the British*, 3rd. ed. (1952); L.A. MILLS, *Ceylon Under British Rule 1795–1932* (1933); E.F.C. LUDOWYK, *The Modern History of Ceylon* (1966), a study of the 19th and 20th centuries; T. ABEYASINGHE, *Portuguese Rule in Ceylon, 1594–1612* (1966), an authentic study of a period of Portuguese rule based on Portuguese and Sinhalese sources; C.R. DE SILVA, *The Portuguese in Ceylon 1617–1638* (1972), a detailed study of a period of Portuguese rule based on Portuguese and Sinhalese sources; S. ARASARATNAM, *Dutch Power in Ceylon 1658–1687* (1958), a study of political, economic, and social effects of Dutch rule in Ceylon; L.S. DEWARAJA, *A Study of the Political, Administrative and Social Structure of the Kandyan Kingdom of Ceylon 1707–1760* (1972), a pioneer study of the last independent Sinhalese kingdom; R. PIERIS, *Sinhalese Social Organization: The Kandyan Period* (1956), an analytical study of Kandyan Sinhalese society from the 16th to the 18th century; K.M. DE SILVA (ed.), *History of Ceylon*, vol. 3, *From the Beginnings of the Nineteenth Century to 1948* (1973), results of recent research on British Ceylon brought together in a collection of studies by specialists; W.I. JENNINGS, *The Economy of Ceylon*, 2nd ed. (1951), a survey of Ceylon's economy at the time of independence, and *The Constitution of Ceylon*, 3rd ed. (1953); W.H. WRIGGINS, *Ceylon: Dilemmas of a New Nation* (1960), an analysis of developments in Ceylon after independence; R.N. KEARNEY, *Communalism and Language in the Politics of Ceylon* (1967); C.A. WOODWARD, *The Growth of a Party System in Ceylon* (1969), a study of politics in Ceylon; A.J. WILSON, *Politics in Sri Lanka 1947–1973* (1974), a comprehensive thematic survey; J. JUPP, *Sri Lanka: Third World Democracy* (1978), an analysis of the process of establishment of democratic politics in Sri Lanka.

(S.Ara.)

Cézanne, Paul

Paul Cézanne was one of the most brilliant and revolutionary painters in the history of art. His art, misunderstood and discredited by the public during most of his life, grew out of Impressionism and eventually challenged all the conventional values of painting in the 19th century through its insistence on personal expression and on the integrity of the painting itself. So unique were Cézanne's vision of the world and his conception of art that he has been called the father of modern painting.

Paul Cézanne was born on January 19, 1839, in Aix-en-Provence in southern France, to a well-to-do bourgeois family. His difficult childhood was to have an unusually Parents strong effect on his adult life and career. His father, a self-made man and by the time of Paul's birth a successful banker, had a domineering personality that succeeded in terrifying his son into neurosis by the time he was grown and in making him subservient to his father all his life. His mother, almost illiterate, was a kind woman who earned Paul's permanent adoration by defending him against his father. As a result of these conflicts in his upbringing, Cézanne remained terribly sensitive to criticism, subject to violent contradictory emotions, and distrustful and defensive of even his closest friends.

Cézanne received an excellent classical education at the Collège Bourbon in Aix. In 1858, under the direction of his father, who wanted him to become a banker, he entered the law school of the University of Aix-en-Provence. He had no taste for the law, however, having

decided at an early age on some kind of artistic career; and, after two years of vacillation over a course of action, he persuaded his father, with the support of his mother's entreaties, to allow him to study painting in Paris.

Early work in Paris (1861–70). Cézanne's first stay in Paris lasted only five months. The instability of his personality gave way to severe depression almost immediately when he found that he was not so proficient technically as some of the students at the Atelier Suisse, the studio where he began his instruction. He stayed as long as he did only because of the encouragement of Émile Zola, with whom he had formed a close friendship at the Collège Bourbon. Returning to Aix, Cézanne made a new attempt to content himself with working at his father's bank, but after a year he returned to Paris with strengthened resolution to stay. During his formative period, from about 1858 to 1872, Cézanne alternated between living in Paris and visiting Aix, to which he returned periodically to recover from the discouragements of those difficult years.

Friendship with Émile Zola

The early 1860s was a period of great vitality for Parisian literary and artistic activity. The conflict had reached its height between the Realist painters, led by Gustave Courbet, and the official Académie des Beaux-Arts, which rejected from its annual exhibition—and thus from public acceptance—all paintings not in the academic Neoclassical or Romantic styles. In 1863 the emperor Napoleon III decreed the opening of a Salon des Refusés, to counter the growing agitation in artistic circles over painters refused by the Salon of the Académie. The works of the Refusés were almost universally denounced by the critics —a reaction that consolidated the revolutionary spirit of these painters. Cézanne, whose tastes had soon shifted away from the academic, became associated with the most advanced of this group, including Édouard Manet, Camille Pissarro, Claude Monet, Auguste Renoir, and Edgar Degas. Most of these artists were only in their 20s (as was Cézanne) and were just forming their styles; they were to become, with the exception of Manet, the Impressionist school. Cézanne's friend Zola was passionately devoted to their cause, but Cézanne's friendship with these young men was at first inhibited by his touchiness and deliberate rudeness, born of extreme shyness and a moodiness that was offended by their convivial ways. Nevertheless, he was supported by their revolutionary inspiration as he sought to synthesize the influences of Courbet, who pioneered in the unsentimental treatment of commonplace subjects, and the Romantic painter Eugène Delacroix, whose compositions, depending on colour instead of line, greatly impressed Cézanne.

During this period Cézanne began to develop a style that was almost opposite to that of his mature works. It was Early style violent and dark; he painted scenes with harsh extremes of light and shadow and with a looseness and vigour that are remarkable for the time but can be traced to the influence of Delacroix's swirling compositions. The subjects, some taken from literature, are usually Baroque and Romantic in alternating themes of morbidity, eroticism, and terror that are a free expression of the preoccupations of his troubled mind. The sensitive dynamism of this youthful period, with the inner feverishness that it reveals, foreshadows the daring innovations of Fauvism and of modern Expressionism, particularly the works of Maurice de Vlaminck and Georges Rouault. Not all of Cézanne's early paintings are morbid, however, and in his sensitive portraits, and especially a still life entitled "The Black Clock" (1869–71), he shows a growing concern with formal composition, using the heavy dark lines of his style to construct strong, balanced designs. Nevertheless, during this early period in Paris, nature was for him no more than a pretext for transmitting to the spectator the interior visions of the artist.

Impressionist years (1870–78). In July 1870, with the outbreak of the Franco-German War, Cézanne left Paris for Provence, partly to avoid being drafted. He took with him Marie-Hortense Fiquet, a young woman who had become his mistress the previous year and whom he finally married in 1886. The Cézannes settled at Estaque, a small village on the coast of southern France, not far from

Marseilles. There he began to paint landscapes, exploring ways to depict nature faithfully and at the same time to express the feelings it inspired in him. He began to approach his subjects the way his Impressionist friends did; in two landscapes from this time, for example, "Snow at Estaque" (1870–71) and "The Wine Market" (1872), the composition is that of his early style, but already more disciplined, more attentive to the realism of light.

In January 1872 a son, Paul, was born to Cézanne and Marie-Hortense. Soon afterward, at the invitation of Camille Pissarro, Cézanne took his family to live at Pontoise in the valley of the Oise River. There and at the nearby town of Auvers he began seriously to learn the techniques and theories of Impressionism from Pissarro, who of his painter friends was the only one patient enough with his difficult personality to teach him. The two artists painted together intermittently through 1874, taking their canvases all over the countryside and painting out-of-doors, a technique that was still considered radical. From this time on, Cézanne was to devote himself almost exclusively to landscapes, still lifes, and, later, portraits. Pissarro persuaded Cézanne to lighten his colours and showed him the advantages of using the broken bits of colour and short brush strokes that were the trademark of the Impressionists and that Cézanne came to use regularly, although with a different effect, in his later work. Even while under Pissarro's guidance, however, Cézanne painted pictures clearly indicating that his vision was unique and that his purpose was quite different from that of the Impressionists. Although he used the Impressionist techniques, he emphasized the underlying structure of the objects he painted rather than the objective vision presented by the light that emanated from them, which was the main concern of the Impressionists. Already he was composing with cubic masses and architectonic lines; his strokes, unlike those of the Impressionists, were not strewn with colour, but they complemented each other in a chromatic unity. He wished to preserve the vibration of light, but, instead of dissolving forms in it as the Impressionists did, he preferred to emphasize their construction and to build a stable architecture within the painting itself. In doing this he began to achieve his dual ambition of depicting nature and his feelings about it; for, to Cézanne, the meaning of the scenes he saw was involved with his response to their internal structure. His most famous painting of this period, "The Suicide's House" (1872–73), illustrates all of these complex forces at work.

In 1874, with the first official show of the Impressionists, Cézanne returned to Paris. Although the paintings that Cézanne exhibited at the first Impressionist show and at their third show in 1877 were the most severely criticized of any works there, he continued to work diligently, periodically going back to soak up the light of Provence. He made sojourns at Estaque in 1876, and in 1878 at Aix-en-Provence, where he had to endure the insults of his tyrannical father, whose financial help he needed to survive, since his canvases were still not finding buyers. The single exception to this lack of patronage was the connoisseur Victor Chocquet, whose portrait he painted in 1877. After the second Impressionist show Cézanne broke professionally with Impressionism, although he continued to maintain friendly relations with "the humble and colossal Pissarro," with Monet, "the mightiest of us all," and with Renoir, whom he admired. Dismayed by the public's reaction to his works, however, he isolated himself more and more at both Paris and Aix, and he effectively ended his long friendship with Émile Zola, as much because of neurotic distrust and jealousy as from disappointment at Zola's "popular" writing, which his antisocial and single-minded genius found incomprehensible.

Development of his mature style (1878–90). During this period of isolation, from the late 1870s to the early 1890s, Cézanne developed his mature style. "L'Estaque" (Louvre *c.* 1888) is perhaps the first masterpiece of the classic Cézanne. It is a composition of grand and calm horizontals, in which the even up-and-down strokes create a clean prismatic effect and the sea spreads wide its implacable blue. Like all his mature landscapes, this painting has the exciting and radically new quality of simultaneously representing deep space and flat design. Cézanne knew well how to portray solidity and depth; his method is that used by the Impressionists to indicate form: in his own words, "I seek to render perspective only through color." And again,

Design and color are not distinct and separate. As one paints, one draws. The more the colors harmonize, the more the design takes form. When color is at its richest, form is at its fullest.

The intelligence and the eye of the painter were able to strip away that which was diffuse and superimposed in the view of a given mass, in order to analyze its constituent elements. He chose to rediscover a more substantial reality of simple forms behind the glimmering veil of appearances, an almost Platonic conception of the Mediterranean intellect. "Everything in Nature is modeled after the sphere, the cone and the cylinder. One must learn to paint from these simple figures." At the same time, his picture is a shimmering harmony of colour that can be seen as a totally flat design, without depth. Cézanne achieves this effect, as he does in all his mature paintings, by treating all objects—near and far, rough and smooth, rocks, sky, and water—with the same even parallel strokes and by using colours of the same intensity, and often the same combinations of tones, over the entire surface of the canvas, regardless of depth. Other striking landscapes from this period are the prismatic landscapes of Gardanne ("The Mills of Gardanne," 1886, Barnes Foundation, Merion, Pennsylvania) and the series of monumental compositions in which Montagne Sainte-Victoire near Aix becomes a mythical presence ("Mont Sainte-Victoire with Large Pine Trees," 1887, National Gallery of London, and 1885–87, the Phillips Collection in Washington, D.C.).

Cézanne was to use essentially the same approach in his portraits. Some of the best known are a portrait of his son in the National Gallery of Art, Washington, D.C. (1885), "Madame Cézanne in a Yellow Armchair" (1890–94), "Woman with Coffee-Pot" (1890–94), and "The Card Players" (1890–92). This last painting portrays a theme that Cézanne treated in five different versions. Except for the card-player paintings, in which the sober dignity of the men is well expressed, there is no attempt in Cézanne's portraits to hint at the sitter's character. In most cases he treats the background with the same care as the subject and often violently distorts facial colour to bring it in harmony with the total composition. Cézanne also applied his principles of representation in his extraordinary still lifes, of which he painted over 200. He organizes them as though they were architectural drawings, giving the most familiar objects significance and force through the intensity of the colour and the essential simplicity of the form. The compositions are constructed with laborious care, with all the elements, to the smallest detail, inextricably interlocked. Subtle distortions of perspective and form are used freely to achieve perfect balance of design.

In creating the landscapes, portraits, and still lifes of his mature years, Cézanne slowly achieved his purpose in painting: to express ideas and arouse emotions through pure form and colour. Full of the intensity of feeling aroused by his surroundings, his art was also deeply intellectual, a conscious search for solutions to problems of representation. Although he had great admiration for many other painters, he disagreed with the objectives of all but himself; painters that narrated events, as did the Romantics and the old masters, and painters that only represented nature—however perfectly, as did the Impressionists—seemed to him to lack a purity of purpose that only his own art possessed. At the same time, he was not a truly abstract painter, for the ideas of structure that he wished to express were about reality, not design. He was, however, the major source of inspiration for the Cubists Braque, Picasso, and Juan Gris, all of whom were moved by his plastic purity.

After his father's death in 1886, Cézanne was able to be completely independent financially. He had married Marie-Hortense six months earlier and, after a year in

Appren-
ticeship
with
Camille
Pissarro

End of
profes-
sional
association
with
Impres-
sionism

Purpose of
Cézanne's
art

Paris in 1888, he installed her and their son there permanently. Cézanne himself then settled in Aix except for a few visits to the capital, to Fontainebleau, to Giverny, to Jura in Switzerland, and to the home of Claude Monet, where he met the sculptor Auguste Rodin. In 1895 the art dealer Ambroise Vollard set up in his gallery the first one-man exhibition of Cézanne's work (more than 100 canvases), but, although the young artists and some art lovers were beginning to show enthusiasm for his painting, the public remained unreceptive.

Final years. Cézanne's art was increasing in depth, in concentrated richness of colour, and in skill of composition. He felt capable of creating a new vision. From 1890 to 1905 he produced masterpieces, one after another: ten variations of the "Mont Sainte-Victoire," three of the "Boy in a Red Waist-Coat," and the "Bathers" series in which he attempted to return to the classic tradition of the nude and explore his concern for its sculptural effect in relation to the landscape. He was obsessed with his work, which was in itself time consuming since he painted slowly. Cézanne had always had extreme difficulty in getting along with people, and, deeply upset by the death of his mother in 1897, he withdrew gradually

Final
isolation

from his wife and from the friends of his youth. Except for a steady but infrequent correspondence with Pissarro, Monet, and Renoir, he let himself sink into solitude. More and more of his time was spent in Provence—in Aix, in Montbriant with his brother-in-law, at the Tholonet lookout on Montagne Sainte-Victoire, and at Château-Noir. By the turn of the century his fame had begun to spread, and since he was rarely seen by anyone, he became something of a legendary figure. He exhibited at the widely attended annual Salon des Indépendants in 1899 and at the Exposition Universelle held in Paris in 1900, and his works were finally sought after by galleries. The Caillebotte collection opened at the Luxembourg Gallery in Paris with two Cézannes. The Nationalgalerie in Berlin purchased a landscape as early as 1900. Young artists admired him; in 1901, the young Symbolist Maurice Denis painted "Homage à Cézanne," a picture of artists admiring one of his still lifes.

Cézanne's last period, the fruit of intense meditation in solitude, reached the heights of lyricism, which only the greatest artists can attain in their lifetime, in its revelation of life in nature. "The landscape," he said, "becomes human, becomes a thinking, living being within me. I become one with my picture . . . We merge in an iridescent chaos." In the apparent immobility of the Provençal countryside, he found geological forces trapped in the rocks, powerful saps coursing through the trees. With a few light brush strokes, this sick and misanthropic old man, shut up in his studio, was able to breathe life into the last Mont Sainte-Victoire paintings (1898–1902, Hermitage in Leningrad; 1904, Philadelphia Museum of Art) and the views of Château-Noir. The last of the great "Bathers" paintings (1900–05, Philadelphia Museum of Art), in which he succeeds in integrating monumental nudes with a landscape in his structural vision of reality, was a profound inspiration to the major painters of the 20th century—particularly Picasso, who modelled his "Demoiselles d'Avignon" after it. The diabetes from which Cézanne had been suffering for a long time became more serious, and he finally succumbed to a harsh chill caught while working in the fields. He died a few days later on October 22, 1906, and was buried in Aix-en-Provence. The following year, a retrospective showing of his works (56 paintings) was held at the Salon d'Automne in Paris and won considerable acclaim.

MAJOR WORKS

PAINTINGS, PORTRAITS, STILL LIFE, and FIGURES: "Uncle Dominic as a Monk" (c. 1866; private collection, New York); "Paul Alexis Reading to Zola" (c. 1869; Museu de Arte, São Paulo, Brazil); "The Black Clock" (1869–71; private collection, Los Angeles); "The Man with a Straw Hat (Portrait of Boyer)" (1870–71; Metropolitan Museum of Art, New York); "Portrait of Chocquet" (1876–77; Lord Rothschild Collection, Cambridge); "Chocquet Seated" (c. 1877; Columbus Gallery of Fine Arts, Columbus, Ohio); "Self-Portrait" (1879–82; Tate Gallery, London); "The Blue Vase" (1883–87; Louvre, Paris); "The Bather" (c. 1885–87; Museum of

Modern Art, New York); "The Card Players" (1890–92; Louvre, Paris); "Tulips and Apples" (1890–94; Art Institute of Chicago, Chicago); "Still Life with Basket of Apples" (1890–94; Art Institute of Chicago, Chicago); "Still Life with Peppermint Bottle" (1890–94; National Gallery of Art, Washington, D.C.); "Bathers" (1890–94; Louvre, Paris); "Still Life with Cupid" (1895; Courtauld Institute Galleries, London); "Still Life with Apples and Oranges" (1895–1900; Louvre, Paris); "The Clockmaker" (c. 1895–1900; Solomon R. Guggenheim Museum, New York); "Still Life with Onions and Bottle" (1895–1900; Louvre, Paris); "Women Bathers" (1895–1905; Philadelphia Museum of Art, Philadelphia); "The Gardener" (c. 1906; Tate Gallery, London).

LANDSCAPES: "The Suicide's House" (1872–73; Louvre, Paris); "View of Auvers" (1874; Art Institute of Chicago, Chicago); "Mont Sainte-Victoire" (1885–87; Metropolitan Museum of Art, New York); "The Bay from l'Estaque" (c. 1886; Art Institute of Chicago, Chicago); "Mountains in Provence" (1886–90; Tate Gallery, London); "Rocks at Fontainebleau" (1894–98; Metropolitan Museum of Art, New York); "The Lake of Annecy" (1896; Courtauld Institute Galleries, London); "Montagne le Victoire from the Bibémus Quarry" (1898–1900; Baltimore Museum of Art, Baltimore).

BIBLIOGRAPHY. The most important source on the life and ideas of Cézanne is the collection of 200 letters by the artist: *Correspondance*, ed. by JOHN REWALD (1937; Eng. trans., 1941).

Biography: Personal accounts include A. VOLLARD, *Paul Cézanne* (1914; Eng. trans., 1924), written by an art dealer who knew the artist during the last 10 years of his life; and JOACHIM GASQUET, *Paul Cézanne* (1921), a literary biography (in French) full of lively anecdotes, written by the son of an old friend of Cézanne. The best biography written originally in English is GERSTLE MACK, *Paul Cézanne* (1935), with a good chronology of the painter. JOHN REWALD, *Paul Cézanne, sa vie, son oeuvre, son amitié pour Zola* (1939; Eng. trans., *Paul Cézanne: A Biography*, 1948, reprinted 1968), has better documentation.

Monographs: The great English critic R.E. FRY in *Cézanne: A Study of His Development* (1927), published many texts and previously unknown photographs: J. MEIER-GRAEFE, *Cézanne und sein Kreis: ein Beitrag zur Entwicklungsgeschichte*, 3rd ed. (1922); F. NOVOTNY, *Cézanne und das Ende der wissenschaftlichen Perspektive* (1938); E. LORAN, *Cézanne's Composition*, 3rd ed. (1963); MEYER SCHAPIRO, *Cézanne* (1952); and L. BRIONGUERRY, *Cézanne et l'expression de l'espace* (1966), study the original element in Cézanne's works. RENE HUYGHE, *Cézanne* (1936), in French; and B. DORIVAL, *Cézanne* (1948; Eng. trans., 1948), settle the chronology of paintings. See also EUGENIO D'ORS, *Cézanne* (1930; Eng. trans., 1936); FRANK ELGAR, *Cézanne* (1968; Eng. trans., 1969); and JACK LINDSAY, *Cézanne: His Life and Art* (1969), which summarize what is today known of the artist. L. VENTURI, *Cézanne, son art, son oeuvre*, 2 vol. (1936), is a catalog indispensable for serious study of Cézanne's works.

(R.Hu.)

Chad

The Republic of Chad (République du Tchad) is an independent landlocked state in north central Africa. It has an area of 495,750 square miles (1,284,000 square kilometres) and a population of about 4,030,000 in 1975. It is bounded on the north by Libya, on the east by The Sudan, on the south by the Central African Republic, and on the west by Cameroon, Nigeria, and Niger. Chad obtained independence from France on August 11, 1960. The capital, N'Djamena (formerly Fort-Lamy; population about 224,000), is almost 1,000 miles (1,600 kilometres) from the West African coastal ports.

Although it is the fifth largest country on the continent, Chad—much of the northern part of which lies in the Sahara—has a population density of only about eight persons per square mile (three persons per square kilometre). Nearly 90 percent of the population lives by agriculture; cotton is grown in the south, and cattle are raised in the central region.

Because of the distance from the sea and the relative lack of transportation, the economy is underdeveloped, and French aid remains important.

The frontiers of Chad, which constitute a heritage from the colonial era, do not coincide with either natural or ethnic boundaries. The country comprises a great diversity of peoples, cultures, and religions; more than 100 languages and dialects are spoken. A guerrilla movement

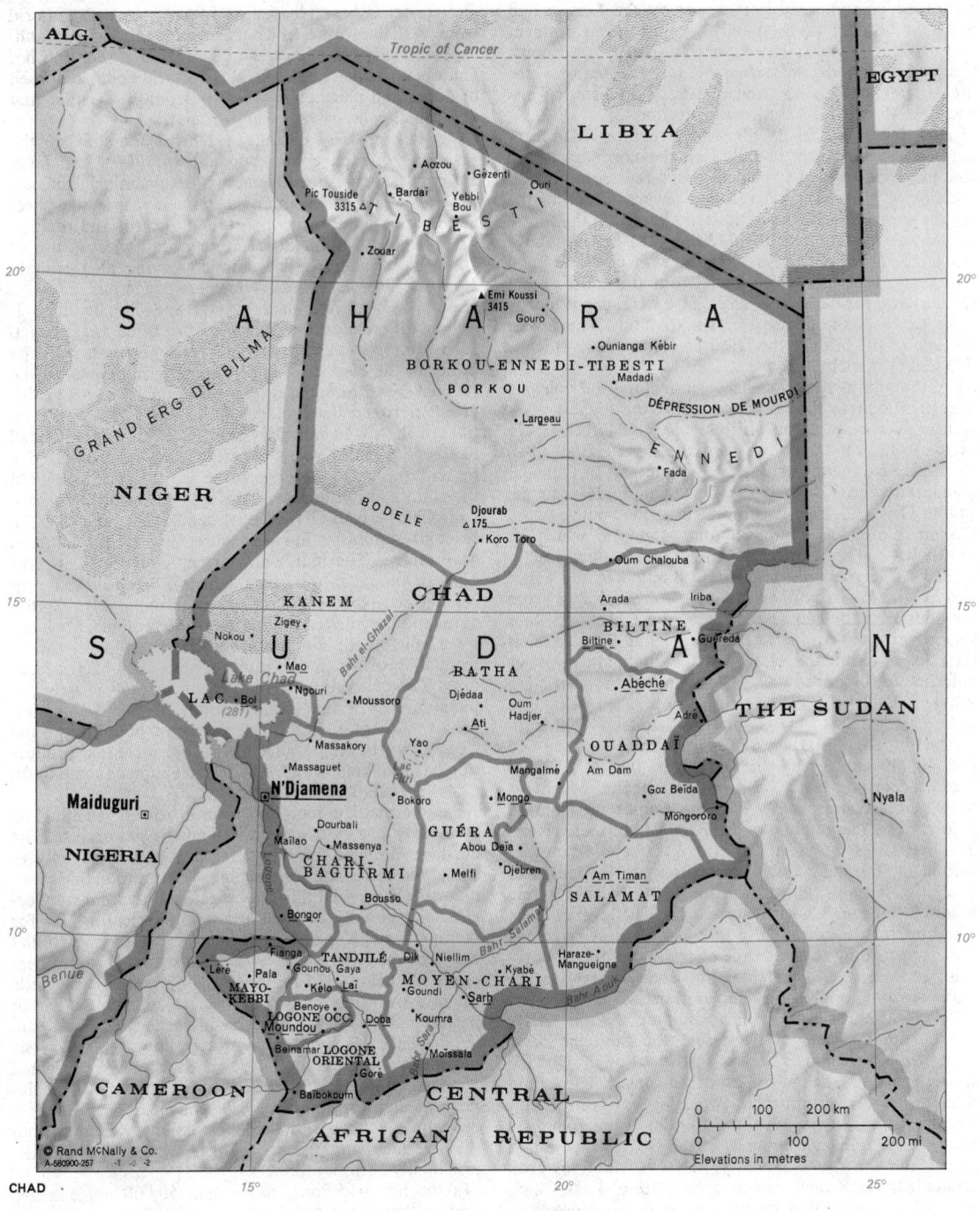

composed of some Muslim groups on the Libyan and Sudanese borders has been active against the government at Fort-Lamy, which has invoked the help of French troops. For coverage of associated physical features, see the articles CHAD, LAKE; and SAHARA. For historical aspects, see the article WEST AFRICA, HISTORY OF.

Relief features. In its physical structure Chad consists of a large basin, bounded on the north, east, and south by mountains. Lake Chad, which represents all that remains of a much larger sea that covered much of the region in earlier geologic periods, is situated in the centre of the western frontier; it is 922 feet (281 metres) above sea level. The Chad Basin is lined with clay and sand sediments, most of which date from the most recent Quaternary period. These sediments were deposited by Lake Chad in the course of its regressions. The lowest altitude of the basin is the Djourâb Depression, which is 573 feet (175 metres) above sea level.

The mountains that rim the basin include the volcanic Tibesti Massif to the north (of which the highest point is Emi Koussi, with an altitude of 11,204 feet [3,415 metres]), the sandstone peaks of the Ennedi Plateau to the northeast, the crystalline rock mountains of Ouaddaï (Wadai) to the east, and the Oubangui Plateau to the south. The semicircle is completed to the southwest by the mountains of Adamawa and Mandara, which lie mostly beyond the frontier in Cameroon and Nigeria.

Chad's river network is virtually limited to the Chari and Logone rivers and their tributaries, which flow from the southeast to feed Lake Chad. The Chari, which is formed by the Gribingui, Bamingui, and Bahr Sara, is later joined from the east by the Bahr Salamat. After entering an ill-defined area of swampland between Niellim and Dourbali, it flows through a large delta into Lake Chad. The Chari is about 750 miles (1,200 kilometres) in length and has a flow that varies between 600 and 12,000 cubic feet per second (17,000 to 340,000 litres), according to the season. The Logone, which for some of its course runs along the Cameroon frontier, is formed by the junction of the Pendé and Mbéré rivers; its flow varies between 170 and 3,000 cubic feet per second (4,800 and 85,000 cubic litres per second), and its course is more than 600 miles (970 kilometres) long before it joins the Chari at Fort-Lamy. The level of Lake Chad fluctuates according to the flow of these rivers, as well as according to the degree of precipitation, evaporation, and seepage. The remaining Chad waterways are either seasonal or are of insignificant size.

Soils. Several types of soil formation occur in Chad, apart from the sand of the desert zone and the sheer rock of the mountainous areas. In the seasonally flooded western regions, such as the Chari, Logone, Salamat, and Guera areas, hydromorphic (waterlogged) soils occur. Tropical iron-bearing soils, red in colour, are found on the exposed folds and mounds of the Ouaddaï mountain slopes; the Koro zone, however, has soils with a low iron content. In the Kanem region (area north of Lake Chad) subarid soils are characteristic, except in the depressions that occur between the dunes on the shores of Lake Chad, where exceptionally rich hydromorphic soils are found.

Climate, vegetation, and animal life. Chad's wide range in latitudes (that extend southward from the Tropic of Cancer for more than 15 degrees) is matched by a climatic range that varies from wet and dry tropical to the hot arid. At the towns of Moundou and Fort-Archambault, in the wet and dry tropical zone, between 32 and 48 inches (800 and 1,200 millimetres) of rain falls annually between May and October. In the central semiarid tropical (Sahel) zone, where Fort-Lamy is situated, between 12 and 32 inches (300 and 800 millimetres) of rain falls between June and September. In the north rains are infrequent, with an annual average of less than one inch (25 millimetres) being recorded at Largeau. Chad thus has one relatively short rainy season. The dry season, which lasts from December to February is cool, after which it becomes very hot until the first rains fall.

Three vegetational zones, correlated with the rainfall, may be distinguished. These are a wet and dry tropical zone in the south, characterized by shrubs, tall grasses, and scattered broad-leaved deciduous trees; a semi-arid tropical (Sahel) zone, in which savanna (grassy parkland) vegetation gradually merges into a region of thorn bushes and open steppe country; and a hot arid zone composed of dunes and plateaus in which vegetation is scarce, and occasional palm oases are to be found.

The tall grasses and the extensive marshes of the savanna zone have an abundant wildlife. Here large mammals, such as the elephant, hippopotamus, rhinoceros, warthog, giraffe, antelope, lion, leopard, and cheetah, coexist with a wide assortment of birds and reptiles. The rivers and the lake are among the richest in fish of all African waters. The humid regions also contain swarms of insects, some of which are dangerous.

Land use. Conditioned by soil and climate, land is put to different uses in each of the three vegetational zones. In the wet and dry tropical zone, farmers cultivate millet in the clay soils, and peanuts (groundnuts) in the sandier areas. Manioc, recently introduced, is also cultivated. Between the latitudes of 11° and 15° N, the retreat of the rivers in the dry season leaves behind flooded depressions called *yaere*, allowing a second crop of "dry season" millet, or *berbere*, to be cultivated. Since 1928 the cultivation of cotton in the area between the Logone and Chari rivers has been encouraged, first by the colonial administration, and since 1960 by the national government. The individual farmer is expected to produce an annual cotton quota, which is then sold to a processing company exercising a total monopoly. Cotton cultivation, while tending to upset the ecological balance by exhausting the soil, has nevertheless resulted in the introduction of a cash economy in place of a barter economy. The cultivation of rice, begun in 1958 in irrigated plots in the Bongor region, south of Fort-Lamy, has proved successful. Improved strains of both cotton and rice have produced higher yields, but increased production has been handicapped by the retention of some traditional agricultural techniques.

The intermediate semi-arid tropical zone is inhabited by both sedentary cultivators and nomadic pastoralists. The northern limit of the bloodsucking tsetse fly, deadly to cattle and the carrier of sleeping sickness to man, is latitude 10° N; beyond this limit extensive stock farming begins, occasionally in association with agriculture, as for example in the Kanem region. The inhabitants raise millet and grow peanuts wherever the mean annual rainfall exceeds 15 inches (375 millimetres). Large herds of cattle migrate over the semi-arid tropical zone in search of pasture and water. In the rich soil bordering Lake Chad, the presence of subterranean water allows three harvests of wheat and corn to be grown each year in irrigated plots called polders. Elsewhere, the seminomadic inhabitants are almost completely dependent upon rainfall; a drought can have serious repercussions, affecting both the livestock and the pastoralists, whose diet consists principally of milk products.

In the hot arid zone, more than 50,000 nomads live among their herds of camels, frequenting palm groves growing in such oases as that at Largeau. Productive economic activity usually takes place only during the rainy season. Rural life is based on a precarious balance between man and environment, and has not been significantly affected by outside influences.

Urban life in Chad is virtually restricted to the capital, Fort-Lamy. Founded in the early years of the 20th century, the city has recently undergone a dramatic growth in population, increasing from 88,000 inhabitants in 1962 to 167,000 in 1972. This growth is not due to a high degree of industrialization, but to the other attractions of urban life. The majority of the population is engaged in commerce. Other major towns, such as Fort-Archambault (pop. 44,000), Moundou (40,000), and Abéché (28,000), are less urbanized than the capital.

People and population. The population of Chad presents a tapestry composed of different languages, peoples, and religions that is remarkable even amidst the variety of Africa. The degree of variety encountered in Chad underscores the significance of the region as a crossroads of linguistic, social, and cultural interchange.

The mountains of Chad

Three vegetation zones

Urban life

Linguistic groups. More than 100 different languages and dialects are spoken in the country. Although many of these languages are imperfectly recorded, the languages may be divided into the following 12 groupings: (1) The Sara-Bongo-Bagirmi group, representing languages spoken by about a million people in southern and central Chad. (2) The Mundang-Tuburi-Mbum languages, which are spoken by several hundred thousand people in the Mayo-Kebbi *préfecture* of southwestern Chad. (3) The Chado-Hamitic group, which is related to the Hausa spoken in Nigeria. (4) The Kanembu-Zaghawa languages, spoken in the north, mostly by nomads. (5) The Maba group, spoken in the vicinity of Abéché, and throughout the Ouaddaï and Biltine *préfectures* of eastern Chad. (6) The Tama languages, spoken in the Abéché, Adré, Goz Béïda, and Am Dam regions. (7) Dagu spoken in the area of Goz Béïda and Am Dam. (8) Some languages of the Central African groups, particularly Sango (which is also the lingua franca of the Central African Republic) are spoken in the south. (9) The Bua group, spoken in southern and central Chad. (10) The Somrai group, spoken in west and central Chad. (11) Mimi and (12) Fur are both spoken in the extreme east.

In addition to this rich assortment, Arabic is also spoken in various forms. The dialects spoken by the nomadic Arabs differ from the tongue spoken by settled Arabs. A simplified Arabic is spoken in towns and markets; its diffusion is linked to that of Islām.

French is the official language of the administration and is used in communications and in instruction, although the national radio network also broadcasts in Arabic, Sara Madjingay, Tuburi, and Mundang. While a regional form of French, showing local linguistic and environmental peculiarities, is spoken widely in the towns, its penetration into the countryside is uneven. Its use is closely linked to the development of education.

Ethnic groups. As might be expected, the linguistic variety reflects an ethnic composition of great complexity. A general classification may nevertheless be made, again in terms of the three regions of Chad.

In the wet and dry tropical zone, the Sara group forms a significant element of the population in the central parts of the Chari and Logone river basins. The Laka and Mbum peoples live to the west of the Sara groups and, like the Gula and Tumak of the Goundi area, are culturally distinct from their Sara neighbours. Along the banks of the Chari and Logone rivers, and in the region between the two rivers, are found the Tangale peoples.

Peoples of the semi-arid tropical zone

Among the inhabitants of the semi-arid tropical zone are the Barma of Bagirmi, the founders of the kingdom of the same name; they are surrounded by groups of Kanuri, Fulani, Hausa, and Arabs, many of whom have come from outside Chad itself. Along the lower courses of the Logone and Chari rivers are the Kotoko, who are supposedly descended from the ancient Sao population that formerly lived in the region. The Buduma and Kuri inhabit the Lake Chad region and, in the Kanem area, are associated with the Kanembu and Tunjur, who are of Arabic origin. All of these groups are sedentary, and they coexist with Daza, Kreda, and Arab nomads. The Hadjeray (of Guera-Massif) and Abou Telfân are composed of refugee populations who, living on their mountainous terrain, have resisted various invasions. On the plains surrounding the Hadjeray are the Bulala, Kuka, and the Midogo, who are sedentary peoples. In the eastern region of Ouaddaï live the Maba, among whom the Kado once formed an aristocracy. They constitute a nucleus surrounded by a host of other groups who, while possessing their own languages, nevertheless constitute a distinct cultural unit. The Tama to the north and the Dadjo to the south have formed their own separate sultanates. Throughout the Ouaddaï region are found groups of nomadic Arabs, who are also found in the Chari-Baguirmi, Salamat, and Guera *préfectures* of central Chad. Despite their widespread diffusion, these Arabs represent a single ethnic group composed of a multitude of tribes. In Kanem other Arabs, mostly of Libyan origin, are also found.

In the northern Chad regions of Tibesti, Borkou, and Ennedi the population is composed of black nomads. Their dialects are related to those of the Kanembu and Kanuri.

Religious groups. The great majority of Muslims are found in the north and east of Chad. Islāmization in Kanem came very early and was followed by the conversion to Islām of the major political entities of the region, such as the sultanates of Wadai, Bagirmi, and Fitri, and—more recently—the Saharan region. Islām is well established in most major towns and wherever Arab populations are found. It has attracted a wide variety of ethnic groups and has forged a certain unity which, however, has not resulted in the complete elimination of various local practices and customs.

Animism flourishes in the southern and most populous part of the country and in the mountainous regions of Guera. The various traditional religions provide a strong basis for cohesion in the villages where they are practiced. Despite a diversity of beliefs, a widespread common feature of traditional religion is the socioreligious initiation of young people into adult society.

In Chad, as elsewhere, Christian missionary work has not affected the Muslim population; it has been directed toward the animist populations in the cities in the western regions south of the Chari River, and in the Guera *préfecture*. There are four Roman Catholic dioceses, with an archbishop at Fort-Lamy. There are some Protestant mission groups, and an effort has been made to form a Chad Evangelical Church.

Chad, Area and Population				
	area		population	
	sq mi	sq km	1963–64 census	1970 estimate
Préfectures				
Batha	34,285	88,800	296,000	327,000
Biltine	18,090	46,850	129,000	143,000
Borkou-Ennedi-Tibesti	231,795	600,350	75,000	83,000
Chari-Baguirmi	32,010	82,910	402,000	454,000
Güera	22,760	58,950	159,000	175,000
Kanem	44,215	114,520	170,000	187,000
Lac	8,620	22,320	115,000	120,000
Logone Occidental	3,355	8,695	190,000	240,000
Logone Oriental	10,825	28,035	236,000	267,000
Mayo-Kebbi	11,625	30,105	486,000	532,000
Moyen-Chari	17,445	45,180	374,000	409,000
Ouaddaï	29,435	76,240	310,000	344,000
Salamat	24,325	63,000	84,000	93,000
Tandjilé	6,965	18,045	228,000	260,000
Total Chad	495,750*	1,284,000	3,254,000†	3,634,000

*Figures do not add to total given because of rounding.   †African population only; de jure.
Source: Official government figures.

The national economy. Cotton is Chad's primary product. Although it is basically an export crop, the processing of raw cotton provides employment for 72 percent of those in industry and accounts for about 80 percent of Chad's export earnings. About 95,000 tons of cotton were harvested in 1970; most of the 35,000 tons of cotton fibre ginned in Chad's 25 processing plants was exported to Europe.

Importance of livestock

Chad's livestock population, which constitutes its second most important economic resource, includes 4,500,-000 cattle and 4,100,000 sheep; these are primarily distributed in the Kanem, Batha, and Ouaddaï *préfectures* of central Chad. Much of this wealth of livestock is not reflected in the national cash economy, however, as only a small proportion of the cattle are sold. A refrigerated meat-processing plant at Fort-Archambault has an annual production of 7,000 tons; it exports meat to the Congo region and Gabon.

Rice is produced in the Mayo-Kebbi *préfecture* of southwestern Chad, and wheat is grown along the shores of Lake Chad; little of either crop is processed commercially. In 1970 peanut production was estimated at 115,000 tons, but of this only 800 tons was processed to make oil. The same year the millet and sorgho harvest was estimated at over 715,000 tons.

Fishing is more important for the nutrition that it supplies than for its commercial significance. Fish are caught in the Lake Chad, Chari, and Logone basins; annual production exceeds 110,000 tons, some of which is exported to Nigeria.

Chad's principal mineral resource is natron (a complex sodium carbonate) that is mined in the Lake Chad and Borkou areas and is used as salt. Annual production is estimated at 4,000 tons, part of which is marketed in Nigeria. There are indications of deposits of gold in the Ouaddaï area, uranium in the Ennedi area, and bauxite near Laï, but no major exploration or exploitation has been launched.

The development of industry is hampered by a shortage of power. Energy is generated by using oil products that have to be imported from Nigeria, although a potential hydroelectric project in the Mayo-Kebbi *préfecture* has been investigated. Oil prospecting is being conducted.

The primary industries, such as cotton ginning, slaughtering, and the milling of wheat and rice, are all associated with agriculture. Secondary industries are few and rely on imported materials.

Transport. Chad's future economic development is primarily dependent upon the establishment of an effective transportation network. There are approximately 7,500 miles (12,000 kilometres) of roads and 12,500 miles (20,000 kilometres) of trails; most of these, however, are impractical for travel during part of the rainy season. Year-round traffic is possible on 1,250 miles (2,000 kilometres) of roads, of which a 100-mile (160-kilometre) stretch between the towns of Massaguet and Maïlao is paved. Three major road axes, forming a triangle joining Fort-Lamy, Fort-Archambault, and Abéché, are under construction. So far only short sections south and west of Fort-Lamy have been completed.

Rivers are of secondary importance, due to great seasonal fluctuations in water levels. The Chari is navigable between Fort-Archambault and Fort-Lamy between August and December, and the Logone is navigable between Mondou and Fort-Lamy in September and October. A rail outlet to the sea would improve prospects for the development of the Chad economy, but the decision as to which route would be the most advantageous is complicated by political, economic, and financial considerations. Two railways have their terminals near the Chad border. Across the Nigerian frontier to the west there is a railhead at Maiduguri, which links up with the Nigerian ports of Lagos and Port Harcourt, thus offering a potential rail link to the sea 1,075 miles (1,725 kilometres) from Fort-Lamy. Across the Sudanese frontier to the east is the railhead at Nyala, which leads eventually to Port Sudan on the Red Sea. A rail connection across Chad from Maiduguri to Nyala would forge a final link in a transcontinental railroad running from the Atlantic to the Red Sea. The projected extension of the Cameroon railroad to Ngaoundéré would offer a possible 1,250-mile (2,000-kilometre) link from Fort-Lamy to Douala, Cameroon. Air traffic plays an important role in the Chad economy, in view of the paucity of alternative means. Fort-Lamy's airport can accomodate large jets, while more than 40 secondary airports exist.

Administration and social conditions. As defined by its constitution, Chad is a secular and social democratic republic of the presidential type. The president, elected by universal suffrage, serves for seven years as chief executive and as head of the army. He is responsible for state appointments, internal and foreign policy, and for the formation of the cabinet. He may take legislative initiative in conjunction with the National Assembly. A single party, the Chad Progressive Party (Parti Progressiste Tchadien) directs and controls the political life of the country. Apart from Chad's own army, military defense is further guaranteed by a defense pact with France.

De facto political developments. In the mid-1960s two guerrilla movements emerged. The Front de la Liberation Nationale du Tchad (Frolinat) was established in 1966 and operated primarily in the north from its headquarters at the southern Libyan oasis of al-Kufrah, while the smaller Front National Tchadien (FNT) operated in the

east-central region. Both groups aimed at the overthrow of the existing government, the reduction of French influence in Chad, and closer association with the Arab states of North Africa. Heavy fighting occurred in 1969 and 1970, and French military forces were brought in to suppress the revolts.

Health. There is a major hospital and clinic at Fort-Lamy, and there are secondary hospitals at Fort-Archambault, Moundou, Bongor, and Abéché. Other health facilities include dispensaries and infirmaries, dispersed throughout the country. The government, in cooperation with the World Health Organization, has developed a health education and training program. Campaigns are conducted against malaria, sleeping sickness, leprosy, and other diseases.

Education. The size of the country, the dispersion of populations, and the occasional reluctance to send children to school, all constitute educational problems that the government is endeavouring to overcome. About 35 percent of the school age population is enrolled. Missions and public education services are responsible for primary education. Secondary and technical education is available in nearly 40 institutions with an enrollment of about 9,000 students. A university is planned, and about 200 Chad students are studying abroad.

Cultural life. With its rich variety of peoples and languages, Chad possesses a valuable cultural heritage. The government encourages cultural activities and institutions. There is a national museum, with a rich collection of prehistoric and traditional artifacts. The Chad Cultural Centre seeks to awaken a conscious interest in national traditions among the population.

Prospects for the future. Primarily an agricultural country, Chad lacks extensive natural resources, sources of energy, a comprehensive transportation network, and a sufficient number of trained personnel. Its population is sparse in relation to its size, and the fact that it still has a subsistence rather than a cash economy hampers further industrialization. There is, in addition, an unfavourable balance of trade. While the government is seeking to overcome these various handicaps by conducting campaigns against illiteracy, improving communications as best it can, and encouraging the diversification of crops, any substantial improvement in the situation depends upon external aid in some form. One such form may be the Inter-African Project for the Development of the Chad Basin, in which Chad is cooperating. Further progress is also dependent to some extent upon the preservation of friendly diplomatic relations with its neighbours.

BIBLIOGRAPHY. INSTITUT NATIONAL TCHADIEN POUR LES SCIENCES HUMAINES, *Bibliographie du Tchad* (1968), more than 2,000 references to books, articles, recordings, and films in the social sciences; *Liste chronologique des études effectuées par l'O.R.S.T.O.M. en République du Tchad* (1970), over 500 references to works in the natural sciences.

General works: HENRI CARBOU, *La Région du Tchad et du Ouadai*, vol. 1, *Études Ethnologiques: Dialecte Toubouri*, vol. 2, *Les Arabes, le Ouadai* (1912), a fundamental work, despite its age; PIERRE HUGOT, *Le Tchad* (1965), a short introductory study; ALBERT LE ROUVREUR, *Sahariens et Sahéliens du Tchad* (1962), a summary of present knowledge on the northern and eastern populations; V. THOMPSON and R. ADLOFF, *The Emerging States of French Equatorial Africa* (1960), an overview of Chad on the eve of independence.

History and archaeology: J.P. LEBEUF, *Archéologie Tchadienne, les Sao du Cameroun et du Tchad* (1962), a basic work on Chadian archaeology, and with A. MASSON DETOURBET, *La Civilisation du Tchad* (1950), a reconstruction of ancient history in the area; J. LE CORNEC, *Histoire politique du Tchad, de 1900 à 1962* (1963), a detailed work on the colonial era and the first years of independence.

Anthropology: JEAN CHAPELLE, *Nomades Noirs du Sahara* (1957), the authoritative study on the Teda.

Linguistics: J.H. GREENBERG, *Languages of Africa* (1963); H. JUNGRAITHMAYR, "Les langues tchado-Chamitiques," in *Les langues du Monde* (1971); ABSI SEAMIR, *Spoken Chad Arabic* (1964); A.N. TUCKER and M.N. BRYAN, "The Non-Bantu Languages of Northeastern Africa," in *Handbook of African Languages*, pt. 3 (1956).

Geography and development: JEAN CABOT, *Le Bassin du Moyen Logone* (1965), an extensive study of the physical and human problems in this region; GEORGES DIGUIMBAYE and ROBERT LANGUE, *L'Essor du Tchad* (1969), a good summary.

Chad, Lake

Lake Chad (French Lac Tchad), in west central Africa, is the largest lake in West Africa and the fourth largest lake on the continent. Its area varies from 3,800 to 9,950 square miles (9,840 and 25,760 square kilometres), and its depths vary accordingly from year to year. It is situated in an immense basin of the same name, at the conjunction of four republics—Chad to the east (which possesses more than half its waters), Cameroon to the south, Nigeria to the southwest, and Niger to the northwest. Lying on the southern fringes of the Sahara, it has been of special interest to geologists, naturalists, and historians.

Geomorphology. Held in by sand dunes, Lake Chad is the remnant of a much larger ancient sea, sometimes referred to as the "Paleochadian Sea," which even as late in geological time as the Quaternary Period (within the last 2,500,000 years) expanded three successive times. It lies 922 feet (281 metres) above sea level in the zone between the desert and the savanna (grassland) known as the Sahel. To the northeast it is bounded by the dead dunes of the Kanem region (Kanem and Lac *préfectures* of Chad), which run northwest to southeast and which are 100 feet (30 metres) or less in height. Throughout this northeastern region the shores of the lake are sharp, clearly shaped into peninsulas and islands, and underlain with channels that follow the lines of the dunes. In the southwest and the southeast, on the other hand, where the tropical rivers, particularly the Komadugu Yobe and the Chari (Shari), flow into the lake, the shores are flat and swampy.

Hydrology. The lake itself is composed of two basins, separated by a ridge known as the Great Barrier, through which there is only a single permanent channel. The basins are shallow, the northern lake being from 13 to 23 feet (4 to 7 metres) deep, and the southern lake being from 10 to 16 feet (3 to 5 metres) deep but sometimes reaching 35 feet (11 metres). Paradoxically, the northern lake, although the deeper, may on occasion dry up altogether because the Great Barrier impedes the circulation of water from the southern basin. Evaporation deprives the lake of an area of water of about seven feet a year. To this must be added smaller losses through infiltration, the movement of water through the basin's surface into the ground. In addition, the lake is slowly filling up with sand carried on the northeast wind; it is also becoming choked by plant growths that include papyrus and ambatch (a leguminous tree associated with the Nile Valley), and is receiving deposits from the Chari River, whose delta advances at the rate of 165 to 330 feet (50 to 100 metres) each year.

Sources of water loss

Depending on the year, the level of the lake rises and its area extends. In 1970, for example, its total area amounted to about 9,400 square miles (about 24,000 square kilometres), while the area of open water was about 8,000 square miles (19,000 square kilometres) and the average depth was almost 13 feet (4 metres). Its highest recorded levels, 922 feet (281 metres) and 932 feet (284 metres), were reached during the 19th century. Low from 1940 to 1950, it again rose until 1958, to the extent of flooding its banks. When the level is high, the southern lake is diverted toward the lowest areas of the basin, the "low countries of Chad," which are in the north, near Borkou. This diversion is a string of basins, called the Bahr el-Ghazal or Soro, which is partially inundated when the lake floods. There is little salt in the waters of the lake, although the waters of the Chari contain 0.04 ounces per cubic foot (40 grams per cubic metre), and evaporation increases the salt content to as much as 0.4 ounces per cubic foot (400 grams per cubic metre) away from the delta. The banks are fertile, and the lake is rich in fish. There has been speculation that the lake may be in danger, in the near future, of disappearing through evaporation, through being filled up, and—finally—through the diversion of the Logone, a tributary of the Chari that

joins it at Fort-Lamy. When in flood, the Logone is diverted westward, in the direction of the lakes Boro, Finaga, and Tikem, into which flow the waters of the Kébé. These lakes empty into the Mayo-Pé, a headstream of the Benue. There does not seem to be any immediate prospect of river capture, however, and it could be prevented. Traffic on the lake is hindered by the waves and by papyrus reeds.

Animal and bird life. Crocodiles and hippopotamuses abound in the lake's waters. On the shores and in the approaches to the lake, bustards, guinea-fowl, and teal provide a plentiful supply of game.

The peoples of the lake. The populations of the lakeshores are mixed, since the lake has at all times been a place of refuge against invaders. The principal groups today are the Buduma, the Kuri, and the Kanembu.

The Buduma. The Buduma, also known as the Yedina, who number a little less than 20,000, are one of the most ancient peoples of the Chad. They are located on the north shore and on the islands west of the 15th meridian. Once veritable pirates, they are now farmers, fishers, and livestock raisers. Their villages, generally located in the middle of an island, are composed of huts of straw or millet stalks. Their activities follow the rhythm of the seasons. From July to October they work at farming on the islands, making use of dikes and dams. They cultivate millet, beans, and gumbo (okra) and sometimes gourds and watermelons. From November to February farming is carried on principally in the polders (areas protected by dikes) on the lakeshore; the herds are moved a little distance from the villages, and the first fishing season occurs. From March to June the cattle herds are moved farther away, maize (corn) is grown, and fishing spreads along the shore. The three principal fishing locations are at the mouth of the Chari, the narrow fairways along the western shore of the Baga Kawa Peninsula, and off the Kindjiri Islands. Fishing expeditions are usually conducted by six canoes, called *kadei*, made of papyrus stalks. They are generally propelled by poling, paddles being used only in deeper waters. The most plentiful fish is the tilapia, weighing two to three pounds. It is sold, always in dried form, in the markets of Nigeria.

Major fishing locations

The Kuri. The Kuri inhabit the islands and shore of the eastern part of the lake. At one time exclusively island dwellers, they today occupy a number of villages on the mainland, but never far from the shore. Their centres are Isseiron on the north shore and Kouloudia on the east shore; they number about 12,000. Island dwellers generally have an affiliation with a village on the shore, but the shore dwellers, who live in conical huts, remain throughout the year in the same village.

The Kuri are excellent farmers, having been the first to drain the polders and utilize their fertile silts. Their fields are composed of little squares about one yard to a side, separated by dikelets and irrigated by channels starting from wells at 100-yard (90-metre) intervals, dug into the water table about six feet (two metres) down. The water is drawn up by a balance-beam system in tightly woven baskets. The Kuri grow wheat, obtaining a high yield. After the wheat harvest in April, the fields are sown with maize.

Their herds consist of cattle and the Arabian zebu (a bovine animal). The Kuri cow is a good milk producer and furnishes much of the food supply, as also do fish. Fishing is slowly being abandoned, however, as also is crocodile hunting, even though it is lucrative.

The Kanembu. The Kanembu number only 3,000 or 4,000. They occupy the dunes, where they build large villages with mound huts of a characteristic pattern. They are adherents of Islām. Formerly fishers, they have abandoned that activity and engage in agriculture and sedentary livestock raising. They draw income from local soda deposits that they own but do not themselves exploit; instead, they collect duties that they impose on the Danoa people for its extraction and transportation.

The Danoa. The Danoa, or Haddad, related to the Kanembu, are a people apart. They are generally looked down upon because they have never been nomads and are not livestock raisers. They are dispersed in the zone extending north from the 13th parallel. They are Muslim and usually adopt the manner of life of the populations among whom they live. They are blacksmiths, ropemakers, dyers, and woodworkers, as well as fishers and hunters.

History. Lake Chad is reputed to have been known by report to Ptolemy and is identified by some writers with the Kura Lake of the Middle Ages. One of the ancient caravan routes across the Sahara from Tripoli (now Tarābulus, Libya) to Kuka in Bornu strikes the lake at its northwest corner; this has, however, today lost much of its former importance. The lake was first known to have been sighted by white men in 1823, when it was reached by way of Tripoli by three Britons, who named the lake Waterloo. Because of an exaggerated belief in its economic importance, there was, during the partition of Africa among European colonial powers in the 19th century, a "race for Lake Chad"; in 1890 to 1893 its shores were divided by treaty among the United Kingdom, France, and Germany. The African republics on the shores of the lake, all of which attained independence in 1960, inherited the political boundaries established by the colonial powers.

Prospects for the future. The lake is not heavily exploited at the present time. Fishing could be of greater significance, particularly in the southeast, or delta, region and off the northeast shores, where such fish food as insect larvae and small fry abound. The lakeshore populations, with the exception to some extent of the Buduma, consider fishing a somewhat poor activity, however, and do not engage in it, except in case of financial necessity. The lakeside populations, most of whom have nomadic traditions, have become increasingly sedentary, thereby opening some prospects for progress in agriculture and animal husbandry. In the Bol region in particular, where the area of the land reclaimed from the lake is constantly growing thanks to dykes built to resist the highest floods, modern techniques have permitted improvement in the cultivation of wheat as well as of corn (maize); the cultivation of potatoes, sugarcane, fruit, vegetables, lucerne grass, and clover is also anticipated. This work is being financed by the European Development Fund and by the World Food Programme, which is an agency established by the United Nations and the Food and Agriculture Organization (FAO).

BIBLIOGRAPHY. GEORGES DIGUIMBAYE and ROBERT LANGUE, *L'Essor du Tchad* (1969), a complete review of the development and potential of the Republic of Chad, with a discussion of fishing commercialization and agricultural perspectives; ALBERT LE ROUVREUR, *Sahariens et Sahéliens du Tchad* (1962), a detailed volume including information on the populations of the islands and shores of Lake Chad; R.K. UDO, *Geographical Regions of Nigeria* (1970), a current study with a chapter devoted to the depression of Chad and to the shores of the lake on the Nigerian side.

(Je.D.)

Chaetognatha

The phylum Chaetognatha comprises a group of small wormlike marine animals with transparent to translucid or opaque arrowshaped bodies, hence their common name arrowworms. The phylum consists of about seven extant genera and one fossil genus. There are more than 50 species, most of which are in the genus *Sagitta*. The size of the Chaetognatha ranges from about three millimetres to more than 100 millimetres; species inhabiting colder waters generally are larger than those from tropical seas. Chaetognatha are hermaphroditic (having both male and female sex organs, or gonads). The body is divided into head, trunk, and tail by two transverse walls or membranes and has lateral fins and a tail fin. Respiratory, circulatory, and excretory systems are not properly developed.

Natural history. *Life cycle.* Chaetognaths are protandric (*i.e.*, male gonads mature earlier than female gonads). Most chaetognaths die after spawning, although some undergo cycles of maturity and often also growth. Cross-fertilization has been observed, the sperm passing from the storage organs called seminal vesicles, which

Size and distribution

open out to the exterior, to the seminal receptacle (tube along the female gonads) of another individual. The eggs are fertilized by the sperm either shortly before or as they are laid, in a part of the duct common to the oviduct and to the seminal receptacle. In several genera (*e.g.*, *Eukrohnia*, and probably also in the genera *Bathyspadella*, *Krohnitta*, and *Heterokrohnia*), mature eggs and larvae are enclosed in a sac formed at the opening of oviducts. In *Pterosagitta*, eggs are laid in a capsule; in *Sagitta*, eggs are discharged into the surrounding water one at a time in several cycles; and in *Spadella*, eggs have an adhesive coat and a stalk and attach to any surface.

Ecology. Chaetognaths are voracious feeders; they consume copepods, euphausiids, fish larvae, medusae, other chaetognaths, cladocerans, amphipods, appendicularias, and eggs and larvae of various animals. Chaetognaths inhabit oceans, seas, and coastal lagoons. Although some species are cosmopolitan, others are restricted to a geographical region or an ocean. Southeast Asia seas have the largest number of species. Epiplanktonic species—*i.e.*, those within 200 metres of the water surface—increase in numbers from the poles to the Equator. Mature chaetognaths inhabit deeper oceanic layers than do the young.

Few chaetognaths have parasites; those that do are more often parasitized in neritic (close to shore) waters than in the open ocean.

Form and function. The body of a Chaetognatha is covered by a cuticle of cells (called collarette when thickened). The head has hooks (curved, grasping spines) covered by a hood or thin fold of skin, which retracts when the arrowworm is catching prey. Head muscles control the movement of hooks, teeth, and mouth; body muscles are longitudinal with some transverse bands. Chaetognaths swim with dartlike movements by contracting the longitudinal muscles and flapping the tail.

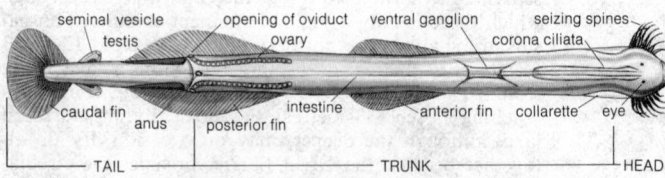

Body plan of arrowworm (*Sagitta bipunctata*).

The nervous system consists of a large cerebral ganglion with sensory nerves (*e.g.*, optic, coronal). The cerebral ganglion is connected with the ventral ganglion by a pair of nerve cords. Additional ganglia and nerves spread along the body. Touch receptors, small, round, ciliated (hairlike) prominences, are scattered over the body.

There is evidence that regeneration of the head and the anterior part of the body occurs; during regeneration, the eyes appear first, then the mouth and hooks. The eyes contain a pigmented central cell, which encloses five clusters of photoreceptor cell processes (or ocelli). A conical body found in the photoreceptor cell either may guide the animal as it swims or act as a resonator. The pigmented central cell may have various shapes (*e.g.*, starlike) in different species. No pigment is present in most deep-sea dwelling species.

The corona ciliata is an olfactory (smell) receptor or chemoreceptor peculiar to the Chaetognatha and is formed by a series of rows of ciliated cells forming a ring or elongated oval at the neck or extending toward the head and the trunk. The digestive tract, which is lined by glandular and absorptive cells, extends from the mouth to the anus and is supported by a mesentery. The central mesentery divides the trunk and tail into two cavities. Trunk and tail regions are filled with a colourless fluid that circulates forward along the body walls and backward in the medial region of the body. Two ovaries, filled with rows of unfertilized eggs, extend along the trunk and are attached to the sides of the body by a mesentery. The seminal receptacle in the oviducts stores sperm after copulation. The testes are located in the tail cavities; a spermduct, or vas deferens, connects the testes with the

The corona ciliata

seminal vesicles, which open out from the body. The ovaries in the trunk, therefore, are isolated from the testes in the tail, with no internal communication between male and female gonads. The seminal vesicles burst when filled with sperm, ejecting the spermatozoa into the surrounding waters or into the seminal receptacle of another individual.

Relationships and classification. The Chaetognatha is an isolated phylum in the animal kingdom; *i.e.*, comparative anatomy and embryology fail to link these animals with any other group. Chaetognaths have been considered as worms, and attempts have been made to relate them to many animal groups (*e.g.*, Heteropoda, Annelida, Nematoda, Arthropoda). They also have been placed taxonomically between Annelida and Nematoda. Structure of the chaetognath eye, however, indicates a probable evolutionary relationship to echinoderms and chordates.

The highest taxonomic rank in the phylum Chaetognatha is the genus. Genera are distinguished by the number, position, and extension of lateral fins and by the teeth. The presence of two pairs of lateral fins separates *Sagitta* from the other genera. Species within each genus are identified by minor differences (*e.g.*, shape and position of anatomical structures). There are at least six other genera of chaetognaths: *Spadella, Eukrohnia, Krohnitta, Heterokrohnia, Bathyspadella,* and *Pterosagitta*. A mid-Cambrian fossil species *Amiskwia sagittiformis* is also known.

BIBLIOGRAPHY. A. ALVARINO, "Chaetognaths," in *Oceanography and Marine Biology*, 3:115–194 (1965), a complete revision of the phylum Chaetognatha; *The Chaetognatha of the NAGA Expedition (1959–1961) in the South China Sea and the Gulf of Thailand*, pt. 1, *Systematics*, in *NAGA Reports*, 4, no. 2:1–197 (1967), analyses of anatomical structures of taxonomic significance and presentation of groups of closely related species to develop evolutionary patterns within the phylum; "Atlantic Chaetognatha: Distribution and Essential Notes of Systematics," *Trab. Inst. Español Oceanogr.*, vol. 37 (1969), a study of Chaetognatha collected by various countries during expeditions in the Atlantic with illustrations and distributional maps for each species; R.M. EAKIN and J.A. WESTFALL, "Fine Structure of the Eye of a Chaetognatha," *J. Cell. Biol.*, 21:115–132 (1964), on the ultrastructure of the eyes of *Sagitta scrippsae* as analyzed with the electron microscope.

(A.Al.)

Chagall, Marc

A folkloristic repertory of images that includes massive bouquets, melancholy clowns, flying lovers, fantastic animals, biblical prophets, and fiddlers on roofs has helped to make the Russian-born painter Marc Chagall one of the most popular of the major innovators in the 20th-century school of Paris. This dreamlike subject matter is presented in rich colours and in a fluent, painterly style that, while reflecting an awareness of such pre-1914 movements as Expressionism, Cubism, and even Abstractionism, remains invariably personal. Although critics have sometimes complained of facile sentiments, uneven quality, and an excessive repetition of motifs in the artist's large total production, there is agreement that at its best it reaches a level of visual metaphor seldom attempted in modern work.

First Parisian period

Chagall was born on July 7, 1887, in Vitebsk, a small city in western Russia not far from the Polish frontier. His family, which included eight children besides himself, was devoutly Jewish and, like the majority of the some 20,000 Jews in Vitebsk, humble without being poverty-stricken; the father worked in a herring warehouse, and the mother ran a shop where she sold fish, flour, sugar, and spices. The boy attended the heder, the Jewish elementary school, and later on he went to the local public school, where instruction was in Russian. He read the Bible, sang in the synagogue, and absorbed some of the ideas of the Ḥasidim, the Jewish mystical sectarians who opposed orthodox rationalism. After learning the elements of drawing at school, he studied painting in the studio of a local Realist, Jehuda Pen, and in 1907 went to St. Petersburg (now Leningrad), where he studied in-

Chagall, photograph by Arnold Newman, 1956.
© Arnold Newman

termittently for three years, eventually under Léon Bakst, who at the time was beginning a brilliant career as a stage designer. Characteristic works of this period of early maturity are the nightmarish "Dead Man," in which a roof violinist is already present, and "My Fiancée with Black Gloves," in which a portrait becomes an occasion for experimenting with an arrangement in black and white.

Birth and early life

In 1910, with a living allowance provided by a St. Petersburg patron, Chagall went to Paris. After a year and a half in rooms in Montparnasse, he moved into a studio on the edge of town in the ramshackle settlement for bohemian artists that was known as La Ruche (the Beehive). He met the avant-garde poets Blaise Cendrars, Max Jacob, and Guillaume Apollinaire, as well as a number of young painters destined to become famous: the Expressionist Chaim Soutine, the abstract colorist Robert Delaunay, and the Cubists Albert Gleizes, Jean Metzinger, Fernand Léger, and André Lhote. In such company nearly every sort of pictorial audacity was encouraged, and Chagall responded to the stimulus by rapidly developing the poetic and seemingly irrational tendencies he had begun to display in Russia. At the same time, under the influence of the Impressionist, Postimpressionist, and Fauvist pictures he saw in Paris museums and commercial galleries, he gave up the usually sombre palette he had employed at home.

The four years of this first stay in the French capital are often considered his best phase. Representative works are the "Self-Portrait with Seven Fingers," "I and My Village," "Hommage à Apollinaire," "Calvary," "The Fiddler," and "Paris Through the Window." In these pictures Chagall is already, in essentials, the artist he will continue to be for the next 60 years. His colours, although occasionally thin, are beginning to have their eventually characteristic complexity and resonance. The often whimsical figurative elements, frequently upside-down, are distributed on the canvas in an arbitrary fashion, producing an effect that sometimes resembles a film montage and can suggest, as it is evidently intended to, the inner space of a reverie. The general atmosphere can imply a Yiddish joke, a Russian fairy tale, or a vaudeville turn. Often the principal personage is the romantically handsome, curly-headed, rather Oriental-looking young painter himself. Memories of childhood and of Vitebsk are already one of the main sources for imagery.

After exhibiting in the annual Paris Salon des Indépendants and Salon d'Automne, Chagall had his first one-man show in Berlin in 1914, in the gallery of the modernist publication *Der Sturm*, and made a strong impression on German Expressionist circles. After visiting the exhibition, he went on to Vitebsk, where he was caught by the outbreak of World War I. Working for the moment in a relatively realistic style, he painted local scenes and a series of studies of old men; examples of the series are "The Praying Jew" and "Jew in Green."

In 1915 he married Bella Rosenfeld, the daughter of a wealthy Vitebsk merchant; among the many paintings in which she appears from this date onward are the depiction of flying lovers entitled "Birthday" and the high-spirited, acrobatic "Double Portrait with a Glass of Wine."

The October Revolution of 1917 found Chagall at first enthusiastic; he became commissar for art in the Vitebsk region and launched into ambitious projects for a local academy and museum. But after two and a half years of intense activity, marked by increasingly bitter aesthetic and political quarrels, he gave up and moved to Moscow. There he turned his attention for a while to the stage, producing the sets and costumes for plays by the Jewish writer Sholem Aleichem and murals for the Kamerny Theatre. In 1922 he left Russia for good, going first to Berlin, where he discovered that a large number of the pictures he had left behind in 1914 had disappeared. In 1923, this time with a wife and daughter, he settled once again in Paris.

Career as printmaker
Chagall had learned the techniques of engraving while in Berlin. Through his friend Cendrars he met the Paris art dealer Ambroise Vollard, who immediately commissioned a series of etchings to illustrate a special edition of Gogol's novel *Dead Souls* and thus launched Chagall on a long career as a printmaker. During the next three years, 107 full-page plates for the Gogol book were executed. But by then Vollard had arrived at another idea: an edition of La Fontaine's *Fables* with coloured illustrations resembling 18th-century prints. Chagall prepared 100 gouaches for reproduction, but it soon became evident that his colours were too complex for the printing process envisaged, and so he switched to black-and-white etchings, completing the plates in 1931. By this time Vollard had come up with still another idea: a series of etchings illustrating the Bible. Sixty-six plates were completed by Chagall by 1939, when World War II and the death of Vollard halted work on the project, and after the war the total was raised to 105. The Paris publisher E. Tériade, picking up at the many places where Vollard had left off, brought out *Dead Souls* in 1948 (with 11 more etchings for the chapter headings, making 118 in all), La Fontaine's *Fables* in 1952 (with two cover etchings, making 102 in all), and the Bible in 1956. Along with these much delayed ventures, Chagall was the producer of a number of smaller collections of engravings, many single plates, and an impressive quantity of coloured lithographs and monotypes.

During the 1920s and the early 1930s, his painting declined in the total of large canvases turned out and also, in the opinion of many critics, in quality; at any rate it became more obviously poetical and more and more popular. Examples are the "Bride and Groom with Eiffel Tower" and "The Circus." With the rise of Hitler, however, and the growing threat of a new world conflict, the artist began to have visions of a very different sort, which are reflected in the powerful "White Crucifixion." Throughout this between-the-wars period he travelled extensively, working in Brittany in 1924, in southern France in 1926, in Palestine in 1931 (as preparation for the Bible etchings), and, between 1932 and 1937, in Holland, Spain, Poland, and Italy. In 1931 he published, in a French adaptation, *My Life*, which he had written earlier in Russian. His reputation as an established modern master was confirmed by a large retrospective exhibition in 1933 at the Kunsthalle, Basel, Switzerland, and by the award in 1939 of the Carnegie Prize.

A refugee from the Nazis
With the outbreak of World War II, he moved to the Loire district of France and then, as the Nazi menace for all European Jews became increasingly real, further and further south. Finally, in July 1941, he and his family took refuge in the United States; with the exception of a summer in Mexico, he spent most of the next few years in New York City or its neighbourhood. In 1942, for the New York Ballet Theatre Company, he did the sets and costumes for the ballet *Aleko*, an all-Russian creation, with the music based on Tchaikovsky's *Trio in A Minor*, the story line from Pushkin's poem "The Gypsies," and the choreography by the Russian Léonide Massine. For

a while Chagall continued in his painting to develop themes he had already treated in France; typical works of this period are the "Yellow Crucifixion" and "The Feathers and the Flowers." But in 1944 his wife Bella died, and memories of her, often in a Vitebsk setting, became a recurring pictorial motif. She appears as a weeping wife and a phantom bride in "Around Her" (1945; Musée National d'Art Moderne, Paris) and, again, as the bride in "The Wedding Candles" (1945; private collection, France) and "Nocturne" (1947; private collection).

In 1945 he designed the backdrops and costumes for a New York production of Igor Stravinsky's ballet *The Firebird*. American art critics and collectors, who had not always been favourably disposed toward his work, were given an opportunity to revise their opinions in a large retrospective exhibition at the New York Museum of Modern Art in 1946 and at the Art Institute of Chicago a few months later. In a lecture, published in 1947 in *The Works of the Mind* by the University of Chicago Press, he explained his intentions:

For the Cubists a painting was a surface covered with forms in a certain order. For me a picture is a surface covered with representations of things (objects, animals, human beings) in a certain order in which logic and illustration have no importance. The visual effect of the composition is what is paramount. . . . I am against the terms "fantasy" and "symbolism." Our whole inner world is reality—perhaps even more real than the apparent world.

The Riviera period
In 1948, after two preliminary visits, he settled again in France, first in the suburbs of Paris and finally on the French Riviera at Vence and nearby Saint-Paul. In 1952 he married Vava Brodsky and began, at the age of 65, what might almost be called a new career—although the familiar, poetic, memory-derived motifs continued to appear in his work. Inspired in part by the nearness of ancient Riviera pottery centres, he began to experiment with ceramics; and, from this experience with three-dimensional forms, he moved on into sculpture. Between 1953 and 1956, without forgetting his native Vitebsk, he produced a series of paintings inspired by his affection for Paris. In 1958 he did the sets and costumes for a production of Ravel's ballet *Daphnis et Chloé* at the Paris Opera. After 1958 he was busy with stained-glass windows, first for the cathedral of Metz and then for the synagogue of the Hadassah-Hebrew University Medical Center in Jerusalem. In 1964 he completed a new ceiling for the Paris Opera, and two years later he completed two large mural paintings, "The Sources of Music" and "The Triumph of Music," for the new home of the New York Metropolitan Opera at Lincoln Center. In 1967 he created the sets and costumes for a Metropolitan Opera production of Mozart's *Magic Flute*. Meanwhile, he continued to turn out easel pictures.

MAJOR WORKS
Paintings
RUSSIA AND PARIS, 1907–22: "The Dead Man" (1908; Marc Chagall Collection, Saint-Paul, France); "My Fiancée with Black Gloves" (1909; Kunstmuseum, Basel, Switzerland); "Sabbath" (1910; Wallraf-Richartz-Museum, Cologne); "The Artist's Father" (1911; private collection, Paris); "I and My Village" (1911; Museum of Modern Art, New York); "Half-Past Three" (1911; Philadelphia Museum of Art); "Hommage à Apollinaire" (1911–12; Stedelijk van Abbemuseum, Eindhoven, The Netherlands); "Calvary" (1912; Museum of Modern Art, New York); "Self-Portrait with Seven Fingers" (c. 1912; Stedelijk Museum, Amsterdam); "The Soldier Drinks" (1912; Solomon R. Guggenheim Museum, New York); "The Fiddler" (1912; Stedelijk Museum); "Paris Through the Window" (1913; Solomon R. Guggenheim Museum); "The Praying Jew" ("The Rabbi of Vitebsk"; 1914; Art Institute of Chicago); "Over Vitebsk" (1914; private collection, Toronto); "Jew in Green" (1914; Charles Im Obersteg Collection, Geneva); "Double Portrait with a Glass of Wine" (1917; Musée National d'Art Moderne, Paris); "Green Violinist" (1918; Solomon R. Guggenheim Museum).

FRANCE, 1922–41: "Birthday" (1915–23; Museum of Modern Art, New York); "The Dream" (1927; Musée d'Art Moderne de la Ville de Paris); "Bride and Groom with Eiffel Tower" (1928; M. Roncey Collection, Paris); "Time is a River Without Banks" ("Le Temps n'a point de rive"; 1930–39; Museum of Modern Art, New York); "Synagogue at Safed" (1931; Stedelijk Museum, Amsterdam); "The Circus" (1931;

Stedelijk Museum, Amsterdam); "Solitude" (1933; Tel Aviv Museum, Israel); "White Crucifixion" (1938; Art Institute of Chicago); "The Cellist" (1939; Stedelijk Museum).

UNITED STATES, 1941–50: "Apparition of the Artist's Family" (1935–47; Marc Chagall Collection, Saint-Paul, France); "Yellow Crucifixion" (1943; Marc Chagall Collection); "The Feathers and the Flowers" ("Les Plumes en fleurs"; 1943; Musée National d'Art Moderne, Paris); "The Juggler" (1943; Art Institute of Chicago).

FRANCE, 1950– : "The Dance" (1950–52; Marc Chagall Collection); "King David" (1951; Marc Chagall Collection); "Saint-Germain-des Pres" (1953; private collection, Paris); "The Roofs" (1953; Marc Chagall Collection); "Portrait of Madame Chagall" (1953; Marc Chagall Collection); "The Circus" (1956; Marc Chagall Collection).

Murals

Ceiling (1964; Paris Opera); murals (1966; Metropolitan Opera, Lincoln Center, New York).

Other works

STAINED GLASS: windows (1958–60; cathedral, Metz); "The Twelve Tribes of Israel" (windows; 1960–61; Hadassah-Hebrew University Medical Center, Jerusalem).

THEATRE DESIGNS: Mural paintings, sets and costumes (1919; Kamerny Theatre, Moscow).

BOOK ILLUSTRATION: Gogol, *Dead Souls* (1948); La Fontaine, *Fables* (1952); Bible (1956).

BIBLIOGRAPHY. FRANZ MEYER, *Marc Chagall* (1961; Eng. trans., 1964), is the most complete biography to its date of publication. LIONELLO VENTURI, *Chagall* (1956); and JEAN CASSOU, *Chagall* (1965), are more accessible accounts, with the emphasis on the painter's aesthetic and philosophical outlook. ROY MCMULLEN, *The World of Marc Chagall* (1968), is a series of critical essays combined with photographs by IZIS, a long-time friend of the artist.

(R.McMu.)

Chamberlain, Joseph

One of the most forceful personalities in British politics in the late 19th century, Joseph Chamberlain, throughout a steady progression from successful businessman to municipal reformer, radical politician, and ardent imperialist, brought a fresh energy and bold imagination to his causes. At the local, national, or imperial level, he was a constructive radical, caring more for practical success than party loyalty or ideological commitment. The ideas with which he is most closely associated—tariff reform and imperial unity—were in advance of his time and pointed the direction that British policy would take in the 20th century.

Born on July 8, 1836, the son of a prosperous shoe manufacturer in London, Chamberlain was reared in an atmosphere of political Liberalism and Nonconformist religion and, eschewing a university career, entered the family business at 16. Two years later he moved to Birmingham to join his cousin's screw-making concern,

Chamberlain, oil painting by Frank Holl, 1886. In the National Portrait Gallery, London.

and there his tycoon characteristics came to the fore. His relentless energy and organizational genius drove out his competitors, and in 1874, at age 38, he was able to retire with a substantial fortune.

Meanwhile he had become involved in civic affairs and was elected mayor of Birmingham in 1873. His pioneer efforts in educational reform, slum clearance, improved housing, and municipalization of public utilities vaulted him into national prominence. At 40, the "gas-and-water Socialist," widely caricatured for his spare frame, incisive features, and ribboned monocle, was one of the most successful men in England.

Wasting no time, in 1876 he was elected to Parliament, where he was distrusted as a Dissenter and an upstart, and his genuinely radical speeches, delivered with a haughty confidence, frightened the Conservatives. Yet his industrial middle class constituency in Birmingham adored him, and his efficient party organization there (the "caucus") turned out big Liberal votes in the Midlands. Known as a wire puller, he became Prime Minister William Ewart Gladstone's lieutenant in the House of Commons and in 1882 was appointed president of the Board of Trade in Gladstone's second ministry (1880–85). Chamberlain, along with fellow radical Sir Charles Wentworth Dilke, led the left wing of the Liberal Party, and in 1885 they stumped the country in support of their "unauthorized programme," calling for a graduated income tax, free education, improved housing for the poor, local government reform, and "three acres and a cow" for agricultural labourers.

During the 1880s, when Irish demands for land reform and an autonomous parliament (Home Rule) increasingly bedevilled British politics and caused a deep rift in the Liberal Party, Chamberlain favoured Irish reform, especially at the local level, and stood with Gladstone in opposition to the use of repressive force in quashing Irish agitation. Chamberlain's instincts, however, were already on the side of imperial unity, and he could not go along with Gladstone in 1885, when the latter committed the party to Home Rule for Ireland. In 1886, when the Home Rule issue came to a vote in Commons, Chamberlain joined with other dissident Liberals (Liberal Unionists) to defeat the government.

The split in the Liberal Party proved permanent; the Conservatives, supported by the Liberal Unionists, dominated British politics for most of the period from 1886 until 1906. Chamberlain used his control of the Liberal Unionists to pressure the Conservatives into adopting a more progressive social policy; before 1892 he had the satisfaction of seeing the Conservatives pass various measures of social reform.

The Conservative hegemony reflected a growing disenchantment with social reform in the country and marked a new emphasis upon empire and foreign affairs. Chamberlain, too, began to abandon his radicalism and turned increasingly to imperialist rhetoric, popular with the increasingly jingoistic industrial masses. In 1895 he joined the Conservative Cabinet of Robert Cecil, 3rd marquess of Salisbury, asking to be made secretary of state for the colonies.

In that office Chamberlain quickly became involved in South African affairs and was accused of complicity in the Jameson Raid, an abortive invasion of the Boer republic of Transvaal by British settlers from the neighbouring Cape Colony (December 1895). Though he was later cleared by a Commons investigation, his anti-Boer stance was evident. When worsening Anglo-Boer relations erupted in the South African War (1899–1902), Chamberlain supported it enthusiastically.

This war, in which Britain was roasted in world opinion as a bully, brought home to Chamberlain the fact that Britain was militarily vulnerable and diplomatically isolated in Europe. Germany, with which he had always wanted an alliance, had proved particularly hostile. In view of Britain's isolation, Chamberlain looked to the self-governing colonies, which had given encouraging support to Britain during the war. Returning from his negotiation of the peace settlement in South Africa in 1902, Chamberlain announced a new tariff scheme that

Birmingham beginnings

Opposition to Home Rule

he hoped would draw Britain and its dependencies together in a kind of common market. Protected by stiff tariffs without and united by preferential tariffs within, the new union would add to Britain's international security, protect manufactures threatened by new competition from the United States and Germany, and raise revenue for social projects at home.

Characteristically, Chamberlain energetically set out to convert his party to the new scheme. When Conservative leader Arthur Balfour, 1st earl of Balfour, refused to commit himself, Chamberlain resigned his cabinet post and from 1903 to 1906 conducted a forceful private campaign, exhorting his listeners to "think imperially." But protection was a political bombshell. Free trade (which to Englishmen meant cheap imported food) had been the touchstone of Britain's conventional wisdom for more than a half century. Liberals everywhere raised the cry of cheap bread, and Conservatives split as irrevocably as the Liberals had 20 years earlier over Home Rule. In the general elections of 1906 the Conservatives and Liberal Unionists went down to a resounding defeat, in great part because of Chamberlain's abandonment of free trade. Chamberlain, however, was reelected in his native Birmingham by an astonishing majority.

It was his last political victory, for shortly after, in July 1906, he suffered a paralytic stroke that left him a helpless invalid for the rest of his life. He lingered on tragically until his death in London on July 2, 1914.

Chamberlain's two sons, Austen and Neville, later rose to national prominence, the former as foreign secretary, the latter as prime minister.

BIBLIOGRAPHY. JAMES L. GARVIN and JULIAN AMERY, *The Life of Joseph Chamberlain*, 6 vol. (1932–69), is the only good full-length work. MICHAEL HURST, *Joseph Chamberlain and Liberal Reunion* (1967), provides the best presentation of Chamberlain's psychology and general character. ROBERT V. KUBICEK, *The Administration of Imperialism: Joseph Chamberlain at the Colonial Office* (1969), is rather incomplete but covers a subject handled inadequately by others.

(Ga.P.)

Chamber Music

In its original sense chamber music refers to music composed for the home, as opposed to that written for the theatre or church; since the "home"—whether it be drawing room, reception hall, or palace chamber—may be assumed to be of limited size, the music is most often composed for a small ensemble, traditionally dispenses with a conductor, and permits no more than one player to a part. Music written for combinations of string or wind instruments, often with a keyboard (piano or harpsichord) as well, and music for voices with or without accompaniment have historically been included in the term.

An essential characteristic of chamber music results from the limited size of the performing group employed: it is intimate music, suited to the expression of subtle and refined musical ideas. Rich displays of varied instrumental colour, and striking effects produced by sheer sonority, play little part in chamber music. In place of those effects are refinement, economy of resources, and flawless acoustical balance.

This article discusses instrumental ensemble music written for groups of two to eight players with one player to a part, and in which string instruments and piano (or harpsichord) supply the principal interest.

HISTORICAL DEVELOPMENT

Origins. Instrumental music designed for home use has existed since about the middle of the 15th century. It became customary in Germany to supply folk-song melodies with two or three countermelodies, to expand and elaborate the whole, and to arrange the result for groups of instruments; original melodies were given similar treatment. The instruments were not often specified, but on the basis of many paintings of the time one may assume that groups of viols of various sizes predominated.

A more important source of later chamber music is to be found in the arrangements of 16th-century chansons (songs of French origin composed usually for four voices on a variety of secular texts), some for voices and lute, others for lute alone. The typical chanson was characterized by contrasts in musical texture and often in metre; the effect of the whole was that of a short composition in several even shorter sections. That sectional form retained in the arrangements later became a striking feature.

The chanson travelled to Italy about 1525, became known as canzona, and was transcribed for organ. The earliest transcriptions differed from the French arrangements in treating the original chanson with greater freedom, adding ornaments and flourishes, and sometimes inserting new material. Soon original canzonas for organ, modelled on the transcriptions, and for small instrumental ensembles, were composed. One such type, characterized by elaborate figurations and ornamented melodies, became influential in England late in the 17th century and played a role in the works of Henry Purcell.

Parallel to the developments that led from the vocal chanson, in France, to the instrumental canzona, primarily in Italy, was the development of the dance suite. Early 16th-century dance tunes in all countries of western Europe usually had appeared in pairs: one was slow, stately in mood, and in duple metre (*i.e.*, with two beats to the measure); the other fast, lively in mood, usually in triple metre, and often melodically similar to the first. Through much of the 16th century, composers in the several countries sought to expand the dance pair into a unified dance suite. Suites based on variations of one movement appeared in England; suites in which each of four dances had its own rhythmic character, melodically based on the first dance, were written in Germany; sets of dances with no internal relationships to each other were common in Italy. The most influential steps were taken in France by composers for the lute or the clavecin (harpsichord). Consisting essentially of four dance forms that were then popular—the allemande, courante, sarabande, and gigue—the suites they composed were based on contrasting tempos, metres, and rhythmic patterns. The French version of the dance suite became the prototype for later chamber-music forms. [margin: Development from dance suites]

Toward the middle of the 17th century the two types of composition—one derived from the canzona and composed in sectional form, the other derived from the dance suite and consisting of several movements—appeared as works for small instrumental ensembles. In Italy small groups of string instruments were often employed in Roman Catholic churches to perform appropriate music; thus canzonas came to be widely used for church purposes. For church use the dance movements were omitted, and what came to be called a church sonata (*sonata da chiesa*) resulted. And a set of *sonate da chiesa* composed in 1667 by Giovanni Battista Vitali marked the beginning of the form as a separate entity.

In the same year Johann Rosenmüller, a German composer working in Venice, published a set of *Sonate da camera cioè Sinfonie . . .* (*Chamber Sonatas, that is, Symphonies . . .*), each consisting of four to six dance movements with an introductory movement (sinfonia) not in dance style. The development of chamber music for the remainder of the century centred upon these two types, *sonata da chiesa* and *sonata da camera*. [margin: Rosenmüller's chamber sonatas]

Instrumental combinations. The first half of the 17th century was marked by considerable variety in the constitution of chamber-music groups. Compositions were commonly for one to four viols, or for combinations of viols and woodwind instruments, most often with a figured-bass accompaniment, a kind of musical shorthand, employed in virtually all music of the period about 1600 to 1750, in which the composer wrote a bass line and inserted figures and other symbols under certain notes. The figures indicated the nature of the desired chord to be improvised over the note—whether major or minor, whether in normal or in inverted position, and so on—and the figured-bass line was designed to be "realized" or played by a harmony instrument (such as a lute, organ, or harpsichord), often with a melody instrument (bass, cello, or bassoon) to reinforce the bass line. The bass line with its figures and the two instruments performing it were called basso continuo or simply continuo.

As early as 1622, the Italian composer Salomone Rossi had begun to specify two violins and *chittarone* (a large lute) in his dance sets; and soon similar combinations were adopted generally. A work written for two violins and bass (continuo) became known as a *sonata a tre* or "trio sonata"—even though four instruments (the three strings and the lute or harpsichord) were usually involved in the performance. Later in the 17th century works for one instrument and continuo appeared also and were called variously solo sonatas, duos, or *sonate a due*. The combinations of violin and continuo or cello and continuo were favoured, and sonatas for those combinations took regular places in the chamber-music field.

Works for two violins and continuo (with harpsichord and bass understood) virtually dominated the field until the middle of the 18th century. About that time the custom of serenading became popular; small groups of instrumentalists strolled the streets of Austrian and Italian cities, performing serenades and divertimentos. The keyboard instrument realizing the continuo proved unwieldy and was soon abandoned. To the three remaining strings a viola was added to fill out the harmonies, the bass was replaced by a cello, and the string quartet emerged. This new combination of two violins, viola, and cello was then adopted by composers of serious music, and from about 1750 the string quartet took its place as the principal medium for chamber music. Owing its development largely to the Austrian composer Joseph Haydn, it has reigned supreme to the present day. About 1760, other combinations for strings alone began to play important but relatively smaller roles in the field: the string trio (violin, viola, cello), string quintet (quartet plus a second viola), and string sextet (quintet plus a second cello) are chief among them.

Meanwhile, as the continuo principle gradually approached obsolescence, the harpsichord (which was superseded by the piano about 1770) took on a new function in chamber music. In works with continuo it had been an accompanying instrument, improvising its part according to the directions indicated in the figured bass; now the keyboard instrument became dominant in new combinations that included one to four strings. The most important of these is the piano trio (piano, violin, cello), the repertory of which includes works from Haydn to the present. Various combinations of piano and one instrument loom almost as large. Toward the end of the 18th century and extending through the 19th, the combinations of piano quartet (piano trio plus viola) and piano quintet (piano and string quartet) give rise to a small but significant repertory ornamented by composers such as Mozart, Beethoven, Brahms, and many others.

Finally, works for individual combinations exist in considerable number after about the 1780s. Representative compositions of that nonstandard group include the clarinet quintets (string quartet and clarinet) by Mozart (K. 581) and Brahms (Opus 115); the *Septet*, Opus 20 (violin, viola, cello, bass, clarinet, bassoon, and horn), by Beethoven; the *Octet*, Opus 166 (as in the septet plus a second violin), the *Trout Quintet*, Opus 114 (violin, viola, cello, bass, and piano), and the *String Quintet in C Major*, Opus 163 (two violins, viola, and two cellos), all by Schubert; and the *Horn Trio*, Opus 40 (violin, horn, and piano), by Brahms. Composers of the 20th century have written works for instrumental groups to which a voice is added.

STRUCTURAL ELEMENTS

Form. A major distinction must be drawn between the prevailing musical forms of the period before about 1750 and those after that date. The earlier forms included primarily the *sonata da chiesa*, which emerged from the instrumental canzona, and the *sonata da camera*, which owed its origin to the dance suite. In the first of these, the several sections that had been taken over from the canzona were gradually extended, cadences (harmonic devices analogous to punctuation marks in prose) were confined largely to ends of sections, and the single-movement form soon dissolved into a set of movements of varying length, tempo, and metre. Toward the 1640s a tendency arose to standardize the number of movements and regularize the contrasts between them; soon a pattern of four movements arranged in slow-fast-slow-fast sequence, with textures based to a large extent on imitative or fugal writing, emerged. The Italian violinist-composer Arcangelo Corelli, with about 38 *sonate da chiesa*, was the most consistent in employing that pattern after about 1680.

The other form, *sonata da camera*, remained less regular. Its parent, the dance suite, had most often contained four movements, but works of three to eight or more movements exist also. When the dance suite adopted the trio-sonata instrumentation and gradually became the *sonata da camera*, it at first maintained that irregularity. Soon, however, it was altered to include a nondance first movement (prelude, preamble, or *intrada*), after which a number of idealized dance forms followed. In keeping with its origin, the *sonata da camera* revealed a relationship to dance rhythms in its several movements (except the first), and homophonic style (*i.e.*, with a single melodic line supported by chords) dominated. The work of Corelli, embodied in 34 *sonate da camera*, again served as a model for later composers.

Toward the end of the 17th century the two forms began mutually to influence each other. The *sonata da chiesa*, with its serious moods set usually in contrapuntal texture (*i.e.*, employing counterpoint, the intertwining of independent melodic lines), adopted some of the lighter and more rhythmic aspects of its rival. Likewise, the *sonata da camera*, light in its total mood and based on dance rhythms, often embodied contrapuntal devices and contained movements that were essentially imitative or fugal in texture and serious in mood. By the end of the 17th century the distinctions between the two types tended to disappear; soon the terms *chiesa* and *camera* were dropped, and the term *sonata a tre* or "trio sonata" prevailed to about 1750. The situation in regard to solo sonatas (for violin and continuo, for example) was similar; they, too, took on common characteristics derived from the contrasting trio-sonata types, and contained both dance metres and contrapuntal textures.

The post-1750 forms, on the other hand, were based on different patterns. A standard pattern of a string quartet consisted of four movements, the first of which was most often cast in sonata form—three-part form containing an exposition of two contrasting melodic ideas, a transition (later elaborated to create a "development section"), and a recapitulation of the first part with changed harmonies. The second movement was generally in slow tempo and could represent one of several forms: another sonata form, a set consisting of theme and variations, or the like. Then followed a movement in triple metre (at first a minuet and later a faster version of that dance called a "scherzo") derived from the dance field and consisting actually of two such idealized dances; the second, called a "trio," usually lighter in texture, was followed by a recapitulation of the first dance. The last movement was a rondo (consisting of a regular alternation of two or more musical ideas, in the form ABABA or ABACA), or a set of variations, or even another sonata form. The whole represents a compound form called a "sonata," although post-1750 and pre-1750 sonatas have few structural elements in common.

The term sonata (in the post-1750 version) can be applied to most of the forms within the field of chamber music as well as to several outside that field. As seen in the compositions of a line of composers from Haydn in the late 18th century to Brahms in the late 19th and beyond, the piano trio, violin sonata, string quintet, and the others are all based essentially on the pattern that characterizes, above all, the string quartet. Even the symphony and the concerto of the post-1750 period are, in effect, sonatas for orchestra. Internal differences exist, of course; the piano trio and the violin sonata, for example, do not always include a dance-derived third movement, which the string quartet and symphony generally do. Conversely, the exposition of the symphony's first movement often contains more than two contrasting themes, and is often preceded by a massive introduction; and the recapitulation is often followed by a large concluding section or coda (literally, "tail"). Similarly, the

Function of the harpsichord

Chamber and church sonatas

Pattern of the string quartet

first movement of a concerto (for piano and orchestra, say) is generally characterized by two expositions—one for the orchestra, the other for the solo instrument. In most other respects, the majority of the larger instrumental forms of the post-1750 period are closely related in their total structure.

Melody. The years about 1600, marking roughly the date when chamber music emerged as a separate branch, also mark one of the major turning points in the evolution of music. Virtually all the factors of music were affected by the developments of the time. A new system of melodic organization (the tonal system, with its major and minor scales) soon assumed a pre-eminent position; the principles of harmony were expanded and systematized; a texture based on the polarity between melody and bass (as opposed to one that had been largely the result of writing intertwined and independent melodies) came to the fore; and the figured bass or continuo was invented (albeit, a few decades earlier) to deal with the new texture. In those new developments all the musical factors continued to be mutually related; but they are considered separately here for the sake of clarity.

The melodies of the canzona, or sonata, at first continued to imitate vocal melodies; easily sung intervals, relatively slow tempos, and undulating stepwise contours were characteristic. Gradually composers began to consider the nature of the instruments they were using and to write melodies appropriate to those instruments. Soon the concept of instrumental idioms was developed; each instrument was given melodies appropriate to its structure. That development is seen most clearly in the many trio sonatas written by Corelli after about 1680.

Harmony as a system

With the emergence of systematized harmony, in which specific functions were given to chords according to their relationships to the tonic (the basic, or root, tone of a given scale), melodies became harmonically directed, moved from one harmonic goal to another, and began to take on regular periodic structure (in units of four measures, eight measures, and so on). Slow movements often adopted elements of vocal style, in which sharp contours were avoided, and the melody followed purely musical or aesthetic laws rather than the laws of textual declamation. The ever-increasing use of harmonic dissonance was reflected in melodic writing through the 18th and 19th centuries. Extreme leaps, angular contours, irregular rhythmic shapes—such characteristics became the common property of all composers.

Harmony. The complex of chords gradually evolved into the system of tonality. Central to that system is the idea that the triad on the first tone of the scale (*i.e.*, the tonic and the third and fifth tones above it) determines the key or tonality (C major, D minor, and so on) around which other chords are grouped. Modulations (shifts to other key centres) became regularized: those to the dominant (five tones above the tonic) and subdominant (five tones below) became the most important. In the period immediately before and after 1800, especially in the works of Beethoven and Schubert, modulations to the mediant and submediant (three tones above and below the tonic, respectively) became characteristic. And throughout the 19th century, modulation to ever more-remote keys was practiced assiduously. Further, chromatic tones—tones not related to the key centre (F sharp or D flat in a C major context, for example)—appeared in increasing numbers; and tones not part of the chord at a given moment (F in a triad on C, for example) were treated more freely. The consequence was a system in which tonality became so ambiguous that it ceased to serve any real function through long passages in the music. Chromatic harmony dominated much music of the late 19th century, and the steps from chromaticism to the atonal and serial systems of the 20th century, in which tonality was entirely abandoned, followed as a matter of course.

Influence of tonality

Texture. Similarly, the element of texture underwent a series of changes. Much music was composed in homophonic style, with a melody supported only by a few chords built above the continuo. Gradually, especially in the trio sonatas, an inner part came to imitate the upper melody to some extent; bits of figuration gave the two upper melodies a degree of independence, and eventually polyphonic texture, composed of two or more intertwining melodies, was restored. That texture reflected the harmonic developments of the time and came under the control of the tonal system with its dissonances, modulations, chromatic embellishments, and all the rest. Mixed textures, partly homophonic and partly polyphonic, became common also; but in general the uppermost melody dominated the structure well past the middle of the 18th century.

Toward the 1770s, with the string quartet an established grouping, increasing attention was given to the inner and lower parts. Viola and cello were occasionally given thematic material, the violins at times played accompanying parts, and detailed writing for all four instruments compensated for the absence of the continuo. The practice of improvising harmonies at the keyboard came to an end, and all parts were obbligati (that is, obligatory). Continued refinement in the writing and equal distribution of musical responsibility to all four instruments resulted in the so-called quartet style, in which the distinction between melody and accompaniment disappeared and no instrument dominated the others. From that point forward, the idea of a soloist in chamber music lost whatever validity it had had earlier; the performers in a chamber-music work became members of a group of equals.

Style. In style, too, there has been a continuing series of changes. "Style" may be defined in this context as the sum of the devices—melodic, structural, harmonic, and all the rest—that a composer consistently employs, that a class of works regularly exhibits, or that a particular age finds most useful for its aesthetic purposes.

In this sense, the majority of chamber-music works composed before 1750 are monothematic in style; those after about 1750 are polythematic. The typical fast movement of a trio sonata, say, consists of a series of phrases largely similar in contour and mood and differentiated primarily by harmonic considerations; whereas the typical sonata-form movement is characterized by having two or more themes embodying sharp contrasts of mood and shape, and further contrasted by means of texture, instrumentation, and harmonic colour. Alternation of dramatic and lyric moods, further, is most often characteristic of post-1750 chamber music.

With the emergence of the string quartet and sonata form toward the middle of the 18th century, thematic materials most often took the shape of relatively long melodies—whatever their contour or mood. Those melodies were then manipulated or repeated in accord with harmonic principles and constituted sections in tonic, dominant, and so on. In the 1780s, and specifically in the quartets Opus 33 by Haydn, certain melodies were so constructed that they could, in effect, be broken apart into fragments or motives, each motive with its own distinctive shape. In the appropriate sections of sonata-form movements—namely, those that connected one thematic section with another, and the large transition that comprised the midsection of the form—the motives were treated separately, manipulated, combined in new ways, served to suggest yet other ideas to the composer; in short, they were "developed."

Thematic development

Such treatment of the motives led to the principle of thematic development and to the practice of motive manipulation. Begun by Haydn, carried forward notably by Beethoven and Brahms, and employed by virtually every other instrumental composer of the 19th century, the principle of thematic development is one of the chief distinguishing marks of late Classical and Romantic instrumental music. Beethoven, however, and after him many other major composers, employed the process somewhat differently from Haydn; he often began with a melodic or rhythmic motive, then let the themes themselves grow out of the motive manipulation.

Use of piano. The repertory of works for piano and strings also grew considerably from the late 18th century onward, and there was considerable modification in the role of the piano in that repertory. The keyboard instru-

Evolution
of role
of piano

ment had entered the field, it will be remembered, after having played a century-long role as the improvising member of the continuo team, in which it provided accompaniments to the other instruments. When it emerged in its new role with written-out parts to play, it at first assumed a dominant position—in violin or cello sonatas and in piano trios alike. Many of the piano trios by Haydn are essentially sonatas for solo piano with accompaniments furnished by violin and cello; the latter often do little more than double the parts given to the pianist's right and left hands, respectively.

Gradually the string parts acquired a degree of independence and became obbligato parts. The final steps toward complete equality were taken across the interval from about 1790 to 1840, especially in the piano trios and quartets of Mozart and Beethoven and in Schumann's *Piano Quintet*, Opus 44 of 1842. In many of those works, particularly the later ones, the piano emerged as one-half of the tonal body with the two, three, or four string instruments providing the other half. Again, as in the string quartets, the concept of soloist versus accompanist has no validity in chamber music with piano. A keyboard player does not "accompany" the strings; he is an equal partner in the ensemble—which marks a major change from the role he played in the 17th and the first half of the 18th centuries.

Romantic practices. Chamber music in the later 19th century became ever more affected by developments in the orchestral field. The rise of professional quartets in the time of Beethoven had the effect of moving chamber music from the confines of the home to the public concert stage. Composers took advantage of the virtuosic attainments of the best performers and wrote music with which the nonprofessional performer could not always cope. Effects requiring consummate technical ability became common; true virtuosity became a general requirement. Further, orchestral effects depending upon sheer volume of sound were often employed; the string quartets and piano trio of Tchaikovsky are examples. And with the rise of descriptive or program music in the orchestral field, extra-musical or nationalistic elements sometimes entered chamber-music works; Smetana's autobiographical string quartet, *Z mého života* (*From my Life*), and certain of Dvořák's compositions containing Czech folk idioms and representing the Czech spirit are typical.

Twentieth-century practices. The overwhelming majority of chamber music composed before about 1900 consists of works that employ instruments in conventional ways. Tones are limited to the pitches in the chromatic scale (*i.e.*, a scale consisting of half steps, C, C sharp, D, D sharp, E, and so through all 12 tones), string instruments are used in the traditional manner, and the piano likewise. A few notable exceptions may be mentioned: in the *Piano Trio No. 1 in D Minor*, Opus 63, by Schumann the strings play a short passage *sul ponticello* ("against the bridge")—that is, play closer to the bridge of the instruments than usual in order to produce the higher overtones and give the pitches an ethereal or veiled quality; in the same composer's *Piano Quartet in E Flat Major*, Opus 47, the cello must retune its lowest string downward a whole step in order to supply a long-held tone beyond the normal range of the instrument. And, in a few works of the time, harmonics are called for: a string is touched lightly at its midpoint or at one of the other nodal positions at one-third or one-quarter of its length, and the harmonic (overtone) thus produced adds a distinctive quality to the music. Such effects, plus the traditional pizzicato (in which the string is plucked rather than set in motion by the bow) are virtually the only exceptions to normal writing.

In 20th-century chamber music, however, the number of purely instrumental effects has been increased; the Hungarian composer Béla Bartók in several of his quartets became the leading exponent of such devices. In his *String Quartet No. 4* (1928), for example, glissandi are required; in such cases the player slides his finger up or down the string to cover the span of an octave or more, and produces a wailing effect. Pizzicati are directed to be performed so that the string slaps back against the fingerboard, to add a percussive effect to the pitch. In works by other composers employing the clarinet, the performer is required to blow through the instrument with its mouthpiece removed while opening and closing the keys at random; this produces the effect of a high-pitched whistling wind along with a semblance of pitch changes. Or again, in the case of brass instruments, the composer's directives call for the player to tap his hand against the mouthpiece, to create a hollow percussive sound.

Pitches themselves are altered on occasion, for tones lying between those of the chromatic scale are sometimes employed; among early exponents of the quarter-tone practice, the contemporary composer Ernest Bloch may be mentioned. In his *Piano Quintet*, and elsewhere, the string performers are required to play certain tones a quarter step higher or lower than written, thereby departing from the scales that had served music for many centuries. Other composers carried the quarter-tone practice further and developed a kind of microtonal music that employs intervals even smaller than quarter-tones.

Use of
quarter-
tones

All such developments give evidence that 20th-century composers continue to seek new means of expression and expand their available resources—thus continuing a practice characteristic of composers in all periods. Two further aspects of that search remain to be considered: the development of new systems of tonal organization and the increasing use of instruments that embody the results of contemporary technology.

Early in the 20th century a number of composers led by Arnold Schoenberg experimented to reach beyond the confines of the tonal system. In a series of chamber-music and other works, Schoenberg gradually arrived at a system in which all 12 tones of the chromatic scale are used as independent entities; concepts of tonic and dominant, of major and minor, and of key centres themselves no longer apply in those works. The 12 tones are arranged in a self-determined series called a "tone row"; certain sections of that row, used vertically, form the chords that supply the harmonic material; the row may be manipulated in accord with self-imposed rules; and the row may be arranged differently for each composition. The system of composing with 12 tones, as Schoenberg referred to his invention, has been modified and enlarged by later composers, the relevant principles have been applied to other elements of music (notably the rhythmic factor); and under a new term, "serial composition," the system has become one of the most influential of the present day.

The other aspect concerns the use of various electronic sound-generating devices called "electronic synthesizers," and of magnetic tape recorders to transmit the results. The composer working with a synthesizer has virtually complete control over the shape and sound of the tones he wishes to produce. He can select tones with characteristics unlike those produced by conventional instruments, noises (that is, sounds with irregular vibration rates) to which a semblance of pitch has been given, or rapid changes in pitch, loudness, duration, and quality beyond the ability of any human mechanism. The new tonal materials, then, can be combined with voices and conventional instruments, or can be used alone. Devices such as the synthesizer have given the composer access to a new world of tonal resources; he still faces the problems of selection, combination, organization, and expressive purpose that have plagued composers since music began. Since his medium of performance is a tape recorder, since human participation in the performance may not be required, and since his composition may contain a few strands or a hundred strands of tone, it becomes impossible to make distinctions between chamber music, orchestral music, or any other genre. Electronic music is, thus, on the way to becoming a completely new type to which traditional classifications do not apply.

Electronic
synthe-
sizers

REPERTORIES

The following sections contain brief accounts of the contributions to the art of chamber music of the major composers.

Late Baroque period, c. 1675–1750. The work of Arcangelo Corelli (1653–1713) in standardizing the two major sonata types of his time has already been discussed. Corelli was of considerable influence on Henry Purcell (c. 1659–95), the most important English composer of his time. Purcell's works include 22 trio sonatas closely allied to the *chiesa* type, and over a dozen "fancies" (that is, fantasies), works of a single movement largely in contrapuntal style for groups of three to seven viols. Another Italian Baroque composer of widespread influence, Antonio Vivaldi (1678–1741), in addition to several hundred concertos for various instruments and orchestra, composed some 75 chamber-music works. Of these, 12 trio sonatas, 16 sonatas for violin and continuo, and about 16 for various other instruments have entered the repertory.

Bach's
contribu-
tions

The contributions of Johann Sebastian Bach (1685–1750) to development of chamber music were noteworthy. In all, Bach's chamber works include 18 sonatas for one instrument (nine for violin, three for viola da gamba, six for flute) and harpsichord, two separate trio sonatas, and two late works of an unusual nature; *Das musikalisches Opfer* (*The Musical Offering*) and *Die Kunst der Fuge* (*The Art of the Fugue*). Half of the sonatas require figured bass; the other half, with written-out keyboard parts, are essentially in three-voice counterpoint: one voice in the solo instrument and two in the keyboard part. *The Musical Offering* consists of 12 canons and fugues for various combinations of two to six instruments and a four-movement trio sonata; the whole is based on a theme given to Bach by Frederick the Great in 1747, upon which Bach improvised in the presence of the King, and which he later elaborated to constitute this "offering." The work is symmetrical in form, reveals Bach's enormous technical skill, and is filled with emotional intensity. *The Art of the Fugue*, Bach's last work, is a set of 19 fugues (the last unfinished) for two to four unspecified instruments. The work is based on one theme that is transformed in systematic fashion in successive movements, and employs two additional themes on occasion. The whole summarizes the contrapuntal practices of the past, contains profound spiritual symbolism, and is unique in music.

The 40-odd chamber works of George Frideric Handel (1685–1759), representing both *chiesa* and *camera* types, contain a wealth of melody and carefully worked-out fugal movements and are filled with the rhythmic drive that represents Handel at his best. Of these about 18 are solo sonatas (with continuo) for various instruments, and some 22 are trio sonatas.

Classical period, c, 1750–1825. The 83 string quartets (of which seven are single-movement arrangements of orchestral pieces titled *The Seven Words of Our Saviour on the Cross* and known as *The Seven Last Words*) by Joseph Haydn (1732–1809) constitute a series in which virtually the entire history of the string quartet is represented. Most of them appeared in sets of six, each under a separate opus number. The earliest sets, Opus 1 and 2, express merely the superficial and diverting elements of Rococo style—the fanciful, ornamental style that was prevalent in the 18th century. From Opus 3 onward the four-movement form is regularized, and in Opus 9 thematic materials begin to reveal details that point to the future. Opus 17 discloses a virtuosic element in its first-violin parts, and lower voices are given only a small share in the thematic work. The latter process comes to full expression in Opus 20, for now cello and viola are entrusted with thematic statements and the quartet style is close at hand.

Haydn's
83 quartets

After a nine-year interval (1772–81) Haydn introduced a "new manner" (his phrase) in the quartets of Opus 33; this resulted in the establishment of the principle of thematic development. Motive manipulation is basic to the texture, and the fully developed sonata form appears. Also in Opus 33 Haydn introduced the scherzo in place of the minuet, but did not continue that practice in later quartets.

The 33 quartets from Opus 50 onward (excepting Opus 51, *The Seven Last Words*) include the masterworks on which Haydn's reputation is so firmly founded. Of them 18 (Opus 50, 54, 55, 64) were composed during the time (c. 1786–90) Haydn was in close contact with Mozart and are characterized by an increasing use of chromaticism to produce poignant effects. The 15 quartets written after Mozart's death (Opus 71, 74, 76, 77, 103) return to the optimistic style that was innate, and they reveal an ever-increasing expressiveness and mastery of detail.

Haydn also composed more than 30 piano trios, eight violin sonatas, and over 60 string trios. While those works contain attractive melodies, they represent a minor aspect of the composer's activity.

Of the 26 string quartets written by Wolfgang Amadeus Mozart (1756–91) the qualities of the last ten are such that they have virtually overshadowed the 16 earlier works. Six of the ten reflect Mozart's first attempts to work in Haydn's "new manner" and reveal how successfully he adopted the principle. The last three, dedicated to King Frederick William II of Prussia, a competent cellist, show Mozart's ability to adapt to the interests of his potential patrons. Here the cello parts reveal something of the virtuosity required of the first violin. Taken together, the last ten quartets are among Mozart's masterpieces.

Of Mozart's eight string quintets, three rise to supremacy. The *String Quintet in C Major*, K. 515 (K. stands for Köchel, a cataloger of Mozart's works), is a model of strength and delicacy, filled with moods reflecting grace and good humour, but also high dramatic tension. Its companion in G minor, K. 516, is characterized by the same strength but is the embodiment of anguish. Two years later Mozart composed the *Clarinet Quintet*, K. 581; now moods of grace, humour, and cheer prevail. The addition of the woodwind instrument enabled Mozart to achieve a high level of brilliance and colour throughout; the *Clarinet Quintet* is one of the monuments of the literature.

Exactly half of Mozart's 32 violin sonatas were composed before his tenth birthday; in them the violin parts do little more than accompany the piano. The last 16 move gradually to a true ensemble texture, which is fully attained in K. 454, K. 481, and K. 526. Two piano quartets, contrasting greatly in mood, are alike in containing a balance between piano and strings. His seven piano trios are somewhat like the violin sonatas in gradually reaching a true ensemble texture. Of the seven, one in B flat major (K. 502), one in E major (K. 542), and one in E flat major for clarinet, viola, and piano (K. 498) rise to greatness in variety of moods, balanced forms, and perfection of detail.

In the works of Ludwig van Beethoven (1770–1827) chamber-music composition takes a central place. His 17 string quartets constitute the backbone of the repertory. The first six take points of departure from the quartet style of Haydn's later works, but far exceed them in strength, occasional boisterousness, and variety of material. Five quartets of Beethoven's middle period represent a great increase in size, depth of expression, and formal freedom. The six last quartets include works that transcend conventional forms and textures. Development techniques and contrapuntal devices play more important roles here; forms are imaginative and fluid, movements are often thematically related, and a range of expression that uncovers new depths of the soul is here disclosed.

The back-
bone of
the
repertory

Beethoven's other chamber music, like the quartets, reveals a gradual increase in the power of the motive to generate thematic sections. This is especially true in the *Three Piano Trios*, Opus 1; the *String Trio in C Major*, Opus 9, No. 3; and the *String Quintet in C Major*, Opus 29. Particularly in the scherzo movements, which Beethoven employs in place of minuets, he generally begins with a one-measure motive, from which most of the thematic material is derived. The *Septet*, Opus 20, together with many of the violin sonatas, the cello sonatas, and a few miscellaneous works, occupy an intermediate stage in this development. Some are based on long melodies that are developed, others on short motives that are manipulated. In virtually every case, however, a masterpiece results.

Early Romantic period, c. 1825–55. Franz Schubert (1797–1828), in about 28 chamber-music works, at first modelled his compositions on those of the Classical period. His restless search for instrumental and harmonic colour soon took him beyond the bounds of Classical style and aligned him with the prophets of Romanticism. Of the eight works in which his mature mastery is so clearly revealed, all but one were composed after 1824. They include the last three string quartets, the *Trout Quintet* for piano and strings, an *Octet* for strings and winds, two piano trios, and the *String Quintet in C Major* with second cello added to the usual quartet.

Schubert's melodic flow

Less concerned with traditional formal structure than other composers of his stature, Schubert relied on unceasing melodic flow coupled with rare harmonic imagination. Typically a melodic section is repeated with changed harmonies, ranging far beyond the usual; the finale of the *Piano Trio in E Flat Major*, Opus 100, is an extreme example. But Schubert also had a keen sense of drama, as the *String Quartet No. 14 in D Minor* (*Death and the Maiden*) exhibits eloquently. Such characteristics (lyrical melody, harmonic variety, and drama) are wonderfully combined in Schubert's last large composition, the *String Quintet in C Major* with two cellos—probably the most perfect work of this composer's short life.

With Felix Mendelssohn (1809–47) a return to Classical ideals of form is seen, coupled, however, with Romantic enthusiasm. Of his about 24 chamber-music works, eight represent the composer at his best; these include five string quartets, two piano trios, and an *Octet* for eight strings. Mendelssohn's contributions include primarily a new kind of light and deft music, heard especially in his scherzos; a rich melodiousness that embraces all sections of the sonata-form movements (hence removing the element of thematic contrast on which musical conflict depends); and scrupulous attention to detail. The scherzo of the *String Quartet No. 4 in E Minor*, Opus 44, No. 2; that of the *String Octet in E Flat Major*, Opus 20; and the finale of the *String Quartet No. 3 in D Major*, Opus 44, No. 1, are among the finest representatives of Mendelssohn's enchanting style.

Robert Schumann (1810–56) represents the best aspects of early Romanticism; these include an interest in tone colour, melodiousness, a free approach to details of form, and subjective expression in which enthusiasm plays a large part. Twelve chamber-music works reflect those aspects in varying degrees. A set of pieces entitled *Märchenerzählungen* (*Fairy Tales*) for piano, clarinet, and viola illustrates the search for new tone colours; the *Piano Quintet*, in which the piano is combined with two violins, viola, and cello (possibly for the first time in the 19th century), does likewise. Three string quartets are melodious, dramatic, brusque, and dreamy in turn. In three piano trios, as in one piano quartet, Schumann's tendency to let the piano dominate the strings is sometimes seen. And in all those works his characteristic impulsiveness and tendency to alternate between forthright and moody expression is characteristic.

Late Romantic period, c. 1855–1900. In chamber music of the last half of the 19th century, only a few dozen works by composers other than Brahms survive in the repertory of the period. A piano quintet, one string quartet, and a single violin sonata by César Franck reveal that composer's fondness for cyclical form, in which successive movements are thematically linked, and for a structural scheme that is based on harmonic manipulation rather than melodic development. Bedřich Smetana (1824–84), in two string quartets and one piano trio, tended toward autobiographical expression in which Czech folk dances played a part. His first quartet, *Z mého života* (*From my Life*), is supplied with a program.

The work of Antonín Dvořák (1841–1904) represents a combination of the finest Romantic writing with a decidedly nationalistic flavour. Of about 30 works of chamber music, nine held an important place in the repertory; these include two string sextets, three quartets, two piano trios, a piano quartet, and a piano quintet. One of the string quartets, the *American*, Opus 96, purports to express Dvořák's impressions of American (including In-

dian) music. Another work, the *Piano Quintet*, Opus 81, marks a high point in the composer's use of attractive melody and rhythmic vitality; it, too, has Czech overtones. And the *Dumky Trio*, Opus 90, contains six dumky (a dumka being a Ukranian folk music form with moods alternating between melancholy and wild abandon); here the element of contrast is stressed to the utmost.

Aleksandr Borodin (1833–87), in the second of his two quartets, combined traces of Russian nationalism with expressions of pure lyricism. Peter Ilich Tchaikovsky (1840–93), with three string quartets (one of them containing the famous "Andante cantabile"), a string sextet, and a big-scale piano trio, often brought moments of orchestral sonority into his chamber music. The *Piano Trio*, Opus 50, is a virtuosic work in two movements—one a lengthy sonata form, and the other a set of brilliant variations—and is primarily elegiac in mood.

It was Johannes Brahms (1833–97), however, who dominated the period. All of Brahms's 24 chamber-music works are highly successful; in all these works Brahms's characteristic balance of emotional and intellectual expression is clearly revealed. Rich sonorities, thick textures, and rhythmic complexity are present everywhere, and the forms are those of the Classical period, somewhat modified in the light of Brahms's temperament and expressive requirements.

Pre-eminence of Brahms

Eloquent melodic writing is most characteristic of his earlier works, notably the *String Sextet No. 1 in B Flat Major*, Opus 18; the *Piano Quartet in G Minor*, Opus 25; and large portions of the *Piano Quintet*, Opus 34. Later works, by contrast, reveal Brahms's increasing concern with motivic and rhythmic development; as a consequence, lyricism plays a smaller role in such works as the two string quartets Opus 51, and the four late works with clarinet, namely the *Clarinet Trio*, Opus 114, the *Clarinet Quintet*, Opus 115, and the two sonatas Opus 120.

The 20th century. As in all times of stylistic change, considerable overlapping of styles occurred at the turn of the 20th century. In chamber music, several composers born in the 19th century carried the modified Late-Romantic style into the 20th. Among the French composers were Gabriel Fauré (1845–1924), who, with ten works, is remembered primarily for a refined and controlled style that is rhythmically subtle; and Vincent d'Indy (1851–1931), represented by about eight works, who reflected the style of César Franck. Likewise the Hungarian Ernő Dohnányi (1877–1960) revealed the strong influence of Brahms in about six works noted for their outspoken melodiousness and contrapuntal excellence. The German Max Reger (1873–1916), with about 36 works, was primarily an exponent of chromatic writing in forms that are derived essentially from the 19th century.

The first step toward the new styles of the 20th century were taken in France by Claude Debussy (1862–1918); his one string quartet (1893) and three sonatas (late works) represent the Impressionistic style based on whole-tone harmony, of which he was an exponent. Somewhat similar are the string quartet and piano trio by Maurice Ravel (1875–1937), with a rich array of tremolos, forms based on repetition of melodic fragments, and many astringent harmonies. In England, on a different path are a string quartet and piano quintet by Sir Edward Elgar (1857–1934) and two string quartets, a string quintet, and a song cycle (*On Wenlock Edge*: for tenor, string quartet, and piano) by Ralph Vaughan Williams (1872–1958). Elgar reveals an intensely personal style; Vaughan Williams uses English folk song, elusive harmonies, and strong rhythms.

The musical styles that have dominated the later 20th century are largely the work of three composers and their respective followers. The most influential was Arnold Schoenberg with his development of the "12-tone style"; but his earlier works were not yet representative of that style. A string sextet, *Verklärte Nacht* (*Transfigured Night*), transferred the form and content of the symphonic poem to the field of chamber music; two string quartets, Opus 7 and 10, are similarly post-Romantic in style, and the second includes a part for soprano voice. A set of 21 short poems for quasi-reciting voice and five instru-

Three major influences

ments, *Pierrot Lunaire*, marked an intermediate stage; and four later works, including the third string quartet, saw the full development of the 12-tone style. In a fourth quartet and a few smaller works the system was carried to completion.

In the *Lyric Suite* for string quartet (1927) Alban Berg (1885–1935), also an Austrian and one of Schoenberg's pupils, brought elements of Romantic expression into the system. And another Austrian pupil, Anton von Webern (1883–1945), sought to develop utmost refinement and consistency, along with brevity. A string quartet, a quartet for violin, clarinet, saxophone, and piano, and a chamber concerto for nine instruments are the principal works that illustrate his methods of extreme economy in the use of all materials. Webern's approach has been of maximum influence on many composers of the present day, and has led to the development of serial writing.

A completely different path was taken by the Hungarian Béla Bartók in six string quartets and a trio, *Contrasts*, for piano, violin, and clarinet. In those works the main thrust has been on harmony (including acrid dissonances that border on atonality), greatly rhythmic drive with many irregular rhythmic patterns (some of them based on eastern European folk song, in which field Bartók was an avid worker), and the development of new instrumental effects. Coupled with such technical elements are fervent expressiveness and, in the slow movements, great repose. The Bartók quartets are among the major chamber-music works of the 20th century.

The third principal influence, that of the Russian-born Igor Stravinsky (1882–1971), was felt perhaps less in chamber music than in orchestral, for Stravinsky composed fewer than a dozen works in the field. Five song cycles for voice and small groups of instruments, several short pieces for string quartet, and a pantomime, *The Soldier's Tale*, for narrator and seven instruments are varied in content and style. An *Octet* for wind instruments (1923) represents a deliberately impersonal style that requires no subjective interpretation on the part of the performers. And a *Septet* for three winds, three strings, and piano (1952) marks Stravinsky's adoption of serial writing, a style that he had consciously rejected earlier.

Other major contributions The German Paul Hindemith (1895–1963), with seven string quartets and more than two dozen sonatas and other works, favoured polyphonic textures, an expanded harmonic scheme, and great rhythmic drive. His style in later works became less dissonant, more lyric, and was characterized by a general lightening of the thick counterpoint that had distinguished his work of the 1940s. His seven works called *Kammermusik* are for larger groups and so do not come within the scope of this article. The French composer Darius Milhaud, in about 18 string quartets, four quintets for various combinations, and a number of other works, for a time espoused the principles of polytonality, the device of employing several keys simultaneously. Characterized by moods that are often pungent, humorous, and even satirical, his works reveal a mixture of dissonant counterpoint, rhythmic flexibility, and graceful expression. His 14th and 15th quartets, independent works in their own right, may be performed simultaneously to form an octet.

Two Russian composers, Sergey Prokofiev (1891–1953) and Dmitry Shostakovich, are represented in the repertory by about 20 works adhering, in the main, to the forms and textures of the 19th century. Both men embrace the new harmonic techniques without departing entirely from Romantic expressiveness. Many of their compositions reveal a sense of humour. Of British composers, Sir William Walton, Lennox Berkeley, Alan Rawsthorne, and Benjamin Britten have made significant contributions to the medium.

The chamber music by American composers has in general reflected the international styles mentioned above. One exception is seen in two quartets, a piano trio, and **American composers** several violin sonatas by Charles Ives (1874–1954), who maintained a style of great originality through his long lifetime. Another exception may be noted in the work of Ernest Bloch (1880–1959), Swiss by birth, but identified with the United States since about 1917. In five string quartets, two piano quintets, and a few smaller works, Bloch brought his Jewish heritage to expression in styles that are robust and varied.

Among the more prominent American composers, a few may be singled out for their notable contributions. Walter Piston, with four string quartets, a piano trio, a quintet for flute and strings, and a piano quintet, is perhaps the most eclectic; his works are basically neo-Classic and are distinguished by elegance and vitality. Roger Sessions, represented principally by two string quartets and a string quintet, has written in an austere, reserved, and strongly dissonant style. Quincy Porter (1897–1966) composed ten string quartets, several quintets for various combinations, and smaller works; they are characterized by warm expressiveness achieved in textures that employ considerable repetition of short motives. The works of Roy Harris are distinguished by forms that depart from 19th-century models; three string quartets and a piano quintet are among his most significant works.

Aaron Copland may be mentioned for a piano trio; a sextet for clarinet, piano, and strings; a piano quartet; and a violin sonata. Those works include variously nationalistic allusions (including Jewish and Latin American), unresolved dissonance, and elements of serial style. William Schuman in four string quartets and smaller works discloses a strongly dissonant style that remains, nevertheless, within the tonal system; his works are rhythmically vital and express great energy.

Elliott Carter, Jr., is best represented by a cello sonata and two string quartets. He employs elements of serial writing, composes in a virtually free rhythmic manner, and employs new instrumental effects in the manner of Bartók; yet his style is a completely individual expression. Leon Kirchner has composed two string quartets, a violin sonata, and a piano trio; unmetrical rhythm is a striking characteristic of his style, along with a variety of harmonies ranging from purely diatonic to atonal, and warm expressiveness is usually present.

Among composers representing the countries of Central and South America, three have risen to international prominence. Heitor Villa-Lobos (1887–1959) has long been the outstanding exponent of Brazilian national idioms, including those of the idigenous Indians. In his many chamber-music works (ten string quartets, several piano trios, and a few sonatas are representative) Villa-Lobos has given expression to those idioms. Carlos Chávez has worked similarly with the idioms of Mexican Indians, but in several of his relatively few chamber-music works, neo-Classical style elements are prominent. Alberto Ginastera, representing Argentina, has stressed the element of rhythm to a high degree in a style that is thoroughly contemporary. **Latin American composers**

AUDIENCES

For well over a century after its inception about 1600, chamber music was supported primarily by the nobility. Aristocratic establishments customarily employed groups of musicians who served as composers, conductors, and performers of a variety of operatic, orchestral, and chamber music; and traditionally the audiences were restricted to the patrons and their guests. Chamber-music concerts were instituted in London in 1672, and seem to have been exceptional for their time, for regularly established professional chamber-music groups did not emerge until about 1810, apparently first in Vienna.

Meanwhile, primarily at certain German university towns in the 1700s, the establishment of collegia musica (music societies) marked the beginning of a movement that brought nonprofessional participation in its wake. Eminent musicians directed those societies in many cases; the Collegium Musicum at Leipzig, for example, was founded by Georg Philipp Telemann and had Bach as its director for a decade after 1729. Audiences were at first restricted to university students; later the general public was admitted, and the rise of the modern chamber-music audience began.

Since the mid-19th century, chamber-music concerts have been a staple of musical life. Many of the best

Famous
quartets

known string quartets (for example, the Joachim Quartet from 1869 to 1907, the Kneisel from 1885 to 1917, the Flonzaley from 1902 to about 1928, the London from 1908 to 1935, the Budapest from 1918 to 1968, and the modern Juilliard, Paganini, Amadeus, and Fine Arts quartets) have travelled throughout the world performing standard as well as contemporary repertories.

This has been paralleled by the continuing activity of informal, nonprofessional groups in virtually all musical centres of the world. The international association, the Amateur Chamber Music Players, publishes a directory in which members grade themselves according to technical ability and experience. Many colleges and universities of the United States stress ensemble activity in their music curricula, and several schools of music are centres of activity in the field.

Music continues to be composed in large quantities, and chamber music will undoubtedly receive the attention of major composers—especially in view of the economic factors that make the performance of new orchestral works so difficult. String quartets are expected to remain the most numerous representatives of the field, largely because of the proven virtues of the medium and because relatively fewer groups that specialize in the performance of trios, quintets, and larger forms are professionally active today. Chamber music remains popular and well-supported, and it is expected to continue to have as significant a role as it has had over the last three and a half centuries.

BIBLIOGRAPHY. WALTER W. COBBETT, *Cobbett's Cyclopedic Survey of Chamber Music*, 2nd ed. by COLIN MASON, 3 vol. (1963), an invaluable and comprehensive work containing analyses and descriptions of works and topics in the field; EDWIN EVANS, *Handbook to Brahms*, vol. 2 and 3, *Chamber and Orchestral Music* (1933–35), contains detailed analyses and comparisons of all of Brahms's chamber-music works, with a general overview of his style; ERNST MEYER, *English Chamber Music* (1946, reprinted 1951), a specialized study devoted primarily to the works of Elizabethan and later 17th-century composers; DONALD FRANCIS TOVEY, *Essays in Musical Analysis: Chamber Music* (1944), a standard work that covers, in nontechnical language, large areas of the repertory; HOMER ULRICH, *Chamber Music*, 2nd ed. (1966), a historical account of the field before Haydn, with descriptive analyses and history of the repertory since 1750.

(H.U.)

Champlain, Samuel de

As the commander of a party of French pioneers in 1608, when the only other Europeans who had any acquaintance with the St. Lawrence River of North America were seasonal fur traders, Samuel de Champlain became the acknowledged founder of Quebec and, as the first governor of French Canada, is known as the "father of New France."

He was probably born a commoner in 1567 at Brouage, a French seaport. He acquired a reputation as a navigator, having taken part in an expedition to the West Indies and Central America, and received an honorary, though unofficial title at the court of Henry IV. In 1603 Champlain accepted an invitation to visit what he called the River of Canada (the modern St. Lawrence River). He sailed, as an observer in a longboat, upstream from the mother ship's anchorage at Tadoussac, a summer trading post, to the site of Montreal and its rapids. His report on the expedition was soon published in France, and in 1604 he accompanied a group of ill-fated settlers to Acadia, a region surrounding the Bay of Fundy.

Champlain spent three winters in Acadia—the first on an island in the St. Croix River, where scurvy killed nearly half the party, and the second and third, which claimed the lives of fewer men, at Annapolis Basin. During the summers he searched for an ideal site for colonization. His explorations led him down the Atlantic coast southward to Massachusetts Bay and beyond, mapping in detail the harbours that his English rivals had only touched. In 1607 the English came to Kennebec (now in Maine) in southern Acadia. They spent only one winter there, but the threat of conflict increased French interest in colonization.

First visit
to Canada

Heading an expedition that left France in 1608, Champlain undertook his most ambitious project: the founding of Quebec. On his earlier expeditions to the St. Lawrence he had been a subordinate, but this time he was the leader of 32 colonists.

Champlain and eight others survived the first winter at Quebec and greeted more colonists in June. Allied by an earlier French treaty with the northern Indian tribes, he joined them in defeating Iroquois marauders in a skirmish on Lake Champlain. That and a similar victory in 1610 enhanced French prestige among the allied tribes, and fur trade between France and the Indians increased. In 1610 he left for France, where he married Hélène Boullé, the 12-year-old daughter of the secretary to the King's chamber.

The fur trade had heavy financial losses in 1611, which prompted Quebec's sponsors to abandon the colony, but Champlain persuaded Louis XIII to intervene. Eventually the King appointed a viceroy, who made Champlain commandant of New France. In 1613 he reestablished his authority at Quebec and immediately embarked for the Ottawa River on a mission to restore the ruined fur trade. The following year he organized a company of French merchants to finance trade, religious missions, and his own exploration.

Commandant of
New
France

Champlain next went to Lake Huron, where native chiefs persuaded him to lead a war party against a fortified village that was located south of Lake Ontario. The Iroquois defenders wounded him and repulsed his Huron–Algonkin warriors, a somewhat disorganized but loyal force who carried him to safety. After spending a winter in their territory, he returned to France, where political manoeuvres were endangering the colony's future. In 1620 the King reaffirmed Champlain's authority over Quebec, but forbade his engaging in personal exploration, directing him instead to employ his talents in administrative tasks.

The colony, still dependent on the fur trade and only experimenting in agriculture, hardly prospered under his care or under the patronage of a new and strong company. English privateers, however, considered Quebec worth besieging in 1628, when England and France were at war. Champlain manned the walls until the following summer, when his garrison exhausted its food and gunpowder. Although he surrendered the fort, he did not abandon the colony. He was taken to England as a prisoner, where he argued that the surrender had occurred after the end of French and English hostilities. In 1632 the colony was returned to France, and in 1633, a year after publishing his seventh book, he made his final voyage across the Atlantic to Quebec.

Only a few more settlers were aboard when his ships dropped anchor at Quebec, but others continued to arrive each year; before he died of a stroke on December 25, 1635, his colony extended along both shores of the St. Lawrence River.

BIBLIOGRAPHY. *Champlain: The Life of Fortitude*, by MORRIS BISHOP (1948), is a full appraisal of Champlain's character and achievements; while *The First Canadian: The Story of Champlain*, by C.T. RITCHIE (1962), is a narrative presentation for younger students. A scholarly treatment by MARCEL TRUDEL appears in the *Dictionary of Canadian Biography*, 1:186–199 (1966). Champlain's own *Works*, 6 vol. (1922–36), translated and published by the Champlain Society, is the chief reference of the biographers.

(C.T.R.)

Ch'ang-an

Ch'ang-an, the historic name of the modern city of Sian (Pinyin romanization Xian) in southern Shensi Province, China, was important in Chinese history as the capital of several ruling dynasties and as a market and trade centre. Although cities have existed in the area since the 11th century BC, the name Ch'ang-an-ch'eng (Walled City of Ch'ang-an) was first used for the Han capital, which was built in 202 BC about seven miles (11 kilometres) northwest of the modern city. The popular name Sian (Western Peace) has been official since the Ming dynasty (1368–1644).

The city, the capital of modern Shensi Province, and a subprovincial-level municipality (*shih*), is located on the loess plain of the Wei Ho (Wei River), bounded on the north, south, and east by mountains. Passes give easy access to the Han and Lower Huang (Yellow) river valleys, to Szechwan and Yunnan provinces and, through Kansu Province, to Central Asia. In 1982 Sian had a population of about 1,500,000.

History. After defeating the Shang King in 1121 or 1027 BC, King Wu Wang of Chou built his capital, Hao Ching (later called Fenghao, site southwest of modern Sian), which flourished until the end of the Western Chou period in 771 BC, when the capital was moved to Lo-yang. Upon the Ch'in unification in 232 BC, Shih Huang Ti ruled at Hsien-yang, approximately 12 miles west of modern Sian. The Former Han dynasty capital of Ch'ang-an-ch'eng, with its population of 250,000 and its more than 50 temples and five palaces within a walled perimeter about six miles square, was one of the greatest cities to be found in the ancient world. It suffered during disturbances preceding Wang Mang's interregnum (AD 9–23), and the Wei Yang Palace was sacked and burned. The Later Han dynasty, established in AD 23, moved to Lo-yang.

For several centuries Ch'ang-an declined, despite its strategic importance to the northwestern barbarian principalities and its adoption as capital by the Western Wei and Northern Chou states in the 6th century. The Sui emperors (581–618) revived it, c. 600, building their new capital on a rectangular plan, about 5.8 by 5.4 miles, around a centre that coincides with modern Sian.

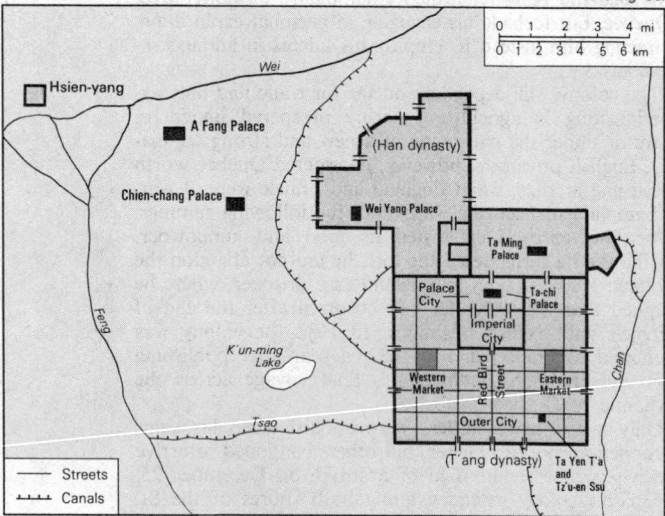

Palace City, Imperial City, and Outer City from Li D.J., *The Ageless Chinese:* Charles Scribner's Sons; remainder from A. Herrmann, *An Historical Atlas of China:* Aldine Publishing Co.

Plan of the city of Ch'ang-an and the surrounding area under the Han and T'ang dynasties.

The T'ang capital

As the T'ang capital, it was expanded and divided into three parts—the Palace City (Kung-ch'eng); the Imperial City (Huang-ch'eng), for the officials; and the Outer City (Wai-kuo-ch'eng; alternatively Ch'ang-an-ch'eng or Ching-shih-ch'eng, both often used for the whole city), for artisans and merchants. The Outer City, consisting of 110 sections, was divided by the Red Bird (Southern) Street into an eastern and a western administrative area, each of which had its own market. The markets and central crossroads were strictly supervised, prices were controlled, and trades occupied separate streets. The population was estimated at 1,000,000, and the splendour and extravagance of Ch'ang-an became a byword in Chinese literature. The city's pleasure quarter, where successful examination candidates had special passes for privileged entry, the foreign diplomats and staffs of more than 4,000, the exotic life, and the great variety of merchandise from throughout Asia all made for a liberal and stimulating urban life. Peony fancying was the rage, and there was much revelry in the city when the blossoms opened in March.

In 904 the city was laid waste when Chu Ch'üan-chung, the founder of the Later Liang dynasty, dismantled buildings in Ch'ang-an and moved the timbers to Lo-yang. Han Chien restored the Imperial City shortly afterward, renaming it Feng-yüan-ch'eng. Early in the Ming period the wall was restored (to a circumference of about 8.5 miles), and a bell tower and corner towers were constructed. In 1644 the first Ch'ing emperor built walls from the central bell tower to the northern and eastern gates to create the Man-chou-ch'eng, a quarter for his Manchu garrison.

Despite vicissitudes, Ch'ang-an's prosperity as a market centre and broker of the Central Asian trade was never seriously affected in the post-T'ang period. In the 13th century Marco Polo described the city, then ruled by Kublai Khan's son Mangalai, as a centre of trade and industry—most notably in silk, gold cloth, and military equipment—and in control of 12 other cities. Marco claimed that the Polos helped the Great Khan reduce Ch'ang-an, after a three-year siege, by supplying him with stone-hurling mangonels; Chinese sources date the event to 1273, when the Polos were still en route to China. Thereafter the city figured little in political history.

Identified historical sites include Lan-t'ien, where Liu Pang, founder of the Former Han dynasty, defeated the Ch'in army (207 BC); the Ch'ing-hua Palace, scene of the dalliance of the T'ang emperor Hsüan Tsung (ruled 712–756) with Yang Kuei-fei; the A Fang Palace of Ch'in; the Wei Yang Palace of Han; and in the T'ang city the ruins of the Ta-chi Palace and the tower of the Tz'u-en Temple. Excavations have revealed a gateway and other remains of the Ta Ming Palace, as well as a gateway and the foundations of a ceremonial building in the Han city. In 1974 archaeologists excavated part of the tomb of Shih Huang Ti about 20 miles northeast of the city. The site contains an army of about 8,000 life-size terra-cotta figures arrayed in battle formation.

Sian. The dowager empress Tz'u-hsi retired to Sian with the boy emperor Te Tsung when the Allies' troops occupied Peking during the Boxer Rebellion (1900). From the 1920s the city was the chief port of entry for Communist ideology reaching China from the Soviet Union. On December 12, 1936, the "Sian incident" occurred. Generalissimo Chiang Kai-shek came to correct the mutinous and anti-Japanese attitude of troops, led by Chang Hsüeh-liang, on whom he was relying for a final campaign against the Communists. Instead, Chang, in league with the Communists, arrested Chiang Kai-shek and his staff. The Generalissimo's subsequent release, at the instance of the Communist leader Chou En-lai, marked the beginning of united resistance against the Japanese and heralded the eventual end of the British, French, and Dutch empires in Southeast Asia.

Following the establishment of the People's Republic of China in 1949, the population of Sian city grew from 503,000 (1949–50) to 787,300 (1953–57); the population of the metropolitan area in the mid-1970s was approximately 2,500,000.

In the redeployment of industry from the vulnerable coastal zone, Sian, together with Lan-chou in Kansu Province, became the chief industrial base in northwestern China. A large electric generating station, using coal from T'ung-ch'uan to the north, was established there, and Sian was later linked to the main electric power grid in Honan Province. The city also became the centre of the manufacture of electrical and electronic equipment and of instruments. It also had a traditional cotton-textile industry and late in the 1950s became the site for one of the largest cotton mills in China. Modern industries also include a steelworks, an electrical machinery plant, and a chemical industry that produces fertilizers and plastics. As the centre of an important agricultural region, Sian is engaged in crop processing, most notably the processing of cotton, wheat, and tea.

Communications have been greatly improved. The Lunghai Railway, joining Sian to central Honan and the coast, reached the city in 1935; it was later extended to Lan-chou in the west, joining the new trunk railway into Sinkiang Uighur Autonomous Region, and rail links were

Historical sites

Under Communist rule

also built to Hsi-ning in Tsinghai Province. In 1958 a line was completed from Pao-chi to the west of Sian across the Tsinling Shan to Szechwan Province.

The city's wide streets have been paved, and many low-rise, Peking-style buildings have been built. At the centre of the old city there are modern high-rise hotels and a telecommunications centre. The Shensi Provincial Museum, housed in a former Confucian temple, is noted for its Pei-lin, an important collection of inscribed stelae and Buddhist sculpture. Sites of interest include the Hsiao-yen t'a (Little Wild Goose Pagoda), Ta-yen t'a (Big Wild Goose Pagoda; 148 feet [45 metres] high), and Ta-tz'u-en ssu (Temple of Great Good Will), constructed during the T'ang dynasty; the Bell Tower and Drum Tower built during the Ming dynasty; the Great Mosque, founded in 742 with the existing buildings dating from the 14th century; and three well-preserved 14th-century city gates. Sian is the seat of Jiaotong University, one of China's largest polytechnic institutions, Northwest Technical University, and numerous other colleges and research institutes.

BIBLIOGRAPHY. There are passing references in such standard works as C.P. FITZGERALD, *China: A Short Cultural History*, 3rd ed. (1961); and W. EBERHARD, *Chinas Geschichte* (1948; Eng. trans., *A History of China*, 1950). R.E. LATHAM, *The Travels of Marco Polo* (1958), is a modern translation of this work, in which the earliest Western references to Ch'ang-an occur; H. MCALVEAVY, *The Modern History of China* (1967), puts the Sian incident well into perspective; contemporary aspects of the city must be gleaned from such works as E. STUART KIRBY (ed.), *Contemporary China, 1962–64*, 6 vol. (1968); and J. WILSON LEWIS, *The City in Communist China* (1971).

(W.W./Ed.)

Chang Chih-tung

Chang Chih-tung (Pinyin romanization Zhang Zhi-dong), Chinese classicist and provincial official of the late Ch'ing period, was one of the foremost reformers of his time. He promoted education, established modern industries, advocated railway construction, and trained Western-style armies.

Chang was born in Hsing-i, Kweichow Province, on September 2, 1837, to a family of scholar-officials, but, in

The Bettmann Archive

Chang Chih-tung, engraving by an unknown artist.

accordance with Chinese custom, he was considered a native of Nan-p'i, Chihli (modern Hopeh) Province, where his ancestors had settled in the 15th century. He was unusually precocious as a student, passing his first-level civil service examinations at the age of 13 and all of the examinations by the time he was 26. His literary talent and the fame he won from it were the foundations on which his career rested.

Chang's career

Chang's experience as an official fell into two broad phases: from 1862 to 1882 he was a scholar and educational director, and from 1882 to 1907 he rose steadily from a provincial to a national leader. Politically he was a supporter of the dowager empress Tz'u-hsi, who in turn favoured him with many promotions. Appointed provincial governor of Shansi in 1882, he became governor general of Kwangtung and Kwangsi in 1884. He was transferred to Hunan and Hupeh in 1889 and remained in that post for 18 years, including three spent on missions to Nanking and Peking. In 1907 he was summoned to the court to become a grand secretary and grand councillor.

Apart from being a capable and benevolent administrator, Chang was deeply concerned with the rejuvenation of China. His life spanned nearly the entire period from the Opium War to the revolution of 1911, an era of unprecedented pressures on China from the West and from Japan. The most pressing problem that Chang and other officials faced was how China might survive and adapt itself to the modern world. In the search for a solution, Chang retained his faith in the traditional Chinese system, but he urged the acquisition of Western knowledge. As his conception of the latter changed, so did the stress of his programs, but his faith in tradition never wavered.

It was for defense reasons that he launched the first iron- and steelworks in China. In his ignorance of metallurgical intricacies, Chang ordered a complete smelting plant from England, without knowing what ore would be available. He also failed to locate the plant near a coal-mining area. Consequently, the works incurred severe losses after production began in 1894. The debacle exposed Chang to ridicule and placed him in political jeopardy.

Chang's transfer to Hunan and Hupeh was occasioned by his proposal to build a railway from Hankow to a point near Peking. The court, in giving its assent, also appointed Chang in charge of the construction. After a long delay the line was completed in 1906. Meanwhile, Chang had set about industrializing the territory under his jurisdiction. Among the industries he founded were a mint, tanneries, tile and silk factories, and paper, cotton, and woollen mills. While on temporary duty in Nanking, he trained a new army with the assistance of German instructors.

In 1895 China fought against Japan and lost, thus demonstrating the ineffectiveness of its previous reforms. This setback turned Chang's attention to education and China's need for better trained bureaucrats. In 1898 he published *Ch'üan-hsüeh p'ien* ("Exhortation to Learning"), in which he both reaffirmed his faith in Confucianism and detailed the measures needed for the acquisition of Western knowledge: study abroad by Chinese students, establishment of a school system, translation of Western and Japanese books, and acquisition of knowledge from foreign newspapers. Accordingly, schools, newspapers, and translation bureaus were established in Hupeh, and students were sent abroad to study; in 1908 the province supported 475 students in Japan and 103 in Western countries.

Contributions to educational reform

At the national level Chang was charged, in 1904, with the task of drafting regulations for the entire school system. The regulations, submitted and approved six months later, consisted of eight volumes that dealt with all aspects of education. These included basic principles, administration, curricula, study abroad, vocational training, and structures of kindergartens and research academies. In order to channel all talent into the school system, Chang repeatedly urged the abolition of the civil service examinations, which was done in 1905. Largely through Chang's persistent efforts, the number of schools and students in China increased 73 and 225 times, respectively, between 1904 and 1909.

A striking feature of Chang's career was his immunity to major political setbacks. The severest test of his political sagacity probably occurred during the Boxer Rebellion in 1900. He was faced, as a loyal official, with the prospect of disobeying the imperial edict declaring war on foreign nations. After consultation with other governors, Chang decided that this decree should not be obeyed because it did not represent the true intention of the throne. Accordingly, Chang and other officials maintained peace in their territories by concluding an agreement with the foreign consuls. As the Boxers collapsed, this action was endorsed and praised by the Empress Dowager.

Chang was married three times, but all his wives died early. He had six sons and four daughters. Chang died on October 4, 1909. In spite of his long tenure of office, he amassed no personal fortune and was not even well-to-do—he pawned his belongings once, when he was a governor general. He was canonized as Wen-hsiang ("Learned and Accomplished"), a coveted posthumous title.

BIBLIOGRAPHY. While many aspects of Chang's life and career remain to be studied, a recent, well-researched book is WILLIAM AYERS, *Chang Chih-tung and Educational Reform in China* (1971). Older are "The Public Career of Chang Chih-tung, 1837–1900," *Pacific Historical Review*, 7:187–210 (1938) and the article on Chang in ARTHUR HUMMEL (ed.), *Eminent Chinese of the Ching Period*, vol. 1, pp. 27–32 (1943), both by MERIBETH E. CAMERON. For a review of Chang's educational efforts, see Y.C. WANG, *Chinese Intellectuals and the West, 1872–1949* (1966).

(Y.C.W.)

Chaplin, Charlie

The English comedian Sir Charles Spencer Chaplin won international fame with his portrayal of a pathetic yet humorous little tramp in American-made silent films. Within two years of his first appearance in motion pictures, in 1914, he had become one of the best known personalities in the nation. By the early 1920s, his box-office appeal was so great that no studio could afford his talents, and he appeared only in films produced by himself. Though he appeared in few films after the advent of sound at the end of the 1920s, his fame scarcely diminished as his early works became recognized as motion-picture classics and found appreciative new audiences.

Brown Brothers

Chaplin as "the Tramp."

Born in London on April 16, 1889, the son of Charles and Hannah Chaplin, music-hall performers who early taught the child to sing and dance, he first appeared on stage at age eight in a clog-dancing act, "Eight Lancashire Lads." Because his father died soon after, and his mother was often in and out of mental institutions, Chaplin's early life was a dreary succession of boarding schools and orphanages, interspersed with occasional stage engagements and periods when he lived in the streets.

When Chaplin was 17 his older half-brother, Sydney, then working for the Fred Karno Company (an English vaudeville organization with a repertory of varied dances, acts, and comedy routines) found a place for him in the troupe. He remained with Karno, performing in numerous music-hall skits, until 1913, when he was signed for the movies by the Keystone Company: Mack Sennett, producer of Keystone's slapstick one-reelers, had noticed Chaplin in New York during a Karno tour. Chaplin's film career began in December 1913 at $150 a week. He never returned to the stage.

Chaplin hit upon his famous costume—derby hat, tight frock coat, baggy trousers, out-sized shoes, moustache, and cane—while making his second picture, *Kid Auto Races at Venice* (1914), though the full pathos and significance of the tramp character had not yet been realized. His comedies were, however, sensationally successful from the start, even though they were made at a rate of two a week. Soon he was allowed to direct all his films, and his salaries soared astronomically: $1,250 a week from Essanay (1915); $10,000 a week, plus a $150,000 bonus for signing, from Mutual (1916); $1,000,000 for eight pictures from First National (1917). Two years later Chaplin—together with two other of the foremost stars of the day, Mary Pickford and Douglas Fairbanks, and the director D.W. Griffith—formed United Artists so that each could produce and distribute his own films independently. After his First National contract ended with *The Pilgrim* (1923), Chaplin produced only for his own company until making *A Countess from Hong Kong* for Universal in 1966.

The tramp character

Chaplin's meteoric rise was due in part to the emergence of the star system—the selling of films on the basis of featured performers rather than titles or plots; indeed, the public's eager reception of the Chaplin screen personality, along with those of Pickford, Fairbanks, and others, did much to establish the system. In *The Tramp* (1915) Chaplin first inserted the note of pathos that was to make his little tramp not only amusing but endearing. As star, director, and writer of his own pictures, he was in a unique position to explore the implications of the character, described by one critic as "the destitute person shown in the perspective of the wealthy." This "little fellow," as Chaplin called him, was developed through such films as *Easy Street* (1917), *Shoulder Arms* (1918), *The Kid* (1921), *The Gold Rush* (1925), *City Lights* (1931), *Modern Times* (1936), and *The Great Dictator* (1940), the latter his first talking picture. It re-emerged, albeit briefly, in the autobiographical *Limelight* (1952).

Chaplin's personal life was often stormy. He was married four times—to three of his leading ladies, Mildred Harris (1918), Lita Grey (1924), and Paulette Goddard (1936), and, in 1943, to Oona O'Neill, daughter of the playwright Eugene O'Neill—and his first two divorces produced sensational headlines, as did a paternity suit in 1944. There were headlines also when, in 1942, Chaplin called for a second front in the war against Germany; his political stance was attacked, in part, on grounds that he had never become a U.S. citizen. His film *Monsieur Verdoux* (1947), a mordant version of the Bluebeard story, angered the American Legion, among others. Pressed by the United States government for back taxes and linked by politicians and newspaper columnists with allegedly subversive causes, Chaplin left the country in 1952. Informed that his re-entry rights would be questioned by the U.S. Department of Justice, he surrendered his re-entry permit at Geneva, Switzerland, in 1953. Thereafter, Chaplin, his wife, and their six children lived at Corsier-sur-Vevey, near Vevey. In 1957 he produced in London *The King in New York*, a comedy laden with sermons against the House Committee on Un-American Activities, inane television commercials, and other aspects of American life. The film brought fresh accusations of pro-Communism, which Chaplin specifically denied. In 1966 he wrote, directed, and appeared briefly in *A Countess from Hong Kong*, starring Marlon Brando and Sophia Loren. In 1972 he returned to the United States to receive a special award from the Academy of Motion Picture Arts and Sciences. He was knighted by Queen Elizabeth II in 1975 and died on December 25, 1977, at Corsier.

Marriages

MAJOR WORKS

Making a Living; Kid Auto Races at Venice; Mabel's Strange Predicament; Between Showers; A Film Johnnie; Tango Tan-

gles; His Favorite Pastime; Cruel, Cruel Love; The Star Boarder; Mabel at the Wheel; Twenty Minutes of Love; Caught in a Cabaret; Caught in the Rain; A Busy Day; The Fatal Mallet; The Knockout; Mabel's Busy Day; Mabel's Married Life; Laughing Gas; The Property Man; The Face on the Bar-room Floor; Recreation; The Masquerader; His New Profession; The Rounders; The New Janitor; Those Love Pangs; Dough and Dynamite; Gentleman of Nerve; His Musical Career; His Trysting Place; Tillie's Punctured Romance; Getting Acquainted; His Prehistoric Past (all 1914); *His New Job; A Night Out; The Champion; In the Park; The Jitney Elopement; The Tramp; By the Sea; Work; A Woman; The Bank; Shanghaied; A Night in the Show* (all 1915); *Carmen; Police; The Floorwalker; The Fireman; The Vagabond; One A.M.; The Count; The Pawnshop; Behind the Screen; The Rink* (all 1916); *Easy Street; The Cure; The Immigrant; The Adventurer* (all 1917); *Triple Trouble; A Dog's Life; The Bond; Shoulder Arms* (all 1918); *Sunnyside* and *A Day's Pleasure* (both 1919); *The Kid* and *The Idle Class* (both 1921); *Pay Day* (1922); *The Pilgrim* and *A Woman of Paris* (both 1923); *The Gold Rush* (1925); *The Circus* (1928); *City Lights* (1931); *Modern Times* (1936); *The Great Dictator* (1940); *Monsieur Verdoux* (1947); *Limelight* (1952); *A King in New York* (1957); *A Countess from Hong Kong* (1966).

BIBLIOGRAPHY. CHARLES CHAPLIN, *My Autobiography* (1964), is surprisingly less revealing of Chaplin the artist, or even of his films and methods of work, than as an insight into the self-made man who also happens to be one of the few creative geniuses of the motion picture medium. CHARLES CHAPLIN, JR., with N. and M. RAU, *My Father, Charlie Chaplin* (1960), a far more personal view than Chaplin is able to give of himself, admirably supplements the autobiography. THEODORE HUFF, *Charlie Chaplin* (1951), is a scrupulously researched, basic study of Chaplin, with emphasis on the films themselves; all of Chaplin's major films are painstakingly and noncritically described, and supplemented by detailed casts and credits. ROBERT PAYNE, *The Great God Pan* (1952), is an eminently readable, sympathetic critical study that focusses less upon Chaplin himself than on the films he made, and that more especially treats in depth the lovable tramp character that Chaplin created and the meanings—mythic, poetic, and sociological—that may be traced through that character.

(A.Kn.)

Charadriiformes

The order Charadriiformes comprises the shorebirds, gulls, auks, and their relatives. These birds form an important and familiar segment of the avifauna of the world's coasts and inland waterways, of the Arctic regions, and of the oceans and their islands. They are mostly strong-flying birds of open country or open water, nesting on the ground and feeding on animal food in or near water. The order is worldwide in distribution, and some species perform the most extensive migrations of any birds.

GENERAL FEATURES

The order is a heterogeneous assemblage of 16 families, linked by similarities in anatomical features (especially skeleton and plumage), and developmental pattern. Better known members of the order fall into three groups, easily recognized on the basis of general body plan. The first of these (the suborder Charadrii), collectively known as shorebirds or waders (Figure 1), includes sandpipers, plovers, lapwings, and a number of less familiar forms. They are primarily birds of shorelines and other open areas, and they walk or wade while feeding. There are about 200 species, varying in size from the least sandpiper, a sparrow-sized bird of about 20 grams (slightly under an ounce), to large curlews of about 640 grams (1½ pounds, near the body size of a small chicken). A second group, the suborder Lari, contains 92 species of gulls, terns, skimmers, skuas, and jaegers. They are long-winged, web-footed birds, the smallest of which is the least tern (*Sterna albifrons*), weighing about 43 grams (1.5 ounces), with a wingspread of about 50 centimetres (20 inches). The largest, the great black-backed gull (*Larus marinus*), weighs about 1,900 grams (a little over four pounds) and has a spread of about 165 centimetres (65 inches). The third and smallest suborder, Alcae, contains 21 species of auks, murres, guillemots, and puffins,

all in a single family, Alcidae. They are compact, streamlined, marine birds with short, narrow wings and webbed feet. Alcids are adapted for swimming on the ocean surface and underwater.

Most charadriiforms have plumage patterns in white, grays, browns, and black, and many have bright red or yellow feet, bills, wattles, eyes, or mouth linings. A few species have both dark and light plumage phases.

Each of the larger families (Laridae, Charadriidae, Scolopacidae) is practically worldwide in distribution, although none of the Scolopacidae breeds in Australia. The skuas and jaegers (Stercorariidae) are found in high latitudes of both hemispheres and are wide-ranging through the world's oceans. Auks and their allies (Alcidae) are widespread in the oceans, islands, and seacoasts of the Northern Hemisphere. They are not related to their similar counterparts of the Southern Hemisphere, the diving petrels and penguins. The oystercatchers (Haematopodidae) are found on coasts of all continents except Antarctica and occur inland in Europe and Asia. A group of families occurs in tropical (or tropical and temperate) regions of the Eastern and Western hemispheres: jacanas (Jacanidae), painted snipes (Rostratulidae), avocets and stilts (Recurvirostridae), thickknees (Burhinidae), and skimmers (Rynchopidae). The coursers and pratincoles (Glareolidae) occur throughout tropical and temperate regions of the Old World, and the crab plovers (Dromadidae) are limited to shores of the Indian Ocean. Seedsnipe (Thinocoridae) are found in southern South America, and northward in the Andes; sheathbills (Chionididae) occur on islands of the southern Atlantic and western Indian oceans and on the southern coast of South America and adjacent Antarctica. Phalaropes (Phalaropodidae) breed in northern regions, and two species winter at sea.

Importance to man. The eggs of murres, puffins, gulls, terns, and lapwings have long been harvested for food. These birds are particularly suitable for such use because many nest in enormous colonies, and because they replace the clutch if the first is taken soon after laying. Several hundred thousand eggs, and sometimes over a million, may be taken from a locality in a single year. Certain colonies, especially those of gulls and terns, have been raided without regard to the future of the colonies, but carefully controlled egging has long been conducted in the Faeroe Islands, Iceland, Greenland, and other northern regions. Adult puffins and other alcids are also harvested with long-handled nets on the Faeroes and in Iceland.

Extravagant exploitation of the great auk for food on its North Atlantic nesting islands by sailors, and later slaughter for the feather trade, probably caused its extinction in the 1840s. Other charadriiform birds, especially terns and gulls, assumed a sudden economic value for decorating women's hats in the latter half of the 19th century, and raiding of breeding colonies in North America almost extirpated several species. Aroused public opinion, hastened by the activities of the newly formed Audubon societies, brought protection to gulls, terns, and other species.

Charadriiform birds have had economic impact in various other ways. California gulls saved the pioneers' crops in Utah during a plague of locusts, and today gulls habitually follow the farmer's plow, consuming exposed grubs and mice. Flocks of noddy terns and other birds serve to guide Hawaiian fishermen to schools of tuna, and the numbers, kinds, and behaviour of the birds may also indicate the size of the fish and the size and depth of the school. Certain shorebirds were once extensively killed for food or sport (causing near extinction of the Eskimo curlew); today woodcock and snipe are hunted under regulation.

Gulls and shorebirds are occasional hazards at airports, where airplanes have been damaged by collisions.

The order as a whole has been the subject of much scientific investigation, leading to important studies on speciation, ecology, ethology, migration, anatomy, and physiology.

Distribution

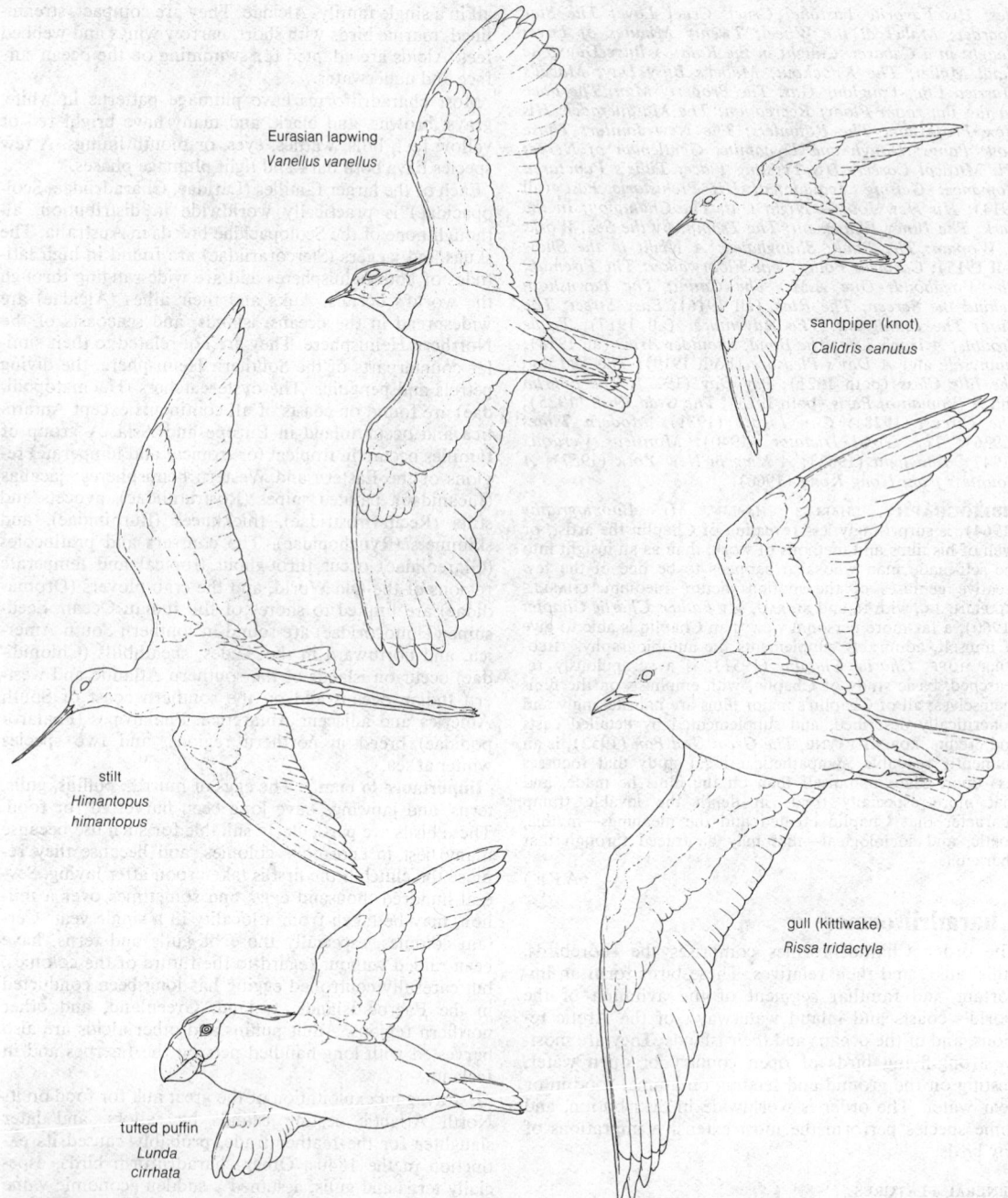

Eurasian lapwing
Vanellus vanellus

sandpiper (knot)
Calidris canutus

stilt
*Himantopus
himantopus*

gull (kittiwake)
Rissa tridactyla

tufted puffin
*Lunda
cirrhata*

Figure 1: Body plans of typical members of major charadriiform groups.
Drawing by G. Tudor

NATURAL HISTORY

Locomotion and feeding behaviour. Most shorebirds inhabit open areas and are strong fliers, some performing extensive migrations that cover long distances over water. A ruddy turnstone (*Arenaria interpres*) banded in the Pribilof Islands was recaptured in the Hawaiian Leeward Islands, 3,770 kilometres (2,325 miles) away, four days later. Gulls, terns, skimmers, skuas, and jaegers spend much of their time on the wing, both in migration and in moving within the breeding or wintering grounds. Immature sooty terns (*Sterna fuscata*) spend several years flying at sea before first coming to land to breed, and Arctic terns (*Sterna paradisaea*) fly each year to and from Antarctic waters after breeding in the Arctic. Gulls are given to soaring and gliding more than the others and are the only members of the suborder Lari that spend considerable time swimming or resting on water. Of the three major charadriiform groups, the alcids spend the least time on the wing, but they are strong, fast fliers for short distances. Outside the breeding season they are pelagic (*i.e.*, living on the open ocean).

The feeding habits of the charadriiforms are as varied as their external appearance. Jacanas inhabit pools and lakes thick with water lilies and other aquatic vegetation. They run agilely on lily pads with prancing steps, supported by their remarkably long toes and claws. While foraging, they turn over lily pads in search of snails, arthropods, and other small animals.

Plovers (Charadriidae) and the crab plover (Dromadidae) usually forage on open ground, relying on sight to locate the invertebrates on which they feed. The foraging bird runs a few steps, pauses with head cocked, then pecks at possible prey or runs again. Most plovers feed during the day, but the crab plover feeds mostly at twilight. Oystercatchers (Haematopodidae) feed largely on mussels, oysters, and marine worms. Depending on the type of mussel bed being exploited, the bird either tears loose a mussel and hammers a hole in the shell or, finding the mussel in water with its shell open, drives the knifelike beak into the open shell, cutting the adductor muscle and preventing the shellfish from closing.

Sandpipers and their relatives (Scolopacidae) use their

Food
habits of
shorebirds

slender bills as forceps to pick up surface invertebrates or (especially in the calidridine sandpipers) for probing in mud. Curlews use their long, down-curved bills for probing crustacean burrows on beaches and worm burrows on mudflats, and for picking up insects and berries on tundra or grassland. Woodcock (*Philohela* and *Scolopax*) also probe, but in woodland soils and leaf litter, feeding extensively on earthworms. Turnstones (*Arenaria*) habitually flip over vegetation, debris, soil, and stones with the straight upper edge of the bill, eating the animal life thus exposed.

Avocets and stilts (Recurvirostridae) feed in shallow water by sweeping the opened bill from side to side over the bottom (avocets) or near the surface (stilts). Stilts also feed by pecking and probing. The ibisbill (*Ibidorhyncha*), a recurvirostrid with a down-curved bill, inhabits Himalayan lakes and rivers and feeds by reaching under rocks in water for insects, mollusks, crustaceans, and worms, sometimes while wading belly-deep. Phalaropes (Phalaropodidae) habitually feed while swimming, and sometimes stir up prey by spinning around.

Coursers and pratincoles (Glareolidae) are insectivorous birds of open country. Coursers feed most actively at night, taking termites, black ants, and other terrestrial arthropods by short dashes. Pratincoles hawk insects on the wing in the manner of swallows.

Sheathbills (Chionididae) inhabit Antarctic regions, where overdependence on one type of food may be disastrous. They subsist on algae; limpets and other mollusks; crustaceans; fish; the eggs and nestlings of penguins, cormorants and other birds; afterbirth and droppings of seals; and human refuse.

The food habits of seedsnipe (Thinocoridae) are unique within the order. These chunky, terrestrial birds eat primarily vegetable matter, such as seeds, buds, shoots, and leaves, for which their short, stout bills are well suited.

Food habits of gulls and relatives The gulls and their relatives (suborder Lari) are more dependent on flight for obtaining their food than are the shorebirds. The strongest fliers are the skuas and jaegers (Stercorariidae), which are gull-like in general proportions but with hooked bills. Stercorariids harass terns, gulls, boobies, and other seabirds until the latter drop or regurgitate food, which is retrieved by the "pirates." On their Arctic or Antarctic breeding grounds these birds prey on insects, rodents, small birds, and the eggs and young of other seabirds.

The diet of gulls (Laridae) is highly varied, including fish, small birds, and rodents, and a wide range of invertebrates, taken by active predation, as well as carrion of all sorts, garbage, and some vegetable material. Many of the larger gulls are not beyond piracy, stealing food from other birds (including members of their own species), and some prey heavily on the eggs and young of other seabirds. Sometimes they hawk insects or break open shellfish by dropping them from a height.

Most terns are smaller than gulls. All have straight, sharp bills and feed chiefly on the wing, by hovering over the water and plunging in for surface fish and crustaceans, by swooping low to pick fish from the water in flight, or by hawking insects over land.

Skimmers (Rynchopidae) feed by day or night. The bird flies over the surface of calm water at speeds up to 30 miles per hour with the long, knifelike lower mandible cutting the water. When the mandible strikes a fish or shrimp, the head doubles under the body and the bill clamps shut. The bird flies upward and swallows the fish in the air or carries it to the nest.

Food habits of alcids Alcids (family Alcidae) are the only charadriiforms adapted for swimming underwater, which they do by propelling themselves with half-open wings. The larger alcids (puffins, murres, auks, and guillemots) feed on small fish and invertebrates, the smaller ones (murrelets and auklets) almost entirely on invertebrates, especially on tiny, free-swimming (planktonic) crustaceans, such as euphausids.

Reproduction. The modes of reproduction in the charadriiforms are only slightly less diverse than the food habits. Nearly all members of the order are ground nesting, laying few eggs (two to four in most families; up to six in jacanas) often with little or no nesting material. Usually the eggs are protectively coloured. Some species nest in crevices or burrows, a few in trees. Many charadriiforms are colonial, with aggregations running to over a million pairs. Sex reversal, in which the female is more brightly coloured than the male and takes a dominant role in courtship, and in which the male incubates the eggs and rears the young, is found in most jacanas, painted snipe, and phalaropes.

Female jacanas are larger and more aggressive than males; after laying, females of some species show no interest in the nest or young, leaving incubation and care of chicks to the male. The nest is a shallow, sodden pile of vegetation that floats among aquatic plants. Chicks are downy and run well when a day old. Both chicks and adults may dive to escape danger and remain submerged (probably clinging to vegetation) with only the bill exposed. Adults have been known to take chicks up to 12 days old under their wings and carry them to a safer location. Jacanas perform injury-feigning displays and other striking displays, sometimes with their broad wings stretched aloft, and they attack other species near the nest.

The female of the Old World painted snipe (*Rostratula benghalensis*) is larger and more brightly coloured than the male, whereas the South American species (*Nycticryphes semicollaris*) shows little sexual dimorphism, although females are slightly larger. As in some jacanas, the female of *Rostratula* is more aggressive in courtship, displaying with spread wing and tail, and she leaves incubation and care of the chicks to the male. The nest is a shallow platform of bent reeds in which the four eggs (two in *Nycticryphes*) are incubated for about 19 days. The downy young take to the water readily.

Phalaropes nest in open tundra, marsh, or sedges near water. Females take the lead role in courtship and aggression, and several may vie for a male and fight among themselves. Copulation occurs on the water. There is no pronounced territorial behaviour around the nest, but a female may drive other females away from her mate. Incubation and care of the brood is performed by the male, and females leave the nesting grounds with the onset of incubation. The chicks are aquatic, swimming within an hour of hatching, and they perform the spinning habit commonly used by adults when feeding in water.

Oystercatchers (Haematopodidae) are noisy, stocky birds of coasts and shores. They are highly gregarious and even perform sexual displays within the flock. One such display is the piping performance involving a number of birds that run toward a central point, holding the bill and neck down and the bill open, uttering a loud piping. Groups also pipe and posture (lowering the bill and neck) in flight. Before copulation the male circles the female in a crouching pose with tail and bill lowered, while the female indicates readiness by raising her tail. All behaviour patterns (except the precopulatory ones) are common to both sexes. Oystercatchers have no strong territorial behaviour at the nest, often tolerating strange birds nearby, but they may return to the same spot with the same mate in successive years. Although pairs separate from the flock to nest, they periodically rejoin communal displays during breeding. The two or three eggs are incubated by both parents. Downy young move to the water's edge where they remain on a feeding territory for at least six weeks and are fed small worms by the parents, who forage within sight in shallow water.

Avocets and stilts (Recurvirostridae) resemble oystercatchers in basic breeding behaviour, although the specific display patterns are different. Avocets nest in small colonies of up to a few hundred pairs, in grassy salt- or freshwater marshes that have substantial areas of shallow open water. Both sexes incubate the four eggs and protect the young. Stilts are somewhat colonial in their nesting, sometimes sharing a marsh with avocets. Stilts perform group displays in the breeding season. The ibisbill lays its eggs among the rocks of glacial streams. When alarmed, it bobs its tail and pumps its head up and down.

Most plovers nest in open areas, relying on their coloration to protect them while incubating or brooding. The solid colour of the back in the true plovers (*Charadrius*) matches the ground, and one or more black bands on the breast and face break the outline of the bird.

Many plovers are somewhat colonial but also exhibit territorial and aggressive behaviour. Some perform song flights during the breeding season, and many have melodious, whistled calls and bob when alarmed. The nest is a scrape or hollow with scant lining, in which four eggs are laid. Incubation is usually shared by the pair and takes from 20 to 30 days, depending upon the species. The chicks feed themselves but are usually protected by both parents by means of alarm calls that elicit crouching in the chicks. Often, parents will feign injury to divert a predator from their young. Many species occur in large postbreeding flocks and migrate great distances.

Crab plovers (*Dromas ardeola*) breed colonially in burrows in sand banks and fashion a nest chamber at the end of the narrow, three-to-five-foot tunnel. Here the bird lays a single, relatively large, white egg. The downy young is fed in the burrow by both parents.

Most pratincoles and coursers nest like plovers. Pratincoles breed in scattered groups, laying two or three eggs in an unlined scrape. They have a distraction display at the nest. The Egyptian plover (*Pluvianus aegyptius*) buries its egg in sand by day and incubates at night. Most glareolids lay two eggs, but the double-banded courser (*Rhinoptilus africanus*) lays only one, often located near antelope droppings, for concealment on otherwise bare ground. In that species, incubation by both sexes lasts about 26 days, and eggshells are removed. The chick has sparse down and is fed for about six weeks, until nearly fledged. A second egg may be laid before the first chick is independent. Adults and young combat the desert heat by panting, and adults also raise dorsal feathers and expose their legs during incubation.

The thickknees frequent dry open ground but within reasonable distance of water. They are cryptically coloured and spend much of the day squatting on their heel joints ("knees") or resting flat on the ground with the legs drawn under the body. On hot days the legs may be extended behind the resting bird, perhaps for heat dissipation. They have large eyes and are active and noisy from dusk until dawn. Their displays include spread wing and tail postures. The one or two eggs are laid on bare ground and are incubated for 25–27 days by the female or by both birds. Both parents attend the downy chicks, which run from the nest a day after hatching and fly when six weeks old.

Sheathbills are the most gull-like of the Charadrii. Their feet are not webbed, but they swim well and fly strongly at sea hundreds of miles from land. Males bow, bob, strut, and coo during courtship. They build bulky nests in holes, burrows, or rock crevices. Their two or three eggs are laid more than a week apart, but incubation begins with the first. As a result, the chicks are of different sizes and rarely does more than the largest one survive. This seemingly wasteful system is an adaptation that allows the sheathbills to fledge the maximum number of young permitted by their fluctuating food supply.

Most members of the Scolopacidae (the largest family of the shorebirds) construct nests on the ground, but several species use the abandoned nests of other birds, in trees or on the ground. Most of the calidridine sandpipers have courtship songs given in flight and are monogamous, but the ruff (*Philomachus pugnax*) is notable for social courtship, performed on the ground, and for promiscuity. Males have a prominent collar of feathers of the head and neck (the "ruff") that are of different colours and patterns in different individuals. They assemble at communal display grounds (the arena or lek) where each bird occupies and defends a site during the day, although an "apprentice" male may be permitted to occupy the same site. Females visit the lek briefly and copulate with one or more birds. There is no pairing, and females assume all domestic responsibilities.

Woodcock and snipe (subfamily Scolopacinae) nest on the ground in dry woods (woodcock) and marshes (snipe). The males of most species perform courtship flights in which some or all of the "song" is produced by specialized wing or tail feathers. Woodcock are largely solitary and nocturnal and are known to fly to safety with a chick carried between their legs.

The subfamily Tringinae is the most diverse of the subgroups of the Scolopacidae. The breeding behaviour of the greenshank (*Tringa nebularia*) includes many features common to a number of shorebirds and provides a useful model for comparison with the behaviour found in the Lari and Alcae.

From their winter quarters throughout much of the Old World temperate regions, greenshanks usually return north each year to the same breeding territory and often to the same mate. Males usually precede females to the breeding grounds, but sometimes they arrive together. Their nesting grounds are in northern Europe and Asia, in flat meadows or swamps near lakes, or in bogs with clusters of trees. The nesting territories vary in size from 100 to 700 acres, and nests may be three to eight kilometres (two to five miles) apart, or as close as a half kilometre. When the territories are relatively small, singing and fighting reaches a high pitch. In aggressive displays, opposing males lean forward with tails fanned, meeting bill to bill. They may then flutter over one another with legs dangling, in leapfrog fashion. Potentially dangerous intruders are met with violent scolding calls, flicks of the open wings, or shaking the half-raised wings. Anxiety is expressed by bobbing and curtseying, or stretching the neck.

Flight songs are performed frequently during courtship and territorial adjustment, intermittently throughout incubation, and less regularly later. The tempo is quickest in unmated birds, which fly high (sometimes out of sight), singing, on downward glides and upward flight, while soaring and circling, sustained bursts of "too-too-too," with other calls interspersed. Unmated males chase other birds in the air. Upon landing the male gives an aggressive display toward other individuals. Males return the display, but females fly off, with the male in wild pursuit, sometimes attaining a great height and ending in a spectacular dive. The female may glide on bowed wings while the male rises and dips over her, dangling one or both legs, or he may flutter over a standing female in leapfrog display. The female invites copulation by tilting forward and squatting, and the male approaches and mounts, sometimes while waving his wings. Copulation is attempted repeatedly by the male before the female becomes receptive.

The male escorts the female to various parts of the territory, but she chooses the nest site and makes a scrape by lowering the breast, turning, and scratching with her feet; she also brings nearby plant material in her bill. A former nest may be reused for three or more years. The site is usually close to a landmark such as a boulder, stump, or tree. On occasion a single male greenshank may command two females that nest 4 to 250 metres apart, or that occasionally lay in the same nest where they may incubate side by side.

A clutch of four speckled and cryptically coloured eggs is laid in late April or early May and is incubated for 23 or 24 days. The eggs are laid at any time of day, and the female is accompanied by the male to the nest during the laying of at least the first eggs. Both members develop incubation patches (featherless areas of skin abundantly provided with blood vessels) on the sides of the breast and across the abdomen, and both share in incubation, although occasionally the male defaults. Duty shifts are most frequent at early morning and evening hours, and males generally incubate at night. The free individual spends its time at feeding grounds—usually a lake or marsh up to eight miles away, where it feeds, preens, or rests, or it may engage in song flights over the territory. The incubating bird sits tightly, even in the presence of danger, but it may spring off the eggs and perform an injury-feigning display. An egg knocked out of the nest is drawn back in by rolling it with the underside of the bill.

Breeding
behaviour
of the
greenshank

When the eggs are pipped the male spends much time perching near the nest. Chicks pipe inside the eggs and the hen calls back; she may or may not enlarge the egg hole by pecking. Immediately after the hatching the adult carries the shells some 50 to 500 metres and drops them, or occasionally eats them. The chicks, covered with protectively coloured down, leave the nest during their first day, running rapidly on relatively large feet. They scatter and squat at the alarm call and rally to gutteral clucking by the parent. The female herds the chicks toward the lake, preceded by the male, who acts as sentry. Chicks may have to cross streams or rivers, and survive cold rains, but they are brooded during storms and at night for about two weeks. They are sometimes taken by weasels, gulls, hooded crows, or other predators. Sometimes the family separates, each parent taking one or more chicks, or one parent may depart, leaving all responsibility to the other. The chicks are feathered and fly at about 26 days of age, but stay near the parents until they are experienced fliers before going their separate ways.

Breeding behaviour of gulls and relatives
The members of the suborder Lari are quite different in breeding behaviour from those of the Charadrii. The herring gull (*Larus argentatus*) is typical of many of the better known gulls. It inhabits subarctic and temperate regions of the Northern Hemisphere. It is not strongly migratory, but most birds shift southward after breeding, and some go as far as Panama, the Hawaiian Islands, the central African coast, northern India, Southeast Asia, and the Philippines.

In winter herring gulls have a daily routine of flying from their social sleeping grounds to the feeding grounds, near which they may rest and preen, returning to the roosting area in the late afternoon. Storms may flood the broad beaches or sandbars that they require for roosting, forcing them to shift many miles in search of a new area.

As spring approaches, the birds drift north to their breeding grounds, over which they may wheel one day only to disappear and return on another day. Eventually the birds land on the dunes or rocky coast that has been their traditional colony. Some stand in pairs, while others are in small groups known as "clubs." Old birds have already paired in February, and they return to their former territories, which are about 30 to 50 metres in diameter. The gulls establish or defend their territories by a number of aggressive displays, which may occasionally lead to fierce fighting.

Threat display of one bird may be met by threat, by anxiety or appeasement postures, or by retreat. The individual is usually dominant on its established territory. One aggressive display is the "oblique with long call," in which the neck is stretched obliquely forward and upward, the wings held slightly out from the body, and a loud, long-drawn call given with the bill wide open. In the silent "upright" threat posture the head is raised, the bill angled downward, the wings held stiffly apart from the body. A bird that approaches an intruder in this posture may increase its speed to a charge, half running and half flying. The intruder usually retreats to his own territory where he, in turn, will perform the upright threat posture. Another aggressive action is "pecking the ground," in which the bird pecks and often tears out moss or grass, which it holds or tosses aside. Tugging at grass is strenuous and occasionally results in a backward tumble. A third threat posture, called "choking," often used by both members of a pair to intimidate another pair, consists of standing with legs bent, breast lowered, head pointed down, and the tongue lowered, while rhythmically jerking the head and uttering a deep call. These displays are effective in intimidating intruders, but occasionally fights break out in which birds peck or hold each other with their bills and pummel each other with their wings. Threat and fighting subside after territories have been established, and groups of neighbours recognize and tolerate each other.

Younger birds, not yet paired, settle in clubs. Here they doze or preen, and sometimes threaten or chase newcomers. Young males perform the "oblique with long call" display, causing other males to avoid them and females to land near them. Females approach males with the neck drawn in and the body and head horizontal, sometimes "head tossing" and uttering a liquid call. Instead of threatening, the male may be induced to walk off with such a female. Aggressive feelings are lessened by a display called "facing away," in which one or both birds, with neck stretched up, abruptly turn the head to the side away from the other bird. Together they make incomplete nest-building movements in a posture that resembles choking. The male may regurgitate half-digested food which the female takes from his mouth and eats. This courtship feeding is repeated during pair formation, but becomes less frequent as copulation becomes more frequent. Copulation is preceded by head tossing and begging calls by both members. The male stretches his neck and mounts the female's back while uttering a hoarse rhythmic call. The female continues to toss her head or may reach up to touch the male's breast while he waves his wings to maintain balance.

Copulations, choking, and courtship feeding may occur at the club, but eventually the pair walks off to establish a territory. They make several hollows (scrapes) with their feet, and begin to build a nest at one of them. Both bring straw and moss, which they may deposit while sitting in the nest with a sideways movement of the head. They scrape and turn in all directions to shape the nest.

The female lays three eggs at two-day intervals. With the first egg one bird (or both) stays at the nest, sitting or standing guard. They incubate in turn, relieving each other after periods of about two to five hours and often bringing new nest material. The arriving bird may call or "choke" and may have to push its reluctant mate off the eggs. If an egg is knocked out of the nest the bird rolls it back in, precariously balancing it with the thin lower edge of its bill. An incubating bird recognizes its returning mate by call even amid the clamour of the colony. Herring gulls apparently do not recognize their own eggs, but return first to the nest site, even if the eggs are placed outside nearby. Incubation lasts about 30 days, including the three-day hatching period after the egg is first cracked. As part of the overall adaptations for concealment of eggs and chicks, gulls defecate at some distance from the nest and carry off the eggshells at hatching.

Defense of the brood lasts several weeks and consists of swoops at intruders, with one or both feet lowered. The alarm call of one bird in the colony alerts the others, but gulls learn not to react to alarm calls of individuals that tend to give false alarms. The chicks are brooded for about three days. They soon peck at the red spot on the adult's bill, which induces the parent to regurgitate food (usually worms) that is held for the chick to eat. Other activities of the chicks are preening, yawning, stretching, scratching, and crouching at the alarm call; later they run from the nest before crouching. Chicks that wander near other adult birds may be pecked to death.

After the chick's juvenile feathers have replaced the down and the bird approaches adult size and shape, its own parents may react aggressively toward it. The chick then adopts a submissive posture—with head withdrawn and body horizontal—similar to that of a female approaching a prospective mate. Full-grown young beg for food by head tossing and high-pitched calls, but they are ignored or rejected as they become independent.

Herring gulls have concealingly coloured eggs, and their nests are widely spaced. The mobbing reaction in which many birds may participate is usually effective in distracting or repulsing a predator before it can extensively damage the colony.

The elaborate display repertoire of the herring gull during the breeding season is duplicated in other species, with some variations, additions, or deletions. The "hooded" gulls, exemplified by the black-headed gull (*Larus ridibundus*) and laughing gull (*L. atricilla*), have a striking "swoop-and-soar" aggressive flight display, and a ground display (called the "forward") wherein the neck is lowered, the head withdrawn and angled upward, and the wings held out from the body.

Several species of gull nest on narrow cliff ledges where they gain protection from predators but have limited space and face constant danger of the eggs or chicks falling off. In the kittiwake (*Rissa tridactyla*) adaptations against predation are reduced—alarm calls are rare, chicks are not camouflaged, defecation occurs on the nest rim, and eggshells are not carried away. Security against falling is achieved by a deep nest cup, smaller clutch (two eggs), and strong claws. The chicks crouch in the nest rather than running out.

The kittiwake is pelagic after breeding, and the swallow-tailed gull (*Creagrus furcatus*) of the Galápagos is semi-pelagic and nocturnal. The gray gull (*Larus modestus*) flies inland to waterless Chilean deserts to breed.

Breeding behaviour of terns

Terns are, in general, smaller than gulls. Most are coastal or pelagic during the nonbreeding season, returning to breed in large colonies on islands, offshore bars, isolated beaches, or on Arctic tundra. The common tern (*Sterna hirundo*) and royal tern (*Thalasseus maximus*) and their relatives nest on the ground, whereas noddies (*Anous*) nest in bushes or on cliff ledges, and the fairy tern (*Gygis alba*) deposits its single egg on the limb of a tree or bush. Nests of *Sterna* and *Thalasseus* may be so closely spaced that neighbouring birds spar with their bills as they incubate.

Displays of terns are more aerial than those of gulls and include "fish flights" in which one bird postures while carrying a fish. Ceremonial transfer of fish occurs during displays on the ground that are important in courtship and for maintenance of the pair bond.

Unlike gulls, most terns do not regurgitate food for the chicks but bring a fish which is fed to the chick, which energetically pecks at the adult's bill. Chicks of royal terns band together soon after leaving the nest and may take to the water when predators approach. Terns are fierce in their mobbing attacks on predators. Like gulls, they often peck and kill chicks that trespass on their territories. Sooty terns (*Sterna fuscata*) have attracted considerable attention from biologists because on Ascension Island in the South Atlantic they breed every 9.6 months and on Christmas Island, in the Pacific Ocean, every six months. Elsewhere they have an annual cycle.

The breeding pattern of skimmers is ternlike. They breed on sandbars in rivers and estuaries in tropical and subtropical regions, forming loose colonies of about 100 to several thousand pairs. The nests are mere hollows in the sand. The eggs usually number three or four and are incubated chiefly by the female. The chicks are fed by both parents, mainly on small fish. In the presence of danger the chicks lie flat or burrow into the sand and may even kick sand onto their backs. Their mandibles are nearly equal length until after fledging, enabling them to pick up fish brought in and dropped by the parents.

Although not strongly colonial in their nesting habits, numbers of skuas (*Catharacta skua*) may nest on the fringes of penguin colonies; in Iceland they nest in clumps of vegetation on great outwash gravel plains. Jaegers (three species of *Stercorarius*) nest on the tundra, where both sexes share in incubating the two eggs. Some species have light and dark phases. They are pelagic and solitary after breeding.

Breeding behaviour of alcids

Alcids breed in island colonies along Arctic and north temperate seacoasts, with the exception of a few murrelets that breed inland on mountains. Even these must remain within flying distance of the sea. The breeding behaviour of the pigeon guillemot (*Cepphus columba*) is fairly typical of the family. This species breeds on islands and coasts of the North Pacific, south to central California. It nests between rocks or in holes in cliffs, uses burrows of other birds, or digs its own tunnels with its bill and feet. Occasionally it nests on an open ledge or in tall grass. Unlike some other alcids, guillemots walk quite well on land.

Birds land at their breeding colonies in British Columbia in early April, at which time they stay only briefly in the early mornings. In general, birds return to the same mate and nest burrow for many years. Full attendance is achieved by the end of June, but even then many birds leave the colony in the afternoon to go to their feeding grounds—shoals that may be several miles distant. Only incubating and brooding birds spend the night at the colony. They drive other birds away from their burrows before egg-laying but are more tolerant later in the season when feeding young. The pair also defends a perch site away from the nest burrow, usually a rock close to the water. On this site, which is used in successive years by the same pair, copulation occurs and the nonincubating bird may rest and preen. About 30 percent of the birds at the colony consists of nonbreeding individuals—yearlings or two-year-olds that were hatched at the colony but are unpaired.

During the pre-egg stage, which lasts about 30 to 60 days, the mated pairs spend much time at the perch sites, but they occasionally visit the nest site or cliff top and join in communal water displays. Their display repertoire includes several alarm reactions—the flight intention call, bill dipping (in water), and a scream delivered with the neck straight up and the bill agape. Among the aggressive and sexual displays are a silent lunge on water or land with bill somewhat open, chases that may be in flight or underwater, and a "hunch-whistle" on shore or water, with tail cocked, the head drawn back, the bill agape, accompanied by piping. A display that may represent appeasement is the "twitter-waggle" in which the bird twitters with the tail raised, wings loose, and head and neck outstretched and wagging sideways. The communal water dances, which occur in the pre-egg stage, involve many birds. Pairs are not always together or both present. The birds move rapidly under water or at the surface propelled both by wings and feet. This behaviour is interspersed with "hunch-whistles" and "twitter-waggles."

Pair formation is indicated by mutual "billing," in which the birds waggle their heads but rarely touch bills, while uttering a twittering trilled song with the bill open, revealing the bright red mouth lining. Copulation is initiated by billing, followed by the male's waddling in a circle, first in one direction, then in the other. The female crouches and the male mounts, resting on his tarsi and fluttering his wings to keep balance; the female may gape, scream, or utter an alarm call. She then rises, throwing off the male, and the birds bill or preen.

The pair cleans debris out of the nest cavity and piles up pebbles, without making a well-defined nest. A normal clutch is two eggs (rarely one), and the birds' brood patches will not accommodate more than two eggs. The second egg follows the first by three days. Incubation lasts for about 32 days, including a two-day interval between cracking and hatching. Steady incubation during the day begins one day after the clutch is complete, but incubation at night may not begin for one or two days more, at which time a single bird begins to sit all night until the early morning exchange. The incubating bird may leave the burrow briefly to defecate, preen, bathe, or drink, but it will not go to the feeding grounds until its mate arrives at the burrow. The downy chicks are fed, beginning the day after hatching, by both parents during their 35-day nestling and fledging period. Their food is mostly fish, including many blennies, sculpins, and sand lances, brought in the parent's bill throughout the daylight hours. The chicks may reject fish that are awkward to swallow or that have sharp spines. Fledged chicks eventually desert the burrow by night and may be coaxed out by a fish dangling in the parent's bill. The young are then independent and they disappear offshore to feed without the parents, who may remain to loaf about the colony during morning hours for several weeks.

Behaviour patterns like those of the pigeon guillemot run through many species with various modifications. Many alcids are burrow nesters, and some (*Uria*) habitually nest on narrow ledges of vertical cliffs, where they rest on their tarsi facing the rock wall. Some murrelets (*Brachyramphus*) nest in rock crevices above the timberline on mountains, and in trees of the taiga zone. Both sexes incubate the one or two eggs and feed the young at the nest site until it is nearly or completely fledged. Other murrelets (*Synthliborhamphus*) are truly nidifugous (precocious), their downy chick taking to the sea within two days of hatching. Many alcids nest in immense colonies of mixed species, which segregate in part according to their specialized needs for nesting and feeding. They migrate to pelagic winter feeding grounds by swimming.

FORM AND FUNCTION

Most members of the Charadriiformes are clearly recognizable as belonging to a particular suborder. Major structural variations occur in the beak and legs, correlated with the mode of feeding and size of food.

Adaptations for flight. Gulls, terns, and skimmers have long, narrow wings, low wing loadings (the ratio of weight to wing area), slow wing beat rates and flight speeds, and moderately developed flight muscles. Alcids, on the other hand, have proportionately shorter wings, high wing loadings, rapid wing beat rates and greater speed (45–55 miles per hour), and large flight muscles. Their wing bones are flattened in adaptation to underwater "flight." The shorebirds lie between the other suborders in flight adaptations; their wings are not adapted for soaring, but they are strong fliers and cover great distances in continuous flight.

The evolution of the wing in the Alcidae has been influenced by the fact that it serves both as an aquatic paddle and as an aerial wing. The wing is partly folded underwater, reducing its area and increasing its mechanical advantage. It is used not to provide lift but to propel the bird in pursuit of prey. To support a bird in air, however, a wing must be larger than the optimum paddle size. This is especially critical in large birds, as body weight is proportional to the cube of linear dimensions and wing area to the square. Body size and flying ability are therefore limited by the need for a small effective paddle. In flightless aquatic species the wing can be relatively small and the bird can be much larger, as in the great auk and in penguins.

Molt. Most Charadriiformes have two molts between breeding periods, which are on an annual cycle in all except some populations of the sooty tern (*Sterna fuscata*). A partial body molt generally precedes breeding, and a complete molt follows breeding. In some species flight feathers of the wing and tail are molted before the fall migration; in others they are retained through the fall migration and molted on the wintering grounds. Still other species stop along the migration route to molt. The ruff (*Philomachus pugnax*) is exceptional in having one complete and two partial molts between breeding cycles.

Major flight feathers of most species are lost gradually and in sequence so that flight is not impaired. Flight feathers of the wing in most Alcidae, however, are molted simultaneously after breeding, with temporary loss of flight but no hindrance to underwater locomotion. One jacana (*Actophilornis*) is also flightless for a brief period.

Adaptations for feeding. As in other birds, the upper jaw as well as the lower jaw can be moved up and down. The lower jaw has special regions of flexibility enabling it to be widened by bowing outward and allowing passage of large prey into the throat in Lari and Alcae.

The shape of the bill varies greatly within the order, in accordance with special feeding methods. The hooked tip in gulls and jaegers facilitates grasping and tearing of food, which cannot be managed by the straight-billed terns. Some species such as the Atlantic puffin, rhinoceros auklet, and fairy tern are able to carry several fish crosswise in the bill while capturing still more. They do this by holding the fish against the roof of the upper jaw with the spiny tongue. The shorebirds exhibit a wide variety of bill types (Figures 2 and 3). Most bills in this group are long and slender, and straight or curved up or down. In the Scolopacidae, the bill is usually slender and flexible; in the Charadriidae, somewhat stouter and less flexible, often slightly swollen at the tip. Among the specialized probers (sandpipers, snipe, and allies), the upper jaw is rigidly attached to the cranium and has a mobile tip with a concentration of tactile sense organs under the rhamphotheca (the horny covering of the beak). The tip of the upper jaw is controlled by jaw muscles and serves

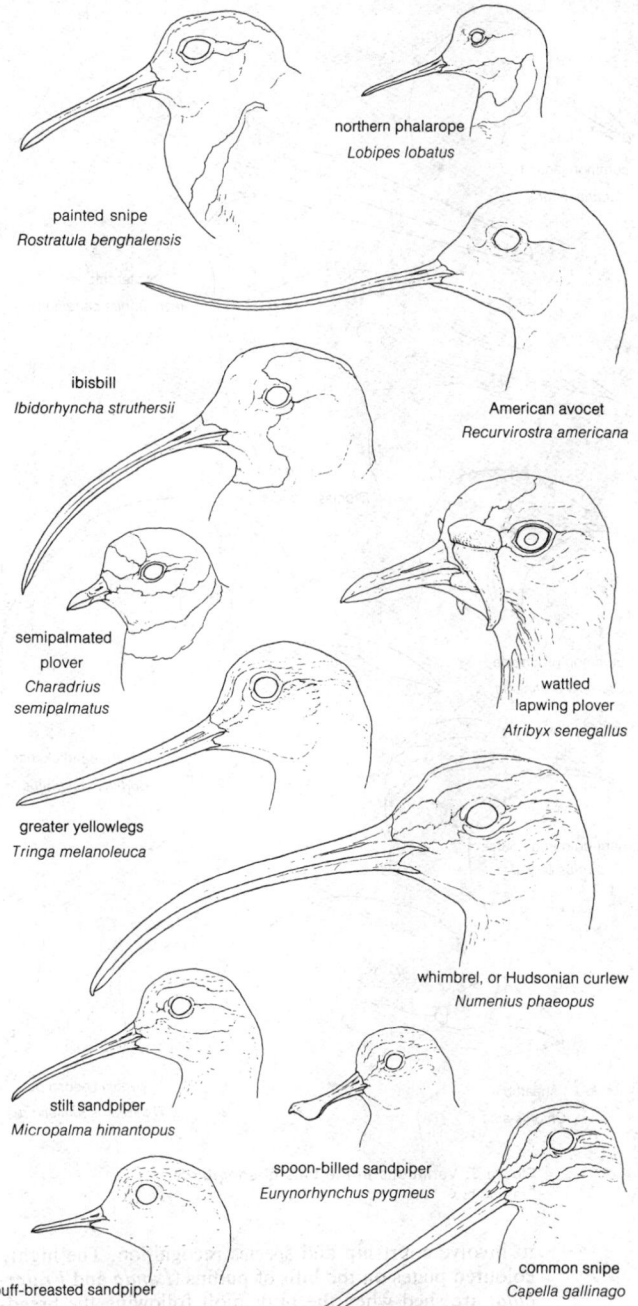

Figure 2: Bill variations among several shorebirds.
Drawing by G. Tudor

painted snipe — *Rostratula benghalensis*

northern phalarope — *Lobipes lobatus*

ibisbill — *Ibidorhyncha struthersii*

American avocet — *Recurvirostra americana*

semipalmated plover — *Charadrius semipalmatus*

wattled lapwing plover — *Afribyx senegallus*

greater yellowlegs — *Tringa melanoleuca*

whimbrel, or Hudsonian curlew — *Numenius phaeopus*

stilt sandpiper — *Micropalma himantopus*

spoon-billed sandpiper — *Eurynorhynchus pygmeus*

buff-breasted sandpiper — *Tryngites subruficollis*

common snipe — *Capella gallinago*

to grasp worms or larvae underground and to inch them along the bill before swallowing.

In one plover (the wrybill, *Anarhynchus frontalis*) the bill curves to the right; in the spoonbilled sandpiper (*Eurynorhynchus pygmeus*) the tip of the bill is broad and spatulate. Oystercatchers have laterally flattened bills, with the tips forming a vertical blade. Seedsnipe have short, conical bills not unlike those of sparrows. Pratincoles have short bills and wide mouths, like those of swallows and swifts.

The Lari show few bizarre modifications of the bill, feathers, or feet. One oddity is the bill of skimmers, in which the upper mandible is streamlined in cross section and laterally compressed. The lower mandible is knifelike and protrudes well beyond the upper. The sharp upper edge of the lower mandible fits into a groove in the upper when the bill is closed (see Figure 4).

Many alcids acquire bill ornamentation or head plumes during the breeding season. The functions of elaborate bill modifications are poorly understood but are believed

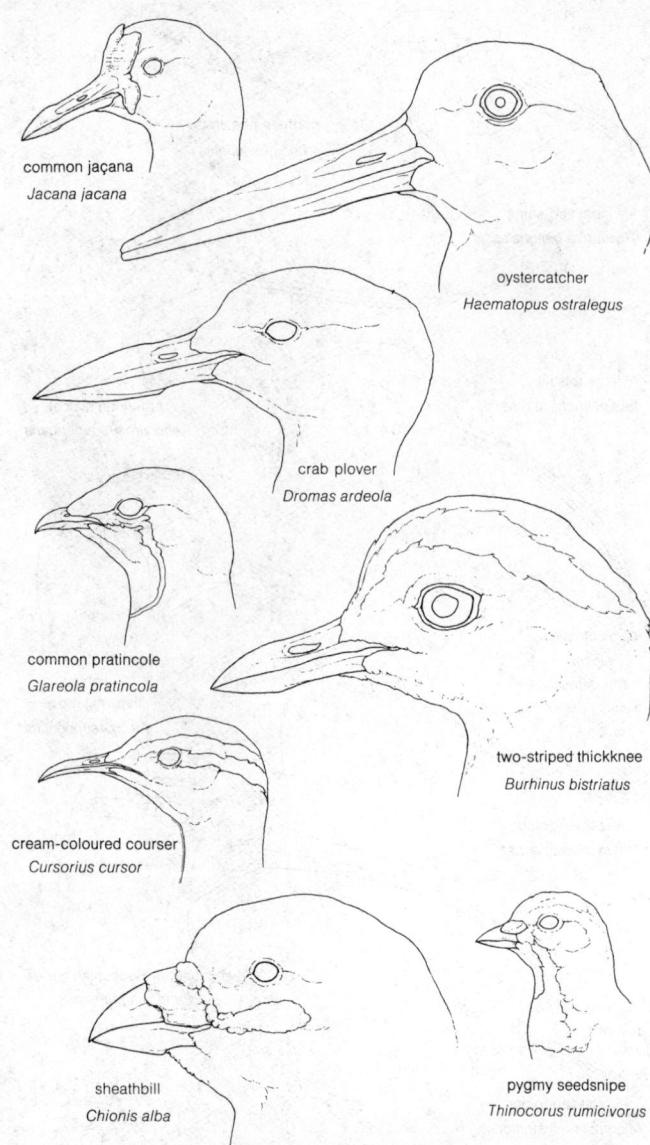

common jaçana
Jacana jacana

oystercatcher
Haematopus ostralegus

crab plover
Dromas ardeola

common pratincole
Glareola pratincola

two-striped thickknee
Burhinus bistriatus

cream-coloured courser
Cursorius cursor

sheathbill
Chionis alba

pygmy seedsnipe
Thinocorus rumicivorus

Figure 3: Variations in the bills of shorebirds.
Drawing by G. Tudor

Presbyornithidae, appear in the lower Eocene rocks of Utah. They are thought to be heavier bodied and more aquatic than present-day avocets, and to represent an ancestral stock from which the avocets and stilts descended. An extinct genus of the Rostratulidae and the modern genus *Limosa* are reported from the middle and upper Eocene of Europe. In the Oligocene are found extinct species in the modern sandpiper genus *Tringa*, in the plover genera *Charadrius* and *Vanellus,* and in extinct genera of the Scolopacidae and Charadriidae. Possible

Drawing by G. Tudor

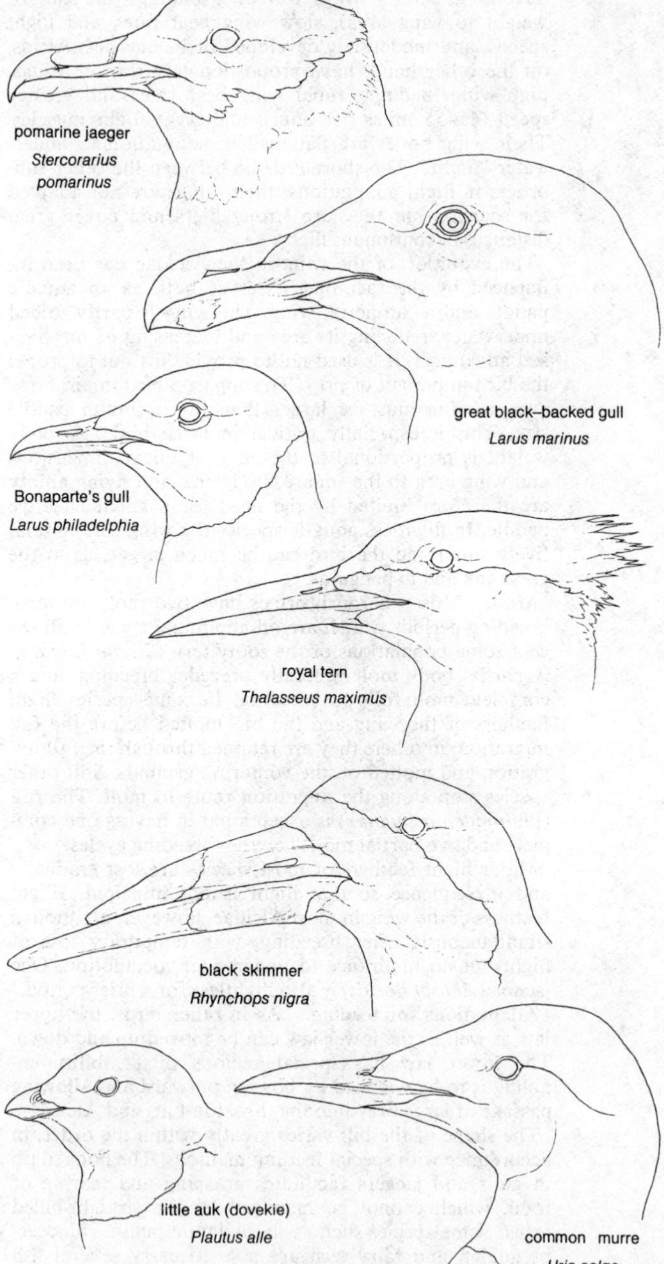

pomarine jaeger
Stercorarius pomarinus

great black–backed gull
Larus marinus

Bonaparte's gull
Larus philadelphia

royal tern
Thalasseus maximus

black skimmer
Rhynchops nigra

little auk (dovekie)
Plautus alle

common murre
Uria aalge

tufted puffin
Fratercula corniculata

crested auklet
Aethia cristatella

Figure 4: Variation in the bill among Lari and Alcae.

to involve courtship and species recognition. The highly coloured plates on the bills of puffins (*Lunda* and *Fratercula*) are shed when the birds molt following the breeding season. In alcids that feed on zooplankton (tiny, free-floating animals), such as the least auklet (*Aethia pusilla*) and the dovekie or little auk (*Plautus alle*), the bill is relatively wide, the tongue large and fleshy, the palate broad with numerous horny projections, and the throat provided with an expandable pouch.

Many charadriiform birds drink saltwater. The ionic balance of their blood is maintained not only by the kidneys but by supraorbital glands (called nasal or salt glands) that lie in grooves in the skull over the eyes, discharging their salty excretion through the nostrils.

EVOLUTION AND PALEONTOLOGY

The earliest known Charadrii are represented by miscellaneous bones from the Upper Cretaceous rock layers of Wyoming, considered to constitute a family, the Cimolopterygidae, of the Charadrii. These bones, comprising two genera and four species, show closest resemblance to the avocets. Of similar age, but extending into middle Eocene times, are the Paleotringinae of the Scolopacidae, known from fossil deposits in New Jersey and Wyoming. These consisted of five species in a single genus of poorly known, large shorebirds, represented by fragmentary limb bones. Other probable relatives of the avocets, the

relatives of the jacanas were the Rhegminornithidae from lower Miocene times of Florida; features of the tarso-metatarsus suggest that these birds had a large hindtoe. Other discoveries from the Miocene are extinct genera of the Scolopacidae, Charadriidae, Haematopodidae, and Burhinidae, and extinct species of four contemporary genera. Pliocene finds include the Recent *Bartramia* and *Micropalama* and an extinct genus of oystercatcher. Pleistocene deposits have added extinct species of four living genera, extinct genera of Scolopacidae and Charadriidae, and many examples of species still living today.

Within the Lari, extinct genera of the Laridae are reported from the Paleocene, Oligocene, Miocene, and Pleistocene, and an extinct genus of tern occurred in the Pleistocene. *Larus* and *Sterna* first appear in Miocene deposits—*Stercorarius* in the Pleistocene. Numerous modern species of Lari have been found in Pleistocene deposits.

The earliest of the auklike birds known at present were members of the alcid subfamily Nautilornithinae from the lower and upper Eocene of Utah. Represented by wing and leg bones, these birds are inferred to have had longer limbs than present forms and to have been less well adapted for flight underwater than are contemporary species. The Miocene produced the first known species of *Uria* and *Cerorhinca*, and an extinct genus of alcid. The murrelet genus *Brachyrhamphus* and the auklet genus *Ptychorhamphus* first appeared in the Pliocene, along with an extinct genus. Fascinating finds from the Pliocene are some very flattened wing bones (humeri) that exhibit features at both ends resembling those of penguins. These birds, the Mancallinae, were undoubtedly flightless and more specialized for underwater wing propulsion than was the now extinct great auk.

From this record of fossil Charadriiformes it appears that considerable adaptive radiation (diversification) has occurred and disappeared in the past. Modern families probably had their origins in Paleocene times or earlier, and many modern genera were well represented by the Oligocene and Miocene. Modern species date chiefly from the Pleistocene, and many facts concerning the distribution and differentiation of northern subspecies and species are explainable in terms of isolation during the periods of Pleistocene glaciation.

CLASSIFICATION

Features used in classification. The order Charadriiformes can be characterized by a variety of anatomical, behavioral, or other features, not all of which are necessarily applicable to any one species, genus, or family, and no one of which is necessarily found throughout the order. One complex of characters may evolve relatively rapidly in one group, another complex in another. It is impossible to reflect all of these relationships in a single classification, and one must expect continued change in any classification with increasing knowledge of living birds and of fossils. The classification below follows that of the American ornithologist Alexander Wetmore.

Annotated Classification.

ORDER CHARADRIIFORMES

Palate schizognathous; upper jaw schizorhinal (except Burhinidae and *Pluvianus*); lachrymal bone fused to ectethmoid; cervical vertebrae 15 or 16; dorsal vertebrae opisthocoelous or heterocoelous; two carotid arteries (except *Synthliborhamphus*); oil gland feathered; syrinx (vocal organ) tracheobronchial; wing diastataxic (except *Philohela*); aftershaft present; down feathers present on adults. Eggs usually pyriform (*i.e.*, somewhat pointed at one end). Chicks downy and nidifugous, pseudonidifugous, or nidicolous. About 312 species; worldwide.

Suborder Charadrii

Hypotarsus complex (with canals), coracoid bones usually separate, depressions for supraorbital grooves usually small or absent; basipterygoid processes and occipital foramina usually present; furcula without hypocleideum; adult downs on pterylae only. Young nidifugous (precocious).

Family Cimolopterygidae

Fossil only. Known only from Upper Cretaceous strata of Wyoming. Four species; medium-sized shorebirds.

Family Jacanidae (jacanas)

7 species. Small to medium-sized birds with showy plumage, moderately long, straight bills, and long legs. Some with wattles or lappets, a horny forehead plate, and wing spurs. All with extremely elongated toes and long, straight claws. Occipital foramina and supraorbital grooves lacking; coracoids overlapping; rectrices 10. Females larger than males. 7 species; worldwide tropical and subtropical; length about 16–53.5 cm (6–21 in.).

Family Rhegminornithidae

Fossil only; lower Miocene strata of Florida. One species; medium-sized birds.

Family Rostratulidae (painted snipe)

Small birds with cryptically patterned plumage, long slender bill, and moderately long legs. Female larger and brighter than male. Occipital foramina present; sternum narrow, with single pair of notches. Crop present in *Rostratula*; trachea convoluted in female but not in male. Two genera; one in southern South America, one in Africa, southern and eastern Asia, Australia; length 19–24 cm (7½–9½ in.).

Family Haematopodidae (oystercatchers)

Medium-sized birds with black, brown, or white plumage in bold patterns, or solid blackish brown. Bill long and wedge-shaped, bright red; legs moderately long, stout. Three toes. Supraorbital grooves large; tarsus covered with small, hexagonal scales. Four species, inhabit most temperate and tropical seacoasts, and inland water bodies in Europe and Asia; length 38–51 cm (15–20 in.).

Family Recurvirostridae (avocets, stilts, and ibisbill)

Moderately large birds with long bills, legs, and necks. Plumage in bold, simple patterns of black and white, gray, chestnut, or buff. Bill straight, recurved, or decurved. Toes webbed in *Recurvirostra*. Legs covered with reticulate scales. Plumage of underparts dense. 7 species worldwide in temperate and tropical regions, one species in Himalayas; length 29–48 cm (11–19 in.).

Family Presbyornithidae

Fossil only. Two genera of large shorebirds from the lower Eocene of Utah.

Family Charadriidae (plovers, lapwings)

Small to medium-sized birds. Mostly with bold (but often concealing) plumage patterns of solid blacks, gray, browns, and white; many with one or two chest bands. Some with wattles and wing spurs. Bill usually short, with a swollen tip. Legs moderately long to long, with reticulate scale pattern. Hindtoe usually absent. About 61 species; worldwide; length about 15–40 cm (6–16 in.).

Family Scolopacidae (snipe, woodcock, sandpipers, turnstones, and allies)

Small to medium-sized birds, mostly finely patterned in buff, browns, chestnut, black, gray, and white. Bill moderate to very long and slender; straight, decurved, or recurved; one with spatulate tip. Legs short to long, usually with transverse scales front and back. Hindtoe usually present and elevated. About 82 species; worldwide; length 12.5–61 cm (5–24 in.).

Family Phalaropodidae (phalaropes)

Small, densely feathered birds with straight slender bills, moderately long legs, lobed toes, and flattened tarsi. Females larger and brighter than males. Three species; Arctic and subarctic regions of Northern Hemisphere; migrating to temperate regions; length 19–25 cm (7½–10 in.).

Family Dromadidae (crab plover)

Medium-sized bird of white and black plumage. Legs long and covered with reticulate scales. Bill strong, laterally compressed, and pointed. Nostrils pervious; basipterygoid processes absent; 15 cervical vertebrae; dorsal vertebrae heterocoelous. One species; coasts of Indian Ocean and southern Red sea; length 38 cm (15 in.).

Family Burhinidae (thickknees)

Medium-sized birds with cryptically patterned plumage of brown, gray-brown, black, and white. Bill stout, short to moderately long. Tarsus reticulate. Upper jaw holorhinal; basipterygoid processes and occipital foramina absent; coracoids overlapping. Large eyes. Nine species; temperate and tropical regions of Eurasia, Africa and Australia; New World tropics; length 35–52 cm (14–20 in.).

Family Glareolidae (pratincoles and coursers)

Pratincoles are short-billed long-winged birds with moderately long legs and forked tails; coursers have longer bills, shorter wings and tail, and long legs. Plumage patterned in olive, brown, gray, chestnut, black, and white. Legs have rectangular scales front and back. Occipital fontanelles absent; basipterygoid processes absent in adult; dorsal vertebrae heterocoelous; 15 cervical vertebrae. 17 species; Africa, southern Eurasia, and Australia; length 15–25 cm (6–10 in.).

Family Thinocoridae (seedsnipes)

Small to medium-sized birds, cryptically patterned in brown, buff, gray, white, and black. Bill short and conical, legs short, wings long and pointed. Nostrils operculate; crop present; vomer broad; basisphenoidal rostrum thick; no basipterygoid processes or occipital fontanelles. Four species; southern South America and north in Andes; length 17–28 cm (7–11 in.).

Family Chionididae (sheathbills)

White birds of moderate size, short legs, and stout bill, with horny sheath over nostrils. No occipital fontanelles or basipterygoid processes; large supraorbital grooves; thick plumage; short carpal spurs on wing. Two species; inhabit islands of extreme southern Atlantic and Indian Oceans; length 35–43 cm (14–17 in.).

Suborder Lari

Hypotarsus simple (grooved but without canals); coracoids in contact (except in Stercorariidae); supraorbital grooves large; basipterygoid processes absent (present but small in young); occipital foramina absent in adults; furcula with hypocleideum; adult downs on both pterylae and apteria; anterior toes usually fully webbed, hind toe absent or minute; young tardily nidifugous (leave nest when half grown).

Family Stercorariidae (skuas, jaegers)

Medium-sized to large birds of solid brown, or brown, white, and black plumage. Bill moderately long, stout, hooked, with a horny dorsal plate. Wings long and pointed; tail with elongate central feathers in some. Legs rather short, toes webbed. Ceca well developed; coracoids not overlapping. 4 species; Arctic and Antarctic; length 43–61 cm (17–24 in.).

Family Laridae (gulls, terns)

Small to large birds, with solid plumage patterns of white, gray, black or sooty brown. Legs, eyes, and bill often brightly coloured in red or yellow. Wings long and pointed; tails of terns often long and deeply forked. Legs moderate to short. Bill short to moderately long; stout and somewhat hooked in gulls, more slender and pointed in terns. Front toes webbed. Sternum with two pairs of notches, ceca small. Rhamphotheca simple (without horny plates). About 85 species; worldwide; length 20–76 cm (8–30 in.).

Family Rynchopidae (skimmers)

Medium-sized birds with long, pointed wings, short legs, and a large bill. Bill deep and extremely flattened, lower mandible knifelike and longer than upper. Plumage black or blackish brown above, white below. Bill red or yellow, sometimes with black tip. Front toes webbed. Pupil closes to vertical slit. Three species; irregularly distributed in tropical and temperate rivers, lakes and seashores; length 37–51 cm (14½–20 in.).

Suborder Alcae

Large supraorbital grooves with intervening space narrowed to ridge; basipterygoid processes absent in adults; occipital fontanelles present; haemapophysis of dorsal vertebrae large; sternum long and narrow with long rounded metasternum. Anterior toes fully webbed, hindtoe absent. Wing bones flattened. Young downy nidicolous or nidifugous.

Family Alcidae (auks, murres, puffins and relatives)

Small to large, dense-plumaged, short-winged, aquatic birds. Plumage black, gray, or brown, usually white below. Many have ornamental bill and head plumes. Legs set far back; tail short. 7 or 8 pairs of ribs attach on sternum. 21 species; coasts of northern oceans; length 16–76 cm (6–30 in.).

Critical appraisal. The Charadriiformes are thought to be related to the Gruiformes and to the Columbiformes. Certain intermediate or aberrant families have been removed from or added to the Charadriiformes by various taxonomists. The Belgian ornithologist R. Verheyen considered the Thinocoridae with the Pteroclidae (sand grouse) as a suborder of the Turniciformes, which he placed between the Columbiformes (pigeons and doves) and Galliformes (pheasants and relatives). It has been argued on behavioral and morphological evidence that the Pteroclidae are charadriiform rather than columbiform, but most authorities retain them in the Columbiformes on anatomical grounds. Verheyen allied the Jacanidae with two gruiform families (Rhynochetidae, Eurypygidae) as an order related to the rails and Charadriiformes. P.R. Lowe united the charadriiform and gruiform birds into a single order—the Telmatomorphae—placing the Thinocoridae as a link between the gruiform and charadriine members. Other families that have been

variously placed in the Charadriiformes or Gruiformes are the Otididae (bustards, see GRUIFORMES), Burhinidae, and Glareolidae.

With undue emphasis on similarities resulting from convergent evolution taxonomists at various times have allied the Lari closely with the Procellariiformes, and the Alcae with other diving birds (penguins, diving petrels, grebes, and loons). Such relationships are at best distant and poorly understood.

Within the widely accepted limits of the Charadriiformes as presented here there are different opinions about the rank (superfamily, family, subfamily, or tribe) of various groups and about their internal relationships. Pending further evidence from comparative anatomy, physiology, biochemistry, and behaviour, the major groups within the suborders are here given family rank.

BIBLIOGRAPHY. C.G. LOW, *The Literature of the Charadriiformes from 1894–1928*, 2nd rev. and enl. ed. (1931); H. SEEBOHM, *The Geographical Distribution of the Family Charadriidae* (1888), a classical, well-illustrated monograph that includes the Scolopacidae.

Form and function: J. BÉDARD, "Adaptive Radiation in Alcidae," *Ibis*, III:189–198 (1969), on feeding adaptations; F.A. HARTMAN, "Locomotor Mechanisms of Birds," *Smithson. Misc. Collns.*, vol. 143, no. 1 (1961); R. MEINERTZHAGEN, "The Speed and Altitude of Bird Flight," *Ibis*, 97:81–117 (1955); and R.W. STORER, "Evolution in the Diving Birds," *Proc. XII Int. Orn. Congr.*, pp. 694–707 (1960), on locomotor adaptations; R.L. ZUSI, "Structural Adaptations of the Head and Neck in the Black Skimmer (*Rynchops nigra* Linnaeus)," *Publs. Nuttall Orn. Club*, no. 3 (1962), a technical discussion of feeding behaviour and adaptations.

Natural history: Many short accounts of the natural history occur in regional books. A.C. BENT has written on the life histories of the North American diving birds, gulls and terns, and shorebirds, published in the *Bull. U.S. Natn. Mus.*, no. 107, 113, 142, and 146 (1919, 1921, 1927, and 1929). R.H. DRENT, "Breeding Biology of the Pigeon Guillemot, *Cepphus columba*," *Ardea*, 53:99–160 (1965); R.C. MURPHY, *Oceanic Birds of South America*, vol. 2 (1936), a readable discussion of many southern species; D. NETHERSOLE-THOMPSON, *The Greenshank* (1951), a very complete life history account; R.S. PALMER, "A Behavior Study of the Common Tern (*Sterna hirundo hirundo* L.)," *Proc. Boston Soc. Nat. Hist.*, 42:1–119 (1941); N. TINBERGEN, *The Herring Gull's World* (1953), an exceptionally clearly written behavioral study; G.D. STOUT (ed.), *The Shorebirds of North America* (1967), excellent illustrations and detailed species accounts.

Fossils and evolution: P. BRODKORB, "Catalogue of Fossil Birds: Part 3 (Ralliformes, Ichthyornithiformes, Charadriiformes)," *Bull. Fla. St. Mus. Biol. Sci.*, 2:99–220 (1967); K. LAMBRECHT, *Handbuch der Palaeornithologie*, 8 vol. (1933), the major sources of general information on charadriiform fossils.

Classification: W.J. BOCK, "A Generic Review of the Plovers (Charadriinae, Aves)," *Bull. Mus. Comp. Zool. Harv.* vol. 118, no. 2 (1958), on the function and value of traditional taxonomic characters; J.R. JEHL, JR., "Relationships in the Charadrii (Shorebirds): A Taxonomic Study Based on Color Patterns of the Downy Young," *Mem. S. Diego Soc. Nat. Hist. 3* (1968), a discussion of a taxonomic character not previously stressed; P.R. LOWE, "An Anatomical Review of the 'Waders' (Telmatomorphae) with Special Reference to the Families, Subfamilies and Genera Within the Suborders Limicolae, Grui-Limicolae, and Lari-Limicolae," *Ibis*, 13th ser., 1:712–771 (1931), an important classification based mainly on anatomy; M. MOYNIHAN, "A Revision of the Family Laridae (Aves)," *Am. Mus. Novit.*, no. 1928 (1959), the basis for many current classifications of gulls and terns; J.L. PETERS, *Check-list of Birds of the World*, vol. 2 (1934), the distribution of all species; R. RIDGWAY, "The Birds of North and Middle America," *Bull. U.S. Natn. Mus.*, no. 50, pt. 8 (1919), taxonomic characters of the order, families, genera, and species.

(R.L.Z.)

Chardin, Jean-Baptiste-Siméon

Although Jean-Baptiste-Siméon Chardin was an artist whose style had all the refinement, charm, and grace of 18th-century French art, he stood apart from his contemporaries, both in his technique, which remained that of the self-taught craftsman unaffected by a traditional academic education, and in his subject matter—mainly still lifes and family scenes. A discoverer of the daily world, he painted it tirelessly and with a deceptive simplicity that masked his acute power of observation. He knew, seemingly, how to give life to mundane reality without concessions to rhetorical pretensions, anecdote, or gratuitous technical virtuosity. Through truth, Chardin attained a wholesome and honest poetry that is distinguished by its restraint and tranquillity.

Alinari

Chardin, self-portrait, pastel, 1775. In the Louvre, Paris. 46.36 cm × 38.1 cm.

Early training and career

Born in Paris on November 2, 1699, Jean-Baptiste-Siméon Chardin never really left his native quarter of Saint-Germain-des-Prés. Little is known about his training, although he worked for a time with the artists Pierre-Jacques Cazes and Noël-Nicolas Coypel. In 1724 he was admitted to the Académie de Saint Luc as a master painter. His true career, however, did not begin until 1728 when, thanks to the court painter Nicolas de Largillière (1656–1746), he became a member of the Académie Royale de Peinture et de Sculpture, to which he offered "La Raie" ("The Skate") and "Le Buffet," both now at the Louvre.

Although not yet established, he was beginning to gain a reputation. In 1731 he married Marguerite Saintard, and two years later the first of his figure paintings appeared, "Dame cachetant une lettre" ("Lady Sealing a Letter"). From then on Chardin alternated between paintings of *la vie silencieuse*, ("the silent life") or scenes of family life such as "Le Bénédicité" ("The Grace"), and half-figure paintings of young men and women concentrating on their work or play such as "Le Jeune dessinateur" ("Young Man Drawing") and "L'Enfant au toton" ("Child with Top," Louvre). The artist often repeated his subject matter and there are often several original versions of the same composition. Chardin's wife died in 1735, and the estate inventory drawn up after her death reveals a certain affluence, suggesting that by this time Chardin had become a successful painter.

In 1740 he was presented to Louis XV, to whom he offered "La Mère laborieuse" ("Mother Working") and "Le Bénédicité," both now in the Louvre. Four years later, he married Marguerite Pouget, whom he was to immortalize 30 years later in a pastel that hangs in the drawing collection of the Louvre. These were the years when Chardin was at the height of his fame. Louis XV, for example, paid 1,500 livres for "La Serinette" ("The Bird-Organ"), perhaps the painting that is today in the Frick Collection in New York. Chardin continued to rise steadily on the rungs of the traditional academic career. His colleagues at the academy entrusted him, first unofficially (1755), then officially (1761), with the hanging of the paintings in the Salon (official exhibition of the academy), which had been held regularly every two years since 1737 and in which Chardin had participated faithfully. It was in the exercise of his official duties that he met the Encyclopaedist and philosopher Denis Diderot, who would devote some of his finest pages of art criticism

to Chardin, the "grand magicien" he admired so much.

An anecdote illustrating Chardin's genius and his unique position in 18th-century European painting is told by one of his greatest friends, the engraver Charles-Nicolas Cochin, who wrote a letter shortly after Chardin's death to Haillet de Couronne, the man who was to deliver Chardin's eulogy to the Académie de Rouen, of which Chardin had been a member.

Unique qualities of his mature work

One day, an artist was making a big show of the method he used to purify and perfect his colors. Monsieur Chardin, impatient with so much idle chatter, said to the artist, "But who told you that one paints with colors?" "With what then?" the astonished artist asked. "One uses colors," replied Chardin, "but one paints with feeling."

He was nearer to the feeling of meditative quiet that animates the rustic scenes of the 17th-century French master Louis Le Nain than to the spirit of light and superficial brilliance seen in the work of many of his contemporaries. His carefully constructed still lifes do not bulge with appetizing foods but are concerned with the objects themselves and with the treatment of light. In his genre scenes he does not seek his models among the peasantry as his predecessors did; he paints the petty bourgeoisie of Paris. But manners have been softened, and his models seem to be far removed from Le Nain's austere peasants. The housewives of Chardin are simply but neatly dressed and the same cleanliness is visible in the houses where they live. Everywhere a sort of intimacy and good fellowship constitute the charm of these modestly scaled pictures of domestic life that are akin in feeling and format to the works of Jan Vermeer, the Dutch master of the 17th century.

Despite the triumphs of his early and middle life, Chardin's last years were clouded, both in his private life and in his career. His only son, Pierre-Jean, who had received the Grand Prix (prize to study art in Rome) of the academy in 1754, committed suicide in Venice in 1767. And then too, the public's taste had changed. The new director of the academy, the all-powerful Jean-Baptiste-Marie Pierre, in his desire to restore historical painting to the first rank, humiliated the old artist by reducing his pension and gradually divesting him of his duties at the academy. Furthermore, Chardin's sight was failing. He tried his hand at drawing with pastels. It was a new medium for him and less taxing on his eyes. Those pastels, most of which are in the Louvre, are highly thought of in the 20th century, but that was not the case in Chardin's own time. In fact, he lived out the remainder of his life in almost total obscurity, his work meeting with indifference. On December 6, 1779, he died forgotten.

Last years

It was not until the middle of the 19th century that he was rediscovered by a handful of French critics, including the brothers Edmond and Jules de Goncourt, and collectors (the Lavalard brothers, for example, who donated their collection of Chardins to the Musée de Picardie in Amiens). Especially noteworthy is the LaCaze Collection donated to the Louvre in 1869. Today Chardin is considered the greatest still-life painter of the 18th century, and his canvases are coveted by the world's most distinguished museums and collections.

MAJOR WORKS

Among the 400-odd works of Chardin, either actually attributed to the master or attributed to him in historical documents, are "La Raie" ("The Skate," 1727–28; Louvre, Paris); "Le Buffet" (1728; Louvre, Paris); "Attributes of the Sciences" (1731; Musée Jacquemart-André, Paris); "Attributes of the Arts" (1731; Musée Jacquemart-André, Paris); "The Copper Fountain" (Louvre, Paris); "Dame cachetant une lettre" ("Lady Sealing a Letter," 1733; Berlin-Dahlem Museum); "Woman Drinking Tea" (Hunterian Museum, Glasgow; "Sketching Youth Sharpening Pencil" (1737; Louvre, Paris); "Scouring Maid" (1738; Hunterian Museum, Glasgow); "The Provider" (1739; Louvre, Paris); "Le Bénédicité" ("The Grace," 1740; Louvre, Paris); "Pipe and Drinking Glasses" (Louvre, Paris); "A Vase of Flowers" (National Gallery of Scotland, Edinburgh); "The Jar of Olives" (1760; Louvre, Paris); "Dessert" (1763; Louvre, Paris); "The Wild Duck" (1764; Museum of Fine Arts, Springfield, Massachusetts); "The Attributes of Music" (1765; Louvre, Paris); "The Attributes of the Arts" (1765; Louvre, Paris); "Portrait of Chardin" (pastel, 1771; Louvre, Paris); "Portrait of

Mme. Chardin" (pastel, 1775; Louvre, Paris); "Portrait of Chardin with Eye Shades" (pastel, 1775; Louvre, Paris).

BIBLIOGRAPHY. The main work on Chardin is still that of G. WILDENSTEIN, *Chardin: biographie et catalogue critiques* (1933). G. WILDENSTEIN, *Chardin*, rev. by D. WILDENSTEIN (Eng. 1969), is the first comprehensive work on Chardin in English. See also PIERRE ROSENBERG, *Chardin: étude biographique et critique* (1963; Eng. trans., *Chardin: Biographical and Critical Study*, 1963).

(P.M.R.)

Charlemagne, Emperor

Charlemagne (Carolus Magnus, Charles the Great) as king of the Franks (768–814) conquered the Lombard kingdom in Italy, subdued the Saxons, annexed Bavaria to his kingdom, fought campaigns in Spain and Hungary, and, with the exception of the Kingdom of Asturias in Spain, southern Italy, and the British Isles, united in one superstate practically all the Christian lands of western Europe. In 800 he assumed the title of emperor. Besides expanding its political power, he also brought about a cultural renaissance in his empire. Although this *imperium* survived its founder by only one generation, the medieval kingdoms of France and Germany derived all their constitutional traditions from Charles' monarchy. Throughout medieval Europe, the person of Charles was considered the prototype of a Christian king and emperor.

By courtesy of the Musee du Louvre, Paris

Charlemagne, bronze statue, 9th century. In the Louvre, Paris.

Early years. Charles was born probably in 742 (on April 2), the elder son of Pepin III, also called Pepin the Short. Pepin and his older brother, Carloman, had just jointly assumed the government of the Frankish kingdom as *maior domus*, or "mayor of the palace." The dynasty, later called Carolingian after Charlemagne, had originated in the Meuse-Moselle region on the borders of modern France, Germany, Belgium, and The Netherlands. In the course of a few generations, it had, as mayors of the palace to the Merovingians, gained control of the entire Frankish kingdom. Charlemagne's grandfather, Charles Martel, reconstituted a realm that had been on the point of breaking up, and, without infringing on the royal prerogatives of the otherwise powerless Merovingians, he had in effect bequeathed the empire to his sons, Pepin and Carloman, like a family inheritance.

Charles grew to manhood while his father was engaged in acquiring sole sovereignty and the kingship. On Carloman's retirement to a monastery, Pepin eliminated the latter's sons from the government. Having thus prepared the way, he had himself proclaimed king in 751, after dethroning the Merovingians. An oracular response by

Pope Zacharias furnished the ecclesiastical approbation for thus shunting aside the former reigning house, which had been held sacred. Zacharias' successor, Stephen II, arrived in the Frankish kingdom during the winter of 753–754, in order to seek help against the Lombards who were attacking Rome. As the reigning monarch's oldest son, Charles, then about 12 years of age, travelled ahead to welcome the Pope, who anointed him king, along with his father and his brother Carloman, thus sanctioning the new dynasty. The political alliance between the Franks and the Pope against the Lombards was affirmed on the same occasion. When his father subdued Aquitaine (France south of the Loire) in a series of yearly campaigns beginning in 760, reasserting the integrity of the Frankish kingdom all the way to the Pyrenees, Charles repeatedly accompanied the army.

Alliance with the papacy

These youthful experiences probably contributed to the formation of Charles' character and to the formulation of his aims. He shared with his father an unbending will to power, a readiness to fight resolutely against external enemies and to increase his domains, and the determination to rule by himself even if it meant usurping the rights of close relatives. Charles early acknowledged the close connection between temporal power and the church; he had a high regard for the church and the king's duty to spread the Christian faith and, while asserting royal suzerainty over the church, considered himself accountable to God for the Christians entrusted to him.

King of the Franks. In accordance with old Frankish custom, the kingdom was divided on Pepin's death in 768 between his two sons. It was not long, however, before a strong rivalry sprang up between the brothers: with his mother's support, Charles concluded, with the Lombard king Desiderius, whose daughter he married, and with his cousin Duke Tassilo of Bavaria, alliances directed against Carloman.

On Carloman's sudden death in 771, Charles was able to make himself sole ruler of the kingdom, unopposed by his young nephews, whose rights he ignored. When Carloman's widow with her children and a few remaining supporters had fled to the Lombard court, and King Desiderius, breaking his alliance with Charles, put pressure on the Pope to anoint Carloman's sons as Frankish kings, Charles was forced to come to the aid of Pope Adrian I. He marched on the Lombard capital, Pavia, and after its fall made himself king of the Lombards. His brother's sons, who had fallen into his hands, disappeared. While the siege of Pavia was still in progress, Charles journeyed to Rome, where he celebrated Easter 774 with the Pope and reiterated, in St. Peter's Basilica, his father's promise to transfer to papal rule large sections of Italy. But he actually enlarged the Pope's lands only slightly, assuming for himself the sovereignty over the entire Lombard kingdom.

Expansion in Italy

Charles had fought the pagan Saxons, in what is now Lower Saxony and Westphalia, in retribution for their attacks on the lower Rhine region, as early as 772, before the first Italian campaign. From 775 on, however, it was his goal to subdue the whole Saxon tribe, converting it to Christianity and integrating it into his kingdom. This aim appeared to have been realized after several campaigns culminating in declarations of allegiance by the Saxon nobility and mass baptisms performed in 775–777. A diet held in 777 in Paderborn sealed the submission of the Saxons. Among those attending the diet had been some Arab emissaries from northern Spain who sought Charles' aid in their uprising against the Umayyad *amīr* of Córdoba. In the summer of 778 Charles advanced into Spain and laid siege to Saragossa, without, however, being able to take the city. Retreating across the Pyrenees, the Frankish army was badly mauled by the Basques. Roland, warden of the Breton march, who died on this occasion, was later immortalized in legend and poetry.

This defeat marks the end of the first period of Charles' rule, the period of vigorous expansion. Within a decade he had become the sole ruler of the Franks, conquered the Lombard kingdom, visited Rome, subdued the Saxons, invaded Spain. Henceforth he was concerned with defending and safeguarding his quickly won gains (which were to be extended only on the right bank of the Rhine), while consolidating the state internally and protecting cultural life and the rule of law.

Not long after Charles' defeat in Spain, the Saxons rose up once more. The war against them became the longest and most cruel war fought by the Franks. In Charles' eyes, the resistance of this people that had undergone baptism and signed a treaty of allegiance amounted to political high treason and religious apostasy. These offenses called for severe punishment, and 4,500 Saxons were reported to have been executed en masse in 782. New outbreaks occurred after 792, and the last Saxons were not vanquished until 804. Between 772 and 804, Charles took the field against the Saxons no less than 18 times. In the end he carried out his aim of not only subjecting them to his rule but also incorporating them fully into his empire. Given the indissoluble tie between temporal power and the Christian faith, this meant that they had to be converted. But the violent methods by which this missionary task was carried out had been unknown to the earlier Middle Ages, and the sanguinary punishment meted out to those who broke canon law or continued to engage in pagan practices called forth criticism in Charles' own circle, for example by Alcuin, his adviser and head of his palace school.

Subjuga-
tion of the
Saxons

When, in 788, Charles deposed his cousin Duke Tassilo III of Bavaria, who had acknowledged the Frankish kings as feudal lords, he in effect deprived of its independence the last of the German tribes beyond the Rhine. The Bavarians, who had long been Christians, were now directly integrated into the empire. The West Germanic tribes of the Alemanni, Bavarians, Saxons, and Thuringians thus found themselves for the first time gathered into one political unit. Charles' conquests on the right bank of the Rhine were, however, not limited to the Germanic tribes. Making Ratisbon (Regensburg), the residence of the Bavarian dukes, his base, he conducted several campaigns, partly under his own command, against the Avar kingdom (in modern Hungary and Upper Austria). The remaining Avar principalities and the newly founded Slav states of the Danubian region drifted into a loose dependence on the Franks, whose sovereignty they more or less acknowledged.

Expansion
of Charles'
realm

The gigantic expansion of the Frankish state, raising it far above the tribal states of the early Middle Ages, entailed qualitative as well as quantitative changes. Yet the idea of bestowing on Charles the Roman title of emperor arose only at a very late stage and out of a specific political constellation. While the Eastern, or Byzantine, Empire laid claim to universal recognition, the popes, constitutionally still subjects of Byzantium, were opposed to the iconoclastic religious policies of the Eastern emperors. Moreover, under the protection of Charles, Pope Adrian sought to erect an autonomous domain over central Italy, the more so as the Byzantines, abandoning for all practical purposes Rome and Ravenna, were asserting their rule only in Sicily and the southernmost edge of Italy. The papacy's desire for independence found a significant expression in the Donation of Constantine, a forgery dating probably from the first few years of Adrian's reign and purporting to legitimize these papal aims in the name of the first Christian emperor, Constantine I the Great. Charles paid a second visit to Rome in 781, when he had the Pope crown his young sons Pepin and Louis as kings of the Lombards and Aquitanians and gained de facto recognition of his Italian position from the Byzantine empress Irene, the mother of Constantine VI. The entente that existed between Charles and Byzantium came to an end after a Frankish attack on southern Italy in 787.

Emperor of the West. In the end, local Roman conflicts brought about the clarification of the city's constitutional position. In May 799, Pope Leo III was waylaid in Rome by personal enemies. He took refuge at the court of Charles, who had him conducted back to the city and who in November 800 came to Rome himself, where he was received with imperial honours. Before

Charles and a synod, Pope Leo cleared himself under oath of the charges made by his enemies. During Christmas mass in St. Peter's, the Romans acclaimed Charles emperor, whereupon the Pope crowned and perhaps anointed him.

Corona-
tion in
Rome

The imperial title was by nature a Roman dignity. While the acclamation represented the juridically conclusive act, it was the coronation at the hands of the Pope that, though of no constitutional importance, was to acquire for the Franks great significance. The Pope had been determined to make Charles emperor, deciding to a large extent the outward form; yet Charles was surely not surprised by these events. His famous statement quoted by one of his favourites, the Frankish historian Einhard, that he would not have set foot in church that Christmas if he had known the Pope's intention, implies a criticism of the ceremony initiated by the Pope, as well as a formal expression of humility. The crowning had been preceded by negotiations. While Charles' imperial rank was legally substantiated by the fact of his dominion over the western part of the old Roman Empire, the desire to counteract the petticoat rule of the empress Irene (who had dethroned and blinded her son in 797) also played a role. Residing in Rome four months and pronouncing sentence on the Pope's enemies as rebels guilty of lese majesty, Charles grasped the imperial reins with a firm hand. Likewise, after his return to Aachen (Aix-la-Chapelle), he promulgated laws in full consciousness of his rank as emperor.

Byzantium braced itself for the usurper's attack, but Charles merely wished to see his new rank and his dominion over Rome recognized in negotiations; he gained his point in 812 when the emperor Michael I acknowledged him as emperor, though not as emperor of the Romans. While the imperial title did not bring Charles any additional powers, his control of Rome was now legitimized, and the estrangement of the papacy from Byzantium and its rapprochement with the Franks, a major historical event that had been initiated in 754, was rendered incontrovertible. A significant result of this development was the tradition to which Charles' assumption of the imperial title and function gave rise: all medieval concepts of empire and all the bonds between the constitutional traditions of the Franks and the later Holy Roman Empire with the Roman Empire founded by Augustus were based on the precedent of Charles' imperial title and position.

Court and administration. The creation of the empire was chiefly legitimized by Charles' efforts to raise its cultural level internally. When Charles came to power, the Frankish kingdom's cultural, administrative, and legal institutions were still relatively undeveloped. The Frankish king, for example, possessed no permanent residence. In the summer months he travelled about, deciding political issues and dispensing justice in assemblies of spiritual and temporal lords; above all, summer was the season for military campaigns. During the winter, from Christmas to Easter and sometimes longer, the king lived and held court at one of the imperial palaces. Charles especially favoured those situated in the Frankish heartland: only rarely did he spend the winter in one of the newly won territories, in encampment in Saxony, in Ratisbon, or in Rome. Not until 794 did Aachen, which the aging monarch liked because of its warm springs, become the court's abode, indeed almost a residence, during every winter and often even in summer. Here Charles built, partially with materials imported from Rome and Ravenna, the court church that is still standing, as well as the palace whose walls were incorporated into the 14th-century city hall.

Charles'
peripatetic
court

Charles' court consisted of his family, of the clergy in his personal service, who were called the king's *capella*, and of temporal officials, among them the count palatine, the seneschal, and the master of the royal household. These men were occasionally joined, on an informal basis, by other spiritual or temporal men of rank who spent some time in the ruler's presence. For Charles had the ambition to make his court the intellectual, as well as the political and administrative, centre of the realm and accordingly summoned prominent scholars from all parts of the empire and even from abroad. Among these the most important were Einhard and Alcuin.

With the help of these and other literary men, Charles established a court library containing the works of the Church Fathers and those of ancient authors, and he founded a court academy for the education of young Frankish knights. Last but not least, he himself took part with his family and the learned and lay members of his entourage in a cultivated social life that afforded him entertainment no less than instruction. His mother tongue was an Old High German idiom, besides which he presumably understood the Old French dialect spoken by many Franks; as a grown man, he also learned Latin and some Greek, had historical and theological writings, including St. Augustine's *City of God*, read aloud to him, and acquired a rudimentary knowledge of mathematics and astronomy.

The Carolingian renaissance

The court's cultural interests, however, extended beyond the intellectual gratification of a small circle, such as the exchange of verses and letters. Efforts were also made to raise the level of religious observance, morality, and the process of justice throughout the empire. The clearest and most famous instance of this was the *Epistula de litteris colendis*, dating presumably from 784–785 and compiled in Charles' name by Alcuin. Its main argument lies in the assertion that the right faith—indeed, every right thought—must be clothed in the appropriate form and language, lest it be falsified; hence, the prescription of intensive study of Latin language and literature for all monastic and cathedral schools. The spiritual and literary movement called the "Carolingian renaissance" had many centres, especially in the empire's monasteries; but it cannot be evaluated without reference to Charles' court and to his endeavour to call on the best minds of the whole world, setting them to work in the education of the clergy and, in the final instance, of the whole people. The court's theological knowledge and intellectual self-confidence are reflected in the *Libri Carolini*, a comprehensive treatise written about 791 in Charles' name and directed against the Council of Nicaea (787), at which Greeks and papal plenipotentiaries had countenanced the practice of iconolatry; at the same time, the *Libri Carolini* did not spare the iconoclasts.

Through this court, Charles ruled and administered his empire and dispensed justice. Once or twice a year at least, the court and the chief magistrates and nobles from all parts of the empire joined in a general assembly held either in the Frankish heartland or in one of the conquered territories. It is indicative of the unique structure of the Carolingian Empire that one cannot draw clear distinctions between an assembly of the armed forces, a constitutional assembly of the nobility, and a church synod: juridical, military, and ecclesiastical affairs were invariably discussed at one and the same time by the representatives of the nobility and the clergy. Above them all towered the figure of Charlemagne.

Internal administration

On the local level the ruler was represented in every region by counts and bishops. Liaison between these and the court was maintained through royal messengers who travelled about at Charles' command, usually in pairs made up of a civil servant and a clerical dignitary. Royal commands did not have to be written out, although Charles' decrees (capitularies) increasingly came to be recorded in writing, at first rather imprecisely, in the last two decades of his reign; the forms coined by the "renaissance" gained ground only with time. Charles respected the traditional rights of the various peoples and tribes as a matter of principle, and, after he became emperor, he had many of them recorded. The capitularies served partly as complements to tribal laws, partly as regulations applying to the most disparate aspects of public and private life, and in part also as specific instructions issued to royal messengers, counts, bishops, and others. Punitive decrees against highwaymen, dispositions concerning military levies, orders for the people to take an oath of allegiance to the emperor or to teach all Christians to recite the Lord's Prayer, are found intermingled in the capitularies with jurisdictional dispositions and regulations about the internal organization of monasteries; temporal and spiritual problems are rarely treated separately. Taken as a whole, the legal documents of Charles' reign bear witness to a great concern, born of profound moral and religious convictions, with the administration of justice and with public enlightenment, but they show discrepancies between the ideal and reality.

Limitations of his rule. Charles' organization of the empire was, however, not without its defects and limitations. The sovereign's power was restricted only by theoretical principles of law and custom, not by institutions or countervailing forces. Significantly, the records report little about opposition movements and conspiracies, which, in fact, did exist. A rebellion that Thuringian counts launched against Charles in 786 can perhaps be explained as ethnic opposition to the centralism of the Franks. More ominous was an aristocratic conspiracy that in 792 attempted to place on the throne the hunchback Pepin, Charles' only son from his first marriage, which was later declared invalid; yet here, too, the political concepts and motives remain unknown. These events and, more clearly still, the history of the empire under Charles' successor, Louis, show the extent to which the political system had been designed for one person on whose outstanding abilities everything depended and with whose disappearance it threatened to collapse. Their self-confidence enhanced by Charles' educational policy, the clergy could not accept for all time his theocracy without opposing it with their own political and religious principles. The temporal nobility that had built the empire with the Carolingians could be firmly tied to the dynasty only as long as new conquests held out the prospect of new spoils and fiefs; if these failed to materialize, there remained only the care of one's properties in the different regions and the hope of gaining advantages from party strife. External expansion, however, could not advance substantially beyond the borders reached by 800; in fact, economic and technical resources were insufficient to hold together and administer what had already been won and to defend it against foreign enemies. Charles' empire lacked the means by which the Romans had preserved theirs: a money economy, a paid civil service, a standing army, a properly maintained network of roads and communications, a navy for coastal defense. Already in Charles' lifetime, the coasts were being threatened by the Normans. In 806 Charles planned a division of the empire between his sons, but after the death of the elder two he crowned Louis of Aquitaine his coemperor and sole successor at Aachen in 813. It was only a few months later that Charles himself died there on January 28, 814.

Personality and influence. Charlemagne's posthumous fame shone the more brightly as the following generations were unable to preserve the empire's internal peace, its unity, and its international position. Even after the Carolingian dynasty had become extinct, political tradition in the East Frankish (German) kingdom and empire, as well as in the West Frankish (French) kingdom, drew sustenance from the example set by Charlemagne. Under Otto I, Aachen became the city in which the rulers of Germany were crowned, and, at Frederick I Barbarossa's request, the antipope Paschal III canonized Charlemagne in 1165. In France the Capetians, beginning with Philip II Augustus, revived the traditions that had grown up around Charlemagne. The controversial question whether the Germans or the French were the true successors of Charlemagne was kept alive through the Middle Ages and into modern times. Napoleon called himself Charlemagne's successor; after the end of World War II, discussions of a united, Christian, "occidental" Europe invoked his model. Hand in hand with these political traditions went those in popular legend and poetry, culminating in the Roland epics. Nor did Charlemagne's fame stop at the boundaries of what was once his empire; some Slavic languages derived their term for "king" from his name (Czech *král*, Polish *król*, etc.).

Charles left no biographical document; his personality can be constructed only from his deeds and the reports

Character
and
appearance

left by contemporaries. This is how Einhard, who lived at the court from about 795 on, described Charlemagne's character and appearance in his famous *Vita Karoli:* "He had a broad and strong body of unusual height, but well-proportioned; for his height measured seven times his feet. His skull was round, the eyes were lively and rather large, the nose of more than average length, the hair gray but full, the face friendly and cheerful. Seated or standing, he thus made a dignified and stately impression even though he had a thick, short neck and a belly that protruded somewhat; but this was hidden by the good proportions of the rest of his figure. He strode with firm step and held himself like a man; he spoke with a higher voice than one would have expected of someone of his build. He enjoyed good health except for being repeatedly plagued by fevers four years before his death. Toward the end he dragged one foot."

The strength of Charlemagne's personality was evidently rooted in the unbroken conviction of being at one with the divine will. Without inward contradiction, he was able to combine personal piety with enjoyment of life, a religious sense of mission with a strong will to power, rough manners with a striving for intellectual growth, and intransigence against his enemies with rectitude. In his politically conditioned religiosity, the empire and the church grew into an institutional and spiritual unit. Although his empire survived him by only one generation, it contributed decisively to the eventual reconstitution, in the mind of a western Europe fragmented since the end of the Roman Empire, of a common intellectual, religious, and political inheritance on which later centuries could draw. Charlemagne did not create this inheritance single-handedly, but one would be hard put to imagine it without him. One of the poets at his court called him *rex pater Europae*—"King father of Europe." In truth, there is no other man who similarly left his mark on European history during the centuries of the Middle Ages.

BIBLIOGRAPHY. EINHARD, *Vita Karoli Magni,* ed. by O. HOLDER-EGGER (1911), ed. by L. HALPHEN (1938), Eng. trans. by S.E. TURNER, *The Life of Charlemagne* (1880, reprinted 1960), the famous biography of one of Charlemagne's closest collaborators—a character analysis rather than an account of events; D.A. BULLOUGH, *The Age of Charlemagne* (1965), a modern presentation for the general reader by a good specialist; "Europae Pater: Charlemagne and His Achievement in the Light of Recent Scholarship," *English Historical Review,* 85:59–105 (1970), a report on recent scholarship; H. FICHTENAU, *Das karolingische Imperium* (1949; *The Carolingian Empire,* 1957); *Karl der Grosse: Lebenswerk und Nachleben,* ed. by W. BRAUNFELS, 4 vol. and index (1965–67), an international compendium of 74 contributions by various experts (mostly in German with some articles in French, English, and Italian), representative of the present-day state of research.

(P.Cla.)

Charles IV, Emperor

Charles IV, German king and king of Bohemia from 1346 to 1378 and Holy Roman emperor from 1355, was the most learned sovereign of his time. He gained more through diplomacy than others did by war, and through purchases, marriages, and inheritance he enlarged his dynastic power. Under Charles's rule Prague became the political, economic, and cultural centre—and eventually the capital—of the Holy Roman Empire. Indeed, from his reign until the 18th century it was understood that the German imperial crown was based on the crown of the king of Bohemia.

Early life

Charles was born in Prague on May 14, 1316. He was the eldest son of the Bohemian king John of Luxembourg and Elizabeth, the sister of the last native Bohemian king. In 1323 he joined the French court, where he married Blanche, the sister of Philip VI of France. One of his teachers in Paris was the future pope Clement VI. In 1330 Charles's father summoned him to Luxembourg, and in 1331 he headed the administration of his father's provisional acquisitions in northern Italy. Two years later his father appointed him margrave of Moravia and captain general of Bohemia. In his autobiography Charles told of the difficulties he had in redeeming the

Charles IV, portrait bust by Petr Parléř, 14th century. In the triforium of St. Vitus' Cathedral, Prague.

Foto Marburg

pawned royal castles, towns, and mansions, in building up an army, and in suppressing the influence of the nobility, which had grown during his father's absence. But Charles's administrative ability only aroused John's suspicion, and he was dismissed in 1335. After a reconciliation Charles was assigned to missions outside Bohemia, but his competence as a statesman and diplomat made him increasingly indispensable to his father. In 1341 John, now blind, introduced him, as his successor, to an assembly of prelates, nobility, and gentry, representatives of the royal towns, and ambassadors of Breslau; in 1343 John entrusted him with the administration of the country. One year later, due to Charles's efforts, Pope Clement VI raised the bishopric of Prague to an archbishopric, thus giving the Bohemian countries ecclesiastical autonomy. At the same time, the foundation stone of St. Vitus' Cathedral, built under the direction of Charles, was laid on the Hradčany. Meanwhile, negotiations were initiated to elect Charles of Luxembourg German king in place of the Bavarian emperor Louis IV, who had been excommunicated by the Pope in 1324. Charles did not gain the throne until 1346, when he was elected by five out of seven electors and had taken all the oaths the Pope had demanded. William of Ockham, one of the greatest medieval theologians and scholars, called Charles *rex clericorum* ("king of the clergy"). Louis, however, refused to acknowledge Charles and maintained that he was the rightful king.

At first the coexistence of two German kings had no bad consequences. But after Charles took part in a war against England, in which his father died at the Battle of Crécy (1346), he became king of Bohemia and prepared to attack Louis. Although Louis IV died in the following year, his followers elected anti-kings until Charles won them over peaceably. By granting privileges to the towns in southern Germany, he gained their support; and by using diplomatic skill, he managed to make friends in the north as well. Soon he was generally recognized as the only German king. His main concern, however, lay in the Bohemian countries—his Luxembourgian dynastic power—which provided his greatest source of strength.

King of
Bohemia

In 1347 Charles was crowned king of Bohemia by the new archbishop in Prague. Within a few months he issued a new law of coronation and defined the constitutional position of the king in the state: Bohemia became a hereditary monarchy in which the law of succession of the first-born son and his descendants was to be valid and binding; in case of the extinction of the male lineage, the law of succession devolved upon the daughters. Later, Charles's testamentary contracts (1364) with the Habsburg family in Austria and the Árpáds in Hungary were the bases on which the Austro-Hungarian monarchy was formed. In 1348 Charles founded the first university in central Europe to possess the same rights and liberties as did the universities of Paris and Bologna. At the same time the foundation stone was laid near Prague for another of Charles's projects—Karlštejn castle, where the imperial crown jewelry and the insignia of the crown of Bohemia were placed. In 1354 Charles led an army into Italy to secure recognition of the authority of the House of Luxembourg and of the patrimonial dominions of Bohemia. Early in 1355 he received the Iron Crown of Lombardy in Milan, and that Easter he received the imperial crown in Rome. At that time a Florentine contemporary described Charles as a medium-sized man, black-haired and broad-faced, with his upper body bent forward. He is said to have fetched the imperial crown and then returned to Prague, leaving the Italians embroiled in their own domestic problems. Petrarch was very much disillusioned by Charles.

The Golden Bull

Back in Prague, Charles issued the decree known as the Golden Bull, a kind of imperial constitution. It regulated the election of the German king by seven electors, who, privileged with special rights, became *domini terrae*, real sovereigns; and above all stood the king of Bohemia. Charles's last wish was to secure the succession to the throne for his eldest son, Wenceslas. After long and difficult negotiations, Wenceslas was elected the German king.

Charles died on November 29, 1378, in Prague and was buried in St. Vitus' Cathedral.

Charles IV was a generous patron of arts and science, especially in Prague, and ardently supported church building and the establishment of charitable institutions. He was interested in the early Humanism, which especially came to influence his government, and was also influential in the development of the German written language.

BIBLIOGRAPHY. BEDE JARRETT, *The Emperor Charles IV* (1935), is a competent survey; also useful is SAMUEL H. THOMSON, "Learning at the Court of Charles IV," *Speculum*, 25:1–20 (1950). GRAY C. BOYCE and WILLIAM H. DAWSON, *The University of Prague: Modern Problems of the German University in Czechoslovakia* (1937), presents a one-sided account. K. PFISTERER and W. PUESS (eds.), *Karoli IV. vita ab eo ipso conscripta* (1950), encompasses the years 1331–46.

(H.Pr.)

Charles V, Emperor

The last emperor to aspire to the medieval ideal of universal empire, Charles V, Holy Roman emperor from 1519 to 1556, left a life's work representing an achievement of rare integrity and consistency, however circumscribed it may have been by personal inhibitions and external obstacles.

Charles faced a fourfold task in his role as emperor, as king of Spain and Naples, and as ruler of Milan, the Netherlands, and the ever-expanding "isles and terra firma" of the New World. The emperor in him was inspired by the idea of reasserting the tradition of a spiritually and politically united Christian world, itself an archaic program that seemed essentially medieval. The Spanish and German sovereign in him laboured under the burden of having to expel Islām from Europe and the Mediterranean, a problem that harked back to the Christian Crusades yet could be successfully solved only through the most up-to-date economic and strategic means. Similarly ambivalent in nature was the New World's incorporation into the Christian community of nations; while the unprecedented newness of the task made it the most modern of those that Charles had to face, the very concept entailed a duty that was in many ways already archaic: that of making the New World Christian and Spanish, much like the reconquered portions of the Iberian Peninsula. An additional difficulty was that everything had to be done literally from the beginning, when it came to absorbing into his empire—politically, administratively, and economically—territories that had never been subjected to such organization. In contrast, the struggle for supremacy in Europe, during which Charles spent several decades fighting against his rival, the King of France, showed him to be very much a man of his own century.

Early years. Charles was born on February 24, 1500, in Ghent (Flanders), the son of Philip I the Handsome, king of Castile, and Joan the Mad, and the grandson of

Charles V, oil painting by Titian, 1548. In the Bayerische Staatsgemäldesammlungen, Munich.
By courtesy of the Bayerische Staatsgemaldesammlungen, Munich

Emperor Maximilian I and Mary of Burgundy, as well as of the "Catholic Kings" Isabella I the Catholic, of Castile, and Ferdinand II the Catholic, of Aragon. After his father's death in 1506, Charles was raised by his paternal aunt Margaret of Austria, regent of the Netherlands. His spiritual guide was the theologian Adrian of Utrecht, a member of the *devotio moderna*, a religious and educational reform movement promoting literacy among the masses; his worldly mentor, the Sieur de Chièvres, was a Francophile Burgundian. Charles's mother tongue was French; but, although he did not learn it until after his 16th birthday, he mastered Spanish so well that it soon became his favourite language.

At the age of 15, he assumed the rule over the Netherlands. His scope of activities soon widened. After the death of his maternal grandfather, Ferdinand II, in 1516, Charles was proclaimed sovereign of Spain, together with his mother (who, however, suffered from a nervous illness and never reigned). In September 1517 he landed in Spain, a country with whose customs he was unfamiliar and whose language he was as yet barely able to speak. There he instituted, under Burgundian influence, a government that was little better than foreign rule. When his election as king of Germany in 1519 (his paternal grandfather, the Habsburg emperor Maximilian I, having died) recalled him to Germany, Charles left behind him, after some two and one-half years in Spain, a dissatisfied and restless people. Adrian, whom he had installed as regent, was not strong enough to suppress the revolt of the Castilian cities (*comuneros*) that broke out at this point. Making the most of their candidate's German parentage and buying up German electoral votes (mostly with money supplied by the powerful Fugger banking family), Charles's adherents had meanwhile pushed through his election as emperor over his powerful rival, Francis I of France.

King of Spain

Political history of his reign. In October 1520 Charles was accordingly crowned king of Germany in Aachen, assuming at the same time the title of Roman emperor-elect. In the spring of 1521, the imperial Diet before which Luther had to defend his theses assembled at Worms. The reformer's appearance represented a first challenge to Charles, who had his own confession of faith, beginning with a sweeping invocation of his Catholic ancestors, read out to the Diet. Rejecting Luther's doctrines in the Edict of Worms, Charles declared war on Protestantism.

Gradually, the other chief task of his reign also unfolded: the struggle for hegemony in western Europe, a legacy of his Burgundian forefathers. Long before, the grand design of his ancestor Charles the Bold had come to naught in the fight against the French Valois, Louis XI. Now the great-grandson was brought face-to-face with the main problem of his great-grandfather's existence. It was to become a fateful problem for Charles also.

Struggle for supremacy with Francis I

After defeating Duca Massimiliano Sforza at Marignano in 1515, the reigning Valois, Francis I, compelled him, in the Treaty of Noyon, to renounce his claim to the Duchy of Milan. The vanquished Sforza turned for help to Pope Leo X and Charles V, with whom he concluded a treaty in 1521. Despite the outbreak of war with France, Charles hurried back to Spain, where his followers had meanwhile gained the upper hand over the *comuneros*. Even though he granted an amnesty, the young monarch proved to be an intransigent ruler, bloodily suppressing the revolt and signing 270 death warrants. These actions were nevertheless followed by a rapid and complete rapprochement between the pacified people and their sovereign; in fact, it was during this second and protracted sojourn in Spain (1522–29) that Charles became a Spaniard, with Castilian grandees replacing the Burgundians. There soon developed an emotionally tinged understanding between Charles and his Spanish subjects that was to be steadily deepened during his long rule. Henceforth, it was primarily the material resources of his Spanish domains that sustained his far-flung policies and his Spanish troops who acquitted themselves most bravely and successfully in his wars.

In 1522 his teacher Adrian of Utrecht became pope, as Adrian VI. His efforts to reconcile Francis I and the Emperor failed, and three years later Charles's army defeated Francis I at Pavia, taking prisoner the King himself. The victory assured Spanish supremacy in Italy. Held in the alcazar of Madrid, the royal captive feigned agreement with the conditions imposed by Charles, even taking the Emperor's oldest sister, Eleanor, the dowager queen of Portugal, for his wife and handing over his sons as hostages. But, as soon as he had regained his freedom, Francis rejected the terms of the Treaty of Madrid of January 1526. That same year, in which Francis I, Pope Clement VII, Venice, and Milan united against Charles in the League of Cognac, also saw an ominous deterioration in eastern Europe, even though at first the Habsburg dynasty gained two further crowns.

With the accession of Süleyman the Magnificent to the sultanate in 1520, Turkish pressure on Europe increased once more. The Sultan threatened not only Hungary but also those hereditary provinces of the Habsburgs that, by Charles's agreement in 1522 with his brother Ferdinand, henceforth belonged to the younger branch of the Habsburgs. When Louis II of Hungary and Bohemia was defeated and killed by the Turks in the Battle of Mohács in August 1526, Ferdinand assumed this throne both as the childless former monarch's brother-in-law and by virtue of the treaty of succession concluded in 1491 between his own grandfather and Louis' father, Vladislov II. After this, the Turkish danger became the Habsburgs' foremost concern on land, as it had been on the seas ever since Charles's accession to the throne of Spain. Although Charles realized that his first duty as emperor of Christendom lay in warding off this peril, he found himself so enmeshed in the affairs of western Europe that he had little time, energy, and money left for this task. In 1526 Charles married Isabella, the daughter of King Manuel I of Portugal.

In early 1527, instead of fighting the infidel, Charles's Spanish troops and his German mercenaries marched against the Pope, his enemy since the establishment of the League of Cognac. Mutinous and with their pay in arrears, they entered the defenseless city of Rome and looted it during the infamous Sack of Rome (May 1527). The Pope, having surrendered to the mutinous troops, was now ready for any compromise. The newly started war between the Emperor and France also came to a close when the mother of Francis I approached Margaret of Austria, the Emperor's aunt, through whose mediation the "ladies' peace" of Cambrai was concluded in August 1529. The status quo was preserved: Charles renounced his claim to Burgundy, Francis his claims to Milan and Naples. The Pope, having made peace with Charles, met him in Bologna; there, he crowned him emperor in February 1530. It was to be the last time that a Holy Roman emperor was crowned by a pope.

In 1530, Charles, attempting to bring about a reformation within the Catholic Church through the convocation of a universal council, also tried to find a modus vivendi with the Protestants. The Catholics, however, replied to the Confession of Augsburg, the basic confessional statement of the Lutheran Church, with the Confutation, which met with Charles's approval. The final decree issued by the Diet accordingly confirmed, in somewhat expanded form, the resolutions embodied in the Edict of Worms of 1521. This, in turn, caused the Protestant princes to close ranks in the following year in the Schmalkaldic League. Faced with renewed Turkish onslaughts, the Emperor granted some concessions in return for armed support against the enemy. In 1532 a large army under Charles's personal command faced Süleyman's forces before the city of Vienna, but the order to give decisive battle was withheld. Instead, the Emperor returned to Spain in 1533, leaving his brother Ferdinand behind as his deputy.

By taking up his grandfather Ferdinand of Aragon's project of conquering North Africa, Charles endeavoured to undertake by sea what he had omitted to do on land. The attempt to repulse the corsair (and Turkish general) Barbarossa (Khayr ad-Dīn) was nonetheless no more than a marginal operation, since Charles's capture of Ḥalq al-Wādī and Tunis (1535) did nothing to diminish the strength of Süleyman's position. In 1532, on the other hand, a decisive change could have been brought about at Vienna.

Fighting Turks and Protestants

From Africa, the Emperor sailed to Naples, entering Rome in 1536 to deliver his famous political address before Pope Paul III and the Sacred College of Cardinals, in which he challenged the King of France (who had meanwhile invaded Savoy and taken Turin) to personal combat. When Francis declined, Charles invaded Provence in an operation that soon faltered. Through the Pope's intercession, peace was concluded in May 1538.

Intent on suppressing the open revolt that had broken out in Ghent, his native city, the Emperor himself went to the Netherlands. The country's regent, Charles's sister, Mary of Hungary, had proved incapable of settling the conflict between herself and the city, which jealously guarded its prerogatives. On his arrival in February 1540, Charles revoked Ghent's privileges, had 13 leading rebels executed, and gave orders to build a fortified castle. Once again his actions, as severe as those he had taken against the *comuneros* in 1522, were crowned by success. Toward the German Protestants, on the other hand, he showed himself conciliatory; in 1541 the Diet of Regensburg granted them major concessions, even if these were later rejected by both the Pope and Luther. Although Ferdinand, having lost his Hungarian capital in August 1541, pleaded for a land campaign against Süleyman, Charles again decided on a naval venture, which failed dismally after an unsuccessful attack on Algiers.

When Charles enfeoffed his son Philip with Milan, the King of France, enraged because he had hoped to regain indirect control of Milan himself, rearmed and declared war in August 1542. Fighting broke out the following year, even though the Pope had finally convoked, in Trent, the council for which the Emperor had been pressing. Once again Charles's precarious financial situation partially accounted for the failure of his plans. His finances were in a perpetually unsettled state. The "Indian" possessions in America were, of course, in an uninterrupted state of expansion throughout his entire reign, marked by, among other ventures, the conquest of Mexico and the conquest of Peru, but they did not yet form an organic part of the Spanish body politic. The gold from the Indies did not add up to any sizable sum at the time. Only in 1550 did 17 Spanish ships provide the Emperor with 3,000,000 ducats and others with a like sum in the earliest significant monetary transfusion from the New World. The silver mines of Potosí were not exploited systematically until the 1550s, so that their revenue arrived too late for Charles. In 1516 the floating debt amounted to 20,000 livres; by 1556 it had risen to 7,000,-000. In 1556, the exchequer owed 6,761,272 ducats. Thus, the campaign of 1543–44, inadequately financed, bogged down. It was to no avail that the French and imperial armies faced one another in the field in November 1543 and again in August 1544. As in 1532, when Charles had faced the Turks before Vienna, neither side cared to open hostilities, with the result that the peace of Crepy (September 1544) again more or less confirmed the status quo.

The Council of Trent did not open until December 1545, but Paul III had earlier offered Charles men and money against the heretics. When the Protestant princes failed to put in an appearance at the imperial Diet of Regensburg in 1546, the religious and political situation turned critical once again. Charles prepared for war, realizing that he neither commanded the allegiance of the German people, a majority of which tended toward the new faith, nor owned any appreciable portion of the German lands within the empire. His attempt to connect Austria with the Netherlands, by means of a land bridge through Württemberg, had failed in 1534.

In a battle that decided the whole campaign and placed his archenemies at his mercy, the Emperor (who had been attacked by the German princes the previous September) defeated the Protestants at Mühlberg in April 1547. Ill much of the time, he spent the following year at Augsburg, where he succeeded in detaching the Netherlands from the imperial Diet's jurisdiction while yet assuring their continued protection by the empire. Also in Augsburg, he drew up his "political testament" for Philip and reorganized the Spanish court. The Diet of Augsburg furthermore saw the publication of the "Interim," a formula conciliatory to the Protestants but retaining the Roman Catholic ritual, in general. Although Charles believed that he had granted far-reaching concessions to the people and the Protestant authorities in this document, his main concern was to make the Protestants return to the Catholic Church. While the Pope naturally confirmed it, the "Interim" was "rejected to his face" in largely Protestant Germany.

Decline and death. North Germany was now on the brink of revolt. The new king of France, Henry II, was eagerly awaiting an opportunity to renew the old rivalry between the houses of Valois and Burgundy, while the German princes believed that the moment was at hand to repay Charles for Mühlberg. After a secret treaty was signed in October 1551 between Henry II, Albert II Alcibiades, margrave of Brandenburg, and Maurice, elector of Saxony, Maurice in January 1552 ceded to France the cities of Metz, Toul, and Verdun, thus handing over imperial lands. When Maurice tried to capture the Emperor himself, the latter barely managed to escape by fleeing from Innsbruck over the Brenner Pass to Villach in Carinthia. He soon gathered reinforcements, but the changed political situation compelled him to ratify an agreement made between his brother Ferdinand and the rebels, according to which the new Protestant religion was to be granted equal rights with Roman Catholicism. Charles's attempt to retake Metz that fall ended in a complete fiasco, with Burgundy capitulating to Valois and the Emperor defeated in his struggle for hegemony in western Europe.

In order to save what he could of this hegemony, Charles, already severely racked by gout, tried new paths by preparing the ground for his widowed son's marriage with Mary I of England. It looked for a while as if his great hopes were about to be fulfilled, the joining of north and south and the realization of the dream of a universal empire. But, even though Philip married Mary in July 1554, the English Parliament emphatically refused to crown him. Since Mary remained childless, Charles's hopes came to naught. After an abortive last

Equal rights for Protestants

campaign against France, he prepared for his abdication, renouncing, in 1555 and 1556, his claims to the Netherlands and Spain in favour of Philip and those to the imperial crown in Ferdinand's favour. Disembarking in Spain at the end of September 1556, he moved to the monastery of Yuste, which he had long ago selected as his final refuge, in early February 1557. There he laid the groundwork for the eventual bequest of Portugal to the Habsburgs after King Sebastian's death with the help of his sister Catherine, grandmother of Sebastian and regent of Portugal. He aided his son in procuring funds in Spain for the continuation of the war against France, and he helped his daughter Joan, regent of Spain during Philip's absence in the Netherlands, in persecuting Spanish heretics. Charles died on September 21, 1558, at Yuste.

Assessment. Not only the task but the man to whom it was given had a dual nature. By background and training, Charles was a medieval ruler whose outlook on life was stamped throughout by a deeply experienced Catholic faith and by the knightly ideals of the late chivalric age. Yet, his sober, rational, and pragmatic thinking again mark him as a man of his age. Although Charles's moral uprightness and sense of personal honour make it impossible to regard him as a truly Machiavellian statesman, his unswerving resolve and his refusal to give up any part whatsoever of his patrimony are evidence of a strong and unconditional will to power. More than that, it is precisely this individual claim to power that forms the core of his personality and explains his aims and actions.

Charles's abdication has been variously interpreted. While many saw in it an unsuccessful man's escape from the world, his contemporaries thought differently. Charles himself had been considering the idea even in his prime. In 1532 his secretary, Alfonso de Valdés, suggested to him the thought that a ruler who was incapable of preserving the peace and, indeed, who had to consider himself an obstacle to its establishment was obliged to retire from affairs of state. Once the abdication had become a fact, St. Ignatius of Loyola had this to say:

> The emperor gave a rare example to his successors . . . in so doing, he proved himself to be a true Christian prince . . . may the Lord in all His goodness now grant the emperor freedom.

In this last, metaphysically tinged period of his life, Charles's freedom consisted in his conscious and conscientious preparation for the *buen morir*, for a lucid death.

BIBLIOGRAPHY. The following are the most important among the publications dealing with the very numerous documents and sources on Charles's life and reign: KARL LANZ (ed.), *Correspondenz des Kaisers Karl V.*, 3 vol. (1844–46); *Staatspapiere zur Geschichte Kaiser Karls V.* (1845); and *Aktenstücke und Briefe zur Geschichte Kaiser Karls V.*, in *Monumenta Habsburgica*, vol. 1 (1853). Of Charles's instructions and testaments (that outweigh, in their importance for our understanding of his thoughts and deeds, even the personal correspondence), only one document has survived in the original. The secret instructions to Philip, however, set down in 1543 in Palamós, are found reprinted in W. MAURENBRECHER, *Forschungen zur deutschen Geschichte*, vol. 2 (1863); the "Political Testament" (Avisos o Instrución) 1548, in PRUDENCIO DE SANDOVAL, *Historia de la vida y hechos del emperador Carlos V*, vol. 3 (1955–56).

Apart from Sandoval's work the most important narrative source among many is the biography (up to 1551), written in a very vivid style and true to fact, of Charles's court historiographer, ALONSO DE SANTA CRUZ, *Crónica del Emperador Carlos Quinto*, 5 vol. (1920–25). Modern treatments of Charles's life are equally numerous. KARL BRANDI, *Kaiser Karl V.*, 3rd ed., 2 vol. (1941; Eng. trans., *The Emperor Charles V: The Growth and Destiny of a Man and of a World Empire*, 1938), is considered the classic account of his life, unsurpassed in the plasticity of its style, its solid informativeness based on a very extensive study of the sources, its profound historical knowledge, and its high literary level. A lively complement to this work is ROYALL TYLER, *The Emperor Charles the Fifth* (1956). Of fundamental importance for the whole economic and financial background is RAMON CARANDE, *Carlos V y sus Banqueros*, 3 vol. (1949–67), an extensive account of this topic. The authoritative analysis of the intellectual and political background is JOSE ANTONIO MARAVALL, *Carlos V y el Pensamiento político del Renacimiento* (1960). MANUEL GONZALEZ ALVAREZ, *La España del Emperador Carlos V* (1966), represents what is probably the most recent all-inclusive description of the emperor's life, work, and reign.

(M. de F.)

Charles VII of France

At the beginning of Charles VII's reign (1422), France, suffering from defeat during the Hundred Years' War, was dominated by the English and their Burgundian allies. Together with Joan of Arc, he became a symbol of resistance to the enemy and the hope of liberation. By war and diplomacy, Charles succeeded in making peace with Burgundy and eventually in expelling the English from almost all of France. Aided by able and energetic counsellors, he renovated the administrative structures of the French monarchy.

Giraudon

Charles VII, portrait by Jean Fouquet (c. 1420–81). In the Louvre, Paris.

Charles VII was born February 22, 1403, the 11th child of King Charles VI and his wife, Isabella of Bavaria. Indulged by his mother, he was permanently marked by his childhood at the French court, where intrigue, luxury, a taste for the arts, extravagance, and profligacy all prevailed at the same time. Crises caused by his father's insanity were frequent. In May 1413 rioting Parisians invaded the Hôtel Saint-Paul, where he lived. Toward the end of that year, he was betrothed to Mary of Anjou, the nine-year-old daughter of Louis II of Anjou, king of Naples, and his wife, Yolande of Aragon. Charles went to live in Anjou, where Yolande, energetic and accustomed to rule, established her influence over him. In 1416, he became captain general of Paris and began to participate in the royal council, where Louis of Anjou played a prominent role.

On the death of his elder brother in April 1417, Charles became dauphin (heir to the throne) at the age of 14. He was named lieutenant general of the kingdom, but his mother left Paris and allied herself with John the Fearless, duke of Burgundy. On May 29, 1418, the Burgundians occupied the capital, and Charles had to **Assumption of regency** flee to Bourges. There he put himself at the head of the Armagnac party (rivals of the Burgundians) and at the end of 1418 assumed the title of regent for the deranged Charles VI. Faced with the threat of the English, who had invaded France, and the demands of the English king, Henry V, who claimed the French crown, Charles attempted to reconcile his differences with the Duke of Burgundy. They concluded a pact of friendship at Pouilly on July 2, 1419, but, in the course of another meeting at Montereau on September 10, the Duke was killed by the Armagnacs in Charles's presence. On December 24 the Duke's successor, Philip the Good, utilizing powers conferred on him by Charles VI, concluded a general truce

with the English, excluding the Armagnacs and sealing the Anglo-Burgundian alliance. In 1420 the Treaty of Troyes recognized Henry V as heir to the French throne, excluding Charles. Charles's supporters, however, included not only the Armagnacs but also the "party of the King," which backed his claim to the succession. These people set up an administration in Poitiers and Bourges the jurisdiction of which extended over all of France south of the Loire River, except for the English part of Guyenne. In April of 1422 Charles celebrated his marriage at Bourges. He then resumed warfare, occupied La Charité, and threatened Burgundian territory, though still avoiding any major confrontation with the Anglo-Burgundian armies.

On the death of his father on October 21, 1422, Charles assumed the title of king of France. His worst difficulties were of a financial nature: the taxes voted by the States General (representative assembly) were insufficient for his needs; he mortgaged his lands and lived by borrowing from financiers and nobles, such as Georges de La Trémoille. His army was repulsed at Verneuil in August 1424, and he tried once again to effect a reconciliation with the Duke of Burgundy; but his efforts were frustrated by the memory of John the Fearless' murder. In 1425, influenced by his mother-in-law, he dissociated himself from the Armagnacs. Arthur de Richemont, brother of John V, duke of Brittany, and brother-in-law of the Duke of Burgundy, became constable of France; he endeavoured to bring about peace, but the negotiators were still unable to come to an agreement in 1427. The English and the Burgundians revived the war and gained ground. Richemont was disgraced and replaced by La Trémoille, who sought only his own fortune. On October 12, 1428, the English laid siege to Orléans. Charles was 25 years old at this time. For 12 years he had known only war and the worst of intrigues. He could neither reconquer his kingdom nor conclude peace with the Burgundians. Discouraged, he thought of retiring to Spain or of ceding to English pressure. But the defense of Orléans became for the French a symbol of their struggle against the enemy. Joan of Arc, the visionary peasant girl from Lorraine, travelled across the country to fortify the King's intentions to fight for France. He received her at Chinon in February 1429. **Meeting with Joan of Arc** She restored the French army's confidence, and they liberated Orléans. On July 17, after a victorious journey with his army, Charles was crowned at Reims, in spite of his counsellors' misgivings. Through the efforts of Yolande, La Trémoille was then forced out of the council, and Richemont was restored to favour. In 1435, after protracted negotiations, Philip of Burgundy concluded a separate peace with France at Arras: the King condemned the murder of Philip's father, and the Duke recognized Charles as his sovereign. A new phase then opened up in Charles's life. At the age of 32, he seemed to have achieved maturity. He worked regularly with his counsellors. Between 1425 and 1439, he gradually acquired the permanent right to levy taxes that previously had to be approved by the States General, thus gaining financial independence. The merchant Jacques Coeur, court banker, master of the mint, and adviser to the king, did much to expand French commerce in the Mediterranean before he fell from favour in 1451.

The administration of the realm was reorganized, and in 1438 Charles promulgated the Pragmatic Sanction of Bourges, limiting papal authority over the church in France. The Sanction also increased the King's control over the granting of ecclesiastical revenues. The discipline of the army was improved and methods of recruitment made more efficient by the ordinances of 1439, 1445, and 1448. In 1437, the King took command of his armies again for the first time since his coronation and returned to Paris, which had been liberated from the English the previous year. The power of the nobility was lessened by his reforms; encouraged by the Duke of Burgundy—and especially by Charles's son, the dauphin Louis (later King Louis XI)—they formed a coalition against the King (the Praguerie). Charles reacted skillfully and energetically, and the rebellion was put down

(1440). To counter such intrigues, to end the destruction caused by the Écorcheurs (bands of mercenary soldiers then ravaging the country), and also because of a stalemate in diplomatic negotiations with England, Charles renewed the war in 1441 both north of Paris and in Guyenne, in the southwest. In 1444, negotiations finally brought a general truce, but no permanent peace was concluded, and hostilities were resumed in 1449; the King's cousin, Jean d'Orléans, comte de Dunois, was placed in charge of operations. Charles campaigned successfully in Normandy and took possession of its capital, Rouen, on November 20, 1450. In 1453, after the victory of Castillon and the surrender of Bordeaux, Guyenne returned to France after having been associated with England for three centuries.

The King's last years were troubled. The reconquered areas were restive under the yoke of royal administration, and the princes still posed a dangerous threat to the royal power: the revolt of Jean V, comte d'Armagnac, and the treason of Jean II, duc d'Alençon, were severely repressed. Philip of Burgundy dreamed of dominating France, and the Dauphin, who was approaching 40, had difficulty in concealing his impatience to reign. The King died at Mehun-sur-Yèvre on July 22, 1461, at the age of 58; he had reigned for 38 years and eight months.

Charles VII's reign was one of the most important in the history of the French monarchy. Although France had lost the economic prosperity and commercial importance it had enjoyed in the preceding centuries and the great nobles had become independent during the long partisan struggles of the Hundred Years' War period, Charles was able to begin the work of reunifying the kingdom by rallying the peoples' loyalty to himself as the legitimate king. Later, when the national feeling, revived by foreign occupation, had crystalized around him, he introduced financial and military reforms to strengthen the revived power of the monarchy. His action in obtaining a posthumous reversal of Joan of Arc's condemnation (1456) was perhaps less inspired by a concern for justice than to justify the circumstances surrounding his coronation. Charles has often been accused of apathy. He did require constant encouragement from courageous and intelligent counsellors, such as Yolande of Aragon, Richemont, Joan of Arc, and his mistress Agnès Sorel; and he certainly had no taste for dangerous adventures, prestigious operations, or sumptuous exhibitions. His innate indolence and his shyness— as well as his good sense and wisdom—induced him to prudence, notably in his foreign policies (as when he refused to participate in a crusade urged on him by the Pope). He was adept at minimizing papal influence over the internal affairs of his kingdom.

Like his cousin of Burgundy, he was pleasure loving, especially toward the end of his life, had influential mistresses (Agnès Sorel and, after her death in 1450, Antoinette de Maignelay), and had no fixed residence, travelling from one castle to another.

He also patronized the arts, surrounding himself with men of letters and intellectuals.

He always preferred peace to war, and his conciliatory policy—he repeatedly pardoned towns that collaborated with the English—contributed much toward restoring unity to his country.

BIBLIOGRAPHY. The standard biographies of Charles VII are VALLET DE VIRIVILLE, *Histoire de Charles VII, roi de France, et de son époque: 1403–1461*, 3 vol. (1862–65); and GASTON DU FRESNE DE BEAUCOURT, *Histoire de Charles VII*, 6 vol. (1881–91); though old, these works have not been superseded. Chronicles of Charles's own time may also be consulted: JEAN CHARTIER, *Chronique de Charles VII, roi de France*, new ed. by VALLET DE VIRIVILLE, 3 vol. (1858); THOMAS BASIN, *Histoire de Charles VII*, ed. by CHARLES SA-MARAN, 2 vol. (1933–44).

(Y.L.)

Charles I of Great Britain

Charles I, king of Great Britain and Ireland from 1625 to 1649, by attempting to impose his authoritarian rule on a people with growing aspirations for political and religious liberty, brought about a civil war that ended with his execution by his subjects. He was born in the palace at Dunfermline on November 19, 1600, the second surviving son of James VI of Scotland and Anne of Denmark. Charles was a sickly child, and when his father became king of England in March 1603, he was temporarily left behind in Scotland because of the risks of the journey. Devoted to his elder brother, Henry, and to his sister, Elizabeth, he became lonely when Henry died (1612) and his sister left England in 1613 to marry Frederick V, elector of the Rhine Palatinate (see also JAMES I OF GREAT BRITAIN).

Charles I, triple portrait by Sir Anthony Van Dyck, 1635. In Windsor Castle.

All his life Charles had a Scots accent and a slight stammer. Small in stature, he was less dignified than his portraits by the Flemish painter Sir Anthony Van Dyck suggest. He was always shy and struck observers as being silent and reserved. His excellent temper, courteous manners, and lack of vices impressed all those who met him, but he lacked the common touch, travelled about little, and never mixed with ordinary people. A patron of the arts (notably of painting and tapestry; he brought both Van Dyck and another famous Flemish painter, Peter Paul Rubens, to England), he was, like all the Stuarts, also a lover of horses and hunting. He was sincerely religious, and the character of the court became less coarse as soon as he became king. From his father he acquired a stubborn belief that kings are intended by God to rule, and his earliest surviving letters reveal a distrust of the unruly House of Commons with which he proved incapable of coming to terms. Lacking flexibility or imagination, he was unable to understand that those political deceits that he always practiced in increasingly vain attempts to uphold his authority eventually impugned his honour and damaged his credit.

In 1623, before succeeding to the throne, Charles, accompanied by the duke of Buckingham, King James I's favourite, made an incognito visit to Spain in order to conclude a marriage treaty with the daughter of King Philip III. When the mission failed, largely because of Buckingham's arrogance and the Spanish court's insistence that Charles become a Roman Catholic, he joined Buckingham in pressing his father for war against Spain. In the meantime a marriage treaty was arranged on his behalf with Henrietta Maria, sister of the French king, Louis XIII.

Conflict with Parliament. In March 1625, Charles I became king and married Henrietta Maria soon afterward. When his first Parliament met in June, trouble immediately arose because of the general distrust of Buckingham, who had retained his ascendancy over the new king. The Spanish war was proving a failure and Charles offered Parliament no explanations of his foreign policy or its costs. Moreover, the Puritans, who advocated extemporaneous prayer and preaching in the Church of England, predominated in the House of Commons, whereas the sympathies of the King were with what came to be known as the High Church Party, which stressed the value of the prayer book and the maintenance of ritual. Thus antagonism soon arose between the new king and the Commons, and Parliament refused to vote him the right to levy tonnage and poundage (customs duties) except on conditions that increased its powers, though this right had been granted to previous monarchs for life.

The second Parliament of the reign, meeting in February 1626, proved even more critical of the King's government, though some of the former leaders of the Commons were kept away because Charles had ingeniously appointed them sheriffs in their counties. The failure of a naval expedition against the Spanish port of Cádiz in the previous autumn was blamed on Buckingham and the Commons tried to impeach him for treason. To prevent this, Charles dissolved Parliament in June. Largely through the incompetence of Buckingham, the country now became involved in a war with France as well as with Spain and, in desperate need of funds, the King imposed a forced loan, which his judges declared illegal. He dismissed the chief justice and ordered the arrest of over 70 knights and gentlemen who refused to contribute. His highhanded actions added to the sense of grievance that was widely discussed in the next Parliament.

By the time Charles's third Parliament met (March 1628), Buckingham's expedition to aid the French Protestants at La Rochelle had been decisively repelled and the King's government was thoroughly discredited. The House of Commons at once passed resolutions condemning arbitrary taxation and arbitrary imprisonment, and then set out its complaints in the Petition of Right, which sought recognition of four principles—no taxes without consent of Parliament; no imprisonment without cause; no quartering of soldiers on subjects; no martial law in peacetime. The King, despite his efforts to avoid approving this petition, was compelled to give his formal consent. By the time the fourth Parliament met in January 1629, Buckingham had been assassinated. The House of Commons now objected both to what it called the revival of "popish practices" in the churches and to the levying of tonnage and poundage by the King's officers without its consent. The King ordered the adjournment of Parliament on March 2, 1629, but before that the speaker was held down in his chair and three resolutions were passed condemning the King's conduct. Charles realized that such behaviour was revolutionary. For the next 11 years he ruled his kingdom without calling a Parliament.

Dissolution of Parliament

In order that he might no longer be dependent upon parliamentary grants, he now made peace with both France and Spain, for, although the royal debt amounted to over £1,000,000, the proceeds of the customs duties at a time of expanding trade and the exaction of traditional crown dues combined to produce a revenue that was just adequate in time of peace. The King also tried to economize in the expenditure of his household. To pay for the Royal Navy, so-called ship money was levied, first in 1634 on ports and later on inland towns as well. The demands for ship money aroused obstinate and widespread resistance by 1638, even though a majority of the judges of the court of exchequer found in a test case that the levy was legal.

These in fact were the happiest years of Charles's life. At first he and Henrietta Maria had not been happy and in July 1626 he peremptorily ordered all of her French entourage to quit Whitehall. After the death of Buckingham, however, he fell in love with his wife and came to value her counsel. Though the King regarded himself as responsible for his actions—not to his people or Parliament but to God alone according to the doctrine of the divine right of kings—he recognized his duty to his subjects as "an indulgent nursing father." If he was often indolent, he exhibited spasmodic bursts of energy, principally in ordering administrative reforms, although little impression was made upon the elaborate network of private interests in the armed services and at court. On the whole, the kingdom seems to have enjoyed some degree of prosperity until 1639, when Charles became involved in a war against the Scots.

The early Stuarts neglected Scotland. At the beginning of his reign Charles alienated the Scottish nobility by an act of revocation whereby lands claimed by the crown or the church were subject to forfeiture. His decision in 1637 to impose upon his northern kingdom a new liturgy, based on the English Book of Common Prayer, although approved by the Scottish bishops, met with concerted resistance. When many Scots signed a national covenant to defend their Presbyterian religion, the King decided to enforce his ecclesiastical policy with the sword. He was outmanoeuvred by a well-organized Scottish covenanting army, and by the time he reached York in March 1639 the first of the so-called Bishops' Wars was already lost. A truce was signed at Berwick-upon-Tweed on June 18.

On the advice of the two men who had replaced Buckingham as the closest advisers of the King—William Laud, archbishop of Canterbury, and the earl of Strafford, his able lord deputy in Ireland—Charles summoned a Parliament that met in April 1640—later known as the Short Parliament—in order to raise money for the war against Scotland. The House insisted first on discussing grievances against the government and showed itself opposed to a renewal of the war; so, on May 5, the King dissolved Parliament again. The collection of ship money was continued and so was the war. A Scottish army crossed the border in August and the King's troops panicked before a cannonade at Newburn. Charles, deeply perturbed at his second defeat, convened a council of peers on whose advice he summoned another Parliament, the Long Parliament, which met at Westminster in November 1640.

The new House of Commons, proving to be just as uncooperative as the last, condemned Charles's recent actions and made preparations to impeach Strafford and other ministers for treason. The King adopted a conciliatory attitude—he agreed to the Triennial Act that ensured the meeting of Parliament once every three years—but expressed his resolve to save Strafford, to whom he promised protection. He was unsuccessful even in this, however. Strafford was beheaded on May 12, 1641.

Charles was forced to agree to a measure whereby the existing Parliament could not be dissolved without its own consent. He also accepted bills declaring ship money and other arbitrary fiscal measures illegal, and in general condemning his methods of government during the previous 11 years. But while making these concessions, he visited Scotland in August to try to enlist anti-parliamentary support there. He agreed to the full establishment of Presbyterianism in his northern kingdom and allowed the Scottish estates to nominate royal officials.

Meanwhile, Parliament reassembled in London after a recess and on November 22, 1641, the Commons passed by 159 to 148 votes the Grand Remonstrance to the King, setting out all that had gone wrong since his accession. At the same time news of a rebellion in Ireland had reached Westminster. Leaders of the Commons, fearing that if any army were raised to repress the Irish rebellion it might be used against them, planned to gain control of the army by forcing the King to agree to a militia bill. When asked to surrender his command of the army, Charles exclaimed "By God, not for an hour." Now fearing an impeachment of his Catholic queen, he prepared to take desperate action. He ordered the arrest of one member of the House of Lords and five of the Commons for treason and went with about 400 men to enforce the order himself. The accused members escaped, however, and hid in the City. After this rebuff the King left London on January 10, this time for the north of England. The Queen went to Holland in February to raise funds for her husband by pawning the crown jewels.

A lull followed, during which both Royalists and Parliamentarians enlisted troops and collected arms, although Charles had not completely given up hopes of peace. After a vain attempt to secure the arsenal at Hull, in April the King settled in York, where he ordered the courts of justice to assemble and where royalist members of both houses gradually joined him. In June the majority of the members remaining in London sent the King the Nineteen Propositions, which included demands that no ministers should be appointed without parliamentary ap-

Bishops' Wars and the Long Parliament

proval, that the army should be put under parliamentary control, and that Parliament should decide about the future of the church. Charles realized that these proposals were an ultimatum; yet he returned a careful answer in which he gave recognition to the idea that his was a "mixed government" and not an autocracy. But in July both sides were urgently making ready for war. The King formally raised the royal standard at Nottingham on August 22 and sporadic fighting soon broke out all over the kingdom.

Civil War. In September 1642 the Earl of Essex, in command of the parliamentarian forces, left London for the midlands, while Charles moved his headquarters to Shrewsbury to recruit and train an army on the Welsh marches. During a drawn battle fought at Edgehill near Warwick on October 23, the King addressed his troops in these words: "Your king is both your cause, your quarrel, and your captain. The foe is in sight. The best encouragement I can give you is that, come life or death, your king will bear you company, and ever keep this field, this place, and this day's service in his grateful remembrance." Charles I was a brave man but no general and he was deeply perturbed by the slaughter on the battlefield.

In 1643 the royal cause prospered, particularly in Yorkshire and the southwest. At Oxford, where Charles had moved his court and military headquarters, he dwelt pleasantly enough in Christ Church College. The Queen, having sold some of her jewels and bought a shipload of arms from Holland, landed in Yorkshire in February and joined her husband in Oxford in mid-July. Both by letters and by personal appeal she roused him to action and warned him against indecision; "delays have always ruined you," she observed. The king seems to have assented to a scheme for a three-pronged attack on London —from the west, from Oxford, and from Yorkshire—but neither the westerners nor the Yorkshiremen were anxious to leave their own districts.

In the course of 1643 a peace party of the parliamentarian side made some approaches to Charles in Oxford, but these failed and the Parliamentarians concluded an alliance with the Scottish covenanters. The entry of a Scottish army into England in January 1644 thrust the King's armies upon the defensive and the plan for a converging movement on London was abandoned. Charles successfully held his inner lines at Oxford and throughout the west and southwest of England, while he dispatched his nephew, Prince Rupert, on cavalry raids elsewhere. For about a year the King's forces had the upper hand; yet eventually he put out a number of peace feelers. These came to nothing, but he was cheered by reports that his opponents were beginning to quarrel among themselves.

The year 1645 proved to be one of decision. Charles may have had some foreboding of what was to come, for in the spring he sent his eldest son Charles into the west, from where he escaped to France, and rejoined his mother who had arrived there the previous year. On June 14 the highly disciplined and professionally led New Model Army organized and commanded by Sir Thomas Fairfax with Oliver Cromwell (*q.v.*) as his second-in-command, defeated the King and Prince Rupert at the Battle of Naseby. This was the first of a long row of defeats the King's forces suffered through the summer and fall. Charles returned to Oxford on November 5, and by the spring of 1646 Oxford was surrounded. Charles left the city in disguise with two companions late in April and arrived at the camp of the Scottish covenanters at Newark on May 5. But when the covenanters came to terms with the victorious English Parliament in January 1647, they left for home, handing over Charles I to parliamentary commissioners. He was held in Northamptonshire, where he lived a placid, healthy existence and, learning of the quarrels between the New Model Army and Parliament, hoped to come to a treaty with one or the other and regain his power. In June, however, a junior officer with a force of some 500 men seized the King and carried him away to the army headquarters at Newmarket.

After the army marched on London in August, the King was moved to Hampton Court, where he was reunited

Capture of Charles

with two of his children, Henry and Elizabeth. He escaped on November 11, but his friends' plans to take him to Jersey and thence to France went astray and instead Charles found himself in the Isle of Wight, where the governor was loyal to Parliament and kept him under surveillance at Carisbrooke Castle. There Charles conducted complicated negotiations with the army leaders, with the English Parliament, and with the Scots; he did not scruple to promise one thing to one side and the opposite to the other. He came to a secret understanding with the Scots on December 26, 1647, whereby the Scots offered to support the King's restoration to power in return for his acceptance of Presbyterianism in Scotland and its establishment in England for three years. Charles then twice refused the terms offered by the English Parliament and was put under closer guard, from which he vainly tried again to escape.

In August 1648 the last of Charles's Scottish supporters were defeated at the Battle of Preston and the second Civil War ended. The army now began to demand that the King should be put on trial for treason as "the grand author of our troubles" and the cause of bloodshed. He was removed to Hurst Castle in Hampshire at the end of 1648 and thence taken to Windsor Castle for Christmas. On January 20, 1649, he was brought before a specially constituted high court of justice in Westminster Hall.

Charles I was charged with high treason and "other high crimes against the realm of England." He at once refused to recognize the legality of the court because "a king cannot be tried by any superior jurisdiction on earth." He therefore refused to plead but maintained that he stood for "the liberty of the people of England." The sentence of death was read on January 27; his execution was ordered as a tyrant, traitor, murderer, and public enemy. The sentence was carried out on a scaffold erected outside the banqueting hall of Whitehall on the morning of Tuesday, January 30, 1649. The King went bravely to his death, still claiming that he was "a martyr for the people." A week later he was buried at Windsor.

Execution of the King

BIBLIOGRAPHY. There is no up-to-date scholarly biography of this king, but a good popular biography by CHRISTOPHER HIBBERT, entitled *Charles I* (1968), is readable and reliable. A sound appreciation of Charles I may be found in DAME VERONICA WEDGWOOD'S two books: *The King's Peace, 1637–1641* (1955), and *The King's War, 1641–1647* (1958), and also in her *Trial of Charles I* (1964). A valuable account of Charles I's imprisonment on the Isle of Wight is given in JACK D. JONES, *The Royal Prisoner* (1965); and an illuminating discussion of Charles I's attitude toward peace negotiations in B.H.G. WORMALD, *Clarendon: Politics, History and Religion, 1640–1660* (1951). For Charles I as a connoisseur of the arts, see SIR CLAUDE PHILLIPS, *The Picture Gallery of Charles I* (1896).

(M.As.)

Charles II of Great Britain

Charles II, the son of Charles I, England's "Martyr King," only succeeded in recovering the throne of Great Britain and Ireland 11 years after the execution of his father. His political adaptability and his knowledge of men enabled him to steer his country through the convulsions of the struggle between Anglicans, Catholics, and dissenters that marked much of his reign.

Charles II, the eldest surviving son of Charles I and Henrietta Maria of France, was born at St. James's Palace, London, on May 29, 1630. His early years were unremarkable, but before he was 20 his conventional education had been completely overshadowed by the harsh lessons of defeat in the Civil War against the Puritans and subsequent isolation and poverty. Thus Charles emerged into precocious maturity, cynical, self-indulgent, skilled in the sort of moral evasions that make life comfortable even in adversity.

But though the early years of tawdry dissipation have tarnished the romance of his adventures, not all of his actions were discreditable. He tried to fight his father's battles in the west of England in 1645; he resisted the attempts of his mother and his sister Henrietta Anne to convert him to Catholicism and remained openly loyal to his Protestant faith. In 1648 he made strenuous efforts to

Birth and early years

Charles II, painting by Sir Peter Lely, c. 1675.
In the collection of the Duke of Grafton.
By courtesy of the Duke of Grafton and the Royal
Academy of Arts

save his father; and when, after Charles I's execution in 1649, he was proclaimed Charles II by the Scots in defiance of the English republic, he was prepared to go to Scotland and swallow the—stringently anti-Catholic and anti-Anglican—Presbyterian Covenant as the price for alliance. But the sacrifice of friends and principles was futile and left him deeply embittered. The Scottish Army was routed by the English under Oliver Cromwell at Dunbar in September 1650, and in 1651 Charles's invasion of England ended in defeat at Worcester. The young king became a fugitive, hunted through England for 40 days but protected by a handful of his loyal subjects until he escaped to France in October 1651.

His safety was comfortless, however. He was destitute and friendless, unable to bring pressure against an increasingly powerful England. France and the Dutch United Provinces were closed to him by Cromwell's diplomacy and he turned to Spain, with whom he concluded a treaty in April 1656. He persuaded his brother James to relinquish his command in the French Army and gave him some regiments of Anglo-Irish troops in Spanish service, but poverty doomed this nucleus of a royalist army to impotence. European princes took little interest in Charles and his cause, and his proffers of marriage were declined. Even Cromwell's death did little to improve his prospects. But George Monck, one of Cromwell's leading generals, realized that under Cromwell's successors the country was in danger of being torn apart and with his formidable army created the situation favourable to Charles's restoration in 1660. Most Englishmen now favoured a return to a stable and legitimate monarchy, and although more was known of Charles II's vices than his virtues, he had, under the steadying influence of Edward Hyde, his chief adviser, avoided any damaging compromise of his religion or constitutional principles. With Hyde's help, Charles issued in April 1660 his Declaration of Breda, expressing his personal desire for a general amnesty, for liberty of conscience, an equitable settlement of land disputes, and full payment of arrears to the army. The actual terms were to be left to a free parliament, and on this provisional basis Charles was proclaimed king in May 1660. Landing at Dover on May 25, he reached a rejoicing London on his 30th birthday.

Restoration settlement

The unconditional nature of the settlement that took shape between 1660 and 1662 owed little to Charles's intervention and must have exceeded his expectations. He was bound by the concessions made by his father in 1640 and 1641, but the Parliament elected in 1661 was determined on an uncompromising Anglican and royalist settlement. The Militia Act of 1661 gave Charles unprecedented authority to maintain a standing army and the Corporation Act of 1661 allowed him to purge the boroughs of dissident officials. Other legislation placed strict limits on the press and on public assembly, and the 1662 Act of Uniformity created controls of education. An exclusive body of Anglican clergy and a well-armed landed gentry were the principal beneficiaries of Charles II's restoration.

But within this narrow structure of upper-class loyalism there were irksome limitations on Charles's independence. His efforts to extend religious toleration to his Nonconformist and Roman Catholic subjects were sharply rebuffed in 1663, and throughout his reign the House of Commons was to thwart the more generous impulses of his religious policy. A more pervasive and damaging limitation was on his financial independence. Although endowed with an estimated annual income of £1,200,-000, Charles had to wait many years before his revenues produced such a sum, and by then the damage of debt and discredit was irreparable. Charles was incapable of thrift; he found it painful to refuse petitioners. With the expensive disasters of the Anglo-Dutch War of 1665–67 the reputation of the restored king sank to its lowest level. His vigorous attempts to save London during the Great Fire of September 1666 could not make up for the negligence and maladministration that led to England's naval defeat in June 1667.

Charles cleared himself by dismissing his old adviser, Edward Hyde, earl of Clarendon, and tried to assert himself through a more adventurous foreign policy. So far, his reign had made only modest contributions to England's commercial advancement. The Navigation Acts of 1660 and 1663, prompted by the threat to British shipping of the rise of the Dutch carrying trade, were valuable extensions of Cromwellian policies; and the capture of New York in 1664 was one of his few gains from the Dutch. But although marriage to Princess Catherine of Braganza of Portugal in 1661 brought him the possession of Tangier and Bombay, they were of less strategic value than Dunkirk, which he sold to Louis XIV in 1662. Charles was, however, prepared to sacrifice much for the alliance of his young cousin. Through his sister Henrietta Anne, duchess of Orléans, he had direct contact with the French court, and it was through her that he negotiated the startling reversal of the Protestant Triple Alliance (England, the Dutch United Provinces, Sweden) of 1668. By the terms of the so-called "Secret Treaty of Dover" of May 1670, England and France not only joined in an offensive alliance against the Dutch, but Charles promised to announce his conversion to Roman Catholicism. If this provoked trouble from his subjects he was assured of French military and financial support. Charles saw to it that the conversion clause of the treaty was not made public.

Foreign policy

This clause, the most controversial act of Charles II's reign, can be explained as a shortsighted bid for Louis XIV's confidence, but in this it failed. Louis neither welcomed nor believed in Charles's intentions, and in the event, it was only upon his deathbed that Charles was received into the Roman Catholic Church. But Charles had now fatally compromised himself. Although he later attempted to pursue policies independent of Louis he remained bound to him by inclination and the fear of blackmail. More seriously, he had lost the confidence of his subjects, who deplored the French alliance and distrusted the whole tendency of Charles's policies.

Other circumstances deepened Englishmen's discontent with their king. By the 1670s, the miscarriages of the Queen had reduced hopes that Charles would have a legitimate heir, and in 1673 the second marriage of his brother James, duke of York, to Mary of Modena, increased the possibility of the Catholic line of succession, for James's conversion to the Roman Church was wellknown. But, it was for his autocratic character as much as for his religion that James was feared as his brother was not, and it was on his brother's behalf that Charles eventually had to face the severest political storm of his reign.

The Popish Plot of 1678 was an elaborate tissue of fictions built around a skeleton of even stranger truths. The allegations of Titus Oates, a former Anglican cleric who had been expelled from a Jesuit seminary, that Catholics planned to murder Charles to make James king, seemed confirmed by scraps of evidence of which Charles was justifiably skeptical. But he was obliged to bow before the gusts of national hysteria that sought to bar his brother from the line of succession. Between 1679 and 1681 Charles nearly lost control of his government. Deprived of his chief minister, the Earl of Danby, who had been compromised by his negotiations with France, the King had to allow the Earl of Shaftesbury and his Whig supporters, who upheld the power of the Parliament—men whom he detested—to occupy positions of power in central and local government. Three general elections produced three equally unmanageable parliaments; and although Charles publicly denied the legitimacy of his first son, the Protestant Duke of Monmouth, he had to send his Catholic brother James out of the country and offer a plan of limitations that would bind James if he came to the throne. The plan was unacceptable to the Whigs and to James, and when Charles fell seriously ill in the summer of 1679 there was real danger of civil conflict.

But Charles kept his nerve. He defended his Queen against slanders, dismissed the intractable parliaments and recovered control of his government. His subjects' dread of republican anarchy proved stronger than their suspicion of James, and from March 1681, when he dissolved his last Parliament, Charles enjoyed a nationwide surge of loyalty almost as fervent as that of 1660. He had made yet another secret treaty with France and in addition to a French subsidy could now count upon a healthy public revenue. Reforms at the Treasury, which he had inaugurated in 1667, provided the crown with a firm basis of administrative control that was among Charles II's most valuable legacies to English government.

As a result of these actions, Charles, who died on February 6, 1685, at Whitehall in London, was able to end his reign in the kind of tranquil prosperity he had always sought.

Believing that "God will never damn a man for allowing himself a little pleasure," he had made quite sure of his own share and left at least 14 illegitimate offspring, of whom only James, duke of Monmouth, played any part in English politics. Mistresses like Barbara Villiers, duchess of Cleveland, and Louise de Kéroualle, duchess of Portsmouth, were always costly and often troublesome, but Charles probably paid a smaller price for his amours than for his laziness. He was tall and active and loved riding and sailing but, although robust enough to outsit his advisers at the Council board, he hated routine and prolonged application. This failing undermined the effectiveness of his government and led to his dependence on France. But the relaxed tolerance he brought to religious matters in the end may have contributed more to the stability of his reign than was lost by his shifty insincerity.

Charles fully shared the interests of the skeptical, materialist century that saw the foundation of the Royal Society under his charter, and he did something to foster technological improvements in navigation and ship design. The sincerity of his interest in England's naval advancement is held by some historians to be the most important of his redeeming features, although, like his reputation for wit and high intelligence, it may not stand up to close examination. Any verdict on Charles is therefore controversial. A contemporary wrote of him that "he had as good a claim to a kind interpretation as most men," and on this basis it may be agreed that his image as a man remains more attractive than his reputation as a king.

BIBLIOGRAPHY. The more colourful aspects of the life of Charles II have attracted numerous biographers, but few can be relied upon for an accurate, original, and unromantic appraisal. By far the most popular account is still SIR ARTHUR BRYANT, *King Charles II*, rev. ed. (1955). Based on wide reading and a pronounced sympathy for its subject, it is a vivid and generous vindication of Charles II against the unfavourable "whig" interpretation of his reign. Most professional scholars, however, remain unconvinced by Bryant's view. J.P. KENYON, *The Stuarts: A Study in English Kingship*, 2nd ed. (1967), contains a short but pungent dissection of Charles II's character. MAURICE P. ASHLEY, *Charles II: The Man and the Statesman* (1971), has some critical insights; but the most penetrating assessment of Charles and his interpreters is in a pamphlet by K.H.D. HALEY, "Charles II," The Historical Association, General Series No. 63 (1966). This up-to-date scholarly review should be compared with the assessment of a statesman who knew Charles well, GEORGE SAVILE (the marquess of Halifax), *A Character of King Charles the Second*, first published in 1750, ed. by J.P. KENYON in *Halifax: Complete Works* (1969).

(H.G.R.)

Charles III of Spain

King of Spain from 1759 to 1788, Charles III, considered one of the "enlightened despots" of the 18th century, introduced numerous reforms in Spain and the Spanish colonial empire in an attempt to restore Spain's declining prestige and power.

Charles was born in Madrid on January 20, 1716, the first child of Philip V's marriage with Isabella of Parma. Charles ruled as duke of Parma, by right of his mother, from 1732 to 1734 and then became king of Naples. On the death of his half-brother Ferdinand VI in 1759—after a useful apprenticeship of 25 years as an absolute ruler—he became king of Spain and resigned the crown of Naples to his third son, Ferdinand I.

By courtesy of the Museo del Prado, Madrid

Charles III, oil painting by Anton Raphael Mengs (1728–79). In the Prado, Madrid.

Charles III was convinced of his mission to reform Spain and make it once more a first-rate power. He brought considerable qualities to the task. In spite of a fanatical addiction to hunting, his frugality and his application to the business of government impressed foreign observers as well as his own subjects. His religious devotion was accompanied by a blameless personal life and a chaste loyalty to the memory of his wife, Maria Amalia of Saxony, who died in 1760. On the other hand, he was so highly conscious of royal authority that he sometimes appeared more like a tyrant than an absolute monarch. His greatest quality, however, was his ability to select effective ministers and continually to improve his government by bringing in men of outstanding quality, notably the Conde de Aranda and the Conde de Floridablanca. While conferring with them regularly, Charles was wise enough to give them sufficient freedom of action.

Failure
of his
foreign
policy

The survival of Spain as a colonial power and, therefore, as a power to be reckoned with in Europe was one of the main objects of Charles's policy. His foreign policy, however, was not successful. Fearing that a British victory over France in the Seven Years' War would upset the balance of colonial power, he signed the Family Compact with France—both countries were ruled by branches of the Bourbon family—in August 1761. This brought war with Great Britain in January 1762. Charles overrated his own strength and prospects and those of his ally. Sharing in the defeat, he lost Florida to England and revealed Spanish naval and military weakness. In the American Revolution, Charles III was caught between a desire to embarrass his colonial rival, which accounts for his undercover aid to the American revolutionaries from 1776, and fear for his own American possessions, which led him to offer his mediation in 1779. When Great Britain refused his conditions, he declared war, but, at the same time, he refused to recognize United States independence. Charles was more successful in strengthening his own empire. Commercial reforms, designed to open new routes and new ports for trade between Spain and the colonies, were undertaken from 1765. Territorial readjustments were carried out in the interest of defense, and a modern administrative organization—the intendant system, of French origin and already operating in Spain itself—was introduced. The intendants, who had executive, judicial, and military power, improved local administration and linked it directly with the crown rather than with the viceroy. Released from the former commercial restrictions, secured against attack, and with the prospect of better administration, the Spanish Empire under Charles III assumed a new look.

Domestic
reforms

In Spain Charles was concerned to make himself more absolute and therefore better able to undertake reform. His ecclesiastical policy was conditioned by his determination to complete the subordination of the church to the crown. He allowed no papal bulls or briefs in Spain without royal permission. He particularly resented the Jesuits, whose international organization and attachment to the papacy he regarded as an affront to his absolutism. Suspecting their loyalty and obedience to the crown in the American colonies, he also chose to believe that they were the instigators of the violent riots in Madrid and elsewhere in 1766. After a commission of investigation, he ordered their expulsion from Spain and the colonies (1767). In 1773, cooperating with the court of France, Charles succeeded in procuring from the papacy the complete suppression of the society. But Charles's opposition to papal jurisdiction in Spain also led him to curb the arbitrary powers of the Inquisition, while his desire for reform within the church caused him to appoint inquisitors general who preferred persuasion to force in ensuring religious conformity.

Charles III improved the agencies of government through which the will of the crown could be imposed. He completed the process whereby individual ministers replaced the royal councils in the direction of affairs. In 1787, with the assistance of Floridablanca, he coordinated the various ministries by establishing a council of state whose regular meetings could produce a concerted policy. He tightened crown control of local government by stimulating his intendants and giving the Council of Castile supervision of municipal finances. The objective of his government was to create the conditions in which industry and trade could improve. By the end of his reign, Spain had abandoned its old commercial restrictions and, while still excluding foreigners, had opened up the entire empire to a commerce in which all its subjects and all its main ports could partake. Protected against foreign competition, the native cotton industry grew rapidly, and the state itself intervened in the production of luxury goods. Charles III's agrarian policy, however, timid in face of landed interests, failed to deal with the greatest obstacles to agricultural progress and to the welfare of the rural masses in Spain—large untilled estates and legally unalterable succession in the inheritance of landed property. In fact, strength, rather than welfare,

was the aim of Charles III. Within these limits he led his country in a cultural and economic revival, and, when he died, in Madrid, on December 14, 1788, he left Spain more prosperous than he had found it.

BIBLIOGRAPHY. RICHARD HERR, *The Eighteenth-Century Revolution in Spain* (1958), a modern account of the political, socio-economic, and cultural achievements of the reign; JOHN LYNCH, *Spanish Colonial Administration, 1782–1810* (1958), includes an account of the colonial reforms of Charles III; R.J. SHAFER, *The Economic Societies in the Spanish World, 1763–1821* (1958), for information on the economic and social conditions in Spain and the empire; V. RODRIGUEZ CASADO, *La política y los políticos en el reinado de Carlos III* (1962), a political analysis by a Spanish expert on the reign.

(Jo.Ly.)

Charles XII of Sweden

Charles XII of Sweden is best known for his contribution to his country's defense in the Great Northern War, in which he resisted a coalition of Russia, Denmark-Norway, and Saxony-Poland for 18 years. His death in 1718 helped to weaken Sweden's position, and supremacy in the Baltic passed to Russia. Charles XII was, however, also a ruler of the early Enlightenment era, promoting domestic reforms of significance.

Charles XII, oil painting by David von Krafft after J.D. Swartz, 1706. In Gripsholm Castle, Sweden.

He was born on June 17, 1682, the second child and eldest (and only surviving) son of Charles XI of Sweden and Ulrika Eleonora of Denmark. His early childhood was happy and secure, but the close family circle was broken by his mother's death in 1693. Charles XI's chief consolation was a close companionship with his heir, and from this time onward Prince Charles accompanied his father on travels of inspection and on all kinds of official occasions. After his father's death in April 1697, Charles XII had to take on the burden of absolute kingship—he was the first and only Swedish king born to absolutism—when he was barely 15 years old. Charles XI had stipulated a regency, but the regents proved anxious to obtain the new king's concurrence in all decisions, and the Riksdag called in November 1697 declared him of age.

Charles XII had been carefully prepared for his task by excellent tutors and governors. He was, however, exceptionally strong willed and gave repeated proof of his obstinate adherence to those standards he accepted from the religious and moral teaching of his family and his governors. In adolescence a personal program for toughening physique—in particular, his intrepid horsemanship and his predilection for risks—worried the old and staid among the courtiers. He had been open and confiding;

but on succeeding to the crown he assumed a noncommittal behaviour in public, though in private he was much influenced by the instructions that his father had left for his political guidance and by the counsel of his father's advisers.

After negotiations for Charles's marriage to a Danish cousin, the daughter of Christian V, were begun on Denmark's initiative, Charles's advisers held back until the outcome of Danish negotiations with other powers were known. These negotiations led in fact to a coalition between Denmark, Saxony, and Russia that, by attacking Sweden in the spring of 1700, began the Great Northern War. The speedy success hoped for by the three allied powers did not materialize, and rumours of rebellion by the Swedish nobility against the absolutist monarchy, in case of war, proved false. The early campaigns—the descent on Zealand (August 1700), which forced Denmark out of the war; the Battle of Narva (November 1700), which drove the Russians away from the Swedish trans-Baltic provinces; and the crossing of the Western Dvina River (1701), which scattered the troops of Augustus II (elector of Saxony and king of Poland)—were all planned and directed by the officers whom Charles had inherited from his father; but the King, while developing his military skill, gave valuable help in fostering morale by his courage, his religiously coloured optimism, and his faith in the cause of Sweden as the victim of a concerted attack.

Military leader, 1700–09

Charles's responsibility in planning and executing armed operations constantly increased, so that from 1702 he became the superior of most of his officers. Also from 1702 he began to take a greater part in political decisions, his senior advisers having died or retired through ill health. Most significant of these personal decisions was that to fight Augustus II in Poland and to transform Poland from a divided country, where Augustus had both partisans and opponents, into an ally and a base for the final campaign against Russia. This transformation was to be accomplished by dethroning Augustus and substituting a Polish-born king willing to cooperate with the Swedes. By the time this program had been brought to success and Stanisław Leszczyński elected king of Poland —Augustus being forced to accept the settlement by a Swedish invasion of Saxony in September 1706—Charles XII had matured both as a general and as a statesman.

Charles was not unmindful of Sweden's role in central and western Europe; his support of the Silesian Protestants against the Catholic Habsburg emperor was firmly based on the Swedish guarantee of the Peace of Westphalia, and he continued that policy of the "balancing role" between the great coalitions of the west to which Swedish rulers and statesmen since 1660 had aspired in the hope of achieving prestige and territory by armed mediation in suitable circumstances. His first necessity in 1706, however, was to secure Sweden's position in relation to Russia, which, under Peter I the Great, had from 1703 onward made good use of Charles XII's campaigns in Poland to train its army and undertake a piecemeal conquest of the Swedish east Baltic provinces. Charles's troops left Saxony to invade Russia in the late autumn of 1707. They won the Battle of Hołowczyn in July 1708, but Russian scorched-earth tactics forced Charles to abandon his route to Moscow and turn instead into the Ukraine. Thereafter, the Russians interfered successfully with the Swedes' communications, and by the summer of 1709 Charles XII had no choice between accepting battle with the Russians or withdrawing once more into Poland. Though wounded in the foot and unable to lead the army in person, Charles chose battle and attacked the Russian fortified camp at Poltava on July 8 (June 27, old style; June 28, Swedish style). The attack failed, and three days later the bulk of the Swedish Army surrendered to the Russians at Perevolochna. Charles was by then already on his way to Turkish-held territory, where he hoped to find allies.

Years in Turkey, 1709–14

Turkey's desire to reconquer Azov from Peter the Great augured well for its cooperation with Charles XII, but —in spite of four Turkish declarations of war against Russia—as the army expected from Sweden never arrived, the Swedish king was unable to pursue his plans vigorously.

He became the object of Turkish intrigues and in February 1713 had to fight a regular battle, the *kalabalik* of Bender (modern Bendery, in the Moldavian S.S.R.), to avoid a plot to deliver him into the hands of Augustus of Saxony, now restored in Poland. The closing of the Turko-Habsburg frontier due to the plague, and the determination of the anti-French alliance in the War of the Spanish Succession to prevent Sweden from using its bases in Germany to attack its enemies further circumscribed Charles XII's freedom of action in these years. The Swedish council, virtually in charge of affairs at home during his absence, was preoccupied with threats to Sweden from Denmark.

The administrative and financial reforms that Charles promulgated from Turkey in order to distribute the burden of the war effort fairly and to increase both resources and efficiency were largely sabotaged and were put into effect only after his return to Swedish Pomerania in November 1714 (having ridden incognito through Habsburg and German lands in 14 days and nights).

For more than a year, Charles fought a delaying action in Pomerania to keep Swedish troops on German soil as long as possible, attempting to restore the prestige of Swedish arms, to keep the war away from Sweden itself, and to prepare his diplomatic offensive for splitting the coalition, augmented after 1714 by Hanover and Prussia. A subsidy treaty with France, intrigues with the Jacobites (the adherents of the exiled branch of the Stuart monarchs) to threaten the Elector of Hanover in his position as king of England, and separate negotiations with the enemies averted the danger to Sweden once Charles, in December 1715, had been forced to leave Stralsund and Wismar.

Decline of Swedish power

From 1713 onward Charles had realized that sacrifice of territory would be necessary but was set on retaining Sweden's great power status either by ceding land for money for a given number of years only, not in perpetuity, or by allowing outright cession only as the price for guaranteed and considerable military help. He argued that any satisfactory peace on these lines could only be gained if military action backed up the diplomatic effort; to some extent, therefore, all negotiations, and especially those with the Russians at Åland throughout the year 1718, were designed to gain time. By the autumn of 1718, Charles XII had collected an army of 60,000 men, but his strategic plan was never fully unfolded, for at the siege of Fredrikshald (Halden), at an early stage in the invasion of Norway, he exposed himself to fire from the fortress and on November 30, 1718, was fatally shot through the head. Rumours that he had been killed by someone from his own side began to circulate shortly after his death. The debate on this question continues, but the weight of available evidence favours the view that Charles XII was killed by an enemy bullet.

Assessment

Charles XII was not the simple and uneducated soldier-king he has often been made out to be. His intellectual pursuits were many and varied. He was always interested in architecture and in painting; he could quote contemporary Swedish poetry and liked to argue theology and philosophy. His real bent was mathematical and scientific. He became increasingly occupied with new ideas in administration, and many of his administrative reforms were far ahead of their time.

Charles's character was complex. Kindhearted, he had to steel himself to say no; yet by virtue of his own sacrifices and devotion to duty, he demanded considerable sacrifices of those classes in Sweden who were lukewarm about the war effort once the years of bad fortune set in after 1709. A youthful longing for romantic love had to be buried in the harsh life of the soldier and produced the ascetic leader whose habits of bachelorhood grew upon him to the extent that those around him hardly credited his reiterated "I'll marry after the war is over." Affectionate to his family, he was torn in two by the factions within it that his own childlessness tended to produce.

In military matters Charles learned from experience to insist on utter secrecy and kept even his own officers guessing until the last moment. He had a good eye for the strategic battleground and insisted on personal leadership in battle, believing that the phlegmatic and cautious Swedish peasant would only fight well when seeing his king sharing the dangers of the battle.

Firmly believing in his responsibility to God, Charles held that the fortunes of war had taught him that one could not always be lucky, but one could always be honourable. He was against double-dealing and against the easy pledging of one's word only to break it at the first suitable opportunity. A self-righteous contempt for the behaviour of rulers that did not fit into his own moral code is evident. He lacked insight into men's motives, probably because of his early assumption of the crown; and having been born to absolutism, he did not realize the strength of the anti-absolutist forces in Sweden. He had, however, no illusions about his real power. "They will not obey me now when I am alive," he said once in answer to an appeal to settle the succession: "how can I expect them to obey me when I am dead?"

BIBLIOGRAPHY. R.M. HATTON, *Charles XII of Sweden* (1968), offers a one-volume modern study of the King as a person and as a ruler. Of the review articles on this biography, the following may be mentioned since they add specifically to the historical argument: J.H. PLUMB in *The New York Times Review of Books* (June 22, 1969); and MICHAEL ROBERTS in the *English Historical Review*, 84:796–801 (1969). A three-volume German work by OTTO HAINTZ, *König Karl XII. von Schweden* (1958, with reprints of vol. 1 and 2 originally published in 1935 and 1951), concentrates on the military history of the reign. A briefer book, *The Life of Charles XII* (U.S. title, *The Sword Does Not Jest;* 1960), consists of an abbreviated version of the Swedish two-volume, beautifully written, but historically less valuable study by FRANS G. BENGTSSON, *Karl XII:s levnad* (1935–36). This book virtually ignores the domestic reform work of the King since Bengtsson wrote at a time when this had not been evaluated. Many scholars, Swedish, Russian, Polish, Danish, French, Turkish, and German, have contributed to knowledge of the period; their books and articles may be found in the select bibliography and notes to the Hatton biography (*op. cit.*).

(R.M.H.)

Charles XIV John, of Sweden and Norway

A prominent French Revolutionary general and a marshal of the empire under Napoleon, Jean Bernadotte's gifts as military leader and as administrator led to his election as crown prince of Sweden and, in 1818, to his accession to the throne as King Charles XIV.

By courtesy of the Svenska Portrattarkivet, Stockholm

Charles XIV John, oil painting by Fredrik Westin, 1824. In Gripsholm Castle, Sweden.

He was born on January 26, 1763, at Pau, France, the son of a lawyer. At the age of 17 he enlisted in the French army. By 1790 he had become an ardent supporter of the Revolution and rose rapidly from sublieu-

tenant in 1792 to brigadier general in 1794. During the campaigns in Germany, the Low Countries, and Italy he restrained his troops from plundering and gained a reputation as a disciplinarian. Bernadotte first met Napoleon Bonaparte in 1797 in Italy. Their relationship, at first friendly, was soon embittered by rivalries and misunderstandings.

In January 1798 Bernadotte was expected to succeed Bonaparte in command of the army of Italy but instead was appointed ambassador to Vienna until April, when his mission ended. On August 17, 1798, having returned to Paris, he married Désirée Clary, Napoleon's former fiancée and the sister-in-law of Joseph Bonaparte, Napoleon's older brother.

Bernadotte campaigned in Germany during the winter following his marriage, and from July to September 1799 he was minister of war. His growing fame, however, and his contacts with the radical Jacobins irritated Emmanuel Joseph Sieyès—one of the five members of the government of the Directory that ruled France from 1795 to 1799—who engineered his removal. In November 1799 Bernadotte refused to assist Bonaparte's coup d'etat that ended the Directory but neither did he defend it. He was a councillor of state from 1800 to 1802 and became commander of the army of the west. In 1802 he fell under suspicion of complicity with a group of army officers of republican sympathies who disseminated anti-Bonapartist pamphlets and propaganda from the city of Rennes (the "Rennes plot"). Although no evidence has been found that he was involved, it is clear that he would have favoured constitutional limitation of the powers of Napoleon, who had in 1799 become the first consul—to all intents and purposes, dictator of France—or even his overthrow. In January 1803 Bonaparte appointed Bernadotte minister to the United States, but Bernadotte delayed his departure because of rumours of approaching war between France and England and remained inactive in Paris for a year. When, on May 18, 1804, Napoleon proclaimed the empire, Bernadotte declared full loyalty to him and, in May, was named marshal of the empire. In June he became the military and civil governor of the electorate of Hanover, and while in office he attempted to set up an equitable system of taxation. This did not prevent him from beginning to accumulate a sizable fortune with the "tributes" he received from Hanover and the Hanseatic city of Bremen.

In 1805 Bernadotte was given command of the I Army Corps during the Austrian campaign. Difficulties delayed his march toward Vienna, and in the battle at Austerlitz, in which Napoleon defeated the combined Russo-Austrian forces, the corps played a dramatic but somewhat minor role. Napoleon gave Bernadotte command of the occupation of Ansbach (1806) and in the same year made him prince of Pontecorvo. Bernadotte and his corps did not participate actively in the battles of Jena and Auerstädt (October 1806), in which the French routed the Prussian army, but nevertheless he was given enlarged responsibility in the Polish campaign, and in January 1807 he defeated the Russians at Mohrungen. In July 1807 Bernadotte was named governor of the occupied Hanseatic cities of northern Germany. He was scheduled to lead a campaign against Sweden, but this was abandoned, and in 1809 he took part in the Austrian campaign as commander of the IX Army Corps. In the Battle of Wagram, in which the French defeated the Austrians, he lost more than one-third of his soldiers and then returned to Paris "for reasons of health" but obviously in deep disfavour. Napoleon, however, put him in command of the defense of the Netherlands against the threatened British invasion; Bernadotte ably organized the defense. The British expedition to the Dutch island of Walcheren, however, was fatally weakened by disease and had to withdraw. When Bernadotte returned to Paris, political suspicions still surrounded him, and his position remained uncertain.

Despite the distrust of French politicians, however, dramatic new possibilities now opened up to him: he was invited to become crown prince of Sweden. In 1809 a

Military career in France

palace revolution had overthrown King Gustav IV of Sweden and had put the aged, childless Charles XIII on the throne. The Danish prince Christian August had been elected crown prince but died suddenly in 1810, and the Swedes turned to Napoleon for advice. The Emperor, however, was reluctant to exert a decisive influence, and the initiative fell to the young Swedish baron Carl Otto Mörner. Mörner approached Bernadotte since he respected his military ability, his skillful and humane administration of Hanover and the Hanseatic towns, and his charitable treatment of Swedish prisoners in Germany. The Riksdag (diet), influenced by similar considerations, by their regard for French military power, and by financial promises from Bernadotte, abandoned other candidates; and on August 21, 1810, Bernadotte was elected Swedish crown prince. On October 20 he accepted Lutheranism and landed in Sweden; he was adopted as son by Charles XIII and took the name of Charles John (Karl Johan). The Crown Prince at once assumed control of the government and acted officially as regent during the illnesses of Charles XIII. Napoleon now tried to prevent any reorientation of Swedish foreign policy and moreover sent an immediate demand that Sweden declare war on Great Britain; the Swedes had no choice, but though technically in a state of war between 1810 and 1812, Sweden and Great Britain did not engage in active hostilities. Then in January 1812, Napoleon suddenly occupied Swedish Pomerania.

Charles John was anxious to achieve something for Sweden that would prove his worth to the Swedes and establish his dynasty in power. He could, as many Swedes wished, have regained Finland from Russia, either by conquest or by negotiation. Political developments, however, prompted another solution, namely the conquest of Norway from Denmark, based on a Swedish alliance with Napoleon's enemies. An alliance was signed with Russia in April 1812, with Great Britain in March 1813—with the British granting a subsidy for the proposed conquest of Norway—and with Prussia in April 1813. Urged by the allies, however, Charles John agreed to take part in the great campaign against Napoleon and to postpone his war with Denmark. The Crown Prince landed his troops at Stralsund, Germany, in May 1813 and soon took command of the allied army of the north. Although the Swedish troops contributed to the allied successes, Charles John intended to conserve his forces for the war with Denmark, and the Prussians bore the brunt of the fighting.

After the decisive Battle of Leipzig (October 1813), Napoleon's first great defeat, Charles John succeeded in defeating the Danes in a swift campaign and forced King Frederick VI of Denmark to sign the Treaty of Kiel (January 1814), which transferred Norway to the Swedish crown. Charles John now had dreams of becoming king or "protector" of France, but he had become alienated from the French people, and the victorious allies would not tolerate another soldier in charge of French affairs. Bernadotte's dream dissolved, and his brief visit to Paris after the armistice was not glorious.

New difficulties recalled him to Scandinavia. The Norwegians refused to recognize the Treaty of Kiel, and in May 1814 a Norwegian assembly adopted a liberal constitution. Charles John conducted an efficient and almost bloodless campaign, and in August the Norwegians signed the Convention of Moss, whereby they accepted Charles XIII as king but retained the May constitution. Thus, when force might have imposed any system on the Norwegians (for a time at least), the Crown Prince insisted on a constitutional settlement.

At the Congress of Vienna (1814–15), Austria and the French Bourbons were hostile to the upstart prince, and the son of the deposed Gustav was a potential pretender to the throne. But, thanks to Russian and British support, the status of the new dynasty was undisturbed, and in Sweden its opponents were very few. Upon the death of Charles XIII on February 5, 1818, Charles John became king of Sweden and Norway, and the former republican and revolutionary general became a conservative ruler.

His failure to learn Swedish increased his difficulties, yet his experience, his knowledge, and his magnetic personal charm gave him preponderant political influence. Though blunt in speech, he was cautious and farsighted in action. His foreign policy inaugurated a long and favourable period of peace, based on good relations with Russia and Great Britain. In domestic affairs, farsighted legislation helped the rapid expansion of Swedish agriculture and the Norwegian shipping trade; in Sweden, the famous Göta Canal was completed, postwar financial problems were solved, and during the reign both countries enjoyed a rapid increase in population. On the other hand, the King's autocratic tendencies, restrictions on the liberty of the press, and his reluctance to introduce liberal reforms in commercial and industrial policy and in the organization of the Swedish Riksdag led to a growing opposition that culminated during the late 1830s and led to some demands for his abdication. In Norway there was opposition to the Swedish predominance within the union and to the royal influence over the legislature. But the King rode out the storms, and the 25th anniversary of his succession to the throne in 1843 was an occasion for successful royalist propaganda and popular acclaim. Charles John died on March 8, 1844.

BIBLIOGRAPHY. The standard biography is TORVALD TORVALDSON HOJER, *Carl XIV Johan*, 3 vol. (1939–60), based on French, Swedish, and other archival materials. The first volume, which deals with the French period, was translated into French in 1943. Two other biographies are: in English, D.P. BARTON, *Bernadotte*, 3 vol. (1914–25); and in French, G. GIROD DE L'AIN, *Bernadotte chef de guerre et chef d'Etat* (1968). Many works, mainly in Swedish but sometimes in other languages (for instance, F.D. SCOTT, *Bernadotte and the Fall of Napoleon*, 1935), deal with special aspects of Charles XIV's foreign and domestic policy. His policy in 1812 especially has been very much debated. Bibliographical information may be found in Höjer's biography; and in S. CARLSSON, *Svensk historia*, 3rd ed., vol. 2 (1970).

(S.C.O.C.)

Charles the Bold, Duke of Burgundy

Charles the Bold, or le Téméraire, was the last of the great dukes of Burgundy. Under him, the Burgundian state attained its greatest power. He was born at Dijon on November 10, 1433, the son of Duke Philip the Good and Isabella of Portugal. French by his paternal ancestry, the Count of Charolais, as he was at first styled, was brought up in the French manner as a friend of the Dauphin, afterward Louis XI of France, who spent five years in Burgundy before his accession. Charles was married in 1457 to Isabella (died 1465), daughter of Charles I of Bourbon. Though he had shown no hostility to France before taking over the government of Burgundy, during his father's last illness, on his father's death (June 15, 1467), he became duke and gave rein to an overriding ambition to make Burgundy wholly independent of France and to raise it, if possible, to a kingdom.

Charles was almost entirely successful until 1474. He extended his possessions, organized them as a state, and freed them from French control. Much annoyed by Louis XI's acquisition of Burgundian territory on the Somme River, he entered upon a lifelong struggle against Louis and became one of the principal leaders of the League of the Public Weal, an alliance of the leading French magnates against Louis. Charles forced Louis to restore to him the territory on the Somme in the Treaty of Conflans (October 1465) and to promise him the hand of his daughter Anne of France, with Champagne as dowry. Louis continued to encourage the towns of Dinant and Liège to revolt against Burgundy. But Charles sacked Dinant (1466), and the Liégeois were defeated in battle and deprived of their liberties after the death of Philip the Good (1467). Charles, moreover, outdid Louis by obtaining the alliance of Edward IV of England, whose sister Margaret of York he married as his third wife (July 1468). Louis now tried negotiations with Charles at Péronne (October 1468). There, in the course of the discussions, Charles was informed of a fresh revolt of the Liégeois, again aided by Louis. Looking on Louis as a trai-

Charles the Bold, portrait by Rogier van der Weyden, *c.* 1460. In the Gemäldegalerie, West Berlin.

By courtesy of the Staatliche Mussen Preussischer Kulturbesitz Gemaldegalerie Berlin (West)

tor, Charles nevertheless negotiated with him but at the same time forced him to remove Flanders, Ghent, and Bruges from the jurisdiction of the Paris *parlement* (superior court) and to assist in quelling the revolt; Liège was destroyed, and the inhabitants were massacred. The truce, however, was not lasting. Louis commanded Charles to appear before the *parlement* of Paris and seized some of the towns on the Somme (1470–71). The Duke retaliated by invading Normandy and the Île-de-France, ravaged the country as far as Rouen, but failed in an attack on Beauvais (1471-72). Another truce was made (November 1472), and Charles decided to wait, before renewing his attempt, for assurances of further help from Edward IV and for the solution of the problem of the eastern border of his states.

Charles wished to extend his territories as far as the Rhine and to make them into a single unit by acquiring the lands bordered by Burgundy, Luxembourg, and the Netherlands. Losing no opportunity, he purchased the county of Ferrette, the landgraviate of Alsace, and some other towns from the archduke Sigismund of Austria in 1469; he secured for himself the inheritance of the old Duke Arnold of Gelderland in 1473. To achieve his territorial aims, it remained for him only to subdue Cologne and the Swiss cantons and to get Lorraine from René II (René of Vaudémont).

Meanwhile, Charles had been reorganizing his army and the administration of his territories. Statutes promulgated at Thionville (1473) instituted companies of four squadrons, at his expense, and made rules for discipline and tactics; Charles also had many excellent guns cast. He hired soldiers and took many Italian condottieri (mercenary captains) into his service. Intending to centralize the government, he created by statute a single *chambre des comptes* to control ducal finances for the Netherlands, a *chambre du trésor* to survey the administration of his own domain, and a *chambre des généraux* to control the collection of taxes. He exacted very heavy taxes indeed from the estates general (parliament), which became a regular institution in his territories. To administer justice, he established a court called the *grand conseil* at Malines, with jurisdiction to supersede that of the *parlement* of Paris, and another that met alternately at Beaune and at Dole.

It remained for Charles to acquire a royal title. For a short time he entertained designs on the crown of the Holy Roman Empire, but this he renounced. On the other hand, he believed that he had persuaded the emperor Frederick III, in the course of conversations at Trier,

Administrative reforms (margin note)

to agree to crown him king of Burgundy. The royal insignia were ready and the ceremony arranged, when Frederick precipitately fled by night (September 1473). He probably was suspicious of the ambitious Charles.

In less than three years, Charles's dream vanished. The crown had slipped through his fingers. He was obliged to give up his plan of taking the little town of Neuss, which he had unsuccessfully besieged for 11 months (July 1474 to June 1475), from the citizens of Cologne. Moreover, the Treaty of Picquigny (August 29, 1475), concluded by Edward IV and Louis XI, made certain the defection of his English ally. Attacked by René of Lorraine, who had signed an agreement with Louis XI (August 1474), and by a coalition of the Swiss, Sigismund of Austria and the towns on the upper Rhine, Charles took Nancy in November 1475; but, in March and June 1476, he was defeated by the Swiss, at Granson and at Morat. In October he lost Nancy. Then, on January 5, 1477, a further battle was fought outside Nancy, and Charles himself was killed; his mutilated body was discovered some days later.

The fragility of his achievement is proved by its rapid disintegration during the minority of Marie, his daughter by Isabella of Bourbon. Yet Charles the Bold was not merely a belated representative of the chivalrous spirit; he was a man of wide knowledge and culture, already a prince of the Renaissance. His haste, his lack of adaptability, and his obstinacy lost him much more than did his visionary approach and his boldness.

BIBLIOGRAPHY. The excellent work by J. BARTIER, *Charles le Téméraire*, rev. ed. (1970), with abundant illustrations, an appendix on the historical, literary, and mythical interpretations of the subject, and a critical bibliography, may be considered definitive. This book is far superior to its predecessors: J.F. KIRK, *History of Charles the Bold, Duke of Burgundy*, 3 vol. (1864–68), well informed but an apology for Charles; R. PUTNAM, *Charles the Bold, Last Duke of Burgundy, 1433–1477* (1908); M. BRION, *Charles le Téméraire, grand duc d'Occident* (1947); and P. FREDERIX, *La Mort de Charles le Téméraire, 5 janvier 1477* (1966).

(M.J.Mo.)

Charles Martel

Charles Martellus (Charles the Hammer), an illegitimate son of a mayor of the palace (see below) of the Frankish kingdom of Austrasia, between 725 and 741 achieved the difficult goal of reuniting the Frankish kingdom. A man of valiant determination, ambition, and ability, he strove incessantly to consolidate his power.

After the death of Dagobert I in 639, there had been no king of any worth in the Frankish kingdom. All of them were of the Merovingian line—idle, slothful, and bent on ease and luxury. The burden of rule lay upon the mayors of the palace, who in reality governed Austrasia, the eastern part of the Frankish kingdom, and Neustria, its western portion. These mayors controlled not only routine in the royal palace but also the political, social, and commercial life of the Franks.

Neustria bitterly resented its conquest and annexation in 687 by Pepin of Herstal, mayor of Austrasia and father of Charles Martel, at the Battle of Tertry (Testry), near Péronne.

When in 714 Pepin of Herstal died, he left as heirs three grandsons, his legitimate children all being dead. Until his grandchildren came of age, Plectrude, Pepin's widow, was to hold power. As an illegitimate son, Charles Martel was entirely neglected in the will. But he was young, strong, and determined, and a struggle for control at once began between him and Plectrude.

Both Charles and Plectrude faced rebellion throughout the Frankish kingdom when Pepin's will was made known. The King, Chilperic II, was in the power of Ragenfrid, mayor of the palace of Neustria, who joined forces with an enemy of the Franks, Radbod, king of the Frisians in Holland, in order to eliminate Charles. Plectrude managed to imprison Charles, but he escaped, gathered an army, defeated King Chilperic and Mayor Ragenfrid, and conquered the hostile Neustrians. His success made resistance by Plectrude and the Austrasians useless; realizing the spirit and power of young Charles, they submitted, and by 719 Charles alone governed the Franks as mayor. Peace and order reigned in Austrasia and Neustria, so that by 724 Charles was free to deal with hostile elements elsewhere. This involved expeditions against the Saxons and the peoples of the lands near the Rhine and the Danube.

Charles next crossed the Loire into Aquitaine, where one Eudes (Odo) was duke. Eudes, once an ally of Charles, had become disloyal and promptly called to his aid the Saracens, Moors from Africa, who, entering Spain in 711, had soon conquered it and were now (732) threatening Gaul. Led by their king, 'Abd ar-Rahmān, they marched for Bordeaux, there to burn churches and to plunder. From Bordeaux they went across Aquitaine to Poitiers. It was outside this city that Charles Martel came upon them and put them to flight.

Battle of Poitiers (732)

In 733 Charles forced Burgundy to yield to his rule, and in 734 he subdued the Frisians. During 735 word arrived that Eudes was dead, and Charles marched rapidly across the Loire to make his power felt around Bordeaux. In 736 he fought to secure his conquest of Burgundy, and there were further engagements against the Saracens during the 730s.

Critics of Charles Martel's policies have pointed out that he robbed the church of its lands and money in order to reward his supporters. Yet he worked hard for the church and made gifts of great value to several abbeys, especially to Saint-Denis on the outskirts of Paris. He also gave aid and protection to two English missionaries: St. Willibrord in Utrecht in the Netherlands and St. Boniface, who organized heathen Germany for the faith.

Charles declined, however, to respond to pleas for military aid from Pope Gregory III, who was beset by the Lombards (739). The Lombards had supported Charles against the Saracens, and he would have been unwise to antagonize them. Though the Pope sent magnificent gifts, even the keys of St. Peter's tomb, and Charles replied with priceless offerings, he gave no promise of aid.

At this time his health was failing, and in 741 he retired to his palace at Quierzy-sur-Oise, where he died soon after. Before his death he divided the Merovingian kingdom between his two legitimate sons, Pepin and Carloman. He had maintained the fiction of Merovingian rule all of his life, refraining from transferring the royal title to his own dynasty.

BIBLIOGRAPHY. ELEANOR DUCKETT, *Anglo-Saxon Saints and Scholars* (1947, reprinted 1967), and *The Wandering Saints of the Early Middle Ages* (1964); THOMAS HODGKIN, *Italy and Her Invaders, 376–814 A.D.*, vol. 7 (1899, reprinted 1967), giving much information in detail; J.M. WALLACE-HADRILL, *The Barbarian West, 400–1000*, 3rd rev. ed. (1967); *The Fourth Book of the Chronicle of Fredegar, with Its Continuations* (1960); and *The Long-Haired Kings and Other Studies in Frankish History* (1962), all indispensable, especially *The Fourth Book*, with original Latin and English translation. See also the *Cambridge Medieval History*, vol. 2 (1964).

(E.S.D.)

Chaucer, Geoffrey

Geoffrey Chaucer, the outstanding English writer before Shakespeare, is among England's greatest poets. He contributed importantly in the second half of the 14th century to the management of public affairs as courtier, diplomat, and civil servant. In that career he was trusted and aided by three successive kings—Edward III, Richard II, and Henry IV. But it is his avocation—the writing of poetry—for which he is remembered. Perhaps the chief characteristics of Chaucer's works are their variety in subject matter, genre, tone, style, and in the complexities presented concerning man's pursuit of a sensible existence. Yet his writings also consistently reflect an all-pervasive humour, combined with serious and tolerant consideration of important philosophical questions. From his writings Chaucer emerges as poet of love, both earthly and divine, whose presentations range from lustful cuckoldry to spiritual union with God. Thereby, they regularly lead the reader to speculation about man's relation both to his fellows and to his Maker, while simultaneously providing delightfully entertaining views of the frailties and follies, as well as the nobility, of mankind.

Chaucer, portrait miniature painted after the poet's death. In the British Museum (Harley Ms. 4866).
By courtesy of the trustees of the British Museum

Forebears and early years. Chaucer's forebears for at least four generations were middle class English people whose connection with London and the court had steadily increased. John Chaucer, his father, was an important London vintner and a deputy to the king's butler; in 1338 he was a member of Edward III's expedition to Antwerp, in Flanders, now part of Belgium, and he owned property in Ipswich, in the county of Suffolk, and in London. He died in 1366 or 1367 at the age of 53. The name Chaucer is derived from the French word *chaussier*, meaning a maker of footwear. The family's financial success derived from wine and leather.

Although *c.* 1340 is customarily given as Chaucer's birth date, 1342 or 1343 is probably a closer guess. No information exists concerning his early education, although doubtless he would have been as fluent in French as in English. He also became competent in Latin and Italian. His writings show his close familiarity with many important books of his time and of earlier times.

Chaucer first appears in the records in 1357, as a member of the household of Elizabeth, countess of Ulster, wife of Lionel, third son of Edward III. Geoffrey's father presumably had been able to place him among the group of young men and women serving in that royal household, a customary arrangement whereby families who could do so provided their children with opportunity for the necessary courtly education and connections to advance their careers. By 1359 Chaucer was a member of Edward III's army in France and was captured during the unsuccessful siege of Reims. The King contributed to his ransom, and Chaucer served as messenger from Calais to England during the peace negotiations of 1360. Chaucer does not appear in any contemporary record during 1361–65. He was probably in the King's service, but he may have been studying law—a not unusual preparation for public service, then as now—since a 16th-century report implies that, while so engaged, he was fined for beating a Franciscan friar in a London street. On February 22, 1366, the King of Navarre issued a certificate of safe-conduct for Chaucer, three companions, and their servants to enter Spain. This occasion is the first of a number of diplomatic missions to the continent of Europe over the succeeding ten years, and the wording of the document suggests that here Chaucer served as "chief of mission."

Capture at the siege of Reims

By 1366 Chaucer had married. Probably his wife was Philippa Pan, who had been in the service of the Countess of Ulster, and who entered the service of Philippa of Hainault, queen consort of Edward III, when Elizabeth died in 1363. In 1366 Philippa Chaucer received an annuity, and later annuities were frequently paid to her through her husband. These and other facts indicate that Chaucer married well.

In 1367 Chaucer received an annuity for life as yeoman of the king, and in the next year he was listed among the King's esquires. Such officers lived at court and performed staff duties of considerable importance. In 1368 Chaucer was abroad on a diplomatic mission, and in 1369 he was on military service in France. Also in 1369 he and his wife were official mourners for the death of Queen Philippa. Obviously, Chaucer's career was prospering, and his first important poem—*Book of the Duchess*—seems further evidence of his connection with persons in high place.

First important poem

That poem of more than 1,300 lines, probably written in late 1369 or early 1370, is an elegy for Blanche, duchess of Lancaster, John of Gaunt's first wife, who died of plague in September 1369. Chaucer's close relationship with John, which continued through most of his life, may have commenced as early as Christmas 1357 when they, both about the same age, were present at the Countess of Ulster's residence in Yorkshire. For this first of his important poems, Chaucer used the dream-vision form, a genre made popular by the highly influential 13th-century French poem of courtly love, the *Roman de la rose*. Chaucer translated that poem, at least in part, probably as one of his first literary efforts, and he borrowed from it throughout his poetic career. The *Duchess* is also indebted to contemporary French poetry and to Ovid, Chaucer's favourite Roman poet. Nothing in these borrowings, however, will account for his originality in combining dream-vision with elegy and eulogy of Blanche with consolation for John. Also noteworthy here—as it increasingly became in his later poetry—is the tactful and subtle use of a first-person narrator, who both is and is not the poet himself. The device had obvious advantages for the minor courtier delivering such a poem orally before the high-ranking court group. In addition, the *Duchess* foreshadows Chaucer's skill at presenting the rhythms of natural conversation within the confines of Middle English verse and at creating realistic characters within courtly poetic conventions. Also, Chaucer here begins, with the Black Knight's account of his love for Good Fair White, his career as a love poet, examining in late medieval fashion the important philosophic and religious questions concerning the human condition as they relate to both temporal and eternal aspects of love.

Diplomat and civil servant. During the decade of the 1370s, Chaucer was at various times on diplomatic missions in Flanders, France, and Italy. Probably his first Italian journey (December 1372 to May 1373) was for negotiations with the Genoese concerning an English port for their commerce, and with the Florentines concerning loans for Edward III. His next Italian journey occupied May 28 to September 19, 1378, when he was a member of a mission to Milan concerning military matters. Several times during the 1370s, Chaucer and his wife received generous monetary grants from the King and from John of Gaunt. On May 10, 1374, he obtained rent free a dwelling above Aldgate, in London, and on June 8 of that year he was appointed comptroller of the customs and subsidy of wools, skins, and tanned hides for the Port of London. Now, for the first time, Chaucer had a position away from the court, and he and his wife had a home of their own, about a ten-minute walk from his office. In 1375 he was granted two wardships, which paid well, and in 1376 he received a sizable sum from a fine. When Richard II became king in June 1377, he confirmed Chaucer's comptrollership and, later, the annuities granted by Edward III to both Geoffrey and Philippa. Certainly during the 1370s fortune smiled upon the Chaucers.

Appointment as comptroller of the customs

So much responsibility and activity in public matters appears to have left Chaucer little time for writing during this decade. The great literary event for him was that, during his missions to Italy, he encountered the work of Dante, Petrarch, and Boccaccio, which was later to have profound influence upon his own writing. Chaucer's most important work of the 1370s was *Hous of Fame*, a poem of over 2,000 lines, also in dream-vision form. In some ways it is a failure: it is unfinished, its theme is unclear, and the diversity of its parts seems to overshadow any unity of purpose; but it gives considerable evidence of Chaucer's advancing skill as a poet. The eight-syllable metre is handled with great flexibility; the light, bantering, somewhat ironic tone—later to become one of Chaucer's chief effects—is established; and a wide variety of subject matter is included. Further, the later mastery in creation of memorable characters is here foreshadowed by the marvellous golden eagle who carries the frightened narrator, "Geoffrey," high above the Earth to the houses of Fame and Rumour, so that as a reward for his writing and studying he can learn "tydings" to make into love poems. Here, too, Chaucer's standard picture of his own fictional character emerges: the poet, somewhat dull-witted, dedicated to writing about love but without successful personal experience of it. The comedy of the poem reaches its high point when the pedantic eagle delivers for Geoffrey's edification a learned lecture on the properties of sound. In addition to its comic aspects, however, the poem seems to convey a serious note: like all earthly things, fame is transitory and capricious.

The middle years: political and personal anxieties. In a deed of May 1, 1380, one Cecily Chaumpaigne released Chaucer from legal action: "both of my rape and of any other matter or cause." Rape (*raptus*) could at the time mean either sexual assault or abduction; scholars have not been able to establish which meaning applies here, but, in either case, the release suggests that Chaucer was not guilty as charged. He continued to work at the Customs House and in 1382 was additionally appointed comptroller of the petty customs for wine and other merchandise; but in October 1386 his dwelling in London was leased to another man, and, in December of that year, successors were named for both of his comptrollerships in the customs—whether he resigned or was removed from office is not clear. Between 1382 and 1386 he had arranged for deputies—permanent in two instances and temporary in others—in his work at the customs. In October 1385 he was appointed a justice of the peace for Kent, and in August 1386 he became knight of the shire for Kent, to attend Parliament in October. Further, in 1385 he probably moved to Greenwich, then in Kent, to live. These circumstances suggest that, for some time before 1386, he was planning to move from London and to leave the Customs House. Philippa Chaucer apparently died in 1387; if she had suffered poor health for some time previously, that situation could have influenced a decision to move. On the other hand, political circumstances during this period were not favourable for Chaucer and may have caused his removal. By 1386 a baronial group led by Thomas of Woodstock, duke of Gloucester, had bested both Richard II and John of Gaunt—with whose parties Chaucer had long been associated—and usurped the King's authority and administration. Numerous other officeholders—like Chaucer, appointed by the King—were discharged, and Chaucer may have suffered similarly. Perhaps the best view of the matter is that Chaucer saw which way the political wind was blowing and began early to prepare to move when the necessity arrived.

Death of Philippa Chaucer

The period 1386–89 was clearly difficult for Chaucer. Although he was reappointed justice of the peace for 1387, he was not returned to Parliament after 1386. In 1387 he was granted protection for a year to go to Calais, in France, but seems not to have gone, perhaps because of his wife's death. In 1388 a series of suits against him for debts began, and he sold his royal pension for a lump sum. Also, from February 3 to June 4, 1388, the Merciless Parliament, controlled by the barons, caused many leading members of the court party—some of them Chaucer's close friends—to be executed. In May 1389, however, the 23-year-old King Richard II regained control, ousted his enemies, and began appointing his supporters to office. Almost certainly, Chaucer owed his next public office to that political change. On July 12, 1389, he was appointed clerk of the king's works, with executive responsibility for repair and maintenance of royal buildings, such as the Tower of London and Westminster Palace, and with a comfortable salary.

Although political events of the 1380s, from the Peasants' Revolt of 1381 through the Merciless Parliament of 1388, must have kept Chaucer steadily anxious, he produced a sizable body of writings during this decade, some of very high order. Surprisingly, these works do not in any way reflect the tense political scene. Indeed, one is tempted to speculate that during this period Chaucer turned to his reading and writing as escape from the difficulties of his public life. The *Parlement of Foules*, a poem of 699 lines, is a dream-vision for St. Valentine's Day, making use of the myth that each year on that day the birds gathered before the goddess Nature to choose their mates. Beneath its playfully humorous tone, it seems to examine the value of various kinds of love within the context of "common profit" as set forth in the introductory abstract from the *Somnium Scipionis* (*Dream of Scipio*) of Cicero. The narrator searches unsuccessfully for an answer and concludes that he must continue his search in other books. For this poem Chaucer also borrowed extensively from Boccaccio and Dante, but the lively bird debate from which the poem takes its title is for the most part original. The poem has often been taken as connected with events at court, particularly the marriage, in 1382, of Richard II and Anne of Bohemia. But no such connection has ever been firmly established. The *Parlement* is clearly the best of Chaucer's earlier works.

The Consolation of Philosophy, written by the Roman philosopher Boethius (early 6th century), a Christian, was one of the most influential of medieval books. Its discussion of free will, God's foreknowledge, destiny, fortune, and true and false happiness—in effect, all aspects of the manner in which the right-minded individual should direct his thinking and action to gain eternal salvation—had a deep and lasting effect upon Chaucer's thought and art. His prose translation of the *Consolation* is very carefully done, and in his next poem—*Troilus and Criseyde*—the influence of Boethius' book is pervasive. Chaucer took the basic plot for this 8,239-line poem from Boccaccio's *Filostrato*.

Some critics consider *Troilus and Criseyde* Chaucer's finest work, greater even than the far more widely read *Canterbury Tales*. But the two works are so different that comparative evaluation seems fruitless. The state of the surviving manuscripts of *Troilus* shows Chaucer's detailed effort in revising this poem. Against the background of the legendary Trojan War, the love story of Troilus, son of the Trojan king Priam, and Criseyde, widowed daughter of the deserter priest Calkas, is recounted. The poem moves in leisurely fashion, with introspection and much of what would now be called psychological insight dominating many sections. Aided by Criseyde's uncle Pandarus, Troilus and Criseyde are united in love about halfway through the poem; but then she is sent to join her father in the Greek camp outside Troy. Despite her promise to return, she gives her love to the Greek Diomede, and Troilus, left in despair, is killed in the war. These events are interspersed with Boethian discussion of free will and determinism. At the end of the poem, when Troilus' soul rises into the heavens, the folly of complete immersion in sexual love is viewed in relation to the eternal love of God. The effect of the poem is controlled throughout by the direct comments of the narrator, whose sympathy for the lovers—especially for Criseyde—is ever present.

Also in the 1380s Chaucer produced his fourth and final dream-vision poem, the *Legend of Good Women*, which is not a success. It presents a "Prologue," existing in two versions, and nine stories. In the "Prologue" the god of love is angry because Chaucer had earlier written about so many women who betrayed men. As penance, Chaucer must now write about good women. The "Prologue" is noteworthy for the delightful humour of the narrator's self-mockery and for the passages in praise of books and of the spring. The stories—concerning such women of antiquity as Cleopatra, Dido, and Lucrece—are brief and rather mechanical, with the betrayal of women by wicked men as a regular theme; as a result, the whole becomes more a legend of bad men than of good women. Perhaps the most important fact about the *Legend*, however, is that it shows Chaucer structuring a

long poem as a collection of stories within a framework. Seemingly the static nature of the framing device for the *Legend* and the repetitive aspect of the series of stories with a single theme led him to give up this attempt as a poor job. But the failure here must have contributed to his brilliant choice, probably about this same time, of a pilgrimage as the framing device for the stories in *The Canterbury Tales*.

Last years. Chaucer's service as clerk of the king's works lasted only from July 1389 to June 1391. During that tenure he was robbed several times and once beaten, sufficient reason for seeking a change of jobs. In June 1391 he was appointed subforester of the king's park in North Petherton, Somerset, an office that he held until his death. He retained his home in Kent and continued in favour at court, receiving royal grants and gifts during 1393–97. The records show his close relationship during 1395–96 with John of Gaunt's son the Earl of Derby, later King Henry IV. When John died in February 1399, King Richard confiscated John's Lancastrian inheritance; then in May he set forth to crush the Irish revolt. In so doing, he left his country ready to rebel. Henry, exiled in 1398 but now duke of Lancaster, returned to England to claim his rights. The people flocked to him, and he was crowned on September 30, 1399. He confirmed Chaucer's grants from Richard II and in October added an additional generous annuity. In December 1399 Chaucer took a lease on a house in the garden of Westminster Abbey. But on October 25, 1400, he died. He was buried in the Abbey, a signal honour for a commoner.

Chaucer's great literary accomplishment of the 1390s was *The Canterbury Tales*. In it a group of about 30 pilgrims gather at the Tabard Inn in Southwark, across the Thames from London, and agree to engage in a storytelling contest as they travel on horseback to the shrine of Thomas à Becket in Canterbury, Kent, and back. Harry Bailly, host of the Tabard, serves as master of ceremonies for the contest. The pilgrims are introduced by vivid brief sketches in the "General Prologue." Interspersed between the 24 tales told by the pilgrims are short dramatic scenes presenting lively exchanges, called links and usually involving the host and one or more of the pilgrims. Chaucer did not complete the full plan for his book: the return journey from Canterbury is not included, and some of the pilgrims do not tell stories. Further, the surviving manuscripts leave room for doubt at some points as to Chaucer's intent for arranging the material. The work is, nevertheless, sufficiently complete to be considered a unified book rather than a collection of unfinished fragments. Use of a pilgrimage as a framing device for the collection of stories enabled Chaucer to bring together people from many walks of life: knight, prioress, monk; merchant, man of law, franklin, scholarly clerk; miller, reeve, pardoner; wife of Bath and many others. Also, the pilgrimage and the storytelling contest allowed presentation of a highly varied collection of literary genres: courtly romance, racy fabliau, saint's life, allegorical tale, beast fable, medieval sermon, alchemical account, and, at times, mixtures of these genres. Because of this structure, the sketches, the links, and the tales all fuse as complex presentations of the pilgrims, while, at the same time, the tales present remarkable examples of short stories in verse, plus two expositions in prose. In addition, the pilgrimage, combining a fundamentally religious purpose with its secular aspect of vacation in the spring, made possible extended consideration of the relationship between the pleasures and vices of this world and the spiritual aspirations for the next, that seeming dichotomy with which Chaucer, like Boethius and many other medieval writers, was so steadily concerned.

For this crowning glory of his 30 years of literary composition, Chaucer used his wide and deep study of medieval books of many sorts and his acute observation of daily life at many levels. He also employed his detailed knowledge of medieval astrology and subsidiary sciences as they were thought to influence and dictate human behaviour. Over the whole expanse of this intricate dramatic narrative, he presides as Chaucer the poet, Chaucer

Composition of the Parlement of Foules

Theme of Troilus and Criseyde

Failure of the Legend of Good Women

The Canterbury Tales

the civil servant, and Chaucer the pilgrim: somewhat slow-witted in his pose and always intrigued by human frailty but always questioning the complexity of the human condition, always seeing both the humour and the tragedy in that condition, and always trying to discover the right way for existence on this Earth. At the end, in the "Retractation" with which *The Canterbury Tales* closes, Chaucer as poet and pilgrim states his conclusion that the concern for this world fades into insignificance before the prospect for the next; in view of the admonitions in "The Parson's Tale," he asks forgiveness for his writings that concern "worldly vanities" and remembrance for his translation of the *Consolation* and his other works of morality and religious devotion. On that note he ends his finest work and his career as poet.

Descendants and posthumous reputation. Information concerning Chaucer's children is not fully clear. The probability is that he and Philippa had two sons and two daughters. One son, Thomas Chaucer, who died in 1434, owned large tracts of land and held important offices in the 1420s, including the forestership of North Petherton. He later leased Chaucer's house in Westminster, and his twice-widowed daughter Alice became duchess of Suffolk. In 1391 Chaucer had written *Treatise on the Astrolabe* for "little Lewis," probably his younger son, then 10 years old. Elizabeth "Chaucy," probably the poet's daughter, was a nun at Barking in 1381. A second probable daughter, Agnes Chaucer, was a lady-in-waiting at Henry IV's coronation in 1399. The records lend some support to speculation that John of Gaunt fathered one or more of these children. Chaucer seems to have had no descendants living after the 15th century.

For Chaucer's writings the subsequent record is clearer. His contemporaries praised his artistry, and a "school" of 15th-century Chaucerians imitated his poetry. Over the succeeding centuries, his poems, particularly *The Canterbury Tales*, have been widely read, and, since about the middle of the 19th century, the number of scholars and critics who devote themselves to the study and teaching of his life and works has steadily increased.

MAJOR WORKS
Information concerning dates of composition of the extant manuscripts, and of the first printings of the various works can also be found in the book by Hammond cited in the Bibliography.

LONGER POEMS (in probable order of composition): *Book of the Duchess; Hous of Fame* (unfinished); *Parlement of Foules; Troilus and Criseyde; Legend of Good Women;* prologue, two versions; *The Canterbury Tales:* consisting of The Prologue (The General Prologue), "The Knight's Tale," "The Miller's Tale," "The Reeve's Tale," "The Cook's Tale," "The Man of Law's Tale," "The Wife of Bath's Tale," "The Friar's Tale," "The Summoner's Tale," "The Clerk's Tale," "The Merchant's Tale," "The Squire's Tale," "The Franklin's Tale," "The Second Nun's Tale," "The Canon's Yeoman's Tale," "The Physician's Tale," "The Pardoner's Tale," "The Shipman's Tale," "The Prioress's Tale," "The Tale of Sir Thopas" and "The Tale of Melibeus" (Chaucer's contributions to the tales told by his fellow-pilgrims, the latter in prose), "The Monk's Tale," "The Nun's Priest's Tale," "The Manciple's Tale," and "The Parson's Tale" (in prose), and ending with Chaucer's "Retractation."

Not all the tales are complete; several contain their own prologues.

SHORTER POEMS: *Anelida and Arcite* (unfinished); *Complaint of Chaucer to his Empty Purse; Lines to Adam Scriven,* his scribe; *Truth, Fortune,* and *Gentilesse;* and letters in verse to Henry Scogan and to Buxton.

PROSE: *The Consolation of Philosophy* (*Boethius*) (trans. from Boethius' *De consolatione philosophiae*); *Treatise on the Astrolabe.*

BIBLIOGRAPHY. Complete reference to publications concerning Chaucer and his works is provided by the following: E.P. HAMMOND, *Chaucer: A Bibliographical Manual* (1908, reprinted 1935); D.D. GRIFFITH, *Bibliography of Chaucer, 1908–1953* (1955); W.R. CRAWFORD, *Bibliography of Chaucer, 1954–63* (1967); in the annual bibliographies in *Publications of the Modern Language Association* (international coverage since 1956); and in *The Chaucer Review* (1966–) with even wider coverage than in *PMLA.* The best selective bibliography is A.C. BAUGH (comp.), *Chaucer* (1968). Manuscripts of Chaucer's works are described, and their locations given, in the book by Hammond listed above. An up-to-date listing of

locations will be included in the revision now in preparation of J.E. WELLS, *A Manual of the Writings in Middle English 1050–1400* (1916; nine suppl., 1919–51). From 1868 to 1926 the Chaucer Society in England published 155 volumes of important Chaucerian texts and commentaries. In the United States the Chaucer Group of the Modern Language Association sponsors *The Chaucer Review*, and also the Chaucer Library, editions of his source-books as he probably knew them.

Editions: The early printed editions of the *Works* are by PYNSON (1526), THYNNE (1532, 1542, and 1545?), STOW (1561), SPEGHT (1598, 1602, and 1687), and URRY (1721); those of the *Canterbury Tales* alone are by CAXTON (*c.* 1478 and *c.* 1484), PYNSON (*c.* 1492), WYNKYN DE WORDE (1495? and 1498), MORELL (1737), and TYRWHITT (1775–78). The most important 19th-century edition is W.W. SKEAT, *The Complete Works of Geoffrey Chaucer*, 7 vol. (1894–97). The three most widely used student editions are F.N. ROBINSON, *The Works of Geoffrey Chaucer*, 2nd ed. (1957); E.T. DONALDSON, *Chaucer's Poetry: An Anthology for the Modern Reader* (1958); and A.C. BAUGH, *Chaucer's Major Poetry* (1963). Scholarly editions, based on all manuscripts, are J.M. MANLY and EDITH RICKERT, *The Text of the Canterbury Tales*, 8 vol. (1940); and R.K. ROOT, *The Book of Troilus and Criseyde* (1926). Two easily available recent editions of the *Tales* are A.C. CAWLEY, *The Canterbury Tales* ("Everyman's Library," 1958); and R.A. PRATT, *Selections from the Tales of Canterbury, and Short Poems* ("Riverside Editions," 1966).

Modernizations: J.S.P. TATLOCK and PERCY MACKAYE, *The Complete Poetical Works of Geoffrey Chaucer* (1912; reprinted as *The Modern Reader's Chaucer*, 1966), expurgated, in prose; THEODORE MORRISON, *The Portable Chaucer* (1949), major selections in verse; NEVILL COGHILL, *The Canterbury Tales* (1951), in verse; R.M. LUMIANSKY, *The Canterbury Tales* (1954) and *Troilus and Criseyde* (1952), both in prose.

Biography and criticism: A.A. KERN, *The Ancestry of Chaucer* (1906); J.R. HULBERT, *Chaucer's Official Life* (1912); M.M CROW and C.C. OLSON (eds), *Chaucer Life-Records* (1966)—these two scholars are now preparing a definitive biography; M.B. RUUD, *Thomas Chaucer* (1926); M.H. SPIELMANN, *The Portraits of Chaucer* (1900); D.S. BREWER, *Chaucer*, 3rd ed. (1965), a brief, up-to-date treatment of Chaucer's life and works; G.G. COULTON, *Chaucer and His England*, 8th ed. (1963), the 14th-century historical background; C.F.E. SPURGEON, *Five Hundred Years of Chaucer Criticism and Allusion, 1357–1900*, 7 vol. (1914–24; 3 vol., 1925, reprinted 1960); W.L. ALDERSON, "A Check-List of Supplements to Spurgeon's Chaucer Allusions," *Philological Quarterly*, 32:418–427 (1953); G.L. KITTREDGE, *Chaucer and His Poetry* (1915), essays on aspects of the poetry; R.K. ROOT, *The Poetry of Chaucer* (1922, reprinted 1957), a detailed treatment of the life and works; W.C. CURRY, *Chaucer and the Mediaeval Sciences* (1926); J.M. MANLY, *Some New Light on Chaucer* (1926), contemporaries seen as possible models for some of Chaucer's characters; J.L. LOWES, *Geoffrey Chaucer and the Development of His Genius* (1934), essays on Chaucer's poetic career; P.V.D. SHELLY, *The Living Chaucer* (1940), a critical assessment of the poetry; CHARLES MUSCATINE, *Chaucer and the French Tradition* (1957); D.W. ROBERTSON, *A Preface to Chaucer* (1962), essays on aspects of Chaucer's thought; BERYL ROWLAND (ed.), *Companion to Chaucer Studies* (1968), essays on the life and works; W.F. BRYAN and GERMAINE DEMPSTER (eds.), *Sources and Analogues of Chaucer's Canterbury Tales* (1941); M.A. BOWDEN, *A Commentary on the General Prologue to the Canterbury Tales* (1948); RALPH BALDWIN, *The Unity of the Canterbury Tales* (1955); R.M. LUMIANSKY, *Of Sondry Folk: The Dramatic Principle in The Canterbury Tales* (1955); S.B. MEECH, *Design in Chaucer's Troilus* (1959); HELGE KOKERITZ, *A Guide to Chaucer's Pronunciation* (1954).

(R.M.Lu.)

Chekhov, Anton

A major playwright and often regarded as the greatest of all short-story writers, the Russian author Anton Pavlovich Chekhov was a master of laconic precision, who probed below the surface of life, laying bare the secret motives of his characters. Chekhov's best works lack complex plots and neat solutions. Concentrating on apparent trivialities, they create a special kind of atmospheric mood, sometimes termed haunting or lyrical. Chekhov describes the Russian life of his time using a deceptively simple technique devoid of obtrusive literary devices and is regarded as the outstanding representative of the late 19th-century Russian realist school.

Boyhood and youth. The third of five children, Anton Pavlovich Chekhov was born in Taganrog, Russia, on

Chekhov, 1902.
David Magarshack

January 29 (January 17, old style), 1860. His father was a struggling grocer and pious martinet who had been born a serf. He compelled the boy Anton to serve in his shop, also conscripting him into a church choir, which he himself conducted. Despite the kindness of his mother, childhood remained a painful memory to Chekhov, although it later proved to be a vivid and absorbing experience that he often invoked in his works. While he sometimes complained that Taganrog was intolerably boring, it was more lively than many other Russian provincial centres. Situated on the Sea of Azov in south Russia, this small port included in its population many sailors of various nationalities. There was also a thriving theatre.

After briefly attending a local school for Greek boys, Chekhov entered the town *gimnaziya* (high school) in 1869, where he remained for ten years. There he received the best standard education then available—thorough but unimaginative and based on an intensive study of the Greek and Latin classics, which left him with a lifelong dislike of these subjects. During his last three years at school Chekhov lived alone and supported himself by coaching younger boys; his father, having gone bankrupt, had moved with the rest of his family to Moscow to make a fresh start. Chekhov graduated from school at the age of 19, a lively and sociable youth. Although he had not distinguished himself academically, he had read widely in the town library and was a frequent theatregoer. He was recognized for his skill in improvising comic amateur dramatics and for his ability to mimic teachers and priests. As a schoolboy he also wrote some comic sketches (which have not survived).

In the autumn of 1879 Chekhov joined his family in Moscow, which was to be his main base until 1892. He at once enrolled in the university's medical faculty, graduating in 1884 as a doctor. By this time he was already the economic mainstay of his family, for his father could only obtain poorly paid employment, while the two elder brothers, Aleksandr and Nicolay, a journalist and an artist, respectively, led bohemian lives and provided little financial help. As unofficial head of the family Anton showed great reserves of responsibility and energy, cheerfully supporting his mother and the younger children through his free-lance earnings as a journalist and writer of comic sketches—work that he combined with arduous medical studies and a busy social life.

First fame as writer Chekhov began his writing career as the author of scurrilous and facetious anecdotes for humorous journals, of which many flourished and languished during this period. He signed his early work pseudonymously, often as "Antosha Chekhonte," a school nickname. By 1888, when he abandoned this pseudonym, he had become widely popular with a "lowbrow" public and had already produced a body of work more voluminous than all his later and more celebrated writings put together. And he had, in the process, turned the short comic sketch of about 1,000 words into a minor art form. He had also experimented in serious writing, providing studies of human misery and despair strangely at variance with the frenzied facetiousness of his comic work. Gradually this serious vein absorbed him, and by 1887 it was beginning to predominate over the comic.

Literary maturity. Chekhov's literary progress during his early 20s may be charted by the first appearance of his work in a sequence of St. Petersburg publications, each successive vehicle being more serious and respected than its predecessor. In 1880 he made his debut in a weekly, *Strekoza* ("Dragonfly"), and publications in other ephemeral magazines followed. He obtained a firm foothold in 1882 in *Oskolki* ("Fragments"), a humorous journal but one less frivolous in tone. Two daily papers, the *Peterburgskaya gazeta* ("St. Petersburg Gazette"; 1885) and *Novoye vremya* ("New Time"; 1886), marked further promotions and permitted Chekhov to develop his serious and tragic vein alongside the comic. Finally, in 1888, Chekhov published his first work in a leading literary review, *Severny Vestnik* ("Northern Herald"). With the work in question—a long story entitled "The Steppe"—he at last turned his back on comic fiction and on the "Antosha Chekhonte" period. "Steppe," an autobiographical work describing a journey in the Ukraine as seen through the eyes of a child, is the first among over 50 stories published in a variety of journals and selections between 1888 and his death in 1904. It is on this corpus of later stories, but also on his mature drama of the same period, that Chekhov's main reputation rests. In retrospect, some of his earlier works appear as the sweepings from an experimental writer's laboratory floor. They include several hundred items, among which is a full-length detective novel, *The Shooting Party* (1884), and also an early play—inordinately long, undated and untitled, but sometimes known as *Platonov*—in which the youthful Chekhov can already be observed dimly pioneering the techniques of his maturity. By contrast with these freaks, such poignant early stories as "The Schoolmaster" (1886), "The Kiss," and "Volodya" (both 1887) are worthy to stand comparison with his mature work.

Although the year 1888 first saw Chekhov concentrating almost exclusively on short stories serious in conception, humour—now underlying—nearly always remained an important ingredient. There was also a concentration on quality at the expense of quantity, the number of publications dropping suddenly from over a hundred items a year in the peak years 1886 and 1887 to only 10 short stories in 1888. Besides "Steppe," Chekhov also wrote several profoundly tragic studies at this time, the most notable of which was "A Dreary Story" (1889), a penetrating study into the mind of an elderly and dying professor of medicine. The ingenuity and insight displayed in this *tour de force* was especially remarkable, coming from an author so young. The play *Ivanov* (1887–89) culminates in the suicide of a young man nearer to the author's own age. Together with "A Dreary Story," this belongs to a group among Chekhov's works that have been called clinical studies. They explore the experiences of the mentally or physically ill in a spirit that reminds one that the author was himself a qualified—and remained a sporadically practising—doctor. The death, in 1889, of his feckless but sympathetic elder brother Nikolay—from tuberculosis, the disease that was to kill Chekhov himself in due course—contributed to this pessimistic phase, which has sometimes been mistakenly regarded as typifying the man and his work as a whole.

However worried he may or may not have been about the purpose of existence in the late 1880s, Chekhov was certainly much concerned about the purpose of his art. Many critics had begun to reprimand him, now that he was sufficiently well-known to attract their attention, for holding no firm political and social views, and for failing to endow his works with a sense of direction. Russian critics and readers, then no less than now, were accustomed to regard imaginative writers as teachers of the art of living as well as exponents of the art of letters.

Such expectations irked Chekhov, who was unpolitical, philosophically uncommitted, and ill at ease with abstract

Serious fiction

Sakhalin expedition

pseudoprofundities. In early 1890 he suddenly sought relief from the irritations of urban intellectual life by undertaking a one-man sociological expedition to a remote island, Sakhalin. This is situated nearly 6,000 miles east of Moscow, on the other side of Siberia, and was notorious as an Imperial Russian penal settlement. Chekhov's journey, undertaken before work on the Trans-Siberian railroad had even begun, was a long and hazardous ordeal by carriage and river boat. After arriving unscathed, studying local conditions, and conducting a census of the islanders, he returned by sea via Hong Kong and Ceylon to publish his findings as a research thesis, which retains an honoured place in the annals of Russian penology: *The Island of Sakhalin* (1893–94).

Shortly after returning from Sakhalin, Chekhov paid his first visit to western Europe in the company of A.S. Suvorin, a wealthy newspaper proprietor and the publisher of much of Chekhov's own work. Sociable and hospitable though Chekhov was, he had but few intimate friends, and it may be noted that Suvorin—for a long time his closest associate—was a man 26 years older than himself. Their friendship caused Chekhov some unpopularity, owing to the politically reactionary character of Suvorin's daily newspaper, *Novoye vremya*. Eventually Chekhov broke with Suvorin over the attitude taken by *Novoye vremya* toward the notorious Dreyfus affair of 1894–1906, in which a French-Jewish army officer was framed and victimized by French conservative and anti-Semitic forces. But though Chekhov championed Dreyfus, he never became a political "progressive." Attaching supreme importance to freedom, both political and artistic, he seemed to see a menace to liberty in all excessively politically minded persons, whether of the right or of the left.

> View of the Dreyfus case

During the years just before and after his Sakhalin expedition Chekhov had continued his experiments as a dramatist. His *Wood Demon* (1888–89) is a long-winded and ineptly facetious four-act play, which somehow, by a miracle of art, became converted—largely by cutting—into *Uncle Vanya*, one of his three greatest stage masterpieces. The conversion—to a superb study of aimlessness in a rural manor house—took place at some time unestablished between 1890 and 1896. Other dramatic efforts of the period include several of the uproarious one-act farces known as vaudevilles: *The Bear, The Proposal, The Wedding, The Anniversary*, and others. Though written in 1888-91, these correspond in spirit to the early "Antosha Chekhonte" stories, a vein he had abandoned except in works for the stage.

Melikhovo Period: 1892–98. After helping, both as doctor and as medical administrator, to relieve the disastrous peasant famine of 1891–92, Chekhov bought a country estate in the village of Melikhovo, about 50 miles south of Moscow. This was his main residence in the years 1892–98, providing a home for his aging parents, as also for his sister Mariya, who acted as his housekeeper and remained unmarried in order to look after her brother. Chekhov himself soon became prominent in the local community, raising money to build village schools and frequently besieged by peasants who insisted on receiving medical treatment. Chekhov also kept open house for the many friends from Moscow, St. Petersburg, and elsewhere who visited him in the country—often to the detriment of his literary work. Yet, despite the many distractions, his Melikhovo period was the most creatively effective of his life so far as short stories were concerned, for it was during these six years that he wrote "The Butterfly," "Neighbours," (1892), "An Anonymous Story" (1893), "The Black Monk" (1894), "Murder," and "Ariadne" (1895), among many other masterpieces. Village life now became a leading theme in his work, most notably in "Peasants" (1897). Undistinguished by plot, this short sequence of brilliant sketches created more stir in Russia than any other single work of Chekhov's, partly owing to his rejection of the convention whereby writers commonly presented the Russian peasantry in sentimentalized and debrutalized form.

Continuing to provide many portraits of the intelligentsia, Chekhov also described the commercial and factory-owning world in such stories as "A Woman's Kingdom," (1894) and "Three Years" (1895). As has often been recognized, Chekhov's work provides a panoramic study of the Russia of his day, and one so accurate that it could even be used as a sociological source (it was, after all, the work of a scientifically trained observer).

Yet another theme of the Melikhovo period was a polemic contained in certain stories attacking by implication the teachings of Leo Tolstoy, the well-known novelist and thinker, and Chekhov's revered elder contemporary. Himself once (in the late 1880s) a tentative disciple of the Tolstoyan simple life, and also of nonresistance to evil as advocated by Tolstoy, Chekhov had now rejected these doctrines. He illustrated his new view in one particularly outstanding story: "Ward Number Six" (1892). Here an elderly doctor shows himself nonresistant to evil by refraining from remedying the appalling conditions in the mental ward of which he has charge—only to be incarcerated as a patient himself through the intrigues of a subordinate. In "My Life" (1896) the young hero, son of a provincial architect, insists on defying middle class convention by becoming a house painter, a cultivation of the Tolstoyan simple life that Chekhov portrays as misconceived. In a later trio of linked stories, "The Man in a Case," "Gooseberries," and "About Love" (1898), Chekhov further develops the same theme, showing various figures who similarly fail to realize their full potentialities. As these pleas in favour of personal freedom illustrate, Chekhov's stories frequently contain some kind of submerged moral, which, however, is far from saying that he ever worked out a comprehensive ethical or philosophical doctrine, whether along anti-Tolstoyan or any other lines.

> Influence of Tolstoy

Despite his rejection of Tolstoy's teaching, Chekhov always retained a warm admiration for Tolstoy as a man and as an artist. It was in 1895 that he first met the great novelist. A friendly but critical admirer of his younger colleague's work, Tolstoy once said that he disliked Chekhov's plays even more than Shakespeare's.

The Seagull is Chekhov's only dramatic work dating with certainty from the Melikhovo period. First performed in St. Petersburg on October 17, 1896 (O.S.), this four-act drama, misnamed a comedy, was badly received; indeed, it was almost hissed off the stage. Chekhov was greatly distressed and left the auditorium during the second act, having suffered one of the most traumatic experiences of his life and vowing never to write for the stage again. Two years later, however, the play was revived by the newly created Moscow Art Theatre (on December 17, 1898), enjoying considerable success and helping to re-establish Chekhov as a dramatist. *The Seagull* is a study of the clash between the older and younger generations as it affects two actresses and two writers, some of the details having been suggested by episodes in the lives of Chekhov's friends.

Yalta Period: 1899–1904. In March 1897 Chekhov had suffered a lung hemorrhage caused by tuberculosis, symptoms of which had become apparent considerably earlier, though the medically qualified victim chose to ignore them. Now forced to acknowledge himself a semi-invalid, Chekhov sold his Melikhovo estate and built a villa in Yalta, the Crimean coastal resort. From then on he spent most of his winters there or on the French Riviera, cut off from the intellectual life of Moscow and St. Petersburg. This was all the more galling since his plays were beginning to attract serious attention, successful performances of *Uncle Vanya* by the Moscow Art Theatre following those of *The Seagull*. Moreover, Chekhov had become attracted by a young actress, Olga Knipper, who was appearing in his plays, and whom he eventually married in 1901.

> Marriage

A detached, reticent, and seemingly unemotional person, Chekhov had always attracted women and had enjoyed the friendship of many, yet without pursuing a strenuous love life. The name of only one mistress (Lydiya Yavorskaya) is known, and that affair was short-lived. A lengthier involvement, with Lika Mizinova, was more passionate on the young woman's side than on Chekhov's. His marriage to Olga Knipper probably marked the only profound love affair of his life. But since Knipper continued to pursue her acting career, husband and wife lived apart during most of the winter months, and there were no children of the marriage. Uneventful as Chekhov's sex life may appear, the psychological implications of sexual involvement are an important theme in his mature fiction, and not least in his "Lady with the Dog" (1899), perhaps the best known of all his stories.

Never a successful financial manager, Chekhov attempted to regularize his literary affairs in 1899 by selling the copyright of all his existing works, excluding plays, to the publisher A.F. Marx for 75,000 rubles, an unduly low sum. In 1899–1901 Marx issued the first comprehensive edition of Chekhov's works, in ten volumes, after the author had himself rejected many of his juvenilia. Even so, this publication, reprinted in 1903 with supplementary material, was unsatisfactory in many ways.

Toward the end of his life Chekhov became friendly with Maksim Gorky—ten years his junior, but already a popular young author, Chekhov gave Gorky much detailed advice on the technique of fiction writing. In 1902 Chekhov resigned, in protest, an appointment as honorary academician by the Imperial Russian Academy of Sciences, after hearing that the Emperor Nicholas II had refused to permit Gorky—a revolutionary—to receive the same honour.

Last plays

Chekhov's Yalta period saw a decline in the production of short stories and a greater emphasis on drama. The two last plays—*Three Sisters* (1900–01) and *The Cherry Orchard* (1903–04)—were both written for the Moscow Art Theatre. But much as Chekhov owed to the theatre's two founders, Vladimir Nemirovich-Danchenko and Konstanin Stanislavsky, he remained dissatisfied with such rehearsals and performances of his plays as he was able to witness. Repeatedly insisting that his mature drama was comedy rather than tragedy, Chekhov grew distressed when producers insisted on a heavy treatment, overemphasizing the—admittedly frequent—occasions on which the characters inveigh against the boredom and futility of their lives. Despite Stanislavsky's reputation as an innovator who had brought a natural, nondeclamatory style to the hitherto overhistrionic Russian stage, his productions were never natural and nondeclamatory enough for Chekhov, who wished his work to be acted with the lightest possible touch. And though Chekhov's mature plays have since become established in repertoires all over the world, it remains doubtful whether his craving for the light touch has been satisfied except on the rarest of occasions. Yet oversolemnity can be the ruin of *Three Sisters*, for example—the play in which Chekhov so sensitively portrays the longings of a trio of provincial young women.

Insisting that his *Cherry Orchard* was "a comedy, in places even a farce," Chekhov offered in this last play a poignant picture of the Russian land-owning class in decline, portraying characters who remain comic despite their very poignancy. The first performance, in Moscow on January 17, 1904 (O.S.), was itself converted into a tragicomic drama when the author—coughing uncontrollably, already a dying man and in any case one who had always abominated fuss—was brought to the theatre and compelled to listen to a series of grandiloquent speeches honouring (inaccurately) the 25th anniversary of his writing début.

Chekhov died on the night of July 14–15 (July 1–2 O.S.), 1904, in the German spa of Badenweiler at the age of 44; physically he was a broken man, but his literary powers were seemingly unimpaired. Already celebrated by the Russian literary public at the time of his death, he did not become internationally famous until the years after World War I, by which time the translations of Constance Garnett and others had helped to publicize his work, which has found many admirers and imitators among authors writing in English. Among these, John Middleton Murry, Sherwood Anderson, Ernest Hemingway, Bernard Shaw, Katherine Mansfield, and J.B. Priestley are only a few of those who have claimed, or have been credited with, a debt to Chekhov. Yet his elusive, superficially guileless style of writing—in which what is

Assessment

left unsaid often seems so much more important than what is said—has defied effective analysis by literary critics, as well as effective imitation by creative writers. Nor does Chekhov lend himself ideally to cinematic treatment, though many films, both Soviet and non-Soviet, have been based on his stories and plays.

It was not until 40 years after his death, with the issue of the 20-volume *Polnoye sobraniye sochineny i pisem A.P. Chekhova* ("Complete Works and Letters of A.P. Chekhov") of 1944–51, that Chekhov was at last presented in Russian on a level of scholarship worthy—though with certain reservations—of his achievement. The eight volumes of this edition contain his correspondence, amounting to several thousand letters. Outstandingly witty and lively, they belie the legend—commonly believed during the author's lifetime—that he was hopelessly pessimistic in outlook. As samples of the Russian epistolary art Chekhov's letters have been rated second only to Pushkin's by the literary historian D.S. Mirsky. Though Chekhov is still chiefly known for his plays, critical opinion now shows signs of establishing the stories—and particularly those written after 1888—as an even more significant and creative literary achievement.

MAJOR WORKS

PLAYS (ONE-ACT FARCES): *Medved* (1888; *The Bear*); *Predlozheniye* (1889; *The Proposal*); *Svadba* (published 1889, performed 1890; *The Wedding*); *Yubiley* (1891; *The Anniversary*). (FULL-LENGTH PLAYS): *Ivanov* (performed 1887, revised and published 1889; Eng. trans.); *Chayka*, performed St. Petersburg and published in *Russkaya mysl* (1896; revised and performed Moscow, 1898; revised text published 1904; *The Seagull*); *Leshy* (1889; *The Wood-Demon*); *Dyadya Vanya* (1897; *Uncle Vanya*); *Tri sestry* (performed and published 1901, revised 1902; revised text published 1904; *Three Sisters*); *Vishnyovy sad* (1904; *The Cherry Orchard*).

STORIES: Most of Chekhov's stories were first published in newspapers or periodicals. A number were revised for publication, with others previously unpublished, in the collections *Pystrye rasskazy* (1886; *Motley Stories*); *Nevinnye rechi* (1887; *Innocent Tales*); *V sumerkakh* (1887; *In the Twilight*); and *Rasskazy* (1889; *Stories*). Chekhov further revised 240 stories for publication in the first complete edition of his works, 1889–1901. Almost all of them have been translated into English. Among them are the following (with dates of first publication): "Barynya" (1882; "The Mistress"); "Radost" (1883; "Joy"); "Doch Albiona" (1883; "A Daughter of Albion"); "Tragik" (1883; "A Tragic Actor"); "Khameleon" (1884; "A Chameleon"); "Drama na okhote" (1884; "The Shooting Party"); "Gore" (1885; "Sorrow"); "Yeger" (1885; "The Huntsman"); "Prishibeyev" (1885; "Sergeant Prishibeyev"); "Panikhida" (1886; "The Requiem"); "Uchitel" (1886; "The Schoolmaster"); "Kto vinovat?" (1886; "Who Was to Blame?"); "Toska" (1886; "Misery"); "Khoroshiye lyudi" (1886; "Excellent People"); "Grisha" (1886; Eng. trans.); "Anyuta" (1886; Eng. trans.); "Sobytiye" (1886; "An Incident"); "Verochka" (1887; Eng. trans.); "Volodya" (1887; Eng. trans.); "Kashtanka" (1887; Eng. trans.); "Potšeluy" (1887; "The Kiss"); "Tyf" (1887; "Typhus"); "Vragi" (1887; "Enemies"); "Pripadok" (1888; "A Nervous Breakdown"); "Step" (1888; "The Steppe"); "Pari" (1888; "The Bet"); "Skuchnaya istoriya" (1889; "A Dreary Story"); Tragik po nevole (1889–90; "An Unwilling Martyr"); "Gusev" (1890; Eng. trans.); "Duel" (1890; Eng. trans.); "Palata No. 6" (1892; "Ward No. 6"); "Strakh" (1892; "Terror"); "Sosedi" (1892; "Neighbors"); "Poprygunya" (1892; "The Grasshopper"); "Zhena" (1893; "The Wife"); "Chorny monakh" (1894; "The Black Monk"); "Ubiystvo" (1895; "The Murder"); "Tri goda" (1895; "Three Years"); "Ariadna" (1895; "Ariadne"); "Moya zhizn" (1896; "My Life"); "Dom s mezoninom" (1896; "An Artist's Story"); "Muzhiki" (1897; "Peasants"); "V rodnom uglu" (1897; "At Home"); "Kryzhovnik" (1898; "Gooseberries"); "Chelovek v futlyare" (1898; "The Man in a Case"); "Sluchay iz praktiki" (1898; "A Doctor's Visit"); "Ionych" (1898; Eng. trans.); "O lyubvi" (1898; "About Love"); "Dushechka" (1899; "The Darling"); "Dama s sobachkoy" (1899; "The Lady with the Lapdog" or "The Lady with the Dog"); "V ovrage" (1900; "In the Ravine"); "Arkhierey" (1902; "The Bishop"); and "Nevesta" (1903; "The Betrothed"), Chekhov's last story.

TRANSLATIONS: *The Oxford Chekhov*, containing Eng. trans. of all Chekhov's major works, 9 vol. (1964–), ed. and trans. by Ronald Hingley, is the definitive translation. The first comprehensive English translation was by Constance Garnett, in *The Plays of Tchekov*, 2 vol. (1923), and *The Tales of Tchehov*, 13 vol. (1916–22). There are translations of *The Sea-*

gull, *Uncle Vania, Three Sisters,* and *The Cherry Orchard* by
Elisaveta Fen, in *Chekhov: Plays* (1959), and of *The Lady
with the Lapdog and Other Stories* (1960), both in the
Penguin Modern Classics series.

BIBLIOGRAPHY

Bibliographies: ANNA HEIFETZ (comp.), *Chekhov in En-
glish: A List of Works by and about Him* (1949); RISSA
YACHNIN, *The Chekhov Centennial Chekhov in English: A
Selective List of Works by and about Him, 1949–1960* (1960).

*Selections of Chekhov's letters: Letters of Anton Tchehov
to his Family and Friends,* trans. by CONSTANCE GARNETT
(1920); *Letters on the Short Story, the Drama and Other
Literary Topics,* selected and ed. by LOUIS S. FRIEDLAND
(1924); *The Letters of Anton Pavlovitch Tchehov to Olga
Leonardovna Knipper,* trans. by CONSTANCE GARNETT (1926);
The Selected Letters of Anton Chekhov, ed. by LILLIAN HELL-
MAN, trans. by SIDONIE LEDERER (1955).

Biographical studies: DANIEL GILLES, *Tchékhov; ou le
Spectateur désenchanté* (1967; Eng. trans., *Chekhov: Observer Without Illusion,* 1968), is the most useful of the
longer biographies; also useful are DAVID MAGARSHACK, *Chekhov: A Life* (1952); and ERNEST J. SIMMONS, *Chekhov: A
Biography* (1962). RONALD HINGLEY, *Chekhov* (1950, reprinted 1966), is a shorter study combining biography and
criticism.

Critical studies: MAURICE VALENCY, *The Breaking String*
(1966), is the best full-length study of Chekhov's drama;
DAVID MAGARSHACK, *Chekhov the Dramatist* (1952), may also
be consulted. THOMAS WINNER, *Chekhov and His Prose*
(1966), is a helpful but somewhat pedestrian study of the
short stories. OLIVER ELTON, *Chekhov* (1929); and WILLIAM
GERHARDI, *Anton Chekhov* (1923), offer suggestive critical
ideas. W.H. BRUFORD, *Chekhov and His Russia* (1948), admirably sets the subject in its social context.

(R.F.Hi.)

Chekiang

Chekiang (Ze-jiang in Pin-yin romanization), the second
smallest province of the People's Republic of China, is
also one of the most densely populated and affluent. Its
area is 39,300 square miles (101,800 square kilometres),
and its population (1970 estimate) is 31,000,000. A
coastal province, it is bounded by the East China Sea
(Tung Hai) on the east and by the provinces of Kiangsu
on the north, Fukien on the south, Anhwei on the west,
and Kiangsi on the southwest. The provincial capital is
Hangchow.

Chekiang has for many centuries been one of the great
cultural and literary centres of China. Its landscape is renowned for its scenic beauty. The name of the province
derives from its principal river, the Che Chiang (meaning
Crooked River), formally known as the Ch'ien-t'ang
Chiang at the estuary of Hangchow Bay, and Fuch'un
Chiang inland. Chekiang is the leading Chinese province
in farm productivity and in the tea and fishing industries.

History. Before the 8th century BC western Chekiang
was a part of the ancient state of Wu (Kou-wu), while
eastern Chekiang was the land of Yüeh tribes. In about
the 6th century BC the two subregions became the rival
kingdoms of Wu and Yüeh. The heartland of the Wu
state lay in southern Kiangsu Province, whereas that of
Yüeh occupied the coastal area to the south of the
Ch'ien-t'ang Chiang Estuary where it merges into Hangchow Bay. Yüeh and Wu engaged in constant warfare
from 510 until 473 BC, when the Yüeh conquered Wu,
after which the victorious kingdom became a dominant
power in the Chinese feudal empire, nominally headed
by the Chou dynasty. Yüeh was itself subsequently subjected, first by the kingdom of Ch'u in 334 BC and then by
the kingdom of Ch'in in 223 BC.

Yüeh (consisting of Chekiang and Fukien) was quasi-
independent during the two Han dynasties (206 BC–AD 8
and AD 23–220). Chekiang later formed a part of the
kingdom of Wu (220–280). During the T'ang and Sung
dynasties (618 to 907; 960 to 1279), Chekiang was divided into Che-hsi (Western Chekiang) and Che-t'ung
(Eastern Chekiang), which became the traditional geographic divisions of the province. Lin-an (modern Hangchow) was made capital of the Chinese Empire during
the Southern Sung dynasty (1126–1279).

Hangchow's population in 1275 was estimated at more
than 1,000,000. Marco Polo (1254–1324), who visited the
city, described it as the finest and noblest in the world.
Odoric of Pordenone (c. 1286–1331) also visited the city,
which he called Camsay, then renowned as the greatest
city of the world, of whose splendours he, like Marco
Polo and the Arab traveller Ibn Baṭṭūtah (1304–1368/9
or 1377), gave notable details. Chinese, Mongols, Nestorian Christians, and Buddhists from different countries
lived together peaceably in the city during this period.
Hangchow continued to be a great cultural centre until
1862, when it was destroyed during the Taiping Rebellion. Of its citizens, 600,000 were slaughtered, while the
rest either drowned themselves in the Hsi Hu (West
Lake) and the canals or else perished from starvation and
disease. Hangchow did not fully recover from this disaster, but it was eventually rebuilt and underwent gradual
modernization. During World War II, Chekiang was occupied by the Japanese. It was little affected by the civil
war of 1946–49 except for the general deterioration of
morals and economic conditions.

Physical geography. *The landscape.* The northwestern
section of the province (Che-hsi) lies within the fertile
Yangtze River Delta, with its labyrinth of rivers and
canals; its coastal lowlands are protected by dikes. The
southern edge of T'ai Hu (Great Lake) forms part of its
northern border with Kiangsu. The greater part of Chekiang Province lies to the south of Hangchow Bay and is
largely mountainous. It has a rocky and deeply indented
coast, dotted with numerous islands. This part is in fact
a continuation of the mountain ranges of Fukien, which
run roughly parallel to the coast. In eastern Chekiang,
mountains occupy 93 percent of the land surface, while
another 1 percent consists of low hills. Only 6 percent is
level land, distributed along Hangchow Bay, the Fu-ch'un
Chiang Valley, and the Ta-ch'i Valley, in southern Chekiang. Most of the province's arable lands—consisting of
alluvial plains of great fertility—are found in these three
areas.

Rivers, harbours, and islands. The chief river of the
province is Fu-ch'un Chiang (Che Chiang), the drainage
basin of which comprises 40 percent of the total area of
the province. Its length is about 250 miles, measured
from Cha-k'ou (Entrance to the Lock) to its source. The
river has, in fact, two headstreams, one coming down
from the southwestern highlands and flowing through the
broad Lan Chiang Valley and the other rising in Anhwei
Province and passing through Chien-te in Chekiang and
other cities. On the latter tributary is located the Hsin-an
Chiang hydroelectric power plant, which has a capacity
of 580,000 kilowatts and is one of the largest in East
Asia. After the confluence of the two tributaries, the river
is called successively T'ung Chiang (River of Tung Trees)
and Fu-ch'un Chiang (the River of Abundant Spring).
Farther downstream, after it is joined by the T'ung Ch'i,
a mountain stream, it is called Ch'ien-t'ang Chiang and
flows from Hangchow to the sea. The Ch'ien-t'ang Chiang
Estuary tidal bore (tidal wave) takes the form of a high
wall that rushes forward with a thunderous roar. Best
seen just after the full moon and at its highest in the
autumn (late September–early October), the bore is a
famed tourist attraction. Along the estuary are miles of
sea dikes that have been built throughout the ages to protect the rich rice lands of the delta. The Fu-ch'un Chiang
and its tributaries are navigable by small steamers for
more than 300 miles. The mouth of the river is, however,
too shallow for coastal steamships.

The other rivers of some importance are the Yung
Chiang, which flows past Ning-po; the Ling Chiang,
which flows into T'ai-chou Wan (Bay); the Ou-Chiang,
which flows into Wen-chou Wan; and the Ou Chiang's
four principal tributaries, the Ta Ch'i (the Large Stream),
the Hsiao Ch'i (the Small Stream), the Hao Ch'i (the
Good Stream), and the Lung-ch'üan Ch'i (the Eminent
Flowing Stream), which together form the second largest
river system of the province. Although these mountain
streams flow swiftly through rocky channels and gorges,
they are navigable to skillful boatmen using sampans
(small, roofed boats propelled by sculling) right up to the
mountains.

The delta lands and the mountains

The Ch'ien-t'ang Chiang

Coastal islands

Hangchow Bay is almost as broad at its entrance as the Yangtze Estuary but is obstructed by a cluster of 400 islands known as the Chou-shan Ch'ün-tao (Chusan Archipelago). The largest island, Chou-shan Tao (Chusan), is 21 miles long and 50 miles in circumference, with an area of about 202 square miles. Chou-shan is a major coastal fishing centre. On P'u-t'ao Shan, a renowned scenic island east of Chou-shan, is one of the sacred mountains of Buddhism that once attracted pilgrims from all over East Asia.

The Chekiang coast has numerous natural harbours. More than 18,000 islands—36 percent of all the islands of China—have been counted along the Chekiang coast.

Climate. Chekiang has a humid subtropical climate, controlled chiefly by monsoonal airflows, modified by local influences. Considerable differences exist between the coast and the hinterland, between the lowlands and the highlands, and between the north and the south, particularly in winter. Thus, Hangchow, in western Chekiang, has an average January temperature of 39° F (4° C), while that of Wenchow (Warm City), on the coast, is about 46° F (8° C). Summer is hot throughout the province; the average July temperature at Hangchow is 82° F (28° C), while that at Wenchow is 84° F (29° C)—a difference of only 2°.

Annual rainfall throughout the province is over 40 inches. The hilly interior has more precipitation than the coast. The coast is frequently visited by devastating typhoons, particularly during late summer and early autumn.

Vegetation. The vegetation of the northern, or T'ai Hu, plain differs from that of the rest of the province. The lake plain, covered with rich alluvial soil, is an open land of rice fields and rural settlements, dotted with some shade and ornamental trees. The original or natural vegetation disappeared centuries ago when the land was cleared for cultivation.

Mountain vegetation

The vegetation of the hilly and mountainous parts of the province, south of the T'ai Hu plain, consists primarily of mixed evergreen broadleaf and coniferous forests grown on gray-brown podzolic (infertile forest) soils at the higher elevations and on red and yellow lateritic (leached, iron-bearing) podzolic soils on the lower slopes. There is an abundance of such trees as the laurel, pine, cypress, and beech. Besides the ubiquitous bamboo, the tung tree, which supplies valuable oil, is widely distributed in the upper Fu-ch'un Chiang Valley.

Animal life. The province has an animal life typical of the subtropical forest zone and characterized by great diversity; it includes monkeys, anteaters, the southern heron, water turtles, many frogs, and numerous southern birds. There are many invertebrates, among which subtropical insects predominate, although tropical insects characteristic of southern Asia are also found.

Population. The mid-1953 census recorded about 23,000,000 inhabitants of the province. By 1957 numbers had increased to 26,000,000 and by 1970 to 31,000,000, an increase of 8,000,000 in 17 years, or an annual growth rate of about 2 percent. Among the most densely populated provinces of China, Chekiang has a population density (1970) of close to 800 persons per square mile.

Patterns of settlement. Only about 15 percent of the population lives in cities and towns. The capital and largest city, Hangchow—located in western Chekiang—had 800,000 inhabitants in 1970; it is followed in size by the port cities of Ning-po and Wenchow, both in eastern Chekiang, which claimed 300,000 and 250,000 inhabitants, respectively, in 1970. Four other important cities have populations ranging from 50,000 to 150,000; these are Shao-hsing and Chin-hua, in eastern Chekiang, and

Cities and towns

Chia-hsing and Wu-hsing, in western Chekiang. Of these seven most important cities, three are located in the Tai Hu plain (Hangchow, Chia-hsing, and Wu-hsing) and three along the coast. Chin-hua alone is located in the interior, being situated near the geographic centre of the province and serving as the chief distribution centre of southwestern Chekiang.

All of the seven urban centres have a long history; the oldest is Shao-hsing, which dates back to the 6th century BC. Hangchow, as noted, was the capital of the Chinese Empire during the 12th and 13th centuries. It was, however, only after the Opium War (1839–42) and the opening of Ning-po to foreign trade that the modernization of the cities—particularly Hangchow, Ning-po, and Wenchow—began. All seven of the cities have developed modern industries.

There are also more than a dozen cities with over 30,000 inhabitants each, another 50 with over 10,000 inhabitants each, and 100 smaller towns. The 160-odd towns distributed throughout the province include the 63 county (*hsien*) capitals, which are located mostly on the agricultural plains and valley bottoms. Most of them are also local commercial centres. Since 1949 some small-scale local industries have been built in some of the towns located in rural areas. Some local centres are developing into larger and more modern towns.

There is a marked contrast between the densely populated plains and the sparsely populated uplands. Thus, two-fifths of the population in the province is concentrated in the T'ai Hu plain and in the southern coastal region of Hangchow Bay. The rural population density reaches from about 1,000 to 1,500 per square mile in the arable plains along the route of the Chekiang–Kiangsi railway and in the valley bottomlands of the lower Ou, Ling, and other rivers of southeastern Chekiang, where the density is among the highest in China. The higher uplands, on the other hand, generally have densities of less than 260 per square mile and—in the less accessible areas—less than 130 per square mile. The low hill tracts have densities between 260 and 520 per square mile.

Population distribution

The population along the Chekiang coast numbers about 500,000, with the greatest concentration occurring in the Ning-po–Chou-shan area. About 140,000 people engaged in obtaining salt from seawater live chiefly on the shores of Hangchow Bay.

Ethnic composition, language, and religion. The ethnic composition of the population is overwhelmingly Chinese (Han). Those belonging to ethnic minorities number slightly over 80,000, consisting chiefly of Yü tribesmen living in the mountainous area of southern Chekiang, in the Wen-chou and Chin-hua areas (*ti-ch'ü*) along the Fukien border. The Yü tribesmen, of whom a greater number live in Fukien Province, have their own language, although most of them also understand Chinese. They grow paddy rice in terraces on hillslopes; farm work is done by both men and women. There are also small numbers of Manchus and Muslims (Hui) scattered in the cities and towns. The former are mostly descendants of Manchu soldiers garrisoned in Chekiang before the overthrow of the Manchu dynasty in 1911. With the exception of the Muslims and some Christians, the religious affiliation of the entire population in the province may be characterized as a complex of Taoism, Confucianism, and Buddhism. This form of religion is generally tolerated by the people's republic, though the monks are required to engage in productive work to earn a living.

Religious affiliations

Administration and social conditions. Chekiang Province is one of the primary administrative divisions of the People's Republic of China. It is subdivided into 11 secondary administrative units consisting of three municipalities (*shih*) under the direct jurisdiction of the province and eight areas (*ti-ch'ü*)—Chia-hsing, Shao-hsing, Ning-po, Chou-shan, T'ai-chou, Wen-chou, Chin-hua, and Li-shui. The three municipalities consist of the enlarged Hang-chou Shih—which controls seven counties (*hsien*), as well as the city of Hangchow—and the two important seaport municipalities of Ning-po Shih and Wen-chou Shih. The subprovince-level administrative areas are subdivided into a total of 63 counties (*hsien*).

Since 1958 the administrative unit below the county has been the commune. Theoretically, each commune is administered by an elected commune committee, but the real power lies in the commune party committee, which is part of the Chinese Communist Party (CCP) hierarchy. Each commune is divided into production brigades,

Communes, brigades, and teams

which own the land as well as the means of production; the brigade branch committee is the local control body of the party apparatus. The brigade itself is divided into production teams, which form the lowest level administrative unit; each administers an average of 20 to 40 households or else a *chieh-tao* (residential street grouping) within a town. The production team has become the basic economic-accounting unit of rural China.

All administrative units, from the province downward, are theoretically governed by assemblies elected through indirect elections but actually run by local party leaders. The Chekiang Party Committee was re-established in 1971, after the turmoil of the Cultural Revolution of the late 1960s.

The economy. Chekiang is one of the more prosperous of China's provinces, leading the country in farm productivity, in sericulture (the raising of silkworms to produce raw silk), in the tea industry, in the fishing industry, and in a number of famous handicraft industries. Many modern manufacturing plants have been established or greatly enlarged since the establishment of the people's republic.

Because of the province's hilly topography, its arable area is estimated at only about 20 percent of its land surface, amounting to about 5,500,000 acres. Two-fifths of the cultivated land lies in northern Chekiang, where it is located in the Yangtze Delta, and on the southern shore of Hangchow Bay. About 60 percent of the T'ai Hu plain is under cultivation. About 78 percent of Chekiang's arable land is irrigated—one of the highest ratios in eastern or southern Asia.

Agriculture. Chekiang farmers practice a diversified form of agriculture. About two-thirds of the arable land is used to 'grow staple food crops—rice, wheat, barley, corn (maize), and sweet potatoes. The rest of the farmland grows either green fertilizer crops or such industrial crops as cotton, jute, ramie (a shrub yielding a fibre used for textiles), rapeseed, sugarcane, and tobacco. Soybeans, vegetables, and crops used for animal feed are also grown. Most farmers also raise pigs and poultry on their small private plots, and many also raise fish in village ponds, reservoirs, or lakes, and rear silkworms during the slack farming season in spring. In the well-watered hilly areas, tea is grown. All these activities provide a second income for peasant households.

Rice and tea cultivation

Rice is the chief staple food and is grown widely throughout the province, although the well-watered northern plains constitute the most productive area. Rice acreage represents 40 percent of the total area under cultivation.

Both single-cropping and double-cropping systems are followed in paddy (rice field) cultivation. Since the establishment of the people's republic, double-cropping of rice has been vigorously promoted, and its share in the rice acreage has increased from a quarter to half of the total.

Chekiang produces about 20 percent of China's output of tea. There are four principal tea districts. The Hangchow district produces the famous Lung-ching (Dragon Well) green tea. The P'ing-shui district has the largest tea acreage and the highest production of made (processed) tea. The other two districts are Chien-te, in the southwest, and Wen-chou—which includes the subdistricts of Jui-an, Yung-chia, and T'ai-shun—in the southeastern hilly region. The total acreage amounts to 167,-000 acres; it is estimated there is at least an equivalent amount of hilly land also suitable for tea growing but not now in use. World War II caused serious damage to the tea industry: tea gardens were abandoned, aging shrubs were not replaced, and the yield was reduced by half. After the war, and especially during the 1950s, a systematic rehabilitation and development program was undertaken. Improved methods of tea cultivation and processing were introduced and new orchards established.

Sericulture

Sericulture is another of Chekiang's traditionally famous industries. Silkworm rearing is engaged in by a large number of rural households. In the districts of Wuhsing (Hu-chou) and Te-ch'ing, both the T'ai Hu plain, sericulture accounts for 25 to 30 percent of the total agricultural income. The T'ai Hu plain itself accounts for 58 percent of the mulberry acreage and 86 percent of the silkworm-cocoon production. Secondary districts are located in the northeast and the northwest. These areas, which have a long history of sericulture, yield a consistently high quality of silk from the cocoons. A new sericultural district has been established in the southwest (Chin-hua Special District). Chekiang has 260,000 acres of mulberry orchards and a cocoon output of 65,000,000 pounds, which constitutes about 36 percent of the national total. The industry, like the tea industry, suffered serious damage during World War II and the civil war that followed. Despite vigorous measures to restore production, the output has not yet reached the prewar level.

Handicrafts. A flourishing handicraft industry is located mostly in rural villages; it employs almost 600,000 workers. Nationally and internationally known products include the porcelain of Lung-ch'üan, the silk umbrellas and tapestry of Hangchow, embroideries, laces, cross-stitchings, wood carvings, stone carvings, clay sculpture, inlay ware, and a host of other products of Chinese folk art, many of which are exported.

Fisheries. The Chekiang coast lies at the convergence of western Pacific warm and cold currents. Its rivers carry rich organic material into the shallow waters above the continental shelf. As a result, many kinds of fish come there to spawn. In 1957 about 30,000 vessels were fishing in those waters, and Chekiang's saltwater-fishing catch amounted to almost 550,000 tons. More than 100 varieties of fish are found there. Important commercial catches include drums (or croakers), cutlass fish, and cuttlefish. The principal fishing banks are located near Cha-p'u, in Hangchow Bay, the Chou-shan Ch'ün-tao, Shih-pu Tao, T'ai-chou Wan, and Wen-chou Wan. Ningpo is the chief fishing port. Most of the fishing vessels are wooden junks, which sometimes find themselves at the mercy of typhoons. The replacement of these vessels by powered craft, together with the surveying of fish life and migration patterns, holds the key to the future development of the fishing industry.

Saltwater fishing

A flourishing aquiculture industry has been developed, producing kelp, the edible red algae Porphyra (used in making soups and condiments), mussels, scallops, clams, oysters, crabs, and other marine products. Freshwater fishes are raised in inland waters throughout the province.

Transportation. *River traffic.* The rivers play an important role in the province's transport; about half of the total freight volume travels on these inland waterways. The remainder of the freight volume is moved mostly by road, though heavier goods are often moved by rail, especially for longer distances. Coastal shipping accounts for only four percent of the total freight volume.

Railroads and highways. The Shanghai-Hangchow railway is the most important trunk line, connecting western Chekiang with East and North China. The Chekiang–Kiangsi line links Chekiang with South and Central China. The Hangchow–Ning-po railway connects the southern littoral of Hangchow Bay with the Chekiang–Kiangsi and the Shanghai–Hangchow lines. A branch line from Ning-po to Ch'uan-shan, on the coast opposite Chou-shan Tao, was completed in 1957. There is also a branch line from Chin-hau to T'ung-kuan to serve the Hsin-an Chiang damsite and the giant hydroelectric power complex located there. A modern highway network with its primary centre at Hangchow connects the province with the cities of Shanghai and Nanking and with the provinces of Anhwei and Fukien.

Ports and harbours. Among the many harbours on the Chekiang coast are Ting-hai Chiang on Chou-shan Tao, Chen-hai (the port of Ning-po), Hsiang-shan Chiang (Nimrod Sound), San-men (Three Entrances) Wan, T'ai-chou Wan, and Wen-chou Wan.

Cultural life. During the Southern Sung dynasty (1126–1279) the political and cultural centre of China moved from the north to western Chekiang. The Hangchow area became the homeland of a galaxy of famous painters (including a Sung emperor), as well as of calligraphers, poets and essayists, philosophers, and historians. The beauty of Hangchow, the Southern Sung capital, was immortalized by the landscape painters Hsia Kuei and Ma Yüan.

Chekiang has had a long educational and literary tradition. During the Great Proletarian Cultural Revolution (1966–69), 36 institutions of higher learning were closed down. In 1970 six colleges and universities in Chekiang were reported to be enrolling students. Education and cultural life have been undergoing radical change since the Cultural Revolution. Mass media includes Radio Hangchow and a controlled press.

BIBLIOGRAPHY. The most comprehensive contemporary regional economic monograph is the collective work, SUN CHING-CHIH (ed.), *Economic Geography of the East China Region (Shanghai, Kiangsu, Anhwei, Chekiang)* (Eng. trans. 1961). The best atlas available on the Chinese People's Republic is *Kung-fei ch'ieh-chü-hsia ti Chung-kuo ta-lu fen-sheng ti t'u* (1966), a reproduction of the maps and geographical description of provinces in *Chung-kuo fen sheng ti t'u* (*Provincial Atlas China*, 1964), with critical commentaries and supplementary data. *Nagel's Encyclopedia-Guide to China* (1968) includes reports on the observations of young French sinologists during their visit to China. The U.S.S.R. ACADEMY OF SCIENCES, INSTITUTE OF GEOGRAPHY, *The Physical Geography of China* (1965; orig. pub. in Russian, 1964), is the best work on the subject in a Western language.

(F.Hu.)

Chelonia

Turtles are members of the Chelonia, an ancient order of reptiles chiefly characterized by a shell that encloses the vital organs of the body and more or less protects the head and limbs. Although there has been much confusion over the scientific as well as the common name of the group, most scientists now accept the term Chelonia rather than Testudines or Testudinata. Two common names are in wide use: "tortoise" and "turtle." "Tortoise" is applied in the British Isles to all members of the group except the few marine species, all of which have paddle-shaped limbs. "Turtle" has long been much more broadly applied in the United States, with the addition of "terrapin" for some edible species. Usage both in the British Isles and in the United States has left the group without a general name comparable to "bird" or "mammal." The American Society of Ichthyologists and Herpetologists standardized the common names of the reptiles of the United States, assigning "turtle" to all of those with a shell. "Tortoise" is employed secondarily for the slow-moving terrestrial species, primarily those of the genera *Testudo* and *Gopherus*.

NATURAL HISTORY

Food habits

Most turtles prefer a varied diet. Fibrous parts of plants are avoided because the jaws are not sharp enough to cut well and are entirely incapable of grinding. Small invertebrates, such as worms, snails, slugs, insects, thin-shelled bivalves and crayfishes and other crustaceans make up the bulk of the animal food. Large aquatic turtles are able to catch fish and occasionally a few birds and small mammals.

Turtles have been toothless for more than 150,000,000 years, but in some modern types the moderately sharp and jagged edges of the horny jaws function as teeth. Food is chewed, the claws of the forelimbs often assisting in manipulation, until it is reduced to fragments that can be swallowed.

A few turtles have special ways of securing prey. The gigantic alligator snapping turtle (*Macrochelys temmincki*) of the southern United States has a wormlike lure on the floor of the mouth with which it entices prey into its open jaws. The grotesque matamata, or fringed turtle (*Chelys fimbriata*) of South America has, on the neck and chin, soft projections with which, apparently, it detects the presence of prey by water movements. The floor of the large throat is quickly lowered as the head thrusts forward, the mouth agape. Water rushing into the mouth takes the unwary prey with it.

Turtles, like other reptiles, can survive long fasts, being able to live on weekly or even monthly feedings; however, when food is readily available, they may eat frequently and grow very fat. The rate of digestion varies with the temperature. In the wild, they probably maintain a relatively constant temperature by seeking suitable surroundings, which may require constant activity. Turtles drink readily, and some store water in cloacal bladders, an ability that allows them to survive long droughts.

Copulation is usually preceded by a courtship highly characteristic for a species or related group of species. The male's part may include various types of head-waving, antics such as lunging at the female while roaring, or, in some aquatic species, gracefully swimming backward in front of her while stroking her lores (cheeks) with the excessively long nails of his forelimbs. The penis, paired in snakes and lizards, is single in turtles.

The most unusual aspect of turtle reproduction is the ability of females to lay fertile eggs for years after a single mating; among higher animals the rule that copulation must precede each pregnancy has few exceptions. In the diamondback terrapin (*Malaclemys*), fertile eggs may be laid for as many as four years after copulation. In a controlled experiment, ten old females were penned without the males they had been living with. During the first season after penning, they laid 124 eggs, all but one of which hatched; during the fourth season they deposited 108 eggs, only four of which hatched, however.

Both terrestrial and aquatic turtles lay their eggs on land. The female usually selects a sunny place for the nest. She then digs a hole about as deep as her hind-limbs are long, into which she deposits round or elliptical, whitish eggs, the shells of which may be either flexible or brittle, but never pigmented like bird eggs. Several clutches may be laid in a season, though this is by no means the rule. A clutch may have more than 200 eggs (as in some sea turtles) or as few as one. The sea turtles and the largest tortoises lay eggs about two inches in diameter, whereas nearly all of the other turtles lay much smaller ones.

Egg-laying behaviour

Many nests are carefully constructed and hidden; a few are crudely made. The most spectacular laying is that of the sea turtles. The female green turtle (*Chelonia mydas*), for instance, crawls up the beach to a point above high tide and excavates a shallow depression, using all four flippers, then digs an egg pit in the bottom of the depression. The sand is removed by hind flippers, used alternately. During this delicate procedure the flipper must be curled and gently lowered to get its load, a feat often accomplished without loss of sand. A final flip sends the sand directly backward and clear of the hole. She then deposits the eggs, usually two at a time, and carefully covers them. Before leaving she obliterates the exact site by flinging sand about with the front flippers. The entire process consumes a few hours.

The period of incubation depends to an appreciable extent on the temperature. After the nest is completed, the mother appears to take no further interest in it, or, for that matter, in the hatchlings. As a result, the nest is often robbed of eggs, and freshly hatched turtles, whose shells are still soft, are frequently preyed on by large birds and small mammals. Again, in the case of the sea turtles, favoured beaches may become the centre of aggregation of countless animals, devouring the hatchlings as they scurry down the beach. Even in the water they are not safe, since predacious fishes lurk there.

These shelled reptiles outlive all other vertebrates, including man, the longest-lived mammal. A marked eastern box turtle (*Terrapene carolina*) of the U.S. survived 138 years in the wild. There is good evidence of a turtle of another species having lived more than a century and a half. Turtles do not grow very slowly; maturity is reached in less than ten years, and growth in a large species may be more rapid than in man himself.

Longevity

Age estimates are sometimes made by counting the growth rings on the horny shields of the shells, but this method is of little practical value, because the rings become indistinct with maturity. Size is sometimes untrustworthy as an indication of age.

Although scientific evidence is lacking, turtles appear to depend heavily on their sense of smell. Their sight

Senses

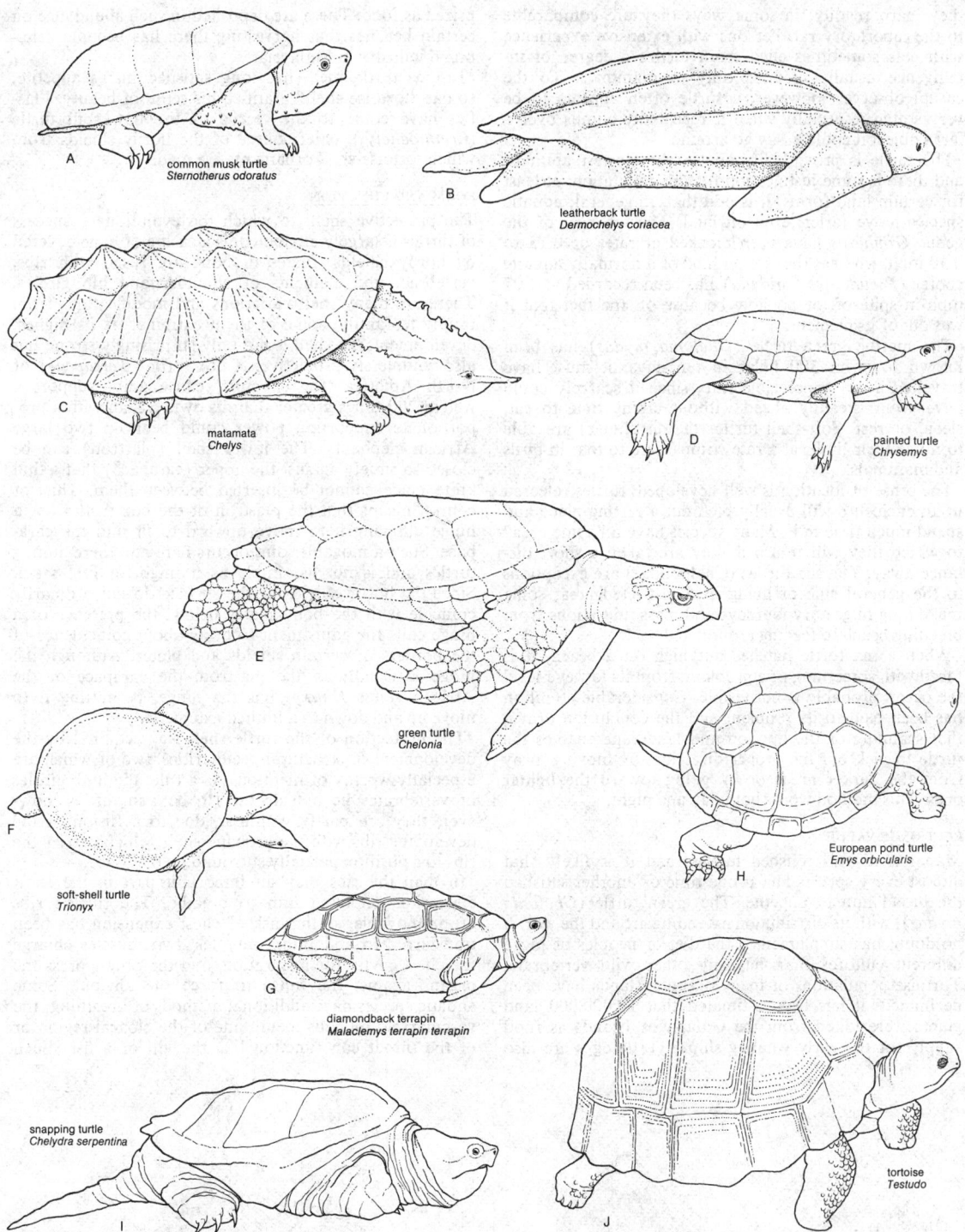

Representative chelonians.

Drawing by M. Moran based on (all except *Sternotherus* and *Malaclemys*) J.Z. Young, *The Life of Vertebrates*, 2nd ed. (1962); The Clarendon Press, Oxford

A common musk turtle *Sternotherus odoratus*

B leatherback turtle *Dermochelys coriacea*

C matamata *Chelys*

D painted turtle *Chrysemys*

E green turtle *Chelonia*

F soft-shell turtle *Trionyx*

G diamondback terrapin *Malaclemys terrapin terrapin*

H European pond turtle *Emys orbicularis*

I snapping turtle *Chelydra serpentina*

J tortoise *Testudo*

is good. They easily distinguish differences in intensity of light and they recognize at least four colours: blue, green, yellow, and red, especially the last, which often figures in the adornment of the turtles themselves. In experimental situations they learn to choose among these colours and among various complex black-and-white patterns to receive reward or avoid punishment. The receptors of the eye are all cones, which are responsible for colour recognition. Many semi-aquatic species can make alterations in curvature of the lens for vision under water, but only the eyes of sea turtles are fully adapted for such vision.

Turtles respond readily to vibrations of the substratum, but those of the air are another matter. Casual observations do not suffice to evaluate turtle hearing and even scientific workers have disagreed. Experiments reported in 1915 by an American indicated that turtles do hear, but this was contradicted in 1925 by a Japanese. A few years later a Soviet investigator concluded that turtles do hear, but his paper was published only in the U.S.S.R. and largely ignored elsewhere. It was not until 1966 that two Americans settled the problem by showing that at least some turtles hear only low frequencies, ranging from about 20 to about 1000 vibrations. The corresponding figures for man are 20 to 20,000, a fact that may help to explain the difficulty of arriving at a suitable conclusion for the turtle.

Turtles seldom emit sounds, except when courting or mating; even then they do little more than grunt or roar. Exceptions are a few sea turtles that can give a loud cry under extreme provocation.

Experiments on the intelligence of turtles indicate that

they learn readily; in some ways they are comparable to the laboratory rat. Persons with extensive experience with pets sometimes elicit from turtles a degree of intelligence usually credited only to mammals. To the casual observer, however, a turtle often appears to be very stupid, especially when it repeatedly climbs over a large object it could easily go around.

The turtle is proverbially one of the slowest animals, and there is some justification for this reputation, at least for certain land forms. It is odd that, in general, aquatic species move faster, even on land. The tortoises of the genus *Gopherus* have been clocked at rates of 0.13 to 0.30 mph, whereas the rate on land of a normally aquatic cooter (*Pseudemys floridana*) has been recorded at 1.07 mph in spite of, or possibly because of, the fact that it was out of its element.

The marine green turtle (*Chelonia mydas*) has been known to swim 300 miles in ten days; it must have travelled at an appreciable rate, since it scarcely could have swum steadily ahead without taking time to eat, sleep, or rest. Soft-shell turtles (Trionychidae) are able to move their limbs at a rate comparable to that in birds and mammals.

The sense of location is well developed; turtles released in an enclosure will usually pick out a resting place and spend much time in it. Many species have a "home area" to which they will return if they are taken a short distance away. The sea turtles (Cheloniidae) are exceptions to the general rule of living in a restricted area; some make long migratory journeys and mass migrations from breeding beach to feeding ground and back.

When a sea turtle hatches out high on a beach, it is faced with something of a problem; from its low eye-level the ocean probably is not visible. Considerable attention has been paid to its problem and the conclusion drawn that scanning of the horizon and landscape enables the turtle to pick out the proper direction, by moving away from the darker areas or by going toward the lighter ones. This method works both day and night.

ECONOMIC VALUE

Man has always relished turtles, and it is likely that almost every species has at one time or another satisfied the broad human appetite. The green turtle (*Chelonia mydas*), with its distribution extending around the world, no doubt has supplemented the diet of peoples of more different cultures than has any other wild vertebrate. Tortoise populations of many oceanic islands have been decimated; it has been estimated that 10,000,000 land giants were taken from the Galápagos Islands as food supply for the early whaling ships. Turtle eggs are also prized as food. These are deposited in such abundance on certain beaches that harvesting them has become a national industry in Malaysia.

Just as turtle meat has long satisfied man's appetite, so has "tortoise shell" gratified his sense of beauty. Plastics have come to the rescue of the hawksbill turtle (*Eretmochelys*), chief source of the horny shields from which tortoise-shell ornaments are made.

FORM AND FUNCTION

The protective shell, to which the evolutionary success of turtles is largely attributed, is a casing of bone covered by horny shields. Plates of bone are fused with ribs, vertebrae, and elements of shoulder and hip girdles. There are many shell variations and modifications from family to family, some of them extreme. At its highest development, the shell is not only surprisingly strong but also completely protective. A box turtle (*Terrapene*) of North America, for example, can readily support a weight 200 times greater than its own; a man with a proportionate supporting power could bear up two large African elephants. The lower shell (plastron) can be closed so snugly against the upper (carapace) that a thin knife blade cannot be inserted between them. This, of course, means that the plastron of the box turtles has a hinge allowing it to move upward to fit into the carapace. Such a movable joint occurs here and there among turtles and is not as simple as it might at first seem. Since the horny shields of the surface do not ordinarily coincide with the bony plates below, the presence of a hinge calls for adjustment to bring about coincidence of the borders of certain shields and plates. Although the hinge is usually in the plastron, the carapace of the African genus *Kinixys* has the hinge, permitting it to move up and down to a limited extent.

The protection of the turtle shell was acquired by the development of structural peculiarities, two of which are especially worthy of mention. As a rule, the limb girdles of vertebrates lie outside the rib box; in turtles, however, they are partly within it, due to a fusion of the developing ribs with the growing shell, which carries the ribs to a position partially surrounding the limbs.

In man the ribs play an important part in the chest expansion, enabling him to breathe. The turtle's ribs are immovable, so the task of chest expansion has been transferred to abdominal muscles; two muscles enlarge the chest cavity for inspiration, and the others press the organs against the lungs to force the air out. Some aquatic species have additional methods of breathing: the vascularized mucous membrane of the cloacal region or of the throat can function like the gill of a fish. Such

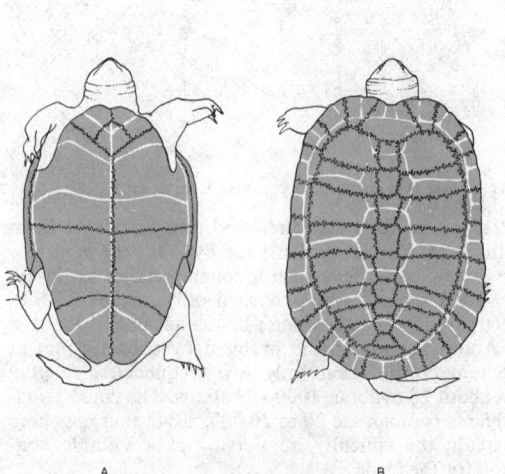
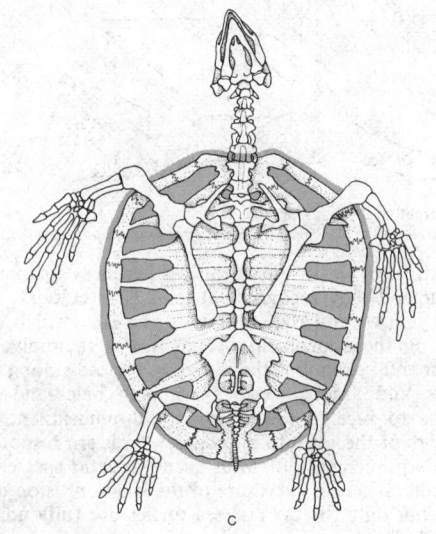

Turtle skeleton.
(A) Plastron and (B) carapace, showing the relationship between bony and horny shells in a freshwater turtle. Shaded parts show horny shell; black lines indicate joints in underlying bone. (C) Relationship between the dermal bones (plastron and carapace) and the axial skeleton in a marine turtle.

accessories to ordinary respiration enable turtles to lie quietly submerged for hours or even days.

The vertebral column, with very little to support, underwent drastic modification. The trend in turtles, in contrast to that in most other reptiles, has been to reduce the number of vertebrae. The ability to retract the head into the shell is related to the retention of eight specialized vertebrae. The result is that the neck has almost as many vertebrae as does the central part of the column (between neck and tail). The manner in which the neck bends is of importance in classification (see below).

Turtles run the gamut in size. The Atlantic leatherback (*Dermochelys coriacea*), largest of living kinds, may weigh more than ¾ ton and measure 12 feet from the tip of one front flipper to that of the other. An extinct marine giant, *Archelon*, of the family Protostegidae, was probably much larger, and an extinct land turtle of Asia (*Colossochelys atlas*) had a shell 7 feet long. The largest living tortoises may weigh more than 500 pounds.

At the opposite extreme, the adults of some species weigh less than a pound and have a shell less than five inches long. The shell length of most adult turtles falls between 5 and 15 in.

ORIGIN AND EVOLUTION

Origin of turtles

The evolution of the turtle is one of the most remarkable in the history of vertebrates. Unfortunately, the origin of this highly successful order is obscured by the lack of early fossils, although turtles leave more and better fossil remains than do other vertebrates. By the middle of the Triassic Period (about 200,000,000 years ago) turtles were numerous and in possession of basic turtle characteristics. Teeth are lacking in all living turtles, but were present in a few fossils. The teeth of even the Triassic turtles were oddly placed, apparently having been confined to the palate. Intermediates between turtles and cotylosaurs, the primitive reptiles from which turtles probably sprang, are entirely lacking. The most likely link is a small, toothed reptile (*Eunotosaurus*) of the Permian Period of southern Africa. The skull roof of *Eunotosaurus* is not known, but the shoulder and pelvic girdles were overlapped by the ribs, possibly a beginning of the condition found in turtles.

By courtesy of the Peabody Museum of Natural History, Yale University

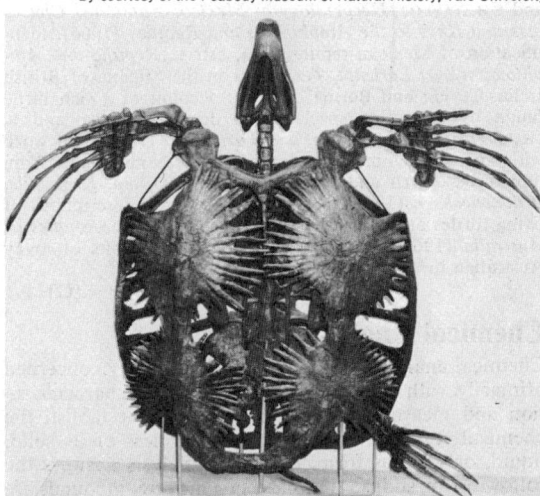

Skeleton of the Cretaceous marine turtle *Archelon*, height 325 cm (10 ft 8 in).

Many turtles today live in marshes and swamps and it is likely that this way of life has been a common one throughout their history. A fairly large group has become terrestrial, but a stronger tendency has been in the opposite direction, toward aquatic life. The extreme development of aquatic types has been large marine species with limbs turned into paddles. The shell may become modified and reduced as seen in the gigantic leatherback (*Dermochelys*), in which the horny shields are gone and the shell has become leathery.

While some reptiles flourished and vanished (as the dinosaurs), others persisted, some as once-successful groups and a few as initiators of expanding groups (snakes and lizards). The turtles, however, have plodded a stolid and steady course through evolutionary time, changing very little in basic structure.

CLASSIFICATION

Distinguishing taxonomic features. The suborders and superfamilies of the Chelonia are defined primarily on the basis of the completeness of the skull and degree of posterior emargination. The most obvious diagnostic feature separating the two modern suborders is the manner of folding the neck (vertical or horizontal) when the head is withdrawn. Family distinctions are based primarily on characters of the skull and shell.

Annotated classification. The classification presented here is adapted from A.S. Romer, 1956 and 1966. Three unimportant fossil families have been omitted from the first two suborders.

ORDER CHELONIA
Reptiles with temporal region of skull complete or emarginate, but without true fenestrae. 18 presacral vertebrae, typically 8 cervicals and 10 dorsals; 2nd to 8th dorsals fused to neural elements of carapace (when present). Shoulder girdle internal to ribs and shell. Clavicles and interclavicle incorporated in shell.

†**Suborder proganochelydia**
Fossil only.

†*Superfamily Proganochelyoidea*

†*Family Proganochelyidae.* Skull solidly roofed, sculptured. 7 cervicals. Teeth present. Oldest and most primitive of true turtles. Found only in the Late Triassic of Europe. Presumably amphibious.

†**Suborder Amphichelydia**
Fossil only. Skull roof complete, rarely emarginate from behind. Little or no retraction of neck. Teeth absent. Suborder includes the more primitive turtles, which were almost entirely Mesozoic and lacked the distinctive features of the cryptodires and pleurodires.

†*Superfamily Pleurosternoidea*
Skull generally elongate, sculptured, or tuberculate; roof at times moderately emarginate. 8 cervicals. Chiefly amphibious but some marine.

†*Family Pleurosternidae.* Temporal region well roofed. Common aquatic chelonians of the Jurassic and Lower Cretaceous. Europe and North America. About 10 genera.

†*Family Plesiochelyidae.* Temporal roof completed by enlarged postorbital. Jurassic and Cretaceous. Europe and Asia. Ancestral to the following family. 2 genera.

†*Family Thalassemyidae.* Temporal region usually less roofed than in foregoing families. Initial development, in the Upper Jurassic, of an important marine group; also Cretaceous. Europe and Asia.

†*Superfamily Baenoidea*
Skull short. Neck possibly a little retractile. Includes forms leading to cryptodires.

†*Family Baenidae.* Skull roof complete. Upper Cretaceous to Eocene. North America.

†*Family Meiolaniidae.* Skull roof complete and with protuberances. Upper Cretaceous to Pleistocene. South America and Australian region.

†*Family Eubaenidae.* Skull roof emarginate. Transitional to cryptodires. Upper Cretaceous. North America.

Suborder Cryptodira
Temporal region of skull frequently emarginate from behind; if completely roofed, probably secondarily so. Neck retracted in a vertical plane. Shell primitively complete, but elements lost or reduced in aquatic, especially marine, species. These are the dominant turtles of today.

Superfamily Testudinoidea
Temporal region usually reduced. Bony shell usually complete and always covered by horny shields.

Family Dermatemydidae. Central American river turtle. Temporal region emarginate from behind. 1 Recent species in Central America and Mexico; others from Late Cretaceous and Early Tertiary of North America. Size medium; adult length to 25 cm.

Family Chelydridae. Common and alligator snapping turtles. Head proportionately large, shell, especially plastron, reduced. Temporal region emarginate. Inhabit swamps, rivers, and shallow lakes of North and a little of South America. Aggressive but not dangerous to man. Miocene to Recent. Adult size: Common snapper 20–46 cm, 5–30 kg; alligator snapper 42–70 cm, 18–100 kg.

Family Kinosternidae. Mud and musk turtles. Plastron often reduced and in some, singly or doubly hinged. Some exude a disagreeable odour when handled. Pliocene to Recent. Aquatic. Widespread in New World temperate and tropical regions. 21 living species, adult length 7–20 cm.

Family Testudinidae. Terrestrial turtles, or tortoises. Shell usually with high dome; hinged plastron in 1 species. Temperate and tropical regions of all continents except Australia; also on islands of eastern Africa and Galàpagos Islands. 40 living species; moderate to large size; adult length 20–100 cm, weight 1–200 kg.

Family Platysternidae. Big-headed turtle. Broad, flat plastron; large head. Inhabits moving streams in southeastern Asia. 1 species; adult length about 15 cm.

Family Emydidae. This family contains most of the familiar turtles. Temporal region primitively and usually emarginate from behind; bony carapace and horny covering complete. Abundant in Northern Hemisphere; a few species in South America and Africa. Eocene to Recent. About 76 living species; adult length 7–22 cm.

Superfamily Chelonioidea

Marine turtles. Temporal region well roofed. Limbs generally paddle-like.

†*Family Toxochelyidae.* Nasal bones small or absent (except in one genus). Upper Cretaceous to Eocene. North America and Europe.

†*Family Protostegidae.* Powerful beak, jaws with large crushing surfaces. Upper Cretaceous to Oligocene of North America and Europe. Some species very large, length up to 4 m (12 ft; *Archelon*).

Family Cheloniidae. Modern sea turtles. Secondary palate, formed by vomer and palatine bones. Distribution worldwide in warmer oceans. Fossils from Cretaceous of Europe, North America, Africa and Asia. 5 to 6 living species; adult length 60–210 cm; weight 20–500 kg. Most are economically important, for eggs and meat.

Superfamily Dermochelyoidea

Family Dermochelyidae. Leatherback turtle and fossil species. Shell of leatherback without horny plates but with prominent ridges of cornufied skin down the back. Worldwide in warm seas. Eocene to Recent. Adult leatherback very large, length to 225 cm, weight to 600 kg.

Superfamily Carettochelyoidea

Family Carettochelyidae. New Guinea plateless turtle and fossil species. Upper Cretaceous to recent; fossils from North America, Europe, and Asia.

Superfamily Trionychoidea

Family Trionychidae. Soft-shell turtles. Horny shields absent; considerable bony carapace supporting flexible leathery covering of the back. Temporal region widely open. Flat, round body; webs between toes. Nostrils in a projecting snout. Fossils from Cretaceous. Freshwater habitats on temperate and tropical parts of continents except South America and Australia. Adult length 5–60 cm.

Suborder Pleurodira

Temporal roof may be emarginate from behind, and is invariably emarginate from below. Neck retracted in a horizontal plane.

Family Pelomedusidae. Side-necked turtles. Skull moderately emarginate behind, variably so below. Aquatic habitats in Africa, Madagascar, and South America. Fossils from Cretaceous onward, all continents except Australia. Adult shell length 20–75 cm.

Family Chelyidae. Snake-necked turtles. Skull slightly emarginate behind, greatly from below. Head and neck may be half of total length. Fossils few, Pliocene to Recent. Present distribution: Australia and South America. Family includes all living land and freshwater turtles of Australia. Adult shell length 12–40 cm.

†Suborder Eunotosauria

Known from a single partial specimen from Middle Permian of South Africa. 10 dorsal vertebrae known, 8 with expanded ribs. Incomplete carapace with dermal ossifications (in rows). Shoulder and pelvic girdles overlapped by ribs. Upper skull unknown; palate with marginal and palatal teeth.

†*Family Eunotosauridae.* Characters are as for the suborder.

Critical appraisal. This classification now has wide acceptance. The chief difference of opinion has been in regard to the modern soft-shell types such as the aquatic trionychid group and especially the marine leatherback (*Dermochelys*) with its highly atypical leathery shell. The leatherback has, in fact, been considered very primitive and consequently assigned to subordinal rank, rather than being placed among the cryptodires.

There is no certainty that *Eunotosaurus* is ancestral to turtles, but the adaptations of its vertebrae and ribs suggest that it is on an evolutionary line leading toward the turtles.

BIBLIOGRAPHY. G.A. BOULENGER, *Catalogue of the Chelonians, Rhynchocephalians, and Crocodiles in the British Museum (Natural History)*, new ed., (1889), an early standard description of the turtles of the world; A.F. CARR, *Handbook of Turtles: The Turtles of the United States, Canada, and Baja California* (1952), a detailed account including copious notes on habits, *So Excellent a Fishe: A Natural History of Sea Turtles* (1967), a readable account of Carr's study of the living green turtle; E.H. COLBERT, *Evolution of the Vertebrates: A History of the Backboned Animals Through Time* (1955), an authoritative work by a specialist who writes simply and clearly; R. CONANT, *A Field Guide to Reptiles and Amphibians of the United States and Canada East of the 100th Meridian* (1958), a useful field guide with illustrations of virtually all species and subspecies, as well as 248 distribution maps; P.E.P. DERANIYAGALA, *The Tetrapod Reptiles of Ceylon*, vol. 1, *Testudinates Marine and Terrestrial and Crocodilians* (1939), the biology of many Asian turtles; J.A. OLIVER, *The Natural History of North American Amphibians and Reptiles* (1955), a good book for the general reader; C.H. POPE, *The Reptiles of China* (1935), descriptions of many Asiatic forms, *Turtles of the United States and Canada* (1939), profusely illustrated with excellent photographs; P.C.H. PRITCHARD, *Living Turtles of the World* (1967), a brief but complete guide with many illustrations in colour; J.J. PARSONS, *The Green Turtle and Man* (1962), a fascinating history of the exploitation of the green turtle; A.S. ROMER, *Osteology of the Reptiles* (1956), an authoritative classification of reptiles, *Vertebrate Paleontology*, 3rd ed., (1966), contains a good summary of chelonian fossil history; N. de ROOIJ, *The Reptiles of the Indo-Australian Archipelago*, vol. 1, *Lacertilia, Chelonia, Emydosauria* (1915), a classic work on Australasian reptiles; H.M. SMITH and E.H. TAYLOR, *Herpetology of Mexico: Annotated Checklists and Keys to the Amphibians and Reptiles* (1966), identification of Mexican reptiles; M.A. SMITH, *Reptilia and Amphibia*, vol. 1, *Loricata, Testudines* in the "Fauna of British India, Ceylon and Burma" (1931), account of a rich turtle fauna by a leading specialist; J. de C. SOWERBY and E. LEAR, *Tortoises, Terrapins, and Turtles* (1872), an old work with many magnificent coloured illustrations made from life; H. WERMUTH and R. MERTENS, *Schildkröten, Krokodile, Brückenechsen* (1961), a German work with descriptions of living turtles and many illustrations; E. WORRELL, *Reptiles of Australia* (1963), contains accounts of the habits of many Australian turtles.

(C.H.P.)

Chemical Analysis

Chemical analysis is that branch of chemistry concerned primarily with the techniques of chemical characterization and measurement; its function is to establish the chemical composition of matter, regardless of its solid, liquid, or gaseous form. Chemical analysis answers the following questions: (1) what elements or compounds are present? (qualitative analysis); (2) how much is present or how pure is it? (quantitative analysis); (3) which chemical fragments can be identified and measured as to quantity? (functional group analysis); and (4) how are the elemental parts and functional groups arranged? (structural and stereochemical analysis).

The forms of matter to be investigated range from simple (pure) elements or compounds to complex mixtures; they may be of organic or inorganic origin; they may be of low molecular weight or have molecular weights as high as tens of millions. An analysis may involve the use of a few grams of sample (macroscale) or less than $\frac{1}{10,000,000}$ of a gram (sub-microscale), and methods exist for even smaller amounts. Analyses are based on mathematical expressions of biological, chemical, or physical principles; they may involve simple glassware costing ten cents or complex instrumentation costing $100,000.

Different authorities have defined the subject in different ways. At the end of the 19th century the German chemist Wilhelm Ostwald emphasized the application of science to the art involved in the identification of different substances and the determination of their composition. Fifty years later the development of a rigorous methodology gave the foundation of reliable analytical procedures. In the 20th century there has been a tendency to define analytical chemistry as a branch of chemical research directed toward the development and improvement of practical analytical procedures.

The most important details of any problem in analytical chemistry are (1) the validity of the sample to be analyzed, (2) the method used to analyze it, (3) the accuracy of the result, and (4) the cost of the analysis in money and time. A standardized analytical procedure can be carried out by relatively unskilled personnel, an important economic factor that has led to the modern distinction between "chemical analysis" and "analytical chemistry." In essence, the performance of an analysis according to detailed instructions is an art demanding care, patience, practice, and technical expertise; usually it is entrusted to an analyst who may not have a thorough understanding of the chemistry or scientific basis of the principle involved but who carries out the instructions of the analytical chemist who is responsible for devising the method in use and for supervising the training of the lesser skilled, lower paid operators, coordinating their activities, and evaluating their results.

Chemical analysis today largely employs methods developed since 1945; this article gives prominence to the principles on which these methods are based, and places important classical techniques in proper perspective.

GENERAL CONSIDERATIONS

Historical background. The chemical balance is of such early origin that it was ascribed to the gods in the earliest documents available. The use of standard weights, made of stone, and the first "institute of standards," supervised by priests, are traced to Babylonian times (2600 BC). Two nonmetals, sulfur and carbon, and seven metals (copper, gold, iron, lead, mercury, silver, tin) and their alloys were used in ancient times; the value of silver and gold probably gave the major incentive for the acquisition of analytical knowledge. In the 4th century BC, the purity of gold samples was estimated from the extent of the yellow marks they made on a touchstone.

Pliny the Elder (AD 23–79) appears to have described the first wet test: an extract of gallnuts turns black if iron sulfate is an adulterant in copper sulfate.

The English natural philosopher Robert Boyle is credited with the introduction of the term analysis in the chemical sense. He distinguished between mixtures and compounds, used acid–base indicators, used hydrogen sulfide as a reagent, and defined elements in the modern sense in his book *The Sceptical Chymist* (1661).

Gravimetric analysis probably originated toward the end of the 17th century with a German physician-chemist, Friedrich Hoffmann (of Halle, the Younger), who precipitated chlorides with silver nitrate and sulfates with lime. The innovations, inventions, and discoveries in techniques are legion and often difficult to credit, but a list of major contributions in the 18th century would include, chemical microscopy, flame tests for the alkali metals, the blowpipe and bead tests for qualitative analysis, and titrimetric analysis. Although many chemists became involved from this time onward, the most important names associated with the development of titrimetry in the 19th century are Joseph-Louis Gay-Lussac in France, Robert Bunsen in Germany, and Karl-Friedrich Mohr, also in Germany, who introduced oxalic acid as a titrant and devised the modern form of the burette (1853). The only major advance in titrimetry in the 20th century has been the introduction of complexometric techniques.

Antoine-Laurent Lavoisier, the French chemist, who

died in the French Revolution, is accepted as the founder of quantitative analysis through his extensive use of the balance. Others among main contributors in the 19th century were Justus von Liebig of Germany and Jean-Baptiste-André Dumas of France. Although organic elemental analysis was revolutionized before 1900, a successful method for determining oxygen was not developed until 1939. Micromethods and sub-micromethods are 20th-century developments.

Inorganic aspects of analysis were developed before 1800, with introduction of the term stoichiometry. Jöns Jacob Berzelius of Sweden in the early 19th century was the dominant influence.

Gas analysis was pioneered by Bunsen in Germany and Marcellin Berthelot in France. This field has been revolutionized since 1952 by chromatography.

Electrochemical methods were first devised by the German chemist Clemens Winkler in the 19th century; the first potentiometric titrations were reported at the end of that century. As physicists progressed with studies of electricity, chemists were quick to exploit the development of several electrochemical-instrumental methods of analysis. The polarograph was an outstanding invention in 1922.

The development of the spectroscope by the German chemists Gustav Robert Kirchhoff and Bunsen in 1859 led to the discoveries of new elements. Although flame photometry was suggested in the 19th century, it was first effectively applied in 1928. Advances in physics at the start of this century led to the utilization of X-rays and ultraviolet and infrared radiation in chemical analysis, and they became the basis of powerful instrumental methods, as has the mass spectrograph (1920). Radiochemical methods proliferated in the period 1945–60 as a result of the developments in nuclear technology.

Since 1950, important techniques based on resonance phenomena, on atomic absorption and fluorescence, and on laser, ion, and electron probes have been developed. All these and the trend toward increased automation and computerization depend on the recent advances in electronics technology.

Perhaps the greatest impact on all branches of chemical analysis since 1940, however, has been made by the application of chromatographic principles, first described in 1903, aspects of which were developed in 1941 (partition chromatography), 1944 (paper chromatography), and 1952 (gas chromatography). Molecular-sieve chromatography (gel filtration, gel permeation chromatography) and thin-layer chromatography were introduced about 1956.

General approach to chemical analysis. Chemical analysis has to answer every conceivable question arising from the identity and composition of matter; *i.e.*, of everything in existence. Typical questions are: What is it? How pure is it? What are its major constituents? Does it contain traces of *X*? Chemical analysis is primarily a service function with the object of trying to give the information requested as efficiently as possible.

In addition to purely qualitative and quantitative analyses relating to the composition of the material, analysis of its properties may be required; *e.g.*, molecular structure, biological activity, or physical properties such as the molecular weight, boiling point, freezing point, osmotic pressure, and surface tension.

Although there are some analytical measurements for which only one method is valid in particular circumstances (*e.g.*, a nondestructive method may be imperative if the object is of value), the steadily increasing intensity of scientific effort over the past 100 years has produced a wide range of methods for most common analyses. The choice of method may lie between a classical wet method or a modern instrumental one; the methods vary in sensitivity, selectivity, speed, and accuracy, and their applicability may depend on some other specific component being absent. Sometimes there is no choice available; *e.g.*, if less than a critical amount of sample is supplied or if an official or referee method is specified. The latter is essential in any legal dispute or when goods are being tested for conformity to specification. It is rare for two different chemical methods to give identical results or for a physical method to give precise agreement with a chemical method.

PRINCIPAL STAGES IN CHEMICAL ANALYSIS

The main steps in a complete analysis are (1) collecting the sample, (2) deciding what analytical data are required, (3) making a preliminary examination of the sample, (4) selecting the most appropriate analytical method, (5) converting the sample or component in question into the state to which the analytical method can be applied, (6) performing the actual determination, and (7) calculating the results in a form that answers the questions asked.

Sampling. Every stage in the above scheme is important, but everything depends on the fact that the sample is truly representative of the whole that it represents.

Sampling is the process of obtaining a small portion possessing all the essential physical and chemical characteristics of the entire batch from which it was extracted. Some materials are relatively easy to sample: a small bag of household sugar, a bottle of brandy, or a tank of hospital oxygen. More difficulty is encountered in obtaining a representative 25-gram (about one-ounce) sample from a 25-ton shipment of coal or wheat. The accepted ways of achieving representative sampling are based on statistical procedures.

There are no general sampling methods applicable to all types of material. Specialized methods depend on whether a gas, liquid, or solid is involved. In the sampling of solids, particle size is an important variable, and the problem can be much more difficult than for liquids or gases, in which a uniform, homogeneous condition usually—but not necessarily—exists. Mechanical devices are available for sampling large volumes of material; in many industrial processes, continuous sampling or monitoring may be possible; *e.g.*, of the cyanide or mercury level in a waste effluent or of radioactive substances in a nuclear-reactor coolant.

Preparation of samples for analysis. Inadvertent chemical or physical modification of the sample must be avoided during its preparation for analysis. Biological substances are particularly susceptible to such changes, and it may be difficult to establish that the component under test has not suffered some transformation during the preparation stages. The analyst can only try to achieve extraction or preparation under the mildest conditions possible. A useful check is to put the product isolated through a second, identical extraction cycle; if the re-extracted product is identical to that first extracted, there can be some confidence in its acceptability for analysis. Extraction without modification is difficult for some materials, and some irreversible change in solubility, molecular size and shape, or other property may have to be tolerated if progress is to be made at all; if the nature and extent of the change is understood, allowance can be made in the interpretation of the results.

As examples of the pitfalls that analysts must avoid, samples to be analyzed for heavy metals should not be pulverized in an iron mortar; solutions to be analyzed for alkali metals should not be stored in glass vessels; solutions containing silver should not be exposed to light; carbohydrates or proteins should not be extracted with hot anhydrous solvents.

Errors and evaluation of results. An understanding of the different types of error and how they arise is extremely important. Analysts must be conversant with the terms absolute and relative error, accuracy, precision, average, range, standard deviation, coefficient of variation, and confidence limits for the mean.

Errors may be indeterminate or determinate. The former are accidental, random errors of chance that account for a proficient analyst finding values such as 21.6, 21.7, 21.5, and 21.6 in four attempts at a simple analysis. Determinate errors may be operative, personal, instrumental, or methodic. The last named (also known as chemical errors) are inherent in all chemical systems of measurement; reactions may not go to completion or may involve equilibria; precipitates in gravimetric procedures usually have small but finite solubility; chemicals are rarely

100 percent pure, and the trace impurities can cause disproportionately high errors. Instrumental errors arise from internal or external effects on measurements made with any instrument—*e.g.*, with a maladjusted balance, or inaccurate weights, or a recorder with a drifting base line; such faults should of course be rectified, and instrumental error is more correctly reserved for errors that arise from design characteristics of instruments. Personal errors result from failure of the analyst to overcome personal perceptual and cognitive inabilities; *e.g.*, lack of sensitivity in judging certain colours. Operative errors occur when necessary attention to analytical practice or experimental detail is not given; *e.g.*, precipitates not dried at the recommended temperature. In these the analyst is culpable.

At the outset of any analytical procedure, it is essential for the analyst to contemplate the various steps he will carry out, assign reasonable magnitudes to the experimental values likely to become involved (volumes of solutions, weights of samples and of products), and so proceed to estimate the maximum possible error likely to occur. This technique pinpoints the critical stage of the procedure; *i.e.*, that expected to give the largest individual contribution to the error. Particular care can then be directed to that stage or perhaps an alternative approach devised; in particular, time need not be wasted by excessive care over stages contributing little toward the error.

How does the analyst know that the procedure yields reasonable results? He carries out replicates (reproducible duplicates, preferably on widely differing amounts of sample); carries out the procedure without the sample in order to allow for the impurities present in the reagents; makes comparative tests with other methods; and carries out determinations on pure chemicals, synthetic test mixtures, or analytical standards; *i.e.*, substances carefully selected and tested for homogeneity and for which an agreed value has been established from the independent results of many laboratories. There is also the standard-addition method, in which a known weight of a pure specimen of the substance under test is added to the sample to be analyzed. If the recovery of the material added (*i.e.*, the difference between the values for the analysis of the sample before and after the addition of the standard) is correct, there can be some confidence that the answer for the sample itself is also satisfactory.

Separation methods. Although any physical or chemical property can be made the basis for a qualitative or a quantitative method of analysis, very few tests are specific (valid for one substance or element only, even in the presence of others), and thus analysis is not generally possible without prior separation of the desired component from others that respond to the procedure used. Quite a few analytical tests are selective (valid for a small number of substances or elements, which therefore are not differentiated, in the presence of all others). The availability of a specific or a selective reagent may obviate a gross separation.

There are two main approaches in separation methods: (1) physical segregation of the required component from all others, or at least from those that will interfere in the analytical procedure selected, and (2) chemical modification of the potential sources of interference so that their chemical activity is effectively suppressed.

Several separation methods depend on transfer of matter from one phase to another. Some of these are sufficiently selective and efficient to allow the desired transfer to be effected by a single application (*e.g.*, volatilization, electrodeposition, precipitation). Other methods are effective only as multistage processes (*e.g.*, fractional distillations, ion exchange, and chromatographic processes).

Precipitation. Precipitation is the process of depressing the solubility of a dissolved substance to the extent that it separates from the solution. It may be brought about by changing the substance to a less soluble one by a chemical reaction or by decreasing the dissolving power of the solvent. Precipitation by chemical reaction constitutes the basis for the classical group-separation system of qualitative inorganic analysis. A simple example is the

---

Representative samples

Types of errors

Tests of accuracy

separation of silver, mercury, and lead as a group from other common metals; the addition of dilute hydrochloric acid forms the chlorides of all metals present, but the chlorides only of silver, mercury, and lead are insoluble in excess dilute hydrochloric acid.

Phase distribution. Under this classification there are important modern methods; *e.g.*, ion exchange, solvent extraction, countercurrent distribution, and chromatographic methods. The most common ion exchangers are polymeric cross-linked resins (usually made in the form of tiny beads to increase permeability to solvents) that have cationic (positively charged) or anionic (negatively charged) sites. Resins with both kinds of sites or mixtures of resins can also be used. A column of a cation-exchange resin is first activated by washing with acid, then with water, to remove excess acid. If a solution containing, for example, sodium or potassium ions is then passed through the column, these cations displace an equivalent amount of hydrogen ions from the anionic sites in the resin; the displaced hydrogen ions appear in the solution emerging from the column, and a quantitative result can be obtained by titration of the hydrogen ions. Solvent extraction takes advantage of the different solubilities of substances in two liquids that are not soluble in one another. If two materials, *A* and *B*, are both soluble in water, but only *A* is soluble in ether, *A* may be separated from *B* by stirring or shaking the water solution with ether, allowing the layers to settle, and removing the ether layer. The effectiveness of this process is expressed by the distribution coefficients of the two substances in the chosen solvents. For each substance, the distribution coefficient is the ratio of its solubilities in the two solvents; two substances having widely different distribution coefficients can be separated readily by solvent extraction. Countercurrent distribution is essentially a method of repetitive solvent extraction, in which a stream of the extracting solvent, flowing in one direction, is continually mixed with and separated from a stream, flowing in the opposite direction, of a solution of the mixture of substances to be separated. Substances having distribution coefficients that differ only slightly can be separated by this procedure.

Ion-exchange resins

Chromatography is a technique for separating the components of mixtures by taking advantage of their different distribution coefficients between a continuously moving liquid or gaseous "mobile phase" and a "stationary phase," which may be a solid, a liquid supported on a solid, or a gel. The separation process usually involves placing a suitable amount of the mixture at the top of the chromatographic device (a paper strip or a column containing the stationary phase), then allowing a suitable solvent mixture or other mobile phase to flow through it. The separated components emerge in the mobile phase.

Paper chromatography

In paper chromatography a sheet or strip of porous paper is the support for the stationary phase. The sample is applied as a small spot on the paper, and the mobile phase can either descend or ascend through the paper, causing different components of the sample to separate, because they migrate at different rates. The choice of solvent system is rather empirical, although effective mobile phases for most separations that have to be effected in analysis are now well-known. Paper chromatography is sometimes carried out in two dimensions: after treatment with one mobile phase, the paper is dried, turned through 90°, then treated with a different mobile phase. Paper chromatography is widely used for separating all types of organic and inorganic compounds.

In thin-layer chromatography, the stationary phase (often alumina) is applied as a slurry to glass plates, to which it adheres on drying. The sample is applied as a spot or streak and separated as in paper chromatography. Very sharp separations can be obtained in short times with simple apparatus, and the recovery of separated components from the alumina is easily achieved.

For column chromatography, a long, narrow, tubular column is packed with the stationary phase (cellulose powder, charcoal, alumina, ion-exchange resin, etc.). The separation of some classes of materials—*e.g.*, polysaccharides—is difficult to detect, but a possible solution is to convert the substances to coloured forms by treatment with reactive dyestuffs prior to chromatographic separation.

Molecular-sieve chromatography

Molecular-sieve chromatography is a technique by which substances can be separated on the basis of differences in their molecular size and shape. The column is packed with a porous gel, glass, or silica preparation; these substances have pores of closely controlled size that act as sieves. The larger molecules cannot pass through the pores and travel down the column by the shortest route possible, emerging quickly. The smaller molecules can pass through the pores and gain access to internal volumes; they therefore percolate down through the column by a longer path length and emerge more slowly. The technique is widely used for proteins, polysaccharides, and synthetic polymers.

Of all the chromatographic techniques, gas chromatography has probably made the greatest impact. Test mixtures are added as suitable solutions to prepared columns (which may be of glass, copper, or stainless steel) positioned in a thermostatically controlled oven. An inert carrier gas sweeps the vaporized test mixture through the column, which is usually packed with a porous inert support coated with an involatile liquid (silicone oils, polyesters, polyglycols). The gas emerging from the column passes through a sensitive, high-speed detector that registers the presence of the separated components of the sample. For well-characterized systems, the identity of a component can be correlated with the time required for it to appear under standardized operating conditions. Positive identification, however, requires more rigorous evidence, such as that obtainable by subjecting the fractions to infrared spectrophotometry or mass spectroscopy.

Complex formation and masking. In its simplest terms, an interfering substance is excluded from chemical activity in solution by the addition of an ion with which it preferentially forms a complex ion; *e.g.*, iron (III) can be masked by the addition of either fluoride or cyanide, which give the complex anions $(FeF_6)^{3-}$ or $[Fe(CN)_6]^{3-}$, respectively, so that there is no longer free iron available to interfere with the analysis of some other component.

Other methods. Differences in particle size, mass, and density give rise to separations by simple filtration, sieving, differential sedimentation, flotation, centrifugation (the ultracentrifuge is important in the study of natural and synthetic polymers), dialysis, and molecular-sieve chromatography. Magnetic, thermal, and electrical methods have limited applicability. Simple illustrations are the separation of magnetic from nonmagnetic metals and the analysis of copper in its alloys by electrodeposition on a preweighed platinum cathode. Biological materials often can be separated by taking advantage of the different rates at which they migrate under the influence of an electric field.

PRINCIPLES OF ANALYTICAL METHODS

Analytical methods can be classified most conveniently according to whether they are (1) qualitative or quantitative, (2) applicable to organic or inorganic substances, (3) based on chemical, physicochemical, or physical principles, (4) classical or instrumental, (5) carried out on samples that can be classified as macro (10^{-1} g), semimicro (10^{-1}–10^{-3} g), micro (10^{-3}–10^{-6} g), sub-micro (10^{-6}–10^{-8} g), nanogram (10^{-9} g), or picogram (10^{-12} g), or (6) deal with major (greater than 1 percent), minor (0.01–1 percent), or trace (less than 0.01 percent) components of the sample. Authorities differ in the specific figures they quote for these scales of analysis. Other clarifications should also be made. Some tests can form the basis for both qualitative and quantitative procedures; classical (*e.g.*, volumetric or gravimetric) methods are also instrumental in the sense that at least a balance is usually required. By "instrumental analysis" is understood the use of a modern, sophisticated instrument, such as a spectrophotometer or a mass spectrometer.

Classical (or "wet") methods. *Inorganic qualitative analysis.* There are separate systematic schemes for dealing with the identification of cations (*e.g.*, Fe^{3+}, Ca^{2+}, K^+) and of anions (*e.g.*, SO_4^{2-}, Cl^-). Because the schemes depend on chemical processes occurring in solutions, insoluble substances require pretreatment of some kind, such as fusion with oxidizing or nonoxidizing alkaline or acidic fluxes, to render them soluble before the schemes can be applied. There are many preliminary tests of great value: analysts can deduce much from what happens when a sample is heated alone or in the presence of simple reagents; from a visual or a microscopic study of the solid sample; and from flame tests, observed either with the naked eye or with the aid of a simple hand spectroscope. After these preliminary tests, the sample must be prepared for series of chemical treatments by dissolution in the least acidic solvent possible. There is the possibility of chemical modification of the sample at this early stage; indeed, it is impossible to avoid on occasion. Sometimes chemical modification is used deliberately to achieve solubility or effect a separation.

The tests for anions are more difficult and less systematic than those for cations, yet successful analysis for cations is dependent on correct identification of the anions. The classical analysis for the common cations is based on their separation into the following groups: Group I—chlorides of lead, silver, mercury; Group II—sulfides of copper, lead, mercury, bismuth, cadmium, arsenic, antimony, tin; Group III—hydroxides of iron, chromium, aluminum; Group IV—sulfides of cobalt, manganese, nickel, zinc; Group V—carbonates of calcium, barium, strontium. Subseparations within these groups are then possible, and discrete tests are applied finally for sodium, potassium, lithium, magnesium, and ammonium cations.

Inorganic quantitative analysis. This covers the determination of the percentage composition of inorganic materials, *i.e.*, those based on any of the elements with the exclusion of carbon. It is therefore a vast part of chemical analysis and virtually impossible to summarize briefly.

The main chemical methods of quantitative analysis involve gravimetry and titrimetry (volumetric analysis). Gravimetric methods have declined steadily in use since World War II; although accurate, they are slow. Basically, the constituent to be determined is precipitated from solution as an insoluble derivative that can be isolated, dried, and weighed. This insoluble derivative is preferably a compound of definite composition, coloured, crystalline, very insoluble, and stable at an appropriate drying temperature.

Titrimetric methods are based on finding (by burette) the volume of a reagent of known concentration (a standard solution) required to react quantitatively with a known amount of the substance being analyzed. A method of detecting the end point (equivalence point) of a volumetric reaction is required. Some systems are self-indicating; that is, some intrinsic change in colour occurs at the end point, as in titrations with potassium permanganate, when the first drop of titrant in excess imparts a permanent pale pink colour to the solution. More frequently, however, a chemical indicator is required, such as phenolphthalein or methyl red for acid–base titrations or diphenylamine or phenanthroline for redox (oxidation–reduction) systems. The function of an indicator is to give a sharp change in colour immediately after the true equivalence point has been reached. There are many special types of titration, but it is always essential that a quantitative relationship should exist between the titrant and the substance being determined and that the reaction be rapid.

Analysis for the rarer elements. Major technological changes in recent years have resulted in increased utilization of many of what were known earlier as rare elements. Some examples are the use of titanium, zirconium, hafnium, niobium, tantalum, vanadium, tungsten, and molybdenum in metallurgical developments of special alloys for aeronautics and space exploration; boron, rare earth and transuranic elements have been studied extensively in atomic-energy programs and silicon, germanium, gallium, and indium in modern electronics. Other rarer elements (*e.g.*, beryllium) have been studied in connec-

tion with rocket-propellant research or research into aspects of pollution. The recent lunar-exploration programs have further stimulated analytical research.

Although there are classical separation schemes for the analysis of rarer elements, more rapid and sensitive methods are now in demand: chromatography, ion exchange, solvent extraction, atomic absorption and other spectroscopic techniques, complexometry, polarography, and other electrochemical procedures are all used frequently in this field of analysis.

Organic qualitative analysis. Organic chemistry is the study of the compounds of carbon (excluding carbonates). There are more compounds of carbon than there are of all the other elements added together. Carbon combines very commonly with hydrogen, oxygen, and nitrogen; frequently with sulfur, phosphorus, and the halogens; and relatively infrequently with other elements.

Organic compounds are distinguished from inorganic by their behaviour on heating in air. The experienced analyst can tell much from the ease of initiation of combustion, smokiness of flame, formation of acidic reaction gases, and deposition of any residue.

The presence of carbon and hydrogen is most simply shown by heating a small amount of the substance being tested with an excess of dry, powdered copper(II) oxide in a large, dry test tube. Carbon dioxide and hydrogen are the primary products. The carbon dioxide is detectable by the formation of insoluble calcium carbonate with limewater; the hydrogen reacts with the copper oxide to form water, which condenses on the upper, cold, dry surface of the tube. Lassaigne's test, used to detect the presence of nitrogen, halogens, and sulfur, involves fusion with metallic sodium; sodium cyanide (nitrogen), sodium halide (halogens), or sodium sulfide (sulfur) is formed if any of these elements is present. Standard inorganic tests for cyanide, halides, and sulfide are then applied. Phosphorus is detected by fusing the organic substance with a mixture of sodium peroxide and carbonate. The phosphorus is converted to phosphate, which is then detected by the standard colorimetric reaction with ammonium molybdate in nitric acid. The presence of metals in organic compounds is determined by standard inorganic tests.

Organic quantitative analysis. This falls into two distinct sections—elemental analysis and functional-group analysis.

The element analyses most often required are for carbon, hydrogen, nitrogen, sulfur, phosphorus, and the halogens. The determination of metals is made by a quantitative ashing technique. Carbon and hydrogen are analyzed by modifications of Liebig's method (1831): combustion in excess of oxygen effects quantitative conversion to carbon dioxide and water, which can be determined by absorption in weighing tubes containing chemical absorbents. Nitrogen is commonly determined by the Dumas method (combustion and conversion to elemental nitrogen, the volume of which is measured) or by the Kjeldahl method (conversion to ammonium sulfate, from which ammonia is steam distilled and determined titrimetrically). Sulfur, halogens, and phosphorus are now commonly determined by the Schöniger oxygen-flask technique (combustion in a flask filled with oxygen); after combustion, the reaction products are dissolved by adding distilled water to the flask, in which the final titrimetric or colorimetric procedure is carried out.

The most common functional group analyses involve the determination of alkoxy (*e.g.*, methoxy, ethoxy), hydroxyl, acetyl, epoxy, amino, carboxyl, peroxy, nitro, cyano, and active hydrogen groups. These demand more analytical skill but give a more rigorous assessment of the percentage purity of a compound than can be obtained from elemental analysis. As an indication of a typical functional-group analysis, Zeisel's method for alkoxy groups involves reaction of the compound with hydriodic acid; the methoxy groups are converted quantitatively to methyl iodide, which can be absorbed and determined titrimetrically.

Instrumental methods. *Optical methods. There are* about 20 distinct analytical techniques based on optical

Group separation of metals

Indicators

Nitrogen, halogens, and sulfur in organic compounds

phenomena: some are of such great importance in general chemical analysis that no modern laboratory could function without them; others are restricted in application to particular compound classes. Taken together, however, the optical methods of analysis form the most widely used group of instrumental physicochemical methods.

Colorimetry

Given the gifts of a good pair of eyes and natural daylight, anyone should be able to distinguish between a solution of copper(II) sulfate pentahydrate (blue) and sodium chloride (colourless); and anyone should be able to tell which of two copper(II) sulfate pentahydrate solutions is the more concentrated; *i.e.*, the more intensely coloured of the two. These are applications of colorimetry; *i.e.*, of optical phenomena involving changes that are manifest in the visible part of the spectrum. The basic requirements for this approach to analysis are a source of light (the sun in this case) and a detector (the human eye). Sunlight (white light) is composite—*i.e.*, the additive effect of light of many wavelengths (colours); these wavelengths can be separated from each other by dispersion devices (prisms, gratings). In many optical methods of analysis, chemicals are studied with the aid of monochromatic radiation; *e.g.*, the light from a sodium or mercury lamp, or from a laser.

Why do solutions of copper(II) sulfate pentahydrate and sodium chloride have different colours when examined in sunlight? The sodium salt does not absorb any of the wavelengths in sunlight at all; the copper salt absorbs radiation of all wavelengths except the blue, so that only the blue component can be reflected or transmitted to the detector. This difference in absorption characteristics results from the different electronic structures of sodium and copper atoms. By replacing the human eye with an electronic device such as a photocell or the even more sensitive combination of a photomultiplier and an amplifier, the sensitivity of measurement can be greatly increased.

The range of colours to which the human eye is sensitive, from red to violet, is only a very narrow range of the electromagnetic spectrum of radiation. Of progressively decreasing wavelength (*i.e.*, increasing frequency and, hence, more energy) are the ultraviolet, X-ray, γ-ray, and cosmic-ray regions of the electromagnetic spectrum. Of progressively increasing wavelength are the infrared and microwave regions. All these regions are used in chemical analysis: whether a molecule absorbs in the ultraviolet or microwave part of the spectrum depends on the structural features of the molecule; that is, on which elements are involved and on the structural arrangements of the atoms in the molecule.

Spectrochemical methods. Spectrochemical methods, which are important modern instrumental techniques, may involve examination of the emission of radiation by molecules that have been suitably excited by heat or some other form of energy; or the absorption of radiation of particular wavelengths by molecules; or, less commonly, the reflection of radiation. Radiant energy can be absorbed by certain molecules and subsequently re-emitted in a modified form; as a result, fluorescence, phosphorescence, and Raman spectra (extra spectrum lines produced when light is scattered by passing through transparent substances) occur. These techniques are also useful analytically.

The other optical phenomena of analytical use involve optical rotation (polarimetry), optical rotatory dispersion (ORD), and refraction. Light-scattering measurements can be made on suspensions or colloidal solutions by nephelometry, in which the measurement is made at right angles to the incident beam, or by turbidimetry, in which the transmitted light is measured. By measuring the intensity of the scattered light at different angles to the incident beam, the molecular weights of polymers can be obtained. All these methods are important in certain fields of analysis, but they are not general, and space does not permit their further discussion.

When some elements are heated strongly, light having a unique distribution of wavelengths is radiated. This behaviour forms the basis of emission spectroscopy, an extremely sensitive, accurate, and rapid automatic method for the qualitative and quantitative analysis of mixtures of many nonmetallic and metallic elements.

A cheaper and more convenient form of emission spectroscopy is flame photometry, applicable to substances that emit visible or ultraviolet light when their solutions are sprayed as a fine mist into a flame. The method is particularly suitable for the alkali and alkaline-earth metals, but a good-quality flame photometer can be used to determine more than 30 of the elements, with detection limits frequently lower than one part per million. Colorimetry involves measurement of the intensity of absorption of visible light. It is therefore restricted to the analysis of coloured substances or substances that can be converted conveniently into coloured derivatives. Standard solutions are prepared to find the concentration of solution that gives exactly the same colour intensity as the test substance under carefully standardized conditions. More accurate and sensitive results are obtained with simple instruments, such as the Duboscq colorimeter, which requires only one standard solution to be made up: colour match is achieved by a system of plungers that effectively change the depths of solution viewed in the comparison cells. The Lambert–Beer law relates the intensity of absorption of a solution to the concentration and effective depth of solution in an absorption cell. Absorption of microwaves (radiation having wavelengths between one centimetre and 100 centimetres) is characteristic of some gaseous molecules. It gives valuable structural information but is not of general analytical importance. Certain specific wavelengths that depend on the structure of the compound under test are absorbed when a beam containing all wavelengths of infrared radiation is passed through a suitably prepared specimen of almost any organic or inorganic compound (the main exceptions are diatomic gases such as oxygen, nitrogen, and hydrogen, and the alkali halides). The most useful range of wavelengths is that between 2.5 and 16 microns (one micron = 10^{-6} metre). (These wavelengths often are expressed by the wave number, the number of waves in one centimetre: radiation having a wavelength of 10 microns has 1,000 waves per centimetre, or a wave number of 1,000 cm^{-1}.) Solids, liquids, and gases can be examined, and mixtures can be analyzed. Both carbon dioxide and water vapour absorb strongly in the infrared region and must be excluded from the apparatus. Sensitive quantitative analyses can be carried out, but perhaps the greatest use of this technique has been in the qualitative identification of organic compounds. Structural information concerning the presence and, more importantly, absence of certain functional groups is obtained; for example, hydroxyl groups absorb in the 3,300–3,600 cm^{-1} region, cyano groups in the 2,200–2,250 cm^{-1} region, and carbonyl groups in the 1,650–1,800 cm^{-1} region. From 650–1,500 cm^{-1} the absorption spectrum of a compound is a unique "fingerprint" that differs from that of any other compound. The interpretation of spectra is a specialized skill that requires much experience.

Infrared spectrometry

Electrons in the molecules that have structures involving unsaturated bonds can absorb quanta of energy corresponding to electromagnetic radiation in the region of the spectrum from 180 to 400 nanometres (the ultraviolet region). The major application of ultraviolet spectrometry is in the analysis of aromatic compounds, vitamins, and other biochemical molecules, although the technique is useful for many inorganic molecules. As in the case of modern infrared instrumentation, ultraviolet spectrometers scan the entire spectrum range automatically and produce a graph of the intensity of absorption in relation to the wavelength.

Ultraviolet spectrometry

Atomic-absorption spectroscopy was introduced in 1955, and applications of the technique have grown steadily since then. By 1971 it was possible to make very sensitive and specific analyses of about 60 elements by this method. A solution of the compound under analysis is sprayed into a flame, in which a reservoir of atoms in various energized states is formed. A beam of radiation is passed through the atom reservoir: if copper is being determined, a copper-containing source must be used to give a beam of radiation of exactly the same wavelengths as those emitted by the energized atoms. Absorption of energy therefore occurs; the amount of energy absorbed can be detected electronically and is directly proportional to the number of atoms present.

Atomic-fluorescence spectroscopy has become very important since 1955 and gives very sensitive analyses of metals such as zinc, mercury, cadmium, magnesium, and silver.

Raman spectroscopy is another technique, in which the radiation scattered in a direction perpendicular to that of the incident beam is measured. The spectra are complementary to infrared spectra, and the technique has experienced a revival and extension in recent years as a result of the development of laser sources of radiation.

X-ray and electron diffraction are specialized methods of great value in determining molecular structures. Electrons have a much more restricted penetration than X-rays and can be used only to examine gases, very thin films, and surface layers. The introduction of computer techniques has allowed the X-ray method to be applied to very complex protein and polysaccharide molecules.

X-ray fluorescence (XRF) is a nondestructive method of elemental analysis widely used for metallurgical and geological specimens. Qualitative and quantitative analyses are possible for elements with atomic number greater than 12, although several lighter elements can be analyzed if ancillary equipment is available. When an element is irradiated with X-rays of appropriate wavelength, X-rays of a different wavelength, characteristic of the element, are emitted. Complex mixtures can usually be analyzed without prior separation of the components, as in the determination of additives or contaminants in motor oils. Samples are best examined in solution, but very finely powdered samples can be used. There is, unfortunately, a lack of sensitivity for some elements, as compared with other methods.

Mass spectrometry. The principles of mass spectrometry are described in the article of that title. To summarize, molecular ions are produced from the sample by a beam of electrons produced by a hot filament. The ions are accelerated electrically to form a beam that is deflected magnetically into separate beams according to the mass-to-charge ratio of the ions involved. These beams can be made to pass through series of slits to reach the ion-collector electrode separately. The "time of flight" spectrometer operates on a different principle: the charged particles are separated by their different velocity of escape from the accelerator stage.

Mass spectroscopy is an important analytical technique of great sensitivity and accuracy. It gives quantitative results for major and minor components of mixtures, gives determinations of molecular weights and of isotopic abundances, and is widely used in the analysis of complex organic molecules. It is one of the few techniques with the sensitivity required to analyze the very small fractions often obtained from chromatographic processes. The mass spectrum ("cracking pattern") of a compound, like the infrared spectrum, is unique and gives unequivocal proof of the identity of a substance. Solid, liquid, and gaseous samples can be analyzed, and its rapidity makes it useful for monitoring process gas streams that alter rapidly.

Magnetic-resonance spectrometry. This technique has revolutionized, since about 1955, the structural analysis of organic compounds and certain classes of inorganic materials. The sample must be soluble in one of a range of solvents containing deuterium atoms in place of hydrogen in order to eliminate interference with the signals from hydrogen atoms in the sample under test.

Nuclear magnetic resonance The nuclei of certain atoms (*e.g.*, the common isotopes of hydrogen, nitrogen, fluorine, and phosphorus but not of carbon or oxygen) act as tiny bar magnets. These nuclei can therefore be influenced by strong external magnetic fields; quantum considerations dictate that they must become aligned either toward or against the applied field. If radiation of the appropriate frequency for absorption is passed through the specimen, the energy absorbed causes transitions from the one alignment to the other; the nuclei are then said to be in resonance. Mea-

surements of the frequency and extent of the absorption by the nuclei form the basis of analysis. The field strength of the magnet must be constant and uniform to within one part in 10^8. Field strengths of 14,000 gauss (the electromagnetic unit of magnetic induction) or 23,500 gauss commonly are used; the corresponding irradiation frequencies required to produce resonances are approximately 60 megahertz (one hertz is one cycle per second) and 100 megahertz.

In a fixed external magnetic field, the exact radio frequency at which a nucleus absorbs depends upon its stereochemical location in the molecule concerned, because the electrons in that molecule produce local fields that cause shielding effects, which vary from position to position within the molecule. In essence, the different hydrogen nuclei, for example, in a complex molecule can be distinguished and the nature of their immediate environment identified in terms of a value termed the chemical shift. For hydrogen atoms, distinction can be made among aliphatic, olefinic, acetylenic, aromatic, aldehydic, amino, amido, hydroxylic, phenolic, and carboxylic environments.

Electron spin resonance (ESR) spectroscopy is a resonance technique (also known as electron paramagnetic resonance) applicable to species having unpaired ("odd") electrons, and it is useful for the analysis of free radicals, molecules in triplet states (having two unpaired electrons), and certain transition metal ions and complexes.

Thermometric methods. When substances are heated, physical changes and chemical reactions or decompositions take place; the nature of these and the temperatures at which they occur are characteristic of the substances under test.

Differential thermal analysis Differential thermal analysis is based on the change of temperature of a sample when heat is supplied at a constant rate. Complex changes in the solid sample, which may either liberate heat (exothermic reaction) or abstract heat (endothermic reaction), can occur; the responses of many substances in this procedure are therefore fairly complex, characteristic patterns. This technique has the advantage that the data can be obtained automatically over long periods by continuously recording instruments, and it is used frequently in the analysis of metallurgical, mineralogical, and polymeric samples.

Thermogravimetry is based on the thermo-balance, which records continuously the change in weight of a sample as it is heated. The temperature at which loss in weight occurs and the extent of that loss can give useful analytical data for polymers and other classes of material.

Pyrolysis has been used increasingly in recent years to characterize polymeric materials. The sample is heated to the temperature at which decomposition to simple gaseous compounds takes place: these products are analyzed by gas chromatography or mass spectrometry.

Calorimetry, cryoscopy, and ebulliometry are examples of other thermal methods available for analytical purposes, but they are not used extensively.

Radiochemical methods. Radioactivity is dealt with in a separate article, and therefore there is no discussion here of the types of radioactive emission, half-lives, methods of detection and measurement, occurrence of radioactive isotopes, safety precautions, etc.

Following the impetus given to nuclear-energy programs and radiochemistry in the 1940s, analytical methods based on aspects of radioactivity have become widely used, because of their unparalleled combinations of selectivity and sensitivity. It is not unusual for analysis to be performed on as little as 10^{-15} gram of material. Although the cost of radiochemicals and of the irradiation of chemicals in nuclear reactors is high, the cost of laboratory counting equipment is comparatively low. Safety precautions additional to those in any chemical laboratory are always required; for many substances these precautions are easily met, but for the more dangerous isotopes very special remote-handling equipment and biological shielding are required.

Radiometric analysis is used to analyze substances on the basis of their small natural content of some radioactive isotope; *e.g.*, natural samples of potassium contain a very small proportion of the isotope potassium-40, which is a β emitter of long half-life (1.28×10^9 years). Another modification of this method is to analyze a nonradioactive substance by converting it to a radioactive form; *e.g.*, chloride ions can be determined with great sensitivity by the addition of radioactive silver nitrate, which leads to the deposition of radioactive silver chloride. The analysis can be based on the radioactivity of the latter or on the decrease in radioactivity of the silver nitrate added.

Activation analysis
Activation analysis takes advantage of the fact that many elements become radioactive when irradiated with neutrons in a nuclear reactor. The active isotopes formed vary widely in terms of their half-lives, and a decay curve is obtained by plotting the intensity of radioactivity against time. From this and supplementary data (such as identifying the different γ radiations present) the composition of the original mixture of elements can be found. The sensitivity obtainable depends on the neutron-capture cross section of the element involved, the intensity of the neutron source, and the half-life of the isotope produced.

The method of isotope dilution can be employed to determine the amount of some element, E, in a mixture. A small, known amount of a radioactive isotope of E is incorporated into the mixture; the element E, including the added radioactive isotope, is then separated from the mixture, and its radioactivity is determined. It is then a simple calculation to establish the concentration of E in the original mixture, on the assumption that there is no difference in the percentage recoveries of E and its isotope from the mixture.

Electrochemical methods. In potentiometric analysis, the concentration of a solution is determined in terms of the measurable electrical potential; the electronic circuitry used is designed so that the measurement is made under conditions in which no current flows. The instrumental measurement of pH (the negative logarithm of the hydrogen ion, H^+, concentration; *i.e.*, a measure of the acidity or alkalinity of a solution) is based on potentiometry. Ion-selective electrodes, sensitive to the activity of a particular ion in solution, are available for hydrogen ions, fluorides, the alkali metals, calcium, silver, etc., and these have greatly extended the analytical utility of potentiometry. Potentiometric titration is frequently used to locate end points in terms of the change in electromotive force of a suitable galvanic cell caused by the addition of known volumes of titrant. By means of simple electronic circuitry, this principle can be extended so that titrations can be done automatically.

The conductivity (reciprocal of resistance) of a solution depends on the identity of the ions present and their concentration. Analytical applications include the titration of mixtures of weak and strong acids, determination of rates of reaction, solubilities of slightly soluble salts, and the end points for titrations in which precipitates or slightly ionized compounds are formed.

Oscillometry (high-frequency titrimetry) determines changes in composition by measuring changes in dielectric constant or conductivity: these can be detected by applying high-frequency alternating signals to electrodes, which can be external to the cell containing the solution under test.

In voltammetry, a small, inert electrode (usually of gold or platinum) is used in conjunction with a larger electrode, at which the corresponding current density is very small, so that the current flowing depends on the rate of transfer of electroactive material (ions or molecules that can be oxidized or reduced at the electrode) from the bulk of the solution to the smaller electrode. If a large excess of an inert electrolyte (*e.g.*, potassium chloride) is present, the rate of transfer becomes almost completely diffusion controlled (limited only by the rate at which the particles move through the solution, rather than by the rate at which the electrochemical reaction occurs). Voltammetry is useful for the analysis of both organic and inorganic compounds, and it can be carried out (1) with variable voltage, (2) with variable current, or (3) at

constant current (a special case known as chronopotentiometry). For each of these methods, a graph of the relationship between current and voltage is an S-shaped curve from which the identity and the concentration of the electroactive substance may be determined.

Polarography
Polarography is an important technique that can be regarded as a special case of voltammetry. A large, nonpolarizable reference electrode is used in conjunction with a small, polarizable electrode of special design—a capillary tube—from which small drops of mercury emerge at regular, short intervals into the solution. The voltage across these two electrodes is swept; the "half-wave potential" at which the required chemical reaction begins and the magnitude of the resulting "diffusion current" give a basis for qualitative and quantitative analysis. Although either electro-oxidizable or electroreducible substances can be examined, the dropping mercury electrode usually is connected to form the cathode (the negatively charged electrode, at which electrons are available to reduce oxidized substances); in the electrolysis of metal ions, the ions are reduced to the metal itself, which amalgamates with (*e.g.*, dissolves in) the drops of mercury. This method is nondestructive and sensitive and applicable to inorganic and organic molecules. Only very small volumes of dilute solutions are required, and the method is applicable to mixtures. Several instrumental variations of the basic principle have been developed.

Amperometry utilizes the principles of polarography and conductometry and is useful for detecting end points in slow or incomplete reactions involving precipitations and complexometric reactions. In an amperometric titration (sometimes called a polarometric titration because a simple polarographic dropping mercury electrode and reference electrode form the essential circuitry required), the change in the diffusion current at a convenient applied voltage is measured in relation to the volume of titrant. The diffusion current decreases linearly to a minimum at the equivalence point, then increases as excess of titrant is added.

Coulometry involves the direct application of Faraday's laws of electrolysis: when a single electrode reaction occurs at 100 percent current efficiency, the number of equivalents of the substance involved is directly proportional to the number of faradays (one faraday is equal to about 96,500 coulombs) of electricity consumed. In direct (primary) coulometry, the substance under test reacts directly at an electrode at a constant applied voltage. As the reaction proceeds, the current decreases. It is frequently preferable to work at constant current. Indirect (secondary) coulometry is more widely used. The quantity of electricity required to generate a low concentration of a titrant is found, this titrant reacting stoichiometrically (*i.e.*, quantitatively), as it is formed, with the substance being analyzed.

Electrodeposition (electrogravimetry) is a simple technique frequently used for copper, transition metals, and noble metals. The test solution is electrolyzed exhaustively at constant voltage or (more commonly) at constant current; the increase in weight of the working electrode (usually a mesh of platinum carefully prepared so that the metal will be electrodeposited in a firm layer) is determined. Efficient stirring is required to prevent concentration polarization. Metals can be separated if their standard electrode potentials differ by about 0.25 volt and if the electrolysis is carried out at a voltage midway between those electrode potentials.

Physical methods. The determination of vapour density, vapour pressure, depression of freezing point, and elevation of boiling point, which lead to the determination of molecular weight, are important techniques, but they are not now used very frequently. The determination of viscosity and osmotic pressure also lead to the determination of molecular weight and are especially useful in the study of colloidal systems such as natural polymers (starch, cellulose, pectin, proteins) or synthetic polymers (polyethylene, nylon) of high molecular weight. Surface tension, sedimentation rates, and particle size distribution are also frequently determined for materials of these classes.

Electrical properties are also widely used; the dielectric constant and dipole moment are useful analytical properties for organic molecules. The refractive index can be measured very accurately and is a very useful way of testing the purity of compounds or measuring the concentration of solutions.

Optically active molecules have the ability to rotate the plane of polarized light. The magnitude and direction of the rotation can be measured with great accuracy by a polarimeter, and this form of analysis is widely used for sugars and polysaccharides.

Other important physical methods of analysis include the determination of calorific values, heats of combustion, activation energy, and reaction rates. Mixtures of similar components that are difficult to separate conveniently frequently can be analyzed in terms of the different rates of reaction of the components. The rates of chemical reactions can be increased by small amounts of catalysts, and a useful method of finding the concentration of some substances is to find a reaction for which the substance acts as a catalyst, then measure its concentration in terms of the increased rates of reaction.

BIBLIOGRAPHY. I.M. KOLTHOFF and P.J. ELVING (eds.), *Treatise on Analytical Chemistry*, in several parts and volumes (1959–), is an authoritative series that treats the broad field comprehensively. H.A. LAITINEN, *Chemical Analysis* (1960), is an excellent text for topics such as equilibria, titrimetry, precipitation processes, electrochemistry, statistical evaluation of data, errors, and sampling. LOUIS MEITES and H.C. THOMAS, *Advanced Analytical Chemistry* (1958), is especially valuable for its coverage of electrochemistry, spectrometric methods, radiochemistry, ion-exchange, and chromatographic methods. RONALD BELCHER, *Submicro Methods of Organic Analysis* (1966), gives the essential details of methods for working with samples weighing less than one milligram. D.R. BROWNING (ed.), *Electrometric Methods* (1969), contains a brief but fairly rigorous treatment of the fundamental principles of these techniques. MAX DONBROW, *Instrumental Methods in Analytical Chemistry*, 2 vol. (1966–67), surveys electrochemical and optical methods. Specialized topics are covered by ERICH HEFTMANN, *Chromatography*, 2nd ed. (1967); WILLIAM RIEMAN and H.F. WALTON, *Ion Exchange in Analytical Chemistry* (1970); SIDNEY SIGGIA, *Quantitative Organic Analysis Via Functional Groups*, 3rd ed. (1963); and E.S. STERN and C.J. TIMMONS, *Gillam and Stern's Introduction to Electronic Absorption Spectroscopy in Organic Chemistry*, 3rd ed. (1970).

(D.M.W.A.)

Chemical Bonding

Chemical bonds hold atoms together in various kinds of associations, such as those in molecules, crystals, and metals. In every neutral atom the number of positive charges on the nucleus (the atomic number) holds an equal number of negatively charged electrons clustered about the nucleus in a pattern characteristic for each element. Chemical bonds result when the electron structure of an atom is altered sufficiently to link it with the electron structure of another atom or atoms. All chemical reactions are explained according to changes in the electron structures of the atoms, whether bonds are made or broken. Various types of bonds are known but they are all explained in terms of quantum mechanics.

NONQUANTUM TREATMENT OF CHEMICAL BONDING

Early theories of chemical bonds. The idea that matter is made up of a large number of discrete particles somehow linked together dates back to Roman times, but it did not attain significance as a scientific hypothesis until the early part of the 18th century, when physical scientists interpreted the behaviour of gases in terms of simple kinetic (pertaining to motion) theory. Later in the same century, chemists began to weigh carefully all reactants and all products (gravimetric measurement) of chemical changes and were able to formulate laws governing such changes. Among these was the law of constant composition, which stated that a pure compound always has the same composition. John Dalton, an English chemist, hypothesized, early in the 19th century, that these chemical observations were most readily explained by what he called an atomic theory, according to which all atoms of

(margin) Dalton's atomic theory

the same element were identical to each other and different from the atoms of all other elements and, in the formation of compounds, atoms of the elements, being indivisible, were joined together in simple whole numbers. Thus, the elements carbon and oxygen formed a compound, carbon monoxide, and also a compound, carbon dioxide. Using symbols, if C represents a single carbon atom and O an oxygen atom, the two compounds have the chemical formulas CO and CO_2, respectively, and such formulas represent single molecules. (Another oxide of carbon, C_3O_2, was discovered later.) Clearly, because all molecules of a given compound were the same, the law of constant composition was explained. These terms came into general usage, however, only decades after Dalton's original work had been published. Discoveries like that summarized in Avogadro's law—that equal volumes of all gases at the same temperature and pressure have equal numbers of molecules—enabled molecular weights to be determined on an arbitrary scale of comparisons in which the hydrogen atom was given a mass of one; later, the standard became oxygen, with a mass of 16 and, recently, by international agreement, carbon was selected for the standard (the isotope carbon-12). This basic knowledge of molecular masses was a necessary preliminary to theories concerning the nature of the chemical bonds holding atoms together in molecules.

Valence. About the middle of the 19th century, the first modern theory introduced the concept of valency to represent the combining capacity of an atom with a number: the valence of an element was the number of hydrogen atoms each atom of the element could combine with. Hydrogen was selected as the unit element because a single atom of hydrogen could never be found to combine with more than one atom of any other element. Thus, atoms of elements that combined with only one hydrogen atom were said to have a valency of 1, for example, chlorine (symbol Cl), while, for example, oxygen, nitrogen, and carbon (symbols O, N, C) had valencies of 2, 3, and 4, respectively. The compounds formed with hydrogen could then be represented quite simply by the numbers of symbols for the elements involved: hydrogen chloride, HCl; water, H_2O; ammonia, NH_3; methane, CH_4. Other molecules were also capable of such simple representation: an oxygen molecule was O_2; carbon dioxide, CO_2, etc.

Electrovalent bond. Early in the 19th century it was realized that there were two types of compounds, later termed electrovalent and covalent. The former, when dissolved in water, were capable of conducting an electric current, while the latter were not. As it became clear that electrically neutral atoms could acquire electrical charges, the concept developed that a charged atom was an independent particle; it was given the name ion and symbolized with a plus or minus superscript, indicating the charge, following the symbol for the element. Thus, the sodium atom could produce a positively charged sodium ion, symbolized as Na^+. Likewise, chlorine could produce negative ions, symbolized Cl^-. If this ionization occurred in a water solution, the ions were stable, so that the compound sodium chloride (common salt) could be regarded as composed of sodium and chlorine ions: Na^+Cl^-. In the first quarter of the 20th century it was shown that even solid crystals of sodium chloride consisted of an assembly of independent sodium and chloride ions arranged in an orderly fashion, so that the positive ions were always balanced by negative ions. All electrovalent compounds have this general structure.

(margin) Discovery of ions

Covalent bond. Covalent compounds do not involve ions. It was observed that two molecules, each made up of the same number of similar atoms (*e.g.*, methylacetylene and allene, both having the formula C_3H_4) could be chemically and physically different. Compounds having the same composition but different properties were named isomers. The only possible explanation for isomerism is that the molecules had different arrangements of the atoms and that these different arrangements were capable of a considerable persistence. An empirical hypothesis was needed to describe how the atoms were joined together, and so the chemical bond, or the covalent bond, was proposed. For many years nothing at all was known about the structure of the covalent bond, but a great deal of information was assembled about its properties. In one representation of the bond it was a line, and the symbol for each atom had as many lines attached to it as the atom had valences. Thus sodium was symbolized Na—, chlorine was Cl—, oxygen —O—, carbon, =C=. In a molecule, a single bond between two atoms consisted of one line from each symbol, but the two lines between bonded atoms were shown simply as a single shared line. Thus, the molecule C_3H_4 could be represented as having either of two possible structures in which all bonds were covalent (each carbon atom has a valency of 4 and each hydrogen of 1):

$$H-\overset{\displaystyle H}{\underset{\displaystyle H}{\overset{|}{\underset{|}{C}}}}-C\equiv C-H \quad \text{or} \quad \overset{\displaystyle H}{\diagdown}C=C=C\overset{\diagup\displaystyle H}{\diagdown_{\displaystyle H}}$$

Difficulties of early theories

Many covalent compounds, particularly in the realm of organic chemistry, could be explained most satisfactorily in this manner, though there were some difficulties. Carbon dioxide, CO_2, was clearly O=C=O, for instance; but how was carbon monoxide, CO, to be explained if carbon had a valency of 4 and oxygen a valency of 2? There were other similar difficulties, but the overall success was so great that the few difficulties were not allowed to invalidate the theory.

Stereoisomers. Toward the end of the 19th century, it became necessary to consider the arrangements of atoms in three dimensions. It was necessary to suppose that the four bonds from a carbon atom were directed from the central nucleus to the four corners of a regular tetrahedron, in order to explain why molecules having four different groups attached to the same carbon atom had isomers. It was realized that, if four different groups were attached tetrahedrally to the same carbon atom, two different molecules, which were mirror images of one another, were possible; for example, the carbon atom joined to four atoms signified by P, R, S, and Q can have the following different structures:

$$\overset{\displaystyle P}{\underset{\displaystyle S}{\overset{|}{R\diagup C\diagdown Q}}} \qquad \overset{\displaystyle P}{\underset{\displaystyle S}{\overset{|}{Q\diagup C\diagdown R}}}$$

The C and P atoms lie in the plane of the page, S projects upward from the page and R and Q lie behind. Substances of this type of mirror-image organization have the same chemical properties but differ in certain physical properties.

The effect of the discovery of the electron. At the end of the 19th century, it was realized that covalent bonds had direction and possessed a considerable spatial rigidity. Further, it became clear that they also possessed a certain degree of independence of one another; *e.g.,* the carbon–hydrogen bonds in compounds as different as methane and chloroform, (formulas CH_4 and $CHCl_3$, respectively) behaving in a similar manner. It was at this stage in history that the English physicist J.J. Thomson discovered the electron. It was soon realized that the covalent bond consisted of electrons being shared and that electrovalent bonds resulting from the formation of ions took place by electron transfer from one atom to another. The subsequent development of the theory of chemical bonding is therefore almost entirely a development of its electronic interpretation.

Early electronic theory of valency. Experiments early in the 20th century showed that atoms were mostly empty space, being made up of a small, heavy nucleus with positive charge around which at a distance were clustered the much lighter negatively charged electrons, the number of which was equal to the positive charge on the nucleus—*i.e.,* to the atomic number of the element, which is the basis of the periodic table of the elements.

Periodic properties of the elements. The modern periodic table of the elements, proposed in the 1860s (see PERIODIC LAW; CHEMICAL ELEMENTS), was based on the relative atomic weights of the elements, and it contributed to the theories of chemical reaction. Early in the 20th century, the basis for the periodic table became the nuclear and electronic structure, and chemical bonding, since then, has been understood with reference to this arrangement of the elements, which emphasizes valence properties as a function of the electronic structure. If the 105 known elements are arranged in sequence according to their atomic numbers (the number of protons in the nucleus) their chemical and physical properties will be periodic; that is, similarities in properties will recur at regular intervals in the sequence of elements. Thus, elements that form a certain type of strong acid with hydrogen (fluorine, chlorine, bromine, iodine) do not directly follow one another in the sequence but are separated by a recurring number of other elements. The sequence may be broken up, therefore, into periods, and, when these are placed horizontally under one another, vertical groups of elements will have similar properties. This is so because the internal structure of atoms, as they become larger and more massive, have recurring similarities. The electrons are grouped into arrangements called shells and subshells, each shell having a maximum number it can hold. Their arrangement is largely the result of quantum mechanical effects summarized in the so-called Pauli principle. The energy required to remove an electron is an important property. Some elements tend to lose electrons easily and thereby be left with a net positive charge; these are the metals. Nonmetallic elements have a great affinity for electrons and will accept them into their structure, thereby acquiring a net negative charge. Such charged atoms are called ions. This tendency to gain or lose electrons, with resulting changes in the total energy, forms the basis of one type of chemical bonding.

The periodic table and the elements

The noble gases, members of Group 0 in the periodic table (helium, neon, argon, etc.), have key positions in the sequence of elements because their electron structures are the most stable. All other elements tend toward this arrangement, gaining, losing, or sharing electrons to achieve it and forming compounds or ions to do so. (The empirical formulas for compounds are simply a numerical count of the atoms that are bonded together through electron structures, the atoms being represented by their symbols, followed by the number present in the molecule; for example, sulfuric acid is written H_2SO_4, which means two atoms of hydrogen, one atom of sulfur, and four atoms of oxygen.)

Structure of the noble gases

Shell theory and ionic bonds. The behaviour of the lighter elements suggests that the orbiting electrons occur in shells at various distances from the nucleus. The helium atom, for instance, atomic number 2 (see periodic table), contains two electrons. Apparently this arrangement must have a high stability, because the helium atom forms no chemical compounds; *i.e.,* it is not disrupted by collisions with other atoms. The lithium atom, atomic number 3, however, with three electrons, readily loses one electron to form an ion that still contains two electrons and is also very stable. (Ions are represented by the symbol for the element with the number of the positive or negative charges written as a superscript: *e.g.,* lithium ion is written Li^+; magnesium ion, Mg^{2+}; oxygen ion, O^{2-}.) The next element showing behaviour similar to that of helium is neon, the atom of which contains ten electrons arranged in a stable inner shell of two (like those of helium) and an outer shell of eight electrons that is also very stable. Moreover, this number of electrons is attained also in the stable ions of oxygen (O^{2-}), fluorine (F^-), sodium (Na^+), and magnesium (Mg^{2+}), showing again the high stability of this outer shell of eight electrons, sometimes called the octet. Oxygen has six outer electrons but its ion has gained two, making a total of eight; fluorine has seven outer electrons, but it gains one in forming the ion; sodium, with 11 electrons, one outermost, loses that one to form a positive ion with only eight electrons outermost; magnesium loses two electrons to form its ion with eight. The argon atom, atomic number 18, contains 18 electrons, and the stability of this number is demonstrated by the formation of the ions of sulfur (S^{2-}), chlorine (Cl^-), potassium (K^+),

Stability of octet shell arrangement

and calcium (Ca^{2+}). The electron configuration of these ions may be assumed to consist of three shells containing two innermost, eight central, and eight outermost electrons, respectively. With this structure, the formation of the simple electrovalent compounds is understandable as being a consequence of electron transfer. The process is illustrated in the following equation of the reaction between sodium, Na, and fluorine, F; the dots represent electrons in the outermost shell only:

$$Na\cdot + \cdot\ddot{\underset{\cdot\cdot}{F}}\colon \longrightarrow [Na]^+ + [\colon\ddot{\underset{\cdot\cdot}{F}}\colon]^-$$

Such an electron transfer usually requires heat energy (*i.e.*, the reaction is usually endothermic), but the ultimate stability of electrovalent compounds, in the solid state, resides in the lowering of energy (called the ionic lattice energy of the crystal) resulting from the interionic electrostatic forces (of attraction between opposite charges and repulsion between similar charges) so that, overall, the total energy of the products is less than that of the reactants, and the energy falls. In solution, the overall lowering of the energy results from the separation by water molecules of the ions, a process called solvation. If a sodium atom were to form the ion Na^{2+}, the energy required to remove the second electron would be considerably larger than that required to remove the first, because the second electron would have to come from the inner, closed shell of eight in the ion Na^+, and the nucleus, still with its total of 11 positive charges, would hold each of those eight with greater affinity than the outermost electron is held when there are 11 electrons. Consequently, even though the electrovalent compound $Na^{2+}(F^-)_2$ would have a higher lattice energy than the compound Na^+F^-, this would not be large enough to compensate the energy required to form the ion Na^{2+}. In fact, the compound NaF_2 is unknown, being impossible in terms of energy content. The stability of the shell of eight provides a most satisfactory guide for the formation of ions for elements with atomic numbers less than 21 (the atomic number of the element scandium, Sc).

The Lewis
structures

Octet and covalent bond. The above consideration led G.N. Lewis, a U.S. chemist, to emphasize the importance of the group of two and the group of eight electrons, called the pair and the octet. He used their stability, together with the concept of "electron sharing," in explaining covalent compounds. It was supposed that a covalent bond consisted of two electrons, one provided by each atom. Each of the shared electrons contributed to the outermost shells of both atoms and thus stability was achieved, just as in electrovalent compounds, with a shell of two for hydrogen and of eight for carbon, nitrogen, oxygen, fluorine, and the corresponding elements of the second short period in the periodic table, silicon, phosphorus, sulfur, and chlorine. Below are examples of electronic covalent structures, using dots to represent outer-shell electrons, for the compounds with the empirical formulas CH_3NH_2, CH_2O, HF, and HOCl:

It was supposed that the octet was made up of four pairs which were either shared or unshared (lone pairs), each of the four pairs being disposed tetrahedrally (at the four corners of a tetrahedron) around the atom. A tetrahedral distribution of covalent bonds of carbon and silicon atoms was postulated, as well as the pyramidal arrangement for nitrogen and phosphorus atoms and a nonlinear arrangement for oxygen and sulfur atoms.

Coordinate bond. In some cases, electron-pair bonds could be formed with both electrons being donated by one atom only. Such a bond was called a coordinate bond and may be illustrated by a group of compounds called the oxo acids of chlorine. Using dots for the outer-shell electrons, the structures are:

To indicate covalent bonds, a line was used, and the symbol usually employed for the coordinate bond was an arrow indicating the donation of the electrons, so that the oxo acids of chlorine could also be written as:

The assumed stability of the octet provided a most successful hypothesis for elements of low atomic number, and certain earlier difficulties were removed. Carbon monoxide, for instance, could have the structure

$$\colon C\colon\colon\colon O\colon \quad \text{or} \quad C\overset{\shortmid}{\underset{\shortmid}{\equiv}} O$$

Some difficulties remained, however; nitrogen oxide (NO), nitrogen dioxide (NO_2), and chlorine dioxide (ClO_2), each of which contains an odd number of electrons, are violations of the electron-pair concept.

In addition, the fluorides of phosphorus, PF_5, and sulfur, SF_6, were known. Since the bonds in these compounds behaved as single bonds, the most likely electronic structures were:

Expansion
of the
octet

Such a configuration required the assumption that the second shell could be expanded beyond the octet. (This discussion is still concerned with elements lighter than argon.) Empirically it appeared that the limit of this expansion was six pairs, the groupings SF_6, PF_6^-, and SiF_6^{2-} being known, but no molecules or ions that required an outermost bonding shell with more than 12. The sulfate ion, SO_4^{2-}, could then be represented by:

Nevertheless, the employment of the Lewis electron-pair bond was still based largely on empiricism and, in fact, it was only slightly less empirical than the 19th-century chemical bond, but its electrical character did serve to guide, in most important ways, the assembly of empirical knowledge. A particularly important example lay in the field of organic chemistry, where physical organic chemists were able to interpret subtle differences in behaviour by considering the polarization and polarizability (*i.e.*, the unequal distribution of charges to produce concentrations, or poles, of positive and negative charge) of the electronic bond; it led to concepts (such as the inductive effect) that have been vitally important during the last fifty years.

This phase in the history of chemical-bond theory ended with quantum mechanics and the provision of the basic equation governing electronic behavior. The application of the equation proved so difficult that empirical development continued to be a most important aspect of research.

Before studying the effect of quantum mechanics it is necessary to consider the earlier quantum theory and its importance to the understanding of atomic structure, a necessary precursor to the understanding of molecular structure and chemical bonding.

Atomic structure and bonding. In the first decades of the 20th century, development within the physical sciences was dominated by the quantum theory proposed in 1900 by Max Planck, a German physicist. Niels Bohr, a Danish physicist, and, later, others applied the quantum theory to atomic structure.

Electron arrangement. It was concluded that because energy was absorbed in finite quanta, or measurable units, by electrons, only certain electron orbits could occur; *i.e.*, an electron could not have energy in any amount but only in multiples of a finite quantity. These quantized orbits were designated and distinguished from one another by three quantum numbers that finally assumed

The
quantum
numbers

the following pattern. The principal quantum number, n, was related primarily to the size of the orbit and could have any integral value. These are the "shells," designated from innermost outward as K, L, M, N, O, P, etc. The subsidiary quantum number, designated as l, was related to the shape of the orbit. It could have the integral values for a given value of n from 0 to $(n-1)$, and it measured the angular momentum (resulting from orbital motion) of the electron. The third quantum number, designated m, was related to the orientation of the orbit and represented a magnetic property. It could have the integral values for any given value of l from $-l$ to $+l$. The letters s, p, d, f (sometimes called subshells) have come to be used to represent the value of the l quantum number, being equivalent to $l = 0, 1, 2, 3$, respectively. Hence, an orbit having $n = 3$ and $l = 1$ is described by the symbol $3p$. There are three such orbits, $3p_{-1}$, $3p_0$, and $3p_1$, in which the magnetic quantum number is given as a subscript. In atoms containing a number of electrons, the order of binding of the orbits is $1s, 2s, 2p, 3s, 3p, 4s, 3d, 4p, 5s, 4d, 5p, 6s, 4f, 5d, 6p, 7s$. Later it became necessary to assume that the electron had an intrinsic angular momentum (*i.e.*, it had a spin). A fourth quantum number had to be added, called the spin quantum number, which measured the orientation of this spin angular momentum about a given axis, prescribed, say, by a magnetic field; the spin angular momentum could have only two values, and two values of the spin quantum are, therefore, possible; these are designated as plus or minus one-half ($\pm\frac{1}{2}$). From spectroscopic and other evidence, Wolfgang Pauli, an Austrian physicist, concluded that it was impossible for two electrons in an atom to have the same four quantum numbers. As a consequence, each orbit had a capacity of two electrons spinning in different directions, each called an orbital. Accordingly, every electron in any atom can be defined according to the position it occupies in terms of the four quantum numbers. When an electron's energy was increased, it acquired different quantum numbers. The s orbitals could each hold two electrons; a set of np orbitals, with a given value of n, could hold six; a set of nd, ten, and a set of nf, 14. Atomic structures, defined by occupancy of orbitals, were then formed according to the principle whereby a number of electrons appropriate to the given atom or ion were "fed" into the sets of orbitals in order of their energy, each receiving electrons up to its capacity. The number of electrons in any subshell is indicated by a superscript, thus: $2s^2$ means two electrons in the s subshell of the second (L) shell; $3d^6$ means six electrons in the d subshell of the third (M) shell. The electronic structures of atoms occupying key positions in the periodic table are given in their ground, or least energy, states in the table herewith.

The stability of the electron pair in helium and in bonded hydrogen is accounted for by the completion of the $n = 1$ shell. The stability of the octet for elements in the next period (ending with neon) is caused by the completion of the $n = 2$ shell (one $2s$ and three $2p$ orbits). In the next period (ending with argon), the stability of the octet is caused by the filling of the $3s$ and $3p$ orbits. In these elements, however, the $3d$ orbits are also available, and it has been proposed that this is why the shell can be expanded beyond four pairs. This is not possible with the $n = 2$ shell, because the l quantum number is limited to 0 and 1 when $n = 2$. Consequently, nitrogen does not form pentavalent compounds whereas phosphorus does.

The stable
configura-
tion

Ion formation by transition elements. The formation of ions by the transition elements will now be examined. These are the elements in the centre of the table and they are classified as metals; *i.e.*, they tend to lose electrons in chemical reactions. Iron forms two simple ions: Fe^{2+} and Fe^{3+}. The electronic structure of the neutral iron atom, Fe, is $1s^2 2s^2 2p^6 3s^2 3p^6 3d^6 4s^2$; that of iron(II) ion (the iron atom having lost two electrons), Fe^{2+}, is $1s^2 2s^2 2p^6 3s^2 3p^6 3d^6$, and that of iron(III) ion (the atom having lost three electrons), Fe^{3+}, is $1s^2 2s^2 2p^6 3s^2 3p^6 3d^5$. There is no question here of losing electrons to achieve an octet structure as former theory assumed. The removal of one electron from an iron atom requires a considerable energy, the removal of a second more, of a third still more, and so on. There is no sudden rise, however, in the energy to remove a further electron as there was with sodium's second electron (discussed above). With the iron atom, electrons are being removed from $4s$ and $3d$ levels, the binding energies of which are not very different. The rise occurs because successive electrons are being withdrawn from an ion that has successively increasing, unbalanced positive charges. In forming a series of compounds with chlorine (the iron chlorides), the electrons removed from iron are trans-

Whole Orbital Occupation for the Least Energy States of a Number of Elements

element	1s	2s	2p	3s	3p	3d	4s	4p	4d	4f	5s	5p	5d	6s	6p	7s
Hydrogen	1															
Helium	2															
Lithium	2	1														
Elements between lithium and neon omitted																
Neon	2	2	6													
Sodium	2	2	6	1												
Elements between sodium and potassium omitted																
Potassium	2	2	6	2	6		1									
Elements between potassium and scandium omitted																
Scandium	2	2	6	2	6	1	2									
Elements between scandium and zinc omitted																
Zinc	2	2	6	2	6	10	2									
Gallium	2	2	6	2	6	10	2	1								
Elements between gallium and rubidium omitted																
Rubidium	2	2	6	2	6	10	2	6			1					
Elements between rubidium and yttrium omitted																
Yttrium	2	2	6	2	6	10	2	6	1		2					
Elements between yttrium and palladium omitted																
Palladium	2	2	6	2	6	10	2	6	10							
Elements between palladium and indium omitted																
Indium	2	2	6	2	6	10	2	6	10		2	1				
Elements between indium and cesium omitted																
Cesium	2	2	6	2	6	10	2	6	10		2	6		1		
Elements between cesium and lanthanum omitted																
Lanthanum	2	2	6	2	6	10	2	6	10		2	6	1	2		
Cerium	2	2	6	2	6	10	2	6	10	2	2	6		2		
Elements between cerium and ytterbium omitted																
Ytterbium	2	2	6	2	6	10	2	6	10	14	2	6		2		
Lutetium	2	2	6	2	6	10	2	6	10	14	2	6	1	2		
Elements between lutetium and mercury omitted																
Mercury	2	2	6	2	6	10	2	6	10	14	2	6	10	2		
Thallium	2	2	6	2	6	10	2	6	10	14	2	6	10	2	1	
Elements between thallium and francium omitted																
Francium	2	2	6	2	6	10	2	6	10	14	2	6	10	2	6	1
Elements following francium omitted																

Role of lattice energy

ferred to chlorine to give chloride ions. One can envisage the formation of the following iron chloride compounds, with their formulas: iron monochloride, Fe^+Cl^-; iron dichloride, $Fe^{2+}(Cl^-)_2$; iron trichloride, $Fe^{3+}(Cl^-)_3$; iron tetrachloride, $Fe^{4+}(Cl^-)_4$; etc. The lattice energy (that required to separate an ion from the lattice of ions forming the solid crystal) of these compounds (all are salts) would increase steadily. The question is, therefore: to what extent can the lattice energy outweigh the energy required to transfer an electron from the iron atom to the chlorine atom? The monochloride, FeCl, is unknown because the gain in lattice energy in forming the dichloride, $FeCl_2$, from FeCl is much more than sufficient to outbalance the energy to remove the second electron from the iron atom. At the next stage (going from $FeCl_2$ to the trichloride, $FeCl_3$), the energies are fairly evenly balanced, so both can be prepared. But the energy required to remove the fourth electron is so great that the increase in lattice energy between $FeCl_3$ and the tetrachloride, $FeCl_4$, would be inadequate to provide it. Hence, $FeCl_4$ is an impossible compound, energetically. Consequently, only the $FeCl_2$ and $FeCl_3$ forms are known.

The existence of such variable valency in the other transition elements can be explained in a similar way. The valency differences are single when simple ions are formed. The energy required to produce very highly charged ions is usually prohibitive for simple electrostatic reasons so that vanadium (V), for example, forms the ions V^{2+} and V^{3+}, but it is tetravalent only in the oxide VO_2, and shows a valency of 5 in such compounds as $VOCl_3$. The relative stability of the different valency states depends on the energy required to remove the electrons. In the series of transition elements iron, cobalt, nickel (Fe, Co, Ni), of increasing atomic number, electrons become increasingly difficult to remove, so that, while the ions Fe^{2+} and Fe^{3+} have comparable stability, the cobalt ion Co^{3+} is more difficult to form, and the nickel ion Ni^{3+} is extremely difficult to form. With the next element, the copper ion Cu^{3+} is unknown, and, in fact, it becomes possible to form the ion Cu^+ in addition to the ion Cu^{2+}.

Complex ions. Another feature of transition-metal ions is the ease with which they form complex ions. Thus, the iron(II) ion Fe^{2+} combines with cyanide ions, CN^-, to give the hexacyanoferrate(II) ion, $Fe(CN)_6^{4-}$. The Fe^{2+} ion has 12 fewer electrons than the next inert gas, krypton. Six electron-pair coordinate links from the cyanide ions to the iron, therefore, provide for the metal atom the same electron shell as that for krypton. The

Ligands

role of the cyanide ion in donating electrons to the iron ion makes the cyanide a ligand, which is defined in any compound as the atom or ion that provides some or all of the bonding pair of electrons to a central atom. Also, from Fe^{3+} the hexacyanoferrate(III) ion, $Fe(CN)_6^{3-}$, is formed, in which the iron atom is associated with a number of electrons that is one short of that for krypton. Many other complex ions are known in which the ligands can all be regarded as being bound to the central positive ion by lone pairs on the ligand, though the extent to which these are incorporated into the electron shells of the central atom varies.

The shape of these complexes has aroused great interest. Ions such as $Fe(CN)_6^{4-}$ are octahedral; that is, the attached groups are located at the corners of an octahedron. Ions such as tetrachloromercurate(II), $HgCl_4^{2-}$, are tetrahedral, but tetracyanonickelate(II), $Ni(CN)_4^{2-}$, is square planar. The explanation of these shapes will be considered later. More recently, interest has shifted from the shape to the study of the spectra (*i.e.*, the spectroscopic analysis of radiation absorbed and emitted by molecules gives evidence concerning their structure) of these complexes.

QUANTUM-MECHANICAL TREATMENT OF CHEMICAL BONDING

The early electronic theory of valency was, as has been said, largely empirical, and the older quantum theory was, in many respects, arbitrary. It dealt quantitatively with a few atomic properties, but it was completely unsuccessful in selecting quantized molecular orbits or making any calculations of the energies of electrons in molecules. Then, in 1924, Louis de Broglie, a French physicist, examined the possibility that particles such as electrons might show, in addition to properties of matter, other properties that were explicable only in terms of wave propagation. That electrons had wave properties was demonstrated by diffraction experiments (see ELECTRON). This observation was followed, in 1926, by a wave equation proposed by Erwin Schrödinger, an Austrian physicist, that provided, for the first time, an equation capable, in principle, of calculating the energy of any electronic system in any potential field. (Werner Heisenberg, a German physicist, simultaneously devised an equivalent scheme.) Hence, the energies of atoms and molecules could be calculated, in principle, exactly. Moreover, the equation allowed immediate approximate calculation. Researchers using this new wave mechanics obtained a value for the dissociation energy of the hydrogen molecule that was about three-quarters of the true one. No comparable success had ever been achieved before, yet, in less than ten years, others calculated this dissociation energy almost exactly. The discovery of the electron in 1897 had revealed the material of the chemical bond, but the introduction of quantum mechanics was perhaps even more important because, with it, the mechanics, dynamics, and energetics of these electrons could be, in principle, calculated exactly. The difficulty lay in the labour and length of such calculations, even for systems containing only two nuclei and only five or six electrons. In fact, progress with exact calculations has been very slow, and even with fast and high-capacity computers, it remains extremely slow. Consequently, less than exact quantum-mechanical calculations involving various approximations and varying degrees of empiricism have assumed great prominence, and new procedures and fresh variants of existing approximations are being proposed and tested all the time. Moreover, the new mechanics has naturally modified the scientific attitude to certain physical models and has introduced new ones. Though qualitative instead of quantitative, these attitudes are of great importance. Unfortunately, the natural desire to describe the quantum-mechanical phenomena in essentially classical and pictorial terms has produced a jargon such that those with little knowledge of quantum mechanics often have difficulty in separating the concepts that arise as a consequence of the approximations from those that are fundamental.

Atomic and molecular states and orbitals. Max Planck's quantum theory, in the hands of Danish physicist Niels Bohr, showed that stationary energy states could exist for atoms. Associated with each stationary state of the hydrogen atom (containing one electron) was an orbit, which was designated by three quantum numbers, n, l, and m; *i.e.*, each orbit was defined by a combination of three numbers representing different kinds of energy states. In atoms with more than one electron, the various electrons moved in several of these orbits, which were, by definition, associated with fixed energy levels; that is, they were quantized orbits. Quantum mechanics does not permit the degree of spatial precision implied by an orbit and, therefore, the orbits are replaced by the concept of orbitals.

In the 1930s a U.S. physicist, Robert Sanderson Mulliken, and others studied molecular energy states and the form of electron orbitals in molecules rather than in atoms. They concerned themselves first with symmetrical diatomic molecules (*e.g.*, those consisting of two atoms, of the same or different elements with comparable electronegativities), relating molecular orbitals to those of the component atoms of the molecule and tracing the changes that occur during the transition of configurations from those of widely separated atoms through the molecule to the united atom produced when the two nuclei became coincident—*i.e.*, fused into one nucleus. Schematic representations of the formation of united-atom orbitals from separated-atom orbitals and the corresponding energy relations are given in Figure 1 and Figure 2.

To understand schematic representation of chemical

Wave equation

Stationary state

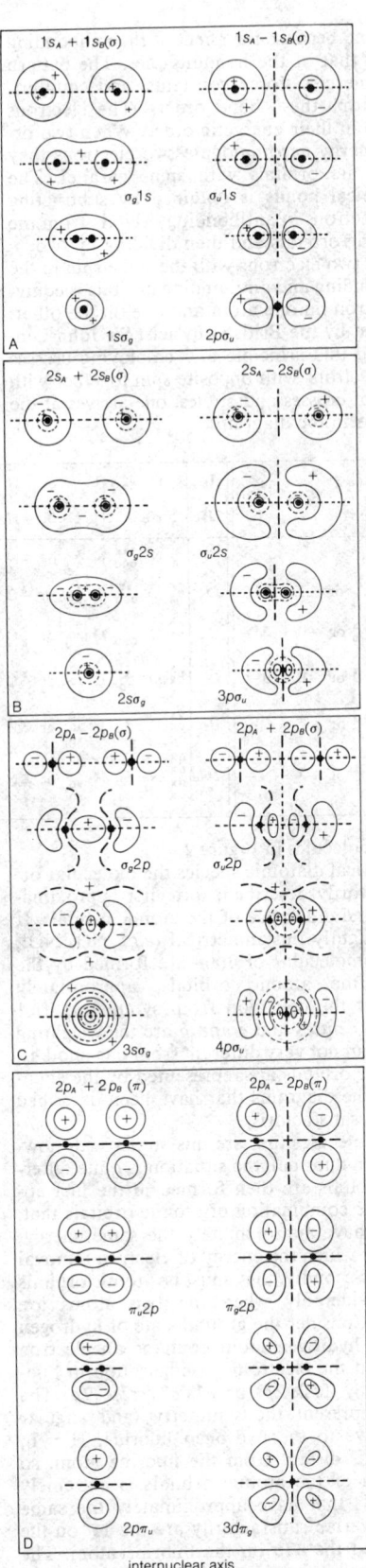

Figure 1: *Transition from separated-atom orbitals to united-atom orbitals for symmetric diatomic molecules.*
(A) Separated 1s orbitals to 1s (bonding) and 2p (antibonding) in the united atom. (B) Separated 2s orbitals to 2s (bonding) and 3p (antibonding). (C) Separated σ2p orbitals to 3s (bonding) and 4p (antibonding). (D) Separated 2pπ orbitals to 2p (bonding) and 3d (antibonding). These diagrams show general form of changes and are not accurate in detail.

bonding, a wider background is required than can be given in this article. (For such information see the articles PERIODIC LAW; ATOMIC STRUCTURE; ENERGY; ELECTRON; MECHANICS, QUANTUM.) When two atoms initially separated are brought together to form a molecule, the electrons in their outermost electron shell (*i.e.*, the electrons farthest from the nucleus), also called the valence electrons, and, in some cases, electrons from an inner shell combine, usually in pairs, and constitute the chemical bond (a covalent bond) that holds the atoms together. The valence electrons in the separated atoms occupy orbitals within the electron shell, designated as *s*, *p*, *d*, and *f*, orbitals corresponding to some orientation with respect to the nucleus (*e.g.*, an *s* orbital is spherically symmetrical; each of the three *p* orbitals is symmetrical about an axis running through the nucleus). An electron shell represents an energy level; integers called the principal quantum number (n) represent an ordering of the electron shells according to increasing energy levels. The letters K, L, M, N, etc., are also used to represent the ordering of the electron shells; *i.e.*, K represents $n = 1$; L represents $n = 2$. In atoms with fewer electrons, the orbitals within a shell have energies that are only slightly different from one another. For atoms with more electrons (hence more electron shells), the energy values of some orbitals, usually the *d* and *f* orbitals in a certain shell, overlap with the next higher energy shell. A complete description of an atomic orbital consists of a designation of the electron shell followed by the type of orbital—*i.e.*, 1s for the *s* orbital in the K ($n = 1$) shell.

Covalent bond in terms of orbitals

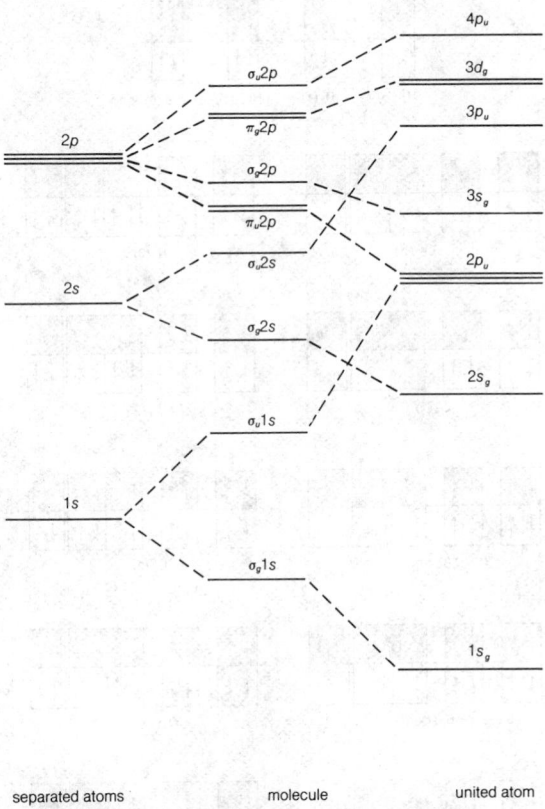

separated atoms   molecule   united atom
Figure 2: Energy level relationships, not drawn to scale. (See text.)

When two atoms unite to form a molecule, certain orbitals combine, forming a new orbital that encompasses the two atomic nuclei (a molecular orbital). One way in which a molecular orbital is formed is by the combination of similar atomic orbitals. Each pair of similar orbitals (*e.g.*, 1s on each atom) leads to two molecular orbitals; one is the sum of the two atomic orbitals creating a new orbital that encompasses the two nuclei, but the other is the difference of the two orbitals creating a new orbital consisting of two parts, each one on either side of the two nuclei (in physical terms, this type of orbital

Anti-
bonding
orbitals

is nodal). The molecule whose bonding electrons occupy orbitals with a node tends to be unstable, and this type of orbital is called an antibonding orbital. Molecular orbitals are represented by the same symbols used for atomic orbitals (*e.g.*, *s*, *p*, *d*, etc.) together with the Greek symbols sigma (σ) or pi (π) corresponding to symmetrical or antisymmetrical orbitals, a symmetrical orbital being one that does not change its sign when rotated about an axis lying in the molecular plane. Occasionally, the Greek symbols are also included in the description of atomic orbitals. The subscripts *g* and *u* are used to distinguish between bonding and antibonding orbitals.

Figure 3 shows the pattern of orbitals and the energy levels in a given state of a given molecule. In assigning electrons to the orbitals, each electron will be repre-

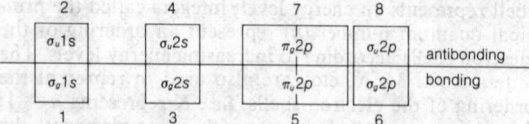

Figure 3: Orbital patterns. Numbers represent order on an energy scale. Compare Figures 1 and 2.

sented by an arrow, the orientation of spin ($+\frac{1}{2}$ or $-\frac{1}{2}$) being indicated by the direction of the arrow (up or down). Figure 4 shows the orbital occupation for the ground states of H_2^+, H_2, He_2^+, He_2, Li_2^+, Li_2, $2Be$, B_2, C_2, N_2^+, N_2, O_2^+, O_2, O_2^-, F_2, and $2Ne$. Two helium atoms

do not form a bond because the effect of the antibonding electrons cancels that of the bonding ones. The pattern of dissociation energies, force constants, and equilibrium lengths confirms these bond orders. The electrons enter the orbitals in their energetic order. When two orbitals of equal energy accommodate two electrons they occupy the separate orbitals with spins parallel. The number of chemical bonds is obtained by subtracting the number of electrons in antibonding orbitals from the number in bonding orbitals and then dividing by two.

The presence of two electrons with the same spin in the corresponding bonding and antibonding orbitals is equivalent to one electron on one atom and one on the other, as was pointed out by the British physicist Sir John Lennard-Jones. Using this principle and employing crosses and circles for electrons with opposite spin together with a line for a pair of crosses and circles, one arrives at the chemical formulas in the diagram:

[Table of chemical formulas with crosses and circles for diatomic species: H_2^+, He_2^+, Li_2^+, Li_2, $2Be$, B_2, C_2, N_2^+ in left column; H_2, $2He$, N_2, O_2^+, O_2, O_2^-, F_2, $2Ne$ in right column]

for the diatomic molecules in Figure 2.

Symmetrical
diatomic
molecules

In these symmetrical diatomic species the molecular orbitals are satisfactorily described, to a first approximation, by the sum and difference of the atomic orbitals. If the molecule is slightly unsymmetrical (*e.g.*, NO, NO^+, or CO), then the molecular orbitals are formed by the combination of the atomic orbitals, appropriately weighted to reflect the deviation from symmetry; if A and B are the two centres and a and b are the weighting factors not equal but not very different from one another, then the molecular orbitals are represented by the equation $a\psi_A \pm b\psi_B$. The diagrams that have been described so far can be used satisfactorily.

With diatomic molecules that are unsymmetrical, however (*e.g.*, hydrogen fluoride), the situation is quite different. Molecular orbitals are then formed in the first approximation by the combination of atomic orbitals that, in the first place, have approximately the same energy; that is, orbitals for which the energy of electron removal is about the same. Secondly, they must be atomic orbitals that overlap considerably when the two atoms are brought together. Consider the ground state of hydrogen fluoride, HF; the hydrogen atom contains an electron in a $1s$ orbital, and the electronic configuration in fluorine is described by $1s^2 2s^2 2p^5$ or $\sigma 1s^2 \sigma 2s^2 \pi 2p^4 \sigma 2p$. The Greek symbols represent the symmetry (and angular momentum) relative to the hydrogen fluoride, H — F, axis; the H atom is distant from the fluorine atom, so that the distortion of the atomic orbitals is extremely small. The orbitals that have approximately the same energy and that overlap satisfactorily are the $1s$ on the hydrogen atom and the $\sigma 2p$ on the fluorine atom. The molecule of hydrogen fluoride will, therefore, be described by: $1s\sigma_F^2 2s\sigma_F^2 2p\pi_F^4 \sigma 2p_{HF}^2$, and the corresponding chemical formula is $-\overset{..}{F}-H$ (the K shell on the fluorine atom being omitted). There will be, of course, an antibonding orbital that is the difference of the orbitals $2p\sigma_F$ and $1s\sigma_H$ corresponding to the bonding orbital that has been labelled $\sigma 2p_{HF}$.

The description used above for hydrogen fluoride constitutes a first approximation. The orbitals of the hydrogen fluoride molecule, $1s\sigma_F$, $2s\sigma_F$, and $\sigma 2p_{HF}$, all have the

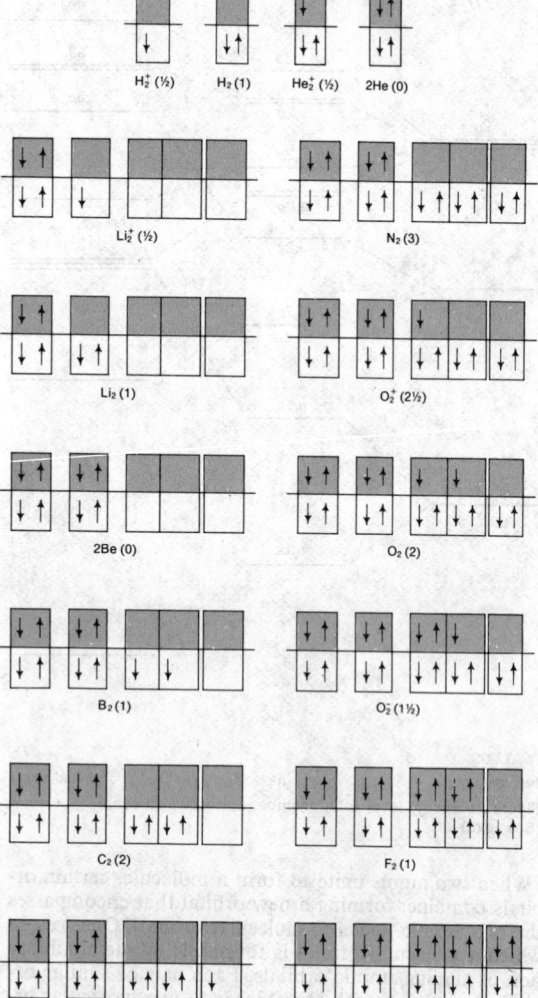

Figure 4: Orbital occupation of lowest states of several symmetrical diatomic systems containing from one to twenty electrons. Number of chemical bonds shown in parentheses. The shaded boxes represent antibonding orbitals; the unshaded boxes, bonding orbitals.

same symmetry with respect to the hydrogen fluoride axis. They are axially symmetric. A better description will be obtained by allowing mixing of some orbitals. The $1s\sigma_F$ orbital (K shell) is, however, so much lower in energy than the others that it will not mix in very much. If $2s\sigma_F$ and $2p\sigma_F$ are combined with the same sign, the resulting orbital projects more towards the proton, while if they are combined with opposite sign, the resulting orbital projects away from the proton. The improved orbitals are formed by the addition of all the atomic orbitals, as shown in the equation, in which a, b, and c represent the weighting factors: $a2s\sigma_F + b2p\sigma_F + c1s\sigma_H$, where a is smaller than b and c, and by the difference of the two orbitals of the fluorine atom, $d2s\sigma_F - e2p\sigma_F$, d being much greater than e (a to e are all positive). The first orbital accommodates the bonding pair (*i.e.*, the electron pair that constitutes the chemical bond between hydrogen and fluorine), the latter the lone pair on the fluorine atom. The bond diagram, therefore, is not altered. The combinations of $2s\sigma_F$ and $2p\sigma_F$ are called hybrid orbitals, and the procedure of mixing atomic orbitals in this way is termed hybridization. In this case the bonding orbital is formed by combining a $2s2p$ hybrid orbital on fluorine with a $1s$ orbital on hydrogen.

The hydrogen molecule. Before proceeding to polyatomic molecules, the results of various quantum-mechanical treatments of the hydrogen molecule consisting of two hydrogen atoms will be described. The simple molecular-orbital (MO) function of this most simple of all molecules leads to an energy (*e.g.*, a weighted mean energy) value lower (by about 70 kilocalories per molecular weight in grams, or kilocalories per mole) than that of two free hydrogen atoms (the true value being 109.5 kilocalories per mole). An important theorem of molecular quantum mechanics (the variation theorem) states that this weighted mean energy must be greater than the true energy of the system. Hence, the calculated dissociation energy for the hydrogen molecule must be too small. The best dissociation energy that can be obtained using a treatment in which both electrons occupy the same molecular orbital without any allowance for the effect of interelectron repulsion on electron distribution is 85 kilocalories per mole.

The first treatment of the hydrogen molecule was by the German physicists Walter H. Heitler and Fritz London, one year after Schrödinger published his equation, and it was startling in its significance in that it showed that a calculation based on the new mechanics yielded a molecular dissociation energy of the right order of magnitude. The wave function consisted of two terms. In the first, one electron occupied the $1s$ orbital on one hydrogen atom and the other occupied the $1s$ orbital on the other atom. In the second, which was added to the first, the electrons were interchanged. In effect this function favoured the electrons being situated at opposite ends of the molecule, compared with the simple molecular-orbital function, which used the same orbital for both electrons. Later, the scale of the two atomic functions was adjusted to minimize the energy. The dissociation energy was then calculated to be 87 kilocalories per mole. This shows how strong is the mutual tendency of the electrons to repel one another and stay apart, and how important, therefore, is the allowance that must be made for such electron correlation. By including only the terms that locate the electrons in separate atomic orbitals the Heitler–London treatment rather overdid this correlation; terms were added to the Heiter–London function that assigned both electrons to the same atomic orbital, then weighting this structure to minimize the energy. This was described by the phrase covalent–ionic resonance, meaning that the true structure lay between the two extremes or that the structure could be best described by assuming that its details were considered a combination of two possible structures, one ionic and the other involving an idealized non-polar covalent bond. The terms in the Heitler–London equations were taken to represent the truly covalent form, using a line to represent the pair of bonding electrons: H—H. Assigning both electrons to the same atom is symbolized as an association of negative and positive ions: H^-H^+ and H^+H^-. Linus Pauling, a U.S. chemist, proposed the name resonance for this mixing of wave functions, the mixing being used to achieve a better total wave function.

Consequently, though it appeared first in time, the Heitler–London function is perhaps best regarded as one that includes (in fact, overincludes) some allowance for electron correlation in the simple molecular-orbital function. Later, electron correlation was added specifically in the function, values involving the interelectron separation being included. This was first done in the mid-1930s to achieve a dissociation energy only slightly less than the true value. This magnificent achievement was improved 25 years later by researchers who obtained a dissociation energy more precise than the existing experimental value.

Such accurate calculations cannot be performed for systems containing more than three or four electrons, so that the above methods cannot be extended to more complex species of molecules. Also, the Heitler–London method (the valence-bond method) cannot be extended as simply to polyelectronic systems as can the molecular-orbital method. Consequently, molecular quantum mechanics in the post-World War II period has been almost entirely based on the molecular-orbital method. An additional reason for this is that orbitals that are unoccupied are given by conventional molecular-orbital calculations. This means that electronic excitation can be described, and, hence, the spectra of molecules can be discussed and even predicted (the absorption and emission of electromagnetic radiation, such as light, is related to changes in occupation of the electron orbitals; the pattern of emitted or absorbed radiation is called the spectrum, and it is studied by spectroscopic methods). In fact, one development that has been associated with the growth of the molecular-orbital method has been an increased interest in visible and ultraviolet spectra, though it is not easy to say which is cause and which is effect.

The simple molecular-orbital function for the hydrogen molecule is that in which both electrons are assigned to the same orbital. If the two atoms are labelled A and B, then their electrons occupy the $1s_A$ and $1s_B$ orbitals; in the molecule they occupy the orbital that can be most simply designated by $(1s_A + 1s_B)$. In the same way that the Heitler–London function was improved by adding ionic terms to covalent terms (resonance), the simple molecular-orbital function can also be improved by adding other functions that involve assigning electrons to other molecular orbitals. This procedure is called configuration interaction, but in principle it is the same as resonance. For instance, a second function in which both electrons are assigned to the antibonding orbital ($1s_A - 1s_B$) can be added with a weight or value which minimizes the energy. Additional configuration, to an extent that is limited only by the availability of computer time and capacity, can be used by assigning both electrons to the $2s$ bonding orbitals or both to the $2s$ antibonding orbital. In addition, the configuration that include p orbitals can be used. The use of configuration interaction serves to adjust the precise spatial form (the three-dimensional geometric shape) of the wave function and also to allow for electron correlation. It is a procedure that has come to be widely used in calculations for polyatomic molecules.

Simple polyatomic molecules. It is best to begin a study of polyatomic molecules with those symmetric molecules consisting of two hydrogen atoms bonded to a single atom of any element with an atomic number between those of beryllium (Be) and oxygen (O) in the periodic table. If H represents the hydrogen atoms and A the other atom, then HAH is the formula. As with diatomic (two-atom) molecules, the molecular orbitals are constructed by taking linear combinations of atomic orbitals (LCAO). The K-shell orbital (the innermost shell, for which $n = 1$, and containing only two electrons, both in the s orbital) on the atom A is little changed in molecule formation, so that the valence-, or outermost, shell atomic orbitals (in the case of these elements the L shell, for which $n = 2$) to be combined with one another are

Hybridization

Covalent-ionic resonance

The molecular spectrum

the two atomic orbitals of the hydrogen atom, designated as $1s_H'$ and $1s_H''$, and the $2s$ and $2p$ orbitals on the atom of element A.

If the HAH molecule is bent, there are two planes of symmetry; one of the whole molecule cutting through HAH, and another one perpendicular to the first plane and passing through the A atom only, thus dividing the two AH bonds on either side onto opposite sides of the plane. Molecular orbitals must be symmetric or antisymmetric to this plane. The contributing atomic orbitals remain the same. These orbitals can be diagrammed, and a study of the diagrams enables certain predictions to be made.

In beryllium hydride, BeH_2, there are four electrons outside the K shell ($n = 1$), and the molecule is linear. Lithium hydride ion, LiH_2^+, has two electrons outside the K shell and is probably bent, and it is better to write it as a combination of the lithium ion and a hydrogen molecule: Li^+H_2. The fifth electron in boron hydride, BH_2, makes the molecule bent, the third orbital (for the fifth electron) strongly favouring a nonlinear form. The molecule of the hydride of carbon, CH_2, with no unpaired electrons (singlet) is also bent. On the other hand, the lowest (triplet) state of CH_2 (with two unpaired electrons) is linear, which could not be anticipated directly from the diagram. The hydride of nitrogen, actually the amine radical NH_2, with seven electrons, and the hydride of oxygen, actually water, OH_2, with eight electrons outside the K shell, are both bent, as would be expected from the diagram. It is interesting that the angles formed by the two hydrogens in CH_2, NH_2, and OH_2 are almost the same ($104°$, $103\frac{1}{4}°$, $104\frac{1}{2}°$), confirming that the effect of filling the fourth ($2p$) orbital in the L shell has no effect on shape; it remains a $2p$ atomic orbital whether the molecule is linear or bent.

Diagrams of a similar kind that have been drawn for other systems have proved to be extremely useful and have maintained their basic correctness extraordinarily well with the passage of time.

In the case of diatomic molecules, the situation outlined was that two electrons with parallel spins (*i.e.*, unpaired electrons) occupying corresponding bonding and antibonding orbitals could be regarded equally as occupying the component atomic orbitals, which are, in fact, the sum and difference of the bonding and antibonding orbitals. Analogously, in the present case with three atoms, electrons with the same spin occupying the two bonding orbitals can equally be regarded as occupying sum and difference orbitals. Likewise, the nonbonding orbitals in the bent molecule can be transformed into two equivalent orbitals capable of accommodating lone pairs. In this way it is possible to arrive at an equal formulation that does, however, correspond to the more classical concepts of chemical bonds. The correspondence between this and the conventional molecular-orbital formulation can be shown. These two formulations are equal to one another. The first, the simple molecular-orbital formulation, is the more suitable one for discussing and describing electron excitation and electron removal and addition. The latter is more suitable for considering more conventional chemical behaviour, which historically has been more usually examined on the basis of localized chemical bonds. If the description of two electrons occupying the same bond orbital is modified to resemble that used by Heitler and London for the bond in the hydrogen molecule, then the conventional valence-bond molecular wave function is obtained.

The compound acetylene, C_2H_2, containing four atoms, can be treated in the same way. The $1s$ orbitals on the two hydrogen atoms and the $2s$ and $2p$ orbitals on the two carbon atoms combine together to give three molecular orbitals that are symmetric to the central plane and three that are antisymmetric to the central plane. Of the first group, two are bonding (one mainly C–H bonding and the other mainly C–C bonding), while one is antibonding. Of the second group, one is mainly C–H bonding, while two are antibonding. The three bonding orbitals contain electron pairs and can be transformed to give an alternative description based on localized C–H

and C–C bond orbitals. The degenerate pair of $2p$ orbitals on the two carbons combine to give a degenerate pair of C–C-bonding orbitals and a degenerate pair of antibonding orbitals. The bonding pairs are filled. Consequently, the C–C bond is a triple bond.

The next example is ozone, a molecule consisting of three oxygen atoms, O_3. Two end atoms of oxygen are bonded to a central one. The arrangement is nonlinear, and all the bonding and nonbonding orbitals are fully occupied, while the antibonding orbitals are empty. Combinations that give localized orbitals can be made. If each localized orbital is represented by a line, the disposition of these orbitals will show that two orbitals are bonding and five are nonbonding. Again, the bonding and nonbonding orbitals contain electron pairs. These orbitals are referred to, rather loosely, as the pi or π-orbitals; however, it is not possible to transform the description based on the filled π-bonding and π-nonbonding orbitals into one single localized description, though it is possible to transform the molecular-orbital description into a combination of localized descriptions.

Quantum-mechanical calculations. The first molecular quantum-mechanical calculation was that of Heitler and London for the hydrogen molecule. As stated earlier, this has been improved with the help of the variation theorem, so that now an effectively exact treatment of the hydrogen molecule exists. Extension of such exact methods to other molecules has been extremely slow, even though the speed and capacity of computers has greatly increased.

Approximate treatments are basically of two kinds: (1) nonempirical, in which calculations are based on an approximate wave-function but an exact expression for the potential and kinetic energies, the success depending on the completeness and flexibility of the function and the art and skill with which it is chosen; (2) empirical, in which a full or approximate energy expression may be used together with an approximate wave function, the values of integrals being chosen to reproduce certain experimental results (some integrals are often set equal to zero) and these used to derive others.

The best known empirical calculations are those that treat the π-orbitals of certain types of molecules called conjugated (butadiene, benzene, naphthalene, pyridine, etc.) using a method called linear combinations of atomic orbitals. This treatment simplifies the calculation to the point that only integrals involving orbitals on the same and adjacent atoms are used, others being assumed to be zero. Moreover, the treatment considers each electron separately, giving the energy as a sum of one-electron energies. This treatment is an extremely simple one, and it yields bond energies, ionization potentials, charge distribution, and other quantities. Improved and developed by many workers, it has been extremely valuable in the development of the quantitative and semiquantitative application of quantum mechanics. The changes introduced usually involved increased complexity and the inclusion of integrals that earlier treatments had omitted. Allowance was also made increasingly for the effect of neighbouring atoms.

Self-consistent field method. In the first decade of quantum mechanics, what is called the self-consistent field method for treating atoms was developed. Using a system of successive approximation, each occupied orbital was determined to satisfy the Schrödinger equation for the nuclear field plus that arising from the averaged distribution of the other electrons. Originally, electron exchange was not included in the function, but this was added later in a special form and has been extended to molecules. The molecular orbitals are constructed from a set of atomic orbitals. The more of these that are included in the basis set, the better is the accuracy achieved. A minimum basis set contains the smallest possible number of atomic orbitals. Calculations have been carried out, using minimum basis sets, for a number of molecules containing atoms of the first and second short periods in the periodic table, and questions of bonding have been investigated; calculations with larger basis sets have been made for simple molecules. Bond lengths and other properties are obtained in satisfying agreement with experiment. Such self-consistent field calculations approach the best that can be achieved by functions that assign electrons to molecular orbitals in pairs, and they approach this limit more closely the larger the basis set. The effect of electron repulsion between orbitals is included, but the mutual effect within the pairs is not. The method must always, therefore, be limited, and, in fact, because of this, occasionally it fails completely. The diatomic fluorine molecule, F_2, for example, is calculated to be unstable relative to two fluorine atoms. The difference between the best value for the calculated energy and the true energy is called the correlation energy; it is a measure of the energy reduction arising from the tendency of the electrons within the pairs to keep apart.

Extension of method. In order to make it possible to extend the self-consistent field method to larger molecules of greater chemical interest, various empirical developments have been made. To begin with, all integrals involving overlap distributions arising from different atomic orbitals were set equal to zero; however, this was found to be an excessive simplification, and, at the present time, various empirical methods that involve an intermediate neglect of differential overlap are being developed and employed. They have achieved considerable success, sometimes as an aid to interpretation and sometimes in providing useful numerical results. It should be stressed that their strength lies in their empirical approach, which derives the values of the integrals used from appropriate experimental data. The reason they have great merit is that all electrons are included. Further developments along these lines may be expected during the next few years.

Many special methods have been introduced, but all too frequently the greater complexity limits their range of application. Special mention ought to be given to empirical and nonempirical methods of attempting to determine electron correlation energy so that the power of the self-consistent field method can be made more useful.

The ultimate aim, of course, must be to increase the range of accurate calculations, and some of the work done suggests that progress is possible. It is quite clear, however, that at present only approximate methods, both of an empirical and of a nonempirical kind, are available for many species of great chemical interest.

Other bonding effects. The most important types of chemical bonding to the chemist are electrovalent and covalent. There is an important special kind, however, in some molecules, called hydrogen bonding. It occurs, for example, in the association of two water molecules in which one hydrogen of one molecule is oriented toward the oxygen of the other molecule. It is also present in a particularly strong form in the hydrogen difluoride ion, HF_2^-, in which the hydrogen nucleus, or proton, lies between the two fluorine atoms. The dissociation energy of most hydrogen bonds is about five kilocalories per mole, which is approximately one-tenth that of most covalent bonds. The hydrogen bond results when the hydrogen atom in a molecule carries a residual positive charge and the receptor atom in the other molecule is negative and contains lone electron pairs. Hydrogen bonding may be intermolecular, as shown in the above example, or intramolecular, as in *o*-chlorophenol, the hydrogen of the hydroxyl being attracted by a lone pair on the neighbouring chlorine atom. Association resulting from hydrogen bonding can produce increased viscosity and increased boiling point in liquids, and it can be of great importance in crystalline structures (*e.g.*, ice and oxalic acid), as well as in such organic molecules as proteins.

Metallic bonds. The bonding in metals and alloys is another form of internuclear binding with distinctive properties. In this case, the valence-shell electrons are strongly delocalized and, therefore, treatments concentrating on this feature are important. The overlap of orbitals of the array of atoms in a solid metal produces bands of energy levels, the constituent orbitals of which are often only partly filled. Electronic properties (*e.g.*, conductivity) have been treated successfully using this approach.

Bonds in crystals. In solids and liquids instantaneous polarization forces between atoms and molecules, called van der Waals forces, are important. They provide the cohesive forces in the crystals of covalent compounds, and they are also important in the interaction of non-bonded atoms in molecules. They do not produce what is normally understood to be a chemical bond, however.

There has been great interest recently in stereospecific reactions, in which there is a close relationship between the three-dimensional geometry of reactants and products. The relation observed can be explained by considering the symmetry of the molecular orbitals and the requirement that the new bond must be formed by the overlap of those lobes of the contributing orbitals that have the same sign. The interpretation of these results has provided one of the great recent triumphs of molecular-orbital theory.

EXPERIMENTAL OBSERVATIONS OF BONDING

From measured heats of combination and other laboratory data, it is possible to derive the heats of formation of molecules from atoms. This can lead to a set of bond energies. It is found that the energy of a particular bond (*e.g.*, the carbon–hydrogen bond) remains fairly constant through a range of molecules. Discrepancies between heats of formation calculated by transferring the value of bond energies in one molecule to another and observed values led to concepts such as resonance.

Molecular dipole moments (the electrical moment of a molecule that has one end positive, the other equally negative) obtained by measuring dielectric constants reflect the overall electron distribution and have been used to assess quantum-mechanical calculations of molecular structures. Changes of dipole moments during molecular vibrations are also useful in the discussion of charge distribution. Molecular polarizabilities and their changes upon distortion as derived from spectroscopic studies (specifically, Raman spectra) also provide information about electronic structures.

Molecular shape, bond length, and bond angles are particularly important in the consideration of electronic structures. There is, in carbon–carbon bonds, for example, a relation between observed bond length and calculated bond order. The interpretation of these quantities has been most important in the development of the application of quantum mechanics to molecular structure. Experimental methods used, include spectroscopy, and electron, neutron, and X-ray diffraction.

The nuclei can be used to probe the electronic structures of molecules; for instance, in nuclear magnetic resonance spectroscopy (the study of radiation absorbed by the nucleus when it is placed in a magnetic field), the nuclear magnetic moment (the nucleus acting as a magnet) interacts with the surrounding electrons, called the electron cloud, and the position of absorption (*i.e.*, the chemical shift) can be used to obtain information about this electron cloud and the way in which it is affected by bonding. Other interactions of the nucleus and the electric field at the nucleus can also be used to obtain information about the surrounding electrons. Experimental data are obtained from microwave spectra. The radiation absorbed on reorienting electron spin can be used to study the spin distribution within a molecule. This is valuable for checking the wave functions of radicals (groups of atoms containing an odd number of electrons). Also, particularly for inorganic complex ions, measurements of magnetic susceptibility are valuable for determining such quantities as the number of electrons possessing unpaired spins. These data are invaluable in the determination of electronic structures.

Since the 1960s the distribution of the energy of electrons ejected from molecules by quanta of electromagnetic radiation has been widely studied. Called photoelectron spectroscopy, it provides the best means of determining molecular-orbital energies and has proved invaluable because the results obtained experimentally are related directly to those obtained from molecular-orbital calculations. Ultraviolet and visible spectra give differ-

Margin notes:

Trends in calculating molecular bond structures

Hydrogen bonding

Stereospecific reactions

ences of energies between molecular-orbital energies and are therefore also valuable for obtaining information of a similar kind. In fact, the growth of molecular-orbital calculations has been encouraged by their ability to interpret the energies of electronic excitation and removal.

There are, therefore, many methods for making observations on the spatial distribution of the electrons and their energies. Because the electrons provide chemical bonding, such observations are of direct importance to understanding the phenomenon. The development of further understanding of electronic structure and chemical bonding depends, therefore, on bringing together the quantum-mechanical theory of electronic behaviour and those molecular properties that are most directly related in one way or another to the electronic distribution.

BIBLIOGRAPHY

Historical works: G.N. LEWIS, "The Atom and the Molecule," *J. Am. Chem. Soc.*, 38:762–785 (1916), the electron-pair bond concept introduced by its originator; N.V. SIDGWICK, *The Electronic Theory of Valency* (1927), a clear statement of the pre-quantum mechanics position; LINUS PAULING, *The Nature of the Chemical Bond and the Structure of Molecules and Crystals*, 3rd ed. (1960), the pre-war position.

Basic works: H. EYRING, J.E. WALTER, and G.E. KIMBALL, *Quantum Chemistry* (1944), an explanation of the techniques of quantum chemistry; F.O. RICE and E. TELLER, *The Structure of Matter* (1949), for the general reader; Y.K. SYRKIN and M.E. DYATKINA, *Structure of Molecules and the Chemical Bond* (1950; orig. pub. in Russian, 1946), based on Pauling's approach; C.A. COULSON, *Valence*, 2nd ed. (1961), an introduction to the semiquantization application of quantum mechanics; K.S. PITZER, *Quantum Chemistry* (1953), an account of the qualitative importance of quantum mechanics; E. CARTMELL and G.W.A. FOWLES, *Valency and Molecular Structure* (1956), for the general reader; J.W. LINNETT, *Wave Mechanics and Valency* (1960), a simple introduction; *The Electronic Structure of Molecules* (1964), description of a particular approach; J.C. SLATER, *Electronic Structure of Molecules* (1963), a lengthy analysis; J.C. SPEAKMAN, *A Valency Primer* (1968), a qualitative introduction for the beginner; M.W. HANNA, *Quantum Mechanics in Chemistry*, 2nd ed. (1969), an introductory book.

Chemical Compounds, Classifications of

A chemical compound is a substance made up of identical molecules containing atoms of two or more elements. Millions of chemical compounds are known; millions more probably exist in nature; and still other millions may be synthesized in the laboratory. The known compounds differ from one another in almost every conceivable way. Some, such as water, are colourless; others, the dyes and pigments, embody every colour of the rainbow. Some are light gases at ordinary temperatures; others, dense solids. Some are chemically inert; others, so unstable that they exist for only fractions of a second. In order to deal with the bewildering mass of diverse information about this multitude of substances, chemists have devised a number of classification schemes. These provide rational ways of organizing all chemical compounds, known or still to be discovered, into related groups of similar and dissimilar substances.

In any systematic classification, of course, chemical compounds must themselves be distinguished from other forms of matter. Most matter encountered by man in his everyday life consists of mixtures of two or more basic substances. Generally, such mixtures can be separated by physical means—as, for example, salt is separated from seawater when the water is evaporated. The basic, or pure, substances themselves are either atoms, or aggregates of atoms, of elements or molecules of compounds. Because the molecules of compounds contain atoms of several elements, compounds can be broken down into their elements by chemical reactions.

Molecular formulas represent the compositions of compounds in terms of the specific elements that constitute them—that is, in terms of what is called their elemental composition. Such formulas consist of the chemical symbols of the elements involved, along with numerical subscripts that indicate the numbers of atoms of each kind in the molecules. Thus, the formula for water, H_2O, in-

dicates that a molecule of water contains two atoms of hydrogen and one of oxygen.

Among the most useful schemes for the classification of chemical compounds are those based on (1) the elemental composition of the compound, (2) the types of bonds that exist between the atoms in their molecules, and (3) the varieties of chemical reactions they undergo. Several other, less important classification methods are used for certain special purposes.

Classification by elemental composition. *Organic compounds.* Early in the 19th century, chemists began to classify chemical compounds found in or produced by living organisms as organic. By contrast, compounds from nonliving sources, such as minerals, were classified as inorganic. Like the biological materials from which they come, organic compounds, such as sugar or alcohol, either burn or char when heated in air; inorganic compounds, such as limestone or table salt, either are inert toward heating or undergo specific characteristic transformations not associated with decomposition. Although it has been known since 1828 that typical organic compounds can be synthesized in the laboratory from inorganic compounds without the involvement of living organisms, the name organic still is used to refer to this group of compounds. Generally, organic compounds are simply compounds of carbon—except for simple compounds containing only carbon and oxygen and minerals, such as limestone or marble. Compounds involving elements other than carbon are classed as inorganic.

Though carbon is only one element among 105, it is thought that the number of carbon compounds is larger than the number of compounds of all other elements put together. Carbon atoms form strong bonds with the atoms of nonmetals, such as hydrogen, oxygen, nitrogen, and chlorine, but the large number of carbon compounds is due to the fact that carbon atoms also are able to form strong bonds with other carbon atoms. The atoms of no other element bond to one another to the same extent or in the same variety of ways as carbon atoms do. Carbon atoms join together in chains or rings that function as molecular backbones to which atoms of other elements are attached. These chains can vary in length from two carbon atoms, as in ethane (symbolized by the formula C_2H_6), a component of natural gas, to hundreds of thousands of carbon atoms, as in polyethylene, a manufactured polymer used to make household utensils and fibres. Each carbon atom in any chain has attached to it a variety of atoms or groups of atoms, which may also be other carbon chains. Molecules consisting of simple carbon chains have been called aliphatic ever since the early discovery that they occurred in fatty substances (Greek *aleiphar-*, "fat"). In contrast, certain compounds consisting of chains of carbon atoms whose ends are joined to form rings, of which a prototype molecule is benzene, C_6H_6, are called aromatic compounds, a name originally chosen because of the odour associated with coal tar, in which such molecules typically are found. The discovery that benzene is a ring of six carbon atoms, rather than a chain, was one of the dramatic breakthroughs in 19th-century science. Generally, aliphatic and aromatic compounds behave quite differently, and the subclassification of organic compounds into these two large families, aliphatic and aromatic, is a natural one. Ring compounds are also called cyclic compounds.

Organic compounds often contain special groups of atoms called functional groups, which readily undergo chemical reaction. Because these functional groups dominate the chemistry of the compounds that contain them, they provide a convenient way of classifying organic compounds. Alcohols, ethers, aldehydes, ketones, and carboxylic acids are typical examples of organic compounds classified by the functional groups they contain.

Inorganic compounds. The periodic table provides the chemist with his most comprehensive scheme for classification of the elements. Consequently, it also serves as a starting point for the classification of inorganic compounds, which, as mentioned above, are compounds of elements other than carbon. One convenient way to classify inorganic compounds is by grouping together all of

(margin) Organic compounds

(margin) Aliphatic and aromatic compounds

the compounds of a particular element. This is especially useful with compounds containing atoms of only two elements (binary compounds), which are designated commonly by the suffix -ide. Thus, the compound sodium chloride (symbolized by the formula NaCl), or table salt, is formed by the combination of the metallic element sodium (Na) with the nonmetallic element chlorine (Cl). Chlorides of other metallic elements are known, and the general class of chlorides often are grouped together. This type of classification can easily be extended to other elements of the chlorine family in the periodic table, which form compounds similar to the chlorides. Members of this family are known as halogens (salt formers). Consequently, the binary compounds formed by this family of elements are called by the generic name halides. Familiar examples of halides are sodium fluoride (NaF), the material added to drinking water to prevent tooth decay, and silver iodide (AgI), a substance used in making photographic films.

Other examples of classifying together the binary compounds of a single element are the binary compounds of hydrogen, known as hydrides, those of oxygen, called oxides; and those of sulfur, called sulfides. Like the halogen elements, most elements within a single vertical file, or group, of the periodic table form similar compounds. For example, all of the elements of the family known as the alkali metals form similar chlorine compounds, which are known collectively as the alkali chlorides. Similarly, the elements of the family known as the alkaline-earth metals form oxygen compounds known as the alkaline-earth oxides.

Similar principles apply to the classification of inorganic compounds composed of more than two elements. In naming these compounds, suffixes and prefixes are employed along with roots. The suffix -ate, for example, often is used to indicate that an element contains a number of oxygen atoms bound to it. Thus, sodium sulfate is the name of the compound with the formula Na_2SO_4 (consisting of sodium, sulfur, and oxygen), and calcium silicate is $CaSiO_3$ (calcium, silicon, and oxygen). Sulfates and silicates are recognizable classes of compounds, and, again, classes such as the alkali sulfates and the alkaline-earth silicates often are discussed.

Organometallic compounds. The great number and variety of potential combinations among the atoms of the elements make it impossible for any classification scheme to put all possible compounds into mutually exclusive categories. Thus, it is found that many metal atoms, most frequently encountered in inorganic substances, can also combine with compounds generally classed as organic. The resulting organometallic, or metallo-organic, compounds are widespread among substances essential to living systems. Hemoglobin, the vital oxygen-carrying constituent in the blood of higher animals, is a large, carbon-containing molecule in which an iron atom is combined. Chlorophyll, similarly essential to green plants, has a magnesium atom imbedded in a large organic molecule. Vitamin B_{12} is an organometallic compound containing cobalt. But organometallics are not restricted to compounds found in nature. Many new synthetic varieties are produced each year. The compound tetraethyllead, formula $Pb(C_2H_5)_4$ (one atom of lead bonded to four groups, each consisting of two atoms of carbon and five of hydrogen), is a synthetic organometallic compound that has found wide use as an additive to gasoline.

Nonstoichiometric compounds. One of the tenets of the atomic theory, on which much of chemistry is based, is that, when elements combine, they do so in such a manner that the ratio of the numbers of atoms of elements is integral. This rule is implied in typical molecular formulas. For example, the formula Al_2O_3 for the substance aluminum oxide means that atoms of aluminum combine with atoms of oxygen in the exact ratio of 2:3 to form this compound. The ratio of elements in a compound is revealed by the analysis of any pure sample of it. Any compound found to contain atoms of elements in whole-number ratios is said to be a stoichiometric (Greek: "element measuring") compound. A great ma-

jority of compounds, including nearly all organic compounds, fall into this class. There is, however, another class of compounds, nonstoichiometric compounds, in which the relative numbers of elemental atoms are not integral. The class includes, particularly, the oxides and sulfides of certain metals. For example, accurate analyses have shown that the number of zinc atoms relative to sulfur atoms in zinc sulfide, ZnS, can actually exceed the predicted 1:1 ratio of the formula by 0.03 percent. Similarly, the analysis of a sulfide of cerium suggests a formula $Ce_{2.7}S_4$, which means that the ratio of cerium to sulfur is in the proportion of 2.7:4. The electricity-conducting properties of such nonstoichiometric substances make them increasingly important as components of solid-state devices used in the electronics industry.

Classification by bond type. *Ionic compounds.* In the chemical reaction by which sodium chloride is formed from sodium atoms and chlorine atoms, the sodium atoms each lose an electron (the basic, negatively charged particle present in all atoms and also free in space), and the chlorine atoms each gain one. The consequence of this kind of electron transfer is that the compound formed exists as an aggregate of particles of matter bearing electrical charges, or ions. Forces of electrical attraction hold, or bond, the positively charged sodium ions in a matrix of negatively charged chloride ions, and vice versa. This form of bonding, ionic bonding, is characteristic of all salts. Certain hydrides (*e.g.*, sodium hydride) and oxides (*e.g.*, magnesium oxide) also have properties —such as high melting point and electrical conductivity in solution—that classify them as saltlike, or ionic, compounds.

Covalent compounds. An alternate, nonionic process, however, is involved in the combination of certain atoms to form compounds. In this process, electrons are shared between atoms, producing bonds, which are referred to as covalent bonds, between them. Covalent bonding occurs when carbon atoms combine in organic compounds and between nonmetal atoms when they combine into molecules. Such bonding results in the formation of covalent molecules, typical examples of which are methane (CH_4), a constituent of natural gas, and water (H_2O). Covalent molecules are complete entities, not electrically charged fragments like ions, and their aggregation into large samples is the consequence of the attractive forces between molecules, rather than electrostatic attraction. Generally speaking, intermolecular forces are weaker than electrostatic forces. As a result, the molecules of covalent compounds are pulled apart more easily than ions are and therefore the melting points of covalent compounds are lower than those of ionic compounds.

The mechanism of covalent-bond formation leads in some cases to the formation of huge, extended molecules involving thousands to millions of atoms. These macromolecules (macro-, "large") are also referred to as polymers (poly-, "many"; -mers, "parts"). The familiar plastics encountered in thousands of everyday uses are polymers. Polyethylene, Plexiglas, and nylon are examples. These are huge organic molecules formed by the combination of many small units. Varieties of macromolecules important to living organisms are proteins, enzymes, carbohydrates, and nucleic acids, such as deoxyribonucleic acid (DNA). All of these are polymers held together by covalent bonds. There are also some inorganic materials that properly can be classed as covalent macromolecules. Quartz (SiO_2) and other silicon-containing minerals, such as clays, have many chemically identical small units bonded together in two- and three-dimensional networks.

Coordination compounds. There are many perfectly stable compounds the structures of which are such that they can form even more stable compounds by adding other molecules. Such addition compounds are called coordination compounds. An example is expressed by the equation

$$CuSO_4 + 4NH_3 \rightarrow Cu(NH_3)_4SO_4,$$

which indicates that one molecule of cupric sulfate ($CuSO_4$), also written copper(II) sulfate, and four mole-

Margin notes:

Hydrides, oxides, and sulfides

Hemoglobin and chlorophyll

Variation in ratios of elements

Macromolecules

Donation of electrons

cules of ammonia (NH_3) combine to produce the coordination compound tetramminecopper(II) sulfate. In the process, four covalent bonds are formed between the four ammonia molecules and the copper ion. In each of these bonds, a pair of electrons on the ammonia molecule is shared with the copper ion. In such bonds, the electrons are donated by only one of the two atoms, rather than coming from both atoms, as in typical covalent bonds. A great variety of coordination compounds is formed by the so-called transition elements, *i.e.*, metallic elements found in the central portion of the periodic table. An important example of a coordination compound is the one formed when carbon monoxide attaches to the iron atom in hemoglobin of the blood. This stable compound robs hemoglobin of its oxygen-carrying ability. For an organism in which a major percentage of the hemoglobin molecules have become converted to such compounds, the consequence is death.

Classification by chemical reactivity. A natural consequence of the accumulation of information about the behaviour of chemical compounds is the recognition of similarities in their chemical properties. This recognition leads to classification on the basis of chemical reactivity, a classification that generally correlates well with classifications based on chemical structure.

Acids, bases, and salts. Very early in the development of chemistry, it was recognized that a type of reaction common to many substances is their ability to act as acids. Vinegar, for example, is a natural product that behaves as it does because it contains an organic acid, acetic acid. Acids generally have the property of imparting a characteristic colour to certain dyestuffs used as indicators. The indicator litmus, for instance, turns from blue to pink in acidic solutions. Acids also have a corrosive effect on many metals and produce hydrogen gas as a result of the action. This observation suggests that acids are hydrogen-containing compounds, as, indeed, most of them are. The so-called mineral acids are aqueous solutions of compounds derived from inorganic materials; typical mineral acids are hydrochloric acid (HCl), sulfuric acid (H_2SO_4), and nitric acid (HNO_3).

Bases, on the other hand, are a class of compounds capable of reacting with acids to neutralize their acidity. They, too, impart a characteristic colour to indicator dyes; litmus turns from pink to blue in solutions of bases. Alkali hydroxides—*e.g.*, sodium hydroxide, (NaOH), commonly called lye—and alkaline-earth oxides—*e.g.*, calcium oxide (CaO), familiarly called lime—are typical bases. Two neutralization reactions are shown in the following equations:

$$HCl + NaOH \rightarrow HOH + NaCl;$$
$$H_2SO_4 + CaO \rightarrow HOH + CaSO_4.$$

In the first equation, hydrochloric acid is neutralized with sodium hydroxide to give water and sodium chloride, common table salt. In the second reaction, sulfuric acid comes together with calcium oxide to form, again, water and a salt, in this case, calcium sulfate. From these reactions and many others like them, it can be generalized that acids as a class react with bases as a class to produce water and a third class of substances, salts.

Some substances, however—ammonia, for example—are capable of neutralizing acids without giving water as a product. The reaction of ammonia with nitric acid can be written

$$NH_3 + HNO_3 \rightarrow NH_4NO_3.$$

In this reaction, a molecule of ammonia is seen to combine with a hydrogen ion (H^+) from the acid in a manner similar to the way in which oxygen (or an oxygen–hydrogen group) combines with hydrogen in the above examples. One definition of bases, then, calls them the class of compounds capable of accepting hydrogen from acids. Ammonium nitrate (NH_4NO_3) is another example of a salt, the product of the neutralization of an acid by a base.

To enlarge the classification, there are compounds containing no hydrogen that are also capable of reacting with bases. Boron trifluoride (BF_3) is such a compound.

It reacts with ammonia to produce a neutral compound, much like a salt: $NH_3 + BF_3 \rightarrow H_3NBF_3$. The structural interpretation of this reaction is that the boron atom accepts a share in a pair of electrons from the nitrogen atom of ammonia. A covalent bond is formed between boron and nitrogen. This reaction suggests another definition of acids and bases: acids are compounds capable of accepting a pair of electrons; bases are compounds capable of donating a pair of electrons.

Acids as electron recipients

Oxidizing and reducing agents. Another frequently employed classification of chemical compounds is based upon their behaviour in so-called oxidation–reduction reactions. Such reactions are ones in which the combining capacity (valence) of several of the components is changed by the reaction. A simple example is:

$$2Cu \text{ (copper)} + O_2 \text{ (oxygen)} \rightarrow 2CuO \text{ (copper[II] oxide).}$$

In this reaction, two atoms of copper are said to be oxidized to two molecules of copper(II) oxide by a molecule of oxygen. In the process, the valence of the copper atoms has been changed from 0 in the uncombined element to $+2$ in the compound. At the same time, the valence of oxygen has been reduced from 0 in the elemental form to -2 in the compound. A comparable result can be accomplished by reacting copper with sulfuric acid:

$$Cu + H_2SO_4 \rightarrow CuO + SO_2 + H_2O.$$

In this reaction, copper again is oxidized; and sulfuric acid is the oxidizing agent, being reduced to sulfur dioxide in the process. (The valence of sulfur changes from $+6$ in sulfuric acid to $+4$ in sulfur dioxide.) There is a certain complementarity in this classification scheme: in oxidation–reduction reactions, oxidizing agents always are reduced; reducing agents invariably are oxidized.

Because examples of oxidation and reduction are so numerous in all branches of chemistry, the classification of substances as oxidizing or reducing agents is important. The results of many reactions can be anticipated before they are carried out by recognizing the degree to which the compounds involved exhibit oxidizing or reducing tendencies.

Nonchemical (trivial) classification schemes. It is hardly surprising that, in any study as vast as the examination of all kinds of matter, there are a great many classification schemes based simply on convenience. Thus, for example, classification based upon the physical state of a pure substance divides all substances into the categories gases, liquids, and solids. Although such a classification may be useful, it reflects little about the essential structure or reactivity of a material. For example, the familiar forms of the compound, the formula of which is H_2O, are solid ice, liquid water, and gaseous steam. The compound itself, however, is chemically identical in all three forms. Another nonchemical basis for classification may be the source of a compound. Thus, natural compounds are found in nature; synthetic compounds are produced in laboratories or factories. Natural compounds may be further classified as terrestrial, meteoric, or lunar, depending on their origin. Again, however, it is important to recognize that a pure compound isolated from any one source is chemically identical with the same compound from any other source. It is in this sense that the chemist considers all such nonchemical classification schemes as trivial.

Natural and synthetic compounds

BIBLIOGRAPHY. Because the discussion in this entry ranges widely over the whole field of chemistry, the reader seeking additional information will do well to choose a book in which the level of discussion matches his prior familiarity with the subject. Three typical sources, written at different levels, are: R.W. PARRY *et al.*, *Chemistry: Experimental Foundations* (1970), a secondary-school text; D.B. MURPHY and V. ROUSSEAU, *Foundations of College Chemistry* (1969), a college-level text; and R.B. HESLOP and P.L. ROBINSON, *Inorganic Chemistry*, 3rd ed. (1967), an advanced treatise.

(W.F.K.)

Chemical Compounds, Inorganic

Inorganic chemical compounds may be defined as compounds of the chemical elements other than carbon. As chemical compounds, they conform to the general requirement of being pure substances composed of two or more elements. (An element is the simplest form of a pure chemical substance, and all the atoms of a pure element have the same gross chemical properties.)

Origin of the term inorganic

In the early stages of the development of chemistry, considerable emphasis was placed on the origins of the various substances. Those substances clearly derived from living organisms were referred to as organic, whereas those that had in no known way been associated with living organisms were described as inorganic. Since the common substances derived from living matter are composed predominantly of the elements carbon, nitrogen, oxygen, and hydrogen—especially carbon—much of the chemistry of those elements was reserved for the field of organic chemistry, organic compounds being chiefly those substances in which varying amounts of hydrogen, oxygen, or nitrogen are combined with carbon. Inorganic chemistry, then, encompasses the bulk of the chemistry of all the remaining elements, a total of 101 (if the four elements found most extensively in organic compounds are excluded; see Figure 1). In addition, there exist compounds of carbon, hydrogen, oxygen, and nitrogen that are strictly inorganic, and there are many inorganic compounds formed by combination of various of these elements with other known elements.

period \ group	Ia	IIa	IIIb	IVb	Vb	VIb	VIIb	VIII	VIII	VIII	Ib	IIb	IIIa	IVa	Va	VIa	VIIa	0
1	1 H																1 H	2 He
2	3 Li	4 Be											5 B	6 C	7 N	8 O	9 F	10 Ne
3	11 Na	12 Mg											13 Al	14 Si	15 P	16 S	17 Cl	18 Ar
4	19 K	20 Ca	21 Sc	22 Ti	23 V	24 Cr	25 Mn	26 Fe	27 Co	28 Ni	29 Cu	30 Zn	31 Ga	32 Ge	33 As	34 Se	35 Br	36 Kr
5	37 Rb	38 Sr	39 Y	40 Zr	41 Nb	42 Mo	43 Tc	44 Ru	45 Rh	46 Pd	47 Ag	48 Cd	49 In	50 Sn	51 Sb	52 Te	53 I	54 Xe
6	55 Cs	56 Ba	57 La *	72 Hf	73 Ta	74 W	75 Re	76 Os	77 Ir	78 Pt	79 Au	80 Hg	81 Tl	82 Pb	83 Bi	84 Po	85 At	86 Rn
7	87 Fr	88 Ra	89 Ac **	104 *Rf*	105 *Ha*													

* 6	58 Ce	59 Pr	60 Nd	61 Pm	62 Sm	63 Eu	64 Gd	65 Tb	66 Dy	67 Ho	68 Er	69 Tm	70 Yb	71 Lu
** 7	90 Th	91 Pa	92 U	93 Np	94 Pu	95 Am	96 Cm	97 Bk	98 Cf	99 Es	100 Fm	101 Md	102 No	103 Lr

Figure 1: The periodic table of the elements.

CHEMICAL BONDING IN INORGANIC COMPOUNDS

The atoms of the elements that are combined in an inorganic compound may be bound to each other by a variety of kinds of chemical bonds, as the attractive forces that hold atoms together are called. These are most broadly separable into three categories: covalent bonds, electrovalent bonds, and metallic bonds. Within certain of these categories, there are also a few other bond types that must also be recognized.

Sharing of electron pairs

Covalent bonding. A covalent bond involves the binding together of two atoms of either the same element or of two different elements by the sharing of two electrons (an electron pair). This type of bond is illustrated by the formation of the compound hydrogen fluoride from its constituent atoms of hydrogen and fluorine, as shown in the following chemical equation:

$$\underset{\text{hydrogen atom}}{\mathrm{H}\cdot} \quad + \quad \underset{\text{fluorine atom}}{\cdot\underset{..}{\ddot{\mathrm{F}}}:} \quad \longrightarrow \quad \underset{\text{hydrogen fluoride molecule}}{\mathrm{H}:\underset{..}{\ddot{\mathrm{F}}}:} .$$

In this equation, atoms of hydrogen and fluorine are represented (as is customary) by their chemical symbols, H and F, respectively; the dots represent electrons in the outermost shells of the atoms of the elements (every atom being made up of electrons in concentric shells around a central nucleus). As is generally true in chemical equations, the starting materials are written to the left of an arrow (which points in the direction of the reaction) and the products to the right.

Since every atom has a definite electron capacity in its outermost shell of electrons (also called the valence shell), each of the combining atoms must be able to accommodate the shared electrons within its valence shell. Very commonly, the number of electrons that can be accommodated is eight. This is the so-called rule of eight (or octet rule), and it comes about because the two lowest energy subshells in any major electron shell are the *s* (electron capacity of two) and *p* (electron capacity, six) subshells (with the letters serving only to designate the subshells and having no other pertinent meaning).

The rule of eight

The formulas of the covalent compounds water (H_2O, O being an atom of oxygen) and ammonia (NH_3, N being an atom of nitrogen) reflect the rule of eight (as does that of hydrogen fluoride, above). This circumstance is shown in the equations below, in which the numbers of electrons in the free atoms reflect the electronic structures of the free elements, whereas the number of electrons assigned to each element in the compounds includes those not involved in bonds as well as those utilized by that element in covalent bonding.

$$\underset{\text{hydrogen atoms}}{2\mathrm{H}\cdot} \quad + \quad \underset{\text{oxygen atom}}{\cdot\underset{\cdot}{\ddot{\mathrm{O}}}:} \quad \longrightarrow \quad \underset{\text{water molecule}}{\mathrm{H}:\underset{\mathrm{H}}{\underset{..}{\ddot{\mathrm{O}}}}:}$$

$$\underset{\text{hydrogen atoms}}{3\mathrm{H}\cdot} \quad + \quad \underset{\text{nitrogen atom}}{\cdot\underset{\cdot}{\dot{\mathrm{N}}}:} \quad \longrightarrow \quad \underset{\text{ammonia molecule}}{\mathrm{H}:\overset{\mathrm{H}}{\underset{\mathrm{H}}{\underset{..}{\ddot{\mathrm{N}}}}}:}$$

Electron configuration. A free hydrogen atom has the electronic configuration designated $1s^1$, in which the first number indicates the number of the shell proceeding outward, the letter designates the type of subshell, and the superscript represents the number of electrons involved. The valence-shell configuration for oxygen is $2s^22p^4$ and that for nitrogen is $2s^22p^3$. In its covalent compounds, hydrogen effectively has the configuration $1s^2$, whereas the configurations of both oxygen and nitrogen in covalent compounds are $2s^22p^6$.

The closed-shell configuration of hydrogen

The closed-shell configuration of bonded hydrogen ($1s^2$) thus contains only two electrons, rather than eight; there is one important respect, however, in which this closed-shell configuration closely resembles those of such other covalently bonded elements as oxygen and nitrogen in their compounds water and ammonia ($2s^22p^6$). In each case, the bonded element has gained a share in a sufficient number of electrons to have the same configuration as the nearest noble gas (or Group 0 element) in the periodic table (see Figure 1). With hydrogen, this element is helium (configuration $1s^2$), whereas with oxygen and nitrogen it is neon ($2s^22p^6$). One may conclude that when an element obeys the rule of eight, it has assumed a noble gas configuration.

For elements having atomic numbers greater than 10 (the elements customarily being arranged in order of increasing atomic number—a value equivalent to the number of electrons in the neutral atom), the valence shell contains a *d* subshell in addition to the *s* and *p* subshells. Many compounds of these elements reflect the fact that more than eight electrons can be accommodated in the outermost shells.

Electronegativity. The ability of two atoms to share electrons depends on their having comparable relative abilities to attract electrons. This affinity for electrons depends ultimately on the charge on the nucleus of the atom as moderated by the other electrons in the atom. It is commonly estimated by a quantity called the electronegativity, which increases from left to right and from bottom to top in the periodic table (Figure 1). If two covalently bonded atoms have identical electronegativities, they share the electron pair equally. The bond is then said to be nonpolar, and the molecule is described as being homopolar (or nonpolar). If the electronegativities of the two atoms are not equal, the electron pair of the covalent bond is shared unequally. This causes one of the

Polarity

atoms to have a slight excess of negative charge and the other a slight excess of positive charge. Such a bond is called polar, and the molecule is described as being heteropolar (or simply polar). Polar and nonpolar molecules have different properties.

Formation of ions

Electrovalent bonding. Electrovalent bonding occurs when the electronegativity difference between two atoms (elements) is so great that electron sharing is not possible. In this case, one atom takes electrons away from the other, and the two atoms are converted to charged particles called ions. The resulting ions have opposite charges, and they are attracted to each other by the resulting electrostatic force (positive–negative attraction). An example of how ions can be considered to be formed from neutral atoms is shown below in the reaction of sodium with fluorine:

$$\text{Na·} \quad + \quad \text{·}\ddot{\text{F}}\text{:} \quad \longrightarrow \quad \text{Na}^+ \quad + \quad \text{:}\ddot{\text{F}}\text{:}^-$$

$$
\begin{array}{cccc}
(3s^1) & (2s^22p^5) & (2s^22p^6) & (2s^22p^6) \\
\text{sodium atom} & \text{fluorine atom} & \text{sodium ion} & \text{fluoride ion}
\end{array}
$$

A great difference between such ion–ion bonds and ordinary covalent (non-ionic) bonds is the fact that the electrostatic bond is not restricted to a single pair of atoms. Every negative ion attracts every other positive ion in its vicinity, and vice versa. This generalized attraction results in the formation of ionic crystal lattices (extended structures built up of positive and negative ions) by solid electrovalent compounds. For an example see Figure 2, representing the structure of sodium chloride (NaCl) crystal.

The number of electrons transferred between atoms is usually in accord with the rule of eight, as illustrated in the examples below:

$$\text{·Ca·} \quad + \quad \text{·}\ddot{\text{O}}\text{:} \quad \longrightarrow \quad \text{Ca}^{2+} \quad + \quad \text{:}\ddot{\text{O}}\text{:}^{2-}$$

$$
\begin{array}{cccc}
(4s^2) & (2s^22p^4) & (3s^23p^6) & (2s^22p^6) \\
\text{calcium} & \text{oxygen} & \text{calcium ion} & \text{oxygen ion} \\
\text{atom} & \text{atom} & &
\end{array}
$$

$$\text{3Li·} \quad + \quad \text{·}\ddot{\text{N}}\text{·} \quad \longrightarrow \quad \text{3Li}^+ \quad + \quad \text{:}\ddot{\text{N}}\text{:}^{3-}.$$

$$
\begin{array}{cccc}
(2s^1) & (2s^22p^3) & (2s^2) & (2s^22p^6) \\
\text{lithium atom} & \text{nitrogen atom} & \text{lithium ion} & \text{nitrogen ion}
\end{array}
$$

Polar molecules, such as those of water, bind to ions by attractive forces between the partially separated charges (dipoles) of the polar molecules and the free charges of the ions. When sodium chloride and other salts dissolve in water, their ions interact with the molecules of solvent by means of ion–dipole forces, as shown in Figure 3 (Left).

Molecules that have unsymmetrical electronic arrangements (dipoles) are commonly referred to as polar because their extremities bear opposite charges, which are indicated by the symbols $\delta+$ and $\delta-$. Various examples of polar molecules and their respective dipoles are provided below:

$$
\overset{\delta+}{\text{H}}\overset{\delta-}{-}\text{F} \qquad\qquad \overset{\delta+}{\text{H}}\diagdown\text{O}^{2\delta-}\diagup\overset{\delta+}{\text{H}}
$$

hydrogen fluoride $\qquad\qquad$ water

$$
\overset{\delta+}{\text{Cl}}\overset{\delta-}{-}\text{F} \qquad\qquad \overset{2\delta-}{\text{S}}\diagup\text{O}^{\delta-}\diagdown\text{O}^{\delta-}
$$

chlorine fluoride $\qquad\qquad$ sulfur dioxide

Polar molecules attract each other by aligning their charges so that those of opposite sign are adjacent. Dipole–dipole forces provide the intermolecular attractions that hold the molecules of many solids and liquids together, as shown in Figure 3 (Right). Certain molecules with polar bonds do not have dipole moments because of

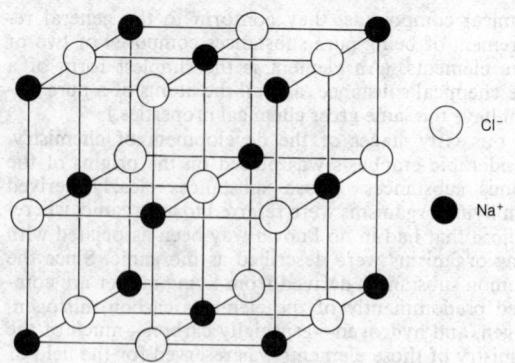

Figure 2: Ionic structure of sodium chloride in a three-dimensional array.

the cancelling of dipoles. Carbon dioxide, CO_2, provides an example:

$$
\overset{\delta-}{\text{:}\ddot{\text{O}}} = \overset{2\delta+}{\text{C}} = \overset{\delta-}{\ddot{\text{O}}\text{:}} \text{.}
$$

Polar molecules with hydrogen atoms at their positive extremities often form very strong ion–dipole and dipole–dipole bonds. This is particularly true when the second element in the compound is strongly electronegative, as are fluorine, oxygen, and nitrogen. These linkages are called hydrogen bonds and are responsible for the unusually large mutual attractions of the molecules of such compounds as hydrogen fluoride, water, and ammonia (when compared to their higher molecular weight analogues: hydrogen chloride, hydrogen sulfide, and phosphine, respectively). Comparisons of the heat of vaporization (the amount of heat needed to vaporize a standard quantity) of the hydrogen halides and of water and its heavier analogues show that more heat is needed to vaporize the lightest member of each series, and hence the strength of the dipole–dipole attractions is markedly greater for these compounds (more heat being required to overcome stronger attractions).

Hydrogen bonds

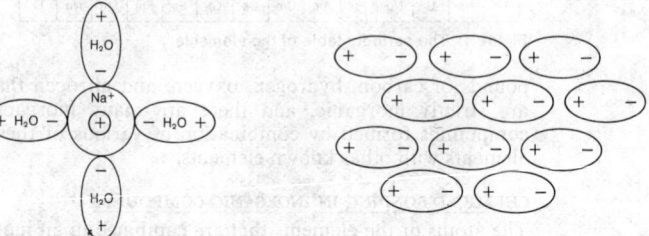

Figure 3: (Left) Attraction of water molecules to a sodium cation by ion–dipole forces. (Right) Alignment of dipoles in a liquid or solid phase containing polar molecules.

The nature of the forces holding the particles together in solids determines the physical and chemical properties of those substances, as shown in Table 1. Ion–ion forces and metallic bonding (the attractive force between atoms in metals) are usually extremely strong. Ion–dipole and dipole–dipole forces are not so strong, and the so-called

class of solid	nature of bonds	physical properties	example
Ionic	ion–ion (electrovalent)	hard, brittle, high mp and bp, melt conducts electricity	NaCl, CaF₂, LaF₃
Giant molecular	covalent	very hard, high mp, and bp, nonconductor	diamond, boron nitride, carborundum
Polar molecular	dipole–dipole	moderately soft, intermediate mp, nonconductor	water, ammonia, ether
Metallic	metallic bonds	great variety in hardness, mp, and bp, malleable, ductile, electrical conductors	elemental metals; e.g., Ag, Cu, Fe, Na, Hg, W
Nonpolar molecular	van der Waals	very soft, low mp and bp, nonconductor	naphthalene, CCl₄, N₂, Ar

Table 1: Binding Forces and Properties of Solids

van der Waals forces (weak attractions between nonpolar molecules) are weakest of all.

More subtle variations in properties than are implied in Table 1 are illustrated by the melting points of the fluorides for the horizontal series (period) of elements in the periodic table, beginning with sodium: 988° C, sodium fluoride; 1,266° C, magnesium fluoride; 1,291° C, aluminum fluoride; −90.2° C, silicon tetrafluoride; −83° C, phosphorus pentafluoride; −50.5° C, sulfur hexafluoride. In this series of compounds, the covalent nature of the molecular structures increases in proceeding to the right.

NOMENCLATURE OF INORGANIC COMPOUNDS

Binary compounds.   There are several acceptable ways of naming binary compounds (compounds of only two elements). The choice of which is used depends on the complexity of the chemistry of the elements in the particular compound and the complexity of the structure of the compound itself.

Order of names

For compounds of electropositive elements (that is, those with only positive oxidation states) that do not have variable valences, such as the alkali and alkaline-earth elements, the name is composed of the unmodified name of the electropositive element followed by that of the electronegative element (the element with negative oxidation state), the latter having its name modified in a phonetically useful way to end in "-ide." The simple compound of sodium and chlorine (NaCl), for example, is called sodium chloride; that between calcium and sulfur (CaS) is calcium sulfide; that between magnesium and nitrogen (Mg_3N_2) is magnesium nitride; and the compound formed between aluminum and boron (AlB_{12}) is known as aluminum boride.

Names incorporating oxidation states

In cases in which several oxidation states are possible for the electropositive element in a binary compound, a roman numeral is added in parentheses after the name of the electropositive element. Thus, the compound with the molecular formula $FeCl_2$ is known as iron(II) chloride, whereas the compound with the formula $FeCl_3$ is referred to as iron(III) chloride. Similarly, CuCl is copper(I) chloride; $SnBr_4$ is tin(IV) bromide; NO_2 is nitrogen(IV) oxide; and SF_6 is sulfur(VI) fluoride. This system replaces an older system in which electropositive elements were given different suffixes to indicate the oxidation state. In the older system, for example, iron(II) chloride was called ferrous chloride and iron(III) chloride was known as ferric chloride.

Alternatively, when compounds incorporating different combinations of the same two elements are known, Latin and Greek prefixes are used to indicate the proportions of elements present in a given compound. A series of compounds named by this method are given in Table 2.

Table 2: Some Compounds Named Using Prefixes To Indicate Proportions

molecular formula	name
N_2O	dinitrogen oxide
N_2O_3	dinitrogen trioxide
N_2O_4	dinitrogen tetroxide
N_2S_5	dinitrogen pentasulfide
S_2Cl_2	disulfur dichloride
Al_2Cl_6	dialuminum hexachloride
ClO_3	chlorine trioxide

Names indicating ratios

This system is also often used more loosely to indicate the ratios of elements combined in a substance rather than its exact molecular formula. Thus the name aluminum trichloride (and the formula $AlCl_3$) indicates the composition of the substance but not its true molecular formula (which is generally thought to be Al_2Cl_6). Furthermore, manganese dioxide, MnO_2, exists in a saltlike lattice (see below *Structural classification of inorganic compounds*) rather than as discrete molecules as the name suggests.

The binary acids may either be named as typical binary compounds (hydrogen chloride for HCl, hydrogen sulfide

for H_2S) or they may be given the prefix hydro- and the suffix -ic acid (thus hydrochloric acid for HCl, and hydrosulfuric acid for H_2S).

Certain classes of binary compounds have systems of nomenclature based on common names. This is especially true of hydrogen derivatives, both neutral and charged, as shown in Table 3.

Table 3: Common Names of Hydrogen Compounds

neutral compound		cation		anion	
formula	name	formula	name	formula	name
H_2O	water	H_3O^+	hydronium	OH^-	hydroxide
NH_3	ammonia	NH_4^+	ammonium	NH_2^-	amide
N_2H_4	hydrazine	$N_2H_5^+$	hydrazinium	—	—
B_2H_6	diborane	—	—	BH_4^-	tetrahydridoborate
SiH_4	silane	—	—	—	—

Compounds with common names

The hydrides of boron are named as boranes by indicating the number of boron atoms with a Latin or Greek prefix and the number of hydrogens with a numerical suffix. Examples are given in Table 4.

Table 4: Names and Formulas of Some Boranes

formula	name
B_2H_6	diborane-6
B_5H_9	pentaborane-9
B_5H_{11}	pentaborane-11
$B_{18}H_{22}$	octadecaborane-22

Ternary compounds.   Generally, ternary compounds (compounds of three elements) can be considered as oxygen acids or their salts. The names of most common oxygen acids are relatively unsystematically derived from old discarded nomenclature systems. Familiarity, however, requires retention of these names. Systematic names can be assigned on the basis of coordination-compound nomenclature (see below *Coordination compounds*); these, however, often are sufficiently cumbersome that the common names are preferred. A list of common names of well-known ternary acids—and the related anions (negative ions)—is included in Table 5.

Table 5: Common Names of Acids and Their Anions

formula	name of acid	name of anion	formula of anion
H_3BO_3	orthoboric acid*	borate	BO_3^{3-}
H_2CO_3	carbonic acid	carbonate	CO_3^{2-}
HNO_3	nitric acid	nitrate	NO_3^-
HNO_2	nitrous acid	nitrite	NO_2^-
H_3PO_4	orthophosphoric acid*	phosphate	PO_4^{3-}
$H_4P_2O_7$	pyrophosphoric acid	pyrophosphate	$P_2O_7^{4-}$
$H_5P_3O_{10}$	triphosphoric acid	triphosphate	$P_3O_{10}^{5-}$
$(HPO_3)_n$	metaphosphoric acid	metaphosphate	$(PO_3^-)_n$
$(HPO_3)_3$	trimetaphosphoric acid	trimetaphosphate	$(PO_3^-)_3$
H_3PO_3	phosphorous acid	phosphite	HPO_3^{2-}
H_3PO_2	hypophosphorous acid	hypophosphite	$H_2PO_2^-$
H_2SO_5	peroxosulfuric acid	peroxysulfate	SO_5^{2-}
$H_2S_2O_6$	dithionic acid	dithionate	$S_2O_6^{2-}$
H_2SO_4	sulfuric acid	sulfate	SO_4^{2-}
H_2SO_3	sulfurous acid	sulfite	SO_3^{2-}
$H_2S_2O_3$	thiosulfuric acid	thiosulfate	$S_2O_3^{2-}$
$HClO_4$	perchloric acid	perchlorate	ClO_4^-
$HClO_3$	chloric acid	chlorate	ClO_3^-
$HClO_2$	chlorous acid	chlorite	ClO_2^-
$HClO$	hypochlorous acid	hypochlorite	ClO^-
$HMnO_4$	permanganic acid	permanganate	MnO_4^-

*Prefix often omitted.

Salts—ternary compounds involving other elements in place of the hydrogen of the parent acids—are named according to the rules for binary compounds, with the anion from the acid playing the role of the more electronegative constituent. If one or more atoms of hydrogen remains, hydrogen is named as a second electropositive constituent. Examples of such salts are given in Table 6.

Table 6: Names and Formulas of Salts Based on Ternary Acids

formula	name
KNO_3	potassium nitrate
$NiSO_3$	nickel(II) sulfite
$KHSO_4$	potassium hydrogen sulfate
$Na_2H_2P_2O_7$	disodium dihydrogen pyrophosphate

The occurrence of water, or similar molecules, in the composition of a material is indicated by adding to the end of the name the word hydrate for water (or, for example, ammoniate for ammonia) with a Latin or Greek prefix to indicate the number of molecules present. Examples of names of materials of this kind are given in Table 7.

Table 7: Names of Hydrated and Ammoniated Compounds

formula	name
$Na_2SO_4 \cdot 10H_2O$	sodium sulfate decahydrate
$NiSO_4 \cdot 7H_2O$	nickel(II) sulfate heptahydrate
$PtCl_4 \cdot 2NH_3$	platinum(IV) chloride diammoniate

Coordination compounds. A coordination compound is composed of one or more complex structural units, each of which has a central atom bound directly to a surrounding set of groups called ligands. Nomenclature of coordination compounds requires a knowledge of these structural relationships. Many ligands bind to the central atom through only one atom; these are called monodentate ligands. Ligands that bind through two atoms (*e.g.*, ethylenediamine, $NH_2CH_2CH_2NH_2$) are described as bidentate, those that have three points of attachment are called tridentate, and so on.

As in simple compounds, the cation is named first, regardless of whether it is complex (that is, coordinated) or simple. Also, when the anion is complex, it takes the suffix "-ate." Furthermore, the oxidation state of the central atom is indicated at the end of the name of the constituent (cation or anion) of which it is part.

In formulas of coordination compounds, the symbol for the central atom is placed first; in names of coordination compounds, the name of the central atom is placed last. The ligands are cited in sequence: anions first, then neutral ligands, finally cationic ligands (which are relatively rare). Within these groupings, alphabetical order is acceptable, but hydride ion (H⁻), oxide ion (O^{2-}), and hydroxide ion (OH⁻) are usually placed first in the sequence given. When these and other anions are coordinated, they are given the suffix -o (as hydrido, oxo, and hydroxo). The numbers of the various ligands are indicated by Latin and Greek prefixes. The presence of water as a ligand is indicated by the term aquo, while ammonia is denoted by ammine. Examples of the application of these rules are given in Table 8.

Table 8: Names of Some Coordination Compounds

formula	name
$Li[AlH_4]$	lithium tetrahydridoaluminate
$Na_2[CoH(CN)_5]$	sodium hydridopentacyanocolbate(III)
$[CoCl_2(NH_3)_4]Cl$	dichlorotetraamminecobalt(III) chloride
$[Ni(H_2O)_6]SO_4 \cdot H_2O$	hexaquonickel(II) sulfate monohydrate

When the names of the ligands are complicated, as in bi-, tri-, and higher polydentate ligands, the number of ligands is indicated by the less common prefixes bis-, tris-, tetrakis-, pentakis-, and so on, to indicate two, three, four, five, and so on, ligands of the kind named. The portion of the name following the prefix is set off with parentheses. Examples are dicyanotetrakis(methylisonitrile)iron(II) for the compound with formula $Fe(CN)_2(CH_3NC)_4$; and tris(ethylenediamine)cobalt(III) nitrate for $[Co(NH_2CH_2CH_2NH_2)_3](NO_3)_3$.

STRUCTURAL CLASSIFICATION OF INORGANIC COMPOUNDS

Salts. The compounds formed by the chemical union of strong metals (elements at the left-hand side of the periodic table, of which the most metallic are the alkali metals, Group Ia) with strong nonmetals (elements at the right-hand side of the table, of which the most nonmetallic are the halogens, Group VIIa) provide the simplest examples of salts. These include sodium chloride (common table salt) and all the other compounds of alkali metals and halogens, called halides, such as lithium fluoride, potassium bromide, rubidium chloride, and cesium iodide, as well as the halides of many other elements—for example, magnesium fluoride, calcium chloride, and lanthanum fluoride. These halides are most clearly electrovalent in nature. The oxides of these elements (binary compounds with oxygen), the sulfides (binary compounds with sulfur), and the nitrides (binary compounds with nitrogen) are also electrovalent.

Most other binary compounds (compounds made of two elements) are either clearly composed of molecules (rather than ions) or else the character of their bonding is open to question. Commonly such materials are partially covalent in nature.

Electrovalent substances form solid crystals that are described in terms of ionic lattices. In these lattices, the positive ions are surrounded by negative ions, and the negative ions, in turn, are surrounded by positive ions. In any particular ionic lattice, a definite number of ions of one kind is arrayed about those of the second kind, and vice versa. This number is called the coordination number. In the sodium chloride lattice, the coordination number of both the cation (positive ion), the sodium ion, and the anion (negative ion), the chloride ion, is 6. The halide salts of most of the alkali metals crystallize in this same lattice form. The main exceptions are the cesium salts (*e.g.*, cesium chloride), which have a lattice in which the coordination number of both ions is 8 (see Figure 4).

Ionic crystal lattices

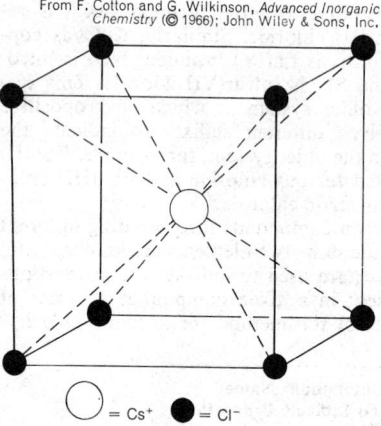

From F. Cotton and G. Wilkinson, *Advanced Inorganic Chemistry* (© 1966); John Wiley & Sons, Inc.

○ = Cs⁺   ● = Cl⁻

Figure 4: Cesium chloride structure.

The anions and cations have the same coordination numbers only in structures in which the same numbers of the two kinds of ions are present. In the lattice of calcium fluoride (CaF_2), the coordination number of the calcium cation is 8, whereas that of the fluoride anion is 4 (see Figure 5).

When salts melt, the geometric constraint of the crystal lattice is overcome, with the result that the individual ions become relatively free to move. This produces the typical fluid nature of liquids. The fact that the ultimate particles of the molten salt are charged makes it possible to pass an electric current through such melts. When such conductance occurs, the ions migrate through the liquid toward the electrode of opposite charge, thereby constituting an electric current. In water solutions, the covalent water molecules separate the ions so that they can move independently. Consequently, such solutions are also electric conductors.

Oxides, anhydrides, acids, and bases. The physical properties and chemical behaviour of the oxides of the

Ligands

elements provide a scheme for systematizing much of the chemistry of inorganic compounds. The gases of low atomic number—helium, neon, and argon—do not form stable oxides. The oxides of the early elements in any period of the table (such as sodium and calcium oxide) are typically electrovalent, or saltlike, as evidenced by their high melting and boiling points. In contrast, the oxides of the last members of a given period in the table are characteristically discrete molecular structures held together by covalent bonds and with only weak forces between the molecules, as evidenced by their low melting points and easy volatilities (for example, phosphoric anhydride and sulfur trioxide). The oxides of the elements in the centre of a period are intermediate in bond type and physical properties.

From F. Cotton and G. Wilkinson, *Advanced Inorganic Chemistry* (© 1966); John Wiley & Sons, Inc.

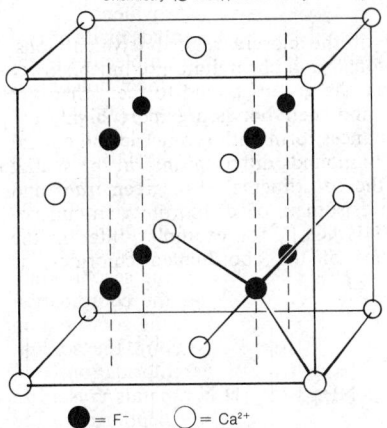

= F⁻   ○ = Ca²⁺

Figure 5: **Calcium fluoride (fluorite) structure.**

The contrast in properties of the oxides of the elements extend also to their chemical behaviour. Oxides of the alkali and alkaline-earth elements (and of a few other metals, the ions of which have low valences—that is, low charges) are basic in character and react with water to form ionic hydroxides. A good example of this behaviour is the action of sodium oxide on water to give sodium hydroxide:

$$Na_2O + H_2O \longrightarrow 2NaOH.$$

sodium oxide   water   sodium hydroxide

Basic oxides

Sodium hydroxide actually is composed of sodium (Na^+) and hydroxide (OH^-) ions. Basic (the chemical opposite of acidic) character is associated with the presence of hydroxide ions in aqueous solutions. Bases neutralize acids, change the colours of certain dyes (red litmus turns blue in bases), and absorb gaseous carbon dioxide to form carbonates. The reaction of sodium hydroxide with carbon dioxide to give sodium carbonate is shown below:

$$2NaOH + CO_2 \longrightarrow Na_2CO_3 + H_2O.$$

sodium hydroxide   carbon   sodium   water
                   dioxide   carbonate

Solutions of bases feel "slick" to the touch because of the destructive action of bases on skin tissue; and they taste bitter (although, of course, tasting is not advisable).

The oxides of the last members of a period, especially in high oxidation states (that is, high valence), are acidic in character. Aqueous solutions of acids contain hydronium ions (H_3O^+). They neutralize bases, turn blue litmus red, destroy carbonates, and react with active metals, forming salts and evolving hydrogen. They also have a sour taste. The reaction of a typical strong acid, sulfuric acid, with metallic zinc to give a salt, zinc sulfate, and free hydrogen is shown below:

Acidic oxides

$$Zn + H_2SO_4 \longrightarrow ZnSO_4 + H_2.$$

zinc   sulfuric   zinc   hydrogen
       acid   sulfate

Standard definitions of acids and bases recognize the

typical behaviour mentioned above and characterize the neutralization reaction as the production of a salt and water. In fact, sodium hydroxide exists in solution as sodium and hydroxide ions, and nitric acid exists as hydronium and nitrate ions; the neutralization process involves the reaction of hydronium ions and hydroxide ions to form water molecules.

In addition to the oxides mentioned above, binary hydrides of strong nonmetals are also acids. In a solution of hydrogen chloride in water, for example, almost all of the hydrogen chloride has reacted with water to form the hydronium and chloride ions:

$$H_2O + HCl \longrightarrow H_3O^+ + Cl^-.$$

water   hydrogen   hydronium   chloride
        chloride   ion   ion

Hydrochloric acid is a strong acid because of its almost complete dissociation to the ionic form. In solutions of acetic acid (vinegar), however, most of the acid is present as discrete molecules of acetic acid rather than as ions, and this substance is, therefore, a weak acid. Some acids have more than one replaceable—or acidic—proton (hydrogen ion): phosphoric acid (H_3PO_4), for example, has three, and sulfuric acid (H_2SO_4) has two.

According to the more general Brønsted acid–base theory (which is named after its first proponent, the Danish chemist Johannes Nicolaus Brønsted), an acid is defined as a proton donor, whereas a base is a proton acceptor. Neutralization is then the transfer of a proton from an acid to a base. In the reaction of gaseous ammonia (NH_3)—a base—with gaseous hydrogen chloride (HCl) —an acid—to form electrovalent ammonium chloride (NH_4Cl), neutralization has produced a new acid, NH_4^+, and a new base, Cl^-:

Acid–base theories

$$NH_3 + HCl \longrightarrow NH_4^+ + Cl^-.$$

ammonia   hydrogen   ammonium   chloride
          chloride   ion   ion

The new acid and base are both weaker than were the original reactants. Because of neutralization, the strongest acid that can exist in water is the hydronium ion (H_3O^+); similarly, the strongest base that can exist in water is the hydroxide ion (OH^-).

Another useful theory of acids and bases is the Lewis theory (named for the U.S. chemist Gilbert Newton Lewis), which specifies that a base is an electron-pair donor and an acid is an electron-pair acceptor. The "donated" electron pair is shared by the donor and the acceptor. According to this definition, water ($H_2\ddot{O}:$), hydroxide ion ($H\ddot{O}:^-$), ammonia ($:NH_3$), and chloride ion ($:\ddot{C}l:^-$) are all Lewis bases. The most obvious Lewis acids (other than the proton H^+) are ions and atoms that have fewer electrons than required by the rule of eight. Boron trifluoride (BF_3), for example, has only six valence electrons and is capable of combining with a fluoride ion ($:\ddot{F}:^-$) to form the tetrafluoroborate ion (BF_4^-). The boron atom in this ion obeys the rule of eight.

The oxides that form acids in aqueous solutions traditionally have been called acid anhydrides. The reaction of such an anhydride with water produces an acid, as in the following example with sulfur trioxide, SO_3:

$$SO_3 + H_2O \longrightarrow H_2SO_4.$$

sulfur   water   sulfuric
trioxide   acid

Coordination compounds. The formation of a metal ion from an atom involves the loss of some or all of its valence electrons; as a result, metal ions in general react vigorously with such electron-pair donors (Lewis bases) as water and ammonia and the chloride, nitrate, and cyanide ions, among others. The reaction of silver ion with ammonia, for example, takes place as follows:

$$Ag^+ + 2NH_3 \longrightarrow (H_3N:Ag:NH_3)^+$$

silver   ammonia   diamminesilver ion
ion

Coordinate
bonds

When both electrons for bond formation come from one of the atoms, the linkage is called a coordinate bond. Once formed, a coordinate bond is simply a polar covalent bond (identical to those produced when one electron comes from each atom).

Coordination number. Each metal ion forms a certain number (or numbers) of coordinate bonds; this is its coordination number. Every coordination number requires a certain set of vacant orbitals (mixed or hybridized orbitals) on the central metal ion, and these orbitals are directed toward the corners of a regular geometric shape, a polygon or polyhedron (a planar or a three-dimensional figure) as shown in Table 9. In coordination compounds, the groups bound to the central ion are called ligands.

Table 9: Coordination Numbers, Hybridized Orbitals, and Coordination Geometries

coordination number	hybridized orbitals	geometric structure	
2	sp	linear	
3	sp^2	trigonal planar	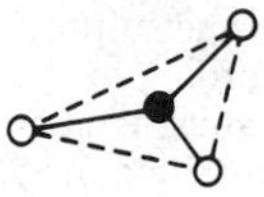
4	sp^3	tetrahedral	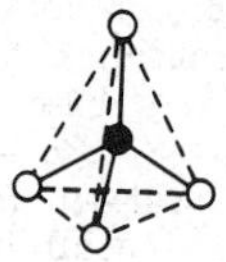
4	dsp^2	square planar	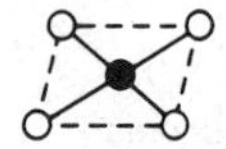
5	dsp^3	trigonal bipyramidal	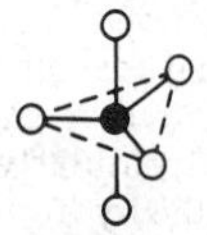
6	d^2sp^3	octahedral	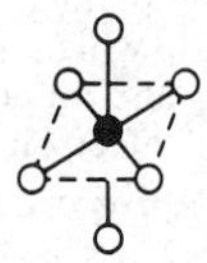

The coordinate bonds of divalent and trivalent ions, especially of the first transition series (the elements in the central part of the fourth period of the table) are frequently highly polar, and this fact is reflected in many of their properties. Thus, the bivalent ions of copper, nickel, and cobalt form many beautifully coloured coordination compounds, which are also distinguished by the common occurrence of unpaired electrons in their structures. The colours of many gemstones derive from these ions. The ionic formulation of the bonding in these compounds (e.g., as the hydrated ions $Ni(H_2O)_6^{2+}$, $Cu(H_2O)_4^{2+}$) is also supported by the very great rates at which the compounds undergo substitution and precipitation reactions.

All theories of bonding of the octahedral complexes of these ions show that their $3d$ orbitals have been split into a pair of higher energy levels and a set of three lower energy levels. The separation between these levels depends on the bonding ability of the ligands. With strong ligands the energy separation is so great that all the electrons possible go into the lower orbitals. This produces the low spin forms of the ions having the electronic configurations $3d^4$ through $3d^7$. Smaller energy intervals—i.e., weaker ligands—produce the high spin forms of the compounds in question. Low spin complexes behave as if they

were more highly covalent than high spin complexes (see Figure 6).

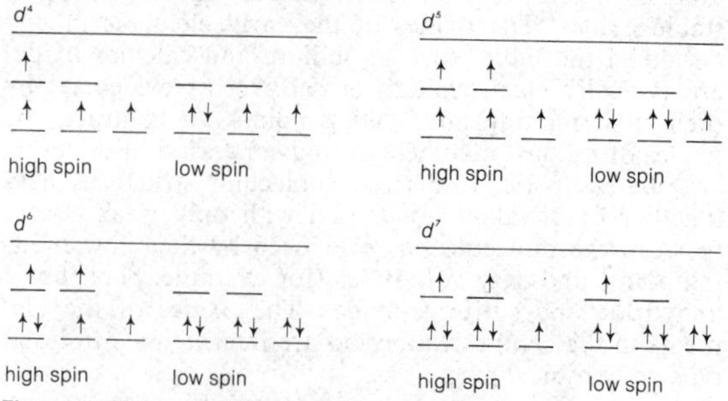

Figure 6: The low spin and high spin configurations of d^4, d^5, d^6, and d^7 octahedral ions (see text).

Isomers. Some of the closely related trivalent ions, notably those of cobalt and chromium, are much slower to exchange or lose the groups bound to them than are the divalent ions, and their bonds are more highly covalent. These substances form both geometric and optical isomers (that is, compounds differing only in the spatial arrangements of the constituents). The green *trans* and violet *cis* geometric isomers of dichlorotetraamminecobalt(III) ion $[Co(NH_3)_4Cl_2]^+$, for example, differ in the relative orientations of the coordinated chlorides, as shown below:

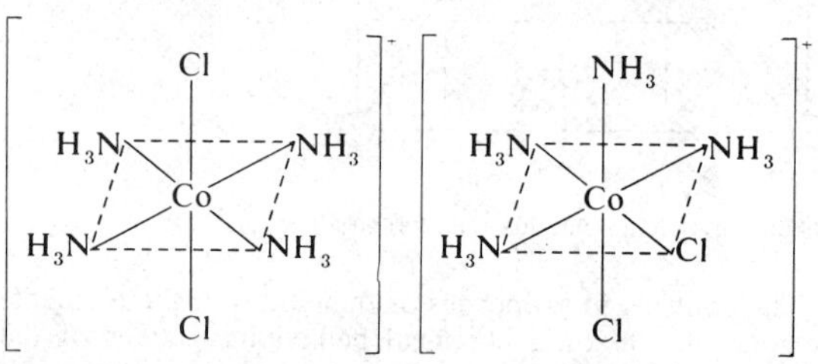

trans isomer   *cis* isomer

The term *trans* is used for the compound in which the two chlorine atoms are across from one another, and the term *cis* is used for the compound in which the two are adjacent. Optical isomers (those that differ the way the right- and left-hand gloves do) of octahedral ions most commonly occur among the so-called chelate derivatives. Chelating ligands are defined as those that bind to the metal ion at more than one site; for example, ethylenediamine ($NH_2CH_2CH_2NH_2$) binds to the cobalt(III) ion through both of its nitrogen atoms. The cobalt(III) complex, containing three molecules of ethylenediamine, forms nonsuperimposable mirror-image isomers, as shown below:

Chelates

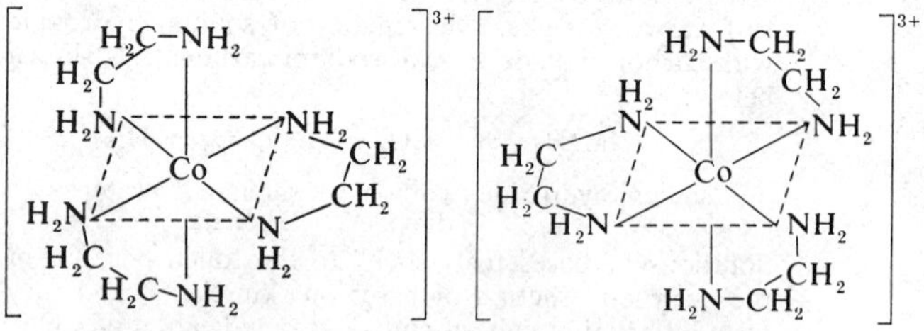

mirror image isomers of $[Co(NH_2CH_2CH_2NH_2)_3]^{3+}$

The heavier transition element ions, such as the platinum(IV), rhodium(III), and ruthenium(II) ions, tend to exhibit a higher degree of covalency. Consequently, unpaired electrons are not so common in the compounds of these groups of elements; as a result, their colours are not as brilliant, and they are slower to undergo reactions.

Transition-element oxides. Transition-element compounds involving oxidation states of +4 or higher usually contain either oxygenated anions of general formula MO_n^{m-} (in which M represents the metallic element, n the number of oxygen atoms, and m the number of negative charges) or fluorinated complexes, MF_p^r (in which p is the number of fluorine atoms and r the number of negative charges). Most ligands other than the oxide or fluoride ions are too easily oxidized to survive while bound to the highly oxidizing central ions. The oxide ion stabilizes higher states than does fluoride; for example, the oxygen-containing ions of highest oxidation state (indicated by roman numerals) of manganese and iron are, respectively, manganate(VII) and ferrate(VI), whereas the corresponding fluoro ions are hexafluoromanganate(IV) and hexafluoroferrate(III). This is almost certainly a result of double-bond formation between the oxide ion and the metal ion, the oxide ion donating shares in two pairs of electrons to the metal. The fluoride ion is too electronegative to donate electrons in this fashion.

Low oxidation states occur with so-called back-bonding ligands, such as carbon monoxide or trialkylphosphines—back-bonding ligands being those that have vacant orbitals that can share electron pairs donated by the metal ion. The carbonyls (compounds in which carbon monoxide is the ligand) of the free metal atoms are most typical of this class of compound; for example, tetracarbonyl-nickel $[Ni(CO)_4]$, octacarbonyldicobalt $[Co_2(CO)_8]$, and pentacarbonyliron $[Fe(CO)_5]$. In all cases reduction to still lower oxidation states can be accomplished; *e.g.*, tetracarbonylcobaltate($-$I) $[Co(CO)_4]^-$ and tetracarbonylferrate($-$II) $[Fe(CO)_4]^{2-}$.

Organometallic compounds. A direct bond between a carbon atom and a metal atom is the defining feature of an organometallic compound. The simplest examples contain carbon–metal sigma bonds—a sigma bond being the usual kind of single covalent bond, in which the orbitals of the bonding atoms overlap along the straight line connecting the atomic centres. An example of this kind of compound is the substance methylmagnesium bromide (belonging to the class of substances known as Grignard reagents after their discoverer, the French chemist Victor Grignard). The formation of metal–carbon sigma bonds may be viewed as the union of an alkyl radical $R\cdot$ (in which R is any hydrocarbon group) with a metal atom (such as $Li\cdot$), as in the following equation:

$$R\cdot \quad + \quad Li\cdot \quad \longrightarrow \quad R:Li \ .$$

| alkyl radical | lithium atom | alkyllithium compound |

Alternatively, the reaction may be considered as the coordination of a carbanion (R^-) with a metal cation (such as Li^+), as follows:

$$R:^- \quad + \quad Li^+ \quad \longrightarrow \quad R:Li \ .$$

| carbanion | lithium | alkyllithium compound |

Organometallic compounds can also be formed when a metal ion binds to the pi electrons of double-bonded carbon derivatives. These complexes include ethylene derivatives, in which the pi electrons of ethylene are donated to a platinum atom. A pair of d electrons from the platinum atom are back-donated into the pi antibonding (or unused) orbital of the ethylene molecule. Organic molecules having two, three, or four double bonds can form corresponding numbers of bonds with a given metal atom. Therefore, butadiene and cyclobutadiene form two organometallic bonds, benzene forms three, cyclopentadienyl anion forms three, and cyclooctatetraenyl dianion forms five. Two examples of this type of bonding are:

cyclobutadiene-tricarbonyliron   benzenetricarbonylchromium

Allyl groups (with the structural formula $CH_2=CHCH_2^-$) simultaneously form the equivalent of one sigma bond and one pi bond with a metal atom. In fact, however, both bonds appear to be identical, and, consequently, the allyl group may be treated as a pi-complexing anion that forms two bonds with a metal atom.

The alkali and alkaline-earth-metal alkyls contain highly polar carbon–metal bonds (M^+R^-), and the reactions of those with higher atomic numbers are characteristic of carbanions. Covalency is greater for the lighter members because of the greater polarizing power of the smaller cations. The beryllium and lithium alkyls have high molecular weights, indicating that they form polymeric structures, such as that shown below:

The apparent penta covalency (three to hydrogen and two to beryllium atoms) of the carbon atoms in such bridged structures may either be the result of electrovalent bonding or it may reflect the presence of a three-centred electron-deficient bond (a special type of bond, such as in boron hydrides; see below *Catenates*). The elements in Group IIb of the periodic table (zinc, cadmium, and mercury) form sigma-bonded metal alkyls with great covalent properties. Such compounds as diethylzinc $[Zn(C_2H_5)_2]$ and dimethylmercury $[Hg(CH_3)_2]$ are strictly molecular (non-ionic) in their properties. The former is one of the most volatile of metallic compounds, boiling at $118°$ C ($244°$ F).

The alkyls of aluminum are similar to those of beryllium and lithium, whereas those of thallium (in the same group as aluminum but in a later period of the table) resemble those of mercury. As might be expected from their position in the group with carbon (which forms more stable molecular-type compounds than any other element), the sigma-bonded organometallic compounds of the Group IVa elements are quite unreactive. Silicon, germanium, and tin alkyls are typically stable molecular substances.

Sigma bonds between transition metal atoms and carbon atoms are stable only in the presence of such back-bonding ligands as phosphines, carbon monoxide, and unsaturated nitrogen-containing groups. The biologically important substance, vitamin B_{12}, contains a carbon–cobalt sigma bond.

The formation of compounds with stable organometallic pi bonds is restricted to transition elements. Substances containing such bonds are especially useful in a variety of catalytic processes. A process known as hydroformylation, for example, produces propionaldehyde (an important industrial chemical) from small molecules. The process is shown in the following equation:

$$CH_2{=}CH_2 + CO + H_2 \xrightarrow[\text{catalyst}]{HCo(CO)_4} CH_3CH_2C{\overset{O}{\underset{H}{\diagdown}}}.$$

| ethylene | carbon monoxide | hydrogen | propionaldehyde |

The same type of coordination catalysis is involved in the low-pressure polymerization of olefins (to produce plastics).

Catenates. The ideal covalent bond is a nonpolar one between two atoms of the same element; in this case, the electron pair is equally attracted to both atoms. The phenomenon of like atoms joining together by covalent bonds is called catenation (Latin *catena*, "chain"), and it reaches a maximum with carbon, giving rise to a great many compounds of this type. The other elements of Group IVa in the table show increasingly diminished abilities to undergo catenation (silicon much less than carbon, germanium and tin somewhat less than silicon, and lead least of all). Silicon forms the series of compounds denoted by the general formulas Si_nH_{2n+2} and Si_nX_{2n+2} (in which n is any integer and X = Cl, F). The structures below represent low-molecular-weight examples of the two series:

Margin notes:
Sigma bonds in organometallic compounds

Pi bonds in organometallic compounds

Organometallic compounds as catalysts

$$H-Si-Si-Si-H \qquad F-Si-Si-F$$

(with H substituents on each Si, and F substituents on each Si respectively)

Catenation in Groups Va and VIa

The elements of Group Va of the table show relatively little tendency to catenate. Hydrazine ($NH_2–NH_2$) is the only hydride of nitrogen containing only nitrogen–nitrogen single bonds. Among Group VIa elements, sulfur is unique in its ability to self-link; it forms several series of linear covalent molecules of the types represented by the following general formulas: HS_nH, ClS_nCl, and $HO_3SS_nSO_3H$. Salts of polysulfide anions (S_n^{2-}) are also well characterized. Structures are given below for representative compounds in these various classes:

dihydrogen disulfide   polysulfide anion

tetrathionic acid

Some of the polysulfide ions are able to form chelate rings in which the sulfur atoms at each end of the chain are coordinated to one metal ion.

Boron is unique among Group IIIa elements in its ability to form catenates; the self-linkage of boron, however, is not restricted to typical boron–boron covalent binding. A few such compounds do exist, including diboron tetrachloride:

diboron tetrachloride

Although the simple hydride diborane (B_2H_6) was once thought to have a similar structure, it actually involves a distinctive three-centre, electron-deficient bond, in which one electron pair is shared between three atoms, two borons and one hydrogen atom:

diborane

The ability of boron to form three-centre bonds in addition to normal covalent linkages leads to the formation of a number of boron hydrides with complicated structures. Although the simplest boron hydrides (for example, diborane) are extremely reactive toward oxygen and all solvents containing replaceable protons (such as water and alcohols), certain of the anions with cagelike structures (such as $B_{10}H_{10}^{2-}$ and $B_{12}H_{12}^{2-}$) are remarkably unreactive.

The carboranes are compounds similar to these anions except that two carbon atoms have replaced two of the boron atoms. Several of the carboranes with basket-like structures form pi complexes with metal ions that are very similar to the organometallic compounds with pi bonds described above.

Cluster compounds

Compounds in which the self-linking of elements has produced compact structures are referred to as cluster compounds. Catenation of metallic elements can yield both simple linear units and clusters. Though a number of representative metals apparently can produce metal–metal bonds under the right conditions, only mercury forms such species in aqueous mediums. The diatomic mercurous ion (Hg_2^{2+}) is unique in this regard. Given the right ligands (attached groups), however, most transition elements (those in the centre of the periodic table) can form metal–metal bonds. The carbonyls of iron and manganese provide examples of metal–metal bonds that are, respectively, accompanied by, and not accompanied by, bridging groups, as shown below:

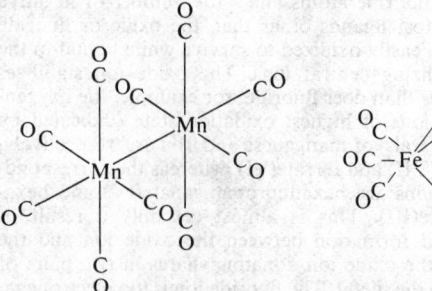

decacarbonyldimanganese   tri-μ-carbonylbis(tricarbonyliron)

In the case of the rhenium halides with the formula $Re_2X_8^{2-}$, molecular orbital theory has been used to explain the unusually short rhenium–rhenium-bond distance in terms of a quadruple bond between the two rhenium atoms. Clusters occur with mutual bonding of three metal atoms [$Os_3(CO)_{12}$, Nb_3Cl_8], four metal atoms [$Co_4(CO)_{12}$], and six metal atoms [$Rh_6(CO)_{16}$ and $Mo_6X_8^{4+}$].

Other inorganic polymers. A polymer is a substance with a molecular structure containing repeating units; commonly, molecules with varying numbers of the repeating units are present, with the result that most polymer samples exist as a distribution of molecules having different molecular weights. Whereas the repeating methylene unit (CH_2) is the simplest and most familar among organic polymers, the unit $–O–SiY_2–$ (in which $Y = O^-$ or OH) is the parent of many inorganic structures, especially certain minerals. Orthosilicic acid, $Si(OH)_4$, polymerizes by the elimination of water to form a vast array of structures, known as polymeric silicates, as shown by the following equation for the formation of a double molecule, or dimer; repetition of the process leads to progressively longer molecules.

Polymeric silicates

These polymers are best known in certain minerals. Long chains of $–SiO_3–$ units, for example, are found in the minerals enstatite, which conforms to the general formula $MgSiO_3$, and in spodumene, $LiAl(SiO_3)_2$. Other minerals, called amphiboles, and including such substances as tremolite, $Ca_2Mg_5(Si_4O_{11})_2(OH)_2$, contain double-stranded long chains in which the repeated unit is $S_4O_{11}^{6-}$. These substances are fibrous in character (asbestos being a good example), and the chains are held together by the cations. Mica and talc are two-dimensional sheet polymers of silicon and oxygen, whereas feldspar and zeolites are rigid, three-dimensional polymers of similar type. Silicates also form such cyclic materials as $Si_3O_9^{6-}$, the structure of which is shown below:

cyclic silicate anion

The most useful of man-made inorganic polymers are the siloxanes (also known as silicones), which use the basic structural unit of the silicate minerals, $–OSiY_2–$, with—however—the Y's being methyl groups. Simple examples of these structures are:

CH₃ — Si — O — Si — CH₃ (structure diagram)

$$CH_3-Si-O-Si-CH_3$$

CH₃ ~ Si — O — Si — O — Si — O — Si — O — Si — CH₃.

Siloxanes are chemically unreactive and thermally stable.

Phosphoric acid (H_3PO_4) and sulfuric acid (H_2SO_4) resemble orthosilicic acid (H_4SiO_4) in undergoing polymerization reactions, but the polymers designated by the formulas $H_2S_2O_7$ and $H_2S_3O_{10}$ are extremely sensitive to moisture. Sulfur trioxide, SO_3, exists in trimeric cyclic and linear polymeric forms.

Polyphosphates and polysulfates

The polyphosphates are somewhat more stable than polysulfates, and long chain structures similar to the single-stranded silicates are known. The lower molecular weight anions, $(O_3P-O-PO_3)^{4-}$ and $(O_3P-O-PO_2-O-PO_3)^{5-}$, are the most important. Cyclic phosphates are also known. Tungsten and molybdenum form a remarkable series of polyacids in which cluster-type polymerization occurs through oxygen bridges.

Phosphorus forms a series of compounds of the formula $(PNX_2)_n$, which can exist in both cyclic and linear polymeric forms, as shown below:

cyclic form   linear polymeric form

Polymers held together by coordination have also been prepared. A substance that found early use in producing coated polarizing lenses had the structure shown:

(Ni–S–C=N structure diagram)

Special nonmetallic derivatives. Oxygen forms metal salts containing the peroxide ion O_2^{2-}, the superoxide ion O_2^-, or the ozonide ion O_3^-. The last two are powerful oxidizing agents, whereas the peroxide ion can act either as an oxidizing or as a reducing agent.

Oxygen fluorides

Oxygen is assigned positive oxidation states only when it is combined with fluorine, the most electronegative of all elements. The compounds formulated as OF_2, O_2F_2, O_3F_2, and O_4F_2 are all strong oxidizing agents, and all are likely to react violently with most other substances. Trioxygen difluoride, O_3F_2, for example, is even more reactive than elemental fluorine. The great oxidizing strengths of these materials has led to interest in them as potential oxidizers for rocket fuels.

The binary compounds of hydrogen with elements at the right of the periodic table (Group IVa to VIIa) have already been discussed. The hydrides of the strong metallic elements are typical salts containing the hydride ion, H^-. The alkali-metal hydrides (e.g., lithium and sodium hydride) have the same crystal structure as sodium chloride. The hydride ion also forms many complexes, especially with the electron-deficient hydrides of the Group IIIa elements. The formation of lithium borohydride is shown below:

$$2LiH + B_2H_6 \longrightarrow 2LiBH_4 .$$

lithium hydride   diborane   lithium borohydride

The complex hydride lithium aluminum hydride is an especially important reducing agent (that is, one that provides electrons) in chemical syntheses.

Interhalogen compounds

The halogens react among themselves to form a remarkable series of molecular interhalogen compounds (such as iodine chloride, bromine trifluoride, and iodine pentafluoride) and interhalogen ions (such as those formulated

as I_3^-, ICl_4^-, BrF_4^-). The structures of these substances have been of theoretical importance because unshared pairs of electrons on the central atoms play a part in determining the geometries of the molecules, as shown in the following diagrams:

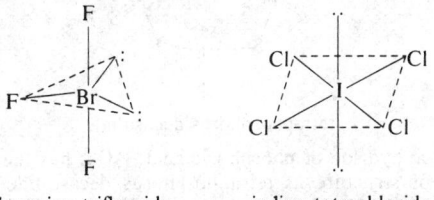

bromine trifluoride   iodine tetrachloride

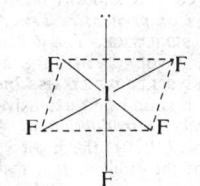

iodine pentafluoride

The fluorides of sulfur contrast strongly with those of oxygen. Sulfur tetrafluoride is a moderate fluorinating agent, and the hexafluoride can be used effectively as a dielectric material (one that does not conduct electricity) because of its great thermal stability and chemical inertness.

Reprinted by permission of the publisher, from *Chemistry: A Study of Matter* by Alfred B. Garrett, W. Thomas Lippincott, and Frank Verhoek (Lexington, Massachusetts, Ginn and Company, a Xerox Company, 1968)

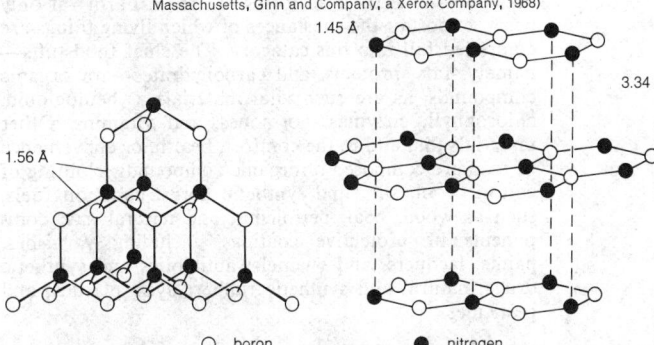

○ boron   ● nitrogen

Figure 7: The structure of boron nitride, BN, illustrating its macromolecular nature and similarity to diamond and graphite. (Left) The arrangement of boron and nitrogen atoms in the diamond form of BN. (Right) The arrangement of boron and nitrogen atoms in the graphite form of BN.

Boron and nitrogen are on opposite sides of carbon in the periodic table, and they occur in one-to-one ratios in a series of materials that resemble elemental forms of carbon (diamond and graphite) and certain hydrocarbons (see Figure 7).

The compounds of sulfur and phosphorus, tetraphosphorus trisulfide (P_4S_3), tetraphosphorus pentasulfide (P_4S_5), tetraphosphorus heptasulfide (P_4S_7), and tetraphosphorus decasulfide (P_4S_{10}), appear to have strange formulas; they can all be understood, however, on the basis of a single structural principle. White phosphorus is composed of discrete P_4 tetrahedra, and the various sulfides are derived from these by the addition of sulfur atoms either along the edges or at the apexes of the structure (as shown below), all such locations being filled in tetraphosphorus decasulfide:

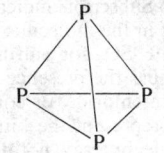

white phosphorus   tetraphosphorus trisulfide

tetraphosphorus decasulfide

The anhydride of phosphoric acid, P_4O_{10}, has the same type of structure as tetraphosphorus decasulfide (with oxygen atoms replacing sulfur atoms).

BIBLIOGRAPHY. F.A. COTTON and G. WILKINSON, *Advanced Inorganic Chemistry: A Comprehensive Text*, 2nd ed. (1966), the standard text; N.V. SIDGEWICK, *The Chemical Elements and Their Compounds*, 2 vol. (1950), the classic compilation; C.S.G. PHILLIPS and R.J.P. WILLIAMS, *Inorganic Chemistry*, 2 vol. (1965–66), a sound and extensive survey of the field; P.J. and B. DURRANT, *Introduction to Advanced Inorganic Chemistry*, 2nd ed. (1970), the most recent relatively thorough presentation of the subject; H.J. EMELEUS and A.G. SHARPE (eds.), *Advances in Inorganic Chemistry and Radiochemistry*, vol. 1 (1959–), annual reviews on specific aspects of inorganic chemistry; INTERNATIONAL UNION OF PURE AND APPLIED CHEMISTRY, *Nomenclature of Inorganic Chemistry* (1959), commission report on internationally accepted methods of naming inorganic compounds.

(D.H.B.)

Chemical Compounds, Organic

Organic chemical compounds can be defined roughly as compounds of carbon. They are of great importance to mankind—indeed, to all forms of life on Earth—if only because most of the substances of which living things are composed fall into this category. The chief foodstuffs—namely, fats, proteins, and carbohydrates—are organic compounds, as are such vital materials as hemoglobin, chlorophyll, enzymes, hormones, and vitamins. Other materials that add to the comfort, health, or convenience of man are composed of organic compounds: clothing of cotton, wool, silk, and synthetic fibres; common fuels, such as wood, coal, petroleum, and natural gas; components of protective coatings, including varnishes, paints, lacquers, and enamels; antibiotics and synthetic drugs; natural and synthetic rubber; dyes; plastics; and pesticides.

GENERAL CONSIDERATIONS

Chemical compounds are substances made up of identical molecules—that is, of unique combinations of atoms of two or more chemical elements. Each atom consists of a nucleus surrounded by electrons—electrons being the smallest stable particle of matter, each of which bears the smallest possible unit of negative charge. The nucleus of an atom carries one or more positive charges (equal and opposite to the unit of negative charge on the electron). The nucleus accounts for most of the weight of the atom, and its composition increases in complexity with increasing atomic weight. The electrons are bound to the nucleus by the attraction between the positive and negative charges. In every atom (in its free, or uncombined, state) the number of electrons surrounding the nucleus is equal to the number of positive charges on the nucleus; hence, the atom is electrically neutral.

Molecular formulas
The compositions of compounds are shown by molecular formulas, in which the atoms are represented by the chemical symbols for the elements—for example, C for carbon, Cl for chlorine, H for hydrogen, N for nitrogen, Na for sodium, O for oxygen, and S for sulfur (see further the article CHEMICAL ELEMENTS). Subscripts indicate the number of atoms of each element in the molecule, as in the formulas H_2O for water and H_2SO_4 for sulfuric acid. (The absence of a subscript implies the presence of only one atom, as in NaCl for sodium chloride, or common salt.) Such molecular formulas represent the kinds and numbers of atoms in a molecule but say nothing about the order or the way in which the atoms are linked.

Chemical compounds are grouped broadly into two classes, organic and inorganic. In general, no chemist would hesitate in classifying a given chemical compound in one or the other of these groups. Yet it is difficult to give a concise definition of either class. The reason is that several factors are involved. Although organic compounds commonly are defined as compounds of carbon, there are many other compounds classed as inorganic that do contain carbon. The distinction is made chiefly on the basis of the kinds of bonds (attractive forces between atoms) in the compounds in question.

Types of chemical bonds
Chemical bonds. These bonds may be divided into two principal types, ionic bonds and covalent bonds. Atoms on the left-hand side of the periodic table of the elements—as the standard classification scheme of the chemical elements is called (see PERIODIC LAW)—can lose electrons more easily than they can gain them and (somewhat ambiguously) are called electropositive, whereas atoms on the right-hand side of the table, except for the last column of inert gases, are able to gain electrons more readily than they lose them and are called electronegative. Chemical bonds can be formed by the transfer of one or more electrons from an electropositive atom to an electronegative atom, the transfer leaving a positive charge on the atom that has lost an electron and a negative charge on the atom that has gained the electron. The charged particles that result from such transfers are called ions, and the attractive force between the oppositely charged ions is called an ionic bond. In general, the transfer of electrons between atoms in this way leads to a much more stable situation (as far as the overall energy of the system is concerned) than when the atoms are isolated, so much so that free atoms do not exist in nature on the Earth's surface under normal conditions.

Ionic bonds. The charge on each ion is dispersed evenly in all directions. Hence ionic bonds are nondirectional. The numerous ions in a substance are held together in a crystal lattice, a three-dimensional framework that extends throughout the crystal, its overall dimensions equalling those of the crystal itself. The structure of any particular crystalline substance depends on the size of the particles and the charges on them. Strictly speaking, then, there is no molecule of the substance sodium chloride, although its formula usually is written as NaCl; instead, there are only sodium ions (Na^+) and chloride ions (Cl^-) held together in a crystal lattice in which each sodium ion is surrounded by six chloride ions and each chloride ion by six sodium ions, all of which are equidistant from one another.

Properties of ionic compounds
Because of the strong electrostatic forces between the constituent ions, ionic compounds have high melting points. Sodium chloride, for example, melts at 801° C (about 1,470° F). In the molten state, the ions in an ionic substance are sufficiently free to move that they are able to conduct an electric current. Furthermore, when such a substance is placed in water, it may dissolve if the crystal lattice forces are not too great, with disruption of the crystal lattice. Water molecules are electric dipoles (that is, they have positive and negative ends), and they attach themselves to the exposed charges on the surface ions of a crystal. The electrostatic forces (positive–negative attractions) between the surface ions and those of the interior are weakened, and, as a result, hydrated ions of the substance pass into solution. These hydrated ions no longer have a strong attraction for each other, because of the electrically insulating property of the water; hence, the hydrated ions are free to move, and the aqueous solution is able to conduct an electric current.

Covalent bonds. Obviously, two like atoms of a single element have no tendency to transfer electrons from one to the other (neither nucleus being more attractive than the other toward electrons). Yet many diatomic molecules of like elements are well known, including hydrogen, H_2, and chlorine, Cl_2. In these instances, the combined charges of two positive atomic nuclei exert a stronger overall pull on the outer valence electrons than could a single nucleus alone; the result is that the outer electrons from both atoms encompass both nuclei, and the two atoms are held together. The type of bond formed is called a covalent, or an electron-pair, bond, and the resulting combination of atoms is a true molecule that does not bear an overall electrical charge. Chemical compounds with covalent bonds between the atoms also form between the atoms of unlike elements, when circumstances do not favour the complete transfer of electrons between the atoms to form ions.

Since the surface of a covalently bonded molecule is essentially covered by electrons, the natural tendency would seem to be for such molecules to repel one another. Other types of attractive forces between the molecules, however, come into play and tend to hold such molecules together, but these forces are much weaker than those between ions in a crystal lattice. Because of the relatively weak forces between their molecules, compounds having only covalent bonds lack the extreme rigidity of the crystal lattice and are either gases, liquids, or low-melting solids. Hydrogen is a gas that can be liquefied under pressure at very low temperatures, and the solid melts at −259° C (−434° F). Of the halogen elements, fluorine, F_2, and chlorine, Cl_2, are readily liquefied gases; bromine, Br_2, is a liquid at ordinary temperatures and pressures; and iodine, I_2, is a solid that melts at 113.5° C (236° F). In general, solid compounds with only covalent bonds melt below 300° C (about 600° F). The atoms of typical organic compounds are held together by covalent bonds. Those organic compounds that do not melt below 300° C usually decompose when heated to higher temperatures, because the bonds eventually are broken, and the molecule itself is disrupted.

Properties of covalent compounds

The special case of the carbon atom. The carbon atom is unique among elements in its tendency to form covalent bonds, not only with other elements but also with itself. Because of its position midway in the second horizontal row, or period, of the table, carbon is neither an electropositive nor an electronegative element; it therefore is more likely to share electrons than to gain or lose them. Moreover, for elements in its period, carbon has the maximum number of outer shell electrons (four) capable of forming covalent bonds. (Other elements, such as phosphorus and cobalt, are able to form five and six covalent bonds, respectively, with other elements, but they lack carbon's ability to bond indefinitely with itself.) The four bonds of the carbon atom are directed to the corners of a tetrahedron (a solid figure with four corners) and make angles of about 109.5° with each other. The result is that carbon atoms not only can combine with one another indefinitely to give compounds of extremely high molecular weight, but the molecules formed have a three-dimensional structure that leads potentially to an infinite variety of different molecules. At present there are approximately ten times as many carbon compounds of known structure as there are compounds of all the other elements of the periodic table combined. It is the abundance of the covalent compounds of carbon, as well as their unique character, that justifies their characterization as a separate group, called organic compounds, whereas the compounds of all other elements that do not contain carbon are classed together as the inorganic compounds.

Elements other than carbon. The elements other than carbon that usually are present in organic compounds, in the order of decreasing frequency, are hydrogen, oxygen, nitrogen, chlorine, and sulfur; in addition, many compounds are known that contain other elements. An illustration of the variety and complexity of organic compounds can be found in the latest complete formula index of *Beilsteins Handbuch der organischen Chemie* (a standard reference source for information on organic compounds, which, however, covers the chemical literature only through 1929); the compound with the simplest formula listed in the *Beilstein* index has the molecular formula CHN, and that with the largest number of carbon atoms has the formula $C_{304}H_{582}O_{27}$. To cite a more recent instance, the first biannual formula index of *Chemical Abstracts* (a standard contemporary reference source) for 1969 lists the molecular formula $C_{783}H_{1,235}N_{221}O_{218}S_2$. Molecular weights can be calculated from molecular formulas by adding the atomic weights of the atoms present. The molecular weight of CHN, for example, is (approximately) 12 + 1 + 14, or 27, and that of $C_{783}H_{1,235}N_{221}O_{218}S_2$ is 12 × 783 + 1 × 1,235 + 14 × 221 + 16 × 218 + 32 × 2, or 17,277. When the molecules of one kind or a few relatively simple kinds of compounds bond together to form giant structures, the process is called polymerization; the giant molecule, or macromolecule, is a polymer, and its components are monomers. Polyethylene is a polymer of ethylene molecules only; polyester fibres of two monomers, while proteins are polymers of about twenty different amino acids. The average molecular weights of organic polymers can run into millions, a further indication of the large size of the molecules of certain organic compounds.

CLASSIFICATION AND NOMENCLATURE

Fortunately, despite the large number of organic compounds, a relatively simple systematic nomenclature has been adopted internationally that can be applied to the less complex—and hence the great majority—of organic compounds. This system was inaugurated by an international congress held in Geneva in 1892 and modified and extended at a meeting of the International Union of Chemistry held at Liège, Belgium, in 1930; since 1949, further development of the system has been continued under the auspices of the International Union of Pure and Applied Chemistry (IUPAC).

The IUPAC system

Fundamentally, the IUPAC system is based on a nomenclature for compounds that contain only carbon and hydrogen—that is, the hydrocarbons. Those hydrocarbons that contain the maximum possible number of hydrogens are called saturated hydrocarbons, and their names end in the suffix -ane. Organic compounds are divided broadly into acyclic compounds, in which the carbon atoms are joined to one another in linear or branched fashion, and cyclic compounds, which contain rings, or circular structures, formed by joining together the ends of a row of atoms.

Alkanes and cyclanes. The acyclic saturated hydrocarbons as a class are called alkanes, and the cyclic compounds as a class are called cyclanes.

Structural formulas

The structures of organic compounds commonly are represented by structural formulas, which show not only the kinds and numbers of atoms present in the molecule but also the way in which the atoms are linked by the covalent bonds—information that is not given by simple molecular formulas. (With most inorganic compounds, the use of structural formulas is not necessary, because only a few atoms are involved, and only a single arrangement of the atoms is possible.) In the structural formulas of organic compounds, dashes are used to represent the covalent bonds. Atoms of the individual elements are represented by their chemical symbols as in molecular formulas. Examples of structural formulas of simple alkanes and cyclanes are given below:

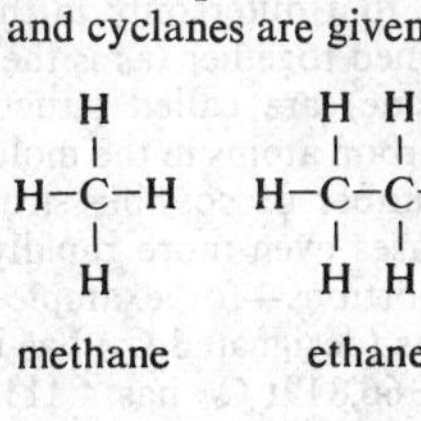

methane ethane

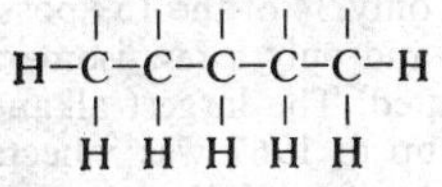

or $CH_3CH_2CH_2CH_2CH_3$

pentane

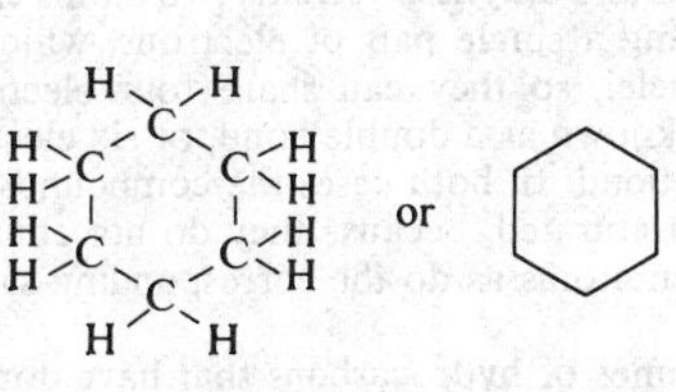

cyclohexane

Because so many hydrogen atoms appear in the various formulas when they are fully written out, it is customary to indicate simply the order of the carbon atoms with the number of hydrogens attached to each carbon indicated by a subscript as in molecular formulas, as shown in the alternate formula of pentane (above). Moreover, with cyclic compounds the rings are often indicated merely by polygons, each apex of which is considered to be a carbon atom bearing as many hydrogen atoms as needed for saturation.

In order to facilitate the naming of more complicated compounds, hydrocarbon groups that have one less hydrogen atom than the alkane are called alkyl groups, and their names have the same root as the corresponding alkane but end in the suffix -yl. Thus, CH_3- is known as a methyl group, and CH_3CH_2-, or simply C_2H_5-, is ethyl. The positions of such groups in the parent hydrocarbon —that is, the hydrogen atoms of the parent alkane that they replace—are indicated by numbers (numbering beginning at one end of a chain or at a fixed position on the ring), as in the examples below:

2,2,4-trimethylpentane   1-methyl-3-ethylcyclohexane

Before the introduction of the systematic names for organic compounds, other names frequently were used. These nonsystematic names, usually known as common names, often are used, and in this article such names will be given in parentheses following the systematic name.

Common names
For simple alkanes containing one to three carbon atoms, only one structure is possible, but, with the alkane that has four carbon atoms, two different structures are possible. This suggests that two different compounds— with the same molecular formula, C_4H_{10}, but with different structural formulas—are possible. Indeed, two such compounds are known. One boils at $-0.5°$ C ($31°$ F) and the other at $-12°$ C ($10°$ F). The former has been shown to have the structure corresponding to butane, whereas the second corresponds to methylpropane. The structures of both compounds are shown below:

$$CH_3CH_2CH_2CH_3 \qquad CH_3CHCH_3$$
$$CH_3$$

butane (*n*-butane)   methylpropane (isobutane)

Two or more compounds that have the same molecular formula but differ in molecular structure and, hence, in at least one chemical or physical property are called isomers. Isomers that differ only in the order in which the atoms are joined together (as is the case with butane and methylpropane) are called structural isomers. As the number of carbon atoms in the molecule of an alkane increases, the number of possible structural isomers of the alkane increases even more rapidly, until it reaches astronomic proportions—for example, the alkane with five carbon atoms (designated C_5) has three isomers; C_{10} has 75; C_{20} has 366,319; C_{30} has 4,111,846,763; and C_{40} has 6.25×10^{13}. By 1967 all of the predicted alkanes through the decanes (C_{10}), but only 34 of the 159 possible undecanes (C_{11}) were known; and only a few isomers of higher alkanes had been isolated. The largest alkane of known structure synthesized up to 1967 was *n*-hectane, $C_{100}H_{202}$, with a molecular weight of 1,402.

Structural isomers
Alkenes and alkynes. Just as two atoms can be bonded by sharing a single pair of electrons, which encompass both nuclei, so they can share four electrons, to give what is known as a double bond, or six electrons, to give a triple bond. In both cases the compounds are referred to as unsaturated, because they do not contain as many hydrogen atoms as do the corresponding saturated compounds.

The names of hydrocarbons that have double bonds in the molecules all end in the suffix -ene. The position of the double bond is indicated by a number (beginning from one end of the chain or a fixed position in a ring). Examples of various compounds with double bonds are shown below:

ethene (ethylene)   1-butene   2-butene

$$\overset{4}{C}H_3\overset{3}{C}H_2\overset{2}{C}H=\overset{1}{C}H_2 \qquad \overset{4}{C}H_3\overset{3}{C}H=\overset{2}{C}HC\overset{1}{H_3}$$

cyclohexene   or

Surprisingly, two substances corresponding to the structure of 2-butene are known. Whereas there is relatively free rotation of atoms or groups about a single bond, rotation about a double bond cannot take place. The two carbon atoms joined by a double bond and the four atoms attached to them all lie in a plane. This fixed arrangement of atoms gives rise to a new type of isomerism, known as stereoisomerism. Stereoisomers have the same structure but differ in the arrangement of the atoms in space. Those compounds that have like groups (or specially designated groups) on the same side of a double bond are called *cis*, and those with like groups on opposite side are *trans*. A comparison of the *cis*- and *trans*-2-butenes with the single isomer of 1-butene is given below:

Stereoisomerism

cis-2-butene   *trans*-2-butene   1-butene

It easily can be seen that 1-butene cannot exist in two forms because it has two like groups attached to one of the doubly bonded carbon atoms. This type of stereoisomerism is called geometrical isomerism because of the geometrical difference between the isomeric forms.

A second major form of stereoisomerism is known as optical isomerism, which occurs when four different groups are bonded to a carbon atom. Such an atom is known as an asymmetric carbon atom. Optical isomers differ in the spatial arrangement, known as the configuration, of their parts. The difference between members of a pair of simple optical isomers is similar to the difference between right- and left-hand gloves; that is, they are not superimposable. Unlike structural isomers and geometrical isomers, optical isomers that are mirror images, called enantiomorphs, are physically identical in all respects—except for one particular property, the ability to rotate plane-polarized light. Each of a pair of enantiomorphs rotates plane-polarized light to the same extent but in opposite directions when measured under identical conditions. One form, which rotates light to the right, is designated as the *d* (for dextrorotatory) form; the other, which rotates to the left, is the *l* (or levorotatory) form. An example of a pair of optical isomers with one asymmetric carbon atom is the *d*- and *l*-lactic acids. In these formulas the asymmetric carbon atom is in the plane of the paper, the carboxyl (CO_2H) and the methyl (CH_3) groups behind the plane of the paper, and the hydrogen atom (H) and the hydroxyl group (OH) in front of the plane of the paper.

d-lactic acid [(+)-lactic acid]   *l*-lactic acid [(−)-lactic acid]

Because the sign of rotation bears no relationship to the spatial arrangement of the groups and because confusion has arisen concerning the symbols for the two properties, the designations *d*, *l*, D, and L no longer are recommended. Dextrorotation is designated by the symbol $(+)$, and levorotation by $(-)$. Except for physical identification, however, it is the configuration and not the sign of rotation that is important to chemists and biologists. In order to designate uniquely the configuration of compounds containing one or more asymmetric carbon atoms, each such atom in a molecule now is classified as *R* (Latin *rectus*, "right") or *S* (Latin *sinister*, "left") according to specific rules advanced in 1956. According to these rules $(-)$-lactic acid has the *R* configuration.

Hydrocarbons that contain a triple bond are called alkynes; their names end in -yne. Examples are:

$$H - C \equiv C - H \qquad CH_3CH_2 - C \equiv C - H \qquad CH_3 - C \equiv C - CH_3.$$

ethyne	1-butyne	2-butyne
(acetylene)	(ethylacetylene)	(dimethylacetylene)

The four atoms involved in a triple bond are arranged in linear fashion, and the structure cannot give rise to stereoisomers. A ring compound may contain a triple bond, but because the normal bond angles in the ring resist more than minimal distortion, the ring must have at least eight carbon atoms before it will permit the inclusion of a triple bond.

The alkanes and cyclanes do not react with other chemicals under ordinary conditions; for example, they are unaffected by bromine in the absence of light, they are not oxidized by solutions of potassium permanganate, and they are not affected by treatment with concentrated sulfuric acid (which can, therefore, be used to remove other organic impurities). Alkenes, cyclenes, and alkynes, on the other hand, react readily with these reagents; for instance, these classes all add bromine rapidly at room temperature.

The reaction of an alkene or alkyne with bromine can be represented, as all chemical reactions are, by balanced equations, in which the number of atoms on the right of an arrow is equal to the number of atoms on the left. The reactants are placed on the left of the arrow and the products on the right. The direction in which the arrow points indicates the direction in which the reaction proceeds; a double arrow indicates that the forward and reverse reactions both occur, with the result that the products and reactants are in equilibrium. In many in-

Chemical reactions (margin)

stances, as in the addition of bromine to double and triple bonds, the reaction, for all practical purposes, goes to completion in one direction, although it is written as an equilibrium because it is, in principle, reversible.

$$CH_3 - CH = CH - CH_3 + Br_2 \rightleftharpoons CH_3 - CHBr - CHBr - CH_3$$

2-butene	2,3-dibromobutane

$$CH_3 - C \equiv C - CH_3 + 2Br_2 \rightleftharpoons CH_3 - CBr_2 - CBr_2 - CH_3$$

2-butyne	2,2,3,3-tetrabromobutane

Compounds with functional groups. Atomic groupings within molecules that are responsible for the varying chemical properties of organic compounds, such as the double and triple bonds, are known as functional groups. The further classification and nomenclature of organic compounds is based on these groups.

If the symbol R is used to represent either hydrogen or an alkyl group, the general classes of organic compounds can be represented by attaching the proper number of R groups to the functional groups that distinguish the various classes. Alkenes, for example, can be represented by the general formula shown below:

$$\begin{array}{cc} R & R \\ \diagdown \quad \diagup \\ C = C \\ \diagup \quad \diagdown \\ R & R \end{array}$$

(If one of the R groups in a class must be hydrogen, it is so indicated.) The functional group is indicated by either a suffix or a prefix added to the name of the corresponding alkane, as shown in Table 1. Before a vowel, the terminal *e* of the alkane is elided. For simpler compounds, common names generally are used.

Polyfunctional compounds have more than one functional group. Hydroxycarboxylic acids, ketocarboxylic acids, and aminocarboxylic acids are common natural products. More complicated compounds with numerous mixed functions frequently are encountered.

Aromatic compounds. A second class of cyclic hydrocarbons must also be noted, namely the aromatic hydrocarbons, of which benzene (C_6H_6) is the simplest example. This compound is characterized by a planar ring of six carbon atoms, none of which bears more than one hydrogen atom. Normally this structure would seem to be that of an unsaturated compound (as substances with double and triple bonds are called),

Structure of benzene (margin)

Table 1: Some Classifications of Organic Compounds According to Functional Group

class	function and name	general formula	suffix	prefix	examples
Alcohols	$-OH$, hydroxyl	$R - OH$	-ol	hydroxy-	C_2H_5OH, ethanol; C_6H_5OH, phenol; $HOCH_2CH_2OH$, 1,2-dihydroxyethane
Halogen compounds	$-X =$ chlorine, bromine, or iodine	$R - X$		chloro-, bromo-, or iodo-	$CH_3CH_2CHClCH_3$, 2-chlorobutane (*sec*-butyl chloride)
Ethers	$RO-$, alkoxyl	$R - O - R$		alkoxy-	$C_2H_5OCH_3$, methoxyethane (ethyl methyl ether)
Carboxylic acids	$-COOH$, carboxyl	$R - COOH$	-oic acid		CH_3COOH, ethanoic acid (acetic acid)
Ketones	$C=O$, carbonyl	$R - CO - R$	-one	oxo- (keto-)	$CH_3CH_2CH_2COCH_3$, 2-pentanone $CH_3COCH_2CH_2COOH$, 4-oxopentanoic acid
Aldehydes	$-C=O$, aldehyde	$RCHO$	-al	formyl-	$CH_3CH_2CH_2CHO$, butanal (*n*-butyraldehyde) $HCOCH_2CH_2COOH$, 3-formylpropanoic acid
Esters	$-C-OR$, alkoxycarbonyl	$R - COOR'$	alkyl... -oate		$CH_3COOC_2H_5$, ethyl ethanoate (ethyl acetate)
Amines	$-NH_2$, amino	RNH_2	-amine	amino-	CH_3CHCH_3, 2-aminopropane NH_2 (isopropylamine)
Thiols (mercaptans)	$-SH$, sulfhydryl	RSH	-thiol	mercapto-	C_2H_5SH, ethanethiol (ethyl mercaptan) $HSCH_2CH_2COOH$, 3-mercaptopropanoic acid
Sulfonic acids	$-SO_2H$, sulfonic acid	RSO_2H	-sulfonic acid		$CH_3CH_2CH_2SO_2H$, propanesulfonic acid

six hydrogens being missing from a typically saturated compound, but benzene shows none of the unsaturated chemical properties of alkenes or alkynes. Also, the hydrogens of benzene can be replaced by other groups more readily than is true for other classes of hydrocarbons. Furthermore, if the benzene ring contained three double bonds, two isomeric 1,2-disubstitution products should exist, which would differ in the location of the double bonds with respect to the substituents, as shown in the following two formulations:

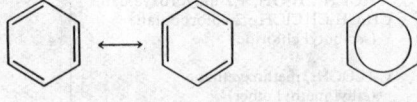

hypothetical isomers of disubstituted benzenes

in which Z is used to represent the substituents without regard to their nature (which is not important to the argument). The failure of all attempts to isolate such isomers of disubstituted benzenes led the German chemist Friedrich August Kekule to postulate in 1872 that the three double bonds in the two expected forms of benzene were in dynamic equilibrium, as shown below:

Kekule representation of
benzene isomers in equilibrium

The Kekule hypothesis, however, hardly accounts for the nonreactivity of the double bonds or for the fact that benzene is more stable than would be expected for a compound with three double bonds. Current theory describes the benzene molecule as a resonance hybrid of two Kekule forms—that is, as a form that shows characteristics of both forms but is identical to neither. Alternatively, the benzene molecule can be described in terms of electron pathways (designated pi orbitals) that encompass all six cabon atoms. Representations of these two descriptions of benzene are given below, the two resonance forms being connected by a single double-headed arrow and the pi-electron system being represented by a circle within the hexagon ring of the benzene molecule:

resonance forms   pi-orbital formulation
of benzene   of benzene

Higher molecular weight members of the aromatic hydrocarbon family can have two or more aromatic rings fused—that is, joined in such a way that two or more carbon atoms are common to two or more rings. Usually, the carbon atoms of the rings and the peripheral hydrogens are not indicated, as in these formulas of representative aromatic compounds with multiple rings:

or

naphthalene, $C_{10}H_8$

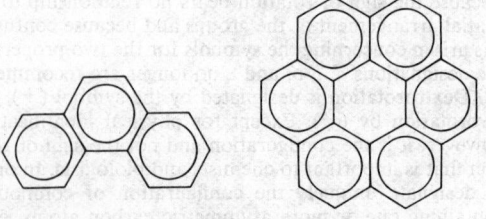

phenanthrene, $C_{14}H_{10}$ coronene, $C_{24}H_{12}$

As with alkanes, aromatic compounds can be converted to derivatives, in which alkyl groups or functional groups replace aromatic hydrogens. If the functional group is attached directly to the aromatic ring, the properties of the group may be changed qualitatively by interaction with the aromatic ring, and the functional group, in turn, may influence markedly the properties of the remaining hydrogens of the aromatic ring. Phenol, C_6H_5OH, for example, an aromatic hydroxyl compound, is much more acidic than ethanol, C_2H_5OH, a saturated hydroxyl compound, and the hydrogens in certain positions of the benzene ring of phenol are much more readily displaced by halogen atoms (atoms of chlorine, bromine, or iodine) than are the hydrogens of benzene (see below *Substitution reactions*).

Functional derivatives of aromatic compounds

Heterocyclic compounds. Still another large group of organic compounds is that classed as heterocyclic. In these compounds, some element other than carbon replaces one or more carbon atoms of the ring. Heterocyclic compounds may be of either the cyclane type or the aromatic type. A few examples of each are given in the formulas shown below. As with other classes of organic compounds, functional groups rather than hydrogen atoms may be present.

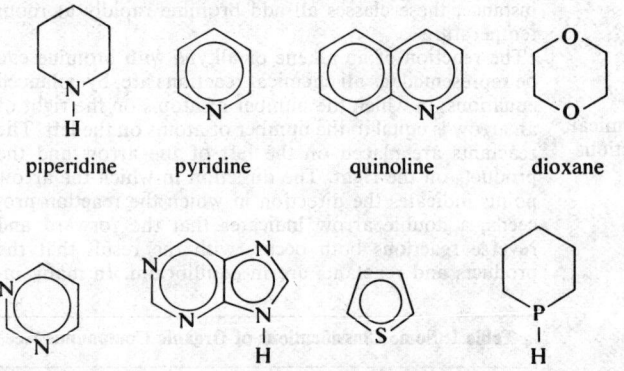

piperidine   pyridine   quinoline   dioxane

pyrimidine   purine   thiophene   phosphacyclohexane

PREPARATION AND PURIFICATION

Organic compounds are either derived from natural products or prepared by synthesis. The natural sources of organic compounds are plants and animals or fossil fuels, such as coal and petroleum. Synthesis is the use of chemical reactions to build larger molecules from smaller ones or to rearrange the atoms in a molecule to give new molecules.

Sources of organic compounds

The destructive distillation of coal to produce coke yields a liquid mixture called coal tar, which once was the chief source of aromatic compounds. Thermal decomposition of ethane, propane, and higher petroleum products is used to give alkenes of lower molecular weight; and the catalytic reforming of gasoline and kerosene fractions (which results in cyclization and the removal of hydrogen) now also yields aromatic hydrocarbons.

Fats, carbohydrates, and proteins not only are important as food substances but also yield fatty acids, sugars, and amino acids. Cellulose from cotton or wood can be converted to synthetic fibres, plastics, and explosives. Many important medicinals, such as the alkaloids and vitamins, as well as some dyes, flavours, and perfumes, are extracted from plants. Synthesis, however, accounts for most organic compounds, the initial starting points for which are chiefly the alkenes and the aromatic hydrocarbons. The chemical reactions of the various classes of organic compounds, many of which are of synthetic utility, are described below (see below *Chemical reactions*).

Separation methods

Most natural products and the products of synthetic reactions are mixtures that must be separated into the pure components. The procedures most commonly used are distillation, crystallization, and extraction with solvents. For the more difficult separations, selective adsorption and the various types of chromatography, a separation procedure based on differential adsorption of substances on various solid supporting materials, are used. Electrophoresis and ionophoresis, two processes that depend on the relative rates of migration in an electric field, can be used for charged particles.

It probably is fair to say that no ordinary compound is ever entirely free of foreign molecules as impurities. The degree of purity of any particular substance depends on the effort that is made to remove the last traces of impurities, and the effort expended generally depends on the use to be made of the compound. Compounds prepared for use as food additives or medicinal agents, for example, may need more extensive purification than those intended merely for industrial use. Once a compound is obtained as homomolecular (that is, in a form in which all the molecules present are identical) as is reasonably possible, it may be analyzed qualitatively for the elements present and then quantitatively for each element to determine the relative amounts of it in the molecule. The final step in establishing the molecular formula of the compound in question is the determination of the molecular weight. Today, in modern chemical laboratories, all of these analytical operations are carried out by specialists in microanalysis rather than by organic chemists.

Determination of structure

Once the molecular formula of a compound is established, the structure of the compound—that is, the order in which the atoms are attached to each other—must be elucidated. First, the kind and number of functional groups are determined. Then the molecule is broken down stepwise by known chemical reactions to smaller molecules of known structure. From the various bits of evidence, a structure is postulated in much the same way as a jigsaw puzzle is put together. This process has been greatly accelerated since about 1940, due to the development of physical procedures that use sophisticated electronic apparatus to secure information concerning molecular structure. Therefore, the determinations of ultraviolet and infrared spectra (light-absorption patterns), nuclear-magnetic-resonance spectra (patterns produced by magnetic effects on atomic nuclei), and mass spectra (separations of compounds—and fragments produced from them—on the basis of their relative mass) all play an important role in investigating the structures of relatively complex molecules. The use of radioactive isotopes of the various elements is fairly common, particularly in the study of organic reactions and in biochemical research on the way in which organic compounds are synthesized by living organisms.

The final proof of structure of a new organic compound is the synthesis of the supposed structure by known reactions from smaller molecules of known structure. Chemists have been able to arrive at the structure and configuration of substances with extraordinarily complex molecules, such as cholesterol, $C_{27}H_{46}O$, penicillin G, $C_{16}H_{18}N_2SO_4$, and chlorophyll *a*, $C_{55}H_{72}N_4O_5Mg$, by investigating their chemical and physical properties—and those of their degradation products. They also have been able to rebuild these molecules step by step from smaller molecules and in the end obtain compounds identical in all respects with the original product. This fact is the most convincing evidence of the soundness of the theories concerning the ways in which the various atoms are attached to one another in organic molecules.

PHYSICAL PROPERTIES

Since all compounds with a given functional group have approximately the same chemical properties, the differences among members of a given class of organic compound are largely differences in their physical properties. Boiling points, melting points, and solubility in various solvents are used most frequently to characterize a particular compound. Density, vapour pressure, and viscosity also often are measured. The most characteristic physical property of an organic compound, however, is its infrared absorption spectrum—that is, the particular pattern of wavelengths of light absorbed in the infrared region of the electromagnetic spectrum. If two products have identical infrared spectra, they almost certainly are identical compounds.

Factors that raise boiling points

Boiling point. In general, the boiling points of compounds with similar structures increase with increasing molecular weight. For simple, monofunctional, straight-chain compounds, the boiling point increases by about 20° C (36° F) for each additional carbon atom. Alkanes with four carbon atoms or fewer are gases at room temperature. For the higher molecular weight compounds, the boiling point rises from 36° C (97° F) for pentane, C_5H_{12}, to 287° C (548° F) for hexadecane, $C_{16}H_{34}$. Branching of the carbon chain lowers the boiling point. Thus, 2-methylbutane boils at 28° C (82° F) and 2,2-dimethylpropane at 9.5° C (49° F).

With the exception of double bonds, functional groups in a compound cause the boiling point to be higher. The chief factors that raise the boiling points of compounds above those of the corresponding alkanes are hydrogen bonding (attraction through secondary bonds involving hydrogen atoms attached to oxygen or nitrogen) and dipole–dipole interaction (attraction between polarized molecules). Both of these factors cause a degree of adhesion between individual molecules, hence making it more difficult to separate them. Table 2 (below) lists the boiling points of some simple compounds of approxi-

Table 2: Boiling Points and Specific Gravities of Some Simple Organic Compounds

common name	formula	molecular weight	boiling point (°C)	specific gravity at 20° C
n-Butane	$CH_3CH_2CH_2CH_3$	58	−0.5	0.58
Methyl ethyl ether	$CH_3OCH_2CH_3$	60	10.8	0.73
Ethyl chloride	CH_3CH_2Cl	64	12.3	0.90
Ethyl mercaptan	CH_3CH_2SH	62	35.0	0.84
n-Propylamine	$CH_3CH_2CH_2NH_2$	59	49.0	0.72
Propionaldehyde	CH_3CH_2CHO	58	49.0	0.81
Acetone	CH_3COCH_3	58	56.0	0.79
n-Propyl alcohol	$CH_3CH_2CH_2OH$	60	98.0	0.80

mately the same molecular weight in the order of increasing boiling points.

Melting point. The melting points of solids increase with an increase of the forces holding the molecules in the crystal lattice. These forces depend on how readily the molecules fit together, a process that is influenced by the functional groups present and by the size and shape of the molecules. Usually, the more symmetrical the molecule, the higher the melting point of the compounds. Other generalizations have been made for certain types of compounds, but few predictions can be made concerning the melting points of most compounds.

Solubility. The solubility of one organic compound in another is the result of the intermingling of like and unlike molecules, whether they be gases, liquids, or solids. The extent to which compounds are mutually soluble depends on how nearly the attractive forces between like molecules match the attractive forces between unlike molecules. Thus, gases are all miscible with each other, because there is little in the way of attractive force even between the like molecules of a particular gaseous substance. The liquid alkanes are miscible in all proportions because the attractive forces between the like alkane molecules are much the same as between the unlike molecules. The liquid alkanes dissolve solid alkanes of lower molecular weights, but the solubility of the solid compounds decreases with increasing molecular weight, chiefly because the force with which the molecules are held in the crystal lattice increases with increasing molecular weight.

At the other extreme, water molecules are practically insoluble in liquid alkanes, and alkanes in water. In these cases, hydrogen bonding (secondary attraction by way of hydrogen atoms) of the water molecules to each other is many times stronger than the attractive forces between water molecules and alkane molecules, and there is little tendency to intermingle.

On the other hand, the lower alcohols, amines, and carboxylic acids are soluble in water for much the same reason that sodium chloride is soluble in water. Water molecules form hydrogen bonds not only with themselves but also with the hydroxyl group of alcohols and the amino group of amines and can hydrate the carboxylic-acid group and its ions, thus tending to equalize the attractive forces between the different molecules. For straight-chain alcohols with more than four carbon atoms and carboxylic acids with more than six carbon atoms, hydration is less effective in equalizing the attractive forces, and solubility of these compounds in water rapidly decreases. These considerations give rise to the old rule of thumb that "like dissolves like"; that is, the more closely organic compounds resemble one another in composition and structure, the greater is their mutual solubility.

Density and viscosity. The density of alkanes is lower than that of all other organic compounds, all alkanes being lighter than water. For liquids, a commonly cited datum is the specific gravity at 20° C (68° F); that is, the density of the substance at 20° C compared to that of water at 4° C (39° F); among the alkanes, the specific gravity varies from 0.63 for pentane (C_5H_{12}) to 0.77 for hexadecane ($C_{16}H_{34}$). The specific gravity increases with the introduction of atoms of elements that have a higher atomic weight than carbon (see Table 2) and with the increase of the ratio of the mass of such atoms to the mass of the rest of the molecule. Thus, ethyl chloride (C_2H_5Cl, $Cl/C_2H_5 = 1.2$) has a higher specific gravity, 0.90, than ethyl alcohol, 0.80 (C_2H_5OH, $OH/C_2H_5 = 0.6$); and 1,2-dichloroethane, at 1.26 (ClC_2H_4Cl, $Cl/CH_2 = 2.5$), is denser than water.

The viscosity of liquids depends on the ease with which molecules can slip past each other. Viscosity usually increases with increasing chain length of organic molecules because of the increased attraction between the molecules and the increased possibility of mutual entanglement.

CHEMICAL REACTIONS

Equilibria and rates of reaction

Most organic reactions are reversible to a greater or lesser extent; that is, the products of the reaction react with one another to regenerate the original reactants. In equilibrium reactions, the most important features are (1) the position of equilibrium, namely the ratio of products to reactants when chemical equilibrium is reached, and (2) the rate of reaction, or the speed at which the reaction takes place. The position of equilibrium is governed by the relative concentrations of reactants, the temperature, and the free energy change for the reaction —that is, the relative energy content of the reactants and products. The rate of reaction is influenced by the nature of the reactants, their concentrations, the temperature, the presence of catalysts or inhibitors, and the type of solvent used (if the reaction is carried out in solution). Acid–base reactions that involve readily ionized acids, for example, are extremely fast. When covalent bonds must be broken, however, the rate of the reaction at room temperature usually is very slow.

Since the rates of chemical processes approximately double for each 10° C (18° F) rise in temperature, organic reactions usually are carried out at elevated temperatures. In those instances in which high temperatures adversely affect the position of equilibrium, catalysts are sought that will make it possible for the reaction to proceed at reasonable rates and at as low a temperature as possible. Because both the forward and reverse reactions depend on the concentrations of the reactants, a desired reaction often can be made to go to completion by removing one of the products of the reaction; water, for

example, may be removed by distillation or by the addition of a dehydrating agent. Since about 1940, chemists have become increasingly aware of the effect of solvents on the rates of reactions. Rate increases of over 1,000,000-fold have been produced merely by changing the solvent.

Types of reactions

Because of the large number of different parent organic compounds and different functional groups, many types of organic reactions are possible. Some of the more important types are acid–base, addition, substitution, displacement, hydrolysis, pyrolysis, condensation, polymerization, and molecular-rearrangement reactions.

Acid–base reactions. Acids may be defined as compounds that can transfer a proton (a hydrogen atom that lacks an electron) to a base and a base as any entity with an unshared pair of electrons (and therefore capable of accepting a proton). In acid–base reactions a proton is transferred from an acid to a base, as shown in the following equation

$$H:A + :B \rightleftharpoons H:B^+ + :A^-,$$

in which HA represents any acid and B any base.

If HA and B are neutral molecules, the product is a positive ion and a negative ion and is known as a salt. A specific example is shown below, in which acetic acid is the acid involved, ethylamine is the base, and ethylammonium acetate is the resulting salt.

$$CH_3COOH + :NH_2C_2H_5 \longrightarrow CH_3COO^- + {}^+NH_3C_2H_5$$

acetic   ethylamine   ethylammonium
acid   acetate

Degrees of acidity and basicity

Varying degrees of acidity—that is, variations in the ease of removal of the proton—are possible, ranging from the extremely strong sulfonic acids to the virtually nonacidic alkanes; and varying degrees of basicity—or attraction for the proton—ranging from the extremely strongly basic alkide ion, R^-, to the extremely weakly basic sulfonate ion, RSO_2O^-, are also possible.

Addition reactions. The addition of one molecule to another to give a single new molecule is an important class of reactions. Illustrative is the addition of bromine to ethylene.

$$H_2C = CH_2 + Br_2 \longrightarrow H_2CBrCH_2Br$$

ethylene   bromine   1,2-dibromoethane

Substitution reactions. The replacement of hydrogen on carbon by another group generally is referred to as substitution. A typical substitution reaction is the synthesis of chlorobenzene from benzene and chlorine using ferric chloride as catalyst, as shown below:

benzene   chlorine   ferric   chlorobenzene   hydrogen
                   chloride   chloride

Displacement reactions. The direct replacement of one functional group by another generally is classed as a displacement reaction. A simple displacement of one halogen atom (chlorine) by another (iodine) in acetone as solvent is shown below:

$$CH_3CH_2CH_2Cl + Na^+I^- \longrightarrow CH_3CH_2CH_2I + Na^+Cl^-.$$

propyl   sodium   propyl   sodium
chloride   iodide   iodide   chloride

Hydrolysis. The scission (or cleavage) of a molecule by reaction with water, with insertion of the elements of water into the final products, is called hydrolysis. An example is the acid-catalyzed hydrolysis of ethyl acetate:

$$CH_3COOC_2H_5 + H_2O \overset{H^+}{\rightleftharpoons} CH_3COOH + HOC_2H_5.$$

ethyl   water   acetic   ethyl
acetate   acid   alcohol

This reaction is typical of reversible reactions that do not go to completion. When one mole (the quantity with a weight in grams numerically equal to the molecular weight) of ethyl acetate and one mole of water react, only about one-third of the ethyl acetate is converted to acetic acid and ethyl alcohol. A greater degree of conversion may be produced by using an excess of water. However, a more practical procedure is to promote the reaction by a strong base, which reacts irreversibly with the acetic acid formed and, therefore, forces the reaction to completion.

Pyrolysis. Pyrolysis is the decomposition of a molecule by heat. The pyrolysis of carbon tetrachloride is a good example:

$$2CCl_4 \xrightarrow{800-900°\,C} Cl_2C = CCl_2 + 2Cl_2 \,.$$

carbon tetrachloride   tetrachloro-ethylene   chlorine

Condensation. The formation of a carbon–carbon bond between two molecules, with the elimination of a small molecule such as water or alcohol, generally is called a condensation reaction. An example follows:

$$CH_3COOC_2H_5 + CH_3COOC_2H_5$$

ethyl acetate   ethyl acetate

$$\xrightarrow[]{^-OC_2H_5} CH_3COCH_2COOC_2H_5 + C_2H_5OH.$$

ethyl acetoacetate

Polymerization. Polymerization refers to the formation of compounds of high molecular weight—that is, polymers—from many smaller molecules (monomers) by addition or condensation reactions. Examples of both types are given below:

Addition polymerization:

$$x CH_2 = CH_2 \xrightarrow[\substack{titanium \\ tetrachloride, \\ trialkyl- \\ aluminum}]{TiCl_4, AlR_3} (-CH_2CH_2-)_x \quad x = 7{,}000 \text{ to } 29{,}000$$

ethylene   polyethylene   molecular weight = 200,000 to 800,000

Condensation polymerization:

$$y HOCH_2CH_2 - O - CO - \bigcirc - COOH$$

ethyleneglycol monoterephthalate

$$\xrightarrow{heat} (-OCH_2CH_2 - O - CO - \bigcirc - CO-)_y + (y-1)H_2O$$

Dacron   y = 80 to 130
molecular weight = 15,000 to 25,000

Molecular rearrangement. Molecular rearrangements are redistributions of atoms or groups within molecules. An example is the heat-induced rearrangement of allyl phenyl ether to 2-allylphenol, as shown:

allyl phenyl ether   2-allylphenol

Numerous subclassifications of the above reactions, such as alkylation, acylation, esterification, ammonolysis, oxidation–reduction, nitration, chlorination, sulfonation, and disproportionation, also are used by chemists.

PRODUCTION

The production of organic chemical compounds has become an important branch of industry and permeates every aspect of everyday life. Table 3 summarizes the total United States production of synthetic organic chemical products for 1969 as compiled and classified by the United States Tariff Commission. No comparable breakdown for world production of synthetic organic chemical

Table 3: U.S. Production of Synthetic Organic Chemical Products (1969)

classification	production in short tons
Crude products from petroleum and natural gas (for chemical conversion)	35,657,689
Cyclic intermediates	14,285,435
Dyes	120,104
Synthetic organic pigments	30,505
Medicinal chemicals	100,017
Flavour and perfume materials	60,195
Plastics and resin materials	9,338,124
Rubber-processing chemicals	151,714
Synthetic rubbers	2,262,028
Plasticizers	691,115
Surface-active agents (detergents and wetting agents)	1,950,510
Pesticides and related products	552,190
Miscellaneous chemicals	37,859,989

products is available. The United Nations *Statistical Yearbook* for 1970 gives the 1969 preliminary figures by countries for two of the above classes, namely synthetic rubbers, and plastics and resins. Table 4 lists these data for the six largest producers.

Table 4: Chief Producers of Synthetic Rubbers and Plastics and Resins (1969)

	production in short tons	
	synthetic rubbers	plastics and resins
France	302,500	1,450,900
West Germany	321,500	4,382,900
Japan	578,000	4,733,300
U.S.S.R.	*	1,598,300
U.K.	300,300	1,463,000
U.S.	2,514,600	9,000,900
World total	5,219,500	25,345,000

*Not given.

Many of these synthetic organic compounds, as well as many waste compounds produced during their manufacture, are dumped eventually on the land and into the rivers, where they resist the chemical reactions that break down naturally produced organic structures. In addition, many noxious synthetic compounds, designed for the control of plants and insects, also are impervious to natural agents, and even low concentrations of these compounds threaten all forms of life. Thus, an increasing problem in organic chemistry is the ultimate disposal of synthetic products.

A recent trend in organic chemistry has been that of greater knowledge of the mechanisms of reactions, a field dominated by the methods of physical chemistry. A trend in biology has been toward increasing use of knowledge concerning molecular structure. Thus, organic chemistry is now a field in which knowledge of physics and knowledge of biological processes meet.

BIBLIOGRAPHY. E.H. RODD (ed.), *Chemistry of Carbon Compounds*, 10 vol. (1951–62; 2nd ed. by S. COFFEY, 1964–), is the most extensive general text on organic chemistry in English. *Beilsteins Handbuch der organischen Chemie* is the only source in any language that attempts to cover the chemical and physical properties of all organic compounds with references to the original literature. The fourth edition of 27 volumes published during the years 1918–37 covers all known organic compounds through 1909. Publication of the first supplement of 31 volumes covering the years 1910–19 began in 1928 and was completed in 1938. The second supplement of 31 volumes covers 1920–29. It was published between 1941 and 1957. General indexes cover all of the literature through 1929. Thirty-five volumes of the third supplement covering 1930–49 have been published through 1970. It appeared to be about 90 percent complete at that time. Until a general index is published for this supplement, the indexes to each volume must be used. *Chemical Abstracts*, published by the AMERICAN CHEMICAL SOCIETY, Washington D.C., is a weekly journal that summarizes world literature in all branches of chemistry. A collective formula index was published covering the years 1920–46. It was followed by supplementary indexes for 1947–56, 1957–61, and 1962–66. For data from 1967 to date, there are semi-annual indexes. R.C. WEAST (ed.), *Handbook of Chemistry and Physics*, 49th ed. (1968–69), lists the common physical properties for 13,621 organic compounds. The *Nomenclature of Organic Chemistry*, 2nd ed. (1966), published by the INTERNATIONAL UNION OF PURE AND APPLIED CHEMISTRY, provides the internationally approved rules of nomenclature. The introduction to the index of *Chemical Abstracts*, vol. 56 (1962), discusses the naming of organic compounds followed for indexing purposes. See also R.S. CAHN, *An Introduction to Chemical Nomenclature* (1959); and the UNITED STATES TARIFF COMMISSION, *Synthetic Organic Chemicals* (1970), for production information.

(C.R.No.)

Chemical Elements

Chemical elements are the fundamental materials of which all matter is composed. From the modern viewpoint, a substance that cannot be decomposed into simpler substances by ordinary chemical processes is, by definition, an element. At present there are 105 known chemical elements. Elements can combine with one another to form a wide variety of more complex substances called compounds. The number of possible compounds is almost infinite; perhaps a million are known, and more are being discovered every day. When two or more elements combine to form a compound, they lose their separate identities, and the product has characteristics quite different from those of the constituent elements. The gaseous elements hydrogen and oxygen, for example, with quite different properties, can combine to form the compound water, which has altogether different properties from either oxygen or hydrogen. Water clearly is not an element because it consists of, and actually can be decomposed chemically into, the two substances hydrogen and oxygen; these two substances, however, are elements because they cannot be decomposed into simpler substances by any known chemical process. Most samples of naturally occurring matter are physical mixtures of compounds. Seawater, for example, is a mixture of water and a large number of other compounds, the most common of which is sodium chloride, or table salt. Mixtures differ from compounds in that they can be separated into their component parts by physical processes; for example, the simple process of evaporation separates water from the other compounds in seawater.

Historical development of the concept of element. The modern concept of an element is unambiguous, depending as it does on the use of chemical and physical processes as a means of discriminating elements from compounds and mixtures. The existence of fundamental substances from which all matter is made, however, has been the basis of much theoretical speculation since the dawn of history. The ancient Greek philosophers Thales, Anaximenes, and Heracleitus each suggested that all matter is composed of one essential principle—or element. Thales believed this element to be water; Anaximenes suggested air; and Heracleitus, fire. Another Greek philosopher, Empedocles, expressed a different belief—that all substances are composed of four elements: air, earth, fire, and water. Aristotle agreed and emphasized that these four elements are bearers of fundamental properties, dryness and heat being associated with fire, heat and moisture with air, moisture and cold with water, and cold and dryness with earth. In the thinking of these philosophers all other substances were supposed to be combinations of the four elements, and the properties of substances were thought to reflect their elemental compositions. Thus, Greek thought encompassed the idea that all matter could be understood in terms of elemental qualities; in this sense, the elements themselves were thought of as nonmaterial. The Greek concept of an element, which was accepted for nearly 2,000 years, contained only one aspect of the modern definition—namely, that elements have characteristic properties.

In the latter part of the Middle Ages, as alchemists became more sophisticated in their knowledge of chemical processes, the Greek concepts of the composition of matter became less satisfactory. Additional elemental qualities were introduced to accommodate newly discovered chemical transformations. Thus, sulfur came to represent the quality of combustibility, mercury that of volatility or fluidity, and salt that of fixity in fire (or incombustibility). These three alchemical elements, or principles, also represented abstractions of properties reflecting the nature of matter, not physical substances.

The important difference between a mixture and a chemical compound eventually was understood, and in 1661 the English chemist Robert Boyle recognized the fundamental nature of a chemical element. He argued that the four Greek elements could not be the real chemical elements because they cannot combine to form other substances nor can they be extracted from other substances. Boyle stressed the physical nature of elements and related them to the compounds they formed in the modern operational way.

In 1789 the French chemist Antoine-Laurent Lavoisier published what might be considered the first list of elemental substances based on Boyle's definition. Lavoisier's list of elements was established on the basis of a careful, quantitative study of decomposition and recombination reactions. Because he could not devise experiments to decompose certain substances, or to form them from known elements, Lavoisier included in his list of elements such substances as lime, alumina, and silica, which now are known to be very stable compounds rather than elements. That Lavoisier still retained a measure of influence from the ancient Greek concept of the elements is indicated by his inclusion of light and heat (caloric) among the elements.

Seven substances recognized today as elements (*i.e.*, gold, silver, copper, iron, lead, tin, and mercury) were known to the ancients because they occur in nature in relatively pure form. They are mentioned in the Bible and in an early Hindu medical treatise, the *Caraka-saṃhitā*. Sixteen other elements were discovered in the second half of the 18th century, when methods of separating elements from their compounds became better understood. Eighty-two more followed, after the introduction of quantitative analytical methods.

The atomic nature of the elements. Paralleling the development of the concept of elements was an understanding of the nature of matter. At various times in history, matter has been considered to be either continuous or discontinuous. Continuous matter is postulated to be homogeneous and divisible without limit, each part exhibiting identical properties regardless of size. This was essentially the point of view taken by Aristotle when he associated his elemental qualities with continuous matter. Discontinuous matter, on the other hand, is conceived of as particulate—that is, divisible only up to a point, the point at which certain basic units called atoms are reached. According to this concept, also known as the atomic hypothesis, subdivision of the basic unit (atom) could give rise only to particles with profoundly different properties. Atoms, then, would be the ultimate carriers of the properties associated with bulk matter.

The atomic hypothesis is usually credited to the Greek philosopher Democritus, who considered all matter to be composed of atoms of the four elements—earth, air, fire, and water. But Aristotle's concept of continuous matter generally prevailed and influenced thought until experimental findings in the 16th century forced a return to the atomic theory. Two types of experimental evidence gave support to the atomic hypothesis: first, the detailed behaviour of gaseous substances and, second, the quantitative weight relationships observed with a variety of chemical reactions. The English chemist John Dalton was the first to explain the empirically derived laws of chemical combination by postulating the existence of atoms with unique sets of properties. At the time, chemical combining power (valence) and relative atomic weights were the properties of most interest. Subsequently numerous independent experimental verifications of the atomic hypothesis were carried out, and today it is universally accepted. Indeed, in 1969 individual uranium and thorium atoms

(margin notes)
Elements, compounds, and mixtures

Lavoisier's list of elements

The atomic hypothesis

Periodic Table of the Elements

group	Ia	IIa	IIIb	IVb	Vb	VIb	VIIb	VIII			Ib	IIb	IIIa	IVa	Va	VIa	VIIa	0

Period 1

1 1.00797 **H** 1s¹ hydrogen

2 4.0026 **He** 1s² helium

Period 2

3 6.939 **Li** 1s²2s¹ lithium
4 9.0122 **Be** 1s²2s² beryllium
5 10.811 **B** 1s²2s²2p¹ boron
6 12.01115 **C** 1s²2s²2p² carbon
7 14.0067 **N** 1s²2s²2p³ nitrogen
8 15.9994 **O** 1s²2s²2p⁴ oxygen
9 18.9984 **F** 1s²2s²2p⁵ fluorine
10 20.183 **Ne** 1s²2s²2p⁶ neon

Period 3

11 22.9898 **Na** [Ne]3s¹ sodium
12 24.312 **Mg** 3s² magnesium
13 26.9815 **Al** 3s²3p¹ aluminum
14 28.086 **Si** 3s²3p² silicon
15 30.9738 **P** 3s²3p³ phosphorus
16 32.064 **S** 3s²3p⁴ sulfur
17 35.453 **Cl** 3s²3p⁵ chlorine
18 39.948 **Ar** 3s²3p⁶ argon

Period 4

19 39.102 **K** [Ar]4s¹ potassium
20 40.08 **Ca** 4s² calcium
21 44.956 **Sc** 3d¹4s² scandium
22 47.90 **Ti** 3d²4s² titanium
23 50.942 **V** 3d³4s² vanadium
24 51.996 **Cr** 3d⁵4s¹ chromium
25 54.938 **Mn** 3d⁵4s² manganese
26 55.847 **Fe** 3d⁶4s² iron
27 58.933 **Co** 3d⁷4s² cobalt
28 58.71 **Ni** 3d⁸4s² nickel
29 63.54 **Cu** 3d¹⁰4s¹ copper
30 65.37 **Zn** 3d¹⁰4s² zinc
31 69.72 **Ga** 3d¹⁰4s²4p¹ gallium
32 72.59 **Ge** 3d¹⁰4s²4p² germanium
33 74.922 **As** 3d¹⁰4s²4p³ arsenic
34 78.96 **Se** 3d¹⁰4s²4p⁴ selenium
35 79.909 **Br** 3d¹⁰4s²4p⁵ bromine
36 83.80 **Kr** 3d¹⁰4s²4p⁶ krypton

Period 5

37 85.47 **Rb** [Kr]5s¹ rubidium
38 87.62 **Sr** 5s² strontium
39 88.905 **Y** 4d¹5s² yttrium
40 91.22 **Zr** 4d²5s² zirconium
41 92.906 **Nb** 4d⁴5s¹ niobium
42 95.94 **Mo** 4d⁵5s¹ molybdenum
43 (98) **Tc** 4d⁵5s² technetium
44 101.07 **Ru** 4d⁷5s¹ ruthenium
45 102.905 **Rh** 4d⁸5s¹ rhodium
46 106.4 **Pd** 4d¹⁰5s⁰ palladium
47 107.870 **Ag** 4d¹⁰5s¹ silver
48 112.40 **Cd** 4d¹⁰5s² cadmium
49 114.82 **In** 4d¹⁰5s²5p¹ indium
50 118.69 **Sn** 4d¹⁰5s²5p² tin
51 121.75 **Sb** 4d¹⁰5s²5p³ antimony
52 127.60 **Te** 4d¹⁰5s²5p⁴ tellurium
53 126.904 **I** 4d¹⁰5s²5p⁵ iodine
54 131.30 **Xe** 4d¹⁰5s²5p⁶ xenon

Period 6

55 132.905 **Cs** [Xe]6s¹ cesium
56 137.34 **Ba** 6s² barium
57 138.91 **La** * 5d¹6s² lanthanum
72 178.49 **Hf** 4f¹⁴5d²6s² hafnium
73 180.948 **Ta** 4f¹⁴5d³6s² tantalum
74 183.85 **W** 4f¹⁴5d⁴6s² tungsten
75 186.2 **Re** 4f¹⁴5d⁵6s² rhenium
76 190.2 **Os** 4f¹⁴5d⁶6s² osmium
77 192.2 **Ir** 4f¹⁴5d⁷6s² iridium
78 195.09 **Pt** 4f¹⁴5d⁹6s¹ platinum
79 196.967 **Au** 4f¹⁴5d¹⁰6s¹ gold
80 200.59 **Hg** 4f¹⁴5d¹⁰6s² mercury
81 204.37 **Tl** 4f¹⁴5d¹⁰6s²6p¹ thallium
82 207.19 **Pb** 4f¹⁴5d¹⁰6s²6p² lead
83 208.980 **Bi** 4f¹⁴5d¹⁰6s²6p³ bismuth
84 (210) **Po** 4f¹⁴5d¹⁰6s²6p⁴ polonium
85 (210) **At** 4f¹⁴5d¹⁰6s²6p⁵ astatine
86 (222) **Rn** 4f¹⁴5d¹⁰6s²6p⁶ radon

Period 7

87 (223) **Fr** [Rn]7s¹ francium
88 (226) **Ra** 7s² radium
89 (227) **Ac** ** 6d¹7s² actinium
104*** (261) **Rf** rutherfordium
105*** **Ha** hahnium

6 * (Lanthanides)

58 140.12 **Ce** [Xe]4f⁵d⁰6s² cerium
59 140.907 **Pr** 4f³5d⁰6s² praseodymium
60 144.24 **Nd** 4f⁴5d⁰6s² neodymium
61 (147) **Pm** 4f⁵5d⁰6s² promethium
62 150.35 **Sm** 4f⁶5d⁰6s² samarium
63 151.96 **Eu** 4f⁷5d⁰6s² europium
64 157.25 **Gd** 4f⁷5d¹6s² gadolinium
65 158.924 **Tb** 4f⁹5d⁰6s² terbium
66 162.50 **Dy** 4f¹⁰5d⁰6s² dysprosium
67 164.930 **Ho** 4f¹¹5d⁰6s² holmium
68 167.26 **Er** 4f¹²5d⁰6s² erbium
69 168.934 **Tm** 4f¹³5d⁰6s² thulium
70 173.04 **Yb** 4f¹⁴5d⁰6s² ytterbium
71 174.97 **Lu** 4f¹⁴5d¹6s² lutetium

7 ** (Actinides)

90 232.038 **Th** [Rn]5f⁰6d²7s² thorium
91 (231) **Pa** 5f²6d¹7s² protactinium
92 238.03 **U** 5f³6d¹7s² uranium
93 (237) **Np** 5f⁴6d¹7s² neptunium
94 (242) **Pu** 5f⁶6d⁰7s² plutonium
95 (243) **Am** 5f⁷6d⁰7s² americium
96 (247) **Cm** 5f⁷6d¹7s² curium
97 (247) **Bk** 5f⁹6d⁰7s² berkelium
98 (249) **Cf** 5f¹⁰6d⁰7s² californium
99 (254) **Es** 5f¹¹6d⁰7s² einsteinium
100 (253) **Fm** 5f¹²6d⁰7s² fermium
101 (256) **Md** 5f¹³6d⁰7s² mendelevium
102 (254) **No** 5f¹⁴6d⁰7s² nobelium
103 (257) **Lr** 5f¹⁴6d¹7s² lawrencium

*** data are currently in dispute

acid-base properties of higher-valence oxides:

● strongly basic   ▶ weakly basic   ◁ weakly acidic   ◉ equal relative strength   ○ strongly acidic

cubic, face centred;   ⊠ cubic, body centred;   ◇ diamond;   ▯ cubic;   ⬡ rhombohedral;   ▯ tetragonal;   ▱ orthorhombic;   ⬡ monoclinic

— solid under normal conditions   ⌇ liquid under normal conditions   ···· gas under normal conditions   = synthetically prepared

were actually observed by means of an electron microscope.

The structure of atoms. Atoms of elemental substances are themselves complex structures composed of more fundamental particles called protons, neutrons, and electrons. Experimental evidence indicates that, within an atom, a small nucleus, which generally contains both protons and neutrons, is surrounded by a swarm, or cloud, of electrons. The fundamental properties of these subatomic particles are their weight and electrical charge. Whereas protons carry a positive charge and electrons a negative one, neutrons are electrically neutral. The diameter of an atom (about 10^{-8} centimetre) is 10,000 times larger than that of its nucleus. Neutrons and protons, which are collectively called nucleons, have relative weights of approximately one atomic mass unit, whereas an electron is only about $\frac{1}{2,000}$ as heavy. Because neutrons and protons occur in the nucleus, virtually all of the mass of the atom is concentrated there. The number of protons in the nucleus is equivalent to the atomic number of the element. The total number of protons and neutrons is called the mass number because it equals the relative weight of that atom compared to other atoms. Because the atom itself is electrically neutral, the atomic number represents not only the number of protons, or positive charges, in the nucleus but also the number of electrons, or negative charges, in the extranuclear region of the atom.

The chemical characteristics of elements are intimately related to the number and arrangement of electrons in their atoms. Thus, elements are completely distinguishable from each other by their atomic numbers. This realization leads to another definition of an element, namely, a substance, all atoms of which have the same atomic number.

The existence of isotopes. Careful experimental examination of naturally occurring samples of many pure elements shows that not all the atoms present have the same atomic weight, even though they all have the same atomic number. Such a situation can occur only if the atoms have different numbers of neutrons in their nuclei. Such groups of atoms—with the same atomic number, but with different relative weights—are called isotopes. The number of isotopic forms that a naturally occurring element possesses ranges from one (*e.g.*, fluorine) to as many as ten (*e.g.*, tin); most of the elements have at least two isotopes. The atomic weight of an element is usually determined on large numbers of atoms containing the natural distribution of isotopes, and, therefore, it represents the average isotopic weight of the atoms constituting the sample. More recently, precision mass-spectrometric methods have been used to determine the distribution and weights of isotopes in various naturally occurring samples of elements.

Classifications of the elements. *The periodic table.* When the elements are arranged in order of increasing atomic number, there occurs a regular variation, and a periodic recurrence, of chemical and physical properties. This phenomenon is called the periodic law. The Figure is a typical arrangement of elements illustrating the periodic law, elements in the same vertical columns having similar properties. Originally the elements were arranged in periodic classifications, or periodic tables, as they are called, on the basis of their experimentally observed properties; but essentially the same arrangement results from consideration of the distribution and number of extranuclear electrons possessing similar energies.

Electrons may be described in terms of the relative average positions they occupy in an atom or in terms of their relative energies. These descriptions of electron behaviour can be obtained by a combination of theoretical arguments (see MECHANICS, QUANTUM) with experimental results (see SPECTROSCOPY, PRINCIPLES OF). The characteristic energies of electrons in an atom are useful for classification purposes because the electrons are grouped in terms of energy and location into narrow zones, often called shells. Each energy zone contains a characteristic number of electrons, and all atoms exhibit the same zones. The electronic structures of the known elements

are accounted for by seven such shells, numbered 1–7 in order of increasing distance from the nucleus. Each main shell is divided into subshells, or sets of orbitals, that differ somewhat in energy. The first main shell consists of one orbital, designated $1s$, having a capacity of two electrons. The second shell comprises a $2s$ orbital, which can hold two electrons, and three $2p$ orbitals, which can hold six more; the third shell has one $3s$, three $3p$, and five $3d$ orbitals, with room for two, six, and 10 electrons, respectively. Higher-numbered shells contain still larger numbers of orbitals. The energies of the subshells are such that electrons fill the $4s$ orbitals before entering the $3d$; overlaps such as this result in partial filling of higher-numbered shells before the lower-numbered ones are completed. Groups of orbitals with similar energies are the following: $1s$; $2s$, $2p$; $3s$, $3p$; $4s$, $4p$, $3d$; $5s$, $5p$, $4d$; $6s$, $6p$, $5d$, $4f$. The numbers of electrons filling these groups (2, 8, 8, 18, 18, 32) are the numbers of elements in the first six periods of the table rather than the set 2, 8, 18, 32, 50, 72, which would correspond to completion of each main shell before beginning the next. The periodic classification places elements with similar electron arrangements in vertical columns; thus, each element in a column has the same electronic arrangement in its outermost, or valence, shell. Because the kinds of compounds an element will form are dictated by its electronic arrangement (see CHEMICAL BONDING), all the elements in any vertical column have similar chemical properties and are called families or groups, which are generally designated by roman numerals. This classification of elements into families is extremely useful. All elements of the first group of the table, for example, are metals of the same general type, reacting with water to form the same kinds of products (called bases). The intensity of the reaction, however, varies in a regular manner down the group. Lithium, the first member, reacts slowly, but the rate of reaction increases progressively until it become explosive with the elements further down in the group, such as rubidium and cesium.

Hydrogen, the element with atomic number 1, has unusual properties. In many of its compounds and reactions it resembles the elements in Group Ia, but in other instances it appears to be a member of Group VIIa. For this reason, hydrogen may be considered in a group by itself or it may be assigned to both Group Ia and Group VIIa.

Many of the groups are designated commonly by the name of the first member. The elements in Group IIIa, for example, generally are called the boron group elements. Some groups, however, have special names that are of historical significance. Thus, the Group Ia elements are known as the alkali metals; the Group IIa elements are the alkaline-earth metals; the Group VIIa elements, the halogens; and the Group 0 elements, the noble gases. The block of elements in the centre of the periodic classification (atomic numbers 22–29, 40–47, and 72–79) is called the transition elements, and the horizontal series with atomic numbers 57–71 and 89–103 are called the lanthanides and actinides, respectively. (For discussion of the individual groups, see HYDROGEN AND ITS COMPOUNDS; ALKALI METALS AND THEIR COMPOUNDS; ALKALINE-EARTH METALS AND THEIR COMPOUNDS; TRANSITION ELEMENTS AND THEIR COMPOUNDS; BORON GROUP ELEMENTS AND THEIR COMPOUNDS; CARBON GROUP ELEMENTS AND THEIR COMPOUNDS; NITROGEN GROUP ELEMENTS AND THEIR COMPOUNDS; OXYGEN GROUP ELEMENTS AND THEIR COMPOUNDS; HALOGEN ELEMENTS AND THEIR COMPOUNDS; NOBLE GASES AND THEIR COMPOUNDS; RARE-EARTH ELEMENTS AND THEIR COMPOUNDS; and ACTINIDE ELEMENTS AND THEIR COMPOUNDS.)

Other chemical and physical classifications. It is useful to classify elements according to whether they are metals or nonmetals. Metallic elements are lustrous, malleable, ductile, and good conductors of heat and electricity. In contrast, nonmetals have a dull appearance, are brittle if solid, and are poor conductors of heat and electricity. The nonmetals occupy the right-hand side of the periodic table (extending farther to the left in the upper periods than the lower) whereas the metals are found on

Margin notes:

Composition of atoms

Electronic structures of atoms

Metals and nonmetals

the lower left-hand side. A diagonal line extending from boron to astatine separates the metals from the nonmetals. Elements along the line have a mixture of metallic and nonmetallic characteristics. Silicon, for example, has a metallic luster but is a very poor conductor of electricity compared to typical metals. Elements with properties intermediate between the metals and nonmetals are called metalloids. Metals and nonmetals have distinctly different chemical properties. In chemical compounds containing only atoms of one metal and one nonmetal, the metal atoms form the positively charged species, whereas the nonmetal atoms are negatively charged. Also significant is the difference in behaviour with water of the oxides of metals and nonmetals. Thus, aqueous solutions of nonmetal oxides are acidic, whereas those of metal oxides are basic (the chemical opposite). Metalloid oxides dissolve in water to give solutions that can be either acidic or basic; such compounds are said to be amphoteric.

Certain methods of classifying elements on the basis of chemical properties are not strictly related to the groups in which the elements appear. Such classification schemes illustrate the fact that useful horizontal as well as vertical relationships exist in the periodic table. Thus, the transition elements, either as a whole or as three horizontal series, are often considered together when chemical properties are discussed. The transition elements in each horizontal series exhibit much less variation in atomic size than do the elements in other parts of the same periods, leading to a similarity in chemical and physical properties. The lanthanide and actinide elements exhibit an even greater similarity for the same reason. The metallic elements in Groups Ia and IIa are often classed together because they are markedly more reactive than the other metallic elements. At the other extreme, elements of the platinum group—including ruthenium, rhodium, palladium, osmium, iridium, and platinum—are chemically inert, as are silver and gold; these elements are collectively designated the noble metals because they do not readily enter into combination with other elements.

Of all the 105 known elements, 11 are gaseous, 2 are liquid, and the remainder are solids under ordinary conditions. Except for hydrogen and mercury, the gaseous and liquid elements occur in the right-hand part of the periodic table, the region associated with the nonmetallic elements.

The physical characteristics of the elements provide convenient means of identification. The melting points of the various elements range from $-272°$ C (for helium) to greater than $3,500°$ C (for carbon in the form of diamond). Properties such as boiling points, electrical conductivity, and thermal conductivity also can be used for identification because they are unique for each element. Perhaps the single most useful characteristic for identifying an element is its pattern of light absorption, or emission, which is called a spectrum (see SPECTROSCOPY, PRINCIPLES OF). An element exhibits its own characteristic spectrum whether it exists in the free state, in a mixture, or in chemical combination with other elements. Since the intensity of the spectrum is dependent upon the amount of the element contained in the sample, the spectrum also can be used as a means for quantitative analysis of the elements. There are several chemical methods for estimating the percentage of an element present in a sample; these, however, require a detailed knowledge of the chemistry of the element in question (see CHEMICAL ANALYSIS).

All naturally occurring elements with atomic numbers greater than 83 are radioactive; these constitute the three families of radioactive elements (*i.e.*, the uranium, thorium, and actinium series), the elements of which are converted from one to another by radioactive processes. In addition, several naturally occurring isotopes of the lighter elements are radioactive. The atomic nuclei of all radioactive elements are unstable and emit highly energetic particles. In the process, the number of protons in the nucleus changes, and the atom is transformed into one of a different element. The half-life of a radioactive isotope

is the time required for half of any amount of the isotope to disintegrate by radioactive decay. The common modes of decay of radioactive isotopes are loss of beta or alpha particles or the capture of an electron. The loss of a beta particle, or electron, from the nucleus increases the atomic number by one unit; the loss of an alpha particle, or helium nucleus (two protons and two neutrons), decreases the atomic number by two units; and the process of electron capture, in which an electron from an inner shell is drawn into the nucleus, corresponds to a decrease of atomic number by one unit. Eleven radioactive synthetic, or man-made, elements (see TRANSURANIUM ELEMENTS) have not as yet been found in nature and the presence of two nontransuranium elements has not been verified absolutely. Although the remaining elements generally are not considered to be radioactive, some do have radioactive isotopes that exist naturally in very small concentrations, and more than 1,000 radioactive isotopes of these elements have been prepared in the laboratory.

Distribution of the elements. Estimates of the terrestrial and cosmic abundance of the elements are obtained primarily from spectroscopic evidence and from chemical analysis of meteorites and terrestrial matter. It is generally assumed that the chemical composition of meteoritic matter is approximately the same as that of the Sun and other fixed stars, except for volatile elements, which are lost readily from meteorites. The most striking feature in these data is the overwhelming abundance of the lightest elements, hydrogen and helium. Furthermore, elements with even atomic numbers are more abundant than their odd-numbered neighbours. If the universe began with a gigantic explosion, as some cosmologists believe, many of the chemical elements may have been formed at that time. Others have been and are being formed continually in the interiors of the stars by nuclear reactions (see CHEMICAL ELEMENTS, ORIGIN OF).

The most abundant element on earth is oxygen. It occurs in the uncombined state in the air and combined in the form of compounds such as water and metal oxides (silica, magnesia, alumina, and ferrous oxide), which constitute most of the earth's solid matter. Although most of the elements occur in chemically combined form, there are some notable exceptions: oxygen; nitrogen; the noble gases; and certain metals such as silver, copper, and gold (see ELEMENTS, GEOCHEMICAL DISTRIBUTION OF).

Over 99 percent of the matter of living organisms is composed of just ten elements: oxygen (62 percent), carbon (20 percent), hydrogen (10 percent), nitrogen (3 percent), calcium (2.5 percent), phosphorus (1.14 percent), chlorine (0.16 percent), sulfur (0.14 percent), potassium (0.11 percent), and sodium (0.10 percent). These elements, together with magnesium, iron, manganese, copper, zinc, boron, molybdenum, iodine, and cobalt, are recognized as essential to plant and animal life, although some are needed only in trace amounts. It has been suggested that silicon, aluminum, nickel, gallium, fluorine, barium, and strontium also are necessary, but conclusive evidence on this point is not available. Oxygen in the form of water is the most abundant element in both plant cells (75 percent water), and animal cells (67 percent water).

Separation and technological importance of the elements. The methods used to separate the elements vary widely. As mentioned above, some elements, such as gold, oxygen, nitrogen, and the rare gases, occur naturally in their elemental form. These can be separated on the basis of differences in physical properties. The gaseous elements present in air, for example, can be separated from one another because they boil at different temperatures. Thus, pure air can be liquefied and the mixture fractionally distilled to give pure samples of the constituent elements. Most elements, however, occur naturally in chemical combination, and their separation becomes a problem of separating and decomposing the compounds. The separation of mixtures of compounds of several elements can be very difficult if the elements—and hence their compounds—have very similar properties. In these cases the separation techniques must take advantage of the slightly different properties of the com-

Man-made elements

Terrestrial abundance

Solid, liquid, and gaseous elements

pounds. Once relatively pure compounds are obtained, appropriate chemical processes must be employed to liberate the elements from their compounds. The action of electricity on aluminum oxide dissolved in an appropriate solvent, for example, produces pure aluminum metal. In general, economic factors determine the most appropriate method for isolating an element from its naturally occurring forms.

Uses of the elements

Nearly all of the elements have achieved some degree of technological importance. The metals, especially iron (and the alloys it forms with many of the transition elements), aluminum, and magnesium, are used as construction materials. The active metals find extensive use in the large-scale commercial preparation of carbon-containing compounds, as do the active nonmetals such as the halogens. Oxygen, produced by the liquefaction of air, is widely used in the manufacture of steel and many other industrial processes. Carbon-containing compounds are processed on a broad scale for use as fuels, plastics, and fibres. Even the rarer elements such as iridium and platinum are employed commercially as catalysts, and little-known lanthanides, such as yttrium and europium, are used in making colour-television picture tubes.

BIBLIOGRAPHY. E. FARBER, *The Evolution of Chemistry* (1952), a history of ideas, methods, and materials from a chemist's viewpoint; M.E. WEEKS and H.J. LEICESTER, *Discovery of the Elements*, 7th ed. (1968), a description of the events, both human and technical, surrounding the discovery of each of the elements and the implications on the ideas of the day; E.S. GILREATH, *Fundamental Concepts of Inorganic Chemistry* (1952), a short technical description of modern ideas concerning atomic structure, periodic relationships, and radioactivity.

(J.J.L.)

Chemical Elements, Origin of

One of the oldest problems in man's speculation about the universe has to do with the nature of matter, its origins, and the processes by which it forms an apparently infinite variety of substances. The notion that everything has derived from a primal substance was formally stated first in philosophical rather than metaphysical terms in Greece. Thales of Miletus (6th century BC) taught that all things are made of water in various degrees of concentration. Later Greek philosophers chose *aēr* (mist, vapour, air) as the basic material of the world, whereas others argued for fire. In the 5th century BC, all four were called primary substances or roots by Empedocles. Finally, Aristotle named them as the four elements, to which he added a fifth element, or quintessence, which underlay all matter and of which the perfect heavenly bodies were made. This view dominated Western thought for over 2,000 years.

The four elements of ancient thought

A related question has had to do with whether or not matter is infinitely divisible. Another Greek philosopher, Leucippus (5th century BC), is credited with the idea of an ultimate particle that could not be made smaller, the atom (Greek *atomos*, "indivisible"), but it was his student Democritus who elaborated an atomic theory of matter. The theory was rejected by Aristotle, who thought that it conflicted with the theory of the four elements, and it was forgotten or ignored save by a few writers until the 19th century.

From the early Christian Era, alchemists based their ideas and actual experiments in chemistry, medicine, and metallurgy upon the four or five, sometimes as many as seven, elements, and especially on the "qualities" of the elements (hot, cold, dry, wet) that supported their theories and visions concerning the transmutation of one kind of substance into another, for example, "base" metals into gold and aging bodies into youthful ones. Not until the end of the 18th century did laboratory experimentation in Europe shed the mystical, metaphysical wrappings of alchemical beliefs and practices—and goals. The most difficult aspect of alchemy to reject was the conviction that elements were, somehow, basic matter without the familiar, mundane properties of ordinary matter. Scattered efforts to define chemical changes more objectively ran against the limitations imposed on elements by old ideas, and, culminating these efforts, a French chemist, Antoine Lavoisier, in 1789 published the first scientific list of elements. He recognized 23. Soon after, in England, another chemist, John Dalton, formulated an atomic theory of the structure of matter that, though it was ignored for the next 50 years, eventually became the basis of modern atomic theory. The study of chemical reactions, electrochemical phenomena, electrical discharges, radioactivity, X-rays, light, crystal formation, the synthesis of organic compounds, and a host of other specific realms of research gradually revealed the structure and properties of atoms.

GENERAL CONSIDERATION OF ATOMIC AND NUCLEAR STRUCTURES

In the most general sense, elements are composed of atoms that are characteristic for each element and that consist of subatomic particles bonded into a unit capable of linking with other atoms by means of alterations in their structures and changes in their energies. The origin of the elements, therefore, cannot be explained without reference to knowledge of atomic structures, and this can be done only briefly here. For detailed study, see ATOMIC STRUCTURE; PARTICLES, SUBATOMIC; NUCLEUS, ATOMIC; ELECTRON; CHEMICAL ELEMENTS; PERIODIC LAW; SPECTROSCOPY, PRINCIPLES OF.

All atoms are composed of a nucleus with a number of positive charges, surrounded by an equal number of negatively charged electrons. The nucleus consists of two kinds of subatomic particles of about the same mass, protons and neutrons, both called nucleons. The number of protons (each carrying a single positive charge) is the same in all the atoms of an element and is called the atomic number, but not all atoms with the same atomic number have identical numbers of neutrons and, therefore, not all atoms of an element have the same mass. These varieties or species of atoms are called the isotopes of an element. The arrangement of electrons orbiting around the nucleus is orderly and periodic; *i.e.*, if the elements are listed in order of increasing atomic number, certain electronic structures recur regularly. This periodicity is the basis of the periodic table of the elements. All chemical properties are determined by the electronic structures of atoms; atoms tend to rearrange their electrons into the more stable configurations, which include several types of bonds between atoms. The hundred-odd elements combine into millions of known compounds and the number possible seems to be almost infinite. Just as the properties of atoms are determined by their electronic structures, so the properties of compounds are determined by the specific manner in which the multiple structures are fitted together. All of the electrons of an atom can be removed by such sufficiently powerful destructive forces as high heat and strong electrical and magnetic fields. A naked nucleus, with its concentrated positive charges, attracts all electrons it encounters to become an atom again. Atoms that have lost or gained electrons are called positive or negative ions.

The mass of a nucleus is always less than the sum of the masses of its constituent nucleons when they are not bonded together, a reflection of the equivalence of mass and energy—*i.e.*, the fact that under certain conditions the mass of a particle may be converted into energy and a quantity of energy may be converted into mass. The equivalence is stated in Einstein's equation: if E is the energy produced when a mass m is transformed (or vice versa), then the energy equals the mass multiplied by the square of the speed of light, symbolized as c. The equation is written $E = mc^2$. Because the speed of light is 186,000 miles per second, no matter how small m is, when it is multiplied by c^2 it will still produce a relatively enormous value for E.

Structure of the nucleus

On being bound into a nucleus, a fraction of the mass of each nucleon is transformed into energy. The more massive the nucleus—*i.e.*, the larger the number of nucleons—the greater the loss of mass per nucleon in elements lighter than iron and in iron itself. In iron, atomic number 26 (atomic number is the number of protons in the nucleus, mass number is the sum of protons and neutrons), nucleons have less mass than in any other element. In atoms heavier than those of iron, there is a reversal; *i.e.*, the loss of mass per nucleon is progressively less with larger nuclei. If a large nucleus is split into parts that are still larger than iron nuclei, nucleons in the two new nuclei will have less mass than they had in the heavier one; the fission of a heavy nucleus therefore releases energy. Fission of a light element does not release energy but requires energy to be added; if elements lighter than iron are split, the nucleons must acquire mass in order to remain bonded into the product nuclei. On the other hand, if two small nuclei are forced to unite, or fuse, to produce a single nucleus that is still smaller than iron, each nucleon must lose energy because in the resulting heavier nucleus (still lighter than iron) each has a smaller mass than it had in the two lighter nuclei. In this way the fusion of light elements releases energy.

Fusion The fundamental reaction that produces the huge amounts of energy radiated by the Sun and most other stars is the fusion of the lightest element, hydrogen, its nucleus having a single proton, into helium, the second lightest and second most abundant, with a nucleus consisting of two protons and two neutrons. In many stars the production of helium is followed by the fusion of helium into heavier elements, up to iron. The still heavier elements cannot be made in energy-releasing fusion reactions; an input of energy is required to produce them (see below *Processes producing elements heavier than hydrogen; neutron capture*).

The proportion of different elements within a star—*i.e.*, its chemical composition—is gradually changed by nuclear fusion reactions. This change is initially concentrated in the central regions of the star where it cannot be directly observed, but it alters some observable properties of the star, such as brightness and surface temperature, and these alterations are taken as evidence of what is going on in the interior. Some stars become unstable and discharge some transmuted matter into interstellar space; this leads to a change in the chemical composition of the interstellar medium and of any stars subsequently formed. The main problem concerned with the origin of the chemical elements is to decide to what extent the chemical composition of the stars seen today differs from the initial chemical composition of the universe and to determine where the change in chemical composition has been produced. Reference is made below to the chemical composition of the universe, but most of the observations refer to our own and neighbouring galaxies.

<u>OBSERVED ELEMENT ABUNDANCES IN VARIOUS LOCATIONS</u>

The relative numbers of atoms of the various elements are usually described as the abundances of the elements. The chief sources of data from which information is gained about present-day abundances of the elements are observations of the chemical composition of stars and gas clouds in the Galaxy, which contains the solar system and part of which is visible to the naked eye as the Milky Way; of neighbouring galaxies; of the Earth, Moon, and meteorites; and of the cosmic rays.

Stars and gas clouds. Atoms absorb and emit light, and the atoms of each element do so at specific and characteristic wavelengths; a spectroscope spreads out these wavelengths of light from any source into a spectrum of bright-coloured lines, a different pattern identifying each element; when light from an unknown source is analyzed in a spectroscope, the different patterns of bright lines in the spectrum reveal which elements emitted the light. Such a pattern is called an emission, or bright-line, spectrum. When light passes through a gas or cloud at a lower temperature than the light source, the gas absorbs at its identifying wavelengths and a dark-line, or absorption, spectrum will be formed.

Thus, absorption and emission lines in the spectrum of light from stars yield information concerning the chemical composition of the source of light and of the chemical composition of clouds through which the light has travelled. The absorption lines may be formed either by interstellar clouds or by the cool outer layers of the stars.

Spectroscopic analysis

The chemical composition of a star is obtained by a study of absorption lines formed in its atmosphere.

The presence of an element can, therefore, be detected easily, but it is more difficult to determine how much of it there is. The intensity of an absorption line depends not only on the total number of atoms of the element in the atmosphere of the star but also on the number of these atoms that are in a state capable of absorbing radiation of the relevant wavelength and the probability of absorption occurring. The absorption probability can, in principle, be measured in the laboratory, but the whole physical structure of the atmosphere must be calculated to determine the number of absorbing atoms. Naturally, it is easier to study the chemical composition of the Sun than of other stars, but, even for the Sun, after many decades of study, there are still significant uncertainties of chemical composition. The spectra of stars differ considerably, and originally it was believed that this indicated a wide variety of chemical composition. Subsequently it was realized that it is the surface temperature of a star that largely determines which spectral lines are excited and that most stars have similar chemical compositions.

There are, however, differences in chemical composition among stars, and these differences are important in a study of the origin of the elements. Studies of the processes that operate during stellar evolution enable estimates to be made of the ages of stars. There is, for example, a clear tendency for very old stars to have smaller quantities of elements heavier than helium than do younger stars. This suggests that the Galaxy originally contained little of the so-called heavy elements (elements beyond helium in the periodic table); and the variation of chemical composition with age suggests that heavy elements must have been produced more rapidly in the Galaxy's early history than now. Observations are also beginning to indicate that chemical composition is dependent on position in the Galaxy as well as age, with a higher heavy-element content near the galactic centre.

In addition to stars, the Galaxy contains interstellar gas and dust. Some of the gas is very cold, but some forms hot clouds, the gaseous nebulae, the chemical composition of which can be studied in some detail. The chemical composition of the gas seems to resemble that of young stars. This is in agreement with the theory that young stars are formed from the interstellar gas.

Solar system. Direct observations of chemical composition can be made for the Earth, the Moon, and meteorites, although there are some problems of interpretation. The chemical composition of the Earth's crust, oceans, and atmosphere can be studied, but this is only a minute fraction of the mass of the Earth, and there are many composition differences even within this small sample. Some information about the chemical properties of the Earth's unobserved interior can be obtained by the study of the motion of earthquake waves and by the Earth's magnetic field, which originates in the interior. At present, direct observations have been made of only a small fraction of the Moon's surface. Meteorites suffer from heating in the Earth's atmosphere, so that what is found on Earth is not necessarily the original chemical composition of the meteorites, especially for the volatiles, light gases that are easily lost. When allowance is made for the loss of volatile light gases and for effects of chemical separation, it seems quite possible that the overall chemical composition of the Earth, Moon, Sun, and the meteorites is essentially the same and that they have a common origin.

All atoms of an element have the same number of protons but may have varying numbers of neutrons, and each of such type, or species, of atom is called an isotope. Thus, hydrogen has three isotopes, one with only a proton for a nucleus, another with one proton and one neutron, and a third, radioactive, isotope with one proton and two neutrons. Some elements have as many as eight naturally occurring isotopes on Earth; their proportion worldwide is constant as a result of mixing effects.

Isotopic abundances

Isotopic abundances can essentially be observed only on the Earth, the Moon, and in meteorites. If elemental abundances are the same in the Earth and stars, isotopic

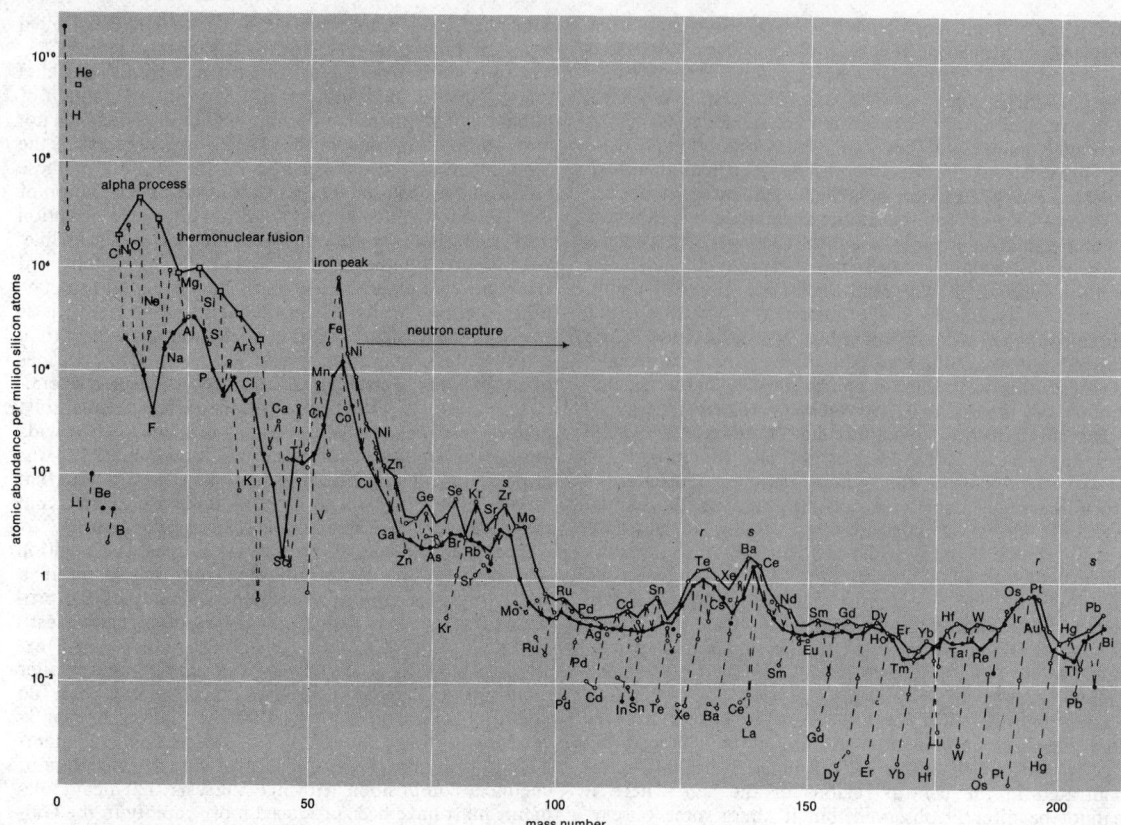

Nuclear abundances plotted against atomic mass number. Filled circles represent nuclei with odd mass numbers; open circles, even mass numbers; open squares, nuclei that can be reduced to helium nuclei (alpha particles). Broken lines join isotopes of given elements; upper solid line at left joins alpha-particle nuclei; upper solid line at right joins nuclei with even mass numbers; the lower solid line joins those with odd mass numbers. The letters *r, s* refer to elements formed by the rapid and slow neutron-capture processes.

This diagram first appeared in *New Scientist*, vol. 26, 1965, B. Pagel

abundances are likely to be the same. Theories predict the relative production of the different isotopes, and it is desirable to be able to compare these with observation. The study of terrestrial abundances of radioactive elements yields information about the age of the solar system, which is discussed below.

Cosmic rays.   High energy electrons and atomic nuclei known as cosmic rays reach the Earth from all directions in the Galaxy. Their chemical composition can be observed only to a limited extent, but this can give some information about their place of origin and possibly about the origin of the chemical elements. The cosmic rays are observed to be proportionately richer in heavy elements than are the stars, and they also contain more of the light elements lithium, beryllium, and boron, which are very rare in stars. One particularly interesting suggestion is that transuranium nuclei may have been detected in the cosmic rays. Uranium is element 92, the most massive naturally occurring on Earth; 13 elements beyond uranium (called the transuranium series) have been created artificially. All transuranium nuclei are highly unstable, which would seem to indicate that the cosmic rays must have been produced in the not too distant past.

Summary of observations.   The chemical composition of all objects in the universe is not quite the same, and not all elements can be observed in any one object, even if they are present. Nevertheless, the compositions of many objects are sufficiently similar to make it worthwhile to try to construct a typical table of abundances. Such compilations have been made by several authors and the best known, the work of the American physicists Hans Suess and Harold Urey, is shown in the figure. Although this dates from 1956, and later compilations differ in some details, its general character is not in dispute.

The main properties shown in the abundance table are quite clear. Hydrogen and helium are much more common than all of the other elements. There is a gradual decline toward higher atomic number with a great under-

abundance of lithium, beryllium, and boron. There is a significant peak in the region of iron, the element with the highest fractional binding energy, and the decline continues to higher atomic number with some subsidiary peaks. These peaks are associated with nuclei containing 50, 82, or 126 neutrons; the theory of nuclear structure predicts that these nuclei should be particularly stable, and these numbers are known as "magic" numbers.

PROCESSES PRODUCING ELEMENTS
HEAVIER THAN HYDROGEN

As mentioned above, energy can be released by either nuclear fusion or fission reactions and there will be a tendency for material to be gradually converted into elements with maximum binding energy. As observations suggest that hydrogen and helium are much more abundant than other elements, and there is an abundance peak near iron, it is generally supposed that heavy elements have been built up from light elements. In addition, some sites in which element transmutations can occur are known; for example, the interiors of stars tend to get hotter as they evolve, and a succession of nuclear reactions provides the energy that they radiate. Whether or not stars are the site of major nucleosynthesis, some nucleosynthesis certainly occurs there.

Atomic nuclei interact through two strong forces. Because they have positive electric charges, they repel one another, but there is also a very short range strong nuclear interaction that is attractive. This may cause fusion reactions to occur if the nuclei ever approach close enough for it to be operative. To overcome the electrical repulsion, the particles must be moving rapidly, as they will be if the material is at a high temperature. The overcoming of the electrical repulsion leads to what are known as thermonuclear reactions. Heavy nuclei have higher electric charges than light nuclei, and a higher temperature is required for reactions between them. The rate of thermonuclear reactions depends on density as well as temperature, but the temperature dependence is much more critical.

Reaction stages reflecting increasing temperature. If one imagines a mixture of light elements gradually heated up, a succession of nuclear reactions occurs that is described below.

Hydrogen burning. Hydrogen is converted into helium by a succession of nuclear reactions that change four protons into a helium nucleus, two positrons, and two neutrinos. (A positron is a particle like an electron but with a positive charge; a neutrino is a particle with no charge and negligible mass.) Two different reaction chains exist. In the proton–proton chain the helium nucleus is built up directly from protons. In another series of reactions that involve carbon and nitrogen, called the carbon–nitrogen cycle, the nuclei of carbon and nitrogen are used as catalysts to transform hydrogen into helium; protons are successively added to carbon or nitrogen until a helium nucleus can be emitted by them and the original carbon or nitrogen nucleus reproduced. Both of these reactions occur at temperatures of about 10,000,000° to 20,000,000° K (10,000,000° K is approximately 18,000,000° F).

Helium burning. At temperatures of about 100,000,000° to 200,000,000° K (1 to 2 × 10⁸° K), three helium nuclei can fuse to form carbon. This reaction takes place in the following way: two helium nuclei combine to form an unstable isotope of beryllium, which has an extremely short life; rarely, a third helium nucleus can be added to form carbon before the beryllium decays. Subsequently, a fourth helium nucleus may combine with carbon to give oxygen. The relative amounts of carbon and oxygen produced depend on the temperature and density at which helium is burned.

Carbon and oxygen burning. At temperatures between 5×10^{8}° K and 10^{9}° K, pairs of carbon and oxygen nuclei can fuse to produce such elements as magnesium, sodium, silicon, and sulfur.

Silicon burning. Further heating of the material leads to a complicated set of nuclear reactions whereby the elements produced in carbon and oxygen burning are gradually converted into the elements of maximum fractional binding energy; *e.g.*, chromium, manganese, iron, cobalt, and nickel. These reactions have collectively been given the name silicon burning because an important part of the process is the breaking down of silicon nuclei into helium nuclei, which are added in turn to other silicon nuclei to produce elements such as nickel and the others noted above.

Reversible nuclear reaction equilibrium. Finally, at temperatures around 4×10^{9}° K, an approximation to nuclear statistical equilibrium may be reached. At this stage, although nuclear reactions continue to occur, each nuclear reaction and its inverse occur equally rapidly, and there is no further overall change of chemical composition. Thus, the gradual production of heavy elements by nuclear fusion reactions is balanced by distintegrations, and the buildup process effectively ceases once the material is predominantly in the form of iron and its neighbouring elements of the periodic table. Indeed, if further heating occurs, a conversion of heavy nuclei to light nuclei follows in much the same way as occurs in the ionization of atoms when they are heated up. The elements heavier than iron cannot be produced by fusion reactions between light elements; an input of energy is required to produce them.

Neutron capture. It is believed that these heavier elements, and some isotopes of lighter elements, have been produced by successive capture of neutrons. Two processes of neutron capture may be distinguished: the *r*-process, rapid neutron capture; and the *s*-process, slow neutron capture. If neutrons are added to a stable nucleus, it is not long before the product nucleus becomes unstable and the neutron is converted into a proton. Outside a nucleus, a neutron decays into a proton and an electron by a process called beta decay (β-decay). Inside a nucleus it can be stable if the nucleus does not contain too many neutrons. In slow neutron capture, neutrons are added at a rate such that whenever an unstable nucleus is formed, it beta-decays before another neutron

can be added. If neutrons can be added more rapidly, as in the *r*-process, the unstable nuclei formed cannot decay before additional neutrons are added until a nucleus is eventually produced that will not accept a further neutron. This nucleus, however, will eventually be subject to beta decay, thus permitting further neutron capture.

It can be imagined that neutron capture could proceed at an arbitrary rate, giving a mixture of the two processes, but, when the possible sites where neutron-capture reactions could take place are considered, it appears that a fairly clean-cut division between the two processes can be made. If the neutron capture occurs during a quiet stage of stellar evolution, there will be ample time for beta decays to occur, and an *s*-process will result. If neutron capture occurs in an explosive situation, the time scale will be so short that the reaction will have to be an *r*-process. The *r*-process produces the most neutron-rich isotopes of the heavy elements, while those isotopes produced by the *s*-process tend to have relatively more protons. The naturally radioactive nuclei are produced by the *r*-process. The neutron-capture processes appear to give a simple explanation of the magic-number abundance peaks mentioned earlier.

Two small groups of nuclei are not readily fitted into either the sequence of nuclear fusion reactions or the neutron-capture processes. These are nuclei with very low relative abundances. One group consists of the light-nuclei lithium, beryllium, and boron, together with the heavy stable isotope of hydrogen, deuterium. These nuclei are destroyed by nuclear fusion reactions at temperatures lower than that needed to convert hydrogen into helium, and they are bypassed by the production of carbon from helium. The other group consists of the most proton-rich isotopes of some heavy elements, which cannot be produced by the addition of neutrons. Two rather rare or inefficient processes would suffice to produce these isotopes, but there is no complete agreement about what these processes are. It has been suggested that the heavy, proton-rich isotopes might be produced by a process of proton capture and that lithium, beryllium, and boron have been produced by the breakdown of heavier nuclei. A recent suggestion is that they are produced in interstellar space by collisions between cosmic-ray protons and interstellar carbon, nitrogen, and oxygen.

REGIONS IN WHICH ELEMENT SYNTHESIS TAKES PLACE

A discussion of how the present chemical composition of the universe has arisen brings to light two distinct questions: what was the initial chemical composition and what alterations have occurred since creation. Ideally, by working backwards, the initial composition can be deduced from the present composition and a life-history, but this approach is overambitious. The initial composition predicted by simple cosmological theory can then be tested for compatibility with present observations. Element production in the universe as a whole can be discussed first; production in stars and other objects in the Galaxy is treated in the sections that follow.

Element production in the universe as a whole. Hydrogen and helium are overwhelmingly the most abundant elements in the objects of which there is direct knowledge, and, as some buildup of heavy elements occurs in stars, the working hypothesis is usually adopted that the initially created matter contained only light elements. Theories differ only as to whether the initial composition was pure hydrogen or whether there was also a substantial amount of helium.

It is usual to try to devise the simplest theory that can account for the small number of reliable observations of agreed cosmological significance. This need not imply a conviction that the universe is simple, but, rather, that it is easiest to work out the consequences of simple theories and there is a better chance of discovering contradictions with observations before too much time has been wasted on detail. The simplest assumption, made in several theories, about the initial chemical composition is that it was pure hydrogen, the hope being that it can be shown that all other elements have been synthesized during the lifetime of the universe.

Rapid and slow processes of neutron capture

In the steady-state theory, in which matter is assumed to be continuously created, the initial composition is arbitrary, although supporters of the steady-state theory have always hoped that production of pure hydrogen would give a consistent picture of the universe. In the big-bang theory, which has received much attention in recent years, there is considerably less freedom of choice. Observations of distant galaxies suggest that the universe is expanding and, if this is so, that galaxies may have been very close together about 10,000,000,000 years ago. In the big-bang theory it is assumed that the universe was created at that time and, in the simplest version, that at its creation the universe was very hot as well as very dense. Nuclear reactions in the early stages of the expansion lead to a rather well-defined initial chemical composition for the universe.

Although there are more complicated big-bang theories than the one just mentioned, there is only one arbitrary quantity in the simplest theory, and assignment of some arbitrary specified value to any one of the unknowns will determine the others. If, for example, the density of the universe is specified at some temperature (perhaps 10^{10} K), the subsequent life history of the universe is, in principle, determined. For a wide range of values of this density, the chemical composition after the initial phase is a mixture of hydrogen and helium, with between 20 percent and 30 percent by mass in the form of helium. Most study in recent years has been concerned with trying to decide whether an initial chemical composition devoid of helium or one with 25 percent helium is most likely to be consistent with present observations.

There are two particular reasons why interest in the big-bang theory has recently been stimulated. The first **Observed** is concerned with the observed helium content of objects **helium** in the Galaxy. It is not always easy to estimate the he- **content** lium abundance in a star or gas cloud, but most estimates have indicated helium abundances greater than 25 percent by mass. Such values would fit in well with most of the helium being primeval and a small admixture having been produced in stars in the galactic lifetime. The second reason for interest in the big-bang theory is the discovery that very short radio waves, microwaves, are observed to be reaching the Earth from all directions in space. According to the big-bang theory, the universe was filled with radiation in its early stages and most of this radiation has never subsequently been absorbed. As the universe has expanded, the radiation has been shifted toward longer wavelengths by the Doppler effect, a change in wavelength brought about by motion of the source with respect to the observer. As a result of this effect, the radiation created by the big bang would be expected to appear today as microwaves of just the type that have been observed.

The big-bang theory not only predicts that all objects, except those in which the helium can have been destroyed, should have a minimum of about 25 percent helium but that the microwave radiation should have a particular distribution with frequency known as the Planck form. The theory can be proved false either if objects are discovered with a substantially smaller amount of helium than 25 percent or if the microwave spectrum does not have the Planck form. Several observations have been made which suggest that the theory is false, but to date none of them appears to be conclusive.

Element production in stars. A substantial amount of nucleosynthesis must have occurred in stars. It was stated above that a succession of nuclear fusion reactions takes place as the temperature of the stellar material rises. Theories of stellar evolution indicate that the internal temperatures of stars first rise during their life history and eventually fall after reaching a maximum value. For very low-mass stars, the maximum temperature may be too low for any significant nuclear reactions to occur, but for stars as massive as the Sun or greater, most of the sequence of nuclear fusion reactions described above can occur. Moreover, a time scale for stellar evolution is derived in theories of stellar evolution that show that stars substantially more massive than the Sun can have completed their active life history in a time short compared with the age of the universe derived from the big-bang cosmological theory.

This result implies that stars more massive than the Sun, which were formed very early in the life history of the Galaxy, could have produced some of the heavy elements that are seen today but that stars much less massive than the Sun could have played no part in this production. Unless the Galaxy is very much older than is generally believed, such low mass stars, even if formed with the Galaxy, would still be at an early stage in their evolution because changes within them proceed at a relatively slow pace. If there has been substantial heavy-element production in stars, a sufficient fraction of the earliest stars formed must have been relatively massive.

If substantial nucleosynthesis has occurred in stars, could such a process have produced all of the heavy elements that are observed today and possibly all of the helium inside the stars? A vital point is the following: if the heavy elements produced in stars are to influence what is observed, they must be expelled from the interiors of the stars in which they are produced and incorporated into future generations of stars, in which they can be observed subsequently. Unfortunately, direct **Mass loss** knowledge of mass loss from stars is fragmentary; steady **in stars** loss of mass is observed in some stars, and a few are observed to explode catastrophically, as in the explosion of a supernova. At present it is only possible for a very rough estimate to be made of the rate of exchange of matter between stars and the interstellar medium.

Supernovae are believed to be stars reaching the end of their evolution, and many astronomers believe that a supernova explosion is the main process whereby heavy elements produced inside stars are returned to the interstellar medium. In addition, because a supernova explosion is the most violent type of event regularly observed in galaxies, it is believed that cosmic rays must also be produced in the explosion. Some rough estimates follow. The mass of the Galaxy is believed to be between 10^{11} and 2×10^{11} solar masses, and perhaps 2×10^9 solar masses are heavy elements. If these heavy elements were produced steadily in a galactic lifetime of about 10^{10} years, one-fifth of a solar mass of heavy elements must have been produced each year. Counts of supernovae in nearby galaxies suggest that there might be one supernova explosion per large galaxy about every 30 years. If all the heavy elements are produced in supernovae, about six solar masses are required from each explosion. Although these numbers are very uncertain, this amount seems too large, but it could be reduced if the frequency of supernovae is very much higher in young galaxies. The possibility remains that a significant quantity of heavy elements may be produced by a very large number of less spectacular stars or by much more massive objects that are mentioned below.

If there has been a gradual production of heavy elements, recently formed stars should contain more than old stars. It is possible to identify some stars which have formed quite recently. The light output of stars rises as a rather high power of their mass according to a mass–luminosity relation that is valid for the vast majority of stars whose masses are known, while their supply of nuclear energy is only directly proportional to the mass. This means that the more massive stars complete their life history much more rapidly than low-mass stars and that the brightest stars observed today cannot be more than a few million years old at the most. The heavy-element content of the young stars is greater than that of many old stars, perhaps because of a gradual increase in the heavy-element content of the interstellar medium from which stars are formed. Observations show that only the very oldest stars have an extremely small amount of very heavy elements in their visible layers, and it appears that element production must have been much more rapid when the Galaxy was young than it is now. There may indeed have been a much higher frequency of supernovae. Recent observations suggest also that chemical composition is a function of a star's place of origin as well as its age. In particular, the production of heavy elements may have been higher near the centre of the Galaxy than elsewhere (see below *Element production in massive objects*).

Although the first nuclear reaction to occur in stars is the conversion of hydrogen into helium, all of the helium that is observed today can hardly have been produced in ordinary stars, the more so if all objects contain more than about 25 percent helium by mass. Considering the relative amounts of helium and heavier elements, observations indicate that the total mass of helium may be ten times greater than that of the heavier elements; if all elements other than hydrogen have been produced in stars, the relative production of helium and heavier elements must have just this value. As stars evolve, however, the conversion of hydrogen into helium is followed by the conversion of helium into heavier elements. At all stages in a star's evolution there will be a region where the temperature is suitable for the conversion of hydrogen into helium, but it appears that there will be only a thin shell of helium separating the regions in which hydrogen has not yet been converted into helium and the region where helium has been burned into heavy elements. The possible chemical composition of a highly evolved star is a series of layers of different chemical composition. The central region would contain elements such as iron and nickel with layers of successively lighter elements surrounding it and the outermost layer containing essentially only hydrogen or hydrogen and helium. A very special type of mass loss would be required to expel ten times as much helium as heavy elements from these different layers into interstellar space.

It is also difficult to see how the full amount of helium could have been produced. If a quarter of the galactic mass, originally hydrogen, has been converted into helium, it can be shown that essentially all of the mass must have passed through at least one generation of massive stars. The total energy release under such a circumstance would imply that the Galaxy was very much more luminous in the past—one hundred times more luminous for the first 10 percent of its lifetime, for example.

Element production in massive objects. Although there is no direct evidence for the existence of stars more than about 50 times as massive as the Sun, there is no obvious reason why much more massive objects should not exist. If they were sufficiently massive, they would not behave as ordinary stars because their gravitational attraction would be so strong that not even the energy released by conversion of hydrogen into helium would prevent such supermassive stars from continuing to collapse rapidly. According to present theoretical ideas, if such a collapse is spherically symmetrical, nothing can prevent the supermassive object from collapsing to an extremely high or infinite density; but, if it is asymmetrical—because it is, for example, rapidly rotating—there is some possibility that the catastrophic collapse, called an implosion, might be followed by explosion. At the high-density, high-temperature phase of such an object, some nucleosynthesis (manufacture of nuclei from smaller nuclei) would occur, primarily of helium but with a small amount of heavier elements according to the arguments given early in this article. Such objects have been suggested as a possible important source of helium.

There is some observational evidence that explosions on a very much greater scale than single supernovae are occurring in galaxies. In some peculiar galaxies that are strong emitters of radio waves, there is evidence that explosions have thrown a large quantity of gas hundreds of thousands of light-years into intergalactic space. Such galactic explosions may not be related to the theoretical supermassive objects mentioned above, but it is difficult to believe that some nucleosynthesis does not take place during the phases of extreme conditions that must occur in such objects. The suggestion that heavy-element abundances may be higher near the centre of the Galaxy could be related to a past explosion there.

RADIOACTIVE CHRONOLOGIES

Radioactive elements in the Earth, the Moon, and in meteorites can provide useful information about the ages of these objects and about the dates of formation of the heavy elements themselves. The elements uranium and thorium gradually decay into lead, different isotopes of lead arising from the various isotopes of uranium and thorium; some isotopes of lead are, however, not produced by any radioactive decay process. When the rocks of the Moon or the Earth's crust or the meteorites solidified, further chemical separation of the radioactive elements and their decay products was prevented. By studying the relative amounts of the radioactive isotopes and their decay products, it is possible to obtain an estimate of when the rocks solidified. Estimates can also be made using radioactive isotopes other than uranium and thorium.

The results of these discussions indicate that the meteorites, or at least the parent body of the meteorites, solidified between 4.5×10^9 and 4.6×10^9 years ago. It is possible to speak with such confidence of this age because two isotopes of uranium and one of thorium have very different decay times that bracket that value. There is no unique age for the rocks of the Earth's crust because there has been considerable volcanic activity during the Earth's history and rocks have solidified at all stages. All indications are that the oldest rocks have ages of the same order as the ages of the parent bodies of the meteorites. Only a very small region of the Moon's surface has been studied so far, but it has been found to have very old rocks of age up to about 4.5×10^9 years. No conclusions can be drawn about the date of solidification of the Moon from these few observations, as nothing is known about its past geological history, but they are certainly not inconsistent with the view that the Earth, the Moon, and meteorites have a similar age and origin.

It has also been found possible to obtain information about the time of formation of the radioactive elements. Assuming that both radioactive nuclei and their stable neighbours are produced by the neutron-capture process discussed earlier, theory predicts a relative production rate for all of the nuclei. The radioactive nuclei can be divided into three groups: short-lived, medium-lived, and long-lived, where short-lived means considerably less than the believed age of the universe and long-lived means comparable with that age. If radioactive nuclei are produced and decay steadily, the total amount of a short-lived isotope reaches a steady value. In meteorites, one can study the decay products of such short-lived nuclei and can discover their abundance when the meteorites were formed. This amount is lower than the expected value, suggesting that nucleosynthesis ceased in the solar system material about 2×10^8 years before the meteorites and planets solidified.

Study of the decay products of nuclei with medium decay rates indicates that their abundance is higher than if nucleosynthesis has occurred at a constant rate throughout galactic history. This suggests that the solar system material was significantly enriched in heavy elements shortly before the cessation of nucleosynthesis—that is, before the Sun and planets were formed. Finally, the very long-lived isotopes give information about the total time scale of nucleosynthesis that is not inconsistent with the galactic age estimated by other methods.

Although there is not unanimous agreement concerning these results, it appears that it is, in principle, possible to obtain a considerable amount of information about the past rate of nucleosynthesis and possibly about the types of objects in which it has occurred. In particular, it may eventually be possible to decide whether most element production has occurred in a large number of supernovae or in a much smaller number of massive objects.

BIBLIOGRAPHY

Semi-popular treatments: W.A. FOWLER, *Nuclear Astrophysics* (1967); G. GAMOW, *The Creation of the Universe*, rev. ed. (1961); F. HOYLE, *Frontiers of Astronomy* (1955).

Elementary text: R.J. TAYLER, *The Origin of the Chemical Elements* (1972).

Advanced texts: L.H. ALLER, *The Abundance of the Elements* (1961); D.D. CLAYTON, *Principles of Stellar Evolution and Nucleosynthesis* (1968); H. REEVES, *Stellar Evolution and Nucleosynthesis* (1968).

(R.J.T.)

Marginal notes: Layers of elements • Collapse in supermassive stars • Radioactive nuclei

Chemical Engineering

Chemical engineering is the development of processes and the design and operation of plants in which materials undergo changes in physical or chemical state on a technical scale. Applied throughout the process industries, it is founded on the principles of chemistry, physics, and mathematics. The laws of physical chemistry and physics govern the practicability and efficiency of chemical-engineering operations. Energy changes, deriving from thermodynamic considerations, are particularly important.

Mathematics is applied increasingly, not only in the use of other sciences but also as a basic tool in optimization and modelling. Optimization means arranging materials, facilities, and energy to yield as productive and economical an operation as possible. Modelling is the construction of theoretic mathematical prototypes of complex process systems, commonly with the aid of computers.

Early development. Chemical engineering is as old as the process industries. Its heritage dates from the fermentation and evaporation processes operated by early civilizations. But modern chemical engineering emerged with the development of large-scale, chemical-manufacturing operations in the second half of the 19th century. Throughout its development as an independent discipline, chemical engineering has been directed toward solving problems of designing and operating large plants for continuous production.

Manufacture of chemicals in the mid-19th century consisted of modest craft operations. Increase in demand, public concern at the emission of noxious effluents, and competition between rival processes provided the incentives for greater efficiency. This led, through amalgamations, to the emergence of combines with resources for larger operations and caused the transition from a craft to a science-based industry. The result was a demand for chemists with knowledge of manufacturing processes, known as industrial chemists or chemical technologists. The term chemical engineer was in general use by about 1900. Despite its emergence in traditional chemicals manufacturing, it was through its role in the development of the petroleum industry that chemical engineering became firmly established as a unique discipline. The demand for plants capable of operating physical separation processes continuously at high levels of efficiency was a challenge that could not be met by the traditional chemist or mechanical engineer.

A landmark in the development of chemical engineering was the publication in 1901 of the first textbook on the subject, by George E. Davis, a British chemical consultant. This concentrated on the design of plant items for specific operations. The notion of a processing plant consisting of a number of operations, such as mixing, evaporation, and filtration, and of these operations being essentially similar, whatever the product, led to the concept of *unit operations*. This was first enunciated by the U.S. chemical engineer Arthur D. Little in 1915 and formed the basis for a classification of chemical engineering that dominated the subject for the next 40 years. The number of unit operations—the building blocks of a chemical plant—is not large. The complexity arises from the variety of conditions under which the unit operations are conducted.

In the same way that a complex plant can be divided into basic unit operations, so chemical reactions involved in the process industries can be classified into certain groups, or *unit processes* (*e.g.*, polymerizations, esterifications, and nitrations), having common characteristics. This classification into unit processes brought rationalization to the study of process engineering.

Modern chemical engineering. Valuable as the unit approach proved to be, it suffered from the disadvantage inherent in such classifications: a restricted outlook based on existing practice. Since World War II, closer examination of the fundamental phenomena involved in the various unit operations has shown these to depend on the basic laws of mass transfer, heat transfer, and fluid flow. This has given unity to the diverse unit operations

and has led to the development of chemical-engineering science in its own right; as a result many applications have been found in fields outside the traditional chemical industry.

Mass transfer is the basis for the design and operation of equipment for the separation of homogeneous mixtures. Such separations are usually achieved by the creation or addition of a second phase, either immiscible (not soluble) or only partially miscible with the original, followed by partition of the components between the two phases. Thus distillation involves creation of a vapour phase by heating a liquid, the components partitioning between the two phases with the more volatile concentrating in the vapour. Solvent extraction and ion exchange are examples involving addition of a second phase. All are traditional unit operations. Examination of the basic interphase transfer processes (transfer between phases) shows the rates of these all to be governed by the same diffusion laws.

Most operations involve addition or withdrawal of energy in the form of heat, and adequate provision must be made for this. Heat transfer between two materials may involve the basic processes of conduction, convection, and radiation, either separately or in combination. Laws from physics governing rates of heat transfer by these mechanisms have been used to develop design procedures having a fundamental rather than a merely empirical basis.

Fluid flow of either gases or liquids appears in most unit operations. The energy loss of a fluid in passing over a solid is a key consideration and governs factors as diverse as loss in pressure of a gas flowing along a pipe and the rate of percolation of liquid through a cake of solid particles in a filter. There are important differences in the flow properties of liquids depending on whether these are Newtonian or non-Newtonian; that is, whether they follow classical laws or depart from them.

Design for many operations involves simultaneous consideration of mass transfer, heat transfer, and fluid flow. In recent years, it has been recognized that these can themselves be approached in a unified manner and has led to the emergence of the subject of transport phenomena.

Until recently, plants for the processing of solids have been designed by essentially empirical methods. The study of powder technology, however, is now yielding information of a fundamental nature on, among other things, the flow properties of solids.

The application of chemical kinetics, in conjunction with transport phenomena and thermodynamics, for the design of industrial reactors (containers in which a chemical reaction takes place) comprises the subject of chemical reaction engineering. The speed of a reaction governs the time necessary for the reactants to remain in contact in order to produce the desired conversion. Many important processes involve the use of a solid catalyst and are then classified as heterogeneous. Chemical-reaction engineering is essential for transition of batch laboratory processes to continuous reactors suitable for large-scale operation.

Thermodynamics plays a vital cohesive role in chemical engineering. It is concerned with equilibrium situations (situations where a steady-state condition has been established) and not with the rates of processes. It provides knowledge of energy changes occurring and gives guidance as to the practicability of certain processes. It governs partition equilibria (equilibria between phases) exploited in separation techniques and provides the basis for correlating equilibrium data. This is a prerequisite to the use of computers for mass-transfer calculations. In chemical-reaction engineering, thermodynamics also provides information on the temperature dependence of chemical equilibria.

Study of the fundamental phenomena upon which chemical engineering is based has necessitated their description in mathematical form and has led to more sophisticated mathematical techniques than in the unit operations era. The advent of digital computers has allowed otherwise laborious design calculations to be performed rapidly, opening the way to accurate optimization of industrial processes. Variations due to different parameters, such as energy source used, plant layout, and environmental factors, can be predicted accurately and quickly so that the best combination can be chosen.

Control is a vital consideration, especially for safe continuous operation of a plant. Design of a control system demands identification of the independently controllable parameters. A prerequisite is continuous measurement of key process variables, among them temperature, pressure, acidity, and chemical composition. Suitable automatic controls actuated by these measurements are then installed on the appropriate lines. Consideration must be given to the process dynamics to ensure a rapid response without causing instability. Such a control system is essentially static. Any deviations will cause loss of product quality.

Computer control of plant performance

In complex plants, more precise and dynamic control can be achieved using computers, thus allowing safe operation at the limit of plant performance. Computers are used to predict the change in performance that will arise from any detected variation in conditions. They then can calculate the change in controllable parameters necessary to annul the effect of the deviation and feed this information to the appropriate controllers so that product quality is kept constant.

Applications of chemical engineering. The fundamental principles of chemical engineering underlie the operation of processes extending well beyond the boundaries of the chemical industry. As a result, chemical engineers are employed nowadays in a diverse range of operations outside traditional areas. Plastics, polymers, and synthetic fibres involve chemical-reaction engineering problems in their manufacture, with fluid flow and heat transfer considerations dominating their fabrication. The dyeing of a fibre is a mass-transfer problem. Pulp and paper manufacture involve considerations of fluid flow and heat transfer. While the scale and materials are different, these again are found in modern continuous production of foodstuffs. The pharmaceuticals industry (both fine chemicals and biochemical products) presents chemical-engineering problems, the solutions of which have been an essential prerequisite to the availability of modern drugs. The nuclear industry makes similar demands on the chemical engineer, particularly for fuel manufacture and reprocessing. This is but one facet of metals processing, which extends from steel manufacture to separation of rare metals. Despite variation in the scale of operation, exploitation of chemical-engineering principles provides a common link.

Further applications of chemical engineering are found in the fuel industries. In the 1950s and 1960s, considerable numbers of chemical engineers have been involved in space exploration, from the design of fuel cells to the manufacture of propellants. Looking to the future, it is probable that chemical engineering will provide the solution to at least two of the world's major problems: supply of adequate fresh water in all regions through desalination of seawater and environmental control through prevention of pollution.

Professional requirements and education. The basic chemical-engineering qualification is a bachelor's degree. Courses are available at most U.S. and Canadian universities and are four years in duration. In Britain, the duration is normally three years. Cooperative education programs, usually one year longer and including practical experience in industry, are available in all three countries and are becoming increasingly popular. In Britain they are known as sandwich courses because they are sandwiched between job experiences. The pattern of education in these countries, and also in Japan and Australia, is essentially the same; it includes basic courses in mathematics, physics, and chemistry, followed by the study of chemical-engineering principles. Many students continue after the bachelor's level, taking a master's degree in a further one to two years by a combination of advanced lecture courses and research. Master's courses are particularly common in North America and are increasing in frequency in Britain. Bachelor's courses in engineering technology have been introduced recently in the U.S. and

Britain's "sandwich courses"

have led to pressure for the master's degree to become the basic professional qualification.

In European countries outside Britain, chemical engineering has been slow to gain recognition as an independent discipline. It is usually taken as a sequel to a comprehensive course in chemistry or mechanical engineering. In France the term for chemical engineering is *génie chimique*. In Germany, *chemische Technologie* and *Verfahrenstechnik* are used to designate the chemical and mechanical orientations of the subject, respectively. These courses are longer in duration and are roughly equivalent to the master's level. Nominally five years in duration, most students take about seven years to graduate. In contrast to practice in the U.S. and Britain, many examinations are conducted orally. Successful completion leads to the award of a diploma as an "Engineer," the term then being used as a formal title of address.

In all countries, doctorate degrees are awarded for original research, usually over a period of three to five years and often including some formal course work.

Functions in industry. Chemical engineers are employed in the design and development of both processes and plant items. In each case, data and predictions often have to be obtained or confirmed with pilot experiments. Plant operation and control is increasingly the sphere of the chemical engineer rather than of the chemist. Chemical engineering provides an ideal background for the economic evaluation of new projects and, in the plant construction sector, for marketing. All of these functions provide routes to management posts, and many executives in the process and process-equipment industries hold chemical-engineering qualifications.

Registration and professional societies. The Society of Chemical Industry, founded in England in 1881, provided one of the earliest forums for those interested in the problems of exploiting chemistry on an industrial scale. The first professional society specifically for chemical engineers was the American Institute of Chemical Engineers, founded in 1908. A corresponding body, the Institution of Chemical Engineers, was established in Britain in 1922. Its activities also cover Australia. Chemical engineering in Canada is covered by the Chemical Institute of Canada. The American Chemical Society is active in the chemical-engineering field with meetings and publications but does not act as a professional body. The European Federation of Chemical Engineering plays a coordinating function in the chemical-engineering world. In addition to societies from all western European countries, chemical-engineering bodies in most other parts of the world are corresponding members.

The chemical-engineering institutions set standards for the profession. The American Institute of Chemical Engineers is active in accrediting university departments. The Institution of Chemical Engineers also acts as an independent examining body. In certain states and provinces in the U.S. and Canada, engineers must be registered before practicing, either by examination or exemption through an appropriate qualification. Corporate membership of the Institution of Chemical Engineers entitles the holder to the description "Chartered Engineer."

BIBLIOGRAPHY. Classic works include: G.E. DAVIS, *A Handbook of Chemical Engineering*, 2 vol. (1901, 2nd ed. 1904), the first textbook on this subject; and W.H. WALKER, W.K. LEWIS, and W.H. McADAMS, *The Principles of Chemical Engineering*, 2nd ed. (1927), a text with thorough coverage of basic principles. Current information may be found in: J.H. PERRY (ed.), *Chemical Engineers' Handbook*, 4th ed. (1963), a comprehensive handbook with much valuable data on systems; H.W. CREMER *et al.*, *Chemical Engineering Practice*, 12 vol. (1956–65), a reference work with each section written by a specialist; and J.M. COULSON and J.F. RICHARDSON, *Chemical Engineering*, 2nd ed., 3 vol. (1964–71), a general textbook covering both basic fundamentals and their applications.

(C.Ha.)

Chemical Industry

Although the chemical industry may be described simply as the industry that uses chemistry and manufactures chemicals, this definition is not altogether satisfactory because it leaves open the question of what is a chemical. Definitions that have been adopted for statistical economic purposes vary from country to country. Also, the Standard International Trade Classification, published by the United Nations, includes explosives and pyrotechnic products as part of its chemicals section. But the classification does not include the man-made fibres, although the preparation of the raw materials for man-made fibres is unquestionably as chemical as any branch of manufacture could be.

The complicated characteristics of the chemical industry.   The scope of the chemical industry is in part shaped by custom rather than by logic. The petroleum industry is usually thought of as separate from the chemical industry, for in the early days of the industry in the 19th century crude oil was merely subjected to a simple distillation treatment. Modern petroleum industrial processes, however, bring about chemical changes, and some of the products of a modern refinery complex are chemicals by any definition. The term petrochemical is used to describe these chemical operations, but because they are often carried out at the same plant as the primary distillation, the distinction between petroleum industry and chemical industry is difficult to maintain.

The influence of custom rather than logic

Metals in a sense are chemicals because they are produced by chemical means, the ores sometimes requiring chemical methods of dressing before refining; the refining process also involves chemical reactions. Such metals as steel, lead, copper, and zinc are produced in reasonably pure form and are later fabricated into useful shapes, much as is the case with plastics. Yet the steel industry, for example, is not considered a part of the chemical industry. In modern metallurgy, such metals as titanium, tantalum, and tungsten (also called wolfram) are produced by processes involving great chemical skill, yet they are still classified as primary metals.

The boundaries of the chemical industry, then, are somewhat confused. Its main raw materials are the fossil fuels (coal, natural gas, and petroleum), air, water, salt, limestone, sulfur or an equivalent, and some specialized raw materials for special products, such as phosphates and the mineral fluorspar. The industry converts these raw materials into primary, secondary, and tertiary products, a distinction that is based on the remoteness of the product from the consumer, the primary being the most remote. The products are most often end products only as regards the chemical industry itself; a chief characteristic of the chemical industry is that its products nearly always require further processing before reaching the ultimate consumer.

Thus, paradoxically, the chemical industry is its own best customer. An average chemical product is passed from factory to factory several times before it emerges from the chemical industry into the market.

The self-competitive nature of the industry

The industry is also its own chief competitor because the same product can often be made in a number of different ways. Phenol, for example, can be made from benzene (which itself can be obtained either from coal or from petroleum) by at least four different processes, and it can also be made from other raw materials. The methods that are used for the manufacture of the alkalies, caustic soda and sodium carbonate, have changed drastically several times. So have the methods that are used for the manufacture of sulfuric acid, the largest staple of the chemical industry.

There are many routes to the same product, and many uses for the same product. The largest use for ethylene glycol, for example, is as an automobile antifreeze, but it is also used as a hydraulic brake fluid. Further processing of ethylene glycol leads to many derivatives that are used as additives in the textile, pharmaceutical, and cosmetic industries; as emulsifiers in the application of insecticides and fungicides; and as demulsifiers for petroleum. The fundamental chemicals, such as chlorine or sulfuric acid, are used in so many ways as to defy a comprehensive listing. Cyanides are used in fumigation, in the case hardening of steel parts, in electroplating, in extracting gold from its ores, in separating lead and zinc minerals when they

occur together in ores, and in making further chemical products.

Not only is the industry its own chief competitor, but frequently many chemicals compete for the same use. As a base to make a foamed plastic, polyurethane and polystyrene compete. As an alkali, caustic soda, soda ash, and sometimes lime are in competition; as an acid, sulfuric acid, hydrochloric acid, and others frequently vie with each other. Many different plastics, fibres, and synthetic elastomers (products having rubber-like properties) compete for very similar uses.

Because of the competitiveness within the chemical industry and among the chemicals, the chemical industry spends large amounts on research, particularly in the highly industrialized countries. The percentage of revenue spent on research varies from one branch to another; companies specializing in large-volume products that have been widely used for many years spend less, whereas in the newer fields, competition can be met only by intensive research efforts. As a result, change is the rule in the chemical industry. Of the many products of the chemical industry, more than one-half were not known on a commercial scale in the 1940s. In the pharmaceutical industry change has been exceptionally striking; more than 90 percent of modern medicinal products were not available prior to 1955.

Importance of change

Economic aspects.   In most fields the United States is the largest producer of chemicals. West Germany, the United Kingdom, France, Italy, and some other European countries are also large producers, and so is the Soviet Union. During the 1960s Japan came into prominence as a very large producer in a number of areas. Japan ranks second in capital investment, as shown in the following table.

Dollar Investment* in the Chemical Industry, 1978 ($000,000)	
United States	6,310
Japan	2,147
West Germany	1,923
United Kingdom	1,841
Italy	1,398
France	1,233
Canada	1,036

*Gross fixed-capital formation.
Source: UN, *Yearbook of Industrial Statistics*, Vol. I, 1979.

To place these figures in perspective, it is necessary to note that investment in the chemical industry as a percentage of total investment in a given country may range from 5 to 15 percent for the less developed countries; for the industrial countries it averages about 6 to 8 percent. For some of the underdeveloped countries this percentage can fluctuate widely; for example, the installation of one sizable fertilizer factory could change the percentage markedly in a specific country.

Earlier in the 20th century there was a marked distinction between economies that were based on coal as a fossil fuel and those based on petroleum. Coal was almost the unique source of the aromatic hydrocarbons (see below *Aromatic hydrocarbons*). Two forces, however, have worked together to change this situation. First, aromatics can now be obtained from petroleum, and all hydrocarbon raw materials are now almost interchangeable; second, modern transportation technology makes possible very large-scale shipments by sea, not only of petroleum, crude or in various stages of refinement, but also of natural gas, refrigerated and condensed to a liquid.

Statistics from the chemical industry as a whole can be very misleading because of the practice of lumping together such products as inexpensive sulfuric acid and expensive dyes or fibres; included in some compilations are cosmetics and toiletries, the value of which per pound may go up almost astronomically. Chemical industry statistics

Lack of reliable statistics

from different countries may have different bases of calculation; the basis also may change from time to time in the same country. An additional source of confusion is that in some cases the production is quoted, not in tons of the product itself, but in tons of the content of the important component. Thus, nitrogenous fertilizers are quoted as tons of nitrogen, even though the actual substance may be ammonia (82 percent nitrogen), ammonium sulfate (21 percent nitrogen), or some other form. In the following discussion, these possible sources of confusion are noted, and the statistics are given for order-of-magnitude comparison.

Sulfuric acid is by far the largest single product of the chemical industry. World production was of the order of 130,000,000–140,000,000 tons annually by the late 1970s. The world production of sugar, a chemical substance in extremely pure form, is about three-quarters that of sulfuric acid, but it is a product of agriculture and not considered part of the chemical industry.

Divisions of the chemical industry

The beginning of the chemical industry might be taken either as the historical beginning or as the raw materials that are to undergo transformation. But to begin with each of the raw materials and follow it through would soon lead to complications. It would also be necessary to consider the end product that emerges from some process and is handed to another industry or to the consumer. For purposes of simplicity then, various divisions of the chemical industry, such as heavy inorganic and organic chemicals, fine chemicals, and various families of end products, will be described in turn, and separately, although it should be borne in mind that they interact constantly. In some cases, discussion of a raw material will follow at a considerable distance, but an occasional glance at the end products will help to understand to what places, in terms of the final consumer, the whole process is directed.

The first division to be discussed is the heavy inorganic chemicals, starting at the historical beginning of the chemical industry with the Leblanc process. The terms heavy chemical industry and fine chemical industry, however, are not precisely exclusive, because numerous operations fall somewhere between the two classes. The two classes at their extremes, however, do correlate with other differences. For example, the appearance of two kinds of plants is characteristically different. The large-scale chemical plant is characterized by large pieces of equipment of odd shapes and sizes standing independent and immobile. Long rows of distilling columns are prominent, but because the material being processed is normally confined in pipes or vessels, no very discernible activity takes place. Few personnel are in evidence.

The light chemical industry is entirely different; it involves many different pieces of equipment of moderate size, often of stainless steel or lined with glass or enamel. This equipment is housed in buildings that correspond to those for assembling light machinery. Numerous personnel are present. Both types of plant require large amounts of capital.

HEAVY INORGANIC CHEMICAL INDUSTRY

Production of sodium carbonate and other alkalies. In 1775 the French Academy of Sciences offered an award for a practical method for converting common salt, sodium chloride, into sodium carbonate, a chemical that was needed in substantial amounts for the manufacture of both soap and glass. Nicolas Leblanc, a surgeon with a bent for practical chemistry, invented such a process. His patron, the Duc d'Orléans, set up a factory for the process in 1791, but work was interrupted by the French Revolution. The process was not finally put into industrial operation until 1823 in England, after which it continued to be used to prepare sodium carbonate for almost 100 years.

The Leblanc process. The first step in the Leblanc process was to treat sodium chloride with sulfuric acid. This treatment produced sodium sulfate and hydrogen chloride. The sodium sulfate was then heated with lime-stone and coal to produce black ash, which contained the desired sodium carbonate, mixed with calcium sulfide and some unreacted coal. Solution of the sodium carbonate in water removed it from the black ash, and the solution was then crystallized. From this operation derives the expression soda ash that is still used for sodium carbonate.

It was soon found that when hydrogen chloride was allowed to escape into the atmosphere, it caused severe damage to vegetation over a wide area. To eliminate the pollution problem, methods to convert the dissolved hydrogen chloride to elemental chlorine were developed. The chlorine, absorbed in lime, was used to make bleaching powder, for which there was a growing demand.

Because calcium sulfide contained in the black ash had a highly unpleasant odour, methods were developed to remove it by recovering the sulfur, thereby providing at least part of the raw material for the sulfuric acid required in the first part of the process. Thus the Leblanc process demonstrated, at the very beginning, the typical ability of the chemical industry to develop new processes and new products, and often in so doing to turn a liability into an asset.

The ammonia soda (Solvay) process. The Leblanc process was eventually replaced by the ammonia-soda process (called the Solvay process), which was first practiced successfully in Belgium in the 1860s. In this process, sodium chloride as a strong brine is treated with ammonia and carbon dioxide to give sodium bicarbonate and ammonium chloride. The desired sodium carbonate is easily obtained from the bicarbonate by heating. Then, when the ammonium chloride is treated with lime, it gives calcium chloride and ammonia. Thus, the chlorine that was in the original sodium chloride appears as calcium chloride, which is largely discarded (among the few uses for this compound is to melt snow and ice from roads and sidewalks). The ammonia thus regenerated is fed back into the first part of the process. Efficient recovery of nearly all the ammonia is essential to the economic operation of the process. The loss of ammonia in a well-run operation is no more than 0.1 percent of the weight of the product.

Electrolytic process. Later in the 19th century the development of electrical power generation made possible the electrochemical industry. This not clearly identifiable branch of the chemical industry includes a number of applications in which electrolysis, the breaking down of a compound in solution into its elements by means of an electric current, is used to bring about a chemical change. Electrolysis of sodium chloride can lead to chlorine and either sodium hydroxide (if the NaCl was in solution) or metallic sodium (if the NaCl was fused). Sodium hydroxide, an alkali like sodium carbonate, in some cases competes with it for the same applications, and the two are interconvertible by rather simple processes. Sodium chloride can be made into an alkali by either of the two processes; the difference between them is that the ammonia soda process gives the chlorine in the form of calcium chloride, a compound of small economic value, while the electrolytic processes produce elemental chlorine, which has nearly innumerable uses in the chemical industry, including the manufacture of plastic polyvinyl chloride, the plastic material produced in the largest volume. For this reason the ammonia soda process, which displaced the Leblanc process, also has been displaced. The older ammonia soda plants continue to operate very efficiently, but no new ammonia soda plants have been built.

Other important processes. The need for sodium carbonate in the manufacture of soap and glass that led to the Leblanc process also led to the creation of the alkali industry and the chlor-alkali industry, another of the historic landmarks of the chemical industry.

Production of sulfuric acid. The process for the preparation of sulfuric acid resulting from the Leblanc process might be regarded as its most important long-term contribution.

Chamber process. When sulfur is burned in air, sulfur dioxide is formed, and this, when it is combined with water, gives sulfurous acid. In order to form sulfuric acid, the dioxide is combined with oxygen to form the trioxide,

Plant
appear-
ance

Chlorine
for
bleaching
powder

A use fo
calcium
chloride

which is then combined with water. A technique to form the trioxide, called the chamber process, developed in the early days of the operation of the Leblanc process. In this technique, the reaction between sulfur dioxide and oxygen takes place in the presence of water and of oxides of nitrogen. Because the reaction is rather slow, sufficient residence time must be provided for the mixed gases to react. This gaseous mixture is highly corrosive, and the reaction must be carried out in containers made of lead.

Contact process. Lead is a material awkward to use in construction, and the process cannot deliver acid more concentrated than about 78 percent without special treatment. Therefore, the chamber process has been largely replaced by the contact process, in which the reaction takes place in a hot reactor, over a platinum or vanadium compound catalyst, a substance that increases the speed of the reaction without becoming chemically involved.

Uses. Of the very large world production of sulfuric acid, almost half goes to the manufacture of superphosphate and related fertilizers. Other uses of the acid are so multifarious as almost to defy enumeration, notable ones being the manufacture of high-octane gasoline, of titanium dioxide (a white pigment, also a filler for some plastics, and for paper), explosives, rayon, the processing of uranium, and the pickling of steel.

Sources of sulfur. Because sulfuric acid is indispensable to so many industries, its primary raw material is of the greatest importance. The needed sulfur is obtainable from a number of sources. Originally, sulfur came chiefly from certain volcanic deposits in Sicily. By the beginning of the 20th century this source was insufficient, but the supply was augmented by sulfur that occurs underground in the southern United States. This sulfur is not mined but is recovered by the so-called Frasch process, in which the sulfur is melted underground by hot water and the mixture brought to the surface in liquid form (see, for further details, SULFUR PRODUCTS AND PRODUCTION).

Other sources of sulfur include the ore iron pyrite, an iron–sulfur compound that can be burned to produce sulfur dioxide, and some natural gases, called sour gas, that contain appreciable quantities of hydrogen sulfide. Certain metal sulfides, such as those of zinc and copper, are contained in the ores of those metals. When these ores are roasted, sulfur dioxide is given off. Sulfur is usually shipped in its elemental form rather than in the form of sulfuric acid. One ton of sulfur converts to three tons of sulfuric acid, and the pure sulfur is easier to ship than the corrosive acid. Sulfur also has many other uses, directly as a fungicide and indirectly in the manufacture of insecticides, dyes, and rubber.

Under some circumstances, the sulfuric-acid stage of manufacture can be avoided. Ammonium sulfate, a fertilizer, is normally made by causing ammonia to react with sulfuric acid. In many parts of the world, abundant supplies of calcium sulfate in any of several mineral forms can be used to make the ammonium sulfate by combining it with ammonia and water. This process brings the sulfur in the calcium sulfate deposits into use, and in the early 1970s methods were being worked out to obtain elemental sulfur from these deposits. Because deposits of calcium sulfate throughout the world are very extensive, development of such a process would make the available resources of sulfur almost limitless.

The sulfur present in low percentages in fossil fuels is a notorious source of air pollution in most industrial countries. Removal of sulfur from crude oil adds to the sulfur supply and reduces pollution. It is less easy to remove the sulfur directly from coal, but in the early 1970s the most economical solution appeared to be to burn the coal and then remove the sulfur dioxide from the flue gases.

Abundance of calcium sulfate supplies

FINE CHEMICAL INDUSTRY

So far the classical heavy chemical industry, heavy in the sense that very large tonnages are produced, has been considered primarily. The heavy chemical industry is also raw-materials oriented, starting from simple raw materials and delivering intermediate product chemicals. Another branch of the chemical industry that produces smaller volumes of higher priced products is termed the fine chemical industry. Because two of its main branches are dyes and pharmaceuticals, it is heavily consumer-oriented.

Dyes. Although the first synthetic dye, mauve, was obtained in 1856 by an Englishman, Sir William Henry Perkin, the dye industry grew first in Germany. German chemists during the last half of the 19th century developed most of the dye classes and many of the individual dyes that are used today. The very first synthetic dyes were made from the organic chemical aniline, obtained from coal tar, and the terms aniline dyes and coal tar dyes were at one time appropriate. For a long time, dyes have been obtained from coal-derived materials other than aniline and are now obtained from petroleum by lengthy chemical processes.

All industrialized countries have a dye industry, and dyes have been developed for every conceivable purpose in addition to their original use in the textile industry. Among modern developments is that of the "shocking" or fluorescent dyes that give out more light than falls on them, an excess radiation made possible because they convert the invisible ultraviolet radiation in daylight to visible light. Such dyes are useful for signalling purposes. There are dyes also made to conform to extremely rigid specifications so that they may be legally used in foods, drugs, and cosmetics (see also DYES AND DYEING).

Pharmaceuticals. The use of synthetic substances rather than natural ones for medicinal preparations is comparatively new. The term chemotherapy was first used by the German medical research worker Paul Ehrlich in the early years of the 20th century, referring to the synthesis of new compounds that were toxic to the invading micro-organisms but not to the host organism. The development of new pharmaceuticals is a lively branch of chemical research, and the variety of compounds used is even greater than in the field of dyes. An unusual feature of this branch of the chemical industry is that the raw materials, in some cases, are not the usual coal- and petroleum-derived products; the antibiotics are produced by a fermentation process in which a micro-organism is allowed to proliferate on a suitable material. The antibiotic is then isolated and in some cases is chemically modified (see also PHARMACEUTICALS, PRODUCTION OF).

HEAVY ORGANIC CHEMICALS

The heavy chemical industry, in its classical form, was based on inorganic chemistry, concerned with all the elements except carbon and their compounds, but including, as has been seen, the carbonates. Similarly the light chemical industry uses organic chemistry, concerned with certain compounds of carbon such as the hydrocarbons, combinations of hydrogen and carbon. In the late 1960s the phrase heavy organic chemicals began to be used. There is no precise definition of what production volume qualifies as heavy. The organic chemicals benzene, phenol, ethylene, and vinyl chloride are usually considered heavy. Benzene and phenol are related chemically, and they are also related to toluene and the xylenes, which can be considered together as part of the aromatic group of organic chemicals, the aromatic compounds being most easily defined as those with chemical properties like those of benzene.

Aromatic hydrocarbons. *Benzene.* Chemically, the hydrocarbon benzene, which forms the basis of the aromatics, is a closed, six-sided ring structure of carbon atoms with a hydrogen atom at each corner of the hexagonal structure. Thus a benzene atom is made up of six carbon (C) atoms and six hydrogen (H) atoms, and has the chemical formula C_6H_6. Benzene has long been an industrial chemical. Mauve, the first synthetic dye, was made from it. Benzene at that time was obtained from the carbonization (heating) of coal, which produces coke, combustible gas, and a number of by-products, including benzene. Carbonization of coal to produce illuminating gas dates back in England to the very early years of the 19th century. The process is still employed in some countries, but more and more use is being made of natural gas (see also COAL PROCESSING). The carbonizing process is also used (with slight modifications) to produce metallurgical coke, indispensable for the manufacture of iron and hence steel. The supply of benzene from the carbonizing process, however, is not sufficient to meet the demand. For every ton of coal carbonized only about two to three pounds (0.9 to 1.35 kilograms) of benzene are obtained.

The shortage of aromatics first became evident during World War I, when toluene was in great demand for the manufacture of trinitrotoluene, or TNT, the principal explosive used then. Methods were worked out to obtain toluene from petroleum. Much later, after World War II, benzene and all the other aromatics derived from it were needed in far greater quantities than metallurgical coke could supply, and by far the greater part of these aromatics now comes from petroleum.

Toluene. Toluene differs from benzene in that one of the hydrogen atoms is replaced by a special combination of carbon and hydrogen called a methyl group ($-CH_3$). The xylenes have two methyl groups in different positions in the benzene ring, and thus all aromatics are to some extent interchangeable. In fact, one of the uses for toluene is to produce benzene by removing the methyl group (dealkylation).

All of these hydrocarbons are useful as gasoline additives because of their antiknock properties.

Toluene is also used as a solvent. The expression "as a solvent," which occurs frequently in describing the uses for chemicals, covers a multitude of applications. The substance dissolved is usually also organic, and the process is used in coatings, adhesives, textiles, pharmaceuticals, inks, photographic film, and metal degreasing. An application that reaches the ultimate consumer is dry cleaning (although the solvent used here is not toluene, but other hydrocarbons or chlorohydrocarbons). Toluene has a multitude of other uses, such as in the polyurethane plastics and elastomers discussed below.

Xylene. The three isomeric xylenes (isomeric means that they have exactly the same number and kind of atoms but are arranged differently) occur together, and with them is another isomer, ethylbenzene, which has one ethyl group ($-C_2H_5$) replacing one of the hydrogen atoms of benzene. These isomers can be separated only with difficulty, but numerous separation methods have been worked out. The small letters *o-*, *m-*, and *p-* (standing for *ortho-*, *meta-*, and *para-*) preceding the name xylene are used to identify the three different isomers that vary in the ways the two methyl groups displace the hydrogen atoms of benzene. *Ortho*-xylene is used mostly to produce phthalic anhydride, an important intermediate that leads principally to various coatings and plastics. The least valued of the isomers is *meta*-xylene, but it has uses in the manufacture of coatings and plastics. *Para*-xylene leads to polyesters, which reach the ultimate consumer as polyester fibres under various trademarked names.

Benzene itself is perhaps the industrial chemical with the most varied uses of all. Figure 1 shows some in outline form; for example, several routes are shown to phenol, itself an important industrial chemical. Special emphasis has been given to the numerous alternative routes to nylon-6 and nylon-6,6, considered later.

Products derived from the aromatic hydrocarbons. In transforming benzene to the products obtained from it, other raw materials are required; for example, ethylene for the production of styrene, and sulfuric acid for the production of benzenesulfonic acid. It would have unduly complicated Figure 1 to attempt to show all of these; chlorine, however, has been shown entering at several places. Chlorine will be encountered in many operations discussed below.

The diagram of Figure 1 is drastically simplified. Many applications of benzene are not shown. In some cases, alternative starting points to the end product sidetrack benzene. For example, to obtain styrene from benzene

Margin note: Uses of solvents

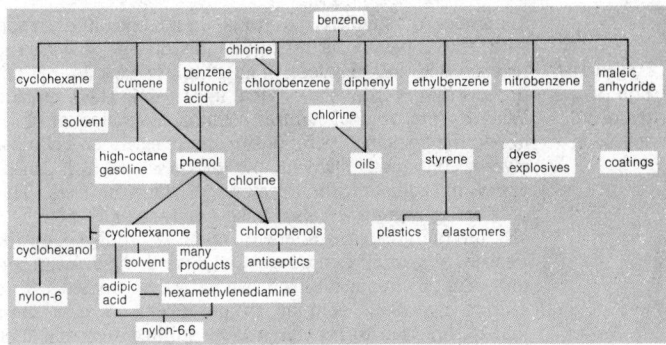

Figure 1: Intermediate and end products from raw benzene.

the route passes through ethylbenzene; but ethylbenzene is found in a mixture with its isomers, the xylenes; the ethylbenzene that is separated from the xylene mixture can be used in the manufacture of styrene.

Polymers. Figure 1 shows synthetic fibres (two kinds of nylon); coatings, plastics, and elastomers (synthetic products having rubberlike properties) are also mentioned. All these groups of substances have one thing in common—they are all polymers (substances composed of large molecules formed from smaller ones), produced by applications of a rapidly growing branch of chemistry, polymer chemistry, established in the early 1930s. Until then classical chemistry had been confined to substances of low molecular weight; that is, composed of a rather small number of atoms held together by valence bonds. For example, common salt can be represented as NaCl, one sodium (Na) atom and one chlorine (Cl) atom held together by electrovalence; cane sugar, a rather complicated molecule for classical chemistry, is composed of carbon (C), hydrogen (H), and oxygen (O), represented by the formula $C_{12}H_{22}O_{11}$, having 45 atoms attached to one another in the molecule. Many natural substances have far higher molecular weights than this; they consist of a much larger number of atoms, all attached as valence connections. The arrangement of such molecules is not random, however; a considerable measure of simplicity is provided by the atoms being arranged in an intelligible pattern with a repeating unit. The name polymer is taken from the Greek, *poly* meaning "many" and *meros*, "part." As an example, the structure of natural rubber can be represented as made up of a large number of repeating units of the form:

$$-CH_2 \qquad CH_2-$$
$$C = CH$$
$$CH_3$$

There may be hundreds, or thousands, of such repeat units in one chain (see also POLYMERS).

Cellulose. An important natural polymer is cellulose, the repeating unit of which is $-C_6H_{10}O_5-$. Cellulose is the principal component of the woody parts of trees and of the fibrous stems of a very large number of plants. Wood cellulose has been used for hundreds of years in the manufacture of paper; the noncellulosic components are washed away after a chemical treatment, and the remaining fibres are caused to interlock, forming the paper. Cotton, still the most important of all fibres, consists of almost pure cellulose.

Polymers were actually at work before understanding and application of polymer chemistry came to be. All the natural fibres, wool, silk, and linen, as well as cotton, are polymers. In paint, the formation of a stable, coherent coating is due to the polymerization of certain naturally occurring oils. A solid material derived from cellulose by nitration and known as celluloid was popular throughout the last third of the 19th century. Because of its high flammability, it was displaced early in the 20th century by less flammable plastics based on phenol.

Several ways have been found to dissolve the cellulose obtained from cotton or from wood. The resulting solution is extruded through a fine aperture, a spinneret (or

Margin note: Growth of polymer chemistry

Regeneration of dissolved cellulose

a number of spinnerets), into a liquid bath that reacts with the solvent, destroying its dissolving power, and regenerating the cellulose. The cellulose yielded by this process differs from the original in one important respect. Whereas the original natural cellulose consisted of short fibres, the spinning operation for the regenerated cellulose gives a continuous filament, the thickness of which can be varied by adjusting the apertures of the spinnerets. This product is rayon (see also FIBRES, MAN-MADE).

By far the greatest amount of rayon is produced by the viscose, or xanthate, process. Cellulose derived from cotton, or more frequently from wood, is first treated with a sodium hydroxide solution to produce a swollen mass that is shredded to provide a large surface area and then aged. The shredded and aged material is treated with carbon disulfide, forming the compound cellulose xanthate and giving a syrupy solution that is referred to as viscose. The viscose solution, after ripening or aging, is extruded into an acid solution to regenerate the cellulose.

Carbon disulfide is made by the reaction of carbon and sulfur. Carbon comes from natural gas, and the sulfur may be supplied in the elemental form, as hydrogen sulfide, or as sulfur dioxide. The chief uses of carbon disulfide are for the manufacture of rayon and for regenerated cellulose film (see below *Film materials*). These two products are made in such large quantity that carbon disulfide is a heavy chemical, by any standard.

The size of the giant cellulose molecule, the polymer, is reduced in the process. In native cellulose the chains are uneven in length, but range from about 3,500 to 10,000 of the basic unit, in this case $- C_6H_{10}O_5 -$. After regeneration the chains are no more than 400–500 units in length.

The importance of this process is that the source of the cellulose is no longer just the tuft of white fibres that surrounds the cotton seeds, but the greater part of the trunk of an entire tree. In general terms, a properly managed tree-growing program will yield two to three times as much cellulose as the same acreage planted to cotton.

Rayon finishes

A rayon factory is also far more versatile than the cotton plant. Rayon originally gave a lustrous, shiny fabric. In modern production, however, much rayon is made with a dull finish by incorporating a white pigment into the spinning solution. Coloured pigments can also be added, giving spin-dyed fibre of exceptional colour fastness.

Annual world production of rayon by the early 1980s was about 1,300,000 tons, greater than that of any other fibre except jute or cotton. Of this total the two largest producers, the United States and Japan, produce about one-fifth and one-seventh, respectively.

Some other fibres, sometimes referred to as regenerated cellulose, also are produced by reconstituting natural fibres. Cuprammonium rayon uses as a solvent the deep blue solution obtained by adding ammonia to a solution of copper sulfate. Cuprammonium is produced in moderate quantities for special purposes. Another very important fibre is acetate. For this fibre, the cellulose is brought into solution with acetic acid and acetic anhydride; in the spinning process, the acetate is not removed, but remains in the fibre as cellulose acetate.

In these and related fibres, the long-chain polymer structure is provided by nature, and is only modified (and partially degraded) by chemical applications. They are thus referred to as semi-man-made fibres. For other fibres, the chemist starts with ordinary chemicals, of quite low molecular weight, and builds up a chain. These constitute the fully manmade fibres.

Polyamides (nylons). Development of the synthetics began with the pioneering work in polymer chemistry of Wallace H. Carothers of the United States in the 1920s and 1930s. Studying the buildup of long molecules with various repeating units, he found that in many cases the most suitable size was a unit containing six carbon atoms with oxygen and hydrogen atoms. In general, only the end elements of such a unit entered into the reaction, and so the four centre carbon atoms could be ignored. In adipic acid, for example, the complete formula is:

$$HOOC - CH_2 - CH_2 - CH_3 - CH_2 - COOH.$$

Because only the end elements are important, this formula can be written:

$$HOOCCH_2CH_2CH_2CH_2COOH.$$

Other organic compounds may be similarly treated. Hexamethylenediamine is a six-carbon compound (with hydrogen and nitrogen), having the formula $H_2N(CH_2)_6NH_2$. These end elements can react with the end elements of adipic acid to form an amide having an end element of the form $-CONH_2$. The two six-carbon compounds (adipic acid and hexamethylenediamine) can therefore react with each other, end to end, indefinitely, to give a compound of the form:

$$[- NH(CH_2)_6NHOC(CH_2)_4CO -]_x.$$

Such a compound is a polyamide. There are a number of such polyamides, all of which are referred to as nylon. The one represented above is nylon-6,6, meaning that there are six carbon atoms in the component that terminates at each end in $-COOH$ and also six carbon atoms in the other component that terminates twice in $-NH_2$. As a variation, it is possible to put the $-COOH$ and the $-NH_2$ at opposite ends of the same molecule. When this material is caused to react with itself, in head-to-tail fashion, the resulting compound differs slightly in the arrangement of the O and the NH_2 group. Another polyamide is designated nylon-6, meaning that only one component is used, and it has six carbon atoms. These nylons are manufactured and made into fibre; they have very similar properties. Their raw material structure and the manner of obtaining them are shown in Figure 1. They are very versatile fibres, and improvements on them constantly have been made. There is also nylon-11, which has only one component with 11 carbon atoms.

Polyesters, acrylics, and elastomers. Several other fully man-made fibres are manufactured on a large scale. Important among these are the polyesters, derived from *p*-xylene. The acrylic fibres (Orlon, Acrilan, and Zefran are well-known trademarks) can be made into fine, fluffy fabrics suitable for sweaters and blankets, and they are also used industrially where chemical resistance is required. Another full synthetic is spandex, an inherently elastic fibre.

The great advances in the science of polymers since Carothers' work was established have led to enormous improvements not only in fibres but in other applications. Much depends upon the way in which the long polymer chains fit together, or interact. It has been implied that they form straight lines; this implication is intended only to show which atoms are connected with one another by valence bonds. The long chains are not straight, but zigzagged, and the long zigzag has a tendency to curl up upon itself. In some cases, cross-linking takes place; that is, an actual valence connection is formed between some of the atoms in neighbouring chains. Such a product is rigid. A common example is the white of an egg, a colourless, liquid substance. On heating, it quickly becomes opaque, white, and comparatively solid, by cross-linking of the protein molecules.

Significance of chain formation in polymers

Short of actual valence connections between the atoms, neighbouring chains in a polymer can have varying degrees of interaction. If the shape of the successive atoms is such that neighbouring chains fit together neatly, local crystallinity results. A fairly high degree of crystallinity is requisite for a fibre. If the crystallinity is low, the chains, if pulled straight, have a tendency to return to the original coiled condition; this results in an elastomer, or rubber-like material. Intermediate crystallinity gives plastics, which can range from soft, squashy material to rigid products.

Saturated and unsaturated hydrocarbons. Because of the complicated interlocking network of the chemical industry, it will be helpful to return briefly to the original raw materials. Earlier the aromatic group of organic chemicals was described; contrasted with these are the aliphatics, of which a number of quite simple chemicals are of great industrial importance.

The simplest organic chemicals are the saturated hydrocarbons methane (CH_4), ethane (C_2H_6 or $H_3C - CH_3$), propane (H₃C — CH₂ — CH₃), and others. These are useful as fuels but are chemically rather unreactive; and so in order to process them to give further chemicals, they are "cracked" by means of a heat treatment to convert them to unsaturated hydrocarbons. These contain less hydrogen than the saturated hydrocarbons, and they contain one or more double valence bonds, or triple valence bonds, connecting carbon atoms. Some of the most important of the unsaturated hydrocarbons industrially are acetylene (HC ≡ CH), ethylene (H₂C = CH₂), propylene (H₃C — CH = CH₂), and butadiene (H₂C = CH — CH = CH₂). An idea of the raw materials for these hydrocarbons and a highly simplified diagram of their products are given in Figure 2.

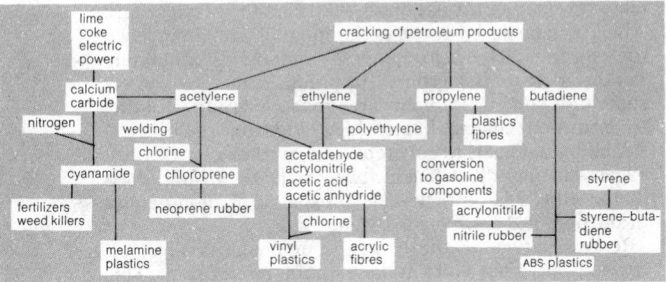

Figure 2: Some of the more important unsaturated hydrocarbons; their origin and final products.

Ethylene. Ethylene, one of the largest volume organic chemicals, can be produced either together with acetylene or with propylene. It gives rise to a large number of products, many in large volume. Some of the more important have been lumped together in a box (Figure 2): acetaldehyde, acrylonitrile, acetic acid, acetic anhydride, the list bringing together substances that have complex interrelations. These relations would come to light if this box were magnified and examined closely. These substances, however, also can be made from acetylene, and acetylene also can be made from a completely different source, calcium carbide.

Acetylene. The raw materials for calcium carbide are shown in Figure 2 as lime, coke, and electric power. Thus calcium carbide is a more suitable source of acetylene in a country that has hydroelectric power but lacks petroleum reserves. The largest producer of acetylene is West Germany, which produced 248,000 tons annually during the late 1970s; the United States and Italy are other major producers.

Calcium carbide generates acetylene when acted upon by water. This process can be done on a small scale to produce acetylene that is suitable for illumination because of its extremely bright flame. Acetylene is also made on a large scale for chemical conversion, as shown in Figure 2. Acetylene is also used for oxyacetylene welding because when burned with oxygen it produces an extremely high temperature.

Acetylene and ethylene have been in competition for chemical industrial uses. During the 1950s acetylene was widely used as a chemical raw material, and methods were worked out for obtaining it from hydrocarbon sources, as shown in Figure 2. Later ethylene became in general more economical, and the use of acetylene as a raw material has therefore declined. Calcium carbide, a raw material for acetylene, however, has other uses. When treated with nitrogen, it gives calcium cyanamide, valuable as a fertilizer and weed killer, and at the same time a raw material for the production of melamine, used in making some modern plastics (see on the left in Figure 2). Other products from acetylene, ethylene, and other unsaturated hydrocarbons marked, in their main outlines, in Figure 2 show that these processes provide a wide variety of raw materials for various plastic, elastic, and fibrous products.

Propylene. Propylene is not produced in as large volume as ethylene and is mostly used chemically. It is an important raw material for a number of detergents. It leads to derivatives that are used in antiknock gasoline

Competition between acetylene and ethylene

additives. It can also be polymerized to a product with uses generally similar to those of polyethylene. When made into a fibre, polypropylene is especially useful for carpets.

Plastics. *Amino resins.* Plastics and related substances represent an enormous field (see also PLASTICS AND RESINS). Melamine (produced from calcium cyanamide) is reacted with formaldehyde (obtained from methanol) to give a polymer that is typical of the amino resins. These resins can either be worked further into plastic molded parts, or they can be used as adhesives or as textile coatings.

Vinyls. The entry vinyl plastics in Figure 2 covers a wide field (vinyl refers to the group CH₂ = CH —). Polyvinyl chloride, the most important member of the group, was produced in the late 1970s at a rate of about 1,800,000 tons annually both in the United States and in Japan; West Germany, France, and Italy also are substantial producers. It can be produced in rigid form or, by the use of plasticizers, in flexible form, and can be used for almost any hard object or for coatings or films. It is widely used for pipe because it is not corroded by water or by many chemicals. Another vinyl, polyvinyl acetate, is used together with polyvinyl chloride for phonograph records and in other applications. Polyvinyl acetals have a very specialized use as the transparent adhesive binding of two layers of glass to make safety glass.

Ethylene can be used as the raw material for the vinyls. Ethylene itself, however, forms a major polymer; world production by the late 1970s was about 36,000,000 tons annually. Polyethylene, called polythene in some countries, was discovered in the 1930s as a result of the study of the effect on ethylene of high pressure. In the product made in this way, the chains of carbon atoms have branches at intervals. There is also a polyethylene, made at lower pressures with suitable catalysts, in which there are substantially no branches. This latter material, frequently referred to as high-density polyethylene, has a higher density, a higher melting point, and greater toughness than other polyethylenes. The uses of the two types vary slightly, according to their properties, but there is considerable overlap. Polyethylene is widely used for translucent, nonbreakable bottles, in cable coverings, as a coating for paperboard milk cartons, in the manufacture of toys and seats for chairs in auditoriums, and as a clear film. It is also made into a fibre used in making rope for marine applications; its density (even the high-density form) is less than that of water, so that it floats.

Uses of polyethylene

Elastomers. Butadiene (Figure 2) is partly used to produce plastics and partly to produce elastomers, a field related to that of plastics. The elastomers were at first regarded as synthetic substitutes for natural rubber. As has often happened with synthetic substitutes, however, a number of different varieties were developed; some were actually better than natural rubber in some ways and others better in other ways, and so it was soon realized that what had been developed was not so much a replacement as a supplement. Of the total, natural plus synthetic rubber, the percentage of synthetic varies in the industrial countries from about 55 percent to about 90–95 percent. Annual world production of synthetic rubber by 1980 was about 9,600,000 tons. The United States is the largest producer, followed by Japan, West Germany, France, Canada, and the United Kingdom.

Interest in a synthetic material that could be used in automobile tires began in Germany as early as World War I, when supplies from the tropical, rubber-producing countries were cut off. A synthetic rubber of a sort was produced that could be used for tires, although the vehicle had to be jacked up when not in motion to prevent developing a flat spot on the tires. Much research in Germany and the United States led to the development, shortly before World War II, of several elastomers. The most important of these, and by far the best for tires, was made of a copolymer of 75 parts of butadiene and 25 parts of styrene. This synthetic was first known as GR-S (Government Rubber–Styrene) but later came to be called SBR—styrene-butadiene rubber. It is produced in far greater quantity than any of the other synthetics. It is better than natural rubber in some respects, but poorer in others. It is often used in blends with other rubbers.

Figure 2 also shows that acrylonitrile can be copolymerized with butadiene (roughly one-third acrylonitrile, two-thirds butadiene) to form nitrile rubber (NBR). This synthetic has different properties from other synthetics, and is used for rubber hose, tank lining, conveyor belts, gaskets, and wire insulation. Acrylonitrile and styrene, together with butadiene, form a terpolymer, called ABS, which is useful for high-impact-strength plastics.

Acrylonitrile contains nitrogen, and therefore is decidedly different in chemical constitution from natural rubber, which contains only carbon and hydrogen. Natural rubber has a repeating unit of five carbon atoms. By starting with the unsaturated hydrocarbon isoprene (C_5H_8), a polymer can be made with the spatial arrangement of the atoms the same as in natural rubber and with very similar properties. This polymer is sometimes referred to as synthetic natural rubber. Another hydrocarbon elastomer starts with isobutylene (C_4H_8) and gives butyl, a rubber characterized by resistance to oxygen and impermeability to gases, which is used in inner tubes, cable insulation, and as a coating for fabrics.

Imperme-ability of butyl rubber

Figure 2 shows that acetylene is the raw material for chloroprene (C_4H_5Cl), which is converted into neoprene, another versatile elastomer of exceptional properties. There are also rubberlike products containing sulfur, known in the United States as the thiokols. A related group, containing carbon, sulfur, and oxygen, the sulfones, are tough plastic materials.

Film materials.   Most of the above-mentioned groups of chemicals that can be used either as plastics or elastomers can also be made into the form of coherent films. In the more highly industrialized countries there is a very high demand for films for wrapping purposes, largely for food, and also in the building construction industry. The requirements for a film vary greatly. For many food products the wrapping film must have the ability to "breathe"; that is, it must have some permeability to water vapour and also to oxygen. Films can be developed with high permeability, or with none at all. In some applications the film should be self-sealing. Films can be made of any thickness, and for some purposes extreme toughness is required. Paper, or treated paper, has of course been used for many of these purposes for many years, but it has such disadvantages as low strength, particularly when wet, and it is difficult to make it transparent. Cellophane was produced commercially starting in the 1920s; its transparency attracted attention at once, beginning a revolution in wrapping materials.

Cellophane is regenerated cellulose. It is like viscose rayon, except that it is extruded flat, instead of in the form of a fibre. It is still very popular, but is highly sensitive to water and to changing humidity. Many other polymers now supplement it and compete with it. Polyethylene makes fine, tough films; there is no sharp distinction between a thin extrusion, useful for a wrapping film, and thicker products used for nonbreakable bottles. Many vinyl products are used in films, as are polystyrene, polyesters, and nylon. A chemical derivative from natural rubber, chlorinated rubber, gives films of extraordinary stretchability.

From coherent films that can stand by themselves, it is a short step to one of the components of a paint. In the days before chemical technology, commercial paints were based on linseed oil as a film-former. A number of inorganic materials were available as pigments, one of the cheapest being iron oxide, which gives a dull red colour, still widely used for painting farm buildings. Linseed oil and the pigment made a mixture that was too thick, so that it was normally thinned with turpentine.

The thinner in paint is the component that has undergone least change. Turpentine, obtained from pine trees, and sometimes as a by-product in the manufacture of paper, is still used. A petroleum distillate, however, is cheaper and equally effective. The thinner completely evaporates very shortly after the paint is applied. In latex paints, the paint itself is in the form of minute droplets in water, and water is the thinner.

The film-former, on the other hand, does not "dry" by evaporation. Linseed oil, obtained from the seeds of the flax plant, is a polyunsaturate because it is rich in unsaturated bonds, and so are various other oils that can be used, such as tung oil, soybean oil, oiticica oil, and tall oil, a by-product of paper manufacture. In all these oils, in several places in the molecule, two carbon atoms are connected by double bonds. Such a molecule can react with oxygen from the air, and with itself, forming a polymer; in so doing it changes from a liquid to a coherent, permanent film. Polymer chemistry has added many other materials as possible film-formers. Vinyls, polystyrene, amino resins, even nylon, in fact most of the plastic materials shown in Figure 2 can be modified to be film-formers for coatings. Perhaps the most typical class for coating formation, however, is the alkyd resins, which are made by reacting compounds containing two (or more) −COOH groups with compounds containing two or more −OH groups. In practice, there is always some of a component with three reactive groups, leading to branched chains, interlocking with one another, a structure that leads to coherent solid products.

The principal dibasic acid (two −COOH groups) used in the alkyds is phthalic acid, in the form of its anhydride, obtained from *ortho*-xylene.

Representative of the −OH component is glycerol, formed as a by-product in the manufacture of soap. This source of supply is inadequate, so that glycerol is also manufactured from propylene, which contains the same three-carbon starting point.

Modern paints using the purified, synthetic ingredients have done away with the once characteristic paint odour, and they also dry much more quickly because of the incorporation of small quantities of chemical products called metallic soaps, compounds of organic acids with cobalt, manganese, lead, or iron.

The pigments used in paints and industrial coatings constitute a very diverse group. For some pigment purposes organic colorants, similar to those used in dyes, can be used. More often the coating pigments are inorganic, and require a different group of raw materials from those that have been considered so far. The most important pigment is plain white, which occurs not only in white paints but also in many off-white and pastel shades. The most widely used white pigment was formerly white lead, a mixed hydroxide and carbonate of lead, but it had two disadvantages: it was inclined to darken because of the formation of lead sulfide in atmospheres that are somewhat polluted with hydrogen sulfide, and it was toxic. Having a sweetish taste, as lead salts often do, it was a prevalent hazard in old buildings where small children lived. Especially for this reason white lead has been largely replaced in modern white paint by a white pigment based on titanium dioxide.

Poisonous pigments

Titanium is comparatively light, exceptionally strong for its weight, and has good resistance to corrosion and to heat. These properties make it extremely valuable in airplane construction and other applications. The ores of titanium are abundant and well distributed, and are worked for some of the industrially valuable compounds as well as for the metal. Titanium dioxide, for example, has specialized uses in electrical equipment, although its main value is as a white pigment, for which its properties are nearly ideal.

There are also white extender pigments (see also DYESTUFFS AND PIGMENTS). These pigments, white when seen alone, exhibit a much less intense white when mixed with the film-former, and therefore have far less covering power than the white opaque pigments. The extender pigments include such substances as calcium carbonate, calcium sulfate, some kinds of clay, and silica. When extender pigments are added to opaque pigments, cost is reduced and there are favourable properties.

Other metal compounds furnish coloured pigments. Iron gives red, brown, and yellow pigments. A well-known bright red pigment is the oxide of lead known as red lead. Cadmium compounds contribute red and yellow; cobalt gives violets and blues. Chromates are yellow or orange, and also confer resistance to corrosion; thus these pigments are often seen in the undercoats applied to bridges or other metal structures. Another kind of pigment is furnished by the metallic powders of aluminum, bronze, lead, and zinc.

Black is a most important pigment colour. Some compounds of iron are black pigments. Another source is lampblack, a substance made by partial combustion of various vegetable products. The outstanding black pigment, however, is the versatile product known as carbon black.

Carbon black

Carbon black is one of the most important of the industrial chemical products. Total world production by the late 1970s was about 4,800,000 tons annually, with a large number of countries producing it. Carbon black is considered an inorganic petrochemical because it is made from natural gas or petroleum residues. There are several processes involving either incomplete combustion (burning off the hydrogen of a hydrocarbon, such as methane, and leaving the carbon) or by externally applied heat in a furnace, splitting the hydrocarbon into hydrogen and carbon.

The most important of all the uses of carbon black is in compounding rubber that is to be used in tires. The average tire of a passenger automobile contains approximately four pounds (two kilograms) of carbon black. Carbon black is not only used as a pigment but also is employed in printing ink, an ink that is little different from an applied coating. Carbon black creates the principal difficulty in the recycling of newsprint because no practical way has yet been found to destroy the black ink. A specialized use of carbon black is as an additive to phonograph records. A special form of carbon black, one that is derived from acetylene, has its principal use in conventional dry-cell batteries.

Uses of typical end products

COMPONENT ELEMENTS OF FERTILIZERS AND THEIR USES

Fertilizers represent one of the largest market commodities for the chemical industry. Between 1970 and 1979 fertilizer production doubled, reaching a world production of 125,000,000 tons by 1979. Already a large industry in all of the industrialized countries, it is a very important industry for introduction as early as possible into developing countries.

The crucial elements that have to be added to the soil in considerable quantities in the form of fertilizer are nitrogen, phosphorus, and potassium, in each case in the form of a suitable compound. These are the major fertilizer elements, or macronutrients. Calcium, magnesium, and sulfur are regarded as secondary nutrients; and it is sometimes necessary to add them. Numerous other elements are required by different soils only in trace quantities; certain soils may be deficient in boron, copper, zinc, or molybdenum, making it necessary to add very small quantities of these elements. As a great industry, however, fertilizers are based on the three elements mentioned above.

Nitrogen is present in vast quantities in the air, making up about 78 percent of the Earth's atmosphere. It enters the chemical industry as ammonia, produced through fixation of atmospheric nitrogen. For phosphorus and potassium, it is necessary to find mineral sources and to convert them into a form suitable for use. These three elements are not used in fertilizer only; they also have other uses and interact with other facets of the chemical industry, making a highly complicated picture. A schematized overview of some of these interactions is presented in Figure 3.

Potassium. The simplest part of this diagram is the portion representing potassium. The element potassium is seventh in order of abundance in the Earth's crust, about the same order as sodium, which it resembles very closely in its properties (see also SODIUM AND POTASSIUM PRODUCTS AND PRODUCTION). Although sodium is readily available in the sodium chloride in the ocean, however, most of the potassium is contained in small proportions in a large number of mineral formations, from which it cannot be economically extracted. When the use of potassium salts as fertilizers began in the second half of the 19th century, it was believed that Germany had a monopoly with the deposits at Stassfurt, but many other workable deposits of potassium salts were later found in other parts of the world. World production of potash (a term covering all potassium salts) by the late 1970s was around 26,000,000–29,000,000 tons annually. World reserves are adequate for thousands of years at this rate of use, with very large deposits occurring in the Soviet Union, in the province of Saskatchewan in Canada, and in both East and West Germany.

Resemblance of potassium to sodium

Potassium chloride is the principal commercial form of potash, and some potassium nitrate is also produced. Approximately 90 percent of the production of these chemicals goes to the production of fertilizers. For other purposes, the similar sodium salts are cheaper, but for a few special uses potassium has the advantage. Some ceramic uses require potassium, and potassium bicarbonate is more effective than sodium bicarbonate in extinguishing fires. Only a small amount of potassium metal is made. Some of it is converted into potassium superoxide, a source of oxygen in self-contained breathing apparatus; and some of it is mixed with sodium to form a liquid mixture that has been investigated as a heat-transfer medium in nuclear reactors.

Phosphorus. Phosphorus presents a somewhat more complicated picture. It has many uses other than in fertilizers. By far the largest source is phosphate rock, although some use is made of phosphatic iron ore, from which the phosphorus is obtained as a by-product from the slag. World production of phosphate rock, for all purposes, by the early 1980s was about 149,000,000 tons annually. As with potassium, there are extensive reserves. The largest deposits are in North Africa (Morocco, Algeria, Tunisia), the United States (largely Florida), and the Soviet Union, but there are also sizable deposits in numerous other countries.

Phosphate rock is found in deposits of sedimentary origin, laid down originally in beds on the ocean floor. The rock consists largely of the insoluble tricalcium phosphate, together with some other materials, including some fluorine. To be used as a fertilizer, phosphate must be converted to a form that is soluble in water, even if only slightly so.

Phosphoric acid (H_3PO_4) has three hydrogen atoms, all of which are replaceable by a metal. Tricalcium phosphate, in which all three of the hydrogen atoms are replaced by calcium, must be converted to the soluble form, monocalcium phosphate, in which only one hydrogen atom is replaced by calcium. The conversion is done by sulfuric acid, which converts the phosphate rock to superphosphate, widely used as fertilizer. This operation requires large tonnages of sulfuric acid.

The fertilizer industry is not only a matter of manufacturing the right chemical but also of distribution, getting the right material to the right place at the right time. Fertilizers are made centrally, but must be distributed over a large agricultural area. A fertilizer factory is, typically, a large installation, characterized by enormous storage silos; the product is manufactured throughout the year, but it requires considerable space to store it until the few weeks during which it is distributed to farms for application to the soil.

Manufacturing considerations

The weight of the superphosphate is greater than that of the original phosphate rock by the amount of the sulfuric acid added. The superphosphate also carries the dead

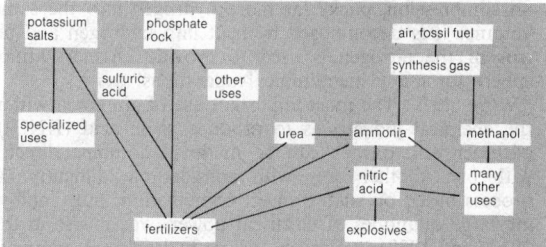

Figure 3: Major interactions of fertilizer products and their uses.

weight of the calcium sulfate that is formed in the manufacturing process. This dead weight can be reduced by replacing sulfuric acid with phosphoric acid (itself obtained by the action of sulfuric acid on phosphate rock, followed by separating the products; or else by an electric furnace process). This process results in triple superphosphate, in which all the calcium originally in the phosphate rock appears as calcium monophosphate. The useful content of the fertilizer, expressed as the percent of phosphoric oxide, is increased from 20 percent in ordinary superphosphate to about 45 percent in the triple variety, resulting in a better than twofold reduction in the amount of material that must be distributed to provide a given amount of the useful oxide.

Instead of using either sulfuric acid or phosphoric acid to treat the phosphate rock, nitric acid can be used. One of the resulting products, calcium nitrate, is a fertilizer, thus one of the many varieties of mixed fertilizers can be obtained. Instead of neutralizing phosphoric acid with calcium, which contributes nothing but dead weight, ammonia can be used, giving ammonium phosphate, in which both ends of the molecule contribute fertilizer elements. Such improvements in fertilizers are constantly taking place.

Many other compounds of phosphorus are used. One group is comprised of phosphoric acid and various phosphates derived from it. The acid is used in soft drinks for its pleasant taste when sweetened and its nutritive value. Other food applications include the use of disodium phosphate in processed cheese and of phosphates in baking powder, flameproofing, and the treatment of boiler water in steam plants. An important use of some of the phosphates is in detergents.

Elemental phosphorus has many allotropic forms. White phosphorus is used in rodent poison, and by the military for smoke generation. Red phosphorus, comparatively harmless, is used in matches. Ferrophosphorus, a combination of phosphorus with iron, is used as an ingredient in high-strength, low-alloy steel. In addition, the many organic compounds of phosphorus have varied uses, including those as additives for gasoline and lubricating oil, as plasticizers for plastics that otherwise would be inconveniently rigid, and, in some cases, as powerful insecticides, related to nerve poisons.

Nitrogen. The production of nitrogen not only is a major branch of the fertilizer industry but it opens up a most important segment of the chemical industry as a whole. World production of nitrogen (in various compounds) by the early 1980s was about 78,000,000 tons (actual nitrogen content) annually; about 80 percent of the production is used in fertilizers, leaving a sizable segment for the general chemical industry.

Farm manure long supplied enough nitrogenous fertilizer for agriculture, but late in the 19th century it was realized that agriculture was outgrowing this source. A certain amount of ammonium sulfate was available as a by-product of the carbonization of coal, and the large deposits of sodium nitrate discovered in Chile were helpful for a time. The long-range problem of supply, however, was not solved until just before World War I, when the researches of Fritz Haber in Germany brought into commercial operation the method of ammonia synthesis that, in principle, is still used. The immediate motivation for this great development was Germany's need for an indigenous source of nitrogen for military explosives. The close interrelation between the use of nitrogen for fertilizers and for explosives still persists.

Haber process for ammonia

Because nitrogen comprises 78 percent of the air, there is a little more than 11 pounds of nitrogen over every square inch of the earth's surface. Nitrogen, however, is a rather inert element and does not combine easily with any other element. Haber succeeded in getting nitrogen to combine with hydrogen by the use of high pressure, moderately high temperatures, and a catalyst.

The hydrogen for ammonia (NH_3) is usually obtained by the decomposition of water (H_2O). This process requires energy, in some cases supplied by electricity, but more often from fossil fuels. In some cases the hydrogen is obtained directly from the fossil fuel.

Haber used coke as a fuel. Carbon can burn either to carbon dioxide or, if the supply of air is kept short, to carbon monoxide, by a process that is known as the producer gas reaction. The gaseous product is a mixture of carbon monoxide with the nitrogen that was originally in the air.

The red-hot coke can also be heated with steam to yield carbon monoxide and hydrogen, a product known as water gas. On cooling, the water condenses out, leaving a mixture of carbon monoxide and hydrogen. It is also possible to cary out a water-gas shift reaction by passing the water gas with more steam over a catalyst, yielding more hydrogen, and carbon dioxide. The carbon dioxide is removed by dissolving it in water at a pressure of about 10 atmospheres; it can also be used directly. Starting from water gas, and converting a certain proportion of the carbon monoxide to carbon dioxide and hydrogen, it is possible to arrive at a mixture of carbon monoxide and hydrogen in any proportion.

Synthesis gas. In Figure 3 the words synthesis gas have been shown as the source of two products, ammonia and methanol. It is not quite the same synthesis gas in the two cases, but they are closely related. The mixture of carbon monoxide and hydrogen described above is the synthesis gas that is the source of methanol. But ammonia requires nitrogen, which is obtained from the producer gas by causing it to undergo the water-gas shift reaction, yielding hydrogen. Ammonia requires much more hydrogen, which is obtained from water gas subjected to the water-gas shift. By appropriate mixing, ammonia synthesis gas of exactly the right composition can be obtained.

Water-gas shift reaction

The above description is a simplified account of how synthesis gas, either for ammonia or for methanol, is obtained from fossil fuel as a source of energy, but it gives an idea of the versatility of the operations. There are many possible variations in detail, depending largely on the particular fuel that is used. The nitrogen industry, which has grown steadily since shortly after World War I, was originally based largely on coke, either from coal or lignite (brown coal). There has been a gradual change to petroleum products as the fossil fuel. As is true with many other branches of the chemical industry, the latest trend is to move to natural gas.

The carbon dioxide removed during the preparation of the synthesis gas can be reacted with ammonia, often at the same plant, to form urea, $CO(NH_2)_2$. This is an excellent fertilizer, highly concentrated in nitrogen (46.6 percent). Urea also is useful as an additive in animal feed since it provides the nitrogen necessary for the formation of meat protein. Urea is also used for an important series of resins and plastics by reaction with formaldehyde, derived from methanol.

Ammonia can be applied as a fertilizer in numerous forms, ranging from the application of liquid ammonia beneath the surface of the soil, or solutions of ammonia in water (also containing other fertilizer ingredients), or as ammonium nitrate, or other products from nitric acid, which itself is derived from ammonia. Ammonia also has other uses within the chemical industry. The small amount of ammonia consumed in the course of making sodium carbonate by the ammonia soda process formerly amounted to a considerable volume. Ammonia is used in one process for making rayon, as a refrigerant in large commercial refrigeration establishments, and as a convenient portable source of hydrogen. Hydrogen can be compressed into cylinders, but ammonia, which forms a liquid on compression, packs far more hydrogen into the same volume; it is decomposed by heat into hydrogen and nitrogen; the nitrogen is used to provide an inert atmosphere for many metallurgical operations.

Ammonia as a source of hydrogen

Nitric acid. The most important use of ammonia within the chemical industry is to produce nitric acid (HNO_3). Nitrogen and oxygen can be made to combine directly with one another only with considerable difficulty. A process based on such a direct combination, but employing large quantities of electrical power, was in use in the 1920s and 1930s in Norway, where hydroelectric power is readily available. It has not proved economical in modern conditions.

Ammonia burns in air, or in oxygen, causing the hydrogen atoms to burn off, forming water and leaving free nitrogen. With the aid of a catalyst, platinum with a small percentage of the related metal rhodium, ammonia is oxidized to oxides of nitrogen that can be made to react with water to form nitric acid.

Nitric acid, when treated with ammonia, gives ammonium nitrate, a most important fertilizer. Ammonium nitrate, moreover, is also an important constituent of many explosives (q.v.). Three fundamental explosive materials are obtained by the process of nitrating (treating with nitric acid, often in a mixture with sulfuric acid): cellulose, obtained from wood, gives cellulose nitrate (formerly called nitrocellulose); glycerol gives glyceryl trinitrate (formerly called nitroglycerin); and toluene gives trinitrotoluene, or TNT. Another explosive ingredient is ammonium picrate, derived from picric acid, the relationship of which appears more clearly in its systematic name, 2,4,6-trinitrophenol.

A minor but still important segment of the explosives industry is the production of detonating agents, or such priming compositions as lead azide [$Pb(N_3)_2$], silver azide (AgN_3), and mercury fulminate [$Hg(ONC)_2$]. These are not nitrates or nitro compounds, although some other detonators are, but they all contain nitrogen, and nitric acid is involved in their manufacture.

Related to the explosives are the rocket propellants. A rocket-propelled missile or spacecraft launch vehicle must carry both reactive components (fuel and oxidizer) with it, either in different molecules, or in the same molecule. Rocket propellants essentially consist of an oxidant and a reductant. The oxidant is not necessarily a derivative of nitric acid, but may also be liquid oxygen, ozone (O_3), liquid fluorine, or chlorine trifluoride (see also ROCKETS AND MISSILE SYSTEMS).

Other uses for nitric acid not related to explosives or propellants include the use of cellulose nitrate in coatings. Without a pigment it forms a clear varnish much used in furniture finishing. With a pigment it forms brilliant shiny coatings referred to as lacquers. At one time a fibre similar to rayon was made from cellulose nitrate.

Nitrating benzene (Figure 1) yields nitrobenzene, which can be reduced to aminobenzene, better known as aniline. Aniline can also be made by reacting ammonia with chlorobenzene, obtained from benzene. Benzene and ammonia are required in either case. Similar treatment applied to naphthalene ($C_{10}H_8$) results in naphthylamine.

Synthetic dyes from petrochemicals Both aniline and naphthylamine are the parents of a large number of dyes, but synthetic dyes are usually petrochemical in origin (see also DYES AND DYEING). Aniline, naphthylamine, and the other dye intermediates lead also to pharmaceuticals, photographic chemicals, and chemicals used in rubber processing.

The above account gives an idea of the importance, not only for fertilizers but for many other products, of the process known as fixation of atmospheric nitrogen; that is, taking nitrogen from the air and converting it into some form in which it is usable. The tremendous increase in the production of fertilizers has led to the construction of huge ammonia plants. In the early 1960s the normal capacity of such a plant was about 200 tons of nitrogen per day. In the early 1970s plants were built to fix 1,000 tons of nitrogen per day, and plants of 1,500 tons per day were operating by the late 1970s. The plants must have available a source of fossil fuel, but petroleum and natural gas are easily transported, so that there is a tendency to locate the plants near the ultimate destination of the product, usually a major agricultural region.

A typical plant comprises all the equipment for the preparation of the synthesis gas on the requisite scale, along with equipment for purifying the gas. In the synthesis of ammonia (but not of methanol) any compound of oxygen is a poison for (reduces the effectiveness of) the catalyst, and so traces of carbon dioxide and carbon monoxide must be carefully removed. Compressing the gas to the desired pressure requires extensive engineering equipment: the higher the pressure the greater the yield, but the higher the actual cost of compression. The higher the temperature the lower the yield, but the temperature cannot be lowered indefinitely to obtain better yields because lower temperatures slow down the reaction. The temperature used is of the order of 500° C (930° F). The choice of temperature and of pressure is a carefully worked out compromise to give optimal results. The yield equals the amount of nitrogen and hydrogen that combine to form ammonia in any one pass through the converters. Only a fraction is converted each time, but after each pass the ammonia is removed and the remaining gas is recycled. Atmospheric nitrogen contains about 1 percent argon, a totally inert gas, which must be removed from time to time so that it does not build up in the system indefinitely. There is also usually a nearby nitric acid factory and equipment for producing ammonium nitrate in the exact grain size that is needed for convenient application as fertilizer.

Optimization of temperature and pressure

The growing plants of agricultural crops do not receive all of their nitrogen from synthetic fertilizer. A proportion is supplied by natural means. Some plants, notably beans, have a symbiotic relationship with nitrifying bacteria that are able to "fix" the nitrogen in the air and to combine it into a form available for plant life. This natural synthesis takes place without the necessity for pressures of several hundred atmospheres or of high temperatures. In many laboratory syntheses of natural products, great success has been obtained by quiet reactions, without extreme conditions, by a process of following nature gently, rather than by brute force. Research has been conducted to synthesize ammonia by processes that more nearly resemble the natural formation, and an easier approach to fixation of atmospheric nitrogen has been undertaken.

ALCOHOLS AND THEIR DERIVATIVES

Methanol. The important product methanol (Figure 3) is obtained from synthesis gas in the form of carbon monoxide and hydrogen (sometimes carbon dioxide and hydrogen). The terms methyl alcohol and methanol are synonymous, the former being used more in Great Britain and the latter expression universal in U.S. industry. The term wood alcohol indicates that this alcohol was formerly obtained by the distillation of wood.

Methanol is a large-volume chemical; about half of the production goes to making formaldehyde (CH_2O), a very reactive chemical with a large number of uses. A small amount of formaldehyde comes from nonmethanol sources, via the direct oxidation of hydrocarbons. Methanol also enters into the production of various plastics; leads to such useful derivatives as methyl chloride, a solvent for inks and dyes; and is used in the purification of steroidal and hormonal medicines.

Formaldehyde. The greatest uses of formaldehyde are in the formation of important groups of plastics, the urea–formaldehyde resins and the phenol–formaldehyde resins. In addition, it is used as a fungicide and as a preservative, in paper and textile treatments, and in the synthesis of further products.

Ethanol and its products. Methanol (CH_3OH) is the simplest of the alcohols. The next number of the series, called either ethanol or ethyl alcohol (CH_3CH_2OH), has two carbon atoms. It is most familiar as the active constituent of fermented beverages, but it is also widely used in industry. When intended for human consumption it is always produced by fermentation of some suitable material to form beer, or wine, or distilled spirits of various kinds. For industrial use it is sometimes produced by fermentation from some cheap material, such as molasses, but more often is made from ethylene by causing it to combine with water under the influence of a catalyst, which may be sulfuric acid or phosphoric acid.

A major industrial use of ethanol is to convert it by oxidation into acetaldehyde (CH_3CHO). Ethanol could have been shown in Figure 2 between ethylene and the block containing acetaldehyde and several related chemicals. Ethanol is also used in the preparation of various derivatives, such as ethyl chloride (used in the production of tetraethyl lead), in the course of making various plastics, and in the usual further syntheses.

Acetaldehyde made from ethanol is generally used in the next step by the same company, most often in the same plant, so that the ethanol is really an intermediate alcohol that is used at once. For other uses, ethanol is often shipped from one plant to another. Alcohol intended for human consumption, however, is in all countries subject to a tax, which would make the cost of ethanol prohibitive for any industrial use. Industrial alcohol, therefore, is denatured by the addition of small amounts of substances that are carefully chosen to be highly unpleasant in taste and hard to remove but that do not interfere with the intended industrial use.

Other alcohols. In the alcohols with three carbon atoms, there are two possible structures, or isomers. One is called *n*-propyl alcohol (or 1-propanol), the other isopropyl alcohol (or 2-propanol).

The alcohol 1-propanol, not manufactured in very large quantities, has major use in printing inks. The alcohol 2-propanol, on the other hand, is manufactured in the million-ton range. It is made from propylene by a process similar to that used to convert ethylene to ethanol, and manufacture of 2-propanol by this process initiated the petrochemical industry in the 1920s.

The principal use of 2-propanol is in the manufacture of acetone, which is used extensively as a solvent and as a starting material in the manufacture of numerous other organic compounds. Smaller amounts of 2-propanol are converted to other chemical products or used as a solvent, as rubbing alcohol, or as a denaturing agent for ethyl alcohol.

Manufacture of higher alcohols Higher alcohols—that is, with more than three carbon atoms—too numerous to detail here, are also manufactured. Mention should also be made of the dihydric alcohol, ethylene glycol. This chemical is produced in large volume, and is made from ethylene by an indirect route. Its principal use is in antifreeze mixtures for automobile radiators. It is also used in brake fluids and has numerous derivatives used in resins, paints, and explosives and in the manufacture of polyester fibres. Similar reactions for propylene generate propylene glycol, the principal use of which is as a moistening agent in foods and tobacco.

HALOGENS AND THEIR COMPOUNDS

In this section a group of closely related elements will be treated, giving examples of the different ways in which they are used in the chemical industry. The group is the halogens: chlorine, fluorine, bromine, and iodine. All these elements are highly reactive chemically, but their properties form a graded series, fluorine being the most reactive and iodine the least. Details of their chemistry are covered in the articles HALOGEN ELEMENTS AND THEIR COMPOUNDS and ORGANIC HALOGEN COMPOUNDS.

From the point of view of industrial chemistry, the most important of the halogens is chlorine, which is available in huge quantities from sodium chloride (common salt; see SALT AND SALT PRODUCTION).

(A.St.)

Chlorine. *Uses.* The first large-scale use of chlorine was in the manufacture of bleaching powder for use in making paper and cotton textiles. Bleaching powder was later replaced by liquid chlorine, which also came into widespread use as a germicide for public water supplies. The principal use of chlorine is in making chemical compounds. Important inorganic chemicals made by direct action of chlorine on other substances include sulfur chloride, thionyl chloride, phosgene, aluminum chloride, iron(III) chloride, titanium(IV) chloride, tin(IV) chloride, and potassium chlorate.

Organic chemicals made directly from chlorine include derivatives of methane (methyl chloride, methylene chloride, chloroform, and carbon tetrachloride), chlorobenzene and *ortho*- and *para*-dichlorobenzenes, ethyl chloride, and ethylene chloride.

Commercial preparation. Of several processes that have been used for the manufacture of chlorine, the oldest employed the reaction of hydrochloric acid with manganese dioxide. The procedure was inefficient, and its commercial application was short-lived.

Deacon process A process introduced around 1868 by the English chemist Henry Deacon was based on the reaction of atmospheric oxygen with hydrochloric acid, which was available as a by-product of the Leblanc process for making soda ash; when the Leblanc process became obsolete, the Deacon process fell into disuse.

The chlor-alkali industry—in which chlorine and caustic soda (sodium hydroxide) are produced simultaneously by electrolytic decomposition of salt (sodium chloride)—has become the principal source of chlorine. In the two important versions of the electrolytic process, brine is the electrolyte (in which the passage of electric current occurs by the movement of charged particles called ions), and graphite rods are the anodes (positive terminals). The difference between the two processes derives from the distinct behaviour of iron and of mercury when those metals are used as cathodes (negative terminals).

In brine the two substances susceptible to chemical reduction (see OXIDATION–REDUCTION REACTIONS) are positively charged sodium ions and neutral water molecules. At a reversible cathode (see ELECTROCHEMICAL REACTIONS and THERMODYNAMICS, PRINCIPLES OF), the reduction of sodium ions requires a higher voltage than does the reduction of water molecules, and application of a voltage high enough to reduce sodium ions would effect reduction of a considerable amount of water but of a very small number of sodium ions. The reaction occurring at the surface of an iron cathode is represented by the following equation: Effect of different cathode materials

$$2H_2O \ + \ 2e^- \ \longrightarrow \ 2OH^- \ + \ H_2$$

water   electron   hydroxide   hydrogen

ion   gas

At a mercury cathode, on the other hand, appreciable reduction of water requires a much higher voltage than that needed at an iron cathode. This so-called overpotential is so great that the electrode voltage can be raised to the amount needed for the reduction of sodium ions without affecting the water molecules.

Passage of a direct electric current through brine is attended by chemical changes at the surfaces where the electrodes come in contact with the electrolyte. At the graphite anode, chloride ions present in the dissolved salt are converted by oxidation to elemental chlorine, which is led away through a vent. At the iron cathode, reduction of water takes place, according to the equation shown above. The hydrogen gas is removed, while the hydroxide ions remain in the solution. The net result is that chloride ions and water are consumed and chlorine gas, hydrogen gas, and hydroxide ions are produced. Complete conversion of chloride to hydroxide is not practical, but as brine is continuously introduced at the top of the cell, a solution containing nearly equal amounts of salt and caustic soda is withdrawn at the bottom. Purification of the effluent liquor yields solid sodium hydroxide containing only a small amount of salt.

Successful production of chlorine and caustic soda in these cells requires that the two products be segregated, because upon mixing they would react with one another. The chlorine is kept away from the caustic by interposing a diaphragm between the electrodes: such cells are commonly called diaphragm cells.

In the other main variant of the chlor-alkali process, the so-called mercury cell is employed. The cathode in such a cell is a shallow layer of mercury flowing across the bottom of the vessel; graphite anodes extend down into the brine electrolyte. A powerful direct current is caused to pass between the graphite rods and the mercury surface. At the anodes, chloride ions are converted to chlorine gas, as in the diaphragm cell; the reaction occurring at the mercury cathode, however, differs from that at an iron cathode. Positively charged sodium ions in the brine migrate to the mercury surface, where the voltage is high enough to reduce them to sodium metal without reducing the water because of the above-noted overpotential of mercury. The metallic sodium formed at the cathode dissolves in the mercury, and the solution (called an amalgam) flows out of the cell into another vessel, where it is brought into contact with water, which reacts with the sodium to form sodium hydroxide and hydrogen. Mercury cell

The overall result of operating a mercury cell is the same as that of operating a diaphragm cell: sodium chloride and water are changed into sodium hydroxide, chlorine, and hydrogen. Use of the mercury cell, however, makes it possible to generate the sodium hydroxide in the absence of salt, so that evaporation of the caustic liquor produces solid sodium hydroxide completely free of sodium chloride. The higher purity of the product makes it more desirable for certain applications, notably in the manufacture of rayon.

(J.V.K.)

Fluorine. *Aluminum refining.* The fluorine industry is intimately related to the production of aluminum. Alumina (aluminum oxide, Al_2O_3) can be reduced to metallic aluminum by electrolysis when fused with a flux consisting of sodium fluoroaluminate (Na_3AlF_6), usually called cryolite. After starting the process, the cryolite is not used up in massive quantities, but a small supply is needed to make up for inevitable losses. Cryolite is a rare mineral, however, found in small quantities in the Soviet Union, Spain, and the United States. Cryolite deposits in Greenland were utilized for more than 100 years but had been exhausted by 1963. It has other uses in glass, in enamels, and as a filler for resin-bonded grinding wheels.

The supply problem was solved by the development of synthetic cryolite. For this synthetic, however, a source of fluorine was needed. Fluorine is actually somewhat more abundant in the Earth's crust than chlorine, but most of it is distributed in various rocks in very small quantities. In a form available to the industrial chemist, it is much scarcer than chlorine. Until the 1960s almost the only source was fluorspar (CaF_2), a mineral long known and used as a flux in various metallurgical operations. It is still so used, in quantities larger than before, because the processes that have come into greatest use for making steel, the basic oxygen process and the electric furnace, use two to three times as much flux as the earlier open-hearth furnaces did. For this need, and to supply the fluorine branch of the chemical industry, world production of fluorspar was, by the early 1980s, about 4,600,000 metric tons annually; Mexico and the Soviet Union are the largest producers. The mineral fluorspar is widely distributed, but the supplies of good quality ore are not large; it has been found necessary to use lower grade ores, making the processing more expensive. A very large reserve that can be tapped for fluorine is the 3 percent or so that is present in some phosphate rock.

Refrigerants. These inorganic uses, as a flux and in the manufacture of aluminum, formerly comprised almost the whole of the fluorine industry. The organic fluorine industry, a separate branch, began in the late 1920s with the discovery by Thomas Midgley, Jr., of the United States, of the fluorine-containing refrigerants. A new refrigerant was needed for the domestic refrigerators that were just beginning to be produced on a large scale. Ammonia was unsuitable because even a very minute leak would give an unpleasant smell, and breakdown would release poisonous quantities of the gas. Although many fluorine compounds were known to be poisonous, Midgley found some that were remarkably nontoxic. They also had the physical properties required for a refrigerant, and were totally odourless.

The most used of these is Freon 12 (CCl_2F_2), dichlorodifluoromethane; also used is Freon 22 ($CHClF_2$), chlorodifluoromethane. Several analogous compounds containing carbon, fluorine, chlorine, and sometimes hydrogen are available.

Isotope separation. The next advance in the fluorine industry was connected with the development of the atomic bomb during World War II. It was necessary to separate the small proportion of the fissionable isotope uranium-235 from other, nonfissionable uranium isotopes. This separation could be done by diffusion, working with uranium hexafluoride, a gas. Fluorine at that time was made only occasionally on a small laboratory scale, and it had a reputation for intense chemical reactivity and for being difficult to handle. The solution to the problem of large-scale preparation of elemental fluorine, which required the development and introduction of novel, fluorine-resistant materials of construction, made this important element generally available. Fluorine manufacture is now routine.

Sources of fluorine

Other uses have been developed: as a component in some rocket propellants; for the preparation of the extremely reactive interhalogen compounds, such as chlorine trifluoride (ClF_3), used for cutting steel; and for the preparation of sulfur hexafluoride, an extremely stable gas that has been employed as an insulator in electrical applications.

Propellants and other uses. Aerosol propellants (see PACKAGING) include several inorganic gases as well as some of the halogenated hydrocarbons that are employed as refrigerants; they are used as the inert carrier material in spray cans of insecticide, starch, deodorants, hair spray, and other materials. Nonstick frying pans have been coated with a fluorocarbon resin, the best known of which is polytetrafluoroethylene. There are several other fluorocarbon and fluorinated hydrocarbon resins, some of which have highly specialized applications in the aerospace industry.

Nonstick coating for utensils

Fluorinated compounds are also used in textile treatments; some are soil-release agents that make fabric easy to wash. The salt sodium fluoroacetate is an extremely powerful rodenticide; it has been reported to give good control of rats, but it must be used with great care. Sodium bifluoride is used as a laundry sour; it also removes iron stains without weakening the fabric.

A minor but important use of fluorine in some countries is in the fluoridation of drinking water in the interest of dental health.

Bromine. The properties of bromine are significantly different from those of fluorine and chlorine, and it is far less abundant. It was discovered in the early 19th century in the form of its salts (bromides) in the bitterns that remained after evaporating seawater and extracting the sodium chloride. Bromine was obtained later from Stassfurt, Germany, as a by-product in the production of potassium salts and from other salt deposits and salt lakes. Its main use was originally for bromides in medicine, still a minor use. Bromine first became of industrial importance with the development of the modern photographic process, in which the light-sensitive material is an emulsion of minute particles of silver bromide (together with silver chloride, or iodide, or both) in gelatin.

Tetraethyl lead was another of Thomas Midgley's discoveries in the 1920s. Long the only effective agent in preventing "knock" in gasoline engines, tetraethyl lead is now supplemented by tetramethyl lead, a similar compound. Although the knock problem was solved, a method was needed to get all traces of lead out of the engine cylinder. This removal was achieved by the addition of small quantities of a scavenger, ethylene dibromide, often in a mixture with ethylene dichloride.

For a time the expanding world automobile industry threatened a scarcity of bromine, obtained from brines from the Great Lakes region and Searles Lake in the southwestern United States, and from the Dead Sea, which contains about 0.5 percent bromine. To meet the demand it was necessary to turn to seawater, which contains about 70 parts per million bromine.

Bromine obtained from brines

To produce bromine from seawater, large volumes of water must be processed. A preferable site for the operation is a neck of land projecting into the ocean so that water can be taken from one side and discharged to the other, avoiding the problem of processing the same water. The water is made acid with a little sulfuric acid and then treated with chlorine, which releases bromine from the bromides.

A current of air removes the bromine as a very dilute mixture of bromine with air. The bromine is absorbed in sodium carbonate, after which treatment with sulfuric acid releases the bromine again in a much more concentrated form.

By far the greater part of the bromine produced is converted to ethylene dibromide by treatment with ethylene. Most of the ethylene dibromide is used in gasoline as a scavenger for lead; but it also is used as a fumigant, as a solvent for certain gums, and for further syntheses. The next most important bromine compound is methyl bromide, which is used as a fumigant, sometimes as a fire extinguisher, and for further syntheses.

Iodine. Iodine enters the chemical industry on a smaller scale. World production by the late 1970s was not much more than 11,500 tons annually. The largest producer is Japan, where iodine is obtained from seaweed. Seawater contains only about 0.05 parts per million iodine, but some species of seaweed concentrate this iodine manyfold, so that commercial extraction of the iodine is possible.

The most important industrial use of iodine compounds is the small amount of silver iodide used with silver bromide in photography. Iodine is important also in medicine (though this is not a large-scale use) in the treatment of certain thyroid conditions, and it is added to common table salt to prevent such conditions. It is also used directly as a disinfectant. Iodine is a component of a few useful dyes. The laboratory chemist frequently makes use of iodine, or its compounds, in synthesis and also in analysis. Crystalline silver iodide is useful in cloud seeding.

BIBLIOGRAPHY. Encyclopaedic coverage of every aspect of the chemical industry is provided by: the *Encyclopedia of Chemical Technology*, 3rd ed. (1978–), in progress; *Ullmanns Enzyklopaedie der technischen Chemie*, 4th ed. (1972–), 24 volumes on completion; and *Thorpe's Dictionary of Applied Chemistry*, 4th ed., 12 vol. (1937–56). The first edition of Thorpe, in 2 volumes (1890–93), is a historical classic.
Books covering the technology of the chemical industry include: R.N. SHREVE, *Chemical Process Industries*, 4th ed. (1977); and E.R. RIEGEL, *Handbook of Industrial Chemistry*, ed. by JAMES A. KENT (1974). Works covering the chemical industry from the industrial and statistical point of view include: CONRAD BERENSON (ed.), *The Chemical Industry: Viewpoints and Perspectives* (1963); JULES BACKMAN, *The Economics of the Chemical Industry* (1970); ORGANISATION FOR ECONOMIC CO-OPERATION AND DEVELOPMENT, *The Chemical Industry ...* (annual); UNITED NATIONS, ECONOMIC COMMISSION FOR EUROPE, *Market Trends and Prospects for Chemical Products*, 2 vol. (1978); and ALFONS METZNER, *Die chemische Industrie der Welt*, vol. 1, *Europa*, vol. 2, *Uebersee* (1955).
Good coverage of sections of the chemical industry is provided by: W.L. FAITH, D.B. KEYES, and R.L. CLARK, *Industrial Chemicals*, 4th ed. (1975), a description of the economics and technology of 137 chemical products; THEODORE P. PECK, *Chemical Industries Information Sources* (1979), a comprehensive guide to sources of information for the chemical industries; WILLIAM GARDNER, *Chemical Synonyms and Trade Names: A Dictionary and Commercial Handbook Containing over 35,000 Definitions*, 8th ed. (1978), a source of chemical terms and proprietary trade names; P.H. GROGGINS, *Unit Processes in Organic Synthesis*, 5th ed. (1958); E. KILNER and D.M. SAMUEL, *Applied Organic Chemistry* (1960).

(A.St.)

Chemical Kinetics, Principles of

Chemical reactions are explained in terms of the atomic structure of matter and of the energy changes that can take place in atoms, bonding them into molecules or breaking up molecules to free or to rebond atoms into different molecules. Chemical reactions may be slow or fast, complicated or relatively simple, and the modes by which they proceed are the subject of chemical kinetics. (Details of the background required for an understanding of the kinetics of chemical reaction may be found in the articles CHEMICAL REACTIONS; ATOMIC STRUCTURE; CHEMICAL BONDING; and MOLECULAR STRUCTURE.)

Preliminary considerations. In a broader view, molecules have a tendency to react with each other to produce other kinds of molecules on condition that the product molecules have less free energy than the reacting molecules had; *i.e.*, the products lie at a lower level of free energy than the reactants. An analogy is that of water always flowing downhill since, in the Earth's gravitational field, water at a higher level gives up energy as it falls to a lower level. Thus, all reactions for which the free energy, symbolized by ΔG, is negative have a tendency to occur. Accordingly, measurements of energy change suffice to indicate whether there will be a tendency for particular products to form when specific reactants are brought together under variable conditions. How fast a reaction will occur, however, depends on what sort of channels are available for the system to traverse in passing from the higher to the lower free energy state, and a study of the nature and effectiveness of these channels is best begun with a generalized symbolization of a reaction.

In an actual reaction in which molecules of a substance A react with molecules of a substance B to form the molecules of substances C and D, usually the reverse reaction is also possible; that is, molecules of C and D react under suitable conditions to form molecules of A and B. If A, B, C, and D represent single molecules of those substances, a chemical equation may be written for the reaction: $A + B \rightleftharpoons C + D$, the half arrows indicating that the reaction is reversible. Of course, if molecules A and B are to react they must first collide, and certain other conditions must also obtain. The number of collisions will be proportional to the concentrations of A and B molecules; if the amount of A is doubled, twice as many encounters will take place. The same is true if the amount of B is doubled. Thus, a change in the concentrations of the substances will change the number of collisions, and the more numerous these collisions are per second, the faster the reaction will proceed (assuming that other determining factors, such as temperature, remain constant). Thus, the rate of the reaction, or its speed, can be calculated by simply multiplying the concentrations. If concentration is signified by bracketing the symbols for the molecules, $[A]$, $[B]$, $[C]$, and $[D]$, and if v_f symbolizes the forward rate, or the speed of reaction to the right in the equation, then this rate equals the product of the concentrations and of a proportionality factor, k_f, also called the specific reaction-rate constant: $v_f = k_f[A][B]$. Similarly, the backward rate is given by the equation $v_b = k_b[C][D]$. When the two rates are the same—*i.e.*, when $v_f = v_b$—the reaction, or, more correctly, the dynamic system of the two reactions, is said to be in equilibrium and $k_f[A][B] = k_b[C][D]$. Rearranging the equation, a ratio is obtained equal to a constant K, called the equilibrium constant; *i.e.*, the product of the concentrations of the products divided by the product of the concentrations of the reactants is equal to the forward reaction-rate constant divided by the backward reaction-rate constant:

$$\frac{[C][D]}{[A][B]} = \frac{k_f}{k_b} = K.$$

Rates of chemical reactions

This is known as the reaction-equilibrium equation. The equilibrium constant K, in view of the energy changes necessary for a reaction to proceed, further relates to the free energy, ΔG, which in turn relates to the forward and backward free energy of activation. The energy of activation is a measure of the energy that the reacting molecules must have in order to react, and it is specific for each reaction. Molecules may collide forever without reacting, and all the familiar solids, liquids, and gases consist of molecules in intimate contact but not reacting. Activation energy for the burning of paper, for example, can be provided to the paper molecules by the flame of a match, itself stable until the heat from friction on the head provides enough energy to activate the chemical reaction of the ingredients. The activation energies, therefore, of the forward (ΔG_f) and backward (ΔG_b) reactions are related to the free energy by the equation $\Delta G = \Delta G_f - \Delta G_b$.

Thoughtful chemists have been impressed by the growth of crystals and of living things for centuries, but the first recorded, quantitative measurement of the rate of a chemical reaction was made in 1850, when it was noted that the plane of a beam of polarized light, passed through a solution of sucrose, was rotated by the solution and that the amount of rotation changed with time. This indicated that a chemical reaction was changing the sucrose into a new species of molecule (which rotated the polarized light to a different extent). The change in the concentration of sucrose can be measured and then related to the passage of time in order to yield a specific rate constant for the reaction.

Early approaches to kinetics

It was found that the rate of any reaction depends not simply on the concentration of the reactants but on these concentrations raised to various powers. This principle is known as the law of mass action. It was pointed out by the Norwegian chemists C.M. Guldberg and P. Waage around 1864–67 and precisely stated by a Dutch physical chemist, Jacobus Henricus van't Hoff, in 1877. In 1889 Svante Arrhenius, a Swedish chemist, published his conclusions that molecules must get into an active state before they can become reactive (*i.e.*, their energies must be raised to activation levels before they will react). Van't Hoff had already obtained the result for the equilibrium constant, K, by calculations involving the energy of reaction, the absolute temperature, and the gas constant (derived from energy relationships observed in the behaviour of gases). Accordingly, Arrhenius was able to formulate an equation (named after him) for the specific rate constant of a chemical reaction that included the energy of activation.

Factors that affect the rate of reaction. Any change in the relative positions of atoms or molecules, such as the deformation of a solid, that takes place with an activation energy (*i.e.*, only after the energies of the reacting molecules have been increased to specific levels) is governed by the same general reaction-equilibrium equation (see above) as ordinary chemical reactions. Examples of solid reactions are the burning of rocket propellants and explosives by detonation, plastic deformation, phase transformations—such as freezing—and certain kinds of catalytic reactions. Many reactions that take place rapidly in the liquid state are sluggish or fail to take place at all in the gas phase.

Solvent. Conspicuous among these are changes that involve ionization (the breaking up of a substance into positively and negatively charged atoms or groups of atoms, called ions, and into electrons). Such reactions are greatly promoted by a solvent with high dielectric (electrically insulating) constant, such as water or dimethyl sulfoxide. Ions are also formed, however, in gases, such as the effluent gas from a burning rocket and as products of the oxidation of acetylene in the oxyacetylene torch. The temperatures involved are usually in the range from 2,000° to 2,500° C (3,600° to 4,500° F). Thus, certain reactions occurring at high temperatures can build up unstable ions at low concentrations in contrast to the heat-stable dissolved ions formed in high concentrations in ionizing solvents. Polar (*i.e.*, exhibiting positive and negative charges) surfaces, such as that of sodium chloride (common table salt), also promote the ionization of polar substances—such as chloroform, acetone, etc.—on their surface, as is shown by the reaction products formed. In fact, many organic reactions occur by the formation of positive (called carbonium) ions in solution. Although the ions are present in very low concentration, careful electrical conductance measurements as well as a study of the products of reaction provide unmistakable evidence of ionization. When a metal is bound to an organic radical (a stable fragment of an organic molecule), there is a marked tendency for the molecule to decompose into a positive metal ion and a negative organic radical (called a carbanion) containing a negatively charged carbon.

Temperature. The effect of temperature on rates of reaction is important. Ordinarily, raising the temperature 10° (Celsius) approximately doubles most but not all reactions. This is because the chance that molecules are sufficiently energy rich to have achieved activation level and undergo reaction is greatly increased by an increase in temperature.

Pressure. Similarly, increasing the pressure on systems in which a reaction in the liquid or solid state is taking place usually changes the rate of reaction. Thus, if the reacting molecules in the activated state occupy more space than when they are not activated, an increase in the pressure will decrease the relative concentration of the activated state as compared with the nonactivated reactants and so slow down the rate of reaction. When the activated state is less voluminous, the rate of reaction will be increased by pressure. This is in accord with the Le Chatelier principle, which states that any system in equilibrium is shifted by a change in property, such as pressure or temperature, in such a direction as to reduce the stress of that change on the system. High pressure, for example, makes diamonds more stable to heat than graphite (diamond and graphite are the two crystalline forms of carbon) but, in spite of this, the transformation between graphite and diamond is slowed in either direc-

tion by pressure because the activated state of a carbon atom is more voluminous than a carbon atom in either diamond or graphite.

The effect of pressure on gaseous reactions is quite different. Here pressure always increases the concentration of reactants (*i.e.*, the number of molecules of gas per unit volume) and so increases the rate of all resulting reactions that involve more than one gaseous reactant because the frequency of forming the activated state is thereby increased. The pressure effect, which becomes important for condensed (solid and liquid) phases, is related to a difference between the actual volume of tightly packed reactants and the volume of the activated state. This effect is present for gases, too, but it plays an insignificant role in comparison to the role played by increase of concentration.

Catalysts. In catalytic reactions a minute amount of a substance (the catalyst) is added to the mixture of reactants to alter the rate of reaction enormously, usually increasing it, without being itself used up. If the catalyst is not soluble in the reaction mixture, the reaction takes place on the surface of the catalyst at activation levels far lower than are necessary without the catalyst. Thus, surface atoms are involved, and if one or more reactants are gaseous, the pressure effect will act to increase the concentration of reactants, as in a gas, and this will overshadow other pressure effects.

Collisions. Further development of the theory of reaction rates calls for elucidation of the Arrhenius equation. The collision theory, though incomplete, represented a notable advance for such reactions. For example, a hydrogen gas molecule, H_2, reacts with a gaseous iodine molecule, I_2, to give hydrogen iodide molecules, HI, according to the equation $H_2 + I_2 = 2HI$. It can be demonstrated that to exchange atoms in this reaction, the activated state is a four-atom complex in which the hydrogen molecule is sandwiched between two attacking iodine atoms formed by the dissociation of an iodine molecule. The activation energy is equal to the work expended in building the activated complex of atoms and consists of the energy required to dissociate an iodine molecule into atoms plus additional energy expended by the two iodine atoms in the breaking of the hydrogen-molecule bond. Since the activated state consists of the four atoms in collision exactly as it would if it were formed by the direct collision of a hydrogen molecule with an iodine molecule, it necessarily obeys the same collision formula; *i.e.*, a formula that calculates the number of collisions per second (here, between H_2 and I_2) and the chance that such a collision will be energetic enough to be successful. The collision formula is quite accurate for some reactions, but for others the predicted rate exceeds the experimental value by a factor of 10^8. This has led to the rewriting of the formula to include an empirical steric factor; *i.e.*, a factor related to the actual molecular structure.

Early attempts to understand first-order reactions also ran into difficulties. It was supposed that individual molecules got into the activated state through absorbing radiant energy (called the radiation hypothesis), but this was soon found to be much too slow. It was then (1922) pointed out that activation by collisions alone would explain unimolecular reactions on condition that deactivation of the activated molecules, also by collision, was much faster than the rate at which they were used up in reaction. This point of view was developed (1928) into a useful theory.

In the reaction between hydrogen and chlorine molecules (H_2 and Cl_2) to form hydrogen chloride, HCl, the equation is $H_2 + Cl_2 \rightarrow 2HCl$, and it might be supposed that the same course would be followed as in the reaction between hydrogen and iodine, but this is not so. The preliminary dissociation into chlorine atoms, $Cl_2 \rightarrow 2Cl$, is followed by the reactions $Cl + H_2 \rightarrow HCl + H$ and $H + Cl_2 \rightarrow HCl + Cl$; these two processes constitute a chain reaction because a product of each is a starting material for the other. This chain is prevented from becoming infinitely long by chain-breaking reactions involving atom recombinations with another molecule or a surface, symbolized as M, such as $Cl + Cl + M \rightarrow Cl_2 + M$ and $H + H + M \rightarrow H_2 + M$. That the chain of reactions may be very rapid is shown by shining light on a hydrogen–chlorine mixture causing it to explode: the heat evolved as the chain reaction proceeds does not have time to diffuse away through the walls of the vessel before it raises the temperature of the reaction mixture to a point at which the resulting pressure bursts the container.

Factors that affect the order of the reaction. The degree to which the concentration of a reactant enters into the equation for the rate of reaction is called the order, with respect to this reactant. Thus, in the equation $H_2 + I_2 \rightarrow 2HI$, the reaction is of the first order with respect to each of the concentrations $[H_2]$, $[I_2]$.

In this example, the order of the reaction agrees with the stoichiometry—*i.e.*, the mass relationship. This is frequently not true, however; for example, the stoichiometry of the equations $H_2 + Cl_2 \rightarrow 2HCl$ and $Cl_2 \rightarrow 2Cl$ is the same, yet, because hydrogen and chlorine react by way of a chain of reactions, the reaction order is quite different. Thus, the equation $Cl + H_2 \rightarrow HCl + H$ is half order with respect to Cl_2 and first order with respect to H_2, while the equation $H + Cl_2 \rightarrow HCl + Cl$ is half order with respect to H_2 and first order with respect to Cl_2, so that the order of the overall chain process is complicated and dependent upon the conditions under which it occurs. In general, there is no way of deducing the order of reaction from the stoichiometry of the equation that expresses the overall process. Much of the effort devoted to the study of reaction rates goes into the establishing of the mechanism of the rate-determining step or steps. The overall order of reaction is further complicated if the surfaces catalyze the reaction.

The degree to which the rate of reaction is influenced by a particular catalytic surface is determined by actually varying the ratio of reactant collisions with the surface to collisions with gaseous molecules. This is readily done for glass surfaces by packing the reactant vessel with glass wool; by varying the amount of glass wool it is easy to multiply manyfold the amount of surface with which reactants collide. If the packing produces no noticeable effect when the overall rate is large, it is safe to ignore the effect of the vessel's surface in the absence of packing and to interpret the rate as occurring entirely in the gas phase. Conversely, if the effect of packing is to speed up or slow down the reaction, it is possible to study the surface-catalyzed reaction.

The order of reaction under one set of conditions may be completely altered if the conditions are changed, even though there is no change in mechanism. (The mechanism of a reaction is the set of atomic or molecular encounters and motions that accounts for every step of the conversion of starting materials to products.) If one reactant is in great excess over the others, for example, it will not seem to vary and may be left out of the rate equation altogether, even though the other concentrations may change by orders of magnitude. The reaction order is thus not to be confused with what is called the molecularity of the reaction: the molecularity is the number of molecules of each kind in the activated complex. For each elementary rate process the molecularity is fixed, and only a shift to a new mechanism can change it. When the molecularity of a substance in the activated state exceeds its molecularity in the stoichiometric equation for the reaction, that substance is said to be acting as a catalyst. Also, when a process occurs by a chain of reactions, the order with respect to a particular reactant may be fractional or even negative. Only when the effects of wide variations in the concentrations of the reactants and other conditions in a reaction have been studied is it possible to be confident that an observed order of reaction does in fact represent the molecularity of the activated state. As shown below, in more complicated cases, such as in chain reactions, the whole idea of associating a unique integral order with a rate of reaction ceases to be useful.

The equilibrium constant. A fundamental question that must be answered if chemical processes are to be controlled is not only how fast a system reaches equilibrium but under what circumstances equilibrium yields the particular product sought in recoverable amounts. This question is comparatively easy to answer for phase transformations. Thus, to obtain ice, water must be cooled below the freezing point. Even this, however, is not quite as simple as it sounds, since by increasing the pressure, the temperature at which ice melts increases. There are seven kinds of ice; *i.e.*, water freezes into seven different forms. It happens that ordinary ice is readily obtained by cooling, but if one of the other seven kinds is wanted, in general not only must the system be cooled but the pressure must be adjusted so that it falls in the range of stability of the ice that is sought. A similar problem occurs when diamonds are made from graphite. A diamond is unstable at ordinary temperatures and pressures, but the rate at which it changes into graphite is far too slow to cause worry. If the pressure is increased to 15,000 atmospheres (one atmosphere equals about 14.7 pounds per square inch), graphite becomes unstable and tends to change into diamond at room temperature. As before, however, the rate is much too slow to be interesting unless a catalyst is added or the temperature is greatly increased. The work, or the free energy, required to change graphite into diamond can be calculated according to a thermodynamic equation that relates measurements of temperature, pressure, and volume; at pressures and temperatures when the two phases are in equilibrium, the work required to change one phase into the other is zero. Thus, thermodynamics predicts how temperature and pressure can be manipulated to make a desired phase stable.

A dramatic example of the consequences of studying an equilibrium is the case represented by the equation $3H_2 + N_2 \rightarrow 2NH_3$. Historically, this study has had awesome consequences because, had German scientists not discovered and used this reaction in the Haber process for making ammonia in 1914, Germany would have been dependent on Chile saltpetre for explosives, and a blockade by the Royal Navy might have made World War I impossible.

Using thermodynamics, the equilibrium constant can be calculated from the pressures of hydrogen, nitrogen, and ammonia, and the work required to change three moles of hydrogen and one mole of nitrogen into two moles of ammonia can be obtained as a function of pressure and temperature. Thus, the circumstances required to produce recoverable amounts of ammonia can be determined. In other words, thermodynamics indicates whether a reaction is possible and kinetics, the speed with which it will occur.

Complex reactions. Chemical reactions proceed by all physically possible mechanisms, and the measured rate is the sum of all the possible rates. Often, one mechanism under a given set of conditions is so much faster than all others as to allow the latter to be ignored, without appreciably affecting the accuracy of the calculations. It is in this sense that a preferred mechanism can be defined, and, theoretically, the preferred mechanism can be singled out only by estimating all rates and selecting the highest. If two velocities are equal at some temperature and much faster than all others, the one with the steepest temperature coefficient will be the important one at high temperatures and the other at low temperatures. In a case in which there are only two reactions in a sequence, and they become equal at some temperature, the one with the lowest temperature coefficient will dominate at low temperatures while the other dominates in the high-temperature range. This temperature dependence provides a ready way of distinguishing between two reactions acting sequentially and in parallel.

Mass spectrography provides a beautiful example of competing reactions. When a molecule is struck by a fast electron or an energetic photon, it is frequently left as a positive ion in an energy-rich state. The mass spectrograph is designed so it records the final product ions about 10^{-6} second after the primary ionization. In the meantime, the parent ion is breaking into all of the various possible products at rates that can be calculated

Thermo-
dynamics
and
kinetics

Effects of
surfaces

Competing
reactions

from changes in bond energies, and the percentage of each product ion formed can be calculated.

If a reaction intermediate is formed that can attack more than one species, the relative amounts of products are in proportion to the rates of reaction with the various species.

If a solid is thought of as a giant molecule, its action as a catalyst does not differ in principle from that of a homogeneous catalyst. When the atoms of a solid metal have their electron shells only partly filled, as in the transition elements, the crowded electrons leak into these partly empty shells during the period of intense electron congestion of the activated complex and, in the course of doing so, lower the activation energy speeding up the reaction.

On the other hand, certain ionic substances, such as clays, can act by breaking hydrocarbons into positive and negative ions, which then reassemble into molecules with new properties.

Enzymes are molecules that occur in living systems and that have structural groups that facilitate reactions, as do ordinary catalysts. One view of their behaviour is that they have the additional property of mechanically straining certain bonds lying between two attachments to the enzyme and giving the distorted bond an increased reactivity. This same strain, resulting from changes in the shape of the protein molecules, is promoted by environmental changes and is exhibited in muscles, in the receptors of taste and smell, and in various immune reactions. Study of these conformation changes reveals that they are volume changes because pressure changes slow down or speed up the process in question.

Chain reactions are another interesting aspect of chemical reactions, and it can be shown that there is no single simple order of reaction for a chain of reactions.

Detonations proceed by a quite different mechanism. A simple model will help explain how an energy-rich molecule may be made to yield its energy to reinforce a decaying shock wave, which is the essence of a detonation (see illustration).

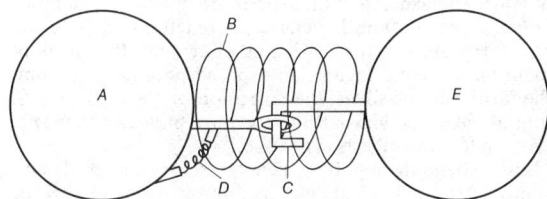

Model of molecular structure that explains detonation (see text).

The two parts of a molecule A and E may be thought of as being separated by a compressed spring B. If the amplitude of vibrations reaches a critical value, corresponding to the activation energy, so that during compression of B the spring D flips the catch C, then A and E will fly apart with the energy stored in the compressed spring B —i.e., the heat of reaction.

Mechanism of detonations

If many such molecules are close packed to form a cylinder and a sharp blow is delivered to one end of the cylinder, a compression wave will pass along the cylinder axis. This shock wave will pass over molecules having random phases and random amplitudes, and some of them will absorb the extra energy that permits them to flip their catch—i.e., to react. If the high pressure and high temperature of the shock wave remain, all of the molecules will react. These reacting molecules release their heat of reaction to enhance the energy in the shock wave. The energy released to the actual movement (called translational degrees of freedom of the molecules) determines the pressure and temperature of the shock wave, and that energy will just balance the energy flowing into the internal degrees of freedom during the period (called the steady state) when the shock wave is advancing at a fixed speed. Since sound is a wave of compression, the detonation will travel through the medium with the velocity of sound of molecules in the shock wave. If the diameter of the detonating cylinder is finite, an ap-

preciable amount of the energy driving the shock wave leaks out through the side, decreasing the shock-wave velocity. The magnitude of this velocity decrease provides a method of measuring the length of the reaction zone.

Principles of methods for studying chemical kinetics. *Measurement of reaction rates.* When reactions proceed at rates that permit making the measurements, many methods of study can be employed. The problem is one of measuring composition by some physical or chemical procedure. If the rate is fast compared with available methods of measurement, it may still be followed by interrupting the reaction by a sudden change—such as lowering the temperature, removal of the catalyst or one of the reactants, or by adding an inhibitor, a substance that drastically slows down a reaction, in effect, a catalyst with a negative effect. Common methods involve measurement of pressure changes, volume changes, and conductivity; more sophisticated methods include polarimetry; circular birefringence; refractometry, colorimetry, and spectrophotometry; potentiometry; polarography; and mass spectrometry. For a method to be useful the property being measured must change (i.e., increase or decrease) with the extent of reaction, preferably in a linear or near-linear fashion—i.e., in direct ratio.

Flowing systems

The study of a continuous flow of reactants through solid catalysts has long been common practice. Since the contact time can be varied, the method provides a way of measuring fast catalytic processes widely applicable in industry. In certain systems, the chemical reaction proceeds to completion within the time required for physical mixing of the reactants. One fruitful method of studying such a system is to displace it from equilibrium by sudden temperature or pressure increases, but some rates are too high or too low to be measured by any method.

Competition methods, used to measure fast reactions, are exactly what the term implies: the reaction is made to compete with a physical process having a known rate, or an equilibrium is displaced by a perturbation (disturbing effect), and the shift in equilibrium (equilibration) measured directly. In polarography, for example, this competition is between the formation of a reducible ion (an ion capable of acquiring electrons, thereby raising its negative charge) and its diffusion to the cathode. Most available information on electron transfer between transition-metal complexes has been found in this way. Proton magnetic resonance is illustrative of a method applicable to various nuclei having magnetic moments (the property comparable to the magnetism of a minute bar magnet). Measuring nuclear magnetic resonance is much like measuring the precession of a spinning top in a gravitational field.

Determining the order of reactions. A general picture of how reactions take place will help in attaching the proper importance to a determination of an order of reaction. The potential energy between any collection or grouping of atoms is a function of the smallest number of distances that fix the configuration of the group complex. If the potential energy is plotted as a function of the distances required to fix the configurations, a potential hypersurface in configuration space is obtained. Although this hypersurface ordinarily involves more than three dimensions, it will be convenient to use the language of three dimensions. Molecules represent valleys or basins on this surface, and a chemical reaction corresponds to passing from one low region to the other over the intermediate barriers. There are, in general, several passes that can be taken between low regions, and the traverse through a particular pass may involve crossing over a succession of passes separated by more or less deep depressions. These depressions are intermediate compounds. If one of these passes along a traverse is enough higher than any other along the traverse, and enough lower than for any other traverse, this particular pass will constitute the point of no return for this reaction, and the molecularity will also be the order of the reaction, provided all reactants are nearly enough at the same concentration so that their concentrations all change measurably during the reaction. If these condi-

Reaction pathways

tions are not fulfilled, there is no unique activated complex and the order of reaction involves some kind of blend of rates for a variety of activated complexes, which can only accidentally be a measure of the molecularity of a particular activated complex. In chain reactions, the measured rate is a blend of a variety of rates, in general involving elementary processes from different potential surfaces. Accordingly, for such reactions, only by changing conditions drastically can a particular elementary process be made sufficiently prominent in the overall process to allow the corresponding specific rate constant to be determined. When the overall rate for a chain reaction is broken into its elementary mechanisms, difficult though this may be, they are all found to involve the concentration of the separate reactants in the activated complex to an integral power.

Only for the simplest of reactions can one expect the measured order to reveal the molecularity of an elementary reaction. Nevertheless, by skillfully arranging conditions the specific rates of many elementary processes have been determined. For an elementary reaction, the reactants are in effective equilibrium with the activated complex. If equivalent amounts of reactants are chosen, the reactants will always remain in a fixed proportion with respect to each other.

Elucidating reaction mechanisms. Even for very complex living systems, some observable property is controlled by a rate-determining step. It is often possible to gain real insight into what is happening by studying the effect of increasing the temperature and pressure and by changing the composition of the system. This is illustrated by studies made on bioluminescence. Luminescent bacteria give off almost no light at the freezing point; as the temperature is raised the luminescence goes through a maximum near 20° C (68° F), depending on the species, and again sinks to near zero at blood temperature. The luminescence is caused by the oxidation of luciferin by oxygen, in the presence of the enzyme luciferase, a reaction in which oxygen molecules accept electrons from the luciferin. In the process, two protons (hydrogen nuclei, or hydrogen ions with positive charge) from the reduced luciferin go into solution and the remaining two electrons are picked up by oxygen with the help of the enzyme luciferase. Nine times out of ten the oxygen picks off the less tightly bound electrons of the luciferin molecule, but once out of ten times it picks off a lower lying electron (one bonded more tightly into the structure), leaving one in a higher level, which then drops into the hole below, emitting a quantum of light. The intensity of the emitted light measures the overall rate of reaction, which in turn depends principally on the state of the enzyme. Thus, there is a ready means of studying the state of a representative oxidative enzyme *in vivo*.

Luminescence provides penetrating insight into many aspects of biology. The rise in luminescence with temperature is to be expected of a chemical reaction involving an activation energy. The maximum in luminescent intensity followed by a decline in luminescence arises from inactivation of the enzyme, causing a steep drop with temperature that more than overbalances the increase in the rate of the remaining enzyme that is still active. Because the enzyme in the activated complex is more voluminous than the free native enzyme, the increase it causes in hydrostatic pressure decreases the light intensity in the low temperature range lying below the luminescence maximum. Above the maximum, the hydrostatic pressure increases the light intensity because the inactive enzyme is more voluminous than it is in the activated complex.

Chemicals such as the alcohols, the ethers, urethane, and even the noble gas xenon under high pressure introduce hydrophobic (water-repelling) groups into cells and cause the enzymes to unfold and become inactive in a way that is parallel to anesthesia. On the other hand, the substances sulfanilamide and *p*-aminobenzoic acid inhibit luminescence by competing with the reactants for the prosthetic groups, and they are without influence on the unfolding of the enzyme. These results were all deduced from a quantitative fitting of equilibrium theory and acti-

vated complex theory to the data and are borne out by work on the purified luciferase and luciferin.

It is convenient to think of solids as giant molecules and of their plastic deformation as a molecular isomerization (*i.e.*, as the same components forced into a spatial rearrangement), to which reaction rate theory applies just as it does to any other molecule. A stress on a solid, whether an electrical or mechanical one, always acts to lower the energy of activation for deformation. Only when the stresses are small is the relaxation (*i.e.*, the return of the deformed solid to its original structure) proportional to the stress, and two or more stresses then—and only then —obey reciprocal relations as defined by thermodynamics. Reaction-rate theory, however, is applicable for both large and small stresses. In fact, all deformations of matter involving activation energies can be studied and predicted using reaction-rate theory.

BIBLIOGRAPHY. SAMUEL GLASSTONE, KEITH J. LAIDLER, and HENRY EYRING, *The Theory of Rate Processes* (1941), the earliest comprehensive treatment of the theory of absolute reaction rates; HENRY and EDWARD M. EYRING, *Modern Chemical Kinetics* (1963), a popular presentation of reactive rate theory; ARTHUR A. FROST and RALPH G. PEARSON, *Kinetics and Mechanism*, 2nd ed. (1961), a useful general text covering many aspects of chemical reactions; HENRY EYRING, "The Activated Complex in Chemical Reactions," *J. Chem Phys.*, 3:107–115 (1935), the first general presentation of activated complex or transition state theory.

(H.Ey.)

Chemical Reactions

The phenomenon of change, noted by everyone almost continuously and said by some to be the only unchanging aspect of the material universe, is the context in which all of the sciences find their place, including the study of chemical reactions. A chemical reaction is a process of change during which either two or more substances both change or one substance changes into at least two other substances. Thus, when wood burns, the substances present initially, wood and oxygen in the atmosphere, are converted in a chemical reaction to water vapour, carbon dioxide, and ash. All combustions are chemical reactions. Other types of familiar chemical reactions include decay, fermentation, the hardening of cement, the development of a latent image in an exposed photographic film, the tarnishing of silver, the corrosion of steel, the evolution of gas when vinegar and soda are mixed, the synthesis of nylon, the digestion of food.

Basic phenomena. In a general sense, material substances can undergo change in three ways: a change of position, called movement; a change of form, such as the freezing of liquid water; and a change of substance, a chemical reaction. Some classify changes of form as chemical reactions, but, historically, the term chemical reaction has been applied only to changes of substance. The application to change of form is discussed below. Using the historical definition, each different chemical reaction displays the same unique characteristics.

Transformation. Thus, in a chemical reaction the substances originally present disappear, and substances that were not initially present appear. Factually, however, it is more descriptive to say that properties that were initially observable are no longer observed, and properties not originally observable are now noted. In combustion, a substance called wood, with its unique properties (fibrous, less dense than water, generally light- or dark-brown in colour), and oxygen, with its unique properties, all of which were capable of detection before combustion occurred, cannot be detected after combustion. Instead, after combustion, only the properties of water vapour, carbon dioxide, and ash can be detected.

Conservation of mass. Chemical reactions display another essential quality. Although substances change in a chemical reaction, within limits that can be measured the total mass does not change. That is, the mass of wood and oxygen that disappears in a combustion is equal to the mass of water vapour, carbon dioxide, smoke, and ash that appears. In ordinary chemical reactions, this loss of mass as the reactants vanish is equal to the gain of mass as the new substances form. Because this effect is

*Biolumi-
nescence*

universal, it has been presumed to be fundamental, an indication that there is some common, universally applicable reason that applies to all material substances.

Fixed composition. Further, substances formed in chemical reactions display another universal but more specific characteristic. For example, water is formed as one of the products in hundreds of quite different chemical reactions, but, without exception, it contains only the elements hydrogen and oxygen and always in the same proportion: the mass of oxygen is eight times as great as the mass of hydrogen. That is, the composition of water is independent of the particular chemical reaction by which it might have been formed. Parallel phenomena are observed with other substances: whenever carbon dioxide is formed as a product, the mass ratio of carbon to oxygen is always 3 to 8; for ammonia (a gas, not the liquid called ammonia), the ratio of its constituent elements, nitrogen and hydrogen, is always 14 to 3. (Precise measurements reveal minor variations in the mass ratio that are understood in terms related not to chemical reaction but to nuclear composition; see ISOTOPES.)

Energy effects. Finally, in all but a very few chemical reactions, energy is either absorbed or evolved. It is often evolved as heat, as in combustion, but also in other forms, such as electrical energy during the chemical reaction in a battery when it is switched on to operate a flashlight or portable radio. The amount of energy evolved depends on the mass of the products formed. For twice the mass of product formed, in two otherwise identical chemical reactions, exactly twice as much energy is evolved. The same relationship applies to reactions during which energy is absorbed rather than evolved.

General definition

A chemical reaction can now be defined more explicitly as a process of change in which the substances originally present, called reagents, are changed into substances with other properties, called products, in such a way that, first, there is no observable change in the total mass; second, whenever the same product is formed by a different process of change, that product exhibits the same mass ratio of components; and, third, almost always, energy is either absorbed or evolved in an amount that is directly related to the mass of the products formed.

These facts have two important consequences. First, they can be used to infer universally applicable, theoretical principles to account for some (eventually, hopefully all) of the reasons why chemical reactions occur and for some of the details of the process, thereby increasing understanding of the material universe. Second, these facts and the related uncertain but usable theories can be used to alter man's environment for either his benefit or his detriment. Examples abound. The chemical industry manufactures beneficial substances, such as polymeric fibres (*e.g.*, nylon) and elastomers (synthetic rubber), dyes, other polymers (plastics), metallic alloys, fertilizers, paints, insecticides, drugs, ceramics, and fuels; but these manufactures also cause undesired effects upon man's ecological system, creating problems that demand further application of chemistry as well as other branches of knowledge.

Growth of major theories concerning chemical reactions. Chemical reactions were known to prehistoric man, and it is possible to conjecture that he speculated upon their cause. In ancient Greek civilization this speculation led to a qualitative supposition that matter is perhaps composed of individual particles. Not until late in the 17th century, however, did theory and philosophical speculation became conjoined in the first of many far-reaching attempts to explain chemical reactions. A German chemist, Georg Ernst Stahl, basing his ideas upon earlier and less specific suggestions, postulated that during combustion a substance, which he named phlogiston, escaped from the burning fuel into the air, the fuel losing weight. Thus if a drinking glass is inverted over a burning candle, the flame dies out in a short time, because, it was postulated, the air within the glass becomes saturated with phlogiston. According to these ideas, because ash remains after combustion, wood is composed of phlogiston and ash. Because no ash is left when a candle burns,

Phlogiston theory

candle wax is obviously pure phlogiston. Therefore it should be possible to prepare wood in a chemical reaction between wood ash and candle wax. This prediction of the phlogiston theory failed. It failed in more startling ways, as well. When metals burn, for example, their ash is greater in mass than the original metal. To explain this, it was suggested that phlogiston possessed the quality of negative mass, which is a direct contradiction of its other postulated properties.

Additional evidence that led to the downfall of the phlogiston theory was accumulated by several workers, among whom Carl Wilhelm Scheele, in Sweden, and Joseph Priestley, first in England and later in North America, can be mentioned particularly. Independently, each discovered a gas (actually oxygen), but both failed to recognize the significance of their discovery. Priestley in particular maintained his belief in phlogiston until his death. At about the same time, however, near the end of the third quarter of the 18th century, Antoine Lavoisier, in France, independently discovered the same gas, and he recognized its significance. He postulated that combustion was a chemical reaction involving two substances, one, a component of the air, which he named *oxigine* (oxygen), and the other a combustible substance, such as candle wax, wood, or metal.

Shortly after the beginning of the 19th century, John Dalton in England postulated that matter is composed of small, indivisible, and unalterable particles called atoms and that in a typical chemical reaction groups of atoms initially conjoined in some way became disassociated and then rejoined in new arrangements. The observed disappearance of properties and the appearance of new properties were thus explained by the theory that the properties of a substance depend upon its atomic composition. Centuries earlier, others had expressed ideas that were very similar, but Dalton was able to convince his contemporaries of the probable validity of his postulate.

Dalton's atomic theory

Of equal importance was Dalton's concept that each atom of any single element was identical in every respect to every other atom of that same element. As a consequence, the masses of the atoms are quantitatively revealed in the ratio of the masses of the components of a substance. Thus, because the mass of oxygen in water is eight times that of the mass of hydrogen, it can be said that one atom of oxygen is eight times as massive as one atom of hydrogen, on condition that one particle (today denoted by the word molecule) of water is composed of one atom each of hydrogen and oxygen. As Dalton recognized, however, one particle of water might be composed of some other number of hydrogen and oxygen atoms— for example, two atoms of hydrogen and one atom of oxygen—then the relative masses of oxygen and hydrogen atoms would be 8 to ½ or, in whole numbers, 16 to 1.

During this same period, other facts obtained in laboratory studies, particularly those of Joseph-Louis Gay-Lussac, in France, suggested that, although the masses of gases that reacted with each other showed no simple consistency, the volumes of those reacting gases did demonstrate a certain simplicity. For example, eight grams of oxygen reacted with one gram of hydrogen, and 14 grams of nitrogen reacted with three grams of hydrogen; but, when measured at equal temperatures and pressures, the volume of hydrogen was found to be exactly twice that of the volume of oxygen in the reaction to form water, and the volume of hydrogen was found to be exactly three times that of nitrogen in the reaction to form the gas ammonia. Apparently, this small integer volume relationship hinted at an as yet unknown fundamental property of matter. Amedeo Avogadro in Italy suggested that this property could be explained by the assertion: All gases at the same temperature, pressure, and volume will contain the same number of particles, which may or may not be single atoms. His suggestion was not well received, but Avogadro's pupil, Stanislao Cannizzaro, carried out further studies, in the light of which it became reasonable to state that water molecules contain two atoms of hydrogen, ammonia molecules three atoms of hydrogen, hydrogen chloride molecules one atom of hydrogen, and, for each, some number of atoms of other elements. These compositions are symbolized today by formulas in which the symbols for the elements represent single atoms. Thus, water is H_2O, the subscript 2 indicating two atoms of hydrogen and a subscript of 1 being understood for one atom of oxygen. For ammonia, the formula is NH_3: one atom of nitrogen and three atoms of hydrogen in each molecule. For hydrogen chloride (Cl being the symbol for chlorine), HCl: one atom of each. Approximately 50 years after the initial publication of Avogadro's ideas and largely through the efforts of Cannizzaro, Avogadro's hypothesis, or theory, as it is more commonly called today, was accepted by most scientists. (Modern methods of analysis have established that the actual number of molecules in a quantity of any substance equal in mass in grams to the molecular weight of the substance—*e.g.*, 18 grams of water—is 6.02×10^{23}, called Avogadro's number.)

Avogadro's number

Facts revealed by intensive laboratory examination of other properties of matter (*e.g.*, magnetism, electricity, radiations) led to theoretical conclusions that atoms are not indivisible but are themselves composed of still smaller parts, or particles. One of these parts is a negatively charged particle named the electron (the meaning of "negative charge" is still unknown except for broad generalities), and another is a positively charged particle called the nucleus. The interaction of electrons from different atoms, often conjointly as electron pairs, with the positively charged nuclei of each of the atoms, constrains them to group together in fixed ways as molecules. Not all substances, however, are molecular. For example, salt, a compound of sodium and chlorine, consists of an aggregation of charged particles called ions. In particular, salt is an aggregation of any number of sodium ions and of an equal number of chloride ions. A sodium ion is derived from a sodium atom by the loss of one electron; a chloride ion is derived from a chlorine atom by the gain of one electron. Still other nonmolecular aggregations are believed possible. Diamond is an aggregation of any large number of carbon atoms arranged in a unique three-dimensional configuration in a repetitive manner, much as the design of wallpaper is repetitive in two dimensions. In this respect, salt is like diamond; its ions are arranged in any single crystal of salt as a repetitive pattern not unlike a three-dimensional chessboard might be imagined, in which black and white squares represent sodium and chloride ions, respectively.

With this information, a more recently developed definition of a chemical reaction can be stated. Thus, if atoms are held together, or bonded, in molecules or in other types of aggregations by electron interactions, then in a chemical reaction these bonds are broken (by the absorption of energy) and, either simultaneously or subsequently, new electronic interactions develop as other bonds are formed (with the release of energy). Hence, distinct from the historically developed ideas, a chemical reaction can now be defined as a process of change in which some bonds are broken and different bonds are formed. This definition includes all processes that involve a change of substance as well as many of the processes that involve a change of form, such as the freezing of water.

Energy considerations. If the energy absorbed in bond rupture exceeds the energy released by the formation of new bonds, then overall the chemical reaction is observed to be energy absorbing. The converse is true for cases in which the energy absorbed is less than the energy released. In a very few instances the overall absorbed and released energies are equal in magnitude.

Types of reaction. Chemical reactions can be classified into three types: exoergic (or exothermic) if, overall, energy is evolved; endoergic (or endothermic) in the converse cases; and aergic (or athermic; *i.e.*, without energy change) for rarer cases.

In every case, however, energy must be supplied to the reactants in order to initiate the breaking of bonds before other bonds can be formed because a stable bond will not of itself degenerate. In general, therefore, all chemical reactions, even exoergic or aergic, require the introduction of energy in some form from an external source in order to begin. The initiating energy, called activation energy, is sometimes supplied as heat from another, already initiated exoergic chemical reaction. Thus, to set fire to paper the activation energy can be supplied by a burning match, for which the activation energy was generated by a chemical reaction of the materials in the match head, for which activation energy was supplied as heat generated from frictional effects when the match head was rubbed upon a suitable surface.

The required energy may be furnished, instead, as electrical energy, as for the endoergic decomposition of water into hydrogen and oxygen, the electrical energy being obtained from generators driven by turbines, which are in turn powered by falling water. In still other instances the requisite energy is supplied in the form of light, which can be thought of as consisting of discrete particles of electromagnetic energy, called photons. Photons that give rise to the sensation of red have less energy than photons that give rise to the sensation of orange, and these have less energy than photons that produce the sensation of yellow, and so on. Photons of lesser energy and photons of greater energy than those that comprise the range of visible colours are known and are called infrared and ultraviolet photons, respectively. If a photon of the particular quantity of energy needed to break a particular chemical bond passes near enough to that bond, it is probable that that photon will cease to exist and its energy will be absorbed by that bond as it breaks. Reactions that can be initiated in this manner are called, appropriately, photochemical reactions. The best known photochemical reaction is actually a series of consecutive reactions that takes place in the green leaves of plants through the influence of sunlight. These reactions, called photosynthesis, involve the consumption of carbon dioxide from the atmosphere and of water present in the plant, with the production of oxygen, released to the atmosphere, and of cellulose and starch (or sugar), which remain within the plant structure.

Use of electrical energy

Catalytic reactions. For reasons not yet well understood, many chemical reactions can be initiated with a lesser activation energy than normally required when they are conducted in the presence of special foreign substances called catalysts; such a reaction is said to be catalyzed. Chlorophyll is a catalyst in the photochemical reaction of plants. Enzymes are involved as catalysts in the metabolic processes (chemical reactions) that occur in living tissue; the enzyme pepsin, present in the stomach, catalyzes the breakup of large protein molecules into smaller molecules.

A sugar cube will sputter but not burn when a match flame is applied to its surface, but very small amounts of substances called rare-earth oxides act as catalysts for this particular combustion; the oxides are present in trace amounts in tobacco ash, and a cube lightly coated with tobacco ash will burn if heated with the flame of a match.

At one time it was thought that the driving force, the cause of the spontaneity of chemical reactions, the reason, so to speak, why wood burns or cement hardens or an egg congeals when it is cooked, could be attributed to energy relationships such as those discussed above.

Entropy. It is now known that these energy relationships are indeed related to the rapidity or slowness of any particular chemical reaction, but the reason a chemical reaction occurs, at any speed, is attributed to changes in what is called the entropy both of the substances involved in the reaction and of the surroundings not otherwise involved in the chemical reaction itself. Entropy is the measure of that energy that is associated with disorder in any system; it is a concept developed in thermodynamics to take into consideration the fact that not all types of energy can be manipulated to do work. Thus, in any isolated system, entropy tends to increase; *i.e.*, the portion of energy that is not available for work is transformed into the energy of disorder. Consider, for example, the reaction in which wood combines with oxygen: water vapour, carbon dioxide, and ash are formed, and heat is evolved. The entropy of the wood and oxygen is relatively small, while the entropy of the products is larger; that is, for the substances themselves, entropy has increased. The evolved heat also causes an increase in the entropy of the surroundings that absorb that heat. Hence, overall, for the substances and for the surroundings, entropy has increased. Unless overall there is an increase in entropy, a chemical reaction cannot occur. In the synthesis of water from hydrogen and oxygen, to be described more fully below, the entropy of the product, water, is less than the entropy of the reagents, hydrogen and oxygen. The heat evolved in this reaction, however, is sufficient to increase the entropy of the surroundings more than the decrease of entropy suffered by the substances themselves; overall, that is, entropy increases. For this reason the reaction is spontaneous.

Modern views and classification systems. When the science of chemistry began, only the masses of the reagents and products could be measured. This early emphasis upon mass and, practically speaking, the weighing of samples influenced the theories of chemical reaction. As understanding developed, measuring instruments more sophisticated than balances and volumetric glassware were designed, particularly as a consequence of developments in physics. Today, it is possible to measure with precision and reliability a variety of subtle effects, ranging from the absorption and emission of energy as heat, as photons, or as electrical energy to detection of almost unimaginably small amounts of reagents. In gen-

Concerns of modern theoretical research

eral, modern chemical theoretical research is concerned with either the mechanism of a chemical reaction (called kinetics, or kinetics and mechanisms, or the dynamics of chemical reactions) or with the construction of mental or physical models of the structure of matter (called structural chemistry). In addition, applications of both new and old theory are made with the consequent introduction of new or improved substances useful in commerce. There is perhaps no single case today for which all of the theoretical details can be completely described, and only a vague distinction can be made between theoretical and applied chemistry.

Various other classifications and types of chemical reactions exist, derived largely from a theoretical viewpoint. They are not, however, all-inclusive, as are the classifications of chemical reactions as exoergic, endoergic, and aergic. Thus, a synthesis reaction may also be an oxidation–reduction reaction. Some acid–base reactions may also be ionic reactions, or precipitation reactions.

Synthesis. A synthesis reaction, in the simplest sense, involves elements as reagents and the formation of a compound (a substance composed of more than one element) as the product, often as the only product. Iron, symbolized as Fe, reacts with sulfur, S, to form iron sulfide, FeS, as shown by this chemical equation: $Fe + S \rightarrow FeS$. Thus, the plus sign on the left symbolizes "reacts with"; the arrow signifies "forms," "produces," or "yields."

In addition to symbolizing the substances, iron, sulfur, and iron sulfide, the symbols used in a chemical equation also specify the amounts of substances that react and are produced. Thus, Fe represents 55.85 grams of iron, S represents 32.06 grams of sulfur, and FeS represents 87.91 grams of iron sulfide. That is, the chemical equation given above summarizes laboratory-measured fact: 55.85 grams of iron will react with exactly 32.06 grams of sulfur to form exactly 87.91 grams of iron sulfide. If other amounts are used, say one-fifth as much iron, 11.17 grams, no matter how much sulfur was present in excess, only one-fifth of 32.06 grams would be consumed and one-fifth as much product formed. The converse is true (in round numbers): if half as much sulfur is available, 16 grams, then half as much iron would react, 28 grams (approximately), and about 44 grams of iron sulfide would be formed. The calculation of the amounts of reagents consumed and of products formed comprises the branch of chemistry called stoichiometry.

As a second example of synthesis, the following equation describes the synthesis of water from its elements:

$2H_2 + O_2 \rightarrow 2H_2O$. Here, a new feature of a chemical equation appears, the stoichiometric factor, 2, preceding the symbols for hydrogen molecules, H_2 (two atoms in each molecule), and water molecules. That is, in the laboratory it has been observed that four grams of hydrogen react with 32 grams of oxygen to produce 36 grams of water. The symbol for one gram of hydrogen in the form of atoms is H; the symbol for two grams of hydrogen in molecular form is H_2. In the reaction described by the equation, then, the symbol $2H_2$ represents four grams of hydrogen in the form of molecules. Analogously, the symbol H_2O without the 2 represents 18 grams of water molecules.

These quantities—H, or one gram of hydrogen atoms, H_2, or two grams of hydrogen molecules, H_2O, or 18 grams of water molecules, Fe, or 56 (approximately) grams of iron atoms, S, or 32 grams of sulfur atoms— are called moles of these substances. Thus, one mole of

The mole unit

hydrogen atoms weighs one gram; one mole of water molecules weighs 18 grams; one mole of iron sulfide molecules weighs 87.91 grams. In each of these instances and in all others that could also have been mentioned as additional examples, the same number of particles is understood to be specified. Thus, one mole of hydrogen molecules contains 6.02×10^{23} (602,000,000,000,000,-000,000,000) molecules (Avogadro's number, see above); one mole of iron atoms is 6.02×10^{23} atoms; one mole of water molecules is 6.02×10^{23} molecules; and so on. With this kind of stoichiometric emphasis, the equation describing the synthesis of water can be read as: two moles of hydrogen molecules react with one mole of oxygen molecules to form two moles of water molecules. The same stoichiometric emphasis is usually applied to the equations for other types of chemical reactions, described below.

Decomposition. Decomposition reactions are chemical reactions in which chemical species break up into simpler parts. The decomposition of the gas ammonia is represented by the equation $2NH_3 \rightarrow N_2 + 3H_2$; or, in terms of a single mole of ammonia, $NH_3 \rightarrow \frac{1}{2}N_2 + \frac{3}{2}H_2$, read as: one mole of ammonia molecules decomposes to form one-half mole of nitrogen molecules and three-halves of a mole of hydrogen molecules.

Compounds need not break down into elements in a decomposition reaction. For example, ammonium carbonate, $(NH_4)_2CO_3$, decomposes into ammonia, carbon dioxide (CO_2), and water, according to the equation $(NH_4)_2CO_{3(s)} \rightarrow 2NH_{3(g)} + CO_{2(g)} + H_2O_{(g)}$.

The subscripts in parentheses indicate the physical state of the substances, *s* for solid, *g* for gaseous, *l* for liquid.

Polymerization. Polymerization reactions are not unlike synthesis reactions in that simpler substances combine to form more complex substances. The term polymerization, however, is restricted to chemical reactions in which the product is composed of many, hundreds or thousands, of the simpler reagent species. The polymerization of terephthalic acid, $HO_2C(C_6H_4)CO_2H$, with ethylene glycol, $HOCH_2CH_2OH$, to form the polymer called Dacron in fibre form or Mylar in sheet form, is represented by the equation

$$n\ HO_2C(C_6H_4)CO_2H + n\ HOCH_2CH_2OH \rightarrow$$
$$[\ldots OC(C_6H_4)CO_2CH_2CH_2O \ldots]_n + 2n\ H_2O$$

in which *n* signifies a large number of moles (and $2n$ twice that number of moles): the dotted extensions at either end of the repetitious polymeric molecule symbol signify further extensions of the same pattern. The polymer ends eventually with a $HO_2C(C\ldots)$ at the left and a $\ldots CH_2OH$ at the right end.

Chain reactions. A chain reaction is a series of reactions in which the product of each step is a reagent for the next. Many polymerization reactions are chain reactions. A simpler example, however, is found in the synthesis of hydrogen bromide. The overall synthesis equation is $H_2 + Br_2 \rightarrow 2HBr$. The details by which this synthesis occurs are believed to involve a series of reactions beginning with $Br_2 \rightarrow 2Br$, which is endoergic. Some of the bromine atoms will recombine, however, in the reverse exoergic reaction, $Br + Br \rightarrow Br_2$, but not all do so. If a bromine atom instead moves in such a way as to meet and interact with a hydrogen molecule, another reaction will occur: $Br + H_2 \rightarrow HBr + H$. This hydrogen atom then can either react with a bromine molecule: $H + Br_2 \rightarrow HBr + Br$; or with an HBr molecule, already formed: $H + HBr \rightarrow H_2 + Br$.

Note that HBr is formed and the chain is propagated by the two reactions $Br + H_2 \rightarrow HBr + H$ and $H + Br_2 \rightarrow HBr + Br$; each recurrence of this sequence converts one molecule of hydrogen and one of bromine to two molecules of hydrogen bromide and generates other atoms that reinitiate the sequence, thus continuing the chain. Finally, after most of the hydrogen and bromine molecules present have reacted, the chain-termination reaction, $Br + Br \rightarrow Br_2$, predominates, with the formation of trace amounts of bromine molecules. Here, the symbols used in the equations represent atoms and molecules rather than moles of atoms and molecules. Stoichiometric application is not as appropriate for these details as it is for the overall synthesis equation.

Substitution, elimination, addition. Substitution reactions are reactions in which a molecule is changed by the loss of one or more atoms and the gain of one or more other atoms that in a sense substitute for those that are lost. For example, chloroform, $CHCl_3$, reacts with antimony trifluoride, SbF_3, to form the useful compound monochlorodifluoromethane, $CHClF_2$. The incomplete, nonstoichiometric equation, emphasizing only the substitution, is $CHCl_3 + SbF_3 \rightarrow CHClF_2$. Two fluorine atoms are substituted for two chlorine atoms in this equation. The product substance undergoes a further reaction when heated strongly: $2CHClF_2 \rightarrow C_2F_4 + 2HCl$.

This reaction is an example of an elimination reaction; in this case, a hydrogen atom and a chlorine atom are eliminated as molecular hydrogen chloride, HCl. In the presence of hydrogen peroxide or other catalysts, this compound, tetrafluoroethylene, C_2F_4, polymerizes to form the well-known substance Teflon, $(CF_2)_n$, or $\ldots CF_2CF_2CF_2CF_2CF_2CF_2CF_2CF_2 \ldots$.

Addition reactions, as the name implies, are reactions in which atoms are added to a molecule. If the added atoms are hydrogen atoms, the addition reaction is called a hydrogenation reaction. For example, many different vegetable oils can be hydrogenated. The product is a solid that can be used as shortening in the preparation of food. Oleic acid, $C_{18}H_{34}O_2$, serves as an example: $C_{18}H_{34}O_2 + H_2 \rightarrow C_{18}H_{36}O_2$. This reaction and the hydrogenation of other vegetable oils are usually carried out in the presence of a specific catalyst, finely divided porous nickel; for this process to be economically effective, the hydrogen must be under high pressure.

Oxidation–reduction. Oxidation–reduction reactions form another class of important chemical reactions. For example, the generation of electric current by the use of a so-called dry cell or by a storage battery can occur only by means of an oxidation–reduction reaction that takes place within the battery. (The chemical reactions that take place inside any typical battery remain unknown in detail.) In the more recently developed mercury cell, constructed out of zinc (Zn) metal, usually in the form of a cuplike container, in which mercury monoxide, HgO, water, and other substances are enclosed, in the region near the electrode marked with a plus sign, a reduction reaction occurs (the electron itself is represented by the symbol e^-, which can be taken to indicate [stoichiometrically] a mole of electrons): $e^- + HgO + H_2O \rightarrow Hg + 2OH^-$.

This equation is called a reduction half-equation because it symbolizes the gain of electrons by the reagents, mercury monoxide and water, to form the products, mercury metal, Hg, and hydroxide ion, OH^-. At the corresponding negative electrode, an oxidation reaction occurs, electrons being lost during the formation of product from the reagent. The reaction is symbolized in the oxidation half-equation $Zn + 2OH^- \rightarrow ZnO + H_2O + 2e^-$.

In addition to the disappearance of hydroxide (OH^-) ion, zinc is also consumed. Hence, the cell will certainly cease to function when the enclosing cup, made of zinc, has disappeared. Further, the reduction half-equation states

that, as this cell is discharged, metallic mercury is produced within the cell.

Acid–base reaction. Although the classes of chemical reaction have by no means been exhausted, the final class to be mentioned here is acid–base reaction. One definition of an acid is that it is a substance that gives up a proton; *i.e.*, a hydrogen ion, H^+ (a hydrogen atom with its single electron removed). Vinegar is largely composed of water and acetic acid, CH_3COOH. The hydrogen atom on the right end, as depicted here, can be lost as an ion with the electron remaining behind on the acetate residue, now to be identified as an acetate ion $(CH_3COO)^-$. $CH_3COOH \rightarrow (CH_3COO)^- + H^+$.

The ionization of acetic acid, however, will not occur unless a base is present. A base is defined as a substance that tends to take protons from acids. Water is a suitable base, taking the proton to become a hydronium ion, $H_3O^+ : CH_3COOH + H_2O \rightarrow (CH_3COO)^- + H_3O)^+$.

In water solution, sodium bicarbonate, $NaHCO_3$ (common baking soda), forms dispersed sodium ions, Na^+, and bicarbonate ions $(HCO_3)^-$, for the most part. Bicarbonate ions are bases, and they tend to take hydrogen ions from hydronium ions, which act as an acid, to form carbonic acid, $H_2CO_3 : (H_3O)^+ + (HCO_3)^- \rightarrow H_2O + H_2CO_3$. The carbonic acid is unstable at ordinary temperatures; most of it decomposes into water and gaseous carbon dioxide: $H_2CO_3 \rightarrow H_2O + CO_2$.

Separation and analysis. Broadly, the techniques used to investigate chemical reactions often require that the products of the reaction first be separated, because they are usually formed together within the same enclosure, such as a test tube. Separation techniques often involve the precipitation of one of the products; *i.e.*, by means of a second chemical reaction, a product of the first is altered by addition of or elimination of one or more atoms, so that this new substance can be separated, perhaps by the addition of a liquid in which only it is soluble or in other ways.

Following separation, the product is identified by its properties. For example, water can be identified by its freezing point or its refractive index (a measure of the ratio of the velocities of light when it passes through one medium compared to another) or its elemental composition of 8 to 1 oxygen to hydrogen mass ratio or by the energy of particular photons that it absorbs when exposed to photons of different energies. *Identification of products*

An example of a simple case indicates in a general-sense a procedure that might be followed. If the amount of acetic acid present in a particular brand of vinegar is to be measured, one first prepares a solution of a base of known concentration, such as baking soda. Then, a measured volume of vinegar is put into a suitable reaction vessel, and, drop by counted drop, the solution of base is added. The volume of base solution added, including the last drop that caused the evolution of gas (carbon dioxide), would serve as a measure (in an approximate way) of the amount of acetic acid in the measured volume of vinegar originally put into the reaction vessel. For more precise work, a solution of hydroxide ion base, made by dissolving sodium hydroxide, NaOH, in water at a known concentration, would be used. In this instance, a few drops of coloured indicator solution, such as the red-coloured liquid made by steeping red cabbage in hot water, would be added to the vinegar before adding the solution of base. The chemical reaction is complete when the indicator, which is dispersed throughout the liquid, changes colour upon the addition of one drop more of base solution. Of course, the procedures currently used to elucidate the details of chemical reactions are considerably more sophisticated, but the principle is the same.

BIBLIOGRAPHY. W.F. KIEFFER, *Chemistry: A Cultural Approach* (1971), an introductory text for the interested person who is uninstructed in science; H.G. CASSIDY, *Sciences Restated: Physics and Chemistry for the Non-Scientist* (1970), a philosophical approach, with emphasis upon the past and future contributions of physics and chemistry to culture; C.H. LANGFORD and R.A. BEEBE, *The Development of Chemical Principles* (1969), outstanding in clarity and rigour, but more advanced than Kieffer or Cassidy; C.H. LANGFORD, *The Meaning of a Chemical Formula*, one of a series of audiotape lectures (with accompanying booklet) on the interaction between a formula and the facts that support it, emphasizing how symbols function as a tool in reasoning (in prep.); J.A. CAMPBELL, *Why Do Chemical Reactions Occur?* (1965), a well-written exposition centred upon the title theme; E.L. KING, *How Chemical Reactions Occur* (1964), an elementary treatment of kinetics and mechanisms, chain reactions, activation energy, and the use of laboratory instruments; J.A. YOUNG, *Chemical Concepts* (1963), a programmed instruction treatment of stoichiometry and related topics; *Selected Principles of Chemistry* (1963), a programmed instruction treatment of oxidation–reduction reactions, the concept of dynamic equilibrium, and kinetics and mechanisms.

(J.A.Y.)

Chemical Reactions, Mechanisms of

The mechanisms of chemical reactions are the detailed processes by which chemical substances are transformed into other substances. The reactions themselves may involve the interactions of atoms, molecules, ions, electrons, and free radicals, and they may take place in gases, liquids, or solids—or at interfaces between any of these.

The study of the detailed processes of reaction mechanisms is important for many reasons, including the help it gives in understanding and controlling chemical reactions. Many reactions of great commercial importance can proceed by more than one reaction path; knowledge of the reaction mechanisms involved may make it possible to choose reaction conditions favouring one path over another, thereby giving maximum amounts of desired products and minimum amounts of undesired products. Furthermore, on the basis of reaction mechanisms, it is sometimes possible to find correlations among systems not otherwise obviously related. The ability to draw such analogies frequently makes it possible to predict the course of untried reactions. Finally, detailed information about reaction mechanisms permits unification and understanding of large bodies of otherwise unrelated phenomena, a matter of great importance in the theory and practice of chemistry.

Reasons for study

Generally, the chemical reactions whose mechanisms are of interest to chemists are those that occur in solution and involve the breaking and reforming of covalent bonds between atoms—covalent bonds being those in which electrons are shared between atoms. Interest in these reactions is especially great because they are the reactions by which such materials as plastics, dyes, synthetic fibres, and medicinal agents are prepared, and because most of the biochemical reactions of living systems are of this type. In addition, reactions of this kind generally occur in time scales convenient for study, neither too fast nor too slow, and under conditions that are easily manipulated for experimental purposes. Lastly, there are a number of techniques by which the mechanisms of such reactions can be investigated.

Chemical reactions involve changes in bonding patterns of molecules—that is, changes in the relative positions of atoms in and among molecules, as well as shifts in the electrons that hold the atoms together in chemical bonds. Reaction mechanisms, therefore, must include descriptions of these movements with regard to spatial change and also with regard to time. The overall route of change is called the course of the reaction, and the detailed process by which the change occurs is referred to as the reaction path or pathway.

Also important to the study of reaction mechanisms are the energy requirements of the reactions. Most reactions of mechanistic interest are activated processes—that is, processes that must have a supply of energy before they can occur. The energy is consumed in carrying the starting material of the reaction over an energy barrier. This process occurs when the starting material absorbs energy and is converted to an activated complex or transition state. The activated complex then proceeds to furnish the product of the reaction without further input of energy—often, in fact, with a release of energy. Such considerations are important to an understanding of

reaction mechanisms because the actual course that any reaction follows is the one that requires the least energy of activation. This reaction course is not always the one that would seem simplest to the chemist without detailed study of the different possible mechanisms.

The study of reaction mechanisms is complicated by the reversibility of most reactions (the tendency of the reaction products to revert to the starting materials) and by the existence of competing reactions (reactions that convert the starting material to other than the desired products). Another complicating factor is the fact that many reactions occur in stages in which intermediate products (intermediates) are formed and then converted by further reactions to the final products. In examining chemical reactions it is useful to consider several general subjects: (1) factors that influence the course of chemical reactions, (2) energy changes involved in the course of a typical reaction, (3) factors that reveal the mechanism of a reaction, and (4) the classification of reaction mechanisms. With this information in mind it is then possible to look briefly at some of the more important classes of reaction mechanisms (The articles ACID-BASE REACTIONS AND EQUILIBRIA; ELECTROCHEMICAL REACTIONS; and OXIDATION-REDUCTION REACTIONS deal with the mechanisms of reactions not described in this article.)

Difficulties in studying reactions

GENERAL CONSIDERATIONS

Factors influencing the course of reaction. *The reactants.* In analyzing the mechanism of a reaction, account must be taken of all the factors that influence its course. After the bulk chemical constituents have been identified by ordinary methods of structure-determination and analysis, any prereaction changes involving the reactants, either individually or together, must be investigated. Thus, in the cleavage of the substance ethyl acetate by water (hydrolysis), the actual reagent that attacks the ethyl acetate molecule may be the water molecule itself, or it may be the hydroxide ion (OH^-) produced from it (see below).

Identification of constituents

The hydrolysis of ethyl acetate can be represented by the following equation:

$$CH_3\overset{\displaystyle O}{\overset{\|}{C}}-OC_2H_5 + H_2O \longrightarrow CH_3\overset{\displaystyle O}{\overset{\|}{C}}-OH + C_2H_5OH$$

ethyl acetate   water   acetic acid ethyl alcohol

in which the structures of the molecules are represented schematically by their structural formulas. An arrow is used to indicate the reaction, with the formulas for the starting materials on the left and those of the products on the right. In the structural formulas, the atoms of the elements are represented by their chemical symbols (C for carbon, H for hydrogen, O for oxygen), and the numbers of the atoms in particular groups are designated by numeral subscripts. The chemical bonds of greatest interest are represented by short lines between the symbols of the atoms connected by the bonds.

Important to this reaction is an equilibrium involving the cleavage of the water molecules into positively and negatively charged particles (ions), as follows:

$$2H_2O \rightleftharpoons H_3O^+ + OH^-$$

water   hydro-   hydrox-
         nium   ide
         ion   ion

In this equation, the numeral in front of the symbol for the water molecule indicates the number of molecules involved in the reaction. The composite arrow indicates that the reaction can proceed in either direction, starting material being converted to products and vice versa. In practice, both reactions occur together and a balance, or equilibrium, of starting materials and products is set up. The significance of this equilibrium for the hydrolysis of ethyl acetate is that any of the three entities (water molecules, hydronium or hydroxide ions) may be involved in the reaction, and the mechanism is not known until it is established which of these is the actual participant. This often can be established if it is possible to determine the relative amounts of the three in the reaction medium and if it can be shown that the rate of the reaction depends upon the amount (or concentration) of one of them. Under certain conditions the hydrolysis of ethyl acetate is found to involve water molecules (as shown in the equation above); in other cases, hydroxide ion is involved.

The transition state. The transition state, or activated complex, is the fleeting molecular configuration that exists at the top of the energy barrier that the reactants must surmount to become the products. Strictly it is not a component of the reaction system and it cannot be examined directly in the way that an intermediate (however unstable) can because it lasts no longer than the duration of a molecular collision. The transition state may have properties of its own, not reflected in those of the starting materials or of the products and of the reaction, and so it is of vital importance in determining the course of reaction. Inference concerning the nature of the transition state is the essence of mechanistic study.

The solvent. The solvent, or medium in which the reaction occurs, may perform the mechanical, but often vital, role of allowing otherwise immiscible reactants to come together rapidly. Among the important groups of solvents, each with its own special type of behaviour, are hydroxylic solvents (those the molecules of which contain hydroxyl [-OH] groups, such as water and alcohols), dipolar aprotic solvents (those the molecules of which show a separation of electrical charge but do not easily give up a proton, or positive hydrogen ion; *e.g.*, acetone), and nonpolar solvents (those the molecules of which do not show charge separation; *e.g.*, hexane).

In dissolving the reactants, the solvent may interact with any or all of them, and it may be involved in the transition state for any reaction available for the system.

Solvent interactions

If the solvent interacts more powerfully with the transition state than with the reactants, it facilitates the reaction. The solvent itself, of course, may be one of the reactants, and this circumstance introduces special problems because of the difficulty of distinguishing experimentally between its functions as a reagent and as an environment for the reaction.

Catalysts. Catalysts are substances that speed up a reaction by facilitating a particular mechanism—sometimes by influencing an existing prereaction and sometimes by making a new process energetically favourable. Their presence or absence frequently determines the course a reaction may take, simply because one of a number of competing reactions is, or is not, favoured. (Most catalysts are changed chemically while they speed up a reaction: sometimes—but not always—they are consumed; sometimes they are reformed and so appear to be unchanged in concentration during a reaction.)

The products. All reactions are reversible in principle, and the nature of the products of the reaction can affect the reaction course in a number of ways. When the position of equilibrium is unfavourable, for example, the accumulation of products may cause a reversal of the reaction. In such circumstances, the physical removal of the products (either through their volatility or insolubility, for example) facilitates the completion of the forward process. Sometimes, too, one of the products acts as a catalyst or as an inhibitor, behaviour that strongly influences the course of the reaction.

The reaction conditions. The conditions under which some reaction occurs, including such variables as the temperature and concentrations of reactants, also are important in determining the course of the reaction. For reactions that have a high energy barrier between reactants and products, the rate is highly responsive to change in temperature, and such reactions become more likely at increased temperatures, so that the minor products of a reaction often appear in larger proportion at higher temperature.

Similarly, the concentration of reagents can be important to the course of a reaction, especially if two mechanisms are available that involve different numbers of molecules in the transition states. Higher concentrations of a particular reagent favour those mechanisms in which

greater numbers of molecules are involved in the transition state. The pressure applied to the reacting system also may be significant; partly because it has an effect on concentration, and partly because mechanisms involving closely associated transition states become more favourable at high pressures. The latter relationship comes about because associated transition states are those in which several molecules or ions are brought close together (and therefore take up less space), a situation that is encouraged by increased pressures.

Importance of concentration of reagents

Energy changes involved in the course of a reaction. Collisions between molecules are rapid; therefore, reactions that occur spontaneously whenever the reagents collide are fast at ordinary concentrations. A reaction may be restricted in rate by its dependence on the occurrence of molecular collisions, however, because, for example, the reagents are present in such small amounts that reactions can only occur when they happen to encounter one another. Such a reaction is said to be diffusion-controlled because it is dependent on the process of diffusion to bring the molecules together. In such cases, the viscosity of the medium is relevant; the more viscous, or "thick," the medium, the more difficult the diffusion and the slower the reaction.

As noted above, however, most reactions involve a rate-limiting energy barrier, and it is the nature of this barrier and of the molecular configuration at its top that determines the mechanism. Diagrams of energy changes during the course of reaction often are used to illustrate the energetic aspects of the reaction. An example of a possible energy diagram for a hypothetical one-stage process, the dissociation in a solution of a covalent molecule designated E–N, into its ions, E⁺ and N⁻, is shown in Figure 1.

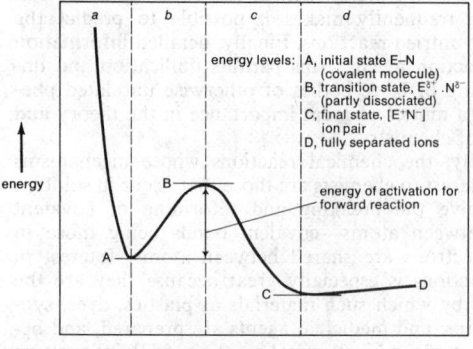

Figure 1: Possible energy diagram for the dissociation of a covalent molecule, E–N, into its ions E⁺ and N⁻ (see text).

In this diagram the energy is plotted against a reaction coordinate—a spatial relationship that varies smoothly during the course of the reaction—in this case the distance between the portions of the molecule designated E and N. At the left-hand energy minimum of Figure 1, the bond between E and N is fully formed; if energy is applied to excite the system in such a way that E and N are brought even closer together (region *a* of Figure 1), the atomic nuclei repel, with the result that energy rises steeply. Alternatively, excitation energy, such as thermal energy from collisions with other molecules, may stretch the bond, and the energy curve then moves into region *b*. The E–N bond is thereby weakened steadily until the transition state is reached. This point, as can be seen in Figure 1, has the maximum energy on the reaction coordinate. At the same time, this point represents the minimum energy required to convert the reactants into the products. The curve shown should be considered as only a planar section of a three-dimensional energy surface relating to the various possible spatial relations among the components of the reaction. The passage of the reactants from the initial state to the products then can be thought of as analogous to the climb from a valley (the initial state) through the lowest mountain pass leading to a second valley (the products). Thus, although the transition state represents a peak on the single curve depicted, it really represents a secondary minimum (or pass) in the energy surface. From the top of this pass (the transition state), the molecule can only descend, losing energy by collision. In doing so it may revert to the starting materials, or it may dissociate to give the products (region *c* in Figure 1). The products in the case of the reaction chosen are the ions E^+ and N^-, which are held together by electrostatic attraction as an ion pair at the right hand minimum of the graph; beyond this point, further separation of the ions involves the consumption of energy (region *d*). In principle, the products may lie at higher or (as shown) at lower energy than that of the initial state. The mechanism of a reaction such as this may be considered to be completely defined when the structures and energy properties of the starting materials, the products, and the transition state are known.

Ultimately, it should become possible to compute the properties of the molecules solely from the properties of their constituent atoms and also to deduce the transition states for any of the reactions these molecules may undergo. For a few simple situations, approaches already have been made to definitions of mechanism in this degree of detail. Systems involving several atoms, however, require a many-dimensional representation of the reaction course instead of the two-dimensional description shown in Figure 1. The problems of computation, and of testing theory against experiment, then become enormous. Nonetheless, attempts have been made to deal with some simple reactions of systems involving up to about five atoms.

Multistage. For a reaction involving several distinct stages, a more complicated description of the reaction course also is necessary. Figure 2 gives an example of

Computation from atomic structures

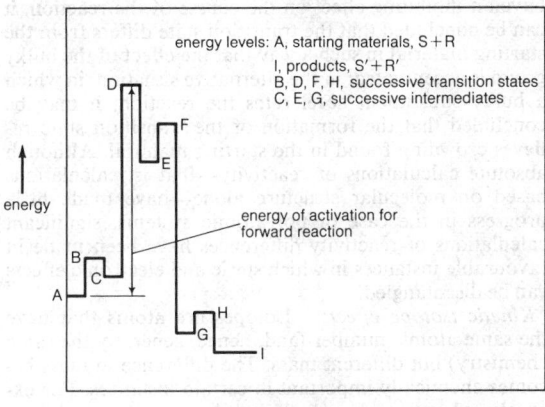

Figure 2: Energy levels in a hypothetical multistage reaction (see text).

such a situation. This hypothetical reaction is reversible, with three successive intermediate complexes formed between the reactants. Unlike the case of the simpler situation above, the physical process that best approximates what is happening along the reaction coordinate changes from stage to stage across the diagram.

The highest point on the energy diagram (Figure 2) corresponds to the energy of the transition state of the rate-limiting step in the reaction—that is, the slowest step in the reaction, the one that governs, or limits, the overall rate. The rate of reaction is independent of the nature and number of the intermediates that lie before this transition state on the reaction coordinate. Progress along the reaction coordinate cannot be identified with the time course of the reaction because any individual pair of reactants may reside for an appreciable time in the partially activated state represented by one of the intermediate complexes before final reaction is achieved. Once the reactants have passed the rate-limiting transition state they must lose energy (usually by collision with other molecules) to reach the final state. In a sense the reaction coordinate in this type of reaction may be thought of as representing the chemical course of the reaction (rather

than a spatial or a time course). If the diagram represents the only reaction of the system, then it is possible to apply the so-called principle of microscopic reversibility, which states that the course taken by reverse action will be statistically identical with that taken by the forward reaction. This principle is not, however, applicable to a reaction giving several different products not at equilibrium with one another.

Principle of microscopic reversibility

Factors that reveal the mechanism of a reaction. *Chemical and stereochemical nature of reactants, intermediates, and products.* The stoichiometry of a reaction consists of the chemical formulas and relative molecular proportions of starting materials and products. Obviously these have a bearing on the mechanism of the reaction, for the overall reaction course must proceed from starting materials to the products. The stoichiometry of the reaction may be misleading, however, because the participants in the overall reaction may not be involved directly in the rate-limiting step.

The discovery of intermediates in the course of a reaction is important because these point to the existence of distinct stages, the mechanism of each of which must then be determined. The identification of intermediates that persist only briefly or that are present in only small amounts depends on the availability of powerful, sensitive, and rapid experimental techniques. For this purpose, a number of specialized instrumental procedures (including ultraviolet, infrared, magnetic resonance, and mass spectrometry) are widely used to supplement the more usual chemical and physical methods.

The identification of a new chemical substance formed transiently in a reaction mixture, however, does not unambiguously imply that that substance is an intermediate in the reaction. In many cases a newly found material is only a temporary repository of the proportion of the reactants, and ultimately produces the products by first reverting to the starting material.

The identification of the products of a reaction also helps to define the reaction course, because the mechanism in question clearly must account for their formation. Mechanistic theory has been greatly facilitated by the development of powerful methods of separation and purification based on chromatography (separation of compounds on the basis of their relative degrees of adsorption to certain solid substances, such as starch or silica) and also by modern methods available for the analysis of small quantities of materials. These spectroscopic procedures are often used, as is another instrumental method, called polarimetry.

Identification of products

An important consideration with regard to the products of the reaction is whether the reaction is under kinetic or thermodynamic control. A reaction is said to be kinetically, rather than thermodynamically, controlled, when the products are formed in proportions different from those that would prevail at equilibrium between the same products under the same conditions. Thermodynamic control leads to the equilibrium ratio of the products. Often, though not invariably, reactions under kinetic control give a greater amount of the thermodynamically less stable of two possible products; if thermodynamic control is then established, the products shift to their equilibrium proportions, which might give a misleading picture of the reaction course. Hence inferences concerning the nature of the transition state can be drawn from the nature of the products only with a good deal of circumspection.

In determining the mechanism of a reaction, one of the major problems is to deduce the spatial or three-dimensional changes that occur to the molecules involved as they proceed from their initial state through the intermediate stages and transition states to the final products. Knowledge about such changes generally can be deduced from knowledge of the stereochemistry (three-dimensional structures) of the starting materials, intermediates, and final products (provided these are obtained under kinetic control). Information of this kind is obtained by determinations of optical activity and analysis of the structures of the compounds by standard means.

In certain instances information about the movement of

atoms between molecules during the course of a reaction can be gained by using compounds containing isotopes of certain of the atoms. These isotopes behave much like the ordinary atoms they replace, but they can be identified by their behaviour. For example, in the hydrolysis of ethyl acetate (see above *The reactants*), it is crucial to a determination of the mechanism to be able to establish which of the two reactants (ethyl acetate or water) provides the oxygen atom that ends up in the product ethyl alcohol. In this case, the use of water labelled with oxygen-18 reveals that the oxygen atom in the alcohol comes from the ethyl acetate molecule.

Kinetic order. The possibilities that need to be considered for the transition state having been limited by determination of the chemical structures of the participants, the most powerful method of obtaining further information is the use of the kinetic method; *i.e.*, the study of the effect of reaction conditions on the rate of reaction. Experimental methods that have been used in kinetic studies include most of the known methods of chemical separation and analysis. Techniques that involve removing samples from the reaction mixture at intervals or stopping the reaction and analyzing for starting material or product are common for reactions with half-lives down to about a minute. For faster reactions, methods involving rapid scanning and automatic recording of some characteristic property of the reacting mixture, such as absorption of light at a particular wavelength, recently have become important. Other procedures for following exceptionally fast reactions include the controlled supply of a reagent within extremely small concentration limits, sometimes by electrolytic procedures (the use of an electric current to produce precise amounts of the substance), and sometimes by carrying out the reaction under conditions in which separate flowing streams of the reactants come together to insure rapid mixing. So-called relaxation procedures, in which a system in equilibrium is very rapidly perturbed and its rate of relaxation to the original or to some new equilibrium state is observed, also have been applied to the study of reactions of extremely small half-lives.

The mechanistic information to be obtained from the observed kinetic behaviour of a system derives from the fact that, for an activated process, the transition state can be considered to be in thermodynamic equilibrium with the starting materials except with respect to its motion along the reaction coordinate. It follows that the rate of reaction is approximately proportional to the product of the concentrations of those substances that comprise the transition state. If the concentrations of all but one reactant are held constant while the concentrations of that reactant are changed, then the variation in rate with the concentration changes will establish how many molecules of that particular reactant are involved in the transition state. This figure is called order of reaction with respect to the reactant in question. A full description of the composition of the transition state then requires identification of the orders of reaction with respect to each of the reactant.

Although straightforward in principle, the application of this method involves some difficulties. Sometimes (for example, with ionic solutes in solvents of low polarity), the concentrations of the reagents are not truly representative of their influence on the reaction rate. The kinetic order then does not properly represent the composition of the transition state. The power of the kinetic method is often greatly increased when the rate of reaction can be followed by more than one method. In such instances, it frequently has been found that unexpected differences reveal the intervention of previously unsuspected intermediates.

Environmental effects. Changes in the environment (such as the composition of the solvent) frequently influence the course of the reaction by affecting the relative stabilization of the initial state and the transition state. Large changes in the polar character (charge distribution) of the solvent, for example, may have an effect on the course of the reaction if there is a substantial change in polarity between the reactants and the transition state.

Structure–reactivity relations. An observed correlation of changes in a reaction rate with systematic changes in the structure of one of the reactants often reveals the movements of electrons between atoms as the reactants shift toward the transition state. Systematic changes in structure usually are brought about by selecting a particular molecular system and varying a portion of it (such as, for example, the substituents on a benzene ring). The effects of each variant on the rates of several different reactions are determined experimentally, and the results plotted on graphs, the values resulting from a particular molecular variation in one reaction being measured along one axis and those of the same variation in the other reaction along the other axis. A straight-line relationship indicates that the molecular changes are affecting the rates of the two reactions in related ways. The slope of the line gives a comparison of the relative response of the two systems to the given change in structure; and the sign of the slope tells whether a particular structural change favours both reactions, or favours one while disfavouring the other. The observed effects generally can be correlated with the electronic nature of the molecular variants introduced. For example, if a substituent in the molecule tends to donate electrons toward the reactive centre in the molecule, and this change favours the reaction, it can be concluded that an electron-rich centre is involved in the transition state.

Electronic effects of the above kinds can be complicated by spatial, or steric factors. (A reaction is said to be sterically hindered when the transition state is more congested than the initial state and to be sterically accelerated when the reverse is true.) When suitable allowance is made for the above electronic influences, structural changes can be used to help define the detailed geometry of the transition state. Thus if large or bulky substituents have an inhibiting effect on the course of the reaction, it can be concluded that the transition state differs from the starting material in such a way that the effect of the bulky group is accentuated; in the alternative situation, in which a bulky substituent accelerates the reaction, it may be concluded that the formation of the transition state relieves crowding found in the starting material. Although absolute calculations of reactivity—that is, calculations based on molecular structure alone—have made little progress in the case of polyatomic systems, significant calculations of reactivity differences have been made in favourable instances in which steric and electronic effects can be disentangled.

Kinetic isotope effects. Isotopes are atoms that have the same atomic number (and, hence, generally the same chemistry) but different mass. The difference in mass becomes chemically important in certain instances. For example, when a carbon–hydrogen bond is replaced by a carbon–deuterium bond (deuterium being an isotope of hydrogen with about twice the mass), the vibrational frequencies of that bond are changed. The vibrational stretching frequency, for example, of a bond between two atoms gives an approximate measure of the bonding forces holding those two atoms together, the effective masses of the two atoms being allowed for. If the character of the carbon–hydrogen bond is altered between the normal state and the transition state, the change from hydrogen to deuterium may have an effect on the relative stabilities of the normal and the transition states, and also, therefore, an effect on the rate of reaction. Such effects, called kinetic isotope effects, operate when only one bond is concerned in such a way that bonds involving the heavier isotope are broken with more difficulty than those involving the lighter isotope. Isotope effects are large only for the isotopes of hydrogen; but, with heavier elements, even small differences can give important information about the mechanism, provided that sufficiently precise methods are available for their measurement.

Classification of reaction mechanisms. There is no one generally agreed and completely satisfactory method of classifying mechanisms; individual authors have often adopted their own nomenclature and symbolism. There are, however, a number of useful classification principles that should be noted.

Side notes:

Effects on reaction rates

Correlation of rate with structural change

Carbon-hydrogen and carbon-deuterium bonds

Homolysis and heterolysis. When a covalent bond (a nonionic chemical bond formed by shared electrons) is made up of two electrons, each of which is supplied by a different atom, the process is called colligation; the reverse process, in which the electrons of a covalent bond are split between two atoms, is known as homolysis. These reactions are shown schematically by the equation:

$$A\cdot + B\cdot \underset{\text{homolysis}}{\overset{\text{colligation}}{\rightleftharpoons}} A:B$$

in which A and B represent the separate atoms (or groups), the single dots represent electrons, and the double dots represent the electron pair that comprises the bond. The products of a homolysis reaction are called free radicals, and all such processes are said to have homolytic or free-radical mechanisms.

If, on the other hand, a covalent bond is formed by a pair of electrons, both of which come from one of the two reagents, the process may be described as coordination, and its reverse is heterolysis. Coordination and heterolysis are shown schematically by the equation:

Covalent bond breaking

$$N: + E \underset{\text{heterolysis}}{\overset{\text{coordination}}{\rightleftharpoons}} N:E$$

in which the dots indicate the electron pair and the letters N and E represent the atoms (or groups) that, respectively, donate and accept the electrons (*see* below for special significance of the letters N and E). Reactions of this kind are said to have heterolytic mechanisms.

Nucleophilicity and electrophilicity. In a heterolytic reaction, the unit that carries the electron pair (designated N: above) is nucleophilic; *i.e.*, it seeks an atomic nucleus to combine with. Conversely, the other unit in the reaction (designated E) is electrophilic: it seeks to combine with a pair of electrons. An electrophilic reaction mechanism is one that involves an electrophilic reagent attacking a nucleophilic substrate. Because every such reaction involves both an electrophilic substance and a nucleophilic substance, it must be agreed arbitrarily which unit is the reagent and which the substrate. Often this agreement is made on the basis of molecular size, the larger sized material being classed as the substrate.

In certain reactions, in which movements of electrons are concerted and cyclic, it is not possible to identify any one reagent, or even any one particular atom or set of atoms in the molecule, as electrophilic or nucleophilic. Such processes are classified as electrocyclic.

Molecularity. The mechanism of an individual stage of a reaction can be described as unimolecular, bimolecular, and so on, according to the number of molecules necessarily concerned in covalency change in the transition state. As an extension of this classification, the number of molecules involved in the rate-limiting step of a several-stage reaction also can be used for classification of the overall reaction. Ambiguities and blurred distinctions arise when there are strong interactions between the solvent and the initial or transition state, or when two stages of a reaction are so near in rate that they become jointly rate-determining. Nevertheless, classifications based on molecularity are widely used.

Intermolecularity and intramolecularity. The distinction between intermolecular and intramolecular processes is often useful. In intermolecular reactions, covalency changes take place in two separate molecules; in intramolecular reactions, two or more reaction sites within the same molecule are involved.

Nature of catalysis. Classification also can be made on the basis of the mode of catalytic action. In ester hydrolysis, as the hydrolysis of ethyl acetate (above), for example, distinction can be made between mechanisms in which catalysis is brought about by protons (hydrogen ions), or by acids in general; by hydroxide ion, or by bases in general; or finally by enzymes.

Kinetic order. The kinetic order of a reaction is best considered as an experimental quantity related to (but not identical with) the number of molecules of any reactant involved in the transition state. It may for various reasons reveal only a part of what is happening in the

rate-limiting transition state, one reason being that the concentrations of the components of the transition state may not all change with progress of the reaction. Establishing that a reaction is of the first order kinetically (that is, behaves as though only one molecule of the reactant is involved in the transition state) with respect to one of the components, for example, seldom reveals whether or not one or more molecules of solvent also is involved in the transition state. This is so because the solvent is present in such large amounts that its concentration does not change effectively with the course of the reaction. For this reason, the order with respect to an individual component may sometimes be useful for classification, but for the overall reaction molecularity is the more fundamental quantity.

Importance of molecularity

Time sequence of events. The time sequence of events in a chemical reaction also provides a means of classification. In some mechanisms, the bond-making and bond-breaking processes occur together and are said to be concerted; in others, the individual stages are discrete, with recognizable intermediates occurring between them, and it may be necessary to specify not only that the mechanism is stepwise, but also the order in which the steps occur.

COMPARATIVE SURVEY OF SELECTED REACTION MECHANISMS

For the following incomplete and abbreviated survey of reaction mechanisms, several mechanisms important in the development of mechanistic study have been chosen.

Nucleophilic substitutions at saturated carbon centres. The term substitution refers in general to the replacement of any group in a molecule by any other group. Saturated carbon centres are carbon atoms at which no multiple bonds occur, and nucleophilic substitutions—those brought about by nucleus-seeking reagents—can occur at such carbon atoms by either of two main mechanisms, bimolecular and unimolecular.

Bimolecular. In bimolecular nucleophilic substitution reactions in which the substrate is attacked at a saturated carbon atom, the starting material has a tetrahedral structure and the transition state has a trigonal bipyramidal structure (both of which are shown below). Each individual act of substitution produces a product of inverted (*i.e.*, mirror-image) stereochemical configuration.

A typical bimolecular substitution reaction is shown by the equation:

Inversion of structure

$$
\underset{\text{starting material}}{\overset{C_6H_5}{\underset{CH_3}{H-C-Br}}}
\;\underset{-N^-}{\overset{+N^-}{\rightleftharpoons}}\;
\underset{\text{transition state}}{\overset{(C_6H_5)}{\underset{H\quad CH_3}{N^+\cdots C\cdots Br^{+-}}}}
\;\underset{+Br^-}{\overset{-Br^-}{\rightleftharpoons}}\;
\underset{\text{product}}{\overset{C_6H_5}{\underset{CH_3}{N-C-H}}}
$$

in which the chemical symbols represent atoms of the elements as above (with Br the symbol for an atom of bromine and N the symbol for any nucleophilic agent). This equation differs from the earlier ones in that a three-dimensional representation of the structures is intended. The three-dimensional effect is achieved by considering that the bonds represented by ordinary solid lines lie in the plane of the paper, bonds represented by dashed lines project to the rear, and bonds represented by dark triangles project to the front. A further unique feature of this equation is that the representation of the transition state shows half bonds (bonds in the process of being formed or broken), which are indicated by dotted lines. In addition, in the transition state, half negative charges are indicated by the symbols "½ −." The mechanism of this reaction is characterized by entry of the nucleophilic reagent from one side of the substrate molecule and departure of the bromide ion from the other side. The resulting change in configuration of the substrate has been likened to the turning inside out of an umbrella, with the transition state representing that precise moment when the ribs are essentially vertical in the course of their passage from one side of the structure to the other. The reaction is synchronized, or synchronous, in that entry of the nucleophile and departure of the leaving group occur simultaneously. It is bimolecular in that one molecule each of substrate and nucleophile are involved in the transition state; and it is stereospecific in that the stereochemical outcome of the reaction is invariably the same.

This bimolecular mechanism occurs with a wide range of structures. It often can be characterized by second-order kinetics, *i.e.*, by reaction rates that are dependent on the concentrations of both the substrate and the nucleophilic reagent. The transition state is highly congested, so that effects of steric hindrance are large. Otherwise, however, structural changes produce a variable response because of the conflicting electronic requirements of the bond-forming and bond-breaking processes. Bimolecular nucleophilic substitutions with rearrangement of the bonding skeleton also are known.

Unimolecular. Unimolecular nucleophilic substitution reactions proceed by a two-stage mechanism, in which heterolysis precedes reaction with the nucleophile. The following equation is a typical example:

starting material   transition state   intermediate

products

in which the symbols are the same as in earlier equations, with the addition of delta plus ($\delta+$) and delta minus ($\delta-$), which indicate partial positive and negative charges respectively. The significant consideration in this reaction mechanism is the initial separation of the bromide ion (by way of a transition state showing partial separation of the ion) to give a free positively charged organic ion (carbonium ion). This step is the rate-determining step of the reaction and, because it involves only a molecule of the substrate, the reaction is unimolecular. The second stage of the reaction is the interaction of the intermediate carbonium ion with the nucleophile to give the products of the reaction.

The unimolecular reaction is characterized experimentally by first-order kinetics *i.e.*, by a rate that depends only on concentration of the substrate (and not the nucleophile); by the absence of effects of steric hindrance; by powerful facilitation of the reaction by the presence of electron-releasing groups attached to the reaction centre; and by variable, and often diagnostic, stereochemistry. Inversion of stereochemical configuration (change from one configuration to the mirror-image configuration) often is found, accompanied by racemization (production of both mirror images). The extent of racemization depends on the life of the intermediate carbonium ion, longer lived ions leading to more extensive racemization (because the symmetrical ion is exposed to attack from either side).

In an important group of structures, a group not formally involved in the overall reaction interacts with a carbonium ion centre to form an intermediate, which then reacts with the nucleophile to give a product of the same stereochemical configuration as the starting material. This behaviour can be represented by the equation:

G=participating or neighbouring group

R_1, R_2, R_3, and R_4=substituents

In the first demonstrations of this behaviour, the participating group (G) was a carboxylate anion group, which can be represented in chemical symbols as:

Many examples with other substituents have become known subsequently, and the phenomenon is often described as neighbouring-group participation.

A frequent consequence of reaction through intermediates having carbonium ionic character is that some of the products have rearranged skeletal structures. In this equation, the symbol Cl represents a chlorine atom.

$$(CH_3)_3C-CH_2Cl \xrightarrow{-Cl^-} [(CH_3)_3C-CH_2^+]$$

1-chloro-2,2-di-   intermediate
methylpropane   carbonium ion

$$\longrightarrow [(CH_3)_2C^+-CH_2CH_3] \xrightarrow{+OH^-} (CH_3)_2C(OH)-CH_2CH_3$$

rearranged   *tert*-amyl alcohol
carbonium ion

The fundamental difference between the transition states in the bimolecular and unimolecular mechanisms is the degree of covalent bonding between the nucleophile and the substrate in the transition state. In the unimolecular mechanism such bonding is negligible; in the bimolecular case, it has essentially reached the half-bond status. In borderline situations, the matter is difficult to resolve, a number of intermediate cases being known, and there has been much controversy as to the validity of the distinction between the bimolecular and the unimolecular mechanisms. Experimentally, however, clear examples of each class have been established.

Nucleophilic substitution at unsaturated carbon centres. Unsaturated carbon centres—including those involving ordinary carbon–carbon double bonds and those involving the extended cyclic systems of alternate single and double bonds known as aromatic rings—are not easily attacked by nucleophilic reagents unless they have been denuded of electrons by electron-attracting substituents. A two-stage process that includes addition of the nucleophile followed by expulsion of a negatively charged (anionic) group is the course normally taken for substitutions at aromatic centres. The presence of the aromatic ring enforces the geometry of the product, and the reaction is favoured by electron-withdrawing groups, such as the nitro (–NO₂) group, which help to accommodate the negative charge on the intermediate. An example of this type of reaction is the displacement of fluoride ion from 2,4–dinitrofluorobenzene by nucleophiles such as ethoxide ion.

2,4–dinitrofluorobenzene   intermediate

2,4–dinitrophenyl ethyl ether

In this equation fluorine atoms are indicated by the chemical symbol F; nitro groups (consisting of one nitrogen and two oxygen atoms) are indicated by the symbols –NO₂; normal benzene rings (of six carbon atoms, each of which carries a single hydrogen atom) are indicated by regular hexagons with circles in them; and benzene rings containing disrupted electronic structures are indicated by hexagons with partial dotted circles.

Substitution reactions at ordinary double bonds (olefinic bonds) also take place by a two-stage process. When the two stages in the reaction occur synchronously or in very quick succession, the product has the same geometrical

Neighbouring-group participation

Resistance of unsaturated carbon centres to nucleophilic reagents relationship that existed in the starting material. If, however, the anionic intermediate has sufficient lifetime, rotation about the new carbon–carbon single bond can precede loss of the negatively charged group, resulting in production of two products of differing molecular geometry—that is, products in which the substituents are differently situated with respect to the double bond.

starting material   intermediate anion

product with unchanged geometry   product with changed geometry

X = a halogen atom: fluorine, chlorine, bromine, or iodine

If the intermediate anion takes up a hydrogen ion (proton) and then loses hydrogen and halogen simultaneously (concerted elimination), the reaction then is said to be following an addition–elimination sequence. Examples of such reactions are known, particularly in situations in which the double bond includes an atom other than carbon. In aromatic systems, the reverse situation, in which elimination occurs, followed by addition, also is found. Finally, unimolecular mechanisms of substitution also are known to take place at particularly activated unsaturated centres. For example:

$$Ar-C(Br)=CH_2 \xrightarrow{-Br^-} Ar-C^+=CH_2 \xrightarrow{+OEt^-} Ar-C(OEt)=CH_2$$

in which the symbol Ar represents a benzene ring or other aromatic system.

Electrophilic substitution at unsaturated carbon centres. Because of its wide applicability, particularly to aromatic systems, electrophilic substitution is a reaction of great importance and has been much studied. Reaction by any one of several mechanisms is possible. One of the more common is shown here; reactions in this general category consist of replacement of a group designated Y (often a hydrogen atom) in an aromatic molecule by an electrophilic agent (see above, *Classification of reaction mechanisms; Nucleophilicity and electrophilicity*) designated E. Both substituents can be any one of a large number of groups (*e.g.*, hydrogen atoms, or nitro, bromo, or *tert*-alkyl groups).

Importance of electrophilic substitution in aromatic systems

starting material   pi complex   intermediate carbonium ion

second pi complex   product

In this equation, Y represents a substituent on the ring, and the arrow proceeding from the centre of the ring indicates coordination.

As shown, the reaction begins with formation of a so-called pi complex, in which the electrons associated with the aromatic ring, or other unsaturated centre (pi electrons), coordinate weakly with the electrophile. This complex forms rapidly in an equilibrium preceding the

rate-determining step. The rate-determining step itself leads to a carbonium ion (positively charged carbon ion) intermediate and then by way of a second pi complex to the product. Examples are known in which the removal of the proton from the carbonium ion intermediate (to form the second pi complex) becomes rate-determining.

Reactivity by this mechanism is dominated by the electrophilic character of the reagent (E); it also, however, responds powerfully to changes in structure of the organic substrate. As would be expected, substituents that release electrons toward the reaction site facilitate the reaction, and those that withdraw electrons retard reaction. These effects are very specific with regard to the position at which the modifying group is introduced.

Steric (spatial) effects generally are smaller than electronic effects in determining the characteristics of reaction by this mechanism; but they are not negligible. Direct steric hindrance and steric acceleration both have been found with suitably placed large substituents and reagents, and indirect effects arising because one group interferes with the orienting power of another also are known.

Substitution with accompanying rearrangement of the double-bond system is another established reaction path. An example is shown below in which the positions of chlorine attachment and proton loss were established by isotopic labelling.

Substitutions with rearrangement

isobutylene   intermediate

methallyl chloride

Addition–elimination and indirect substitution reactions also can occur and are responsible for a number of unusual products formed in aromatic substitution reactions. Examples of these reaction sequences are shown below:

anthracene   intermediate

9–acetoxyanthracene

aniline   phenylnitramine   o-nitroaniline

Addition reactions. Reactions in which a multiple bond between two atoms becomes partly or fully saturated by covalent attachments at both centres are called addition reactions. Many mechanisms are known for such reactions; most of them are variants of four basic mechanisms, which differ chiefly in the sequence of events that occur.

With initial electrophilic attack. Addition reactions beginning with electrophilic attack include many additions to olefins (compounds with double bonds), some additions to acetylenes (compounds with triple bonds), and some additions to compounds with other multiple bonds. There is a close relationship between this mode of addition and the electrophilic substitutions discussed in the preceding section, as shown by this general representation of the reaction:

$$\overset{\frown}{CH_3CH{=}CH_2} + H^+ \longrightarrow CH_3\overset{+}{C}HCH_3 + Cl^-$$

propylene proton intermediate carbonium ion chloride ion

(not $CH_3CH_2\overset{+}{C}H_2$)

$$\longrightarrow CH_3CHClCH_3;$$

2-chloropropane

(not $CH_3CH_2CH_2Cl$

1-chloropropane)

in which the arrows on the olefin structure indicate the flow of electrons toward the terminal carbon, which attracts the electrophilic proton because it becomes an electron-rich centre. Electrophiles, which can be effective either as positive ions (E^+) or in combination with a nucleophile (E-N), include protons (H^+), carbonium ions (R_3C^+), positively charged halogen ions (Cl^+, Br^+, I^+), nitronium ions (NO_2^+), nitrosonium ions (NO^+), and many others. In general, any nucleophile can complete the reaction. When the first stage of the reaction (addition of the electrophile) is rate-determining, the rate responds powerfully to electron-release to the reaction centre, and this factor determines selectively the orientation of initial attack with respect to the double bond. Thus propylene reacts with hydrogen chloride many times

$$CH_2{=}CH_2 + H^+ \longrightarrow CH_3\overset{+}{C}H_2 + Cl^- \longrightarrow CH_3CH_2Cl$$

ethylene proton intermediate carbonium ion chloride ion ethyl chloride

faster than ethylene does, and the product is exclusively 2–chloropropane, rather than 1–chloropropane, because the concentration of electrons on the terminal carbon determines that the electrophilic proton finds it easier to attack that carbon rather than the central carbon atom.

Addition by this mechanism can be accompanied by substitution and by rearrangement as alternative reactions of the carbonium ionic intermediate. Characteristically, the ratios of product are kinetically controlled (see above). Reactions by this mechanism can be complicated by the intervention of intermediates that are more complicated structurally. Neighbouring-group interaction can modify the structure of the intermediate toward a bridged structure, and thus determine the stereochemistry of addition.

Although it is common to find that the first stage of this sequence is rate-determining, in some cases the rate-limiting transition state lies later along the reaction path. It also is possible for the two stages to be concerted, with the electrophilic and nucleophilic fragments (E and N) of the reagent E–N acting either as still covalently bound or as separate kinetic entities (E^+ and N^-). Especially in acid-catalyzed additions to carbon–oxygen and carbon–nitrogen double bonds, the first stage of the reaction can become rapidly reversible, and the mechanistic characteristics of the reaction are then appropriately modified.

With initial nucleophilic attack. The reverse mode of addition, in which a nucleophile initiates attack on the multiply bonded carbon atom, is less easily realized in simple systems; but it does occur with acetylenes, and it also is the basis of reactions that occur when the centre of attack is denuded of electrons. For example, the formation of substances called cyanohydrins from carbonyl compounds (materials with carbon-oxygen double bonds) occurs as follows:

$$R_1R_2C{=}O \underset{-CN^-,\ \text{slow}}{\overset{+CN^-}{\rightleftharpoons}} R_1R_2C(CN){-}O^- \underset{+OH^-,\ -H_2O}{\overset{+H_2O,\ -OH^-}{\rightleftharpoons}} R_1R_2C(CN){-}OH$$

carbonyl compound intermediate cyanohydrin

in which the curved arrow indicates the movement of electrons in the carbonyl group. Initial attack on carbon by the nucleophilic cyanide ion in this case is facilitated by the electron withdrawal by the oxygen atom (shown by the curved arrow in the formula). Such electron withdrawal also can be transmitted along a series of alternate double and single bonds (a conjugated system), with resultant addition to the ends of the system.

Electrocyclic. In a third class of additions, both portions of the attacking reagent combine simultaneously with the substrate. Reactions of this kind sometimes retain predominantly electrophilic or predominantly nucleophilic character, as can be shown by structural and environmental effects. In a number of important cases, however, quite different behaviour is observed. For example, the addition of cyclopentadiene to 1,4-benzoquinone follows second-order kinetics and proceeds at nearly the same rate in the gas phase and in solvents of widely differing polar character.

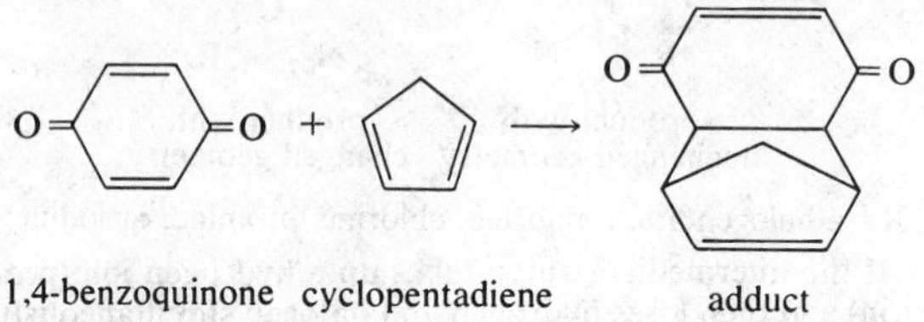

1,4-benzoquinone cyclopentadiene adduct

In this equation the polygons represent rings of carbon atoms (one at each corner) with double bonds between certain atoms as shown. There must, therefore, be little development of charge in the transition state, and the formation of the two new single bonds and the accompanying electronic movements must be well synchronized. A large number of such reactions are known; they are characterized by a remarkable stereospecificity (stereochemical specificity), controlled in part by steric effects and in part by the stereo-electronic characteristics of the combining double-bond systems.

Synchronized reactions

Homolytic. Additions by free-radical mechanisms also are well known. They replace the concomitant polar additions most easily when homolytic (decomposition of a compound into two neutral atoms or radicals) fission of the reagent can be readily catalyzed and when the radicals produced as intermediates sustain chain processes. Addition of hydrogen bromide to olefins falls into this class. Equations (1)–(4) describe the main part of the sequence; reactions (2) and (3) are repeated many times before reaction (4) or some other reaction intervenes to break the chain. As a result, one act of initiation results in many molecules of product.

(1) $HBr \longrightarrow H\cdot + Br\cdot$ (chain-initiating step)

(2) $Br\cdot + CH_3CH{=}CH_2$
$\longrightarrow CH_3\dot{C}HCH_2Br$ (chain-propagating step)

(3) $CH_3\dot{C}HCH_2Br + HBr$
$\longrightarrow CH_3CH_2CH_2Br + Br\cdot$ (chain-propagating step)

(4) $CH_3\dot{C}HCH_2Br + H\cdot$
$\longrightarrow CH_3CH_2CH_2Br$ (chain-terminating step)

The reaction can give an orientation of substituents opposite to that found in electrophilic addition [which in the above example would produce $CH_3CH(Br)CH_3$]; and in suitable cases it can be just as stereospecific.

Elimination reactions. Elimination reactions can be treated formally as the reverse of additions. The simplest examples of this class of reactions are the olefin-forming 1,2-eliminations—that is, elimination of substituents from adjacent carbon atoms—but eliminations to give other types of double bonds are equally well known. Again, 1,3-eliminations—eliminations of substituents from carbon atoms separated by a third carbon—give compounds with three-membered rings of carbon atoms (cyclopropanes). Furthermore, the so-called conjugate eliminations occur when one or more double bonds are inserted between carbon atoms bearing the substituents that are eliminated; the result of such eliminations is a system of alternating double and single bonds (a conjugated system). Finally, there also are fragmentation reactions, in which two small fragments are lost from the organic molecule. Of these reaction types, only the 1,2-eliminations will be discussed here, it being understood that examples of the mechanisms may be found, as appropriate, in other types of elimination reactions.

Concerted, bimolecular. Concerted bimolecular eliminations are characterized by second-order kinetics; they occur readily with powerful nucleophiles. A favoured stereochemical course (*trans*-elimination) involves a particular geometry, as shown, which requires that in the starting material the eliminated units be situated on opposite sides of the molecule. The olefinic product then

starting material   olefin product

must have the particular structure shown, rather than that of its geometric isomer. The relative extent to which the various bonds are formed and broken in the transition state varies considerably with the substrate.

Stepwise, bimolecular. If removal of the electrophilic fragment precedes the loss of the nucleophile, the reaction becomes stepwise and involves a carbanionic intermediate.

starting material   carbanion   olefin product
                      intermediate

Reaction by this path, which sometimes can be characterized by exchange of protons between the solvent and the starting material, is less stereospecific than the reaction by the concerted mechanism. This lessened stereospecificity is caused by the carbanion intermediate not maintaining the rigid geometry characteristic of the concerted mechanism.

Carbonium ion intermediates   *Stepwise, unimolecular.* A carbonium ion produced by heterolysis (decomposition of a compound into oppositely charged particles or ions) may lose a proton, thereby effecting a 1,2-elimination reaction:

starting material   carbonium ion   olefin product

Such eliminations, which generally accompany nucleophilic substitutions, are promoted by electron-release to the carbonium-ion centre. The loss of the proton usually occurs in such a way as to give predominantly the thermodynamically more stable of the alternative products.

Cyclic. Some cyclic eliminations are fully concerted, but in others the loss of a nucleophilic or of an electrophilic component can be dominant. For example, the gasphase pyrolysis (destructive heating) of alkyl halides shows the orientation and structure effects characteristic of unimolecular stepwise elimination reactions in solution. In such cases, the transition state (shown below), though still cyclic and preserving the stereochemistry, must involve greater stretching of the carbon–chlorine than of the carbon–hydrogen bond.

transition state

Nucleophilic replacements in complexes of metals. Stable compounds with more than four groups bonded to a central atom (the situation commonly encountered in compounds of carbon) are formed by elements in the second and higher rows of the periodic table of the elements. Mechanisms of reactions of these compounds therefore become more complex on stereochemical grounds alone. Furthermore, the energy levels of electron paths (orbitals) which can accommodate the bonding electrons of the reacting atom have become closer in these compounds, and reactions involving the formation of new bonds by expansion of the valency shell of this atom often become more readily accessible. For example, nucleophilic attack on carbon tetrachloride is slow, whereas that on silicon tetrachloride is fast, because in the former compound the attacked atom (carbon) has reached its maximum stable coordination number (indicative of the size of the valence shell), whereas in the latter, the central atom (silicon) has not, and its valency shell can be expanded simply by the attachment of a nucleophile. A similar difference in the mechanisms of reactions of metal complexes is found, depending on whether or not the metal atoms are free to engage in valence-shell expansion.

Expanding the valence shell

Unimolecular, in octahedral complexes. Octahedral complexes of metals of the first transition series (elements from scandium to zinc) have reached their maximum stable coordination number, six. Accordingly, many of their replacement reactions are believed to occur by dissociation to give an intermediate having only five groups bonded to the reaction centre. Several different types of kinetic behaviour have been recognized. The initial stage may be a rate-determining dissociation of the cobalt complex shown below, in which methanol is the solvent, "en" is ethylene diamine ($H_2NCH_2CH_2NH_2$), and N^- can be any of a variety of nucleophiles, including bromide, thiocyanate, and nitrate ion.

$$[Co(en)_2Cl_2]^+ \xrightarrow[slow]{-Cl^-} [Co(en)_2Cl]^{2+} \xrightarrow[fast]{+N^-} [Co(en)_2ClN]^+$$

Alternatively the dissociative stage can be a pre-equilibrium, as in many replacements of water, as shown in the reaction below.

$$[Co(NH_3)_5(OH_2)]^{3+} \underset{+H_2O}{\overset{-H_2O}{\rightleftharpoons}} [Co(NH_3)_5]^{3+} \xrightarrow{+N^-} [Co(NH_3)_5N]^{2+}$$

The stereochemistry of these reaction paths is of great mechanistic significance, and varies both with the nature of the central metal atom and the nature of the attached groups (ligands).

Bimolecular, in square planar complexes. Square planar four-coordinated complexes differ from their octahedral six-coordinated analogues in that they generally undergo bimolecular associative, rather than dissociative, nucleophilic displacements. Thus, for many reactions involving replacement of a ligand by a nucleophile in complexes of platinum(II) ions, a kinetic effect proportional to the concentration of the nucleophile can be identified, showing that the nucleophile is involved in the transition state. Furthermore, the stereochemical specificity of such reactions, as shown below, can be accommodated readily in terms of the five-coordinated associated intermediate, whereas a dissociative mechanism would be expected to result in the formation of a mixture of the two geometric isomers.

Kinetic evidence

four-   five-coordinated   preferred   geometrical
coordinated   intermediate   product   isomer
complex

A ligand across from, or *trans* to, a replaceable group has a much greater influence on the rate of substitution than does the same substituent next to, or *cis* to, the replaceable group, and this *trans* effect helps to define the nature of the bonding in the transition state, because it suggests that only the *trans* substituent is in the same plane as the associated and departing group in the intermediate.

BIBLIOGRAPHY. Classic books and reviews of historical importance include: J.W. BAKER, *Tautomerism* (1934); A.F. HOLLEMAN, *Die Direkte Einführung von Substituenten in Benzolkern* (1910). Faraday Society Discussions: "Mechanism and Chemical Kinetics of Organic Reactions in Liquid Systems," *Trans. Faraday Soc.*, 37:601–804 (1941); "Reaction Kinetics," *ibid.*, 34:1–265 (1938). L.P. HAMMETT, *Physical Organic Chemistry*, 2nd ed. (1970); and C.K. INGOLD, "Principles of an Electronic Theory of Organic Reactions," *Chem. Rev.*, 15:225–274 (1934).

Books of general interest include: C.K. INGOLD, *Structure and Mechanism in Organic Chemistry*, 2nd ed. (1969); J.H. RIDD (ed.), *Studies on Chemical Structure and Reactivity* (1966); M.S. NEWMAN (ed.), *Steric Effects in Organic Chemistry* (1956); F. BASOLO and R.G. PEARSON, *Mechanisms of Inorganic Reactions*, 2nd ed. (1967); R. BRESLOW, *Organic Reaction Mechanism*, 2nd ed. (1969); C.H. LANGFORD and H.B. GRAY, *Ligand Substitution Processes* (1966); A. STREITWIESER, JR., *Molecular Orbital Theory for Organic Chemists* (1961); A.A. FROST and R.G. PEARSON, *Kinetics and Mechanism*, 2nd ed. (1961); S. GLASSTONE, K.J. LAIDLER, and H. EYRING, *The Theory of Rate Processes* (1941); S.W. BENSON, *The Foundation of Chemical Kinetics* (1960); R.P. BELL, *The Proton in Chemistry* (1959); L. MELANDER, *Isotope Effects on Reaction Rates* (1960); J.E. LEFFLER and E. GRUNWALD, *Rates and Equilibria of Organic Reactions* (1963); and R. STEWART, *The Investigation of Organic Reactions* (1966).

Books of specialized interest include: C.A. BUNTON, *Nucleophilic Substitution at a Saturated Carbon Atom* (1963); D. BETHELL and V. GOLD, *Carbonium Ions* (1967); J. MILLER, *Aromatic Nucleophilic Substitution* (1968); R.O.C. NORMAN and R. TAYLOR, *Electrophilic Substitution in Benzenoid Compounds* (1965); P.B.D. DE LA MARE and J.H. RIDD, *Aromatic Substitution, Nitration and Halogenation* (1959); P.B.D. DE LA MARE and R. BOLTON, *Electrophilic Additions to Unsaturated Systems* (1966); and D.V. BANTHORPE, *Elimination Reactions* (1963).

Current information may be found in the following series: *Progress in Physical Organic Chemistry* (1963–); *Advances in Physical Organic Chemistry* (1963–); *Progress in Stereochemistry* (1954–); *Topics in Stereochemistry* (1967–); and in reviews on various topics in *Annual Reports on the Progress of Chemistry*, published by the Chemical Society, London; and *Chemical Reviews* (bimonthly), published by the American Chemical Society.

(P.B.D. de la M.)

Chemical Separations and Purifications

Since ancient times, man has used methods of separating and purifying chemical substances for improving the quality of his life. The extraction of metals from ores and of medicines from plants is older than recorded history. In the Middle Ages the alchemists' search for the philosophers' stone (a means of changing base metals into gold) and the elixir of life (a substance that would perpetuate youth) heavily involved separation. In the industrial and technological revolutions, separations and purifications have assumed major importance. During World War II, for example, one of the main problems of the Manhattan Project, which led to the atomic bomb, was the separation of uranium-235 from uranium-238. Many industries now find separations indispensable: the petroleum industry separates crude oil into products used as fuels, lubricants, and chemical raw materials; the pharmaceutical industry separates and purifies natural and synthetic drugs to meet health needs; the mining industry is based on separation and purification of metals.

Separations and purifications also find their places in medicine and the sciences. In the life sciences (biology, pharmacology, etc.) many advances can be directly traced to the development of each new separation method. The first step in understanding the chemical reactions of life is to learn what substances are present in samples obtained from biological sources. The complexity of these mixtures is shown by the fact that more than 300 compounds have been identified in urine. Identification first requires isolation by separation. Modern medicine depends upon purifications, such as that performed by the artificial kidney, and separations, such as those involved in clinical analysis of biological fluids.

BASIC CONCEPTS OF SEPARATIONS

This article is concerned with separations of the smallest subdivisions of matter, such as atoms, molecules, and small particles (sand, minerals, bacteria, etc.). Such processes start with a sample in a mixed state (composed of more than one substance) and transform it into new samples, each of which—in the ideal case—consists of a single substance. Separation methods, then, can be defined as processes that change the relative amounts of substances in a mixture. In chemical methods, one may start with a completely homogeneous mixture (a solution) or a heterogeneous sample (*e.g.*, solid plus liquid); in the act of separation, some particles are either partially or totally removed from the sample.

Reasons for making separations. There are two general reasons why separations are performed. First, the mixture may contain some substance that it is desirable to isolate from the rest of the mixture: this process of removing substances considered to be contaminants is called purification. For example, in the manufacture of synthetic drugs, mixtures containing variable proportions of several compounds usually arise. The removal of the desired drug from the rest of the mixture is important if the product is to have uniform potency and is to be free of other components that may be dangerous to the body.

The second reason for performing separations is to alter the composition of a sample so that one or more of the components can be analyzed. For example, the analysis of air pollutants to assess the quality of the air is of great interest, yet many of the pollutants are at a concentration level too low for direct analysis, even with the most sensitive devices. Pollutants can be collected by passing samples of air through a tube containing an adsorbent material. By this process the pollutants are concentrated to a level such that straightforward analysis and monitoring can take place. In a second example, several impurities in a sample may interfere with the analysis of the substance of primary interest. Thus, in the analysis of trace concentrations of metals in rivers, organic substances can cause erroneous results. These interferences must be removed prior to the analysis.

Classification of separations. There are a variety of criteria by which one can classify separations. One is based on the quantity of material to be processed. Some methods of separation (*e.g.*, chromatography) work best at very small concentration levels of sample, while others (*e.g.*, distillation) are more suited to large-scale operations.

One may also classify separations on the basis of the physical or chemical phenomena utilized. These phenomena can be divided into two broad categories: equilibrium and rate (kinetic) processes. Table 1 lists a num-

Table 1: Separations Based on Phase Equilibria

gas–liquid	gas–solid	liquid–solid	liquid–liquid
distillation	adsorption	precipitation	extraction
gas–liquid	sublimation	zone melting	partition
chromatography	molecular	crystallization	chromatography
foam fractionation	sieves	ion exchange	
		adsorption	
		exclusion	
		clathration	

ber of chemical separation methods based on equilibria, and Table 2 indicates those methods based on rate phenomena.

Separations based on equilibria. All equilibrium methods considered in this article involve the distribution of substances between two phases that are insoluble in one another. As an example, consider two insoluble liquids (*e.g.*, benzene and water). If a coloured compound is

Table 2: Separations Based on Rate Phenomena

barrier separations	field separations	other
membrane	electrophoresis	enzyme
filtration	ultracentrifugation	degradation
dialysis	electrolysis	molecular
ultrafiltration		distillation
electrodialysis		
reverse osmosis		

Industrial and military importance

placed in the water and the two phases are mixed, colour appears in the benzene phase, and the intensity of the colour in the water phase decreases. These colour changes continue to occur for a certain time, beyond which no changes take place, no matter how long or vigorously the two phases are mixed. Because the dye is soluble in the benzene as well as in the water, the dye is extracted into the benzene at the start of the mixing. But just as the dye tends to move into the benzene phase, so it also tends to be dissolved in the aqueous phase. Thus dye molecules move back and forth across the liquid–liquid interface. Eventually, a condition is reached such that the tendencies of the dye to pass from benzene to water and from water to benzene are equal, and the concentration of the dye (as measured by the intensity of its colour) is constant in the two phases. This is the condition of equilibrium. Note that this is not a static condition but rather a dynamic one, for many molecules continue to pass through the liquid–liquid interface (although of equal number in both directions).

Distribution coefficient

The condition of equilibrium in this example can be described in terms of the distribution coefficient, K, by the equation

$$K = \frac{\text{concentration of dye in the benzene phase}}{\text{concentration of dye in the water phase}},$$

in which the concentrations in the equilibrium state are considered. For $K = 1$, there are equal concentrations of the dye in the two phases. If K were larger, more dye would be found in the benzene phase at equilibrium. At $K = 100$, 99.01 percent is in the benzene, and only 0.99 percent is in the water (assuming equal volumes of the two liquids). For certain purposes, this condition might be considered to represent essentially complete removal of the dye from water, but more often $K = 1,000$ is selected (i.e., 99.9 percent removal).

Separation results when the distribution coefficient values for two substances (e.g., two dyes) differ from one another. Consider K = 100 for one substance and K = 0.01 for a second substance: then, upon reaching equilibrium, 99 percent of the former substance will be found in the benzene phase, and 99 percent of the latter substance will be found in the aqueous phase. It is clear that this sample is rather easily separated by liquid–liquid distribution. The ease of the separation thus depends on the ratio of the two distribution coefficients, α (some-

Separation factor

times called the separation factor):

$$\alpha = \frac{K_2}{K_1},$$

in which K_1 and K_2 are the respective distribution coefficients of components 1 and 2. In the above example, $\alpha = 10,000$. In many other cases, α can be very small, close to unity (α is defined such that it is always unity or greater): then separation is difficult, requiring very efficient methods. Part of the art of separations is finding conditions that produce large separation factors of pairs of substances.

In Table 1 most of the important chemical equilibrium separation methods are subdivided in terms of the two insoluble phases (gas, liquid, or solid). The example previously cited involved extraction (liquid–liquid). Each of the other methods is described in the course of this article.

Separations based on rates. Rate separation processes are based on differences in the kinetic properties of the components of a mixture, such as the velocity of migration in a medium or of diffusion through semipermeable barriers.

The separation of mixtures of proteins often is difficult because of the close similarity of the chemical structures of such molecules. When proteins are dissolved in water, they ionize (form electrically charged particles). Both positive and negative electrical charges can occur on various parts of the complex molecule, and, depending on the acidity or alkalinity of the solution, a protein molecule as a whole will be either positively or negatively charged. For a given set of solution conditions, the net charges on different proteins usually are unequal.

Electrophoresis takes advantage of these charge differences to effect a separation. In this method, two electrodes are positioned on opposite sides of a paper, starch gel, or other appropriate supporting medium. A salt solution is used to moisten the medium and to connect the electrodes electrically. The mixture to be separated is placed in the centre of the supporting medium, and an electrical potential is applied. The positively charged proteins move toward the negatively charged electrode (cathode), while the negatively charged proteins migrate toward the positively charged electrode (anode). The migration velocity in each direction depends not only on the charge on the proteins but also on their size: thus proteins with the same charge can be separated.

This example demonstrates the separation of charged species on the basis of differences in migration velocity in an electric field. The extent of such a separation (based on the rate of a process) is time-dependent, a feature that distinguishes all such separations from those based upon equilibria.

The velocity can be either positive or negative: it depends not only on the size and electrical charge of the molecule but also on the conditions of the experiment (e.g., voltage between the two electrodes). In analogy to equilibrium methods, the separation factor can be defined as the ratio of migration velocities for two proteins,

$$\alpha = \frac{v_2}{v_1}.$$

The extent of separation (i.e., how far one protein is removed from another) depends on the different distances traversed by the two proteins:

$$\text{extent} = v_2 t - v_1 t,$$

in which t is the time allowed for migration. Thus the extent of separation is directly proportional to the time of migration in the electric field.

Another major category of rate separation methods is based on the diffusion of molecules through semipermeable barriers. Besides different charges, proteins also have different sizes, and this latter property can be used as the basis of separation. If a vessel is divided in half by a porous membrane, and a solution of different proteins is placed in one section and plain water in the other, some of the proteins will be able to diffuse freely through the membrane, while others will be too large to fit through the holes. Still others will be able to just squeeze through the holes and so will diffuse more slowly through the membrane. In reality there is distribution of hole sizes, so that most protein molecules can diffuse through the membrane if given sufficient time. In any event, the extent of separation will be dependent on the time allowed for diffusion to take place.

Diffusion through membranes

Table 2 lists the various barrier separation methods discussed in this article. The differences in the methods involve the type of substances diffusing through the semipermeable barrier and whether an external field or pressure is applied across the membrane to influence the diffusion.

Particle separations. Up to this point, only separations at the molecular level have been mentioned. Separations of particles are also important in both industry and research. Particle separations are performed for one of two purposes: (1) to remove particles from gases or liquids or (2) to separate particles of different sizes. The first reason underlies many important applications. The electronics industry requires dust-free "clean rooms" for assembly of very small components; the household vacuum cleaner uses a stream of air to pick up particles of dust and dirt, which are separated from the air prior to its release in the room. The second purpose deals with the classification of particles from samples containing particles of many different sizes. Many technical processes using finely divided materials require that the particle size be as uniform as possible. The more important particle separation methods are filtration, sedimentation, elutriation, centrifugation, particle electrophoresis, electrostatic precipitation, flotation, and screening, which are described in a later section.

Single-stage versus multistage processes. As shown earlier, ease of separation in equilibrium methods is based on the value of the separation factor, α. When this value is large, separation is easy, requiring little input of work. Thus, if α lies between 100 and 1,000, a single equilibration in liquid–liquid extraction is sufficient to separate at the level of 90 percent or higher. This type of process, in which the equilibration is carried out only once, is called a single-stage process.

If the separation factor is smaller, separation is more difficult: more work must be done on the system to achieve the desired separation. This result can be accomplished by repeating the equilibration process many times, such a method being called a multistage process.

To better envision this, consider a liquid–liquid extraction experiment in which the volumes of the two liquid phases (A and B) are equal and in which equal amounts of two components, 1 and 2, are present in one of the phases (say A). If $K_1 = 0.5$ and $K_2 = 2.5$, then $\alpha = 5$, according to the previous definition. After equilibration, 66.7 percent of component 1 and 28.5 percent of component 2 remain in the original liquid phase (A), because $K_1 = 0.5 = 33.3/66.7$ and $K_2 = 2.5 = 71.5/28.5$; so that the concentration ratio in this phase has gone from unity to 66.7/28.5, or 2.3. If the extracting liquid phase (B) is removed and replaced with an equal portion of fresh liquid (B) containing none of components 1 and 2, and a second extraction is performed, 44.4 percent of component 1 and 8.1 percent of component 2 are left in the original phase (A). The concentration ratio has increased from 2.3 to 5.5; however, note that there is less of components 1 and 2 in the original phase. If the equilibration is carried out again with fresh solvent (B), the original phase contains 29.6 percent of component 1 and only 2.3 percent of component 2, a concentration ratio of approximately 13. Thus the purity of component is increased by repeating the process of equilibration.

Before examining multistage separations in more detail, consider an alternate procedure, by which component 2 (with $K = 2.5$) could be removed from the original liquid phase. Three consecutive extractions with fresh solvent result in the removal of $100 - 2.3 = 97.7$ percent of the component. Instead of three separate equilibrations, what would happen if one extraction were performed, using the same volume of liquid B used in the three consecutive extractions? It can be calculated that only 88 percent of component 2 would be extracted in this case. Thus, repeated equilibrations with a small amount of solvent remove more material than a single extraction with a large amount. This fact has important practical application.

Returning to the separation of two components, the experiments described are quite wasteful of material. While the concentration ratio is 13, only 30 percent of the concentrated component remains in the original phase. It seems clear that the extracted phase should not be discarded. The separation can be performed without loss of either component by employing a sequence of extractions: each vessel in a series is half filled with the denser, or lower, liquid phase (without components 1 and 2). The mixture is added to the lower phase (A in the above example) of the first vessel, and fresh upper phase (B) is added in the correct amount; after shaking to achieve equilibrium, the upper phase is transferred to the second vessel, and fresh upper phase is added to vessel 1. Vessels 1 and 2 are both equilibrated, and the upper phases are moved along the train, one vessel at a time.

In this experiment, component 2 (with $K = 2.5$) will move more quickly down the train of vessels than component 1. After a large number of transfers, the different migration velocities of the two components result in complete separation. The number of transfers required to achieve complete separation is dependent on the value of the separation factor (α) of the two components; the smaller the value is, the larger must be the number of tubes.

This discontinuous, multistage, liquid–liquid extraction scheme has been highly refined: an especially designed apparatus is used to permit automatic operation. This method has played an important role in biochemistry for preparation of purified materials. In advanced models of this machine, the lower phase is transferred to the left after each equilibration, and the upper phase is transferred to the right; the sample is initially placed in the central vessel of the train. Because flow of the two solvents occurs in both directions, this mode of operation is called countercurrent.

PRINCIPLES OF SPECIFIC METHODS

Equilibrium separations. *Distillation.* Distillation, a method of separation based on differences in the boiling points of substances, has been known for centuries. The essential operation in distillation is the boiling of a liquid; converting it into a vapour, which is then condensed to a liquid that is collected separately rather than allowed to flow back into the original liquid.

Above the surface of any pure liquid (or solid) substance, a definite amount of its vapour is present. The concentration of the vapour and, therefore, the pressure it exerts increase as the temperature is raised. When the pressure of the vapour equals the pressure of the surroundings (one atmosphere in an open vessel at sea level), the substance boils: bubbles of vapour form within the liquid and rise to the surface. Above the surface of a mixture, the vapour contains all the substances present in the mixture, each making a contribution to the total pressure exerted by the vapour. The boiling point of the mixture is the temperature at which the total vapour pressure equals the pressure of the surroundings. In general, the composition of the vapour above a liquid mixture differs from that of the liquid: the vapour contains a larger proportion of the substance having the lower boiling point. This difference in composition of the two phases is the basis of separations effected by distillation. If the boiling points are widely different, only the component of lowest boiling point makes an appreciable contribution to the vapour, and condensation of the vapour provides practically pure material.

Separation by distillation, thus, is based on gas–liquid equilibrium, differing from the previously cited example of liquid–liquid extraction in that the phases are constituted from the components themselves. The ease of separation is obviously based on the differences in the boiling points of the substances; because boiling point is related, to a first approximation, to the molecular weight of the substance, distillation separates on the basis of weight (or size) of molecules. If the boiling points are close together, it is not possible to make a complete separation of two components in a single stage process, as the component of higher boiling point enters the vapour phase before the lower boiling component is completely removed. Such a case necessitates a multistage operation, which can most conveniently be achieved by placing a column above the boiling liquid solution. This glass column contains some loosely packed material (*e.g.*, glass beads), and the hot vapours from the boiling solution partially condense on the surfaces. The condensed liquid flows back toward the solution until it meets rising hot vapours, whereupon the more volatile portion of the returning liquid revaporizes, and the less volatile part of the rising vapour condenses. Thus in the column there occurs a multistage operation, the eventual outcome of which is that the component of lower boiling point concentrates at the upper part of the column and that of higher boiling point in the lower part. Condensation of the vapour at the top of the column provides material much richer in the component having the lowest boiling point.

Distillation finds its greatest application in the large-scale separation of liquid mixtures, as in petroleum-refining plants, where crude oil is distilled into fractions having various boiling points, such as gasoline, kerosene, and lubricating oils. The large towers in refineries are efficient distillation columns that effect sharp separation of the fractions. Distillation is a procedure essential to the chemist, who uses it to purify synthetic products. In general, however, because of its inability to handle small quantities of material or to separate closely similar compounds, the current use of distillation for difficult separations is limited.

The multistage process

Liquid–vapour equilibrium

Chromatography. Chromatography, an extremely powerful separation technique, was developed by Mikhail Tsvet (also spelled Tswett), a Russian botanist, in 1906. Tsvet separated the pigments of plants, hence the name chromatography (literally: graphs of colours). Application of this method has been developed to the extent that coloured substances represent only a minor fraction of the substances separated; however, the name has remained.

Chromatography is a separation process involving two phases, one stationary and the other mobile. Its principle is closely related to that of multistage liquid–liquid extraction, covered earlier in this article. Typically, the stationary phase is a porous solid (*e.g.*, glass, silica, alumina) that is packed into a glass or metal tube. The mobile phase flows through the packed bed or column. The sample to be separated is injected at the beginning of the column and is transported through the system by the mobile phase. In their travel through the column, the different substances distribute themselves according to their relative affinity for the two phases. The rate of travel is dependent on the values of the distribution coefficient, the components more soluble in the stationary phase requiring larger time periods for elution (complete removal from the column). Thus, separation is based on differences in distribution behaviour reflected in different migration times through the column. As in repetitive extraction, the larger that the separation factor is for a pair of components, the shorter will be the column necessary to resolve them. Chromatography is analogous to multistage extraction, except that in chromatography there are no discontinuous steps but rather a continuous flow.

Gas chroma- tography

By the mid-20th century, gas chromatography probably had become the principal separation technique in the laboratory, as the result of its speed, resolving power, and especially its sensitivity. Since both gas–liquid and gas–solid chromatography (GLC and GSC) depend on vaporization, they are best suited to compounds that can be vaporized without suffering decomposition.

As already noted, GLC involves vapour–liquid equilibrium but is unlike distillation in that the phases consist of components other than those to be separated. The gas phase is considered to be a carrier, transporting the components of the sample along the column in a manner analogous to the moving phase in liquid–liquid extraction. Either helium or hydrogen usually is used as the carrier gas, although nitrogen is sometimes used. The stationary liquid phase is coated on a solid support that is packed into the column. Most frequently the solid support is a diatomaceous earth. (For further coverage of this topic, see the article CHROMATOGRAPHY.)

Special adsorbents called molecular sieves are used in certain separations. These materials contain pores of approximately the same dimensions as small molecules. Advantage can be taken of this property in the separation of molecules having linear structures from molecules having bulky structures. The former can readily get into the pores, but the latter are unable to penetrate. This is an example of an exclusion mechanism of separation (based on shape differences). Molecular sieves also play an important role in the drying of gases: water, a very polar substance (*i.e.*, its positive and negative electrical charges are unevenly distributed within the molecule), is readily adsorbed on the particles, but less polar gases are not retained.

Sublimation, another method of gas–solid distribution, is not used very often. In sublimation a solid evaporates without passing through the liquid state; thus it is somewhat analogous to distillation, in that both methods involve evaporation. In the case of a solution made up of two solids, it is possible to separate the two components if the vapour pressures of the solids are different. Since not all substances sublime, the applicability of the method is limited.

Crystallization and precipitation. Crystallization is a technique that has long been used in the purification of substances. Often, when a solid substance (single compound) is placed in a liquid, it dissolves. Upon adding more of the solid, a point eventually is reached beyond which no further solid dissolves, and the solution is said to be saturated with the solid compound. The concentration (that is, the amount of the solid dissolved in a given volume of the solvent) of the saturated solution depends upon the temperature, in most cases a higher temperature resulting in a higher concentration.

These phenomena can be employed as a means of effecting separation and purification. Thus, if a solution saturated at some temperature is cooled, the dissolved component begins to separate from the solution and continues to do so until the solution again becomes saturated at the lower temperature. Because the solubilities of two solid compounds in a particular solvent generally differ, it often is possible to find conditions such that the solution is saturated with only one of the components of a mixture. Upon cooling such a solution, part of the less soluble substance crystallizes alone, while the more soluble components remain dissolved.

Crystallization, the process of solidifying from solution, is highly complex. Seed particles, or nuclei, form in the solution, and other molecules then deposit on these solid surfaces. The particles eventually become large enough to fall to the bottom of the container. In order to achieve a high purity in the crystallized solid, it is necessary that this precipitation take place slowly. If solidification is rapid, impurities can be entrapped in the solid matrix. Entrapment of foreign material can be minimized if the individual crystals are kept small. Best results are obtained by cooling the solution slowly while stirring the liquid. Stirring promotes the formation of many nuclei, so that many small crystals form, rather than a few large ones. It is sometimes necessary to add a seed crystal to the solution in order to begin the crystallization process: the seed crystal provides a solid surface on which further crystallization can take place. (Additional coverage of this topic appears in the article CRYSTALLIZATION AND CRYSTAL GROWTH.)

Chemical precipi- tation

The term precipitation sometimes is differentiated from crystallization by restricting it to processes in which an insoluble compound is formed in the solution by a chemical reaction. It often happens that several substances are precipitated by a given reaction. To achieve separation in such cases, it is necessary to control the concentration of the precipitating agent, so that the solubility of only one substance is exceeded. Alternatively, a second agent can be added to the solution to form stable, soluble products with one or more components in order to suppress their participation in the precipitation reaction. Such compounds, often used in the separation of metal ions, are called masking agents.

Precipitation was used for many years as a standard method for separation and analysis of metals. By the mid-20th century, however, it had been replaced by selective and sensitive instrumental methods that directly analyze many metals in aqueous solutions.

Zone melting. Another separation procedure based on liquid–solid equilibria is zone melting, which has found its greatest use in the purification of metals. Purities as high as 99.999 percent often are obtained by application of this technique. Samples are usually in a state of moderate purity before zone melting is performed.

The zone-melting process is easy to visualize. Typically, the sample is made into the form of a thin rod, from two to ten feet or more in length. The rod, confined within a tube, is suspended either horizontally or vertically, and a narrow ring that can be heated is positioned around it. The temperature of this ring is held several degrees above the melting point of the solid, and the ring is caused to travel very slowly (a few inches per hour) along the rod. Thus, in effect, a melted zone travels through the rod: liquid forms on the front side of this zone, and solid precipitates on the rear side. Because the freezing point of a substance is depressed by the presence of impurities, the last portion of a liquefied sample to freeze is enriched in the impurities. As the molten zone moves along, therefore, it becomes more and more concentrated with impurities. At the end of the operation, the impurities are found solidified at the end of the rod, and the impure section can be removed by simply cutting it off.

High purities can be achieved through multistage operation, either by recycling the ring several times or by using several rings in succession.

Liquid–solid adsorption and ion exchange. Liquid–solid adsorption is similar to gas–solid adsorption in that the equilibrium involves a distribution between a three-dimensional phase (gas or liquid) and a two-dimensional phase (solid surface). Thus, many of the types of separations are similar for the two methods. Separations are based on the properties of classes of compounds; *e.g.*, amines (alkaline) from alcohols (neutral), esters (neutral) from acids, etc. Because in liquid–solid adsorption there is no step (such as vaporization) strongly affected by molecular weight, separations within a given class of compounds are poor.

Liquid–solid chromatography, used by Tsvet, is the oldest of the chromatographic methods. Until the mid-20th century, the experimental procedure had not changed much from its original form. A vertical tube one to two metres long and one centimetre wide was filled with adsorbent particles roughly 100–200 microns in diameter (one micron $= 10^{-6}$ metre). The sample was introduced at the top of the column, and the mobile liquid phase was allowed to flow down the column. The solution emerging from the bottom of the tube was collected in fractions for analysis or subsequent use. In general, this method was characterized by poor efficiency, slow separations, and poor reproducibility. By means of later developments, including the use of smaller tubes, smaller adsorbent particles, and high liquid velocities, speeds and efficiencies comparable to those of gas chromatography have been achieved.

Liquid–solid adsorption chromatography also can be performed on thin, flat plates (thin-layer chromatography, or TLC). TLC is inexpensive and rapid but not as sensitive or efficient as column chromatography. In practice, the adsorbent is spread on a glass plate and dried. The sample is applied as a spot near one end of the plate, which is placed (vertically) in a shallow reservoir containing the mobile phase. As the mobile phase travels up the plate by capillary action, the sample dissolves in the liquid, and its components are transported up the plate to new positions at varying distances from the starting point.

Ion-exchange chromatography is a subdivision of liquid–solid chromatography, but its importance is such that it deserves special mention. As the name implies, the process separates ions (electrically charged atoms or groups of atoms); the basis of the separation is the varying attraction of different ions in a solution to oppositely charged sites on a finely divided, insoluble substance (the ion exchanger, usually a synthetic resin). In a cation-exchange resin all the sites are negatively charged, so that only positive ions (cations) can be separated; an anion-exchange resin has positively charged sites.

An important application of ion exchange is the removal of dissolved iron, calcium, and magnesium ions from hard water. The negative sites on a cation exchanger are first neutralized with sodium ions by exposure to a strong solution of common salt (sodium chloride); when the hard water is passed through the resin, the undesirable ions in the water are replaced by sodium ions.

Exclusion and clathration. Differences in the sizes of molecules can be the basis for separations. An example of these techniques is the use of molecular sieves in gas–solid chromatography. Exclusion chromatography (or gel-permeation chromatography) has proved effective for the separation and analysis of mixtures of polymers (large molecules formed by combining many smaller molecules). In this method the largest molecules emerge from the chromatographic column first because they are unable to penetrate the porous matrix of the support. Smaller molecules appear later because they can traverse the whole porous matrix. A column can be calibrated with polymer samples of known molecular weight so that the time required for emergence of the unknown mixture can be used to deduce the molecular weights of the components of the sample as well as their proportions; such molecular weight distributions are very important characteristics of polymers. Exclusion chromatography also finds use in the separation of mixtures of proteins, which are natural polymers.

In clathration, separation also is based on fitting molecules into sites of specific dimensions. Upon crystallizing from solution, certain compounds form cages (on the molecular scale) of definite size. If other substances are present in the liquid solution and they are small enough, then they will be entrapped in the cage; larger components will be excluded. This method has been used in large-scale processes for separating chemicals made from petroleum.

Rate separations. *Field separations.* Electrophoresis, described in an earlier section of this article, finds its most important application in the separation of proteins for analysis. It is also possible to use it in a preparative mode. In this case, the sample is continuously fed (with a salt solution) at the top centre of a vertically mounted sheet of paper. As the sample flows down the paper, it is subjected to an electrical potential at right angles to the flow. The various species disperse across the paper depending on their charge and mobility and drop from the coarsely serrated bottom edge of the paper into receivers.

Ultracentrifugation involves separation on the basis of the centrifugal force created by very rapid rotation (50,000 revolutions per minute or more). Different species, depending on their masses, will settle at different speeds under these conditions. Ultracentrifugation finds its greatest use in the separation of polymeric materials, such as proteins and nucleic acids.

Electrolytic separations and purifications are effected by taking advantage of the different voltages required to convert ions to neutral substances. A particularly important example of this method is the refining of copper. Copper ores typically contain minor amounts of other metals that are not removed by the initial processes that reduce the ores to the metal. A slab of the impure copper and a sheet of pure copper are placed in a vessel containing a solution of sulfuric acid in water, and the two pieces of copper are connected to a source of direct electric current, so that the pure copper becomes the cathode (negatively charged electrode) and the impure copper becomes the anode (positively charged). The anode dissolves, the metal atoms becoming positive ions that migrate through the solution to the cathode. The voltage between the electrodes is regulated so that, as the metal ions arrive at the cathode, only the copper ions are reduced to metal atoms, which deposit on the cathode. Some of the original impurities, such as zinc and nickel, remain as their ions in the solution, because their conversion back to neutral metal atoms requires a higher voltage than that of the system; other impurities, such as silver and gold, never dissolve at all, but, as the atoms around them dissolve, they fall to the bottom of the vessel as a slime from which they can be recovered by other processes.

Barrier separations. Several separation methods depend upon penetration of molecules through semipermeable membranes. Membrane filtration involves simple migration resulting from a concentration difference on the two sides of the membrane. In ultrafiltration, this diffusion through the membrane is accelerated by means of a pressure difference. In electrodialysis, an electrical field accelerates the migration.

Unrestricted migration of the individual components of a solution results in equalization of the concentration of each component throughout the solution. All the components take part in this process: there is just as much tendency for the solvent to diffuse from regions where its concentration is high (and the solution is therefore dilute) to regions where its concentration is low (and the solution is concentrated) as there is for the dissolved substance to diffuse from regions where it is concentrated to those where it is dilute. In many separations, attention is focussed on the tendency of the dissolved particles to migrate, while the corresponding tendency of the solvent particles to migrate is largely ignored. Osmosis, however, is a phenomenon in which only the solvent is free to migrate through a membrane that separates two regions of different composition. The solvent, driven by its tendency

Thin-layer chromatography [margin]

Electrolytic refining [margin]

Osmosis [margin]

to move from the region where its concentration is higher, passes from the dilute solution into the concentrated one and would continue to do so indefinitely if the liquid levels on the two sides of the membrane remained the same. But, as the solvent passes through the membrane, the amounts of the two solutions become unequal, and the resulting difference in pressure eventually brings the migration to a stop. This pressure difference is called the osmotic pressure of the solution.

In a separation technique called reverse osmosis, a pressure is applied opposite to and in excess of the osmotic pressure to force the solvent through a membrane against its concentration gradient. This method is an effective means of concentrating impurities, recovering contaminated solvents, cleaning up polluted streams, and desalinizing seawater. Dialysis, a technique frequently used in biochemistry, is a membrane-separation method used for removing dissolved salts (small particles) from solutions of proteins or other large molecules.

Enzyme-catalyzed reactions. Enzymes are highly specific biological catalysts capable of discriminating between molecules having similar structures. One compound may be chemically changed in the presence of an enzyme, while another, otherwise inseparable from the first, is not affected. This selectivity has been used as a basis of separation; the method is not frequently used but may be invoked when two very closely related molecules cannot be separated by other means.

Particle separations. *Sedimentation.* Particles such as viruses, colloids, bacteria, and small fragments of silica and alumina may be separated into different fractions of various sizes and densities. Suspensions of relatively massive particles settle under the influence of gravity, and the different rates can be exploited to effect separations. To separate viruses and the like, it is necessary to employ much more powerful force fields, such as those produced in an ultracentrifuge (500,000 times gravity).

Filtration and screening. In filtration, a porous material is used to separate particles of different sizes. If the pore sizes are highly uniform, separation can be fairly sensitive to the size of the particles, but the method is most commonly used to effect gross separations, as of liquids from suspended crystals or other solids. To accelerate filtration, pressure usually is applied. Screening is similar to filtration, but it is usually applied to dry particles rather than to a slurry or a suspension of a solid in a liquid. A series of sieves is stacked, with the screen of largest hole size at the top. The mixture of particles is placed at the top, and the assembly is agitated to facilitate the passage of the particles through successive screens. At the end of the operation, the particles are distributed among the sieves in accordance with their particle diameters.

Elutriation. Elutriation is a method of separation of particles. The particles are placed in a vertical tube in which water (or other fluid) is flowing slowly upward. The particles fall through the water at speeds that vary with their sizes and densities. If the flow rate of the water is slowly increased, the most slowly sinking particles will be swept upward with the fluid flow and removed from the tube. Intermediate particles will remain stationary, and the largest or densest particles will continue to migrate downward. The flow can again be increased to remove the next size of particles. Thus, by careful control of flow through the tube, particles can be separated according to sizes.

Particle electrophoresis and electrostatic precipitation. As the name implies, particle electrophoresis involves the separation of charged particles under the influence of an electric field; this method is used especially for the separation of viruses and bacteria. Electrostatic precipitation is a method for the precipitation of fogs (suspensions of particles in the atmosphere or in other gases): a high voltage is applied across the gas phase to produce electrical charges on the particles. These charges cause the particles to be attracted to the oppositely charged walls of the separator, where they give up their charges and fall into collectors.

Flotation. There are a few methods that use foams to achieve separations. In these, the principle of separation is adsorption on gas bubbles or at the gas–liquid interface. Two of these methods are foam fractionation, for the separation of molecular species, and flotation, for the separation of particles. When dissolved in water, a soap or detergent forms a foam, if gas is bubbled through the solution. Collection of the foam is a means of concentrating the soap. Because proteins produce foams, foam fractionation has also been used to concentrate these substances. The value of the method lies in its speed and in the fact that no heat is applied during the process (proteins usually are damaged by heat). The method is not very selective, however.

Flotation is a process in which particles are carried out of a suspension by a foam. In this case, a soap or other chemical agent first adsorbs on the surface of the particle to increase its ability to adhere to small air bubbles. The clinging bubbles make the particle light enough to float to the surface, where it can be removed. By proper selection of the chemical, particles having similar densities but different compositions can be separated. This method is extremely important in concentrating the valuable constituents of minerals before chemical processing to recover the metals present.

BIBLIOGRAPHY. B.L. KARGER, L.R. SNYDER, and G. HORVATH, *An Introduction to Separation Science* (1973), a modern treatment of theory and practice, with emphasis on small-scale operation; J.A. DEAN, *Chemical Separation Methods* (1969), deals with separation methods in analysis; C.T. KENNER and R.E. O'BRIEN, *Analytical Separations and Determinations: A Textbook in Quantitative Analysis* (1971), up-to-date treatment of classical methods; ERICH HEFTMANN (ed.), *Chromatography*, 2nd ed. (1967), especially useful for applications of chromatography to organic and biochemical mixtures; E.S. PERRY and C.J. VAN OSS (eds.), *Progress in Separation and Purification* (annual since 1968), a continuing series of chapters by experts in specialized fields; J.J. KIRKLAND (ed.) *Modern Practice of Liquid Chromatography* (1971), an up-to-date appraisal of a rapidly changing field; WILLIAM RIEMAN III and H.F. WALTON, *Ion Exchange in Analytical Chemistry* (1970), broad coverage of applications of ion exchangers in analysis; ROBERT LEMLICH (ed.), *Adsorptive Bubble Separation Techniques* (1972), the only book on this technique; HELMUT DETERMANN, *Gelchromatographie* (1967; Eng. trans., *Gel Chromatography, Gel Filtration, Gel Permeation, Molecular Sieves: A Laboratory Handbook*, 2nd ed., 1969), the best available presentation of ion-exclusion methods; E.W. BERG, *Physical and Chemical Methods of Separation* (1963), a good overview of separation science, but somewhat out of date.

Periodicals: Separation Science (bimonthly) deals with all aspects of separation techniques; *Analytical Chemistry* (monthly) treats separations as part of analytical procedures for chemical compounds; *Journal of Chromatographic Science, Journal of Chromatography,* and *Chomatographia* (all monthly) deal specifically with chromatography; *Industrial and Engineering Chemistry* (monthly) often treats separations from the industrial viewpoint.

(B.L.K.)

Chemical Synthesis, Principles of

Chemical synthesis is concerned with the construction of complex chemical compounds from simpler ones. Several million compounds have been synthesized, and their number is being added to at the rate of some hundreds of thousands every year.

GENERAL CONSIDERATIONS

The purpose of synthesis. A synthesis usually is undertaken for one of three reasons: first, to meet an industrial demand for a product. For example, ammonia is synthesized from nitrogen and hydrogen and used to make, among other things, ammonium sulfate, employed as a fertilizer; vinyl chloride is made from ethylene and used in the production of polyvinyl chloride (PVC) plastic. In general, a vast range of chemical compounds is synthesized for applications as fibres and plastics, pharmaceuticals, dyestuffs, herbicides, insecticides, and other products.

Second, an enormous number of compounds of considerable molecular complexity occur naturally, in both living organisms and their degradation products; examples are proteins (in animals) and alkaloids (alkaline materials found in plants). The syntheses of these natural products have usually been undertaken in the context of the determination of the structures of the compounds; if a material is deduced to have a particular structure on the basis of its chemical reactions and physical properties, then the finding that a compound synthesized by an unambiguous method for this structure is identical to the natural product provides confirmation of the validity of the assigned structure.

Third, a synthesis may be carried out to obtain a compound of specific structure that does not occur naturally and has not previously been made, in order to examine the properties of the compound and thereby test theories of chemical structure and reactivity.

Atomic structure and bonding. An appreciation of the problems involved in chemical synthesis requires an introductory knowledge of the atomic and molecular structure of matter, details of which are treated in the articles ATOMIC STRUCTURE; MOLECULAR STRUCTURE; and CHEMICAL BONDING; only a brief summary of these topics can be presented here. The text returns to chemical synthesis in the section *General approach to synthesis*.

All substances are composed of atoms of one or more of the chemical elements, of which there are more than 100. Every atom is composed of a nucleus surrounded by electrons. The nucleus is composed of protons, particles with a single positive electrical charge, and neutrons, with no electrical charge. The chemical identity of an atom is determined by the number of protons in its nucleus. The number of electrons in a neutral atom is the same as the number of protons; the electrons are particles with very little mass, but each has a single negative charge. They occupy regions of space, or shells, that differ in shape and in average distance from the nucleus. Certain distributions of electrons around a nucleus are more stable than others, the most stable generally being those in which the outermost occupied shell contains eight electrons. Electrons in this shell, however, are least strongly attracted to the nucleus and are the ones affected by ordinary chemical processes; they are referred to as valence electrons. If valence electrons are removed, the remaining structure, with a net positive charge, is called a cation. Similarly, if electrons are attracted by nuclei, the new structure will bear a net negative charge: it is called an anion. Many compounds are made up of ions (both cations and anions), and their structures are determined by ionic bonds, which arise from the mutual attractions of the oppositely charged components of the compound.

The composition of a chemical compound is represented by a formula, in which the chemical symbol of an element stands for one atom of that element and subscripts denote the proportions of the different kinds of atoms present in the compound. Sodium chloride, or common salt, for example, is composed of equal numbers of sodium atoms, symbol Na, and chlorine atoms, symbol Cl; its formula is NaCl.

Pairs of atoms may form a covalent bond by sharing two valence electrons. For example, two hydrogen atoms, each with one electron available for sharing (monovalent), can form a bond to one another giving a stable combination, a hydrogen molecule, H_2, or they can bond to a divalent oxygen atom to form water, H_2O. Molecules often are represented by structural formulas in which each atom is designated by its chemical symbol and each pair of electrons that constitutes a bond by a line (*e.g.*, $H-Cl$). In synthesis, this system of notation is invaluable, enabling concise representations of the structures of complicated compounds.

Most synthesis is carried out to obtain organic compounds; *i.e.*, compounds containing carbon. The carbon atom is tetravalent: it can form bonds to four other atoms, which are situated at the four corners of a tetrahedron of which the carbon atom is the centre. For simplicity and ease in representing compounds and their reactions, common groupings of atoms often are indicated without utilizing the appropriate bonding "lines," as in methyl chloride, CH_3-Cl, in which the carbon atom is attached to one chlorine and three hydrogen atoms. The

methyl group, CH_3 takes its name from the compound methane, CH_4.

An atom that has at least two electrons available for sharing can share two with another such atom in a double bond; for example, two of the four valence electrons of a carbon atom can be shared with another carbon atom and the other two with hydrogen atoms, as in ethylene, represented as $CH_2=CH_2$, or two can be shared with oxygen and the other two with hydrogen, as in formaldehyde, $H_2C=O$. Likewise, three electrons can be shared in a triple bond, as in the molecule of nitrogen, $N\equiv N$, or that of acetylene, $HC\equiv CH$. No compound is known, nor is likely to be found, in which carbon forms a quadruple bond.

The chemistry of carbon usually is considered separately from that of the other elements, largely because of the vast number of compounds that it forms. This in turn stems from the fact that carbon atoms form stable bonds with each other; thus, propane, $CH_3-CH_2-CH_3$, with a chain of three carbon atoms, is stable, but the analogous compound formed by nitrogen, $NH_2-NH-NH_2$, is not. Compounds occur with long chains of carbon atoms—for example, there are chains with about 20 carbon atoms in the naturally occurring fats—as well as with branched chains and rings of atoms; *e.g.*,

2-methylbutane   cyclohexane   benzene

GENERAL APPROACH TO SYNTHESIS

There is, then, an essentially limitless range of compounds that are capable of being synthesized. In practice, the synthesis of a preselected compound is made possible by particular chemical groupings undergoing transformations that, while they are dependent upon the conditions applied to the compound, are largely independent of the structure of the remaining part of the molecule. Thus, the combination of a knowledge of the structure of the compound to be synthesized and the general types of transformation that compounds undergo enables a synthesis to be planned. The general approach, cut to its barest essentials, is to examine the structure of the desired end product—for example, *Z*—and to deduce the structure of some (slightly simpler) compound—for example, *Y*—that should be capable of transformation into *Z* by a reaction of known type. A possible precursor of *Y* is sought in similar manner, and in this way the chain of compounds is extended until a compound, *A*, is reached that is available for the work; the necessary transformations, beginning with *A* and ending with *Z*, are then carried out. Most individual steps in the sequence result in a change in only one bond; some result in changes in two bonds at a time, but it is rare for more extensive changes to occur.

Evaluation of a synthetic method. Three factors must be borne in mind when evaluating a particular synthetic plan. The first is cost, of far greater importance in industrial, large-scale synthesis than in laboratory work in which a particular synthesis may be carried out only once, as in the total synthesis of a naturally occurring compound, and which in any case is likely to be on a relatively small scale.

Second, the yield in each step must be considered. A step in a synthesis may be theoretically possible but in practice almost impossible to achieve. For example, a proportion of the reactant may be converted into a different product by an alternative process that competes with the desired one, some of the product may undergo a subsequent reaction, or some of the product may be lost in the separation processes required for its isolation in a pure state. The yield is usually defined, on a percentage basis, as the number of molecules of product obtained when 100 could in principle have been formed. A yield of about 80 percent or more is generally considered good,

Composition of the nuclei

Organic compounds

Importance of yield

but some transformations can prove so difficult to achieve that even a yield of 10 or 20 percent may have to be accepted.

Naturally, the yield of a process affects the cost of the product, because the shortfall from a 100 percent yield represents wasted material. In addition, yield can be of the utmost importance in determining whether or not a synthesis is a practicable possibility, because the overall yield of a synthesis is the product of the yields of the individual steps. If these intermediate yields are mostly low, the ultimate product may not be obtainable in the necessary amount from the available starting material.

Finally, consideration must be given to the rate at which each step in the planned sequence occurs. In many instances, a desired reaction is possible in principle but in practice takes place so slowly as to be ineffective. It is then necessary to investigate whether the rate can be increased to a practicable level by altering the conditions of the reaction—for example, by raising the temperature or by adding an extra species that increases the rate without altering the nature of the reaction.

The factors that have been briefly mentioned above as important in determining the course of a synthesis will now be considered in detail.

Availability of starting materials. All syntheses must be planned so as to start with available materials. A few elements occur naturally and require only a simple separation process for their isolation; examples are oxygen and nitrogen in the atmosphere and the metals gold and silver. Most metals occur, however, as minerals, in combined form, and an appropriate chemical extraction process must be applied if the element itself is required.

Sources of starting materials

The main source of organic compounds is now petroleum, which has superseded coal. Petroleum consists mainly of straight-chain alkanes (hydrocarbons of general formula C_nH_{2n+2}, such as methane, CH_4, ethane, CH_3CH_3, propane, $CH_3CH_2CH_3$, etc.) with up to about 125 carbon atoms in the chain, together with smaller quantities of cyclic alkanes and aromatic hydrocarbons such as benzene; the proportions vary from one oil field to another. The mixture is separated by fractional distillation, based on the fact that the compounds in the mixture have different boiling points. From the resulting compounds, others are formed by chemical processes; for example, the compounds containing 16–20 carbon atoms are passed through a catalyst, a fine powder made of silica and aluminum oxide, and heated at 450°–500° C (850°–950° F), resulting in the formation of smaller compounds including olefins (compounds containing the unit $\rangle C = C \langle$) such as ethylene, a process called catalytic cracking. From such processes a large number of compounds is available on an industrial scale, at prices that range upward from a few cents per pound.

Planning the synthesis. *Possible synthetic routes.* As has been noted, the usual approach is to work backward in a stepwise fashion until an available starting material is reached.

If, for example, the compound sought, again labelled Z, is an olefin, a possible precursor is an alcohol because it is known that olefins can be obtained (among other ways) from alcohols by removal of water (dehydration). One route to an alcohol is by reaction of one of a group of compounds called Grignard reagents with a compound containing the carbonyl group $\rangle C = O$; an appropriate combination in this case would be the compounds U + V, the Grignard reagent U being available from the compound T. As the materials T and V are available in most laboratories, one possible scheme for synthesizing Z is now complete:

$$C_6H_5-Br + Mg \longrightarrow C_6H_5-Mg-Br$$
$$\quad\quad T \quad\quad\quad\quad\quad\quad U$$

$$C_6H_5-Mg-Br \;+\; CH_3-\underset{\underset{O}{\|}}{C}-CH_3 \;\longrightarrow\; C_6H_5-\underset{\underset{CH_3}{|}}{\overset{\overset{CH_3}{|}}{C}}-O-Mg-Br$$
$$\quad\quad U \quad\quad\quad\quad V \quad\quad\quad\quad\quad\quad\quad\quad W$$

$$C_6H_5-\underset{\underset{CH_3}{|}}{\overset{\overset{CH_3}{|}}{C}}-O-Mg-Br + H_2O \longrightarrow C_6H_5-\underset{\underset{CH_3}{|}}{\overset{\overset{CH_3}{|}}{C}}-OH + MgBrOH$$
$$\quad\quad W \quad\quad\quad\quad\quad\quad\quad\quad\quad\quad\quad Y$$

$$C_6H_5-\underset{\underset{CH_3}{|}}{\overset{\overset{CH_3}{|}}{C}}-OH \longrightarrow C_6H_5-\underset{\underset{CH_2}{\|}}{C}-CH_3 + H_2O.$$
$$\quad\quad Y \quad\quad\quad\quad\quad\quad\quad Z$$

Other possibilities would certainly be considered. First, there is an alternative alcohol, S, from which the product could be derived; working backward from S, by way of the appropriate Grignard reagent, gives a possible route from P. P is unlikely to be available in the laboratory, however; if it is not, it requires synthesis, for example, from O. At this stage it is realized that the planned synthesis is longer than that from T and V, and, unless some specific advantage can be seen—for example, much better yields, which are unlikely in this case—it is discarded.

$$C_6H_5-CH_2-CH_3 + Br_2 \longrightarrow C_6H_5-CHBr-CH_3 + HBr$$
$$\quad\quad O \quad\quad\quad\quad\quad\quad\quad\quad\quad P$$

$$C_6H_5-CHBr-CH_3 + Mg \longrightarrow C_6H_5-\underset{\underset{Mg-Br}{|}}{CH}-CH_3$$
$$\quad\quad P \quad\quad\quad\quad\quad\quad\quad\quad\quad Q$$

$$C_6H_5-\underset{\underset{Mg-Br}{|}}{CH}-CH_3 + CH_2=O \longrightarrow C_6H_5-\underset{\underset{CH_2-O-Mg-Br}{|}}{CH}-CH_3$$
$$\quad\quad Q \quad\quad\quad\quad\quad\quad\quad\quad\quad R$$

$$C_6H_5-\underset{\underset{CH_2-O-Mg-Br}{|}}{CH}-CH_3 + H_2O \longrightarrow C_6H_5-\underset{\underset{CH_2-OH}{|}}{CH}-CH_3 + MgBrOH$$
$$\quad\quad R \quad\quad\quad\quad\quad\quad\quad\quad\quad S$$

$$C_6H_5-\underset{\underset{CH_2-OH}{|}}{CH}-CH_3 \longrightarrow C_6H_5-\underset{\underset{CH_2}{\|}}{C}-CH_3 + H_2O$$
$$\quad\quad S \quad\quad\quad\quad\quad\quad\quad\quad Z$$

Second, a precursor to Z other than the alcohols Y and S would be considered. For example, a possibility is N. The most obvious route to N, however, is from the alcohol Y, so that this method would simply involve an extra, unnecessary step compared with the route involving the conversion of Y into Z directly.

$$C_6H_5-\underset{\underset{Br}{|}}{\overset{\overset{CH_3}{|}}{C}}-CH_3 + NaOH \longrightarrow C_6H_5-\underset{\underset{CH_2}{\|}}{C}-CH_3 + NaBr + H_2O$$
$$\quad\quad N \quad\quad\quad\quad\quad\quad\quad\quad\quad Z$$

Evaluation of alternatives. Once a scheme with the minimum number of transformations in it has been selected, attention must be given to three other questions for each of the individual steps.

The first of these is whether the step will succeed as planned in this particular case. For example, reaction with the Grignard reagent was chosen because it is known that normally a Grignard reagent reacts with a compound containing the carbonyl group to give an alcohol. Some exceptions to this are also known, however; if, for example, the carbon atom in the carbonyl group is attached to two very bulky groups, the Grignard reagent can be prevented from reaction. Therefore, an examination must be made of any grounds for suspecting that the reaction might fail.

The second question is whether any unwanted transformation will occur at the same time. It frequently happens that there are two or more positions in a compound with which a particular agent can react. In such cases, unless that position at which reaction is desired is much more reactive than the others, it is necessary to modify the other positions to prevent them from reacting. This technique, called protection, is described in more detail later.

The third question is whether the operations required are practicable in the laboratory. For example, some reactions require very high pressures, and the necessary equipment is not widely available; others involve hazards that can be adequately dealt with only in highly specialized laboratories, as in the case of radioactive materials.

The problems in planning a synthesis increase rapidly with the degree of complexity of the target molecule for two reasons: first, the number of possible combinations of steps that must be considered in reaching a decision as to the best route quickly multiplies; for example, if there were two ways in which the final step could be effected, two for the preceding step, and so on, then the number of possibilities to consider is 32 for a five-step synthesis, over 1,000 for a ten-step synthesis, and so on. Second, as the molecule becomes more complex, the possibility of finding a reagent that will effect a desired transformation without bringing about unwanted processes is reduced. Even the most thoughtfully conceived scheme can founder because there was no hint from any previous observation that a particular step would fail as a result of a combination of factors specific to the target molecule in question and never previously encountered. It can be readily appreciated that some of the more complex compounds that have been synthesized—for example, the steroid cholesterol, the alkaloid strychnine, and the plant material chlorophyll—have each taken many man-years of highly skilled effort for their achievement. The failure of a step in a synthesis, perhaps formation of a product different from the one intended, can sometimes be turned to advantage in revealing a new aspect of reaction mechanism that can be applied in later syntheses.

The protection of reactive positions. A plan to effect reaction at a particular position in a compound with a specific reagent can be thwarted if in the molecule there is another position or group that preferentially reacts with that reagent. In such cases it is sometimes possible to block this more reactive position temporarily, while the planned reaction is carried out. The technique is to introduce another reagent that converts the more reactive grouping into a derivative that is inert to the desired reagent; the latter can then be introduced so as to react at the intended position, and finally a third reaction is used to reconvert the blocked position to its original form.

Factors affecting reaction rate. Some reactions take place instantaneously at room temperature simply on mixing the reagents. This is especially true of reactions between inorganic salts; for example, when an aqueous solution of silver nitrate is mixed with one of sodium chloride, silver chloride immediately precipitates from the solution. The underlying reason for this rapidity is that these compounds both contain ions that move freely in solution and collide frequently with each other; collision between a silver ion and a chloride ion can result in the two particles staying together and gradually coagulating with other such pairs as a precipitate, because silver chloride is insoluble in water.

Reactions of covalent compounds In contrast, the reactions of covalently bonded compounds usually occur slowly at room temperature. The reason is that one or more of these bonds generally has to be broken, and energy is required for that process; the energy is normally supplied in the form of heat but in some circumstances can be supplied as visible or ultraviolet light. The reaction of iodomethane, CH_3I, with sodium hydroxide, $NaOH$, in solution, to give methanol, CH_3OH, and sodium iodide, NaI, is exemplary. Sodium hydroxide is an ionic compound containing Na^+ and OH^- ions, and its reaction with iodomethane consists of the formation of a covalent bond between the oxygen atom of OH^- and the carbon atom of CH_3I while at the same time the C–I bond breaks, the two electrons in the bond remaining with the iodine atom, which consequently becomes an iodide ion. The first requirement for reaction to

occur is a collision between the OH^- ion and CH_3I, but it is also necessary that the molecules possess enough kinetic energy on collision in order to supply the amount necessary for bond breaking. At room temperature only a small proportion possess the required amount of energy, but as the temperature is raised the average amount of kinetic energy of the particles increases and, with it, the proportion of molecules that possess enough energy for reaction. The critical amount of energy—*i.e.*, the activation energy—varies from reaction to reaction, and so does the dependence of the rate on temperature, but, as a rough guide, for many reactions the rate doubles for each 10° C (18° F) rise in temperature.

The physical state of the reactants also has to be considered. Two solids do not react at a significant rate because when they are put in contact the rate at which the molecules diffuse from one into the other and thereby collide with each other is negligible. In both gases and liquids, however, collisions occur millions or billions of times a second; consequently, a solid reactant is usually brought into the liquid state by heating, or, if its melting point is undesirably high, it is dissolved in a solvent. A commonly employed method is to dissolve the reactants in a solvent, such as water or benzene, and then to heat the solution at its boiling point.

Reactions in liquids

Reactions in the gas phase, which are mostly of industrial concern, can be carried out in temperature-controlled furnaces. For example, in the Haber process for the manufacture of ammonia, a mixture of nitrogen and hydrogen is heated at a pressure of 300 atmospheres and a temperature of about 500° C (950° F).

Catalysis. Many reactions occur too slowly even at elevated temperatures to be practicable procedures, but their rates can sometimes be enormously increased by the addition of a catalyst (defined broadly as a material that speeds a reaction but is unchanged at the end of it).

Catalysts can be divided into two categories—heterogeneous and homogeneous; the former group are solids suspended in a solution of the reactants or over which gaseous reactants are passed, and the latter are materials that are soluble in the reaction medium.

A simplified interpretation of the ability of a heterogeneous catalyst, usually a metal, to increase the rate of a reaction is that molecules of each reactant become adsorbed on its surface in close proximity, and their internal bonds become weakened somewhat so that reaction is facilitated. Homogeneous catalysts, on the other hand, almost always take part chemically in the reactions they catalyze but are regenerated at the end of the process. Metallic compounds have proved valuable as catalysts for organic reactions, including those of industrial importance. The key to success with these catalysts lies in the transient formation of an intermediate compound.

Activation. Closely akin to catalysis is the activation of a compound by a slight modification of one of its groups.

An activating influence of a different type occurs in reactions of inorganic complexes of platinum, and it is useful to consider this behaviour in detail. Platinum exists in salts as the ion Pt^{2+}, usually bonded to four molecules or ions located at the corners of a hypothetical square of which platinum is the centre:

$$\begin{array}{ccc} A & & B \\ & \diagdown Pt \diagup & \\ D & & C \end{array}$$

The ease with which a particular group, A, for example, is replaced by another group is much more strongly dependent upon the nature of the group opposite (*trans*) to it, C, than on those adjacent to it, B and D. This *trans* effect can be exploited in synthesis, as, for example, in the preparation of the two stereoisomers of the compound $PtCl_2(NH_3)_2$:

$$\begin{array}{cccccc} Cl & & NH_3 & & Cl & & NH_3 \\ & \diagdown Pt \diagup & & & & \diagdown Pt \diagup & \\ Cl & & NH_3 & & H_3N & & Cl \end{array}$$

Here, use is made of the fact that a chloride ion, Cl^-, exerts a greater *trans* effect than does ammonia, NH_3; that is, the group *trans* to chloride is more readily replaced than is that opposite ammonia. Consequently, when the complex ion $PtCl_4^{2-}$ is treated with twice its amount of ammonia, the second molecule of ammonia preferentially occupies a position adjacent to the first, giving the *cis* stereoisomer,

$$\begin{bmatrix} Cl & Cl \\ & Pt \\ Cl & Cl \end{bmatrix}^{2-} \xrightarrow{NH_3} \begin{bmatrix} Cl & Cl \\ & Pt \\ Cl & NH_3 \end{bmatrix}^{-} \xrightarrow{NH_3} \begin{bmatrix} Cl & NH_3 \\ & Pt \\ Cl & NH_3 \end{bmatrix} ;$$

but reaction of the complex $Pt(NH_3)_4^{2+}$ with chloride ion preferentially gives the *trans* stereoisomer,

$$\begin{bmatrix} H_3N & NH_3 \\ & Pt \\ H_3N & NH_3 \end{bmatrix}^{2+} \xrightarrow{Cl^-} \begin{bmatrix} H_3N & NH_3 \\ & Pt \\ H_3N & Cl \end{bmatrix}^{+} \xrightarrow{Cl^-} \begin{bmatrix} Cl & NH_3 \\ & Pt \\ H_3N & Cl \end{bmatrix} .$$

Isolation and purification of products. The product of a synthesis is normally contaminated with reagents used in the synthesis, by-products, and possibly some unchanged starting material; these contaminants must be removed in order for a pure sample to be obtained. In a multistep synthesis, it is normally desirable to purify the product from each step before proceeding to the next. Various techniques for isolation and purification are available.

If the product is soluble in a liquid such as ether, and the contaminants are not but are soluble in water (with which ether is essentially immiscible), the product can be obtained by partition. In this procedure the mixture is put in contact with the two solvents, and the lower (aqueous) layer is run out through a tap at the bottom of the separating vessel; the remaining ether solution of the product is warmed to boil off the ether. This process separates most organic materials (usually soluble in ether) from inorganic salts (most are soluble in water); any remaining organic impurities must be removed by other methods.

Liquids often can be purified by distillation. If the impurities have boiling points markedly different from that of the product, simple distillation suffices; but if the boiling point differences are less than about 80° C, fractional distillation is necessary. In this process the vapour from the boiling mixture passes up through a vertical column packed with glass beads or the like and is condensed when it emerges. The most volatile component emerges first; the remaining components follow in the order of increasing boiling points.

Solids usually can be purified by recrystallization, exploiting the fact that most of them become increasingly soluble in a given solvent as the temperature is raised. The mixture is heated in a suitable solvent, filtered to remove contaminants that are insoluble in that solvent, and allowed to cool. After the required material has crystallized, it is filtered from the solution, leaving the more soluble contaminants in the solution.

Purification also can be effected by chromatography. In one form of this technique, suitable for solids and liquids, the mixture is dissolved in a solvent, and the solution is poured onto the top of a vertical column of a powdered solid such as aluminum oxide held in a glass tube. Each component of the mixture has a particular tendency to be held to (adsorbed upon) the surface of the solid and a particular solubility in the solvent. The stronger the adsorption, the more slowly the component passes through the column, and the greater the solubility, the more rapidly it passes, so that different components emerge at the bottom of the column after different intervals. In a second form of chromatography—gas chromatography—suitable for gases and volatile liquids and solids, the mixture is vaporized before being carried through the column by a stream of gas. The column is heated to prevent condensation, and each component emerges as a gas from the end of the column after a characteristic time interval.

RECENT DEVELOPMENTS IN SYNTHETIC METHODS

The art of chemical synthesis is a constantly evolving one in which new approaches and techniques are developed to meet new challenges. There are two recent developments of a novel kind that are likely to become of increasing importance.

First, it has been shown that synthetic schemes can be efficiently planned with the aid of a computer. The input consists of the various methods for transforming particular types of grouping into others, together with the known information as to the suitability of each process in particular structural situations. For any particular target molecule, the computer can then select various synthetic schemes and can choose between these on the basis of such factors as ease of handling, likely yields, or other considerations.

Second, the practicability of the automation of synthesis has been proved for the case of polypeptides. Briefly, polypeptides and proteins are polymers (*q.v.*) that occur in living systems, and they are best synthesized from amino acids, species that contain both carboxylic acid groups and amino groups. In the laboratory, however, problems arise. First, amino acids do not react together readily; it is necessary to activate the carboxylic acid group of one molecule by converting it into some suitable function that will react readily with the amino group of the second molecule. Second, the activated group is approximately as likely to react with the amino group of another molecule of the same type as with that of a molecule of the second amino acid. To obviate this problem, the amino group of the first molecule is first protected by the application of a suitable reagent. The sequence of operations, then, is to protect one amino acid at its amino end, activate it at its carboxylic acid end, and treat it with the second amino acid; the protecting group is then removed, and a third amino acid, likewise protected at its amino end and activated at its carboxylic end, is introduced; the synthesis continues with repetition of this cycle. The outstanding problem has been that, after each chemical operation, it has been necessary to purify the intermediate product so as to prepare it for the next operation, and this has not only been considerably time-consuming but has also resulted in the loss of material at each step; since dozens or even hundreds of steps are needed, the procedure has proved impracticable for very large molecules. The advance, simple in concept and remarkably effective in practice, has been to attach the first amino acid in the sequence, by means of a reaction generating a covalent bond, to an insoluble solid. The second amino acid, duly protected and activated, is introduced, and, after reaction, soluble reagents and by-products are simply removed by washing the solid, the protecting group is removed by chemical reaction and washing, and the next amino acid is introduced. No purifications other than washing are necessary until the final polypeptide, having been removed from the solid by chemical reaction, is purified. The losses normally sustained during conventional purification methods are thereby avoided, so that yields are high, and each of the individual steps can be carried out in quick succession.

Moreover, apparatus can be designed so that the fairly small number of reagents needed, including each amino acid in its protected and activated form, can be automatically delivered into the reaction vessel at the appropriate time, according to a predetermined program based on the particular polypeptide required.

For the isolation, purification, and identification of products, see CHEMICAL SEPARATIONS AND PURIFICATIONS; CHEMICAL ANALYSIS; SPECTROSCOPY, PRINCIPLES OF; and MOLECULAR STRUCTURE.

BIBLIOGRAPHY. J.B. HENDRICKSON, D.J. CRAM, and G.S. HAMMOND, *Organic Chemistry*, 3rd ed. (1970), ch. 23, "Organic Synthesis," deals with the strategy underlying synthesis; R.B. WOODWARD, "Synthesis," in *Perspectives in Organic Chemistry*, ed. by A.R. TODD (1956), illustrates the diversity of complex molecules that occur naturally and some general considerations pertaining to their synthesis; E.J. COREY, "General Methods for the Construction of Complex Molecules," *Pure*

Automated synthesis

Appl. Chem., 14:19–37 (1967), deals with the logic of synthesis and with methods of formulating practicable synthetic plans; R.B. MERRIFIELD, "Solid-Phase Peptide Syntheses," *Endeavour*, 24:3–7 (1965), describes a recent development, referred to in the article; E.J. COREY, "Computer-Assisted Analysis of Complex Synthetic Problems," *Q. Rev. Chem. Soc.*, 25:455–482 (1971).

(R.O.C.N.)

Chemistry

As an intellectual discipline, chemistry has two primary thrusts: one, to determine and to elucidate the physical and chemical properties of substances, and the other, to develop and control chemical processes to attain specific goals. In this discussion, the word substance is restricted to either an element such as hydrogen gas or a compound such as water. According to this restricted use of the word, wood is not a substance but a complex array of many substances. Even a single fibre of wood is a complex system of many compounds. The number of substances possible is almost without limit. A few common substances are water (H_2O); octane (C_8H_{18}); ammonia (NH_3); sodium chloride ($NaCl$); nitrogen monoxide, or nitric oxide (NO); neon (Ne); and sucrose ($C_{12}H_{22}O_{11}$). The notation H_2O is the chemist's symbol (formula) for water: it denotes the smallest unit of water, the molecule, widely distributed in space as water vapour. The water that constitutes fog and clouds, including the cloud that may be observed above a teakettle, is made up of large—very large—numbers of molecules of water held together in small droplets. Hydrogen and oxygen are elements, and water is a compound. Each molecule of water is made up of two atoms of hydrogen and one atom of oxygen. The smallest unit of oxygen gas, the molecule, in the Earth's atmosphere is diatomic, O_2. H_2O and O_2 are molecular formulas. Under the high-energy conditions of the Sun's surface, oxygen is monoatomic, and its molecular formula is simply O. Some molecules, particularly those in biological systems and plastics, are very large and contain thousands of atoms.

The
chemical
equation

Chemical reactions, also called chemical transformations, entail the conversion of one or more substances into one or more different substances. The substances that react are called reactants, and the substances formed are called products. Hydrogen gas, H_2, reacts with oxygen gas, O_2, under appropriate conditions to produce water. This chemical reaction may be indicated by $H_2 + O_2 \rightarrow H_2O$, read as H-two reacts with O-two to form H-two-O. The term appropriate conditions implies that hydrogen gas and oxygen gas can exist together at some temperature and pressure without reacting but that under other circumstances, such as a higher temperature or in the presence of a catalyst, a reaction does occur. The most common way to carry out this reaction would be to use the hydrogen gas as a fuel in a burner and to ignite the gas with a match. The reaction of the hydrogen gas with the oxygen of the air continues as a very hot blue flame.

In a chemical reaction the atoms are regrouped to form different substances. Atoms are not destroyed and not converted into atoms of other elements in chemical reactions. The number of molecules of hydrogen and the number of molecules of oxygen that react must give an integral number of molecules of water. The smallest numbers of molecules that could meet this requirement of conservation of atoms are two molecules of hydrogen and one molecule of oxygen: $2H_2(g) + O_2(g) \rightarrow 2H_2O(l)$. This statement is the chemical equation for the reaction. It states very specifically what substances react and what substances are formed. It also states the minimum number of molecules of each substance that could take part in the reaction. It is an equality only in the bookkeeping sense of the number of atoms of each element present before the reaction and after the reaction. Energy is released during this particular reaction, usually as heat and light, and three molecules of reactants end up as two molecules of product. The letters (g) and (l) indicate that, under the conditions of the reaction, both reactants are gases and the product is a liquid.

The reactivity of hydrogen with oxygen is a chemical property of hydrogen and of oxygen. Oxygen gas and nitrogen gas do not react under atmospheric conditions. This lack of reactivity is a chemical property of both oxygen and nitrogen. Nitrogen gas and oxygen do react under the conditions of high temperature and pressure that exist in an automobile engine. The product formed is usually nitrogen monoxide, NO, but other oxides of nitrogen, such as nitrogen dioxide, NO_2, can be produced depending on the temperature, the pressure, and the relative amounts of nitrogen and oxygen present. Herein lies one of the major sources of pollution of the atmosphere.

Universality of
chemical
reactions

Anything that can be confined to a container and weighed is either a single substance or a collection of substances. Anything that can be touched, tasted, or smelled is made up of one or more substances. All biological responses, including the responses to touch, sound, light, smell, and taste, involve chemical change, usually a series of chemical changes. With the exceptions of nuclear reactions, the transport of substances from one place to another, and the conversion of one phase into another (such as the freezing of a liquid), all changes are chemical changes. Clearly chemistry occupies a central position in natural phenomena and in the processes that are the basis of a technological society.

GENERAL CONSIDERATIONS

The subdivisions of chemistry. The field of chemistry encompasses the study of an uncounted and theoretically almost unlimited number of compounds. By the early 1970s there must have been more than 1,000,000 individuals working on chemical problems in independent, academic, industrial, and government laboratories throughout the world for a myriad of personal, social, economic, and political reasons. In systematizing chemical knowledge and activities by grouping together related compounds, related systems, related methods, and related goals, a number of subdivisions of chemistry have developed. These subdivisions provide the basis of organization of academic curricula and literature and of bringing together scientists who share common interests.

During the first half of the 20th century, undergraduate curricula were almost exclusively organized into courses in inorganic, analytical, organic, and physical chemistry and biochemistry, which were usually studied in that order. This organization of subject material is still apparent in many college catalogs, but it is difficult to defend and, accordingly, many attempts are being made to organize academic programs along other lines.

Organic and inorganic chemistry. Organic chemistry and inorganic chemistry are subdivisions based upon the elements present in the compounds. Organic chemistry is the chemistry of carbon compounds, which, of course, also contain elements other than carbon, such as hydrogen, oxygen, sulfur, nitrogen, phosphorus, and chlorine. Inorganic chemistry encompasses all substances that are not organic. The separation of the study of carbon compounds from the rest of chemistry is defensible on the basis of the sheer numbers of carbon compounds that are of great interest and that not only have been but are still being intensively studied. The structure of the carbon atom is unique among atoms and makes possible this great array of compounds, which are stable under atmospheric conditions on Earth but are also sufficiently reactive to make possible a great variety of chemical change.

Physical chemistry. Physical chemistry is a method of approach to any chemical system, either a single substance or a mixture of substances, without regard to whether the substances are organic or inorganic or both. Physical chemistry includes the study of all properties that can be measured, the development of experimental methods and instruments to make the measurements, the rationalization of measurements that have been made, the development of theories (particularly theories that can be expressed mathematically), and the prediction of the values of properties that can be checked by experimental measurements.

Analytical chemistry. Analytical chemistry is the identification of the substances present in a sample and the determination of the quantity of one or more substances in a sample. In principle, the simplest approach would be to isolate a compound of known composition and weigh it. In practice, this approach is seldom used because the problem associated with attaining an essentially complete separation may lead to an extremely complicated or at least time-consuming undertaking. Modern analytical methods tend to be based on the use of instruments to measure a physical property of the ion or molecule. In many cases such measurements can be made without carrying out a separation of that substance from the sample. The science of analytical chemistry is concerned with the development of methods and of instruments and with the testing of the reliability of these methods for various-sized samples under a variety of conditions, including the presence of other substances that might interfere. Recent interest in pollution has led to marked increases in the development of methods suitable for the detection and measurements of trace amounts of substances not only in air, water, and foods but also in biological systems.

New importance of analytical chemistry

Biochemistry. Biochemistry is the chemistry of biological systems. Biochemical studies range all the way from the identification of compounds present at particular biological sites to very comprehensive investigations of the detailed mechanism by which compounds are transformed from one into another, with particular attention to the energy changes associated with each of these transformations. Recent advances in biochemistry and even greater advances expected in the future are the consequence of the present high levels of instrumentation and of general knowledge of chemical transformation.

The study of a given substance may be an appropriate study for an organic chemist, an inorganic chemist, a physical chemist, an analytical chemist, and a biochemist. Hemoglobin has been and still is such a substance. The organic chemist is an expert on the properties of groups of atoms such as occur in organic molecules; the inorganic chemist, on the properties of the various charge states of iron in the hemoglobin; the physical chemist, on the determination of structures and elucidating the nature of the bonding; the analytical chemist, on methods of blood analysis; and the biochemist has the overall knowledge of the role of the hemoglobin in biological transformations.

Many attempts have been and are being made to organize curricula along other lines. One of the newer approaches is to organize chemistry around structure, dynamics, and synthesis.

Classification of subjects. *Chemical Abstracts*, a publication of the American Chemical Society (ACS), Washington, D.C., very briefly summarizes new books, new patents, and the articles of chemical and chemical engineering interest in over 1,000 journals and other periodicals. These abstracts required 137,183 pages exclusive of indexes in 1970; the total publication for that one year including the annual indexes required 50 inches of linear shelf space. As of July 1971, *Chemical Abstracts* grouped its coverage into 80 fields, which in turn were grouped under five main sections:

Chemical Abstracts' organization of the field

Biochemistry. In the biochemistry section are the following topics: history, education, and documentation; general biochemistry; enzymes; hormones and related substances; radiation biochemistry; biochemical methods; plant biochemistry; microbial biochemistry; non-mammalian biochemistry; animal nutrition; mammalian biochemistry; mammalian pathological biochemistry; immunochemistry; toxicology; pharmacodynamics; fermentations; foods; plant-growth regulators; pesticides; fertilizers, soils, and plant nutrition.

Organic chemistry. Covered under organic chemistry are the following: general organic chemistry; physical-organic chemistry; aliphatic compounds; alicyclic compounds; noncondensed aromatic compounds; condensed aromatic compounds; heterocyclic compounds (one hetero atom); heterocyclic compounds (more than one hetero atom); organometallic and organometalloidal compounds; terpenoids; alkaloids; steroids; carbohydrates; synthesis of amino acids, peptides, and proteins.

Macromolecular chemistry. The macromolecular section includes synthetic high polymers; plastics manufacture and processing; plastics fabrication and uses; elastomers, including natural rubber; textiles; dyes, fluorescent whitening agents, and photosensitizers; leather and related materials; coatings, inks, and related products; cellulose, lignin, paper, and other wood products; industrial carbohydrates; fats and waxes; surface-active agents and detergents.

Applied chemistry and chemical engineering. The applied chemistry and chemical engineering section covers the following subjects: apparatus and plant equipment; unit operations and processes; industrial inorganic chemicals; propellants and explosives; petroleum, petroleum derivatives and related products; coal and coal derivatives; mineralogical and geological chemistry; extractive metallurgy; ferrous metals and alloys; nonferrous metals and alloys; ceramics; cement and concrete products; air pollution and industrial hygiene; sewage and wastes; water; essential oils and cosmetics; pharmaceuticals; pharmaceutical analysis.

Physical and analytical chemistry. The last of the five main categories is physical and analytical chemistry, which abstracts studies of general physical chemistry; surface chemistry and colloids; catalysis and reaction kinetics; phase equilibria, chemical equilibria, and solutions; thermodynamics, thermochemistry, and thermal properties; crystallization and crystal structure; electric phenomena; magnetic phenomena; spectra by absorption, emission, reflection or magnetic resonance, and other optical properties; radiation chemistry, photochemistry and photographic processes; nuclear phenomena; nuclear technology; electrochemistry; inorganic chemicals and reactions; inorganic analytical chemistry; organic analytical chemistry.

Undoubtedly the classification system reflects the evolutionary process of *Chemical Abstracts* itself and the number of publications that have appeared on particular topics. Even so, it is interesting to note the degree to which the subdivisions discussed under academic curricula have been disproportionated. For example, inorganic chemistry appears only twice in the titles of the 80 sections.

Classification within the profession. The members of the American Chemical Society have organized 26 divisions within the society to sponsor programs at national meetings and activities appropriate to professional groups. Here again the titles reflect the evolutionary process, but they also reflect the areas of interest that have brought chemists together, as can be seen in the alphabetical list of divisions:

American Chemical Society divisions

Agricultural and food chemistry; analytical chemistry; biological chemistry; carbohydrate chemistry; cellulose, wood, and fibre chemistry; chemical education; chemical literature; chemical marketing and economics; colloid and surface chemistry; fertilizer and soil chemistry; fluorine chemistry; fuel chemistry; the history of chemistry; industrial and engineering chemistry; inorganic chemistry; medicinal chemistry; microbial chemistry and technology; nuclear chemistry and technology; organic chemistry; organic coatings and plastic chemistry; pesticide chemistry; petroleum chemistry; physical chemistry; polymer chemistry; rubber chemistry; water, air, and waste chemistry.

In this article the discussion of chemistry is organized along still another pattern: the physical properties and structure of pure substances, chemical transformations, and the chemistry of complex systems.

Impact of chemistry on society. Advances in chemistry extend comprehension of the nature of physical and biological systems and the processes by which they change. In so doing, they enhance the dignity of humanity as intellectual beings. These same advances provide much of the knowledge on which technological societies are based, and that knowledge has been applied to extend the life-span and to change the manner in which mankind lives. Such knowledge also enables societies to make choices on the development of technologies and the controls to be placed upon them. With the advances in scientific knowledge, the number of options open to a society increases, and the choices it makes increasingly reflect the value judgments of that society.

The most obvious distinction between the developed and the developing nations is the level of technology. Scientific and technological knowledge is a necessary condition for technological development. The priorities set by each society, as well as the economic limitations and political stability of that society, also influence the rate and direction of development.

The IUPAC. The International Union of Pure and Applied Chemistry (IUPAC) is a voluntary association of organizations each representing the chemists of one of 44 nations. IUPAC promotes continuing cooperation among chemists of member nations, organizes a large variety of international conferences, and establishes international standards for physical constants, units, and nomenclature.

The education of a chemist. The activities of chemists are extremely varied, and the education of an individual chemist can be viewed only as an enabling process. The broader and the more intense that an individual's education, both formal and informal, is, the greater will be the number of professional options open. Since breadth and depth are in a sense incompatible, the individual must choose the manner in which to structure an education that starts in the formal educational system and extends throughout the professional years. The responsibilities of a chemist to make social, economic, and political judgments both as an individual and as a part of some organization indicate the essential place of the humanities and the social sciences in the education of the chemist. At the secondary school level the ideal program for most students in the United States is four years of mathematics and one year of biology, one year of physics, and one year of chemistry (or the equivalent of these three years of science in an integrated program), along with his own and foreign languages, history, and social sciences.

Many scientific companies employ promising high school graduates and give them on-the-job training in specific technical operations that are essential to the activities of that company. An increasing number of academic institutions are developing two-year college programs for chemical technicians. Chemical technicians play an important part in many industries, and merit is recognized. There are, however, limitations on the responsibilities a technician can accept without broader training in the theoretical basis of the science.

The more usual pattern is for a student to take a degree in chemical engineering in a four- or five-year college program or a degree in chemistry in a four-year college before seeking employment. For a number of years, students have been encouraged, even required, to take prescribed and rather specialized programs in mathematics, physics, and chemistry at the undergraduate level. The present trend is toward greater flexibility and the encouragement of broader programs, not only in the sciences but also in the humanities and the social sciences. There is also a growing trend to encourage students to make a broad chemistry major the base for professions such as law, politics, journalism, and business administration.

Advanced degrees in chemistry

The doctor of philosophy degree and the doctor of science degree are largely research degrees and are the standard routes to a career as a research chemist. In addition to the traditional fields of biochemistry and analytical, inorganic, organic, and physical chemistry, degrees in fields such as pharmacology and biophysics may be essentially degrees in chemistry. German is the language most frequently required for advanced study. Strength in mathematics and physics is essential for advanced work in physical chemistry and is an asset in many others. An increasing number of specialties in the future are expected to be in chemical systems such as the oceans and the cell rather than in the traditional fields.

THE METHODS OF CHEMISTRY

As with all relatively mature sciences there are two approaches: one, intellectual or theoretical, the other, experimental. The theoretical approach frequently provides direction for experimental studies. Experimental results set the boundaries within which the theoretical approach develops concepts, hypotheses, theories, and models. The fashion changes in the use of the terms concept, hypothesis, theory, and model. The term model is the current vogue. The intellectual approach and the experimental approach are interdependent, and one is not fruitful for long without the other.

Theoretical approaches. A variety of theoretical approaches have been and are being used to correlate and rationalize the great masses of experimental results that have been and are being accumulated. Quantum mechanics starts with a simple model for the atom and through highly mathematical methods generates more and more detailed models for the atom and also more and more detailed models for molecules. Thermodynamics is an elegant mathematical structure that deals with transformation of directly observable quantities of matter—*i.e.*, on a strictly macroscopic scale—and that in no way depends on a model of the atom. The structure is based upon three postulates known as the laws of thermodynamics, which are accepted as true because they rationalize the observed facts and because there is no evidence to indicate they are not true. Statistical mechanics is again an elegant mathematical structure. It starts with the microscopic and on the basis of statistics predicts the properties of the macrosample.

Use of models. An old and very familiar example of the use of models is in the development of knowledge of gases. Experimental studies in the 17th and 18th centuries yielded results that could be summarized by stating that the product of the pressure and the volume is proportional to the absolute temperature. This relationship has been put in the form of the equation: $PV = kT$, in which P is the pressure, V the volume, T the absolute temperature, and k a proportionality constant that depends on the sample. Such a statement is a law, an exact statement of what has been observed experimentally to be true. To rationalize an empirical statement such as that law is intellectually challenging, and in response to the challenge the kinetic molecular theory of gases slowly developed. Along the way further experimental work was indicated and carried out. On the basis of those results Amedeo Avogadro, the Italian physicist, in 1811 postulated that equal volumes of gases under the same conditions of temperature and pressure contained the same number of molecules regardless of the identity of the molecules. This concept provoked further experimental work that led to a system of atomic weights and a more comprehensive gas law that applied to all gases regardless of the identity of the molecules. The kinetic molecular theory (model) proposed to rationalize this law specified simply that the molecules have no volume, have no forces between them, and move with an average kinetic energy of translation that is directly proportional to the absolute temperature. Precise measurements demonstrated deviations from this simple gas law, called the ideal gas law, and necessitated further modifications in the kinetic molecular theory that recognized not only the volume of the molecules but also the forces that exist between molecules.

Models are proposed with the expectation that they will be useful in directing experimental work. They are expected to undergo continuous modification. If the model holds up under continuous testing, this in no sense proves that the model coincides with reality but only that the model is consistent with the available experimental facts. There are many models in chemistry, but the models of most significance are those of the atom and the manner in which it bonds to form compounds.

Gas models

The development of computers has revolutionized many areas of research. They are, of course, a great convenience in processing large quantities of data, but the principal value of doing so has been to aid in investigating models and designing experiments. In making calculations based upon models, the chemist frequently needs several parameters such as bond angles, bond lengths, and reaction velocity constants that must have definite values but whose actual values are not known and cannot be directly determined experimentally. If an experimen-

Use of computers in investigating models

tally measurable quantity can be mathematically formulated in terms of these parameters and the computer properly instructed (programmed) within the limitations of that computer, the computer will carry out a great multiplicity of evaluations of the experimentally measurable quantity for a range of values for each parameter. In this manner, curves can be simulated for rather complex relations and checked against the actual experimental curve. A good fit gives creditability to a set of values for these parameters.

In a similar manner, experimental conditions that can be set arbitrarily may be treated as parameters to determine the particular combination of experimental conditions that should give the most significant results.

Atomic structure. Modern atomic theory considers the atom to consist of a nucleus and an atmosphere of electrons, also called a swarm of electrons. The nucleus is very compact, very dense, and positively charged. (For the purpose of this article, it will be adequate to consider the nucleus of an atom simply as an aggregate of protons and neutrons.) During a chemical reaction the composition of the nucleus remains unchanged but the distribution of electrons does change. The electronic atmosphere of the atom is a diffuse distribution of electrons, and in modern theories no effort is made to specify either the position or the motion of individual electrons within the atom. Instead, the electronic atmosphere is considered in terms of the most probable distribution of the moving, negatively charged electrons, or, in other words, in terms of the charge density at particular distances and directions from the nucleus. Chemical reactions are discussed in terms of changes in the electron distribution in atoms. In an isolated atom the distribution of electron charge is oriented with respect to the nucleus of that one atom. In the combination of two or more atoms, the distribution of electronic charge is determined by more than the one nucleus, and the resultant distributions of charge in relation to these nuclei are the chemical bonds that determine the properties of the new substance.

The unit charge most frequently used by the chemist is the charge of the electron, minus one, written -1. The charge on the proton is equal in magnitude and opposite in sign, plus one, or $+1$. The neutron is neutral. The atom has a net charge of zero: the number of electrons equals the number of protons. This number is called the atomic number and is the unique characteristic of all atoms of that element. The atomic number of carbon, for example, is 6, which means that all atoms of carbon have a total of six protons in their nuclei. The nuclei of carbon atoms also contain from six to eight neutrons. These different varieties of carbon are designated as ^{12}C (read C-twelve, often written carbon-12), ^{13}C (carbon-13), and ^{14}C (carbon-14), and as a group they are referred to as the three isotopes of carbon. The numbers 12, 13, and 14, called mass numbers of the isotopes, are equal to the sum of the neutrons and the protons in the nucleus.

Quantum mechanics. The quantum-mechanical approach to the atom treats matter as a wave phenomenon and is based on an equation known as the Schrödinger wave equation—a postulate that has been neither derived nor proved. The equation seems to be complex but is not so different from other wave relations and essentially equates total energy within the atom to the sum of the kinetic and potential energy arising from the relative motions and positions of its component particles. Meaningful solutions of the equation are obtained only under the condition that the total energy may not assume all arbitrary values but only a set of discrete values; in other words, the energy of the system can change only by definite amounts, called quanta. The solutions of this equation become very complex for atoms other than the very simplest because of the great multiplicity of interactions: between the nucleus and the electrons (attractive) and between the electrons themselves (repulsive). The hydrogen atom, with its one proton and one electron, is the simplest of atoms; thus an exact solution is comparatively easy. The models obtained for the simpler atoms are extrapo-

Schröding-er wave equation

lated in a very approximate manner to more complex atoms.

The solution of the Schrödinger equation predicts the existence of a series of energy states, called quantum levels, for the atom. This series is rather complex and is expressed by the physicist in terms of four sets of quantum numbers: the principal, the azimuthal (also called orbital), the magnetic, and the spin quantum numbers. The chemist, however, tends to express these relations in terms of the principal quantum numbers 1, 2, 3, etc., and a set of orbitals (regions of highest probability of finding electrons) associated with each of these principal quantum levels. This difference is purely one of notation. The characteristics of the orbitals and the restrictions on the number of orbitals associated with each principal quantum level are the consequence of the relation of the azimuthal and the magnetic quantum numbers to the principal quantum numbers. The orbitals corresponding to the first four values of the azimuthal quantum number are designated by the letters s, p, d, and f.

The solutions of the Schrödinger equation are not concerned with the motion of the electrons but instead give information about these energy levels and the probability of the electron being in a particular volume of space, or of the density of charge at particular points in space. As the principal quantum number increases, the charge distribution is further extended into space. The s orbital has a charge distribution that depends only on the distance from the nucleus. All principal quantum numbers have one s orbital. The p orbitals have a more specific orientation of charge distribution. For any one p orbital, the region of high charge distribution is oriented with respect to an axis passing through the nucleus, and it is frequently referred to as an hourglass distribution. This phrase correctly implies the orientation as far as an axis is concerned, but it incorrectly implies that the electrons are confined to a specific volume. For a given principal quantum number of 2 or higher, there may be a maximum of three p orbitals, p_x, p_y, and p_z, oriented at right angles to each other along the x-axis, the y-axis, and the z-axis, with the nucleus and the constricted portions of the "hourglasses" at the origin. The five d orbitals, which are associated with principal quantum numbers 3 or higher, have more elaborate charge distributions, which are also definitely oriented in space. Each orbital can accommodate a maximum of two electrons. Associated with each electron is a fourth quantum number, the spin quantum number, which can have only two values, $\frac{1}{2}$ and $-\frac{1}{2}$. If two electrons occupy the same orbital, they have different spin values and are said to be paired or to have antiparallel spins.

The magnificent order of the details of this quantum model of the atom is fascinating, and its power to rationalize experimental results is impressive. The distribution of electrons of six elements—helium, neon, argon, krypton, xenon, and radon—is of particular interest. These, called the noble gases, are the most unreactive elements, and their electron structures are of particular significance as points of reference in discussing the compounds formed by other elements (see PERIODIC LAW).

Valence bond approach. The most significant questions in chemistry concern the nature of the chemical bond and deal with, for example, why elements form compounds, why some elements form similar compounds while others form quite different types of compounds, and why molecules react with molecules to form other molecules. One approach to these questions is through the valence bond model. It starts with atomic orbitals, the spatial distribution of electrons within the atoms, and modifies these in such a way as to fill atomic orbitals by sharing electrons between two nuclei. For example, the chlorine atom, atomic number 17, is one electron short of having the three $3p$ orbitals filled. If the one electron in the $3p$ orbital of one atom joins in a cooperative venture with the one electron in a $3p$ orbital of a second atom, the two electrons are shared by both atoms and become identified with both of the partly filled p orbitals. The negative electron charge density between the two positive nuclei is considered to be the basis of holding

The covalent bond

the two nuclei together with a characteristic spacing between the nuclei. In more formal terms, the sharing of the electrons is discussed in terms of the overlap of atomic orbitals, and the distance separating the nuclei when attractive and repulsive forces balance is discussed as the bond length for the chlorine, Cl_2, molecule. Such a bond formed by the sharing of two electrons between two nuclei is known as a sigma (σ) bond. The molecule BrCl can also be described in a similar manner because bromine, atomic number 35, has again only one electron in a p orbital, in this case a p orbital of principal quantum number 4, denoted $4p$. There is, however, one significant difference: the chlorine and bromine atoms do not share the electron pair equally, and the two ends of the molecule have very slightly different charge distributions. The chlorine end of the molecule is slightly negative with respect to the bromine end of the molecule, and the chlorine–bromine covalent bond is said to be polar. The chlorine–chlorine covalent bond is nonpolar.

Bonding with hydrogen

Hydrogen, atomic number 1, enters into bonding in a similar manner, with the exception that the electron that is shared is a $1s$ electron. This electron is considered as pairing with the lone electron in one of the three $3p$ orbitals of chlorine to form a σ-bond in the molecule HCl. The chlorine atom is much more electronegative than the hydrogen, and the covalent bond is very definitely polar. In the water molecule, one hydrogen atom is considered to bond through an electron in one $2p$ orbital (such as p_x) of the oxygen atom, and the second hydrogen atom is considered to bond through an electron in another $2p$ orbital (such as p_y) of the oxygen atom. The third $2p$ orbital (p_z) of the oxygen already has a pair of electrons, referred to as an unshared electron pair. In each of the four molecules, each atom attains the electron configuration of a noble gas: hydrogen attains the helium structure, oxygen the neon structure, chlorine the argon structure, and bromine the krypton structure.

In the consideration of molecules that contain three or more atoms, spatial orientation of the atoms is of prime importance. Water, H_2O, was discussed in terms of the sharing of the $1s$ electron in each hydrogen atom with the one electron in a $2p$ orbital of the oxygen atom. Thus, two $2p$ orbitals (p_x and p_y) of the oxygen atom are involved. These two $2p$ orbitals are at right angles to each other, and this simple picture predicts that the three nuclei must have a fixed orientation in space and that the angle HOH would be 90°. It is comparatively unimportant that the value predicted does not correspond exactly to the experimental value of about 104°. This discrepancy simply indicates that the model has to be extended. This is done by modifying the atomic orbitals by a process known as hybridization, which is beyond the scope of this presentation.

Molecular orbital approach. A second quantum-mechanical approach to the nature of covalent bonding is called the molecular orbital approach; it goes back to the Schrödinger equation and is an attempt to obtain solutions for the much more complicated situation in which there are at least two nuclei and a larger number of electrons. This process again gives a set of energy levels and information concerning the charge densities throughout the molecule. This approach is usually stated in mathematical terms and is consequently less generally understood. It is successful in predicting energy levels that can be correlated with the experimentally observed visible and ultraviolet absorption spectra. Each molecular orbital can again (as in atomic orbitals) accommodate a maximum of two electrons. Some energy levels in the molecule correspond to more stable energy states than those in the separate atoms; such orbitals are referred to as bonding molecular orbitals. Other energy levels in the molecule are less stable than those in the separate atoms; these orbitals are referred to as antibonding molecular orbitals. In order to have a stable molecule, it is necessary that the number of electrons in bonding orbitals exceed the number of electrons in antibonding orbitals. This approach has been successful in rationalizing the stability of certain combinations of atoms and the instability of other combinations. It has been par-

ticularly successful in rationalizing the existence of molecules containing odd numbers of electrons, such as that of nitric oxide, NO, with a total of 15 electrons, and in rationalizing the magnetic properties of some substances such as liquid oxygen, O_2, which is very strongly attracted by a magnetic field (paramagnetic).

The ionic chemical bond

In compounds such as sodium chloride, NaCl, unequal sharing of electrons is carried to the extreme by a complete transfer of an electron. The sodium in the compound then has ten electrons and 11 protons, as compared with the 11 electrons and the 11 protons in the sodium atom, and consequently it has a net charge of $+1$ and is called the sodium ion, Na^+. The chlorine in the compound NaCl has 18 electrons and 17 protons, as compared with the 17 electrons and 17 protons in the chlorine atom, and consequently has a net charge of -1 and is called the chloride ion, Cl^-. The sodium ion is isoelectronic with (has the same electronic structure as) the neon atom, and the chloride ion is isoelectronic with the argon atom. The bonding in sodium chloride results from the attraction of opposite charges and is said to be ionic as contrasted to covalent bonding in molecules, and the compound is classified as an ionic compound.

Experimental approach. *Instrumentation.* Many separations and observations and all measurements depend upon instruments. Burettes, balances, calorimeters, barometers, potentiometers, Geiger counters, all have been available and extensively used for many years. During the 1950s and 1960s, routine testing, teaching, and research laboratories were revolutionized by the many new instruments that became readily available. For the most part these new tools made use of the rapid advances that had been made in solid-state physics and electronic engineering. With these instruments, operations can be carried out on smaller samples—and more quickly—and measurements can be made with higher precision and in greater variety. As a consequence, more comprehensive studies are made, more subtle problems are attacked, and more complicated systems are investigated.

Functions of instruments

Measuring instruments serve two functions. One is to measure known single substances simply to determine the properties of that substance. For example, the measurement of the absorption of light (electromagnetic wave radiation) gives both the frequency of the light absorbed and the degree to which the incident light is absorbed, usually expressed as absorbance (a defined quantity that relates the intensity of the light incident to the sample and the intensity of the light that emerges from the sample). The frequency can be interpreted in terms of the energy levels for the molecule and the types of transitions that occur in that compound. The absorbance can be interpreted in terms of the probability of the transition occurring. In this type of study the measurements are being used in the physical-chemical sense of pursuing the structure of the molecule and the nature of the chemical bond. The other use of such instruments is to carry out measurements to identify the substances present and to determine the quantity of those substances or, more frequently, to determine the concentration of solutions. For these cases the instrument is purely a convenient analytical tool.

Atomic weights and the mole. Carbon-12, or the ^{12}C isotope of carbon, is taken as the reference point in modern chemistry for the experimental determination of the masses of atoms of all elements and is therefore the basis of all quantitative relations in chemistry. This isotope of carbon has been assigned the mass of exactly 12 atomic mass units (amu). By the use of a mass spectrometer, the mass of any isotope of any element is compared with that of the mass of carbon-12 and assigned the appropriate mass in atomic mass units. For example, the atomic mass of the isotope sulfur-32, ^{32}S, is 31.97207 amu. (An atom of this isotope of sulfur weighs approximately eight-thirds (32/12) times as much as an atom of the isotope carbon-12.)

In the laboratory, where weighings are usually made in terms of grams, the chemist thinks in terms of masses that are numerically equal to the mass of the atom in atomic mass units but are expressed in terms of grams.

This quantity of carbon-12 is called one mole of carbon-12. Exactly 12 grams of carbon-12 must contain a certain number of atoms of carbon. That number has been given the name Avogadro's number. The concept of a number of this type, a fixed or constant number of units in one mole, is fundamental to all quantitative considerations in chemistry. Obviously, 31.97207 grams of sulfur-32 must contain the same number of atoms of sulfur-32 as exactly 12 grams of carbon-12 contains of carbon-12. The numerical value of Avogadro's number must be experimentally determined and is consequently subject to experimental error. The currently accepted value is 6.0225×10^{23}, although the experimental values obtained by some methods may deviate from this by as much as 1 percent. The magnitude of this number is so large that it is difficult to comprehend.

The chemist almost invariably works with natural mixtures of isotopes, and consequently the mass that is significant to the chemist is the mass of Avogadro's number of atoms of the element taking into consideration the normal abundance of the various isotopes. For carbon this mass is 12.01115 ± 0.00005 grams, with the uncertainty in the figure not arising from lack of exactness in laboratory measurements but from the variation in isotopic abundances between various samples.

The mole is the chemist's unit of quantity. A mole of hydrogen atoms contains Avogadro's number of atoms of hydrogen and weighs 1.00797 grams. A mole of diatomic hydrogen molecules contains Avogadro's number of H_2 molecules and weighs 2.01594 grams.

The equation for the reaction of hydrogen with oxygen, which was explained in terms of two molecules of hydrogen reacting with one molecule of oxygen, may equally well be read in terms of two moles of hydrogen reacting with one mole of oxygen to give two moles of water. Converted to weights, this statement becomes 4.03188 grams of hydrogen reacts with 31.9988 grams of oxygen to give 36.0307 grams of water. The ideal gas equation, previously stated as $PV = kT$, is usually stated in terms of the number of moles, n, of gas present: $PV = nRT$, in which R, the universal gas constant, is entirely independent of the identity of the gas.

The mass of a proton is approximately one atomic mass unit. The mass of a neutron is approximately one atomic mass unit. The mass of the electron is very small by comparison.

Separation of mixtures. Mixtures may be separated by the ancient and familiar processes of filtration, distillation, sublimation, and extraction, provided that the mixture contains only a few substances and that these substances have marked differences in melting points, vapour pressures (volatilities), or solubilities. When the mixture contains substances having closely similar properties, the problem becomes more difficult, and more elaborate equipment and more precise controls of conditions become necessary.

Variations in the degree to which substances tend to adsorb on surfaces are the bases of a variety of chromatographic methods of separation. These methods have had increasingly widespread use in recent years—particularly with small samples of very similar compounds. In all of these methods the sample, either a gas solution or a liquid solution, is carried over a surface by either a carrier gas or a liquid solvent. The degrees to which the substances in the sample are adsorbed on the surface determine the degrees by which the various substances are retarded in their forward motion over the surface. These relative retardations cause the different substances to emerge in the carrier fluid after different lengths of time and thus lead to separations that can be remarkably complete even for very similar compounds that may be very difficult to separate by any other method. Even a not-too-sensitive gas chromatograph can demonstrate that the gas phase above a ripe banana contains in excess of 100 compounds. It does not, however, identify the compounds, and the quantity of each compound is indeed small. Identification depends upon the empirical calibration of the instrument by measuring the times of appearance of known compounds.

The separation of mixtures such as those in natural systems presents special problems because of their complexity and numbers of large molecules. Separations of these mixtures may be based upon the differences in the masses of the molecules, the sizes of the molecules and ions, and the charge on ions and may be carried out by methods known as centrifugation, dialysis, electrodialysis, and electrophoresis. To achieve a complete separation is indeed difficult, and the degree of purity of the substances separated may be the major consideration.

Measurement of physical properties. The measurements of the physical properties of mixtures parallel those for single substances. Interest in the properties of mixtures centres on the relation of the property of the mixture to the properties of the pure substances and also to the composition or concentration of the mixture. Some properties such as the absorption of electromagnetic radiation are additive: each substance absorbs in the usual fashion, and the total absorbance is the sum of the absorbances that each of the substances would have if present alone in the solution at the same concentration. Other properties are closely related to the relative number of molecules of each substance in the mixture.

In terms of current models all physical properties of a pure substance are a manifestation of the structure and the mass of the atoms, of the spatial orientation and bonding between the atoms within the molecules or ions, of the mass and the dimensions of the molecules or ions, and the spatial orientation and the forces between the molecules or ions. All physical properties are therefore of interest to chemists, and those properties that yield results useful in further developing models or as a basis of analytical work are extensively studied.

In addition to such rather obvious properties as melting point, boiling point, density, and solubility in specific solvents, the chemist is particularly diligent in measuring the response of the substance to a magnetic field, to an electric field, to electromagnetic wave radiation, to a change in temperature, and to various combinations of these simultaneously. All of these procedures involve subjecting the substance to different energy situations. Only a very few physical properties and the instruments used to determine them will be mentioned here.

A combination of a sensitive analytical balance and a large magnet to produce the magnetic field (a Gouy balance) is used to measure the force produced by a magnetic field on a sample that is brought into it. An attractive force is interpreted as meaning that there are unpaired electrons in the molecules or ions. A repulsive force is a clear indication of the absence of unpaired electrons. Substances of the first type are said to be paramagnetic, and the second type said to be diamagnetic. A capacitor and standard bridge circuit are used to investigate the distribution of charge in molecules, and the results are interpreted in terms of the polarity of bonds, bond lengths, and bond angles in molecules.

The study of the absorption of electromagnetic wave radiation has been particularly fruitful, and important information on properties of substances is obtained using radio waves, microwaves, infrared light, visible light, ultraviolet light, and X-rays (listed in order of increasing energy, or increasing frequency or decreasing wavelength). All spectrophotometers (instruments for measuring the absorption of different types of radiation) are alike in that there must be a source of radiation, a means of selecting one frequency or a narrow frequency range for the measurement, a means of placing the sample in the path of the radiation, and a means of detecting the change in the intensity of the radiation produced by its passage through the sample. The experimental details of various operations depend upon the frequency of the electromagnetic radiation.

X-ray-diffraction equipment and electron microscopes belong to a discussion of the effects of electromagnetic radiation on substances, particularly on solids, but these instruments are not spectrophotometers. X-ray-diffraction measurements are interpreted in terms of the loci of the nuclei of the atoms. The electron microscope gives more detail than that obtainable with the best optical microscope and is used to investigate the dimensions of very large molecules and the characteristics of surfaces.

Modern mass spectrometers are precision instruments used to determine the ratio of the mass of an ion to the charge of that ion. These instruments are used in the determination of atomic weights and also to study ions containing several atoms. Such ions can be produced by fragmenting molecules. From the information obtained it is possible to reason back, at least in part, to the structure of the original molecule.

Various calorimeters are useful in determining the heat capacities of a given phase, the heat gained or lost in the transition from one phase to another. The recent development of differential-scanning calorimeters has both reduced the size of the sample required for measurements and also increased the precision of the measurements.

Geiger counters and scintillation counters are useful in studying samples that contain radioactive isotopes such as carbon-14. These isotopes undergo spontaneous nuclear reactions (reactions that cause changes in the nucleus of the atom) that lead to the formation of ions that are detected and counted by these instruments.

Physical properties and structure of pure substances. The most obvious property of any substance at room temperature is the phase in which it exists. If the substance is ionic, like sodium chloride, it has a high melting point: all positive ions attract all negative ions, particularly those nearby, and it requires a great deal of energy to give these ions the capacity to move past each other in the liquid phase and a great deal more energy for the ions to break free of contact with each other and exist in the vapour phase. Covalent substances are strongly bonded within the molecule, but the attractive forces between the molecules are comparatively small. Attractive forces between the molecules do exist, however; otherwise all covalent substances would be gases or powders of molecular dimensions. The attractive forces between molecules hold liquids and most solids together. The nature of these attractive forces between molecules is related to the distribution of charge within the molecules.

Some molecules—as carbon dioxide—have polar bonds, but the molecule as a whole is nonpolar. This apparent contradiction arises from the molecular symmetry, which allows the effect of the charges at its two ends to cancel. The carbon–oxygen bonds are polar, but the molecule is linear with the carbon in the centre. Since the two ends of the molecule are alike, there are only limited attractive forces between two molecules. Water, on the other hand, is not a linear molecule. The two polar bonds do not counterbalance, and the molecule as a whole is polar: the oxygen end of one molecule attracts the hydrogen of another to such a degree that aggregates of molecules of water are held together by these attractive forces, which are designated as hydrogen bonds. Heavy molecules have comparatively low velocities and frequently exist as solids or liquids.

An impressive array of physical measurements led to the formulation of well-defined, three-dimensional models of many molecules and ions long before the concepts of atomic structure and the chemical bond developed. For example, the physical (and chemical) properties of many carbon compounds were rationalized in terms of a carbon atom that formed four bonds with four other atoms uniformly distributed in space around the central carbon atom. The compound CH_2Cl_2 may be written as

$$Cl-\overset{\overset{\textstyle H}{|}}{\underset{\underset{\textstyle Cl}{|}}{C}}-H \quad \text{or} \quad Cl-\overset{\overset{\textstyle H}{|}}{\underset{\underset{\textstyle H}{|}}{C}}-Cl$$

to indicate the four bonds to the central carbon atom, but a three-dimensional model made with five gumdrops (of three different colours) and four bits of toothpick gives a much more informative model. A uniform distribution in all of space around the carbon gumdrop clearly demonstrates that all bond angles ($\angle$ HCH, $\angle$ HCCl, and $\angle$ ClCCl) are equal to approximately 109° and that there

is only one possible arrangement of these five atoms in space. The formulas written out above could very easily have been misinterpreted to indicate two arrangements: the first to give a polar molecule and the second to give a nonpolar molecule. The rationalization of the formation by carbon of four very specifically oriented sigma bonds is attained through a quantum-mechanical approach.

Another compound of carbon, hydrogen, and chlorine has the formula $C_2H_2Cl_2$ and properties that indicate the structure

$$\overset{\textstyle H}{\underset{\textstyle Cl}{\diagdown}}C=C\overset{\textstyle Cl}{\underset{\textstyle H}{\diagup}}.$$

All six nuclei lie in a plane, and all bond angles are approximately 120°. The two carbon atoms are said to be doubly bonded. The quantum-mechanical rationalization of a double bond is made in terms of one ordinary sigma bond (high charge density along the line of centres) and one pi (π) bond. The pi bond is similar to the sigma bond in that it involves a sharing of electrons between the two nuclei, but the charge density is high above and below the plane of the six nuclei and low along the line of centres of the two carbon nuclei.

The distance between the nuclei of two doubly bonded carbon atoms is shorter than that of two singly bonded carbon atoms. There are two other compounds that have the formula $C_2H_2Cl_2$:

$$\overset{\textstyle H}{\underset{\textstyle Cl}{\diagdown}}C=C\overset{\textstyle H}{\underset{\textstyle Cl}{\diagup}} \quad \text{and} \quad \overset{\textstyle H}{\underset{\textstyle H}{\diagdown}}C=C\overset{\textstyle Cl}{\underset{\textstyle Cl}{\diagup}}.$$

The three compounds have different properties and are said to be structural isomers. Many elements form covalent bonds, usually single bonds, but double and triple bonds are also common. One bond is considered to be a sigma bond; the others, pi bonds.

The significance of stereochemical (spatial) relations cannot be overemphasized. These are particularly significant in biological systems and are the basis of an approach to chemotherapy. Scale models of atoms that can be snapped together to build models of molecules are standard chemist's and biologist's equipment.

Interpretation of some physical measurements. *Electromagnetic wave interaction.* The interaction of electromagnetic wave radiation with substances provides a wealth of experimental information that can be interpreted in great detail in terms of various models. In the process of absorption, the ion or molecule increases in energy by the energy of the photon (the unit of light) absorbed. Each compound is very selective about the frequencies of the light it absorbs, because the energy of the photon must be just the right amount for the molecule or ion to go from one energy state to another.

Light absorbed in the infrared region of the spectrum produces a change in the rotational motion of the molecule as a whole or a change in the vibrational motion of the atoms with respect to each other. The energies involved in molecular rotation give information concerning the dimensions of the molecule, and those in the vibration give information concerning the properties of the bonds and the bond angles. The frequencies absorbed in the infrared region are particularly useful in identifying compounds and groups of atoms in molecules.

Light absorbed in the ultraviolet or visible frequency range (very high energy per photon as compared with the infrared region) changes the relation of an electron to the rest of the molecule or ion. The energy of the photon absorbed indicates the difference in energy between two states of the molecule or ion. The situation is complicated by the fact that the molecule or ion absorbs photons that have the right amount of energy to effect one electronic transition and also at the same time one or more vibrational or rotational (or both) transitions. The net result is that the molecules in the sample absorb a range of frequencies rather than a

Phases of matter

Isomers

Selectivity of photon absorption

group

Periodic table of the elements.

single frequency, and ultraviolet and visible spectra exhibit broad regions of absorption. The electrons that require the least energy to be transferred and consequently cause absorption in the visible region are as follows: a single electron in an atomic or molecular orbital, one of a pair of electrons in an atomic orbital associated with a high principal quantum number (commonly called an unshared pair of electrons or nonbonding electrons), and electrons in pi (π) molecular orbitals. Sigma-bond electrons are not readily transferred to higher energy levels.

Magnetic-field effects. A great deal of very detailed information about the more subtle relations in molecules and ions is obtained through nuclear magnetic resonance (NMR) and electron spin resonance (ESR) measurements. Some nuclei and all unpaired electrons have spin moments and are aligned by a magnetic field according to two, and for some nuclei more than two, energy states. The absorption of electromagnetic radiation effects a net transition from a lower energy state to a higher energy state. The energy required for the transition—and consequently the frequency absorbed—is dependent on the strength of the magnetic field, so that both the frequency of the absorbed radiation and the strength of the magnetic field must be determined. NMR measurements have been particularly useful in determining the manner in which several nuclei with magnetic moments interact with each other in the same molecule or ion. The characteristic patterns of very sharp absorption lines are often used to identify groups of atoms within molecules or ions. Among the nuclei with magnetic moments are hydrogen, carbon-13, nitrogen-15, and fluorine-19.

Periodic table of the elements. A great amount of information about both the physical properties of elements and the types of compounds they form is correlated by a listing of the elements in order of increasing atomic number in a tabular form that emphasizes the periodic recurrence of elements of similar properties (see the Figure). The periodic table (see PERIODIC LAW) has served not only to correlate experimental facts but also to direct research and to guide the development of models of the structure of atoms and molecules. The elements in the column to the extreme right are mono-atomic gases, the noble gas group. The elements in the next column, the halogen group or family, exist at room temperature and pressure as diatomic molecules—fluorine and chlorine as gases, bromine as a volatile liquid, and iodine as a volatile solid. The halogens form ions with a single negative charge like the chloride ion Cl^-, with one electron more than the neutral atom. The elements in the next column, the oxygen family, form ions with a charge of -2, having two electrons more than the atoms, but none of the elements in the next column, the nitrogen family, forms ions with a charge of -3.

The elements in the column to the extreme left, except hydrogen, are metals, the alkali metals, and form ions with a charge of $+1$, like the sodium ion Na^+, with one electron less than the atom. The elements in the second

Group properties (margin note)

column from the left are metals, the alkaline earths, and form ions with a charge of $+2$; and the elements in the next column, with the exception of boron, form ions with a charge of $+3$. All of the ions mentioned above are isoelectronic with the nearest noble gas.

The elements in the upper right-hand portion of the table, with the exception of the noble gases but including boron, silicon, arsenic, and tellurium, form tremendous numbers of compounds with hydrogen and with each other. The bonding within these compounds is covalent but with unequal sharing of the electrons between the atoms unless the two atoms bonded are of the same element. In general the closer the element is to a noble gas, the greater is the tendency of that atom to dominate in the electron-sharing process, but, within a family (column), the smaller atoms dominate.

CHEMICAL TRANSFORMATIONS

In the study of a chemical reaction, the chemist may seek to answer a number of questions including (1) whether a particular combination of substances reacts, (2) under what conditions the reaction or reactions occur, (3) how the products can be isolated, (4) how the products can be identified, (5) whether more than one set of products is formed and, if so, whether a specific set of products can be obtained by a careful selection of conditions, (6) how rapidly the reaction proceeds, (7) how the rate of the reaction or reactions is influenced by light, by the addition of other substances, by a change of temperature, by a change in pressure, or by a change in concentration, (8) what the mechanism is by which the reaction proceeds, (9) whether the reaction proceeds until the quantity of one reactant is reduced to zero or, if not, where it stops, (10) what energy changes accompany the reaction, and (11) how all of the above can be rationalized.

Goals of chemical research (margin note)

Great ingenuity is used in solving these problems, but there is no reaction for which all of these questions have been fully answered, even though the bibliography for some reactions exceeds a thousand journal articles. If the goal of a study is to prepare a particular compound, the answers to the first five questions may suffice. Each additional answer provides fundamental information about the nature of the reaction and may provide the basis for selecting better experimental conditions for synthesis. All of the other considerations fall into the province of physical chemistry: chemical kinetics, questions (6), (7), and (8); thermodynamics, (9) and (10); and statistical mechanics and quantum mechanics, (11). Rationalizations may be approached in a highly qualitative manner, but the ultimate aim is an exact mathematical treatment.

Chemical equilibrium. A closed chemical system at constant temperature frequently reaches a steady state, showing no evidence of further reaction occurring even though there is a measurable quantity of each reactant present. This situation is an equilibrium; *i.e.*, the rate at which the products are reacting to give the starting materials is equal to the rate at which the forward reaction is occurring. Removal of either a reactant or a product from the reaction mixture reduces the rate of either the forward reaction or of the reverse reaction, and a net reaction again occurs until a new state of equilibrium is established with a new set of concentrations and a new pair of equal but opposite rates.

Any system in equilibrium can be described by a mathematical expression known as the equilibrium constant, K_{eq}. This expression is a fraction. Its numerator is a product of terms related to the concentrations or pressures of the chemical products. The denominator is a product of terms related to concentrations or pressures of the reactants. The numerical value of the equilibrium constant depends only on the temperature of the equilibrium mixture and the substances involved in the equilibrium. Since the products appear in the numerator and the reactants appear in the denominator of the equilibrium-constant expression, the numerical value for the equilibrium constant is high for those reactions in which there is a high conversion of reactants to products before equilibrium is established. The equilibrium constant states, in a very concise and a very precise manner, the tendency for a particular combination of substances to produce a particular set of products at a particular temperature. It states nothing, however, in regard to the time needed to establish equilibrium.

Energy changes. The energy changes that accompany chemical reactions can be expressed in a number of ways. The change in the enthalpy (also called heat content), H, and the change in the Gibbs free energy, symbol G, will be considered here for reactions under conditions of constant pressure and constant temperature. These two restrictions make the following a very limited approach to the whole topic, but conditions of constant temperature frequently are the conditions under which studies are made. In order for some reactions, called endothermic, to proceed at constant temperature, heat must be transferred to the system. The heat content of the system increases, and the change in enthalpy, ΔH, for the system is positive. For other reactions, called exothermic, the temperature tends to rise as the reaction proceeds. The heat that would have to be removed from the system to maintain the constant temperature is the change in the enthalpy of the system. The change in enthalpy, ΔH, for an exothermic reaction thus is negative. For the reaction $2H_2(g) + O_2(g) \rightarrow 2H_2O(l)$, $\Delta H = -136,640$ calories at $25°$ C for every two moles of liquid water formed. For the reverse reaction $2H_2O(l) \rightarrow 2H_2(g) + O_2(g)$ at $25°$ C, $\Delta H = +136,640$ calories for every two moles of liquid water decomposed.

The Gibbs free energy change. The free energy change associated with a reaction is a more fundamental quantity as far as chemical reactions are concerned. It is also more difficult to comprehend since it cannot be directly observed or measured. For a very special experimental situation, in which each reactant and each product is held at a specified pressure or specified concentration called unit activity, the free energy change is called the standard free energy change and indicated in the ΔG symbol by a superscript small circle, $\Delta G°$. The standard free energy change, $\Delta G°$, is related to the equilibrium constant (K_{eq}) for that temperature by an equation in which R is the constant that appears in the ideal gas equation and T is that absolute temperature; the product of these is multiplied by the logarithmic value of K_{eq}:

$$\Delta G° = -2.303RT \log_{10}K_{eq}.$$

If the numerical value of K_{eq} is greater than 1, log K_{eq} is positive and $\Delta G°$ is negative: the standard free energy of a system decreases (runs down) for chemical reactions that give a high yield of products in a closed system. For those reactions that give a low yield of products in a closed system, the equilibrium constant is less than 1, log K_{eq} is negative, and the standard free energy change is positive.

The change in the standard free energy for the reaction to form liquid water at $25°$ C ($298°$ K), $\Delta G°$, is $-113,-380$ calories, and the corresponding equilibrium constant is equal to the inverse of the product of the pressures in atmospheres (P_{H_2} and P_{O_2}), raised to the required power:

$$K_{eq} = \frac{1}{P_{H_2}{}^2 P_{O_2}} = 1 \times 10^{82}.$$

For the reaction to decompose liquid water at $25°$ C into its elements, $\Delta G° = +113,380$ calories and

$$K_{eq} = \frac{P_{H_2}{}^2 P_{O_2}}{1} = 1 \times 10^{-82}.$$

The entropy change. Standard free energy change and standard enthalpy change ($\Delta H°$) are related by

$$\Delta G° = \Delta H° - T\Delta S°,$$

in which T is again the absolute temperature. Entropy is expressed in calories per degree. For the reaction to form liquid water, these relations are $-113,396$ calories $= -136,640$ calories $- (298$ degrees $\times [-78.0]$ calories/degree), and $\Delta S°$, the change in entropy, is -78.0 calories per degree for the formation of the two moles of liquid water. The entropy of a system is related to the degree of disorder in a system. Three molecules of gas with only two atoms in each molecule is a less ordered system than two molecules of three atoms each in the liquid phase. In this reaction there has been an increase in order, which correlates with the decrease in entropy of the system.

A gas has a higher entropy (a greater degree of disorder) than the same substance as a liquid at the same temperature. In turn, the liquid has a higher entropy than the crystalline solid at the same temperature. When Humpty-Dumpty fell off the wall, he suffered a large increase in entropy, too.

A high yield of products is obtained when the decrease in free energy is large. The largest decrease goes along with an exothermic change and an increase in disorder in the system: the energy of the system runs down, and the system becomes more chaotic.

Kinetics of reaction. The kinetics of chemical reactions are difficult to study experimentally because it is necessary to measure the changing concentration of at least one reactant or one product as the reaction proceeds. The results of the kinetic measurements also are difficult to interpret: the reaction mechanism is frequently complex and may depend upon surface conditions (even the wall of the container) and upon trace amounts of substances that do not appear in the chemical equation for the total reaction.

The experimental study seeks to determine the dependency of the rate of the reaction on the temperature and also its dependency on the concentrations of reactants. The simplest situations occur in all-gas systems and in single-phase liquid systems (the so-called homogeneous systems) when the rate at which one of the products appears, or the rate at which one of the reactants disappears, is directly proportional to the concentration of each reactant raised to a small integral power including 0 as well as 1 or 2 (the x and y in the following rate expression). In such a case the rate is a product of such concentration values and of a proportionality constant, k, called the velocity constant, which is characteristic of the system at a particular temperature:

rate = k[concentration of reactant A]^x × [concentration of reactant B]^y.

The larger the value of k is, the faster will be the reaction. For many reactions the rate equation is quite complicated, involving a sum of terms and fractional values for x and y.

The question of the probability of a collision between two molecules leading to a reaction is of considerable interest. One approach is to consider whether the orientation of the molecules is such that proper atoms in the respective molecules come into contact; the other approach is to consider whether the molecules collide with sufficient energy to stretch old bonds and initiate the formation of new bonds. These are questions that can be considered by statistical mechanics.

Essentially all reactions proceed more rapidly (have larger values for k) at higher temperatures; none proceeds more slowly. This dependency on temperature is discussed in terms of a concept of an activation energy, E_A,

Margin notes:

Heats of reaction

The driving force for a chemical reaction

The rate equation

Activation energy

which is necessary for a reaction to occur. E_A is evaluated by experimentally determining the velocity constants for several temperatures. E_A may be zero for a few reactions that do not involve the breaking of any bonds, but in general the rate of a reaction increases with temperature, and E_A is positive. If the average kinetic energy of molecules is directly proportional to the absolute temperature and only those molecules colliding with some minimum amount of kinetic energy react chemically, an increase in temperature increases the fraction of the collisions that lead to reaction.

The direct reaction of hydrogen molecules with oxygen molecules has too high an activation energy to be significant near room conditions, and a mixture of these gases can remain together indefinitely even though the free energy change indicates the reaction is spontaneous. The mixture is metastable, but, once the reaction is initiated by a spark to give either H atoms or O atoms, a series of reactions, which continues to generate these atoms, proceeds rapidly and attains explosive violence, particularly if the mixture contains two molecules of hydrogen for each molecule of oxygen. This reaction, under controlled conditions, is a very effective power source for rockets.

The same overall reaction may be carried out in quite a different fashion in a fuel cell. The hydrogen gas flows to one porous carbon block partly immersed in an aqueous solution of potassium hydroxide, and the oxygen flows to a second carbon block, also partly immersed. If the two blocks are connected outside the solution with a metal conductor, the following two reactions occur with the electrons, e^-, being conducted from one block to the other by the metal conductor:

$$2H_2 + 4OH^- \rightarrow 4H_2O + 4e^-$$
$$4e^- + O_2 + 2H_2O \rightarrow 4OH^-.$$

The total reaction is the sum of the two:

$$2H_2 + O_2 \rightarrow 2H_2O.$$

This process is the source of electric power on many spaceships. The mechanism is entirely different from the gas-phase reaction, and different energies of activation are involved.

Surprising rate equations can be rationalized in terms of reaction mechanisms that involve a series of simple reactions. A reaction such as $A + B \rightarrow AB$ is sometimes markedly accelerated by a substance, C, that does not appear in the equation of the overall reaction. The mechanism can be thought of as being a two-step sequence

Catalytic
processes

$$A + C \rightarrow AC$$
$$AC + B \rightarrow AB + C;$$

the sum of the two is:

$$A + B \rightarrow AB,$$

in which the activation energy of each step is less than the activation energy for the single-step reaction. A higher proportion of the collisions in each step proceeds to products, and the overall stepwise reaction is faster than the single-step reaction. Such an accelerating substance is called a catalyst. This is the role of enzymes in biological systems. Other substances, known as inhibitors, act in quite a different way to combine with an intermediate substance in a reaction mechanism and thus block the reaction mechanism.

Although the presence of a catalyst greatly accelerates the reaction and consequently gives a larger experimental value for the velocity constant, k, for the reaction, the presence of a catalyst in no way affects the numerical value of the equilibrium constant, K_{eq}, for the reaction, because a catalyst for the forward reaction is also a catalyst for the reverse reaction.

The energy needed to make some reactions occur is usually supplied simply by heating the reaction mixture. Energy can also be supplied electrically and by electromagnetic wave radiation. In both cases changes may be brought about by entirely different mechanisms, and reactions may be brought about that require an increase in free energy. For example, the thermal decomposition of water into hydrogen and oxygen is not practical under laboratory conditions, but this transformation can be easily brought about by electrolysis.

The irradiation of a reaction mixture with either visible or ultraviolet light of the appropriate frequency to be absorbed by a reactant provides the most selective method of providing the energy to promote reaction.

Chemistry of complex systems. The term complex systems refers to both natural systems and engineered systems. Natural systems include the geochemical systems and the biochemical systems and all of the systems produced from these by natural processes: the liquid and solid portions of the planets and the stars; and all plants and animals including the parts thereof both living and dead. The engineered complex systems include all those produced from the above in engineering processes and include not only the end products such as foods, textiles, building materials, and fertilizers and the complex systems involved in the production of drugs, pure metals, and drinking water but also the complex systems discharged into local ecological systems.

Complex systems are not so different from simple systems containing only a few substances: thermodynamics applies equally well to the energy changes associated with transformations; chemical bonding is the same in compounds; and chemical kinetics follow the same laws. There are, however, more substances, more simultaneous reactions, more possibilities for catalysis, and a much more complex balance of energy changes, as one reaction may provide the energy for another reaction. The changes that occur are more difficult to determine experimentally, harder to rationalize, and the processes are harder to control.

Biological systems are largely made up of carbon compounds distributed in, or saturated with, water. The properties of these systems are to a larger degree the consequence of both the unique properties of the water molecule and the unique structure of the carbon atom.

BIBLIOGRAPHY. Among the many excellent texts are: MICHELL J. SIENKO and ROBERT A. PLANE, *Chemistry*, 4th ed. (1971); and GEORGE C. PIMENTEL and RICHARD D. SPRATLEY, *Understanding Chemistry* (1971), two that are unusually readable and that provide more than adequate background for further reading; HAROLD G. CASSIDY, *Sciences Restated: Physics and Chemistry for the Non-Scientist* (1970); and WILLIAM F. KIEFFER, *Chemistry: A Cultural Approach* (1971), which emphasizes the philosophical and humanitarian aspects of the science. A quick and readable introduction to the three-dimensional character of molecules, including the large molecules of biological significance, is JAMES C. SPEAKMAN, *Molecules* (1966). Other comparatively nontechnical treatments of the significance of the spatial distribution of atoms, molecules, and ions are STANLEY W. ANGRIST and LOREN G. HEPLER, *Order and Chaos: Laws of Energy and Entropy* (1967); MARTIN GARDNER, *The Ambidextrous Universe* (1964); and A.I. KITAIGORODSKII, *Order and Disorder in the World of Atoms* (1967; Eng. trans. of the 4th Russian ed. of 1966).

Chemistry, a journal published by the American Chemical Society for high school and first-year college students, has widely diverse articles of interest to even professional scientists. The *Scientific American*, a journal for the intelligent layman, has excellent articles dealing with chemical developments of current interest.

Two reports of studies dealing with the relation of science and society are the AMERICAN CHEMICAL SOCIETY, *Cleaning Our Environment: The Chemical Basis for Action* (1969); and the NATIONAL ACADEMY OF SCIENCES, *Technology: Processes of Assessment and Choice* (1969). J. CALVIN GIDDINGS and MANUS B. MONROE (eds.), *Our Chemical Environment* (1972), is a selection of recent articles that have appeared in newspapers, popular magazines, and the publications of scientific societies.

LOUISE B. YOUNG (ed.), *The Mystery of Matter* (1965), is a compilation of selections from the writings of scientists and philosophers from Lucretius and Dalton to Einstein and Jeans. IAN G. BARBOUR (ed.), *Science and Religion* (1968), is a well-chosen compilation of essays. JACOB BRONOWSKI, *Science and Human Values* (1956), deals with intellectual inquiry, creativity, and human dignity.

The American Chemical Society periodically publishes *Selected Titles in Chemistry* (3rd ed. 1972), an annotated bibliography of several hundred books suitable for high school and college students—and for the general reader.

(A.J.Ha.)

Chemoreception

All animals react to chemicals in the environment, initially through a sensory process called chemoreception. The process begins when chemical stimuli come in contact with chemoreceptors, specialized cells in the body that convert (transduce) the immediate effects of such substances directly or indirectly into nerve impulses. A nerve cell (neuron) that makes a direct conversion is called a primary receptor; a cell that is not a neuron but that responds to stimulation by inducing activity in an adjacent nerve cell is called a secondary receptor.

General considerations

TYPES OF CHEMORECEPTORS

In man two distinct classes of chemoreceptors are recognized: taste (gustatory) receptors, as found in taste buds on the tongue; and smell (olfactory) receptors, embedded high in the lining (epithelium) of the nasal cavity. These respond to different classes of chemicals: gustatory receptors to water-soluble materials (*e.g.*, salt) in direct contact with them and olfactory receptors to generally water-insoluble, vaporous materials that may arise from a distant source, such as a neighbour's kitchen. The receptors themselves are also different; gustatory receptors are specialized epithelial cells (secondary receptors) with neurons branching among them, while olfactory receptors are nerve cells (primary receptors) with fibres leading to the brain (see SENSORY RECEPTION, HUMAN).

In all air-breathing vertebrates (*e.g.*, reptiles, birds, and mammals) the two classes of chemoreceptors are easily identifiable. In fish gustatory organs are on the fins and even the tail, as well as in and near the mouth, all still recognizable as taste buds. The nostrils in fish do not usually open into the mouth, but they are lined with olfactory epithelium. Much lower concentrations of chemicals are needed to elicit responses in fish for smell than for taste. These concentrations are similar to those for air breathers, permitting separate identification of the chemical senses for aquatic and terrestrial vertebrates.

For some invertebrates (*e.g.*, worms), however, distinctions between taste and smell receptors may not emerge. Chemoreceptors of these animals are structurally different from those of vertebrates, and their locations on the body are different. It has been held that invertebrate animals have only one chemical sense, with different sensitivities for various chemicals, as measured by the lowest concentrations (thresholds) of chemicals that can be received. Terrestrial invertebrates, particularly insects, do exhibit separable chemoreceptive capacities, however; additional study seems likely to reveal similar distinctions for other invertebrates. For these animals, the terms distance chemoreceptors and contact chemoreceptors are preferred by many biologists over the terms (*e.g.*, smell and taste) used in human physiology. Separation of these seems feasible because contact chemoreceptors are usually stimulated by nonvolatile, water-soluble chemicals, while distance chemoreceptors typically respond to volatile, oil-soluble chemicals. In addition, thresholds for stimulation of distance chemoreceptors are usually very much lower than those for contact chemoreceptors. Generally the behavioral results of contact chemoreception are feeding, mating, or the deposit of eggs, while those of distance chemoreception are orientation or movement of the animal toward or away from a volatile chemical.

Aquatic animals and terrestrial species with mucus-secreting skins are generally sensitive to chemicals all over the body, reacting with avoidance. This sensitivity has been called the common chemical sense. Man and other terrestrial vertebrates have a remnant of this receptor system that responds to irritants in the mucous membranes of the mouth, eyes, and genital organs. Common chemical receptors are thought to be free nerve endings (branching structures, or dendrites, of nerve cells) in the skin or in moist membranes. Even on the basis of relatively few studies, the common chemical sense is known to be separable from the sense of pain, and thus it is considered as a separate sensory capacity.

Receptors for humidity, particularly well studied in insects, may or may not be chemoreceptors. There is no question that some animals can orient toward or away from regions of high or low atmospheric humidity. The question is whether this is true hygroreception (*i.e.*, stimulation of the receptor by moisture-saturation deficit) or is stimulation by water acting as an odorous chemical. While the matter is far from settled, it seems that some insects and possibly mammals actually may be able to smell water, while others have true hygroreceptors.

In common speech the word taste refers to what is more correctly designated as flavour. For man, flavour sensations represent integration in the central nervous system (*e.g.*, the brain) of a complex of stimuli: gustatory, olfactory, common chemical, tactile, thermal, even painful. When carefully studied in other species (*e.g.*, a few other mammals and a few insects), reactions to foods seem to be similar to those of man, with multidimensional stimulation involved in food preferences.

ADAPTIVE FUNCTIONS OF CHEMORECEPTION

For most animals, chemical stimuli are leading sources of information about the environment; even man relies heavily on chemoreception for food selection. Species identification, mate finding, courtship, and mating are also chemically directed among most animals.

Food procurement. Foods are generally located by reception of odours they emit, sampled for palatability by both contact and distance chemoreception, fed upon only if they supply appropriate chemical stimuli during feeding, and laid aside either when the animal is full or when the animal's threshold of response for the stimulating chemical rises above the intensity of stimulation provided by the foods.

At least four classes of chemicals are recognized that affect feeding behaviour: (1) attractants: odours eliciting movement *toward* the source; (2) repellents: odours that prompt the animal to move *away* from the source; (3) feeding stimulants (phagostimulants): tastes and odours that induce the animal to feed; and (4) feeding deterrents (antifeedants): tastes and odours that inhibit feeding behaviour. Chemicals in foods that attract animals or that induce feeding are not necessarily nutritionally valuable in themselves; in food plants, the stimulants often are so-called secondary plant substances (*e.g.*, odorous essential oils) that provide little nourishment. Among animals that are preyed upon as food, the stimulants are often traces of odorous materials present on the body surface. Indeed, animals will feed on nutritionally worthless materials that have been experimentally impregnated with appropriate phagostimulants. Ordinarily, however, specific feeding stimulants are part of an animal's natural food (see also FEEDING BEHAVIOUR).

Symbiotic relationships. Most parasites do not just blunder onto their hosts but, rather, orient themselves toward suitable animals or plants. Little is known about the guiding stimuli for most parasites, but for some the odour of the host acts as an attractant, and the taste of the host's body surface functions as a feeding stimulant. Parasitic wasps that lay their eggs on wood-boring insects, for example, locate their targets in logs through olfactory signals. The wasp then drills into the log with a complex egg-laying structure (ovipositor) on the end of which are contact chemoreceptors that allow the insect to sample the prospective host to determine whether or not it is already parasitized. Animals that establish nonparasitic (mutualistic or commensalistic) relationships also find each other by chemical clues; or at least the mobile member of a pair finds the nonmobile member through chemoreception. Sea anemones that attach themselves to shells housing hermit crabs, for example, detect the proper shells with contact chemoreceptors on their tentacles. Annelid worms that are commensal (feeding together) with starfish or sea urchins to which they cling locate the latter by chemicals given off by the hosts.

Communication. Many animals release chemicals that influence other individuals behaviorally or at least physiologically. Usually produced by glands, these chemical communication signals have been named pheromones

Fish that taste with their tails

Flavour

Chemoreception among parasitic wasps

because they seem to act somewhat like hormones inside an animal's body. Females of some moths, for example, produce scents that attract males from great distances (a behavioral effect). Queen honeybees give off a chemical (so-called queen substance) that suppresses ovarian development in worker bees (a physiological effect). Basically the general classes of information that are coded in chemical signals are concerned with species or individual identification, with social communication, and with sexual or reproductive activity.

Ovarian suppression in bees

In aggregating as groups or in dispersal, animals depend on their ability to identify species or individuals. Thus, honeybees scent-mark their own hive and areas around it with odours that uniquely identify that particular insect community for its members. Many mammals are individually territorial, marking the boundaries of their territories with special glandular secretions (*e.g.*, deer), with body odours (*e.g.*, bears), or with urine (*e.g.*, dogs).

Chemical signals facilitate cooperation among social insects and many mammals. When their colony is endangered, for instance, ants, bees, and wasps alert the group with alarm odours. They also deposit chemicals that serve as guidance signals to indicate the way to sources of food or to living quarters.

Most of the sexual signals that animals produce at all stages of mating are chemical. Females of many mammalian species, for example, produce specific odours that attract only males of the same species. Male bumblebees mark leaves or sticks with a scent that induces females of their species to tarry for mating. In many species mating itself is stimulated in one or both sexes by special chemicals produced by the partners. Male tree crickets, for instance, produce a glandular secretion on which the female feeds during mating.

Orientation. Besides being oriented toward or away from food or mates, many animals are guided to suitable habitats by chemicals emanating from plants or from other environmental features. Fish such as salmon, which return from the ocean to lay their eggs in freshwater, generally come back to the specific stream where they themselves were hatched, guided by the odour of the stream. Other fish recognize their nesting areas by odours produced by plants in the vicinity.

Protection against predators. A most effective form of chemical protection is found in marine slugs and snails that produce strong acid secretions when disturbed. These secretions can injure other animals. Many species of animals produce chemicals that are repellent without necessarily being dangerous; for example, stinkbugs, millipedes, skunks, and some earthworms produce strongly smelling or bitter-tasting secretions when disturbed. An animal that causes a predator to become ill long after contact is not thereby directly protected. If the prey has a special taste or smell, however, the predator that samples it and later sickens learns to avoid the taste or smell, thus sparing other members of the species upon which it might otherwise prey.

Repellents of stinkbugs and skunks

Survey of chemoreception in the animal kingdom

Detailed evidence of chemoreception is available for only insects and mammals. Indeed, chemoreception has been studied in depth for only three or four species of insects and four or five species of mammals. For most animals data for secure generalizations are lacking.

LOWER INVERTEBRATES

Protozoa. Protozoans, even though they are single-celled, behave as if they had a nervous system. They are sensitive to chemicals in the environment and usually select some foods in preference to others. Carbon dioxide dissolved at low concentrations attracts many protozoans and may be the agent that leads them to foods. Some protozoans (*e.g.*, *Spathidium*), however, can locate specific foods at a distance, presumably by a chemical sense. Ciliates (*e.g.*, *Paramecium*) are most sensitive to chemical stimulation at the anterior (front) end; the receptors are probably special cilia (hairlike structures). *Paramecium* takes nonfoods, such as carmine particles, but soon "learns" to stop this, the change in behaviour persisting

for some days. In some ciliates (*e.g.*, *Vorticella*) that reproduce by exchanging genetic material between individuals (conjugation), a motile partner (conjugant) swims to a stationary individual. The swimmer is attracted from up to a millimetre away by a chemical produced by the fixed partner. All of these behaviour patterns performed by only one cell are nevertheless similar to those of multicellular animals.

Cnidaria (Coelenterata). Chemoreception is doubtless the most crucial receptive capacity of cnidaria (*e.g.*, *Hydra* and jellyfish), but little is known about the organs involved. Sensitivity to food chemicals is greatest near the mouth and tentacles, but specialized organs remain to be described. Almost all receptors are free nerve endings in the integument (body surface). *Hydra* exhibits feeding behaviour when stimulated by such chemicals as reduced glutathione or tyrosine. This reaction occurs in about half of the tests with weak solutions (1×10^{-6} molar) of these substances. Reduced glutathione acts similarly on the Portuguese man-of-war (*Physalia*) and some other coelenterates called marine hydroids. Amino acids other than tyrosine induce a feeding response in some coelenterates: valine and glutamine in sea anemones and proline in some hydroids and corals.

The feeding sequence of coelenterates is highly coordinated, despite the presence of only a very primitive kind of nervous system called a nerve net. Contact with food causes discharge of stinging or entangling structures (nematocysts), the reaction being released by a combination of chemical and tactile stimuli. The tentacles then draw the prey into the mouth. This response may be evoked by release of glutathione or amino acids from the injured prey.

Other behaviour patterns of coelenterates have been little studied. Anemone fish (*e.g.*, *Amphiprion*) live safely among the tentacles of sea anemones that kill other fishes. Seemingly the mucous coat of the anemone fish develops a chemical that inhibits the discharge of nematocysts, although other interpretations of observations made so far are possible. Many marine coelenterates that live in immobile groups shed sperms or eggs (depending on their sex) synchronously, the activity probably being regulated by chemicals given off by some individuals that trigger discharge in others. A swimming sea anemone, when touched by a starfish that feeds upon it, releases its hold and swims away. Identification of the predator starfish is specifically chemical. Reactions of coelenterates to chemical stimuli are far from stereotyped, a wide range of responses being observable.

Platyhelminthes. Flatworms (Platyhelminthes) have two major life-styles—free-living (turbellarians) and parasitic (tapeworms and flukes)—and their reactions vary accordingly.

For some free-living flatworms (*e.g.*, freshwater planarians) the locations of chemoreceptors in the body are known, but their structure is not. Planarians locate foods at a distance, and their behaviour during this process indicates that earlike protuberances (the auricles) on the head bear the receptors. Water currents elicit orientation movements, the animals crawling upstream when thus stimulated, as if they were making an olfactory response. Removal of a structure called the auricular groove abolishes planarian responses to foods; the receptor organs in the groove are thought to be ciliated glandular patches of nerve cells. Upon reaching food, the worm makes contact with its anterior end and with the tip of its pharynx (proboscis). Ingestion then may or may not occur, the reaction resembling selective taste (gustatory) responses of other animals. The tip of the worm's proboscis has receptors; indeed, an isolated pharynx cut away from the rest of the body will feed on appropriate foods.

Flatworms have been experimentally subjected to stimulation with many pure chemicals, most at concentrations not likely to be encountered in nature. The animals are usually attracted by relatively weak solutions and repelled by high concentrations. They respond to natural food juices and experimentally to pure amino acids and their derivatives. A worm called *Dugesia* reacts positively to such chemicals as lysine and glutamine, negatively

Reactions of flatworms to pure chemicals

to aspartic acid, asparagine, and α-keto-glutaric acid, and gives no observable response to hydroxyproline and glutamic acid. Planarians of different species, when mixed together in the same tank of water, can be separated by species through differences in their chemical-recognition behaviour. These distinctive chemically mediated reactions indicate well-developed sensory function for the planarian nervous system.

Little evidence is available about chemical sensitivity among tapeworms and flukes. Tapeworms are said to have only tactile organs, but supporting evidence is almost nil. Adult flukes obviously find their way to specific organs in the bodies of animals they parasitize, but the sensory mechanisms are unknown. The free-swimming stages (miracidia and cercariae) in the life cycle of flukes find their hosts effectively, but there is no general agreement on how this is done. Some workers hold that they swim at random and enter whatever body they encounter; others say that the flukes swim at random but select the host on contact; still others claim that they orient toward the host before contact. Perhaps different species of flukes vary in their behaviour, but the evidence is too sparse to draw general conclusions.

Nematoda. For a phylum with so many commercially and medically important parasites (as well as free-living species), the lack of studies on chemoreception in roundworms (nematoda) is surprising. The integument of these roundworms is supplied with many types of receptors, mostly free nerve endings. These are concentrated anteriorly, particularly on structures around the mouth called papillae. Nematode papillae could be chemoreceptors, but the possibility is supported by no direct evidence. Some roundworms have specialized glandulo-neural structures (amphids at the anterior end of the body and phasmids at the posterior end) that have been claimed to be chemoreceptive, again without critical verifying evidence.

Except for nematodes that parasitize plants, no agreement has been reached on how these animals find their hosts or foods or how they form "social" aggregations, as some free-living species of roundworms do. Parasitic nematodes may attack the roots of plants in response to a chemical attractant in the roots. In some cases the attractant is found to be carbon dioxide that stimulates the worms at a distance, with some other chemical acting on contact. The possibility that control of some agriculturally destructive pests may be achieved by changing the chemical environment in the soil is drawing increased attention to behavioral studies of these nematodes.

Echinodermata. These marine animals (*e.g.*, starfish, sea urchins, sea cucumbers) have also been little studied. They are generally sensitive to chemicals, seemingly most acutely at the tips of their myriad tubular "feet" (podia). Only free nerve endings are present in the integument (skin) of most echinoderm species, but sea cucumbers have sensory pits on their tentacles with more specialized nerve endings. The concentration of primary sensory cells in the integument of many echinoderms is truly striking, upwards of 4,000 per square millimetre being reported for certain starfish. These endings may be multisensitive (to a number of chemicals), or they may be functionally differentiated although structurally they appear to be identical.

Reports of studies of chemical reactions among echinoderms are few and spotty. These animals respond positively to natural foods and to some food chemicals (such as glutamic acid) at a distance, and they feed on specific items on contact. They avoid harmful chemicals (*e.g.*, injurious acids and salts). They also form specific aggregations, possibly through chemical responses to their fellows, and are known to spawn synchronously as a result of chemicals released during the process.

Annelida. Annelids (*e.g.*, leeches and earthworms) are sensitive to chemicals all over the body; they are selective in feeding, but no specialized chemoreceptors are yet known for them. Three types of nerve endings in the skin of these animals have been claimed to be chemoreceptive, but without direct evidence: (1) primary sensory cells concentrated at the anterior end, up to 700 per square

millimetre in front of the mouth (on the prostomium) of an earthworm; (2) branching free nerve endings in the skin, possibly mechanoreceptors rather than chemoreceptors; and (3) special concentrations of nerve endings, called integumental sense organs. Some "hairy" marine annelids (polychaets) have a so-called nuchal organ near the head, ranging in complexity from a simple ciliated pit to an elaborate set of folds covering many of the ringlike segments (somites) that form the body. The nuchal organ has been reported as chemoreceptive, but no direct evidence has been produced.

Chemoreception among annelids has been studied mainly by dipping them into or flooding them with various solutions and noting withdrawal or by feeding them natural and man-made foods. The animals respond appropriately, so that thresholds for eliciting responses have been determined. What these mean in the lives of the worms is generally obscure; as usual, low concentrations of many substances are accepted or produce positive responses, whereas high concentrations are rejected or repel. Studies of nerve impulses picked up from receptors in the skin of the body wall have been made with earthworms. The receptors, still unidentified, produce impulses when stimulated with appropriate concentrations of table salt, quinine, and acids, but they fail to respond to ordinary sugar (sucrose). The prostomium, however, does have receptors that are sensitive to sucrose solutions.

Feeding, selection of places on which to settle by some marine annelids, and selection of soil by earthworms have been shown to be chemically mediated. Commensal polychaetes (*e.g.*, *Podarke*) distinguish the organisms with which they live through chemicals coming from their hosts. Synchronous spawning occurs in many anchored (sessile) marine worms, being mediated through the release of signal chemicals. Release of sperms by breeding males of *Platynereis*, a swimming marine polychaete, requires chemical stimuli from the female. Earthworms incorporate an alarm chemical in the mucus given off when they are roughly handled; the effect is to repel other earthworms for as long as several months thereafter.

Mollusca. More information about chemoreception among mollusks (*e.g.*, snails, clams, squids) is available than there is for the groups discussed so far; but these animals comprise a large phylum, and very few species have been studied.

Chemical sensitivity is generally distributed over the mollusk's body, being greatest at the mouth, tentacles, front of the foot, and along the edge of its thin, capelike mantle. The receptors, although not identified with certainty, are thought to be variously branched free nerve endings. Body regions known to be most sensitive to chemicals have high concentrations of these cells. These regions are: (1) tentacles—a variety of projections on various parts of the body; (2) osphradia—ridges or projections near the front of the mantle cavity, best studied in marine gastropods (*e.g.*, snails and slugs); (3) abdominal receptors at the base of the siphons in bivalves (*e.g.*, oysters and mussels); and (4) olfactory pockets behind the eyes in cephalopods (*e.g.*, octopuses and nautiluses). Other organs have been designated as chemoreceptors, but with no critical evidence: (1) so-called subradular organs in the mouths of lower mollusks; (2) a structure called Hancock's organ in some gastropods; and (3) rhinophores (once identified as "olfactory" tentacles) of some gastropods called opisthobranchs. The last, however, are almost certainly established as receptors for water currents rather than as chemoreceptors.

Most of the physiological studies with mollusks have been on reactions to food or to foreign chemicals. Octopuses have been blinded and then trained or conditioned to respond to pure chemicals with specific behaviour patterns. Studies of orientation to or acceptance of feeding stimulants have shown that tentacles and osphradia bear receptors for odorous materials and that receptors near the mouth initiate feeding. Thus separation of contact from distance chemoreception among these animals seems probable; but, until specific receptors are identified

The chemoreceptive "feet" of starfish

Blinded octopuses

through their nerve impulses, the distinction remains conjectural. Although nerve-impulse studies have been made with at least two gastropods (*Aplysia* and *Buccinum*), specific receptors have not been identified thus far. The osphradium has finally been shown to bear chemoreceptors (a matter long debated), and reactions to food extracts and chemicals in natural foods have been studied.

Location of food or prey by many species of mollusks involves what suggests distance chemoreception, generally through the tentacles. Some carnivorous land snails detect and follow (by "tasting") the slime trail left by the prey. Specific "social" aggregations are common among marine bivalves; some of these are brought about by the settling of bivalve larvae near chemically detected members of their group (conspecifics). Chemically regulated synchronous spawning is common among marine mollusks. Land snails and slugs find mating partners by following their slime trails by "tasting" them. Limpets and other snails that live close to the shore emerge to feed when seawater splashes on them at low tide; the sense organs involved differentiate seawater from rain.

Many bivalves and gastropods react strikingly to chemicals from their predators such as starfish or enemy mollusks. Herbivorous marine snails, for example, move rapidly away from predators as soon as they touch them. A freshwater snail (*Physa*), when touched by a leech, swings its shell back and forth and then drops to the bottom. These reactions are induced by specific chemicals; the skin of echinoderms, for instance, has yielded such a material, the extract being found to resemble a group of chemicals called saponins.

ARTHROPODA

In the Arthropoda, which includes more than two-thirds the total number of all individual animals alive, detailed chemoreceptive studies have been reported for less than ten species of insects and five species of crustaceans; reliable information about other arthropods (*e.g.*, sow bugs and centipedes) is rudimentary. Many of these latter animals have hairs on their outer surface (exoskeleton) that may be chemosensory, since they are similar to those known to be chemoreceptive in insects and crustaceans.

Responses to food and mates, supposedly chemically mediated, have been described for millipedes, centipedes, and a number of arachnids (*e.g.*, spiders). Electrophysiological studies of chemoreceptors have been made with the horseshoe crab (king crab, *Limulus*) found on many beaches. The receptors are in spines on the legs and chilaria (flaps behind the mouth) of the animal. Each sense organ has from six to 15 nerve cells that respond or fire when bathed in clam juice or in solutions of amino acids. A tick (*Ornithodoros*), when fed through an artificial membrane, accepts glucose solutions with such substances as reduced glutathione, adenosine triphosphate, and nicotinamide-adenine-dinucleotide; glutamic acid inhibits feeding behaviour in this arachnid. Among some wandering spiders, the male locates the female by the scent of her silken dragline, which serves to identify species and sex. Contact chemoreceptors at the tips of the spider's legs are the sensitive structures. These observations represent a good sample of the scattered work to date with arthropods other than insects and crustaceans.

Crustacea. Crustaceans include such arthropods as crabs, lobsters, shrimps, barnacles, and many other forms. For a number of crustacean species, reactions to food chemicals or other substances have been used to locate the body regions that bear chemoreceptors. The list is impressive. Distance chemoreceptors are borne on the antennae and the smaller antennules, specialized structures (esthetascs) on the tips of the antennules being particularly sensitive (Figure 1). Contact chemoreceptors are borne chiefly on the tips of the walking legs, the mouthparts, antennules, tail flap (telson), walls of the gill chambers, and, in some species, on the general body surface.

Locations and structure of chemoreceptors. The sense organs in these regions are various, but only the esthe-

Margin note, left: Chemoreceptors of horseshoe crabs, ticks, and spiders

Figure 1: Hermit crab in shell, showing antennae (long and thin) and antennules (held vertically between eyes) with esthetascs (specific chemoreceptors) along edges near tips.
Hubert Frings

tascs have been shown electrophysiologically to be chemoreceptive. Scattered over the body are so-called funnel canals (or pore organs), which are assumed to mediate avoidance reactions to high concentrations of chemicals. Also widely distributed over the body, particularly on the appendages, is a variety of hairlike structures that are similar in appearance to known chemoreceptors of insects. Short blunt projections, resembling certain specialized receptors (basiconic sensilla) of insects, on the body wall of terrestrial isopods (*e.g.*, wood louse or pill bug) are also assumed to be chemoreceptive. The esthetascs at the tips of the antennules are groups of hairlike or spinelike structures. Receptors in these produce nerve impulses when stimulated with a variety of chemicals. Each esthetasc hair receives 100–500 nerve endings from cells aggregated in a ganglion-like structure at its base. The nerve endings, as revealed by the electron microscope, have a cilia-like pattern of fibrils, characteristic of the primary chemoreceptors of insects and vertebrates. The outer layer (cuticle) of the esthetascs is very thin, but it has no openings through it, as does the cuticle of the sensory hairs of insects.

Most studies on chemoreception among crustaceans have been made on a few species of crabs and crayfish, with food selection or reactions to chemicals as indicators of reception. Tests before and after removal of parts of the body have led to the discovery of the chemoreceptor locations. There have been a few recent electrophysiological studies with only a very limited number of species.

Responses. In general, crustaceans respond to a wide range of chemicals, negatively at high concentrations and positively at low. In many species, although the body regions that bear chemoreceptors have only one structural type of sensory hair, reactions to different chemicals vary. The antennae of crayfish, for example, have only one distinguishable type of hair, yet the antennae have distance chemoreceptors functionally resembling those of insects and vertebrates, as well as contact chemoreceptors. This has led some to suggest that there is no differentiation between "taste" and "smell" in these animals, merely differences in thresholds. Nevertheless, the behaviour patterns of crayfish stimulated by different classes of chemicals are different. Receptors in the antennules of a shrimp (*Crangon*) respond electrophysiologically to coumarin (usually considered an odour substance) at concentrations of 0.0001–0.00005 percent, to salt (NaCl) at 1.3–7.2 percent, to acetic acid at 0.01 percent, and to quinine chloride at 0.001–0.0005 percent. The observed differences are sufficient to put coumarin in a separate ("smell" or distance) class from the other (contact or "taste") chemicals, as it is for insects and mammals. Thresholds for the other three substances are on the same order as they are for insects and mammals. Thus, although two structurally different receptors have not been distin-

Margin note, right: Questions of the distinction between "taste" and "smell" in crustacea

guished for crustaceans, these animals still show evidence of two types of chemoreception (distance and contact), as in insects and vertebrates. Perhaps the structural similarity of crustacean antennal hairs masks functional differences in their nerve cells.

Behavioral significance of crustacean chemoreception. Chemically modifiable behaviour patterns are widespread among crustaceans and have received considerable study. Feeding responses usually occur in two steps: (1) response to chemicals from food at a distance, mediated through receptors on the antennae, antennules, and sometimes the tips of the legs; and (2) acceptance or rejection upon contact with receptors on the antennae, legs, and mouthparts. Barnacles have receptors that mediate feeding responses when stimulated with glutamic acid, proline, or potassium ions. It is believed that these materials initiate ingestion when they are released from prey that is punctured by spines on the entrapping legs of the barnacles. Electrophysiological studies on specialized appendages (dactyls) of the crab (*Cancer*) show that these respond to a variety of amino acids. Among crabs that feed on fish, the receptors respond to trimethylamine oxide and betaine, both chemicals found in fish flesh.

Parasitic and commensal crustaceans respond to chemicals from their hosts. Receptors on the antennules of commensal shrimps initiate nerve impulses when stimulated with fluid discharges (effluents) from their mollusk or echinoderm hosts. Communication by chemicals within any crustacean species is presumably common in the group but has been little studied. Swimming barnacle larvae aggregate specifically, attracted by a chemical given off by settled (fixed) individuals of the same species. This eventually makes reproduction possible among these fixed animals, since their eggs are fertilized internally. Sperms from one barnacle are transferred by a long penis to a neighbouring individual, this being feasible only because the animals aggregate. Sex pheromones have been reported for certain crabs. When ready to moult to sexual maturity, a female crab (*Portunus*) releases a chemical in her urine that attracts the male. In many species of crabs, the male is attracted from a distance by pheromones but uses his contact chemical sense for final identification of the female before mating.

Reactions to environmental chemicals are almost universal in crustaceans. Intertidal barnacles, like intertidal mollusks, respond when splashed with seawater by opening and becoming active, and they react to freshwater by closing tighter. The receptors that mediate this behaviour are along the edges of the mantle. Terrestrial isopods (sow bugs) select places that have specific humidities, the preferences varying with species and other environmental conditions. The receptors have been called osmoreceptors (since they conceivably respond to osmotic pressure), but there is no proof that they are distinct from ordinary chemoreceptors.

Insecta.   Among the insects, only the blow fly (*Phormia*), the honeybee (*Apis*), and a few species of caterpillars and moths have been given detailed chemoreceptive study. Otherwise studies are scattered, in detail on only one aspect for some species, in others wide-ranging but without detail. Chemoreception in whole orders of insects has been almost entirely neglected; *e.g.*, among Neuroptera (*e.g.*, ant lions), Trichoptera (caddisflies), Odonata (dragonflies), Mecoptera (scorpionflies), and Plecoptera (stoneflies). For *Phormia* and *Apis*, however, investigative evidence rivals that available for man and rat; and understanding of the mechanisms of taste for *Phormia* is better than that for mammals.

Locations and structure of insect chemoreceptors. There is general agreement as to the parts of the insect body that bear chemoreceptors. Distance chemoreceptors are usual on the antennae and on the palpi of the mouthparts. For most insects, the antennae are probably the major locations of these receptors. In the honeybee, each antenna has about 500,000 receptor cells, most of them probably chemoreceptive, the remainder being mechanoreceptive (for tactile stimuli) and thermoreceptive (for temperature). Contact chemoreceptors are on the following structures: external mouthparts, pharyngeal wall

(inner mouth), and ovipositor (egg-laying organ) in both chewing and sucking insects; tarsi (feet) and antennae in sucking species. A form of common chemical sense has been reported for insects but has been poorly studied. The receptors seem to be generally distributed over the animal's body, but they are still unidentified.

Regions of the insect body known to bear chemoreceptors have many types of so-called hair sensilla, named on the basis of their shape (Figure 2). The following types of sensilla are known from critical behavioral or electrophysiological studies to be chemoreceptive: (1)

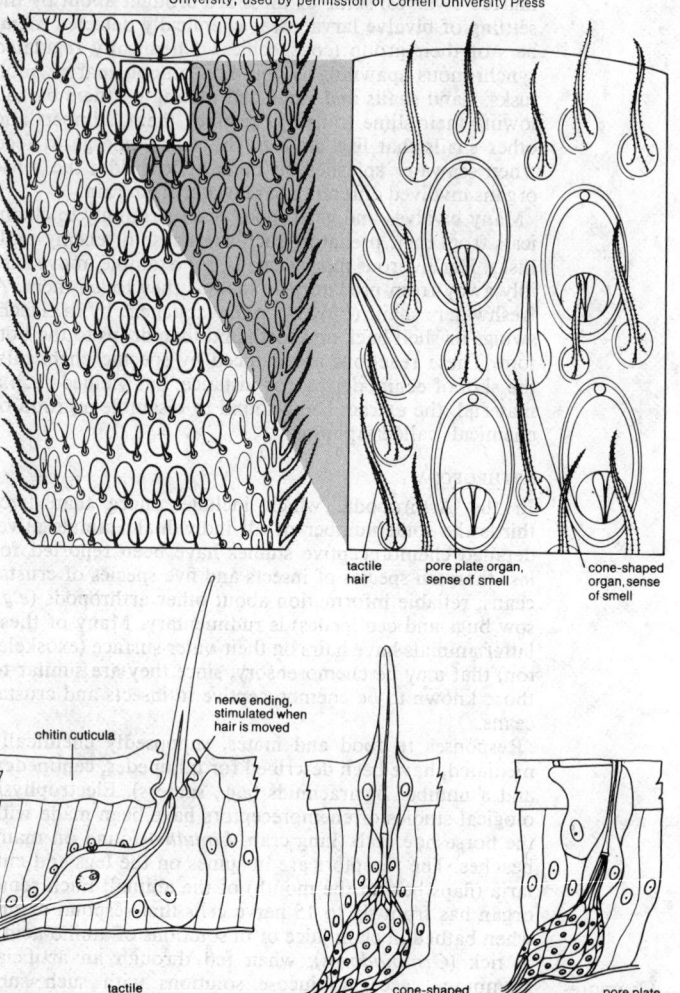

tactile hair   pore plate organ, sense of smell   cone-shaped organ, sense of smell

chitin cuticula

nerve ending, stimulated when hair is moved

tactile organ   cone-shaped organ   pore plate organ

Figure 2: (Top) Segment of worker honey bee antenna; (bottom) cross sections of the antenna's sensory organs.

trichodea (hairs), distance and contact reception; (2) basiconica (pegs), distance and contact; (3) coeloconica (pegs in pits), distance; and (4) placodea (pore-plates), distance.

The following types of structures are suspected of being chemoreceptive: (1) sensilla ampullacea (flasklike pits), distance; (2) sensory patches in the pharynx, contact; and (3) free nerve endings in hairs and integument, common chemical sense.

The shapes of the sensilla are not fully reliable indicators of function. Trichoid sensilla, particularly, are active not only in both distance and contact chemoreception, but also in thermoreception and mechanoreception. Electrophysiological recording of impulses from specific sensilla should help settle the matter. The designations by shape also are not entirely precise, for many types of insect "hairs" are intermediate between typical long thin types and short blunt pegs, and some have extensive modifications of the walls.

In the central cavity of the hair or peg, chemoreceptive

sensilla have terminal strands from neuron cell bodies at the base of the sensillum. The nerve cells are usually few in number, and their terminal strands (dendrites) branch variously to lead eventually to micropores (detectable only by electron microscopy) in the walls of the hair or peg. The taste hairs (labellar hairs) on the end of the extensible proboscis of the blow fly (*Phormia*) have been studied most thoroughly. Each of these has three to five neurons that send their dendrites to the micropores, plus a mechanoreceptive neuron with its dendrite attached to the base of the hair. The discovery of these micropores (formerly the exoskeleton of insects was thought to be imperforate) has necessitated considerable reinterpretation of experimental results.

Insect chemoreceptive processes. In the physiology of chemoreception among insects, many types of studies have been made—unfortunately, however, usually scattered among different species. Behavioral studies of feeding responses and other reactions to chemical substances at a distance and in contact, coupled with experimental removal of body parts and similar manipulations, have produced a large published literature. A few insects have been trained to give special reactions to chemical stimuli, the honeybee having been most extensively conditioned chemoreceptively. Some beetles, wasps, ants, flies, and cockroaches have also been studied in this way. Nerve impulses induced by chemical stimulation of the labellar hairs of *Phormia* have been detected electrophysiologically, representing the first time (1955) that a chemoreceptor of any animal was so studied. Since then, electrophysiological studies have been numerous, but mostly with relatively few species of Diptera (true flies) and Lepidoptera (moths and butterflies).

Among selected examples from the history of research on the functions of insect chemoreceptors, studies before 1950 had shown that the principal loci of distance ("olfactory") chemoreceptors are the antennae and that the end organs (terminal structures) are basiconic sensilla and pore-plates. Determinations of response thresholds, differing with the testing conditions, showed that the classes of chemicals to which insects respond at a distance are about the same as those that elicit responses from vertebrates. (The thresholds for series of chemicals are in the same general order for both groups of animals, although absolute values often differ widely.) Some species of insects are found to have distance chemoreceptors on structures other than the antennae, mainly the palpi of the mouthparts. The exact receptors and their properties were little understood in the 1950s.

Since about 1960, electrophysiological studies have yielded major data about the distance chemoreceptors of insects. Nerve impulses are recorded from the antennal nerves to produce so-called electroantennograms. The major species studied are silkworm moths, both the commercial silkworm (*Bombyx mori*) and the giant silkworms (Saturniidae). Males of these species find their prospective mates by means of a special scent given off by the females; receptors on the antennae of males are remarkably sensitive to these special compounds. *Bombyx* males have about 40,000 sex-odour receptor cells on each antenna, with endings in various hairs and pegs. These structures are generally tuned to specific odours and so are called "odour specialists." They can be stimulated with odorant concentrations as low as 100 molecules of the given chemical per cubic centimetre of air. Females of the *Bombyx* species have distance chemoreceptors that are not so tuned; instead, the cells respond to a wide variety of chemicals, being called "odour generalists." The generalist type of receptor cell can respond both by increased neural firing (excitation) or by decreasing firing (inhibition).

Among caterpillars that feed on plants, odours are detected by similar sensilla on the short antennae. These structures are generalists, each responding to a variety of compounds. Their responses, however, differ in a number of ways: (1) latency, the time needed for response after a stimulus is presented; (2) rate of increase in frequency of firing; (3) rate of adaptation, such as loss of responsive capacity as stimulation continues; and (4) alternation of

increase and decrease in the frequency of neural firing. Although there are only a few receptors present in the antennae of such a caterpillar, distinctive patterns of these four modes of response to different compounds represent a kind of code that the central nervous system of the animal seems to interpret as, at least, acceptable or unacceptable chemical stimulation.

After many years of behavioral studies on contact chemoreceptive processes among insects, electrophysiological methods have dominated the field since 1955. In many cases these continue to be supplemented by corresponding behavioral observations. The blow fly (*Phormia*) has become the "standard" subject, just as the fruit fly (*Drosophila*) has served in genetics. The labellar hairs of *Phormia* are known to be contact chemoreceptors; when its tip is inserted into a capillary tube containing a sapid solution, the hair responds with electrical changes that may be picked up through the solution. Thus the animal's responses to specific chemical substances can be readily monitored. An extensive mass of data has been gathered with this fruitful system.

Besides having a mechanoreceptive cell at its base, the blowfly's labellar hair has dendrites from four or five sensory cells. Each of these makes electrical responses that distinguish the cell as one of at least four types: (1) salt receptor (or cation receptor), once called L fibre because it produces large spikelike patterns of electrical activity on the recording screen; this cell is stimulated by positively charged ions (cations such as Na^+) and by acids and mediates behavioral rejection in water-satiated flies; (2) anion receptor, stimulated by negatively charged ions, and mediating rejection under all circumstances; (3) water receptor, once called W fibre; this structure fires when stimulated by water and mediates its acceptance by the animal; and (4) sugar receptor, once called S fibre because of its small electrical spike; stimulated by sugars, it mediates their acceptance by the fly.

Thus, rejection or acceptance of sapid solutions largely depends on the blow fly's receptors. A sugar solution causes one set of receptors to fire to bring about extension of the animal's proboscis and to stimulate feeding activity. A solution containing salt or acid stimulates another set of receptors to fire to inhibit extension of the proboscis and of feeding behaviour.

The stimulating thresholds for a great number of chemicals have been determined with the blow fly, and some general rules have been propounded. The stimulative effectiveness of cations and anions is proportional to the effective intensity of the electrical field generated by the given ion. At least for cations, stimulative effectiveness also seems correlated with the speed at which they move in solution (*i.e.*, their ionic mobilities). The data suggest that the receptor is stimulated by penetration or adsorption of the chemical on the surface; so far neither ionic mobility nor electrical field has been shown to be the only factor that affects thresholds. Rejection of alcohols and of other organic compounds by blow flies seems to be mediated by inhibition of the animal's sugar receptors. Stimulative effectiveness increases with carbon-chain length in a given series of chemicals up to about 11 carbon atoms. The effectiveness seems best correlated with the comparative solubility of the substance in water and oil, suggesting that penetration of the receptor surface is involved in stimulation. The effectiveness of sugars shows no obvious relationship to any of their chemical or physical properties but loosely seems to depend on their nutritional utility to the insect. Lactose, one sugar that is not adequate for nourishing flies, for example, does not stimulate the sugar receptor. Most stimulating are fructose, sucrose, and glucose, in that order; this is the order of their sweetness as tasted by man. In spite of the large amount of data available, however, neither the exact mechanisms of stimulation nor the details of their interrelationships has been worked out for these insects.

Among the so-called pseudotracheae ("false air ducts") on the labellar pads at the tip of the proboscis of these flies are short peglike sensilla (the interpseudotrachea papillae). Studied electrophysiologically, the papillae show evidence of bearing four kinds of receptors: (1) a

Electrical activity of silkworm antennae

Extension of the proboscis

mechanoreceptor; (2) a sugar receptor; (3) a salt receptor having other sensitivity as well; and (4) one with chemosensory function unknown as yet, although some data suggest that it may respond to amino acids. Specifically, the labellar hairs do not respond to amino acids, yet amino acids are ingested by blow flies.

The electrophysiological activity of taste receptors in *Phormia* has been correlated with the feeding behaviour of the animal. Attraction to foods from a distance is olfactory, mediated by receptors on the fly's antennae and palpi. Extension of the proboscis (at rest it is folded into the head capsule) is brought about by stimulation of sugar receptors, usually in tarsal hairs, sometimes in labellar hairs. Extension can be inhibited by appropriate stimulation of other sensory fibres by salts, acids, or repellent organic compounds. Stimulation of the labellar sugar receptors brings about sucking as long as stimulation of the other fibres is not too intense or provided that inhibition by other organic substances is not too great. Feeding behaviour is maintained and its level of activity is determined by stimulation of labellar and interpseudotracheal sugar receptors. The higher the concentration of sugar in solution, the more avid the fly becomes and the longer it feeds. As feeding proceeds, the sugar receptors adapt to stimulation, finally no longer firing above their resting levels, and feeding ceases. After this, chemoreceptors in the blowfly's foregut take over and shut off feeding behaviour until the meal is moved out. How widely this *Phormia* scheme will be found to operate remains to be seen, but, as studied so far, it seems generally to hold for other insects.

Behavioral significance of insect chemoreception. Studies on feeding behaviour among insects are extensive. Some insects are strictly monophagous (eating only one food); at the other extreme there are highly polyphagous insects (that eat almost any organic matter). Most insects, however, fall between these rare extremes, showing restricted food preferences that depend on the presence of specific marker chemicals (feeding stimulants) in acceptable items of diet.

Insects engage in a tremendous variety of mutual and commensal relationships; to do so they must find symbiotic partners. Many cases of chemical orientation to partners are recorded, usually in connection with the important communication signals of insects. Host finding by insects that parasitize other animals is likewise influenced or determined by chemical signals. Mosquitoes, for instance, find suitable hosts (*e.g.*, human picnickers) by sensing lactic acid, carbon dioxide, and moisture on the victim's skin, as well as by detecting his body heat and movement.

Chemical communication is probably universal among insects; it is certainly of major importance for the largest and best known groups. The possible practical use by man of sexual communication chemicals (pheromones) produced by insects (or made synthetically) in the control of these animals has led to extensive studies of materials that induce their sexual behaviour.

Social insects (*e.g.*, termites, bees, wasps, and ants) have been known for some time to use chemicals to scent the nest and to recognize individual members of the community. Advances in chemical analysis have facilitated the isolation and identification of many of these compounds. Some of these undoubtedly affect more than the insect's transient behaviour; the so-called queen substance of honeybees (trans-9-oxy-2-decenoic acid), for instance, suppresses development of ovaries in worker bees, thus producing (when the swarm is not too large) a community with only one functional female. Similar chemicals are also used for trail marking and as guidance marks to food sources. In ants and stingless bees, deposits of secretions from the mandibular ("jaw") glands (containing such chemicals as geraniol, citral, various terpenes, and methyl ketones) function as guidance spots in the environment to direct fellows to food sources. The most thoroughly studied pheromones of insects are those used for sexual attraction and activation. Specific sexual attractants have been identified in about 250 species of insects. All but about 60 of these are Lepidoptera (moths

and butterflies); most of the others are Coleoptera (beetles and weevils). In about 200 of these species, females attract males, and, in about 50 species, males attract females. Generally the attractant substances are what chemists call substituted hydrocarbons, with chain lengths of between eight and 17 carbon atoms in the molecule. It has been theorized that molecules that will allow sufficient structural variety while still being stimulating to insects should have chains of ten to 17 carbon atoms and molecular weights of 180 to 300. Most of the active substances studied thus far fall within these limits.

Synthetic chemicals that act like the natural pheromones have been prepared for many insect species; these are mainly acetates with chains of 12–16 carbon atoms. Reactions of insects' olfactory receptors to these materials are remarkably specific. In field tests, male moths distinguished the specific chemicals of their own females when these substances were mixed with 26 other pheromones from different species of moths. In the laboratory, where concentrations may be made much higher than in the field, males may confuse some of the compounds, but not under natural conditions. Small differences in molecular structure or configuration can be highly significant. One molecular mirror image (trans isomer) of the Propylure molecule, a substance that attracts pink bollworm males, is active; the other mirror image (the cis isomer) does not attract, yet it masks the trans form when mixed with it.

Remarkably small concentrations of these pheromones can elicit behavioral responses. What was once thought to be the gypsy moth pheromone (isolated in tiny quantities from an extract of hundreds of thousands of female moths) and its synthetic version (Gyplure) have now been found to be inactive in themselves. The active principle seems to be some still unknown impurity present in even more minuscule amounts in the original extracts.

Insect pheromones are thought to be excellent prospects for pest control because of their attractant properties. Unfortunately, most attract males, and even a few fertilized females can maintain a population. At present, the major use of these materials is in population sampling; for instance, male cotton boll weevils (which emit substances called terpenoids) are used in traps to attract females in making a census of their population.

The use of pheromones in insect control is complicated by the finding that high concentrations repel and low concentrations attract. Thus, if high concentrations are used in insect traps to get wide coverage, the animals may be repelled when they get near. Furthermore, a pheromone used in baiting a trap must compete with the attractant from living members of the species. Many pheromones have multiple effects, depending not only upon their concentrations but on environmental factors as well. The so-called Nassonoff gland pheromone of honeybees, for example, consisting mainly of terpenes, serves the insects for attracting workers and queens, for marking food sources, in marking the hive, in scenting prospective hive locations by scouts, and in gathering swarms in flight. Thus, different behavioral reactions to the same pheromone can occur under different circumstances.

As a possible way out of many difficulties, it has been suggested that pheromones could be used to flood given locations with odour. This could fatigue the chemoreceptors of the insects and prevent them from finding mates; their sexual communication channel would be jammed. So far, the few tests of this idea that have been made in the field have not yielded very promising results. Except for short-term, geographically restricted effects, as among insects that live in warehouses where farm products are stored, pheromones for insect control have yet to fulfill earlier optimistic expectations.

Besides responding to food and communication odours, insects are oriented by a variety of other environmental chemical factors. Humidity responses have been extensively studied, but whether the receptors react to water vapour or are hygroreceptors (responding to lack of water) is much debated, with no general agreement. Places for laying eggs are selected by many insects (*e.g.*, mos-

Prey location by mosquitoes *(margin note)*

Use of pheromones in insect control *(margin note)*

quitoes and parasitic wasps) by chemical sampling of the prospective sites. Some plant chemicals and a number of synthetic materials repel various insects. There seems to be no generally occurring repellent for all insects, nor has any special relationship between chemical composition and olfactory repellency been discovered.

Protection of man and other mammals from attack by mosquitoes, fleas, ticks (which are arachnids, not insects), and other bloodsucking arthropods has been sought in chemical repellents. Tens of thousands of organic compounds have been tested as insect repellents, mainly for use against mosquitoes. Besides repelling at adequate levels when put on a part of the body that attracts the pests, the compound should not irritate the skin nor be otherwise harmful and should have a reasonable rate of evaporation. In the face of such criteria, few practical repellents have been found. Among those in common use are such substances as dimethyl phthalate, Indalone, Rutgers-612, benzyl benzoate, and Deet; the last is widely used, since it repels many arthropods—mosquitoes, fleas, and ticks. Repellent substances also have been sought among the many warning and alarm chemicals produced by insects, but most of these prove to be irritating to the skin or nose of mammals.

Alarm signals among ants Alarm pheromones have been studied most intensively in ants, which produce them with special glands to alert their colonies to invaders or to other dangers. The active materials are generally related to hydrocarbons, often ketones; citral and its relatives are important components. Some of these chemicals are also constituents of social and sexual pheromones. Honeybees produce an alarm scent that contains citral and isoamylacetate, among other materials. Formic acid, produced by specialized glands of ants, is found to excite both ants and bees. All of these materials function to alert members of an insect colony when the community is threatened. Other insects (*e.g.*, some beetles) produce strongly repellent chemicals that serve to ward off predators. These chemicals range from apparently harmless but strongly odorous substances to such toxic materials as hydrocyanic acid gas. Among bombardier beetles the ejected spray is even heated by chemical action to about the boiling point of water.

CHORDATA

Besides the familiar vertebrates (animals with backbones), the phylum Chordata includes some smaller creatures sometimes called protochordates. Little indeed is known about chemoreception in such protochordates (*e.g.*, the lancelets and tunicates) beyond that they seem to show some selection of food and location and that they respond negatively to a variety of foreign chemicals. A group of what are commonly called lower vertebrates is the cyclostomes, such round-mouthed aquatic forms as lampreys and hagfish. Cyclostomes have a well-developed nasal tract, with a single median (central) nostril; they can locate their prey by smell, but otherwise almost nothing is established about their chemical senses. For this reason, the bulk of attention given here to chordate chemoreception will be confined to the five main divisions of vertebrates: fish, amphibians, reptiles, birds, and mammals.

General vertebrate chemoreception. *Gustatory receptors.* The taste buds of vertebrates are secondary sense organs (*i.e.*, sensilla) derived from epithelial cells (Figure 3). Their structure has been well studied by electron microscopy, but in relatively few species (mostly mammals). Each vertebrate taste bud seems to consist of a number of cells of three or four types, but there is some debate as to their exact classification. One widely held view is that the taste bud has four types of cells: so-called supporting cells, sensory cells (the true receptors), basal cells (supplying replacements for old sensory cells), and another type of unknown function. Attempts have been made to designate developmental stages of these types and to view some of them as stages in the development of others, thus giving rise to at least five classes. The sensory cells are continually replaced, each cell having an average life span (at least for rat, mouse, and rabbit)

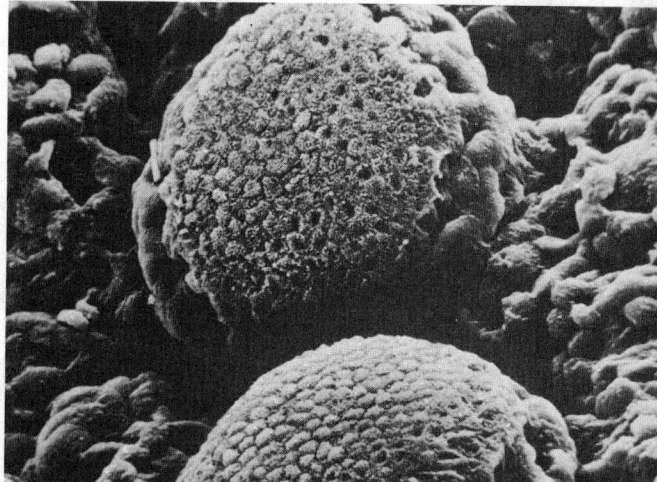
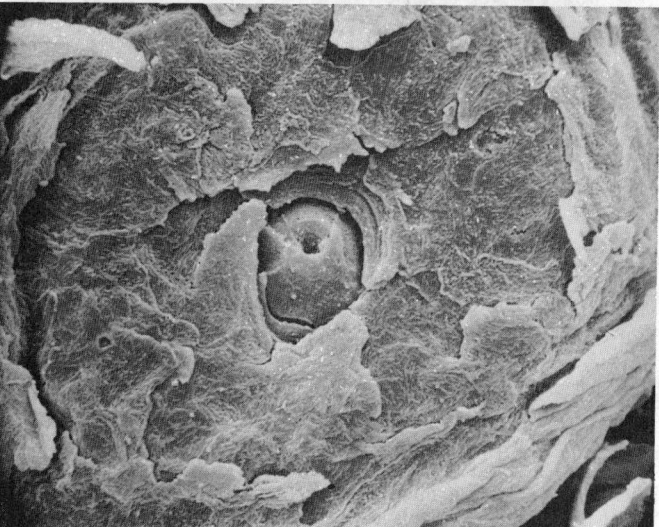

Figure 3: Scanning electron micrographs of (top) two frog fungiform papillae (magnified about 515 X), and (bottom) taste bud with pore projecting through surface of rat fungiform papilla (magnified about 850 X).
(Top) P. Graziadei, (bottom) L.M. Beidler, Florida State University

of about ten days (Figure 4). Each taste bud is innervated by up to 50 nerve fibres entering from below and branching into 200 or more branches to form a basket-like set of dendrites. Presumably chemical stimuli produce electrical changes in the sensory cells of the taste bud, these activating the afferent neurons nearby to generate nerve impulses.

Taste buds of reptiles, birds, and mammals are confined mainly to the upper surface of the tongue, with a few on the pharyngeal walls. In amphibians (*e.g.*, frogs) they are more numerous on the pharyngeal walls and present also on the cheeks and lips. In fish, taste buds are present also on the fins and in some species on the tail. In all cases, vertebrate taste buds are innervated from cranial nerves, mostly the facial and the glossopharyngeal.

Olfactory receptors. Among vertebrates these are the cells of the olfactory epithelium in the nasal cavities. They are primary receptors, true nerve cells the fibres of which form the olfactory nerve leading to the lobe of the brain that mediates the sense of smell. The structure of the cells of this epithelium, as seen with an ordinary (light-wave) microscope, appears remarkably similar for all vertebrates. Electron microscope studies reveal much more structural detail but have not changed the general interpretations. There are three fundamental cell types in the olfactory membrane: receptor cells, supporting cells, and basal cells; in addition, numerous gland cells furnish a mucous covering for the epithelium. Ramifying (branching) among the cells are very delicate terminal fibres of neurons leading to the brain through the tri- **Olfactory cell types**

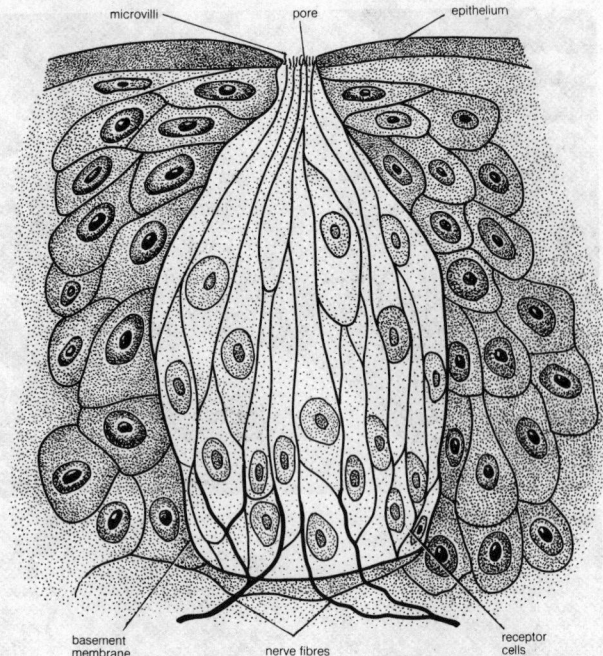

microvilli — pore — epithelium

basement membrane — nerve fibres — receptor cells

Figure 4: Microscopic section of taste buds of circumvallate papilla.

Adapted from A.J.D. De Lorenzo, "Ultra-Structure and Histophysiology of Membranes" in Y. Zotterman (ed.), *Olfaction and Taste* (1963); Pergamon Press

geminal nerve. These are thought to be receptors of the common chemical sense, responding chiefly to irritants. The olfactory receptor cells have terminal cilia, which are fused into olfactory rods projecting outward.

Man has about 40,000 sensory cells per square millimetre of olfactory epithelium, while the rabbit has about 120,000 per square millimetre, with an estimated total of 100,000,000 such cells. (Fish average between 45,000 and 95,000 per square millimetre, the eel having a total of about 800,000.) A significant discovery made with the electron microscope is that the olfactory sensory cells seem to be synaptically related. Such an arrangement would permit the cells to interact through mutual excitation and inhibition, thus allowing versatility of response at the receptor level itself.

The olfactory epithelium forms at least one wall of the nasal cavity of vertebrates. In fish, the nasal cavities are mostly paired pits or tubes just in front of the eyes, each with two nostrils, one anterior, the other posterior. In terrestrial vertebates, the paired nasal cavities have external openings, the nostrils (external nares), and paired or unpaired internal openings (internal nares) into the mouth or pharynx. In all cases, water or air is moved through the nasal cavity and over the olfactory epithelium.

Another olfactory receptor of many vertebrates is the so-called Jacobson's organ (vomeronasal organ). This structure is variously developed; absent in fish, birds, and some mammals, it is highly developed in lizards and snakes. Nerve fibres from this organ lead to the accessory olfactory lobe of the brain and so are closely related to the primary olfactory system.

Common chemical receptors. Mucous membranes in vertebrates have receptors that respond to the presence of chemicals rather indiscriminately and, when stimulated, tend to evoke avoidance reactions from the animal. In mammals these common chemical receptors are restricted to the mucous membranes of the nose, mouth, pharynx, eyes, and genital organs. Free nerve endings in the olfactory epithelium of mammals are believed to respond to irritant chemicals.

Free nerve endings   In fish and larval amphibians, free nerve endings all over the animal's body seem to be sensitive to chemicals, their excitation eliciting avoidance reactions. These free nerve endings send their fibres to the central nervous system through spinal nerves. The free nerve endings of the head region enter the brain via the trigeminal nerve. These widely responsive receptors are vitally·important

in enabling the animals to escape from harmful chemicals in the environment, but relatively few studies have been made on them.

Process of gustation (taste). Among vertebrates other than man, the usual types of behavioral studies (*e.g.*, involving feeding responses) have been made, and training or conditioning procedures also have been used. Gustatory thresholds for detection, acceptance, and rejection have been determined. In more recent years electrophysiological techniques have been most numerous. Human reactions to tasted chemicals can be studied by experiments involving recognition of materials and verbal specification of preference or aversion. Aside from man, the animals most studied are frog, monkey, rabbit, rat, and cat; the investigations have focussed on taste qualities and on the action of sapid substances.

During the 19th century it was widely held that there are four primary taste qualities (salt, sweet, sour, and bitter) and that all other gustatory experiences represent combinations of these. Some investigators have added to these an alkaline and a metallic taste, but others claim that they are not primary qualities. On the assumption that there are four primary taste qualities, chemicals supposedly exemplifying each of the classes (NaCl for salt, sugars for sweet, acids for sour, and alkaloids for bitter) have been applied to the tongues of man and laboratory animals in attempts to find regions of selective sensitivity or (by electrophysiological tests) to locate different types of taste receptors.

Unfortunately taste buds are compound structures, and their neural connections are complex. At any rate, impulses recorded from nerves, or even from single taste buds, fail to give direct evidence about what the individual receptor cells can do. While recordings can be made by inserting fine wires into individual taste buds, the exact cell sampled is not known. It is clear, however, that vertebrate taste receptor cells are not classifiable as sugar, cation, anion, and water receptors as they are among insects. Some vertebrate cells respond to a fairly narrow range of chemicals, but most do not; those cells that respond to salts may also react to acids and sugars, or even water. Certain regions of the tongue tend to be selectively sensitive (*e.g.*, the tip of the human tongue seems highly responsive to sweet chemicals, but not uniquely so). It is no longer expected that, by studying impulses in single gustatory nerves, specific salt, sweet, sour, and bitter receptor cells will be discovered. It seems that patterns of response (rather than specific receptor activation) set up among the sensory cells on the tongue mediate the different taste sensations in man.

As in the case of insects, there is no general agreement on how sapid substances stimulate vertebrate taste receptors. For related series of organic chemicals, stimulative effectiveness is proportional to carbon-chain length up to some maximum and is also related to the comparative solubility of the substance in water and oil. Among inorganic materials, cations generally seem to have stimulative effects that are proportional to their mobilities, but there is great variability in response to the same ions from one vertebrate species to another. Sweet substances are not chemically definable; at least there is no obvious relation of taste with molecular structure. Although many sugars apparently stimulate the same receptors, man and other mammals often can easily distinguish one sugar from the other. Activation or inhibition of receptor cells occurs upon stimulation with different materials. The idea of four primary taste qualities or senses (modalities) has semantic utility, but it has not proved useful as a central dogma in understanding fundamental mechanisms of taste.

Process of olfaction. Studies of smell reception among vertebrates have been similar to those with taste, with electrophysiological methods dominating modern research. The literature on the subject is large, particularly with respect to man.

While attempts have been made to categorize odours in classes that could be considered primary, they have not produced a generally accepted system. The smallest number of primary odour qualities suggested is four, but more than 30 have been offered by some theorists. Attempts to relate odours to chemical structure or to other generalizable physical characteristics of odorous materials have not succeeded. Studies on mechanisms of stimulation of olfactory cells have similarly given rise only to theories, none generally acceptable.

The most active research on human olfaction is concerned with attempts to link odours, such as those of foods or perfumes, with specific chemical structures. Newer analytical techniques, as with insect pheromones, have facilitated the determination of the chemical composition of odorous materials present in the tiny amounts typical of natural products. By these means, extracts from foods can be separated into components with characteristic odours and chemically identified. From the standpoint of olfactory physiology, these studies emphasize the immense capacity of individual olfactory cells to detect a tremendous variety of chemical materials.

From white bread alone, for example, approximately 70 odorants have been identified, including alcohols, organic acids, esters, aldehydes, and ketones. From coffee, 103 separable volatile compounds have been isolated and many chemically identified; it is estimated that at least 150 substances contributing to the flavour of coffee will be discovered. Since many of these are present in extremely minute quantities, the capabilities of the human olfactory epithelium, usually regarded as having low sensitivity as compared with that of other mammals, seem remarkable. For substances called mercaptans (*e.g.*, **Skunk** in the skunk odorant), only about 40 receptor cells in the **odour** human nose need be stimulated by no more than nine molecules each to give a detectable odour sensation.

Chemoreception in the main vertebrate divisions. *Fish.* Structure, location, and innervation of fish chemoreceptors are like those of terrestrial animals; thus separation into distance and contact chemoreceptive channels is possible. Taste buds are more widely distributed over the body in fish than in terrestrial vertebrates. In teleosts (*e.g.*, herring, trout, perch) they occur not only in the mouth and pharynx but also on the lips and regions nearby, on whisker-like barbels where present, on fins, and (in some fishes) on the tail. These taste buds are all innervated by branches of the facial nerve. The olfactory epithelium in the fish is in nasal cavities through which water passes; the nasal cavities do not, except in lungfish, open to the mouth. There is no true Jacobson's organ, although some authors believe that structures near the nostrils may represent a rudiment of this organ (Figure 5).

Feeding behaviour among fish, as with all animals, is determined primarily by the chemical senses, smell being used to find food and taste to determine final palatability. Odours from foods excite movement in hungry fish, but true orientation toward food requires a current to indicate direction.

Social and sexual chemical signals are widespread among fish, though they are probably not as important as visual and possibly acoustic signals. In darkness, or for blindfish in light, species odours are important in schooling. Species differentiation may be excellent; a minnow (*Phoxinus*) can be trained to distinguish 14 different species of fish by their odours, even when the odours are offered in up to 15 different combinations. Mouthbreeders, fishes that hold eggs and young in the mouth, are able to distinguish their own offspring from those of others by odour. Some fish chemically mark their nests with mucus. Redfin shiners, fishes that lay their eggs in the nests of green sunfish, find these nests by the sunfish odour.

Some fish have remarkable powers of olfactory orientation to specific geographic locations. Minnows can distinguish the galaxy of odours of aquatic plants in their home streams and return to them when displaced. The most noteworthy of homing fish are salmon and eels, which return to the freshwater (where they began life) after some years in the sea. Each fish returns to the precise stream in which it was hatched. Many experiments have shown that this is possible only because they sense the odour of the natal stream. Apparently a form of learning called imprinting occurs in these baby fish. The

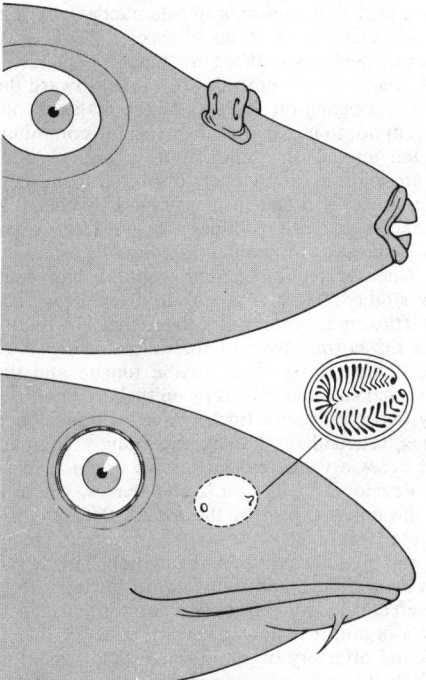

Figure 5: *Nostrils of marine fishes.*
(Top) Puffer (*Tetraodon*) with nostrils on "tentacles."
(Bottom) Cod (*Gadus*) with typical form of nostrils (insert shows detail of folds in nasal cavity).
From J.A. Nicol, *The Biology of Marine Animals;* Sir Isaac Pitman and Sons Limited

hatchlings learn (or are imprinted) to associate the particular odour of a specific stream with home base. Orientation to the mouths of the streams from the sea requires some other talents as well; but, once the fish enters its home river, it unerringly finds its way to the headwaters where it started life.

Among the earliest reports of animal warning odours was that of the so-called *Schreckstoff* (German for "fright substance") given off by agitated fish. Injured fish produce chemicals that alarm other members of their own species, generally causing them to flee. The material is detectable to fish at extremely low concentrations. Some predators have turned this to their advantage; for example, sharks can detect the odour of an injured fish and swim toward it. In the hope that some chemicals besides those naturally occurring could repel sharks from swimmers, considerable effort has been expended to try to find **Shark** a suitable shark repellent. So far the results have not been **repellents** promising, but compounds that are remarkably effective in stimulating other fishes have been found; for example, phenacyl bromide repels teleosts at 0.01 part per million, but unfortunately it does not do this to sharks.

Amphibians. In spite of the widespread use of frogs in physiology laboratories, understanding of chemoreception in amphibians is extremely meagre, particularly as related to their normal life. The gustatory organs are typical taste buds not only on the tongue and walls of the mouth and pharynx but also variously distributed on the lips. The nasal cavities of urodeles (*e.g.*, salamanders, newts) are relatively simple, but those of anurans (toads and frogs) are complex, with three chambers. The olfactory epithelium is of the usual type; in *Triton*, a salamander that lives both in water and air, cells of the olfactory epithelium have long cilia when the animal is an air breather and short cilia when it is a water breather. The Apoda, wormlike amphibians that are blind, have well-developed nasal cavities and olfactory epithelium. The organ of Jacobson in urodeles is a mere grooved channel in the nasal cavity, but in anurans it forms one chamber of the three nasal cavities.

As usual, feeding is chemically mediated, at least in part, although anurans mostly use their eyes for food capture. There have been few studies on chemicals that determine feeding among amphibians. Chemical communication is probably dominant in salamanders, odours of females attracting males in many species. Females of aquatic salamanders are induced to mate by chemicals produced by males. The chemicals are wafted toward the females by tail-wagging on the part of the males. Frogs and toads seem not to use chemical signals for communication, relying instead on auditory and possibly visual signals. As among fish, salamanders displaced from their home stream are able to find their way back by chemical sensing. Tadpoles, like fish, produce a *Schreckstoff* when injured, its discharge causing other tadpoles to scatter.

Reptiles. Chemoreception among reptiles has been very poorly studied. The major physiological work has been with turtles, mostly with objectives that are totally unrelated to the normal lives of the animals. The taste buds of the turtle are restricted to the tongue and the walls of the pharynx; the olfactory epithelium is in the nasal cavity. All reptiles but turtles have well-developed nasal cavities, crocodilians having exceedingly complex

Jacobson's organ in reptiles

cavities and accessory sinuses. Jacobson's organ reaches its acme of development in lizards and snakes, where it opens into the anterior part of the mouth. Nearby, the lacrimal ducts (tear ducts) open, thus irrigating Jacobson's organ and possibly aiding in its function. This organ is absent in crocodilians and indistinct in turtles. While there has been considerable argument about the function of Jacobson's organ, it is now generally believed that it acts as a second olfactory organ in snakes and lizards at least. The forked tongue of some snakes can be inserted into the openings (inside the mouth) of Jacobson's organ, thus bringing chemical particles picked up on the tongue into contact with the olfactory epithelium. All snakes cannot do this, however, and apparently in some species the materials are dissolved off the tongue in the secretion from the lacrimal glands and thus brought to the organ.

Feeding behaviour among reptiles is probably determined to a large extent by chemical stimuli, but there have been few verifying studies. Some snakes find their prey by using the sense of smell, as is shown when newborn young of some snake species attack objects scented with extracts from the skin of species upon which they prey. The receptors involved in this case are in Jacobson's organ. Some predatory snakes cannot trail their prey when this organ is destroyed.

Communication in lizards, turtles, and crocodilians seems to be mostly by visual signals, although some tortoises have glands that secrete chemicals, which they distribute in their territories. Male snakes track females by detecting an odour on their skin; the male will not court his prospective mate if his nostrils are plugged. Rattlesnakes react defensively to the odour of king snakes; conversely, the predatory king snakes track rattlesnakes by their odour. Snakes seem to be more reactive to olfactory stimuli than are other reptiles; nevertheless, reasonable generalizations about the role of chemoreception in the lives of reptiles can only be expected to come from much more study than these animals have had to date.

Birds. General opinion among ornithologists is that birds are predominantly auditory and visual creatures; certainly among birds these senses are usually well developed. This opinion, however, has led to a possibly unwarranted lack of interest in chemical reception among birds. There is growing evidence that chemoreceptors are well developed in at least some birds. The receptors are well-known: taste buds on the tongue and olfactory epithelium in a rather uncomplicated nasal cavity. The olfactory lobe of the brain in many birds (*e.g.*, kiwis, albatrosses) is large, suggesting a high degree of olfactory sensitivity. Birds have no organ of Jacobson.

Early observations on birds in the field led to the belief that their chemical senses were poorly developed, or even totally absent. Later studies, though few and scattered, suggest otherwise, however. Birds taste water before drinking or bathing, for instance, and their thresholds for rejection are similar to those for mammals. Indeed, birds drink water containing some chemicals at concentrations higher than those they tolerate in bathing water. The bathing thresholds may be well below thresholds for gustatory stimulation of mammals. The large olfactory brain areas of many birds certainly indicate that older ideas about their being olfactorily impoverished need re-examination. The few recent studies that have been made show that birds do, indeed, have an olfactory sense. Quail, for instance, can be trained easily to respond to odours and apparently can mark feeding locations by scent from their bodies, much as mammals do. The chemical senses and the place of chemoreception in the lives of birds—as well as reptiles and amphibians—deserve much more study than they have received up to now.

Mammals. Chemoreceptively, mammals are the best studied of vertebrates by far, and man is probably the most studied of all, although experimental techniques that can be used with blowflies (*Phormia*) and rats are inappropriate for humans. The taste buds of mammals are mostly on the upper surface of the tongue, on so-called vallate, foliate, and fungiform papillae. Some taste buds are also on the palate and in the walls of the pharynx. The olfactory epithelium lies dorsally in the nasal cavity, which in most mammals is extensive and complicated. Bony structures (conchae) subdivide the nasal passages, and sinuses extend into the bones of the mammalian skull. Aquatic mammals alone have relatively small olfactory areas. Jacobson's organ is absent in aquatic mammals, bats, and primates (*e.g.*, monkeys and humans). In almost all other mammals the organ is in the nasal septum (central dividing wall), being small but functional. In a few groups of mammals, Jacobson's organ opens into the mouth cavity through special (nasopalatine) ducts.

Mammalian feeding behaviour is dominated by the chemical senses; indeed, mammals generally are activated and oriented primarily by chemical stimuli. Food finding usually involves olfaction, and food testing involves gustation and olfaction together. Flavours of foods seem to determine acceptance or rejection in all mammals. (Flavour refers to the combined experience of taste, smell, texture, and temperature.)

Flavour testing of foods for human use is an important factor in the economics of commercial food processing.

Flavour testing

Therefore an extensive literature exists on the techniques and results of flavour testing and on the production of synthetic flavouring materials. The gustatory organs supply rather restricted information to the brain, but the olfactory receptors supply a vast set of information. As an example of the wide array of volatile chemicals in foods, strawberries contain at least 35 chemical constituents contributing to their odour. These vary from time to time and with conditions in the same berry; for example, crushing converts some materials present in the intact fruit to other substances. The human olfactory organ easily detects these subtle changes, and responses in the brain are thereby affected.

It seems clear that the most important communication signals of mammals are chemical. Social aggregation and territoriality are guided by marking scents secreted by a variety of special glands in different places on the animals' bodies (*e.g.*, on the flanks, back, belly, and near the anus). The secretions are wiped onto objects or sprayed over terrain or are deposited by discharge of urine and feces at particular locations. Almost all mammals chemically mark their nesting or resting areas and quickly detect intruders. Members of a flock or herd (*e.g.*, of sheep) identify one another mainly by scent, apparently producing not only the species scent but also an odour distinctive of that flock or herd alone. Man's use of incense and perfumes in social and religious activities is probably rooted in the basic mammalian pattern of odour sharing within a group.

Similarly, chemical sexual signals are general among mammals. When their nostrils are plugged, male rhesus monkeys and males of some herbivores (*e.g.*, cattle) show no interest in females in heat. Among mice, the odour of strange males (from other communities of mice) interferes with the normal development of fertilized eggs in females; yet, signs of sexual arousal (estrus) can be induced in female mice and other rodents by the odour of a strange male. In probably all terrestrial mammals, arousal of the estral state in females is in response to odours produced by the male genital glands. While fastidious people often may say that sexual odours do not exist for man, the widespread use of perfumes (which supply masked sexual odours) attests to the importance to man of chemical channels in sexual communication.

Orientation to chemical cues is also general among mammals. Many mammals find water or home territories, even when far from them, by the sense of smell. As with fish, it is probable that the total odour complex from soil and plants of a region is detected by mammals.

Mammalian alarm odours

Alarm odours are part of the general communication system of most mammals. Many herbivores have special glands that release odours that alarm the herd when the animals are frightened. Similarly the odour of blood is repellent to many mammals. Many animals (e.g., skunks) have warning odours that repel prowling predators. The tendency of mammals to discharge feces or urine when frightened is also adaptive, for these may act as olfactory repellents to enemies.

Man seems to be an unusual mammal in his limited use of the sense of smell. Other land mammals use olfactory function as their primary sensory basis for interacting with the environment. The sensitivity demonstrated for the human nose with respect to flavour discrimination suggests that even man relies much more than he realizes on the array of olfactory stimuli reaching him from the environment as sources of information.

Theories of chemoreceptor action

Attempts to create theoretical concepts to explain the actions of chemicals on chemoreceptors have generally been directed toward answering one, or both, of two questions:

1. What characteristics of chemical molecules are critical in producing responses by receptor cells?
2. What molecular characteristics elicit the experiences of particular tastes and smells?

There is still no generally accepted answer for either of these. The theoretical constructs developed have been somewhat different for taste and smell.

TASTE (CONTACT CHEMORECEPTION)

Many kinds of actions of sapid substances at gustatory receptor cells have been postulated, and some evidence has supported each. Unfortunately, much evidence militates against each. The most widely accepted possible mechanisms for stimulation of gustatory receptors are the following: (1) chemical reactions at the cell surface; (2) adsorption of molecules on the cell surface; (3) penetration of substances into the cell; (4) enzymatic reactions at the cell surface; and (5) protein bonding in the cell membrane.

Not all of the many adherents of theory (1) select the same type of chemical reaction at the receptor-cell surface. A few physicochemical models of the theory have been proposed, but none fits all the data. The adsorptive theory (2) is probably most widely believed now; while a wide spectrum of data fits this well, not all of the evidence is explained. The penetration theory (3) is supported by correlations between the oil–water solubility and stimulative effectiveness of sapid substances, but the mechanism seems to be too slow and too long lasting. The enzymatic theory (4) can be made to explain almost any data, if one just imagines the existence of the right enzymes (yet to be discovered). Nevertheless, the temperature independence of taste stimulation militates strongly against it, for enzymatic reactions are strikingly influenced by temperature. The protein-bonding theory (5) is weakened, as is the penetration theory (3), because these processes would be slow to reverse; otherwise good fits with data can be obtained by postulating the existence of appropriate proteins.

Some correlation between human taste responses and chemical composition has been found for sweet, salty, and sour substances, but the results are much less clearcut for bitter materials. Most substances do not have one of the four simple tastes, and there are other suggested primary taste qualities, the validity of which has not been settled. Almost all investigators who have studied contact chemoreception in detail have come to doubt the validity of any theory of four primary tastes, at least for mammals. More recent electrophysiological data, although gathered mainly by workers who originally adopted the concept of four primary qualities as their guide, do not support the theory. Individual receptors (except labellar hairs of blowflies) are generally not excited by only one of the four presumed primary categories of sapid compounds. The intergrading of tastes for a large series of chemical compounds and the variety of electrical response patterns of receptors obtained in the laboratory suggest more of a continuum of taste-response patterns in a population of receptor cells than the existence of four specialized receptors for primary gustatory qualities.

SMELL (DISTANCE CHEMORECEPTION)

Theories of olfactory stimulation are even less satisfactory than are those for taste. The events that have been suggested as occurring at the receptor cell to trigger off an olfactory response include the following: (1) chemical reactions at the cell surface; (2) solution of odorant molecules at the surface, thus altering surface tension; (3) radiant energy from an odorant affecting the cell without actual contact of the chemical molecule with the cell; (4) adsorption of the odorant on the cell surface; (5) effect of molecular internal vibrations (molecular resonance) on some aspect of cellular function; (6) enzymatic reactions; (7) penetration of odorant molecules with disruption of receptor-cell membranes; and (8) effect on an olfactory chemical or pigment within the receptor cell, similar to the effect of light on visual pigments such as visual purple (rhodopsin) within the retina of the eye.

Stages in the olfactory response

As would be expected with this array of olfactory theories (and not all proposed ideas are included), there is even less agreement than in the case of taste. The first, fourth, sixth, and seventh of these theories of smell are similar to their counterparts suggested for taste and have the same strong and weak points. The solution theory (2) seems too slow, particularly in accounting for recovery of olfactory sensitivity after adaptation to an odorant has occurred. There is no good positive evidence for olfactory theories based on radiant energy (3) or on olfactory pigments (8). Neither the molecular-resonance theory (5) nor the penetration theory (7) has even majority acceptance right now, although the idea that adsorption (4) is the critical step in stimulation seems to attract adherents.

Attempts to find and name odour primaries have proved more difficult than in the case of postulated taste primaries. A major stumbling block is that none of the theorized primary odour qualities can be related to specific classes of chemical compounds. The postulated primary odours have received such names as: foul, fruity, ethereal, fragrant, resinous, and burnt. The number varies from as few as four primaries to as many as 32, the most usual number being six or eight.

Some current theories relating olfactory experience to chemical or physical characteristics of odorous materials rely upon some postulated selection of primary odours; others do not. Although the first class of theories is based upon attempts to relate specific odours to particular chemicals, no reasonable correspondence between chemical structure and odour has yet been found. Attempts to correlate solubilities or other physicochemical characteristics with odours have been equally unsuccessful. Because many workers believe that the first step in olfactory excitation is adsorption of odorants on the surface of receptor cells, extensive studies have been made on correlations between odour and adsorptive behaviour of chemical compounds at interfaces between water and lipids (e.g., fats or oils). The correlation is surprisingly good in some cases and poor in others. By changing postulated cell-surface characteristics, good correspondence with experimental data can sometimes be obtained, but the theory then potentially seems to fit any data and therefore is suspect.

Theory of
molecular
shape

Two newer, widely discussed theories are based, at least in part, on molecular shape rather than on chemical structure alone. One theory is based on the assumption that odorant molecules puncture the receptor-cell surface, thus releasing ions, and that the ability to puncture the surface depends not only upon the molecule's chemical properties but also on its shape. The olfactory quality experienced is believed to be the result of differential ability of molecules to puncture the receptor cells, determined by the size and shape of the molecules, and by differential rates of healing of the punctures by the cell. Not enough observational data are available on the fundamental events assumed here to make evaluation possible.

An alternative theory starts with the postulate that there are only seven primary odours, each of which results from the fitting of molecules of seven specific sizes and shapes into special receptor sockets imagined to exist on the cells. Thus molecules of compounds with a similar odour should have similar size and shape, and proponents of this idea believe that this is so. Others, however, find situations that are inexplicable by this "socket" theory. A most critical objection to this theory is that it is impossible to code the tremendous variety of definable smells with a system of only seven units. This has led some investigators to postulate many more than seven primary odours, separable molecular shapes for all of which have yet to be discovered.

Still another theory (5) of odour qualities starts from observations of high correlations between low-frequency molecular vibrations (resonances) and odours. This theory assumes different primary receptor cells, the number still unknown but probably relatively large. The primaries, in this case, are not postulated ahead of time (a priori). Since the theory depends on experimental evidence for its detailed development, only time will tell how or if the correlations will emerge. It is not assumed that the molecular characteristics being measured (e.g., resonances called Raman spectra) are in themselves the stimulative factors; instead it is theorized that they are accompaniments of molecular energy characteristics that are the actual factors in olfactory stimulation. Thus, the unspecified molecular vibrational characteristics are postulated as acting upon energy-transfer mechanisms in the cell membrane or as determining orientation of odorant molecules on the cell surfaces.

None of these theories of smell at present has wide enough acceptance to be said to be the dominant idea. The general attitude is one of wait and see, while proponents of each gather data. Only further research will decide whether any one of these, or none, fits the observed evidence. Theories of gustatory qualities, starting with widely accepted agreement on primary tastes, and those on olfaction, starting without a generally accepted scheme of primary modalities, have now come to about the same conceptual turning point.

BIBLIOGRAPHY. J.E. AMOORE, *Molecular Basis of Odor* (1970), a technical discussion of molecular shapes and odours; M. BEROZA (ed.), *Chemicals Controlling Insect Behavior* (1970), technical reports at a symposium on pheromones and defensive secretions of insects; T.H. BULLOCK and G.A. HORRIDGE, *Structure and Function in the Nervous Systems of Invertebrates*, 2 vol. (1965), a monumental review of invertebrate sensory physiology and neurophysiology, with extensive bibliographies; V.G. DETHIER, *The Physiology of Insect Senses* (1963), a technical review, with sections on chemoreception; H. and M. FRINGS, *Animal Communication* (1964), a semipopular survey, including sections on chemical signalling in the animal kingdom; R. HARPER, E.C. BATE SMITH, and D.G. LAND, *Odour Description and Odour Classification* (1968), a technical review of odour theory and practical schemes of classification; T. HAYASHI (ed.), *Olfaction and Taste II* (1967), technical reports at a symposium on vertebrate chemoreception, especially electrophysiological and electron microscope studies, and discussion of theories; J.W. JOHNSTON, D.G. MOULTON, and A. TURK (eds.), "Communication by Chemical Signals," *Advances in Chemoreception*, vol. 1 (1970), a technical discussion of the field; M.R. KARE and O. MALLER (eds.), *The Chemical Senses and Nutrition* (1967), technical reports at a symposium, mostly on human chemoreception, with an extensive bibliography on taste for the years 1566–1966; W.W. KILGORE and R.L. DOUTT (eds.), *Pest Control: Biological, Physical, and Selected Chemical Methods* (1967), technical reviews by specialists, including chapters on pheromones, repellents, and antifeedants; H. KLEEREKOPER, *Olfaction in Fishes* (1969), a semipopular review especially on orientation by odours; L. and M. MILNE, *The Senses of Animals and Men* (1962), a popular survey of senses and behaviour; R.W. MONCRIEFF, *The Chemical Senses*, 3rd ed. (1967), a standard technical reference on chemoreception in vertebrates, particularly man; G.H. PARKER, *Smell, Taste, and Allied Senses in the Vertebrates* (1922), a classic summary of earlier research and theories; H.W. SCHULTZ, E.A. DAY, and L.M. LIBBEY (eds.), *Symposium on Foods: The Chemistry and Physiology of Flavors* (1967), technical reports at a symposium, particularly on chemical analysis for odorants in foods; see the *Scientific American* for excellent semipopular articles on many aspects of chemoreception (February 1964, August 1964, June 1967, May 1968, and February 1969); T.A. SEBEOK (ed.), *Animal Communication* (1968), technical reviews by specialists, with chapters on chemical signalling; E. SONDHEIMER and J.B. SIMEONE (eds.), *Chemical Ecology* (1970), technical reviews by specialists on effects of environmental chemicals on animals, including chapters on plant feeding stimulants, communication signals, defense chemicals, and fish orientation; T.H. WATERMAN (ed.), *The Physiology of Crustacea*, vol. 2 (1961), technical reviews by specialists, including chapters on senses and behaviour; V.B. WIGGLESWORTH, *The Principles of Insect Physiology*, 6th ed. (1965), a standard textbook in the field, including a chapter on chemoreception; K.M. WILBUR and C.M. YONGE (eds.), *The Physiology of Mollusca*, vol. 2 (1966), technical reviews by specialists, including chapters on chemoreception and behaviour; G.E.W. WOLSTENHOLME and J. KNIGHT (eds.), *Taste and Smell in Vertebrates* (1970), technical reports at a symposium, particularly on morphology of receptors, electrophysiology, and theories; D.L. WOOD, R.M. SILVERSTEIN, and M. NAKAJIMA (eds.), *Control of Insect Behavior by Natural Products* (1970), technical reports at a symposium particularly concerned with methods of research on feeding stimulants, deterrents, and pheromones; R.H. WRIGHT, *The Science of Smell* (1964), a semitechnical discussion of odour theories, particularly the molecular vibration theory; Y. ZOTTERMAN (ed.), *Olfaction and Taste* (1963), technical reports at a symposium, particularly on morphology, electrophysiology, and theories.

(H.W.F.)

Chemotherapeutic Drugs

Chemical compounds that destroy infectious agents in animals, including man, are called chemotherapeutic drugs. The term chemotherapy is a controversial one; in one sense, it means treating diseases with chemical agents. This definition is too broad in scope, however, since all drugs used in medicine could be included in such a definition. A widely accepted meaning of the term chemotherapy is based not only on etymology but also on historical tradition. The founder of chemotherapy, the German bacteriologist Paul Ehrlich, wanted to develop specific chemical compounds with a selective toxicity for the causative agents of diseases so that they could be completely eliminated. In this sense, chemotherapeutic drugs are agents that are used to treat infectious diseases caused by bacteria, viruses, fungi, protozoans, and helminths. The term chemotherapy now includes the treatment of cancer with drugs.

HISTORICAL BACKGROUND

The use of chemotherapeutic drugs actually began hundreds of years ago. Cinchona bark, for example, was used in South America for the treatment of malaria as early as the 17th century. Quinine, the main active component of cinchona bark, still is used as an antimalarial drug. Ehrlich, after observing the selective staining of malarial parasites by such dyes as methylene blue in the late 19th century, eventually discovered arsphenamine (Salvarsan), which was the most effective drug for the treatment of syphilis until the introduction of the antibiotic drug penicillin.

Despite early success with the chemotherapeutic approach in treating diseases, however, few useful drugs were developed before 1935, and these were limited to the treatment of syphilis and a variety of tropical diseases. The turning point in chemotherapy occurred in

Development
of the
chemotherapeutic
approach

1935 with the synthesis of a red dye, prontosil, a compound of the sulfonamide drug group; prontosil resulted from research, directed by Gerhard Domagk, a German chemist and pathologist, on the antibacterial action of azo dyes. The successful use of prontosil in experimentally introduced streptococcal infections in mice was significant because, until that time, there was no known synthetic drug that could cure general bacterial infections in man. The interest created by the development of prontosil resulted in the synthesis of a large number of sulfonamide drugs and revolutionized the treatment of bacterial infections. The synthesis of sulfonamide drugs was followed by the discovery of antibiotics. Penicillin, described and named by Sir Alexander Fleming in 1929, was shown to be effective in treating human bacterial infections by Sir Howard Walter Florey and Ernst Boris Chain in 1941; after penicillin, new antibiotics and chemotherapeutic drugs were developed. Isoniazid and para-aminosalicylic acid, for example, became valuable supplements to the antibiotic drug streptomycin in treating tuberculosis; chloroquine, primaquine, and pyrimethamine were used as antimalarial drugs; and piperazine, diethylcarbamazine, bephenium, niridazole, and thiabendazole became important drugs in treating diseases caused by parasitic worms. Antiviral and anticancer chemotherapy show promise.

Until the discovery of chemotherapeutic drugs, man had to rely entirely on sanitation and immunological approaches in defending himself against diseases. The additional defenses provided by chemotherapy, therefore, often are of vital importance. Prevention and treatment of diseases in man, animals, and plants is not, however, the only benefit that has been derived from chemotherapy; applications of chemotherapy also have contributed to understanding control mechanisms and other functions at the cellular level.

ESSENTIAL FEATURE OF CHEMOTHERAPEUTIC DRUGS

Sites and nature of action. Chemotherapeutic drugs have a selective effect on specific causative agents of disease but do not injure the cells of the host. In general, one of three basic reasons usually accounts for the selective effect. The chemotherapeutic drug may have an affinity for the infective agent and accumulate in it, or it may block some biochemical process necessary for survival of the infective agent but not the host. The latter is the most common reason for the selective action of chemotherapeutic drugs. In addition, unequal distribution of a drug in the body of a host may contribute to its success in treating an infectious disease; for example, sulfonamide drugs, which accumulate in higher concentration in the urine than in the blood, are valuable in treating infections of the urinary tract.

Absorption, metabolism, excretion, and toxicity. An ideal chemotherapeutic drug would be completely nontoxic, absorbed easily when taken by mouth, unaltered by metabolic processes, and excreted efficiently and completely. Although no known agent fulfills all of these criteria, many drugs have been modified chemically in attempts to approach these ideal objectives; the absorption and excretion of the sulfonamide drugs, for example, have been modified by changing the structure of the drug molecules using chemical methods.

The extent of metabolism and the rate of excretion influence the duration of action of a drug in the body. A drug with a long-lasting action is advantageous in situations in which prevention of infections for relatively long periods of time (*e.g.*, one or several weeks) is desirable. In most cases, however, a drug that remains in the body only a short time is preferred for two reasons. If adverse effects (*e.g.*, allergic reactions) develop, it is important that the drug be eliminated in a short time; in addition, the amount of a drug in the body is easier to regulate if small doses are administered frequently.

The toxicity of chemotherapeutic drugs is variable. Even the antibiotic penicillin, which is essentially nontoxic to most mammalian cells, may cause allergic reactions that have serious, sometimes fatal, consequences.

In most cases, however, the clinically useful chemotherapeutic drugs are less toxic to human cells than they are to infective agents.

CHEMOTHERAPEUTIC TREATMENT OF PARASITIC DISEASES

Anthelmintic drugs. Although drugs for treating helminthic infections (*i.e.*, those caused by parasitic worms) have long been known, many ancient remedies (*e.g.*, chenopodium oil, carbon tetrachloride, thymol, pelletierine, santonin) have been replaced as more effective, and less toxic, drugs have been developed. One ancient anthelmintic drug, an aspidium oleoresin extracted from a male fern plant, however, is still used to treat some tapeworm infections.

Although they are sometimes found in other organs, parasitic worms are most common in the intestinal tract of man and other animals. Anthelmintic drugs effective in eliminating worms from the intestinal tract are not so successful in treating helminthic infections involving other organs. Systemic infections caused by certain trematode parasites (*e.g.*, schistosomes) and nematode parasites (*e.g.*, filaria, trichinella), for example, do not respond to chemotherapy; most roundworms (phylum Nematoda) and tapeworms (phylum Platyhelminthes), common causative agents of intestinal helminthic infections, however, are eliminated effectively by chemotherapeutic drugs. Diethylcarbamazine citrate is effective in treating filariasis infections caused by nematode parasites such as *Wuchereria bancrofti*, *Brugia malayi*, and *Loa loa*. Adverse effects following the use of this anthelmintic drug generally result from the release of products from the dying filarial parasites. Piperazine citrate and pyrvinium pamoate (an orange-red dye) are safe and effective drugs used to treat roundworm infections caused by certain nematode species. Bephenium hydroxynaphthoate, a synthetic drug used to treat hookworm infections caused by the nematode *Ancylostoma duodenale*, occasionally may cause nausea and diarrhea. Tetrachlorethylene, related chemically to carbon tetrachloride, is much less toxic than the latter and is used to treat hookworm infections caused by *Necator americanus*. Tetrachlorethylene may cause nausea, dizziness, headache, and liver damage. Thiabendazole has been useful in treating a variety of roundworm infections, including those caused by the nematodes *Ascaris lumbricoides*, *Necator americanus*, *Ancylostoma duodenale*, and *Enterobius vermicularis*, as well as infections in man caused by dog and cat roundworms. Other anthelmintic drugs include hexylresorcinol, suramin sodium, niclosamide, and lucanthone hydrochloride.

Quinacrine hydrochloride (Atabrine), a synthetic drug originally used as an antimalarial drug, now is more often used as an anthelmintic drug, especially in the treatment of tapeworm infections caused by the beef tapeworm (*Taenia saginata*), the pork tapeworm (*Taenia solium*), the dwarf tapeworm (*Hymenolepis nana*), or the fish tapeworm (*Diphyllobothrium latum*). Quinacrine may cause adverse reactions such as nausea, headache, and dizziness. A number of drugs containing the chemical element antimony (*e.g.*, antimony potassium tartrate, antimony sodium dimercaptosuccinate, antimony sodium gluconate, stibophen), and used to treat certain schistosome infections, may have serious side effects.

Antimalarial drugs. Since the 17th century, malaria has been treated with extracts of cinchona bark, whose antimalarial ingredient is quinine. Research stimulated by the slight chemotherapeutic activity of the dye methylene blue against the malarial parasite *Plasmodium* culminated around 1930 in the synthesis by German chemists of a large number of potential antimalarial compounds, including pamaquine and quinacrine (Atabrine). When supplies of quinine from Southeast Asia were no longer available to many countries during World War II, quinacrine became the most important antimalarial drug, even though it had many limitations. The necessity for a better antimalarial drug resulted in the examination of more than 15,000 compounds; two promising drugs, chloroquine and primaquine, eventually became important curative drugs for certain forms of malaria. Another antimalarial drug, chloroguanide, was developed in Great Britain.

Although synthetic antimalarial drugs are effective in the treatment of malaria, treatment now is more complex than it was during the hundreds of years that quinine alone was used. Selection of the proper antimalarial drug now is complicated not only by the fact that there are at least six drugs available but also because complex factors such as the species of the causative parasite and its resistance to certain drugs in some geographic areas must be considered.

Quinine, an alkaloid compound that can be extracted from the bark of the cinchona tree, has a nitrogen-containing component known as a quinoline ring; some of the most useful synthetic antimalarial drugs also are quinoline compounds. Although it has been synthesized in the laboratory, quinine is obtained more economically from its natural sources. The drug generally is used as a sulfate or hydrochloride salt. Quinine sulfate is available in tablet form for oral administration; a hydrochloride salt solution is used for injections. Despite the synthesis of newer antimalarial drugs, quinine still is used to treat infections caused by parasites that have become resistant to synthetic drugs such as chloroquine. Large doses of quinine, however, cause a series of symptoms referred to as cinchonism; these symptoms include ringing of the ears, headache, nausea, and disturbances of vision. Very large doses of quinine may cause deafness and blindness.

Chloro-
roquine

Chloroquine is the most generally used synthetic antimalarial drug and has replaced quinine and quinacrine (Atabrine) in the treatment of many types of malaria. Available in tablet form for oral administration and as a hydrochloride salt solution for injection, chloroquine is useful as a suppressive antimalarial drug and is used by individuals who enter an area in which malaria is known to occur. Chloroquine-resistant strains of causative organisms of malaria (*Plasmodium* species) have appeared in some parts of South America and Southeast Asia, and other antimalarial drugs (*e.g.*, quinine, pyrimethamine, Dapsone, sulfadiazine) have replaced chloroquine for treating malaria in these regions. Chloroquine has some adverse effects. Nausea, itching of the skin, and headache, for example, may occur following its use. Skin eruptions and damage to cornea and retina of the eye, however, are less frequently occurring toxic effects.

The mechanism of chloroquine action may be related to its tendency to form complexes with cellular nucleic acids (*i.e.*, deoxyribonucleic acid [or DNA] and ribonucleic acid [or RNA]), which comprise the hereditary material of cells and initiate protein synthesis. Although nucleic acids have similar essential functions in both parasite and host cells, the parasite has a greater affinity for the drug than the host cells. As a result, the drug, present in parasitized cells in larger quantities than in normal red blood cells of the host, destroys the parasite but has little effect on noninfected cells.

Developed during World War II, chemically related to an older antimalarial drug (pamaquine) but not so commonly used as chloroquine, primaquine has some unique properties. It is one of the few drugs that cures malaria caused by the organism *Plasmodium vivax;* simultaneously, however, it may cause severe anemia in certain individuals. Primaquine, orange red in colour, is available in tablet form for oral administration.

Two antimalarial drugs, chloroguanide and pyrimethamine, act in a similar way on malarial parasites. Both drugs interfere with the metabolism of folic acid, thereby blocking in the malarial parasite a variety of folic-acid-requiring reactions. Inhibition of folic-acid synthesis is injurious to both bacteria and plasmodia because these micro-organisms cannot use folic acid unless they synthesize it. Since sulfonamide drugs act in a similar way (see below *Sulfonamide drugs*), chloroguanide and pyrimethamine also increase the effectiveness of sulfonamide drugs and sulfone drugs used to treat malaria. Both chloroguanide and pyrimethamine are available in tablet form for oral administration. Although organisms re-

sistant to these drugs also may develop, pyrimethamine is used to treat cases of malaria in which the causative *Plasmodium* strain has become resistant to chloroquine.

Although primarily antibacterial in action, sulfadiazine and Dapsone are valuable in treating malaria in which the causative organism is resistant to chloroquine. These drugs are discussed more fully below in relation to the chemotherapy of bacterial infections.

Amebicides and other protozoacidal drugs. The protozoan parasite *Entamoeba histolytica* causes intestinal diseases that range from conditions lacking symptoms to those in which dysentery occurs. In addition, the parasite may invade body tissues and cause abscesses in various organs, particularly the liver. Amebicidal drugs are generally of two types. Intestinal amebicides destroy amoebas found in the intestinal tract. A much smaller number of such drugs act as chemotherapeutic drugs by destroying parasites that have entered cells in tissues outside the intestine; these drugs are called extra-intestinal amebicides. The intestinal amebicides include iodine-containing quinoline drugs, compounds containing arsenic (called arsenicals), and several antibiotics. The extra-intestinal amebicides include an alkaloid compound called emetine and chloroquine.

Types of amebicidal drugs

The destruction of amoebas in the intestinal tract is important not only to eliminate symptoms such as diarrhea but also to prevent recurrences of the illness and dissemination of the parasites into tissues in which they can cause serious complications. Because most intestinal amebicides are poorly absorbed if taken by mouth, they are found in high concentrations in the intestinal contents. High intestinal concentrations of these drugs injure the motile forms (called trophozoites) of the parasite *E. histolytica;* the cyst forms of the amoeba are eliminated with the intestinal contents. For complete elimination of an intestinal infection, prolonged treatment with intestinal amebicides is required.

Synthetic iodine-containing quinoline compounds (*e.g.*, chiniofon, iodochlorhydroxyquin, diiodohydroxyquin) are yellow or yellow brown in colour; only partially absorbed from the gastrointestinal tract after oral administration, these drugs are among the oldest and safest intestinal amebicides known. Arsenicals (*e.g.*, carbarsone and glycobiarsol), in tablet or capsule form, may be effective intestinal amebicides because they injure the trophozoites. Many antibiotics are used to treat intestinal amebiasis. The most useful ones, the tetracyclines, exert a direct inhibitory effect on the multiplication of the amoebas. They may also affect the parasite by altering the intestinal flora. Other antibiotics (*e.g.*, paromomycin), although highly amebicidal, are not as widely used for this purpose as are tetracyclines.

Two drugs, emetine and chloroquine, may be used to destroy trophozoites of *E. histolytica* after they have invaded the liver and other organs. The intestinal amebicides are ineffective, however, in treating extraintestinal amebiasis.

Emetine is an alkaloid compound obtained from ipecac, which is the dried root of *Cephaelis ipecacuanha*, a plant native to Brazil. Ipecac has been used in South America for centuries to treat diarrhea; it was not until 1912, however, that the lethal effect of emetine on *E. histolytica* was first demonstrated. Emetine hydrochloride, a white crystalline water-soluble powder, is always administered by injection since it produces nausea if taken orally. Emetine inhibits the multiplication of the motile forms of *E. histolytica*, probably by blocking protein synthesis in the parasite. Although it exerts favourable chemotherapeutic action in extraintestinal amebiasis, emetine also has adverse effects on mammalian cells. Patients who receive emetine injections frequently show at least some adverse effects on the heart, skeletal muscles, and gastrointestinal tract. Although it is far from being an ideal drug, emetine hydrochloride is the most effective drug known thus far for treating liver abscesses caused by *E. histolytica*. Emetine is valuable also in curing acute amoebic dysentery, probably because it destroys parasites within the walls of the intestine.

Although chloroquine is used primarily as an antimalarial drug, it is useful also in treating liver abscesses caused by *E. histolytica*. The drug concentrates in liver tissue and may be used instead of emetine without the many side effects of emetine. Chloroquine often is administered after emetine has been given for several days.

Other proto-zoacidal drugs

A group of chemicals known as nitroimidazole compounds have powerful inhibitory activity against a variety of protozoans. The most important of these drugs, metronidazole or 1-(2-hydroxyethyl)-2-methyl-5-nitro-imidazole, is the first drug known that, when taken by mouth, can cure infections in both males and females caused by *Trichomonas vaginalis*. It is probable that the drug also may be useful in treating other protozoan infections. The mechanism of action of metronidazole, a white crystalline powder, is not yet known with certainty; it is known, however, that the drug inhibits the activity of several specific enzymes. The drug produces disagreeable side effects in humans who have recently ingested alcohol.

CHEMOTHERAPEUTIC TREATMENT OF MICROBIAL DISEASES

Effective treatment of microbial diseases has been an important achievement of chemotherapeutic research. Although the most powerful antimicrobial agents used are antibiotics, this section emphasizes treatments with chemotherapeutic drugs that are not derived from living organisms. (For a detailed discussion of the treatment of microbial diseases with antibiotics see ANTIBIOTIC.)

Following the successful introduction in 1935 of the sulfonamide drug prontosil, numerous infections considered incurable before that time yielded to the chemotherapeutic approach. Despite significant achievements, however, some problems remain that have not yet been solved by drugs, while others have been created by new approaches to the treatment of infections.

Sulfonamide drugs. The chemotherapeutic effect of the sulfonamide drug prontosil resides in the sulfanilamide (*i.e.*, *p*-amino-benzenesulfonamide) portion of the molecule. After this fact was established, thousands of new sulfonamide, or sulfa, drugs, many superior to prontosil, were synthesized. One sulfonamide drug may be considered superior to another as a result of variations in solubility, differences in potency against certain bacteria, or persistence in the body following administration of a single dose. There are only slight differences in antibacterial potency among the sulfonamide drugs; in addition, one sulfonamide drug inhibits about the same range of bacterial species as another.

Absorption of the sulfonamide drugs from the gastrointestinal tract and their excretion by the kidneys in urine differ in extent among individual drugs. Some sulfonamide drugs (*e.g.*, sulfasuxidine, sulfathalidine), absorbed only slightly from the gastrointestinal tract, are commonly referred to as intestinal antiseptics because they affect only bacteria in the intestinal tract. Sulfonamide drugs such as sulfadiazine, on the other hand, are absorbed efficiently but also are metabolized and excreted rapidly. These drugs, therefore, must be administered several times a day. Some longer acting synthetic sulfonamide drugs, which may have to be administered as infrequently as once a day, also have been involved in serious hypersensitivity reactions. In such cases, long persistence of the drug in the body is a disadvantage.

In general, sulfonamide drugs do not dissolve readily in acid solutions (*e.g.*, urine). Since they are excreted from the kidney in urine, therefore, many sulfonamide drugs are not excreted properly and remain in the urinary tract; this is one disadvantage associated with their use. Sulfonamide drugs (*e.g.*, sulfisoxazole) more soluble in urine than others, however, have been synthesized.

Biological antago-nism

The mode of action of a sulfonamide drug is an example of biological antagonism. A sulfonamide drug is an antimetabolite for certain bacteria because it has a molecular structure similar to that of a compound (*i.e.*, para-aminobenzoic acid) required by the bacteria to synthesize a metabolite (*i.e.*, folic acid) essential for growth. The mechanism of action of sulfonamide drugs not only explains their ineffectiveness in the presence of yeast extract, pus, and other materials containing para-aminobenzoic acid (PABA) but also provides a reason for their selective toxicity against certain bacterial species and their lack of toxicity for mammalian cells. Sulfonamide drugs prevent the incorporation of PABA into the essential metabolite folic acid in certain species of bacteria. Since these bacteria must synthesize folic acid but are prevented from doing so by the antagonistic action of the sulfonamide drug, the bacteria cannot divide. On the other hand, mammalian cells can not synthesize folic acid from PABA; they require folic acid that is already formed. The presence of a sulfonamide drug in mammalian cells, therefore, has no effect on their folic-acid content.

Research on the sulfonamides has influenced the synthesis of many useful drugs. Discovery of hypoglycemic sulfonylureas, for example, which are used in the treatment of diabetes; benzothiadiazine diuretics, which are used to increase water excretion by the kidneys; antihypertensive drugs, which are used to reduce blood pressure; and certain antimalarial drugs have resulted from interest in the sulfonamide drugs.

The large number of bacterial species susceptible to the sulfonamide drugs contrasts with the restricted number of infections for which these drugs now are used. The reason is that many other chemotherapeutic agents and antibiotics now are used to treat infections formerly treated by the sulfonamide drugs. The sulfa drugs now are recommended for the treatment of certain urinary tract infections, infectious ulcers caused by venereal disease, certain infections of the eyes (*i.e.*, trachoma), certain types of meningitis (*i.e.*, inflammation of the membranes investing the brain and spinal cord), and in association with the treatment of certain forms of malaria. Generally, sulfonamide drugs are used with higher frequency in regions of the world in which medical care has not yet been fully developed and the selection of antibiotics based on laboratory studies cannot be carried out; in these areas, the simplicity of use and low cost of sulfonamide drugs are advantageous.

Although the sulfonamide drugs are important either alone or in association with other drugs for treating a large number of infections, bacteria tend to develop resistance to them. The value of sulfonamide drugs in the chemotherapy of various diseases, therefore, must be re-evaluated at intervals; after several decades of use, for example, the sulfonamide drugs may lose their effectiveness in treating gonococcal, meningococcal, and streptococcal infections. In addition, although the toxicity of the sulfonamide drugs for mammalian cells is low, and experimental animals such as mice tolerate very large doses, some patients (1 to 5 percent) manifest adverse effects that range from skin rashes to drug fever.

Antileprotic drugs. The treatment of leprosy was unsuccessful for hundreds of years. After the discovery of the sulfonamide drugs, however, the related sulfone drugs were found to be useful in treating this disease. The sulfone drugs used in the treatment of leprosy include diaminodiphenylsulfone (Dapsone), sulfoxone sodium (Diasone), and solapsone (Sulphetrone); all are available in tablet form for oral administration. When they are used for long periods of time, sulfone drugs effectively reverse the course of leprosy. The mode of action and adverse effects of the sulfone drugs probably are similar to those of the closely related sulfonamide drugs. Although the sulfone drugs are more effective in treating leprosy than are the sulfanilamide drugs, the reasons for this difference are not yet clear.

Antituberculotic drugs. Infections caused by the tubercle bacillus, *Mycobacterium tuberculosis*, were unaffected by chemotherapeutic drugs until the discovery of the antibiotic streptomycin. Although several sulfone drugs now used as antileprotics showed promise against the tubercle bacillus, they are not usually used to treat human tuberculous infections. The turning point in antituberculotic chemotherapy was the demonstration by the Nobel Prize winner Selman A. Waksman in 1943 of the

Strepto-mycin

powerful action of streptomycin against the tubercle bacillus. Very small amounts of streptomycin inhibited the multiplication of the bacillus; in addition, streptomycin could eliminate tuberculous infections in guinea pigs and aided in the recovery of patients who were suffering from tuberculous meningitis, a fatal disease until that time. The striking success that was achieved with streptomycin was tempered, however, by its toxic effects and the tendency of the tubercle bacillus to develop streptomycin-resistant strains. The development of the chemotherapeutic agent para-aminosalicylic acid (PAS), although only slightly antituberculotic when administered alone, helped delay the development of resistant strains of the tubercle bacillus when it was used in conjunction with streptomycin. The drug isoniazid (INH) is used with other preventive and curative drugs to increase their effectiveness. In addition to these standard antituberculotic drugs, a number of secondary drugs (e.g., ethionamide, pyrazinamide, ethambutol, cycloserine, and viomycin) serve as additional defenses against tuberculous infections. Streptomycin kills a variety of bacteria, including the tubercle bacillus. Its selective toxicity for bacteria is relative, however, since it also can damage the auditory nerve in humans. Streptomycin also may cause allergic reactions (e.g., skin rashes and fever) in its users. Streptomycin is administered by intramuscular injection because the drug is not absorbed when taken by mouth.

Para-aminosalicylic acid (PAS) and some of its salts are used in tablet form to treat tuberculosis. Although PAS inhibits the multiplication of certain strains of M. tuberculosis, it has no effect on most bacterial species. The selective effect of PAS on the tubercle bacillus is difficult to explain since the inhibitory action of the drug is antagonized by para-aminobenzoic acid; this condition suggests that PAS has a mechanism of action which is similar to that of the sulfonamide drugs. PAS also has been used with drugs other than streptomycin to treat tuberculosis. Disadvantages of PAS include toxic and allergic side effects; some of them (e.g., gastrointestinal upsets), almost impossible to avoid, are especially troublesome since the drug is effective only when administered in large doses.

Isoniazid (INH), or isonicotinic acid hydrazide, which was first used in the early 1950s, is available as tablets or syrup for oral administration; an injectable preparation also is used occasionally. Although isoniazid is active in the prevention and the treatment of infections that are caused by M. tuberculosis, these micro-organisms tend to develop isoniazid-resistant strains; for this reason the drug generally is used in combination with streptomycin or para-aminosalicylic acid. The mechanism of isoniazid action is not yet completely understood. Some of its toxic effects may be prevented by administering the vitamin pyridoxine, which does not, however, prevent the beneficial effects of the drug. The metabolism of isoniazid in humans is an example of a pharmacogenetic abnormality. The rate at which isoniazid undergoes a specific metabolic change in the body is controlled by the hereditary material of the cell. As a result, most of the people who use this drug belong to one of two groups: slow isoniazid inactivators and rapid isoniazid inactivators. The slow inactivators, because they are unable to metabolize the drug rapidly, build up higher concentrations of the drug in the bloodstream and thus are more likely to develop toxic effects than are rapid inactivators who are on the same dosage schedule.

Secondary drugs

Use of secondary drugs in treating tuberculosis is limited by their adverse reactions. These drugs are important, however, if the tubercle bacillus develops strains resistant to the standard drugs (i.e., streptomycin, PAS, and INH) or if they fail to achieve a desired therapeutic objective. Secondary antituberculotic drugs include cycloserine, ethambutol, ethionamide (structurally related to isoniazid), pyrazinamide, and viomycin (a Streptomyces antibiotic).

Antibiotic drugs. Antibiotics may be considered true chemotherapeutic agents; their derivation from living organisms does not provide them with any properties not possessed by synthetic drugs. Many antibiotic drugs, although they originate from growth cultures of living organisms, subsequently are modified by chemical means. Semisynthetic penicillins, for example, represent chemical modifications of 6-aminopenicillanic acid, which is isolated from cultures of the mold *Penicillium*. Antibiotics are discussed in the separate but related article ANTIBIOTIC.

THE USE OF CHEMOTHERAPEUTIC DRUGS IN THE TREATMENT OF CANCER

The success of chemotherapy in treating parasitic and microbial diseases is based on exploiting an essential difference in structure or function between invading organisms and host. A chemotherapeutic drug that is effective against a specific infection usually is discovered accidentally, after research shows that the invading organisms are more vulnerable to the drug than is the host. A similar series of events occurs in cancer chemotherapy. The small but different susceptibilities of malignant cells, as compared with normal cells, to a variety of drugs may eventually result in successful cancer chemotherapy. Although drugs used in cancer chemotherapy may be beneficial, they do not generally cure the disease. An exception is methotrexate, a folic-acid antagonist, which has a curative effect in the treatment of choriocarcinoma (usually in the ovary) in women. Drugs used in cancer chemotherapy include alkylating agents (e.g., nitrogen mustards), antimetabolites (e.g., folic-acid antagonists), plant alkaloids, antibiotics (e.g., actinomycin D), hormones, and radioactive isotopes.

BIBLIOGRAPHY. A. ALBERT, *Selective Toxicity*, 6th ed. (1979); a thorough discussion of the history and principles of chemotherapy; P.H. BELL, J.F. BONE, and R.O. ROBLIN, JR., "Relationship of Structure to Activity of Sulfanilamide-type Compounds," *J. Amer. Chem. Soc.*, 66:847 (1944), a classic study; J. BURCHENAL, "Some Problems Basic to Cancer Research, with Particular Reference to Chemotherapy," *Cancer Res.*, 23:1186–90 (1963), and with J.R. BURCHENAL, "Chemotherapy of Cancer," *Chemistry*, 50:11–17 (July/August 1977); P. FILDES, "A Rational Approach to Research in Chemotherapy," *Lancet*, 1:955–957 (1940), the theory of competitive inhibition as an approach to chemotherapy; A. GOLDIN and F. HAWKING (eds.), *Advances in Chemotherapy*, vol. 1 (1964), historical perspectives in chemotherapy; L.S. GOODMAN and A. GILMAN, "Chemotherapy of Parasitic Disease," "Chemotherapy of Microbial Diseases," and "Chemotherapy of Neoplastic Diseases," in *The Pharmacological Basis of Therapeutics*, 6th ed. (1980), authoritative discussions of chemotherapeutic drugs; R.S. MITCHELL, "Control of Tuberculosis," *New Eng. J. Med.*, 276:842 (1967); *Proceedings* of the INTERNATIONAL CONGRESS OF CHEMOTHERAPY, convened every two years, collections of papers on recent research.

(A.Go.)

Cheng Ch'eng-kung

Better known to people in the West as Koxinga (or Coxinga), Cheng Ch'eng-kung (in Pinyin romanization Zheng Cheng-gong) in the 17th century led a prolonged resistance by pro-Ming-dynasty Chinese forces in Fukien Province against the Manchu conquerors of China. His most lasting achievement was the expulsion of the Dutch from Taiwan and the establishment of Chinese control over that island.

Cheng Ch'eng-kung was born on August 28, 1624, to a Japanese woman in the small seacoast town of Hirado, near Nagasaki in Japan. His father, Cheng Chih-lung, was a maritime adventurer who made a fortune through trade and piracy in the Taiwan Straits.

Cheng Ch'eng-kung was raised by his mother in Japan until the age of seven, when his father, having been given an official position in maritime defense by the Ming dynasty, recalled him to the ancestral home in southern Fukien. There, separated from his mother, Cheng was given the conventional scholarly Confucian education, entering the Imperial Academy of Learning at Nanking in 1644.

With the fall of the southern capital to the invading Manchus the next year, young Cheng retired with his father to Fukien, where Cheng Chih-lung's military power was the basis for setting up the Prince of T'ang as pretender to the Ming throne. It was at this juncture that, as a sign of special favour, the Ming Prince conferred the imperial surname, Chu, upon the youthful Cheng Ch'eng-

Recognition by the Ming pretender

kung. Thus originated his most commonly used title, Lord of the Imperial Surname—in Chinese Kuo Hsing Yeh, corrupted by the Dutch into Koxinga.

When Manchu forces entered Fukien, his father succumbed to their offers of preferment under the new Ch'ing dynasty (the dynastic name of the Manchus) and abandoned the fragile Ming court at Foochow. The Prince of T'ang was captured and killed; but Cheng Ch'eng-kung, resisting his father's orders to abandon a lost cause, vowed to restore the Ming dynasty and began to build up land and naval forces for that purpose.

Over the next 12 years the Manchu's preoccupation with larger Ming remnants in the southwest, plus Cheng's considerable strategic and organizational talents, allowed Cheng to build a strong position on the Fukien coast, centred on the islands of Amoy and Quemoy. Although this region was in effect his personal kingdom, he continued to use Ming reign titles and to acknowledge the suzerainty of the last Ming pretender—the Prince of Kuei in southwest China. He also consistently refused blandishments of rank and power from the Manchus, even those supported by personal entreaties from his father.

In 1659 Cheng launched his most ambitious military campaign, a maritime expedition with more than 100,000 troops up the Yangtze River. With large Manchu forces still campaigning in the south, he achieved remarkable initial success, smashing through the lower Yangtze defenses to the gates of Nanking. There, however, mistaken strategy and failure to heed his field commanders' advice led to a disastrous defeat.

Forced back to his original base of Amoy, Cheng was still unbeatable at sea; but the collapse of Ming resistance in the southwest and the Ch'ing's new policy of forced inland emigration of the coastal population put him in a dangerous position. In these circumstances he hit upon the plan of taking Taiwan from the Dutch as a secure rear base area.

Invasion of Taiwan

In April of 1661 he landed on Taiwan near the main Dutch stronghold at Anping (near the present-day city of Tainan) with a force of more than 25,000 men. After a nine-month siege, the small Dutch garrison capitulated and were allowed to leave Tainan safely with their personal possessions. Cheng followed this military success by setting up an effective civil administration based on Tainan and settling the island with his soldiers and with refugees brought from Fukien. His larger ambitions on the mainland and half-formed plans for ousting the Spaniards from the Philippines, however, were cut short by his premature death on June 23, 1662.

His son, Cheng Ching, used the Taiwan base to sustain the anti-Manchu struggle for another 20 years. But after his death in 1681, the Cheng kingdom on Taiwan fell to a Ch'ing invasion fleet in 1683. This defeat ended the longest lived of the Ming restorationist movements.

Thus Cheng's plans ultimately failed, but his posthumous reputation has grown to remarkable proportions. In Japan the famous 18th-century playwright Chikamatsu's *Battles of Koxinga* made Cheng as well-known to Japanese audiences as Othello is to the English. In Europe, lurid Dutch accounts of the fall of Formosa (Taiwan) established Cheng as one of the few Chinese historical figures to bear a latinized name. In his own country he soon became a popular deity and cultural hero to the early Chinese settlers of Taiwan—Kai Shan Sheng Wang, the Sage King Who Settled the Country. On the official level, in 1875 the Ch'ing court recognized its old protagonist as a paragon of loyalty and established an official temple to him on Taiwan.

Later reputation

The development of modern Chinese nationalism in the 20th century has put Cheng Ch'eng-kung in the front ranks of China's historical heroes. To the anti-Manchu revolutionaries of the early 1900s he was a natural forebear. To Republican-period nationalists he was a symbol of resistance against foreign invaders. And in midcentury he continued to receive the accolade of "national hero" from both Chinese governments—from the Nationalists on Taiwan for his determination to restore proper Chinese rule and from the Communists on the mainland

mainly for his great victory over Western (Dutch) imperialism.

In his own day a martyr to a lost cause, Cheng Ch'eng-kung became a hero to all sides in modern Chinese politics, although to each for a different reason.

BIBLIOGRAPHY. EARL SWISHER, "Chêng Ch'êng-kung," in A.W. HUMMEL (ed.), *Eminent Chinese of the Ch'ing Period, 1644–1912*, vol. 1, pp. 108–110 (1943, reprinted 1964), is a very brief but reliable biography. See also the articles on Cheng Ching and Cheng Chih-lung. W. CAMPBELL, *Formosa Under the Dutch* (1903), is still the most detailed English-language account of the Cheng regime on Taiwan. DONALD KEENE (ed.), *The Battles of Coxinga, Chikamatsu's Puppet Play, Its Background and Importance* (1951), although entirely unreliable historically, is of interest for the Japanese image of the hero.

(R.C.C.)

Cheng Ho

Cheng Ho (in Pin-yin romanization, Jeng Ho), a Chinese admiral of the early 15th century, commanded seven naval expeditions to the Indian Ocean almost a hundred years before the Portuguese reached India by sailing around Africa. The son of a ḥājjī, a Muslim who had made the pilgrimage to Mecca, Cheng Ho was born Ma San-pao in K'un-ming, Yunnan Province, about 1371. His family claimed descent from an early Mongol governor of Yunnan and a descendant of King Muḥammad of Bukhara. The family name Ma was derived from the Chinese rendition of Muḥammad. In 1381, when he was about ten years old, Yunnan, the last Mongol hold in China, was reconquered by Chinese forces led by generals of the newly established Ming dynasty. The young Ma Ho, as he was then known, was among the boys who were captured, castrated, and sent into the army as orderlies. By 1390, when these troops were placed under the command of the Prince of Yen, Ma Ho had distinguished himself as a junior officer, skilled in war and diplomacy; he also made influential friends at court.

Background and early years

In 1400 the Prince of Yen revolted against his nephew, the Yün-wen emperor, becoming the Yung-lo emperor in 1402. Under the Yung-lo administration, the war-devastated economy of China was soon restored. The Ming court then sought to display its naval power to bring the maritime states of South and Southeast Asia in line.

For 300 years the Chinese had been extending their power out to sea. An extensive seaborne commerce developed to meet the taste of the Chinese for spices and aromatics and the need for raw industrial materials. Chinese travellers abroad, as well as Indian and Muslim visitors, widened the geographic horizon of the Chinese. Technological developments in shipbuilding and in the arts of seafaring reached new heights by the beginning of the Ming.

The Emperor having conferred on Ma Ho, who had become a court eunuch of great influence, the surname Cheng, he was henceforth known as Cheng Ho. Selected by the Emperor to be commander in chief of the missions to the "Western Oceans," he first set sail in 1405, commanding 300 ships and 27,000 men. The fleet visited Champa (now South Vietnam), Siam, Malacca, and Java; then through the Indian Ocean to Calicut, Cochin, and Ceylon (now Sri Lanka). Cheng Ho returned to China in 1407.

The naval expeditions

On his second voyage, in 1409, Cheng Ho encountered treachery from King Alagonakkara of Ceylon. He defeated his forces and took the King back to Nanking as a captive. In 1411 Cheng Ho set out on his third voyage. This time, going beyond the seaports of India, he sailed to Hormuz on the Persian Gulf. On his return he touched at Samudra, on the northern tip of Sumatra.

On his fourth voyage Cheng Ho left China in 1413. After stopping at the principal ports of Asia, he proceeded westward from India to Hormuz. A detachment of the fleet cruised southward down the Arabian coast, visiting Djofar and Aden. A Chinese mission visited Mecca and continued to Egypt. The fleet visited Brava and Malindi and almost reached the Mozambique Channel. On his return to China in 1415, Cheng Ho brought the envoys of over 30 states of South and Southeast Asia to pay homage to the Chinese Emperor.

During Cheng Ho's fifth voyage (1417–19), the Ming fleet revisited the Persian Gulf and the east coast of Africa. A sixth voyage was launched in 1421 to take home the foreign emissaries from China. Again he visited Southeast Asia, India, Arabia, and Africa. In 1424 the Yung-lo emperor died. In the shift of policy the new emperor, Hung-hsi, suspended naval expeditions abroad. Cheng Ho was appointed garrison commander in Nanking, with the task of disbanding his troops.

Cheng Ho's seventh voyage left China in the winter of 1431, visiting the states of Southeast Asia, the coast of India, the Persian Gulf, the Red Sea, and the east coast of Africa. He returned to China in the summer of 1433. Since Cheng Ho's name no longer appears in historical chronicles after that date, he may have died about that time.

Assessment Cheng Ho was the best known of the Yung-lo emperor's diplomatic agents. Although some historians see no achievement in the naval expeditions other than flattering the Emperor's vanity, these missions did have the effect of extending China's political sway over maritime Asia for half a century. Admittedly, they did not, like similar voyages of European merchant-adventurers, lead to the establishment of trading empires. Yet, in their wake, Chinese emigration increased, resulting in Chinese colonization in Southeast Asia and the accompanying tributary trade, which lasted to the 19th century.

BIBLIOGRAPHY. There is no definitive biography of Cheng Ho. The following titles tell only about his travels, though they give aspects of his life in passing. The best is still CHENG HO-SHENG, *Cheng Ho i-shih hui-pien* (1947). As to Western-language sources, J.J.L. DUYVENDAK's short book, *China's Discovery of Africa* (1949), originally a speech delivered in London, is the best general work on the subject of Chinese naval expeditions of early Ming.

(J.-p.L.)

Ch'en Tu-hsiu

Ch'en Tu-hsiu (in Pin-yin romanization, Chen Du-xiu), the founder of the Chinese Communist Party and an important leader in the Chinese intellectual and cultural revolution, is most noted for his devastating attacks upon traditional Chinese ethical, social, and literary ideals. With the establishment of the "New Youth" monthly under his editorship, in 1915, he vigorously promoted the adoption of Western thought and social systems—epitomized by science and democracy—and gave impetus to the celebrated May Fourth Movement. Named after the date of the massive student protests in 1919 against the Chinese government's weak policy toward Japan and the Shantung resolution of the Versailles Peace Conference, which was going to transfer German rights in China to the Japanese, the May Fourth Movement launched an intellectual, social, and political revolution.

Early education and career Ch'en was born to a wealthy family in Huaining County, Anhwei Province, on October 8, 1879. His father, who had passed the first degree in the civil service examination and served as an official in the military office in Manchuria, died when Ch'en was a few months old. The youngest of four children, Ch'en was brought up by his mother and educated in the Chinese Classics and traditional literature in turn by his grandfather, several private tutors, and, finally, by his brother. In 1896 Ch'en passed the first civil service examination summa cum laude in Huaining and the next year passed the second in Nanking. His experience in the examinations, however, convinced him of the irrelevance of the traditional educational and governmental systems in the 20th century and prompted him to become a social and political reformer. Consequently, he entered the renowned Ch'iu-shih (Truth-Seeking) Academy in Hangchow, where he studied French, English, and naval architecture.

In 1901, at the age of 22, Ch'en, after delivering speeches against the Manchu regime in the capital of his home province, fled to Nanking. He went to Japan the next year for study, enrolling at the Tokyo Higher Normal School. Upon his return to China in 1903 he assisted friends in establishing the subversive *National Daily News* in Shanghai, which was quickly suppressed by the authorities. He then went back to Anhwei in 1904, where he established a periodical to promote the use of the vernacular in writing. In 1906 Ch'en again went to Japan and studied at Waseda University in Tokyo but returned to Anhwei in the same year to teach at a high school and establish another vernacular periodical in Wu-hu. During his stay in Japan, Ch'en refused to join the revolutionary party led by Sun Yat-sen, because he did not wish to accept nationalism, which was one of its tenets. According to some reports, in the following year Ch'en went to study in France and became an enthusiastic admirer of French culture. Upon his return to China in 1910 he visited Manchuria for a short time before teaching at the Army Elementary School in Hangchow. After the overthrow of the Manchu monarchy and the establishment of the republic in 1911, Ch'en became secretary general to the military governor of Anhwei Province and, concurrently, dean of the provincial higher normal school. After taking part in the unsuccessful second revolution against Pres. Yüan Shih-k'ai in 1913, he fled to Japan, where he helped to edit "The Tiger" (*Chia-yin tsa-chih*), a liberal Chinese magazine calling for political reforms.

Role in the intellectual revolution The period of Ch'en's greatest influence on Chinese thought and politics began on his return to China in 1915, when he established the monthly "Youth Magazine" in Shanghai, later renamed "New Youth" (*Hsin ch'ing-nien*). In its pages he proposed that the youth of China undertake a vast intellectual, literary, and cultural revolution to rejuvenate the nation. Many of the young writers who contributed to the monthly—among them Hu Shih, a liberal promoter of the vernacular literature, Lu Hsün, a leading short story writer and essayist, Li Ta-chao, Ch'en's chief collaborator in the Chinese Communist Party, and Mao Tse-tung—were later to become important intellectual and political leaders.

Between 1916 and 1927, in the absence of a strong central power, numerous warlords arose in most parts of the country, whose armed quarrels all but rent China. Ch'en's revolutionary mission thus assumed even greater importance; when, in 1917, he was appointed dean of the School of Letters at the Peking National University, he took care to gather around him many liberal and progressive professors and students. With their help, he established the short-lived radical "Weekly Critic" (*Mei-chou p'ing-lun*) in December 1918. Their "new thought" and "new literature" dominated the May Fourth Movement. Because of his prominent role in the movement, however, Ch'en was forced to resign his post and was imprisoned for three months from June to September 1919.

The Russian Revolution of 1917 impressed Ch'en as a way of modernizing an underdeveloped country, and shortly after his release he was converted to Marxism in Shanghai. There, in May 1920, with a handful of followers, Ch'en founded the Chinese Communist Party, of which he was elected secretary general. (The founding date was officially set later as July 1921 by the present party leadership.) He remained in that post as the party's undisputed leader for seven years, often regarded as "China's Lenin." In December 1920, in an effort to promote his Communist views, Ch'en accepted the invitation of the rebel military governor of Kwangtung to become head of the education board of the provincial government in Canton. In the fall of 1922, Ch'en established the influential "Guide Weekly" (*Hsiang-tao chou-pao*) as a successor to the "New Youth," which he had converted into a Communist organ two years earlier. After his attendance at the Fourth Congress of the Comintern (the international organization of Communist parties) in Moscow in November–December 1922, Ch'en reluctantly carried out the order of the Comintern to head his party's collaboration with the Kuomintang (the Nationalist Party founded by Sun Yat-sen); he was elected to that party's Central Committee in January 1924. A year later, when the right wing of the Kuomintang launched its attack on the Communists, Ch'en repeatedly proposed to withdraw en masse from the Nationalist Party but was overruled by the Comintern. After the collaboration col-

Foundation of the Chinese Communist Party

lapsed in 1927, the Comintern blamed Ch'en for the failure of the alliance with the Kuomintang and had him removed from his position of leadership. In November 1929, he was expelled from the party. For several years, with the support of the Chinese Trotskyists and other Communist dissenters, he tried to regain influence in the party but failed.

On October 15, 1932, Ch'en was arrested by the foreign administration of Shanghai, where he had been residing since 1927. Extradited to Nanking, he was tried and in 1933 sentenced to 15 years in prison by the Nationalist government. After the outbreak of the Sino-Japanese War, he was released on parole in August 1937. Ch'en moved from place to place until the end of 1938, when he arrived in the wartime capital, Chungking, where he taught for a while in a junior high school. In poor health and with few friends, he retired to Chiang-ching, a small town west of Chungking, where he died on May 27, 1942.

A fearless protester, Ch'en rejected China's traditional values and saw Marxism as a means to achieve a "mass democracy" with the broad labouring masses as its base. He recognized, however, the significant role played by the bourgeoisie in the Chinese revolution that he hoped to achieve. During the last years of his life, Ch'en, still a Socialist, denounced Stalin's dictatorship, and defended such democratic institutions as an independent, nonpartisan judiciary, opposition parties, the free press, and free elections.

BIBLIOGRAPHY. HOWARD L. BOORMAN (ed.), *Biographical Dictionary of Republican China*, vol. 1 (1967); DONALD W. KLEIN and ANNE B. CLARK, *Biographic Dictionary of Chinese Communism, 1921–1965* (1971), contain basic biographies. CHOW TSE-TSUNG, *The May Fourth Movement: Intellectual Revolution in Modern China* (1960), and *Research Guide to the May Fourth Movement* (1963), provide detailed accounts (and bibliography) of Ch'en's background and activities during 1915–25.

(T.-t.C.)

Chess

Chess, a game for, usually, two players, uses a checkered board and specially designed pieces. Each player moves in accordance with fixed restrictions on the movement of each type of piece, attempting to force the opponent's principal piece, the King, into a position where it is unable to escape capture (checkmate). In French the game is Échecs; Spanish Ajedrez; German Schachspiel; Russian Shakhmat; late Latin Ludus Scaccorum; from the Persian *shāh*, "king"—also *māt*, "dead." Because of its previous pre-eminence among intellectual pastimes favoured by the upper classes, it is also called the Royal Game. It originated in India, or China, during or before the 6th century from ancient forms, derivations of which may still persist in certain regional variants, such as Chinese, Korean, Japanese, Malay, and Burmese Chess. The game spread westward through Persia to Arabia and thence to western Europe, where it also acquired a patron goddess, Caissa, the Muse of Chess, first appearing in a poem by Sir William Jones in 1763.

Chess has been likened to the logistics and conduct of war (*e.g.*, F.K. Young: *Chess Generalship*, Boston, 1910) in a somewhat inconclusive interpretation of the Chess features of attack and defense, aiming at the surrender of the opponent's King. Nevertheless, the game is only a rather limited simulation of war or, in Freudian terms, a sublimation of that aggressive impulse. More likely, the game contains elements of Indian symbolism and other allegories (see below *Origin of Chess*). The game of Chess as defined here is the present version so recognized in almost all parts of the globe and under the auspices of the World Chess Federation, the international governing body of the game.

Following a description of the Chessboard and the Chessmen, this article includes the history of Chess, the characteristics of the game, the development of modern Chess, types of Chess competition including governing bodies and events, Chess composition including problems, Chess sets, designs, and pieces, and Chess and thought.

The Chessboard. The Chessboard consists of 64 squares, coloured alternately light and dark, arranged in eight vertical rows called files and eight horizontal rows called ranks. The rows, or lines, of squares of the same colour that crisscross the Chessboard are called diagonals. The players—or opponents—are called White and Black (regardless of the actual colours of the Chess set). The players are seated opposite each other with the board placed between them, so that each player has a white corner square at his right hand. In printed diagrams (as illustrated in Figure 1), the Black side is by

Figure 1: Diagram showing position of Chessmen at beginning of game. Queen's Rook (QR); Queen's Knight (QN); Queen's Bishop (QB); Queen (Q); King (K); King's Bishop (KB); King's Knight (KN); King's Rook (KR). The Chessmen in front of these pieces are the Pawns.

convention on top, with the White Pawns imagined to be moving upward, the Black Pawns downward. The conventional Chessboard consists of black (or brown) and white (or beige) squares.

The Chessmen or Chess set. Each opponent has a set of 16 men, one set light in colour for the White side, the other dark for the Black side, both placed facing each other (see Figure 1). The first row is occupied by the "pieces," distinguished by their shapes into five kinds: King, Queen, Rook, Bishop, Knight, abbreviated in conventional notation: K, Q, R, B, N. The men in front of these pieces, positioned in the second row, are called Pawns, abbreviated P. Though the term piece or pieces is often interchanged for the word Chessmen, in an accurate sense it should exclude Pawns and apply only to the pieces standing in the first row. To avoid ambiguity, the pieces and Pawns together are sometimes designated as the material.

HISTORY

Origin of Chess. Sir William Jones, the creator of Caissa (see above), in his essay "On the Indian Game of Chess" (*Asiatic Researches*, 1790), maintained that Hindustan was the cradle of Chess, the game having been known since ancient times by the name of Chaturaṅga; that is, the four (*chatur*) *aṅga*(s), or parts of an army, said to be elephants, horses, chariots, and foot soldiers. Jones's essay is substantially a translation of the *Bhaviṣya-Purāṇa* (550 BC), a tractate on "moralities" including a purported description of a four-handed game of Chess played with dice. He argued that Chaturaṅga was introduced into Persia in the 6th century AD and thence as Shatranj (or Shitranj) into Arab lands. H.J.R. Murray, in his authoritative *History of Chess* (1913, reprinted 1962), concluded that Chess is a descendant of an Indian game transmitted to the West in the shape it had assumed sometime in the 7th century.

To this version has been added a hypothesis that attributes the origin, structure, and attraction of Chess to certain elemental ancient symbolisms. In a thesis published in the official Chess organ and magazine *FIDE* (1964, No. 2 and 4; and 1965, No. 2) a Yugoslav, Pavle Bidev, attempted to link the development of Chess (and

Origins; relation to symbolism and ritual

board games in general) genetically to secret magical and religious rituals of ancient times. He connected the geometrical progressions inherent in the Chessboard and the moves with numerical symbolism, the choice of Chessmen and their movement with cosmic elements, and the total interplay of the men on the board with allusions to astronomy and the universe. He also drew comparisons to the summations in the so-called magic squares, passed on from India by the Muslims, and their various parallels with Chess moves and some Knight's tours (Chess constructions in which a Knight makes a circuit of the board touching each square once). All of these symbolisms are taken as projected into the framework of war board games such as Chess.

Allegorically, a multitude of parables and metaphors has been woven around Chess for centuries, and Chess motifs have had a particular attraction for iconography (see below *Chess sets, designs, and pieces*).

Early history. The game was most likely passed on to the Spaniards by the Muslims, and to the Italians by the Byzantines, and thus made its way further into Europe. It became a favourite pastime of the aristocracy, whereas the clergy frowned on it as a wasteful and compulsive detraction from spiritual commitment.

After the game's entry into Europe, its rules, moves, and laws gradually underwent important changes that increased the range of the pieces and speeded the course of the game. Although the King seems to have had the same move as at present, the faster manoeuvre of castling (see below *The moves*) dates no further back than the first half of the 17th century. The Queen has undergone changes in name, sex, and power. In Shatranj the piece was called *farz* or *firz*, meaning "counsellor," or "general." The French may have changed it into *fierce*, *fierge*, and *vierge* ("virgin"), which, if true, might explain its becoming a female. Another and less speculative account has it that formerly a Pawn on reaching an eighth square was elevated in value and became a *farz* and not any other piece—a promotion that was of the same kind as that in Draughts (or Checkers; in French, Dames). Thus the Pawn became a *dame* or Queen as in the latter game, and thence *dama*, *donna*, etc.

The Queen formerly moved only one square diagonally and was consequently the weakest piece on the board. The immense power now possessed by her seems not to have been conferred until about the middle of the 15th century.

The Bishop, who once could move only two squares diagonally, may now traverse the length of a whole diagonal. Among the Persians this piece was called *pil*, "elephant," but the Arabs, not having the letter *p* in their alphabet, wrote it *fil* or, with their definite article, *al-fil*, whence *alfiere* (Italian) and perhaps *fol* and *fou* (French). The term Bishop seems to match parallel development of an otherwise different northern European nomenclature and styling of carved Chessmen. He was the next in command and a force assisting the "counsellor" or "minister" (the Queen) and has become the accepted term in northern Europe and in English usage.

The Rook, despite its rotund shape, is the sketched condensation of the Indian chariot, protecting the army's flank. The molding, development, and meaning of Chess pieces are subject to extensive, special literature (see below *Chess sets, designs, and pieces*).

CHARACTERISTICS OF THE GAME

The moves. *Pieces.* The King moves in any direction, one square at a time. The Queen, Rook, and Bishop are "long-range" pieces that can cover all the distance across the board in any direction as long as they are not obstructed. The Rook moves on the rank and files, the Bishop on the diagonals; the Queen combines the powers of Rook and Bishop inasmuch as it moves on any open line. The Knight's move consists of a peculiar L-shaped movement, moving over two squares at a time, one of which is straight, the other diagonal, and thus "jumping" over any Black or White man that might occupy any of these intermediate squares. Any piece other than a Pawn captures in the same way as it moves; that is, it may

capture an enemy man standing on a square to which the capturing man may legally move. The capturing piece replaces the captured man on the same square, and the captured man is removed from the board.

Pawns. The Pawn has several peculiarities. It moves only forward and, when not capturing, advances only on the file. For the first advance from its initial square on the second rank, the Pawn has the option of moving one or two squares, but thereafter it may move only one square at a time. If it reaches the eighth rank, farthest from the owner, the Pawn is immediately replaced by a Queen, Rook, Bishop, or Knight of the same colour, at the option of the owner. This Cinderella-type transformation, called promotion, is also called queening because the usual choice is a Queen, the most powerful piece. If for a particular reason the chosen substitute is not a Queen but a minor piece, the change is called an underpromotion. A Pawn may promote even though the piece chosen to replace it had not been removed from the board by capture—*e.g.*, a player may have two or more Queens or other pieces—but promotion to a King is not permitted.

Of all Chessmen, only the Pawn captures differently from its noncapturing move. It captures to either square that is adjacent diagonally forward. If a Pawn makes the double advance for its first move, an adverse Pawn that could have captured it had the first Pawn moved only one square may capture it en passant (*i.e.*, in passing); but this en passant capture may be made only on the immediate turn, not later.

Castling. Castling is a compound move of the King and one Rook (the Rook was formerly also called the Castle) that may be made, if at all, only once in a game. The move is executed by moving the King two squares toward the Rook and then placing the Rook on the square passed over by the King. Either Rook may be used in castling. The move is legal only if neither the King nor the Rook has yet moved from its original square, if all the squares between them on the rank are vacant, if no adverse piece commands the two squares nearest the King on the side on which castling is to be carried out, and if the King is not in check (threatened with capture on the opponent's next move).

Promotion, castling, and en passant capture are the only exceptions to the otherwise strictly geometrical norms of movement, but these exceptions create a great range of permutations of calculable moves.

Evaluation of pieces and Pawns. Rating the value of the Pawn as 1, the fighting power of the pieces is approximately: Knight 3, Bishop 3, Rook 5, Queen 9. While Knight and Bishop are often rated equal, two Bishops are usually stronger than two Knights. This scale provides a measure of whether material equality is disturbed by an exchange of captures of unlike pieces, whereby any gain may be potentially decisive. Tactical considerations, however, often override the abstract evaluations. Sacrifices of material are often made for long-range positional advantage. The conduct of the game thus becomes subject to both qualitative and quantitative interplay in a fight of mind over matter.

Object of play. The game is won by capturing the adverse King. A threat to capture the King is a check. The only ways of meeting a check are to move the King, capture the attacker, or interpose a man on the line of check. The capture of the King is never consummated and remains symbolic—when the King is attacked ("in check") and cannot escape by any of the aforementioned means, then he is checkmated (or "checkmate") and the game ends forthwith. Often, games end by resignation when it is obvious that ultimate defeat cannot be avoided.

Drawn games. A game is drawn by reason of: (1) inability of either player to checkmate, (2) perpetual check, (3) triple recurrence of an identical position with the same player having the move, (4) absence of material exchange or any Pawn move within a sequence of 50 moves, with certain exceptions if so laid down before the game, (5) stalemate, whereby a player can make no legal move although his King is not in check, or (6) mutual agreement by players, although in some instances this requires assent by a referee.

Marginal notes:

Changes in names, moves, and powers of the pieces

The exceptions: promotion, capturing en passant, and castling

Phases of the game. The game generally is divided into an opening, middle game, and end game.

The opening. This stage of the game, starting with the first move, aims at developing or mobilizing an optimal number of men in a coordinated manner for the purposes of attack, while maintaining a secure position for one's own King and not prematurely compromising one's own defense. The choice and sequences of White's moves and Black's replies form distinctive patterns called variations, lines, attacks, defenses, and, in more complex formations, systems, methods, and the like. Their course has been subject to codification called opening theory, which uses Chess notation for identification and employs a certain basic terminology, which, however, varies in some detail from country to country according to alleged priorities of analysis. Called the Chess bible, the most widely known compendium in the field of opening theory is *Modern Chess Openings*, edited and periodically updated by Walter Korn, a United States authority on Chess. The selection of a particular opening is based as much on experience or fashion as on subjective predilections or psychological considerations. It has an important bearing on the strategies of the middle game.

Patterns of moves

The middle game. When the end of pre-analyzed branches of opening theory has been reached and the mobilization of material completed, winning strategies may be devised by the opponents. This phase, with substantial forces still on the board, is the most dynamic part of the game. It allows for either combinative "attacking" manoeuvres that might lead to a quick decision or pressure resulting in certain technical advantage favourable for the end game. Explanations of the elements of tactics and strategies and of the interplay of combinatory planning and positional judgment have for practical purposes been attempted by Max Euwe, Reuben Fine, Edward Lasker, Luděk Pachman, and others (see below *Bibliography*).

The end game. The final phase of the game, unless it terminates before then, is entered when a considerable reduction in forces normally rules out a combinative attack. What counts instead is the players' technical skill in maximizing an often minimal edge, or exploiting a very precarious majority of Pawns, or achieving greater dominance in space to achieve victory. Conversely, a seemingly lost game might skillfully be held to a draw. This is the phase in which the King might begin to play a very active role. The very precise end-game techniques have been exhaustively charted, above all by André Chéron in *Lehr- und Handbuch der Endspiele* (vol. 1–4, Berlin, 1960–70)—an extension of his original French work (Lille, 1952)—that also quotes a large number of end-game studies (see below *Chess composition*). Entirely pragmatical is Reuben Fine's voluminous yet very compact *Basic Chess Endings* (Philadelphia, 1941).

Books devoted to the end game

Codes of notation. With a game ready to commence, its course may, and often must, be recorded by means of one of various methods of notation.

Descriptive notation. Descriptive notation is used in all the Americas, the British Commonwealth and Ireland, and in the Iberian Peninsula. Each square has an individual designation (see Figure 2), each file carries the name of the piece originally posted on its first rank, with the ranks numbered from 1 to 8 away from the player. The board is alternately seen from the point of view of White or Black, according to which player's move it is. Each rank thus has a dual designation according to the colour of the moving man. A move is written in a given form; *e.g.*, "1 P–QB4" in which "1" is the number of the move, "P" (Pawn) the initial of the moving man, followed (after the hyphen) by "QB4," meaning the fourth square in the file headed by the Queen's Bishop; that is, the square to which the piece moves. The number of the rank is counted from the player's side, on the diagram upward for White, downward for Black. After a comma (or in a separate column), Black's corresponding part of the move is recorded in the same manner. Indication of K side or Q side is omitted when no ambiguity would result; *e.g.*, "B–B4" suffices if only one of the player's Bishops can reach the fourth square along the file named for a Bishop.

	a	b	c	d	e	f	g	h	
8	QR1 **QR8**	QN1 **QN8**	QB1 **QB8**	Q1 **Q8**	K1 **K8**	KB1 **KB8**	KN1 **KN8**	KR1 **KR8**	8
7	QR2 **QR7**	QN2 **QN7**	QB2 **QB7**	Q2 **Q7**	K2 **K7**	KB2 **KB7**	KN2 **KN7**	KR2 **KR7**	7
6	QR3 **QR6**	QN3 **QN6**	QB3 **QB6**	Q3 **Q6**	K3 **K6**	KB3 **KB6**	KN3 **KN6**	KR3 **KR6**	6
5	QR4 **QR5**	QN4 **QN5**	QB4 **QB5**	Q4 **Q5**	K4 **K5**	KB4 **KB5**	KN4 **KN5**	KR4 **KR5**	5
4	QR5 **QR4**	QN5 **QN4**	QB5 **QB4**	Q5 **Q4**	K5 **K4**	KB5 **KB4**	KN5 **KN4**	KR5 **KR4**	4
3	QR6 **QR3**	QN6 **QN3**	QB6 **QB3**	Q6 **Q3**	K6 **K3**	KB6 **KB3**	KN6 **KN3**	KR6 **KR3**	3
2	QR7 **QR2**	QN7 **QN2**	QB7 **QB2**	Q7 **Q2**	K7 **K2**	KB7 **KB2**	KN7 **KN2**	KR7 **KR2**	2
1	QR8 **QR1**	QN8 **QN1**	QB8 **QB1**	Q8 **Q1**	K8 **K1**	KB8 **KB1**	KN8 **KN1**	KR8 **KR1**	1
	a	b	c	d	e	f	g	h	

Figure 2: *Descriptive and algebraic systems of notation.* The descriptive system names the file after the piece on the first rank, as the KR file at extreme right. The ranks are counted away from the player whose piece moves. In the algebraic system the files are lettered a to h, from White's left to right, and the ranks are numbered 1 to 8 from White to Black. In diagrams the bottom edge is always the White side. In this diagram, heavy type indicates system from White's side, lighter type is system as seen from Black's side.

The symbol x, as in PxP, indicates a capture and signifies "takes." The symbols ch and + stand for check and O–O or O–O–O for castles King's side or castles Queen's side, respectively. Symbols that may be added to a notation include: (!) best, or a good move; (?) questionable, or a poor move; and (e.p.) en passant.

Algebraic (or continental) notation. In algebraic notation the files are lettered a to h from White's left to right; the squares along the file are numbered 1 to 8. Each of the 64 squares thus has its own designation, a letter and a number that remain constant whether White or Black is recording the move (see Figure 2). An initial move is recorded; *e.g.*, 1 Ng1–f3, which indicates (1) that it was White's first move, (2) the piece moving, (3) the number of the square of departure and, after the hyphen, (4) the number of the square of destination. In the case of a Pawn move, the Chessman's initial is, however, omitted and the move becomes simply "c2–c4." The algebraic notation can be further condensed by omitting the square of departure. Thus 1 Ng1–f3 becomes 1 Nf3 and 2 c2–c4 becomes 2 c4. The symbol : is used for "takes." A stylized cross(†) stands for check. The algebraic notation is of Muslim origin and is more precise and space saving than the descriptive one. Its use prevails in Europe. The name and abbreviation for each Chessman, which differs in each language, may be replaced by its decorative symbol (see Figure 1), thus making the printed game record more universally legible.

International codes. The numerical postal Chess notation is widely used by correspondence Chess players. Each square carries a two-digit number. The so-called Uedemann code, wherein each square is identified by two letters, has been employed for cable and radio matches.

Conduct of the game. The game is played according to the Laws of Chess (or Chess Code) as formulated by the World Chess Federation. These include not only the basic rules but also special regulations that apply to official tournaments and matches (see below *Competition*). Some of the more important of these regulations are those covering a touched piece, the time limit for a move, and the adjournment of a game.

The Laws of Chess

A touched piece. Unless preceded by the warning "I adjust" (French *j'adoube*), a piece touched must be moved or captured, and a completed move shall not be retracted.

Time limit. In tournament play each player must make a given number of moves in a given period of time, specified in advance, called the time limit.

Adjournment. If a game is not finished by the closing time designated for the session, it is adjourned.

Other provisions. Disputes between players are decided by the referee (or umpire) or by the tournament director or directors or ultimately by the World Chess Federation. A proviso formalized by FIDE in 1968 allows champions and contenders the legitimate use of a second, to advise them on stratagems and help analyze and evaluate positions during adjournments. The privilege of using seconds was extended also to grand masters on the occasion of important international events.

DEVELOPMENT OF MODERN CHESS

Evolution of modern play. The first professional Chess manuscripts were written in the 15th century by the Spaniard Lucena. His compatriot Ruy López de Segura was the first to merit recognition as a Chess analyst. In 1561 he wrote *Libro de la invención liberal y arte del juego del Axedrez* ("Book of the Liberal Invention and Art of Playing Chess"). In the 17th century, Gioacchino Greco was the leading Spanish master. Spain was rivalled by Italy, with Paolo Boi, Damiano, Giovanni Leonardo da Cutri, Giulio Polerio, Alessandro Salvio, and others as leading players. It was a time when Chess and Chess masters were held in high esteem.

In the 18th century the centre of prominence shifted north. The leading spirit was François-André Philidor of France, by profession a musician and composer; he was trained by M. de Kermar, sieur de Légal, the star of the Café de la Régence in Paris, which was the focus of French Chess until early in the 20th century. In 1747 Philidor visited England and defeated Philip Stamma, a noted Arab player, eight games to one and one draw. In 1749 he published his *Analyse du jeu des échecs*, a book that went through more editions and translations than any other work on the game. Philidor travelled much, but never to Italy, the only country in which he could have found opponents of first-rate skill—*e.g.*, Ercole del Rio, G.B. Lolli, and D.L. Ponziani. Blindfold Chess play, already exhibited in the 8th century by Arab and Persian experts, was taken up afresh by Philidor, who on many occasions played three games simultaneously without sight of board or men. These exhibitions were given in London at the London Chess Club in St. James's Street. Philidor's legacy was sustained in the early 19th century by A.-L.-H. Lebreton Deschapelles, who also was an expert Whist player, and by Charles Mahé de La Bourdonnais. After 1843, however, when Pierre-Charles Fournié de Saint-Amant lost a match to Howard Staunton of England, the French school of Chess fell into decline.

The middle of the 19th century witnessed new interest throughout the world, producing formidable players and competitive events. In 1851 Staunton was defeated by Adolf Anderssen of Germany, who in turn lost a match in 1858 to an American, Paul Morphy, whose career was short but meteoric. Morphy learned Chess at the age of 10 and, at the age of 13, beat the United States champion, the Hungarian-born J.J. Löwenthal. After touring Europe, Morphy returned to the United States in 1859 and gradually gave up Chess. Challenged no further, Anderssen remained at the helm till 1866, when he was beaten in a match by Wilhelm Steinitz, born in Prague in 1836. Steinitz lived in London from 1862 to 1882 and then in the United States, where he became naturalized. He died in New York in 1900 in abject poverty.

Steinitz was dethroned as champion in 1894 by Emanuel Lasker, a native of Berlinchen, Germany (now Barlinek, Poland), after which central Europe moved to the forefront of Chess activity. It held on to its lead until the 1930s, when the United States again entered the international scene, winning in the period 1931–37 all four of the scheduled International Team tournaments. Some of the participants of the U.S. teams were Isaac Kashdan, Reuben Fine, and Samuel Reshevsky, who arrived in New York in 1920 and, from 1936 onward, was several times U.S. champion until Bobby Fischer assumed this distinction more or less continuously. In the U.S. Championship of 1963, among 12 participants, Fischer, at the age of 20, scored 11 straight wins out of 11 possible points.

Historically, Benjamin Franklin popularized Chess in North America by writing a treatise in 1786 entitled *The Morals of Chess*. It dealt extensively with Chess etiquette and the educational value of Chess playing. Although this aesthetic outlook fitted in with the mores of the period, it gradually has become outdated with the emergence of more fiercely competitive tendencies (see below *Chess and thought*).

In the late 19th and early 20th centuries United States Chess was still outside the mainstream, but it produced some powerful personalities, especially in Harry Nelson Pillsbury and Frank J. Marshall. At an international tournament in Hastings, East Sussex, in 1895, the 23-year-old Pillsbury finished first in front of the strongest players of the era. Marshall also held a long-lasting record in simultaneous play (Montreal, 1922, against 156 opponents, with 129 wins, 21 draws, and six losses).

During the early years of the 20th century, the Western Hemisphere started developing the "Chess machine." José Raúl Capablanca of Havana, who at the age of 13 defeated Cuba's leading master, J. Corzo, captured the world championship from Emanuel Lasker in 1921 and kept the title until 1927, when he lost it to the Russian-born French Chess genius Alexander Alekhine

Meanwhile, the Soviet Union, which until 1940 had had only five grand masters, developed a vast number of outstanding players (*e.g.*, Mikhail Botvinnik, Isaac Boleslavsky, Igor Bondarevsky, Aleksandr Kotov, Vyacheslav Ragozin, and others) and defeated the U.S. by a great margin in a radio match in 1945. The Soviet Union's entry changed the complexion of the game in many respects. Not until the late 1960s was that country's supremacy consistently challenged by powerful Yugoslav masters and by an increasing number of strong Western players. A match—U.S.S.R. versus the Rest of the World —conducted in Belgrade in 1970 was won by the Soviet Union by the narrowest margin, 20½ to 19½, with each of the 10 contestants playing four games against his opponent.

One of the Belgrade participants was the U.S. champion, Bobby Fischer, who beat the former world champion, Tigran Petrosyan of the Soviet Union, with a 3:1 score. Also in 1970 Fischer won tournaments with commanding margins in Zagreb, Palma (in Majorca), and Buenos Aires, beginning a drive toward the world championship. In the first of three elimination matches in 1971, he disposed of Mark Taimanov, of the Soviet Union, 6:0 and, by the same score, Bent Larsen of Denmark. The third contest with Petrosyan ended 6½ to 2½ in Fischer's favour, opening the way for him to challenge the world champion, Boris Spassky of the Soviet Union. At Reykjavík, Iceland, in 1972, he won the championship by 12½ points to 8½, with Spassky resigning in the 21st game. Fischer forfeited the title in 1975, and the Soviet challenger, Anatoly Karpov, was declared the world champion. In 1978 Karpov successfully defended the title against a challenge from Viktor Korchnoi, a Soviet defector.

Theories of play and illustrative games. The development of Chess has gone through several stages, from the early conception of a symbolistic spatial game; through the phase of the self-reliant probers; the chivalrous period of reckless attack with its spirit of naïveté and pure enjoyment of a leisurely pastime; to the epoch of gruelling professional contest, of a craftsmanship based on a tremendous heritage, and a huge proliferation of events providing constant training.

Today's systemization of Chess may be dated from Philidor's *Analyse*, undertaken when the French Encyclopaedists rang in the age of reason, and the approach to Chess changed from an empirical (and glorified) phase to a theoretical one. Philidor pointed out the importance of the Pawns as fighting units. Hitherto, attention had been paid almost exclusively to the pieces for purposes of attack because of their greater range and mobility. Adding Pawn power, the effect of sustained attack was greatly increased, and it inaugurated a first era of "brilliant" Chess (*i.e.*, Chess exhibiting impressive imagination), culminating in Anderssen. At the same time, the pervasive tendency to attack caused a certain disregard of

Early books and masters

The resurgence of interest in Chess in the 19th century

American and Soviet masters

Philidor's use of Pawns in emphasis on attack

sound defensive principles. The inviting offer and acceptance of a sacrifice became almost a convention.

In one of his most famous games, since known as the "Immortal Game," played against Kieseritzky in London in 1851, Anderssen sacrificed a Pawn and both Rooks in three successive moves (17–19) and, three moves later (22), sacrificed his Queen—to win the game with checkmate on move 23 (see Illustrative game no. 1, especially note d).

Illustrative game no. 1

White Anderssen	Black Kieseritzky	White Anderssen	Black Kieseritzky
1 P–K4	P–K4	13 P–R5	Q–N4
2 P–KB4	PxP	14 Q–B3	N–N1
3 B–B4	P–QN4	15 BxP	Q–B3
4 BxNP	Q–R5ch	16 N–B3	B–B4
5 K–B1	N–KB3	17 N–Q5	QxP
6 N–KB3	Q–R3	18 B–Q6 (c)	BxR (d)
7 P–Q3	N–R4 (a)	19 P–K5	QxRch
8 N–R4	P–QB3	20 K–K2	N–QR3
9 N–B5	Q–N4	21 NxPch	K–Q1
10 P–KN4	N–B3	22 Q–B6ch!	NxQ
11 R–N1 (b)	PxB	23 B–K7mate	
12 P–KR4	Q–N3		

(a) Threatens N–N6ch, but the sortie is premature, and a developing move—e.g., B–N2—was called for.
(b) Commencing a combination inspired by the precarious position of Black's Queen.
(c) The key move of White's sanguine combination.
(d) Black cannot resist challenging White to show him how to win with two Rooks down. However, after the sober 18 . . . QxRch; 19 K–K2, Q–N7! White's scheme would have failed.

Following Philidor's creed of concerted attack, Morphy added the idea of prior simple but rapid development, of economically moving each piece only once, although onto a predetermined ideal square, of opening up lines and then going over to the attack. The fast open treatment, with less emphasis on defense, favoured the attacker's chances because of the advantage of having the first move.

It took a thinker, in the person of Steinitz, to formulate sounder positional standards. He used restraint in the opening, kept his position more closed, less vulnerable, and better defendable, blunting the furor of his opponent's attacks till the opening initiative had begun to evaporate. His strategy paid off against a very resourceful player of the period, Mikhail Chigorin, called the father of Russian Chess. Chigorin was a thorough, but less rigid, theoretician.

Attempts at codifying theory, especially of openings, started with Staunton's *The Chess Player's Handbook* (1847) and *The Chess Player's Companion* (1849). Steinitz's methodology was further strengthened by the researches of the German Siegbert Tarrasch, who enriched the theory of the Queen's Pawn openings. The Queen's Pawn openings offered slower development but more persistent positional pressure, with the Pawn centre remaining stabler than in the 1 P–K4 overture. Tarrasch formulated the principle that the occupation of the centre squares by Pawns or pieces secures for them a maximum radius of influence, which, after slow and methodical buildup, almost necessarily results in success.

Lasker, who profited from all these ideas, remained somewhat aloof from dogma and orthodoxy and regarded a Chess game as a struggle between personalities. He often made moves that "according to book" were inferior but that had the effect of upsetting an opponent's expectations, plans, and equilibrium. Among masters, such tactics needed of course a degree of subtle virtuosity and finesse. Lasker's credo is contained in his *Common Sense in Chess* (1895).

While thoroughness, coupled with considerable ability, secured leading places in the foreground for Tarrasch and his contemporaries, it was the genius of Capablanca that created the living image of smooth perfection. In his prime, he combined unerring positional judgment with incredible speed of comprehension and unsurpassed mastery of end-game technique. Capablanca's international career began in 1914, when he placed second after Lasker in a tournament at St. Petersburg (now Lenin-

grad). Their encounter was Lasker's last convincing win over Capablanca, who from 1916 till 1924 never lost a game. At Havana in 1921 Capablanca took the world champion's crown from Lasker and kept it till 1927, when Alekhine's imaginative neo-romanticism proved superior to Capablanca's supratechnical formulas.

With classical standardization at a seeming zenith, a reaction had been in the making, spearheaded by the so-called hypermodern school. Its earlier prophet was a Baltic master, Aron Nimzowitsch, whose works *Mein System* and *Die Blockade* (1925) pioneered ideas of containment and centralization that went even beyond Tarrasch's theorems but, on the other hand, came up with some very original criticism, which was taken up by younger experimentalists: Gyula Breyer, Efrim Bogolyubov, Richard Réti, and Savielly Tartakover. This group replaced the usual procedure of occupying the centre of the board with a principle of influencing and controlling the centre from a distance. Their ideas resulted in an entirely new complex of so-called Indian openings. The hypermoderns refrained from making early Pawn-moves that might create an irreversible commitment to a set strategy. Instead they manoeuvred so as to retain more options of opening and middle-game strategy. It was no longer taboo to move the same piece more than once in the opening (actually this taboo had been sporadically ignored by Steinitz and Chigorin). The foremost product of this new trend was the Russian expert Alexander Alekhine. The Illustrative games no. 2 and no. 3, with some of the champion's own notes, provided instructive insight into the Chess mind.

Illustrative game no. 2

White Ståhlberg	Black Alekhine	White Ståhlberg	Black Alekhine
1 P–Q4	N–KB3	17 KR–Q1	QR–Q1
2 P–QB4	P–K3	18 P–QR4 (b)	P–B5! (c)
3 N–QB3	B–N5	19 P–R5	PxKP
4 Q–N3	P–B4	20 QxKP	N–B4
5 PxBP	N–B3	21 Q–B3	P–Q3!
6 N–B3	N–K5	22 PxP	PxP
7 B–Q2	NxQBP	23 N–K1	P–K4 (d)
8 Q–B2	P–B4	24 R–R7	N–Q5!
9 P–QR3	BxN	25 Q–K3	R–Q2
10 BxB	O–O	26 R–R2	R/2–KB2
11 P–QN4	N–K5	27 P–B3	R–B5 (e)
12 P–B3	P–QN3!	28 B–Q3	Q–R4 (f)
13 B–Q3	NxB	29 B–B1	Q–N4! (g)
14 QxN	B–N2	30 R–KB2	P–KR3! (h)
15 O–O	N–K2 (a)	31 K–R1	RxBP!
16 K–B2	Q–K1	32 Resigns.	

"(a) It certainly looks risky to leave the central dark squares without adequate defence—but something had to be done to prevent White from increasing his pressure in the middle by means of P–QB5.
(b) This advance takes too much time and thus permits Black to build the ensuing instructive attack. Better would have been 18 Q–K5, P–B5! 19 Q–B7! BxN; 20 BxB, PxP; 21 PxP, N–B4 with the double intention 22 . . . NxKP and 22 . . . N–R5. Although White would not have time to exploit Black's weak Queen's side, he would still have been able to protect his King —for the moment the most important problem!
(c) From now, on, and until the end, all Black's moves are very exactly timed. It is hardly possible to replace any of them by a better one.
(d) Securing the square Q5 for the Knight. The weakness of the dark squares has been, without apparent effort, transformed into strength.
(e) One would suppose that this Pawn, besides being protected by its neighbor, and easily supported by 3 - 4 pieces, cannot possibly form a welcome objective for Black's attack. And yet White's KB3 will be captured, almost inevitably. It was certainly the unusualness of Black's winning stratagem which induced the judges to award this game the Brilliancy Prize.
(f) Threatening 29 . . . P–K5! etc.
(g) With the main threat 30 . . . RxBP! forcing the win of the Queen. White's answer is forced.
(h) A terrible move in its simplicity. Black threatens 31 . . . RxP! 32 QxQ, RxR; etc. Or if 31 Q–Q2, BxP; 32 NxB, NxNch; 33 RxN, RxR; 34 QxQ, RxBch; 35 RxR, RxRch; 36 KxR, PxQ; 37 K–K2, K–B2; 38 K–B3, K–K3; 39 K–K4, P–QN4! with a won pawn-endgame. White's next move does not change anything." (Game notations are adapted from Alexander Alekhine, *My Best Games of Chess, 1924–1937.* Used by permission of the publishers, G. Bell & Sons, Ltd.)

Opening theory

Hypermodern theories of containment and centralization

Illustrative game no. 3

	White Alekhine	Black Reshevsky		White Alekhine	Black Reshevsky
1	P–K4	N–KB3	19	N–R4	B–R4!
2	P–K5	N–Q4	20	P–B4!	B–B2
3	N–KB3	P–Q3	21	P–N3	P–B3
4	P–Q4	B–N5	22	PxP	Q–K3
5	P–B4	N–N3	23	P–KR3!	KR–N1
6	B–K2	PxP	24	B–Q4	NxKP
7	NxP	BxB	25	Q–QB3!	N–Q2
8	QxB	QxP	26	P–B5!	KR–K1
9	O–O	QN–Q2	27	P–QN4!	N–N1
10	NxN	NxN?	28	P–N6ch	BxN
11	N–QB3	P–QB3	29	PxB	QxQRP
12	B–K3	Q–K4	30	Q–KN3!	R–Q2
13	QR–Q1	P–K3	31	B–B5	Q–B2
14	Q–B3!	O–O–O!	32	R–R1	Q–N3
15	BxP	Q–R4	33	Q–R2!	R–K4
16	B–Q4	Q–KB4	34	R–R8	R–Q7
17	Q–N3	P–K4	35	R–Nch!	KxR
18	B–K3	B–N5	36	QxRch! and mate in 3 moves (a)

Alekhine's comments on the development of the game are illuminating. Only his final note is cited here:
"(a) Although in all objectivity I had to blame my 17th move (which by the way is accompanied in the Tournament Book by an !) I must admit that the final attack of this game gave me (and I hope will give the readers) much more pleasure than a scientifically correct, but purely technical exploitation of a Pawn majority on the Queen's side would do. After all, Chess is *not only* knowledge and logic!" (*ibid.*)

The use of a "combination"

In Illustrative game no. 3, the U.S. representative Samuel Reshevsky employed the defense carrying Alekhine's name. The chain of moves starting with 35 RxNch! is a lucid illustration of a "combination." This initial sacrificial keymove forcibly lures the Black King into a situation in which he will find himself mated, if a White Rook or Queen can force unobstructed access to the eighth rank. The Queen's sacrifice (35 . . . KxR) 36 QxRch, PxQ (else Black is mated in two moves) clears the line for White's Rook, 37 R–B8ch, and, after two futile interpositions, 37 . . . Q–K1; 38 RxQch R–Q1; 39 RxR mates, as foreseen on White's 35th move.

In 1914 Alekhine placed joint first with A. Nimzowitsch in the All-Russian Championship and first in the first Soviet Championship of 1920. He subsequently left the Soviet Union, became a French citizen, and started his brilliant career toward the world title. Badly affected by excesses of alcohol and nicotine, he briefly lost the title in 1935 to the Dutch Chess analyst and writer Max Euwe. Euwe's success resulted in an immense upsurge of Chess and Chess publications in The Netherlands. In 1937 strong-willed Alekhine regained supremacy and held it until his death in exile in Portugal in 1946. Alekhine's style of play was profound, dramatic, and elegant.

With the emergence, in 1948, of a new champion by means of a match tournament, a profound change occurred in both the personalities and the nature of participation. Broadly put, European Chess had been primarily an intellectual pastime of the middle class. Its strongest proponents were often gentlemen-amateurs. Many of its editors, writers, and masters and almost all champions were more or less scholastically trained. Whereas many enthusiasts originated from European coffeehouse Chess, the financial support came from wealthy sponsors; so much so that during the late 19th and until the middle of the 20th century, separate workmen's Chess federations were founded in many European countries, which had little impact beyond being fraternities of players. The first break with this tradition came with the highly utilitarian and pragmatical style as developed by the Americans after World War I. The next shock came from eastern Europe.

The Soviet Chess revolution

Botvinnik's assumption of the championship, in 1948, was the climax of a powerful concentration in the U.S.S.R. on Chess promotion, numerical enrollment, and massive state aid (see below *Chess teaching and ideology*). Before 1940, the Soviet Union had only five grand masters, but the increase in tournaments and space lavishly accorded to Chess literature and analyses produced a vast number of outstanding Chess masters of high calibre. To remain near the top required ever more intimate knowledge of the deeply analyzed and extensive opening theory; of all stratagems of the middle game; of accurate end-game technique; and of an opponent's idiosyncrasies. All three phases of the game became one fully integrated strategy. Ever more time had to be devoted to preparation and to literary activity. Lastly, physical fitness and stamina were essential in order to survive the frequency and tempo of competition. All this created a new discipline, with specialists engaged in a perpetual contest and with the supremacy of any individual maintained only precariously. Virtuosity rose, and victory rested on the ability constantly to develop special individual traits of taking risks in situations of sustained suspense—as was typical for M. Tal—or to manoeuvre patiently until the opponent became just a little careless—the forte of superstrategist T. Petrosyan and others.

In individual matches and tournaments the competitor's predilections are the criteria for a winning campaign. The frequent involvement of whole groups of U.S.S.R. masters sometimes tended to subordinate such considerations imperceptibly to the grand design of a team bent also on collective triumph.

By 1970 competitive resistance to Soviet Chess saturation began to make itself felt, with interest and ambition reintensified elsewhere. A breed of "ultramoderns" revived, but on a higher plateau, some of the old "hypermodern" experimentations. For further refined opening weapons, they improved on the flexibility of the "flank" openings that were typical for an early fianchetto development of the Bishops (as a move to QN2 or KN2, from which the centre can be controlled) and coupled with Pawn attacks just to the left or right of the centre. Utmost attention was paid to the possibility of sudden transpositions into other opening stratagems, which would push the opponent off balance into unprepared lines and upset any strategic conceptions. A typical exponent was the Danish ("existentialist") grand master Bent Larsen. Another challenger to the Soviet Union's leadership emerged in Fischer, who became world champion in 1972. Illustrative game no. 4 is neither player's "best" but is a vivid example of a powerful clash of fantasies. The analyses in the notes hint at the complex calculations inherent in such difficult encounters. Even though some of the comments are postmortem analyses, the intuitive grasp of the complex possibilities is truly astonishing.

Illustrative game no. 4

	White Fischer (U.S.)	Black Tal (U.S.S.R.)		White Fischer	Black Tal
1	P–K4	P–K3	12	B–QN5! (c)	B–Q2 (d)
2	P–Q4	P–Q4	13	O–O	O–O–O (e)
3	N–QB3	B–N5	14	B–N5? (f)	NxKP! (g)
4	P–K5	P–QB4	15	NxN	BxB (i)
5	P–QR3	B–R4	16	NxP (j)	BxR!
6	P–QN4!	PxQP	17	NxR	RxB
7	Q–N4	N–K2	18	NxKP	RxP +!
8	PxB	PxN	19	K–R1! (k)	Q–K4 (l)
9	QxNP	R–N1	20	RxB	QxN (m)
10	QxP	QN–B3	21	KxR	Q–N5 +
11	N–B3 (a)	Q–B2 (b)	22	Drawn by perpetual check.

"(a) 11 P–B4 bolsters the center but shuts in the QB and weakens the dark squares.
(b) On 11 . . . QxP; 12 N–N5! R–B1; 13 P–B4 (followed by the advance of the KRP) ties Black up.
(c) Harmoniously pursuing development without losing time. Also playable is 12 B–KB4, B–Q2; 13 B–K2, O–O–O; 14 Q–Q3, QxRP; 15 O–O, R–N5; 16 B–N3 (Unzicker–Dückstein, Zürich 1959).
(d) Not 12 . . . RxP; 13 K–B1! R–KN1; 14 R–KN1! RxR+; 15 KxR, and Black's King remains hemmed in the center while White merely marches his KRP to victory.
(e) After the game Petrosian suggested 13 . . . NxKP; but 14 NxN, QxN; 15 BxB+, KxB; 16 Q–Q3! keeps White on top (if 16 . . . Q–K5? 17 QxQ, PxQ; 18 P–B3! wins a Pawn).
(f) I simply underestimated the force of Tal's reply. Correct is 14 BxN! BxB (if 14 . . . QxB; 15 B–N5, P–Q5; 16 P–KR4! or 14 . . . NxB; 15 R–K1, followed by B–N5 and P–KR4 with a decisive bind); 15 QxP, P–Q5 (unsound is 15 . . . RxP+; 16 KxR, P–Q5; 17 K–N1, R–N1+; 18 N–N5); 16 QxP, B–Q2 (16 . . . K–N1; 17 N–N5 is hopeless); 17 QxN, RxP+; 18 KxR, B–R6+; 19 KxB, QxQ; 20 B–N5 and White soon consolidates to victory.

(g) Setting off a dazzling array of fireworks! I thought Tal was merely trying to confuse the issue.

(h) Originally I had intended 15 BxB+ but saw that after 15 . . . RxB; 16 NxN (if 16 BxN, NxN+; 17 K–R1, QxP+), QxN; 17 BxN, R–R1! Black regains his piece with greater activity: e.g. 18 QR–K1, RxQ; 19 RxQ, RxB and the compact center Pawns far outweigh White's passed KRP. Not playable is 15 BxN? NxN+; 16 K–R1, R–R1!

(i) Playing for a win. After 15 . . . QxN; 16 BxN, R–R1; 17 KR–K1! QxR+; 18 RxQ, RxQ; 19 BxR, KxB!; 20 BxB, KxB; 21 R–K3! bails White out.

(j) White could still have kept some tension with 16 BxN, QxB (if 16 . . . QxN? 17 KR–K1); 17 KR–K1, etc.

(k) The saving move. Not 19 KxB? RxP!; 20 Q–B7 (if 20 NxQ, RxQ wins a piece), R–R8+! produces a winning attack from nowhere! [*A characteristic of Tal's!* W.Ko.]

(l) On 19 . . . Q–QB5; 20 QxN, R–N1; 21 N–B4! holds nicely (if 21 . . . QxN? 22 Q–K6+, K–B2; 23 QxR).

(m) On 20 . . . R–N3; 21 QxN, RxN; 22 Q–B8+, R–K1; 23 Q–B3 is in White's favor." (From Bobby Fischer, *My 60 Memorable Games.* Copyright © 1969 by Bobby Fischer. Reprinted by permission of Simon & Schuster.)

Fischer's impact seemed to unfold from an early concentration on Chess exclusively, without allowance for any other distraction. He not only mastered all the facets of the game but also made the pursuit of Chess truly professional.

COMPETITION: GOVERNING BODIES AND EVENTS

World Chess Federation. The World Chess Federation, officially the Fédération Internationale des Échecs, or FIDE, is the body with which almost all countries are affiliated. It controls world Chess events and is in charge of the revision and interpretation of the rules of the game. Every year it holds a congress and every two years supervises the International Team Tournament, held in a sponsoring country, with each country represented by a team of four players with two reserves. It also organizes the World Championship and various other events.

The FIDE Qualification Committee investigates and recommends the awarding of titles as they concern competitions (except in the field of Chess composition). Selection of candidates is assisted by the use of the International Rating (grading) System.

FIDE meetings and decisions are publicized in the multilingual volumes of the Yugoslav *Chess Informant* that appears every six months. It reports, with brief notes, selected games from events of the preceding semi-annual period.

Since 1950, a prerogative of FIDE is the official award of various titles, including those of international grand master; international master; international judge, or umpire, whose foremost function is as referee in tournaments; international master of Chess composition; and international judge of Chess compositions. Judges, selected by the Permanent Commission of the FIDE for Chess compositions, are responsible for the regular publication of albums containing the best compositions of a given genre and period. The judges' conduct is governed by the "Kodex" adopted at the commission's congress in Piran, in 1958.

FIDE-sponsored competitions. *International team championships.* International Team Tournaments, also known as Chess Olympics or Olympiads or World Team Championships, started informally in 1924 as an event confined to amateurs and endowed with the (Lord and Lady) Hamilton-Russel Cup. After the first official tournament in the series was held in London in 1927 with Hungary finishing first, Denmark second, and Great Britain third, it quickly became a popular, hotly contested, official affair. For record of International Team Championship winners, see SPORTING RECORD in the *Ready Reference and Index.*

Individual world championships: men. When Alekhine died in 1946 officially undefeated, the World Chess Federation assumed arrangements for orderly acquisition of the title and regular challenges. In 1948 FIDE organized a match tournament between five leading contenders, which was won convincingly by Mikhail Botvinnik of the U.S.S.R. Since 1965, the statute has provided for cycles of qualifying tournaments and knockout matches to produce a contender every three years to challenge the champion. For list of world champions since 1866, see SPORTING RECORD in the *Ready Reference and Index.*

Individual world championships: women. While there is no segregation of sexes in Chess events, a separate status has officially been accorded to women on higher level competition. When the first Women's World Championship title was established in 1927, it was won and retained by Vera Menchik of Great Britain, a master in her own right, who, however, was the first—and so far last—participant also in regular international grandmaster tournaments, often downing some of the strongest men. She perished in a bombing raid in London in 1944. After the war a cycle similar to that determining the men's championship was organized, the first winner (1950) being L. Rudenko of the U.S.S.R. For winners since 1950, see SPORTING RECORD in the *Ready Reference and Index.*

Other international contests. Other international contests include the World Correspondence Chess Championship, the World Junior Championship, the World Students' Team Championship, the European Team Championship, and the International Chess Composition and Solving Tourneys (see below *Chess composition*).

National federations. *Structure.* In English-speaking regions, the largest governing bodies are the United States Chess Federation (USCF), the British Chess Federation (BCF), with which the Scottish and Irish Chess associations maintain close liaison, and the Canadian, Australian, and New Zealand Chess federations. Each maintains an official rating list (see below *Rating methods*), organizes important events, and represents its country within the framework of FIDE. The USCF annually conducts the U.S. Championship for men and women, the U.S. Open Championship, the U.S. Amateur Championship, Speed Chess tournaments, and Postal Chess tournaments, and supports students' and other Chess competitions. A similar breakdown prevails in England—*e.g.*, the British Postal Chess Federation, the Chess Education Society.

Rating methods. Each federation maintains an official Rating List (in Britain Grading List) of members' playing strength and relative standing, broken down into various categories, from ordinary players up to grand masters. The systems used in the United States, Great Britain, and also West Germany all classify a player's performance by the score he achieves against his opponents, with some degree of weighting attached to latest performances. The rating systems apply mainly to over-the-board play, not to postal Chess.

The Soviet Union, in consequence of its numerical strength, has a demanding qualification system. To become a master, a Soviet player has to work his way up through five classes and finally score 45 percent or better in an all-master tournament. Even then his games have to be examined by a committee as to the quality of his play. A candidate can also become a master by beating a master in a match. In other words, the candidate has to prove himself to be a stronger player than a good many established players to gain the title. The title is not necessarily given for life, and its holder may be called upon to re-establish his title by winning a match or by partaking in a tournament and placing sufficiently high. These conditions, which favour specialization as against recreation per se, and the existence of an examining committee, were in line with doctrine (see below *Chess teaching and ideology*).

Membership. There is an immense gap between the number of members belonging to the Soviet Chess federation and the numbers affiliated with Chess federations in other countries. Federation members in the Soviet Union number 3,200,000, whereas the United States figure, for example, is about 15,000, and that of Great Britain is about 8,000. Examples of memberships in other countries include West Germany, between 45,000 and 50,000; The Netherlands, 16,000; East Germany, 30,000; Hungary, 36,000; Yugoslavia, about 22,000; Czechoslovakia, 25,000; and Poland, 10,000. These generalized membership figures, however, reflect the fact that Chess

[margin note left] International Team Tournaments

[margin note right] National championships

activity in eastern Europe is thoroughly institutionalized, whereas in some countries, and especially in the United States, there is a great deal of informal interest and activity outside the federations. If this were not so, the periodic good results obtained by American players—many of whom are only semiprofessionals—would be hard to explain. These figures are subject to fluctuations due to decreased or accentuated interest.

Organization of Chess events. Chess tournaments usually are conducted either as round-robin or elimination events. A round-robin tournament is a contest in which every player plays against every other participant. Often they are "double-round" events, whereby each opponent is once White, once Black. A knockout or elimination tournament consists of several rounds in which the losers or low scorers are eliminated in each of the successive rounds.

The Swiss tournament system The Swiss system is a method of pairing a large number of contestants in tournament play in the first round and matching equal or nearly equal higher or lower scorers against each other in subsequent rounds. No player is ever matched with the same opponent more than once. For example, 150 contestants may play in 12 rounds, of which there might be two, or even three, in a day. The system was first utilized at Zürich in 1895. After a period of disuse it became very popular throughout the United States, Canada, and Great Britain.

Exhibitions. *Simultaneous.* In a simultaneous exhibition an expert plays a game against each of several participants. He progresses from board to board, thinking and moving as rapidly as he can so as to complete all games as quickly as possible. Often such a display is more one of physical stamina than of Chess quality, yet it requires master strength to ensure a favourable percentage against strong adversaries. A record number of 400 games was played by the Swedish grand master Gideon Ståhlberg at Buenos Aires in 1941, with 364 wins, 22 losses, and 14 draws. Displays may also be by one expert against a few groups of consulting players.

Blindfold Chess. In blindfold Chess a player does not see the board and men but is told the opponent's move by a third party who also makes the moves on the board as directed by the blindfolded player. The ability to visualize the position and moves of a single game without sight of the board is frequent among expert players but becomes an onerous feat with three or more simultaneous engagements. In Philidor's age it was considered Records in blindfold chess incredible that he was able to play three such games simultaneously, but this performance has since been exceeded by Alekhine, Flesch, Najdorf, Réti, Sämisch, and others. Qualitatively, Pillsbury did well in Hannover, Germany, in 1902, when he played and won 21 such games against an array of German master candidates. Quantitatively, Miguel Najdorf broke this record in 1947 in São Paulo, Brazil, with 45 games, winning 39, drawing four, and losing two.

Blindfold play, not permitted in the Soviet Union, is often regarded as a stunt that does not add to intrinsic Chess values. Still, it has its fascinations, and outstanding proof of an almost photographic memory and kaleidoscopic imagination was given in 1945 at an exhibition by Reuben Fine in New York. He played blindfolded against four masters simultaneously at a speed of ten seconds a move.

Lightning Chess. Lightning Chess, also known as speed Chess, rapid transit, or blitz, is fast Chess with a severe time limit. It may be played in groups or teams, round by round, with timekeepers advising the opponents at intervals of five to ten seconds that it is their turn to move under penalty of prompt forfeiture. In individual blitz games each player is allowed a fixed time—*i.e.*, five or seven or ten minutes—to complete his game, and, if he goes over his time, he loses even if he has a winning position.

Correspondence Chess. There are means of conducting a game other than by facing an opponent in person across the board. But, whereas the principles of the game remain the same, the change in the elements of time control and physical absence rather than presence creates subtly different criteria. Correspondence Chess, also called postal Chess or Chess by mail, may be practiced by players located in places remote from populated areas or for the purpose of more thorough analysis than is possible in combative fight across the board and with the greater limitations of time control. Chess by courier has been practiced since the origin of the game. Frederick II and Voltaire indulged; one of the first large-scale matches, a consultation one, was between London and Edinburgh between 1824 and 1828. Postal Chess has its own rating systems, associations, specific rules of conduct, and its own periodicals.

Variants, sometimes called electronic Chess, include individual or team tournaments and matches conducted by cable (or telegraph), telephone, radio, and by relays connecting computers (see below *Chess and automation*).

CHESS COMPOSITION

Chess compositions, generally, are abstractions based on a planned idea or a combination of such ideas (or themes), involving elements of strategy, difficulty, beauty, or surprise to achieve the desired result. Composers construct artificial situations that bring such elements into focus, using only as much material as is essential for the execution of a particular idea. Compositions are of three types: end-game studies, orthodox problems, and the type known as Fairy Chess, or heterodox problems.

End-game studies. End-game studies (or composed endings) usually carry the condition "White to win" (symbolized by +) or White to draw (in which the symbol = is used), always against Black's strongest resistance. The end-game studies of earlier composers were mostly didactic-analytical, but with an exceptional content. Systematic development began in the 19th century, producing a rich harvest of classical, or natural, end-game studies. Many of these were published in 1910–11. Another comprehensive anthology appeared in 1938 and covered a wide range of neo-romantic forms of study. Most examples still adhered to the credo that a study should resemble a true game ending and be plausible. Composition No. 1 (see Figure 3), an example of a nat-

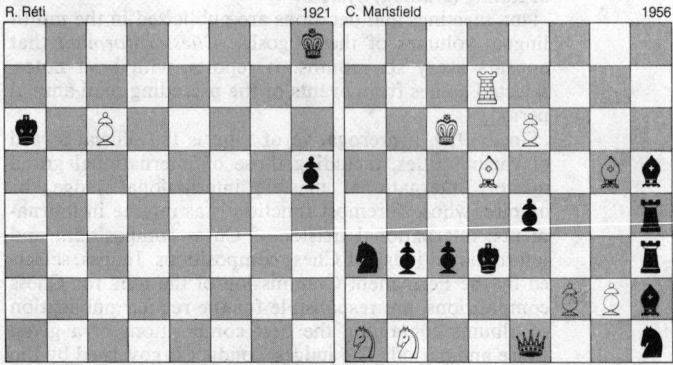

R. Réti   1921   C. Mansfield   1956

Figure 3: *Chess problems.*
(Left) Draw; (right) mate in two.

ural study of monolithic simplicity, was created by R. Réti's classic end-game study Réti in 1921. The position is a sheer loss for White, whose King seems unable to catch Black's advanced Pawn, which threatens to queen, while his own Pawn is under imminent threat of capture by Black's King. Yet, White draws through a triangular manoeuvre, which allows a lucid insight into the geometry of Chess moves; that is: 1 K–N7! P–R5; 2 K–B6! P–R6; 3 K–K6! P–R7; 4 P–B7, K–N2; 5 K–Q7 drawn; or 2 . . . K–N3; 3 K–K5, with either 3 . . . KxP; 4 K–B4! catching the Pawn, or 3 . . . P–R6; 4 K–Q6, again protecting the White Pawn. Recent creations, by reason of near exhaustion or repetition of natural concepts, assume a thematic character—*e.g.*, perpetual attack, positional draw, or other rhythmical motions perfected by Soviet composers between 1935 and 1970. Another modern group of studies consists of a variety of multiple promotions and underpromotions. They already begin to border on the area of formal exercises.

Orthodox problems. Orthodox problems are situations constructed to display an idea, or combination of ideas, that leads to forced mate in a specified number of moves. The first recorded problems were Arabian *manṣūbāt*—i.e., practical game endings stipulating mate in a given number of moves, usually not less than six. The modern era of problem composition began during the middle of the 19th century and developed into a highly diversified and rigidly structured endeavour, with a strictly defined nomenclature for all the techniques involved.

The most popular form of an orthodox problem is the so-called two-mover (with the symbol #2 meaning mate in 2), and the three-mover (#3) a close second. Problems revolve around a wide variety of themes that may be defined by their functions or by the name of the composer who invented or specialized in one of them. According to the first move (the key), the problem could be a threat problem or, if the opening move contains no immediate threat, a waiting move or block problem. Comins Mansfield, dubbed the "genius of the two-mover" by White, is represented by Composition No. 2 (see Figure 3). The problem is difficult to solve. Three tries (1 P–N4? or 1 P–N3? or 1 P–B4?) fail against best defense: the key is 1 P–B3!

One of the most versatile and imaginative problem makers was Sam Loyd, of the United States, who composed the bulk of his Chess production before the age of 20. His style was characterized by the humorous, the spectacular, and the unexpected. Loyd's tradition was to some extent continued by W. Shinkman, who also excelled in long-movers (see below *Fairy Chess*), but the most influential supporter of American—and international—problem activity was the U.S. composer Alain White, who compiled a classified collection (now in the hands of a group of British custodians) of over 150,000 problems and edited the "Christmas Series" of over 30 books on problem art. He was an organizer of the Good Companion Chess Problem Club, a society of prominent problemists from many countries. Somewhat in contrast to the universal emphasis on thematic richness, the Bohemian (Czech) school insisted on utmost clarity and economy in the use of any material, with every man on the board playing a vital role in the final position, which had to be a model mate or rather a variety of them contained in one problem. This severe demand helps in tightening the structure of some given theme and altogether conveys a feeling of rare beauty. Unfortunately, in a two-mover it requires crude sacrificial types of key, and the applicable matrices were soon exhausted; its ideal application lay with the three- (and four-) mover.

In the second quarter of the 20th century, the drive for maximum effects resulted in the successful creation of many a task, as a problem is called when its composer has surpassed a maximum effect previously achieved; or has attained the maximum effect obtainable within a specific theme. Concurrently, some problemists kept searching for still newer patterns, and two Soviet composers, E. Rukhlis and L. Zagoruyko, came out with new angles and themes, consequently named after them. But otherwise, the Soviet composer supreme is the mathematician L.I. Loshinsky, who is at home in almost any construction of two- or three-movers. Much pioneering has also been done by the younger British composers M. Lipton, R.C.O. Matthews, and John Rice, who summarized the latest problem developments in their joint publication *Chess Problems: Introduction to an Art* (1963). Longer problems (or more-movers) have for some time been cultivated by the German school and the late Hungarian O. Blathy. Another aspect of problem solving might be based on retrograde analysis as a mandatory requirement in a situation in which the soundness or inadmissibility of a key or try has to be proved from the reconstruction of preceding moves. This category and some of the lengthier more-movers are often artificial enough to be better classified under Fairy Chess than among orthodox constructions.

Retrograde analysis

Fairy Chess. Fairy Chess (or heterodox problems) deviates from some of the orthodox conventions but has been recognized by FIDE as a legitimate discipline. The modifications might concern: (1) the mode of outcome: instead of a "direct" mate in "x" moves, it might be a "self"-mate, or a "help"-mate, or a problem subject to other conditions or restrictions; (2) the introduction of new, unconventional pieces that add new categories of play; (3) alterations of the board, providing a change in dimensions that also include cylinder Chess, or multi-dimensional Chess.

Rudiments of such experimentation are present in early Chess periods, and Loyd and Shinkman laid the groundwork for Chess "puzzles" that raised the curtain on modern "fairies." But the concentrated exploration of their immense range dates from T.R. Dawson (1889–1951), editor of the British *Fairy Chess Review*.

CHESS SETS, DESIGNS, AND PIECES

Chessmen. Early Indian Chessmen were miniature reproductions of the animals or persons whose name they bore. Many were of ordinary shape, cheap to produce, for use by the common player. Other tastes were reflected in models elaborately carved, mostly in ivory.

The Arabic specimens of the next epoch show less individual carving and more uniform cylindrical design, distinguished rather by size and shape. This difference is due to the Islāmic prohibition of images of men and animals. Individual luxury manifested itself in the employment of costlier materials, and valuable models of Chessmen made of rock crystal or semiprecious stones have been preserved in museums and private collections.

Styles and symbolism of Chessmen

In Europe, commoners were initially barred from playing Chess and Chessmen represented royal warriors or had ritualistic and other ideological meaning. Craftsmen produced ornate pieces, mostly of bone, hardwood, metal, or ceramics, with delicately finished Chessboards to match. A modern prototype of this trend is a Soviet porcelain set depicting Communists versus capitalists (1930). Chess utensils were exported wholesale by the Chinese, earlier examples including lavishly carved and rather impractical figurines. Twentieth-century craftsmanship ranges from costly Italian alabaster sets to Impressionistic styles made from bolts and nuts, metal turnings, or other non-traditional materials. For utility (and in larger size for tournament use), a few typical patterns of Chessmen made of wood or plastics have become standard on account of their clear colour contrast, circular contours for all-round unobstructed vision, proper weight and stability, and the right proportions of size and height of the men to the dimensions of standard-size boards. Most popular are the so-called Staunton pattern, squat and solid; the Czech Club set, with slim bodies but with a wide, firm base; and the French set, fully cylindrical and somewhat tall. The French set seems closest to being the descendant of the original Oriental designs. A tasteful replica of this style has been maintained in the contemporary Yemenite Jewish pieces made from woven silver wire, gold-plated for use by Black.

Chess ornamentation. Chess motifs have exerted a particular fascination for the applied arts and often acquire expression quite independent of the conduct of the actual game. Either as symbols or telling a story, Chess objects have been reproduced on copperplate engravings, on carpets and tapestry, in reliefs and mosaics, and on parchments and on canvases of famed artists—in recent times by Paul Klee, Juan Gris, Samuel Bakh, and others. Commemorative coins have been minted, postage stamps issued, greeting cards printed, and merchandise advertised, all bearing Chess insignia.

CHESS AND THOUGHT

Psychology. As a distinct mental process, Chess has been subjected to observation, the object being the player's mind, the *modus operandi* in Chess, and any activating factors inherent in the game in a figurative sense. The methods of approach have undergone various stages as consonant with the thinking of each epoch. During the Middle Ages, numerous tractates were devoted to the symbolical or allegorical explanation of the game of Chess as symptomatic of the alleged social condition of the time. One of the earliest manuscripts is attributed to

Allegorical and psychological explanations

the Lombard Jacobus de Cessolis (*c.* 1300). Mixing satire and instruction, he drew comparisons between the goals of life and the pursuit of Chess. His and similar future works are labelled "Moralities," and Benjamin Franklin's *Morals* were a kind of offshoot.

After the turn of the 19th century, there appeared some German works on Chess written in the vein of speculative philosophy. They were followed by pamphlets of psychoanalytical precept (*e.g.*, by Reuben Fine, Ernest Jones, *et al.*), dealing also with aspects of psychosis. But the ambiguity of these concepts and their absence of true clinical diagnoses precluded reliable conclusions. The first experimental methods were applied in 1894 by the Parisian Alfred Binet, who focussed on the phenomenal ability of some experts to play blindfold, but his findings were distorted, inasmuch as he overrated the function of memory and nonvisual imagery so prevalent in blindfold Chess but not so essential in normal over-the-board play. The next group testing was conducted in 1925 at the Moscow Laboratory for Experimental Psychology and Psychotechnic. Basically, these tests destroyed those fallacies that had exaggerated a Chess player's specific and presumably superior talent in logic and created instead a "psychogram" of his personality. This contained a balanced variety of factors rather than one or another particular trait that would induce Chess ability.

Subsequently, a very complete methodology of this thinking process was compiled by Chess master A.D. de Groot in *Thought and Choice in Chess* (1965). De Groot reaffirmed that the Chess expert does *not* "think faster" or explore infinitely more possibilities than a weaker player. The better player's advantage "stems from his superior selective search heuristics, based on knowledge and experience" (Herbert A. Simon, *IBM Journal*, 1968).

Literature. Much of the golden age of allegory and fantasy is found in memoirs of wit and entertainment or in interesting compilations such as Norman Knight, *Chess Pieces; An Anthology in Prose and Verse* (1949); Walter Korn, *The Brilliant Touch in Chess* (1966); Fred Reinfeld, *The Treasury of Chess Lore* (1951) and, in collaboration with Irving Chernev, *The Fireside Book of Chess* (1949); and, finally, Jerzy Gizycki's massive illustrated almanac *Chess Throughout the Ages* (1960–67).

In the realm of novels, some are based on veiled realities—*e.g.*, Frances Parkinson Keyes's romanticized biography of Paul Morphy, *The Chess Players* (1960); or Anthony Glyn's *Dragon Variation* (1969), a story of players' compulsions. Most other works of fiction are lacking, in that they fail to present plausible versions of the Chessplayer's psyche.

Libraries and collections of Chess literature

The volume of literature, past and present, has reached huge proportions, much of it concentrated in a few extensive libraries that continuously kept adding new publications. The largest body of Chess literature, with 115,000 volumes of books, magazines, and manuscripts, is the John G. White collection in the Cleveland (Ohio) Public Library. The next largest is the Bibliotheca van der Linde-Niemeijeriana in the Koninklijke Bibliotheek (Royal Library), The Hague, which also houses A. Rueb's collection of end-game studies. Both libraries have marketed catalogs of their collections.

Copyright. Proprietorship and copyright in Chess have been marginal problems, with active competitions treated as a public spectacle under rules of free reporting; ownership of games, their compilation, and dissemination have not been established. The legal aspects of the problem were dealt with by Walter Jung in his *Gibt es ein Urheberrecht am Schachspiel* (Erlangen University, 1931). With the advent of television broadcasting and of substantially larger investments in Chess events, a different approach to the rights of distribution was developing.

Chess and numbers. Most explorations of the relationship between Chess and numbers evolve from special conditions and their consequences rather than from any strictly mathematical formulas. True, special arithmetical and geometrical conditions may be dealt with in Fairy Chess; calculations of possible progressions and permutations are inherent in arriving at certain positions after a number of given moves; or domination of the Chessboard by given pieces is the theme in a variety of configurations. The analysis of the mathematical structure of the game in the sense of modern mathematics, however, has not yet been undertaken because of its extremely peculiar character and great difficulty. To quote from F. Le Lionnais and E. Maget's very scholarly *Dictionnaire des échecs* (Presses Universitaires, Paris, 1967):

The data of the game, and its heterogeneousness . . . make it difficult to suggest . . . a mathematical framework. The regular form of the board is delusive . . . it may be a Cartesian product but otherwise the ranks, files and diagonals are not just straight lines, there are no parallels, no perpendiculars, no distance between squares (except in Maximum problems), no relationships in measurement, no affinity, no projection, no topological structure, and no "geometry" except in an imaginary sense. . . . If the inventory of the mathematical structures constituting the game of chess could be resolved, it might provide the tools for the construction of a procedure (*algorithm*) which would infallibly decide the best move (if any!) in whatever position *without* [*as different from computer technology*—W.Ko.] having to exhaust the pyramid of possibilities in all its totality.

E. Zermelo (1912) demonstrated that the game of Chess is "decidable," and F.E. Borel maintained that a "stratagem" was always possible, but so far no exhaustive algorithm or theorem has been worked out by mathematicians.

Chess teaching and ideology. Apart from reliance on straightforward books, texts resembling the syllabus of a teaching machine have been tried with varied success. The most concerted impact has come, however, from the organized mass basis on which Chess has been put in the Soviet orbit since the 1920s, when it was resolved that Chess could not be apolitical and must be aligned to "dialectic realism." Education to Chess was spread through all strata of the social organism via youth centres, school Chess circles, trade unions, armed forces, and other agencies, with a structure in depth by age groups and achievement.

The Soviet Chess-education program

This supreme effort channelled energy into a preoccupation with Chess and created a branch of cultural diplomacy, officially supervised in all its communications whether domestic or abroad. Thus resulted a well-controlled near-dominance in international Chess affairs and literature with purposeful foreign penetration through subsidized translations from Soviet-area publications; extending great influence to matters of organization and reportage and to the choice of nomenclature; and gaining international prestige at small investment. In some fashion, the historical path of the "moralities" was continued with a new pedagogic tenet. This accented the beneficial intellectual qualities of Chess, its capability of arriving at logical conclusions and forecasts, and its values for training and thoroughness—making creative work dependent on analytical ability and collective teamwork. This excessive emphasis on formalistic instruction and strict schematized patterns of thought disregarded the potential supplementary factors of intuitive, visually oriented, and unshackled artistic impulses that might be another ingredient in making important social or cultural contributions. Nevertheless, the connection between the determinable factors in Chess, in decision making, and in human behaviour has lately crystallized into an independent element (see below).

Chess and automation. Rapid advances in technology, electronics, and in the computer field have their influence on Chess in two directions. One is toward improvement within the handling of Chess by making use of modern technics. The other, quite opposite, direction is toward utilization of Chess and Chess players as the object of research in other fields.

Chess technics. These have involved, for example, the indexing and recording of moves and positions by means of classification methods, such as Ray Kooyman's adapted Royal McBee Punch Hole System; or the (French) System Balbo, which uses a combination of numerical and letter symbols; and the (Belgian–Dutch) System Lipchitz, which suggests a decimal classification for openings and move-by-move tabulation of game scores.

Electronic data processing

These methods are slow, although they offer the advantage of some individual control; but they may eventually be replaced by electronic data processing covering information storage and retrieval via memory banks with (tele-) transmittal, translation, and multimedia reproduction of any desired Chess material, providing an unbroken chain from inception to publication.

A smooth operation is ultimately dependent also on the manner of immediate electronic recording of moves as made, with electronic (or magnetic) impulses coordinating the moves and time control. The first public test of the feasibility of such synchronization took place during the first U.S. Computer Chess Championship in New York City in 1970. This was a three-round Swiss tournament between six different computer programs. The "conductor" made the moves on a diagram-like video screen by means of a pointer (a "light pen"), which activated the "moves" on the screen and was capable of starting a fully computerized process if so desired.

Chess and computers. While disputes were raging about the nature of Chess (Is it an avocation or an educational subject? Should it be classified as game, sport, science, or art?), it became one of the first activities to enter the electronic age. Certain factors were conducive to making Chess a foremost test case for experimentation in effective computer programming. Some of them were the definite and controllable rules of an intricate game; the assumed ability to evaluate difficult positions within a defined "map"—*i.e.*, the Chessboard; the logical, yet in its complexity almost "infinite," variety of possibilities—and all this within a seemingly rational process of planning and decision making.

The pilot project of thoroughly formalizing Chess via computer programming was initiated by Claude Shannon of the Bell Telephone Laboratories. Shannon visualized the use and extension of such programs as an instrument for pinpointing the principles at work in long-range planning, forecasting, and decision making; as an end in developing management systems and techniques of information; as a means of increasing the knowledge of the workings and the theory of probabilities; and as a tool to gain more exact insight into the master player's thought processes and their reduction to mathematical form—and consequently to arrive at general norms governing human thought and behaviour within the environment. As an immediate goal, Shannon's efforts laid some of the foundations for the use of computers, their adaptation to intellectual multireaction, the performance of logical inferences, and their mastery by the computer circuit and switching systems.

Basically, the game of Chess is an "inexact problem," which a computer is taught to solve by means of an exact program. The problem itself is inexact because no computer can at present calculate the 10^{120} possible games within any available period of computer time. Therefore, the method of selecting a move is still heuristic, dependent on the efficiency of the program to discard obvious statistical irrelevancies and extract only the pertinent alternatives. At the same time the computer must employ all strategic and qualitative considerations built into its program and must be able in due course to learn from and correct its own miscalculations. It is at this point that two experts in Chess and computer science are at variance. Former world champion Botvinnik, of the Moscow Institute of Power Engineering, advocates realistically that the course of straightforward games will ultimately and conclusively be mastered by a computer. On the other hand, former world champion Euwe avers, in theoretical disagreement, that supreme mastery of Chess rests forever with the human brain. While the groundwork for guidelines started as far back as 1949, it has been only since 1967 that the efficiency of constructed programs has begun to be tested by comparing the programs with each other. They still show crude defects, but also "brilliant" flashes.

A sample computer game

Illustrative game no. 5 (see below), between computers of the Moscow Institute of Theoretical and Experimental Physics and of Stanford University, California, showed Soviet programming to be somewhat better.

Illustrative game no. 5 (cable match, 1966–67)

	White Moscow Institute	Black Stanford University		White Moscow Institute	Black Stanford University
1	P–K4	P–K4	10	Q–Q3 (b)	N–B4
2	N–KB3	N–QB3	11	Q–Q5	N–K3?
3	N–B3	B–B4?	12	P–B5	N–N4??
4	NxP	NxN	13	P–KR4	P–KB3
5	P–Q4	B–Q3	14	PxN	PxP
6	PxN	BxP	15	RxP!! (c)	R–B1
7	P–B4 (a)	BxN+	16	RxP	P–B3
8	PxB	N–B3	17	Q–Q6	RxP
9	P–K5	N–K5	18	R–N8+	R–B1 (d)
			19	QxR mate.	

(a) Two of the guidelines written into the program obviously were "attack" and "control of the centre."
(b) The computer "sees" the threat 10 . . . Q–R5 + ; 11 P–N3, NxNP; Black in turn must suffer from crossed wires, as he plays quite aimlessly even for a freshman robot! His 12th move is an outright blunder.
(c) Probably the first computer "spectacular." If now 15 . . . RxR; 16 Q–N8 + , K–K2; 17 BxP mate.
(d) Useless, although 18 . . . K–B2; 19 B–B4 also mates.

During the period following this game, researchers produced much more sophisticated programs and gained "style" experience. Elimination of the ever so subtle mistakes that occur in human nature may be achieved by the electronic brain. This in turn severely curtails the frontiers of so-called creativity as based merely on prior human error or exposes it as being simply forgotten "routine" that can be recalled from the memory bank.

Even if Botvinnik's prognosis thus becomes feasible, however, it is just as plausible to assume that even "synthetic playing" would, in response, create vistas of posed problem solving "in reverse," lead to the acceptance of added dimensions in Chess, and simply legitimize the interest in the phase of Chess now called heterodox, just to mention a few future prospects. Finally, the untapped mass of population of the Far East and the Indian subcontinent—the cradle of Chess—may come forward with vast sources of Chess manpower.

BIBLIOGRAPHY

Introductory: I. CHERNEV and K. HARKNESS, *An Invitation to Chess* (1945, reissued 1972); C.H.O'D. ALEXANDER, *A Book of Chess*, ed. by DEREK BIRDSALL (1973).

Official regulations: M.E. MORRISON (ed.), *Official Rules of Chess* (1975), giving rules of the World Chess Federation (FIDE) and the United States Chess Federation (USCF); BRITISH CHESS FEDERATION, *Year Book of Chess* (annual), regulations of Great Britain.

Openings: W. KORN, *Modern Chess Openings*, 12th ed. (1980); Y. ESTRIN and V.N. PANOV, *Comprehensive Chess Openings*, 3 vol., 5th ed. (1973; Eng. trans. from the Russian, 1980).

Middle game: EDWARD LASKER, *Modern Chess Strategy*, 3rd ed. (1968); L. PACHMAN, *Complete Chess Strategy*, 3 vol. (Eng. trans. from the Czech, 1975–78); M. EUWE and H. KRAMER, *Het middenspel* (1952; Eng. trans., *The Middle Game*, 2 vol., 1964–65).

Treatises: L. PACHMAN, *Modern Chess Strategy* (1958; Eng. trans. from the Czech, 1963), and *Modern Chess Tactics*, 2 vol. (1962–64; Eng. trans. from the Czech, 1968–73).

Game collections: S. TARTAKOWER and J. DU MONT, *500 Master Games of Chess* (1952); A. HOROWITZ, *The Golden Treasury of Chess*, rev. ed. (1969); A. ALEKHINE, *107 Great Chess Battles* (Eng. trans. from the Russian, 1980); V. KORCHNOI, *Viktor Korchnoi's Best Games* (1978).

Chess composition: (End-game studies): W. KORN, *American Chess Art: 250 Portraits of Endgame Study* (1975); H.M. LOMMER, *1357 End-game Studies* (1975). (Problems): C. MANSFIELD and B. HARLEY, *Modern Two-Move Chess Problems* (1959); J. RICE, *An ABC of Chess Problems* (1970). (Fairy Chess): A. DICKENS, *A Guide to Fairy Chess* (1969); K. FABEL and C.E. KEMP, *Chess Unlimited* (1969).

Chess teachings and ideology: D. BRONSTEIN, *The Chess Struggle in Practice* (Eng. trans. from the Russian, 1978); W. KORN, "Chess Teaching and Learning; on Teaching Machines," *Chess Review* (June 1967); D.J. RICHARDS, *Soviet Chess: Chess and Communism in the USSR* (1965); GEORG KLAUS, "Wozu ist Schach gut?", *Schach*, no. 8 (August 1969).

Chess pieces: The development and transformation of Chessmen have been chronicled and illustrated in: D.M. LIDDELL, *Chessmen* (1937); A. HAMMOND, *The Book of Chessmen*

(1950); H. and S. WICHMANN, *Schach: Ursprung und Wandlung der Spielfigur in Zwölf Jahrhunderten* (1960; Eng. trans., *Chess: The Story of Chesspieces from Antiquity to Modern Times*, 1964); A.E.J. MACKETT-BEESON, *Chessmen* (1968); and METROPOLITAN MUSEUM OF ART, *Chess: East and West, Past and Present* (1968).

Chess and automation: D. LEVY, *Chess and Computers* (1976); P.W. FREY (ed.), *Chess Skill in Man and Machine*, rev. ed. (1979); M.M. BOTVINNIK, *Computers, Chess and Long-range Planning* (1968; Eng. trans. from the Russian, 1970).

Reference: J. GAIGE, *Chess Tournament Cross-Tables, 1851–1920*, 3 vol. (1971–72); B. KAŽIĆ, *International Championship Chess: A Complete Record of FIDE Events* (1974); H. GOLOMBEK (ed.), *Chess: A History* (1976); *Golombek's Encyclopedia of Chess* (1977).

Periodicals and Chess columns: British Chess Magazine and *Chess* (England), *Chess Life & Review* (U.S.), all monthly; *New York Times* (triweekly); *New Statesman* (weekly); *EG*, for end-game (quarterly), both England.

(W.Ko.)

Chiang Kai-shek

Chiang Kai-shek (in Pinyin romanization Jiang Jieshi), Chinese soldier and statesman, head of the Nationalist government of China from 1928 to 1949 and subsequently head of a Chinese government in exile on Taiwan, was born on October 31, 1887, into a moderately prosperous merchant and farmer family in the coastal province of Chekiang. He prepared for a military career, first (1906) at the Paoting Military Academy in North China and subsequently (1907–11) in Japan. From 1909 to 1911 he served in the Japanese Army, whose Spartan ideals he admired and adopted. More influential were his youthful compatriots whom he met in Tokyo; plotting to rid the motherland of its alien Manchu dynasty, they converted Chiang to republicanism and made him a revolutionary.

In 1911, upon hearing of revolutionary outbreaks in China, Chiang returned home and helped in the sporadic fighting that led to the overthrow of the Manchus. But the revolutionists soon lost control of the new republic by handing its presidency to Yüan Shih-k'ai. Yüan, aiming at personal rule, used his office to crush the party that had put him into it. The revolutionists struck back; but their Second Revolution soon collapsed, and in 1913 Chiang fled to Japan, where he remained with one interruption until the end of 1915. Meanwhile, Yüan discredited himself, especially by an attempt to restore the monarchy with himself as emperor. Chiang returned to participate in the "third revolution," which, by dashing Yüan's hopes of founding another dynasty, saved the republic.

After these excursions into public life, Chiang relapsed into obscurity. For two years (1916–17) he lived in Shanghai, where he apparently belonged to the Green Gang (Ch'ing-pang), a secret society involved in financial manipulations. In 1918 he reentered public life by joining Sun Yat-sen, the leader of the Nationalist Party, or Kuomintang. Thus began the close association with Sun on which Chiang was to build his fame. Sun's chief concern was to reunify China, which the downfall of Yüan had left divided among warring military satraps. Having wrested power from China's alien dynasty, the revolutionists had lost it to indigenous warlords.

Chiang joined the southern armies as a major general but could not gain control of them, for they were actually warlord troops that supported the Kuomintang only because Sun had struck bargains with their commanders. Each side intended to outwit the other, so that treachery followed treachery. Often outmanoeuvred by their confederates, the revolutionists found their southern base insecure; twice they had to abandon it and return to the north. They needed an army of their own, and, to build up an army, they needed foreign help. Presently they turned to the Soviet Union, the only foreign power to have shown their cause any sympathy. Chiang visited the Soviet Union in 1923 to study Soviet institutions, especially the Red Army. Back in China after four months, he became commandant of a military academy established on the Soviet model at Whampoa near Canton. Soviet advisers poured into Canton, and the Chinese Communists were admitted into the Kuomintang. Chiang read

Chiang Kai-shek.
Camera Press—Pix from Publix

Marx and Lenin and, like many Asian patriots of the time, seized on Lenin's doctrine of imperialism—according to which Western capitalism had prolonged its life only by expanding into colonial territories—as the clue to his country's weakness and poverty. Thereafter Leninism coloured his outlook, but it did not make him tolerant of any efforts to sovietize his own country. The Chinese Communists made such efforts as they gained strength, especially after Sun's death in 1925. Chiang, who, with the Whampoa army behind him, was the strongest of Sun's heirs, met this threat with consummate shrewdness. By alternate shows of force and of leniency, he prevented a Communist coup without losing Soviet support. Moscow supported him until 1927, when, in a bloody coup of his own, he finally broke with the Communists.

Meanwhile, Chiang had gone far toward reunifying the country. Commander in chief of the revolutionary army since 1925, he had launched a campaign against the warlords in the following year. This drive ended only in 1928 when he entered Peking. A new central government with Chiang at its head was established at Nanking. In October 1930 Chiang became a Christian, apparently at the insistence of the powerful westernized Soong family, whose youngest daughter, Mei-ling, had become his second wife. But compared with the Japanese and the Leninist influence on his thinking, that of Christianity remained minor. Chiang stood committed to a program of social reform, but most of it remained on paper, partly because his control of the country always remained precarious. In the first place, the warlords, whom he had neutralized rather than crushed, still disputed his authority. The Communists posed another continuing threat, having withdrawn to rural strongholds and formed their own army and government. In addition, Chiang faced certain war with Japan, which, after seizing Manchuria (Northeast Provinces) in 1931, showed designs upon China proper. Chiang decided not to resist the Japanese until after he had crushed the Communists—a decision that aroused many protests, especially since the Communists continued to elude him. To give the nation more moral cohesion Chiang revived the state cult of Confucius and in 1934 launched a campaign, the so-called New Life Movement, to inculcate Confucian morals. Simultaneously, he promoted Western notions of hygiene and urged conscious emulation of the Japanese as models of Spartan discipline.

War with Japan broke out in 1937, and for more than four years China fought alone. The effort nearly broke the country's endurance, and Chiang repeatedly received advice to negotiate a separate peace. But he stood firm, and China stayed alone in the war until it was joined by the Allies in World War II when, with the exception of the Soviet Union, they declared war on Japan in 1941. China's reward was an honoured place among the victors as one of the Big Four. But internally Chiang's govern-

Rise to power

Efforts to reunify the country

Exile on
Taiwan

ment showed signs of decay, which multiplied as it resumed the struggle against the Communists. Civil war recommenced in 1946; by 1949 Chiang had lost continental China and the People's Republic of China was established. Chiang moved to Taiwan and continued to fight the Communists in the Formosa Strait. In 1955 the U.S. signed an agreement with Chiang's Nationalist government on Taiwan guaranteeing its defense. Beginning in 1972, however, the value of this agreement and the future of Chiang's government were seriously called in question by the growing rapprochement between the U.S. and the People's Republic of China.

Among the reasons for Chiang's defeat, one frequently cited is the corruption that he countenanced in his government. But corruption is a normal concomitant of most governments. Nor can Chiang's downfall be ascribed to personal failings alone. Insofar as these contributed,

Assessment

however, none proved more fatal than his loss of flexibility in dealing with changing conditions. Growing more rigid, he became less responsive to popular sentiment and to new ideas. He came to prize loyalty more than competence and to rely more on personal ties than on ties of organization. His dependence on a trusted clique also showed in his army, in which he favoured narrow traditionalists over many abler officers. But to list Chiang's failings is not to deny his historical significance, which emerges from the contradictions that he combined in himself. Soldier and politician, revolutionary and traditionalist, Christian and Confucian, anti-Communist with a Leninist bias, Chiang embodied the crosscurrents and confusion of a transitional period in Chinese history. He died on April 5, 1975, and was succeeded as leader of the Nationalists by his son Chiang Ching-kuo.

BIBLIOGRAPHY. "Chiang Kai-shek" in HOWARD L. BOORMAN and RICHARD HOWARD (eds.), *Biographical Dictionary of Republican China,* vol. 1 (1967), the most objective and comprehensive assessment of Chiang as a person and as a leading figure in Chinese politics after 1924; HOLLINGTON K. TONG, *Chiang Kai-shek: Soldier and Statesman,* rev. ed. (1953), Chiang's official biography, originally published in Shanghai in 1937, an interesting work by Chiang's former press chief, although based, by its very nature and purpose, on the premise that its hero is "the greatest soldier-statesman of our time on the Continent of Asia"; PICHON P.Y. LOH, *The Early Chiang Kai-shek: A Study of His Personality and Politics, 1887–1924* (1971), on Chiang's early years, particularly his intellectual development; *China's Destiny,* authorized Eng. trans. by WANG CHUNG-HUI (1947), easily the most revealing of Chiang's own works—provides a survey of his political and economic outlook including sweeping societal changes such as the collectivization of agriculture, since carried out by his Communist successors; *The Collected Wartime Messages of Generalissimo Chiang Kai-shek, 1937–45,* 2 vol. (1946; reprinted in 1 vol., 1969), essential reading for anyone interested in Chiang primarily as a wartime leader; *Soviet Russia in China: A Summing-Up at Seventy,* rev. ed. (1965), contains primarily, as its title indicates, Chiang's official alibi for having lost control of the Chinese mainland—also contains some of Chiang's fond recollections of the Soviet military mission that helped him to achieve power in the period 1924–27 and hence holds genuine historical interest as well; JOSEPH W. STILWELL, *The Stilwell Papers* (1948), by Chiang's chief-of-staff from 1942 to 1944, is one of the most often cited indictments of Chiang's qualities as a statesman and military leader during World War II.

Chicago

Until the 1830s a minor trading post at a swampy river mouth near the southwestern tip of Lake Michigan, Chicago used its strategic location as the interior land and water hub of the expanding United States to bring it to its present position as the second most populous city of the United States and the centre of one of the world's richest industrial and commercial complexes. It is, thus, of classic interest as the largest European-implanted city ever to rise in the continental interior of the Western Hemisphere. But at the same time, its achievements are distinctly characteristic of the United States, and its problems are the problems of the modern United States; in a sense it may be—as a series of observers has called it—the typical U.S. city.

The relation of this youthful city to its environment is also noteworthy. Throughout its history, Chicago and the surrounding counties of what became its metropolitan area, now containing two-thirds of the population of Illinois, have existed as almost a separate entity—politically, socially, and spiritually—from the largely rural areas of "Downstate" Illinois. The attitudes and lives of the early settlers in and around the city, mainly from the Northeastern states or from Europe, were in contrast to those of Downstaters, many of whom came from Appalachian or Southern states. While Chicago was, for example, a major supplier of goods and manpower to the Union during the Civil War, southern Illinois experienced an unsuccessful but strong movement toward secession and alliance with the Confederacy. This alienation continued to plague the political and social life of both city and state into the 1970s. (For information on related topics, see the article ILLINOIS.)

THE CHARACTER OF CHICAGO

A by-product of Chicago's growth on the raw frontier of U.S. industry was its reputation as a city in which "anything goes," a city whose name became an international byword for underworld violence during and after the Prohibition era of the 1920s and early 1930s. The high tolerance of its citizenry for human frailty was revealed, at least in the opinion of some observers, by the large vote that in 1970 re-elected the county assessor, when for several weeks prior to the elections he had been accused by the news media of having, for years, systematically under-assessed the commercial properties of wealthy supporters of his party, thus theoretically shifting the tax burden to owners of small homes. In the words of a University of Chicago theologian, commenting on the revelations shortly thereafter that Chicago and Downstate politicians of both parties had profited enormously from ownership of racetrack stocks, "Someplace else it might be shocking. . . . Children grow up here knowing things are rigged and fixed."

Among recent events that brought the city international notoriety were riots in the black ghetto of the West Side in 1968 following the assassination of Martin Luther King, Jr.; during the riots the mayor suggested that the police "shoot to kill" arsonists and looters. A few months later, confrontations between young protesters and Chicago police during the Democratic National Convention —called later, by a presidential commission, a "police riot"—also attracted international attention.

However much Chicago's political and social life may have deserved the brickbats of its numerous critics, there is little disagreement that the city's physical presence is stunning (although the exigencies of the marketplace often conquered civic pride in preserving the great landmarks of its past). Chicago arose from the ashes of its fiery immolation in 1871 to spawn the skyscraper as well as many of the other major innovations of modern architecture. Its striking skyline, containing some of the world's tallest buildings, rises along a narrow lakeside strip.

Urban vistas

Behind this impressive facade lies a sprawling industrial city, its monotony accentuated by the flat Middle Western landscape and by a repetitive gridiron pattern of streets broken only by the radial avenues that cover old Indian trails to the northwest and southwest and the great freeways and railroad lines that for many years have made the city a major hub of commerce. The whole mass reaches out over the former prairie, spilling over city limits into an irregular and continuously expanding belt of suburbs and industrial satellites and coalescing into a vast region that had become the home of well over 7,-500,000 persons by the 1970s.

The magnificent downtown lakeside strip nevertheless remains the focus of attention in the mind of resident, commuter, and visitor alike. A person strolling up Michigan Avenue in the 1970s passes the green acres of Grant Park (in the downtown area), with its neoclassical Art Institute building and well-hidden tracks of the Illinois Central Gulf Railroad; the central building of the Chicago Public Library, the arched rooms and hallways of which were decorated with fine mosaic work of a past era; and seemingly unending excavations to be topped with still further cloud-tickling ventures in one of the world's greatest skyscraper complexes—for eventual enwrapment within the urban smog, blown aloft from power plants, steel factories, oil refineries, and other indicators of municipal well-being. From the bridge over the Chicago River, the stroller would be confronted with what many regard as one of the most beautiful and open urban spaces in the world, stretching along both sides of what once was the river's estuary. North of the river along Michigan Avenue is "the Magnificent Mile"—Chicago's answer to New York City's Fifth Avenue in commercial elegance—which includes the Water Tower, the medieval stone turrets of which survived the conflagration of 1871 to become an eccentric monument to civic nostalgia.

Outside these areas of downtown Chicago, the stroller would find a complex city mirroring the ethnic and racial diversity of U.S. life. Chicago in the 1970s remained essentially the "blue-collar" city characterized by the poet Carl Sandburg as the "city of big shoulders," heavily populated by the descendants of workingmen from the streets and soils of the 19th-century Europe and of former slaves from the United States' Deep South. The latest influx—that of Spanish-speaking residents—has added further to the complexity.

Civic disasters of the 19th and 20th centuries

Its widely scattered ethnic neighbourhoods (often mutually antagonistic) and its suburbs retained memories of a long series of disasters, running from the time of the Great Fire itself. In the 19th century, these included the police assault on strikers that claimed six lives, the apparently retaliatory bomb throwing (attributed to anarchists) that killed seven policemen, and the ensuing reaction against German-American leaders, all associated with the Haymarket Square Riot. Many other bitter, often fatal, disputes occurred in the steel, railroad, packinghouse, and other industries. These were followed by the catastrophic Iroquois Theatre Fire; the sinking of the cruise-ship "Eastland" in the Chicago River, drowning more than 800 persons; the gangsterism and intermittent mayhem evoked by mention of Al Capone, John Dillinger, and the St. Valentine's Day Massacre; the televised violence attendant upon the 1968 Democratic convention; and a continuing succession of major and minor municipal corruptions. At the same time, "the windy city"—a meteorologically correct nickname nevertheless derived from the inflated claims of the early municipal "boosters"—could and did lay claim to a distinguished list of citizens who had significantly enriched the intellectual, artistic, and social life of the United States.

The "second city" syndrome

A minor but strangely persistent cottage industry existed among Chicago intellectuals—in an attempt to explain the city to itself (and sometimes to apologize for it). This collective enterprise examined and polished all facets of what was called the "second-city" mentality, a viewpoint that could both puff civic endeavour to surpass New York City as well as excuse its laggard behaviour in such areas as the arts. Since it seemed unlikely that Chicago's population—more than 3,300,000 in the city proper in 1970—would ever reach that of New York or that the city could ever support the diverse activities of its Eastern rival, it is probable that this homegrown exercise in self-disparagement will continue to entertain Chicagoans and the city's millions of tourists and conventioneers for many years to come.

Whatever the future of Chicago's reputation, it seems likely that the economic and political power of the city will continue to enable it to play a major role in national and international affairs. Like many other North American cities, however, it faces a difficult future when gauged by the quality of life it offers to its peoples, whether they reside in affluent suburbs or in decaying inner-city neighbourhoods. (R.Do.)

THE HISTORY OF CHICAGO

Settlement and early activity. In 1673 the French explorers Louis Jolliet and Jacques Marquette followed an Indian portage to the mudflats over which a Y-shaped river flowed. Its leg emptied into Lake Michigan, while its arms reached nearly to the drainage basin of the Mississippi River system, thus virtually linking two great North American waterways. The meaning of the Indian name for the region remains controversial—skunk, wild onion, or powerful.

Trappers, traders, and adventurers used the area for portage and barter throughout the 18th century, and in 1795 the United States obtained a six-mile-square area about the river mouth. The first known non-Indian settler was Jean-Baptist Point Sable (or Pointe du Sable), son of a wealthy Quebec merchant and a black. Ft. Dearborn, built in 1803 to protect merchant interests, was destroyed in 1812 and all but one of its military and civilian population killed in an Indian raid. Rebuilt in 1816, the fort was occupied until the 1830s. Outside its walls, a cluster of traders' shacks and log cabins grew up, but the settlement attracted little interest even after Illinois, with most of its population in the central and southern regions, became a state in 1818.

The opening of the Erie Canal in 1825, joining the Atlantic states and the Great Lakes, shifted the main axis of westward movement northward from the Ohio River route, with Chicago the principal western terminus. The county of Cook located its seat at the small community, and the regional federal land office opened there. Numerous retail stores opened to outfit newcomers to the West, and the volume of animal pelts and products for Eastern markets increased. Small wooden cottages and rooming houses provided added living space for a population of about 4,200 in 1837, the year Chicago became incorporated as a city.

Emergence as a rail centre

Chicago's geographical potentiality as a water gateway was fulfilled by completion (in 1848) of the Illinois and Michigan Canal, linking the Great Lakes and Mississippi systems and providing for eastward-bound produce of the hinterlands and westward-bound people. Rails soon joined water as a major carrier, and Chicago further capitalized on its strategic position. A pair of westbound lines tied into Chicago in 1852, and by 1856 it had become the nation's chief rail centre. A belt line connected the radiating trunk lines by 1856, and commuter service to outlying neighbourhoods and suburbs began. By 1869 Chicago was the hub of the transcontinental route.

Explosive economic growth. Industry followed the rails. By the late 1850s, lake vessels carried iron ore from the Upper Michigan ranges to the blast furnaces of Chicago. Located convenient to transportation between the forests of the Upper Great Lakes and the growing settlements of the Middle West, Chicago became the nation's major lumber-distributing centre by the 1880s. The railroads brought farm produce from west and south, and Chicago's Board of Trade became the nerve centre of the commodities market. The railroads also hauled cattle, hogs, and sheep to Chicago for slaughtering and packing, a city industry from the 1830s to the late 1960s. The consolidated Union Stock Yards, largely bankrolled by nine railroads and the owners of several other Chicago stockyards opened on Christmas Day, 1865.

Chicago now emerged as the major city of the Middle West. Its 1880 census found over 500,000 inhabitants, a 17-fold increase over the almost 30,000 of 1850, for the first time exceeding St. Louis in population. It was the site of the 1860 Republican National Convention—the first for the new party—at which Illinoisan Abraham Lincoln won the presidential nomination. Local real-estate values were booming. Native U.S. and northern European immigrants, drawn by Chicago's factories and carried by the Chicago-anchored rail network, continued to pour into the city.

The Great Chicago Fire

Four square miles of Chicago, including the business district, were destroyed by fire on October 8–9, 1871. Starting in the southwest, fed by wooden buildings and pavements and favoured by a long dry spell, flames spread northeastward, leaping the Chicago River and dying out only when they reached Lake Michigan on the North Side. In their course about 300 lives were lost, 90,000 people were made homeless, and nearly $200,-000,000 in property was destroyed.

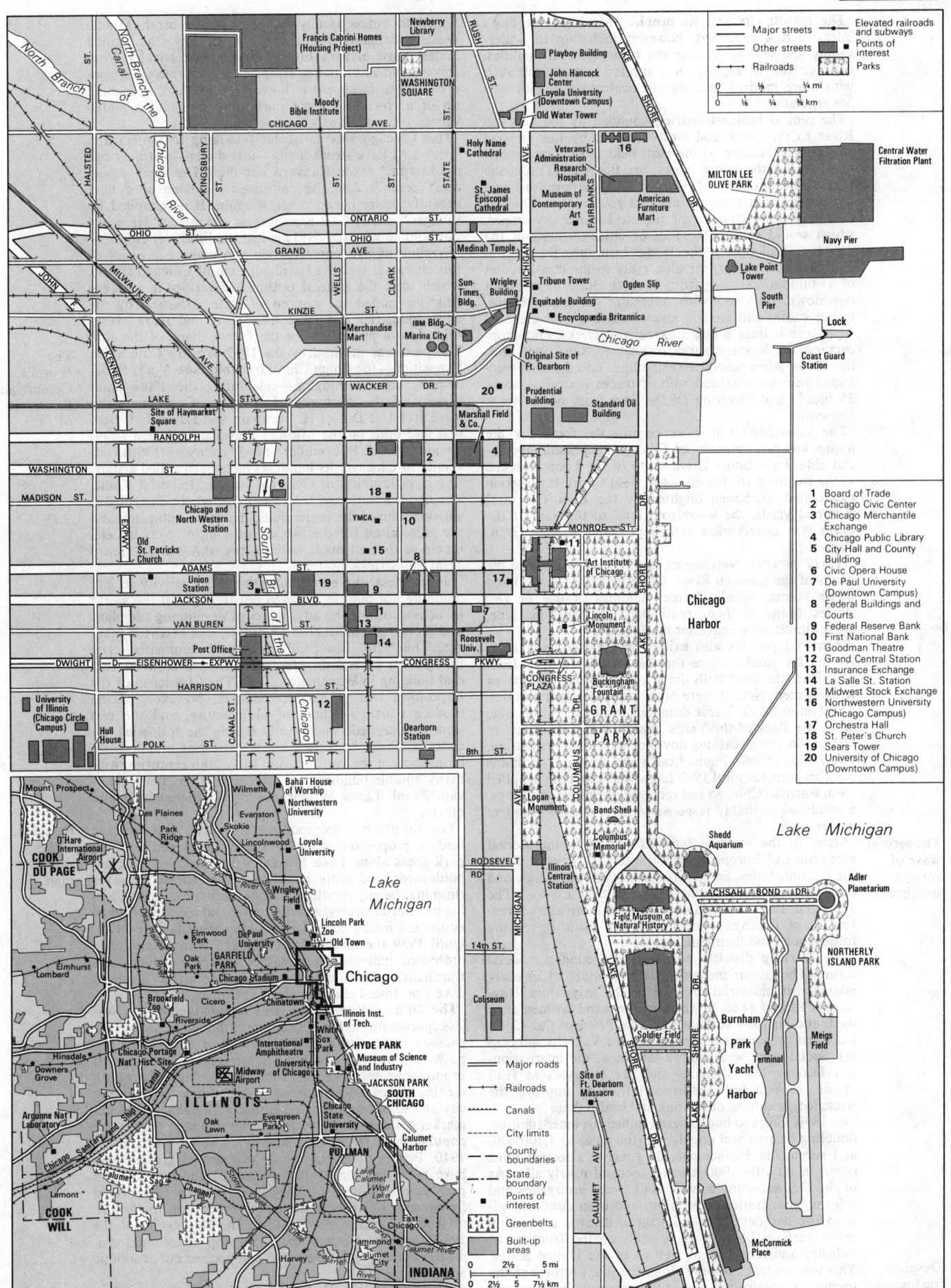

Central Chicago and (inset) its metropolitan area.

The rebuilt city and its people. Much of the city's infrastructure remained, however, including its water-supply and sewage systems and transportation facilities. Chicago rebuilt rapidly in a similar pattern, although with more modern buildings in conformance with new fire regulations.

The central business district, bounded by the Chicago River to the north and westward and by the railroad along the lakeshore to the east, held the major department stores, the larger banks, the Board of Trade, the regional headquarters of rising national corporations, and the centres of commerce, law, and government. The district was the birthplace of the steel-frame skyscraper, which would change the face of cities throughout the world. Completion of the Home Insurance Building in 1885 led during the next nine years to the construction of 21 buildings varying from 12 to 16 stories throughout downtown. Railroads with commuter passenger service, horse, cable, and electric street railways, and elevated rapid-transit lines brought executives, clerks, and shoppers into the downtown area, nicknamed "the Loop" since the 1890s, when several elevated lines into the area were joined into an overhead web of tracks encircling some 35 blocks and receiving feeder lines from north, west, and south.

The Lake Michigan shore became the focus for the homes and civic pursuits of Chicago's economic and social elite. Lake Shore Drive north of the Loop emerged as the mainline for society—the Gold Coast, it was soon nicknamed. Although blighted by the Illinois Central Railroad yards, the waterfront land to the east of the Loop was nevertheless landscaped and named Grant Park.

Heavy industry, warehouses, and rail yards crowded the banks of the Chicago River. Close by were the workingmen's homes, usually frame buildings of one or two stories. Many of them, particularly on the West Side, arose almost overnight after the 1871 fire.

Industrial pockets also existed at Chicago's outskirts. At the far south, where the Calumet River met Lake Michigan, the steel mills drew a polyglot community of workingmen. Nearby were other industrial communities. The Union Stock Yards dominated another South Side area, the Back-of-the-Yards district made infamous in Upton Sinclair's scathing novel of industrial oppression, *The Jungle* (1906). Public health and sanitary conditions were an outrage: until 1900 Lake Michigan both supplied fresh water to Chicago and received its untreated sewage, a condition probably responsible for the city's frequent epidemics.

Many of the working families arrived in the second great wave of European immigration: the Russian Jews, the Italians, Poles, Serbs, Croatians, the Bohemians, and other groups from southern and eastern Europe. The 1890 and 1900 censuses showed that more than three-fourths of Chicago's population was made up of the foreign born and their children.

The working districts were fertile ground for social action. The labour movement left the mark of its early attempts at industrial organizing: the mysterious Haymarket Riot of 1886, in which workers and lawmen alike died, and an 1894 strike against the Pullman Car Company, led by pioneer organizer Eugene V. Debs and others. Social work was another influence: the internationally famous Jane Addams and her followers at Hull House, a West Side settlement, tried to improve the wretched conditions of housing and health there.

By 1890, Chicago had annexed numerous inner suburbs, doubling its area and population (the latter to 1,100,000) and surpassing Philadelphia as America's second most populous city. By 1900 it was a focus of nearly all parts of the U.S. economy as well as of social insurgency and reform, immigration, education, and even culture. Chicago also had developed a flavour of its own, a brawling spirit, perhaps because of its years on the frontiers of industry and morality, as well as of the United States. This was evident not only along the dingy streets of the immigrant ghettos but also in the corporate boardrooms, where the sons and grandsons of early Chicagoans con-

tinued to amass family fortunes as the brash Middle Western captains of industry. In the city, the United States' most elegant brothel entertained royalty from abroad and millionaires from the newly sprawling suburbs. These facets were, however, less than an iceberg tip of a rowdiness some parts of which had a gilded veneer, other parts of which were quite open.

This Chicago was particularly striking to writers and visitors. "I have struck a city—a real city—and they call it Chicago," wrote Rudyard Kipling. "The other places don't count." And, he continued, "Having seen it, I urgently desire never to see it again. It is inhabited by savages." Later, Carl Sandburg would write, "Here is a tall bold slugger set vivid against the little soft cities."

Symbols of civic consolidation. A major expression of this character was the Burnham Plan of Chicago (1909), which took the general outlines of turn-of-the-century Chicago, added the notions of style possessed by the city's industrial and mercantile elite, and froze everything into a projection for the future shape of the city. The plan was inspired by the 1893 World's Columbian Exposition—for which Chicago outbid New York, Philadelphia, and Washington—celebrating the 400th anniversary of the discovery of America. Coordinated by local architect Daniel H. Burnham and Edward H. Bennett and built on the Midway Plaisance adjacent to oil tycoon John D. Rockefeller's newly endowed (1890) University of Chicago, its buildings have been called a startling stylistic union of Classical Greece, Imperial Rome, Renaissance Italy, and Bourbon Paris, wholly improbable yet symbolic of the pretensions, the naïve optimism, and the admiration for the proper ordering of complex elements of the self-made millionaires who had developed great industries.

Nonetheless, the exposition stimulated activity in city planning not only in Chicago but throughout the world by demonstrating the advantages of developing site plans and groups of buildings in an orderly and aesthetic manner. The "City Beautiful" movement dominated civic thought for several decades, influencing even some federal building in Washington, D.C. The Classicism of the Exposition was in marked contrast, however, to the modern Chicago School of architecture, and the two trends proceeded concurrently during the following decades. Chicago became a world centre of architectural innovation in the late 19th and early 20th centuries, with many notable buildings by Dankmar Adler, Louis Sullivan, Frank Lloyd Wright, Henry H. Richardson, and others.

The Burnham Plan, sponsored by civic and business leaders, proposed many subsequently developed features: park areas along Lake Michigan that included beaches, boulevards, and yacht basins; a belt of forest preserves rimming the city for close-in rustic recreation; the widening of arterial streets; a civic centre; and a double-decked boulevard in the central area along the Chicago River. Until 1939 the quasi-official Chicago Plan Commission promoted individual features of the plan, which, like Burnham's admonition, "Make no little plans," came to have a profound effect on physical Chicago.

The 20th century. Chicago's population growth was less spectacular in the 20th century, though industrial expansion associated with World Wars I and II and the postwar prosperity continued to attract newcomers. Most pronounced was the influx of blacks from the South seeking industrial employment. A building boom in the city and suburbs terminated abruptly following the stock-market collapse of 1929, and during the next decade the population increased only slightly, to about 3,400,000 in 1940. Possibly contributing to this slowed growth may have been the worldwide notoriety of Chicago (only in part deserved) as the playground of such underworld figures as Al Capone during Prohibition era, the failure of several Chicago banks during the Depression of the 1930s, and the allegedly powerful grip of criminal syndicates in following decades on many aspects of economic and political life.

After World War II, construction was slow to resume until the election of Mayor Richard J. Daley in 1955.

Massive rebuilding programs became a hallmark of his terms in office, including an almost total alteration of the skyline of the Loop and adjacent areas.

As in most cities, the downtown area, nevertheless, suffered from a continuing decline in other functions, including retailing, entertainment, and wholesale distribution, while rapid expansion of those activities took place on the periphery of the city and in suburban areas. The 1970 census revealed that, for the first time, the city itself had less than one-half of the metropolitan population.

THE CONTEMPORARY CITY

Chicago proper occupies 228.1 square miles (590.8 square kilometres) and had a population early in the 1970s of over 3,300,000, down 5.2 percent since 1960. It is the focus of the six-county Chicago Standard Metropolitan Statistical Area (SMSA) of 3,719 square miles. Contiguous and closely related to the Chicago SMSA is the Gary–Hammond–East Chicago SMSA in Indiana, embracing 938 square miles, which had in the early 1970s a population of over 600,000, an increase of 10.4 percent since 1960. The two adjacent metropolitan areas form the Chicago–Northwestern Indiana Standard Consolidated Area.

The natural and human environment. *Surface features and climate.* Chicago's site is generally level, rising from Lake Michigan, 579 feet (176 metres) above sea level, to slightly over 600 feet in outlying portions of the city. Most of Chicago is built on a plain, the remnant of postglacial Lake Chicago, formed when the retreating continental glacier blocked normal northeastward drainage through the St. Lawrence Valley 10,000 to 12,000 years ago. Outlying portions of the metropolitan area, formed from material deposited by the glaciers, rise to over 700 feet.

The narrow Chicago River extends one mile inland from Lake Michigan, where it splits, dividing the city into North, West, and South sides. Its original flow was into Lake Michigan, but completion of the Chicago Sanitary and Ship Canal in 1900 reversed it since the bottom of the canal is below the surface of Lake Michigan. Near the southeastern corner of the city, the Calumet River was reversed by the Calumet Sag Channel, completed in 1922 and enlarged as a modern barge route from 1955–72. The two waterways join southwest of the city and receive treated sewage effluent from three plants of the Metropolitan Sanitary District of Greater Chicago, as well as wastes from industrial plants and outlying areas. During high runoff the rivers occasionally revert to their original lakeward drainage, and some flooding occurs in low-lying areas.

The climate is subject to rapid changes of weather as successions of air masses pass from west to east. Lake Michigan tends to mitigate extremes, with lower temperatures in summer and higher in winter generally occurring close to the lake. January temperatures average about 25° F (−4° C) and July 75° F (24° C). Annual precipitation averages about 33 inches, and heavy snows occasionally disrupt local transportation.

Layout of the city. Chicago meets its suburbs in a ragged pattern of boundaries on three sides, while on the east the curving lakefront retreats from southeast to northwest. The Loop area just south of the river was platted on a gridiron pattern in 1830 following specifications of the Northwest Ordinance of 1787. This plan was followed to some degree in the rest of the city, though it was broken often by radial avenues (some following old Indian trails leading to the river mouth) and other features of the Burnham Plan, rail lines and yards, industrial sites, parks, and the like.

The building boom that began in the mid-1950s extended the highly concentrated business district westward from the Loop and, in the 1970s, into the Near West Side beyond the river's south branch. Many new skyscrapers radically altered the city's skyline. North Michigan Avenue, initially developed following completion of a Michigan Avenue Bridge in 1920, and adjacent Near North sites experienced much high-rise commercial and residential building in the 1960s, culminating in the

City and regional populations and areas

The 100-story John Hancock Center, dominating the skyline of Chicago's North Side along Lake Michigan. The glass-walled apartment buildings at right were designed by Ludwig Mies van der Rohe.
By courtesy of the John Hancock Mutual Life Insurance Company

100-story John Hancock Center. A combination office–shopping–apartment–garage structure, it was, at completion, the world's second-tallest building. In 1970 construction began on a 110-story building (Sears Tower) just west of the Loop, and a skyscraper complex was begun over the Illinois Central lakefront tracks northeast of the Loop, including the 80-story Standard Oil (of Indiana) Building. Office-building construction kept Chicago unchallenged as the headquarters centre of the Middle West.

Grant Park, in downtown Chicago, is joined by Lincoln Park on the North Side and Jackson Park on the South Side, both stretching for miles along the lakefront. Inland the city had an impressive park system as well.

Principal industrial areas lay along the Chicago River, its two branches, and in the Calumet region to the southeast, as well as along railroad lines and in satellite cities, such as Waukegan, Aurora, Joliet, and Chicago Heights in Illinois and the Gary–Hammond–East Chicago complex in Indiana, up to 40 miles from downtown Chicago. In South Chicago, along and near the Calumet River and along the lakefront in adjacent Indiana, are many oil refineries and iron and steel, chemical, and fabricating plants. The first steel plant in the area was established at the entrance of the Calumet River in 1880, followed by additional large plants nearby and at Indiana Harbor in the early 1900s. Gary was established as a major steel-producing centre in 1906. In the 1960s two large steel plants were established at Burns Harbor, east of Gary in the Indiana Dunes area. Meanwhile, the principal terminal of the Great Lakes–St. Lawrence Seaway overseas shipping route was developed after 1956 by the Chicago Regional Port District in Lake Calumet, six miles down the Calumet River from Lake Michigan.

The people and patterns of settlement. The proportion of foreign-born population declined steadily in both Chicago and its metropolitan area, reaching, respectively, 11.1 and 8.1 percent in 1970. The principal countries of origin were Poland, Germany, Italy, Russia, Sweden, and

Patterns of industrial and suburban growth

Ireland. The concentrations of Irish and of eastern and southern European groups helped to make Chicago's Roman Catholic archdiocese the largest in the nation.

Although there were a few blacks in Chicago from the earliest period of the city's growth, immigration was accelerated during and after World War I. The black population increased from 232,000 in 1930 to more than 1,100,000 in 1970, when it represented nearly one-third of the city's population and nearly 18 percent of that of the eight-county Standard Consolidated Area.

North of the Loop, the Lake Shore Drive mansions were being replaced rapidly by equally luxurious high-rise apartment buildings that by the 1970s extended this new lakefront Gold Coast almost to the city's border. Behind this strip, especially on the Near North Side, lay a narrow band of two- and three-story apartment buildings and older homes occupied largely by families of professional people and single persons.

An area around the University of Chicago on the South Side formed one of the city's major intellectual communities, though it was virtually surrounded by one of the most blighted sections of the black ghetto. Other universities contributing to local social patterns were DePaul and Loyola on the North Side and the Chicago Circle Campus of the University of Illinois, the construction of which in the 1960s uprooted much of the old Italian community southwest of the Loop.

Ethnic communities, city and suburban

Many ethnic and racial groups continued to form more or less homogeneous communities in various parts of the city. The Irish, long in control of the city's politics, were widespread, and a predominantly Irish region on the South Side had, in the early 1970s, spawned the last four mayors of Chicago—all Democrats. Chicago's Polish community, the largest in the nation, remained heavily concentrated on the Near Northwest Side. Swedish and German neighbourhoods reached through the North and Northwest sides, Bohemian Czechs spread into the southwestern suburb of Cicero, while Greeks gathered just west of the Loop.

Heavily Jewish populations were characteristic of the Far North and the adjoining suburbs of Lincolnwood and Skokie. Chinese and Japanese communities were concentrated on the South and North sides, respectively, while the nation's second-largest urban enclave of American Indians shared its poverty with Appalachian whites in the Mid-North. Groups of Chicagoans with Spanish surnames found shelter in deteriorating neighbourhoods in various parts of the city.

The majority of these ethnic communities had lost most of their distinctive character by the 1970s as the newer generations became homogenized into U.S. life. Foreign tongues remained in evidence, however, together with restaurants and stores that added flavour to the Chicago neighbourhoods.

Black settlement

The original main axis of black settlement was along mass-transit lines, especially through the South Side, where access to industrial employment was favourable. During and after World War II the South Side "black belt" expanded within the city and into adjacent suburbs, while additional areas of the West Side, once heavily Jewish, and parts of the Near North were occupied by blacks. Both in city and suburbs, most new black areas previously had been occupied by first or second generations of foreign origin who either left already deteriorating neighbourhoods or fled a growing influx of blacks.

Residential suburbs first grew up along the principal rail lines, but in recent years much suburban development has taken place, commonly at lower densities, in the areas between the earlier radial axes. A suburban real-estate boom in 1869 created new communities that were able to absorb many of the persons burned out by the 1871 fire. Among these was Riverside, west of the city, laid out in irregular streets and with exemplary planning, which enabled the community to retain its character to the present. Such lakeside communities as Evanston, Winnetka, and Lake Forest began a growth that in the 20th century made the North Shore the most prestigious of suburban areas. To the west, Oak Park had similar growth.

Among developments that encouraged residential deconcentration after World War II were new express highways; expansion of industries outside the city; huge regional shopping centres the sales of which rivalled those downtown; O'Hare International Airport (later annexed to the city) and its surrounding complex of hotels, motels, shopping centres, office buildings, and industrial districts; nuclear-research facilities, including the Argonne National Laboratory and a huge atomic research complex near Batavia; and many communities and "new towns," the first of which, Park Forest, was begun in 1947 30 miles south of the Loop and contained, in 1970, over 30,000 residents.

Economic life. Chicago's economy is one of the most diversified in the nation. Its balance between industry and commerce, between durable and nondurable goods, and between white-collar and blue-collar employment renders it less vulnerable than many other areas to economic recessions.

Components of the economy. In the late 1960s the metropolitan area had approximately 14,000 manufacturing establishments with about 1,000,000 employees and an annual payroll of about $8,000,000,000. The leading categories of manufacturing, measured by employment and by payrolls, were, in order, electrical equipment and supplies, non-electrical machinery, fabricated metal products, printing and publishing, food and kindred products, primary-metals industries, and chemicals and allied products.

Among the electrical products in which Chicago leads the nation are radio and television receivers, telephones, and many types of household appliances. Basic to Chicago's economy is the primary-metals industry, the largest component of which is the manufacture of iron and steel. In 1954 the Chicago area surpassed Pittsburgh as the nation's leading producer of these products, and by the late 1960s steel production in the metropolitan area was about one-fifth of total United States production.

The blue-collar and white-collar economy

This industry is dependent upon low-cost water transportation for basic raw materials. Large lake vessels bring iron ore from the Lake Superior area and eastern Canada and limestone, used as a blast-furnace flux, from Michigan; Appalachian coking coal arrives by rail. Lake Michigan furnishes a significant source of water, as well as area for plant expansion on landfill. During the 1960s, major problems of the industry in the region were the necessity for substantial investments to conform to air- and water-pollution control standards and the competition of foreign steel imported through the St. Lawrence Seaway.

Chicago's steel supply and its strategic situation as the major transportation node of the continent enabled it to assume leadership in manufacture of a wide variety of machinery and fabricated metal products, ranging from diesel-electric locomotives to printing presses, material-handling equipment, and earth-moving machinery to agricultural machinery. In the 1960s more than one-half of the area's industrial employment was engaged in metal-working manufacturing, including both machinery and metal fabrication.

A wide variety of chemicals and allied products serve both industrial and consumer markets. Closely associated are several large petroleum refineries, principally in the Calumet area and northwestern Indiana.

Chicago's printing establishments include several of the world's largest. Many nationally distributed magazines and mail-order catalogs, as well as a substantial proportion of telephone directories, are produced in these plants. Enormous quantities of paper, much of it from Canada, reach Chicago by water. The city ranks second to New York in the white-collar aspects of publishing, though it tends to specialize in such areas as educational materials, encyclopaedias, and professional and trade publications. It was also the home office of several major advertising and public relations firms.

Situated between the agricultural Middle West and the urban–industrial Northeast, Chicago remains a leader in food processing, although by the early 1970s the Union Stock Yards had terminated all meat-packing activities.

Related commercial activities of nationwide importance include trading in commodities futures on the Chicago Board of Trade and the Chicago Mercantile Exchange and associated brokerage offices and related establishments.

Convention facilities

Chicago has more trade shows, conventions, and fairs than any other city; about 1,000 such events attract some 1,300,000 persons annually. The Merchandise Mart, with most of its 4,000,000 square feet of floor area devoted to wholesaling activities, was for many years the world's largest commercial building. Other facilities, such as the American Furniture Mart, serve specialized wholesaling industries. Convention and trade-show facilities include concentrations of hotels and motels, notably in the downtown area and in the vicinity of O'Hare Airport, together with McCormick Place convention hall, on the South Side lakefront, opened in 1970 to replace a smaller facility destroyed by fire. Other centres include the International Amphitheatre, the scene of several national political conventions, in which another notable event is an annual International Livestock Exposition.

Chicago is the site of a Federal Reserve Bank, established in 1914. Most large banks are in the Loop area, and, because Illinois prohibits branch banking, the outlying neighbourhoods and suburbs are served by smaller banks, currency exchanges, and savings-and-loan associations. The city is also the site of the Midwest Stock Exchange and offices of most major brokerage houses. Many insurance companies are in the city or suburbs, including the nation's two largest automobile insurers.

Transportation. In addition to Chicago's standing as a major inland port and the United States' railroad hub, O'Hare International Airport is the world's busiest. By the late 1960s the older, smaller Midway Airport had been pressed into service again to relieve congestion, and various federal, state, and municipal bodies were concerned with the projected need for a third airport by about 1980. Chicago lost many intercity passenger trains before and after the advent of the quasi-public Amtrak system in 1971. Its several commuter lines serving suburbs to the north and west were widely regarded, however, as the finest in the nation in terms of comfort, punctuality, and overall service.

The freeway system built after World War II had become congested by the 1970s, as had the lakefront drive, which reached nearly from the northern to southern city limits and provided scenic views of both lake and city skyline. In the same period the elevated, subway, and surface lines of the Chicago Transit Authority had become increasingly debt ridden in spite of its having one of the nation's highest fare structures.

Administration. The spiritual chasm between Chicago and the rest of Illinois is perhaps widest in the political and social spheres and deepest in the struggles between city hall and the state government in Springfield. Chicago Democrats and Downstate Republicans found few issues over the years that could be debated on a basis other than that of partisan politics. Until the one man, one vote reapportionment of the legislature in the 1960s, the whip was usually in the hands of the sparsely populated Downstate counties. In addition, the growth in population and wealth of the suburbs in recent decades created a second front on which Chicago, like most large U.S. cities, was forced to wage a defensive campaign against a growing drain on its human and financial resources.

City and regional government. Routine operation and long-range planning in the Chicago SMSA is complicated by the continuous proliferation of overlapping administrative and taxing units of government. In addition to the more than 400 incorporated municipalities and the unincorporated areas under administration of the counties, the SMSA has over 700 special districts—elementary and high school and community college, park, forest preserve, drainage, sanitary, and the like—established to circumvent state-imposed limitations on borrowing. Such authorities as public housing, ports, transit, and highways operated without taxing power. State and federal funds and, when appropriate, user charges supplemented local outlays.

Overlap of administrative institutions

The Northeastern Illinois Planning Commission (NIPC), created by the state in 1957, coordinates much planning, especially among suburban governments. All projects involving federal aid must conform to the NIPC comprehensive plan adopted in 1968 for the six Illinois counties of the SMSA.

Administration of the city. Chicago's government long has been handicapped by an unwieldy structure not adapted to efficient administration of a modern urban region. Power is concentrated in a strong mayor who presides over a Council of aldermen representing the city's 50 wards. The mayor, with Council approval, also appoints members of the Board of Education, Park District, Housing Authority, and other special-purpose boards and commissions.

Political life. This formal scattering of power long has nurtured an informal but highly structured and disciplined political machine in Chicago that was brought to its peak of efficiency during the administration of Mayor Richard J. Daley, widely regarded as "the last of the big-city bosses" well before his re-election to a fifth four-year term in 1971. As chairman of the Cook County Democratic Party, he wielded great power beyond the city limits and was recognized as the predominant voice in the statewide party and a major power in the national Democratic Party. A deeply entrenched patronage system in all areas of government was moved into its highest gears for elections, and accusations and denials of voting irregularities were a constant feature of Chicago's political life. Opponents often charged that city building inspectors and other officials employed statutory sanctions to enforce party loyalty or punish disaffection and that the Council, in spite of a scattering of liberal independent and Republican aldermen, served as little more than a rubber stamp for mayoral programs.

Patronage and the "Organization"

Although Chicago administrations, both Democratic and Republican, had had a reputation for roughhouse politics since the 19th century and internal scandals were frequent, the foundations of the present-day "Organization," as it is called by its adherents, were laid during the brief term (1931–33) of Anton Cermak, a Bohemian immigrant who quickly mastered the politics of Chicago's ethnic ghettos, opposed the Prohibition that was unpopular with immigrant workers, and carefully balanced Democratic slates and platforms among the many ethnic, labour, and business interests. Innovative programs for municipal conservation and rebuilding renewal that were begun during the reformist administration of Martin Kennelly (1947–55) were moved ahead rapidly only after Daley's accession in 1955. Since then, an unofficial alliance of labour unions, civic and business leaders (often suburbanites), and party faithful from the precinct level upward, with heavy voting support from the blue-collar and ethnic communities, has maintained the Organization's hold on Chicago's political and social life.

The social milieu. The tremendous growth and spread of its black population and the concomitant flight of middle and upper class whites and of commerce to the suburbs probably has been the most dominant feature of Chicago's social picture since World War II and especially since the early 1960s. The city's few black aldermen tended to align themselves with the Organization and bring it the votes of the black community. A growing Spanish-speaking community, without political representation in the early 1970s, intensified the situation. The impact of these factors was felt most heavily in housing, although pressing needs in education and in health and welfare services increasingly forced the city to look to state and federal sources for relief. These requests intensified hostilities between city and state governments, especially when the latter was controlled by Republicans. In Chicago the socially conservative administration, with its most consistent voting support in the black neighbourhoods, often was accused of paying greater heed to highways, commercial construction, and maintenance of the social status quo than to the improvement of living and employment conditions. An impassioned opposition was for a time conducted by black groups such as Operation Breadbasket, an economic activity of the Southern Chris-

Social and political interactions

tian Leadership Conference founded by Martin Luther King, Jr. It mounted campaigns, often in conjunction with white-controlled businesses and citizen groups, to achieve greater economic and political power for the black community, but by the early 1970s it had become divided internally. The Chicago Council on Urban Opportunity had some success in its programs, but its ties to the Democratic organization made it suspect to many of the more militant black leaders. A so-called Chicago Plan for equal job opportunities in the trades, announced by Mayor Daley in 1969, had little implementation in its early years.

Housing. A fundamental clash of values became apparent in the 1960s when Mayor Daley, in rebutting a charge that Chicago was the United States' most segregated city, declared that the city had no ghettos. Numerous restrictive real-estate practices, however, long had been in effect in Chicago, intensified by a six-day race riot in 1919 that killed at least 38 persons. Scores of incidents occurred in following years. The inevitable outward explosion of the black community after World War II was abetted by unscrupulous real-estate operators but opposed by "block organizations" and other militant white-citizen groups, especially on the South and West sides.

By 1970 the Chicago Housing Authority had built about 40,000 units of low-rent housing, mainly as massive high-rise apartment projects that, in the view of many persons, tended to intensify the crime, isolation, and other evidences of life in the slums they were intended to replace and to epitomize the worst aspects of racial and socio-economic segregation. Private institutions, such as the Illinois Institute of Technology on the South Side, had better fortune with privately financed middle-income housing projects. A combination of redevelopment, conservation, and social programs in the area centred on the University of Chicago became a prototype for treatment of changing urban communities.

In 1971 the city's participation in the federally funded Model Cities program was jeopardized by the administration's reluctance to locate low-rent public housing in predominantly white neighbourhoods. At the same time, a number of the suburbs, many of which had fair-housing laws, resisted such housing and were largely unreceptive to pleas for housing aid from the city.

Education. The racial patterns of Chicago's public schools reflected neighbourhood residential patterns, with few attempts at integration and a relatively low standing in comparison with nationwide achievement standards. Both they and the Catholic parochial schools, which made up the nation's largest private-school system, teetered on the brink of financial calamity by the early 1970s and provoked intense city–state political feuds. Notable within the Chicago community-college system were the innovative approaches to black education at Malcolm X College.

Higher education

In higher education, the University of Chicago long has been among the nation's most prestigious institutions. Both the Illinois Institute of Technology and Northwestern University, the latter with campuses in Evanston and Chicago, had national reputations, while Loyola and DePaul universities were major Catholic institutions. Roosevelt University, in downtown Chicago, founded in 1945, offered a diverse curriculum especially geared toward an urban student body. The Chicago Circle Campus of the University of Illinois complemented the main campus in Champaign–Urbana.

Health and welfare. Chicago is among the United States' major medical- and dental-training centres, and its hospitals and research facilities are of high quality. A high proportion of trained personnel leave the area, however, creating an overall shortage in both city and state. As in many cities, service to the poor remained deficient, heavily encumbered by partisan political controversy. Publicly supported Cook County Hospital, one of the nation's largest, often found itself embroiled in political and financial crises that tended to affect its services, while neighbourhood clinics in black and Spanish-speaking areas, staffed mainly by young doctors and med-

ical students, were in frequent conflict with the politically run Board of Health.

Welfare services were broad but enmeshed in problems of overlapping city, county, state, and federal funding and supervision that often victimized those on aid rolls. Hull House, the best known privately operated welfare agency, continued in its several centres a legacy dating from its founding by Jane Addams in 1889, when it became a prototype for similar community-oriented settlement houses across the nation.

Cultural life and institutions. *The arts.* Its reputation as a boisterous and crassly commercial city notwithstanding, Chicago has fostered a robust artistic life throughout most of its history. It was a major theatre centre during the late 19th and early 20th centuries, and, before the discovery of Hollywood in the first decade of this century, it was the cradle of the infant U.S. motion-picture industry. During the 1950s the Second City troupe began a series of theatrical innovations that were to provide many new directions and talents to the entertainment world. The Goodman Theatre, long a nationally recognized school of theatre affiliated with the Art Institute, initiated a resident professional company in 1970. At the same time, numerous avant-garde companies proliferated, especially in the young-oriented sections of the city, and city and suburban "dinner theatres" attained some artistic acclaim.

Theatrical and musical life

The status of the Chicago Symphony Orchestra as one of the world's major musical ensembles was reinforced with critical enthusiasm after the appointment of Georg Solti as conductor in 1969. Chicago opera revived when the Lyric Opera was founded in 1954 to provide Chicago with brief but regular seasons of opera of a high calibre. Chicago's place in literature was at its highest in the early decades of the 20th century, especially with the publication of *Poetry* magazine, which profoundly altered the face of modern literature. Although many Chicago writers have gained renown, the city's peculiar literary genius showed itself most prominently in the field of journalism —from bucolic, Middle Western homily to stinging social and political commentary.

Although Chicago and environs incubated the most outstanding examples of modern domestic and commercial architecture—by Dankmar Adler, Louis Sullivan, Frank Lloyd Wright, and others—the city's record in preserving its landmarks was a depressing one. The razing of Sullivan's Stock Exchange Building in 1971 epitomized to conservationists and historians a callousness toward the city's aesthetic heritage that already had replaced numerous architectural landmarks with more profitable but uninspired buildings.

Architecture

In the early 1970s architectural Chicago remained among the finest of the world's large cities, but its plan and skyline were threatened by an increasing number of conventionalized structures indifferently adapted from the buildings of Ludwig Mies van de Rohe, an innovative genius who had renewed Chicago's architectural history in the years following World War II.

Museums and related institutions. Its many and diversified collections of painting, sculpture, prints, photographs, and handicrafts ranked the Art Institute of Chicago among the major museums of the world. In addition, its school of the arts, including the Goodman Theatre, made it an important training centre for the fine arts. The Museum of Contemporary Art, opened in 1967, provided Chicagoans with a complementary point of view through its revolving exhibitions of the leading edge of artistic endeavour. In striking contrast to these institutionalized programs, independent artists and groups transformed the sides and fronts of many buildings in black and Spanish-speaking areas into huge murals symbolizing communal or racial solidarity. Summer art fairs throughout the city and suburbs provided both professional and amateur artists with opportunities for income.

The exhibitions of the Museum of Science and Industry, housed in a huge remnant of the 1893 world's fair, were rivalled in the U.S. only by Washington's Smithsonian Institution. The public displays and research activities of the Field Museum of Natural History place it among the leading scientific institutions of the world. With the Shedd Aquarium, The Adler Planetarium, the Art Institute, and acres of landscaped lawn and shrubbery in Grant Park, it is part of the long lakeside refreshment of Chicago.

Recreations. For the more affluent Chicagoans, leisure was to be enjoyed in Wisconsin, Michigan, or other states, rarely in Downstate Illinois. Closer to home, the park system was supplemented by forest preserves located along the original city limits and in suburban areas of Cook County. Sandy beaches provided summertime sunshine in intermittent patches along Lake Michigan, though civic and privately owned encroachments, as well as distance, limited access for many Chicagoans. Professional sports sparked civic enthusiasm for the White Sox and Cubs in baseball, the Bears in football, the Black Hawks in hockey, and the Bulls in basketball. For Chicagoans and conventioneers alike, the many entertainments available along the neon-lit streets in the Near North nightclub area were a continuous attraction.

Journalism. In the early 1970s Chicago's four major daily newspapers were the most to be found in any U.S. city. Ownership was concentrated in only two corporations, however, and the competing afternoon dailies were dependent for survival on their morning counterparts. The *Chicago Sun-Times* and the *Chicago Daily News* tended to a centre-to-liberal position politically, whereas the staunch conservatism of the *Chicago Tribune*, which had become legendary in U.S. journalism, was somewhat less evident in the thin tabloid *Chicago Today*. The *Daily Defender* was directed to the black community. Neighbourhood weeklies proliferated throughout the city, while the polished publications of the North Shore suburbs appeared in a unique magazine format.

PROBLEMS AND PROSPECTS

In the 1970s, Chicago, like most other large U.S. cities, faced a complex of problems that challenged many of the existing political, administrative, and other institutions and practices. The city retained its primacy among the cities of interior North America with respect to commercial and industrial activity, transportation, and culture; but the deconcentration of many of these activities, along with a high proportion of the middle- and upper-income population, to suburban areas intensified the administrative, fiscal, and racial problems of the city proper. Although the central business district experienced a boom in office-building construction, many of the other functions, including retail and wholesale trade, entertainment, and manufacturing, were expanding within the metropolitan area at a much greater rate than in the city, while at the same time the city's essential welfare, protective, and other services were threatened by a relatively declining economic growth.

The diversity of the economic base, however, made the city less vulnerable than many others to economic fluctuations. Physically, the central area was being rapidly transformed by new skyscrapers, while on the fringes of the central area a program of action hopefully more sensitive than the large-scale urban renewal of previous decades was evolving. Under the impetus of federally prescribed planning processes, metropolitan planning, centring in the Northeastern Illinois Planning Commission, and city planning, under the Chicago Department of Development and Planning, constituted an important model —in spite of the fact that the city proper had not made significant progress toward solution of its racial, educational, and social problems.

Tensions between city and suburbs were increased by the racial differences, and the city's schools had not been able to arrest the general deterioration in the effectiveness of many of their programs. Air and water pollution continued to constitute major challenges, although city, state, and federal regulations and their enforcement began to make notable improvement in the quality of the city's air and water. In spite of these challenges, Chicago continued to maintain its position as the most important economic and cultural centre of the Middle West.

Margin note: Paradox of physical growth and economic uncertainty

BIBLIOGRAPHY. General works include IRVING CUTLER (ed.), *The Chicago Metropolitan Area: Selected Geographic Readings* (1970); the FEDERAL WRITERS' PROJECT, *Illinois*, rev. ed. (1947); and HARRY HANSEN, *The Chicago* (1942), in the "Rivers of America Series." The *Chicago Guide* (monthly) provides a worthy history of artistic and cultural events in the city, while JORY GRAHAM, *Chicago: An Extraordinary Guide* (1968), details the city's monuments, neighbourhoods, restaurants, and the like. Aspects of Chicago's history are covered in HERMAN KOGAN and ROBERT CROMIE, *The Great Fire: Chicago, 1871* (1971), a photographic and textual treatment; HAROLD M. MAYER and RICHARD C. WADE, *Chicago: Growth of a Metropolis* (1969), a photographic, cartographic, and textual treatment of the geographic evolution of the city and metropolitan area; and BESSIE L. PIERCE, *A History of Chicago*, 3 vol. (1937–57), a comprehensive treatment of the political, social, and economic history of the city. Demographic and economic studies include O.D. and B. DUNCAN, *The Negro Population of Chicago: A Study of Residential Succession* (1957), an account of the spread of Negro-occupied areas. LOUIS WIRTH, *The Ghetto* (1928, reprinted 1956); and HARVEY W. ZORBAUGH, *The Gold Coast and Slum: A Sociological Study of Chicago's Near North Side* (1929), both classic studies of Chicago communities. The CENTER FOR URBAN STUDIES, UNIVERSITY OF CHICAGO, *Mid-Chicago Economic Development Study*, 3 vol. (1966), is a comprehensive study of the economic and developmental problems of the inner city, with recommendations. EZRA SOLOMON and ZARKO G. BILBIJA, *Metropolitan Chicago: An Economic Analysis* (1959), is basic but now somewhat outdated. Materials on Chicago politics and government include: LLOYD LEWIS and HENRY JUSTIN SMITH, *Chicago: The History of Its Reputation* (1929); LEVERETT S. LYON et al., *Modernizing a City Government* (1954); PETER H. ROSSI and ROBERT A. DENTLER, *The Politics of Urban Renewal: The Chicago Findings* (1961); MIKE ROYKO, *Boss* (1971), a stinging attack on the Democratic Organization of Mayor Daley; and OVID DEMARIS, *Captive City* (1969), a somewhat sensationalized account of the interactions between the organized crime syndicate and politics in Chicago. Basic works on city and regional planning are DANIEL H. BURNHAM and EDWARD H. BENNETT, *Plan of Chicago* (1909); the CHICAGO DEPARTMENT OF DEVELOPMENT AND PLANNING, *Comprehensive Plan of Chicago* (1966); and the NORTHEASTERN ILLINOIS METROPOLITAN AREA PLANNING COMMISSION, *The Comprehensive General Plan for the Development of the Northeastern Illinois Counties Area* (1968). The city's architectural heritage is covered in IRA J. BACH, *Chicago on Foot* (1969); CARL W. CONDIT, *The Chicago School of Architecture* (1964); and ARTHUR SIEGEL, *Chicago's Famous Buildings: A Photographic Guide to the City's Architectural Landmarks and Other Notable Buildings* (1965).

(H.M.M.)

Ch'ien-lung

The reign (1735–96) of Hung-li, known from 1736 as Ch'ien-lung (in Pin-yin romanization Qian-long), fourth emperor of the Manchu (Ch'ing) dynasty (1644–1911), was one of the longest and most brilliant in China's entire history. Until the 20th century, Ch'ien-lung was looked upon as an enlightened sovereign ruling over a remarkably prosperous and well-administered empire, as a friend of the arts and of letters, and as a great builder with a mind open to ideas from the outside world. This picture of a philosopher-emperor, drawn by the Jesuit fathers who resided at the court of Peking, stimulated 18th-century Western philosophers and strengthened their aspirations toward an enlightened monarchy. But modern historical research, both Chinese and Western, appraises Ch'ien-lung's reign less favourably. Here, emphasis is on the excessive financial burden of the numerous military expeditions and lavish expenditures of the court, the corruption that was eating away at the administration at the close of the 18th century, and the tyranny of a reign in which censorship was exercised in a particularly destructive manner. Although Ch'ien-lung remains one of the great sovereigns of Chinese history, he nonetheless left an empire seriously weakened and ill-prepared to resist the impact from the West that was to strike it in the middle of the 19th century.

Margin note: Modern reappraisal of the reign

Youth and education. When born on September 25, 1711, he was named Hung-li. On October 7, 1735, on the eve of the death of the Yung-cheng emperor (reigned 1723–35), of whom he was the fourth son, Hung-li was declared the heir apparent, since Imperial Chinese tradi-

Ch'ien-lung, colour on silk by an unknown artist, 19th century. In the Metropolitan Museum of Art, New York.
By courtesy of the Metropolitan Museum of Art, New York, Rogers Fund, 1942

tion ignored the rules of primogeniture. In fact, in keeping with the wish of his grandfather, the K'ang-hsi emperor (reigned 1661–1722), Hung-li had been secretly designated Yung-cheng's successor shortly after the latter had ascended the throne. K'ang-hsi had noticed the outstanding qualities of his grandson and had decided to do his best to prepare him for his future task. Hung-li was given a carefully planned education, including the teachings of the eminent scholar Fu-min. He then was initiated into affairs of state and, in 1733, was made a prince of the first degree. He ascended the throne on October 18, 1735, at 24 according to the Western system, though 25 according to the Chinese system, and was to rule under the regnal title of Ch'ien-lung for more than 60 years.

Appearance and character.   Nearly six feet tall, with a frank and penetrating gaze, Ch'ien-lung was of slender build, with an upright bearing that he kept even in old age. A member of the ambassadorial staff of Lord Macartney in 1793 noted that the Emperor "walked firm and erect." He had a very vigorous constitution, was an excellent horseman and a remarkable archer, and loved hunting and long excursions into the country. Two years before his death, he was still able to take part in a hunting expedition.

His well-organized daily life followed the rhythm of protocol whether he was in Peking, in Jehol (in northeastern China, cradle of the dynasty), or in his palace (*yüan*) of Yüan Ming Yüan near Peking. He rose at 6 o'clock in the morning, took a bath, then had a quick breakfast alone. He then studied the reports and memos brought to him by his ministers, after which he received officials and gave them his instructions. At 2 o'clock in the afternoon, again alone, he had a meal that lasted about a quarter of an hour, choosing a few of the dishes prepared in the Imperial kitchens. After an hour's rest, the Emperor spent the afternoon reading, painting, practicing calligraphy, writing verses, or holding discussions with the best scholars. Sometimes he would receive the Empress or some member of his family. He had no evening meal, taking only some light refreshment and abstaining from any alcoholic beverage.

Though he was frugal and methodical, Ch'ien-lung was in no sense a killjoy. He was amiable by nature, enjoyed

The emperor's frugal life

having theatrical performances at court, and, at the new year, would open the walks of the palace grounds to hawkers and mountebanks, strolling about with obvious pleasure in the carnival atmosphere.

In private life, he was deeply attached to his first wife, the empress Hsiao-hsien, whom he had married in 1727 and by whom he had (in 1730) a son whom he wished to see his successor but who died in 1738. His second wife, Ula Nara, was elevated to the dignity of empress in 1750, but in 1765 she renounced living at the court and retired to a monastery, doubtless because of a disagreement with the Emperor.

Ch'ien-lung had 17 sons and ten daughters by his concubines. One of the latter, Hsiang-fei, or the "Perfumed Consort," was, according to popular legend, the grand passion of Ch'ien-lung. The widow of a prince from Yarkand (in Central Asia, now Sinkiang Province), she had been taken prisoner in 1759 by the Imperial armies. Although Ch'ien-lung lavished attentions upon her, even building her a small mosque, a Turkish bath, and a Muslim bazaar to remind her of her native country, the legend assures us that she always refused herself, threatening to kill the Emperor if he approached her. After two years, taking advantage of the Emperor's absence, the Dowager Empress gave Hsiang-fei the order to commit suicide. Ch'ien-lung's filial piety was not affected by this event, and he continued to show deference toward his mother, whom he visited frequently until her death in 1777.

Dynastic achievements.   In the 18th century, a considerable expansion of arable lands, a rapidly growing population, and good administration brought the Ch'ing dynasty to its highest degree of power. Under Ch'ien-lung, China reached its widest limits. In the northeast, decisive results were achieved by successive military expeditions (1755–60). Campaigns against the turbulent Turkish and Mongolian populations eliminated the danger of invasion that had always threatened the Chinese Empire and culminated in the creation of the New Province (Hsin-chiang, modern Sinkiang, in northwest China), which enlarged the empire by about 600,000 square miles (1,600,000 square kilometres). In the South, campaigns were less successful, but Chinese authority was nonetheless reinforced by them. An anti-Chinese revolt at Lhasa, Tibet, was easily put down (1752), Ch'ien-lung tightening his grip on a Tibet where real power passed from the Dalai Lama to two Chinese high commissioners. This brought an end to incursions on the Tibetan frontiers by Gurkhas from Nepal (1790–92), who now agreed to pay regular tribute to Peking. Campaigns against native tribes in rebellion from the west of Yünnan (the southwest corner of China) in 1748, then against Burmese tribes in 1769, ended in failure, but new expeditions finally crushed the Yünnan rebels in 1776. Burma itself, weakened by internal conflicts and by struggles with Siam, agreed in 1788 to pay tribute to Peking. In Annam, where rival factions were in dispute, the Chinese armies intervened in 1788–89, at first victoriously but later suffering heavy defeats. The new ruler of Hanoi was nevertheless willing to recognize that his kingdom was a tributary state. In the east, a serious rebellion on the island of Taiwan was crushed in 1787. The enormous cost of these expeditions seriously depleted the once healthy finances.

Still more serious was the bad management, the extravagance, and the corruption that marked the last two decades of Ch'ien-lung's reign and weakened the empire for some time to come. During the early years of his reign, Ch'ien-lung was assisted by the four regents designated by his father, the Yung-cheng emperor. Two of these were astute statesmen: the Chinese Chang T'ing-yü, who was given in 1739 the title of grand guardian but from whom the Emperor progressively withdrew his confidence, and the Manchu Oêr-t'ai, who was appointed grand tutor in 1745 but who died the same year. Ch'ien-lung was sole ruler from 1750 to 1780, his ministers either upholding his policies or not daring to disagree with the evermounting expenses of the court. Ch'ien-lung was 65 years old when he noticed a young officer, Ho-

The "Perfumed Consort"

shen, whom he was to make the most powerful person in the empire. In a few years, Ho-shen was given considerable responsibilities, and his son married the Emperor's favourite daughter. Under Ho-shen, who was intelligent but thirsty for power and wealth and completely without scruples, nepotism and corruption reached such a point, especially during Ch'ien-lung's last years, that the dynasty was permanently harmed.

Ch'ien-lung maintained blind confidence in his favourite. The Chia-ch'ing emperor, who succeeded Ch'ien-lung, had to wait for the old emperor's death before he could have Ho-shen arrested, relieve him of all his responsibilities, order the confiscation of his property, and grant him the favour of a suicide by reason of his blood ties with the Imperial family.

Contributions to the arts. The role of Ch'ien-lung in the arts and letters of his time was a considerable one. He himself wrote abundantly in prose as well as in verse. Even if he was not with certainty the author of the many poems (more than 40,000) that have been attributed to him, he was nonetheless constantly seeking literary glory and supervised the regular publication of his works. They are today more appreciated for their historical interest than for their poetic value.

But the name of Ch'ien-lung remains attached to the most important compilation of texts realized in Chinese history, where such enterprises are traditional. In 1772, Ch'ien-lung ordered that a choice be made of the most important texts in the four traditional divisions of Chinese learning—classical works, historical works, philosophical works, and belles lettres. The *Ssu-ku ch'üan-shu* ("Complete Library in the Four Branches of Literature") involved scrutiny of entire libraries, both Imperial and private, and was carried on for ten years under the direction of the scholars Chi yün and Lu Hsi-hsiung, the Emperor himself intervening on several occasions in the choice of texts. Seven handwritten series of the 36,275 volumes of the *Ssu-ku ch'üan-shu* were distributed, between 1782 and 1787, among the principal Imperial palaces (Peking, Jehol, Mukden, and Yüan-ming Yüan) or were placed in libraries open only to scholars. The descriptive catalog of *Ssu-ku ch'üan-shu* remains an essential bibliographic guide for the study of classical Chinese literature.

But this positive contribution to Chinese literature was combined with harsh censorship. In 1774, Ch'ien-lung ordered the expurgation or destruction of all seditious books; that is, all those containing anti-Manchu declarations or allusions. As the examinations of the works took place, an index was drawn up, and, between 1774 and 1788, provincial governors received renewed orders to have the public or private libraries in their provinces checked. It has been estimated that about 2,600 titles were ordered to be destroyed. Nevertheless, several hundred works were preserved because there happened to be a copy in a Japanese or Korean library or in the library of some influential Manchu. The *Ssu-ku ch'üan-shu* itself was revised on several points after its completion, at the expense of the compilers, after the Emperor had discovered in it some texts that he considered seditious.

The flowering of the arts that had occurred under the K'ang-hsi and Yung-cheng emperors continued with Ch'ien-lung. Architecture, painting, porcelain, and particularly jade and ivorywork flourished with a final brilliance, for later Chinese artisans produced only for export.

Like his grandfather, Ch'ien-lung protected artists. He granted a reprieve to the excellent calligrapher Chang Chao, who was in prison awaiting execution (1736), and entrusted him with important functions. He was particularly appreciative of the painting talents of certain European missionaries who lived at the court, such as Castiglione and Jean-Denis Attiret. He also admired the knowledge and skill of the Jesuit fathers who constructed various machines and mechanical devices, though he regarded the latter as no more than a source of intellectual satisfaction and a means of creating amusing objects.

Ch'ien-lung devoted the greatest attention to the beauti-

Ho-shen [margin note]

The Ssu-ku ch'üan-shu [margin note]

fication of the Yüan-ming Yüan near Peking. He was to reside there more and more often, and he considered the ensemble formed by its numerous pavilions, lakes, and gardens as the Imperial residence *par excellence*. He increased the estate and erected new buildings. At his request, several Jesuit missionaries built residences and gardens in a modified Italian style (Baroque and Rococo —roughly corresponding with the 17th- and 18th-century architecture—but with Chinese roofs) around fountains similar to those of Versailles in France. Ch'ien-lung chose 40 remarkable views of Yüan-ming Yüan, which two Chinese artists were commissioned to paint and for which he himself composed 40 poems. They were published in two volumes in 1745.

Ch'ien-lung had a passion for architecture and spent large sums on new constructions or on restorations such as those of the temples of Heaven and of agriculture in Peking. He professed to have regretted these expenditures, but he probably did so without much conviction.

Relations with the West. Ch'ien-lung maintained China's traditional attitude to the outside world. The excellent personal relationships that he enjoyed with the Jesuits residing in Peking did nothing to modify the Imperial reserve regarding Catholicism. Catholic preaching remained officially forbidden after the "Rites Controversy"—a quarrel over the compatibility of ancestor worship with Catholicism—that pitted the Pope's legate against the K'ang-hsi emperor at the beginning of the 18th century. Although the work of the missionaries continued to be tolerated in the provinces, it frequently met with strong hostility from the local authorities, and the total number of congregations declined greatly. The British authorities later tried in vain to widen commercial contacts with China, but these remained confined to the port of Canton. A mission extraordinary led by Lord Macartney was received by the Emperor in September of 1793, but the demands it presented were rejected.

Abdication. After having reigned for 60 years, Ch'ien-lung, out of respect for K'ang-hsi, whose reign had lasted 61 years, announced on October 15, 1795, that he was designating his fifth son, Yung-yen, to succeed him. On February 9, 1796, the Chinese new year, the new reign took the title of Chia-ch'ing. But, out of deference, the customs of the years of the Ch'ien-lung reign were upheld in the palace until the death of the old emperor (February 7, 1799). He had, in fact, held real power until this time, which makes his actual reign the longest in all Chinese history. He was given the temple name of Kao-tsung and the posthumous name of Ch'un Huang-ti. His tomb, to the northeast of Peking, is called Yü-ling.

Patronage of the arts [margin note]

BIBLIOGRAPHY. SIMON HARCOURT-SMITH, "The Emperor Ch'ien-lung, 1735–1799," *History Today*, 5:164–173 (1955), an informative article; ARTHUR W. HUMMEL, *Eminent Chinese of the Ch'ing Period, 1644–1912* (1943), contains a scholarly article on Hung-li. See also SIR EDWARD BACKHOUSE and JOHN O. BLAND, *Annals and Memoirs of the Court of Peking (from the 16th to the 20th Century)* (1914); HOPE DANBY, *The Garden of Perfect Brightness: The History of Yuan Ming Yuan and of the Emperors Who Lived There* (1950); L. CARRINGTON GOODRICH, *The Literary Inquisition of Ch'ien-lung* (1935); SVEN HEDIN, *Jehol: City of Emperors* (1933); and CARROLL BROWN MALONE, *History of the Peking Summer Palaces Under the Ch'ing Dynasty* (1934).

(Ro.Pe.)

Childhood Diseases

The most characteristic features of the diseases of childhood relate to the phenomenon of change, either in the child himself or in his immediate environment. Changes in the child related to growth and development are so striking that it is almost as if the child were a series of distinct yet related individuals as he passes through infancy, childhood, and adolescence. Changes in the environment occur as the surroundings and contacts of the totally dependent infant become those of the progressively more independent child and adolescent. This article reviews the scope of diseases that affect children, with particular emphasis on the ways in which the unique attributes of the growing child and special aspects of his environment serve as modifiers.

The age span of concern to physicians who specialize in diseases of childhood begins with the fetus and extends through the whole period of adolescence.

Although, for the most part, the diseases of childhood are similar to those of the adult, there are several important differences. For example, certain specific disorders, such as erythroblastosis—a red-cell-destroying disease arising from incompatibility between the blood of the fetus and that of the mother—and precocious puberty are unique to children, and others, such as acute nephritis—inflammation of the kidney—are common in children and infrequent in adults. At the same time, some diseases that are common in adults are infrequent in children. These include essential hypertension (high blood pressure of unknown cause), diseases of the coronary arteries (*i.e.*, the arteries that supply blood to the heart), and gout. Finally, a major segment of pediatric disease concerns congenital anomalies, both functional and structural. The recognition and treatment of these diseases and attempts to prevent them comprise a major part of pediatric practice.

Apart from variations in disease due to differences between children and adults, certain other features of diseases in children need to be emphasized. Infectious disorders are prevalent and remain a leading cause of death, although individual illnesses are often mild and of minor consequence. Most instances of the common communicable diseases, such as measles, chickenpox, mumps, and poliomyelitis, are encountered in childhood. Disorders of nutrition, still of great concern, especially but not exclusively in less medically developed countries, are of extreme importance to the growing and developing organism. The unique nutritional requirements of children make them unusually susceptible to deficiency states: vitamin-D deficiency causes rickets, a common disorder of children in underdeveloped countries, and only rarely causes any disease in adults.

The major environmental hazards that endanger the health of young children are either unavoidable, as in air pollution, or accidental, as in poisoning and in traffic injuries. Older children, especially adolescents, are exposed, as are adults, to environmental hazards, such as cigarette smoking, alcohol, and drugs, that they deliberately seek.

DIAGNOSIS AND GENERAL CONSIDERATIONS OF TREATMENT AND PREVENTION

Diagnosis of the diseases of childhood involves special considerations and techniques; for example, in evaluating genetic disorders, not only the patient but his entire family may need to be examined. Inapparent environmental causes of diseases, such as poisonings, must be considered and investigated, by methods that at times resemble those of a detective. Diseases of the fetus may derive directly from disorders of the mother or may be caused by drugs administered to her. Diagnostic techniques have been developed that permit sophisticated examination of the fetus despite its apparent inaccessibility in the uterus. Withdrawal of a small amount of the fluid, called amniotic fluid, that surrounds the fetus permits examination of cells of the fetus as well as the fluid itself. Chromosomal and biochemical studies at various stages of development may help to anticipate problems in the postnatal period; they may indicate the need for immediate treatment of the fetus by such techniques as blood transfusion; or they may lead to the decision to terminate pregnancy because serious, untreatable fetal disease has been recognized. Other specialized techniques permit examination of the fetus by X-ray, electrocardiography, and electroencephalography (methods for observing and recording the electrical activity of the heart and the brain, respectively). Fetal blood can be obtained for analysis, and certain techniques permit direct viewing of the fetus.

In examination of the infant, inaccessibility is no special problem, but his small size and limited ability to communicate require special techniques and skills. Of even more importance, however, is the fact that adult norms cannot be applied to younger age groups. Pediatric diagnosis requires knowledge of each stage of development, with regard not only to body size but also to body proportions, sexual development, the development and functioning of organs, biochemical composition of the body fluids, and the activity of enzymes. The development of psychological and intellectual functioning is equally complex and requires special understanding. Since the various periods of growth and development differ so markedly from one another, they are divided for convenience into the following stages: intrauterine (the period before birth); neonatal (first four weeks), infant (first two years), preschool (two to six years), early school (six to ten years for girls, six to 12 for boys), prepubescent (ten to 12 for girls, 12 to 14 for boys), and adolescent (12 to 18 for girls, 14 to 20 for boys). Only if appropriate norms are established for each stage of development can the child's condition be adequately evaluated and the results of diagnostic tests properly interpreted. Thus, it is of no concern if a 12-month-old infant is unable to walk alone, although some infants are able to do so at nine months of age. The crucial question is at what age one becomes concerned if a developmental milestone has not been reached. Five-year-old boys average 43 pounds (20 kilograms) in weight but may vary from 34 to 53 (15 to 24 kilograms). The hemoglobin level that is of no concern in the three-month-old infant may reflect a serious state of anemia in the older child. The blood levels of certain enzymes and minerals differ markedly in the rapidly growing child from those in the late adolescent, whose growth is almost complete. Failure of a 15-year-old girl to have achieved menarche (the beginning of menstruation) may be indicative of no abnormality in sexual development but requires thoughtful consideration and careful evaluation.

Treatment of childhood disease requires similar considerations with regard to various stages of growth and development. Variation in drug dosage, for example, is based not only on body size but also on the distribution of the drug within the body, its rate of metabolism, and its rate of excretion, all of which change during various stages of development. The inability of infants and small children to swallow pills and capsules necessitates the use of other forms and alternate routes of administration. Drug toxicity of importance at one stage of development may be of no concern at another; for example, the commonly used antibiotic tetracycline is usually avoided in treatment of the young child because it is deposited in teeth in which enamel is being deposited and stains them. When permanent teeth are fully formed, the deposition of tetracycline no longer occurs. The delayed consequences of certain forms of treatment, especially with radioactive isotopes—substances that give off radiation in the process of breaking down into other substances—might be of no consequence in the case of an elderly person with a life expectancy of ten or 20 years but might deter one from the use of such treatments for the infant with his whole life before him. Finally, the nutritional requirements of the growing child must be considered when treatment of disease requires modification of the diet or administration of drugs that may affect the absorption or metabolism of essential nutrients.

The outlook for recovery from diseases in children often is better than it is for adults, since the young organism has an additional capacity of growth that may counteract the adverse influences of disease. The bony fracture that results in permanent deformity in the adult, for example, may heal with complete return to structural normality in the child, as continued growth results in remodelling and reshaping of the bone. Ultimately, the infant who has one kidney removed because of infection or tumour most likely will have entirely normal renal (kidney) function because the remaining kidney will increase its size and functional capacity with growth. In contrast, removal of one kidney in the adult usually results in a residual functional capacity equal to 70 to 75 percent of that of two normal kidneys.

Thus, being in a period of growth and development may favourably affect the course of a disease. The converse may also be true, however, and the child may be more susceptible than the adult to the adverse effects of disease. The rapidly growing and maturing central nervous system, for example, is particularly susceptible to injury; also, children may react unfavourably to psychological stresses that are tolerated readily by more mature individuals.

Prevention of childhood disease

In the general consideration of childhood diseases, a final aspect that merits emphasis is the role of prevention. The major factors responsible for the decline in infant and childhood mortality rates over the past decades have been the development and application of preventive measures. In the United States, for example, in the past half century the death rate for infants under one year of age has decreased until it is scarcely more than a tenth of the former rate. Although socioeconomic factors, such as better maternal nutrition and obstetrical care and better housing, have played a role, the change is due primarily to the introduction of sterilization of infant feeding formulas and the development of techniques of immunization against the common infectious diseases of infancy. In comparison to the favourable effect of these and other preventive measures, an increased capacity to treat diseases, even with such powerful tools as the antibiotic drugs, has had relatively little impact. Just as important as the development of public health measures is their practical application: underutilization of established procedures and techniques for prevention of disease is a major health problem, especially (but not exclusively) in less medically developed countries.

DISEASE-AFFECTING DIFFERENCES BETWEEN CHILDREN AND ADULTS

Disturbances in growth may be among the most striking consequences of disease in children. An obvious example of this effect is total growth failure, which is seen in almost every serious disease of infants and children. Local retardation or disturbance in growth patterns may be equally striking. Osteomyelitis, an infection of bone, may, for example, result in retardation or cessation of growth at that site, with subsequent severe asymmetry between the affected limb and its normal counterpart. Enlargement of the heart as the result of cardiac disease may cause gross distortion of the chest, as the growing ribs adapt to the abnormal shape of the heart.

Anatomical differences. Many differences in the manifestations of disease in children and adults can be ascribed to differences in anatomical structure and in biochemical, immunological, and physiological function. Less well understood are the consequences of differences in psychological functioning. In general, the younger the child, the more striking these differences are.

Not only is the child's body smaller than that of the adult, but it has different proportions; for example, the sitting height of the newborn infant represents about 70 percent of total body length. With rapid growth of the extremities, sitting height decreases to about 57 percent of the body length at three years of age and, finally, as growth proceeds more slowly, to the adult proportion of about 50 percent. In addition to differences in body proportions, there are marked differences in body composition. As examples, in newborn infants muscle mass constitutes approximately 25 percent of total body weight, compared to 43 percent in adults. Total body water, which accounts for 90 percent of early fetal weight, represents 75 percent of body weight at birth, drops to about 60 percent by one year of age, and then declines gradually to reach the adult figure of 55 percent. The higher proportion of body water, due almost entirely to a relatively greater volume of fluid outside the cells, affects the response of the infant, particularly to disturbances in water balance.

Hyperplasia and hypertrophy

Another notable characteristic of growth relates to increases in cell number (hyperplasia) versus increases in cell size (hypertrophy). Hyperplasia accounts for early fetal growth. In the latter stages of fetal life, both hyperplasia and hypertrophy contribute to the increasing size of the fetus. Postnatal growth results almost entirely from hypertrophy.

There are many examples of differences in anatomical

structure that affect manifestations of disease. In assessing the health of the infant with cardiac or pulmonary (lung) disease, his thinner chest wall, the relatively more horizontal position of the heart, and the more rapid cardiac and respiratory rates must be taken into account. The thin abdominal wall of the infant permits palpation—examination by touching with the fingers—of the kidneys, which in older subjects usually can be felt only if they are abnormally large. In the infant, with the bones of the skull still not fused together, obstruction to the flow of cerebrospinal fluid may result in striking enlargement of the head, referred to as hydrocephalus. In the older child, when the sutures have fused, such enlargement is not possible, and the manifestations of spinal-fluid obstruction are similar to those of the adult, including severe headache and visual difficulties as a result of increased intracranial pressure. The primary manifestation of mumps is a painful swelling of the parotid and other salivary glands. In children, involvement of the testes or ovaries occurs only rarely, a phenomenon related in some way to the state of immaturity of these organs. In contrast, in the adult, particularly in the male, severe sex-gland involvement is commonly encountered. In children exclusively, there is a condition in which certain of the growth centres of bone undergo necrosis (tissue death). Although the cause is unknown, it appears to be related to the stresses of growth, particularly with regard to changes in the blood supply to the bone. Necrosis of the head of the femur, called Legg–Calvé–Perthes disease, is a striking example of this disorder.

Physiological differences. Physiological differences between children and adults that cause differences in the manifestations of disease include all the various functional, endocrine, and metabolic features of the growing and maturing organism. A major characteristic in this regard is the limited ability of the infant to maintain homeostasis (a stable internal environment) during illness because of his greater metabolic and nutritive requirements. Moreover, most of the first year of life is characterized by immaturity of renal function, the capacity of the kidneys to respond to the stresses of disease being less than later in life. As a consequence, with any degree of stress, metabolic abnormalities are likely to be more severe in the infant than in the older child.

The liver of the newborn child also demonstrates certain features of immaturity. Of particular importance is its limited capacity to excrete bilirubin, a product of the breaking down of hemoglobin. In certain conditions in which there is a rapid rate of destruction of red blood cells, the inability of the liver to excrete the added load of bilirubin may result in a large increase in the concentration of this substance in the blood; the bilirubin concentration, if high enough, can cause severe brain damage known as kernicterus. Since immaturity of the brain also contributes to the infant's increased susceptibility to this disorder, the disorder is rarely encountered outside of the neonatal period, even in subjects with severe liver disease.

The ability of the young infant to metabolize and to excrete certain drugs is limited by the immaturity of the liver and of the kidney, and drug dosage must be adjusted accordingly.

Immunologic responsiveness

The immunologic responsiveness of the infant is qualitatively and quantitatively different from that of the older child and adult. Although the differences in antibody response cannot be related specifically to differences in the capacity of the infant to withstand infection, they certainly must play some role. On the other hand, many of the clinical features of infectious diseases occurring during the first two or three years of life appear to be related to the fact that these are infections occurring for the first time.

DISEASES PECULIAR TO THE NEWBORN INFANT

Diseases transmitted through the placenta or due to placental dysfunction. Infectious diseases of the fetus are caused by many different types of organisms, including viruses, bacteria, spirochetes, and protozoa (toxoplasmosis). Most of these infections are the result of infection of the mother, the infectious agents being transmitted through the placenta (the temporary organ by means of which the fetus receives nourishment and discharges waste) by way of fetal circulation. Bacterial infection is most often associated with premature rupture of the membranes and infection of the amniotic fluid.

Maternal rubella (German measles) occurring during the first eight weeks of pregnancy is associated with congenital malformation of the fetus in more than 50 percent of cases, the figure decreasing to about 20 percent by the 16th week and dropping sharply thereafter. Infection of the fetus with a virus of the cytomegalovirus type involves many organs, has a high fatality rate, and may result in severe brain damage in infants who survive. Infection by the intracellular parasite *Toxoplasma gondii* produces a disease called toxoplasmosis, which may cause death or may result in microcephalus (abnormal smallness of the head), hydrocephalus (excessive accumulation of fluid in the brain cavities), or mental retardation. Congenital syphilis may have a variety of effects in the infant, including involvement of the skin, liver, spleen, lymph nodes, and kidneys. Malformations of the bones and teeth appear later, and severe involvement of the central nervous system may become apparent after many years.

The entire nutrient supply of the fetus derives from the mother. Although maternal deficiency states may, therefore, be reflected by parallel deficiencies in the fetus, in general the needs of the fetus will be met ahead of those of the mother, and an adequate amount of a given nutrient may be supplied to the fetus, despite maternal deficiency. Mild to moderate deficiencies of iron or calcium in the mother, for example, are not usually associated with deficiencies in the fetus. On the other hand, protein and caloric malnutrition may be associated with decreased fetal size. In experimental animals, maternal zinc deficiency is associated with a high incidence of fetal malformation.

Placental insufficiency

Deficiencies in the fetus may also arise from placental dysfunction (malfunctioning). The consequences of abnormalities of the placenta depend upon the time of onset and the severity of placental inadequacy. Serious placental insufficiency early in pregnancy may result in the death of the fetus. It is also likely that placental insufficiency can be a factor in decreasing fetal growth. Toward the end of pregnancy, placental dysfunction is associated with premature delivery or evidence of varying degrees of fetal distress, ranging from yellow staining of the skin to fetal wasting and to signs of severe lack of oxygen.

Drugs administered to the mother may pass through the placenta and have important effects on the fetus. A most dramatic and devastating example of this effect was the induction of severe fetal malformations (phocomelia) by the maternal ingestion of the apparently harmless drug thalidomide. Anesthetics, analgesics (pain relievers), sedatives, antihypertensive drugs, and antibiotics all may have adverse effects on the fetus. Congenital goitres (enlargement of the thyroid) have been produced by administration of antithyroid drugs to the mother. It is now clear that adverse effects on the fetus must be considered whenever drug therapy of the mother is contemplated.

Injuries incurred during birth. The physical trauma of delivery may result in a number of injuries to the infant. Of little consequence is the diffuse soft-tissue swelling of the scalp referred to as caput succedaneum. Abrasions and ecchymoses (black-and-blue spots) may result from the use of forceps. Bleeding under the periostium (the covering membrane) of one of the cranial bones may be associated with skull fracture. Injuries to the spinal cord are rare, but injuries of peripheral nerves as a result of traction on the head are not uncommon. Such injuries include Erb's paralysis, with weakness of the arm and shoulder because of damage to the fifth and sixth cervical nerves, and Klumpke's paralysis, with weakness of the hand from damage to the seventh and eighth cervical nerves. Injury to the phrenic nerve, with paralysis of the diaphragm—the muscular partition between the chest and the abdomen—and facial-nerve injury resulting in facial palsy also are encountered. In the vast majority of such instances of peripheral-nerve injury, recovery is complete.

Fractures of bones, particularly the collarbone, and injury to viscera also may occur during delivery. Severe injury, such as rupture of the liver, may cause death.

An extremely important form of birth injury is that associated with lack of oxygen (anoxia). Fetal anoxia may occur from inadequate oxygenation of the mother, low blood pressure in the mother, or abnormalities in the uterus, placenta, or umbilical cord that result in inadequate blood flow to the fetus. After birth, anoxia may result from blood loss, shock, or inadequate respiration. Clinical manifestations of anoxia include decreased activity, slowing of the heart, and blueness of the skin (cyanosis). Severe anoxia may cause death of the newborn infant, although recovery is more common. The major significance of anoxia is that it may result in brain damage if prolonged for more than a few minutes.

Prematurity. Infants born prior to 37 weeks of gestation are considered to have been born early and are referred to as premature. Infants who at birth weigh 2,500 grams (about 5.5 pounds) or less are considered to be of low birth weight and either are prematurely born or have had less than the expected rate of growth within the uterus. Often, it is not possible to determine gestational age (the age of the infant from the time of conception), and therefore prematurity is diagnosed by birth weight alone. It is important, however, to attempt to distinguish between the premature infant and the mature infant that is small for gestational age.

Definition of prematurity

Infants whose weight is low at birth account for as many as 10 to 15 percent of births among low socioeconomic groups and as few as 4 to 5 percent of births among those of higher socioeconomic status. Overall, about 8 percent of infants born in the United States fall into the low-birth-weight category. Since the majority of these infants truly are premature, the importance of this classification is the association between prematurity, neonatal mortality, and numerous complications of growth and development.

Early delivery may interfere with adaptation to life (life outside the womb) in that many organ systems will not be fully developed. The infant who is large and only slightly immature is entirely capable of surviving after birth and statistically does as well as the full-term infant; the very small premature infant, below 1,000 grams (about 35 ounces) in weight, has a high fatality rate and is prone to the many complications of prematurity.

The complications encountered in coping with extrauterine existence involve primarily the respiratory and gastrointestinal systems. In addition to anatomical immaturity of the lungs, a handicapping feature of the premature infant may be a lack of a substance called a surfactant, which plays an important role in permitting the air spaces, or alveoli, of the lungs to remain open. Surfactant appears in some fetuses at 24 weeks' gestation but is absent in others until about 30 weeks.

Inability to suck adequately and limitations in the capacity to digest foodstuffs and absorb them through the intestinal tract provide other serious handicaps for the premature infant. To circumvent these problems, infants may be fed (by stomach tube) specially prepared formulas tolerated by even the smallest of infants.

The relatively large surface area of the small premature infant and his inability to maintain body temperature may require his being kept in an incubator. In addition to temperature control, the incubator makes it possible to provide extra oxygen to the infant who has respiratory difficulties, although this must be done with care because excessive oxygen may lead to damage to the eyes, a condition known as retrolental fibroplasia.

Survival of premature infants

As indicated above, the prematurely born infant is considerably less likely to survive than are full-term infants. Premature infants, accounting for less than 8 percent of all live births, account for two-thirds of infant deaths. Even after the first year of life, the mortality rate among infants with low birth weights is greater than among infants with birth weights above 2,500 grams. The cause of this increased rate is not completely known, although a higher prevalence of congenital anomalies accounts for some of the difference. Moreover, retarded intellectual development and other abnormalities of the nervous system are more common in such infants, particularly those with birth weights of less than 1,500 grams (3.3 pounds). The majority of infants with low birth weights remain small throughout the childhood years, which may reflect a continued pattern of slow growth, first evidenced in the uterus.

Congenital anomalies. The infant may be born with any of a wide variety of defects. These may involve the bones and muscles, the nervous system, the sense organs, the digestive tract, the heart and blood vessels, the blood itself, the excretory system, the reproductive system, metabolic processes, or the chromosomes. Accounts of the anomalies may be found in BIRTH DEFECTS AND CONGENITAL DISORDERS and in the articles on the diseases of the various systems (*e.g.*, CARDIOVASCULAR SYSTEM DISEASES AND DISORDERS).

Metabolic disturbances. Infants of diabetic mothers represent a unique group with special metabolic problems. Intrauterine death is common and unexplained. The placenta often is abnormal. The infants at birth generally are large and have large organs, a condition referred to as macrosomia. Respiratory distress and low levels of sugar in the blood (hypoglycemia) are common complications, and low blood levels of calcium and renal-vein thrombosis (blood-clot formation) seem to occur more often than would be expected by chance.

Neonatal hypoglycemia is a relatively common disorder, particularly among infants whose birth weight is low. Fifteen percent of hypoglycemic infants have associated abnormalities of the central nervous system. In most instances hypoglycemia is transient and responds readily to treatment. In the unusual case of persistent hypoglycemia the infant may die.

Tetany of the newborn, a condition that appears within a few days after birth, is characterized by increased neuromuscular irritability, with muscular twitching, tremors, and convulsions. In most cases, the blood concentration of calcium is abnormally low, and that of inorganic phosphate is abnormally high. In some infants the disorder appears to be due to a low concentration of magnesium in the blood. The infant's condition is usually dramatically improved by the intravenous administration of calcium. The disorder is transient, so that treatment with oral calcium supplements can be discontinued after one or two weeks.

Respiratory disturbances. Numerous abnormalities of respiratory function are commonly encountered in the newborn infant. One of the most severe, called the idiopathic respiratory distress syndrome, or hyaline membrane disease, is the most common cause of death in the newborn, especially in premature infants, occurring in 0.5 to 1 percent of all deliveries. It is encountered commonly in infants of diabetic mothers and after cesarean section (delivery through the wall of the mother's abdomen), although it also occurs in full-term infants without any apparent predisposing cause. Soon after birth, infants begin to take rapid, shallow breaths and can be shown by appropriate tests to be exchanging air (*i.e.*, absorbing oxygen and exhausting carbon dioxide) only poorly. They may die within a few hours or may have a protracted course over a period of several days, with later demise or gradual improvement and recovery. The cause is unknown, although numerous causal mechanisms have been suggested. Treatment is directed at relieving the symptoms and includes correction of an associated acidosis, administration of oxygen, and assisting the infant to breathe. The recovery rate may be as low as 50 percent in premature infants, although the outcome in full-term infants is usually favourable.

Pneumonia is the most common pulmonary cause of death in infants dying after 48 hours. The onset is either within hours after birth, in infants whose infection is contracted from the mother, or after 48 hours of life,

Hyaline membrane disease

when the infection is acquired in the nursery. Infants show signs of difficulty in breathing and may have either an increase or, more frequently, a decrease in body temperature. Often there is an associated infection of the blood (septicemia). Treatment consists of the administration of carefully selected antibiotics in appropriate dosages and respiratory support.

Infants may inhale meconium (a semisolid discharge from the infants' bowels) during the course of delivery, leading to obstruction of the upper airway. Clearing the airway with suction, the administration of oxygen, and general respiratory support are usually effective in promoting recovery within two to three days.

Leakage of air into the pleural space (between the membrane lining the chest and that enveloping the lungs and other thoracic organs), with consequent partial or complete collapse of the lung (pneumothorax), bleeding into the lung, and failure of expansion of the lung (atelectasis), also causes respiratory failure in the newborn infant. Prompt recognition and treatment often are necessary to ensure survival.

The lungs are insufficiently developed in some small premature infants. Respiratory symptoms are noted after the first week of life and progress slowly, reaching a maximum intensity four to eight weeks after onset. In infants who recover, the symptoms gradually improve over weeks or months. Treatment is directed toward relief of symptoms. The fatality rate varies between 25 and 50 percent.

Cardiac disturbances. Cardiac disturbances in the newborn are related primarily to congenital malformations of the circulatory system, described in CARDIOVASCULAR SYSTEM DISEASES AND DISORDERS. Lesions such as complete transposition of the great vessels (so that the pulmonary artery arises from the left lower chamber of the heart and the aorta from the right) may result in death soon after birth. Other lesions, such as large ventricular septal defects (holes in the wall between the two lower chambers of the heart), may cause difficulties in breathing and feeding, with subsequent failure to grow and evidence of increasing inability of the heart to function adequately. Severe heart lesions, however, can exist in the newborn without causing any symptoms.

Blood diseases. The diseases affecting the blood of newborn infants include diseases of the red blood cells (particularly the anemias, which involve an inadequate level of functioning hemoglobin—the oxygen-carrying pigment—in the blood), of the white blood cells (particularly the leukemias, fatal diseases of the blood-forming organs that result in enormous increases in the numbers of particular types of white cells), and of the clotting factors (*e.g.*, hemophilia). These diseases and others that affect the blood of the newborn are touched upon below, in the sections dealing with diseases associated with later infancy and childhood, and are covered in BLOOD DISEASES. Erythroblastosis fetalis, a disease in which the red blood cells of the fetus are destroyed because of an incompatibility between the infant's blood and that of the mother, is described in ALLERGY AND ANAPHYLACTIC SHOCK.

Infections. The newborn infant is subject to the ordinary infections and, in addition, to infection with commonly encountered organisms such as *Escherichia coli* and *Staphylococcus aureus*, which are not usual causes of serious infection in older age groups. Infection may be acquired by the fetus in the uterus, during delivery, or later, in the nursery. The most commonly encountered serious infections are pneumonia, meningitis (inflammation of the coverings of the brain and spinal cord), septicemia (infection of the bloodstream), diarrhea, and peritonitis (inflammation of the membrane that lines the abdomen and covers the abdominal organs). Often the infant shows few signs of the disease other than poor feeding, irritability, or slight fever. Since the newborn infant's resistance to infection is poor, early diagnosis and treatment are particularly important. Often, treatment is given even when infection is merely suspected.

Common infections

Gastrointestinal disturbances. Vomiting, a common symptom among newborn infants, may be due to intestinal obstruction or to overfeeding or may occur without apparent cause. Continuous relaxation or contraction of the muscle governing the opening between the stomach and the intestine may cause vomiting. The former condition, called chalasia, is infrequent. The latter—pyloric stenosis—may occur at any time in early infancy and usually requires surgical treatment.

Meconium ileus, intestinal obstruction by masses of meconium in the newborn period, occurs almost exclusively in infants with cystic fibrosis, an inherited disease that affects many glands, including particularly the pancreas. The diagnosis is made provisionally from the symptoms and from X-rays and is confirmed by surgery. Recovery, except in some instances of perforation of the intestine, is the rule.

Jaundice in the newborn does not ordinarily involve abnormal mechanisms but is related to an imbalance between the rate of destruction of red blood cells and the metabolism of hemoglobin to bilirubin and the rate of excretion of bilirubin in the bile; there is a resultant temporary elevation of bilirubin level in the blood. Jaundice may, however, be due to septicemia, to several different diseases of the liver, or to obstruction of the ducts through which bile flows into the intestinal tract. Abnormally high bilirubin levels have also been found in association with breast feeding; it is an extremely rare condition resulting from the presence of an unusual substance in the milk of the mother.

The significance of jaundice depends on the underlying cause and the amount of excess bilirubin in the blood. In extreme cases, bilirubin can be deposited in brain cells, resulting in severe nerve-cell damage, called kernicterus. This condition is encountered most often in infants with erythroblastosis fetalis. Brain damage can usually be prevented by means of exchange transfusions (in which most of the infant's blood is replaced with blood from donors), which in the most severe case may need to be repeated many times.

Kernicterus

Disturbances of the kidneys and of fluid and electrolyte homeostasis. The kidneys of the newborn infant are entirely capable of maintaining homeostasis, or balance, of fluids and electrolytes in normal circumstances, adapting readily, for example, to the various formulas utilized in infant feeding, despite the wide range of solute content and the consequent large variation in the excretory load imposed. (Electrolytes, in this context, are substances that in solution become ionized; that is, are given a positive or negative electrical charge.) In situations of stress, however, abnormalities in the regulation of salt and water balance and of acid–base metabolism are common. Limitations in the excretory capacity of the newborn infant's kidneys require adjustment of drug dosage and fluid therapy.

The most common disorders of the kidneys and urinary tracts encountered in the neonatal period are congenital anomalies, touched upon in BIRTH DEFECTS AND CONGENITAL DISORDERS. Formation of blood clots in renal veins, with impairment of renal function, occurs most often in young infants, particularly in the offspring of diabetic mothers. Such infants usually recover when only one kidney is involved and may recover even when both kidneys are affected.

Various forms of nephritis (inflammation of the kidneys) are infrequently encountered in young infants. One of the most common of these, congenital nephrosis, is a disease in which large amounts of protein are lost in the urine, with consequent development of severe, generalized edema (accumulation of fluid in the tissues). The outlook for recovery in congenital nephrosis and in other forms of nephritis in young infants is extremely poor.

Although uncommon, infections of the kidneys and urinary tracts do occur in young infants. They are difficult to recognize clinically but, if diagnosed early and treated promptly, respond well to treatment, unless there is an associated congenital obstructive lesion. Kidney failure, as a result of dehydration, circulatory insufficiency (inadequate circulation of blood), and septicemia, is rarely encountered in the young infant. The outlook for recovery depends upon the severity of the kidney damage.

Disturbances of the central nervous system. Many congenital malformations of the nervous system are apparent at birth. Acquired conditions, including those secondary to insufficient oxygen and bleeding, are touched upon above in the subsection on birth injuries. Meningitis (inflammation of the coverings of the brain and spinal cord) may occur in the newborn. Unfortunately, the diagnosis is often delayed because of the lack in young infants of characteristic symptoms and findings. The common causative organisms, *Escherichia coli* and certain other bacilli, are particularly resistant to currently available antibiotic therapy.

DISEASES ASSOCIATED WITH LATER INFANCY AND CHILDHOOD

Infectious diseases. Infectious diseases are by far the most common disorders of childhood. The significance of these disorders and the role they play in pediatric morbidity and mortality vary widely among different populations and in different parts of the world. For example, infantile diarrhea, associated with poor sanitation, contamination of food supplies, and malnutrition, remains a leading cause of death in most medically underdeveloped countries. Among the higher socioeconomic groups in these countries, diarrheal disease is common, but a fatal outcome is rare.

Infantile diarrhea

There is similar marked variation in the frequency of occurrence of the common contagious diseases of childhood. Properly applied programs of immunization have nearly eradicated these diseases in populations with high standards of medical care. Diseases such as tetanus and smallpox, which are now completely preventable, remain major causes of death in children and adults in certain areas of the world.

All of the various types of infectious disease, which can involve virtually every organ and part of the body, are encountered in children. Their clinical features and courses are usually no different from the same diseases in adults, although, in general, children recover with fewer aftereffects than older patients, and the common communicable diseases tend to be less severe.

Measles (rubeola) is a viral disease transmitted by the respiratory route, with an incubation period of ten to 14 days. The initial symptoms include a runny nose, conjunctivitis (inflammation of the membrane lining the eyelids and covering part of the front of the eye), cough, and a characteristic eruption on the mucous membranes of the mouth (Koplik spots). The characteristic rash then appears on the skin, usually beginning over the neck and the face, and spreads to the rest of the body. There is no treatment. Recovery is the rule, although serious neurologic complications and secondary bacterial infections of the lungs may occur.

German measles, or rubella, is a milder disease, also viral, with an incubation period of 14 to 21 days. Its major significance is the likelihood of its causing severe malformations of the fetus if contracted by the mother during the first three months of pregnancy.

Exanthem subitum, also called roseola infantum, a common disease of infants and young children, is probably due to a virus that has not yet been identified. Characteristically, there are several days of high fever without other noticeable symptoms. After three or four days, the fever rapidly disappears, and a typical generalized rash appears. This usually lasts only a few hours.

Chickenpox (varicella) is a highly contagious viral disease with an incubation period of 13 to 17 days. At the start there is mild to moderate fever, followed by a generalized eruption of papules, small, solid elevations that appear in crops, initially small and red, becoming vesicular (*i.e.*, becoming small blisters). After several days, no new lesions develop, and the vesicles gradually crust over and heal. Severe itching usually accompanies the rash.

Mumps is a viral disease of the parotid and other salivary glands, which has an incubation period of 14 to 24 days. The predominant feature of the disease is painful swelling of the parotid glands, which are below and in front of the ears. The pancreas and gonads (sex glands) may also be involved, although rarely in children.

Smallpox
Smallpox is an acute, highly contagious, viral disease with an incubation period of ten to 16 days. It is characterized by a three-day pre-eruptive period of fever, which is followed by a generalized eruption. The eruption is more marked on the face and extremities than on the trunk. It quickly passes through papular and vesicular stages to the pustular stage. With recovery, the pustules (pus-filled elevations of the skin) usually dry after eight to ten days and form scabs. Fatality rates in untreated cases vary with the severity of the illness from as high as 90 percent or more to less than 8 percent. Although new drugs are effective in reducing the mortality rate, the basis of control of smallpox is vaccination.

Tuberculosis, a disease that mainly affects the lungs, but can also involve other organs of the body, continues to be a major world health problem. As countries improve public-health standards and increase their socio-economic level, the illness and mortality from this disease decrease steadily. In children, tuberculosis appears mostly in a primary form consisting of a small localized lesion of the lung that either heals completely or remains quiescent for many years. Only infrequently among children does the disease extend to involve other parts of the lung or other parts of the body, such as bones, kidney, or the central nervous system. Miliary tuberculosis, a generalized form of infection, and tuberculous meningitis are the most severe forms of the disease and have an extremely high mortality, although recovery may occur with proper treatment. Among children, these forms most commonly occur in infants. As with other diseases, tuberculosis is better prevented than treated. A form of immunization (BCG—bacille Calmette–Guérin—vaccine) is utilized in areas of the world in which the disease is endemic; *i.e.*, constantly present. In other areas, control depends on prevention of contacts and early identification and treatment, if necessary, of infected individuals. A variety of antibiotic agents are effective in treatment, particularly the drug isoniazid.

The immunologic system of the body is responsible for the defense against infectious disease. This highly complex system involves the production of several types of antibody, the destruction of infecting organisms by white blood cells in a process called phagocytosis, and a variety of cellular mechanisms involving the complement system (complement is an enzyme-like substance in the blood). Congenital defects of each part of the immunologic system have been described. The most striking feature of these diseases is the inability of the patient to combat infection. Thus, untreated patients with some forms of agammaglobulinemia (lack of gamma globulin in the blood) may die from overwhelming infection in infancy or early childhood.

Diseases of the digestive system and liver. Abdominal pain, one of the commonest symptoms of childhood, can be indicative of many gastrointestinal disorders but usually occurs without evidence of disease. Recurrent abdominal pain without detectable disease may be a psychosomatic disorder.

Acute appendicitis is the commonest lesion requiring abdominal surgery in children. It occurs in all age groups, although it is rare in extremely young infants. It is twice as common in boys as in girls. The clinical manifestations (abdominal pain, vomiting, fever) in older children are similar to those in adults. In infants and younger children, the systemic manifestations are more severe, and rupture of the appendix is more frequent.

Intus-
susception
Intussusception is a condition encountered in the first and second years of life in which one section of intestine doubles (invaginates) into the section next distant from the stomach. Gastrointestinal bleeding and symptoms of obstruction result. Sometimes the intussusception is eliminated by administration of a barium enema. Surgical correction are more usually required, however.

Meckel's diverticulum is an outpouching of a segment of the small intestine. In infants and children it may be the site of an ulcer that produces painless intestinal bleeding, which may be severe and recurrent. The diverticulum is removed by surgery if it is identified or strongly suspected as the source of intestinal bleeding.

Foreign bodies in the intestinal tract often occur in small children. Foreign bodies lodged in the esophagus must be removed. Objects small enough to pass through the esophagus into the stomach usually will pass through the entire intestinal tract, and no treatment is necessary.

Congenital aganglionic megacolon (congenital enlargement of the colon with absence of ganglia), also called Hirschprung's disease, is a disorder of infancy and early childhood. The absence of groups of nerve cells (ganglia) that control peristalsis (the wavelike motions that propel the intestinal contents) and the consequent stagnation of the bowel contents cause enlargement of the section of colon immediately above the section lacking nerve cells. Treatment consists of surgical removal of the aganglionic section.

The celiac syndrome includes a large group of disorders in which there are abnormalities of intestinal absorption. The first indications of the presence of a major disorder of this group, called celiac disease, or gluten-induced enteropathy, are chronic diarrhea, with large, bulky, greasy stools, and malnutrition. Celiac disease is caused by a peculiar sensitivity to gluten, a component of grain flours. The onset is usually between six and 18 months of age, and there is complete recovery when gluten is removed from the diet.

In so-called disaccharidase deficiencies there is a specific disturbance in the enzymatic activity required for the transport of one or more of the commonly ingested sugars. Diarrhea and malabsorption result. When the carbohydrate that cannot be transported is removed from the diet, there is prompt remission of all symptoms.

Viral hepatitis (inflammation of the liver due to infection with a virus) has its highest incidence but lowest mortality rates among children of school age. It is the major viral disease that has not yet been brought under control by programs of immunization, although a vaccine for one form of viral hepatitis was thought to be near in the early 1970s. Two forms of the disease have been recognized, initially distinguished by their clinical characteristics, now recognized to be caused by two different viruses. Serum hepatitis has an incubation period of 60 to 160 days and is gradual and unnoticed in onset. Infectious hepatitis has an incubation period of 14 to 40 days and usually has an abrupt onset. Fever, headache, and feelings of ill health are followed by loss of appetite, nausea, and vomiting. Jaundice ensues, and the liver is enlarged and tender. Improvement usually is noted in a few weeks' time. In children, complete recovery is common.
Types of viral hepatitis

Congenital malformations of the gastrointestinal tract and liver are described in BIRTH DEFECTS AND CONGENITAL DISORDERS. Other conditions are covered in DIGESTIVE SYSTEM DISEASES.

Deficiency diseases. Malnutrition, although uncommon in the medically well-developed countries of the world, remains an enormous pediatric problem elsewhere in the world. In addition, specific nutritional disturbances are encountered regularly in all populations.

Malnutrition may occur as a consequence of inadequate or improper intake of food. Muscle wasting, stunted growth, pallor, increased susceptibility to infection, and fatigue result. A special form of malnutrition, in which the intake of calories is adequate but that of protein is not, is referred to as kwashiorkor; it is the most prevalent and the most severe form of malnutrition in the world today. Kwashiorkor primarily affects children from six months to five years of age, the onset usually coinciding with discontinuation of breast feeding. The affected children are small, have excess fluid in their tissues, and often have enlarged livers. They have unusual pigmentation of the skin and sparse, reddish hair. Permanent aftereffects of kwashiorkor, especially on the intellectual functions, are matters of great concern.
Kwashiorkor

Rickets is a disorder secondary to deficiency of vitamin D. The major consequence is bone disease, with defective growth of the epiphyseal cartilage. (This cartilage, present in several bones, especially near the ends of the long bones of the arms and legs, ossifies as a person matures.)

Scurvy occurs as a consequence of a deficiency of vitamin C. Clinical manifestations include bone disease, irritability, and bleeding under the skin and mucous membranes.

Pellagra is due to a deficiency of niacin and is manifested clinically by diarrhea, dermatitis, and dementia.

Riboflavin deficiency results in lesions of the skin and corners of the mouth, with a peculiar smoothing of the tongue.

Beriberi is a consequence of thiamine deficiency. The major clinical features often relate to cardiac impairment. Defects in the functioning of the nervous system also are common.

Deficiency of vitamin A results in ocular abnormalities, growth retardation, anemia, and dermatitis.

Respiratory system diseases. The common cold, or acute nasopharyngitis, the most common respiratory disease in children, is caused by a large number of viruses and may be complicated by superimposed bacterial infection. There is no specific treatment.

Tonsillitis, as all acute infections of the tonsils are called, is more properly considered a part of the acute-pharyngitis (throat-inflammation) syndrome. Enlargement of the tonsillary tissue as a result of recurrent infection often leads to the decision to remove the tonsils, a course many physicians now believe is rarely indicated for any reason. Enlarged tonsils are not the cause of irritability, poor appetite, or poor growth.

Enlargement of the adenoids (lymphoid tissue in the nasal part of the pharynx) as a result of recurrent infection can result in mouth breathing and a so-called adenoidal facial appearance, the most conspicuous feature of which is the constantly open mouth. By blocking the eustachian tube, it can contribute to infections of the middle ear (otitis media) and to hearing loss. In children with chronic middle-ear disease and a specific type of hearing loss, removal of adenoids may be indicated.

Croup is an inflammatory disease of the larynx (voice box) or epiglottis (the plate of cartilage that shuts off the entrance into the larynx during the process of swallowing), most often caused by viral infection; it is encountered in infants and small children. Inflammation and swelling of the vocal cords lead to respiratory obstruction, particularly in the inspiratory phase, and a croupy cough, which sounds like the bark of a puppy. Treatment is directed toward the maintenance of adequate intake of oxygen and exhausting of carbon dioxide. In rare instances, tracheostomy, the cutting of an opening into the trachea, is necessary.

Allergic rhinitis (inflammation of the nasal passages) is the most common allergic disorder of childhood. Seasonal allergic rhinitis, or hay fever, due to sensitization to house dust, pollen, or molds, is characterized by attacks of sneezing, nasal itching, and a watery nasal discharge during the season when the specific allergens are prevalent. Similar symptoms are present in perennial allergic rhinitis but without seasonal pattern. In addition to inhalants, sensitization to specific foods may underly the disorder. Treatment consists of avoidance of the substances causing the reaction, desensitization, and use of decongestant drugs and antihistamines; *i.e.*, drugs that, by inactivating the histamine given off by injured cells, suppress many of the symptoms of an allergic attack.

Asthma

Asthma is a common allergic disorder of children that affects the bronchi and bronchioles (the large and small air passages in the lungs). Spasm, edema, and abnormal secretion of mucus result in obstruction of the lower respiratory tract and characteristic wheezing and laboured breathing. Inhalant allergens, particularly dust, molds, and pollens, and foods may play important causal roles. Psychologic stress may be a precipitating factor, and attacks of asthma may result from emotional struggles between parent and child. Viral and bacterial infection of the respiratory tract also may play a role. Treatment of the attack is directed at relieving the symptoms. Long-term management includes avoidance of substances that cause the attacks, desensitization, and psychologic support. The outlook generally is good, only 10 percent of children continuing to have severe asthma into adult life.

Sinusitis, otitis, bronchitis (inflammation of the sinuses, the ears, and the bronchi, respectively), and pneumonia all occur commonly in children and do not differ in essential detail from the same diseases in adults. Other conditions that affect children and adults alike are described in RESPIRATORY SYSTEM DISEASES.

Endocrine system diseases. Congenital hypothyroidism (subnormal secretion by the thyroid glands, also called cretinism) is an especially important endocrine disease of infancy in that failure to identify and treat it early may result in severe mental retardation. It is due either to an absence of the thyroid or to a metabolic disturbance in the normal functioning of the gland. Abnormalities shown by affected infants include slow growth, yellowish discoloration of the skin, constipation, feeding and respiratory difficulties, and a large tongue. Early diagnosis and proper therapy with thyroid drugs results in dramatic improvement, with rapid disappearance of all signs and symptoms of disease.

Congenital adrenal hyperplasia is a group of conditions in which there is a defect in the production of normal adrenocortical-steroid hormones (secretions of the cortex, or outer substance, of the adrenal glands). Excessive stimulation of the cortex of the adrenals by a pituitary hormone (adrenocorticotropic hormone, or ACTH) results in abnormal enlargement of the glands and overproduction of androgenic (masculinizing) adrenal hormones. As a result, there may be abnormal development of the genitalia of females in utero and evidence of excessive androgenic effect in either sex during infancy, with accelerated growth, premature appearance of pubic hair, and enlargement of the phallus.

Precocious puberty includes a large group of conditions in which there is premature onset of sexual development. Although precocious puberty can result from disease of the brain, adrenals, or gonads, in most instances no underlying disease can be detected.

Overactivity of thyroid function, or hyperthyroidism, is uncommon in children; it occurs more frequently in girls than in boys. Affected persons exhibit nervousness, weight loss, irritability, and hyperactivity. Usually there is enlargement of the thyroid gland. A variety of drugs that suppress thyroid function is available. In some instances, surgical removal of most of the thyroid gland is indicated.

Pituitary or adrenal insufficiency results in a complex disturbance of many body functions, usually requiring urgent treatment. Therapy consists of administration of those hormones that are not being produced in sufficient quantity.

Diabetes insipidus

A specific lack of antidiuretic hormone, which is normally produced in the hypothalamus (a nerve centre at the upper end of the brainstem, which is an extension of the spinal cord into the brain) and released into the blood from the posterior pituitary, results in diabetes insipidus, or an inability to concentrate solutes in the urine. Symptoms include excessive urination, thirst, and dehydration. There is usually no detectable cause, although some cases occur after the development of brain tumours. The symptoms are controlled by administration of posterior pituitary preparations.

Nervous-system diseases. Congenital anomalies of the nervous system are common. They include microcephaly, an abnormally small head due to limited brain growth, and hydrocephalus, in which there is or has been an increase in the volume of cerebrospinal fluid associated with increased pressure. The obvious evidence of the latter condition is the large size of the head. Some infants with hydrocephalus die before birth. After birth, the condition may arrest spontaneously. The major treatment is relief of pressure by diversion of the spinal fluid or surgical correction of any obstruction. The prevention of progressive damage is the goal of therapy. Meningocele, a condition in which there is a protrusion of the covering of the spinal cord (meninges) with or without neural elements through a defect in the spinal column, is frequently accompanied by hydrocephalus.

Mental retardation is a major pediatric problem, recognizable in about 0.5 percent of preschool children. The number in certain school populations rises to as high as 5 to 10 percent. Mild retardates, children with intelligence quotients (IQ) between 50 and 75, are educable and trainable and constitute between 85 and 90 percent of the total number of retarded children.

The static encephalopathies constitute a group of conditions of diverse causation leading to permanent nervous-system abnormalities that do not become worse. They may appear to progress, however, as dysfunction becomes more obvious with increasing age or as the defects interfere with normal development. If only the motor areas of the brain are involved, cerebral palsy results. More diffuse cerebral involvement is associated with mental retardation.

Children are subject to numerous degenerative diseases of the nervous system. Most of these are of unknown cause and are untreatable.

Tumours of the brain are among the most common tumours of childhood, being exceeded in frequency only by leukemia. Of the brain tumours, the most frequently occurring is the medulloblastoma, a cancer arising in the cerebellum and having its peak incidence around five years of age. Symptoms include vomiting, headache, and double vision. Treatment is unsatisfactory, and permanent recovery is rare.

Convulsive disorders in children are common. As many as 5 percent of children have a seizure at least once during their lifetime. So-called febrile seizures occur in association with high fever. They are most common between six months and three years of age, and there is a high familial incidence. Spontaneous recovery is usual. Epilepsy, or recurrent seizures, has a prevalence of about 0.5 percent. There are many known causes, but in most cases none is found. Treatment with anticonvulsant drugs is successful in suppressing seizures in most cases.

Familial dysautonomia

In familial dysautonomia, a peculiar disorder of infants and children, there is reduced or absent production of tears during crying, intermittent high blood pressure, postural hypotension (low blood pressure upon standing up), coldness of the hands and feet, excessive sweating, relative indifference to pain, and mental and physical retardation. Most affected children are of Jewish origin. To take effect, the abnormal gene must be inherited from both parents.

Blood diseases. Virtually all the recognized blood diseases of adults are encountered in children. Of particular importance are the conditions in which abnormal types of hemoglobin are formed. The abnormal hemoglobin present in sickle-cell anemia, also called sickle-cell disease and sicklemia, must be inherited from both parents to cause the disease, the effects of which include hemolytic anemia (anemia involving destruction of red blood cells and release of their hemoglobin) and recurrent crises with episodes of painful swelling of the hands and feet, abdominal pain, and increase of the anemia. Persons who have inherited the defect from one parent and are said to have the sickle-cell trait constitute approximately 10 percent of the American Negro population. There are a number of other abnormal hemoglobins. Thalassemia, or Cooley's anemia, is a condition in which there is severe, progressive hemolytic anemia, beginning at about six months of age. The disease, most common in individuals of Mediterranean extraction, is caused by a deficient production of adult hemoglobin (hemoglobin A). Repeated transfusion of blood and, in certain instances, removal of the spleen are the only available treatments.

Hereditary spherocytosis and hereditary elliptocytosis cause hemolytic anemia because of abnormalities in the structure of the red blood cell. A number of abnormalities in red-blood-cell enzymes also can lead to increased red-cell destruction.

The commonest form of anemia in infants and children is caused by iron deficiency. Fetal stores of iron usually prevent development of anemia during the first six months of life, but it is common thereafter, when the diet may not be adequate to meet the high requirements for iron. Apart from pallor, children usually are well, although they may show irritability and lack of appetite

and have a rapid heartbeat. Treatment consists of the administration of iron and modification of the diet to include sufficient iron to prevent recurrence.

Leukemia is a fatal, neoplastic (cancerous) disorder of the leukocyte precursors (*i.e.*, young forms) of the white blood cells in the blood-forming tissues. The incidence in childhood is about four cases per 100,000 population. It is the most common malignant disease of children, with a peak onset between three and four years of age. Eighty to 90 percent of the cases are of the lymphoblastic type. (Lymphoblasts are precursors of lymphocytes.) Clinical manifestations include anemia, thrombocytopenia (deficit of blood platelets), and infiltration of various organs of the body with leukemic cells. A number of drugs are available for the treatment of leukemia. Remission (disappearance of symptoms) can be induced in about 90 percent of children with acute lymphoblastic leukemia. Half of these survive 20 to 22 months and 10 percent about 45 months. At present, less than 1 percent of all cases can be considered cured.

Leukemia

Thrombocytopenia is a disorder characterized by a tendency toward bleeding because of a decrease in circulating platelets. (The platelets help to stop bleeding in two ways: they contain a clotting factor, and they serve to block rents in blood-vessel walls.) There are several known causes, but the causes of most cases remain unknown. Treatment consists of replacement of blood loss when there is a major hemorrhage, transfusion of platelets for emergency management, and, in selected cases, administration of adrenocortical steroids and removal of the spleen. Prompt spontaneous recovery occurs in 80 to 90 percent of cases within three months from the onset of illness.

Congenital disorders of the coagulation process usually became manifest during infancy or early childhood. The most common of these is hemophilia, a disease caused by deficiency in a specific coagulation factor. The disease is manifested only in males who have inherited the trait from both parents and occurs in about one of every 10,000 male births. Treatment consists of measures to control bleeding locally, transfusion of blood when necessary, and replacement of the coagulation factor by the administration of plasma or a factor concentrate.

There are a number of other bleeding disorders caused by deficiencies in various of the clotting factors.

Skin diseases. Diaper dermatitis, a common affliction of infants, is due to contact with wet diapers, allergy to various soap products, poor local hygiene, and sensitive skin. Treatment consists of prompt changing of diapers, local cleansing of the skin, and application of local medicaments.

Eczema is a common condition, encountered most often in infancy and characterized by reddening of the skin, papules, oozing, and crusting with intense itching. The lesions often appear first on the cheeks and then develop on other areas, particularly the insides of the elbows and the knees. Treatment includes attention to any underlying allergic causes and local application of a variety of different medications, especially adrenocortical-steroid ointments.

Impetigo contagiosa is a superficial infection of the skin with *Staphylococcus aureus* or hemolytic streptococci. Vesicular or pustular lesions exude moisture and become crusted. Untreated, the lesions tend to become widespread and may involve any area of the skin or the scalp. Treatment consists of keeping the affected areas clean and local or systemic administration of antibiotics. Impetigo often is caused by beta hemolytic streptococci, organisms that may cause disease of the kidneys (acute nephritis) or the heart (acute rheumatic fever).

Pigmented nevi, or moles, are common lesions in childhood. They vary in type from flat, brownish areas to elevated, dome-shaped, blue- or black-coloured lesions. They are removed surgically for cosmetic reasons or if they cannot be distinguished from lesions that may become cancerous. The vascular nevus usually is present at birth or develops during infancy as a flat, irregular, reddened area, especially common on the face or back of the neck, or as a sharply demarcated, reddened, raised

Pigmented nevi

tumour (strawberry mark). The cavernous hemangioma is a subcutaneous collection of vessels with normal but bluish overlying skin. These lesions all have a tendency to disappear spontaneously.

A variety of fungal infections of the skin are encountered in children. These include tinea capitis, or ringworm of the scalp; tinea corporis, infection of the skin; and tinea pedis, or athlete's foot.

Cardiovascular-system diseases. The most common cardiovascular disorders in children are congenital heart defects and rheumatic heart disease, described in CARDIO-VASCULAR SYSTEM DISEASES AND DISORDERS.

The majority of disorders of cardiac rate and rhythm in childhood are benign, although they may be indicative of more serious underlying heart disorders. Paroxysmal atrial tachycardia, the most important disturbance in children, is characterized by a steady, rapid heart rate, which in infants may exceed 300 per minute. If the disorder persists, heart failure usually ensues. Treatment with digitalis is usually successful in restoring a normal rhythm.

Pericarditis and myocarditis, inflammation of the sac enclosing the heart and of the heart muscle, are caused by a variety of infectious agents; they may result from systemic diseases. The most common cause is acute rheumatic fever. Symptoms include pain, fever, and evidence of heart failure. Treatment and prospects of recovery depend on the underlying cause.

Bacterial endocarditis (bacterial infection of the heart lining) occurs most frequently in children with pre-existing heart disease. The most common organism is the alpha streptococcus, which accounts for 80 percent of cases. Common symptoms are fever, a sense of ill health, and fatigue; more specific symptoms, such as chest pain, are less common. The outlook depends on the sensitivity of the infecting organism to antibiotic drugs, the age of the affected child, and the type of underlying heart disease.

Diseases of the kidneys and urinary tract. Infection, the most common disorder of the urinary tract in both children and adults, occurs predominantly in females. The most frequent infection is cystitis, a superficial infection of the lining of the bladder, but pyelonephritis, infection of the kidney, is not uncommon. *Escherichia coli* is the organism responsible in 80 percent of the cases. Symptoms of cystitis include urgency, frequency, painful urination, and suprapubic pain (pain just above the frontal pelvic bones). Pyelonephritis may be without symptoms or may cause fever, back pain, and shaking chills. Treatment is with antibiotics. Investigation for underlying congenital abnormalities is especially important in children. Recurrence can be anticipated in 50 to 60 percent of cases.

The presence of bacteria in the urine without manifestation of symptoms, observed in about 1 percent of school-girls, may be associated with an increased frequency of urinary-tract abnormalities and of subsequent attacks of pyelonephritis.

Congenital malformations of the kidneys, ureters, bladder, and urethra, all important lesions in children, are covered in BIRTH DEFECTS AND CONGENITAL DISORDERS.

Of the various forms of glomerulonephritis (kidney disease in which there is inflammation of the glomeruli—the knots of minute blood vessels in the capsules of the nephrons, the functioning units of the kidneys), the one most commonly encountered in children is acute post-streptococcal nephritis. This disorder occurs as a late complication of infection with certain strains of group A beta streptococci. The onset is heralded with blood in the urine, excess fluid in the tissues, or headache due to high blood pressure. Spontaneous recovery ordinarily occurs, and there is no evidence that children with acute streptococcal nephritis have a predisposition to renal disease as adults. Persons with severe disease may, however, have brain involvement and heart failure. A rare patient with unusually severe disease may suffer irreversible kidney damage early and fail to recover.

The nephrotic syndrome is a group of symptoms that occur as a consequence of any kidney disease; character-

Cystitis and pyelonephritis

istically, there is excretion of great amounts of protein in the urine, and generalized edema occurs in the absence of evidence of glomerulonephritis or systemic disease. Most of these children respond to treatment with adrenocortical steroids and ultimately recover. The outlook in children with the nephrotic syndrome associated with glomerulonephritis and other systemic diseases is much worse, and there is a high fatality rate. Congenital nephrosis is an especially severe form that may be apparent at the time of birth. There is no effective treatment, and infants do not usually survive beyond the first year of life.

All forms of glomerulonephritis described in adults are seen also in children. If sufficient information is available, most instances of hereditary nephritis can be shown to have their onset in childhood.

Disorders of specific tubular functions (*i.e.*, functioning of the nephrons) are encountered in infants and children. Nephrogenic diabetes insipidus is a disease of male infants in which there is failure of the kidney to respond to antidiuretic hormone, with consequent inability to concentrate urine. The symptoms are polyuria (copious urine), polydipsia (excessive thirst), and chronic dehydration. Renal tubular acidosis occurs in both males and females and includes various abnormalities in the renal mechanisms for acid excretion. Growth retardation is the most striking clinical feature. The Fanconi syndrome is a group of diseases in which there are multiple abnormalities in renal-tubular function. In one of these, cystinosis, there is progressive impairment in renal function with ultimate death. Renal glycosuria is a benign condition in which there is an isolated tubular abnormality in reabsorption of glucose, with consequent excretion of large amounts of glucose in the urine. It may be confused with diabetes mellitus.

Children with renal failure and uremia (nitrogenous wastes in the urine) can now be treated with hemodialysis (use of semipermeable membranes—the artificial kidney) and renal transplantation. The major role of dialysis in children appears to be to support patients until a transplant can be performed. Transplantation of a kidney from a living, related donor yields the best results, but many children have had successful transplants of kidneys from cadavers.

Hemodialysis and kidney transplant

Other diseases. Diabetes mellitus is a metabolic disorder with a prevalence in children under 15 years of age in the United States of 40 cases per 100,000 population. The most striking clinical features, elevated levels of glucose in the blood and increased excretion of glucose in the urine, are due to an inability to metabolize glucose normally. Abnormalities in fat and protein metabolism are also present, however. Control of the abnormal handling of glucose by daily administration of insulin and some restrictions of diet can keep most children asymptomatic and enable them to lead normal, healthy lives. Even the best control does not prevent the vascular and neurologic complications that occur later in the course of the disease, however. The outcome, therefore, is unsure, and the majority of persons with onset of diabetes mellitus in childhood appear to develop significant complications in adult life and to have a reduced life expectancy.

Fibrocystic disease, also called cystic fibrosis of the pancreas and mucoviscidosis, is a disorder that affects many organ systems. Estimates of incidence vary from one in 3,700 to one in 1,000 live births. It is rare among Negroes and Orientals and is transmitted as a recessive trait. The cause is unknown, but the disease appears to start with the secretion of unusually thick and sticky mucus. Meconium ileus in infants with fibrocystic disease and caused by intestinal obstruction from viscid meconium has already been mentioned. Pulmonary involvement may be apparent in the newborn infant or may develop during childhood, with repeated bouts of obstruction, atelectasis (collapse of the lungs), and ultimate bronchiectasis (chronic dilation and degeneration of bronchi and bronchioles). Pancreatic insufficiency leads to a malabsorption syndrome, with fatty, bulky stools and malnutrition. The liver may be involved. Abnormality of the sweat glands is evidenced by a high salt content of the sweat, which, in hot weather, may lead to salt depletion and collapse. Treatment is directed toward the many organs involved, particularly with regard to obstructive and infectious lesions of the respiratory tract. Inhalation of various types of mist, postural drainage of the lungs, and use of antibiotics are all helpful. Regulation of diet and administration of pancreatic enzymes contribute to the maintenance of adequate nutrition. No treatment of the liver involvement is available. The ultimate outlook is grave, although therapy has been successful in markedly prolonging life. Many affected persons survive into their teens and even early adult life.

Accidents, also, must be mentioned as responsible for many illnesses and deaths among children.

DISEASES AND DISTURBANCES ASSOCIATED WITH ADOLESCENCE

Adolescence is the period of development that begins with the onset of sexual maturation and continues through the transition state from childhood to young adulthood. The beginning is biologically defined by the onset of puberty, usually during the tenth to 13th year. The end is less definable and, depending upon environmental factors, may be as early as 16 years or as late as 20. In addition to rapid anatomical and physiological changes occurring during adolescence, the period is one of rapid psychosocial and psychosexual change, with tremendous turmoil generated over feelings of inadequacy, increase in sexual and aggressive drives, internal disorganization, and the attempt to attain self-control.

During adolescence, body weight almost doubles, and an additional 25 percent in height is gained. Secondary sexual characteristics appear, menstruation begins in girls, and spermatogenesis (sperm formation) and fertility are established in boys. The adolescent establishes a sense of identity and achieves a degree of independence that ultimately prepares him to take his place in adult society. It is expectable, therefore, that the major disorders of adolescence concern problems of growth, sexual development, and psychological disturbances.

Disturbances of growth Disturbances of growth chiefly concern short stature in boys and tall stature in girls. Although organic and genetic causes of short stature in boys must all be considered, most relatively short but otherwise healthy children are simply late maturers. Graphic plots of height gain with age reveal steady, normal progression but a delayed pubertal growth spurt, concordant with the delay in sexual maturation. With further sexual maturation, acceleration in growth will occur, and adult height within normal limits will be achieved. In certain instances, the psychological handicap of delayed adolescence is so great that treatment directed toward earlier attainment of the pubertal growth spurt is warranted. The administration of androgenic substances to accelerate growth requires care, because excessive treatment, which produces immediate results, can lead to loss of ultimate height as skeletal maturation is more rapid than linear growth.

Excessive height in girls produces similar psychological handicaps. Many of these girls are early maturers, initially outstripping their peers in height; however, with early sexual and skeletal maturation, their linear growth stops at an adult height well within normal limits. In the unusual instance of the girl in whom it can be predicted that ultimate height will be truly excessive, hormone therapy may be indicated to decrease ultimate height by accelerating sexual and skeletal maturation.

Sexual development The sequence of sexual development in girls is extremely variable. Widening of the bony pelvis, growth of the nipples and breasts, changes in external and internal genitalia, and the menarche occur sequentially as pituitary gonadotrophin (sex-gland-stimulating hormone) causes ovarian release of estrogen (female sex hormone). Axillary (armpit) and pubic hair and some of the changes of the external genitalia develop under the stimulus of androgens of adrenal origin. Since these arise from a different source of pituitary stimulation, there is considerable variation among girls in the relationship of their appearance and, for example, development of the breasts. Recognition of this is of extreme importance to avoid anxiety based on "abnormal" sexual development.

Menstruation in adolescence is characterized by many functional disturbances, including oligomenorrhea (scant menstruation), amenorrhea (absent menstruation), menorrhagia (excessive bleeding), and dysmenorrhea (painful menstruation). Amenorrhea requires a thorough evaluation for possible organic abnormality, such as hypogonadism (underfunctioning sex glands), absence of the uterus, or obstruction to the menstrual flow. In most instances, skipped menstrual periods during the first year or so after the menarche reflect the common, normal irregularity of menstruation during early adolescence. Later in adolescence, transitory amenorrhea may be associated with stress, such as onset of the school year, the taking of examinations, or moving to a new home. Treatment is not usually required.

Sexual development in boys usually follows a more predictable sequence, although there is great variation in the time of onset of puberty and the time of achievement of full sexual maturation. Stimulation of the testes by pituitary gonadotrophins results in the release of the hormone testosterone, which causes growth of the internal and external genitalia, development of pubic, axillary, and facial hair, changes in the larynx that result in deepening of the voice, and increased statural growth and muscular development. In about half of all boys, noticeable swelling of mammary-gland tissue occurs midway through adolescence. When the enlargement of the breasts is great enough to engender concern, it is called gynecomastia. In most instances, the enlargement disappears spontaneously. Occasionally, surgical correction of extreme degrees of gynecomastia is required.

Adolescent goitre is an enlargement of the thyroid in the absence of evidence of underactivity or overactivity of the gland. It is much more common in girls than in boys. In most instances, there is spontaneous regression of the enlargement before it causes concern. In the girl with extreme thyroid enlargement, treatment with a thyroid preparation suppresses pituitary release of thyroid-stimulating hormone, putting the thyroid at rest and permitting it to decrease in size.

Acne is a disturbing skin condition of adolescence due to androgenic stimulation of the sebaceous glands. Treatment is directed toward local cleansing and prevention of follicular plugging with sebum. In older girls, treatment with estrogen to suppress sebaceous-gland growth and activity may succeed.

Psychological disturbances The psychological disturbances of adolescence are universal and protean, ranging from minor emotional upsets to schizophrenia—from mild feelings of inadequacy to suicide. The sexual and aggressive impulses of the preadolescent period are complicated by the advent of physical and sexual maturity. Both an inability to control urges and desires and an excessive degree of self-control are characteristic. Some adolescents remain too dependent upon their parents; others attempt to achieve independence too quickly. Overcompensation, overintellectualization, and overreaction are usual. As many as 10 percent of adolescents may have psychological disturbances of a serious enough nature to interfere with their functioning and the development of social relations. This may become manifest in psychoneurotic behaviour, psychosomatic complaints, enuresis (involuntary urination), scholastic underachievement or dropping out of school, delinquency, or addiction to drugs or alcohol.

BIBLIOGRAPHY. The major pediatric texts in use today are H.L. BARNETT, *Pediatrics*, 15th ed. (1972); and W.E. NELSON (ed.), *Textbook of Pediatrics*, 9th ed. (1969).

(C.M.E./H.L.B.)

Children's Literature

Children's literature first clearly emerged as a distinct and independent form of literature in the second half of the 18th century, before which it had been at best only embryonic. During the 20th century, however, its growth has been so luxuriant as to make defensible its claim to be regarded with the respect—though perhaps not the solemnity—due any other recognized branch of literature.

The article is divided into the following sections:

I. Nature and significance of children's literature

DEFINITION OF TERMS

"Children." All potential or actual young literates, from the instant they can with joy leaf through a picture book or listen to a story read aloud, to the age of perhaps 14 or 15, may be called children. Thus "children" includes "young people." Two considerations blur the definition. Today's young teenager is an anomaly: as with the pre-19th-century child, his environment pushes him toward a precocious maturity. Thus, though he may read children's books, he also, and increasingly, reads adult books. Second, the child survives in many grown-ups. As a result, some children's books (e.g., Lewis Carroll's *Alice in Wonderland*, A.A. Milne's *Winnie-the-Pooh*, and, at one time, Munro Leaf's *The Story of Ferdinand*) are also read widely by adults.

"Literature." In the term children's literature, the more important word is literature. For the most part, the adjective imaginative is to be felt as preceding it. It comprises that vast, expanding territory recognizably staked out for a junior audience, which does not mean that it is not also intended for seniors. Adults admittedly make up part of its population: children's books are written, selected for publication, sold, bought, reviewed, and often read aloud by grown-ups. Sometimes they seem also to be written with adults in mind, as for example the popular French *Astérix* series of comics parodying history. Nevertheless, by and large there *is* a sovereign republic of children's literature. To it may be added five colonies or dependencies: first are "appropriated" adult books satisfying two conditions—they must generally be read by children and they must have sharply affected the course of children's literature (Daniel Defoe's *Robinson Crusoe*, Jonathan Swift's *Gulliver's Travels*, the collection of folktales by the brothers Jacob and Wilhelm Grimm, the folk-verse anthology *Des Knaben Wunderhorn* ["The Boy's Magic Horn"], edited by Achim von Arnim and Clemens Brentano, and William Blake's *Songs of Innocence*); second are books the audiences of which seem not to have been clearly conceived by their creators (or their creators may have ignored, as irrelevant, such a consideration) but that are now fixed stars in the child's

literary firmament (Mark Twain's *Adventures of Huckleberry Finn*, Charles Perrault's fairy tales, and J.R.R. Tolkien's *Lord of the Rings*); third, picture books and easy-to-read stories commonly subsumed under the label of literature but qualifying as such only by relaxed standards (though Beatrix Potter and several other writers do nonetheless qualify); fourth is Lilliputian in area—first-quality children's versions of adult classics (Walter de la Mare's *Stories from the Bible*, perhaps Howard Pyle's retellings of the Robin Hood ballads and tales, and, finally, there is the domain of once oral "folk" material that children have kept alive—folktales and fairy tales; fables, sayings, riddles, charms, tongue twisters; folksongs, lullabies, hymns, carols, and other simple poetry; rhymes of the street, the playground, the nursery; and, supremely, *Mother Goose* and nonsense verse.

Five categories often considered children's literature are excluded from this article. Broadest of the excluded categories is that of unblushingly commercial and harmlessly transient writing, including comic books, much of which, though it may please young readers, and often for good reasons, is for the purposes of this article notable only for its sociohistorical, rather than literary, importance. Second, all books of systematic instruction are barred except those sparse examples (*e.g.*, the work of John Amos Comenius) that illuminate the history of the subject. Third, excluded from discussion is much higher literature not originally intended for children: from the past, Jean de La Fontaine's *Fables*, James Fenimore Cooper's Leatherstocking tales, Sir Walter Scott's *Ivanhoe*, Charlotte Brontë's *Jane Eyre*, Alexandre Dumas' *Three Musketeers*, Rudyard Kipling's *Kim;* from the modern period, Marjorie Kinnan Rawlings' *Yearling*, J.D. Salinger's *Catcher in the Rye*, *The Diary of Anne Frank*, Thor Heyerdahl's *Kon-Tiki*, Enid Bagnold's *National Velvet*. A fourth, rather minor, category comprises books about the young where the content but not the style or point of view is relevant (Sir James Barrie's *Sentimental Tommy*, William Golding's *Lord of the Flies*, F. Anstey's [Thomas Anstey Guthrie] *Vice Versa*). Finally, barred from central, though not all, consideration is the "nonfiction," or fact, book. Except for a handful of such books the bright pages of which still influence or which possess artistic merit (Hendrik Willem van Loon's *Story of Mankind*, Cornelia Meigs's biography *Invincible Louisa*), this literature should be viewed from its socio-educational-commercial aspect.

Categories often considered children's literature

THE CASE FOR A CHILDREN'S LITERATURE

Many otherwise comprehensive histories of literature slight or omit the child's reading interests. Many observers have made explicit the suspicion that children's literature, like that of detection or suspense, is "inferior." They cannot detect a sufficiently long "tradition"; distinguish an adequate number of master works; or find, to use one thoughtful critic's words, "style, sensibility, vision."

Others, holding a contrary view, assert that a tradition of two centuries is not to be ignored.

Though the case for a children's literature must primarily rest on its major writers (including a half dozen literary geniuses), it is based as well on other supports that bolster its claim to artistic stature.

Children's literature, while a tributary of the literary mainstream, offers its own identifiable, semidetached history. In part it is the issue of certain traceable social movements, of which the "discovery" of the child (see below) is the most salient. It is independent to the degree that, while it must meet many of the standards of adult literature, it has also developed aesthetic criteria of its own by which it may be judged. According to some of its finest practitioners, it is independent, too, as the only existing literary medium enabling certain things to be said that would otherwise remain unsaid or unsayable. The nature of its audience sets it apart; it is often read, especially by pre-12-year-olds, in a manner suggesting trance, distinct from that of adult reading. Universally diffused among literate peoples, it offers a rich array of genres, types, and themes, some resembling grown-up

Scholarship and criticism

progenitors, many peculiar to itself. Its "style, sensibility, vision" range over a spectrum wide enough to span matter-of-fact realism and tenuous mysticism.

Other measures of its maturity include an extensive body (notably in Germany, Italy, Sweden, the U.S.S.R., and Japan) of commentary, scholarship, criticism, history, biography, and bibliography, along with the beginnings of an aesthetic theory or philosophy of composition. Finally, one might note its power to engender its own institutions: publishing houses, theatres, libraries, itinerant storytellers, critics, periodicals, instruction in centres of higher learning, lectureships, associations and conferences, "book weeks," collections, exhibitions, and prizes. Indeed, the current institutionalizing of children's literature on an international scale has gone so far, some feel, as to cast a shadow on the spontaneity and lack of self-consciousness that should lie at its heart.

SOME GENERAL FEATURES AND FORCES

The discovery of the child. A self-aware literature flows from a recognition of its proper subject matter. The proper subject matter of children's literature, apart from informational or didactic works, is children. More broadly, it embraces the whole content of the child's imaginative world and that of his daily environment, as well as certain ideas and sentiments characteristic of it. The population of this world is made up not only of children themselves but of animated objects, plants, even grammatical and mathematical abstractions; toys, dolls, and puppets; real, chimerical, and invented animals; miniature or magnified humans; spirits or grotesques of wood, water, air, fire, and space; supernatural and fantasy creatures; figures of fairy tale, myth, and legend; imagined familiars and Doppelgänger; and grown-ups as seen through the child's eyes—whether Napoleon, Dr. Dolittle, parents, or the corner grocer. That writers did not detect this lively cosmos for two and a half millennia is one of the curiosities of literature. At any moment there has always been a numerous, physically visible, and audible company of children. Whether this sizable minority, appraised as literary raw material, could be as rewarding as the adult majority was never asked.

And so, almost to the dawn of the Industrial Revolution, children's literature remained recessive. The chief, though not the only, reason is improbably simple: the child himself, though there, was not seen. Not seen, that is, as a child.

In preliterate societies he was and is viewed in the light of his social, economic, and religious relationship to the tribe or clan. Though he may be nurtured in all tenderness, he is thought of not as himself but as a pre-adult, which is but one of his many forms. Among Old Testament Jews the child's place in society replicated his father's, molded by his relation to God. So too, in ancient Greece and Rome, the child, dressed in the modified adult costume that with appropriate changes of fashion remained his fate for centuries to come, was conceived as a miniature adult. His importance lay not in himself but in what Aristotle would have called his final cause: the potential citizen-warrior. A girl child was a seedbed of future citizen-warriors. Hence classical literature either does not see the child at all or misconstrues him. Astyanax and Ascanius, as well as Medea's two children, are not persons. They are stage props. Aristophanes scorns as unworthy of dramatic treatment the children in Euripides' *Alcestis*.

Throughout the Middle Ages and far into the late Renaissance the child remained, as it were, *terra incognita*. A sharp sense of generation gap—one of the motors of a children's literature—scarcely existed. The family, young and old, was a kind of homogenized mix. Sometimes children were even regarded as infrahuman: for Montaigne they had "neither mental activities nor recognizable body shape." The year 1658 is a turning point. In that year a Moravian educator, Comenius, published *Orbis Sensualium Pictus* ("The World of Pictures"), a teaching device that was also the first picture book for children. It embodied a novel insight: children's reading should be of a special order because children are not scaled-down adults. But the conscious, systematic, and successful exploitation of this insight was to wait for almost a century.

It is generally felt that, both as a person worthy of special regard and as an idea worthy of serious contemplation, the child began to come into his own in the second half of the 18th century. His emergence, as well as that of a literature suited to his needs, is linked to many historical forces, among them the development of Enlightenment thought (Rousseau and, before him, John Locke); the rise of the middle class; the beginnings of the emancipation of women—children's literature, unlike that for grown-ups, is in large measure a distaff product; and Romanticism, with its minor strands of the cult of the child (Wordsworth and others) and of genres making a special appeal to the young (folktales and fairy tales, myths, ballads). Yet, with all these forces working for the child, he still might not have emerged had it not been for a few unpredictable geniuses: William Blake, Edward Lear, Lewis Carroll, George MacDonald, Louisa May Alcott, Mark Twain, Collodi, Hans Christian Andersen. But, once tentatively envisaged as an independent being, a literature proper to him could also be envisaged. And so in the mid-18th century, what may be defined as children's literature was at last developing.

Beginnings of children's literature

Shifting visions of the child. Even after the child had been recognized, his literature on occasion persisted in viewing him as a diminutive adult. More characteristically, however, "realistic" (that is, nonfantastic) fiction in all countries regarded the discovered child in a mirror that provided only a partial reflection of him. There are fewer instances of attempts to present the child whole, in the round, than there are (as in Tolstoy or Joyce) attempts to represent the whole adult. Twain's Huck Finn, Erich Kästner's Emil (in *Emil and the Detectives*), Vadim Frolov's Sasha (in *What It's All About*), and Maria Gripe's delightful Josephine all exemplify in-the-round characterization. More frequently, however, children's literature portrays the young as types. Thus there is the brand of hell of the Puritan tradition; the moral child of Mrs. Trimmer; the well-instructed child of Madame de Genlis; the small upper class benefactor of Arnaud Berquin; the naughty child, modulated variously in Catherine Sinclair's *Holiday House* and in the books of Comtesse de Ségur, E. Nesbit, Dr. Heinrich Hoffmann (*Struwwelpeter*), and Wilhelm Busch (*Max und Moritz*); the rational child of Maria Edgeworth; the little prig of Thomas Day's *Sandford and Merton;* the little angel (Frances Hodgson Burnett's *Little Lord Fauntleroy*); the forlorn waif (Hector Malot's *Sans Famille*); the manly, outdoor child (Arthur Ransome's *Swallows and Amazons*); the down-with-adults revolutionary of some of Kenneth Grahame; etc. The rationale behind these shifting visions of childhood is akin to Renaissance theories of "humours" or "the ruling passion." Progress in children's literature depended partly on abandoning this mechanical, part-for-the-whole attitude. One encouraging note in realistic children's fiction of the second half of the 20th century in all advanced countries is the appearance of a more organic view.

Slow development. A third universal feature: children's literature appears later than adult and grows more slowly. Only after the trail has been well blazed does it make use of new techniques, whether of composition or illustration. As for content, only after World War II did it exploit certain realistic themes and attitudes, turning on race, class, war, and sex, that had been part of general literature at least since the 1850s. This tardiness may be due to the child's natural conservatism.

Realistic themes and attitudes

Fourth, the tempo of development varies sharply from country to country and from region to region. It is plausible that England should create a complex children's literature, while a less developed region (the Balkans for example) might not. Less clear is why the equally high cultures of France and England should be represented by unequal literatures.

The didactic versus the imaginative. The fifth, and most striking, general feature is the creative tension resulting from a constantly shifting balance between two forces: that of the pulpit-schoolroom and that of the imagination. The first force may take on many guises. It may stress received religious or moral doctrine, thus generating the Catholic children's literature of Spain or the moral tale of Georgian and early Victorian England. It may bear down less on morality than on mere good manners, propriety, or adjustment to the prevailing social code. It may emphasize nationalist or patriotic motives, as in Edmondo De Amicis' post-Risorgimento *Cuore* (*The Heart of a Child*) or much Soviet production. Or its concern may be pedagogical, the imparting of "useful" information, frequently sugarcoated in narrative or dialogue. Whatever its form, it is distinguishable from the shaping spirit of imagination, which ordinarily embodies itself in children's games and rhymes, the fairy tale, the fantasy, animal stories such as Kipling's *Jungle Books*, nonsense, nonmoral poetry, humour, or the realistic novel conceived as art rather than admonition.

Children's literature designed for entertainment rather than self-improvement, aiming at emotional expansion rather than acculturation, usually develops late. *Alice in Wonderland*, the first supreme victory of the imagination (except for *Mother Goose*), did not appear until 1865. Frequently the literature of delight has underground sources of nourishment and inspiration: oral tradition, nursery songs, and the folkish institutions of the chapbook and the penny romance.

While the didactic and the imaginative are conveniently thought of as polar, they need not always be inimical. *Little Women* and *Robinson Crusoe* are at once didactically moral and highly poetical. Nevertheless, many of the acknowledged classics in the field, from *Alice* to *The Lord of the Rings*, incline to fantasy, which is less true of literature for grown-ups.

II. The development of children's literature

CRITERIA OF DEVELOPMENT

Keeping these five general features of development in mind, certain criteria may now be suggested as helpful in making a gross estimate of the degree of that development within any given country. Some of these criteria are artistic. Others link with social progress, wealth, technological level, or the political structure. In what seems their order of importance, these criteria are:

1. Degree of awareness of the child's identity (see above).

2. Progress made beyond passive dependence on oral tradition, folklore, and legend.

3. Rise of a class of professional writers, as distinct from moral reformers, schoolteachers, clerics, or versatile journalists—all those who, for pedagogical, doctrinal, or pecuniary reasons turn themselves into writers for children. For example, a conscious Italian literature for young people may be said to have begun in 1776 with the Rev. Francesco Soave's moralistic "Short Stories," and largely because that literature continued to be composed largely by nonprofessionals, its record has been lacklustre. It took more than a century after the Rev. Francesco to produce a *Pinocchio*. And only in the 20th century, as typified by the brilliant work of a professional like Gianni Rodari (*e.g.*, *Telephone Tales*), did children's literature in Italy seem to be getting into full stride.

4. Degree of independence from authoritarian controls: church, state, school system, a rigid family structure. Although this criterion might be rejected by historians of some nations, one must somehow try to explain why the Spanish, a great and imaginative people, took so long—indeed until 1952—to produce, in Sanchez-Silva, a children's writer of any notable talent.

5. Number of "classics" the influence of which transcends national boundaries.

6. Invention of new forms or genres and the exploitation of a variety of traditional ones.

7. Measure of dependence on translations.

8. Quantity of primary literature: that is, annual production of children's books and, more to the point, of good children's books.

9. Quantity of secondary literature: richness and scope of a body of scholarship, criticism, reviewing.

10. Level of institutional development: libraries, publishing houses, associations, etc.

To these criteria some might add a vigorous tradition of illustration. But that is arguable. While Beatrix Potter's words and pictures compose an indivisible unit, it is equally true that a country may produce a magnificent school of artists (Czechoslovakia's Jǐrí Trnka, Ota Janeček, and others) without developing a literature of matching depth and variety.

THE CRITERIA APPLIED: THREE EXAMPLES

West versus East. The first application of such standards reveals the expected: a gap separating the achievement of the Far East from that of the West. Some Eastern literatures (New Guinea) have not advanced beyond the stage of oral tradition. Others (India, the Philippines, Ceylon, Iran) have been handicapped by language problems. Professional children's writers are rarer than in the West: according to D.R. Kalia, former director of the Delhi Public Library, "No such class exists in Hindi." In Japan, authoritarian patterns—filial piety and ancestor worship—have operated as brakes, though far less since World War II. A low economic level and inadequate technology discourage, in such countries as Burma, Sri Lanka (Ceylon), and Thailand, the origination and distribution of indigenous writing. A towering roadblock is the tendency to imitate the children's books of the West.

It is true that this vast Eastern region, considered as a whole, has produced a number of works ranking as "classics." Most advanced is Japan. Its literature for children goes back to the late 19th century and by 1928 was established in its own right. Japan's "discovery" of the child seems to have been made directly after World War II. In Iwaya Sazanami, Japan has its Grimm; in Ogawa Mimei, perhaps its Andersen; in the contemporary Ishii Momoko, a critic and creative writer of quality; in Takeyama Michio's *Harp of Burma* (available in English), a high-quality postwar controversial novel. But, though less markedly in Japan, the basic Oriental inspiration remains fixed in folklore (also, in China and Japan, in nursery songs and rhymes), and the didactic imperative continues to act as a hobble. By most criteria the development of Eastern (as compared with Western) children's literature still appears to be sparse and tentative.

Japanese development

North versus south. In western Europe there is a sharp variation or unevenness, as between north and south, in the tempo of development. This basic feature was first pointed out by Paul Hazard, a French critic, in *Les livres, les enfants et les hommes* (Eng. trans. by Marguerite Mitchell, *Books, Children and Men;* Boston: The Horn Book, Inc., 1944; 4th ed., 1960): "In the matter of literature for children the North surpasses the South by a large margin." For Hazard, Spain had no children's literature; Italy, with its *Pinocchio* and *Cuore*, could point only to an isolated pair of works of note, and even France in order to strengthen its claims had to include northern Frenchmen: Erckmann-Chatrian, Jules Verne —and the classic Comtesse de Ségur came from Russia.

Hazard wrote in the 1920s. Since then the situation has improved, not only in his own country, but in Italy and in Portugal. Yet he is essentially correct: the south cannot match the richness of England, Scotland, Germany, and the Scandinavian countries. To re-enforce his position the United States might also be adduced, noting that the Mason–Dixon line is (though not in the field of general literature) a dividing line: the American South, even including the Uncle Remus stories, has supplied very little good children's reading. As for nursery literature, though analogous rhymes are found everywhere, especially in China, the English *Mother Goose* is unique in the claims made for it as a work of art.

Why is the north superior to the south? The first criterion of development may be illuminating. It simply restates Hazard's dictum: "For the Latins, children have never been anything but future men. The Nordics have understood better this truer truth, that men are only grown-up children." ("Adults are obsolete children," says the American children's author "Dr. Seuss.") Hazard does not mention other factors. Historically, the south has

Superiority of northern literature

shown greater attachment to authoritarian controls. Also up to recent times it has depended heavily on reworked folklore as against free invention. Besides there is the mysterious factor of climate: it could be true that children in Latin countries mature faster and are sooner ready for adult literature. In France a special intellectual tradition, that of Cartesian logic, tends to discourage a children's literature. Clear and distinct ideas, excellent in themselves, do not seem to feed the youthful imagination.

Latin America. Once more applying the chosen criteria, familiar patterns are recognizable: unevenness, as compared with the United States; belatedness—in Argentina the *cuento infantil* is hardly detectable before 1900; and especially an unbalanced polarity, with didacticism decidedly the stronger magnet. The close connection of the church with the child's family and school life has tended to encourage a literature stressing piety, and this at a time when the West, at least in its northern latitudes, is concerned less with the salvation than with the imagination of the child. Fantasy emerged only in the 1930s, in Brazil and in Mexico, where a Spanish exile, Antonio Robles, continued to develop his inventive vein. And realistic writing about the actual life of the young evolved even more deliberately, being generally marked by a patriotic note. Though understandable and wholesome, this did not seem to help the cause of the imagination.

Folklore has been vigorously exploited, often by scholars of high repute. It is largely influenced by the legendry of Spain. Cuba, however, has produced interesting Afro-American tales for children; Argentina offers some indigenous folk stories and tales of gaucho life; and Central America is rich in native traditional verse enjoyed by children. Guatemala, in particular, possesses a large body, still largely unworked, of Mayan legends.

Characteristics of Latin American literature

Latin American literature in general displays a special characteristic, part of its Iberian heritage: a partiality for linguistic decoration, which is unpalatable to the relatively straightforward taste of the young reader. Also the Latin American view of the child remains tinged with a sentimentality from which many European countries and the United States had by 1914 more or less freed themselves. Thus verse for children, a medium specially cultivated in Latin America, has run to the soft, the sweet, even the lachrymose rather than to the gay, the humorous, or the sanguine—moods more congenial to the child's sensibility. This is true even of the children's verse of the Nobel Prize-winning poet Gabriela Mistral. To these two weaknesses one must add a third: the practical difficulty involved in the fact that most families cannot afford books. The absence of a powerful middle class has had a retarding effect.

Children in Latin America often complain that the authors write not for them but for their parents. They are given *lectura* ("reading matter") rather than *literatura*, which is but to say that in Latin America the admonitory note, considered so useful by church, state, and parent, continues to be sounded.

In summary, and applying the criteria: some less advanced Latin American countries can hardly be said to have a children's literature at all. Others have produced notable writers: Brazil's José Bento Monteiro Lobato, Argentina's Ana Maria Berry, Colombia's Rafael Pombo, Uruguay's Horacio Quiroga. Yet the quality gap separating Latin American children's literature from that of its northern neighbour is still wide.

III. The major literatures: historical sketches

ENGLAND

Overview. The English have often confessed a certain reluctance to say good-bye to childhood. This curious national trait, baffling to their continental neighbours, may lie at the root of their supremacy in children's literature. Yet it remains a mystery.

But, if it cannot be accounted for, it can be summed up. From the critic's vantage point, the English (as well as the Scots and the Welsh) must be credited with having originated or triumphed in more children's genres than any other country. They have excelled in the school story, two solid centuries of it, from Sarah Fielding's *The Governess; or, The Little Female Academy* (1745) to, say, C. Day Lewis' *The Otterbury Incident* (1948) and including such milestones as Thomas Hughes's *Tom Brown's School Days* (1857) and Kipling's *Stalky & Co.* (1899); and the boy's adventure story, with one undebatable world masterpiece in Stevenson's *Treasure Island* (1883), plus a solid line of talented practitioners, from the Victorian Robert Ballantyne (*The Coral Island*) to the contemporary Richard Church and Leon Garfield (*Devil-in-the-Fog*); the "girls' book," often trash but possessing in Charlotte M. Yonge at least one writer of exceptional vitality; historical fiction, from Marryat's vigorous but simple *Children of the New Forest* (1847) to the even more vigorous but burnished novels of Rosemary Sutcliff; the "vacation story," in which Arthur Ransome still remains unsurpassed; the doll story, from Margaret Gatty and Richard Henry Horne to the charming fancies of Rumer Godden and the remarkable serious development of this tiny genre in Pauline Clarke's *Return of the Twelves* (1962); the realism-cum-fantasy novel, for which E. Nesbit provided a classic, and P.L. Travers a modern, formulation; high fantasy (Lewis Carroll, George MacDonald, C.S. Lewis, Alan Garner); nonsense (Carroll again, Lear, Belloc); and nursery rhymes. In Jonathan Swift's *Gulliver's Travels* and Daniel Defoe's *Robinson Crusoe*, the English furnished two archetypal narratives that have bred progeny all over the world, and in Mary Norton's Tom-Thumb-and-Gulliver-born *The Borrowers* (1952) a work of art. In Leslie Brooke (*Johnny Crow's Garden*) and Beatrix Potter (*e.g., The Tale of Peter Rabbit*) they have two geniuses of children's literature (and illustration) for very small children—probably the most difficult of all the genres. In poetry they begin at the top with William Blake and continue with Christina Rossetti, Robert Louis Stevenson, Eleanor Farjeon, Walter de la Mare, A.A. Milne, and James Reeves. In the mutation of fantasy called whimsy, Milne (Winnie-the-Pooh) reappears as a master. In the important field of the animal story, Kipling, with his *Jungle Books* (1894, 1895) and *Just So Stories* (1902) remains unsurpassed. Finally the English have produced a number of unclassifiable masterpieces such as Kenneth Grahame's *Wind in the Willows* (which is surely more than an animal story) and several unclassifiable writers (Mayne and Lucy Boston, for example).

Genres of English children's literature

The social historian, surveying the same field from a different angle, would point out that the English were the first people in history to develop not only a self-conscious, independent children's literature but also the commercial institutions capable of supporting and furthering it. He would note the striking creative swing between didacticism and delight. He would detect the sources in ballads, chapbooks, nurses' rhymes, and street literature that have at critical moments prompted the imagination. What would perhaps interest him most is the way in which children's literature reflects, over more than two centuries, the child's constantly shifting position in society.

Prehistory (early Middle Ages–1712). "Children's books did not stand out by themselves as a clear but subordinate branch of English literature until the middle of the 18th century." At least one critic has used "prehistorical" to designate all children's books published in England up to 1744, when John Newbery offered *A Little Pretty Pocket Book*.

Before that, and as far back as the Middle Ages, children came in contact with schoolroom letters. There was the Anglo-Saxon theologian and historian the Venerable Bede, with his textbook on natural science, *De natura rerum*. There were the question-and-answer lesson books of the great English scholar Alcuin; the *Colloquy* of the English abbot Aelfric; the *Elucidarium* of the archbishop of Canterbury Anselm, often thought of as the first "encyclopaedia" for young people. Not until the mid-14th century was English (the genius of which somehow seems fitter than Latin for children's books) thought of as proper for literature. (For his son "litel Lowis" Geoffrey Chaucer wrote in English the "Treatise on the Astrolabe"

(1391). The English child was also afflicted, in the 15th and 16th centuries, by many "Books of Courtesy" (such as *The Babees Boke, c.* 1475), the ancestors of modern, equally ineffective manuals of conduct.

Along with these instructional works, there flourished, at least from the very early Renaissance, an unofficial or popular literature. It may not have been meant for children but—no one quite knows how—children managed to recognize it as their own. It included fables, especially those of Aesop; folk legends, such as those in the much read *Gesta Romanorum;* bestiaries, which, along with Aesop, may be ancestral to that flourishing children's genre, the animal story; romances, often clustering around King Arthur and Robin Hood; fairy tales, of which Jack the Giant Killer was the type; and nursery rhymes, probably largely orally transmitted. Perhaps the most influential underground literature consisted of the chapbooks, low-priced folded sheets containing ballads and romances (*Bevis of Southampton*, which was a model for the later *Pilgrim's Progress*, and *The Seven Champions of Christendom* [1597] were favourites), sold by wandering hawkers and peddlers. They fed the imagination of the poor, old and young, from Queen Anne's reign almost through Queen Victoria's. These native products of fancy were, in the early 18th century, reinforced by the first English translations of the classically simple French fairy tales of Charles Perrault and the more self-conscious ones of Madame D'Aulnoy.

Against this primitive literature of entertainment stands a primitive literature of didacticism stretching back to the early Middle Ages. This underwent a Puritan mutation after the Restoration. It is typified by that classic for the potentially damned child, *A Token for Children* (1671), by James Janeway. The Puritan outlook was elevated by Bunyan's *Pilgrim's Progress* (1678), which, often in simplified form, was either forced upon children or more probably actually enjoyed by them in lieu of anything better. Mrs. Overtheway (in Juliana Ewing's *Mrs. Overtheway's Remembrances*, 1869), recalling her childhood reading, refers to it as "that book of wondrous fascination." A softened Puritanism also reveals itself in Bunyan's *Book for Boys and Girls: or, Country Rhymes for Children* (1686), as well as the *Divine and Moral Songs for Children* by the hymn composer Isaac Watts, whose "How doth the little busy bee" still exhales a faint endearing charm.

The entire pre-1744 period is redeemed by two works of genius. Neither *Robinson Crusoe* nor *Gulliver's Travels* was meant for children. Immediately abridged and bowdlerized, they were seized upon by the prosperous young. The poorer ones, the great majority, had to wait for the beginning of the cheap reprint era. Both books fathered an immense progeny in the children's field. Defoe engendered a whole school of "Robinsonnades" in most European countries, the most famous example being Wyss's *Swiss Family Robinson* (1812–13).

On the whole, during the millennium separating Alcuin from Newbery, the child's mind was thought of, if at all, as something to be improved; his imagination as something to be shielded; his soul as something to be saved. And on the whole the child's mind, imagination, and soul resisted, persisted, and somehow, whether in a dog-eared penny history of *The Babes in the Wood* or the matchless chronicle of Gulliver among the Lilliputians, found its own nourishment.

From "T.W." to "Alice" (1712?–1865). Napoleon called the English a "nation of shopkeepers," and in England art may owe much to trade. Children's literature in England got its start from merchants such as Thomas Boreman, of whom little is known, and especially John Newbery, of whom a great deal more is known. Research has established that at least as early as 1730 Boreman began publishing for children (largely educational works) and that in 1742 he produced what sounds like a recreational story, *Cajanus, the Swedish Giant.* Beginnings of English children's literature might be dated from the first decade of the 18th century, when a tiny 12-page, undated book called *A Little Book for Little Children* by "T.W." appeared. It is instructional but, as the critic Percy Muir

says, important as the earliest publication in English "to approach the problem from the point of view of the child rather than the adult." In sum, without detracting from the significance of Newbery, it may be said that he was merely the first great success in a field that had already undergone a certain amount of exploitation.

The elevation of the publisher-bookseller-editor Newbery (who also sold patent medicines) to the position of patron saint is an excusable piece of sentiment. Perhaps it originated with one of his hack writers who doubled as a man of genius. In Chapter XVIII of *The Vicar of Wakefield* (1766), Oliver Goldsmith lauds his employer as "the philanthropic bookseller of St. Paul's Churchyard, who has written so many books for children, calling himself their friend, but who was the friend of all mankind." There is no reason to believe that Newbery was anything but an alert businessman who discovered and shrewdly exploited a new market: middle class children, or rather their parents. Nevertheless this was a creative act. In 1744 he published *A Little Pretty Pocket Book.* Its ragbag of contents—pictures of children's games, jingles, fables, "an agreeable Letter to read from Jack the Giant Killer," plus a bonus in the form of "a Ball and a Pincushion"—are of interest only because, addressing itself single-mindedly to a child audience, it aimed primarily at diversion. Thus children's literature clearly emerged into the light of day.

The climate of Newbery's era was nevertheless more suited to a literature of didacticism than to one of diversion. John Locke's *Some Thoughts concerning Education* (1693) is often cited as an early Enlightenment emancipatory influence. But close inspection of this manual for the mental conditioning of gentlemen reveals a strong English stress on character building and practical learning. Locke thinks little of the natural youthful inclination to poetry: "It is seldom seen that anyone discovers mines of Gold or Silver in Parnassus." He does endorse, as a daring idea, the notion that a child should read for pleasure, and he recommends Aesop. But the decisive influence was not Locke's. It came from across the Channel with Rousseau's best seller *Émile* (1762). What is positive in Rousseau—his recognition that the child should not be too soon forced into the straitjacket of adulthood—was more or less ignored. Other of his doctrines had a greater effect on children's literature. For all his talk of freedom, he provided his young Émile with an amiable tyrant for a teacher, severely restricting his reading to one book, *Robinson Crusoe.* It was his didactic strain, exemplified in the moral French children's literature of Arnaud Berquin and Madame de Genlis, that attracted the English.

They took more easily to Rousseau's emphasis on virtuous conduct and instruction via "nature" than they did to his advocacy of the liberation of personality. Some writers, such as Thomas Day, with his long-lived *Sandford and Merton*, were avowedly Rousseauist. Others took from him what appealed to them. Sarah Kirby Trimmer, whose *Fabulous Histories* specialized in piety, opposed the presumably free-thinking Rousseau on religious grounds but was in other respects strongly influenced by him. The same is true of Anna Laetitia Barbauld, with her characteristically titled *Lessons for Children.* But Mary Martha Sherwood could hardly have sympathized with Rousseau's notion of the natural innocence of children; the author of *The History of the Fairchild Family* (1818–47) based her family chronicle on the proposition (which she later softened) that "all children are by nature evil." Of all the members of the flourishing Rousseauist or quasi-Rousseauist school of the moral tale, only one was a true writer. Maria Edgeworth may still be read. In one of her most famous stories, "The Purple Jar," Rousseau's stress on experience rather than book learning is interestingly reflected.

Though the tone varies from Miss Edgeworth's often sympathetic feeling for children to Mrs. Sherwood's Savonarolan severities, one idea dominates: a special literature for the child must be manufactured in order to improve or reform him. The reigning mythology is that of reason, a mythology difficult to sell to the young.

Yet during the period from John Newbery's *Little Pretty Pocket-Book* to Lewis Carroll's *Alice in Wonderland*, children's literature also showed signs of antisolemnity. In verse there was first of all William Blake. His *Songs of Innocence* (1789) was not written for children, perhaps indeed not written for anyone. But its fresh, antirestrictive sensibility, flowing from a deep love for the very young, decisively influenced all English verse for children. Yet the poetry the young really read or listened to at the opening of the 19th century was not Blake but *Original Poems for Infant Minds* (1804), by "Several Young Persons," including Ann and Jane Taylor. The Taylor sisters, though adequately moral, struck a new note of sweetness, of humour, at any rate of nonpriggishness. Their "Twinkle, twinkle, little star," included in *Rhymes for the Nursery* (1806), has not only been memorized but actually liked by many generations of small children. No longer read, but in its way similarly revolutionary, was *The Butterfly's Ball and the Grasshopper's Feast* (1807), by William Roscoe, a learned member of Parliament and writer on statistics. The gay and fanciful nonsense of this rhymed satiric social skit enjoyed, despite the seeming dominance of the moral Barbaulds and Trimmers, a roaring success. Great nonsense verse, however, had to await the coming of a genius, Edward Lear, whose *Book of Nonsense* (1846) was partly the product of an emergent and not easily explainable Victorian feeling for levity and partly the issue of a fruitfully neurotic personality, finding relief for its frustrations in the noncontingent world of the absurd and the free laughter of children.

Lear's nonsense verse

In prose may be noted, toward the end of the period under discussion, the dawn of romantic historical fiction, with Frederick Marryat's *Children of the New Forest* (1847), a story of the English Civil War; and of the manly open-air school novel, with Thomas Hughes's *Tom Brown's School Days* (1857). A prominent milestone in the career of the "realistic" children's family novel is *Holiday House* (1839), by Catherine Sinclair, in which at last there are children who are noisy, even naughty, yet not destined for purgatory. Though Miss Sinclair's book does conclude with a standard deathbed scene, the overall atmosphere is one of gaiety. The victories in the field of children's literature may seem small, but they can be decisive. It was a small, decisive victory to have introduced in *Holiday House* an Uncle David, whose parting admonition to his nieces and nephews is: "Now children! I have only one piece of serious, important advice to give you all, so attend to me!—Never crack nuts with your teeth!"

A similar note was struck by Henry (later Sir Henry) Cole with his *Home Treasury* series, featuring traditional fairy tales, ballads, and rhymes. The fairy tale then began to come into its own, perhaps as a natural reaction to the moral tale. John Ruskin's *King of the Golden River* (1851) and William Makepeace Thackeray's "fireside pantomime" *The Rose and the Ring* (1855) were signs of a changing climate, even though the Grimm-like directness of the first is partly neutralized by Ruskin's moralistic bent and the gaiety of the second is spoiled by a laborious, parodic slyness. More important than these fairy tales, however, was the aid supplied by continental allies: the English publication in 1823–26 of the Grimms' *Fairy Tales;* in 1846 of Andersen's utterly personal fairy tales and folktales; in the '40s and '50s of other importations from the country of fancy, notably Sir George Dasent's version of the stirring *Popular Tales from the Norse* (1859), collected by Peter Christen Asbjørnsen and J.E. Moe. Though the literature of improvement continued to maintain its vigour, England was readying itself for Lewis Carroll.

Coming of age (1865–1945). In 1863 there appeared *The Water-Babies* by Charles Kingsley. In this fascinating, yet repulsive, "Fairy Tale for a Land-Baby," an unctuous cleric and a fanciful poet, uneasily inhabiting one body, collaborated. *The Water-Babies* may stand as a rough symbol of the bumpy passage from the moral tale to a lighter, airier world. Only two years later that passage was achieved in a masterpiece by an Oxford mathe-matical don, the Reverend Charles Lutwidge Dodgson (Lewis Carroll). *Alice's Adventures in Wonderland* improved none, delighted all. It opened what from a limited perspective seems the Golden Age of English children's literature, a literature in fair part created by Scotsmen: George MacDonald, Andrew Lang, Robert Louis Stevenson, Kenneth Grahame, James Barrie.

The age is characterized by a literary level decisively higher than that previously achieved; the creation of characters now permanent dwellers in the child's imagination (from Alice herself to Mary Poppins, and including Long John Silver, Mowgli, intelligent Mr. Toad, and—if Hugh Lofting, despite his American residence, be accepted as English—Dr. Dolittle); the exaltation of the imagination in the work of Carroll, MacDonald, Stevenson, E. Nesbit, Grahame, Barrie, Hudson, Lofting, Travers, and the early Tolkien (*The Hobbit* [1938]); the establishment of the art fairy tale (Jean Ingelow with *Mopsa the Fairy* [1869]; Dinah Maria Mulock Craik with *The Little Lame Prince* [1875]; Mrs. Ewing with *Old Fashioned Fairy Tales* [1882]; Barrie's *Peter Pan* [1904]; and the exquisite artifices of Oscar Wilde in *The Happy Prince, and Other Tales* [1888]); the transmutation and popularization, by Andrew Lang, Joseph Jacobs, and others, of traditional fairy tales from all sources; the development of a quasi-realistic school in the fiction of Charlotte M. Yonge (*Countess Kate*); Mrs. Ewing (*Jan of the Windmill*); and Mrs. Molesworth; and, furthering this trend, a growing literary population of real, or at least more real, children (by E. Nesbit and Ransome).

The Golden Age in English children's literature

It is further characterized by the rapid evolution of a dozen now-basic genres, including the school story, the historical novel, the vacation story, the "group" or "gang" novel, the boy's adventure tale, the girl's domestic novel, the animal tale, the career novel (Noel Streatfeild's *Ballet Shoes*, 1936), the work of pure whimsy (A.A. Milne's *Winnie-the-Pooh*, 1926); the solution, a brilliant one by Beatrix Potter and a charming one by L. Leslie Brooke, of the problem of creating literature for prereaders and beginning readers; and the growth of an impressive body of children's verse: the lyric delicacy of Christina Rossetti in *Sing-Song* (1872), the accurate reflection of the child's world in Stevenson's *Child's Garden of Verses*, the satirical nonsense of Hilaire Belloc in his *The Bad Child's Book of Beasts* (1896), the incantatory, other-worldly magic of Walter de la Mare with his *Songs of Childhood* (1902) and *Peacock Pie* (1913), the fertile gay invention of Eleanor Farjeon, and the irresistible charm of Milne in *When We Were Very Young* (1924).

Finally it is characterized by the dominance in children's fiction of middle and upper middle class mores; the appearance, in the late 1930s, with Eve Garnett's *The Family from One End Street*, of stories showing a sympathetic concern with the lives of slum children; the reflection, also in the 30s, of a serious interest, influenced by modern psychology, in the structure of the child's vision of the world; the rise, efflorescence, and decline of the children's magazine: *Boy's Own Magazine* (1855–74), *Good Words for the Young* (1867–77), *Aunt Judy's Magazine* (1866–85), and—famous for its outstanding contributors—*The Boy's Own Paper* (1879–1912); the beginning, with F.J.H. Darton and other scholars, of an important critical-historical literature; institutionalization, commercialization, standardization—the popularity, for example, of the "series"; and the dominating influence of the better English work on the reading taste of American, Continental, and Oriental children.

During these 80 years a vast amount of trash and treacle was produced. What will be remembered is the work of a few dozen creative writers who applied to literature for children standards as high as those ordinarily applied to mainstream literature.

Contemporary times. If the contemporary wood cannot be seen for the trees, it is in part because the number of trees has grown so great. The profusion of English, as of children's books in general, makes judgment difficult. Livelier merchandising techniques (the spread of children's bookshops, for example), the availability of cheap paperbacks, improved library services, serious and even distinguished reviewing—these are among the post-World War II institutional trends helping to place more books in the hands of more children. Slick transformation formulas facilitate the rebirth of books in other guises: radio, television, records, films, digests, cartoon versions. Such processes may also create new child audiences, but that these readers are undergoing a literary experience is open to doubt.

Among the genres that fell in favour, the old moral tale, if not a corpse, surely became obsolescent but raised the question whether it was being replaced by a subtler form of didactic literature, preaching racial, class, and international understanding. The standard adventure story too seemed to be dying out, though excellent examples, such as *The Cave* (U.S. title, *Five Boys in a Cave* [1950]), by Richard Church, continued to appear. The boy's school story suffered a similar fate, despite the remarkable work of William Mayne in *A Swarm in May* (1955). Children's verse by Ian Serraillier, Ted Hughes, James Reeves, and the later Eleanor Farjeon, excellent though it was, did not speak with the master tones of a de la Mare or the precise simplicity of a Stevenson. In science fiction one would have expected more of a boom; yet nothing appeared comparable to Jules Verne.

Conversely, there was a genuine boom in fact books: biographical series, manuals of all sorts, popularized history, junior encyclopaedias. Preschool and easy-to-read beginners' books, often magnificently produced, multiplied. So did specially prepared decoys for the reluctant reader. After the discovery of the child came that of the postchild: conscientiously composed teen-age and "young adult" novels were issued in quantity, though the quality still left something to be desired. A 19th-century phenomenon—experimentation in the juvenile field by those who normally write for grown-ups—took on a second life after World War II. Naomi Mitchison, Richard Church, P.H. Newby, Richard Graves, Eric Linklater, Norman Collins, Roy Fuller, C. Day Lewis, and Ian Fleming, with his headlong pop extravaganza *Chitty Chitty Bang Bang* (1964), come to mind.

A post-World War II stress on building bridges of understanding was reflected both in an increase in translations and in the publication of books, whether fiction or nonfiction, dealing responsibly and unsentimentally with the sufferings of a war-wounded world. One example among many was Serraillier's *Silver Sword* (1958), recounting the trans-European adventures that befell four Polish children after the German occupation. *The Silver Sword* was a specialized instance of a general trend toward the interpretation for children of a postwar world of social incoherence, race and class conflict, urban poverty, and even mental pathology. Such novels as John Rowe Townsend's *Gumble's Yard* (1961); *Widdershins Crescent* (1965); *Pirate's Island* (1968); Eve Garnett's *Further Adventures of the Family from One End Street* (1956); and Leila Berg's *Box for Benny* (1958) represented a new realistic school, restrained in England, less so in the United States, but manifest in the children's literature of much of the world. It failed to produce a masterpiece, perhaps because the form of the realistic novel must be moderately distorted to make it suitable for children.

In two fields, however, English postwar children's literature set new records. These were the historical novel and that cloudy area comprising fantasy, freshly wrought myth, and indeed any fiction not rooted in the here and now.

There was fair reason to consider Rosemary Sutcliff not only the finest writer of historical fiction for children but quite unconditionally among the best historical novelists using English. A sound scholar and beautiful stylist, she made few concessions to the presumably simple child's mind and enlarged junior historical fiction with a long series of powerful novels about England's remote past, especially that dim period stretching from pre-Roman times to the coming of Christianity. Among her best works are *The Eagle of the Ninth* (1954), *The Shield Ring* (1956), *The Silver Branch* (1957), *The Lantern Bearers* (1959), and especially *Warrior Scarlet* (1958).

Not as finished in style, but bolder in the interpretation of history in terms "reflecting the changed values of the age," was the pioneering Geoffrey Trease. He also produced excellent work in other juvenile fields. Typical of his highest energies is the exciting *The Hills of Varna* (1948), a story of the Italian Renaissance in which Erasmus and the great printer Aldus Manutius figure prominently. Henry Treece, whose gifts were directed to depicting violent action and vigorous, barbaric characters, produced a memorable series of Viking novels of which *Swords from the North* (1967) is typical.

This new English school, stressing conscientious scholarship, realism, honesty, social awareness, and general disdain for mere swash and buckle, produced work that completely eclipsed the rusty tradition of Marryat and George Alfred Henty. Some of its foremost representatives were Cynthia Harnett, Serraillier, Barbara Leonie Picard, Ronald Welch (pseudonym of Ronald O. Felton), C. Walter Hodges, Hester Burton, Mary Ray, Naomi Mitchison, and K.M. Peyton, whose "Flambards" series is a kind of Edwardian historical family chronicle. Leon Garfield, though not working with historical characters, created strange picaresque tales that gave children a thrilling, often chilling insight into the 18th-century England of Smollett and Fielding.

In the realm of imagination England not only retained but enhanced its supremacy with such classics as *Tom's Midnight Garden* (1958), by Ann Philippa Pearce, a haunting, perfectly constructed story in which the present and Victoria's age blend into one. There is the equally haunting Green Knowe series, by Lucy M. Boston, the first of which, *The Children of Greene Knowe*, appeared when the author was 62. The impingement of a world of legend and ancient, unsleeping magic upon the real world is the basic theme of the remarkable novels of Alan Garner. Complex, melodramatic, stronger in action than in characterization, they appeal to imaginative, "literary" children. Garner's rather nightmarish narrative *The Owl Service* (1967) is perhaps the most subtle.

Finally there is a trio of masters, each the architect of a complete secondary world. The vast Middle Earth trilogy *The Lord of the Rings* (1954–55), by the Anglo-Saxon and Middle English language scholar J.R.R. Tolkien, was not written with children in mind. But they have made it their own. It reworks many of the motives of traditional romance and fantasy, including the Quest for the grail, but is essentially a structure, conceivably but not inevitably allegorical, of sheer invention on a staggering scale. It is also a sociocultural phenomenon, selling 3,000,000 copies in nine languages and functioning, for a certain class of American teen-agers, as a semisacred cult object.

Tolkien's fellow scholar, C.S. Lewis, created his own otherworld of Narnia. It is more derivative than Tolkien's (he owes something, for example, to Nesbit), more clearly Christian-allegorical, more carefully adapted to the tastes of children. Though uneven, the seven volumes of the cycle, published through the years 1950 to 1956, are exciting, often humorous, inventive, and, in the final scenes of *The Last Battle*, deeply moving.

The third of these classic secondary worlds is in a sense not a creation of fantasy. The four volumes (1952–61) about the Borrowers, with their brief pendant, *Poor Stainless* (1971), ask the reader to accept only a single impossibility, that in a quiet country house, under the grandfather clock, live the tiny Clock family: Pod, Homily, and their daughter Arrietty. All that follows from this premise is logical, precisely pictured, and carries absolute conviction. Many critics believe that this miniature world so lovingly, so patiently fashioned by Mary Norton will last as long as those located at the bottom of the rabbit hole and through the looking glass.

UNITED STATES

Overview. Compared with England, the United States has fewer peaks. In *Huckleberry Finn*, of course, it possesses a world masterpiece matched in the children's literature of no other country. *Little Women*, revolutionary in its day, radiates a century later a special warmth and may still be the most beloved "family story" ever written. Though *The Wonderful Wizard of Oz* has been recklessly compared with *Alice*, it lacks Carroll's brilliance, subtlety, and humour. Nonetheless, its story and characters apparently carry, like *Pinocchio*, an enduring, near-universal appeal for children. To these older titles might be added *Stuart Little* (1945) and *Charlotte's Web* (1952), by E.B. White, two completely original works that appear to have become classics. To this brief list of high points few can be added, though, on the level just below the top, the United States bears comparison with England and therefore any other country.

The "law" of belated development applies in a special way. From Jamestown to the end of the Civil War, American children's literature virtually depended on currents in England. In the adult field Cooper and Washington Irving may stand for a true declaration of independence. But it was not until the 1860s and '70s, with Mary Mapes Dodge's *Hans Brinker*, Louisa May Alcott's *Little Women*, Lucretia Hale's *Peterkin Papers*, Mark Twain's *Tom Sawyer*, and *St. Nicholas* magazine, that children's literature finally severed its attachment to the mother country. In the marketplace, however, a uniquely American note was sounded much earlier, the first of the Peter Parley series of Samuel Goodrich having appeared in 1827.

In certain important fields, the United States pioneered. These include everyday-life books for younger readers; the non-class-based small-town story such as *The Moffats* by Eleanor Estes; the Americanized fairy tale and folktale such as *Uncle Remus* (1880), not originally meant for children, and Carl Sandburg's *Rootabaga Stories* (1922); beginners' books such as Dr. Seuss's *The Cat in the Hat* (1957); and the "new realism." One might maintain that American children's literature, particularly since World War II, is bolder, more experimental, more willing to try and fail, than England's. Moreover, it set new standards of institutionalization, "packaging," merchandising, and publicity, as well as mere production, especially of fact books and "subject series."

Prehistory (1646?–1865). The prehistoric annals are short and simple. Dominated by England, native creativity—to refer only to books with even the thinnest claim to literary quality—amounted to little. The Puritan view of the unredeemable child obtained almost into the era of Andrew Jackson. Jonathan Edwards put it neatly: unrepentant children were "young vipers and infinitely more hateful than vipers." More moderate notions also existed. Imported English ballads and tales, even a few "shockers," were enjoyed by the young vipers. But in general, from John Cotton's *Spiritual Milk for Boston Babes* (1646) through the Civil War, the admonitory and exemplary tract and the schoolmaster's pointer prevailed. Occasionally there is the cheerful note of non-improvement, as in Clement Moore's "Visit from St. Nicholas" (1823), sounding against the successful lesson-cum-moral tales of Peter Parley (Goodrich) and the didactic "Rollo" series of Jacob Abbott. The latter's *Franconia Stories* (1850–53), however, showing traces of Rousseau and Johann Pestalozzi, is the remote ancestor of those wholesome, humorous pictures of small-town child life in which American writers excelled after World War I. Affectionately based on the author's own memories, they occasionally reveal children rather than improvable miniatures of men.

The children's magazines of the early 19th century did their best to amuse as well as instruct the young. Sara Josepha Hale's "Mary Had a Little Lamb" appeared in *The Juvenile Miscellany* (1826–34). The atmosphere was further lightened by *Grandfather's Chair* (1841) and its sequels, retellings of stories from New England history by Nathaniel Hawthorne. These were followed in 1852–53 by his redactions, rather unacceptable today, of Greek legends in *The Wonder Book for Girls and Boys* and *Tanglewood Tales for Girls and Boys.* Hawthorne's death date (1864) coincided roughly with a qualified subsidence of the literature of the didactic.

Peaks and plateaus (1865–1940). During the period from the close of the Civil War to the turn of the century an Americanized white, Anglo-Saxon, Protestant, Victorian gentility dominated as the official, though not necessarily real, culture. At first glance such a climate hardly seems to favour the growth of a children's literature. But counterforces were at work: a vigorous upsurge of interest, influenced by European thinkers, in the education and nurture of children; the dying-out of the old Puritanism; and the accumulation of enough national history to stimulate the imagination. To these forces must be added the appearance in Louisa May Alcott of a minor genius and in Samuel Clemens (Mark Twain) of a major one.

American materialism (and also its optimism) expressed itself in the success myth of Horatio Alger, while a softened didacticism, further modified by a mild talent for lively narrative, was reflected in the 116 novels of Oliver Optic (William Taylor Adams). But a quartet of books appearing from 1865 to 1880—heralded a happier day. These were Mary Mapes Dodge's *Hans Brinker, or the Silver Skates* (1865), which for all its Sunday-school tone, revealed to American children an interesting foreign culture and told a story that still has charm; Louisa May Alcott's *Little Women* (1868; vol. ii, 1869; and its March family sequels), which lives by virtue of the imaginative power that comes from childhood truly and vividly recalled; Lucretia Hale's *Peterkin Papers* (1880), just as funny today as a century ago, perfect nonsense produced in a non-nonsensical era; and Thomas Bailey Aldrich's *Story of a Bad Boy* (1870). This, it is often forgotten, preceded *Tom Sawyer* by seven years, offered a model for many later stories of small-town bad boys, and is a fair example of the second-class classic. But it took *Tom Sawyer* and *Huckleberry Finn* to change the course of American writing and give the first deeply felt vision of boyhood in juvenile literature.

To these names should be added Frank Stockton (whose *Ting-a-Ling Tales* [1870] showed the possibilities inherent in the invented fairy tale) and especially the writer-illustrator Howard Pyle. His reworkings of legend (*The Merry Adventures of Robin Hood*, 1883; the King Arthur stories, 1903–1910, and his novels of the Middle Ages [*Otto of the Silver Hand*, 1888; and *Men of iron*, 1892]) exemplify perfectly the romantic feeling of his time, as does the picture of Shakespeare's England drawn by John Bennett in *Master Skylark* (1897).

The sentimentality that is sometimes an unconscious compensatory gesture in a time of ruthless materialism expressed itself in the idyllic *Poems of Childhood* (1896), by Eugene Field, and the rural dialect *Rhymes of Childhood* (1891), by James Whitcomb Riley. These poems can hardly speak to the children of the second half of the 20th century. But it is not clear that the same is true of the equally sentimental novels of Frances Hodgson Burnett. It is easy to smile over *Little Lord Fauntleroy* (1886) or her later and superior novels, *A Little Princess* (1905) and *The Secret Garden* (1911). Back of the absurd sentimentality, however, lies an extraordinary narrative skill, as well as an ability to satisfy the perennial desire felt by children at a certain age for life to arrange itself as a fairy tale.

The development of a junior literature from 1865 to about 1920 is ascribable less to published books than to two remarkable children's magazines: *The Youth's Companion* (1827–1929, when it merged with *The American Boy*) and the relatively nondidactic *St. Nicholas* magazine (1873–1939), which exerted a powerful influence on its exclusively respectable child readers. (It is surely needless to point out that up to the 1960s children's literature has been by and for the middle class.) These magazines published the best material they could get, from England as well as the United States. For all their gentility, standards, including that of illustration, were high. The contributors' names in many cases became part of the canon of world literature. To the children of the last quarter of the 19th and first quarter of the 20th century, the periodical delivery of these magazines presumably meant something that film and television cannot mean to today's children. The magazines were not "media." They were friends.

Appropriately the new century opened with a novelty: a

Dominance of Victorian gentility

Contributions of Howard Pyle

Development of a junior literature

successful American fairy tale. *The Wonderful Wizard of Oz* (1900) is vulnerable to attacks on its prose style, incarnating mediocrity. But there is something in it, for all its doctrine moralism, that lends it permanent appeal: a prairie freshness, a joy in sheer invention, the simple, satisfying characterization of Dorothy and her three old, lovable companions. Several of the sequels—but only those bearing L. Frank Baum's name—are not greatly inferior.

Auspiciously opened, the century underwent for the next two decades a rather baffling decline. Some institutional progress was made in library development, professional education, and the reviewing of children's books. Much useful work was also accomplished in the field of fairy-tale and folktale collections. But original literature did not flourish. There were Pyle and Mrs. Burnett and the topflight nonsense verses of the phenomenal Laura E. Richards, whose collected rhymes in *Tirra Lirra* (1932) will almost bear comparison with those of Edward Lear. Much less memorable are the works of Lucy Fitch Perkins, Joseph Altsheler, Ralph Henry Barbour, Kate Douglas Wiggin, Eliza Orne White, and the two Burgesses—Thornton and Gelett. During these dim American decades, de la Mare, Miss Potter, Kipling, Barrie, Grahame, and E. Nesbit were at work in England.

During the period between world wars new trails were blazed in nonfiction with van Loon's *Story of Mankind* and V.M. Hillyer's *Child's History of the World* (1922). The *Here and Now Story Book*, by Lucy Sprague Mitchell, published in the 1920s, was the first real example of the "direct experience" school of writing, but it is more properly part of the chronicle of pedagogy than of literature. The small child was far better served by a dozen talented writer-illustrators, such as Wanda Gág, with her classic *Millions of Cats* (1928) and other delightful books; and Ludwig Bemelmans, with *Madeline* (1939) and its sequels. Other distinguished names in the important and growing picture-book field were Marjorie Flack, Hardie Gramatky, James Daugherty, the d'Aulaires, and Virginia Lee Burton.

In the field of comic verse and pictures for children of almost all ages, Dr. Seuss (Theodore Geisel), starting with his *And to Think that I Saw It on Mulberry Street* (1937), continued to lead, turning out so many books that one tended to take him for granted. His talent is of a very high order.

Literature of the 1920s and '30s

The 1920s and '30s produced many well-written historical novels, striking a new note of authority and realism, such as *Drums* (1925, transformed in 1928 into a boy's book with N.C. Wyeth's illustrations), by James Boyd, and *The Trumpeter of Kracow* (1928), by Eric Kelly. The "junior novel" came to the fore in the following decade, together with an increase in books about foreign lands, minority groups, and a boom in elaborate picture books. Children's verse was well served by such able practitioners as Dorothy Aldis and Rosemary and Stephen Vincent Benét, with their stirring, hearty ballad-like poems collected in *A Book of Americans* (1933). But the only verse comparable to that of Stevenson or De la Mare was the exquisite *Under the Tree* (1922), by the novelist Elizabeth Madox Roberts, a treasure that should never be forgotten.

At least three other writers produced work of high and entirely original quality. Two of them—Florence and Richard Atwater—worked as a pair. Their isolated effort, *Mr. Popper's Penguins* (1938), will last as a masterpiece of deadpan humour that few children or adults can resist. The third writer is Laura Ingalls Wilder. Her *Little House* books, nine in all, started in 1932 with *The Little House in the Big Woods*. The entire series, painting an unforgettable picture of pioneer life, is a masterpiece of sensitive recollection and clean, effortless prose.

Work of quality was contributed during these two lively decades by authors too numerous to list. Among the best of them are Will James, with his horse story *Smoky* (1926); Rachel Field, whose *Hitty* (1929) is one of the best doll stories in the language; Elizabeth Coatsworth, with her fine New England tale *Away Goes Sally* (1934); and the well-loved story of a New York tomboy in the 1890s, *Roller Skates* (1936), by the famous oral storyteller Ruth Sawyer.

Contemporary times. Since the 1930s the quality and weight of American children's literature were sharply affected by the business of publishing, as well as by the social pressures to which children, like adults, were subjected. Intensified commercialization and broad-front expansion had some good effects and some bad ones as well.

For any book of interest to adults, publishers constructed a corresponding one scaled to child size. The practice of automatic miniaturization stimulated a pullulation of fact books—termed by an unsympathetic observer "the information trap"—marked by a flood of subject series and simplified technology. Paperbacks and cheap reprints of juvenile favourites enlarged the youthful reading public, just as the multiplication of translations widened its horizon. More science fiction was published, a field in which the stories of Robert Heinlein and *A Wrinkle in Time* (1962), by Madeleine L'Engle, stood out. An increase was also noticeable in books for the disadvantaged child and in work of increasingly high quality by and for blacks. In the early 1950s, children's book clubs flourished, though they appeared to be on the wane little more than a decade later. Simple narration using "scientifically determined vocabulary" also seemed to decrease in popularity. There was a marked tendency to orient titles, fiction and nonfiction, to the requirements of the school curriculum. Another trend was toward collaborative "international" publishing. This had the double effect of cutting colour-plate costs and promoting blandness, since it was important that no country's readers be offended or surprised by anything in text or illustration. Still another alteration took place in the conventional notion of age and grade levels. Teen-agers reached out for adult books; younger children read junior novels.

The most striking development was the growth of the "realists," most of them as earnest as Maria Edgeworth, a few of them lighter fingered, with a fringe of far-outers. The latter were fairly represented by Nat Hentoff in *Jazz Country* (1965), for example, and Maria Wojciechowska in *The Rotten Years* (1971). Teen-age fiction as well as nonfiction dealt mercilessly with ethnic exploitation, poverty, broken homes, desertion, unemployment, adult hypocrisy, drug addiction, sex (including homosexuality), and death. A whole new "problem" literature became available, with no sure proof that it was warmly welcomed. The aesthetic dilemmas posed by this literature are still to be faced and resolved. The new social realist story often had the look of an updated moral tale: the dire consequences of nondiligence were replaced by those of pot smoking.

Growth of "realist" fiction

Nevertheless such original works as *Harriet the Spy* (1964) and *The Long Secret* (1965), by Louise Fitzhugh, showed how a writer adequately equipped with humour and understanding could incorporate into books for 11-year-olds subjects—even menstruation—ordinarily reserved for adult fiction. Similarly trailblazing were the semidocumentary novels of Joseph Krumgold: *. . . And Now Miguel* (1953), *Onion John* (1958), and *Henry 3* (1967), the last about a boy with an I.Q. of 154 trying to get along in a society antagonistic to brains. The candid suburban studies of E.L. Konigsburg introduced a new sophistication. Her 1968 Newbery Medal winner, *From the Mixed-up Files of Mrs. Basil E. Frankweiler*, was original in its tone and humour.

As for the more traditional genres, a cheering number of high-quality titles rose above the plain of mediocrity. The nonfantastic animal story *Lassie Come Home* (1940), by Eric Knight, survived adaptation to film and television. In the convention of the talking animal, authentic work was produced by Ben Lucien Burman, with his wonderful "Catfish Bend" tales (1952–67). The American-style, wholesome, humorous family story was more than competently developed by Eleanor Estes, with her "Moffat" series (1941–43) and *Ginger Pye* (1951); Elizabeth Enright, with her Melendy family (1941–44); and Robert McCloskey, with *Homer Price* (1943)—to name only three unfailingly popular writers. Text-and-picture books for the very young posed an obdurate challenge: to create literature out of absolutely simple materials. That challenge, first sucessfully met by Beatrix Potter, attracted Americans. The modern period produced many enchanting examples of this tricky genre: *The Happy Lion* (1954) and its sequels, the joint work of the writer Louise Fatio and her artist husband, Roger Duvoisin; the "Little Bear" books, words by Else Holmelund Minarik, pictures by Maurice Sendak; and several zany tours de force by Dr. Seuss, including his one-syllable revolution *The Cat in the Hat* (1957). The picture books of Sendak, perhaps one of the few original geniuses in his restricted field, were assailed by many adults as frightening or abnormal. The children did not seem to mind.

Fiction about foreign lands Fiction about foreign lands boasted at least one modern American master in Meindert De Jong, whose most sensitive work was drawn from recollections of his Dutch early childhood. A Hans Christian Andersen and Newbery winner, he is best savoured in *The Wheel on the School* (1954), and especially in the intuitive *Journey from Peppermint Street* (1968). The historical novel fared less well in America than in England. *Johnny Tremain* (1943), by Esther Forbes, a beautifully written, richly detailed story of the Revolution, stood out as one of the few high points, as did *Innocent Wayfaring* (1943), a tale of Chaucer's England by the equally scholarly Marchette Chute. Poetry for children had at least two talented representatives. One was the eminent poet-critic John Ciardi, the other David McCord, a veteran maker of nonsense and acrobat of language.

In fantasy, the farcical note was struck with agreeable preposterousness by Oliver Butterworth in *The Enormous Egg* (1956) and *The Trouble with Jenny's Ear* (1960). The prolific writer-illustrator William Pène Du Bois has given children nothing more uproariously delightful than *The Twenty-one Balloons* (1947), merging some of the appeals of Jules Verne with those of Samuel Butler's *Erewhon* and adding a sly humour all his own. Two renowned *New Yorker* writers, James Thurber and E.B. White, developed into successful fantasists, Thurber with an elaborate series of ambiguous literary fairy tales such as *The Thirteen Clocks*, White with his pair of animal stories *Stuart Little* and *Charlotte's Web* that for their humanity and uninsistent humour stand alone. The vein of "high fantasy" of the more traditional variety, involving magic and the construction of a legendary secondary world, was represented by the five highly praised volumes of the Prydain cycle (1964–1968) by Newbery Medal winner Lloyd Alexander.

Two other works of pure imagination gave the 1960s some claim to special notice. The first was *The Phantom Tollbooth* (1961) by Norton Juster, a fantasy about a boy "who didn't know what to do with himself." Not entirely unjustly, it has been compared to *Alice*. The second received less attention but is more remarkable: *The Mouse and His Child* (1969), by Russell Hoban, who had been a successful writer of gentle tales for small children. But here was a different affair altogether: a flawlessly written, densely plotted story with quiet philosophical overtones. It involved a clockwork mouse, his attached son, and an unforgettable assortment of terribly real, humanized animals. Like *Alice* and *The Borrowers*—indeed like all major children's literature—it offered as much to the grown-up as to the young reader. With this moving, intellectually demanding fantasy the decade ended on a satisfactory note.

GERMANY (AND AUSTRIA)

A. Merget's *Geschichte der deutschen Jugendliteratur* ("History of German Children's Literature") appeared in 1867, some years before the Germans had much children's literature to consider, a demonstration of Teutonic thoroughness. By two criteria—degree of awareness of the child's identity and level of institutional development —Germany leads the world. It has built a vast structure of history, criticism, analysis, and controversy devoted to a subject the chief property of which would appear to be its charm rather than its obscurity. One estimate has it that in West Germany alone there are over 300 associations dedicated to the study and promotion of children's literature. Such conscientiousness, nowhere else matched, such a serious desire to relate the child's reading to his nurture, education, and *Weltanschauung*, has an admirable aspect. But by attaching juvenile books too closely to the theory and demands of pedagogy, it may have constricted a marked native genius.

Historical influences The dominant historical influences roughly coincide with those that have affected German mainstream literature, though, as expected, they were exerted more slowly. The Reformation, stressing the Bible, the catechism, and the hymnbook, bent the literature of childhood toward the didactic, the monitory, and the pious. The Enlightenment, however, did something to help toward the identification of the child as an independent being. With this insight are associated the educational theories of J.B. Basedow, J.F. Herbart, and Friedrich Froebel. One fruit of the movement was *Robinson der Jüngere* (1779; "The Young Robinson"), by Joachim Heinrich Campe, who adapted Defoe along Rousseauist lines, his eye sharply fixed on what he considered to be the natural interests of the child. Interchapters of useful moral conversations between the author and his pupils were a feature of the book. Campe's widespread activities on behalf of children, though less commercially motivated, recall Newbery's.

Rationalism, piety, and the German partiality for disciplined conduct were modified by the influence of two crucial works, not intended for children but soon taken over by them. Both are part of the Romantic movement that swept Germany and much of the Continent during the early 19th century. *Des Knaben Wunderhorn* (1806–08; "The Boy's Magic Horn"), a collection of old German songs and folk verse, included many children's songs, or songs that were so denominated by the editors, Achim von Arnim and Clemens Brentano. The effect of the book was to retrieve for Germany much of its rich folk heritage, to promote a new emotional sensibility, and to draw attention to the link, as the Romantics thought, binding folk feeling to the child's vision of the world. *Des Knaben Wunderhorn* became a part of German childhood, as La Fontaine's *Fables* in France and *Mother Goose* in England had become a part of growing up in those countries. It helped inspire several excellent writers of verse for children: A.H. Hoffmann von Fallersleben; August Kopisch; the writer-illustrator Count Franz Pocci, the first German to write nonsense verse for the young; F.W. Güll; and later poets such as Paula and Richard Dehmel.

German fairy tales Just as *Des Knaben Wunderhorn* became a source of poetry, so the epochal folktale collection of the brothers Grimm helped to develop a school of prose fairy-tale writers. Not all of these Romantics wrote with children in mind. But some of the simplest of their tales have become part of the German child's inheritance. In today's presumably practical era, they are once more in favour. Among these masters of the "art" *Märchen* are E.T.A. Hoffmann; C.M. Brentano; Ludwig Tieck; de la Motte Fouqué, author of *Undine;* and Wilhelm Hauff, whose talents are most nearly adapted to the tastes of children.

Two curious half-geniuses of comic verse and illustration wrote and drew for the hitherto neglected small child. *Struwwelpeter* ("Shock-headed Peter"), by the premature surrealist Heinrich Hoffmann, aroused cries of glee in children across the continent. Wilhelm Busch created the slapstick buffoonery of Max and Moritz, the ancestors of the Katzenjammer Kids and indeed of many aspects of the comic strip.

The second half of the 19th century saw an increase in commercialized sentimentality and sensation and a corresponding decline in quality. The bogus Indian and Wild West tales of Karl May stand out luridly in the history of German children's literaure. Up to about 1940, 7,500,000 of his books had been sold to German readers alone. (Emilio Salgari in Italy, G.A. Henty in England, and "Ned Buntline" in the United States, who were contemporaneously satisfying the same hunger for the suspenseful, did not approach's May's talent for fabrication without the slightest root in reality.)

It may have been May and others like him who roused an educator, Heinrich Wolgast, to publish in 1896 his explosive *Das Elend unserer Jugendliteratur* ("The Sad State of Our Children's Literature"). The event was an important one. It advanced for the first time the express thesis that "Creative children's literature must be a work of art"; Wolgast resolutely decried nationalistic and didactic deformations. He precipitated a controversy the echoes of which are still audible. On the whole his somewhat excessive zeal had a wholesome effect.

Two post-Wolgast poets of childhood worthy of mention, both artists, are Christian Morgenstern, whose macabre, pre-Dada poetry for adults later came into vogue, and the lesser-gifted Joachim Ringelnatz. The nondidactic note they sounded in modern times was strengthened by a whole school of children's poets. No other country produced work in this difficult field superior to the finest verse of the multitalented James Krüss, and especially Josef Guggenmos, whose lyric simplicity at times recalls Blake. Guggenmos also has to his credit a translation of *A Child's Garden of Verses*, in itself an original work of art.

Between the world wars, prose showed few high points and, after the advent of Hitler, many low ones. *Der Kampf der Tertia* (1927; "The Third-form Struggle"), by Wilhelm Speyer, was Germany's excellent contribution to the genre of the school story. Erich Kästner's *Emil and the Detectives* (1929) ranked not only as a work of art, presenting city boys with humour and sympathy, but as an immediate classic in an entirely new field, the juvenile detective story (Mark Twain's awkward *Tom Sawyer, Detective* [1896] may be ignored). Kästner, the dean of German writers for children, won an international audience with a long series of stories of which the thesis-fable *Die Konferenz der Tiere* (1949; Eng. trans. *The Animals' Conference*, 1949) is perhaps the funniest as well as the most serious.

Post-World War II literature Post-World War II literature, recovering from the Nazi blight, was strong in several fields. In realistic fantasy there is *Vevi* (1955), by the Austrian Erica Lillegg, an extraordinary tale of split personality, odd, exciting, even profound. Michael Ende's *Jim Knopf und Lucas der Lokomotivführer* (1961; Eng. trans. *Jim Button and Luke the Engine Driver*, 1963) has more than a touch of *Oz*; and both Kästner and Krüss have made agreeable additions to the realm of fantasy.

In the domain of the historical novel, Hans Baumann is a distinguished name. Lacking the narrative craft of Miss Sutcliff, whose story lines are always clean and clear, he matched her as a scholar and mounted scenes of great intensity in such novels as *Die Barke der Brüder* (1956; Eng. trans. *The Barque of the Brothers*, 1958) and especially *Steppensöhne* (1954; Eng. trans. *Sons of the Steppe*, 1958), a tale about two grandsons of Genghis Khan. His narrative history of some exciting archaeological discoveries, *Der Höhlen der grossen Jäger* (1953; Eng. trans. *The Caves of the Great Hunters*, 1954; rev. ed., 1962), is a minor classic. Mention should be made of Fritz Mühlenweg, a veteran of the Sven Hedin expedition of 1928–32 to Inner Mongolia and the author of *Grosser-Tiger und Kompass-Berg* (1950; Eng. trans. *Big Tiger and Christian*, 1950). A long, richly coloured narrative of a journey made by two boys, Chinese and European, through the Gobi Desert, it should stand as one of the finest adventure stories of the postwar years.

One general conclusion regarding West German children's literature after 1945 was that the native genius, which had been impeded by pedagogical theory and nationalist dogma, again appeared to be in free flow.

In East Germany, production was conditioned by the association with the U.S.S.R., and it appeared to be recapitulating the developments in children's literature that had occurred in the Soviet Union after 1917. Socialist realism was the basic food offered to the literary appetites of young East Germans.

SCANDINAVIA

Sweden. Scandinavia, but especially Sweden, inevitably suggests a question as to why a group of small,

sparsely populated countries ranks directly after England and the United States for the variety, vigour, and even genius of its children's literature. Hazard's north–south theory describes; it does not explain. A few possible factors may be listed: the inspiration of the master Andersen—yet he does not seem greatly to have inspired his homeland; the appearance in 1900 of the Swedish Ellen Key's two-volume *Barnets århundrede* (Eng. trans. *The Century of the Child*, 1909), pivotal in the history of the discovery that children really exist; a general modern atmosphere of social enlightenment; welfare statism tempered by regard for the individual; a school and library system, notably in Sweden, of extraordinary humanity and efficiency; perhaps even the long, lively career of the Stockholm Children's Theatre, a centre of creative activity. Yet the mystery persists. Since the first half of the 19th century, Scandinavia produced Andersen, Zacharias Topelius, Jørgen Moe, Henrik Wergeland, Helena Nyblom, Selma Lagerlöf, Elsa Beskow, Astrid Lindgren, Tove Jansson, Maria Gripe, Anna Lisa Warnlöf, Lennart Hellsing, Karin Anckarsvärd, Inger Sandberg, plus a school of critics and historians second only to that of Germany, plus so many talented illustrators to satisfy the needs of the beginning reader and the pointing age.

Children's literature in Sweden for centuries reflected that of Germany, of which Sweden was a cultural province during the Reformation and even through the Enlightenment period. The historian Göte Klingberg traced some kind of religious-instructive reading for children back to 1600. There is a record, though the manuscripts have vanished, of children's plays produced at the country manors during the 1700s and into the following century. The tradition of children's theatre has always been stronger in Sweden than elsewhere in Europe.

True Swedish national literature A true native literature is usually dated from 1751–53, when the tutor Count Carl Tessin wrote his "An Old Man's Letters to a Young Prince" (Gustav III), in which instruction was tempered by the first fairy tales written for Swedish children. The German influence, however, persisted until about the middle of the 19th century, when Fredrika Bremer, traveller and feminist, tried to stimulate the work of indigenous children's writers. The dominant influence of the Finnish-born but basically Swedish Topelius, of Hans Christian Andersen, and of the romantic spirit in general was felt at this time. Later in the century two followers of Andersen—Helena Nyblom and Anna Wahlenberg—enriched the tradition of the fairy tale. The former's *Sagokrans* (1903; Eng. trans. *The Witch of the Woods*, 1968), preserves a rare charm.

The great landmark, however, is Miss Lagerlöf's world classic *Nils Holgerssons underbara resa genom Sverige*, 2 vol. (1906–07; Eng. trans. *The Wonderful Adventures of Nils*, 1907; *Further Adventures of Nils*, 1911). Written (at the request of the state ministry of education) as a school geography, it is the rare example of an officially commissioned book that turned out to be a work of art. *Nils*, for all its burden of instruction, is a fantasy. At the same time, a realistic breakthrough was achieved by Laura Fitinghoff, whose historical novel about the famine of the 1860s, *Barnen från Frostmofjället* (1907; Eng. trans. *Children of the Moor*, 1927), ranks as a classic.

According to the historian Eva von Zweigbergk, didacticism ("diligence, obedience, and moderation") obtained up to the 1920s, though she also views the period 1890–1915 as Sweden's Golden Age. It included not only *Nils* but the emergence of a school of creators of picture books for small children headed by Elsa Beskow, whose work in pictures and text, extending over the years from 1897 to 1952, was decisive in its influence. This premodern period also saw many good writers for grown-ups devoting their talents to juvenile fiction. The sailing story *Mälarpirater* (1911; "The Pirates of Lake Mälaren"), by the novelist Sigfrid Siwertz, is a still-remembered example.

The period from 1940 on has called forth a bewildering array of talented writers and artist-writers. In the field of humour and nonsense there are Åke Holmberg, with his parodic Ture Sventon detective series; the outstanding poet Lennart Hellsing, with *Daniel Doppsko* (1959); Astrid Lindgren, successful in a half dozen genres but perhaps best known as the creator of the supergirl Pippi Longstocking; Gösta Knutsson, with her well-liked *Pelle svanslös* (1939; Eng. trans. *The Adventures of the Cat Who Had No Tail*). The psychological realistic novel, delving deeply into the inner lives of children, has been developed by Maria Gripe, whose *Hugo and Josephine* trilogy may become classic; Gunnel Linde's *Tacka vet jag Skorstensgränd* (1959; Eng. trans. *Chimney-Top Lane*, 1965); and Anna Lisa Warnlöf, writing under the pseudonym of "Claque," whose two series about Pella and Fredrika show an intuitive understanding of lonely and misunderstood children.

Harry Kullman and Martha Sandwall-Bergström are among the few Swedish writers who have used working class industrial backgrounds successfully. Kullman is also a historical novelist. The prolific Edith Unnerstad has written charming family stories, with a touch of fantasy, as has Karin Anckarsvärd, whose *Doktorns pojk'* (1963; Eng. trans. *Doctor's Boy*, 1965) is a quietly moving tale of small-town life in the horse-and-buggy days. The Sandbergs, Inger and Lasse, have advanced the Beskow tradition in a series of lovely picture books. Fantasy has been well served by Lindgren, Edith Unnerstad, Holmberg, Hellsing, and others. Children's poetry is a lively contemporary art, one distinguished poet being Britt G. Hallqvist.

By most criteria of development the Swedes rank high among those creating a children's literature that is both broad and deep.

Norway. Norway cannot boast a genius of worldwide fame. But, beginning with the 1830s when a new literary language, based on spoken Norwegian, was forged, Norway has possessed an identifiable children's literature. From 1837 to 1844 Asbjørnsen and Moe, the Grimms of Norway, published their remarkable collection of folk stories, and thus created not only a literary base on which the future could build but a needed sense of national identity. Moe also wrote specifically for children. His poems are part of Norwegian childhood, and his nature fantasy *I brønden og i tjernet* ("In the Well and the Lake," 1851) made Viggo and his little sister Beate familiar for more than a century. Equally enduring are the fairy tales and children's verse of Norway's greatest poet Henrik Wergeland.

Golden Age of Norwegian literature

The Norwegian critic Jo Tenfjord believes that the 30 years from 1890 to 1920 represented a golden age. With this period are associated Dikken Zwilgmeyer, author of the "Inger Johanne" series about a small-town little girl; Barbra Ring, creator of the popular "Peik" stories and of a play *The Princess and the Fiddler*, which was produced yearly at the National Theatre in Oslo; Gabriel Scott; and the fairy-tale writer Johan Falkberget.

Among the more prominent and well-loved moderns are Halvor Floden, whose most famous work, centred on a gypsy waif, is *Gjenta fra lands vegen* ("The Girl from the Road"); the nonsense versifier Zinken Hopp; the poet Jan-Magnus Bruheim, three of whose collections have won state prizes; Finn Havrevold, whose tough-minded boys' teen-age novel *Han Var Min Ven* became available in English translation as *Undertow* in 1968, and who also wrote successfully for girls; Leif Hamre, specializing in air force adventures; the prolific, widely translated Aimée Sommerfelt, whose works range from "puberty novels" to faraway stories set in Mexico City and northern India; Thorbjørn Egner, who is the author of, among other books, a tiny droll fantasy, *Karius and Baktus* (1958; Eng. trans. 1962), which will actually persuade small children to brush their teeth; and Alf Prøysen, creator of Mrs. Pepperpot, a delightful little old lady who never knows when she is going to shrink to pepperpot size. Fantasy of this kind seems less characteristic of contemporary Norway than does the realistic novel, especially that designed for older children.

Denmark. Without Hans Christian Andersen, Danish children's literature might have fared better. It is not that his countrymen deify him, as much as it is that the outside world does. Indeed, because modernized versions of his tales do not exist, his now rather antiquated Danish tends to outmode him. Yet his gigantic shadow must have intimidated his literary descendants, just as Dante and Cervantes intimidated theirs. Doubtless other forces also account for the sparseness and relative conventionality of Danish children's literature.

The earliest books were written for the children of the nobility. Not till the passage of the Education Act of 1814 did the poorer ones have access to any suitable reading matter, and this, obedient to the prevailing European fashion, was dour in tone. The climate, of course, relaxed when Andersen appeared with his phenomenal series, still the finest of their kind, of invented or reworked fantastic tales. In 1884 H.V. Kaalund published a picture book of "Fables for Children" based on the popular verse narratives (1833) of a Thüringian pastor, Wilhelm Hey. Three years later an unidentified Danish humorist added three cautionary tales to a translation of six *Struwwelpeter* stories. Though it does not seem to have appeared as a picture book until 1900, Christian Winther in 1830 wrote a pleasing trifle, with an unusual fantastic touch, called "Flugten til Amerika" ("Flight to America"). It is still ranked as a classic. Such are some of the 19th-century oases.

Denmark's general tendency has been to over-rely on translations or adaptations, drawn especially from its neighbour Germany. As against this, it can point to an excellent original tradition of nursery and nonsense rhymes. The first such collection, made as early as 1843, stimulated not only Andersen but such other 19th-century figures as Johan Krohn, whose "Peter's Christmas" remains a standard seasonal delight. The tradition is relayed to the 20th century by Halfdan Rasmussen, whose collected *Bjørnerim* ("Verse for Children") won the 1964 Danish Children's Book Prize, and Ib Spang Olsen, with his nonsense picture book *The Boy in the Moon* (1962). As for the complementary prose tradition of fireside tales, Denmark had to wait (Andersen was artist, not scholar) for its Grimm until 1884, when a collection made by Svend Grundtvig, son of N.F.S. Grundtvig, a great bishop-educator, was posthumously published.

Early nursery and nonsense rhymes

As compared with other Scandinavian countries, post-World War II developments lagged. Picture books exhibited much more originality than did teen-age literature. Jytte Lyngbirk's girls' novels, notably the love story "Two Days in November," however, are well reputed, as are the realistic fictions, laid against an industrial background, of Tove Ditlevsen. Perhaps Denmark's boldest original talent is Anne Holm, who aroused healthy controversy with her (to some) shocking narrative of a displaced boy's journey to Denmark, the novel *David* (1963; Eng. trans. *North to Freedom*, 1965).

Some informed observers ascribe Denmark's only moderate performance to domination by the teaching profession, to the lingering influence of conventional didacticism, and to the lack of the economic-social forces that stimulate professional writers. As late as 1966 the Minister of Culture commented on the scarcity of Danish juvenile authors, and this at a time when the rest of Scandinavia was, as it remained, in the full flood of the modern movement.

Finland. Although its language and people are not of European origin, Finland is loosely conceived as part of the Scandinavian bloc. Only since December 6, 1917, has it been formally independent. During much of its history Swedish was the language of the educated class. Thus its two outstanding premodern children's writers, the father figure Zacharias Topelius and Anni Swan, wrote their fairy tales and folktales primarily for a Swedish-reading audience. Their works however were promptly translated into Finnish and became part of the native heritage. The same is true of the contemporary Tove Jansson, 1966 Andersen Medal winner, whose series of novels about the fantastic self-contained world of Moomintrolls, though less successful with English-reading children, enchants young readers throughout northern and central Europe.

The labours of Topelius in the children's field and of Elias Lönnrot (compiler of the great Finnish epic-miscellany the *Kalevala*, 1835) in the field of national folklore constituted the soil from which Finnish children's literature was eventually to derive nutriment. But that literature emerged as an identifiable whole only after World War I. It is largely folktale rooted. Indeed this small country became an international focus of folklore research. One student has said that it probably possesses the largest number of folktales in existence, some 30,000 of them. In the early 1960s a fairy tale competition yielded 795 manuscripts, a phenomenal statistic in view of Finland's sparse population.

Finland, despite the fact that its language tends to limit its audience, is part of the main current of children's literature, even though only Jansson has won anything like an international reputation. Two children's poets, Aila Meriluoto and Kirsi Kunnas, have achieved renown.

FRANCE

Overview. The French themselves are not happy with their record. Writing in the late 1940s, critic Jean de Trigon, in *Histoire de la littérature enfantine, de ma Mère l'Oye au Roi Babar* (Paris, Librairie Hachette, 1950) said: "The French have created little children's literature. They have received more than they have given, but they have assimilated, adapted, transformed. The two are not the same thing, for one must love childhood in general if one is to please children other than one's own." In 1923 Marie-Thérèse Latzarus tolled the passing bell in *La littérature enfantine en France dans la seconde moitié du XIXᵉ siècle* (Paris; Les Presses Universitaires de France): "Children's literature, more's the pity, is dying." And in 1937, in their introduction to *Beaux livres belles histoires*, the compilers Marguerite Gruny and Mathilde Leriche wrote: "Children's literature in France is still poor, despite the earnest efforts of the last decade."

Surely Trigon was too severe. Even more surely Mlle Latzarus has proved a false Cassandra. As for the compilers, the very decade they scorned saw at least three magnificent achievements. The first was Jean de Brunhoff's. Equally talented as author and artist, in 1931 he gave the world that enlightened monarch Babar the Elephant, one of the dozen or so immortal characters in children's literature. The next year saw the start of Paul Faucher's admirable Père Castor series, imaginatively conceived, beautifully designed educational picture books for the very young—not literature, perhaps, but historically comparable to Comenius. Finally, in 1934 appeared the first of Marcel Aymé's miraculous stories about two little girls and the talking animals whose adventures they shared. These grave-comic fantasies were later collected as *Les Contes du chat perché* (1939; Eng. trans. *The Wonderful Farm*, 1951; *Return to the Wonderful Farm*, 1954), and, along with de Brunhoff and Faucher, were enough to make the decade great.

But there are no other decades to match it. There does exist a disproportion between French literary genius as a whole and the children's literature it has been able to produce. The explanation is uncertain. Mme Le Prince de Beaumont, an adventurous 18th-century lady who wrote over 70 volumes for the young, thought that children's stories should be pervaded by "the spirit of geometry." It is possible that the blame for France's showing might in part be laid on a persistent Cartesian spirit, reinforced by rationalist and positivist philosophies. The Cartesian does not readily surrender to fancy, especially of the more wayward variety. And so, even counting Charles Perrault, the later Charles Nodier, and the contemporary Simone Ratel and Maurice Vauthier, a dearth of first-rate fairy tales may be noted. Cartesians would tend to be weak also in children's verse, in nonsense of any sort, in humour (despite Babar), even in the more imaginative kind of historical novel exemplified by Hans Baumann in Germany and Rosemary Sutcliff in England. Perhaps French children's literature has been restrained by a Catholicism or by a Protestantism that continued to insist on the edifying when mainstream literature had already freed itself from explicit moralism. It may not even be true, as Trigon thinks, that the French have fruitfully assimilated the children's literature of foreign countries. *Alice* has more or less bewildered them; *Huckleberry*

Finn has never been digested. The child's cause was not much aided by the triumph of a post-Napoleonic bourgeois cast of thought—or by the wave of post-1871 nationalism.

It is a complicated problem. But perhaps the heart of it lies in the value the French set on maturity. For them childhood at times has seemed less a normal human condition than a handicap. The children themselves have often seemed to feel the pressure, which may account for the fact that they absorb French adult books precociously. The French came much later than did many other countries to the discovery of the child as a figure worthy of the most sensitive understanding; that is what makes Père Castor so important. One is not surprised to note the comparatively recent date (1931) of a study by Aimé Dupuy, translatable as *The Child: A New Character in the French Novel*.

Historical sketch. If one skips Jean de La Fontaine, whose *Fables* (1668; 1678–79; and 1693), though read by the young, were not meant for them, French children's literature from one point of view begins with the classic fairy tales of Charles Perrault. These were probably intended for the salon rather than the nursery, but their narrative speed and lucidity commended them at once to children. The fairy tales of his contemporary Mme d'Aulnoy, like many others produced in the late 17th and early 18th centuries, are hardly the real thing. With a Watteau-like charm, they taste of the court, as does the *Télémaque* of François Fénelon, a fictionalized lecture on education.

Rousseau, as has been noted, did make a difference. *Émile* at least drew attention to what education might be. But the effect on children's literature was not truly liberating. His disciple, Mme de Genlis, set a stern face against make-believe of any sort; all marvels must be explained rationally. Her stories taught children more than they wanted to know, a circumstance that endeared her to a certain type of parent. Sainte-Beuve, to be fair, called her "the most gracious and gallant of pedagogues." One of her qualities, priggishness, was energetically developed by Arnaud Berquin in his *Ami des enfants*. Berquin created the French equivalent of the concurrent English bourgeois morality. In effect, he unconsciously manufactured an adult literature for the young, loading the dice in favour of the values held by parents to be proper for children. Yet one must beware of judging Berquin or his equally moralistic successor Jean-Nicolas Bouilly by today's standards. Children accepted them because they were the best reading available; and Anatole France's tribute in *Le Petit Pierre* (1918) shows that they must have exerted some charm.

The didactic strain, if less marked than in England or Germany, persisted throughout most of the 19th century. To it, Mme de Ségur, in her enormously popular novels, added sentimentality, class snobbery, but also some liveliness and occasional fidelity to child nature. Her "Sophie" series (1850s and 60s), frowned on by modern critics, is still loved by obstinate little French girls. *Sans Famille* (1878), by Hector Malot, a minor classic of the "unhappy child" school, also continues to be read and is indeed a well-told story. But the century's real writer of genius is of course Jules Verne, whose first book, *Un Voyage en ballon*, was originally published in 1851 in a children's magazine, *Le Musée des Familles*.

The period was lively enough. Production was vast. Children's magazines flourished, particularly the remarkable *Magasin d'Éducation et de Récréation*, brilliantly edited by Jules Hetzel. Writers of the stature of George Sand, Alphonse Daudet, and Alexandre Dumas *père* were not too proud to write for children. Much worthy, though transient, work was produced along with a mass of mediocrity, as was the case also in England and the United States. But on the whole, as the century drew to a close, French children might have been better served, even though one critic sees the apogee as occurring between 1860 and 1900.

From the turn of the century to the close of World War II, a number of superior works were produced. The books of de Brunhoff and Faucher have already been

---

[margin left:] Criticism of French children's literature

[margin right:] Perrault's fairy tales

Early
20th-
century
French
literature

cited. A remarkable picture of prehistoric life by J.-H. Rosny (pseudonym of J.-H.-H. Boex) appeared in 1911 and has proved so durable that in 1967 an English translation, *The Quest for Fire*, appeared. *Patapoufs et filifers*, by André Maurois, a gentle satire on war, has lasted (Eng. trans. *Pattypuffs and Thinifers*, 1948; reissued 1968). His fantastic *Le Pays des 36,000 volontés* is almost as popular. The famous dramatist Charles Vildrac has done much to advance the cause of French children's literature. Two pleasant stories of his, remotely decended from *Robinson Crusoe, L'Isle rose* and its sequel *La Colonie*, appeared in the 1920s and 1930s. In 1951 his now-classic comic animal tale *Les Lunettes du lion* won immediate success (Eng. trans. *The Lion's Eyeglasses*, 1969). On a high literary level, not accessible to all children, was *Le Petit Prince* (1943, both French and English, *The Little Prince*) by the famous aviator-author Antoine de Saint-Exupéry. The very vagueness of this mystical parable has lent it a certain magnetism. Finally, it is necessary to mention a field in which the French proved incomparable: the comic strip combining action and satire, conceived on a plane of considerable sophistication. Hergé's *Tintin* started in the 1930s and sold over 25,000,000 copies. Also successful was the later and even more unconventional *Astérix* series.

Production after 1945 so multiplied that to single out names is bound to involve some injustice. A few, however, by reason either of the originality of their talent or the scope of their achievement, stand out. One is Maurice Druon, whose *Tistou of the Green Fingers* (1957; Eng. trans. 1958), a kind of children's *Candide*, demonstrated how the moral tale, given sufficient sensitivity and humour, can be transmuted into art. Perhaps the most original temperament was that of Henri Bosco, author of four eerie, haunting Provençal novels about the boy Pascalet and his strange involvements with a gypsy companion, a fox, and a dog in a shifting, legend-shrouded natural world. It may be that time will rate these books, like those of the English writer Walter de la Mare, among the finest of their kind. Bosco's *L'Enfant et la rivière* (1955; Eng. trans. *The Boy and the River*, 1956), *Le Renard dans l'île* (1956; Eng. trans. *The Fox in the Island*, 1958), and *Barboche* (1957; Eng. trans. 1959) are notable.

Sound, realistic novels, almost free of excess moralism, were written by at least a dozen reputable authors. Among them Colette Vivier (*The House of the Four Winds*), Paul-Jacques Bonzon (*The Orphans of Simitra*), and Étienne Cattin (*Night Express!*) were distinguished. The domain of the imaginative tale was well represented by Maurice Vauthier, especially by his *Ecoute, petit loup*. Among those noted for their prolific output as well as the high level of their art two names emerged. One is Paul Berna, who has worked in half a dozen genres, including detective stories and science fiction. His *Cheval sans tête* (1955) was published in England as *A Hundred Million Francs*, and in the United States as *The Horse Without a Head*, and was made into a successful Disney film. A "gang" story, using a hard, unemotional tone that recalls Simenon, it may be the best of its kind since *Emil and the Detectives*.

The death of René Guillot removed a deeply conscientious and responsible artist. Guillot, though probably not of the first rank, was not far below it. He left over 50 widely translated novels for the young and about ten nonfiction works. For his entire body of work he received in 1964 the Andersen Prize. His finest achievements in the adventure novel, based on his experiences in Africa, include *The White Shadow* (1948) and *Riders of the Wind* (1953).

Children's verse has at least one delightful practitioner in Pierre Gamarra. His *Mandarine et le Mandarin* comprise Fontainesque fables of notable drollery and high technical skill. Maurice Carême aso has some repute as a children's poet. In summary, contemporary French activity seems a bit lacking in colour and versatility. But one solid achievement must be registered: the 19th century's legacy was decisively rejected and at last a natural child prevailed in the imaginative work of the best French contemporaries.

RUSSIA/SOVIET UNION

Pre-Revolutionary Russian literature

Here history breaks cleanly into two periods: pre-1917 and post-1917. In pre-Revolutionary Russia may be observed a most dramatic illustration of the disproportion that may exist between a children's and a mainstream literature. Beyond question the latter is one of the greatest of the modern world. But Russia's pre-1917 children's literature is anemic. It does include the fables of Ivan Krylov; a great treasury of Russian folktales (*skazki*) assembled by A.N. Afanasyev; the epic tales (*byliny*) sung or told to children; the classic by Pyotr Yrshov, *Konyok gorbunok* (1834; Eng. adaption by Ireene Wicker, *The Little Hunchback Horse*, 1942); and other stories and poems enjoyed by small Russians but not originally designed for them. To this folk material should be added the McGuffeyish moral tales that Tolstoy wrote for his four graded readers. There is also the poet-translator Vasily Zhukovsky, praised by the respected critic Vissarion Belinsky as one of the few poets of the century, part of whose work was dedicated to children.

On the whole, however, pre-Revolutionary Russia could make only a few feeble gestures toward the creation of an independent children's literature. The submerged peasantry relied on the fireside tale teller. The middle class, while far stronger than is generally recognized, was in no position to stimulate or support a literature for its children. The privileged class looked to the West: the children read Mme de Genlis. Thus it came about that the child was recognized later in Russia than in other parts of western Europe. The critic and children's writer Korney Chukovsky speaks of the "indifference" with which "early childhood was regarded in the past." He then points out that attitudes have changed, so that now the child is "an adored hero."

The Revolution was the watershed. After 1917 Soviet children's literature developed more or less in accord with the necessities of the state. This is not to say that it became identical with Soviet propaganda. Indeed one of the finest teen-age novels, Vadim Frolov's *Chto k chemu* (Eng. trans. *What It's All About*, 1965), is quite untouched by dogma of any kind. Soviet children's literature, and especially its vast body of popularized science and technology for the young, however, was in general governed by the ideals of "socialist realism," the idolization of the "new Soviet man" (as in the widely read works of Boris Zhitkov and Arkady Gaydar), the exaltation of the machine over the irresponsible furniture of fairyland, and especially a revised version of the pre-18th-century miniature adult view of the child: he now becomes a potential Soviet citizen and architect of the Communist future.

Juvenile fiction and biography have naturally tended to cue themselves into the crucial episodes of Soviet history. But the theory underlying this basically nationalist literature (suggesting similar developments in Italy and England in the latter half of the 19th century) is by no means clear-cut. The most influential thinker was Maksim Gorky, who during the 1920s called for "creative fantasy," for children's stories "which make out of the human being, instead of a willess creature or an indifferent workman, a free and active artist, creator of a new culture." He asked for books that would encourage the child to become "a knight of the spirit." Gorky's essays are a curious, endearing mixture of Marxist doctrine (with a utopian slant) and quite standard Western humanistic ideas. It is in Kornei Chukovsky's remarkable book *Malenkiye deti ot duukh do pyati* (1925; Eng. trans. *From Two to Five*, 1963), however, that the opposition of two familiar forces, entertainment and instruction, can be sensed most clearly. The tension is typically expressed in Chukovsky's account of the Soviet war over the fairy tale, the opposition to which reached its high point in the 1920s and 1930s. "We propose," wrote one journalist in a Moscow magazine in 1924, "to replace the unrealistic folktales and fantasies with simple realistic stories taken from the world of reality and from nature." Chukovsky, himself a writer full of humour and invention, opposed this view, as had Gorky before him. The struggle still continues, in Soviet Russia as elsewhere.

Gorky's contributions

Though rich in folklore drawn from its many peoples and languages, the Soviet Union remains weak in the realm of fantasy. A fairy play such as Marshak's *Krugly god* (Eng. trans. *The Month Brothers*, 1967) seems (at least in English) fatally heavy handed, and there is no encouragement in another of his imaginative efforts, *Seven Wonders*. Nor has Soviet Russia so far given to the world a children's classic of universal appeal to match the dozens of great Russian works of literature that are now part of the adult world's cultural heritage. That children's literature in the Soviet Union is vigorous, varied, and motivated by a genuine concern for the child is undoubted. But it is hard to imagine a Soviet "Narnia" series, a Soviet *Borrowers*.

It is not difficult to see that contemporary children's literature in Russia is lively, copious, and probably enjoyed. It is much more difficult for those who have no Russian to judge its value. Occasionally in translation one will come across something as superb as the beautiful nature and animal tales in *Arcturus the Hunting Hound and Other Stories* (1968), by Yury Kazakov. But one can only record, without judging, the vast production of such popular children's writers as Samuil Marshak, Sergey Mikhalkov, Lev Kassil, and N. Nosov. Especially notable is the popularity of poetry, whether it be the work of such past generation writers as Vladimir Mayakovsky or that of the contemporary Agniya Barto. Apparently Russian children read poetry with more passion and understanding than do English-speaking children. The mind of the Soviet child is carefully looked after. He is provided with books, often beautifully illustrated, at prices the West cannot match. "Demand from them as much as possible, respect them as much as possible," says Anton Makarenko, the theorist of children's literature.

BIBLIOGRAPHY

Historical, critical: (*Europe*): BETTINA HURLIMANN, *Europäische Kinderbücher in drei Jahrhunderten*, 2nd ed. (1963; Eng. trans., *Three Centuries of Children's Books in Europe*, 1968). (*England*): GILLIAN AVERY, *Nineteenth Century Children: Heroes and Heroines in English Children's Stories 1780–1900* (1965); FLORENCE V. BARRY, *A Century of Children's Books* (1922, reprinted 1968); MARCUS CROUCH, *Treasure Seekers and Borrowers: Children's Books in Britain 1900–1960* (1962); F.J. HARVEY DARTON, *Children's Books in England: Five Centuries of Social Life* (1932); ROGER LANCELYN GREEN, *Tellers of Tales: British Authors of Children's Books from 1800 to 1964*, rev. ed. (1965); PERCY MUIR, *English Children's Books, 1600 to 1900* (1954); M.F. THWAITE, *From Primer to Pleasure: An Introduction to the History of Children's Books in England, from the Invention of Printing to 1900* (1963); JOHN ROWE TOWNSEND, *Written for Children: An Outline of English Children's Literature* (1965). (*Canada*): SHEILA EGOFF, *The Republic of Childhood: A Critical Guide to Canadian Children's Literature in English* (1967). (*Anglo-American mainly*): CORNELIA MEIGS et al., *A Critical History of Children's Literature: A Survey of Children's Books in English from Earliest Times to the Present*, rev. ed. (1969). (*Germany*): IRENE DYHRENFURTH-GRAEBSCH, *Geschichte des deutschen Jugendbuches*, 3rd rev. ed. (1967); H.L. KOSTER, *Geschichte der deutschen Jugendliteratur* (1968). (*Sweden*): EVA VON ZWEIGBERGK, *Barnboken I Sverige 1750–1950* (1965). (*France*): MARIE-THERESE LATZARUS, *La Littérature enfantine en France dans la seconde moitié du XIXᵉ siècle* (1923); JEAN DE TRIGON, *Histoire de la littérature enfantine de ma Mère l'Oye au Roi Babar* (1950). (*Italy*): PIERO BARGELLINI, *Canto alle rondini: Panorama storico della letteratura infantile*, 6th ed. (1967); GIUSEPPE FANCIULLI, *Scrittori per l'infanzia*, 3rd ed. (1968); LOUISE RESTIEAUX HAWKES, *Before and After Pinocchio: A Study of Italian Children's Books* (1933). (*Spain*): CARMEN BRAVO VILLASANTE (ed.), *Historia de la literatura infantil española* (1963). (*Latin America*): CARMEN BRAVO VILLASANTE, *Historia y antología de la literatura infantil iberoamericana*, 2 vol. (1966); DORA PASTORIZA DE ETCHEBARNE, *El cuento en la literatura infantil, ensayo crítico* (1962).

General: RICHARD BAMBERGER, *Jugendlektüre*, 2nd ed. (1965); ELEANOR CAMERON, *The Green and Burning Tree: On the Writing and Enjoyment of Children's Books* (1969); KORNEI CHUKOVSKY, *From Two to Five*, rev. ed. (1968; Eng. trans. of the 20th Russian ed. of 1968); HANS CORNIOLEY, *Beiträge zur Jugendbuchkunde* (1966); MARGERY FISHER, *Intent upon Reading: A Critical Appraisal of Modern Fiction for Children* (1961); PAUL HAZARD, *Les Livres, les enfants et*

les hommes (1932; Eng. trans., *Books, Children and Men*, 4th ed., 1960); ENZO PETRINI, *Avviamento critico alla letteratura giovanile* (1958); LILLIAN H. SMITH, *The Unreluctant Years: A Critical Approach to Children's Literature* (1953); DOROTHY M. WHITE, *Books Before Five* (1954).

Bibliographical: VIRGINIA HAVILAND, *Children's Literature: A Guide to Reference Sources* (1966); ANNE PELLOWSKI, *The World of Children's Literature* (1968).

Biographical: BRIAN BOYLE (ed.), *The Who's Who of Children's Literature* (1968); MURIEL FULLER (ed.), *More Junior Authors* (1963); STANLEY J. KUNITZ and HOWARD HAYCRAFT (eds.), *The Junior Book of Authors*, 2nd ed. rev. (1951).

Illustration: BETTINA HURLIMANN, *Die Welt im Bilderbuch* (1965; Eng. trans., *Picture-Book World*, 1968); LEE KINGMAN, JOANNA FOSTER, and RUTH GILES LONTOFT (comps.), *Illustrators of Children's Books: 1957–1966* (1968); DIANA KLEMIN, *The Art of Art for Children's Books: A Contemporary Survey* (1966); BERTHA E. MAHONY et al. (comps.), *Illustrators of Children's Books 1744–1945* (1947); BERTHA MAHONY MILLER et al. (comps.), *Illustrators of Children's Books, 1946–1956* (1958).

(C.Fa.)

Children's Sports and Games

Since children learn chiefly by imitating, it is natural that in their basic play they should emulate the actions of their elders and the supposed deeds of national or mythical figures of whom they have heard tell. Thus children pretend to be mothers and fathers, hospital nurses, soldiers, policemen, robbers, presidents, pop stars, witches, and fairies. Boys play with toy weapons, automobiles, hobbyhorses, and building bricks. Girls play with dolls, mimicking the actions of their mothers; they dress up, pretending to be princesses or beauty queens; they enact special events, as christenings, weddings, funerals.

Although make-believe weapons and dolls are universal and have a considerable history (Greek girls in the 5th century BC had jointed dolls similar to those of today), the precise form of children's imitative play varies according to the life and conditions of the country in which they live. As the English anthropologist Edward B. Tylor pointed out in his *Primitive Culture* (1871; new ed. 1958):

> The Esquimaux children's sports are shooting with a tiny bow and arrow at a mark, and building little snow-huts, which they light up with scraps of lamp-wick begged from their mothers. Miniature boomerangs and spears are among the toys of Australian children; and even as the fathers keep up as a recognised means of getting themselves wives the practice of carrying them off by violence, so playing at such Sabine marriage has been noticed as one of the regular games of the little native boys and girls.

Distinction needs to be made, however, between pure play and the playing of games. When children are simply playing, whether on their own or with others, they divert themselves according to the inclination of the moment. But players in a game must submit to predetermined rules; for a game ordinarily involves some form of contest, whether of skill, strength, or chance, or a combination of these elements. Thus children pretending to be cowboys, prancing about as if on steeds, may simply be playing; but children taking part in Cowboys and Indians will engage in combat and will, for the sake of fairness, observe certain rules or prohibitions, no matter how rudimentary and unformulated. Similarly, children shutting their eyes and making believe they are blind will merely think it amusing when they bump into each other. But when one child is blindfolded in the game of Blind Man's Buff and catches another player, that player may be obliged by the rules to take the blindman's place and will not be relieved of the bandage over his eyes until he, in his turn, has caught someone else. The children are now taking part in a recognized game and are, in fact, letting themselves be governed by a set of rules that are not dissimilar if the game is played in the United States or the U.S.S.R., or in countries as various as Chile, China, Japan, Papua, India, and Ethiopia. Further, they are playing a game that was a favourite in the Middle Ages and that was described by Julius Pollux in the 2nd century AD.

Distinction between play and games

"Children's Games," an oil painting by Pieter Bruegel, 1559, depicts 78 forms of juvenile recreation, many extant, of which 30 are identified in the diagram at left.
By courtesy of (top) the Kunsthistorisches Museum, Vienna

1. Knucklebones, or jacks
2. Playing with dolls
3. Make-believe christening
4. Carry my lady to London
5. Hobbyhorse
6. Making mud pies
7. Bowling hoops
8. Blowing up a pig's bladder balloon
9. Buck, buck
10. Playing store

11. Mumblety-peg
12. Building with bricks
13. Bounce the baby
14. Leapfrog
15. Tug-of-war
16. Odds or evens
17. Running the gauntlet
18. Blind man's buff
19. King of the mountain
20. Tilting

21. Riding a fence
22. Wedding procession
23. Walking on stilts
24. Tipcat
25. Marbles
26. Wrestling
27. Crack-the-whip
28. Piggyback
29. Whipping tops
30. Fraü Rose

Factors
affecting
play

The balance of this article examines the history of children's sports and games and discusses the four major categories of games children play: adult-sponsored games; child-transmitted games; party or family games; and manufactured games.

History. Although it may be presumed, from such evidence as exists, that the games children played in ancient Egypt and classical antiquity were similar to those children play today, the evidence is indicative rather than concrete; and it should not be thought that the games most popular with children today were necessarily those most played in the past or are likely to be the oldest. It is observable that when a sport or game grows in popularity it tends to become increasingly formal and time-consuming, until eventually it ceases to be a pleasure. In the Middle Ages the game of Base or Bars, a catching or capturing game in which individual members of two teams chase and are chased by individuals of the opposing team, seems to have been one of the most popular of communal games among young people in western Europe. Today, Prison Base is little played other than as an adult-sponsored game in schools. Similarly, the game in which members of opposing sides invade each other's territory and attempt to run off with flags or possessions (a game having warlike names: Capture the Flag in the United States, French and English in Britain, and Guerra francese in Italy) is no longer the prominent game it was in the 19th century; while the chasing game Barley-break, one of the most popular of games in Shakespeare's day, has disappeared so completely that it is now uncertain even how it was played.

Another factor affecting children's play is the change that takes place over the years in the social climate. Just as in most countries bearbaiting and cockfighting are no longer esteemed by adults, so the juvenile pursuits of throwing at cocks (particularly at Shrovetide, just before Lent), of tying cans to cats' tails, of attaching birds or insects to the ends of threads and making them fly, and of crushing snails together to try which shell is the strongest have largely become sports of the past. Indeed it is noticeable that games of fortitude, in which players regularly hit each other about the head or kick each other on the shins as part of the game are generally losing their appeal in more civilized or comfort-loving communities.

On the other hand, changes in physical environment have not been found to have the deep effect on children's play that might be expected. Certainly the speed and density of modern traffic makes street play dangerous, and top spinning and games of tipcat, in which one player with a bat struck a tapered wooden peg (the cat) and as it flew up batted it as far as possible while the other players tried to retrieve it, are not now seen in the centres of great cities as they were in the 19th century. But some streets have always been dangerous for children to play in, even in the days of horsedrawn traffic; and when a once-quiet street becomes crowded, children have a way of moving on to less frequented streets or to vacant lots or wasteland. Up to a point, children are quick to adapt (if they cannot play Wood-Tag because there is no wood, they play Touch-Colour; if they have not a wooden wicket, an empty can serves just as well), and provided a city possesses unused plots and open spaces children are usually well able to entertain themselves. Difficulty arises, however, when a city is so highly developed for industrial or residential purposes that little vacant land remains for spontaneous recreation. The provision of swimming pools, ice rinks, and sports fields are useful principally for participation in adult-sponsored sports (see below). In consequence the idea of creating "junk" or "adventure" playgrounds, originating in Scandinavia, has been adopted in many European and American cities. In populous districts, sites are fenced off, to which children alone have entry. The sites are left rough and are supplied with waste timber and other junk so that children may light fires, build huts, and erect structures to clamber upon. Such play places require the attendance of professional wardens or youth leaders, and, satisfactory as they are to

many children, these confined reserves are, of course, only substitutes for the child's natural play places and are not in themselves an ideal recreational facility.

During the past four centuries the repertoire of children's games has been affected most of all by the technological innovations that have made new sports and pastimes possible. Whereas hoops were known to the ancient Greeks, as also to the Romans, who used to fix bells on them, kites appear to have been unknown to the Western world until introduced from China, and flying them did not become a common juvenile pastime until the beginning of the 17th century. Swings were known to the Minoans on the island of Crete about 1600 BC and appear to be popular in every quarter of the globe; but rope skipping, despite some statements to the contrary, does not appear to have become general until the 16th or early 17th century. As far as the playground is concerned, the greatest technological innovation has been the introduction of rubber. Although bouncing balls of a kind, whether inflated animal-bladders or spheres stuffed with resilient material, have been known since antiquity, it was not until the production of the India-rubber ball and, more especially, of the sponge-rubber ball marketed in 1920 that the rapid and elaborate ball-bouncing games of today became possible, in some of which a single player keeps two or more balls bouncing at once.

Technological change versus longevity

Nevertheless, despite such changes, sufficient evidence is available to show that the longevity of some of the games is remarkable. The game commonly played with five jackstones (knucklebones, jacks, or small stones), which are tossed up and caught on the palm or the back of the hand, is known to have been played in ancient Greece. It is clearly depicted, for instance, on a vase of 400 BC and also on a wall painting from Pompeii, now in the National Museum at Naples, as well as being described by Pollux. The game in which two sides face each other, neither side knowing which is to chase the other until a coin, disk, or shell has been tossed or a particular word uttered, was referred to by Plato and was so well known in Italy in the 2nd century that it became proverbial to say that fortune might change "at the turn of a shell." This game continues to be played in Italy, as also in the rest of Europe and in America. The game in which a player is hit from behind by each of the other players until he guesses correctly who last hit him (a game known in Great Britain for several centuries as "Hot Cockles" and in France as "La Main chaude") is another game described by Pollux and was probably the sport the men guarding Jesus had in mind when, after blindfolding him, they "slapped him, saying, Prophesy to us, you Christ! Who is it that struck you?" (Matt. 26: 67–8). Further, this game appears to be depicted on the wall of a tomb of the 12th dynasty (c. 2000 BC) at Beni Hassan in Middle Egypt.

Even so, assertions about the prehistoric origin of the more ceremonial games, especially those games embodying verbal formulas, should be regarded with caution. The likelihood of children's singing games in the Western world preserving words or actions of pagan ritual has, on the whole, been overemphasized. Recent research has revealed that the antiquity is doubtful even of some of the spell-like gibberish elimination rhymes that children repeat, for example:

> Eeny, meeny, macca, racca,
> Ere, ree, dominacca,
> Icaracca, omaracca,
> Om, pom, push.

It seems that the only games that can be regarded as possibly retaining vestiges of past significance are those that have survived in more than one culture with little change both in the actions of the game and in the verbal formula. Examples are the singing games "Looby-loo" and "Oats and Beans and Barley grow," which, it may be noted, are in the medieval *carole* (chain or ring dance) form, and the melodramatic games of Rich and Poor, Frau Rose, and Witch or Mother, the Cake is burning, known in Sicily as "Mamma caduta dal monte," in each of which children are taken one by one from their mother.

Adult-sponsored games. By adult-sponsored games may be understood, firstly, the infant games that a mother or nurse communicates to the child on her knee, being simple amusements usually involving face, fingers, or toes, as "Bo-peep," "Handy Dandy," and "This little pig went to market"; and, secondly, those games and sports in which adults encourage schoolchildren to participate, such as baseball, basketball, boxing, cricket, football, golf, hockey, lacrosse, tennis, and many other sports, on the premise that they give healthy exercise, build moral stamina, teach team spirit, and keep the children out of mischief. Participation in these games is not looked upon as childish, and the games speedily inculcate adult values. Indeed, success in them can bring social prestige to the player, honour to the child's school or club, and reputation to the teacher. It is ordinarily assumed that the child, whether a good player or not, will continue to play these games after reaching maturity, or at least remain interested in them. It is noticeable that the number of games and sports with official rules has increased with the extension of education; that instruction in them (now often given by professional coaches) is becoming more technical earlier in the child's life; and that the competitive element is being taken increasingly seriously, particularly in the emergent countries.

As a relief from these official games it also happens that teachers and other adults often remember a minor game they played when young and teach it to the children in their charge during recreational or physical training periods. Thus the teaching of certain memory games, team races, and partner duels (*e.g.*, wrestling using only one hand) have become almost an integral part of Boy Scout, Girl Scout and Girl Guide, youth club, Sunday school, and similar movements. At the beginning of the present century, as part of the folk song revival in many countries, children's traditional singing games were taught in schools as being natural and graceful games for girls to play. In Great Britain this was an understandable sequel to the cult for manly sports developed in the 19th century at Eton, Harrow, and others of the leading schools for boys. Books written to give children ideas for games to play were published throughout the 19th century, the best known being William Clarke's *The Boy's Own Book*, 1828, which went through more than 20 editions in Great Britain and the United States during the next 20 years and was still in print in 1880, and for girls, *The Girl's Own Book*, 1832, by the American authoress L.M. Child, which was almost equally successful. It is not evident, however, that these works had great influence on children's play, since games are more readily transmitted by oral than written instruction. The mainstream of children's play seems to have flowed almost wholly independently of the printed word.

Child-transmitted games. It will be appreciated that the rules of almost all games other than "manufactured games" (see below) were at first orally communicated, open to regional variation, and subject to local improvisation. Thus in the century before the rules of baseball were formulated by the Knickerbocker Club in 1845 and long before league games were organized, youngsters in both North America and Great Britain commonly played versions of the game under such names as Rounders, Round Ball, Feeder, Goal Ball, and One-, Two-, Three-, and Four-Old Cat, as well as Baseball (a name recorded in Maidstone, England, in 1700). Indeed, games that have no official rules are the games that children of 5–11 years tend to enjoy most, and they are the games that are the most interesting to the folklorist and the most valuable for understanding the nature of childhood.

These games are, in the daytime, chiefly played with schoolfellows in school playgrounds and, in the evening, with neighbourhood children in the vicinity of the home. The characteristics of these games are that they need no preparation, little or no equipment, no special ground, no umpires, no fixed number of players, and no set length of playing time. Most of the games are viable even though

played for only five minutes. The best known of these games, including tag, hide-and-seek, marbles, hopscotch, leapfrog, piggyback fighting, and Buck, Buck (or Johnny on the Pony), have virtually worldwide distribution. In addition, in all countries and localities where children do not engage in a round of domestic and agricultural duties when at home, they play a host of minor guessing, chasing, running, and catching games, often bearing exotic local names, as All the Birds in the Air, Bunny in the Hole, Fairy Footsteps, and Farmer, Farmer, may we cross your golden water?, which are largely unknown to the adult world and yet are as traditional as the better known games. Further, city and country children alike have a predilection for playing in the dark, both because seeking and hunting games become more exciting and because, after dark, children can engage in sports in which the focal point of the fun is the aggravation of the adult world. In fact pranks played upon pedestrians and householders sometimes take on ritual form and are manifestations of long-accepted calendrical license, of which an example is Trick or Treat at Halloween.

Examination has also shown that the manner in which children enforce their code of fair play, even when engaged in their wilder sports, and in particular the terms they use for challenging, for giving warning, and for opting out of a game, tend to remain constant from generation to generation of children, and even from century to century. In every play group, however, there is superficially a conflict between innovation and tradition. Whereas many of the games, and their rules, may be old, the doggerel rhymes employed in the games may be modern. Thus girls showing their traditional skill in the jump rope may time their jumps with a bawdy rhyme about the latest television hero. Nevertheless the impression children give of their inventiveness can be deceptive. Investigations have shown that a seemingly contemporary song, sung by youngsters in World War II:

> When the war is over Hitler will be dead,
> He hopes to go to heaven with a crown upon his head.
> But the Lord said No! You'll have to go below,
> There's only room for Churchill so cheery-cheery-oh,

was merely an echo of a song sung in the streets during the First World War, beginning:

> When the war is over and the Kaiser's dead;

and this same formula has, most recently, been reworded to celebrate the fictional demise of a well-known pop singer. Thus children may be less creative in their play than they appear to a casual observer and, indeed, less original than they themselves think they are.

Party games. Party or family games are those that take place at social gatherings, usually but not necessarily indoors. Their characteristic is not merely that knowledge of them may be transmitted as frequently from adult to child as from child to child but that adults and children can generally take part in them on equal terms. Indeed the giving of parties exclusively for children became customary only in the 19th century. Before that young people and adults attended social gatherings together, or the party was exclusively for adults. The games that were played—sometimes when the guests had tired of dancing—may today seem puerile; yet their adult origin is certain, and not so long ago they were enjoyed by prince and commoner alike. Thus Samuel Pepys in 1669 tells of the Duke of York (later James II) and the Duchess "with all the great ladies sitting upon a carpet, on the ground, there being no chairs, playing at 'I love my love with an A, because he is so and so: and I hate him with an A, because of this and that:' and some of them, but particularly the Duchess herself, and my Lady Castlemayne, were very witty." As well as intellectual games, guessing games, and quizzes, the forerunners of the games later popular on radio and television, other round games much played included memory games, in which the players had to repeat ever-lengthening nonsensical verses; games of nimbleness, such as Spinning the Trencher, in which a player must try to catch a spinning plate or platter before it stops; and amusements in which,

Values
attributed
to sports
and games

Characteristics of informal leading

for instance, a solemn countenance had to be maintained throughout the game. These games involved the paying and redeeming of forfeits, which were a high point of the evening's entertainment. Party games also include games giving rise to theatricals, such as Charades and Dumb Crambo, and games for which prizes can be awarded, as Hunt the Thimble and Musical Chairs. Further, some sports are a traditional feature of parties held to celebrate particular festivals in the year, as ducking for apples at Halloween and snatching raisins from burning brandy at Christmas.

Manufactured games. The manufacture of games specifically for the young started under the idea, propagated by John Locke and others, of "teaching through sport." Toward the end of the 17th century, primers began to appear under such alluring but inaccurate titles as *The Child's Delight* (1671); but in 1742 Mary Cooper published *The Child's New Play-Thing*, which contained at the end a folding sheet of letters, backed by alphabetical verses ("A was an Archer and shot at a Frog"), which were "to be cut into single Squares for Children to play with." The practice of teaching through play was further extended in the second half of the 18th century with the manufacture of race games played on maps, for example *A Journey Through Europe, or The Play of Geography*, which was invented and published by a schoolmaster, John Jefferys, in 1759; and in the next decade it was realized that another effective manner of teaching geography was to cut out the countries on a map and get children to fit them together. By the end of the century "dissected" maps and pictures mounted on board (*i.e.*, jigsaw puzzles) had become an accepted feature of home entertainment.

Although manufacturers have never been unmindful of the appeal that an educational game has for the gift-buying parent and have sometimes been highly successful in combining amusement with instruction, as in the card game "The Counties of England" (*c.* 1875) and in a number of spelling games, an increasing number of games during the 19th century were manufactured purely for juvenile amusement. Many of the popular commercially produced games have been part of the regular stock of toy and sports shops for several generations—for instance, the pegboard game or solo puzzle "Solitaire," which dates from the 18th century; Happy Families, played with picture cards designed by Sir John Tenniel (*c.* 1860); and the board games Snakes and Ladders (*c.* 1870), Halma (*c.* 1880), and Ludo (*c.* 1896; see also BOARD AND TILE GAMES). One of the most successful of manufactured board games has been Monopoly (1933).

BIBLIOGRAPHY. No one volume contains, or could contain, all the sports and games known to children. *Children's Games in Street and Playground* by I. and P. OPIE (1969), contains the majority of informal games, together with their histories and analogues in different countries. Supporting documentation may be found in P.G. BREWSTER, *American Nonsinging Games* (1953); B. SUTTON-SMITH, *Folkgames of Children* (1972); O. KAMPMULLER, *Oberösterreichische Kinderspiele* (1965); and MATIZIA MARONI LUMBROSO, *Giochi descritti e illustrati dai bambini* (1967). For games played in the 19th century, and in particular for singing games, see W.W. NEWELL, *Games and Songs of American Children* (1883, reprinted 1963); A.B. GOMME, *The Traditional Games of England, Scotland, and Ireland*, 2 vol. (1894–98, reprinted 1964). For children's terminology, seasonal games, and pranks, see I. and P. OPIE, *The Lore and Language of Schoolchildren* (1959). For games in the Orient see S. CULIN, *Korean Games, with Notes on the Corresponding Games of China and Japan* (1895, reprinted as *Games of the Orient*, 1958); and in antiquity, L.A.V. BECQ DE FOUQUIERES, *Les Jeux des anciens* (1869).

(P.O./I.O.)

Chile

The Republic of Chile, situated on the Pacific coast of South America, is a long narrow country, stretching about 2,700 miles (4,350 kilometres) southward from latitude 17°30′ S and averaging only about 110 miles in width. It has an area of 292,257 square miles (756,942 square kilometres) and, at the beginning of the 1980s, a population of some 11,100,000. It is bounded on the north by Peru and Bolivia, on its long eastern border by Argentina, and on the west by the Pacific Ocean. Chile also exercises sovereignty over Easter Island, the Juan Fernández Islands, and other islands, all in the South Pacific Ocean. Chile claims domain over the ocean up to 200 nautical miles from its coast and also claims a part of Antarctica (between longitude 53° and 90° W).

Chile's topography is dominated by the Andes mountains, which run north to south throughout the entire length of the country. It is a land of climatic and geographic extremes and is subject to violent storms, volcanic eruptions, and sudden earthquakes originating along major faults on the floor of the Pacific. Much of northern Chile is a desert; the central part of the country is an agreeable region in which more than 90 percent of the population live and in which the capital city—Santiago—is located. Southern Chile is an inhospitable region, cold, wet, and with a very limited economic potential. Chile has a predominantly agricultural economy but is a leading producer of copper and of nitrates. (For associated physical features, SEE ANDES MOUNTAIN RANGES; ATACAMA DESERT; and EASTER ISLAND; see also ANTARCTICA, and the city article SANTIAGO; for historical aspects, see CHILE, HISTORY OF.)

THE LANDSCAPE

Physical geography. The distinctive characteristics of Chile's surface configuration are the latitudinal division of the country into three parts (northern, central, and southern regions) and the longitudinal division of the country into the Andes mountains to the east; the intermediate depression, or longitudinal valley, in the centre; and the coastal mountain range to the west. The central lowlands, which are bisected at many points by mountain spurs or other natural barriers running east–west, disappear south of latitude 40° S. In consequence, Chile offers tremendous contrasts in the relief of its principal terrains, often within a small space.

The three main regions

The Chilean Andes. Along its entire 2,700-mile length, the high Andes mountains represent both a physical and a human dividing line. The Chilean Andean system is compact, contains sharp breaks in its slopes, and reaches dizzying heights.

As far south as latitude 33° S, the Andes frequently reach heights between 16,500 and 19,500 feet (5,000 and 6,000 metres); peaks include Llullaillaco, 22,051 feet, and Ojos del Salado, 22,572 feet. Farther south, the elevation decreases, but even in Patagonia, in the extreme south, heights of more than 6,500 feet are reached; Cerro Sarmiento has an altitude of 7,544 feet and the Cordillera Darwin an altitude of 7,997 feet. The part of the Andes situated in Chile is characterized by sedimentary and crystalline rocks and volcanic materials; its interior sections reflect action that was both glacial and periglacial (associated with the margin of a glacier). The numerous volcanoes and accumulated lava formations and ashes reflect geologic events occurring in the Tertiary Period (from 65,000,000 to 2,500,000 years ago), as well as in recent times (within the last 10,000 years). The dismemberment of the Patagonian Andes and marks of glaciation on the mountains provide evidences of glacial erosion.

Rivers follow steep courses down the mountains and erode the humid western slopes. As a result, deep valleys are common; they are sometimes terraced and have plains that facilitate penetration of the Andean mass.

The Chilean Andes may be divided into three sections. From the north to latitude 27° S are the wide Andes plateaus, which are prolongations of the Bolivian plateaus in the northeast.

Zones of the Chilean Andes

Between 27° S and 42° S rise the central Andes, which are narrower than those in the north and which include the most populated area of Chile; there, the mountains include a large extension of rock sedimentation from the Mesozoic Era (from 225,000,000 to 65,000,000 years ago) and the Tertiary Period. It is thus easy to distinguish between the high crystalline (granitic) and volcanic core and external formations, which are affected by volcanic deposits. The Andean mountain passes most frequently used (Aconcagua, Pehuenche, Lonquimay, Puyehue) are also found in this section.

Teaching through play (margin note)

In the southern Andes, glacial activity dominated the formation of the surface during the Quaternary Period (from 2,500,000 years ago to the present) and continues to do so. About 7,000 square miles of ice remain, and fjords and Andean lakes are common.

The intermediate depression. The intermediate depression between the Andes and the coastal ranges lacks the continuity of the mountain system. In Norte Chico, the desert fringe of southern Atacama province, the depression is replaced by ridges of mountains and transverse valleys; in Puerto Montt, its longitudinal slope disappears beneath the sea.

A natural receptacle for materials coming from the Andes, the depression has been filled by alluvial, fluvioglacial, or moraine sediments, according to the region. The alluvial deposits are extremely important in the centre of the country, where there are mineral-rich collections of debris laid down by rivers as they enter the depression from the Andes. The depression forms the principal plains area in Chile and is the focal area for land communications as well as the most populated and developed part of the country.

The coastal cordillera. On the western flank of the intermediary depression, the coastal mountain system looks like a smaller replica of the Andes; it has not, however, been subjected to movements of the Earth's crust or volcanic action and does not include glacial formations. Although made of older materials than the Andes, these ranges have not been independent of the Andes in their geomorphological evolution. The masses of visible Cretaceous granites (dating from the period of 136,000,000 to 65,000,000 years ago) form part of a topography that is also characterized by basins full of decomposed materials and by transverse drainage systems. In such areas intensive agriculture has resulted in exhaustion of the soil and the formation of badlands (highly eroded areas nearly devoid of vegetation) in Ñuble and Concepción provinces, for example. Locally, the cordillera along the ocean shore has been subjected to erosion; terraces of marine origin dating from the Quaternary Period have been formed. Especially in central Chile, however, the coastal ranges form an obstacle to communications, blocking access to the sea.

Drainage. Because of the country's peculiar configuration, most of Chile's rivers are short and flow from east to west. Most of them originate in the Andes and successively cross the intermediate depression and the coastal mountain range. The coastal ranges also form a watershed and are the source of some small rivers. As with the climate, the rivers have different characteristics in different regions; their volume of flow progressively increases from north to south. In the desert region, most of the rivers (except, notably, the Río Loa) do not reach the sea; their sources are uncertain, and they run spasmodically. In the central region, where snow and rain feed the rivers, their volume of flow is more regular, although most of them follow uncertain courses. In the so-called Mediterranean climatic region, the river system is fed by thawing ice; from the Río Bío-Bío south, however, rivers originate as a result of the rains. In Patagonia, a barren tableland extending into Magellenas province in southern Chile, snowstorms and rain combine to supply the more important rivers, which flow westward to the Pacific.

The rivers in Chile do not have the same economic significance that they have in the other South American countries. Only the Río Valdivia is of importance for communications. The rivers have nonetheless been important in terms of settlement and are vital sources of water in the desert and central regions; they are also the basis of developmental planning of a number of regions, such as the area through which the Bío-Bío flows. From Cautín south, the pre-Andean lakes form a tourist attraction, being the most outstanding characteristic of a beautiful landscape.

Soils. Chile's soils vary in character from north to south. In the desert region, such soils as exist are made up of gravel and of sand cemented with calcium sulfate. In the Mediterranean climatic region of Chile, brown soils without lime or calcium are present on top of alluvial deposits in the longitudinal valley; they are especially suited to grain cultivation. Alternating with these soils are the poorer soils formed by deposits of volcanic ash. South of the Río Bío-Bío, diverse varieties of humid soils are found, including brown-red (lateritic) soils, volcanic-ash soils, and dark gray (podzolic) soils; all are usually good for forestry.

The climate. Because of its latitudinal range, Chile has all types of climatic conditions except tropical types. Nonetheless, a temperate climate generally predominates.

Annual rainfall statistics provide criteria for climatic differentiation, varying both with latitude and altitude. North of 30° S latitude, there is practically no rainfall. In the so-called Mediterranean region (32° to 37° S), precipitation ranges from 14 inches (360 millimetres) in Santiago to 51 inches in Concepción. In Valdivia, farther south, it reaches 93 inches, and still farther south it reaches amounts unequalled in any other nontropical region of the world—amounting to 161 inches in the islands of western Patagonia (about 47° S). The presence of two mountain ranges, which act as climatic screens, and the prevalence of rain-bearing winds from the Pacific determine rainfall along the two western slopes, especially in the Pacific region of Patagonia.

In the central and southern regions, where there is sufficient humidity, the rainy period coincides with the Southern Hemisphere winter (May to July). There is, however, much latitudinal variation; for example, the dry period lasts for eight months (September to April) in Santiago, but only for three (December to February) in Valdivia.

The Chilean climate is generally only moderately warm because of the nearness of the sea and the influence of the cold Humboldt Current. The highest monthly temperatures are registered in the northern desert: Arica, 66° F (19° C), and Antofagasta, 63° F (17° C). They then decrease toward the south—Santiago, 59° F (15° C); Temuco, 54° F (12° C); and Puerto Montt, 52° F (11° C). No area has rigorous cold, the coldest area being Punta Arenas, 36° F (2° C).

Average annual temperatures in Chile, throughout most of the year, are moderate; in interior localities not influenced by altitude, the average is 50° F (10° C).

Taking all climatic characteristics and factors into consideration, three distinct regions—northern, central, and southern—may be distinguished.

The northern desert. Running from the north to 27° S latitude, the aridity of this region is primarily caused by the high-pressure belt over the Pacific around latitude 30° S and the cold Humboldt Current. The area covered by the anticyclone (circulation of winds around the central region of high atmospheric pressure) blocks the movement of low-pressure systems and favours formation of a mass of homogeneous, stable, tropical Pacific air, totally inhibiting precipitation. In addition to lack of rain, of drainage systems, and of permanent vegetation, the Chilean desert is distinguished by its moderate average temperatures, which vary from 55° to 59° F (13° to 15° C) in July to 68° to 70° F (20° to 21° C) in January. Temperature variations depend only upon the direct heat of the Sun, and differences result from atmospheric humidity. Humidity is singularly high along the coast—a circumstance that results in lower temperatures in that part of the desert that is near the ocean. Elsewhere in the desert dry air favours marked daily variations—amounting to 47° F (26° C) in Canchones—as well as intense sunshine.

Central Chile. The climate as well as the annual average temperature in central Chile is characteristic of midlatitudinal areas. There are distinct seasonal changes in the climate, which varies from a Mediterranean type with a marked dry season between the Aconcagua and Ñuble provinces to a temperate and humid type of climate on the coast and all western-facing slopes between Ñuble and Chiloé. Temperatures are moderate; the difference between the averages in San Felipe, in San Felipe province, in north central Chile, and Castro, in Chiloé province, in the south central region, is only 7° F (4° C). During the coldest month (June) in both cities the temperature does not drop below 45° F (7° C), although the two cities are

The rivers

Rainfall patterns

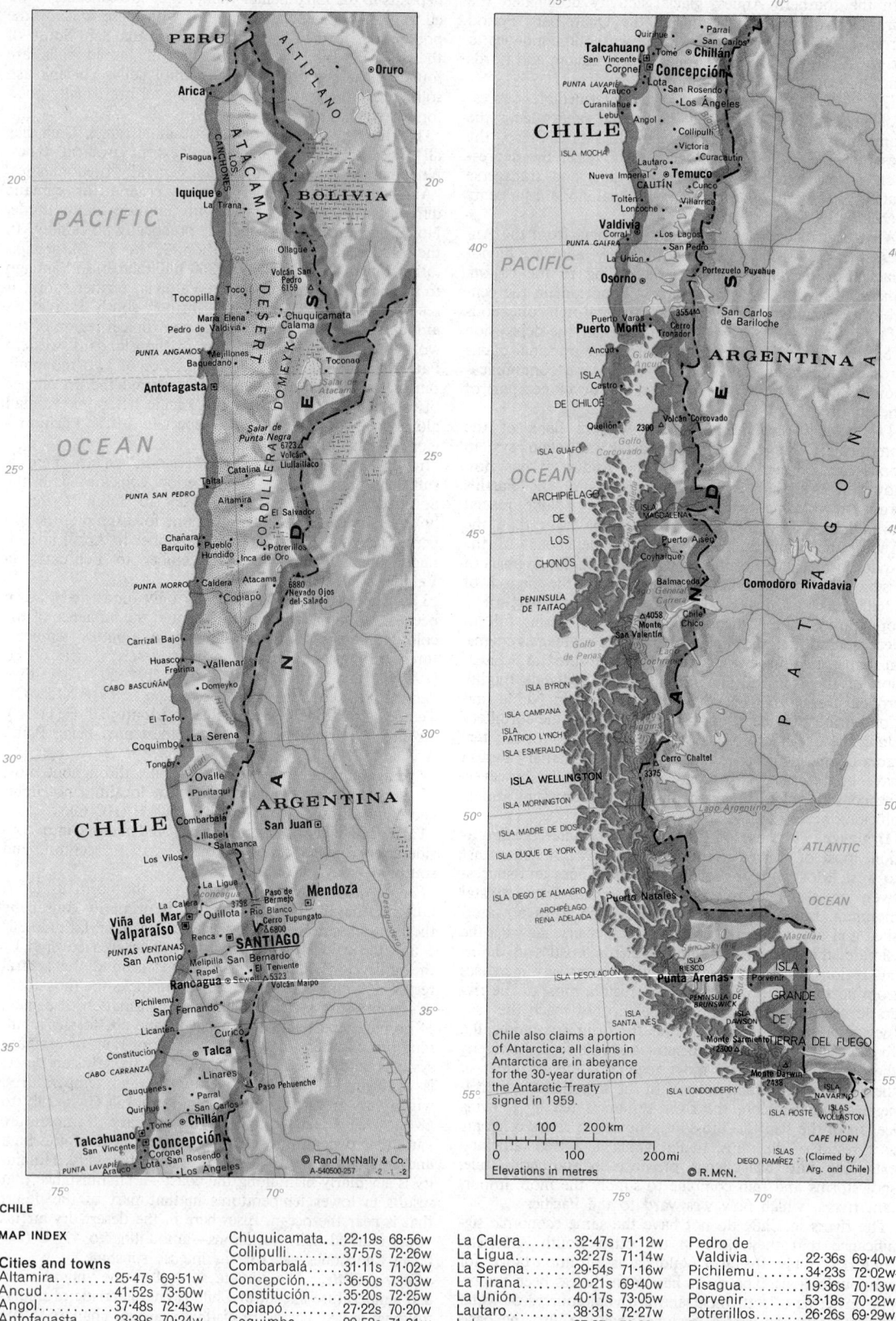

© Rand McNally & Co.
A-540500-257

Chile also claims a portion
of Antarctica; all claims in
Antarctica are in abeyance
for the 30-year duration of
the Antarctic Treaty
signed in 1959.

0   100   200 km
0   100   200 mi
Elevations in metres   © R. McN.

CHILE

MAP INDEX

separated by 10° of latitude. Bad weather—in the form of low temperatures and rain—occurs in winter (May to August) and is a distinctive characteristic of the region. The rains are cyclonic (associated with the circulation of winds around a central region of low atmospheric pressure) and originate in low-pressure systems that come from the polar region. The rains move northward as the anticyclonic (high-pressure) system, which prevails in winter, weakens.

Southern Chile. The extreme south usually has cold temperatures resulting from the year-round passage of disturbances associated with the cyclonic low-pressure belt, from the continual westerly winds, and from the heavy rainfall that occurs along the Pacific coasts. Despite these factors, at no season in continental Chile do monthly temperatures average less than 32° F (0° C).

Vegetation and animal life. Like the soils and the climates, Chile's vegetation is subject to north–south variation. In the northern desert region, vegetation has adapted to the aridity; even in the driest desert region, there is some vegetation cover (*Prososis tamaruge*). The desert area has interesting varieties of cactus, as well as shrubs and spiny brambles. Steppes (treeless plains), with thorny shrubs and inferior grass covering, predominate in the so-called Mediterranean region. The thickets are, however, beginning to disappear, because of the use of the shrubs for firewood by the local agricultural population. South of the Río Bío-Bío, mixed forests of *Nothofagus* (false beech), *Oblicua*, and evergreen laurel are found. The trees growing along the Frontier region and in the green rain forest of Valdivia province constitute Chile's principal source of timber. In Patagonia the cold steppes are primarily covered with grasses that provide grazing for livestock.

The animal life of Chile lacks the richness of other regions of South America because the barrier of the Andes, which scarcely has a pass below the snow line, has restricted animal migrations. Among the most interesting animal species are those living on the northern plateaus; they include such members of the camel family as the llama (*Lama glama*), the alpaca (*Lama pacos*), and the vicuña (whose dense silky fleece is the finest wool known). Among the rodents, the chinchilla has been so much hunted for its fur that it is now virtually extinct. Also decimated by hunters are some of the Andean mammals, such as the puma, the guanaco (a type of llama), and the huemul—a member of the deer family native to Chile and represented on the national coat of arms. Other animals are the Andean wolf, the foxlike chilla, and the spike-horned pudu (the smallest deer known). The Chilean bullfrog is a source of food.

Traditional regions. Geography and tradition have combined to divide Chile into seven regions. From north to south these are Norte Grande (Great North), Norte Chico (Little North), Núcleo Central (Central Nucleus), Bío-Bío, La Frontera (the Frontier), Los Lagos (the Lake region), and Los Canales (or Patagonia; the Canal region).

Norte Grande, consisting of Arica, Iquique, Tocopilla, Antofagasta, and El Loa provinces, is an arid region whose residents are vitally dependent on water from the Andes. The coastal cities—such as Iquique, Tocopilla, and Antofagasta, as well as the mining settlements of the interior—are obliged to bring their water across the desert from the Andes. Settlement of the region dates from the 19th century, and the population has been of a pioneer nature, engaged in exploiting the area's mineral deposits. Economic activity is export oriented. Chuquicamata, the location of one of the largest copper deposits in the world, is in this region and has contributed to the growth of Calama (92,000 residents), the port of Antofagasta (185,000), and Tocopilla (36,000). The oldest form of mining has been for nitrates, for which the entire region was once famous; the industry, however, is now beset by increasing competition and government control. Anchovy fishing has diversified the region's economy; fish flour and powder are made from the fish. Tourism has become increasingly important, with the principal tourist attractions being the desert itself, the warm-water beaches of Arica and Antofagasta, and a famous religious centre at La Tirana.

The Norte Chico region consists of Chañaral, Copiapó, Huasco, Elqui, Limarí, and Choapa provinces. A semi-arid region, it has prolonged periods of extreme dryness; one such period occurred in 1968 to 1969. The population is primarily concentrated in the irrigated valleys of Copiapó, Huasco, Elqui, and Limarí·or is dispersed in groups in the mountainous areas, where they engage in prospecting

Norte
Grande

for minerals. Cities comparable to those of central Chile are found in the valleys; they include Copiapó, Vallenar, Ovalle, and La Serena. Agriculture, goat raising, and iron and copper mining are the principal economic activities. The area is famous for pisco (a kind of brandy that is usually associated with Peru), as well as for the production of fruit early in season. Tourism is an important economic activity and is based on beach resort areas, reservoirs, and religious shrines.

The Central Nucleus

The Núcleo Central, or Central Nucleus, extends from the province of Valparaíso down through Linares. This is the hub of the nation's activity, in part because of the prevalence of the Mediterranean type of climate, with its long dry season. Due to the presence of the country's principal cities (including the national capital), the concentration of the bulk of the population, good agricultural production, and developing industries, this region is of fundamental importance. The area's traditional agricultural base (up to half of the population is engaged in agriculture) has been characterized by a feudal pattern of land-ownership, with large haciendas (estates) covering about three-fourths of Chile's arable land. Massive land redistribution in the 1970s resulted in decreases in productivity, and by the early 1980s some 20 percent of the land had been returned to its original owners.

Central Chile has been an urban area since ancient times. Most of its cities were founded during the Spanish colonial era; each was planned around a central *plaza de armas* (square of arms) and was built of materials such as adobe (sun-dried brick), which would deteriorate. These characteristics are changing, however, as urbanization brings taller buildings, greater population densities, and an increase in subsidiary economic activities, as well as serious housing problems, a lack of facilities, and deteriorating social conditions. The nation's manufacturing industry is concentrated in the cities of the region.

The Bío-Bío region, which extends from Ñuble to Malleco, lies within the borders of Mediterranean Chile and consists of the entire area drained by the Río Bío-Bío, which is one of the largest rivers in the country. The primary city of the region is Concepción, an industrial centre that has grown enormously since 1950, when the Huachipato steelworks began to operate. Other industries include the manufacture of cellulose (from pine trees), cement, refined petroleum and petrochemicals, and textiles.

La Frontera, or the Frontier region, is colder and more humid. The land itself has been settled only since the latter half of the 19th century, although a unique characteristic of the region is the remnant of its aboriginal Mapuche, or Araucanian, population, which lives in missions; their circular thatched huts, called *rucas*, lend a picturesque aspect to the area. The farms of the region, which is known as the granary of Chile, are large, and wheat is the major crop; cultivation is extensive, and irrigation is not necessary.

Los Lagos, or the Lake region, consists of Valdivia, Osorno, and Llanquihue provinces. Valdivia is known for its rainfall—which, distributed throughout the year, amounts to about 80 inches annually. The land is reminiscent of northern Europe; substantial German colonization took place between 1860 and 1880, especially in the vicinity of Valdivia and Puerto Montt. At the foot of the Andes are many lakes and volcanoes, which attract tourists. Economic activity is based largely on timber obtained from the forests and on dairy farming. Milk-pasteurizing plants dominate the economy of many of the area's towns and cities.

Los Canales (the Canal region) in Patagonia extends from Chiloé to Antártica Chilena. It has a predominantly cold climate, with heavy rainfall along the Pacific coastal zone. Except in Chiloé, where the population dates from colonial times, the area is still in the process of being settled. The province of Aisén is particularly noted for its developmental potential and is thus called the "final frontier." The population density is about 2.4 persons per square mile; most of the residents live in cities or towns. Economically, the region is of peripheral importance; sheep raising for the export of wool, which has been practiced since the 19th century, is the primary activity. Since 1945 oil has been produced in Magallanes province; it is refined, outside the area, in Concón and Concepción. The distances, the isolation, and the lack of both roads and railroads limit the development of the region.

THE PEOPLE

Groups historically associated with Chile. Chileans are descended from racial groups that intermixed during the colonial era: indigenous peoples who lived in Chile before the Spanish colonization (Diaguitas; Picunches; Mapuches, or Araucanians; Huilliches; Pehuenches; and Cuncos) and colonists (Spaniards from Andalucía, Extremadura, Castile, and Leon) who arrived during the 16th and 17th centuries. Basques predominated in the 18th-century Spanish migrations to Chile and brought about major changes in economic and political life. Few blacks were taken to Chile, largely because there was no speculative, agrarian economy based on the use of manual labour. Chileans are still an ethnically homogeneous group, since no important migrations have taken place since the colonial period.

Ethnic homogeneity

Chile remained on the margin of the large international population migrations during the republican era, partly because of the distance from Europe, partly because the Andes mountains were a barrier to transport, and partly because of the lack of an official immigration policy. (The official encouragement of the German colonization in the Los Lagos region during the second half of the 19th century was exceptional.) Unorganized immigration has been of little importance; the 1970 census showed that foreigners—principally Spaniards, Argentines, Germans, and Italians—formed only 1 percent of the total population.

The result of racial intermixture has been the development of a primarily mestizo people—a people of mixed European and American Indian ancestry. The population as a whole has a strong sense of cultural unity, which can be traced to the predominance of both the Spanish language and the Roman Catholic religion. The only significant minority consists of the Mapuche (Araucanian Indian) people of the frontier area. By the late 1970s the indigenous population in Chile, consisting of Mapuches for the most part, numbered about 616,000.

Geographically, 92 percent of all Chileans live between Copiapó and Puerto Montt; some 70 percent of these live within the area known as Mediterranean Chile. This region has the highest population density in the country. By contrast, the northern and southern extremities of Chile are noted for their low population densities (three persons per square mile in the desert region of Norte Chile and fewer than one person per square mile in Patagonia).

The concentration of population in the central part of the country can be attributed to a decided preference on the part of the people for living in the intermediate depression instead of in the mountain areas. The lack of population in the Andes is worth noting; the coastal cordillera, even though it has older settlements and a somewhat larger population density, also remains much less populated than the longitudinal valley.

From 1940 to 1980 Chile's urban population grew constantly; in the early 1980s it represented more than 80 percent of the total population. Santiago is the principal urban centre, followed by Valparaíso and Concepción.

Urban population growth

Santiago, with a population of almost 3,500,000 residents, is the national metropolis, overshadowing all the other cities in size. Valparaíso and Concepción each have more than 500,000 residents. Other Chilean cities serve primarily local functions and seldom have more than 200,000 residents. The northern and southern territorial extremes (the desert and Patagonia) are decidedly more urban than rural in their settlement pattern, though they have no cities of more than regional importance. Rural population patterns predominate, however, in almost every province located between the cities of Concepción, in the Bío-Bío region of central Chile, and Chiloé, on the Isla Grande de Chiloé in the Puerto Montt region. The attraction of the big cities is shown by the number of migrants they draw; Santiago attracts migrants from all the provinces and especially from rural areas. The Metropolitan Region of Santiago grew at an annual rate of 2.5

Chile, Area and Population				
	area		population	
	sq mi	sq km	1970 census	1980 census*
Regions				
Región de Tarapacá	22,422	58,073	175,000	239,000
Provinces				
Arica	6,535	16,925	96,000	124,000
Iquique	15,887	41,148	79,000	115,000
Región de Antofagasta	48,381	125,306	252,000	313,000
Provinces				
Tocopilla	6,326	16,385	31,000	36,000
Antofagasta	25,478	65,987	148,000	185,000
El Loa	16,577	42,934	73,000	92,000
Región de Atacama	30,219	78,268	153,000	199,000
Provinces				
Chañaral	9,521	24,660	37,000	48,000
Copiapó	13,337	34,452	63,000	82,000
Huasco	7,361	19,066	53,000	68,000
Región de Coquimbo	15,308	39,647	340,000	417,000
Provinces				
Elqui	5,904	15,290	166,000	207,000
Limarí	5,512	14,277	112,000	135,000
Choapa	3,892	10,080	62,000	75,000
Región de Valparaíso	6,324	16,378	967,000	1,231,000
Provinces				
Valparaíso	1,057	2,739	571,000	735,000
San Antonio	624	1,641	74,000	92,000
Quillota	623	1,613	145,000	182,000
Petorca	1,819	4,711	43,000	54,000
San Felipe	961	2,489	82,000	102,000
Los Andes	1,167	3,022	50,000	64,000
Isle de Pascua	63	163	2,000	2,000
Región del Libertador General Bernardo O'Higgins	6,920	17,924	495,000	568,000
Provinces				
Cachapoal	3,506	9,079	320,000	377,000
Colchagua	3,415	8,844	175,000	191,000
Región del Maule	11,783	30,518	619,000	707,000
Provinces				
Curicó	2,891	7,487	159,000	175,000
Talca	4,353	11,276	248,000	289,000
Linares	4,539	11,756	213,000	243,000
Región del Bío-Bío	13,903	36,007	1,253,000	1,474,000
Provinces				
Ñuble	4,668	12,091	320,000	356,000
Concepción	1,276	3,305	577,000	711,000
Arauco	2,023	5,240	99,000	113,000
Bío-Bío	5,935	15,370	258,000	293,000
Región de la Araucanía	12,538	32,472	600,000	657,000
Provinces				
Malleco	5,442	14,095	177,000	193,000
Cautín	7,095	18,377	423,000	464,000
Región de los Lagos	26,656	69,039	748,000	863,000
Provinces				
Valdivia	7,132	18,472	278,000	320,000
Osorno	3,566	9,236	160,000	184,000
Llanquihue	7,029	18,205	119,000	231,000
Chiloé	8,928	23,125	111,000	128,000
Región Aysén del General Carlos Ibáñez del Campo	41,373	107,153	49,000	63,000
Provinces				
Aysén	22,201	57,480	40,000	53,000
General Carrera	4,790	12,406	7,000	7,000
Capitán Prat	14,381	37,247	2,000	3,000
Región de Magallanes y de la Antártica Chilena	43,363	112,311	89,000	109,000
Provinces				
Ultima Esperanza	17,695	45,831	14,000	16,000
Magallanes	14,284	36,995	68,000	84,000
Tierra del Fuego	11,384	29,485	6,000	7,000
Región Metropolitana de Santiago	5,331	13,808	3,134,000	4,265,000
Total Chile†	284,519‡	736,903‡	8,884,000‡	11,103,000‡

*Estimates. †Excluding 490,243 sq mi (1,269,723 sq km) of the Chilean Antarctic Territory and Chileans reported living there in 1970 (998) and 1980 (1,141). ‡Figures do not add to total given because of rounding. Source: Official government figures.

percent during the 1970s, with internal migrants constituting a large percentage of the population influx.

Emigration patterns are strongest in the regions of Valparaíso and Concepción, in central Chile, and Puerto Montt, further south.

Demography. According to census figures, the population in 1952 was about 5,930,000. It increased to about 7,370,000 in 1960, rose again to 8,850,000 in 1970, and was more than 11,100,000 by 1980.

The annual rate of population increase during the 1970s was 1.7 percent. Since immigration is insignificant, this growth must be attributed to internal factors, such as the relatively high annual birth rate that in 1979 was 21.5 per

1,000 population; and the declining death rate, which in 1979 was 6.8 per 1,000 population, as compared with rates of 25.9 in 1935 and 12.3 in 1960. By the late 1970s the infant mortality rate in Chile had fallen to almost 38 per 1,000 population, less than half the 1960 figure, but it remained one of the highest rates in South America.

Improvements in the standard of living have raised life expectancy to 62 years for men and 69 years for women. The Chilean population is basically young; about 45 percent of the people are under 20 years of age. Thus, a high proportion of the population is dependent upon those who are economically active, and a heavy responsibility is borne by the government for the expansion of educational facilities.

In the early 1980s the economically active population numbered close to 3,700,000 (about 33 percent of the total population) and was primarily engaged in providing services; agricultural and industrial occupations were next in importance.

THE NATIONAL ECONOMY

Chile has been plagued continually by inflationary pressures and economic imbalances. The economy is essentially dependent on copper, the country's chief export, with capital goods the principal import. Industrial development has been promoted, and as a result, some light industrial goods are produced within the country. During the early 1970s sweeping governmental reforms in almost every sector of the economy were accompanied by severe drops in production, while inflation rose drastically. During the mid-1970s cutbacks were made in government expenditures, many business restrictions and controls were abolished, and a search for foreign investments and loans was begun as a new government attempted to bring the economy under control.

Natural resources. Chile has placed increasing emphasis on developing its many natural resources. The country is rich both in raw materials and in the sources of energy needed for economic development. Mineral resources are varied and are intensively exploited. The reserves of copper in Chile are estimated at about 107,000,000 tons, the largest in the world. Annual production reached almost 1,177,000 tons in 1980, with operations concentrated in the arid zone and along the length of the Andes from Concepción province to the central part of the country. Molybdenum (a silver-white metal with a high melting point derived from the large copper deposits) became Chile's principal export product after copper when, in 1979, export value increased more than fourfold as a result of a spectacular rise in the international price. Reserves are estimated to total about 2,700,000 tons. Iron also is an important mineral. High-quality (60-percent pure) iron deposits are found in Norte Chico as well as along the coast, which facilitates exportation. Reserves amount to about 1,000,000,000 tons. Nitrate deposits, which have played an important role in Chile's economic history, are located in the low interior desert, extending for about 450 miles from Pisagua, in the vicinity of 19° S, to Chañaral, at about 27° S. Reserves are estimated to total slightly less than 1,000,000,000 tons, although production has dropped to less than 1,000,000 tons annually.

In addition to these principal products, Chile has many metallic and nonmetallic deposits, mined in varying degrees and found in various areas of the country, especially in the extreme north. These resources include gold, silver, manganese, lead, zinc, mercury, apatite (a mineral used in manufacturing phosphate fertilizers), limestone (the source of the cement industry), marble, and gypsum. Among its sources of energy, Chile has coal, petroleum, and natural-gas deposits, as well as a considerable hydroelectric potential. Reserves of soft (subbituminous and lignite) coal total 1,150,000,000 tons and have been obtained from underwater deposits in the Arauco Gulf south of Concepción since the 19th century.

Oil and natural gas are extracted on Tierra del Fuego Island in the south and along the northern shore of the Strait of Magellan. Production in the early 1980s was at the rate of 11,860,000 barrels of crude oil and 191,000,000,000,000 cubic feet (5,000,000,000,000 cubic metres) of natural gas annually. Oil production meets less than one-fifth of the country's oil requirements, however, and the remainder must be imported.

The hydro-electric potential
Favourable conditions for hydroelectric development exist in the Andes, where the Empresa Nacional de Electricidad (National Electric Company) has installed plants at Chapiquiña, Sauzal, Cipreses, El Abanico, El Toro, and Pullinque. Hydroelectric development has been extended to the coastal mountain range as well, while thermoelectric power plants are located in central Chile, at Renca, in Santiago, and at Punta Ventanas, in Valparaíso. Altogether Chile has an installed capacity of about 3,000,000 kilowatts, half of which is hydroelectric.

From the Río Bío-Bío south, climatic conditions favour the development of natural forests. Chile has about 50,000,000 acres (20,000,000 hectares) of forests, almost one-third of which are exploited commercially. The primary tree species, which are used for making lumber and panelling, are the coigue, oak, rauli (beech), ulmo (elm), tepa (laurel tree), and Araucanian pine (monkey puzzle tree). Pine for the manufacture of paper and pulp is taken from rapid-growth forests in central Chile and the Bío-Bío region.

Mining. Mining is the mainstay of the Chilean economy; it is important for its contribution both to external commerce and to domestic industrial development. Copper, molybdenum, iron, nitrates, and other mining products make up about 60 percent of the total value of national exports. Although mining accounts for about 12 percent of the gross domestic product, it provides employment for only 78,000 people, about 2 percent of the working population.

Copper now plays the role in the Chilean economy that was played by nitrates until World War I; copper production amounted to almost 1,177,000 tons in 1980. The industry was originally developed by large amounts of North American capital during the first few decades of the 20th century. Small-scale copper mining is carried on by numerous individual miners, or *pirquineros*, in the foothills of Norte Chico and in the coastal mountains of central Chile. Medium-sized mining enterprises consist of companies with a larger investment capacity and with their own treatment plants. Together, the small and medium-sized producers have an output of about 150,000 tons of refined copper annually. Large-scale mining produces more than 900,000 tons annually.

Traditionally in the hands of foreign or mixed-ownership corporations, the principal copper-producing corporations were nationalized in 1971. Although the government has initiated various programs to encourage foreign companies to reinvest, by the late 1970s the vast bulk of Chile's copper output was still produced by mines that were being operated by the Chilean government body, Corporacion Nacional de Cobre de Chile (CODELCO-Chile). The large companies appraise the low-quality deposits found in various parts of the Andean mountain range (at Chuquicamata, El Salvador, Río Blanco, and El Teniente). The copper ore is then mined, together with quantities of other materials, by strip-mining (as at Chuquicamata) or by tunnelling (as at Sewell). The ore is converted into electrolytic copper or is "blistered" (fire refined) and is then sent to such ports as Antofagasta, Barquito, or San Antonio for shipment.

The iron and coal industries
The annual production of iron ore amounts to about 11,000,000 tons, and by the late 1970s an expanding domestic market consumed more than 30 percent of the iron produced. The coal industry in Chile is beset by overemployment and high exploitation costs. Annual production declined steadily throughout the 1970s, amounting to about 70,000 tons by 1980.

Although the Chilean government has retained control over the mineral operations in copper, coal, nitrates, and iron ore, it has encouraged private capital to expand output in copper, petroleum, and natural gas, as well as other resources. The National Planning Office (ODEPLAN) emphasizes resource development, including foreign investment.

Agriculture. Agriculture is the second largest employer in Chile, with about 570,000 workers, or 20 percent of the total labour force during the late 1970s, but it produces less than 10 percent of the gross domestic product. Although it forms a basic sector of the national economy, agriculture in Chile is scarcely developed; as a result, the country imports large amounts of agricultural products annually.

Agricultural production in Chile during the 1970s was affected by shifting governmental policies. Agrarian reform, involving nationalization of large farms, in 1970-71 nearly resulted in chaos. Farm production also declined due to bad weather, strikes, and organizational problems. By the mid-1970s agrarian policies had been almost completely reversed by the new government. About 20 percent of the farms that had been nationalized were returned to their original owners; the Chilean economy, including agriculture, was opened to unrestricted foreign competition; and the government ended price supports for domestic agricultural products. By 1980 agriculture had the lowest growth (3 percent) of any sector of the economy.

Traditionally, the principal agricultural products have been cereals (particularly wheat), potatoes, corn (maize), beans, sugarbeets, and sunflowers. Vineyards are common in the Mediterranean region; they cover some 267,000 acres and produce about 150,000,000 gallons (568,000,000 litres) of wine annually.

Stock raising has been one of the most underdeveloped activities in rural areas, partly because of poor technology and inefficient breeding. There has been, however, vigorous expansion of the output of poultry meat, pork, and mutton, as well as a rise in the production of beef.

Industry. Manufacturing, like agriculture, declined in output and employment when the government nationalized the industry in the early 1970s. Although rapid growth began in mid-decade, manufacturing activity by the late 1970s had not reached earlier levels. Manufacturing employs some 13 percent (374,000 people) of the labour force in Chile and accounts for about 20 percent of the gross national product. Industry is dependent on both market and labour factors and is thus concentrated around the principal urban centres—Santiago, Valparaíso, and Concepción.

Light industries, manufacturing such items as textiles, food products, and clothing, are most common, although there are some plants manufacturing electronic and other types of equipment and automobiles. Other plants process sugarbeets and produce cellulose and paper. The fishing industry was the most rapidly growing production activity during the late 1970s. In 1979 Chile produced about 672,000 tons of fishery products, more than double the 1970 production figure.

Trade and finance. Trade patterns changed substantially during the late 1970s, as Chile had a marked drop in trade with the United States and increased imports from Latin-American countries. The balance-of-payments deficit rose steadily during the early 1970s, but as a result of new commercial and fiscal policies adopted in 1973, Chile's foreign markets expanded and exports more than tripled by 1980.

Mining products are the most important commodities sold abroad, followed by industrial goods and agricultural products. The country's principal markets are West Germany, Japan, and the United States. Industrial supplies and machinery make up more than half of total imports. In spite of a decline in the trade deficit, the balance of payments remains unfavourable, in part because of increases in interest payments.

Foreign trade

The national monetary unit is the peso. The Central Bank of Chile, established in 1925, is the official state bank; it implements the internal banking policies of the government and also conducts foreign trade. The State Bank of Chile seeks to promote production and to stimulate savings.

Within the Chilean economic system, the private and public sectors collaborate, with the private sector contributing an increasing percentage of the total investments. Private businesses are generally organized in the form of *sociedades anónimas* (literally "anonymous societies"), which are similar to United States corporations and which participate in all areas of economic activity.

Since 1925 the state has increasingly intervened in both the social and the economic domains. The Corporation for Production Growth was created in 1939 in order to formulate a development plan and to stimulate economic activity in general. In 1967 the National Planning Office was created. The tendency toward direct state involvement was reinforced under the administration of Eduardo Frei Montalva (1964–70) and was further expanded under the Marxist administration of Salvador Allende (1970–73). The Allende administration involved the state in virtually every sector of Chile's economy. It ordered wage increases of 40 percent, froze prices, and instituted far-reaching agricultural and industrial reforms.

The trend toward increasing state involvement ended in 1973, however, when a four-man military junta, led by Gen. Augusto Pinochet Ugarte, overthrew Allende's government and established a rightist authoritarian state. Under the military regime the National Planning Office promotes a mixed economy in which the government assumes only those functions that cannot be performed by the private sector. In accordance with these policies, Pinochet cut government expenditures by 20 percent, returned many of the nationalized farms and production firms to private hands, and abolished most price controls. Although inflation dropped and the economy improved considerably, problems such as unequal distribution of income and very high unemployment (officially 13.8 pecent in 1980, but unofficially reported to be as high as 30 percent) have persisted.

Transportation and communication. Chile's geographical shape constrains its means of communication and the flow of its traffic. In the central region the intermediate depression provides a natural path, some 550 miles long, that both road and railway builders have taken advantage of. Between Arica, in the north, and Santiago, the highway is used more than the antiquated railway. South of Puerto Montt all land communications disappear, and only air or sea travel is possible.

The highway network covers almost 80,000 miles, with about 10,000 paved. The principal route is the Pan-American Highway, which connects Arica with Quellón on Chiloé Island—a total distance of more than 2,100 miles. Other heavily travelled routes include those connecting Santiago with the ports of San Antonio and Valparaíso. The latter route has been considerably shortened because of the construction of the Lo Prado Tunnel through the coastal cordillera. The most important international road connects Santiago with Mendoza, Argentina. International roads also connect Iquique with Oruro, Bolivia; Antofagasta with Salta, Argentina; La Serena with San Juan, Argentina; and Osorno with San Carlos de Bariloche, Argentina. An indication of the notable development of the highway system is the increasing number of vehicles on the roads. Bus and trucking companies have become competitive with the railroads.

Railways   Consisting of a northern and a southern network of different gauges, the railway system has about 6,300 miles of track. The northern network, using a one-metre gauge, runs between La Calera and Iquique; the southern network, using four different gauges, runs between La Calera and Puerto Montt. The most travelled sections connect Santiago and Valparaíso and Santiago and Puerto Montt; both sections are electrified. Most of the railway system is under the control of the Empresa de los Ferrocarriles del Estado (State Railway Enterprise). The most important international rail line connects Los Andes and Mendoza.

Coastal shipping has grown in importance, partly as a result of the increase in tonnage of the national merchant marine and partly because of the modernization of some of the country's ports. Sea transportation is generally supervised by one of three state authorities, with various private companies participating.

Chile's busiest port of entry is Valparaíso. The principal export centres are the ports of Huasco, Guayacán, and San Vicente. These export centres handle the shipping of minerals.

A state airline, Línea Aérea Nacional de Chile, serves the entire country and handles the bulk of Chile's air traffic. The line uses both jet and turboprop planes and links Chile with various other Latin-American countries as well as with the United States, Europe, and Tahiti (via Easter Island). Chile has more than 350 airports, of which five accommodate international traffic. Pudahuel Airport in Santiago is the most important terminal for foreign airlines.

The government-controlled National Telecommunications Enterprise, established in 1964, owns the telephone and telegraph network almost in its entirety.

ADMINISTRATION AND SOCIAL CONDITIONS

Governmental structure. Chile is a constitutional republic, divided into 12 regions and a metropolitan area. The country has been under military rule since the coup in September 1973. Great authority and responsibility are exercised by the president, who is elected to an eight-year term of office and may not be reelected. Chile's only legislative body is the Congress, which represents the entire nation.

A new constitution was approved by a plebiscite in 1980, at which time Chilean voters also approved an eight-year extension of General Pinochet's presidential term. The military junta has the power to appoint him for another eight years. The president of the republic, who must be native born and at least 30 years of age, is the chief executive, head of the government, and commander in chief of the armed forces. The president is elected by direct vote of citizens over 18 years of age. There are no literacy requirements for voting. If no candidate obtains a majority of the vote, the Congress chooses between the two candidates with the largest numbers of votes. The ministers of state are appointed by the president.

According to the new constitution, legislative powers reside fundamentally with the national Congress (one of the oldest parliaments on the continent), which consists of an upper chamber of 27 senators elected for eight-year terms and a lower chamber of 120 deputies elected for four-year terms. The sections of the constitution referring to these elections, however, are effective as of 1989, until which time legislative power is invested in the four-man military junta.

The administration of the state is the responsibility of the president of the republic, assisted by the ministers of state. Each ministry has particular services to perform and supervises a number of autonomous institutions.

The constitution provides for a general comptroller, who is responsible for legislation concerning income (for example, minimum wages), for investing public funds, and for judging the legality of decrees relating to money matters and all administrative questions.

The president directly appoints the *intendentes* (chief administrative officials) in each of the country's 40 provinces. Each *intendente* represents the president and acts as governor in those provinces in which capitals are located. Governors appoint subdelegates to oversee subdelegations, or *comunas* (municipalities), which are subdivisions of the provinces. The *comunas* are governed by a *municipalidad* (municipal council), made up of *regidores* (councilmen), who are elected by direct vote. *Regidores* serve four-year terms and choose a mayor from among themselves. For cities of more than 100,000 residents, the mayor is named by the president of the republic.

Political parties. The Partido Nacional and the Democracia Radical are two of the largest conservative parties in Chile. Both were formed in the late 1960s, though they have their origin in parties dating from the 19th century. The Partido Nacional resulted from the fusion of two traditional parties, the Liberals and Conservatives. The Partido Democracia Radical is an offshoot of the old Radical Party.   Principal political blocs

The Christian Democratic Party has traditionally had the largest electoral base in Chile. It came to power in 1964 under the leadership of Pres. Eduardo Frei and began the process of change and reform known as the freedom revolution (*revolución en libertad*). It was the principal opposition party during the Allende administration.

Socialist politics in the country were formerly represented by a coalition of parties known as the Popular Unity (Unidad Popular). The coalition consisted of the Socialist

Party (established in 1933), the Communist Party (1922), the Radical Party (1863), as well as the Social Democrats, the Alianza Popular Independiente, and the Movimiento de Acción Popular Unitaria (MAPU). This coalition won the presidency for Allende in 1970.

In 1973 the junta suspended the activities of all political parties and declared all Marxist political parties unlawful. Both the Christian Democratic Party and Popular Unity were forced underground (their operations being moved abroad), and many Communist and Socialist leaders were arrested and either exiled or killed. The regime later became somewhat more tolerant of criticism. The arrests of political opponents declined, and some Chileans forced into exile after the 1973 coup were allowed to return to Chile. An estimated 40,000 people, however, still remained in exile by the early 1980s.

Justice and the military. Although the chief executive makes appointments to the judiciary and has the power to make transfers of judges within their jurisdictions, the judiciary has generally been considered the most independent of the three branches of government. Since the military coup, however, courts-martial have replaced the judiciary for many political offenses. The court system is headed by a 13-member Supreme Court of Justice, with more than a dozen Courts of Appeal.

The armed forces in Chile total about 90,000 men. All able-bodied Chilean men are obliged to serve in the Chilean Army, which is a national militia; women serve on a volunteer basis. Recruits receive two years of training, after which they are placed in the army reserve, estimated to number about 160,000. The Chilean Air Force includes jet fighters, bombers, and fighter bombers; its personnel number about 15,000. The Chilean Navy has several cruisers, destroyers and destroyer escort vessels, and submarines, as well as a number of patrol vessels and auxiliary craft.

Education. The educational system was organized during the mid-19th century by Chileans who were influenced primarily by the French educational methods of their day. Later, with the creation of the Pedagogical Institute in 1889, a generation of German teachers contributed to the development of Chile's educational tradition. Still later arose a strong national pedagogic movement, which has continued.

Traditionally, the educational system has been organized on three levels—primary, secondary, and university. Substantial modifications to the system were introduced in 1965, which resulted in increased educational opportunities. By the early 1970s, enrollment of students had risen by 46 percent, to a total of almost 2,700,000, and by the early 1980s there were about 3,000,000 students enrolled in Chilean schools. The primary level, known as Enseñanza Básica Obligatoria, has been expanded into an eight-year program; the secondary level, Enseñanza Media, has been reduced to a four-year program. Secondary schools are either scientific and humanistic or technical and professional in orientation. The 1965 reforms also introduced fundamental changes in terms of the quality of education, including new study programs, the improvement of teaching courses, and new teaching materials and texts.

The universities
Chile's universities are renowned throughout Latin America. They include the Universidad de Chile (the official university), the Universidad Católica de Chile, and the Universidad de Santiago de Chile, all in Santiago and regional centres; the Universidad de Concepción; the Universidad Católica de Valparaíso; the Universidad del Norte (Antofagasta); and the Universidad Austral de Chile (Valdivia).

Social welfare. Social and labour legislation in Chile originated in 1924, when the first important social-welfare laws were passed, dealing with labour contracts and with mandatory accident and health insurance. The Código del Trabajo (Labour Code) enacted in 1931 systematized the initial social-welfare legislation, forming the basis of labour–management relations.

The Allende government encouraged labour organizations as a part of its campaign to expand the public, or "social," sector of the economy. By late 1972 agricultural

unions alone claimed almost 280,000 members—a larger membership than all of the organized labour movement at the end of 1964. There were, however, widespread strikes and demonstrations by labour throughout the early 1970s.

The military regime that took control in 1973 imposed a radically different system of industrial relations. Pinochet's government repressed major labour organizations and prohibited strikes, collective bargaining, and political activity by unions. It was not until 1979 that a new labour code was instituted, authorizing the resumption of collective bargaining and restoring the right to strike, with limitations.

The social security system in Chile has been steadily expanded by successive governments. In 1981 a social security program was established within the private sector under the Administradoras de Fondo de Pensiones. Employees are given the choice of registering with the new program or remaining with the established system administered by the state. By the early 1980s, 800,000 of the 1,500,000 employees in the social security system were covered by the new program.

The National Health Service (Servicio Nacional de Salud), established in 1952 as a subsidiary of the Ministry of Health, was reorganized by the military government to provide services from local, decentralized health units. Per capita expenditures in health by the government have been increased. In 1979 there was one doctor for every 1,060 people. There are state and university hospitals and private hospitals and clinics.

Between 1965 and 1970, 260,000 residential units of various types were constructed, with both the Housing Ministry and the National Savings and Loan System participating in the drive to build new housing. Public investment decreased significantly, however, during the early 1970s resulting in an enormous drop in construction activity. Recovery began in 1977 and accelerated by 1979, with the majority of the activity shifting to the private sector in accordance with government policy.

Cultural life. In the creative arts, Chile boasts such The arts universally known poets as Gabriela Mistral, Pablo Neruda (both winners of the Nobel Prize for literature), and Nicaner Parra; such concert musicians as Claudio Arrau; painters such as Roberto Matta Echaurren; and sculptors such as Marta Colvin. Because of the lack of a rich indigenous background, patrons of the arts have favoured the European tradition. Chilean art, however, has a distinctive personality of its own. Folk arts include ceramics, weaving, and horsehair handicrafts.

Chile's long tradition of press freedom was ended in 1973. Since the assumption of power by the military, censorship has been in force. In the early 1980s the country had 27 daily newspapers, six of which were published in Santiago. There were about 200 radio stations, and television was broadcast by one state-owned and three university-owned stations.

Prospects for the future. There are both positive and negative aspects to Chile's social and economic situation. The life-span had increased to 66 years by the early 1980s, and the infant mortality rate, while still high among Latin-American countries, had decreased by half. Pinochet's administration brought the soaring inflation rates of the mid-1970s down to a manageable level and induced steady growth in the gross national product. Much of this economic boom, however, has been concentrated among the wealthy and upper middle classes; many formerly state-supported businesses have closed, and the unemployment rate remains extremely high. Rapid urbanization has resulted in severe housing shortages among the lower income groups, and the average diet in Chile remains nutritionally poor.

Chile must resolve these fundamental problems in order to establish a more just balance between distinct social classes, as well as to promote economic development that can underwrite further social progress. Under the military government Chileans lost many of the freedoms they enjoyed under previous administrations, and, although the military rulers had begun to ease political repression by the early 1980s, they were doing so only very slowly.

BIBLIOGRAPHY

General: GILBERT J. BUTLAND, *Latin America: A Regional Geography,* 3rd ed. (1972); J.P. COLE, *Latin America: An Economic and Social Geography* (1965), both books contain a chapter on Chile; ANIBAL PINTO *et al., Chile, hoy* (1970); CORPORACIÓN DE FORMENTO DE LA PRODUCCIÓN, *Geografía económica de Chile,* 6 vol. (1950–66), the most complete geographic study published on Chile; PEDRO CUNILL, *Geografía de Chile,* 7th ed. corrected (1978), a well-documented overview of Chile; CARLOS RUIZ FULLER, *Geología y yacimientos metalíferos de Chile* (1965); JEAN BORDE, *Les Andes de Santiago et leur avant-pays* (1966); LUIS LLIBOUTRY, *Nieves y glaciares de Chile* (1956), an excellent work that discusses the Andean glaciation in Chile; GILBERT J. BUTLAND, *The Human Geography of Southern Chile* (1957); SERGIO SEPÚLVEDA, *Regiones geográficas de Chile* (1962), a systematic presentation of regional variations—human, physical, and economic.

Economy and transportation: JEAN BORDE and MARIO GONGORA, *La evolución de la propiedad rural en el valle del Puangue,* 2 vol. (1956), a historical-geographic study of land division since colonial times; JOSÉ CADEMARTORI, *La economía chilena: un enfoque marxista* (1968); INSTITUTO DE ECONOMÍA DE LA UNIVERSIDAD DE CHILE, *La economía de Chile en el período 1950–1963,* 2 vol. (1963); OFICINA DE PLANIFICACIÓN NACIONAL, *Política de desarrollo nacional* (1968); ANÍBAL PINTO, *Chile: una economía difícil* (1964); ALBERT A. BLUM (ed.), *International Handbook of Industrial Relations* (1981), contains an informative chapter on Chile.

Administration and social conditions: RICARDO MADRID CRUZ-COKE, *Geografía electoral de Chile* (1952); RICARDO DONOSO, *Las ideas políticas en Chile* (1946); JAIME EYZAGUIRRE, *Historia constitucional de Chile* (1956); ALBERTO EDWARDS, *La Fronda aristocrática,* 6th ed. (1966); ALBERTO EDWARDS and EDUARDO FREI, *Historia de los partidos políticos chilenos* (1949); SERGIO GUILISASTI, *Partidos políticos chilenos,* 2nd ed. (1964); ARMAND MATTELART, *Atlas social de las comunas de Chile* (1965); ARMAND MATTELART and MANUEL A. GARRETÓN, *Integración nacional y marginalidad: un ensayo de regionalización social de Chile* (1965); PHILIP O'BRIEN (ed.), *Allende's Chile* (1976), a well-documented collection of essays on the accomplishments and on the failings of the Allende administration.

(S.S.G./Ed.)

Chile, History of

From the beginning of their conquest of Chile in 1536, it took the Spanish forces 70 years to subdue the indigenous population; and the subjugation of the Araucanian tribes, which occupied the central southern region of the country, never was completed.

Chilean historians of the 19th century considered the period succeeding the conquest—the colonial period—to have been unimportant. Such an interpretation, however, did not take into consideration the social, economic, and cultural aspects of Chilean history, which even the most modern historiography has failed to appreciate fully.

The origin of two of the most important characteristics of modern Chile developed during the colonial centuries. The first is the relative homogeneity of the people, which the sparse European immigration of the 19th and 20th centuries failed to alter significantly. This homogeneity is due substantially to the early growth of the mestizo (mixed Indian and European) population and to epidemics of diseases brought by the Europeans, which decimated the Indian population. In the 18th century the process of homogenization accelerated so rapidly that by the first decade of the 19th century the composition of the Chilean population was substantially the same as it is today.

Origin of the landed oligarchy

The second characteristic is the economic, social, and political influence exerted by the oligarchy of the great landlords. After the conquest the Spaniards received land lots, not larger than 500 acres (200 hectares), on which they used indigenous labour, especially to raise cattle that were exported to Peru. During the 17th and 18th centuries the descendants of the conquerors and the wealthy merchants were oriented toward the acquisition of land; they amassed enormous territorial units (known as haciendas), which, due to the exploitation of the Indians and later of the mestizos, assured their owners of high incomes. Land-ownership was the basic element of social prestige, and it remained so during the 19th century and a good part of the 20th century.

Thus, when the Chilean independence movement began (*c.* 1810), society had a dichotomic structure: on one side was the upper class—the landlords, the Spanish bureaucrats, and the merchants; on the other, the labourers. There was no true bourgeoisie, even during the 19th century, which explains why the upper class had a monopoly on political power after independence had been achieved.

Members of the upper class, the oligarchy, were aware of the inferior state to which they had been condemned by their Spanish rulers. They were convinced that once freed from the yoke of Spain, they could increase their wealth by expanding their commerce, which had previously been limited to trade with Spain and Peru.

Thus the desire for nationhood was influenced more by practical motives than by ideology, though the influence of the North American and French revolutions was of course also a factor.

CHILE FROM 1810 TO 1920

The immediate occasion of independence in Chile, as in the rest of Latin America, was the French invasion of Spain in 1808. In 1810 a provisional Chilean government was established. It ruled for two years, until Spanish forces arrived and ousted it. Bernardo O'Higgins and other Chilean leaders fled to Argentina, where they won support from the Argentine leader José de San Martín.

Early national history, 1817–30. A combined Argentine and Chilean army defeated the Spaniards at Chacabuco on February 12, 1817. O'Higgins was nominated Chilean head of state (February 17) and served as such (with the title of *director supremo*) until 1823.

The Chilean oligarchy had little sympathy with O'Higgins, who favoured abolishing their privileges. They accepted him, however, because he was supported by the army and because of dangers posed by Spaniards still in Peru and parts of Chile (Valdivia and the island of Chiloé) and by guerrillas loyal to the Spanish monarchy.

Opposition to O'Higgins began to make itself heard once the Chilean–Argentine army expelled the Spaniards from Peru; it increased after 1822, when the Chileans succeeded in driving the remaining Spaniards from Chile. O'Higgins' attempt, by means of a new constitution, to concede a larger political role to the oligarchy did not increase his support, and general unrest and poor harvests forced him to abdicate in 1823.

The years 1823–30 were troubled by an internal political split between the oligarchy and the army; 30 successive governments held office, and a variety of political experiments were tried. Rivalries developed between federalists and centralizers and between authoritarians and liberals.

To the political chaos was added financial and economic disorder and an increase in lawlessness that tended to strengthen the authoritarian members of the oligarchy. Rival political factions were eliminated in 1829 when authoritarians, with the help of a part of the army, were able to install a junta (collegial government) that nominated José Tomás de Ovalle as provisory president. Actual power, however, was held by Diego Portales, who, as either a cabinet member or a private citizen, ruled as a virtual dictator.

The conservative hegemony, 1830–61. During the next 30 years, Chile established its own definitive organization, made possible by a compromise among the members of the oligarchy. Portales played an important role in the compromise, and a new constitution achieved as a result (1833) remained the basis of Chilean political life until 1920–30. It created a strong central government, responsive to the influence of the landowning class which controlled the parliament.

Basis of Chilean political life, 1833–1930

Consolidation of conservative factions. The establishment of this new political structure united the different factions that had brought Ovalle and later Joaquín Prieto to power. The new government was strengthened by a successful war against the Peruvian-Bolivian Confederation (1836–39), during which it broadened its support by reinstating army officers ousted when the conservatives had seized power in 1829–30.

Economic prosperity. The government of Prieto and the two succeeding governments, those of Manuel Bulnes and Manuel Montt dedicated, themselves to developing the economy. Their first and most pressing need was to re-establish the state finances, exhausted by the war. To this end, measures were taken to expand the principal source of state income—foreign trade. A free port was created at Valparaíso to encourage trade by foreign, especially British, merchants. These measures, however, would not have worked if Chilean products had not found new markets abroad. The discovery of gold in California (1848) and in Australia (1853) assured Chilean grain a vast market, as the populations of those two areas expanded. The production of silver and copper increased in response to an increased European demand, thereby increasing the wealth of the state and the dominant class. The economic development helped overcome political disagreements and aided the consolidation of internal peace.

Political stability and economic prosperity opened the way to modernization: the construction of the first railroads began, new roads were opened, and the harbours were improved. The government tried also to develop education, though largely for upper class children. The University of Chile was founded, and foreign scholars were recruited to foster geological, botanical, and economic studies.

The development of commerce attracted numerous foreign entrepreneurs (British, French, and North American), who came to dominate the import-export trade. Few members of the oligarchy dealt with commerce, and most ships flying the Chilean flag were foreign-owned.

Political diversification. The increase of wealth that especially favoured the oligarchy and foreign merchants also contributed to a diversification of the ruling class; the development of mining production in the north and of agriculture in the south created new fortunes, whose owners soon made their entry into the political world. An attempted coup d'etat, the "revolution of 1851," failed but was an indication of the political awakening of these new elements. A new development among younger members of the traditional oligarchy was the growth of liberalism and the appearance of political clubs around the middle of the century.

The impact of these forces was felt inside the political establishment, so much so that a minor conflict between the state and the church over the right to make ecclesiastical appointments was sufficient to break the unity of the dominant political class. The crux of the dispute was the question of whether the state had the right to control the church. The oligarchy was divided into two groups: conservatives, who defended the traditional privileges of the church; and nationalists, who maintained the supremacy of the state. A part of each group, dissatisfied by the authoritarian government of President Montt, united and created a separate faction, the liberals.

The widening of liberal influence, 1861–91. The period after 1860, known as "Liberal Republic," saw the emergence of many rival political groups whose common characteristic—following an unsuccessful armed insurrection by radicals in 1859—was an attempt to gain power by peaceful means.

Political factions. After 1855 the conservative element, supporting the hegemony of the church, had allied with the liberals in opposing President Montt's disregard of the oligarchy. The radicals joined the alliance against Montt, while continuing to fight the temporal power of the church. José Joaquín Pérez (1861–71), although elected with the support of the "nationalists," governed with the help of the liberal-conservative alliance. A division in the dominating political classes occurred about 1872, when the liberals started to draw away from the conservatives; the liberals favoured secularization, and freedom of religion and education; they succeeded in ending the Roman Catholic Church's monopoly in religious matters.

European influences. The fight to secularize the state helped to modernize Chile and opened the country to European influences in cultural activities and civil reforms. Young members of the economic and political oligarchy began to travel and study in Europe. They brought back many political, literary, and scientific ideas.

This new political and cultural opening toward Europe was linked to closer economic relations, especially with Great Britain, Chile's main trading partner. The British began to invest directly into Chile, supplying the capital needed to bring about the construction of railroads and the modernization of ports and public services. Many Englishmen travelled to Chile, and their diplomatic representatives had great influence, which they used to obtain economic privileges greater than those given to other foreigners.

The increase of imports and the payment of interest from loans aggravated an already weak balance of payments position and resulted in a continuing devaluation of the Chilean peso in relation to the British pound sterling. The annual inflation rate during this period was more than 8 percent.

The War of the Pacific (1879–84). The need to improve its balance of payments position attracted Chile to saltpetre mines situated along the Chilean border in the Bolivian province of Antofagasta and in the Peruvian provinces of Tarapacà and Arica. Ill-defined borders and oppressive measures allegedly taken against the Chilean migrant population in these territories furnished Chile with a pretext for invasion. Chile defeated the Peruvian and Bolivian army and annexed these provinces.

The War of the Pacific had broad repercussions. Because Britain and, to a lesser degree, France and Germany had strong commercial interests in the saltpetre mines, they threatened to intervene. The United States, hoping to keep the European powers from extending their influence in the Pacific, offered to resolve the conflict by mediation; Chile refused the United States' offer, fearing it would have to give up its territorial gains. Finally, support given by Germany to the Chilean position impeded further European intervention.

The war had weakened Chilean finances, and the economic situation continued to worsen. During the presidency of José Manuel Balmaceda (1886–91) the government tried to claim the revenues from the saltpetre mines and thus to assert major responsibility in economic matters. Nearly all of the oligarchy, however, was looking for a weaker rather than a stronger central power and objected to this attempt to strengthen the executive. The clash was resolved in a brief civil war, which ended with Balmaceda's abdication.

The parliamentary republic, 1891–1920. The coalition that overthrew Balmaceda resulted from a large political regrouping of all those who wanted to strengthen the parliament; thus, after the civil war Chile's presidential republic was converted into a parliamentary republic. This meant that the oligarchy, which had extended itself into commerce and banking, needed only to assure itself of control of parliament—and thus of the various ministries—to dominate the political life of the country. In order to remain in office, governments now had to have the confidence of the parliament. What emerged was a continual struggle for power among the factions, which began to organize themselves as real political parties.

Growth of the middle and lower classes. The period between 1891 and 1920 was one of intense political activity that saw the formation of new political parties and tendencies that tried to express the political desires of the middle and lower classes. The development of a state bureaucracy and the growth of the railroads and of commerce favoured the formation of social groups with urban concerns, rarely linked to the landed oligarchy, and increasingly aware of their possible political roles.

A proletariat developed in the saltpetre mines, in the large public utility enterprises (railways, gas, electricity), and in the many factories that began to appear in the urban centres, especially in Santiago. The first strikes to obtain better salaries and working conditions occurred during this period.

The Radical Party. The radical political faction—born as a dissenting wing of the liberals and striving toward the secularization of the country—became a party in 1888 and tended progressively to become the spokesman of the growing middle class; it adopted evolutionary socialism as an ideological base.

Margin notes:

Rise of the liberals

Balance of payments crisis

Organization of political parties

The Democratic Party. The Democratic Party (formed 1887) was led by Malaquías Concha, who spoke for the needs of the artisans and a part of the urban proletariat. Founded by former radicals, this party differed from the Radical Party only in the particular accent it gave to the problem of public education.

The Socialist Party. Marxist ideology had begun to spread among Chilean workers. The first socialist group, founded in 1897, advocated anarchism and a worker-controlled economy. It became the Socialist Party in 1901, but had a fleeting life. The increase of strikes and dissatisfaction of the mining proletariat, however, led to a new Socialist Party, formed in the mining zone in 1912, which influenced workers and university students and advocated an international class struggle.

Decline of the ruling class. The radicalization of the parties of the left was largely caused by the ruling class's neglect of Chile's complex economic and social problems. The ruling class, concerned with protecting its own interests, failed to introduce needed reforms, and as a result the political instability already evident in the late 19th century grew worse. The traditional parties—the Liberals and Conservatives—were unable to adapt to the country's changing situation.

Economic dissatisfaction

Along with the growing political and social problems, the economic situation also worsened. Loans obtained from Britain and, after 1916, from the United States served more to pay the interest on previous debts and to cover state expenses than to allow productive investments. The country consumed more than it produced, and this was translated into an annual inflation rate of more than 10 percent and to the constant devaluation of the currency in relation to the pound sterling and the dollar. Agrarian production barely kept pace with home consumption, but the large landowners were unable to introduce techniques to increase it. On the other hand, industrial development was blocked by insufficient capital and by a lack of entrepreneurial spirit.

CHILE SINCE 1920

Political uncertainty, 1920–38. In the decade 1920–30 inflation menaced the middle and lower classes, and dissatisfaction increased. The discontent of these classes rapidly extended to the army officers, who had a middle class origin. The traditional political class was aware of the growing dissatisfaction but was unable to control it.

Military takeover. A pretext for army intervention came when parliament approved a raise in senators' salaries at a time when a series of special social laws were still awaiting discussion. On September 5, 1924, a representative of the officers asked the president of the republic, Arturo Alessandri Palma, to intervene for quick approval of the social laws. A frightened parliament approved 16 new social laws in three days. Alessandri, considering himself a prisoner of the military, resigned on September 8. The military seized power and kept it until the following year, when they returned it to Alessandri.

Reduction of legislative power. When President Alessandri returned to office in 1925, he deluded himself in believing that he could restore calm by eliminating the parliamentary form of government. To this end he launched a new constitution that reintroduced a presidential republic and reduced legislative power.

New presidential republic

In the period between 1924 and 1932, 21 cabinets were formed and dissolved. These were years of profound crises, marked by attempts to create a new political structure by replacing the oligarchy with a new political elite. Under the military dictatorship of Carlos Ibáñez del Campo (1927–31), new economic reforms were tried: new industrial products were developed, the saltpetre mines were partially nationalized, public works were begun, and public education was improved. But these reforms did not touch the economic power of the oligarchy, which remained the principal political force.

Effects of the world depression. The world depression of the 1930s was very difficult for Chile's economy because the international demand and the prices for saltpetre and copper were reduced. The country was forced to reduce imports dramatically, which in turn reduced

national production. Incomes diminished, while public expenditures grew. Middle and lower class discontent increased to the point where people were ready to support any potential solution. Meanwhile, the military officers, led by Col. Carlos Ibáñez del Campo, remained in a state of agitation, opposing the oligarchy and the socialist groups and favouring a type of Fascist corporate state.

The economic crisis of the 1930s and the continued dissatisfaction of the middle class permitted the traditional political forces to regain power. They remained in office only briefly, from July 1931 to June 1932, under the presidency of Juan Esteban Montero Rodríguez, because the economic crisis was so strong that every attempted improvement failed. Power was then gained by a civilian-military coalition that formed the Socialist Republic (from June to September 1932). By the end of 1932, however, the most acute phase of the economic crisis had passed; elections were held, and Arturo Alessandri was returned to the presidency.

Return to constitutional normality. Alessandri's second term (1932–38) was characterized by a return to constitutional normality and by the return to power of the old ruling class. Alessandri tried to restore state finances, badly weakened by the crisis. His economic measures attempted to increase mining production, create a central bank, and stimulate industrial production. Public works eased part of the existing unemployment. Social discomfort diminished, but it did not disappear.

The Radical presidencies, 1938–52. The return to constitutional government did not resolve Chile's serious problems. The discontent of the proletariat, and especially of the middle class which was removed from power, was manifested in elections. In the presidential election of 1938 the Radical candidate, Pedro Aguirre Cerda, won, with the support of a coalition of the left. From 1934 to 1938 the number of voters increased by 66 percent, while Chile's total population (1930–40) increased by only 16 percent. The sudden rise in participation in the political process resulted largely from middle class discontent.

The presidencies of Cerda and Ríos. The period of Radical presidencies can be divided in two parts, separated by 1946. The first part included the presidencies of Cerda (1938–41) and Juan Antonio Ríos (1942–46). Cerda represented the middle class; his triumph came through the support of a popular front, which included the Radical, Socialist, and Communist parties (the last having split with the Socialist Party in 1919) and also the left-inspired Labour Confederation.

Cerda's program included agrarian reform and measures for increasing industrial output. The Corporación de Fomento de la Producción (Corfo) was created in 1939 to reduce imports and thus diminish the trade deficit by developing peasant industry, mainly ironworks, and by producing consumer and intermediate goods.

Cerda and Ríos tried to carry out reforms and, when these failed, tried to apply palliatives. Party strength in parliament remained stable, and power management was difficult due to the lack of a decisive majority.

This inactive period in internal affairs was largely caused by World War II; Chile remained neutral until 1942, when, in a common action with other Latin American countries, it declared war on Germany, Italy, and Japan. World War II and the Korean War of the early 1950s benefitted Chile's economy; an increased demand for copper permitted a rise in incomes, which facilitated the expansion of public education and aided industrial development, thus helping to increase production.

The presidency of Gabriel González Videla. During the period from 1946 to 1952, the president was Gabriel González Videla, also of the Radical Party, who gained a plurality with the support of the Communists. The Socialist Party denounced an offer of alliance, however, and the popular front could not be reconstituted. González Videla's first cabinets, between 1946 and 1948, included Communist ministers; but the international Cold War and Chile's internal troubles soon forced González Videla toward the right, and after 1948 he ruled with the support of the Conservative and Liberal parties.

Economic links with the United States, which had grown after the economic crisis of the 1930s, were strengthened after World War II; between 1945 and 1950, United States investments in Chile increased from $414,000,000 to $540,000,000, largely in copper production. By 1952 the United States had loaned $342,000,000 to the Chilean government. The exchange of technicians and professors helped tighten technical and cultural links between the two countries.

Recovery of the political right

The presidency of González Videla saw the strong political recovery of the right. The Radical presidents had failed to reform Chile's economic and social situations. Between 1941 and 1949 the Conservative Party grew from 17 to 22.7 percent of parliament, and the Liberal Party from 13.9 to 17.9 percent, while the strength of the Radical Party diminished from 21.7 to 19.9 percent, and that of the Communist Party dropped from 11.8 to 10.2 percent. In 1948 a new law declared the Communist Party to be illegal.

During the 14 years of Radical rule, the major development had been the creation of the Corporación de Fomento and the resulting industrial development. Between 1940 and 1952 Chile's population rose from 5,000,000 to 6,350,000, with the strongest increase in urban areas, which accounted for 52 percent of the total population in 1940 and 60 percent in 1952. Production rose during this period by a rate very close to the rise in population. But social inequities were not reduced.

Political stagnation, 1952–64. Various conditions explain the victory in 1952 of the former dictator Gen. Carlos Ibáñez del Campo. Under Radical rule the middle class had affirmed itself as a social group without injuring the economic power of the landed oligarchy, which by then had even greater control over the banks and industry. The lower classes, however, had become even poorer under the Radical presidencies. In 1949 the vote was granted to women, and the electorate thus expanded from 631,257 in 1946 to about 1,000,000 in 1952.

Ibáñez was the candidate of a heterogeneous front consisting of socialists, the right wing, and the partisans of authoritarianism and supported by a middle class concerned only with defending its acquired privileges. With the victory of Ibáñez there began a type of political rule previously unknown in Chile—populism.

The return of Ibáñez. Ibáñez had promised to rule with a strong hand and if necessary to eliminate the parliament; but during his six years as president, he ruled with the support of the parties of the traditional right, and this prevented any attempt at reform. The government of Ibáñez retained the policy of state intervention in the economy and industrial matters inaugurated by the Radical cabinets.

The presidency of Jorge Alessandri Rodríguez. Ibáñez was succeeded (1958–64) by the son of Arturo Alessandri Palma, Jorge Alessandri Rodríguez, who won the support of the Conservative and Liberal parties. To satisfy popular demands without altering profoundly the structures of the country, he launched a vast program of public works that helped absorb the large number of unemployed, which in the region of Santiago included 30 percent of the active population. At the same time he tried to reduce the high inflation rate (about 60–70 percent yearly), to augment the productive capacity of the country by reducing taxes on business enterprises, and to stimulate industrial growth by expanding the home market through public expenditure.

The government placed restrictions on salary increases; salaries thus rose more slowly than prices, which continued to increase by about 30 percent yearly. This alienated the voters, and the government had to call for the support of the Radical Party in order to stay in power.

New political groupings. Popular discontent aided the return of the Marxist-inspired Socialist and Communist parties and produced an electoral loss of the parties of the right and the centre that corresponded with the rise of those of the left. The Christian Democrat Party (Partido Demócrata Cristiano), a reform party founded in 1957, enjoyed the biggest increase—from 15.9 percent in 1961 to 22 percent in 1963.

The Christian Democrat Party

The Christian Democrat Party grew out of the Conservative Party. In 1938 a group of young conservatives had left their party to form the Falange Nacional, whose model was the Spanish Falange. In 1957 the Falange Nacional fused with the Social Christian Party (which had also seceded from the Conservatives) to form the Christian Democrat Party, whose program tended toward serious reforms in the archaic economic, political, and social structures.

The Communist Party regained strength peacefully, through a popular front that included all the leftist parties. Its design contrasted with that of the Socialist Party, which insisted that election was not the only way to power and rejected alliances with the non-Marxist left.

At the end of Alessandri Rodríguez' rule the right-wing parties were so weakened that their electoral strength was practically cut in half in the 1965 elections; in order to remain on the political scene, they joined together to form the National Party (Partido Nacional), which in the new parliament represented 12.5 percent of the electoral force. Also discredited was the Radical Party, which in 1965 obtained only 13.3 percent of the parliamentary votes. The Christian Democrats received 42.3 percent of the votes in 1965.

A common point existed between the Christian Democrat Party and the Marxist parties—the wish to eliminate the old economic and political oligarchy and to try to rescue the country from its chronic underdevelopment by more decisive action in the agrarian sectors.

A period of change, 1964–73. In the presidential election of 1964 the Christian Democrat candidate, Eduardo Frei Montalva, obtained 56 percent of the votes.

The presidency of Frei Montalva. Frei's program, synthesized in the slogan "Revolution in Freedom," promised a series of reforms for developing the country by raising the incomes of the lower classes. To attain this aim, Frei and the Christian Democrats instituted a program of "Chilenization," by which the state took control of copper, Chile's principal resource, acquiring 51 percent of the shares of the big United States copper companies in Chile. They thus intended to increase incomes, with which they planned to permit industries to develop; they also planned a vast agrarian reform by which to reduce the imports of agricultural products. Frei also promised decisive state intervention and reform in banking, which was largely controlled by the political right. Frei's programs would have destroyed the power of the right, which, although beaten politically, had retained its economic strength.

Reforms to aid the lower classes

The Frei administration, at least during its first years, counted on strong support from the middle class. But the government alienated much of the middle class by trying also, by a program of cultural development and by reforms in public education, to obtain the support of the enormous mass of peasants and of the urban underemployed, until then on the margin of the political scene.

In 1967, with the support of the Socialist and Communist parties, an agrarian reform law was approved that enabled the government to expropriate uncultivated land and limited to 190 acres the land that could be conserved by each owner. Peasant cooperatives were to be established on these lands, and the state was empowered to teach the peasants better farming techniques. Agrarian reform, however, proceeded slowly because of its costly emphasis on better housing and agricultural equipment and on an irrigation system. By 1970 about 5,000,000 acres had been expropriated.

The socialist experiment. The reformist program of the Frei government gave rise to a number of expectations among the poorer people, driving them toward an active role in political life. This increase in political participation brought about further radicalization not only of the Communist and Socialist parties but also of some of the Radicals and Christian Democrats. In 1969 this cluster of parties and left-wing groups converged into the Popular Unity (Unidad Popular) coalition, proposing as its candidate for the presidency Salvador Allende Gossens, a Socialist, who was elected president of the republic the following year.

The
Popular
Unity
Party

The Popular Unity program envisaged the eventual transition to socialism, which was to be accomplished through the end of domination of mining and finance by foreign capital, expanded agrarian reform, and more equal distribution of national income favouring the poorer classes. The accomplishments of this program were responsible for the electoral advance of Popular Unity in the local elections of 1971 and in the general elections of 1972, a success that can be essentially explained by growing popular support.

Between 1970 and 1972, however, support of the Popular Unity government by the middle class declined, as a consequence of difficulties in the economy, which featured a complex and not always consistent reorganization resulting from the nationalization of U.S.-owned copper mines —the main resource of economic production—and of a number of heavy industries. Difficulties in maintaining production levels were further augmented by boycotts on the side of foreign capital, mainly American, and the reduction of agricultural production as a consequence of agrarian reform. Inflation and stagnation of production were propitious to the growth and regrouping of the forces that opposed the socialist experiment. The oligarchy, the right-wing Partido Nacional, and the centre Christian Democrats finally joined their efforts and supported the anti-government trends in the armed forces.

The military dictatorship, from 1973. On September 11, 1973, the armed forces staged a coup. Allende died during a military assault on the presidential palace, and the military officers installed a junta composed of three generals and an admiral, with Gen. Augusto Pinochet Ugarte as president. At the outset the junta received the whole-hearted support of the oligarchy and of a sizable part of the middle class and the right-wing movements; the Christian Democrats were largely neutral. This support by moderate political forces can be explained by their deluded belief that a dictatorship represented a transitional stage necessary to restoring the status quo as it had been before 1970. Very soon they were to bow to the fact that the military officers now in power had their own political objectives, which included the repression of all left-wing and centre political forces. The Christian Democrat, National, and Democratic Radical parties were "recessed," and the Communists, Socialists, and Radicals were proscribed. In 1977 all the traditional parties were dissolved and a private enterprise economy was reinstated.

The politics of the military government, though encouraging the development of a new and dynamic entrepreneurial class, caused unemployment, decline of real wages, and, as a consequence, worsening of the standard of living of the lower and middle classes. The international economic crisis exacerbated this situation and impeded return to democratic government. In 1975 the junta attempted to legitimate its rejection of "ideological pluralism" by forming a National Unity Movement (Movimento de Unidad Nacional, or MUN).

Chilean culture and education. In the 20th century the state, by means of a Ministry of Public Education and the national universities, made itself the chief promoter of cultural development. To the national universities, with numerous campuses, were added Catholic and private secular institutions. Several national universities also developed research activities in history, literature, and science. Until 1969 the universities were the centres for scientific research; in that year the National Commission for Scientific and Technological Research was created, a state institution charged with supporting research in both private and university centres.

After 1930 the humanities enjoyed an important revival and the social disciplines a noticeable development, influenced, after 1960, by cultural exchanges with the United States and western Europe. The collaboration of economists and sociologists enabled the government to make deep analyses of national problems: the Frei administration created the ODEPLAN, a state institution charged with the study of problems related to economic and social planning, which saw a great development in the Allende administration.

The development of public and private education permitted the formation of a highly qualified body of intellectuals and technicians, whose skills were often in short demand; many were forced to emigrate, and after 1973 a major emigration took place.

BIBLIOGRAPHY

Chile from 1810 to 1920 (Political aspects): SIMON COLLIER, *Ideas and Politics of Chilean Independence, 1808–1833* (1967); H. BLAKEMORE, *British Nitrates and Chilean Politics 1886–1896* (1974); F.B. PIKE, *Chile and the United States, 1880–1962* (1963). (*Economic and social aspects*): F.W. FETTER, *Monetary Inflation in Chile* (1931); G.M. MCBRIDE, *Chile: Land and Society* (1936); A.J. BAUER, *Chilean Rural Society from the Spanish Conquest to 1930* (1975). (*Cultural aspects*): W.R. CRAWFORD, *A Century of Latin-American Thought,* rev. ed. (1961).

Chile since 1920 (Political aspects): PAUL W. DRAKE, *Socialism and Populism in Chile, 1932–52* (1978); BARBARA STALLINGS, *Class Conflict and Economic Development in Chile, 1958–1973* (1978); F.B. PIKE, *op. cit.* (*Economic and social aspects*): MARKOS MAMALAKIS, *The Growth and Structure of the Chilean Economy: From Independence to Allende* (1976); STEFAN DE VYLDER, *Allende's Chile: The Political Economy of the Rise and Fall of the Unidad Popular* (1976); F.W. FETTER, *op. cit.*; A.J. BAUER, *op. cit.*

(M.A.Ca.)

China

China is the largest of all Asian countries and has the largest population of any country in the world. It covers an area of 3,691,500 square miles (9,560,900 square kilometres), which is approximately one-fourteenth of the land area of the world; among the major countries of the world, it is surpassed in area only by the Soviet Union and Canada, and it is larger than either the United States or Brazil. Its population—officially estimated to number about 960,000,000 in 1978—represents a fifth of the world's total population; statistically speaking, there is one Chinese for every four persons of any other nationality. Both in area and in population, Europe (excluding the Soviet Union) is only half the size of China. In general terms, a Chinese province may thus be equated to a country of Europe. The Chinese province of Kiangsi, for example, while only one-third the size of Sweden, has more than triple Sweden's population, while the province of Kiangsu, with only one-fifth of the area of Spain, has nearly one and a half times Spain's population. Four of China's 21 provinces and two of its autonomous regions are larger in area than France.

The People's Republic of China, a country in East Asia, stretches for about 3,100 miles (5,000 kilometres) from east to west and about 3,400 miles (5,500 kilometres) from north to south. Its land frontier is about 12,400 miles and its coastline is 8,700 miles in length. It is bounded by the Mongolian People's Republic to the north; the Soviet Union and North Korea to the northeast; the Yellow Sea and the East China Sea to the east; the South China Sea to the southeast; Vietnam, Laos, Burma, India, Bhutan, and Nepal to the south; Pakistan to the southwest; and Afghanistan and the Soviet Union to the west. In addition to the 12 countries that border directly on China, China also faces Japan across the Yellow Sea, and in the southeast it looks toward the Philippines beyond the South China Sea.

Geographically, the large island of Taiwan (Formosa) is treated, along with the other 3,415 islands lying off the Chinese mainland, in this article. Information on all other matters concerning Taiwan will be found in a separate article of that title.

In the early 1970s, China had 29 administrative units directly under the central government; these consisted of 21 provinces (excluding Taiwan), five autonomous regions, and three municipalities (Peking, Shanghai, and Tientsin). Peking, the capital of the People's Republic, is also the cultural, economic, and communications centre of the nation. Shanghai is the largest industrial and commercial city and also the leading port.

With more than 4,000 years of recorded history, China is one of the few existing countries that also flourished economically and culturally in the earliest stage of world civilization. In the century preceding 1950, however, it experienced an era of dire anarchy and decrepitude. Un-

The country's geographical setting

der regimes that often proved to be inefficient and corrupt, it remained helpless as foreign powers nibbled at its territory and resources and as its humiliated people struggled for bare subsistence. Although it was called an "independent country," its status and condition resembled that of a foreign colony. The revolution, occurring after World War II, was a cataclysm that changed China overnight. The establishment of the Communist government in China in 1949 marked the beginning of a new era and created a new pattern of political geography. By the early 1970s, China had developed into a superpower, ranking unchallenged as one of the three most influential countries in the world. See also the articles HONG KONG; TAIWAN; city articles on CANTON; CHUNGKING; HARBIN; LHASA; MUKDEN; NANKING; PEKING; SHANGHAI; TAIPEI; TIENTSIN; and WU-HAN; also see articles on individual Chinese provinces and autonomous regions. For associated physical features, see AMUR RIVER; BRAHMAPUTRA RIVER; CHINA SEA; EVEREST, MOUNT; GOBI (DESERT); HIMALAYAN MOUNTAIN RANGES; HSI CHIANG (RIVER); KOKO NOR (LAKE); KUNLUN MOUNTAINS; TAKLA MAKAN (DESERT); TARIM RIVER; TIEN SHAN (MOUNTAINS); YALU RIVER; YANGTZE RIVER; HUANG HO (RIVER); and YELLOW SEA.

Four Chinese geographical terms—*shan*, meaning "mountains"; *ling*, meaning "mountains," "ridge," or "pass"; *chiang* and *ho*, meaning "river"—are employed, as appropriate, in this article, divided as follows:

I. The landscape

THE NATURAL ENVIRONMENT

Relief. The relief of China is high in the west and low in the east; consequently, the direction of flow of the major rivers is generally eastward. The surface may be divided into three steps, or levels. The first level is represented by the Plateau of Tibet, which is located in both Tibet and Tsinghai and which, with an average height of well over 13,000 feet, is the loftiest highland area in the world. The western part of this region, the Ch'iang-t'ang, has an average height of 16,500 feet and is known as the "Roof of the World." The second step lies to the north of the Kunlun Mountains and Ch'i-lien Shan-mo and (farther south) to the east of the Chiung-lai Shan and Taliang Shan. Here the mountains descend sharply to heights of between 6,000 and 3,000 feet above sea level, after which basins intermingle with plateaus. This step includes the Mongolian Plateau, the Tarim Basin, the Loess Plateau (loess is a yellow-gray dust deposited by the wind), the Szechwan Basin, and the Yunnan–Kweichow highland region. The third step extends from the east of the Ta-hsiang Shan, T'ai-hang Shan, and Wu Shan ranges and from the eastern perimeter of the Yunnan–Kweichow highland region to the China Sea. Almost all of this area is made up of hills and plains lying below 1,500 feet.

The most remarkable feature of China's relief is the vast extent of its mountain chains; the mountains, indeed, have exerted a tremendous influence on the country's political, economic, and cultural development. According to a rough estimate, about one-third of the total area of China consists of mountains. China possesses the world's highest mountain and largest plateau, in addition to extensive coastal plains. The five major landforms—mountain, plateau, hill, plain, and basin—are all well represented. The complex natural environment and rich natural resources of the country are closely connected with the varied nature of its relief.

The topography of China is marked by many splendours. Mt. Everest (29,028 feet, or 8,848 metres, high), known to the Chinese as Chu-mu-lang-ma Feng and located at the border between China and Nepal, is the highest peak in the world. The lowest part of the Turfan Depression in the Sinkiang Uighur Autonomous Region —Ai-ting Hu (Lake Ai-ting)—is 505 feet (154 metres) below sea level. The total range of height is thus almost 30,000 feet.

The fact that highlands that rise 15,000 feet above sea level account for more than one-fifth of the total land area of the country has directly affected climate and soil and has indirectly influenced land utilization.

Relief has dictated the development of China in many respects. The civilization of China originated in the southern part of the Loess Plateau (which in its totality covers Shensi Province and also extends into east Kansu, west Shansi, and west Honan), and from there it extended outward until it encountered the combined barriers of relief and climate. The long protruding corridor, commonly known as the Kansu or Hosi Corridor, illustrates this fact. South of the corridor is the Tibetan Plateau, which was too high and too cold for the civilization of China to gain a foothold. North of the corridor is the Gobi, a desert, which also formed a barrier. Consequently, Chinese civilization was forced to spread along the corridor, where melting snow and ice in the Ch'i-lien Shan-mo provided water for oasis farming. The westward extremities of the corridor became the meeting place of the ancient East and West.

The ancient political centre of China was subsequently, for a long time, located along the lower reaches of the Huang Ho (Yellow River). Because of the barrier formed by topography, however, it was very difficult for the central government, except when represented by unusually strong dynasties, to gain complete control over the entire country. In many instances, the Szechwan Basin, an isolated region in southwest China about twice the size of Scotland, well-protected by high mountains and self-sufficient in agricultural products, became an independent

The three altitudinal levels

The influence of relief on historic development

kingdom. A comparable situation often arose in the Tarim Basin. Linked to the rest of China only by the Kansu Corridor, the basin is even more remote than that of Szechwan, so that, when the central government was unable to exert its influence, oasis states were established; only the three strong dynasties—the Han (206 BC to AD 220), the T'ang (AD 618 to 907), and the Ch'ing (1644 to 1911)—were capable of controlling the region.

Apart from the three altitudinal zones already mentioned, it is possible—on the basis of geological structure, climatic conditions, and differences in geomorphological development—to divide China into three major topographical regions. These are the eastern, northwestern, and southwestern zones, which form the three basic regions of China. The eastern zone is a region shaped by the rivers, which have eroded landforms in some parts and have deposited alluvial plains in others; its climate is monsoonal (characterized by seasonal rain-bearing winds). The northwest region is arid and eroded by the wind; it forms an inland drainage basin. The southwest is a cold, lofty, and mountainous region, containing intermontane plateaus and inland lakes.

The three basic regions may be further subdivided into second-order geographical divisions. The eastern region contains ten of these (the Northeast Plain, the Ch'ang-pai Shan, the North China Plain, the Loess Plateau, the Shantung Hills, the Tsinling Shan, the Szechwan Basin, the Southeast Mountains, the plains of the Middle and Lower Yangtze, and the Nan Ling); the southwest contains two (the Yunnan–Kweichow highland region and the Tibetan Plateau); and the northwest contains three (the Tarim Basin, the Dzungarian Basin, and the Tien Shan).

The eastern region *The Northeast Plain.* The Northeast Plain, which is the largest in the country, is located in the region formerly known as Manchuria. It consists of an undulating plain split into northern and southern halves by a low divide of from 500 to 850 feet high. Drained in its northern part by the Sungari River and tributaries and in its southern part by the Liao Ho, the Northeast Plain is also known as the Sung–Liao Plain and the Manchurian Plain. Most of the area has an erosional rather than a depositional surface, but it is covered with a deep soil. The plain has an area of about 135,000 square miles. Its basic landscapes are forest-steppe, steppe, meadow-steppe, and cultivated land; its soils are rich and black, and it is a famous agricultural region. The river valleys are wide and flat and have a series of terraces formed by deposits of silt. During the flood season, the rivers overflow their banks, inundating extensive areas.

The Ch'ang-pai Shan. To the southeast of the Northeast Plain is a series of ranges comprising the Ch'ang-pai Shan, the Chang-kuang-ts'ai Ling, and the Wan-ta Shan. They are collectively known as the Ch'ang-pai Shan, or Long White Mountains; broken by occasional open valleys, they reach altitudes of between mostly 1,500 and 3,000 feet. In some parts the scenery is characterized by rugged peaks and precipitous cliffs. The highest peak is the volcanic cone of Pai-t'ou Shan (9,003 feet, or 2,744 metres), which has a beautiful crater lake at its snow-covered summit. As one of the major forest areas of China, the region is the source of many valuable furs and famous medical herbs. Cultivation is generally limited to the valley floors.

The North China Plain. This is the second-largest plain of China and has an area of about 135,000 square miles. Most of the plain lies at heights below 150 feet, and the relief is monotonously flat. Formed by enormous sedimentary deposits brought down by the Huang Ho and Huai Ho from the Loess Plateau, the Quaternary deposits alone (*i.e.*, those from 10,000 to 2,500,000 years old) reach thicknesses of from 2,500 to 3,000 feet. The river channels, which are higher than the surrounding locality, form local water divides, and the areas between the channels are depressions in which lakes and swamps are found. In particularly low and flat areas, the underground water table often fluctuates from between five and six and a half feet, resulting in the formation of meadow swamp and, in some places, saline soils. A densely populated area that has long been under settlement, this plain has the highest proportion of land under cultivation of any region in China.

The Loess Plateau. This plateau forms a unique region of loess-clad hills and barren mountains situated between the North China Plain and the deserts of the west. In the north, the Great Wall of China (a defensive fortification about 1,500 miles long, much of which dates from the 3rd century BC) forms the boundary, while the southern limit is the Tsinling Shan, in Shensi Province. The average altitude of the surface is between 4,000 and 5,000 feet, but individual ranges of bedrock are higher, reaching 9,285 feet (2,830 metres) in the Liu-p'an Shan. Most of the plateau is covered with loess to thicknesses of between 150 and 650 feet. In northern Shensi Province and eastern Kansu Province, the loess may reach a thickness of 800 feet. The loess is particularly liable to erosion by water; ravines and gorges are consequently found crisscrossing the plateau. It has been estimated that ravines cover approximately one-half of the entire region, with erosion reaching depths of from 300 to 500 feet and, in some places, more than 650 feet.

The Shantung Hills. These hills are basically composed of Archean (early to middle Precambrian) crystalline shales and granites and of Lower Paleozoic sedimentary rocks (*i.e.*, between 395,000,000 and 570,000,000 years old). Faults have played a major role in creating the present relief, and, as a result, many hills are horsts (blocks of the Earth's crust uplifted along faults), while the valleys form the grabens (blocks of the Earth's crust that have been downthrown along faults). The Chiao-lai Plain divides this region into two parts. The eastern part is lower, lying at heights averaging less than 1,500 feet, with only certain peaks and ridges rising to 2,500 feet and (rarely) to 3,000 feet, and only one mountain, Lao Shan, reaching a height of 3,707 feet (1,130 metres). The western part is slightly higher; the highest peak is T'ai Shan (5,026 feet, or 1,532 metres), a mountain that is sacred as a symbol of the divine election of the ruling house of China. The Shantung Hills meet the sea along a bold and rocky shoreline.

The Tsinling Shan. The Tsinling Shan in Shansi Province, is the greatest mountain chain east of the Tibetan Plateau. It consists of a high and rugged barrier extending from Kansu to Honan and dividing China proper into two parts—North and South. The altitude of the mountains is between 3,000 and 10,000 feet. The western part is higher, with the highest peak, T'ai-pai Shan, rising to 13,474 feet (4,107 metres). The Tsinling Shan consists of a series of parallel ridges, all running a little south of east, separated by a maze of ramifying valleys whose canyon walls often rise sheer to a height of 1,000 feet above the valley streams. Division between North and South China

The Szechwan Basin. This basin (also known as the Red Basin) is one of the most attractive geographical regions of China. With an area of about 75,000 square miles, the basin is surrounded by mountains, which are higher in the west and north. Protected against the penetration of cold northern winds, the basin is much warmer in the winter than the plains of Southeast China, even though they are situated more to the south. Except for the Ch'eng-tu plain, the region is very hilly. In the eastern half of the basin are numerous folds, forming a series of ridges and valleys that trend northeast to southwest. The lack of arable land has obliged farmers to cultivate the slopes of the hills, on which they have built terraces that frequently cover the slopes from top to bottom. The terracing has slowed down the process of erosion and has made it possible to cultivate additional areas by using the steeper slopes—some of which have grades up to 45° and more.

The Southeast Mountains. Southeastern China is bordered by a rocky shoreline backed by picturesque mountains. In general, there is a distinct structural and topographic trend from northeast to southwest. The higher peaks may reach an altitude of about 5,000 to 6,500 feet. The rivers are short and fast flowing and have cut steep-sided valleys. The chief areas of settlement are on narrow stripes of coastal plain where rice is produced. Along

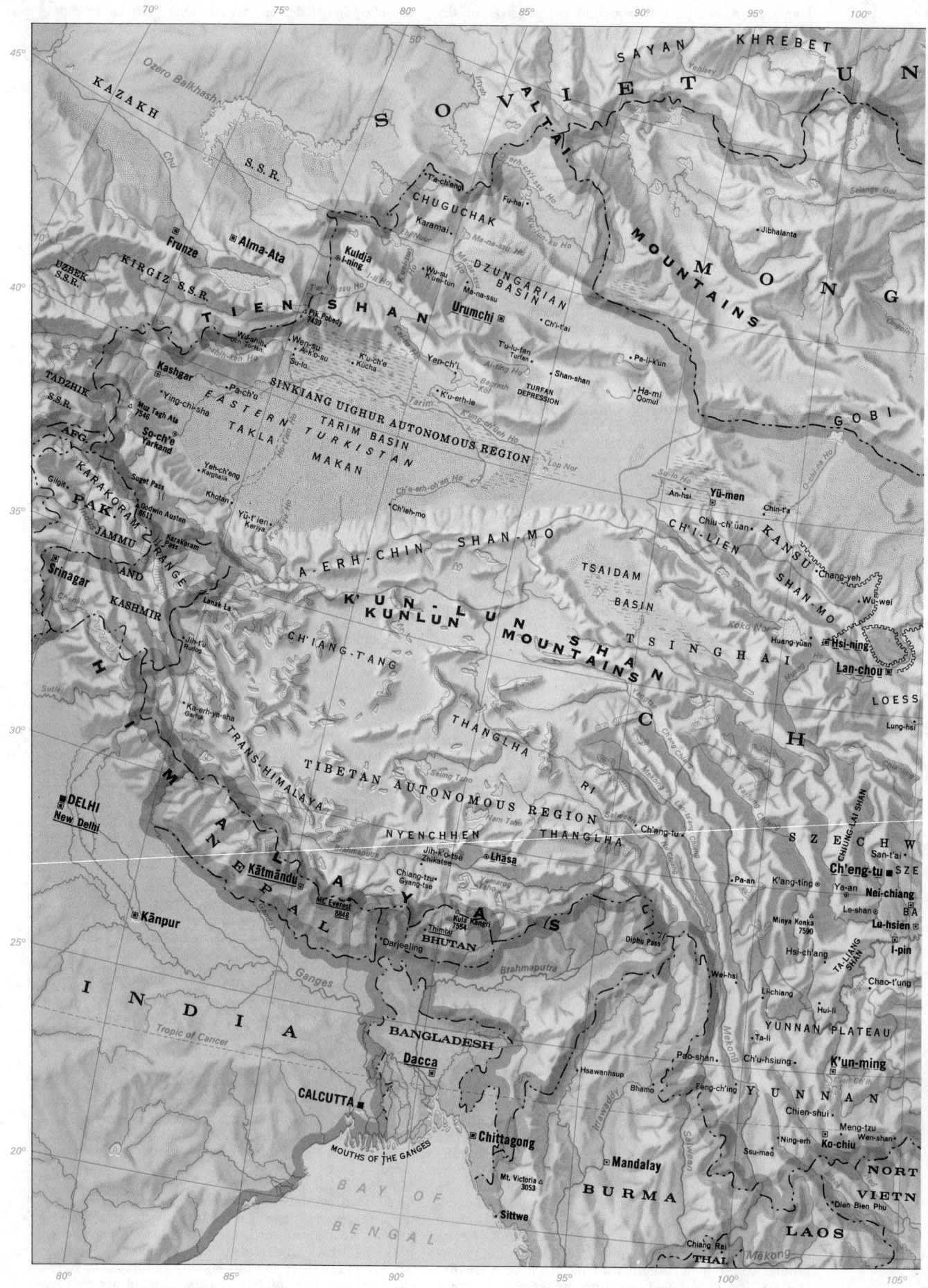

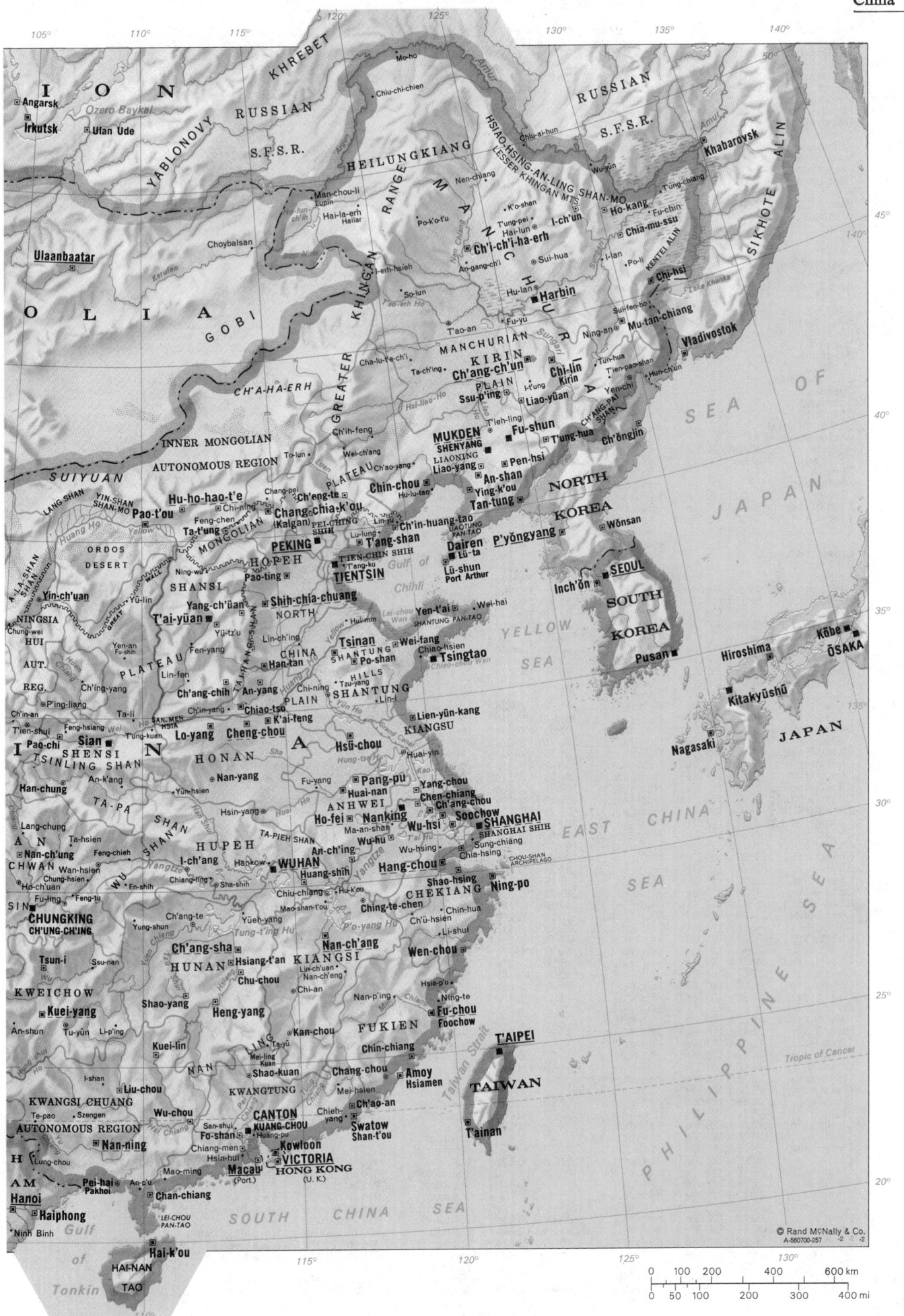

Angarsk
Irkutsk
Ulan Ude
KHREBET
YABLONOVY
RUSSIAN
S.F.S.R.
Ozero Baykal
RANGE
HEILUNGKIANG
GREATER
KHINGAN
RUSSIAN
S.F.S.R.
Amur
Chiu-chi-chien
Mo-ho
Chiu-ai-hun
HSIAO-HSING-AN-LING SHAN-MO
LESSER KHINGAN MTS.
Khabarovsk
SIKHOTE ALIN
Ulaanbaatar
MONGOLIA
Choybalsan
Kerulen
Hai-la-erh
Hailar
Hai-lun
Man-chou-li
Lupin
Hu-lun-ch'ih
K'o-shan
Nen-chiang
T'ung-pei
I-ch'un
Po-k'o-t'u
Ch'i-ch'i-ha-erh
An-gang-ch'i
Sui-hua
I-lan
Wu-yün
Fu-chin
Chia-mu-ssu
T'ung-chiang
Chi-hsi
KENTEI ALIN
GOBI
CH'A-HA-ERH
So-lun
Hsi-liao Ho
Cha-lu-te-ch'i
Ta-ch'i
T'ao-an
Fu-yü
Hu-lan
Harbin
Ning-an
Suifen-ho
Mu-tan-chiang
Lake Khanka
Vladivostok
INNER MONGOLIAN
AUTONOMOUS REGION
PLATEAU
To-lun
Ch'ih-feng
Wei-ch'ang
T'ao-an
Ch'ang-ch'un
KIRIN
Ssu-p'ing
Kirin
Chi-lin
Liao-yüan
Tun-hua
Tien-pao-shan
Yen-chi
Hun-ch'un
Ch'ŏngjin
SEA OF JAPAN
SUIYUAN
LANG SHAN
YIN-SHAN
SHAN-MO
Pao-t'ou
Hu-ho-hao-t'e
Ch'ing-te
Chang-pei
Ch'ao-yang
Chin-chou
Hu-lu-tao
Tieh-ling
MUKDEN
SHENYANG
Fu-shun
LIAONING
Liao-yang
An-shan
Ying-k'ou
Tan-tung
T'ung-hua
CH'ANG-PAI
SHAN
Wŏnsan
NORTH KOREA
A-LA-SHAN
SHAN
Yin-ch'uan
NINGSIA
HUI
AUT.
REG.
ORDOS
DESERT
Chung-wei
Yü-lin
Ta-t'ung
(Kalgan)
Feng-chen
GREAT WALL
MONGOLIAN
HOPEH
Pao-ting
Ning-wu
Chang-chia-k'ou
PEI-CHING
SHIH
Hsin
Lu-lung
Hsi-
T'ang-shan
T'IEN-CHIN SHIH
T'ang-ku
Lü-ta
Dairen
P'yŏngyang
SOUTH KOREA
Inch'ŏn
SEOUL
Ch'in-huang-tao
TAOTUNG
PAN-TAO
PEKING
T'ien-tsin
TIENTSIN
Lü-shun
Port Arthur
Gulf of
Chihli
Pao-chi
Ch'in-an
T'ien-shui
SHENSI
TSINLING SHAN
SHANSI
Yen-an
Fu-shih
Lin-fen
PLATEAU
Fen-yang
Yang-ch'üan
T'ai-yüan
Yü-tz'u
Shih-chia-chuang
NORTH
CHINA
Lin-ch'ing
Hui-min
Yen-t'ai
Wei-hai
SHANTUNG PAN-TAO
YELLOW
SEA
Pusan
Hiroshima
Kitakyūshū
Kōbe
ŌSAKA
Nagasaki
JAPAN
Ch'ing-yang
P'ing-liang
Ta-li
Feng-hsiang
Wei
T'ung-kuan
Ch'in-yang
An-yang
Ch'ang-chih
Chiao-tso
K'ai-feng
Lo-yang
Cheng-chou
HONAN
SHANTUNG
HILLS
Han-tan
Tsinan
Po-shan
Chiao-hsien
Tsingtao
Chiao-chou Wan
Wei-fang
Tzu-yang
Lin-i
Grand Canal
Yün Ho
Lien-yün-kang
KIANGSU
Han-chung
Lang-chung
AN
Nan-ch'ung
Ta-hsien
Feng-chieh
Wan-hsien
Chung-hsien
Ho-ch'uan
Fu-ling
Feng-tu
CHUNGKING
CH'UNG-CH'ING
Tsun-i
KWEICHOW
Kuei-yang
An-shun
Tu-yün
Li-p'ing
TA-PA
SHAN
I-ch'ang
Hankow
Huang-shih
WUHAN
HUPEH
TA-PIEH SHAN
An-ch'ing
Ma-an-shan
Wu-hu
Wu-hsing
Sung-chiang
Chia-hsing
SHANGHAI
SHANGHAI SHIH
Hang-chou
CHEKIANG
Ning-po
Nan-yang
Fu-yang
Huai-nan
ANHWEI
Ho-fei
Nanking
Chen-chiang
Ch'ang-chou
Soochow
Wu-hsi
Yang-chou
Pang-pu
Huai-yin
Hsü-chou
Hsin-yang
Hung-tse Hu
Hao
Kao-
An
CHINA
PLAIN
Sha
HUNAN
Ch'ang-te
Yüeh-yang
Tung-t'ing Hu
Ch'ang-sha
Hsiang-t'an
Chu-chou
HUNAN
Heng-yang
Shao-yang
Ch'ang-sha
Yung-shun
Ssu-nan
Mao-shan-t'ou
Chiang-ling
Sha-shih
Hu-k'ou
Ching-te-chen
Ch'ü-hsien
Li-shui
KIANGSI
Nan-ch'ang
P'o-yang Hu
Lin-ch'uan
Nan-ch'eng
Chi-an
Wen-chou
Ning-te
Hsia-p'u
Shao-hsing
Kuei-lin
Liu-chou
NAN
LING
Mei-ling
Kuan
Shao-kuan
Chang-chou
Mei-hsien
Ch'ao-an
Amoy
Hsiamen
Swatow
Shan-t'ou
T'ainan
TAIWAN
T'AIPEI
Tropic of Cancer
Fu-chou
Foochow
FUKIEN
Chin-chiang
Kan-chou
Nan-p'ing
KWANGSI CHUANG
Wu-chou
Te-pao
Szengen
AUTONOMOUS REGION
Nan-ning
Lung-chou
Pei-hai
Pakhoi
An-p'u
Chan-chiang
Mao-ming
Hsin-hui
San-shui
Fo-shan
CANTON
KUANG-CHOU
Huang-tu
Chiang-men
Chieh-
yang
KWANGTUNG
Kowloon
VICTORIA
HONG KONG (U.K.)
Macau (Port.)
Hanoi
Haiphong
Ninh Binh
Gulf
of
Tonkin
Lung-chou
HAI-NAN
TAO
Hai-k'ou
SOUTH CHINA SEA
EAST CHINA SEA
CHOU-SHAN
ARCHIPELAGO
T'ai Hu
PHILIPPINE SEA
Taiwan Strait
© Rand McNally & Co.
A-560700-257 -2 -2

| 0 | 100 | 200 | 400 | 600 km |

| 0 | 50 | 100 | 200 | 300 | 400 mi |

the coast there are numerous islands, where the fishing industry is well developed.

Plains of the Middle and Lower Yangtze. East of I-ch'ang, in Hupeh Province, a series of plains of uneven width are found along the Yangtze River, or Ch'ang Chiang. The plains are particularly wide in the delta area and in places where the Yangtze receives its major tributaries—including large areas of lowlands around the lakes of Tung-t'ing, P'o-yang, T'ai, and Hung-tse, which are hydrologically linked with the Yangtze. The region is an alluvial plain; the accumulation of sediment was laid down by the rivers throughout long ages. There are a few isolated hills, but for the most part the land is level, lying mostly below 150 feet. Rivers, canals, and lakes form a very dense network of waterways. The surface of the plain has been converted into a system of flat terraces, which descend in steps along the slopes of the valleys.

The Nan Ling. Nan Ling is composed of many ranges of mountains running from northeast to southwest. These ranges form the watershed between the Yangtze to the north and the Chu Chiang (Pearl River) to the south. The main peaks along the watershed are above 5,000 feet, and some are well over 6,500 feet. But a large part of the lands to the south of Nan Ling is also hilly; flatland does not exceed 10 percent of the total area. The Chu Chiang Delta is the only extensive plain in this region and is also the richest part of South China. The coastline is rugged and irregular, but less so than that of the southeast coast. There are many promontories and protected bays, including that of Hong Kong (*q.v.*). The

principal river is the Hsi Chiang (*q.v.*), which rises in the highlands of eastern Yunnan and southern Kweichow.

The Yunnan–Kweichow highland region. This region comprises the northern part of Yunnan and the western part of Kweichow; its edge is highly dissected. Yunnan is more distinctly a plateau and contains larger areas of rolling uplands than Kweichow, but both parts are distinguished by canyon-like valleys and precipitous mountains. The highest elevations lie in the west, where Tiehchi'ang Shan rises to 12,080 feet (3,682 metres). In the valleys of the major rivers, elevations drop to 1,300 to 1,600 feet. Particularly sharp differences in elevation and the greatest ruggedness of relief occur in the western part of the region, in the gorges of the large rivers. In the eastern part, karst processes (creating sinks, ravines, and underground streams in the limestone landscape) have developed very strongly. Scattered throughout the highlands are small lake basins, separated by mountains.

The Tibetan Plateau. This great massif occupies about one-fourth of the whole country. A large part of the plateau lies at elevations above 13,000 to 15,000 feet. The border ranges of the plateau are even higher, with individual peaks rising to heights of 23,000 to 26,000 feet. The interior slopes of these border mountains, as a rule, are gentle, while the exterior slopes are very steep. In its eastern and southern periphery, great rivers—such as the Yangtze, Huang Ho, Mekong, Salween, Indus, and Brahmaputra—find their sources. Only in the low valleys, chiefly along the Brahmaputra Valley, are there centres of human settlement.

Tsaidam is the largest, as well as the lowest, basin in the Tibetan Plateau, but it is also the highest basin in China. The broad northwestern part of the basin lies at elevations from 8,800 to 10,000 feet; the narrow southeastern part of the basin lies between 8,500 and 8,800 feet. Within the basin there is a predominance of gravel, sandy and clay deserts, semideserts, and salt wastes.

The Tarim Basin. North of the Tibetan Plateau, and at the much lower level of about 3,000 feet, lies the Tarim Basin. It is hemmed in by great mountain ranges: the Tien Shan on the north, the Pamir Knot on the west, and the Kunlun Mountains on the south. From these heights, glacier-fed streams descend, only to lose themselves in the loose sands and gravels of the famous Takla Makan Desert, which occupies the centre of the basin. The Takla Makan is one of the most barren of the world's deserts; only a few of the largest rivers, such as the Tarim and Ho-t'ien, cross the desert, but even their flow is not constant, and they have water throughout their entire courses only during the flood period. The area of the basin is about 215,000 square miles, and its elevations are from 2,500 to 4,600 feet above sea level. Its surface slants to the southeast, where the Lop Nor (a lake) is situated in the Sinkiang Uighur Autonomous Region.

The Dzungarian Basin. North of the Tarim Basin is another large depression, the Dzungarian. It is enclosed by the Tien Shan on the south, while to the northeast it is cut off from the Mongolian People's Republic by the Altai Mountains. The surface of the basin is flat, with a gentle slope to the southwest. The larger portion of the land lies at elevations between 1,000 and 1,500 feet, and in the lowest part the elevation drops to 620 feet. In general the main part of the basin is covered by a broad desert with moving barchan (crescent-shaped) dunes; only in certain parts are they retained by vegetation. The largest rivers of this basin are the O-erh-ch'i-ssu and the Wu-lun-ku, which flow down from the Altai Mountains, and the Ma-na-ssu and K'uei-tun, which descend from the Eastern Tien Shan.

The Tien Shan. The Chinese part of the Tien Shan consists of a complex system of ranges and depressions in which two major groups of ranges—the northern and southern—may be distinguished; they are separated by a strip of intermontane depressions that is broken up by the interior ranges. Ancient metamorphic rock (formed under heat and pressure) comprises the larger portion of the ranges in the interior zone; Paleozoic (from 225,000,-000 to 570,000,000 years old) sedimentary and igneous–sedimentary beds form its north and south chains, while Mesozoic (from 65,000,000 to 225,000,000 years old) sandstones and conglomerates fill the intermontane depressions in the interior zone and comprise the foothill ridges. The height of the main chains of the Eastern Tien Shan is between 13,000 and 15,000 feet, with individual peaks exceeding 16,000 feet; the interior chains reach 14,500 feet. In the western part, where there is adequate precipitation, large glaciers are formed, reaching a length of more than 20 miles. Large rivers with much water, such as the T'e-k'o-ssu Ili and its tributaries, begin their courses here. With predominant Alpine meadow steppe, this area is one of the best grazing lands of China.

The coast and coastal waters. The Chinese government has declared the breadth of China's territorial sea to be 12 nautical miles. This provision applies to all territories of China, including the Chinese mainland and the coastal islands. The coast of China contrasts greatly between South and North. To the south of the bay of Hangchow, the coast is rocky, and indented with many harbours and offshore islands. To the north, except along the Shantung and Liaotung peninsulas, the coast is sandy and flat.

Drainage. The three principal rivers of China, all of which flow generally from west to east, draining into the China Sea, are the Huang Ho, or Yellow River (*q.v.*), the Yangtze (*q.v.*), and the Hsi Chiang (*q.v.*). The Huang Ho, which rises in the Kunlun Mountains, is the northernmost of the three; it drains into the Gulf of Chihli, north of the Shantung Peninsula. The Yangtze, the longest river in the country, rises in the Tibetan Highlands and

flows across central China, draining into the East China Sea north of Shanghai. The Hsi Chiang, the southernmost of the three, rises in the Yunnan–Kweichow highlands and empties into the South China Sea via the Chu Chiang Delta, at Canton.

Table 1: The Major Rivers of China*			
	length (mi)	drainage area (sq mi)	annual runoff (cu ml)
Yangtze River (Ch'ang Chiang)	3,716	705,298	243.7
Hsi Chiang (West River)	1,216	168,815	87.8
Amur River (Hei-lung Chiang)	1,771†	332,785†	34.8
Salween River (Nu Chiang)	957	46,300‡	18.5
Min Chiang	359	21,620	14.9
Huang Ho (Yellow River)	3,011	297,680	11.6
Red River (Yüan Chiang)	408	31,614	9.9
Huai Ho	675	81,080	8.2
Liao Ho	836	83,010	4.7
Yalu River	491	12,359‡	4.0
Hai Ho	602	80,500	1.7
Tumen River	324	8,826	1.4

*Figures are those of source cited, and may differ from figures given elsewhere for the same rivers. †This is the total length; approximately two-thirds of the river's course runs along the present frontier of China and the Soviet Union. The total drainage area of the Amur River is 711,972 sq mi, of which 47 percent is on the Chinese side. ‡Both the drainage area and average annual runoff are for the Chinese portion of the river only. Source: C.S. Chen, *China*, vol. I, part 4, 1971.

China has more than 5,000 rivers with individual drainage areas of more than 40 square miles. The total runoff (amount of water they carry away) annually is estimated at 3,000,000,000,000 tons, of which 95.5 percent drains directly into the sea and 4.5 percent disappears inland. Of the total runoff, more than 80 percent drains into the Pacific Ocean, 12 percent into the Indian Ocean, and only 0.3 percent into the Arctic Ocean.

The distribution of surface water in China is extremely uneven. Only a small part of the country has enough water all the year round. Much of the country has an abundant runoff but only during the rainy summer, when enormous surpluses of water are received. From the southeast to the northwest, the surface water decreases as mountainous features increase. A vast area of the northwest lacks water throughout the year.

The mountains of the southeast and the mountainous islands of Taiwan (*q.v.*) and Hainan have the most abundant surface water. Over the year they receive more than 60 inches of precipitation (in some places even more than 80 inches), of which almost two-thirds constitutes the runoff, so that a dense drainage network has developed. The amount of runoff is highest in the southeast, exceeding 40 inches. In western Hunan, where annual precipitation is from 47 to 55 inches, the runoff amounts to between 24 and 35 inches; on the Kweichow highlands, it is between 20 and 24 inches, and, in the Szechwan Basin, it amounts to only between 12 and 16 inches. Farther west, in the source area of the Huang Ho, the runoff is between four and eight inches. In the Tsaidam Basin, it is only between two and four inches, and, in the true deserts, it is usually less than 0.4 of an inch. The arid climate of the northwest is reflected in the landscape of the dry steppes, which is characterized by richer grasses in the east, while in the west the landscape gradually changes to bare deserts.

In the lower reaches of the Yangtze, the Chu Chiang Delta, and the Ch'eng-tu plain, a very dense network of waterways has been developed. In the North China Plain and the Northeast Plain, most of the rivers have a linear flow, and tributaries are few and unconnected. In the inland drainage area, there are very few rivers because of scanty precipitation. Extensive areas such as the Tarim Basin and northeastern Kansu Province are often completely void of runoff. In these regions, the rivers are dependent upon melted snow and ice; in consequence, they are mostly small ones and are found only in mountains and mountain foothills. As they drain farther and farther away from the mountains, most of them eventually disappear in the desert, while some form inland lakes. Because the northern part of the Tibetan Plateau is a cold desert, the rate of evaporation is slow, so that a denser network of rivers has developed; most of them, however, run into glaciated depressions, forming numerous lakes.

Chinese geographers use a line drawn from the Tsinling Shan to the Huai Ho as the dividing line separating South and North China. Because of its flat relief and early agricultural development, the area north of this line contains 62 percent of China's cultivated land; paradoxically, however, because of scanty and erratic precipitation, the average annual runoff north of this line accounts for only 14 percent of the total for the country as a whole.

Soils. Because of its vast and diverse climatic conditions, China has a wide variety of soils. Indeed, all the soils of the Eurasian continent, except the soils of the tundra and the highly leached podzolic-gley soils of the northern taiga, are found in China. As a result of the difference in climatic conditions between the drier and cooler North and the wetter and hotter South, soils may be grouped into two major classifications. Generally speaking, the soils north of the Tsinling Shan–Huai Ho line are pedocals (calcareous) and are neutral to alkaline in reaction; those south of this line are pedalfers (leached noncalcareous soils), which are neutral to acid.

Apart from the great plateaus and high mountains to the southwest, marked soil zones are formed in China according to differences in climate, vegetation, and distance from the sea. The east and southeast coastal region is covered by the forest zone associated with a humid and semihumid climate, while the north and northwest inland regions mostly belong to the steppe zone, as well as to the semidesert and desert zone associated with a semi-arid and arid climate. Between these two broad soil zones lies a transitional zone—the forest-steppe zone, where forest soils merge gradually with steppe soils.

Between the pedocals of the north and the pedalfers of the south lie the neutral soils. The floodplain of the Yangtze below the Three Gorges is overlain with a thick cover of noncalcareous alluvium. These soils, sometimes classified as paddy (rice-growing) soils, are largely neutral and, for the most part, are exceedingly fertile and of good texture. The paddy soil is one of the unique types of cultivated soils; it has been formed over a long period of time under the specific conditions of rice cultivation.

Along the coast of North China are belts of saline and alkaline soil. They are associated with a combination of poor drainage and aridity, where the rainfall is insufficient either to dissolve or to carry away the salts in solution. Thought is being given to the possibility of reclaiming these saline areas.

The adverse effects of nature on the soil have been further intensified by centuries of concentrated cultivation that has resulted in an almost universal deficiency of nitrogen and of organic matter. The shortage of organic matter is due primarily to the habitual use by farmers of crop stalks and leaves for livestock feed and fuel. The animal manure and night soil used for fertilizer contain too small an amount of organic matter to compensate for the loss of nutrients in the soil. The soils are also often deficient in phosphorus and potassium, but these deficiencies are not so widespread or so severe as that of nitrogen.

At one time, half of the territory of China may have been covered by forests, but now only about 8 percent of the country is forested. Extensive forests in central and southern China have been cleared for farmlands, with the

inevitable accompaniment of excessive erosion of soils from the hillsides and soil deposition in the valleys. Farmers consequently construct level terraces, supported by walls, in order to hold back water for rice fields, thus effectively controlling erosion. Wherever elaborate paddy terraces have been built, soil erosion is virtually absent, and stepped terraces have become one of the characteristic features of the rural landscape.

Excessive grazing and destruction of the grass cover by man can also result in soil removal. With the valuable crumb structure broken down and porosity lost, the topsoil may be easily washed away through erosion in the rainy season; if the region happens to be a dry one, the wind produces the same effect. The Loess Plateau, constantly buffeted by rain and wind, is especially vulnerable

to soil erosion, which results in a distinctive landscape. Steep-sided gullies, some of which may be several hundred feet deep, cut the plateau into fantastic forms of relief. The damage done by heavy rain in summer is caused not only by the loss of the topsoil but also by the frequent floods resulting from the silt-laden riverbeds.

Climate. *The air masses.* China lies in the southeast of Asia, the world's largest continent, and faces the Pacific, the world's largest ocean. Between the Pacific and this part of Asia, there is a seasonal movement of air masses. The polar continental air mass, originating in Siberia, dominates a large part of China during the winter, while the tropical Pacific air mass exerts its influence during the summer. In China, the sharply varied climatic conditions prevailing in summer and in winter result from the interaction of these two air masses, which are entirely different in nature.

The Siberian air mass, which is quite stable, is extremely cold and dry and often has marked layers of temperature inversion. After crossing the Mongolian Plateau, the air mass spreads southward and begins to invade North China, where it undergoes a series of rapid changes; its temperature rises slightly, and its stability decreases. During the day it may be quite warm, but at night, or in shaded places, the cold is often unbearable. In general, the diurnal (daily) range of temperature is over 18° F (10° C); in extreme cases, it may exceed 45° F (25° C). North China is dry because it is affected by this air mass most of the time.

The prevailing winter wind blows from November through March; it changes direction as it moves to the south. In northern and northeastern China its direction is from the northwest; in eastern China, it comes from the north; and in the southeastern coasts, it is from the northeast.

The height of the winter wind belt usually does not exceed 13,000 feet. As it moves to the south, the height decreases; in Nanking it is about 6,500 feet, and in South China it is less than 5,000 feet. Tsinling Shan becomes an effective barrier to the advance of the cold waves to the south, particularly in the western section, where the average altitude of the mountains is mainly between 6,500 and 9,000 feet.

In the descent of 3,000 feet from the Mongolian Plateau to the North China Plain, the Siberian air is warmed adiabatically (*i.e.*, it undergoes a change of pressure but without gain or loss of heat). This sharp drop of altitude also intensifies the air's dryness. As the Siberian air moves to the south, the warming of the lower layer occurs much more rapidly, and this results in the great soil dryness characteristic of this time of the year. Therefore, in Nanking, which is 530 miles to the south of Peking, the relative humidity of the Siberian air increases by 50 percent. The aridity of the air is the basic factor accounting for clear weather and an abundance of sunshine during the winter months in northern China.

In China, the tropical Pacific air mass is the chief source of the summer rainfall. When it predominates, it may cover the eastern half of China and penetrate deep into the border areas of the Mongolian Plateau and onto the eastern edge of the Tibetan Plateau. In summer, the Siberian air mass retreats to the western end of Mongolia, although it occasionally extends southward and sometimes may reach the Huai Ho Valley, which constitutes a battleground between the tropical Pacific and Siberian air masses in summer.

The movement of the two air masses is of immense significance to the climate of central and North China. In summer, when the tropical air mass predominates, the frontal zone between the two shifts northward; as a result, North China receives heavier rainfall. When the southeastern monsoon slackens, however, the frontal zone moves southward, and central China receives more rainfall, as a result of which floods may occur. The summer rainfall in North China is mainly the result of the interaction between these two air masses.

The activity of the tropical Pacific air mass in winter is confined to the southeast coastal areas; during this season, therefore, drizzle quite frequently occurs in the hilly areas south of the Wu-ling Shan, and dense fog often appears in the morning.

Besides these two air masses, three other air masses also play their parts in the making of the climate of China. These are the equatorial continental air mass (a highly unstable southwest monsoon), the polar maritime air mass, and the equatorial maritime air mass. Furthermore, as China is a vast country with complex topography, the interaction between the air masses and relief produces many different types of climate.

Temperature. The temperature generally decreases from south to north. The mean annual temperature is above 68° F (20° C) in the Chu Chiang Valley. It decreases to between 59° and 68° F (15° and 20° C) in the middle and lower reaches of the Yangtze; to about 50° F (10° C) in North China and the southern part of Sinkiang; and to 41° F (5° C) in the southern area of the Northeast, the northern part of Sinkiang, and places near the Great Wall. It drops to below 32° F (0° C) in the northern part of Heilungkiang. The annual range of temperature between the extreme south and north is about 86° F (30° C). With few exceptions, January is the coldest month, and July the hottest.

South of the Tsinling Shan–Huai Ho line, the mean January temperature increases progressively, rising from 32° F (0° C) to 72° F (22° C) on the southern coast of Hainan Island. Snow rarely falls, and the rivers do not freeze. North of this line, the temperature drops from 32° F (0° C) to −18° F (−28° C) in the northern part of Heilungkiang. The difference in January temperature between the extreme north and south is as much as 90° F (50° C). No country in the world shows a greater contrast in temperature between its southern and northern borders.

In April, the mean temperature for the whole of China is above 32° F (0° C) with the exception of the extreme north of Heilungkiang. During this time, the mean temperature for the Northeast Plain is between 36° and 46° F (2° and 8° C), and, for the extensive plain between Peking and Shanghai, it is between 54° and 59° F (12° and 15° C). South of the Nan Ling, the mean temperature is well over 68° F (20° C). Along the coast of southern Kwangtung, willows start to bud in late January, but in Peking the budding of willows comes as late as early April—a difference of about 70 days.

In summer, the range of temperature between North and South China is quite small. In July the difference in temperature between Canton and Peking is only about 5° F (3° C), and the isotherms in July are roughly parallel to the coastline. In July, the isotherm of 82° F (28° C) embraces an extensive area. The hottest place in China is to be found along the valleys in the Middle and Lower Yangtze. The mean July temperature of Nan-chang and Ch'ang-sha is well over 84° F (29° C), and in many years it is above 86° F (30° C).

In North China, autumn is generally cooler than spring; the mean October temperature in Peking is about 55° F (13° C), and in April the mean temperature is about 57° F (14° C). In South China, the reverse is true. The mean October temperature in Canton is 75° F (24° C); in April the mean temperature is only about 70° F (21° C).

The middle and lower reaches of the Huang Ho are the areas where China's civilization and agriculture first developed. There, the seasonal rhythm is well marked, and the duration of each season is evenly spaced. In other parts of China, however, there are variations between different regions in the duration, as well as in the starting and closing dates, of each season. In northern Heilungkiang summer is nonexistent, while in southern Kwangtung there is no winter. In K'un-ming, on the Yunnan Plateau, the climate is fine throughout the year; there, spring and autumn together make up 310 days, and winter lasts less than two months.

In general, south of the Tsinling Shan–Huai Ho line, the mean daily temperature seldom falls below freezing, so that farming can be practiced all through the year. In the Yangtze Valley, two crops a year are usually grown, but, north of the Great Wall, only one crop a year is grown.

South of the Nan Ling, the mean daily temperature exceeds 50° F (10° C) all the year round, but, in the north of the Heilungkiang, the total number of days with temperatures of above 50° F (10° C) drops to less than 120 days.

Rainfall. The distribution of rainfall in China generally decreases from the southeast to the northwest. The annual precipitation of certain places along the southeastern coast amounts to over 80 inches. The Yangtze Valley receives about 40 inches. Further north, in the Huai Ho Valley, the annual rainfall decreases to 30 inches. In the lower reaches of the Huang Ho, only 20 inches of precipitation are received annually. The Northeast obtains much more precipitation than the North China Plain, where, along the Southeast Mountains, as much as 40 inches is received.

The southeast monsoon has lost much of its moisture by the time it reaches the northern part of the Loess Plateau, where the annual precipitation is reduced to about between 12 and 20 inches. Northwest of a line linking the Greater Khingan Range, Yin-shan Shan-mo, Lang Shan, Ch'i-lien Shan-mo, and the A-erh-chin Shan-mo, the annual precipitation is less than ten inches. This is because these regions are far from the sea, and the southern monsoon is prevented from reaching them by high mountains; only grasslands, therefore, are found there. In western Inner Mongolia, the Kansu Corridor, and the Tarim Basin, the annual precipitation is even less than four inches. These are areas of true desert, where sometimes not a single drop of rain is received for several years.

The Dzungarian Basin and the I-li Valley of northern Sinkiang are open to the influences of the westerlies; precipitation there is heavier. The precipitation of the Tibetan Plateau, like that of China as a whole, decreases from southeast to northwest. The valleys in the southeastern part of the plateau receive more than 40 inches of precipitation, while the eastern edge of the plateau receives 20 inches annually. But in the enclosed basin in the north—the Tsaidam—the annual precipitation is only between from four to ten inches.

The high variability of rainfall is another characteristic of the climate of China. Usually, the less the rainfall, the greater the variability; this fact has a close connection with the high frequency of drought and flood in China. Spring rain is of immense significance to farming in China; unfortunately, spring is the season with the highest variability. In South China, the variability exceeds 40 percent; along the Yangtze, it is around 45 percent; and in North China, it is over 50 percent. The variability of a very large area in North China exceeds 70 percent in some places; east of Peking, for example, the rainfall variability in spring may even exceed 80 percent. In the central parts of the Yunnan–Kweichow highlands, the variability of spring rain also exceeds 80 percent.

Rain falls mostly in the summer months, when plants need water the most. This is an important asset for farmers, but the rainfall in summer is usually too intense. In June many places south of the Yangtze receive an average daily rainfall of more than eight-tenths of an inch; in some cases, the rainfall may even exceed an inch. In North China, the daily rainfall is less than six-tenths of an inch. In July, when the frontal zone shifts northward, cyclones (circulation of winds around centres of low atmospheric pressure) are much more active in North China than in South China, and North China begins to receive heavier rainfall. More than half of the North China Plain records eight-tenths of an inch of daily rainfall. In some places, as much as an inch to an inch and a fifth of rain may fall daily. During this time areas south of the Yangtze are covered by the tropical Pacific air mass, so that the weather becomes comparatively stable, and the amount of rainfall usually decreases, while the average rainfall intensity is less than that of June; a large area receives less than six-tenths of an inch. The intensity of August rainfall is in general less than that of July. With the exception of the southeast coastal regions, rainfall in other places in August seldom reaches eight-tenths of an inch.

The temperature pattern

Rainfall distribution

In the southeastern coastal regions, around Foochow and Swatow, the maximum daily rainfall may even approach 12 inches. This fact is clearly related to the high frequency of typhoons (tropical cyclones) striking this part of the coastal area of China. Typhoons usually arrive during the period from May to November; July, August, and September are the three months when typhoons are the most frequent.

In May typhoons usually strike the coast south of Swatow. Later in June, the typhoons shift northward, arriving between Swatow and Wenchow. After July, typhoons begin to invade areas north of Wenchow. August is the month with the highest frequency of typhoon invasions. Over one-third of the typhoons reaching China arrive in this month. After September, the frequency of typhoons decreases, and the pattern again shifts southward. In October typhoons usually land south of Wenchow; the late typhoons arriving in November and December strike the coast to the south of Swatow.

Vegetation and animal life. Types of natural vegetation and their floristic composition are quite diverse. The total number of seed plants in China is about 30,000 species, representing 2,700 genera; more than 200 of these genera are restricted to China. There are about 2,500 species of forest trees, and, among flowering plants, 95 percent of the known woody group are to be found. Many of them are trees of economic importance, such as tung oil trees, camphor trees, lacquer trees, star anise (yields an oil used as a flavouring additive), and privet. That no insurmountable topographic barriers, such as large stretches of desert, exist between the tropical, temperate, and semi-frigid zones, that wind systems alternate in winter and summer, and that cyclones frequently occur are all factors that contribute to the variety and intermixture of tropical and temperate plants in China. If the vegetation of Heilungkiang Province in the north and Kwangtung Province in the south are compared, it is hardly possible to find a single common plant species, with the exception of certain weeds. In the taiga of the northern border of China or in the high mountains, however, there are many plant species also found inside the Arctic Circle, while, in the Chinese tropics, there are species that also grow below the Equator. From the ecological point of view, the tropical forests of South China, however, do not in general differ greatly from those of Indonesia and other Southeast Asian countries, while the desert and steppe vegetation of northwestern China is closely akin to that found in Mongolia or to that in Kazakhstan, in the Soviet Union. Furthermore, the Chinese taiga of the frontier area near the Soviet Union in no way differs from that of Siberia.

Travelling in China, one may encounter practically all types of natural vegetation indigenous to the Northern Hemisphere, with the exception only of that of the polar tundra. There are mangrove swamps along the shores of the South China Sea; tropical rain forests on Hainan Island and in the south of Yunnan; and elsewhere there are desert, steppe, meadows, and savannas, as well as regions where tropical and temperate coniferous, broad-leafed evergreen, and deciduous plants prevail.

On China's high mountains—for example, those in the proximity of the Himalayas—there exists a rich and varied stock of Alpine and sub-Alpine vegetation, extending until the limit of their vertical distribution is reached; above this, only sterile rocks, glaciers, and permanent snow are usually to be found.

In accordance with the character of the plant life and vegetation, China may be divided—roughly along a diagonal from the southwest to the northeast—into two sharply different parts: the dry Northwest and the humid Southeast. The tropical area, adjoining the humid Southeast, is geographically related more to Southeast Asia.

In the Northwest, where desert-like conditions prevail, there are vast areas of very sparse drought-resisting vegetation; within these areas in the low-lying land and depressions are patches of salt-tolerant plants, notably in the Dzungarian, Tsaidam, and Gobi regions. Skirting the southern edge of the Gobi is a wide belt of grassland.

(C.-S.Ch.)

Profusion of vegetation and a variety of relief have fostered the development of a great diversity of animal life and have permitted the survival of animals elsewhere extinct. Notable among such survivals are the great paddlefish of the Yangtze, the small species of alligator in eastern and central China, and the giant salamander (related to the Japanese giant salamander and the American hellbender) in western China. The diversity of animal life is perhaps greatest in the ranges and valleys of the Tibetan border, to which region the giant panda is confined. The takin, or goat antelope, numerous species of pheasants, and a variety of laughing thrushes are to be found in all the Chinese mountains. China seems to be one of the chief centres of dispersal of the carp family and also of Old World catfishes.

The regional affinities of Chinese animal life are complex. In the Northeast there are resemblances to the animal life of the Siberian forests. Animals from Central Asia inhabit suitable steppe areas in northern China. The life of the great mountain ranges is Palearctic (relating to a biogeographic region that includes Europe, Asia north of the Himalayas, northern Arabia, and Africa north of the Sahara), but with distinctively Chinese species or genera. To the southeast the lowlands and mountains alike permit direct access to the eastern region. This part of China presents a complete transition from temperate-zone Palearctic life to the wealth of tropical forms distinctive of southeastern Asia. Tropical types of reptiles, amphibians, birds, and mammals predominate in the southernmost Chinese provinces. (K.P.S.)

THE LANDSCAPE UNDER HUMAN SETTLEMENT

Rural settlement patterns. Except in the mountains and hills, an overwhelming majority of the rural settlements of China consist of sizable compact (nucleated) villages. The formation of such rural settlements is related not only to the increasing population and to a long historical background but also to water supply (the practice of drilling deep wells, for instance) and to defense (especially against the attack of bandits in former days). Many of the big villages have no urban atmosphere at all, even with populations of several thousand.

Frequent but irregular markets may be held between the settlements to enable the peasants to barter their agricultural produce. These gatherings are usually held every three or ten days and, in some instances, every other day or every other month, depending on local commercial needs. They are also called by different names in different regions. Those in Kwangtung and Kwangsi are called *hsu;* those in the North China Plain, *chi* or *tien;* those in the Yunnan–Kweichow highland region, *kai;* and those in the Szechwan Basin and its southeastern adjoining districts, *ch'ang.*

Compact villages are the rule on the North China Plain. A village of average size has from 500 to 700 people. About 20 to 30 villages are served by a rural town in an area of about 20 square miles. Villages are fairly evenly distributed and are connected with each other by footpaths and cart tracks. Houses are built close together and are mostly made of sun-dried brick or pounded earth. Many of the market towns or even big villages are surrounded by walls. The number and length of the streets depend on the town's size and the nature of the terrain; some streets are merely narrow lanes.

Rural landscapes of central and southern China are dominated by rice fields. The Yangtze Delta has almost every type of human settlement, from the single farmstead to the fairly large market town. Villages to the south and east of T'ai Hu (T'ai Lake) in Kiangsu Province are mainly compact, with populations between 1,000 and 1,500; they are located one to two miles apart. Compact villages in central China, particularly on the Lower Yangtze, are larger than those of North China; many have a few shops that serve not only the villagers but also the dispersed residents nearby. In the centre of dozens of such villages is a market town, which collects rural produce and distributes manufactured goods. Communication among the villages is mainly by boat, along the dense net of waterways. The most elegant structures in the landscape are the numerous stone bridges that span streams and canals. In the Ch'eng-tu plain of the Szechwan Basin, a large part of the population lives in isolated farmsteads or scattered hamlets, surrounded by thickets of bamboo and broad-leafed trees. The rural settlements on the southeastern coast, especially in the deltaic plains, are mostly compact villages.

Cave dwellings are another distinctive feature of the Chinese rural landscape. They are common on the Loess Plateau, and particularly in northern Shensi, western Shansi, and southeastern Kansu, where the loess is thick and timber is scarce. The cave dwelling requires little timber and has the further advantage over a surface structure of being cooler in summer and warmer in winter.

Urban settlement patterns. Urbanization and industrialization are often closely related. The 1953 census reported 102 places with a population of more than 100,000 and nine cities with a population exceeding 1,000,000 each. The urbanization trend in China accelerated after 1953 as the government intensified its efforts to convert the country into an industrial power. Some indications of this rapid growth are given by the fragmentary reports that, between 1953 and 1970, the number of cities with populations of more than 1,000,000 had grown from nine to 21. One source indicated that the total urban population of China in 1964 was 130,000,000, which represented an increase of 80 percent over the 1953 figures. The 1970 city estimates cited in Table 2 appear to refer to the urban centres of the municipalities and so differ from UN and official Chinese estimates, which refer to the entire municipality.

The dramatic change in the urban landscape is the result of the rapid development of modern manufacturing industries and of communications. In the early 1970s, many new towns and cities were being built around manufacturing and mining centres. In the more remote areas of China, the first appearance of railways and highways contributed to the rapid growth of some entirely new

Table 2: Cities Having a Population over 500,000

	1953	1970
Shanghai	6,204,000	7,000,000
Peking	2,768,000	5,000,000
Tientsin	2,694,000	3,600,000
Shen-yang	2,300,000	2,800,000
Wu-han	1,427,000	2,560,000
Chungking	1,772,000	2,300,000
Canton	1,599,000	2,200,000
Nanking	1,092,000	1,750,000
Harbin	1,163,000	1,670,000
Dairen	766,000	1,650,000
Sian	787,000	1,500,000
Lan-chou	397,000	1,450,000
T'ai-yüan	721,000	1,350,000
Tsingtao	917,000	1,300,000
Ch'eng-tu	857,000	1,200,000
Ch'ang-ch'un	855,000	1,200,000
K'un-ming	699,000	1,100,000
Tsinan	680,000	1,100,000
Fu-shun	679,000	1,080,000
An-shan	549,000	1,050,000
Cheng-chou	595,000	1,000,000
Hangchow	697,000	960,000
T'ang-shan	693,000	950,000
Pao-t'ou	149,000	900,000
Tzu-po	184,000	850,000*
Ch'ang-sha	651,000	820,000
Ch'i-ch'i-ha-erh	345,000	750,000
Shih-chia-chuang	373,000	730,000
Soochow	474,000	720,000
Kirin	435,000	700,000
Su-chou	373,000	700,000
Foochow	553,000	680,000
Nan-ch'ang	398,000	650,000
Kuei-yang	271,000	650,000
Wu-hsi	582,000	650,000
Ho-fei	184,000	630,000
Huai-nan	287,000	600,000
Nan-ning	195,000	550,000
Hu-ho-hao-t'e	148,000	500,000

*Largely as a result of territorial expansion of the city limits.
Source: C.S. Chen, *China*, vol. II, part 3, 1971.

towns, such as Karmo, Shih-ho-tze, and Sze-chuan-ho. For larger cities, Urumchi (capital of the Sinkiang Uighur Autonomous Region), Lan-chou (Kansu), and Pao-t'ou (Inner Mongolian Autonomous Region) provide examples of extremely rapid expansion. The population of Urumchi increased from about 141,000 in 1953 to 450,-000 in 1968. Lan-chou lies midway between Southeast and Northwest China. Although a railway first reached Lan-chou only in 1952, by the early 1970s it was served by four main rail lines and several major highways and was expected to become one of the leading industrial centres in the interior. The population of the city increased from 397,000 in 1953 to 1,450,000 in 1970. Pao-t'ou was a bleak frontier town of traders, artisans, and immigrant farmers, but its population rose from 149,-000 in 1953 to 900,000 in 1970; it is now the third-largest steel centre in China, surpassed in size only by An-shan and Wu-han.

II. People and population

ETHNIC AND LINGUISTIC GROUPS

China is a multinational country, with a population composed of a large number of ethnic and linguistic groups. Almost all its inhabitants are of Mongoloid stock. The basic classification of the population is therefore not so much ethnic as linguistic. According to the 1953 census, the Han Chinese, the largest group, numbered about 547,000,000—almost 94 percent of the total population. They outnumbered the minority groups or minority nationalities in every province or autonomous region except Tibet and Sinkiang. The Han, therefore, forms the great homogeneous mass of the Chinese people, sharing the same culture, the same traditions, and the same written language. The 53 minority groups, spreading over approximately 60 percent of the total area of the country, numbered only about 35,000,000, or about 6 percent of the total population, in 1953. Where these minority groups are found in large numbers, they have been given some semblance of autonomy and self-government; autonomous areas of several types have been established on the basis of the geographical distribution of nationalities.

The Han
Chinese

The People's government takes great credit for its treatment of these minorities, including care for their economic well-being, raising of their living standards, provision of educational facilities, the promotion of their national languages and cultures, and the raising of their levels of literacy, as well as for the introduction of a written language where none existed previously. In this connection it may be noted that, of the 50-odd minority languages, only 20 had written forms before the coming of the Communists, and only relatively few written languages —for example, Mongolian, Tibetan, Uighur, Kazakh, Tai, and Korean—were in everyday use. Other written languages were used chiefly for religious purposes and by a limited number of persons. Educational institutions for national minorities are a feature of many large cities, notably Peking, Wu-han, Ch'eng-tu, and Lan-chou.

Four major language families are represented in China —the Sino-Tibetan, Altaic, Indo-European, and Austro-asiatic. The Sino-Tibetan family, both numerically and in the extent of its distribution, is the most important; within this family, Han Chinese is the most widely spoken language. Although unified by their tradition, the written characters of their language, and many cultural traits, the Han Chinese speak several mutually unintelligible dialects and display marked regional differences. By far the most important Chinese tongue is the Mandarin, or *p'u-t'ung hua*, meaning "generally understood language." By 1970, it was said that more than 90 percent of the Chinese people already understood or used Mandarin, and increasing efforts were being made to teach and publicize the use of this standard speech in other dialect areas. There are three variants of Mandarin. The first of these is the northern variant, of which the Peking dialect, or Peking *hua*, is typical and which is spoken to the north of the Tsinling Shan–Huai Ho line; as the most widespread Chinese tongue, it has long seemed the most likely basis for a national language. The second is the western variant, also known as the Ch'eng-tu or Upper Yangtze

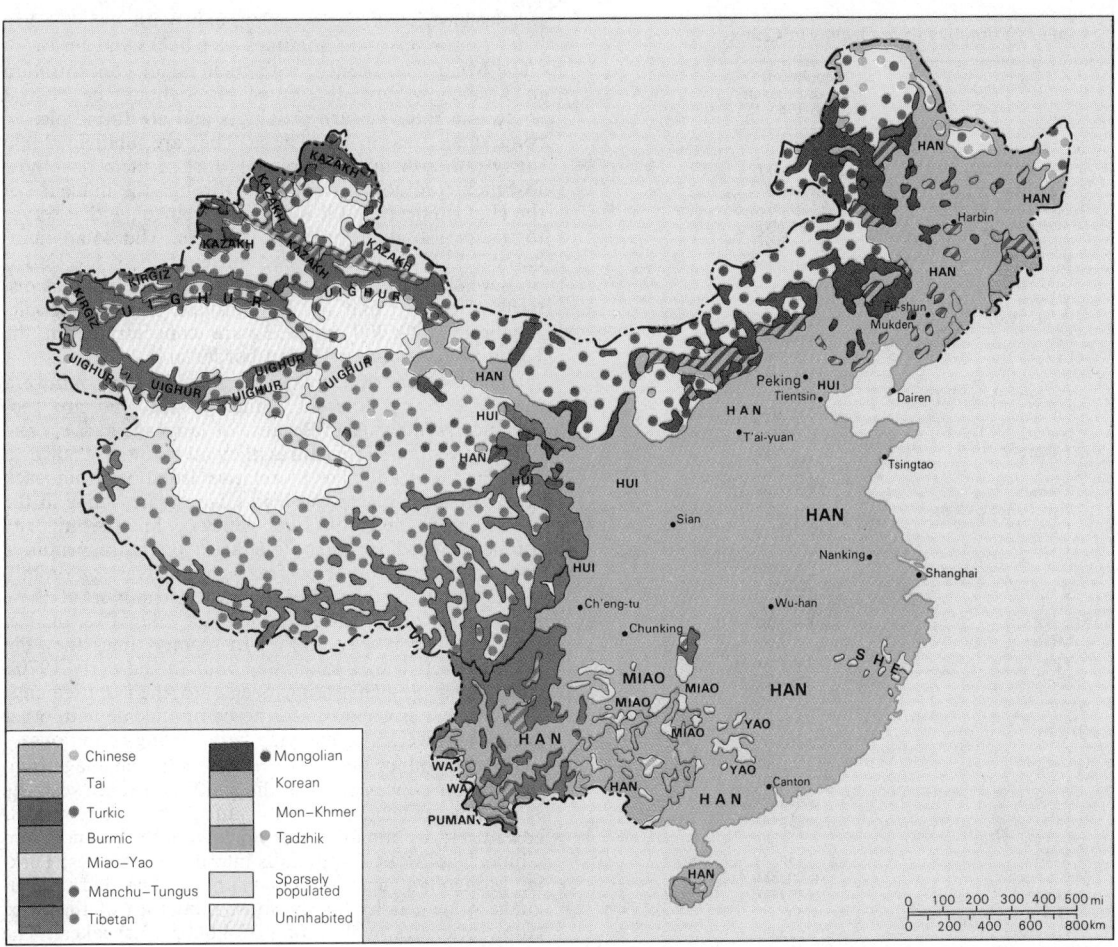

General ethnic composition of China.

variant; this is spoken in the Szechwan Basin and in adjoining parts of Southwest China. The third is the southern variant, also known as the Nanking or Lower Yangtze variant, which is spoken in northern Kiangsu and in southern and central Anhwei.

Related to Mandarin are the Hunan, or Hsiang, dialect, spoken by about 26,000,000 people in central and southern Hunan, and the Kan dialect, used by 15,000,000 people. The Hweichow dialect, spoken by 7,000,000 people in southern Anhwei, forms an enclave within the southern Mandarin area.

Less intelligible to Mandarin speakers are the dialects of the southeast coastal region, stretching from Shanghai to Canton. The most important of these is the Wu dialect, spoken by about 50,000,000 persons in southern Kiansu and in Chekiang. This is followed, to the south, by the Fuchow, or Min, dialect of northern and central Fukien, which is spoken by about 10,000,000 people; and by the Amoy–Swatow dialect of southern Fukien and easternmost Kwantung, with more than 15,000,000 speakers (excluding those in Taiwan). The Hakka dialect of southernmost Kiangsi and northeast Kwangtung is spoken by at least 20,000,000 people, who have a rather scattered pattern of distribution. Probably the best known of these southern dialects is Cantonese, which is spoken by about 35,000,000 people in central and western Kwangtung and in southern Kwangsi—a dialect area in which a large proportion of overseas Chinese originated.

In addition to the Han Chinese, the Manchus and the Hui (or Chinese Muslims) also speak Mandarin and use Chinese characters. The Huis are descendants of Chinese who adopted Islām when it penetrated into China in the 7th century. According to the 1953 census, there were 3,-559,000 Hui, out of a total of 10,000,000 Muslims in China. They are intermingled with the Hans throughout much of the country. Although widely dispersed, their heaviest concentration is in the Northwest, particularly in the Ningsia Hui Autonomous Region and in Kansu,

The Manchus and the Hui

where nearly one-third of the Hui reside. Other Hui communities are organized as autonomous districts (*tzu-chih-chou*) in Sinkiang and as autonomous counties (*tzu-chih-hsien*) in Tsinghai, Hopeh, Kweichow, and Yunnan. There has been a tendency in recent years for the Hui people to move from their scattered settlements into the area of major concentration, possibly because, as firm adherents of Islām, this facilitates intermarriage with persons of the same faith.

According to the 1953 census, there were 2,419,000 Manchus, who declared themselves to be descendants of the Manchu warriors that invaded China in the 17th century and founded the Ch'ing dynasty (1644 to 1911). Ancient Manchu is virtually a dead language, and Manchus have been completely assimilated into Chinese culture. They are found mainly in North China and the Northeast, but they form no separate autonomous areas above the commune level. The Koreans of the Northeast, who numbered 1,120,000 at the time of the 1953 census and who form the Yen-pien Korean Autonomous District in eastern Kirin, cannot be assigned with certainty to any of the standard language classifications.

The Chuangs, with 6,611,000 persons at the time of the 1953 census, are China's largest minority group. More than 90 percent of them live in the Kwangsi Chuang Autonomous Region, where they account for about 28 percent of the total population. They are also represented in national autonomous areas in neighbouring Yunnan and Kwangtung. They depend mainly on the cultivation of rice for their livelihood. In religion they are animists, worshipping particularly the spirits of their ancestors. The Puyi group, numbering almost 1,250,000 in 1953, are concentrated in southern Kweichow, where they share an autonomous district with the Miao group. The T'ung group, who numbered 690,000 in 1953, are settled in small communities in Kwangsi and Kweichow; they share with the Miao group an autonomous district set up in southeast Kweichow in 1956. The Tai group are con-

The Chuangs

Table 3: Ethnolinguistic Groups in China

	population (estimates given between 1955–65)
Sino-Tibetan	
Sino-Tibetan	709,024,000
Han Chinese	681,650,000
Hui (Chinese Muslim)	3,930,000
Tibeto-Burman	8,664,000
Tibetan	2,776,000
Yi (Lolo)	3,260,000
Pai (Minchia)	680,000
T'uchia	600,000
Hani (Woni)	540,000
Lisu	310,000
Lahu	180,000
Nasi (Moso)	150,000
Chingpo (Kachin)	110,000
Ch'iang	42,000
Nu	13,000
Tulung	2,700
Tai	11,140,000
Chuang	7,780,000
Puyi (Chung-chia)	1,310,000
T'ung	820,000
Thai	500,000
Li	390,000
Nung	180,000
Shui	160,000
Miao-Yao	3,640,000
Miao	2,680,000
Yao	740,000
She	220,000
Altaic	
Altaic	8,916,000
Turkic	4,545,000
Uighur	3,900,000
Kazakh	530,000
Kirgiz	68,000
Salar	31,000
Uzbek	11,000
Yuku	4,600
Mongolian	1,909,000
Mongol	1,640,000
Tung	150,000
Tu (Mongor)	63,000
Daghur (Daur)	50,000
Paoan	5,500
Manchu-Tungus	2,462,000
Manchu	2,430,000
Sibo	21,000
Evenki (Solon)	7,200
Oronchon (O-lun-chun)	2,400
Hoche (Nanay)	600
Indo-European	
Tadzhik (Tajiks)	15,000
Austro-Asiatic	
Mon-Khmer	295,000
Wa (Kawa)	280,000
Puman (Pulang)	15,000

omous District of northern Yunnan (with 385,000 Yi). They raise crops and sometimes keep flocks and herds.

The Miao–Yao branch, with their major concentration in Kweichow, are distributed throughout the central south and southwestern provinces and are found also in some small areas in East China. They are subdivided into many rather distinct groupings. Most of them have now lost their traditional tribal traits through the influence of the Han Chinese, and it is only their language that serves to distinguish them as tribal peoples. The Miao numbered 2,511,000 in 1953; two-thirds of them are settled in Kweichow, where they share two autonomous districts with the T'ung and Puyi groups. The Yao people, numbering 640,000 in 1953, are concentrated in the Kwangsi–Kwangtung–Hunan border area.

In some areas of China, especially in the southwest, there are many different ethnic groups who are geographically intermixed. Because of language barriers and different economic structures, they all maintain their own cultural traits and live in relative isolation from each other. In some places the Han Chinese are active in the towns and in the fertile river valleys, while the minority peoples depend for their livelihood on more primitive forms of agriculture or on grazing their livestock on hillslopes and mountains. The vertical distribution of these peoples is in zones—usually the higher they live, the less complex is their way of life. In former times they did not mix well with one another, but in the early 1970s, with highways penetrating deep into their settlements, they had better opportunities to communicate with other groups and were also enjoying better living conditions.

While the minorities of the Sino-Tibetan language family are thus concentrated in the south and southwest, the second major language family—the Altaic—is represented entirely by minorities in northwestern and northern China. The Altaic family falls into three branches; Turkic, Mongolian, and Manchu–Tungus. The Turkic language branch is by far the most numerous of the three Altaic branches, with a total of 4,600,000 speakers. The Uighur numbered 3,640,000 in 1953, forming the largest Turkic minority. They are distributed over chains of oases in the Tarim Basin and in the Dzungarian Basin of Sinkiang. They mainly depend on irrigation agriculture for a livelihood. Other Turkic minorities in Sinkiang are splinter groups of nationalities living in Soviet Central Asia, including Kazakhs and Kirgiz. All these groups are adherents of Islām. The Kazakhs and Kirgiz are pastoral nomadic peoples, still showing traces of tribal organization. The Kazakhs live mainly in northwestern and northeastern Sinkiang as herders, retiring to their camps in the valleys when winter comes; they are established in the Ili Kazakh Autonomous District. The Kirgiz are highmountain pastoralists and are concentrated mainly in the westernmost part of Sinkiang.

The Mongolians, who are by nature a nomadic people, are the most widely dispersed of the minority nationalities of China. Most of them are inhabitants of the Inner Mongolian Autonomous Region. Small Mongolian and Mongolian-related groups of people are scattered throughout the vast area from Sinkiang through Tsinghai and Kansu and into the provinces of the Northeast (Heilungkiang, Kirin, and Liaoning). In addition to the Inner Mongolian Autonomous Region, the Mongolians are established in two autonomous districts in Sinkiang, a joint autonomous district with Tibetans and Kazakhs in Tsinghai, and several autonomous counties in the western area of the Northeast. Some of them retain their tribal divisions and are pastoralists, but in the early 1970s large numbers of Mongolians were engaged in sedentary agriculture, and some of them combined the growing of crops with herding. The tribes, who are dependent upon animal husbandry, travel each year around the pastureland—grazing sheep, goats, horses, cattle, and camels—then return to their point of departure. A few take up hunting and fur trapping in order to supplement their income. The Mongolian language consists of several dialects, but in religion it is a unifying force; most Mongolians are believers in Tibetan Buddhism.

A few linguistic minorities in China belong to neither

The Altaic language family

centrated in southern Yunnan and were established in two autonomous districts—the Hsi-shuang-pan-na Thai Autonomous District, whose population is related most closely to the Tais of northern Thailand, and the Te-hung Thai-Chingpo Autonomous District, whose Tais are related to the Shan people of Burma. The Li of Hainan Island form a separate group of the Chinese-Tai language branch. They numbered 330,000 in 1953 and share with about 30,000 Miao people a district in southern Hainan.

Tibetans numbered about 2,776,000 in 1953 and are distributed over the entire Tsinghai–Tibetan plateau, about 1,275,000 living in the Tibetan Autonomous Region. Outside Tibet, Tibetan minorities are constituted in autonomous districts and autonomous counties. There are five Tibetan autonomous districts in Tsinghai, two in Szechwan, and one each in Yunnan and Kansu. The Tibetans still keep their tribal characteristics, but few of them are nomadic. Though essentially farmers, they also raise livestock and, as with other tribal peoples in the Chinese far west, also take to hunting to supplement their food supply. The major religion of Tibet has been Tibetan Buddhism since about the 17th century; before 1959 the social and political institutions of this region were still largely based on this faith. The Yi numbered about 3,-255,000 in 1953; many were concentrated in the Liangshan Yi Autonomous District of southern Szechwan (with about 800,000 Yi) and in the Ch'u-hsiung Yi Auton-

of the two major language families. The Tadzhiks of westernmost Sinkiang are related to the population of the Tadzhik Soviet Socialist Republic and belong to the Iranian branch of the Indo-European family. The Kawa people of the Chinese–Burmese border area belong to the Mon–Khmer branch of the Austroasiatic family.

DEMOGRAPHY

Population growth. Historical records show that, as long ago as 800 BC, in the early years of the Chou dynasty, China was already inhabited by about 13,700,000 people. Down to the last years of the Western Han dynasty, around 2 BC, comparatively accurate and complete registers of population were kept, and the total population in that year was given as 59,600,000, living in 12,-200,000 households, with an average of 4.87 persons per household. This first Chinese census was intended mainly as a preparatory step toward the levy of a poll tax. Being aware that a census might work to their disadvantage, many members of the population managed to avoid reporting; this explains why all subsequent population figures were unreliable until 1712. In that year the Emperor declared that an increased population would not be subject to tax; population figures thereafter gradually became more accurate.

The census of 2 BC

It was during the later years of the Northern Sung dynasty, in the early 12th century, when China was already in the heyday of her economic and cultural development, that the total population began to exceed 100,000,000. Later, when uninterrupted and large-scale invasions took place from the north, China again suffered from internal troubles that led to a diminution of her population. When national unification returned with the advent of the Ming dynasty, the census was at first strictly conducted. According to a registration compiled in 1381, China possessed a total of 59,900,000 persons, distributed in 10,-600,000 households, with an average of 5.62 persons per household. The total figure came quite close to the one registered in 2 BC.

From the 15th century onward, the population of China increased steadily; this increase was interrupted only by wars and natural disasters in the middle part of the 17th century. During the 18th century, China enjoyed a lengthy period of peace and prosperity, characterized by continual territorial expansion and an accelerating population increase. By 1762, China had a population of more than 200,000,000, and, by 1803, this had increased to 302,000,000. In 1834 the figure rose still further to 401,-000,000. It should be noted that during this period there was no concomitant increase in the amount of cultivable land. Hence, from this time on, land hunger began to make itself felt.

From the early 19th century, China again suffered from internal strife and foreign invasions, marking a period of more than a century in which population growth was slowed.

Birth and mortality rates. In common with some Asian countries, but contrary to Western experience, men in China outnumber women. The 1953 census reported that 51.8 percent of the population was male, and 48.2 percent female; in other words, for every 100 females there were 107.7 males. This situation was in contrast to that in, for example, the United States, where in the same year there were only 98.9 males per 100 females. The 1953 census also revealed that about 505,000,000 Chinese—almost 87 percent of the total population—lived in rural areas. The term rural area, as used in the census, meant either a place with a population of 2,000 or less or a place inhabited by a population of more than 2,000, of whom 50 percent were peasants or were in one way or another engaged in agriculture. A place with a population of more than 2,000, of whom 50 percent were nonagricultural, was defined as a town.

The male–female ratio

In 1964, a second census, covering a much wider range of investigation than the first census of 1953, was conducted. The result of this census, however, had not yet been officially announced in the early 1970s. Unofficial sources reported that the total population of China given by the census was 713,000,000.

According to the 1957 registration, the average birth rate was 34 per 1,000, and the average death rate was 11 per 1,000. Hence, the rate of natural increase at that time was about 23 per 1,000. In urban areas the birth rate was higher and the death rate lower than in rural areas.

Since 1949, sanitation and medical care have greatly improved, epidemics have been brought under control, and the younger generation has become much healthier. Even more important has been the rapid extension of public hygiene and the cult of cleanliness throughout the country. The result has been that, while the number of births has remained fairly constant, the death rate—estimated at about 27 to 30 per 1,000 in the early decades of the 20th century and at 18 per 1,000 in 1952—by the early 1970s had fallen to about 15 per 1,000, and was continuing to fall.

The reduction of infant mortality rates was even more striking. The infant mortality rate for the whole country fell from more than 200 per 1,000 in 1949 to 81 per 1,000 in 1956. After 1956 the infant mortality rate in rural areas dropped to less than 100 per 1,000, while that in the major urban areas fell to less than 40 per 1,000.

The fall in infant mortality

The fast-increasing population of China poses a major food-supply problem for the government. In the period 1954 to 1958—the five years after the 1953 census—the average annual population increase was 17,000,000, which was equivalent to the total population of East Germany or of Romania. Faced with difficulty in obtaining an adequate food supply and in combatting the generally low standard of living, the authorities began a drive for birth control in the years 1955 to 1958. For some reason, the campaign was called off in mid-1958 but was resumed again in 1962, at which time late marriages were advocated. Once again contraception was advised; the need for family planning, including the proper spacing of childbirth and the care of the mother's health, rather than the curbing of number, was stressed. The ages of marriage recommended are 23 to 27 for women and 25 to 29 for men. Earlier marriages are condemned on the basis that they are physically and mentally harmful to the health of parents and children and that they distract youth from study and productive work. In addition to late marriage, smaller families have been vigorously advocated throughout the country. The three-child family has been declared ideal, and abortion is once again available under liberal provisions. Although in the early 1970s there were some reports that food and cloth rations and maternity leave were not granted after the fourth child, these potentially repressive measures apparently were not strictly applied.

Population distribution. Because of complex natural conditions, the population of China is quite unevenly distributed. Population density varies strikingly, with the greatest contrast occurring between the eastern half of China and the lands of the west and the northwest. Many areas in the eastern coastal plain and deltas have, on the average, a population density of more than 1,250 persons per square mile, and the lowland areas alongside the major rivers and lakes may have a density of from 750 to 1,000 persons per square mile. Exceptionally high population densities—for example, of more than 1,500 persons per square mile—occur in the Yangtze Delta, in the Chu Chiang Delta, and on the Ch'eng-tu plain of western Szechwan Basin. Most of the high-density areas are coterminous with the alluvial plains on which intensive agriculture is centred.

In contrast, the extensive western and frontier regions, which are almost as large as the whole of Europe, are all sparsely populated. These regions, having on the average less than one person per square mile, occupy about one-half of the total area of the country. The three largest administrative divisions of Sinkiang, Tibet, and Tsinghai have a combined area of 1,385,900 square miles —nearly two-fifths of the national total—yet this vast area is inhabited by only about 11,400,000 persons, who constitute only 1.6 percent of the nation's total. In sharp contrast, the five provinces of Hopeh, Honan, Shantung, Kiangsu, and Anhwei have a combined area of only

Table 4: China, Area and Population

	area		population	
	sq mi	sq km	1957 estimate†	1970 estimate
Autonomous regions *(tzu-chih-ch'ü)*				
Inner Mongolia	163,900	424,500	4,200,000	7,000,000
Kwangsi Chuang	92,700	240,100	21,400,000	24,000,000
Ningsia Hui	65,600	170,000	1,800,000	2,200,000
Sinkiang Uighur	635,800	1,646,700	5,600,000	8,000,000
Tibet	471,700	1,221,700	1,300,000	1,300,000
Municipalities *(shih)*				
Peking	6,900	17,800	4,000,000	7,600,000
Shanghai	2,200	5,800	6,900,000	10,800,000
Tientsin	1,500	4,000	3,200,000	4,300,000
Provinces *(sheng)*				
Anhwei	54,000	139,900	33,600,000	35,000,000
Chekiang	39,300	101,800	25,300,000	31,000,000
Fukien	47,500	123,000	14,700,000	20,000,000
Heilungkiang	272,300	705,300	16,100,000	25,000,000
Honan	64,400	166,800	48,700,000	50,300,000
Hopeh	74,300	192,400	41,500,000	43,000,000
Hunan	81,300	210,600	36,200,000	38,000,000
Hupeh	72,400	187,500	30,800,000	33,700,000
Kansu	238,100	616,600	13,300,000	13,000,000
Kiangsi	63,600	164,700	18,600,000	25,000,000
Kiangsu	39,500	102,300	45,200,000	47,000,000
Kirin	104,900	271,700	13,800,000	20,000,000
Kwangtung	81,700	211,500	35,900,000	42,800,000
Kweichow	67,200	174,000	16,900,000	20,000,000
Liaoning	88,600	229,500	26,100,000	29,500,000
Shansi	60,700	157,200	16,000,000	20,000,000
Shantung	59,300	153,600	54,000,000	57,000,000
Shensi	75,600	195,800	18,100,000	21,000,000
Szechwan	219,700	569,000	72,200,000	70,000,000
Tsinghai	278,400	721,100	2,100,000	2,100,000
Yunnan	168,400	436,200	19,100,000	23,000,000
Total China	3,691,500	9,560,900*	646,600,000	731,600,000

*Converted area figures do not add to total given because of rounding.
†1957 population figures have been adjusted to reflect post-1957 territorial-administrative changes.
Source: Official government figures; US Central Intelligence Agency.

291,500 square miles, or about 8 percent of the nation's total land area, yet these provinces are inhabited by a population totalling 232,300,000, or about 32 percent of the national total. The sparsely populated areas of the western and the northern frontier are relatively isolated from the central areas both by distance and by natural barriers. Extensive uninhabited areas include the extremely high (over 15,000 feet) northern part of Tibet, the sandy wastes of the central Tarim and eastern Dzungarian basins in Sinkiang, and the barren desert and mountains east of Lop Nor, where China exploded its atomic and hydrogen bombs.

Settlement of the frontier regions In the 1960s the government became increasingly aware of the importance of the frontier regions and initiated a drive for former servicemen and young intellectuals to settle there. Consequently, the population has increased, following the construction of new railways and highways that traverse the wasteland; a number of small mining and industrial towns have also sprung up.

Internal migration. Migrations have often occurred throughout the history of China. Sometimes they took place chiefly because there was a famine or political disturbance; as a result of this, an area already intensively cultivated would be depopulated, after which people in adjacent crowded regions would move in to occupy the deserted land. Sometime between 1640 and 1646, a peasant rebellion broke out in Szechwan, resulting in a great loss of life. Subsequently, people from Hupeh and Shensi entered Szechwan to fill the vacuum, and the movement continued until the 19th century. Again, during the middle of the 19th century, the Taiping Rebellion caused another large-scale relocation of population. Many people in the Lower Yangtze were massacred by the opposing armies, and the survivors suffered from starvation because their food supplies had been plundered. After the defeat of this peasant rebellion, people from Hupeh, Hunan, and Honan moved into the depopulated areas of Kiangsu, Anhwei, and Chekiang, where farmland was lying uncultivated for want of labour. Similar examples are provided by the Nien Rebellion in Shensi and Kansu,

in the 1860s and 1870s, and by the great Shensi famine of 1877 to 1878.

It is historically evident that many major and longer lasting Chinese population movements have tended to be toward the south. Had it not been for the influence of foreign powers in the middle years of the Ch'ing dynasty (1644–1911), more of the surplus population of northern China would have migrated south and would thus have contributed to the development of vast areas there. Unfortunately, this southward migration route was often blockaded, and the migrants had to go toward the north, the northeast, and the northwest. All of these movements, excepting the one toward the northeast, were by no means massive and were usually attended by tribulations.

In recent history, the domestic movement of the Han Chinese to the Northeast, formerly known as Manchuria, is the most significant. The Manchu dynasty was established in 1644, yet, even before its establishment, Manchu soldiers launched raids into North China and captured Chinese labourers, who were then obliged to settle in the Northeast. The Chinese settlement in Manchuria did not last long, however, for in 1668 the area was closed to further Chinese migration by an Imperial decree, though Chinese migrants still continued, somewhat clandestinely, to move to the north of the Great Wall, and the ban placed on Chinese migration, despite its frequent renewals, was never effectively enforced. This situation continued until 1850, by which time Chinese settlers had secured a position of dominance in their colonization of Manchuria. The ban was later partially lifted, partly because the Manchu rulers were harassed by disturbances among the teeming population of China proper and partly because the Russian Empire time and again tried to invade sparsely populated and thus weakly defended Manchuria. The ban was finally removed altogether in 1878, but settlement was encouraged only after 1900.

With Manchuria open to the Han Chinese, the population increased as expected—by 1904 it had reached 17,-000,000, including the Manchus. The increase in population was stimulated by several incentives. The physical setting of the region was conducive to agricultural development, and the well-developed transportation system and subsequent industrial growth helped to provide ample employment opportunities. While other northern provinces were experiencing high population pressures, civil strife, heavy taxation, and famine, there was affluence and relative peace in Manchuria. In the 1920s, the region therefore attracted poor people from such northern provinces as Shantung, Hopeh, and Honan.

The great influx of people into Manchuria has been especially pronounced since 1923, and incoming farmers have rapidly brought a vast area of virgin prairie under cultivation. About two-thirds of the immigrants entered Manchuria by sea, and a third came overland. On account of the severity of the winter weather and migrants' strong attachment to their native place, migration in the early stage was highly seasonal. The movement of farmers from Hopeh and Shantung usually started in February and continued through the spring. After the autumn harvest a large proportion of the farmers returned south. In the years from 1923 to 1929, the arrivals numbered about 5,000,000, of whom approximately half remained as permanent settlers. The three Manchurian provinces of Liaoning, Kirin, and Heilungkiang had a population totalling about 34,000,000 in 1930—a figure that rose to 47,000,-000 at the time of the 1953 census and that was estimated to have risen to about 74,500,000 by 1970.

With industrial development in Manchuria and the consequent rise of urban centres, the nature of the migration changed. No longer was the movement primarily one of agricultural resettlement, based substantially on an exodus from the overcrowded areas of North China; instead, it became essentially a rural-to-urban movement of interregional magnitude, as Manchuria developed into the main industrial region of China. In the 20 years from 1923 to 1943, official records indicated an average net increase by migration in the population of Manchuria of about 1 percent per year. For several years following 1945, there seemed to be a time when the migration to

The migration to Manchuria

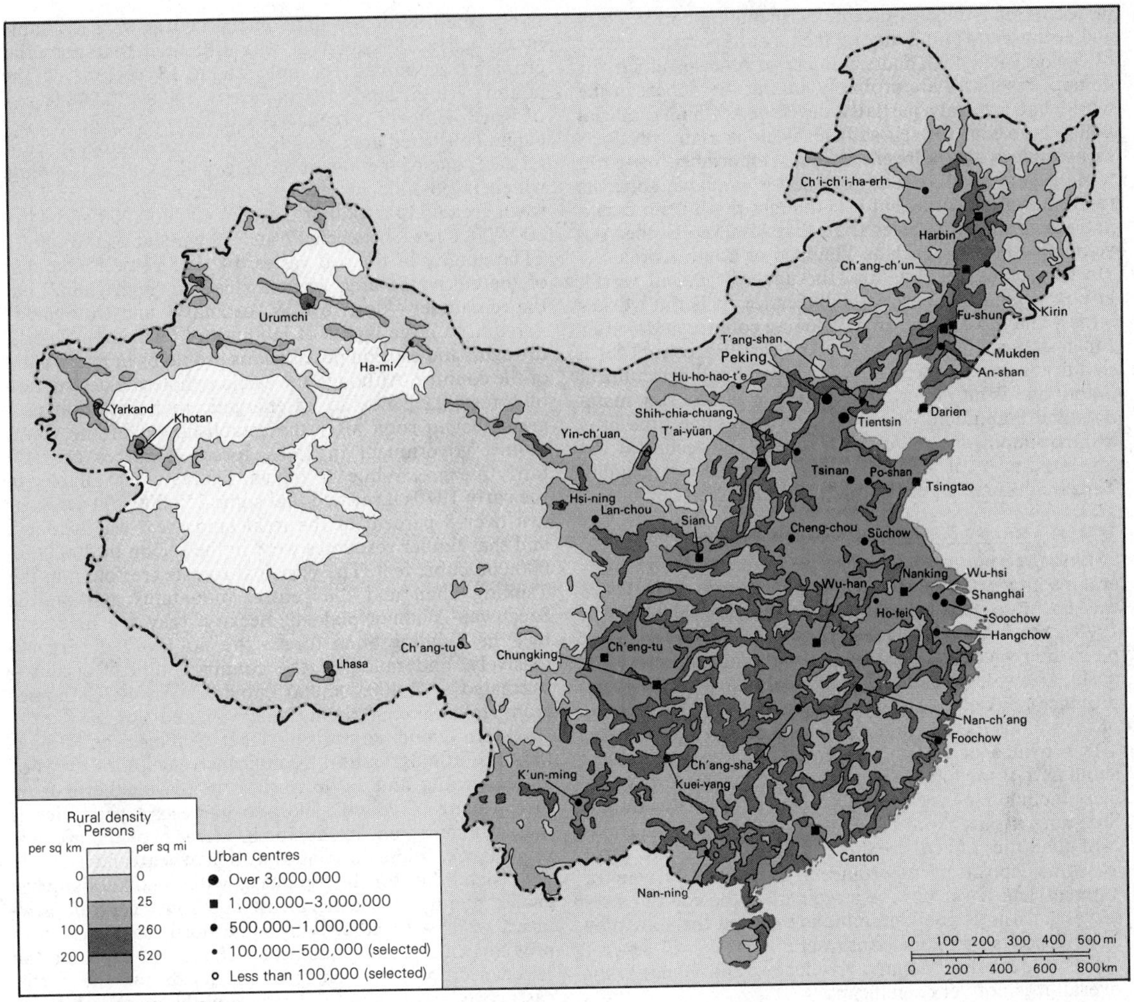

Population density of China.
By courtesy of the Central Intelligence Agency

Rural density
Persons

per sq km	per sq mi
0	0
10	25
100	260
200	520

Urban centres
● Over 3,000,000
■ 1,000,000–3,000,000
● 500,000–1,000,000
• 100,000–500,000 (selected)
○ Less than 100,000 (selected)

Settling
the virgin
lands

the Northeast had stopped for a while or else had reversed itself to become a migration to North China from Manchuria; by 1949, however, the migration toward the Northeast had started again.

Although the Northeast has been the most promising region for development, the government has also tried to promote settlement on unused lands elsewhere, not always with success. Statistical figures issued by official sources indicated that the people who settled on virgin lands in the years 1949 to 1955 totalled only about 600,-000. Thus, in 1956 plans were made to quicken the tempo of the movement; in that year alone, the Ministry of Interior reported that 725,000 people had moved to the new lands. Of this total, 432,000—mostly from Honan, Hopeh, Shanghai, Peking, and Tientsin—were reported to have settled in Inner Mongolia, Heilungkiang, Kansu, Tsinghai, and Sinkiang; the remaining 293,000 were relocated within their own provinces, including Kwangtung, Fukien, Chekiang, Kiangsu, Kirin, and Liaoning.

According to a 1958 plan, 530,000 were to be further resettled, and 230,000 out of this number were to be moved interprovincially, mostly from Shantung and Honan to Heilungkiang and Kansu; settlers who had already settled in Heilungkiang, Kansu, Tsinghai, and Inner Mongolia in the two previous years were to be joined by about 140,000 of their dependents. In subsequent years, however, the frontierward migration groups seemed to have changed in their composition. Instead of being household-size migration groups, the later migrants were mostly unmarried youths, city workers, unmarried managerial personnel, and discharged servicemen. Such migrants, however, represent only a tiny proportion of the population of the areas from which they come.

Although in the early 1970s complete statistical figures were lacking, it nevertheless was apparent that such mi-

gration was still continuing. As these frontier areas were all situated along the border of the Soviet Union, which had become increasingly antagonistic toward China after ideological tensions developed, such migrations have been increasingly influenced by China's policy.   (C.-S.Ch.)

III. The national economy

Despite its huge population, China's role in the world economy is relatively small. Notwithstanding its rapid economic growth since the establishment of the People's Republic, China is still a developing country; it is likely to remain so for some time before it achieves its ambition of becoming an advanced industrial nation. Agriculture, which provides the livelihood of the bulk of the population, is still relatively antiquated in its methods. It is underchemicalized, undermechanized, and highly vulnerable to the vagaries of nature, with the result that yields are comparatively low and output is not always sufficient to feed the population.

Because of its size, however, China is the world's largest producer of rice and tung oil and is among the principal sources of wheat, tobacco, soybeans, peanuts (groundnuts), and cotton. In the early 1970s, its industry was capable of turning out a wide range of products, and its machine-building sector was in a position to meet the larger part of domestic demand for machinery. The country also possesses a number of advanced engineering plants that are able to manufacture an increasing range of sophisticated equipment, including nuclear weapons and an Earth satellite.

Most of China's industrial output, however, is still provided by relatively backward and ill-equipped factories, and the technological level and quality standards of industry as a whole are fairly low. In spite of this, the country is one of the world's largest producers of a number of

The technological level

industrial and mineral products—including cotton cloth and antimony—and is among the most important sources of cotton yarn, coal, and a number of other products. Its mineral resources are probably among the richest in the world but are only partially developed. China's official policy is to aim for self-sufficiency in as many products as possible with the result that its importance in world trade is very small. No information is available about its total national income, but it is thought that its per capita national product is lower than that of several other developing countries, such as Thailand or South Korea.

In the context of Asia and the underdeveloped world, however, China is of great significance. It is the world's largest and most powerful developing country and—after Japan—Asia's largest economic power. It accounts for a significant part of the region's industrial and agricultural output and is an important market for certain raw materials and manufactured products. At the same time, it is a fairly important source of financial and technical aid for a number of underdeveloped countries, including Tanzania, Zambia, Pakistan, and Sri Lanka (Ceylon).

THE EXTENT AND DISTRIBUTION OF RESOURCES

Mineral resources. China is well endowed with mineral resources, the most important of which is coal. There was no up-to-date information on reserves in the early 1970s, but it was thought that total coal reserves might be in the region of 1,500,000,000,000 tons. Although deposits are widely scattered (some coal is found in every province), Soviet geologists estimate that some 70 percent of the total is located in the northern part of the country. The province of Shansi, in fact, is thought to contain about half of the total; other important coal-bearing provinces include Heilungkiang, Liaoning, Kirin, Hopeh, and Shantung. Apart from these northern provinces, significant quantities of coal are present in Szechwan, and there are some deposits of importance in Kwangtung, Kwangsi, Yunnan, and Kweichow. A large part of the country's reserves consists of good bituminous coal, but there are also large deposits of lignite. Anthracite is present in several places (especially Liaoning, Kweichow, and Honan), but overall it is not very significant.

China's oil resources, which are about 2 percent of the world's total, are located in the Northeast and in Sinkiang, Kansu, Tsinghai, and Szechwan. Shale oil is found in a number of places, especially at Fu-shun in Liaoning, where the deposits overlie the coal reserves, as well as in Kwangtung.

Although no reliable estimates are available, it is now thought that China's iron-ore resources are very significant; the indications are, however, that except for one or two deposits, quality is relatively poor. Iron ore is found in most provinces, and there are reserves on the island of Hainan.

Reserves of ferroalloys

With the exception of nickel, chrome, and cobalt, China is well supplied with ferroalloys, and has considerable reserves of manganese. Reserves of tungsten are also known to be fairly large; according to some estimates they are the largest in the world. Reserves of molybdenum, on the other hand, are not very significant.

Copper resources are moderate, and high-quality ore is present only in a few deposits. New discoveries have been reported from the Ningsia Hui Autonomous Region. Although some lead and zinc is available, reserves are inadequate for the country's needs. Bauxite resources are thought to be plentiful. China's antimony reserves are the largest in the world. There is little information available about mercury, although it is thought that reserves are fairly large. Tin resources are plentiful, and there are fairly rich deposits of gold. Uranium reserves are not precisely known. There are important deposits of phosphate rock in a number of areas, and resources are thought to be very large. Pyrites (common brass-yellow material) occur in several places; Liaoning, Hopeh, Shantung, and Shansi have the most important deposits. China also has large resources of fluorspar, gypsum, asbestos, and cement.

Agricultural resources. As a result of topographic and climatic features, the area suitable for cultivation is rela-

tively small. No up-to-date official figures were available in the early 1970s, but it was estimated that potential cropland accounted for only about 15 percent of the country's total land area of nearly 2,400,000,000 acres, of which 10 to 13 percent was cultivated. This gave a per capita cultivated area of only a little more than a third of an acre, one of the lowest in the world. Double cropping, which is possible in several provinces, could bring the sown area up to a total of between 400,000,000 and 440,-000,000 acres—between 17 and 19 percent of the total.

The quality of the soil varies. In 1958 some 30 percent of the cultivated area was classified as "high yield," but the remainder—described as "ordinary" and "low yield" —required large inputs of labour and fertilizers. Floods, drought, and erosion pose serious problems in many parts of the country. Although the earlier wholesale destruction of forests gave way to an energetic reafforestation program, begun soon after the establishment of the Communist government in 1949, forest resources are still fairly meagre. While no official figures are available, in the early 1970s it seemed that some 250,000,000 acres, or just over 8 percent of the total land area, was wooded, and that timber resources were in the region of 200,000,-000,000 cubic feet. The principal forests are found in the Tsinling Shan and the central mountains and on the Szechwan–Yunnan plateau. Because they are inaccessible, the Tsinling Shan forests are not worked very extensively, and much of the country's timber output— estimated at 1,400,000,000 cubic feet in 1970—comes from Heilungkiang, Kirin, Szechwan, and Yunnan.

Western China, comprising Tibet, Sinkiang, and Tsinghai, has little agricultural significance except for areas of oasis farming and cattle raising. In the southern provinces, many of which yield two harvests a year, rice is the dominant crop. In the north, wheat is of the greatest importance, while in central China wheat and rice vie with each other for the top place. Millet and kaoliang are grown mainly in the northeast and some central provinces, which—together with some northern areas—also provide considerable quantities of barley. Most of the soybean crop is derived from the north and the northeast; corn is grown in the centre and the north, while tea comes mainly from the hilly areas of the southeast. Cotton is grown extensively in the central provinces; but the north and to a lesser extent the southeast also produce significant quantities. Tobacco comes from the centre and parts of the south.

Hydroelectric resources. In view of China's extensive river network and mountainous terrain, there is ample hydroelectric potential. The total is estimated at around 580,000,000 kilowatts, of which only about 1 percent was utilized in the early 1970s. According to Soviet estimates, about 70 percent of total hydroelectric capacity is in the southwest, where coal supplies are poor but demand for energy is still relatively restricted. Potential in the Northeast is fairly small, but it was here that the first hydroelectric stations were built (by the Japanese). As a result of considerable seasonal fluctuations in rainfall, the flow tends to drop during the winter, forcing many power stations to operate at less than normal capacity, while in the summer floods often interfere with production. Since the early 1950s, much attention has been paid to hydroelectric development and by the early 1970s a large number of new stations had been built. Important plants include Ku-mo-tsin (with a capacity of about 209,000 kilowatts), Feng-men (570,000 kilowatts), and Mu-tan Chiang (383,-000 kilowatts), all in the northeast; and Liu-chia and San-men (1,000,000 kilowatts each) and Hsin-an-chiang (with a capacity of 650,000 kilowatts) in Chekiang. It is unofficially estimated that hydroelectricity accounts for from 20 to 30 percent of total generating capacity and production, although in view of the scarcity of official information, these figures must be treated with some caution.

Hydroelectric stations

SOURCES OF NATIONAL INCOME

Agriculture. The importance of agriculture in the Chinese economy is difficult to assess. There are no official figures, and until recently it was widely assumed that the agricultural sector accounted for 30 to 50 percent of the country's gross national product. Early in 1971, however, Chou En-lai, premier of the People's Republic, revealed that the value of agricultural and industrial output stood at U.S. $30,000,000,000 and $90,000,000,000, respectively, which would indicate that—after allowing for the contribution of other sectors of the economy—agriculture's share must have been well below 30 percent. The basis and coverage of these figures are, however, not known. Information was equally scanty about the size of the agricultural labour force, but in the early 1970s it seemed reasonable to assume that about 60 to 70 percent of the economically active population was engaged in this sector. Agriculture also plays an extremely important part in exports; in 1970, for example, between 50 and 60 percent of China's sales to the developed Western countries consisted of farm and related products.

The communes

The farming community is organized into communes made up of production brigades and production teams. The commune itself, whose leadership is elected by the members, acts as the basic unit of government in the countryside, coordinates the work of the production brigades, runs major projects that require large inputs of capital and labour, provides a variety of services used by both the production brigades and teams, and provides education, health, welfare, culture, and a range of other similar services. The production brigade coordinates the work of the production teams and runs a large number and variety of small industrial enterprises, the principal objective of which is to support agriculture. The basic accounting and production unit is the production team; this is responsible for planning output in accordance with the commune's broad plan and for deciding how income is utilized. Recent estimates of the number of communes in China vary from 60,000 to 74,000. Their size is far from uniform; some consist of no more than a few thousand members cultivating a few hundred acres, but there are also those that work at least 25,000 acres and have a membership of 100,000 people. Apart from the communes, there are also a number of state farms on which employees are paid a wage instead of receiving their income from the profits. In 1960, there were about 2,500 such farms, with 2,800,000 employees and a land area of 13,000,000 acres. By 1964, their number was put at 6,400 (2,000 of which were described as "big"), working more than 10,000,000 acres of crop fields. It is thought that many more were established during the second half of the 1950s, especially on reclaimed land. The army runs a number of state farms.

In 1958 agricultural cooperatives were merged with each other to form communes; the role and organization of the communes then underwent considerable change. During the first few years, the commune had considerable authority over its main constituent parts, and attempts were made to eliminate most manifestations of individualism and even privacy. Thus, the small private plots of the members were taken away, and communal food halls and even living quarters were set up in several areas. This was very strongly resented by the membership and had a serious effect on labour discipline and morale. Combined with highly unfavourable weather conditions, this led to a very large drop in agricultural output. It is estimated that in 1960 total grain output was only between 150,000,000 and 160,000,000 tons; and although the official figure of 270,000,000 tons claimed for the previous year was almost certainly a gross exaggeration, there is no doubt that the 1960 outcome represented a serious deterioration in the situation. As a result of the agricultural crisis, the authorities were forced to relax the discipline of the communes and to give greater responsibility to production brigades and production teams. Some communes were reduced in size, private plots were restored, greater stress was placed on experience and expertise as opposed to political and ideological merit, and a greater role was given to material incentives. Food halls and other obvious manifestations of communal living were abolished.

At the same time, the usual Communist policy of starving agriculture of resources was reversed. There was a vast transfer of urban population (probably involving tens of millions) to the countryside, and industry was ordered to devote its energies to increasing the output of those products that were of direct relevance to the needs of agriculture. As a result, farm production began a slow recovery and—despite the upheaval of the Cultural Revolution from 1966 to 1969—the grain crop was claimed to have reached an all-time record of 246,000,000 tons in 1971. Record production levels were also claimed for cotton and a number of other industrial crops as well as for the meat, livestock, and fisheries sectors. In the early 1970s agricultural policy remained relatively pragmatic. As usual, much emphasis was placed on "putting revolution in command" and on developing "political consciousness"; but the importance of private plots, private livestock, and other sideline activities, as well as the role of material incentives, was also stressed.

Stimulating agricultural production

Despite considerable efforts in the field of fertilizer and agricultural-machinery production in the early 1970s, Chinese agriculture was still seriously lacking in chemicals and farm machinery. According to Premier Chou En-lai, the output of chemical fertilizers was in the region of 14,000,000 tons; this—supplemented by imports of 3,000,000 to 4,500,000 tons—covered between 50 and 55 percent of total requirements. There is no information on the number of tractors in use. It seemed highly unlikely, however, that this exceeded 200,000 (in terms of 15 horsepower units), which would be only about a quarter of what had been officially stated to be necessary in the early 1950s. There was also a lack of other types of farm machinery; for the most part the Chinese peasant still depended on simple, nonmechanized farming implements. Good progress had been made in increasing water conservancy and irrigation. In 1958, officials claimed that 170,000,000 acres were irrigated. It later became clear, however, that only a small part of this area could be given adequate protection against drought; and in the early 1970s, it was estimated that adequate irrigation facilities covered some 100,000,000 to 110,000,000 acres—less than half of the land under cultivation.

Farm machinery

Rice is China's most important crop; other crops of significance include wheat, potatoes, sugar beet, oilseeds, cotton, tea, and tobacco. Since 1961 China has been buying large quantities of wheat and other cereals from other countries. In the early 1970s, for example, total grain purchases amounted to about 5,000,000 tons a year.

Mining. The most important coal-producing areas are Liaoning, Heilungkiang, Kirin, Hopeh, and Shansi. Two of the country's largest coal-producing centres are located at Fu-shun and Fou-hsin, both in Liaoning; there are also a number of small production centres in the same province. In Heilungkiang, industry is concentrated in the Chi-hsi and Hao-kang areas; in Hopeh the large K'ai-luan coalfield is significant. Shansi's largest producer is Ta-t'ung, whereas in Anhwei Province, Huai-nan is of particular significance. It is estimated that even the smallest of all these producing areas has an output of between 7,000,000 and 10,000,000 tons a year and that the output of the largest may be as high as 25,000,000 tons a year. Other mines of importance include T'ung-hua and Liao-yüan (both in Kirin Province), Ching-hsing and Feng-feng (both in Hopeh), Hung-yüan (Szechwan), P'ing-ting-shan (Honan), and P'ing-hsiang (Kiangsi).

In order to ensure a more even distribution of coal supplies and to reduce the strain on the less than adequate transport network, the authorities have for some time been pressing for local self-sufficiency and for the development of a large number of small, commune-run mines all over the country. This campaign was particularly energetically pursued after the so-called Cultural Revolution of 1966 to 1969, with the result that by the early 1970s thousands of small pits had been established. Their importance in terms of total output was difficult to establish, although it was known that in some provinces (especially in those with relatively meagre resources) they provide 30 to 40 percent of the total. As a result of their growth, China was beginning to achieve a better regional balance in the output of coal. Thus, it was claimed that the provinces of Kiangsu, Chekiang, Anhwei, Fukien, Kiangsi, Hupeh, Hunan, and Kwangtung were virtually self-sufficient and that several other traditionally coal-deficient provinces were capable of satisfying a rapidly growing share of their requirements. No recent national or provincial production figures were, however, available. In 1957, officials put output at 130,-000,000 tons, and by 1960 this was said to have risen to 425,000,000 tons. It was, however, likely that, in common with other "great leap" production figures, this was a gross overexaggeration; and it was thought that in the early 1970s output was between about 300,000,000 and 350,000,000 tons.

Oil production

The most important oil-producing area, the Ta-ch'ing field in Heilungkiang, was discovered in the late 1950s and now probably accounts for about one-third of China's total oil output. Second in importance is the Karamai field in Sinkiang, followed by the old but still fairly productive Yü-men field in Kansu. Of two other smaller producing areas, Tsaidam in Tsinghai seems to have failed to live up to original expectations, as does Nan-ch'ung in central Szechwan, where oil was first discovered in 1958. Oil discoveries have also been claimed near Chin-chou in Liaoning and in Yunnan, but no further details have been made available. Mao-ming, in Kwangtung, is probably the most important area producing shale oil. Despite a fairly rapid growth in the industry, output and usage of oil was still very low in the early 1970s; according to Premier Chou En-lai, production in 1970 totalled 20,000,000 tons, which was sufficient to meet domestic requirements. There was little information about natural gas. Some was known to be produced in Szechwan, but its importance in the country's total energy supplies was thought to be minute.

An important part of the total output of iron ore comes from a half a dozen or so producing centres. These include the An-shan and Pen-ch'i area of Liaoning, where there are large reserves of hematite (ferric oxide, a red-coloured iron ore) and magnetite (an iron ore that is strongly attracted by a magnet) ores; the Ma-an-shan area of Anhwei; Ta-yeh near Wu-han in neighbouring Hupeh; and east Hopeh. Production is also significant in the Hsüan-hua area of northwest Hopeh, where the quality of the ore is relatively high, and around Pao-t'ou in Inner Mongolia. As with coal, considerable attention has been given to the development of small iron-ore mines. Despite fairly rapid development since 1965, however, in the early 1970s their combined importance still appeared to be relatively small. It was nevertheless known that production had been increasing at a rapid rate; in 1970, for example, overall output was claimed to have increased by 43 percent since 1969. No official production figures were, however, available; and unofficial estimates put current output at from 40,000,000 to 60,000,000 tons.

Manganese output was unofficially estimated at just over 1,000,000 tons a year, which was more than adequate to meet domestic requirements. Most of this came from the Ch'ang-sha area of Hunan and from Kwangsi and Hupeh, but significant quantities were also mined in Kwangtung, at Tsun-i in Kweichow, Luan-p'ing in Hopeh, and in the northeast. Trading partners' statistics show that significant quantities of tungsten are exported. The principal producing areas are in Hunan, Kwangtung, Kiangsi, and Kwangsi. Outside observers put concentrate output in the late 1960s at around 15,000 tons, which would make China the world's largest producer. Molybdenum output—estimated at about 1,500 tons—is more than enough to meet home demand. It is mined in a number of places, including Fukien, Chekiang, Sinkiang, and in the Tsinling Shan. Vanadium is produced at Ch'eng-te and Luan-p'ing in Hopeh and in Liaoning.

Copper resources are underexploited. The most important producing area is thought to be Tien-pao-shan in Kirin Province, followed by Chuang-ho in neighbouring Liaoning and T'ung-liang in Szechwan. Copper is also extracted in Yunnan and Kweichow, but the importance of these deposits is not clear. Smelter output is unofficially estimated at around 110,000 tons, which probably falls short of home requirements. The country is also deficient in lead and zinc; these are mined at Hunan, at

Tien-pao-shan in Kirin (where they occur in conjunction with copper), at Fu-shun, and at several other places in Liaoning and in Yunnan. Outside estimates of production are in the region of 100,000 tons for lead (metal content) and between 100,000 and 150,000 tons for zinc (metal content). The aluminum industry is not well developed, largely because of the shortage of electric power; there are deposits around Pen-ch'i in Liaoning, Po-shan in Shantung, and in Yunnan, Fukien, and Kweichow, as well as on Hainan.

Antimony production—at an estimated 12,000 tons in 1970—is higher than in any other country except South Africa and possibly Bolivia, and allows large-scale exports. A significant part of total output is derived from the Hsi-k'uang-shan area of Hunan, but some quantities are also mined in Kweichow, Kwangtung, Kwangsi, and Yunnan. Mercury production—probably in the region of 2,000,000 pounds—is thought to allow considerable exports. The most important producing areas include Tu-yüh in Kweichow, and west Hunan, as well as Szechwan and Kwangsi provinces. The bulk of the total output of tin comes from the large Kochiu field in southern Yunnan, which extends into Burma and Malaysia. Some tin is also produced at Kuei-lin, in Kiangsi. According to unofficial estimates, output is in the region of 25,000 tons (metal content). Gold reserves are located at Mo-ho and a number of other places in Heilungkiang, as well as in Szechwan, Kirin, Sinkiang, and Shantung; United States estimates put likely production at 60,000 troy ounces, the bulk of which is probably derived from Heilungkiang. There is a veil of secrecy over uranium mining activities; but according to reports from the United States, producing areas include Mao-shan-t'ou and Chu-shan, both in Kiangsi Province, and at Hsia-chuang in Kwangtung.

China also produces a fairly wide range of nonmetallic minerals. One of the most important of these is salt, which is derived from coastal evaporation sites in Kiangsu, Hopeh, Shantung, and Liaoning. There are also extensive salt fields in Szechwan, Ningsia, and the Tsaidam Basin. In 1969, output was estimated at 15,000,000 tons but was believed to have risen to about 20,000,000 by 1970. Phosphate rock is produced mainly in Hupeh and Kweichow, but there are important deposits in a large number of other areas.

Industry. The development of industry has been given considerable attention since the advent of the Communist regime, as a result of which rapid growth had occurred by the early 1970s. Official figures, available up to 1958, show that in the period from 1950 to 1958, gross industrial production, starting from a very low base, recorded a sevenfold increase. It is, however, known that the official index was seriously distorted by double counting and other statistical imperfections, and outside estimates —derived from other official data—put the true rate of growth at only some 320 percent.

The years 1959 and 1960 saw further improvements, but by 1961 the effects of the agricultural crisis and the withdrawal of Soviet aid were beginning to be felt. Unofficial estimates suggest that output during this and the following year fell back to 1957 levels; and although the subsequent years saw a recovery, the 1960 peak is unlikely to have been reached once more until 1966. In 1967 and 1968, industrial production was adversely affected by the Cultural Revolution, which led to large-scale absenteeism, to the sabotage of industrial installations, and to the wholesale removal of experienced and qualified technical personnel. In view of contradictory official statements, the extent of the damage is difficult to assess; but it seems reasonable to assume that in 1967 the level of output was some 30 to 35 percent below that of 1966.

Industrial results of the Cultural Revolution

Since 1967, growth has been the order of the day and—judging by the production gains claimed by the various provinces—it seems likely that output in 1971 was about 35 percent higher than the previous peak of 1966. According to official figures, in 1961, industry contributed 55 percent of the combined gross output of industry and agriculture; but by 1970 the value of industrial production reached U.S. $90,000,000, accounting for 75 percent of the combined total for industry and agriculture.

Industrial policies and priorities have seen a number of changes since the early 1950s. During the First Five-Year Plan period (1953 to 1957), the main emphasis was on the development of the heavy industries and the capital-goods industries and the construction of large capital-intensive projects, many of which were built with Soviet financial and technical assistance. This policy, however, imposed a considerable strain on the country's limited capital resources; and during the Great Leap Forward, beginning in 1958, there was a shift to small "backyard" production units, which utilized local capital and made intensive use of labour.

This policy at first was claimed to have resulted in a spectacular increase in production, but by 1960 it had become clear that a significant part of the "backyard" output was of unacceptably low quality and was produced at a disproportionate cost; many of these small units were then closed down. This action coincided with a general revision of economic priorities forced by the crisis in agriculture and the withdrawal of Soviet financial and technical assistance. The net result was a shift of resources and people to agriculture and a general retrenchment in industry, including a virtual halt to all large-scale capital construction and the closing down of several large plants. By 1963 and 1964, however, the worst effects of the harvest failures were over, and industry's share of investment had begun to increase.

There has been a further move in this direction during subsequent years, but care has been taken not to repeat the earlier mistake of starving agriculture of resources. Since the Cultural Revolution, there has been considerable emphasis on increasing the importance of small factories and on achieving local self-sufficiency in as many products as possible. This campaign, however, is different from the backyard production drive of the Great Leap period in that much attention is paid to quality and cost. The importance of small factories—the number of which appears to have increased rapidly during the last years of the 1960s—is probably greatest in the production of chemical fertilizers, agricultural implements, simple agricultural machinery, textiles, coal, cement, and a wide range of consumer goods. Another important aspect of current industrial policy is the accent on self-reliance, dictated in part by the shortage of foreign exchange, which rules out large-scale imports of machinery and technology, but also by the realization that sophisticated foreign equipment and technology is often ill-suited to the needs of the Chinese economy, which is characterized by an acute shortage of capital and a relatively plentiful supply of labour.

Steel output Among the various industrial branches, iron, steel, and coal are regarded as the most important. According to Japanese estimates, crude-steel output amounted to 23,000,000 tons in 1972—over four times as much as at the end of the First Five-Year Plan. There has been a steady improvement in the quality and range of the industry's products, but a significant part of domestic demand, especially for special steels, can be satisfied only through imports. In 1970, nearly a fifth of China's purchases from countries in western Europe and over 40 percent of China's imports from Japan was made up of iron and steel products. Much of the country's output comes from a small number of producing centres; the largest is An-shan in Liaoning, followed by Shanghai, Wu-han (in Hupeh), Ma-an-shan (Anhwei), Pao-t'ou (Inner Mongolia), Pen-ch'i (Liaoning), and Chungking (Szechwan).

The engineering industry has also been receiving considerable official attention. On the one hand, much stress has been laid on raising the technical standard of some important enterprises in order to ensure an adequate supply of relatively sophisticated equipment for the few large and advanced industrial projects, whereas on the other a high priority is assigned to increasing the output of relatively simple products in demand by agriculture and industry. Engineering plants and workshops can be found all over the country, but the main engineering centres include Shanghai, Canton, Harbin, Loyang, and Tientsin.

The principal preoccupation of authorities in the chemical industry is to expand the output of chemical fertilizers, plastics, and synthetic fibres. In 1970, fertilizer output was said to have reached 14,000,000 tons and was expected to rise to between 30,000,000 and 35,000,000 tons by the mid-1970s. In the consumer-goods sector, the main emphasis was on textiles and clothing, which also formed an important part of Peking's exports. The industry tended to be scattered all over the country, but there were a number of important textile centres, including Shanghai, Canton, and Harbin. According to Premier Chou En-lai, 9,300,000,000 yards of cotton cloth were produced in 1970. This was some 70 percent more than in 1957 and made China the world's largest cotton cloth manufacturer.

Energy. It is estimated that something like 85 to 90 percent of China's total energy requirements are derived from coal. Despite a fairly rapid development of the fuel and power industries, energy supplies in the early 1970s were still inadequate to meet demand; hence the constant appeals for maximum economy in the use of coal, electricity, and oil. In 1957, a total of 19,300,000,000 kilowatt-hours of electricity was produced, while installed capacity was 4,500,000 kilowatts. By the early 1970s, progress had been fairly rapid in the building of both thermal and hydroelectric plants, with the result that generating capacity may have risen into the region of 15,000,000 to 16,000,000 kilowatts (25 to 28 percent of which may have been hydroelectric), and production may have amounted to about 70,000,000,000 kilowatt-hours. There was no evidence that China had any nuclear power stations operating on a commercial basis.

Finance. As in most other Communist countries, financial institutions are owned by the state. The principal instruments of fiscal and financial control are The People's Bank of China and the Ministry of Finance, both subject to the authority of the General Office for Finance and Trade of the State Council. The People's Bank, which replaced the Central Bank of China in 1950 and gradually took over private banks, fulfills many of the functions of Western central and commercial banks. It issues the currency, controls circulation, extends loans to enterprises and organizations and plays an important role in disbursing budgetary expenditures. At the same time, it conducts ordinary banking transactions and acts as a savings bank for the public. Furthermore, it handles the accounts, payments, and receipts of enterprises, government organizations and other bodies, which enables it to exercise detailed supervision over their financial and general performance in the light of the state's economic plans.

It is also responsible for foreign trade and other overseas transactions (including remittances by overseas Chinese), but these functions are exercised through the Bank of China, which maintains branch offices in a number of European and Asian countries.

The responsibilities of the Ministry of Finance include the collection of taxes, the preparation of annual financial plans and the distribution of a large part of budgetary investment funds, except those intended for the agricultural sector, which are administered by the Agricultural Bank of China under the direct control of the General Office for Finance and Trade of the State Council. At lower levels, rural financial administration is in the hands of the rural credit cooperatives, which draw their resources from the banks and from deposits by the peasants. Another important financial institution is the People's Construction Bank of China, responsible for investment planning and for providing capital funds for certain industrial and construction enterprises. A number of foreign banks maintain offices in China; these include the Chartered Bank, the Hong Kong and Shanghai Banking Corporation, as well as a number of overseas Chinese banks.

State finances The Chinese have not published any details about state finances since 1960. It is known, however, that the annual budget covers a very large part (80 to 85 percent) of total receipts and expenditures and that it includes the spending of the local authorities. The principal sources of revenue are taxes and the profits of state enterprises; according to recent reports, profits account for nearly 70 percent of the total, whereas taxes bring in about 30 percent. There are no recent figures showing the breakdown of state expenditure. In the early 1960s nearly two-thirds of the total was devoted to the economy, whereas the bulk of the remainder was allocated to social and welfare services and defense. It is thought, however, that a part of total expenditure listed under economic headings was in fact defense related.

Foreign trade. China does not publish foreign-trade statistics, and any estimate of its imports and exports must be derived from trading partners' returns. These show that the country is a very small foreign trader in relation to its size and economic potential; it is estimated, for example, that during 1971 Peking's foreign trade totalled only U.S. $4,500,000,000, which was about two-thirds that of Hong Kong. Nor has growth in trade been remarkable. As a rule, Peking puts considerable emphasis on maintaining a balance or earning a surplus in as many overseas markets as possible; and over the period from 1960 to 1969 it is thought to have accumulated a trade surplus of around $1,000,000,000. Peking's other sources of foreign exchange include remittances by overseas Chinese and sales of gold on the London market. These were particularly heavy in the early and the late 1960s.

Table 5: China's Trade with Selected Countries
($000,000)

	exports to China		imports from China	
	1970	1971	1970	1971
Developed countries				
Japan	568.9	578.6	253.8	323.3
West Germany	167.2	138.6	84.4	95.4
United Kingdom	107.0	69.3	80.5	77.2
France	80.7	112.7	69.9	71.3
Italy	57.0	59.2	63.1	64.3
The Netherlands	21.9	17.5	26.7	11.6
Developing countries				
Hong Kong	10.6	10.2	467.0	549.6
Singapore	22.7	15.2	125.9	132.9
Pakistan	39.3	27.3	27.8	32.8
Sri Lanka (Ceylon)	42.3	41.5	48.6	47.4
Egypt	22.6	46.4	16.2	21.4
The Sudan	17.3	36.8	11.6	20.5
Morocco	7.2	18.5	11.0	11.9
Communist countries				
Romania	71.8	...	62.0	...
East Germany	42.0	44.0	35.7	39.0
Soviet Union	24.9	...	21.7	...

Source: OECD and national-trade statistics.

The direction of China's foreign trade has undergone marked changes since the early 1950s. In 1950 more than 70 percent of the total was accounted for by trade with the non-Communist world, but by 1954—the year after the end of the Korean War—the situation was completely reversed, and the Communist share stood at around 74 percent. During the subsequent few years, the Communist world lost some of its earlier importance, but it was only after the Sino-Soviet breach in 1960—which resulted in the cancellation of Soviet credits and the withdrawal of Soviet technicians—that the non-Communist world began to see a rapid improvement in its position. In 1965, Peking's trade with fellow Socialist countries made up only some 30 percent of the total and this was thought to have declined even further, to just over 20 percent, by 1970. In the Communist bloc, China's largest trading partner is Romania, followed by East Germany, Poland, Czechoslovakia, and the Soviet Union. In the non-Communist world, pride of place is held by Japan, which—despite frequent Chinese attempts to use trade as a means of influencing Tokyo's foreign policy—experienced an increase of 75 percent in its sales to Peking between 1968 and 1970. In second place is Hong Kong (whose regular trade deficit with the mainland is one of China's important sources of foreign exchange), followed

by West Germany, France, Singapore, the United Kingdom, and Italy. In the early 1970s, China and the United States carried on some minor trade, and—in view of the gradual reappraisal of American policy towards Peking—more commercial contacts were considered likely for the future. Although China trades with a large number of developing countries, the amounts involved are small.

A significant part of Peking's trade with the less developed world is financed through credits, grants, and other forms of assistance. In 1971 it was estimated that, since 1952, China had pledged between about $2,000,000,000 and $2,500,000,000 in foreign aid, although—because of political differences and the inability to deliver in every case the type of goods required—only a part of this had been disbursed. At first, from 1953–55, aid went mainly to North Korea and North Vietnam and some other Communist states; but from the mid-1950s onward, large amounts—mainly grants and long-term, interest-free loans—were promised to politically uncommitted developing countries. The principal aid efforts were made in Asia—especially to Indonesia, Burma, Pakistan, and Ceylon (now Sri Lanka)—but large loans were also granted in Africa (Ghana, Algeria, Tanzania, etc.) and in the Middle East (Egypt). Peking's most impressive foreign-aid project to date is the Tanzam Railroad, linking Tanzania and Zambia. In the early 1970s this was being built with Chinese technical and financial assistance; the total cost is not yet known, but by 1971 a loan of U.S. $350,000,000 had already been pledged. *Trade through aid*

Precise details about the composition of China's foreign trade are not available, but it is known that agricultural products play a very important role in both exports and imports. On the basis of statistics published by Peking's principal trading partners, it is estimated that 35 to 45 percent of its total sales abroad is made up of such products, the most important of which are tea, rice, and vegetables. A further 40 to 45 percent is accounted for by sales of manufactured products (especially textiles and some other consumer goods); the remainder is made up of raw materials such as minerals (tin, tungsten, mercury, and antimony) and a range of traditional Chinese export products such as tung oil, feathers, and bristles. Imports of farm products account for 35 to 40 percent of the total, the bulk of which consists of wheat and other grains that have been purchased mainly from Australia and Canada. Raw materials and semimanufactured products for industry come next in importance (fertilizers, iron and steel, nonferrous metals, cotton, and rubber), whereas purchases of machinery and equipment make up 10 to 15 percent.

A more precise commodity breakdown of China's trade with the countries of western Europe, which constitutes about 25 percent of the total, shows that in 1970, 67 percent of western European shipments were accounted for by sales of manufactured products, of which iron and steel, nonferrous metals, and machinery and equipment were the most important. Chemicals, including plastics and chemical fertilizers, made up a further quarter, and the share of foodstuffs (mainly cereals) was 3 percent. Sales of machinery and transport equipment accounted for about 20 percent, comparable to the early 1960s, when China bought a number of complete industrial plants in the west. Western European purchases from China included crude materials—such as oilseeds, nuts and kernels, textile fibres, hides, skins, and minerals—which accounted for 44 percent of the total. Manufactured goods (mainly textile yarn) were responsible for a further 30 percent, but imports of food constituted only 18 percent. *Trade with western Europe*

Until 1968, the unit of exchange in China's trade with the non-Communist world was the pound sterling, but following its devaluation in 1967 Peking began to use French francs for trading purposes. When, however, in 1968 the franc also weakened, sterling regained at least part of its previous role. In the early 1970s, sterling was still used on a fairly wide scale; but growing use was also made of the Chinese yuan, which Peking describes as "the most stable currency in the world." Foreign trade is a state monopoly and is conducted through a number of foreign-trade corporations specializing in broad product groups. Western businessmen report that the Chinese are always scrupulous in observing the provisions of trade and loan agreements.

THE MANAGEMENT OF THE ECONOMY

The role of the government. The government plays an all-important role in the economy; there is no private sector to speak of. The bulk of the country's industry is owned and run by the state; the service trades are controlled by the government or the closely regulated cooperatives; and finance and related services are a government monopoly. At the same time, agriculture is in the hands of the state farms and the communes, which operate within fairly narrow confines laid down by the authorities. The communes are responsible for the running of small plants, but these activities are also subject to control by the provincial authorities. A form of private enterprise is tolerated only in respect of collective farmers' private plots—the area of which seldom exceeds 5 percent of the communes' total holdings—and in the handicraft industry, the bulk of which is in collective hands. There are also a few enterprises in industry that are in joint state and private ownership. These are normally operated by the private partner in return for a wage and some interest payments on capital but are subject to close supervision by the government. The state also lays down detailed economic policy, prepares and executes long- and short-term economic plans, fixes a large number of physical production targets, determines the number of employees and the level of remuneration, and fixes the price of a very large number of products and services. It also controls investment and its distribution among the various branches of the economy and is directly concerned with a number of large investment projects.

The effective exercise of such detailed control over the economy requires an army of bureaucrats and a highly complicated chain of command, stretching from the top down to the individual enterprise level. The highest economic authority in the country is the State Council, which has a number of specialized offices dealing with economic matters (such as trade and finance, industry, and communication) and whose members are both ministers and leading figures of the political bureau of the Communist Party. This is in direct control of a number of commissions and committees, which are charged with formulating and executing economic policy. The most important of these are the State Planning Commission, which is responsible for the preparation of long-term plans, and the State Economic Commission, whose two principal tasks are to look after annual planning and to maintain a balance between the supply and allocation of raw materials in state-controlled enterprises. There is also a State Capital Construction Commission, concerned with investment planning, as well as a General Bureau for the Supply of Raw Materials and a State Scientific and Technological Commission. The State Planning and Economic commissions and the General Bureau for the Supply of Raw Materials maintain a number of local offices, most of which operate at provincial and county level. The indications are that these are not just simple branches controlled by the head office but are partly under the influence of local government organs, the most important of which is the local revolutionary committee.

Overall control over the various industrial branches is exercised by the 14 or so industrial ministries, eight of which deal with different areas of machine building (including conventional and nuclear weapons). Their influence over individual enterprises varies quite considerably. Up to 1958, central control was extremely strict, but by the end of that year some 80 percent of industrial enterprises were put under the jurisdiction of local authorities. The first half of the 1960s saw some moves toward greater centralization, but the effect of the Cultural Revolution, which seriously damaged the country's administrative structure, was to enhance local independence. In the early 1970s the position appeared to be that most of the larger enterprises were under the direct control of the central ministries, but the supervision of small and me-

Organizations controlling the economy

dium-sized enterprises was the responsibility of the local revolutionary committees. The agricultural activities of the communes were controlled by the Ministry of Agriculture and the provincial authorities; since the Cultural Revolution most of these seemed to have enlarged their already extensive powers in this field. Control over financial and other matters, however, was fairly centralized and was enforced through the Ministry of Finance and The People's Bank of China, which was also charged with the detailed supervision of industrial and some other enterprises.

As far as the extent of central or provincial control over the various units of production is concerned, the position seems to vary from sector to sector. State farms are, on the whole, fairly closely supervised; but the communes appear to be free to take a number of important decisions as long as they fulfill the state procurement quotas and conform to other principal features of the plan. The independence of most industrial enterprises is, however, considerably more limited. There appears to be no standard list of mandatory targets or indicators that must be fulfilled—the number and nature of these probably varies according to the size and importance of the enterprise concerned—but the evidence is that, on the whole, individual managements have little freedom of action. Thus, the quantity and range of goods to be produced is specified by the superior authority, as are the principal inputs, the number of employees, and the total wage bill. In addition, enterprises have little say in the prices received for their products and, since their investment funds are allocated from above, they have very little part in determining how this should be spent. They are also given certain technical targets to fulfill, and—before the Cultural Revolution—they were expected to fulfill a certain profit target. Whether this was still in force or not was not known in the early 1970s, although it seemed clear that material incentives—which other Communist countries are using on an increasing scale—no longer existed. The degree of control over commune-run small industrial plants was thought to be very much less thorough, although there were some signs that provincial and county revolutionary committees were taking steps to enhance their influence over their activities.

Economic policy is based on a series of five-year plans. At the top of the planning mechanism is the State Planning Commission which—in accordance with the instructions of the State Council—prepares broad plans covering the output of principal commodities, investment, and similar aspects. This plan is then passed down to the regions through the appropriate ministries and the local planning bodies, which are expected to make detailed plans in respect of their areas and industries, including production targets for those items for which no central figure is given. This is done through consultation with individual enterprises, whose influence on plan targets varies from region to region and from industry to industry. When the plans are completed, they are forwarded to the central ministries and planning authorities. This is followed by considerable cross-checking, balancing and aggregating, and—when the final plan is approved by the State Council—it becomes the official framework for economic policy.

The five-year plans

Taxation. Virtually all of the government's revenue is derived from taxes and the profits of state-owned enterprises. During the early 1960s, taxes accounted for 60 to 65 percent of the total; but in the early 1970s reports suggested that this had shrunk to only about 30 percent and that the share of enterprise profits had expanded to nearly 70 percent. One reason for this appeared to have been a change in the enterprises' financial obligations to the state. In the mid-1960s most of these were allowed to retain a small share—probably averaging about 5 percent—of their profits; but by the early 1970s it seemed that they were required to pass on the whole of their net earnings to the authorities. The most important tax was the general industrial and commercial tax, which was levied on total sales or on business income. In 1960, this brought in about three-quarters of all tax revenue, but by 1971 there were some indications that it might have lost some of its earlier importance. Agriculture's contribution to the state coffers took the form of profit payments by the state farms and a tax on the communes that amounted to from 5 to 7 percent of the value of their total output. There was little information about other taxes and levies; in the early 1960s these included a variety of license fees and a selectively levied income tax, the yield from which was not very significant. It was known, however, that in 1971 personal incomes were no longer subject to tax, and it was likely that a number of other earlier levies had also been abolished. Most receipts that did not enter into the state budget were collected by the local authorities. These were thought to include a supplement to the general industrial and commercial tax and a range of other charges, such as admission fees to local amenities and a variety of license fees.

Trade unions. Chinese trade unions are organized on a broad industrial basis. Membership is open to those who rely on wages for the whole or a large part of their income—a qualification that excludes most agricultural workers except those employed by the state farms. In theory, membership is not compulsory, but in view of the unions' role in the distribution of social benefits, the economic pressure to join is considerable. In the mid-1960s, there were 16 unions, with a combined membership of about 21,000,000. The lowest unit is the enterprise union committee; the indications are that these committees must be formed in every enterprise with more than ten employees. There is some uncertainty about the total number of such units—in 1954 it was put at 200,000, but in 1965 official reports spoke of only 160,000. Individual trade unions also operate at provincial level, and there are trade union councils that coordinate all union activities within a particular area and operate at county, municipal, and provincial levels. At the top of the movement is the All-China Federation of Trade Unions, which discharges its functions through a number of regional federations. The income of the unions is derived from membership fees averaging about 1 percent of wages, in addition to a contribution from the employers, who are also required to contribute to the labour insurance fund.

Authority
of the
unions

In theory, the appropriate trade union organizations are consulted on the level of wages as well as on wage differentials, but in practice their role in these and similar matters is insignificant. They do not engage in collective bargaining—not at all surprising, since their principal duties include assisting the party and promoting production. In fulfilling these tasks, they have a role in enforcing labour discipline and in promoting and organizing Socialist emulation campaigns. From the point of view of the membership, the most important activities concern the social and welfare services. Thus, it is the unions that look after industrial safety, organize social and cultural activities, and provide services such as clinics, rest and holiday homes, hostels, libraries, and clubs, which are available free or at preferential rates to members. They also administer old-age pensions, workers' insurance, disability benefits and a number of other welfare schemes. Although the trade unions have not escaped the general upheaval created by the Cultural Revolution, they appear to have passed through without any drastic changes in their organizations or functions.

Contemporary economic policies. The 1950s and 1960s saw a number of far-reaching changes in China's economic policies and priorities. During the First Five-Year Plan period (1953 to 1957), emphasis was concentrated on rapid industrial development, partly at the expense of other sectors of the economy. The bulk of the state's investment was channelled into the industrial sector, while agriculture, which occupied over 80 percent of the economically active population, was forced to rely on its own meagre capital resources for a substantial part of its fund requirements. Within industry, investment was concentrated on the heavy industrial and the capital-goods sectors, and the needs of the light and consumer-goods industries were largely ignored. Iron and steel, electric power, coal, heavy engineering, building materials, and basic chemicals were given first priority; in accordance with Soviet practice, the aim was to construct large, sophisticated, and highly capital-intensive plants rather than to rely on less expensive and less advanced medium-sized projects.

Despite the low level of investment in other sectors of the economy, this program could not be financed out of domestic resources, and a large number of the new plants (about 150 in all) were built with Soviet technical and financial assistance. The policy led to a rapid growth in heavy industry, but just a few months after the introduction of the Second Five-Year Plan in 1958—which was to be on the same lines as its predecessor—the policy of the Great Leap Forward was announced. In agriculture, this involved the formation of the communes, the abolition of private plots, and the increasing of output through greater cooperation and greater physical effort. In industry, the construction of large plants was to continue; but it was to be supplemented by a huge small-industry drive, making use of a large number of small, simple, locally built and run plants. The Chinese peasant, however, was not ready for the communes; and the resulting deterioration in labour morale, combined with unusually unfavourable weather, led to a spectacular drop in agricultural production. At the same time, the indiscriminate backyard production drive failed to achieve the desired effects and yielded large quantities of expensively produced, substandard goods. These difficulties were aggravated by the withdrawal of Soviet aid and Soviet technicians, who made a point of taking their blueprints with them. In consequence, by 1960 the country faced an economic crisis of the first order.

The response of the authorities was a complete about-face in policy. Private plots were restored, the size of the communes was reduced, and greater independence was given to the production team, which corresponded closely to the traditional village. There was also a mass transfer of labour from industry to the countryside and—under a new slogan—"Agriculture is the foundation and industry is the leading factor of the economy"—industrial investment was slashed in order to free resources for farm production. Within the industrial sector, priorities were reversed. Funds devoted to the previously all-important heavy industry were curtailed, which led to the closing down of some factories and the suspension of a large number of half-finished construction projects. At the same time, industrial branches of direct interest to agriculture (such as fertilizers and farm machinery) were given greater attention, as were those producing consumer goods.

This policy, which led to an immediate improvement in the agricultural situation, was maintained more or less unchanged up to 1963. By that time, however, the worst effects of the disastrous Great Leap experiment were over, and it became possible to re-direct some resources to the capital-goods industry. As a result, industrial production and construction gathered some momentum, but care was taken to avoid the earlier mistake of sacrificing food production to iron and steel and similar industries. The relatively pragmatic policy of retaining certain material incentives was also maintained, although the role of these appears to have been very much less important in industry than in agriculture. Then, in 1966, a new experiment, the "Great Proletarian Cultural Revolution" began, which led to serious violence, widespread factional rivalry and the removal of a large number of experienced party, government, and factory officials. Unlike the Great Leap, the Cultural Revolution did not have an explicit economic philosophy; except for the general call to "put politics in command," no clear guidelines were issued as to the kind of economic policies to be pursued. There were numerous attacks on "selfishness," "economism," and the principle of "material incentives"; but because of the obvious split at the top and a virtual breakdown of central authority in large parts of the country, the attacks were rarely carried to their logical conclusion. Nevertheless, industrial production was badly hit by the strife, and by 1967 the most frequently heard slogan was one which invited people to grasp both production and revolution. In order to stabilize the situation, the army assumed

The Great
Leap
Forward

a greater and greater role; but during 1967 and part of 1968, economic policy varied from area to area, according to the political tendencies of the local leaders concerned. By the end of 1969, however, order was generally re-established, and most provinces were under the control of the army-dominated provincial revolutionary committees. They pursued a fairly pragmatic economic policy, which had a beneficial effect on both industry and agriculture.

By mid-1970 the Cultural Revolution was to all intents and purposes over, and it was clear that the economic policies of the pre-1966 period had survived relatively unscathed. In the countryside, private plots, sideline activities, and material incentives continued to play a part; and there was no evidence—despite several years of good harvests—that there was any intention to cut resources devoted to this sector. In industry, there was emphasis on the need for technical expertise, and the brief anti-expert campaign of early 1970 appeared to have disappeared without a trace. It seemed, however, that material incentives had been abolished but that the effect might not be serious since their scope was fairly limited even before 1966. Another important aspect of current industrial policy was the emphasis devoted to small industries and to self-reliance. Day after day it was stressed that, for both economic and defense reasons, there was a need for a network of small industrial plants that were capable of satisfying local demand for as many products as possible. From a strategic point of view, the argument was that with local self-sufficiency the enemy would be lost in a "people's war," whereas the economic justifications centred on the fact that these plants could be set up with relatively little (local) capital and could make a significant contribution to easing the strain on the country's weak transport system. It was recognized that labour productivity in such plants was relatively low; but in view of the fact that capital was scarce and labour was plentiful, this did not seem to worry the authorities. There was, however, little similarity between the current small-industry campaign and the backyard production drive of the Great Leap. Although a number of small plants closed after the Great Leap were allowed to re-open, there was much more emphasis on efficiency, economy, and planning than in 1957 to 1959; and the signs were that the local authorities were anxious to strengthen their control over small-scale industrial activities.

Problems and prospects. In the early 1970s, no official information was available about the targets of the 1971 to 1975 Five-Year Plan; but—judging by the confident tone of the press and official announcements—the authorities expected a rapid growth in the economy. In the light of current conditions, this confidence seemed to be justified. Thus, as a result of a series of good harvests, grain output was now higher than ever before, reserves were at record levels, and the material conditions of the rural population were better than for some time. Similarly, industry appeared to have more than made up the loss caused by the Cultural Revolution, and there was evidence that capital construction activities, which were particularly hard hit, were being given increasing attention. At the same time, it seemed certain that the Cultural Revolution had not resulted in any significant leftward shift in economic policy, nor were there any reasons for expecting such a shift in the near future. All in all, the Chinese economy was in a fairly strong position, and most of the essential conditions of rapid growth seemed to be present. Although renewed factional rivalry and political instability could not be ruled out, the moderates —supported by the army—seemed to be firmly in control; and the chances of a leftist comeback—which would almost certainly lead to a revision of economic policy— were thought to be fairly remote.

The 1971 to 1975 Five-Year Plan

The aim of the current five-year plan seemed to be rapid, but balanced, growth. In agriculture, the principal objectives probably include a further increase in the output of food and cash crops as well as an improvement in the meat-supply position by stepping up collective and private pig-raising activities. Further efforts were expected in order to minimize the effects of unfavourable weather conditions, which would involve a significant extension of the water conservancy, irrigation, and flood defense facilities. At the same time, considerable emphasis was likely to be put on stepping up the supply of chemical fertilizers and agricultural machinery and on a continuous improvement in farming techniques. In the industrial sector, the principal stress would probably be given to iron and steel, coal, engineering and chemicals; but growth in these branches was not expected to be at the expense of the light-goods and consumer-goods industries. The indications were that the role of small enterprises would be further enhanced; but the authorities' control over their operations would be strengthened in order to ensure minimum quality and performance standards. Efforts would also be made to improve the technical standard of the large, advanced enterprises; but the use of foreign technology would be much more selective than before 1966. Foreign trade was expected to continue its growth at a steady if unspectacular rate; efforts to gain influence in the uncommitted world by economic means were also likely to be stepped up. (E.I.U.)

IV. Transportation and communications

OVERALL PATTERNS

Great emphasis has been placed on the development of transport, because it is closely related to the development of the national economy, the consolidation of the national defense system, and the strengthening of national unification.

Since 1949 China's transport and communications policies, influenced by political, military, and economic considerations, have experienced changes of emphasis in different periods. Thus, during the national rehabilitation from 1949 to 1952, the primary concern was to repair existing lines of communication, to give priority to military transport needs, and to strengthen political control. During the First Five-Year Plan (1953 to 1957) new lines were built, while at the same time old lines were improved. During the Great Leap Forward (1958–59) it was discovered that transport capacity could not keep pace with industrial development; consequently, the improvement of regional transportation became the responsibility of the general population, and many small railways were constructed. After 1963 emphasis was placed on developing transportation in rural and mountain areas, and especially in forested areas, in order to help promote agricultural production; simultaneously the development of international communications was energetically pursued, and the scope of ocean transport was broadened considerably.

Transport-development policy

The rapid development of transportation and communications since 1949, apart from accelerating industrial and agricultural production and facilitating the exchange of materials, has also enabled the central government effectively to control the whole country. The application of modern techniques during this period has enabled the government to exert a more effective and thorough control than any of the strong dynasties of former times was able to do. By 1971 China had about 25,500 miles (41,000 kilometres) of railways open to traffic, more than 400,000 miles (650,000 kilometres) of highways, 100,000 miles (160,000 kilometres) of inland waterways, and 28,000 miles (45,000 kilometres) of civil air routes. Initially, as China's railways and highways were mostly concentrated in the coastal regions, communications to the interior were inconvenient. During the 1970s this situation was gradually being rectified, as efforts to establish a more balanced development were pursued. The newer railways and highways were to be found in the remote border areas of the Northwest and Southwest.

COMPONENT SYSTEMS

Railways. Because railways can conveniently carry a greater volume of goods over long distances than can road transport, they are of especial importance in China's transportation system. Estimates for 1971, for example, gave total volume of goods carried by modern means of transport exceeding 1,300,000,000 tons, of which 620,000,000 tons, or nearly 50 percent, were carried by railways. In 1958 about 78 percent of all freight carried and about 47 percent of all passengers (representing 350,000,000 out of a total of 740,000,000) were carried by rail. In terms of distances travelled, more than 70 percent of the total of passenger mileage represented travel by rail.

During the First Five-Year Plan more than 16 percent of total investment was set aside for transport, the postal service, and telecommunications; about 10 percent of this was for railways. In 1960, out of 21 percent of total investment for transport and communications, more than 15 percent was for railways.

Railway construction began in China in 1876, when British merchants built a line from Shanghai to the nearby town of Wu-sung; soon after being opened to traffic, however, it was bought by the Chinese government and removed to Taiwan because of strong opposition from the local people. By 1948, however, China had 58 separate railway lines, with a total length of about 14,-500 miles, or about 15,500 miles including branch lines. Of this total, about 44 percent was in the Northeast, about 33 percent to the north of the Yangtze River, and about 23 percent to the south of the Yangtze. Because the water-transport network was well developed in the Yangtze Basin, the construction of railways was relatively difficult there, while at the same time the need for rail communications was less necessary. By 1949, after eight years of the Sino-Japanese War, followed by four years of civil war, the rail network in operation had been reduced to a length of 13,000 miles.

By 1952 the total length of railways had been restored to about 15,000 miles, of which about 800 miles represented new lines. By the end of the First Five-Year Plan more than 3,000 miles of new railways had been built, including 22 new lines of narrow-gauge forest railways, making a total length of 19,500 miles.

Since 1958 some minor changes have occurred in railway-construction policy. On the one hand attention has been paid to the needs of the eastern region of China, while on the other hand emphasis has been laid upon the improvement of the original railway system, including such measures as bridge building, laying double tracks, and the use of long rails. Priority has also been given to the electrification of certain important rail links, such as the line from Pao-chi, in Shensi Province, to Ch'eng-tu, in Szechwan Province, from Peking to Pao-t'ou in the Inner Mongolian Autonomous Region, and Pao-t'ou to Ta-t'ung in Shansi Province. These new links were constructed as part of the Second Five-Year Plan (1958–62).

The small railways

All railways in China are owned by the state. Apart from those operated by the state, there are also small local railways that link mines, factories, farms, and forested areas, thus forming a network supplementing that of the state railways. The construction of these smaller railways is sponsored by the central government; technical assistance is provided by the state railway system. While these small railways can be built more quickly and cheaply than larger ones and consequently have developed more rapidly, they are often temporary or transitional in nature.

The first such small railway was built in Shansi Province in 1958, and by the end of 1959 more than 400 separate lines totalled 3,700 miles, of which about 1,500 miles were open to traffic. By 1962 the total length had increased to about 6,000 miles. In the early 1970s it was expected that these lines would often be replaced by regular railways, as some had already been. In addition to the small railway system, about 500 miles of special railways had also been built.

Since 1960 the railway system in the Northwest and Southwest has been greatly developed. Hundreds of thousands of Railway Corps and civilian workers were mobilized to construct the major lines of Lan-hsin (running from Lan-chou in Kansu Province to Sinkiang Uighur Autonomous Region), Lan-ching (from Lan-chou to Tsinghai Province), Chuan-chien (from Szechwan Province to Kweichow Province), Chien-kuei (from Kweichow Province to Kwangsi Chuang Autonomous

Region), Hsiang-chien (from Hunan Province to Kweichow Province), Nei-kun (from Nei-chiang in Szechwan Province to K'un-ming in Yunnan Province), and Chengkun (from Ch'eng-tu in Szechwan Province to K'un-ming), as well as to carry out the survey of the Ching-tsan (Tsinghai–Tibet) railway. In the early 1970s new lines were extending into parts of the country as yet unopened, particularly in the Northwest, where new regions were being linked to the national market and opened up for development. The best example was the line built from Lan-chou westward into the Tsaidam Basin, which was expected to develop as an oil region. These new developments, which are coordinated on a national level, contrast to the pattern prevailing before World War II, when foreign-financed railroads were built in different places without any attempt at coordination or at standardization of the transport and communications system. At that time, virtually no railroad system existed to the west of a line from Pao-t'ou (Inner Mongolia) through T'ienshui (Kansu Province) to K'un-ming (Yunnan Province).

By 1965 the total length of railways in China (counting double tracks as a single length and excluding narrowgauge and local small railways) was 22,300 miles, while the total length of rails totalled more than 37,000 miles. Apart from the Tibetan Autonomous Region, all other provinces and autonomous regions were accessible by rail. Thus, supplemented by other means of transport, the initial stage of the country's basic transport network had been completed.

In the early 1970s China's rail network consisted of the following 15 main lines:

1. The Peking to Mukden railway links the capital, Peking, with Mukden (q.v.), in Liaoning Province, via Tientsin (q.v.), T'ang-shan (Hopeh), and Shan-hai-kuan (Liaoning), with a total length of 524 miles. The line was once more opened to double-track service in 1954 and is the most important railway connecting North and Northeast China. Another line, also from Peking to Mukden but running further north, through Ch'ao-yang (Liaoning), has also been built.

2. The Harbin to Dairen (or Harbin to Port Arthur) railway is 588 miles long, running from Harbin (q.v.), in Heilungkiang Province, to Dairen (Liaoning), via Ch'angch'un (Kirin), Mukden, and An-shan (Liaoning). With a big seaport as its terminus, it links the Sungari River and Liao Ho basins, passing through the region most important for heavy industry. The line was completely restored to double-track service in 1957 and is the main transport artery in the Northeast (formerly called Manchuria).

The Peking to Canton railway

3. The Peking to Canton railway has a total length of 1,442 miles—756 miles from Peking to Hankow on the north bank of the Yangtze and 686 miles from Wuch'ang on the south bank of the Yangtze to Canton (q.v.). The railway passes over the Yangtze bridge at Wu-han, which, opened in 1957, is 6,478 feet long, and transverses four major river basins from north to south—those of the Huang Ho (Yellow River), the Huai Ho, the Yangtze (Ch'ang Chiang), and the Chu Chiang (Hsi Chiang). The line is double tracked and, like the Tientsin to Shanghai railway, is an important artery of north to south communication. Express service from Canton to Peking takes 37 hours.

4. The Tientsin to Shanghai railway links two of the largest commercial and industrial centres in China. The line, 819 miles long, is double tracked; the distance from Tientsin to P'u-k'ou, in Kiangsu Province (on the north bank of the Yangtze opposite Nanking), is 626 miles, while from Nanking to Shanghai the distance is 193 miles. Between P'u-k'ou and Nanking the line crosses the famous Yangtze bridge (completed in 1968) at Nanking, the 8,083-foot-long (2,464-metre) passage taking only 11 minutes as against the early train-ferry crossing that took two hours. The line is the most important rail link between North and East China.

5. The Peking to Lan-chou railway has a total length of 1,119 miles, comprising the 505-mile rail link from Peking to Pao-t'ou, and the 614-mile link from Pao-t'ou to Lan-chou. Providing the connection between two new

Air, rail, and water transport routes and ports in China. Major highways often run parallel to rail and water routes.
By courtesy of the Central Intelligence Agency

industrial centres, the line is important in promoting the economic development of Inner Mongolia and the Northwest region.

6. The Lan-chou to Lien-yün-kang railway, also known as the Lunghai Railway, was begun at the port of Lien-yün-kang, in Kiangsu Province, reaching Sian, in Shensi Province, in 1916, T'ien-shui (Kansu) in 1950, and Lan-chou in 1952. Its total length is 1,075 miles, of which 856 represent the distance from Lien-yün-kang to T'ien-shui, while that from T'ien-shui to Lan-chou is 219 miles. The section from Lien-yün-kang (Kiangsu) to Lien-hua-ssu (Shensi) is double tracked.

7. The Lan-chou to Urumchi railway, also known as the Lan-hsin railway, is an extension of the Lunghai Railway which was first planned as an extension to the Soviet border. Opened for traffic to Urumchi in the Sinkiang Uighur Autonomous Region in 1963, it is 1,186 miles long. The final section running through the Tien Shan represents a great engineering feat. The line is both politically and economically important; large oil fields lie on both sides of the track, and oil refineries are established at Lan-chou. In the early 1970s, the line was extended to Shih-ho-tzu in the Dzungarian Basin of the Sinkiang Uighur Autonomous Region.

8. The Shanghai to Chu-chou railway passes through Hangchow (Chekiang) and Nan-ch'ang (Kiangsi) and then joins the Peking to Canton railway at Chu-chou (Hunan). The route runs roughly parallel to the Yangtze River but some distance south of it. Of the total length of 707 miles, 122 miles are from Shanghai to Hangchow and 585 miles from Hangchow to Chu-chou. A branch line also runs from Ying-t'an (Kiangsi) to the ports of Amoy and Foochow, both in the southeast coastal province of Fukien.

9. The Chi-ning to Erh-lien railway, 210 miles long, runs from the Peking to Pao-t'ou railway at Chi-ning, in Inner Mongolia, to Erh-lien-hao-t'e, on the border with the Mongolian People's Republic, forming the Chinese section of the Chi-ning to Ulaanbaatar railway, which, completed in 1954, connects with both Mongolia and the Soviet Union. The journey from Peking to Moscow via this route is two and a half days, or 707 miles, shorter than by the circuitous route through the Northeast.

10. The Pao-chi to Chungking railway, 728 miles long, consists of two sections, the first of 415 miles from Pao-chi (Shensi) to Ch'eng-tu (Szechwan) and the second of 313 miles, lying entirely within Szechwan Province, from Ch'eng-tu to Chungking. The second section runs across the Szechwan Basin, connecting the rich Ch'eng-tu plain with the industrial centre and Yangtze port of Chungking. Completed in 1951, this line gave Szechwan —one of the most populous and richest provinces of China—its first railway.

11. The Chungking to Chan-chiang railway runs southward, via Kuei-yang (Kweichow), Tu-yün (Kweichow), Liu-chow (Kwangsi Chuang Autonomous Region), and Li-t'ang (also in Kwangsi), to the port of Chan-chiang, on the eastern shore of the Luichow Peninsula in Kwangtung Province. This 955-mile line provides the Szechwan Basin with a shorter outlet to the sea than that to the east and has greatly contributed to the development of the Southwest region of China.

12. The Heng-yang to P'ing-hsiang railway, also known as the Hunan to Kwangsi railway, 774 miles long, runs from Heng-yang (Hunan), on the Peking to Canton railway, to Yu-i Kuan, or the Friendship Gate, on the Sino-North Vietnamese border, via Kuei-lin, Lui-chow, and Nanning, all located in the Kwangsi Chuang Autono-

The rail system in Szechwan

mous Region. It is the principal line connecting China and North Vietnam.

13. The Ch'eng-tu to K'un-ming railway, 636 miles long, runs southward via Hsi-ch'ang (Szechwan), along the An-ning Ho Valley, across the Chin-sha Chiang (Chin-sha River), and through the Lung-ch'uan Chiang Valley to I-p'ing-lang (Yunnan). Turning eastward to Kun-ming, the line provides a rail link with a second route connecting China with North Vietnam.

14. The Man-chou-li to Sui-fen-ho railway, built between 1898 and 1903, forms part of the old Trans-Siberian Railroad. The line, 922 miles long, runs from Man-chou-li (Heilungkiang) near the Soviet border across the northeastern region of China to Sui-fen-ho (Heilungkiang), northwest of Vladivostok. For convenience of management, it is divided at Harbin into eastern (Pin-sui line) and western (Pin-hsien line) sections.

15. The Mukden to Tan-tung line is one of several railways running southeastward to North Korea from Harbin, Ssu-ping (Kirin), and Mukden. The Mukden to Tan-tung line is the shortest and the most important for transport, carrying the most freight. The 160-mile line begins from Su-chia-t'un on the Harbin to Darien railway, about 12 miles south of Mukden, and runs eastward to the border city of Tan-tung, which has connections to P'yŏngyang, the capital of the Democratic People's Republic of Korea.

Coal has long been the principal railway cargo. Around 1960 coal accounted for about 40 percent of the total annual railway freight. The rather uneven distribution of coalfields in China make it necessary to transport coal over long distances, especially between the north and south. Other commodities carried in significant quantities are grains, iron, steel, cotton, fertilizer, and building materials. Coal, steel, grains, and cotton are estimated to represent more than 60 percent of the freight carried by the railway system.

Road networks. The first modern highway in China was built in 1913 in Hunan Province, from Ch'ang-sha to Hsiang-t'an. Although there were 80,000 miles of highways in China in 1949, only 50,000 miles were open to traffic. During the period of economic rehabilitation, highway repairs, rebuilding, and new construction brought the total length of highways open to traffic by 1953 to 78,500 miles.

During the First Five-Year Plan, the length of newly constructed or rebuilt highways amounted to about 94,-750 miles. By 1957 the total length of highways in China had reached 157,500 miles, while that of all-weather highways was more than 80,000 miles, or more than half of the total.

The most striking achievement in highway construction was the roads built on the cold and high Tsinghai–Tibetan plateau. With the support of the People's Liberation Army, the Chinese workers, after overcoming various physical obstacles, within a few years built three of the highest and longest highways in the world, thus markedly changing the transport pattern in the western border regions of China while at the same time promoting economic and cultural development in areas with minority populations and strengthening the national defense system.

Of the three highways, one runs across Szechwan into Tibet (1,411 miles; completed in 1954); another runs from Tsinghai to Tibet (1,305 miles; completed in 1954); another runs from Sinkiang to Tibet (752 miles; completed in 1957). The Tsinghai–Tibet route, improved and shortened to 1,218 miles in 1956, has an average altitude of more than 13,000 feet, while T'ang-ku-la Shan-k'ou (T'ang-ku-la Pass), the highest point, is 16,994 feet (5,180 metres) above sea level. The Sinkiang–Tibet highway runs at a height of more than 13,000 feet for about 567 miles of its length and at a height of more than 16,400 feet for 80 miles. Driving speed is limited to about 12 miles an hour, and the whole journey takes five days.

During the Second Five-Year Plan, which coincided with the Great Leap Forward, the development of many more roads was urgently demanded. With the emergence

The three highways into Tibet

of people's communes and the proclamation of the slogan "Communications to be operated by all the people," a campaign for highway construction by the masses was launched. From the second half of 1958 to the first half of 1959, the length of highways built totalled almost 100,000 miles, of which more than 60,000 were constructed by the people's communes, although few roads were paved. By 1960 the whole country had 325,000 miles of highways, of which 156,000 were paved and 169,000 unpaved; travel on the unpaved roads often presents difficulties during the rainy season. By the early 1970s, 97 percent of the *hsien* (administrative units resembling counties) in China were accessible by motor vehicles.

Both the Manchurian Plain and the North China Plain are covered with a dense network of highways—a fact clearly related to their level terrains and to the relatively few rivers in these regions.

Highway building has taken the form of a national movement. By 1964, for example, the province of Kwangtung had almost 20,000 miles of highways, while 85 percent of its rural communes were accessible by motor vehicles. In 1971 the total length of highways in Chekiang Province was about 7,500 miles, while much progress was being made in road building in relatively undeveloped forest areas. Thus in 1965 there were only about 650 miles of highways in the province's mountain areas, while by 1970 their length had increased to more than 2,350 miles—between three and four times as much.

The most important influence on transport development since the early 1960s has been the policy shift giving priority to agriculture in resource development. Since 1962 the development of local transport facilities has been emphasized, and rubber-tired wheelbarrows, improved carts, and bicycles have been mass-produced for use by the rural population on the new highways and improved village roads. By 1964 the two hilly southwestern provinces of Szechwan and Kweichow had completed a road-building program that brought almost every county (*hsien*) into the highway network. By 1964, also, highway mileage in the plateau province of Tsinghai totalled more than 9,500 miles—32 times the mileage in 1949. Most rural highways, linking the administrative centres of the counties with rural communes and with production brigades, were built after 1958.

The rural road-building program has aimed at the opening up of commercial routes to the villages to facilitate the transport of locally produced goods. The wide dispersion and seasonal and variable nature of agricultural production, as well as the large numbers of relatively small shipments involved, explains the preferability of trucks for shipping. Similarly, trucks best bring consumer goods, fertilizers, and farm machinery and equipment to rural areas.

The highways of China may be divided into three categories: (1) state, provincial, or regional highways of political, economic, or military importance; (2) local highways of secondary importance, operated by counties or communes; (3) special-purpose highways, mostly managed by factories, mines, state farms, or forestry units. Certain specifically important highways are constructed and maintained by the central government. The Sinkiang Production and Construction Corps, for example, participated in building the highway from Sinkiang to Tibet.

When large-scale highway construction was in progress, China also began to develop its petroleum and motor-vehicle industries. The first two motor-vehicle manufacturing plants, with designed capacities of 30,000 and 60,000 vehicles per year, respectively, began to operate during the First Five-Year Plan. The first plant at Ch'ang-ch'un was completed in 1957. By 1970, apart from Tibet and Ningsia Hui Autonomous Region, all other provinces and autonomous regions could make their own motor vehicles. According to the accepted principles of self-reliance and local initiative, in which indigenous and modern methods are combined, technical innovation was applied to motor-vehicle manufacture. Attention was also paid to the use of local materials, and adaptations were made to local circumstances so that ve-

Motor-vehicle production

hicles produced suited local conditions, such as the low temperatures and thin atmosphere on the plateaus.

The foundation of the local motor-vehicle industry was generally simple, usually an extension of motor-vehicle repair shops. Each shop or factory produces vehicles of various types to serve the needs of the locality. The regional agency, instead of the central government, is responsible for supplying raw materials and machines. It is envisaged that future motor vehicles needed in each local area should be produced by each area. Vehicles produced by the large state automotive factories, including those at Ch'ang-ch'un, Shanghai, Peking, Harbin, Nanking, and Chi-nan, are distributed by the central government to state enterprises and military units. Special vehicles may also be built by the state at these plants. Thus, the Shanghai Automotive Factory has produced 32-ton self-loading motor vehicles for mining purposes, as well as 150-ton tow trucks; Harbin has produced large 150-horsepower trucks for forest use.

To strengthen highway transport, many large bridges have been renovated and built, such as the Liu Chiang bridge (1,994 feet [608 metres] long) in Liu-chou (Kwangsi Chuang Autonomous Region), completed in 1969; the Pei Chiang bridge (3,296 feet [1,005 metres]) in Ying-te (Kwangtung), completed in 1971; and Wu-lung Chiang bridge in the lower Min Chiang near Foochow (Fukien), completed in 1971. The reinforced concrete Wu-lung Chiang bridge has the longest span in China—1,797 feet (548 metres).

Waterways. The high cost of construction prevents railways from being built extensively, and rail-transport conditions are often congested. Freight volume carried by highways is limited, and they are not suitable for bulky goods. The water-transport potential is great; it is, however, far from being fully developed. To relieve land transport and to make more use of water transport, the central government has proclaimed the slogan of "linking various streams and rivers; connecting places in all directions," and it has launched a program to establish a national network of waterways. A national water-transport office has been instituted within the Ministry of Communications with separate departments for southern waterway, northern waterway, and marine transport. All provinces and autonomous regions have also established sections for water transport in their planning offices. The marine-transport department is further divided into northern and southern China marine-transport sections, operated, respectively, by the Shanghai Marine Transport Bureau and by Kwangtung Province. Since 1960 emphasis has also been laid on the development of ocean shipping.

In China more than 100,000 miles of inland waterways are open to navigation with many more used for the transport of timber and bamboo. The distribution of waterways is chiefly within central and South China, except for a few navigable streams in the Northeast. In the period immediately after 1949, however, there were only about 46,000 miles of inland waterways, of which only about one-third was open to steamship navigation. Before 1949 the peak annual freight volume carried by modern steamers and barges did not exceed 12,640,000 tons. To develop inland water transport during the years of economic rehabilitation (1949–52), a quarter of all appropriations for navigational construction was invested in building harbours, wharves, and storehouses. On the inland waterways the piers, barges, and conveyance facilities at the Yangtze ports of Nanking (Kiangsu), Wu-hu (Anhwei), An-ch'ing (Anhwei), and Huang-shih and Hankow (both in Hupeh) were successively restored. Simultaneously, emphasis was placed on dredging certain channels of the main rivers.

Dredging channels for river navigation

During this period the navigation channel on the lower course of the Yangtze was dredged, especially the silt clogging the channel about three miles upstream from P'u-k'ou, the north bank port opposite Nanking. The project, begun in 1950, aimed at removing islets, strengthening the embankments, and opening a navigation channel from about 600 to 1,200 feet wide in midstream. By 1952 the sandy island of Pai-sha at the port of Nanking, originally about 25 feet above water, had been cleared and dredged until it was six feet below the surface; simultaneously the new navigation channel in midriver had been opened and the main stream diverted away from the north bank, thereby ensuring the safety of the piers at P'u-k'ou.

Other activities during this period included the dredging of the Li-chiao navigation channel on the Chu Chiang (Pearl River), which provided access to Canton. The entire navigation channel of the Sungari River, a tributary of the Amur River and the most important inland waterway in Northeast China, was also dredged. The Sungari, originally a shallow river with a rocky bed and many shoals, had more than 20 shoals and other navigational impediments removed between 1950 and 1952 so that fully loaded steamers could sail down the river unimpeded.

Navigational-assistance facilities have also been installed on the main rivers. For example, since 1950 the 428-mile navigation channel of the Sungari River between Harbin and Tung-chiang (at the river's confluence with the Amur) has been equipped with more than 900 night-navigation signals and about 200 navigational buoys. More than 300 lightships, beacons, or flashing buoys have been installed in the navigation channel of the Yangtze. Also, in channels where navigation is more difficult, such as the shallow channel at T'ung-ling (in Anhwei) and Chang-chia Chou between Chiu-chiang (Kiangsi) and Chiang-yu (Hupeh), a special mechanized junk is stationed to take regular soundings and to lay bamboo rafts, lighted at night, that indicate the navigation channel. In the hazardous section of the Three Gorges on the Yangtze, not only have the original navigation facilities been restored but night-navigation light signals have also been installed on the 400-mile stretch from I-ch'ang (Hupeh) to Chungking.

By 1952 inland waterways in China had increased to 59,000 miles, of which 18,900 miles could handle steamships. The volume of freight was estimated at more than 30,000,000 tons, of which 14,000,000 were carried by steamships and barges, exceeding the peak annual volume of freight carried before World War II.

Under the First Five-Year Plan the primary aim in water transport was to develop river navigation, including a planned increase of river-steamship tonnage by 280,000 tons and increased river-barge capacity, especially on the Yangtze. Port facilities at Shanghai, Hankow, and Chungking were greatly expanded, and a special telephone system was installed along the entire navigation route. To ensure freighting of coal from the Huainan area (south of the Huai Ho) via the Huai-nan railway for export down the Yangtze, the new river port of Yü-ch'i-k'ou (Anhwei) was extended and mechanized.

From 1953 to 1957 work to improve the middle course of the Yangtze was also undertaken. Teams specializing in engineering control, detonation, dredging, and surveying were sent not only to the hazardous Matang Shui-tao between An-ching (Anhwei) and Chiu-chiang (Kiangsi) but also to the Tien-hsing-chou Shui-tao (Hupeh) in the middle course, where the river bed is subject to frequent changes, as well as to the channel between I-ch'ang and Chungking, which had many reefs. Their efforts by 1957 had not only made the middle and lower course of the Yangtze fully navigable at night but also the Szechwan section. Such river ports as I-ch'ang, Huang-shih (in Hupeh), and Nanking were equipped with scores of loading and unloading machines, lifts, overhead trains, cable cars, and loading trucks. The 1,700-mile waterway from I-pin in Szechwan to the mouth of the Yangtze has become navigable by day and night throughout the year. When the Yangtze is high in summer, it is navigable from its mouth to Hankow for ships of up to 10,000 tons, as far as I-ch'ang for ships of up to 6,000 tons, and as far as Chungking for ships of up to 3,000 tons.

Such other rivers as the Chu Chiang, Min Chiang, Huai Ho, Hai Ho, and Amur River were also dredged and were in use to varying extents. Hence, by 1957 the length of navigable waterways had reached more than

89,000 miles, an increase of more than 50 percent over the 1952 figure.

A planning conference on river waterways was held in 1958, at which it was decided to link the main waterways and their tributaries and to use long-term national planning on river-network development to serve industrial needs, taking water conservation into account and coordinating development with railways and highways. Since the Great Leap Forward, civilian workers by millions have often been mobilized to work on the waterways during the winter and early spring slack season.

The 15 principal waterways
By 1961 the 15 principal navigation waterways opened to navigation included the Yangtze, Chu Chiang, Huai Ho, Huang Ho, Grand Canal (Yün Ho), Chia-ling Chiang, Han Shui, Min Chiang, Fou Chiang, Chiu-lung Chiang, Red River, Hai Ho, Chia-lu Ho, Sungari River, and Amur River, with particular emphasis being laid on the first five.

By the early 1970s many cable-hauling stations had been established at rapids on the upper course of the Yangtze and of its major tributaries, such as the Wu Chiang. Boats sailing against the current are hauled over the rapids with strong steel cables attached to fixed winches, thus augmenting their loading capacity, increasing speed, and saving time. Such improvements have permitted 21 regular steamship services, both passenger and cargo, to be operated on the Yangtze. The number of ships anchored in the Yangtze's 200-odd ports has been reduced and the flow of river traffic correspondingly increased.

On the Hsi Chiang, as well as the dredging of the waterways from Canton to Chiang-men, Kai'-ping, Shih-chi, and Pan-yü, all to the south of Canton, and on the Ch'en-ts'un waterway the Li-yu-ho Sha-tao has also been opened, shortening the distance from Canton to Wuchow by almost 40 miles. Navigation signals have also been installed on the river's principal and major branch navigation channels.

The Yangtze, the most important artery in China's waterway network, is also one of the most economically important rivers in the world. Together with its tributaries, it accounts for about 40 percent of the nation's waterways, while the volume of the freight it carries represents half of the total volume carried by river transport. The Hsi Chiang is second in importance only to the Yangtze, being the major water-transport artery in South China. Ships of 1,000 tons can sail up the Hsi Chiang to Wuchow, while shallow-water steamships and wooden boats can sail up the middle and upper courses of the Hsi Chiang, Pei Chiang, Tung Chiang, and their tributaries.

The Yangtze and the Hsi Chiang are not icebound in winter. While by 1962 the Sungari River flowing across the Manchurian Plain had become navigable for half of its course, it is, nevertheless, icebound from November through March; traffic is, however, very busy from April to October. The Amur, Sungari, and Ussuri rivers with their tributaries form a network of waterways totalling about 12,500 miles in length.

In the past the Huang Ho had little navigation, especially on its middle and lower courses, but it was reported in 1964 that mechanized junks had begun navigation along the middle course, the Hua-yüan-k'ou in Honan. On the upper course and lower course of the Huang Ho, the channel from Chung-wei in Ningsia Hui to Pao-t'ou in Inner Mongolia had been improved by 1955, and navigation opened between Ho-ch'ü (Shansi) and Pao-t'ou, as well as between Lo-k'ou and Sun-chia-k'ou in Shantung. After completion of the water-conservation project at San-men Hsia (San-men Gorge) in Honan, the 490-mile-long section from Menghsien (Honan) to the mouth of the river is expected to be navigable in the 1970s by 200-ton boats. The planned clearing of the entire course of the Huang Ho will allow 500-ton tugboats to ply between Lan-chou (Kansu) and the mouth of the river.

The Grand Canal
The Grand Canal, the only major Chinese waterway running from north to south, passes through the river basins of the Hai Ho, Huang Ho, Huai Ho, Yangtze, and Ch'ien-t'ang Chiang in its 1,105-mile length from Peking to Hangchow. One of the greatest engineering projects in China, equal in fame to the Great Wall, it is the world's longest artificial waterway; some of its sections follow the natural course of the river, while other sections have been dug by hand. Work on the canal began in the early 5th century BC and was completed by the end of the 13th century AD, taking altogether 1,779 years to complete. It forms a north-to-south communications and transport link between the most densely populated areas in China. From the latter part of the 19th century, however, because of political corruption and mismanagement, it gradually became silted up, and the higher section in Shantung became blocked. In 1958 a Grand Canal planning committee was formed to restore navigation and water conservation on the canal by mobilizing several hundred thousand people to work on three different sections concurrently. Thus the Grand Canal, silted up for more than a century, was subsequently reopened to navigation, this time also by larger modern craft. The canal is important in the north–south transport of bulky goods, thus facilitating the nationwide distribution of coal and foodstuffs.

Port facilities and shipping. China has a coastline 8,700 miles long, which is indented by some 100 large and small bays, with about 20 deepwater harbours, most of them ice-free throughout the year. The long coastline passes through seven provinces, two municipalities, and one autonomous region, the extensive hinterlands and rich produce of which provide the basis for marine-transport development, which is the responsibility of the Ministry of Communications.

From 1950 to 1959 state investment in port construction accounted for 30 percent of the total investment in water-transport construction. In addition to new port construction older ports have been rebuilt and extended. Such ports as Dairen, Port Arthur, Ying-k'ou, Ch'in-huang-tao, all in Liaoning, T'ang-ku (Hopeh), Lien-yün-kang (Kiangsu), Shanghai, Hsiang-shan (Chekiang), Lo-hsing-E'a, Foochow, Amoy, all in Fukien, Swatow, Huang-pu, Chan-chiang, Ching-lan, all in Kwangtung, and Tung-fang and Yü-lin, both on Hainan Island, have all been extended. Among these, Dairen, Ch'in-hung-tao, T'ang-ku, Shanghai, Huang-pu, and Chan-chiang can accommodate ships of up to 10,000 tons. For these six ports the degree of mechanization or semi-mechanization in loading and unloading has increased from 25 percent in 1957 to about 70 percent in 1962. In Shanghai, for example, where it once took three days for 500 people to unload a 10,000-ton coal ship, in the early 1970s most of the work was done by machinery operated by 40 people.

Progress has also been made in port-construction planning, as at Chan-chiang in the south and T'ang-ku in the north. From 1955 to 1957 Chan-chiang was equipped with deepwater piers, medium-sized piers, special-purpose piers, storehouses, cargo yards, railways, roads, and other facilities, while in 1970 a new deepwater pier was built to enable four 10,000-ton ships to anchor at once, and new navigation signals were installed to facilitate the entry and exit of shipping. Thus, Chan-chiang was becoming the second largest port of South China in the 1970s and a focal point for commodities from nearby areas. After the gradual completion of the railway network in the Southwest, the hinterland of Chan-chiang has greatly expanded.

By 1959 the new port of T'ang-ku, near Tientsin, had become a leading artificial port in the north; in the early 1970s its three deepwater piers could accommodate 20 10,000-ton ships concurrently, with most loading and unloading being done by machines.

Because of tension with Taiwan, the section of the coastwise route from Wenchow (Chekiang) to Swatow (Kwangtung) still has no normal shipping. Coastal shipping is divided into two principal navigation zones, the northern and southern marine districts. The northern district extends from Wenchow to Tan-tung (Liaoning) with Shanghai as its centre. Shipping lanes run from Shanghai to Dairen, Tientsin, Chin-huang-tao, Tsingtao (Shantung), Lien-yün-kang, Ning-po (Chekiang), and Wenchow. The southern district extends from Swatow to Pei-hai (Kwangsi) with Canton as the centre. Shipping

Northern and southern navigation zones

lanes run from Canton to Swatow, Chan-chiang, Hai-k'ou, and Yü-lin; and they have been extended to Hong Kong, and to Haiphong in North Vietnam. Altogether some 60 scheduled or nonscheduled routes exist, and in the early 1970s the number of passengers and cargo ships was increasing annually. China's commercial shipping fleet has also grown quickly, totalling about 1,100,000 tons by 1971, in addition to a considerable tonnage of chartered foreign ships, as well as numerous junks.

In the early 1970s water-transport development continued to receive considerable emphasis. Dredging and improvement of inland waterways have proved an important aid to economic reconstruction, while capital and maintenance costs for water transport are much lower than for railway transport. From 1962 onward, coal and coke going from North China to Shanghai were routed through ports to relieve the burden on the Shanghai to Tientsin railway and other rail lines. By 1964 the coastal shipping lines' capacity north of Shanghai had increased more than 100 percent since 1957.

In 1961 China established an Ocean Shipping Corporation and subsequently signed ocean-shipping agreements with many countries, thus laying the foundation for the development of ocean transport. Most of the oceangoing routes begin either from the new port of T'ang-ku, Shanghai, Dairen, Tsingtao, Huang-pu or from Chan-chiang. Shanghai, the leading port of China since the early 19th century, maintains its position in all forms of water transport.

Civil aviation. Aviation development is particularly suited to a country such as China, with such an extensive territory and such a varied terrain. Chinese civil aviation has two major categories: air transport, which mainly handles passengers, cargoes, and mail, travelling on both scheduled or nonscheduled routes; and special-purpose aviation, which mainly serves industrial and agricultural production by aerial photography, aerial prospecting, insect-pest control, fertilizer dissemination, forest surveying, and bush-fire control.

By 1950 emergency transport air routes had been opened from Peking to Tientsin, Canton, and Chungking. By 1952 nine air routes linked 23 domestic and foreign cities. Peking, Shanghai, Tientsin, Canton, Lanchou, and Mukden one after another started scheduled flights. All the air routes together then amounted to more than 8,100 miles.

During the First Five-Year Plan the aim of civil aviation was primarily to extend air routes; to strengthen the link between Peking and other important cities, as well as remote border areas; to develop special-purpose flights, serving the needs of agriculture, forestry, and geological prospecting; to increase the number of large transport airplanes; and to build the Central Airport in Peking. By 1957 the civil air routes had increased to 16,400 miles. With Peking as the centre, 42 important cities and industrial areas in China and neighbouring countries were linked. In addition, with Peking, Shanghai, Canton, and Urumchi as regional centres, an aviation-coordinating agency was formed to link major and local air routes. Air-transport links between China and some 30 countries were also arranged.

After 1958 progress became even faster, with many new routes being opened. By 1959 air-route mileage had increased to 22,300. With Peking as the centre of the network, 72 major cities in China and abroad were connected. By the end of 1960 the air routes had further increased to more than 30,000 miles. By 1964, 56 domestic air routes linked 70 cities to form an air network centred on Peking. In the 1970s many mountainous and border areas that in the past appeared very remote could be reached in a few hours, and travel between various cities was even quicker. For example, a scheduled flight from Peking to K'un-ming takes only four hours—a distance of about 1,365 miles. In April 1971 the unduplicated route mileage on 75 routes totalled 28,000 miles.

In its early stages international aviation mainly depended on Soviet support; originally all principal international air routes passed through Moscow, where transit was made by Soviet planes. For example, according to the Sino-Soviet Regular Aviation Agreement of 1955, scheduled flights between Peking and Irkutsk, Peking and Moscow, Urumchi and Alma-Ata, and the nonscheduled route from Mukden and Harbin to Chita (Russian S.F.S.R.) were linked to Moscow by Soviet civil air services, whence air links extended to European capitals and other parts of the world. Because of the deterioration of the Sino-Soviet relationship, China opened new international air routes to western Europe and other places without passing through Moscow. Thus, in addition to the original Sino-Soviet, Sino-Korean, Sino-Mongolian, Sino-Vietnamese, and Sino-Burmese routes, by the early 1970s air-transport routes had been opened with Pakistan, Cambodia, Indonesia, and France, while the Sino-Pakistani airline, from 1964 onwards, also scheduled flights to various places in Pakistan, western Asia, Europe, and Africa.

Airport construction has increased greatly since Peking's modern airport was built in 1958. In 1964 expanded international airports were completed at Shanghai and Canton. Although airplanes, including various types of military aircraft, have long been made by China, yet in the early 1970s civil airliners for long-distance flights were still mostly purchased abroad. In 1972 the Chinese sealed an agreement with Boeing Company, the U.S. airplane manufacturer, for the purchase of ten of their 707 jet passenger planes. In addition China bought six British jets and placed an order for three of the Anglo-French Concordes.

When special-purpose aviation first began to operate in 1952, it was restricted to patrolling and protecting forests. Later the functions of special-purpose aviation were greatly expanded. For example, aerial prospecting has been carried on in various parts of Inner Mongolia and on the middle and lower reaches of the Yangtze Valley. Aerial photographic surveys have also provided the necessary topographic, geomorphological, and water-resource data for the Huang Ho conservation project, for the construction of the San-men Hsia Dam, and for opening up the wilderness in Sinkiang.

Special-purpose aviation

Aviation has also been of importance for agriculture. Apart from spraying insecticides to control such pests as locusts, airplanes are also used to transport Sinkiang sheep, silkworms from the T'ai Hu area of Kiangsu, fish fry from the Yangtze, and seedlings for improved varieties of crops. In 1966, for example, airplanes were used for afforestation in Fukien Province, while in the same year millions of fish fry were scattered from the air at low altitudes over lakes in Anhwei.

Airfields for special-purpose aviation have been constructed in all China's provinces and autonomous regions, numbering more than 100 in the early 1970s, of which 15 are used for locust control. Special-purpose airfields may also be used for emergency landings and, in case of war, could easily be converted to military use.

Posts and telecommunications. Posts and telecommunications were established rapidly in the 1950s and 1960s. In 1950 the Ministry of Posts and Telecommunications was established within the central government, with branch bureaus in all provinces, municipalities, and autonomous regions and with offices in all counties (*hsien*), smaller municipalities (*shih*), and districts (*ch'ü*). By 1952 the principal posts and telecommunications network centred on Peking, and links to all large cities had been established; later, the network was extended to the border areas and into most villages. By 1964, 44,000 places provided postal and telecommunications service, out of which 38,000 places were located in the countryside. Also, 48,000 more offices, 35,000 of them in rural areas, sold postage stamps. All county administrative centres in the country had major branch offices. In addition, there were some 90,000 transit points for mail and newspapers throughout the country.

From 1956 onwards, telecommunications routes were extended more rapidly. To increase efficiency, the same lines are used for both telegraphic and telephone service, while teletype and television services were also added.

By 1957 telephone-line service extended over more than 445,000 miles and by 1960 over 744,000. By 1963 telephone wire had been laid from Peking to the capitals of

Telephone service

all provinces, autonomous regions, and large cities, while capitals of all provinces and autonomous regions were connected to the administrative seats of the counties and smaller municipalities and to larger market towns; altogether, about 95 percent of the rural people's communes and more than 60 percent of production brigade headquarters could be reached by telephone. By the early 1970s, all the people's communes could be reached by telephone, as also could more than 90 percent of production brigades.

Immediately following 1949, telecommunications, whether by telegraph or telephone, mainly used wire; by the 1970s, however, radio-telecommunications were increasingly used. In 1956 the first automatic speed teletype was installed on the Peking to Lhasa line. By 1964 such machines had been installed in ten cities, Peking, Shanghai, Mukden, Urumchi, Lhasa, Ch'eng-tu, Chungking, Foochow, Canton, and Hai-k'ou. Radio-television service has also been installed in major cities, and radio-teleprinters are widely used.

Postal service

Great progress was made in improving the postal service under the First Five-Year Plan. By 1957 regular postal routes extended over some 1,300,000 miles. Postal service was also developed in the rural areas. Besides extending rural postal routes, the problem of delivering mail to places below the county level was solved by enlisting the aid of the population. From 1954 onward, a system of mail delivery by rural postmen was tried out in agricultural cooperatives, and in 1956 this system was extended throughout the country. By 1959 the plan of "connecting each *hsien* by post" was completed, and the basic postal network was formed. By the early 1970s, on the average, 19,000,000 copies of newspapers and magazines and 5,500,000 letters were sent out every 24 hours through this postal network. Mail sent from Peking to capitals of various provinces and to autonomous regions takes only three days at most. More than half of the capitals of provinces and of autonomous regions receive Peking newspapers on their day of publication. By 1963 the postal-route mileage had increased to 1,773,000 and reached 97 percent of the seats of all rural communes and some 80 percent of the production brigades.

(C.-S.Ch.)

V. Administration, social conditions, and cultural life

THE STRUCTURE OF GOVERNMENT

The constitutional framework. *The constitution of 1975.* The People's Republic of China (abbreviated hereafter as CPR) has had three basic constituent instruments since 1949. The constitution adopted by the Fourth National People's Congress on January 17, 1975, supplanted the first constitution, adopted in 1954. The latter had replaced the organic laws of the Chinese People's Political Consultative Conference, convened in 1949. The constitution of 1975 consists of a programmatic preamble and 30 operative articles grouped into four chapters.

Chapter 1 (articles 1 to 15), "General Principles," defines the CPR as a "socialist state of the dictatorship of the proletariat led by the working class and based on the alliance of workers and peasants." The Chinese Communist Party is identified as the "core of leadership of the whole Chinese people" and the body through which the "working class exercises leadership over the state." Chapter 2 (articles 16 to 25), "The Structure of the State," defines the organs of state power and administration, including the National People's Congress and its Standing Committee, the State Council, local people's congresses and local revolutionary committees, the special regimes for autonomous areas, and the organs of judicial authority and public security. Chapter 3 (articles 26 to 29), "The Fundamental Rights and Duties of Citizens," and Chapter 4 (article 30), "The National Flag, the National Emblem, and the Capital" complete the document.

The constitution entered into force immediately upon its adoption. The National People's Congress was empowered to amend the constitution, and its Standing Committee, as the permanent organ of the congress, reportedly was assigned the task of compiling a new set of laws.

Presumably such laws, when promulgated, would provide the details on how the various provisions of the constitution were to be implemented. The Supreme People's Court, which is politically responsible to the congress and reports to it, has none of the functions of a constitutional court.

While the constitution of 1954 was considered the basic law of the land until its replacement in 1975, many of its provisions were in abeyance during the Cultural Revolution: the National People's Congress and its Standing Committee did not meet, the elected chairman of the CPR did not perform his functions, and the People's Courts and other judicial organs were generally inactive during the extended period in which extraconstitutional revolutionary committees exercised authority within central government organs and at territorial levels below the centre. Drafts of a new state constitution were circulated for internal discussion after the party Central Committee called, in 1970, for the convening of the Fourth National People's Congress "at an appropriate time." In the interval, a skeletal state apparatus survived in highly attenuated form. Central government ministries were consolidated and then revitalized after 1970 under Premier Chou En-lai, but central policy direction was exercised directly by the party centre. In Marxist–Leninist–Maoist constitutional theory, "state" describes the relationship between dominant and subordinate social classes, and the state apparatus is regarded as a flexible "superstructure" through which the dominant classes exercise authority during the "transition" to a future Communist society. The 1954 constitution was adopted for a "period of transition to socialism" based on a "worker–peasant alliance" but with acknowledgment of status for remaining elements of the "national bourgeoisie" and "petty bourgeoisie." The last two underwent severe attrition during the Cultural Revolution and generally were excluded from the reorganized committees. Meanwhile changes in the local form of government with the establishment of people's communes in 1958 began a process of altering the state form of 1954. Thus, throughout the period of that constitution, questions were raised as to whether a new constitution more appropriate to the new conditions should not be enacted. The revised draft adopted at the Fourth National People's Congress in 1975 brought the programmatic and structural revisions of the constitution into line with these new conditions.

Concept of "state"

The most important changes in the new draft were abolition of the position of chairman of the state, the establishment of the party's leadership over the central government administration, the placement of control of the armed forces under the chairman of the party Central Committee, and the inclusion among "the fundamental rights and duties of citizens" of the freedom to strike. The descriptions of the central government system and of local administration, below, deal with the formal constitutional arrangements adopted in 1975. It was clear, however, in the first months after the adoption of the new constitution, that additional changes would continue to render many features of the constitution inoperative.

The National People's Congress. The governmental system of the CPR is based on the unitary principle. The National People's Congress, "the highest organ of state power under the leadership of the Chinese Communist Party," exercises legal authority over provinces, national autonomous areas, and local governments and administrations. All state organs observe the principle of "democratic centralism," which nominally renders people's congresses (and their revolutionary committees) responsible to the lower congresses ("democracy") but actually permits higher level congresses and their administrations to prescribe mandatory policies for lower level organs ("centralism"). Within the central government, the powers of the National People's Congress nominally extend to all other organs, the senior personnel of which are selected by the congress and are subject to recall by it "on proposal of the Central Committee of the Chinese Communist Party." The principle of unity of power, rather than separation, governs the assignment of particular functions to all state organs.

Democratic centralism

The National People's Congress is a unicameral body with membership in the first two congresses (1954–58 and 1959–63) of approximately 1,200. That number was more than doubled to approximately 3,000 for the third congress (1964–75) and totalled 2,864 for the fourth congress in 1975. A single session of the third congress was held from December 1964 to January 1965, and the first session of the fourth congress met in Peking from January 13 to 17, 1975. Congressional deputies are chosen for five-year terms (that may be extended under special circumstances) by "the provinces, autonomous regions, municipalities directly under the central government, and the People's Liberation Army." In the fourth congress, worker, peasant, and soldier deputies accounted for 72 percent of the total. The rest were government officials ("cadres"), intellectuals, patriotic personages, and "returned" overseas Chinese. Twenty-two percent of the deputies were women, and deputies were selected to represent both China's minority nationalities and Taiwan province.

Franchise The franchise is held by all citizens aged 18 and above, except persons deprived of these rights by law. The qualification was employed during the period of voter registration in the 1950s and '60s to exclude "counter-revolutionaries and politically hostile elements." The individual right to vote, however, is exercised only in elections of people's congresses at the basic levels. The form of the vote is not specified. Deputies elected to the basic level (commune and town) people's congresses elect the members of the county (*hsien*), municipal, and prefectural people's congresses. The National People's Congress is chosen by the provincial congresses or their equivalent. The congresses of the rural people's communes and towns serve for a term of two years, those of the county level three years, and the provincial and national levels five years.

The National People's Congress has formal authority over all important matters affecting the life of the nation. It makes laws, approves the national economic plan, examines and approves the state budget and final state accounts, and supervises the workings of the State Council. The Standing Committee of the National People's Congress exercises the functions of the congress between its annual sessions. It is reported to meet monthly, has the authority to convene the sessions of the congress, interpret laws, enact decrees, dispatch and recall diplomatic representatives abroad, receive foreign diplomatic envoys, and ratify and denounce treaties. The chairman of the Standing Committee thus exercises many of the functions of chief of state. This became especially so under the 1975 constitution, which eliminated the position of chairman of the CPR. On the proposal of the party Central Committee, the National People's Congress selects the members of the State Council: premier, vice premiers, ministers, and ministers heading commissions.

The State Council. The State Council, called the Central People's Government, is the highest administrative organ of the state. It exercises the characteristic functions of a national administration, with broad powers for formulating and issuing administrative and legal measures and decisions, supervising the work of ministries and commissions and the lower level organs of state, and drafting and implementing the national economic plan and state budget. Its precise composition and that of its organs varies as changes are made in the number of ministries and commissions and the political position of the vice premiers shifts. Chou En-lai served as premier from the founding of the CPR until his death in 1976.

Before the Cultural Revolution, the administrative apparatus under the State Council developed into a complex bureaucratic structure of some 90 ministries, commissions, and other central organs. In the Cultural Revolution, revolutionary committees took control of most units of both central and local administration (in varying degrees of totality); ministers and department heads were supplanted by committees, large numbers of functionaries accused of bureaucratic behaviour or revisionist beliefs were removed from office (temporarily or permanently), and previously established lines of responsibility became blurred. Premier Chou En-lai, while sometimes severely criticized, retained his position and used his reputation and skill to keep many basic central functions alive. In this process the army came to play a more active role in state policy making. By early 1972 at least 17 ministries, three commissions, and 15 other agencies had been restructured and substantially retrenched in structure and personnel. At the time of the fourth congress the number of bodies at the ministerial level had been increased to 29.

Regional, provincial, and local government. For administrative purposes, China is divided into 21 provinces, five autonomous regions, and three municipalities under direct central control (see Table 4). The provinces, which date back to ancient China, have their own deep historical and cultural traditions, and provincial separatism frustrated the efforts of earlier governments to modernize the country. The Chinese Communist Party (CCP) developed explicit policies calculated to counteract provincialism, but it incurred criticism because of the predominance of CCP members from a small number of provinces (especially Hunan) in its higher echelons. The national autonomous regions and other areas reflected the CCP policy of seeking to minimize "Great Han" nationalism and to accord cultural autonomy, though not political independence, to areas in which national minority peoples predominate.

The provinces

In their turn, the provinces are basically divided into approximately 170 areas, or prefectures (*ti-ch'ü*) and some 2,000 units at the county (or the equivalent) level, many of which also have independent traditions. At the next successive lower level the municipalities are divided into municipal districts, and the units of county level are divided into approximately 50,000 communes. People's congresses and their revolutionary committees are set up at each of these levels and are required to "ensure the execution of laws and decrees in their respective areas; lead the socialist revolution and socialist construction in their respective areas; examine and approve local economic plans, budgets, and final accounts; maintain revolutionary order, and safeguard the rights of citizens."

The Chinese Communist Party. *Party development.* The Chinese Communist Party was formally established at the First Congress of the Chinese Communist Party in Shanghai in 1921. National party congresses were held thereafter at irregular intervals. Between 1921 and the later 1970s the CCP had increased from 57 to 30,000,000 members, becoming the world's largest Communist party.

It achieved national power on October 1, 1949, by a process of territorial expansion from large rural base areas that remained under its control after the cessation of hostilities in World War II.

Between 1921 and 1935, the CCP was torn by internal and factional differences over such questions as relations with non-Communist elements, relations with the Soviet Union and the Communist International, political–military strategy and tactics, and a number of ideological issues, such as the respective roles of the urban proletariat and the rural peasantry in the revolutionary process. An extraordinary party conference at Tsun-i (Kweichow Province) in 1935 established the leadership of Mao Tse-tung (*q.v.*). Party dissidents were disciplined by him and his principal lieutenant, Liu Shao-ch'i; and the *cheng-feng*, or rectification movement, of 1942–43 had the effect of consolidating Mao's leadership and of establishing his interpretations of Marxism–Leninism as the basic ideological guide for the party's subsequent revolutionary action.

The revised party constitution of August 1973 defined the CCP as "the political party of the proletariat, the vanguard of the proletariat." It declared that the party "takes Marxism–Leninism–Mao Tse-tung Thought as the theoretical basis guiding its thinking" and endorsed Mao's direction of the Cultural Revolution and his idea that "revolutions like this will have to be carried out many times in the future." The programmatic sections of the constitution of 1973 contemplated "a considerably long historical period" for the transition from the socialist society to the "realization of communism" and reaffirmed the Maoist "theory of continued revolution."

CCP view of its nature and role

The major themes for political action following the Cultural Revolution were expressed in these terms:

Throughout this historical period, there are classes, class contradictions, and class struggle, there is the struggle between the socialist road and the capitalist road, there is the danger of capitalist restoration, and there is the threat of subversion and aggression by imperialism [*i.e.*, the United States] and social-imperialism [*i.e.*, the Soviet Union].

The CCP retained its own constitution and administrative systems, but in the post-Cultural Revolution situation these were not so rigorously distinguished from the state and mass organizations as formerly.

Organization and structure. The Cultural Revolution (1966–69) severely shook the entire party apparatus. Political struggle, including factionalism and party–army alliances, undermined the party's former unity. Most party organs at county and provincial levels became inoperative when all-embracing "revolutionary committees" were established in 1967–69, and Mao's direction from a vestigial party centre was performed through improvised organs and channels. By 1969 (1) the former party bureaucracy had been thoroughly discredited and temporarily superseded; (2) the People's Liberation Army (PLA) had assumed strong leadership within the revolutionary committees and was directing many activities formerly reserved for the party bureaucracy; (3) measures were required to deal effectively with a range of personnel problems, at a time of general retrenchment in administrative agencies at all levels, combined with a dramatic increase in party membership; and (4) adjustments between revolutionary committees and the party and state structures created many uncertainties.

Party constitution. The ninth party congress (1969) adopted a brief constitution of 12 articles (in contrast to the 60 articles of the 1956 constitution) and called for a program of "party-building and consolidation." The structures called for in this constitution were essentially reaffirmed in the revised constitution adopted by the 10th party congress (1973). Such party concepts as "democratic centralism" and "unified discipline" were reaffirmed by both constitutions but had uncertain operational meaning as the political struggles initiated in the Cultural Revolution continued. A principal change introduced by the 1969 constitution and continued in 1973 was that party decisions formerly reserved for the party hierarchy were to be made in consultation with the party and nonparty "masses." "Democratic consultation" supplanted "democratic election" as the basis for selecting members of leadership organs of the party at all levels. In the constitution of 1973 it was made "absolutely impermissible to suppress criticism and to retaliate," and the report on the constitution laid even greater stress than in 1969 on the supervision of the party by the masses. Such provision for extraparty involvement produced a series of general guidelines leaving the definitive structure of the party to the vicissitudes of ongoing political developments.

While leaving the structural provisions of the 1969 constitution relatively intact, the 10th party congress in 1973 did make several important revisions that reflected the removal of Lin Piao in 1971 and the subsequent campaign against him. In particular, the new constitution eliminated the previous reference to Lin as Mao's "close comrade-in-arms and successor." It also toned down the language introduced by Lin that excessively praised the "great red banner of Mao Tse-tung Thought" and that specified Mao as the party's "leader."

The National Party Congress. The structural capstone of the CCP hierarchical apparatus remained the National Party Congress, the "highest leading body of the party," to be convened every five years by the Central Committee elected by the preceding congress. The 1956 party constitution had called for the election of the National Party Congress by lower level congresses, but the constitutions of 1969 and 1973 omitted any mention of the details of election procedures. The concept of a five-year congress supplanted the 1956 prescription that congresses elected for five-year periods should hold annual meetings during their tenure. The eighth congress, elected in 1956, had actually held only two sessions between 1956 and 1969 (in 1956 and 1958); the 1969 and 1973 constitutions left undetermined the time and frequency of congressional sessions. It had been typical of National Party congresses that their sessions lasted a few weeks, but the 10th party congress (1973) met for only five days. Before adjourning, the congress elects regular and alternative members of a Central Committee to exercise formal authority over the party until the next congress is convened. The Central Committee in turn elects its chairman, vice chairmen, a Standing Committee of the Central Political Bureau, and the Central Political Bureau (Politburo).

Before 1969 the administrative apparatus of the Central Committee had comprised a secretary general and a large number of functional departments and bureaus, each nominally directed by a Central Committee member. The constitutions of 1969 and 1973 abolished the post of secretary general. The former Central Committee departments were at least temporarily disbanded, and the 1973 constitution simply specified that "a number of necessary organs, which are compact and efficient, shall be set up to attend to the day-to-day work of the party, the government, and the army in a centralized way." The organs officially identified included a general office, departments for international liaison, organization, and united front work, and the Military Commission and party newspaper. A number of other organs for propaganda, social affairs, women's work, and the Communist Youth League were also presumed to function at the central level. Directed by the Standing Committee of the Central Political Bureau, the central party apparatus appeared to be functioning effectively on the basis of greatly reduced personnel and formal structure—in keeping with Mao's predilection for minimizing bureaucratic behaviour that impaired good relations with the masses and inhibited the attainment of major ideological objectives. The 1973 constitution required members on all leading bodies to be elected in accordance with the principle of "combining the old, the middle-aged and the young."

Party membership. The requirements for party membership were modified in the 1969 and 1973 constitutions. Formerly, membership had been "open to any Chinese citizen who works and does not exploit the labour of others" and who passed a rigorous examination by the party branch to which he applied for admission. The requirements of party rebuilding in 1973 called for a reduction of procedural formalities (which had been exploited by the party bureaucracy) and a sharper emphasis on the personal revolutionary characteristics of party members; thus the revised constitution of 1973 opened the party to "any Chinese worker, poor peasant, lower-middle peasant, revolutionary armyman, or any other revolutionary element who has reached the age of 18." In keeping with the dominant cultural revolutionary themes of recognizing revolutionary merit, avoiding local bureaucratism, and reducing sectarianism, the admitting party branch had to "seek the opinions of the broad masses inside and outside the party" concerning an applicant's qualifications. Party membership remained highly selective in keeping with the "vanguard" principle, but measures were applied to avoid the self-conscious "elitism" that previously affected the attitudes of many party members toward the general masses. In the report on the 1973 constitution special emphasis was laid on the training of "millions of successors for the cause of proletarian revolution."

Party control and government. In CCP doctrine, the party assumes the leadership of social and political transformation directed to the ultimate transition to a Communist society. In principle, the party contemplates the "elimination of classes, state authority, and party" (Mao Tse-tung, June 30, 1949). During the pre-Communist phase, it considers the "state institutions of people's democratic dictatorship and its laws" as "superstructure" that performs a role in social transformation (Mao Tse-tung, February 27, 1957), under party direction. The dual structures of party and state have been mutually reinforced and noncompetitive, because: (1) state administrative personnel in influential positions have been party members; (2) the state constitution (1975) authorized party leadership over state organs; (3) leadership organs of state authority that may have included non-Communists have contained (in accordance with party practice) party committees or "leading party groups" to provide political and ideological direction; (4) basic constituent acts and legislative enactments were drafted and proposed by the party organizations, and important state policies were often published jointly by the State Council and the party Central Committee; (5) a system of controlled selection of members of the National People's Congress ensured party control over its membership; and (6) the national system of publicity and information was controlled by the propaganda department of the party. While conflicts between party and state functionaries have occurred, any effort to undermine the role of the party has been quickly denounced and reversed. Many major programs, such as the establishment of a system of people's communes (1958), the Cultural Revolution itself (1966), and the subsequent major campaigns (including the establishment of revolutionary committees), were undertaken on the direct initiative of the party, which felt no obligation to have them enacted into formal public law or to seek approval of the state apparatus.

Such basic party–state relations and patterns of action survived the Cultural Revolution and were even strengthened, despite important organizational changes. The Mao-dominated party centre initiated and encouraged the attacks on aberrant members of the state bureaucracy during 1966–69 that led to a substantial dismantling of the state administrative apparatus, without reference to formal action by state courts or other control authorities. The manifold problems requiring solution after the Cultural Revolution involved no challenge by the state to the party and were handled mainly as political–organizational–administrative questions to be resolved according to the judgment of the party leadership. For a time the army did appear to challenge that leadership, at least until the death of Lin Piao in 1971. But thereafter the party reasserted its dominant position, despite its own internal difficulties and the tentative or experimental quality of institutions and practices that came to life during the Cultural Revolution. Even though the character of the party itself underwent changes during this period, its basic responsibility for leadership of the state and other social structures found clear expression in both the party and state constitutions.

Justice. "The law of the people's state is a weapon . . . to be used to punish subversive elements of all sorts" (*People's Daily*, March 25, 1952), and People's Courts are politically responsible to, and report to, the "permanent organs" of the people's congresses that appoint them at different levels. The Organic Law on the People's Courts (September 21, 1954) assigned final appellate jurisdiction to a Supreme People's Court, which also exerts judicial control over Local People's Courts, Intermediate People's Courts, and such Special People's Courts as may be appointed for specific purposes from time to time. The constitution of 1975 continued this system. Until it was abolished in 1959, the Ministry of Justice was the principal agency concerned with the administrative assignment of judicial personnel, but these functions thereafter were centralized under the Supreme People's Court. Judges are chosen from among "those who have been tempered in the revolutionary struggle." Some are workers, peasants, and soldiers; some, but not all, are graduates of law schools. A deliberate attempt is made to have old, middle-aged, and young judges in the courts.

People's Courts exercise criminal and civil jurisdictions so as

to safeguard the people's democratic system, maintain public order, protect public property, protect the rights and legitimate interests of citizens, and ensure the smooth progress of the socialist construction and socialist transformation of the country (Organic Law, article 3).

The procedures followed in criminal cases are generally the same as those in civil cases. There is an investigation of the case ("prosecution") by the police, then a follow-up inquiry ("verification") by the court, the trial, and the verdict. Only those accused of serious crimes, unlike the

People's Courts (margin note)

parties in civil or petty criminal cases, normally are kept in jail prior to trial and are escorted to the court by the police. Witnesses are not sworn, and normally no lawyers (who no longer exist as a separate profession) are engaged. The system does not provide for jury trials, but selected citizens in the courtroom are always assigned participating roles. Each case reportedly is judged on the basis of its social impact and in respect to the attitude of the accused.

Public prosecutions, once maintained by a Supreme People's Procuratorate (Organic Law of September 21, 1954), are now under the organs of public security at various levels. According to the constitution, the "mass line must be applied in procuratorial work and in trying cases." The essentially political character of the judicial organs was further suggested by Vice Premier Chang Ch'un-ch'iao in 1973: The proletarian state

Political character of judicial organs (margin note)

suppresses the reactionary classes and elements and those who resist socialist transformation and oppose socialist construction, and suppresses all treasonable and counter-revolutionary activities; and secondly, it protects our country from subversion and possible aggression by external enemies.

The Ministry of Public Security maintains a national police organization, which is supported by rural and urban militia and the garrison forces of the People's Liberation Army and, together with the People's Courts, forms the backbone of the apparatus of the "dictatorship of the proletariat." The "six codes" of the former Kuomintang government were annulled in 1949, but no subsequent codification of criminal and civil law was promulgated.

The armed forces. The People's Liberation Army (PLA) is the unified organization of all Chinese land, sea, and air forces. Known as the Red Army (until 1937) and as the 8th Route Army and New 4th Army (and 18th Army Group) during the Sino-Japanese War, the PLA adopted the new name when the civil war resumed in 1946. The history of the PLA is officially traced to the Nan-ch'ang Uprising of August 1, 1927; the army fought under the "8-1" red flag (bearing the characters for "eight" and "one," commemorating the birth of the Liberation Army on August 1, 1927) until 1949, and August 1 is celebrated as PLA day. The PLA developed as the armed force of the CPR, the CCP Military Commission exercises political control, and Mao Tse-tung's military lectures and essays of 1936–38 strongly influence its doctrines. A system of political commissars, with full military status, is maintained throughout the PLA.

The PLA is recruited on the principle of compulsory military service (law of July 30, 1955) by all males who attain the age of 18. Women may register for medical, veterinary, and other technical services. Eligible men are required to register before July 1 of the year they reach 18. Basic service is for a two- to six-year period, which may be extended. Because the PLA is estimated to include about 3,500,000 persons, the annual call-up is fewer than 1,000,000, perhaps less than one-tenth of those eligible. Technical information concerning the operation of the system is restricted. Demobilized servicemen are carried in a ready reserve, which is reinforced by a standby reserve of veterans and by the urban and rural militias.

Shortly after the Ministry of National Defense was established in 1954, an officer system based on the Soviet model was adopted (1955). Under Defense Minister P'eng Te-huai, the PLA was modernized with Soviet equipment, and its officer cadres became more highly professional. Largely because P'eng Te-huai advocated the primacy of defense requirements over those of the Socialist revolution, the Central Committee in 1959 removed him from his post. His emphasis on regularization and modernization of the armed forces was said to violate Mao Tse-tung's doctrines about "people's war," the military primacy of revolution-oriented personnel over weapons and matériel, the role of the army in production activity, the importance of a mass militia, and the mass line system of command relations. After his departure, the social and political work of the PLA was emphasized, and, after new regulations governing political activities within the PLA were issued and implemented in 1963, the armed forces were held before the party and the country as models of

Politicization of the PLA (margin note)

organization, discipline, and working style. A system was adopted for assigning senior officers to temporary duty as ordinary soldiers; the general political department of the PLA emerged as the leading component in the military system of administration; and, to heighten still further the image of a "people's army," all military ranks and rank insignia were abolished in 1965. Later that year, Lin Piao, the defense minister, published his *Long Live the Victory of People's War!* as an authoritative statement of Maoist military doctrines. At the outset of the Cultural Revolution, it became apparent that the movement to politicize the PLA had not wholly converted all leading elements in the military establishment: leading military figures were removed from their posts in 1966 and 1967, and several other former marshals and central military bureaucrats, as well as regional and provincial commanders and political commissars, became targets of public Red Guard condemnations and were relieved of their duties.

As a presumed model of political rectitude and loyalty to Chairman Mao, the PLA performed a central role during the Cultural Revolution. In the guise of reforming its own work in the fields of art and literature, the PLA generated policies and regulations that became general directives. As deputy supreme commander of the Cultural Revolution, Lin Piao became the principal spokesman and aide-de-camp of Chairman Mao, and he produced the *Quotations from Chairman Mao Tse-tung*, which became the standard reference manual for all revolutionary activists. The *Liberation Army Daily* became the most authoritative organ of the Maoist press, taking priority over the Central Committee's own organs (*People's Daily* and *Red Flag*); and the Cultural Revolution's "small group of the PLA" assumed large responsibilities for directing the course of the revolution. In 1967 Mao Tse-tung called upon the PLA to "support the revolutionary Left," and it became deeply embroiled in assisting the organization of revolutionary committees and their seizures of power, in maintaining order between competing revolutionary organizations, and in purging from its own ranks those who sympathized with Mao's opponents. Its instructions were to avoid recourse to military force and to rely principally upon its political cadres in its propaganda and educational work. Mao and Lin Piao insisted that "the party must control the gun," and, with all its internal difficulties, the PLA appeared more cohesive and responsive to central direction than the lower echelons of the CCP. The mass base of the PLA and its political working style combined to make it a leadership component of the Maoist system of general social organization.

Arma-
ment

In the field of military technology, the Chinese armed forces became largely dependent upon internal resources after the withdrawal of Soviet aid in 1960. Increasing amounts of matériel, including ships and aircraft, were produced in China. Official Chinese sources reported that the Soviet Union agreed in 1957 to supply technical assistance for the manufacture of nuclear weapons but that such aid was discontinued in 1959. The Chinese remained committed to the development of nuclear weapons and exploded their first nuclear bomb in October 1964. China rejected the Nuclear Test-Ban Treaty, signed by the United States, the Soviet Union, and Great Britain in 1963, proposing instead the "complete prohibition and thorough destruction of nuclear weapons" (government statement, July 31, 1963). This was reaffirmed on October 16, 1963, when the government declared that "China will never at any time and under any circumstances be the first to use nuclear weapons." China continued to test and deploy nuclear weapons and by late 1966 had developed a ballistic missile. It exploded its first hydrogen bomb in 1967. Meanwhile, a military doctrine that would relate China's growing nuclear arsenal to the strategy and tactics of "people's war" remained to be announced. China refused to sign the Treaty on the Non-proliferation of Nuclear Weapons, but in 1973 it did adhere to the additional protocol II of the Treaty for the Prohibition of Nuclear Weapons in Latin America (1967).

The chairman of the party Central Committee is commander in chief of the armed forces and chairman of the Military Commission of the Central Committee. Under a chief of staff, the PLA maintains general political and general logistics departments and special command organizations for the navy, air force, and other service branches. The minister and vice ministers in the Ministry of National Defense, department heads, and regional commanders are nearly all members of the CCP Central Committee. The territorial organization of the PLA consists of 11 military regions (with headquarters in principal cities), each with jurisdiction over one to four provincial military districts (with headquarters in provincial capitals). The National Defense Scientific and Technological Commission has responsibility for weapons research and development.

Military
organiza-
tion

Divisions are grouped into some 40 armies. An army is usually assigned to each of the 11 military regions, in each of which the military commander also commands air and naval forces and the civil militia. Altogether, the PLA in the mid-1970s consisted of about 210 divisions, including 121 infantry, 40 artillery, 10 armoured, three cavalry, and four airborne divisions. The PLA is augmented by the People's Militia, the most advanced members of which receive substantial military training. Their number is estimated to be between 5,000,000 and 8,000,-000.

In the mid-1970s naval personnel numbered about 275,-000 (including 28,000 marines and 30,000 members of the Naval Air Force). Naval forces were divided into three groups—the North Sea Fleet, the East Sea Fleet, and the South Sea Fleet. Naval strength included 56 submarines, 18 destroyers and destroyer escorts, and several hundred smaller armed craft, together with numbers of auxiliary vessels.

The air force had an estimated strength in the mid-1970s of about 4,250 combat aircraft, divided into regiments of jet fighters and some regiments of tactical bombers in addition to transport, helicopter, and reconnaissance units. Each regiment consisted of three squadrons. Air force personnel numbered about 250,000.

Overall, China's military forces continued steadily to become modernized. Civil defense programs, enlisting large numbers of civilian volunteers, were pressed in many large cities. Estimates of annual CPR defense expenditures varied, but the annual budget was thought to exceed $32,800,000,000, or about 11 percent of the country's gross national product. In the transition following Mao Tse-tung's death in 1976, the new party chairman, Hua Kuo-feng, assigned greater urgency to modernizing both the military and industrial sectors. Although CPR officials reportedly concurred on the priority given to some weapons programs, they openly debated competing formulas for attaining these twin goals.   (J.W.Le.)

SOCIAL SERVICES AND SOCIAL CONDITIONS

Education. During the First Five-Year Plan period (1953 to 1957), overall enrollment in Chinese educational institutions at all levels reportedly increased about 33 percent from 54,000,000 to 71,000,000. By the 1960s the total had risen to more than 100,000,000. Educational policy is generally directed by the propaganda department of the CCP Central Committee, but the principal administration is vested in a Ministry of Education.

Educational policy strongly reflects the political objectives of the CCP. Mao Tse-tung asserted, on February 27, 1957: "Not to have a correct political point of view is like having no soul. . . . Our educational policy must enable everyone who gets an education to develop morally, intellectually and physically and become a cultured [*i.e.*, literate], socialist-minded worker." Following a Central Committee Conference on Educational Work in 1958, Lu Ting-yi, a member of the CCP Politburo, declared:

Our state is a proletarian dictatorship, a socialist state. Our education is not bourgeois, but socialist education. . . . The educational policy of the Chinese Communist party has always been that education should serve the politics of the working class and be combined with productive labour; and to apply this policy, education must be led by the Communist party. . . . We believe there are only two kinds of knowledge in the world. One is knowledge of the class struggle. . . .

The other kind of knowledge is the knowledge of the struggle for production, that is, the knowledge men gain in their struggle against nature. . . . The philosophy of dialectical materialism provides men with a correct way of thinking.

In 1957 and 1958 strong emphasis was placed upon compulsory "socialist education" at all school levels and for all elements of the population, under a special curriculum prescribed by the propaganda department. Extensive indoctrination was maintained concerning the necessity for combining "redness" with "expertness"—in large part to overcome rightist and "bourgeois" tendencies in educational and intellectual circles. Especially after 1958, students and faculty in all educational institutions were required to engage in productive activity, either establishing their own factories and workshops or being assigned to work in factories, on farms, and in other enterprises.

A policy of decentralization introduced in 1958 to 1959 made the people's communes responsible for maintaining local schools and colleges, including "commune universities" in which experienced peasants acted as "professors." During the retrenchment following the failure of the Great Leap Forward, many students in middle schools and colleges were assigned to agricultural production, thus deferring (or terminating) their studies; students in urban schools were also affected by the policy of reducing urban populations in 1962. In 1961 to 1962 emphasis on learning about Communism was somewhat reduced in favour of technical studies, but by 1963 emphasis on "class education" was found at all levels of the system.

"Half-work, half-study" schools

"Half-work, half-study" middle schools were developed experimentally in the late 1950s and were more widely popularized (to include "half-work, half-study" primary schools and colleges) in the mid-1960s. In them the regular labour of students in agriculture or handicrafts provided financial support for schools and colleges, the curricula of which were strongly influenced by technical emphases. Part-time education in basic literacy for peasants and in technical subjects for trade-union members had long been featured in Chinese Communist education; the further proliferation of part-time schools produced effects that could not be carefully assessed because comprehensive educational statistics were no longer being published.

Early in the Cultural Revolution (1966), the Central Committee decided to close the middle schools and institutions of higher education, pending a thorough reform of admissions procedures, curricula, and examination systems. The school closing, which also affected elementary schools, released students and faculty to participate in Red Guard activities, which were first manifested in sweeping condemnations of "bourgeois academic" values in the educational system. Many faculty and staff members were exposed to ideological reform, and not all survived the process. An attempt to resume classes in the elementary and middle schools in the spring of 1967 was only a partial success, but, in such schools as opened then and later, nearly all formal curricula were abandoned in favour of intensive reading of the works of Mao Tse-tung as a basic means for learning "revolutionization." Several universities resumed classes in the fall of 1967, before the promised reforms had been completed, on the basis of experimental procedures intended to expunge the remnants of bourgeois pedagogy.

A new "proletarian educational line" began to be implemented with the reopening of several technical and scientific institutions in 1969–70, but for several years thereafter liberal-arts types of institutions were only slowly reopened. The key to the new policy was the substitution of tests of "proletarian revolutionary" character for admission, replacing national examinations that emphasized formal tests of earlier academic achievement. In the case of Tsinghua University (the premier institution of higher learning and the model for many others), admission in 1970 was based on recommendations of "the masses" in localities where candidates had demonstrated their production skills and political activism. Graduation from lower middle school was expected, but proletarian elements lacking that degree of formal education might also be admitted. Representatives of the working masses, students, faculty and staff became involved in a thorough curricular reorganization, in programs of team-teaching that placed as much emphasis upon performance in the school's factories, farms, and other productive enterprises as in the classroom; the period of instruction was shortened, and measures were taken to insure against inculcation of elitist attitudes (principally by requiring graduates to return to production activities in their original localities). Notable was the shift from courses in "political study," developed before 1966, to the experience of students in production activities working side-by-side with workers, peasants, and soldiers—judged to be a better means of inculcating "proletarian revolutionary" habits and ways of thinking.

Elementary education was to be reduced to five years, and in elementary and secondary schools students also were expected to participate in some degree of productive activity—at rising levels of sophistication. Factories also were encouraged to establish their own schools.

(H.A.S./Ed.)

Health. Government policy has laid particular emphasis on providing medical service and undertaking sanitation measures in the countryside. Medical personnel stationed in cities are encouraged to go into the country to serve people there; medical teams circulate regularly in rural areas. Among these are the so-called barefoot doctors—who, in effect, are normally shod except when working in rice paddy areas during the wet season; these doctors are given intensive training for relatively short periods in order that they may work in country areas. In the province of Shantung in 1970, for example, it was reported that medical teams totalling 20,000 were regularly visiting rural districts, while about 2,400 medical staff and 4,000 medical college graduates had settled in the country.

Apart from this, the People's Liberation Army also sends large numbers of medical personnel to serve people and soldiers in rural areas; it also helps to train the barefoot doctors and to assist communes to develop the cooperative medical-care system, which provides virtually free medical care, with people paying only a very small sum each month in return. Many small pharmaceutical factories have also been built.

In the earlier part of the 20th century, China was notorious for its filthy environment; today, however, standards of scrupulous cleanliness are maintained. Because of progress made in medical science and in sanitation, it is claimed that almost all major communicable diseases have disappeared—an exception being schistosomiasis, a parasitic disease affecting the blood. The two major diseases now threatening the lives of the Chinese are, first, cancer and, second, heart diseases (especially arteriosclerosis, or hardening of the arteries).

Since 1949 China has reported remarkable achievements in medical science, including the discovery of how to produce a purified synthetic insulin, the replanting of broken fingers and arms, the use of moxibustion (burning of cones of wormwood leaves on designated anatomical spots), and of new techniques in anesthetic surgery.

The use of acupuncture

In addition, the time-honoured Chinese medical treatment known as acupuncture (treatment by the insertion of needles at specified points in the body) is widely used to cure malignant diseases, to treat deafness and muteness, and to cure other ailments. By virtue of its simplicity, acupuncture is welcomed and widely practiced in the countryside.

Social conditions. Because of population pressure on the land, the standard of living of the Chinese people is lower than that in Western countries. Before the revolution that culminated in 1949, however, not only was Chinese society generally poor, but it also contained considerable extremes of poverty and wealth, with most of the wealth concentrated in the hands of a few. This inequality led to severe social tension. Only a few out of the immense total population had received higher education, and these educated people formed a clique apart.

Because of political conditions, knowledge was rarely applied.

Wages and cost of living. According to a statement by Premier Chou En-lai in 1971, China's gross national income (representing the total value of industrial and agricultural production) is equivalent to U.S. $120,000,000,-000, or U.S. $150 per person. Because of different statistical methods used and great variations in the cost of living, however, these figures are of little use for comparative purposes. The monthly income of an average worker is equivalent to about U.S. $30, and the monthly salary of graduates fresh from university is even lower, although both groups enjoy an adequate living standard. The average income of members of rural communes is still lower, but their living conditions are also satisfactory.

Social changes. Since the drastic changes in China's political and social system, the family life and ethical concepts of the Chinese are also undergoing changes. The traditional structure of the Chinese family was centred around the guardian, who controlled the family's production, income, and expenditure and who possessed much authority. The Confucian concept of ethics lays great stress on the role of the family. Academic success, for example, was considered to bring fame to one's family and to reflect honour upon one's ancestors. Most women did not participate in social production and were not economically independent. Sons and daughters, as dependents on the father and the elder brother, were expected to show strict obedience. Because the family structure was a bulwark of the system of privately owned wealth, it was viewed by the new regime as being not in accord with Socialism and hence became a target for reform.

In the reformed Chinese family, the absolute authority of the guardian no longer exists. Each adult member of the family is given equal status. The management of family finance must be democratic, with discussion open to all. Children in the family have more right to speak than in the past and may even criticize their parents; the idea that children are reared to support their parents in old age is considered out-of-date.

The status of women. The status of women has been changed greatly. The marriage law promulgated in 1950 advocates equality of men and women and freedom of marriage; marriages are no longer arranged by parents. Nurseries, kindergartens, public canteens, and homes for the aged have been widely established, gradually relieving women from family work and enabling them to participate in production. In the people's communes women account for about half the agricultural labour force. In the cities women are also habitually engaged in productive work. Women also participate in political and scientific work and in military (including air force) service and are employed in heavy industry. Women are also numbered among the members and alternate members of the Central Committee of the CCP.

Between 1951 and 1959 the number of woman students at universities and colleges increased fivefold, from 35,-000 to 180,000. In the Chinese Academy of Medical Science, female scientists and technicians are approximately equal in number to male. In 1962 the An-shan Iron and Steel Corporation employed some 600 female engineers, planners, and technicians. (C.-S.Ch.)

The role of women

CULTURAL LIFE

Since the early 20th century China has experienced the most momentous transformation in its history, affecting every aspect of life: economic, social, political, intellectual, ethical, and cultural. Early changes were at first sporadic, the automatic result of infiltration of alien ideas and foreign commodities. One of these was the gradual introduction of modern industry, which in turn led to the rise of trade unions, thereby eroding the old guild system. The advent of modern education in the 1920s also played an important role in disrupting traditional society.

These forces were greatly expanded with the establishment of the Communist regime and its ideal of continuous revolution. Borrowing Soviet techniques of political organization, the Chinese Communists attempted to bring the entire population under political, social, and psychological control in their effort to remold the society and the economy. Although the governmental and political structure appears to many Westerners to be totalitarian and repressive, it has been seen since the Cultural Revolution to be flexible and responsive to the masses. Political indoctrination is an important factor of all phases of life, but in the mid-1970s it was estimated that only one-seventh of the population belonged to the party-controlled mass organizations, such as the trade unions. The agricultural commune movement of the 1950s has yielded to dissatisfaction, and private plots, private livestock, and material incentives are now allowed. The Communist Party does maintain overall control of the economy, but local administration seems to have increased.

The *Quotations from Chairman Mao Tse-tung* is perhaps the most widely read book (and a powerful political tool), but its strictures have been accompanied by improvements in the economy, education, health, and public works that were sorely needed.

PROSPECTS FOR THE FUTURE

The political, social, and cultural revolutions since 1949 have produced tremendous changes, and they are still taking place. The role of the family, of women, and of education have all been transformed, while political pressures have created an entirely new pattern of individual and group behaviour. The Chinese Communists are mobilizing the population in an extensive program of economic development aimed at transforming China from an agricultural nation into one of the world's leading industrial powers.

In the 1970s, especially after the People's Republic gained recognition from the United Nations in 1971, the relative isolation that China had maintained began to experience modification. It also became increasingly clear that relations between China and other nations, especially the big powers, would in the future do much to determine the pattern of events in the remaining years of the 20th century. (Ed.)

BIBLIOGRAPHY.

The land and people: The following works provide introductions to their subjects: KEITH M. BUCHANAN, *The Transformation of the Chinese Earth* (1970); T.R. TREGEAR, *A Geography of China* (1965); A. KOLB, *East Asia: China, Japan, Korea, Vietnam,* Eng. ed. (1971); and C.S. CH'EN, "Population Growth and Urbanization in China, 1953–1970," *Geog. Rev.,* No. 1 (1973). PING-CHIA KUO, *China,* 3rd ed. (1970), also provides a general introduction. Materials on physical geography are surveyed in *The Physical Geography of China* (Eng. trans. 1967), mainly based on recent Chinese investigations, published in two volumes by the Institute of Geography, U.S.S.R. Academy of Sciences; STANLEY D. RICHARDSON, *Forestry in Communist China* (1966); C.S. CH'EN et al., *Climatic Classification and Climatic Regions in China* (1956). Studies of the population of China include TA CHEN, *New China's Population Census of 1953 and Its Relations to National Reconstruction and Demographic Research* (1957); and SRIPATI CHANDRASEKHAR, *China's Population,* 2nd ed. (1960). Two general surveys are C.T. HU et al., *China: Its People, Its Society, Its Culture* (1960), with a topical bibliography; and THEODORE SHABAD, *China's Changing Map,* 2nd ed. (1972). Useful atlases are the *Atlas of the People's Republic of China* (Peking, 1958); and the *People's Republic of China Atlas,* published by the United States Central Intelligence Agency.

The economy: The two best analyses of Chinese economic development are AUDREY G. DONNITHORNE, *China's Economic System* (1967); and C.S. CH'EN, "China," in the *World Atlas of Agriculture,* vol. 2 (1971). Some attempts to appraise the situation include NAI-RUENN CHEN, *The Chinese Economy Under Communism* (1969); C.S. CH'EN, "The Sugar Industry of China," *Geog. J.,* vol. 137, part 1 (March 1971), "The Petroleum Industry of China," *Die Erde,* No. 3–4 (1972), and *The Agricultural Regions of China,* Special Bulletin, American Institute of Crop Ecology (1970); the JOINT ECONOMIC COMMITTEE OF THE UNITED STATES CONGRESS, *An Economic Profile of Mainland China* (1968), a collection of studies by China specialists; BARRY M. RICHMAN, *Industrial Society in Communist China* (1969), a study of China's economic development and management in comparison with India, the U.S.S.R., Japan, and the United States; EDWARD L. WHEEL-

WRIGHT and BRUCE MCFARLANE, *The Chinese Road to Socialism: Economics of the Cultural Revolution* (1970); and YUAN-LI WU, *The Economy of Communist China: An Introduction* (1965).

Transportation and communications: Information on railway, air, and highway communication may be found in general works on the Chinese economy (see above). Y.L. WU, *The Spatial Economy of Communist China: A Study on Industrial Location and Transportation* (1967), treats transportation in the context of developmental economics, with some statistical support. References to transportation also appear in NAI-RUENN CHEN, *The Economy of Mainland China, 1949–1963: A Bibliography of Materials in English* (1963). The many studies of the role of transportation in the history of Western influence upon China and upon regional economics are well exemplified in SHUN-HSIN CHOU, "Railway Development and Economic Growth in Manchuria," *China Quarterly*, no. 45, pp. 57–84 (1971). Current information compiled from Chinese press reports appears in the annual reports on China published by the Union Research Institute (Hong Kong). Articles on transportation appear intermittently in *Peking Review* (weekly), and Chinese press materials dealing with transportation and communication are given in the several translations series of the American Consulate General in Hong Kong. In the absence of a monographic literature of the subject, several journal articles offer helpful insights: V.D. LIPPIT, "Development of Transportation in Communist China," *China Quarterly*, no. 27, pp. 101–119 (1966); R.L. POWELL, "The Role of the Military in China's Transportation and Communication Systems," *Current Scene*, pp. 5–12 (February 7, 1972); and BERNHARD GROSSMANN, "The Background of Communist China's Transport Policy," in *Symposium on Economic and Social Problems of the Far East*, pp. 46–54 (1963).

Administration, social conditions, and cultural life: JOHN K. FAIRBANK, *The United States and China*, 3rd ed. (1971), a standard survey of the Chinese social and political environment, with emphasis on elements useful for American understanding of Chinese developments; WILLIAM HINTON, *Fanshen: A Documentary of Revolution in a Chinese Village* (1966), an eyewitness account of 1948 revolutionary activity in a village in Shansi, setting out the factors of social conflict that assisted the Communist take-over; HO PING-TI and TANG TSOU (eds.), *China's Heritage and the Communist Political System in China in Crisis*, vol. 1 (1968), critical analysis and evaluation of the Chinese political system during the early phase of the Cultural Revolution—articles by 13 academic specialists; JOHN WILSON LEWIS (ed.), *Party Leadership and Revolutionary Power in China* (1970), analyses by 12 specialists of the early impact of the Cultural Revolution on the Chinese Communist leadership and its policies, with historical perspectives; FRANZ SCHURMANN, *Ideology and Organization in Communist China* (1966), a full-scale attempt to evaluate Communist ideology and institutions on the eve of the Cultural Revolution from a sociological perspective; RICHARD H. SOLOMON, *Mao's Revolution and the Chinese Political Culture* (1971), a close examination of Mao's thought applied to the problems of political socialization of the masses in Communist China; JACK GRAY (ed.), *Modern China's Search for a Political Form* (1969), a scholarly symposium; JOHN M.H. LINDBECK (ed.), *China: Management of a Revolutionary Society* (1971), a series of specialized studies of cultural, ideological, and institutional change; JAN MYRDAL, *Rapport från kinesisk* (1963; Eng. trans., *Report from a Chinese Village*, 1965), detailed observations (including census and family budgets) of village life during 1962 in an "old" liberated village near Yenan in Shensi Province, and its sequel, written after a return visit by the author, *The Revolution Continued* (1971); THOMAS W. ROBINSON (ed.), *The Cultural Revolution in China* (1971), five specialized studies of the origin and development of the Cultural Revolution, with emphasis on conflicting elements of political power.

(C.S.Ch./H.A.S.)

China, History of

The present article tracing the history of China from the Old Stone Age to the present is divided into the following sections:

I. Prehistoric period and Shang dynasty

PREHISTORY AND ARCHAEOLOGY

To the Chinese scholar up to the 20th century, archaeology was closely linked with historical and literary studies. Archaeological materials were valued according to whether they verified or illustrated the past as encompassed in the Classics and annals. Epigraphy was all-important, while objects without inscriptions were neglected. Thus scriptless documents were neglected in China until Westerners began to organize explorations in the early 1920s. Their activities, soon shared by the Chinese themselves, resulted in geological, paleontological, and archaeological discoveries of the utmost importance. After World War II field work was conducted on a large scale under the Communist authorities, and a good deal of the rapidly accumulating material was published in journals and monographs.

Paleolithic in North China. The site of Chou-k'ou-tien, 30 miles (48 kilometres) southwest of Peking, first investigated in 1921 and in part excavated between 1923 and 1939 and again after 1949, has fossiliferous deposits ranging from the Miocene to the end of the Pleistocene and contains the remains of *Sinanthropus pekinensis*, a hominid that ranks in age with the closely related *Pithecanthropus* of Java. The geologically oldest identified artifact from Chou-k'ou-tien is estimated to date about 500,000 years back in time. An advanced stone technique is indicated in flaked tools still of preloessic age but from a geologically younger period. Whether these superior tools also were made by *Sinanthropus* is a question that cannot safely be answered.

At the so-called Upper Cave of Chou-k'ou-tien were found remnants of the Late Pleistocene loess formation. Four human skulls found there revealed what has been termed an early *Homo sapiens asiaticus*. Cultural remains suggest a burial place of some stage comparable with the Magdalenian.

In 1954 another Lower Paleolithic site was found at Ting-ts'un in Shansi. The artifacts as well as the osteological remains represent a stage comparable with that of the younger period at Chou-k'ou-tien.

Ordos industries.   Several important Upper Paleolithic sites have been discovered along the southern fringe of the Ordos Steppe, the area skirted by the great bend of the Huang Ho. They belong in their entirety in the Late Pleistocene but vary in age. None of them yielded skeletal remains of man. A series of extremely hard quartzite implements, mostly made of round pebbles chipped along one edge, as well as some flakes, came from the basal gravels underneath the loess. Finds of this category were reported from a number of other sites. In the loess stratum itself, two dwelling places and workshop sites were explored: Shui-tung-kou, close to the Huang Ho, opposite Ningsia, and Sjara-osso-gol, in southeastern Ordos. Shui-tung-kou is a loess-filled depression, stretching east–west for ten miles (16 kilometres), where five hearths with ashes and a great number of artifacts were located at various depths. A rich and diversified stoneworking industry suggests a stage more developed than that of the aforementioned group; yet more primitive tools occurred in the same assemblage. The materials used, chert and silicified limestone, were taken from the gravel of streams embedded in the yellow loam that later was buried under renewed deposits of wind-carried loess dust. The site of Sjara-osso is remarkable for the extraordinary depth of the fossil-bearing beds of dune sands and lacustrine clayey sediments overlying the Paleolithic floor and for the smallness of the stone implements. Typologically, this "micro-industry" is considered by the 20th-century French archaeologist Henri Breuil as advanced beyond the Shui-tung-kou stage. But it is separated from the Neolithic horizon of the same site by no less than 180 feet (55 metres) of deposits, sands, and sandy clays rich in fossils. The absolute age of Shui-tung-kou and Sjara-osso is about 100,000 years and is separated from the final phase at Chou-k'ou-tien by about another 100,000 years. The Upper Cave of Chou-k'ou-tien follows much later—about 25,000 BC.

Mesolithic phase.   A Mesolithic phase comparable with that of post-Pleistocene Europe has not been identified in China proper. In the southerly region of Kwangsi, however, a possibly Mesolithic culture was discovered in cave deposits of perhaps still Late Pleistocene Age, but it is devoid of remains of extinct animals or any strongly fossilized bones. Polished or only partly polished stone implements and pottery are absent. The stage is comparable with—and probably related to—the early Bacsonian of neighbouring Tongking (Vietnam).

In the northern borderlands—Mongolia and Manchuria—geographic and climatic conditions of the postglacial period apparently favoured the development and spread, over millennia, of a culture of hunters and later of primitive farmers, who left abundant traces of their culture in microlithic tools made of fine minerals such as jasper, agate, carnelian, chalcedony, and flint. The foremost site in Mongolia is that of Shabarakh-Usu in the Gobi desert. Widely diffused to the east, into Manchuria and southward (Ordos), and no doubt related to Siberian microlithic cultures, this Shabarakh, or Gobi, culture corresponds in part to the Tardenoisian and Azilian of Europe. In China, microlithic chipped implements are scarcely encountered to the south of the line of the (erected much later) Great Wall; it appears as though this gigantic fortification followed a cultural borderline of hoary age and remarkable stability. A cluster of 15 dune-dwellers' stations of possibly the Late Mesolithic to Early Neolithic Period was discovered in eastern Shensi, however, in 1956. It is an assemblage without either pottery or agricultural tools. The finds consist of chipped microliths and larger forms that are said to resemble Mousteri-

[margin: Shui-tung-kou and Sjara-osso-gol]

[margin: Microlithic cultures]

an types. This Sha-yüan assemblage may represent a southern outpost of the Shabarakh culture of the Mongolian Plateau.

Neolithic stage.   A gradual transition toward a primitive Neolithic culture of sedentary farmers and husband-

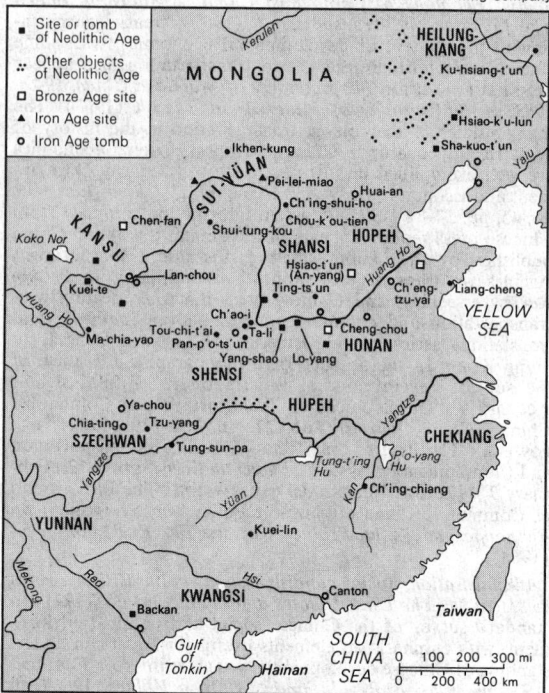

Adapted from A. Herrmann, *An Historical Atlas of China* (1966); Aldine Publishing Company

Principal sites of prehistoric and Shang China.

men can be observed at two sites in the Ch'eng-te region—Lin-hsi and Ulan Hada (now Ch'ih-feng). The artifacts at Lin-hsi include crude rhyolithic pebble tools and blades as well as nuclei of fine siliceous rocks occurring side by side with grinding stones and pestles, usually made of granite. A few hoelike implements and perforated round pebbles were recovered. Polished implements were rare, and true axes, or celts, were absent. The pottery encountered was handmade and poorly fired. Bones of domesticated horse, ox, and sheep, but none of wild game, were found. Similar conditions prevail at the site to the south of the "red rock," which gave Ulan Hada its name. In addition, this site yielded rather advanced types in stone as well as pottery, the later age of which seems unquestionable but could not be ascertained stratigraphically.

The "Mongolian Neolithic," typified by the presence of microliths, agricultural tools, and some pottery such as those from Lin-hsi, extends northward into northern Manchuria, where it shows a stronger dependence on fishing and hunting; farther west it was traced in the Gobi (later Shabarakh) and southwest in the Ordos. This culture, which must have comprised the wide territories to the north of the yellow clay, or loess, of China proper and to the south of the Siberian forest zone, seems to have vanished without further local developments, presumably because of desiccation and the resulting desert-like conditions. Some traces of it were found in sites spreading between western Kansu and the Gulf of Liao-tung, where a new Late Neolithic culture with painted pottery and polished stone tools also developed. These "mixed sites" evidence an expansion of the new culture into the southern fringes of the territory previously and perhaps still held by the makers of the microliths.

The rare case of what appears to be an intrusion in Ch'i-chia-p'ing, in south Kansu, of north Eurasian Kammkeramik, a ware with comb-stamped ornaments entirely foreign in China, probably belongs in the period preceding the appearance of the painted pottery.

Yang-shao Painted Pottery culture.   The period between the Late Paleolithic of the Upper Cave at Chou-k'ou-tien and the appearance of the Painted Pottery, or Yang-shao, culture in North China, a period of many millennia, is archaeologically obscure. There are few finds to shed light on that long period. Climatic conditions may account largely for this hiatus. The final Pleistocene, when the loess formation was still in progress, was a cold and semi-arid phase; afterward, in postglacial times, the river valleys and plains may have been swamplands.

Discovery of the Yang-shao civilization

In 1921 at Yang-shao-ts'un, the Swedish archaeologist J.G. Andersson discovered a civilization that appeared in c. 2500 BC of numerous, large, populous villages whose inhabitants were hunters, stock raisers, and farmers and were skilled carpenters and weavers. Their excellent ceramics, with few or no equals at that time, indicate that the then inhabitants of Honan and Kansu had developed a generally high standard of civilization. There must have been, by some means or other, new inventions or the introduction of new ideas from abroad—a rather sudden impetus that allowed the rapid spread of a fast-growing population. Further explorations revealed that this culture had covered the wide area between western Kansu and northern Honan, with extensions into Szechwan, Ch'eng-te, in Hopeh Province, and Liaoning and that the ancient settlements were close to the Hsi-ning, T'ao, Wei, upper Chia-ling, and Han rivers, and to the Huang Ho, where it flows eastward after the great Ordos bend. This discovery shows that China falls in line with west Asian and Indian sequences; not only does there appear in China a painted ware but, exactly as in the west, this ware is gradually replaced by a burnished black ware. The discovery was, however, a complicated process and has not yet been clarified by field work. The observations made are summarized briefly below.

Stratigraphy. In most of the dwelling sites explored, the cultural stratum was rather shallow, except in two very large ancient villages—Hsi-yin-ts'un (southwestern Shansi) and Yang-shao. Judged by the occurring types of pottery shards, no clear subdivision or stratigraphic sequence was seen in either place. Andersson stated that Yang-shao represents one single cultural stage comprising both painted and burnished black wares. The only stratigraphic change noted at Hsi-yin-ts'un was a slight increase in the percentage of the black shards as compared with the painted shards in the upper layers; the percentage of the cruder pottery, gray and reddish, with or without cord impression, remained constant throughout.

In a few northern Honan sites, excavated by staff members of the Academia Sinica in 1931 and 1932, a stratigraphic sequence of painted pottery overlaid by black pottery and, topmost, gray Shang pottery was observed. In other sites in northern as well as western Honan, however, black pottery associated with, or overlaid by, gray pottery—but with no trace of painted pottery—was found to be a recurring and typical assemblage. Field observations made in the upper Wei Ho Valley by W.C. P'ei in 1947 indicated that ceramic wares of that area—the main route from Kansu to Honan—suggest three stages, early, middle, and late, characterized by painted pottery, first of good style, then of degenerate style, and, finally, by utter decay and disappearance. From Kansu came the finest of the painted ceramics but little of stratigraphic interest (see also ASIANS, PREHISTORIC).

Some inferences can be drawn. In Honan and Shensi the painted ware preceded but apparently overlapped with the black pottery, and the latter, in turn, preceded a Bronze Age gray ware. In Kansu, where the black pottery seems almost absent, the Yang-shao ware is older than both the Hsin-tien ware of the beginning metal age and the (unpainted) Ch'i-chia ware, unknown in Honan.

Painted pottery styles. The phenomenon of clearly differentiated styles of ornament was observed only in Kansu. Named after type sites in Kansu, most of these styles suggest an evolutionary sequence and, consequently, relative dates: (1) Pan-shan; (2) Ma-ch'ang; (3) Hsin-tien; and (4) Sha-ching.

Evolutionary sequence at Kansu

The Pan-shan style is distinguished by an amphora type of noble shape and with exquisitely painted ornaments, among which a design of rotary S curves running hori-zontally around the vessel predominates. Other common patterns are rhombic checkers, diamonds, zigzags, and a gourd motif. A tomb excavated at Pien-chia-kou (Pan-shan T'ao-erh Ho Valley) contained the skeleton of a man of about 40, in a flexed position and sprinkled with ochre.

The Ma-ch'ang wares are of reddish clay and are painted, sometimes carelessly, with black ornaments such as large concentric circles, rhombic T hooks, and large meander bands consisting of parallel lines; the spiral patterns have disappeared.

It was with the pottery of the following Hsin-tien stage that some minor bronze objects came to light, none of them typically Chinese (Shang). These Hsin-tien wares retain the meander as the predominating motif of their sparse decoration, while their shapes depart from the Pan-shan–Ma-ch'ang tradition. Sha-ching, the fourth phase, appears to have derived from Hsin-tien.

More closely comparable with the ornamental designs found in Shansi, among which stand out large, flower-like, sweeping patterns, are decorations from minor find spots in south Kansu. Their exact relationship to the styles of the above-described sequence is not fully clarified, but it appears likely that they postdate the Pan-shan style; they presuppose the spiral motif, which here is transformed into free and asymmetrical curvilinear patterns foreign to the geometric development of the Ma-ch'ang phase.

Ma-chia-yao and Lo-han-t'ang in central Kansu, two large dwelling sites, exhibit designs that may well stand midway between Pan-shan and the south Kansu styles. Closely connected with the latter are painted wares uncovered at two western Honan sites, Miao-ti-kou and San-li-ch'iao, which typify two successive stages. Miao-ti-kou I displays the flowerlike patterns in dynamic and elegant examples; Miao-ti-kou II, about contemporary with San-li-ch'iao I, reduces those patterns to simplified, angular motifs, which continue into the further impoverished designs of San-li-ch'iao II, where there appear gray and blackish unpainted wares regarded as forerunners of the subsequent black-pottery types.

Complexity of the Yang-shao culture

As new material is uncovered, however, the picture of the Yang-shao culture becomes increasingly complex, necessitating continuous reappraisals. Excavations in 1953 and 1955 at the site of a large Neolithic village at Pan-p'o-ts'un (in Shensi Province), for instance, brought to light some previously unparalleled pottery designs in addition to rich architectural remains, including kilns, which for the first time give evidence of a long-continued occupation.

It may be said that after a splendid manifestation in Shansi (Ching-ts'un and Hsi-yin-ts'un), decline set in in west Honan (Yang-shao-ts'un), followed by a rapid decay in north Honan; so that a loss of diversity and freshness becomes the more noticeable moving farther eastward.

Stone implements. The four tools characteristic of the Pan-shan phase, according to Andersson, are heavy axes of rectangular cross section with rounded-off corners, flat adzes, small adzes, and rectangular or trapezoidal knives with one or two perforations. There are pendants and beads of jade, amazonite, turquoise, and marble and perforated disks of jade, which in more regular shapes reappear in Shang and Chou times. The techniques of sawing and drilling hard stones thus were familiar to those vase painters. The occurrence of composite tools such as bone knives set with small flint blades points to connections with the Gobi microlithic cultures.

Lung-shan Black Pottery complex. As noted above, black ware is associated with the painted ceramics in Shansi and Honan. In the eastern provinces of Shantung, Kiangsu, Anhwei, and Chekiang, however, only black wares are found, with no traces of painted pottery. A culture or cultural phase traceable through this black ware became known through the excavation in 1930 and 1931 at Ch'eng-tzu-yai, in west Shantung.

Specimens of characteristic black pottery bowls were unearthed not only in Shantung but also as far south as the Hangchow Bay and in westerly Szechwan. Sparse occurrences of black pottery have been reported from outlying regions such as northwest Kansu, south Szechwan, and Port Arthur. The centres of the Black Pottery culture appear to have been located in Shantung and the Huai Ho Valley, areas held by tribes that as late as the Chou dynasty had not yet been assimilated.

Similarities between the Lung-shan and Shang cultures

It is certain that the Lung-shan culture preceded the Bronze Age level of An-yang (north Honan), site of the last Shang capital, and that several Lung-shan features were retained in the Shang culture: bone oracles, shapes of vases (in gray Shang pottery and in bronze), and tamped-earth structures.

It appears, moreover, that the pottery of the later Lung-shan phase was barely distinguishable from the typical Shang ware—a thick-walled gray ware made with pad and beater (wound with cord)—but whether this was the result of an internal evolution or an assimilation to the emerging Shang culture with dissimilar potting traditions is an open question. That the known early Shang sites overlie Lung-shan settlements implies continuity.

Chronology and Western connections. An earlier Lung-shan I without metal was found to be separated by a thin, sandy layer from a later Lung-shan II with scarce bronze objects at Ch'eng-tzu-yai. Lung-shan II probably belongs in the early Shang period (c. mid-16th–early 13th century BC), and, accordingly, Lung-shan I probably begins around 1800 BC. Consequently, the final phase of the Painted Pottery culture must be placed about 2000 BC at the latest.

Both the painted Yang-shao and the black Lung-shan ceramics point to early contacts with western Asia, where possible prototypes of similar shapes, ornamentation, and techniques are widespread. In the case of the Painted Pottery, moreover, an apparent want of archaic forerunners (hence the phenomenon of a sudden unfolding) makes it almost necessary to think of outside stimuli. These may have come from Iran, where similar shapes occur, dating from around 2000 BC, or from south Russia, where both shape and decor offer striking parallels to the Chinese types. For the black pottery, close similarities to north Iranian and east Caspian types dating from about 2000 BC seem to warrant actual connections through cultural transmissions. Even a type of tripod with hollow legs, widely regarded as uniquely and specifically Chinese, occurs as far west as Anatolia.

The approximate dates of the relevant western Asian and European material agree fairly well with the rough estimates permitted by the Chinese evidence.

Late Neolithic of South China. The beginning of exploration in South China dates only from about 1932, along the coast between Hong Kong and Swatow. Numerous reconnaissances undertaken during the 1950s make it clear that South China was lagging behind the North. The evidence collected from no fewer than 159 sites along the lower Yangtze River shows that as late as the Western Chou period (c. 1122–771 BC) these parts had not advanced beyond a Chalcolithic phase. The commonest ceramic ware of the epineolithic Hu-shu culture (after the eponymic site of Hu-shu-chen, about 20 miles [32 kilometres] southeast of Nanking) is a coarse sandy-red

Northern influences

ware in shapes that reveal influences from the North, as do sparser blackish wares. The later phase is distinguished by a hard-fired grayish ware with stamped patterns derived from Chou bronze ornaments. This stamped ware is found throughout the coastal provinces, in Chekiang, Kiangsi, Fukien, Kwangtung, and Hong Kong during the centuries of Eastern Chou to Han (771–202 BC and after).

Most of the stone implements current in North China occur in the South also. Occasionally a stone imitation of some typical Shang or Chou bronze weapon is encountered in a seemingly Neolithic assemblage. The shouldered ax, less common in the North, is found in many sites between Nanking and Canton. Most typical is the stepped adz with a tang of elliptic cross section distinctly set off from the angular body, a boatbuilders' tool that forms one important link with Neolithic Formosa, the Philippines, and Polynesia, while it seems to have remained unknown in northern China.

Early Bronze Age in North China. Until excavations at Chengchow (Honan, south of the Huang Ho), concepts of the early Bronze Age depended on the material excavated at several sites near An-yang in northern Honan, known as the Ruins of Yin (Yin-hsü). Yin, the last capital of the Shang dynasty, lasted from 1301 to 1050 BC, according to the chronology of the *Bamboo Annals,* or 1388–1122 in the computation of Liu Hsin, 7 BC. The year 1300, therefore, was the archaeologically safe upper limit for the Bronze Age chronology of Shang China. Scanty occurrences of primitive metal objects from Painted Pottery sites in remote Kansu and Ch'eng-te (Jehol), which probably are older than 1300 BC, shed little light on what happened in the Shang domain before An-yang.

The discovery at Chengchow of an older Shang city (identified with the ancient Ao) in no fewer than 24 scattered localities, excavated from 1951 onward by the Archaeological Research Institute of the Chinese Academy of Sciences, reveal a pre-An-yang bronze phase. Four Shang levels have been recognized at Chengchow, preceded by a Lung-shan level in some of the sites. The latest level corresponds to the An-yang phase; but in the main the Chengchow strata end where An-yang begins. Thus it appears that at Chengchow was a large Shang settlement, indeed a walled city, whose flourishing period occurred during the earlier phase of the dynasty, more precisely the period of the tenth Shang king, Chung-ting, who made Ao his capital, and his successors down to P'an-keng, who abandoned the city in favour of Yin.

Discoveries at Chengchow

Of the architectural remains, the ancient city wall, built in layers of pounded earth and about 66 feet (20 metres) in its greatest width at the base, is most impressive. Within and without the wall were numerous pits for dwelling and storage, as well as foundations of houses, which by their stratigraphic positions and varying designs suggest occupation through many successive generations. Ceramic factories and kilns, workshops of bone carvers, and several bronze foundries were found. The Erh-li-kang site of Chengchow yielded oracle bones, but only two of them were inscribed; it would appear, therefore, that writing was practiced on a limited scale and not until toward the end of the pre-An-yang period. The bronze objects and vessels from Chengchow compare with those of early style from An-yang. More primitive than the typical Shang bronzes, the vessels are still close to pottery shapes, and their decoration is of an archaic cast.

The bulk of the finds consists of ceramic wares—the typically gray, heavy, cord-marked Shang wares, sometimes with elaborately carved patterns like those of the bronzes. On the basis of the typological correlation of the pottery, finds at such other localities as Lo-yang (Honan), Hsing-t'ai (Hopeh), and Liu-li-ko in Hui-hsien (Honan) are also considered pre-An-yang. Bronze is always rare in these early settlements (see also below, *Beginnings of the Chinese Civilization: Shang, or Yin*).

Measured by the wealth and character of the finds at An-yang, however, the foregoing stages amount to little more than vague promises of a breaking away from the Neolithic traditions with their parallels in western Asia and in Europe. During the last three centuries of Shang rule in Yin, Chinese civilization appeared, for the first time, distinct from other ancient civilizations, in a process that, if no longer unheralded, seems sudden and unpredictable. Even so, some of the Shang people's most significant cultural possessions were paralleled in the west and ultimately may have come thence: the horse-drawn war chariot, the idea of a script, and the technique of bronze casting as such. The form they took, however, is uniquely Chinese.

Emergence of a distinct Chinese civilization

Excavations by the Academia Sinica in 15 campaigns (October 1928–June 1937) in an area stretching more than three miles along the Huan River to the west of An-yang revealed many individual sites of varying age and importance.

Clear links with older cultures exist in the case of the gray pottery—which in a coarsened fashion continues the black-pottery traditions—and in the case of many types of bronze vessels, the shapes of which were dependent on then-current pottery prototypes. Also connected with ceramic traditions is a limited but common repertory

Shang
white
pottery

of geometric ornaments, found on gray pottery and bronzes as well as on a peculiar new kind of ceramic ware, the Shang white pottery, a heavy, hard-fired whitish ware distinguished by its carved décor.

The same white pottery, on the other hand, marks a departure, being carved in a technique foreign to the Neolithic potters and decorated also with animal images of an abstract, heraldic style that is one of the Shang novelties in archaic bronzes as well as on carved bones and ivories. A bone-carver's tradition looms as the uniting agency behind the abstract animal imagery in all those mediums including wood, but the origins of this tradition are unknown. Another new feature is small animal sculptures in jade; they have no precursors in Neolithic sites, while in a general way they are reminiscent of much earlier animal amulets in stone such as were unearthed at Ur, Erech (Warkā), Tepe Gawra, and Khafaje in Mesopotamia.

Among the magnificent bronze weapons of the Shang are types of tanged axes that appear to be autochthonously Chinese. Others are suggestive of foreign connections: some rarer types of shaft-hole axes recall designs current in Mesopotamia, Luristan, and Persia; spearheads, socketed celts, and certain kinds of daggers and knives have close analogies in east Russia, Siberia, Mongolia, and the Ordos Steppe inside the great bend of the Huang Ho. Conditions thus seem to repeat a pattern observed when dealing with the Neolithic painted ceramics, which likewise point toward south Russia and the ancient Near East as centres of diffusion.

The true standard of Shang culture, however, was attained in sacrificial bronzes developed in the few centuries at An-yang. The technical excellence and the monumental designs of these vases, which were used in the ancestral temples of the aristocracy, are unmatched in the ancient world.

Ordos bronzes. On the evidence of numerous stray finds of bronze objects, the Ordos region and adjacent Inner Mongolia form part of the geographical and cultural continuum of the Eurasian steppe belt, an area that was to remain alien to that of the Chinese culture. The Ordos bronzes have close affinities in the Bronze Age inventory of central and south Siberia and south Russia, and after they became known in the 1920s were rightly recognized as related to Scythian art. Older, pre-Scythian strains, however, also are present in Ordos art. In fact, it seems that the Bronze Age sequence established for Siberia is fully answered by the Ordos bronze material so far known, whereas correspondences with Shang art appear to be limited to the weapons mentioned above. These types belong, in Siberia, in the periods called Andronovo (c. 1500–1300 BC) and Karasuk (c. 1300–700 BC). It is the influence of these cultures, including early Ordos, that in the author's opinion accounts also for the lesser bronze finds in several Kansu and Ch'eng-te Painted Pottery sites.

The
Karasuk
phase

The Karasuk phase is archaeologically important in that it offers early examples of what is known as the Eurasian animal style. This culture has been explained as the result of an amalgamation with Mongoloid elements, which, absent in the older Andronovo population, were traced in the skeletal remains of the Minusinsk area of southern Siberia. Even so, most of the Karasuk inventory, whether metal tools or pottery, is linked with Andronovo, and the animal sculptural adornments of daggers and knives (which might be taken as testimony of influences from An-yang or the Shang cultural sphere at large) agree so well with older Siberian animal sculpture in stone, antler, and bone that there is little need to look to China for their origin, particularly because the comparable specimens from An-yang appear to be novelties with no background of native traditions. An attempt at disentangling these Bronze Age Chinese-Siberian relations suffers because of the lack of excavations in the Ordos region. Evidence rests with stray finds of metal tools and chronology; thus it can only be assumed that metallurgy came to China from the northwest, ultimate filiations with Mesopotamia notwithstanding.

Perhaps no other single factor so aptly illustrates the

degree of obscurity in regard to the pre-An-yang period as does the Chinese script. Appearing in the archaic but essentially developed system of the oracle inscriptions on tortoise shells and animal bones found in one of the An-yang sites, this script, an eminent achievement of Chinese civilization, undoubtedly presupposes some span of time prior to An-yang for its evolution. Yet the only trace of pre-An-yang ideographic writing is that found on the two inscribed oracle bones unearthed at Chengchow and dating from near the end of the pre-An-yang period. It is justifiable, therefore, to conceive of the creation of the Chinese script as at some time during the obscure two centuries or so before An-yang, a creation that, save perhaps for the basic idea of writing, was entirely indigenous. (Ma.L.)

BEGINNINGS OF THE CHINESE CIVILIZATION

Origins. The origins of the Chinese people and their civilization are still undetermined. It is unlikely that the people were of one original stock or that the civilization spread from one centre either within or outside the modern boundaries. More likely, many different ethnic groups and many separate centres of primitive culture gradually merged and mingled to produce the civilization that has been continuously unfolding and spreading over this continental region. As noted above, the Neolithic culture in China bore fundamental resemblances to the Neolithic in many parts of Eurasia but also had some distinctive features. In different parts of China, moreover, there were from early times regional variations. There was apparently a continuity of population from Neolithic times into the historic period, and there are some evidences of cultural continuity as well. But the sources of information available allow no simple conclusion about the connection between the civilization of China and other ancient centres to the west.

Merging
of
primitive
cultures

The oldest Chinese historical literature, in the *Shu Ching* ("Classic of History" or *Book of Documents*)— parts of it the so-called ancient text, a late forgery—and the earliest extant collection of ancient songs and poems, the *Shih Ching* ("Classic of Odes" or *Book of Songs*), cannot be depended upon for information earlier than the 1st millennium BC, and much of that is by no means uncontested. The earliest documents in even these books show a civilization already far removed from primitive conditions and contain no certain proof of either a native or a foreign origin for the Chinese. Archaeological researches in Central Asia have disclosed extremely ancient seats of culture east of the Caspian and have suggested the possibility of migrations from what is now Sinkiang and Mongolia, possibly from farther west, and also of very early transmission of some art forms from western Asia and southeastern Europe. The excavations in China proper described above have revealed, in this regard, only that clear glimpses of what can be called with assurance Chinese culture are caught first in the present area of Honan, Shantung, and Shensi, that at the time from which there are remains it was already old, and that it and the people who possessed it were probably the result of several strains from different parts of Asia. Much, and perhaps most, of Chinese culture may have developed in China itself.

Legends. Chinese legends about earliest times are not of much use for history because they come from late literature that may have been modified for political or social purposes. Of ten figures of most ancient times, cited in the 1st millennium, only three are of real significance: Fu Hsi, Shen Nung, and Huang Ti. All three were sages as well as rulers and sacrificed on T'ai Shan, a mountain of hoary antiquity even in the time of Confucius, who lived in its shadow. Fu Hsi taught people to hunt, while Shen Nung cultivated the five grains, invented the plow, and established markets. Huang Ti stands out most prominently, for during the period of the Chou, men in the royal house and in the feudal states revered him as primal ancestor. His inventions included boats and oars and the fire drill. With fire he cleared the hills and the plains of their trees and brush, and he rid the country of wild beasts, making cattle breeding possible. He even in-

Significant
early
legendary
figures

stituted music among his officials. Two royal houses earlier than the Shang are mentioned in the texts—Yü and Hsia—but their historicity has not been determined. If they did exist they may have been roughly contemporaneous with the Late Neolithic stage. The traditional dates for Hsia are 2205–1766 BC, but one prominent Chinese scholar revised this to 2183–1751, and another (following the oldest text of the *Bamboo Annals*, or *Chu shu chi nien*) put them at 1994–1524.

Shang, or Yin (c. 1766–c. 1122 BC). In this age, though made more secure by archaeology, the dating is still uncertain. The orthodox school puts it at 1766 to 1122, the 20th century scholar Tung Tso-pin at 1751 to 1112, and others either at 1558–1051 or 1523–1027. Settlements of the Shang have been identified all the way from Sian in the west to Tsinan in the east.

Chengchow. According to early literature the royal house successively occupied several seats, and archaeology seems to support this tradition. One may have been the walled town discovered at Chengchow (see above). In addition to tombs, workshops of several kinds distinguish the area. Notable among these are pottery kilns. Clay stamps for impressing decorated designs were located in the debris. Some of the pottery pieces show indications of having been made with the potter's wheel. No painted ware has turned up. Some black pottery occurs, but none as fine as that discovered at Lung-shan, west Shantung, in a Late Stone Age site (see above). White pottery is completely absent, but there is glazed ware with a brownish body, which must have been fired at high temperature.

Shops for casting bronze also existed. Here were fashioned such objects as arrowheads, knives, fish hooks, socketed axheads, awls, and ritual vessels. In the tombs lay examples of the *ko*, or halberd (a chief weapon of the Shang), hairpins, washbasins, and vessels for liquor. There were artifacts made of bone, stone, shell, ivory, jade, and gold; among the first, made of bone of oxen, were pieces used for oracular purposes, as were a few tortoise carapaces. Other bones with incised characters may represent the first appearance of script in China. Obviously this was an important city, but though it reveals the first certain beginnings of the use of bronze in China, its cultural level is below that which followed.

An-yang. Some time around the 14th century BC (1401 according to orthodox dating, 1397 or 1315, according to others) a Shang ruler named Pan (or P'an)-keng is said to have moved his capital to Yin by the Huan River near modern An-yang, and there he and his successors remained for more than 250 years. The town and its tombs have yielded evidences of a civilization both brilliant and barbaric. Bronze had come into its own, as had glazed pottery and the fine white ware. Wood carving also was probably advanced, for the bronzes seem to have been based on wood originals. Carving in stone, jade, marble, bone, and ivory was far advanced. Objects of bronze and bone sometimes were inlaid with turquoise or mother-of-pearl.

While the poor may have continued to live as their ancestors did, the patricians built large timber houses with roofs supported on rows of wooden pillars with stone or bronze bases. Palaces, government offices, and ancestral shrines also were erected. The craft of building must have been well advanced, for numerous architectural terms are found in contemporary inscriptions.

An-yang tombs The tombs, many of the finest probably for members of the royal house, are magnificently constructed and furnished. One such tomb—26 feet (eight metres) long, 39 feet (12 metres) wide, 26 feet deep—with 17 sacrificial pits, had two sloping passages opening out from its north and south walls. The pits contained bodies of decapitated human beings, dogs, and horses. Its grave furniture included ceremonial vessels of bronze, stone, and pottery; bronze weapons and bridle fittings; stone, jade, and bone ornaments, and a musical stone or chime of gray limestone with a tiger design on its face. Other tombs revealed occasional chariot burials.

Social system. The royal house that ruled from Yin was obviously important. At its apogee the kingdom was probably bounded by the sea on the east, the Yangtze River on the south, Shensi on the west, and southern Hopeh on the north. The king was assisted by a hierarchy of nobles. His state was largely a kind of tribute-collecting machine; hence there were numerous wars with peoples on its borders. Succession was irregular; of 38 successions, 19 were from father to son, 14 from elder brother to younger brother, and five deviated from both practices. Queens were of some consequence; the one who bore the heir apparent, might, after her decease, be awarded her own shrine in the family temple and be worshipped as an ancestress. The kings, with one or two exceptions, were not war leaders but intermediaries between man and unseen powers. The king's ancestors were ostensibly the real power; he consulted them through his diviners and sacrificed to them. Ti was the supreme god, whose aid was invoked indirectly for good harvests and success in war. Lesser divinities included the god of wind (called Ti's messenger), of the river (Yellow), of earth, of the sun (worshipped at sunrise), of the moon, of the six clouds, and of Yüeh (T'ai Shan). Whether ancestor worship went beyond the royal house has not been determined. (For ritual and sociological function, see ANCESTOR WORSHIP.) **Ancestor worship**

Calendar. The calendar was important to the Shang, for the chief industry was agriculture and the king had to inform the people of the right times for sowing and reaping. The appropriate functionaries understood lunation; the character for month is the moon. The month was normally 30 days in length, two months making a 60-day cycle, with 360 days in a year. Intercalation (bringing the calendar in line with the solar year) was practiced; in the time of Wu-ting (orthodox dates of reign, 1324–1266 BC) an intercalary month was added when necessary at the end of the year and called the 13th month. Tsu-chia, his third son by his third queen (traditional dates, 1258–26 BC), placed the intercalary month after any month when it was required and called it the same as the month just preceding. It was an awkward but a stable calendar. One Chinese scientist has ascertained from study of a period of 152 years (1313 to 1161, according to his reckoning) that the mean length of a solar year was 365¼ days. In the time of Wu-ting, days were divided into seven parts; in Tsu-chia's, into ten. This is one of the several indications that the Chinese leaned toward the decimal system from earliest times, and with remarkable consistency carried it forward in measurements of all sorts. As a result of this concern for calendrical reckoning, the chief astrologer and recorder of events (for long he was the same man) came to have an important place; and the recording of lunar eclipses, considered a portent of evil, and other celestial phenomena began. Eclipses of the moon were reported to the capital even from distant states, and several stars and planets (the one now known as Jupiter, for example) are mentioned in the inscriptions.

Warfare. In warfare nobles led armies of 3,000 to 5,000 men, but there are notices of 23,000 and 30,000 concurrent conscripts. The nobles, armed with bronze spears and halberds and protected by shields and helmets, rode in chariots drawn generally by two horses, though four-horse vehicles were also known. The troops were supplied chiefly with composite bows that shot arrows tipped with points of bronze, bone, or stone. An inscription on a bone dated in the 12th century BC tells of a successful military campaign against a state on the western marches, in which the booty included 1,570 prisoners, two chariots, 180 shields, 15 pieces of armour, and a few arrows. **Military weapons and equipment**

Industry and commerce. In farming the peasantry used hoes and mattocks, shod with stone or shell, spades, and a foot plow. Millet, apparently the only common cereal indigenous to China, was the chief crop; wheat and some rice may have been introduced about this time. In addition to domesticated animals known earlier, goats and fowl were added to the economy. Tamed elephants were used to assist in heavy building operations. Some irrigation was practiced. Commerce may be taken for granted, since much of what was found at An-yang and much of what the people required came from elsewhere. Seashells and salt probably derived from the Shantung coast; some of the tortoise shells came from the Yangtze Valley and beyond, possibly as far south as the Malay Peninsula; tin and lead and some copper were imported from the south and southeast; cinnabar (a principal ingredient of red paint) was produced in Szechwan; and turquoise derived from outside the Shang sphere. More conspicuous examples are jade, probably mined in Khotan, and cowrie shells—chief medium of exchange— which may have come from as far distant as the Maldive Islands. Shang tradesmen were so well known that the name *Shang jen* ("Shang man") became standard for merchant. Textiles included silk and hemp cloth; names for these and such words as dress, shawl, fur, silkworm, and mulberry are given in the inscriptions, and traces of silk have been identified in wrappings for precious weapons. Names for a number of musical instruments (mostly wind and percussion) also are known, as are a few examples of stone chimes, ocarinas, and bells.

Script. Of highest importançe among the archaeological discoveries are the bones and tortoise carapaces employed both for sacred and profane use. More than 162,-000 of these are scattered in public and private collections around the world. The biggest discovery came in 1936, when 17,096 were located in a single pit. A few bones lay among a great mass of tortoise shells, 300 of them complete. The inscriptions on a large percentage were incised against a scorched area, but some also were written with a brush, using cinnabar or black fluid. A number of the inscriptions reveal a king consulting the oracle and getting replies that at times are signed by the diviner. There are also records of receipts and historical records dealing with events of the royal court; these are not scorched. The diviners wrote sometimes from right to left, sometimes left to right, probably to suit the "oracle signs"; the recorders or archivists, however, wrote in the same way as at present, from top to bottom. About 3,000 different characters have been identified, but only about 1,400 are readable. The idea of script, long known in Babylonia and Egypt, may have come from outside; but the Chinese examples, found incidentally on bronze and other hard surfaces, except for the simplest pictograms, are conspicuously different from the writing of the people of the Tigris and Euphrates and Nile valleys and of the island of Crete. Chinese characters of the Shang period may be divided into three types: pictographs, ideograms, and phonograms. By 1100 BC they had already developed over a stretch of several hundred years.
(L.C.G.)

II. The Chou and Ch'in dynasties

THE HISTORY OF CHOU (1122–221 BC)

The Chou people — The origin of the Chou royal house is lost in the mists of time. Although the traditional historical system of the Chinese contains a Chou genealogy, no dates can be assigned to the ancestors. The first ancestor was Hou Chi, literally translated "lord of millet." He appears to have been a cultural hero and agricultural deity rather than a tribal chief. The earliest plausible Chou ancestor was Tan Fu, the grandfather of Wen Wang. Prior to and during the time of Tan Fu, the Chou people seem to have migrated to avoid pressure from strong neighbours, possibly nomadic people to the north. Under the leadership of Tan Fu, they settled in the valley of the Wei Ho in the present province of Shensi. Their city had palaces and ancestor temples with walls and foundations of pounded earth. The fertility of the Wei Ho Valley loess soil apparently made a great impression on these people, who had already been engaged in farming when they entered their new homeland. A walled city was built, and a new nation was formed.

Chou and Shang. The name Chou appears often in the oracle bone inscriptions of the great Shang kingdom, sometimes as a friendly tributary neighbour and at others as a hostile one. Marriages were occasionally made between the two ruling houses. The Chou also borrowed the arts of their more cultivated neighbour, such as bronze casting. The Chou royal house, however, had already conceived the idea of replacing Shang as the master of China—a conquest that took three generations. Although the conquest was actually carried out by his sons, Wen Wang should be credited with molding the Chou kingdom into the most formidable power west of Shang. He also provided a plan for conquering Shang, based on an intricate and extensive system of alliances with other states, which were either conquered or persuaded to accept Chou hegemony. Wen Wang extended the Chou sphere of influence to the north of the Shang kingdom and also made incursions to the south, thus paving the way for the final conquest by Wu Wang.

Wen Wang and Wu Wang — In Chinese historical tradition Wen Wang was depicted as intelligent and benevolent, a man of virtue who won popularity among his contemporaries and expanded the realm of the Chou. His son, Wu Wang, though not as colourful as his father, was always regarded as the conqueror. In fact, Wu, his posthumous name, means "martial." But the literary records indicate that the Chou actually controlled two-thirds of all China at the time of Wen Wang, who continued to recognize the cultural and political superiority of the Shang out of feudal loyalty. There is not enough evidence either to establish or to deny this. A careful historian, however, will tend to take the Chou subjugation to the Shang as a recognition of Shang strength. It was not until the reign of the last Shang ruler, Ti Hsin, that the kingdom exhausted its strength by engaging in large-scale campaigning against nomads in the north and against a group of native tribes in the east. At this time Wu Wang organized the first probing expedition and reached the neighbourhood of the Shang capital. A full-scale invasion soon followed. Along with forces of the Chou, the army was made up of the Chiang, southern neighbours of the Chou, and of eight allied tribes from the west. The Shang dispatched a large army to meet the invaders. The pro-Chou records say that, after the Shang vanguard defected to join the Chou, the entire army collapsed, and Wu Wang entered the capital without resistance. Yet Mencius, the 4th-century-BC thinker, cast doubt upon the reliability of this account by pointing out that a victory without enemy resistance should not have been accompanied by the heavy casualties mentioned in the classical document. One may speculate that the Shang vanguard consisted of remnants of the eastern tribes suppressed by the Shang ruler Ti Hsin during his last expedition and that their sudden defection caught the Shang defenders by surprise, making them easy prey for the invading enemy. The decisive battle took place in 1111 BC (as tabulated by Tung Tso-pin, although it is commonly dated at 1122, and other dates have also been suggested). Wu Wang died shortly after the conquest, leaving a huge territory to be consolidated. This was accomplished by one of his brothers, Chou Kung, who served as regent during the reign of Wu's son, Ch'eng Wang.

The defeated Shang could not be ruled out as a potential force, even though their ruler, Ti Hsin, had immolated himself. Many groups of hostile "barbarians" were still outside the sphere of Chou power. The Chou leaders had to yield to reality by establishing a rather weak control over the conquered territory. The son of Ti Hsin was allowed to organize a subservient state under the close watch of two other brothers of Wu Wang, who were garrisoned in the immediate vicinity. Other leaders of the Chou and their allies were assigned lands surrounding the old Shang domain. But no sooner had Chou Kung assumed the role of regent than a large-scale rebellion broke out. His two brothers, entrusted with overseeing the activities of the son of Ti Hsin, joined the Shang prince, and it took Chou Kung three full years to reconquer the Shang domain, to subjugate the eastern tribes, and to re-establish the suzerainty of the Chou court.

These three years of extensive campaigning consolidated the rule of the Chou over all of China. An eastern capital was constructed on the middle reach of the Huang Ho as a stronghold to support the feudal lords in the east. *The Chou states* — Several states established by Chou kinsmen and relatives were transferred further east and northeast as the vanguard of expansion, including one established by the son of Chou Kung. The total number of such feudal states mentioned in historical records and later accounts varies from 20 to 70; the figures in later records would naturally be higher since enfiefment might take place more than once. Each of these states included fortified cities. They were strung out along the valley of the Huang Ho between the old capital and the new eastern capital, reaching as far as the valleys of the Huai and Han rivers in the south and extending eastward to the Shantung Peninsula and the coastal area north of it. All these colonies mutually supported each other and were buttressed by the strength of the eastern capital, where the conquered Shang troops were kept, together with several divisions of the Chou legions. Ancient bronze inscriptions make frequent mention of mobilizing the military units at the eastern capital at times when the Chou feudal states needed assistance and reinforcements.

The Chou feudal system. The feudal states were not contiguous but, rather, were scattered at strategic locations surrounded by potentially dangerous and hostile nations. The fortified city of the feudal lord was often the only area that he controlled directly; the state and the city were therefore identical, both being *kuo*, a combination of city wall and weapons. Satellite cities were established at convenient distances from the main city in order to expand the territory under control. The satellite cities bred more satellite cities by a process of subinfeudation, developing a feudal network and consolidating the position of the feudal states collectively.

The scattered feudal states gradually acquired something like territorial solidity as the neighbouring populations established closer ties with them, either by marriage or by accepting vassal status; the gaps between the fortified cities were thus filled by political control and by cultural assimilation. This created a dilemma for the Chou central court. On the one hand, the evolution of the feudal network buttressed the structure of the Chou order. On the other hand, the strong local ties and parochial interests of the feudal lords tended to pull them away from the centre. Each of these opposing forces became at one time or another strong enough to affect the history of the Chou order.

For about two centuries, Chou China enjoyed stability and peace. There were wars against the non-Chou peoples of the interior and against the nomads along the northern frontier, but there was little dispute among the Chinese states themselves. The southern expansion was successful, and the northern expansion worked to keep the nomads away from the Chinese areas.

The changing strength of the feudal order can be seen from two occurrences at the Chou court. In 841 BC, the nobles jointly expelled Li Wang, a tyrant, and replaced him with a collective leadership headed by the two most influential nobles until the crown prince was enthroned. In 771 BC, the Chou royal line was again broken when Yu Wang was killed by invading barbarians. The nobles apparently were split at this time, because two courts ensued headed by two princes, each of whom had the support of part of the nobility. One of the pretenders, P'ing Wang, survived the other; but the royal order had lost prestige and influence. The cohesion of the feudal system had weakened. Thereafter, it entered a new phase traditionally known as the Ch'un Ch'iu ("Spring and Autumn") period (722–481 BC).

In the Ch'un Ch'iu period there is a gradual dilution of the familial relationship among the nobles. A characteristic of the Chou feudal system was that the extended family and the political structure were identical. The line of lordship was regarded as the line of elder brothers, who, therefore, enjoyed not only political superiority but also seniority in the family line. The head of the family not only was the political chief but also had the unique privilege of offering sacrifice to and worshipping the ancestors, who would bestow their blessings and guarantee the continuity of the heavenly mandate. After the weakening of the position of the Chou king in the feudal structure, he was not able to maintain the position of being the head of a big family in any more than a normal sense. The feudal structure and familial ties fell apart, continu-

ing in several of the Ch'un Ch'iu states for various lengths of time with various degrees of modification. Over the next two centuries the feudal-familial systems gradually declined and disappeared.

In the first half of the Ch'un Ch'iu period, the feudal system was a stratified society, divided into ranks as follows: the ruler of a state; the feudal lords who served at the ruler's court as ministers; the *shih* (roughly translated as "gentlemen") who served at the households of the feudal lords as stewards, sheriffs, or simply as warriors; and, finally, the commoners and slaves. The state ruler and the ministers were clearly a superior class, and the commoners and slaves were an inferior class; while the class of *shih* was an intermediate one in which the younger sons of the ministers, the sons of *shih*, and selected commoners all mingled to serve as functionaries and officials. The state rulers were, in theory, divided into five grades; in reality, the importance of a ruler was determined by the strength of his state. The ministerial feudal lords, however, often had two or three grades among themselves, as determined by the lord–vassal relationship. In general, each state was ruled by a group of hereditary feudal lords who might or might not be of the same surname as that of the state ruler. The system was not stable in the Ch'un Ch'iu period, and everywhere there were changes.

The first important change occurred with the advent of interstate leadership. For several decades after 722 BC, the records show chiefly battles and diplomatic manoeuvres among the states on the central plain and in the middle and lower reaches of the Huang Ho Valley. These states, however, were too small to hold the leadership and too constricted in the already crowded plain to have potentiality for further development. The leadership was soon taken over by states on the peripheral areas.

The first to achieve this leadership was Huan Kung (reigned 685–643 BC), the ruler of the state of Ch'i on the Shantung Peninsula. He successfully rallied around him many other Chinese states to resist the pressure of non-Chinese powers in the north and south. While formally respecting the suzerainty of the Chou monarchy, Huan Kung adopted a new title of "overlord" (*pa*). He convened interstate meetings, settled disputes among states, and led campaigns to protect his followers from the intimidation of non-Chinese powers.

After his death, the state of Ch'i failed to maintain its leading status. The leadership, after a number of years, passed to Wen Kung of Chin (reigned 636–628 BC), the ruler of the mountainous state north of the Huang Ho. Under Wen Kung and his capable successors, the overlordship was institutionalized until it took the place of the Chou monarchy. Interstate meetings were held at first during emergencies caused by challenges from the rising southern state of Ch'u. States answering the call of the overlord were expected to contribute and maintain a certain number of war chariots. Gradually the meetings became regular, and the voluntary contribution was transformed into a compulsory tribute to the court of the overlord. The new system of states under the leadership of an overlord developed not only in north China under Chin but also in the south under Ch'u. Two other states, Ch'in and Ch'i, while not commanding the strength of the formidable Chin and Ch'u, each absorbed weaker neighbours into a system of satellite states. A balance of power emerged among the four states of Ch'i, Ch'in, Chin, and Ch'u. The balance was occasionally tipped when two of them went to war, and then restored by the transference of some small states from one camp to another.

A further change began in the 5th century BC, when the states of Wu and Yüeh far to the south suddenly challenged Ch'u for hegemony over the southern part of China, at a time when the strong state of Chin was much weakened by an internecine struggle among powerful magnates that subsequently split Chin into three contending powers. Wu got so far as to claim overlordship over north China in an interstate meeting held in 482 BC after defeating Ch'u. But Wu's hegemony was short-

Social ranks

Rivalry among the Chou states

lived; it collapsed after being attacked by Yüeh. Although Yüeh held the nominal overlordship for a brief period, the decline of Chin, Ch'in, and Ch'i, weakened by internal disturbances, and the paralysis of Ch'u after a series of defeats, made the balance-of-power system unworkable.

A half century of disorder followed. Small states fell prey to big ones, while in the big states usurpers replaced the old rulers. When the chaos ended, there were seven major powers and half a dozen minor ones. Among the seven major powers, Chao, Han, and Wei had formerly been parts of Chin; the Ch'i ruling house had changed hands; and Ch'in was undergoing succession problems. The only "old" state was Ch'u. Even Ch'u, a southern state, had become almost completely assimilated to the northern culture (except in art, literature, and folklore). The minor powers had also changed: some had retained only small portions of their old territories; some had new ruling houses; and some were new states that had emerged from non-Chinese tribes. The long period of power struggle that followed is known as the Chan Kuo ("Warring States") period (481–221 BC).

SOCIAL, POLITICAL, AND CULTURAL CHANGES

The centuries from the 8th century BC to 221 BC witnessed the painful birth of a unified China. It was a period of bloody wars and also of far-reaching changes in politics, society, and intellectual outlook.

The decline of feudalism. The most obvious change in political institutions was the replacement of the old feudal structure by systems of incipient bureaucracy under monarchy. The decline of feudalism took its course in the Ch'un Ch'iu period, and the rise of the new order may be seen in the Chan Kuo period. The Chou feudalism suffered from a continual dilution of authority. As a state expanded, its nobility acquired vassals, and these in turn acquired their own vassals. The longer this went on, the more diluted became the family tie, and the more dependent the ruler became on the combined strength of the vassals. At a certain point the vassals might acquire an advantageous position, and the most dominant figures among them might eclipse the king. The Chou royal house perhaps reached the turning point earlier than the other feudal states. The result was the shrinkage of the Chou royal domain and royal influence when P'ing Wang moved his court to the east. The ruling houses of other states suffered the same fate. Within a century after the Chou court moved to the east, the ruling houses in most of the feudal states had changed. Sometimes a dominating branch replaced the major lineage; sometimes a powerful minister formed a strong vassaldom and usurped the authority of the legitimate ruler. Bloody court intrigues and power struggles eliminated many established houses. The new power centres were reluctant to see the process continue and therefore refused to allow further segmentation and subinfeudation. Thus, the feudal system withered and finally collapsed.

Urbanization and assimilation. At the same time a process of urbanization was occurring. Minor fortified cities were built, radiating out from each of the major centres, and other towns radiated from the minor cities. From these cities and towns, orders were issued, and to them the resources of the countryside were sent. The central plain along the Huang Ho Valley was the first to be saturated by clusters of cities. This is probably the reason why the central states soon reached the maximum of their influence in the interstate power struggle: unlike the states in peripheral areas, they had no room to expand.

The period of urbanization was also a period of assimilation. The non-Chou population caught in the reach of feudal cities could not but feel the magnetic attraction of the civilization represented by the Chou people and Chou feudalism. The bronze inscriptions of the Western Chou (c. 1122–771 BC) refer to the disturbances of the "barbarians," who could be found practically everywhere. Those were the non-Chou groups scattered in the open spaces. The barbarians in inland China were forced to integrate with one or another of the contenders in the in-

terstate conflicts. Their lands were annexed; their populations, moved or absorbed. The strength of the large states owed much to their success at incorporating these non-Chinese groups. By the time of the unification of China in the 3rd century BC, there was virtually no significant concentration of non-Chinese groups north of the Yangtze Valley and south of the steppe. Bronze pieces attributable to non-Chou chiefs in the late Ch'un Ch'iu period show no significant difference in writing system and style from those of the Chinese states.

The assimilation of the Ch'u civilization in the south was another story. The Ch'u culture was markedly different. For some centuries Ch'u was the archenemy of the Chinese states, yet the nobles of the Ch'u acquired enough of the northern culture to enable their envoy to the courts of the north to cite the same verses and observe the same manners. The Ch'u literature that has survived is the fruit of these two distinctive heritages.

To the north were the nomadic peoples of the steppe. As long as they remained divided, they constituted no threat, but under strong leaders, able to forge a nomadic empire challenging the dominance of the Chinese, there were confrontations. The "punitive" action into the north during the reign of Hsüan Wang (827–782 BC) does not seem to have been very large in scope; both sides apparently had little ambition for territorial aggrandizement. Cultural exchange in the northern frontier region was far less than the assimilation that occurred in the south along the Yangtze Valley, and it was mainly concerned with techniques of cavalry warfare.

The rise of monarchy. As states grew in both population and area, there were internal political changes. The most basic change was in the pattern of the delegation of power. Under feudalism, authority had been delegated by the lord to the vassal. The new state rulers sought ways of maintaining and organizing their power.

In the state of Chin, the influence of kinsmen of the ruling house had been trimmed even before Wen Kung established his overlordship. Wen Kung reorganized the government, installing his most capable followers in the key posts. He set up a hierarchical structure that corresponded to the channels of military command. Appointments to these key positions came to be based on a combination of merit and seniority, thus establishing a type of bureaucracy that was to become traditional in Chinese government.

The Ch'u government was perhaps the oldest true monarchy among all the Ch'un Ch'iu states. The authority of the king was absolute. Ch'u was the only major state in which the ruling house survived the chaotic years of the Chan Kuo period.

Local administration went through a slow evolution. The prefecture system developed in both Chin and Ch'u was one innovation. In Chin there were several dozens of prefects across the state, having limited authority and limited tenure. The Chin prefect was no more than a functionary, in contrast to the feudal practice. In Ch'u similar local administrative units grew up. New lands taken by conquest were organized into prefectures governed by ranking officials who were evidently appointed by the king. The prefecture system of Chin and Ch'u was to become the principal form of local administration in the Chan Kuo period.

By that time practically all the major states had chancellors. A chancellor acted as the leader of the court, which was composed of numerous officials. Whereas in the feudal state the officials had been military officers, the more functionally differentiated court of the Chan Kuo period usually had a separate corps of civil-service personnel. Local administration was entrusted to prefects, who served limited terms. Prefects were often required to submit annual reports to the court so that the ruler could judge their performance. Regional supervisors were sometimes dispatched to check the work of the prefects, a system developed by the later Chinese Imperial government into the "censor" system. Fiefs of substantial size were given to very few people, usually only to close relatives of the ruler. There was little opportunity for anyone to challenge the sovereignty of the state. The majority of the government employees were not relatives of the ruler, and some of them might not even be citizens of the state. Officials were paid in grain, or perhaps in a combination of cash and grain. Archives were kept by scribes on wooden blocks and bamboo strips. These features indicate the emergence of some form of bureaucracy.

The new pattern was the result of the efforts of many reformers in different states. Both practical men and theoreticians helped to form the new structure, which, though still crude, was the forerunner of the large and complex bureaucracy of later Chinese dynasties.

New methods of warfare

Military technique also underwent great changes in the Chan Kuo ("Warring States") period. In the feudal era, war had been a profession of the nobles. Lengthy training was needed to learn the technique of driving and shooting from a chariot drawn by horses. There was also an elaborate code of behaviour in combat. The nature of war had changed by the late Ch'un Ch'iu ("Spring and Autumn") period. The nobility had given way to professional warriors and mercenaries. In some states special titles of nobility were created for successful warriors, regardless of their origin. Foot soldiers were replacing the war chariot as the main force on the battlefield. The expansion of the major states into mountainous areas and the rise of the southern powers in an area of swamps, lakes, and rivers increased the importance of the infantry.

Battles were fought mostly by tens of thousands of foot soldiers, aided by cavalry units; war chariots apparently served only auxiliary roles, probably as mobile commanding platforms or perhaps as carriers. The hordes of foot soldiers were mainly commoners. All the Chan Kuo powers seem to have had conscription systems to recruit able-bodied male citizens. The organization, training, and command of the infantry required experts of a special type. The Chan Kuo period produced commanders who conducted battles involving several thousand men, with lines extending hundreds of miles. A few treatises on the principles of warfare still survive, one of the most celebrated being *Ping fa* (*The Art of War*). By the end of the Chan Kuo period, the major battles were all commanded by professional soldiers.

Cavalry warfare developed among the northern states, including Ch'in, Chao, and Yen. One of the rulers of Chao even ordered his soldiers to adopt the nomadic dress with its narrow sleeves and trousers. The Ch'in cavalrymen were generally drawn from the northern and northwestern border areas, where there were constant contacts with the steppe peoples. The rise of Yen from a rather obscure state to a major power probably owed much to its successful adoption of cavalry tactics, as well as to its northern expansion.

Economic development. Important changes occurred in agriculture. Millet had once been the major cereal food in the north, but gradually, over the centuries, wheat grew in importance. Rice, a plant imported from the south, was extended to the dry soil of the north. The soybean in a number of varieties proved to be one of the most important crops. Chinese farmers gradually developed a kind of intensive agriculture. Soil was improved with the use of organic fertilizers. The fallow system was replaced by planting in carefully regulated rows. The importance of plowing and seeding at the proper time was stressed (especially in the fine-grained loess soil of north China). Frequent weeding was done throughout the growing season. Farmers also knew the value of rotating crops to preserve the fertility of the soil; soybeans were often part of the rotation. Although iron had been used to cast implements in the 5th century BC (probably even as early as the 8th century BC), those discovered by archaeologists are of rather inferior quality. Plows were pulled by men more often than by animals.

Agriculture

As population pressure forced the extension of cropland, irrigation became necessary. In the late years of the Ch'un Ch'iu period and in the Chan Kuo period, irrigation works of considerable scale were constructed in many states. Some of these projects were built to drain swampy areas; some for the purpose of leaching out alkaline soil and replacing it with fertile top soil; and others, in the south and in the Szechwan Basin, for carrying water into the rice paddies. The irrigation systems unearthed by archaeologists in recent decades indicate that these were small-scale works carried out for the most part by state or local authorities.

Another significant change in the economic sphere was the growth of trade among regions. Coins excavated in scattered spots show, by their great variety, that active trade had been extended to all parts of Chou China. Great commercial centres had arisen. The new cities brought a demand for luxuries. The literary records as well as the archaeological evidence show that wealthy persons had possessions made of bronze and gold, silver inlays, lacquer, silk, ceramics, and precious stones. The advancement of ferrous metallurgy led to the earliest recorded blast furnace and the earliest steel. The Chinese had been casting bronze for over 1,000 years; turning to iron, they became very skillful at making weapons and tools. The Han historian Ssu-ma Ch'ien (writing about 100 BC) told of men making fortunes in the iron industry.

Trade

The Chan Kuo period witnessed the demise of the old feudal regimes and their replacement by centralized monarchies. The feudal nobility fell victim to power struggles within the states and to conquest by stronger states. During the Ch'un Ch'iu period these parallel processes drastically reduced the numbers of the nobility.

In the late Ch'un Ch'iu period there arose a new elite class, composed of the former *shih* class and the descendants of the old nobility. The members of this class were distinguished by being educated, either in the literary tradition or in the military arts. The *shih* provided the administrators, teachers, and intellectual leaders of the new society. The philosophers Confucius (551–479 BC), Mencius (c. 371–289 BC), Mo-tzu (or Mo Ti, 5th century BC), and Hsün-tzu (c. 298–c. 230 BC) were members of the *shih* class, as were also a large proportion of high-ranking officials and leaders of prominence. The interstate competition that drove rulers to select the most capable and meritorious persons to serve in their courts resulted in an unprecedented degree of social mobility.

Emergence of a new intellectual elite

The populace, most of whom were farmers, also underwent changes in status. In feudal times the peasants had been subjects of their lords. They owned no property, being at most permitted to till a piece of the lord's land for their own needs. The ancient texts tell of the "well-field" system, under which eight families were assigned 100 *mou* (15 acres, or six hectares) each of land to live on while collectively cultivating another 100 *mou* as the lord's reservation. As farming became more intensive, there was a transition to individual ownership. This can be seen in the growth of the practice of taxing farmers according to the amount of their land. By the time of the Chan Kuo period, the land tax had become a common practice. By paying taxes, the tiller of the field acquired the privilege of using the land as his own possession, which perhaps was the first step toward private ownership. As states expanded and as new lands were given to cultivation, an increasing number of "free" farmers were to be found tilling land that had never been part of a lord's manor. With the collapse of the feudal structure, farmers in general gradually ceased to be subjects of a master and became subjects of a state.

A similar transformation occurred among the merchants and craftsmen, who gradually passed from being household retainers of a lord to the status of independent subjects. Thus, the feudal society was completely reshaped in the two centuries preceding the Ch'in unification.

Cultural change. These great political and socioeconomic changes were accompanied by intellectual ferment, as men tried to adjust themselves to a rapidly changing world. Ideas about the proper relationships between members of society were naturally questioned when the old feudal order was shaken, and, in this period, the great teacher Confucius (*q.v.*) elaborated the social concepts that were to become normative for later Chinese civilization. In place of rigid feudal obligations, he posited an order based on more universal human relationships (such as that between father and son) and taught that ability and moral excellence, rather than birth, were what fitted a man for leadership.

The great thinkers who followed Confucius, whether or not they agreed with his views, were all conditioned by his basic assumptions. Mo-tzu, who started out as a Confucianist, based his system on a concept of universal love that was largely an extension of the Confucian idea of humanity; the "worthy man" he recommended as the ideal leader was a development of Confucius' notion of excellence, combining virtue and ability (see MO-TZU). Even the individualist thinkers known as Taoists, who did not follow Confucius, formulated their teachings as a rebuttal to his system.

Confucius and other pre-Ch'in thinkers viewed the traditional political institutions of China as bankrupt and tried to devise a rationale for something to replace them. Some, such as Confucius, put their main emphasis on the quality of the ruling elite group; others, such as Shang Yang (see below *Struggle for power*) and Han-fei-tzu (died 233), regarded a well-organized governing mechanism as the only way to an orderly society. The development of the new centralized monarchical state after the middle of the Ch'un Ch'iu period is not only the embodiment of the ideas of these various thinkers but also the working premise in the context of which they elaborated their theories. The high degree of social and political consciousness that characterized most of the pre-Ch'in philosophical schools set the pattern for the close association of the intellectual with government and society in later China.

The burgeoning commercial life of the period also had its influence in other spheres, especially in the prevalence of contractual relationships. Thus, a minister would roam from one court to another, "selling" his knowledge and service to the most accommodating prince, and the quality of his service was determined by the treatment he received. This kind of contractual relationship remained common in China until the tide of commercialism was ended by the restriction of commercial activity under Han Wu Ti in the 2nd century BC.

In the Ch'un Ch'iu period, the local cultures of China were blended into one common civilization. Through contacts and interchanges, the gods and legends of one region became identified and assimilated with those of other regions. Local differences remained, but, from this time on, the general Chinese pantheon takes the form of a congregation of gods with specific functions, a celestial projection of the unified Chinese empire with its bureaucratic society.

Bold challenges to tradition have been rare in Chinese history, and the questioning and innovating spirit of the Ch'un Ch'iu period was to have no parallel until the ferment of the 20th century, after two millennia had elapsed under the domination of Confucian orthodoxy.

THE CH'IN EMPIRE (221–206 BC)

The Ch'in state. The history of the Ch'in dynasty may be traced back to the 8th century BC. When the Chou royal house was re-established at the eastern capital in 770 BC, the Ch'in ruling house, according to the Ch'in historical record, was entrusted with the mission of maintaining order in the previous capital. This may be an exaggeration of the importance of the Ch'in ruling house, and the Ch'in may have been only one of the ruling families of the old nations who recognized Chou suzerainty and went to serve the Chou court. The record is not clear. In the old annals Ch'in did not appear as a significant power until the time of Mu Kung (reigned 659–621 BC), who made Ch'in the main power in the western part of China. Although Ch'in attempted to obtain a foothold in the central heartland along the Huang Ho, it was blocked by the territories of Chin. After a number of failures to enter the eastern bloc of powers, Ch'in had to limit its activities to conquering, absorbing, and incorporating the non-Chinese tribes and states scat-

The early Ch'in

tered within and west of the big loop of the Huang Ho. Ch'in's success in this was duly recognized by other powers of the Ch'un Ch'iu period, so that the two superpowers Ch'u and Chin had to grant Ch'in, along with Ch'i, the status of being overlord in its own region. The eastern powers, however, regarded Ch'in as a "barbarian" state because of the non-Chinese elements it contained.

Ch'in played only a supporting role in the Ch'un Ch'iu power struggle; its location made it immune to the cutthroat competition of the states in the central plain. Ch'in, in fact, was the only major power that did not suffer battle within its own territory. Moreover, being a newly emerged state, Ch'in did not have the burden of a long-established feudal system; this allowed it more freedom to develop its own pattern of government. As a result of being "underdeveloped," it offered opportunity for eastern-educated persons; with the infusion of such talent, it was able to compete very well with the eastern powers, yet without the overexpanded ministerial apparatus that embarrassed other rulers. This may be one reason why Ch'in was one of the very few ruling houses that survived the great turmoil of the late Ch'un Ch'iu period.

A period of silence followed. Even the Ch'in historical record that was adopted by the historian Ssu-ma Ch'ien yields almost no information for a period of some 90 years in the 5th century BC. The evidence suggests that Ch'in underwent a period of consolidation and assimilation during the years of silence. When it re-emerged as an important power, its culture appeared to be simpler and more martial, perhaps because of the non-Chinese tribes it had absorbed.

Struggle for power. Until the 5th century BC, China was dominated by the central-plain power Wei, a successor to Chin, and by the eastern power Ch'i, a wealthy state with a new ruling house. Ch'in remained a secondary power until after the great reforms of Hsiao Kung (361–338 BC) and Shang Yang (Wei Yang).

Shang Yang, a frustrated bureaucrat in the court of Wei, went westward seeking a chance to try out his ideas. In the court of Ch'in he established a rare partnership with Hsiao Kung in the creation of the best organized state of their time. Shang Yang first took strong measures to establish the authority of law and royal decree. The law was to be enforced impartially, without regard to status or position. He convinced the Ch'in ruler that the rank of nobility and the privileges attached to it should be awarded only to those who rendered good service to the state, especially for valour in battle. This deprived the existing nobility of their titles and privileges, arousing much antagonism in the court.

Shang Yang's reforms

One of his most influential reforms was the standardization of local administration. It was a step toward creating a unified state by combining various localities into counties, which were then organized into prefectures under direct supervision of the court. This system was expanded to all China after unification in 221 BC.

Another measure taken by Shang Yang was the encouragement of production, especially in agriculture. Farmers were given incentive to reclaim wasteland; game and fishing reserves were also opened to cultivation. A shortage of labour was met by recruiting able-bodied men from neighbouring states, especially from Han, Chao, and Wei. This policy of drawing workers to Ch'in had two consequences: an increase of production in Ch'in and a loss of manpower in the neighbouring states. In order to increase incentives, the Ch'in government levied a double tax on any male citizen who was not the master of a household. The result was a breakdown of the extended-family system, since younger children were forced to move out and establish their own households. The nuclear family became the prevalent form in Ch'in thereafter. As late as the 2nd century BC, Han scholars were still attacking the Ch'in family structure as failing to observe the principle of filial piety, a cardinal virtue in the Confucian moral code. Shang Yang also standardized the system of weights and measures, a reform of some importance for the development of trade and commerce.

Under the joint labours of Hsiao Kung and Shang Yang, Ch'in grew wealthy and powerful. After Hsiao Kung's death, Shang Yang fell victim to political enemies, notably the resentful Ch'in nobility, and was put to death. Ironically, however, the Ch'in policies remained generally the same after his death.

What remained of the Chou royal court still survived, ruling over a fragmentary domain: poor, weak, and totally at the mercy of the contending powers. It was commonly felt that China ought to be unified politically, although the powers disagreed as to how it was to be done and on who was to be the universal king. Hui Wang, son of Hsiao Kung, claimed the royal title in 325 BC. The adoption of the royal title by Ch'in, of course, was a challenge to Ch'i and Wei. Ch'in pursued a strategy of dividing its rivals and individually defeating them. Ch'in would appeal to the self-interest of other powers in order to keep them from intervening in a military action it was taking against one of its neighbours. It would befriend the more distant states while gradually absorbing the territories of those close to it.

Ch'in strategy

Within half a century, Ch'in had acquired undisputed predominance over the other contending powers. It continued manoeuvring in order to prevent the others from uniting against it. A common topic of debate in the courts of the other states was whether to establish friendly relations with Ch'in or to join with other states in order to resist Ch'in's expansion. The Ch'in strategists were ruthless: all means, including lies, espionage, bribery, and assassination, were pressed into the service of their state.

For a time the eastern power Ch'i had seemed the most likely to win. It defeated Wei, crushed Yen in 314 BC, and annexed Sung in 286 BC. But Ch'i was overturned by an allied force of five states, including Ch'in. Chao, the power with extensive territory in the northern frontier, succeeded Ch'i as the most formidable contender against Ch'in. In 260 BC, a decisive battle between Ch'in and Chao destroyed Chao's military strength, although Ch'in was not able to complete its conquest of Chao for several decades.

The empire. When Ch'in succeeded in unifying China in 221 BC, its king claimed the title of first sovereign emperor, Shih Huang Ti. He was a strong and energetic ruler, and, although he appointed a number of capable aides, the emperor remained the final authority and the sole source of power.

The reforms of Shih Huang Ti

Shih Huang Ti made a number of important reforms. He abolished the feudal system completely and extended the administration system of prefectures and counties, with officials appointed by the central government sent into all of China. Circuit inspectors were dispatched to oversee the local magistrates. China was divided into some 40 prefectures. The empire of Shih Huang Ti was to become the traditional territory of China. In later eras China sometimes held other territories, but the Ch'in boundaries were always considered to embrace the indivisible area of China proper. In order to control this vast area, Shih Huang Ti constructed a network of highways for the movement of his troops. Several hundred thousand workers were conscripted to connect and strengthen the existing walls along the northern border. The result was a complex of fortified walls, garrison stations, and signal towers extending from the Chihli Gulf westward across the pastureland of what is today Inner Mongolia and through the fertile loop of the Huang Ho to the edge of Tibet. This defense line, known as the Great Wall, marked the frontier where the nomads of the great steppe and the Chinese farmers on the loess soil confronted each other. Yet the Emperor failed in another great project, the digging of a canal across the mountains in the south to link the southern coastal areas with the main body of China.

Shih Huang Ti and his capable chancellor, Li Ssu, unified and simplified the writing system and also codified the law.

All China felt the burden of these 11 years of change.

Millions of men were dragooned to the huge construction jobs, many dying on the long journey to their destination and others fleeing. Rich and influential men in the provinces were compelled to move to the capital. Weapons were confiscated. Hundreds of intellectuals were massacred for daring to criticize the Emperor's policies. Books dealing with subjects other than law, horticulture, and herb medicine were kept out of public circulation because the Emperor considered such knowledge to be dangerous and unsettling. These things have contributed to make Shih Huang Ti appear the archtyrant of Chinese history.

Some of the accusations levelled against him by historians are perhaps exaggerated, such as the burning of books and the indiscriminate massacre of intellectuals. Shih Huang Ti himself claimed in the stone inscriptions of his time that he had corrected the misconduct of a corrupted age and given the people peace and order. Indeed, his political philosophy did not deviate much from that already developed by the great thinkers of the Chan Kuo period and adopted later by the Han emperors, who have been generally regarded as benevolent rulers.

Shih Huang Ti was afraid of death. He did everything possible to achieve immortality. Deities were propitiated, and messengers were dispatched to look for an elixir of life. Yet death overtook him on one of his tours of the empire in 210 BC, only 11 years after taking the Imperial title.

Fall of the Ch'in dynasty

His death led to the fall of his dynasty. The legitimate heir was compelled to commit suicide when his younger brother usurped the throne. Capable and loyal servants, including Li Ssu and Gen. Meng T'ien, were put to death. Erh Shih, the second emperor, lasted only four years. Rebellion broke out in the Yangtze River area when a small group of conscripts led by a peasant killed their escort officers and claimed sovereignty for the former state of Ch'u. The uprising spread rapidly as old ruling elements of the six states rose to claim their former titles. Escaped conscripts and soldiers who had been hiding everywhere emerged in large numbers to attack the Imperial armies. The second Emperor was killed by a powerful eunuch minister, and in 206 BC a rebel leader accepted the surrender of the last Ch'in prince. (C.-y.H.)

III. The Han dynasty

The Han dynasty was founded by Liu Pang, who assumed the title of emperor in 202 BC. Eleven members of the Liu family followed in his place as effective emperors until AD 9. In that year the dynastic line was interrupted by Wang Mang, who established his own regime under the title of Hsin. In AD 25 the authority of the Han dynasty was reaffirmed by Liu Hsiu, who reigned as Han emperor until 57. Eleven of his descendants maintained the dynastic succession until 220, when the rule of a single empire was replaced by that of three separate kingdoms. While the whole period from 202 BC to AD 220 is generally described as that of the Han dynasty, the terms Western (or Former) Han and Eastern (or Later) Han are used to denote the two subperiods. During the first period, from 202 BC to AD 8, the capital city was situated at Ch'ang-an, in the west; in the second period, from AD 23 to 220, it lay further east at Lo-yang.

The four centuries in question may be treated as a single historical period by virtue of dynastic continuity, for apart from the short interval of 9–23, Imperial authority was vested in successive members of the same family. The period, however, witnessed considerable changes in Imperial, political, and social development. Organs of government were established, tried, modified, or replaced, and new social distinctions were brought into being. Chinese prestige among other peoples varied with the political stability and military strength of the Han house; and the extent of territory that was subject to the jurisdiction of Han officials varied with the success of Han arms. At the same time, the example of the palace, the activities of government, and the growing luxuries of city life gave rise to new standards of cultural and technological achievement.

Ch'in
and Han
dynasties
compared

China's first Imperial dynasty, that of Ch'in, had lasted barely 15 years (221–206 BC) before its dissolution in the face of rebellion and civil war. By contrast, Han formed the first long-lasting regime that could successfully claim to be the sole authority entitled to wield administrative power. The Han forms of government, however, were derived in the first instance from those of its immediate predecessor, the Ch'in dynasty; and these, in turn, incorporated a number of features of the government that had been practiced by the kingdoms of the pre-Imperial age. The Han empire left as a heritage a practical example of Imperial government and an ideal of dynastic authority to which its successors have always aspired. But the Han period has been credited with more success than is its due; it has been represented as a period of 400 years of effective dynastic rule, punctuated by a short period of usurpation by a pretender to power; and it has been assumed that Imperial unity and effective administration advanced steadily with each decade. In fact, there were only a few short periods marked by dynastic strength, stable government, and intensive administration. Several reigns were characterized by palace intrigue and corrupt influences at court; and on a number of occasions the future of the dynasty was seriously endangered by outbreaks of violence, seizure of political power, or a crisis in the Imperial succession.

DYNASTIC AUTHORITY AND THE SUCCESSION OF EMPERORS

Western Han. Since at least as early as the Shang (or Yin) dynasty (c. 1766 to c. 1122 BC), the Chinese had been accustomed to acknowledging the temporal and spiritual authority of a single leader and its transmission within a family, at first from brother to brother and later from father to son. Some of the early kings had been military commanders, and they may have organized the corporate work of the community, such as the manufacture of bronze tools and vessels. In addition, they acted as religious leaders, appointing scribes or priests to consult the oracles and thus assist in taking major decisions covering communal activities, such as warfare or hunting expeditions. In succeeding centuries the growing sophistication of Chinese culture was accompanied by demands for more intensive political organization and for more regular administration; as kings came to delegate tasks to more officials so was their own authority enhanced and the obedience that they commanded the more widely acknowledged. Under the kingdoms of Chou (c. 1122 BC

to 256 BC) an association was deliberately fostered between the authority of the king and the dispensation exercised over the universe by Heaven, with the result that the kings of Chou, and, later, the emperors of Chinese dynasties, were regarded as being the Sons of Heaven.

From 403 BC onward seven kingdoms other than Chou were established as the ruling authorities in different parts of China, each led by its own king or duke. In theory, the king of Chou, whose territory was by now greatly reduced, was recognized as possessing superior powers and moral overlordship over the other kingdoms, but practical administration lay in the hands of the seven kings and their professional advisers, or of the well-established families that were settled on the land. After a long process of expansion and take-over, a radical change was brought about in Chinese politics in 221 BC; for the kingdom of Ch'in had succeeded in eliminating the power of its six rivals and establishing a single rule that was acknowledged in their territories. According to later Chinese historians, this success had been achieved and the government of the Ch'in empire was thereafter maintained by oppressive methods and the rigorous enforcement of a harsh penal code; but this view probably was coloured by later political prejudices. Whatever the quality of Ch'in Imperial government was, the regime scarcely survived the death of the first Emperor (210 BC). The choice of his successor was subject to manipulation by statesmen, and local rebellions soon developed into large-scale warfare. Liu Pang, whose family had not so far figured in Chinese history, emerged as the victor of two principal contestants for power. Anxious to avoid the reputation of having replaced one oppressive regime by another, he and his advisers endeavoured to display their own empire—of Han—as a regime that had relieved the people of China from cruelty and suffering and whose political principles were in keeping with a Chinese tradition of liberal and beneficent administration. As yet, however, the concept of a single centralized government that could command obedience universally was still subject to trial. In order to exercise and perpetuate its authority, therefore, Liu Pang's government perforce adopted the organs of government, and possibly many of the methods, of its discredited predecessor.

The authority of the Han emperors had been won in the first instance by force of arms, and both Liu Pang and his successors relied on the loyal cooperation of military

Events
immediately
preceding
the foundation of
the Han
dynasty

Adapted from A. Herrmann, *An Historical Atlas of China* (1966); Aldine Publishing Company

China under the Han emperor Wu Ti (c. 100 BC), and (inset) China at the end of the Ch'un Ch'iu period (c. 500 BC).

leaders and on officials who organized the work of civil government. In theory, and to a large extent in practice, the emperor remained the single source from whom all powers of government were delegated. It was the Han emperors who appointed men to the senior offices of the central government and in whose name the governors of the commanderies (provinces) collected taxes, recruited men for the labour corps and army, and dispensed justice. And it was the Han emperors who invested some of their kinsmen with powers to rule as kings over certain territories or divested them of such powers in order to consolidate the strength of the central government.

The Imperial succession

The succession of emperors was hereditary, but it was complicated by a system of Imperial consorts and the implication of their families in politics. Of the large number of women who were housed in the palace as the emperor's favourites, one was selected for nomination as the empress; and while it was theoretically possible for an emperor to appoint any one of his sons heir apparent, this honour, in practice, usually fell on one of the sons of the empress. Changes could be made in the declared succession, however, by deposing one empress and giving the title to another favourite; and sometimes, when an emperor died without having nominated his heir, it was left to the senior statesmen of the day to arrange for a suitable successor. Whether or not an heir had been named the succession was often open to question, as pressure could be exerted on an emperor over his choice. Sometimes a young or weak emperor was overawed by the expressed will of his mother or by anxiety to please a newly favoured concubine.

Throughout the Western and the Eastern Han periods, the succession and other important political considerations were gravely affected by the members of the Imperial consorts' families. Often the father or brothers of an empress or a concubine were appointed to high office in the central government. Alternatively, senior statesmen might be able to curry favour with their emperor or consolidate their position at court by presenting a young female relative for the Imperial pleasure. In either situation the succession of emperors might be affected; jealousies would be aroused between the different families concerned; and the actual powers of a newly acceded emperor would be overshadowed by the females in his entourage or their male relatives. Such situations were particularly likely to develop if, as happened on a number of occasions, an emperor was succeeded by an infant son.

The Imperial succession was thus frequently bound up with the political machinations of statesmen, particularly as the court grew more sophisticated and statesmen acquired coteries of clients engaged in factional rivalry. On the death of the first emperor, Liu Pang (195 BC), better known under his title of Kao Tsu, the palace came under the domination of his widow. Outliving her son, who had succeeded as emperor under the title of Hui Ti (reigned 195–188), the empress dowager Lü arranged for two infants to succeed consecutively. During this time (188–180) she issued Imperial edicts under her own name and by virtue of her own authority as empress dowager. She set a precedent that was to be followed in later dynastic crises—e.g., when the throne was vacant and no heir had been appointed; in such cases although statesmen or officials would in fact determine how to proceed, their decisions were implemented in the form of edicts promulgated by the senior surviving empress.

The empress Lü appointed a number of members of her own family to highly important positions of state, and clearly hoped to substitute her own family for the reigning Liu family. But these plans were frustrated on her death (180) by men whose loyalties remained with the founding Emperor and his family. Liu Heng, better known as Wen Ti, reigned from 179 to 157. He soon came to be regarded as one of three outstanding emperors of Western Han (with Kao Tsu and Wu Ti), thanks to the personal qualities attributed to him and to the stable government of his reign. He was credited with the ideal behaviour of a monarch reigning according to later Con-

fucian doctrine; i.e., he was supposedly ready to yield place to others and to hearken to the advice and remonstrances of his statesmen, and to eschew personal extravagance. It can be claimed with some justification that his reign saw the peaceful consolidation of Imperial power, successful experimentation in operating the organs of government, and the steady growth of China's material resources.

Accomplishments of Wu Ti's reign

The third emperor of Western Han to be singled out for special praise by traditional Chinese historians was Wu Ti (reigned 140–87), whose reign was the longest of the whole Han period. His reputation as a vigorous and brave ruler derives from the long series of campaigns fought chiefly against the Hsiung-nu (northern nomads) and in Central Asia. But Wu Ti never took a personal part in the fighting. The policy of taking the offensive and extending Chinese influence into unknown territory resulted not from the Emperor's initiative but from the stimulus of a few statesmen, whose decisions were opposed vigorously at the time. Thanks to the same statesmen, Wu Ti's reign saw a more intensive use of manpower and exploitation of natural resources. This depended on more active administration by Han officials. Wu Ti participated personally in the religious cults of state far more actively than his predecessors and some of his successors. And it was during his reign that the state took new steps to promote scholarship and develop the civil service.

From c. 90 BC it became apparent that Han military strength had been overtaxed, and a policy of retrenchment was begun in military and economic policies. The last few years of the reign were darkened by a dynastic crisis arising out of jealousies between the Empress and heir apparent on the one hand, and a rival Imperial consort's family on the other. Intense and violent fighting took place in Ch'ang-an in 91, and the two families were almost eliminated. Just before Wu Ti's death a compromise was reached whereby an infant who came from neither family was chosen to succeed. This was Chao Ti (reigned 86–74). The stewardship of the empire was vested in the hands of a regent, Huo Kuang. This shrewd and circumspect statesman had seen service in government for some two decades, and even after his death his family retained a dominating influence in Chinese politics until 64 BC. Chao Ti, who died in 74, had been married to a granddaughter of Huo Kuang; his successor, who was brought to the throne at the invitation of Huo Kuang and other statesmen, proved unfit for his august position and was deposed after a reign of 27 days. Huo Kuang, however, was able to contrive his replacement by a candidate whom he could control or manipulate. This was Hsüan Ti (reigned 73–49), who began to take a personal part in government after Huo Kuang's death in 68. The new Emperor had a predilection for a practical rather than a scholastic approach to matters of state. While his reign was marked by a more rigorous attention to implementing the laws than had recently been fashionable, his edicts paid marked attention to the ideals of governing a people in their own interests and distributing bounties where they were most needed. The move away from the realistic policies of Wu Ti's statesmen was even more noticeable during the next reign (Yüan Ti; 48–33).

In the reigns of Ch'eng Ti (32–7), Ai Ti (6–1 BC), and P'ing Ti (1 BC–AD 5) the conduct of state affairs and the atmosphere of the court were subject to the weakness or youth of the emperors, the lack of an heir to succeed Ch'eng Ti, and the rivalries between four families of Imperial consorts. It was a time when considerable attention was paid to omens. Changes that were first introduced in the state religious cults in 32 BC were alternately countermanded and reintroduced in the hope of securing material blessings by means of intercession with different spiritual powers. To satisfy the jealousies of a favourite, Ch'eng Ti went so far as to murder two sons born to him by other women. Ai Ti took steps to control the growing monopoly exercised by other families over state affairs. It was alleged at the time that the deaths of both Ch'eng Ti, who had enjoyed robust health, and P'ing Ti, not yet 14 when he died, had been arranged for political reasons.

In the meantime, the Wang family had come to dominate the court. Wang Cheng-chün, who had been the empress of Yüan Ti and mother of Ch'eng Ti, exercised considerable powers not only in her own capacity but also through several of her eight brothers. From 32 to 7 BC five members of the family were appointed in succession to the most powerful position in the government, and the status of other members was raised by the bestowal of nobilities. The empress dowager lived until AD 13, surviving the decline of the family's influence under Ai Ti, who sought to restore a balance at court by honouring the families of other consorts (the Fu and Ting families). Wang Mang (q.v.), nephew of the empress dowager Wang, restored the family's position during the reign of P'ing Ti. After the latter's death, Wang Mang was appointed regent during the reign of an infant; but in AD 9 he assumed the Imperial position himself, under the dynastic title of Hsin.

The regime of Wang Mang

Insofar as he took Imperial power from the Liu family, Wang Mang's short reign from 9 to 23 may be described as an act of usurpation. His policies were marked both by traditionalism and innovation. In creating new social distinctions he tried to revert to a system allegedly in operation before the Imperial age, and some of his changes in the structure of government were similarly related to precedents of the dim past. He appealed to the poorer classes by instituting measures of relief, but his attempts to limit the size of landed estates and to ban the sale of slaves antagonized the more wealthy members of society. Experiments in new types of coinage and in controlling economic transactions failed to achieve their purpose of increasing the resources of state, which were depleted by campaigns fought against the Hsiung-nu. The last years of his reign were dislocated by the rise of dissident bands in a number of provinces; several leaders declared themselves emperor in different regions, and in the course of the fighting Ch'ang-an was entered and damaged. Later it was captured by the "Red Eyebrows," one of the most active of the robber bands; and Wang Mang was killed in a scene of violence played out within the palace buildings.

Eastern Han. The Han house was restored by Liu Hsiu, who reigned as Kuang Wu Ti from 25 to 57. Another member of the Liu house who contested his claim and was actually enthroned for two years had been killed in the course of turbulent civil fighting. Ch'ang-an had been virtually destroyed by warfare, and the new emperor established his capital at Lo-yang.

Kuang Wu Ti completed the defeat of rival aspirants to the throne in 36. As had occurred in Western Han, dynastic establishment was followed by a period of internal consolidation rather than expansion. The new Emperor resumed the structure of government of the Western Han emperors, together with the earlier coinage and system of taxation. The palace once more promoted the cause of scholarship. Eunuchs had come to the fore in the Han palace during Yüan Ti's reign, and several had succeeded in reaching powerful positions. Kuang Wu Ti's policy was to rid the government of such influences, together with that of the families of Imperial consorts. Under Ming Ti (58–76) and Chang Ti (77–88) China was once more strong enough to adopt a positive foreign policy and to set Chinese armies on the march against the Hsiung-nu. To prevent the incursions of the latter, and possibly to encourage the growth of trade, Han influence was again brought to bear in Central Asia. Chinese prestige reached its zenith around 90 and fell markedly after 125.

Beginnings of Han decline

Dynastic decline can be dated from the reign of Ho Ti (88–105), when the court once more came under the influence of consorts' families and eunuchs. The succession of emperors became a matter of dexterous manipulation designed to preserve the advantages of interested parties. The weakness of the throne can be judged from the fact that, of the 12 emperors of Eastern Han, no less than eight took the throne as infants aged between 100 days and 15 years. There was an increasing tendency for the growth of factions whose members, like the families of Imperial consorts, and the eunuchs, might choose to place their own interests above those of the state.

During the last 50 years of Eastern Han, north China became subject to invasion from different sides; and, as was observed by several philosopher statesmen, the administration became corrupt and ineffective. Powerful regional officials were able to establish themselves almost independently of the central government. Rivalry between consorts' families and eunuchs led to a massacre of the latter in 189, and the rebel bands that arose included the Yellow Turbans who were fired by beliefs in supernatural influences and led by inspired demagogues. Soldiers of fortune and contestants for power were putting troops in the field in their attempts to establish themselves as emperors of a single united China. By 207 Ts'ao Ts'ao had gained control over the north; and had he not been defeated by Sun Ch'üan at the battle of the Red Cliff, which later became famous in Chinese literature, he might well have succeeded in establishing a single dynastic rule. Other participants in the fighting included Tung Cho, Liu Pei, and Chu-ko Liang. The situation was resolved in 221 when Ts'ao P'ei, son of Ts'ao Ts'ao, accepted an instrument of abdication from Hsien Ti, last of the Han emperors (acceded 189). Ts'ao P'ei duly became emperor of a dynasty styled Wei, whose territories stretched over the northern part of China and whose capital was at Lo-yang. At the same time, Liu Pei was declared emperor of the Shu Han dynasty, thereby maintaining the fiction that as a member of the Liu family he was continuing its rule over the Han dynasty, albeit in the restricted regions of Shu in the southwest (capital at Ch'eng-tu). In the southeast there was formed the third of the Three Kingdoms, as the period from 220 to 264 has come to be described. This was the kingdom of Wu, with its capital at Chien-yeh, under the dispensation of Sun Ch'üan.

THE ADMINISTRATION OF THE HAN EMPIRE

The structure of government. One of the main contributions of the Han dynasty to the future of Imperial China lay in the development of the civil service and the structure of central and provincial government. The evolutionary changes that subsequently transformed Han polity beyond recognition were not directed at altering the underlying principles of government but at applying them expediently to the changing dynastic, political, social, and economic conditions of later centuries. One of the problems faced by Han governments was the recruitment of able and honest men to staff the civil service of an empire. Despite the recent reform of the script, which facilitated the drafting of documents, considerable training was still needed before sufficient competence could be attained. While the dynasty remained susceptible to crisis, factionalism, and revolt there was no means of ensuring the loyal service of the men appointed to high offices. Recruitment to the Han civil service was partly by recommendation or sponsorship. Officials were invited to present candidates who possessed suitable qualities of intelligence and integrity, and at certain times provincial units were ordered to send a quota of men to the capital at regular intervals. At times candidates were required to show evidence of their intelligence and integrity and to submit answers on questions of policy or administration. They might then be kept at the palace to act as advisers in attendance, or they might be given appointments in the central government or in the provinces, depending upon their success. But at this time there was no regular system of examination and appointment such as was evolved in the time of the Sui and T'ang dynasties.

Recruitment of civil servants

Posts in the Han civil service carried set stipends, which were paid partly in cash and partly in grain. There was a total of 12 grades, ranging from that of clerk, earning 100 measures of grain annually, to the most senior minister of state, whose stipend was described as "a full 2,000 measures." There was no division in principle between men serving in the central offices or the provincial units. Promotion could be achieved from one grade of the service to the next, and, in theory, a man could rise from the humblest to the highest posts.

In theory, and partly in practice, the structure of Han government was marked by an adherence to regular hierarchies of authority, by the division of specialist responsibilities, and by a duplication of certain functions. By these means it was hoped to avoid excessive monopoly of power by individual officials. The uppermost stratum of officials or statesmen comprised two, and at times, three men—the chancellor, the Imperial counsellor, and, sometimes, the commander in chief. These men acted as the emperor's highest advisers and retained final control over the activities of government. Responsibility was shared with nine ministers of state whose stipend was lower than that of the three senior advisers, and who cared for matters such as religious cults, security of the palace, adjudication in criminal cases, diplomatic dealings with foreign leaders, and the collection and distribution of revenue. Each minister of state was supported by a department staffed by directors and subordinates. There were a few other major agencies; these ranked slightly below the nine ministries and were responsible for specialist tasks. Functions were duplicated so as to check the growth of power. Occasionally, for example, two chancellors were appointed concurrently. Similarly, financial matters were controlled by two permanent ministries: the Department of Agriculture and Revenue, and the Lesser Treasury.

The foregoing structure of regular organs of government was known as the "Outer Court." With the passage of time it became balanced by the growth of a secondary seat of power known as the "Inner Court." This grew up from members of the secretariat, and had started as a subordinate agency in the Lesser Treasury. The secretariat officials had acquired direct access to the emperor and could thus circumvent the more formal approaches required by protocol of other officials. The secretariat rose to prominence during the latter part of the first century BC and was at times staffed by eunuchs. Its members were sometimes distinguished by the bestowal of privileged titles that conveyed a mark of Imperial favour without specific administrative responsibility. The highest of these titles was that of supreme commander, and when this title was accompanied by the right or the Imperial instruction to assume leadership of the secretariat, the powers of the incumbent outweighed those of the highest ministers of the Outer Court. An official thus named could effectively control decisions of state, to the discomfiture of senior officials such as the chancellor. It was in this capacity that Wang Mang and his four predecessors had been able to assert their power without fear of check.

Provincial government
At the outset of the Han dynasty very large areas were entrusted as kingdoms to the emperor's kinsmen while the central government administered the interior provinces as commanderies. But by c. 100 BC, the Imperial government had deprived the kingdoms of their strength, and most of their lands had been incorporated as commanderies under the central government. Although the kingdoms survived in a much reduced form until the end of the period, their administration came to differ less and less from that of the commanderies, which formed the regular provincial units. Each commandery was controlled by two senior officials, the governor and the commandant, who were appointed by the centre. Commanderies could be established at will: by dividing larger into smaller units; by taking over the lands of the kings; or by establishing organs of government in regions only recently penetrated by Chinese officials. But provincial government was not necessarily pervasive throughout the lands where commandery offices existed. Nevertheless, the Han period saw a steady advance in provincial government. During Kao Tsu's reign there were 16 commanderies, but by the end of Western Han the number had risen to 83. A comparable number existed in Eastern Han.

Each of the commanderies consisted of some ten or 20 prefectures, the size of which corresponded to that of English counties. The prefect's headquarters were situated in a walled town, from which his administration was extended and his officials were sent to collect taxes, settle disputes, or recruit able-bodied men for service. The prefectures were themselves subdivided into districts. The

commanderies included a number of nobilities, to which responsibility for tax collection and the maintenance of order had been made over. Nobles received such privileges in return for services rendered and were entitled to retain a proportion of the tax. The number of nobilities varied very considerably, sometimes totalling several hundred. The system was used as a political instrument for reducing the power of the kings, supplementing a shortage of trained civil servants, and rewarding military officers, civil officials, and treating surrendered enemy leaders. Special arrangements were instituted for provincial government at the periphery of the empire. Agencies of a specialist nature were set up both here and in the provinces of the interior, with responsibilities for, for example, supervision of the salt and iron industries, manufacture of textiles, fruit growing, sponsored agriculture, or control of passage in and out of the frontier.

From 106 BC the government tried to supervise the work of provincial officials more directly. A total of 14 regional inspectors was appointed, with orders to visit the commanderies and kingdoms of a specified area and to report to the central government on the efficiency of officials, the degree of oppression or corruption, and the state of popular affection or disaffection. The inspectors were graded considerably lower than the governors whose work they observed, and they reported their findings directly to the centre. Although the arrangement was not yet tantamount to the creation of a limited number (about 20) of very large provinces, such as came about from about the 13th century, it may have facilitated the establishment of separatist provincial regimes at times of dynastic decline.

The command of the armed forces was also arranged so as to avoid giving excessive powers to a single individual. General officers were usually appointed in pairs, and in times of emergency, or when a campaign was being planned with a defined objective, officers were appointed for a specific task; when their mission was fulfilled, their commands were brought to a close. At a lower level there existed a complement of colonels whose duties were defined so as to cover smaller scale activities. In addition the governors and commandants of the commanderies were sometimes ordered to lead forces. The commandants were also responsible for training conscript soldiers, setting them to maintain internal discipline and to man the static lines of defense; these latter were situated only in the north and northwest.

Command of the armed forces

The Han armies drew their recruits from conscripts, volunteers, and convicts. Conscripts, who formed the majority, were men aged 23 (at times 20) to 56. They were obliged to serve for two years, either under training or on active service. This duty devolved on all able-bodied males other than those who had acquired privileges of rank or those who could pay for substitutes. The latter practice was probably rare. In addition, men were liable for recall to the colours in times of emergency. Volunteers were the sons of sons of privileged families who probably served as cavalrymen; and convicts were sometimes, but not frequently, drafted to work out their terms of sentence in the army. There is ample evidence to show that Han commanders used to draw on Central Asiatic tribesmen as recruits, and the tribesmen were particularly valuable as skilled cavalrymen. There also are a number of cases of foreigners who served with distinction as officers. While little is known of the organization of armies on campaign, garrison forces were divided into separate commands consisting of perhaps four companies. Each company had a strength of some 40 or 50 sections, grouped, for combat purposes, in platoons. Each section mustered one officer and up to five men.

The practice of government. As the final arbiter of power, the emperor—and at times the empress dowager—issued edicts declaring the Imperial will. Such instructions often took the form of repeating officials' proposals with a note of approval. Some edicts were couched as comments on the current situation, and called in general terms for an improvement in the quality of government, or for more vigorous attempts to achieve a just administration. The emperor also issued formal deeds of investiture to kings or noblemen and letters of appointment for senior officials. Edicts were circulated to the relevant authorities for action, together with books of other regulations such as the statutes and ordinances, laying down entitlements for services rendered to the state and penalties for infringing its prohibitions. Officials could suggest methods of government by submitting written memorials, and there were occasions when an emperor called a conference of senior statesmen and asked their views on topical problems.

The Han governments regularly issued calendars to enable the community to adjust its work to the seasons and officials to maintain their records correctly. Regular means of transport were kept for the use of officials travelling on business and for the conveyance of official mail from one office to another. Provincial and local officials were responsible for two regular counts without which government could not proceed: the census of the population and the register of the land and its production. Returns, which were submitted for the number of households and individuals and for acreage under the plow, eventually found their way to the capital. Two counts that have been preserved record the existence of some 12,-400,000 households and 57,000,000 individuals (AD 1), and 9,500,000 households and 48,000,000 individuals in AD 140. It may be noted that at the time of the latter count parts of north China were probably under alien domination, which would have prevented officials from conducting their work efficiently. Administrative limitations also affected the collection of taxes, two main forms of which were the land tax and the poll tax. The land tax was levied in kind at a thirtieth (sometimes a fifteenth) part of the produce, the assessment depending partly on the quality of the land. Poll tax was usually paid in cash and varied with the age and sex of the members of the household. Other taxes were levied in respect to wealth and by means of property assessments.

Use of the census

In addition to service in the army, able-bodied males were liable to one month's service annually in the state labour corps. Under the direction of local officials the men were set to work that included building palaces and Imperial mausoleums, the transport of staple goods such as grain and hemp, and the construction of roads and bridges. There were occasions when conscript labour was used to repair breaches in the river banks or dikes; and men were sent to work in the salt and iron industries after these were taken over by the state.

State monopolies

The establishment of state monopolies for salt and iron was one of several measures taken in Wu Ti's reign to bring China's resources under the control of the government. Agencies were set up c. 117 BC to supervise mining, manufacturing, and distribution, and to raise revenue in the process. The measure was criticized on the grounds both of principle and expedient, and was withdrawn for three years from 44 BC; and by the middle of the first century AD the industries had reverted in practice to private hands. Final measures to standardize the coinage and to limit minting to the agencies of state were taken in 112 BC; and, with the exception of Wang Mang's experiments, the copper coin of a single denomination, minted from Wu Ti's reign onward, remained the standard medium of exchange. Little is known of the work of other agencies that were established in Western Han to stabilize the prices of staple commodities and to regulate their transport. Such measures had been the answer of Wu Ti's government to the problem of moving goods from an area of surplus to one of shortage.

The government ordered migrations of the population for several reasons. At times such a migration was intended to populate an area artificially—the city of Hsien-yang during the Ch'in empire, for example, and the state-sponsored farms of the border lands. Alternatively, if the defense of the periphery was impractical, the population was sometimes moved away from danger; and distressed folk were moved to areas where they could find a more prosperous way of life.

From about 100 BC it was evident to some statesmen that very great disparities of wealth existed and that this was most noticeable in respect of land ownership. Some

philosophers looked back nostalgically to an ideal state in which land was said to have been allotted and held on a basis of equality, thereby eliminating the wide differences between rich and poor. Despite several suggestions it was only in Wang Mang's time that an attempt was made to limit landholding and slaveholding. But the attempt failed because of political and economic instability, and the accumulation of land continued without hindrance during Eastern Han. In the last half century or so of the dynasty, country estates were acquiring retainers and armed defenders, almost independently of the writ of government. As a result, the great families came to exercise greater power than the duly appointed officials of state.

The Han, like the Ch'in, government ruled by dispensing rewards for service and exacting punishment for disobedience and crime. Rewards consisted of exemptions from tax; material bounties of gold, meat, spirits, or silk; amnesties for criminals; and orders of honour. The latter were bestowed either individually or to groups. There was a scale of rank of 20 degrees, and with the receipt of several of these awards cumulatively a man could rise to the eighth place in the scale. The more senior orders were given for specified acts of valour, charity, or good administration usually to officials, and the highest of the orders was that of the nobility. In addition to conferring social status, the orders carried with them legal privileges and freedom from some of the statutory obligations for tax and service.

In theory, the laws of Han were binding on all members of the population, and some incidents testify to the punishment of the highest in the land. But some privileged persons were able to secure mitigation of sentences. Nobles, for example, could ransom themselves from most punishments by forfeiting their nobilities. Han laws specified a variety of crimes, including those of a social nature such as murder or theft, those that infringed the Imperial majesty, and offenses that were classed as gross immorality. There was a regular procedure for impeachment and trial; and some difficult cases could be referred to the emperor for a final decision. The punishments to which criminals were sentenced included exile, hard labour, flogging, castration, and death. In the most heinous cases the death sentence was carried out publicly; but senior officials and members of the Imperial family were usually allowed to avoid such a scene by committing suicide. After the death penalty a criminal's goods, including members of his family, were confiscated by the state. Such persons then became slaves of the state and were employed on menial or domestic tasks in government offices. If the government did not need their services, they could be sold as slaves to the houses of the great landowners (see CHINESE LAW).

Han law

RELATIONS WITH OTHER PEOPLES

Simultaneously with the rise of the Ch'in and Han empires, some of the nomadic peoples of Central Asia, known as the Hsiung-nu, succeeded in achieving a measure of unity under a single leader. As a result, while the Chinese were consolidating their government, the lands lying to the north of the empire, and the northern provinces themselves, became subject to incursion by Hsiung-nu horsemen. One of the achievements of the Ch'in dynasty had been the unification of the several lines of defense into a single system of fortification. By keeping that wall, or line of earthworks, manned, the Ch'in dynasty had been free of invasion. With the fall of Ch'in and China's subsequent weakness, the wall fell into a state of disrepair and lacked a garrison. Until about 135 BC Han governments were obliged to seek peaceful relations with the Hsiung-nu, at the price of gold, silk, and even the hand of a Chinese princess. But with the initiation of strong policies by Wu Ti's governments China took the offensive in an attempt to throw back the Hsiung-nu to Central Asia and to free the northern provinces from the threat of invasion and violence. By 119 BC campaigns fought to the north of Chinese territory had attained this objective; and after a short interval it was possible to send Han armies to advance in the northeast (modern Korea), the south (modern Vietnam), and the southwest. As a result of the campaigns fought from 135 BC onward, 18 additional commanderies were founded, and organs of Han provincial government were installed as outposts among peoples who were unassimilated to a Chinese way of life.

Relations with the Hsiung-nu

Chinese government was by no means universally accepted in these outlying regions. But despite large losses and expenditures incurred in fighting the Hsiung-nu, the Chinese were able to mount expeditions into Central Asia from c. 112 BC. The defensive walls were reoccupied and renamed, and by c. 100 BC were extended to the northwest as far as Tun-huang. Chinese travellers, whether diplomats or merchants, were thus able to proceed under protection as far as the Takla Makan Desert. It was at this juncture that were pioneered the trade routes that skirted the desert and that are known collectively as the Silk Road.

The success of Chinese arms in these remote areas was short-lived. Long lines of communication made it impossible to set up garrisons or colonies in the forbidding country to the west of Tun-huang. Diplomatic moves were made to implant Chinese prestige more firmly among the communities that were situated around the Takla Makan Desert and controlled the oases; for it was necessary for the Chinese to win those peoples' support, thus denying it to the Hsiung-nu. In a few cases the Chinese resorted to violence or plots to remove a leader and to replace him with a candidate known to favour the Han cause. A more usual procedure was to marry one of the alien leaders to a Chinese princess, with the intention that he should in time be succeeded by an heir who was half-Chinese. These endeavours and the military ventures met with partial success. While the Chinese position in Central Asia was subject to question, relations with the Hsiung-nu leaders varied. The visit of a Hsiung-nu leader to Ch'ang-an in 51 BC was hailed as a mark of Chinese success; but the ensuing decades were by no means free from fighting. Chinese prestige suffered a decline toward the end of Western Han and recovered only during the reigns of Ming Ti and Chang Ti, when the Han government was once more strong enough to take the field. Pan Ch'ao's campaigns in Central Asia (from AD 94) succeeded in reestablishing the Chinese position, but again the full strength of Chinese prestige lasted only for a few decades. During Eastern Han, China suffered invasion from the northeast as well as from the north. The settlement of Hsiung-nu tribesmen inside China, south of the wall, was a disruptive factor in the second and third centuries, to the detriment of Imperial unity.

The Han expansion into Central Asia has been represented by the Chinese as a defensive measure designed to weaken the Hsiung-nu and to free China from invasion. Allowance must also be made for commercial motives. Some of Wu Ti's statesmen were well aware of the advantages of exporting China's surplus products in return for animals and animal products from Central Asia; and there is evidence that Chinese silk was exported at this time. No attempt can be made to estimate the volume of trade, and as the transactions were conducted through Parthian middlemen, no direct contact was made by this means between Han China and the world of Rome and the Mediterranean. China's export trade was sponsored by the government and not entrusted to private merchants.

The earthworks formed a boundary separating the Chinese provinces from the outside world. Traffic was controlled at points of access, not only to check incoming travellers to China but also to prevent the escape of criminals or deserters. At the same time, a ban was imposed on the export of certain goods such as iron manufactures and weapons of war. The wall also formed a protected causeway along which travellers to the west could be conducted safely. Watch stations were erected in sight of each other to signal the approach of the enemy; and the garrison troops were trained and disciplined to a high degree of professional ability. Meticulous records were kept to show how government stores were expended and rations issued; routine signals were relayed

along the line and daily patrols were sent out to reconnoitre. The troops were organized in regular formations and hierarchies of command, and schedules of work were kept to show the tasks on which each man was engaged.

As a result of the campaigns and of diplomatic activity, China's immediate contacts with other peoples grew brisker. Many of the Hsiung-nu and other neighbouring leaders who had surrendered to Han arms were given nobilities and settled in the interior of the empire. Chang Ch'ien had been the pioneer who had set out c. 130 BC to explore the routes into Central Asia and North China, and as a result of his report and observations Han advances were concentrated in the northwest. In AD 97 Chinese envoys were frustrated in an attempt to visit the western part of the world, but a mission from Rome reached China by ship in 166. The first record of official visitors arriving at the Han court from Japan is for the year AD 57.

Contacts with Rome and Japan

CULTURAL DEVELOPMENTS

The Han emperors and governments posed as having a temporal dispensation that had received the blessing of Heaven together with its instructions to spread the benefits of a cultured life as widely as possible. By a cultured life the Chinese had in mind a clear distinction between their own settled agriculture and the delights of the cities, as opposed to the rough and hardy life spent in the saddle by the nomads of Central Asia. The growth of Han government both depended upon and encouraged the development of literary accomplishment, scholastic competence, religious activity, scientific discovery, and technological achievement.

Han administration required a proliferation of documents. Official returns were sometimes kept in duplicate, and each agency kept running files to record its business. Following the reform of the script that had been evolved before the Han period, there was developed a new style of writing suited to the compilation of official documents. These were mostly written on wooden strips, which were bulky and fragile. Silk was used for luxury purposes. A major development in world history occurred in China in AD 105 when officials reported to the throne the manufacture of a new substance. Although the use of paper can be traced to this incident, it was some three or four centuries before the earlier materials were completely superseded. In the meantime, the demands of a growing civilization had increased the written vocabulary of the Chinese. The first Chinese dictionary compiled c. AD 100, included more than 9,000 characters, with explanations of their meanings and the variant forms used in writing.

The discovery of paper

In an attempt to break with earlier tradition, the Ch'in government had taken certain steps to proscribe literature and learning. Han governments stressed their desire to promote these causes as part of their mission. In particular, they displayed a veneration for works with which Confucius had been associated, either as a collector of texts or as an editor; and from the reign of Wen Ti on orders were given to search for books lost during the previous dynasty. Knowledge of texts such as the "Classic of Poetry," the "Classic of History," the "Classic of Changes," and the "Spring and Autumn" Annals became a necessary accomplishment for officials and candidates for the civil service. To support an argument laid before the throne, statesmen would find a relevant quotation from these works; already in the 1st century BC the tradition was being formed whereby the civil service of Imperial China was nurtured on a Classical education. On two occasions (51 BC and AD 79) the government ordered official discussions about the interpretation of texts and the validity of differing versions; and in AD 175 a project was completed for inscribing an approved version on stone tablets, so as to allay scholastic doubts in the future. In the meantime, and still before the invention of paper in AD 105, a collection of literary texts had been made for the Imperial library. The catalog of this collection, which dates from the start of the Christian Era, was prepared after comparison of different copies and the elimination of duplicates. The list of titles has been preserved and constitutes China's first bibliographical list. The works are classified according to subject, but unfortunately a high proportion have been lost. The importance of these measures lies not only in their intrinsic achievement but also in the example they set for subsequent dynasties.

The prose style of Han writers was later taken as a model of simplicity, and, following the literary embellishments and artificialities of the 5th and 6th centuries, deliberate attempts were made to revert to its natural elegance. Examples of this direct prose may be seen in the Imperial edicts and in the memorials ascribed to statesmen, and above all in the text of the standard histories themselves, in which such documents of state were incorporated. The compilation of the standard histories was a private undertaking in Han times, but it already received Imperial patronage and assistance. History was written partly to justify the authority and conduct of the contemporary regime and partly as a matter of pride in Chinese achievement. Further examples of prose writing are the descriptions of protocol for the court. One of the earliest acts of Han government (c. 200 BC) had been to order the formulation of such modes of behaviour as a means of enhancing the dignity of the throne; and one of the latest compilations (c. AD 175) that still survives is a list of such prescriptions, drawn up at a time when the dynasty was manifestly losing its majesty and natural authority. Some of the emperors were themselves composers of versified prose; their efforts have also been preserved in the standard histories.

Religious practices

The emperor was charged with the solemn duty of securing the blessings of spiritual powers for mankind. One of the nine ministries of state existed to assist in this work of mediation, but from the time of Wu Ti onward the emperor himself began to play a more active part in worship and sacrifice. These cults were initially addressed to the Five Powers, which were associated with yellow and four other colours; to the Supreme Unity; and to the Lord of the Soil. In 31 BC these cults were replaced by sacrifices dedicated to Heaven and Earth. The sites of worship were transferred to the southern and northern outskirts of Ch'ang-an city, and a new series of altars and shrines was inaugurated. On two occasions (110 BC and AD 56) the Han emperor paid his respects to supreme powers and reported on the state of the dynasty at the summit of Mt. T'ai. Wu Ti's desire for immortality or for the quickening of his deceased favourites led him to patronize a number of intermediaries who claimed to possess the secret of making contact with the world of the immortals. From such beliefs, and from a fear of the malevolent influences that the unappeased souls of the dead could wreak on mankind, a few philosophers, such as Wang Ch'ung (AD 27–c. 100), reacted by propounding an ordered and rational explanation of the universe. But their skepticism received little support. Sometime during the 1st century AD the faith of the Buddha had reached China, propagated in all probability by travellers who had taken the Silk Road from north India. The establishment of the first Buddhist foundations in China and the first official patronage of the faith followed shortly. From the 2nd century AD there arose a variety of beliefs, practices, and disciplines from which alchemy and scientific experiment were to spring, and which were to give rise to Taoist religion.

Most of the cultural attainments of the Han period derived from the encouragement of the palace and the needs of officials. A textbook of mathematical problems was probably compiled to assist officials in work such as land assessment; fragments of a medical casebook were concerned with the care of troops and horses serving on the northwestern frontier. Water clocks and sundials were used to enable officials to complete their work on schedule. The seismograph constructed by Chang Heng (AD 132) was probably concerned with the interpretation of earthquakes as a sign of Heaven's wrath, and with the distribution of relief to the areas affected by such disasters. The palace demanded the services of

artists and craftsmen to decorate Imperial buildings with paintings and sculptures, to design and execute jades, gold wares and silver wares, and lacquer bowls for use at the Imperial table. Intricate patterns were woven in multicoloured silks and turned out by looms in the Imperial workshops. On a more mundane level, technology served the cause of practical government. The state's ironwork factories produced precision-made instruments and weapons of war; and the state's agencies for the salt industry supervised the recovery of brine from deep shafts cut in the rocks of west China. Water engineers planned the construction of dikes to divert the flow of excess waters, and the excavation of canals to serve the needs of transport or irrigation; and in many parts of the countryside there was seen a sight that was to remain typical of the Chinese landscape up to the 20th century—a team of two or three peasants sitting astride a beam and pedalling the lugs of the "dragon's backbone" so to lever water from the sluggish channels below to the upper levels of the cultivated land. (Ed.)

IV. The Six Dynasties

POLITICAL DEVELOPMENTS

The division of China. *The Three Kingdoms (AD 220–264).* By the end of the 2nd century AD, the Han empire had virtually ceased to exist. The repression of the Taoist rebellions of the Yellow Turbans and related sects marked the beginning of a period of unbridled warlordism and political chaos, from which three independent centres of political power emerged. In the north, all authority had passed into the hands of the generalissimo and "protector of the dynasty," Ts'ao Ts'ao; in AD 220 the last puppet emperor of the Han officially ceded the throne to Ts'ao Ts'ao's son, who thereby became the legitimate heir of the empire and the first ruler of the Wei dynasty. Soon afterward, two competing military leaders proclaimed themselves emperor, one in the far interior (Shu Han dynasty, in present-day Szechwan Province) and one in the south, behind the formidable barrier of the Yangtze (the empire of Wu, with its capital at present-day Nanking). The short and turbulent period of these "Three Kingdoms," filled with bloody warfare and diplomatic intrigue, has ever since been glorified in Chinese historical fiction as an age of chivalry and individual heroism.

The Wei, Shu Han, and Wu dynasties

In fact, even Wei, the strongest of the three, hardly represented any real political power. The great socioeconomic changes that had started in the Later Han period had transformed the structure of society to such an extent that all attempts to re-establish the centralized bureaucratic state—the ideal of the Ch'in and Han dynasties—were doomed to failure. The great families—aristocratic clans of great landowners, entrenched in their fortified estates under the protection of their private armies of serfs and clients—had survived the decades of civil war and even increased their power. This process, sometimes (but inappropriately) called a "refeudalization" of Chinese society, created conditions that were to remain characteristic of medieval China. The Han system of recruiting officials on the basis of talent was replaced by a network of personal relations and patronage. The hierarchy of state officials and government institutions was never abolished, but it became monopolized by a few of aristocratic clans, who filled the highest offices with their own members and the minor posts with their clients.

Wei succeeded in conquering Shu Han in 263, but two years later a general of the dominant Ssu-ma clan overthrew the house of Wei and founded the Western Chin dynasty (265). Wu could maintain itself until 280, when it was overrun by the Chin armies.

The role of Wu was extremely important: it marks the beginning of the intensive Sinicization of the region south of the Yangtze, which before that time had been a frontier area, inhabited mainly by primitive tribes. The rise of a great administrative and cultural centre on the lower Yangtze paved the way for future developments: after the north was lost to barbarian invaders (311), Nanking was to become the capital of Chinese successor states

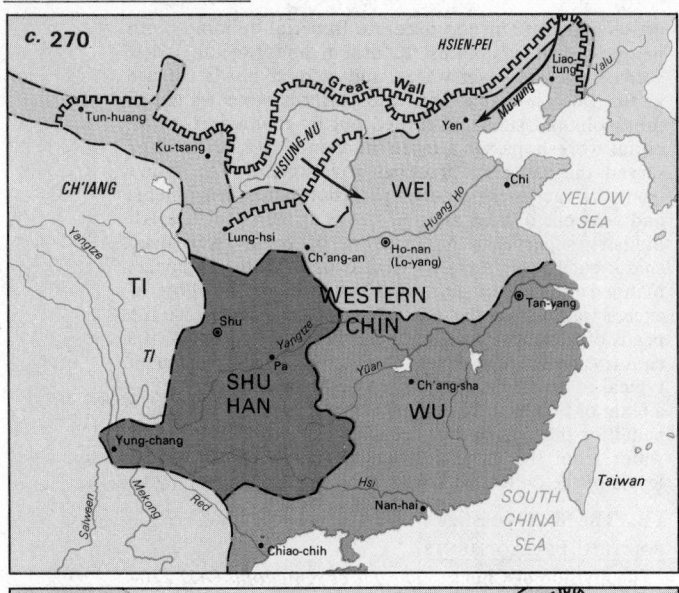

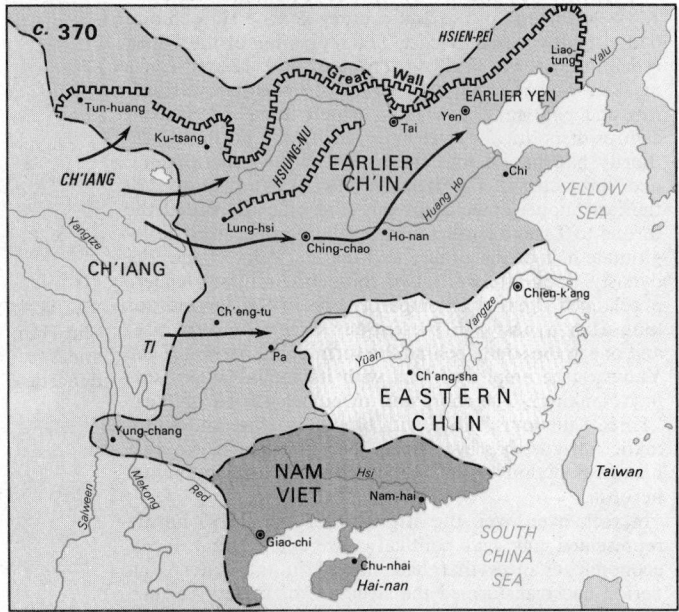
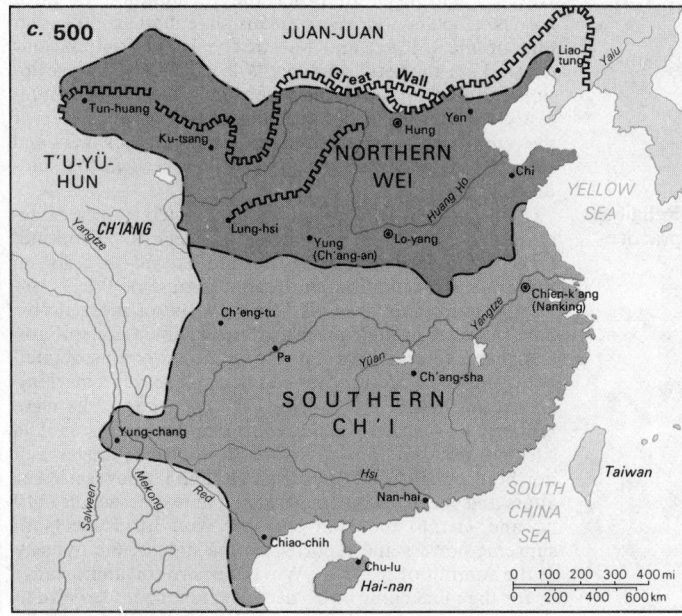

China in the Six Dynasties period.

From (all but bottom right) M. Penkala, *A Correlated History of the Far East*, maps by Edward Penkala, F.R.G.S.;
(bottom right) E. Reischauer and J. Fairbank, *East Asia: The Great Tradition*, copyright ©1958 and 1960 by Edwin O.
Reischauer and John K. Fairbank, published by Houghton Mifflin Company

and the focus of Chinese civilization for more than 250 years.

The Western Chin (AD 265–317). This was a period of relative order and prosperity, a short interlude between the turbulent age of the Three Kingdoms and the devastating barbarian invasions. The empire had been nominally reunited (AD 280), and for a short time the central government attempted important fiscal and political reforms, mainly intended to curb the power of the great families. Contacts with the oasis kingdoms of Central Asia and the Indianized states of the far south (Funan and Champa) were resumed, and in 285 the Chin court even sent an envoy to distant Fergana in Central Asia to confer the title of king on its ruler—a grand Imperial gesture reminiscent of the great days of Han. But this ghost of the Han empire disappeared almost as soon as it had been evoked. Within two decades the Chin disintegrated through the struggles of rival clans, followed by an internecine war between the various Ssu-ma princes. The familiar signs of the end of the "dynastic cycle" appeared: collapse of the central government, decentralized military control of the provinces, famine, large-scale banditry, and messianic peasant movements.

The era of barbarian invasions and rule. For the first time, the power vacuum was filled by non-Chinese forces. In 304, a Sinicized Hsiung-nu (Hun) chieftain assumed the title of king of Han and started the conquest of northern China with his nomadic hordes. Operating from bases in western and southern Shansi, the Hsiung-nu armies, supported by local Chinese rebels, conquered the ancient homeland of Chinese civilization; the fall and destruction of the two capitals, Ho-nan (Lo-yang) (311) and Ching-chao (Ch'ang-an) (316), ended Chinese dynastic rule in the north for centuries. Although in the far northeast, in present-day Kansu, and in the inaccessible interior (Szechwan), Chinese local kingdoms did occasionally succeed in maintaining themselves for some time, the whole North China Plain itself became the scene of a bewildering variety of "barbarian" states, collectively known in Chinese historiography as the Sixteen Kingdoms.

The Eastern Chin (317–419) and later dynasties in the south (419–589). During the whole medieval period, it was the lower Yangtze region, the former territory of Wu, that remained the stronghold of a series of "legitimate" Chinese dynasties with Chien-k'ang (Nanking) as their capital. In 317, a member of the Chin Imperial family had set up a refugee regime at Chien-k'ang, mainly consisting of members of the exiled northern aristocracy. From the beginning, the Chin court was completely at the mercy of the "great families." Government in the Chinese south became a kind of oligarchy exercised by

The "barbarian" states of the north and the refugee states of the south

ever-changing groups and juntas of aristocratic clans. The so-called Six Dynasties (actually five: Eastern Chin, 317–419; Liu-Sung, 420–479; Southern Ch'i, 479–502; Liang, 502–557, and Ch'en, 557–589; the earlier kingdom of Wu, 222–280, is counted as the sixth) were politically and militarily weak and constantly plagued by internal feuds and revolts. Their annihilation (in 589) was postponed only by the internal division of the north and by the protection afforded by the Yangtze. As so often in Chinese history, however, political weakness was coupled with cultural brilliance: in literature, art, philosophy, and religion, the Nanking dynasties constitute one of the most creative period in Chinese cultural history. They reached their highest flowering under the long and relatively stable reign of the great protector of Buddhism, Emperor Wu of the Liang dynasty (502–549). To the very end, the opposition to the north remained alive, but occasional attempts to reconquer the ancient homeland were doomed to failure. The final reunification of China was to start from the northern plains, not from Nanking.

The Sixteen Kingdoms in the north (304–589). The term Sixteen Kingdoms traditionally denotes the plethora of short-lived non-Chinese dynasties that after 316 came to rule the whole or parts of northern China. The many ethnic groups involved included ancestors of the Turks (such as the Hsiung-nu, probably related to the Huns of late Roman history, and the Chieh), the Mongolians (Hsien-pei), and the Tibetans (Ti and Ch'iang). Most of these nomadic peoples, relatively few in number, had to some extent been Sinicized even before their ascent to power. In fact, some of them, notably the Hsiung-nu, had already since late Han times been allowed to live in the frontier regions within the Great Wall.

The "barbarian" rulers thus set up semi-Sinicized states, in which the foreign element constituted a military aristocracy and the nucleus of the armed forces. Since in administrative matters they lacked all experience, and their own tribal institutions were not adapted to the complicated task of ruling a large agrarian society, they had to make use of traditional Chinese ways of government. In doing so, they faced the dilemma that has ever since confronted foreign rulers on Chinese soil: the tension that existed between the need to preserve their own ethnic identity (and their position as *Herrenvolk*), on the one hand, and, on the other, the practical necessity of using Chinese literati and members of prominent Chinese families in order to rule at all. In spite of various and sometimes highly interesting experiments, most of these short-lived empires did not survive this tension. Significantly, the only one that proved to have more lasting power and that was able to unify the whole of northern China, the "Toba" or Northern Wei (386–534), was completely Sinicized within one century. In the late 5th century the court even forbade the use of the original Toba language, dress, customs, and surnames. This policy of conscious, acculturation was further symbolized by the transfer of the Northern Wei capital from the northern frontier region to the ancient Imperial residence of Lo-yang.

Thus, toward the end of the period of division, the north had become more homogeneous as the result of a long process of adaptation. The most important factor in this process may have been the rehabilitation of the Chinese agrarian economy under the Northern Wei, stimulated by fiscal reform and redistribution of land (c. AD 500). The landed gentry again became the backbone of society, and the primitive rulers of nomadic origin simply had to conform to their way of life. Another factor may be sought in the intrinsic superiority of Chinese upper class culture: in order to play the role of the "Son of Heaven," the barbarian court had to adopt the complicated rules of Chinese ritual and etiquette. In order to surround themselves with an aura of legitimacy, the foreign conquerors had to express themselves in terms of Chinese culture. In doing so, they invariably lost their own identity. History has repeated itself again and again: in this respect the 4th- and 5th-century Chieh and Toba were but the forerunners of the Manchu rulers in the 19th century.

Soon after 520, the Wei empire disintegrated into various rivalling successor states, also ruled by ancestors of the Mongolians that had been thoroughly Sinicized. North China again became a vast battlefield for several decades. The Northern Chou (557–581), strategically based in the rich basin of the Wei, succeeded in reunifying the north (577). Four years later, Yang Chien, a general of mixed Chinese and "barbarian" descent (but claiming to be a pure-blooded Chinese), usurped the throne and founded the Sui dynasty. And in 589, after having consolidated his regime, he crossed the Yangtze and overthrew the last of the Chinese dynasties at Nanking. After almost four centuries of division and political decay, China was again united under one central government, which, in spite of its short duration, would lay the foundation of the great T'ang empire.

INTELLECTUAL AND RELIGIOUS TRENDS

Confucianism and philosophical Taoism. The social and political upheaval of the late 2nd and 3rd centuries AD was accompanied by an intense intellectual activity. During most of the Han period, Confucianism, as the official ideology, had provided the government with a standard code of morals and ritual behaviour, regulating the relations between ruler and subject and the social conduct of the individual.

At the beginning of the 3rd century, however, Confucianism had lost much of its prestige: it had obviously failed to save the empire from disintegration or to safeguard the privileges of the ruling elite. Disappointed members of the scholar-official class started to look for other ways and means. Thus, in the 3rd century there was a curious revival of various all-but-forgotten schools of thought: Legalism, with its insistence upon harsh measures, intended to re-establish law and order; Moism and the ancient school of Dialecticians; and, above all, a renewed interest in the earliest Taoist philosophers, Lao-tzu and Chuang-tzu. In general, this movement did not mean a return to ancient Taoist quietism and consequently a rejection of Confucianism itself: with the breakdown of the elaborate scholastic doctrine that had formed the official Han ideology, Confucianism had been deprived of its metaphysical superstructure, and this vacuum was now filled by a whole set of philosophical ideas and speculations, largely of Taoist provenance.

Within this movement, two trends came to dominate the intellectual life of the cultured minority. One of these was closely related to the practical affairs of government and stressed the importance of social duties, ritual, law, and the study of human characteristics. This mixture of Confucian and Legalist notions was called *ming-chiao*, "the doctrine of names" ("names" in ancient Confucian parlance designating the various social functions—father, ruler, subject, etc.—that an individual could have in society). The other trend was marked by a profound interest in ontological and metaphysical problems: the quest for a permanent substratum (called *t'i*, "substance") behind the world of change (called *yung*, "function"). It started from the assumption that all temporally and spatially limited phenomena—anything "nameable," all movement, change, and diversity, in short, all "being"— is produced and sustained by one impersonal principle, which is unlimited, unnameable, unmoving, unchanging, and undiversified. This important movement, which found its scriptural support both in Taoist and in drastically reinterpreted Confucian sources, was known as Hsüan Hsüeh ("Dark Learning"); it came to reign supreme in cultural circles, especially at Nanking during the period of division, and represented the more abstract, unworldly, and idealistic tendency in early medieval Chinese thought.

The partisans of Hsüan Hsüeh undoubtedly still regarded themselves as true Confucianists. To them, Confucius was no more the great teacher who had fixed the rules of social behaviour for all times but was the enlightened sage who had inwardly recognized the ultimate reality but had kept silent about it in his worldly teachings, knowing that these mysteries cannot be expressed in words. Hence, his doctrine was supposed to be an expedi-

Sinicization of the foreign conquerors

Ming-chiao and Hsüan Hsüeh

ent, a mere set of ad hoc rules intended to answer to the practical needs of the times. This concept of "hidden saintliness" and the "expedient" character of the canonical teachings came to play a very important role in upper class Buddhism (see below).

Because Hsüan Hsüeh is sometimes referred to by the term Neo-Taoism, it must be noted that it was both created by and intended for literati and scholar-officials —not Taoist masters and hermits. The theories of such thinkers as Hsi K'ang (223–262), who, with their quest for immortality and their extreme antiritualism, were much nearer to the spirit of Taoism, hardly belong to the sphere of Hsüan Hsüeh, and the greatest Taoist author of this period, Ko Hung (c. 250–330), was clearly opposed to these mystic speculations.

The popularity of Hsüan Hsüeh was closely related to the practice of "pure conversation" (ch'ing-t'an), a special type of philosophical and rhetorical discussion that was much in vogue among the cultured upper class from the 3rd century on. In the earliest phase, the main theme of such discussions—a highly formalized critique of the personal qualities of well-known contemporaries—still had a concrete function in political life ("characterization" of persons was the basis of recommendation of clients for official posts and had largely taken the place of the earlier methods of selection of officials by court examinations). By the 4th century, however, ch'ing-t'an meetings had evaporated into a refined and very exclusive pastime of the aristocratic elite, a kind of salon in which "eloquent gentlemen" displayed their ability in expressing some philosophical or artistic theme in elegant and abstruse words. It is obvious that much of Hsüan Hsüeh had become divorced from the realities of life and afforded an escape from it.

True Confucianism had thus lost much of its influence. In the occupied North, the early, not yet Sinicized "barbarian" rulers were mainly interested in Confucianism as a system of court ritual; ideologically, they were more attracted by the magical powers of Buddhist and Taoist masters. In the South, the disillusioned aristocratic exiles, doomed by circumstances to lead a life of elegant inactivity, had little use for a doctrine that preached the duties of government and the regulation of human society as its highest goals. In general; Confucianism had become so closely associated with the ideals of officialdom that it could be fully realized only in a situation of Imperial unification and centralized government. In this period of internal division and political weakness, it had to hibernate; soon after the Sui had reunited the empire, it would wake up again (see CONFUCIANISM; see also CONFUCIANISM, HISTORY OF; CHINESE RELIGION; and CHINESE PHILOSOPHY).

Taoism. The suppression of the Yellow Turbans and other Taoist religious movements in AD 184 had left the Taoist church in a decapitated state. With the elimination of its highest leadership, the movement had fallen apart into many small religious communities or parishes, each led by a local Taoist master (Tao-shih), assisted by a council of wealthy Taoist laics. Under such circumstances, local Taoist masters could easily become leaders of independent sectarian movements. They could also, in times of unrest, use their charismatic power to play a leading part in local rebellions. In the early medieval period, Taoism at the grass-roots level continued to play this double role: it had an integrating function by providing spiritual consolation and ritualized forms of communal activity, but it could also play a disintegrating role as a potential source of subversive movements. The authorities naturally were well aware of this. Taoist rebellions periodically broke out in this period; and, although some masters occasionally became influential at court, the governments, both northern and southern, maintained a cautious reserve toward the Taoist religion. It was never stimulated and patronized to an extent comparable with Buddhism.

It would be wrong to speak of Taoism as a popular religion. Taoism counted its devotees even among the highest nobility. In view of the expensive ceremonies, the costly ingredients used in Taoist alchemy (notably cin-

Development of sectarian movements

nabar), and the almost unlimited amount of spare time required from the serious practitioner, one may assume that only the well-to-do were able to follow the road towards salvation. But they were mostly individual seekers; in the 3rd and 4th centuries, there gradually grew a distinction between individual (and mainly upper class) Taoism and the popular, collective creed of the simple devotees. In fact, Taoism has always been a huge complex of many different beliefs, cults, and practices. Most of these can be traced back to Later Han times; after the 3rd century they were more and more influenced by Buddhism.

The basic ideal of Taoist religion—the attainment of bodily immortality in a kind of indestructible "astral body" and the realization of the state of hsien, or Taoist "immortal"—remained alive. It was to be pursued by a series of individual practices: dietary control; gymnastics; the performance of good deeds; meditation and visualization of the innumerable gods and spirits that were supposed to dwell inside the microcosmos of the body. Famous literati, such as the poet Hsi K'ang (223–262) and the calligrapher Wang Hsi-chih (321–379), devoted much of their life to such practices. They combined various methods, ranging from mystic self-identification with the all-embracing Tao to the use of charms and experiments in alchemy.

The other, collective, and more popular form of Taoism, practiced in the communities or parishes throughout the country, was characterized by communal ceremonies (chai, "fasting sessions," and ch'u, "banquets"), held by groups of Taoist families under the guidance of the local master, both on fixed dates and on special occasions. The purpose of such meetings was the collective elimination of sins (evil deeds being considered as the main cause of sickness and premature death) through incantations, deafening music, fasting, and the display of penance and remorse. The gatherings sometimes lasted several days and nights, and, according to the indignant reports of their Buddhist adversaries, they were ecstatic and sometimes even orgiastic. The allegation of sexual excesses and promiscuity may have been stimulated by the curious fact, unknown in Confucian and Buddhist ritual, that in Taoist meetings both men and women took part.

The Taoist parish as an organization and the Taoist master who led it relied on two sources of income: the presents made by devotee families at ceremonial gatherings and the regular "heavenly tax," or yearly contribution of five bushels of rice, which every family was due to pay on the seventh day of the seventh month. The office of Taoist master was hereditary, within one family; in the early centuries, Taoist priests usually married. Because Buddhist influence also increased at this humble level, however, the Tao-shih more and more came to resemble the Buddhist clergy, especially since most Taoist priests, at least from the 5th century on, went to live in Taoist monasteries with their wives and children. In the 6th century, when Buddhism became paramount, some Taoist leaders introduced celibacy; in Sui times the unmarried state had become general, and the Taoist clergy with its monks and nuns had evolved into a counterpart of the Buddhist sangha.

In spite of their resemblance or, perhaps, because of it, the two creeds were bitterly opposed throughout the period. Taoist masters were often involved in anti-Buddhist propaganda and persecution. As an answer to Buddhist claims of superiority, Taoist masters even developed the curious theory that the Buddha had been only a manifestation of Lao-tzu, who had preached to the Indians a debased form of Taoism, which naturally should not be reintroduced into China; this theme can be traced in Buddhist and Taoist polemic literature from the 4th to the 13th centuries.

In general, one must conclude that Taoism, compared with Buddhism and Hsüan Hsüeh, played a secondary role. The best minds of the period were attracted to Buddhism, which far surpassed Taoism in philosophical depth and coherence. Unlike Buddhist monasteries, the Taoist clerical communities never developed great eco-

Popular Taoist ceremonies

nomic power, nor did they became great centres of learning (see TAOISM; TAOISM, HISTORY OF).

Buddhism. This period was the Buddhist age of China. Several factors contributed to the extraordinary expansion and absorption of the foreign religion after about 300, both in the Chinese South and in the occupied North. A negative factor was the absence of a unified Confucian state, which naturally would be inclined to suppress a creed the basic tenets of which (notably the monastic life and the pursuit of individual salvation outside family and society) were clearly opposed to the ideals of Confucianism. The popularity of Hsüan Hsüeh was a positive and powerful factor. Especially in the South, Mahāyāna Buddhism, thoroughly amalgamated with Hsüan Hsüeh, was preached by cultured monks in the circles of the Nanking aristocracy, where it became extremely popular. Another stimulus for the growth of Buddhism was the relative safety of the monastic life, both for the masses and the gentry. In a countryside devastated by war and rebellion, innumerable small peasants preferred to give up their independence and to avoid the scourges of heavy taxation, forced labour, and deportation by joining the large estates of the nobility as serfs, where they would get at least a minimum of protection. This process of tax evasion, coupled with the extension of the manorial system, also stimulated the growth of Buddhist monasteries as landowning institutions, peopled with both monks and families of hereditary temple serfs. By the beginning of the 6th century, the monasteries had become an economic power of the first order, which, moreover, enjoyed special privileges (such as exemption from taxes). This, indeed, became the main source of tension between clergy and government and occasionally led to anti-Buddhist movements and harsh restrictive measures imposed upon the Buddhist church (446–452 and again in 574–578).

The rise of Buddhism

The monastic life attracted many members of the gentry as well. In these times of turmoil, the official career was beset with dangers, and the monastery offered a hiding place to literati who tried to keep clear of the intrigues and feuds of higher gentry circles; thus the ancient Chinese ideal of the retired scholar merged with the new Buddhist ideal of the monastic life. Many large monasteries thereby became centres of learning and culture and so became even more attractive to members of minor gentry families, for whom the higher posts in government in any event would be unattainable. Buddhist institutions offered a kind of "internal democracy"—a fact of great social importance in the history of class-ridden medieval China. Finally, Buddhism was patronized by most of the "barbarian" rulers in the North. At first, they were mainly attracted by the pomp and magical power of Buddhist ritual, practices that may have accorded well with their own aboriginal cults. Later, other motivations were added to this. Unwilling to rely too much upon Chinese ministers with their following of clan members and clients, they preferred to make use of Buddhist masters, who as unmarried individuals were totally dependent on the ruler's favour. Ideologically, Buddhism was less "Chinese" than Confucianism, especially in the North, where the connections with central Asia constantly reinforced its international and universalistic character. This peculiar "Sino-barbarian" nature of northern Buddhism with its foreign preachers and its huge translation projects strongly contrasts with the South, where Buddhism in the 4th century was already fully domesticated.

Because of all these circumstances, the large-scale development of Chinese Buddhism started only after the barbarian invasions of the early 4th century. In the 3rd century, the picture did not basically differ from Han times: there are indications that Buddhism was still largely a religion of foreigners on Chinese soil (apart from some activity involving the translation of Buddhist scriptures). But, by the 4th century, the picture was changing. At the southern Chinese court in Nanking, there was forming a clerical elite of Chinese monks and propagators of a completely Sinicized Buddhism, strongly amalgamated with Hsüan Hsüeh, and their sophisticated creed was being spread among the southern gentry. Starting at Nanking and in northern Chekiang (the Hangchou region), this trend was further developed in the late 4th and early 5th centuries in other centres throughout the middle and lower Yangtze Basin.

The highest flowering of this uniquely "Chinese" type of Buddhism took place in the early 5th century under the great patron of the *saṅgha*, Emperor Wu of the Liang dynasty (reigned 502–549). He himself took the Buddhist vows and soon afterward ruthlessly persecuted Taoism, at the same time ordering all imperial relatives, courtiers, and officials to become Buddhists. On the eve of the reunification, southern China had become almost a Buddhist state.

In the North, the climax of Buddhist activity and Imperial patronage occurred under the Northern Wei, especially after the beginning of their policy of conscious Sinicization. The Toba court and the great families vied with each other in building temples and granting land and money to the monasteries; the monumental cave temples at Yün-kang are lasting proof of this large-scale Imperial protection. This also had its dark side: in the North the Buddhist clergy became closely tied with secular government, and the lavish treatment of the church was counterbalanced by repeated attempts at government control. It may also be noted that the North remained open to influences brought by travelling monks from central Asia, and an enormous amount of Indian Buddhist texts of all schools and eras was translated.

Popular Buddhism

Little is known of the beginnings of popular Buddhism. Among the masses, there was, to judge from Taoist materials, an intense mingling of Buddhist and popular Taoist notions and practices, such as communal festivals and the worship of local Taoist and Buddhist saints. At this level, simple devotionalism was no doubt far more influential than the scriptural teachings. It is also quite probable that the oral recital of Buddhist scriptures (mainly edifying tales) had already inspired the development of vernacular literature. (For further discussion, see also BUDDHISM, HISTORY OF.)

In any event, the constant amalgamation of Buddhism, Taoism, and innumerable local cults was to continue for centuries, eventually producing an amorphous mass of creeds and practices collectively known as Chinese popular religion. (E.Z.)

V. Sui and T'ang dynasties

THE SUI (581–618)

The Sui dynasty that reunified China after nearly four centuries of political fragmentation, during which the North and South had developed in quite different ways, played a part far more important than its short span would suggest. In the same way that the Ch'in rulers of the third century BC had unified China after the Warring States period, so the Sui brought China together again and set up many institutions that were to be adopted by their successors, the T'ang. In doing so, however, like the Ch'in they overstrained their resources and fell. As in the case of the Ch'in, traditional history has judged the Sui somewhat unfairly; it has stressed the harshness of the Sui regime and the megalomania of its second emperor, giving too little credit for its considerable positive achievements.

Reign of Yang Chien

Yang Chien, (Sui Wen Ti), the Sui founder (reigned 581–604), was a high-ranking official at the Northern Chou court, a member of one of the powerful northwestern aristocratic families that had taken service under the successive non-Chinese royal houses in northern China and had intermarried with the families of their foreign masters. The Northern Chou had recently (577) reunified northern China by the conquest of the rival northeastern dynasty of Northern Ch'i. But political life in the northern courts was extremely unstable. The succession of an apparently deranged and irresponsible young emperor to the Chou throne in 578 set off a train of court intrigues, plots, and murders. Yang Chien was able to install a child as puppet emperor, and then to seize the throne for himself.

In control of all of northern China, and in command of formidable armies, he immediately set about establishing order within his frontiers. He built himself a grand new capital, Ta-hsing, close to the site of the old Ch'in and Han capitals, a city erected very quickly with a prodigal use of compulsory labour. This great city remained (under the name Ch'ang-an) the capital of the T'ang and the principal seat of government until the beginning of the 10th century.

He also took quick action to protect the frontiers of his new state. China during the 6th century had a formidable northern neighbour in the Turks (T'u-chüeh), who controlled the steppe from the borders of Manchuria to the frontiers of the Byzantine and Sāsānid empires. At the time of Yang Chien's seizure of power, the Turks were splitting into two great empires, an eastern one dominating the Chinese northern frontier from Manchuria to Kansu, and a western one stretching in a vast arc north of the Tarim Basin into Central Asia. Yang Chien encouraged this split by supporting the khan of the western Turks, Tardu. Throughout his reign he also pursued a policy of encouraging factional strife among the eastern Turks. At the same time he strengthened his defences in the north by repairing the Great Wall. In the northwest, in the area around the Koko Nor, he defeated the T'u-yü-hun people, who from time to time raided the border territories.

By the late 580s Yang Chien's state was stable and secure enough for him to take the final step toward the reunification of the whole country. In 587 he dethroned the emperor of the Later Liang, the state that had ruled the middle Yangtze Valley as a puppet of the Northern Chou since 555. In 589 he overwhelmed the last southern dynasty, the Ch'en, which put up only token resistance. Several rebellions against the Sui regime subsequently broke out in the South, but these were easily quelled by the Sui general Yang Su. Yang Chien now ruled over a firmly reunited empire.

Yang Chien's institutional reforms. His achievement consisted of much more than strengthening and reunifying the empire. He provided it with uniform institutions and established a pattern of government that survived into the T'ang dynasty and beyond. A hard-working administrator, he employed a number of extremely able ministers who combined skill in practical statecraft with a flexible approach to ideological problems. They revived the Confucian state rituals to win favour with the literati and establish a link with the empire of the Han; and at the same time they fostered Buddhism, the dominant religion of the South, attempting to establish the emperor's image as an ideal Buddhist saint–king.

Yang Chien's lasting success, however, was in practical politics and institutional reforms. In the last days of the Northern Chou he had been responsible for a revision of the laws, and one of his first acts on becoming emperor was to promulgate a penal code, the New code of 581. In 583 his ministers compiled a revised code, the K'ai-huang code, and administrative statutes. These were far simpler than the laws of the Northern Chou, and more lenient. Considerable pains were taken to ensure that local officials studied and enforced the new laws. Toward the end of Yang Chien's reign, when neo-Legalist political advisers gained ascendancy at court, the application of the laws became increasingly strict. The K'ai-huang code and statutes provided the pattern for the T'ang code, the most influential body of law in the history of the Far East.

The central government under Yang Chien developed into a complex apparatus of ministries, boards, courts, and directorates. The conduct of its personnel was supervised by another organ, the censorate. The emperor presided over this apparatus, and all orders and legislation were issued in his name. He was assisted by the heads of the three central ministries who acted as Counsellors on State Affairs (I kuo-cheng). This system later provided the basic framework for the central government of the early T'ang.

Even more important, he carried out a sweeping reform and rationalization of local government. The three-level system of local administration inherited from Han times had been reduced to chaos during the 5th and 6th cen-

The legal code (margin)

turies by excessive subdivision; there were an enormous number of local districts, some of them with not more than 100 families. Yang Chien created a simplified structure in which a much reduced number of counties were directly subordinated to prefectures. He also rationalized the chaotic rural administrative units into a uniform system of *hsiang* comprising 500 households each. Appointments to the chief offices in prefectures and counties were now made by the central government, rather than filled by members of local influential families as had been the practice. This reform ensured that local officials would be agents of the central government. It also integrated local officials into the normal pattern of bureaucratic promotion, and in time produced a more homogeneous civil service.

Local government (margin)

Since the registration of population had fallen into chaos under the Northern Chou, a careful new census was carried out during the 680s. It recorded the age, status, and landed possessions of all the members of each household in the empire. On the basis of this census, the land allocation system employed under the successive northern dynasties since the end of the 5th century was reimposed. The tax system also followed the old model of head taxes levied in grain and silk at a uniform rate. The taxable age was raised, and the annual period of labour service to which all taxpayers were liable was reduced.

Yang Chien's government, in spite of his frontier campaigns and vast construction works, was very economical and frugal. By the 590s he had accumulated great reserves, and when the Ch'en territories were incorporated into his empire he was in a position to exempt the new population from ten years of taxes to help ensure their loyalty.

The military system, likewise, was founded upon that of the northern dynasties; the Imperial forces were organized in militias. They served regular annual turns of duty but lived at home during the rest of the year and were largely self-supporting. Many troops were settled in military colonies on the frontiers to make the garrisons self-sufficient. Only when there was a campaign did the costs of the military establishment soar.

Integration of the South. The second Sui emperor, Yang Ti (reigned 605–618), has been depicted as a supreme example of arrogance, extravagance, and personal depravity who squandered his patrimony in megalomaniac construction projects and unwise military adventures. This mythical Yang Ti was to a large extent the product of the hostile record written of his reign shortly after his death. His reign began well enough, continuing the trends begun under Yang Chien. A further revision of the law code with a general reduction of penalties was carried out in 607. The census of 609 showed a registered population of 50,000,000 persons.

Reign of Yang Ti (margin)

Yang Ti's principal achievement was the integration of the South more firmly into a unified China. There is little evidence that the South was ever completely brought into line with all the administrative practices of the North; the land allocation system seems unlikely to have been enforced there, and it is probable that the registration of the population, the essential foundation for the whole fiscal and military system, was only incompletely carried out in the old Ch'en territories. But Yang Ti himself was personally very much involved with the South. Married to a princess from the southern state of Liang, he had spent 591–600 as viceroy for the southern territories; their successful integration into the Sui empire after the initial wave of risings was largely due to his administration and to the generally clement policies employed in the former Ch'en territories.

His identification with the southern interest was one of the reasons why he began the establishment of an examination system, based upon the Confucian Classical curriculum, as a means of drawing into the bureaucracy scholars from the southern and northeastern elites that had preserved traditions of Confucian learning. Hitherto, the court had been dominated by the generally less cultivated aristocratic families of mixed blood from northwestern China.

Yang Ti also attempted to weaken the predominance of the northwest by building a second great capital city at Lo-yang on the border of the eastern plains. This capital was not only distant from the home territories of the northwestern aristocrats, but also easily provisioned from the rich farmlands of Hopeh and Honan. The new city was constructed in a great hurry, employing vast numbers of labourers both in building and in transporting from the south the timber and other materials required. Yang Ti also built new palaces and an immense Imperial park, again with a prodigal use of labour.

Development of the canals

His next grandiose plan aimed at unifying the empire was to develop still further the canal system his father had begun in the metropolitan region, and to construct a great canal linking Ho-nan (Lo-yang) with the Huai Ho and with the southern capital Chiang-tu at Yang-chou on the Yangtze. Much of this route followed either existing rivers or ancient canals, but it was still an immense undertaking that employed masses of forced labourers working under conditions of appalling hardship. In 605 water transport was opened between the capital at Lo-yang and the Yangtze. In 610 the canal system was extended south of the Yangtze to Hangchow. At the same time, in preparation for campaigns in Manchuria and on the Korean frontier, another great canal was built northward from Ho-nan to the vicinity of the modern Peking. By 611 the whole eastern plain had been given a canal system linking the major river systems of northern China and providing a trunk route from the Yangtze Delta to the northern frontier. The construction of these waterways was inordinately expensive, caused terrible suffering, and left a legacy of widespread social unrest; but in the long term the transportation system was to be a most important factor in the maintenance of a unified empire.

Further hardship was caused by the mass levies of labour required to rebuild and strengthen the Great Wall in Shansi in 607 and 608 as a precaution against the resurgent eastern Turks.

Foreign affairs under Yang Ti. In addition to these far-sighted construction works, Yang Ti also pursued a very active foreign policy. An expedition to the south established sovereignty over the old Chinese settlement in Tongking, and over the Champa state of Lin-i in central Nam Viet. Several expeditions were sent to Taiwan. Relations with Japan were opened. The T'u-yü-hun people were driven out of Kansu and eastern Turkistan, and Sui colonies were established along the great western trade routes. The rulers of the various petty local states of Central Asia, and the king of Kao-ch'ang (Turfan) became tributaries. A prosperous trade with Central Asia and the West grew up.

Relations with the Turks

The principal foreign threat was still posed by the Turks. These had now been completely split into the eastern Turks, who occupied most of the Chinese northern frontier, and the immensely powerful western Turks, whose dominions stretched westward to the north of the Tarim Basin as far as Sāsānid Persia and Afghanistan. During the early part of Yang Ti's reign the western Turks, whose ruler, Ch'u-lo Khan, was half-Chinese, were on good terms with the Sui. In 610, however, Yang Ti supported a rival, She-kuei, who drove out Ch'u-lo and took service, with an army of 10,000 followers, at Yang Ti's court. When Sui power began to wane after 612, the western Turks under She-kuei gradually replaced the Sui garrisons in Central Asia and established control over the states of the Tarim Basin. The eastern Turks had been on good terms with the Sui, their khans being married to Chinese princesses. In 613 P'ei Chü, Yang Ti's principal agent in dealing with the foreign states of the north, attempted unsuccessfully to dethrone the eastern Turkish khan and split up his khanate. Relations with the Turks deteriorated, and in the last years of his reign Yang Ti had to contend with a hostile and extremely powerful neighbour.

Campaigns in Korea

His most costly venture was a series of campaigns in Korea. At that time Korea was divided into three kingdoms, of which the northern was the most important and powerful. It was hostile to the Chinese and refused to pay homage to Yang Ti. Yang Ti made careful preparations

for a punitive campaign on a grand scale, including construction of the Yung-chi-ch'ü canal from Ho-nan to Peking. In 611, the canal was completed; a great army and masses of supplies were collected, but terrible floods in Hopeh delayed the campaign. During 612, 613, and 614 Yang Ti campaigned against the Koreans. The first two campaigns were unsuccessful, and were accompanied by the outbreak of many minor rebellions in Shantung and southern Hopeh. The severe repression that followed led to outbreaks of disorder all over the empire. In 614 yet another army was sent into Korea and threatened the capital at P'yŏngyang, but had to withdraw without a decisive victory. These futile campaigns distracted Yang Ti's attention from the increasingly vital internal problems of his empire, involved an immense loss of life and material, and caused terrible hardships among the civilian population. They left the Sui demoralized, militarily crippled, and financially ruined.

At this point, Yang Ti decided to secure his relations with his northern neighbours. His envoy P'ei Chü had continued to intrigue against the eastern Turkish khan, in spite of the fact that the Sui were no longer in a position of strength. When, in the summer of 615, Yang Ti went to inspect the defenses of the Great Wall, he was surrounded and besieged by the Turks at Yen-men; he was rescued only after a month of peril.

Rebellions and uprisings soon broke out in every region of the empire. Late in 616 Yang Ti decided to withdraw to his southern capital of Chiang-tu (in the Yang-chou area), and much of northern China was divided among rebel regimes contending with one another for the succession to the empire. Yang Ti remained nominally emperor until the spring of 618, when he was murdered by members of his entourage at Chiang-tu. But from 617 the real powers in China were the various local rebels: Li Mi in the area around Ho-nan, Tou Chien-te in the northeast, Hsüeh Chü in the far northwest, and Li Yüan (who remained nominally loyal but had established a local position of great power) in Shansi. At the beginning of 617 Li Yüan inflicted a great defeat on the eastern Turks and thus consolidated his local power in the impregnable mountainous area around T'ai-yüan. In the summer of 617 he raised an army and marched on the capital with the aid of the Turks and other local forces. Ch'ang-an fell, after a five-week siege, at the end of 617. Hsüeh Chü's northwestern rebels were crushed, and the armies of Li Yüan occupied Szechwan and the Han River Valley. A Sui prince was enthroned as "emperor," while Yang Ti was given the title of "retired emperor." In the summer of 618, after Yang Ti's death, Li Yüan deposed his puppet prince and proclaimed himself emperor of a new dynasty, the T'ang.

Fall of the Sui dynasty

EARLY T'ANG (618–624)

When Li Yüan became emperor (reigned 618–626), he was still only one among the contenders for control of the empire of the Sui. It was several years before the empire was entirely pacified. After the suppression of Hsüeh Chü and the pacification of the northwest, the T'ang had to contend with three principal rival forces: the Sui remnants commanded by Wang Shih-ch'ung at Ho-nan (Loyang), the rebel Li Mi in Honan, the rebel Tou Chien-te in Hopeh, and Yü-wen Hua-chi, who had assassinated the previous Sui emperor Yang Ti and now led the remnants of the Sui's southern armies. Wang Shih-ch'ung set up a grandson of Yang Ti at Ho-nan as the new Sui emperor. Yü-wen Hua-chi led his armies to attack Ho-nan, and Wang Shih-ch'ung persuaded Li Mi to return to his allegiance with the Sui and help him fight Yü-wen Hua-chi. Li Mi defeated Yü-wen Hua-chi's armies but depleted his own forces seriously. Wang Shih-ch'ung, seeing the chance to dispose of his most immediate rival, took over Ho-nan and routed Li Mi's forces. Li Mi fled to Ching-chao (Ch'ang-an) and submitted to the T'ang. In the spring of 619 Wang Shih-ch'ung deposed the puppet Sui prince at Ho-nan and proclaimed himself emperor.

Li Yüan's struggle for control

The T'ang armies gradually forced him to give ground in Honan, and by 621 Li Yüan's son Li Shih-min was besieging him in Ho-nan. At this time Wang Shih-ch'ung attempted to form an alliance with the most powerful of all the Sui rebels, Tou Chien-te, who controlled much of Hopeh and who had completed the defeat of Yü-wen Hau-chi's forces in 619. He held the key area of southern Hopeh, where he had successfully resisted both the T'ang armies and the forces of Wang Shih-ch'ung and Li Mi. Tou now agreed to come to the aid of the beleaguered Wang Shih-ch'ung, but in the spring of 621 Li Shih-min attacked his army before it could lift the siege, routed it, and captured Tou. Wang Shih-ch'ung then capitulated. The T'ang had thus disposed of the two most powerful rivals in the empire and extended their control over most of the eastern plain, the most populous and prosperous region of China.

This was not the end of resistance to the T'ang conquest. Most of the surrendered rebel forces had been treated leniently, and their leaders were often confirmed in office or given posts in the T'ang administration. Tou Chien-te and Wang Shih-ch'ung, however, were dealt with severely, Tou being executed and Wang Shih-ch'ung murdered on his way to exile. At the end of 621 Tou Chien-te's partisans in the northeast again rebelled under Liu Hei-t'a, and recaptured most of the northeast. He was finally defeated by a T'ang army under the crown prince Chien-ch'eng at the beginning of 623. The prolonged resistance in Hopeh, and the comparatively harsh T'ang conquest of the region, was the beginning of resistance and hostility in the northeast that continued to some degree throughout the T'ang dynasty.

Resistance was not confined to the northeast. Liu Wu-chou in the far north of Shansi, who had been a constant threat since 619, was finally defeated and killed by his former Turkish allies in 622. In the south, during the confusion at the end of the Sui, Hsiao Hsien had set himself up as emperor of Liang, controlling the central Yangtze region that embraced Kiangsi, Kwangtung, and Annam. The T'ang army descended the Yangtze from Szechwan with a great fleet and defeated Hsiao Hsien's forces in two crucial naval battles. In 621 Hsiao Hsien surrendered to the T'ang, who thus gained control of the central Yangtze and the far south. The southeast was occupied by another rebel, Li Tzu-t'ung, based in Chekiang. He, too, was decisively defeated near Nanking at the end of 621. As had been the case with Hsiao Hsien's dominions, the southeast was incorporated into the T'ang empire with a minimum of fighting and resistance. A last southern rebellion by Fu Kung-shih, a general who set up an independent regime at Nanking in 624, was speedily suppressed. The empire was now completely pacified and unified under the T'ang house.

Administration of the state. The T'ang unification had been far more prolonged and bloody than the Sui conquest. That their regime lasted for nearly three centuries rather than three decades, as with the Sui, was largely the result of the system of government imposed on the conquered territories. The emperor Li Yüan's role in the T'ang conquest was understated in the traditional histories compiled under his successor Li Shih-min (reigned 627–649), which portrayed Shih-min as the prime mover in the establishment of the dynasty. Shih-min certainly played a major role in the campaigns, but Li Yüan was no figurehead. Not only did he direct the many complex military operations; he also established the basic institutions of the T'ang state, which proved practicable not only for a rapidly developing Chinese society but also for the first centralized states in societies as diverse as those of Japan, Korea, Vietnam, and the southwestern kingdom of Nan Chao.

The T'ang pattern of central control

The structure of the new administration resembled that of Yang Chien's time with its ministries, boards, courts, and directorates. Most of the highest ranks in the bureaucracy were filled by former Sui officials, many of whom had been the new emperor's colleagues when he was governor in T'ai-yüan, or by descendants of officials of the Northern Chou, Northern Ch'i or Sui, or of the royal houses of the northern and southern dynasties. There was no radical change in the dominant group at court. The T'ang were related by marriage with the Sui royal house,

and a majority of the chief ministers were related by marriage either to the T'ang or Sui Imperial families. The emperor's court was composed very largely of men of similar social origins. At this level the T'ang in its early years, like the Sui before it, continued the pattern of predominantly aristocratic rule that had dominated the history of the northern courts.

Li Yüan also continued the pattern of local administration established under the Sui, and maintained the strict control exercised by the central government over provincial appointments. In the first years after the T'ang conquest, many prefectures and counties were fragmented to provide offices for surrendered rebel leaders, surrendered Sui officials, and followers of the emperor. But these new local districts were gradually amalgamated and reduced in number, and by the 630s the pattern of local administration was very similar to that under the Sui. The merging of the local officials into the main body of the bureaucracy, however, took time; ambitious men still looked upon local posts as "exile" from the main current of official promotion at the capital. Until well into the 8th century, many local officials continued to serve for very long terms and the ideal of a regular circulation of officials prevailed only gradually.

Local government in early T'ang times had a considerable degree of independence, but each prefecture was in direct contact with the central ministries. In the spheres of activity that the administration regarded as crucial—registration, land allocation, tax collection, conscription of men for the army and for corvée duty, and the maintenance of law and order—prefects and county magistrates were expected to follow centrally codified law and procedure. They were, however, permitted to interpret the law to suit local conditions. Local influences remained very strong in the prefectures and counties. Most of the personnel in these divisions were local men, many of them members of hereditary families of petty functionaries.

Fiscal and legal system. Li Yüan inherited a bankrupt state, and most of his measures were aimed at simple and cheap administration. His bureaucracy was very small, both at the central and local levels. The expenses of government were largely met out of endowments of land attached to each office, the rents from which paid office-running expenses and salaries; by interest on funds of money allocated for similar purposes; and by services of taxpayers who performed many of the routine tasks of government as special duties, being exempted from tax in return.

Land distribution followed the equal allocation system used under the northern dynasties and the Sui. Every taxable male received a grant of land, part of which was returnable when he ceased to be a taxpayer at 60, part of which was hereditary. The disposal of landed property was hedged around with restrictive conditions. Great landed estates were limited to members of the Imperial clan and powerful officials, to various state institutions, and to the Buddhist foundations. Although some land was hereditary, and more and more passed into the hereditary category with the passage of time, the lack of primogeniture meant that land holdings were fragmented among all the sons in each generation, and thus tended to be small. It is unlikely that the system was ever enforced to the letter in any region, and it was probably never enforced at all in the South. But as a legal system governing registration of landed property and its disposal, it remained in force until An Lu-shan's rebellion in the 8th century.

Land distribution

The tax system based on this land allocation system was also much the same as that under the Sui and preceding dynasties. Every adult male paid a head tax in grain and cloth and was liable to 20 days of work for the central government (normally commuted into a payment in cloth) and to a further period of work for the local authorities. This tax system collected revenues exclusively from the rural population, and left out of account trade and the urban communities. It also bore more heavily upon the poor, since it ignored the economic status of the taxpayer.

Coinage

The Sui had made a somewhat desultory attempt to provide China with a unified coinage. Li Yüan set up mints and began the production of a good copper currency that remained standard throughout the T'ang era. But cash was in short supply during most of the 7th century and had to be supplemented by standard-sized lengths of silk. Counterfeiting was rife, particularly in the Yangtze Valley where the southern dynasties had supported a more highly monetized economy, and where the governments had to a considerable degree exploited commerce as a source of revenue.

Li Yüan also undertook a new codification of all centralized law, completed in 624. It comprised a code that embodied what were considered basic, unchanging normative rules, prescribing fixed penalties for defined offences; statutes, comprising the general body of universally applicable administrative law; regulations, or rules supplementary to the code and statutes; and ordinances, detailed procedural laws supplementing the statutes and issued by the departments of the central ministries. Under the early T'ang, this body of codified law was revised every 20 years or so. The systematic effort to maintain a universally applicable codification of law and administrative practice was essential to the uniform system of administration that the T'ang succeeded in imposing throughout their diverse empire. The T'ang code proved remarkably durable. It was still considered authoritative as late as the 14th century, and was used as a model by the Ming. It was also adopted with appropriate modifications in Japan in the early 8th century, and by the Koreans and the Vietnamese at a much later date.

Li Yüan (or Kao Tsu, his posthumous title) thus laid down, in the very first years of the 7th century, institutions that survived until the middle of the 8th century. These provided strong central control, a high level of administrative standardization, and very economical administration.

THE PERIOD OF T'ANG POWER (626–755)

Reign of T'ai Tsung

Two of Li Yüan's sons were rivals for the succession: the crown prince Chien-ch'eng and Li Shih-min, a brilliant general who had played a large part in the wars of unification. Their rivalry, and the factional strife it generated, reached a peak in 625–626 when it appeared that Chien-ch'eng was likely to succeed. In a military coup, Li Shih-min murdered Chien-ch'eng and another of his brothers, and forced his father to abdicate in his favour. He succeeded to the throne in 626 and is known by his posthumous title as T'ai Tsung, one of the most famous rulers in Chinese history (see T'ANG T'AI TSUNG).

The "era of good government." The reign of T'ai Tsung (627–649), known traditionally as the "era of good government of Chen-kuan," was not notable for innovations in administration. Generally, his policies developed and refined those of his father's reign. The distinctive element was the atmosphere of his administration and the close personal interplay between the sovereign and his unusually able team of Confucian advisers. It approached the Confucian ideal of a strong, able, energetic, yet fundamentally moral king seeking and accepting the advice of wise and capable ministers, advice that was basically ethical rather than technical.

His reign saw the beginnings of some important changes in political organization that were to continue throughout the 7th century. The court remained almost exclusively the domain of men of aristocratic birth. But T'ai Tsung attempted to balance the regional groups among the aristocracy so as to prevent the dominance of any single region. They comprised the Kuan-lung group from the northwest, the Tai-pei group from Shansi, the Shan-tung group from Hopeh, and the southern group from the Yangtze Valley. The most powerful Hopeh clans were excluded from high office and remained aloof, but T'ai Tsung employed members of each of the other groups and of the lesser northeastern aristocracy in the highest administrative offices as well as in his consultative group of scholars.

A second change was the use of the examination system on a large scale. The Sui examinations had already been

re-established under Kao Tsu, who had also revived the Sui system of high-level schools at the capital. Under T'ai Tsung the schools were further expanded and new ones established. Measures were taken to standardize their curriculum; an official orthodox edition of the Classics with a standard commentary was completed in 638. The schools at the capital were restricted to the sons of the great families and of high-ranking officials. Other examination candidates, however, came from the local schools. The examinations were in principle open to all, but they provided relatively few new entrants to the bureaucracy since most officials entered as sons of officials of the upper ranks. The examinations demanded a high level of education in the traditional curriculum and were largely used as an alternative method of entry by younger sons of the aristocracy and by members of lesser families with a scholar-official background. Moreover, personal recommendation, the lobbying of examiners, and often a personal interview by the emperor played a large part. The main effect of the examination system in T'ang times was to afford access to the upper levels of the bureaucracy for members of locally prominent clans, and in the long term to break the monopoly of political power held by the upper aristocracy. The employment of persons dependent for their position on the emperor and the dynasty, rather than upon birth and social standing, made it possible for the T'ang emperors to establish their own power and independence.

The examination system

In the early years there was a great debate as to whether the T'ang ought to reintroduce the feudal system used under the Chou and the Han, by which authority was delegated to members of the Imperial clan and powerful officials and generals who were enfeoffed with hereditary territorial jurisdictions. T'ai Tsung eventually settled on the strictly centralized form of government through prefectures and counties staffed by members of a unified bureaucracy. The T'ang retained a ⸰nobility, but their "fiefs of maintenance" were merely areas the revenues of which were earmarked for their use and gave them no territorial authority.

T'ai Tsung continued his father's economic policies. He attempted to cut down the bureaucratic establishment at the capital and drastically reduced the number of local government divisions. The country was divided into ten provinces, which were not permanent administrative units but "circuits" for occasional regional inspections of the local administrations; these tours were carried out by special commissioners, often members of the censorate, sent out from the capital. This gave the central government an additional means of ensuring the standardization and efficiency of local administration. Government remained comparatively simple and cheap. Measures to ensure tax relief for areas stricken by natural disasters, and the establishment of relief granaries to provide adequate reserves against famine, helped to ensure the prosperity of the countryside. T'ai Tsung's reign was a period of low prices and general prosperity.

T'ai Tsung was also successful in his foreign policy. In 630 the eastern Turks were split by dissension among their leadership and by the rebellion of their subject peoples, the Tölös and the Uighurs. Chinese forces invaded their territories, totally defeated them, and captured their khan. Many of the surrendered Turks were settled along the Chinese frontier, and many took service in the T'ang armies. A similar policy of encouraging internal dissension was also practiced against the western Turks, who split into two separate khanates for a while. In 642–3 a new khan re-established a degree of unified control with Chinese support and agreed to become a tributary of the Chinese. To seal the alliance, T'ai Tsung married him to a Chinese princess.

Foreign policy under T'ai Tsung

The eclipse of Turkish power enabled T'ai Tsung to extend his power over the various small states of the Tarim Basin. By the late 640s Chinese power, and a Chinese military administration, had extended westward even beyond the limits of modern Chinese Turkistan. To the north, the region of the Orhon and to the north of the Ordos, the T'ang armies defeated the Tölös, former vassals of the eastern Turks, and these also became T'ang vassals in 646. The T'u-yü-hun in the region around Koko Nor caused considerable trouble in the early 630s. T'ai Tsung invaded their territory in 634 and defeated them, but they remained unsubdued and invaded Chinese territory several times.

The Chinese western dominions now extended farther than in the great days of the Han. Trade developed with the West, with Central Asia, and with India. The Chinese court received embassies from Sāsānid Persia and from the Byzantine Empire. The capital was thronged with foreign merchants and foreign monks and contained a variety of non-Chinese communities. The great cities had their Zoroastrian, Mazdean, and Nestorian temples, along with the Buddhist monasteries that had been a part of the Chinese scene for centuries.

T'ai Tsung's only failure in foreign policy was in Korea. The northern state of Koguryŏ had sent tribute regularly, but in 642 there was an internal coup; the new ruler attacked Silla, another T'ang vassal state in southern Korea. T'ai Tsung decided to invade Koguryŏ, against the advice of most of his ministers. The T'ang armies, in alliance with the Khitan in Manchuria and the two south Korean states Paekche and Silla, invaded Koguryŏ in 645 but were forced to withdraw with heavy losses. Another inconclusive campaign was waged in 647, and the very end of T'ai Tsung's reign was spent in building a vast fleet and making costly preparations for a final expedition.

T'ai Tsung's last years also saw a decline in the firm grasp of the emperor over politics at his court. In the 640s a bitter struggle for the succession developed when it became clear that the designated heir was mentally unstable. The court split into factions supporting various candidates. The final choice, Li Chih, prince of Chin (reigned 649–683; posthumous title Kao Tsung) was a weak character, but he had the support of the most powerful figures at court.

Rise of the empress Wu. Kao Tsung was 21 when he ascended the throne. In his first years he was dominated by the remaining great statesmen of T'ai Tsung's court, above all by the Emperor's uncle Chang-sun Wu-chi. But real power soon passed from Kao Tsung into the hands of the empress Wu, one of the most remarkable women in Chinese history. Wu had been a low-ranking concubine of T'ai Tsung. She was taken into Kao Tsung's palace, and after a series of complex intrigues managed in 655 to have the legitimate empress Wang deposed and herself appointed in her place. The struggle between the two was not simply a palace intrigue. Empress Wang, who was of noble descent, had the backing of the old aristocratic faction and of the great ministers surviving from T'ai Tsung's court. Empress Wu came from an eastern family of considerably lower standing which had strong connections with the Sui, and seems to have been supported by the eastern aristocracy, by the lesser gentry, and by the lower-ranking echelons of the bureaucracy.

But her success was largely due to her skill in intrigue, her dominant personality, and her utter ruthlessness. The deposed Empress and another Imperial favourite were savagely murdered, and the next half century was marked by recurrent purges in which she hounded to death one group after another of real or imagined rivals. The good relationship between the Emperor and his court, which had made T'ai Tsung's reign so successful, was speedily destroyed. Political life became precarious and insecure, at the mercy of the Empress' unpredictable whims. The first victims were the elder statesmen of T'ai Tsung's reign, who were exiled, murdered, or driven to suicide in 657–9. In 660 Kao Tsung suffered a stroke and remained in precarious health for the rest of his reign. During his illness Empress Wu took charge of the administration.

Although utterly unscrupulous in politics, she backed up her intrigues with policies designed to consolidate her position. In 657 Lo-yang (Ho-nan-fu), the geographical centre of Wu's family, was made the second capital. The whole court was frequently transferred to Lo-yang, thus removing the centre of political power from the home region of the northwestern aristocracy. Ministries and

(margin) Skillful intrigue of the empress Wu

court offices were duplicated; Lo-yang had to be equipped with all the costly public buildings needed for a capital. Eventually, Empress Wu took up permanent residence in Lo-yang. She was obsessed by superstition, symbolism, and religion. One favourite magician, sorcerer, or monk followed another. For symbolic reasons the names of all offices were changed, and the emperor took the new title of "Heavenly Emperor."

The bureaucracy was rapidly inflated to a far greater size than in T'ai Tsung's time, many of the new posts being filled by candidates from the examination system who now began to attain the highest offices and thus to encroach on what had been the preserves of the aristocracy. Another blow at the aristocracy was struck by the compilation in 659 of a new genealogy of all the empire's eminent clans, which ranked families according to the official positions achieved by their members rather than by their traditional social standing. Needless to say, the first family of all was that of Wu. The lower ranks of the bureaucracy, among whom the Empress found her most solid support, were encouraged by the creation of new posts, by greater opportunities for advancement, and by salary increases.

The Chinese were engaged in foreign wars practically throughout Kao Tsung's reign. Until 657 they waged continual war against the Turks, finally defeating them and placing their territories as far as the valley of the Oxus under a Chinese protectorate in 659–661. Kao Tsung also waged repeated campaigns against Koguryŏ (Korea) in the late 650s and 660s. In 668 the T'ang forces took P'yŏngyang, the capital, and Koguryŏ was also placed under a protectorate. But in 676 the Chinese withdrew their forces to southern Manchuria, and Korea was increasingly dominated by the rapidly expanding power of the southern Korean state of Silla.

The eastern Turks, who had been settled along the northern border, rebelled in 679–81 and were quelled only after widespread destruction and heavy losses to the Chinese forces.

The most serious foreign threat in Kao Tsung's reign was the emergence of a new and powerful force to the west, the Tibetans (T'u-fan), a people who had exerted constant pressure on the northern border of Szechwan since the 630s. By 670 the Tibetans had driven the T'u-yü-hun from their homeland in the Koko Nor Basin. The northwest had to be increasingly heavily fortified and garrisoned to guard against their repeated raids and incursions. After a series of difficult campaigns, they were finally checked in 679.

When Kao Tsung died in 683 he was succeeded by the young Chung Tsung, but Empress Wu was made empress dowager and immediately took control over the central administration. Within less than a year she had deposed Chung Tsung, who had shown unexpected signs of independence, and replaced him by another puppet emperor, Jui Tsung, who was kept secluded in the Inner Palace while Empress Wu held court and exercised the duties of sovereign.

In 684 disaffected members of the ruling class under Li Ching-yeh raised a serious rebellion at Yang (Yang-chou) in the south, but this was speedily put down. The Empress instituted a reign of terror among the members of the T'ang royal family and the officials, employing armies of agents and informers. Fear overshadowed the life of the court. Wu herself became more and more obsessed with religious symbolism, erecting in 688 a Ming T'ang (Hall of Light)—the symbolic supreme shrine to Heaven described in the Classics—a vast building put up with limitless extravagance. In 690 the Empress proclaimed that the dynasty had been changed from T'ang to Chou. She became formally the empress in her own right, the only woman sovereign in China's history. Jui Tsung, the Imperial heir, was given the surname Wu; everybody with the surname Wu in the empire was exempted from taxation. Every prefecture was ordered to set up a temple in which the monks were to expound the notion that the Empress was an incarnation of Buddha. Lo-yang became the "Holy Capital," and the state cult was ceremoniously transferred there from Ching-chao (Ch'ang-an). The

(margin) Empress Wu enthroned

remnants of the T'ang royal family who had not been murdered or banished were immured in the depths of the palace.

Destructive and demoralizing as the effects of her policies must have been at the capital and at court, there is little evidence of any general deterioration of administration in the empire. By 690 the worst excesses of her regime were past. In the years after she proclaimed herself empress she retained the services and loyalty of a number of distinguished officials. She remained, however, susceptible to the influence of a series of worthless favourites and after 700 gradually began to lose her grip on affairs.

The external affairs of the empire had meanwhile taken a turn for the worse. The Tibetans renewed their warfare on the frontier. In 696 the Khitan in Manchuria rebelled against their Chinese governor and overran part of Hopeh. The Chinese drove them out, with Turkish aid, in 697. The Chinese reoccupied Hopeh under a member of the Empress' family and carried out brutal reprisals against the population. In 698 the Turks in their turn invaded Hopeh, and were only driven off by an army under Chung Tsung, who had now been renamed heir apparent in place of Jui Tsung.

New taxes

The expenses of the empire began to call for new taxes. These took the form of a household levy—a graduated tax based on a property assessment upon everyone from the nobility down, including the urban population—and a land levy collected on an acreage basis. These new taxes were to be assessed on the basis of productivity or wealth, rather than on a uniform per capita basis. Some tried to evade taxes by illegally subdividing their households to reduce their liabilities. There was a large-scale migration of peasant families fleeing from oppression and heavy taxation in the Hopeh and Shantung area. This migration of peasants, who settled as unregistered squatters on vacant land in central and southern China and no longer paid taxes, was accelerated by the Khitan invasion in the late 690s. Attempts to stop it were ineffectual.

By 705 the Empress, who was now 80, had allowed control of events to slip from her fingers. The bureaucratic faction at court, tired of the excesses of her latest favourites, forced her to abdicate in favour of Chung Tsung. The T'ang were restored.

Chung Tsung, however, had a domineering wife, the empress Wei. When he died in 710, probably poisoned by her, she tried to establish herself as ruler as the empress Wu had done before her. But the future Hsüan Tsung, with the aid of Empress Wu's formidable daughter, the princess T'ai-p'ing, and of the palace army, succeeded in restoring his father, Jui Tsung (the brother of Chung Tsung), to the throne. The Princess now attempted to dominate her brother the emperor, and there followed a struggle for power between her and the heir apparent. In 712 Jui Tsung ceded the throne to Hsüan Tsung but retained in his own hands control over the most crucial areas of government. A second coup, in 713, placed Hsüan Tsung completely in charge and resulted in Jui Tsung's actual retirement and in the princess T'ai-p'ing's suicide.

Reign of Hsüan Tsung

Prosperity and progress. Hsüan Tsung's reign (712–756) was the high point of the T'ang dynasty (see T'ANG HSUAN TSUNG). It was an era of wealth and prosperity that saw institutional progress along with a flowering of the arts. Political life was at first dominated by the bureaucrats recruited through the examination system who had staffed the central government under Empress Wu. But a gradual revival of the power of the great aristocratic clans tended to polarize politics, a polarization that was sharpened by the Emperor's employment of a series of aristocratic specialists who reformed the empire's finances from 720 onward, often in the teeth of bureaucratic opposition.

After 720 a large-scale re-registration of the population produced a greatly increased number of taxpayers and restored state control over vast numbers of unregistered families. The new household and land taxes were expanded. In the 730s the canal system, which had been allowed to fall into neglect under Empress Wu and her suc-

cessors, was repaired and reorganized so that the administration could transport large stocks of grain from the Yangtze region to the capital and to the armies on the northern frontiers. The South was at last financially integrated with the North. By the 740s the government had accumulated enormous reserves of grain and wealth. The tax and accounting systems were simplified, taxes and labour services reduced. A serious attempt was at last made to deal with the deficiencies of the coinage.

Some important institutional changes accompanied these reforms. The land registration, reorganization of transport, and coinage reform were administered by specially appointed commissions holding extraordinary powers. These commissions were mostly headed by censors, and they and the censorate became centres of aristocratic power. The existence of these new offices reduced the influence of the regular ministries, enabling the emperor and his aristocratic advisers to circumvent the normal channels and procedures of administration.

Dominance of the aristocracy

After 736 the political dominance of the aristocratic element was firmly re-established. An aristocratic chief minister, Li Lin-fu, became a virtual dictator, his powers increasing as Hsüan Tsung in his later years withdrew from active affairs into the pleasures of life in the palace and the study of Taoism. In the latter part of his reign Hsüan Tsung, who had previously strictly circumscribed the power of the palace women to avoid a recurrence of the disasters of Empress Wu's time and had also excluded members of the royal family from active politics, faced a series of succession plots. In 748 he fell deeply under the influence of a new favourite, the Imperial concubine Yang Kuei-fei. In 751–752 one of her relatives, Yang Kuo-chung, thanks to the Emperor's personal favour, rapidly rose to rival Li Lin-fu for supreme power. After Li's death in 752 Yang Kuo-chung dominated the court. He had not, however, Li's ability or his experience and skill in handling people.

Military reorganization. The most important new development in Hsüan Tsung's reign was the growth in the power of the military commanders. During Kao Tsung's reign the old militia system had proved inadequate for frontier defense and had been supplemented by the institution of permanent armies and garrison forces quartered in strategic areas on the frontiers. These armies were made up of long-service veterans, many of them non-Chinese cavalry troops, settled permanently in military colonies. Although these armies were adequate for small-scale operations, for a large-scale campaign an expeditionary army and a headquarters staff had to be specially organized and reinforcements sent in by the central government. This cumbersome system was totally unsuitable for dealing with the highly mobile nomad horsemen on the northern frontiers.

Hostility of the Turks and Tibetans

At the beginning of Hsüan Tsung's reign the Turks threatened to become again a major power, rivalling China in Central Asia and along the borders. Mo-ch'o, the Turkish khan who had invaded Hopeh in the aftermath of the Khitan invasion in the time of Empress Wu and had attacked the Chinese northwest at the end of her reign, turned his attention northward. By 711 he controlled the steppe from the Chinese frontier to Transoxiana, and appeared likely to develop a new unified Turkish empire. When, in 716, he was murdered, his flimsy empire collapsed. His successor, Bilge kaghan, tried to make peace with the Chinese in 718, but Hsüan Tsung preferred to try to destroy his power by an alliance with the southwestern Basmil Turks and with the Khitan in Manchuria. Bilge, however, crushed the Basmil and attacked Kansu in 720. Peaceful relations were established in 721–722. Bilge's death in 736 precipitated the end of Turkish power. A struggle among the various Turkish subject tribes followed, from which the Uighur emerged as victors. In 744 they established a powerful empire that was to remain the dominant force on China's northern border until 840. Unlike the Turks, however, the Uighur pursued a consistent policy of alliance with the T'ang. On several occasions Uighur aid, even though offered on harsh terms, saved the dynasty from disaster.

The Tibetans also were hostile in the early part of Hsüan Tsung's reign, invading the northwest year after year from 714 on. In 727–729 the Chinese undertook large-scale warfare against them, and in 730 a settlement was concluded. But in the 730s fighting broke out again, and the Tibetans began to turn their attention to the T'ang western territories in the Tarim. Desultory fighting continued on the border of Kansu until the end of Hsüan Tsung's reign. From 752 onward the Tibetans acquired a new ally in the Nan Chao state in Yunnan, which enabled them to exert a continuous threat along the entire western frontier.

The
frontier
com-
manders

In the face of these threats, Hsüan Tsung organized the northern and northwestern frontiers from Manchuria to Szechwan into a series of strategic commands or military provinces under military governors who were given command over all the forces in a large region. This system developed gradually and was formalized in 737 under Li Lin-fu. The frontier commanders controlled enormous numbers of troops: nearly 200,000 were stationed in the northwest and Central Asia and over 100,-000 in the northeast; there were well over 500,000 in all. The military governors soon began to exercise some functions of civil government. In the 740s a non-Chinese general of Sogdian and Turkish origin, An Lu-shan, became military governor first of one and finally of all three of the northeastern commands, with 160,000 troops under his orders. An Lu-shan had risen to power largely through the patronage of Li Lin-fu. When Li died, An became a rival of Yang Kuo-chung. As Yang Kuo-chung developed more and more of a personal stranglehold over the administration at the capital, An Lu-shan steadily built up his military forces in the northeast. The armed confrontation that followed (see below) nearly destroyed the dynasty.

The 750s had seen a steady reversal of T'ang military fortunes. In the far west the overextended Imperial armies had been defeated by the Arabs in 751 on the Talas. In the southwest a campaign against the new state of Nan Chao in Yunnan had led to the almost total destruction of an army of 50,000 men. In the northeast the Chinese had lost their grip on the Manchuria–Korea border with the emergence of the new state of Parhae in place of Koguryŏ, and the Khitan and Hsi peoples in Manchuria constantly caused border problems. The Tibetans in the northwest were kept in check only by an enormously expensive military presence. The principal military forces were designed essentially for frontier defense.

Thus the end of Hsüan Tsung's reign found the state in a highly unstable condition, with central government dangerously dependent on a small group of men operating outside the regular institutional framework, and with an overwhelming preponderance of military power in the hands of potentially rebellious commanders on the frontiers, against whom the Emperor could put into the field only a token force of his own and the troops of those commanders who remained loyal.

THE LATE T'ANG (755–907)

The An
Lu-shan
Rebellion

The rebellion of An Lu-shan in 755 marked the beginning of a new period. At first the rebellion had spectacular success. It swept through the northeastern province of Hopeh, captured the eastern capital at Ho-nan (Lo-yang) early in 756, and took the main T'ang capital, Ch'ang-an, in July of the same year. The Emperor fled to Szechwan, and on the road his consort Yang Kuei-fei and other members of the Yang faction who had dominated his court were killed. Shortly afterward, the heir apparent, who had retreated to Ling-wu in the northwest, himself usurped the throne. The new emperor, Su Tsung (reigned 756–762), was faced with a desperately difficult military situation. The rebel armies controlled the capital and most of Hopeh and Honan. In the last days of his reign Hsüan Tsung had divided the empire into five areas, each of which was to be the fief of one of the Imperial princes. Prince Yung, who was given control of the southeast, was the only one to take up his command; during 757 he attempted to set himself up as the independent ruler of the crucially important economic heart of the empire in the

Huai and Yangtze valleys but was murdered by one of his generals.

An Lu-shan himself was murdered by a subordinate early in 757, but the rebellion was continued, first by his son and then by one of his son's generals, Shih Ssu-ming, and his son Shih Ch'ao-i. Not until 763 was it finally suppressed. The rebellion had caused great destruction and hardship, particularly in Honan. The final victory was made possible partly by the employment of Uighur mercenaries, whose insatiable demands remained a drain on the treasury well into the 770s; partly by the failure of the rebel leadership after the death of Shih Ssu-ming; partly by the policy of clemency adopted toward the rebels after the decisive campaign in Honan in 762. The need for a speedy settlement was urged by the growing threat of the Tibetans in the northwest. The latter, allied with the Nan Chao kingdom in Yunnan, had exerted continual pressure on the western frontier and in 763 occupied the whole of modern Kansu. Late in 763 they actually took and looted the capital. They continued to occupy the Chinese northwest until well into the 9th century.

Provincial separatism. The postrebellion settlement not only pardoned several of the most powerful rebel generals but also appointed them as Imperial governors in command of the areas they had surrendered. Hopeh was divided into four new provinces, each under surrendered rebels, while Shantung became the province of An Lu-shan's former garrison army from P'ing-lu in southern Manchuria, which had held an ambivalent position during the fighting. Within these provinces the central government held very little power. The leadership was decided within each province, and the central government in its appointments merely approved *faits accompli*. Succession to the leadership was frequently hereditary. Three of the ruling families were of non-Chinese origin. For all practical purposes, the northeastern provinces remained semi-independent throughout the later part of the T'ang era. They had been among the most populous and productive parts of the empire, and their semi-independence was not only a threat to the stability of the central government but also represented a great loss of revenue and potential manpower.

Breakdown
of the
central
machinery

Provincial separatism also became a problem elsewhere. With the general breakdown of the machinery of central administration after 756, many of the functions of government were delegated to local administrations. The whole empire was now divided into provinces for routine administration, the governors of which had wide powers over their subordinate prefectures and counties. The new provincial governments were of two main types. In northern China (apart from the semi-autonomous provinces of the northeast, which were a special category) most provincial governments were military, their institutions closely modelled on those set up on the northern frontier under Hsüan Tsung. The military presence was strongest in the small frontier-garrison provinces that protected the capital Ch'ang-an from the Tibetans in Kansu and in the belt of small heavily garrisoned provinces in Honan that protected China—and the canal from the Huai and Yangtze valleys, on which the central government depended for its supplies—from the semi-autonomous provinces. Military governments were also the rule in Szechwan, which continued to be menaced by the Tibetans and the Nan Chao, and in the far south in Ling-nan. In central and southern China, however, the provincial government developed into a new organ of the regular civil bureaucracy. The civil governors of the southern provinces were regularly appointed from the bureaucracy, and in time it became customary to appoint to these posts high-ranking court officials who were temporarily out of favour.

All the new provinces had considerable latitude of action, particularly during the reigns of Su Tsung and Tai Tsung, when central power was at a low ebb. There was a general decentralization of authority. The new provinces had considerable independence in the fields of finance, local government, law and order, and military matters.

Under Tai Tsung (reigned 762–779) the court was dominated by the emperor's favourite, Yüan Tsai, and by the

Reign of
Tai Tsung

eunuchs who now began to play an increasing role in T'ang politics. A succession of eunuch advisers not only rivalled in influence the chief ministers, but even exerted influence over the military in the campaigns of the late 750s and early 760s. Under Tai Tsung the decay of the regular offices of the administration and the irregularities encouraged by Yüan Tsai and his clique, in the appointment of officials, led to an increasing use of eunuchs in secretarial posts and to their increasing dominance over the Emperor's private treasury.

The central government did achieve some success in finance. The old fiscal system with its taxes and labour services had been completely disrupted by the breakdown of authority and by the vast movements of population. The revenues became more and more dependent upon additional taxes levied on cultivated land or on property. Increasingly the government attempted to raise revenue from the urban population. But its survival depended upon the revenues it drew from central China, from the Huai Valley, and from the lower Yangtze. These revenues were sent to the capital by means of a reconstructed and improved canal system maintained out of the new government monopoly on salt. By 780 the salt monopoly was producing a major part of the state's central revenues, in addition to maintaining the transportation system. The salt and transportation administration was controlled by an independent commission centred in Yang-chou near the mouth of the Yangtze, and this commission gradually took over the entire financial administration of southern and central China.

Taxes and rebellion
The weak Tai Tsung was succeeded by a tough, intelligent, activist emperor, Te Tsung (reigned 780–805), who was determined to restore the fortunes of the dynasty. He reconstituted much of the old central administration and decided on a showdown with the forces of local autonomy. As a first step he promulgated a new system of taxation under which each province was assessed a quota of taxes, the collection of which was to be left to the provincial government. This was a radical measure, for it abandoned the traditional concept of head taxes levied at a uniform rate throughout the empire and also began the assessment of taxes in terms of money.

The semi-independent provinces of the northeast saw this as a threat to their independence, and, when it became apparent that Te Tsung was determined to carry out consistently tough policies toward the northeast, even denying them the right to appoint their own governors, the Hopeh provinces rose. From 781 to 786 there was a wave of rebellions not only in the northeastern provinces but also in the Huai Valley and in the area of the capital itself. These brought the T'ang even closer to disaster than had the An Lu-shan rising. The situation was saved because at a crucial moment the rebels fell out among themselves and because the south remained loyal. In the end, the settlement negotiated with the governors of Hopeh virtually endorsed the preceding status quo, although the court made some marginal inroads with the establishment of two small new provinces in Hopeh.

After this disaster, Te Tsung pursued a very careful and passive policy toward the provinces. Governors were left in office for long periods, and hereditary succession continued. But the latter part of Te Tsung's reign was a period of steady achievement. The new tax system was gradually enforced and proved remarkably successful; it remained the basis of the tax structure until Ming times. Revenues increased steadily, and Te Tsung left behind him a wealthy state with great reserves. Militarily, he was also generally successful. The Tibetan threat was contained. Nan Chao was won from its alliance with the Tibetans. The garrisons of the northwest were strengthened. At the same time, Te Tsung built up a powerful new palace army, giving the central government a powerful striking force—numbering 100,000 men by the end of his reign. Command was given to the eunuchs.

The death of Te Tsung in 805 was followed by the very brief reign of Shun Tsung, an invalid monarch whose court was dominated by the clique of Wang Shu-wen and Wang P'ei. They planned to take over control of the palace armies from the eunuchs but failed.

The struggle for central authority. Under Hsien Tsung (reigned 806–820) the T'ang regained a great deal of its power. Hsien Tsung, a tough and ruthless ruler who kept a firm hand on affairs, is chiefly notable for his successful policies toward the provinces. Rebellions in Szechwan (806) and the Yangtze Delta (807) were quickly put down. After an abortive campaign (809–810) that was badly bungled by a favourite eunuch commander, the court was again forced to compromise with the governors of Hopeh. A fresh wave of trouble came in 814–817 with a rebellion in Huai-hsi, in the upper Huai Valley, that threatened the canal route. This uprising was crushed and the province divided up among its neighbours. The P'ing-lu army in Shantung rebelled in 818 and suffered the same fate. Hsien Tsung thus restored the authority of the central government throughout most of the empire. His success was based largely upon the palace armies. The fact that these were controlled by eunuchs placed a great measure of power in the emperor's hands. Under his weak successors, however, eunuch influence in politics proved a disaster. **Reign of Hsien Tsung**

Hsien Tsung's restoration of central authority involved more than military dominance. It was backed by a series of institutional measures designed to strengthen the power of the prefects and county magistrates as against their provincial governors, by restoring to them the right of direct access to central government and giving them some measure of control over the military forces quartered within their jurisdiction. An important financial reform was also carried out: the provincial government no longer had first call on all the revenue of the province, some of the revenue going directly to the capital. The government also began the policy, continued throughout the 9th and 10th centuries, of cutting down and fragmenting the provinces. It strengthened its control over the provincial administrations through a system of eunuch army supervisors, who were attached to the staff of each provincial governor. These eunuchs played an increasingly important role, not merely as sources of information and intelligence but as active agents of the emperor, able to intervene directly in local affairs.

The balance of power within the central government had, however, been considerably changed. The emperor Te Tsung had begun to delegate a great deal of business, in particular the drafting of edicts and legislation, to his personal secretariat, the Hanlin Academy. Although the members of the Hanlin Academy were handpicked members of the bureaucracy, this eventually placed the power of decision and the detailed formulation of policy in the hands of a group dependent entirely upon the emperor, thus threatening the authority of the regularly constituted ministers of the court. The influence of the eunuchs also began to be formalized and institutionalized in the palace council; this provided the emperor with another personal secretariat, which had close links with the eunuch command of the palace armies.

The eunuch influence in politics increased. Hsien Tsung was murdered by some of his eunuch attendants, and henceforth the chief eunuchs of the palace council and the palace armies intervened in nearly every succession to the throne; in some cases they had candidates enthroned in defiance of the previous emperor's will. But the apogee of eunuch power was brief, ending with the accession of Wu Tsung in 840. He and his successors continued to rely upon the eunuchs but seem to have been comparatively little influenced by them. The emperor Wen Tsung (reigned 827–840) sought to destroy the dominance of the eunuchs; his abortive schemes only demoralized the bureaucracy, particularly after the "Sweet Dew" coup of 835, which misfired and led to the deaths of several ministers and a number of other officials. **The eunuchs**

The reign of Wu Tsung (840–847) saw another major rebellion, this time in southern Shansi, and a financial crisis. Wu Tsung, a committed Taoist, attempted to raise revenues by suppressing Buddhism. All but a select few of the monastic foundations were closed, their lands and property confiscated and sold off, their slaves manumitted, and their clergy laicized. Although these measures were rescinded immediately after Wu Tsung's death, when many monasteries were restored, Chinese Buddhism had been dealt a deadly blow, from which it never fully recovered.

Growing chaos in the late 9th century

In the second half of the 9th century the central government became progressively weaker. In I Tsung's reign (859–873) the first signs of discontent and rebellion appeared in the Yangtze Valley and the south. The situation was complicated by a costly war against the Nan Chao kingdom on the borders of the Chinese protectorate in Annam, which later spread to Szechwan and dragged on from 858 until 866. After the suppression of the invaders, part of the garrison force that had been sent to Ling-nan mutinied and, under its leader Pang Hsün, fought and plundered its way back to Honan, where it caused widespread havoc in 868 and 869, cutting the canal linking the capital to the loyal Yangtze and Huai provinces. In 870 war broke out again with Nan Chao. I Tsung was succeeded by Hsi Tsung, a boy of 11 who was the choice of the palace eunuchs. He reigned from 873 to 888.

Honan had several times suffered serious floods. In 874, following a terrible drought, a wave of peasant risings began. The most formidable of them was led by Huang Ch'ao, who marched south and sacked Canton and then marched to the north where he took Lo-yang in late 880 and Ch'ang-an in 881. Although Huang Ch'ao's forces were eventually driven off with the aid of Sha-t'o Turks, the T'ang court was now virtually powerless and its emperor a puppet manipulated by rival military leaders. The dynasty lingered on until 907, but the last quarter century was dominated by the generals and provincial warlords. With the progressive decline of the central government in the 880s and 890s, China fell apart into a number of independent kingdoms. Unity was not restored until after the establishment of the Sung dynasty in 960.

THE INFLUENCE OF BUDDHISM

The T'ang emperors officially supported Taoism because of their claim to be descended from Lao-tzu, but Buddhism continued to enjoy great favour through most of the period, especially under Empress Wu. The famous pilgrim Hsüan-tsang, who went to India in 629 and returned in 645, was the most learned of Chinese monks and introduced new standards of exactness in his many translations from Sanskrit. The most significant development in this time was the growth of new indigenous schools that adapted Buddhism to Chinese ways of thinking. Most prominent were the syncretistic T'ien-t'ai school, which sought to embrace all other schools in a single hierarchical system (even reaching out to include Confucianism), and the radically antitextual, antimetaphysical southern Ch'an (Zen) school, which had strong roots in Taoism. The popular preaching of the salvationist Pure Land sect was also important. After the rebellion of An Lu-shan, a nationalistic movement favouring Confucianism appeared, merging with the efforts of T'ien-t'ai Buddhism to graft Buddhist metaphysics on to Classical doctrine and lay the groundwork for the Neo-Confucianism of the Sung era.

In 843–845 Wu Tsung, a fanatical Taoist, decided to suppress Buddhism. One of his motives was economic. China was in a serious financial crisis, which Wu Tsung and his advisers hoped to solve by seizing the lands and wealth of the monasteries. The suppression was far-reaching: 40,000 shrines and temples were closed; 260,-000 monks and nuns were returned to lay life; vast acreages of monastic lands were confiscated and sold off. The suppression was short-lived, but irreparable damage was done to Buddhist institutions. Buddhism had already begun to lose intellectual momentum, and this attack upon it as a social institution marked the beginning of its decline in China.

The monastic communities

There were several types of monastic community. Official temples set up by the state had large endowments of land and property and large communities of monks who chose their own abbot and other officers. There were vast numbers of small village temples, shrines, and hermitages; these were often privately established, had little property, and were quite vulnerable to state policies. There were also private temples or "merit cloisters" established by great families, often in order that the family might donate their property and have it declared tax-exempt.

The monastic community was free of all obligations to the state. It was able to hold property without the process of division by inheritance that made the long-term preservation of individual and family fortunes almost impossible in T'ang times. It acquired its wealth from those taking monastic vows, from gifts of pious laymen, and from grants of lands by the state. The lands were worked by monastic slaves, by dependent families, by lay clerics who had taken partial vows but lived with their families, or by tenants. Monasteries also operated oil presses and mills. They were important credit institutions supplying loans at interest and acting as pawnshops. They provided lodgings for travellers, operated hospitals and infirmaries, and maintained the aged.

Perhaps their most important social function was primary education. The temples maintained their own schools, training the comparatively large proportion of the population who, although not educated to the standards of the Confucian elite or of the clergy, were nevertheless literate.

TRENDS IN THE ARTS

In literature the greatest glory of the T'ang period was its poetry. By the 8th century, poets had broken away from the artificial diction and matter of the court poetry of the southern dynasties and achieved a new directness and naturalism. The reign of Hsüan Tsung (712–756)—known as Ming Huang, the Brilliant Emperor—was the time of the great figures of Li Po, Wang Wei, and Tu Fu. The rebellion of An Lu-shan and his own bitter experiences in it brought a new note of social awareness into the later poetry of Tu Fu. This appears again in the work of Po Chü-i (772–846), who wrote verse in clear and simple language. Toward the end of the dynasty a new poetic form, the *tz'u,* in a less regular metre than the five-word and seven-word *shih* and meant to be sung, made its appearance. The *ku-wen,* or "ancient style," movement grew up after the rebellion of An Lu-shan, seeking to replace the euphuistic "parallel prose" then dominant. It was closely associated with the movement for a Confucian revival. The most prominent figures in it were Han Yü and Liu Tsung-yüan. At the same time came the first serious attempts to write fiction, the so-called *ch'uan-ch'i,* or "tales of marvels." Many of these T'ang stories later provided themes for the Chinese drama (for further development, see also CHINESE LITERATURE).

T'ang poet

The patronage of the T'ang emperors and the general wealth and prosperity of the period encouraged the development of the visual arts. Though few T'ang buildings remain standing, contemporary descriptions give some idea of the magnificence of T'ang palaces and religious edifices and the houses of the wealthy. Buddhist sculpture shows a greater naturalism than in the previous period, but there is some loss of spirituality. Few genuine originals survive to show the work of T'ang master painters such as Wu Tao-hsüan, who worked at Ming Huang's court. As a landscape painter the poet Wang Wei was a forerunner of the *wen-jen,* or "literary man's," school of mystical nature painting of later times. The minor arts of T'ang, including ceramics, metalwork, and textiles, give expression to the colour and vitality of the life of the period (see also VISUAL ARTS, EAST ASIAN). Printing appeared for the first time during T'ang. Apparently invented to multiply Buddhist scriptures, it was used by the end of the dynasty for such things as calendars, almanacs, and dictionaries.

Visual arts

SOCIAL CHANGE

Decline of the aristocracy. The late T'ang period saw the beginnings of social changes that did not reach their culmination until the 11th century. The most important of these was the change in the nature of the ruling class. Although in the early T'ang era the examination system had facilitated the recruitment into the bureaucracy of persons from lesser aristocratic families, the great majority of the bureaucracy had continued to come from the established elite. Social mobility increased after the An Lu-shan Rebellion, with the emergence of the provincial governments, which recruited their staffs in many cases from soldiers of very lowly social origins, and with the establishment of the specialized finance commissions, which also recruited a large part of their personnel by irregular appointment, often from the commercial community. The contending factions of the 9th-century court also employed irregular appointments to secure posts for their clients and supporters, many of whom came from comparatively lowly backgrounds.

Although the old aristocracy retained a grip on political power until very late in the dynasty, its exclusiveness and hierarchical pretensions were rapidly breaking down. They were finally extinguished in the Five Dynasties period (907–960), when the old strongholds of aristocracy in the northeast and northwest became centres of bitter military and political struggles. The aristocracy that survived did so by merging into the new official-literati class; this class was based not on birth but on education, office holding, and the possession of landed property.

At the same time there was a return to servile relationships at the base of the social pyramid. Sheer economic necessity led many peasants either to dispose of their lands and become tenants or hired labourers of rich neighbours or to become semiservile dependents of a powerful patron. Tenancy, which in early T'ang times had most often been a temporary and purely economic agreement, now developed into a semipermanent contract requiring some degree of personal subordination from the tenant.

Population movements. Censuses taken during the Sui and T'ang dynasties provide some evidence as to population changes. Surviving figures for 609 and for 742 represent two of the most complete of the earlier Chinese registrations of population. They give totals of around 9,000,000 households, or slightly more than 50,000,000 persons. Contemporary officials considered that only about 70 percent of the population was actually registered, so that the total population may have been about 70,000,000 persons.

Between 609 and 742 a considerable redistribution of population took place. The population of Hopeh and Honan fell by almost a third because of the great destruction suffered at the end of the Sui era and in the invasions of the 690s. The population of Ho-tung (modern Shansi) and of Kuan-chung and Lung-yu (modern Shensi and Kansu) also fell, though not so dramatically. The population of the south, particularly the southeastern region around the lower Yangtze, took a leap upward, as did that of Szechwan.

Whereas under the Sui the population of the Great Plain (Hopeh and Honan) had accounted for more than half of the empire's total, by 742 this had dropped to 37 percent. The Huai–Yangtze area, which had contained only about 8 percent of the total in 609, now contained a quarter of the entire population, and Szechwan's share jumped from 4 percent to 10 percent of the total, exceeding the population of the metropolitan province of Kuan-chung. The increase in the south was almost entirely concentrated in the lower Yangtze Valley and Delta and in Chekiang. The far south, the coastal provinces, and the valleys of Hunan and Kiangsi remained sparsely peopled.

Although there are no reliable population figures from the late T'ang era, the general movement of population toward the south certainly continued; there were considerable increases in the population of the area south of the Yangtze, in modern Kiangsi and Hunan, and in Hupeh. The chaos of the last decades of the T'ang dynasty completed the ruin of the northwest. After the destruction of the city of Ch'ang-an in the Huang Ch'ao rebellion, no regime ever again established its capital in that region.

The new provincial officials and local elites were able to establish their fortunes as local landowning gentry largely because after 763 the government ceased to enforce the system of state-supervised land allocation. In the aftermath of the An Lu-shan and later rebellions, large areas of land were abandoned by their cultivators;

other great areas of farmland were sold off on the dissolution of the monastic foundations in 843–846. The great landed estate managed by a bailiff and cultivated by tenants, hired hands, or slaves became a widespread feature of rural life. Possession of such estates, previously limited to the established families of the aristocracy and the serving officials, now became common at less exalted levels.

Growth of the economy. The 8th and 9th centuries were a period of growth and prosperity. The gradual movement of the population away from the North, with its harsh climate and dry farming, into the more fertile and productive South meant a great overall increase in productivity. The South still had large areas of virgin land. Fukien, for example, was still only marginally settled along the coastline at the end of T'ang times. During the latter half of the T'ang, the Huai and lower Yangtze became a grain-surplus area, replacing Hopeh and Honan. In the period from 763 to the mid-9th century, great quantities of grain were shipped from the South annually as tax revenue. New crops, such as sugar and tea, were grown widely. The productivity of the Yangtze Valley was increased by double-cropping land with rice and winter wheat and by the development of new varieties of grain. Whereas in early T'ang times the chief silk producing areas had been in the northeast, after the An Lu-shan Rebellion silk production began to increase rapidly in Szechwan and the Yangtze Delta region.

A boom in trade soon followed. The merchant class threw off its traditional shackles. In early T'ang times there had been only two great metropolitan markets, in Ch'ang-an and Lo-yang. Now every provincial capital became the centre of a large consumer population of officials and military, and the provincial courts provided a market for both staple foodstuffs and luxury manufactures. The diversification of markets was still more striking in the countryside. A network of small rural market towns, purely economic in function and acting as feeders to the county markets, grew up. At these periodic markets, held at regular intervals every few days, travelling merchants and peddlers dealt in the everyday needs of the rural population. By the end of the T'ang period these rural market centres had begun to form a new sort of urban centre, intermediate between the county town, with its administrative presence and its central market, and the villages.

The growth of trade brought an increasing use of money. In early T'ang times silk cloth had been commonly employed as money in large transactions. When the central government lost control of the major silk-producing region in Hopeh, silk was replaced in this use by silver. The government neither controlled silver production nor minted a silver coinage. Silver circulation and assay were in the hands of private individuals. Various credit and banking institutions began to emerge: silversmiths took money on deposit and arranged for transfers of funds; a complex system of credit transfers arose by which tea merchants would pay the tax quota for a district, sometimes even for a whole province, out of their profits from the sale of the crop at Ch'ang-an and receive reimbursement in their home province.

The increasing use of money and of silver also affected official finance and accounting. Taxes began to be assessed in money. The salt monopoly was collected and accounted for entirely in money. The government also began to look to trade as a source of revenue—to depend increasingly on taxes on commercial transactions, levies on merchants, transit taxes on merchandise, and sales taxes.

The most prosperous of the merchants were the great dealers in salt, the tea merchants from Kiangsi, the bankers of the great cities and particularly of Ch'ang-an, and the merchants engaged in overseas trade in the coastal ports of Yang-chou and Canton. Foreign trade was still dominated by non-Chinese merchants. Canton had a large Arab trading community. The northern coastal traffic was dominated by the Koreans. Overland trade to Central Asia was mostly in the hands of Sogdian and later of Uighur merchants. Central Asian, Sogdian, and

The southward migration

Expansion of the grain crop

The merchants

Persian merchants and peddlers carried on much local retail trade and provided restaurants, wine shops, and brothels in the great cities. Only in the 9th century did the foreign influence in trade begin to recede.

In the late T'ang many officials began to invest their money (and official funds entrusted to them) in commercial activities. High officials took to running oil presses and flour mills, dealing in real estate, and providing capital for merchants. The wall between the ruling class and the merchants that had existed since the Han period was rapidly breaking down in the 9th century, and the growth of urbanization, which characterized the Sung period, had already begun on a wide scale. (D.C.T.)

VI. The Five Dynasties and the Ten Kingdoms

Unlike the earlier Six Dynasties period (AD 220–618), the brief period of disunity in the 10th century known as the Five Dynasties did not bring about sharp breaks in the evolution of Chinese culture. In the social, political, economic, and cultural areas many long-term trends of change that already had been set in motion continued and made subsequent Chinese society characteristically different from that of the past. Most historians tend to view the several centuries from the late T'ang through the

Sung as a great divide. From that standpoint, the Five Dynasties interlude was merely a transient stage; its military and political upheavals were but manifestations of deep underlying changes and of factors that further accelerated the process of change. Though the T'ang empire was dismembered, the ideal of Imperial unification, deeply rooted in tradition, survived. Several governors, one after the other, reorganized their provincial structure and extended it into the neighbouring regions in North China, historically the central arena of contest, aspiring to establish a new focus of central power if not national hegemony.

THE FIVE DYNASTIES

Chu Wen emerged as the initial contender. While consolidating his strength on the strategic plains along the Huang Ho (Yellow River) and connecting them with the vital transportation system of the Grand Canal, he made the significant choice of locating his base at Pien, in modern Honan; it later became K'ai-feng, the Northern Sung capital. Pien's lack of historical prestige was balanced by the ancient capital, Lo-yang, a short distance to the west, which was still the nation's cultural centre. Chu Wen's short-lived Later Liang dynasty, founded in 907, was su-

Adapted from A. Hermann, *An Historical Atlas of China,* Aldine Publishing Company, 1966

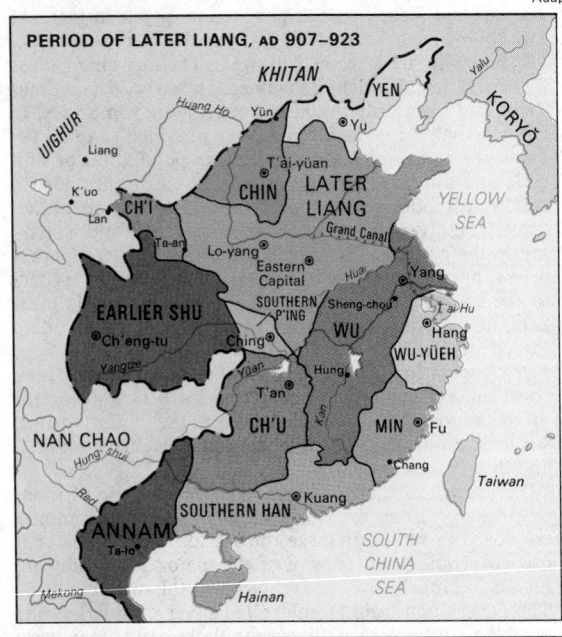

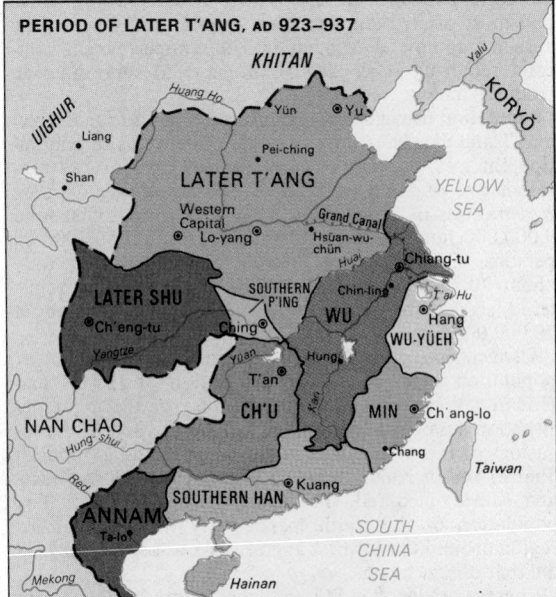

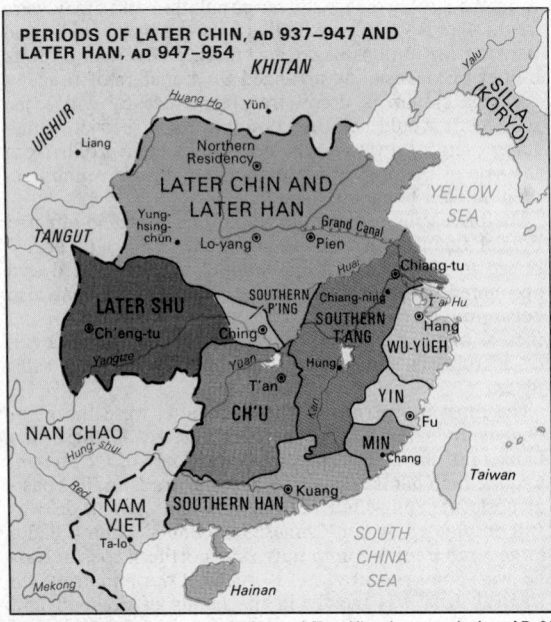

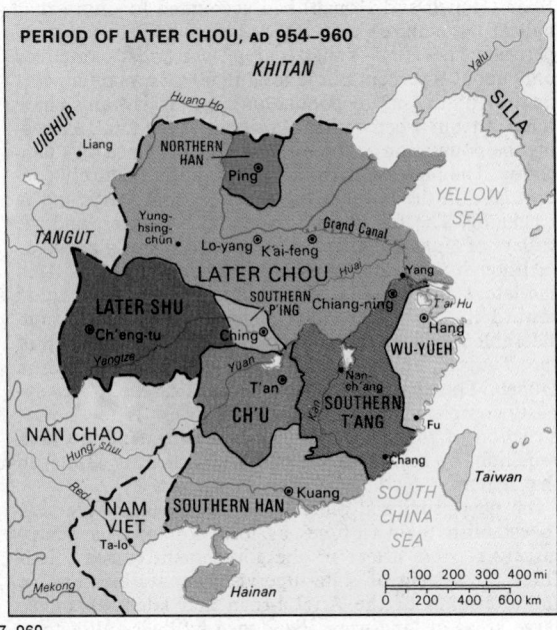

China during the Five Dynasties and Ten Kingdoms period *c.* AD 907–960.

perseded only 11 years after his murder by the Later T'ang in 923, by the Chin in 937, by the Han in 947, and by the Later Chou in 954; hence the term Five Dynasties. These rapid successions by usurpation came to an end only with that of the Sung, which finally succeeded in establishing another lasting empire and in taking over much, though not all, of the former T'ang empire.

Changes in the political process

Beneath the surface, however, were the continuous efforts of a reintegrative political process that not only heralded the coming of the new empire but also helped to shape its political system. In this respect the successive usurpers moved like a relay team along the tortuous road back to unification. These militarists expanded their personal power by recruiting peoples of relatively humble social origins to replace the earlier aristocrats. Such recruits owed personal allegiance to their masters, upon whose favours their political positions remained dependent, thus presaging the rise of absolutism.

Rather than being discarded, the T'ang administrative form underwent expedient alterations to enable the new type of officials, promoted because of merit from regional posts to palace positions, to exert their political skill, especially in military administration, in supervising the nearby provinces and gradually bringing them under direct control. The top priorities went to the securing of fiscal resources, salt monopoly, tribute transport, and in particular new tax revenues, without which the military domination would have been hard to sustain and political expansion impossible. Eventually, a pattern of centralizing authority emerged. Fiscal and supply officials of the successive régimes went out to supervise provincial finances and the local administration. The minor militarists, heretofore the local governors in control of their own areas, had to submit themselves to such reintegrative measures under double pressure: the inducement of the politically accommodative carrot, which allowed them to keep their residual power, and the militarily threatening stick of palace army units commanded by special commissioners, which were sent on patrol duty into their areas. The way was thus paved, in spite of occasional detours and temporary setbacks, for the ultimate unification.

The seemingly chaotic period was in fact less chaotic than other rebellious times, except from the standpoint of the aristocrats, whose pre-eminent status disappeared along with the loss of their large estates, usually taken over piecemeal by their former managers. The aristocratic dominance in Chinese history was gone forever; a new bureaucratic era was about to begin.

THE TEN KINGDOMS

On the frontier, the far-reaching influence of T'ang culture had stimulated the rise of the nomadic, semi-nomadic, and pastoral peoples. From then until the Ch'ing dynasty, which arose in the 17th century, China consisted of two parts: the North, militarily strong, and the South, economically and culturally wealthy. Ten independent kingdoms emerged in China—the Tangut and Khitan in the North, and eight smaller kingdoms in the South.

Differences between North and South

The Tangut. In the northwestern corner, the Tangut, a Tibetan people, inhabited the region between the far end of the Great Wall in modern Kansu and the Huang Ho bend in Inner Mongolia. Their semi-oasis economy combined irrigated agriculture with pastoralism. Their control over the terminal of the famous Silk Road made them middlemen in trade between Central Asia and China. As a state religion they adopted Buddhism; but in government and education they followed the T'ang model, and they devised a written script for their own language. This richly mixed culture blossomed, as evidenced by the storing at the Tun-huang caves of an unparalleled collection of some 10,000 religious paintings, manuscripts, and books in Chinese, Tibetan, Uighur, and other languages; these remained unknown to the world until their discovery in 1900. In 1038 the Tanguts proclaimed their own kingdom of Hsi Hsia, which survived with remarkable stability a series of on-and-off border clashes with the neighbouring states in North China over the course of two centuries. The kingdom's end came

with the Mongols, who made the first nomadic conquest that took all parts of China.

The Khitan. To the north at the time of the Five Dynasties rose the seminomadic but largely pastoral Khitan, who were related to the eastern Mongols. The word Khitan (or Khitai) is the source of Cathay, the name for North China in medieval Europe (as reported by Marco Polo), and of Kitai, the Russian name for China. The Khitan founded the Liao empire (947–1125) by expanding from the border of Mongolia into both southern Manchuria (Northeastern Provinces) and the 16 prefectures below the Great Wall. The Liao made Yen-ching (modern Peking) its southern capital, thus starting its history as a capital city, and claimed to be a legitimate successor to the T'ang. They incorporated their own tribes under respective chieftains and, with other subdued tribes in the area, formed a confederation, which they transformed into a hereditary monarchy. Leadership always remained in the hands of the ruling tribe, the Yeh-lü, who for the sake of stability shifted to the Chinese clan system of orderly succession.

The Liao economy was based on horse and sheep raising and on agriculture. Millet was the main crop, and salt, controlled by government monopoly, was important. There were also such other riches as iron produced by smelters. The Liao employed an effective dual system of administration. Against the danger of being absorbed by Sinification, they had one administration for their own people that enforced tribal laws, maintained traditional rites, and largely retained the steppe style of food and clothing; deliberately avoiding the use of Chinese, they added to their particular branch of the Mongolian language two types of writing—a smaller one that was alphabetical and a larger one related to Chinese characters. A second administration governed the farming region by the old T'ang system, complete with the T'ang official titles, examination system, tax regulations, and use of the Chinese language. The laws of the second administration enforced the established way of life, including such practices as ancestral worship among the Chinese subjects. The status of Chinese subjects varied. Free subjects had opportunities for upward mobility into the civil service, while others ranged from partial liberty to bondage and slavery.

Dual system of administration

Though honouring the Confucian philosophy, the Liao rulers patronized Chinese Buddhism. Their achievements were generally military and administrative rather than cultural. They were eventually overthrown by the Juchen, another semi-nomadic and semipastoral people who originated in Manchuria, swept across North China, ended the Northern Sung as well, and established the Chin dynasty (1112–1234). This new and much larger empire in North China followed the same pattern of dual government as well as acculturation but at a much higher cultural level. It went down with the coming of the Mongols.

Kingdoms in the South. More crucial to the future of Chinese culture, however, were changes that evolved at the southern end of the country. In the Yangtze River Valley and in areas farther south existed eight of the Ten Kingdoms through all or part of this period: the Wu (907–937), the Southern T'ang (937–975), the Southern P'ing (907–963), the Ch'u (927–951), the Earlier Shu (907–925) and the Later Shu (934–965), the Min (909–944), the Southern Han (907–971), and the Wu-yüeh (907–978), the last significantly located in China's most rapidly advancing area—in and near the lower Yangtze Delta.

While some of these separate regimes achieved relative stability, none attained enough strength to strive for unification. Of great interest nonetheless were the regional developments in South China, in the upper Yangtze region in southwest China, and in the lower Yangtze region in southeast China. In South China the Min kingdom in modern Fukien and the Southern Han in modern Kwangtung and Kwangsi sharply reflected cultural differences. Along the coast, sea trade expanded, promoting both urban prosperity and cultural diversity. On land, wave after wave of refugees moved southward, settling along rivers and streams and in confining plains and mountain

Regional developments

valleys, using a frontier agriculture but with highly developed irrigation and land reclamation, usually pushing aside the aboriginal minorities, earlier settlers, and previous immigrant groups. This process turned South China into a cultural chessboard of great complexity, with various subcultural pieces sandwiched between one another, many of which eventually evolved along different lines.

In southwest China the valley of modern Szechwan presented an interestingly different picture of continuous growth. Usually protected from outside disturbances and invasions by the surrounding mountains, it enjoyed peace and prosperity except for one decade of instability between the Earlier and Later Shu. The heritage of the T'ang culture not only survived there but, assisted by advancing technology, reached out toward new horizons. The beautiful landscape continually inspired the best talents to infuse a refreshing vitality into old-style poetry and essays. This region was a stronghold of Taoist religion, and the people inserted into the ancient scholarship an admixture of Taoist philosophy. Buddhism was not far behind. The intellectual trends there foreshadowed an eclectic synthesis of the three major teachings—Confucianism, Taoism, and Buddhism—in a nationwide pattern. The Buddhist monasteries with large estates were usually among the first to introduce new and better technology. On the economic scene a lack of copper was met by an increasing output of iron through more efficient methods and an elementary division of labour in production. When the limited number of copper coins could no longer cope with the growing volume of trade, iron currency briefly went into circulation. Another way of dealing with the mounting demand for more money and credit was an ingenious device called flying money, first used among merchants and then adopted in the form of official notes issued by the salt monopoly government agencies; this was the forerunner of paper currency as the legal tender of the subsequent Sung period. It was closely related to the use of movable type in printing. The best printing in the country during the Five Dynasties and the Sung came from the regions of Szechwan and Fukien.

Leadership of the Yangtze Delta

From the Five Dynasties on, southeast China, especially its core region of the Yangtze Delta, began to lead the country in both economic prosperity and cultural refinement. In this region fertile soil, irrigation networks, and highly selective crops combined to create the best model of intensive farming. Labelled by some scholars as a creek culture, it had interlocking streams, rivers, and lakes to feed an ever-increasing number of markets, market towns, cities, and metropolitan areas, where many farm products were processed into an ever-expanding variety of consumer goods as well as highly valued articles. Such development enhanced regional trade, stimulated other regions to adopt specialization, and became part of an overseas trade.

Linking economics with aesthetics were the "four treasures" of a scholar's study: brush-pen, paper, ink stick, and ink slab, the best of which came from the area between the western shores of T'ai Hu (Lake T'ai) and the neighbouring corner of modern Anhwei. Other evidence of refined culture was abundant. Upon the surrender of the last Southern T'ang ruler, himself a renowned poet, the unexcelled royal library in the capital at Nanking was moved to the North; along with it went many officials who were skilled in art, literature, and bibliography. The surrender of the Wu-yüeh kingdom, slightly farther south, followed the same pattern. Moreover, refined culture developed away from the coast in such inland mountainous areas as modern Kiangsi, which shortly thereafter produced internationally coveted porcelain and where many great artists and scholar-officials attained positions of cultural leadership. Thereafter, southeast China retained its cultural excellence. At the end of the Northern Sung period, the Southern Sung based itself in this very area and located its capital at Hang-chou, the former capital of the Wu-yüeh.

As traditional histories stress, this period of disunity definitely had its dark side: militarism, wars, disintegration of the old order, and an inevitable lowering of moral standards. The guiding ideology of Confucianism was sadly weakened. Paradoxically, however, many changes were creeping out of darkness; and soon came the dawn of a new era.

VII. The Sung dynasty

NORTHERN SUNG (960–1126)

The Northern Sung (also known simply as the Sung) did not have an honourable beginning. Its founder, Chao K'uang-yin (T'ai Tsu), the commander of the capital area and inspector general of the Imperial forces, simply usurped the Chou, the last of the Five Dynasties.

Unification. Though a militarist himself, Chao ended militarism as well as usurpation. Even his own coup was skilfully disguised to make it appear that the popular acclaim staged by the rank and file left him with no choice. Masterful in political manoeuvring, Chao, as emperor (reigned 960–976), did not destroy other powerful generals as had many previous founding rulers. Instead, he persuaded them to give up their commands in exchange for honorary titles, sinecure offices, and generous pensions—an unheard-of arrangement in Chinese history. With a shrewd appreciation of the war-weariness among the population, he stressed the Confucian spirit of humane administration and the reunification of the whole country. To implement this policy, he took power from the military governors, consolidated it at court, and delegated it (even the supervision of military affairs) to able civilians; but no official was regarded as above suspicion. A pragmatic civil service system evolved, with a flexible distribution of power and elaborate checks and balances. Each official had a titular office, indicating his rank but not his actual function, a commission for his normal duties, and additional assignments or honours. This seemingly confusing formula enabled the ruler to remove an official to a lower position without demotion of rank, to give an official a promotion in rank but an insignificant assignment, or to pick up a low ranking talent and test him on a crucial commission. Councillors controlled only the civil administration because the division of authority made the military commissioner and the finance commissioner separate entities, reporting directly to the ruler, who coordinated all important decisions. In decision making the Emperor received additional advice from academicians and other advisers—collectively known as opinion officials—whose function was to provide separate channels of information and to check up on the administrative branches. Similar checks and balances existed in the diffused network of regional officials: circuit intendants in charge of civil administration; fiscal intendants; intendants for such vital functions as tribute transport, state monopolies, and state trade; judicial intendants; and military intendants, whose circuit boundaries did not coincide with those of the civil circuits. Below these intendants were the prefects, varying in grade according to an area's size and importance; each prefect was assisted and checked on by one or two vice administrators and a host of specialized subordinates for various functions. Under the all-powerful "Son of Heaven," no bureaucrat could gather much authority except by the Emperor's delegation or in abnormal circumstances.

Following Confucian ideals, T'ai Tsu lived modestly, listened to his ministers, and curbed excessive taxation. The rising prestige of his régime preceded his conquests. He also absorbed the best military units under his own command and disciplined them in the same Confucian style. His superior force notwithstanding, he embarked upon a reunification program by mixing war with lenient diplomatic or accommodative terms that assured defeated rivals of generous treatment. A well-planned strategy first took Szechwan in the southwest in 965, the extreme south in 971, and the most prosperous lower Yangtze area in the southeast one year before his death, making the reunification nearly completed. The Wu-yüeh, the sole survivor among the Ten Kingdoms, chose to surrender without a war in 978.

T'ai Tsu's sudden death left a speculative legend of assassination, though it was probably caused by his heavy drinking. The legend stemmed from the fact that his young son was denied the orderly succession. Instead,

End of militarism and usurpation

the Emperor's younger brother, who had acquired much experience at his side, seized the throne. With reunification accomplished in the South, the new emperor, T'ai Tsung (reigned 976–997) turned northward to fight the Khitan empire, only to suffer a disastrous defeat (986) and a personal narrow escape. A relative shortage of horses and grazing grounds to breed them, in contrast to the strong Khitan cavalries, was not the only reason for the defeat. It also resulted from a deliberate policy of removing generals from their armies, subordinating officers to civilians, concentrating strength in Imperial units, and leaving provincial armies unduly weak, as well as from a spreading complacency and a decline of martial spirit.

Defeat by the Khitan empire

The Sung never achieved a military prowess comparable to that of the Han or the T'ang. It did not even succeed in penetrating Indochina; the independent kingdoms of Nan Yüeh and Nan-choa merely agreed to pay token respect as vassal states. Satisfied with its prestige in East Asia, China from then on suffered from geographical isolation, especially from Central Asia, whence had come many cultural stimulations. Combined with a natural pride in internal advancements, China's cultural ethnocentrism deepened.

Consolidation. Under the third emperor, Tseng Tsung (reigned 998–1022), the Sung achieved consolidation. A threatening Khitan offense was directly met by the Emperor himself. A few battles assured neither side of victory. The two empires pledged peaceful coexistence in 1004 through an exchange of sworn documents that had a modern ring of international treaty. The Khitan gave up its claim to a disputed area it had once occupied below the Great Wall; and the Sung agreed to a yearly tribute: 100,000 units (a rough equivalent of ounces) of silver and 200,000 rolls of silk. It was a modest price for the Sung to pay for securing the frontier.

The Emperor thereafter turned to self-aggrandizement and the strengthening of his absolutist image by claiming a Taoist charisma. Prompted by magicians and ingratiating high officials, he proclaimed that he had received a sacred document directly from Heaven. He ordered a grand celebration with elaborate rites, accompanied by reconstructed music of ancient times; and he made a tour to offer sacrifices at Mt. T'ai, following a Han dynasty precedent. His hope for longevity, however, was in vain. After his death, frictions arose between his wife, the empress dowager, who was acting as regent, and Emperor Jen Tsung (reigned 1023–63), his teen-aged son by a palace lady of humble rank. Following the death of the empress dowager, the Emperor divorced his empress, who had been chosen for him by and had remained in sympathy with the old lady. The divorce was unjustifiable in Confucian morality and damaging to the Imperial image; it aroused a storm of protests among idealistic bureaucrats but to no avail.

Growth of the bureaucracy

By this time the bureaucracy had attained a much higher quality than at the Sung's beginnings. Well-regulated civil service examinations brought new crops of excellent scholar-officials. The sponsorship system, which discouraged favouritism by putting responsibility upon the sponsors for the official conduct of their appointees, also insured deserving promotions and carefully chosen appointments. Many first-rate officials—especially those from the South whose families had no previous bureaucratic background—upheld the Confucian ideals. These new officials were critical not only of palace impropriety but also of bureaucratic malpractices, administrative sluggishness, fiscal abuses, and socio-economic inequities. Respecting absolutism, they focussed their attacks upon a veteran chief councillor, whom the Emperor had trusted for years. Factionalism developed because many established scholar-officials, mostly from the North, with long bureaucratic family backgrounds, stood by their leader, the same chief councillor.

A series of crises proved the complaints of the idealists justified. After half a century of complacency, peace and prosperity began to erode. This became apparent in the occurrence of small-scale rebellions near the capital itself; in the disturbing incapability of local governors to restore order by themselves; and in a dangerous penetra-

tion of the northwestern border by Hsi Hsia, which rejected its vassal status and declared itself an independent kingdom. The Khitan took advantage of the changing military balance by threatening another invasion. The idealistic faction, put into power under these critical circumstances in 1043–44, effectively stopped the Hsi Hsia on the frontier by reinforcing a chain of defense posts and made it pay due respect to the Sung as the superior empire (though the Sung no longer claimed suzerainty). Meanwhile, the peace with Khitan was reinsured by an increase in yearly tribute.

The court also instituted administrative reforms, stressing the need for emphasizing statecraft problems in civil service examinations, eliminating patronage appointments for family members and relatives of high officials, and enforcing strict evaluation of administrative performance. It also advocated reduction of compulsory labour, land reclamation and irrigation construction, organization of local militias, and a thorough revision of codes and regulations. Though mild in nature, the reforms hurt vested interests. Shrewd opponents undermined the reformers by misleading the Emperor into suspecting that they had received too much power and were disrespectful of him personally. With the crises eased, the Emperor found one excuse after another to send most reformers away from court. The more conventionally minded officials were returned to power.

Despite a surface of seeming stability, the administrative machinery once again fell victim to creeping deterioration. When some reformers eventually returned to court, beginning in the 1050s, their idealism was modified by the political lesson they had learned. Eschewing policy changes and tolerating colleagues of varying opinions, they made appreciable progress by concentrating upon the choice of better personnel, proper direction, and careful implementation within the conventional system; but many fundamental problems remained unsolved. Mounting military expenditures did not bring greater effectiveness; an expanding and more costly bureaucracy could not reverse the trend of declining tax yields; and, during the brief reign of Ying Tsung (1064–67), relatively minor disputes and deliberately exaggerated issues over mere ceremonial matters embroiled the bureaucracy in mutual and bitter criticism.

Creeping deterioration of the administration

Reforms. Shen Tsung (reigned 1068–85) was a reform emperor. Originally a prince reared outside the palace, familiar with social conditions and devoted to serious studies, he did not come into the line of Imperial succession until adoption had put his father on the throne before him. Shen Tsung's reign responded vigorously (and rather unexpectedly, from the standpoint of many bureaucrats) to the evolving needs for change that were troubling the established order, some of which were approaching crisis proportion. Cautiously keeping his monarchial role above partisan politics, he made the scholar-poet Wang An-shih his chief councillor and gave him full backing in sweeping reforms. Known as the new laws, or new policies, these reform measures set up regulatory systems that amounted to drastic institutional changes. In sum, they achieved administrative effectiveness, fiscal surplus, and military strength. Wang's famous "Ten Thousand Word Memorial" outlined the philosophy of the reforms. Contrary to conventional Confucian views, it upheld assertive governmental roles; but its ideal remained basically Confucian in the belief that economic prosperity would provide the essential social environment and that such an environment would in turn promote moral well-being.

Never before had the government undertaken so many economic activities. The Emperor empowered Wang to institute a top-level office for fiscal planning, which supervised the Commission of Finance, previously beyond the jurisdiction of the chief councillor. The government squarely faced the reality of a rapidly spreading money economy by increasing the supply of currency. The state became involved in trading, buying specific products of one area for resale elsewhere (thereby facilitating the exchange of goods), stabilizing prices whenever and wherever necessary, and making a profit itself. This did not

Economic gains from the reforms

displace private trading activities. On the contrary, the government extended loans to small urban and regional traders through state pawnshops—a practice somewhat like modern government banking but unheard-of at the time. Far more important, if not controversial, was the institution of providing government loans at the interest rate, low for the period, of 20 percent to the whole peasantry during the sowing season, thus assuring their farming productivity and undercutting their habitual dependency upon usurious loans from the well-to-do. The government also maintained granaries in various cities to insure adequate supplies on hand in case of emergency need. The burden upon rich and poor alike was made more equitable by a graduated tax scale based upon a reassessment of the size and the productivity of the landholdings. Similarly, compulsory labour was converted to a system of graduated tax payments, along with which the government instituted a hired-labour service program that at least theoretically controlled underemployment in farming areas. Requisition of various supplies from guilds was also replaced by cash assessments, with which the government bought what it needed at a fair price.

Wang's reforms achieved increased military power as well. To remedy the Sung's military weakness, the villages were given the duty of organizing militias, under the old name of *pao-chia*, to maintain local order in peacetime and to serve as army reserves in wartime. To reinforce the cavalry, the government procured horses and assigned them to peasant households in northern and northwestern areas, in consideration for which one member of the family had the privilege of serving in the army with his horse. Various weapons were also developed. As a result of these efforts, the empire eventually scored some minor victories along the northwestern border.

The gigantic reform program required an energetic bureaucracy, which Wang attempted to create—with mixed results—by means of a variety of policies: promotion of a nationwide state school system; establishment of specialized training in such utilitarian professions as the military, law, and medicine, which were neglected by Confucian education; placing a strong emphasis on interpretations of Classics, some of which Wang himself supplied rather dogmatically for statecraft applications in civil service examinations; demotion and dismissal of dissenting officials (thus inadvertently creating more conflicts in the bureaucracy than necessary); and provision of strong incentives for better performances by clerical staffs, including merit promotion into bureaucratic ranks.

Opposition to the reforms

The magnitude of the reform program was matched only by the bitter opposition to it. Determined criticism came from the groups hurt by the reform measures: large landowners, big merchants, and moneylenders. Noncooperation and sabotage arose among the bulk of the bureaucrats, drawn as they were from the landowning and otherwise wealthy classes. Geographically, the strongest opposition came from the traditionally more conservative northern areas. Ideologically, however, the criticisms did not necessarily coincide with either class background or geographic factors. They were best expressed by many leading scholar-officials, some of whom were northern conservatives while others were brilliant talents from Szechwan. Both the Emperor and Wang failed to reckon with the fact that, by its very nature, the entrenched bureaucracy could tolerate no sudden change in the system it had been accustomed to. It also reacted, with valid reasons, against the overconcentration of power at the top, which neglected the art of distributing and balancing power among government offices, and the overexpansion of governmental power in society.

Without directly attacking the Emperor, the critics attacked the reformers for deviations from orthodox Confucianism. It was wrong, the opponents argued, for the state to pursue profits, to assume inordinate power, and to interfere in the normal life of the common people. It was often true as charged that the reforms, and the resulting changes in government, brought about the rise of unscrupulous officials; an increase in high-handed abuses in the name of strict law enforcement; unjustified discrimination against many scholar-officials of long experience;

intense factionalism; and resulting widespread miseries among the population—all of which were in contradiction to the claims of the reform objectives. Particularly open to criticism was the rigidity of the reform system, which allowed little regional discretion or desirable adjustment for differing conditions in various parts of the empire.

In essence the reforms augmented growing trends of both absolutism and bureaucracy, in the long run injurious to the general welfare. Even for the short run, the cost of the divisive factionalism that the reforms generated turned out to have disastrous effects. To be fair, Wang was to blame for his overzealous if not doctrinaire beliefs, his low tolerance for criticism, and his persistent support of his followers even when some of their errors were hardly in doubt. Nonetheless, it was the Emperor himself who was ultimately responsible because of his determination to have the reform measures implemented, his ignoring of loud remonstrances, his disregard of friendly appeals to have certain measures modified, and his continuation of the reforms after Wang's retirement.

Effects of the reforms

The traditional historians, by studying documentary evidence alone, overlooked the fact that scholar-officials rarely openly criticized an absolutist emperor, and they generally echoed the critical views of the conservatives in assigning the blame to Wang—a revisionist Confucian in public, a profound Buddhist practitioner in his old age, and a great poet and essayist of historical fame.

Decline and fall. Factionalism proved fatal. The Imperial system not only malfunctioned, but it also disintegrated. Essential to good government in China, a lesson learned through trial and error since Han and T'ang times, was careful balancing of power in the bureaucracy, through which the absolutist ruler acted and from which he received a variety of advice and information. The demonstrated success of this principle in early Northern Sung so impressed later scholars that they described it as the art of government. It became a lost art, however, in the reform zeal and more so in the subsequent eagerness to do away with the reforms.

The reign of Che Tsung (1086–1100) began with a regency under another empress dowager, whose sympathies for the conservatives recalled them to power. An antireform period, which lasted until 1093, saw most of the reforms rescinded or drastically revised. Though men of integrity, the conservatives offered few constructive alternatives in trying to make the established order of pre-reform days work again. They achieved a relaxation of tension and a seeming stability but without preventing old problems from recurring. Some conservatives objected to turning the clock back, especially by swinging to the opposite extreme; but their voices were silenced. As usual, once the young Emperor took control he undid what the deceased empress dowager had done; the pendulum swung once again to a restoration of the reforms, a period that lasted to the end of the Northern Sung. In such repeated convulsions, the government could not escape dislocation, and the society became demoralized. Moreover, the restored reform movement was a mere ghost without its original idealism. Enough grounds were found by conservatives out of power to blame the reforms for the fall of the dynasty.

Antireform period

Perennial factionalism aside, deterioration spread through the successive layers of government. The next emperor, Hui Tsung (reigned 1100–25), was a great patron of the arts and an excellent artist himself. Such qualities, however, did not make him a good ruler. Indulgent in pleasures and irresponsible in state affairs, he misplaced his trust in favourites. Those in power knew how to manipulate the regulatory system to obtain excessive tax revenues. At first the complacent Emperor granted more support to government schools everywhere; the objection that this move might flood the already crowded bureaucracy was dismissed as not seeing the significant gains it would bring in popular support among scholar-officials. Then the Emperor built a costly new Imperial garden with paradise-like landscaping exuberant with Taoist atmosphere. When his extravagant expenditures put the treasury in deficit, he rescinded scholarships in government schools. Support for him among scholar-officials soon vanished.

Alliance
with the
Juchen

More serious was carelessness in war and diplomacy. Disregarding the treaty and coexistence with the Liao empire, the Sung, allied with the expanding Juchen from Manchuria, made a concerted attack to destroy it. The Sung commander, contrary to long-held prohibition, was a favoured eunuch; under him and other unworthy generals, military expenditures ran high, but army morale was low. The fall of Liao was cause for court celebration. But because the Juchen had done most of the fighting, they accused the Sung of not doing its share and denied it certain spoils of the conquest that the two parties had agreed upon. The Juchen, riding the momentum of victory, soon turned upon the Sung. At this point the Emperor chose to abdicate, giving himself the title of Taoist "emperor emeritus" and leaving the critical state of affairs largely in the unprepared hands of his son, Ch'in Tsung (reigned 1125–26), while seeking safety and pleasure himself by touring the Yangtze region.

Below such a court the quality of the bureaucracy declined, although the cost of its maintenance kept rising. Factionalism degenerated into sheer nepotism, promoting laxity and corruption. Appointments and promotions, by the abuse of the sponsorship system, usually went to the highest bidders. To get new posts, some officials borrowed money from merchants. Honest officials who refused to oblige the demeaning demands of their superiors found it hard to escape criticism or to make ends meet; if dismissed, they waited in vain for other assignments. Meanwhile, hardship posts that no one wanted remained vacant. The state examinations, previously well regulated, also suffered because of notorious cheating.

The reform movement had enlarged both the size and duties of the clerical staff. The anti-reform period brought a cutback but also a confusion that presented manipulative opportunities to some clerks. Supervision was difficult because officials stayed only a few years, whereas clerks remained in office for long periods. Bureaucratic laxity spread quickly to the clerical level. Bribery for appointments either went to them or through their hands. It was they who made cheating possible at examinations, using literary agents as intermediaries between candidates and themselves.

End of the
Northern
Sung

The Juchen swept across the Huang Ho plain and found the internally decayed Sung an easy prey. During their long siege of K'ai-feng (1126) they repeatedly demanded ransoms in gold, silver, jewels, other valuables, and general supplies. The collapsing court, whose emergency call for help brought only undermanned reinforcements and untrained volunteers, obliged the invaders' demands and ordered the capital residents to follow suit. Finally, an impoverished mob plundered the infamous Imperial garden for firewood. Yet the court had a mental fixation on the magic of financial power to buy peace. The Juchen lifted the siege briefly. But once convinced that local resources were exhausted and that the régime, even with the return of the Emperor Emeritus, no longer had the capability of delivering additional wealth from other parts of the country, the invaders changed their tactics. Suddenly taking the two emperors and the entire Imperial house as captives and exiling them to Manchuria, they put a tragic end to the Northern Sung.

SOUTHERN SUNG (1126–1279)

The Juchen could not extend their conquest beyond the Yangtze, and the areas there remained united. The Huai Ho Valley, with its winding streams and crisscrossed marshlands, made cavalry operations difficult. Though the invaders penetrated it without sustained occupation and raided several parts below the Yangtze, they found the weather there too warm and humid for them. Moreover, the farther they went, the stronger was the resistance they met. These areas had been leading the country in productivity and population and therefore in defense capability. Besides, the Juchen felt concerned about the areas in the rear that they had already occupied, where one after another of their puppet rulers had failed to secure popular support and the Juchen had been forced to consolidate control by setting up their own administration, following the Liao model of dual government.

Survival and consolidation. Despite the fall of the Northern Sung, Confucian loyalty survived and the majority of scholar-officials found it unacceptable to identify themselves even culturally with the alien conquerors. The same was generally true at the grassroots level, among numerous roving bands: former volunteer militias, army units that had disintegrated, and bandits who had arisen during the disorder. As time went on, both civilians and military men turned toward the pretender to the throne, Kao Tsung. He was the only son of the former emperor Hui Tsung who had been absent from K'ai-feng and thus spared captivity.

As the founder of the Southern Sung, Kao Tsung devoted his long reign (1127–62) to the arduous task of putting the pieces together. He rediscovered the lost art of his ancestors: recruiting bureaucrats, securing fiscal resources, and extending centralized control. Starting with no more than a few thousand troops, however, he had to place a much greater reliance on sophisticated politics, which he often artfully disguised. By praising the old, established ways of his predecessors, he pleased the conservatives who remained opposed to the reform system. In reality he merely modified the system he had inherited where it had obviously failed and pragmatically retained the parts that were working. Though he honoured the scholar-officials who had refused to serve under the puppet rulers, he was also glad to have those who had compromised their integrity in so serving. While he denounced the notorious favourites who had misled his father, he used the excuse of being broad-minded in picking many of their former subordinates for key positions, especially those experienced in raising tax revenues. A new network of officials called the fiscal superintendent generals was set up in each region, but they reported directly to court. Urban taxes were increased; they were easier to collect than rural revenues, and prosperous cities did not suffer much from the imposition. The high priority placed on fiscal matters, though not publicized as in the previous reform period in order to avoid a bad image, persisted throughout the Southern Sung, which was a long era of heavy taxation.

Use of
sophisti-
cated
politics

Some officials, anxious for the recovery of the central plains, wished to have the capital located in Nanking, on the Yangtze, or farther up the river in central China. Kao Tsung discreetly declined such advice because these locations were militarily exposed. Instead, he chose Hang (present Hangchow), which he renamed Lin-an ("temporary safety"). Protected by the coastline and by the mountain ranges at its back, it was a more secure retreat. It was popularly referred to as the place of Imperial headquarters (Hsing-tsai), later known to Marco Polo as Quinsai. Economically, it had the advantage of being at the corner of the lower Yangtze Delta, the wealthy core of the new empire.

The Southern Sung, through continuous development, eventually became wealthier than the Northern Sung. Though its capital was near the sea—the only such case among Chinese empires—and international trade increased, the country was not sea oriented. Kao Tsung maintained a defensive posture against periodic Juchen incursions from the north and meanwhile proceeded to restore Imperial authority in the hinterland as far west as the strategic Szechwan and in parts of Shensi to its immediate north.

No less important was the need for adequate military forces. Neither conscription nor recruitment would suffice. Because his position was militarily weak but financially strong, Kao Tsung adopted the *chao-an* policy, which offered peace to the various roving bands. The government granted them legitimate status as regular troops with ample supplies, and it overlooked their minor abuses in local matters. Thus, the size of Imperial forces swelled, and the problem of internal security was largely settled. The court then turned its attention to the control of these armies, which was inseparable from the issue of war or peace with the Juchen.

Kao Tsung did not want to prolong the war; he valued

Quest for
peace and
security

most the security of his realm. A few minor victories did not convince him that he could hope to recover North China. On the contrary, he saw in war a heavy drainage of available resources, at the risk of eventual defeat. Nor did he feel comfortable with the leading generals, on whom he would have to rely in case the war went on. He had to get around the critics at court, however, who found the Juchen peace terms humiliating and unacceptable: in addition to an enormous yearly tribute, the northern enemy demanded that the Southern Sung formally admit, with due ceremonials, to the inferior status of a vassal state. The shrewd Emperor found an impeccable excuse for accepting the terms by claiming filial piety; he sought the return of his mother from captivity. To this, no Confucianist could openly object. Significantly, Kao Tsung refrained from asking the release of former emperor Ch'in Tsung; such a move would have called into question the legitimacy of his succession.

A dramatic crisis occurred in 1141. On the eve of concluding peace negotiations, Kao Tsung decided to strip the three leading generals of their commands. The generals, summoned to the capital on the pretext of rewarding their merits, were promoted to military commissioners, while their units were reorganized into separate entities directly under Imperial control. Two of the generals reconciled themselves to the nominal honours and sizable pensions. But the third, Yo Fei or Yüeh Fei, openly criticized the peace negotiations. He was put to death on a trumped-up charge of high treason. He later became the subject of a great legend, in which he was seen as a symbol of patriotism. At the time, however, his elimination signified full internal and external security for the court.

Relations with the Juchen. In spite of Kao Tsung's personal inclination, his artful guiding hand, and the success of his efforts to consolidate the empire, the impulse remained strong among many idealistic Confucianists to attempt to recover the central plains. Even when silenced, they were potentially critical of court policies. Kao Tsung eventually decided to abdicate, and he left the matter to his adopted heir; but he retained control from behind the throne. The new emperor, Hsiao Tsung (reigned 1163–89), sympathetic to the idealists, appointed several of them to court positions and command posts. Information about a Juchen palace coup and alleged unrest in the Juchen empire, particularly in the parts recently occupied, led to a decision to resume the war. An initial Sung attack was repulsed with such heavy losses that even regrouping took some time to accomplish; but sporadic fighting went on for nearly two years in the Huai Valley and reflected in effect a military stalemate, which resulted in a significant change in the new peace formula of 1165. The vassal state designation was dropped, and the Southern Sung attained a nearly equal footing with the Juchen, except that it had to defer to the latter empire as the senior one.

Resumption
of war

After the death of Kao Tsung in 1187, Hsiao Tsung followed the precedent of abdication. The international peace was kept during the brief reign of his son, Kuang Tsung (reigned 1190–94); but it was broken again in 1205, during the reign of his grandson, Ning Tsung (reigned 1195–1224). The 40-year span of continuous peace dimmed the memory of difficulties in waging war. A new generation, nurtured by a flourishing Confucian education and with a renewed commitment, tended to underestimate enemy strength and to think once more about recovering the central plains. The Southern Sung again initiated a northward campaign; and again it met with defeat. The event left no doubt that the Juchen empire's hold over North China was far beyond the military capability of the southern empire alone. And it was also obvious that the Chinese population in North China consisted of new generations that were brought up under alien domination and were accustomed to it.

The Juchen, in establishing their Chinese-style Chin empire, occupied a broader geographic region in the farming country than had any previous nomadic or pastoral conquerors. The migration of their own people in large numbers notwithstanding, they were proportionally a smaller minority than their Khitan predecessors, for they ruled a much larger Chinese population. Because they formed a small minority in their own empire, their tribesmen were kept in a standing army that was always prepared for warfare. Though quartered among their farming subjects, they were expected to respond to the command of their captains at short notice. In the military service the Juchen language was kept alive, and no Chinese-style names, clothing, or customs were permitted. They realized that protecting their separate ethnic and cultural identity was an indispensable prerequisite to maintaining military superiority.

Politically, however, it was necessary for the Juchen rulers to familiarize themselves with the higher culture of their Chinese subjects in order to manage state affairs. Without allowing much Chinese participation in the government, they shrewdly deflected the interests of their Chinese subjects toward the pursuit of such peaceful arts as printing, scholarship, painting, literature, and, significantly, the development of drama for widespread entertainment (these trends continued under the Mongols and contributed new enrichment to the Chinese culture). In spite of the Juchen efforts, time was on the side of the majority culture, which gradually absorbed the dominant minority. The transplanted tribesmen, after settling on farmland, could not avoid being affected by the Chinese way of life, particularly during long periods of peace.

Economically, the Juchen were no match for the Chinese. In time a number of Juchen became tenants on Chinese-owned land; some were reduced to paupers. Their economic decline altered social relations. Eventually they were permitted intermarriage, usually with parties wealthier than themselves. Their military strength also sagged. Understrength became the accepted pattern; captains of "hundreds" often could put no more than 25 men into the field and captains of "thousands" had no more than four or five such nominal "hundreds" under them. Their ruling class followed a parallel decline, with the interest in government affairs deflected to Confucian norms, Chinese Classics, T'ang- and Sung-style poetry. The rulers found little use for the two styles of Juchen script that their ancestors had devised.

Juchen
assimila-
tion

Assimilation was only partly completed, however, at the time of the third war. The Juchen still not only retained their military edge over the Southern Sung but had also revived the ambition of southward expansion. An offer was made to the governor of Szechwan, who decided to turn against the court in faraway Lin-an and to become king of a vassal state allied with the Juchen. The civilian officials around him, however, took quick action and ended his separatist rebellion. Though a passing danger, it highlighted the fact that the Southern Sung consolidation was not entirely secure; peace was preferred.

Though the peace terms involved little substantive change in the pattern between the two empires, procedurally the Southern Sung had to oblige a firm Juchen demand for a self-demeaning act. Han T'o-chou, the Sung councillor responsible for the initiation of the war, was assassinated and his head was sealed in a box and delivered to the Juchen court—a disgraceful violation of Confucian values and an outrageous departure from the Sung tradition of never putting high officials to death. Traditional historians made little criticism of this case, however, largely because Han T'o-chou had previously committed an unforgivable offense by persecuting the leading Confucian school and thus, in their minds, hardly deserved sympathy.

The court's relations with the bureaucracy. Kao Tsung set the style for all subsequent Southern Sung emperors. The first two emperors in the Northern Sung, both strong militarists, had towered above the relatively modest bureaucracy they had created; most of their successors had found little difficulty in maintaining a balance in the bureaucracy. The circumstances under which the Southern Sung came into being, however, were quite different. Kao Tsung faced tough competition in building up a loyal bureaucracy, first with the two puppet rulers in the North and then from the dual administration the Juchen empire set up. He became keenly aware that a cautious handling of bureaucrats was essential. Later, the attempted rebellion in Szechwan taught his successors the same lesson.

Kao
Tsung's
handling
of bureau-
crats

Kao Tsung was an attentive student of history who consciously emulated the restoration by the Later Han (AD 23–220) and defined his style as a gentle approach. This meant using bureaucratic tactics to deal with the bureaucrats themselves. The gentle approach proved helpful in maintaining a balance at court and thus protecting councillors and Imperial favourites from the criticism of opinion-officials. Absolutism had grown since the middle of the Northern Sung; the emperors had delegated much more power than before to a few ranking councillors. Similarly, Imperial favourites— *e.g.*, eunuchs, other personal attendants of the emperor, and relatives of the consorts—gained influence.

The "opinion-officials" by virtue of their rank or conviction wished to have their voices heard against those who abused power and influence; as a result of the factionalism that had plagued the late Northern Sung, their effectiveness had declined and never recovered. But as long as absolutism was qualified by Confucian values and the monarch cherished a Confucian image, he had to learn to deal with some adverse opinions; he often resorted to sophisticated delaying tactics. Well adapted to bureaucratic style, the Southern Sung emperors listened to criticism with ostensible grace, responded appreciatively, and made it known they had done so, as good Confucian rulers should, but without taking concrete action. Sometimes an emperor would either order an investigation or express a general agreement with the criticism, thereby preventing the critics from making an issue of it by repeated remonstrances. On other occasions the emperors would listen to the critics and commend them for their courage; but the court would explicitly forbid the circulating of private copies of the criticisms among other scholar-officials, to avoid stirring up a storm. More subtly, sometimes the court would announce an official version of such criticism, leaving out the most damaging part. Likewise, rectifying edicts that followed the acceptance of criticism often had little substance. Reconciliation at court was another technique; an emperor would deliberately, if not evasively, attribute criticism to probable misunderstanding, assemble the parties in dispute, ask them to compose their differences, caution those under attack to mend their ways, and suggest to the critics that their opinions, though valid, should be modified. The handling of severe critics who refused to change their stand required different tactics. Seemingly accepting their adverse opinion, the court might reward them by promotion to a higher position, whose functions did not include the rendering of further advice. Rarely did the court demote or punish opinion-officials, especially those with prestige; sometimes it would not even permit them to resign or to ask for a transfer. Any such move tended to damage the court's valuable Confucian image. On sensitive issues the emperors were likely to invoke their absolutist power, but this was usually handled gently, by quietly advising the opinion-officials to refrain from commenting on the issues again.

Under this bureaucratized style of the court, the institution of opinion-officials degenerated. Often the emperors appointed their own friends to such posts; but just as often, when the emperors hinted that they were displeased with certain ministers, the opinion-officials dutifully responded with unfavourable evidence, thus furnishing the court with grounds for dismissals. Such Imperial manipulations served manifold purposes: safeguarding absolutist power and its delegation to various individuals, maintaining a non-absolutist pretension, and keeping the bureaucracy in balance.

The chief councillors. The later Southern Sung emperors preferred not to take on the awesome burden of managing the huge and complex bureaucracy. Most of them were chiefly concerned with security and the status quo. The Southern Sung court delegated a tremendous amount of power and thus had a series of dominant chief councillors; none of them, however, ever was a potential usurper. No bureaucrat during the Sung era had a political base, a hereditary hold, or a personal following in any geographic area. In addition, the size of the bureaucracy and fluidity of its composition precluded anyone from controlling it, as distinct from keeping it under controlled balance. The tenure of chief councillor was essentially dependent upon the ultimate sanction of the emperor. At times even the chief councillor had to reaffirm his loyalty along with the other bureaucrats. Loyalty in absolutist terms being another name for submission, the court, bureaucratized as it was, retained its supreme position beyond challenge.

Delegation
of power
in the
Southern
Sung
court

Nevertheless, the history of Southern Sung politics had much to do with powerful chief councillors, increasingly so as time went on. Kao Tsung at first had a rapid succession of ranking ministers, but none of them measured up to the difficult task at hand: external security through peace with the northern empire, and internal security by undermining the power of leading generals. Only the chief councillor Ch'in Kuei did both; moreover, he increased tax revenues, strengthening the fiscal base of the court and enriching the private Imperial treasury. For these merits, he was given full support to impose tight control over the bureaucracy as long as he lived. Powerful as he was, he avoided doing anything that might arouse Imperial suspicion. He had many dissident scholar-officials banished from court but only with Imperial sanction; he accommodated many bureaucrats, even those who neither opposed nor followed him; but he made many of them jealous of his great power and of the rapid promotions he gave to his son and grandson. Ch'in Kuei's chief failure, however, was to underestimate his bureaucratized master, who turned out to be an even more masterful politician than he was. Upon Ch'in Kuei's death, the Emperor shifted all blame to him and recalled from banishment some of his opponents, thus restoring in time a balance in the bureaucracy.

After his voluntary abdication, Kao Tsung retained his power by using Hsiao Tsung more or less as a chief councillor. Hsiao Tsung subsequently failed to find a firm hand among his successive ministers, and the great burden on himself was probably one reason that he chose to abdicate. His son, Kuang Tsung, was mentally disturbed, unresponsive to bureaucratic consensus, and pathetically dominated by his consort. He turned against Hsiao Tsung and even refused to perform state funeral rites when the retired Emperor died—an unprecedented default that shocked the court. The solution was equally unprecedented; the Empress Dowager, the palace personnel, and the ranking ministers agreed to force his abdication. Through the crisis, Han T'o-chou, mentioned above in connection with the renewed war against the Juchen, moved rapidly into power. Related originally to the Empress Dowager and again to a new consort, he received deferential treatment from Ning Tsung. He was made the chief councillor; but he found it hard to control many bureaucrats who objected to his lack of scholarly qualifications, questioned his political ability, and criticized his nepotistic appointments. Reacting to the hostility, he made first a crucial mistake and then a fatal one. First, he banned a particular school of Confucian idealists, led by Chu Hsi (see below *The rise of Neo-Confucianism*). This proved unpopular, even among neutral scholar-officials. After he rescinded the ban, he attempted to recruit support and to reunite the bureaucracy by initiating the war. The defeat in the war made him a sacrificial lamb in the sue for peace. His failure basically stemmed from too much reliance on absolutistic support without enough attention paid to the gentle approach that was essential in dealing with the bureaucracy.

Rise of
Han
T'o-chou

After an interlude, Shih Mi-yüan emerged as the dominant chief councillor of long tenure. Coming from a bureaucratic family background, he understood the gentle approach and the importance of accommodating various kinds of bureaucrats in order to achieve a political balance. Promoting on merit and refraining from nepotism, he restored considerable stability. He recognized that the ideological prestige the followers of Chu Hsi had won had become a political factor, and he appointed some of their prominent leaders to highly respectable posts but without giving them real power. Like the emperors he served, he wanted to have both authority and a good political image. Because Ning Tsung had no son, the chief councillor helped him adopt two heirs. When the Emperor died without designating an heir apparent, Shih Mi-yüan arbitrarily decided in favour of the younger one, which was contrary to the normal order of succession but had the backing of palace-connected personnel.

Both Li Tsung (reigned 1225–64) and his successor Tu Tsung (reigned 1265–74) indulged excessively in pleasure, though much of it was carefully concealed from the public. Shortly after the death of Shih Mi-yüan, the role of dominant chief councillor went to Chia Ssu-tao. Though denounced in history, he actually deserves much credit. He dismissed many incompetents from the palace, the court, the bureaucracy, and the army. He curbed excessive corruption by instituting minor administrative reforms. His strict accounting made the generals personally liable for misappropriation of funds. A system of public fields was introduced, cutting into the concentration of landownership by requisitioning at a low price one-third of large estates beyond certain sizes and using the income for army expenditures when the government faced external danger and fiscal deficit. These measures, however, hurt the influential elements of the ruling class, making Chia unpopular. He too had failed to practice the gentle approach. His ill fame in history nominally resulted from defeats by the Mongols, though he did muster strong defenses; but actually he was denounced by those who had defected to the enemy and later reconciled their guilt by placing the blame on him.

Except in name, the several dominant chief councillors were nearly actual rulers by proxy. They ran the civil administration, supervised both state finance and military affairs, and controlled most scholar-officials by some varying combination of gentle accommodation and high-handed pressure. The emperors, however, kept their separate Imperial treasury—from which the government in deficit had to borrow funds—and their private intelligence information to check upon the chief councillors. Potential competitors always existed in the bureaucracy, however, ready to criticize the chief councillors whenever state affairs went badly enough to displease or disturb the emperors. The chief councillors had enormous power only by virtue of the Imperial trust, and that lasted only as long as things went tolerably well.

The bureaucratic style. Regular posts in the Southern Sung civil service numbered about 20,000 without counting numerous sinecures, temporary commissions, and a slightly larger number of military officers. Besides eliminating most patronage privileges, by which high officials were entitled to obtain an official title for a son or other family member, the court occasionally considered a general reduction in the size of the bureaucracy. But the vested interests always opposed it. Those who entered government service seldom dropped out or were thrown out. Meanwhile, new candidates waiting for offices came in waves from state examinations, from extra examinations on special occasions, from graduation from the National Academy, from special recommendations and unusual sponsorship; others gained official titles because their families contributed to famine relief or to military expenditures. Thus, the ever-increasing supply of candidates far exceeded the vacancies.

According to Confucian theory, any prosperity that made possible more books in print, schools, and availability of a better educated elite was all for the good. But the original Confucian ideal intended to have the elite serve the society in general and the community in particular rather than flood the bureaucracy. The rising educational standards would theoretically make the competition at examinations harder and raise the average quality of degree holders as well as of bureaucratic performance. With the scarcity of vacant posts, however, the competition for degrees—sought in order to rise in the bureaucracy—became perverted. The decisive factors in appointments became influence, favouritism, and bribery instead of integrity and quality.

The bureaucracy had another problem. The Confucian ideal of government by moral example, influence, and

persuasion did not exist in administrative reality; the state was, after all, a legalistic institution that functioned according to its laws. Nor did the laws work well. The complexity of Southern Sung society, plus bureaucratic and clerical manipulations, made inevitable a jungle-like proliferation of rules and regulations, supplementary codes, and confusing interpretations. Once an exception was made, always in the name of Confucian precepts, a precedent was available to justify partially comparable and remotely similar cases. Now and then the government issued a revised set of law books to bring the whole complex up-to-date, only to find soon that it, too, was soon behind times. A major reform might have altered the state of affairs, but after the lesson learned in the Northern Sung the idea of reform was taboo. The government merely struggled to get along in a tolerable manner. The conservatives resisted change and believed that a gradual approach was the only sure way to move toward good government. There were some incremental improvements; but these did not arrest the general downward drift.

The most a scholar-official could do was to keep things quiet and perhaps maintain the appearance that there was no serious trouble. The bureaucratic style was to follow the accustomed ways in accordance with proper procedure, find expedient solutions based upon certain principles in spirit, make reasonable compromises after due consideration of all sides, and achieve smooth reconciliations of divergent views. To protect one's own career record it was essential to engage in time-consuming consultations with all appropriate offices and to report to all concerned authorities so that everyone else would have a share of responsibility. Anyone who criticized the bureaucratic style would be going against the prevalent mode of operation, namely, mutual accommodation. Even the emperor took on the bureaucratic style. When one edict did not take effect, the court repeated it, clarified it, and then stressed that strict enforcement was called for, as if such had not originally been the intention.

The picture was not entirely dark, however. Evasions and deviations notwithstanding, the letter of the laws and the formalities of procedures had to be fulfilled, and definite limits were set on official negligence and misconduct. For example, suppressing evidence or distorting information were, beyond doubt, punishable offenses. Minor juggling of office accounts went on, but outright embezzlement was never permissible. Expensive gifts were customary and even expected, but an undisguised bribe was hardly acceptable. The refined art of the bureaucratic style was not sophistry and hypocrisy alone; it required a circumspect adherence to the commonly accepted substandard norms, without which the maintenance of government would have been impossible.

The clerical staff. The norms for the native clerks beneath the bureaucrats were even lower, especially in local government. Some 300 clerks in a large prefecture or nearly 100 in a small one were placed under the supervision of a few officials. The clerks had numerous dealings with various other elements in the community, whereas the officials, being outsiders, rarely had direct contacts. Holding practically lifelong tenure after benefitting from the cumulative experience of their fathers and uncles before them, the clerks knew how to operate the local administrative machinery far better than did the officials, who stayed only a few years before moving elsewhere. Under honest, strict, and hardworking magistrates, the clerks would recoil—but only briefly—because such magistrates would soon either gain promotion for their remarkable reputations, or their strict insistence on clean government would become intolerable to their superiors, colleagues, subordinates, and influential elements in the community who had connections with high circles. Though all bureaucrats complained of clerical abuses, many connived with the clerks and none had a viable alternative to the existing situation. One significant suggestion was to replace the clerks with the oversupply of examination candidates and degree holders, who presumably had more moral scruples. But this solution had no chance of being considered because it implied a down-

Denuncia-
tion
of Chia
Ssu-tao

Legal
problems

Clerical
abuses

grading of the status of those who considered themselves to be either potential or actual members of the ruling class.

The law did place definite limits on clerical misbehaviour. But when a clerk was caught in his wrongdoing, he knew enough to save himself—taking flight before arrest, getting a similar job elsewhere under a different name, defending himself through time-consuming procedures, appealing for leniency in sentencing, requesting a review, or applying for clemency on the occasion of Imperial celebrations. What prevented clerical abuses from getting worse was not so much official enforcement of legal limits as it was the social convention in the community. For themselves as well as for their descendants, the clerks could ill afford to overstep the socially acceptable limits.

The net result of a large bureaucracy and its supporting clerical staff, accommodating one another in various defaults, malfunctions, and misconduct within loose limits led to a declining tax yield, tax evasion by those who befriended colluding officials and clerks, and an undue shift of the tax burden onto those least able to pay.

The rise of Neo-Confucianism.   Meaningful within this dismal context was the rise of the particular school of Neo-Confucianism led by Chu Hsi. The Neo-Confucian upsurge beginning in the late T'ang embraced many exciting extensions of classical vision. Noteworthy during the Northern Sung was the emergence of a new Confucian metaphysics that was influenced by Buddhism and that borrowed freely from Taoist terminology, while rejecting both religions. Of relevance to Southern Sung political and social conditions was its continuous growth into a well-integrated philosophical system that synthesized metaphysics, ethics, social ideals, political aspirations, individual discipline, and self-cultivation.

The best thinkers of the early Southern Sung were disillusioned by the realization that previous Neo-Confucian attempts had failed. Reforms that had sought to apply statecraft had ended in abuses and controversies. The spread of education had not coincided with an uplifting of moral standards. The loss of the central plains was a great cultural shock, but to talk of recovering the lost territory was useless unless it was preceded by a rediscovery of the true meaning of Confucianism. Moreover, threatened by the Juchen adoption of the same heritage, the Sung survival lay in an exclusive claim of both legitimacy and orthodoxy. Such a claim required that their new departures be interpreted as reaffirmation of ancient ideals. Thus, the intellectual trend that developed under Chu Hsi's leadership was at first referred to as Tao Hsüeh (the School of True Way) and later as Li Hsüeh (the School of Universal Principles). Education, to the thinkers of this school, meant a far deeper self-cultivation of moral consciousness, the ultimate extent of which was the inner experience of feeling at one with universal principles. These men, who might be described as transcendental moralists in Confucianism, also made a commitment to reconstruct a moral society—to them the only conceivable foundation for good government. With missionary-like zeal, they engaged in propagation of this true way and formed moral-intellectual fellowships. Chu Hsi, the great synthesizer, ranked the Classics in a step-by-step curriculum, interpreted his foremost choices, collectively known as the *Four Books*, summed up a monumental history in a short version full of moralistic judgments, prepared other extensive writings and sayings of his own, and opened the way for an elementary catechism, entitled the "Three Word Classics," which conveyed the entire value system of this school in simple language for what approximated mass education.

Many idealistic scholars flocked to Chu Hsi, his associates, and his disciples. Frustrated and alienated by the prevalent conditions and demoralizing low standards, these intellectuals assumed a peculiar archaic and semi-religious lifestyle. Prominent in scholarship, educational activities, and social leadership and filling some relatively minor government posts, they asserted their exclusive ideological authority with an air of superiority, much to the displeasure of many conventional Confucianists.

Though they were not keen about politics, the prestige they acquired was an implicit threat to those in power. The chief councillor Han T'o-chou was particularly alarmed when he found some of his political adversaries sympathetic to and even supporting this particular school. A number of other bureaucrats at various ranks shared Han's alarm; one after another, they accused this school of being similar to a subversive religious sect, calling it a threat to state security and attacking its alleged disrespect for the court. The school was proscribed as false learning and un-Confucian. Several dozen of its leaders, including Chu Hsi, were banished, some to distant places. Thenceforth, all state examination candidates had to declare that they had no connection with the school.

Most historical accounts follow the view that the controversy was another factional strife, but that was not quite the case; neither did the attackers form a cohesive group, except for their common resentment toward this school; nor was the school itself an active group in politics. The conflict was in fact one between two polarized levels—political power and ideological authority. The nature of the Confucian state required that the two should converge, if not coincide.

The persecution boomeranged by making heroes out of its victims and arousing sympathy among neutral scholar-officials. Realizing his mistake a few years later, Han lifted the ban. Most historical accounts leave an erroneous impression that, once the ban was removed, the Chu Hsi school of Neo-Confucianism by its pre-eminence soon gained wide acceptance, which almost automatically raised it to the coveted status of official orthodoxy. But in reality the rise to orthodoxy was slow and achieved by political manipulation, occasioned by an internal crisis of Imperial succession and then by the external Mongol threat. Shih Mi-yüan, the chief councillor who made Li Tsung emperor, created circumstances that forced the elder heir to commit suicide. This was damaging to the image of the court and to that of Shih himself. Mending political fences, he placed a few of the school's veteran leaders in prestigious positions in order to redress the balance of the bureaucracy. In 1233, the year before the Mongol conquest of Juchen, the Mongols honoured Confucius and rebuilt his temple in Peking. In 1237 their emerging nomadic empire, already occupying a large portion of North China, reinstituted a civil service examination, thus claiming that it, too, was a Confucian state. Threatened both militarily and culturally, the Southern Sung made Chu Hsi's commentaries official, his school the state orthodoxy, and its claim the legitimate version—that the true way of Confucius had been lost for more than 1,000 years and the line of transmission was not resumed until, inspired by the early Northern Sung masters, Chu Hsi re-established it. This implied that whatever Confucianism the Mongols took over was but a pale imitation and without legitimacy (see CONFUCIANISM, HISTORY OF).

Internal solidarity during the Southern Sung decline. Honouring the Chu Hsi school did not stop further deterioration of the Southern Sung administration and its long-standing military weakness. Despite its weakness, however, the Sung maintained an effective defense against the Mongols for four decades—the longest stand against Mongol invasions anywhere. But the Sung capital, Lin-an, finally fell in 1276 without much fighting, after high-ranking officials and officers had fled. The empire finally came to an end in 1279, when its last fleet was destroyed near Kuang-chou (modern Canton) and a loyal minister with the boy pretender to the throne committed suicide by jumping into the sea—a unique act at the last stand of a land empire.

For years before the fall of the Southern Sung, heavy taxation along with inflation of paper currency, concentration of landownership, bureaucratic laxity, clerical abuses, and lack of justice for the poor peasants tended to make internal rebellions highly probable. There were, in fact, some local uprisings, but, remarkably, there was no large rebellion. Most historical accounts attribute this to patriotism because the war against the Mongols was for cultural rather than merely dynastic survival. Though

Chu Hsi and his followers

The government's response to Chu Hsi

partly true, this was not the only reason. The impressive internal solidarity involved many other factors: (1) the government mobilized the resources of the wealthiest region, the lower Yangtze, without overburdening other parts; (2) the tax burden and the emergency requisitions fell mostly upon the prosperous urban sectors rather than on rural areas, the backbone of the empire; (3) scholar-officials in many areas, in spite of their shortcomings, were sophisticated in the art of administration, moving quickly to put down a small uprising before it got larger, or offering accommodative terms to induce some rebel leaders to come over while dividing the rest. Finally, the Neo-Confucian values had pervaded the country through more books, more schooling, and more efforts by Neo-Confucianists to promote moral standards, community solidarity, and welfare activities, and through widespread Neo-Confucian roots planted at the local levels by half-literate storytellers, makeshift theatres, and travelling companies in various performing arts. The peasants were probably far more Confucian in their belief and behaviour, without the sophisticated compromise and distortions of the urban population. In the final analysis, the internal solidarity of the Southern Sung existed not so much with the régime but in the minds of the vast majority of Chinese peasants. The Mongols eventually overlorded the peasants but never destroyed their solidarity; under Mongol occupation, the evolution of Chinese culture went on.

Factors in Southern Sung solidarity

SUNG CULTURE

The changes in Sung China were great enough to raise the question whether its culture was innovative and perhaps "modern" in character or an enrichment of the established pattern. An agricultural revolution produced plentiful supplies for a population of more than 100,000,000—by far the largest in the world at the time. Acreages under cultivation multiplied in all directions, stretching across sandy lands, climbing uphill, and pushing back water edges. A variety of early ripening rice, imported during the 11th century from Champa in modern Cambodia, shortened farming time to below 100 days, making two crops a year the norm and three crops possible in the warm South. Among other new crops the most important was cotton, which provided clothing for rich and poor alike; silk and hemp were also important. Improved tools, new implements, and mechanical devices that raised manpower efficiency were widely used and found their way into guidebooks used by the literate community leaders. Mineral productivity of such products as gold, silver, lead, and tin also increased. Consumption of iron and coal, the latter known to Marco Polo as black stone, grew at a faster rate from 850 to 1050 than that in England during the first two centuries of its industrial revolution. The Chinese never invented the joining of the two resources, however, to generate mechanical power, and no such technological breakthrough occurred.

The agricultural revolution of the Sung

Manufacturing made tremendous headway within the skill-intensive pattern, but with the aid of new devices, better processing, a beginning of division of labour, and expertise. Skills and products entered into diversified specialization. High quality earthenware progressed to genuine porcelain, which attained international fame. Though information on ordinary handicrafts was available in handbooks and encyclopædias, advanced skills were guarded as trade secrets. Specialization in production and regional trade stimulated mutual growth.

Improved transportation

Transportation facilities improved, allowing production away from the sources of supplies and making products available to distant parts. The state maintained highways, with staffed stations at convenient stops, for official travel and a courier service network, the latter being an index of centralized government control. Along the highways and branching byways stood private hostels and inns frequented by private traders. Rivers carried tribute vessels and barges, private shipping, transfer crafts, fishing boats, and pleasure yachts. Large ships with multiple decks were propelled by fast-moving wheels paddled by manpower; many sailed on the high seas, aided by accurate compasses, charts, and instruments as well as by experience in distant navigation. The expanding sea trade, apart from that with Japan and Korea, moved southward and linked up with activities of merchants from Islāmic Persia and Arabia. Some Chinese merchants began to settle in Southeast Asia. For the first time in history, Chinese naval forces assumed a vital military role, though China had not become a sea power.

An advanced money economy was everywhere in evidence. Many cultivated lands produced cash crops. By 1065 the Northern Sung government was taking in annual cash tax payments that were 20 times what the T'ang had received in 749. The income of the Southern Sung consisted of more cash revenues than grain and textile receipts. The economy had progressed to such a state that it needed more means of exchange. Merchants used drafts, called flying cash, and certificates of deposits made elsewhere. State monopoly agencies in salt and tea followed with their respective certificates, which were as good as money. The government first permitted printed paper money for limited regional circulation and then authorized it as nationwide legal tender (China was the first country to do so).

Busy transactions approached a commercial revolution, carried on by rapid calculations on the abacus, another specialized service skill that remained unmatched until the appearance of adding machines and computers. Cities changed; the T'ang pattern of walled-in blocks, each for a particular trade, broke down, and stores appeared in various parts of the urban area and trade guilds proliferated. Though official documents and scholarly essays carried a downgrading tone toward commercial activities, Sung China became a society of wholesalers, shippers, storagekeepers, brokers, travelling salesmen, retail shopkeepers, and peddlers. Urban life reached a new intensity. The populations of several metropolitan areas approached 1,000,000, and a dozen other cities ranged from 250,000 to 500,000.

Changes in urban life

Crowding was serious. Houses usually had narrow frontages. Fires became frequent and disastrous. Neighbourhood fire squads, with water-containers at hand, could not prevent destruction, and some fires lasted several days. Nonetheless, prosperity was the keynote of urban life. Teahouses, wine shops, exquisite cuisines, and catering service for private parties existed in multitude and variety. Pleasure grounds provided daily amusement and festival merriment with acrobats, jugglers, wrestlers, sword swallowers, snakecharmers, fireworks, gambling, performing arts of all sorts, puppet shows, storytellers, singing girls, and professionally trained courtesans. Upper class families enjoyed higher culture, with such diversions as music, pets, intricate games, tasteful hobbies, calligraphy, painting, and poetry. Noticeably declining were hunting, horseback riding, and polo, the latter a traditional pastime of some T'ang aristocrats. Gentility displaced sportsmanship. The prosperous cities also provided easy prey for pickpockets and professional thieves. Inasmuch as pauperism appeared in cities, parallel to rural underemployment and unemployment, the government undertook relief and such welfare measures as orphanages, nursing homes for the aged poor, charitable graveyards, and state pharmacies.

The maintenance of the economy depended on favourable central locations. According to a popular saying of the time, the Southern Sung capital of Lin-an had "vegetables from the east, water from the west, wood from the south, and rice from the north." Streams also worked as a sewage system, serviced by scavengers who formed their own guild. Additional supplies of clean water came from reservoirs fed by mountain springs and lake overflows and from neighbourhood wells.

Expansion of knowledge

Knowledge expanded because of specialization. Medicine embraced such skills as acupuncture, obstetrics, dentistry, laryngology, ophthalmology, and treatment of rheumatism and paralysis. The demand for improvement in technology, aided by certain concerns of the Neo-Confucian philosophy, helped to promote numerous investigations approaching science. Literacy spread with printing, which evolved from rubbing through block printing to the use of movable type that facilitated large quantity production at reduced cost. A large number of scholars achieved high standing through Classical studies, newly developed archaeology, philosophical interpretations, statecraft ideas, classical forms of poetry, an evolving lyric poetry called *tz'u*, which had its origin in singing, and written versions of popular songs, called *san-ch'u*. Of greatest influence on scholar-officials in succeeding generations was a masterful prose style that was original and creative but that was always used in the name of reviving ancient models. Diversified and specialized developments widened knowledge so much that scholars compiled voluminous histories, collected works, comprehensive handbooks, compendiums, and encyclopædias. Fine arts also reached new heights.

In describing the Sung culture, the term early modern has often been applied, because it not only advanced beyond the earlier pattern in China and far ahead of the rest of the world at the time but it also had many startlingly new features that approximated later developments in Western Europe. This characterization, though helpful to highlight and appreciate the Sung progress, tends to be misleading. The so-called early modern stage did not pave the way for more modernity later on. On the contrary, the Sung pattern attained cultural stability, giving rise to the myth of an unchanging China.

The two seemingly conflicting images stemmed from the basic fact that modern-style advances took place alongside the strengthening of older trends. The private land estates, ever-growing in size, held down innumerable tenants by traditional bonds, outright exploitation, and abuses of legal rights, which the government did not seek to protect. Sumptuary regulations continued to differentiate between the clothing, housing, and ceremonials of different social classes. Sex segregation, instead of loosening, became tighter than before. Sex inequality was more lopsided than the past, reinforced by Neo-Confucian morality and its rigidity. Particularly notorious was the spread of foot-binding, which was never justifiable in Neo-Confucianism itself.

So tenacious were the cultural traditions that most changes remained within the broad limits of traditional directions. For example, the combined powers of dominant absolutism and increasing bureaucracy kept under their control the vast growth in manufacturing and trading; this was a major factor in retarding the potential development of capitalism. The institutional framework as evolved during the Sung remained unchanged until the 19th century.

Stable as it was, however, the Sung heritage of Chinese culture was far from being stagnant. Relying upon ancient origins, it became the new fountainhead that dominated the succeeding centuries. The neo-traditional period from the Sung to the eve of modern revolutions saw incremental changes that interweaved old and new trends. These changes inwardly pervaded the society and deepened their influence among the vast peasantry, making the whole culture ever more integrated, continuous, and stable and thus tenaciously resistant to other changes that were sudden, drastic, and fundamentally different.

(J.T.C.L.)

VIII. The Yüan dynasty

THE MONGOL CONQUEST OF CHINA

Genghis Khan rose to supremacy over the Mongol tribes in the steppe in 1206, and within a few years he attempted to conquer northern China. By securing the allegiance of the Tangut state of Hsi Hsia in what are now Kansu and northeastern Tibet (1209), he disposed of a potential enemy and prepared the ground for an attack against the Chin state of the Juchen in northern China.

Preparations for war against Chin

At that time the situation of Chin was precarious, because in 1206–08 the Juchen had been exhausted by a costly war against their hereditary enemies, the Sung. Discontent among the non-Juchen elements of the Chin population (Chinese and Khitan) had increased, and not a few Chinese and Khitan nobles defected to the Mongol side. Genghis Khan, in his preparation for the campaign against Chin, could therefore rely on a number of foreign advisers who were familiar with the territory and the conditions of the Chin state.

Invasion of the Chin. The Mongol armies started their attack in 1211, invading from the north in three groups; Genghis Khan led the centre group himself. For several years they pillaged the country; finally, in 1214, they concentrated upon the central capital of the Chin (what is now Peking). Its fortifications proved difficult to overcome, so the Mongols concluded a peace and withdrew. Shortly afterward, the Chin emperor moved his capital to K'ai-feng (now in Honan Province). Genghis Khan considered this a breach of the armistice; a renewed attack brought large parts of northern China under Mongol control and finally resulted in the capture of Ta-tu (Peking; 1215). The Mongols had had little or no experience in siege craft and warfare in densely populated areas; their strength had been chiefly in cavalry attacks. The assistance of defectors from the Chin state probably contributed to this early Mongol success. In subsequent campaigns, the Mongols relied even more upon the sophisticated skills and strategies of the increased number of Chinese under their control.

After 1215 the Chin were reduced to a small buffer state between the Mongols in the north and Sung China in the south, and their extinction was but a matter of time. The Mongol campaigns against Hsi Hsia in 1226–27 and the death of Genghis Khan in 1227 brought a brief respite for Chin, but the Mongols resumed their attacks in 1230.

The Sung Chinese, seeing a chance to regain some of the territories they had lost to the Juchen in the 12th century, formed an alliance with the Mongols and besieged K'ai-feng in 1232 (the defenders fought with a kind of flamethrower—one of the earliest recorded instances for the use of fire weapons). The Emperor of Chin left K'ai-feng in 1233, just before the town fell, and took up his last residence in Ts'ai Prefecture (Honan); but this refuge was also doomed. In 1234 the Emperor committed suicide, and organized resistance ceased. The southern border of the former Chin state—the Huai Ho—now became the border of the Mongol dominions in northern China.

Invasion of the Sung. The next decades saw an uneasy coexistence between the Mongols in northern China and the Sung state in the south. The Mongols resumed their advance in 1250 under the Grand Khan Möngke (Mangu) and his brother Khublai Khan—grandsons of Genghis Khan. Their armies outflanked the main Sung defenses on the Yangtze River and penetrated deeply into southwestern China, conquered the independent Tai state of Nan Chao (in what is now Yunnan Province), and even reached present-day North Vietnam. Möngke died in 1259, and Khublai succeeded him; Khublai sent an ambassador, Hao Ching, to the Sung court with an offer to establish peaceful coexistence. Hao did not reach the Sung capital of Lin-an (now Hangchow), however, but was interned at the border and regarded as a simple spy. The many letters that Hao Ching from his confinement addressed to the Sung government in pursuit of his diplomatic mission remained unanswered.

Mongol penetration into southwestern China

The Sung chancellor, Chia Ssu-tao, considered the Sung position strong enough to risk this affront against Khublai; he thus ignored the chance offered by Khublai and instead tried to strengthen the military preparations against a possible Mongol attack. He secured military provisions by a land reform that included the confiscation of land from large owners, but this alienated the greater part of the landlord and official class. The Sung generals, whom Chia distrusted, also had grievances, which may explain why a number of them later surrendered to the Mongols without fighting.

From 1268 on, the Mongols, this time assisted by numerous Chinese auxiliary troops and technical specialists, attacked on several fronts. The prefectural town of Hsiang-yang on the Han River was a key fortress, blocking the access to the Yangtze River. The Mongols besieged Hsiang-yang for five years (1268–73). (Marco Polo in his book boasts that his father and uncle built catapults for the Mongols at Hsiang-yang, but Chinese sources indicate that the siege artillery was under the direction of Arab engineers from Iraq.) The Chinese commander finally surrendered in 1273, after he had obtained a solemn promise from the Mongols to spare the population; and he took office with his former enemies.

Khublai Khan's warning to his forces not to engage in indiscriminate slaughter seems to have been heeded to a certain extent. Several prefectures on the Yangtze River surrendered; others were taken after brief fighting. In January 1276, Mongol troops reached Lin-an. Last-minute attempts by the Sung court to conclude a peace failed, and the Mongol armies took Lin-an in February. The reigning Sung empress dowager and the nominal emperor—a boy—were taken to Ta-tu and granted an audience by Khublai Khan.

National resistance in the Sung state continued, however, and loyalists retreated with two Imperial princes into the southern province of Fukien and from there to the region of Kuang-chow. In 1279 the last remnants of the court fled the mainland by boat, and eventually, a faithful minister drowned himself and the last surviving Imperial prince in the ocean. When organized resistance ceased soon afterward, foreign invaders controlled the whole Chinese empire for the first time in history.

CHINA UNDER THE MONGOLS

Mongol government and administration.   After their initial successes in northern China in 1211–15, the Mongols faced the problem of how to rule and extract material benefits from a largely sedentary population. They were assisted by Khitan and Chinese and even Juchen renegades; these defectors were treated as "companions" (*nökör*) of the Mongols and were given positions similar to the higher ranks of the steppe aristocracy—their privileges included the administration and exploitation of fiefs considered as their private domain.

Early Mongol rule.   The government system during the early years of the Mongol conquest was a synthesis of Mongol military administration and a gradual return to Chinese traditions in those domains ruled by former subjects of the Chin state. The most important office or function in Mongol administration was that of the *darughatchi* (or seal bearer), whose powers were at first all-inclusive; only gradually were subfunctions entrusted to specialized officials in accordance with Chinese bureaucratic tradition. This refeudalization of northern China along Mongol lines with a slight understructure of Chinese-type bureaucrats lasted for many years.

The central administration of Mongol China was largely the creation of Yeh-lü Ch'u-ts'ai, originally a Chin state official of Khitan extraction who had acquired a profound Chinese scholarship and had become one of Genghis Khan's trusted advisers. Yeh-lü continued to serve under Ögödei, who became grand khan in 1229, and persuaded him to establish a formal bureaucracy and to replace indiscriminate levies with a rationalized taxation system along Chinese lines. An important part of Yeh-lü's reforms was the creation of the Chung-shu sheng (Central Secretariat), of which he became the first head (the Central Secretariat represented a bureaucratic body that could centralize the civilian administration and achieve some continuity).

The territory was divided into provinces, and the provincial administrations were chiefly responsible for regularized taxation. The people had to pay a land tax and a poll tax, either in kind (textiles and grain) or in silver. Merchants had to pay a sales tax. Monopolies on wine, vinegar, salt, and mining products were also introduced. All this enabled the treasuries of the Mongol court to accumulate considerable wealth.

In spite of the success of his economic policy, Yeh-lü's influence decreased during his later years. One reason was bitter opposition from the Mongol feudatories and from those Chinese, Juchen, and Khitan nobles who were used to ruling independently in their appanages, which they exploited at will. Also, Ögödei himself apparently lost interest in the internal conditions of the Mongol dominion in China. During the 1230s, Muslims

from the Near East had already begun to fill the higher positions at the Mongol court, and their ruthless exploitation of the Chinese created widespread resentment of Mongol rule. A relapse into feudal anarchism seemed inevitable, and Yeh-lü's reforms fell into temporary abeyance. China was ruled more or less like a colony by the foreigners and their allies.

Changes under Khublai Khan and his successors.   Khublai Khan's ascendancy in 1260 marked a definite change in Mongol government practice; Khublai moved the seat of Mongol government from Karakorum in Mongolia to the Shang-tu (Upper Capital) near modern To-lun in Inner Mongolia, and in 1267 the official capital was transferred to Peking, or Ta-tu (Great Capital), as it was then called. Under its Turkicized name, "Cambaluc" (Qan Balya, "the Khan's town"), Peking became known throughout Asia and even Europe. But, true to nomad traditions, the Mongol court continued to move between these two residences—Shang-tu in summer and Ta-tu in winter. With the establishment of Peking as the seat of the central bureaucracy, Outer Mongolia and Karakorum no longer remained the centre of the Mongol empires. Mongolia began to fall back to the status of a northern borderland, where a nomadic way of life continued and from where Mongol grandees, dissatisfied with the growing Sinicization of the court, repeatedly engaged in rebellions.

Khublai, who even prior to 1260 had surrounded himself with Chinese advisers, was still the nominal overlord of the other Mongol dominions (*ulus*) in Asia; but his Chinese entourage persuaded him to accept the role of a traditional Chinese emperor. A decisive step was taken in 1271, when the Chinese dominion was given a Chinese dynastic name—Ta Yüan, the Great Yüan. The name "Yüan" was in itself, however, a departure from Chinese traditions. All earlier Chinese dynasties were named after ancient feudal states or geographic terms; even the Khitan and the Juchen had followed this tradition by naming their states Liao (after the Liao River in Manchuria) and Chin (Gold, after the name of a river in Manchuria that had a Juchen name meaning "gold"). Yüan (Primeval) was the first nongeographic name of a Chinese dynasty since Wang Mang, who established the Hsin dynasty (AD 9–23); it was chosen from a passage in the Chinese *I Ching* ("Classic of Changes") and was, therefore, a purely literary name.

During the 1260s the central bureaucracy and the local administration of the Chinese empire were remodelled on Chinese lines. The Central Secretariat remained the most important civilian authority, with specialized agencies such as the traditional six ministries of finance, war, officials, rites, punishments, and public works. The Shu-mi yüan (Military Council) was another institution inherited from previous dynasties. A Yü-shih t'ai (Censorate) was originally created for remonstrations against the emperor and criticism of policies; but it became more and more an instrument of the court itself and a tool to impeach and eliminate other members of the bureaucracy. In the main, the territorial divisions followed Chinese models, but the degree of local independence was much smaller than it had been under the Sung; the provincial administrations were actually branches of the Central Secretariat and were therefore called *hsing chung-shu sheng* ("moving central secretariats"). The structures of the various provincial administrations throughout China were smaller replicas of the Central Secretariat. According to a Chinese source, in 1260–61 the lower echelons in the Central Secretariat were mostly Chinese; the high offices, however, even if they had traditional Chinese names, were reserved for non-Chinese. Surprisingly, Khublai Khan had few Mongols in high administrative positions; apparently suspicious of some of his tribal leaders, he preferred absolute foreigners. The military sphere was affected least by the attempts to achieve a synthesis between Chinese and native ways of life; there the Mongol aristocracy remained supreme.

Too many antagonistic social and ethnic groups existed within the government to secure a stable rule. The traditional Chinese value system had largely disappeared, and

The Mongols' use of defectors

Foundation of the Yüan dynasty

no political ethics had replaced it. The personalized loyalty ties focussed on the ruler; the companionship of *nökör* relations was not enough to amalgamate the heterogeneous ruling group into a stable body, and a decline in efficiency resulted. This unbalanced system of government could function only under a strong ruler; under a weak or incompetent emperor, disintegration was certain.

The former scholar-bureaucrats of China remained to a great extent outside the governmental and administrative structure; only minor positions were open to them. The Mongols never made full use of the administrative potential of the scholar-bureaucrats, fearing their competence and abilities. The ruling foreign minority in China was more an elite of the colonialist type than a part of the Chinese social system.

The basic unwillingness of the Mongols to assimilate with the Chinese is shown clearly by their attempts to cement the inequalities of their rule. After the Sung empire had been conquered, the whole population of China was divided into four classes. The first class was the Mongols themselves, a tiny minority but privileged in every respect. Next came the *se-mu jen* ("persons with special status"), such confederates of the Mongols as Turks or Near Eastern Muslims. The third group was called the *han-jen* (a term that generally means Chinese but that was used to designate the inhabitants of northern China only); this class included the Chinese and other ethnic groups living in the former Chin state, as well as Hsi Hsia, Juchen, Khitan, Koreans, Po-hai, and Tangut, who could be employed in some functions and who also formed military units under Mongol leadership. The last group was the *man-tzu*, an abusive term in Chinese, meaning "southern barbarian," which designated the former subjects of Sung China, the majority group of the whole Chinese empire. The lowest stratum in Yüan China was the slaves, whose numbers were quite considerable. The slave status was hereditary, and only under certain conditions could a slave be freed.

Over 80 percent of the taxpayers came from the *man-tzu* group, which was generally barred from holding higher office (only rarely would one of them rise to some prominence). The Mongols and the *se-mu jen* were tax-exempt and enjoyed the protection of the law to a higher degree than did the *han-jen* and *man-tzu*.

The formal distinction between various ethnic groups and the corresponding graded status was no Mongol invention but a social differentiation inherited from the Chin state. In the same way, many institutions were taken over from the Chin. Law in Yüan China was based partly on the legislation of the Chin and partly on traditional Chinese law; but Mongol legal practices and institutions also played a great role, particularly in penal law. The Yüan legal code has been preserved in the dynastic history, *Yüan shih;* in addition, many rules, ordinances, and decisions of individual cases are collected in such compilations as *Yüan tien-chang*, which throw much light not only on the legal system but also on social conditions in general.

Mongol and Chinese dualism was also reflected in the problem of administrative documents and languages. Few of the ruling Mongols knew Chinese, and the number who mastered the Chinese script was still smaller. Even during the later years of the Yüan, the number of Mongols and other foreigners who knew Chinese remained comparatively small. On the other hand, very few Chinese bothered to learn the language of the conquerors. Administration and jurisdiction, therefore, had to rely largely on interpreters and translators. Mongol was the primary language; most decisions, ordinances, and decrees were originally drafted in Mongol, and a Chinese interlineary version was added. This Chinese version was in the colloquial language instead of the formal documentary style, and it followed the Mongol word order so that these Chinese versions must have seemed barbaric to the native literati. Many of these Chinese versions have survived in such collections as *Yüan tien-chang*.

Economy. The Mongol conquest of the Sung empire had for the first time since the end of T'ang reunified all

China. Sung China had been trading with its neighbours, the Liao and Chin, but trade was strictly controlled and limited to authorized border markets. The Mongol conquest therefore reintegrated China's economy. The Mongol administration, in its desire to utilize the resources of the former Sung territory, the most prosperous part of China, tried to promote internal trade and aimed at a fuller integration of North and South. The Peking region was dependent on grain transports from the south, and large quantities of food and textiles were needed to keep the Mongol garrisons. The Grand Canal, which had linked the river systems of the Yangtze, the Huai, and the Huang Ho since the early 7th century AD, was repaired with conscripted corvée labour under supervision of Chinese hydraulic engineers—an action entirely within Chinese tradition. This was preceded, however, by another measure in the field of economic communications that was unorthodox in Chinese eyes: in about 1280, concessions for grain transport overseas were granted to some private Chinese entrepreneurs from the southeastern coastal region (some Chinese government officials were traditionally antagonistic toward private trade and enterprise, an attitude that the ruling Mongols did not share). These private shipowners transported in their fleets grain from the lower Yangtze regions to northern Chinese harbours and from there to the capital. Early in the 14th century, however, these private fleet owners, who had made huge fortunes, were accused of treason and piracy, and the whole action was abolished; the Mongol government never replaced them with government fleets.

Another factor that contributed to the flourishing internal trade in China was the unification of currency. The Sung and Chin had issued paper money, but only in addition to bronze coins, which had remained the basic legal tender. The Yüan government was the first to make paper money the only legal currency throughout the empire. This facilitated financial transactions in the private sector as well as in the state treasuries. As long as the economy as such remained productive, the reliance on paper money as the basic currency had no detrimental effects. Only when the economy began to disintegrate under the last Mongol ruler did the paper money became gradually valueless and inflation set in. One reason for the paper currency might have been that much bronze and copper was used for the Buddhist cult and its statues, another that metal ores in China proper were never in sufficient quantity to guarantee the founding of enough coins to supply a national economy serving about 80,000,000 people.

Religious and intellectual life. The Mongols did not try to impose their own religion (a cult of Heaven, the forces of nature, and shamanistic practices) on their subjects. This gave comparative freedom to the existing religions in China. Under the Chin dynasty, several popular Taoist sects had flourished in northern China, and Genghis Khan had apparently been impressed by the Taoist patriarch Ch'ang-ch'un. In 1223 Genghis Khan granted to Ch'ang-ch'un and his followers full exemption from taxes and other duties demanded by the government; this was the first of a series of edicts granting special privileges to the clergy of the various religions in China.

For some time it seemed as if Chinese Taoism would win favour with the Mongol rulers at the expense of Chinese Buddhism. The Buddhists, however, also profited from the open-minded attitude at the court; they tried to win influence within the Imperial family, prompted by the fact that many Buddhist institutions had been occupied by the Taoists, who relied on Mongol favour. Under the grand khan Möngke, several discussions were held between the Taoist and the Buddhist clergy, ending in a ruling that the former Buddhist temples should be returned to their original purpose. Imperial orders also outlawed some apocryphal Taoist texts, in which Buddhism was presented as a branch of Taoism and the Buddha as a reincarnation of Lao-tzu, the mythical founder of Taoism. But Taoism as such continued to exist under the Yüan, and the fiscal privileges originally granted to the Taoist followers of Ch'ang-ch'un were extended on principle to all clergies.

Buddhism. The spokesmen of Chinese Buddhism under the early Mongol rulers came from the Dhyāna sect (meditation Buddhism). Their high intellectuality and refined aestheticism, however, did not appeal to the Mongols, who felt more attracted by the mixture of magic practices, rather nebulous metaphysics, and impressive symbolism in the visual arts of Tibetan Buddhism. Khublai Khan appointed a young Tibetan lama known by the honorific name of 'Phags-pa as Imperial teacher (*ti-shih*); 'Phags-pa became the head of the Buddhist church in all Mongol dominions, including China. A special government agency to deal with Buddhism was established in 1264 and served as a sort of bureau for the Imperial teacher; it was in charge not only of Buddhist affairs in general but also of Tibetan affairs, although Tibet remained outside the administration of China proper, and no Mongol garrisons were ever established in Tibet. Tibetan politicians had thus succeeded in winning over the Mongol court and in retaining a more than just nominal independence.

After the conquest of Sung China, a special agency for the supervision of Buddhism in southern China was established and placed under the control of another Tibetan lama. There thus existed two supervisory offices for Buddhism—one in Ta-tu for northern China and Tibet and one in Hangchow for southern China. The southern office caused great resentment among Chinese Buddhists and the population at large by its brutal and avaricious procedures, seizures of property, and extortions from the population. Throughout the Yüan dynasty, complaints continued against the arrogant behaviour of Tibetan lamas. (Under the last emperor, Tibetan clerics introduced the court to sexual rites calling for intercourse with consecrated females—practices not unfamiliar in Indian and Tibetan cultures but shocking to the Chinese elite.)

Complaints against Tibetan lamas

Although Buddhism had won a victory among the ruling minority of China, it was a foreign rather than a Chinese Buddhism. The national varieties of Buddhism, especially meditation Buddhism, continued to exist, and monasteries in southern China sometimes became islands of traditional civilization where monks and lay Buddhists alike cultivated poetry, painting, and all the intellectual pastimes of the Chinese literati class; but, on the whole, Chinese Buddhism suffered from the general conditions in the Yüan empire. The exemption from taxes and corvée labour attracted many persons to monastic life for purely utilitarian reasons, and, the more society disintegrated, the more people sought refuge behind the monastery walls. In about 1300, the number of monks throughout China was about 500,000, and it must have grown during the last decades of Mongol rule. Monks played a great role in the rebellions to which the Yüan empire eventually succumbed; also, the first Ming emperor had been a monk for some time.

Foreign religions. Tibetan lamaism always remained outside Chinese civilization, as did other imported religions. A certain number of Muslims came to China, all from the Near East or from Central Asia. The Turkic Öngüt tribe was largely Nestorian Christian. Many tombstones have been preserved with a bilingual Turkic and Chinese inscription, but none of these believers seems to have been Chinese by origin; a census taken about 1300 in Chen-chiang (in present Kiangsu Province) lists the Nestorians together with foreign nationalities. The number of Nestorian Christians in China was so great that in 1289 a special agency for their supervision was established in Peking. Manichaeism, which had spread to China under the T'ang, had become extinct under the Yüan as an organized religion; but some Manichaean communities were probably absorbed by messianistic Buddhist sects such as the White Lotus sect, group that attracted many followers among the Chinese lower classes.

Confucianism. Confucianism—insofar as it can be considered as a religion—had a difficult stand under Mongol rule. Confucian scholars enjoyed the benefits extended to the clergy of all religions; but what hit the Chinese cultural elite hardest was the discontinuation of literary examinations, which had for many centuries been the basis for selection of officials and for their privileged

position within state and society. A certain Confucianization took place under Khublai Khan; Chinese rituals were performed for a while in the dynastic temple (*t'ai-miao*), erected in Peking in 1263, and some lip service was paid to Confucius and to the study of the Classics. In fact, however, most of the rites observed at the court were either Buddhist–lamaist or inherited from the Mongol nomad past. The emperor Buyantu (ruled 1311–20), who showed a more than average interest in Chinese civilization, reintroduced the examination system in 1313, but it remains doubtful how well the examinations functioned. They certainly did not guarantee an official career, as those under the Sung and, to a certain extent, under the Chin had done.

Discontinuation of literary examinations

The system of the Yüan, as introduced in 1313, provided different types of curricula for Mongols, other foreigners (*se-mu jen*), and Chinese; also, the requirements were different—Chinese had to show their complete mastery of the curriculum, whereas Mongols and other foreigners could get away with a mediocre performance. This inequality was even formalized for the candidates who were to be admitted to the state academy (*kuo-tzu chien*). The first examinations were held in the presence of the Emperor in 1315, and, of the 300 persons granted the title of doctor (*chin-shih*), 75 were Mongols, 75 were other foreigners, 75 were northern Chinese (*han-jen*), and 75 came from southern China; they all received official positions within the bureaucracy, Mongols the higher and Chinese the lesser posts. The positions of power within the hierarchy remained in the hands of the Mongols and other foreigners.

Under Buyantu, for the first time, the interpretation and commentaries of the Neo-Confucian school were made obligatory. This cemented Neo-Confucian ideology not only among the Chinese literati who wished to pass an examination but also for future generations. Chinese Confucian orthodoxy from the 14th to the 19th century therefore rested largely on the foundations it had received under the Yüan. In spite of all this, Classical scholarship under the Yüan did not produce a single remarkable work; the Confucian scholars were content with expounding the doctrines laid down by the Sung philosophers.

Literature. Chinese literature also shows conservative tendencies. To compose poetry remained a favourite pastime of the educated class, but no great works or stylistic innovations were created. During the last chaotic decades of the Yüan, some notable poets emerged, such as the versatile Yang Wei-cheng and the bold and unconventional Kao Ch'i.

Many prose works dealing with contemporary events and persons were composed under the Yüan, but these were notable for their content, not their literary merit. Surprisingly harsh criticism and satire against the Mongols and also undisguised Sung loyalism found expression, presumably because the Mongols as a group were uninterested in what the Chinese wrote in Chinese and, moreover, were mostly unable to read it. Some writers collected rare or interesting and piquant items and transmitted many aspects of Sung culture to future generations. The lament for the refinement and grandeur of the Sung is a constant theme in Yüan writings.

Criticism and satirization of the Mongols

In historiography, the early Yüan period was relatively unproductive. The intellectual climate was not conducive to the creation of historical works on the scale of the Sung period. Several works of private historiography were written, dealing chiefly with the last phase and eventual downfall of the Sung—events that, in the eyes of the educated Chinese, had to be explained somehow; and as usual the explanation was sought in the neglect of the traditional Confucian values under the last Sung rulers. The official dynastic histories for the Sung, Liao, and Chin were compiled in 1343–45 by a committee of mostly Chinese historians. These compilations led to a debate on the principle of legitimate succession. A number of scholars had the opinion that the Sung was a legitimate dynasty up to the year 1279 but that border states such as the Liao and Chin empires were not legitimate enough to merit their own history, The committee, however, did not give in, and so the three states each received their own history, a fact that allows modern scholars to study the Chinese multistate system in the 10th–13th centuries from several sides. Because of a huge mass of historical material that had survived in Ta-tu (for the Liao and Chin) and Hangchow (for the Sung), the compilation was achieved quickly. Later Chinese critics have called the three histories superficial and stylistically inferior; the haste with which the work was done certainly prevented a thorough revision of the original documentary materials, but it also prevented much distortion and harmonization so that the source value of these histories must be regarded as relatively high.

Popular literature

In urban society a literature in the vernacular language began to flourish, untrammelled by rigid norms of formalistic or ideological orthodoxy. Novels and stories were written for the amusement of a wide-reading public. And dramatic literature reached such a peak in Yüan China that later literary criticism regarded the Yüan as the classical age for operatic arias (*ch'ü*, a word that also means a full opera, with arias and chanted recitativo). The collection *Yüan ch'ü hsüan* ("Selection from Yüan Operas"), with 100 opera librettos, gives ample evidence for the creativity and vitality of Chinese dramatic literature. This phenomenon may perhaps be considered as evidence that under the Yüan a certain urbanization took place and something like a kind of bourgeoisie emerged because dramatic literature and colloquial novels found their clientele chiefly among the merchant and artisan classes.

Foreigners, chiefly of Turkic or Persian origins, also contributed to Chinese literature under the Yüan; they tried to emulate the traditional Chinese culture. They wrote poetry and painted in the Chinese way in order to distinguish themselves in fields where they could gain prestige among the educated Chinese. All the foreigners who wrote in Chinese seem to have avoided any reference to their foreign origin or creed. Nothing, in fact, could be more Chinese than their productions. Even foreigners who, like the Persians, came from a country with a considerable literary tradition of their own never attempted to introduce their native forms, subject matter, or religions. No literary symbiosis seemed possible; and, although China was exposed to more external influences under the Yüan than ever before, Chinese literature shows little effects from such contacts with the outside world. It is perhaps symptomatic that under the Yüan no literary works from other civilizations were translated into Chinese and that practically no translations of Chinese Classical and historical works into Mongol have survived. There seemed to be only the alternatives of complete rejection of Chinese civilization, as practiced by most Mongols, or wholesale absorption by Chinese culture.

Yüan China and the West. As mentioned above, Mongol rulers favoured trade in all their dominions. In China too, they eliminated state trade controls that had existed under the Sung and Chin, so that internal and external trade reached unprecedented proportions. It seems, however, that China's transcontinental trade with the Near East and Europe was in the hands of non-Chinese (Persians, Arabs, Syrians). Silk, the Chinese export commodity *par excellence*, reached the Near East and even Europe via the caravan routes across Asia; Chinese ceramics were also exported, chiefly into the Islāmic countries. The Asian countries concentrated their European trade largely with the Italian republics (*e.g.*, Genoa, Venice). To the Italians, trade with the East was so important that the *Practica della Mercatura*, a handbook on foreign trade, included the description of trade routes to China.

Early Chinese contacts with Europe and the Near East

Direct contacts between China and Europe were insignificant, however, in spite of China's being a part of an empire stretching from Ta-tu to southern Russia. Chinese historical and geographic literature had little to say about the European parts of the Mongol Empire; in the official dynastic history of the Yüan, references to foreign countries are limited to countries such as Korea, Japan, Vietnam, Burma, and Champa, with which China had carried on trade or tributary relations for centuries,

and there are some scattered data on Russia. For some time a Russian guards regiment existed in Ta-tu, and some Russian soldiers were settled in military colonies in what is now eastern Manchuria. As a whole, however, the civilizations of Europe and China did not meet, although contacts were made easy; Europe remained for the Chinese a vague region somewhere "beyond the Uighurs."

More important were the contributions from the Muslim countries of the Near East, chiefly in the fields of science and technology. During the reign of Khublai Khan, Arab–Persian astronomy and astronomical instruments were introduced into China, and the Chinese astronomer Kuo Shou-ching operated an observatory. Nevertheless, the basic conceptions of astronomy remained Chinese, and no attempt was made to adopt the Near Eastern mathematical and theoretical framework. Similarly, Near Eastern physicians and surgeons practiced successfully in China, but Chinese medical theory remained uninfluenced by Western impacts. In geography a Chinese world map of the 14th century incorporates Arabic geographical knowledge into the Chinese world view. It shows not only China and the adjacent countries but also the Near East, Europe, and Africa; the African continent is already given in its actual triangular shape. But this knowledge probably never spread beyond a limited circle of professional geographers, whereas it is certain that the Sinocentric world conception continued unchallenged under the Yüan dynasty; no curiosity of what lay beyond the Chinese borders was aroused. For the countries to be reached by sea (such as Southeast Asia and India), Chinese works of the Yüan offer only a poor extract from the Sung work *Chu-fan-chih* ("Description of the Barbarians") of *c.* 1225.

The situation is different regarding European knowledge of China. The Mongol advance into eastern Europe had given Europeans an acute awareness that actual people lived in regions hitherto shrouded in vague folkloristic legends and myths; the Islāmic world had become a reality to Europeans with the first Crusades. It was, therefore, only natural that the Roman Catholic Church looked for potential converts among the obviously non-Muslim people of Asia. After Franciscan envoys brought back information on what was known as Cathay (China) in the mid-13th century, Pope Nicholas IV, a former Franciscan, dispatched a Franciscan mission to the court of the Grand Khan in Ta-tu (known in Europe as Cambaluc). The missionaries formed the nucleus of a Catholic hierarchy on Chinese soil: Cambaluc became the seat of an archbishopric, and in 1323 a bishopric was established in Ch'üan-chou. A famous Franciscan missionary was Odoric of Pordenone, who travelled in China in the 1320s; his reports—together with letters written by other Catholic missionaries—brought first-hand information on China to medieval Europe and today throw some light on the earliest missionary work in China. The Franciscan mission, which had to compete with the Nestorian clergy, was carried on more by the foreigners in China than by the Chinese themselves. The friars preached in Tatar, which means either Mongol or Turkish, and apparently won no Chinese converts. Significantly, no Chinese source mentions the activities of these missionaries; the Chinese probably regarded the Franciscans as one of the many strange, foreign sects, perhaps an outlandish variety of Buddhism. Archaeological evidence of the presence of Europeans and of Roman Catholicism has been discovered only recently, in Yang-chou (in present Kiangsu Province), on a Latin tombstone dated 1342 and recording the death of an Italian lady whose name suggests some relation to a Venetian family engaged in trade with Asia.

European knowledge of China

Only the last direct contact between the papal see and Yüan China can be corroborated by both Western and Chinese sources. In 1336 a group of Alani Christians in Ta-tu sent a letter to Pope Benedict XII, who sent John of Marignola with a mission to the Mongol court. The mission reached the summer capital, Shang-tu, in 1342. Chinese sources have recorded the date of its audience as August 19, 1342. The country from where the envoys came is given by the Chinese source as Fu-lang, a Chinese version of the name Farang (Franks), which was used as a general term for Europeans in the Near East. The arrival of envoys from what must have seemed the end of the world so impressed the court that an artist was commissioned to paint a portrait of the battle horse that Marignola had brought as a present; this portrait was still extant in the 18th century but is now lost. Chinese literati wrote many eulogies on the portrait of the horse; the country of Fu-lang, however, did not interest the Chinese poets, and the whole embassy of Marignola is invariably described in terms that point to an unbroken Sinocentric attitude. Thus, the contact between the pontiff and the Mongol court remained without further consequence. The end of Mongol rule over China and the strong nationalism of the Ming dynasty also doomed the Catholic missions of the 14th century. The reports of Marco Polo, on the other hand, inaugurated for Europe the era of discoveries and created a new vision of the world, with China as a part.

Chinese
influence
in Asia

Although China as a separate cultural entity was only realized dimly and gradually in the European West, Chinese influences spread under the Yüan dynasty to other parts of Asia. Chinese medical treatises were translated into Persian, and Persian miniature painting in the 13th and 14th centuries shows many influences of Chinese art. Chinese-type administration and chancellery practices were adopted by various Mongol dominions in Central Asia and the Near East. It has even been suggested that the invention of gunpowder and of printing in Europe was due to a sort of stimulus diffusion from China, although a direct influence from China via the Near East cannot be proved.

Chinese civilization itself remained very much what it had been before the Yüan dynasty, and a certain cultural isolationism remained a distinctive element. Neither the self-image of the Chinese nor China's position in the world had changed very drastically. The change and challenges to which China had been exposed under the Yüan, however, can explain many of the characteristic traits of Ming history.

The end of Mongol rule. The basic dilemma of Mongol rule in China—the Mongols' inability to achieve a durable identification with Chinese civilian institutions and to modify the military and colonialist character of their rule—became more apparent under Khublai's successors and reached a maximum under Togon-temür, the last ruler of the Yüan dynasty. Togon-temür himself was not unfriendly toward Chinese civilization, but this could not alter the contempt of many leading Mongols for Chinese civilian institutions. For centuries, China had known clique factionalism at the court, but this was mostly fought with political means, whereas Mongol factionalism usually resorted to military power. Militarization gradually spread from the Mongol ruling class into Chinese society, and not a few dissatisfied Chinese leaders established regional power based on local soldiery. The central administration, headed by a weak emperor, proved incapable of preserving its supremacy.

Thus, the military character of Mongol rule paved the way for the success of Chinese rebels, some of whom came from the upper class, while others were messianistic sectarians who found followers among the exploited peasantry. The Mongol court and the provincial administrations could still rely on a number of faithful officials and soldiers, and so the progress of the rebel movement in the 1350s and 1360s remained slow. But the rebel armies who had chosen Nan-ching (Nanking) as their base took Ta-tu in 1368; the Mongol emperor fled to Shang-tu and later to Outer Mongolia, followed by the remnants of his overthrown government.

The Mongols remained a strong potential enemy of China for the next century, and the Genghis Khan clan in Mongolia continued to regard itself as the legitimate rulers of China. The century of Mongol rule had some lasting effects upon the government of China—Imperial absolutism and a certain brutalization of authoritarian rule, inherited from the Yüan, were features of the succeeding Ming government. (H.Fr.)

IX. Ming dynasty

POLITICAL HISTORY

Ineptitude on the throne, bureaucratic factionalism at court, rivalries among Mongol generals, and ineffective supervision and coordination of provincial and local administration had gravely weakened the Yüan dynasty government by the 1340s. And in 1351 disastrous flooding of the Huang and Huai river basins aroused hundreds of thousands of long-oppressed Chinese peasants into open rebellion in northern Anhwei, southern Honan, and northern Hupeh provinces. Capitalizing on the breakdown of Yüan control, rebel movements spread rapidly and widely, especially throughout central China; and by the mid-1360s large regional states had been created that openly flouted Yüan authority: Sung in the Huai basin, under the nominal leadership of a mixed Manichaean-Buddhist secret-society leader named Han Lin-erh; Han in the central Yangtze valley, under a onetime fisherman named Ch'en Yu-liang; Hsia in modern Szechwan, under an erstwhile general of the rebel Han regime named Ming Yü-chen; and Wu in the rich Yangtze Delta area, under a former Grand Canal boatman named Chang Shih-ch'eng. A onetime salt trader and smuggler named Fang Kuo-chen (1319/20–74) had simultaneously established an autonomous coastal satrapy in modern Chekiang province. While Yüan chieftains contended with one another for dominance at Ta-tu (modern Peking) and in the North China Plain, these rebel states to the south wrangled for survival and supremacy. Out of this turmoil emerged a new native dynasty called Ming (1368–1644).

Back-
ground
of the
founding
emperor

Chu Yüan-chang, founder of the new dynasty, came from a family of physiognomists from K'ai-feng city who in Yüan times had deteriorated into itinerant tenant farmers in northern Anhwei (see Hung-wu). Orphaned by famine and plague in 1344, young Chu was taken into a small Buddhist monastery near Feng-yang city as a lay novice. For more than three years he wandered as a mendicant through the Huai basin; then he studied for the Buddhist priesthood in his monastery. In 1352, after floods, rebellions, and Yüan banditry-suppression campaigns had devastated and intimidated the whole region, Chu was persuaded to join a Feng-yang branch of Han Lin-erh's uprising. He quickly made himself the most successful general on the southern front of the rebel Sung regime, and in 1356 captured and set up his headquarters in Nanking, a populous and strategically located city on the Yangtze River. There he began assembling a rudimentary government and greatly strengthened his military power. Between 1360 and 1367, still nominally championing the cause of the Sung regime, his armies gained control of the vast central and eastern stretches of the Yangtze valley, absorbing first the Han domain to the west of Nanking and then the Wu domain to the east. He also captured the Chekiang coastal satrap, Fang Kuo-chen. Chu then announced his intention of liberating all China from Mongol rule and proclaimed a new dynasty effective with the beginning of 1368. The dynastic name Ming, meaning "brightness," reflects the Manichaean influences in the Sung-revivalist Han Lin-erh regime under which Chu had achieved prominence.

Vigorous campaigning in 1368 drove the Mongols out of Shantung, Honan, and Shansi provinces and from Ta-tu itself, which was occupied by Ming forces on September 14 and simultaneously extended Ming authority through Fukien and Hunan into Kwangtung and Kwangsi provinces on the south coast. In 1369–70 Ming control was established in Shensi, Kansu, and Inner Mongolia; and continued campaigning against the Mongols thereafter extended northwestward to Hami—the gateway to Central Asia (1388)—northeastward to the Sungari River in Manchuria (1387), and northward into Outer Mongolia beyond Karakorum, almost to Lake Baikal (1387–88). In operations to the west and southwest, Ming forces destroyed the rebel Hsia regime in Szechwan in 1371, wiped out major Mongol and aboriginal resistance in Kweichow and Yunnan in 1381–82, and pacified troublesome aboriginal tribesmen on the Sino-Burmese border in 1398. Thus, by the end of Chu Yüan-chang's 30-year reign in 1398 his new dynasty controlled the whole of modern China proper and dominated the northern frontier regions from Hami, through Inner Mongolia and into northern Manchuria.

The dynastic succession. The Ming dynasty, which encompassed the reigns of 16 emperors, proved to be one of the stablest and longest dynasties of Chinese history. Rulers of Korea, Mongolia, Chinese Turkistan, Burma, Siam, and Vietnam regularly acknowledged Ming overlordship, and at times tribute was received from as far away as Japan, Java and Sumatra, Ceylon and South India, the East African coast, the Persian Gulf region, and Samarkand. Modern Chinese honour the Ming emperors especially for having restored China's international power and prestige, which had been in decline since the 8th century. The Ming emperors probably exercised more far-reaching influence in East Asia than any other native rulers of China, and their attitude toward the representatives of Portugal, Spain, Russia, Britain, and Holland who appeared in China before the end of their dynasty was a condescending one.

Ming era names

For the first time in Chinese history the Ming rulers regularly adopted only one era name (*nien-hao*) each; the sole exception was the sixth emperor, who had two reigns separated by an interval of eight years. Because of this era-name practice, which was perpetuated under the succeeding Ch'ing dynasty, modern writers, confusingly but correctly, refer to Chu I-chün, for example, by that personal name, or as Ming Shen Tsung, or as the Wan-li emperor, and sometimes, incorrectly but conveniently, simply as Wan-li, as if the era name were a personal name.

1. T'ai Tsu, temple name of Chu Yüan-chang, born 1328, reigned 1368–98; era name Hung-wu.

2. Hui Ti, temple name of Chu Yün-wen, grandson of T'ai Tsu; b. 1377, r. 1398–1402; era name Chien-wen.

3. Ch'eng Tsu, temple name of Chu Ti, son of T'ai Tsu; b. 1360, r. 1402–24; era name Yung-lo.

4. Jen Tsung, temple name of Chu Kao-chih, son of Ch'eng Tsu; b. 1378, r. 1424–25; era name Hung-hsi.

5. Hsüan Tsung, temple name of Chu Chan-chi, son of Jen Tsung; b. 1398, r. 1425–35; era name Hsüan-te.

6. Ying Tsung, temple name of Chu Ch'i-chen, son of Hsüan Tsung; b. 1427, r. 1435–49, era name Cheng-t'ung; restored 1457–64, era name T'ien-shun.

7. Ching Ti, temple name of Chu Ch'i-yü, brother of Ying Tsung; b. 1428, r. 1449–57; era name Ching-t'ai.

8. Hsien Tsung, temple name of Chu Chien-shen, son of Ying Tsung; b. 1447, r. 1464–87; era name Ch'eng hua.

9. Hsiao Tsung, temple name of Chu Yu-t'ang, son of Hsien Tsung; b. 1470, r. 1487–1505; era name Hung-chih.

10. Wu Tsung, temple name of Chu Hou-chao, son of Hsiao Tsung; b. 1491, r. 1505–21; era name Cheng-te.

11. Shih Tsung, temple name of Chu Hou-tsung cousin of Wu Tsung, grandson of Hsien Tsung; b. 1507, r. 1521–66; era name Chia-ching.

12. Mu Tsung, temple name of Chu Tsai-kou, son of Shih Tsung; b. 1537, r. 1566–72; era name Lung-ch'ing.

13. Shen Tsung, temple name of Chu I-chün, son of Mu Tsung; b. 1563, r. 1572–1620; era name Wan-li.

14. Kuang Tsung, temple name of Chu Ch'ang-lo, son of Shen Tsung; b. 1582, r. only one month in 1620; era name T'ai-ch'ang.

15. Hsi Tsung, temple name of Chu Yu-chiao, son of Kuang Tsung; b. 1605, r. 1620–27; era name T'ien-ch'i.

16. Chuang-lieh-ti, canonical name given by Manchus to Chu Yu-chien, brother of Hsi Tsung; b. 1611, r. 1627–44; era name Ch'ung-chen; canonized by various Ming loyalists as Ssu Tsung, Huai Tsung, and I Tsung.

The founding emperor, T'ai Tsu, was one of the strongest and most colourful personalities of Chinese history. His long reign established the governmental structure, policies, and tone that characterized the whole dynasty. After his death in 1398 his grandson successor Hui Ti, trying to assert control over his powerful uncles, provoked a rebellion on the part of the Prince of Yen and was overwhelmed in 1402. The Prince of Yen, posthumously titled Ch'eng Tsu (see Yung-lo), took the throne for himself and proved to be vigorous and aggressive. He subjugated Nam Viet (present North Vietnam), personally campaigned against the reorganizing Mongols in the north, and sent large naval expeditions overseas, chiefly under the eunuch admiral Cheng Ho (*q.v.*), to demand tribute from rulers as far away as Africa.

For a century after Ch'eng Tsu the empire enjoyed stability, tranquillity, and prosperity. But state administration began to suffer from exploitative domination of weak emperors by favoured eunuchs: Wang Chen in the 1440s, Wang Chih in the 1470s and 1480s, and Liu Chin from 1505 to 1510. Jen Tsung, Hsüan Tsung, and Hsiao Tsung were, nevertheless, able and conscientious rulers, in the Confucian mode. The only serious disruption of the peace occurred in 1449 when the eunuch Wang Chen led Ying Tsung into a disastrous military campaign against the Oyrats (Western Mongols). The Oyrat leader Esen Taiji ambushed the Imperial army, captured the emperor, and besieged Pei-ching (modern Peking). The defense minister, Yü Ch'ien, forced him to withdraw unsatisfied and for eight years dominated the government with emergency powers. When the interim emperor, Ching Ti, fell ill in 1457 Ying Tsung was restored, having been released by the Mongols in 1450 to live in disgraced retirement. Yü Ch'ien was then executed as a traitor.

Conflict with the Western Mongols

Wu Tsung and Shih Tsung were among the less esteemed Ming emperors. Wu Tsung was an adventure-loving carouser, Shih Tsung a lavish patron of Taoist alchemists. For one period of 20 years, during the regime of an unpopular grand secretary named Yen Sung, Shih Tsung withdrew almost entirely from governmental cares. Both emperors cruelly humiliated and punished hundreds of officials for their temerity in remonstrating.

China's long peace ended in Shih Tsung's reign. The Oyrats, under the vigorous new leadership of Altan Khan, were a constant nuisance on the northern frontier from 1542 on; in 1550 Altan Khan raided the suburbs of Pei-ching itself. During the same era Japan-based sea raiders repeatedly plundered China's southeastern coast. Such sea raiders, a problem in Yüan times and from the earliest Ming years, were suppressed in Ch'eng Tsu's reign, when the Ashikaga shogunate offered nominal submission to China in exchange for generous trading privileges. But eventually changes in the official trade system provoked new discontents along the coast, and during the 1550s corsair fleets looted the modern Shanghai-Ning-po region almost annually, sometimes sending raiding parties far inland to terrorize cities and villages throughout the whole Yangtze Delta. Although coastal raiding was not totally suppressed, it was brought under control in the 1560s. Also in the 1560s Altan Khan was repeatedly defeated, so that he made peace in 1571. For the next decade, during the last years of Mu Tsung and the early years of Shen Tsung, there was a high level of governmental stability. The court was dominated by the outstanding grand secretary of Ming history, Chang Chü-cheng; and capable generals such as Ch'i Chi-kuang restored and maintained effective military defenses.

In 1592, when Japanese forces under Hideyoshi invaded Korea, Ming China was still strong and responsive enough to campaign effectively in support of its tributary neighbour. But the Korean war dragged on indecisively until 1598, when Hideyoshi died and the Japanese withdrew. It made heavy demands on Ming resources and apparently precipitated a military decline in China.

The reign of Shen Tsung was a turning point of Ming history in other regards as well. Partisan wrangling among civil officials had flared up in the 1450s in reaction to Yü Ch'ien's dominance and again in the 1520s during a prolonged "rites controversy" provoked by Shih Tsung on his accession; after Chang Chü-cheng's death in 1582, it became the normal condition of court life. Through the remainder of Shen Tsung's long reign a series of increasingly vicious partisan controversies absorbed the energies of the officialdom, while the harassed emperor abandoned more and more of his responsibilities to eunuchs. The decline of bureaucratic discipline and morale continued under Kuang Tsung, whose sudden death after a reign of only one month in 1620 fuelled new conflicts. Hsi Tsung was too young and indecisive to provide needed leadership. In 1624 he finally gave almost totalitarian powers to his favourite, Wei Chung-hsien, the most notorious eunuch of Chinese history. Wei brutally purged hundreds of officials, chiefly those associated with a reformist clique called the Tung-lin party, and staffed the government with sycophants.

The threat from the Manchus

A new threat had meantime appeared on the northern frontier. The Manchus, quiet occupants of far eastern Manchuria from the beginning of the dynasty, were aroused in 1583 by an ambitious young leader named Nurhachi; and during Shen Tsung's latter years they steadily encroached on central Manchuria. In 1616 Nurhachi proclaimed a new dynasty, and overwhelming victories over Ming forces, in 1619 and 1622, gave him control of the whole northeastern segment of the Ming empire, down to the Great Wall at Shan-hai-kuan.

Chuang-lieh-ti tried to revitalize the deteriorating Ming government. He banished Wei Chung-hsien but could not quell the partisan strife that was paralyzing the bureaucracy. The Manchus repeatedly raided within the Great Wall, even threatening Pei-ching in 1629 and 1638. Taxes and conscriptions became more and more oppressive to the Chinese population, and banditry and rebellions spread in the interior. The Ming government became completely demoralized. Finally, a domestic rebel named Li Tzu-ch'eng captured the capital in April, 1644. Chuang-lieh-ti committed suicide. The Ming commander at Shan-hai-kuan accepted Manchu help in an effort to punish Li Tzu-ch'eng and·restore the dynasty, only to have the Manchus seize the throne for themselves.

Ming loyalists ineffectively resisted the Manchu Ch'ing dynasty from various refuges in the South for a generation. Their so-called Southern Ming dynasty principally included the Prince of Fu (Chu Yu-sung, era name Hung-kuang, d. 1646), the prince of T'ang (Chu Yü-chien, era name Lung-wu, d. 1646), the Prince of Lu (Chu I-hai, no era name, d. 1662), and the Prince of Kuei (Chu Yu-lang, era name Yung-li, d. 1662). The loyalist coastal raider Cheng Ch'eng-kung (Koxinga) and his heirs held out on Taiwan until 1683.

GOVERNMENT AND ADMINISTRATION

Local government. The Ming state system was built upon a foundation of institutions inherited from the T'ang and Sung dynasties and modified by the intervening dynasties of conquest from the North, especially Yüan. The distinctive new patterns of social and administrative organization that emerged in Ming times persisted, in their essential features, through the Ch'ing dynasty into the 20th century.

At local and regional levels the traditional modes and personnel of government were perpetuated in ad hoc fashion in the earliest Ming years, but as the new empire became consolidated and stabilized T'ai Tsu imposed highly refined control structures that—in theory and probably also in reality—eventually subjugated all Chinese to the throne to an unprecedented and totalitarian degree. The Ming law code, promulgated in final form in 1397, reinforced the traditional authority and responsibility of the paterfamilias, considered the basis of all social order. Each family was classified in a hereditary status category, the chief categories being civilian, military, and artisan; and neighbouring families of the same category were organized into groups, for purposes of self-government and mutual help and surveillance. Thus civilians were grouped in "tithings" of ten families, and these, in turn, were grouped in "communities" totalling 100 families, plus ten additional prosperous households, which, in annual rotation, provided community chiefs who were intermediaries between the citizenry at large and the formal agencies of government. This li-chia (later called pao-chia) system of social organization served to stabilize, regulate, and indoctrinate the populace under relatively loose formal state supervision.

Social organization

As in earlier times, formal state authority at the lowest level was represented by court-appointed magistrates of counties (hsien), and each cluster of neighbouring counties was subordinate to a supervisory prefecture (fu) normally governed from and dominated by a large city.

Government at the modern provincial (sheng) level, after beginnings in Yüan times, was now regularized as an intermediary between the prefectures and the central government. There were 13 Ming provinces, each as extensive and populous as modern European states: Shantung, Honan, Shansi, Shensi (incorporating modern Kansu), Szechwan, Hukuang (comprising modern Hupeh and Hunan), Kiangsi, Chekiang, Fukien, Kwangtung, Kwangsi, Kweichow, and Yunnan. Nam Viet (modern North Vietnam) was a 14th province from 1407 to 1428. The large regions dominated by the great cities Pei-ching (in modern Hopeh) and Nan-ching (Nanking in modern Kiangsu and Anhwei) were not subordinated to provincial-level governments but for administrative supervision were "directly attached" (chih-li) to the capital establishments in those cities; they are normally referred to as the northern and southern metropolitan areas (Pei Chih-li and Nan Chih-li). Nan-ching was the national capital until 1420. Thereafter Pei-ching was the capital, but Nan-ching retained special status as auxiliary capital.

Ming provincial governments consisted of three coordinate agencies with specialized responsibilities for general administration, surveillance and judicial affairs, and military affairs. These were the channels for routine administrative contacts between local officials and the central government.

Central government. In its early form the Ming central government was dominated by a unitary Secretariat. The senior executive official of the Secretariat served the emperor as a chief counsellor, or prime minister. Suspected treason on the part of the chief counsellor Hu Wei-yung in 1380 caused T'ai Tsu to abolish all executive posts in the Secretariat, thus fragmenting general-administration authority among the six functionally differentiated, formerly subordinate ministries of Personnel, Revenue, Rites, War, Justice, and Works. This so-called abolition of the Secretariat left the emperor as the central government's sole coordinator of any significance, strengthened his control over the officialdom, and, in the view of many later scholars, gravely weakened the Ming state system.

Especially prominent among other agencies of the central government was a Censorate, which was charged with the dual functions of maintaining disciplinary surveillance over the whole officialdom and of remonstrating against unwise state policies and improprieties in the conduct of the emperor. Equally prominent were five chief military commissions, each assigned responsibility, jointly with the Ministry of War, for a geographically defined segment of the empire's military establishment. There was originally a unitary Chief Military Commission paralleling the Secretariat; but in the 1380s its authority was similarly fragmented. The hereditary soldiers, who were under the administrative jurisdiction of the chief military commissions, originated as members of the rebel armies that established the dynasty, as surrendering enemy soldiers, in some instances as conscripts, or as convicted criminals. They were organized and garrisoned, principally along the frontiers, near the capital, or in other strategic places, but also throughout the interior, in units called guards and battalions. Whenever possible, such units were assigned state-owned agricultural lands so that, by alternating military duties with farm labour, the soldiers could be self-supporting. The "military families," in compensation for providing soldiers in perpetuity, enjoyed exemptions from labour services levied by the state on civilian families and benefitted to some extent from special land-tax treatment. Each guard unit reported to its Chief Military Commission at the capital through a provincial-level Regional Military Commission. Soldiers from local guards were sent in rotation to the capital for special training or to the Great Wall or another area of comparable military importance for active patrol and guard duty. At such times, as on large-scale campaigns, soldiers served under tactical commanders who were on ad hoc duty assignments, detached from their hereditary posts in guard garrisons or higher echelons of the military service.

Military organization

Later innovations. In the 15th century new institutions were gradually devised to provide needed coordination both in the central government and in regional administration. Later emperors found T'ai Tsu's system of highly centralized power and fragmented government structure inefficient and inconvenient. Litterateurs of the traditional and prestigious compiling and editing agency called the Hanlin Academy came to be assigned to the palace as secretarial assistants, and they quickly evolved into a stable Grand Secretariat (Nei-ko) through which emperors guided and responded to the ministries and other central government agencies. Similarly, the need for coordinating provincial-level affairs led to the delegation of high-ranking central government dignitaries to serve as regional commanders (tsung-ping kuan) and governor-like grand coordinators (hsün-fu) in the provinces. Finally, clusters of neighbouring provinces came under the supervisory control of still more prestigious central government officials, known as supreme commanders (tsung-tu), whose principal function was to coordinate military affairs in extended, multiprovince areas. As the dynasty grew older, as the population expanded, and as administration became increasingly complex, coordinators proliferated even at subprovincial levels in the form of circuit intendants (tao-t'ai), who were delegated from provincial agencies as functionally specialized intermediaries with prefectural administrations.

Recruitment by competitive examinations

To an extent unprecedented except possibly in Sung times, Ming government was dominated by nonhereditary civil-service officials recruited on the basis of merit demonstrated in competitive written examinations. Hereditary military officers, although granted ranks and stipends higher than their civil-service counterparts and eligible for noble titles rarely granted to civil officials, always found themselves subordinate to policy-making civil servants except in the very early years of the dynasty. Members of the Imperial clan, except in the earliest and latest years of the dynasty, were forbidden to take active parts in administration; and the Ming practice of finding Imperial consorts in military families effectively denied Imperial in-laws access to positions of significant authority. High-ranking civil officials were customarily able to place one son each in the civil service by hereditary right, and, beginning in 1450, wealthy civilians often were able to purchase nominal civil-service status in government fund-raising drives. But persons entering the service in such irregular ways rarely had notable, or even active, careers in government. In the early decades of the dynasty, before competitive examinations could provide sufficient numbers of trustworthy men for service, large numbers of officials were recruited directly from government schools, or through recommendations by existing officials; and such recruits often rose to eminence. But after about 1400, persons entering the civil service by avenues other than examinations had virtually no hope for successful careers.

In a departure from traditional practices, but in accordance with the Yüan precedent, there was only one type of examination given in Ming times. It required a general knowledge of the Classics and history, the ability to relate Classical precepts and historical precedents to general philosophical or specific political issues, and competence in traditional forms of literary composition. As in Yüan times, interpretations of the Classics by the Chu Hsi school of Neo-Confucianism were prescribed. By the end of the Ming dynasty the writing of examination responses had become highly stylized and formalized in a pattern called "the eight-legged essay" (pa-ku-wen), which, in subsequent centuries, became notoriously repressive of creative thought and writing.

Local schools

Beginning in T'ai Tsu's reign, the government sponsored county-level schools, in which state-subsidized students prepared for the civil-service examinations. Especially talented students could be promoted from such local schools into programs of advanced learning and probationary service at a National University in the capital. Especially after 1500, there was a proliferation of private academies in which scholars gathered to discuss philosophy and students were also prepared for the examinations. Education intendants from provincial headquarters annually toured all localities, examining candidates who presented themselves and certifying those of "promising talent" (hsin-ts'ai) as being qualified to undertake week-long examination ordeals that were conducted every third year at the provincial capitals. Those who passed the provincial examinations, normally called licentiates (chü-jen), could be appointed directly to posts in the lower echelons of the civil service. They were also eligible to compete in triennial metropolitan examinations conducted at the national capital. Those who passed were given degrees often called doctorates (chin-shih) and promptly took an additional palace examination, nominally presided over by the emperor, on the basis of which they were ranked in order of excellence. They were registered as qualified officials by the Ministry of Personnel, which assigned them to active-duty posts as vacancies occurred. While on duty they were evaluated regularly by their administrative superiors and irregularly by touring inspectors from the Censorate. It was normally only after long experience and excellent records in low- and middle-grade posts, both in the provinces and in the capital, that an official might be nominated for high office and appointed by personal choice of the emperor.

Although acceptance into, and success in, the civil service (which in Ming times came to be considered the most highly esteemed goal for all) were achievements nominally determined solely by demonstrated scholastic and administrative abilities, other factors inevitably intruded to prevent the civil-service system from being wholly "open." Differences in the economic status of families made for inequalities of educational opportunity and, consequently, inequalities of access to civil-service careers. The sons of well-to-do families clearly had advantages, and men of the affluent and cultured southeastern region so threatened to monopolize genuinely "open" scholastic competitions that regional quotas for passers of the metropolitan examinations were imposed by the government, beginning in 1397. Once in the service, moreover, one's advancement or even survival often depended on shifting patterns of favouritism and factionalism. Modern scholarship strongly suggests, nevertheless, that "new blood" was constantly entering the Ming civil service, that influential families by no means monopolized or dominated the service, and that men regularly rose from obscurity to posts of great esteem and power on the basis of their merit. Social mobility, as reflected in the Ming civil service, was very possibly higher than in Sung times and was clearly higher than in the succeeding Ch'ing era.

Weaknesses of Ming government

The Ming pattern of government has generally been esteemed for its stability under civil-service dominance, its innovative creativity in devising new institutions to serve changing needs, and its suppression of separatist warlordism on one hand and disruptive interference by Imperial clansmen and palace women on the other. It suffered, however, from sometimes vicious factionalism among officials, from recurrences of abusive influence on the part of palace eunuchs, and from defects in its establishment of hereditary soldiers. The military system not only failed to achieve self-support but stagnated steadily, so that from the middle of the 15th century on, it had to be supplemented by conscripts and, finally, all but replaced by mercenary recruits. Most notoriously, the Ming state system allowed emperors to behave capriciously and abusively toward their officials. Despite their high prestige, officials had to accept being ignored, humiliated, dismissed, or subjected to bodily punishment, and to risk being cruelly executed (sometimes in large numbers), as suited the Imperial fancy. Power was concentrated in the hands of the Ming emperors to a degree that was probably unparalleled in any other long-lived dynasty of Chinese history, and the Ming emperors often exercised their vast powers in abusive fashions.

FOREIGN RELATIONS

Whereas in Ming times the Chinese organized themselves along wholly bureaucratic and tightly centralized lines the Ming emperors maintained China's traditional feudal-seeming relationships with foreign peoples. These included the aboriginal tribespeople of south and southwest China, who often rose in isolated rebellions but were gradually being assimilated. The Chinese took for granted that their emperor was everyone's overlord and that de facto (mostly hereditary) rulers of non-Chinese tribes, regions, and states were properly his feudatories. Foreign rulers were thus expected to honour and observe the Ming ritual calendar, to accept nominal appointments as members of the Ming nobility or military establishment, and, especially, to send periodic missions to the Ming capital to demonstrate fealty and present tribute of local commodities. Tributary envoys from continental neighbours were received and entertained by local and provincial governments in the frontier zones. Those from overseas were welcomed by special maritime trade superintendencies (*shih-po ssu*, often called offices of trading ships) at three key ports on the southeast and south coasts: Ning-po in Chekiang (for Japanese contacts), Ch'üan-chou in Fukien (for contacts with Taiwan and the Liu-ch'iu or Ryukyu Islands), and Kuang-chou (modern Canton) in Kwangtung (for contacts with Southeast Asia). The frontier and coastal authorities forwarded foreign missions to the national capital, where the Ministry of Rites offered them hospitality and arranged for their audiences with the emperor. All envoys received valuable gifts in acknowledgement of the tribute they presented. They also were permitted to buy and sell private trade goods at specified, officially supervised markets, both in the capital and on the coasts and frontiers. Thus, copper coins and luxury goods (notably silks and porcelains) flowed out of China, and pepper, other spices, and similar rarities flowed in. On the western and northern frontiers the principal exchange was in Chinese tea and steppeland horses. On balance, the combined tribute and trade activities were highly advantageous to foreigners—so much so that the Chinese early established limits for the size and cargoes of foreign missions and prescribed long intervals that must elapse between missions.

Aims of foreign policy

The principal aim of Ming foreign policy was political: to maintain China's security and, especially, to make certain the Mongols could not threaten China again. To this end, as has been noted, T'ai Tsu repeatedly sent armies northward and northwestward to punish resurgent Mongol groups and prevent any reconsolidation of Mongol power. Ch'eng Tsu was even more zealous: he personally campaigned into the Gobi five times, and his transfer of the national capital from Nan-ching to Pei-ching, completed in 1421 after long preparations, was largely a reflection of his great concern about the frontier. Ch'eng Tsu's successors were less zealous than he in this regard, but they were vigilant enough so that the Great Wall was restored and expanded to its present-day extent and dimensions. Frontier defense forces, aligned in nine defense commands stretching from Manchuria to Kansu, kept China free from Mongol incursions, except for occasional raiding forays such as those by Taiji Esen and Altan Khan.

The fact that the Mongols could not reunite themselves was a fortunate circumstance for Ming China. As early as Ch'eng Tsu's time the Mongols were divided into three groups that were often antagonistic to one another. They were the so-called Western Mongols or Oyrats (also known as Eleuthes, Kalmycks, or Dzungars), the Eastern Mongols or Tatars, and a group in modern Jehol Province known as the Urianghad tribes. The Urianghad tribes surrendered to T'ai Tsu and were incorporated into China's frontier defense system under a Chinese military headquarters. Because they served Ch'eng Tsu as a loyal rear guard during his rebellion against Hui Ti, Ch'eng Tsu rewarded them with virtual autonomy, withdrawing the Chinese command post from their homeland behind the Great Wall. Subsequently, Hsüan Tsung similarly withdrew the command post that T'ai Tsu had established at the Mongols' old extramural capital, Shang-tu. These withdrawals isolated Manchuria from China proper, terminated active Chinese military control in modern Inner Mongolia, and exposed the Pei-ching area in particular to the possibility of probing raids from the nearby steppes. They reflected an essentially defensive Chinese posture in the north, which by late Ming times allowed the Oyrats to infiltrate and dominate Hami and other parts of the northwestern frontier, and the Manchus to rise to power in the northeast.

As for foreign peoples other than the Mongols, the Ming attitude was on the whole unaggressive: so long as they were not disruptive, the Ming emperors left them to themselves. T'ai Tsu made this his explicit policy. Even though he threatened the Japanese with punitive expeditions if they persisted in marauding along China's coasts, he dealt with the problem by building strong fortresses and coastal-defense fleets that successfully repulsed the marauders. T'ai Tsu did send an army to subdue Turfan in 1377 when the Turko-Mongol rulers of that oasis region rebelled and broke China's traditional transport routes to the west. But he refused to intervene in dynastic upheavals in Nam Viet and Korea (Koryŏ), and he was unmoved by the rise of the Turko-Mongol empire of Timur in the far west at Samarkand, even though Timur murdered Chinese envoys and planned to campaign against China.

Ch'eng Tsu was much more aggressive. He sent the eunuch admiral Cheng Ho on massive tribute-collecting voyages into Southeast Asia, the Indian Ocean, the Persian Gulf, and as far as East Africa. On one early voyage Cheng Ho intervened in a civil war in Java and established a new king there; on another, he captured the hostile king of Ceylon and took him prisoner to China. Ch'eng Tsu also reacted to turbulence in Nam Viet by sending in an expeditionary force that incorporated the area directly into the Ming domain as a province in 1407.

After Ch'eng Tsu's time the Ming government reverted to T'ai Tsu's unaggressive policy toward foreign states. Nam Viet was abandoned in 1428 after protracted guerrilla-style resistance had thoroughly undermined Chinese control there. A new civil war in Nam Viet provoked the Chinese, after long and agonized discussion, to prepare to intervene there again in 1540; but the offer of ritual submission by a usurper gave the Chinese an opportunity to avoid war, and they welcomed it. On only two other occasions were Ming military forces active outside China's borders: in 1445–46, when Chinese troops pursued a rebellious border chief into Burma despite Burmese resistance; and in 1592–98, when the Ming court undertook to help Chosŏn (Korea) repulse Japanese invaders, in a long and costly effort.

In order to preserve the government's monopolistic control of foreign contacts and trade, and, at least in part, to keep the Chinese people from being contaminated by "barbarian" customs, the Ming rulers prohibited private dealings between Chinese and foreigners and forbade any private voyaging abroad. The rules were so strict as to disrupt even coastal fishing and trading, on which large populations in the south and southeast had traditionally depended for their livelihood. Such unrealistic prohibitions were unpopular and unenforceable, and from about the middle of the 15th century Chinese readily collaborated with foreign traders in widespread smuggling, for the most part officially condoned. By late Ming times, also, thousands of venturesome Chinese had migrated to become mercantile entrepreneurs in the various regions of Southeast Asia and even in Japan. In efforts to enforce its laws the Ming court closed all maritime trade superintendencies except the one at Kuang-chou early in the 16th century, and by the 1540s had begun to reinvigorate coastal defenses against marauders throughout the southeast and the south.

These circumstances shaped the early China coast experiences of the modern Europeans, who first appeared in Ming China in 1514. The Portuguese had already established themselves in southern India and at Malacca, where they learned of the huge profits that could be made in the regional trade between the China coast and Southeast Asia. Becoming involved in what the Ming court considered smuggling and piracy, the Portuguese were not welcomed to China; but they would not be rebuffed, and by 1557 had taken control of a settlement at

Tribute-collecting voyages of Ch'eng Tsu's reign

the walled-off end of a coastal peninsula (modern Macao) and were trading periodically at nearby Kuang-chou. In 1575 Spaniards from Manila visited Kuang-chou in a vain effort to get official trading privileges, and soon they were developing active though illegal trade on the Kwangtung and Fukien coasts. Representatives of the Dutch East India Company, after unsuccessfully trying to capture Macao from the Portuguese in 1622, took control of coastal Taiwan in 1624 and began developing trade contacts in nearby Fukien and Chekiang provinces. In 1637 a squadron of five English ships shot its way into Kuang-chou and disposed of its cargoes there. Russia, meanwhile, had sent peaceful missions overland to Pei-ching, and by the end of the Ming dynasty the Russians' eastward expansion across Siberia had carried them finally to the shores of the Pacific north of the Amur River.

Missionary activities

Christian missionaries from Europe were handicapped by the bad reputation their trader countrymen had acquired in China, but the Jesuit tactic of accommodating to local customs eventually got them admitted to the mainland. Matteo Ricci (*q.v.*) was the successful pioneer, beginning his work, in 1583, well trained in the Chinese language and acquainted with Confucian learning. By the time of his death in 1610, despite hostility in some quarters, Jesuit communities were established in many cities of south and central China, a church had been built in Pei-ching under Imperial patronage, and Christianity was known and respected by many Chinese scholar-officials. Before the end of the dynasty, Jesuits had won influential converts at court (notably the grand secretary Hsü Kuang-ch'i, or Paul Hsü), had produced Chinese books on European science as well as theology, were manufacturing Portuguese-type cannon for Ming use against the Manchus and they also held official appointments in China's Directorate of Astronomy, which had the important responsibility of determining the official calendar. Both European technology and European ideas were beginning to have some effect on China, albeit still very limited.

ECONOMIC POLICY AND DEVELOPMENTS

Population. Ming China's northward orientation in foreign relations was accompanied by a flow of Chinese migrants from the crowded South back into the vast North China Plain, and by a concomitant shift in emphasis from an increasingly urban and commercial way of life back to a predominantly rural and agrarian pattern. Thus, demographic and economic trends that had characterized China for centuries—the southward movement of population and the urbanization and commercialization of life—were arrested or even reversed.

Migration to the North

The North China Plain had been neglected since early Sung times, and its rehabilitation became a high-priority project of the early Ming emperors. The Ming founder's ancestral home was in the North, and his son Ch'eng Tsu not only won the throne from a personal power base in the newly recovered North but moved the national capital from Nan-ching to Pei-ching. Securing the northern frontier was the major political goal of both of these emperors, and both had reasons for being somewhat suspicious of southerners and hostile toward them. In consequence, both emperors regularly moved well-to-do city dwellers of the Yangtze Delta region to northern towns for their cultural adornment, resettled peasants from the overpopulated southeast into the vacant lands of the North for their agrarian redevelopment, and instituted water-control projects to restore the productivity of the Huang and Huai river basins. (Notable among these were thousands of engineering contributions toward rehabilitating and extending the Grand Canal, which reopened in 1415.) Colonists were normally provided with seeds, tools, and animals and were exempted from taxes for three years. The numerous army garrisons that were stationed in the North for defense of the frontier and of the post-1420 capital at Pei-ching were also given vacant lands to develop and were encouraged to become self-supporting. Such government measures were supplemented, following political reunification, by popular migration into the relatively frontier-like and open North.

Rehabilitation of the North was no doubt also facilitated by the new availability of sorghum for dryfield planting. All these elements in combination produced a substantial revival of the North. Whereas in Yüan times censuses credited the northern provinces with only one-tenth of the total Chinese population, by the late 16th century they claimed 40 percent of the registered total; and until the late Ming years they were productive enough to sustain themselves as well as most of the large frontier defense forces. Suspension of government incentives late in the 15th century caused the northwest to enter upon a long agrarian decline, so that Shensi Province eventually became impoverished and bandit-infested. Support of the frontier defenses consequently became an increasing burden on the central government.

During the migrations back to the North, the registered populations of the largest urban centres of the southeast declined. Between 1393 and 1578 Su-chow (Soochow) declined from 2,355,000 to 2,011,000; Nan-ching from 1,193,000 to 790,000; Sung-chiang from 1,219,000 to 484,000; Chekiang Province from 10,487,000 to 5,153,000; and Kiangsi Province from 8,982,000 to 5,859,000. Despite this evening-out trend in the regional distribution of population, however, the South, and especially the southeast, remained the most populous, the wealthiest, and the most cultured areas of China in Ming times. Such great southeastern cities as Nan-ching, Su-chou, and Hang-chou (Hangchow) remained the major centres of trade and manufacturing, of entertainment, and of scholarship and the arts. Pei-ching was their only rival in the North—solely because of its being the centre of political power.

Population changes

Although official census figures suggest that China's overall population remained remarkably stable in Ming times at a total of about 60 million, modern scholars have estimated that there was, in fact, substantial growth, probably to a total well over 100 million and perhaps almost as high as 150 million in the early 17th century. Domestic peace and political stability in the 15th century clearly set the stage for great general prosperity in the 16th century. This can be accounted for in part as the cumulative result of the continuing spread of early ripening rice and of cotton production—new elements that had been introduced into the Chinese economy in Sung and Yüan times. The introduction in the 16th century of food crops originating in America (peanuts, maize, and sweet potatoes) created an even stronger agrarian basis for rapidly escalating population growth in the Ch'ing period.

Agriculture. Neo-feudal land-tenure developments of late Sung and Yüan times were arrested with the establishment of the Ming dynasty. Great landed estates were confiscated by the government, fragmented, and rented out; and private slavery was forbidden. In the 15th century, consequently, independent peasant landholders predominated in Chinese agriculture. But the Ming rulers were not able to provide permanent solutions for China's perennial land-tenure problems. As early as the 1420s the farming population was in new difficulties despite repeated tax remissions and other efforts to ameliorate its condition. Large-scale landlordism gradually reappeared, as powerful families encroached upon the lands of poor neighbours. Sung-style latifundia do not seem to have reemerged, but by the late years of the dynasty, sharecropping tenancy was the common condition of millions of peasants, especially in central and southeastern China, and a new gulf had opened between the depressed poor and the exploitative rich. The later Ming government, though it issued pronouncements lamenting the plight of the common man in an endless stream, never undertook any significant reform of land-tenure conditions. Indeed, the government itself, especially in the 16th century, repeatedly transformed peasants into oppressed tenant farmers by assigning huge tracts to empresses, princes, Imperial in-laws, and various Imperial favourites, whose business agents were the most callous of all landlords.

Taxation. The Ming laissez-faire policy in agrarian matters had its counterpart in fiscal administration. The Ming state took the collection of land taxes—its main

Collection
of land
taxes

revenues by far—out of the hands of civil-service officials and entrusted this responsibility directly to well-to-do family heads in the countryside. Each designated tax captain was, on the average, responsible for tax collections in an area for which the land-tax quota was 10,000 piculs (one picul = 138 pounds) of grain. In collaboration with the *li-chia* community chiefs of his fiscal jurisdiction, he saw to it that tax grains were collected and then delivered, in accordance with complicated instructions: some to local storage vaults under control of the county magistrate, and some to military units, which, by means of the Grand Canal, annually transported more than 3,000,000 piculs northward to Pei-ching and the frontier garrisons. In the early Ming years venal tax captains seem to have been able to amass fortunes by exploiting the peasantry. Later, however, tax captains normally faced certain ruin because tax-evading manipulations by large landlords thrust tax burdens increasingly on those least able to pay and forced tax captains to make up deficiencies in their quotas out of their personal reserves.

The land-tax rate was highly variable, depending not on the productivity of any plot but on the condition of its tenure, which might be as freehold or as one of several categories of land rented from the government. The land tax was calculated together with labour levies or corvée, which, though nominally assessed against persons, were assessed against land in normal practice. Corvée obligations also varied widely and were usually payable in paper money or in silver rather than in actual service. Assessments against a plot of land might include several other considerations as well, so that a farmer's tax bill was a complicated reckoning of many different tax items. Efforts to simplify land-tax procedures in the 16th century, principally initiated by conscientious local officials, culminated in the universal promulgation of a consolidated-assessment scheme called "a single-whip" (*i-t'iao-pien*) in 1581. Its main feature was the reduction of land tax and corvée obligations to a single category of payment in bulk silver or its grain equivalent. This reform was little more than a bookkeeping change at best, and it was not universally applied. Land-tax inequities were unaffected, and assessments rose sharply and repeatedly from 1618 to meet spiralling costs of defense.

Many revenues other than land taxes contributed to support of the government. Some, such as mine taxes and levies on marketplace shops and vending stalls, were based on proprietorship; others, such as salt taxes, wine taxes, and taxes on mercantile goods in transit, were based on consumption. Of all state revenues, more than half always seem to have remained in local and provincial granaries and treasuries; and of those forwarded to the capital, about half seem normally to have disappeared into the emperor's personal vaults. Revenues at the disposal of the central government were always relatively small. Prosperity and fiscal caution had resulted in the accumulation of huge surpluses by the 1580s, both in the capital and in many provinces; but thereafter the Sino-Japanese war in Chosŏn, unprecedented extravagances on the part of the long-lived emperor Shen Tsung, and defense against domestic rebels and the Manchus bankrupted both the central government and the Imperial household.

Coinage. Copper coins were the original Ming monetary units and remained in use throughout the dynasty. Paper money was issued from 1375 and was used for various kinds of payments and grants by the government, but it was always nonconvertible and, consequently, lost value disastrously. It would, in fact, have been utterly valueless except that it was prescribed for the payment of certain types of taxes. The exchange of precious metals was forbidden in early Ming times, but gradually bulk silver became common currency, and after the middle of the 16th century, government accounts were reckoned primarily in taels (ounces) of silver. By the end of the dynasty silver coins produced in Mexico, introduced by Spanish sailors based in the Philippines, were becoming common on the south coast.

Because the last century of the Ming dynasty saw the emergence of a genuine money economy, and because

concurrently there developed some relatively large-scale mercantile and industrial enterprises under private as well as state ownership (most notably in the great textile centres of the southeast), some modern scholars have considered the Ming age one of "incipient capitalism" from which European-style mercantilism and industrialization might have evolved had it not been for the Manchu conquest and expanding European imperialism. It would seem clear, however, that private capitalism in Ming times flourished only insofar as it was condoned by the state, and it was never free from the threat of state suppression and confiscation. State control of the economy—for that matter, of society in all its aspects—remained the dominant characteristic of Chinese life in Ming times as earlier.

CULTURE

The predominance of state power also marked the intellectual and aesthetic life of Ming China. By requiring use of their interpretations of the Classics in education and in the civil-service examinations, the state prescribed the Neo-Confucianism of the great Sung thinkers Ch'eng I and Chu Hsi as the orthodoxy of Ming times; by patronizing or commandeering craftsmen and artists on a vast scale, it set aesthetic standards for all the minor arts, for architecture, and even for painting; and by sponsoring great scholarly undertakings and honouring practitioners of traditional literary forms, the state established norms in these realms as well. It has consequently been easy for subsequent historians of Chinese culture to categorize the Ming era as an age of bureaucratic monotony and mediocrity. But the stable, affluent Ming society, in fact, proved irrepressibly creative and iconoclastic. Drudges by the hundreds and thousands may have been content with producing second-rate imitations or interpretations of T'ang and Sung masterpieces in all genres, but independent-minded thinkers, artists, and writers were striking out in many new directions. The final Ming century, especially, was a time of intellectual and artistic ferment akin to the most seminal ages of the past.

Philosophy and religion. Taoism and Buddhism by Ming times had declined into ill-organized popular religions, and what organization they had was regulated by the state. State espousal of Chu Hsi thought, and state repression of noted early litterateurs, such as the poet Kao Ch'i (1336–74) and the thinker Fang Hsiao-ju (1357–1402), made for widespread philosophical conformity during the 15th century. This was perhaps best characterized by the scholar Hsüeh Hsüan's (1389–1464) insistence that the Way had been made so clear by Chu Hsi that nothing remained but to put it into practice. Philosophical problems about man's identity and destiny, however, especially in an increasingly autocratic system, rankled in many minds; and new blends of Confucian, Taoist, and Buddhist elements appeared in a sequence of efforts to find ways of personal self-realization in contemplative, quietistic, and even mystical veins. These culminated in the antirationalistic individualism of the famed scholar-statesman Wang Shou-jen, or Wang Yang-ming (1472–1529), who denied the external "principles" of Chu Hsi and advocated striving for wisdom through cultivation of the innate knowledge of one's own mind and attainment of "the unity of knowledge and action." Wang's followers carried his doctrines to extremes of self-indulgence, preached to the masses in gatherings resembling religious revivals, and collaborated with so-called mad Ch'an Buddhists to spread the notion that Confucianism, Taoism, and Buddhism are equally valid paths to the supreme goal of individualistic self-fulfillment. Through the 16th century intense philosophical discussions were fostered, especially in rapidly multiplying private academies (*shu-yüan*). Rampant iconoclasm climaxed with Li Chih (1527–1602), a zealous debunker of traditional Confucian morality, who abandoned a bureaucratic career for Buddhist monkhood of a highly unorthodox type. Excesses of this sort provoked occasional suppressions of private academies, occasional persecutions of heretics, and sophisticated counterarguments from tradi-

Role of
the state in
intellectual
life

tionalistic, moralistic groups of scholars, such as those associated with the Tung-lin Academy near Su-chou who blamed the late Ming decline of political efficiency and morality on widespread subversion of Chu Hsi orthodoxy. The zealous searching for personal identity was only intensified, however, when the dynasty finally collapsed and China came under the rule of new alien conquerors, the Manchus.

Fine arts. In the realm of the arts, the Ming period has long been esteemed for the variety and high quality of its state-sponsored craft goods—cloisonné and, particularly, porcelain wares. The sober, delicate monochrome porcelains of the Sung dynasty were now superseded by rich, decorative polychrome wares. The best known of these are of blue-on-white decor, which gradually changed from floral and abstract designs to a pictorial emphasis. From this eventually emerged the "willow-pattern" wares that became export goods in great demand in Europe. By late Ming times, perhaps because of the unavailability of the imported Iranian cobalt that was used for the finest blue-on-white products, more flamboyant polychrome wares of three and even five colours predominated. Painting—chiefly portraiture—followed traditional patterns under Imperial patronage, but independent gentlemen-painters became the most esteemed artists of the age, especially four masters of the Su-chou area: Shen Chou (1427–1509), Ch'iu Ying (16th century), T'ang Yin (1470–1523), and Wen Chengming (1470–1559). Their work, always of great technical excellence, gradually became less and less academic in style; and out of this tradition, by the late years of the dynasty, emerged a widespread conception of the true painter as a professionally competent but deliberately amateurish artist bent on individualistic self-expression. Notably in landscapes, a highly cultivated and somewhat romantic or mystical simplicity became the approved style, perhaps best exemplified in the work of Tung Ch'ich'ang (1555–1636).

Literature and scholarship. As was the case with much of the painting, Ming poetry and belles-lettres were deliberately composed "after the fashion of" earlier masters, and groups of writers and critics earnestly argued about the merits of different T'ang and Sung exemplars. No Ming practitioner of traditional poetry has won special esteem, though Ming literati churned out poetry in prodigious quantities. The historians Sung Lien (1310–81) and Wang Shih-chen (1526–90) and the philosopher-statesman Wang Yang-ming were among the dynasty's most noted prose stylists, producing expository writings of exemplary lucidity and straightforwardness. Perhaps the most admired master was Kuei Yu-kuang (1506–71), whose most famous writings are simple essays and anecdotes about everyday life—often rather loose and formless but with a quietly pleasing charm, evoking character and mood with artless-seeming delicacy. The rampant iconoclasm of the final Ming decades was mirrored in a literary movement of total individual freedom, championed notably by Yüan Tsung-tao (1560–1600); but writings produced during this period have subsequently been denigrated as being insincere, coarse, frivolous, and so strange and eccentric as to make impossible demands on the readers.

The importance of popular fiction

The late Ming iconoclasm did successfully call attention to popular fiction in colloquial style. In retrospect, this must be reckoned the most significant literary work of the late Yüan and Ming periods, despite its being disdained by the educated elite of the time. The late Yüan-early Ming novels *San Kuo chih yen-i* (*Romance of the Three Kingdoms*) and *Shui-hu chuan* (*The Water Margin*, also known in translation as *All Men Are Brothers*) became the universally acclaimed masterpieces of the historical and picaresque genres, respectively. Sequels to each were produced throughout the Ming period. Wu Ch'eng-en, a 16th-century local official, produced *Hsi-yu chi* ("Travels to the West"), known in translation as *Monkey*), which became China's most treasured novel of the supernatural; and late in the 16th century an unidentifiable writer produced *Chin P'ing Mei* (*Golden Lotus*), a realistically Rabelaisian account of life and love among the bourgeoisie, which established yet another genre for the novel. By the end of the Ming period iconoclasts such as Li Chih and Chin Sheng-t'an (d. 1661), both of whom published editions of *Shui-hu chuan*, made the then astonishing assertion that this and other works of popular literature should rank alongside the greatest poetry and literary prose as treasures of China's cultural heritage. Colloquial short stories also proliferated in Ming times, and collecting anthologies of them became a fad of the last Ming century. The master writer and editor in this realm was Feng Meng-lung (1574–1645), whose creations and influence dominate the best-known anthology, *Chin-ku ch'i-kuan* ("Stories Old and New"), published in Su-chou in 1624.

Operatic drama, which had emerged as a major new art form in Yüan times, enjoyed continuing popularity throughout the Ming dynasty, and Yüan masterpieces in the tightly disciplined four-act *tsa-chü* style were regularly performed. Ming contributors to the dramatic literature were most creative in a more rambling, multiple-act form known as "southern drama" or as *ch'uan-ch'i*. Members of the Imperial clan and highly respected scholars and officials such as Wang Shih-chen and particularly T'ang Hsien-tsu (1550–1617) wrote for the stage. A new southern opera aria form called *k'un-ch'ü*, originating in Su-chou, became particularly popular and provided the repertoire of sing-song girls throughout the country. Sentimental romanticism was a notable characteristic of dramas written in Ming times.

Ming scholarship

Perhaps the most representative of all Ming literary activities, however, were voluminous works of sober scholarship in many realms. Ming literati were avid bibliophiles, both collectors and publishers. They founded many great private libraries, such as the famed T'ien-i-ko collection of the Fan family at Ning-po. They also began producing huge anthologies (*ts'ung-shu*) of rare or otherwise interesting books and thus preserved many works from extinction. The example was set in this regard by an Imperially sponsored classified anthology of all the esteemed writings of the whole Chinese heritage completed in 1407 under the title *Yung-lo ta-tien*. Its more than 11,000 volumes being too numerous for even the Imperial government to consider printing, it was preserved only in manuscript copies. Private scholars also produced great illustrated encyclopaedias, including: *Pen-ts'ao kang-mu* (late 16th century), a monumental materia medica listing 1,892 herbal concoctions and their applications; *San-ts'ai t'u-hui* (1609) on architecture, tools, costumes, ceremonies, animals, amusements, etc.; *Wu-pei chih* (1621) on weapons, fortifications, defense organization, and war tactics; and *T'ien-kung k'ai-wu* (1637) on industrial technology. Ming scholars also produced numerous valuable geographical treatises and historical studies, including more than 2,000 local and provincial histories or gazetteers. Among the true creative milestones of Ming scholarship, which pointed the way for the development of modern critical scholarship in early Ch'ing times, were the following: a work questioning the authenticity of sections of the ancient *Shu Ching* ("Classic of History") by Mei Tsu (16th century), a phonological analysis of the ancient *Shih Ching* ("Classic of Poetry") by Ch'en Ti (1541–1617); and a dictionary by Mei Ying-tso (17th century) that for the first time classified Chinese characters under 214 radicals and subclassified them by number of brushstrokes—the arrangement of most standard modern dictionaries (see also LITERATURE, EAST ASIAN).

One of the great all-round literati of Ming times, representative in many ways of the dynamic and wide-ranging activities of the Ming scholar-official at his best, was Yang Shen (1488–1559). Yang won first place in the metropolitan examination of 1511, remonstrated vigorously against the caprices of the emperors Wu Tsung and Shih Tsung, and was finally beaten, imprisoned, removed from his post in the Hanlin Academy, and sent into exile as a common soldier in Yunnan Province in the far southwest. But he produced poetry and belles-lettres in huge quantities, as well as a study of bronze and stone inscriptions through history, a dictionary of obsolete characters, suggestions about the phonology of ancient Chinese, and a classification of fish in Chinese waters.

(C.O.Hu.)

X. The Ch'ing dynasty

EARLY CH'ING

The rise of the Manchus.   The Manchus, the rulers of the Ch'ing dynasty, were descendants of the Juchen tribes of Manchuria who in the 11th century had founded the Chin dynasty. After 1403 the Ming dynasty Yung-lo emperor applied to them the so-called commandery system, under which the hereditary tribal chiefs were given an official title and subjected to Ming control. This system worked so well as a divide-and-rule tactic that, until the rise of Nurhachi (1559–1626), no powerful core of leadership emerged among the Juchen tribes. But in the middle of the 16th century there began to appear many fortified castles scattered throughout Manchuria as tribal centres, which signified development of more sophisticated forms of agriculture and commerce.

The Juchen agriculture was conducted by slaves they had captured on the Chinese and Korean borders; their commerce depended largely upon their trade with China. They exported to China ginseng roots, furs, and pearls in exchange for Chinese cloth, grains, metalworks, and other goods. The Ming aimed to control the Manchus by tying in their trade with the tributary system.

Emerging from one of the three commanderies of Chien-chou, Nurhachi annexed the other two in 1588; by 1616 he had unified most of the main Juchen tribes. This was not only a military but also a political and a diplomatic achievement. His success, however, was supported indirectly by a corrupt Ming official in Liao-tung, Li Ch'eng-liang, with whose connivance he succeeded in monopolizing the Manchu trade with China. In 1619 Nurhachi gained a decisive victory over the Ming army at Sarhu, east of Fu-shun, and in 1621 he seized the important cities of Liao-yang and Mukden; he made the latter city his capital in 1625.

Unification of the main Juchen tribes

In 1626 Nurhachi's son Abahai ascended the throne. Soon he attacked Chosŏn (Korea) and secured a trade mart at the mouth of the Yalu River, which enabled him to obtain Korean as well as Chinese goods. He ventured on an expedition in 1634 against the Chahar tribe of Inner Mongolia; this also made his China trade easier. In 1636 he was installed as emperor by the Manchus, Mongols, and the Chinese in Manchuria, and adopted the name Ch'ing, or "pure"; but Korea refused to recognize his new position. Abahai thus embarked on a second campaign to Korea, making it a vassal state of the Ch'ing with a large annual tribute.

Manchu entrance to Peking.   In China the Ming army, preoccupied with the invading Manchus, lost its chance to suppress roving bandits from Shensi Province who ravaged several provinces north of the Yangtze River. By 1635 Li Tzu-ch'eng and Chang Hsien-chung had emerged as the most prominent among these bandit leaders. In 1644 Chang set up a new state in Szechwan. Li returned to Shensi in 1643 and established a state at Hsi-an (Sian); then he marched to Peking (Pei-ching) and seized it in late April 1644, terminating the Ming dynasty. A Ming general, Wu San-kuei, sought Manchu assistance to retaliate against Li Tzu-ch'eng. Dorgon, the regent and an uncle of the Manchu Fu-lin, who ruled as the Shunchih emperor, defeated Li near Shan-hai Kuan and marched to Peking, where he declared the Manchu rule of China. Fu-lin became the first Ch'ing emperor of China.

Beginning of Manchu rule in China

Early resistance to the Manchus.   Li Tzu-ch'eng was driven to Hsi-an and fled to Hupeh, where he was killed in 1645. But his followers moved to Hunan, where they were incorporated into the army of a Ming loyalist. Chang Hsien-chung was also killed by Ch'ing troops in 1647, but his adherents moved to Kweichow and Yunnan.

In the southeast a few Ming princes were installed by the loyalists at Nan-ching (Nanking) and other coastal cities. But most of them soon surrendered to the advancing Manchu force. Chu Yu-lang, who had set up his re-

gime in the province of Kwangtung, extended his power to the southwestern provinces by absorbing the vast number of Li Tzu-ch'eng's remnants. In 1651 a coalition was formed with Chang Hsien-chung's followers. In 1659, however, the Ch'ing army secured the province of Yunnan, driving Chu to Burma.

Many of the groups, scattered over the country, that had risen up against the Ming in its last years, now turned their hostilities toward the new regime. Thus, huge hordes of the abused and dislocated commoners of the late Ming period joined the anti-Ch'ing movement and confronted the new dynasty with a long and difficult task of pacification. The Chinese generals and troops played an important role in coping with this resistance; the most distinguished among them was Wu San-kuei. He pacified Yunnan and governed it and Kweichow semi-independently from Peking, a situation that eventually became incompatible with the Ch'ing regime. In 1673 Wu launched a rebellion that quickly spread to the several adjoining provinces. It was joined in 1674 and 1676, respectively, by Keng Ching-chung in Fukien and Shang Chih-hsin in Kwangtung who, together with Wu, were called the three feudatories.

The rebel camp was curbed by Wu San-kuei's lack of positive policy and Keng's and Shang's dropping out. In Fukien Ch'ing took advantage of the feud between Keng and Koxinga's successor and restored Kwangtung Province by the end of 1677. This weakened Wu's position in Hunan, his foremost front; he died in 1678 soon after assuming the title of emperor. The Ch'ing restored Yunnan in 1681, terminating the great rebellion which had lasted for eight years and had its repercussion even in Inner Mongolia, Vietnam, and Tibet. Again the Chinese officers and troops were more meritorious in the field than the Manchus.

Early Ch'ing institutions.   The early Manchu state was based on the banner (military company) system, a transition from tribalism to a monarchial autocracy under which every Manchu tribesman was enlisted in a banner; at first there were four Manchu banners, which later expanded to eight. During Abahai's rule, this system was extended to the Mongols and the Chinese under his control. Chinese institutions were widely introduced by Abahai, and the Ming administrative practices were mostly adopted upon the Manchu arrival in Peking; but group leadership, in which the leaders of the banners shared in the top decision-making, was still preserved though partially modified to suit the Chinese institutions. But the Yung-cheng emperor (ruled 1723–35) was a reformer; he established the Grand Council (Chün-chi Ch'u), a body of advisers that worked closely and confidentially with the emperor, a prototype of what later developed as a supreme decision office, in 1731 (variously dated between 1726 and 1732); he also abolished the tight control of a banner chief over his bannermen, thus giving the emperor direct control, for the first time, over every bannerman.

The banner system

Another specific Ch'ing institution was the Court of Colonial Affairs (Li-fan yüan), which developed from the Mongolian Office and later came to handle relations with Tibet, Ch'ing-hai, Eastern Turkistan, and Russia. Unlike other offices, its main staffs were exclusively filled by Manchus and Mongols.

The core of the Ch'ing army was the banner force, which, before the Taiping Rebellion, numbered roughly 200,000 men. About half of these troops were stationed in and around the capital, and the rest were garrisoned in the provinces. There was another army called "Green Standards," which was recruited from the Chinese and totalled about 600,000. It was indeed unprecedented in Chinese history that the Ch'ing could control the vast empire with only some 800,000 troops.

In the K'ang-hsi (ruled 1661–1722) and Yung-cheng eras an epoch-making reform was made in the tax system: in 1713 the total number of the adult males (*ting*) liable to labour service (payable in money) was frozen; the amount of labour assessment thus fixed was merged with the land tax during the Yung-cheng period in almost all the provinces and localities. This innovation removed the former malpractice of imposing the *ting* tax on landless people.

Institutionally, the local officials could not dispense with some degree of surtaxing in the name of charges on "wastage and loss," which, however, tended to be arbitrarily increased. To prevent such a tendency, the Yung-cheng emperor legalized and limited the surcharges and at the same time invented a new system of official salary called *yang-lien* ("nourishing integrity") allowance. The reform had two aims: to prevent officials' embezzlement of public funds and to protect the taxpaying commoners from arbitrary squeeze by the officials. The emperor also used spies and encouraged high officials to communicate directly and secretly with him about provincial affairs, using palace memorials, a form of communication whose beginnings go back to the K'ang-hsi reign. By these efforts, Ch'ing rule was much consolidated.

Early foreign relations. The early Ch'ing, preoccupied with the conquest of China and the consolidation of their rule, also had to face problems on and beyond China's borders.

Russia. Russian eastward expansion, beginning in the late 16th century, was remarkable; Russians appeared on the Amur River in 1650 and fortified Albazin in 1651. But the Ch'ing lacked the power to cope with Russia until they were freed from the war with the three feudatories in 1681. In 1689 the Treaty of Nerchinsk between the Ch'ing and Russia, defined the Siberian–Manchurian borders along the Amur and Stenovoi Mountains to the sea and providing for periodic visits of Russian caravan traders to Peking. Another Sino-Russian treaty at Kiakhta in 1727 further defined the Siberian–Mongolian borders and regulated private trade at Kiakhta.

The main items of trade in the early period were Russian furs, gold, silver coins, European woolens, and Chinese silk and cotton cloth. But, after the turn of the 19th century, Russian cloth and Chinese tea became the main items of trade at Kiakhta, which reached the zenith of its prosperity in the 1830s and 1840s.

Mongolia, Tibet, and Eastern Turkistan. In the early Ch'ing period, western Mongolia lay beyond Peking's control; a move for unity emerged in the first half of the 17th century. Dga'-ldan, a chieftain of the Dzungar tribe of western Mongolia, began a conquest of Eastern Turkistan after 1672 as the first step in a plan to establish a Buddhist kingdom extending over all the Mongols and Tibetans in support of the fifth Dalai Lama of Tibet. By 1690 Dga'-ldan had reached Ulan-butung in Jehol, where he harassed the Ch'ing army and then returned north. But in 1696 the Ch'ing emperor led a vast army to Outer Mongolia and defeated Dga'-ldan.

In Tibet a scandal involving the sixth Dalai Lama gave the Dzungars under Cevang Rabdan, who had usurped his uncle Dga'-ldan's power, an opportunity for intervention. In 1717 Cevang's forces attacked Tibet. The Ch'ing emperor, fearing a hostile coalition including the Tibetans and Mongols, sent a counterexpedition to Tibet, which expelled the Dzungars from Lhasa in 1720. In 1723 the Ch'ing subdued a Ch'ing-hai Mongolian revolt supported by the Dzungars and secured the Ch'ing-hai area, the main gateway to Tibet.

In 1739 Cevang Rabdan's successor, Dga'-ldan Cereng, made peace with the Ch'ing and established the Altai Mountains as the border between the two nations. After Dga'-ldan Cereng's death in 1745, the Dzungars were torn by internal strife and were completely destroyed by the Ch'ing in 1755–58.

With the fall of the Dzungars, an independence movement was staged by the Muslims in the Tarim Basin. But by 1760 the Ch'ing suppressed the movement and established control over the area by granting official status to the former rulers of its oasis states. At this time the Ch'ing came into contact with the khanates to the west and around the Pamir massif—Khokand, Kazakh, Bukhara, Badakhshan, and Afghan—and treated them as irregular tributary states.

It was necessary for the Ch'ing, as conquerors and rulers of China, to secure the cooperation of the Mongols, who had many social and cultural affinities with the

(margin: Border treaties)

Manchus, and at the same time to restrain them from emerging as a hostile power that might bring pressure on the frontiers. Effective for this purpose was the banner system, which the Manchus used to reorganize the Mongol society under their control. Also effective was the Manchus' warm treatment of the Yellow Sect of Lamaism, which had appealed to the Mongols since the late 16th century. The early Ch'ing relationship with Tibet was, therefore, a partnership between a secular patron of religion and a spiritual leader. But after the expedition of 1720 the Ch'ing assumed the role of Tibet's protector against foreign aggressors.

Throughout Chinese history the confrontation with the northern nomad or semi-nomad nations had been of crucial importance. The Hsiung-nu, T'u-chüeh, and Mongols had struggled with China in the Han, T'ang, and Sung–Ming periods, respectively but with the fall of the Dzungars in the mid-18th century, China was for the first time freed from northern pressure, a situation that greatly contributed to the peace and prosperity of mid-Ch'ing China. The advance to Eastern Turkistan was also an outstanding Ch'ing contribution, following precedents in the Han, T'ang, and Yüan periods.

(margin: Freedom from northern pressures)

Nepal. A new Nepalese dynasty founded by the Gurkhas in 1768 sent two expeditions to Tibet, in 1788–89 and 1791–92, to force the Tibetans to accept their trade demands. Because the Tibetans were weak, the Ch'ing intervened; in 1792 an expedition was sent to chastise the Gurkhas, marching close to the Nepalese capital of Katmandu. Though unable to gain a decisive victory, it secured from the Gurkhas a promise to send a quinquennial tributary mission to China and intensified Ch'ing control over Tibet. Thus, by the end of the 18th century, Ch'ing control of the territories composed of the five nations—the Han, the Manchus, the Mongol, the Muslims, and the Tibetans—was completed.

Burma. In the early Ch'ing period there was no contact between Burma and China. After Alaungpaya established a new Burmese dynasty (1752), Burma seized the Tai capital of Ayutthaya in 1767, causing disorders among the Shan principalities on the Yunnan borders. The Ch'ing sent three unsuccessful expeditions to Burma in 1766–70. In 1788, however, Burma sought to establish a tributary relationship with the Ch'ing. Accordingly, the Ch'ing installed Bodawpaya as king of Burma, obliging him to send a decennial mission and permitting him to trade with China. Burmese kings, however, regarded themselves as equal to the Chinese emperors.

Tai or Siam. The first Ch'ing–Tai contact was made in 1652, and regulations for the Tai's tributary relations were laid down in 1665 and continued until 1852. It is notable that the Ch'ing promoted Sino-Tai overseas trade with the aim of importing rice from Siam because of a rice shortage in the coastal provinces. Laos and Sulu also maintained tributary relationships with the Ch'ing in 1729–1853 and 1727–63, respectively.

Vietnam. When the Manchus entered China, there existed in Dai Viet (Vietnam) two opposed powers—the Le dynasty at Hanoi, whose real power rested with the Trinh family, and the princely Nguyen family at Hue, which ruled the central and southern parts of the country. After formal Ch'ing–Vietnamese relations had begun, with the Ch'ing investiture of a Le emperor in 1667, some disputes occurred concerning the Yunnan borders and the numerous Chinese emigrants smuggled from Kwangsi to Nam Viet; but no serious conflict ensued.

In 1771 a rebellion was started by Nguyen Nhac and his two brothers, from the native hamlet of Tayson. In 1788 the youngest brother, Nguyen Hue, advanced northward and occupied Hanoi, driving the last Le emperor to the Kwangsi border, where he asked for Ch'ing help. The Chien-lung emperor sent an expedition, but it was smashed by Nguyen Hue's furious counterattack early in 1789. Instead of retaliating, the Ch'ing emperor invited Nguyen Hue to Peking, hoping to turn him into an obedient vassal; but the latter sent a double and thus tricked the emperor out of the title of king of Nam Viet.

Ryukyu. Ryukyu's tributary status and trade with the Ch'ing began in 1654. But Ryukyu's independence had been only a fabrication after the conquest of the island in 1609 by the Shimazu family of Satsuma, a feudal lord in Kyushu, Japan. This reality was, or ought to have been, known to the Ming and Ch'ing Chinese, because it is clearly recorded in the authoritative "History of the Ming Dynasty."

Korea. Ch'ing relations with Chosŏn (modern Korea) were far deeper than those of other tributary states. Not only the king of Chosŏn but also the queen and heir apparent were invested; exchanges of missions between Peking and Seoul were more frequent and cultural connections, far closer than elsewhere.

In contrast to the success in the north, the Ch'ing intervention in the southern nations was abortive, as seen in Nepal, Burma, and Vietnam. Yet the unequal tributary relationships were preserved, partly because the neighbour nations wished to stabilize the borders and to maintain trade with China by establishing official intercourse in whatever form.

Early Western contacts. Conspicuous among the early Ch'ing–Western contacts was the Rites Controversy, a dispute over the propogation of Christianity and its compatibility with Chinese traditional rites and ceremonies. Jesuits tried to maintain harmony with the religious and conventional traditions of China; this policy, however, was opposed in the 1630s by newly arriving Dominicans and Franciscans. A papal fact-finding mission to China in 1705 was ill-fated because it had to publicize in China the Roman decision of 1704, condemning Chinese rites. The final anti-rite decision of Rome was brought to China in 1715. The K'ang-hsi emperor could no longer trust Rome, and he determined to ban Christianity when another papal legate came to China in 1720–21 to promulgate the 1715 decision. But in a vast country like China the missionaries could continue their work, though in disgrace and with sporadic persecutions, for more than a century. As a result of the controversy the door was closed on Christianity, which thus never became integrated with Chinese culture as Buddhism had through a long process of adjustment and domestication.

After 1684 the Ch'ing maritime trade gradually improved from its early stagnation. In the mid-18th century, however, the Chinese brought Western trade under the so-called Canton system, placing many restrictions on trade and traders coming to China. A new feature was added to China's trade with the West in the 18th century by the steady increase in the export of Chinese tea by the British East India Company. Meanwhile, with Great Britain's passage of the Commutation Act in 1784, the duties on tea in Britain were reduced to about one-tenth of the previous high rate of over 100 percent. This blocked the smuggling of tea by European competitors and placed the British in the foremost position among the Western nations trading at Canton (then Kuang-chou). Yet they had many complaints about the Chinese trade system, which they hoped to improve by negotiation. In addition to the company, by the 1790s, emerging industrial capitalists in Great Britain were calling for a commercial mission to China to search for a market in Asia.

Following the abortive mission of Charles Cathcart who had died on his way to China in June 1788, Lord Macartney was dispatched with the first commercial mission to China; under the auspices of the British government and with the lukewarm support of the company, he arrived at Tientsin in 1793. The Ch'ien-lung emperor, however, treated Macartney merely as a tribute-bearer and had no thought of changing the Chinese system of foreign trade.

Mid-Ch'ing society and economy. During the 100-odd years of domestic peace from the annexation of Taiwan in the late 17th century to the end of the 18th century, China witnessed remarkable social and economic developments. The age certainly deserves the name of *Pax Sinica.*

Agriculture. To the province of Hunan, which had become a main rice-producing area in the late Ming era, were added Szechwan, Kwangsi, and Taiwan as important rice producers. Wheat and barley were disseminated to the marginal land during the late Ming and early

Ch'ing periods. The introduction and spread of the American-originated crops of maize, sweet potatoes, and peanuts enabled utilization of the hilly and mountainous regions of central and southern China. Cultivation of tea, cotton, tobacco, and other commercial crops was widespread. Great landlords were rare in the north, but in the centre and south, landownership was increasingly concentrated among a handful of landowners. The tenants were increasingly exploited as competition for land intensified; they were also squeezed by usurers. In due course they began to campaign for nonpayment or reduction of rent in the late years of the Ch'ien-lung period (1736–96).

Crafts and industries. Crafts and industries attained their heights during the 18th century. Copper and lead mining in Yunnan and other western provinces were prosperous, as were pottery and porcelain industries at Ching-te-chen in Kiangsi and tea-processing, salt-making, and cotton- and silk-cloth industries in the lower Yangtze region. Su-chou (Soochow), Sung-chiang, Hu-chou (modern Wu-hsing), Hang-chou (Hangchow), and Canton were the leading textile centres, some of them with large-scale dyeing and calendering factories. Some of these used an advanced division of labour and are said to have attained the stage of factory production. In commerce, the most active were the Shansi and Anhwei merchants, who had been eminent since the Ming time. The Anhwei were particularly prosperous not only with the lucrative government-monopolized salt business at Yang-chou but also in managing banking and retail and other trade, with an extensive network of agents all over the country. The brisk Ch'ing commerce was stimulated by the influx into China of large sums of silver and copper from abroad, which increased the amount of money in circulation. The silver imported into China by the Europeans and Americans in the late Ming and the Ch'ing periods is roughly estimated at 200,000,000 taels, the silver, gold, and copper from Japan at no less than 200,000,000 (gold converted to silver by 1:10), the silver brought annually by the Chinese workers at the mines in Burma and Nam Viet at several million during the Ch'ien-lung period.

The important investors were anonymous officials. Big enterprises in the Ch'ing period were connected directly or indirectly with the official class and were managed with government support; consequently they were influenced by the political, social, and cultural needs and considerations of the official and gentry class, and this restrained the free exercise of industrial rationalism. For example, the salt merchants at Yang-chou, the champions of Ch'ing commercialism, wasted much money on extravagant entertainments; they assisted the artists and scholars; they squandered money on welcoming the Ch'ien-lung emperor, who often visited the southeastern cities. Industry's golden age, however, was gone with the end of the Ch'ien-lung era.

Meanwhile peasants were often victimized by the increasing monetization of the economy, for example, because of usury and the increased investment of merchant and official wealth in land accumulation, and by the upward trend of the commodity price; the price of rice and cotton cloth, for example, rose by about five times during the second half of the 18th century. Nevertheless, they at least enjoyed a fairly high standard of living during the century.

Population growth. The rapid population growth of China in the 18th century was unprecedented. The population in 1600 is roughly estimated at 150,000,000. Thereafter came the devastation of half a century, and it is doubtful whether the level for 1600 was recovered by 1700. But with the coming of peace in 1683, the increase was prodigious, reaching about 313,000,000 by 1794 and 430,000,000 by 1850. While this was a sign of prosperity, it began to have the reverse effect in the last years of the 18th century.

Migration was directed to Manchuria, Taiwan, eastern Kwangtung, and Hainan. But the main target of immigration was western China, including Szechwan, western Hupeh highlands, the adjacent Han Ho Basin, and southern Shensi. Szechwan Province had mostly recovered

Margin notes:

The Rites Controversy

The *Pax Sinica*

Immigration to western China

from the late Ming and early Ch'ing depopulation by the end of the K'ang-hsi era; but the wave of immigration continued to flow into Szechwan in defiance of the Yung-cheng emperor's effort to check the tide. The Ch'ien-lung emperor followed a policy of laissez faire, which allowed vast numbers of poor men and drifters from the densely populated coastal region to move to Szechwan and the adjoining area. Immigrants' lives became increasingly insecure with the passage of time.

Bureaucrats versus commoners. The early Ch'ing budget was miserably imbalanced. The revenue was limited because of the declared exemption of the late Ming surtaxes, and expenditures were enormous because of military requirements during the conquering years. But the difficulty was overcome by the simple way of life of the emperors and their fellow Manchus. Then followed the zenith, where China's favourable situation vis-à-vis its northern neighbours contributed to the improvement in government finance, commercial and industrial progress, and stabilization of the commoners' lives. But on the other hand the intensified money economy and the laissez-faire mood of the late Ch'ien-lung period raised the consumer level of the ruling class and stimulated its greediness. After the 1760s increasing numbers of officials were punished for bribery or other scandals.

Religious associations and secret societies. Popular religious movements had been active since the Sung period. In general, these movements were syncretic, composed of Buddhism at the centre, along with some Confucian and Taoist teachings. Revolts by the White Lotus sect (Pai-lien chiao), during Yüan and Ming times, caused the government to ban to the popular association in general. This sect had, as a religious element, the cult of the Maitreya, the future Buddha. This primarily peaceful organization turned into a revolutionary one, perhaps because of a lack of a consistent system of beliefs, its magical ingredients, and the presence of some of the characteristics of secret societies.

There were other secret societies of anti-regime character, typical of which was the Heaven and Earth Society (T'ien-ti hui). Presumably, it was first founded during the years 1775–85 in southern Fukien and brought to Taiwan, where it provided the organizational basis for the rebellion of Lin Shuang-wen (1786–88). Originally, the secret societies were poor men's means of self-defense, but as the 18th century reached its close with ever

Increasing popular discontent increasing distress among the people, their activities began to attract attention as a source of social unrest.

The White Lotus Rebellion (1796–1804). Bandits, called *kuo-fei*, had constantly ravaged heavily populated Szechwan since the early years of the Ch'ien-lung era. In the last years of the era a great many salt smugglers and forgers swarmed into eastern Szechwan; they were the products of the social unrest and a source of further trouble in the region. The White Lotus sect had been increasingly attracting the frustrated people of this area, and it rose up first in Hupeh in 1796 and spread to Szechwan via Shensi. In rising it was joined by a large number of *kuo-fei* bandits, salt smugglers, and coiners, who played an important role in fighting the government army.

After their stockades had been destroyed by the Imperial force, the rebels resorted to guerilla tactics. To cope with them, the Imperial forces had to help villagers improvise earthworks into which they could move for self-defense. This task required a long time and vast expense. The pacifiers' camp was weak and had to employ numerous local militias, some of whom, however, joined the rebels in 1803, retarding the pacification until the spring of 1805.

The White Lotus Rebellion, caused by many social and political grievances, marked a turning point in the history of the Ch'ing dynasty. It inflicted two blows to the Ch'ing. First, the use of the vast number of local militia exposed the ineffectiveness of the government army, affecting the prestige of the dynasty. Second, the Ch'ing finance was damaged. The Ch'ien-lung era saw a financial boom, with a surplus of 70,000,000–80,000,000 taels at the end of the era; but the rebellion

cost about 120,000,000 taels. The gap between the surplus and the expense was filled by contributions from the salt merchants and by other irregular levies. With the rebellion, the Ch'ing prosperity was gone forever.

Intellectual trends. The progress in Classical studies during the Ch'ing period was unprecedented in Chinese history. In contrast with the abstract discourses of the late Ming period, the leading early Ch'ing scholars—*e.g.*, Ku Yen-wu, Huang Tsung-hsi, and Wang Fu-chih—advocated a learning suited to practical affairs. This reaction was more or less motivated by their political purpose of restoring the Ming. After 1656 the Ch'ing began to suppress the intellectuals' anti-Ch'ing movement, and the anti-Ch'ing associations, called *fu-she,* were gradually disbanded or neutralized. Subsequently, the K'ang-hsi emperor encouraged scholars to seek knowledge for its own sake, and the Yung-cheng emperor called the anti-Manchu racism contrary to the Confucian idea of rule by virtue; they thus helped to turn the intellectuals' political-mindedness to an academic climate of research for the sake of research, a new trend that was called textual criticism, or empirical research, because of its emphasis on textual or other evidences. Represented by Hui Tung and Tai Chen, the new school flourished in the Ch'ien-lung and Chia-ch'ing (ruled 1796–1820) periods, producing many excellent works in Classical studies.

Classical studies

The Ch'ien-lung emperor far surpassed his father and grandfather in sponsoring the compilation of the Chinese Classics. The famous "Complete Works of Four Treasuries" was compiled in the decade after 1772 by about 300 scholars, who edited some 3,500 works in more than 36,000 volumes. But this work was accompanied by a dismal aspect—the suppression of the undesirable works of anti-Ch'ing savour, often causing a "literary inquisition."

Among the Western sciences introduced by the Jesuit missionaries, astronomy and mathematics were favourably accepted and applied by the Chinese scholars to the study of Classics. This trend was also stimulated by the K'ang-hsi emperor's high esteem for Western science. But after the Rites Controversy, the Western studies were discouraged, and Chinese students turned back to the traditional learning. Significantly, according to a French Jesuit's report from China in the early 18th century, the main reason for the lack of natural science in China was the lack of any reward, of any social or political prominence given to scientists and technicians (an attribute of a society where the Confucian literati and their ideas were predominant).

Representing the other Ch'ing cultural assets were *Hung lou meng* (*Dream of the Red Chamber*) and *Liao-chai chih-i* (*Strange Stories from a Chinese Studio*) in the field of popular literature; porcelain of superior beauty made at Ching-te-chen during the Yung-cheng and Ch'ien-lung years; architectural masterpieces, such as the old summer palace outside Peking, with its Western-style fountain, and the Lamaist temples of Jehol—all of which represent the grandeur of *Pax Sinica*.

Dynastic degeneration. The official exploitation of the commoners in the late Ch'ien-lung years gained momentum through the Chia-ch'ing and the Tao-kuang (ruled 1821–50) eras. Beginning in the early Chia-ch'ing years, the court repeatedly blamed the officials for the loss of provincial and local government funds and ordered them to make up the lost sums, inevitably resulting in increased levies on the commoners. Government expenditures showed a steady increase, particularly for the Huang Ho and Grand Canal conservancy, which gave the officials concerned opportunities for pocketing public funds. The result was fiscal imbalance, the only solution of which was an increase in the popular burden. Thus, in the last years of the Chia-ch'ing period, the court was faced with the possibility of a disaster occasioned by popular discontent.

Upon his accession to the throne, the Tao-kuang emperor attempted to suspend the arbitrary surtax—a reform attempt similar to that made by the Yung-cheng emperor. This time, however, high officials opposed the Emperor's effort, and the situation was left to grow even worse. In addition the Tao-kuang era saw a noticeable increase in famine-relief expenditures, but most of these were siphoned off by officials, leaving the victims unheeded. Heavy burdens caused rural labourers to neglect the dredging of canals and waterways necessary for agriculture. In the late Tao-kuang years agriculture deteriorated because of poor irrigation, a phenomenon seen also in the late Ming time.

Turmoils in the early 19th century

China was beset with many turmoils, beginning in the Chia-ch'ing period. Besides the White Lotus Rebellion in central China, pirates ravaged the southeastern coast for a long time. The Tay Son leader of Vietnam, Nguyen Hue, encouraged and protected them; but the founder of the Nguyen dynasty, Nguyen Phuc Anh, resorted to an anti-pirate policy. This led the pirates to shift their activity from Kwangtung to the coast of Fukien and Chekiang, where they could find cooperators in the secret-society adherents. Generally, the officials were lax in pursuing the pirates, because they wanted a share of the pirates' loot. Thus, piracy survived for more than 20 years, until the chief of the Fukien pirates was drowned in 1809, and the remnants were dispersed the next year.

At the end of 1813 there occurred, in northern China, a revolt of the T'ien-li chiao (Heavenly Reason Society), which had many followers in the northern provinces and in Inner Mongolia. The ringleaders, Li Wen-ch'eng and Lin Ch'ing, mapped out a scheme for seizing Peking; but it failed after four months' fighting.

The increasing number of Chinese immigrants gathered in the southwestern region of the Miao tribe during the Ch'ien-lung period had sharpened racial friction, which flared up in an anti-Chinese uprising of the Miao tribe in the Kweichow Province in 1795 and soon spread to western Hunan. Though it was put down in 1797, Miao unrest continued until 1816.

The Chia-ch'ing era saw many other disturbances staged by secret societies and religious sects; anti-rent and anti-tax outbursts became more frequent. Though the Tao-kuang period saw no large-scale uprising, local unrest became more pervasive and chronic.

The unrest and disorder in the first half of the 19th century can be explained by the aftermath of the remarkable population growth, the effects of the money economy, and the intensified exploitation of the common people by officials and gentry—all of which acted to disrupt the agrarian society of China. To these problems were added a drain of silver caused by the increasing importation of opium, the Opium War (see below), and a resultant war indemnity that further dislocated the popular livelihood. Thus, the chaos of the late Ch'ing period was caused by the political, social, and economic deterioration that had haunted the past dynasties, but this time was accelerated by the military and commercial penetration of the West.

LATE CH'ING

The opium question

Western challenge, 1839–60. The opium question, the direct cause of the first Sino-British clash in the 19th century, began with a late 18th-century British attempt to counterbalance their unfavourable China trade with traffic in Indian opium. After having monopolized the opium trade in 1779, the East India Company's government started in the 1780s to have the opium sent from India to buyers in China. In 1819 the company began to handle larger amounts of opium, resulting in a sharp rise in the amount of the drug brought to China. The resulting drain of silver from China involved serious economic and social repercussions. The Peking court repeatedly banned the importing of opium, but without success, because the prohibition itself promoted corruption among the officials and soldiers concerned. There was no possibility of the opium question being solved as a domestic affair.

After the turn of the 19th century, the main vehicle of opium smuggling was the country traders who were allowed only to manage the inter-Asian trade under the company's license. Without protection from the company, they cultivated the opium market in China on their own. They defied the opium ban in China and gradually became defiant toward Chinese law and order in general, having nothing in mind but making money.

After Parliament revoked the East India Company's monopoly in 1834, William John Napier was appointed chief superintendent of British trade in China and arrived at Canton. He tried to negotiate with the Canton authorities on equal footing, but the latter took his behaviour as contrary to the established Sino-foreign intercourse. His mission failed.

In Peking a proposal to relax the opium restraint, made in 1836, acquired support from many quarters. But the Tao-kuang emperor appointed a radical patriot, Lin Tse-hsü, as Imperial commissioner for an anti-opium campaign. Arriving at Canton in March 1839, Lin confiscated and destroyed more than 20,000 chests of opium. Skirmishes began after September between the Chinese and the British.

The Opium War and its aftermath. In February 1840 the British government decided on an expedition, and Rear Adm. George Elliot was appointed first commissioner and plenipotentiary to China. In June, 16 British warships arrived in Hong Kong and sailed northward to the mouth of Pei Ho to press China with its demands. No agreement was reached. In May 1841 the British attacked the walled city of Canton and received a ransom of $6,000,000, an operation that provoked a counterattack on the part of the Cantonese. This was the beginning of a continuing conflict between the British and the Cantonese.

The Ch'ing had no effective tactics against the powerful British navy. They retaliated merely by setting burning rafts on the enemy's fleet; and they encouraged people to take the heads of the enemies, for which they offered a prize. The Imperial troops were powerless; the Green Standard troops were more eager to abuse the civilians than to fight the enemy. To make up the weakness, local militias were urgently recruited; but they were useless. The British proclaimed that their aim was to fight the government officials and soldiers who abused the people, not to make war against the Chinese population. And indeed there was a deep rift between the government and people, of which the British could easily take advantage, a weakness in Ch'ing society that became apparent in the crisis of the war.

Elliot's successor, Henry Pottinger, arrived at Macau in August and campaigned northward, seizing Amoy, Ting-hai, and Ning-po. Reinforced from India, he resumed action in May 1842 and took Wu-sung, Shanghai, and Chinkiang (Chen-chiang). Nanking yielded in August, and peace was restored with the Treaty of Nanking.

The Treaty of Nanking

The main provisions of the Treaty of Nanking were the cession of Hong Kong, the opening of five ports to British trade, the abolition of the cohong system of trade, equality of official recognition, and an indemnity of $21,000,000. This was the result of the first clash between China, which had regarded foreign trade as a favour given by the Celestial Empire to the poor barbarians, and the British, to whom trade and commerce had become "the true herald of civilization."

The Treaty of Nanking was followed by two supplementary arrangements with the British in 1843. In July 1844 China signed the Treaty of Wanghia with the United States and, in October, the Treaty of Whampoa with France. These arrangements made up a complex of foreign privileges by virtue of the most-favoured-nation clauses (guaranteeing trading equality) conceded to every signatory. All in all, they provided a basis for such later evils as the loss of tariff autonomy, extraterritoriality (exemption from the application or jurisdiction of local law or tribunals), and the free movement of missionaries.

With the signing of the treaties—which began the so-called treaty-port system—the Imperial commissioner Ch'i-ying, newly stationed at Canton, was put in charge of foreign affairs. Following a policy of appeasement, his dealing with foreigners started fairly smoothly. But contrary to the British expectation, the amount of trade dropped after 1846; and, to their dissatisfaction, the question of opium remained unsettled in the postwar arrangements. The core of the Sino-Western tension, however, rested in an anti-foreign movement in Kwangtung.

Anti-foreign movement. A Sino-British discrepancy existed at the signing of the Treaty of Nanking as to whether or not foreigners were allowed to enter the walled city of Canton. Though Canton was declared open in July 1843, the British faced Cantonese opposition. After 1847 trouble rapidly increased, and as a result of an incident at nearby Fo-shan, a promise was given the British that they would be allowed to enter the city in 1849. Yet troubles continued. As a result of his inability to control the situation, Ch'i-ying was recalled in 1848 and replaced with the less compliant Hsü Kuang-Chin. As the promised date neared, the Cantonese demonstrated against British entry. Finally, the British yielded, and the anti-foreigners won a victory despite the fact that the Peking court conceded a "temporary entrance" into the city.

After the Cantonese resistance in 1841, the gentry in Kwangtung began to build a more organized anti-foreign movement, promoting the militarization of the village society. The city of Canton was also a centre of diffusion of xenophobia because the scholars at the city's great academies were proclaiming the Confucian theory that uncultured barbarians should be excluded. The inspired anti-foreign mood also contained a strong anti-government sentiment and perhaps a tendency toward provincialism; the Cantonese rose up against the barbarians to protect their own homeland, without recourse to the government authorities.

In the strained atmosphere in Canton, where the xenophobic governor general Yeh Ming-ch'en was inciting the Cantonese to annihilate the British, the "Arrow" incident occurred in October 1856; the Canton police seized the "Arrow," a Chinese-owned but British-registered ship flying a British flag, and charged its Chinese crew with piracy and smuggling. The British consul Harry Parkes sent a fleet to fight its way up to Canton. French forces joined the venture on the plea that a missionary had been officially executed in Kwangsi Province. The British government sent an expedition under Lord Elgin as a plenipotentiary. The Russians and the Americans abstained but sent their representatives for diplomatic manoeuvring. At the end of 1857 an Anglo-French force occupied Canton; in March 1858 they took the Ta-ku fort and marched to Tientsin.

Anglo-French occupation of Canton

Foreign gains. The Ch'ing representatives had no choice but to comply with the demands of the British and French; the Russian and American diplomats also gained the privileges their militant colleagues secured by force. During June, four Tientsin treaties were concluded.

In 1859, when the signatories arrived off the Ta-ku fort on their way to sign the treaties in Peking, they were repulsed, with heavy damage inflicted by the gunfire from the fort. In 1860 an allied force invaded Peking, driving the Hsien-feng emperor (ruled 1851–62) out of the capital to Jehol. A younger brother of the emperor, Prince Kung, was appointed Imperial commissioner in charge of negotiation. But the famous summer palace was destroyed by the British in October. Following the advice of the Russian negotiator, Prince Kung exchanged ratification of the 1858 treaties; in addition, he signed new conventions with the British and the French. The American and Russian negotiators had already exchanged the ratification in 1859, but the latter's diplomatic performance in 1860 was remarkable.

Russian interests in the East had been activated in competition with the British effort to open China. A Russian spearhead, directed to Kuldja (Ili) by way of the Irtysh River route, resulted in the Sino-Russian Treaty of Kuldja in 1851, which opened Kuldja and Chuguchak (Tarabagatai) to Russian trade. Another drive was directed to the Amur watershed under the initiative of Nikolay Muraviev, who had been appointed governor general of eastern Siberia in 1847. By 1857 Muraviev had sponsored four expeditions down the Amur; in the third one, in 1856, the left bank and lower reaches of the river had actually been occupied by the Russians. In May 1858 Muraviev pressed the Ch'ing

general I-shan to sign a treaty at Aigun, by which the territory on the northern bank of the Amur was ceded to Russia, and the land between the Ussuri River and the sea was placed in joint possession by the two nations, pending further disposition. But Peking refused to ratify the treaty. When the Anglo-French allies attacked North China in 1860, the Russian negotiator Ignatiev acted as China's friend and mediator in securing the evacuation of the invaders from Peking. Soon after the allies had left Peking, Ignatiev secured, as a reward for his mediatory effort, the Sino-Russian Treaty of Peking, which confirmed the treaty of Aigun and ceded to Russia the territory between the Ussuri and the sea.

The 1858–60 treaties extended the foreign privileges given by the post-Opium War arrangements and confirmed or legalized the developments in the treaty-port system. The worst effects for the Ch'ing authorities were not the utilitarian rights, such as trade, commerce, and tariff, but the privileges that affected the moral and cultural values of China. The right to propagate Christianity threatened the Confucian values, the backbone of the Imperial system. The permanent residence of foreign representatives in Peking signified an end to the long established tributary relationship between China and other nations. The partial collapse of the tribute system meant a loss of the emperor's virtue, a serious blow to dynastic rule in China.

Effects of the treaties of 1858–60

During the turbulent years 1858–60, the Ch'ing bureaucracy was divided between the war and peace parties; and it was the peace party's leaders—Prince Kung, Kuei-liang, and Wen-hsiang—who took charge of negotiating with the foreigners. But they did so because the imminent crisis forced them to and not as a matter of principle.

In 1861, in response to the settlement of the foreign representatives in the capital, the Tsungli Yamen (a Chinese government office) was opened to deal with foreign affairs, with a main staff filled by the peace-party leaders. The Ch'ing officials themselves, however, deemed this as still keeping a faint silhouette of the tribute system.

The delay and difficulty in the Ch'ing adjustment to the West may possibly be ascribed to both external and internal factors. The Chinese must have seen the Westerners who had appeared in China as purveyors of poisonous drugs, as barbarians in the full sense of the word, from whom they could learn nothing. But the Chinese staunchly held to their tradition, which also had two aspects—ideological and institutional. The core of the ideological aspect was the Confucian distinction between China and foreign nations. The institutional aspect had recently been much studied, however, and precedents in Chinese history had been found, for example, of treaty ports with foreign settlements, consular jurisdiction, and employment of Westerners as imperial personnel, etc.; thus, the Chinese regarded the Western impact as an extension of their tradition rather than as a totally new situation that necessitated a new adjustment. And at least until 1860 the Ch'ing leaders remained withdrawn in the shell of tradition making no effort to cope with the new environment by breaking the yoke of the past.

Popular uprising. The third quarter of the 19th century saw a series of uprisings, again as a result of social discontent.

The Taiping Rebellion. In the first half of the 19th century, the province of Kwangtung, the homeland of the Taiping, was beset with accelerating social unrest. After the Opium War, government prestige declined, and officials lost their capacity to reconcile communal feudings. The greatest among such conflicts was that between the native settlers and the so-called guest settlers—the Hakkas, who had migrated to Kwangtung and Kwangsi from central China in olden times. The Association of the God Worshippers (Pai shang-ti hui) was founded by Hung Hsiu-ch'üan, creator of a new religion, and his protégé Feng Yün-shan, an able organizer. His followers were collected from among miners, charcoal workers, and poor peasants in central Kwong-si, most of whom belonged to the Hakkas. In January 1851 a new state named Tai-p'ing T'ien-kuo (Celestial Kingdom of Great Peace) was declared in the district of Kuei-p'ing in Kwangsi with the chief of the state, Hung Hsiu-ch'üan, proclaimed Heavenly King. That September their base was shifted to the city of Yung-an, where they were besieged by the Imperial army until April 1852. Then they broke the siege and rushed into Hunan; absorbing some secret society members and outlaws, they dashed to Wu-han, the capital of Hupeh, and proceeded along the Yangtze to Nanking, which they captured in March 1853 and made their capital.

Taiping religion

The core of the Taiping religion was a monotheism tinged with fundamental Protestant Christianity. But it was mixed with a strong anti-Manchuism and an intolerant attitude toward the Chinese cultural tradition. This politico-religious complex firmly supported the fighting spirit of the Taiping. They gave away all their belongings to the "general treasury," which was supposed to be shared by them alike; this system attracted the distressed people and lured them to the Taiping cause. The origin of many Taiping religious ideas, morals, and institutions can be traced to China's tradition; but the Taiping's all-out anti-regime struggle, motivated by strong religious beliefs and a common sharing, also had precedents in earlier religious rebellions.

After the Taiping settled in Nanking, village officials were appointed, and redistribution of farm land was planned in accordance with an idea of primitive communism. But in fact the land reform was impracticable, and the village officials' posts were mainly filled by the former landlords or the clerks of the local governments, and the old order in the countryside was not replaced by a new one in which the oppressed people could dominate.

In May 1853 the Taiping sent an expedition to northern China, which reached the neighbourhood of Tientsin but finally collapsed during the spring of 1855. After this, the Yangtze Valley provinces were the main theatre of struggle. Of the government armies in those years, the Green Standards were too ill disciplined, and not much could be expected of the bannermen. The Ch'ing government had no choice but to rely on the local militia forces, such as the "Hunan Braves" (later called the Hunan Army), organized by Tseng Kuo-fan in 1852, and the "Huai braves" (later called the Huai Army), organized by Li Hung-chang in 1862. These local armies were composed of the village farmers, inspired with a strong sense of mission for protecting the Confucian orthodoxy, and used for wider operations than merely protecting their own villages. The necessary funds for maintaining them were provided initially by local gentry.

The Taiping were gradually overwhelmed, and with the capture of An-ch'ing, the capital of Anhwei, in October 1861 by the Hunan Army, the revolutionary cause was doomed. But the fall of Nanking was accelerated by the cooperation of Chinese mercenaries equipped with Western arms, commanded by an American, Frederick T. Ward, a Briton, Charles G. Gordon, and others. The fall of Nanking in July 1864 marked the end of one of the greatest civil wars in world history.

The fall of Nanking

The main cause of the Taiping failure was internal strife among the top leaders in Nanking. Not only did they give themselves over to luxury but also their energy was exhausted and their leadership lost by a fratricidal conflict that occurred in 1856. In addition, religious fanaticism, though it inspired the fighters, became a stumbling block because it countered the rational and elastic attitude necessary to handle delicate military and administrative affairs. The intolerance toward traditional culture also alienated the gentry and the people alike. Presumably, the failure of the land-redistribution policy also estranged the landless paupers from the Taiping cause.

The Nien Rebellion. Often in the first half of the 19th century, plundering gangs, called *nien*, ravaged northern Anhwei, southern Shantung, and southern Honan. In mid-century, however, their activities were suddenly intensified, partly by the addition to their numbers of a great many starving people who had lost their livelihood from repeated Huang Ho floods in the early 1850s, and partly because they became emboldened by the Taiping advance to the north of the Yangtze. From 1856 to 1859 the Nien leaders consolidated their bases north of the Huai Ho by winning over the masters of the earthwall communities, which had been organized for self-defense against the Taiping. The Nien strategy was to use their powerful cavalry to plunder the outlying areas and carry the loot to their home bases.

Many influential clans, with all their members, joined the Nien cause; and among the Nien leaders, the clan chiefs played an important role. Gentry of lower strata also joined the Nien. The greater part of the Nien force consisted of poor peasants, although deserters from the government-recruited militias and salt smugglers were important as military experts. The real cause of their strength was supposed to have been the people's support and sympathy for their leaders; but there was difficulty in creating a power centre, because the Nien's basic social unit was the earthwall community, where a powerful master exercised autonomy. In 1856 Chang Lo-hsing received the title of "Lord of the Alliance" of the Nien, but he was far too weak to form a centre. Imperial pacification was launched by the general Seng-ko-lin-ch'in, who led a powerful cavalry into the affected area in 1862; but his pursuit was ineffective, and the general himself was killed in Shantung in May 1865. Thus, the last Imperial crack unit disappeared. Tseng Kuo-fan succeeded Seng as general and enforced a policy of detaching the earthwall masters from their men and of employing the latter as his troops. Finally, Li Hung-chang succeeded Tseng in 1866 and set up encirclement lines along the Huang Ho and the Grand Canal, by means of which he destroyed the revolts in 1868.

Muslim rebellions. Muslim rebellions in Yunnan and in Shensi and Kansu originated from clashes between the Chinese and Muslims in those provinces. Religious antipathy must be taken into account, but more important were the social and political backgrounds. In the frontier provinces the late dynastic confusions were felt as keenly as elsewhere, which aggravated the problems between the Chinese and the Muslims. Yunnan had been haunted by Muslim–Chinese rivalries since 1821, but in Shensi small disturbances had been seen as early as the Ch'ien-lung period. Government officials supported the Chinese, and the Muslims were obliged to rise up against both the Chinese and the authorities.

Clashes between Chinese and Muslims

A rivalry between the Chinese and Muslim miners in central Yunnan triggered a severe clash in 1855, which developed into a slaughter of a great many Muslims in and around the provincial capital of K'ung-ming the following April. This caused a general uprising of Yunnan Muslims, which lasted until 1873. Lack of a unified policy weakened the Muslims, and the rebellion was brought to an end partly through the pacifiers' policy of playing the rebel leaders off against one another.

Another Muslim uprising, in Shensi in 1862, promptly spread to Kansu and Eastern Turkistan and lasted for 15 years. The general cause of the trouble was the same as in Yunnan, but the Taiping advance to Shensi stimulated the Muslims into rebellion. The first stage of the uprising developed in the Wei Ho Valley in Shensi; in the next stage the rebels, defeated by the Imperial army, fled to Kansu, which became the main theatre of fighting. Encouraged by the Nien invading Shensi at the end of 1866, the core of the rebel troops returned to Shensi, and sporadic clashes continued in the two provinces. In the last phase, Tso Tsung-t'ang, a former protégé of Tseng Kuo-fan, appeared in Shensi and succeeded in pacifying the area in 1873.

In Shensi and Kansu there were many independent Muslim leaders; but they had neither a common headquarters nor unified policy, and there were no all-out revolutionaries. Pacification was delayed because the Imperial camp was preoccupied with the Taiping and the Nien and could not afford the expenditure needed for an expedition to the remote border provinces.

Effects of the rebellions. To meet the large popular uprisings, the Ch'ing authorities had to rely on local armies, which were financed by the provincial and local gentry class. To meet this need, a likin was started in 1853. The provincial governor generals and governors came to enlarge their military and financial autonomy, bringing about a trend of decentralization. Moreover, the locus of power shifted from the Manchus to those Chinese who had played the main part in putting down the rebellions. The Hunan Army was gradually disbanded after the fall of Nanking; but the Huai Army, after its success against the Muslims, served as a strong basis for the political manoeuvres of its leader, Li Hung Chang, until its defeat and collapse in the Sino-Japanese War in 1894–95.

Shift of power away from the Manchus

These rebellions brought immeasurable damage and devastation to China. Both the Taiping and the pacifiers were guilty of brutality and destruction, and victimized 40 to 80 percent of the population in the lower Yangtze provinces. A contemporary estimate of 20,000,000 to 30,000,000 victims is certainly far less than the real number. Prior to the Taiping war, this area had been losing much of its surplus population; but thereafter it was settled by immigrants from less damaged areas. Its ruined industry and agriculture had not fully recovered even by the beginning of the 20th century. In the area of the Muslim rebellions, devastation and population decrease was sharp.

During the first half of the 19th century, a number of natural disasters left large hordes of starving victims who had no choice but to join the Taiping and other rebel groups. The worst of these calamities was a drought that attacked the northern provinces of Shansi, Shensi, and Honan in 1877–78 and caused hardship for between 9,000,000 and 13,000,000 people. These disasters were a serious setback to China, which had just begun to promote industrialization to cope with the Western challenge.

The self-strengthening movement. Upon the Hsien-feng emperor's death at Jehol in 1861, his anti-foreign entourage entered Peking and seized power; but Tz'u-hsi, the mother of the newly enthroned boy emperor Tsai-ch'un (ruled as the J'ung-chih emperor 1862–75), and Prince Kung succeeded in crushing their opponents by a coup d'état in October. There emerged a new system in which the leadership in Peking was shared by Tz'u-hsi and another empress dowager, Tz'u-an, in the palace and by Prince Kung and Wen-hsiang, with the Tsungli yamen as their base of operation. The core of their foreign policy was expressed by Prince Kung as "overt peace with the Western nations in order to gain time for recovering the exhausted power of the state."

Foregn relations in the 1860s. The Tsungli yamen had two offices attached to it; the Inspectorate General of Customs and the Language School, called T'ung-wen-kuan. The former was the centre for the Maritime Custom Service, administered by Western personnel appointed by the Ch'ing. The latter was opened to train the children of bannermen in foreign languages, and, later, some Western sciences were added to its curriculum; but the quality of candidates for the school was not high. Similar schools were opened in Shanghai and Canton.

A superintendent of trade for the three northern ports (later known as high commissioner for *pei-yang*, or "northern ocean") was established in 1861 at Tientsin, parallel to a similar, existing post at Shanghai (later known as high commissioner for *nan-yang*, or "southern ocean"). The creation of the new post was presumably aimed at weakening the foreign representatives in Peking by concentrating foreign affairs in the hands of the Tientsin officials.

In 1865–66 the British strongly urged the Ch'ing authorities to make domestic reforms and to become Westernized. Prince Kung asked the high provincial officials to submit their opinions about the proposed reforms. The consensus advocated diplomatic missions abroad and the opening of mines but firmly argued against telegraph and railway construction. Against this background, a roving mission was sent to the United States in 1868, which then proceeded to London and Berlin. This first mission abroad was a success for China, but its very success had an adverse effect on China's modernization by encouraging the conservatives, who learned to regard the Westerners as easy to manipulate.

First mission abroad

The Anglo-Chinese Treaty of Tientsin provided for its revision in the year 1868, for which the Ch'ing could negotiate with due preparations and in a mood of peace for the first time after the Opium War. The result was the Alcock Convention of 1869, which limited the unilateral most-favoured-nation clause, a sign of gradual improvement in China's foreign relations; but under pressure from British merchants in China, the London government refused to ratify it. The resentment engendered by the refusal, together with an anti-Christian riot at Tientsin in 1870, brought an end to the climate of the Sino-foreign cooperation that had prevailed in the 1860s.

The post-Opium War arrangements forced China to remove the ban on Christianity, but the Peking court tried to keep the fact secret and encouraged provincial officials to prohibit the religion. The pseudo-Christian Taiping movement furthered the anti-Christian move on the part of royalists. Under such circumstances, anti-Christian riots had spread throughout the country culminating in the Tientsin Massacre in 1870, in which a French consul and two officials, ten nuns, and two priests died, and in which three Russian traders were killed by mistake. At the negotiating table, the French sternly demanded the lives of three responsible Chinese officials as a preventive against further such occurrences; but the Ch'ing negotiators, Tseng Kuo-fan and Li Hung-Chang, were successful at least in refusing the demanded execution. After the incident, however, Tseng was denounced for his infirm stand and Prince Kung's political influence began to wane in the growing anti-foreign climate.

As to the nature of the anti-Christian movement, there are various interpretations: some emphasize the anti-foreign Confucian orthodoxy, while others stress the patriotic and nationalistic reaction against the missionaries' attempt to Westernize the Chinese. Still others point to the Christian support of the oppressed in their struggle against the official and gentry class. What is clear, however, is that Christianity sowed dissension and friction in the already disintegrating late Ch'ing society and undermined the prestige of the Ch'ing dynasty and the Confucian orthodoxy.

Industrialization for self-strengthening. Stimulated by the military training and techniques exhibited during the Westerners' cooperation against the Taiping and supported by Prince Kung in Peking, a movement called T'ung-chih Restoration was launched by the anti-Taiping generals Tseng Kuo-fan, Li Hung-chang, and Tso Tsung-t'ang, who sought to consolidate the Ch'ing power by introducing Western technology. The ideological champion of the movement was Feng Kuei-fen, who urged "the use of the barbarians's superior techniques to control the barbarians," and proposed to give the gentry stronger leadership than before in local administration.

Introduction of Western technology

In the first period of modern industrial development (1861–72), effort was focussed on the manufacture of firearms and machines, the most important enterprises being the Kiangnan Arsenal in Shanghai (established in 1865), the Tientsin Machine Factory (established in 1867, expanded in 1870), and the Foochow Shipyard (1866). There were many other smaller ones, and 60,000,000–70,000,000 taels were spent on them during the years 1865–1910. But the output was disappointing—the Foochow Shipyard, for example, built 15 vessels during the five years after 1869 as scheduled, but thereafter it declined and was destroyed in 1884 during the Sino-French War—and the weapon industry was significant not so much for its direct military purpose as for the introduction of Western knowledge and techniques through the many educational facilities that were attached to the installation.

In the second period (1872–94), weight shifted from the weapons industry to a wider field of manufacture, and the operation shifted from direct government management to a government-supervised and merchant-managed method. Leading among the several enterprises of the second period were the China Merchants' Steam Navigation Company (1872) and the K'ai-p'ing Coal Mines (1877). The officials and gentry supplied capital to them, but the chief investors were the compradors (Chinese agents employed by foreign firms in China) who, acting as a link between Chinese commerce and the foreign firms in the treaty ports, accumulated vast wealth. These enterprises were sponsored by high provincial officials—the central figure was Li Hung-chang—but their management was left to joint operation by shareholders' representatives and the lower officials appointed by the sponsors.

Management, however, was beset with bureaucratic malpractices. The seat of decision-making and responsibility was obscure; business was spoiled by nepotism and corruption; the sponsors tended to use the enterprises as a basis for their regional power. The central government was not only unable to supply capital but also looked for every opportunity to exploit these enterprises as it had exploited the monopolistic salt business after which those companies were modelled. Under such circumstances, the enterprises inevitably slid into depression after some initial years of apparent success.

Though active in supplying capital and managerial personnel to the new enterprises, the compradors themselves had many shortcomings—e.g., embezzlement, speculation, and lack of technical training and knowledge. Each comprador belonged to an exclusive community by strong family or regional ties that focussed his concerns on his community rather than on national interests.

These shortcomings were deeply rooted in the late Ch'ing social conditions and more than offset the many efforts to construct and maintain the new enterprises. Thus, the Chinese society as a whole did not show a structural change until 1911.

Changes in outlying areas. With the decline of the Ch'ing power and prestige, beginning in the early 19th century, China's peripheral areas began to free themselves from the Ch'ing influence.

Eastern Turkistan. To the west of Kashgaria in Eastern Turkistan, a khanate of Khokand emerged in Ferghana after 1760 as a powerful caravan trade centre. When Muslim rebellion spread rapidly from Shensi and Kansu to Eastern Turkistan, a Khokandian adventurer, Yakub Beg, seized the opportunity to invade Kashgaria and established power there in 1865; he soon showed signs of advancing to the Ili region in support of the British in India. In Ili rebel Muslims had set up an independent power at Kuldja in 1864, which terrorized the Russian borders in defiance of the Sino-Russian Treaty of 1851. The Russians, therefore, occupied Kuldja in 1871 and remained there for ten years.

Having subdued the Kansu Muslim rebellion in 1873, Tso Tsung-t'ang captured Urumchi in August 1876 and restored the whole region northward to the Tien Shan range, except for the Kuldja area, and painstakingly recovered Kashgaria at the end of 1877.

Li Hung-chang hoped to regain Ili through negotiation. A treaty for the restitution of Ili, signed at Livadia in October 1879, was extremely disadvantageous to China. Upon returning home amid a storm of condemnation, the Chinese negotiator Ch'ung-hou was sentenced to death; the Russians considered this to be inhuman and they stiffened their attitude. But the minister to Britain and France, Tseng Chi-tse, son of Tseng Kuo-fan, succeeded in concluding a treaty at St. Petersburg in February 1881 that was more favourable yet still conceded the Russians many privileges in Eastern Turkistan.

Though at a cost of nearly 58,000,000 taels in expedition and indemnity, the northwest was finally restored to China, and in 1884 a new province, Sinkiang, was established over the area, which had never before been integrated into China.

Nepal and Tibet. The border dispute between Nepal and British India, which sharpened after 1801, had caused an Anglo-Nepalese War of 1814–16 and brought the Gurkhas under British influence. During the war the Gurkhas sent several missions to China in vain expectation of assistance. During political unrest in Nepal after 1832, an anti-British clique seized power and sought assistance from China and to form an anti-British common front with the Ch'ing, then fighting the Opium War. But this, too, was rejected. Jang Bahadur, who had be-

come premier of Nepal in 1846, decided on a pro-British policy; taking advantage of the Taiping uprising in China, he invaded Tibet in 1855 and gained many privileges there. Though Nepal sent quinquennial missions to China until 1906, the Gurkhas had not recognized Chinese suzerainty.

Ch'ing control of Tibet reached its height in 1792. But thereafter China became unable to protect Tibet from foreign invasion. When an army from northern India invaded western Tibet in 1841, China could not afford to reinforce the Tibetans, who expelled the enemy on their own. In 1844, when a coup d'état occurred in Lhasa, China was a mere bystander. In 1855, when the Gurkhas invaded Tibet, China was unable to protect the latter. Tibet thus tended to free itself from Ch'ing control.

Burma. In 1867 the British gained the right to station a commercial agent at Bhamo in Burma, from which they could explore the Irrawaddy up to the Yunnan border. A British interpreter accompanying a British exploratory mission to Yunnan was killed by local tribesmen on the Yunnan–Burma border in February 1875. The British minister in China, Thomas Wade, seized the opportunity to force China to comply with the Cheefoo Convention (1876), which further enlarged the British rights by opening more Chinese ports to foreign trade and agreeing to a mission to delineate the Yunnan–Burmese border, though the London government put off its ratification until 1885. Kuo Sung-tao, appointed chief of a mission of apology to Britain, arrived in London in 1877. He was the first Chinese resident minister abroad, and within two years China opened embassies in five major foreign capitals.

When the last king of Burma, Thibaw, tried to join with France and Italy to stave off the British pressure, Britain sent an ultimatum in October 1885, seized the capital of Mandalay, and annexed the country in January 1886. During the final bargaining with the British, the Burmese king ignored his tributary relations with the Ch'ing; yet China proposed that the Burmese royal court be preserved even nominally so that it could send a decennial mission to China. Britain refused; but in a convention signed in July 1886 it agreed that the Burmese government should send to China a decennial envoy selected from the Burmese people. This outdated practice, however, was buried in 1900.

Vietnam. In 1802 a new dynasty was founded in Vietnam (Dai Viet) by Nguyen Phuc Anh, a member of the royal family of Nguyen at Hue, who had expelled the short-lived Tay Son regime and had unified the country. The Ch'ing, under the emperor Chia-ch'ing, recognized the new dynasty as a *fait accompli*, but a controversy arose as to a name for the new country. Nguyen Phuc Anh demanded the name Nam Viet, but the Ch'ing recommended Vietnam, reversing the two syllables. Finally an agreement was reached, and Nguyen Phuc Anh became king of Vietnam.

During the rule of the second and third kings of Vietnam (1820–41), the persecution of Christians was accelerated. France resorted to arms after 1843 and, by the treaty of 1862 signed at Saigon, received three eastern provinces of Cochin China besides other privileges concerning trade and religion. In time, French attentions were focussed on the Tongking Delta, into which the Red River (the Songkoi) flows, providing easy access to Yunnan. But the region was beset with many disorderly gangs escaped from China, among which was the Black Flags under the command of Liu Yung-fu, a confederate of the Taiping. After a small French force had occupied some key points in Tongking in 1873, a treaty was signed at Saigon in March 1874 that stipulated the sovereignty and independence of Vietnam. Though this clause implied that China could not intervene in Vietnamese affairs, the Tsungli yamen failed to file a strong protest. In 1880, however, the Ch'ing claimed a right to protect Vietnam as its vassal state. Against the French occupation of Tongking in 1882–83 and France's proclamation of protectorate status for Vietnam (under the name of Annam) in the treaty of Hue of August 1883, the Ch'ing deployed its army in the northern frontier of Tongking.

Meanwhile, parallel efforts for peaceful settlement were made; but they all ended in failure, and both countries made preparations for war.

Sino-French warfare

In August 1884 French warships attacked Foochow and destroyed the Chinese fleet and dockyard there. Thereafter, however, the French navy and army were stalemated, and an armistice was reached in the spring of 1885. By the subsequent definitive treaty, the French protectorate of Vietnam was recognized, terminating the historical Sino-Vietnamese tributary relationship.

In this crisis, the attitude of the Ch'ing headquarters fluctuated between advocates of militancy and appeasement. Meanwhile, Li Hung-chang and Tseng Kuo-ch'üan were reluctant to mobilize their *pei-yang* and *nan-yang* navies in accordance with orders from Peking.

Japan and Ryukyu. Three years after the beginning of the Meiji Restoration (a period of political change in Japan) in 1868, a commercial treaty was signed between China and Japan, and it was ratified in 1873. Understandably it was reciprocal, because both signatories had a similar unequal status vis-à-vis the Western nations. The establishment of the new Sino-Japanese relations was warmly supported by Li Hung-chang and Tseng Kuo-fan, who advocated positive diplomacy toward Japan.

In 1872 the Meiji government conferred on the last king of Ryukyu, Shō Tai, the title of vassal king, and in the following year took over the island's foreign affairs. In reprisal for the massacre of shipwrecked Ryukyuans by Taiwanese tribesmen in 1871, the Tokyo government sent a punitive expedition to Taiwan. Meanwhile the Japanese sent an envoy to Peking to discuss the matter, and the Ch'ing agreed to indemnify Japan. In 1877, however, the Ryukyu king asked for Ch'ing intervention to revive his former tributary relations with China; Sino-Japanese negotiations were opened at Tientsin in regard to Ryukyu's position, and an agreement was reached in 1882. But the Ch'ing refused to ratify it, and the matter was dropped.

Korea and the Sino-Japanese War. In Korea (Chosŏn) a boy king, Kojong, was enthroned in 1864 under the regency of his father Taewŏn-gun, a vigorous exclusionist. In 1866 they began a nationwide persecution of Christians and repulsed the French and Americans there. The Ch'ing, although uneasy, did not intervene.

After the Meiji Restoration, Japan made many efforts, all in vain, to open new and direct intercourse with Korea. The main reasons for the failure were such trifles as some offensive words in letters addressed by the Japanese government to Korea, or Japanese envoys coming to Korea in Western-style dress, which was unacceptable to the Koreans. With a slightly improved Korean attitude toward foreigners, a Japanese envoy began talks at Pusan in 1875, but the parley was protracted. Japan impatiently sent warships to Korea; these sailed northward to Kanghwa Bay, where gunfire was exchanged between the Japanese vessels and a Korean island fort. The Treaty of Kanghwa was signed in 1876, in which Korea was defined as an independent state on an equal footing with Japan. On this occasion, Japan sent an envoy, Mori Arinori, to China to report on recent Korean affairs. China insisted that though Korea was independent, China could come to the support of its vassal state (Korea) in a crisis, an interpretation that Mori saw as contrary to the idea of independence in international law.

Sino-Japanese competition

From this time on, the Ch'ing strove to increase their influence in Korea; they helped open Korea to the United States and supported the efforts of pro-Chinese Koreans for modernization. But in Korea, a powerful conservatism and xenophobia provided the basis for the resurgence of Taewŏn-gun. In July 1882 he expelled Queen Min and her clique and burned down the Japanese legation. The Ch'ing dispatched an army to Korea, arrested Taewŏn-gun, and urged the King to sign a treaty with Japan. Thus, the Ch'ing claim for suzerainty was substantiated.

In December 1884 another coup was attempted by a group of pro-Japanese reformists, but it failed because of the Ch'ing military presence in Korea. From these two incidents, Ch'ing political influence and commercial privileges emerged much stronger, though Japan's trade in Korea far surpassed that of China in the late 1880s.

In 1860 a Korean scholar, Ch'oe Che-u, founded a popular religion called Tonghak (Eastern Learning). By 1893 it had turned into a political movement that attracted a vast number of paupers under the banner of anti-foreignism and anti-corruption. They occupied the southwestern city of Jŏn-ju in late May 1894. Both China and Japan sent expeditions to Korea, but the two interventionists arrived to find the rebels at Jŏn-ju already dispersed. To justify its military presence, Japan proposed to China a policy of joint support of Korean reform. When China refused on the ground that this was counter to Korean independence, a clash seemed inevitable. On July 25 the Japanese navy defeated a Chinese fleet in the Kanghwa Bay, and on August 1 both sides declared war. Japan gained victories in every quarter on land and sea.

During the crisis the Ch'ing power centre was again divided. The *pei-yang* navy was less powerful than it appeared, lacking discipline, unified command, and the necessary equipments of a modern navy.

In February 1895 Li Hung-chang was appointed envoy to Japan; he signed a peace treaty at Shimonoseki on April 17, whose main items were recognition of Korean independence; indemnity of 200,000,000 taels; and the cession of Taiwan, the Pescadores Islands, and the Liao-tung Peninsula. Six days later, however, Russia, Germany, and France forced Japan to restore the peninsula; Japan formally relinquished it on May 5, for which China agreed to pay 30,000,000 taels. Gaining China's favour by this intervention, the three powers suddenly began to press China with demands, which gave rise to a veritable scramble for concessions.

Reform and upheaval. Immediately after the triple intervention, Russia succeeded in 1896 in signing a secret treaty of alliance with China against Japan, by which Russia gained the right to construct the Chinese Eastern Railway across northern Manchuria. In November 1897 the Germans seized Chiao-chou Bay in Shantung and forced China to concede them the right to build two railways in the province. In March 1898 Russia occupied Port Arthur and Dairen on Liao-tung Peninsula and obtained the lease of the two ports and the right to build a railway connecting them to the Chinese Eastern Railway. Vying with Russia and Germany, Britain leased Wei-hai-wei in Shantung and Kowloon on the coast opposite Hong Kong and forced China to recognize the Yangtze Valley as being under British influence. Following suit, Japan put the province of Fukien under its influence, and France leased Kuang-chou Bay and singled out three southwestern provinces for its sphere of influence. Thus, China was placed on the brink of partition, arousing a keen sense of crisis in which the Hundred Days' Reform of 1898 was staged.

The scramble for concession

The Hundred Days' Reform of 1898. The advocates of the Self-Strengthening movement had regarded any institutional or ideological change as needless. But after 1885 some lower officials and comprador intellectuals began to emphasize institutional reforms and the opening of a parliament and to stress economic rather than military affairs for self-strengthening purposes. But for the Peking court and high officials in general the necessity of reform had to be proved on the basis of the Chinese Classics.

The outstanding reform leader and ideologist was K'ang Yu-wei (1858–1925), who grounded reformism on the Classics. He used what he considered authentic Confucianism and Buddhist canons to show that change was inevitable in history and, accordingly, that reform was necessary. Another important reformist thinker, T'an Ssu-t'ung (1865–98) relied more heavily on Buddhism than K'ang did and emphasized the people's rights and independence. Liang Ch'i-ch'ao (1873–1929) was an earnest disciple of K'ang but later turned toward people's rights and nationalism under the influence of Western philosophy. The fact that some of these late Ch'ing thinkers turned to Buddhism and Taoism shows that the two religions, with their emphasis on individualism and humanism, played important roles in criticizing Confucian orthodoxy.

In April 1895, when Japanese victory appeared inevitable, K'ang began to advocate institutional reform. In

August, K'ang, Liang, and other reformists founded a political group called Society for the Study of National Self-Strengthening. Though this association was soon closed down, many study societies were created in Hunan, Kwangtung, Fukien, Szechwan, and other provinces. In April 1898 the National Protection Society was established in Peking under the slogan of protecting state, nation, and national religion. Against this background, K'ang won over the Kuang-hsü emperor (ruled 1875–1908) to radical reformism, and the latter started radical and hasty reforms on June 10, which lasted for about 100 days until September 20. The reform movement produced no practical results, although it brought forth a shower of decrees for institutional reforms. Finally, the conservatives were provoked to a sharp reaction when they learned of a reformist's plot to remove the arch-conservative empress dowager Tz'u-hsi. On September 21 the Emperor was detained, and the Empress Dowager took over the administration, putting an end to the reform movement.

Failure of the reform movement

The immediate cause of the failure lay in the power struggle between the Emperor and Tz'u-hsi. But from the beginning prospects for reform were dim, because most high officials were cool toward or opposed to the movement. In addition, the reformist–conservative confrontation overlapped with the rivalry between the Chinese and the Manchus, who considered the Chinese-sponsored reform as disadvantageous to them. As for the reformists themselves, their leaders were few in number and inexperienced in politics, and their plan was too radical.

Among the local movements for reform, that in Hunan was the most active. After 1896, journals and schools were opened there for popular enlightenment; but K'ang's radical reformism aroused strong opposition, and the Hunan movement was shattered at the end of May 1898.

Though it failed, the reform movement had a few important repercussions: it produced some degree of freedom of speech and association, furthered the dissemination of Western thought, and stimulated the growth of private enterprises.

The Boxer uprising, 1900. The crisis of 1896–98 stirred a furious anti-foreign uprising in Shantung. It was staged by a band of people called I-ho ch'uan (Righteous and Harmonious Fists), who believed in the invulnerability of a mysterious boxing art. The group's origin is generally supposed to have been in the White Lotus Society, though a recent study explains it as a self-defense organization founded in the years of the Taiping war. The Boxers (as they were called in the West) increased their membership in the strong anti-foreign sentiment aroused by the German advance in Shantung. Recruits came mainly from among the peasants, whose peace and subsistence were seriously threatened by the foreign interests and by communities of Chinese Christian converts. Others who joined the Boxers were the unemployed Grand Canal bargemen and disbanded Green Standard troops and local militiamen. In addition, the Boxers' expansion was closely connected with natural calamities in North China: after 1895 the Huang Ho flooded almost annually, and serious drought attacked North China in 1899–1900, leaving a vast number of starvelings.

Not confident of suppressing the large popular uprising, the court assumed a neutral policy, stating that Christians and non-Christians had to be treated equally. On the part of the Boxers, there emerged, sometime in the autumn of 1899, a move to gain access to the court under the slogan of "support for the Ch'ing and extermination of foreigners." Presumably in May 1900 the Ch'ing government changed its policy and gave secret support to the Boxers.

Government support of the Boxers

Tz'u-hsi's inclination toward war was stepped up on June 9, when she was convinced of the dependability of the Boxers' art, and on June 19, when she became incensed over a false report that the foreign powers required her to return administration to the Emperor. The Boxers' eight-weeks' siege of the foreign legations began on June 20; a day later, Tz'u-hsi declared war by ordering provincial governors to take part in the hostilities.

An international reinforcement of some 2,000 men left Tientsin in June for Peking, but on the way it was resisted by the Boxers and forced back to Tientsin. The foreign powers, therefore, sent an expedition of some 19,000 troops, which marched to Peking and seized the city on August 15. Tz'u-hsi and the Emperor fled to Sian.

The two governor generals in the southeastern provinces, Liu K'un-i and Chang Chih-tung, who together with Li Hung-chang at Canton had already disobeyed Peking's anti-foreign decrees, concluded an informal pact with foreign consuls at Shanghai on June 26, to the effect that the governor generals would take charge of the safety of the foreigners under their jurisdiction. At first the pact covered the five provinces in the Yangtze River region, but later it was extended to three coastal provinces. Thus, the foreign operations were restricted to Chihli, along the northern coast.

Developing from an anti-Christian struggle, the Boxer upheaval turned to naïve but furious destruction of all things foreign, which the people believed were the real source of their troubles. The uprising had an aspect of being patriotic and a national Chinese movement. But, viewed from another angle, the Boxers were driven to fanaticism and lacked a headquarters capable of controlling the numerous small leaders. The intellectuals had no thought of organizing the people more effectively.

The United States, which had announced the commercial Open Door Policy in 1899, made a second declaration of the policy in July 1900, including the preservation of the territorial and administrative entity of China. The United States, with its newly acquired territory in the western Pacific, helped protect its own commercial interests in China by preserving Chinese territorial integrity from the other major powers. This provided a basis for the Anglo-German agreement (October 1900) for preventing further territorial partition, to which Japan and Russia consented. Thus, partition of China was avoided by mutual restraint among the powers.

The final settlement of the disturbance was signed in September 1901. The indemnity amounted to 450,000,000 taels to be paid over 39 years with an interest rate of 4 percent. Moreover, the settlement demanded the establishment of permanent guards and the dismantling of the Ta-ku and other forts from Peking to the sea, a humiliation that made an independent China a mere fiction. In addition, the southern provinces were actually independent during the crisis. These occurrences meant the collapse of the Ch'ing prestige.

Collapse of Ch'ing prestige

After the uprising Tz'u-hsi had to declare that she had been misled into the war by the conservatives and that the court was neither anti-foreign nor anti-reformist and would promote reform measures, an incredible statement in view of the court's suppression of the 1898 reform movement.

Reformist and revolutionist movements at the end of the dynasty. Sun Yat-sen, a commoner with no background of Confucian orthodoxy, educated in Western-style schools in Hawaii and Hong Kong, went to Tientsin in 1894 to meet Li Hung-chang and present a reform program but was refused an interview. This event supposedly caused his anti-dynastic attitude. Soon he went to Hawaii where he founded an anti-Manchu fraternity called the Hsing-chung hui (Revive China Society). Returning to Hong Kong (Hang-chiang), he and some friends set up a similar society under the leadership of his associate Yang Ch'ü-yün. After an abortive attempt to capture Canton in 1895, Sun sailed for England and then went to Japan in 1897, where he found much support. Tokyo became the revolutionaries' principal base of operation.

After the collapse of the Hundred Days' Reform, K'ang Yu-wei and Liang Ch'i-ch'ao had also fled to Japan. An attempt to reconcile the reformists and the revolutionaries became hopeless by 1900—Sun was slighted as a secret-society ruffian, while the reformists were more influential among the Chinese in Japan and the Japanese.

The two camps competed in collecting funds from the overseas Chinese as well as in attracting secret-society members on the mainland. The reformists strove to unite with the powerful secret Ko-lao hui (Society for Brothers and Elders) in the Yangtze River region. In 1899 K'ang's followers organized the Tzu-li chün (Independence Army) at Hankow, in order to plan an uprising; but the scheme ended unsuccessfully. Early in 1900 the Revive China Society revolutionaries also formed a kind of alliance with the Brothers and Elders, called the Revive Han Association. This new body nominated Sun as its leader, a decision that caused him also to assume, for the first time, the leadership of the Revive China Society. The Revive Han Association started an uprising at Hui-chou, in Kwangtung, in October 1900, which failed after two weeks' fighting with Imperial forces.

After the Boxer disaster, Tz'u-hsi reluctantly issued a series of reforms, including the abolition of the civil-service examination, the establishment of modern schools, and the sending of students abroad. But these measures could never repair the damaged Imperial prestige; rather, they inspired more anti-Manchu feeling and heightened the revolutionary tide. But there were other factors that intensified the revolutionary cause. First, the introduction of Social Darwinist ideas by Yen Fu after the Sino-Japanese War countered the reformists' theory of change based on the Chinese Classics. Second, the

Spread of revolutionary ideas

Western and revolutionary thoughts came to be easily and widely diffused by means of journals and pamphlets published in Tokyo, Shanghai, and Hong Kong, which began to mushroom at the turn of the 20th century.

Nationalists and revolutionists had their most enthusiastic and numerous supporters among the Chinese students in Japan, whose numbers increased rapidly between 1900 and 1906. The Tsungli yamen sent 13 students to Japan for the first time in 1896; the figure rose to about 1,000 in 1903 and to some 8,000 in 1905–06. Many of these students began to organize themselves for propaganda and immediate action for the revolutionary cause.

In 1902–04 revolutionary and nationalistic organizations, including the Chinese Educational Association, the Society for Revival of China, and the Restoration Society, appeared in Shanghai. The anti-Manchu tract "Revolutionary Army" was published in 1903, and more than 1,000,000 copies were issued.

Dealing with the young intellectuals was a new challenge for Sun Yat-sen, who hitherto had concentrated on mobilizing the uncultured secret-society members. He had also to work out some theoretical planks, though he was not a first-class political philosopher. The result of his response was the Three Principles of the People—nationalism, democracy, and socialism—the prototype of which came to take shape by 1903. He expounded his philosophy in America and Europe during his travels there in 1903–05, returning to Japan in the summer of 1905. The activists in Tokyo joined him to establish a new organization called the United League (T'ung-meng hui); under Sun's leadership, the intellectuals increased their importance.

Sun Yat-sen and the United League. Sun's leadership in the League was far from undisputed. His understanding that the support of foreign powers was indispensable for Chinese revolution militated against the anti-imperialist trend of the young intellectuals. Only half-heartedly accepted was the principle of people's livelihood, or socialism, one of his three people's principles. Though various evaluations are given to his socialism, it seems certain that it did not reflect the hopes and needs of the commoners. (For a fuller discussion of Sun's ideology see section XII below.)

Ideologically, the League soon fell into disharmony; Chang Ping-lin (1869–1936), an influential theorist learned in the Chinese Classics, came to renounce the people's principles; some others deserted to anarchism, thus leaving anti-Manchuism as the only common denominator in the League. Organizationally, too, the League became divided; a Progressive Society (Kung-chin hui), a parallel to the League, was born in Tokyo in 1907, and a branch of this new society was soon opened at Wu-han with the ambiguous slogan of "equalization of human right." The next year Chang Ping-lin attempted to revive the Restoration Society.

Constitutional movements after 1905. Japan's victory in the Russo-Japanese War (1904–05) aroused a cry for constitutionalism in China. Unable to resist the intensifying demand, the court decided, in September 1906, to adopt a constitution and, in November the same year, reorganized the traditional six boards into 11 ministries in an attempt to modernize the central government. It promised to open the consultative provincial assemblies in October 1907 and proclaimed, in August 1908, the outline of a constitution and a schedule of nine-year tutelage period before its full implementation.

Effect of the Russo-Japanese War

Three months later the strangely coinciding deaths of Tz'u-hsi and the Emperor were announced and a boy who ruled as the Hsüan-te emperor 1908–12 was enthroned under the regency of his father, the second Prince Chün. These deaths, followed by that of Chang Chih-tung in 1909, almost emptied the prestige of the Ch'ing court. The consultative provincial assemblies were convened in October 1910 and became the main base of the furious movement for immediate opening of a consultative national assembly, with which the court could not comply.

The gentry and wealthy merchants were the sponsors of constitutionalism; they had been striving to gain the rights held by foreigners. Started first in Hunan, the so-called right-recovery movement spread rapidly and gained noticeable success, reinforced by local officials, students returned from Japan, and the Peking government. But finally the recovery of the railroad rights ended in a clash between the court and the provincial interests.

The retrieval of the Hankow–Canton line from the American China Development Company in 1905 tapped a nationwide fever for railway recovery and development. But difficulty in raising capital delayed railway construction by the Chinese year after year. The Peking court therefore decided to nationalize some important railways in order to accelerate their construction by means of foreign loans, hoping that the expected railway profits would somehow alleviate the court's inveterate financial plight. In May 1911 the court nationalized the Hankow–Canton and Szechwan–Hankow lines and signed a loan contract with the four-power banking consortium. This incensed the Szechwan gentry, merchants, and landlords who had invested in the latter line, and their anti-Peking remonstrance grew into a province-wide uprising. The court moved some troops into Szechwan from Hupeh; some other troops in Hupeh mutinied and suddenly occupied the capital city of Wu-han on October 10, now the memorial day of the Chinese revolution.

Peasant uprisings. The commoners' standard of living, which had been deteriorating since the beginning of the 19th century, was further dislocated by the mid-century civil wars and foreign commercial and military penetration. The heavy budgetary imbalance caused by the wars and indemnities of the late 19th century imposed on the tax-paying commoners a heavy burden, sometimes 10 to 20 times heavier than the prescribed tax quota. For those miserably exploited commoners—they can be roughly defined as peasantry—the preparations for constitutionalism were nothing but an additional squeeze. Thus, popular uprisings had taken place in many quarters before the whole Yangtze River region was affected by floods in 1910 and a large horde of starving people rose up at Chang-sha, the capital of Hunan, demanding cheaper rice. Again in 1911, nearly half the empire was affected by a crop failure and the Yangtze region was full of homeless starvelings.

Burden of the tax-paying commoners

The 1911 Revolution. The 1911 Revolution was not triggered by the United League itself but by the Hupeh army troops urged on by the local revolutionary bodies not incorporated in the League. An accidental exposure of a mutinous plot forced a number of junior officers to choose between arrest or revolt in Wuhan. The revolt was initially successful because of the determination of lower level officers and revolutionary troops and the cowardice of the responsible Manchu and Chinese officials. Within a day the rebels had seized the arsenal and the governor general's offices and had gained possession of the provincial capital, Wu ch'ang. With no nationally known revolutionary leaders on hand, the rebels coerced a colonel, Li Yuan-hung, to assume military command, although his role was only that of a figurehead. They persuaded the Hupeh provincial assembly to proclaim the establishment of the Chinese republic; T'ang Hua-lung, the assembly's chairman, was elected head of the civil government.

After this initial victory, a number of historical tendencies converged to bring about the downfall of the Ch'ing dynasty. A decade of revolutionary organization and propaganda paid off in a sequence of supportive uprisings in important centres of central and south China; these occurred in recently formed military academies and in newly created divisions and brigades, in which many cadets and junior officers were revolutionary sympathizers. Secret-society units also were quickly mobilized for local revolts. The anti-revolutionary constitutionalist movement also made an important contribution; its leaders had become disillusioned with the Imperial government's unwillingness to speed the process of constitutional government, and a number of them led their respective provincial assemblies to declare their provinces independent of Peking or actually to join the new republic. T'ang Hua-lung was the first among them. As a product of the newly emerging nationalism, there was widespread hostility among Chinese toward the alien dynasty. Many had absorbed the revolutionary propaganda that blamed a weak and vacilating court for the humiliations China had suffered from foreign powers since 1895. Therefore, there was a broad sentiment in favour of ending Manchu rule. Also, as an outcome of two decades of journalizing discussion of "people's rights," there was substantial support among the urban educated for a republican form of government. Probably the most decisive development was the recall of Yüan Shih-k'ai, the architect of the elite Peiyang Army, to government service to suppress the rebellion when its seriousness became apparent.

After the collapse of the Huai Army in the Sino-Japanese War, the Ch'ing government had striven to build up a new Western-style army, among which the elite corps trained by Yüan Shih-k'ai, former governor general of Chih-li, had survived the Boxer uprising and emerged as the strongest force in China. But it was, in a sense, Yüan's private army and did not easily submit to the Manchu court. Yüan had been retired from officialdom at odds with the regent prince Chün; but on the outbreak of the revolution in 1911, the court had no choice but to recall him from retirement to take command of his new army. Instead of using force, however, he played a double game—on the one hand, he deprived the floundering court, step by step, of all its power; on the other, he started to negotiate with the revolutionaries. At the peace talks that opened at the end of the year, Yüan's emissaries and the revolutionary representatives agreed that the abdication of the Ch'ing and the appointment of Yüan to the presidency of the new republic were to be formally decided by the National Assembly. But this was renounced by Yüan, probably because he hoped to be appointed by the retiring Manchu monarch to organize a new government rather than nominated as chief of state by the National Assembly. (This is a formula of the Chinese dynastic revolution called *ch'an-jang*, which means the peaceful shift in rule from a decadent dynasty to a more virtuous one.) But events turned against him, and the presidency was given to Sun Yat-sen, who had been appointed provisional president of the republic by the National Assembly. In February 1912 the Ch'ing court proclaimed the decree of abdication, which contained a paragraph purporting that Yüan Shih-k'ai was to organize a republican government to negotiate with the revolutionists on unification of North and South; this portion was a fabrication inserted by Yüan into the last Imperial document. Thus, the Ch'ing dynasty ended its 296-year rule with no legitimate successor.

End of the Ch'ing dynasty

THE ROLE OF THE MANCHUS IN CHINESE HISTORY

The Manchus' simple way of life and their vitality enabled them to endure the hardship of the conquering years and seem to have acted as a cure for the moral decadence of the late Ming officialdom. By the mid-18th century China developed favourable relations with the Inner Asian nations, which helped bring about an unprecedented social stability and economic progress in the mid-Ch'ing years. The commercial and industrial progress, however, involved Chinese society in a money economy, in which the officials, gentry, and landlords began to exploit the common people increasingly heavily. The morale of officials was also undermined during the years of peace and prosperity. The result was the unrest and turbulence that began at the end of the 18th century.

In place of the waning importance of Inner Asian relations, the second half of the 18th century saw deepening commercial ties with the West, headed by the British. Unfortunately, however, China clashed with Britain over the opium trade.

The Ch'ing defeats in the wars with the West and the shift in the military leadership from the Manchus to the Chinese in pacifying the popular uprisings in the third quarter of the century exposed the Ch'ing powerlessness. The Chinese then launched a self-strengthening movement by introducing merely the technological aspect of Western civilization. But in the end the movement fell short of paving a way to China's industrialization.

The Ch'ing border system and its relations with neighbour nations gradually collapsed during the 19th century, at the end of which the Ch'ing were defeated by Japan in a struggle for hegemony in Korea. Then followed the threat of partition of China by Imperialist powers, which instilled a keen sense of crisis in the Chinese. As a countermeasure, intellectuals staged an institutional reform; but the court and the conservatives reacted and aborted it. The people of Shantung rose up against the foreigners in retaliation, to which the court and the conservatives gave rash support that ended in fiasco. These misdoings deprived the court of its *raison d'être* as rulers of China.

This situation fed the revolutionary cause with fuel. But the revolutionaries lacked cohesion, discipline, and a clear-cut program to deal with the dislocated masses. Certainly, the revolutionaries contributed much toward disseminating anti-Manchu sentiment, but they were too feeble to seize power by their own force. The Ch'ing was overthrown neither by the revolutionaries nor by peasant leaders but by a trick played by the military politician Yüan Shih-k'ai and by the withdrawal of loyalty to the regime by the gentry who held positions of leadership in Chinese society. It may be that the Ch'ing dynasty fell of its own as the result of the powerlessness and ineptitude, revealed repeatedly after the mid-19th century, of imperial institutions and ideology. A way to improve the dishonourable foreign relations, one of the most important problems facing the late Ch'ing, was found in the last years of the dynasty in the form of the rights recovery movement. But the problem of how to stabilize the life of the masses was left for solution to the leaders of Republican China. (C.Su.)

XI. The republican period

THE DEVELOPMENT OF THE REPUBLIC (1912–20)

The first half of the 20th century saw the gradual disintegration of the old order in China and the turbulent preparation for a new society. Foreign political philosophies undermined the traditional governmental system, nationalism became the strongest activating force, and civil wars and Japanese invasion tore the vast country and retarded its modernization.

Although the revolution ushered in a republic, China had virtually no preparation for democracy. A three-way settlement ended the revolution—abdication by the dynasty; relinquishment of the provisional presidency by Sun Yat-sen in favour of Yüan Shih-k'ai, regarded as the indispensible man to restore unity; and Yüan's promise to establish a republican government. This placed at the head of state an autocrat by temperament and training, and there had been no agreement as to distribution of powers in the new government.

Early power struggles. The first years of the republic saw a continuing contest between Yüan and the former revolutionaries over where ultimate power should lie.

The contest began with the election of parliament (also called the National Assembly) in February 1913. The Nationalist Party (Kuomintang), made up largely of former revolutionaries, won a commanding majority of seats. Parliament was to produce a permanent constitution. Sung Chiao-jen, the main organizer of the Kuomintang's electoral victory, advocated executive authority in a cabinet responsible to parliament rather than to the president. On March 20, 1913, Sung was assassinated; the confession of the assassin and later circumstantial evidence strongly implicated the Premier and, possibly, Yüan himself.

Parliament tried to block Yüan's effort to get a "reorganization loan" (face value $125,000,000) from a consortium of foreign banks, but in April Yüan concluded the negotiations and received the loan. He then dismissed three Nationalist military governors. That summer, revolutionary leaders organized a revolt against Yüan, later known as the Second Revolution, but his military followers quickly suppressed it. Yüan then coerced parliament into electing him formally to the presidency, and he was inaugurated on October 10, the second anniversary of the outbreak of the revolution. By then his government had been recognized by most foreign powers. When parliament promulgated a constitution placing executive authority in a cabinet responsible to the legislature, Yüan revoked the credentials of the Kuomintang members, charging them with involvement in the recent revolt. He dissolved parliament on January 10, 1914, and appointed another body to prepare a constitution according to his own specifications. The presidency had become a dictatorship, and it soon appeared that Yüan was planning to restore the Imperial system with himself on the throne.

China in World War I. With the outbreak of World War I in August, Japan joined the side of the Allies and seized the German leasehold around Kiaochow Bay, together with German-owned railways in Shantung. China was not permitted to interfere.

Japanese gains. Then on January 18, 1915, the Japanese government secretly presented 21 demands directly to Yüan. Japan sought, in effect, to make China its dependency.

Yüan skillfully directed the negotiations by which China tried to limit its concession, while at the same time searching for foreign support. The European powers, locked in war, were in no position to restrain Japan. The United States was unwilling to intervene. The Chinese public, however, was aroused. Most of Yüan's political opponents supported his resistance to Japan's demands. On May 7, 1915, Japan gave Yüan a 48-hour ultimatum, forcing him to accept the terms as they stood at that point in the negotiations.

Japan gained extensive special privileges and concessions in Manchuria and confirmation of its gains in Shantung from Germany. The Han-Yeh-P'ing mining and metallurgical enterprise in the middle Yangtze Valley was to become a joint Sino-Japanese company. China promised not to alienate to any other power any harbour, bay, or island on the coast of China nor to permit any nation to construct a dockyard, coaling station, or naval base on the coast of Fukien, the province nearest to Japan's colony of Taiwan.

Yüan's attempts to become emperor. After resolving this difficult foreign policy problem, Yüan resumed his plans for enthronement. The Japanese government began to "advise" against this move in October and induced

its allies to join in opposing Yüan's plan. Additional opposition came from the leaders of the Kuomintang and of the Progressive Party. In December Ch'en Ch'i-mei and Hu Han-min, two followers of Sun Yat-sen, who was actively scheming against Yüan from his exile in Japan, began a movement against the monarchy. More significant was a military revolt in Yunnan Province, led by Gen. Ts'ai O, a disciple of Liang Ch'i-ch'ao, and by the governor of Yunnan, T'ang Chi-yao. Joined by Li Lieh-chün and other revolutionary generals, they established a Hu kuo chün (National Protection Army) and demanded that Yüan cancel his plan. When he would

not, the Yunnan army invaded Szechwan and Kwangsi in January 1916, hoping to bring the southwestern and southern provinces into rebellion and then induce the lower Yangtze provinces to join them. The Japanese government covertly provided funds and munitions to Sun and the Yunnan leaders. One by one military leaders in Kweichow, Kwangsi, and parts of Kwangtung declared the independence of their provinces or districts. By March the rebellion had assumed serious dimensions, and public opinion was running strongly against Yüan.

A third source of opposition came from Yüan's direct subordinates, generals Tuan Ch'i-jui and Feng Kuo-chang, whose powers Yüan had attempted to curtail. Now, when he called upon them for help, they both feigned illness. On March 22, with the tide of battle running against his forces in the southwest, public opposition in full cry, and his closest subordinates advising peace, Yüan announced the abolition of the new empire. His opponents, however, demanded that he give up the presidency as well. The revolt continued to spread, with more military leaders declaring the independence of their provinces. The issue became that of succession should Yüan retire. The president, however, became gravely ill; he died on June 6 at the age of 56.

Yüan's four years had serious consequences for China. The country's foreign debt was much enlarged, and a precedent had been established of borrowing for political purposes. The country was becoming fractured into competing military satrapies—the beginning of warlordism. Yüan's defiance of constitutional procedures and his dissolution of parliament set precedents that were often later repeated. There was much disillusionment with the republican experiment; China continued to be a republic in name, but arbitrary rule based upon military power was the political reality.

Gen. Li Yuan-hung, the vice president, succeeded to the presidency, and Gen. Tuan Ch'i-jui continued as premier, a position he had accepted in April. A man of great ability and ambition and supported by many generals of the former Peiyang Army, Tuan quickly began to gather power into his own hands. Li favoured the restoration of parliament and a return to the provisional constitution of 1912. Parliament reconvened on August 1; it confirmed Tuan as premier but elected Gen. Feng Kuo-chang, the leader of another faction of the Peiyang Army, as vice-president. The presidential transition and restoration of parliament had by no means answered the underlying question of where predominant governing power lay.

Conflict over entry into the war. In February 1917 the American government severed diplomatic relations with Germany and invited the neutral powers, including China, to do the same. This brought on a crisis in the Chinese government. Li opposed the step, but Tuan favoured moving toward entry into the war. Parliamentary factions and public opinion were bitterly divided. Sun Yat-sen in Shanghai argued that entering the war could not benefit China and would create additional perils from Japan. Under heavy pressure, parliament voted to sever diplomatic relations with Germany, and Li was compelled by his premier to acquiesce. When the United States entered the war in April, Tuan wished China to do the same but was again opposed by the President.

Tuan and his supporters demanded that China enter the war and that Li dissolve parliament. On May 23, Li dismissed Tuan; he then called upon Gen. Chang Hsün, a power in the Peiyang clique and also a monarchist, to mediate. As a price for mediation, Chang demanded that Li dissolve parliament, which he did reluctantly on June 13. The next day Chang entered Peking with an army and set about to restore the Ch'ing dynasty. Telegrams immediately poured in from military governors and generals denouncing Chang and the coup; Li refused to sign the restoration order and called upon Tuan to bring an army to the capital to restore the republic. Li requested that Vice President Feng assume the duties of president during the crisis and then took refuge in the Japanese legation. Tuan captured Peking on July 14; Chang fled to asylum in the Legation Quarter. Thus ended a second attempt to restore the Imperial system.

Tuan resumed the premiership, and Feng came to Peking as acting president, bringing a division as his personal guard. The two powerful rivals, each supported by an army in the capital, formed two powerful factions —the Chihli clique under Feng and the Anhwei clique under Tuan. Opposed neither by Li Yuan-hung nor by the dissolved parliament, Tuan pushed through China's declaration of war on Germany, which was announced on August 14, 1917.

Formation of a rival southern government. Meanwhile, in July, Sun Yat-sen, supported by part of the Chinese navy and followed by some 100 members of parliament, attempted to organize a rival government in Canton. The initial costs of this undertaking, termed the Movement to Protect the Constitution, probably were supplied by the German Consulate in Shanghai. On August 31 the rump parliament in Canton established a military government and elected Sun commander in chief. Real power, however, lay with military men, who only nominally supported Sun. The southern government declared war on Germany on September 26 and unsuccessfully sought recognition from the Allies as the legitimate government. A Hu fa chün (Constitution Protecting Army) made up of southern troops launched a punitive campaign against the government in Peking and succeeded in pushing northward through Hunan. Szechwan also was drawn into the fight. Tuan tried to quell the southern opposition by force, while Feng advocated a peaceful solution. Tuan resigned and mustered his strength to force Feng to order military action; Gen. Ts'ao K'un was put in charge of the campaign and drove the southerners out of Hunan by the end of April 1918. In May the southern government was reorganized under a directorate of seven, in which military men dominated. Sun therefore left Canton and returned to Shanghai. Although his first effort to establish a government in the South had been unsuccessful, it led to a protracted split between South and North.

Wartime changes. Despite limited participation, China made some gains from its entry into the war, taking over the German and Austrian concessions and cancelling the unpaid portions of the Boxer indemnities due its enemies. It was also assured a seat at the peace conference. Japan, however, extended its gains in China. The Peking government, dominated by Tuan after Feng's retirement, granted concessions to Japan for railway building in Shantung, Manchuria, and Mongolia. These were in exchange for the Nishihara loans, amounting to nearly $90,-000,000, which went mainly to strengthen the Anhwei clique with arms and cash. Japan also made secret agreements with its allies to support its claims to the former German rights in Shantung and also induced the Peking government to consent to these. In November 1917 the United States, to adjust difficulties with Japan, entered upon the Lansing–Ishii Agreement, which recognized that because of "territorial propinquity . . . Japan has special interests in China." This seemed to underwrite Japan's wartime gains.

Important economic and social changes occurred during the first years of the republic. With the outbreak of the war, foreign economic competition with native industry abated and native-owned light industries developed markedly. By 1918 the industrial labour force numbered some 1,750,000. Modern-style Chinese banks increased in number and expanded their capital.

Modernization and nationalism. A new intelligentsia had also emerged. The educational reforms and the ending of the governmental examination system during the final Ch'ing years enabled thousands of young people to study sciences, engineering, medicine, law, economics, education, and military skills in Japan. Others went to Europe and the United States. Upon their return they took important positions and were a modernizing force in society. Their writing and teaching became a powerful influence on upcoming generations of students. In 1915–16 there were said to be nearly 130,000 new-style schools in China with more than 4,000,000 students and

The rise of a new intelligentsia

nearly 200,000 teachers. This was mainly an urban phenomenon, however; rural life was barely affected except for a gradual increase in tenancy and a slow impoverishment that sent rural unemployed into cities and the armies or into banditry.

An intellectual revolution. An intellectual revolution took place during the first decade of the republic, sometimes referred to as the New Culture Movement. It was led by many of the new intellectuals, who held up for critical scrutiny nearly all aspects of Chinese culture and traditional ethics. Guided by concepts of individual liberty and equality, a scientific spirit of inquiry, and a pragmatic approach to the nation's problems, they sought a much more profound reform of China's institutions than had resulted from self-strengthening or the republican revolution. They directed their efforts particularly to China's educated youth.

In September 1915, Ch'en Tu-hsiu, who had studied in Japan and France, founded *Hsin ch'ing nien* ("New Youth") magazine to oppose Yüan's Imperial ambitions and to regenerate the nation's youth. This quickly became the most popular reform journal, and in 1917 it began to express the iconoclasm of new faculty members in Peking National University (Peita), which Ch'en had joined as dean of the College of Letters. Peita, China's most prestigious institution of higher education, was being transformed by its new chancellor, Ts'ai Yüan-p'ei, who had spent many years in advanced study in Germany. Ts'ai made the university a centre of scholarly research and inspired teaching. The students were quickly swept into the New Culture Movement. A proposal by Professor Hu Shih, a former student of John Dewey, that literature be written in the vernacular language (*pai-hua*) rather than in classical style, won quick acceptance. By 1918 most of the contributors to "New Youth" were writing in *pai-hua*, and other journals and newspapers soon followed suit. Students at Peita began their own reform journal, *Hsin ch'ao* ("New Tide"). A new experimental literature inspired by Western forms became highly popular, and scores of new literary journals were founded.

Riots and protests. On May 4, 1919, patriotic students in Peking protested the decision at the Versailles Peace Conference that Japan should retain defeated Germany's rights and possessions in Shantung Province. Many students were arrested in the rioting that followed. Waves of protest spread throughout the major cities of China. Merchants closed their shops, banks suspended business, and workers went on strike to pressure the government. Finally, the government was forced to release the arrested students, to dismiss some officials charged with being tools of Japan, and to refuse to sign the Treaty of Versailles. This outburst helped spread the iconoclastic and reformist ideas of the intellectual movement, which was renamed the May Fourth Movement. By the early 1920s China was launched on a new revolutionary path.

The May Fourth Movement

THE INTERWAR YEARS (1920–37)

Beginnings of a national revolution. This new revolution was led by the Nationalist Party (Kuomintang) and the Communist Party (Kungch'antang, or CCP).

The Kuomintang. The Kuomintang had its origins in the earlier T'ung-meng hui (United Party) against the Manchus. Sun Yat-sen and a small group of veterans were stimulated by the patriotic upsurge of 1919 to rejuvenate the moribund party Sun had formed in 1914. The party's publications took on new life as the editors entered the current debates on what was needed to "save China." Socialism was popular among Sun's followers.

The formation of an effective party took several years, however. Sun returned to Canton late in 1920, when Gen. Ch'en Chiung-ming drove out the Kwangsi militarists. Another rump parliament elected Sun president of a new southern regime, which claimed to be the legitimate government of China. In the spring of 1922 Sun attempted to launch a northern campaign as an ally of the Manchurian warlord, Chang Tso-lin, against the Chihli clique, which by now controlled Peking. Ch'en, however, did not want the provincial revenues wasted in internecine wars. One of Ch'en's subordinates drove Sun from the presidential residence in Canton on the night of June 15–16, 1922. Sun took refuge with the southern navy, and he retired to Shanghai on August 9. He was able to return to Canton in February 1923; he then began to consolidate a base under his own control and to rebuild his party.

The Chinese Communist Party. The CCP grew directly from the May Fourth Movement. Its leaders and early members were professors and students who came to believe that China needed a social revolution and who began to see Soviet Russia as a model. Chinese students in Japan and France had earlier studied socialist doctrines and the ideas of Karl Marx, but the Russian Revolution of 1917 stimulated a fresh interest in keeping with the enthusiasm of the period for radical ideologies. Li Ta-chao, the librarian of Peking National University, and Ch'en Tu-hsiu were the CCP's cofounders.

In March 1920 word reached China of Soviet Russia's revolutionary foreign policy enunciated in the first Karakhan manifesto, which promised to give up all special rights gained by tsarist Russia at China's expense and to return the Russian-owned Chinese Eastern Railway in Manchuria without compensation. The contrast between this promise and the Versailles award to Japan that had touched off the 1919 protest demonstrations could scarcely have been more striking. Although the Soviet government later denied such a promise and attempted to regain control of the railway, the impression of this first statement and the generosity still offered in a more diplomatic second Karakhan manifesto of September 1920 left a favourable image of Soviet foreign policy among Chinese patriots.

Russian influence

Russia set up an international Communist organization, the Comintern, in 1919 and sent Grigory Voitinsky to China the next year. Voitinsky met Li Ta-chao in Peking and Ch'en Tu-hsiu in Shanghai, and they organized a Socialist Youth League, laid plans for a Communist Party, and started recruiting young intellectuals. By the spring of 1921 there were about 50 members in various Chinese cities and in Japan, many of them former students who had been active in the 1919 demonstrations. Mao Tse-tung, a protégé of Li Ta-Chao, had started one such group in Chang-sha.

The CCP held its First Congress in Shanghai in July 1921, with 12 or 13 attendants and with a Dutch Communist—Hendricus Sneevliet, who used his Comintern name, Maring, in China—and a Russian serving as advisers. Maring had become head of a new bureau of the Comintern in China, and he had arrived in Shanghai in June 1921. At the First Congress, Ch'en Tu-hsiu was chosen to head the party.

The CCP spent the next two years in recruiting, publicizing Marxism and the need for a national revolution directed against foreign imperialism and Chinese militarism, and in organizing unions among railway and factory workers. Maring was instrumental in bringing the Kuomintang and the CCP together in a national revolutionary movement. A number of young men were sent to Russia for training. Among the CCP members were many students who had worked and studied in France, where they had gained experience in the French labour movement and with the French Communist Party; Chou En-lai was one of these. Other recruits were students influenced by the Japanese Socialist movement. By 1923 the party had some 300 members, and there were perhaps between 3,000 and 4,000 in the ancillary Socialist Youth League.

Communist–Nationalist cooperation. By then, however, the CCP was in serious difficulty. The railway unions had been brutally suppressed, and there were few places in China where it was safe to be a known Communist. In June 1923 the Third Congress of the CCP met in Canton, where Sun Yat-sen provided a sanctuary. After long debate this congress accepted the Comintern strategy pressed by Maring—that Communists should join the Kuomintang and make it the centre of the na-

tional revolutionary movement. Sun had rejected a multiparty alliance but had agreed to admit Communists to his party, and several, including Ch'en Tu-hsiu and Li Tao-chao had already joined the Kuomintang. Even though Communists would enter the other party as individuals, the CCP was determined to maintain its separate identity and autonomy and attempt to control the labour union movement. The Comintern strategy was for an undetermined period of steering the Nationalist movement and building a base among the Chinese masses, followed by a second stage—a Socialist revolution in which the proletariat would seize power from the capitalist class.

By mid-1923 Russia had decided to renew the effort to establish diplomatic relations with the Peking government. Lev Karakhan, the deputy commissar for foreign affairs, was chosen as plenipotentiary for the negotiations. In addition to negotiating a treaty of mutual recognition, Karakhan was to try to regain for Russia control of the Chinese Eastern Railway. On the revolutionary front, Russia had decided to assist Sun in Canton with an initial allocation of $2,000,000 (about U.S. $950,000) Mexican and to send a team of military men to help train a revolutionary army in Kwangtung. By June, five young Russian officers were in Peking for language training. More importantly, the Russian leaders selected an old Bolshevik, Mikhail Borodin, as their principal adviser to Sun Yat-sen. The Russian leaders also decided to replace Maring with Voitinsky as principal adviser to the CCP, which had its headquarters in Shanghai. Thereafter three men—Karakhan in Peking, Borodin in Canton, and Voitinsky in Shanghai—were the field directors of the Soviet effort to bring China into the anti-imperialist camp of "world revolution." The offensive was aimed primarily at the positions in China of Great Britain, Japan, and the United States.

The arrival of Soviet advisers

Reactions to warlords and foreigners. These states, too, were moving toward a new, postwar relationship with China. At the Washington Conference (November 1921–February 1922), eight powers agreed to respect the sovereignty, independence, and territorial and administrative integrity of China, to give China opportunity to develop a stable government, to maintain the principle of equal opportunity in China for the commerce and industry of all nations, and to refrain from taking advantage of conditions in China to seek exclusive privileges. The powers also agreed to steps leading toward China's tariff autonomy and to the abolition of extraterritoriality. Japan agreed separately to return the former German holdings in Shantung, although under conditions that left Japan with valuable privileges in the province. For a few years thereafter Great Britain, Japan, the United States, and France attempted to adjust their conflicting interests in China, cooperated in assisting the Peking government, and refrained, on the whole, from aiding particular Chinese factions in the recurrent power struggles. But China was in turmoil, with regional militarism in full tide. Furthermore, a movement against the "unequal treaties" (see below) began to take shape.

Militarism in China. During the first years of the republic China had been fractured by rival military regimes to the extent that no one authority was able to subordinate all rivals and create a unified and centralized political structure. The South was detached from Peking's control; but even the southern provinces, and indeed districts within them, were run by different military factions (warlords). Szechwan was a world in itself, divided among several military rulers. The powerful Peiyang army had split into two major factions whose semi-independent commanders controlled provinces in the Yangtze Valley and in the North; these factions competed for control of Peking. In Manchuria, Chang Tso-lin headed a separate Fengtien army. Shansi Province was controlled by Yen Hsi-shan. Each separate power group had to possess a territorial base from which to tax and recruit. Arms were produced in many scattered arsenals. Possession of an arsenal and control of ports through which foreign-made arms might be shipped were important elements of power. Most of the foreign

The rival military regimes of republican China

powers had agreed in 1919 not to permit arms to be smuggled into China, but this embargo was not entirely effective.

The richer the territorial base, the greater the potential power of the controlling faction. Peking was the great prize because of its symbolic importance as the capital and because the government there regularly received revenues collected by the Maritime Customs Service, administered by foreigners and protected by the powers. Competition for bases brought on innumerable wars, alliances, and betrayals. Even within each military system there was continuous conflict over spoils. To support their armies and conduct their wars, military commanders and their subordinates taxed the people heavily. Money for education and other government services was drained away; revenues intended for the central government were retained in the provinces. Regimes printed their own currency and forced "loans" from merchants and bankers. This chaotic situation partly accounts for the unwillingness of the maritime powers to give up the protection that the treaties with China afforded their nationals.

The foreign presence. As a result of several wars and many treaties with China since 1842, foreign powers had acquired a variety of unusual privileges for their nationals. These were the "unequal treaties," which patriotic Chinese bitterly opposed. Hong Kong, Taiwan, and vast areas in Siberia and Central Asia had been detached from China. Dependencies such as Korea, Outer Mongolia, Tibet, and Annam had been separated. Leaseholds on Chinese territory were granted to separate powers—such as the southern part of the Liaotung Peninsula to Japan; the Kiaochow territory in Shantung, which Japan had seized from Germany; the New Territories to the adjacent British Crown Colony of Hong Kong; and the Kwangchow Bay area to France. In most major cities there were concession areas, not governed by China, for the residence of foreigners. Nationals and subjects of the "treaty powers" were protected by extraterritoriality (*i.e.*, they were subject to the civil and criminal laws of their own countries and not to Chinese law); this extended to foreign business enterprises in China, providing a great advantage in competition with Chinese firms, which was enhanced when foreign factories or banks were located in concession areas under foreign protection. The Chinese had to compete with foreign ships in Chinese rivers and coastal waters, with foreign mining companies in the interior, and with foreign banks that circulated their own notes. Foreign trade also had a great advantage in that there could be no protective tariff to favour Chinese products.

Christian missionaries operated many schools, hospitals, and other philanthropic enterprises in China, all protected by extraterritoriality. The separate school system, outside of Chinese governmental control, was a sore point for Nationalists, who regarded the education of Chinese youth as a Chinese prerogative. There were bodies of foreign troops on Chinese soil and naval vessels in its rivers and ports to enforce treaty rights. Bound by a variety of interlocking treaties, the Chinese government was not fully sovereign in China. Past regimes had accumulated a vast foreign debt against which central government revenues were pledged for repayment. All this was the foreign imperialism against which the Kuomintang launched its attack after being reorganized along Bolshevist lines.

Reorganization of the Kuomintang. The Kuomintang held its First National Congress in Canton, January 20–30, 1924. Borodin, who had reached Canton in October 1923, quickly began to advise Sun in the reorganization of his party. He prepared a constitution and helped draft a party program as a set of basic national policies. Delegates from throughout China and from overseas branches of the party adopted the program and the new constitution.

Kuomintang goals

The program announced goals of broad social reform and a fundamental readjustment of China's international status. Its tone was nationalistic; it identified China's enemies as imperialism and militarism. It singled out farmers and labourers as classes for special encouragement but also appealed to intellectuals, soldiers, youth, and women. It threatened the position of landlords in relation to tenants and of employers in relation to labour. Western privileges were menaced openly.

The constitution described a centralized organization, modelled on the Russian Communist Party, with power concentrated in a small, elected group and with a descending hierarchy of geographical offices controlled by executive committees directed from above. Members were pledged to strict discipline and were to be organized in tight cells. Where possible they were to penetrate and try to gain control of such other organizations as labour unions, merchant associations, schools, and parliamentary bodies at all levels. Sun was designated as leader of the party and had veto rights over its decisions. The Congress elected a central executive committee and a central supervisory committee to manage party affairs, and confirmed Sun's decision to admit Communists, though this was opposed by numerous party veterans, who feared the Kuomintang itself might be taken over. A few Communists, including Li Ta-chao, were elected to the executive committee.

The executive committee set up a central headquarters in Canton. It also decided to strengthen the party throughout the country by deputizing most of its leaders to manage regional and provincial headquarters and by recruiting new members. A military academy was planned for training a corps of young officers, loyal to the party, who would become lower-level commanders in a new national revolutionary army that was to be created. Borodin provided funds for party operations, and Soviet Russia promised to underwrite most of the expenses of and to provide training officers for the military academy. Chiang Kai-shek (*q.v.*) was chosen to be the first commandant of the academy and Liao Chung-k'ai to be the party representative, or chief political officer.

From February to November 1924 Sun and his colleagues had some success in making the Kuomintang's influence felt nationally; they also consolidated the Canton base, although it was still dependent upon mercenary armies. The military academy was set up at Whampoa, on an island south of Canton, and the first group of some 500 cadets was trained. In September, Sun began another northern campaign in alliance with Chang Tso-lin against Ts'ao K'un and Wu P'ei-fu, who now controlled Peking. The campaign was interrupted, however, when Wu's subordinate, Feng Yü-hsiang, betrayed his chief and seized Peking on October 23, while Wu was at the front facing Chang Tso-lin. Feng and his fellow plotters invited Sun to Peking to participate in the settlement of national affairs, while Feng and Chang invited Tuan Ch'i-jui to come out of retirement and take charge of the government. Sun accepted the invitation and departed for the North on November 13. Before he arrived in Peking, however, he fell gravely ill with incurable cancer of the liver. He died in Peking on March 12, 1925.

Struggles within the two-party coalition. After Sun's death the Kuomintang went through a period of inner conflict, although it progressed steadily, with Russian help, in bringing the Kwangtung base under its control. The conflict was caused primarily by the radicalization of the party under the influence of the Communists. They organized labour unions and peasant associations and pushed class struggle and the anti-imperialist movement.

Clashes with foreigners. On May 30, patriotic students, engaged in an anti-imperialist demonstration in Shanghai, clashed with foreign police. The British captain in charge ordered the police to fire upon a crowd that he believed was about to rush his station. Some 12 Chinese were killed, including students. This aroused a nationwide protest and set off a protracted general strike in Shanghai. A second incident occurred on June 23, when French and British marines exchanged fire with Whampoa cadets who were part of an anti-imperialist parade, killing 52 Chinese, many of them civilians, and wounding at least 117; which side had fired first became a matter of dis-

Organization of the executive committee

pute. This set off a strike and boycott against Britain, France, and Japan, which was later narrowed to Britain alone. The strike and boycott, led mainly by Communists, lasted for 16 months and seriously affected Hong Kong's trade. These incidents intensified hostility toward foreigners and their special privileges, enhanced the image of Soviet Russia, and gained support for the Kuomintang, which promised to end the unequal treaties. By January 1926 the Kuomintang could claim some 200,000 members. The CCP also benefitted; its membership grew from less than 1,000 in May 1925 to about 10,000 by the end of that year.

Kuomintang opposition to radicals. The two parties competed for direction of nationalist policy, control of mass organizations, and recruitment of new members. Under Russian coaching, the Communist strategy was to try to split the Kuomintang, drive out its conservative members, and turn it to an ever more radical course. In August 1925, Kuomintang conservatives in Canton tried to stop the leftward trend. One of the strongest advocates of the Kuomintang's Russian orientation, Liao Chung-k'ai, was assassinated. In retaliation, Borodin, Chiang Kai-shek, and Wang Ching-wei deported various conservatives. As a countermove, a group of Kuomintang veterans in the North ordered the expulsion of Borodin and the Communists and the suspension of Wang Ching-wei; they set up a rival Kuomintang headquarters in Shanghai. The left-wing leaders in Canton then held a Second National Congress in January 1926, confirming the radical policies and the Russian alliance. But as the Russian presence became increasingly overbearing, as the Canton–Hong Kong strike and boycott dragged on, and as class conflict intensified in the south, opposition to the radical trend grew stronger, particularly among military commanders.

Chiang Kai-shek, now commander of the National Revolutionary Army, took steps in March to curb the Communists and to send away several Russian officers whom he believed were scheming with Wang Ching-wei against him. In a readjustment of party affairs, Communists no longer were permitted to hold high offices in the central headquarters, and Wang Ching-wei went into retirement in France. Chiang also demanded Russian support of a northern military campaign and the return of Gen. V.K. Blücher as his chief military adviser. Blücher, who used the pseudonym Galen in China, was a commander in the Red Army who had worked with Chiang in 1924 and 1925 in developing the Whampoa Military Academy and forming the National Revolutionary Army. Blücher returned to Canton in May and helped refine plans for the northern expedition, which began officially in July, with Chiang as commander in chief.

The northern expedition. In the northern expedition the outnumbered southern forces were infused with revolutionary spirit and fought with great elan. They were assisted by propaganda corps, which subverted enemy troops and agitated among the populace in the enemy's rear. Russian military advisers accompanied most of the divisions, and Russian pilots reconnoitered the enemy positions. The army was well financed at the initial stages because of fiscal reforms in Kwangtung during the previous year, and many enemy divisions and brigades were bought over. Within two months the National Revolutionary Army gained control of Hunan and Hupeh, and by the end of the year it had taken Kiangsi and Fukien. The Nationalist government moved its central headquarters from Canton to the Wu-han cities of the Yangtze. By early spring of 1927, revolutionary forces were poised to attack Nanking and Shanghai.

The political situation, however, was unstable. Hunan and Hupeh were swept by a peasant revolt marked by violence against landlords and other rural power holders. Business in the industrial and commercial centre of the middle Yangtze, the Wu-han cities, was nearly paralyzed by a wave of strikes. Communists and Kuomintang leftists led this social revolution. In January the British concessions in Hankow and Kiukiang were seized by inflamed Chinese crowds. The British government had

just adopted a conciliatory policy toward China, and it acquiesced in these seizures, but it was readying an expeditionary force to protect its more important position in Shanghai. Foreigners and many upper-class Chinese fled from the provinces under Nationalist control. The northern armies began to form an alliance against the southerners.

Conservative Kuomintang leaders in Shanghai mobilized against the headquarters in Wu-han. And there was a deep rift within the revolutionary camp itself; the leftists at Wu-han, guided by Borodin, pitted themselves against Chiang and his more conservative military supporters, who were also laying plans against the leftists. Resolutions of the CCP's Central Committee in January 1927 showed apprehension of a counterrevolutionary tide against their party, Soviet Russia, and the revolutionary peasant and workers' movement; they feared a coalition within the Kuomintang and its possible alliance with the imperialist powers. The central leadership resolved to check revolutionary excesses and give all support to the Kuomintang leadership at Wu-han. Others within the CCP, notably Mao Tse-tung, disagreed; they believed the mass revolution should be encouraged to run its course.

Expulsion of Communists from the Kuomintang. The climax of the conflict came after Nationalist armies had taken Shanghai and Nanking in March. Nanking was captured on March 23, and the following morning Nationalist troops looted foreign properties, attacked the British, American, and Japanese consulates, and killed seven foreigners. In Shanghai a general strike led by Communists aroused fears that Chinese might seize the International Settlement and French concession, now guarded by a large international expeditionary force. Conservative Kuomintang leaders, some army commanders, and Chinese business leaders in Shanghai encouraged Chiang to expel the Communists and suppress the Shanghai General Labour Union. On April 12–13, gangsters and troops bloodily suppressed the armed pickets of the General Labour Union and arrested many Communists. Similar suppressions were carried out in Canton, Nanking, Nanchang, Foochow, and other cities under military forces that accepted Chiang's instructions. The Kuomintang conservatives then established a rival Nationalist government in Nanking.

Wang Ching-wei had returned to China via Russia. Arriving in Shanghai, he refused to participate in the expulsions and went secretly to Wu-han, where he again headed the government. In July, however, the leftist Kuomintang leaders in Wu-han, having learned of a directive by Stalin to Borodin to arrange for radicals to capture control of the government, decided to expel the Communists and invite the Russian advisers to leave. The leftist government thereby lost important bases of support; furthermore, it was ringed by hostile forces and cut off from access to the seas, and it soon disintegrated.

The CCP went into revolt. Using its influence in the Cantonese army of Chang Fa-k'uei, it staged an uprising at Nanchang on August 1 and then attempted an "Autumn Harvest" uprising in several central provinces. Both efforts failed. In December Communist leaders in Canton started a revolt known as the Canton Commune. They captured the city with much bloodshed, arson, and looting; but this uprising was quickly suppressed, also with much slaughter. Between April and December, the CCP lost most of its membership by death and defection. A few score leaders and some scattered military bands then began the process of creating military bases in the mountains and plains of central China, remote from centres of Nationalist power.

The now more conservative Kuomintang resumed its northern expedition in the spring of 1928 with a reorganized National Revolutionary Army. In the drive on Peking it was joined by the National People's Army under Feng Yü-hsiang, part of the Kwangsi army, and the Shansi army of Yen Hsi-shan. In early June they captured Peking, from which Chang Tso-lin and the Fengtien army withdrew for Manchuria. As his train neared Mukden, Chang died in an explosion arranged by a few

Japanese officers without knowledge of the Japanese government. Japan did not permit the Nationalist armies to pursue the Fengtien army into Manchuria, hoping to keep the northeastern provinces (Manchuria) out of Nationalist control. By the end of the northern expedition the major warlords had been defeated by the Nationalists, whose armies now possessed the cities and railways of eastern China. On October 10 the Nationalists formally established a reorganized National Government of the Republic of China, with its capital at Nanking.

National control of eastern China

The Nationalist government from 1928 to 1937. The most serious immediate problem facing the new government was the continuance of military separatism. The government had no authority over the vast area of western China and even regions in eastern China were under the rule of independent regimes that had lately been part of the Nationalist coalition. After an unsuccessful attempt at negotiations, Chiang launched a series of civil wars against his former allies. By 1930 one militarist regime after another had been reduced to provincial proportions and Nanking's influence was spreading. Explained in materialistic terms, Chiang owed his success to the great financial resources of his base in Kiangsu and Chekiang and to foreign arms. Quick recognition by the foreign powers brought the Nationalist government the revenues collected by the efficient Maritime Customs Service; when the powers granted China the right to fix its own tariff schedules, that revenue increased.

The Nationalists did much to create a modern government and a coherent monetary and banking system and to improve taxation. They expanded the public educational system, developed a network of transportation and communication facilities, and encouraged industry and commerce. Again it was urban China that mainly benefitted; little was done to modernize agriculture or to eradicate disease, illiteracy, and underemployment in the villages, hamlets, and small towns scattered over a continental territory. With conscription and heavy taxation to support civil war, rural economic conditions may have grown worse during the Nationalist decade.

The Nationalist government during its first few years in power had some success in reasserting China's sovereignty. Several concession areas were returned to Chinese control, and the foreign powers assented to China's resumption of tariff autonomy. Yet these were merely token gains; the unequal treaties were scarcely breached. The country was in a nationalistic mood, determined to roll back foreign economic and political penetration. Manchuria was a huge and rich area of China in which Japan had extensive economic privileges, possessing part of the Liaotung Peninsula as a leasehold and controlling much of south Manchuria's economy through the South Manchurian Railway. The Chinese began to develop Hulutao, in Liaotung, as a port to rival Dairen and to plan railways to compete with Japanese lines. Chang Hsüeh-liang, Chang Tso-lin's son and successor as ruler of Manchuria, was drawing closer to Nanking and sympathized with the Kuomintang's desire to rid China of foreign privilege.

For Japan, Manchuria was regarded as strategically and economically vital. Many Japanese had acquired a sense of mission that Japan should lead Asia against the West. The worldwide depression had hurt Japanese business, and there was deep social unrest in the villages and cities. Such factors influenced many army officers to regard Manchuria as the area where Japan's power must be consolidated, especially officers of the Kwantung Army, which protected Japan's leasehold in the Liaotung Peninsula and the South Manchurian Railway.

Japanese aggression. In September 1931 a group of officers in the Kwantung Army set in motion a plot to compel the Japanese government to extend its power in Manchuria. The Japanese government was drawn, step by step, into the conquest of Manchuria and the creation of a regime known as Manchoukuo. China was unable to prevent Japan from seizing this vital area (see MAN-CHURIA, HISTORY OF). In 1934, after long negotiations, Japan acquired the Soviet interest in the Chinese Eastern Railway, thus eliminating the last legal trace of the Rus-

sian sphere of influence there. During 1932–35 Japan seized more territory bordering on Manchuria. In 1935 it attempted to detach Hopei and Chahar from Nanking's control and threatened Shansi, Suiyüan, Shantung. The National government's policy was to trade space for time in which to build military power and unify the country. Its slogan "Unity before resistance" was directed principally against the Chinese Communists.

War between Nationalists and Communists. In the meantime, the Communists had created 15 rural bases in central China, and they established a soviet government on November 7, 1931. Within the soviet regions the Communist leadership expropriated and redistributed land and in other ways enlisted the support of the poorer classes. The Japanese occupation of Manchuria and the localized war around Shanghai in 1932 distracted the Nationalists and gave the Communists a brief opportunity to expand and consolidate. But the Nationalists soon forced the Red armies to abandon their bases and retreat. Most of the later Communist leaders, including Mao Tse-tung, Chu Teh, Chou En-lai, Liu Shao-ch'i, and Lin Piao, marched and fought their way across western China. By the middle of 1936 the remnants of several Red armies had gathered in an impoverished area in northern Shensi, later known as the Yenan region.

The Long March

During this Long March the CCP began to develop a new political strategy—a united front against Japan. It was first conceived as an alliance of patriotic forces against Japan and the National government; but as Japan's pressure on China and the pressure of the Nationalist armies against the weakened Red armies increased, the Communist leaders began to call for a united front of all Chinese against Japan alone. Virtually all classes and various local regimes supported this, and the Communists moderated their revolutionary program and terminated class warfare in their zone of control.

Chiang was determined, however, to press on with his extermination campaign. He ordered the Manchurian army under Chang Hsüeh-liang, now based in Sian, and the Northwestern army under Yang Hu-ch'eng to attack the Communist forces in northern Shensi. Many officers in these armies sympathized with the Communist slogan, "Chinese don't fight Chinese"; they preferred to fight Japan, a sentiment particularly strong in the homeless Manchurian army. Chang Hsüeh-liang was conducting secret negotiations with the Communists and had suspended the civil war. In December 1936 Chiang Kai-shek flew to Sian to order Chang and Yang to renew the anti-Communist campaign. Under pressure from subordinates, Chang detained Chiang on the morning of December 12 (this became known as the Sian Incident).

Chiang's insistence on fighting the CCP

The united front against Japan. Fearing that if Chiang were killed China would be plunged into renewed disorder, the nation clamoured for his release. The Soviet Union quickly denounced the captors and insisted that Chiang be freed (the Soviet Union needed a united China opposing Japan, its potential enemy on the east). The CCP leaders also decided that Chiang's release would serve China's interests as well as their own, if he would accept their policy against Japan. Chou En-lai (q.v.) and several other Communist leaders flew to Sian to try to effect this. Chang Hsüeh-liang finally agreed to free his captive, with the understanding that Chiang would call off the civil war and unite the country against the invader. On Christmas day Chiang was freed. For Chang Hsüeh-liang, the outcome was 25 years of detention.

The two Chinese parties began protracted and secret negotiations for cooperation, each making concessions. But it was not until September 1937, after the Sino-Japanese war had begun, that the National government published the CCP's promises to strive for Sun Yat-sen's Three Principles of the People, to abandon its policies of armed revolt and forcible confiscation of land, to abolish the soviet government, and to place Communist troops under government command.

THE WAR AGAINST JAPAN (1937–45)

The Sino-Japanese War. On July 7, 1937, a minor clash between Japanese and Chinese troops near Peking finally led the two nations into war. The Japanese government tried for several weeks to settle the incident locally, but China's mood was highly nationalistic and public opinion clamoured for resistance to further aggression. In late July, new fighting broke out. The Japanese quickly took Peking (renamed Peiping by the Nationalists) and captured Tientsin. On August 13, savage fighting broke out in Shanghai. By now the prestige of both nations was committed, and they were locked in a war.

Phase one. As never before in modern times, the Chinese united themselves against a foreign enemy. China's standing armies in 1937 numbered some 1,700,000 men, with 500,000 in reserve. Japan's naval and air superiority were unquestioned. But Japan could not commit its full strength to campaigns in China; the main concern of the Japanese army was the Soviet Union, while for the navy it was the United States.

During the first year of the undeclared war, Japan won victory after victory against sometimes stubborn Chinese resistance. By late December, Shanghai and Nanking had fallen. But China had demonstrated to the world its determination to resist the invader; this gave the government time to search for foreign support. China found its major initial help from the Soviet Union. On August 21, 1937, the U.S.S.R. and China signed a nonaggression pact, and the Soviet Union quickly began sending munitions, military advisers, and hundreds of aircraft with Soviet pilots. Japanese forces continued to win important victories. By mid-1938 Japanese armies controlled the railway lines and major cities of northern China. They took Canton on October 12, stopping the railway supply line to Wu-han, the temporary Chinese capital, and captured Hankow, Hanyang, and Wuchang on October 25–26. The Chinese government and military command moved to Chungking in Szechwan, farther up the Yangtze and behind a protective mountain screen.

At the end of this first phase of the war, the National government had lost the best of its modern armies, its air force and arsenals, most of China's modern industries and railways, its major tax resources, and all the ports through which military equipment and civilian supplies might be imported. But it still held a vast though backward territory and had unlimited manpower reserves. So long as China continued to resist, Japan's control over the conquered eastern part of the country would be difficult.

Phase two: stalemate and stagnation. During the second stage of the war (1939–43) the battle lines changed very little, although there were many engagements of limited scale. Japan tried to bomb Free China into submission; Chungking suffered repeated air raids in which thousands of civilians were killed. In 1940 Japan set up a rival government in Nanking under Wang Ching-wei. But the Chinese would not submit. Hundreds of thousands migrated to west China to continue the struggle. Students and faculties of most eastern colleges took the overland trek to makeshift quarters in distant inland towns. Factories and skilled workers were re-established in the west. The government rebuilt its shattered armies and tried to purchase supplies from abroad.

In 1938–40 the Soviet Union extended credits for military aid of $250,000,000, while the United States, Great Britain, and France granted some $263,500,000 for civilian purchases and currency stabilization. Free China's lines of supply were long and precarious; when war broke out in Europe shipping space became scarce. After Germany's conquest of France in the spring of 1940, Britain bowed to Japanese demands and temporarily closed Rangoon, Burma, to military supplies for China (July–September). In September 1940 Japan seized control of northern Indochina and closed the supply line to Kunming. The Soviet Union had provided China its most substantial military aid, but when Germany attacked Russia in June 1941, this aid virtually ceased. By then, however, the United States had sold China 100 fighter planes—the beginning of an American effort to provide air protection.

In addition to bombing, the civilian population in Free China endured great hardships. Manufactured goods were scarce, and hoarding drove up prices. The government did not have the means to carry out rationing and price control, though it did supply government employees with rice. The government's sources of revenue were limited, yet it supported a large bureaucracy and an army of more than 3,000,000 conscripts. The government resorted to printing currency inadequately backed by reserves. Inflation grew until it was nearly uncontrollable. Between 1939 and 1943, the morale of the bureaucracy and military officers declined. Old abuses of the Chinese political system reasserted themselves—factional politics and corruption, in particular. The protracted war progressively weakened the Nationalist regime.

The war had the opposite effect upon the CCP. The Communist leaders had survived ten years of civil war and had developed a unity, camaraderie, and powerful sense of mission. They had learned to mobilize the rural population and to wage guerrilla warfare. In 1937 the CCP had about 40,000 members and the poorly equipped Red Army numbered perhaps 100,000. By agreement with the National Government, the Red Army was renamed the Eighth Route Army (later the 18th Group Army); Chu Teh and P'eng Te-huai served as commander and vice commander, and Lin Piao, Ho Lung, and Liu Po-ch'eng were in charge of its three divisions. The Communist base in the northwest covered parts of three provinces with a backward economy and a population of about 1,500,000. Operating within the general framework of the united front against Japan, the leaders of the Eighth Route Army adopted a strategy that used their experience in guerrilla warfare. They sent small columns into areas of northern China that the Japanese army had overrun but lacked the manpower to control; there they incorporated remnant troops and organized the population to supply food, recruits, and sanctuaries for guerrilla units attacking small Japanese garrisons.

Early in the period of united resistance, the government permitted the creation of the New Fourth Army from remnants of Communist troops left in Kiangsi and Fukien at the time of the Long March. Commanded by Gen. Yeh T'ing, with Hsiang Ying, a Communist, as chief of staff, this force of 12,000 officers and men operated behind Japanese lines near Shanghai with great success. Its strategy included guerrilla tactics, organizing resistance bases, and recruitment. This army grew to more than 100,000 by 1940; by then it operated in a wide area on both sides of the lower Yangtze.

Thus the CCP revitalized itself. It recruited rural activists and attracted patriotic youths from the cities and systematically strengthened the ranks by continuous indoctrination and by expelling dissident and ineffective party members.

Renewed Communist–Nationalist conflict. There were numerous clashes between Communists and Nationalists as their military forces competed for control of enemy territory and as the Communists tried to expand their political influence in Nationalist territory through propaganda and secret organizing. Though both sides continued the war against Japan, each was fighting for its own ultimate advantage. Bitter anti-Communist sentiment in government circles found its most violent expression in the New Fourth Army Incident of January 1941.

The government had ordered the New Fourth Army to move north of the Huang Ho and understood that its commanders had agreed to do so as part of demarcation of operational areas. But most of the army had moved into northern Kiangsu (south of the Huang Ho) and, together with units of the 18th Group Army, was competing with government troops for control of bases there and in southern Shantung. Yeh T'ing and Hsiang Ying stayed at the army's base south of the Yangtze. Apparently believing that Yeh did not intend to move northward, government forces attacked the base on January 6, 1941. The outnumbered Communists were defeated, Yeh T'ing and some 2,000 others were captured, Hsiang Ying was killed, and both sides suffered heavy casualties. Ignoring Chiang's order to dissolve the New Fourth Army, the Communist high command named Ch'en I as its new commander and Liu Shao-ch'i as political commissar.

Marginal notes:

Early Japanese victories

Communist guerrilla warfare

The danger of renewed civil war caused widespread protest from China's civilian leaders. The People's Political Council, a multiparty advisory body formed in 1938 as an expression of united resistance, debated the issue and later tried to mediate. Neither the Kuomintang nor the CCP was willing to push the conflict to open civil war in 1941. The government deployed many of its best divisions in positions to prevent the Communist forces from further penetration of Nationalist-held territories.

The international alliance against Japan. The United States had broken the Japanese diplomatic code, and by July 1941 it knew that Japan hoped to end the undeclared war in China and was preparing for a southward advance toward British Malaya and the Netherlands Indies, planning first to occupy southern Indochina and Thailand even at the risk of war with Britain and the United States.

American aid to China. One American response was presidential approval on July 23 of a recommendation that the United States send large amounts of arms and equipment to China, along with a military mission to advise on their use. The underlying strategy was to revitalize China's war effort as a deterrent to Japanese military and naval operations southward.

The Nationalist army was ill equipped to fight the Japanese in 1941. Its arsenals were so lacking in nonferrous metals and explosives that they could not produce effectively. The maintenance of millions of ill-trained and under-equipped troops was a heavy drain on the economy. There was no possibility that the United States could arm such numbers from its limited stocks while building up its own forces and assisting many other nations. Furthermore, there was a formidable logistics problem in shipping supplies along the 715-mile (1,150-kilometre) Burma Road, which extended from Chungking to Lashio, the Burma terminus of the railway and highway leading to Rangoon.

The U.S. military mission

By December 1941 the United States had sent a military mission to China and had implicitly agreed to create a modern Chinese air force, to maintain an efficient line of communications into China, and to arm 30 divisions. Japan's bombing of Pearl Harbor brought the United States into alliance with China, and Great Britain joined the Pacific War as its colonial possessions were attacked. This widening of the Sino-Japanese conflict lifted Chinese morale, but its other early effects were harmful. With the Japanese conquest of Hong Kong on December 25, China lost its air link with the outside world and one of its principal routes for smuggling supplies. By the end of May 1942, the Japanese held most of Burma, having defeated the British, Indian, Burmese, and Chinese defenders. Now China was almost completely blockaded. The United States granted China a loan of $500,000,000, and Great Britain stated its willingness to lend £50,-000,000. But there was little else China's allies could do wihout an effective supply route.

The solution was found in an air route from Assam, India, to Kunming in southwest China—the dangerous "Hump" route along the southern edge of the Himalayas. In March 1942, the China National Aviation Corporation (CNAC) began freight service over the Hump, and the United States began a transport program the next month. But shortages and other difficulties had to be overcome, and not until December 1943 were cargo planes able to equal the tonnage carried along the Burma Road by trucks two years before. This was much less than China's needs for gasoline, arms, munitions, and other military equipment.

Conflicts within the international alliance. China's alliance with the United States and Great Britain was marked by deep conflict. Great Britain gave highest priority to the defeat of its main enemy, Germany. The United States Navy in the Pacific had been seriously weakened by the Japanese air attack at Pearl Harbor and required many months to rebuild. During the winter of 1941–42 the grand strategy of the United States and Great Britain called for the defeat of Germany first, then an assault across the Pacific against Japan's island empire. China was relegated to a low position in American strategic planning. America aimed to keep China in the war and enable it to play a positive role in the final defeat of Japan on the continent. Chiang Kai-shek, on the other hand, envisaged a joint strategy by the United States, the British Commonwealth, and China over the whole Pacific area, with China playing a major role. He demanded an equal voice in Allied war planning, which he never received. From the fundamentally different outlooks of President Chiang, the British prime minister Winston Churchill, and the American president Franklin D. Roosevelt and because of the divergent national interests of China, the British Commonwealth, and the United States, there followed many controversies that had powerful repercussions in China and led to frustrations and suspicions among the partners.

After the fall of Burma, a controversy developed over whether the principal Chinese and American effort against Japan should be devoted to building up American air power based in China or to reform of the Chinese army and its training and equipment for a combat role. Chiang advocated primary reliance on American air power to defeat Japan. Several high-ranking American generals, on the other hand, emphasized creation of a compact and modernized Chinese ground force able to protect the airfields in China and to assist in opening an overland supply route across northern Burma. Already in India, the United States was training two Chinese divisions from remnants of the Burma campaign, plus artillery and engineering regiments (this became known as X-Force). Also in training were Chinese instructors to help retrain other divisions in China. Both air development and army modernizing were being pushed in early 1943, with a training centre created near Kunming to re-energize and re-equip select Chinese divisions (called Y-Force), and a network of airfields was being built in southern China. This dual approach caused repeated conflict over the allocation of scarce airlift space.

Chinese-U.S. disagreements

By the end of 1943 the China-based American 14th Air Force had achieved tactical parity with the Japanese over central China, was beginning to bomb Yangtze shipping, and had conducted a successful raid on Japanese airfields on Taiwan. A second training centre had been started at Kweilin to improve 30 more Chinese divisions (Z-Force). The campaign to open a land route across northern Burma, begun from the Assam end, had run into serious difficulty. At the Cairo Conference in November, Chiang met Churchill and Roosevelt for the first time. The Cairo Declaration promised the return of Manchuria, Taiwan, and the Pescadores Islands to China and the liberation of Korea. The three allies pledged themselves to "persevere in the . . . prolonged operations necessary to procure the unconditional surrender of Japan." These words, however, concealed deep differences over global strategy. American planners now realized that Japan might be approached successfully through the south and central Pacific and that Russia would enter the war against Japan after Germany's defeat; hence, the importance of China to American grand strategy declined. Churchill was unwilling to use naval resources, needed for the forthcoming European invasion, in a seaborne invasion of Burma to help reopen China's supply line. Yet Chiang had demanded a naval invasion of Burma as a condition to committing the Y-Force to assist in opening his supply line. Shortly after Cairo, Churchill and Roosevelt agreed to set aside the seaborne invasion of Burma, and when Chiang learned of this he requested enormous amounts of money, supplies, and air support, asserting that otherwise Japan might succeed in eliminating China from the war. The United States did not accede, and Chinese–American relations began to cool.

Phase three: approaching crisis (1944–45). China was in crisis in 1944. Japan faced increasing pressure in the Pacific and threats to its supply bases and communications lines in China as well as to nearby shipping. Its response was two-fold—first, to attack from Burma toward Assam to cut the supply lines or capture the airfields at the western end of the Hump, and, second, to capture the railway system in China from north to south and seize the eastern China airfields used by the U.S.

The British and Indian army defeated the Japanese attack on Assam (March–July 1944) with help from transport planes withdrawn from the Hump. But the Japanese campaign in China, known as Ichigo, showed up the weakness, inefficiency, and poor command of the Chinese armies after nearly seven years of war. During April and May the Japanese cleared the Peking–Hankow railway between the Huang Ho and the Yangtze. Chinese armies nominally numbering several hundred thousand men were unable to put up effective resistance. Peasants in Honan attacked the collapsing Chinese armies, their recent oppressors.

The second phase of the Ichigo campaign was a Japanese drive southward from Hankow and northwestward from Canton to take Kweilin and open the communication line to the Indo-China border. By November the Chinese had lost Kweilin, Liuchow, and Nanning, and the Japanese were approaching Kweiyang on the route to Chungking and Kunming. This was the high water mark of Japan's war in China. Thereafter, it withdrew experienced divisions for the defense of its over-extended empire, and China finally began to benefit from the well-trained X-Force when two divisions were flown in from Burma in December to defend Kunming.

Meanwhile, the Chinese government was involved in a crisis of relations with the United States, which contended that the Chinese army must be reformed, particularly in its command structure, and that lend-lease supplies must be used more effectively. There were also many subsidiary problems. The American general Joseph Stilwell, the executor of disagreeable American policies in China, had developed an unconcealed disdain for Chiang, whom he nominally served as chief of staff. Stilwell was an effective troop commander, and Roosevelt requested that Chiang place Stilwell in command of all Chinese forces. In terms of Chinese politics, in which control of armies was the main source of power, President Chiang's compliance was virtually inconceivable. He declined the request and asked for Stilwell's recall. Roosevelt agreed, but thereafter his relations with Chiang were no longer cordial. Stilwell was replaced by Gen. Albert C. Wedemeyer, a more tactful man and an excellent staff officer.

Nationalist deterioration. The military weakness in 1944 was symptomatic of a gradual deterioration that had taken place in most aspects of Nationalist Chinese public life. Inflation began to mount alarmingly as the government pumped in large amounts of paper currency to make up its fiscal deficits. Salaries of government employees, army officers, teachers, and all those on wages fell far behind rising prices. For most, this spelled poverty amid growing war weariness. Dissatisfaction with the government's policies spread among intellectuals. Inflation gave opportunities for some groups to profit through hoarding of needed goods, smuggling of high value commodities, black market currency operations, and graft. Corruption spread in the bureaucracy and the armed forces.

As the war dragged on, governmental suppression of dissidence grew oppressive. Secret police activity and efforts at thought control were aimed not only against Communists but also against all influential critics of the government or the Kuomintang.

Communist growth. The Communist armies were growing rapidly in 1943 and 1944. According to American war correspondents visiting the Yenan area in May 1944 and to a group of American observers that established itself there in July, the Communists professed allegiance to democracy and to continued cooperation with the National Government in the war effort. There was convincing evidence that the areas under Communist control extended for hundreds of miles behind Japanese lines in north and central China.

This situation was the result of many factors. Communist troop commanders and political officers in areas behind Japanese lines tried to mobilize the entire population against the enemy. Party members led village communities into greater participation in local government than had been the case before. They also organized and

controlled peasants' associations, labour unions, youth leagues, and women's associations. They linked together the many local governments and the mass organizations and determined their policies. Because of the need for unity against Japan, the Communist organizers tended to follow reformist economic policies. The party experimented with various forms of economic cooperation to increase production; one of these was mutual-aid teams in which farmers temporarily pooled their tools and draft animals and worked the land collectively. In areas behind Japanese lines some mutual-aid teams evolved into work and battle teams composed of younger peasants; when danger threatened, the teams went out to fight as guerrillas under direction of the local Red army, and, when the crisis passed, they returned to the fields. The party recruited into its ranks the younger leaders who emerged from populist activities. Thus, it penetrated and to some extent controlled the multitude of villages in areas behind Japanese lines. As the Japanese military grip weakened, the experienced Communist armies and political organizers spread their system of government ever more widely. By the time of the CCP's Seventh Congress in Yenan (April–May 1945), the party claimed to have an army of more than 900,000 and a militia of more than 2,000,000. It also claimed to control areas with a total population of 90,000,000. These claims were disputable, but the great strength and wide geographical spread of the Communist system of organization was a fact.

Communist economic policy

Efforts to prevent civil war. Between May and September of 1944, representatives of the government and the CCP carried on peace negotiations at Sian. The main issues were the disposition, size, and command of the Communist armies; the relationship between Communist-organized regional governments and the National Government; and problems of civil rights and legalization of the CCP and its activities in Nationalist areas. Suggestions for a coalition government arose for the first time. No settlement was reached, but it appeared that the antagonists were seeking a peaceful solution. The U.S. vice president Henry Wallace visited Chungking in June and had several discussions with Chiang, who requested American assistance in improving relations between China and the U.S.S.R. and in settling the Communist problem.

In September 1944 Patrick J. Hurley arrived as Roosevelt's personal representative. Hurley attempted to mediate, first in discussions in Chungking and then by flying to Yenan on November 7 for a conference with Mao Tse-tung. But the positions of the two sides could not be reconciled, and the talks broke off in March 1945. Between June and August, Hurley resumed protracted discussions, both indirect and in conferences with high-level representatives from both sides. Each side distrusted the other; each sought to guarantee its own survival, but the Kuomintang intended to continue its political dominance, while the CCP insisted upon the independence of its armies and regional governments under whatever coalition formula might be worked out.

The Pacific war ended on August 14, 1945, and the formal Japanese surrender came on September 2. China rejoiced, and President Chiang's prestige stood very high. Yet the country faced enormously difficult problems of reunification and reconstruction and a future clouded by the dark prospect of civil war. (For other aspects of the Sino-Japanese War, see JAPAN, HISTORY OF; WORLD WARS.)

CIVIL WAR (1945–49)

In a little more than four years after Japan's surrender, the CCP and the Peoples Liberation Army conquered mainland China, and, on October 1, 1949, the People's Republic of China was established, with its capital at Peking. The factors that brought this about were many and complex and subject to widely varying interpretation, but the basic fact was a Communist military triumph growing out of a profound and popularly based revolution. The process may be perceived in three phases: (1) from August 1945 to the end of 1946, the Nationalists and

Chinese military weaknesses

Communists raced to take over Japanese-held territories, built up their forces, and fought many limited engagements while still conducting negotiations for a peaceful settlement; (2) during 1947 and the first half of 1948, after initial Nationalist success, the strategic balance turned in favour of the Communists; (3) the Communists won smashing victories in the latter part of 1948 and 1949.

A race for territory. As soon as Japan's impending surrender was known, the commander of the Communist armies, Gen. Chu Teh, ordered his men, on August 11, to move into Japanese-held territory and take over Japanese arms, despite Chiang's order that they stand where they were. The United States aided the Chinese government by flying many divisions from the southwest to occupy the main eastern cities, such as Peking, Tientsin, Shanghai, and the prewar capital, Nanking. The American navy moved Chinese troops from South China to other coastal cities, and landed 53,000 marines at Tientsin and Tsingtao to assist in disarming and repatriating Japanese troops but also to serve as a counterweight to the Russian army in southern Manchuria. Furthermore, the American general Douglas MacArthur ordered all Japanese forces in China proper to surrender their arms only to forces of the National Government. They obeyed.

U.S. aid to the Nationalists

Immediately after the surrender, the Communists sent political cadres and thousands of troops into Manchuria. This had been planned long in advance. Gen. Lin Piao became commander of the newly organized force (the Northeast Democratic Allied Army), which incorporated "puppet" troops of Manchoukuo and began to recruit volunteers; it got most of its arms from Japanese stocks taken over by the Russians.

Manchuria (the Northeast Provinces) was a vast area, with 40,000,000 population, the greatest concentration of heavy industry and railways in China, and enormous reserves of coal, iron, and many other minerals. The Soviet Union had promised the National Government to withdraw its occupying armies within 90 days of Japan's surrender and to return the region to China. The government was determined to control Manchuria, which was vital to China's future as a world power. But Lin Piao's army attempted to block the entry of Nationalist troops by destroying rail lines and seizing areas around ports of entry.

The struggle for Manchuria

Soon the two sides were locked in a fierce struggle for the corridors into Manchuria, although negotiations were underway in Chungking between Mao and Chiang for a peaceful settlement. The Soviet army avoided direct involvement in the struggle, but it dismantled much industrial machinery and shipped it to the Soviet Union together with hundreds of thousands of Japanese prisoners of war. By the end of 1945 the Nationalists had positioned some of their best American-trained armies in southern Manchuria as far north as Mukden, a strategic rail centre to which Nationalist troops were transported by air. The government's hold was precarious, however, because the Communist 18th Group Army and the New Fourth Army had regrouped in North China, abandoning areas south of the Yangtze after a weak bid to take Shanghai. By the end of 1945 Communist forces were spread across a band of provinces from the northwest to the sea. They had a grip on great sections of all the railway lines north of the Lunghai, vital supply lines for Nationalist armies in the Tientsin-Peking area and in Manchuria. The National government held vast territories in the south and west and had re-established its authority in the rich provinces of the lower Yangtze Valley and a few important North China cities; it had also assumed civil control on Taiwan.

Attempts to end the war. Peace negotiations continued in Chungking between Nationalist and Communist officials after Japan's surrender. An agreement reached on October 10 called for the convening of a multiparty Political Consultative Council to plan a liberalized postwar government and to draft a constitution for submission to a national congress. Still, the sides were far apart over the character of the new government, control over the Communist liberated areas, and the size and degree of autonomy of the Communist armies in a national mili-

tary system. Hurley resigned his ambassadorship on November 26, and the next day Pres. Harry S. Truman appointed Gen. George C. Marshall (q.v.) as his special representative, with the specific mission of trying to bring about political unification and the cessation of hostilities in China.

Marshall arrived in China on December 23. The National government proposed the formation of a committee of three, with Marshall as chairman, to end the fighting. This committee, with generals Chang Chun and Chou En-lai as the Nationalist and Communist representatives, met on January 7, 1946. It agreed on January 10 that Chiang and Mao would issue orders to cease hostilities and halt troop movements as of January 13 midnight, with the exception of government troop movements south of the Yangtze and into and within Manchuria to restore Chinese sovereignty. The agreement also called for the establishment in Peking of an executive headquarters, equally represented in by both sides, to supervise the cease-fire.

Cease-fire agreement

This agreement provided a favourable atmosphere for meetings in Chungking of the Political Consultative Council, composed of representatives of the Kuomintang, the CCP, the Democratic League, the Young China Party, and nonparty delegates. From January 10 to 31, 1946, the Council issued a series of agreed recommendations regarding governmental reorganization, peaceful national reconstruction, military reductions, a national assembly, and the drafting of a constitution. President Chiang pledged that the government would carry out these recommendations, and the political parties stated their intention to abide by them. The next step was meetings of a military subcommittee, with Marshall as adviser, to discuss troop reductions and amalgamation of forces into a single national army; these resulted in an agreement to reduce the government and Communist forces to 90 and 18 divisions respectively within one year, with an eventual further reduction to 60 divisions, of which ten would come from the Communist army. This army was to be divorced from politics.

Early 1946 was the high point of conciliation. It soon became clear, however, that implementation of the various recommendations and agreements was being opposed by conservatives in the Kuomintang, who feared the dilution of their party's control of the government, and by Nationalist generals, who objected to the reduction of their armies. The Communists attempted to prevent the extension of Nationalist military control in Manchuria. On March 17–18, a Communist army attacked and captured a strategic junction between Mukden and Changchun, the former Manchoukuo capital; on April 18, Communists captured Changchun from a small Nationalist garrison directly after the Soviet withdrawal. On that day Marshall returned to China after a trip to Washington, and resumed his efforts to stop the spreading civil war.

Resumption of fighting. Each side seemed convinced that it could win by war what it could not achieve by negotiation—dominance over the other. Despite the efforts of Chinese moderates and General Marshall, fighting resumed in July in Manchuria, and in North China the Nationalists attempted massive drives in Kiangsu and Shantung to break the Communist grip on the railways. The Communists launched a propaganda campaign against the United States, playing upon the nationalistic theme of liberation; they were hostile because of the extensive U.S. military and financial assistance to the National Government at the very time that Marshall was mediating. The Chinese government had become increasingly intransigent, confident of continued American help.

To exert pressure and to try to keep the United States out of the civil war, Marshall in August imposed an embargo on further shipment of American arms to China. By the end of the year, however, he realized that his efforts had failed. In January 1947 he left China, issuing a statement denouncing the intransigents on both sides. All negotiations ended in March; the die was cast for war.

In the latter half of 1946, government forces made impressive gains in North China and Manchuria, capturing

165 towns from the enemy. Buoyed by these victories, the government convened a multiparty National Assembly on November 15, despite a boycott by the CCP and the Democratic League. The delegates adopted a new constitution, which was promulgated on New Year's Day. The constitution reaffirmed Sun Yat-sen's Three Principles of the People as the basic philosophy of the state; and called for the five-fold division of powers among the executive, legislative, judicial, control, and examination *yüan* ("governmental body"); and the four people's rights of initiation, referendum, election, and recall. The way was prepared for election of both central and local officials, upon which the period of Kuomintang tutelage would end.

Economic problems of the National government

The National Government struggled with grave economic problems. Inflation continued unabated, caused principally by government financing of military and other operations through the printing press: approximately 65 percent of the budget was met by currency expansion and only 10 percent by taxes. Government spending was uncontrolled; funds were dissipated in maintaining large and unproductive garrison forces. Much tax revenue failed to reach the treasury because of malpractices throughout the bureaucracy. Inflation inhibited exports and enhanced the demands for imports. The government had to import large amounts of grain and cotton, but in the months immediately after Japan's surrender it also permitted the import of luxury goods without effective restrictions. As an anti-inflationary measure, it sold gold on the open market. These policies permitted a large gold and U.S. currency reserve, estimated at $900,000,000 at the end of the war, to be cut in half by the end of 1946. Foreign trade was hampered by excessive regulation and corrupt practices.

The spiraling effects of inflation were somewhat curbed by large amounts of supplies imported by the United Nations Relief and Rehabilitation Administration, chiefly food and clothing, a wide variety of capital goods, and materials for the rehabilitation of agriculture, industries, and transportation. In August 1946 the United States sold to China civilian-type army and navy surplus property at under 20 percent of estimated procurement cost of $900,000,000. In spite of these and other forms of aid, the costs of civil war kept the budget continuously out of balance. Speculation, hoarding of goods, and black market operations as hedges against inflation continued unabated. The constant depreciation in the value of paper currency undermined morale in all classes dependent upon salaries, including troops, officers, and civilian officials.

By contrast, it appears that in their areas, mostly rural, the Communists practiced a Spartan style of life close to the common people. Morale remained high in the army and was continuously bolstered by indoctrination and effective propaganda. As they had during the war years, Communist troops tried in many ways to win support of the masses. In newly occupied areas social policy was at first reformist rather than intraclass revolutionary.

In Manchuria, Lin Piao was forging a formidable army of veteran cadres from North China and natives of Manchuria, now well equipped with Japanese weapons. By 1947 the Communists' Northeast Democratic Allied Army controlled all Manchuria north of the Sungari, the east, and much of the countryside in the Nationalist stronghold in the South. There the Nationalists had most of their best trained and equipped divisions; but the troops had been conscripted or recruited in China's southwest, and they garrisoned cities and railways in a distant land. Beginning in January 1947, Lin Piao launched a series of small offensives. By July the Nationalists had lost half their territory in Manchuria and much materiel; desertions and casualties, caused by indecisive Nationalist leadership and declining troop morale, reduced their forces by half. Lin Piao was not yet strong enough to take Manchuria, but he had the Nationalist armies hemmed up in a few major cities and with only a tenuous hold on the railways leading southward.

The tide begins to shift. The strategic initiative passed to the People's Liberation Army sometime in 1947. In midsummer Liu Po-ch'eng started moving toward the Yangtze; by late in the year the Communists had concentrated strong forces in central China. Ch'en I operated on both sides of the Lunghai, east of Kaifeng; Liu Po-ch'eng was firmly established in the Ta-pieh Shan on the borders of Anhui, Honan, and Hupeh, northeast of Hankow; and Ch'en Keng had another army in Honan west of the Peking–Hankow railway. These groups cut Nationalist lines of communication, destroyed protecting outposts along the Lunghai and Pinghan lines, and they isolated cities.

By the end of 1947 the government forces, according to American military estimates, still numbered some 2,700,-000 facing 1,150,000 Communists. But the Nationalists were widely spread and on the defensive. In November, Mao Tse-tung (*q.v.*) established the Communist capital at Shihchiachuang, a railway centre leading from the Peking–Hankow railway into Shansi; this was a measure of the consolidation of the Communist position in North China. In a report to the CCP Central Committee on December 25, 1947, Mao exuded confidence:

> The Chinese people's revolutionary war has now reached a turning point. . . . The main forces of the People's Liberation Army have carried the fight into the Kuomintang Area. . . . This is a turning point in history.

A land revolution. One reason for Communist success was the social revolution in rural China. The CCP was now unrestrained by the multi-class alliance of the united front period. In the middle of 1946, as civil war became more certain, the party leaders had launched a land revolution. They saw land redistribution as an integral part of the larger struggle; by encouraging peasants to seize the landlords' fields and other property, the party apparently expected to weaken the government's rural class base and strengthen its own support among the poor. This demanded a decisive attack upon the traditional village social structure. The party leaders believed that to crack the age-old peasant fear of the local elite and overcome traditional respect for property rights required unleashing the hatred of the oppressed. Teams of activists moved through the villages, organizing the poor in "speak bitterness" meetings to struggle against landlords and Kuomintang supporters, to punish and often to kill them, and to distribute their land and property. The party tried to control the process in order not to alienate the broad middle ranks among the peasants; but land revolution had a dynamism of its own, and rural China went through a period of terror. Yet apparently the party gained from the revolutionary dynamism; morale was at fever pitch and for those who had benefitted from land distribution there was no turning back.

The decisive year, 1948. The year 1948 was the turning point. In central China, Communist armies of 500,-000 men proved their ability to fight major battles on the plains and to capture, though not always hold, such important towns on the Lunghai as Loyang and Kaifeng. In North China they encircled Taiyuan, the capital of Shansi, took most of Chahar and Jehol, provinces on Manchuria's western flank, and recaptured Yenan, which had been lost in March 1947. The decisive battles were fought in Shantung and Manchuria, where the forces of Ch'en I and Lui Po-ch'eng and those under Lin Piao crushed the government's best armies. For the government it was a year of military and economic disasters.

The turning point in the war

In Shantung, despite the departure of Ch'en I's forces, Communist guerrillas gradually reduced the government's hold on the railway from Tsingtao to Tsinan; they penned up about 60,000 government troops in the latter city, an important railway junction. Instead of withdrawing this garrison southward to Hsuchow, the government left it, for political reasons, to stand and fight. Then Ch'en I's forces returned to Shantung and overwhelmed the dispirited Tsinan garrison on September 24. This opened the way for a Communist attack upon Hsuchow, the historic northern shield for Nanking and a vital railway centre.

Beginning in December 1947, a Communist offensive severed all railway connections into Mukden and isolated the Nationalist garrisons in Manchuria. The govern-

Lin Piao's final offensive

ment armies went on the defensive in besieged cities, partly out of fear that demoralized divisions would defect in the field. Instead of withdrawing from Manchuria before it was too late, the government tried unsuccessfully to reinforce its armies and to supply the garrisons by air. With the fall of Tsinan, Lin Piao launched his final offensive. He now had an army of 600,000, nearly twice the Nationalist force in Manchuria. He first attacked Chinchow, the government's supply base on the railway between Tientsin and Mukden; it fell on October 17. Changchun fell three days later. The great garrison at Mukden then tried to retake Chinchow and Changchun and to open the railway line to the port of Yingkow. In a series of battles, Lin Piao's columns defeated this cream of the Nationalist forces. By early November the Nationalists had lost some 400,000 men as casualties, captives, or defectors.

The government's military operations in the first part of 1948 produced ever larger budget deficits through the loss of tax receipts, dislocation of transportation and productive facilities, and increased military expenditures. Inflation was out of control. In August the government introduced a new currency, the gold yuan, to replace the old notes at the rate of 3,000,000 for one, promising drastic reforms to curtail expenditures and increase revenue. Domestic prices and foreign exchange rates were pegged, with severe penalties threatened for black market operations. The people were required to sell their gold, silver, and foreign currency to the government at the pegged rate; large numbers did so in a desperate effort to halt the inflation. In Shanghai and some other places, the government used Draconic methods to enforce its decrees against speculators, but it apparently could not control its own expenditures nor stop the printing presses. Furthermore, the government's efforts to fix prices of food and commodities brought about an almost complete stagnation of economic activity, except for illicit buying and selling at prices far above the fixed levels. Some army officers and government officials were themselves engaged in smuggling, speculation, and other forms of corruption. Then came the loss of Tsinan and knowledge of the threat in Manchuria. During October the final effort to halt inflation collapsed, with shattering effect to morale in Nationalist-held cities. Prices started rocketing upward once more.

Communist victory. Between early November 1948 and early January 1949, the two sides battled for the control of Hsuchow. General Chu Teh concentrated 600,000 men under Ch'en I, Liu Po-ch'eng, and Ch'en Keng near that strategic centre, which was defended by Nationalist forces of similar size. Both armies were well equipped, but the Nationalists had a superiority in armour and were unopposed in the air. Yet poor morale, inept command, and a defensive psychology brought another disaster to the National Government. One after another its armies were surrounded and defeated in the field. When the 65-day battle was over on January 10, the Nationalists had lost some 500,000 men and their equipment. The capital at Nanking would soon lie exposed.

With Manchuria and most of the eastern region south to the Yangtze in Communist hands, the fate of Tientsin and Peking was sealed. The railway corridor between Tientsin and Kalgan was now hopelessly isolated. Tientsin fell on January 15 after a brief siege, and Fu Tso-i surrendered Peking on the 23rd, allowing a peaceful turnover of China's historic capital and centre of culture.

Thus, during the last half of 1948, the Communist armies had gained control over Manchuria and northeastern China nearly to the Yangtze, except for pockets of resistance. They now had a numerical superiority and had captured such huge stocks of rifles, artillery, and armour that they were better equipped than the Nationalists for land warfare.

Political shifts in 1949

Great political shifts occurred in 1949. Chiang Kai-shek retired temporarily in January, turning over to the vice president, Gen. Li Tsung-jen, the problem of holding together a government and trying to negotiate a peace with Mao Tse-tung. But Li's peace negotiations (February–April) proved hopeless. The Nationalists were not prepared to surrender; they still claimed to govern more than half of China and still had a large army. General Li tried to secure American support in the peace negotiations and in the military defense of South China, but the American government clung to its basic policy of noninvolvement in China's civil war and internal political problems.

When peace negotiations broke down, Communist armies crossed the Yangtze virtually unopposed; the Nationalist Government abandoned its undefensible capital on April 23 and moved to Canton. In succession, Communist forces occupied Nanking (April 24), Hankow (May 16–17), and Shanghai (May 25). The Nationalists' last hope lay in the south and west. But Sian, a long-time Nationalist bastion and the gateway to the northwest, had fallen to Gen. P'eng Te-huai on May 20.

During the last half of 1949 powerful Communist armies succeeded in taking the provinces of south and west China. By the end of the year only the islands of Hainan, Taiwan, and a few offshore positions were still in Nationalist hands, and only scattered pockets of resistance remained on the mainland. The defeated National government re-established itself on Taiwan, to which Chiang had withdrawn early in the year, taking most of the Government's gold reserves and the Nationalist air force and navy. On October 1, with most of the mainland held by the People's Liberation Army, Mao proclaimed the establishment in Peking of the government of the People's Republic of China.

(C.M.Wi.)

XII. Development of Kuomintang and Chinese Communist ideologies

ORIGINS AND BACKGROUND OF MODERN IDEOLOGIES

Social and political conditions. The ideologies of both the Nationalist Party (Kuomintang) of China and the Communist Party of China came eventually to be expressed in universal terms, as ideologies tend to be; but they can be understood only in relation to the social conditions and political circumstances that produced them. They were attempts to solve the specific problems of China as its radical politicians saw them; and many ideas that are expressed in these positive universal terms represent, historically, negative reactions to what was seen to be undesirable in China's circumstances, its traditions, and its modern social and political development. Although modern Chinese ideologies have expressed an attempt to find solutions to China's problems, it would be too much to say that the starting point of Chinese thought was an objective view of these problems. The problems, as seen, had already been through a process of refraction. The problem of land tenure, for example, though serious in China, was probably both economically and politically far less important than other problems; for, in comparison with most other premodern agricultural countries of the world, China was still largely a land of owner-operator peasants, not of landlords and tenants. Yet land tenure was accepted as the key social problem. The problems involving foreign economic operations in China were also seen in a slanted way; Sun Yat-sen's naïve appraisal of China's total payments made to foreigners, without consideration of the services provided in return, or the new opportunities that foreign enterprise provided, is characteristic. In the same way, the marginal losses of sovereignty that China suffered through extraterritoriality, foreign administration of its customs, and the destruction of the tribute relationship between China and the countries on its borders, although infinitely less odious and harmful than the colonial fate of most of Asia and Africa, produced in China a myth of Western imperialism held with passionate intensity and invulnerable to facts, expressing more the high pride of the Chinese in their traditionally dominant position among their neighbour nations than the severity of actual foreign control. This myth of economic imperialism became the shibboleth of modern Chinese patriotism and the major premise of all Chinese political thought.

The chronic problem of China was the insecurity of the nation's frontiers and of its sovereignty, dramatized in a long series of disastrous defeats at foreign hands from

Myths and realities

1840 onward. Successive defeats, with their renewed revelation of weakness, marked the stages of radicalization of Chinese political thought. The Opium Wars in the 1830's and 1850's produced the Self-Strengthening movement; the shocking defeat of the new, modern armed forces at the hands of the Japanese in 1894 gave rise to the Reform Movement of 1898; the proven helplessness of China in the face of Japan in 1919 set the stage for the May Fourth Movement; and the Japanese occupation of large areas of China after 1937 was perhaps the greatest single factor in the creation of popular nationalism in China, under the leadership of Communist guerrilla soldiers. To this helplessness in the face of foreign aggression was added the inability, from World War I to 1949, to secure effective reunification of China. To many Chinese, the relations between foreign powers and provincial warlords made these two problems one, with foreign intrigue as the major factor in preventing unification, and internal division being the principal cause of weakness in the face of foreign power.

The twin problems of warlords and foreign powers

The radicalization of thought. Diagnosis of China's condition, however, changed over time. The solution of one problem revealed another lying beneath it. The Self-Strengtheners hoped to preserve China by adopting the military techniques of the enemy, but with as little industrial development as possible. Their successors associated with the Reform Movement of 1898 had come to appreciate that technological change could not be confined to the military sphere, and that technological change and economic strength were dependent upon legal, political, and social changes that would provide security and encouragement for modern entrepreneurs. The revolutionaries rejected Manchu constitutionalism as a sham and affirmed that the decisive act would be the removal of the alien Manchu rulers: if China were ruled by Chinese, everything would be possible. The replacement of the Manchu monarchy by a parliamentary republic, however, created nothing except corruption and confusion on an even greater scale; and many Chinese—for example, Liang Ch'i-ch'ao—expressed their belief that institutional change on Western models could not in itself improve China, because Chinese traditional social and political attitudes were inimical to the operation of parliamentary institutions. Out of the failure of the parliamentary regime and the subsequent division of China came support for Sun Yat-sen's idea of a three-stage development of revolution—from (1) military rule in the wake of the defeat of the warlords, through (2) a period of one-party political tutelage, to (3) the gradual extension upward, from the local governments to the centre, of democratic, representative institutions. Finally, Sun himself came to accept, in common with almost all politically conscious Chinese of his time, that political weakness, economic stagnation, and social privilege formed a vicious circle that could be broken only by radical social revolution for which the Russian Revolution provided the main example.

The broadening of the political public. In another respect also, the revolution gradually deepened, as China's effective political public grew to embrace new groups and classes. The Self-Strengtheners were established high officials; the 1898 Reformers were distinguished graduates and therefore potential officials, operating under the protection of a part of the establishment. The revolutionaries of 1911 represented a wider Chinese public, but still a very limited one: the revolutionary leaders were students who had studied abroad; the rank and file were drawn largely from the secret societies; and the financial backers were largely members of the emigrant Chinese communities in Southeast Asia and North America. In terms of class this support was by no means narrow, yet it consisted of elements alienated in one way or another from Chinese society as a whole, by the choice of a Western education abroad, by association with secret societies (which themselves represented alienated elements in society), or by emigration.

The "alienated" in the Chinese revolution

The May Fourth Movement demonstrated a new range of possibilities in the widening of the Chinese political public. Although led by radical students, it gained sup-

port from the merchant classes of China and the new modern working class in the treaty ports. In this, it illustrated in a dramatic way what had begun to happen within the Nationalist Party at the same time, as membership of the party spread throughout China's cities (though unevenly, because of warlord repression) until its emigrant and returned-student elements and its secret-society auxiliaries were outweighed by representatives of urban China generally.

The final stage of political mobilization brought in the peasants. This stage developed through the peasant movements of the 1920s and 1930s. The Hunan-Hupeh peasant revolt of 1927, for instance, drew the attention of Mao Tse-tung and proved to be one of the key experiences in his development; thereafter there was a long and widening association of the Chinese Communist Party with the rural areas of China. The ruthless policies pursued by the Japanese occupation forces during the subsequent war also inspired guerrilla and peasant nationalism and loyalty to the Communists.

Economic developments. These changes in political ideas and political allegiance were accompanied by, and influenced by, contemporary social and economic changes. Again, the objective facts are not only difficult to ascertain but were subject to distortion from the political ideas about them. It was widely believed that the Chinese traditional economy was rapidly heading for collapse, that handicrafts were being destroyed by privileged competition from foreign, machine-made imports, and that growing landlordism was prejudicing agriculture to the point that a significant proportion of China's arable land was being deserted and agricultural production falling. Sun Yat-sen even believed that China's population had decreased during the decades of imperialism by about 90,000,000. None of this was generally true, although there was much hardship in particular localities; but all of it was widely accepted and formed part of the mythology of modern Chinese politics and one of the uncriticized assumptions of political ideology. It is true that in many areas landlords were becoming absentees, and the traditional patron-client relationship of owner and tenant was being weakened; that agricultural taxes generally were multiplying and becoming ever more oppressive; that there was probably, in those parts favoured by access to large urban markets, a certain commercialization and polarization of rural life; that a new element of precariousness (as well as new opportunities) had been introduced in some areas through new connections with world markets; that silk exports had collapsed largely through the inefficiency of the peasant producer; and that new enterprise was made all but impossible in the areas repeatedly devastated by warlord fighting. But, on the other hand, in the more favoured areas of the country, and especially in those cities where foreign power could preserve the peace, there was very rapid economic growth and modernization comparable in scale and pace with development in Japan. Whatever the balance, however, it is true that Chinese society was in a state of change sufficiently rapid to produce almost universal discontent, whether arising from distress or from the frustration of new aspirations. For the young radicals who preached the need for great changes in the local branches of the Nationalist Party, or in the new Tientsin trade unions, or in the Shanghai merchant guilds, or in the seminars of Peking University, or in the peasant associations of Kwangtung, a sympathetic audience was never lacking; and as continued disorder was fed by increasing protest and increasing repression, the audiences grew.

Elements of rapid economic growth

The new consensus. In these circumstances, there developed a consensus, based essentially on a new feeling of common nationality but including a large measure of agreement on the nature of China's problems and on the appropriate solutions. It was agreed that China's greatest problem was weakness in the face of the great industrial powers; that the first stage of change must be the reunification of the country; that, for this purpose, a strong one-party government supported by a politically committed army was the first necessity; that the succeeding period would be one of tutelage under this one-party government, in which dictatorial control over resistant elements would be exercised on behalf of "the people"; that both economic improvement and social justice demanded that this new political power would be used to secure, with or without compensation, the redistribution of the land to the cultivators, and the organization thereafter of some type of cooperative agriculture to increase the size of the average unit of cultivation; that industry would have to be built up largely through the initiative of the state; and that the "unequal treaties" would be abrogated, if necessary by unilateral Chinese action. Most of this came to be beyond dispute, or at least beyond public disavowal.

It had also come to be generally accepted that to carry out these tasks would demand more than a vigorous and modern-minded elite and more than formally representative government. All parties were agreed upon the need for mass mobilization and gradual political education in order to create a modern political consciousness. All parties recognized that this would involve an attack on traditional values and behaviour; and all were, to a greater or lesser extent, ambiguous in their attitudes toward these traditions. To save the nation by destroying everything that identified it as a nation was a solution hard to accept. The development of contrasting Nationalist and Communist ideologies after the breakdown of the first united front in 1927 expressed itself largely in contrasting evaluations of the national past.

In all ideological and political aspects of Chinese life, the pace of change was striking. Yesterday's radical, publishing in fear of his life and anathematized even in the moderate press, was the pillar of today's establishment. The "generation gap" was not so much between biological generations as between this year's graduates and those of the next year. The traditionalist intellectual entourage of Chiang Kai-shek in 1930 was composed of iconoclasts of 1920. It is perhaps natural that China has become the home of the concept of permanent revolution, and not surprising that the political theory of Chairman Mao emphasizes the ideas that today's revolutionary leaders will falter and fail and be overtaken and replaced, that political leadership is an endless process of recruitment, and that all political institutions are relative and temporary.

China's ideological inheritance. The Chinese tradition had ceased in most respects to be creative for some centuries, smothered under Ming absolutism and under the exploitation of the alien Manchu (Yüan) dynasty that sought to secure loyalty from the Chinese. Change still continued in Chinese life, though at a slower pace than in Europe, and the diversification of the tradition by dissenting scholars had, indeed, never been so wide as it was during the Manchu dynasty; but Manchu control was such that these heretical scholars made little or no impact on their contemporaries and often feared to publish their more radical works. Some of them, however, were rediscovered in the 20th century, and provided much of the Chinese rationalization for modern changes: the iconoclastic writings of K'ang Yu-wei, the leader of the Reform Movement of 1898, were based very largely on those of 18th-century predecessors.

It is important to remember that China and Japan, unlike those Asian nations that became colonies in the full sense, kept their own written language, modernized it and expressed modern ideas in it. There is, therefore, a continuity in Chinese and Japanese thought that is absent in the case of many other Asian nations. Even the most un-Chinese idea had to be expressed in a language already encrusted with two thousand years of associations, a language that makes distinctions where European languages do not and that does not make distinctions where European languages do. Thus, it is difficult in Chinese to distinguish between "politics" and "administration," between "will" and "purpose," or between "liberalism" and "license." The Sinification of Western social theories, including Marxism, began with the very act of translating them into the language developed to express Confucianism.

Confucianism itself, however, as the doctrine of a civilization of great age and immense richness, was many-sided and full of ambiguities. One could say that modern China's political inheritance was not so much a system of political ideas as a number of ambivalent pairs of ideas.

The central paradox of the Chinese tradition was that while Chinese government was totalitarian, in the sense that the government was empowered to intervene in almost any aspect of life, Chinese society, on the contrary, was based upon self-government by autonomous families and clans, grouped in villages and local communities that enjoyed a high degree of autonomy. The Legalist and Taoist polarity of Chinese philosophy, indeed, expresses this ambivalence, with orthodox Confucianism providing an uneasy compromise between these two extremes. Related to this is the paradox that, while the legitimation of Imperial authority in China was moral (in that the emperor's position was a sacerdotal one), philosophy in China nevertheless maintained the idea of a right of rebellion if the emperor's rule was bad or ineffective: the loss of the Mandate of Heaven would be shown pragmatically by the very fact of widespread and successful rebellion.

Related to these ambiguities is the further ambiguity that although the Chinese have always accepted a theory of government by an intellectual elite, authorized by education to wield the totalitarian power of the emperor, Chinese life at the same time has been characterized by far greater development of self-government through non-elite voluntary associations, guilds, and fraternities of all kinds, than was the case in almost any other premodern society.

These same paradoxes also expressed themselves in the fact that while the Chinese, vis-à-vis other peoples, have been intensely conscious of themselves as a nation (though united by culture rather than by race), this nationalism has not expressed itself in a sense of high obligation to their fellow citizens as Chinese, so that national responses have been prejudiced severely by the extremely localized nature of Chinese loyalties.

At a more personal level, there is a contrast between the extreme conformism of China, inculcated by the ritualization of social relationships and by sumptuary legislation, and the great stress in Chinese philosophy on sincerity and self-knowledge. This is perhaps the result of Buddhist influence.

There is another contrast which is produced by the gap between the ideals of the system and its actual performance. The careerism inevitable in a society in which public office was the only path to advancement caused the mandarin elite to be the object of popular cynicism, fear, and hatred. Chinese administration was impaired by the reluctance of the population to have contact with the official elite.

In contrast to this, the myth of unlimited opportunity to rise through the public examinations lived stubbornly on, in spite of the fact that upward social mobility was by no means high.

Finally, and perhaps most important of all, there is a very great contrast between the extremely hierarchical organization of Chinese society and the egalitarianism of fraternities, secret societies, and other groups. Here the contrast is a result of straight reaction, the egalitarianism of the societies representing an escape from the pressures of elaborately structured family and social relationships.

At the psychological level, the stress upon harmony contrasts with the outbursts of unlimited violence, which are just as characteristic of Chinese life. The repression of even moderate aggression leads eventually to such outbursts. What is missing is the ability to handle conflict and direct it to constructive purposes.

THE POLITICAL IDEAS OF SUN YAT-SEN

Sun Yat-sen's (*q.v.*) ideas were highly ambiguous in their policy implications; but his view of China's predicament was simple and straightforward. The nation's continued existence was in doubt:

Japan . . . if she should strike . . . could destroy China any day. . . . The U.S. could destroy China within one month after a rupture; . . . in two months at the most, England

Need for mass mobilization

Paradoxes and ambiguities in Chinese thought

could wipe out China. . . . France, like England, could destroy China within two months. . . . Why has China survived to the present? . . . Because the strength of the different nations in China has become a balance of power, which makes it possible for China to go on existing. . . . Is not this kind of dependence on others just 'gazing at Heaven and casting lots?' . . . It is only necessary that the diplomats of the different countries meet in one place and sign; in one day the signing of a document . . . would wipe out China.

He said further, "China, if she is to be crushed by political and economic power . . . will hardly last ten more years."

Sun
Yat-sen's
three
principles

Sun's San Min Chu-i, or Three Principles of the People, consisted of (1) nationalism, or the liberation of China from foreigners; (2) democracy, or government by the people and for the people; and (3) livelihood, or economic security for all the people. The explicit purpose of the three principles was simple:

They will elevate China to an equal position among the nations, in international affairs, in government, and in economic life, so that she can permanently exist in the world.

The principle of nationalism was therefore primary; the principles of democracy and of livelihood were largely means to nationalist ends, rather than ends in themselves.

The principle of nationalism.

We have the greatest population and the oldest culture. . . . But . . . we are the poorest and weakest state in the world. . . . If we do not earnestly promote nationalism and weld together our four hundred million people, we face . . . the destruction of our race.

To Sun Yat-sen, China's weakness sprang essentially from a lack of national consciousness:

the unity of the Chinese people has stopped at the clan and has not extended to the nation. . . . Clansmen who would ignore the downfall of the country will fight to the death to protect "the continuity of blood and food of the lineage"; let them see that *this* is endangered in China's danger.

To support this analogy, Sun embraced a legend of Chinese racial purity, whereby, apart from 10,000,000 of national minorities, the Chinese were united not only by common customs, religion, and language, but also by common blood. He was thus attempting to evade the fact that the Chinese, under their broad cultural identity expressed in Confucian values, were racially and culturally very diverse, and that these diversities were and still are a major obstacle to stable national unity. The Chinese nation, if such it is, is in fact the result of a long, imperfect, and still far from complete process of the acculturation of varied aboriginal peoples by a Han minority who were the bearers of "Chinese" culture; nation-building has been and must be an important facet of any modernizing revolution in China.

Sun at this time believed that the building of a sense of nationhood from the roots upward was the only hope of a united China with a single will. This would mean building, first, family loyalty, then clan loyalty, and finally national loyalty. In expressing this idea, Sun typically echoed the rhythm and language of a key passage of Confucius' "Great Learning," which every Chinese with the most minimal education knew by heart and which Sun himself emphasized later as the central idea of Chinese morality.

Sun's
emphasis
on China's
traditional
heritage

Sun believed that, to achieve nationhood, China must depend upon its own great traditional morality and learning. Science would have to be learned from outside (though he emphasized the great contributions to the development of science formerly made by China); but China's own morality, and her own developed political philosophy, were superior to those of foreigners. The traditional morality stressed filial devotion and loyalty, kindness and love, faithfulness and justice, harmony and peace. Sun conceded that in kindness and love, the Chinese had been "less active in performance" than those foreigners whose charity in China exceeded the charity of the Chinese themselves; and he was concerned that, with the disappearance of the symbol of loyalty—the emperor—many Chinese had become confused as to where their loyalties should lie and found it difficult to give loyalty to an abstract "nation." With respect to ancient virtues

other than loyalty, however, Sun believed that the Chinese were still pre-eminent.

Of these virtues, filial devotion "covers almost the whole field of human activity. . . . It is still indispensable." Thus, Sun still accepted the traditional analogy between family relationships determined by the authority of the head of the family, and social and political relationships beyond the family—an emotional pattern which the next generation of revolutionaries, the students of May Fourth, would attempt to repudiate as the source of all that was evil and ineffective in the traditional political culture. This passage, however, was to become the text of Chiang K'ai-shek's New Life Movement and the crux of right-wing philosophy in China.

In one other important respect, Sun sought to base the new nationalism upon the ancient learning. He quoted the same key passage in the "Great Learning":

The ancients who wished to illustrate illustrious virtue throughout the kingdom, first ordered well their own states. Wishing to order well their states, they first regulated their families. Wishing to regulate their families, they first cultivated their persons. Wishing to cultivate their persons, they first rectified their hearts. Wishing to rectify their hearts, they first sought to be sincere in their thoughts. Wishing to be sincere in their thoughts, they first extended to the utmost their knowledge. Such extension of knowledge lay in the investigation of things.

China was to be based, in the last analysis, upon the self-cultivation of the individual. This faith in individual morality and self-cultivation, as has often been observed, has passed into Communism in China, and given it a strongly moral emphasis in contrast to the amoral, "scientific" nature of Marxism.

The principle of democracy. Sun's main argument in favour of "democracy" was really only an argument in favour of republicanism, as the best guarantee against the renewal of personal despotism and struggles for power among rival leaders. He pointed out that whereas Western countries have had civil wars over religion and over freedom, "China in her thousands of years has had but one kind of war, the war for the throne." He then examined the concepts of liberty and equality that underlie Western democracy and concluded that neither was particularly applicable in China. Liberty was not a demand of the ordinary people in China; it was a concept they did not understand. China had never suffered from the extremes of autocracy as had the West. China's problem was not too little liberty, but too much:

The aims of our revolution are just the opposite of the aims of the revolutions of Europe. . . . We . . . must break down individual liberty and become pressed together into an unyielding body like the firm rock which is formed by the addition of cement to sand.

He felt that the Kuomintang failed to check Yüan Shih-k'ai because the provinces would not work together, and he deplored student strikes and riots as symptoms of excessive liberty.

Liberty . . . means the freedom to move about within an organised group. . . . On no account must we give more liberty to the individual; let us secure liberty instead for the nation.

The
problem of
excesses of
liberty

Sun's attitude toward liberty was not, however, essentially authoritarian; it expressed a dilemma common to politically underdeveloped states. The precondition of effective liberty, as Sun intuitively saw, is a national government strong enough to impose on all what has been agreed by all. Inability to secure acceptance and implementation of reforming legislation is a major obstacle to development in almost all the poor countries of Asia; and this, in spite of Sun Yat-sen, was to be the fate of the Kuomintang itself. Chinese Communist commentary on democratic centralism, as well as on mass-line political style, is essentially concerned with this problem also; and much of Mao's political theory and style reflect his experience of it. As regards equality, Sun argued that China had too much rather than too little. China had never been aristocratic; "only the Emperor's rank was hereditary"; consequently, there was no powerful reaction to social stratification as in the West. His argument was the familiar one that men are not equally endowed with ability; and on this basis he developed briefly an elitist theory based upon the idea that

there are those who know and understand beforehand, those who know and perceive afterwards, and those who do not know and perceive—the discoverers, the promoters, and the practical men.

His ideal government was one that put the discoverers in power, though under democratic sanctions.

Strong government is both desired and feared; this is the dilemma of democracy everywhere, said Sun. "We must not be afraid, as Western peoples are, that the government will be too strong and get from under our control." Sun believed that Western democracy, which gave the people only the right to elect, did not provide adequate safeguards against excessive or corrupt government; and experience of merely representative government in China had been disastrous:

the members of the Chinese parliament have become mere swine, filthy and corrupt, worse than the world has ever seen before. . . . China has not only failed to learn well from Western democracy, but has been corrupted by it.

On the other hand, he stressed that, although elections were not enough, the people nevertheless must have the right of suffrage, recall, initiative, and referendum. This is not necessarily a contradiction of his insistence on strong government. Government should be obeyed, but legislation and policy should be as much under popular control as possible.

The problems of authority and power

Sun's institutional proposals were based upon a distinction between authority and power (the legitimation of government as opposed to its exercise); they were an attempt to provide a government whose writ would be accepted but which would be under popular control, which in fact, by representing the national interest, could secure obedience from sectional interests. On the basis of this distinction between authority and power, Sun proposed a form of government divided, not into three powers, but five: legislature, executive, and judiciary, plus the power of examination of candidates for office, and the power of supervision of government organs. The addition of these two powers makes little logical sense; they represent a concession to Chinese traditions. Both of these extra powers seem to have been meant to be exercised in relation to the executives of government rather than the policy makers, the bureaucrats rather than the elected politicians. But Sun was quite vague on their powers. In his lectures on the Three Principles, he did not elaborate upon them.

The principle of livelihood. If Sun's concepts of democracy were ambiguous, his concept of "people's livelihood" was even more open to a variety of conflicting interpretations. He was a leader in a party that included both radical elements and elements conservative in everything except the need for renewed unity and strength, and thus he could not afford to be too specific. His lectures on livelihood therefore abound with contradictions, which he attempted to conceal under striking but imprecise aphorisms.

Sun's ambiguous views on Communism

His statements concerning Communism form the heart of these contradictions. On the one hand, he condemned the basic features of Marxism and denied that history is determined by material forces or that social progress is the consequence of class struggle. Marx, he said, is the pathologist, not the physiologist of society. He argued that Marxism had no relevance to China's social situation: in China there were no rich and poor, only different degrees of poverty; there was as yet no capitalist class of any significance, and very few large landlords, and little overt discontent over land tenure. Finally, he argued that the Western countries had succeeded in reconciling class conflicts arising from capitalism to a considerable extent by social and industrial reform, public ownership of transport and communications, direct taxation, and socialized distribution: "Society progresses, then, through the adjustment of major economic interests rather than through the clash of interests." On the other hand, he insisted that

the Principle of Livelihood is socialism, it is Communism, it is the Great Commonwealth. . . . Communism is an ideal of Livelihood, while the Principle of Livelihood is practical Communism. . . . The Principle of Livelihood aims at the equalisation of the financial resources in society. So we consider the principle of Livelihood to be the same thing as socialism or communism.

There is a corresponding ambiguity in Sun's positive proposals for the economy. The slogan "land to the tiller" implied the expropriation of the Chinese landlords, but this was to come about only when "the Principle of Livelihood is fully realised"; in the shorter term, reduction of rents and "protection and encouragement" for the peasants was all that was proposed. In the field of industry, capital was to be regulated, and state capital provided.

The blend of Sun's ideas. Sun's positive ideas can be briefly summarized. The aim was the survival of the Chinese nation. The immediate problem was the unification of China. The problems of unification were the lack of effective national loyalties and the inability of the political regimes to enforce unity. The ideal was a government whose writ would extend everywhere; this took precedence over democratic freedoms, and the new political authority was conceived in explicitly elitist terms with the ordinary citizen enjoying a relatively passive role, under tutelage in the first stages. Only after the establishment of an effective government and after this period of political education from above, were democratic rights to be fully extended to China. Democratic government would be extended gradually upward from the local communities, not only as part of a process of increasing experience of self-government, but as part of the creation of a sense of common national identity and interest. During the predemocratic, tutelary period, the new government would expropriate the profits accruing from rising urban land values to launch a program of state-sponsored industrialization in cooperation with controlled private and foreign capital, while encouraging increases in agricultural production by lowering rents and ensuring greater security of tenure. In total, these theories of Sun's foreshadow the later theories of "guided democracies" for postcolonial Asia and Africa. Sun would seem to have anticipated, in China, many of the problems that the underdeveloped new states of Asia and elsewhere have faced since World War II.

Sun's theories as a foretoken of "guided democracy"

Sun's ideas were wide enough for both right-wing and left-wing to claim the succession from him. His ideas of democracy were so ambivalent that they could be interpreted equally as a plea for mass-mobilization politics or as a plea for a disciplined revolution from above. His ideas of the role of the party, in a similar way, might be cited to justify its being used primarily as an educational force or as the cadre of a quasi-totalitarian government. His attitude toward Chinese culture was equally ambiguous. Although no one saw more clearly than he the obstacles that China's existing political culture put in the path of the development of a state at once effective and popular, he yet felt himself obliged to stress the continuing vitality of traditional morality and Classical learning. Again, his successors were left free to interpret Sun's views on the "national spirit" according to their own interests and tastes.

THE POLITICAL IDEAS OF CHIANG KAI-SHEK

Chiang Kai-shek's political ideas were most fully expressed in *China's Destiny* (1943), a generation after the writing of Sun Yat-sen's *Three Principles of the People*. Chiang's situation was a different one. First, in the face of the Japanese threat, some measure of national unification had been achieved—although, in fact, this consisted of hardly more than a loose federation of provinces mostly led by warlords who brooked no interference from the Nationalist government in local matters. Second, the Nationalists were no longer in alliance with the Communists (the second united front of 1937 had virtually broken down by 1940–41); on the contrary, they were faced with a Communist state within the state, embracing about one quarter of China's population, led by

Differences between Sun and Chiang

men whose courageous resistance to the Japanese had stolen much of Chiang's thunder as the national leader. Third, Chiang's regime had faced, as Sun in Canton had not had the opportunity to face, the task of reconstructing Chinese society. This changed situation accounts for much of the difference between the ideas of Sun and those of Chiang. Differences of personality, however, account also for much; and most important of all, the Nationalists came increasingly to rely upon the more conservative elements in Chinese society, especially after the Japanese cut the regime off from its original bases in the Westernized, mercantile coastal cities.

The idealization of Chinese tradition. Chiang's view of China's situation is indicated by the title of the first chapter of *China's Destiny*: "The Origins of National Humiliation and the Sources of Revolution." His view of Chinese history is an entirely conventional one: the struggles of the political factions at the end of the Ming dynasty made possible the Manchu conquest, and the Manchus corrupted scholarship and the examination system in the interest of controlling the conquered Chinese. Otherwise, however, the Manchus were worthy successors of Han and T'ang; it is clear enough that Chiang considers them worthy in that they extended China's boundaries, just as these earlier dynasties had done.

To Chiang Kai-shek, China's troubles began with the unequal treaties, especially the treaty tariff, as a result of which "China's economic and financial power fell completely into foreign hands and the lifeblood of the state was cut off." (In fact, honest foreign administration of the Chinese customs had given the Chinese throne a far greater revenue from foreign trade than it had ever had before.) After 1911, instead of bearing firmly in mind that

the main objective was to escape from the bondage of the unequal treaties, and especially to overcome the habits of arrogance, extravagance, immorality, lawlessness, and sycophancy that had been fostered under the unequal treaties,

the public concentrated upon the futile imitation of Western democracy. These ideas reveal the emotional basis of Chiang's political thought. The unequal treaties were the source of all China's ills. They not only hamstrung the exercise of Chinese sovereignty but produced a situation in which Chinese morals were debauched, political unity prejudiced, and the efforts of the nation deflected from its own ways to slavish imitation of foreign culture and institutions.

Chiang was unwilling to admit that China's predicament in any sense sprang from internal faults. Sun Yatsen praised traditional morality and learning; but he did not eulogize China's traditional society, as Chiang Kaishek did:

China's original social structure . . . proceeded from the individual to the clan. From the standpoint of local divisions, it proceeded from the clan to the *pao-chia* and then to the village community. . . . From the administrative regulations governing the individual's conduct in the family, there developed the rules of family propriety and clan regulations. In the *pao-chia* there were *pao* contracts; in the villages and communities there were village agreements and community regulations. The spirit of self-government was sufficient to ensure individual and family good behaviour without depending on legal intervention. The spirit of mutual co-operation was sufficient to ensure planning for the public benefit without the need for government supervision. . . . There were village and community schools. . . . As to dykes and irrigation works, roads and rivers, there were none that were not built or dredged through the joint effort of villages and communities. . . .

But during the past hundred years, as a result of the oppression of the unequal treaties . . . the traditional structure of the family, the village, and the community was disrupted. Mutual help was replaced by competition and jealousy. Public planning was neglected. . . . Social traditions and public morale were gradually destroyed.

This idealization of the traditional national society and the vague accusations that it was destroyed by foreign pressures and influences is perhaps characteristic of the ideology of excolonial nationalist regimes. It lays salve to the national ego, it minimizes attention to internal disruptive forces by over-stressing the responsibility of for-

eign influences for social evils, and it suggests that change can proceed on the basis of traditional ways—that is, with the minimum disturbance of vested interests.

Chiang's nationalist wrath was especially directed at China's modern intellectuals:

For the past hundred years . . . literary theories and political writings . . . glorified selfish desires and the quest for profit. . . . The tradition of emulating the [Chinese] sages was despised by the people. . . . They even praised foreign figures and scorned the history of their own country.

Meanwhile, Chiang believed, as a result of the opium-ridden foreign concessions, "beautiful and prosperous cities became hells of misery and chaos," and China's 5,000-year-old tradition of diligence, thrift, and simplicity, of cotton clothes and a simple diet, of women weaving and men farming, were completely undermined by the opium, gambling, prostitution, and thugs of the concessions.

The pattern of moral and social reconstruction. In these circumstances, political and economic reconstruction, he emphasized, must be based upon social reconstruction, and this in turn depends upon psychological and ethical reconstruction. No doubt is left that this must take the form of the restoration of traditional Chinese morality and the society that (in Chiang's eyes) expressed it:

Our country's sages . . . realised that changes in social traditions and morale determine whether there is order or chaos in the state, and whether the nation survives or is destroyed. . . . Therefore we should emulate the sages, worship the heroes, and follow the precepts of our forefathers. . . . Propriety, righteousness, modesty, and honour are the four pillars of the state. . . . The glories and scope of our ancient Chinese learning cannot be equalled by the history of any of the strong western nations of today . . . a lofty system, superior to any other philosophy in the world.

Psychological reconstruction should therefore

be based on the development of an independent ideology, in which the greatest emphasis must be placed on a revival of the nation's ancient culture. . . . The virtues necessary for national salvation . . . need not be sought abroad . . . we need but revive, expand, and glorify our original system of ethics.

In the interests of this revival of the national spirit, Chiang bitterly attacked the radicals of May Fourth, with their willingness to learn with an open mind from all countries. In this he followed Sun Yat-sen, who wrote "cosmopolitanism is no doctrine for wronged nations"; but Chiang, faced, unlike Sun, with a hostile and powerful Communist movement that was more and more winning the sympathy of China's intellectuals, was more sweeping in his condemnations:

After the May Fourth Movement . . . the educated classes . . . lost their confidence in Chinese culture. . . . [They] had no real knowledge of its enduring qualities. . . . [Academics and teachers were] careless and irresponsible in their lectures, uncritically echoing the popular trend. . . . Their concept of liberty was based on their own selfish desires, while their theory of "democracy" was based on their desire to advance their own material interests.

The intellectuals, in Chiang's view, thus regarded observance of the law as humiliating and resistance to orders as clever.

In the 1930s Chiang sought to achieve this psychological reconstruction of the Chinese nation through the New Life Movement; its object was to "modernize the Chinese people" without, however, changing the national tradition. Inevitably, in defending the New Life Movement, Chiang immediately ran into contradictions: from the national tradition he demanded means of modernization that it was most unlikely to provide; and his exhortations about what had to be done formed a condemnation of the tradition he hoped to revive and use. The Chinese must, he emphasized,

sweep away century-old habits of servile dependence and blind submission. . . . Our citizens must become actively creative, must use their own initiative, and transform their cold apathy into warm enthusiasm for progress. . . . Our young men must aspire to become engineers . . . and . . . seek creativeness and inventiveness through practical work.

Margin notes:

Chiang's criticism of foreign influence and intervention

Chiang's praise of China's old social structure

The New Life Movement

In other words, China must use its traditional culture to break down the stultifying efforts of hierarchical social and family relationships, the bureaucratic fear of taking responsibility for innovation, and the contempt for practical learning, all of which were integral features of that traditional culture. And, Chiang emphasized, it should do so on the basis of filial piety as the model of all other virtues—the behaviour pattern that all Chinese radicals had regarded as the most stultifying factor of all.

Emphasis on political obedience and discipline
What issues from this in practical terms is the suppression of dissent in order to create the unity necessary for strong government: "Democracy . . . depends entirely on government by law and discipline." Four pages of *China's Destiny* are devoted to praise of the great disciplinarians of Chinese history, from Chu-ko Liang to Tseng Kuo-fan; it is especially significant that Chiang should praise the latter, who put down the protosocialist Taiping rebels by creating a disciplined and indoctrinated peasant army, whereas Sun Yat-sen, brought up on legends about the great leader Hung Hsiu-ch'üan, regarded the Taiping as heroic precursors of his own revolutionary movement.

Most nationalist leaders of excolonial regimes, however, have faced the predicament of what to do when there is no tradition of obedience to novel legislation, when indeed there is no conception of the feasibility of new law. The problem of how to get reforming legislation obeyed is one with which Chiang had ample experience; and it was the rock upon which his regime perished.

THE DEVELOPMENT OF MAOIST IDEOLOGY

From the foundation of the Communist Party in 1921 until the breakup of the first united front in 1927, the Communist Party's attempt to form an independent program and ideology was inhibited by the necessity, imposed partly by internal conditions and partly by Comintern policy, of close cooperation with the Nationalist Party. The initial instinctive exclusiveness of the newly founded party, determined to cooperate with none but the fully committed, even to the exclusion of government servants, soon disappeared; and although cooperation with the Nationalists was always uneasy, it was generally accepted as a means to try to secure the unification of the country. Lenin's interest in securing allies for the Russian Revolution among the national liberation movements of Asia and Africa helped to rationalize the alliance between the two Chinese radical parties. The ambiguity of Sun Yat-sen's own position (and the uncertainties as to the future shape of Russian Communism) made the alliance ideologically possible. It was a close alliance, a "bloc within," in which the Communist Party compromised its own independence. The Communists stressed their identification with the anti-imperialist and nationalist aims of the Kuomintang, and within this framework contented themselves with laying particular stress upon propaganda among workers and peasants, which access to the Kuomintang's growing political network enabled them to pursue, building up mass organizations (labour, peasants, women, youth) with great rapidity.

In the attempt to secure the widest possible support for the reunification of the country, however, the Communists had to restrain their mobilization of workers and peasants so as not to appear to threaten those elements of the ruling classes whose cooperation was sought, either by too aggressive trade-union activity or by the encouragement of peasant demands for reduction of rents, security of tenure, or redistribution of land.

The origins of Mao's political theories
The origins of what has since come to be Chairman Mao Tse-tung's characteristic political theory lay in this unstable and frustrating situation. In 1926, when ominous cracks were already showing in the facade of unity, his essay on the "Analysis of the Classes in Chinese Society" began by posing the question that, until then, both parties in the alliance had sought to avoid: "Who are our enemies? Who are our friends?" he asked; "The basic reason why all previous revolutionary struggles in China achieved so little was their failure to unite with real friends to attack real enemies." He then attempted to

answer this question by analysis of classes, their interests, and their consequent attitude toward the revolution. The conclusions were not narrowly sectarian. The only groups excluded from consideration were those that Mao (and most other Chinese radicals) believed were dependent upon foreign power in China—the landlord class and the comprador class (the latter being those Chinese businessmen whose fortunes depended upon foreign economic power and privileges in China). The existence of these classes, he stated, "is utterly incompatible with the aims of the Chinese revolution."

All other classes were potential allies. The middle bourgeoisie, mostly Chinese businessmen frustrated by foreign privileges and economic strength and by warlord disorder, sought to found a bourgeois state; but this was impossible: polarization of Chinese (and world) politics was inevitable, and "the intermediate classes are bound to disintegrate quickly, some sections turning left to join the revolution, others turning right to join the counterrevolution." One year and one month later, as a result of Chiang Kai-shek's Shanghai coup, this prophecy was significantly fulfilled, when Chinese politics were rent down the middle, and the moderates rendered helpless between two armed extremes.

Mao's division of the petty bourgeoisie and semiproletariat
Among the petty bourgeoisie, Mao included the ownerpeasants (those who owned all the land they farmed) as well as independent handicraftsmen, small traders, and poor intellectuals. He divided the petty bourgeoisie into three types, not according to differences in their relation to the means of production, but in terms of whether their economic position was improving or not: those who had a surplus and could hope to improve their position; those who were maintaining their accustomed standards but at the cost of ever-increasing effort; and those whose standard of living was falling. "In normal times," wrote Mao,

these three sections of the petty bourgeoisie differ in their attitude to the revolution. But in times of war . . . not only will the left wing of the petty bourgeoisie join the revolution, but the middle section too may join, and even right-wingers, swept forward by the great revolutionary tide.

Under the term "semi-proletariat," Mao included tenants and semitenants, along with small handicraftsmen, peddlers, and shop assistants, and he asserted that their receptiveness to revolutionary propaganda, too, was proportionate to their poverty, though all were allies of the revolution. The Chinese proletariat, both urban and rural, of course were the leaders. Thus, Mao was not asserting a narrow sectarian theory of the revolution but was affirming that there were circumstances in which all except the landlords, the compradors, and some of the middle bourgeoisie would be willing to support the revolution.

Role of the peasants. Mao's analysis implicitly stressed the very great political importance of the peasants—an importance that Mao was to express not in terms of cold class analysis but with passion, almost with amazement, in his "Report on an Investigation of the Peasant Movement in Hunan." In this report, Mao emphasized not only the critical political importance of peasant discontent, but the forms and characteristics that the peasant movement had taken in Hunan. There, underground agitation ahead of the Kuomintang's revolutionary armies had entailed a peasant movement that, according to Mao (after more than a month's investigation), embraced 2,000,000 peasant households in a dozen counties of the Hsiang Ho Valley. The peasant associations had virtually taken over the government of these areas:

With the collapse of the power of the landlords, the peasant associations have now become the sole organs of authority . . . the top local tyrants and evil gentry have fled. . . . All decisions are made by a joint council consisting of the magistrate and the representatives of the revolutionary mass organisations. . . . At such council meetings the magistrate is influenced by the views of the public organisations and invariably does their bidding. The adoption of a democratic committee system of government should not therefore present much of a problem in Hunan. . . . In a few months the peasants have accomplished what Dr. Sun Yat-sen wanted, but failed, to accomplish in the forty years he devoted to the national revolution.

In a famous passage, Mao summed up the political potential of this movement:

> In a very short time, in China's central, southern, and northern provinces, several hundred peasants will rise like a mighty storm, like a hurricane, a force so swift and violent that no power, however great, will be able to hold it back. They will smash all the trammels that bind them and rush forward along the road to liberation. They will sweep all the imperialists, warlords, corrupt officials, local tyrants, and evil gentry into their graves. Every revolutionary party and every revolutionary comrade will be put to the test, to be accepted or rejected as they decide. There are three alternatives. To march at their head and lead them? To trail behind them, gesticulating and criticizing? Or to stand in their way and oppose them? Every Chinese is free to choose, but events will force you to make the choice quickly.

There has been much controversy over whether or not Mao was heretical in his neglect of the importance of proletarian leadership in this report; but the report can be interpreted as dealing with the peasants as the main force of the revolution, leaving the proletariat as leaders of the revolution by implication. More important, however, is the faith that Mao shows in the effectiveness of spontaneous organization by the people themselves: "every . . . revolutionary comrade will be put to the test, to be accepted or rejected as *they* [the peasants] decide." It is a long way from Lenin and his cool manipulation of social forces and his fear of spontaneity.

Mao's
defense of
peasant
rule in
Hunan

Mao not only insists on the strength of potential peasant revolt but on its effectiveness. To those who represented the situation in Hunan as anarchy, Mao replied, first, that the peasants were carrying out the essential task of the revolution: "the forces of rural democracy have risen to overthrow the forces of rural feudalism. . . . To overthrow these feudal forces is the real objective of the revolution." Then in analyzing their use of force, he insisted that

> in this period it was necessary to establish the absolute authority of the peasants. . . . To put it bluntly, it is necessary to create terror for a while in every rural area . . . but . . . the peasants are clear-sighted. Who is bad and who is not, who is the worst and who is not quite so vicious, who deserves severe punishment and who deserves to be let off lightly—the peasants keep clear accounts, and very seldom has the punishment exceeded the crime.

He was equally impressed by the fact that the peasant associations, although usually led by the poorest peasants, promptly forbade gambling and opium smoking and very successfully put down banditry. Out of this argument against those who were in fear of anarchy, came another characteristic of Maoist thought, which has been a major premise ever since: that the masses, even the most deprived and downtrodden, can be trusted to rise to the responsibilities of power.

Throughout the report, Mao insisted that the seizure of political power was fundamental:

> Once the peasants have their organisation, the first thing they do is to smash the political power and prestige of the landlord class. . . . This . . . is the pivotal struggle. . . . Without victory in this struggle, no victory is possible in the economic struggle to reduce rent and interest, to secure land and other means of production, and so on. . . . The political authority of the landlords is the backbone of all the other systems of authority. With that overturned, the clan authority, the religious authority, and the authority of the husband all begin to totter. . . . No one any longer dares to practise the cruel corporal and capital punishments that used to be inflicted in the ancestral temples. . . . In many places the peasant associations have taken over the temples of the gods as their offices. Everywhere they advocate the appropriation of temple property in order to start schools and to defray the expenses of the associations. . . . As to the authority of the husband, this has always been weaker among the poor peasants because, out of economic necessity, their womenfolk have had to do more manual labour. . . . The women in many places have now begun to organise rural women's associations.

Everything followed, therefore, from the seizure of political authority: not only the possibility of economic changes, but immediate spontaneous movement toward cultural and social change, including the immediate imposition of a frugal and puritanical morality (which Mao has ever since assumed to be a proper expression of poor-peasant dominance) and a burning interest in education. The seizure of power by the armed masses, exercising their initiative through omnicompetent Paris Commune type committees of government, has also remained central to Maoist thought.

The strategy of the "people's war." Mao's report failed to impress either the Wu-han government or the Communist Party, which were trying to minimize the threat of a rupture with Chiang Kai-shek and his armies lower down the Yangtze; but Chiang's coup in Shanghai in 1927 and the Kuomintang's subsequent repudiation of its Communist allies in Wu-han forced the Communists to desperate straits that included—too late—the encouragement of peasant revolt in Hunan. It was when the defeated remnants sought safety on Ching-kang Shan, in much less hopeful circumstances, that the Communists in 1931 set up their first peasant government or "soviet republic." Mao's report of the following year on "The Struggle in the Chingkang Mountains" was an account of the difficulties, rather than of the potentialities, of rural revolution.

Disappointed in his hope of Communist-Kuomintang leadership of a massive peasant revolt throughout China, Mao and his fellow leaders faced the very different problem of survival, surrounded and outnumbered manyfold by hostile armies. Military and political tactics were worked out in these conditions that subsequently passed into the theory of the Chinese Communist movement and determined much of its future political and military organization; the first and classical "people's war" was fought in Kiangsi.

In evolving his military strategy, Mao Tse-tung had to fight against two extreme and contrasting tendencies. One, supported by the Central Committee in Shanghai and backed by the Comintern, was the attempt to use the inadequate armed forces of the soviet area in an attempt to seize Chinese cities. The other, arising inside the ranks of the Chinese Red Army itself and perhaps expressing the older tradition of Chinese banditry, was the tendency to dissipate strength in a roving-band strategy of plundering raids, which were rationalized as a means of spreading the revolutionary message as widely as possible. By persuasive arguments and outright disobedience, Mao and his associates eventually won the right to operate their own strategy. What both these dangerous extremes had in common was that they could not take advantage of the immense strength that a friendly population could give to the small regular forces of the Red Army; the Red Army in the soviet area was the backbone, the mobile corps, of an indoctrinated and armed population. The strength of this system was shown only if the enemy could be drawn into the pro-Communist area, where its every movement was reported to the Communist military leaders, who then, through great mobility made possible by the enthusiasm of its indoctrinated soldiers, could concentrate a locally superior force in secrecy and destroy the enemy piecemeal. The strength of the Red Army was the strength of its popular support. Four successive "extermination campaigns" launched by Chiang Kai-shek between 1930 and 1933 were swallowed up and annihilated by this means. The fifth, in October 1934, was successful only because, with the advice of Otto Braun, the Comintern adviser attached to the soviet, the Communist leaders attempted to fight a conventional positional war, and lost; the temptation to try to halt the enemy on the edge of the now well-consolidated and extensive soviet area was natural, but the price was the destruction of the soviet. Another price paid—by the Comintern—was the decisive destruction of its dominant influence in the Chinese Communist movement, and the confirmation of Mao's leadership.

Factors
hindering
military
strategy

The establishment of Communist political influence, however, was no easy task. The growth of the Communist-held area had to be gradual, limited by the rate at which new territory could be consolidated politically by propaganda, political organization, and land reform favouring the interests of the majority of peasants. The great Hunan peasant movement of 1927–28 had been relatively successful because it had taken place in the wake of the victory of the revolutionary armies, in a province famous for its truculent radicalism, and in the most populated and vital counties, where there existed a particularly bitter issue of harsh tenancy terms. The Kiangsi soviet area to which Mao and his forces fled in 1930 to make their chief base, however, was poor and backward, and the people were afraid of their rulers. In this mountain area, life was extremely localized and the experience of the people limited and narrow. The Red Army's hold on the area was far from secure, and support by the peasants for its revolutionary program brought down a White terror on their heads whenever the Communists retreated. Life was dominated by the clan system, which cut across class lines and inhibited the development of class consciousness. The population was divided into natives and immigrants, at constant loggerheads, so that when the poor immigrant hill farmers supported the Communists, the natives in the valleys automatically took the other side, and the Communist Party found itself made an instrument of communal strife. In these circumstances, the new democratic institutions set up by the Communists, in imitation of the revolutionary committees of Hunan, withered through the apathy and lack of confidence of the population; the decisions were taken not by the committee but by its executive council—often only by the council's three principal officials or even by its chairman alone. Mao's pessimistic account of this situation in his article "The Struggle in the Chingkang Mountains" is so opposed to his description of Hunan conditions as not only to show that he was bitterly conscious of the contrast but also to suggest that he gave it a dialectical significance.

The issue of land reform

The key to the development of Communist influence was social policy, centred upon land reform. The history of Communist land-reform policy at this time is still somewhat obscure and at times contradictory, and Mao's own part in its evolution has been differently evaluated by different writers; but its general evolution is not in doubt. It is of great significance, because the experience gained here was the basis of the great land reform in China launched in the course of the Communist achievement of power, between 1947 and 1953. The Kiangsi legislation of 1933 was used as the basis of the final campaigns.

The soviet administration had begun in 1928 with a rigidly egalitarian and doctrinaire idea of land distribution, by which all land was to be requisitioned and then distributed in equal allotments per head of the population. In view of Chinese rural conditions, this would have prejudiced the interests of the "middle peasants"—those farmers who neither exploited nor were exploited and who were mostly owner-operators, generally holding more than the average landholding of the village. They would suffer from an egalitarian distribution, and to incur their enmity was politically impossible. Moreover, a sweeping reform of this kind would have dangerously disrupted agriculture and prejudiced the already miserable standards of life in this poor area, as well as destroying the farm surplus that was the basis of the Communist economy. It would also have shifted much land into the hands of men who had neither the tools nor the capital—nor sometimes the skill—to farm it successfully.

Mao Tse-tung reacted strongly against this extreme. Mao had already suggested, in 1927, that the most satisfactory compromise would be simply to abolish rent—thus changing tenancy to ownership at a stroke, leaving the pattern of cultivation undisturbed, the middle peasants left in secure possession of their larger than average holdings, and even the rich peasants deprived only of that part of their land rented out to tenants. Gradually, from 1929 on, land policy in the Kiangsi soviet moved in this direction until by 1933 it corresponded very closely to the implications of Mao's 1927 views. This was the basis of the 1950 Agrarian Reform Law.

The modification of land reform in the soviet illustrates the effects upon Chinese Communist ideology of their having early come to rule a state, however small and poor. The survival of the state took precedence over ideological purity. This had two aspects. The first was that the regime's dependence, militarily, on the intelligence and the guerrilla assistance given by a devoted population meant that enemies must be minimized. Mao was even prepared to adopt policies that would at least neutralize if not win over what he vaguely called the "intermediate class"—that is, the ruling class with the exception (largely theoretical) of large landlords. The second aspect was that a healthy economy became vitally important, and in order to achieve this, trade must be protected and encouraged. Hence, Mao and his associates positively disobeyed Central Committee instructions to destroy the bourgeoisie of the soviet area and, on the contrary, prided themselves upon their successful protection of trade. This, too, was the beginning of a stress upon improved production as an integral part of Mao's ideology.

The strategy of maximum economy and efficiency in the border regions. The Kiangsi soviet, though it was destroyed in October 1934, provided the practical and ideological precedents for the Chinese Communists after their Long March to the border regions of far-off Shensi. Circumstances in the border regions after the breakdown of the second united front in 1940 were somewhat similar to those of the earlier soviet, in that the Communist government was dealing with a territory under siege and was dependent for survival on guerrilla warfare. The main difference, however, was that the Communist Party now was attractive because it was leading a nationalist resistance against the Japanese, not because it was leading a social revolution. Its more radical policies, indeed, were suspended for the duration in order to encourage the maximum nationalist support from all classes.

Effects of border region experiences. The border regions provided in many significant ways a microcosm of the Chinese polity as a whole, with the same problems but in sharper focus. The scattered nature of the Communist-held territories presented in a more severe and more urgent form the problems of central control that were fundamental to all Chinese political organization. Recruitment of leaders from two contrasting milieux—subliterate peasant guerrillas, whose experience was local and practical, and educated urban students who could take longer and broader views but whose direct experience of the problems of rural China was nil—represented in a critical form the essential national problem of how to create a leadership at once sophisticated and responsive to mass opinions. The problems of maintaining and developing the border region economy in regions of particularly severe poverty also created a view of economic development very different from the essentially Western, capital-intensive model of Soviet Russia. Such a view was perhaps more appropriate to Chinese conditions of low capital accumulation and plentiful manpower.

Border regions as a microcosm of Chinese society

The critical phase of the development of border region ideology came about as the result of successful Communist attacks against the Japanese—attacks that ended in victory but called down upon the Communist territories far more determined Japanese pressure. The Communists were forced to seek maximum economy and efficiency and did so by intensifying the techniques they had already developed. Maoist ideology as developed in 1942 cannot be understood except in relation to the practical measures then taken to sweat down the bureaucracy, to provide the most effective leadership to the scattered localities under Communist control by transferring leadership personnel to lower levels, and to provide leadership for cooperative economic construction based on the intensive use of labour. In these respects, the 1942 campaign prefigured the social and economic strategies of the Communes and the Great Leap Forward of 1958.

The particular political difficulties were several. First, the considerable political and economic apparatus that had been built up over the years was too expensive and vulnerable to be maintained in the face of increased Japanese pressure. In an editorial written for the "Liberation Daily," September 7, 1942, Mao enlarged on a new slogan, "better troops and simpler administration":

Our enormous war apparatus is suited to past conditions.

Effects of Japanese pressures

... But ... the base areas have shrunk and may continue to shrink for a period, and undoubtedly we cannot maintain the same enormous war apparatus as before. ... But men's minds are liable to be fettered by circumstances and habit from which even revolutionaries cannot always escape. We created this enormous apparatus ourselves, little thinking that one day we would have to reduce it ... we feel reluctant and find it very difficult. The enemy is bearing down on us with his enormous war apparatus, and how dare we reduce ours? ... We can learn from how the Monkey King dealt with Princess Iron Fan ... by changing himself into a tiny insect the Monkey King made his way into her stomach and overpowered her.

The vested interests of officials now obliged to scatter themselves in less prestigious local positions, the tension between old local leaders and young intellectuals sent down to assist them, the reluctance of soldiers and specialists to participate in production of food and cotton, all these problems played a part in the formation of ideology in this phase. Among these problem groups can be mentioned especially the "young Bolsheviks," a group of Communists recently returned from training in Moscow who occupied relatively high positions in the party and presumably had the confidence of the Comintern. These men, with whatever justification, were made the symbols of the orthodox, dogmatic, abstract views, unrelated to border region realities.

Second, severe political problems were posed by the need to maintain revenues in the shrinking Communist areas. The solution was seen to be to concentrate upon increased production rather than simply upon enhanced rates of taxation. This is the starting point of Mao's whole view of economic development, and it was in this context that he first condemned the counterproductive attitude of the mere tax collector, an attitude that he was later to condemn as typical of the Soviet Union—"draining the pond to catch the fish." In the preface to his "Economic and Financial Problems," Mao developed this point:

Financial difficulties can be overcome only by down-to-earth and effective economic development. ... When the government is in very great difficulties, it is necessary to ask the people to bear a heavier burden. ... But while taking from the people we must at the same time help them to replenish and expand their economy ... so that they gain at the same time as they give and moreover gain more than they give.

In his inner-party directive of October 1943, Mao further emphasized this idea:

It is wrong to have a handful of government functionaries busying themselves with collecting grain and taxes, funds and food supplies, to the neglect of organising the enormous labour-power of the rank and file of the Party, the government, and the army, and that of the people, for a mass campaign of production. ... It is wrong simply to exhort people in any base area to endure hardship in the bitter struggle without encouraging them to increase production and thereby try to improve their material conditions.

The practical policies adopted as a result were (1) the full employment of army, party, and government personnel in production, to make their units as nearly self-sufficient as possible; (2) the full implementation of rent-reduction, to stimulate peasant support for party policies; and (3) production campaigns based on mutual aid and cooperation, particularly in land reclamation and the extension of irrigation. The political problem involved was that increased dependence upon economic development based on mass mobilization meant a substantial degree of decentralized management; it meant that success would depend more on persuading people to cooperate than on imposing central planning decisions.

The theoretical discussions that were involved tended to systematize Mao's thinking. The aim was to provide the ethos for a new and closer relationship between various groups in both political and cultural matters. At the same time, it had to provide a stiffer ideological backbone for a newly decentralized system. It had, in a word, to reconcile unified leadership and decentralized management not only of the economy, but of all activities relevant to the war of resistance. Mao's "Speech at the As-

sembly of Representatives of the Shensi-Kansu-Ninghsia Border Region," November 21, 1941, set the framework by insisting on the necessity and the possibility of good working relations between the Communist minority and the general population:

Chinese society is small at both ends and big in the middle ... the great majority of the people consists of the peasants, the urban petty bourgeoisie and the other intermediate classes. No political party that wants to run China's affairs properly can do so unless its policy gives consideration to the interests of these classes. ... Communists should cooperate democratically with non-Party people and must not act arbitrarily and keep everything in their own hands.

In "Some Questions Concerning Methods of Leadership," June 1943, Mao summed up his theory of mass-line politics:

There are two methods which we Communists must employ in whatever work we do. One is to combine the general with the particular; the other is to combine the leadership with the masses.

In any task, if no general and widespread call is issued, the broad masses cannot be mobilised for action. But if persons in leading positions confine themselves to a general call—if they do not personally ... go deeply and concretely into the work called for ... gain experience and use this experience for guiding other units—then they will have no way of testing the correctness or of enriching the content of their general call. ... In the Rectification Movement of 1943, each bureau and sub-bureau of the central committee and each area and prefectural Party committee ... must do the following things, gaining experience in the process. Select two or three units ... from the organisation itself and from other organisations ... in the vicinity. Make a thorough study of these units ... give personal guidance to those in charge to find concrete solutions for the practical problems facing those units. ... This is the method by which the leaders combine leading and learning. ...

Experience in the 1942 Rectification Movement also proves it is essential ... that a leading group should be formed in each unit ... and that this leading group should link itself closely with the masses. ... However active the leading group may be, its activity will amount to fruitless effort by a handful of people unless combined with the activity of the masses. ... In the process of a great struggle, the composition of the leading group in most cases should not and cannot remain entirely unchanged throughout the initial, middle, and final stages; the activists who come forward in the course of the struggle must constantly be promoted to replace those original members of the leading group who are inferior by comparison or who have degenerated. ...

In the practical work of our Party, all correct leadership is necessarily "from the masses, to the masses." This means: take the ideas of the masses (scattered and unsystematic ideas) and concentrate them (through study, turn them into concentrated and systematic ideas), then go to the masses and propagate and explain these ideas until the masses embrace them as their own, hold fast to them, and translate them into action. Then once again concentrate ideas from the masses and once again go to the masses so that the ideas are persevered in and carried through. And so on, over and over again in an endless spiral, with the ideas becoming more correct, more vital, and richer each time. Such is the Marxist theory of knowledge.

The close relation in Mao's mind between mass-line politics and his theory of knowledge is shown not only by the specific reference to the Marxist theory of knowledge in this passage on the mass line, but by the occurrence of an exactly parallel passage that ends his philosophical essay "On Practice":

Discover the truth through practice, and again through practice verify the truth. Start from perceptual knowledge and actively develop it into rational knowledge; then start from rational knowledge and actively guide revolutionary practice to change both the subjective and the objective world. Practice, knowledge, again practice, and again knowledge. This form repeats itself in endless cycles, and with each cycle the content of practice and knowledge rises to a higher level. Such is the whole of the dialectical-materialist theory of knowledge, and such is the dialectical-materialist theory of the unity of knowing and doing.

In his speech at the opening of the new party school on February 1, 1942, Mao discussed this central problem in terms of the process of study, in so far as that process, in his theory, could be separated from practice:

Mass mobilization and decentralized management

Let us first ask, is the theoretical level of our Party high or low? Recently more Marxist-Leninist works have been translated and more people have been reading them. That is a very good thing. But can we therefore say that the theoretical level of our Party has been greatly raised? ... We have not yet examined all the problems of revolutionary practice ... or even the important ones ... and raised them to a theoretical plane. Just think, how many of us have created theories worthy of the name on China's economics, politics, military affairs or culture? ... If all a person can do is to commit Marxist economics or philosophy to memory ... but is utterly unable to apply them, can he be considered a Marxist theorist? No! ... It is necessary to master Marxist theory and apply it, master it for the sole purpose of applying it. ...

It is entirely right for us to esteem intellectuals, for without revolutionary intellectuals the revolution cannot triumph. But we know there are many intellectuals who fancy themselves very learned and assume airs of erudition without realising that such airs are bad and harmful and hinder their own progress. They ought to be aware of the truth that actually many so-called intellectuals are, relatively speaking, most ignorant and the workers and peasants sometimes know more than they do. ... How can those who have only book-learning be turned into intellectuals in the true sense? The only way is to get them to take part in practical work ... to get those engaged in theoretical work to study important practical problems. ...

On the other hand, our comrades who are engaged in practical work will also come to grief if they misuse their experience. ... They must realise that their knowledge is mostly perceptual and partial and that they lack rational and comprehensive knowledge. ...

However, of the two kinds of subjectivism, dogmatism is still the greatest danger in our Party. For dogmatists can easily assume a Marxist guise to bluff, capture, and make servitors of cadres of working-class and peasant origin who cannot easily see through them; they can also bluff and ensnare the naive youth.

Mao's opposition to elitism and bookishness

In subsequent speeches and writings, Mao Tse-tung attacked the related problems of stereotyped party writing and of literature and art that did not meet the needs of the population in the wartime situation. In both cases he extended his essential argument on the need to base all activities upon the existing social and political consciousness of the population, in order to secure their full and enthusiastic participation in the war effort. Much of the argument, though expressed as if universally valid, reflected Mao's opposition to the elitism of Chinese tradition and the extreme bookishness of Chinese education—obstacles to democratic development that were as clearly recognized by Kuomintang writers as by Communist writers.

The pragmatic theses. Although Mao's two philosophical essays, "On Practice" (1937) and "On Contradiction" (1937), show little originality as contributions of Marxist dialectical analysis, their importance lies in the particular emphasis they give, an emphasis related to specific and practical problems. "On Practice" was, in effect, a further attack on abstract intellectual dogma; "On Contradiction" was an attack on those who could not accept that Chinese conditions differed from Soviet conditions, and therefore required solutions based upon the pragmatic study of Chinese problems. Both, however, have a greater significance than this point of departure would suggest. "On Practice" was clearly an attempt to transcend the contradiction between the two great intellectual schools of Marxism and Pragmatism. It offered a theory of knowledge that sought the advantages of the firm assumptions of Marxism, and at the same time the advantages of pragmatic examination of facts.

"On Contradiction," first of all, provided analyses for local cadres who were forced to deal with complex situations at once political, military, and economic, and who needed guidance on how to arrange their manifold urgent tasks in some order of priority and in some workable relationship. The discussions of the universality and the particularity of contradiction, of the principal and the secondary contradictions, and of the principal and the secondary aspects of each contradiction are not merely extravagant logic chopping but have a functional purpose in a decentralized administration conducted largely by ill-educated men. The second aim of "On Contradiction"

was to challenge the traditional Chinese reluctance to engage in conflict and to provide cues on how to indulge in controlled, creative conflict. The third aim of "On Contradiction" was to offer a rationale not for compromise but for transcending or overcoming contradictions. It was necessary to avoid the unprincipled compromises that could smother the radical solutions upon which the modernization of China depended, whether under Communist or any other leadership. This was of vital importance in a situation in which the Communists were making nationalist appeals to classes whose future attitude toward radical change, when the opportunity for it arose again, was not likely to correspond with that of the Communist Party.

Both "On Practice" and "On Contradiction," in fact, deal with how to analyze a complex and changing situation:

> We are opposed to diehards in the revolutionary ranks whose thinking fails to advance with changing objective circumstances. ... These people fail to see that the struggle of opposites has already pushed the objective process forward while their knowledge has stopped at the old stage. ... Marxism-Leninism has in no way exhausted truth but ceaselessly opens up roads to the knowledge of truth in the course of practice. ["On Practice"]
> The fact is that the unity or identity of opposites in objective things is not dead or rigid, but is living, conditional, mobile, temporary, and relative. ["On Contradiction"]

Much of the illustration in both of these articles is drawn from the relations between the Communist Party and the Kuomintang and is directly relevant to differing attitudes within the party on the implications of the united front.

Expression of Mao's political ideas in "On New Democracy"

Many of Mao's political ideas were summed up in "On New Democracy" (written in January 1940), which proposed a political and economic organization for China after the defeat of Japan. Essentially, Mao took the orthodox Communist idea of a two-stage revolution—bourgeois-democratic followed by socialist—and applied it to Chinese circumstances. He reiterated his idea that the revolution could proceed with the support of the whole Chinese nation (except for a tiny minority whose interests were dependent upon foreign support); reflecting on his experience in guiding elected local governments in the wartime Communist areas, he felt that Communist participation after the war could be strictly limited to one-third membership. Economically, new democracy could take the form of a mixed economy of state enterprises, cooperatives, and private business; capitalists could be encouraged to assist in developing the economy, and landlords could be encouraged (through rent-reduction disincentives) to transfer their capital to commerce and industry. By reducing rents, imposing progressive taxation, and encouraging landlords to move into business, Mao and his forces had already achieved a considerable degree of peaceful social change in some of their base areas by the end of World War II, giving substance to the idea that class struggle need not impair national unity and strength. As he would say in "On Coalition Government" (1945):

> Of course there are still contradictions among these classes, notably the contradiction between labour and capital. ... It would be hypocritical and wrong to deny the existence of these contradictions and differing demands. But throughout the stage of New Democracy, these contradictions, these differing demands, will not grow and transcend the demands which all have in common and should not be allowed to do so; they can be adjusted. Given such adjustment, these classes can together accomplish the political, economic, and cultural tasks of the new-democratic state.

In this passage Mao anticipated the spirit of the "nonantagonistic contradictions" that he was to develop in 1957 after the successful socialization of agriculture and business.

COMMON CONCEPTIONS OF ALL
MODERN CHINESE IDEOLOGIES

All wartime and postwar Chinese leaders and thinkers, regardless of their political persuasions, were against piecemeal solutions; they all accepted the idea that poli-

Appeals to comprehensive reform or change

tics must be holistic, that it must constitute a system greater than the sum of its parts, and that it must be dominated by ideology. Action might aim at comprehensive change, or comprehensive revival, but it had to be comprehensive. Mao Tse-tung and others embraced systematic Marxism. Chiang Kai-shek and his entourage embraced an ideology exploiting tradition and explicitly based on the "Great Learning" and linking psychological, ethical, social, political, and economic change in a single process. But in both cases pragmatic piecemeal change was rejected as futile.

Everyone across the spectrum of Chinese politics accepted that the key to successful modernization was some form of mass mobilization; but there were two distinct interpretations of this. The right-wing interpretation was that, because the purpose of this mobilization was to strengthen national feeling, divisive issues should be avoided and dissent discouraged. The left-wing interpretation was that effective mass nationalism was inconceivable without popular participation and without the redress of the manifest injustices of Chinese society; that, in a word, successful nation-building was inseparable from social revolution, because it must be based upon common purpose and common values and, therefore, upon the aspirations of the vast majority. (J.Gra.)

XIII. Communist China and the Nationalist government on Taiwan

The Communist victory in China brought to power revolutionaries committed to the country's fundamental change. They recognized that the contest of arms would be largely supplanted by a political struggle, the outcome of which would determine China's future as a modern industrial nation. In a landmark session of the Communist Party Central Committee only months before the proclamation on October 1, 1949, of the People's Republic of China, the new leaders declared that only the first few steps had been taken toward modernization and that the struggle ahead would be as arduous and challenging as the revolutionary war just ending.

The mood of the losers, then in full flight to the island of Taiwan, sharply contrasted with that of the victors. The last remaining Nationalist footholds were crumbling, and the end of the civil war seemed imminent. Where all predicted the revolutionary transformation of society on the mainland, most observers also anticipated the rapid withering and eventual extinction of the remnant Nationalist forces operating officially after December 8, 1949, from Taipei on Taiwan.

ESTABLISHMENT OF THE PEOPLE'S REPUBLIC
ON THE MAINLAND

When the Communist Party proclaimed the People's Republic, most Chinese understood that the new leadership would be preoccupied with industrialization. A priority goal of the Communist political system was to raise China to the status of a great power. While pursuing this goal, the "centre of gravity" of Communist policy shifted from the countryside to the city; but Mao insisted that the revolutionary vision forged in the rural struggle would continue to guide the party.

In a series of speeches in 1949 Chairman Mao Tse-tung stated that his aim was to create a Socialist society and, eventually, world Communism. These objectives, he said, required transforming consumer cities into producer cities to set the basis on which "the people's political power could be consolidated." This would temporarily require strengthening

> the apparatus of the people's state, which refers mainly to the people's army, the people's police, and the people's courts, for the defense of the nation and the protection of the people's interests.

The four-class coalition

Mao advocated forming a coalition of elements of the urban middle class—the petty bourgeoisie and national bourgeoisie—with workers and peasants, under the leadership of the Communist Party. Theoretically, this four-class coalition would be organized and led by democratic methods of persuasion rather than coercion. Especially

in dealing with the working class and peasant populations, the party and government had to adopt "mass-line" techniques involving continuous, face-to-face contacts and mutual respect between leaders and led. The people's state, in turn, would exercise a dictatorship "for the oppression of antagonistic classes" made up of flexibly defined opponents of the regime.

The authoritative legal statement of this "people's democratic dictatorship" was given in the 1949 Organic Law for the Chinese People's Political Consultative Conference; and at its first session the Conference adopted a Common Program that formally sanctioned the organization of state power under the coalition. Communist leaders, however, argued that this state system based on selective applications of force and on a united front with bourgeois elements was a temporary device. They saw an eventual unity of all Chinese, with their interests expressed by the Communist Party and its officials, called cadres; at that time, in accordance with the principle of democratic centralism (see below), discipline within the populace would be a natural by-product of national consensus and identity with the Communist elite. A new form of government would then emerge.

In 1949 discipline and public order were almost immediately forthcoming, principally because of national exhaustion. The most basic urban functions—production, distribution, supply of water and power, garbage collection, and transportation—had seriously deteriorated in most large cities and in many rural areas during the years of warfare. Following the Communist victory, a widespread urge to return to normality helped the new leadership restore the economy. Police and party cadres in each locality, backed up by army units, began to crack down on criminal activities associated with economic breakdown. Within months it was possible to speak of longer term developmental plans.

The cost of restoring order and building up integrated political institutions at all levels throughout the nation proved important in setting China's course for the next two decades. Revolutionary priorities had to be downgraded, for example, so as to face immediate economic needs. The political transformation of society had to be postponed, as did the implementation of the democratic side of the democratic dictatorship. Land reform did proceed in the countryside: landlords were virtually eliminated as a class; land was redistributed; and after some false starts China's countryside was placed on the path toward collectivization. In the cities, however, an accommodation was reached with non-Communist elements; many former bureaucrats and capitalists were retained in positions of authority in factories, businesses, schools, and governmental organizations. At the time, this and similar pragmatic accommodations were considered temporary expedients, but they affected the long run. The leadership recognized that such compromises endangered their aim of perpetuating revolutionary values in an industrializing society, yet out of necessity they accepted the lower priority for Communist revolutionary goals and a higher place for organizational control and enforced public order.

Loss of popular sympathy

A further cost, less fully appreciated and in a way much more damaging to the maintenance of revolutionary mass-line values, was the gradual loss of popular sympathy that had accrued to the Communists as a party in opposition. In power, Communist cadres could no longer condone what they had once sponsored, and inevitably they adopted a more rigid and bureaucratic attitude toward popular participation in politics. This postconquest conservatism coincided with the demands of members of the party and of the People's Liberation Army for secure political careers as a reward for revolutionary services. Young people quickly realized that they could get ahead on slogans and political activism in campaign periods but otherwise had to rely on advanced education and good connections. That realization also seemed consistent with top-level pressures for bureaucratic expansion. Despite policy statements to the contrary, China was experiencing a proliferation of institutions and governmental networks and a general preoccupation with the symbols of office and red tape. Many Communists, however, considered these changes a betrayal of the revolution; their responses became more frequent and intense, and the issue eventually began to divide the once cohesive revolutionary elite. This development is central to an understanding of China's political history from 1949 to 1972.

Scholars tend to periodize China's history from the formation of the People's Republic in 1949. These postwar periods, which will be discussed here briefly, must be used with caution, however, because their definition depends so much on which events are selected for emphasis. In the 1970s official disapproval concerning many events once remembered with pride caused the party to begin re-evaluating the standard periodization given here.

Reconstruction and consolidation, 1949–52. During this initial period, economic and social programs restored stability, and prewar production levels and plans were set in motion in virtually all fields to begin the transformation to full Communist rule and to build up the base for industrialization. The mood of the leadership remained militant and doctrinaire, in part because of the memories of revolutionary struggle and in part because of the Korean War, which Liberation Army troops—called Chinese People's Volunteers—entered, against United Nations forces, in October 1950. Peking had felt threatened by the northward thrust of UN units and had attempted to halt them by its threats to intervene. These threats were ignored by the United States General Douglas MacArthur, however, and when UN troops under his command reached the Chinese border, Peking acted. By the war's end in July 1953 approximately two-thirds of China's combat divisions had seen service in Korea.

In the three years of war, a "Resist America, Aid Korea" campaign translated the atmosphere of external threat into a spirit of sacrifice and enforced patriotic emergency at home. Regulations for the Suppression of Counterrevolutionaries (February 20, 1951) authorized police action against dissident individuals and suspected groups. A campaign against anti-Communist holdouts, bandits, and political opponents was also pressed. Greatest publicity attended Peking's dispatch of troops to Tibet at about the same time that it intervened in Korea. The distinctiveness and world reputation of the Tibetan culture was to make this a severe test of Communist efforts to complete the consolidation of their power. After several years of unsuccessful attempts at "peaceful liberation," Peking tried to subdue the Tibetans by force, provoking a rebellion in 1959.

In this militant spirit, centrally-initiated programs from late 1951 through 1952 gradually reduced the capitalist hold on the urban economy as well as the number of officials held over in key positions from the Nationalist government. The two principal campaigns in the cities during this period were a Three-Anti campaign within governmental organs to eliminate corruption, waste, and bureaucratism, and a Five-Anti campaign within the business and industrial community to purge those charged with the sins of bribery, tax evasion, theft of state property and economic information, and cheating on government contracts.

Under the Agrarian Reform Law of June 28, 1950, the property of rural landlords had been confiscated and redistributed, which fulfilled a promise to the peasants and smashed a class identified as feudal or semifeudal. The property of traitors, "bureaucrat capitalists" (especially the "four big families" of the Kuomintang—the K'ungs, Soongs, Chiangs, and Ch'ens), and selected foreign nationals was also confiscated, helping end the power of many industrialists and providing an economic basis for industrialization. Programs were then begun to increase production and to lay the basis for long-term socialization.

These programs coincided with a massive effort to win over the population to the leadership. Such acts as a marriage law (May 1, 1950) and a trade-union law (June 29, 1950) symbolized the break with the old society, while mass organizations and the regime's "campaign style" dramatized the new. Many techniques of mass mobiliza-

tion had been initiated and partially tested in Communist base areas before 1949. As the aura of novelty and success wore off and popular sympathy for the Communists waned, propaganda campaigns and mobilization efforts became more common.

The pressures toward national political consolidation and the costly struggle in Korea produced significant consequences. Particularly in northern and northeastern China, leading officials, especially those in charge of the subnational "regional bureaus," were granted near dictatorial powers and urged to exercise them forcibly to impose Communist rule. The northeastern region, the several provinces of Manchuria (now called "Northeast"), witnessed a growing concentration of industrial and military resources during the Korean period, as well as an increased presence of Soviet economic advisers and key elements of China's tiny corps of technicians and specialists. The Northeast's most distinctive organizational characteristic lay in the relative separation of the party, military, governmental, and economic planning structures, whose operation and coordination depended on a single leader, Kao Kang.

In addition to his authoritative regional position, Kao influenced decisions in Peking. He planned the Three-Anti campaign, which was later to be extended throughout the country, and he also took the lead in adapting Soviet techniques to Chinese factory management and economic planning. He promoted these techniques on a national basis when he moved to Peking in late 1952 to set up the State Planning Commission. Working closely with the head of the party's Organization Department, Jao Shu-shih, and other senior officials, Kao allegedly tried to take over the party and to reduce drastically the authority of his potential competitors, notably Liu Shao-ch'i (q.v.) and Teng Hsiao-p'ing (both leading members of party and state organs). At a February 1954 session of the party's Central Committee, Chinese leaders opposed to Kao and Jao precipitated a power struggle that lasted nearly a year. During these months party media played on the themes of unity and cadre discipline as a prelude to the Central Committee's crushing the Kao-Jao clique and eliminating the organizational apparatus associated with it. In April 1955 Teng Hsiao-p'ing and Lin Piao were promoted to the Politburo, where Liu Shao-ch'i had risen to the number two position behind Mao. Within weeks after the National Conference of the party (March 1955) had proclaimed the defeat of the Kao–Jao clique, Peking approved a long-delayed first five-year plan (technically covering the years 1953–57) and active programs for agricultural collectivization and the socialization of industry and commerce.

The period 1949–52 was marked by changes in Soviet influence in China. The officially sanctioned terms of that influence had been worked out in a visit by Mao to Moscow from mid-December 1949 until the following March and were formalized in a Treaty of Friendship, Alliance, and Mutual Assistance (signed February 14, 1950). Years later the Chinese charged that Moscow had failed to give Peking adequate support under that treaty and had left the Chinese to face UN forces virtually alone in Korea. The seeds of doubt concerning Soviet willingness to help China had been sown. Moreover, one of the errors purportedly committed by Kao Kang was his zealousness in using Soviet advisers and promoting the Soviet economic model for development. After the purge of Kao-Jao elements, steps were taken to reduce direct Soviet control in China, particularly their joint ownership of the Chinese Ch'ang-ch'un Railway (the former Chinese Eastern and South Manchurian railways) and of naval facilities at Port Arthur and Dairen. The Chinese also spurned Soviet-style factory management introduced by Kao in favour of a party-dominated system. The applicability of the Soviet model to China and the degree to which its use might become a pretext for Soviet manipulation of China began to be questioned.

Nevertheless, these reductions in Soviet influence were partially counterbalanced by growing Soviet activity in other fields. The Chinese army was reorganized along Soviet lines, with a greater emphasis on heavy firepower

Intervention in the Korean War

Growth of power in the Northeast

Changes in Soviet influence

and mobility. Soviet texts and propaganda materials flooded the country. The U.S.S.R. had earlier extended $300,000,000 credit (used up by 1953); this was followed by a smaller developmental loan in 1954 (used up by 1956). Under these aid programs the Soviets supplied the equipment and technical aid for a large number of industrial projects. The Soviet Union also played a major role in Chinese foreign policy, and most observers assumed that China had accepted Moscow's leadership in the international Communist movement. Coordinating with Stalin, Peking supported revolutionary activity throughout Asia and opposed compromise with neutralist regimes.

The transition to Socialism, 1953–57. The period 1953–57 corresponded to the first five-year plan, which, with Soviet help, began China's rapid industrialization.

Beginning of rapid industrialization

The State Planning Commission linked the construction of large industrial facilities and the opening up of new sources of raw material with the transition of the rural and urban economy to collective and Socialist forms.

Rural collectivization. This transition was most obvious in the countryside. Land reform had already been carried out, and in 1951–53 a national movement toward establishing nearly 10,000,000 mutual-aid teams (covering 70,000,000 households) by the end of 1954, had allowed the Communists to experiment with voluntary forms of agricultural collectivization. Each team brought together small numbers of villagers in a cooperative endeavour to share labour, farm implements, draft animals, and limited capital resources. In many villages such sharing was a common feature in traditional life. The teams, which did not affect private ownership, were formed first on a seasonal or ad hoc basis and then, if successful, on a permanent basis; they were designed to improve the lot of the poor at the expense of the so-called rich peasants.

By 1953 a campaign had been launched to transform these teams into small collectives, called lower-level agricultural producers' cooperatives, averaging 20 to 30 households. The response varied widely, but many farmers who had joined the teams believed that they would gain even further advantages, particularly in respect to credit, tax relief, and farm prices, by pooling their land into cooperatives. In the process, land divided among peasants in land reform gradually became aggregated into larger, more economically efficient units. Government and peasants anticipated substantial returns from what appeared to be a more rational cultivation of the land and a more coherent use of available labour resources. Moreover, the peasants kept title to their small plots and retained the theoretical right to withdraw from the cooperative. Although land in the cooperatives was worked in common, payments were made to each family on the basis of the amount of land donated and labour performed.

In October 1955 cooperativization turned into an intensive national campaign to consolidate the lower-level cooperatives into what were called higher-level or advanced agricultural producers' cooperatives. In the previous stages there had been signs of a return to more traditional forms of village solidarity, and increased returns as well as greater stability had helped elicit the peasant's acquiescence or, in many cases, his enthusiastic approval. There was a more selective and negative reaction to the higher-level cooperative. Evidence suggests that the greatest approval was obtained in areas that had reached a modest but still not advanced level of agricultural and commercial development. Where subsistence agriculture prevailed and few rural markets existed, tradition-bound villagers resisted or failed to support the larger cooperatives; where the most modern commercialization existed, the cooperatives appeared to be too primitive for the peasants to accept with equanimity.

Higher-level cooperatives

The pivotal group in most cases was the middle peasant —a farmer able to live off his own land. The advanced cooperative was particularly disadvantageous to the wealthier peasants because it invested the cooperative itself with title to the land, granting no right of withdrawal, and because wages were based on labour performed, not land contributed. This also made middle peasants resent landless peasants, whom the party was recruiting into the new cooperatives. Also, the advanced form, modelled on the Soviet *kolkhoz*, brought with it the outside political controls that were necessary to extract the agricultural surpluses required to pay for China's capital equipment in its industrialization and to feed the workers moving into the cities to man the growing industries. Many middle peasants actively resisted these changes and the measures for enforcing them, particularly grain rationing, compulsory purchase quotas, and stricter regulations on savings and wage rates.

A vehement debate arose within the Central Committee in 1955 over the urgency of these measures for increased centralization and the degree to which modifications on a local basis could be tolerated. Opposition thus came from both senior officials and middle peasants. Nevertheless Mao personally called for a "high tide of socialization in the countryside" and insisted that it coincide with a full nationalization of urban industries and businesses. As a result Chinese agricultural organization in 1956 reached the approximate level of collectivization achieved in the Soviet Union—a peasant owned his house, some domestic animals, a garden plot, and his personal savings; by the end of 1956, 88 percent of China's peasant households were organized into advanced cooperatives.

Political development. The successful reduction of private ownership in the first years of the "transition to Socialism" was accompanied by a gradual transformation to "more democratic means of leadership." At the outset of its rule in cities and towns, for example, the Communist Party had retained the existing forms of urban control and collective responsibility (*pao-chia*). After the takeover in 1949 real power had been placed in the hands of military control commissions, which gradually turned their functions over to party-dominated civilian governments. Follow-up regulations provided for a fully elaborated urban administration with a number of functional bureaus, as well as for elected councils of representatives. An integrated political regime emerged in each city, which was built pyramid-like from residents groups and committees to street offices and public security stations, and thence to the organs of the district and municipal governments. City officials were jointly responsible to elected congresses, to higher-level administrations, and most especially to the relevant party office.

These basic-level institutions were sufficiently operational by 1954 that the party could establish a nationwide system of people's congresses at the national, provincial, and local levels. On September 20, 1954, the First National People's Congress adopted the first Constitution of the People's Republic of China, somewhat optimistically reformulating the principles of state operation according to a condition of national unity and cooperation in class relationships. The document, however, retained certain dictatorial aspects, in order, it was argued, to deal with remaining domestic and foreign enemies. According to Article 4 of the Constitution, the state system was still to be considered a transitional one. It would rely "on the organs of state and social forces" and use "socialist industrialization and transformation" to insure "the gradual elimination of systems of exploitation and the building of a socialist society." Presumably, the completion of the transformation to a socialist system would lay the foundation for yet another state constitution.

Basic level institutions

The transition to Socialism also had major implications for China's cities. It had become quite clear that the initial emphasis on urban law and order, factory production, and the bureaucratic elite in 1949 had led to building up the cities at the expense of the countryside. Although most Communist leaders insisted that the burdens of industrialization should fall equally on the rural and urban sectors, there is no evidence that these leaders would have tolerated any weakening of the urban build-up. Despite repeated pleas in the 1950s for the cities to share their advantages with surrounding towns and vil-

Rapid
growth
of city
popula-
tions

lages, the attractiveness of the city and the priority given urban development remained obvious, and peasants poured into the cities in a wave that grew as the movement to establish higher-level cooperatives in the countryside intensified. The urban population jumped from over 77,000,000 in 1953 to 99,500,000 in 1957 and to 130,000,000 in 1961; no techniques could be devised to halt the flow.

The pressures on the city thus mounted as it assumed a more central and favoured place. One aspect of the problem affected education. In this period, "transition to Socialism" meant campaigns of mass education to eliminate illiteracy and to train ever larger numbers of people in modern technology. These included the retraining of teachers by means of ideological reform movements, the writing of new textbooks or the translation of Soviet texts, and a mushrooming of adult education programs. While emphasis was placed on a more rigorous Western-style education through high school and university levels for a greater number of youth, the central leadership became concerned over the disinterest of urban youth in perpetuating the ideals of the revolution. Educational programs seemed only to intensify the interest in science and technology, orienting youth toward personal achievement rather than self-sacrifice and devotion to the nation, which might require them to follow less prestigious careers. Many party leaders thus came to feel that, in the transition to Socialism, those who had attended school longest or had otherwise received the most advantages were often the least reliable candidates, ideologically speaking, for higher-level positions or even membership in Communist organizations.

Some top leaders became convinced that their revolutionary ideals were being fundamentally threatened by the emergence of such nonrevolutionary and careerist sentiments among the urban youth and intellectuals. Some even associated these sentiments with the alleged "revisionist" attitudes that by the late 50s and early 60s were becoming manifest in the Soviet Union and eastern Europe. That element of the leadership closest to Mao had sought to rule on the premise that the party could induce rapid change and industrialization without changing its revolutionary values and methods or becoming dominated by apolitical industrial technicians and scientists. These developments fundamentally challenged that hope at the same time that the urban bias brought an increasing frustration among the rural youth and peasants whose sympathies had once substantially undergirded the Communist revolutionary cause.

By the end of this period uncertainty thus began to grow about the wisdom of continuing the city as the centre of gravity, despite the cities' importance as commercial and production centres. The effective nationalization of industrial and business enterprises through the device of joint state–private operation and interest payments to the former owners on state-appraised value of their share complicated the problem. Although industrialists and merchants comprising the national bourgeoisie ceased to exist as a class, they were able to influence the tone of urban life and make the cities even less congenial to the fostering of Communist values. Objectively measured, the society had thus moved closer to the classless ideal; yet many class attitudes and styles persisted. As class labels lost their objective meaning and people learned the proper proletarian vocabulary, the problem of further progress toward a socialist society grew more subtle and more difficult for the leadership.

Domestic policy. Despite the growth of problems, the Communists' confidence in their ultimate success remained high. Substantial economic gains had been recorded in the first five-year plan, and the transition to Socialism had been largely attained by rapid agricultural collectivization and the nationalization of industry and commerce; an atmosphere of success and self-congratulation prevailed at the party's Eighth National Congress (September 1956). At this landmark session the party elite formalized its national leadership apparatus and wrote the party constitution that was to guide the Communist operations for the next decade.

This regularization of the party machinery was necessitated by a steady increase in party membership and a change in its composition during the first seven years of Communist rule. The typical party members before 1949 were the exemplary soldier and the peasant, but after liberation, technicians and educated youths, particularly young workers, were considered the most desirable recruits. In 1951 and 1952 the qualifications for party membership were raised, emphasizing its elitist character and organizational solidarity. By 1956, with recruitment regulations giving preference to university-trained intellectuals, 14 percent of the members were workers, 69.1 percent peasants, 11.7 percent intellectuals, and 5.2 percent of "other" class status. Membership grew from about 4,500,000 in 1949 to almost 10,750,000 in 1956 (by 1961 it had exceeded 17,000,000).

The elitist tone was echoed in official statements of the party Congress on cadre training and organization. As then defined, cadres were individual officials in responsible or leading positions. They might be compared to the officer corps, with state-determined ranks and commensurate salary scales. In theory the Communists stressed the need for constant circulation within the cadre profession. Not all cadres were party members, although substantial effort was made to have all non-party cadres meet party standards. Behind the official doctrine, however, cadre behaviour deviated sharply from Mao's revolutionary ideal. As revealed by various documents that emerged during the Great Proletarian Cultural Revolution, many cadres enjoyed special privileges, acted as petty tyrants, and joined informal networks for protection and advancement. Even at the 1956 Congress some dissatisfaction was expressed concerning the low motivation and qualifications of new party members, and decisions were taken to revitalize revolutionary traditions and to propagandize mass-line doctrines (requiring direct consultation with and attention to the citizenry) that had been forgotten in the first years of rule. A party rectification campaign was launched in 1957 and thence a bold political line that was to set the tone for the next several years.

Policies toward intellectuals changed first. The leadership's policies in the past had reflected considerable ambivalence toward the intelligentsia—on the one hand it required their services and prestige, but on the other it suspected that many were untrustworthy, coming from urban and bourgeois backgrounds and often having close family and other personal ties with the Kuomintang. After 1949 and particularly during the first part of the Korean War, the Central Committee had launched a major campaign to re-educate teachers and scientists and to discredit Western-oriented scholarship. In 1951 the emphasis had shifted from general campaigns to self-reform; in 1955 it had shifted once again to an intensive thought-reform movement, following the purge of Hu Feng, until then the party's leading spokesman on art and literature. This latter movement had coincided with the denunciation of a scholarly study of the *Dream of the Red Chamber*, an 18th-century novel of tragic love and declining fortunes in a Chinese family. Literature without a clear class moral had received blistering criticism, as had any hint that the party should not command art and literature—a theme identified with the ousted Hu Feng. For months thereafter "Hu Feng elements" had been exposed among intellectuals in schools, factories, and cooperatives.

The intensity of these attacks slackened in early 1956. Party leaders publicly discussed the role of intellectuals in the new tasks of national construction and adopted the line of "Let a hundred flowers blossom, a hundred schools of thought contend." Because intellectuals in China were simply high school graduates (intellectuals) and those with college or advanced professional training (higher intellectuals), the policy affected a vast number of people. The "hundred flowers" line explicitly encouraged "free ranging" discussion and inquiry, with the explicit assumption that this would prove the superiority of Marxism-Leninism and speed the conversion of intellectuals to Communism. Their response was gradual and

1956 party
constitu-
tion

The
"Hundred
Flowers"
Campaign

cautious to the party's invitation for free discussion and criticism. Instead of embracing Marxism, moreover, many used the opportunity to translate and discuss Western works and ideas and blithely debated "reactionary" doctrines at the very moment Hungarian intellectuals were triggering a wave of anti-Communist sentiment in Budapest.

Following this initial phase of the Hundred Flowers Campaign, Mao issued what was perhaps his most famous post-1949 speech, "On the Correct Handling of Contradictions Among the People" (February 27, 1957). Its essential message was ambiguous. He stressed the importance of resolving "non-antagonistic contradictions" by methods of persuasion, but stated that "democratic" methods of resolution would have to be consistent with centralism and discipline. He left it unclear when a contradiction might become an "antagonistic" and no-holds-barred struggle. This speech was particularly confusing because its final authoritative version, not published until June, contained explicit limits on the conduct of debate that had been absent in the original. According to the June text, the party would judge words and actions to be correct only if they united the populace, were beneficial to Socialism, strengthened the state dictatorship, consolidated organizations, especially the party, and generally helped strengthen international Communism. These textual manipulations, moreover, led to an unresolved controversy concerning the initial intent of Mao's speech.

The leadership's explanation was that Mao had set out to trap the dangerous elements among the intellectuals by encouraging their criticism of the party and government. An alternative view was that the leaders used the metaphor of the trap to rationalize their reaction to the unanticipated criticism, popular demonstrations, and general anti-party sentiments expressed in the late spring, when the term hundred flowers gained international currency. Whatever the correct explanation, the Communist leaders had encouraged free criticism of the party and its programs, and they had then turned on their critics as rightists and counterrevolutionaries. In June non-Communists who had thrown caution to the winds reaped the full fury of retaliation in an antirightist campaign.

Foreign policy. Chinese foreign policy between 1953 and 1957 reflected the success and greater confidence in domestic programs. By the end of the Korean War the Chinese had begun the long-delayed task of transforming the economy, and they reorganized their military forces along more conventional, Soviet lines. These changes were accompanied, in 1953–55, by major debates concerning the applicability of foreign, especially Soviet, models of industrialization. While taking their principal cues in their foreign policies from domestic developments and generally adhering to the initial pro-Soviet line, the Chinese began to act—on the basis of several important lessons gained during the Korean struggle—to reduce Peking's militant and isolationist attitudes in international affairs. In Korea Peking had recognized that the great costs of the war, the questionable reliability of Soviet military backing, and the danger of direct American retaliation against China had come close to threatening its very existence. Although in preserving North Korea as a Communist state China had attained its principal strategic objective, its leaders understood the costs and risks involved and were determined to exercise a greater caution in their international dealings. Another lesson was that the neutralist states in Asia and Africa were not Western puppets, and it was politically profitable to promote friendly relations with them. These lessons, as reinforced by domestic considerations, led China to take a conciliatory role in the Geneva Conference on Indochina in 1954 and to try to normalize its foreign relations.

Premier Chou En-lai symbolized China's more active diplomatic role at the Asian-African Conference held at Bandung, Indonesia, in April 1955. His slogan was "unity with all," according to the line of peaceful coexistence. This "Bandung line" associated with Chou gained world-

Lessons from the Korean War

wide attention when he told the Bandung delegates that his government was fully prepared to achieve normal relations with all countries, including the United States. As a result of his initiative, ambassadorial talks between China and the United States were begun in Geneva (and later transferred to Warsaw).

Between 1955 and 1957, however, changes in Soviet and American policies caused Chinese leaders to doubt the validity of this more cautious and conciliatory foreign policy. At the 20th Congress of the Soviet Communist Party in 1956, Party Secretary Nikita Khrushchev announced a de-Stalinization policy and set in motion a chain of events that was to lead to a lessening of the Soviet commitment to ideological solidarity above national differences. Antagonisms based on different national traditions, revolutionary experiences, and levels of development, which had been submerged since the 1950 Treaty of Friendship, Alliance, and Mutual Assistance, broke through to the surface. Where once the Chinese had declared their intention to lean toward the Soviet Union, they now began to question how far the Soviet Union would support China and its national interests. Subsequent revelations have indicated that Peking in 1957 obtained Moscow's commitment to supply China with information and material to build nuclear weapons, but that this agreement broke down as the Chinese resisted Moscow's insistence on exercising control over China's defense policy as a quid pro quo and explored a more independent policy.

The new policy can be traced to Mao's statement during a Moscow trip in November 1957 that the "East wind prevails over the West wind." This implied a return to militant struggle. According to some estimates, the change in line was necessitated by America's building up of anti-Communist regimes to encircle China and by the lack of major gains in peaceful coexistence with the Third World neutrals. Other analysts argue that Mao regarded the launching of a Soviet space vehicle (October 1957) and the Sino-Soviet nuclear-sharing agreement as indications that the balance of world forces had changed in favour of Communism.

Return to a militant struggle

At a plenary meeting of the Central Committee convened at that time, a debate on the overall direction of domestic and foreign policy led within months to decisions for a new national policy direction.

New directions in national policy, 1958–61. The pressures behind the dramatic inauguration in 1958 of "three red banners"—the general line of Socialist construction, the Great Leap Forward, and the rural people's communes—are still not fully known. The successful completion of the first five-year plan had resulted in substantial disagreement within the highest leadership over projects for the next plan. There appears to have been increasing impatience with Soviet developmental strategy and a larger concern that reliance on Soviet economic and military aid might result in a gradual erosion of Chinese independence. On the other hand, more philosophical issues were also at stake, for behind the discussion on the optimum rates of economic development, the correct size and location of the social units for development, and the appropriate political mechanisms for monitoring and rectifying personal attitudes during the transition to an independent economy, lay differing philosophies about Communist man. The question was: would modernization lead China down a Western path to Socialism or could the country become something uniquely Chinese?

Even in 1956 a change in emphasis could be detected. The drums began to sound for more intensive political study and for party and governmental cadres to conduct "investigation and research" among the general populace. By the following April the party had received Mao's blueprint for handling "non-antagonistic" class conflict, as well as instructions for a party rectification movement. Communist unity, no longer assumed, was being enforced.

The rectification movement, when transformed into the Hundred Flowers attack on Communist programs and party rule, shattered Mao's presumption that the populace

The party rectification movement

supported his policies. Following the antirightist campaign in the last half of 1957 and the more activist approach toward economic development and international politics, Chinese party leaders proclaimed that a united, politically conscious population could overcome all obstacles in whatever sphere. In this spirit party officials in the winter of 1957–58 scrapped economic programs based on capital investment and Soviet-style planning, and spoke of a turning point that they felt would usher China into the Communist era in advance of all other states. The goals of the second five-year plan (1958–62) consequently had an open-ended quality, making cautious planning and technically oriented planners obsolete. A new political line summarized the change in approach.

This general line of socialist construction was announced at the second session of the Eighth Party Congress (May 1958), which concentrated as much on political slogans as on specific objectives. The general line was defined as "going all out and pressing ahead consistently to achieve greater, faster, better, and more economical results." Special emphasis was placed on political guidance by party cadres of the country's scientists and technicians, who were viewed as potentially dangerous unless they would become fully "Red and expert." The progressive indoctrination of experts would be paralleled by introductory technical training for cadres, thereby in theory transforming the entire elite into political-technical generalists. The 1958 Congress called for a bold form of ideological leadership that could unleash a "leap forward" in technical innovation and economic output. To link the new generalist leaders and the "masses," emphasis fell on sending cadres to the lower levels (*hsia fang*) for first-hand experience and manual labour and for practical political indoctrination.

Mass participation in campaigns, study programs, and "speak bitterness" sessions for the denunciation of "class enemies," already a feature of the Chinese landscape, became a way of life during the Great Leap Forward. The change was especially dramatic in literature and the performing arts. Peasants and workers were encouraged to write poetry, newspaper articles, songs, and scripts for plays. Mao's own poetry became the object of reverent study. Particularly popular among the peasants were small travelling troupes that combined lively drama with propaganda, often humorously. Traditional forms of itinerant drama and local operas underwent political scrutiny and were rewritten to suit the times. Some recalled revolutionary glories or an instructive victory in the land reform or the Korean War; others praised the leadership and its programs and set to song and dance the party's calls for public spiritedness, sanitation, and loyalty to the revolution.

Yet even in the arts, a lack of uniform response could be seen. While many of the changes increased popular participation and innovation, movies and music displayed a greater professional, even Soviet, bias. By the early 1960s the arts evoked considerable controversy, and by the time of the Great Proletarian Cultural Revolution in 1966, the resolution of that controversy in favour of mass participation had become a principal object of Mao's concern.

In the context of the Great Leap Forward, the urban bias of the first eight years was repudiated. The leadership again placed its faith in the peasantry and gave priority to agricultural development. The prototype of the true Communist was thought to be found serving in the villages or in huge water-conservancy projects in the countryside. This man, typically a lower-level party cadre, was heralded as the model for the transformation of the entire society. The decision to shift the "centre of gravity" back to the countryside was thus not a rejection of the objectives of 1950 to build China into a modern industrial state; rather it represented a faith that the human resources for achieving that objective could be found on the farm.

Thus, the general line of 1958 may be seen as a strategy to transform China in accordance with the revolutionary doctrines on which the 1949 victory had supposedly rested. Mao began to resist more actively the erosion of

The Great Leap Forward

revolutionary values in the city, and sought to strengthen them with an alternative instrument for effective social change in the countryside.

The rural people's communes became that instrument. Although more than 1,000 urban communes were temporarily set up in 1959–60, the commune movement was essentially rural-based. Drawing lessons from the experimental consolidation of advanced cooperatives in central China, the communes were designed to become large, self-sufficient organizations that would arrange all activities for the peasants, from farming and marketing to education, administration, and public security. The Central Committee's Resolution on the Establishment of People's Communes in the Rural Areas (August 29, 1958) called for the rapid creation of communes, which would accelerate the transition to state ownership of all property and large-scale agricultural planning. After about six months, the communes were organized hierarchically into production brigades (comparable to the advanced cooperatives) and production teams (comparable to the lower-level cooperatives) throughout most of China, with 24,000 communes averaging 5,000 households each.

There are many interpretations of the changes in rural organization after the communes were first established. One view is that the communes, as initially created, upset ages-old commercial and social patterns and provoked an antagonistic reaction that aggravated, or perhaps caused, social breakdown and widespread starvation during the next so-called three hard years (1959–61). Once again peasants in the less developed rural areas generally considered the commune too advanced, while those around the industrialized regions found it crude or oppressive. Economically it was unsuited for the management of production and social organization in most areas. Politically it ran afoul of the spirit of localism that had gained substantial momentum during the collectivization movement before 1957, making it impossible for commune cadres from the outside to reconcile competing and intense local interests. Hastily conceived, the 1958 commune system in many places remained an aspiration on paper, while in others it faltered under the impact of famine and political unrest. When the pleas of the peasants for food and order went unanswered, they turned on the cadres and in large areas of China joined forces in riots and even rebellions. Many analysts discount these difficulties, however, and argue instead that the communes after initial adjustments helped the countryside survive the "three hard years."

Differences of opinion on the commune were also recorded in the Communist leadership. In August 1959 the Central Committee met in an atmosphere of mounting crisis and recrimination (the meeting is usually referred to as the Lushan Plenum). It was soon discovered that inflated inferences had been drawn from incorrect or falsified "Great Leap" statistics. Even the bad crop weather added to the gloom and encouraged opponents of the more radical domestic and foreign policies, especially a group in the military headed by the minister of defense, P'eng Te-huai. P'eng sent a letter of opinion to Mao outlining his objections to the "short-comings and errors" that had accompanied the formation of the communes. He was especially critical of reliance on mass movements in economic construction, particularly a movement to create backyard steel furnaces. He argued that "putting politics in command is no substitute for economic principles" and implied that a full reappraisal of the Great Leap approach was in order. Branded a right opportunist, P'eng and other members of his clique were drummed out of their leadership positions, and a general purge directed by the new minister of defense, Lin Piao, began a shakeup of the military and of the top political echelons. Many observers consider this the opening act of the thoroughgoing purge that occurred in the Great Proletarian Cultural Revolution seven years later.

The Central Committee acknowledged the need for a readjustment and a strengthening of centralized control. It revitalized the higher- and lower-level cooperatives, now labelled production brigades and production teams.

The rural people's communes

A "three-level system of ownership" eventually emerged, with real power lodged in the production teams. Within a few years the operating system had been shifted from the commune level to the teams, each comprising from 20 to 30 households. The actual state of collectivization thus came to approximate that of 1954 or 1955. Moreover, in 1963–64 the communes were quietly divided into 74,000 new ones, with traditional marketing units taken into account in drawing commune boundaries. Practical compromises were also made in doctrine, and party cadres generally adopted a more localist and pragmatic approach. Mao's dream of a continuing revolution and a breakthrough to the final Communist stage remained unrealized.

Three-level system of ownership

Supporters of Great Leap policies were also confronted at home by the spectre of the very revisionism (deviation from revolutionary Marxism) they had denounced in the Soviet Union. The widening divergence between official pronouncements and Chinese realities was becoming manifest at the moment that Peking was engaged in a growing dispute with Moscow and dissenters within the Central Committee. Relations with the Soviet Union had begun to deteriorate, and the Chinese had declared themselves the world centre of revolutionary orthodoxy. On the defensive, the leadership publicly justified the awkwardness of the situation by blaming bad weather, lower-level cadres, and the Soviets for the economic collapse of 1960. By removing technicians and advisers sent to China during the first five-year plan, Moscow, it was alleged, had deliberately undermined the faltering Chinese economy. Afterward, all efforts to make piecemeal adjustments came to a halt as the economy plummeted into chaos.

Readjustment and reaction, 1961–65. The years 1961–65 did not resemble the three previous ones, despite the persistence of radical labels and slogans. The Chinese themselves were loath to acknowledge the end of the Great Leap period, declaring the validity of the general line of socialist construction and its international revolutionary ("East wind") corollary for one and all.

Reality can be seen, however, in the increasing role of the Chinese military and security personnel. At a top level meeting of the Military Affairs Committee in October 1960 and at one of the rare plenary sessions of the party's Central Committee the following January, the elite gave the highest priority to the restoration of security and national order. Its decision was, first, to gain effective control of the army and then to re-establish political orthodoxy, using soldiers to man indoctrination programs. Party recruitment procedures were tightened, and a major thought-reform movement was launched within the cadres' ranks. The Central Committee also established six supraprovincial regional bureaus charged with enforcing obedience to Peking and bringing the new procedures for control into line with local conditions. The army, now firmly under Lin Piao, took the lead, beginning with a "purification" movement against dissidents within its own ranks. Throughout 1961 and most of 1962 the central officials worked to consolidate their power and to restore faith in their leadership and goals.

In January 1962 the Central Committee convened one of a long series of secret work conferences, in which the implications of these adjustments for the long-run Communist goals were assessed and debated. (In the Cultural Revolution that began some four years later, this conference was said to mark a watershed in Mao's views on the need for renewing class struggle and in his dissatisfaction with many of his comrades in the leadership elite.) By this time Mao, as he later put it, had moved to the "second line" to concentrate "on dealing with questions of the direction, policy, and line of the party and the state." The "first line" administrative and day-by-day direction of the state had been given to Liu Shao-ch'i, who had assumed the chairmanship of the Chinese People's Republic in 1959; additional responsibilities in the first line were given to Teng Hsiao-p'ing, another tough-minded organizer who, as general secretary, was the party's top administrator. By 1962 Mao had apparently begun to conclude that the techniques used by these comrades in the first line not only violated the basic thrust of the revolutionary tradition but also formed a pattern of error that mirrored "modern revisionism" in the Soviet Union.

Assessment of long-run goals

Revelations during the Cultural Revolution also suggest that opposition to Mao and his programs took a sharper and much more organized form within the cultural and educational communities from 1962 on. Essays satirizing the alleged incompetence of the Chinese leader were openly published in journals and newspapers, and some evidence even suggests the existence of a closer relationship between dissident intellectuals and their "protectors" in the top party command.

None of this, however, was evident in 1962 to the outside observer or even, it would seem, to most of the Chinese leadership. There was an outward appearance of confidence, as challenges from within and without were met and overcome. Internally, by cautious moves and by dint of the labour of the population, the economy gradually moved onto the path of recovery, and the morale of the people seemed to improve. In September 1962 the party's Central Committee held another plenary session and called for the consolidation and continued adjustment of the economy, the strengthening of the army and public security forces, the augmentation of the Central Control Commission and Secretariat, and the launching of a national movement for "socialist education."

That movement quickly dominated the countryside and had a major effect on efforts to purify the party's ranks. Socialist education at first had a rather abstract quality, because people had to measure their lives against the "thought of Mao Tse-tung," a slogan that was to grow in popularity. The emphasis was on the need to study Mao's *Selected Works* and to recall the glories of the revolutionary struggle.

Dispute with India

Events on the Sino-Indian border in the fall of 1962 gave this emphasis a more militant cast and helped the People's Liberation Army re-establish discipline and its image. From 1959 to 1962 both India and China, initially as a by-product of a rebellion in Tibet, resorted to military force along their disputed border. On October 12, 1962, a week before the Chinese invaded the disputed border territories held by India, Prime Minister Nehru of India stated that the Indian army was to free all Indian territory of "Chinese intruders." In the conflict that followed, Peking's regiments defeated the Indian army in the border region, penetrating well beyond it. The Chinese then withdrew from most of the invaded area and established a demilitarized zone on either side of the line of control. Thereafter, Sino-Indian tensions continued, with Peking providing small amounts of aid to extremist Indian revolutionary groups and with closer relationships between China and Pakistan, India's enemy. Most significantly, the leadership seized on the army's victory and began to experiment with the possibility of using army heroes as the ideal types for popular emulation.

Increasingly preoccupied with indoctrinating its heirs and harking back to revolutionary days, Peking's leaders closest in outlook to Mao and Lin Piao viewed the soldier-Communist as the most suitable candidate for the second and third generation leadership. Army uniformity and discipline, it was seen, could transcend the divided classes; and all army men could be made to comply with the rigorous political standards set by Mao's leadership.

The militancy of subsequent campaigns to learn from army heroes, or from the People's Liberation Army as a whole, was echoed in international politics. In a tour of Africa in late 1963 and early 1964, Chou En-lai startled his hosts by calling for revolution in newly independent states and openly challenged the Soviet Union for the leadership of the Third World. Simultaneously, China challenged America's alliance system by establishing formal relations with France, and the Soviet Union's system by forming closer ties with Albania.

Peking's main target was Moscow. A Soviet-American crisis in Cuba (October 1962) had coincided with the

The end of
Sino-
Soviet
unity

Sino-Indian struggle, and in both cases the Chinese believed the Soviet Union had acted unreliably and timidly and had become "capitulators" of the worst sort. For the next months polemicists in Peking and Moscow laid their differences before the world in barbed exchanges and lengthy treatises. When the Soviet Union signed a partial Nuclear Test-Ban Treaty with the United States and Great Britain in July 1963, Chinese articles accused the Soviets of joining an anti-Chinese conspiracy.

Confronted by this new strategic situation, the Chinese shifted their priorities to support an antiforeign line and to promote the country's "self-reliance." Mao's calls for "revolutionization" acquired a more nationalistic aspect, and the People's Liberation Army assumed an even larger place in Chinese political life.

These many-sided trends seemed to collide in 1963 and 1964. With the split in the international Communist movement, the party in late 1963 called on intellectuals, including those in the cultural sphere, to undertake a major reformulation of their academic disciplines to support China's new international role. The initial assignment for this reformulation fell to Chou Yang, a party intellectual and deputy director of the Central Committee's Propaganda Department, whose statement of October 26, 1963—officially heralded as providing the guidelines for future research and publication—tried to enlist China's intellectuals in the ideological war against Soviet revisionism and in the struggle for rigidly pure political standards. (Less than three years later, however, Chou Yang was purged as a revisionist and many intellectuals were condemned as Mao's opponents.)

Closely connected with the concerns of the intellectuals were those relating to the party and the Communist Youth League. A drive began to cultivate what one author called "new-born forces," and by mid-1964 young urban intellectuals were embroiled in a major effort by the Central Committee to promote those forces within the party and league; meanwhile their rural cousins were buffeted by moves to keep the Socialist education campaign under the party's organizational control through the use of "work teams" and a cadre-rectification movement.

Mao in the summer of 1964 wrote a document entitled "On Khrushchev's Phoney Communism and Its Historical Lessons for the World," which summarized most of Mao's doctrinal principles on contradictions, class struggle, and political structure and operation. This summary provided the basis for the re-education ("revolutionization") of all youth hoping to succeed to the revolutionary cause. This high tide of revolutionization lasted until early August, when American air strikes on North Vietnam raised the spectre of war on China's southern border. A year-long debate followed on the wisdom of conducting disruptive political campaigns during periods of external threat.

Effects
of the
war in
Indochina

This period may now be interpreted as a time of major decision within China. One ingredient of the debate was whether to prepare rapidly for conventional war against the United States or to continue the revolutionization of Chinese society, which in Mao's view had fundamental, long-term importance for China's security. Those who argued for a postponement of the internal political struggle supported more conventional strategies for economic development and took seriously Soviet calls for "united action" in Vietnam and the establishment of closer Sino-Soviet ties. Their position, it was later alleged, received the backing of the general staff under Lo Jui-ch'ing. With the dispatch of about 50,000 logistical personnel to Vietnam after February 1965, factional lines began to divide the military forces according to ideological or national-security preferences.

Meanwhile some members tried to restore rigid domestic controls. Where Mao in May 1963 had called for an upsurge in revolutionary struggle, other leaders in the following September circumscribed the area of cadre initiative and permitted a free-market system and private ownership of rural plots to flourish. A stifling of the revolutionary upsurge was supposedly evident in regulations of June 1964 for the organization of poor and lower mid-

dle peasant associations, and by early 1965 Mao could point to bureaucratic tendencies throughout the rural areas. In a famous document on problems arising in the course of the Socialist education campaign, usually referred to as the "23 articles," Mao in January 1965 stated, for the first time, that the principal enemy was to be found within the party and once more proclaimed the urgency of class struggle and mass-line politics.

It was in this period of emphasis on self-reliant struggle that China acquired nuclear weapons. China's nuclear programs can be traced to Mao's speech "On the 10 Major Relationships" in April 1956, when he said:

> On such a basis [of national economic construction], our defense construction will progress faster. In this way, we shall have not only many airplanes and guns but also our own atomic bombs in the not too distant future.

Although the Soviet Union supported Chinese nuclear aims for a time, this effort was taken over completely by the Chinese after June 1959. By 1964 the costs of the program had forced a substantial reduction in other defense costs. China's first atomic explosion (October 16, 1964) affected the debate by appearing to support Mao's contention that domestic revolutionization would in no way jeopardize long-term power aspirations and defense capabilities.

China's
first atomic
explosion

Mao's military thinking, a product of his own civil war experiences and an essential component of his ideology, stressed the importance of people's war during the transition to nuclear status. He felt that preparation for such a war could turn China's weaknesses into military assets and reduce its vulnerability. Mao's view of people's war belittled the might of modern advanced weapons as "paper tigers" but recognized that China's strategic inferiority subjected it to dangers largely beyond its control. His reasoning thus made a virtue out of necessity in the short run, when China would have to depend on its superior numbers and the morale of its people to defeat any invader. In the long run, however, he held that China would have to have nuclear weapons to deprive the superpowers of their blackmail potential and to deter their aggression against smaller states.

Lin Piao repeated Mao's position on people's war on September 3, 1965. Lin further argued that popular insurrections against non-Communist governments could succeed only if they took place without substantial foreign assistance. To the extent that indigenous rebels came to depend on outside support, inevitably their bonds with the local populace would be weakened. When this happened, the rebellion would wither for lack of support. On the other hand, the hardships imposed by relying on indigenous resources would stimulate the comradeship and the ingenuity of the insurgents. Equally important, Lin's statement also indicated a high-level decision for China to remain on the defensive.

Lin's speech coincided with yet another secret working conference of the Central Committee, in which the Maoist group reissued its call for cultural revolutionization, this time convinced that the 1964 effort had been deliberately sabotaged by senior party and military officials. Initiated by Mao and Lin, the purge first struck dissident army leaders, especially the chief of staff, Lo Jui-ch'ing; and as the power struggle began, China turned its back on the war in Vietnam and other external affairs. The Lin Piao statement and the September meeting may be taken as the beginning of the Great Proletarian Cultural Revolution.

The Great Proletarian Cultural Revolution, 1966–69. As the clash over issues in the autumn of 1965 became polarized, the army initially provided the battleground. The issues concerned differences over policy directions and their implications for the organization of power and the qualifications of senior officials to lead. Much of the struggle went on behind the scenes; in public it took the form of personal vilification and ritualized exposés of divergent world views or, inevitably, "two lines" of policy. Lin, in calling for the creative study and application of Mao's thought in November and at a meeting of military commissars the following January, consistently placed the army's mission in the context of the national ideological and power struggle. In these critical months the base of operations for Mao and Lin was the large eastern Chinese city of Shanghai; and newspapers published in that city, especially the *Liberation Army Daily*, carried the public attacks on the targets selected.

Attacks on cultural figures. Their first target was the historian Wu Han, who doubled as the deputy mayor of Peking. In a play, Wu had lampooned Mao and lauded the deposed former minister of defense, P'eng Te-huai. The denunciation of Wu and his play on November 10, 1965, constituted the opening volley in an assault on cultural figures and their intellectual products.

During a five-month period in which he remained hidden from public view, Mao expressed particular concern about the education of youth, which he said took too long and was divorced from reality. As the Cultural Revolution gained momentum, Mao turned for support to the youth as well as the army. In seeking to create a new system of education that would eliminate differences between town and country, workers and peasants, and mental and manual labour, Mao struck a responsive chord within the youth; it was their response that later provided him with his best shock troops. As a principal purpose, the Cultural Revolution was launched to revitalize revolutionary values for the successor generation of Chinese young people.

Mao on education

The bureaucrats, however, had different thoughts. They had grown increasingly comfortable in office and resistant to disruption and popular initiative. On February 7, 1966, members of the Central Political Bureau (Politburo), notably P'eng Chen and Lu Ting-yi, issued an "outline report" on carrying out cultural reforms. These same individuals, after the widening of the Vietnam War in 1964, had taken a leading role in bottling up the campaign to revolutionize China's youth and, more for this than for the report, were denounced by Mao and Lin as being "Left in form but Right in essence."

During the spring the attack against authors, scholars, and propagandists emphasized the cultural dimension of the Cultural Revolution. Increasingly it was hinted that behind the visible targets lay a sinister "black gang" in the fields of education and propaganda and high up in party circles. Removal of P'eng and Lu and subsequently of Chou Yang, then tsar of the arts and literature, indicated this was to be a thoroughgoing purge. Clearly, a second purpose of the Cultural Revolution would be the elimination of leading cadres whom Mao held responsible for past ideological sins and alleged errors in judgment.

Attacks on party members. Gradual transference of the revolution to top echelons of the party was managed by a group centred on Mao, Lin, Chiang Ch'ing (Mao's wife), and Ch'en Po-ta (Mao's longtime confidant and propagandist). On May 7, 1966, Mao secretly assigned major responsibilities in cultural and educational affairs to the army and labelled the army a "great school" for the nation. Nine days later, a circular of the Central Committee to its subordinate echelons, as well as to leading party elements in the government, mass organizations, and the army, denounced the "outline report" of February 7, which had "done its best to turn the movement to the right" and was a harbinger of "out-and-out revisionism." Another purpose of the Cultural Revolution, as then conceived, would be a "revolution in the superstructure": a transformation from a bureaucratically run machine to a more popularly based system led personally by Mao and a simplified administration under his control.

Following the May instructions, the educational system received priority attention. "Big-character posters," or large wall newspapers, spread from the principal campuses in Peking throughout the land. University officials and professors were singled out for criticism, while their students, encouraged by the central authorities, held mass meetings and began to organize. In June the government dropped examinations for university admissions and called for a reform of entrance procedures and a delay in reopening the campuses. Party officials and their wives circulated among the campuses to gain favour and to obstruct their opponents. Intrigue and political manoeuvring dominated, although political lines were not at first sharply drawn or even well understood. The centres of this activity were Peking's schools and the inner councils of the Central Committee; the students were the activists in a game they did not fully comprehend.

This phase of the Cultural Revolution ended on August 1, 1966, with the convening of a plenary session of the Central Committee. On August 5, Mao issued his own big-character poster to "Bombard the Headquarters," a call for the denunciation and removal of senior officials. "In the last 50 days or so," his poster said, "some leading comrades from the central down to the local levels have acted in a diametrically opposite way." Three days later a 16-point Central Committee decision was issued, in which the broad outlines for the Cultural Revolution were laid down and supporters were rallied to the revolutionary banner. The immediate aim would be to seize power from bourgeois authorities. The locus of the struggle would be their urban strongholds. Now more than ever, Mao's thoughts, soon to be encapsulated in red, plastic-covered books (*Quotations from Chairman Mao Tse-tung*), were taken as the "compass for action."

Inside the Central Committee, Mao and Lin worked to rally support. Adhering to established protocol, Liu Shao-ch'i, Teng Hsiao-p'ing, and others submitted themselves to self-criticism, issuing confessions as well as statements of loyalty to Mao. The Chairman rejected their statements as insincere and incomplete; the die had been cast for a thoroughgoing reorganization at the top.

Leftist power seizures. The drama on the streets of Peking provided the setting for the party's closed-door sessions. Organized into semimilitary groups called Red Guards, millions of youths poured into Peking to "meet with Chairman Mao" in eight great demonstrations held between August 18 and November 26, 1966. They came from all across China by rail, by bus, or, reenacting the Long March of the '30s, by foot. On the way they stormed through towns and cities, creating local rebellions in their wake, and laid siege to lesser "bourgeois authorities." "To rebel is justified," Mao had said. The students took him at his word, and few escaped his wrath. Factionalism soon became rampant within the Red Guards, characterized by a poster war carried out to prove the righteousness of one's own unit and to reveal the latest evil designs of one's adversaries.

The Red Guards

By late November and early December, Mao felt ready to call on leftists to seize power in cities outside Peking. With the populace and party leadership polarized and with the support of the army, the students, and many lower level cadres, Maoists sounded the call to battle in city after city. Only sporadically did the struggle for power affect the peasantry, though from time to time it was necessary to deter villagers from engaging in disruptive activities.

There was no single pattern to the power seizures. Each had its own characteristic and appeared to turn on conflicting local priorities, policies, and political doctrines; practical issues, masked by hysterical outbursts, were usually at stake. The national press exhorted urban residents to seize municipal power and to engage in a series of campaigns, meetings, and "Mao thought" study programs. The criterion of correctness was professed obedience to Mao, and the goal was a participatory political environment at the municipal levels. The most radical demands were made by youths who—under the guise of public service and political indoctrination—had been shipped to the countryside in earlier programs to reduce pressures on urban facilities. Where the conflict intensified, deaths and injuries were common.

In each struggle an emergency atmosphere prevailed, and Mao's broader purposes often were lost from sight. The Chairman held to his conviction that "revolution is a good thing," though increasing efforts were made to regulate the degree of disruption. The army assumed much of this latter burden, despite Mao's urging it to "support the left." The Cultural Revolution Group under Mao and Lin also received the counsel of caution from Chou En-lai.

These conservative pressures enhanced the power of the army and, to Peking's dismay, fostered localism in some commands. Army cadres whose careers had frequently combined political with military missions were given a mandate to overthrow urban party and state bureaucrats and to purify or eliminate suspected city, provincial, and regional institutions. They quickly occupied pivotal positions in police stations, banks, newspapers, warehouses, factories, and party and state units. For all practical purposes the army, though technically allied with the "revolutionary masses" and "revolutionary cadres," became the provisional government of China. It insulated national security sectors (including defense installations) from the strife and took its responsibilities seriously to consolidate production and ensure "revolutionary order."

Revolutionary committees. The most distinctive institutions to come into existence during the Cultural Revolution were the revolutionary committees, which replaced the local party and state organs and became the instruments for army-dominated rule. How successful they were in establishing a genuinely new order is not fully known. Mass movements for criticism of class enemies became widespread at the time the committees were formed and were supplemented in late 1968 by campaigns that urged the populace to prepare for war, thus perpetuating the atmosphere of fear and crisis. There was also a tendency to encourage the return of veteran workers to their former positions, and generally each place worked out its "three-way alliance" of army men, revolutionary cadres, and revolutionary masses, according to each city's conditions.

These local developments restricted the authority of the national leaders and their capacity to act. So marked was the resistance to Peking in many localities during early 1967 that the Maoists referred to this period as an adverse current in which elements in the country joined forces to "reverse the verdict on the bourgeois reactionary line and headquarters headed by Liu Shao-ch'i." Many army commanders sided with local party officials, and some, especially in western China, attempted to insulate themselves from national control. These and others who attempted to create "independent kingdoms" or "centres within centres" proved difficult to dislodge. Many survived the worst period of upheaval.

In March 1967 the Central Committee reacted with restraint. It laid down guidelines for model revolutionary committees and issued open letters to factory cadres and workers to strengthen labour discipline and oppose anarchism. Closely associated with this, however, was a campaign to discredit Liu, then called China's Khrushchev, and all other officials removed in the political struggles.

During this campaign ultra-leftist elements set loose a wave of terror within the country; meanwhile, in many foreign capitals and in Hong Kong, Red Guards within Peking's embassies and the Chinese communities rioted and attacked officials.

The atmosphere of intensifying crisis reached its peak in July 1967. Clashes between armed groups had broken out in many places, causing casualties and serious disruption of the economy. In the industrial city of Wu-han, the resident military commander attempted to mobilize popularly based forces against the radicals, but the Cultural Revolution Group intervened on the radicals' side. When its urgent directives failed to get the desired response, the group dispatched two senior representatives to straighten things out. They were arrested, and Peking was forced to rush military units to Wu-han to rescue the situation.

Steps to ease disruptions. Following the restoration of national authority in Wu-han, the selective dismissal of regional and unit army commanders was accelerated in all parts of China, and the campaign against Liu was intensified. But the central leadership was deeply disturbed by the implication of the Wu-han events, and soon Mao himself made a secret trip to the areas of central China most infected by the spirit of antagonism toward the Maoist excesses. When his trip was finally announced in late September, the Chairman issued one in a long series of "latest instructions"; his message symbolized the ambiguousness of the central authority and the stalemate between Peking and local dissidents.

Several general trends emerged from this uncertain situation, which lasted from August 1967 until a plenary meeting of the Central Committee in October of the next

year. In the more modern areas of eastern and northern China coalitions of army and Maoist groups rapidly won control but became increasingly conservative as they attempted to govern. In these and many other areas the contests between the various groups ebbed and flowed, and only a few areas could stabilize the governing coalition more or less permanently. With the radical tide receding, new leaders, largely unknown outside China, emerged and formed revolutionary committees throughout the provinces.

As radical voices were gradually stilled—though not without protest and widespread feelings of betrayal—a line associated with Chou En-lai became more manifest. Locally, the increased stress on production under experienced cadres and the use of the army where needed restored a type of order only recently condemned by the Maoist press. Power at the centre rested on a simplified administrative apparatus (one-sixth the size of the former apparatus in Peking, according to Chou in 1971), and deposed cadres were sent to retraining camps.

The end of the Cultural Revolution. In 1968 the society began to return to business, though not as usual. China's regular schools were reopened, although the number of students in higher institutions represented only a small percentage of those three years before. In July yet another of Mao's "latest instructions" approved science and engineering education and called for the "return to production" of all graduates.

By October 1968 Mao had signalled the beginning of a new phase and the end of revolutionary disruption. Formalizing the victory and advocating the establishment of a new party and state system, the Central Committee, by then a body vastly different from that of 1966, authorized political reconstruction.

Reconstruction, 1969–71. The meeting of the Central Committee in October 1968 also closed the era of China's turning inward. Almost immediately, the Foreign Ministry called on the United States to resume ambassadorial discussions with a view toward signing a treaty based on peaceful coexistence. Coming on the eve of the inauguration of Richard M. Nixon as U.S. president, the ministry's statement indicated both the outward turning of the regime and its interest in normalizing its international contacts. During this period Peking negotiated diplomatic relations with a number of countries; and at the 1970 session of the United Nations General Assembly it received, for the first time, a majority vote in its bid to be the sole representative of China in that body.

A number of constraints, however, severely circumscribed China's efforts at accommodation. Overtures to the United States were limited by two obstacles: the U.S. presence on Taiwan and the war in Indochina. Reviewing the events of 1963–68, the Chinese concluded that the United States remained hostile toward China. Moreover, the American-Soviet "duopoly," as Peking called it, presented a continuing threat to Chinese security. Throughout the Cultural Revolution the Chinese had laboured to preserve the integrity of their strategic defense programs and had tested hydrogen weapons as well as components of a missile system. When the Nixon administration singled out the "Chinese nuclear threat" in order to win congressional votes for its various defense programs, Peking could see little likelihood of an early improvement in its relations with the United States.

Conflict with the Soviet Union. The Soviet Union was perceived to be the most serious threat to Chinese interests. In their attempt to influence the leadership of the revolutionary or Third World forces globally, the Chinese had challenged Soviet authority in the Communist world. Particularly significant, the Soviet Union began to revise its estimate of the Chinese challenge, not so much for its ideological influence as for what Chinese national policies meant to the security of the Soviet borders with China. From 1966 to 1968 the Soviet Union had augmented army border units, whose presence had forced Peking in 1968–69 to prepare for the possibility of a Soviet invasion. So tense had the situation become by early 1969 that a small incident could have touched off a border conflict. Indeed, many minor conflicts had already occurred; and

Resistance to Peking

Crisis in Wu-han

Recession of the radical tide

it appeared in March, when Chinese and Soviet units in regimental formation finally clashed (on a remote island—Damansky in Russian, Chen-pao in Chinese—in the Ussuri River on China's northeastern frontier), that war between the two states was only a matter of time. Afterward, the Soviet Union took emergency measures to reorganize and strengthen its military units and by the following August felt sufficiently strong to issue an ultimatum to the Chinese to discuss an agreement demarcating the border. Peking thereupon dropped its conditions for border talks, which were begun formally in October.

The triumph of Maoism. The Ussuri incident was still fresh in memory when the Ninth Congress of the Chinese Communist Party met (April 1-24, 1969). This meeting formally ended a four-decade era of political leadership in China. During the Cultural Revolution the revolutionaries' common bonds of ideological belief, loyalty, and organizational solidarity and their world vision had been shattered. The membership of the ninth congress reflected the downgrading of purely party virtues by the added numbers of military commanders and representatives of the "revolutionary masses" present. More than 70 percent of the eighth Central Committee elected in 1956 had been removed from the ranks of the Communist exalted, while more than 40 percent of the reconstituted ninth committee held military posts.

Changes in party leadership

Both Mao and Lin Piao were named in the new party constitution: Mao the leader, Lin his chosen number-two man and successor. The atmosphere of the congress mirrored the Mao personality cult; "little red books," Mao buttons, songs, banners, statues, and an endless hailing of his name and ideas symbolized his triumph. Mao's political reach, however, was based on personal, charismatic authority, and it could not match the influence of the pre-1966 bureaucracy. Most institutions outside Peking now operated relatively independently. Mao's power had been won at the expense of the centre. Mao seemed to appreciate this, and his actions suggested that his mission was largely educational and inspirational.

Continuing power struggle. These complexities complicated the process of rebuilding local party organizations and stabilizing the revolutionary committees—also prolonged by the continuing conflict among rival factions. Substantial bargaining went on in each locality, sometimes over a period of years, to settle the balance of power. It was with these shifting power groups, many of them dominated by local military commanders, that Peking had to negotiate. The party constitution seemed to legitimize this new situation by allowing the basic levels to bypass many intermediate groupings, reporting directly to the Central Committee and to Mao himself. With the party's lines of authority unsettled, however, the election of a new National People's Congress and the preparation of a new state constitution had to be postponed.

These signs of uncertainty within the party and state mirrored the continuing power struggle in Peking. Each move to reunify the leadership merely reopened the Cultural Revolution's wounds; bitter partisanship could transform any policy issue into an opportunity to settle old scores. Officials associated with the ultra-leftist "May 16" faction (including a Politburo member, Ch'en Po-ta) were among those to falter in the contest. While the outside world could only speculate about the causes of the conflict, its results seemed plain enough: the Politburo's effective membership was cut in half in two years, and many groups or programs denounced in the Cultural Revolution were reinstated. The most unexpected move occurred in the summer of 1971, when Mao's personally chosen successor, Lin Piao, and many senior military figures disappeared. Details of Lin's abortive attempts to assassinate the Chairman freely circulated inside China, as did news of his subsequent death in a plane crash while fleeing the country. To fill Lin's place, Premier Chou En-lai stepped into the number-two position.

Fall and death of Lin Piao

Reconstruction, 1972–76. The demise of Lin Piao thus coincided with a complex period of rebuilding party and state institutions. The campaign to denounce Lin and his associates directly affected this rebuilding process and delayed until 1973 the revision of the party constitution and until 1975 the more major revision of the state constitution. It further intensified the long intraparty debate concerning the balance between organizational leadership and mass participation, military security and economic modernization, central authority and local initiative, and Mao's revolutionary outlook and the requirements for an orderly succession. Though many-sided, the debate and resultant political struggles were characterized as a "struggle between two lines," causing many to believe that the Chinese leadership was split into two competing factions. Whatever the political groupings in China and their internal relations, this period was also shaped by the increasing preoccupation with the succession to Mao Tse-tung and his aging colleagues and with the more bitter struggle with the Soviet Union that was to force China into closer relations with the United States.

This second post-Cultural Revolutionary period of reconstruction appeared to concentrate on setting Peking's priorities according to the answers sought to three major questions: Will the next generation remain true to revolutionary values and thereby continue to build China into a Communist society? Will the party and state institutions guide the course of transition successfully or fall prey to bureaucratic stagnation and "capitalist errors"? Will China continue to be built into a powerful modern state capable of joining the front rank of the world's leaders?

The preoccupation with the first question was to continue to give Chinese political life its "radical" tone. Artists, writers, filmmakers, and performers reminded the people, especially the school-age youth, to preserve revolutionary values and combat bourgeois influences. Slogans such as "self-reliance" and "serve the masses" permeated the campaign to denounce Lin Piao as well as the follow-up campaigns against Confucius and Mencius, against selected plays and historical novels, and generally against "Soviet revisionism." Yet, as planning proceeded for the holding of party and state congresses, "revolutionization" became the battle cry of a band of radical officials close to Mao. These officials were led by Mao's wife, Chiang Ch'ing, and Wang Hung-wen, Chang Ch'un-ch'iao, and Yao Wen-yüan, who together were called the Gang of Four. They brooked no compromise with the ideals of the Cultural Revolution. (Indeed, according to some historical accounts made in the early 1980s the period defined as the Cultural Revolution should be extended from 1966 to 1976 to include the activities of the Gang of Four.)

Gang of Four

The answers to the first question (concerning revolutionary values) were thus affected by the second question (concerning institutionalization). In the process of preparing for the 10th National Party Congress in August 1973 and the Fourth National People's Congress in January 1975, the emphasis was placed on greater centralization under the aegis of the party, whose 28,000,000 members were enjoined to occupy the senior positions in all official organizations, including the army and the mass organizations and at the local levels. Compared to some 15 years before, the party and state apparatus was much more streamlined and efficient; but it was also much more conscious of the conflicting demands on it and increasingly concerned about ensuring the orderly transition to a post-Mao leadership.

This was particularly the case because of difficulty in reaching a consensus concerning the third question: how to build China into a powerful modern nation. In his last major speech, a year before his death in January 1976, Premier Chou En-lai set forth the guidelines for China's modernization. He noted that China at the end of the Fifth Five-Year Plan (1976–80) should have built an "independent and relatively comprehensive industrial and economic system." Thereafter, he said, China would "accomplish the comprehensive modernization of agriculture, industry, national defense, and science and technology before the end of the century." These goals came to be known as the "four modernizations."

The "four modernizations"

Soon after delivering this speech, Chou's terminal illness forced him to turn over day-to-day administration to Teng Hsiao-p'ing, who had been denounced in the Cultural Revolution but who, after his rehabilitation in 1973, had become a senior leader in the party and the ranking vice premier. It thus fell to Teng to weigh the policies needed to implement the four modernizations while carrying out the competing goals of fostering revolutionary struggle and maintaining constitutional order. Almost immediately after Chou En-lai's death, the Gang of Four convinced Mao to remove Teng from office, and, in disgracing him, strengthened their own bid for supreme power. There then erupted a tense intraparty struggle during which Mao declared: "Stability and unity do not mean writing off class struggle; class struggle is the key link and everything else hinges on it." As in the Cultural Revolution, Mao's views and the political storm they engendered spilled over into the public arena, first in press articles and then in riots. The main eruption, in T'ien An Men Square in Peking in April 1976, caused numerous injuries and damage to property and was the proximate cause of Teng's abrupt dismissal from all posts on April 7. Thereupon Hua Kuo-feng, a compromise candidate, was promoted to succeed Chou as premier.

After the Cultural Revolution Hua had risen from the relative obscurity of provincial posts in Hunan to the Central Committee in 1969 and to the Politburo in 1973. Appointed vice premier and minister of public security in January 1975, Hua established the political base that enabled him to succeed first Chou and then Mao Tse-tung (who died on September 9, 1976). For a time Hua's position seemed to be challenged by the Gang of Four, who, using the extended campaign against Teng Hsiao-p'ing, demanded unstinting devotion to revolutionary ideals. In October 1976 Hua deposed the Gang of Four and became chairman of the Central Committee. In the ensuing campaign against alleged supporters of the four and their influence, Hua consolidated his power and reaffirmed the goals embodied in the "four modernizations." (In 1981 a special court convicted the four, as well as six associates of Lin Piao, on charges that included conspiracy, suppression, and persecution.)

During the following months Hua exploited his position as Mao's chosen heir to reassert the primacy of economic development. Beginning in December, his lieutenants convened a series of meetings on major problems—agriculture, defense, communications, and industry—and published for the first time Mao's speech of 1956 "On the 10 Major Relationships." In this way Hua based his new policies both on his own evaluation of selected problems and on the authority of Mao's less doctrinaire ideas.

Hua's decline and Teng's ascendancy, 1976–81. Hua's

Hua's
economic
programs

government, assuming power in late 1976, faced huge problems: a narrow and shaky political coalition, an economy disabled by policies and disruptions of the 1960s, a shattered and outmoded educational system, a managerial force ill-equipped for the modern industrial world, and a disgruntled labour force. Hua's immediate problem stemmed from the party's strained relations with the people. He thus moved first to discredit previous unpopular policies as acts of the Gang of Four and then to lessen dissatisfaction by announcing plans for restoring economic order and wage increases for many in the urban labour force. In 1977–78 he introduced incentive bonuses and other measures to meet increasing consumerism.

Reliance on direct material incentives for the consumer-worker, however, did not touch the more fundamental economic problems, and the pace of the Fifth Five-Year Plan scarcely responded. Hua's priorities thereupon shifted to improving industrial management and increasing investment in key economic construction projects. Most dramatic of all, Hua proclaimed a new 10-Year Plan intended to challenge and mobilize the Chinese people.

Yet, behind the scenes, many senior officials almost immediately deemed the plan unattainable. In fact, the lack of realism symbolized by the plan's major targets was quickly tied to the "line of the 11th Party Congress" (held in August 1977). The congress met shortly after Teng Hsiao-p'ing and other officials, who had led the economy in the past, had been rehabilitated but before they had time to influence economic policies significantly. Their authority had only begun to be felt when the 10-Year Plan was announced. As the power of Teng's new coalition grew, so did the spirit of realism and the ques-

tioning of both the plan and the general directions of national policy.

Within a year that questioning had become rejection and with it the beginning of a new political and economic administration under Teng. The inauguration of that administration and its pragmatic economic line, "readjustment, restructuring, consolidation, and improvement," was formalized at the Central Committee's plenary meeting in December 1978, at which the slogan "seek truth from facts" was adopted.

Rise of
Teng

Over the next three years party and state meetings periodically reevaluated and criticized Mao and Hua, rehabilitated many former officials (including some, such as Liu Shao-ch'i, posthumously), assessed the slow progress of economic readjustment, and strengthened the bureaucracy and the system of leadership. Chao Tzu-yang and Hu Yao-pang replaced Hua as state premier and party chairman, respectively, though Teng continued to wield the real power.

THE NATIONALIST GOVERNMENT ON TAIWAN

Comparisons are inevitably made between the mainland and the Republic of China on Taiwan. The island of Taiwan (q.v., with a population of about 17,700,000 in 1980) would be more properly compared to a single Chinese province than to the entire mainland (970,000,000 people), but this comparison is seldom made. Neither is due allowance made for the different levels of industrialization in 1949. Taiwan from 1895 to 1945 formed part of the Japanese Empire. Consequently, Japanese investment in the island had given it a substantial head start toward industrialization and agricultural modernization. The mainland during the same period had undergone economic chaos and war.

Comparisons aside, economic development on Taiwan from 1949 to 1971 was impressive. It contributed significantly to the Nationalist government's role in international politics and helped shape specific policies emanating from Peking and Taipei, the seat of Chiang Kai-shek's government. Chiang's government in 1953 began a series of four-year economic plans that resulted in an average annual growth rate of per capita national income of more than 4 percent.

When the Nationalist refugees (almost 2,000,000 soldiers and their dependents) arrived in Taiwan in the late 1940s, final defeat seemed only a matter of time. Little outside assistance was forthcoming; and the United States, among others, appeared determined to allow the civil war to run its course toward the eventual destruction of the Kuomintang and the incorporation of Taiwan into the People's Republic. The People's Liberation Army, however, placed priority on mopping up holdout Nationalist units on the mainland and on subduing Tibet. And because Peking lacked substantial capability to land its forces on Taiwan or on such remaining Nationalist-held islands as Quemoy and Matsu close by the mainland, there was no immediate prospect of Chiang's final defeat. His survival until the Korean War provided a decisive respite.

When North Korea invaded the south in June 1950, Pres. Harry S. Truman, assuming Peking's complicity from the outset, interposed the U.S. 7th Fleet between Taiwan and the mainland; during the conflict the United States increased its economic and military aid to Taipei. In the first of several major crises over Quemoy and Matsu, following the Korean War, the United States incorporated the Republic of China into its Pacific defense system. A mutual defense treaty signed December 2, 1954, pledged the United States to the defense of Taiwan and the neighbouring Pescadores Islands for the indefinite future.

U.S. intervention in
Korea

After the Bandung Conference (April 1955) there was substantial hope that Peking might limit its tactics to the "peaceful liberation" of Taiwan. During the initial stages of the post-Bandung talks (begun August 1955) between the United States and China, it seemed that this hope might be formalized in a treaty mutually renouncing the use or threats of force in the Taiwan area. These talks broke down, however, and by 1958 Peking had adopted a more militant approach concerning Taiwan. In August

1958 Peking resumed an artillery bombardment of Quemoy and issued an ultimatum demanding the surrender of the island's Nationalist garrison, an ultimatum broken by the interposition of American naval power and the behind-the-scenes withdrawal of Soviet support. After prolonged shelling, both sides agreed by loudspeaker to continue firing only according to specifically arranged schedules; by 1964 only shells containing propaganda leaflets were used in the artillery exchanges.

The extent of American support for Taiwan proved an important factor in the consolidation and rejuvenation of the Nationalist Party and its governmental organs. This rejuvenation could be measured in many ways. One was the dramatic increase in industrial and commercial construction on Taiwan; another was the improvement of communications and educational facilities. Another could be seen by comparing the 99 members elected to the 10th Central Committee of the Kuomintang to the 74 elected to the ninth committee in 1963—generally, the newer group was younger, better educated, more widely travelled, and much less likely to have been selected because of political connections alone.

Antag-onism between Taiwanese and Chiang's forces

Various attempts were made to solve the problem of Taiwanese and mainlander antagonisms. About 90 percent of Taiwan's population belonged to South Chinese ethnic groups (especially Hokkien and Hakka) that had emigrated long before Chiang's arrival and thus considered his forces as intruders or "out-province" strangers. Because many Taiwanese had cooperated with the Japanese—some in puppet governments in China during World War II—and because the central government had not closely monitored its administrators on Taiwan after 1945, harsh official policies had destroyed much of the bond of "Chineseness" that might have helped ease the Chinese takeover in 1945. Islanders held bitter memories of repression, including the murders of leading Taiwanese in March 1947. By the time Chiang's defeated forces landed on the island, the Taiwanese had experienced so much repression that policies of accommodation between them and the new arrivals would require years to take effect. Over the next two decades efforts were made, many of them successful, to enroll Taiwanese in the civil service and to promote them to junior positions within the army's officer corps. A growing number of municipal and county officials were native Taiwanese, who all along had dominated most of the economy. The government, however, would brook no expression of separatist interests and actively suppressed the highly secretive Taiwanese independence movement.

In its first two decades on Taiwan, the Kuomintang began to lose some of its original militancy. Memories of defeat provided the basis for much Nationalist solidarity during the 1950s and early '60s, and most officials, at least publicly, believed that their presence on the island would be temporary. As younger mainlanders and Taiwanese rose to positions of authority, however, and as the pain of defeat faded, Taiwan itself became more the focus of attention. This change was reflected in a new spirit of confidence and a lessening of tension.

Yet as late as 1971 the strongest voices associated with Chiang and his son and political heir, Chiang Ching-kuo, insisted on the inevitability of reconquest. The approved scenario held that this reconquest would originate in an uprising in China, which would be followed by popular demand for a Nationalist return. The certainty of this future had waned over the years; but in 1965, even with the ideology of counterattack receding decisively as accepted political dogma, the intensification of the Vietnam War and the upheaval during the Cultural Revolution revived the hopes of reconquest for many in the Nationalist Party. These hopes survived the death of Chiang Kai-shek in April 1975 and the assumption of power by his son.

The ideology of counterattack had been explained by Chiang Kai-shek in annual October 10 (the Republic of China's National Day) addresses. Particularly in 1957 and 1962, he described the future Chinese society he wished to create and appealed for support from both sides of the Formosa Strait. The ideology gave Chiang and his government the warrant to remain in office, despite constitu-

tional provisions to the contrary, and to perpetuate police controls under martial law. It was also used to justify a standing military force estimated at 600,000 men, as well as governmental institutions suitable in size for a much larger country.

Although many observers compared such controls to the Communist dictatorship on the mainland, most were equally willing to praise many Nationalist programs, especially land reform. Ch'en Ch'eng, the governor of Taiwan in 1949, launched the "land to the tillers" program and gave responsibility for its operation to the Joint Committee on Rural Reconstruction. This program evolved in three stages during 1949–53: rent reduction, sale of public land, and reduction of land holdings through forced sale. The majority of Taiwan's peasants were given title to the land they worked, and the money acquired by former landowners was invested in the island's industrialization. This indigenous capital, along with foreign aid and investment (especially by overseas Chinese, Americans, and Japanese), helped create one of the highest rates of economic growth in the world.

Despite its success, economic modernization as such was never considered Taipei's main goal. Modernization would provide the necessary basis, it was argued, to build up the power and international prestige of the republic and to assure support from its allies—all required for the eventual counterattack.

U.S. support

The key to external support was the United States, whose policy was indicated by the U.S. position toward the seating question at the United Nations. From 1951 to 1960 the United States was able to muster a majority vote to postpone consideration of resolutions to replace Taipei's representatives with those of Peking. Then a tactical move by the U.S. delegation to require a two-thirds majority on the "important question" of Chinese representation reinforced the opposition. Not until 1970 did Peking's supporters muster a simple majority for their position. America's firmness at the UN and other evidence of U.S. fidelity made Chiang's government confident that its international position was reasonably secure.

This confidence did not spring solely from American backing. Many recently independent countries in Africa and Asia were reluctant to recognize Peking. Nationalist representatives competed directly with those of Peking for support, particularly in Africa, by offering financial and technical assistance. Taipei made considerable political capital out of the dramatic success of Taiwan's industrialization and contrasted the political reform of the Kuomintang at its 1967 congress with the economic stagnation and political upheaval on the mainland. When U.S. involvement in Vietnam was lessened in 1968, Chiang and his subordinates privately expressed misgivings, but they appeared optimistic at the time the Nixon administration assumed office in 1969.

Their hopes, however, were almost immediately dashed by the new U.S. administration's efforts to normalize relations with Peking. Between 1969 and 1971, U.S. restrictions on trade and travel by Americans to China were eased, and Washington began to explore alternatives to opposing Peking's representation in the United Nations. Meanwhile, a number of countries severed diplomatic relations with Taipei. The stage was seemingly being set for a readjustment in the international position of the two Chinese governments.

INTERNATIONAL RELATIONS
AFTER THE CULTURAL REVOLUTION

Peking could claim some credit for its more favourable situation. As noted, in 1969 Mao gave greater attention to international affairs. Consistent with the more complex pressures on domestic decision making, the country's international policies displayed a greater flexibility than before and became more difficult to categorize as "soft" or "hard." While backing down in 1969 in the face of the Soviet ultimatum and even exploring a possible accommodation with the United States early in 1970, China, mainly preoccupied with domestic power struggles associated with Lin Piao, began a major reappraisal of its international position.

Mao's theory of "three worlds." China's perception that the Soviet Union constituted its principle enemy increased steadily after the border conflicts in 1969 and as U.S. power seemed to be diminishing in Asia. Gradually over the next several years a new international line—called the "theory of three worlds"—began to emerge; it was within the framework of this theory that the eventual rationalization for a "united front" with western Europe, Japan, the United States, and China was to be made. (In the formulation approved in the 1980s the First World constituted the Soviet Union and the United States as superpowers, the Third World most of Asia, Africa, and Latin America, and the Second World, or "intermediate zone," Japan and western Europe; at times the U.S. seemed to be ranked in the latter.)

China unexpectedly dramatized the diplomatic side of its changing outlook in early 1971. Buoyed by Communist victories in Indochina and by a more favourable outlook in the United Nations, the Chinese, at the international table-tennis matches in Japan, invited the U.S. table-tennis team to China—the first such official invitation to Americans since the Communists had taken power.

These and subsequent diplomatic initiatives—dubbed "Ping-Pong diplomacy"—had at least two objectives: to outmanoeuvre the Soviet Union and to win support, especially among the Japanese, for China's taking a more active role in the area.

"Ping-Pong diplomacy"

The most dramatic move in Ping-Pong diplomacy came in July 1971, when President Nixon revealed his national security adviser, Henry A. Kissinger, had made a secret trip to Peking and had arranged for the President himself to visit China at a later date. China's new openness and its diplomatic recognition by one capital after another radically altered its international position, as was demonstrated by the vote to seat Peking's representatives in the United Nations on October 25, 1971. Equally significant was the apparent alignment of U.S. and Chinese interests against the Soviet Union and India in the Indo-Pakistani conflict the following December. China pulled back from its active political support of revolutionaries abroad and explored an accommodation with the United States at the very moment that Hanoi was insisting on a firm commitment to its struggle against the United States in Indochina. This turnabout in international affairs was made all the more visible by President Nixon's globally televised eight-day trip to China on February 21–28, 1972. In the final communiqué of the visit, the President and Premier Chou En-lai announced agreement on steps leading toward cultural exchanges, trade, and the eventual normalization of relations. The U.S. president called the trip a historical beginning in the building of "a bridge across 16,000 miles and 22 years of hostility" that had divided the United States and the People's Republic of China.

Sustained by a common concern over Soviet military and political pressures, the normalization of United States–China relations proceeded relatively rapidly in 1972–73 but slowed in the subsequent two years. In April 1973 quasi-diplomatic liaison offices were set up by each government in the other's capital; trade and the exchange of delegations increased.

Consistently with this more amicable relationship, China's Asian policy shifted: the government established diplomatic relations with Japan, urged a rapprochement between North and South Korea, and supported the agreements that brought about a cease-fire in Vietnam in 1973. At the same time, China resisted U.S.–Soviet efforts to attain a more stable détente, especially by strategic arms limitations and in Europe. While actively preparing their defenses for a possible war with the Soviet Union, the Chinese denounced the Soviet Union as contending for global "hegemony," and by the end of the 1970s China was openly advocating an anti-Soviet united front.

For Taipei, Ping-Pong diplomacy and the favourable response to it by the Nixon administration had come as devastating setbacks. Nationalist officials began to prepare the island for greater international isolation, but the post-1973 stalemate in U.S.–China relations, as further complicated by the resignation of Nixon in 1974 and the Communist conquest of Indochina in 1975, provided a temporary reprieve to the island. That reprieve appeared to be over on January 1, 1979, with U.S. establishment of formal diplomatic relations with the People's Republic of China. In the normalization agreement the administration of Pres. Jimmy Carter accepted an end to all official U.S. defense ties with Taiwan and acknowledged Peking's position that there is but one China and that Taiwan is part of China. It thus precluded itself from any future support for an independent Taiwan.

Subsequently, however, the U.S. Congress passed the Taiwan Relations Act, authorizing continued social and economic ties with Taiwan that were to be facilitated by a semi-official American Institute in Taiwan and a corresponding organization from Taiwan in the United States. The United States also unilaterally stated that it would continue to sell defensive arms to Taiwan, a move that complicated Washington–Peking talks concerning greater defense cooperation.

Peking added to these complexities for Taiwan by adopting a conciliatory line on the island's reunification with China. Shortly before his highly publicized 1979 visit to the United States in celebration of normalization, Teng Hsiao-p'ing declared that Taiwan could maintain its own economic systems, its political autonomy, and even its own armed forces after reunification. It would, however, be expected to eliminate symbols of its rival authority (such as its national flag). Taiwan rejected these continuing overtures as propaganda and acted to strengthen its economic, political, and military stability. Thus the uncertainties that had so long characterized China's domestic politics and international relations continued.

(J.W.Le.)

BIBLIOGRAPHY

General readings: EDWIN O. REISCHAUER and JOHN K. FAIRBANK, *East Asia: The Great Tradition* (1960); and ALBERT CRAIG, *East Asia: The Modern Transformation* (1965); OTTO FRANKE, *Geschichte des chinesischen Reiches*, 2nd ed., 5 vol. (1948–65); L. CARRINGTON GOODRICH, *A Short History of the Chinese People*, 4th ed. (1969); JOHN MESKILL (ed.), *An Introduction to Chinese Civilization* (1973).

Prehistoric China and the Shang period: CHI LI, *The Beginnings of Chinese Civilization* (1957), an account by the first Chinese to discover a Neolithic site in China; KWANG-CHIH CHANG, *The Archaeology of Ancient China*, rev. ed. (1968), broad and critical coverage of the many discoveries made throughout China until the Cultural Revolution in 1966; TE-K'UN CHENG, *Prehistoric China* (1959), and its supplement, *New Light on Prehistoric China* (1966), and *Shang China* (1961), systematic treatments by one who has done fieldwork in several parts of China; WILLIAM WATSON, *China Before the Han Dynasty* (1961); ALEKSANDR L. MONGAIT, *Archaeology in U.S.S.R.* (1959; orig. pub. in Russian, 1955).

From the Chou to the Ch'in: CHI LI, *The Formation of the Chinese People* (1928, reprinted 1967), useful for information on the ethnic history of ancient China; KWANG-CHIH CHANG (*op. cit.*), comprehensive treatment of archaeological findings in China from Paleolithic to the Unification; TE-K'UN CHENG, *Archaeology in China*, vol. 3, *Chou China* (1964), a good summary of archaeological discoveries in China; H.G. CREEL, *The Birth of China* (1937), still regarded as one of the standard references, and *The Origins of Statecraft in China*, vol. 1 (1970), the first Western book to include extensive materials from bronze inscription—especially significant on the activities of non-Chou peoples; WOLFRAM EBERHARD, *Conquerors and Rulers*, 2nd rev. ed. (1965), includes chapters on the Chou feudalism; CHO-YUN HSU, *Ancient China in Transition* (1965), a work on the social structure and social mobility in the Chou period, regarded as one of the standard references; PAUL WHEATLEY, *Pivot of the Four Quarters* (1971), a comparative study of urban developments in ancient China and the ancient Middle East; DERK BODDE, *China's First Unifier* (1938), and *Statesman, Patriot, and General in Ancient China* (1940), works covering the effort of the First Emperors and their courts to accomplish unification; FUNG YU-LAN, *A History of Chinese Philosophy*, 2nd ed., 2 vol. (Eng. trans. 1952–53), comprehensively covers the thought of different schools of thinking in ancient China.

The Han period: Translations of historical source material can be found in EDOUARD CHAVANNES, *Les Mémoires historiques de Se-ma Ts'ien* (vol. 1–5, 1895–1905, reprinted 1967; vol. 6, 1969); T'UNG-TSU CH'U, *Han Social Structure* (1972); RAFE DE CRESPIGNY, *The Last of the Han* (1969); HOMER H. DUBS (ed. and trans.), *The History of the Former Han*

Dynasty, 3 vol. (1938–55); ESSON M. GALE, *Discourses on Salt and Iron* (1931, reprinted 1967); and BURTON WATSON, *Records of the Grand Historian of China*, 2 vol. (1961). Monographs on specific topics of Han history include: HANS BIELENSTEIN, *The Restoration of the Han Dynasty*, 3 vol. (1954–67); A.F.P. HULSEWÉ, *Remnants of Han Law* (1955); MICHAEL LOEWE, *Records of Han Administration*, 2 vol. (1967), and *Everyday Life in Early Imperial China During the Han Period 202 B.C.–A.D. 220* (1968), and *Crisis and Conflict in Han China 104 B.C. to A.D. 9* (1974); BURTON WATSON, *Ssuma Ch'ien, Grand Historian of China* (1958); C. MARTIN WILBUR, *Slavery in China During the Former Han Dynasty, 202 B.C.–A.D. 25* (1943); and YING-SHIH YU, *Trade and Expansion in Han China* (1967).

The Six Dynasties: ETIENNE BALAZS, "Les Courants intellectuels en Chine au IIIᵉ siècle de notre ère," *Études Asiatiques*, vol. 2 (1948), the best Western-language study on the rise of "Neo-Taoism" and other schools of thought after the breakdown of the Han empire; KENNETH K.S. CHEN, *Buddhism in China: A Historical Survey* (1964), an extensive history of Chinese Buddhism by an eminent specialist; WOLFRAM EBERHARD (*op. cit.*), technical and at times highly speculative—partly devoted to the aspects of Chinese society under the "barbarian" dynasties; and *Das Toba-Reich Nordchinas: Eine soziologische Untersuchung* (1949), the only Western-language monographic study on the Toba-Wei—controversial, interesting, but highly technical; JACQUES GERNET, *Les Aspects économiques du Bouddhisme . . .* (1956), an indispensable, but rather technical, work on the economic functions of the Buddhist monasteries from the 5th to the 10th centuries; HENRI MASPERO, *Le Taoisme* in *Mélanges posthumes sur les religions et l'histoire de la Chine*, vol. 2 (1950), three essays dealing mainly with early medieval Taoism, still the most important general survey of the Taoist religion of this period, written by a great authority for a general public; HOLMES WELCH, *The Parting of the Way* (1957), a general history of the Taoist movement, with about one-third of the book devoted to the development of Taoist religion in the Six Dynasties period; ARTHUR F. WRIGHT, *Buddhism in Chinese History* (1959), a popular but authoritative survey of Chinese Buddhism as a whole, two chapters of which are devoted to the Six Dynasties period; EMIL ZÜRCHER, *The Buddhist Conquest of China*, 2 vol. (1959), a detailed, rather technical, study of the formation of gentry Buddhism.

The Sui and T'ang: There is no book-length general account of this period in a European language, apart from ANTOINE GAUBIL, "Abrégé de l'histoire chinoise de la grande dynastie Tang," in *Mémoires concernant . . . des Chinois*, vol. 15–16 (1791–1814). This work, actually completed in Peking in 1753, though an extraordinary achievement for its time, is now virtually useless. The most extensive modern account is that in OTTO FRANKE, *Geschichte des chinesischen Reiches*, vol. 2, with copious notes in vol. 3. This is a rather traditional chronological history, which pays little attention to non-political matters, and absolutely none to modern historical writing on the period in Chinese and Japanese. A very full treatment will be contained in *The Cambridge History of China*, vol. 2 (forthcoming). There is very little in print on the political history of the period in Western languages. Two studies by ARTHUR F. WRIGHT, "The Formation of Sui Ideology 581–604," in JOHN K. FAIRBANK (ed.), *Chinese Thought and Institutions* (1957); and "Sui Yang-ti: Personality and Stereotype," in ARTHUR F. WRIGHT (ed.), *The Confucian Persuasion* (1960), are the best available modern works on the Sui. WOODBRIDGE BINGHAM, *The Founding of the T'ang Dynasty: The Fall of Sui and Rise of T'ang* (1941, reprinted 1970), gives a lucid account of the period from 607 to 624. Two books by CHARLES P. FITZGERALD give a somewhat superficial account of the political history of the early T'ang: *The Son of Heaven: A Biography of Li Shih-Min, Founder of the T'ang Dynasty* (1933) and *The Empress Wu*, 2nd ed. (1968). These take no account of modern scholarship. The most important study of T'ang politics is EDWIN G. PULLEYBLANK, *The Background to the Rebellion of An Lu-shan* (1955), which gives a full account of every aspect of the reign of Hsüan-tsung. There is no modern study of the An Lu-shan Rebellion itself, but the two principal sources exist in well-annotated translations by HOWARD S. LEVY, *Biography of An Lu-shan* (1960); and by ROBERT DES ROTOURS, *Histoire de Ngan Lou-chan* (1962). There is no satisfactory account of the following period. The rebellions of the 780s are described briefly in DENIS TWITCHETT, "Lu Chih (754–805)," in ARTHUR F. WRIGHT and DENIS TWITCHETT (eds.), *Confucian Personalities* (1962). The mysterious reign of Shun-tsung has not been subjected to a modern study, but the principal source is translated in BERNARD S. SOLOMON, *The Veritable Record of the T'ang Emperor Shun-tsung* (1955). There is some account of the subsequent reigns in ARTHUR WALEY, *The Life and Times of Po Chü-i, 772–846*

A.D. (1949), but the historical analysis is not very satisfactory. For the period after 847 even the Chinese primary documentation becomes very thin. The only events that have attracted attention from Western scholars are the rebellions; on these see ROBERT DES ROTOURS, "La Révolte de P'ang Hiun," *T'oung Pao*, 56:229–240 (1970); and HOWARD S. LEVY, *Biography of Huáng Ch'ao* (1955). On the Huang Ch'ao rebellion and the subsequent disorders the best account is GUNGWU WANG, *The Structure of Power in North China During the Five Dynasties* (1963). A number of important studies on T'ang political history, taking account of modern Japanese and Chinese scholarship, are included in ARTHUR F. WRIGHT and DENIS TWITCHETT (eds.), *Perspectives on the T'ang* (1973). On T'ang institutions in general there is a very perceptive though somewhat outdated (the book was actually completed in 1951) account in HENRI MASPERO and ETIENNE BALAZS, *Histoire et institutions de la Chine ancienne*, pp. 160–262 (1967). The traditional sources on the administrative system are translated in ROBERT DES ROTOURS, *Traité des fonctionnaires et de l'armée*, 2 vol. (1947–48); and on the examination system in his *Traité des examens* (1932). On finances and general economic problems, see DENIS TWITCHETT, *Financial Administration Under the T'ang Dynasty*, 2nd ed. (1970), which contains a full bibliography. On finance under the Sui, see ETIENNE BALAZS, *Études sur la société et l'économie de la Chine médiévale*, vol. 2 (1954). On general social history, see DENIS TWITCHETT, *Land Tenure and the Social Order in T'ang and Sung China* (1962); and "Merchant, Trade and Government in Late T'ang," *Asia Major*, 14:63–95 (1968), also the relevant sections of ETIENNE BALAZS, *Chinese Civilization and Bureaucracy* (1964). More information is to be found in JACQUES GERNET (*op. cit.*); and in the eyewitness account by a contemporary Japanese monk in EDWIN O. REISCHAUER, *Ennin's Diary* (1955), with a companion volume, *Ennin's Travels in T'ang China* (1955). See also, on the very important evidence from Tunhuang, LIONEL GILES, *Six Centuries of Tunhuang* (1944); and DENIS TWITCHETT, "Chinese Social History from the Seventh to the Tenth Centuries: The Tunhuang Documents and Their Implications," *Past and Present*, 35:28–53 (1966). The following are extremely important for the light they throw on the cosmopolitan nature of T'ang society: EDWARD H. SCHAFER, *The Vermilion Bird: T'ang Images of the South* (1967), *The Golden Peaches of Samarkand: A Study of T'ang Exotics* (1963), and *Shore of Pearls* (1970), dealing with early history of Hainan Island; while a more factual account of Chinese colonization of the south is in HEROLD J. WIENS, *China's March into the Tropics* (1952). The best general account of Chinese relations with her northern neighbours in the steppes is RENE GROUSSET, *L'Empire des steppes*, 4th ed. (1960; Eng. trans., *The Empire of the Steppes*, 1970). On Chinese overseas trade and relations with Southeast Asia, see GUNGWU WANG, *The Nanhai Trade: A Study of the Early History of Chinese Trade in the South China Sea* (1958).

The Five Dynasties period: GUNGWU WANG, *The Structure of Power in North China During the Five Dynasties* (1963), offers a recent outstanding analysis; WOLFRAM EBERHARD (*op. cit.*), suggests sociological interpretations. EDWARD H. SCHAFER, *The Empire of Min* (1954), has the best sinological summary on this kingdom in the south; see also his article, "The History of the Empire of the Southern Han," in *The Silver Jubilee Volume*, Institute of Humanistic Sciences, Kyoto University (1954), an annotated translation of the section in Chinese dynastic history. On conquest dynasties in the north, see KARL A. WITTFOGEL and CHIA-SHENG FENG, *History of Chinese Society: Liao, 907–1125* (1949); and HOK-LAM CHAN, *The Historiography of the Chin Dynasty: Three Studies* (1970). On the Sung period, listings of works in Western languages are available in YVES HERVOUET, *Bibliographie des travaux en langues occidentales sur les Song parus de 1946 à 1965* (1969), and a recent sequel to it, MICHAEL C. MCGRATH, "A Bibliography of Western Language Sources on the Sung, 1966–1970," in *Sung Studies Newsletter*, no. 3 (1971). A useful understanding of contributions by Chinese scholars may be obtained in I-TU JEN SUN and JOHN DE FRANCIS (trans.), *Chinese Social History* (1956); and CHARLES P. FITZGERALD, "The Chinese Middle Ages in Communist Historiography," in ALBERT FEUERWERKER (ed.), *History in Communist China* (1968). Similarly, for a sampling of numerous contributions by Japanese scholars, see SETSUKO YANAGIDA, "Eastern History: China, Five Dynasties, Sung and Yüan," in *Japan at the XIIth International Congress of Historical Sciences in Vienna* (1965); and DENIS TWITCHETT, "Recent Work on Medieval Chinese Social History by Sudō Yoshiyuki," *Journal of the Economic and Social History of the Orient*, 1:145–156 (1957). On the significance of the Sung and varying interpretations, see JAMES T.C. LIU and PETER J. GOLAS (eds.), *Change in Sung China: Innovation or Renovation?* (1969). Further general information is available in the following: E.A. KRACKE, JR.,

Civil Service in Early Sung China, 960–1067 (1953), a monumental work; JAMES T.C. LIU, Ou-yang Hsiu, an Eleventh-Century Neo-Confucianist (Eng. trans. 1967) and Reform in Sung China: Wang An-shih (1021–1086) and His New Policies (1959), both works attempting to relate general trends through historical figures; and BRIAN E. MCKNIGHT, Village and Bureaucracy in Southern Sung China (1971), the best recent account coming down to the later period as well as the local scene. JACQUES GERNET, La Vie quotidienne en Chine, à la veille de l'invasion mongole 1250–1276 (1959; Eng. trans., Daily Life in China on the Eve of the Mongol Invasion, 1250–1276, 1962), provides vivid descriptions.

The Yüan period: (Mongol conquest of China): HENRY DESMOND MARTIN, The Rise of Chingis Khan and His Conquest of North China (1950, reprinted 1971), on Mongol operations against Northern China, now partly superseded; IGOR DE RACHEWILTZ, "Personnel and Personalities in North China in the Early Mongol Period," Journal of the Economic and Social History of the Orient, 9:88–144 (1966), a fundamental study of the Mongol conquest. (Government and political history of the Yüan): OTTO FRANKE, Geschichte des chinesischen Reiches, vol. 4–5 (1948–52), still the most detailed general account of Yüan history in any Western language; ISTITUTO ITALIANO PER IL MEDIO ED ESTREMO ORIENTE, Oriente poliano (1957), a collection of scholarly articles in English, French, and German on various aspects of Yüan China; FRANZ SCHURMANN (ed. and trans.), Economic Structure of the Yüan Dynasty (1956), on fiscal administration; PAUL RATCHNEVSKY, Un Code des Yuan (1937), on the legal system. (Religious and intellectual developments): ARTHUR WALEY (trans.), The Travels of an Alchemist (1931), on Ch'ang-ch'un; FREDERICK W. MOTE, "Confucian Eremitism in the Yüan Period," in ARTHUR F. WRIGHT (ed.), The Confucian Persuasion (1960); CH'EN YUAN, Western and Central Asians in China Under the Mongols (1966), annotated translation of an authoritative Chinese work. (Chinese contacts with Asia and the West): EMIL BRETSCHNEIDER, Mediaeval Researches from Eastern Sources, 2 vol. (1888, reprinted 1910).

Ming dynasty: The standard Chinese source on Ming history is the official dynastic history, Ming-shih (completed 1736). WOLFGANG FRANKE, An Introduction to the Sources of Ming History (1968), describes and evaluates all important Chinese-language sources. Good modern histories of the Ming period have been written in Chinese by LI CHIEH (1962), LI KUANG-PI (1957), and MENG SEN (1957). There is as yet no comprehensive history of Ming China in a Western language, but a good introduction to Chinese life and institutions of the period is LOUIS J. GALLAGHER (trans.), China in the Sixteenth Century: The Journals of Matthew Ricci, 1583–1610 (1953). The eventual collapse of the Ming dynasty is described in JAMES B. PARSONS, The Peasant Rebellions of the Late Ming Dynasty (1970). Political and socio-economic analyses may be found in CHARLES O. HUCKER, The Traditional Chinese State in Ming Times (1368–1644) (1961), The Censorial System of Ming China (1966), and (ed.), Chinese Government in Ming Times: Seven Studies (1969); PING-TI HO, The Ladder of Success in Imperial China (1962) and Studies on the Population of China, 1368–1953 (1959); I-TU JEN SUN and JOHN DE FRANCIS (op. cit.); F.C. LIANG, The Single-Whip Method (I-t'iao-pien fa) of Taxation in China, trans. by Y.C. WANG (1956); and AYAO HOSHI, The Ming Tribute Grain System, trans. by MARK ELVIN (1969). For a brief introduction to early Ming overseas adventures, see J.J.L. DUYVENDAK, China's Discovery of Africa (1949). Aspects of Ming tributary relations with neighbouring peoples are found in Y.T. WANG, Official Relations Between China and Japan, 1368–1549 (1953); T.T. CHANG, Sino-Portuguese Trade from 1514 to 1644 (1934); CHARLES R. BOXER (ed.), South China in the Sixteenth Century (1953); and ARNOLD H. ROWBOTHAM, Missionary and Mandarin: The Jesuits at the Court of China (1942, reprinted 1966). WM. THEODORE DE BARY et al., Self and Society in Ming Thought (1970), deals with Chinese cultural development in Ming times.

The Ch'ing period: (The rise of the Ch'ing Dynasty): IMMANUEL C.Y. HSU, The Rise of Modern China (1970); ROBERT H.G. LEE, The Manchu Frontier in Ch'ing History (1970); SILAS H.L. WU, Communication and Imperial Control in China: Evolution of the Palace Memorial System, 1693–1735 (1970). (Early foreign relations): LUCIANO PETECH, China and Tibet in the Early 18th Century (1950); TORU SAGUCHI, Jūhachi-jūkyū seiki Higashi Torukisutan shakai shi kenkyū ("The Social History of Eastern Turkestan in the 18th–19th Centuries," 1963), with summary in English; CHUSEI SUZUKI, "China's Relations with Inner Asia: The Hsiung-nu, Tibet," in JOHN K. FAIRBANK (ed.), The Chinese World Order (1968); KENNETH S. LATOURETTE, A History of Christian Missions in China (1929); EARL H. PRITCHARD, Anglo-Chinese Relations During the Seventeenth and Eighteenth Centuries (1929) and The Cru-

cial Years of Early Anglo-Chinese Relations, 1750–1800 (1936, reprinted 1970); ANTONIO S. ROSSO, Apostolic Legations to China of the Eighteenth Century (1948); YOSHIRO SAEKI, Shina Kirisutokyō no kenkyū, 4 vol. ("A Study of Christianity under the Ch'ing Dynasty," 1943–49). (Mid-Ch'ing society and economy): CHUNG-LI CHANG, The Chinese Gentry (1955); T'UNG-TSU CHU, Local Government in China Under the Ch'ing (1962); PING-TI HO (op. cit.). (Intellectual and cultural aspects): L. CARRINGTON GOODRICH, The Literary Inquisition of Ch'ien-lung (1935); JOSEPH R. LEVENSON, Confucian China and Its Modern Fate: The Problem of Intellectual Continuity (1958) and "The Abortiveness of Empiricism in Early Ch'ing Thought," Far Eastern Quarterly, 13:155–165 (1954); CH'I-CH'AO LIANG, Intellectual Trends in the Ch'ing Period, trans. by IMMANUEL C.Y. HSU (1959). (Dynastic degeneration): JEAN CHESNEAUX with MARIANNE RACHLINE, Les Sociétés secrètes en Chine, XIXe et XXe siècles (1965); KUNG-CHUAN HSIAO, Rural China: Imperial Control in the Nineteenth Century (1960); PHILIP A. KUHN, Rebellion and Its Enemies in Late Imperial China: Militarization and Social Structure, 1794–1864 (1970). (Western challenges): MASATAKA BANNO, China and the West, 1858–1861: The Origins of the Tsungli Yamen (1964); HSIN-PAO CHANG, Commissioner Lin and the Opium War (1964); W.C. COSTIN, Great Britain and China, 1833–1860 (1937); JOHN K. FAIRBANK, Trade and Diplomacy on the China Coast, 2 vol. (1953); MICHAEL GREENBERG, British Trade and the Opening of China, 1800–42 (1951); IMMANUEL C.Y. HSU, China's Entrance into the Family of Nations: The Diplomatic Phase, 1858–1880 (1960). (The Taipings): VINCENT Y.C. SHIH, The Taiping Ideology: Its Sources, Interpretations, and Influences (1967); FRANZ H. MICHAEL and CHANG CHUNG-LI, The Taiping Rebellion: History and Documents, vol. 1 (1966). (Nien rebellion): SIANG-TSEH CHIANG, The Nien Rebellion (1954); S.Y. TENG, The Nien Army and Their Guerrilla Warfare, 1851–1868 (1961). (Chinese response): ALBERT FEUERWERKER, China's Early Industrialization: Sheng Hsüan-huai (1844–1916) and Mandarin Enterprise (1958); YEN-P'ING HAO, The Comprador in Nineteenth Century China: Bridge Between East and West (1970); MARY C. WRIGHT, The Last Stand of Chinese Conservatism: The T'ung-Chih Restoration, 1862–1874 (1957). (Boxer Rebellion): PAUL A. COHEN, China and Christianity: The Missionary Movement and the Growth of Chinese Antiforeignism, 1860–1870 (1963); VICTOR PURCELL, The Boxer Uprising (1963). (Revolutionary movements at the end of the Ch'ing): MICHAEL GASSTER, Chinese Intellectuals and the Revolution of 1911 (1969); ROBERT A. SCALAPINO and GEORGE T. YU, The Chinese Anarchist Movement (1961); HAROLD Z. SCHIFFRIN, Sun Yat-sen and the Origins of the Chinese Revolution (1968).

The first Republican period: The broadest general and interpretative work is IMMANUEL C.Y. HSU, The Rise of Modern China (1970); more detailed and politically centered is O. EDMUND CLUBB, 20th Century China (1964). There are two excellent collections of biographies of the leading figures of the period: HOWARD L. BOORMAN and RICHARD C. HOWARD (eds.), Biographical Dictionary of Republican China, 4 vol. (1967–71); and DONALD W. KLEIN and ANNE B. CLARKE, Biographic Dictionary of Chinese Communism, 1921–65, 2 vol. (1971). For the revolution of 1911–12 and the early Republican period, scholarly essays offering fresh interpretations are found in MARY C. WRIGHT (ed.), China in Revolution: The First Phase, 1900–1913 (1968). New intellectual and cultural currents are discussed in a classic work, CHOU TSE-TSUNG, The May Fourth Movement: Intellectual Revolution in Modern China (1960). Economic conditions are discussed in R.H. TAWNEY's prophetic and still valuable study, Land and Labour in China (1932, reprinted 1966). On the Nationalist Revolution, see C. MARTIN WILBUR and JULIE LIEN-YING HOW (eds.), Documents on Communism, Nationalism, and Soviet Advisers in China, 1918–1927 (1956). The broadest work treating the history of the Communist movement is CONRAD BRANDT, BENJAMIN I. SCHWARTZ, and JOHN K. FAIRBANK, A Documentary History of Chinese Communism (1952). A stimulating reportorial work is EDGAR SNOW, Red Star over China, rev. ed. (1970); while a broad survey is presented by LYMAN VAN SLYKE, Enemies and Friends: The United Front in Chinese Communist History (1967). Three excellent books on Mao Tse-tung and his role are BENJAMIN I. SCHWARTZ, Chinese Communism and the Rise of Mao (1951); JEROME CH'EN, Mao and the Chinese Revolution (1965); and STUART R. SCHRAM, Mao Tse-tung (1967).

On China's relations with foreign powers, WERNER LEVI, Modern China's Foreign Policy (1953), offers a broad account. An interesting scholarly interpretation is AKIRA IRIYE, After Imperialism: The Search for a New Order in the Far East, 1921–1931 (1965). On relations between China and Russia, an important general work is O. EDMUND CLUBB, China and Russia: The "Great Game" (1971); while a fine study of American policy toward China during a limited period is given in DOROTHY BORG, *The United States and the Far Eastern Crisis of 1933–1938* (1964). F.C. JONES, *Japan's New Order in Asia: Its Rise and Fall, 1937–45* (1954); and F.F. LIU, *A Military History of Modern China, 1924–1949* (1956), provide information on the military aspects of Sino-Japanese relations. A scholarly study of foreign assistance to China during the Sino-Japanese war is ARTHUR N. YOUNG, *China and the Helping Hand, 1937–1945* (1963).

For developments in the Communist regions during the Sino-Japanese war, in addition to general works on the Communist movement cited above, a close factual account based on intelligence studies is LYMAN VAN SLYKE (ed.), *The Chinese Communist Movement: A Report of the United States War Department, July 1945* (1968). CHALMERS A. JOHNSON provides a scholarly interpretation of Communist successes behind Japanese lines in *Peasant Nationalism and Communist Power: The Emergence of Revolutionary China* (1962). Important works dealing with wartime conditions in Nationalist areas are CHANG CHIA-AO, *The Inflationary Sprial: The Experience in China, 1939–1950* (1958); and CHARLES F. ROMANUS and RILEY SUNDERLAND, *The United States Army in World War II: China-Burma-India Theatre*, 3 vol. (1952–58), which is carefully documented and well illustrated. A similar scholarly account, very well written, is BARBARA W. TUCHMAN, *Stilwell and the American Experience in China, 1911–1945* (1970). The final civil war period is covered by LIONEL MAX CHASSIN, *La Conquête de la Chine par Mao Tsé-tung, 1945–1949* (1963; Eng. trans., *The Communist Conquest of China: A History of the Civil War, 1945–1949*, 1965); and interesting interpretative essays are assembled in PICHON P.Y. LOH (ed.), *The Kuomintang Debacle of 1949: Collapse or Conquest?* (1965).

Nationalist and Communist ideology: The most influential work of Sun Yat-sen has been translated under the title *San Min Chu I*, ed. by FRANK PRICE (1927). The most revealing work of Chiang Kai-shek is his *China's Destiny and Chinese Economic Theory*, ed. in English with comments by PHILIP JAFFE (1947). The official translation of Mao Tse-tung's *Selected Works*, 4 vol., is that published by the Foreign Languages Press, Peking (1961). The best introduction to the relations between China's traditional political culture and the problems of change and modernization is R.H. SOLOMON, *Mao's Revolution and the Chinese Political Culture* (1971). The intellectual ferment of the early twenties is well described and documented in CHOU TSE-TSUNG, *The May Fourth Movement* (1960); and the development of Marxist influence in this context is analyzed with imagination and skill in BENJAMIN I. SCHWARTZ, *Chinese Communism and the Rise of Mao* (1951), which also deals with the formation of Mao's ideas up to 1949. STUART R. SCHRAM, *The Political Thought of Mao Tse-tung*, rev. ed. (1969), is the best introduction to Chinese Communist ideology.

China since 1949: The bibliography on contemporary Chinese history is vast and growing rapidly. Although publications on modern China are uneven in coverage and quality, most subjects of interest to the reader have been discussed in the writings of scholars and visitors to China and Taiwan. A comprehensive bibliography of these writings is compiled annually by the *Journal of Asian Studies*. See also O. EDMUND CLUBB, *20th Century China* (1964); JOHN K. FAIRBANK, *The United States and China*, 3rd ed. (1971); A. DOAK BARNETT, *Cadres, Bureaucracy, and Political Power in Communist China* (1967), *China and the Major Powers in East Asia* (1977), and *Uncertain Passage: China's Transition to the Post-Mao Era* (1974); RICHARD BAUM, *Prelude to Revolution: Mao, the Party, and the Peasant Question, 1962–66* (1975), and (ed.), *China's Four Modernizations: The New Technological Revolution* (1980); PARRIS H. CHANG, *Power and Policy in China* (1975); LOWELL DITTMER, *Liu Shao-ch'i and the Chinese Cultural Revolution: The Politics of Mass Criticism* (1974); JÜRGEN DOMES, *Die Ära Mao Tse-tung* (1972; Eng. trans., *The Internal Politics of China, 1949–1972*, 1973); ALEXANDER ECKSTEIN, *China's Economic Revolution* (1977); THOMAS FINGAR (ed.), *China's Quest for Independence: Policy Evolution in the 1970s* (1980); WILLIAM E. GRIFFITH, *The Sino-Soviet Rift* (1964); PING-TI HO and TANG TSOU (eds.), *China in Crisis*, 2 vol. (1968); JOHN WILSON LEWIS, *Leadership in Communist China* (1963), and (ed.), *Party Leadership and Revolutionary Power in China* (1970), and *The City in Communist China* (1971); RODERICK MACFARQUHAR, *The Origins of the Cultural Revolution*, vol. 1, *Contradictions Among the People, 1956–1957* (1974); WILLIAM L. PARISH and MARTIN KING WHYTE, *Village and Family in Contemporary China* (1978); ROBERT SCALAPINO (ed.), *Elites in the People's Republic of China* (1972); STUART SCHRAM *Mao Tse-tung* (1966); FRANZ SCHURMANN, *Ideology and Organization in Communist China*, 2nd ed. enl. (1968); BENJAMIN I. SCHWARTZ, *Communism and China: Ideology in Flux* (1968); MARK SELDEN (ed.), *People's Republic of China: A Documentary History of*

Revolutionary Change (1979); DOROTHY J. SOLINGER, *Regional Government and Political Integration in Southwest China, 1949–1954: A Case Study* (1977); RICHARD H. SOLOMON, *Mao's Revolution and the Chinese Political Culture* (1971); JAMES R. TOWNSEND, *Politics in China*, 2nd ed. (1980); WILLIAM W. WHITSON and CHEN-HSIA HUANG, *The Chinese High Command: A History of Communist Military Politics, 1927–71* (1973); MARTIN KING WHYTE, *Small Groups and Political Rituals in China* (1974); ROXANE WITKE, *Comrade Chiang Ch'ing* (1977); MARGERY WOLF and ROXANE WITKE (eds.), *Women in Chinese Society* (1975).

(L.C.G./C.-y.H./M.Lo./E.Z./D.C.T./J.T.C.L./H.Fr./
C.O.Hu./C.Su./C.M.Wi./J.Gra./J.W.Le.)

China Sea

The China Sea is that part of the western Pacific Ocean bordering the east-southeast portion of the Asian mainland. It consists of two seas, the South China Sea and the East China Sea, which connect through the shallow Formosa Strait between Taiwan and the People's Republic of China.

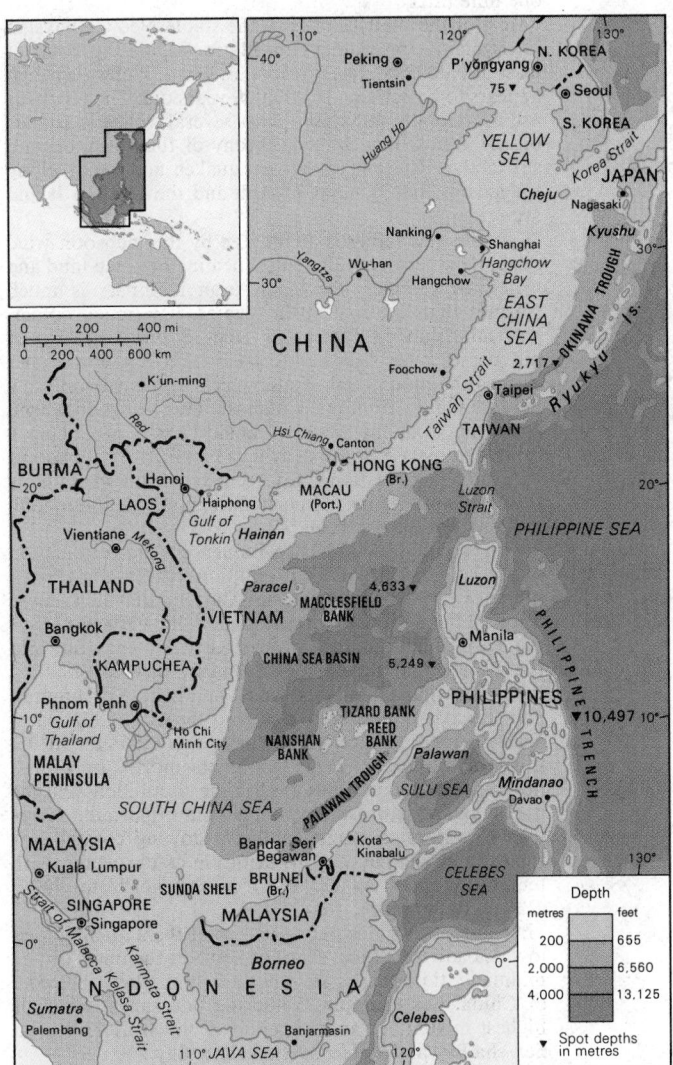

The China Sea.

East China Sea. The East China Sea, or Eastern Sea, known in Chinese as the Tung Hai, extends northeastward from the South China Sea. Eastward it includes waters out to the Ryukyu Island chain; north to Kyūshū, the southernmost of Japan's main islands; northwest to the island of Cheju-do off South Korea; and hence west to the mainland of China. This northern boundary separates the East China Sea from the Yellow Sea.

Physiography. The East China Sea, which has an area of 290,000 square miles (752,000 square kilometres), is largely shallow, with 71 percent of the area less than 650

Boundaries
of the East
China Sea

feet and an average depth of only 1,145 feet. The deeper part is the Okinawa Trough, extending alongside the Ryukyu Island chain, with a large area over 3,300 feet (1,000 metres) deep and a maximum depth of 8,912 feet (2,717 metres). The western edge of the sea is a continuation of the shelf that extends from the South China Sea up to the Yellow Sea. A large number of islands and shoals dot the eastern boundary as well as the area near the Chinese mainland. The shallow shelf areas are covered with sediments from the bordering land masses deposited mainly by the Yangtze and other rivers near the northern part of the sea. Coarser sediments of sand occur farther out, and rocks, muds, and oozes are also found in scattered areas. Seismic profiling indicates that the geological sub-bottom structure is comprised of nearly parallel folds, with rock ridges near the northern limits of the East China Sea, near the edge of the continental shelf, and along the Ryukyus. These have afforded barriers for sediment brought down by the great Huang (Yellow) and Yangtze rivers. Between the ridges the sediment is up to one mile thick.

Most of the shelf belongs to the stable Neo-Cathaysian Geosyncline (or Cathaysian Platform), dating back at least 300,000,000 years or longer. The Okinawa Trough appears to be perhaps 10,000,000 years old. The Ryukyus are a double island chain, with several volcanic islands on the East China Sea side. Many of the volcanoes are still active. Epicentres of earthquakes are found along the axis of the Okinawa Trough and the Ryukyu Island arc.

Climate. Weather is dominated by the monsoon wind system, the result of differential heating between land and water. In summer, the high Asian landmass is much warmer than the sea; in the winter, it is much colder, particularly in the Plateau of Tibet. Summer heating of air masses over Asia builds areas of low pressure and creates the monsoonal winds, which in this season blow predominantly from the southeast. This brings in warm, moist air from the western Pacific Ocean, producing a rainy summer season that is accompanied by typhoons. In winter the situation is reversed: monsoon winds blow predominantly from the north bringing with them cold, dry air from the continent.

Hydrography. Winds also influence water circulation of the Kuroshio (Black) Current, a north-flowing branch of the warm North Equatorial Current that flows near Taiwan. Some of the Kuroshio enters the eastern part of the East China Sea then diverts eastward back out into the Pacific and flows east of Japan. Strengthened by monsoon winds, it is at its widest and fastest in summer, and the axis is displaced well into the East China Sea. This warmed surface water varies from 86° F (30° C) in the south to 77° F (25° C) in the north. In winter, northerly monsoon winds modify the circulation, and the north-flowing Kuroshio, though still important, is reduced in strength, while southerly flowing coastal currents are strengthened. This brings in colder water, with temperatures of 41° F (5° C) in the north to 73° F (23° C) in the south.

Because of the constricting nature of the adjoining Yellow Sea and the funnel shape of some of the inlets on the mainland, tidal ranges are especially high along the coast of China. For example, the spring tide range, which is highest in summer and winter, is as much as 23 feet at San-sha Bay and 36 feet at Hangchow Bay.

Resources and navigation. The East China Sea is a highly marine-organic productive region, with China, Japan, Taiwan, and North and South Korea actively fishing in the area. Most of the fishing is done by small local boats, although larger trawlers are also used. Tuna, mackerel, shrimps, sardines, milk fish, sea breams, croakers, shell fish, and seaweeds are the main resources harvested. The records of fishing intensity correlate well with the preference of bottom fishes for areas of fine-grain, organic-rich sediments that are probably the result of the greater abundance of worms and other small, mud-digesting organisms in the area.

In addition to the local shipping traffic in and out of Chinese and Korean ports, the East China Sea serves as the main shipping route from the South China Sea to Japanese and other North Pacific ports.

South China Sea. The South China Sea, or Nan Hai, is bounded on the west by the Asian mainland, on the south by the southern limit of the Gulf of Thailand and the east coast of Malay Peninsula, and on the east by Taiwan, the Philippines, and Borneo. The southern boundary is a rise in the seabed between Sumatra and Borneo, and the northern boundary stretches from the northernmost point of Taiwan to the coast of Fukien Province, China (the southern limit of the East China Sea). It embraces an area of about 848,400 square miles, with an average depth of 3,740 feet.

Physiography. The major topographic feature is a deep rhombus-shaped basin on the eastern part, with reef-studded shoal areas rising up steeply within the basin to the south (Reed, Tizard, Nanshan banks) and northwest (Paracel Island and Macclesfield banks). The deep portion, called the China Sea Basin, has a maximum depth of 16,452 feet, and an abyssal plain with a mean depth of 14,100 feet. The continental shelf falls off sharply near Luzon and Palawan islands and forms the Palawan Trough near the latter island.

Along the northwest side of the basin to the mainland is a broad, shallow shelf as wide as 150 miles. It includes the Gulf of Tonkin (maximum depth of 269 feet) and the Formosa Strait. The large islands of Hainan and Taiwan are situated on this shelf. To the south, off South Vietnam, the shelf narrows and connects with the Sunda Shelf, one of the largest in the world, which covers the area between Borneo, Sumatra and Malaysia, and includes the southern part of the South China Sea, the Gulf of Thailand, and the Java Sea. This broad trough is about 130 feet deep at its periphery and up to 330 feet in its central part. On the bottom of the shelf is a network of submerged river valleys that converge into the Sunda Depression and then into the China Sea Basin. These valleys and tributaries vary in width up to three miles.

The Sunda Shelf is covered with littoral sediments contributed by submerged valleys. The inner zone of mud is characteristic of the continental shelf near the Mekong and Red River deltas, while the sediment of the deeper parts of the South China Sea is mainly composed of clay. A characteristic part of the sediments in both deep and shallow water is volcanic ash. This is found in layers, derived from large volcanic eruptions in the East Indies, notably the enormous eruption of Krakatoa in 1883, when ash was transported through the entire area by both wind and currents.

The South China Sea has connecting channels. The Formosa Strait on the north is about 90 miles wide, with a depth of about 230 feet. The main deep channel connecting the South China Sea with the Pacific Ocean lies between Taiwan and the Philippines and has a depth of about 8,500 feet. Shallow channels are found on the east along the Philippine Island chain and on the south between Borneo and Sumatra. The western connection to the Indian Ocean is the long Strait of Malacca. At its narrowest part it is 19 miles wide and about 100 feet deep. The South China Sea is the largest "marginal sea" of the western Pacific. Some 1,000,000 to 60,000,000 years ago, it was rifted and collapsed as a result of sea-floor spreading. The China Sea Basin is believed to have dropped 2.5 miles, leaving residual plateaus studded with numerous coral reefs, islets, and banks, some of which are drowned atolls.

Climate. Weather is tropical and largely controlled by monsoons. In summer, monsoonal winds blow predominantly from the southwest; in winter, winds blow from the northeast. Annual rainfall approximates 12.3 feet, and summer typhoons are frequent.

Hydrography. Monsoons control the sea-surface currents as well as the exchange of water between the South China Sea and adjacent bodies of water. In August, the surface flow into the South China Sea is from the south through Karimata and Kelasa (Gasper) straits. Near the mainland the general flow is northeasterly, passing out through the Formosa and Luzon straits. There is a weak countercurrent on the eastern side of the sea. In Febru-

Sea currents and tides *(margin note)*

Boundaries of South China Sea *(margin note)*

Connecting channels *(margin note)*

ary, the flow is generally to the southwest; the strongest flow occurs along the bulging part of Vietnam, with speeds of up to three knots (nautical miles per hour).

The near-surface waters are relatively warm (about 84° F [29° C] in the summer) because of the low latitude and a tendency for the equatorial current to feed warm water into the area. In early summer, wind from the southwest not only moves the surface water to the northeast but causes it to be displaced off the coast. As a result, upwelling areas having colder surface temperatures and higher nutrient content are found off central Vietnam. In winter, the general surface temperature is colder, ranging from about 70° F (21° C) in the north to 81° F (27° C) in the south.

The major rivers draining into the South China Sea are the Hsi Chiang, which enters near Macau; the Red River at Haiphong, North Vietnam; and the Mekong River, near Saigon, South Vietnam. The wet summer season causes the Mekong River to triple its annual average flow, and it causes an even greater relative change in the flow of the Red River.

Resources and navigation. The heavily fished South China Sea is the main source of animal protein for the people living near its shores, providing as much as 50 percent for the densely populated Southeast Asian area. Most abundant are the various species of tuna, mackerel, croaker, anchovy, shrimp, and shellfish. Nearly the entire catch is consumed locally, either fresh or preserved.

Fishing

The main transport route to and from Pacific and Indian ocean ports is through the Strait of Malacca and the South China Sea. In the main, oil and minerals move up the coast, and food and manufactured goods move down. In the mid-1970s some areas in the central South China Sea were still not well sounded, and nautical charts bore the notation "dangerous ground."

Prospects. It was clear in the 1970s that the rapid increase in population density in countries bordering the China Sea would necessitate increased food and other consumer requirements. Inshore fisheries over the continental shelf have nearly reached the economically sustainable limit. The Yellow and East China seas produce 427,000 tons of fish per year and have a potential of 553,000 to 681,000 tons. The South China Sea produces 636,000 with a potential of 765,000 to 850,000 tons. But the deepwater-fish catch should double or triple in these areas, and mollusk farming was expected to increase.

The seaward edge of the continental shelf of the East China Sea appears to coincide with an extension of a folded zone between the islands of Kyūshū and Taiwan. Most of the oil and gas fields on land in the region are associated with this and other similar folded zones. The nature of rock samples and the probable continuation of the folded zones beneath the sea floor suggest that the most favourable location for future submarine oil and gas fields is a wide band along the outer part of the continental shelf that extends into the South China Sea.

BIBLIOGRAPHY. R.W. FAIRBRIDGE, "East China Sea," *Encyclopedia of Oceanography*, pp. 238–243 (1966), on the geology and oceanography of the East China Sea; K.O. EMERY *et al.*, "Geological Structure and Some Water Characteristics of the East China Sea and the Yellow Sea," *Economic Commission for Asia and the Far East (ECAFE) Bull.*, 2:3–43 (1969), on ridges, soundings, and bottom contours; E.C. LAFOND, "South China Sea," *Encyclopedia of Oceanography*, pp. 829–837, includes information on oceanography, climate, and geology; "Physical Oceanography and Its Relation to the Marine Organic Production in the South China Sea," pp. 5–33 in *Ecology of the Gulf of Thailand and the South China Sea: A Report of the Results of the NAGA Expedition (Scripps Inst. Oceanogr. Contr.,* 63–6; 1963); and KLAUS WYRTKI, "Physical Oceanography of the Southeast Asian Waters," *NAGA Report*, vol. 2, *Scientific Results of Marine Investigations of the South China Sea and the Gulf of Thailand. 1959–1961* (1961), both on oceanography.

(E.C.LaF.)

Chinese Law

Chinese law is the law that evolved in China over millennia from earliest times virtually uninfluenced by foreign jurisprudence until the 20th century, when Western

—especially, Western Socialist—law was introduced. Until this modification, China's legal tradition was the longest of any enduring political community in the world.

Much of China's legal history is associated with the great ruling households, or dynasties, which began with the Hsia, the Shang, and the Chou (traditionally, though uncertainly, dated 2205–1766, 1766–1122, and 1122–221 BC, respectively). During these centuries feudalism prevailed. Under the nominal overlordship of the king the country was divided into hundreds of states or tribes, ruled by various classes of lords, all administering their own laws. During the early centuries of the Chou dynasty the king did obtain a certain measure of central justice by having feudal lords bring disputes to his court. But beginning with the 7th century BC the authority of the Chou kings degenerated. The lords began to fight for power, and the hundreds of states were reduced to seven. The ceaseless warfare earned for this period from the 5th to the 3rd centuries BC the name of the "era of Warring States." This was the era, however, that also saw the rise of some of the most influential of Chinese philosophies, including those most important for law—Confucianism and Legalism (see below).

By 221 BC the king of the state of Ch'in had conquered the other six kingdoms and founded the Ch'in dynasty (221–206 BC) proclaiming himself Emperor Shih Huang Ti. He united China under one administrative system and set of laws. No longer was there a cluster of states with nobles swearing (but not observing) fealty to their lord king. China was now in fact an empire, for the emperor appointed administrators to govern the provinces without regard for local loyalties, and he ruled with iron discipline. Indeed, the harshness of laws and punishments under the Ch'in was one of the reasons for its early overthrow by rebel military officers, who established the Han dynasty (206 BC–AD 220).

During the Han dynasty the philosophy of Confucianism was resurrected (it had been proscribed under the Ch'in), but the new rulers nevertheless recognized that a vast empire still required the bureaucratic machinery of imperial control and some kind of unified administration with codified laws—all of which helped to make the country one of the wealthiest, most powerful, and most prestigious of ancient times. The chief subsequent dynasties were the T'ang (AD 618–907), the Sung (960–1279), the Ming (1368–1644), and the Ch'ing, or Manchu (1644–1911). Even during periods of unsettledness and changes of rule, the bureaucratic and legal traditions nevertheless continued to evolve, only slowly adapting to new conditions.

The oldest complete Chinese law code extant, that of the T'ang (the work of a commission of jurists in AD 653) represented the culmination of a long period of systemization and social development. The T'ang code begins with a statement of general principles—types of penalties (death, banishment, and bastinado), tables of relationship, of heinous crimes, and of persons entitled to privilege—and then offers a catalog of offences arranged according to the government departments held responsible, listing the basic penalty for each offense. Succeeding codifications varied the substance of the law somewhat, but the style and layout of the codes remained relatively constant down to the Manchu era (if one excepts the period when China formed part of the Mongol Empire in 1279–1368). In addition to the codes, there had also developed, by the time of T'ang, a well-articulated system of administrative law regulating the activities of government officials through sanctions ranging from merely a bad mark in an official's record to forfeiture of salary or dismissal.

Because the official statutes and penal codes served mainly governmental needs and generally ignored everything else, private needs had to be met by the private or semiprivate jurisdictions within the village, the clan, or the guild. This system remained basically unchanged until the end of the 19th century. A committee to modernize the laws on the German and modern Japanese models (1904–10) produced only a revised version of the Manchu Code, which remained in force until 1931. In that year the Kuomintang government of Chiang Kai-shek set up a legislative commission to work out a provisory constitution and a civil code on Western lines, but the great output of legal texts had no practical use in circumstances of civil war and the Japanese invasion. The People's Republic of China, established in 1949, deliberately rejected the legal system of the parliamentary West and promulgated new sets of laws of a Socialist persuasion (see SOVIET AND SOCIALIST LEGAL SYSTEMS).

Distinguishing features of Chinese jurisprudence. The Chinese legal system incorporated elements of contradictory social philosophies of early China—principally Confucianism and Legalism (or Fa-chia). Both arose as responses to the disorder of the Warring States period, the one emphasizing traditional moral teaching (*li*), the other advocating the introduction of legally stipulated punishments and rewards (*fa*).

Confucianism versus Legalism

The Confucian ideology contained the idea of social harmony based on ordered relationships and a hierarchy of classes and persons. According to Confucianism, it was the duty of rulers and superiors to educate their subjects or subordinates in benevolent and righteous conduct that would be appropriate to particular personal relations and concrete situations and that would be expressed in proper etiquette and reinforced by rituals. Punishment might serve as a deterrent but would generally be reserved for those persons hard to educate or too obtuse to behave properly (not entirely a matter of social class as has sometimes been asserted). Abstract concepts and generalizations were uncongenial to Confucianists; hence also was the idea of law. As against this, the Legalists, or Fa-chia, school advocated uniform objective standards that would be published for all to know and that would not require special gifts of character to understand or to apply; most important, these standards would be enforced by a system of defined rewards and punishments. Such standards or laws would serve the ruler as an instrument of control over his subjects. Whereas Confucianists saw punishment only as an extension of education, the Legalists opposed any cult of benevolence as softening and corrupting. Over the centuries, this opposition between conflicting principles continued.

The Ch'in had leaned toward the Legalist theory as an effective means for strengthening the state and unifying the empire, but the harshness of Ch'in methods made the law unpopular, thus reopening the way to Confucian influence. The dominant political orthodoxy during the succeeding Han dynasty accepted law as a system of punishments but introduced such Confucian ideas as variability according to status and circumstances. The official legal system thus accommodated the Confucianist view that was reluctant to concede law an important position in the state and the more realistic Legalist view that the harsh penal apparatus that had been inherited was useful for dealing with unruly elements and enforcing morality. What the conflicting philosophies had in common were these principles: punishments were necessary as deterrents; inequality and hierarchy were socially desirable; trade was not significant enough to be provided for in law; and moral prescriptions or legal commands, backed by sanctions, would automatically achieve the intended results (this last suggests the failure to see the significance of legal procedures or to wish to improve or develop them). These features were enshrined in the Chinese system. In practice, legal prescriptions served more as models or ideals to be aimed at than as minimum enforcible standards or ways of adjusting conflicting interests.

The role of punishment

The conception of the emperor's divine role in the universe also had its effect on law. The emperor and his representatives were considered responsible to Heaven for any disturbance in the earthly sphere, and, thus, whenever a disturbance did occur, punishment was considered, in effect, a means of restoring the cosmic equilibrium. The very occurrence of a legal case was deemed a disturbance, and thus a sentence of punishment was almost always the outcome. Furthermore, in general, law was understood as a system of punishments applied by officials to people who deserved them, and no distinction ever developed between civil and criminal liability. The law as such took no account of the claims that private persons or groups might wish to make on one another unless a disturbance occurred, when action would be brought to redress that disturbance.

The development of a unified empire brought everyone under one law, but the law recognized the principle of inequality by dividing the people into three ranks below the emperor—the privileged, the commoners, the unfree. It also recognized the gradations of the kinship hierarchy. Officials, whether active or honourably retired, enjoyed certain privileged exemptions with regard to government levies and legal actions; the higher their rank, the more numerous and extensive their privileges. In all cases involving injury, severity of punishment varied according to the relative status of the person concerned; an injury to a person of higher rank or senior in the kinship hierarchy carried a more serious penalty than injury to an equal or inferior (or no penalty at all if the injury was viewed as a legitimate exercise of discipline).

Courts and procedure. All citizens had an obligation to denounce wrongdoers to the magistrate's office of the local prefecture (*hsien*), an office that on certain days of the month served as the court to which individuals first brought their complaints or questions. It was the magistrate's duty to investigate all cases reported within the area of his jurisdiction, to apprehend suspects, and to bring them to justice—that is, to investigate and study the facts and decide under what section of the penal code the case should be entered and what punishment would be appropriate for the accused and any other persons concerned. (Cases involving persons related to the local magistrate had to be transferred to a magistrate of an adjacent jurisdiction.) If there was no section of the code exactly covering the case, the magistrate could resort to analogies suggesting relevant principles of some kind. A catchall section, "Things which ought not to be done," closed any loopholes otherwise left in the code. No appeal was possible to a principle suggested by the precedent of an earlier case, though previous decisions were included in revisions of the code for reference purposes.

The *hsien* magistrate and the administration of justice

Time limits for dealing with cases were specified, but there were virtually no restrictions on the methods that a magistrate might use either in his investigation or in eliciting a confession of guilt, which was required before conviction. Thus it was not unusual for accused persons to be beaten in court or sometimes even tortured. If a plaint proved to be unfounded, an unjustified accuser was liable to suffer the punishment that would have been meted out to the accused if convicted, and the magistrate himself was liable to administrative sanctions for any errors that he committed in applying the code. Most Chinese in consequence were very reluctant to become involved in court proceedings, and magistrates themselves were advised, in unofficial handbooks, to be cautious in accepting cases and to counsel parties to try to reconcile their differences without resort to the court.

Apart from certain categories of persons—such as women, juveniles, the aged, and those entitled to privileges—accused persons were not allowed to be represented in court. Consequently, no profession of defense lawyers, advocates, or counsel developed in China. Excluding those who received fees for writing petitions on behalf of others, the only persons specialized in legal work quasi-professionally were magistrates' legal secretaries. These specialists passed on their expertise to the disciples whom they accepted for training and whom they then recommended to a magistrate for employment as personal legal secretaries. Magistrates depended greatly on the knowledge and experience of these men to save them from errors, and some men could acquire considerable reputation for skill in this work and were relatively well paid. Some secretaries later became magistrates themselves by passing the regular official examinations for entry into the civil service.

Cases were referred upward through a hierarchy of courts roughly corresponding to the state's administrative hierarchy. (Although minor punishments could be administered locally, all cases requiring punishment more serious than beating with a bamboo had to be referred to higher authority according to the gravity of the case. Un-

Referral and appeal to higher courts

satisfied individuals might also appeal to higher courts.) A slight procedural difference was made between cases requiring a ruling concerning personal affairs (marriage, property inheritance, and so on) and those involving prosecution for crimes—a difference not quite the same as the Western distinction between "civil" and "criminal." At the provincial level, cases of the "personal" category were referred to the provincial treasurer's office and went no further, whereas those of the "criminal" category went to the provincial judicial commissioner. Cases beyond the competence of these offices and all cases judged by analogy were referred to the Department of Punishments at the capital, and cases serious enough to merit the death penalty were referred to a court composed of the three chief legal bodies at the capital for a recommendation that was then referred to the emperor himself for final decision. The final decision might be deferred two years, which offered an accused person a chance of surviving until amnesty or final acquittal—if he survived the rigours of Chinese jails.

The scope of Chinese law. *Law of persons.* Because the object of Chinese law was to regulate personal behaviour in the interests of the ruler, it emphasized obligations owed rather than rights enjoyed. Also, because its ethic was based on personal status, the law distinguished between persons according to their relative positions in society.

Emphasis on obligations rather than rights

As noted earlier, there were three officially recognized statuses—privileged, commoner, and unfree. There were in fact two types of legal privilege: the first consisted of a general bureaucratic privilege of exemption from physical punishments, public labour or corvée duty, certain levies, and so on, enjoyed by all who occupied official rank (or were honourably retired) and their families; the second consisted of privileges for various classes of persons who, because of their relation to the emperor or as a reward for illustrious service, were entitled to special consideration and could be tried only with the emperor's consent, unless they forfeited the privilege through treason.

Two forms of servitude existed. The first was official and involved persons and their relatives who were transported to the frontier or malarial regions after being convicted of serious crimes against the state, such as treason or rebellion. The second was domestic and arose from the sale of persons, usually girls and women, in times of distress. The sale was mitigated by the condition that a marriage had to be arranged for the girl on her attaining marriageable age or, if she bore her master a child, that she be treated as a secondary wife. A slave could not marry the daughter of a free man. And it took three generations for liberated slaves to regain completely normal status.

Other kinds of ranks or statuses were stipulated. In a family, for instance, unrelated persons resident in the household had to be assimilated somehow and were given the status of junior family members. By extension, certain other senior–junior relationships were recognized—such as teacher–pupil, employer–hired labourer, abbot–monk—and in all such cases violence was more severely sanctioned if the junior acted against the senior.

Family law. The importance of the family and the wider kinship group was recognized in the Chinese laws governing succession, inheritance, adoption, marriage, and divorce.

The importance of the family in law and culture

The father or senior male member was legally recognized as head of the family or lineage group, with wide authority over its other members and with power, during his lifetime, to dispose of its property. Descent was reckoned through the male line, and succession to the position of head went to the senior male in direct line in the next generation. If a man had no son, he might adopt an heir but only from among members of the next generation in collateral lines. Another method of continuing descent lines was the device of recognizing one male as heir to two lines of descent, in which case he could have a principal wife in each line.

Unmarried women were members of their natal families, but on marriage a woman moved to the family of her husband and was afterward subject to the authority of her husband's parents and seniors. Any property brought by the bride, apart from such items as personal ornaments, was transferred to the ownership of her husband's family. The position of a bride, who became a daughter-in-law, was legally weak, and she could rely on the physical protection of her natal family only if it could risk disfavour. In practice, however, the wife's position strengthened with time, more particularly after the birth of sons and the performance of mourning for her husband's seniors.

Marriage was arranged by formal agreement between the heads of the families concerned, after negotiation usually conducted through a go-between according to generally accepted forms. The agreement was signalized by an exchange of presents. Its terms—specifying, among other things, the period of betrothal—were binding on both parties, and failure to carry them out carried legal penalties. A man might take only one principal wife, but secondary wives were permitted, children of both being recognized as legitimate. It was common for poor families to take a girl into their families as an extra daughter, who, with less ceremony, later became a bride for one of their sons. In another permitted form of marriage, a family without a son could take in a bridegroom for one of its daughters; he then assumed the surname of his wife's family and with it the obligations of a son. Legally, the bride and the groom could not be from families closely related; theoretically, they could not have even the same surname, though this prohibition was not always enforced.

Arrangement of marriage and divorce

Divorce could be arranged without the intervention of state authorities. It was permitted on grounds of incompatibility if the *status quo ante* could be restored—that is, if the woman's family were willing to have her back. A husband could divorce his wife on several grounds, chiefly adultery or conduct unsatisfactory to his parents, but not if she had carried out mourning for his parents or if the material circumstances of the families had changed. An ill-used husband might hand his wife over to justice or sell her, though the law was silent about wives acquired by sale, and presumably this was resorted to only by the poor. A wife deserted and left destitute might file a complaint and apply to the magistrate for permission to remarry.

In addition to legal rules, lineage groups often adopted and enforced their own formal rules and sanctions for the management of their affairs and the discipline of members. These reinforced moral teaching and not uncommonly included a prohibition against crimes also forbidden by state law, including infanticide. Some also forbade members to engage in litigation.

Inheritance. An estate was divided equally among sons, except that the eldest son might receive slightly more, partly because of his extra responsibility in ritual duties and partly because of his usual responsibility to care for an aged mother. The fragmentation of landholdings involved in such a division of inheritance at each generation was avoided by some lineages by the device of setting up a charitable trust. Apart from gifts at marriage, daughters did not normally inherit property, though connections through marital relatives might confer other economic advantages.

Contracts. Formal contractual agreements are known to have existed in Han times and probably date from a much earlier period. Besides betrothal agreements, official law was concerned with land transfers, which had to be officially registered for purposes of taxation. Apart from these matters, agreements were regularly entered into for transactions involving sale of goods, tenancy, and employment of hired labour or apprentices. Issues over these agreements, however, rarely gave rise to court actions; they were customarily negotiated through a third person trusted by both parties, who would guarantee the terms of an agreement and apply appropriate pressure for the fulfillment of the terms. The middleman-guarantor received a fee, usually as a percentage of the value of the transaction. In form an agreement might be written, in which case it would spell out details of the specific transaction and the responsibilities of each party, and the deed itself would be physically divided into two "tallies," one kept by each party. Or the agreement might be an unwritten compact based on customary expectations—such as tenancy according to local custom or the mutual exchange of labour. Care for one's good name, frequently referred to as "face," acted powerfully to ensure compliance with terms of contracts and moral standards alike. Inability to fulfill terms because of insolvency and other reasons would be dealt with by customary mediation or arbitration. In the absence of lawyers, the need to have suitable contacts or go-betweens for purposes of introduction and guarantee involved much concern with keeping a circle of willing acquaintances.

Torts. Law in China concerned itself with deterrence and correction of offenders rather than with providing remedies for those who suffered wrongs. Its provisions regarding commerce and property other than land were meagre; such matters as contract and insolvency were generally left to guilds for regulation according to the local custom of the trade. No action for damages was possible in the official courts. No concept of abstract rights or entitlement developed, though land titles were registered because of tax liabilities. Actions for encroachment or trespass on land or about water rights or disputes about inheritance could be entered for adjudication, but litigation was resorted to only if other means of settlement failed, and the written rules of many lineages and guilds forbade members to engage in such litigation.

Private mediation or pressure or arbitration by ad hoc leaders was preferred, and arbitration of disputes was one important function of leadership everywhere in China; lineages and guilds, for instance, constituted themselves on occasion as courts and applied either their own formally adopted rules or local custom. An unresolved dispute might possibly be transferred through a series of progressively more public agencies, but, even so, only an exceptional dispute ever reached the courts of the administration. The notion of a test case was unknown.

Crime. For reasons no doubt connected with cosmological beliefs, the protection of persons was generally more heavily sanctioned than the protection of property, and apart from land, greater protection was given to public than to private property. Chinese law was rich in the elaboration of crimes of violence and in the minute specification of such offenses according to the method employed and the circumstances. Robbery and breaking accompanied by violence were more seriously treated than theft and trespass. Embezzlement was specifically covered only with regard to public funds. The law also distinguished between crimes that could be pardoned and those that could not, between acts committed intentionally and those occurring accidentally, and, in crimes involving more than one accused person, between principal guilt and accessory or secondary guilt. A number of "bureaucratic" offences were included in the code, such as a misuse of the official seal of a magistrate and misappropriation of public funds. Serious political crimes, such as treason, desertion, and rebellion, involved collective responsibility and included punishment of the relatives of a convicted offender.

Influence of the Chinese legal system. Stemming from a distinct philosophical tradition and unique historical experience, Chinese law retained its own special character until the 20th century. Moreover, China's achievements in law as in other cultural matters strongly influenced neighbouring lands in the Far East. The bordering region of Korea, for instance, was colonized by China for four centuries (1st century BC to 3rd century AD), and the ensuing cultural similarities have been compared with Roman influence on Britain. Certain Korean kingdoms drew up law codes on the Chinese model as part of a deliberate program of Sinicization. In Japan, too, during the 7th century AD, Chinese political institutions were introduced, and laws on the T'ang model were compiled, including a penal code, administrative statutes, and supplementary regulations. Chinese influence revived in Japan in later centuries, and commentary based on the Ming Code was invoked by feudal lords in codifying the

law of their domains; both code and cases were cited even when the substance of these decisions was clearly Japanese. The influence of Confucianism, strong in Tokugawa Japan (1603–1867), undoubtedly led the Japanese to prefer mediation to litigation in interpersonal disputes.

BIBLIOGRAPHY. The chief current work is D. BODDE and C. MORRIS, *Law in Imperial China* (1967), which lists in an annotated bibliography most volumes on the subject of Chinese law, both those written in Western languages and those written in Chinese. Material not covered in this work may be found in G. JAMIESON, *Chinese Family and Commercial Law* (1921).

(S.v.d.S.)

Chinese Mythology

Chinese mythology deals with the actions of gods and other supernatural creatures as they affect man and the world in which he lives. Chinese myths thus explain the origins of things and elucidate the continuing role of supernatural beings in the day-to-day life of the Chinese peoples. This article deals with the functions and role of Chinese mythology, its sources and historical evolution. It includes a detailed presentation of specific myths concerning heaven and earth, man, cultural heroes, animals, and a wide variety of gods.

FUNCTION, ROLE, AND EVOLUTION OF CHINESE MYTHOLOGY

Function and role. In China, as elsewhere, mythology has served to explain the otherwise unexplainable, by attributing the origin and current structure of the universe to the operations of supernatural beings. Chinese myths likewise account for the origin of man and have provided China with an uninterrupted cultural history, which began with quasi-divine saviour-heroes whose superhuman achievements benefitted all successive generations. Mythology also removed the frightful aspects of such terrifying natural phenomena as lightning and thunder by placing individual gods in charge of each natural force and thus making them accessible to men. In addition, numerous other deities are empowered to meet virtually every human need. Gods watch over the city, the field, and the home; they aid examinees, safeguard craftsmen, and protect women in labour. By their mere existence they imbue daily life with a supernatural aura. Mythology also provided the Chinese with perennial models for inspiration and imitation by establishing names and dates for legendary prehistoric rulers of extraordinary virtue. The invisible world of the supernatural is thus inseparable from China's past and current history.

Sources and evolution. Chinese mythology presents a double image: the relatively few myths of antiquity, about which little is known, and the numerous myths of later ages, about which a great deal is known. Though there certainly were myths in ancient China, early Chinese literature does not present, as the literatures of certain other world cultures do, great epics embodying mythological lore. What information exists is sketchy and fragmentary and provides no clear evidence that an organic mythology ever existed; if it did, all traces have been lost. Attempts by scholars, Eastern and Western alike, to reconstruct the mythology of antiquity have consequently not advanced beyond probable theses. Shang dynasty (c. 1766–1122 BC) material is limited to a few inscriptions. Chou dynasty (c. 1122–221 BC) sources are more plentiful, but even these must at times be supplemented by writings of the Han period (206 BC–AD 220), which, however, must be read with great caution. This is the case because Han scholars reworked the ancient texts to such an extent that no one is quite sure, aside from evident forgeries, how much was deliberately reinterpreted and how much was changed in good faith in an attempt to clarify ambiguities or reconcile contradictions. Ancient gods, moreover, rarely if ever appeared in art. It is notable that ancient Chinese culture grew out of a conglomerate of several aboriginal cultures that were vastly different, both in themselves and in their mythological traditions.

The early state of Chinese mythology was also molded

by the religious situation that prevailed in China at least since the Chou conquest (12th century BC), when religious observance connected with the cult of the dominant deities was proclaimed a royal prerogative. Because of his temporal position, the king alone was considered qualified to offer sacrifice and to pray to these deities. Shang Ti (Lord on High), for example, one of the prime dispensers of change and fate, was inaccessible to persons of lower rank. The princes, the aristocracy, and the commoners were thus compelled, in descending order, to worship lesser gods and ancestors. Though this situation was greatly modified about the time of Confucius in the early part of the 5th century BC, institutional inertia and a trend toward rationalism precluded the revival of a mythological world. Confucius prayed to Heaven (T'ien) and was concerned about the great sacrifices, but he and his school had little use for genuine myths.

Nevertheless, during the latter centuries of the Chou (c. 5th century BC), Chinese mythology began to undergo a profound transformation. The old gods, to a great extent already forgotten, were gradually supplanted by a multitude of new gods, many of whom were imported from India with Buddhism or gained popular acceptance as Taoism spread throughout the empire. In the process, many early myths were totally reinterpreted to the extent that some deities and mythological figures were rationalized into abstract concepts and others were euhemerized into historical figures. Above all, a hierarchical order, resembling in many ways the institutional order of the empire, was imposed upon the world of the supernatural. Many of the archaic myths were lost; others survived only as fragments, and, in effect, an entirely new mythological world was created. These new gods generally had clearly defined functions and definite personal characteristics and became prominent in art and literature. They were not the vague, often sexless and colourless gods of old. Many of these new gods are still worshipped in temples or in private homes and have annual festivals that tend to preserve their memory or perpetuate their cult.

Over and above his role as executor of the temporal order, the emperor sanctioned the divine order and created or elevated new gods. At the end of the 2nd century BC, the Han emperor Wu raised T'ai I (Great One, who was probably a secondary tribal deity of southern origin) into the position of highest deity formerly held by Shang Ti. In the 11th century the Sung emperor Chen Tsung named Yü Huang (Jade Emperor)—also known as Lao T'ien Yeh (Old Man Heaven)—to this exalted position, which he retained for the remaining life of Imperial China.

A host of other deities was in this way created or sanctioned by Imperial authority. This investiture was the result in some instances of the emperor's own initiative (at times catalyzed by dreams and visions), in other instances of portents, omens, and events, including induced events that were assumed to be manifestations of a divine power. Further, responding to popular pressure, the emperor frequently sanctioned a deity that had spontaneously found wide acceptance. Deities were thus sometimes taken from local cults and from Buddhism and Taoism. Historical personages were also commonly taken into the pantheon, for Chinese popular imagination has been quick to endow the biography of a beloved hero with legendary and eventually mythological traits. Myth making has consequently been a constant, living process in China. It can be observed, too, that historical heroes and would-be heroes arranged their biographies in a way that lent themselves to mythologizing. Among the best-known historical figures in the official pantheon are the two gods of war, Kuan Yü and Yüeh Fei. The first was a general of one of the contenders for power during the period of the Three Kingdoms (220–264), and the second was a Sung dynasty general who warred against the intruding Chin barbarians (12th century AD).

Imperial investiture guaranteed the gods continuous service, exercised in some cases by the emperor himself, in others by his civilian officialdom. To the extent that the gods were served officially, the hierarchy of the pantheon took on traits of the temporal bureaucracy. To the extent that they were living entities in popular belief, however, these traits tended to be submerged by the proliferation of popular mythologizing, so that even determinedly hierarchically minded emperors were never quite able to enforce a consistent divine order. Outstanding among the figures in this pantheon is T'ai Yüeh Ta Ti (Great Emperor of the Eastern Peak), who had temples all over the empire but resided on Mt. T'ai in Shantung Province, one of the five official holy mountains. He is a manifestation or appointee of Yü Huang (the two are hardly distinguishable in art) and presides over human life and death with a large subordinate officialdom. He procures life for every human being but is also in charge of retribution for human deeds and in this regard also presides over hell (or the 18 hells), where the wicked are taken to task in a most colourful manner. Most of the features of this inferno, including the highest judge in hell, Yen Wang or Yen Lo Wang (the Yama in India), were adopted from Buddhist lore.

TYPES OF MYTHS

Chinese mythology presents a vast array of myths, the central characters of which range in dignity from Shang Ti to lesser gods whose functions are determined by individual worshippers. The myths themselves account for the origin and structure of the universe and for the beginnings of Chinese civilization and culture. In culture myths, superhuman heroes are often assisted by mythological animals. Later myths, reflecting major religious traditions, show an abundance of lower gods, each generally invoked as a patron or protector.

Myths of the cosmos. *Creation of the world.* Although very little remains of ancient Chinese creation myths, there is mention of the world-egg motif and some evidence of the concept of primordial chaos out of which heaven and earth emerged. A more elaborate tradition concerns the separation of heaven and earth. Originally, the gods who dwelled in heaven do not seem to have mixed with the human dwellers on earth. A relaxation of this segregation eventually occurred through the endeavours of shamans and diviners. Human beings first ascended to heaven, then the gods took to descending to earth. Such migrations came to an end when Ch'ih Yu, one of the gods, enlisted the support of human beings in overthrowing Shang Ti. (In Chinese mythology, "original sin" is thus introduced by a god.) Those among men who withheld their support (and were slaughtered in consequence) complained to Shang Ti, who sent heavenly soldiers to squelch the rebellion and then ordered Ch'ung Li (or Ch'ung and Li) to set up a barrier between heaven and earth. According to one tradition, Ch'ung thereafter administered heaven and Li the earth. Nostalgic reminiscences of the time when heaven and earth were mutually accessible to men and gods seem to be the closest Chinese approximation to the concept of paradise.

After the revolt of Ch'ih Yu, heaven and earth were said to be kept apart by an elevation resting on four pillars stationed at the four corners of the world. One day Kung Kung, another villainous god battling for power with the highest deity, fell against one of the heavenly pillars (Mt. Pu-chou) and thereby caused heaven to be slightly slanted ever after. Another tradition introduces Nü Kua, a female deity, who is said to have fashioned, or refashioned, the four pillars by using turtle feet or multicoloured melted rock. The most elaborate Chinese myth concerning the fashioning of the earth (and the origin of man) is comparatively late (the earliest literary evidence is the 3rd century AD). In this myth, probably influenced from India, heaven and earth were forced apart when a certain P'an Ku grew ten feet every day. After his death, the parts of his body were transformed: his breath into wind, his voice into thunder, his eyes into the sun and moon, other parts of his body into mountains, rivers, plants, metals, the soil, and so forth. The lice on his body became the human race. Nü Kua is further credited with fashioning men out of the earth, some with care, others by merely dragging a string through mud. She sometimes appears as the bride or sister of Fu Hsi, China's first

Imperial investiture of gods

Shang Ti and Ch'ih Yu

legendary emperor. Later traditions ascribe demiurgic activities to both of them. Nü Kua's cult as the goddess of marriage and patroness of matchmakers still persists. Another cosmic myth describes Chu Ying (or Chu Lung) as having a human face and the body of a red snake. Day arrives when he opens his eyes; night falls when he closes them; winter and summer depend on the strength of his breath.

The sun and the moon. Among nature myths, sun mythology seems from its remnants to have been particularly rich. One text mentions that Hsi, the son of Li (administrator of the earth), helped his father administer the sun and moon. Hsi had a human face and legs growing out of his head but no trunk or arms. Other texts speak of the goddess Hsi Ho, one of the wives of Ti Chün (apparently a manifestation of Shang Ti), to whom she bore ten suns. In what seems to be the original version of the myth, Hsi Ho bathed the ten suns every morning in a lovely pond to restore their brightness before they set out, one each day, on their journey. The nine suns not on duty would perch on a giant *fu-sang* tree on the eastern edge of the world. The *jo* tree, with its glowing red leaves, was located at the place where the sun set. The sun is described as travelling in a chariot, occasionally drawn by a dragon, with Hsi Ho sometimes as charioteer. Occasionally, a three-legged raven appears in myths about the sun and its journey. The existence now of but one sun is due to the saviour-hero Hou I, the archer (see below).

Ch'ang O   Much less evidence remains of early moon myths, though the loveliness of Ch'ang O (Ch'ang Hsi, Heng O), the moon goddess, has often been celebrated in poems and novels. As the consort of Ti Chün, Ch'ang O gave birth to 12 moons, 11 of which somehow eventually disappeared. In another legend she is called the wife of Hou I; she fled to the moon when he discovered she had stolen the pills of immortality given to him by the gods. Hou I's pursuit was impeded by the hare, who would not permit the irate husband to pass until he promised reconciliation. Each year on the 15th day of the eighth lunar month, Chinese celebrate the memory of Ch'ang O's flight to the moon with the Mid-Autumn Festival (*Chung Ch'iu Chieh*). Round moon cakes are eaten and offered as gifts to friends and neighbours; many go outdoors to look for the outline of a toad on the surface of the moon for, according to one account, Ch'ang O was changed into a toad. There is also evidence of an early male moon god in some of the contributing aboriginal cultures, traces of which can be found in later literature.

Other nature myths. Myths about the origin of other natural phenomena are almost entirely lost, though some names of deities in charge of one or the other aspect of nature are preserved. She Chi, spirits of the soil and grain, were worshipped in very ancient times by China's emperors, for they alone had total responsibility for the country and the earth. Later emperors worshipped the gods of the soil inside the Forbidden City, Peking, on the She Chi T'an (Altar of Earth and Harvests), an altar covered with soil of five colours representing the five spirits of the Earth that reside in mountains and forests, rivers and lakes, tidelands and hills, mounds and dikes, springs and marshes. Hou T'u was first worshipped as Sovereign Earth in 113 BC by the Han emperor Wu. Though this deity seems to be one with She Chi, Hou T'u apparently also had a cult as the spirit of humanity and as the spirit of deceased emperors. Excluded from participation in these Imperial rituals, local communities and single families created their own "place gods" (*t'u-ti*), whose jurisdiction was limited to a single bridge, temple, field, private home, or some other such clearly defined object. Especially at harvest time, offerings were made to these *t'u-ti*, who eventually were represented as an elderly couple.

Myths about man.   *The origin of man.* Though ancient nature myths are relatively few, a lack of detailed myths regarding the origin of man is even more conspicuous. As already noted, one well-known but late tradition relates that mankind came from the lice on the decaying body of P'an Ku, but P'an Ku is described in another tradition as fashioning men from clay, some of whom were damaged by rain and became deformed as a consequence. Nü Kua, the deity who reconstructed the four pillars supporting heaven, was also said to have created men, some with care, others by dragging a string through mud. The same Nü Kua sometimes appears as Nü and Kua, sister and brother, whose union marked the beginnings of the human race. Ti Mu (Earth Mother) and T'ien Lung (Celestial Dragon) are likewise credited with producing all of creation, including man. The impossibility of reconciling these various traditions is typical of Chinese mythology, which has never formed a homogeneous unit.

Imperial clans.   Clan lore has also contributed, to some extent, to the preservation of myths of human origins. Clan genealogies drawn up to legitimize social positions made heavy use of euhemerized cultural heroes and frequently dipped into genuine mythological traditions to sustain supernatural origins. The ancestress of the House of Shang, for instance, was said to have become pregnant by swallowing the egg of the "dark bird," the swallow. The ancestress of the Chou family conceived by stepping into the tracks of a giant. Her son, Hou Chi (Lord of the Millet), was abandoned at some desolate place but grew up under the care of animals or birds and became the founder of the house of Chou. Modern scholars have shown that many seemingly rational clan genealogies can be traced to nature myths. Even later, clan genealogies made use of mythological imagery that is not necessarily specifically Chinese but sometimes of worldwide validity.

Saviour-heroes.   Among Chinese hero myths, that of   Hou I and
Hou I is among the most elaborate. One day the ten suns   Yü the
all appeared simultaneously in the sky, searing the Earth   Great
with scorching heat: Hou I downed nine of the ten suns with white arrows shot from a red bow and thus saved the world from destruction. This remarkable exploit was matched by such other Herculean tasks as saving the world from six destructive monsters. Despite his role as saviour-hero, a strange ambivalence is built into the image of Hou I. The wild-boar monster that he sacrificed, for example, was rejected by Shang Ti, and he appears in other situations as a villain. After marrying Ch'ang O, the heavenly moon goddess, he roamed the woods as a wild huntsman and had illicit relations with the fairy of the Lo Ho (Lo River). When she was called to task by her husband, the sprite of the Huang Ho (Yellow River), Hou I shot him in the head. Threatened by Ch'ang O with banishment to hell, Hou I pursued Hsi Wang Mu (Queen Mother of the West) and charmed her into giving him two pills of immortality to guarantee that he would become not only an immortal but a heavenly fairy. When he foolishly entrusted the pills to Ch'ang O for safekeeping, she made off with them and fled to the moon. Hou I was finally done in by a disciple whom he had trained too well as an expert marksman in archery. The ambivalence that surrounds Hou I can be accounted for by the fact that, like Hercules, he occupies an ambiguous position between the world of the gods and the world of men. Though endowed with superhuman powers, he was not himself among the immortals with whom he maintained various relationships, being married to one and battling with another. Not only was immortality denied him, but Shang Ti would not even accept the sacrifice that would have made him a ruler among men. He thus remained suspended between the heroic and the villainous, a person who at one and the same time made orderly life possible and who infringed upon that order. He is a killer as well as a saviour. Such a figure seems to represent a general mythopoeic (myth creating) trait that takes account of the coincidence of opposite forces.

Another saviour-hero is the key figure in Chinese deluge stories, which abound on all levels of tradition but differ in some important aspects from those prevalent in the West. In Chinese myths the great mass of water that covered the land was a primordial condition that, above all else, prevented man from engaging in agriculture. Because the deluge did not recede of itself, the labours of a hero were required to alleviate the situation. The story of Yü the Great (Tamer of the Flood) has thus been viewed as a myth involving the creation of Chinese society and not as a retribution for sin nor an attempt to destroy mankind.

The original version of the myth is almost entirely shrouded by euhemerization, but it must have run something like this. A man called Kun, ordered to control the flood, planned to accomplish his task by damming up the waters. Toward this end, he stole from heaven a piece of magic soil or mold, variously interpreted as the breathing, the living, or the swelling clod of earth from which plants grow. The theft so angered heaven that the harder Kun worked, the higher the waters rose. Shang Ti, in fact, ordered Kun to be executed on Mt. Yü, a somber place far to the north. When Kun's incorrupted corpse was slit open three years later, his son, Yü the Great, was brought forth. In time Yü sought to reduce the floodwaters by dredging and, after years of strenuous labour, provided outlets to the sea. Besides a host of sprites and spirits who offered Yü assistance, dragons and tortoises were especially helpful because they dragged their tails over the most suitable courses of prospective channels. In this way Yü made the world suitable for agriculture and human habitation. Although one myth recounts that Yü was transformed into a bear, his name is connected above all else with water animals. Not only was he helped by them, but either he or his father was engendered by a water monster, perhaps by the three-legged tortoise, the sprite of the Eastern Sea. Yü myths again reveal the not uncommon ambivalence in which opposites occur, for he is both the horrible monster and the tamer of the flood.

Cultural heroes. China's cultural origins are primary subjects of mythology ("charter myths") and are associated in large measure with legendary emperors whose actual existence is almost as doubtful as the very dubious dates that are traditionally given for their rule. The list is headed by Fu Hsi, a divine being with a serpent's body, who was born miraculously. Some representations show him as a leaf-wreathed head growing out of a mountain. He is said to have discovered the famous Chinese trigrams used in divination and thus to have contributed in some uncertain way to the development of writing. He domesticated animals, taught his people to cook, to fish with nets, and to hunt with weapons made of iron. He instituted marriage and offered the first open-air sacrifice to heaven. Nü Kua, his wife or sister, is naturally enough the patroness of matchmakers and the goddess of marriage.

Shen Nung (Divine Husband man) succeeded Fu Hsi. He was born with the head of a bull and the body of a man. By inventing the cart and plow, by teaching his people to clear the land with fire, and by taming the ox and yoking the horse, Shen Nung is said to have established a stable agricultural society in China (which Yü had to reconstruct after the deluge). Shen Nung cataloged 365 species of medicinal plants that became the basis of later herbological studies. Marvelous tales of his youth relate that he spoke after three days, walked within a week, and could plow a field at the tender age of three.

The third of China's legendary emperors was Huang Ti (Yellow Emperor), whose title indicates that he was born on Earth Element Day (yellow signifying earth). His fame likewise rests on great cultural achievements: he introduced mathematical calculations and organized the calendar into 60-year cycles still used today; he invented money, building blocks, and the compass; he constructed the first Imperial palace and founded the cult of sacrifice by making an offering to Heaven at the first altar raised solely for this purpose. Huang Ti brought bamboo to China, made musical instruments, and designed utensils of wood, metal, and earth. He constructed boats, carriages, and carts for oxen and studied medicine to prolong the life of his people. Many stories assert that Huang Ti's wife, later canonized as Ts'an Nü (Lady of the Silkworm), taught women to breed silkworms and weave fabrics from threads of silk. Among other culture myths, there is one about Lord K'ai, who wore two black snakes in his ears, rode two dragons, visited heaven three times, and brought down to earth the earliest ritualistic songs. And there is also the story of K'uei, who originated music by beating his belly with his tail.

Myths about gods. *Taoist deities.* Chinese religions, especially Taoism and Buddhism, have also been rich sources of mythology. Taoism's preoccupation with immortality, for example, has generated an extensive cycle of myths about Hsi Wang Mu (Queen Mother of the West). Though there is no mention of the moon in later mythology, the Queen Mother is probably no other than Ch'ang O in a new role. In any case, Hsi Wang Mu's cult survived and expanded. She rules over a land of beauty and pleasure in the Kunlun Mountains and is occasionally visited by select mortals. More frequent guests at her banquets are the Pa Hsien (Eight Immortals), all colourful creatures, who feast on the "flat peaches" (*p'an-t'ao*) of immortality that ripen once every 3,000 years in the Queen Mother's garden. Among the Eight Immortals, one rides a marvelous donkey that can be folded when not in use; another can make flowers bloom in an instant. The only girl in the group became etherial by eating mother-of-pearl and now floats at will over hills and valleys.

Tsao Chün (Furnace Prince) is one of numerous other gods belonging to the Taoist tradition. He is an alchemist in charge of the furnaces used to fashion plates of gold that confer immortality on the users. Lei Kung (Duke of Thunder), another Taoist deity, punishes earthly mortals guilty of secret crimes and evil spirits who have used their knowledge of Taoism to harm human beings. When so ordered by heaven, he gouges evildoers with a chisel carried for that purpose. Because Lei Kung is not a beneficent god, he is a fearsome creature with few temples. Those who honour him do so in the hope that he will take revenge on their personal enemies. Lei Kung also carries a drum to produce thunder and has assistants capable of producing other types of heavenly phenomena. Tien Mu (Mother of Lightning), for example, uses flashing mirrors to send bolts of lightning across the sky. Yün T'ung (Cloud Youth) whips up clouds, and Yü-tzu (Rain Master) causes downpours by dipping his sword into a pot. Roaring winds rush forth from a type of goatskin bag manipulated by Feng Po (Earl of Wind), later transformed into Feng P'o-p'o (Madame Wind), who rides a tiger among the clouds.

Buddhist deities. Buddhism has, perhaps, been an even more fertile source of myths than Taoism. Even ancient Chinese dragon lore was enriched with stories of Buddhist *nāga* (mythical serpent deities), and bits and pieces from the Buddhist pantheon were gradually accepted by the Chinese. They increased, for example, to 500 the original 16 (or 18) *arhat*, called *lo-han* in Chinese, Buddhist saints who have attained Enlightenment. Among them may be found one or other of the Chinese emperors, the Italian traveller Marco Polo, and a certain Hsi Ssu T'i, a transformed St. Christopher, who saved the child Jesus from drowning and thus made the very existence of Christianity contingent upon the deeds of a Buddhist saint.

The most important contribution of Buddhism, however, was the *bodhisattva* Avalokiteśvara, known in China as Kuan-yin, or Kuan-shih-yin, the deity of mercy "who hears the cry of the world." Kuan-yin, whose principal virtues are compassion and mercy, is worshipped in the belief that assistance and even miraculous rescue will never be denied to any devotee in a situation involving suffering. Kuan-yin is thus invoked by sailors who fear death from shipwreck and has become the protector of many craftsmen. The wide popularity of Kuan-yin's cult is also partially due to the fact that this deity is also the bestower of offspring. Great confusion and misunderstanding have marked discussions of Kuan-yin's sex. Some scholars hold that originally Kuan-yin was (and in some areas still is) worshipped as a male deity; they find confirmation of this in representations that have a beard and moustache. Others insist that a transformation took place and that Kuan-yin changed from male to female in the course of time. Still others insist that Kuan-yin is above sex and for this reason representations are either deliberately noncommittal or combine male and female characteristics. The common people of China, however, unquestionably view Kuan-yin as the goddess of mercy.

Legendary emperors

Lo-han and Kuan-yin

Local deities. Because nearly every Chinese city or town has its own supernatural magistrate, each Ch'eng Huang (God of the Wall and Moat) has great local importance; he is generally a deified human whose biography has been elaborated and mythologized. In addition to defending a particular town or district, the Ch'eng Huang has jurisdiction over everything related to public welfare: he offers protection from rapacious officials; he intercedes with higher celestial authorities in times of drought and flood; and he helps in the detection and punishment of crime. Lesser local gods make periodic reports to the town's foremost spiritual official. Most Ch'eng Huang have presided over their respective districts for centuries, but some have been replaced when the local people decided that the old gods had neglected their duties. Sometimes a Ch'eng Huang is a person of minor distinction or a minor tragic figure whose charismatic qualities posthumously stimulated the mythologizing tendencies of the populace.

Among household deities, Tsao Shen (God of the Kitchen or Hearth) is the most widely revered. Acting the part of a celestial spy, he observes the behaviour of the family and toward the end of the year ascends to heaven to deliver his annual report. On the eve of his departure, honey is smeared on the lips of his (usually crude) image so that only sweet words can issue from his mouth. He also protects the household from evil spirits, and during his absence the house is particularly vulnerable to haunting. Frequently, he is presented in company with his wife, who is then in charge of household animals. The Men Shen (Gods of the Door), whose martial images are pasted on the two halves of the front gate, are two deified T'ang dynasty generals who protected their emperor from a plot against his life and are expected to perform a similar service for those who worship them.

Gods of professions and of personal success. Because crafts and professions are frequently close-knit groups within society, they have had mythological worlds of their own in which much old lore has persisted. More widely known than either the gods of war or the patroness of matchmakers is Wen Ti (or Wen Ch'ang), the god of literature, who battles for unlucky scholars against magical interference and even against dragons. He is attended by K'uei Hsing, the spirit of a constellation, who was so ugly that the examiner failed him for this reason alone in spite of his brilliance. He now sees to it that gifted scholars receive due recognition. Less brilliant candidates have recourse to another of Wen Ti's assistants, Chu I (Red Coat), who helps them pass examinations by sheer luck. All classes of society honour the three stellar gods, known collectively as Fu-Shou-Lu. Fu Hsing is worshipped as one of many Chinese gods of happiness. Shou Hsing is honoured, especially on birthdays, as the god of longevity, though he has no temples. Lu Hsing, the god of prosperity, has special importance because he can urge promotions and salary increases. Ts'ai Shen, the god (or gods) of wealth, is worshipped by all classes of society in the hope that he can be induced to enter the home of his devotees to bestow some of the riches carried about by his assistants. Large numbers of Chinese also pray to Kuan-yin because she has the power to bestow children. Among numerous factors that determine the relative importance of individual gods is one's position in life, religious beliefs, and local environment.

Myths about animals. Among Chinese animal myths, dragon lore is the earliest and most persistent. The dragon (*lung*) is a beneficent force that dispenses blessings in the supernatural and natural worlds. He moves through the heavens and gathers clouds and moisture to disperse life-giving rains. As such, the dragon has always been venerated and became in time the symbol of China and of Imperial majesty. On the other hand, like rain itself, the dragon can sometimes be destructive and in this respect resembles monsters of Western literature. Occasionally, he guards a hoard of wealth, but a Chinese dragon never eats virgins and is never slain by heroes such as St. George and Siegfried.

In what is perhaps the earliest of China's dragon ballads, the dragon moves from its subterranean watery home to an irrigated field and then, driven by a dearth of water, flies up to heaven to conquer a new empire. He finally overreaches himself in his arrogance. It is said that this causes him regret, but there is no mention of punishment. Legendary rulers of the Hsia dynasty bred dragons, according to one tradition, and feasted on their flesh to ensure continued prosperity for their reign. In later art, the dragon acquired scales, body hair, and a more slender body and sometimes dorsal fins and wings. He can transform himself or make himself invisible at will. Imperial dragons appear with five claws rather than the usual four.

Five-clawed dragons, symbols of Imperial majesty, on a gold jewelled plaque believed to come from the tomb of Emperor Hsüan-te (1426–35). In the British Museum.

The phoenix (*feng-huang*), counterpart of the dragon in later Chinese symbolism, seems to have been unknown in ancient China, though some elements of the phoenix archetype, such as the burning of the nest, occur in connection with other birds. The *Shuo-wen* dictionary (1st or 2nd century AD) describes the *feng-huang* as a composite of many animals whose rare appearance was said to presage some great event or to bear testimony to the greatness of a ruler. Throughout the tradition, a special affinity between the *feng-huang* and music is stressed. Not only is the song of the phoenix particularly musical and full of symbolic meaning, but the *feng-huang* has a special appreciation of human music. For weddings, brides prefer phoenix ornaments because in systematized mythology the phoenix acts as the female counterpart of the male dragon.

The amiable Chinese unicorn (*ch'i-lin*) antedates the *feng-huang* and in ancient times was a harbinger of offspring (one appeared to the mother of Confucius before his birth). The *ch'i-lin* made its first appearance in the garden of Huang Ti in the 27th century BC and gradually turned into a kind of protector of saints and sages. It never walks on verdant grass or eats living vegetation.

Whereas the dragon, the phoenix, and the unicorn are highly fanciful creatures, other animals also frequently appear in Chinese myths: the bear with Yü, the hare with the moon goddess, the tortoise with Fu Hsi, and so on.

STATE OF MYTHOLOGY IN MODERN CHINA

The current state of mythology in China is difficult to determine, for age-old traditions die slowly even when discouraged. One would suspect, however, that such deities as the moon goddess, the kitchen and door gods, and the gods of long life and happiness are still known and honoured. In those regions, moreover, where Buddhism has retained its vitality, Kuan-yin and other Buddhist deities are surely worshipped. In Taiwan, mythological lore is very much alive, for the entire country is caught up in

Dragon, phoenix, and unicorn

the celebrations of all the traditional festivals; and Buddhism is actively practiced by a large percentage of the population. Though the number of Taoists is relatively small, the legendary Jade Emperor, among others, is prominent during the Great Festival (Ta Pai-pai), which is celebrated with elaborate ritual and feasting.

BIBLIOGRAPHY. DERK BODDE, "Myths of Ancient China," in S.N. KRAMER (ed.), *Mythologies of the Ancient World*, pp. 367–408 (1961), a good critical introduction, but limited to five classical myths; CHANG CH'I-YUN, *Chinese History of Fifty Centuries*, vol. 1, *Ancient Times* (Eng. trans., 1962), myths treated as historical material, based upon classical Chinese sources; *Chinese Myths and Fantasies, Retold by Cyril Birch* (1961), very readable versions of the most beloved Chinese myths, based on solid scholarship; ANTHONY CHRISTIE, *Chinese Mythology* (1968), beautifully illustrated, with a short but useful bibliography; BERNHARD KARLGREN, "Legends and Cults in Ancient China," *Bulletin of the Museum of Far Eastern Antiquities*, no. 18, pp. 199–365 (1946), an excellent compilation that makes a distinct division between myth material of the pre-Han period and that of the later periods; *Ku shih-pien (Symposium on Ancient Chinese History)*, 7 vol. (1926–41), an important critical presentation—vol. 7 especially valuable for the classical myths; HENRI MASPERO, "The Mythology of Modern China," in JOSEPH HACKIN, CLEMENT HUART, and RAYMONDE LINOSSIER (eds.), *Asiatic Mythology*, pp. 252–384 (1932, reprinted 1963), a good compilation of material, but of little relevance to classical myths; E.T.C. WERNER, *A Dictionary of Chinese Mythology* (1932), somewhat dated but still very helpful.

(He.W.)

Chinese Philosophy

The keynote in Chinese philosophy is humanism: man and his society have occupied, if not monopolized, the attention of Chinese philosophers throughout the ages. Ethical and political discussions have overshadowed any metaphysical (nature of Being) speculation. It must quickly be added, however, that this humanism does not imply any indifference to a supreme power or Nature. Instead, the general conclusion represented in Chinese philosophy is that of the unity of man and Heaven. This spirit of synthesis has characterized the entire history of Chinese philosophy.

HISTORICAL SKETCH OF CHINESE PHILOSOPHY

Rise of humanism

Roots of Chinese humanism. During the transition from the Shang dynasty (c. 1766–c. 1122 BC) to the Chou, China was changing from tribal to feudal society and from the Bronze Age to the Iron Age. A new economy and a new society required new tools and new talents. The Shang people had prayed to their ancestors for the solution of their problems, but the Chou people turned to man, though they honoured their ancestors no less than the Shang people did. Prayers for rain, for example, gradually gave place to irrigation. Man was in the ascendency. The Shang people had believed in Ti, the tribal "Lord," who was the greatest ancestor and the supreme deity who protected them in battles, sanctioned their undertakings, and sent them rewards and punishments. During the Chou, however, Ti was gradually supplanted by Heaven (T'ien) as the supreme spiritual reality. Its anthropomorphic (or man-patterned) character decreased, and its wishes were now expressed not in unpredictable whims but in the Mandate of Heaven (T'ien Ming). This mandate was absolute and constant, beyond man's control. In time, however, as man grew in importance, it was felt that rewards and punishments depended on man's virtue, for "Heaven is always kind to the virtuous." Thus, man's virtue became the determining factor; man could now control his own destiny (*ming*). Religious sacrifices continued to play a great role in the lives of the people; the meaning of sacrifice however was changing from a magical to an ethical one; that is, from ways to placate spiritual beings to pure expressions of reverence. It was in this atmosphere that the so-called Hundred Schools of thought emerged (6th–3rd centuries BC).

All of the Hundred Schools arose in response to practical conditions. Their philosophers were either government officials or scholars, travelling from one feudal state to another and offering ideas for social reform. Expressing their ideas in conversations, official documents, or short treatises, they set the pattern for later philosophers.

The existential character of Chinese philosophy has created the erroneous impression, however, that it is purely ethical and social and devoid of metaphysics. Though seemingly random and unsystematic, the philosophy of every school was the result of years of serious thinking and formed a coherent and logical whole. It was in each instance built on definite concepts about man and Heaven, whether the latter was interpreted as the Supreme Being or simply as Nature. This is true of all periods.

Periods of development of Chinese philosophy. Historically, Chinese philosophy has gone through four periods: the classical, the Neo-Taoist and Buddhist, the Neo-Confucian, and the modern. In the classical period (6th–3rd centuries BC), the chief concepts were Tao ("the Way"), *te* ("virtue"), *jen* ("humanity, love"), *i* ("righteousness"), *t'ien* ("heaven"), and *yin-yang* (cosmic elements of tranquillity and activity, or weakness and strength, respectively). Every school had its own Way, but the Way of Confucius (551–479 BC) and that of another traditional sage, Lao-tzu (6th century BC), were the most prominent. To Confucius, Tao is the Way of man, the Way of ancient sage-kings, and the Way of virtue. To Lao-tzu, however, Tao is the Way of nature. His concept was so unique that his school later came to be called the Taoist school. For all schools, Tao possesses the two aspects of Yin and Yang; the Tao endowed in man is his virtue; and the greatest virtues, especially for the Confucianists, are *jen* and *i*. Clearly, some concepts are ethical and others metaphysical.

The Neo-Taoist and Buddhist period

In the Neo-Taoist and Buddhist period (3rd–9th centuries AD), there was a radical turn to strictly metaphysical concepts. Going beyond Lao-tzu's characterization of Tao as Nonbeing, the Neo-Taoists concentrated on the question of whether Ultimate Reality is Being or Nonbeing and whether the principle (*li*) underlying a thing was universal or particular. Under their influence, early Chinese Buddhist philosophers directed their attention chiefly to Being and Nonbeing. Subsequently, Buddhist schools introduced from India were divided into corresponding categories, viz., schools of Being and schools of Nonbeing. The question of universality and particularity, or of one and many, led to the development of truly Chinese Buddhist schools, whose concern was the relationship between principle, which combines all things as one, and facts, which differentiate things into the many. In the Neo-Confucian period (11th–19th centuries), all ancient concepts remained basic (as they had been from ancient times), but under Buddhist impact metaphysics was needed to provide a foundation for ethical and social considerations. Consequently, traditional metaphysical concepts such as principle, material force (*ch'i*), Tao, Heaven, the Great Ultimate (T'ai-chi), and Yin–Yang became key elements in the vocabularies of Neo-Confucianism. It was its metaphysical character, in fact, that made Confucianism "new."

It is interesting to note that these three periods represent a dialectical movement: the classical period was concerned chiefly with mundane problems; the Neo-Taoist and Buddhist period was concerned with the transcendent; and the Neo-Confucian period was a synthesis of the two. The modern period, on the other hand (20th century), which consists of the introduction of Western philosophy, a reconstruction of Confucianism, and the application of Marxism, does not seem to conform to any previous pattern. Nevertheless, the humanistic interest and the spirit of synthesis are very much in evidence.

CLASSICAL PHILOSOPHICAL SCHOOLS

Of the Hundred Schools, the most outstanding were six —Confucianism, Taoism, Yin–Yang, Moism, the Dialecticians, and the Legalist school—which may be said to represent four different ways of life; *i.e.*, the Confucian way of man, the Taoist way of Nature, the Moist way of both man and Heaven, and the Legalist way of neither man nor Nature.

Confucianism. Confucianism is rooted in the teachings of Confucius and his followers Mencius and Hsün-tzu.

Confucius. Man is the theme of Confucian teachings: "It is man that can make *Tao* great," Confucius said.

He taught many virtues, such as filial piety, brotherly respect, loyalty, faithfulness, wisdom, love, and courage. The cardinal virtue, however, is *jen*, variously translated as humanity, love, or human-heartedness. Before his time, *jen* had meant a particular virtue, that of benevolence; but Confucius turned it into the universal virtue out of which all particular virtues will come. To him and to his followers, *jen* is simply *jen* (another word for man); *i.e.*, it is what a man should be. Significantly, the Chinese character for the word consists of two parts, one representing the individual and the other human relations or society. The ideal virtue, therefore, involves both the perfect individual and perfect society. This is the goal not only of Confucianism but of all Chinese philosophy.

For Confucius the perfect individual is the superior man, or the *chün-tzu*, literally son of a ruler. Up to his time the superior man had been an aristocrat; but to Confucius the superior man becomes one not because of blood but because of moral excellence. Such a man is "wise, benevolent, and courageous"; he is motivated by righteousness instead of by profit; and he "studies the Way and loves men." Confucius' emphasis was on practice. He left unanswered the question of whether by nature man is good. "By nature men are alike," he said, "but through practice they become different."

Confucius' two immediate followers. The unanswered question led to a diametric opposition between his two major followers, Mencius (*c.* 372–*c.* 289 BC) and Hsün-tzu (313–238 BC). Mencius maintained that man's nature is originally good, for he said that everyone has in him the "four beginnings": humanity (*jen*), righteousness, propriety, and wisdom. Therefore, man possesses the innate knowledge of the good and the innate ability to do good. This, he argued, can be seen in the fact that a child naturally loves his parents and that a man instinctively rushes to save a child about to fall into a well. All moral qualities are inborn and not drilled in from the outside. "All things are complete in oneself," he said. If a person develops his original nature and fully exercises his original mind, he can become a sage. If he does evil, it is not due to his original nature but to his self-destruction. Though Mencius' arguments may seem arbitrary, his doctrine has nonetheless remained orthodox Confucian theory of human nature up to this day.

Hsün-tzu, however, took the directly opposite position. To him the original nature of man is evil. He reasoned that by nature man seeks for gain and is envious. Because conflict and strife inevitably follow, rules of propriety and righteousness were developed to control evil and to train for goodness. Thus, goodness is acquired through artificial efforts. Whereas Mencius called for the development of nature, Hsün-tzu called for its control.

The two Confucian followers were also opposed with reference to society. Confucius understood human relations in moral terms—affection between father and son, righteousness between ruler and minister, attention to their separate functions between husband and wife, proper order between old and young, and faithfulness between friends. Confucius wanted society to be governed by men of virtue who aim at social order and welfare for the people. Both Mencius and Hsün-tzu closely followed these teachings. But whereas Mencius advocated a "humane government," ruled by men with a "humane mind," Hsün-tzu advocated government by law; and whereas Mencius recommended moral examples and moral persuasion, Hsün-tzu recommended discipline.

In the relationship between the individual and society, the ideal for Confucius was their balance and harmony. The ideal is *jen*, a subject Confucius talked about more than any other. "A man of *jen*," he said, "wishing to establish his own character, also establishes the character of others, and wishing to be prominent, also helps others to be prominent." In the end, there will be self-perfection, family harmony, social order, and world peace. Both Mencius and Hsün-tzu adhered to this doctrine strictly. But Mencius also took a step forward by coupling *jen* with righteousness—important for making *jen* specific and concrete. According to *jen*, for example, a person should love all men, as Confucius had taught; but according to righteousness, love should be applied differently in different human relations, each with its specific appropriateness. This is the Confucian doctrine of love with distinctions, often misrepresented in the West as love with degree.

When both the individual and society are in proper order, the Way is said to prevail. The Way, which is the moral law, is rooted in Heaven and is Heaven's mandate (*ming*). Confucius no longer regarded Heaven as the anthropomorphic Ti, who rules and makes decisions for man; instead, Heaven is the Supreme Being who "does not speak" but leaves the Way to operate by itself. He also taught that "without knowing the Mandate of Heaven, one cannot become a superior man." To Mencius, to develop one's nature is to fulfill one's destiny (*ming*), and that is the way to know and serve Heaven. Thus, Mencius carried the spiritual character of Heaven a step further. Hsün-tzu, on the contrary, looked upon Heaven simply as Nature. It does not exist because of ancient sage-kings, he said, nor cease to exist because of evil men. Its course is constant and its operation regular. Fortune and misfortune result from man's own behaviour and have nothing to do with Heaven. Man's duty is to adapt to Nature so as to control it. In this respect, Hsün-tzu pushed Confucian humanism to the extreme and, in his interpretation of Heaven, came close to Taoism.

Taoism and Yin–Yang. The Taoists, of whom Lao-tzu and Chuang-tzu (born 369? BC) were the chief representatives, were as much concerned with human problems as the Confucianists. Like Confucius, Lao-tzu's goal was to become a sage, or in Chuang-tzu's words, a man of "sageliness within and kingliness without." Philosophically, however, the Taoists opposed the Confucianists almost at every turn. As said before, their Way is not the Way of man but that of Nature. According to Lao-tzu, Tao is the course, the principle, the substance, and the standard of all things, to which all of them must conform. It is one and simple, like the uncarved block. In its essence, it is eternal, absolute, and beyond space and time; in its operation, it is spontaneous, everywhere, constant and unceasing, always in transformation, going through cycles and finally returning to its root. It is modelled after Nature and is called the "self-so." It is good like water, always benefitting things without claiming credit. It takes no unnatural action (*wu-wei*), and yet all things flourish. But it is nameless because it is indescribable. Furthermore, it is Nonbeing itself, not in the sense of nothingness but as not being any particular thing. It is out of Nonbeing that Being has come. When it is possessed by an individual thing, it becomes its virtue (*te*, "character"). The ideal life of the individual, the ideal order of society, and the ideal type of government are all modelled after it. In addition to simplicity, spontaneity, and vacuity, a good life is one of tranquillity, which characterizes the natural state; of weakness, which eventually overcomes strength; and above all, of nonaction, which means letting Nature take its own course.

Lao-tzu's naturalism was much enhanced in Chuang-tzu. To him, Tao is not merely Nature; it is "self-transformed" Nature. All things change at all moments. They are all different and even conflicting, but Tao transforms and harmonizes them and combines them into a unity. It is in this stage—of everything following its own nature and yet all forming a harmonious whole—that happiness and freedom are to be found. Therefore, the ideal man, the "true man," does not allow the way of man to interfere with that of Nature, but becomes a "companion of Nature" and forms a unity with Heaven.

The Tao of the Taoist is much more metaphysical than that of the Confucianists. In fact, Lao-tzu was probably the first scholar to put Chinese philosophy on a metaphysical basis. Still, Taoism is by no means indifferent to practical matters. After all, Tao is immanent in the world and always operates there. In the final analysis, it is nothing but the way things should behave. While the Taoists denounced conventional morality, they cherished love, wisdom, peace, and harmony no less than the Confucianists.

Lasting harmony is achieved when Yin and Yang are well balanced. Lao-tzu said that "all things carry the Yin and embrace the Yang, and through the blending of the material force they achieve harmony." The concepts of material force (ch'i), as well as Yin and Yang, were to play an exceedingly important role in Neo-Confucianism (see below). The Yin–Yang concept was also present in Confucianism. In the "Appended Remarks" of the *I Ching* ("Classic of Changes"), attributed to Confucius, it is said, "In the system of change there is the Great Ultimate. It generates the two modes (Yin and Yang)." It is also said, "The successive movements of Yin and Yang constitute the Way (Tao). What issues from the Way is good, and that which realizes it is the individual nature." Here lies the seed of Neo-Confucianism.

Generations from the Great Ultimate

Aside from its presence in Taoism and Confucianism, the Yin–Yang concept was also present in many other ancient schools. Along with it was the theory of five elements or agents—metal, wood, water, fire, and earth—opposing, complementing, or succeeding each other. Tsou Yen (305?–?240 BC) combined the two theories and became the leader of the Yin–Yang school. In the Yin–Yang theory, existence is a dynamic process obeying definite laws, following regular patterns, and evolving a pre-established harmony. Because of Yin–Yang, all things rise and fall, integrate and disintegrate; but all are related, and in the end man and Nature form a unity. Because of the cyclical movement of the five agents, the seasons, history, fortune, and misfortune proceed in cycles. The effects of the doctrine have been far-reaching. The Yin–Yang ideal dictates that in marriage there should be the harmony of the male and female; in landscape painting, that of mountain and water; and in spiritual life, that of humanity and wisdom. Things rotate, but they should do so in harmony.

Other classical schools. Confucianism and Taoism have come down to the present day as the two dominant systems of indigenous Chinese thought. There were three other schools of some importance, however, in classical times: Moism, the Dialecticians, and the Legalist school.

Moism. Actually, Moism, founded by Mo-tzu (5th century BC), was for a long time as prominent as Confucianism. In a way its approach combines those of Confucianism and Taoism. As in Confucius, the Moist Way is that of ancient sages, but its final sanction is Heaven. This makes Moism more religious than any other ancient Chinese philosophical school.

Mo-tzu's notion of universal love

The basic teaching of Mo-tzu is "universal love and mutual benefit." He taught people to love other people's parents, families, and countries as their own. As to benefits, he encouraged everything that contributes to wealth and population, avoiding anything that is wasteful and destructive. He strongly denounced extravagant musical festivals, elaborate funerals, and war. Though the Confucianists completely agreed with the Moist interest in man and his welfare, the two schools were bitter antagonists. Mencius attacked Mo-tzu on two fronts: he said (1) that the Moists were motivated by profit and not by righteousness and were therefore morally wrong; and (2) that, though the doctrine of universal love sounded good, it was actually the way of animals. In his view, if all people treat other people's parents as their own, there will not be any father-and-son relationship to speak of and the whole family system will collapse. This is just as dangerous, Mencius said, as the doctrine of Yang Chu (440?–?360 BC), who was only for preserving himself and would not care for the welfare of the whole empire if he had to sacrifice a single hair in exchange for it. In Yang Chu's case, society is sacrificed for the sake of the individual, just as in the case of Mo-tzu the individual relationship is sacrificed for the sake of the group. Confucianism demanded the balance and harmony of the individual and society.

If Mo-tzu neglected individual relations, Confucius (as Mo-tzu charged) neglected Heaven. Mo-tzu strongly attacked the Confucian teachings of humanity and righteousness—not for advocating them but for failing to recognize that they originated with Heaven. Mo-tzu traced everything to the will of Heaven. Men should love universally, he said, because it is the will of Heaven. What is good is what is beneficial not only to man but also to spiritual beings and not only to spiritual beings but also to Heaven. In Moism the note of Heaven is the strongest of all.

The Dialecticians (School of Names) and the Legalists. The Dialecticians also held the doctrine of universal love. Their philosophy may have been developed for the purpose of explaining or defending that doctrine. To the Confucianists names and actualities—such as titles and functions, words and deeds—must correspond. Hsün-tzu distinguished private, class, and general names and explained the reasons for them. The Taoists, on the other hand, rejected names as being a false representation of reality and were thus the most radical among ancient schools on this issue. Although the Chinese name for the Dialecticians is ming-chia, or School of Names, they discussed not only names but such problems as existence, relativity, space, time, quality, and causes. Whereas Hui Shih (c. 380–c. 305 BC) emphasized relativity and change, Kung-sun Lung (born 380 BC) emphasized the absolute, universality, and permanence. Other thinkers of the school presented paradoxes that showed sameness in diversity and the unity of heaven and earth and all things. Though very small, this was the only school primarily devoted to logical and epistemological problems.

Political absolutism and statecraft

Though ancient Chinese philosophy was built around man and Heaven or Nature, the Legalist school ignored them all; its whole objective was the concentration of power in the ruler. For this purpose, various thinkers advocated the enforcement of law with liberal rewards and heavy punishment, the manipulation of statecraft, and the exercise of power. Han-fei-tzu (died 233 BC) synthesized the three tendencies and became its representative philosopher. The school shared certain concepts with other schools—such as the equality of all men and the necessity for the correspondence of names and actuality—but it had no use for the Taoist natural standard of the Way, the Confucian moral standard of *jen*, and the Moist religious standard of Heaven.

The Legalist school triumphed over the other schools in the 3rd century BC, and its philosophy was put into strict practice during the brief period of the Ch'in dynasty (221–206 BC), when a ruthless totalitarian regime united most of the kingdoms of China and held them in an iron grip by terrorism, the burning of books, and other Orwellian forms of statecraft. Soon thereafter, however, Confucianism began to gain ground and in less than a century became the state doctrine. From then onward it controlled Chinese social and political institutions for some 2,000 years. Philosophy had to grow elsewhere, specifically in Neo-Taoism and Buddhism.

NEO-TAOISM AND BUDDHISM

Neo-Taoism. This heterodox development went in several directions. One was the movement of "pure conversation," an unconventional way of life expressed in elegant, refined, carefree, and witty conversations. Lasting from the 3rd to the 4th century, the movement aimed not only at freedom from vulgarity and worldliness but also at a transcendent reality beyond phenomena and at the meanings beyond words. Thus, the movement had a philosophical undertone that marked the new spirit of the age—a spirit prominent in another more important movement, that of the metaphysical.

In the movement of metaphysical studies (hsüan-hsüeh), called Neo-Taoism in recent days, attention is directed at ultimate reality behind phenomena. To the most brilliant Neo-Taoist, Wang Pi (AD 226–249), who died at the age of 23, ultimate reality is Original Nonbeing (Pen-wu), which is not nothingness or negation of reality but basic and pure reality, transcending all distinctions and descriptions. It is whole, strong, and always correct because of its accord with principle, which underlies all things and thereby unites them as one. In his commentary on the *I Ching*, Wang Pi argues that a man need not go to many particular instances to find a common principle, for any single instance contains the universal principle that combines all as one and whole. In his commentary on the *Tao-te Ching*, he puts principle behind Tao, for Tao is the Way in accordance with principle. Where Lao-tzu spoke of fate or destiny (*ming*), Wang Pi interpreted it in the sense of principle. In all this he raised principle to a higher philosophical level than ever before, anticipating Buddhism and Neo-Confucianism.

Kuo Hsiang (died AD 312), commentator on the *Chuang-tzu*, went in the other direction. Principle is also his central concept, but to him each individual thing has its own particular principle. Thus, different things have different principles, and for this reason everything is natural and self-sufficient. Chuang-tzu's doctrines of self-transformation and the equality of things are here put on a strictly metaphysical basis. Whereas to Wang Pi ultimate reality is Nonbeing, one, and transcendent, to Kuo Hsiang it is Being, many, and immanent. To both of them, however, the sage was not Lao-tzu but Confucius, who was "sagely within and kingly without" and not one who "sits in the forest with folding arms and a closed mouth." The Neo-Taoist movement was not influential but it did, on the one hand, bring Confucianism and Taoism closer together and, on the other, prepared for the development of Buddhist thought in China.

Buddhist philosophy. The development of Buddhist thought in China went through three stages.

Early Buddhist movements. In the first of these stages (3rd and 4th centuries AD), Neo-Taoism had a direct bearing. In the 3rd century there were two movements of Buddhist thought: *dhyāna* ("concentrated meditation") and *prajñā* ("wisdom"). The goal of *dhyāna* was to meditate so as to remove ignorance and delusions, and that of *prajñā* was to obtain the wisdom that things possess no nature of their own. Eventually, Buddhist thinkers came into contact with the Neo-Taoists and began to "match concepts" by equating a Buddhist concept with one in Chinese thought. They concentrated their attention, however, on Being and Nonbeing, basic concepts in Neo-Taoism. The seven Buddhist schools in this period held variously that Being came out of Nonbeing, that matter is "matter as we find it" (or actual things), that mind is Nonbeing in the sense that it is perfectly natural and vacuous without any deliberateness toward things, that phenomena are illusory, or that things are results of combinations of causes.

In the second stage (6th–8th centuries), a number of Indian schools were introduced, especially the Three Treatise school (San-lun) developed by Chi-tsang (549–623) and the Ideation Only school (Wei-shih) founded by Hsüan-tsang (595–664). The former regarded the nature and character of all *dharmas* (elements of existence) as unreal and all differentiations as dissolved in the true middle of emptiness; the latter school regarded the nature and character of *dharmas* as real, being perpetual transformations in the mind. These schools were purely Indian in essence, did not suit the Chinese temperament, and rapidly declined in the 9th century.

Schools of wisdom and concentration. In the meantime, truly Chinese schools were rapidly growing. In the third stage (8th–11th centuries), Chinese Buddhist philosophy developed along the earlier lines of wisdom and concentration. The former led to the T'ien-t'ai and Hua-yen schools and the latter to the meditation school (Ch'an; Japanese Zen).

The T'ien-t'ai school was founded by the monk Chih-i (538–597) in the T'ien-t'ai ("Heavenly Terrace") Mountain in eastern China. Though Chih-i based his authority on an Indian text, the celebrated *Lotus Sūtra*, the fact that the school has no Indian but only a Chinese name indicates its Chinese character. Chih-i accepted the two levels of truth, namely, the level of worldly truth of "temporary names" or *dharmas* dependent on causes for their existence, and the level of absolute truth of emptiness, as taught in the Three Treatise school; but he maintained that being both empty and temporary is the very nature

of *dharmas*. He advocated the "perfect harmony of the three levels"; that is, of the two levels and their combination. In this harmony, the three are one and one is three. The middle path, then, means a synthesis of phenomena and noumena (unseen basic realities). Here transcendence and immanence are harmonized so that "Every color or fragrance is none other than the Middle Path." Since all involves one and one all, the doctrine culminates in the universal salvation of all beings.

The same spirit of synthesis is found in the Hua-yen school, at once the most highly developed and philosophical of all Buddhist schools in China. It is also the most syncretic, most Chinese, and most influential. The school was established by Fa-tsang (643–712) on the authority of the Indian *Avataṃsaka-sūtra* (Chinese *Hua-yen*, "Flowery Splendour"). No Avataṃsaka school ever existed in India; the philosophy was essentially a Chinese product. Its central idea is that of the universal causation of the realm of *dharmas*. According to the theory, the universe consists of four realms: the realm of facts, the realm of principle, the realm of principle and facts harmonized, and the realm of all facts interwoven and mutually identified. Each *dharma* possesses the six characteristics—universality, specialty, similarity, difference, integration, and disintegration—all of which imply and involve one another, so that each *dharma* is at once one and all, and the world is in reality a perfect harmony. Consequently, when one *dharma* rises, all *dharmas* rise with it. In short, the entire universe rises at the same time. The Hua-yen philosophy goes beyond that of T'ien-t'ai in that, whereas in T'ien-t'ai things involve one another, in Hua-yen things by their very nature imply others—such as specialty implying generality and vice versa; thus, the universe is a set of interrelations. As such, it possesses an organic character. The mutual identification of principle and facts represents the highest Buddhist synthesis of phenomenon and noumenon. The influence of this philosophy on the development of Neo-Confucianism was strong and direct.

Equally influential was the Meditation school. The standard saying of the school is "Directly point to the human mind, see one's own nature, and become a Buddha." According to the most revered patriarch, Hui-neng (638–713), the human mind is originally pure. Erroneous thoughts and erroneous attachments are similar to clouds hiding the sun. When they are removed, the original nature will be revealed and great wisdom obtained. The way to discover the original nature is through calmness and wisdom, which are really one. Calmness does not mean not thinking or having nothing to do with the character of *dharmas*; rather, it means not being carried away by thought in the process of thought and being free from attachment to the character of *dharmas* while in the midst of them. When the mind is unperturbed by selfishness or deliberate effort and is left to take its own course, it will reveal its pure nature, and enlightenment will come suddenly. Thus, the mind can apprehend the great truth of this fleeting universe, see the Buddha nature, and achieve salvation. The debt of the school to Taoism is obvious. In its own turn, it vastly affected Neo-Confucianism.

NEO-CONFUCIANISM

The Neo-Confucianists, rejecting the Buddhist emptiness and the Taoist Nonbeing as negative and vague, substituted principle, which they regarded as positive, concrete, and rational. The idea of principle, negligible in ancient Confucianism, can be traced to Neo-Taoism and Buddhism, especially to Hua-yen; but the Neo-Confucian understanding of it and conclusions from it are utterly different.

The man who laid the foundation of Neo-Confucianism was Chou Tun-i (1017–73). Drawing from Taoist doctrines and elaborating on the *I Ching*, he held (see Figure) that the universe evolved from the Ultimate of Nonbeing, which is the same as the Great Ultimate, through the two material forces of Yin and Yang and the Five Agents (metal, wood, water, fire, earth), by the principles of Heaven (male) and Earth (female), to the myriad

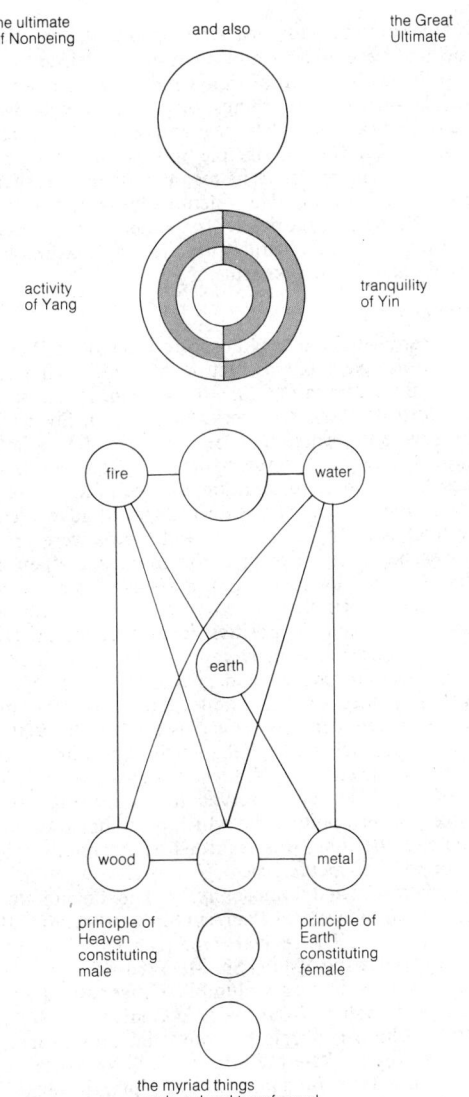

the ultimate of Nonbeing   and also   the Great Ultimate

activity of Yang   tranquility of Yin

fire   water

earth

wood   metal

principle of Heaven constituting male   principle of Earth constituting female

the myriad things produced and transformed

Chou Tun-i's diagram.

things. The five agents are the basis of differentiation of things, whereas Yin and Yang constitute their actuality. Since the two forces are fundamentally one, the many are ultimately one, and the one is actually differentiated into the many, each being correct in its own state of being. The fundamental concepts underlying this philosophy are nature and principle, the basic concepts in Neo-Confucianism. For this reason Neo-Confucianism is called the School of Nature and Principle (hsing-li hsüeh).

The school of principle and the school of mind. The men who developed the concept of principle and made it the central thesis of the movement and thus made Confucianism "new" were the Ch'eng brothers, Ch'eng **The** Hao (1032–85) and Ch'eng I (1033–1107), who first **Ch'eng** built their philosophies primarily on the doctrine of prin- **brothers** ciple and thus inaugurated a kind of Chinese Rational- **and** ism. These brothers argued that for a thing to exist, there **Chu Hsi** must be its principle. "Every blade of grass and every plant has principle," Ch'eng I said. He conceived principle as self-evident, self-sufficient, correct, extending everywhere, and governing all things. It is universal truth, universal order, and universal law. It is laid before man's very eyes and cannot be increased or decreased. Every principle is different but is, after all, principle. "Principle is one but its manifestations are many." Sharing these views, Ch'eng Hao stressed the principle of production and reproduction as the chief characteristic of nature.

The Ch'eng brothers never discussed the Great Ultimate. It was left to Chu Hsi (1130–1200) to "complete" Neo-Confucianism. According to him, the number of definite principles is infinite. As new things appear, new principles are realized. Yet all principles are but one, called the Great Ultimate. In substance, the Great Ultimate is one, but as it functions, it is manifested in the many; *i.e.*, in the innumerable concrete things. Reflecting the Hua-yen metaphor of the ocean appearing in many waves, Chu Hsi said that the Great Ultimate is like the moon. It is one, but its lights are scattered upon rivers and lakes. Thus the Great Ultimate is both the sum total of all principles and principle in its oneness. The material force is the actualizing factor. Operating as Yin and Yang, material force provides the stuff that makes a thing concrete. Things differ because their material endowments are different, and yet things share the same principle. Material force and principle are never separate: there has never been one without the other. In Hua-yen terms, principle and facts are perfectly harmonized. When endowed in man, principle becomes his nature. The standard saying of the Ch'eng–Chu school, often called the school of principle, is that "Nature is principle."

Leading Neo-Confucianists were by no means unanimous in this philosophy. Chang Tsai (1020–77) regarded principle not as above or different from material force but as the law according to which material force operates. To him, material force is the Great Ultimate. In its ultimate state material force is one, the great vacuity; but in its activity and tranquillity, integration and disintegration it is many, the great harmony. The two, however, are really one. Shao Yung (1011–77) agreed with Chang and the Ch'engs that supreme principles govern the universe, but he explained them in terms of number. In his cosmology, change is due to spirit, spirit gives rise to number, number to form, and form to concrete things, thus resulting in a structural universe that can be calculated and objectively known. Nevertheless, both Chang and Shao agree that principle underlies the nature of man and things.

In direct opposition to this doctrine, Lu Hsiang-shan Lu Hsiang- (Lu Chiu-yüan, 1139–1193) and Wang Yang-ming (Wang shan and Shou-jen, 1472–1529) declared that "Mind is principle" Wang and thus championed a kind of Chinese Idealism. Yang-ming Here lies the divergence of Neo-Confucianism into the Ch'eng–Chu school of principle and the Lu–Wang school of mind. Although the school of principle dominated Chinese thought from the 12th century to the 19th, the school of mind posed a strong challenge and almost replaced it from the 15th century to the 17th.

Lu Hsiang-shan refused to accept the distinction between principle and material force. Man's mind is not the function of his nature, as understood by Chu Hsi, but is rather the function of principle itself. The mind is one and is indissoluble. It fills and is identified with the universe. Throughout all ages and in all directions there is the same mind. It is identical with all things, because there is nothing outside the Way (principle) and there is no Way outside things. In short, the mind *is* the universe.

Continuing this line of thought, Wang Yang-ming also equated principle with the mind, by which he meant, however, essentially the will. There would be no principle or things, he argued, if the mind were not determined to realize it. If the will to be filially pious is sincere, for example, the principle of filial piety will become evident and the fact of filial piety will be realized. Thus, things or facts and the mind are the same.

Although the two schools radically differed as to whether nature or mind is principle, they agreed that human nature is originally good, thus reaffirming the tradition from Mencius. In the school of principle, man's nature is originally good because principle, as the source of goodness, is good; and evil arises when feelings are aroused that divert a man from principle. In the school of mind, the mind is originally good and endowed with the innate knowledge of the good and the innate ability to do good, as Mencius had taught long before.

Contrasts and controversies between the schools. On The inves- the question of how to discover principle, the schools tigation of were at great odds. Since for Ch'eng I principles are in things

things, *ke-wu* meant "to investigate things." All things should be investigated. One can investigate, Ch'eng I said, by studying one thing intensively or many things extensively, by reading books, by studying history, and by handling human affairs. Chu Hsi emphasized more the systematic methods of induction and deduction. Both Lu and Wang vigorously opposed Chu's external approach. Since the mind is principle, clearly to investigate things is to investigate the mind. All principles being inherent and complete in the mind, there is no need to look outside. Thus, investigation of things does not mean a rational and objective study of external objects but "to eliminate what is incorrect in the mind so as to preserve the correctness of its original substance." What is needed is to concentrate and be calm. As delusions and evil thoughts are removed, the original purity of the mind will shine. To what extent Wang owed his ideas to the Buddhist meditation school is difficult to determine, but he was severely attacked as a Buddhist in Confucian disguise. Since Wang emphasized the will, he held that a man's will must be sincere before he proceeds to investigate things. In this he stood in direct opposition to Chu Hsi's contention that only after a man has investigated things and obtained knowledge can his will become sincere. Wang also went a step further than Chu Hsi in the relationship between knowledge and action. To Chu Hsi, a man's knowledge and action depend on each other; but to Wang they are the same. Wang said that since all men have the innate ability to do good, they naturally extend their knowledge into action. Knowledge and action are really identical. According to Wang, knowledge is the beginning of action and action the completion of knowledge. No one knows filial piety until he has practiced it. Here are Wang's two famous doctrines—the extension of innate knowledge and the unity of knowledge and action—both new in the history of Chinese thought.

The controversy between Chu Hsi and Wang Yang-ming about investigation of things is one of the most vigorous and celebrated in Chinese history. Actually, it concerned only method and not objective because for all Neo-Confucianists the highest good is *jen*. In the Confucian tradition, *jen* is humanity, the moral quality that makes a person a true man. What is new in Neo-Confucianism is that, whereas the traditional concept did not extend beyond the love of all men, Neo-Confucianism extended it to cover the entire universe and provided it with a metaphysical foundation leading to the cardinal doctrine of "forming one body with heaven, earth, and all things." The Ch'eng brothers added a new note to *jen* by interpreting the word in its other sense, that of seed and growth. *Jen* was then understood to be the chief characteristic of heaven and earth, the production and reproduction of things. This life-giving character is the highest good. Being love in the broadest sense, it should be extended to include all men, all things, and heaven and earth. In Chang Tsai's essay, "Western Inscription," heaven and earth are regarded as the parents of all men, and all men are brothers. In Neo-Confucianism, *jen* has reached the zenith.

Later developments. K'ang Yu-wei (1858–1927) conceived of a world of great unity, in which all possible classes and distinctions are abolished, a Utopia to be gained through the three stages of historical progress from the age of chaos, to that of small peace and, finally, to that of great unity. The philosophical basis of this is *jen*, which he equated with ether and electricity, which create, attract, permeate, and unite all things.

It is true that all Neo-Confucianists have remained faithful to the concepts of principle and *jen;* but revolts against the methods of both the school of principle and the school of mind to achieve them arose in the 17th and 18th centuries, notably in Yen Yüan (1635–1704) and in Tai Chen (1724–77). The introduction of Western knowledge and new historical conditions made the reaction inevitable. The demand was growing to replace philosophical speculation with "investigation on the basis of concrete evidence" and practical learning. Yen considered that principle, nature, destiny, sincerity of the will, and similar subjects close to the hearts of Neo-Confucianists

can be found only in actual learning through the practice of music and ceremonies, the vocation of agriculture, and so forth. Investigation of things meant not the study of principle—whether in things or in the mind—but learning from practical experience and solving practical problems. To Tai Chen, principle was nothing but the order of things, and by things he meant daily affairs, such as drinking and eating. He relentlessly attacked the school of principle in particular for suppressing human desires in favour of an abstract principle of Heaven; yet he fully subscribed to the doctrine of *jen*.

THE 20TH CENTURY

Twentieth-century Chinese philosophy went from Westernization, through a reconstruction of traditional philosophy, to the triumph of Marxist Maoism. In the second and third decades, the works of Darwin, Spencer, and others were translated and the doctrines of Haeckel, Kropotkin, Nietzsche, Schopenhauer, Bergson, Eucken, Descartes, and James, in addition to Plato, Kant, and Hegel, were introduced, each with his special advocates. Later, Whitehead, Royce, Carnap, and others were promoted by earnest if small groups. This movement opened the Chinese eye to new philosophical vistas in metaphysics, logic, and epistemology (theory of knowledge). The general tone was scientific, positivistic, and pragmatic. Of all Western systems, the most influential was Pragmatism, which was introduced and promoted by Hu Shih (1891–1962), leader of the intellectual revolution of 1917. In the "polemic of science versus life" in the 1920s, leading Chinese intellectuals debated the question as to whether or not science could form the basis of a philosophy of life. The debate served to question the supremacy of Western philosophy which, as understood by the Chinese at the time, was regarded as essentially scientific as opposed to metaphysical.

Revival of traditional philosophy. The debate undoubtedly paved the way for the resurgence of traditional Chinese philosophy. The revival came especially in Fung Yu-lan (born 1895) and Hsiung Shih-li (1883–1968).

Trained in philosophy at Columbia University, Fung derived his Rationalism from the Neo-Confucian school of principle, whose concepts he converted into formal, logical ones. In his "New Rationalism," set forth in 1939, there are four fundamental concepts: principle, material force, the substance of Tao, and the Great Whole. The concept of principle is derived from the Ch'eng I–Chu Hsi proposition that "As there are things, there must be their specific principles." To Fung, however, whereas a thing must follow principle, principle does not have to be actualized in a thing. The concept of material force is derived from the Ch'eng–Chu proposition, "If there is a principle, there must be material force." To Fung, it is true that material force, being the material of actualization, is the ground and power of existence; but such force itself does not exist as a thing either in principle or in the actual world. Tao means a "universal operation," the universe of daily renewal and incessant change. Finally, the Great Whole, in which all is one and one is all, is the Absolute. All four are treated as formal concepts and not as assertions about the actual world. Basically, Fung's philosophy is a combination of Neo-Confucianism and Western Realism and logic; but in regarding the world of actuality as secondary, he has really replaced Neo-Confucianism, essentially a philosophy of immanence, with a philosophy of transcendence. From 1936 to 1946, he wrote five books to complete this philosophy, which he has called a "new tradition."

In 1950, soon after the Communist triumph in China, Fung repudiated his own philosophy as Idealistic, abstract, and devoid of historical and practical character. From 1956 to 1963, he was severely attacked for advocating the "method of continuing abstract ideas" in Chinese philosophy and the idea of "form of universality" in Chinese concepts. In 1962–64, under Communist Party guidance, he wrote a new version of his influential *History of Chinese Philosophy* (1934), a version that he said was written from the Marxian point of view. Fung now maintains that Idealism and Materialism have conflicted,

Doctrine of humanity in Neo-Confucianism

Fung Yu-lan's Rationalism

attacked, influenced, and penetrated each other throughout Chinese history; but he also insists that certain Chinese concepts, such as the Confucian *jen*, have a form of universality and that such abstract concepts should be perpetuated. He has remained silent in recent years. Apparently his "new version" still holds.

Hsiung Shih-li's Idealism

Just as the school of mind paralleled the school of principle, so the philosophy of Hsiung Shih-li parallels that of Fung. Hsiung's philosophy is a "new Idealism," which is based on the *I Ching* and, to some extent, on Wang Yang-ming but which is expressed in the terminology of the Buddhist Ideation Only school. According to him, reality is an endless process of production and reproduction, giving rise to a new transformation at every instant. But reality and manifestation, or substance and function, are one. In its closing aspect (when the universe becomes finite, contracts, and assumes a definite form), original substance tends to integrate into matter, whereas in its opening aspect (when the universe becomes free and infinite, expands, and has no formal restrictions), it tends to maintain its own nature and be its own master, and to result in the mind itself. Thus, Hsiung has avoided Chu Hsi's bifurcation of principle and material force and Wang's subordination of material force to the mind and has provided the idea of dynamic change in Neo-Confucianism with a metaphysical foundation. Completely ignored in mainland China, he has had considerable influence among Chinese philosophers abroad.

Marxism. In contemporary China, Marxism is the official philosophy. Marxist thought had been growing in China since the mid-1920s, and by the time of the establishment of the People's Republic in 1949, it had gone through Leninism to Maoism. The official ideology does not prohibit the study of traditional Chinese philosophy but has subjected it to critical evaluation and severe criticism. In 1955 a strong attack was launched against the pragmatist Hu Shih for his "reactionary philosophical thought" and for his undermining of Materialism in Chinese philosophy. From 1957 to the middle of 1960, many debates were carried on and many books and journals published. One topic of debate centred on the nature of the history of Chinese philosophy. Though there was no unanimity of opinion, the "correct" viewpoint was that the history of Chinese philosophy is but a part of the world history of philosophy and as such is a history of the struggle between Materialism and Idealism. The conflict between the theories of the original good and evil character of human nature, the opposition between principle and material force, the contradiction between Being and Nonbeing, and the conflict between names and actuality were given as evidence of this continuous struggle. As such, the history of Chinese philosophy is but the development of Marxism–Leninism in Chinese history. That part of China's philosophical heritage that is Materialistic and possesses a class nature must be continued and promoted. And this must be done under the guidance of Mao Tse-tung's writings.

Materialism versus Idealism

In pursuance of this objective, many naturalistic philosophers were interpreted as Materialists; Materialism in certain philosophers was magnified; and minor Materialists were given a prominence entirely out of proportion to their thought, work, or influence in Chinese history. Chang Tsai, who replaced universal principle with material force as the ultimate reality, Wang Fu-chih (1619–92), who equated concrete things with Tao, and Tai Chen, who revolted against the suppression of human desires, were all hailed as great Materialists.

In this intellectual climate, Lao-tzu and Confucius, as well as other classical philosophers, were critically re-evaluated. In a forum in 1959 and in later publications, some thinkers interpreted the concept of Tao in Materialistic terms on the grounds that Tao is the basic substance of all things, their necessary nature, the law of change, the condition of existence, and the sum total of things. Others argued that the concept of Tao is Idealistic because Tao is indescribable, transcends space and time, comes from Nonbeing, is the One and Absolute, and is spirit. In any case, the official view is that only the Materialistic aspect of Lao-tzu should be continued.

From 1960 to 1962, 13 discussion meetings were held on Confucius. The discussions revolved around four main questions: Confucius' concept of Heaven, whether he was an Idealist, his doctrine of *jen* and rites, and his class standpoint. The discussion on Heaven dealt not so much with the metaphysical nature of Heaven as with the Heavenly mandate, whether it was deterministic or alterable through man's effort. Confucius was described variously as an Idealist and a Materialist, depending upon whether one understood Confucius' Heaven as physical or as the Supreme Being and upon whether or not the Way of Heaven of which Confucius spoke meant physical natural laws. As to *jen* and rites, many felt that the Confucian *jen* meant love for one's own class, that the rites were designed to support slavery, and that both should therefore be attacked and rejected; but Fung Yu-lan insisted that the Confucian *jen* possessed in itself a universal character—*i.e.*, a love for all. Again, the general view was that only the progressive and Materialistic elements should be continued. Other philosophers such as Wang Fu-chih have also been discussed at the forums, but Neo-Confucianism has been virtually ignored both in meetings and in publications.

Mao Tse-tung is not labelled as a philosopher, but his two essays, "On Practice" (1937) and "On New Democracy" (1940), have set the pattern and determined the direction of Chinese philosophy in China. In his "On Practice," he wants people to "discover truth through practice and through practice to verify and develop truth." Though Mao is putting forth the dialectical Materialistic theory of knowledge and doing, one cannot help noticing the influence of the traditional Chinese emphasis on the correspondence of words and deeds and Wang Yang-ming's doctrine of the unity of knowledge and action. In his essay "On New Democracy," Mao says that "the new democratic culture is scientific . . . . and it can never form a united front with any reactionary idealism." A splendid ancient culture was created during the long period of China's feudal society, he said, but "its feudal dross must be thrown away and its democratic essence absorbed." In short, the philosophy in new China must be practical, scientific, democratic, and popular; *i.e.*, for the masses. Philosophers and intellectuals must go to the masses and work on the farms. All abstract concepts, Idealistic theories, and subjectivisms of any kind must be thrown overboard. Instead, philosophy must be practical and aim at the concrete development of society. Thought and practice and intellectuals and the working masses must be united. The effort in China is not to develop any new theory of technical philosophy or produce any individual philosopher but to meet the practical needs of the masses. In terminology and reasoning, this philosophy is sharply different from traditional Chinese philosophy, but there is still the essential agreement that man should occupy the centre of thought.

Thought of Mao Tse-tung

BIBLIOGRAPHY. Chinese philosophy is accessible to the West chiefly through the publications of FUNG YU-LAN and WING-TSIT CHAN. See FUNG YU-LAN, *A History of Chinese Philosophy*, 2nd ed., 2 vol. (Eng. trans. 1952–53), the best treatment of the subject, with ample source materials and authoritative discussions; WING-TSIT CHAN (comp. and trans.), *A Source Book in Chinese Philosophy* (1963; paperback, 1969), sources with introductions and interwoven comments; and H.G. CREEL, *Chinese Thought: From Confucius to Mao Tsê-tung* (1953; paperback, 1960), not a complete history but, with basic doctrines clearly stated and expertly discussed, it is especially useful for the beginner. Other recommended works are: WING-TSIT CHAN, *An Outline and Annotated Bibliography of Chinese Philosophy*, rev. ed. (1969); *Chinese Philosophy, 1949–1963: An Annotated Bibliography of Mainland China Publications* (1967); "Review of 'Chung-kuo che-hsüeh shih hsin-pien,' Vol. I, by Fung Yu-lan," *Journal of Asian Studies*, 24:495–497 (1965), showing changes in Fung's thinking under the Communist regime; *Historical Charts of Chinese Philosophy* (1955); FUNG YU-LAN, *A Short History of Chinese Philosophy* (Eng. trans. 1948); *The Spirit of Chinese Philosophy* (Eng. trans. 1947); HOU WAI-LU *et al.*, *A Short History of Chinese Philosophy* (Eng. trans. 1959), a Maoist interpretation published in Peking.

(W.-T.C.)

Chinese Religion

Chinese religion consists in the beliefs and practices of both the folk religious traditions and the great religious traditions of China (including Taoism, Confucianism, and Buddhism).

Chinese religion may be regarded as essentially an expression of Chinese culture, rather than as several systems of dogma. The Chinese generally did not separate the religious from other aspects of their lives. Exceptions to this were the professional religious, and lay people who joined together in cult societies of religious and quasi-religious character. It is convenient to distinguish between two currents, or levels, of Chinese religion—a folk or popular level and an elite or philosophic one. A single preoccupation, however, dominates Chinese religion: the ancestral cult.

Ewing Krainin

Spirits of the family dead being honoured with offerings of food and incense in a Chinese graveside ceremony in Malaya.

Folk religion. A complex of spiritistic ideas deriving from, and often maintaining the features of, primitive religion has been an important component of religion in China down through the centuries to the present day. Folk religion is not well explored, but its continuing presence is unmistakable. The fact that China was always predominantly a peasant society assured that its folk religion would remain vital. The folk religion absorbed many elements from the more sophisticated systems, such as Confucian and Taoist philosophy and Buddhism, transforming these in the process to suit the level of the common people.

Religion and the literati. The Chinese themselves distinguished between the cults (*chiao*) whose religious inspiration derives from the philosophical sources and the philosophical schools as such (*chia*). The scholarly class prided itself not only upon its literary attainments but upon a rational outlook that set it far above the vulgar masses. The Confucian tradition, which dominated the education of literati from the 2nd century BC on, was humanistic, rationalistic, often overtly agnostic. The classical works of Taoism (*Lao-tzu* or *Tao-te Ching*, and *Chuang-tzu*) were philosophical and poetic. Even many of the texts by Buddhist writers were devoted to philosophical problems underlying religion. Although the literati may not have shared in the grosser superstitions of

the illiterate populace, they too were religious. At the minimum they carried on the ancestral cult, as officials they had many religious duties, and as intelligentsia they formulated the basic concepts as well as the refinements of the Chinese world view.

The history of Chinese religion may for convenience be presented in four major divisions: emergence of Chinese religion; formulation of the Great Tradition; dominance of Buddhism and religious Taoism; renaissance of the Great Tradition; to which may be added a postscript on foreign religions and modern conditions.

Emergence of Chinese religion. Bronze age sites at Chengchou and Anyang in the north-central province of Honan, dating from the 14th century BC, have yielded abundant archaeological evidence concerning religion: tombs, sacrificial remains, ceremonial bronzes, oracle bones. The latter, continuing and refining the Neolithic practice of scapulimancy (bone divination), reveal belief in the postmortem powers of ancestors, and the anxiety of their descendants to placate and receive blessings from them. This evidence, in conjunction with slightly later texts preserved in *Shu Ching* ("Book of History") and *Shih Ching* ("Book of Odes"), indicates that "ancestor worship" was already central in the religion of the royal house. The royal ancestors dwelt in Heaven with the Supreme Ruler, called Ti or Shang Ti. If pleased by the behaviour of their living representative, the ancestors would persuade the Supreme Ruler to send down blessings; if displeased, the converse would take place. How far this ancestral cult was spread among the people is unknown but during early Chou (c. 1122–221 BC) it was certainly common among the aristocratic clans.

While ancestor worship was the warp of Chinese religion, there were other important threads forming the woof: belief in spirits of many sorts, animal, celestial, meteorological, topographical; the cult of the tutelary (guardian) deity of the locality; the conception of fate or destiny; the legitimation of kingship by the Heavenly Mandate of Shang Ti; elaborate rituals (including human sacrifice); the emergence of a specialized profession of divination, which perhaps involved a monopoly of that arcane (mysterious) power, writing. During early Chou the basic cosmological concepts of the Chinese also evolved, although they were not clearly enunciated until the following period.

Formulation of the Great Tradition. This period begins with the philosopher Confucius (551–479 BC) and extends into early Han dynasty (2nd century BC). For religion, as for all else, two historical factors were of supreme consequence: the breakdown of an earlier feudalism with concomitant political chaos and increasing social mobility, and the perfection and popularization of the writing system. The former resulted in a new age of vigorous free thought, while the latter permitted the recording and systematizing of this thought. As if to exemplify the inescapable principle of duality in all things (*yin-yang*), the Great Tradition itself, as formulated in late Chou and early Han, was developed in two opposing, yet complementary, Ways: Confucian and Taoist. Confucianism was formalistic, ritualistic, ethical, familial, and societal in its emphases; Taoism balanced it by affirming the values of asocial individualism, anarchism, mystical experience, and a generally aesthetic response to the cosmos.

The Taoists searched for individual salvation, and by the end of the period they had evolved various techniques—alchemical, yogic (physical and mental discipline), dietary, sexual—for the prolongation of life and even for immortality.

In both the Ch'in dynasty (221–206 BC), which unified China into a polity that lasted until the 20th century, and the early Han dynasty, China's first great empire, religious activity was phenomenal. "Religious Taoism" came of age, especially the quest for immortality; at the same time it was an age of great credulity and superstition—characteristics not only of the spiritistic religion of

Origins of the ancestral cult

Confucianism and Taoism

the peasant masses but of the cosmology of the literate elite as well. The triumph of Confucianism in the mid-2nd century BC was later to become of great importance, for Confucian teachings were proclaimed the Orthodox Way by the state.

Dominance of Buddhism and religious Taoism. Into this vigorous Chinese culture with its diversified religious movements came Indian and Central Asian missionaries, bringing Buddhism. During the first several centuries of the Christian Era, Buddhist missionaries and their converts laboured to translate the *sūtras* (Buddhist scriptures) and to establish monastic centres. Gradually more Chinese embraced the new Way, either by entering the *Saṅgha* (Buddhist order) or by supporting it as devout householders. The decline and fall of the Han Empire by the early 3rd century AD, and the succeeding ages of political division, barbarian encroachments, and the consequent irrelevance of the traditional Confucian official career, contributed to the success of both Taoism and Buddhism.

Taoism developed along several distinguishable, though related, lines: the eclectic philosophy of Neo-Taoism, the techniques of achieving immortality, and the progressive institutionalizing of its professional religious in emulation of Buddhism—this involving monasticism, hagiography (biography of venerated people), iconography, liturgy, and a vast canonical literature. Most important of all was the blending of Taoism with folk religion and the emergence of various cults under charismatic leaders. Notable among these leaders was one Chang Ling, or Chang Tao-ling (2nd century), first in what was to be a continuing line of southern Taoist masters still in existence. The rise of Taoist-inspired cults was the beginning of a salient feature of Chinese history, the close connection between religious societies and political insurrection.

Buddhism, however, captured most of the intellectuals and dominated Chinese thought during the first millennium. Hundreds of thousands of men and women entered the *Saṅgha*, and millions of pious lay people supported it and made it rich. Chinese Buddhism was of the Mahāyāna ("larger vehicle") form, its theoretical position based on the treatises of the South Indian teacher Nāgārjuna (late 2nd century). By the late 7th century assimilation was not only complete but the Indian schools had been supplanted by Chinese schools: T'ien-t'ai and Hua-yen, Ch'ing-t'u (Pure Land) and Ch'an (Yogic Meditation). Ch'ing-t'u and Ch'an were to dominate Chinese Buddhism thereafter.

By the mid-T'ang dynasty (8th and 9th centuries) the continuous opposition of Taoist and Confucian enemies of Buddhism bore fruit. The T'ang dynasty was a new Han, since it was also an empire united under native rule, powerful, and culturally vigorous. Confucianism was again relevant; Confucian training was appropriate for a gentleman's career in state service. The state also looked with alarm on Buddhist institutions and in 845 suppressed them, returning more than 200,000 monks and nuns to lay life, destroying hundreds of monasteries, and confiscating most of the valuables in them. Never again did religion offer a threat to the state in China.

Renascence of the Great Tradition. The revitalization of Confucianism that began in the T'ang dynasty (618–907) reached its culmination in the Sung dynasty (960–1279), with the formulations of the Neo-Confucian philosophers. Neo-Confucian thought produced scholars and philosophers rather than saints and religious leaders. At the same time, the blow dealt to the temporal power of Buddhism seems to have affected its spiritual vitality as well; at least, there were no great Buddhist thinkers and no new schools during all the later centuries. There is no reason to doubt, either, that folk religion continued with undiminished vigour down the centuries, undocumented though much of it is, and though it has barely been studied.

Postscript: foreign religions and contemporary conditions. Many foreign religions came to China, especially during the cosmopolitan T'ang dynasty, the Pax Tatarica of the Yüan dynasty (1279–1368), and the modern period beginning in the late 16th century. During the T'ang dynasty, Iranian religions—Zoroastrianism and Manichaeism—Islām, and so-called Nestorian Christianity were introduced, but only Islām was to have any future in China. During the Yüan dynasty Islām became well established and even dominant in the west and northwest. A few Catholic friars also reached the Mongol capital. None of these foreign religions, however, not even Islām, made any real impression on Chinese civilization.

The arrival of the Jesuit Matteo Ricci at Peking in 1600 began a great Christian missionary movement that has continued to the present. During the 17th and 18th centuries the missions were exclusively Catholic, while since that time Protestants have been the more numerous. Despite a number of conversions among the intellectual class as well as the masses, and despite the undeniable importance of Christian educational and medical work in the past century, Christianity as a religion has hardly reached the assimilable stage and remains foreign. A major, perhaps fatal, handicap has been its close association with the opium pushing, gunboat diplomacy, extra territorial privileges, and generally imperialist policies of Western governments preceding World War II.

In some striking respects Communism played the role of an imported religion, particularly during the 1920s, '30s, and '40s. Political chaos, compounded by the incalculably disruptive effects of modern science and technology, left the Great Tradition in shreds. The ancestral cult and the Confucian-sanctified familial and social systems were shaken by the impact of Western individualistic thought and the conditions of an industrializing economy. The religion of the state had of course disappeared with the end of the empire (1912). Even the deeply rooted spiritistic beliefs and magical practices of the folk religion were slowly undermined as elementary scientific knowledge filtered down to the masses. Western materialism, pragmatism, and technological change served to disrupt traditional patterns. In such an extreme confusion of mind and spirit, Communism seemed to many intellectuals to be the one creed that promised salvation of body and soul for China—and the only one completely "scientific," in accord with the modern age.

After the Communist regime had been established on the mainland, religion, like every other constituent of Chinese culture, became a tool of state policy. Such features as could be utilized to forward the state's aims were manipulated to those purposes; for the rest, it was suppressed or forced underground. In the island province of Taiwan, under the government of the Republic of China, freedom of religion was the policy. Despite an environment of rapid modernization the old religious practices continued to flourish, while Buddhism even seemed to enjoy a renaissance. Foreign missions were numerous and energetic, with over 60 Protestant denominations represented; however, the Roman Catholics appeared to be making the most headway.

Religious roles of Communist ideology

COMMON CONCEPTUAL BASIS OF CHINESE RELIGION

The Chinese world view was based upon a few simple but remarkably fruitful concepts, already found in sketchy form in the oldest texts (*Shu Ching, Shih Ching*, and *Yi* or *I Ching*—the "Book of Changes"—dating from early Chou) and by the late Chou dynasty common property.

Views of the world. Thoughtful men perceived the world of nature and man as a unified whole. The world was a cosmos in the literal sense of the term: a harmony, an order. Man had a special part to play, but he was not, as in the West, an actor for whom the world of nature was merely a stage. His was the task of maintaining the beneficial and harmonious functioning of the cosmos through timely agricultural operations, appropriate ritual practices, and good moral conduct.

The philosophers created no Creator of this cosmos. Its Ultimate Cause was thought to be impossible to conceptualize, and the term *Tao* was used as its conventional designation. The phenomenal world was manifested through the two forces—*yin* and *yang*—somehow proceeding from *Tao*. These forces, like the mysterious positive and negative forces that "explain" the universe of modern science, produced all things through their various interactions and permutations. *Yin* and *yang* were the polar opposites into which all things can be classified, male and female, light and dark, hot and cold, high and low, and so forth. But the cosmos was not static, it was alive, which meant that *change* was its essence. The ceaseless waxing and waning, contracting and expanding, cycling, merging, and counteracting of *yin* and *yang* brought the cosmos into being and kept it moving. The material world resulting from the operations of *yin* and *yang* was seen to be reducible to five basic sorts of phenomena, called *wu hsing:* water, fire, wood, metal, and earth. These also are to be understood not as static building blocks but as active qualities characteristic of all phenomena. As the tangible effects of *yin* and *yang*, they restlessly reacted with each other, mutually transforming one another to produce the incessant flow of natural processes.

Time was also conceptualized. The periodicity of day and night and the seasons were noted, but, more than this, years, months, days, and hours were conceived in a framework of endlessly repeating series. In fact, there were two series, one called the "ten stems," and the other the "twelve branches," each stem and branch being denoted by a different graph. In all Chinese thought from the Han dynasty on, these stems and branches functioned not merely as serial designations but as signs of the auspicious or inauspicious character of the times they marked. While a system of correlations with many other factors (planets, directions, bodily organs, tastes, musical pitches, etc.) was not fully worked out until Han times, it is noteworthy that the stems and branches are already in use on the Shang dynasty oracle bones.

Tao, *yin* and *yang*, the *wu hsing*, the stems and branches, and the correlative systems were the foundation of the Chinese world view down to the present century. While they are found in every aspect of Chinese religion, however, they were not sufficient for religious needs. In early texts the highest supernatural power is personified in Ti or Shang Ti, apparently a tribal deity or perhaps the high ancestor of the ruling house. In the writings of the late Chou thinkers (with the notable exception of Mo Ti) this Supreme Ruler in Heaven has become an almost abstract concept, referred to generally by his dwelling place alone, as Heaven (T'ien).

Views of man in nature. The rationalism of the intellectuals did not reflect the beliefs of the vast majority. For the latter, the supernatural was an invisible but entirely real dimension of this world, peopled with numberless spiritual beings. The benevolent ones were especially the souls of ancestors happy because their descendants gave them the proper postmortem care; the malevolent ones were especially the ghosts of the dead who had been wronged or were neglected by their descendants.

Two elements of the soul (*hun*) Benevolent spirits (*shen*) were constituted of the *yang* elements of the human soul (*hun*), while the ghosts or demons (*kuei*) derived from the *yin* elements (*p'o*). In religious development, then, *yang* and *yin* had come to embody the opposing forces of good and evil.

A remarkable feature of the Chinese notions of soul and afterlife is the concurrent acceptance, without any feeling of incongruity, of an entirely different theory, the contribution of popular Buddhism, which introduced the Indian doctrine of *karman*. According to this doctrine the soul after death journeyed to purgatory, where it was judged, punished until the misdeeds of the past life had been expiated, and then reborn in circumstances suited to the record of that past life.

Views of man in society. The spiritism of Chinese religion is ultimately reducible to the basic beliefs of the ancestral cult. Folk religion and family religion are but different expressions of one outlook. So-called ancestor worship was primary because it molded both the family and clan, and hence Chinese society. The ancestors conferred blessings or sent disaster according to the behaviour of their descendants. Those who were immediate ancestors, the parents, must be served with the utmost filiality. Filial piety (*hsiao*) constituted the cardinal virtue, the basis for the family's governance, and the most powerful force for law and order in the society as a whole. Filiality was demonstrated in practice largely through formal modes of behaviour (*li*), which were designed to emphasize the hierarchial structure of family and clan.

Above the familial level there was the code of ethical imperatives for the "superior men," the elite who governed the people. These had been expounded and exemplified by the Master, Confucius. The ethical principles of the Confucian school—righteousness, loyalty, trustworthiness, modesty, courtesy, frugality, learning, and the like—were summed up in the term *jen*, or moral perfection. These ideals filtered through all of Chinese society, becoming the universal standards of behaviour, rounding out the rules of *li*, and fulfilling the sacred duties of *hsiao*.

COMMON CHARACTERISTICS OF CHINESE RITUAL PRACTICES AND INSTITUTIONS

Rituals of the family religion. In China, as elsewhere, certain moments in the career of the individual and the family were invested with special significance: birth, coming of age, marriage, and death. These moments were much more significant as milestones in the religious history of the family than as merely individual experiences. All of them derived their importance from their connection with the basic duty of filiality (*hsiao*), which required that children devote themselves body and soul to the care of their parents and that above all a grandson must be provided who would carry on the ancestral sacrifices.

Rites surrounding birth. The birth of sons is one of the oldest themes in Chinese prayer, recurring constantly in *Shih Ching* (roughly 100–500 BC). One of these ancient songs tells us that dreaming of bears portends the birth of sons, while dreaming of snakes means daughters. Other early texts emphasize the importance of prenatal influences. The ritual codes do not speak in much detail about the natal ceremonies, but in the case of noble sons it seems that the most important thing was the shaving of the infant's head, and the father formally conferring its name, at the end of the third month.

In later times any number of practices became associated with birth, mostly deriving from the spiritistic beliefs of the folk religion. Many deities were besought to make the womb fruitful, to assist mother and babe at parturition, and to protect the infant. The formal announcement of the new arrival and the first bath are on the third day, as in antiquity, but the ceremony of shaving the head was moved from the third to the end of the first month (at which time the mother is considered to have returned to normal health and the child to be firmly established in this world). Among a host of universal and local customs connected with the new life were the wearing of amulets, casting of horoscopes (the word refers in Chinese context particularly to the influences of the *wu hsing* as these are determined by the stems and branches of the year, month, day, and hour of birth), congratulations by family and friends in the form of gifts symbolic of good health and luck, giving the child derogatory names (to fool evil spirits into thinking it is of too little value to attack), and—most important—presentation of the infant to the ancestors at their tablets on the family altar.

Engagement and marriage. The ceremony marking coming of age is the least important of the Chinese "rites of passage," and the events that really signified maturity were engagement and marriage. Since the purpose of marriage was to ensure the perpetuation of the family line and particularly the ancestral sacrifices, it was too vital a matter to be left to the idiosyncratic whims of the young. The families made all the arrangements through go-betweens, and the couple often saw each other for the first time at their wedding. The engagement,

Fecundity and infant protection

which was binding, was made by exchanging presents and the horoscopes of the boy and girl. After this engagement, even if the prospective groom died before the wedding day, a virtuous girl might consider herself tied by the contract, go through a marriage ceremony with the ghost of the deceased, and remain in his home to serve her parents-in-law.

Every act in the series of formalities constituting the engagement and the marriage was performed on days determined by the almanac to be auspicious. The elaborateness of these formalities would, of course, vary according to the means of the participants, but the following were essential: exchange of betrothal presents, exchange of wedding presents and sending of the bride's trousseau to her new home (*i.e.*, the home of her parents-in-law) in an impressive procession, the conveyance of the bride to the groom's home in a red sedan chair (this nowadays often being replaced by the less picturesque automobile), obeisance of the couple before heaven and earth and the spirits in the groom's ancestral tablets, raising of the bride's veil by the groom, sipping of wine and exchange of cups, sitting side by side on the nuptial bed. The wedding taking place in the groom's family home, the bride was in a sea of strangers, kinsmen of her husband—himself a stranger.

At every step of the wedding symbols of good luck and numerous (male) progeny were in evidence, while care was taken to ward off evil influences. The dominant colour—of the bride's skirt, the sedan chair, the wrappings of wedding presents—was red, symbol of life and felicity. A gift of pomegranates symbolized, by its plentiful seeds, the hope for many sons. A sieve and a mirror carried on the bride's sedan chair were to shield her from malicious spirits, while any that were following her would be scared off at the gateway where she entered her new home by the noise of firecrackers.

Marriage was the destiny of every boy and girl, as inevitable as birth and death themselves. For the girl it meant practically severing her connection with her own family and being enrolled in the family and clan of her husband. The wedding ceremony was only the formal establishment of her marriage; its validation would not be achieved until she had earned it through demonstrating her capabilities as a filial daughter-in-law and bearing the parents-in-law their grandson. Eventually, she in her turn would receive the filial service of her son, daughter-in-law, and grandson, and in the end her spirit tablet would stand on the family altar to receive equal homage with her husband, as the mother and grandmother of descendants in the family line. This status was, in the Chinese view, no empty rationalization to assuage the fear of death. Becoming an ancestor was not the end of life but its commencement.

Death rites and customs. Death was not a traumatic interruption in the normal flow of family life but an integral part of that flow. Death rituals were by far the most important in Chinese religion. They were protracted, momentous, prescribed in exhaustive detail in the canonical codes, and enforced by the criminal law of the state. They were carried out in three stages: the funeral, mourning, and continuing sacrifices to the manes.

An old person was comforted by assurance of a proper funeral, and his children were considered especially respectful if they would procure a good coffin, graveclothes, and even a tomb for the parent while the latter was still in good health. When death was imminent, the person was placed in the main room of the house, where the icons of the family altar were covered to prevent the contamination of evil influences. Once the soul had departed, the entire family commenced a ritualized expression of grief: dressing in sackcloth, letting the hair go unkempt, and wailing. The corpse was garbed ritually in graveclothes by the eldest son. The family in-laws and other kinsmen and friends came to offer consolation in prescribed fashion. A temporary abode for the soul, called the "soul silk," was set up before the corpse and was later carried by the eldest grandson in the elaborate

Funeral ceremonies

funeral procession and then returned to the home. Professional undertakers would arrive to place the body in the coffin properly and to seal it shut. Professional mourners would be engaged to lend volume to the wailing of family members in the funeral procession. Taoist and Buddhist priests played musical instruments and chanted scriptures on behalf of the soul. If the family were rich, the burial itself might be delayed for weeks or months, to allow continual oiling of the coffin and more protracted ceremonies of prayer. Eventually, after the coffin had been escorted to the grave and interred with many additional rites, the soul silk was replaced by a permanent spirit tablet, (*shen-chu*), which joined the other ancestors on the family altar.

Mourning commenced immediately and followed exactly detailed ordinances in the Confucian canon. The length of the mourning period, the sackcloth worn, and the nature of the ascetic observances were precisely proportional to the relationship between the mourner and the deceased. The closest relationship—son to parent, father to heir, adopted heir to certain family members, and (in ancient times) feudal lord to Son of Heaven (as the emperor was titled)—required what was called the Three Years' Untrimmed Mourning (*chan-ts'ui*). In practice this lasted just into the third year. During its initial and most stringent phase, such mourning required the wearing of sackcloth and rush shoes, living in a hut of brush beside the house, pillowing the head on a clod, eating only two bowls of gruel a day, and wailing day and night. With the passage of time the mourner would gradually resume a more normal mode of life. Retirement from the world to carry out this mourning was not only expected of a filial son but was even obligatory under law. No one, not even the highest ministers of state, was exempt from this most sacred demonstration of filiality, which took precedence over every other responsibility.

Dead and buried, the departed one was not forgotten, at least for several generations. Not only was his spirit (the *yang* soul called *hun*) present in the home on the family altar, where it would daily receive gestures of remembrance, such as offerings of food and wine and the burning of incense, but the *yin* soul (*p'o*) in the grave was likewise not neglected. The contentment of the *p'o* was all-important to the living members of the family, for a wrathful *p'o* (known as *kuei*, meaning ghost or demon) endangered the health, happiness, and prosperity of those who offended it. Hence the burial rites had to be properly performed, the grave itself had to be situated auspiciously according to the *feng-shui* (geomantic) lore of the augurs, and several times a year, as directed by the annual calendar of religious festivals, services of remembrance were held, or visits made to the tombs by the family members. In addition, because of the dual theory of soul, it was believed that the deceased spent seven weeks on a dangerous and difficult journey to purgatory, and during this period prayers and sacrifices were especially necessary to assist it. Formal services for this purpose were conducted by both Buddhist and Taoist priests. Finally, in wealthy clans, the spirit tablets of the ancestors of all the constituent families were gathered together under the roof of the clan temple. In this sacred place the kinsmen would hold periodical meetings to pay reverence to the ancestors, to bring genealogical records up to date, and to renew the solidarity of the religious corporation that was the clan.

Communal religion: gods and temples. The reality of the spiritual dimension and the spiritistic beliefs of the masses have already been noted. Benevolent spirits (*shen*) were deities, malevolent spirits were ghosts or demons (*kuei*). Their nature was essentially identical with the *hun* and *p'o* of the ancestor cult—and in fact ultimately derived from these—but they had wider jurisdictions. *Kuei* would seem to have operated purely on an individual basis, but *shen* became tutelary (guardian) deities of a locality, spiritual magistrates of a district, patrons of the various professions, or specialized powers in such crises as sickness or danger. A few became gods

Spirits and ghosts: *shen* and *kuei*

of universal character, popular everywhere in China, and invested with more general powers of protection and benevolence. The birth of a cult and its flourishing or decline depended upon the reputation of the deity for efficacious response to prayer.

Deities were housed in temples designed as palaces, rather than as churches serving congregations. Petitioners could come at any time with requests for advice or help. These temples were built and supported by community efforts, and their size and equipage would therefore vary with the community's resources. The temple might be only a boxlike shrine with a doll-like image or even just a rude inscription behind an altar of a few bricks; at the other extreme it would constitute a huge complex of buildings in a series of courts. Purely Buddhist temples housed only Buddhist icons, but temples of the popular religion might contain a variety of images in addition to the chief deity. Most popular of the great universal deities was the goddess Kuan-yin, who had been transformed by the faith and affection of the masses from the male Mahāyāna Buddhist *bodhisattva* (Buddha-to-be) Avalokiteśvara into a compassionate mother figure. Most omnipresent of the *shen* was the local earth god (T'u-ti), humble in rank, yet closest of all to the daily lives of the people in his capacity as the tutelary deity of hearth, home, and neighbourhood.

People visited the community cult temples as they felt the need. At least once a year the temple festival, held on the birthday of the god, would draw large crowds. The image of the chief deity, flanked by two attendants, sat behind the altar, which was furnished with red candles in tall brass holders, an incense brazier, vases of flowers, and offerings of food and drink. Petitioners bowed or knelt before the images, presenting lighted sticks of incense and perhaps candles. Mock paper money was often burned, particularly to be sent to the souls of relatives in the purgatorial interlude. The deity was often asked to respond negatively or affirmatively to questions concerning proposed courses of action. A response might be obtained mechanically by casting wooden blocks or by drawing printed oracles upon obtaining a number from a bamboo tube of sticks, or the temple might have a resident medium (*chi-t'ung*) through whom the god would communicate with mortals. Many temples of the folk religion had no professional attendants; often those that did made do with caretakers of a very nondescript sort who had little esteem from the parishioners.

Ritual offerings

Imperial worship and state religion. Divine right was the basis of kingship in China as elsewhere. In China it took the form of a "mandate" or commission from Heaven, which could be and often was withdrawn from the incumbent line to be bestowed on another. In other words the emperor was not himself divine, and his divine authority depended upon proper performance of his duties—not only those pertaining to mundane administration but also the rituals that maintained the harmony of Heaven, Earth, and Man.

Heaven (T'ien) and Earth (*Ti*), the great symbols of the cosmos, were the only powers before whom the emperor humbled himself; at the same time only he, as Man's representative, could legitimately perform the ritual worship of those powers. The great altars preserved in Peking today can but suggest the sublimity of the grand ceremonials that used to be performed there under the last dynasties.

The religion of the state was crowned by these rites, but the state religion also operated throughout the empire. In every local seat of government the regulations provided for three types of facilities: memorial halls, of which the Confucian temple was by far the most important; the altars to the gods of land and grain, mountains and rivers, and bereaved spirits; and the temples of various cults that had become so popular that they were adopted into the official liturgy. There was no separate estate of priests to conduct the rites, for this was a routine function of the literati officials.

Understanding and dealing with the supernatural. What was outside of the regular, calculable behaviour of nature had to be coped with by special concepts and procedures. When spiritual beings wished to communicate with men they would do so through a medium. When Heaven and Earth were disturbed by the errant actions of men they gave warning of impending disaster by unnatural phenomena. When the Chinese sought to save themselves from attack by the malevolent spirits that brought accident, disease, and madness, they wore amulets, brought up the artillery of firecrackers and gongs, engaged professional practitioners of magic, made vows of good deeds and offered sacrifices (edibles, incense, candles, mock paper money) to secure the mercy of benevolent deities.

At the same time that such protective actions were taken, men tried to see the reason in apparently unreasonable events. Early rational systems of understanding arose from the same deep-seated human desire to make sense out of the myriad phenomena of the universe as modern science. The Western "pseudosciences" had their Chinese counterparts—astrology, numerology, somatomancy, geomancy, etc. The Chinese systems were conditioned by such all-pervasive concepts as *yin* and *yang*, the *wu hsing*, and the cyclical series.

Practices of religious Taoism and Buddhism. Of all the early systematic efforts at mastering fate, none was so bold as that of religious Taoism. The goal of this system was not merely circumvention of inimical influences from the supernatural realm but the actual attainment of immortality. In view of the many and close correspondences between the Chinese and Western traditions, the term alchemy has been applied to these practices. (See also ALCHEMY.)

Alchemy

Buddhism, highly institutionalized before its arrival in China, provided later Chinese religion with much of its form and ritual. Buddhist iconography, *sūtra* chanting, burning of incense and worship before the image, the saying of "masses" for the souls of the dead, the organization and discipline of monastic life—these, and many other practices, helped to mold Taoism and folk religion alike.

Religion in other social institutions. The major institutions of the traditional Chinese polity included the state, the local communities, and the families and clans. Institutionalized Buddhism and Taoism were permitted but usually subjected to close surveillance. Aside from these there were also craft guilds, commercial organizations, and secret societies. Artisans and merchants had their own special patron deities and were careful to maintain the proper worship services. The secret societies were for the most part secret not because of any subversive intent but simply because Confucian officials regarded sectarian doctrines as heterodox and any group of persons gathered together to perform rituals as potentially dangerous to the government. There was enough truth in this idea to warrant uneasiness among officials, as certain of the secret societies did in fact grow into mass movements and eventually become vehicles for serious political insurrections. The vast majority of sects were, however, small, local, and devoted to purely religious and social purposes. Such sects display the universal human tendency to follow charismatic leaders and popular beliefs that promise salvation. All of these sects would draw, for their doctrines and practices, upon the common stock of concepts about the workings of the cosmos, the familial and ethical imperatives of the Great Tradition, and the liturgical usages of institutionalized Taoism and Buddhism.

CHINESE RELIGIOUS SYMBOLISM

In religious practices. Aside from Neolithic vestiges, whose interpretation must always remain conjectural, the most ancient evidences of Chinese religious symbolism are the bronze vessels of late Shang and Chou dynasties. Technically astounding, these hundreds of individualized works are zoomorphic (in animal form) in ornamentation and sometimes in shape. Although the source of much later Chinese design, they have nothing of the feel of "typical" Chinese art about them. On the contrary, they are sombre, weighty with a spirit of blood sacrifice. Some patterns are realistic enough—one recognizes owls or tigers, elephants or dragons—while some are abstracted, fragmented, and tantalizingly enigmatic.

This spirit of a primitive religion disappeared during the later Chou under the secularizing influences of an age of turmoil, technological progress, and free thought. The changes are reflected in both bronzes and literary remains. In Han and later ages traditional Chinese culture was formulated. The dominant motif of religious symbolism in this traditional culture was the struggle between *yang* and *yin*. At all save the highest philosophical level these two concepts had now become symbols of the benevolent and malevolent spiritual forces acting on man from the unseen dimension. Everything that was conceived to help man in the warfare with evil spirits was a symbol of *yang:* from the blood of a freshly killed cock to the noise of gongs and firecrackers, from the icon of a *shen* to the magical sword of an exorcist, from the writing on a charm or in the pages of scripture to pure springwater, from the invocation of a priest to the lighting of candles and incense. All signs in nature were read as symbols of *yin* and *yang*.

Images and tablets   The most explicit symbols of *shen* were images and tablets. The former may have been introduced by Buddhism, which arrived in China with an already rich repertory of symbols pertaining to Buddhas and *bodhisattvas*, as well as other older Indian ideas: *mudras*, (gestures), *mantras* (sacred syllables), yogic devices, and much else. The spirit tablet *shen-chu* is especially associated with the ancestral cult; it is, however, not simply a symbol but the actual seat of the spirit. Most ancient and fundamental objects of worship—the ancestors, the spirits of Heaven and Earth, the deities of the natural phenomena, the gods of the locality—continued throughout Chinese history to be represented by tablets, at least in rituals of family and state.

In visual arts and literatures.   On the whole, Chinese art and literature do not remain at the level of religious symbolism, yet such symbolism is much in evidence. Calligraphy, the basis of painting, is a purely abstract art of line; but the highest genre of painting itself, the landscape, is an attempt to give visual expression to the unified Chinese cosmology and is entirely symbolic. Many features of Chinese architecture were at least originally symbolic, as for example the north–south orientation found in all important structures from the ancient Shang capital to recent Peking (the city of Peking is itself the greatest example of the north–south orientation). The profusion of carvings, paintings, and other ornamental features of temples and palaces come from myth and legend and the basic cosmological concepts. Sculpture has been practically confined to religious subjects. The decorative arts derive their motifs from nature and these motifs are invested with symbolic meaning. Of course, in the long ages of use many common symbols—trees, flowers, and birds, the Eight Taoist Immortals, the graphs for felicity, longevity, or wealth, rebuses such as the bat or blessings (both pronounced *fu*)—have been more or less emptied of religious meaning and may often be no more than conventional in their significance. The "finer" arts express an intuition that is a blend of the religious, philosophical, and poetic; while the arts in everyday life express more directly the spiritistic outlook of folk religion.

Great religious-philosophical-poetic intuitions are found in poetry, while the beliefs of the masses are more obviously seen in the entertainments of storytellers, which include all sorts of popular religious ideas, such as fate and fortune-telling, magic and miracles performed by Buddhist and Taoist monks, manifestations of gods and ghosts, attainment of immortality by adepts of alchemical art. Several of the major works of fiction—notably *Hsi-yu chi* ("Travels to the West" or *Monkey*), *Chin P'ing Mei* (*The Golden Lotus*) and *Hung lou meng* (*Dream of the Red Chamber*)—are extended parables of suffering and salvation according to Taoist and especially Buddhist views. Even tales that would seem to qualify as little

The relationship of man to nature in Chinese thought, exemplified in a painting by Chou Ch'en, ink on silk, 15th–16th century. In the Museum of Fine Arts, Boston.

By courtesy of the Museum of Fine Arts, Boston, Keith McLeod Fund

more than pornography are given a moralistic justification, since their characters ultimately find religious truth (*e.g., Jou p'u t'uan, The Prayer-Mat of Flesh*).

In other contexts.   The separation out of the religious, as opposed to other components of traditional Chinese culture, is largely an artificial convenience (often a misleading one) for analytical purposes. Chinese life was a whole, an inseparable blend of what the West calls the secular and the religious, all unbeknownst to the Chinese. The innumerable proverbs and maxims, which formed much of the speech and way of thinking and acting of peasant and scholar alike, were a crystallization of the religious convictions of the nation. The mundane life was lived in the midst of spirits whose dimension impinged upon the sensible world. The symbols of ritual occasions carried into daily life.

Symbolism in proverbs, maxims, and the almanac   This intimate association of worldly and supernatural was summed up in the almanac, issued by the state, and found in every household. Calendrical and kabalistic (mystical) information were indistinguishable in its pages, whose detailed advice concerning lucky and unlucky times guided the actions of even the most rationalistic Chinese. There one could see the systematization of the pseudosciences applied to practical living, could learn the homely moral teachings of the Great Tradition, and could find methods of divination and telling one's own fortune. The calendrical structure of the almanac not only provided the weather forecasts essential to agriculturists but also set forth the dates of the annual religious festivals. So vital was all this to the nation that issuance of the almanac was one of the signs of legitimate rule by the dynasty.

BIBLIOGRAPHY. Good introductions to this subject are L.G. THOMPSON, *Chinese Religion* (1969); and C.K. YANG, *Religion in Chinese Society* (1961), a definitive work. For the world-view of Chinese philosophy, see W.T. CHAN, *An Outline and an Annotated Bibliography of Chinese Philosophy*, rev. ed. (1969). For information on ancestor cult and folk religion, see J.J.M. DE GROOT, *The Religious System of China*, 6 vol. (1892–1910, reissued 1964). Other works on folk religion include: H. DORE, *Recherches sur les superstitions en Chine*, 13 vol. (1911–38; Eng. trans., 1914–38, reissued 1968); V.R. BURKHARDT, *Chinese Creeds and Customs*, 3 vol. (1953–58); and D.C. GRAHAM, *Folk Religion in Southwest China* (1961). For state religion, see the work of C.K. YANG; and J.K. SHRYOCK, *The Origin and Development of the State Cult of Confucius* (1932). For Chinese Buddhism the best introduction is J. BLOFELD, *The Wheel of Life* (1959); on history, see K.S. CH'EN, *Buddhism in China* (1964); on Sangha and monachism, see the classic work of J. PRIP-MOLLER, *Chinese Buddhist Monasteries*, 2nd ed. (1968); and H. WELCH, *The Practice of Chinese Buddhism, 1900–1950* (1967). On meditational techniques, see K'UAN-YU LU, *The Secrets of Chinese Meditation* (1964); and C.C. CHANG, *The Practice of Zen* (1959). For religious Taoism the leading Western authority is H. MASPERO; see his "Le Taoïsme," in his *Melanges posthumes sur les religions et l'histoire de la Chine* (1950); also his important article, "Les Procédés de 'nourrir le principe vital' dans la religion Taoïste ancienne," *Journal Asiatique*, vol. 229 (1937). What little is known of the history of religious Taoism is well summarized in H. WELCH, *The Parting of the Way: Lao Tzu and the Taoist Movement* (1957). For the most important text of religious Taoism, see *Alchemy, Medicine, Religion in the China of A.D. 320: The Nei P'ien of Ko Hung* (*pao-p'u tzu*), Eng. trans. by J. WARE (1966). For examples of adepts who achieved immortality, see L. GILES (ed. and trans.), *A Gallery of Chinese Immortals* (1948); for personal experiences of a Western convert, see P. GOULLART, *The Monastery of Jade Mountain* (1961). Samples of religious tracts that have been immensely popular among laymen are given in translations by T. SUZUKI and P. CARUS, *T'ai-Shang Kan-Ying P'ien* and *Yin Chih Wen* (both published 1906, reissued 1950). For the religious situation in the modern century, see W.T. CHAN, *Religious Trends in Modern China* (1953); H. WELCH, *The Buddhist Revival in China* (1968); and R.C. BUSH, JR., *Religion in Communist China* (1970).

(L.G.T.)

Ch'in Shih Huang Ti

Shih Huang Ti ("First Sovereign Emperor") was the creator of the first unified Chinese empire. He was born, with the personal name Cheng, the son of Chuang Hsiang, later king of the state of Ch'in in northwest China, while his father was held hostage in the state of Chao. His mother was a former concubine of the rich merchant Lü Pu-wei, who, guided by financial interests, had managed to install Chuang Hsiang on the throne, even though he had not originally been designated as successor.

King of Ch'in

When Cheng, at the age of 13, ascended the throne in 246 BC, Ch'in already was the most powerful state and was likely to unite the rest of China under its rule. Although looked upon by the central states as a barbarous country, its strong position on the mountainous western periphery (with its centre in the modern province of Shensi) enabled Ch'in to develop a strong bureaucratic government and military organization as the basis of the totalitarian state philosophy known as Legalism.

Until the King was officially declared of age in 238, his government was headed by Lü Pu-wei. Cheng's first act as king was to execute his mother's lover, who had joined the opposition, and to exile Lü, who had been involved in the affair. A decree ordering the expulsion of all aliens, which would have deprived the King of his most competent advisers, was annulled at the urging of Li Ssu, later grand councillor. By 221, with the help of espionage, extensive bribery, and the ruthlessly effective leadership of gifted generals, Cheng had eliminated one by one the remaining six rival states, and the annexation of the last enemy state, Ch'i, in 221, marked his final triumph: for the first time China was united, under the supreme rule of the Ch'in. To herald his achievement the King assumed the sacred titles of legendary rulers and proclaimed himself Ch'in Shih Huang Ti, the "First Sovereign Emperor of Ch'in." With unbounded confidence, he claimed that his dynasty would last "10,000 generations."

As emperor he initiated a series of reforms aimed at establishing a fully centralized administration, thus avoiding the rise of independent satrapies. Following the example of Ch'in and at the suggestion of Li Ssu, he abolished territorial feudal power in the empire, forced the wealthy aristocratic families to live in the capital, Hsien-yang, and divided the country into 36 military districts, each with its own military and civil administrator. He also issued orders for almost universal standardization—from weights, measures, and the axle lengths of carts to the written language and the laws. Construction of a network of roads and canals was begun, and fortresses erected for defense against barbarian invasions from the north were linked to form the Great Wall.

Emperor of China

In 220 Shih Huang Ti undertook the first of a series of Imperial inspection tours that marked the remaining ten years of his reign. While supervising the consolidation and organization of the empire, he did not neglect to perform sacrifices in various sacred places, announcing to the gods that he had finally united the empire, and he erected stone tablets with ritual inscriptions to extol his unprecedented attainment of "highest peace," his incomparable eminence, and his unremitting care for his people. When his pilgrimage was cut short by heavy storms —a misfortune supposedly caused by a local deity—the Emperor, greatly enraged, ordered that the trees of the god's mountain sanctuary be felled and the area be painted red like a criminal.

Another motive for Shih Huang Ti's travels was his interest in magic and alchemy and his search for masters in these arts who could provide him with the elixir of immortality. After the failure of such an expedition to the islands in the Eastern Sea—possibly Japan—in 219, the Emperor repeatedly summoned magicians to his court. Confucian scholars strongly condemned the step as charlatanry, and it is said that 460 of them were executed for their opposition. The continuous controversy between the Emperor and Confucian scholars who advocated a return to the old feudal order culminated in the famous Burning of the Books of 213, when, at Li Ssu's suggestion, all books not dealing with agriculture, medicine, or prognostication were burned, except historical records of Ch'in and books in the Imperial library.

The last years of Shih Huang Ti's life were dominated by an ever-growing distrust of his entourage—at least three assassination attempts nearly succeeded—and his increasing isolation from the common people. Almost inaccessible in his huge palaces, the Emperor led the life of a semidivine being. In 210 Shih Huang Ti died during an inspection tour. He was buried in a gigantic grave hewn out of a mountain and shaped in conformity with the symbolic patterns of the cosmos. The disappearance of his forceful personality immediately led to the outbreak of fighting among supporters of the old feudal factions that ended in the collapse of the Ch'in dynasty and the extermination of the entire imperial clan (206).

Most of the information about Shih Huang Ti's life derives from the successor Han dynasty that prized Confucian scholarship and thus had an interest in disparaging the Ch'in period. The report that Shih Huang Ti was an illegitimate son of Lü Pu-wei is possibly an invention of that epoch. Further, stories describing his excessive cruelty and the general defamation of his character must be viewed in the light of the distaste left by the ultimately victorious Confucians for Legalist philosophy in general. It seems certain that Shih Huang Ti had an imposing personality and showed an unbending will in pursuing his aim of uniting and strengthening the empire. His despotic rule and the draconic punishments he meted out were dictated largely by his belief in Legalist ideas. In

Assessment

using Li Ssu as his adviser and in employing only highly skilled generals he showed remarkable acumen. The constant emphasis in stone inscriptions on the Emperor as the origin and centre of power reveals how conscious Shih Huang Ti was of his role as founder of a new era in history. Political and religious elements, closely related in China's tradition, largely determined his actions. In his pilgrimages, in his palaces laid out according to cosmic designs, in the founding of his "eternal dynasty," and in his quest for immortality, he displayed an ever stronger sense of his unique position.

With few exceptions, the traditional historiography of Imperial China has regarded Shih Huang Ti as the villain *par excellence*, inhuman, uncultivated, and superstitious. Modern historians, however, generally stress the endurance of the bureaucratic and administrative structure institutionalized by Shih Huang Ti, which, despite its official denial, remained the basis of all subsequent dynasties. In the People's Republic of China, especially, he is hailed as an outstanding personality in Chinese history who civilized barbarians and "whose positive efforts hastened the progress of history."

BIBLIOGRAPHY. DERK BODDE, *China's First Unifier* (1938, reprinted 1967), the pioneer study of Li Ssu and Shih Huang Ti; *Statesman, Patriot, and General in Ancient China* (1940), biographies of three men (Lü Pu-wei, Li Ssu, and Meng Tien) who were connected with the emperor's life; EDOUARD CHAVANNES, *Les Mémoires historiques de Se-ma Ts'ien*, vol. 2, pp. 100–246 (1897, reprinted 1967), for a translation in French of Shih Huang Ti's biography; LEONARD COTTRELL, *The Tiger of Ch'in: The Dramatic Emergence of China As a Nation* (1962), an unreliable popularization. An extensive survey of Chinese Communist evaluation of Shih Huang Ti is provided by A.F.P. HULSEWÉ, "Chinese Communist Treatment of the Origins and the Foundation of the Chinese Empire," in *The China Quarterly*, 23:78–105 (1965).

(C.C.M.)

Chiroptera

Bats, which comprise the mammalian order Chiroptera, are the only mammals to have evolved true flight. This ability, coupled with the benefits deriving from their system of acoustic orientation (so-called bat sonar), has made the group a successful one in numbers of species and individuals. About 900 species are currently recognized, belonging to some 174 genera. Many species are enormously abundant. Observers have concluded, for example, that some 100,000,000 female Mexican free-tailed bats (*Tadarida brasiliensis mexicana*) form summer nursery colonies in Texas, where they produce about 100,000,000 young in five large caves. Adult males of this species, although equal in numbers, may not range as far north as Texas. (Individuals of the species also range widely throughout tropical America.) Thus, bats of one species alone number in the hundreds of millions of individuals.

GENERAL FEATURES

Most bats are insectivorous. Little is known of the spectrum of insect species consumed, but the quantities are formidable. The Mexican free-tailed bats of Texas have been estimated to consume about 20,000 tons of insects per year. Bats would thus seem to be important in the balance of insect populations and possibly in the control of insect pests. Some bats feed on fruit and aid in dispersing seeds; others feed on pollen and nectar and are the principal or exclusive pollinators of a number of tropical and subtropical plants. The true vampires of tropical America feed on the blood of large birds and mammals, occasionally becoming significant pests of livestock and sometimes serving as carriers of rabies.

Certain aspects of the physiology of some bats, particularly those involving adaptations for long hibernation, daily lethargy, complex temperature regulation, acoustical orientation, and long-distance migrations, are of interest to experimental scientists.

In tropical countries, in particular, large colonies of bats often inhabit houses and public buildings, attracting attention by their noisiness, guano (droppings), and collective odour. In the West, bats have been the subject of unfavourable myths; in parts of the Orient, however, these animals serve as symbols of good luck, long life, and happiness.

Diversity of structure. All bats have a generally similar appearance in flight, dominated by the expanse of the wings, but they vary considerably in size. The order is usually divided into two well-defined suborders: the Megachiroptera (Old World) and the Microchiroptera (worldwide). Among members of the Megachiroptera, a flying fox, *Pteropus vampyrus*, may have a wingspread of about 1.5 metres (about five feet) and a weight of about one kilogram (2.2 pounds). The largest insectivorous bat is probably *Cheiromeles torquata;* it weighs about 250 grams (about nine ounces). The largest of the carnivorous bats (and the largest bat in the New World) is *Vampyrum spectrum*, with a wingspread of over 60 centimetres (24 inches). The tiny Philippine bamboo bat, *Tylonycteris pachypus meyeri*, has a wingspread of barely 15 centimetres (six inches) and weighs about 1.5 grams (about 0.05 ounce).

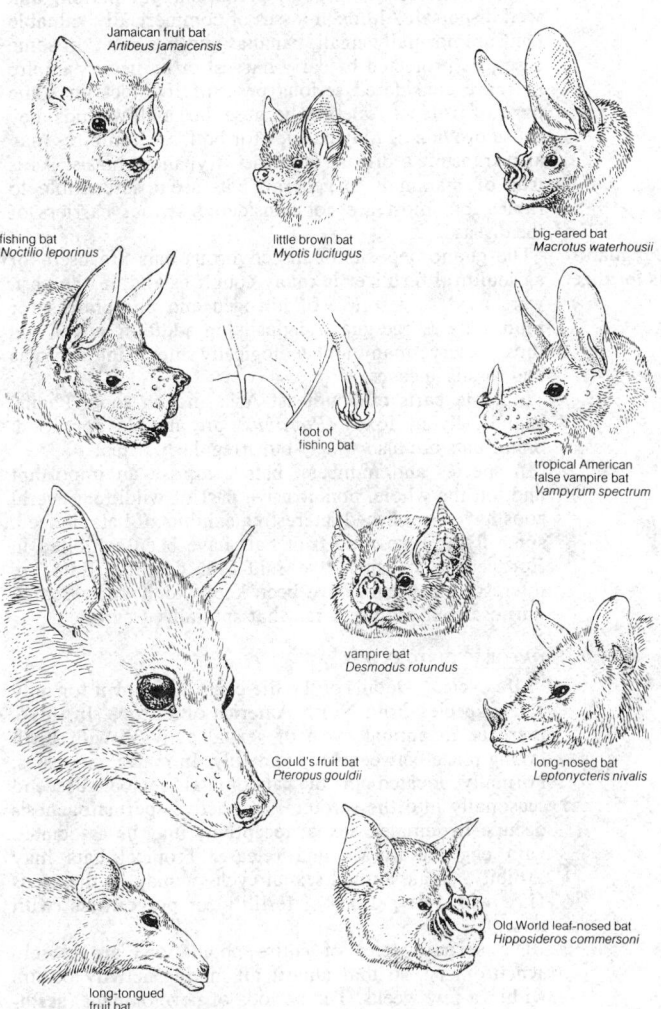

Figure 1: Heads of various bats.

Jamaican fruit bat
Artibeus jamaicensis

fishing bat
Noctilio leporinus

little brown bat
Myotis lucifugus

big-eared bat
Macrotus waterhousii

foot of
fishing bat

tropical American
false vampire bat
Vampyrum spectrum

vampire bat
Desmodus rotundus

Gould's fruit bat
Pteropus gouldii

long-nosed bat
Leptonycteris nivalis

Old World leaf-nosed bat
Hipposideros commersoni

long-tongued
fruit bat
Macroglossus minimus

Bats vary in colour and in fur texture. Facial appearance, dominated by the muzzle and ears, varies strikingly with family and often with genus. In several families, a complex fleshy adornment called the nose leaf surrounds the nostrils. Wing proportions are modified according to modes of flight. The tail and the interfemoral (between the legs) membrane also differ, perhaps with feeding, flight, and roosting habits. Finally, at the roost, bats vary in the postures they assume, particularly in whether they hang suspended or rest on the wall and in the manner in which the wings are folded and used.

Distribution. Bats are particularly abundant in the tropics. In West Africa, for example, 31 genera embracing 97 species have been catalogued; in the United States 15 genera, totalling 40 species, are known. Of the 17 living families, three (the Vespertilionidae, Molossidae, and Rhinolophidae) are well represented in the temperate zones. A few phyllostomatid species range into mild temperate regions. Several vespertilionids range well into Canada.

The Vespertilionidae are found worldwide, excepting only the Arctic and sub-Arctic, Antarctic, and isolated islands. The genus *Myotis* has a range almost equal to that of the order. The Molossidae and Emballonuridae also encircle the earth but are restricted to the tropics and subtropics. The Rhinolophidae extend throughout the Old World, the Hipposideridae and Pteropodidae throughout the Old World tropics, and the Phyllostomatidae throughout the New World tropics and slightly beyond. The other families have more restricted ranges.

IMPORTANCE TO MAN

Bats are important to man primarily because they affect other living things through predation, pollination, and seed dispersal. Although losses of commercially valuable fruit are normally small, bananas and figs must, in some cases, be protected by early harvest or by nets. Vampire bats are considered serious pests of livestock in some parts of tropical America, because the small wounds they cause provide egg-laying sites for botflies. Vampires may also transmit a disease of cattle—trypanosomiasis. As is true of mammals in general, bats seem susceptible to rabies, but most are not considered serious carriers of the disease.

Bat guano as fertilizer The guano deposits of insectivorous bats are used for agricultural fertilizer in many countries and, in the past, were used as a source of nitrogen and phosphorus for munitions. Large guano deposits, in addition, cover and thus preserve many archaeologically interesting artifacts and fossils in caves.

In some parts of Southeast Asia and on some Pacific islands, flying foxes (*Pteropus*) are hunted for food. Small bats are also widely but irregularly eaten.

In species and numbers, bats comprise an important and, on the whole, nonintrusive part of wildlife. Several zoos have established interesting exhibits of bats; indeed, some flying foxes and fruit bats have been exhibited in European zoos since the mid-19th century. Bats are interesting pets and have been kept widely for research purposes but require somewhat specialized care.

NATURAL HISTORY

Life cycle. Details of the life cycle are known for only a few species from North America or Europe. In these, there is an annual cycle of sexual activity, with birth taking place between May and July. In males, the testes, normally located in the abdominal region, descend seasonally into the scrotum, and active spermatogenesis occurs. In females, sexual receptivity may be associated with egg maturation and release. Tropical bats may exhibit a single annual sexual cycle or may be diestrous (*i.e.*, with two periods of fertility) or polyestrous (with many).

The sexual cycles of entire populations are closely synchronized, so that almost all mating activity occurs within a few weeks. The periods of development (gestation), birth, lactation, and fledging are also usually synchronized. Gestation varies in duration: five or six months in *Pteropus*, over five months in *Desmodus*, three months in some small *Hipposideros*, and six or seven to 14 weeks in several small vespertilionid genera. The length of gestation may be influenced by ambient (surrounding) and body temperature.

In several North American and Palaearctic (northern Eurasian) vespertilionids and rhinolophids that hibernate, copulation occurs in the fall, and the sperm are stored in the female genital tract until spring. Ovulation, fertilization, and implantation occur after emergence from hibernation, when the female again has available an abundant food supply and warm roost. The favourable environmental conditions greatly enhance the young bat's chances of survival.

Most bats bear one young, but the big brown bat (*Eptesicus fuscus*) may bear twins, and the red bat (*Lasiurus borealis*) bears litters of one to four.

At birth, the young, who may weigh from one-sixth to one-third as much as the mother, usually have well-developed hindlegs with which they hold on to their mother or to the roost. The wings are very immature. The young, nude or lightly furred, are often briefly blind and deaf. Female bats normally have one pectoral (at the chest) or axillary (at the armpit) mammary gland on each side. Several families that carry their young while foraging also have a pair of false pubic nipples, which the infant may hold in its mouth when its mother flies. The infants are nourished by milk for a period of about five or six weeks in many small Microchiroptera and for five months in *Pteropus giganteus*. By two months of age, most of the Microchiroptera have achieved adult size, having begun to fly and forage three or four weeks earlier.

Nursery roosts In many species, females late in pregnancy migrate to special nursery roosts, in which large numbers of pregnant females may aggregate, usually to the exclusion of nonpregnant females, males, and bats of other species. In some cases, the nursery roosts seem to be chosen for their high temperature, which may derive from the sun, the bats themselves, or from decomposing guano. When foraging, some bats (*Erophylla*) leave their infants hanging quietly, one by one, on the cave wall or ceiling. In other cases (*Tadarida brasiliensis, Natalus*), the closely spaced infants may move about and mingle on the wall. Among others, especially molossids in buildings, the infants may form play groups and rough-and-tumble on the floor. Some bats carry their young with them. Generally, each mother, on returning to her roost, seeks out her own child by position, smell, and acoustical exchange. In the huge nursery colonies of *Tadarida brasiliensis mexicana* and *Miniopterus schreibersii*, however, the mothers appear to feed the first one or two infants they encounter on returning. This is called the milk-herd system.

T.S. Lal—P.I.P.

Mother dog-faced fruit bat (*Cynopterus sphinx*), with clinging young, in flight.

Some bats achieve sexual maturity in the first year; others in the second year. Infant mortality appears to be high. Developmental and genetic errors and disease take their toll, but accidents seem to cause more serious losses —the young may fall from the ceiling or have serious collisions in early flight attempts. A fair number of bats probably fail to make the transition from dependent infants to self-sufficient foragers.

Life-span Adult bats have low mortality. Predation is rarely serious, especially for cave-dwelling species. Disease, parasitic infestation, starvation, and accidents apparently take small tolls. There are records of several big brown (*Eptesicus fuscus*), little brown (*Myotis lucifugus*), and greater horseshoe bats (*Rhinolophus ferrum-equinum*) that have lived more than 20 years. Probably many bats in temperate climates live more than 10 years. Longevity has not been established for tropical species.

Several factors probably contribute to the unusual longevity of bats. Generally isolated roosts and nocturnal flight substantially protect them from predation, from some elements of weather, and from exposure to the sun. The largely colonial way of life may ensure that entire populations experience contagious infection and subsequent immunity; indeed, such a pattern may, in the past, have hastened adaptation to disease. The persistent use of various seasonal roosts probably ensures isolation and security, food and water supply, and access to mates. Many bats, moreover, drop their body temperature at rest. Not only is there a probability that this conserves some cellular "machinery," since metabolism is reduced, but fewer hours need be spent in actively seeking food and water.

Behaviour. *Activity patterns.* Nocturnal activity is a major feature of the behavioural pattern of bats: nearly all species roost during the day and forage at night. Carnivorous bats, vampires, and perhaps fishing bats may have an advantage at night over inactive or sleeping prey. In addition, nocturnal flight protects bats from visual predators, exposure to the sun, high ambient temperature, and low relative humidity. The large area of naked wing skin might mean that bats would absorb rather than radiate heat, if they were active during the day. They would also lose body water required for temperature regulation and would then be forced to forage near water or to carry extra water in flight.

The nocturnal-activity pattern in bats is probably kept in synchrony with changing day lengths by their exposure to light at dusk or dawn. Bats often awaken and fly from the cave exit well before nightfall. Should they be too early, their internal clock may be reset. A few species of bats, *Lavia frons* and *Saccopteryx bilineata*, may forage actively during the day, but little is yet known of their special adaptations.

Locomotion. Flight is the primary mode of locomotion in all bats, although the flight styles vary. Some groups (the Molossidae, for example), adapted for flight in open spaces and often at high altitudes, have long, narrow wings, swift flight, and a large radius of turning. Other bats (the Nycteridae, Megadermatidae, and the Glossophaginae), adapted for hovering as they pick prey off vegetation or feed on flowers, have short, broad wings, slow flight, and a small radius of turning. Some bats take flight easily from the ground: members of the genus *Macrotus* do so simply by flapping, vampires (*Desmodus*) leap into the air and then spread their wings and fly. The molossids, however, roost well above the ground since, on takeoff, they fall before becoming airborne.

Speed in flight

Though flight speeds in nature are hard to measure, four vespertilionid species, carefully observed, have been timed on the average at 11.7 to 20.8 miles per hour. In flight, the posture of each of the four fingers incorporated into the wing is under precise and individual control. Finger and arm postures, which determine the shape, extension, and angle of the wings, govern such actions as turning, diving, landing, and hovering. Except when interrupted by insect catches or obstacles, bat flight paths are straight. Insects may be pursued and captured at a rate of up to two per second; during each catch, the flight path is interrupted and thus appears erratic.

In many cases (especially in the families Nycteridae, Megadermatidae, Rhinolophidae, and Hipposideridae), there is little locomotion other than flight. These bats may move across the cave ceiling from which they hang, by shifting their toehold, one foot at a time. A few genera (especially among the Pteropodidae) may crawl along branches, in a slothlike posture, using their thumb claws as well as their feet. The Emballonuridae and Rhinopomatidae hang on vertical surfaces suspended by their hind claws, but with their thumbs and wrists propped against the surface. In this orientation, they can scramble rapidly up or down and forward or backward, as well as sideways.

Bats of many genera (Vespertilionidae, Molossidae, Noctilionidae, Desmodontidae) walk or crawl on either horizontal or vertical surfaces using hindfeet, wrists, and thumbs. Many move freely either backward or forward, a convenience for entering and leaving crevices. The vampires may also leap from roost to roost. The Thyropteridae and Myzopodidae, as well as the vespertilionid *Tylonycteris*, have specialized wrist and sole pads for moving along and roosting on the smooth surface of leaves or bamboo stalks.

Bats are not known to swim in nature except, perhaps, by accident. When they do fall into the water, however, they generally swim competently.

Roosting. Bats choose a variety of diurnal roosts. Each species favours a particular kind of roost, though this varies with sex, season, and reproductive activity. Many bats favour isolated or secure roosts—caves, crevices in cliff faces, the interstices of boulder heaps, tree hollows, animal burrows, culverts, abandoned buildings, portions of buildings inaccessible to man (*i.e.*, roof, attic, hollow wall), and the hollow core of bamboo stalks. Some species roost externally—on tree trunks or in the branches of trees, under palm leaves, in unopened tubular leaves, or on the surface of rocks or buildings. For some, the darkness, stability of temperature and humidity, and isolation from predators provided by caves and crevices seem essential. Others prefer the heat and dryness of sun-exposed roosts. Many species choose special nursery or hibernation roosts. Buildings are so widely exploited by bats (especially Vespertilionidae, Molossidae, and Emballonuridae) for regular diurnal or nursery roosts that the numbers of many species have probably become more abundant since the advent of architecture. Many bats also occupy nocturnal roosts, often rocky overhangs or cave entrances, for napping, for chewing food, or for shelter from bad weather.

Allan Roberts

Indiana bats (*Myotis sodalis*) hibernating on a cave roof.

Bats are usually colonial; indeed, some form very large cave colonies. Generally, large colonies are formed by bats that roost in dense clusters, pressing against one another, although many roost spaced out, not touching. In trees, *Pteropus* may form outdoor camps numbering hundreds of thousands of individuals. Many species form smaller groups of several dozen to several hundred. Less commonly, bats are solitary; sometimes, the adult female roosts only with its most recent child. Occasionally one sex is colonial, and the other is apparently solitary. Some species regularly form mixed colonies (*e.g.*, *Mormoops* and *Chilonycteris* with *Leptonycteris*, *Monophyllus*, *Carollia*). The advantages of colonial or solitary life and the factors that govern colony size in bats with colonial predilection have not been established.

The roost requirements of many bats, rather precise in terms of light, temperature, and humidity, limit their distribution in space. Some of the Megachiroptera strikingly defoliate the trees on which they roost.

Elaborate communities of other animals are often satellites of cave-bat colonies. Among these are cave crickets, roaches, blood-sucking bugs, a variety of parasites (*e.g.*, fleas, lice, ticks, mites, and certain flies), and dermestid beetles and other insects that feed on cave-floor debris—guano, bat and insect corpses, and discarded pieces of food or seeds. Molds and other fungi are also conspicuous members of the cave-floor community. Bats and their excretions alter the cave environment by producing heat, carbon dioxide, and ammonia.

Migration. Many bats of temperate climates migrate annually to and from summer roosts and winter hibernation sites, with an individual often occupying the same roosts in seasonal sequence each year. Members of the same species may converge on a single hibernation cave or nursery roost from many directions, indicating that the choice of migration direction to and from these caves cannot be genetically determined. Migration time probably is genetically determined (*i.e.*, instinctive) and influenced also by weather conditions and the availability of food. Nothing is known of how migration goals are recognized or how their location is learned by succeeding generations. Female young, of course, are born at a nursery roost and may memorize its location, but how they know where to go at other times of year is not clear.

Separation of male and female migrants

Female Mexican free-tailed bats migrate from Central Mexico to Texas and adjacent states each spring, returning south in the fall. Mating probably occurs in transient roosts during the spring flight. The migration is believed to remove pregnant (and lactating) females to a region of high food supply where they need not compete with males of their own species. Presumably they return to Mexico for its suitable winter climate and food supply and to meet their mates.

The North American red and hoary bats (*Lasiurus borealis* and *L. cinereus*) and the silver-haired bat (*Lasionycteris noctivagans*) migrate in the fall from the northern U.S. and Canada to the southern states, returning in spring. Little is yet known of energy storage, navigation, or other specializations for migrations.

Orientation. Bats of the suborder Microchiroptera orient acoustically by echolocation ("sonar"). They emit short, high-frequency pulses of sound (usually well above the range of human hearing) and listen to the echoes returning from objects in the vicinity. By interpreting returning echoes, bats may identify the direction, distance, velocity, and some aspects of the size or nature or both of objects that draw their attention. Echolocation is used to locate and track flying and terrestrial prey, to avoid obstacles, and possibly to regulate altitude; orientation pulses may also serve as communication signals between bats of the same species. Bats of the megachiropteran genus, *Rousettus*, have independently evolved a parallel echolocation system for obstacle avoidance alone. Echolocation pulses are produced by vibrating membranes in the larynx and emitted via the nose or the mouth, depending upon species. Nose leaves in some species may serve to channel the sound.

The principle of echolocation

The echolocation signals spread in three dimensions on emission, the bulk of the energy in the hemisphere in front of the bat or in a cone-shaped region from the nostrils or mouth. When the sound impinges on an intervening surface (an insect or a leaf, for example) some of the energy in the signal is reflected or scattered, some absorbed, and some transmitted and reradiated on the far side; the proportion of sound energy in each category is a function of wavelength and of the dimensions, characteristics, and orientation of the object. The reflected sound spreads in three dimensions, and some portion of it may impinge on the bat's ears at perceptible energy levels.

Bats' external ears are generally large, probably enhancing their value for detecting direction of incoming signals, and their middle and inner ears are specialized for high-frequency sensitivity. In addition, the bony otic (auditory) complex is often isolated acoustically from the skull, probably enhancing signal comparison by both ears. The threshold and range of hearing have been studied in several genera of bats, and, in each case, the region of maximum sensitivity coincides with the prominent frequencies of the outgoing echolocation signals.

The characteristics of echolocation pulses vary with family and even with species. Echolocation pulses of a substantial number of bat species have been analyzed in terms of frequency, frequency pattern, duration, repetition rate, intensity, and directionality. The prominent frequency or frequencies range from 12 kiloHertz (one kiloHertz is equivalent to 1,000 cycles per second) to about 150 kiloHertz or more. Factors influencing frequency may include bat size, prey size, the energetics of sound production, inefficiency of propagation of high frequencies, and ambient noise levels.

Orientation pulses may be of several types. The individual pulse may include a frequency drop from beginning to end (frequency modulation, FM) or the frequency may be held constant (CF) during part of the pulse, followed by a brief FM sweep; either FM or CF pulses may have high harmonic content. The pulse duration varies with the species and the situation. In cruising flight, the pulses of the Asian false vampire (*Megaderma lyra*) are 1.5 milliseconds (0.0015 second), those of Dobson's mustache bat (*Chilonycteris psilotis*) 4 milliseconds, and those of the greater horseshoe bat 55–65 milliseconds. In goal-oriented flight, such as the pursuit of an insect or the evaluation of an obstacle or a landing perch, the pulse duration is systematically altered (usually shortened) with target distance, sometimes ending with pulses as short as 0.25 millisecond.

During insect pursuit, obstacle avoidance, and landing manoeuvres, there are three phases of pulse output design: search, approach, and terminal. The search phase, during which many bats emit about ten pulses per second, precedes specific attention to a target. In the approach phase, which starts when the bat detects an object to which it subsequently devotes its attention, the bat raises the pulse rate to about 25 to 50 per second, shortens the pulses with decreasing distance, and often alters the frequency pattern. The terminal phase, which often lasts about 100 milliseconds, is characterized by extremely short pulses, repeated as rapidly as 200 or more per second, and ceases as the bat intercepts the target or passes it (the stimulus being, perhaps, the cessation of echoes); another search phase follows. During the brief terminal phase (a fraction of a second), the bat is engaged in final interception (or avoidance) manoeuvres and appears to pay little attention to other objects.

The use of echolocation to gain sensory information requires integration of the vocal and auditory centres of the brain, in addition to sensitive ears. Not only must the nervous system of the bat analyze in a few thousandths of a second the reflected, and thus altered, form of its own pulse, but it must separate this echo from those of other individuals and from others of its own pulses. All of this must be done while the animal (and often the target) is moving in space. In the laboratory, bats have been found to be able to identify, pursue, and capture as many as two fruitflies (*Drosophila*, about three millimetres long) per second, and to locate and avoid wires as fine as 0.1 or even 0.08 millimetre in diameter.

Capabilities of bat sonar

Research has provided some information on the mechanisms of bat sonar. There is evidence that the multiple frequencies of FM or harmonic patterns serve in determining target direction. The relative intensities of the various frequencies will be different at the two ears, allowing the animal to determine target direction when three or more frequencies are received. Target velocity may be measured by constant-frequency bats through the use of the Doppler shift, a change in perceived frequency due to the relative motion of the bat and its target. Changes in pulse–echo timing may provide information on target distance and velocity. The ratio of useful signal to background noise is increased by several mechanisms, including specializations of the middle ear and its ossicles (tiny bones), isolation of the cochlea (the area where sound energy is converted into nerve impulses), and adaptations of the central nervous system.

Food habits. Most bats feed on flying insects. In some cases, prey species have been identified from stomach contents or from discarded pieces under night roosts, but such studies have not yet provided an adequate measure of the spectrum of bat diets.

Insects are identified and tracked in flight by echo-location. Large insects may be intercepted with the wing membranes and pulled into the mouth. Some moths, however, (Noctuidae, Arctiidae) are able to avoid capture by bats.

Some genera of bats (*Macrotus, Antrozous, Plecotus, Nycteris*) feed on arthropods, such as large insects, spiders, and scorpions, which they find on the ground, on walls, or on vegetation. These bats may either land on and kill their prey before taking off with it or pick it up with their teeth while hovering.

Fishing by bats

Three genera (*Noctilio, Pizonyx,* and *Myotis*) include at least one species that catches small fish and possibly crustaceans. All fish-eating species also feed on flying insects or have close relatives who do so. Each is specialized in having exceptionally large hindfeet armed with long, strong claws with which the fish are gaffed.

The Megachiroptera and many of the phyllostomatid genera feed on a variety of fruits, often green or brown in colour; usually such fruits are either borne directly on wood or hang well away from the bulk of the tree and have a sour or musky odour.

The pteropodid subfamily Eonycterinae (and some other fruit bats) and the phyllostomatid Glossophaginae feed, at least in part, on nectar and pollen. Many tropical flowers, adapted for pollination by these bats, open at night, are white or inconspicuous, have a sour, rancid, or mammalian odour, and are borne on wood, on pendulous branches, or held beyond or above the bulk of the plant. The phyllostomatid Phyllonycterinae may also feed on flowers.

Several phyllostomatid and megadermatid genera are carnivorous, feeding on small rodents, shrews, bats, sleeping birds, tree frogs, and lizards. The true vampires, which feed on the blood of large mammals or birds, land near a quiet prospective victim, walk or jump to a vulnerable spot on it where the skin is relatively exposed—the edge of the ear or nostril, around the anus, or between the toes, for example—make a scooping, superficial bite from which the blood oozes freely, and lap the blood with very specialized tongue movements. Each vampire requires about 15 millilitres (about one cubic inch) of blood per night.

The interaction of bats with their food, be it insects, fruit, or flowers, probably has a substantial impact on some biological communities. Many plants are dependent on bats for pollination; other plants benefit from seed dispersal by bats. Moths of two families are known to take evasive or protective action on hearing bat pulses nearby, an adaptation that implies heavy predation.

Maintenance behaviour. Bats are meticulous in their grooming, spending a fair part of the day and night combing and grooming their fur and cleansing their wing membranes. Generally they comb with the claws of one foot, while hanging by the other; they remove the combings and moisten their claws with their lips and tongue. On the wing membranes, in particular, they use the mouth meticulously, perhaps oiling the skin with the secretions of dermal (skin) glands while cleansing it.

Social interactions. Bats often segregate by sex. As noted, in many species, pregnant females occupy special nursery roosts until their young are independent. In some species, the sexes occupy the same general roost but gather in separate clusters. In others, the sexes intermingle or arrange themselves into a pattern within a group—the females centrally, for example, and the males peripherally. Sexual segregation during foraging has been reported for several species. Among bats that migrate over long distances, such as Mexican free-tailed, red, and hoary bats, the sexes may meet only briefly each year.

FORM AND FUNCTION

Anatomical specializations. Bats are mammals with front limbs modified for flight. The fingers, other than the thumb, are greatly elongated and are joined by a membrane that also extends from the posterior border of the forearm and upper arm to the side of the body and leg as far as the ankle or foot. Only the thumb, and

occasionally the index finger, end with a claw. The wing membrane consists of two layers of skin, generally darkly pigmented and naked, between which course blood vessels and nerves. When not fully extended, the wing skin is gathered into wrinkled folds by elastic connective tissue and muscle fibres. Some of the fingers, especially the third, fold over when the bat is not in flight; the wing may then be quite tightly folded or may partly enfold the bat's undersurface. The thumb, always free of the wing membrane, is used for walking or climbing in some species; in others, it is used for handling food. Bats that walk often have pads or suction disks on their thumbs or wrists or both, and many female bats use the thumbs for suspending themselves, hammock fashion, when giving birth.

Structure of the wing

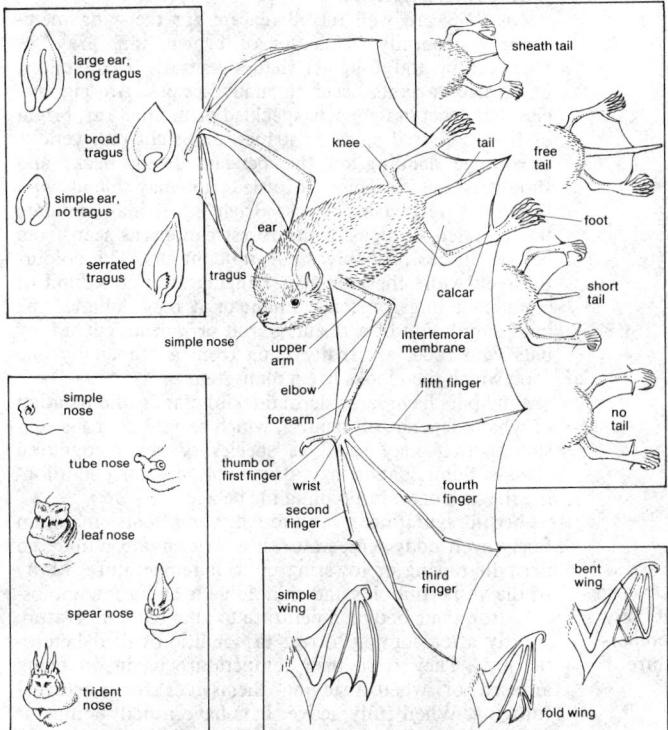

Drawn by R. Keane, based on *Natural History* (October 1958)

Figure 2: Typical microchiropteran bat (*Myotis*). Insets show variations of structures found in other bats.

Wing shape, governed by the relative lengths of the forearm and the fingers, varies greatly, in adaptation to flight characteristics.

Most bats have a membrane, consisting of skin like the wings, that extends between their legs (interfemoral membrane). In the midline, the interfemoral membrane is usually supported, at least in part, by the tail, and the distal edges are often shaped in flight by greatly elongated heel bones. The interfemoral membrane, especially well developed in insectivorous, carnivorous, and fish-eating bats, is less well developed or even absent in the vampires and in fruit- and flower-feeding bats. Many bats in flight, on catching large prey, bring the membrane forward and by flexing the neck and back tuck the prey against and into the membrane while taking a new tooth hold. By this manoeuvre, the bat takes hold of the victim head first and is able to kill or disable it promptly.

At rest, a bat's head is its most striking feature. The pinna (projecting portion) of the external ear usually is extremely large and often funnel shaped. In several genera that feed on terrestrial arthropods, the ears are particularly oversized, probably for ultraprecise directional assessment. The tragus (a projection on the anterior or side of the auditory canal) or antitragus (on the posterior side) may also be conspicuous. The ears are often highly mobile, sometimes flicking back and forth in phase with the production of sonar signals. In some species the ears are immobile, but, in all cases, they probably function jointly for directional analysis.

Bats often have a muzzle of somewhat rodent-like or foxlike proportions but, in many, the face has a pushed-in, pug-dog appearance. In the nectar feeders, the snout is elongated to house the long, extensible tongue. Many bats have a facial ornament, the nose leaf, consisting of skin and connective tissue surrounding the nostrils and extending as a free flap or flaps above the nostrils and in front of the face. The complexity and shape of the nose leaf varies with family; its presence correlates with nasal emission of orientation signals. Thus, it is supposed that the nose leaf influences sound output, perhaps by narrowing the beam, but evidence is sparse.

A bat's neck is likely to be short and relatively immobile, the chest and shoulders large and well muscled, the hips and legs slender.

Most bats are well furred (except for the wing membranes), generally in shades of brown, tan, gray, or black on top and in lighter shades ventrally. Red, yellow, or orange variants occur in many species. Among species that roost in the open, speckled or mottled fur, bright or light-coloured spots or stripes, or bright red, yellow, or orange shading on the pendant head, neck, and shoulders are common. Mottled fur may blend with lichen-covered bark or rock. Bright spots may simulate the speckled sunlight of the forest canopy as seen from below. Stripes probably break up contours. The colouring seen while the animal is hanging may be a kind of countershading for concealment or it may enhance the bat's simulation of a ripening fruit or a dead leaf. Many bats who roost externally hang from a branch by one foot, which then looks like a plant stem.

Many bats have large dermal (skin) glands (the location of which depends on family), which secrete odorous substances that may serve as species or sex recognition signals. Some glands may also supply oils for conditioning the skin or waterproofing the pelage.

Thermoregulation. Although some bats maintain fairly even body temperatures, a large number undergo periodic raising or lowering of their temperature. Many of the vespertilionids and rhinolophids and a few molossids drop their body temperature to ambient temperature shortly after coming to rest (a condition called heterothermy). They raise their temperature again on being aroused or when readying themselves for nocturnal foraging. When fully active, bats have a body temperature of about 37° C (98.6° F). During pregnancy, lactation, and juvenile growth, bats probably thermoregulate differently, more closely approximating stability. The drop in body temperature, if the ambient temperature is relatively low, results in the bat's assuming a lethargic state. Energy is conserved by "turning down the thermostat," but the bat is rendered relatively unresponsive to threats by predators or weather. Heterothermic bats, therefore, generally roost in secluded, isolated sites, often in crevices, and have specializations for arousal. One or more sensory systems and the brain remain sensitive at low temperatures and initiate the necessary heat production for arousal. Heat is generated by the metabolism of brown fat and by shivering.

Many bats that exhibit daily torpor hibernate during the winter and must, therefore, store energy as body fat in the fall, increasing their weight by 50 to 100 percent. They must also migrate from the summer roost to a suitable hibernation site (often a cave); *i.e.*, one that will remain cool and humid but will not drop below freezing throughout the winter. Large populations often aggregate in such caves. Hibernation also involves the suspension of temperature regulation for long periods; adaptations of circulation, respiration, and renal function; and suspension of at least some aspects of diurnal activity. Bats of hibernating species generally court and mate in the fall when the males are at their nutritional peak.

Bats of several tropical families are homeothermic. A spectrum of degrees of homeothermy and heterothermy probably will be discovered in the order.

Digestion and water conservation. Digestion in bats is unusually rapid. They chew and fragment their food exceptionally thoroughly and thus expose a large surface area of it to digestive action. They may begin to defecate 30 to 60 minutes after beginning to feed, thus reducing the load that must be carried in flight.

Some bats live in sun-baked roosts without access to water during the day. They may choose these roosts for their heat, thus conserving body heat, but it is not yet known how they hold their body temperature down without using water. In the laboratory, bats die if body temperature rises above about 40–41° C (104°–106° F).

Senses. Bats have been considered in folklore to be blind. In fact, the eyes in the Microchiroptera are small and have not been well studied as yet. Among the Megachiroptera, the eyes are large, but vision has been studied in detail only in *Pteropus*. These bats are able to make visual discriminations at lower light levels than can man. The Megachiroptera fly at night, of course, and some genera fly below or in the jungle canopy where light levels are very low. Except for *Rousettus*, none are known to orient acoustically.

Studies of several genera of Microchiroptera have revealed that vision is of use in long distance navigation and that obstacles and motion can be detected visually. Bats also presumably use vision to distinguish day from night and to synchronize their internal clock with the local day–night cycle.

The senses of taste, smell, and touch in bats do not seem to be strikingly different from those of related mammals. Smell is probably used as an aid in locating fruit and flowers and possibly, in the case of vampires, large vertebrates. It may also be used for locating an occupied roost, colleagues of the same species, and individuals of the correct sex. Many bats depend upon touch, aided by well-developed facial and toe whiskers and possibly by the projecting tail, to place themselves in comforting body contact with rock surfaces or with colleagues in the roost.

EVOLUTION AND PALEONTOLOGY

The fossil record of bats prior to the Pleistocene (about 2,500,000 years ago) is limited and reveals little about bat evolution. Most fossils can be attributed to living families. Skulls and teeth compatible with early bats are known from the Paleocene (about 60,000,000 years ago), but these fossils may equally well have been from insectivores, from which bats are clearly separable only on the basis of adaptations for flight. By the middle Eocene (45,000,000 years ago) bats with full flight had evolved.

The Chiroptera are readily divided into two suborders—Megachiroptera and Microchiroptera. The Megachiroptera orient visually and exhibit a number of primitive skeletal features. The Microchiroptera orient acoustically. It is not certain that they have a common origin. The suborders either evolved separately from flightless Insectivora or diverged very early in chiropteran history.

The two principal geographic centres of bat evolution appear to be the Australo-Malaysian region, with about 290 species, and the New World tropics, with about 230 species. Comparable ecological niches in the Old and New World are largely occupied by different genera of bats, usually of different families.

CLASSIFICATION

Distinguishing taxonomic features. The order Chiroptera is defined by true flight. The elongated finger bones support the wing membrane. Bats are also characterized by their generally small size, marked pectoral specialization for flight, and relatively weak pelvic and leg development. The ulna is reduced, claws are absent on fingers except for the thumb (and occasionally the second finger), and the knee is directed posteriorly and laterally. The maximum complement of milk teeth is 22 and of permanent teeth, 38; the minimum of permanent teeth is 20. The dental formula indicates the number of pairs of upper and lower incisors, canines, premolars, and molars, respectively, and total number of teeth.

Annotated classification.

ORDER CHIROPTERA
Eighteen living families, 174 genera, and about 900 living species.

Suborder Megachiroptera
One family.

Family Pteropodidae (flying foxes and Old World fruit bats)

Generally large, fruit- or flower-feeding; lack acoustic orientation (except *Rousettus*); ears small, eyes large, vision well-developed; generally roost in trees, often colonial; often show countershading, cryptic markings, or bright fur colours or patterns. Index finger generally clawed, tail short or lacking, interfemoral membrane reduced. Muzzle simple in appearance (except *Hypsignathus*), generally cannot walk but can move along branches in hanging posture. Forearm length varies from 37 mm (*Macroglossus*) to 220 mm (*Pteropus vampyrus*). Teeth modified for fruit- and flower-feeding. Dental formula $\frac{(1-2) \cdot 1 \cdot 3 \cdot (1-2)}{(0-2) \cdot 1 \cdot 3 \cdot (2-3)} = 24-34$. Old World tropics and subtropics, including many Pacific islands; 39 Recent genera, about 154 species.

Suborder Microchiroptera
Seventeen families.

Family Rhinopomatidae (mouse-tailed bats)

Small, insectivorous; tail very long and largely free beyond a narrow interfemoral membrane, forearm very long, ears large, small nose leaf, primitive shoulder girdle. Dental formula $\frac{1 \cdot 1 \cdot 1 \cdot 3}{2 \cdot 1 \cdot 2 \cdot 3} = 28$. Store fat (probably seasonally). Roost on vertical surfaces, probably not in total darkness or isolation. Tropical distribution from northern Africa through southern Asia as far as Sumatra; 1 genus, 3 species. Generally considered to be the most primitive of living Microchiroptera.

Family Emballonuridae (sheath-tailed or sac-winged bats)

Small to medium sized. Ears large but simply shaped, eyes small, muzzle sharp but plain; tail short, perforating dorsal surface of well-developed interfemoral membrane. Several genera have a glandular pouch in the wing extension, anterior to the arm. Relatively unspecialized shoulder girdle and arm articulation. Dental formula $\frac{2 \cdot 1 \cdot 2 \cdot 3}{3 \cdot 1 \cdot 2 \cdot 3} = 34$, $\frac{1 \cdot 1 \cdot 2 \cdot 3}{3 \cdot 1 \cdot 2 \cdot 3} = 32$, or $\frac{1 \cdot 1 \cdot 2 \cdot 3}{2 \cdot 1 \cdot 2 \cdot 3} = 30$. Insectivorous; roost on vertical surfaces, such as tree trunks, cliff faces, cave entrances, and walls. Some favour buildings, especially belfries; some densely colonial but not touching one another; others form small groups or are solitary. Hang suspended from toes with wrists propped against wall. Worldwide tropical distribution (excluding West Indies and some Pacific islands); 12 genera, about 50 species; each genus restricted to either Old or New World.

Family Nycteridae (slit-faced or hollow-faced bats)

Small to medium sized, the humerus and pectoral girdle not greatly specialized, skull with peculiar nasal fossa (depression), cleft nose leaf, and a deep midline facial cleft behind and above the nostrils. Ears large, wings broad, tail long with bifid (split) end, calcars (heel bones) greatly elongated, tail and calcars support well-developed interfemoral membrane. Dental formula $\frac{2 \cdot 1 \cdot 1 \cdot 3}{3 \cdot 1 \cdot 2 \cdot 3} = 32$. Insectivorous, mostly preying on terrestrial forms or those resting on vegetation, rocks, or walls. Cannot walk. Roosts usually dark and humid, some species roosting externally in jungle canopy. Generally form small nontouching colonies, but some are solitary. Distributed through most of tropical Africa, Malaysia, and Indonesia; 1 genus, 13 species.

Family Megadermatidae (false vampires)

Moderately large bats; external ears very large and fused across midline; tragus bifid; nose leaf large with truncated end; eyes relatively large; wings broad, interfemoral membrane well-developed and supported distally by heel bones, no external tail. Females bear false inguinal nipples. Premaxillae lacking; dental formula $\frac{0 \cdot 1 \cdot (1-2) \cdot 3}{2 \cdot 1 \cdot 2 \cdot 3} = 26-28$. Insectivorous, principally on terrestrial arthropods, as in Nycteridae; at least 2 species, *Megaderma lyra* and *Macroderma gigas*, also feed on small vertebrates hunted and taken in the same fashion as arthropod prey. Cannot walk. Form small nontouching colonies usually in dark, secluded caves or abandoned buildings. *Lavia frons* is at least partly diurnal and roost in trees in the savanna and open forest. Central Africa, Southeast Asia, and Australia; 4 genera, 5 species.

Family Hipposideridae (Old World leaf-nosed bats)

Small to large bats. Complex nose leaf with subordinate leaflets and compartments; large ears, widely separated and highly mobile, antitragus well-developed; interfemoral membrane well-developed, tail generally projects slightly beyond distal edge of membrane. Often bear glandular pouch on forehead; females have false inguinal nipples. Dental formula $\frac{1 \cdot 1 \cdot 2 \cdot 3}{2 \cdot 1 \cdot 2 \cdot 3} = 30$. Colour usually drab brownish but red phases not uncommon. Insectivorous, usually on flying insects. Mostly colonial, non-touching, and roosting in humid caves, tree hollows, culverts, or buildings. A few roost externally in branches of trees, a few are solitary. Do not walk. Old World tropics; 9 genera, about 60 species, the genus *Hipposideros* particularly successful in numbers of species and individuals throughout the Old World tropics.

Family Rhinolophidae (horseshoe bats)

Small to moderately large size. Complex nose leaf; large, highly mobile ears, well-developed antitragus; wings short and rounded; well-developed interfemoral membrane, supported by tail; calcanea (backs of heels) weak. Fur generally brown (red phases occur); females bear false inguinal nipples. Dental formula $\frac{1 \cdot 1 \cdot 2 \cdot 3}{2 \cdot 1 \cdot 3 \cdot 3} = 32$. Dark, humid roosts selected, especially caves, but tree hollows, buildings, and culverts as well; generally colonial, nontouching; cannot walk. Insectivorous, usually on flying insects. Old World, including parts of western Europe, the U.S.S.R., and Japan; 2 genera, about 70 species, the genus *Rhinolophus* one of the most successful in species and numbers.

Family Noctilionidae (bulldog bats)

Medium sized. Muzzle heavy but unadorned; lips full; internal cheek pouches; ears large, pointed, and mobile; wings long and narrow. Dental formula $\frac{2 \cdot 1 \cdot 1 \cdot 3}{1 \cdot 1 \cdot 2 \cdot 3} = 28$. Tail well-developed, extending to midpoint of large interfemoral membrane, which is pierced dorsally by tail tip, membrane supported distally by very well-developed calcars and calcanea. Feet large, or very large (*N. leporinus*). Colour dark brown to rufous orange dorsally; musky odour. Walk well, often roost in crevices, tree hollows, attics, grottoes, and caves; colonial, in touching clusters. *Noctilio labialis* feeds on flying insects, as does *N. leporinus*, which also gaffs fish. Tropical America; 1 genus, 2 species.

Family Mormoopidae

Small; insectivorous on flying insects; some walk; all lack nose leaf but have elaborate lip leaves; colour from brown through orange, red, and yellow. Densely colonial in dark caves, colonies often number tens of thousands. Tail and interfemoral membrane well-developed. Dental formula $\frac{2 \cdot 1 \cdot 2 \cdot 3}{2 \cdot 1 \cdot 3 \cdot 3} = 34$. Tropical Central and South America; 3 genera, 9 species.

Family Phyllostomatidae (American leaf-nosed bats)

Small to large size. Nose leaf simply shaped, ears often large and mobile, wings generally short and broad, tail and interfemoral membrane quite varied (from absent to well-developed); dental formula varied, from 26 to 34; fur colour and patterns varied. Diet highly varied, include insectivorous (on flying or terrestrial forms), carnivorous, fruit- and flower-feeding species. Generally do not walk. Colonial, often densely so; generally roost in touching clusters in caves, tree hollows, buildings, culverts, or in the open under bridges, eaves, in the crests of palm trees, or on the underside of palm leaves. Flight swift and straight to hovering. Southwestern U.S. through tropical America; 47 genera, about 120 species.

Subfamily Phyllostomatinae. Medium to large. Nose leaf often of striking size, ears large. Insectivorous, fruit-feeding, or carnivorous. Varied dental formulas. Subfamily may be an artificial grouping.

Subfamily Glossophaginae. Small to medium sized. Small nose leaf, snout elongated; tongue elongated and extensible. Wings broad; hovering flight. Feed on pollen, nectar, fruit.

Subfamilies Carolliinae, Sturnirinae, Stenoderminae. Medium sized. Fruit-feeding; some may be insectivorous. Nose leaves well-developed. Many Stenoderminae have white or light facial stripes, may roost in the open; 2 species alter palm leaves as roosts.

Subfamily Phyllonycterinae. Small bats, endemic to West Indies, probably fruit- and flower-feeding. Legs and feet exceptionally well-developed and body flexible. Beige, maize, or light brown; cave-dwelling; nose leaves very small; snout and tongue moderately elongated.

Family Desmodontidae (vampire bats)

Medium-sized. Small nose leaf. Teeth highly specialized for cutting skin, cheek teeth reduced; dental formula in *Desmodus* $\frac{1 \cdot 1 \cdot 1 \cdot 1}{2 \cdot 1 \cdot 2 \cdot 1} = 20$. Hindlegs and thumbs very well adapted for walking and jumping. Tail absent; interfemoral membrane reduced. Feed on blood of large mammals or birds; roost in caves, hollow trees and culverts; colonial. Most of tropical America, excluding West Indies; 3 genera, 3 species.

Family Natalidae (funnel-eared bats)

Small, slenderly built. Gray, buffy, yellow, or reddish; fur deep. Well-developed tail and interfemoral membrane. Ears large snout plain: dental formula $\frac{2 \cdot 1 \cdot 3 \cdot 3}{3 \cdot 1 \cdot 3 \cdot 3} = 38$. Natalids walk clumsily but do not enter crevices; cave-dwelling, colonial in nontouching groups; feed on flying insects. Central America, and northern South America, West Indies; 1 genus, 4 species.

Family Furipteridae (smoky bats)

Small, delicately built. Thumb vestigial; snout plain; tail long, ending short of distal edge of well-developed interfemoral membrane; legs long; feet small. Dental formula $\frac{2 \cdot 1 \cdot 2 \cdot 3}{3 \cdot 1 \cdot 3 \cdot 3} = 36$. Biology unknown; probably insectivorous. Northern South America; 2 genera, 2 species.

Family Thyropteridae (disk-wing bats)

Second finger reduced to rudiment, base of thumb and sole provided with sucking disk, simple muzzle, ears large; dental formula $\frac{2 \cdot 1 \cdot 3 \cdot 3}{3 \cdot 1 \cdot 3 \cdot 3} = 38$. Insectivorous, roost alone or in small groups, often in still furled banana leaves. Biology poorly known. Central America and northern South America, excluding West Indies; 1 genus, 2 species.

Family Myzopodidae (Old World sucker-footed bats)

Small, plain muzzle, large ears with peculiar mushroom-shaped lobe, dental formula $\frac{2 \cdot 1 \cdot 3 \cdot 3}{3 \cdot 1 \cdot 3 \cdot 3} = 38$. Thumb and sole with adhesive disks, vestigial thumb claw; tail extends free beyond interfemoral membrane; specialized scapulo-humeral articulations. Probably insectivorous (biology unknown); endemic to Madagascar; 1 species.

Family Vespertilionidae (common bats)

Small to medium sized. Muzzle plain; eyes small; ears moderate to large, tragus well-developed; dental formula varied, $\frac{1 \cdot 1 \cdot 1 \cdot 3}{2 \cdot 1 \cdot 2 \cdot 3} = 28$ to $\frac{2 \cdot 1 \cdot 3 \cdot 3}{3 \cdot 1 \cdot 3 \cdot 3} = 38$. Wings generally long and moderately narrow; tail and interfemoral membrane well-developed. All walk well, often entering crevices. Insectivorous, some on flying, some on terrestrial insects; a few (*Pizonyx* and some *Myotis*) eat fishes. Mostly roost in caves, attics, barns, hollow trees, boulder heaps, the twig work of birds' nests, or roof thatching; a few (*Lasiurus*) roost on tree trunks, or in hollow core of bamboo (*Tylonycteris*). Generally colonial in dense, touching clusters; a few solitary. Many temperate species hibernate and migrate; many drably coloured; several that roost externally are spotted (*Euderma*) or speckled (*Lasiurus*). Family worldwide to tree line, including many oceanic islands; some genera (*Myotis*, *Eptesicus*, and *Pipistrellus*) also worldwide; 35 genera, about 290 species.

Family Mystacinidae (New Zealand short-tailed bats)

Small, with simple vespertilionid-like head; highly adapted for walking. Wings fold exceptionally compactly; thumb and toe claws long and sharp; tail perforates interfemoral membrane dorsally. Dental formula $\frac{1 \cdot 1 \cdot 2 \cdot 3}{1 \cdot 1 \cdot 2 \cdot 3} = 28$. Feeds on flying and terrestrial insects. Biology poorly known. New Zealand; 1 species.

Family Molossidae (free-tailed bats)

Robustly built, small to very large. Tail projects well beyond well-developed interfemoral membrane; ears large, rather immobile, often fused to one another, and of very unusual shapes; lips and snout often heavy, eyes tiny. Wings very long and narrow; legs well-developed for walking; toes often bear bristles; dental formula varied from $\frac{1 \cdot 1 \cdot 1 \cdot 3}{1 \cdot 1 \cdot 2 \cdot 3} = 26$ to $\frac{1 \cdot 1 \cdot 2 \cdot 3}{3 \cdot 1 \cdot 2 \cdot 3} = 32$. Often have a conspicuous odour; fur short, usually dark brown or black. Many highly colonial, as many as millions clustering in dense, touching groups; roost pressed against fellows or walls, often in crevices. Occupy caves, tree hollows, and buildings. Walk exceptionally well; many prefer hot, dry roosts. Feed on flying insects; some migrate. Worldwide in tropics and subtropics, with a few species ranging into mild temperate regions; 11 genera, about 90 species (the genus *Tadarida* worldwide).

BIBLIOGRAPHY. G.M. ALLEN, *Bats* (1939, reprinted 1962), a comprehensive view by a naturalist; K.C. ANDERSEN, *Catalogue of the Chiroptera in the Collection of the British Museum*, 2nd ed., vol. 1, *Megachiroptera* (1912), definitive taxonomy of the Megachiroptera; R.W. BARBOUR and W.H. DAVIS, *Bats of America* (1970), comprehensive coverage of North American bats, distribution, natural history, photographs, and taxonomy; A. BROSSET, *La Biologie des Chiroptères* (1966), the most complete, up-to-date review of all bats; R.G. BUSNEL (ed.), *Animal Sonar Systems*, 2 vol. (1967), the most recent important symposium on echolocation and related systems; R.B. DAVIS, C.F. HERREID II, and H.L. SHORT, *Mexican Free-Tailed Bats in Texas* (1962), the most complete published survey of a given species of bats; M. EISENTRAUT, *Aus dem Leben der Fledermäuse und Flughunde* (1957), a review of European bats by an important student of bat natural history and physiology; K. FAEGRI and L. VAN DER PIJL, *The Principles of Pollination Ecology* (1966), the role of bats in pollination; D.R. GRIFFIN, *Listening in the Dark: The Acoustic Orientation of Bats and Men* (1958), the most recent authoritative summary of echolocation; *Echoes of Bats and Men* (1959), a paperback introduction to echolocation; A. NOVICK and N. LEEN, *The World of Bats* (1970), a recent review of bat behaviour and ecology with action photographs; L. VAN DER PIJL, *Principles of Dispersal in Higher Plants* (1969), the role of bats in dispersal of seeds; D.R. ROSEVEAR, *The Bats of West Africa* (1965), an important compilation on the bats of a particular range; H. SAINT GIRONS, A. BROSSET, and M.C. SAINT GIRONS, "Contribution à la connaissance du cycle annuel de la Chauve-souris *Rhinolophus ferrum-equinum* (Schreber, 1774)," *Mammalia*, 33:357–470 (1969), an extensive study of the biology of one European bat species; J. VERSCHUREN, *Ecologie, biologie, et systématique des Cheiroptères* (1957), the primary work on the ecology of bats; B. VILLA-R., *Los murcielagos de Mexico* (1966), an important compilation of knowledge on the bats of Mexico; W. WIMSATT (ed.), *The Biology of Bats* (1971), the definitive current work on bat biology.

(A.N.)

Chondrostei

The Chondrostei comprise one of the three major subdivisions (subclasses, or infraclasses) of the class Actinopterygii, the higher, bony, ray-finned fishes. The chondrosteans first appear in rocks of Middle Devonian Period (about 375,000,000 years ago), and they have persisted to the present time. The only living representatives are the sturgeons and paddlefishes; the living bichirs (polypterids and the closely related reedfish) of Africa are also considered to be chondrosteans by some ichthyologists.

The chondrosteans were most numerous and diversified during the last part of the Paleozoic (ending 225,000,000 years ago) and the beginning of the Mesozoic Eras (beginning 225,000,000 years ago). With the rise of the holosteans and teleosts (the other two major subdivisions of the Actinopterygii) during the Mesozoic, the chondrosteans declined, until by the end of the Cretaceous Period (65,000,000 years ago) they had been reduced to a few genera. The few living chondrosteans are highly specialized and aberrant forms. Their evolutionary history has not been clearly documented. Except for the sturgeon, which is a food fish for man and the source of caviar, they have no economic importance. A study of the living sturgeons, paddlefishes, and bichirs, however, provides some understanding of extinct forms.

Drawing by J. Helmer based on D.S. Jordan, *A Guide to the Study of Fishes*

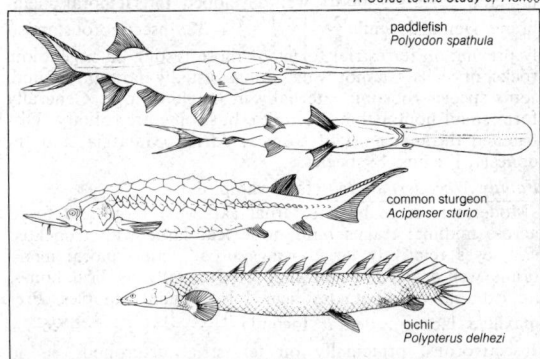

Figure 1: Body plans of modern chondrostean fishes.

General features. The chondrosteans are difficult to characterize as a group, but certain features are common to most of them. Generally the bony adult neurocranium, or braincase, is composed of two divisions, a larger ethmo-otic and a smaller occipital section. In the paddlefishes and sturgeons the braincase is mostly cartilaginous, with a few isolated areas of bone.

The most numerous and widespread Paleozoic chondrostean fishes belong to the order Palaeonisciformes. The earliest known chondrosteans (Cheirolepidae and Stegotrachelidae), from the Middle Devonian of Europe, belong to this group. The palaeonisciforms inhabited a variety of freshwater and marine habitats and are known

Distribution and size range

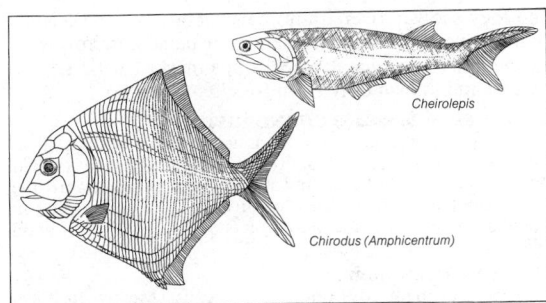

Figure 2: Examples of two chondrosts of the order
Palaeonisciformes.

from all the continents except Antarctica. They reached
their period of greatest number and diversity during the
Carboniferous Period (280,000,000 to 345,000,000 years
ago). Although they persisted with little modification into
the Cretaceous, they began to show a marked decrease in
the Triassic Period (190,000,000 to 225,000,000 years
ago) and, by the end of the Cretaceous, had completely
died out.

Modern sturgeons occur only in the Northern Hemisphere. The common sturgeon (*Acipenser sturio*) is found
on the European coast from Norway to the Mediterranean Sea. A closely related form, probably of the same
species, occurs along the east coast of North America
from the St. Lawrence River to the Gulf of Mexico. *A.
guldenstatii* occurs in western U.S.S.R. east to Lake
Baikal. A smaller species, the sterlet (*A. ruthenus*), inhabits the Black and Caspian seas. *A. stellatus* occurs in
rivers leading to the Black Sea, the Sea of Azov, and the
Caspian Sea. The lake sturgeon of North America (*A.
fulvescens*) occurs in the Mississippi Valley, the Great
Lakes, and northward into Canada. The white, Oregon,
or Sacramento sturgeon (*A. transmontanus*) occurs on the
Pacific Coast of North America from California to
Alaska.

Bichirs (*Polypterus*) and the closely related reedfish
(*Calamoichthys calabaricus*) occur in freshwaters of Central Africa. The Mississippi paddlefish (*Polyodon spath-
ula*), also known as the spoonbill sturgeon, is found in
the Mississippi basin; the Chinese paddlefish (*Psephurus
gladius*), also called the swordbill sturgeon, occurs in the
Yangtze River of China.

The length of some palaeonisciforms may have been as
great as one metre (slightly more than three feet). The
so-called subholosteans—a collective term for a heterogeneous group of chondrostean orders, from Perleidiformes through Parasemionotiformes (see below *Annotated classification*—probably grew to no more than 30
centimetres (about one foot) or so. Most modern sturgeons reach a length of little more than two metres (seven
feet), but the hausen, or beluga (*Huso huso*), has been reported to reach 8.5 metres (28 feet). The Mississippi paddlefish grows to about 1.8 metres (about six feet), but the
Chinese paddlefish sometimes reaches 6.3 metres (about
21 feet) in length. The largest species of bichir grows to
about 70 centimetres (28 inches); the reedfish reaches a
length of 90 centimetres (35 inches).

Natural history. *Reproduction and life cycle.* Marine
sturgeons ascend rivers in spring or summer to deposit
their spawn. They are abundant in the rivers of southern
U.S.S.R. during the two weeks of the upstream migration.
Early in summer the fish migrate into the rivers or toward
the shores of freshwater lakes in large shoals for breeding purposes. The eggs are small and numerous, and the
growth of the young is rapid. After the sturgeon attains
maturity, growth continues at a slow rate for several
years. Some attain great age: observations made in Russia indicate that the hausen may attain an age of 200 to
300 years.

Bichirs initiate courtship by leaping from the water.
Little is known of their spawning habits. Young fish have
external branching gills and are newtlike in appearance.
Paddlefishes breed when seven or eight years old and

spawn during spring floods. The larvae hatch in about
two weeks and feed on their large yolk sac. The paddle,
a long, broad extension of the snout, is absent at birth
but begins to appear after two or three weeks.

Ecology. Sturgeons occur in both salt water and freshwater. Ground feeders, they spend much time foraging,
dragging their tactile, whisker-like barbels over the bottom in search of small invertebrates and fishes. Paddlefishes feed by straining plankton (mostly tiny, drifting
aquatic organisms) through their gill system and have
been described as living plankton nets. Bichirs and reedfish mainly inhabit the edges of streams and flood plains.
They remain concealed by day and forage at night for
worms, insect larvae, crustaceans, and small fishes.

Form and function. *Extinct forms.* Most palaeonisciforms had fusiform (*i.e.*, tapered at both ends)
bodies with blunt snouts; eyes situated far forward; pelvic
fins located at about the middle of the body; dorsal (*i.e.*,
back) and anal (on the lower side) fins nearly opposite
one another on the posterior part of the body; and
heterocercal (*i.e.*, with the top lobe longer than the lower
lobe) caudal fins. With few exceptions, their bodies were
covered with rhomboidal (diamond-shaped) scales, with
or without a dentine layer. The scales articulated with
one another by a peg-and-socket joint; in some groups,
the scales tended to become thin and cycloidal, or
rounded, as in the coccolepids. The rays of the unpaired
fins were usually more numerous than their basal supports, and all the fins were usually bordered by scales
that were generally larger and stronger than other scales
(fulcral scales). A few families, such as the Late Paleozoic
platysomids and amphicentrids, evolved deep, compressed bodies with elongated anal and dorsal fins.

In all palaeonisciforms, the upper jaw was tied to the
cheekbones, which completely covered the area between
the eyes and the gill covers. The jaw suspension may have
had an oblique orientation (associated with a wide mouth
gape) or a nearly vertical orientation (associated with a
relatively smaller gape). The teeth were either rather
well developed or were sometimes practically absent. If
present, they were generally styliform, or needlelike, in
both the upper and lower jaws, and the musculature closing the mouth was rather straplike.

There is reason to believe that the biting mechanism in
palaeonisciforms was less powerful than that of the
holosteans. The arrangement of the fins and the structure
of the tail suggest that manoeuvrability in swimming was
not as great as in either the holosteans or in the teleosts.
Members of the Late Paleozoic order Tarrasiiformes had
an elongated body and was continuous with the dorsal
and anal fins. Haplolepiforms, also of the Late Paleozoic,
had robust paired and unpaired fins and a relatively small
number of unbranched fin rays. Like the palaeonisciforms, the subholosteans ranged from fusiform to deep
bodied.

In some subholosteans, the upper jaw was freed from
the cheek elements and articulated with the skull only in
the snout region. The palate and the cheek were also
modified in such a way that the adductor, or closing,
musculature of the lower jaw could enlarge to provide
greater force in seizing prey. In connection with this, the
upper border of the mandible developed an elevation
(coronoid process) on its posterior part, and the attachment of part of the jaw musculature to this elevation increased the efficiency of the feeding mechanism. In the
dorsal and anal fins, the number of fin rays tended to
equal the number of basal supports, and the caudal fin
became hemiheterocercal (*i.e.*, apparently symmetrical,
but with the vertebral column turned upward and extending into the upper lobe).

Extant forms. The amount of bone in the sturgeon
skeleton is less than that in the ancient forms. The modern sturgeon has bony plates on the head and five rows of
bony shields along the body: one along the back, one on
each side above the pectoral fins, and one on each side
near the belly. The tail fin is heterocercal. The mouth is
subterminal (*i.e.*, behind and below the snout tip), and
this and other specializations are clearly related to bottom feeding. The mouth is toothless and is preceded by

Feeding

Specializa-
tions for
bottom
feeding

four fleshy barbels; the protractile lips have taste buds surrounding them. The form of the snout becomes more blunt and abbreviated with age.

The relationship of the paddlefishes to the sturgeons is not fully understood. The skeleton of the paddlefish, like that of the sturgeon, has lost much of its ossification. The body is fusiform, the fins well developed, and the tail heterocercal. The elongated, paddle-shaped snout, which is composed entirely of cartilage, is one-third to one-half the total body length. The skin is smooth, except for a few scattered vestigial scales. The mouth is subterminal, and the jaw structure, particularly that of the adductor muscles, is suggestive of the palaeonisciform condition.

The bichir is rather elongated in form, the reedfish eel-like; both have hard, diamond-shaped scales. The dorsal fin consists of a few to several separate finlets. The upper body is brown, grayish, or greenish; the lower side often white or yellowish.

Evolution and classification. *Historical development.* The long history of the chondrosteans, which extends over a period of 375,000,000 years, is marked by several important evolutionary events. The first is related to the appearance of the earliest ray-finned fishes, the palaeonisciforms. These fishes possess essentially the same feeding mechanism design and the same pattern, including a fully heterocercal tail, as later forms. The Late Paleozoic Tarrasiiformes and Haplolepiformes are obviously descended from the palaeonisciforms, but they are divergent enough to be regarded as separate orders.

The main groups of holosteans and halecostomes (which gave rise to the teleosts) apparently arose from subholostean-like ancestors during the Permian and Triassic periods. The heterogeneous subholosteans show modifications in the feeding mechanism and in the body that foreshadow the holosteans and halecostomes. Fishes referred to this unnatural group were characteristic of the Triassic Period, although a few families continued into the Jurassic (136,000,000 to 190,000,000 years ago). In general, the subholosteans can be said to show a diversity in the structure of the skeleton that was never attained by the more primitive palaeonisciforms. This diversity suggests the kind of evolutionary "experiments" that must have occurred during the rise of the various families of more advanced actinopterygians.

The origin of the order Acipenseriformes (which includes the sturgeon) is not known, although they were clearly derived from some palaeonisciform groups. Fossils that are without doubt related to the sturgeons and paddlefishes are no older than the Upper Cretaceous (about 65,000,000 to 100,000,000 years ago). Earlier, the history of this order is poorly documented and confused. Both the sturgeons and the paddlefishes became specialized early in their history and have shown only minor diversification since then.

The Polypteriformes, which include the living bichirs (*Polypterus*) and reedfish (*Calamoichthys*) of Africa, show a confusing array of palaeonisciform, holostean, and specialized characters. Some skull and scale features indicate derivation from palaeonisciform ancestors. The palate and jaws, on the other hand, suggest attainment of a nearly holostean-like pattern. However, the specialized fins, including the diphycercal tail, indicate that the polypteriforms have had a long, independent history. Fossil occurrences, which may extend back to the Early Tertiary Period (beginning 65,000,000 years ago), offer no clues to their affinity.

Distinguishing taxonomic features. The approximately 37 families of the Chondrostei are separated from one another, for the most part, on the basis of differences in dermal bone pattern, body shape, and fin form and position.

Two orders, Tarrasiiformes and Haplolepiformes, are quite palaeonisciform-like in many ways but diverge in other ways that clearly set them apart as separate categories.

An advanced group of some 12 orders of unrelated chondrosteans is popularly referred to as subholosteans. The different subholostean families possess various combinations of palaeonisciform and holostean characters,

and they show a diversity in the structure of the skeleton that was never attained in the earlier palaeonisciforms.

Annotated classification. Groups marked with a † are extinct and known only from fossils.

SUBCLASS (or Infraclass) CHONDROSTEI
A group that has undergone various evolutionary diversifications. The orders of the Chondrostei are specialized for certain habitats and ways of life, and many show trends toward the holostean–halecostome level of organization, especially in median fin structure and development of a hemiheterocercal tail.

†Order Palaeonisciformes
Lower Devonian to Middle Cretaceous. Mostly fusiform fishes with heterocercal tail; maxillary bone fixed; limited; many more fin rays than basal elements in the median fins; 37 families of wide distribution, early members freshwater, later marine.

†Order Tarrasiiformes
Carboniferous (about 280,000,000 to 345,000,000 years ago). Palaeoniscid-like, but with elongated body, a diphycercal tail, and dorsal and anal fins continuous with it. One family, Tarrasiidae; Scotland and Illinois.

†Order Haplolepiformes
Upper Carboniferous. Peculiar fishes with stout, unbranched fin rays; large gular (*i.e.*, in the throat region) plates; small opercular (*i.e.*, gill cover) apparatus. One family, Europe and North America.

†Order Perleidiformes
Lower to Upper Triassic. With ganoid (*i.e.*, bony, diamond-shaped, and not overlapping) scales; fin rays equal number of basal supports rather than exceed them; tail hemiheterocercal. Three families; worldwide.

†Order Redfieldiiformes
Lower and Middle Triassic. Like Perleidiformes, but fin rays more numerous than basal elements in dorsal and anal fins. One family, Redfieldiidae, in freshwaters of South Africa, Australia, and North America.

†Order Dorypteriformes
Upper Permian (225,000,000 to 250,000,000 years ago). Deep-bodied, with very modified skull; scales confined to anterior part of trunk. One family, Dorypteridae; Europe, China.

†Order Bobasatraniiformes
Lower Triassic. Body deep, laterally compressed; fin rays slightly more numerous than basal supports; crushing dentition; pelvic fins absent. One family, Bobasatraniidae; marine; widely distributed.

†Order Pholidopleuriformes
Lower to Upper Triassic. Some relatively long and slender; dorsal and anal fins far back on body, origin of anal fin anterior to dorsal fin; fin rays more numerous than basal elements; tail hemiheterocercal; jaw support almost vertical or moderately oblique. One family, Pholidopleuridae; marine and freshwater; wide distribution.

†Order Peltopleuriformes
Upper Triassic. Large eyes; hemiheterocercal tail almost symmetrical externally; dentition weak. Two families, Peltopleuridae and Habroichthyidae; marine, perhaps some plankton feeding; Italy, China.

†Order Platysiagiformes
Lower Triassic to Lower Jurassic. Elongated, fusiform body; tail hemiheterocercal; rays of median fins probably equalled basal elements in number; teeth large, conical. One family, Platysiagidae; marine; probably predacious; Italy and England.

†Order Cephaloxeniformes
Middle to Upper Triassic. Body deep, fusiform; thick head bones and crushing dentition; tail hemiheterocercal. One family, Cephaloxenidae; marine, probably bottom-dwelling mollusc eaters; Italy.

†Order Luganoiiformes
Middle and Upper Triassic. Body fusiform; head somewhat flattened in the horizontal plane; some head bones fused; jaw suspension inclined forward; fin rays apparently equal to basal elements in number; tail hemiheterocercal. One family, Luganoiidae; marine; probably predacious midwater fishes; Italy.

†Order Ptycholepiformes
Middle Triassic to Upper Jurassic. Fusiform body; fin rays of median fins nearly equalling basal elements in number; jaw support almost vertical; teeth small. One family, Ptycholepididae; marine; presumably plankton feeders; Europe.

†Order Saurichthyiformes
Lower Triassic to Upper Jurassic. Elongate, slender; snout elongated; single dorsal fin far back on body, opposite anal

fin; tail with nearly equal lobes; number of scale rows reduced, 1 dorsal, 1 ventral, and 1 along each side; jaw suspension almost vertical; teeth large, conical; jaws long. One family, Saurichthyidae; marine and freshwater; predacious; worldwide. Length about 7–150 cm.

†Order Chondrosteiformes

Lower Triassic to Upper Jurassic. Body scales and skull bones reduced; snout moderately developed, maxillary and opercular bones reduced; jaw support somewhat inclined backward; median fins paleonisciform-like, rays more numerous than basal supports. Probably gave rise to sturgeons. One family, Chondrosteidae; marine; some were suctorial feeders like sturgeons; England.

†Order Parasemionotiformes

Lower Triassic. Near holosteans in dermal skull structure. Two families; marine; Siberia, Greenland, and Madagascar.

Order Acipenseriformes (sturgeons and paddlefishes)

Upper Cretaceous to Recent. Almost no internal ossification; platelike scales in isolated rows (Acipenseridae); snout enlarged and tactile (Polyodontidae); median fins chondrostean in having more fin rays than basal elements; tail heterocercal. Marine and freshwater, bottom suctorial feeders (sturgeons, Acipenseridae; Europe, Asia, North America) and plankton feeders (paddlefishes, Polyodontidae; China and North America). Length (sturgeons) up to 8.5; weight to 1,400 kg (3,080 lbs.).

Order Polypteriformes (bichirs and reedfish)

Pleistocene to Recent. Typical chondrostean characters, such as ganoid scales. Dorsal fin modified into row of finlets; tail diphycercal; freshwater; Africa.

Critical appraisal. Because they are a fairly uniform group, the classification of the Chondrostei is difficult and unsettled. About 37 families are now recognized. The relationships of bichirs and the reedfish are especially controversial. Some authorities place them in a separate subclass; others conclude that they are related to the crossopterygians.

BIBLIOGRAPHY. S.M. ANDREWS *et al.*, "Pisces," in W.B. HARLAND *et al.* (eds.), *The Fossil Record: A Symposium with Documentation*, ch. 26 (1967), a recent classification of fish, with first and last occurrences for each family; E.S. GOODRICH, "*Vertebrata craniata*," fasc. 1, "Cyclostomes and Fishes," in E.R. LANKESTER (ed.), *A Treatise on Zoology* (1909), a classic work on the anatomy of fish that is still useful; D. HEYLER, *Vertébrés de l'autunien de France* (1969), a detailed account of some palaeonisciform fish from a classic locality in France; J.P. LEHMAN, "Etude complementaire des poissons de l'Eotrias de Madagascar," *K. Svenska Vetensk-Akad. Handl.*, 2:1–201 (1952), a detailed study of early Triassic fish from Madagascar; "Super-ordre des Chondrostéens (Chondrostei): Formes fossiles," in P.P. GRASSE (ed.), *Traité de zoologie*, vol. 13 (1958), a comprehensive reference work on the organization and classification of the chondrosteans, and "Actinopterygii," in J. PIVETEAU (ed.), *Traité de paléontologie*, vol. 4 (1966); D.V. OBRUCHEV (ed.), *Fundamentals of Paleontology*, vol. 11, *Agnatha, Pisces* (1967); and A.S. ROMER, *Vertebrate Paleontology*, 3rd ed. (1966), two comprehensive reference works.

(B.Sc./Ed.)

Chopin, Frédéric

Although he wrote little but piano works, many of them brief, Frédéric Chopin ranks as one of music's greatest tone poets by reason of superfine imagination and fastidious craftsmanship. He had the rare gift of composing very personal melodies, expressive of heartfelt emotion but never merely sentimental. Although "romantic" in essence, Chopin's music has none of the expected trappings of Romanticism—there is a classic purity and discretion in everything he wrote and no sign of Romantic exhibitionism. He found within himself and in the tragic history of Poland the chief sources of his inspiration.

He was born on March 1, 1810, at Żelazowa Wola, near Warsaw. His father, Nicholas, had left a modest vineyard-family background in France at 16 to seek his fortune in Poland. There, after working in a tobacco factory and fighting in the National Guard against the Russians in 1794, he became a tutor to various aristocratic families, including the Skarbeks, at Żelazowa Wola, one of whose poorer relations he married. When his son Frédéric was eight months old, Nicholas became a French teacher at the Warsaw lyceum and also taught at one or two military schools.

Chopin, portrait by Eugène Delacroix (1798–1863). In the Louvre (Paris).
Giraudon

Boyhood. Chopin himself attended the lyceum from 1823–26. Even then he had a droll sense of humour, accompanied by a gift for caricature, both of which lasted for life, alongside the uneasier side of a highly sensitive nature. Until he was 13 he studied at home, enjoying the companionship of three sisters and several country boys at the lyceum, who during term time boarded in the Chopin household. For holidays, Chopin often went back with them to their family estates, where he made his first acquaintance with folk music in its natural surroundings, notably mazurkas sung by the peasants. Happiness was shadowed in 1837 by the death of his tubercular youngest sister, Emilia, and by his own delicate constitution. In 1826 his mother had even been driven to take them both to a spa for treatment.

All the family had artistic leanings, and in infancy he was always strangely moved when listening to his mother or eldest sister playing the piano. By six he was already trying to reproduce what he heard or to make up new tunes. The following year he started piano lessons with the 61-year-old Wojciech (Adalbert) Zywny, more violinist than pianist, but an all-around musician with an astute sense of values when it came to weighing Bach, Mozart, and Beethoven against the then fashionable modern school of virtuoso composers. Because of Chopin's exceptional natural facility, his five years of study with Zywny were free of technical drudgery.

Soon, Chopin found himself invited at an early age to play at private soirées. At eight he made his first public appearance at a public charity concert. The following year he played before a famous Italian soprano, Angelica Catalani, who gave him a gold watch. Three years later he improvised on a new kind of piano-organ, the aeolomelodicon (invented by a local musician), in the presence of Tsar Alexander I, who was in Warsaw to open Parliament. Playing was not alone responsible for his growing reputation as a *Wunderkind* ("child prodigy"). At seven he wrote a *Polonaise in G Minor*, which was printed, and soon afterward a march of his appealed to the grand duke Constantine, who had it scored for his military band to play on parade. Other polonaises, mazurkas, variations, écossaises (lively Scottish dances), and a rondo (a piece of music with a reiterated main section) followed, with the result that, when he was 16, his family enrolled him at the newly formed Warsaw Conservatory of Music, directed by the Polish composer Joseph Elsner, with whom Chopin had been studying musical theory for several years. No better teacher could have been found, for, while insisting on a traditional training, Elsner, as a Romantically inclined composer himself, realized that Chopin's individual imagination must never be checked by purely academic demands. Elsner's last report on Chopin, in July 1829, contained the phrase "musical genius." Gradually, it became clear that, despite Warsaw's lively interest in new Italian opera

First public appearance

and visits from such celebrities as Johann Hummel (the German composer and pianist) and Niccolò Paganini, the violinist and composer, Chopin urgently needed wider musical experience. Undeterred by ministerial rejection of their request for financial aid, Chopin's devoted parents found the money to send him off to Vienna.

Visits to Vienna. An introduction from Elsner took Chopin directly to a Viennese publisher, Tobias Haslinger, who agreed to publish Chopin's variations on "Là ci darem" (by Mozart) if Chopin would give an unpaid public performance by way of advertisement. Other new Viennese acquaintances were equally insistent about a platform appearance, including Count Gallenberg, who offered his Kärnthnerthor Theatre, as well as the rival piano makers Graff and Stein, both of whom wanted to lend their instruments. Though unprepared, Chopin agreed to give two concerts in August 1829, following up *Là ci darem* in the first with the *Krakowiak Rondo* in the second, as well as improvising on operatic and Polish folk themes. Although some surprise was shown at his unusually delicate touch, he was an indisputable success and went home in a delirious whirl, fully resolved to return as soon as possible.

First Viennese success

Back in Warsaw, in September 1829, an unforeseen complication arose. Chopin fell in love with Constantia Gładkowska, an attractive and popular young singing student at the Warsaw Conservatory. Shyness limited his encounters; his main recourse was to worship in secret and pour out his heart in music. The human voice (particularly in the context of Italian opera) became his prime source of inspiration at this time, begetting the exquisite melody and irridescent decoration of his nocturnes and even the lyrical sections of two poetically virtuosic piano concertos. In March 1830 he made his official adult Warsaw debut with the *Piano Concerto No. 2 in F Minor*, the slow movement of which he confessed to having written in Constantia's memory. When he introduced his *Piano Concerto in E Minor* to Warsaw later that year, she sang an aria at the same concert. What with Constantia, family ties, exploratory chamber music parties in the house of a local musician, and a congenial visit to the country seat of Prince Radziwiłł (a keen amateur cellist for whom Chopin wrote a polonaise to play with his attractive pianist daughter), he was not able to tear himself away from Warsaw until November 1830 and only then because a friend volunteered to accompany him. The departure was made unforgettable by Elsner, who stopped the coach on the outskirts of Warsaw so that a hand-picked choir could sing a song of farewell he had especially composed for his favourite pupil—almost as if aware that Poland would never see him again.

Once in Vienna, in late November, Chopin quickly found himself back in a varied social round that precluded all loneliness, although disillusionments abounded. This time he discovered that public taste was all too superficial, that Haslinger was wary of risking further publication of Chopin's music, and that no one was in a hurry to invite him to play and, when they did, that it was only at minor events. There was no obvious solution to the problem of further study, and he knew he was costing his parents more than they could afford. Most unsettling of all was the news of the Polish uprising against the Russians. Since his family was unwilling for him to return to fight and the Viennese cared little about his personal nationalistic conflict, he soon resolved to seek the more idealistic atmosphere of Paris, consoling himself, during interminable passport delays, with setting patriotic poems to music and writing turbulent piano solos, such as the *Scherzo in B Minor*, Opus 20, and the *Revolutionary Étude*, Opus 10, No. 12. When he eventually got as far as Stuttgart, in Germany, and heard that Warsaw had fallen to the Russians, his desperation brought him near to breaking point. Despite his outward reserve, there were several times in life when the intensity of his feeling overtaxed a far from robust physical constitution.

Success in Paris. By late September 1831 he was in Paris, overwhelmed by its size and extremes of "splendour and filthiness and virtue and vice," yet immediately aware that nowhere outside Poland would he find more kindred spirits. Introductions from a Viennese friend gave him direct contact with such established figures as the Italian composer Ferdinando Paer, conductor of the court theatre; the Italian composer Luigi Cherubini, director of the Paris Conservatoire; the Italian operatic composer Gioacchino Rossini; and leading instrumentalists. But Chopin quickly found his own milieu among the many Polish émigrés and a younger generation of composers, including Franz Liszt, Hector Berlioz, Felix Mendelssohn, Vincenzo Bellini, and the cellist Auguste Franchomme. In Germany, Schumann, too, immediately hailed him as a representative of the new Romantic age.

Initially, there were problems, professional and financial. After his debut in February 1832 at the salon of the piano maker Camille Pleyel and another concert in the great hall of the Conservatoire in May, he realized with growing despondency that his extreme delicacy at the keyboard was not to everyone's taste in larger spaces. Had his family and Elsner, suspecting professional jealousy, not so forcefully dissuaded him, Chopin might even have agreed to a three-year course of study with the influential pianist Friedrich Kalkbrenner to strengthen and consolidate his technique. But an introduction from Prince Radziwiłł to the wealthy Rothschild banking family later in 1832 suddenly opened up new horizons. With his elegant manners, fastidious dress, and innate sensitivity, Chopin soon found himself a favourite in the great houses of Paris, both as a recitalist at fashionable soirées and as a teacher, able to command very high fees. He described this turn of fortune with a characteristic sophisticated drollness:

Parisian debut

> You at once have more talent if you have been heard at the English or Austrian embassies; you at once play better if Princess Vaudemont has patronized you. . . . You will imagine that I am making a fortune, but my cabriolet and white gloves cost more than that, and without them I should not have *bon ton*.

His new piano works at this time included two startlingly poetic books of études, the *Ballade in G Minor*, the *Fantaisie-Impromptu*, and smaller pieces, among them many mazurkas and polonaises inspired by Chopin's strong nationalist feeling.

The year 1835 was memorable for personal reasons: Chopin had a brief, blissfully happy reunion with his parents in Karlsbad, Bohemia (all of them unaware that they would never meet again), after which he went on to Dresden, in Germany, to see his old Polish friends the Wodzińskis. He discovered that their little daughter, Maria, had become an attractive young girl of 16 who could play the piano and paint. Rejoining them the following summer, it was not long before he and Maria were tenderly and innocently in love, wanting only parental consent for their marriage. But during the following winter, Mme Wodzińska took fright at the increasing rumours she heard about Chopin's ill health: the longed-for summer invitation was not repeated in 1837.

Liaison with George Sand. Deeply upset, Chopin escaped on a brief sight-seeing trip to England in company with his friend Pleyel, only to return to Paris to face the biggest emotional problem of his life. The notorious, provocatively free-living novelist George Sand (Aurore Dupin, or Mme Dudevant), whom he had met in the autumn of 1836 in company with Liszt and some of his literary friends, fell in love with him and openly offered herself to him as his mistress. Loyalty to Maria, reluctance to offend his parents, and dread of Parisian gossip at first deterred him. By the autumn of 1838 he could no longer fight her high-powered arguments against what she regarded as his all-too-naïve moral scruples. Under the pretext of poor health, he set off with her, her 15-year-old son, Maurice, and her eight-year-old daughter, Solange, to winter on the island of Majorca. Renting a simple villa just a few miles outside Palma, they were idyllically happy until the sunny weather broke and Chopin became ill. When rumours of tuberculosis reached the villa owner, they were ordered out and had to throw themselves on the mercy of the French consul until they could move into accommodations in the remote mountain village of Valldemosa—none other than a windswept monastery they had once discovered on an expedition, deserted (after the monks had been disbanded by government order) except for the old apothecary, the sacristan, and a work woman. Its picturesque romanticism immediately appealed to George Sand, whose current novel, *Spiridion*, made rapid strides, despite household problems and meagre comfort.

Chopin, with only a hired Majorcan cottage piano, tried to work, too, and he managed to finish a highly atmospheric set of *Twenty-four Preludes*, the dramatic *Scherzo in C Sharp Minor*, and a nobly tragic *Polonaise in C Minor*. But the cold and damp, malnutrition, peasant suspiciousness of their strange ménage, and his own secret fears and dreads when the wind howled, bells tolled, or mountain birds screeched, reduced him to a critical state of weakness. Although a piano from Pleyel arrived from Paris in January and by February the weather was again good, George Sand realized that only immediate departure would save his life. They arrived at Marseilles, in the south of France, in early March 1839, and, thanks to a skilled physician, Chopin was sufficiently recovered after just under three months for them to start planning a return to Paris.

Summer at Nohant

The summer of 1839 they spent at Nohant, George Sand's dearly loved country house some 180 miles (290 kilometres) south of Paris. Chopin, too, was at first enchanted by the rambling garden where roses grew and nightingales sang; but he knew he was really not suited for country life and by the autumn was pining for Paris. He entrusted an old school friend with the task of ordering new clothes, of finding a valet, and, most important of all, choosing apartments for both himself and George Sand that allowed easy visits yet were totally separate, so as to avoid gossip. After various temporary solutions, they eventually both joined a friend, the wife of the Spanish consul in the Place d'Orléans; all three families maintained separate establishments but were within easy reach for shared meals and many an evening gathering of diplomats, literary figures, and aristocratic patrons of the arts. Chopin, an active member of the Polish Literary Society, was always particularly welcome, not only because of his improvising at the piano but also on account of his lifelong gift for mimicry. There were also frequent visits to the theatre and the opera, still a major source of pleasure and inspiration to Chopin.

In April 1841 he was persuaded to proclaim his return with a semiprivate recital at Pleyel's, followed by another with his cellist friend Franchomme and the mezzo-soprano Pauline Viardot. He was also invited to play for King Louis-Phillippe at the Tuileries Palace. But, despite the material rewards brought by all three concerts, he found the nervous strain too great. As a regular source of income, he again turned to private teaching and was even able to raise his fee to 30 francs, as well as expecting to be fetched and returned by private carriage if a lesson had to be given outside his own house. His method

Chopin's piano method

of teaching permitted great flexibility of the wrist and arm and daringly unconventional fingering in the interests of greater agility, with the production of beautiful, singing tone a prime requisite at nearly all times. There was also a growing demand for his new works, and, since he had become increasingly shrewd in his dealings with publishers, he could afford to live not just comfortably but elegantly.

Health was a recurrent worry. Every summer (except in 1840), George Sand, now increasingly maternal in her attitude toward him, took him to Nohant for fresh air and relaxation. Close friends, such as Pauline Viardot and the painter Eugène Delacroix, were often invited, too. In 1844 even Chopin's sister Louise came to comfort him after the death of their father. Chopin produced much of his most searching music at Nohant, not only miniatures but also extended works, such as the *Fantaisie in F Minor* (composed 1840–41), the *Barcarolle* (1845–46), the *Polonaise-Fantaisie* (1845–46), the *Ballade in A Flat Major* (1840–41), and *Ballade in F Minor* (1842), and the *Sonata in B Minor* (1844). Here, in the country, he found the peace and time to indulge an ingrained

quest for perfection once described (by the older brother of Karl Filtsch, Chopin's most gifted Hungarian pupil) as causing "days of nervous strain and almost frightening desperation. He alters and retouches the same phrase incessantly and walks up and down like a madman." In particular, at Nohant, he seemed anxious to develop his ideas into longer and more complex arguments and even sent to Paris for treatises by the Alsatian musicologist Jean Georges Kastner and Cherubini to strengthen his counterpoint. His harmonic vocabulary at this period also grew much more daring, though never at the cost of sensuous beauty. He valued that quality throughout life as much as he abhorred descriptive titles or any hint of an underlying "programe." Given a more equable temperament, Chopin could have turned these Nohant summers to still richer account, but, suspecting that George Sand's diminishing sexual demands were due to another lover rather than because she had a deep regard for his physical frailty and his work, he grew increasingly moody and petulant—like Prince Karol in Sand's contemporaneous novel *Lucrezia Floriani*. After cumulative domestic upsets, the storm broke. Chopin felt completely unable to return to Nohant in the summer of 1847, and, by the following year, the rift between him and George Sand was complete. Pride prevented either from effecting the reconciliation they both, at heart, so profoundly desired.

Last years. Broken in spirit and still more depressed by the revolution that had broken out in Paris only a few days after the recital he had been persuaded to give on February 16, 1848, at Pleyel's (with Franchomme as his partner in three movements of his new cello sonata), Chopin soon accepted an invitation from Jane Stirling, an adoring Scottish pupil of 44, to visit England and Scotland. Between Easter of that year and August, settled in elegantly expensive rooms big enough to accommodate three different grand pianos immediately placed at his disposal by the makers, he characteristically refused all "establishment" offers, such as a Philharmonic Society engagement, to struggle through an exhausting London round of lessons and appearances at fashionable parties, including one at Stafford House for the Duchess of Sutherland, whose guests included Queen Victoria and Prince Albert. Meetings with such kindred spirits as the Scottish essayist and historian Thomas Carlyle, Charles Dickens, and the soprano Jenny Lind (whom he rarely missed at the opera) slightly eased the strain of contact with so many foreigners for whom he suspected art to be no more than a status symbol, but by midsummer he was exhausted enough to escape to Scotland to rest in the homes of several of Jane Stirling's aristocratic relations near Edinburgh, Glasgow, and Stirling. He broke loose briefly to visit Lady Bellhaven at Wishaw, the Duke and Duchess of Hamilton at Hamilton Palace, and one or two Polish émigrés, including the Prince and Princess Czartoryski; he also undertook recitals in Manchester, Glasgow, and Edinburgh to raise money for his immediate needs. But, increasingly weak, homesick, and embarrassed by his inability to reciprocate Jane Stirling's growing devotion, he was totally unable to compose. As he put it in a letter to an old friend:

Visit to England and Scotland

> You and I are a couple of old cembalos on which time and circumstances have played out their miserable trills. . . . In clumsy hands we cannot give forth new sounds and we stifle within ourselves those things which no one will ever draw from us, and all for lack of a repairer.

Returning to London for three weeks, he played only before a charity ball at the Guildhall for Polish refugees and was back in Paris by November 24. By the following spring his condition had so drastically deteriorated that doctors advised the fresher air of the suburb of Chaillot, a move made possible by much discreet financial help from friends—even his aging mother managed to send 2,000 francs. His sister Louise arrived by August 1849, and after returning to a spacious new apartment in central Paris, he was constantly surrounded by those people he most wanted to see before dying of tuberculosis in the early hours of October 17, 1849.

Although not a conventional churchgoer, he accepted

the last sacraments from a Polish priest and at the end was calm, asking only that his unfinished manuscripts should be destroyed and that Mozart's *Requiem* should be sung at his funeral. This took place at the Church of the Madeleine on October 30, after which the many mourners followed the coffin to the cemetery of Père-Lachaise. When a monument to his memory in the form of a weeping muse with a broken lyre was unveiled a year later, a small box of Polish earth was sprinkled over the grave.

Though Chopin undoubtedly disappointed such men as Elsner by never writing Polish operas, and the exiled patriot Polish poet Adam Mickiewicz, for squandering too much time on drawing-room-oriented Parisian aristocracy, as well as various establishment critics who valued artistic worth only in terms of large-scale academic achievement, he was immediately recognized at his true worth by more discerning contemporaries. His youthful "Là ci darem" variations were at once hailed by Robert Schumann in the famous phrase, "Hats off, gentlemen! a genius!" for a new strain of poetic fancy refertilizing an old virtuoso tradition. Other contemporary critics were astounded, however reluctantly, by the startling originality he reconciled with exquisite craftsmanship. Present-day evaluation, in full recognition that he was more a self-indulgent, beauty-loving poet than an expansive musical moralist or philosopher, places him among the immortals of music by reason of his insight into the secret places of the heart and because of his awareness of the magical new sonorities to be drawn from the piano.

MAJOR WORKS
Piano music

ETUDES: *Twelve Grand Études*, op. 10 (composed 1829–32); *Twelve Études*, op. 25 (1832–36).
SONATAS: *C Minor*, op. 4 (1827); *B Flat Minor*, op. 35 (1839); *B Minor*, op. 58 (1844).
BALLADES: *G Minor*, op. 23 (1831–35); *F Major*, op. 38 (1836–39); *A Flat Major*, op. 47 (1840–41); *F Minor*, op. 52 (1842).
SCHERZOS: *B Minor*, op. 20 (1831–32); *B Flat Minor*, op. 31 (1837); *C Sharp Minor*, op. 39 (1839); *E Major*, op. 54 (1842).
OTHER PIANO MUSIC: *Twenty-four Preludes*, op. 28 (1836–39); *Fantaisie in F Minor*, op. 49 (1840–41); polonaises, including *Polonaise–Fantaisie*, op. 61 (1845–46); nocturnes; impromptus; waltzes; mazurkas.

Orchestral works

Piano Concerto No. 2 in F Minor, op. 21 (1829); *Piano Concerto No. 1 in E Minor*, op. 11 (1830).

Chamber music

Piano Trio in G Minor, op. 8 (1828–29); *Sonata for Piano and Cello*, op. 65 (1845–46).

Songs

Seventeen Polish Songs, op. 74 (published 1855).

BIBLIOGRAPHY. ARTHUR HEDLEY, *Chopin* (1947) and his extended article on Chopin in *Grove's Dictionary* (1954), are the most succinct and reliable modern surveys of life and music, each with a catalog of works. Hedley's *Selected Correspondence of Fryderyk Chopin* (1962), is also the most complete collection of the composer's letters in the English language (drawn from Bronislaw Edward Sydow's larger collection in French and Polish) with detailed annotations and a biographical summary. FREDERICK NIECKS, *Frederick Chopin As a Man and Musician* (1888), long remained the standard study, though for Polish and French readers it was superseded by the further researches of FERDYNAND HOESICK, *Chopin, życie i twórezóśé* (1904; 3rd ed., 2 vol., 1927); and EDOUARD GANCHE, *Frédéric Chopin: sa vie et ses oeuvres* (1913). As for music alone, GERALD ABRAHAM, *Chopin's Musical Style* (1939), is still the most scholarly English counterpart to HUGO LEICHTENTRITT, *Analyse der Chopin'schen Klavierwerke*, 2 vol. (1921–22). ALAN WALKER (ed.), *Frédéric Chopin: Profiles of the Man and the Musician* (1966), a symposium from various writers, is variably stimulating. For background reading, GEORGE SAND, *Histoire de ma vie*, 10 vol. (1856), *Correspondance, 1812–1876*, 4th ed. (1883–95), *Un Hiver à Majorque* (1867), and *Lucrezia Floriani* (1848), are invaluable; while FRANZ LISZT, *F. Chopin* (1851), also has the interest of immediacy. The finest collections of manuscripts and other relics may be found at the Chopin Institute in Warsaw and at the monastery of Valldemosa, Majorca.

(Jo.Ch.)

Choral Music

Music sung by a choir, known as choral music, ranks as one of several musical genres subject to misunderstanding because of false historical perspectives or misinterpretation caused by the confusion engendered by unsolved semantic problems. Choral, chorale, choir, and chorus stand in obvious relationship to one another and are in some respects used interchangeably when a body of singers, for example, is referred to as a choir, a chorus (Latin noun derived from the Greek word *choros*), or a chorale, which properly is a Lutheran hymn tune. The adjective choral may therefore be applied in a general way (choral music, choral technique) or in a specific way (such as Beethoven's *Choral Symphony* and *Choral Fantasia*). The nouns chorale, choir, and chorus are frequently used as adjectives in such expressions as chorale prelude ("choral prelude" is incorrect), choir organ, or chorus part.

The definition of choral music has by circumstance and usage been forced to comprise a far wider area than a comparable definition of an instrumental genre. It is unusual, to say the least, to perform a symphony with only a single instrument to each part, even though the opposite has occasionally happened when a string quartet movement is played by the massed strings of an orchestra. Much music now performed by choirs, however, was originally intended for soloists; and, while the lack of historical authenticity may here be deplored, it is evident that a choral performance of a madrigal (equivalent to an orchestral performance of a string quartet movement) permits many amateur musicians to enjoy, as members of a team, music that might otherwise escape their knowledge.

If a choral performance of genres for several solo voices, such as the madrigal, ballett, villanella, and part-song, results in a more neutral sound and a less personal intensity of expression, it is nevertheless true that the reverse sometimes offers unsuspected advantages, as when a work written for choir alone is performed by a group of soloists. In certain cases the work may take on a new and enhanced aspect because each strand of melody within the texture carries a personal rather than a group expression.

In defining choral music, some attention should also be paid to the enormous variation in the size of choirs. A chamber choir need contain only a dozen voices, certainly not more than 20; whereas a choir assembled for the Handel Festivals in the 19th century or for the Berlioz *concerts monstres* in Paris during the same epoch, might have numbered thousands. Modern traces of such massive choral effects may be found in the *Symphony No. 8 in E Flat Major* (sometimes called *Symphony of a Thousand*) of the Austrian composer Gustav Mahler. This work calls for a large double choir and a separate boys' choir, in addition to a large orchestra and eight soloists. On the other hand, numerous modern choral works, because of their difficulty and complexity, seem to have been composed with a chamber choir in mind, as in the case of *Cinq rechants* (1949) by the French composer Olivier Messiaen.

If there is more than one voice to each part—*i.e.*, to each line of polyphony (music of several voice parts) or strand of melody—the performance is choral, even though the actual sonority may not seem choral in the accepted sense until there are more than five or six voices to a part. Both types of singing may also coexist, since a choir may contain several capable soloists who may at certain points sing as a group without the choir or with the choir as a background. This feature is the choral equivalent of the orchestral concerto grosso, in which a small group of solo instruments alternate or combine with the main body of players. Examples of this may be found in choral music of all types and ages. The medieval rondeau was usually performed by a soloist who sang the verses, with a small choir for the refrain. When the mass became a vehicle for choral performance in the 15th century, the Christe Eleison, certain parts of the Gloria and the Credo, the Benedictus, and the Agnus Dei

Variation in size of choirs

were frequently assigned to a group of soloists within the choir. *The Eton Choirbook* motets demand similar treatment since red and black text is used to differentiate between those sections intended for soloists and those for full choir. Comparable effects may be found in music written for special occasions, oratorios, verse anthems, and settings of the Passion.

Emergence of the choral tradition

Although choirs existed throughout Europe in the Middle Ages, their role was restricted to unison singing of plainchant. Polyphony was the exclusive preserve of soloists. This state of affairs was gradually modified for several reasons. Early forms of musical notation were not precise enough to allow choral performance of even the simplest two-part polyphony. As time went on, improved accuracy in notating pitch and time values permitted some degree of experiment in choral performance.

Knowledge of the subtleties of mensural (precisely measured) music was at first the prerogative of a small number of initiates. The ordinary member of the plainchant choir, or schola, was not expected to understand the notation or to perform music using it. But the teaching of musical theory spread rapidly in the 14th century, and singers became better equipped and educated than they had been at any previous time. The ever-growing wealth of the church also acted to encourage choral performance, since abbeys, cathedrals, parish and collegiate churches, and court chapels vied with each other in the opulence and perfection of their choral establishments. Laws were passed enabling royal chapels to impress (that is, to seek out and enroll) eligible provincial choirboys for the great central establishments, and in consequence every boy was a soloist in his own right, just as were the countertenors, tenors, and basses. Finally, the rapidity with which composers took advantage of this situation, evolving new techniques and adapting old ones, created a tremendous surge of choral activity and composition, which the new art of music printing was to aid even further in the early years of the 16th century. From that time until the present, there has been no abatement of interest in choral music, which is performed at amateur and professional levels throughout the entire world.

SACRED MUSIC

The mass. The ordinary of the mass (consisting of the Kyrie, Gloria, Credo, Sanctus and Benedictus, Agnus Dei, and in some medieval masses also the "Ite, missa est") has been a focal point of choral music for more than 600 years. The earliest masses, such as the four-part setting by the 14-century French composer Guillaume de Machaut, were intended for soloists; remarkable both in musical texture and structure, they are often performed chorally today. In the 15th century this tradition, in which architectonic considerations still held sway, was carried on in the masses of the English composer John Dunstable and his Burgundian contemporary, Guillaume Dufay. The use of a plainchant cantus firmus, or dominating tenor theme, knit together the movements even though they were separated during the liturgy. Modern concert performances and recordings obscure this feature, sometimes to the disadvantage of even the greatest masterpieces, which, with all movements in immediate sequence may sound too concentrated. The Renaissance saw the highest development of the cantus firmus mass, using as the central melodic support not only plainchant but even secular songs, as Josquin's *Missa L'Homme armé super voces musicales* (printed, 1502) or folk songs, as John Taverner's mass, *The Western Wynde* (c. 1520).

Hundreds of composers wrote settings of the ordinary of the mass at this time; some, like the Italian composer Giovanni da Palestrina, wrote more than 100 masses. The Spaniards Cristóbal de Morales and Tomás Luis de Victoria and the Englishmen William Byrd and Thomas Tallis all avoided secular melodies, even though these would have been largely obscured by the texture of the voices. On the other hand, the Netherlanders Orlando di Lasso and Philippe de Monte did not hesitate to draw upon themes of diverse origins. Byrd and his Flemish contemporary Heinrich Isaac also set a considerable amount of the proper of the mass (that part of the liturgy liable to change according to the feast), but such settings remained comparatively rare.

The parody mass found many advocates, since it was possible by this means to base a long work on all voice-parts of a shorter one, such as a motet or a hymn, and by beginning with familiar and recognizable material, to progress gradually into inventive independence. This particular technique may have owed as much to convenience as to a desire to pay homage to another composer.

Addition of instruments

The 16th- and 17th-century Venetian school, especially Giovanni Gabrieli and Claudio Monteverdi, added an instrumental element to the basically choral foundation of the mass. They also occasionally employed two or more choirs to create massive antiphonal effects. Further development of the orchestral mass occurred in the 17th century in the works of the Italian composers Francesco Cavalli and Alessandro Scarlatti and the French composer Marc-Antoine Charpentier, while the polychoral element was brought to a colossal and almost unmanageable pitch by Orazio Benevoli in his mass for the dedication of the Salzburg cathedral (1628) in 53 parts.

In the 18th century, Haydn's early masses, notably the *Missa Sanctae Caeciliae*, lean toward Italian models. His choral writing is robust and sonorous, even though four-part writing is the norm. His later masses emphasize soloists and orchestra but without diminishing the interest of the choral writing. Mozart's early masses tend to be brief (because of the taste and dictates of his archbishop patron), yet the fugal choruses sometimes dispel this impression by their very excellence, as in the *Mass in C Major*, K. 317 (1779; *Coronation Mass*). The unfinished *Mass in C Minor*, K. 427, abounds in magnificent choral music.

Remote in style and function from the Classical Viennese works, J.S. Bach's *Mass in B Minor* (1733–38) was a monument of the preceding Baroque era. It was never intended to be performed as a whole within the liturgy, and its various movements date from different periods of Bach's life. Five-part choral writing is most in evidence, the two soprano lines adding brilliance and edge to a richly contrapuntal (interwoven melody) texture. In the "Sanctus," Bach branches into six-part polyphony, and in the "Osanna" he calls for an eight-voice double choir apt for antiphonal writing.

Beethoven's *Mass in C Major*, Opus 86 (1807), and *Missa Solemnis*, Opus 123 (1823), written in the maturity of the Classical era, are not liturgical, yet they stem from an inner need to carry on a great tradition and to set to music a text of central importance. The role of the choir is central to the work. The composer uses it to produce effects ranging from breathtaking mystery to the utterly grandiose. The masses of the 19th-century Austrian composers Franz Schubert and Anton Bruckner worthily continue the same tradition in their individual ways. The *Petite Messe solennelle* (*Little Solemn Mass;* 1864) of Italian composer Gioacchino Rossini was originally written for soloists, chorus, and an accompaniment of two pianos and harmonium, but it was later scored for full orchestra.

Outstanding among 20th-century masses are those of the English composer Ralph Vaughan Williams, the Czech composer Leoš Janáček (*Glagolitic Mass*, setting an Orthodox text in Old Slavonic), and the Russo-American composer Igor Stravinsky, who is said to have derived his inspiration from Mozart, although some of the effects created by the mixed chorus and wind instruments are more reminiscent of medieval music.

The Missa pro Defunctis ("Mass for the Dead"), or Requiem Mass (often simply called Requiem) also stimulated numerous choral masterpieces, beginning with Jean d'Ockeghem in the late 15th century and continuing through Victoria, Felice Anerio, Scarlatti, Mozart, Luigi Cherubini, Hector Berlioz, Giuseppe Verdi, and Gabriel Fauré to the present century. Johannes Brahms' *Ein deutsches Requiem* (*German Requiem*, 1857–68) is based on the composer's own selection of Biblical texts. The *Requiem* (1914–16) of the early 20th-century British composer Frederick Delius derives its libretto from the 19th-century German philosopher and poet Friedrich

Nietzsche. The *War Requiem*, Opus 66 (first performed, 1962), of the British composer Benjamin Britten makes skillful and impressive use of liturgical texts but also contains secular poetry by Wilfred Owen, killed in World War I. The work as a whole is thus linked with the senseless suffering of war and the idea of sacrifice induced by false patriotism. The choral effects are rich in novelty, originality, and forcefulness. One of the most successful of 20th-century masses for unaccompanied chorus is the *Mass in G Major* (1937) by Francis Poulenc.

Vespers and Anglican services

In the Middle Ages, the service of greatest musical importance, after the mass, was Vespers. Its component antiphons, psalms, hymn, and Magnificat have given rise to much noble choral music, from the time of the Flemish composer Adriaan Willaert in the 16th century, through Monteverdi, Scarlatti, and Mozart. In the Anglican Church, service settings embrace Holy Communion and Morning and Evening Prayer and have been continuously written since the time of Byrd and Tallis. These early services for choir and organ were followed by "verse services," in which solo voices played an important part, combining or alternating with the choir. By the time of the 17th-century British composer Henry Purcell, instruments were accepted as a means to fuller accompaniment, notably in the Chapel Royal, London. But modern composers, except in works for ceremonial use, tend to return to scoring their services for choir and organ.

Motets. Choral music has been enriched for centuries by the composition of motets, which were originally settings of liturgical or Biblical texts. Responsories (liturgical texts originally performed responsively) were of major importance until the great monastic institutions lost their influence in the early years of the 16th century. Subsequently, the choral motet was mainly cultivated in royal and collegiate chapels. Settings of votive antiphons (verses preceding psalms and canticles), frequently, though not exclusively, texts in honour of the Virgin Mary, were popular in the late 15th and early 16th centuries. Many of these compositions demanded a high degree of skill and virtuosity from the choir and its soloists; a noble example is the British composer John Browne's *Stabat Mater*, from *The Eton Choirbook*. An Italian contemporary, Giovanni Spataro, displays a more simple and restrained style in his four-part *Virgo prudentissima*, which nevertheless belongs to the same category of motet.

During the 16th and 17th centuries, the term motet was used in looser connotation, sometimes linked with a few verses of a psalm, sometimes a complete psalm including Gloria Patri (lesser doxology). Many of these longer settings, by 16th-century composers such as Josquin, Willaert, and Lasso, attain the level of symphonic choral writing through their high degree of formal organization and their imaginative vocal scoring. The concertato motet (using contrasting groups of singers and instruments), as developed and perfected in the 17th century by Gabrieli, Monteverdi, Heinrich Schütz, and Scarlatti, added the vivid colours of the orchestral palette to the already highly malleable vocal textures. Pergolesi's *Stabat Mater*, although sometimes performed as a choral work, was originally written with solo voices in mind. Bach's motets, of which *Jesu meine Freude* (*Jesus My Joy; c.* 1723) is a typical and splendid example, return to the a cappella manner of performance. Contrary to one popular conception, this often included instrumental doubling of the voice parts and the use of an organ continuo, an improvised part. Subsequently little used in the Protestant Church, the motet continued to be cultivated by the Catholic composers of Europe and the Americas. Especially worthy of note are the motets and psalm settings of Anton Bruckner, whose *Te Deum* (composed 1881, revised 1883–84) is one of his choral masterpieces. Conservative tastes in much religious music somewhat discouraged the greatest talents from contributing fully to this genre. Stravinsky's *Threni* (on the Lamentations of Jeremiah), for instance, is more frequently heard in the concert hall than in church, as are also Poulenc's *Stabat Mater* (1951) and other liturgical motets of his.

Anthems. The use of the vernacular after the Reformation in England made it necessary for composers to forge a new style of choral music. The elaborate melodic tracery of Robert Fayrfax and John Taverner gave way to a completely unelaborate kind of choral counterpoint designed to allow the English words to be clearly heard. Both Thomas Tallis and William Byrd made outstanding contributions to the development of the anthem. Tallis perfected a style of contrapuntally animated homophony that ensured clarity of declamation, while Byrd experimented with more elaborate textures both in full anthems (for choir alone) and in verse anthems, in which the choir was supported by the organ and sometimes other instruments, allowing solo voices to detach themselves from the main body of singers. Among Byrd's finest verse anthems are *Christ rising again* (for Easter) and *O God that guides the cheerful sun*. Orlando Gibbons carried to a further stage the use of a consort of viols, which accompanies with a rich but discreet body of sound the countertenor and bass soloists in *Glorious and powerful god*. One of the most effective of his full anthems is the seven-part *Hosanna to the Son of David* for Palm Sunday. Thomas Tomkins displays a mastery of twelve-part polyphony in his full anthem *O praise the Lord, all ye heathen*, but for quiet expressive intimacy of thought there is little to surpass *When David heard that Absalom was slain*. Among a considerable number of verse anthems by Tomkins, two of the most inspiring are *My Shepherd is the living Lord* and *Thou art my King, O God*, both of which can be accompanied by organ alone or by organ and string ensemble.

When the monarchy was restored in 1660, Matthew Locke contributed a number of fine anthems to the repertory of the revived Chapel Royal, among them the double-choir setting of *Not unto us, O Lord* and the grandiose, almost Venetian *The king shall rejoice*, scored for three four-part choirs and orchestra. Another eminent musician of the time was Pelham Humfrey, whose verse anthem *By the waters of Babylon* is one of the best examples of its kind. For chromatically expressive music Michael Wise provides an admirable pattern in his *The ways of Sion do mourn*, as does Daniel Roseingrave in his *Lord, thou art become gracious*.

The verse anthem with instruments reached its zenith in the late 17th century in the music of Henry Purcell and John Blow. Much of their music was performed in the Chapel Royal, the choir and consorts of which had improved markedly. Among the most memorable of Purcell's full anthems are the eight-part *Hear my prayer, O Lord* and the five-part *Remember not, Lord, our offences*. His most successful verse anthems frequently make use of short, impressive passages for choir alone, as in the evocation of the turtle's voice in *My beloved spake* and the moving harmonies of "O worship the Lord" toward the end of *O sing unto the Lord*. Blow excels in the antiphony of verse soloists and full choir in *I beheld, and lo, a great multitude*. In his full anthems, such as *God is our hope and strength* and *O Lord God of my salvation*, he sometimes almost equals Purcell in the richness and resource of his eight-part writing.

Of the succeeding generation of composers, William Croft seems most at ease in his full anthems, notably *Put me not to rebuke* and *O Lord, rebuke me not*, two distinct and different works in spite of the similarity of text. Maurice Greene excelled in this style in works such as *God is our hope and strength* and *Acquaint thyself with God*. William Boyce carried on the tradition of sensitive word setting in such works as *I have surely built thee an house* and *O where shall wisdom be found?*.

Although the late 18th and early 19th centuries did not exactly overflow with masterpieces, a trio of composers proved themselves competent craftsmen. *O Lord, look down from heaven* will assure Jonathan Battishill a place in the history of the genre, while the Epiphany anthem *O God, who by the leading of a star* speaks eloquently for Thomas Attwood. Although Samuel Wesley, converted to Catholicism, chose Latin for the greater number of his church compositions, one of these is sometimes sung to its English text, *Sing aloud with gladness*.

Samuel Sebastian Wesley attempted, often with considerable success, to raise up the anthem to a new level of artistry and accomplishment, extending it so as to form a kind of cantata giving freer rein to soloists than was customary in the older type of verse anthem. His finest contributions are perhaps *The Wilderness; Ascribe unto The Lord;* and *O Lord, Thou art my God.* Also noteworthy from this epoch are Sir John Goss's setting of *The Wilderness,* Thomas Attwood Walmisley's *O give thanks,* and the double-choir anthem *O Saviour of the world* by Sir Frederick Gore Ouseley.

Sir Joseph Barnby, Sir John Stainer, and Sir Arthur Sullivan wrote anthems of fair quality, but not until Sir Hubert Parry demonstrated the need for a return to conscientious word setting did new spirit begin to pervade English church music in works such as Parry's double-choir anthem *Lord let me know mine end,* Sir Charles Stanford's similarly scored *Jesus Christ is risen today,* and Charles Wood's *O thou the central orb.* In the 20th century, T.T. Noble's *The souls of the righteous* and John Ireland's *Greater love hath no man* are typical of the earlier period, while *O pray for the peace of Jerusalem* by Herbert Howells and Benjamin Britten's *Hymn to St. Peter* successfully continue a long tradition.

Cantata and oratorio. The cantata, as developed in northern Germany in the 17th century, often relied only upon soloists and a small group of instruments, although the role of the chorus gradually became more important. In more than 200 church cantatas written by J.S. Bach, the chorus often occupies a prominent place and is given music of challenging complexity—frequently on a par with the music of the accompanying instrumental forces. The cantatas use the chorus again in the closing chorale, which is usually a special setting of a hymn tune with orchestral doubling or accompaniment.

Bach's 200 church cantatas

In Italy, the oratorio achieved what was beyond the motet's capabilities by projecting through verse and music a story of Biblical origin that the public could enjoy while learning. Giacomo Carissimi, whose *Jephtha* is still an established classic, led the way to the oratorios of Antonio Vivaldi (*Juditha triumphans,* first performed 1716), Handel (a long series of oratorios written for London, all dramatic in form except for *Israel in Egypt* of 1739 and the *Messiah* of 1741), and Haydn, whose greatest oratorio is *Die Schöpfung* (1798; *The Creation*). The choral contribution to 19th-century oratorios remained at a remarkably high level, enhancing such works as Beethoven's *Christus Am Ölberg* (1803; *Christ on the Mount of Olives*), the perennially popular *Elijah* (1846) of Mendelssohn, Franz Liszt's *Die Legende von der heiligen Elisabeth* (*The Legend of St. Elizabeth*), Berlioz's *L'Enfance du Christ,* Opus 25 (1854), and a series of compositions by the British composer Edward Elgar, culminating in *The Dream of Gerontius* (1900). The oratorio tradition, because of its links with choral bodies, has shown constant renewal and growth in the 20th century. Among outstanding 20th-century oratorios are Frank Martin's *Golgotha* (1949), Arthur Honegger's *Le Roi David* (*King David;* 1921), Sir William Walton's *Belshazzar's Feast* (1931), and Bernard Rogers' *The Passion* (1944). A work in oratorio style, though in a class of its own, is Ernest Bloch's *Arodath Hakodesh* (*Sacred Service*) composed 1930–33 and scored for baritone solo, chorus, and orchestra.

OCCASIONAL MUSIC

In addition to sacred and secular works, a very considerable number of compositions, many of them choral, were written for great occasions of state. These include motets and cantatas based on special texts, suitable for performance in a palace, outdoors on a platform or rampart, in a private chapel, or wherever the occasion demanded. The signing of a peace treaty, a royal marriage, ducal obsequies, consecration, election of a doge—all these and many similar events called for music written to order; since composers have always been happy to receive a commission, the number of occasional works is virtually incalculable.

Soon after St. Mark's, Venice, inaugurated in 1403 a choir of boys from the city, their master Antonio Romano was invited to compose a festive work in honor of the doge. When Francesco Foscari was elected doge in 1423, Christoforo de Monte introduced the choral parts of his motet with brass fanfares. Dufay, asked to produce a stirring work for the consecration of a new cathedral at Patras (now Pátrai) in Greece, scored his *Apostolo glorioso-Cum tua doctrina-Andreas* (1426) for wind ensemble and mixed chorus; but, although the work was undoubtedly performed in the cathedral, the use of an Italian rather than a Latin text places it firmly in the category of occasional music. An equally impressive work by the same composer, *Supremum est mortalibus* (*Supremacy is for the Dead*), was written expressly for the signing of the Treaty of Viterbo in 1433, when Pope Eugenius IV and King Sigismund of Bohemia were both present at the ceremony. Toward the end of the motet, the choir sings, in successive block chords, the names of Pope and King, syllable by syllable. Another peace treaty celebrated in music is that of Bagnolo, Italy, when the Franco-Flemish composer Loyset Compère was commissioned to write the motet *Quis numerare queat* (1484). Imaginative use is made of the chorus throughout this work, even to the extent of the composer's choice of tessitura (high or low part of the voice range): when the chorus sings of the lamentations of the people over the terrors of war, the words are sung by the dark-hued combination of tenors, baritones, and basses in their middle or lower register. A further example of choral writing so disposed as to represent a state of mind is the "Amen" of Isaac's *Optime pastor* (written in 1513 in honour of the newly elected Pope Leo X), where the opulent six-part polyphony suggests the wealth and substance of the Emperor Maximilian I and his desire to impress listeners with a show of temporal power at least the equivalent of the Pope's spiritual power.

Occasional music is sometimes considered of less value than sacred or secular music, even when it stems from a composer of high reputation. Since the work could by definition receive only one formal performance and since it might have been written in a hurry, the theory is that the music must be inferior. There are, however, examples of such works whose music was used for more than one occasion, thanks to the simple but effective process of stripping away the original text and substituting another, or even substituting one name for another. A study of the text of Taverner's motet *Christe Jesu pastor bone* (*Jesus Christ, Good Shepherd*) shows that it must have been intended first as a votive antiphon for St. William of York, then as a paraliturgical prayer for Cardinal Wolsey (Taverner being at one time organist and master of the choristers at Cardinal's College, now Christ Church, at Oxford), and finally as a prayer for Henry VIII. Similarly, the anthem *O Lord, make thy servant Elizabeth our Queen,* written by William Byrd for Queen Elizabeth I, remained in the repertoire of the Chapel Royal for several decades, the name being changed first to James and then to Charles.

Repetition of occasional works

Most events of importance were planned months in advance, and the composer could usually count on being given adequate warning of a new commission. The meeting of Louis XII of France and Ferdinand V the Catholic of Castile at Savona in 1507, for which the French composer Antoine de Févin wrote a superb choral work, *Gaude Francorum regia corona,* was certainly not decided upon at short notice. Nor was the visit of Cardinal Ippolito de' Medici to Venice the result of a sudden decision, for Willaert had ample time to pen his solemn and sonorous motet *Adriacos numero* just as he did in the case of *Haud aliter pugnans,* in honour of King Ferdinand.

A later Ferdinand, who became Holy Roman Emperor Ferdinand III in 1637, commissioned two outstanding choral works by Monteverdi, both of which were published in his *Madrigali guerrieri et amorosi* (*Madrigals of War and Love,* 1638). *Altri canti d'amor* (*Let Others Sing of Love*) is a choral cantata for six voices, bass solo, and instrumental ensemble. The Emperor's military prowess is recounted in considerable detail, with choral imitations of swords clashing and guns firing. His qualities as a leader are also referred to in the ballet *Movete al mio bel suon* (*Move to my Beautiful Sound*), which extols him also as a just and equitable monarch in time of peace—although the Thirty Years' War did not in fact come to an end for several years. The text used by Monteverdi was a reworking of a poem which his friend the Italian poet Ottavio Rinuccini had originally written for Henry IV of France.

Purcell, a composer of occasional music who was also a brilliant choral writer, enriched the history of music with a series of odes and welcome songs beginning in 1680 (*Welcome, vicegerent of the mighty King*) and extending until the year of his death, 1695, which saw the production of the ode for the Duke of Gloucester's birthday, *Who can from joy refrain?* Among the finest of the series, and especially notable for the noble vigour of the choruses, are the odes for Queen Mary's birthday and for the St. Cecilia's Day celebration, 1692.

In France scores of comparable proportions were being written for such occasions as the baptism of the Dauphin (1688), for which Jean-Baptiste Lully set Pierre Perrin's *Plaude laetare* for double chorus and orchestra. Numerous court ceremonies or rejoicings called for large-scale performances of the Te Deum, Marc-Antoine Charpentier and Michel-Richard de Lalande, as well as Lully, providing music of the requisite pomp and proportions. Handel wrote two festive settings of the Te Deum for the Treaty of Utrecht (1713) and the British victory at Dettingen (1743). His royal odes worthily continue the Purcellian tradition, especially in the *Ode for the Queen's Birthday* (1713) for Queen Anne and in two wedding anthems, *This is the Day* (1734) for Princess Anne and *Sing unto God* (1736) for the Prince of Wales.

Although J.S. Bach did not disdain to write occasional music, he followed Handel's practice in the *Occasional Oratorio* (a patriotic piece given in 1746) without ever knowing Handel, by reworking this kind of music to a new text. One of the cantatas Bach supplied for the election of the Leipzig town councillors was deftly changed into a cantata for the 12th Sunday after Trinity; another, destined for the same annual event, *Preise Jerusalem, den Herrn*, (*Praise the Lord, O Jerusalem*) BWV 119 (1723) has been re-edited in modern times with a new text, in imitation of the composer's own practice.

Haydn, in spite of his considerable duties as court conductor and composer, found time to write occasional works of considerable proportions, such as the two-hour birthday cantata. *Applausus* (1768), intended for the Abbot of Zwettl Stadt, Austria. His masses, even though they are liturgical, sometimes border also on the occasional because of their close ties with contemporary events, such as the *Missa St. Bernardi de Offida* (1796) written to celebrate the recent canonization of a Capuchin monk from Offida in Italy. An occasional choral composition of Beethoven's is his *Kantate auf den Tod Kaiser Josephs II* (1790; *Cantata on the Death of the Emperor Joseph II*).

Berlioz, who had toyed with the idea of a large-scale choral and orchestral work to honour Napoleon, eventually had to abandon it but salvaged certain movements and incorporated them into his *Te Deum* (1849). His contemporary, Liszt, was more deliberately productive in this area, enjoying consistently enthusiastic receptions for his choral works of an occasional nature, such as the St. Cecilia antiphon *Cantantibus organis* (for a Palestrina festival in Rome in 1880), the *Missa solennis zur Einweihung der Basilika in Gran* (1855; *Mass for the Dedication of the Basilica at Gran*); the *Hungarian Coronation Mass* for Emperor Francis Joseph I (1867), and a unique composition for male chorus and organ accompaniment, *Slavimo Slavno Slaveni!*, written in 1863 for the millenary of SS. Cyril and Methodius. Also noteworthy are his two cantatas in honour of Beethoven.

The Czech composer Josef Förster achieved widespread recognition in his own country as a master of choral style, and a telling example of this may be heard in the cantata *Mortus fratribus*, written as a kind of requiem after the end of World War I. In Hungary, Zol-

tán Kodály went to texts of a 16th-century Hungarian poet, Michael Veg, for his *Psalmus Hungaricus* (first performed, 1923) celebrating the 50th anniversary of the union of the cities Buda and Pest. For the Paris Exhibition of 1937, the French composer Florent Schmitt composed one of his finest choral works, the *Fête de la lumière* (*Festival of Light*).

In 20th-century England the royal odes appeared less frequently than in the time of Purcell and Handel, yet there are a few choral works worthy of mention—Charles Stanford's *Welcome Song* for the opening of the Franco-British Exhibition (1908), and Sir Arthur Bliss's *Song of Welcome* (1954) for the homecoming of Queen Elizabeth II. Britten's cantata *St. Nicolas*, for tenor solo, mixed chorus, strings, piano, organ, and percussion, was written for the centenary of Lancing College in 1948, and 12 years later he supplied a *Cantata Academica* for the quincentenary of the University of Basel. The score of this work has parts where alternative words may be used for celebrations at other institutions of learning.

SECULAR MUSIC

Since the vast majority of secular vocal works of the Middle Ages and the Renaissance were written with soloists in mind rather than a chorus, this repertory will be dealt with in a later section of this article. A truly secular choral tradition does not really emerge until the 17th century, apart from dramatic works, which are mainly dealt with in the special article OPERA. Choruses were, however, supplied by way of incidental music to plays in the late 16th century; outstanding examples include the music written in 1585 by Andrea Gabrieli for the *Oedipus Tyrannus* of Sophocles and that of Giovanni Giacomo Gastoldi for Battista Guarini's play *Il pastor fido* (1590; *The Faithful Shepherd*). Choruses appear in 17th-century drama from time to time, as well as in masques and comparable extravaganzas. In the age of Lully, Marc-Antoine Charpentier, Purcell, and Matthew Locke, their position is clearly established. Secular cantatas tended for the most part to rely on solo voices, and when the chorus does make its appearance it sometimes consists only of three-part writing, as in Purcell's setting of Abraham Cowley's poem "If ever I more riches did desire."

The majority of Bach's secular cantatas call for solo voices only, in addition to the orchestra. Among those that do make full use of the chorus are *Phoebus and Pan* (*Geschwinde, geschwinde, ihr wirbelnden Winde*, BWV 201; 1731), the *Birthday Cantata* (*Schleicht, spielende Wellen*, BWV 206; 1733), and the *Hunt Cantata* (*Was mir behagt, ist nur die muntre Jagd*, BWV 208; 1716). The choral writing in Handel's secular cantatas and odes tends to be as massive and dignified as in the best of his oratorios, yet they are on the whole less frequently performed in the 20th century; as a group they do not fit easily into any single category. *Athalia* (1733) draws its inspiration and plot from the drama by the 17th-century French playwright Jean Racine; *Il trionfo del tempo e del disinganno* (1708; *The Triumph of Time and Truth*) is an allegory deriving from two of the composer's youthful Italianate compositions; *Alexander's Feast* (1736) and the *Ode for St. Cecilia's Day* (1739) both have texts by the 17th-century English poet Dryden; and the trilogy *L'allegro, Il penseroso, ed il moderato* (1740) is based on the poetry of another Englishman, John Milton.

Those powerful and opposite poles, church and opera, monopolized choral writing for many years, and apart from isolated works of an occasional nature there is little in the truly secular field until Beethoven's *Choral Fantasia* (1808), an unusual work in nine movements, the first seven of which are a set of variations for piano and orchestra. Voices are introduced only in the eighth movement—solo voices at first, singing verses in praise of music by a minor German poet of the early 19th century named Christoph Kuffner, then the choir, so that the previously dominant instrumental texture is gradually and effectively modified to include richly deployed vocal sonorities that assist the work to a climax in the same way as in the later *Choral Symphony*.

Beetho-
ven's
"Choral"
symphony

This gigantic work, the ninth and last symphony by Beethoven, is planned in such a way that the choral finale is the only proper and logical way for it to end, although performances have been given where the finale has been omitted (using the scherzo as ending). The choral finale of the *Ninth Symphony* grows from the fertile soil of its predecessors and becomes a structural, thematic, and aesthetic necessity. It is notoriously difficult to perform, as Beethoven often seems to treat the singers like instruments.

The influence of his *Ninth Symphony* on later symphonic literature was considerable. Beethoven's bravura choral writing sent its echoes to the outer limits of the Romantic era, and there were many subsequent essays in the integration of choral and orchestral forces. In *La Damnation de Faust*, Opus 24 (1846), Berlioz uses the weight of massed voices in an imaginative and dramatic way; in contrast, in his *Roméo et Juliette* symphony the voices tend to serve as an extra dash of colour to the orchestral palette. Brahms made skillful use of the chorus in his *Rhapsodie* (1869) and *Schicksalslied* (*Song of Destiny;* 1871), and Schumann relied upon it throughout his *Das Paradies und die Peri* (*Paradise and the Peri;* 1843), a kind of secular oratorio based on the long poem *Lalla Rookh* (1817) by the Irish poet Thomas Moore. The best of both composers, chorally speaking, is to be found in their many settings of contemporaneous poems for mixed voices, male voice choir, or female choir. Much of this remains little known outside Germany, to the detriment of choral programs that would gain interest from one of Schumann's finely constructed double-choir compositions or from one of Brahms's sensitive settings of the poetry of Ludwig Uhland or Goethe.

The technical demands of the choral sections in Antonín Dvořák's *Svatební košile* (*The Spectre's Bride*), a cantata written for the Birmingham Festival of 1885, are within the capabilities of the amateur choral societies for which it was intended, and in general his treatment of voices shows consideration as well as ingenuity. The macabre plot of this work is a narrative poem by a learned countryman of the composer's, the Czech poet Karel Erben, who achieved fame as a collector of folklore. Czech folk songs and tales exercised a powerful attraction for Dvořák throughout his life, and some of his best choral music consists of settings such as *V přírodě* (*Amid Nature*, 1882) and *Tři sborg* (*Three Slovak Folksongs*, 1877). Czech poetry gave rise to many remarkable compositions among the choral works of Janáček, perhaps the most memorable being the three male-voice choruses written between 1906 and 1909 that were based on poems by Petr Bezruč: *Kantor Halfar* (*Teacher Halfar*), *Maryčka Magdanova*, and *Sedmdesát tisíc* (*The Seventy Thousand*).

In modern Germany and Austria, the most far-reaching attempt to bring together choral and orchestral forces in symphonic literature was that of Gustav Mahler. Unable for three years to find the solution to the problem of a finale for his second symphony, Mahler heard at the funeral of the eminent conductor-pianist Hans von Bülow the *Resurrection* Ode by the 18th-century German poet Friedrich Gottlieb Klopstock. He decided to use this poem as a basis for a choral finale in the *Symphony No. 2 in C Minor* (1894). The use of massed voices for unaccompanied passages, such as the beginning of the ode, and later on with orchestral accompaniment and the collaboration of soprano and contralto soloists, affords ample evidence of Mahler's deep understanding of choral effects and techniques. The role of the choir is considerably less in his *Symphony No. 3 in D Minor* (1896), but it is nonetheless highly artistic and imaginative in the setting of the old popular verses *Es sungen drei Engel* ("Three angels were singing"). The *Eighth Symphony* (1906–07) marks the high point of symphonic choral music not only in Mahler's own output but in the entire history of the symphony as an art form. Instead of saving the chorus for climactic effects in the finale, as in his *Second Symphony* (and as in Beethoven's *Ninth*), Mahler integrates it from the very beginning into the complex and many-hued vocal and in-

The im-
portance
of Mahler

strumental colours—eight soloists, a boys' choir, two large choirs of mixed voices able to project powerful antiphonal effects with orchestra and organ. This *Symphony of a Thousand*, as it is generally called, presents two texts of a complementary and opposing nature: the hymn *Veni creator spiritus* and the closing scene of Goethe's *Faust*. Mahler's inspired use of his colossal forces to enhance, explain, and endow with added meaning the divine and human aspects of the two texts is without parallel. His achievement has not since been matched for sheer virtuosity and impact.

It is true that Arnold Schoenberg's *Gurrelieder* (1900–11) calls for even larger orchestral forces than Mahler's *Eighth Symphony*, although it has never enjoyed as much success. Choirs have preferred other early works of Schoenberg or those of Anton von Webern.

At the opposite end of the scale are the robust, tonal, and extrovert compositions of Paul Hindemith and also of Carl Orff, whose particular genius for setting classical and medieval texts may be seen in his *Catulli Carmina* (1943) and *Carmina Burana* (1937). Modern American choral music has been much enlivened by the contributions of Charles Ives (*An Election* composed in 1920), Randall Thompson, Roger Sessions, and many other eminent composers. Igor Stravinsky, who spent the latter part of his life in the United States, retained his interest in choral writing and constantly sought new ways of presenting the sonorities of a massed group of voices. To his earlier *Les Noces* (1923; *The Wedding*), and *Symphony of Psalms* (1930) for chorus and orchestra, he added the *Cantata on Old English Texts* (1952) on anonymous English poems of the 15th and 16th centuries and *A Sermon, A Narrative, and a Prayer* (1961) which is not a liturgical work, though its text is taken from the New Testament.

Twentieth-century English choral music for secular use finds its best advocates in Ralph Vaughan Williams, whose early setting of *Toward the Unknown Region* (first performed 1907) by the 19th-century American poet Walt Whitman was followed by *A Sea Symphony* (1910) based on material by the same poet. Frederick Delius also drew upon Whitman for his *Sea Drift* (1903) and upon the poems of the contemporary British poet Arthur Symons for his *Songs of Sunset* (1907). Britten's genius for word setting is evident in his *Hymn to St. Cecilia* (1942) and *A Ceremony of Carols* (1942) and in the handling of the boys' choir and mixed chorus in his *Spring Symphony* (1949) which ends with a choral waltz combining syllabic effects and the Old English lyric *Sumer is icumen in*. Outstanding among contemporary Polish choral works are three compositions by Krzysztof Penderecki: *Dimensions of Time and Silence* for chorus and chamber orchestra (published 1961); *Stabat Mater* for three choirs (1962); and *Psalms of David* for choir and percussion (1958).

MADRIGALS AND RELATED FORMS

A considerable amount of music sung by choirs in the 20th century is not really choral music at all, since it was conceived for performance by small groups of soloists and attains its fullest expression only through the individually projected personality of the solo voice. Assignment of these solo lines to a body of singers tends to neutralize this effect of personality, producing instead a weight of tone and an impression of superimposed dynamics and expression which, however carefully cultivated and disciplined, cannot surpass the kind of performance originally envisaged by the composer; yet a reasonable multiplication of voices does no harm to the texture as such, since the harmonies, the interweaving of parts, and the vocal spacing all remain constant. It is also true that a madrigal sung by 50 instead of by only five musicians will be more readily and rapidly understood by those directly involved because a massed performance of a five-part madrigal with ten singers on each line is a more practical proposition than forming ten separate consorts of five soloists. Individual voices, especially in amateur groups, may not possess the technique, the stamina, or the confidence to sustain a part on

Choral
perfor-
mance of
madrigals

their own, but if they sing as a member of a group the likelihood is that they will achieve good results.

Madrigals were originally published for professional singers and for amateur singers of high standard. They were issued not in score, as is the 20th-century custom, but in the form of part books, each one of which contained only the music necessary for one line—soprano, alto, tenor, bass, or any intermediate voice. The quantity printed of each edition was generally modest, with the result that prices were high, and choral performance was ruled out for economic reasons as well as artistic ones. The development of modern methods of engraving and printing music, allied to the creation of a worldwide market for choral works, has brought about a situation directly opposed to that of the Middle Ages and the Renaissance, whereby each singer now has a full score (or vocal score) that is less expensive than the part books printed in earlier times. In consequence, the choral performance of madrigals and related forms has become an economic possibility.

One of the most important predecessors of the madrigal proper was the frottola, which flourished in Italy between 1490 and 1520. In its early stages, the frottola was a song with instrumental accompaniment, with the main melody and text in the uppermost part (usually in the soprano or alto range) and supporting harmonies below. These harmonies were so simple and functional that an entire line could be dispensed with when intabulations for voice and lute were made. Four-part harmony was thus reduced to three, though without any serious loss since the polyphonic element tended to be of minimal importance. In later collections of frottolas, however, a different technique appears: instead of the upper line alone being supplied with text, all four parts join in. These completely texted frottolas were certainly intended to be sung by four singers, possibly, though not necessarily, doubled by instruments; and they could even have been sung by a small chorus.

Contemporary with the frottola were cognate forms such as the German lied, the French chanson, the Spanish villancico, and the English songs for voice and viols. All these began as accompanied songs, and all eventually followed the Italian fashion by dropping the instruments and substituting voices. This process was at first an obvious makeshift and can be detected as such because of the characteristically instrumental nature of the lower three parts, with numerous unvocal skips and contours. Words can be added to lines such as these, but they are often uncomfortable to sing because of the lack of conjunct movement and the paucity of breathing spaces. Occasionally, the added words appear only in one source, often a manuscript copy rather than a printed edition, the earlier sources on the other hand retaining the instrumental nature and function of the alto, tenor, and bass. The songs of Isaac provide clear examples of this gradual change, by which *Tenorlieder* (songs with the tune in the tenor) were transformed into part-songs by the addition of text to the instrumental lines. Some German composers, however, favoured the purely vocal or choral type of performance and made certain that all parts were texted.

Similar tendencies can be seen in France, in Spain, and in England, where many of the court songs written during Henry VIII's reign have text in all voice parts. One of the best known of these, *Passetyme with good cumpanye*, is a part-song for three male voices, written in all probability by the monarch himself. As the century progressed, amateurs began to take an interest in the part-song, which was generally for four voices, and several composers helped to lay the foundation for the English madrigal school. It is worthy of note that Byrd, in his *Psalmes, Sonets, & songs of Sadnes and pietie* (published, 1588), underlaid text to every part but mentioned in his preface that the songs were "originally made for Instruments to expresse the harmonie, and one voyce to pronounce the dittie."

Italian madrigals. The early development of the Italian madrigal was fostered as much by foreigners as by natives, and the considerable contributions made by the

Henry VIII's part-song

16th-century Flemish composers Jacques Arcadelt, Philippe Verdelot and Adriaan Willaert should not be underestimated. Although Willaert's settings of the works of the 14th-century Italian poet Petrarch and other serious Renaissance poets maintain an invariably high contrapuntal interest and are frequently suitable for choral performance, his compositions in the lighter, more homophonic vein, are well worth acquaintance.

Cipriano Rore, another Netherlander adopted by Italy, felt Willaert's influence strongly yet contrived to set new standards in the interpretation of poetry through music and also to encourage an artistic fusion of the contrapuntal and homophonic styles, using them alternately in one and the same composition according to the dictates of the poem. Even his early madrigals show a deep concern for intensity of expression, as in the Petrarch setting for five voices *Hor che'l ciel e la terra*. One of his finest four-part madrigals, *Ancor che col partire*, sets off pairs of voices one against the other. New heights of expression are reached in his descriptive madrigal *Quando lieta sperai* (text by the lady poet Emilia Anguissola), in which a sudden and disappointing change in the weather is perfectly mirrored in the music. The four-part *Datemi pace*, based on a Petrarch sonnet, favours homophony and looks eagerly forward to the bold chromaticism of Pomponio Nenna and Don Carlo Gesualdo. In his maturity, Rore produced a number of remarkably intense madrigals for the court of Parma. One of the finest is his setting of *Dalle belle contrade*, full of powerful contrasts of mood and colour underlining the interplay of direct and indirect speech.

Further experiments in chromaticism were carried out by Nicola Vicentino, whose dramatic setting of *O messaggi del cor*, by the Renaissance poet Ludovico Ariosto, makes highly effective use of a mounting modulatory scheme (changes of key) to enhance the insistent repetition of the opening exclamations. His early madrigals exploit a more classical vein, without ignoring illustrative possibilities. His most typical and fascinating work is nevertheless to be found in such madrigals as *Poichè il mio largo pianto* or *L'aura che il verde lauro* in which Petrarch's verbal puns are suitably matched by Vicentino's harmonic ambiguities. Even more extreme is the Neapolitan composer Pomponio Nenna, whose striking and original harmonies must have made an indelible impression on his pupil Gesualdo. But whereas Gesualdo's chromaticism is often wayward and illogical, that of Nenna tends toward reason and reality. Several of the master's madrigals can be usefully compared with those of his noble pupil that were set to identical texts. *Mercè, grido piangendo*, for example, is treated by Nenna with an enviable intensity of expression heightened by tremendous contrasts of timbre and dynamic; and, although this pattern is followed in Gesualdo's setting (*Book V*, 1611), perhaps with even greater violence, the most favourable musical impression comes from Nenna. His four-part madrigal *La mia doglia s'avvanza* is startling by any standards, for the opening four bars move rapidly from G minor to F-sharp major, D minor, and C-sharp major.

Gesualdo's preoccupation with poems containing diametrically opposed ideas and concepts finds its outlet in his last two books of madrigals (V and VI, both 1611). *Itene, O miei sospiri* not only looks forward in its manneristic treatment of vocal texture and harmony; it looks backward to classical procedures such as the interpolation of rests at the word *sospiri* (sighs), invented much earlier when the quarter-note rest was called *suspirium*. It would be wrong, however, to classify Gesualdo as an extremist on every occasion, for he could often write melting phrases of unforgettable beauty. He can even be witty at times, as in the madrigal about a venturesome mosquito (*Ardita zanzaretta*), which is somewhat in the vein of a vocal scherzo.

Luca Marenzio, one of the most prolific among late 16th-century Italian madrigalists, achieved his high reputation not through experiment but rather through his remarkable sensitivity to words, both as single entities and as the basic elements of a poetic phrase. His balance

Gesualdo's extraordinary range

between the two opposing claims of general mood and particular effect is always perfect, and the mastery of his vocal spacing is probably unrivalled, no matter whether four, five, or six parts are involved.

At the court of Mantua (now Mantova, Italy), two important composers were active toward the very end of the 16th century—Giaches de Wert and Giovanni Giacomo Gastoldi. Each of them, in his own particular way, helped to renew and transform madrigal techniques even though the countless admirers of Marenzio felt that the pinnacles of perfection had already been reached. De Wert's contribution to the new madrigal was in some ways unusual and unexpected, for he approached the dramatic madrigal-poetry in a way that combined realism with clarity. He returned, in fact, to homophonic writing when it was necessary to emphasize a point, allowing the highest voice part to project the melody in what was essentially a kind of "choral recitative." His
Monte-
verdi's
mastery
of the
madrigal
pupil Monteverdi published nine books of madrigals. From the sixth book onward continuo support becomes obligatory, and in consequence solo voices emerge from a choral background with tremendous dramatic effect, especially in the later works. The ballet *Tirsi e Clori* is rich in five-part choral writing of considerable elegance and resource, and the same is true (though in six-part texture) of *Altri canti di Marte. Vago augelletto* contrasts solo and choral writing until the last tutti, when all singers combine in a sonorous statement. Perhaps the greatest Monteverdi work of all is *Hor che'l ciel e la terra*, a six-part madrigal in two sections, with many solos and choral sections accompanied by violins and continuo. Monteverdi rarely surpassed the heights of emotional expressiveness found in this product of his maturity.

Related forms. *German lieder.* At the time of the Italian madrigal's fullest flowering, German composers derived much inspiration from the south while still contriving to retain something of their earlier heritage. The result was often a kind of international style, greatly influenced by Orlando di Lasso, who was as much at home writing Italian madrigals as he was with French chanson and German lieder. His pupils, the Austrian Leonhard Lechner and the German Johann Eccard, developed this style still further, as may be seen in the former's setting of *Wohl kommt der Mai* (*Welcome May*), a lively and optimistic May song full of expressive harmonic colour. The setting by Lasso of the same text is calmer, more homophonic; yet its apparent simplicity and unostentatiousness hides a subtle and skillful mastery of vocal art.

In his five-part lieder, Lasso makes the most of contrasting duets and trios very frequently, as in *Es jagt ein Jäger* a hunting song which serves as an excuse for lightly concealed amatory dalliance. Hans Leo Hassler was obviously fired by Lasso's lead in the sheer variety and latent possibilities of secular vocal style, and much of his best work was done in the dialogue form. A peak of brilliance and energy is reached in his eight-part dialogue for two opposing choral bodies, *Mein Lieb will mit mir kriegen* (*My Love Will Fight Me*), which might be described as a musically stylized battle of the sexes, with blows given and taken freely until the two groups combine to sing of final reconciliation and contentment.

Dialogues in this vein were also cultivated successfully by Christoph Demantius, whose anthology of 1609 contains examples of memorable beauty and charm. In his *Jungfrew, ich het ein' Bitt' an euch* (*Maiden, I have a Request for You*), Demantius allows one four-part choir to represent the girl and the other the boy in a conversation full of innocent affection and honest courtship, the two groups joining at the end to sing goodnight. In his five-part lieder, Demantius sometimes displays a learned touch in his imitative counterpoint, although the general impression is one of Italianate elegance rather than of studious endeavour. It is worthy of note that many of his lieder are strophically conceived, and in consequence he printed the verses complete in each voice part, a feature which has been unfortunately obscured in the modern edition of his works. One of the finest of his lieder is *Lieblich ich hörte singen*, which tells of the Sirens' song

and reproduces its allegedly hypnotic effect by means of flowing melismata in the upper voices.

The dialogue, considered as an art form of the Renaissance and Baroque eras, contains many choral elements. In its earliest form, as exemplified by the dialogues of Willaert, seven voices is the norm, and the texture is not yet clearly separated into two groups. Instead there is a kaleidoscopic impression caused by the skillful deployment of varied groupings. By the time of Andrea Gabrieli, a dialogue such as the popular and erotic *Tirsi morir volea* calls for a trio of high voices representing the girl and a quartet of deeper voices for the man. The amorous interchanges are carefully allocated to the individual groups, and there is no attempt to join them together until the very end. But in a typical dialogue by the younger Gabrieli, *Dormiva dolcemente*, there is no relationship between direct and indirect speech as far as the music is concerned. The setting is in this sense abstract, and the beauty of the dialogue lies in its purely musical architecture and expression.

One of the greatest masters of the French dialogue was
The
dialogues
of
di Lasso
Orlando di Lasso, who set two poems of the 16th-century French poet Pierre de Ronsard in eight-part, double-choir compositions of exceptional quality. *Que dis-tu, que fais-tu?* (1576; *What Are You Saying, What Are You Doing?*) plays off one group against another in a series of sympathetic exchanges culminating in a final chorus praising the constancy of the lovebirds. Another masterpiece of this kind is *O doux parler* (1571), in which the interlocutors are human and the approach of both poet and composer more intensely passionate.

French chansons. The French chanson, one of the most widespread and popular among secular vocal genres in the 16th century, is essentially in miniature form. Unlike the Italian madrigals, which were sometimes composed in sequences of three, four, or more sections, French chansons tend to remain individual in the sense that they are self-contained, epigrammatic, and brief. It is partly for this reason that they have been less explored by 20th-century choral groups, although the language factor must also be taken into consideration.

English madrigals. English madrigals, because of their relatively innocuous texts and their moderate degree of difficulty, have always been a staple diet of choral societies and to an even greater extent of chamber choruses. The 16th- and 17th-century madrigals of William Byrd, Thomas Weelkes, John Wilbye, Thomas Morley, and their contemporaries and successors are too well-known to need elaborate description and too numerous to permit individual discussion. It is nevertheless true that although this repertory may today be considered as generally choral, certain madrigals are better reserved for performance by soloists. The criterion for making such a choice lies often with the text rather than with the music, for a certain degree of personal intensity in the words demands a corresponding projection of individual lines and their message. On the other hand, others are eminently suitable for choral performance.

The glee. After the vogue of the madrigal had disappeared, that of the glee eventually took its place, flourishing from the early 18th century to the middle of the 19th. Like the madrigal, the glee was originally intended for solo voices, but choral performances were by no means infrequent. The word glee, derived from the Anglo-Saxon word for music (*gligge*) does not necessarily imply a composition of a cheerful nature, and many of the best glees in fact express solemn or poetic themes. Samuel Webbe's *Glorious Appolo* and R.J.S. Stevens's *Ye spotted snakes* provide very different, though typical, examples of this vocal genre. Tonality is for the most part simple and unaffected, harmony is robust, and the span of musical thought necessarily brief.

BIBLIOGRAPHY. MANFRED F. BUKOFZER, *Studies in Medieval and Renaissance Music* (1950) and *Music in the Baroque Era* (1947), are both well-established classics, the first volume being of particular importance since it discusses the beginnings of choral music. ALFRED EINSTEIN, *The Italian Madrigal*, 3 vol. (1949, reprinted 1971), is a detailed account of the entire history of the Italian madrigal. The third volume contains hitherto unpublished compositions, EDMUND H. FEL-

LOWES, *English Cathedral Music from Edward VI to Edward VII*, 2nd ed. rev. (1945), and *The English Madrigal Composers*, 2nd ed. (1948), are regarded as classics and are well suited to the general reader as well as to the professional musician. FRANK L. HARRISON, *Music in Medieval Britain* (1958), is the most thorough account of church music in Britain from the earliest times up to the middle of the 16th century. PETER LE HURAY, *Music and the Reformation in England, 1549–1660* (1967), provides especially good coverage for this period. GUSTAVE REESE, *Music in the Renaissance*, rev. ed. (1959), is the finest single-volume study of music from the time of Dufay up to that of Byrd. DENIS W. STEVENS, *Tudor Church Music* (1961), is a study of forms and styles in 16th-century church music.

(D.W.S.)

Chordata

The chordates (phylum Chordata) comprise the vertebrates and several groups of small invertebrate animals. Three common characteristics unify the chordates and distinguish them from all other animals: a rodlike supporting structure, the notochord; openings through the wall of the pharynx; and a hollow nerve cord located on the dorsal side, or back. In addition, the chordate body is divided into segments, and muscle and nerve elements are repeated in successive segments. These characteristics appear early in the development of all chordates, but they may be greatly modified, or eliminated, in adults.

The phylum includes three subphyla: the Urochordata, which are chordate-like only in the larval state; the Cephalochordata (*q.v.*), in which the basic pattern of the phylum is retained throughout life; and the Vertebrata, which have evolved a series of increasingly complex forms. A fourth group, the Hemichordata, is now generally classified as a related, but separate, phylum.

Structure and development. The chordate body consists of a tube (gut) within a tube (body wall), the two layers being separated by a cavity (coelom) lined with mesoderm, one of three basic tissue types that originate in the embryo. The terminus of the gut (anus) is at the site of the blastopore, an opening in the gastrula (*i.e.*, an early two-layered embryonic stage) that marks the point of infolding of the embryonic endoderm (*i.e.*, another basic tissue type), which is to become the future gut lining; the mouth opens later at a different location. On the basis of this characteristic, the chordates are assigned to the deuterostomes, a larger group, which also includes the Echinodermata, the Hemichordata, and the Pogonophora (*qq.v.*). Typically the chordate body is bilaterally symmetrical; *i.e.*, the right and left sides are similar. It is elongated, the anterior–posterior (*i.e.*, head-to-tail) dimension being supported by the notochord. There are sense organs at the anterior end, and a tail extends behind the anus. Swimming is effected by the alternating contraction of blocks of muscle tissue (myotomes) arranged on either side of the notochord.

Lower chordates. The basic characteristics of the chordates are exemplified by the cephalochordate amphioxus, a slender, fishlike animal about five to six centimetres (two inches or slightly more) long. The notochord, which consists of a fibrous sheath filled with a mucus-like material, gives the animal the combination of flexibility and rigidity necessary to permit it to move in and out of the sandy or gravelly sea bottoms on which it lives. Swimming movements are coordinated by a segmental series of dorsal (joined to cord at upper surface) or ventral (joined at lower surface) nerve roots. Though an active swimmer in larval (immature form) stages, the adult amphioxus spends most of its time partly embedded in the sea bottom, with only the anterior end exposed. A circlet of tentacles around the mouth directs a current of water into the pharynx, and oxygen is absorbed by the blood as the water passes out through the gill slits on each side of the pharynx. Organic debris is filtered out of the water, concentrated, and passed to the postpharyngeal gut, where it is digested and absorbed.

Despite its superficial resemblance to fishes and thus to vertebrates in general, amphioxus differs strikingly from vertebrates in lacking a clearly defined head. There is no brainlike enlargement of the nerve cord extending in front of the notochord, and there are no well-defined cephalic (head-region) sense organs. Amphioxus is also peculiar in possessing a group of excretory cells (protonephridia) similar to those found in lower invertebrates but not in echinoderms or vertebrates.

Adult urochordates are sessile (*i.e.*, fixed to the bottom or other surface) or floating marine organisms. They reveal their chordate nature only in the possession of gill slits in the pharynx. The newly hatched urochordate larva, however, is elongated, bilaterally symmetrical, and has a well-developed tail. It has a notochord, nerve cord, and a series of myotomes. The short trunk contains a sensory vesicle enclosing a primitive eye that consists of three lens cells and several pigmented retinal cells. There is also a small gut sac with gill slits and a mouth, but no anus. The larva does not feed but, within about a day, attaches itself by suckers at the anterior end, resorbs its tail, and wraps itself in a fleshy tunic from which protrude a pair of siphons that convey water in and out of the body.

Urochordates and cephalochordates develop from small eggs that contain little yolk. Elongation of the gastrula leads to a larva that is minute but possesses the basic chordate attributes. Vertebrate eggs, with the exception of those of mammals, are laden with a mass of yolk that interferes with the process of cleavage (*i.e.*, cell division in the early embryo). This condition has led to profound modifications in the patterns of cleavage and gastrulation among the vertebrates; yet the early embryo has essentially the form of a chordate—the hollow nerve cord develops early by an infolding of the dorsal surface; pharyngeal openings are established, even in forms that never live in water; and the notochord, though modified in terrestrial forms, invariably appears. Vertebrate embryos are, however, distinguished even at the earliest stages by their high degree of cephalization, or development of the head region: the anterior end of the neural tube (*i.e.*, the primitive dorsal nervous system of the embryo) is expanded into a series of vesicles, or lobes, from which the brain differentiates and the rudiments of the olfactory organs, eyes, and ears appear.

Higher chordates. The vertebrates, in contrast to the lower chordates, exhibit diverse, complex forms derived from the basic chordate plan. New supporting material (bone or cartilage or both) differentiates in all vertebrates and makes possible the development of large body size. In all but the Agnatha, the most primitive vertebrates, a movable jaw with teeth appears, as do two pairs of appendages. The pharyngeal gill slits function as part of the respiratory apparatus in vertebrates that are aquatic in adult or larval life. In terrestrial forms the slits disappear in embryonic life, but the pharynx produces a ventral diverticulum, or pouch, from which the lungs develop.

Lung breathing has been accompanied by profound modifications of the heart. In the aquatic chordates, the heart is a muscular tube, situated below the pharynx, which receives blood from the tissues and drives it upward through the gills, to be supplied with oxygen, before it flows to the tissues again. In air breathers, the heart has become subdivided so that the right side receives blood from the tissues and sends it to the lungs, and the left side receives blood from the lungs and sends it to the tissues. This type of heart is found in modern lungfishes, as well as in reptiles. In the birds and mammals, the subdivision is complete, and freshly oxygenated blood from the lungs passes to all the organs of the body without mixing with any unoxygenated blood. The heightened physical activity thus made possible is also associated with modification of the excretory apparatus. Vertebrate embryos that live in water excrete their nitrogenous wastes (*i.e.*, products of protein metabolism) by way of a few simple pronephric tubules that draw in fluid from the coelom. Adult fishes and amphibians, however, develop an advanced series of mesonephric tubules that collect wastes directly from the bloodstream. Completely terrestrial forms develop a metanephric kidney, in which very large numbers of minute tubules filter the nitrogenous wastes from the blood.

Marginal notes:
Amphioxus: a generalized chordate

Lung breathing

Evolution and classification. *Paleontology.* The interrelations of the chordates and their evolution from nonchordates are speculative subjects, because the soft-bodied lower chordates have left no fossil record. The deuterostome condition (*i.e.*, the separate origins of mouth and anus) indicates that the major invertebrate phylum most clearly related to the Chordata is the Echinodermata. The common ancestor of deuterostomes may have been a sessile or semisessile organism, some descendants of which (Chordata, Hemichordata) developed pharyngeal openings in the larval stage. A commonly accepted view holds that the pharynx thus modified was put to use as a food-collecting organ; the body meanwhile became increasingly specialized for locomotion by development of a streamlined body supported by a notochord and propelled by the contractions of segmentally repeated muscle blocks, the action of which was coordinated by a well-organized nervous system.

Among modern urochordates a larva having the characteristics described above swims briefly in search of a favourable habitat before regressing to the sessile state. In the ancestors of the cephalochordates and vertebrates, on the other hand, the larva probably became sexually mature in its free-swimming state; the cephalochordates have apparently evolved no further than this. The vertebrates, however, have evolved further. Perhaps the most significant use they made of their swimming ability was to move into freshwater, which favoured the evolution of large eggs that could develop safely in quiet pockets of riverbeds and produce larvae of substantial size, which were thus more capable than minute marine larvae of feeding themselves and surviving.

Distinguishing taxonomic features. The Urochordata are set apart on the basis of their distinctive adult structure, and the Cephalochordata are separated from the Vertebrata because they have no skeletal tissue and lack a brain and attendant sense organs. Among the vertebrates, the principal division is between the fishlike forms, which continue to live in water, and the partly (Amphibia) or wholly (Reptilia, Aves, Mammalia) land-living forms. Reptiles produce large eggs that can develop on land, but adults lack the respiratory, circulatory, and other physiological adaptations necessary for the maintenance of constant body temperature and intensive physical activity. Birds and mammals, though specialized in different directions, have circulatory, respiratory, and excretory systems that enable them to support a high level of bodily activity and to maintain constant temperature; their brains are more complex than those of other vertebrates, and they have physical and behavioral characteristics that enable them to care for their young.

Annotated classification. The classification below follows that of the U.S. zoologist Alfred Romer (1970). Groups known only from fossils are indicated by a dagger (†).

PHYLUM CHORDATA
Animals with notochord, dorsal hollow neural tube, gill slits, at least in larval stages; body segmented, bilaterally symmetrical; closed blood system with heart below pharynx.

Subphylum Urochordata (or Tunicata) (tunicates, sea squirts)
Generally sessile (attached) as adults, elaborate gill apparatus, no notochord, reduced nerve cord; motile as larvae, with well-developed notochord and neural tube; see TUNICATA.

Class Ascidiacea
Sessile as adults; solitary or living as colonies within a common tunic (covering).

Class Thaliacea
Adults modified for life in open sea; transparent tunic; propelled by contractions of circular muscle bands.

Subphylum Cephalochordata (amphioxus, lancet)
Small streamlined marine animals; well-developed neural tube and gill apparatus; notochord extends to anterior tip of body; semisedentary as adults; only 2 living genera; see CEPHALOCHORDATA.

Subphylum Vertebrata
Bony or cartilaginous vertebrae supplant notochord; enlargement of brain and attendant sense organs.

Class Agnatha
Fishlike animals without jaws or fins; vertebral column of cartilaginous plates flanking notochord; extant forms (lampreys, hagfishes) have slimy skin without scales; are free-living as larvae but parasitic on higher fishes as adults; fossil forms had bony armour; see AGNATHA.

Class Placodermi
†Extinct fishes, limited to Paleozoic (225,000,000–570,000,-000 years ago) Era; covered with bony plates; had jaw, primitive fins; see PLACODERMI.

Class Selachii (or Chondrichthyes) (sharks, skates, rays, chimeras)
Fishes with completely cartilaginous skeletons, mostly marine; Paleozoic to present; modern forms produce large eggs with much yolk; fertilization internal, young develop within maternal oviducts (*i.e.*, tubes conveying eggs from ovary); see SELACHII.

Class Osteichthyes
Fishes with bony skeletons.

Subclass Actinopterygii. Fishes with fanlike fins consisting of thin dermal rays; some primitive forms (*e.g.*, sturgeon) have reverted to partly cartilaginous skeletons; includes most marine and freshwater fishes.

Subclass Sarcopterygii. Mostly extinct; Paleozoic forms gave rise to terrestrial vertebrates; had fleshy fins consisting of large bony elements and attached musculature; internal nostrils, indicative of lung breathing; 3 living genera of freshwater lungfishes, 1 marine genus.

Class Amphibia
Four-footed, partly terrestrial animals, including frogs, toads, and salamanders, plus larger extinct forms from Triassic (about 190,000,000–225,000,000 years ago) and Late Paleozoic periods; poorly developed lungs, 3-chambered hearts; depend partly on skin and other structures for blood oxygenation; eggs laid in water, hatch as aquatic tadpoles that undergo metamorphosis (transformation) to air-breathing adults; see AMPHIBIA.

Class Reptilia
Very diverse group, dominant in Mesozoic Era (about 65,-000,000–225,000,000 years ago); now represented by turtles, snakes, lizards, and crocodiles; skin protected against drying by horny scales or bony plates; large eggs contain abundant food and water; embryo develops within fluid-filled sac (amnion); young adapted to terrestrial life at hatching; extant forms have metanephric kidney, heart incompletely subdivided into 4 chambers; see REPTILIA.

Class Aves (birds)
Generally small, except flightless types; have feathers, scales on legs, no teeth; well-developed lungs; heart completely subdivided into 4 chambers; maintain constant body temperature of 41° C (106° F); produce small number of large eggs; a few fossils had feathers, teeth, long bony tails; see BIRD.

Class Mammalia
Animals with mammary glands and typically with hair; young develop in uterus, except in 1 order; forebrain greatly enlarged; metanephric kidney; 4-chambered heart; body temperature constant; see MAMMALIA.

Critical appraisal. The Hemichordata were originally classified as a chordate subphylum, but most authorities now assign them to a separate phylum. The great variety of extant fishes and their fossil relatives has led to problems that some authors have attempted to resolve by various types of classifications (see FISH). The Acanthodii, for example, which may include the ancestors of modern fishes, are sometimes placed in a separate class, as are the Actinopterygii and Sarcopterygii.

BIBLIOGRAPHY. E.J.W. BARRINGTON, *The Biology of Hemichordata and Protochordata* (1965), a brief but authoritative account of the characteristics of the lower chordates and their evolution; N.J. BERRILL, *The Origin of Vertebrates* (1955), an important book that has helped to establish the thesis that the urochordate larva represents the prototype from which cephalochordates and vertebrates are derived; L.H. HYMAN, *The Invertebrates*, vol. 5, *Smaller Coelomate Groups* (1959), a classic work treating the hemichordates in extensive detail; C. DAWYDOFF, "Classe de entéropneustes," in P.P. GRASSE (ed.), *Traité de zoologie*, pp. 367–453 (1948), an authoritative account of the form, functions, development, and evolution of the Enteropneusta; A.S. ROMER, *The Vertebrate Body*, 4th ed. (1970), a successful college textbook that includes a detailed classification of vertebrates; J.Z. YOUNG, *The Life of Vertebrates*, 2nd ed. (1962), a wide-ranging work including two informative chapters on the lower chordates.

(Fl.M.)

Choreography and Dance Notation

Although the writing down of dance was originally called *chorégraphie* (from the Greek *choreia*, "dance," and *graphein*, "to write"), later the anglicized form of the word, choreography, came to mean the art of composing dances. Choreography may range from the arrangement of groups on stage, entrances, and exits, to the arrangement of an established dance vocabulary, to selection and modification of movement ideas from other sources, and the creation of new movement sequences. Fields for the application of choreography include recreational dance, ritual dance, and theatrical dance (plays, operas, ballets, films). Dance notation, on the other hand, is the recording of movement on paper by means of signs. Notation systems through the centuries have ranged from a simple memory-aid device to record known material to a highly developed system dealing with subtle variations in all aspects of human movement.

CHOREOGRAPHY

Elements and principles of composition. Lacking a developed system of notation until the 20th century, dance has not yet evolved elements and principles of composition comparable to those existing in music. The structure of dance composition rested on what was visually pleasing and the generally accepted taste of the time. Nevertheless, a few basic rules have emerged based on the limitations in reception and perception of images through the eye. The eye demands periodic, if brief, respite from great activity. Because movement is fleeting, repetition is effective, and memory of a preceding movement will give significance to ones that follow. The use of repetition depends greatly on the spectator's cultural development: the more trained the eye and sophisticated the intellect, the less need for repetition and familiar material. A clear relationship to the musical accompaniment in terms of basic beat or phrasing is required to a greater or lesser degree depending, again, on the spectator. As modern compositions break more and more with traditional structures, the eye and mind are trained to look for and to enjoy other elements and aspects. But certain basic truths remain.

The placement of the dancers on stage and their relation to one another has an intrinsic dramatic effect quite apart from movement. The use of the stage area in conventional proscenium theatres affects any dramatic statement being made. Modern theatres-in-the-round provide radically different conditions for relationship to the audience and, hence, the impact of climatic moments.

Characteristic patterns, particularly floor designs, have been handed down in certain cultures. Examples of this include the straight-line advance and retreat of the earliest hulas in Hawaii and the T design of the ancient *bhārata-nāṭya* of India. The special characteristics of dance in diverse cultures have been ascertained by examining films of ethnic and anthropological material. Such a study, called choreometrics, involves a comparative analysis of the occurrence and frequency of certain choreographic factors (repetition, path of movement, group arrangement, etc.) to determine basic dance-types and similarities between cultures.

Functions of the choreographer

A choreographer may arrange dances for an opera, play, or film for which the story, music, costumes, and scenery have already been selected, or he may be the sole author of every aspect of a theatrical piece, including the selection and training of the dancers, composing the music or aural accompaniment and designing, and overseeing or, indeed, constructing the costumes, sets, and props. More often, however, the role of choreographer falls between these two extremes. Each choreographer has an individual way of working. The initial attack may vary according to the type of work being prepared. There are eight main approaches: (1) an outline of the entrances, exits, and general group arrangement is first sketched with the dancers, after which suitable steps, body, and arm movements are arranged for each phase, and, finally, specific details are added and the movements polished; (2) individual movement themes

which form the core of the choreography are taught first, then arranged and modified with suitable introductions, conjunctions, and conclusions into choreographic sequences; (3) ideas and suggestions are advanced on which dancers improvise, and the choreographer then selects and molds any suitable material into a finished form. Though principal dancers may be given considerable latitude in composing their own variations, the choreographer retains final decision on the total effect; (4) manipulation and distortion of existing dance vocabulary is often a springboard for choreography, "original" movements resulting from changes in the component parts of a familiar step; (5) the music inspires movement patterns as in music "visualization," in which movement expresses visually what the music states aurally; (6) movements spring physically from within as a result of a dramatic, dynamic, or rhythmical spark; as the dancers respond to each movement idea, the choreographer is, in turn, often further inspired by their reaction; (7) manipulation of objects or materials may be the source of dance movement; (8) arrangement and rearrangement of colour in lighting and costume may be the focal point for choreography.

Formal training in choreography has only recently become accepted. In years past, the absence of notated dance scores made any structural study of choreography virtually impossible. The prevailing idea in the ballet world that choreography cannot be taught, that choreographers are born, not made, grew from the fact that choreographers have generally emerged from the ranks of a ballet company. In the U.S., Louis Horst, musical adviser to Martha Graham, evolved courses in dance composition based on pre-Classic and modern forms, and these and other such courses were included in many college and university dance departments. Schools of choreography have been established in the U.S.S.R. and Sweden, but neither makes use of dance notation. A start in choreographic training comparable to the detailed discipline of a musician's compositional training began in London at the Royal Ballet School where Léonide Massine used his modification of the Stepanov notation in his special choreographic course.

Historical developments. In its simplest form, choreography originated with the first group dance. Though a solo dance can be improvised and changed according to the mood of the performer, a dance for two or more needs some coordination. The origins of choreography as an art can be traced to the early 15th century, when the first known professional dancing masters appeared at the Italian courts of the Renaissance. Among their tasks was the arrangement of dances which were part of the elaborate spectacles produced in those courts for entertainment and to enhance the prestige of the ruling prince. Only from the manuscripts that their masters have left has the modern world any knowledge of the steps of the time and of their arrangement into dances. These early *basses* (low) *danses* were fundamentally social, the steps being simple but decorated walking sequences following elaborate floor patterns, designed to show the performers and their elaborate costumes to advantage.

In the early court ballets there was no division between singers, actors, and dancers. Acrobatic dances were popular as well as *balli*, or *balletti*, which often contained pantomimic interplay between performers. Allegorical figures and episodes, then much in vogue, were featured in the celebrated *Ballet comique de la reine* in 1581 at the French court. The entertainment was concluded by the "grand ballet," a formal solemn dance of symmetrical design danced by the courtiers. A knowledge of geometry was expected of choreographers, who sought to reflect in the floor patterns the perfection of the planetary paths, metaphysical ideas being incorporated. With dancing recognized as a necessary social grace, books were published by professional dancing masters, notably Fabritio Caroso's *Il ballarino* (1581), Thoinot Arbeau's *Orchésographie* (1588), and Cesare Negri's *Le gratie d'amore* (1602), which described the manner in which steps should be performed. Choreography was much en-

Origins of choreography as an art

riched at this period through the evolution of dance technique, to which the most famous choreographer of the mid-17th century, Pierre Beauchamps, contributed. He is credited with establishing the five positions of the feet in ballet and also with evolving a system of dance notation on which Raoul Feuillet based a system published in 1700. The retirement of Louis XIV as a dancer heralded the end of the court ballet, which then progressed to the public theatre and evolved into the form of opera-ballet, a series of *entrées* or divertissements linked by a common theme, the best known being *Les Indes galantes* (1735). Through publications using the so-called Feuillet notation, much is known of the dances of this time. Theatrical and social dancing still had much in common, although the technique of the former was more elaborate. Differences between the French and Italian styles were already apparent, the French being concerned more with grace, charm, and elegance, while the Italians stressed virtuosity.

Dancing continued to be combined with speech and song until well into the 18th century, when they gradually separated into two streams, speech and song becoming opera and dancing combining with mime to evolve into the *ballet d'action*. The first *ballet d'action*, *The Loves of Mars and Venus*, by John Weaver, was produced in London in 1717. This work relied on mime and gesture to convey the story, the dances being only patterns and not related to the plot or expressive of the characters dancing them. The concept of the *ballet d' action* was later developed by choreographers such as Franz Hilverding, Jean-Baptiste de Hesse, Noverre, and Angiolini. In its development a considerable influence was exerted by the Italian commedia dell'arte, a popular form of entertainment in which dance and acrobatics were important elements.

18th century. The great French dance reformer of the mid-18th century, Jean-Georges Noverre, set forth Noverre's principles in 1760 a number of principles that have had a lasting effect: a ballet should contain a good plot that can be followed without program notes; good music should be used, preferably a commissioned score; all of the choreography, both for corps de ballet and principals, should be designed to express or assist the development of the theme; stage costume should be historically correct and relate to the scenery. Despite Noverre's ideas, choreography still followed the pattern of set dances interspersed with mime scenes, in the same way that arias were inserted in opera between recitatives. Noverre's rival, Gasparo Angiolini, proved that program notes could be eliminated by choosing stories that were expressed in easily understandable mime set to music.

Theatre choreography of the period had inherited from the court a formal aristocratic style of movement and vocabulary of steps. As the theatregoing public expanded to include more of the middle class, themes based on gods, goddesses, and idealized shepherds and shepherdesses no longer seemed appropriate, and choreographers felt the need to break through to more realistic themes and to adapt to a style more acceptable to their public. One of the first ballets to depict ordinary people with sympathetic realism was Jean Dauberval's *Fille mal gardée* (1789), which dealt with simple human relationships in a rural setting.

19th century. In the early 19th century at Milan, Salvatore Viganò attempted to weld the movements of a large company into a cohesive stage work. Much influenced by Dauberval, Viganò had at first choreographed lighter works, then developed mimed dramas on heroic and historical subjects in which the action was expressed by gestures in strict time with the music. He used the corps de ballet creatively to aid in telling the story.

An important French choreographer of that time, Charles Didelot, who spent most of his career in St. Petersburg (now Leningrad), subordinated everything to the ballet's theme. He studied paintings and pieces of sculpture to glean ideas for beautiful and expressive grouping of the dancers and made imaginative use of stage effects, and was the first choreographer to have groups of dancers fly by means of wires.

As ballet technique developed, male virtuosity came to include high jumps, turns in the air, and beating steps. Pirouettes developed in perfection, achieving a finish not known 50 years before. Costume reforms which Developments in technique introduced shorter and more transparent costumes for women emphasized the line of the body. Elegant line required a greater turn out of the leg and so the 90° turn-out gradually became standard, a change from the usual 45° of Noverre's time. By eliminating the heel from the shoe, women began to rise onto the pointe, if at first only briefly as a feat. Teaching and choreography revolved around perfection in a relatively narrow vocabulary of steps. The improved teaching methods of his time were codified by Carlo Blasis in his teaching manual *Traité élémentaire, théorique, et pratique de l'art de la danse* (1820).

Around 1830 ballet was greatly influenced by the Romantic movement, and the plots mirrored literary fashion, deriving on the one hand from supernatural themes and on the other from exotic sources. The role of the ballerina as a spirit creature was further enhanced by the development of pointe work. The two broad categories of themes were accompanied by two distinct dance styles: for the mortals, realistic, vigorous, and earth-bound movements; for the spirits, a light, aerial style involving steps of elevation and lifts to give the illusion of flight. The more poetic style of choreography required soft, curved, flowing movements of the arms and head.

The two most important choreographers of the period were Jules Perrot and August Bournonville. Perrot was an important innovator in his skillful use of the dance to advance the action, in dance passages called *pas d'action*. Most of his choreography has been forgotten, but some of it remains in *Giselle* (first performed, 1841). The ballets of Bournonville are the purest surviving examples of the choreography of the Romantic period.

The second half of the 19th century witnessed a development in ballet music. Léo Delibes in Paris and Tchaikovsky in Russia set new standards, their ballet scores having independent validity. Tchaikovsky, although given precise instructions by Petipa for the variations and scenes in *The Sleeping Beauty* (1890), even to being told the tempo, mood, and length of each passage, was able to provide a score of high quality, full of melodic invention and rich orchestration, perfectly suited to the accompanying dance.

The development of the female dancer's technique through the use of pointe work, her domination in being Decline of the male dancer the central figure, the superhuman, the unattainable, and her glorification through the themes of the Romantic ballets, relegated the male dancer literally to a supporting role. Leading roles for men became mimed rather than danced. A virtuoso male dancer might appear in a national dance to highlight a scene, with no other part in the ballet. Because of the absence of opportunities, male dancing declined, except in Denmark where Bournonville's ballets provided challenging roles of substance and also in Russia where the indigenous folk dance provided intricate dances for men, requiring great virtuosity. The ideal balance between the roles of male and female in ballet was lost, and display became the principal end of ballet.

In the 1870s and 1880s ballet productions in London included transformation scenes and large corps de ballet moving in unison. In Milan, Luigi Manzotti wrote and produced numerous spectacular, pageant-like ballets in which he stressed the overall dramatic effect rather than relationships between individual people expressed in dance steps and choreographic movement.

The return to ballet as a form concentrating on the dramatic telling of a story through dance came principally in Russia with Petipa's development of the three- or four-act ballet providing a full evening's entertainment. The formula which Petipa established was for each act to contain several pas d'action, character dances, and dances for the corps de ballet. A grand pas de deux climaxed the last act, to be followed by a finale involving all of the dancers who had hitherto appeared. His choreography departed from the Romantic emphasis on content and evolved more and more into a spectacle designed to show off the ballerina to advantage. Technical virtuosity became the springboard for the variations, and the pas de deux were designed to display the brilliance of the woman. The ballerina performed national dances with few appropriate movements, classical ballet technique predominating. Though the changes of formation and groupings were inventive and often beautiful, the dancers ceased to be individuals personally concerned with story or plot.

20th century. The earliest decades of the 20th century saw radical departures from choreography of the past. Two main tendencies emerged: a classical stream impelled by Sergey Diaghilev's influence and a modern stream initiated by Rudolf Laban in Europe and the Denishawn company in the United States.

Ballet choreography under Diaghilev

Diaghilev brought together leading artists and musicians to work for him, thereby changing the whole direction of ballet and raising it to a serious theatrical art. His first choreographer, Michel Fokine, who had already protested against the meaningless traditions and conventions in the Imperial Russian Ballet, was able to put his ideas into practice. He insisted that everything, including the role of the prima ballerina, should contribute to make a cohesive whole. Music should not consist of polkas, waltzes, and galops strung together; there should be complete continuity; the style of movement, costumes, and decor should all suit the style of the period depicted. In developing the one act ballet, Fokine featured dramatic content, but, in *Les Sylphides* (1909), he evolved the mood ballet. Though his choreographic principles remained inviolable, his choice of subject matter varied widely, as can be seen from *The Firebird* (1910), *Le Carnaval* (1910), and *Le Spectre de la rose* (1911). He provided challenging roles for male dancers; he made appropriate and logical use of folk material, rejecting the balletic tradition of performing them on pointe.

Considerable as these changes from the ballets of Petipa were, Diaghilev looked for advances which would parallel the then current developments in art and music. Fokine was artistically fully formed, but Diaghilev was able to groom Vaslav Nijinsky as a choreographer from the beginning, encouraging him to develop such new ideas as the staccato, angular, two-dimensional movement used to Claude Debussy's lyric music in *L'Après-midi d'un faune* (1912) and the primitive—and to the taste of the time—grotesque and ugly movements in *The Rite of Spring* (1913) to the then apparently shocking, dissonant music of Igor Stravinsky. Nijinsky's use of stillness during a strong passage in the music was another new departure, as was his presenting dancers in everyday tennis clothes in his ballet *Jeux* (1913).

Léonide Massine, Nijinsky's successor as Diaghilev's principal choreographer, initiated new ideas in several directions. He excelled not only as a choreographer but also as a performer, portraying characterization through intricate steps and gestures. In his most famous ballet, *Le Tricorne* (1919), he achieved a strong Spanish flavour, and, in his symphonic ballets, mostly produced in the 1930s, he broke through to a new form and explored greater freedom in movement.

George Balanchine first emerged as a strong force at the close of the Diaghilev era, pointing the direction into which his art would develop in *Apollon Musagète* (1928), in which he juxtaposed strictly classical movement with bent, inturned limbs, distortions, and inversions of recognizable actions.

Choreography of George Balanchine

Balanchine's marriage of dance to music was a dominant feature of his accomplishments. As exemplified in *Agon* (1957), music was for him the springboard of the actual steps and movements. Despite his wide range, a Balanchine ballet came to mean specifically an abstract ballet featuring movement for its own sake, the human body being an instrument of movement design, the movement often athletic in nature, with distortion of recognizable balletic steps by broken wrist, ankle, or hip line, and often including intertwining of groups of dancers, or of a few individual dancers' limbs. Partly from economic necessity, Balanchine pared ballet down to movement itself, eliminating large groups, decor, and costume other than practice clothes.

Whereas in Balanchine's story ballets, such as *The Prodigal Son* (1929), choreographic design took first place, the English choreographer Antony Tudor was concerned with intimate personal experience. He created the psychological ballet, which centred on expressing emotional interrelation between real people, as in *Lilac Garden* (1936), which told of a deep love thwarted by a marriage of convenience. Tudor initiated an important departure in his use of expressive gesture, contrasting tenuous unresolved motions and freely flowing passages in scenes between the lovers with technical virtuosity expressing the highlights of their anguish.

In the United States, Agnes deMille, who was also concerned with real people, expressed their moods and foibles through a ballet-based vocabulary blended with stylized, everyday movement patterns made unexpectedly poignant or humorous by contrasting dynamics, breath pauses, suspensions, sudden thrusts, or slow, sustained strength. Her first outstanding ballet, *Rodeo* (1942), made effective use of American square dance to further the story. Though she produced other ballets, deMille's greatest choreographic contribution was the introduction of highly artistic and meaningful dance into Broadway musicals as in *Oklahoma!* (1943). Other choreographers, such as Hanya Holm, Michael Kidd, and Jerome Robbins, followed her lead. Robbins' contribution was epitomized in *West Side Story* (1957). This was the high point in integration of dance with plot, the concept put forward by Noverre but only gradually achieved since his day. Robbins' choreography for *West Side Story* had a worldwide impact, opening up interest in modern jazz as a style suitable for serious choreographic treatment. His gift lay in a blend of musical, spatial, and dynamic sensitivity and his sense of selection and arrangement.

Sir Frederick Ashton, choreographer for the Royal Ballet in England, provided an example of consistently excellent choreography on a range of themes that remained strongly balletic, in spite of experimentation with freer, modern styles. As choreographer for a conservative company, Ashton broke no new ground, unless it was to lead the way back to the full-length ballet form. *Cinderella* (1948), his first essay in this genre, and *Ondine* (1958) are two of his best known works. This lead has been followed by two other British choreographers, John Cranko and Kenneth MacMillan.

In postwar France, Roland Petit broke away from the Paris Opéra Ballet, producing ballets that were fresh, inventive, and dramatic. With his taste and tremendous showmanship, Petit pulled off vivid, sensual ballets, full of action and inventive lifts, as in *Carmen* (1949). Maurice Béjart brought *musique concrète* (music and other sounds electronically distorted and assembled into a time structure) into ballet to accompany his free, inventive use of movement.

The tradition of ballet in Russia, unbroken since 1738, survived the chaos of the Revolution, despite its previous close links with the tsarist court. The classical technique, preserved by such great teachers as Agrippina Vaganova, produced dancers physically strong, with supple spines and fluid arm movements. Choreography continued along the old traditions, untouched by the wave of new ideas engendered by Diaghilev. Despite some experimentation with Cubist ideas and modern themes (often aimed at poking fun at bourgeois capitalism), the full-length ballet treating heroic themes with a strong story line remained the framework. Staging and scenery were realistic, and effective use was made of folk dance to enrich the vocabulary. The influence of Konstantin Stanislavsky could be seen in the range of dramatic expression and the complete immersion of the dancers in their roles. Ballets were often epic in scale, as in Vasily Vainonen's *Flames of Paris* (1932), which told a story of the French Revolution. The greatest ballet of the Soviet regime was Leonid Lavrovsky's *Romeo and Juliet* (1940), produced on a sumptuous scale with every part of the story unfolding through eloquent, expressive choreography.

To an increasing degree in the 20th century, ballet choreography has been influenced by the modern dance developments in Europe and the United States, reaching the point at which modern dance and ballet techniques are studied side by side, and choreography freely uses both.

In Europe Rudolf Laban with his interest in movement on a wide scale liberated dance from any set vocabulary. His concern was not with training the instrument in a limited vocabulary but with the nature of movement itself, particularly its spatial and dynamic properties. In Laban and his followers, such as Mary Wigman, Harald Kreutzberg, and Kurt Jooss, lack of technique was compensated for by dynamic individuality and dramatic projection. Jooss and Sigurd Leeder developed a teaching method that stressed details of technique and control absent in the work at the Wigman school. As a choreographer, Jooss was more lyrical, more airborn, in contrast with Wigman's earthiness and predilection for movements on or close to the floor. Jooss's contribution to choreography was refinement in the complete telling of a complex story through movement alone. In his ballets the story flows on as uninterrupted narrative, total dance. His ballet *The Green Table* (1932) broke new ground in presenting a topical subject—the inevitable outbreak of war and its consequences—as a work of art.

In the United States, at the start of the century, Ruth St. Denis was a pioneer in dance based on ethnic forms. Though she did not study authentic dances of the countries she depicted, her innate understanding of inner content and style produced works of art that were accepted in those countries—in particular in India and Japan. Another aspect of her art, to which her partner Ted Shawn contributed, was the expression of religious themes. Shawn raised the status of male dancers through virile works choreographed for his men's groups.

On leaving Denishawn, Martha Graham found the need to develop a stronger, more disciplined technique. Focussing first on the spine, with movement emanating from the torso, she developed great control and strength, particularly in movements descending to and rising from the floor. From a simple, almost Amazonian technique, she evolved a highly refined style of dance that came to have a worldwide influence on the training of dancers as well as on choreography. A choreographer with a highly developed sense of form, Graham based her earlier works on Americana, as in *Frontier* (1935) and *Appalachian Spring* (1944). Later she portrayed the heroines of Greek tragedies, such as Medea, Jocasta, and Clytemnestra.

Finding a need similar to Graham's, Doris Humphrey, who, with Charles Weidman, left the Denishawn company in 1928, searched for a theory of movement suitable for her developing choreographic ideas. Seeking to rediscover the fundamental laws of motion, rhythms, and dynamics innate in human actions, she evolved a theory that dance movement exists on an arc which ranges from balance to imbalance. Her training technique developed clear-cut forms based on these principles.

Where Graham and Humphrey have contributed classic works in the modern style, a younger generation has broken through to experiment in new forms. Alwin Nikolais developed his own special genre in which he is total author, designing costumes, lights, decor, and props as well as the music and choreography. Focussing on a total blend of sound, colour, and movement, he uses dancers as an integral part of the whole rather than the focal point. The accompanying sound, usually electronic, blends perfectly with the visual action to produce a harmonious whole.

In breaking away from established theatrical dance forms, choreographers of the 1960s resorted to every possible device from motionless dance (four minutes of sitting still) to the freest happenings involving instant improvisation with any materials at hand. In freeing the mind from habitual forms, the computer has been resorted to, the juxtapositions of the items fed into the machine producing unusual and often effective results for which a master hand is still required to instill phrasing, dynamics, and kinetic logic. The most important name in this field is Merce Cunningham, who worked with the avant-garde composer John Cage.

DANCE NOTATION

Though dance notation dates from the late 15th century, it is only in the 20th century that it has become an integral part of dance comparable to the use of notation in music. Dance notation has been a separate subject, few dancers have been able to read and write, and few ballets have been recorded. Over the centuries, as each system of notation in turn fell into disuse, dances recorded in it lay forgotten, being resurrected only by a few specialists.

Until the mid-20th century, dancing—both the teaching heritage and choreographic works—was handed down by memory. Today, with the advent of highly developed systems of movement notation, dance technique is being analyzed and recorded as a classroom aid; dance-literate choreographers are recording ideas ahead of time, drafting the dance score in greater or lesser detail; and ballets are being reconstructed from scores, in many cases by those who have never seen the original work. Thus, dance is beginning to operate in a way similar to music, but the day is yet to come when it will be common for the dancer to be given his notated part and to arrive at the first rehearsal knowing the steps and sequences.

Notation systems. Through the centuries notation systems have included: abbreviations of the names of well-known steps; track drawings, the path across the floor with indication of steps used; visual image through stick figure drawings of a representational, stylized, or abstracted nature; music notation modified to describe direction and the parts of the body; abstract symbols or numbers, or both, representing the basic elements of movement. In describing movement, systems have concentrated on visual representation or on analysis of movement.

A highly developed system must allow not only a choice of description but also gradations in fineness of detail in use of parts of the body, time, direction, ebb and flow of energy, partner work, group movement, and the handling of props. A comprehensive and flexible system provides a means for research into movement of all kinds and a deeper understanding of precise performance of training exercises and subtle variations in performance. Until the mid-20th century, dance notation was used only as a memory aid. With increased use of film and videotapes to serve that function, notation's full potential is being discovered.

Historical developments. It is believed that the ancient Egyptians used hieroglyphs to represent dance movements and that the Romans employed a method of notation for gestures of formal greeting. The earliest manuscript known to be dance notation, however, dates from the late 15th century. In the Renaissance, the *basses* (low) *danses* were recorded through word abbreviations (R for *révérence*, b for branle, etc.), the steps being well known. Emphasis on floor pattern in the formal dances of the 17th century court ballets led to track drawing systems, the most highly developed of which was *Chorégraphie, ou l'art de décrire la danse* (1700; "Choreography, or the Art of Describing the Dance"), credited to Raoul Feuillet. Translated into several languages and with many collections of dances published, this system provided a rich record of the dance of that period, although many details of performance were not notated.

As ballet advanced technically, the Feuillet system was found inadequate, and ballet masters turned to systems based on stick-figure drawings, the first of these being *La Sténochorégraphie*, published in 1852 by the French dancer and choreographer Arthur Saint-Léon. This was followed by a similar though more highly developed system by Albert Zorn, balletmaster in Odessa, whose *Grammatik der Tanzkunst* ("Grammar of the Art of Dancing"), published in 1887, and in an English edition printed in Boston in 1905, was chiefly a book about ballet technique with exercises illustrated in the notation.

The principal disadvantage of a stick-figure system is the lack of accurate indication of continuity in movement and of timing in relationship of actions. This led to devices based on music notes, the element of time being common to dance and music. The first full-fledged system of this kind based on an anatomical analysis was by

Vladimir Stepanov, a dancer at the imperial Mariinsky Theatre (now Kirov State Academic Theatre of Opera and Ballet) in St. Petersburg. His book, *L'Alphabet des mouvements du corps humain (Alphabet of Movements of the Human Body)*, was published in Paris in 1892, and the system was included for a while in the curriculum of the St. Petersburg Imperial School of Ballet and was used to record some 30 ballets in the repertory, a few of which were later reconstructed from the scores for the Sadler's Wells Ballet.

20th century. In breaking away from classical traditions during the early part of the 20th century, dance came to include a far greater range of movement. To record this variety, a system of notation fundamentally applicable to all movement was needed. In England, Margaret Morris, whose interest in movement extended beyond dance into such fields as physical therapy, in 1928 brought out a system based on abstract symbols. In the same year Rudolf Laban published his abstract-symbol system *Kinetographie* in Vienna. In addition to dance, Laban's interest in movement encompassed theatre, sport, anthropology, physical therapy, and industry. The system he originated, known in the United States as Labanotation, was further developed by a number of people concerned with different fields of movement study. Though scientific in its approach to movement and encompassing a wide range in choice of description, the version in general use describes movement in human terms and makes use of conventions to write simply such complex actions as walking and jumping.

The advent of computers resulted in predominantly mathematical systems. That by Noa Eshkol and Abraham Wachmann, published in 1958, analyzes movement anatomically in terms of degrees of circular movement in a positive or negative direction, positions being determined according to two coordinates.

The desire in the dance world for a quick memory aid led to new systems based on visual representation. Outstanding among these was the system of Joan and Rudolf Benesh called choreology, which was adopted in 1955 by the Royal Ballet in London to record its ballets and

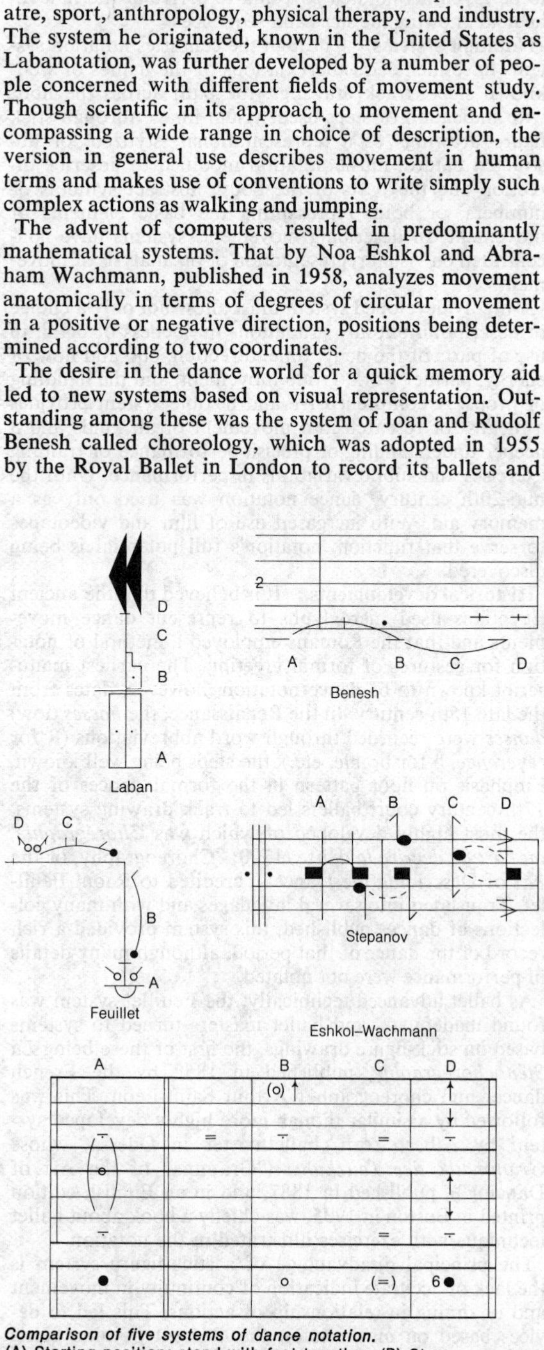

Margin note: Abstract-symbol system

subsequently modified for other types of movement. In the addition of a notator, the Royal Ballet set an example that was soon followed by other companies, and in 1960 the Institute of Choreology was founded to train notators and teachers in the Benesh system.

Personal use of notation by choreographers. The extent to which early choreographers made use of notation is not known. The early-18th-century collections of dances in the Feuillet system were probably recorded after they had become popular. In the 19th century neither Arthur Saint-Léon, who was a prolific choreographer, nor Albert Zorn used their systems as a creative tool. Nor was the system of Russian dancer, Vladimir Stepanov put to such a use, even though many of the Mariinsky Theatre ballets were recorded in it, thanks to the *régisseur's* knowledge of it.

Choreographers have, of course, often made their own notes, which are usually meaningless to others. Bournonville left some written records, which were an amalgamation of names of steps, verbal descriptions, stick figures, and floor plans, but these were a personal memory aid and cannot be considered as a system of notation. Manzotti recorded the floor plans of his spectacular ballets with specially devised symbols, and, more recently, Eugene Loring prepared schematic plans showing entrances and exits and the number of people on stage. Some choreographers work out their ballets in detail in advance but without using a system of notation. Only a choreographer fluent in a system of notation will record actual movement ideas or full sequence on paper, prior to rehearsals.

BIBLIOGRAPHY

Reference books: ANATOLE CHUJOY and P.W. MANCHESTER (eds.), *Dance Encyclopedia*, 2nd ed. rev. and enl. (1967); G.B.L. WILSON, *A Dictionary of Ballet*, 2nd ed. rev. (1961); C.W. BEAUMONT, *Complete Book of Ballets* (1937).

Historical studies: PETER BRINSON and PEGGY VAN PRAAGH, *The Choreographic Art* (1963); IVOR F. GUEST, *The Dancer's Heritage*, 4th ed. (1970); *The Romantic Ballet in England* (1954); and *The Romantic Ballet in Paris* (1966); MARGARET M. MCGOWAN, *L'Art du ballet de cour en France, 1581–1643* (1963); MARIE-FRANCOISE CHRISTOUT, *Le Ballet de cour de Louis XIV, 1643–1672* (1967); LINCOLN KIRSTEIN, *Movement and Metaphor* (1970).

Works on choreography: FABRITIO CAROSO, *Il ballarino* (1581; reprinted 1967); THOINOT ARBEAU, *Orchésographie* (1588; Eng. trans., *Orchesography*, 1925); CESARE NEGRI, *Le gratie d'amore* (1602); JEAN GEORGES NOVERRE, *Lettres sur la danse et sur les ballets*, rev. and enl. ed. (1803; Eng. trans., *Letters on Dancing and Ballets*, 1930); CARLO BLASIS, *Traité élémentaire, théorique, et pratique de l'art de la danse* (1820; Eng. trans., *The Art of Dancing*, 1830); SERGE LIFAR, *Traité de chorégraphie* (1952); MICHEL FOKINE, *Memoirs of a Ballet Master*, ed. by ANATOLE CHUJOY, trans. by VITALE FOKINE (1961); DORIS HUMPHREY, *The Art of Making Dances*, new ed. by B. POLLACK (1959); LA MERI, *Dance Composition* (1965); LOUIS HORST, *Pre-Classic Dance Forms* (1937), and *Modern Dance Forms in Relation to the Other Modern Arts* (1961); ELIZABETH R. HAYES, *Dance Composition and Production for High Schools and Colleges* (1955).

Dance notation: JUANA DE LABAN, "Introduction to Dance Notation," *Dance Index*, vol. 5, no. 4–5 (1946); DERRA DE MORODA, "Die Tanzschrift des 18 Jahrhunderts," *Maske und Kothurn*, 13:21–29 (1967); RAOUL FEUILLET, *Chorégraphie, ou l'art de décrire la danse* (1700); ARTHUR SAINT-LEON, *La Sténochorégraphie* (1852); FRIEDRICH ALBERT ZORN, *Grammatik der Tanzkunst* (1887); VLADIMIR I. STEPANOV, *L'Alphabet des mouvements du corps humain* (1892; Eng. trans., *Alphabet of Movements of the Human Body*, 1958); MARGARET MORRIS, *The Notation of Movement* (1928); ANN HUTCHINSON, *Labanotation: The System for Recording Movement*, 2nd ed. (1970); RUDOLF and JOAN BENESH, *An Introduction to Benesh Dance Notation* (1956); NOA ESHKOL and ABRAHAM WACHMANN, *Movement Notation* (1958).

(A.H.Gt.)

Comparison of five systems of dance notation.
(A) Starting position: stand with feet together. (B) Step forward on the right foot (count 1). (C) Spring into the air. (D) Land to the left, feet together, knees bent (count 2).

Chou En-lai

Chou En-lai (Pin-yin romanization Jou En-lai), who played a leading role in the Chinese Communist Party (CCP) from its beginnings in 1921, became one of the great negotiators of the 20th century and a master of policy implementation, with infinite capacity for details. He survived internecine purges, always managing to retain his position in the party leadership. He has been called affable, pragmatic, and persuasive.

Chou En-lai was born in 1898 to a gentry family in Huaian, Kiangsu Province. He was reared by his uncle in Shao-hsing, Chekiang Province, where he received his elementary education. He graduated from a well-known

P. Ramrakha—Pix

Chou En-lai.

middle school in Tientsin and went to Japan in 1917 for further studies. He returned to Tientsin in the wake of the student demonstrations in Peking that became known as the May Fourth Movement of 1919. He was active in student publications and agitation until arrested in 1920. After his release from jail that fall, he left for France under a work-and-study program. It was in France that Chou made a lifelong commitment to the Communist cause. He became an organizer for the CCP in Europe after its founding in Shanghai in July 1921.

Lifelong commitment to the Communist cause

In the summer of 1924 Chou returned to China and took part in the National Revolution, led by Sun Yat-sen's Kuomintang (KMT, or Nationalist Party) in Canton with CCP collaboration and Russian assistance. Chou was appointed deputy director of the political department of the Whampoa Military Academy, where Chiang Kai-shek was the commandant. Early in 1927 Chou became director of the military department of the CCP Central Committee.

When Chiang's troops were on the outskirts of Shanghai in March 1927, Chou organized the city's workers for massive armed strife. Chiang captured Shanghai and Nanking in April and purged the Communists. Chou escaped to Wu-han, the new centre of Communist power, where the CCP was still working closely with the left-KMT. There, in April 1927, during the party's Fifth National Congress, Chou was elected to the CCP Central Committee and to its Politburo.

In July 1927 the left-KMT split with the Communists. The latter went underground and staged their first armed revolt on August 1—celebrated thereafter as Army Day. Chou was a major planner of the event. The Communists captured Nanchang, Kiangsi, but had to abandon it several days later. Chou retreated to eastern Kwangtung and then escaped to Shanghai via Hong Kong.

In 1928 Chou went to Moscow for the Sixth National Congress of the CCP, held in June–July, and for about a year he was concurrently head of the party's organization department. The Sixth Congress of the Communist International (Comintern), held in Moscow immediately after the CCP congress, elected Chou as an alternate member of the Comintern's Executive Committee.

Later in 1928 Chou returned to China. The CCP centre, operating underground in Shanghai, continued to stress urban uprisings, but Communist attempts to seize major cities failed repeatedly, with great losses. In order to cor-

rect the party line, in April 1930 the Comintern summoned Chou to Moscow, where he was invited to address the 16th Congress of the Communist Party of the Soviet Union—an unprecedented honour for a Chinese Communist.

Back in Shanghai, in January 1931, Chou retained his place in the restructured party hierarchy, which was dominated by students who had returned from the Soviet Union. Later in that year he left Shanghai for Kiangsi, where Chu Teh and Mao Tse-tung had been developing Communist rural bases since 1928. In 1932 the party centre, under increasingly heavy police pressure in Shanghai, also moved to Kiangsi, and Chou succeeded Mao as the political commissar of the Red Army, commanded by Chu Teh.

On occasions during the Kiangsi period, Chou's relations with Mao appeared to be strained. Chiang Kai-shek's campaigns finally forced the Communists to retreat from Kiangsi and other Soviet areas in south central China in October 1934. During this Long March the CCP lost contact with Moscow. Mao gained control of the party apparatus at the Tsunyi Conference of January 1935; he also took over Chou's directorship of the Central Committee's military department. Chou thenceforth faithfully supported Mao's leadership in the party.

Strained relations with Mao

When the retreat ended in northwest China in October 1935, the Yenan period of the Chinese Communist movement began. For the next ten years Chou gained new prominence as the party's chief negotiator, spending much of the time in Nationalist territory as the Communist official representative.

Exploiting the growing national sentiment against Japanese aggression and carrying out Moscow's new so-called popular-front strategy against Fascism, the CCP in late 1935 proposed to unite with the KMT and all patriotic Chinese in order to resist Japan. When in December 1936 Chiang Kai-shek was arrested in Sian by his generals, who wanted to stop the CCP–KMT civil war, Chou immediately flew to the provincial capital of Shensi. When it became known that Moscow favoured the preservation of Chiang as the national leader to resist Japanese militarism, Chou helped obtain his release.

After the outbreak of the Sino-Japanese War in July 1937, the CCP once again formed a united front with the KMT, this time against Japanese invasion. The United States government urged closer KMT–CCP collaboration to help the Allied war effort, after the U.S. entry into the war in December 1941, and it tried to bring the two contending parties together after the war. Two weeks after the Japanese surrender in August 1945, Chou accompanied Mao Tse-tung to Chungking for peace talks with Chiang Kai-shek. When Mao returned to Yenan six weeks later, Chou remained in Chungking to continue the negotiations.

In December 1945 the American general George C. Marshall was sent as special U.S. envoy to China with the mission to mediate the Chinese civil war. Chou served with Marshall on the "Committee of Three" that worked out a cease-fire agreement, but the agreement was not successfully carried out. In Chungking and later in Nanking and Shanghai, Chou won over a group of Chinese intellectuals and politicians who had become disenchanted with the KMT and Chiang's government. Chou's success in carrying out the strategy of united front—now against the KMT government—was a crucial factor in Chiang's eventual downfall after the resumption of full-scale civil war in 1947.

As premier of the Peking government from the beginning of its establishment in October 1949, Chou became the chief administrator of the huge civil bureaucracy of the People's Republic of China. Serving concurrently as foreign minister (1949–58), he also bore heavy responsibilities in foreign affairs and continued to play a key role in diplomacy after relinquishing the post of foreign minister. At a Geneva Conference on Indochina in 1954, Chou made his debut in international conferences as a major diplomat. In April 1955 he scored a personal triumph at an Afro-Asian conference held at Bandung, Indonesia. An emergency trip to Poland and Hungary in

Premier of the Peking government

January 1957 marked the emergence of China's influence in eastern Europe. His first trip to Africa, in December 1964, signified Peking's increasing influence in that part of what came to be called the Third World. After the American envoy Henry A. Kissinger made a dramatic visit to him in Peking in July 1971, Chou's reputation as a diplomat and negotiator was widely noted by the American press.

Chou meanwhile maintained his leading position in the CCP. In 1956 he was elected one of the party's four vice chairmen. Although Lin Piao emerged after the Cultural Revolution of the late 1960s as the only vice chairman of the party, Chou remained the third-ranking member of the Standing Committee of the Politburo. During the Cultural Revolution he played a key role in exercising restraints on the extremists and was probably the single most important stabilizing factor. Avoiding any thrust for supreme personal power, he again came through the "intraparty struggle" unscathed and even unruffled.

Not a theorist, Chou produced no significant theoretical works and contributed little to Communist doctrine. Nevertheless, his voluminous speeches and reports after 1949 provide one of the richest available sources of basic data about China. He died in Peking on Jan. 8, 1976, of cancer.

Chou married Teng Ying-ch'ao in 1925; a student activist turned prominent party member in her own right, Teng was elected alternate member of the CCP Central Committee in 1945 and in 1956 became a full member. She too had a strong influence on the history of the Chinese Communist movement.

BIBLIOGRAPHY. Basic data on Chou En-lai is given in the *Biographic Dictionary of Chinese Communism, 1921–1965*, vol. 1, pp. 204–219 (1971). Two book-length biographies of uneven quality in English are KAI-YU HSU, *Chou En-lai: China's Gray Eminence* (1968); and LI TIEN-MIN, *Chou En-lai* (1970).

(C.-t.H.)

Christian IV of Denmark and Norway

Christian IV, king of Denmark and Norway, led two unsuccessful wars against Sweden and brought disaster upon his country by dragging it into the Thirty Years' War, but is remembered as one of the most popular of Danish kings. He energetically promoted trade and shipping, left a national heritage of fine buildings, and won repute as a plucky, hard-drinking man of grim wit and great resource.

The son of Frederick II of Denmark and Sophia of Mecklenburg, Christian IV was born at Frederiksborg Castle on April 12, 1577. He succeeded to the throne on the death of his father in 1588, but until his coronation in 1596 his country was governed by a regency of four members of the Rigsråd, the privy council, who also supervised his education. He was brought up as a Lutheran and studied Latin, French, Italian, and German as well as mathematics, navigation, drawing, military command, fencing, and dancing.

In 1597 he married Anna Catherine of Brandenburg, mother of his son and successor, Frederick III. She died in 1612, and three years later Christian married Kirsten Munk, a young Danish noblewoman, who remained his wife—bearing him 12 children—until 1630 when she committed adultery with a German count and was banished from the court.

After his coronation Christian succeeded in limiting the powers of the Rigsråd. He kept the most important offices vacant and surrounded himself with an entourage of aristocratic young officers and German officials drawn mainly from his dukedom of Holstein. The Rigsråd was opposed to a war against Sweden, but Christian threatened to declare war in his capacity as duke of Schleswig-Holstein, thus forcing the Rigsråd to sanction plans for a war (1611–13), with the aim of once more uniting Sweden with Denmark. Although Christian won the war, his victory remained essentially inconclusive.

After the war Christian centred his efforts on the economic development of his kingdom; he founded new towns, particularly ports to strengthen defenses, enlarged

Christian IV, oil painting by Pieter Isaacsz, 1612. In Frederiksborg Castle, Denmark.
By courtesy of Det Nationalhistoriske Museum paa Frederiksborg, Denmark

the royal shipyards, and built beautiful buildings and castles in and around Copenhagen. When the Protestant cause in northern Germany was endangered, in 1624, Christian entered the Thirty Years' War, again in opposition to his councillors. His aims were to protect Danish interests in northern Germany, to stop the Swedish king from playing a role in European politics, and to take up the legacy of his father and grandfather as the leading member of the Lutheran Church and its defender against expanding Catholicism. In 1625 he began operations against the Catholic League in Germany led by Tilly, the Bavarian commander in chief, who defeated him at Lutter am Barenberge on August 17, 1626. Tilly's and Wallenstein's troops next invaded and plundered Jutland, thus forcing Christian to form an alliance with the Swedish king Gustavus II Adolphus against the Catholics. After the Swedish–Danish army and fleet had forced Wallenstein to raise the siege of Stralsund, however, Christian severed the alliance and concluded a separate peace with the Holy Roman Emperor at Lübeck in May 1629. Though Christian's prestige and even his faith in himself as a great captain were diminished, he had not lost any lands. After the war he continued to try to impede Swedish progress in northern Germany and to maintain his rights in the Baltic and the North Sea. He repeatedly raised the shipping tolls through The Sound into the Baltic in order to augment his income independently of the Rigsråd, but he thus alienated his old allies, the sea powers of England and The Netherlands. With the help of The Netherlands, Sweden attacked Denmark in December 1643; and by the end of January 1644, Jutland was in their possession. Christian led the defense personally, blockading the Swedish ships for a time, and lost an eye in the naval battle of Kolberger Heide. Although this battle was inconclusive, the Danish fleet was later annihilated by the combined navies of Sweden and Holland, and Christian was compelled to conclude a humiliating peace in August 1645 which cost him possessions in the Baltic, Norway, and Scania. Throughout his reign the Rigsråd and the nobility had opposed his warlike policies and the ensuing strain on finances, and after this defeat even Christian's sons-in-law turned against him, forcing him to accept the increased power of the nobility. A bitter and broken man, Christian IV died at Copenhagen on February 28, 1648, 70 years of age, having ruled his kingdom for more than 50 years.

Christian IV was inclined to occupy himself with every minor detail of his administration while losing sight of the larger problems. Not only did he personally lay down the lines of Denmark's mercantilistic policy, he even es-

Thirty Years' War

Assessment

tablished the import duties; he started state-subsidized and privileged trading companies and manufactures—all of them with no marked success—and insisted on auditing their accounts personally. He founded a new academy for young noblemen, provided funds for the students at the university and built them a new college, personally examined the knowledge of Latin and the religious orthodoxy of the clergymen due for promotion, made designs for new types of guns and tested them himself, inspected the contents of the new arsenals, acted as a judge even in minor cases, and tried out the new ships of his navy. Christian was a great builder and founder of cities. He founded the towns of Kristiania (now Oslo) and Kristiansand in Norway; Kristianstad and Kristianopel in what is now Sweden; Christianshavn in Denmark; and Glückstadt (which was to compete with Hamburg) in Holstein. Evidence of his unremitting industry are his more than 3,000 handwritten letters still preserved, written in an imaginative and vivid Danish prose and teeming with orders and questions on all subjects from the eternal laws of God to the brewing of stronger beer.

BIBLIOGRAPHY. SVEND ELLEHOJ, *Christian 4.s tidsalder, 1596–1660* (1964), is the most recent work to present a view of 17th-century Danish history. The Danish biographical dictionary *Dansk Biografisk Leksikon*, vol. 5 (1934), contains an article on Christian. His holograph letters are published in C.F. BRICKA, J.A. FRIDERICIA, and J. SKOVGAARD (eds.), *Kong Christian den Fjerdes egenhaendige Breve*, 8 vol. (1887–1947). See also J.A. GADE, *Christian IV, King of Denmark and Norway* (1928).

(J.E.)

Christianity

Founded in the 1st century AD by Jesus of Nazareth (the Christ), Christianity has become the largest of the world's religions. Geographically the most widely diffused of all religions, it has a membership of over 1,000,000,000. Its largest groups are the Roman Catholic Church, the Eastern Orthodox churches, and the Protestant churches; in addition to these churches there are several independent churches of Eastern Christianity as well as numerous sects throughout the world.

This article is divided into the following sections:

I. The "essence of Christianity"

THEOLOGICAL DEVELOPMENTS OF THE CONCEPT

Early views. Because of widespread national, social, linguistic, and cultural differences within the early church, questions were raised from the church's very beginning about a common "essence of Christianity." De-

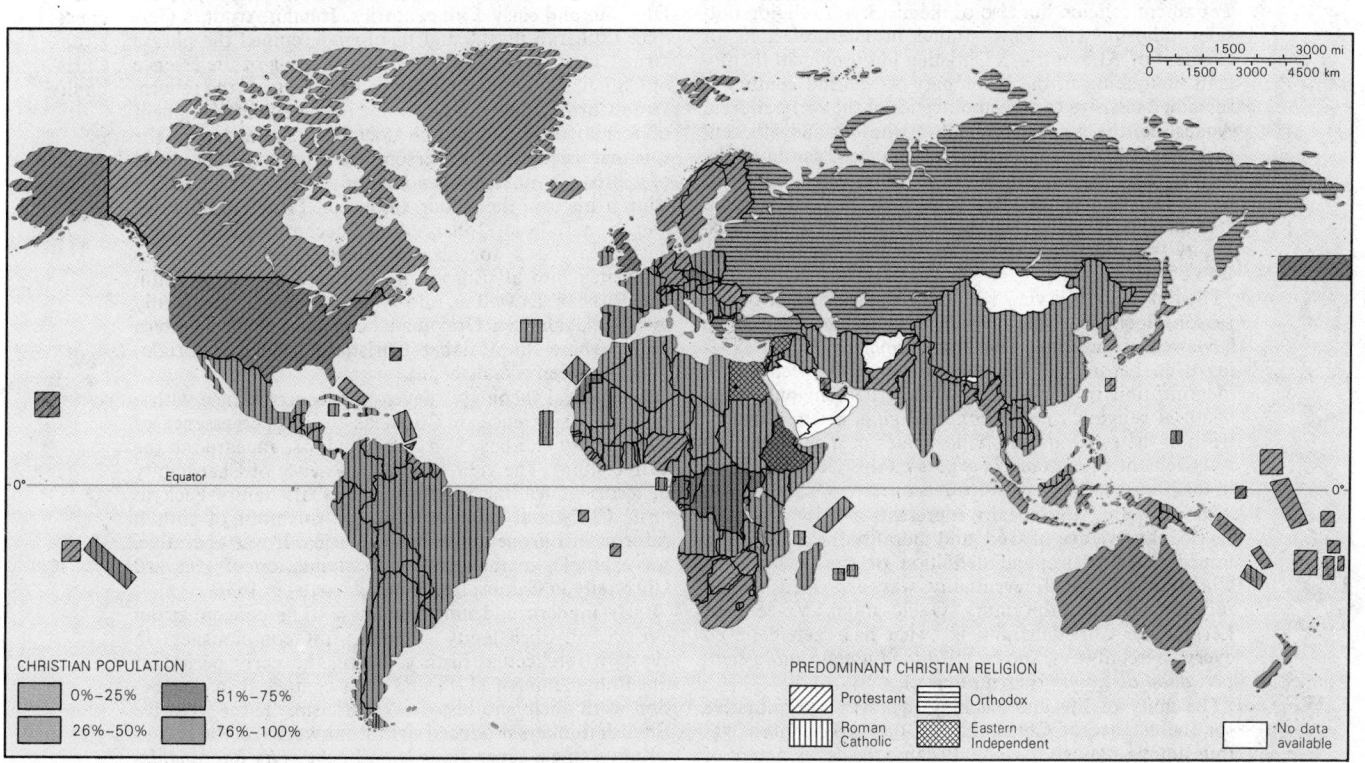

CHRISTIAN POPULATION
0%–25% 51%–75%
26%–50% 76%–100%

PREDOMINANT CHRISTIAN RELIGION
Protestant Orthodox
Roman Catholic Eastern Independent
No data available

World distribution of Christianity by country.

spite these differences, however, early Christians based their interpretations of the "essence of Christianity" on two basic principles: Christianity contained the one eternal truth and the one universal salvation.

The unity of the early church

The early Christians maintained that the unity of the early church, which exhibited a vast array of institutional, theological, and worship forms, consisted not of an external constitutional, dogmatic, and liturgical uniformity but of a "unity of the Spirit" maintained, as noted in the Bible in the Letter of Paul to the Ephesians, "in the bond of peace, . . . just as you were called to the one hope that belongs to your call, one Lord, one faith, one baptism, one God and Father of us all, who is above all and through all and in all."

The concept of "Christianity" (*Christianismos*), which denotes what is meant by "essence," does not appear in New Testament writings. Not until the time of the Apostolic Fathers (*i.e.*, the Christian thinkers of the late 1st and early 2nd centuries) was it used as a Christian parallel to the concept "Judaism" (*Ioudaïsmos*), which the Apostle Paul had used in his Letter to the Galatians, chapter 1, verse 13, to characterize the Jewish way of faith and life. The term Christianity was first used in such a manner by Ignatius, the bishop of Antioch (died *c.* AD 110), in his *Letter to the Magnesians.* Thus, the term Christianity is a rather late Christian neologism used to contrast the beliefs and way of life of Christians with that of both Jews of the synagogue and sectarian Jewish Christians (*i.e.*, Christians who wanted to retain the Mosaic Law).

The tendency toward intellectualizing the concept "Christianity"

From its first formulations, however, there inhered in the concept "Christianity" a certain tendency toward emphasizing the didactic, or theoretical, basis. Philo of Alexandria, a Jewish philosopher of the late 1st century BC and the early 1st century AD, had already interpreted the Jewish religion as "the true philosophy." A projection of this didactic and systematic principle appeared among the Christian Apologists, the intellectual defenders of the Christian faith of the 2nd and 3rd centuries. Though Justin Martyr, a mid-2nd-century philosopher and apologist, praised Christianity in terms of a "true philosophy," he interpreted philosophy as more than a correct manner of knowledge; it also included a correct way of life—*i.e.*, the right kind of morality.

Christianity, interpreted according to the didactic principle, was conceived as the fulfillment not only of Old Testament religion but also of the history of religion outside Judaism. This view—found in interpretations of Clement of Alexandria, a Christian philosophical theologian flourishing in the latter part of the 2nd century—remained decisive for the apologetics of the early church. Augustine, the great theologian of the 4th and 5th centuries, said that the Christian religion was "as old as the world," and earlier, in the 4th century, the church historian Eusebius of Caesarea called the Christian religion "the first, only, and true" religion, meaning that Christianity was inherent in the beliefs of man since the creation of the world.

The linking of this view with the Logos (Word, or divine reason) doctrine of the New Testament—in which Jesus is viewed as the active revelatory principle of God existing even before the creation of the world—led to an identification of Christianity ("the true religion") with "natural religion"; *i.e.*, rational religion, or the seeds of truth in the religions and philosophies outside Christianity. Clement of Alexandria expressed this view succinctly in the phrase "The river of truth is one."

The view that Christianity represents a unity of divine service, knowledge of God, and morality for a long time impeded the conceptual definition of the "essence of Christianity," which eventually was expressed in the formula of the 5th-century Gallic monk Vincent of Lérins: the Christian faith is "what has been believed everywhere, always, and by all" (*quod ubique, quod semper, quod ab omnibus creditum est*).

The unity of life and teaching that was determinative for the essence of Christianity in the early church was thus not maintained for long. Because the development of doctrine along the lines of "true" and "false" religion

involved relationships with numerous heretical groups and external critics, the earlier and less rigid concept of unity was displaced by a tendency toward uniformity in the theological definitions of orthodox church doctrines. According to the German theologian Adolf von Harnack, Christianity became Hellenized—*i.e.*, interpreted according to the categories of Greek philosophy—and theology became increasingly detached from its original relationship to liturgy and ethics.

The tendency toward uniformity in doctrine

Medieval and Reformation views. At the end of this didactic development, which led to the development of that medieval philosophical–theological movement that attempted to balance reason and revelation and was known as Scholasticism, came the Reformation of the 16th century, which viewed the essence of Christianity as grounded in "pure teaching." The unity of life and teaching of Christianity was thus dramatically torn asunder. The process of intellectualization of Christianity concluded in the different confessions of faith of the Protestant churches, as they were formulated in the course of the 16th and 17th centuries, as well as in the 16th-century Tridentine profession of faith of the Roman Catholic Church.

The question of the essence of Christianity was provoked in a special sense by the Reformation, which—in contrast to earlier reforms—led not to a reformation within the Catholic Church but rather to the emergence of a plurality of Protestant churches, each claiming to be the true church carrying on the tradition of the early church. Attempts at reunion forced these churches to reflect upon the possibility of a common faith that they believed the church of the first five centuries had maintained. If all innovations in faith, doctrine, polity, and worship could be reduced to the standards that formed the essential basis of the unity of the ancient church, they believed that reunion might be possible. Such a subsequent reduction, however, turned out to be unfeasible—because Reformation theologians initially restricted reflections upon the essence of Christianity to dogmatic concepts of doctrine. In spite of the constant polemics, Georg Calixtus (died 1656), an irenic German Lutheran theologian, tried to bring about an agreement on the common essence of Christianity on the basis of the formula "Unity in essentials, variety in nonessentials, charity in all things."

In reaction to the rationalistic dogmatic theology of the late 16th and early 17th centuries, Johann Arndt, a German Lutheran mystic and theologian, coined the phrase "true Christianity" as a new understanding of the essence of Christianity. As the spiritual Christianity of the reborn, "true Christianity" consisted not in the acknowledgment of formal orthodox church doctrines, but rather in the spiritual rebirth of a person according to the image of Christ. A unique phenomenon in post-Reformation church history, the "Four Books of True Christianity" (begun in 1606) by Johann Arndt became an ecumenical devotional book for all Christian confessions. It was translated into all European languages, including Latin and Russian, as well as into Arabic, Yiddish, and finally into Malayalam, a Dravidian language of southwestern India, where the Malabar Christians (of Syrian origin) had long been established.

The concept of "true Christianity"

A "mystical theology," developed in accordance with a personal experience of Christ as the proper essence of Christianity and based on Arndt's views, appeared in the 17th century. The view of Arndt's essence of Christianity in terms of leading a degenerated Christianity back to "true Christianity" became the central motif of church reforms in Europe and North America. It was operative, for example, in the articles of foundation of Harvard University in Cambridge, Massachusetts, in 1636.

Early modern and modern views. The concept of an essence of Christianity came to full consciousness in Western intellectual history during the early period of the Enlightenment (17th and 18th centuries) in connection with incipient historical criticism. Three creative English thinkers produced significant works on the matter within a single generation: John Locke, *The Reasonableness of Christianity* (1695); John Toland, *Christianity* not Mysterious (1696); and Matthew Tindal, *Christianity as Old as the Creation* (1730). At the basis of all these works lay the attempt of Enlightenment theology to demonstrate that the essence of Christianity is rational religion, which supposedly was present in all periods of church history. Johann Salomo Semler, an 18th-century German church historian and theologian, was the first to use the phrase "essence of Christianity" in connection with a distinction between private and public religion. He defined private religion as the spiritual-religious and moral life of an individual believer before God—as distinguished from theological dogmatic definitions of legally valid church creeds. In his view the essence of Christianity was, thus, in the area of private religion.

Whereas scholars during the Enlightenment had hoped to discover the essence of Christianity in a basic universal religious principle, Friedrich Schleiermacher, an 18th–19th-century German theologian, emphasized that what is essential in a religion can be discovered only in definite, concrete religion and only at a given time. Schleiermacher thus emphasized that the essence of Christianity cannot be understood as an abstraction apart from its historical form.

With the advent of the 19th and 20th centuries, in which historicism became increasingly important, the question of the essence of Christianity came to be posed as a purely historical question. This direction of scholarship—because its critical assumptions completely renounced the religious or spiritual state of "being inwardly grasped"—led to a total historical relativizing of Christianity. This developed especially after the attempt to ascertain the essence of Christianity through the "life of Jesus" investigations—beginning with the works of the 19th-century German scholar David Friederich Strauss—failed.

Adolf von Harnack's efforts to ascertain the essence of Christianity in terms of the history of dogma gave way to various views of the history of religions approach. In lectures published posthumously in 1932, Nathan Söderblom, a Swedish archbishop, emphasized two especially distinguishing characteristics of Christianity: first, the fact that what is new in Christianity is "not a message, not a teaching, but a historical person, a real human being, Jesus"; and second, the "barbarian idea" of viewing the "wretched fact" of the cross of Golgotha in the divine way of salvation. Also significant was a thesis of a German theologian, Ernst Troeltsch, in *The Absoluteness of Christianity* (1902), holding that Christianity does not need the ideological claim of absoluteness: with its message of the historical uniqueness of the revelation of God in Jesus Christ as the fundamental assumption concerning human salvation, Christianity holds that it can safely afford to enter into competition with the other world religions without suppressing genuine spiritual controversy with an initial ideological claim to absoluteness.

ETHICAL AND OTHER DEVELOPMENTS OF THE CONCEPT

Ethical and ecumenical views. The shifting of the view of the essence of Christianity to the dogmatic area and to systematic theology, as occurred in the medieval and Reformation periods, evoked a response in radical church circles. Such groups defined the essence of Christianity in ethical terms—*i.e.*, in a rejection of the "world" and in an emphatic renunciation of the entanglements in the "old aeon [world]." Since the time of the emergence of medieval moral reform sects and the appearance of radical anti-establishment sects in the Reformation period, Jesus' Sermon on the Mount in chapters 5–7 of Matthew has been taken to be the main guide for the faithful of the radical churches and sects. In the Sermon on the Mount there is an ecumenical aspect that appeals to Christians in a great number of churches, even including some movements (*e.g.*, Pietism) of the territorial (established state) churches of Lutheranism and Calvinism. This ecumenical aspect of the Sermon on the Mount, however, has been opposed by numerous churches. Lutheran and Reformed churches sometimes have held that the ethic of perfection of the Free Churches (*e.g.*, Methodists, Baptists, Congregationalists, and others) is a fun-

damental misunderstanding of the doctrine of justification, which teaches that man can never overcome the sinful condition in this life and thus reach a point of perfection. John Wesley, the 18th-century founder of Methodism who preached the ideal of perfection, was vigorously opposed by Anglican, Lutheran, and Presbyterian churches.

The historical catastrophes of the 19th and 20th centuries—especially the two world wars—helped to bring the question of the essence of Christianity into a new perspective and to renewed significance. In the ecumenical movement of the 20th century, different attempts to reflect upon the common essence of Christianity have been going on simultaneously. On the one side there has been an endeavour to view the essence of Christianity according to its ethic. On this basis, for example, Christian churches joined together, first in Edinburgh (1910), later in Stockholm (1925), in Life and Work conferences. Common ethical substance and activity alone, however, were recognized as not sufficient for the founding of a "pure" community. A formula of faith was also viewed as necessary; this need led to the foundation of the World Council of Churches in Amsterdam in 1948—which emphasized that the essence of Christianity consisted in the common prayer of Christendom: the Lord's Prayer (see also ECUMENISM).

The question of the essence of Christianity, because of historical circumstances, must be posed anew in every era.

Eschatological views. During the course of the 20th century, theology has endeavoured to determine the essence of Christianity from the eschatological (last times) character of the appearance of Jesus and his preaching of the inbreaking rule of God. Following the guidance of the 19th-century Danish philosopher Søren Kierkegaard, theologians holding this thesis have attempted a critical question: "How is Christian existence possible today within this world while sharing in culture, in its problems and blessings, in work as well as in pleasure?" The question of eschatological expectations, however, diverted concepts attempting to comprehend the essence of Christianity from critical existential understanding and rather led to a new understanding. In approximation to Marxist philosophy, the Christian message of the coming Kingdom of God was reduced more and more to the social-ethical and social-utopian contents of the expectation of the Kingdom of God. Along with faith in a personal God, faith in a hereafter was also given up. The Christian faith, according to both internal and external critics, thus became reduced to a principle of hope oriented toward a social-revolutionary program of Marxism. In view of this direction in reflection on the essence of Christianity in the 20th century, the words of Harnack about the Christian religion may still seem appropriate:

He already wounds it who primarily asks what it has achieved for culture and the progress of mankind and wants to accordingly determine its value. The meaning of life always unfolds only in the supra-worldly.

II. Historical background

According to chapter 28, verses 19–20, of the Gospel According to Matthew, Jesus left his disciples with the words

Go therefore and make disciples of all nations, baptizing them in the name of the Father and of the Son and of the Holy Spirit, teaching them to observe all that I have commanded you.

These words have been held to be the missionary commandment or commission of Jesus; he joined to them a universal promise—"Lo, I am with you always, to the close of the age"—thereby promising his disciples to be present in their universal work of salvation until the end of the world.

Not only Christianity but also all other great world religions have promulgated a similar universal salvation claim, along with a missionary consciousness and a global commission. Siddhārtha Gautama, the Buddha ("Enlightened One"), the 6th-century-BC founder of Buddhism, addressed his teachings not only to his fellow Indians but also to all people; Muḥammad, the 6th–7th-century-AD Arabian prophet and founder of Islām, proclaimed his law not only to his fellow tribesmen but also to mankind. Of all the world religions, however, only Christianity was established as a world religion in a total geographical sense.

The phenomenon becomes quite striking when it is recognized that this expansion all over the world (commissioned by Jesus about 2,000 years ago) took place primarily within the last three centuries. Numerous times in the first 1,500 years of Christian history it appeared as if Christianity would disappear.

The study of the process of expansion of Christianity has only quite recently (in the 20th century) undergone a broadly conceived, coherent, and scientific description. In 1902 Harnack wrote a work, later translated as *Mission and Expansion of Christianity in the First Three Centuries*. Scholarship in the history of Christian missions directed its attention beyond the territorial, nationalistic, and European boundaries of Christendom and took into view the total expanse of missions—thus eliminating national ecclesiastical and confessional biases. Between 1937 and 1945 Kenneth Scott Latourette, an American Church historian, published his seven-volume *History of the Expansion of Christianity*, the first great step toward a complete description of the history of the global expansion of Christianity.

The first five centuries

The first 500 years of Christianity represented the period that began with the appearance of the founder of the church, Jesus, and ended with the firm establishment of Christianity as the state religion of the Roman Empire. During this period the church gained acceptance in spite of initial and lengthy opposition from the pagan Roman Empire, and it initiated the first great wave of missions. Christian missionary activity not only made Christianity the prevailing religion in the Hellenistic (Greco-Roman) sphere of culture in the Mediterranean world but also in Syria, Egypt, North Africa, the lands around the Black Sea, Georgia, Armenia, the Persian Empire, Arabia, Abyssinia, and on the Malabar Coast of India.

The 6th–15th centuries

In the period between 500 and 1500, Christianity penetrated the Romance, Celtic, Germanic, and Slavic peoples and established the medieval Roman Catholic culture in the West. At the same time, however, this millennium was the period of Christianity's most stringent confinements. Geographically, the East—the old area of the expansion of Christianity—was lost to Islām and experienced the effects of Buddhist missionary activities. Only a few schismatic churches maintained themselves in isolation upon Asian and African soil. The Holy Land (Palestine), Syria, Asia Minor, North Africa, and parts of Spain were lost, and Sicily and southern Italy were threatened. The Russian Church existed under the control of the Khans of the Mongol and Turkic Golden Horde; and Islām threatened Europe from the west and the south. Assaults on the West by various non-Christian tribes—Avars, Huns, Mongols, and, finally, Turks—convulsed Christendom from the East.

In 1453 Constantinople, the seat of the Eastern Orthodox ecumenical patriarch, fell to the Turks. The Turks soon occupied Bulgaria, Moldavia, Walachia, Hungary, Serbia, and Greece. The borders of Christendom were further pressed inward. The eastern border shifted between the Elbe River and the Carpathian Mountains, the western border between the Pyrenees and the western Atlantic coast. The attempts of Franciscan missionary monks to extend missions to Islāmic peoples in North Africa, Syria, Egypt, and Palestine were not successful. The painstakingly achieved successes of the Crusades (mainly in the 11th–13th centuries), in which the Western counterthrust took place against an advancing Islām, soon became insignificant as defensive efforts. The late Middle Ages marked a low ebb in the history of the expansion of Christianity.

Even inwardly the church seemed near its end—it no longer had the strength for a common undertaking in foreign policy, like that of the Crusades. The popes squandered the financial resources of Christendom, which had been gathered to support the Crusades, on their own papal territories in Italy and on the splendid embellishment of Rome. The self-consciousness of the national states, which were beginning to develop, impeded undertakings in church solidarity. Christianity seemed about to become an insignificant religion confined mainly to parts of Europe. It was precisely this strong compression, however, that elicited an unexpected activation of the expansion of Christianity.

The 16th–20th centuries

After the period of the church's confinement because of the onslaughts of Islām, the self-reflection of the church upon its evangelical task, effected through the Reformation, first gave rise to a second great wave of expansion of Christianity—after a period of 1,000 years of uncertainty and threat. The Reformation not only led to the formation of reformed territorial churches (Anglican, Lutheran, and Reformed) and Free churches but it also provided an impetus for self-reflection and an internal strengthening of the Roman Catholic Church, which undertook vast missionary activities and a reformation in Roman Catholic areas. The expansion of the Roman Catholic Church ensued in the course of the Counter-Reformation under the leadership of the newly organized religious orders—especially the Jesuit order. An important result of the Reformation was the activation of a global expansion of the Roman Catholic Church.

Only later did the Protestant churches of the Reformation turn to missions. In a very short time, however, Protestant missions made up for the Roman Church's lead of 200 years. They introduced an era of expansion of Christianity that in intensity, methodology, and penetration of the peoples affected outstripped the missionary activities of the Roman Catholic Church, especially in North America and in the realms of the British Empire (*e.g.*, South Africa, East Africa, India, the Pacific Islands, New Zealand, and Australia).

From a European point of view, the 18th century, the century of the Enlightenment, was the era of the rationalistic dissolution of Christian dogma and of the beginning of anticlericalism, modern materialism, and atheism; from a global point of view, it was an era of increased expansion of Christianity. The Protestant missionary expansion ensued under the influence of Pietism (a chiefly Lutheran reform movement), Puritanism (a chiefly Calvinistic reform movement in English-speaking areas), and various other revival movements based on Calvinism. From Greenland to the Malabar Coast (in India), wide areas, previously outside the mainstream of Christianity, came within the sphere of influence of the Christian Church.

In the history of the expansion of Christianity, the 19th century has been called the "great century." Christian missions, in this third wave of expansion, succeeded in carrying the Christian Church to the remotest regions of the world. In the 20th century, Christian missions established, in the areas under their care, viable churches led by an indigenous clergy in independent church structures. These indigenous churches have created new types of Christian forms of life and community and have, to some extent, outgrown directions from foreign missionaries. (See also CHRISTIANITY BEFORE THE SCHISM OF 1054; EASTERN ORTHODOXY, HISTORY OF; EASTERN CHRISTIANITY, INDEPENDENT CHURCHES OF; ROMAN CATHOLICISM, HISTORY OF; REFORMATION; PROTESTANTISM, HISTORY OF; PIETISM; and ECUMENISM.)

III. Problems of self-definition

VIEWS ON THE UNITY OF THE CHURCH

Early views on the unity of the church. The self-understanding of the Christian Church has been a matter of intense interconfessional controversy. In individual Christian churches, orthodoxy of teaching, sacramental validity, and polity are all dependent upon their own conceptions of the essence of the church. The view of the unity of the church is most important for them.

The ecclesiology (doctrine of the church) of both the Roman Catholic and Eastern Orthodox churches creates the impression that the unity of the church had expressed itself from the very beginning in a constitutional and dogmatic uniformity. The New Testament, however, as well as early church tradition, indicates that at the beginning of church history there existed not uniformity but rather a multiplicity of concepts about the self-understanding of the Christian Church.

Multiplicity of concepts and forms in the early church

This multiplicity was manifested in the various forms of the church's external structures. In the original Jerusalem community, different kinds of church structure existed. First, there was leadership through James (Iakobos), the brother of the Lord, expressing the principle of linking religious leadership with the family of the founder in a way similar to that of the later Islāmic caliphate. The family principle was still noticeable after the execution of James. Several Jewish-Christian refugee churches in Transjordan (after the fall of Jerusalem in AD 70) were led by relatives (cousins) of the Lord. Second, there was a development of the pre-eminence of Peter, based on the fact that he was the first Apostle to witness the appearance of Jesus as the Resurrected One. Furthermore, there also were the three major Apostles—James, Peter, and John—all of whom were thought of as holding leading positions in the community; and the other Apostles, called by the Lord himself, who assumed positions of leadership.

The Diaspora churches (*i.e.*, those outside Palestine) also showed great differences in structure. Some apparently utilized the principle—appropriated from the Jewish synagogue—of leadership through elders, or presbyters; others were led by free charismatic, or spiritually influential, figures and prophets; and still others by prophets and elected leaders of the congregation (elders, or bishops).

The Apostles, who knew themselves to be authorized by their personal calling through the Lord, appointed bishops and apparently in this way promoted a monarchical church leadership. In the biblical Pastoral Letters (I and II Timothy and Titus) there are described congregations in which bishops and presbyters participate side by side in the church leadership. In a large community, such as Rome, there were several joint bishops.

The concept of the "body of Christ"

Thus—in view of the multiplicity of organizational forms—the unity of the church consisted not in the unity of its polity but rather in the fact that it understood itself as the body of Christ whose head was the living, resurrected Lord. The comparison of a state, a city, or a people with a "body" was also known to ancient political philosophy, but this idea had always been understood figuratively. What was decisively new in the Christian Church's self-understanding was that the inclusion of the faithful in the body of Christ was no longer understood figuratively but rather as real and sacramental. The faithful were believed to participate in his death and in his Resurrection. Together with him they form an undivided, living organism in which there is a mysterious relationship between the individual members that is guaranteed precisely because the resurrected Christ is the head of this body. Among the members of the church there exists not only an external relationship of common worship services and mutual care but also an internal relationship of vicarious suffering and sacrifice, of vicarious atonement.

Moreover, a decisive element of the inclusion of the faithful in the one body of Christ is the belief that physical death does not divide the community. The community of the living and the dead belong together in one body of Christ. The heavenly and the earthly church form a unity that is represented through the risen Lord; in the Eucharist the earthly is joined with the heavenly church in the presence of the resurrected Lord.

Tendencies toward organizational and constitutional unity. This "essential" unity also moved toward an organizational unity, which led to uniformity within the church. From the church's very beginning, different tendencies toward certain types of organizational and constitutional unity entered into a tension with certain tendencies that inclined toward diversity and differentiation.

Variety of tendencies that led to external unity

The tendencies that moved toward a constitutional and an organizational unification, toward a visible external representation of an internal unity, have been: controversies over charismatic leaders, controversies over heresy, persecution, eschatological expectations, and political factors.

The controversy over charismatic leaders. In opposition to itinerant prophets, who, like the Apostles, performed in the churches a function not restricted by region, an increasing exercise of the authority of elected local bishops and presbyters emerged. The monarchical office of bishop had come into prominence as the leading office quite early. The Apostles themselves had appointed bishops as their successors in the churches founded by them, and the large congregations of the early church pointed to episcopal lists of succession that began with the founding Apostles. Bishops not only supervised acts of charity in the congregation and administered the church's wealth but also led the worship services—especially the Eucharist—and instructed both initiates and the faithful. With the bishop lay decisions about the acceptance of a believer into the church, the use of church discipline, the believer's possible expulsion and "delivery unto Satan," readmittance, and judgment of his sins and the degree of punishment for their expiation. Hence, in the course of the 2nd century the episcopal form of polity was adopted relatively uniformly in the church, and charismatic church leadership was gradually suppressed.

The controversy over heresy. The common effort to resist dissenting interpretations of the Christian message led to a unification of teaching, liturgy, and polity. Dealing with heretical beliefs also led to the holding of provincial synods as the initial organs of a centralized church leadership, which was exercised by the bishops.

Persecution. Persecution also contributed to the unification of the church. Imperial laws enacted against the Christians assumed the unity of the Christian Church and its adherents as members of a *religio illicita* ("illegal religion"), and imperial authorities carried out uniform measures directed against bishops, the Scriptures, and individual believers. Persecution, however, strengthened a consciousness of the unity of the church among Christians, who mutually assisted each other through organizations concerned with aiding those arrested, imprisoned, and condemned to labour in the mines. Persecution also led to much necessary travelling by Christians to avoid the Roman law-enforcement officers and mobs, to the acceptance of refugees into local congregations outside regions of acute persecution, and to the formation of a very effective news network among Christians scattered in the various imperial and senatorial provinces (see also ROME, ANCIENT).

Eschatological expectation. Consciousness of the unification of the church during periods of persecution was especially promoted by apocalyptic expectations—based on the view that an intervention by God in history would be accompanied by dramatic, cataclysmic events. The common expectation of the early return of the Lord in glory produced a synchronism of apocalyptic expectation in all the churches of Christendom.

Political factors. The presence of a strong principle of unity in the Christian Church impressed the politically farsighted emperor Constantine in the early 4th century. The lack of success of state suppression against Christians in the Roman Empire was a deciding factor in his turning radically from the hitherto official existing policy of persecution and making the church's principle of unity the basis of the unity of the Roman Empire. Constantine recognized the political implications of the unity of the Christian Church, which had manifested itself victorious by the time of the end of the persecutions.

The influence of the principle of unity

The effects of the unification of church and state on the concept and implementation of unity. This produced a profound alteration in the very idea of the Christian Church: (1) the church was forced into the political boundaries of the Roman Empire, and (2) there was a radical dismantling of Christian apocalyptic expectations. In place of the expectation of the coming Kingdom of God, there emerged a triumphal mood within the church that henceforth understood itself to be an earthly institution allied with the state to maintain order.

The elevation of the Christian Church to the status of the imperial church thus contributed decisively to the final external unification of the church. The imperial church pressed toward elimination of pluralism in church life. The multiformity of church structures was replaced by a uniform episcopal constitution anchored in imperial law. In place of the multiplicity of creeds of the larger churches there appeared a uniform, imperial confession of faith (the Nicene Creed) that was enforced as the legally valid creed for all churches of the empire. A uniform, imperially sanctioned liturgy took the place of the multiplicity of liturgies in the large churches. Monasticism also was standardized in structure.

The levelling process, which a political principle of organization carried into the unity of the "mystical body" of Christ, led, in fact, to destruction of the unity of the church. The imperially unified church was delineated by the territorial boundaries of the Roman Empire. Missionary activity outside the area of the Roman Empire, involving the political sovereignty of the imperial church, thereby drove Christians who lived in Asian lands outside the empire into a national and political opposition to the Roman imperial church.

Destruction of the unity of the church

Unity of faith in the Christian Church came to be viewed as the bond of unity in the empire, and every deviation from orthodoxy—which was fixed through imperial synods—was regarded as a deviation from public order. All spiritual, theological controversies within the imperial church were thus subject to strict imperial laws against heresy. Minorities were threatened, and theological parties courted the favour of the emperor and political authorities in order to suppress theological opponents. There thus resulted an external unification of the church —but only within the borders of the direct sphere of influence of the Roman Empire.

An analogous occurrence of a politically forced levelling of the church was achieved in the 9th century in the Carolingian Empire at the time of the renewal of the idea of the Roman Empire within Germanic-Roman areas. In the Carolingian Empire the original church pluralism also was rigorously eliminated through a centralized imperial church, which linked the Frankish (Germanic) dominion to the Roman papacy. This church had pledged to the pope that it would introduce the Roman model of the church within the Carolingian Empire.

In monasticism, the Benedictine (Italian) form defeated the multiformity of monasticism that had existed in the orders of Celtic-Scotch-Irish origins and of Asia Minor origins. A uniform and imperial Roman liturgy replaced the multiformity of the French, Mozarabic (Spanish), and Ambrosian (the school of St. Ambrose of Milan) liturgies. All such types of unification were enforced by imperial councils.

The most striking attempt at a political guarantee for the unity of the Christian Church was carried out by Spanish, Portuguese, and French Roman Catholic missionaries during the conquest of the American continents in the 16th century. The kings of Portugal and Spain, who were also charged by the pope with the task of missions, prevented Protestant participation in the conquest of the new lands through strict laws. The New World, they claimed, should become and remain Catholic. A church multiformity had already emerged again at this time, however, because of the development of the various Reformation churches in Europe, and the Christianization of North America was achieved under the mark of confessional pluralism.

Standardization through a uniform church language

The tendency toward standardization of the church also was furthered through the use of a uniform church language in a church spread out over several peoples, linguistic areas, and political domains. Thus, the Latin language exercised an exceedingly strong unifying effect on the Roman Catholic Church from the 3rd century to the second Vatican Council (1962–65).

In a similar fashion, the expansion of the Eastern Roman imperial church ensued under the pre-eminence of the Greek language. When the patriarch of Constantinople received from the Ottoman Turkish sultan in the 15th century the assigned task of being the representative of all Orthodox Christians in the Turkish Empire, the Greek patriarchate attempted to set up a Greek cultural autonomy in the provinces of the Orthodox churches in Slavic-, Romanian-, and Arabic-speaking countries. This monop-

olization tendency initiated a fierce nationalistic struggle within the Orthodox Church and accelerated the formation of autocephalic, or self-governing, national churches in Serbia, Macedonia, and Bulgaria.

The Anglican Church, which as the English state church received a privileged position in the British Empire, utilized the English language, the language of *The Book of Common Prayer*, as a unifying church language that helped to link together the various colonies of the British world empire. English eventually established itself as the ecumenical church language in the World Council of Churches and broke the monopolistic position of Latin and Greek.

Tendencies toward organizational, national, and tribal multiformity. *Unity within multiformity.* Within the church from its very beginning—as has been noted— there was a perceptible tendency toward a unity of the church within a multiplicity of forms of doctrine, liturgy, and polity. The diversity of forms first appeared with the multiplicity of charismatic manifestations, which concerned not the natural gifts of the human mind but rather the spiritual, miraculous gifts of the miracles of the Kingdom of God (*e.g.*, healing, exorcism, prophecy, visions). Significantly, Paul used the idea of the church as the body of Christ to characterize the divergency of the gifts of the Spirit, not the divergency of offices within the church. Not until the *First Letter of Clement* (*c.* AD 95) was the organizational principle of the body brought together in such a way that the hierarchical organizational principle of the military was applied to the hierarchical structure of ecclesiastical offices.

Diversity of forms

Linguistic multiformity. The multiformity of charismatic manifestations was directly connected with the large number of languages used in the churches. The outpouring of the Spirit at Pentecost—recorded in the Acts of the Apostles—began with the significance of languages: the Diaspora Jews gathered on the streets of Jerusalem heard, each in his own language, the great deeds of God spoken by the Apostles, who were inspired to perform this miracle by the Holy Spirit. Accordingly, the missionary expansion of Christianity in the early church was accomplished under the aegis of linguistic multiformity.

From the period of the early church on, translation of the Bible and the liturgy into the respective vernacular languages was a significant linguistically creative act. Many of these languages, previously preliterary, for the first time were raised to the ranks of literary languages. The linguistically creative accomplishment of Christian world mission from its earliest period represents one of the greatest of Christianity's contributions to mankind's education and intellectual endeavours.

The translation of Holy Scripture into a vernacular language generally has been based upon the form of the language that was spoken at the time of the translation. Hence, the sacred language and the vernacular language initially corresponded to one another, and the translations of the Bible thus represented a linguistically creative enrichment of the living popular tongue. Use of the Scriptures in worship services, however, generally led to the development of a "sacred" church language that no longer was able to keep up with linguistic development. It rather has remained fixated upon the ancient substratum of the language from the period of the translation of the Scriptures (*e.g.*, Old Church Slavonic in the liturgy of some Eastern Orthodox churches, or the King James Version of the Bible in early 17th-century English). Translation of the Scriptures into popular languages thus is a never-ending task, which must continuously be carried out anew under new charismatic impulses.

Translations of the Bible into popular languages

Multiformity manifested in the voluntaristic principle. The strongest principle of individualization in the church has been shaped by the precept of voluntarism, which was the latest principle to develop. The ideal picture of a voluntary, personal conversion to Christianity, which has frequently been assumed to be the usual form of conversion, was only seldom true in the early church. Frequent conversions of an entire family as a unit, including house slaves (the *familia*), to Christianity occurred in the early church. Christianization also took place in the mass baptisms of entire tribes, such as the Goths, Franks, Anglo-Saxons, and Frisians.

Conversely, there were numerous instances in which Christianity was the representative religion of a foreign political power, against which tribes conducted a political struggle for freedom in the form of a defense of their old tribal religions. The pagan Saxons and Frisians, for example, resisted the Christian Frankish Empire, as did the smaller Slavic border tribes, such as the Wends, against the Christian missions of the German kings.

During the Reformation, the demand to form voluntary churches, as opposed to the principle of territorial churches, in Europe was not accomplished. Attempts of various left-wing (or "radical reform") groups— *e.g.*, Baptists, Mennonites, Schwärmer (fanatics), and Schwenkfelders—to organize themselves into voluntary churches were, in part, suppressed.

The realization of these attempts—accompanied by the death of many martyrs—first succeeded in the Netherlands during the wars of the Protestant Dissenters against the Spanish Catholic occupation forces in the 16th and early 17th centuries, and later in the English Revolution in the 17th century.

VIEWS ON THE HISTORY OF THE CHURCH

Characteristically, the self-definitions of the Christian churches can be distinguished not only according to their conceptions of the unity of the church but also according to their differing views on the history of the church. From the very beginning, two types opposed to one another appear: the first is based upon a view of the continuity of the Christian Church; the second is expressed in the idea of a corruption of original principles and in a demand for a return to the conditions of an idealized "original church."

The concept of continuity. The idea of continuity is directly connected with the formation of an institutional church and with the office of bishop. According to this view, the church is a divine institution that received its teaching and its polity from Jesus Christ himself. The divine-legal institution thus guarantees the continuous preservation of the divine truth entrusted to it within the flux of history. The pledge "I believe . . . in One, Holy, Catholic [Christian], and Apostolic Church" of the Nicene Creed includes a belief in the church as a divine-legal institution. This guarantees the inviolability of church teaching, which for its part is removed from the realm of history and thus knows no "development." The historical self-understanding of the Roman Catholic Church is determined by this idea of continuity and by appeals to the divine founding of the papacy: "You are Peter, and on this rock I will build my church." The Roman Catholic Church views this continuity to be guaranteed by an unbroken line of succession of the followers of Peter upon the Roman episcopal chair.

Similarly, the historical self-understanding of the Eastern Orthodox Church rests both upon the idea that the intact continuity of church teaching and polity is guaranteed by the apostolic succession of bishops and upon the idea of the continuity of church consciousness in the ecumenical synods. The Anglican Church, at least according to the view of its Anglo-Catholic wing, is based upon the continuity of the church as guaranteed through the office of bishop; the Reformation of the 16th century has been viewed by many Anglo-Catholics as an unhealthy disturbance of the apostolic continuity of the English Church.

The concept of discontinuity because of a corruption of original principles. Opposed to the foregoing concept are views of the self-understanding of the church held by the churches of the Reformation, the Free churches, and the sects, which see a far-reaching corruption of Christianity within the institutional church. The notion of corruption can be based upon the very institutionalization of the church itself, upon a deficient understanding of the disciples concerning the words of their master, or upon a decline of the original moral radicalness of the churches in adhering to the demands of

the gospel, especially the precepts of the Sermon on the Mount. Marcion, a 2nd-century heretic, asserted that Jesus' disciples themselves had misunderstood their master, had refashioned his teaching into the Jewish religion of the Law, and had thus corrupted his gospel. Tertullian's turning to the 2nd-century heretical prophetic and moralistic movement known as Montanism was based upon his contention that the church controlled by Rome had become corrupt by permitting a "second repentance" by mortal sinners.

Medieval heretical movements—*e.g.*, the Waldenses and Albigenses—held that the church became corrupted when it was transformed from a persecuted, suffering church in the first three centuries into a conquering imperial church during the Constantinian era. Luther applied the corruption idea to the Roman church of the 16th century and even called the pope the Antichrist, who established himself in the name of Christ upon the throne of his representative in Rome and from there took up his dominion over the church. The revolutionary currents of the Reformation, such as that of the German radical reformer Thomas Muntzer, also based their revolutionary activities upon the idea of ecclesiastical corruption. The corruption idea can be found in the views of the great spiritual and political leaders of the English Revolution, from Oliver Cromwell (died 1658) to the Fifth Monarchy Men (a radical Puritan sect), as well as among the Quakers and Baptists.

The idea of corruption in the church generally has been the basis of every notion of reformation. Those who hold this view believe that the ideal, perfect form of the Christian Church once indeed existed in the "original church," but that a corruption of this church later set in. The reformation task thus consists in reforming the degenerate church according to the image of the original church. This is the basis of every form of "primitivism" (*i.e.*, establishing the conditions that were dominant in the early church), which has been especially strong in the Pentecostal churches of the 20th century. The notions of corruption and primitivism, central to certain basic ideas of Western church history—*renovatio* (renovation), *reformatio* (reformation), *restitutio* (return to a former state)—occasionally are coupled with an emphatic antihistoricism.

Another form of reformational primitivism has attempted to demonstrate that the historical continuity of the church has existed even through periods of corruption, thereby maintaining the idea of the continuity of the church. This tendency has distinguished such reformers as Calvin and Luther from the primitivism of medieval sects.

The continuity and the corruption concepts occasionally complement one another. The Scottish Presbyterian Church, for example, holds to an apostolic succession of presbyters; the presbyterian church order is understood as the principle of order of the original church. According to this view, the Reformation brought about the reestablishment of this original principle of church polity, which had never completely ceased to exist.

Supporters of the Free Church idea viewed America as the "new world," the "wilderness," or the "desert" into which fled the "woman clothed with the sun" (as it had been recorded in chapter 12 of Revelation); *i.e.*, the true church pursued by the dragon of the state church. The American Free Church concept has been molded by the primitivistic idea of a new beginning of church history in a New World, in contrast to the corruption of the church of "Babel" in Europe. Such a primitivistic model of history has the disadvantage of viewing America solely on the basis of concepts of immigrants from Europe, who in the "wilderness" believed they were starting a new chapter in church history, unencumbered by the mistakes of the past. A further disadvantage of this understanding has been that the indigenous history of pre-Columbian America has been fundamentally ignored. The Mormons first tried to demonstrate the continuity of a specific history of salvation on the American continent. According to the Mormons, the "eternal gospel" was preserved throughout all the centuries of early American history

Concepts of continuity and corruption

The concept of corruption as the basis for reformations

Continuity and corruption as complementary concepts

until the appearance of the gospel in the revelation of the *Book of Mormon*. This revelatory book was given to the prophet Joseph Smith (died 1844), the founder of the Church of Jesus Christ of Latter-day Saints. The continuity between the history of salvation of the Old and New worlds, according to Mormon views, is based upon the belief that the original inhabitants of America go back to the Ten Lost Tribes of Israel, which supposedly emigrated from Palestine to America after the fall of the northern kingdom of Israel in the 8th century BC. In this way, a common genealogical root has been asserted for the development of the history of salvation upon the European, Asian, and American continents.

SPECIFIC PROBLEMS OF SELF-DEFINITION

The relationship to Judaism and the Old Testament revelation. *Continuity*. The relationship of Christianity to Judaism was a relationship of both continuity and discontinuity from the very beginning. Continuity was provided by the fact that: (1) Jesus was a Jew; (2) he apparently understood himself as the one who fulfilled the Old Testament promises of salvation about the coming of the messianic Son of man; and (3) this proclamation about him was believed by some of the Palestinian Jews, especially by those who had intense beliefs and expectations about the coming Messiah, such as the disciples of John the Baptist, a prophet and preacher of repentance. The miracles performed by Jesus, which linked the forgiveness of sins with the curing of illnesses and with the exorcism of demons, contributed to a reinforcement of a belief in Jesus as the one who fulfilled the Old Testament promises of salvation. Not only Jesus as the Christ (Messiah) but also the church formed about him were increasingly understood as the fulfillment of the Old Testament promises of salvation. Thus, the holy book of Judaism—the "Old Testament"—became the holy book of the Christian Church. Only gradually was the Jewish canon of Scriptures joined to a carefully selected collection of Christian writings—the "New Testament," whose authority was based upon its apostolic origin.

> **Jesus as the one who fulfilled Old Testament prophecies**

This development was strengthened by Christian missions that expanded, at first, among the synagogues of the Jewish Diaspora, whose missionary activities among non-Jews since the 1st century BC aided the Christian missionary endeavours. The connection with Judaism was further reinforced by the Jewish Christian churches utilizing the Jewish community organization: the presbytery (system of elders), the Holy Scriptures, and the synagogal forms of worship.

Discontinuity. Discontinuity arose because many did not accept that the fulfillment of the Old Testament promise of salvation came in the person of Jesus Christ. Even Jesus, who knew himself to be primarily sent "to the lost sheep of the house of Israel" (as he noted in Matthew, chapter 10, verse 6), had experienced this rejection. A surprising experience for Jesus was that non-Jews—including even members of the Roman army of occupation in Palestine, detested by the Jews both politically and religiously—did accept his message of salvation. In the synagogal communities in which the disciples of Jesus spread their message, many members of the *sebomenoi* (the "God-fearing" sympathizers) and proselytes—former pagans—especially showed themselves to be open to the message of Jesus.

> **Acceptance of Christianity by non-Jews**

The discontinuity finally centred on the question of adherence to the Law, which was decisive for Judaism. In the original Jewish Christian church two opposing views existed side by side: some demanded that converted pagans fully observe the Law, including the rite of circumcision; the so-called apostolic pillars (James, Peter, and John), however, were ready to concede to Paul and his missionary companion Barnabas that missions could be made to pagans and that converts would not have to adhere to the Law in pagan areas. Despite this agreement reached at an "apostolic council" in Jerusalem, however, Paul was exposed to Jewish–Christian countermissions in Galatia and Corinth.

The tension between continuity and discontinuity was expressed by Paul himself. According to Paul, it was not necessary that a believing Gentile become a Jew according to the rituals of the Mosaic Law in order to belong to the people of God, but Jews "according to the flesh" were still subject to the Mosaic traditions. For all men, the saving access to the God of Abraham, Isaac, and Jacob, who is the God and Father of Jesus Christ, was thus freed from the ritualistic and nationalistic "dividing wall" that previously had blocked the way to the Gentiles. Alongside the old Israel there now stands the new spiritual Israel—with both being grafted branches of the same tree.

The church of the 2nd century went through a distinct phase of separation from Judaism and liberation from its Jewish tradition. The main reason for the destruction of Jewish Christianity did not lie in the fact that Jerusalem finally succumbed in its struggle for freedom against Roman domination and that the conquest of Jerusalem by the Roman army under Titus led to the destruction of the Temple, the city, and the extermination and expulsion of its inhabitants. On the basis of prophetic predictions, numerous members of the Jewish Christian community had already left Jerusalem for safety in east Jordan (Pella).

> **Separation from Judaism**

In the Gospel According to John "the Jews," who demanded the crucifixion of Jesus although Pilate found "no crime in him" and "sought to release him," were in disrepute. The other Gospels also tend to excuse the Romans and to attribute the guilt for the death of Jesus to "the Jews." In the face of the assertion of Pilate that "I am innocent of this man's blood; see to it yourselves," the Jewish people exclaim, "His blood be on us and on our children!" (Matthew, chapter 27, verses 24–25). This cry was understood in the ecclesiastical interpretation of later centuries as a spontaneous confession of the collective guilt of the Jews for the death of Jesus.

Both Jewish and Gentile Christians diverged from each other, and both were responsible in this estrangement. Among the Gentile Christians, the idea of the newness of the Christian message of salvation was firmly established—*e.g.*, the "New Testament," the "new commandment," the "new life," the "new life of the Spirit," the "fresh dough," the "new creature," the "new man," the "new way," the "new song," the "speaking in new tongues," the "new Jerusalem," and the "new heaven and the new earth." Marcion, a mid-2nd-century anti-Jewish heretic, conscious of the newness of the Christian message, had promulgated a complete break with the Old Testament tradition and the God encountered therein, thus forcing the church to establish a canon of Scripture. Judaism, departing from its missionary enterprises in the 1st century AD again became a "people" and returned to its consciousness of exclusive election. The renewed consciousness of election by God caused the Jews to view the Christian interpretation of "Scripture" in terms of Christ and the church as presumptuous.

Judaism and Christianity were still identified as one religion in the 1st and 2nd centuries AD by the Roman authorities, who made no effort to distinguish between the two religions. They considered that the Christians were a Jewish sect and thus treated them rather badly because the Roman emperors thoroughly disliked the unruliness of the Jews, who constantly arose in rebellion against Roman supremacy. The Jewish religion in the Diaspora, however, was considered a *religio licita* ("licensed religion") with special rights—*e.g.*, the right to freely practice religious customs and the right to be exempt from participation in the emperor cult. Christianity, on the other hand, soon became a *religio illicita* ("illegal religion"); persecution of Christians was allowed and pursued precisely because they refused to perform the sacrifice to the emperor imposed upon them by law.

> **The concept of a legal religion**

The tensions between Christianity and Judaism stood out all the more after Christianity, under Constantine, was elevated to state religion. The Jewish religion still remained a *religio licita*, but in Palestine, Syria, and the West, Judaism came under the sway of the Christian state and became an object of Christian missions. Specific legislation against "heretics," who turned against the prevailing orthodoxy of the dominant imperial church, were likewise extended to the Jews. The legislation of the emperor Justinian (reigned 527–565)—Corpus Juris Civilis ("Body of Civil Law")—became authoritative for Christian legislation concerning Jews of the Middle Ages.

From the 6th century, Judaism in Europe was constantly subject to the various administrative, law-enforcement, and military measures against heretics and unbelievers during the period of the dominance of the Catholic Church. In the Merovingian (Frankish) realms the Jews were charged with guilt for the victories of the Islāmic armies over the Christians, because they, like the Muslims, denied the divinity of Christ. After the conversion of the Goths in Spain to Catholicism under King Recared (reigned 586–601), the rights of the Jews were greatly limited and their complete expulsion from the realms of the West Goths was planned. The Arabic conquest of the Iberian Peninsula was thus experienced by the Jews as a liberation.

Persecution of the Jews

That Jews and Muslims were placed by Christians in the same category had catastrophic results for Jews during the Crusades. In the first three Crusades (1096–99, 1147, late 12th century), organized and unorganized crusaders and mobs ravaged numerous Jewish ghettos in the bishoprics in the West and on the Rhine, as well as in Bohemia. This caused the great eastern migration of the German Jews toward Poland and Russia. The fourth Lateran Council (1215) prescribed special dress for the Jews and excluded them from public offices. The establishment of the Inquisition and its subordination to the Dominican order, founded by St. Dominic in the 13th century, brought a new wave of persecution because the order set as one of its goals the conversion of the Jews. The 15th-century Hussite wars in Bohemia and wars against the Turks likewise contributed to the persecution of Judaism: in 1450 a Franciscan monk, St. John of Capistrano, preached in southern and eastern Europe not only against the Turks but also against the Jews.

From its beginning the Christian Church viewed missions to the Jews as an obligation. In the Middle Ages these missions frequently took the form of violent conversions. The Inquisition, commissioned with Jewish missions, had both political and law-enforcement means at its disposal. Genuine spiritual debate, however, also occasionally occurred in public disputations between Jewish and Christian theologians. Though these debates were ordered by Christian state or ecclesiastical authorities, they nonetheless contributed to a better mutual understanding. In Spain, the church compelled mass conversions among the Jews, the Marranos (Hebrew *anusim*, "the forced ones"), under the jurisdiction and power of the Inquisition. After the unification of the kingdoms of Aragon and Castile under the two Spanish "Catholic kings," Ferdinand and Isabella, in 1469, and the subsequent conquest of the last Moorish (Muslim) dominion in Granada, there ensued a final expulsion of the Jews from Spain (1492) and Portugal (1497). Many Marranos also left Spain, finding refuge in Navarre, northern France, the Hanseatic towns (along the North Sea and the Baltic Sea), Italy, Greece, and Turkey.

Besides the violent conversions, mostly in the course of persecution, some individual Jews converted to Christianity for reasons of inner conviction. The Catholic Church in every century has recorded Jewish converts among its theologians and bishops.

Some such converts from Judaism, such as Johannes Pfefferkorn (15th–16th centuries), demanded the destruction of Jewish literature, and others attempted to deprive Jews of their social rights.

Modern anti-Semitism

In its most radical form, the discontinuity between Judaism and Christianity led to a fundamentally anti-Jewish attitude that promoted the rise of modern anti-Semitism. Anti-Semitism had its roots not in theology but in a racial doctrine that was supported by a pseudo-scientific transference of biological principles, such as the survival of the fittest, the doctrine of heredity, and the distinctions made between "higher" and "lower" races from the animal world to man. Modern anti-Semitism finally pursued a systematic extermination of the Jews under the hegemony of National Socialism in Germany. Although basically anti-Christian in attitude, National Socialism nonetheless partially appropriated traditional motifs of the ecclesiastical polemic against Judaism as a foundation for its anti-Semitic propaganda. Recognition of the extent of the crimes executed in the name of anti-Semitism later called forth in the Christian churches intensified reflection upon the inner connection between Judaism and Christianity. This in turn led to the creation in all countries of numerous institutions for "Jewish–Christian cooperation" in scholarly and practical areas, on national as well as international levels.

The quest for Jewish roots. Throughout all church history, however, Christian theology has continuously reached back to Jewish biblical scholarship, especially biblical commentaries and translations. Without a knowledge of the Old Testament scholarship of Alexandrian Judaism, the great biblical scholarly achievements of Origen in the 3rd century would not have occurred. His chief intention was to create a secure textual foundation for theological debate with Judaism. Jerome, the 4th-century author of the Latin Vulgate—which subsequently became the canonical text of the medieval church—learned Hebrew from a baptized Jew. Luther, in his German translation of the Old Testament, was likewise advised by Jewish rabbis. The history of Christian exegesis (critical interpretation) of the Old Testament is one of continuous contact with rabbinical exegetical literature. This reciprocal influence also extends to the New Testament. Whereas Judaism occupied itself only polemically with Jesus and early Christianity until its emancipation at the beginning of the 19th century, Jewish scholars in the 19th century began to investigate the genesis of Christianity, especially the figure of Jesus, in terms of agreement or contrast with the Jewish tradition.

Christianity's relationship to Jewish biblical scholarship

Jewish mysticism also exerted a continuous influence upon Christian mysticism in later centuries. The 15th–16th-century Jewish philosopher Judah Abrabanel (also known as Leone Ebreo) combined in his *Dialoghi di amore* ("Dialogues of Love") the mysticism of love of Italian Neoplatonism with the mysticism of the Jewish Kabbala (a mystical tradition) and thus had a great influence upon Christian Baroque mysticism. The Christian Kabbala also represents an especially striking form of the influence of Jewish mysticism. Johannes Reuchlin, a 15th–16th-century German Humanist, became the most significant spokesman for a Christian Kabbala. The *Kabbala Denudata* ("Kabbala Uncovered") by a 17th-century knight, Christian Knorr von Rosenroth, then became an important source of inspiration for radical Pietism (primarily a Lutheran reform movement), particularly for its separatist mystical groups. This direct influence of Jewish mysticism upon Christian piety—from the theosophy of the 18th-century German thinker Friedrich Christoph Oetinger to the metaphysical (nature of reality) thought of the 19th-century German philosopher Friedrich Schelling—has been continued in the 20th century by the Jewish thinkers Leo Baeck and Martin Buber.

Jewish influence on Christian mysticism

The emancipation of Judaism from its ghetto conditions and mentality in the 18th century fundamentally altered the relationship between Christianity and Judaism. After the conferment of civil rights upon Jewish citizens in France by the National Assembly in 1791, and after corresponding legislative steps in other European countries, the characteristic of the Jews as a "nation" was diminished and that of a confession was enhanced. Many Jews viewed the emancipation as an occasion for spontaneous conversions to Christian churches; the Protestant churches, which were considered more liberal, were preferred. Typical was the religious development of the father of Karl Marx, who found an inner connection with the evangelical church of the Rhineland by way of the thought of the great German philosopher Immanuel Kant. On the other hand, Judaism, having become a religious confessional group again, began to develop a missionary consciousness.

The relation to Greece. The encounter of Christianity with Hellenism (Greek culture) became the model, or paradigm, of debate and discussions with high cultures, which were repeated later with other cultures, such as those of India and China. In the 20th century such debates have occurred on a global scale in the sphere of Christian world missions.

The Christian encounter with Hellenism
The influx of the Greek spirit and the connection of the gospel with it was the most significant happening in Christianity of the 2nd century and in succeeding centuries. The process of Hellenization, however, was not limited just to dogma but included other aspects of church activities—*e.g.*, liturgy, polity, ethics, mysticism, and ecclesiastical art, symbolism, and iconography. Late Judaism, like early Christianity, had gone through an intensive process of Hellenization. Philo of Alexandria had introduced the Greek concept of the Logos (Word) into Old Testament theology. He identified the Lord (Kyrios) of the Old Testament with world reason, the principle of order of the cosmos. Christian Apologists in the 2nd and 3rd centuries did not introduce the Greek concept of the Logos into theology but rather identified the Logos with the Messiah–Son of man, who became human in Jesus Christ. This identification of the Logos with the historical form of Jesus Christ became the point at which Greek philosophy fused with the apostolic heritage, and it brought Christianity into Greek culture.

The process was not, on the surface, apparent. Paul had stressed the contrast between the "foolishness" of the gospel and the "wisdom of the world"; he underlined especially the fact that the gospel is "folly to Gentiles" (as noted in I Corinthians, chapter 1, verse 23). Nonetheless, even Paul displayed signs of Hellenistic emphases that were in accordance with the rabbinic traditions of his Jerusalem teacher, and especially used Stoic Greek philosophical terminology that emphasized moderation.

The discovery that the Logos, world reason itself, appeared among men in the form of Jesus Christ exerted a fascinating effect upon the Hellenistic cultural world. Christianity viewed its prehistory as no longer restricted to the Old Testament history of salvation but rather as a part of universal history. The history of Christianity became identical with the history of religion and ideas itself: Christianity was viewed as the universal religion that was as old as the world; it was and is the "religion of Adam." Christians emphasized that throughout the history of the world the Logos has been manifest in ever new forms among all peoples, expressed as the "seminal Logos" (*logos spermatikos*) in all religions and philosophical systems. In Christ, however, the Logos first achieved its full form and appeared as the teacher of the true philosophy among men.

This idea was expanded among the Apologists and especially among the leaders of the catechetical school of Alexandria, who, in that great centre of Hellenistic culture, fostered debates with the Greek spiritual tradition. Clement of Alexandria included among the witnesses to the Logos not only Socrates and Plato but also philosophers and religious thinkers among the Persians, Indians, and Egyptians. In ancient church icons, the Greek philosophers Socrates and Plato are found in the succession of the redeemed, righteous ones whom Christ leads forth from the underworld upon his storming of Hades.

The penetration of the Greek intellectual tradition into Christian thought
The Greek intellectual tradition penetrated into Christian thought—*e.g.*, Platonism, with its idealistic interpretation of reality; Aristotelianism, with its realistic doctrine of being and knowledge; and Stoicism, with its cosmology and ethics. Hellenistic mystery religions and mystery philosophy also exerted an influence upon the formation of Christian liturgy and hymnology. In the controversy between the schools of theology of Alexandria (symbolical) and Antioch (literalistic and historical), the tension between the Neoplatonic tradition of Alexandria and the Aristotelian tradition of Antioch was discharged.

The process of Hellenization was achieved in a powerful and dramatic dialectic. After the victory of Christianity as the state church in the Roman Empire, pagan academies and universities were closed in connection with the tumultuous destruction of pagan temples, and the leaders of the pagan schools of Athens, Alexandria, and Antioch moved to Syria and Persia. Invasions by Germanic tribes, continuing into the 5th century, also led to a reduced pagan (Hellenistic) educational system in the West.

Christianity's encounter with Greek culture became a model case for analogous encounters with other high cultures and their religions in later centuries; *e.g.*, China (Confucianism and Taoism), India (Hinduism), and Japan (Buddhism and Shintō). The translation of the works of Confucius by a French Jesuit, Philippe Couplé (1587), initiated a renewed reflection upon the Logos theology of the Apologists of the early church. The discovery that a powerful empire in China had existed for more than two millennia upon the foundations of an ethic that was so closely related to the "natural ethics" of Christianity appeared as a new and surprising confirmation of the concept of a divine Logos that has manifested itself in all peoples—and not just among those connected with the revelation initiated in the Old Testament tradition. The doctrine of "natural revelation" and of "natural religion" —as found in the works of the Enlightenment philosophers (*e.g.*, Gottfried Wilhelm Leibniz in Germany and John Locke in England)—was influenced by a renewal of interest in the early church's teaching of the "seminal Logos" that had been stimulated by the discovery of the Asian high religions.

Renewed reflection of the Logos theology

During the Renaissance of the 16th century the early Christian heritage was rediscovered along with the pre-Christian Greek intellectual tradition. A German Lutheran Humanist, Philipp Melanchthon, who through his preference for the original Greek text of Aristotle created the basis for a Protestant Neoscholasticism in the sphere of Lutheran orthodoxy, also newly edited numerous works of the early Church Fathers. The Dutch Humanist Erasmus, with his edition of the Greek New Testament, created the foundation for a fresh exegesis of the New Testament.

Based upon Christian humanism—which cultivated studies of both pre-Christian Greek classical literature and Christian Greek literature—attempts at overcoming confessional strife were made by such men as an irenic German theologian, Georg Calixtus, who outlined a program of union upon the basis of the common tradition of the first five centuries ("*consensus quinquesaecularis*") of church history.

A reaction against Christian humanism from the 17th century on ensued among groups that were opposed to the view that the spiritual values of pre-Christianity and Hellenism threatened to de-emphasize or eliminate specifically Christian perspectives of faith, ethical teachings, and forms of life. Such reactions were found in German Pietism, with its attacks upon "Platonic Christianity," and in the educational programs of several radical, revivalistic Free Churches. Dialectical theology, following the teachings of the Danish philosopher Søren Kierkegaard, also endeavoured to emphasize the discontinuity between the message of the gospel and the Hellenistic cultural tradition.

Reactions against Christian humanism

The relation to the Roman state and, by extension, to all states. The early Christian Church passed through several stages in its relationship to the Roman state. These stages, in general, represent a model of the church's relationship with the other states.

The pagan Roman state. Christians of the first three centuries turned decisively against the state religion of Rome, with its cultic rites officiated or governed by state officials, and its priestly functions associated with certain state offices. For Christians, the chief offense lay in the emperor cult, which at first consisted of a cultic veneration of the spirit (*genius*) of the imperial house. Soon, however, the cult stressed the divine worship of the person, or the image, of the ruler. Christians viewed themselves as citizens of the coming heavenly city and as pilgrims and strangers on earth, whose fatherland is in heaven. They also viewed themselves as already set apart, as members of the Kingdom of God, as the "third race," beyond Jews and Gentiles, which was dissolving its ties to this passing world and thereby also to the political order.

Rejection of the emperor cult

Attitudes toward the state were thus ambivalent. On the one hand, the state authorities had been granted a mandate by God to maintain order, which Christians must respect (as Paul required in Romans, chapter 13). On the other hand, the state belongs to "this world," whose "form is passing away" (which Paul noted in I Corinthians, chapter 7, verse 31). In addition to this, the saying of Jesus, "Render therefore to Caesar the things that are Caesar's, and to God the things that are God's" (as recorded in Matthew, chapter 22, verse 21), had an ironic ring: give Caesar the taxes he demands (*i.e.*, the money that bears his image) and "render to God the things that are God's"—namely oneself.

The Roman state and Roman society reacted to these attitudes of Christians with social and political defamation. Christians were considered "godless" (*atheoi*), because their religion could not be fitted into the politically sanctioned pagan religious system and was therefore "illegal." At the same time their cult, which appeared to be analogous to other mystery cults, was morally defamed: the Eucharist was denounced as cannibalism.

The church as a political threat

The Christian community—which was rapidly expanding numerically—became a political threat to the authorities, and official countermeasures resulted. Each individual citizen, as a sign of state loyalty, was required by statutory decree to perform sacrifice before the emperor's image. Christians refused to do so, and the resulting persecution drove them into open opposition to the state. State representatives, on the one hand, developed a persecution psychosis; many Christians, on the other hand, developed a martyr's psychosis, which frequently provoked state authorities. The period of persecution of Christians by the Roman emperors of the 2nd and 3rd centuries was the classical period of Christian martyr-heroism. Confronted with the readiness of members of a religious community for martyrdom—an utterly new phenomenon in the Roman Empire—state officials were perplexed. Initially, vigorous action with radical persecutory measures (*e.g.*, public execution, condemnation to death in the arena, punitive labour in the mines, confiscation of property, and banishment) was attempted. The psychological effects of the numerous martyrdoms upon the public were not noticed by the authorities in terms of their political consequences.

Only in later centuries did anti-Christian states profit from the classical persecutions of Christians in the Roman imperial period. In the 20th century, the Soviet Union and Hitler's Germany, in their measures directed against the church, avoided as much as possible the creation of opportunities for public martyrdoms; instead, they shifted the persecution of Christians to the taciturnity of prisons and concentration camps.

Constantine, in the early 4th century, was the first Roman emperor who recognized the church's resistance against a pagan Roman state established upon the ruler cult as a political factor. Drawing political conclusions from the strength of the church's resistance, he ended the persecution of the church and made it itself the basis for the spiritual unity of the Roman Empire. The church thereby became the partner of the Christian state; this partnership (*harmonia, symphōnia*) became one of the foundations of the Christian empire—first in the Byzantine Empire (4th–15th centuries), then in the Carolingian (8th–9th centuries), and then in the medieval Holy Roman Empire of the German nation that lasted until Napoleon dissolved the imperial unity in 1806.

The three Romes: Rome, Byzantium, and Moscow. In the perspective of the Western church (*i.e.*, Roman Catholic) history, Byzantium appears as the metropolis of the Eastern Roman Empire. It did not submit to Roman papal primacy, and dogmatically and liturgically it entered upon a separate development. According to the historical self-understanding of the Byzantines, on the

The concept of the "new Rome"

other hand, the history of Byzantium, the "new Rome," designates the continuity with, as well as the distinction from, the old Rome. The new Rome was the bearer of the entire fullness of power of the old Rome, but at the same time it was Christian Rome, which actualized the claim to power of the Roman Empire according to the law of Christ.

Constantine attempted to establish Byzantium as the "second Rome"; *i.e.*, as the second capital of the empire. The second Rome, however, quickly became a new

Rome. Contributing to the latter concept was the fact that old Rome was conquered by the Germans. The old Rome was thereby eliminated as a political and administrative centre. The second Rome, Byzantium, became the new Rome, which succeeded to the power and stature of the old Rome. The imperial Council of Constantinople in 381 officially confirmed Byzantium as the new Rome. Byzantium, according to this view of history, was the new, young, and vigorous Rome in contrast to the aging, senile, and moribund Rome of the West.

The delineation of the new Rome vis-à-vis the old Rome was strengthened by two further factors. The Roman popes used the period of political confusion during the popular migrations upon Italian soil both (1) to extend—as their powers permitted—their ecclesiastical claim to dominion, which was henceforth no longer limited by the presence of an emperor; and (2) to raise as well a claim to political leadership in the West.

The pope as leader of the old Rome

The pope, as the leader of the old Rome, engaged in a political coalition with the enemies of the empire—the rulers of the Frankish kingdom. He presumed, on his own authority, to confer the title of emperor upon a Germanic barbarian prince, the Carolingian Charles, although the imperial throne of the Roman Empire in Byzantium was occupied by a legitimate representative. From the Byzantine perspective, the developments in the West appeared as a common rebellion of the bishop of Rome and the western barbarian kings, who reciprocally imparted to themselves power positions and legal titles to which they could lay no legitimate claims. For the first time, the idea of renovation in Byzantium was further developed into the notion of the transfer of the empire from the old to the new Rome.

Until the 9th century, the Byzantine church held fast to its position of equality with the Roman See. The Byzantine patriarch Photius (858–867 and 877–886) tried to denigrate the Roman claims to primacy, arguing that the bishop of Rome had fallen away from the faith and had thereby lost his position of pre-eminence to the see of Constantinople. On the basis of the canon of the Council of Chalcedon (451), the church of Constantinople assumed the privileges of Rome. The Byzantine church asserted that it had been founded by the "first-called" Apostle, Andrew, who was called as an Apostle by the Lord before Peter (claimed by the Romans to be the first bishop of Rome) and for his part first led his brother Peter to the Lord.

In 1453 the new Rome on the Bosporus (Constantinople) fell to the Turks. The Byzantine concept of Rome, however, was not thereby extinguished. The Russian princes of Moscow took over its basic concepts and claims. Russian historical and ecclesiastical consciousness unfolded upon the basis of the idea of Moscow as the "third

Moscow as the "third Rome"

Rome." After Hagia Sophia (the Church of Holy Wisdom)—the spiritual and liturgical centre of the Byzantine imperial church—became a Muslim mosque, the grand duchy of Moscow remained as the last politically independent Eastern Orthodox power, and Russian national and ecclesiastical self-consciousness received an exceptional impetus. The political claim of the Roman world empire as well as the spiritual claim of the Byzantine imperial church were assumed by the Muscovite realm and the Muscovite church. Ivan III in the latter part of the 15th century introduced the two-headed Byzantine imperial eagle into the official Russian coat of arms and assumed the title "Tsar [Caesar] of Russia." The city of Moscow became the new Byzantium, the third Rome. When the tsardom collapsed with the outbreak of the Bolshevik Revolution in 1917, in the midst of the chaos of revolution and the severe church persecutions, the Russian Church revived its patriarchal polity (dismantled by Peter the Great in the 18th century) despite the initially intense resistance of the Bolshevik government against the church and its representative, the patriarch Tikhon.

The relation to the "world." *Christians as distinct from the "world."* Viewed externally, the attitudes of Christians toward the world seem extremely contradictory; viewed internally, they express the characteristic metamorphosis that Christianity passed through in its beginnings and continues to do so in reform movements. In the early period, when Christians believed the coming Kingdom of God to be imminent, their basic attitude to the "world" embodied the view that they were radically distinct from the world. Through the sacrament of Baptism and through the forgiveness of sins, the believing Christian knew himself to be transposed into a new life of godliness that was fundamentally different from the life of the old "world."

In practical terms, the Christian was freed from a series of customs and institutions of the life of the old pagan world. Meat markets, for example, were to a large extent connected with the pagan temples where animal sacrifices were made. Many Christians thus questioned whether or not they should eat "food offered to idols." Christians likewise dissociated themselves from the theatre, the subject of which often was pagan mythology, and from wide areas of pagan art and literature, which similarly exalted pagan myth. They often dissociated themselves from military service, which contained regulations closely connected with the emperor cult; from gymnasium sporting events, which took place in a pagan cultic milieu; and from public bathing establishments. They likewise rejected pagan prostitution, the sex culture of the pagan world, and its many manifestations of degeneration. Other pagan activities, customs, and institutions shunned by Christians were: the circus, with its pornographic performances; gladiatorial fights, in which the defeated were killed in the arena; the theatre; sexual exploitation of female slaves, which—through household slavery—reached into the individual homes; ecstatic dances practiced in the pagan cults; ecstatic music; the use of drugs and narcotics; polygamy and divorce; and gluttony, intemperance, and luxury in clothing. Christians thus set their own resolute and distinct style of life over against the various forms of cultural existence of their pagan environment.

Throughout church history many Christians have found ever new ways of establishing their own distinct style of life over against "the world": avoidance of certain professions (*e.g.*, the military, through conscientious objection; the judicial; brothel keeping); avoidance of certain institutions and cultural forms (*e.g.*, theatre, ballet, to some extent the cinema and television, and obscene and pornographic literature); nonsmoking; avoidance of alcohol or of certain foods (*e.g.*, blood sausage by the Mennonites); and the avoidance of certain clothing fashions interpreted as luxurious and immoral.

Other means by which some Christians distinguish themselves from "the world" have been the struggle against governmental insistence on passports and the stamps of official authorities, including the post office (*e.g.*, stamps, interpreted as the "mark of the beast" among the Russian Old Believers, a schismatic sect); the struggle against forms of politeness (*e.g.*, Quakers refusing to take off their hats before those who are higher placed, because "all men are equal"); and the rejection of shaving. According to the Orthodox view, the beard belongs to the "image of God," and shaving is thus viewed as a desecration of the image of God; hence the Russian Old Believers reject shaving, and the Orthodox priest has an obligation to wear a beard and not to cut his hair. Many Christians likewise have distinguished themselves from others of their cultural milieu by rejecting sorcery, necromancy, and spiritualism; medical science and doctors' care, especially inoculation (by radical faith-healing groups) or blood transfusions (*e.g.*, Jehovah's Witnesses); insurance (fire, hail, and life insurance), because insurance is viewed as a reflection of no-confidence in Divine Providence; lightning rods, because they are regarded as malicious interference with Divine Providence; contraceptive pills (*e.g.*, among radical sects, the Roman Catholic Church, and Mormons); drugs and stimulants (*e.g.*, coffee, tea, and alcohol by the Mormons); and drugs by the so-called "Jesus freaks," a difficult to define religious youth movement in the 20th century. Some reject modern technology; the Amish (a radical Protestant sect) prefer the horse and buggy to the "unbiblical"

Avoidance of certain practices and institutions

automobile. The Roman Catholic Church and some radical sects have rules against divorce, which in this form of protest set them apart from the supposed majority of Western culture.

In the area of music and the arts, some reject organs and instrumental music in the church. The Eastern Orthodox Church regards man as the single instrument for God's praise and has developed choral singing to a high degree. The Eastern Orthodox Church also permits for liturgical use only icons that are two-dimensional projections of the heavenly prototype.

Forms of expression of the Christian style of life. This new style of life has been expressed in three ways. One form is that of a consciously aggressive attitude of rejection of the "world," which sometimes has approached the point of provocation—*e.g.*, in the refusal of Christians to marry, a frequent motif of the saints, and provoked martyrdoms of the early church. After the official victory of Christianity and its state recognition, however, Christian mobs destroyed pagan temples and cultic monuments in riots and even became involved in lynch actions against prominent representatives of paganism.

This attitude of opposition was continued among the radical sects (*e.g.*, the Franciscan Spirituals) of the Middle Ages and by the sects and Free churches of the post-Reformation period that espoused the ideal of poverty over against the accumulation of wealth by the church. The Iconoclasts (image destroyers) also represent a classic case of provocation; *e.g.*, the destroyers of the pagan cultic images and temples in the 3rd through 5th centuries and of Roman Catholic images of Christ and the saints during the Reformation in Germany, England, and the Netherlands.

A second posture toward the world is that of retreat. The "quiet in the land" referred to in Psalms, chapter 35, verse 20, first appeared under this name in the German revival movement of the 18th century associated with Gerhard Tersteegen. The life of quiet withdrawal, however, has been exemplified among the adherents of medieval lay mysticism (*e.g.*, the Beguines and Beghards), the Bohemian Brethren of the 15th century, the baptismal groups of the Reformation period (*e.g.*, Mennonites), the English Puritans and Free Church communities, Pietism, and various revival movements in the United States. In the Roman Catholic Church this attitude of retreat finds expression in the contemplative orders, lay orders, and brotherhoods. The resistance of these groups against the world—including the allegedly worldly tendencies in the established "church"—has been strong and systematic but not provocative; it has also been effective where it has not been consciously recognized.

A third posture is that of a peaceable coexistence with the world on the basis of a far-reaching accommodation with the existing order. This attitude is characteristic of periods when the Christian Church has had to refute the reproach that it was hostile to the state and society in order to gain toleration in state and society. Thus, Christians during the first three centuries had to prove that, although they rejected the emperor cult, they were for order in the state and prayed for the emperor. The Christians of the Soviet Union have had to prove that, although they indeed do not espouse the philosophy of dialectical materialism they do support the Russian Soviet state; a similar accommodation enabled Christians in China to survive. Such an adaptation allows existing legal and social customs to be acknowledged and practiced as long as they do not directly violate Christian propriety.

Within established state or territorial churches, this attitude is established as the norm and leads toward a "cultural Christianity." In cultural Christianity the Christian posture is not inactive; it endeavours, as far as possible, to penetrate all areas of state, society, law, and custom with the Christian spirit. This process, however, is achieved slowly and frequently unnoticed, without revolutionary shock. Christianity thus becomes a "normal" component of state and society.

In the missions field, the transition from the first to the third phase has been accomplished with a certain regularity in the 20th century. Generally, the first-generation

Rejection, retreat, and coexistence

"Cultural Christianity"

Christians in newly missionized lands have been dominated by an emphatic attitude of resistance against the "paganism" of their environment. Frequently, the iconoclasm exhibited in the early church has been repeated in the act of removing images of gods, at least from one's own household. Also repeated have been the abolition of pagan living customs and the avoidance of pagan symbols and pagan cultic flowers, instruments, and rites in the Christian liturgy. Later a period of accommodation generally has followed—mostly from the third generation on—which has displayed a greater tolerance, on the one hand, and a more conscious form of influencing the state and society in the surrounding environment, on the other hand.

The attitude of the churches toward technology has been one of either rejection or accommodation. Several radical Free churches and sects have rejected the development of modern technology as "unworldly" and, as far as possible, made no use of its discoveries (*e.g.*, the Amish). Other sects and churches, however, have been distinguished by the great value they place in the technical perfectionism of their organization and methods of mission, publicity, and education—*e.g.*, techniques used by the great revival organizations in large cities. Here, technology has been regarded as a means entrusted by God to man in the building of the Kingdom of God.

Practical adjustment or nonadjustment to society as it is. The tendencies enumerated above have led to dissimilar forms of practical adjustment or nonadjustment to society.

Absorption of the popular piety of pre-Christian cults

The practical adjustment of the early church to society of late antiquity ensued in such a way that the needs for popular piety in the church itself were, to a large extent, taken into account. Frequently, Christian popular piety transformed pre-Christian cultic customs and religious conceptions into Christian ones, merely veiled them as Christian, or further tolerated them in a context with Christian conceptions and customs (*e.g.*, the carnivals prior to beginning of the fasting of the Lenten season). Many pre-Christian heroic figures and myths live on in Christian saints and saintly legends. This process of practical adaptation, which stands out in the sphere of Roman, Hellenistic, Celtic, and old Slavic culture, can also be observed in the area of more recent missions among the individual tribes and cultures of Asia and Africa.

Practical opposition against adjustment regularly appears at that point where radical reform groups offer resistance to, or separate themselves from, an institutional church that, in their opinion, has betrayed its Christian substance in the process of adaptation. Puritan society of the 17th century, thus, turned against the alleged immorality of the theatre and forced prohibition of theatrical performances on Sunday. The anti-Modernist policies of the Roman Catholic Church under the popes from Pius IX until Pius XII in the 19th and 20th centuries are a classic example of a countermovement against a process of adaptation that was growing. The Roman Catholic Church resisted modern intellectual, scientific, social, and political currents—*i.e.*, materialistic science, theological liberalism, biblical and dogmatic criticism, historicism, Socialism and Communism, the theory of evolution, the separation of church and state, and cremation. It retreated to a line of resistance. Only under Pope John XXIII in the 1960s was the anti-Modernist stance somewhat relaxed, not only in the area of theology, but above all in the attitude toward Socialism, the Communist world view, and the Communist countries.

The conversion of the heathen. Throughout the centuries, the fundamental goal of Christian missions was conversion. The Christian proclamation thereby took over the central demand that the Old Testament already directs to man—"returning to the Lord with all your heart" (as noted in I Samuel, chapter 7, verse 3). This occurs in a threefold sense: (1) turning away from godlessness to the Lord; (2) turning away from false gods to the only true and one God: and (3) turning away of man from his own evil nature. In the Christian proclamation, conversion means detachment from ensnarement in the

The process of conversion

old aeon (world) and its lord, Satan, and turning toward the coming new aeon and its Lord, Christ. This renunciation finds its dramatic, symbolic-sacramental expression in the baptismal liturgy.

For Christian missionary preaching, the conversion of the Apostle Paul became a model case. It was treated fully in preaching, catechetics (instruction), and church iconography. In the evangelist preaching of the various revival movements, which have been strongly oriented toward individualistic conversion, the concept of transformation (as evidenced in Paul's life) was decisively emphasized—*e.g.*, in Pietism, Methodism, and the powerful revival movements of the 19th century that extended from the American Middle West through England to Germany and Russia.

For the most part, the so-called decision for Christ—*i.e.*, the sudden turning point attained by means of a sermon on repentance—is connected with a confession of the sins of one's previous period of life. Thus, in many instances revival movements include a "repentance bench" upon which the confession of sin is given. This older practice led to various forms of modernization of confession. In German Pietism another type of conversion was achieved through the influence of August Hermann Francke in the 17th and early 18th centuries—*i.e.*, conversion as the conclusion of a "struggle for repentance." The latter leads through every abyss of doubt in one's own salvation, indeed even in the existence of God and the reality of the history of salvation. Francke demanded this norm of conversion, for instance, from candidates for ministerial office as a presupposition of successfully completing ministerial studies—which often provided incentives for hypocrisy and insincerity. Nikolaus Ludwig, Graf von Zinzendorf, an 18th-century founder of the Moravian Church, on the other hand, held that conversion cannot be fixed in terms of a single standard type; rather, God has "many ways to draw His own to Himself."

The "struggle for repentance"

Thus, from the outset, along with a sudden conversion type there also has been a slow, progressive type that advanced toward a life centred on the Christian gospel. In addition to these types of conversion, there are a strongly intellectual drive toward an understanding of truth, a strongly emotional need for salvation, or a mixture of intellectual and emotional motives.

Personal conversion has become significant in connection with the development of modern individualism and modern personality consciousness.

The conversion of an entire clan or tribe, in societies so organized, represents an expanded form of conversion of the large family, which was often the case in antiquity. As a rule, the group follows the conversion of the head of the clan. In such cases, Baptism becomes mass Baptism; and there thus exists the danger of a superficial and purely formal Christianization, which makes necessary intensive Christian education afterward. Such instances were characteristic of early medieval missions to the Germans and Slavs, as well as of 19th- and 20th-century missions among African tribes.

Mass conversions

Missions that were intent on external success usually concentrated on winning over the leading personalities of the state. The intention was to bring the masses along afterward. The missions of the Jesuit order in Japan and China were thus largely oriented toward gaining influence at the courts of the emperor or shogun (Japanese ruler). The Jesuits in China were engaged at the imperial court in Peking in an official capacity as court scholars (astronomers or mathematicians). Adjustment to the morals and customs of the Chinese environment led to the so-called Chinese Rites Controversy, in which the opponents of any adjustment to Chinese practices were at first successful in Rome (which occurred under Pope Innocent X, 1645).

The conversion of prominent people to the Christian cause is an old practice of Christian missions; its model is to be found in the New Testament in the deacon Philip's winning of the treasurer of Queen Candace of Ethiopia.

The proper and original missionary activity of Christianity, however, has been directed to the underprivileged

Jesuit missionary to China, Matteo Ricci (left), in Chinese dress with one of his converts, 18th-century engraving by an unknown artist.
Radio Times Hulton Picture Library

Missionary activities to the lower classes of society

classes. Jesus himself understood his activity as fulfillment of the prophecy of Isaiah in chapter 61, verse 1:

The Spirit of the Lord God is upon me, because the Lord has anointed me to bring good tidings to the afflicted; he has sent me to bind up the brokenhearted, to proclaim liberty to the captives, and the opening of the prison to those who are bound.

A great number of slaves, freedmen, and members of the lower classes belonged to the earliest congregations. Hence, tending the poor and social care also received much emphasis in the church. The first church office set up in the early congregations was that of deacon, who was appointed for service to the poor. In later centuries, Christian missions perceived in different ways the duty of taking an interest in the underprivileged classes. Missions by churches of the colonial powers, however, often neglected the underprivileged classes, often because the upper class of the colony, which had converted to Christianity, generally was not desirous of mixing in the church with socially proscribed fellow countrymen. Thus, for example, Indians of higher castes, who converted to the Anglican Church, did not often aid in missions to the lower castes. On the other hand, the Protestant Free Churches took an especially emphatic interest in the underprivileged. Thus, Baptists pursued successful missions among the black slaves of the South in the United States, Methodists and Baptists among the lower castes of India, Pentecostals among the underprivileged classes of South American countries, Adventists and Jehovah's Witnesses among the black population of the Union of South Africa, and the Herrnhuters (Moravians) among the black slaves of the former Danish colonies in the Caribbean and among the Indians of the New England colonies. In Roman Catholic missions, the Franciscans—out of the Franciscan tradition of the ideal of poverty—took an interest in the underprivileged ranks. The Roman Catholic Church developed special forms of missions and missionary societies for this work.

Christian world missions in the 20th century experienced a severe crisis as a result of both world wars. On the one hand, the moral self-claim of the nominally Christian

states and peoples was most strongly compromised by their participation in the military actions of the world wars, which, to a large degree, occurred upon Asian and African soil and in which many troops from colonial areas fought. The lack of influence of Christianity and of the churches upon public life in the West became evident. On the other hand, missionaries coming from the enemy side at the time were interned by the respective occupation forces in the missionary areas affected by the war, and this resulted in a forced independence of many mission churches hitherto subordinate to the leadership of their European mother churches. This development concluded in the formation of independent "younger churches" in the entire sphere of the earlier foreign missions of European and American mother churches. It created a wholly new ecclesiastical map.

The crisis of missions in the 20th century

A complete change in missionary methods also emerged. White missionaries, for example, could no longer serve as the superiors of indigenous churches on behalf of European mother churches. Rather, their function became that of co-workers and specialists who worked on behalf of and as members of the mission churches themselves governed by an indigenous clergy. Within missionary practice, the gospel message was transformed by means of various indigenous idiomatic usages so that Christian congregations could more effectively address persons and institutions of their non-Christian environment. Christian congregations in the newly formed states in Asia and Africa lived, on the one hand, as minorities in a pagan environment, but on the other hand—because of their higher education opportunities in the Christian missionary school systems—assumed positions of importance in the governmental administrations of the African and Asian states.

In the young Asian and African states, Christian missions have seen themselves in a new situation insofar as the indigenous governments sometimes limit admission and residence permits of foreign missionaries. The missionary activity of Christian institutions similarly has been increasingly restricted—*e.g.*, the demand of indigenous governments that the children of non-Christian families receive religious instruction in their native religions at Christian schools and no longer be exposed to Christian "proselytism."

On the other hand, the autonomous younger churches not only have freed themselves from the tutelage of foreign missionaries but also have proceeded to engage in missions on their part, especially among related peoples and tribes. Thus, Indian missionaries work in Africa, Nepal, Indonesia, and the South Seas; Korean missionaries in Thailand; Japanese in Okinawa, Canada, and Latin America; and Filipinos in Okinawa, Indonesia, Thailand, Iraq, and Iran.

Internal dissent. The idea of unity, belonging to the self-understanding of the Christian Church from the beginning, is grounded in the view of the church as the one body of Christ. Christ's "seamless robe" (as noted in John, chapter 19, verse 23) became the symbol of this unity in the theological writings of the early Church Fathers. Nevertheless, from the beginning there appeared within the church deviations that led to cleavages. These concerned worship, discipline, and doctrine. The "Easter controversy," for example, arose after 155 between the Roman Church and the congregations in Asia Minor over the date of Easter. Doctrinal dissent came more and more into the foreground—as a consequence of disputes with Hellenistic philosophy, Gnosticism, and Judaism.

Deviations in worship, discipline, and doctrine

Both the concept of heresy (doctrinal deviation) and the development of punitive procedures against heretics were already current in synagogal Judaism. According to chapter 24, verses 5, 6, and 14, of the Acts of the Apostles, the Jews designated the Jewish Christian group as "heretical." In the Christian churches the distinction between schism and heresy had already been established by the 2nd century. Schism is the refusal to be subordinate to the leadership of the large established church (in the Orthodox Church to the bishop or the synod, in the Roman Catholic Church to the pope). Heresy is offense against doctrine as ascertained by the church that holds the criterion of the traditional apostolic norm of faith. Various motives can initiate the process of disagreement. Early groups (*e.g.*, Jewish Christianity) sometimes remain behind the development of the larger churches. Lower social classes may not feel understood by the larger church, which is in social transformation, and they activate more primitive religious elements against the more "progressive" community. Certain world images become sacralized (*e.g.*, the biblical image of the world in Genesis over against the Copernican world image among fundamentalists).

At first, the church itself permitted heterogeneity in forms of proclamation and worship. Paul, for example, allowed for very differentiated forms of proclamation according to a person's ability to understand—Jews, Greeks, weak, strong, and followers of Peter, James, Apollos—without assuming heresy in these various groups. On the other hand, he turned decisively against offenses against the "faith" or in which "another gospel" or "another Christ" stands out. In such situations, the champion of a dissenting view becomes a "false prophet," from whom the "spirit of Antichrist" speaks. From this point of view, the practice of excommunication in managing willful dissent against the community may be understood. In its strongest form, excommunication is the expulsion of the dissenter from the congregation through anathema (official curse). This is based on the view of the impending return of Christ, who wants to find a pure and holy church, a bride "without spot or wrinkle."

In the Pastoral Letters (I and II Timothy and Titus), "sound doctrine" has already become the standard for judging heresy. The formal "deliverance to Satan" is already known for the exclusion of the heretic. According to Titus, the "factious man"—if he is "perverted" and the admonishment unavailing—is "self-condemned." The practice of admonition and excommunication reaches back to the method of treating heretics as practiced in the synagogue. The appearance of heresies in the 2nd and 3rd centuries initiated a large number of apologetic writings (*e.g.*, Irenaeus of Lyons, *Adversus haereses, c.* 180). Heresy appeared as "sickness" or "pestilence," the church as "hospital," and orthodox doctrine as a "medicine chest."

In the imperial church—especially after the emperor Theodosius in the late 4th century—heresy became a criminal transgression punishable by the state. The enemy of the church was likewise viewed as the enemy of the empire. Thus, bishops at the imperial synods of the 4th to 8th centuries attempted to declare as heretics the minority of dissenters and to eliminate them as enemies of the state. Canonical measures in the Middle Ages for the protection of church orthodoxy were the Inquisition (ecclesiastical courts to deal with offenses against church doctrine and order) and the *Index of Prohibited Books* (a list of books whose contents violated Catholic dogma and whose reading was forbidden to Catholics or was allowable only with the permission of ecclesiastical superiors). The Inquisition was the most powerful weapon of the Roman Catholic Church both in the fight against medieval heretical groups (*e.g.*, the Waldenses, Albigenses, Cathari, Bohemian Brethren) and, above all, in the struggles of the Counter-Reformation against the different currents of the Reformation in the 16th century. At the urging of the Pope, the emperor Frederick II in 1220 combined the imperial ban with excommunication. With Luther, the imperial ban of 1521 followed the bull of excommunication of the same year.

After the separation of church and state in the 19th century, the states no longer placed their forces at the disposal of the church for the execution of death sentences pronounced by the Inquisition, and the Inquisition had to close its own prisons (ordered by Napoleon in 1816). The Inquisition, however, continued to exist in Rome as the Holy Office in the fight against "Modernism." Since the second Vatican Council, however, the Roman Catholic Church has become more restrained in the use of excommunication as well as the use of the *Index* of prohibited books, which was suppressed in 1966.

The old institutions of the Inquisition changed their traditional names but have by no means been abolished; rather, they are still firmly established in Catholic canon law. In the sense of Thomas Aquinas, heresy is understood as opposition to church dogma, to church authority, and to the creed, which is taken as legal norm.

According to Roman canonical law, the excommunicated person is excluded from the church community, but he does not cease being a member of the church and bound to his churchly obligations. He loses the right to attend worship service (other than the sermon), to dispense or receive the sacraments, and to practice the office of godparent, as well as the right to patronage, an active church voting right, the right to a church burial, and the right to all churchly income. Extra-churchly community relationships are also denied the excommunicated person —*i.e.*, Catholic believers are forbidden to cultivate relationships with him even outside the church. The worship service must be broken off upon his appearance in the church.

The Reformation churches viewed heresy theologically as a "spiritual matter"; the Protestant territorial churches demanded, and in countless cases practiced, the punishment of heretics through the authorities in terms of imperial law on heresy (valid until 1649)—as in the persecution of the Baptists, the Sacramentarians, and the anti-Trinitarians. In Protestant lands, the heretic appears as an enemy of the Holy Scriptures, an opponent of the publicly and legally valid church, and thereby as the same as an enemy of the public order. Protestant confessional writings preserved the early church and medieval forms of anathematizing heresy. The Lutheran Reformation retained only the "little anathema" (exclusion from the sacraments). Through excommunication, the public sinner is publicly excluded from the congregation; absolution follows only after public confession of sin. Legal proceedings in Lutheranism were carried out by the consistories after their establishment from 1560 on. In Reformed areas, excommunication is granted to the local consistory, subject to the control of the synod.

In countries and provinces without sovereign church government (*e.g.*, The Netherlands and the United States), intra-church dissent could unfold relatively without risk in the form of new congregational or church establishments. Congregationalism granted the individual congregation a far-reaching autonomy in forms of worship and doctrine. Yet dissenting groups—primarily of a Unitarian character—detached themselves from Congregationalism.

In the formation of new churches through dissenting groups, numerous nontheological factors also frequently play a role. They are connected with changing social structure, financial situations, educational conditions, and the political convictions of the dissenters. The ecumenical movement of the 20th century has been attempting to contribute to overcoming church division precisely through clarification of the nontheological factors.

Christianity as a way of life. The Christian life is expressed in the observance of the special form of Christian ethics, which leads to a distinct form of church discipline; in a definite form of Christian instruction; and in various forms of devotion, prayer, and worship.

The forms of Christian devotion and Christian worship are extraordinarily numerous.

Personal devotion in the form of individual prayer plays a most important role, as does household devotion, in which the family appears as the innermost form of Christian community. Household devotions can take different forms: table grace, morning and evening blessing, and home Eucharists. In the house-churches of previous centuries, the extensive literature of devotional books was mostly read aloud for the family. Modern technical mass media have replaced this literature. Congregational forms of devotion and worship vary immensely, and members of a congregation take part in the congregational life with varying intensity.

In the early churches the priest soon developed a monopoly position in doctrine, worship, church discipline,

---

Margin notes:

The practice of excommunication

Heresy as a criminal transgression

Excommunication in Roman Catholic and Protestant churches

Forms of Christian devotion and worship

and church administration. The Reformation fought against the priestly hierarchy of the Roman Catholic Church with the slogan "the priesthood of all believers," but in Lutheran territorial churches a new monopoly of the minister was created. In the Reformed churches, however, the laity at least achieved a stronger voice within a presbyterian polity. The Free churches enabled the development of the many-sided gifts of the laity in their congregations. Because of currents within the ecumenical movement, more participation of the laity in the worship life of the congregations has been carried out, even in the established state churches.

Whereas in the territorial churches and in the institutional churches of an episcopal type the sermon has been reserved for ordained clergy, the Free churches have allowed lay preaching or, sometimes, only lay preaching. The different types of Bible schools and theological colleges in these churches provide for preparation of lay preachers as well as for ministers. Even the Pentecostal churches encourage theological schooling of their preachers. Under the influence of the Free churches, the Anglican Church has lessened the preaching monopoly of its ordained clergy by allowing lay members to be "readers."

Development of hymnody

In all periods in the history of Christendom, spiritually significant movements have spurred the creation of new songs. In the early church, spiritual life often was expressed in new songs, which appeared as gifts of the Holy Spirit—"Singing psalms and hymns and spiritual songs with thankfulness in your hearts to God" (Colossians, chapter 3, verse 16). The hymnody of the great fasters, penitents, worshippers, and ascetics of the early church was incorporated by congregations into the liturgy. Frequently, the melodies of widespread secular folksongs also became part of the church's liturgical and hymnodic tradition because spiritual texts were attached to them. The Reformation of Luther, Zwingli, and Calvin expressed itself as a charismatic singing movement from its beginning. Luther was the creator of many new songs, which at first appeared as broadsheets and later (1524) were collected in the Wittenberg *Achtliederbuch* ("Eight-Song Book").

Among the Protestant sects and Free churches, the Baptists were especially prominent in creating new church songs—*e.g.*, David Joris' *Spiritual Songbook* (1529–36). Protestant songs gradually influenced song writing in the Roman Catholic Church, which, in part, used Protestant melodies of songs with texts in a Catholic way.

Whereas Protestant orthodoxy preferred songs that had as their content the fundamental truths of Christian faith, Pietism yielded an abundance of songs that expressed the personal experience of faith. Accordingly, it produced numerous private hymnbooks that were used in homes and in private assemblies. On the other hand, its songs of the personal experience of faith also enhanced congregational singing to an extraordinary degree. The Pietist joy in singing exerted a great influence upon the Methodist Church, which, primarily through the songs of Charles Wesley, became a "singing church." Decisive also was the influence of Graf von Zinzendorf, the composer of countless hymns, which in English translation were assimilated into the Methodist hymnbook. The Herrnhuters developed their own style of singing worship services, in which new songs were strung together in free, charismatic succession through intonation of the brothers' and sisters' choirs. A comparison of the hymnbooks of all churches indicates that the hymnbooks are more expressive of the ecumenical aspects of the church than are their creeds, and, moreover, that the churches of the world find their common ground in common spiritual songs rather than in the common theological formulations of their faith.

Congregational singing plays a special role in missions. To a great extent, mission churches are singing churches. In part, this is because their members—on the basis of their own form of religious experience and perception—are seldom open to subtle theological distinctions.

Prayer is the innermost and most personal form of manifestation of Christian piety. The spiritualization and theologization of prayer sometimes has obscured the fact that in the beginning prayer also included an entreating intention. With the call "Maranatha" ("O Lord, come"), the congregation entreated the return of Christ and the end of the world. With the incessantly repeated call, "Kyrie eleison" ("Lord, have mercy"), it implored the mercy of God. Prayer preserved its entreating character in exorcism also, as well as in the short, fervent prayers in every possible situation of distress. In case of need, prayer does not even need to be expressed in logical word order and sentences: "We do not know how to pray as we ought, but the Spirit himself intercedes for us with sighs too deep for words" (Romans, chapter 8, verse 26). In accordance with the basic Christian understanding of the relationship between God and man, a personal association between man and God takes place in prayer. Personal prayer constitutes the fundamental form of all prayer.

Prayer as an expression of Christian piety

Jesus taught his disciples the Lord's Prayer, as the essence of a Christian prayer, with the introductory words: "When you pray, go into your room and shut the door and pray to your Father who is in secret" (Matthew, chapter 6, verse 6). The early church, however, soon adopted rigidly formulated prayers in its worship services. In part they derived from the synagogal tradition of prayer, without thereby excluding free charismatic prayer. The church absorbed the prayers of its great saints, penitents, and ascetics into its liturgy, which in its changeable parts—both in the Sunday and holy day liturgies and in the canonical hours prayers—has a rich treasure of prayers at its disposal.

In the course of the centuries, a copious literature of prayer arose. Numerous prayer books and prayer "schools" have arisen, especially in periods of pietistic movements, as in the *devotio moderna* ("modern devotion," a medieval reform movement), Pietism of the 17th and 18th centuries, and the revival movements of the 18th and 19th centuries.

Protestant orthodoxy has given prayer a didactic meaning. The prayer books created or recommended by it have a strongly dogmatic tone; they attempt to promote spiritual drilling in the correct doctrine. In contrast to this, the radical spiritualist groups of the Reformation demanded and practiced spontaneous prayer. In general, the liturgically formulated church prayer was used in the established territorial and state churches, and spontaneous prayer in the Free churches. The polemics against ecclesiastically formulated prayers often made use of the words of Jesus: "In praying do not heap up empty phrases as the Gentiles do; for they think that they will be heard for their many words. Do not be like them" (Matthew, chapter 6, verses 7–8). Spontaneous prayer, however, is also exposed to the danger of formalism, as it frequently—especially in fundamentalist groups—uses a stereotyped "language of Canaan," which is familiar to the congregation and the employment of which is expected by the one in prayer.

The substance of prayer and the use of the Bible

The substance of prayer is praise, thanksgiving, and intercession. Praise of God, in which the earthly church is united with the heavenly, has as its high point the Trisagion ("Holy, Holy, Holy"), which is written in Revelation, chapter 4, verse 8, and Isaiah, chapter 6, verse 3. The prayer of thanks, which is central to the Eucharist, offers gratitude to God for his work of salvation, for the creation, for the election of God's people to redemption (and especially for the incarnation, death, Resurrection, and exaltation of Christ), and for the arrival of the Kingdom of God. The prayer of intercession was characterized by the Apostolic Fathers (*e.g.*, Justin) as a necessary service for the salvation of the world.

In the "Christian way of life" the Bible plays a decisive role. The Bible has the greatest number of editions of any book of the world; it has been translated into all languages and the most remote dialects. In practical piety an exceedingly multisided task devolves upon the Bible. In the liturgy, it forms the basis for the order of worship through scriptural readings, which express the spiritual substance of holidays. In preaching, it forms the basis for sermonic reflections. Sermons about biblical texts continue to constitute the fundamental forms of Sunday addresses; even the topical sermon, widespread in Anglo-Saxon countries, generally proceeds from a biblical passage or serves as its interpretation. The Bible also forms the basis of religious instruction: instruction for confirmands and for Sunday schools. Its reading aloud was for a long time the subject of evening family devotion. In numberless instances it has been the subject of personal devotion far beyond the realm of baptized members of Christian churches.

The "Christian way of death"

Besides a "Christian way of life" there is also a "Christian way of death." Death is understood by Christians not simply as a biological phenomenon but rather as "the wages of sin." The meditation of death accompanies the Christian exploration of conscience. On the other hand, the redemptive act of Christ appears as the overcoming of death through the Resurrection. "Death is swallowed up in victory" (I Corinthians, chapter 15, verse 54). Christians believe that they participate in the death and resurrection of Christ; they are "baptized into his death" and through him are set "free from the law of sin and death."

Preparation for death plays a great role in Christian life. The "final short hour" is personally and liturgically formed as the farewell of the dying person from family and friends, with blessing and common prayer. The Roman Catholic Church has given the dying person its sacramental consecration through a sacrament of healing, which has also become a sacrament dispensed to the dying. Extreme unction, as the sacrament of healing is called, is connected with confession and absolution. The Reformers rejected extreme unction as a sacrament, because for them the essence of a sacrament lies in its institution by Jesus, and such institution is not ascertainable for extreme unction. The shifting of the dying hour from the private residence to the solitude of hospital rooms, as well as the use of sedative injections, has involved a far-reaching desacralization of dying.

The original form of burial was the interment of Christians during the persecution period in special Christian catacombs—which at the same time were meeting places for divine services—and later in churches or in the churchyard; i.e., the self-contained area surrounding the church. Burial in the vicinity of the altar or in a crypt under the altar, as well as burial in the proximity of graves of saints and martyrs, was preferred. Decisive in these practices is the double notion of the church as the community of the living and the dead and resurrection on Judgment Day, which the Christian community wants to experience together. Burial in the church or in the churchyard thus became a visible expression of the view that the living and the dead are joined in Christ and are not separated through death, but together await his return. Cemeteries were therefore also consecrated by the church. Denial of burial in consecrated earth constituted one of the most severe ecclesiastical punishments.

After the 18th century, the churches accepted, only reluctantly, the separation of cemeteries from the church, which resulted because of ideas developed by Enlightenment thinkers, on the one hand, and population growth, on the other. The Roman Catholic custom of burying monks and members of the religious orders in simple rows of graves with uniform plates or crosses has its analogy in the Protestant realm with the customs associated with Zinzendorf. In opposition to the luxurious, individualistic Baroque grave style, which was also spreading in the Protestant churches, Zinzendorf created for the Herrnhuter Bohemian Brethren plain cemeteries with equal distribution of ground and uniform, unadorned tablets. This form was continued in modern military cemeteries after both world wars.

The problem of cremation

For the first 1,900 years of Christianity, the basic idea of the resurrection of the body allowed burial alone as the form of funeral admissible for the Christian faith. Pagan cremation was practiced in the period of persecution of Christians in the Roman Empire as an anti-Christian punitive measure, so as to mock the faith in resurrection (e.g., the burning of the martyrs of Lyons and the scattering of their ashes in the Rhône in 177). The reintroduction of cremation was first attempted by supporters of the French Revolution in 1797. Freemasons, materialists, and Marxists of the 19th century joined the movement, but the Roman Catholic Church rejected cremation. At the beginning of the 20th century, proletarian freethinkers demanded cremation and withdrawal from the church. After long hesitation, cremation was declared inconsequential as far as salvation is concerned in the Protestant churches. For reasons of hygiene and lack of space, cremation has gained vogue alongside burial in most churches except the Roman Catholic.

Problems of self-definition posed for Christianity since the Enlightenment. Since the Enlightenment, a series of new problems has been posed for the self-understanding of the church. The old confessional forms appeared questionable and had forfeited their credibility through the European wars of religion of the 16th and 17th centuries. As a traditional solution, the view that the true church is the church of the reborn (composed of persons who often left the church that was symbolized by a "stone-building") and those enlightened through the Holy Spirit appeared.

The true church as the church of the reborn and rational criticism

This self-interpretation, however, only provoked a new situation in which no longer the Holy Spirit but rather reason appeared as the criterion of true Christianity. A series of spokesmen of modern Rationalism, such as Johann Christian Edelmann (died 1767) and Johann Konrad Dippel (died 1734), emerged from the circles of the radically, spiritualistically inspired. They discovered that the prologue to the Gospel According to John says nothing other than "in the beginning was Reason [Logos]." This appeared to be the only reliable arbiter in all matters of faith and religion. The period of scientific criticism of dogma thereby began, which began in England in terms of a rationalistic neo-Arianism (anti-Trinitarianism) and Rationalism.

It quickly spread to the Continent, however, and in Germany found expression in the critical history of dogma and then in Old and New Testament textual criticism and in the initial attempts at investigations into the life of Jesus. There soon arose a clear contrast between the traditional faith of the church and the results of historical-critical research in the history of dogma and the New Testament. To the degree that the results of criticism of dogma, church history, and the Bible were diffused among the educated public, a turning away from the church commenced.

The influence of Asian religions, science, and technology

Criticism of the church and of Christianity was reinforced under the influence of the rediscovery of the major Asian religions. At the same time, a process of detachment of the sciences from theology took place—slowly but increasingly. The theological controversies of the Reformation period had already led to a devaluation of Christian cosmology through their restriction of the religious question to the relationship between man and God and through an emphasis on the doctrine of justification. At the beginning of the Enlightenment, theologians were still in a leading position in the sphere of the sciences. They turned to the individual areas of the sciences—such as zoology, botany, mineralogy, geology, astronomy, and physics—in terms of a "physico-theology"; they believed that scientific investigation of the individual areas of creation would contribute to enhancing the praise of the divine glory. Nonetheless, the sciences soon separated themselves from the theological aim.

The estrangement of theology from the sciences reached its high point in the 19th century when anti-ecclesiastical socialism, based upon a philosophical materialism, discovered Darwinism (evolutionism) as "proof" of the correctness of its world view. The struggle between the church and the sciences polarized itself into the opposition between the Christian world view and the Darwinian doctrine of evolution.

This opposition, however, was dismantled by the fact that the concept of "matter," upon which the materialistic scientific world view of the 19th century rested, in the meantime had become questionable itself because of modern knowledge about the structure of the atom. In the 20th century, a new conception has been in the process of being sketched out among numerous scientists. It holds the coexistence of religious and scientific world views to be thoroughly possible and declares the artificial 19th-century polarization of faith and knowledge overcome. Direct attempts at harmonizing Christology and the teaching of evolution—such as was undertaken by the French Jesuit paleontologist Pierre Teilhard de Chardin—have evoked vigorous criticism on the parts of both theology and science.

IV. Major traditional doctrinal issues

THE MEANING OF DOGMA

Dogma, according to the view of the church (*i.e.*, its officially promulgated teachings) is the body of Christian teachings necessary for salvation. Its genesis, however, has been a matter of controversy. According to Adolf von Harnack, a German church historian and theologian, dogma is the reinterpretation of the original message of Jesus and the Apostles in the spirit of Hellenic philosophy —which he judged in fact to be a symptom of the disintegration of Christianity.

The Hellenization of the Christian message

Such a Hellenization did, to a large extent, take place. The definition of the Christian faith as contained in the creeds of the ecumenical synods of the early church indicate that unbiblical categories of Neoplatonic philosophy were used in the formulation of the doctrine of the Trinity, as well as in Christology and the doctrine of man.

The Eastern Orthodox Church, however, views the formation of dogma not as a purely human process (which would have to be judged a falsification of divine truths) but as a divine–human process in which the Holy Spirit, proceeding from God, and the human spirit, proceeding from history, participate. According to this view, the origin of divine revelation in God means that the truths of dogma are divine, eternal, and immutable.

Concepts of dogma in the various churches

Dogma has varying positions in the different churches. Whereas in Protestant churches doctrines and creeds generally are associated primarily with theology and preaching, in the Eastern Orthodox Church dogma is directly related to the liturgical life of the church. The confessions of faith of the Orthodox Church are not to be understood as abstract formulations of a pure doctrine but as hymns of worship incorporated appropriately in the liturgy.

In contrast to the rather definitive dogmatic development in the Roman Catholic Church and Reformation Christianity, a much greater freedom in the interpretation of dogma is guaranteed in the Eastern Church. Even the formulation of a dogma by an ecumenical council in Eastern Orthodoxy does not have a binding legal character until it is received within the total ecumenical church consciousness.

COMPARISON OF DOCTRINAL ORIENTATIONS

Orientation of the Western churches. From their inception, the Western churches have viewed the fundamental relationship between God and man primarily in judicial terms. Characteristically, the Apostle Paul in his letter to the Romans depicted the experience of salvation as justification. The Roman church was strongly Jewish–Christian in character and combined this character without difficulties with the basic orientation of the Roman view of religion—*i.e.*, the relationship between God and man was likewise primarily a judicial one. The legal character of Roman religion was expressed in the fact that the efficacy of the state cult ceremonies was dependent upon the strictest observation of a wide variety of regulations. Later developments of Roman Catholic Christianity depended largely upon the basis of this legal thinking. In Rome was developed the specifically Western sacrament of penance, which is wholly dominated by the idea of justification.

The relationship between God and man as judicial

In the judicial foundation of the sacrament of penance (in which an offender might regain a right relationship with the church through the performance of certain works), later possibilities of corruption are built in (*e.g.*, the indulgence, or remission of temporal punishment upon the granting of absolution by a priest and, perhaps, the payment of a fee or performance of certain works).

The indulgence resulted from a fusion of Roman and German legal thought.

The development of the Western notion of church and of the priesthood is also dominated by the legal concept. The church understands itself as a spiritual–judicial institution, founded by Christ. The priest is the legitimate bearer of this legal order. In the sphere of this kind of legal thinking the papacy and the doctrine of papal primacy developed. The idea of a jurisdictional primacy played a prominent role in the formation of the doctrine of the papacy. Kingly authority passed over to the priestly, the emperor's crown to the episcopal tiara. At the high point of this development, Pope Boniface VIII in 1302 proclaimed himself the highest ruler of the world, to whom Christ has committed both swords, the spiritual and the temporal. This judicial idea is also reflected in the individual priest's consciousness of his office. Ordination by the bishop confers upon the priest a legal authority to administer the sacraments and to exercise the power of the keys. In consciousness of this legal process the priest absolves the sinner from his sins in confession with the words: "I absolve you."

On the basis of this legal consciousness the Western church also developed its own canon law. Canon law in the West penetrated, indeed dominated, the societal sphere of life much more strongly than it did in the Orthodox Church.

Influence of judicial thinking in Western theology and monasticism

Judicial thinking was similarly significant in the theology of the West. Whereas the East never assigned a decisive significance to the justification doctrine—which was based on Roman legal theory and practice—of the Apostle Paul, a North African theologian named Tertullian (*c.* 200) introduced a series of fundamental juridical concepts into theology (*e.g.*, persona—a legal person). For Augustine, the doctrine of justification was the very foundation of his view of the relationship of man to God as well as of his view of sin, guilt, and grace. For Anselm, archbishop of Canterbury in the 11th and 12th centuries, the existing, valid judicial relationship between God and man had to be the basic presupposition of all theological thinking. Anselm believed that he could cogently derive —even for unbelievers—the truth of Christian faith and the necessity of the incarnation of God from the idea of satisfaction (*i.e.*, that one could make satisfaction for a crime against another).

Western monasticism also received its special imprint from judicial thought. Sanctification is believed to be accomplished by practicing "good works" and, particularly, "surplus works" or "works of supererogation"—*i.e.*, those that the saint performs over and above those necessary for the satisfaction of his own sins. Alexander of Hales (died 1245), an English theologian and philosopher, advanced the doctrine that out of the works of satisfaction of Christ, the saints, and the martyrs, the church has collected a "treasury of good works," which the pope properly has at his disposal.

This judicial thinking is even extended to the eschatological expectation and the view of the last things, for it is precisely here that the idea of righteousness takes precedence over the idea of love. At the end of the world stands the radical separation of mankind into the redeemed, who enter eternal blessedness, and the damned, who are delivered over to eternal punishment. According to the Roman Catholic view, the prospects for the sinner are improved by his acceptance of an interim state, in which he can still ameliorate his position vis-à-vis God, before the Last Judgment, through expiation in punishment for his sins. Through indulgences, requiems, and other acts, the church expanded its spiritual–judicial authority even to this realm of the departed souls of purgatory (the state of existence after death in which temporal punishment is meted out).

Orientation of the Eastern churches. In Orthodox piety the mystical aspect of the New Testament proclamation—indeed, Pauline as much as Johannine mysticism— is much more prominent. The main motifs are not justification but rather the deification, sanctification, rebirth, new creation, resurrection, and transfiguration of man, and not just of man but also—and herein lies its char-

Motifs
of the
Eastern
churches

acteristic cosmic feature—of the entire world. The central concept is not the righteousness but the love of God. Thus, a different overall development of religious perception took place in the East, especially noticeable in the conception and development of the sacrament of penance. Since, in the East, the idea of educating the Christian to a life of sanctification is decisive, the juridical conception of penance never gained wide acceptance. Thus, neither the doctrine nor the practice of indulgences was developed in the Eastern Church.

Also, the Eastern Church did not claim power to intervene in the realm of the dead, to loosen or to bind. Eastern Christianity is familiar only with intercession for the dead, because the bond of the faithful who are joined together into the body of Christ is not extinguished even with death.

The legal idea, is, however, present in the Eastern Church's view of the ecclesiastical office, especially in its conception of the episcopal office and apostolic succession. But the Eastern view is embedded in the conception of the church as the mystical body of Christ and of the Holy Spirit as the stream of life of the church. The bishops of the Eastern Orthodox Church have always remained primarily bishops (and not also temporal rulers) of their church and have always preserved the spiritual character of their office—even when, as under Islāmic rule, the function of ethnarchs (official representatives of the Christian portions of the population) was assigned them. The conception that the Orthodox priest has of the essence of his priesthood is, then, not determined through a judicial idea, and in the Orthodox sacrament of penance, the formula of absolution has the form not of a declaration but of a prayer for divine forgiveness.

Judicial features are also absent from the Eastern Church's conception of the sanctification of man and, thereby, of the task of monasticism. In Eastern monasticism, a doctrine of good works or of the "treasure of the church" was never able to arise. Saints were venerated as spiritually gifted personalities who realized in this earthly life the "angelic" life of the heavenly church.

The
incarnation
of God
and the
deification
of man

In Orthodox theology the schema of justification has scarcely played a role. Its chief motif is the incarnation of God and the deification of man. Thus, the emphasis of proclamation lay upon rebirth, the new creation of man, the process of transformation into a new creature, resurrection with Christ, the ascension of man to God, and transfiguration. Only the penetration of Reformation ideas in the 16th and 17th centuries compelled Orthodox theologians to take a position on the doctrine of justification.

In Roman thought, sin is a violation of the legal relationship fixed by God between himself and man. Sin for the Eastern Church, however, is viewed as a contraction of essence, a sickness or infection of the original being of the image of God. Accordingly, redemption is not primarily the restoration of a judicial relationship disturbed by sin but rather a renewal of being, transfiguration of being, completion of being, and deification.

Thus, the idea of love is dominant in Eastern piety. Characteristic of this is a catechetical sermon by St. John Chrysostom (died 407), patriarch of Constantinople, about Christ's parable of the workers in the vineyard as told in Matthew, chapter 20. Still read at Easter in the 20th century from all pulpits of the Orthodox Church, the sermon is a song of triumph about the victory of the boundless love of God:

> You who have fasted and you who have not fasted, rejoice today! The table is laden, enjoy it everyone! The calf is fattened, may no one leave hungry! Everyone partake of the banquet of faith! Everyone partake of the riches of goodness! May no one complain of poverty, for the common Kingdom has appeared.

The conception of the Last Judgment in the Eastern Church did not develop according to the strictly juridical interpretation that was customary in the West. On the contrary, trust in grace and in the "love of man" by the divine Logos, as well as supplication for divine compassion, are dominant. Hence, the Orthodox Church understood only with difficulty, or not at all, the theological

concern of the Western Reformation. It comprehended the Western Reformation only to the extent that it concurred with the latter in its rejection of certain Roman Catholic doctrines and practices—e.g., the doctrine of papal primacy and the demand of priestly celibacy. The central argument about justification was reflected upon by only a few Orthodox theologians educated in the West, such as Cyril Lucaris, and was grafted upon Orthodox theology with but ephemeral success.

GOD THE FATHER

On the basis of their religious experiences, the mystics of Christianity of all eras have concurred in the belief that one can make no assertions about God, because he is beyond all concepts and images. Inasmuch as man is a being gifted with reason, however, the religious experience of transcendence demands historical clarification. Thus, in Christian theology two tendencies stand in constant tension with each other. On the one hand, there is the tendency to systematize the idea of God as far as possible. On the other, there is the tendency to eliminate the accumulated collection of current conceptions of God and to return to the understanding of the utter transcendence of God.

Tendencies
within
Christian
theology
to make
assertions
about God

All great epochs of the history of Christianity are defined by new forms of the experience of God and of Christ. Rudolf Otto, a modern German theologian, attempted to describe to some extent the basic ways of experiencing the transcendence of the "holy." He called these the experience of the "numinous" (the spiritual dimension), the utterly ineffable, the holy, and the overwhelming. The "holy" is manifested in a double form: as the *mysterium tremendum* ("mystery that repels"), in which the dreadful, fearful, and overwhelming aspect of the numinous appears, and as the *mysterium fascinosum* ("mystery that attracts"), by which man is irresistibly drawn to the glory, beauty, adorable quality, blessing, redeeming, and salvation-bringing power of transcendence. All of these features are present in the Christian concepts of God as explicated in the ever new experiences of the charismatic leaders.

Characteristic features of the Christian concept of God. Within the Christian perception and experience of God, definite, characteristic features stand out: (1) the personality of God, (2) God as the Creator, (3) God as the Lord of history, and (4) God as Judge. (1) God, as person, is the "I am who I am" designated in Ex. 3:14. The personal consciousness of man awakens in the encounter with God understood as a person: "The Lord used to speak to Moses face to face, as a man speaks to his friend" (Ex. 33:11). (2) God is also viewed as the Creator of heaven and Earth. The believer thus maintains, on the one hand, acknowledgement of divine omnipotence as the creative power of God, which also operates in the preservation of the world created by him and, on the other hand, trusts in the world, which—despite all its contradictions—is understood as one world created by God according to definite laws, principles, and according to an inner plan. The decisive aspect of creation, however, is that God fashioned man according to his image and made the creation subject to man. This special position of man in the creation, which makes man a co-worker of God in the preservation and consummation of the creation, brings a decisively new characteristic into the understanding of God. (3) This new characteristic is God as the Lord of history, which is the main feature of the Old Testament understanding of God: God selects for himself a special people, with whom he contracts a special covenant. Through his Law he binds this "people of God" to himself; he sets before them a definite goal of salvation—the establishment of his dominion—and through his prophets he has his people admonished through proclamations of salvation and calamity whenever they are unfaithful to his covenant and promise. (4) This God of history also is the God of judgment. The genuinely Israelite belief that God reveals himself in the history of his people leads, with an inner logic, to the proclamation of God as the Lord of world history and as the Judge of the world.

The
special
position of
man in
creation
and history

The specific concept of God as Father. What is decisively new in the Christian, New Testament faith in God lies in the fact that this faith is so closely bound up with the person, teaching, and work of Jesus Christ that it is difficult to draw boundaries between theology (doctrines of God) and Christology (doctrines of Christ). Jesus himself embraced the God of the Hebrew patriarchs (Abraham, Isaac, and Jacob), but he also understood himself as the fulfiller of the promise of the Messiah–Son of man, who is the bringer of the Kingdom of God. The religious experience that forms the basis of the messianic self-understanding of Jesus is the recognition that the Messiah–Son of man is the Son of God.

The special relationship of Jesus to God

The special relationship of Jesus to God is expressed through his designation of God as Father. In prayers Jesus used the Aramaic word *abba* (father) for God, which is otherwise unusual in religious discourse in Judaism; it was usually employed by children for their earthly father, similar to "daddy" in English. This father–son relationship became a prototype for the relationship of the Christian to his God. Appeal to the sonship of God played a crucial role in the development of Jesus' messianic self-understanding. According to the account of Jesus' baptism, Jesus understood his sonship when a voice from heaven said: "This is my beloved Son, with whom I am well pleased." In the Gospel According to John, this sonship constitutes the basis for the self-consciousness of Jesus: "I and the Father are one" (John 10:30).

The belief in the oneness of the Father and the Son. Faith in the Son also brought about a oneness with the Father. The Son became the mediator of the glory of the Father to those who believe in him. In Jesus' high priestly prayer (in John, chapter 17) he says: "The glory which thou hast given me I have given to them, that they may be one even as we are one, I in them and thou in me, that they may become perfectly one." In the Lord's Prayer Jesus taught his disciples to address God as "our Father."

The Father–God of Jesus after Jesus' death and Resurrection becomes—for his disciples—the God and Father of our Lord Jesus Christ (*e.g.*, II Cor. 1:3), who revealed his love through the sacrifice of his Son who was sent into the world. The faithful Christian can thus become the son of God, as noted in Rev. 21:7: "I will be his God and he shall be my son." For the Christian, therefore, faith in God is not a doctrine to be detached from the person of Jesus Christ.

The vision of God (the Beatific Vision) for the great medieval theologians speaking out of their own mystical experience constituted the fulfillment of salvation in the Kingdom of God, which the Son will deliver to the Father.

Transpersonal mystical and mono-Christological tendencies

In the history of Christian mysticism, this visionary experience of the transpersonal "Godhead" behind the personal "God" (as in the works of the medieval mystic, Meister Eckehart)—also called an experience of the "trans-diety," the "divine ground," "groundlessness," the "abyss," and the divine "nothingness"—constantly breaks through and is renewed. Occasionally, this experience of transpersonal divine transcendence has directed itself against the development of a piety that has banalized the personal idea of God so much so that the glory and holiness of God has been trivialized. The attempt of the 20th-century theologian Paul Tillich to reduce the Christian idea of God to the impersonal concept of "ultimate concern," or "what ultimately concerns me," pointed toward an understanding of the pre-personal depths of the transcendence of Godhood.

Nevertheless, in the Christian understanding of Christ as being one with the Father, there is a constant possibility that faith in God will be absorbed in a "monochristism"—*i.e.*, that the figure of the Son in the life of faith will overshadow the figure of the Father and thus cause it to disappear and that the figure of the Creator and Sustainer of the world will recede behind the figure of the Redeemer. The history of Christian piety and of Christian theology has constantly moved in this field of tension. Thus, the primacy of Christology and of the doctrine of justification in Reformation theology led to a depreciation of the creation doctrine and a Christian cosmology. This depreciation accelerated the estrangement between theology and the sciences during the period of the Enlightenment and led to a subsequent materialism. An extreme monochristism occurred in the so-called dialectical theology with which a Swiss theologian, Karl Barth, opposed the cultural Christianity of the 19th and early 20th centuries.

The revelatory character of God. The God of the Bible is the God of revelation; on his initiative he presses toward revelation. The creation of the world is viewed as an expression of God's will toward self-revelation, for even the pagans "knew God." In Paul's so-called Areopagus speech in Athens, he said of God: "Yet he is not far from each one of us, for 'in him we live and move and have our being,' " in allusion to the words of the pagan writer Aratus: "For we are indeed his offspring" (Acts 17:27–28). Here is the beginning of a knowledge of God that, throughout the entire history of Christianity, has manifested itself under the catchphrase of the "natural revelation" of God or his revelation in the "book of nature."

God's bent toward self-revelation

The self-revelation of God presupposes, however, a basic biblical understanding of the existing relationship between God and man. It cannot be separated from the view that God created man according to his image and that in Jesus Christ, who "reflects the glory of God and bears the very stamp of his nature" (Heb. 1:3), the heavenly man has appeared among men as the "last Adam." The inner connection between the "natural" and the biblical revelation takes place through the view of Christ as the divine Logos become human.

Hellenistic thinkers, who influenced Christian theologians, had already been attracted by the emphasis in later Judaism on monotheism and transcendence. This tendency was sketched out earlier in Plato and later Stoicism, but it came to its mature development in Neoplatonism in the 3rd century AD. In the first century Philo of Alexandria had interpreted the Old Testament concept of God in terms of the Logos idea of Hellenistic philosophy, but this Hellenization led to a characteristic tension that was to dominate the entire further history of Christian piety, as well as the Western history of ideas. The Greek idea of God was constructed by the inference from the world to its assumable origin and was governed by the principle of causality: God was viewed as the "first cause."

The tension between monotheism and the Logos doctrine

God as Creator, Sustainer, and Judge. The biblical understanding of God, however, was based upon the idea of the freedom of the Creator, Sustainer, and Judge vis-à-vis the world; the latter also included breaking out of the causal chain through miracles. This led to two specific problems that theology, inspired by Greek philosophy, set for itself: (1) the attempt to prove the existence of God, and (2) the attempt to justify God in view of both the existing shortcomings of the creation and evil in history (*i.e.*, the problem of theodicy). Both attempts have very much occupied the intellectual efforts of Western theology and have inspired the highest of intellectual achievements. The attempt itself, however, already presupposed that the transcendent can submit to rationalization, which, in spite of tremendous efforts, is impossible. Thus, in the course of the history of Christian piety, these attempts were frustrated ever again because of the paradoxical character of the historical revelation of God in Jesus Christ.

The attempts at a theodicy and a justification of God likewise led to no satisfying conclusions. The problem, which was already posed by Augustine and treated in detail by Thomas Aquinas, became of pressing importance in the European Thirty Years' War (1618–48) and its results. At that time the German philosopher Gottfried Wilhelm Leibniz, who created the concept of theodicy, endeavoured to defend the Christian notion of God against the obvious atheistic consequences that were evoked by the critical thinkers of his time. This was because of the behaviour of the Christian churches that were engaged in a war of mutual extermination. The result of such theological efforts, however, was either to declare God himself as the originator of evil, to excuse evil as a consequence of divine "permission" or, instead—as by Hegel—to understand world history as the justification of God ("the true theodicy, the justification of God in history"). These answers satisfied neither the Christian experience of faith nor thoughtful reflection (*e.g.*, the Russian writer Fyodor Dostoyevsky's references to the suffering of children, as in *The Brothers Karamazov*).

The German philosopher Immanuel Kant's critique of the proofs of God's existence, founded upon the fundamental impossibility of the human intellect's achieving insights into the realm of the transcendent (together with the shift of the sciences from their earlier theological foundation into an autonomous sphere of purely experimental experience and research), allowed for an abandonment of the idea of God as a goal worthy of attainment in the 19th century. The German philosopher Ludwig Feuerbach tried, in his philosophy of religion, to unmask the substance of religion as an ideological self-interpretation of man. In the philosophy of dialectical materialism, religion appeared as the "opiate of the people" —the opiate being an attempt of man to expect the solution of his life's difficulties from an imagined God and an imagined hereafter, instead of trying to solve them on his own responsibility here on Earth. Darwinism, with its doctrine of evolution, was brought into the field against the biblical idea of creation and was claimed by dialectical materialism as the most important ally in its fight against the worldview of Christianity. This tack overlooked the fact that the idea of evolution itself had its roots in the genuinely Christian idea of the creation and the history of salvation. English and American theology of the 19th century has demonstrated that the idea of evolution in no way contradicts the Christian concept of creation.

Modern views on God. The theological situation in the 20th century has been characterized by a worldwide tension between the "second illumination" and the "first illumination"—in which 18th-century rationalistic and scientific, or pseudoscientific, concepts and antireligious trends have filtered down to influence the broad masses of the 20th century. Notable scientists of the 20th century, such as Albert Einstein, Max Planck, Max Born, and others, however, have admitted the religious backgrounds of their concepts of life, of the universe, and of man.

Corresponding to recognition of God by the leading thinkers of science, there has been a new surge of experience of God noticeable in the different revival movements in the younger churches of Asia and Africa, as well as in the older churches of America and Eurasia—in the midst of people either de-Christianized or attached to a purely conventional "cultural Christianity." Many would argue that the German philosopher Nietzsche's bombastic message, "God is dead," was correct only insofar as certain traditional intellectual and dogmatic conceptions of God have been in the process of dying away, as if to make room for the discovery of a "greater God." Teilhard de Chardin's strongly attacked views toward a "theology of evolution" are typical of such new attempts to express the experience of God.

Thrusts into the cosmos, which were undertaken through the modern development of astronautics by the United States and the Soviet Union, have for their part contributed to the elimination of the remains of the traditional geocentric conception of the world, which until the 1960s and early 1970s lay at the basis of naïve religious thinking as well as of much Christian theology. Such space programs have also contributed to preparing the way for a new religious feeling for the world and for life, as well as a new conception of God. With a recognition of the unique position of man and his Earth in the cosmos, they also have contributed to raising anew into consciousness the personal characteristic of the Christian conception of God and image of man.

The view that God is not solitary. Since Deism of the 18th century, the progressive intellectualization of the Christian idea of God, which began with medieval Scholasticism, led to banishing God into the frigid solitude of his transcendence—into which he withdrew after the creation and starting of the world machine so as to watch its running from afar.

According to the original Christian understanding of God of the early church, the Middle Ages, and the Reformers, God is not solitary nor does he wish to be alone. He encircled himself with a boundless realm of angels— who are created according to his image, who surround him in free love in a kingdom of graduated, individuated hierarchies, who offer him their praise, and who are active in the universe as the messengers and executors of his will. From the beginning God appears as the centre and ruler of the realm fashioned by him, and the first-created of this realm are the angels. The church of the angels is the upper church; the earthly church joins with them in the "cherubic hymn," the Trisagion ("Holy, Holy, Holy"), at the epiphany of the Lord and the angelic choirs surrounding him in the Eucharist. The earthly church is thus viewed as a participant—coliturgist—in the angelic liturgy. Because the angels are created as free spiritual beings in accordance with the image of God— the first fall takes place in their midst—the first misuse of freedom was in the rebellion of the highest prince of the angels, Lucifer ("Light-bearer"), against God.

According to the view of the Fathers of the early church, teachers of the Middle Ages, and the Reformers, man is only the second-created. The creation of man serves to refill the Kingdom of God with new spiritual creatures who are capable of offering to God the free love that the rebellious angels have refused him. In the realm of the first-created creatures, the angels, there already commences the problem of evil, which appears immediately in the freedom or misuse of freedom.

Satan and the origin of evil. In the Old and New Testaments, Satan (the devil) appears as the representative of evil. The philosophy and theology of the Enlightenment endeavoured to push the figure of the devil out of Christian consciousness as being a product of the mythological fantasy of the Middle Ages. It is precisely in this figure, however, that the Christian idea of God and conception of evil are especially evident. The devil, or Satan, first appears as an independent figure alongside God in the course of the Old Testament history of religion. In the Old Testament evil is still brought into a direct relationship with God himself; even evil, insofar as it has power and life, is effected by God: "I form light and create darkness, I make weal and create woe, I am the Lord, who do all these things" (Isa. 45:7).

Satan represents the demonic side of the divine wrath. In the Book of Job he appears as the partner of God, who on behalf of God puts the righteous one to the test. Only in post-biblical Judaism does the devil become the adversary of God, the prince of angels, who, created by God and placed at the head of the angelic hosts, entices some of the angels into revolt against God. In punishment for his rebellion he is cast from heaven together with his mutinous entourage, which was transformed into demons. As ruler over the fallen angels he henceforth continues the struggle against the Kingdom of God in a threefold function: he seeks to seduce man into sin; he tries to disrupt God's plan for salvation; and he appears before God as slanderer and accuser of the saints, so as to reduce the number of those chosen for the Kingdom of God.

Thus, Satan has a threefold function: he is a creature of God, who has his being and essence from God; he is the partner of God in the drama of the history of salvation; and he is the rival of God, who fights against God's plan of salvation. Through the influence of the dualistic thinking of Zoroastrian religion during the Babylonian Exile (586–538 BC) in Persia, Satan took on features of a countergod in late Judaism. In the writings of the Qumrān sects (who preserved the Dead Sea Scrolls), Belial, the "angel of darkness" and the "spirit of wickedness," appears as the adversary of the "prince of luminaries" and the "spirit of truth." The conclusion of the history of salvation is the eschatological battle of the prince of luminaries against Belial, which ends with judgment upon him, his angels, and men subject to him and ushers in the

Marginal notes:

Modern attempts to abandon the idea of God

Resurgence of a recognition of God

The role of angels

The functions of Satan

Satan leaves the presence of God to test God's faithful servant, Job. Engraving by William Blake, 1825, for an illustrated edition of *The Book of Job.*

cessation of "worry, groaning, and wickedness" and the beginning of the rule of "truth."

In the New Testament, the features of an anti-godly power are clearly prominent in the figures of the devil, Satan, Belial, and Beelzebub—the "enemy." He is the accuser, the evil one, the tempter, the old snake, the great dragon, the prince of this world, and the god of this world, who seeks to hinder the establishment of God's dominion through the life and suffering of Jesus Christ. He offered Christ the riches of this world, if he acknowledges him as supreme lord. Thus, he is the real antagonist of the Messiah–Son of Man, Christ, who is sent by God into the world to destroy the works of Satan.

He is lacking, however, the possibility of incarnation: he is left to rob others in order to procure for himself the appearance of personality and corporeality. As opposed to *philanthrōpia*, the love of man of Christ, who presents himself as an expiatory sacrifice for the sins of mankind out of love for it, Satan appears among early church teachers, such as Basil of Caesarea in the 4th century, as the *misanthrōpos*, the hater of men; vis-à-vis the bringer of heavenly beauty, he is the hater of beauty, the *misokalos*. With Gnosticism, dualistic features also penetrated the Christian sphere of intuitive vision. In the *Letter of Barnabas* (early 2nd century) Satan appeared as "the Black One"; according to the 2nd-century apologist Athenagoras he is "the one entrusted with the administration of matter and its forms of appearance," "the spirit hovering above matter." Under the influence of Gnosticism and Manichaeism (a syncretistic religion founded by Mani, a 3rd-century Persian prophet), there also followed—based on their dualistic aspects—the demonization of the entire realm of the sexual. This appears as the special temptational sphere of the devil; in sexual activity, the role of the instrument of diabolical enticement devolves upon woman. Manichaeistic and Gnostic tendencies, thus, remained as a permanent undercurrent in the church and determined, to a great extent, the understanding of sin and redemption. Satan remained the prototype of sin as the rebel who does not come to terms with fulfilling his godlikeness in love to his original image and Creator but instead desires equality with God and places love of self over love of God.

Gnostic and Manichaean elements in Christian concepts of angels and sin against God

Among the Fathers of the early church, the idea of Satan as the antagonist of Christ led to a mythical interpretation of the incarnation and disguise in the "form of a servant." Through this disguise the Son of God makes his heavenly origin unrecognizable to Satan; he becomes the "bait" cast before Satan, after which Satan grasps because he believes Christ to be an ordinary man subject to his power. In the Middle Ages a further feature was added: the understanding of the devil as the "ape of God," who attempts to imitate God through spurious, malicious creations that he interpolates for, or opposes to, the divine creations.

In church history, the eras of the awakening of a new consciousness of sin are identical with those of a newly awakened sense for the presence of "evil"—as was the case with Augustine, Bernard of Clairvaux, Luther, Calvin, and Wesley. In the Christian historical consciousness the figure of Satan plays an important role, not least of all through the influence of the Revelation to John. The history of salvation is understood as the history of a continuous struggle between God and his antagonist, who with constantly new means tries to thwart God's plan of salvation. The idea of the "stratagems of Satan," as developed by a fortress engineer, Jacobus Acontius (died 1567), had its roots here: the history of the world is a constant attempt of Satan to disrupt the salvation events of God through ever new counterevents. This altercation constitutes the religious background of the drama of world history. Characteristic here is the impetus of acceleration already indicated in the Revelation to John: blow and counterblow in the struggle taking place between God and Satan follow in ever shorter intervals; for the devil "knows that his time is short" (Rev. 12:12), and his power in heaven has already been laid low. On Earth the possibility of his efficacy is likewise limited by the return of the Lord. Hence, his attacks upon the elect of the Kingdom so increase in the last times that God himself is moved to curtail the days of the final affliction, for "if those days had not been shortened, no human being would be saved" (Matt. 24:22). Many of these features are retained in the philosophy of religion of German idealism as well as in Russian philosophy of religion. According to the Russian philosopher Nikolay Berdyayev (died 1948), like the Germans Schelling and Franz von Baader before him, the devil has no true personality and no genuine reality and, instead, is filled with an insatiable "hunger for reality," which he can attain by stealing reality from the men of whom he takes possession. Since the Enlightenment, theology has been occupied with demythologizing the devil and proving his nonexistence. According to the Russian philosopher Vladimir Solovyov (died 1900), this is the devil's most cunning attempt at self-camouflage and thereby the most certain proof of his existence (see also ANGELS AND DEMONS).

Consciousness of sin against God and a renewed sense of evil

GOD THE SON

Dogmatic teachings about the figure of Jesus Christ go back to the spontaneous faith experiences of the original church. The faithful of the early church experienced and recognized the incarnate and resurrected Son of God in the person of Jesus. The disciples' testimony served as confirmation for them that Jesus really is the exalted Lord and Son of God, who sits at the right hand of the Father and will return in glory to consummate his Kingdom.

Different interpretations of the person of Jesus. *The Antiochene school.* From the beginning of the church different interpretations of the person of Jesus have existed alongside one another. The Gospel According to Mark, for example, understands Jesus as the man upon whom the Holy Spirit descends at the Baptism in the Jordan and who is declared the Son of God through the voice of God from the clouds. All later Christological attempts of the theological school of Antioch have followed this line of interpretation. They proceed from the humanity of Jesus and view his divinity in his consciousness of God, founded in the divine mission that was imposed upon him by God through the infusion of the Holy Spirit.

The Alexandrian school. Another view is expressed by the Gospel According to John, which regards the figure

Emphasis on the Logos

of Jesus Christ as the divine Logos become flesh. Here, the divinity of the person of Jesus is understood not as the endowment of the man Jesus with a divine power but rather as the result of the descent of the divine Logos—a pre-existent heavenly being—into the world: the Logos taking on a human body of flesh so as to be realized in history. This view was adopted by the catechetical school of Alexandrian theology. Thus it was that the struggle to understand the figures of Jesus Christ created a rivalry between the theologies of Antioch and Alexandria. Both schools had a wide sphere of influence, not only among the contemporary clergy but also in monasticism and among the laity. Characteristically, Nestorianism (a heresy founded in the 5th century), with its strong emphasis upon the human aspects of Jesus Christ, arose from the Antiochene school, whereas Monophysitism (a heresy founded in the 5th century), with its one-sided stress upon the divine nature of Christ, emerged from the Alexandrian school of theology.

The Christological controversies. The many suggestions for resolving the Christological problem, with which the history of dogma is minutely occupied, cannot be enumerated because of the limitations of space. This is because new intermediate solutions constantly were proposed between the two extreme positions of Antioch and Alexandria. As in the area of the doctrine of the Trinity, the general development of Christology has been characterized by an astonishing plurality of views and formulations. Also, the creeds of the major churches have by no means agreed with each other word for word. After Constantine, the great ecumenical synods occupied themselves essentially with the task of creating, in ever new drafts, uniform formulations binding upon the entire imperial church.

Even the Christological formulas, however, do not claim to offer a rational, conceptual clarification; instead, they emphasize clearly three facts in the mystery of the sonship of God. These are: first, that Jesus Christ, the Son of God, is completely God, that in reality "the whole fullness of deity dwells bodily" in him (Col. 2:9); second, that he is completely man; and third, that these two "natures" do not exist beside one another in an unconnected way but, rather, are joined in him in a personal unity. Once again, the Neoplatonic metaphysics of substance offered the categories so as to settle conceptually these various theological concerns. Thus, the idea of the unity of essence (*homoousia*) of the divine Logos with God the Father assured the complete divinity of Jesus Christ. Thus, the mystery of the person of Jesus Christ could be grasped in the formula: two natures in one person. The concept of person, taken from Roman law, served to join the fully divine and fully human natures of Christ into an individual unity. Christology is not the product of abstract, logical operations but instead originates in the liturgical and charismatic sphere of prayer, meditation, and asceticism. Not being derived primarily from abstract teaching, it rather changes within the liturgy in ever new forms and in countless hymns of worship—as in the words of the Easter liturgy:

Christology as originating in the charismatic sphere

> The king of the heavens appeared on earth out of kindness to man and it was with men that he associated. For he took his flesh from a pure virgin and he came forth from her, in that he accepted it. One is the Son, two-fold in essence, but not in person. Therefore in announcing him as in truth perfect God and perfect man, we confess Christ our God.

Messianic views. Faith in Jesus Christ is related in the closest way to faith in the Kingdom of God, the coming of which he proclaims and introduces. Christian eschatological expectations, for their part, were joined with the messianic promises, which underwent a decisive transformation and differentiation in late Judaism, especially in the two centuries just before the appearance of Jesus. Two basic types can be distinguished as influencing the messianic self-understanding of Jesus as well as the faith of his disciples.

Political messianic concepts. The old Jewish view of the fulfillment of the history of salvation was guided by the idea that at the end of the history of the Jewish people the Messiah will come from the house of David and es-tablish the Kingdom of God—an earthly kingdom in which the Anointed of the Lord will gather the tribes of the chosen people and from Jerusalem will establish a world kingdom of peace. Accordingly, the expectation of the Kingdom has an explicitly innerworldly character. The expectation of an earthly Messiah as the founder of a Jewish kingdom became the strongest impulse for political revolutions, primarily against Hellenistic and Roman dominion. The period preceding the appearance of Jesus was filled with continuous new messianic uprisings in which new messianic personalities appeared and claimed for themselves and their struggles for liberation the miraculous powers of the Kingdom of God. Especially in Galilee, guerrilla groups were formed in which hope for a better future blazed all the more fiercely, because the present was so unpromising. Jesus disappointed the political expectations of these popular circles; he did not let himself be made a political Messiah. Conversely, it was his opponents who used the political misinterpretation of his person to destroy him. Jesus was condemned and executed by the responsible Roman authorities as a Jewish rioter who rebelled against Roman sovereignty. The inscription on the cross, "Jesus of Nazareth, king of the Jews," cites the motif of political insurrection of a Jewish messianic king against the Roman government as the official reason for his condemnation and execution.

Apocalyptic messianic concepts. Alongside this political type of messianic expectation there was a second form of eschatological expectation. Its supporters were the pious groups in the country, the Essenes and the Qumrān community on the Dead Sea. Their yearning was directed not toward an earthly Messiah but toward a heavenly anointed one, who will bring not an earthly but a heavenly kingdom. Fulfillment lies not in the old world but in the future, coming world, for which the main thing is to prepare oneself through repentance. These pious ones wanted to know nothing of sword and struggle, uprising and rebellion. They believed that the wondrous power of God alone creates the new time. The birth of a new eon will be preceded by intense messianic woes and a frightful judgment upon the godless, the pagan peoples, and Satan with his demonic powers. The

Hope for a future world

Anderson—Alinari

Christ risen from the tomb on the third day after death, fresco by Piero della Francesca (c. 1420–92). In the Palazzo Comunale, Sansepolcro, Italy.

Messiah will come not as an earthly king from the house of David but as a heavenly figure, as the Son of God, a heavenly being of the ages, who descends into the world of the Evil One and there gathers his own to lead them back into the realm of light. He will take up dominion of the world and, after overcoming all earthly and supernatural demonic powers, will lay the entire cosmos at the feet of God.

Anticipation of the Resurrection

A second new feature, anticipation of the Resurrection, was coupled with this transcending of the old expectation. According to the old Jewish eschatological expectation, the beneficiaries of the divine development of the world would be only the members of the last generation of mankind who are fortunate enough to experience the arrival of the Messiah here upon Earth; all earlier generations would be consumed with the longing for fulfillment but would die without experiencing it. Ancient Judaism knew no hope of resurrection. In connection with the transcending of the expectation of the Kingdom of God, however, even the Zoroastrian anticipation of resurrection was achieved: the Kingdom of God is to include within itself in the state of resurrection all the faithful of every generation of mankind. Even the faithful of the earlier generations of man will find in resurrection the realization of their faith. In the new eon the Messiah–Son of man will rule over the resurrected faithful of all times and all peoples. A characteristic breaking free of the eschatological expectation is thereby presented. It no longer refers exclusively to the Jews alone; with its transcendence a universalistic feature enters into it.

Jesus—in contrast to John the Baptist (who was a preacher of repentance who pointed to the coming bringer of the Kingdom)—knew himself to be the one who brings fulfillment of the Kingdom itself, because the wondrous powers of the Kingdom of God are already at work in him. He proclaimed the glad news that the long promised Kingdom was already dawning, that the consummation was here. This is what was new: the promised Kingdom, supraworldly, of the future, the coming new eon, already now reached redeemingly into the this-worldly from its beyondness, as a charismatic reality that brings men together in a new community.

Jesus as the Son of man

Jesus did not simply transfer to himself the promise of heavenly Son of man, as it is articulated in the apocryphal *First Book of Enoch*. Instead, he gave this expectation of the Son of man an entirely new interpretation. Pious Jewish circles, such as the Enoch community and other pietist groups, expected in the coming Son of man a figure of light from on high, a heavenly conquering hero, with all the marks of divine power and glory. Jesus, however, linked expectations of the Son of man with the figure of the suffering servant of God (as in Isaiah, chapter 53). He will return in glory as the consummator of the Kingdom. Logos Christology could also associate itself with this self-understanding of Jesus.

The doctrine of the Virgin Mary and holy Wisdom. The dogma of the Virgin Mary as the "mother of God" and "bearer of God" is connected in the closest way with the dogma of the incarnation of the divine Logos. The theoretical formation of doctrine did not bring the cult of the mother of God along in its train; instead, the doctrine only reflected the unusually great role that the veneration of the mother of God already had taken on at an early date in the liturgy and in the church piety of Orthodox faithful.

The expansion of the veneration of the Virgin Mary as the bearer of God (Theotokos) and the formation of the corresponding dogma is one of the most astonishing occurrences in the history of the early church. The New Testament offers only scanty points of departure for this development. Mary completely recedes behind the figure of Jesus Christ, who stands in the centre of all four Gospels. From the Gospels themselves it can be recognized that Jesus' development into the preacher of the Kingdom of God took place in very sharp opposition to his family, who were so little convinced of his mission that they held him to be insane (Mark 3:21). Accordingly, all the Gospels stress the fact that Jesus separated

The Virgin Mary as the Mother of Mercy, panel by Lippo Memmi (c. 1285–c. 1361). In the dome of the Orvieto Cathedral, Italy.
Anderson—Alinari

himself from his family. Even the Gospel of John still preserved traces of Jesus' very tense relationship with his mother. Mary appears twice without being called by name the mother of Jesus; and Jesus himself regularly withholds from her the designation of mother. The harsh saying, "Woman, what have you to do with me?" (John 2:4), is indeed the strongest expression of a conscious distancing.

The opposition of Jesus' family toward him

Nevertheless, with the conception of Jesus Christ as the Son of God, a tendency developed early in the church to grant to the mother of the Son of God a special place within the church. This development was sketched quite hesitantly in the New Testament. Only the prehistories in Matthew and Luke mention the virgin birth, which, however, cannot be combined there with the statements of the preceding genealogical tables. On these scanty presuppositions, the later cult of the mother of God was developed. The view of the virgin birth entered into the creed of all Christianity and became one of the strongest religious impulses in the development of the dogma, liturgy, and ecclesiastical piety of the early church.

Veneration of the mother of God received its impetus when the Christian Church became the imperial church under Constantine and the pagan masses streamed into the church. The peoples of the Mediterranean area and the Near East could not make themselves conversant with the absolute power of God the Father and with the strict patriarchalism of the Jewish idea of God, which the original Christian message had taken over. Their piety and religious consciousness had been formed for millennia through the cult of the "great mother" goddess and the "divine virgin," a development that led all the way from the old popular religions of Babylonia and Assyria to the mystery cults of the late Hellenistic period. Despite the unfavourable presuppositions in the tradition of the Gospels, cultic veneration of the divine virgin and mother found within the Christian Church a new possibility of expression in the worship of Mary as the virgin mother of God, in whom was achieved the mysterious union of

Absorption of the cult of the "great mother"

the divine Logos with human nature. The spontaneous impulse of popular piety, which pushed in this direction, moved far in advance of the practice and doctrine of the church. In Egypt, Mary was, at an early point, already worshipped under the title of the bearer of God (Theotokos)—an expression that Origen already used in the 3rd century. The Council of Ephesus (431) raised this designation to a dogmatic standard. To the latter, the second Council of Constantinople (553) added the title "eternal Virgin." In the prayers and hymns of the Orthodox Church the name of the mother of God is invoked as often as is the name of Christ and the Holy Trinity.

The doctrine of the heavenly Wisdom (Sophia) represents an Eastern Church particularity. In late Judaism, speculations about the heavenly Wisdom—a heavenly figure beside God that presents itself to men as mediatress in the work of creation as well as mediatress of the knowledge of God—abounded. In Roman Catholic doctrine, Mary, the mother of God, was identified with the figure of the divine Wisdom. The process of deifying the mother of God went a step further here, in that Mary is treated like a divine hypostasis (substance), the figure of heavenly Wisdom.

Mary and heavenly Wisdom This process of treating Mary and the heavenly Wisdom alike did not take place in the realm of the Eastern Orthodox Church. For all its veneration of the mother of God, the Eastern Orthodox Church never forgot that the root of this veneration lies in the incarnation of the divine Logos that took place through her. Accordingly, in the tradition of Orthodox theology, a specific doctrine of the heavenly Wisdom, Sophianism, is found alongside the doctrine of the mother of God. This distinction between the mother of God and the heavenly Sophia in recent Russian philosophy of religion (Vladimir Solovyov, Pavel Florensky, W.N. Iljin, and Sergey Bulgakov) developed a special Sophianism. Sophianism did, however, evoke the opposition of Orthodox academic theology. The numerous great churches of Hagia Sophia, foremost among them the cathedral by that name in Constantinople, are consecrated to this figure of the heavenly Wisdom.

GOD THE HOLY SPIRIT

Contradictory aspects of the Holy Spirit. The Holy Spirit appears as the true creative element in the life of the church. It works in an apparently contradictory sense: by virtue of its authority, the Holy Spirit establishes law and breaks law, it institutes order and breaks order, it founds tradition and breaks tradition. It is the conservative as well as the revolutionary principle in church history. It guarantees the continuity of the church, and yet it interrupts this continuity ever again through new creations. Both sides of its activity stand in a characteristic relationship of tension to one another.

The essence of free spontaneity *The principle of continuity.* The essence of the expression of the Holy Spirit is free spontaneity. The Spirit blows like the wind, "where it wills," but where it blows it establishes a firm norm by virtue of its divine authority. The spirit of prophecy and the spirit of knowledge (*gnōsis*) are not subject to the will of the prophet and the enlightened one; revelation of the Spirit in the prophetic word or in the word of knowledge becomes Holy Scripture, which as "divinely breathed" "cannot be broken" and lays claim to a lasting validity for the church.

The Spirit, which is expressed in the various officeholders of the church, likewise founds the authority of ecclesiastical offices. The laying on of hands, as a sign of the transference of the Holy Spirit from one person to another, is a characteristic ritual that visibly represents and guarantees the continuity of the working of the Spirit in the officeholders chosen by the Apostles; it becomes the sacramental sign of the succession of the full power of spiritual authority of bishops and priests. The Holy Spirit also creates the sacraments and guarantees the constancy of their action in the church. All the expressions of church life—doctrine, office, polity, sacraments, power to loosen and to bind, and prayer—are understood as endowed by the Spirit.

The principle of revolution. The same Holy Spirit, however, also comes forth as the revolutionizing, freshly creating principle in church history. All the decisive reformational movements in church history, which broke with old institutions, have appealed to the authority of the Holy Spirit. This is probably the main reason that in the history of church dogma the article of the Holy Spirit has been developed only hesitantly and incompletely in comparison with the Christological article. A characteristic view of the Holy Spirit is sketched out in the Gospel According to John: the outpouring of the Holy Spirit takes place only after the Ascension of Christ; it is the beginning of a new time of salvation, in which the Holy Spirit is sent as the Paraclete (Counsellor) to the church remaining behind in this world. The ecstatic phenomena, which are prominent in the church at Pentecost, are understood as fulfillment of this promise. With this event (Pentecost) the church entered into the period in the Holy Spirit. After a process of institutionalization in the church, opposition against it—through appeal to the Holy Spirit—became noticeable for the first time in Montanism (a prophetic movement in the mid-2nd century). Montanus, a Phrygian prophet and charismatic leader, understood himself and the prophetic movement sustained by him as the fulfillment of the promise of the coming of the Paraclete. In the 13th century a spiritualistic countermovement against the feudalized institutional church gained attention anew in Joachim of Fiore, who understood the history of salvation in terms of a continuing self-realization of the divine Trinity in the three times of salvation: (1) the time of the Father, (2) the time of the Son, and (3) the time of the Holy Spirit. He promised the speedy beginning of the period of the Holy Spirit, in which the institutional papal church, with its sacraments and its revelation hardened in the letter of scripture, will be replaced by a community of charismatic figures, filled with the Spirit, and by the time of "spiritual knowledge." This promise became the spiritual stimulus of a series of revolutionary movements within the medieval church—*e.g.*, the reform movement of the radical Franciscan spirituals and the Hussite reform movement led by Jan Hus in 15th-century Bohemia. Their effects extend to a 16th-century radical reformer, Thomas Müntzer, who substantiated his revolution against the princes and clerical hierarchs with a new outpouring of the Spirit. Quakerism represents the most radical mode of rejection—carried out in the name of the freedom of the Holy Spirit—of all institutional forms, which are regarded as shackles and prisons of the Holy Spirit.

Revolutionary movements appealing to the Holy Spirit

Conflict between order and charismatic freedom. As the fundamentally uncontrollable principle of life in the church, the Holy Spirit considerably upset Christian congregations from the very outset. Paul struggled to restrict the anarchist elements, which are connected with the appearance of free charismata (spiritual phenomena), and, over against these, to achieve a firm order in the church. He attempted to repress the irrational and prerational charismata, especially speaking in tongues, in favour of the rational expression of the Spirit, the sermon; he also pushed for the observance of order as well as control of the charismata in the worship services. This tendency led to an emphasis on ecclesiastical offices with their limited authority vis-à-vis the uncontrolled appearance of free charismatic figures.

The conflict between church leadership resident in the locality and the appearance of free charismatic figures in the form of just arrived itinerant preachers forms the main motif of the oldest efforts for a church order. This difficulty became evident in the *Didachē*, the *Teaching of the Twelve Apostles* (early 2nd century). The authority of the Holy Spirit, in whose name the free charismatic figures speak, does not allow its instructions and prophecies to be criticized in terms of contents; its evaluation had to be made dependent upon purely ethical qualifications. This tension ended, in practical terms, with the exclusion of the free charismatic figures from the leadership of the church. The charismatic continuation of the revelation, in the form of new scriptures of revelation, was also checked. Bishop Athanasius of Alexandria, in his 39th Easter letter (367), selected the number of writings—of apostolic origin—that he considered "canonical." Revelation in the form of Holy Scriptures binding for the Christian faith was thereby considered definitively concluded. The canon, henceforth fixed, can no longer be changed, abridged, or supplemented through new writings of revelation.

In a similar way, individual charismatic offices become institutionalized. A lower degree of consecration—a first stage for priestly ordination—still holds for the exorcist. The teacher (*didaskalos*) also becomes institutionalized. In the Roman Church, only ordained priests are permitted to be church teachers—in contrast to the Eastern Orthodox Church, which up until the 20th century does not require ecclesiastical ordination of a professor of theology.

The article about the Holy Spirit in the church creeds reflects little of these struggles. It suppresses the revolutionary principle of the Holy Spirit. Neither the so-called Apostles' Creed nor the Nicene Creed go beyond establishment of faith in the Holy Spirit and its participation in the incarnation. In the Nicene Creed it is further emphasized that the Holy Spirit is the life-creating power—*i.e.*, the power both of creation and of rebirth—and that the Spirit has already spoken in the prophets.

The emergence of Trinitarian speculations in early church theology led to great difficulties in the article about the Holy Spirit. For the being-as-person of the Holy Spirit, which is evident in the New Testament as divine power and appears only in the figure of the dove at Jesus' Baptism, could not be clearly grasped. Nevertheless, with Athanasius (died 373) the idea of the complete *homoousia* (essence) of the Holy Spirit with the Father and the Son was achieved. This was in opposition to all earlier attempts to subordinate the Holy Spirit to the Son and to the Father and to interpret him—similarly to anti-Trinitarian Christology—as a prince of the angels. According to Athanasius, the Holy Spirit alone guarantees the complete redemption of man: "through participation in the Holy Spirit we partake of the divine nature." In his work *De Trinitate*, Augustine undertook to render the essence of the Trinity understandable in terms of the Trinitarian structure of the human person: the Holy Spirit appears as the Spirit of love, which joins Father and Son and draws man into this communion of love. In Eastern Church theological thought, however, the Holy Spirit and the Son both proceed from the Father. In the West, the divine Trinity is determined more by the idea of the inner Trinitarian life in God; thus, the notion was carried through that the Holy Spirit goes forth from the Father and from the Son. Despite all the efforts of speculative theology, a graphic conception of the person of the Holy Spirit was not developed even later in the consciousness of the church.

The operations of the Holy Spirit. For the Christian faith, the Holy Spirit is clearly recognizable in charismatic figures (the saints), in whom the gifts of grace (charismata) of the Holy Spirit are expressed in different forms: reformers and other charismatic figures. The prophet, for instance, belongs to these charismatic types. The history of the church knows a continuous series of prophetic types, which reaches from New Testament prophets, such as Agabus (in Acts 11:28) through the 12th-century monk Bernard of Clairvaux to such Reformers as Luther and Calvin. Christoph Kotter and Nicolaus Drabicius—prophets of the Thirty Years' War period—were highly praised by the 17th-century Moravian bishop John Amos Comenius. Other prophets have existed in Pietism, Puritanism, and the Anglo-Saxon Free churches.

Prophetic women are especially numerous. In church history they begin with Anna (in Luke 2:36) and the prophetic daughters of the apostle Philip. Others are: Hildegard von Bingen, St. Bridget of Sweden, Joan of Arc, and the prophetic women of the Reformation period (*e.g.*, Christina Poniatovia) and of Pietism.

A further type of charismatic person is the healer, who carried out his function in the early church as an exorcist but who also emerged as a charismatic type in healing personalities of more recent church history (*e.g.*, Vincent de Paul in the 17th century). Equally significant is the

curer of souls type, who exercises the gift of "distinguishing between spirits" in daily association with the people of his environment. This gift is found especially emphasized among many of the great saints of all times. In more recent times, it particularly stands out in Johann Christoph the Elder (died 1880), in Protestantism, and in Jean-Baptiste Vianney (died 1859), the curé of Ars, in Roman Catholicism.

The charismatic wanderer type, who leads his roving life in imitation of Jesus Christ, who "has nowhere to lay his head," was molded through the ideal of "ascetic homelessness." The latter drove Scots–Irish monks, for example, not only through all of Europe but also to the most remote islands of the northern seas and as far as Iceland and Newfoundland. This ideal is still alive today in the Eastern Orthodox Church in the form of the *strannik* ("wanderer"). The "holy fool" type conceals his radical Christianity under the mask of foolishness and holds the truth of the gospel, in the disguise of folly, before the eyes of highly placed personalities: the worldly and the princes of the church who do not brook unmasked truth. This type, which frequently appeared in the Byzantine Church, has been represented especially in Western Christianity by Philip Neri, the founder of the religious order known as the Oratorians, in the 16th century.

The charismatic teacher (*didaskalos*), on the other hand, still appears. Filled with the spirit of intelligence or knowledge of the Holy Spirit, he carries out his teaching office, which does not necessarily need to be attached to an academic position. Many Free Church and ecclesiastical reform movements owe their genesis to such spirit-filled teachers, who are often decried as anomalous. The deacon likewise is originally the holder of a charismatic office of selfless service. This history of Christian *diakonia*, which finds its continuation in modern social service outside the church, is continuously inspired through the appearance of personalities who are filled with the charisma of *diakonia*, serving the sick and socially weak. Alongside such men as the Pietist August Hermann Francke, the Methodist John Wesley, Johann Wichern (the founder of the Inner Mission in Germany), and Friederich von Bodelschwingh (the founder of charitable institutions), important women have appeared as bearers of this charisma (*e.g.*, the English nurse Florence Nightingale and the Salvation Army leader Catherine Booth).

The Holy Spirit that "blows where it wills" has secured for women an effectiveness in the church. In the synagogal worship service, the woman was a mute, darkly veiled participant from behind the nontransparent barriers of the side for women, located in the left-hand section of the worship service area. In the ecstatic worship services of the Christian congregations, women, however, came forth with speaking in tongues, hymns, prayer calls, or even prophecies. Evidently, this innovation in the face of the strict synagogal custom was held admissible on the basis of the authority of the Holy Spirit: "Do not quench the Spirit" (I Thess. 5:19). Inasmuch as the appearance of charismatic women upset traditional concepts, however, Paul returned to the synagogal principle: "the women should keep silence in the churches" (I Cor. 14:34).

Because expressions of free charisma were increasingly suppressed in the institutional churches, the emergence of Pentecostal movements outside the institutional churches and partly in open opposition to them arose. This movement led to the founding of various Pentecostal Free churches at the end of the 19th century and the beginning of the 20th; today, it is represented through numerous independent Pentecostal groups, such as the Church of God and the Assemblies of God. At first scorned by the established churches and devalued as "demonic," the Pentecostal movement has grown to a world movement that is developing strong missionary activity not only in Africa and South America but also in the European countries. In the United States, a strong influence of the Pentecostal movement—which has returned high esteem to the proto-Christian charismata of speaking in tongues, healing, and exorcism—is noticeable

The fixing of revelation in a fixed number of sacred books

The relationship of the Holy Spirit to the Father and the Son

Types of charismatic leaders

in the older churches as well, even in the Roman Catholic, Lutheran, and Anglican. This has occurred especially in liturgy and church music but also in preaching style and the return to faith healing.

THE HOLY TRINITY

The basis for the doctrine of the Trinity. The Christian doctrine of the Trinity has its ultimate foundation in the special religious experience of the Christians in the first communities. This basis of experience is older than the doctrine of the Trinity. It consisted of the fact that God came to meet Christians in a threefold figure: (1) as Creator, Lord of the history of salvation, Father, and Judge, who revealed himself in the Old Testament; (2) as the Lord who, in the figure of Jesus Christ, lived among men and was present in their midst as the "Resurrected One"; and (3) as the Holy Spirit, whom they experienced as the power of the new life, the miraculous potency of the Kingdom of God. The question as to how to reconcile the encounter with God in this threefold figure with faith in the oneness of God, which was the Jews' and Christians' characteristic mark of distinction over against paganism, agitated the piety of ancient Christendom in the deepest way. It also provided the strongest impetus for a speculative theology—an impetus that inspired Western metaphysics throughout the centuries. In the first two centuries a series of different answers to this question stood in juxtaposition; at first none of them was thought through speculatively.

Novosti Press Agency

Testament Trinity, detail from the Four-Part-Icon, Novgorod School, *c.* 1400. In the State Museum of Russian Art, Leningrad.

The diversity in interpretation of the Trinity was conditioned especially through the understanding of the figure of Jesus Christ. According to the theology of the Gospel According to John, the *divinity* of Jesus Christ constituted the departure point for understanding his person and efficacy. The Gospel According to Mark, however, did not proceed from a theology of incarnation but instead understood the Baptism of Jesus Christ as the adoption of the *man* Jesus Christ into the Sonship of God, accomplished through the descent of the Holy Spirit. The situation became further aggravated by the conceptions of the special personal character of the manifestation of God developed by way of the historical figure of Jesus Christ; the Holy Spirit was viewed not as a personal figure but rather as a power and appeared graphically only in the form of the dove and thus receded, to a large extent, in the Trinitarian speculation.

Introduction of Neoplatonic themes. In the Johannine understanding, Christ as the Logos, under the influence of Neoplatonic Logos philosophy, became the subject of a speculative theology; there thus developed a speculative interest in the relationship of the oneness of God to the triplicity of his manifestations. This question was answered through the Neoplatonic metaphysics of being. The transcendent God, who is beyond all being, all rationality, and all conceptuality, divests himself of his divine transcendence; in a first act of becoming self-conscious he recognizes himself as the divine *nous* (mind), or divine world reason, which was characterized by the Neoplatonic philosopher Plotinus as the "Son" who goes forth from the Father. The next step by which the transcendent God becomes self-conscious consists in the appearance in the divine *nous* of the divine world, the idea of the world in its individual forms as the content of the divine consciousness. In Neoplatonic philosophy both the *nous* and the idea of the world are designated the hypostases (essences, or natures) of the transcendent God. Christian theology took the Neoplatonic metaphysics of substance as well as its doctrine of hypostases as the departure point for interpreting the relationship of the "Father" to the "Son" in terms of the Neoplatonic hypostases doctrine. This process stands in direct relationship with a speculative interpretation of Christology in connection with Neoplatonic Logos speculation (see also PLATONISM AND NEOPLATONISM).

The assumption of the Neoplatonic hypostases doctrine meant from the beginning a certain evaluation of the relationships of the three divine figures to one another, because for Neoplatonism the process of hypostatization is at the same time a process of diminution of being. In flowing forth from his transcendent source, the divine being is weakened with the distance from his transcendent origin. Diminution of being is brought about through approach to matter, which for its part is understood in Neoplatonism as non-being. In transferring the Neoplatonic hypostases doctrine to the Christian interpretation of the Trinity there existed the danger that the different manifestations of God—as known by the Christian experience of faith: Father, Son, Holy Spirit— would be transformed into a hierarchy of gods graduated among themselves and thus into a polytheism. Though this danger was consciously avoided and, proceeding from a Logos Christology, the complete sameness of essence of the three manifestations of God was emphasized, there arose the danger of a relapse into a triplicity of equally ranked gods, which would displace the idea of the oneness of God.

Attempts to define the Trinity. *The Arian controversy.* By the 3rd century it was already apparent that all attempts to systematize the mystery of the divine Trinity with the theories of Neoplatonic hypostases metaphysics led to ever new conflicts. The high point, upon which the basic difficulties underwent their most forceful theological and ecclesiastically political actualization, was the so-called Arian controversy. Arius (died 336) belonged to the Antiochene school of theology, which placed strong emphasis upon the historicity of the man Jesus Christ. In his theological interpretation of the idea of God, Arius was interested in maintaining a formal understanding of the oneness of God. In defense of the oneness of God, he was obliged to dispute the sameness of essence of the Son and the Holy Spirit with God the Father, as stressed by the theologians of the Neoplatonically influenced Alexandrian school. From the outset, the controversy between both parties took place upon the common basis of the Neoplatonic concept of substance, which

The revelation of God in three figures

Speculative theology

Emphasis on the historicity of Jesus

was foreign to the New Testament itself. It is no wonder that the continuation of the dispute on the basis of the metaphysics of substance likewise led to concepts that have no foundation in the New Testament—such as the question of the sameness of essence (*homoousia*) or similarity of essence (*homoiousia*) of the divine persons.

The basic concern of Arius was and remained disputing the oneness of essence of the Son and the Holy Spirit with God the Father, in order to preserve the oneness of God. The Son, thus, became a "second God, under God the Father"—*i.e.*, he is God only in a figurative sense, for he belongs on the side of the creatures, even if at their highest summit. Here Arius joined an older tradition of Christology, which had already played a role in Rome in the early 2nd century—namely, the so-called angel-Christology. The descent of the Son to Earth was understood as the descent to Earth of the highest prince of the angels, who became man in Jesus Christ; he is to some extent identified with the angel prince Michael. In the old angel-Christology the concern is already expressed to preserve the oneness of God, the inviolable distinguishing mark of the Jewish and Christian faiths over against all paganism. The Son is not himself God, but as the highest of the created spiritual beings he is moved as close as possible to God. Arius joined this tradition with the same aim—*i.e.*, defending the idea of the oneness of the Christian concept of God against all reproaches that Christianity introduces a new, more sublime form of polytheism.

The angel-Christology of the 2nd century

This attempt to save the oneness of God led, however, to an awkward consequence. For Jesus Christ, as the divine Logos become man, moves thereby to the side of the creatures—*i.e.*, to the side of the created world that needs redemption. How, then, should such a Christ, himself a part of the creation, be able to achieve the redemption of the world? On the whole, the Christian Church rejected, as an unhappy attack upon the reality of redemption, such a formal attempt at saving the oneness of God as was undertaken by Arius.

The main speaker for church orthodoxy was Athanasius of Alexandria (died 373), for whom the point of departure was not a philosophical–speculative principle but rather the reality of redemption, the certainty of salvation. The redemption of man from sin and death is only then guaranteed if Christ is total God and total man, if the complete essence of God penetrates human nature right into the deepest layer of its carnal corporeality. Only if God in the full meaning of his essence became man in Jesus Christ is deification of man in terms of overcoming sin and death guaranteed as the resurrection of the flesh.

Augustine, of decisive importance for the Western development of the Trinitarian doctrine in theology and metaphysics, coupled the doctrine of the Trinity with anthropology. Proceeding from the idea that man is created by God according to his own image, he attempted to explain the mystery of the Trinity by uncovering traces of the Trinity in the human personality. He went from analysis of the Trinitarian structure of the simple act of cognition to ascertainment of the Trinitarian structure both of self-consciousness of man and of the act of religious contemplation in which man recognizes himself as the image of God.

The Trinity as successive phases of revelation. A second model of Trinitarian doctrine—suspected of heresy from the outset—which had effects not only in theology but also in the social metaphysics of the West as well, emanated from Joachim of Fiore. He understood the course of the history of salvation as the successive realization of the Father, the Son, and the Holy Spirit in three consecutive periods of salvation. This interpretation of the Trinity became effective as a "theology of revolution," inasmuch as it was regarded as the theological justification of the endeavour to accelerate the arrival of the third state of the Holy Spirit through revolutionary initiative.

The Athanasian concept of the Trinity. The final dogmatic formulation of the Trinitarian doctrine in the so-called Athanasian Creed (c. 500), *una substantia—tres personae* ("one substance—three persons"), reached back to the formulation of Tertullian. In practical terms it meant a compromise in that it held fast to both basic ideas of Christian revelation—the oneness of God and his self-revelation in the figures of the Father, the Son, and the Holy Spirit—without rationalizing the mystery itself. In the final analysis the point of view thereby remained definitive that the fundamental assumptions of the reality of salvation and redemption are to be retained and not sacrificed to the concern of a rational monotheism.

The Athanasian formula

Characteristically, in all periods of the later history of Christendom in which a rationalistic philosophy was achieved and the history of salvation aspect of the Trinitarian question receded, anti-Trinitarian currents returned. Many, to some extent, consciously rejoined ties with Arius: the Humanist Enlightenment of the 16th century, and the so-called anti-Trinitarians of the Italian Renaissance. A direct connection exists between anti-Trinitarianism and 18th-century research into the life of Jesus. The oldest life of Jesus researchers in the 18th century, such as Venturini, Karl Bahrdt, and Reimarus, who portrayed Jesus as the agent of a secret enlightenment order that had set itself the goal of spreading the religion of reason in the world, were at the same time anti-Trinitarians and pioneers of the radical rationalistic criticism of dogma. The Kantian critique of the proofs of God contributed further to a devaluation of Trinitarian doctrine. In the philosophy of German Idealism, G.W.F. Hegel, in the framework of his attempt to raise Christian dogma into the sphere of the conceptual, took the Christian Trinitarian doctrine as the basis for his system of philosophy and, above all, for his interpretation of history as the absolute spirit's becoming self-conscious. In more recent theology, the doctrine of the Trinity has been actually supplanted by a monochristism, which was achieved among the followers of dialectical theology in Europe and North America.

In the so-called theology of death of God of the 1960s, the faith in a transcendent God, and thereby faith in the Trinity as well, were depreciated. Christian dogma was interpreted purely anthropologically and was reduced to the idea of human togetherness—a delayed victory of a philosophy of religion over Christian dogma, which forgot or gave up its own foundations.

The transcendence of God, however, has been rediscovered by science and sociology; theology in the 1970s has endeavoured to overcome the purely anthropological interpretation of religion and once more to discover anew its transcendent ground. Theology has thereby been confronted with the problem of Trinity in a new form, which, in view of the Christian experience of God as an experience of the presence of the Father, Son, and Holy Spirit, cannot be eliminated.

Rediscovery of the transcendence of God

MAN

The starting point for the Christian understanding of man is the recognition that man is created after the image of God. This idea views God and man joined with one another through a mysterious connection. The incomprehensible, suprasubstantial God wanted an image formed of himself in one of his creatures themselves, and for this he singled out man. Man as the image of God belongs, therefore, to the self-revelation of God in quite a decisive way. In that God is reflected in man, he makes him the partner of his self-realization. God and man belong so closely together with one another that one can say that God and man are intended for each other. For this the statements of the great mystics are of significance. Man finds his fulfillment in God, his prototype, but God also first comes to the fulfillment of his essence in man.

Man as a creature. *The concept of solidarity.* The idea of man as the creature created according to the image of God was already being interpreted in a twofold direction in the early church. For one thing, man, like all other creatures of the universe, is a creation of God. According to his nature, man is thus not divine but he is created out of nothingness; as creature he stands in a relationship of utter dependency on God. He has nothing from himself but owes everything, even his being, exclusively to the will of his divine Creator; he is joined with all other fellow creatures through a relationship of brotherly solidarity. Later, this idea of the solidarity of the creatures among one another almost completely receded behind the idea of the special position of man and his special commission of dominion. The idea of solidarity with all creatures has been expressed and practiced by but few charismatic personalities in the history of Western piety, such as by Francis of Assisi in his "Canticle of the Sun": "Praised be Thou, my Lord, with all Thy creatures, especially with our sister sun."

The concept of superiority. The second aspect of the idea of man as a creature operated very much more emphatically: the superiority of man over all other creatures. God placed man in a special relationship to himself in that he created him in his image; he thereby also assigned him a special commission vis-à-vis all other creatures.

Man as the image of God. Under the influence of the dualistic philosophy of Plato, Christian theology attempted for some time to regard the image of God in man as restricted simply to man's intellectual capability and his faculty of perception. In his work *De Trinitate*, Augustine attempted to ascertain traces of divine Trinity in the human intellect. Christian mysticism overcame this dualistic view of man and understood man in his mind–body entirety as the image of God. The image of God is stamped all the way into the sphere of man's corporeality. The idea of man's creation according to the image of God is already based upon the intention of the Incarnation, the self-representation of God in corporeality. Even according to his somatic (bodily) condition, man is the universal being, in whom the powers and creative principles of the whole universe are combined in a personal unity of spirit, soul, and body.

The Christian understanding of evil is also linked with the idea of human createdness according to the image of God. Evil cannot, in the Christian view, be derived from the dualistic assumption of the contrasts of spirit and body, reason and matter. According to the Christian understanding, the triumph of evil is not identical with the victory of matter, the "flesh," over the spirit. Such a dualistic interpretation has frequently been furthered by the fact that for centuries the Christian understanding of sin, even among many church teachers, was influenced by the philosophical assumptions of Neoplatonic dualism. Moreover, in Augustine there are still the aftereffects of Manichaeism, which—out of the dualistic conceptions of Zoroastrian religion—ultimately viewed the main motive force of sin in "concupiscence"—*i.e.*, the sex drive.

The only genuine departure point for the Christian view of evil is the idea of freedom, which is based in the concept of man as the image of God. Man is person because God is person. The being-as-person of man is the real seal of his being-as-the-image-of-God, and herein lies the true nobility of man that distinguishes him from all other creatures. If the Christian faith is differentiated from other religions through the fact that for the Christian God is person, then this faith takes effect in the thereby resulting consequence that man, too, is person.

God himself has at the same time entered into a great risk in that he has created man as person. The real sign of God as personal being is freedom. When God created man according to his image, he also gave over to him this mark of nobility—*i.e.*, freedom. This alone constitutes the presupposition of love. Only through this freedom can man as partner of God offer his free love to God; only in this freedom can he answer God's love through his free love in return. Love in its fulfilled form, according to the Christian understanding, is possible only between persons; conversely, the person can be realized only in the complete love to another person. Man could use this freedom to offer God, his Creator, his free love.

Yet, in the gift of freedom itself there also lay enclosed the possibility for man to decide against God and to raise himself to the goal of his love. The event that is portrayed in the Mosaic creation story as the Fall of

man (Genesis, chapter 3) is essentially the trying out of freedom, the free decision of man against God. This rebellion of man consists of the fact that he improperly uses his freedom given him by God so as to set himself against God and even to wish to be "like God."

Man's redemption. This special interpretation of sin likewise renders understandable the specifically Christian understanding of man's redemption, namely, the view of Jesus Christ as the historical figure of the Redeemer—*i.e.*, the specifically Christian view of the incarnation of God in Jesus Christ.

Members of non-Christian Asian high religions have found it difficult to understand the fundamental Christian idea of the incarnation. The religious person of the East is inclined to understand the Christian idea of incarnation as an analogy to the Hindu concept of the *avatāra* (best rendered as incarnation). The starting point of the latter is that the divine descends to Earth ever again and is constantly clothed anew in a human figure, in order to reveal the heavenly truth to every era and every people in a manner comprehensible to it. Thus, it was natural to understand the figure of Jesus Christ also as such an *avatāra*, as a form of descent of the divine to mankind. In the realm of Hinduism ever new attempts are found to comprehend Christology in this sense.

The Christian understanding of the incarnation, however, is based upon a fundamentally different idea, which is enclosed in the simple saying of the Gospel According to John: "The Word became flesh" (chapter 1, verse 14). Whereas the *avatāra* concept assumes that the divine appears in the cyclic lapse of time periods—now in this, now in that earthly veil—the incarnation of the divine Logos in Jesus Christ is, according to the Christian view, a definitively *unique* happening; it has an extremely materialistic feature. In Christianity, it is not a transcendent, divine being that takes on the appearance of an earthly corporeality, so as to be manifested through this semblance of a body; instead, God himself *as man*, as member of a definite people, a definite family, at a certain time—"suffered under Pontius Pilate"—enters into the corporeality, carnality, and materiality of the history of mankind. In the midst of history he creates the beginning of a thorough transformation of man that in like manner embraces all spheres of man's being—matter, soul, and mind. Incarnation so constituted did not have the character of veiling God in a human form, which would enable the divine being to reveal a new teaching to man with human words. The incarnation is not the special instance of a cyclic descent of God always occurring afresh in constantly new veils. Instead, it is the unique intervention of God in the history of mankind in which God betakes himself in the figure of a single historical person into man's historical conditions of being, suffers through these historical conditions of being, and overcomes in himself the root of their corruption—the misuse of freedom. He thereby established the dawn of a transformed, renewed, exalted form of human being. He opens a realm in which love to God and to neighbour can be tranquilly fulfilled.

The problem of suffering. Here is raised the decisive question of the place of suffering within the Christian anthropology. Christianity's opponents, and precisely the representatives of the Asian high religions as well, have ever again reproached it with glorifying suffering instead of overcoming it. This reproof seems to many to be not entirely unjustified. There have in fact been eras in the history of Christian piety in which suffering as such underwent a frankly ecstatic glorification. This was especially so in several periods of the Middle Ages, in which the Christian Church was convulsed by the most severe inner and outer crises and Christ predominantly in the figure of the man of suffering.

The starting point for the Christian understanding of suffering is the messianic self-understanding of Jesus himself. A temptation to power and self-exaltation lay in the late Jewish promise of the coming of the Messiah–Son of man. The Gospel According to Matthew described the temptation of Jesus by Satan in the wilderness as a temptation to worldly power. In his novel *The Brothers*

Karamazov Dostoyevsky understood the meaning of this temptation as the attempt at a diabolical perversion of Jesus' divine mission into the role of political, social, and magical world ruler. Jesus himself deeply disappointed his disciples' notions aiming at power and exaltation, in that he taught them, in accordance with Isaiah, chapter 53: "The Son of man will suffer many things." Already in Jesus' announcements of suffering the Christian understanding of suffering is brought clearly to expression: suffering is not the final aim and end in itself in the realization of human destiny; it is the gateway to resurrection, to rebirth, to new creation. This idea receives its clarification from the Christian understanding of sin. Sin as the misuse of man's freedom has led man into total opposition against God, who in return delivers him over to death. Turning to God can therefore take place only when the results of this rebellion are overcome in all levels of human being, all the way to physical corporeality.

The Christian understanding of suffering

In the early church the sign of the cross was not considered a glorification of suffering but a "sign of victory" (*tropaion*) in the sense of the ancient triumphal sign that was set up at the place where the victorious turning point of the battle took place. The cross is likewise considered the "dread of the demons," since as a victory sign it strikes terror into the hitherto ruling demonic powers of the world. An ancient church hymn of the cross speaks of the "cross of the beauty of the Kingdom of God." Christ generally appeared upon early church representations of the cross as the crowned victor, who is manifest at the holy road as the lord of the new eon. The emperor Constantine thus fastened to the standards of the imperial legions the cross, which was considered the victory sign for the community of Christians hitherto persecuted by the Roman Empire, and elevated it to a token of military triumph over the legions of his pagan foes that were assembled under the sign of the old gods.

The crowned victorious Christ

In the Christian understanding, suffering also does not appear—as in Buddhism—as suffering under man's general conditions of existence in this world; it is instead coupled with the specifically Christian idea of the imitation of Christ. The individual Christian is called to become an imitator of Christ; incorporation into the body of Christ is granted to him who subsequently is ready to carry out upon himself Christ's destiny of suffering, death, and resurrection. The early church's characterization of the Christian was that of *Christophoros*—"bearer of Christ." Suffering is an unalterable principle in the great drama of freedom, which is identical with the drama of redemption.

The resurrection of man. Just as clear, however, is the real, indeed materialistic, significance that lies in the Christian understanding of the resurrection. A dualistic understanding of man, which assumes an essential difference in man between the spiritual and the material–bodily side of his existence, necessarily leads to the idea of the immortality of the soul. According to this view, imperishableness belongs to man's spiritual nature alone. The Christian hope, however, does not aim at the immortality of the soul but at the resurrection of the body. Corporeality is not a quality that is foreign to the spiritual. Everything spiritual presses toward corporealization, its eternal figure is a corporeal figure.

The resurrection of the body rather than immortality of the soul

> What help would the highest and greatest moral victory be for man, if the enemy, "death," which lurks in the ultimate depth of man's physical, somatic, material sphere, were not overcome?

The goal of redemption is not separation of the spirit from the body; it is rather the new man in his entirety of body, soul, and mind. The Christian image of man has an essentially corporeal aspect that is based in the idea of the incarnation and finds its most palpable expression in the idea of the resurrection.

The progressive perfection of man. For a long time Christian anthropology in academic theology was dominated by static thinking. Man appeared as a complete being, placed in a finished world like a methodically provided for tenant in a prefabricated, newly built residence ready for occupation. Redemption was understood just as statically: salvation appeared in the teachings of church dogma as restitution and restoration of the lost divine image and often in fact more a patching up of fragments through ecclesiastical remedies than as a real new creation. The New Testament, on the other hand, knows of a progression of salvation in history and indeed of both the individual human being and mankind—a progressive perfection of man. This characteristic stands out already in the proclamation of Jesus. He promises his disciples: "Then the righteous will shine like the sun in the kingdom of their Father. He who has ears, let him hear." (Matt. 13:43). In the Gospel According to John, Jesus promises his disciples an increase of their divine powers that is to exceed even the spiritual powers at work in himself (John 14:12). Similar expectations are also expressed in the First Letter of John: "Beloved . . . it does not yet appear what we shall be, but we know that when he appears we shall be like him, for we shall see him as he is" (chapter, 3 verse 2).

The New Testament concept of the progression of salvation

The idea of the Christian "superman," which was expressed by Montanus, is a result of this view. In connection with the breakthrough of the idea of evolution through Darwin in the areas of biology, zoology, and anthropology, the tendency asserted itself—above all in 19th-century American theology—of interpreting the Christian history of salvation in terms of the evolution and expectation of the future perfection of man in the form of reaching even higher charismatic levels and ever higher means of spiritual knowledge and communication.

In the mid-20th century, these ideas have experienced their actualization through the thought of Teilhard de Chardin, who, from the viewpoint of paleoanthropology, sought to develop a new understanding of Christian anthropology over against the traditional restorative anthropology of ecclesiastical doctrine. Christ is not only the figure in which the incarnation becomes historical event but at the same time the eschatological goal of anthropogenesis (beginning of man), in which the genesis of the universe "converges." This "greater Christ" is the focal point not only of the individual but also of the collective salvation of the "living stones" of the faithful being fit together into his body. In the New Testament Letter of Paul to the Ephesians, the goal of the development of Christendom is already described with the words: "until we all attain to the unity of the faith and of the knowledge of the Son of God, to mature manhood, to the measure of the stature of the fulness of Christ" (Eph. 4:13). Only from the special understanding of Christ, which sees in Jesus Christ the second Adam and inaugurator of the new humanity, do the various definitions of man's being become comprehensible.

The thought of Teilhard de Chardin

The justified man. Since the Reformation of the 16th century in the West, the Christian anthropology of Luther, Zwingli, and Calvin has been oriented primarily toward the schema of justification. The Christian is the one to whom the righteousness of God is ascribed in faith for the sake of the merit of Jesus Christ, which he earned for himself through his expiatory sacrifice on the cross. In the 20th century, however, the schema of justification seems less understandable as the starting point for a Christian anthropology, because Jewish law and the Roman Catholic concept of penance based on Roman law (against which the Reformers fulminated) are scarcely found any more in the religious consciousness of the modern era. Paul only spoke of justification when he becomes "as a Jew to the Jews," but if he spoke to Gentile Christians, then he becomes "as a Greek to the Greeks" and talked to them in ideas and images that are more suitable to the Greek ways of thinking in terms of the mystery religions: the new man, the freed and ransomed man, the new creation, the resurrection with Christ, the process of man's transformation and supraformation, and the sonship and friendship of God.

The new man. Probably no idea and no sentiment in the early church dominated the Christian feeling for life so thoroughly and comprehensively as the consciousness of the newness of the life into which the person viewed himself transposed through his participation in the life and body of Christ. The newness of the Christian mes-

The notion of the newness of life

sage of salvation not only filled the hearts of the faithful but was also striking to the non-Christian milieu. The new man experiences and recognizes the newness of his life as the life of Christ that is beginning to mature in himself, as the overwhelming experience of a new state already now commencing. In the New Testament statements about the new man, it was not a settled, complete new condition that was being spoken of, into which man is transposed through grace, but rather the beginning of a coming new state, the consummation of which will first take place in the future. The new man is one who is engaged in the process of renewal; new life is a principle of growth of the Christian maturing toward his "perfect manhood in Christ." This new man, for his part, works anew as fermenting "leaven" within old mankind, as "fresh dough," and contributes to transforming the old mankind through its fermentation into the state of the Kingdom of God.

The "reborn man." "Rebirth" has often been identified with a definite, temporally datable form of "conversion." Especially the pietistic and revival type of Christianity has contributed to a certain levelling of this concept. In the history of Christian piety a line of prominent personalities experienced their rebirth in the form of a temporally datable and also locally ascertainable conversion event. Fixation upon a single type of experience, however, is factually not justified. There are numerous

Forms of "rebirth" other forms of completion of that mysterious event characterized with the expression rebirth. The mode of experience of rebirth itself is as manifold as the individuality of the person concerned, his special intellectual or emotional endowment, and his special history. The different forms of rebirth experience are distinguished not only according to whether the event sets in suddenly with overwhelming surprise or as the result of a slow process, a "growing," a "maturing," and an "evolution." They are also distinguished according to the psychic capability predominant at the time that thereby takes charge (will, intellect), the endowment at hand, and the personal type of religious experience. With the voluntaristic type, rebirth is expressed in a new alignment of the will, in the liberation of new capabilities and powers that were hitherto undeveloped in the person concerned. With the intellectual type, it leads to an activation of the capabilities for understanding, to the breakthrough of a "vision." With others it leads to the discovery of an unexpected beauty in the order of nature or to the discovery of the mysterious meaning of history. With others it leads to a new vision of the moral life and its orders, to a selfless realization of love of neighbour. In the experience of rebirth, the hitherto existing "old man" is not simply eliminated in his given personality structure and its imitation through heredity, education, and earlier life experiences, but the person affected perceives his life in Christ at any given time as "newness of life."

The liberated man. The condition of the "fallen" man is preferably characterized in the New Testament as

The problem of slavery: internal and external "slavery." It is the slavery of human wilfulness that wants to have and enjoy all things for itself: the slavery of alienated love, which is no longer turned toward God but toward one's own self and the things of this world and which also degrades one's fellow man into the means for egoism and exploitation. The servitude of the person fallen away from God is much more oppressive than mere slavery of the senses and of greed for life. It is the enslavement not only of his "flesh" but also of all levels of his human being, even his "most spiritual."

In a bold reversal of the language of Platonic dualism, Luther expressed it thusly in his commentary to the letter of Paul to the Romans: "The entire man who is not reborn is flesh, even in his spirit; the entire man who is reborn is spirit, even when he eats and sleeps." Only from this perspective do Martin Luther's words about the "Freedom of the Christian Man" (1520) receive their true meaning. The freedom that the Christian receives is the freedom that Christ, the new Adam, gained for him by fighting. The freedom of the Christian man is the freedom reattained in Christ, in which the possibility of the misuse of freedom is overcome.

In the initial centuries of the church, a special significance fell to the evangelical schema of liberation—and to the corresponding schema of ransom—in a society that, in its social structure, was constructed entirely upon the system of slavery. On the one hand, wide strata of the population lived in the permanent state of slavery; on the other hand, on the basis of the prevailing usage of war, even the free population was constantly exposed to the danger of passing into possession of the victor as a slave in case of a conquest. The schema of liberation could therefore count upon a spontaneous understanding.

Freedom alone also makes a perfect community possible. Such a community embraces God and the neighbour, in whom the image of God confronts men in the flesh. Community is fulfilled in the free service of love. Luther probably most pertinently articulated the paradox of Christian freedom, which includes both love and service: "A Christian man is a free lord of all things and subordinate to no one. A Christian man is a submissive servant of all things and subject to everyone." Christian freedom is thus to be understood neither purely individually nor purely collectively. The motives of the personal and the social are indivisibly joined with one another by the idea that each person is indeed an image of God for himself alone, but that in Christ he also recognizes the image of God in the neighbour and with the neighbour as a member in the one body of Christ. Here, too, the evolutive principle of the idea of freedom is not to be mistaken; in it, for example, lay the spiritual impetus to the social and racial emancipation of slaves, as it was demanded by the great Christian champions of human rights in the 18th and 19th centuries and, through unspeakable efforts, pursued and achieved.

The joyous man. Friedrich Nietzsche summarized his critique of the Christians of his time in the words of Zarathushtra (Zoroaster): "They would have to sing better songs to me that I might believe in their Redeemer: his disciples would have to look more redeemed!" The critique is to the point. In the New Testament testimonials, joy appears as the characteristic mark of distinction of the Christian. It is the spontaneous result of being filled with the Holy Spirit and is among the

Joy as a characteristic mark of a Christian main fruits of the Holy Spirit. Joy was the basic mood of congregational gatherings and was often expressed in an exuberant jubilation; it has its origin in the recognition that the dominion of evil is already broken through the power of Christ, that death, devil, and demons no longer possess any claim upon man, and that the forces of forgiveness, reconciliation, resurrection, and transfiguration are already effective in mankind. This principle of the joy of the Christian is most strongly alive in the liturgy of the Eastern Orthodox Church.

The roots of a specifically Christian sense of humour also lie within this joy. Its peculiarity consists of the fact that in the midst of the conflicts of life the Christian is capable of regarding all sufferings and afflictions from the perspective of overcoming them in the future or from the perspective of victory over them already achieved in Christ. In Christian humour, joy is combined with the "freedom of a Christian man," who does not let himself be confused and tempted through cross and suffering but already perceives in the cross and in suffering the eschatological sign of triumph and joy. At one extreme the humour of the Danish philosopher Søren Kierkegaard is too dialectical and too bitter to exhaust the entire fullness of the Christian joy. More of it is found in the "hallelujah" of genuine Negro spirituals.

The charismatic man. In the New Testament the Christian is depicted as the person who is filled with the powers of the Holy Spirit. The view of the gifts of the Spirit stands in a direct relationship with the understanding of man as the image of God. For the believing Christian of the original period of the church, the Holy Spirit was the Spirit of the Lord Jesus Christ, who is already now made manifest in his body, the community of the faithful, as the miraculous principle of life of the new eon. Throughout the centuries the Holy Spirit has remained the ferment of church history—all great reformations and numerous foundings of new churches and

Pope Leo III crowning Charlemagne as emperor, AD 800, manuscript Illumination by Jean Fouquet (c. 1420–c. 1481). In the Bibliothèque Nationale, Paris (Ms. Fr. 6465).
By courtesy of the Bibliotheque Nationale, Paris

Christ himself. In the fellow man he sees, under the wrapping of misery, degeneration, and suffering, the image of the present Lord, who became man, who suffered, died and was resurrected in order to lead mankind back into the Kingdom of God.

In the self-understanding of the Christian community two tendencies battle with one another from the beginning of church history. They lead to completely different consequences in the basic orientation of Christians toward fellow Christians and fellow men.

The one attitude stands under the governing idea of election. God chooses his own out of a mankind existing in opposition to him and erects his Kingdom from the elect. This idea underlines the aristocratic character of the Kingdom of God; it consists of an elite of elect. In the Johannine apocalypse the 144,000 ". . . who have not defiled themselves with women" (Rev. 14:4) constituted the picked troops of the Kingdom of God. For Augustine and his theological successors up to Calvin, the community of the elect is numerically restricted; their number corresponds to the number of fallen angels, who must again be replaced through the matching number of redeemed men so that the Kingdom of God would again be restored numerically as well. The church is here understood as a selection of a few out of the masses of perdition who constitute the jetsam of the history of salvation. A grave endangering of the consciousness of community is concealed in this orientation, for self-righteousness, which is the root of self-love and thereby the death of love of neighbour, easily enters again via this consciousness of exclusive election.

The other attitude proceeds from the opposite idea that the goal of the salvation inaugurated through Jesus Christ can only be redemption of the whole of mankind. According to this view God's love of man (*philanthrōpia*), as the drama of his self-surrender for man's salvation shows, is greater than the righteousness that craves the eternal damnation of the guilty. Since the time of Origen, the great 3rd-century philosophical theologian of Alexandria, this second attitude is found again and again not only among the great mystics of the Eastern Church but also among some mystics of Western Christendom. The teaching of universal reconciliation (*apokatastasis pantōn*) has struck against opposition in all Christian confessions. This is connected with the fact that such a universalistic view easily leads to a disposition that regards redemption as a kind of natural process that no one can evade in the long run. Such an orientation can lead to a weakening or loss of a consciousness of man's moral responsibility before God and neighbour; it contains the temptation to spiritual security and moral indolence.

THE CHURCH

The Christian view of the church was influenced by the Old Testament concept of the *qahal*, the elected people of God of the end time, and by the expectation of the coming of the Messiah in Judaism. The Greek secular word *ekklēsia*, the term used for the church, means an assembly of people coming together for a meeting.

In Christianity the concept received a new meaning through its relationship to the Person of Jesus Christ as the messianic inaugurator of the Kingdom of God: (1) with Christ the elected community of the end time has appeared; (2) the church is the eschatological gift of the Holy Spirit, which already flows through the life of the church (Acts 2:33); (3) the community of the end time consists of those who believe in Jesus Christ—both Jews and pagans; the idea of the elected convenant people (*i.e.*, the Jews) is transferred to the "new Israel"; (4) the church forms the body of its Lord; and (5) the church consists of "living stones," from which its house is "built" (I Pet. 2:5).

Jesus himself created no firm organization for his community; the expectation of the immediate imminence of the Kingdom of God provided no occasion for this. Nevertheless, the selection of Apostles and the special position of individual Apostles within this circle pointed to the beginnings of a structuralization of his community. After the community was constituted anew because

The Holy Spirit as the ferment of the church

sects stand under the banner of new charismatic breakthroughs.

The perfect man. The demand for perfection is frequently repeated in the New Testament and has played a significant role in the history of Christian spirituality. In the Gospel According to Matthew, Jesus directs the demand to his disciples: "You, therefore, must be perfect, as your heavenly Father is perfect" (chapter 5, verse 48). This demand seems to exceed by far the measure of reasonableness for man. Yet, it is meant literally, for it is asserted again in the writings of the New Testament. The meaning of this claim is recognizable only from the understanding of man as the image of God and from the apprehension of Christ as the "new Adam." The perfection of man is the perfection with which he reflects the image of God. He has, to be sure, disfigured this image through willful alienation from his original, but in Christ he recovers the perfection of the image of God.

The idea of the deification of man also points in the same direction. Post-Reformation theology, out of anxiety before "mysticism," struck almost entirely from its vocabulary this concept that originated in the techniques of the mystical experience. In the first one and one-half millennia of the Christian Church, however, the idea of deification constituted a central concept for Christian anthropology. Athanasius created the fundamental formula for the theology of deification: "God became man in order that we become God." In the theology of the early church these words became the basis of theological anthropology. Only the idea of perfection makes understandable a final enhancement of the Christian image of man—the intensification from "child of God" to "friend of God." This appears as the highest form of communion reached between God and man; in it love is elevated to the highest form of personal communication between prototype and image.

Fellow man as the present Christ. That revolutionizing idea, which constitutes the basis of Christian ethics, also becomes comprehensible through the foundation of Christian anthropology in the image of God: in the eye of Christian faith Christ is present in every man, even the most debased. According to Matthew (chapter 25, verses 40 and 45) the Judge of the world says to the redeemed: "Truly, I say to you, as you did it to one of the least of these my brethren, you did it to me," and to the damned: "As you did it not to one of the least of these, you did it not to me." Another saying of the Lord is cited by Tertullian: "If you have seen your brother, you have seen your Lord." For the Christian the fellow man is the present

Christ as present in every man

The relationship of the Christian and Jewish concepts of the people of God

of the impressions made by the appearances of the Resurrected One, the succession of the appearances apparently effected a certain gradation within the community.

The unity of the church, which was dispersed geographically, was understood from the viewpoint of the Diaspora (James I:1—the scattered churches of the new Israel represent "the twelve tribes in the dispersion"). The *Didachē*, or the *Teaching of the Twelve Apostles* (late 1st century), viewed the church in terms of the bread of the Eucharist, whose wheat grains "are gathered from the mountains." The idea of the pre-existence of the divine Logos brought into existence the concept of the pre-existence of the church, which included the view that the world was created for the sake of the church. The earthly church is thus the representative of the heavenly church.

Normative defenses in the early church. Establishment of norms for the church was necessary because diverse kinds of interpretations of the Christian message were conceived under the influence of the religions of late antiquity, especially Gnosticism—a syncretistic religious dualistic belief system that incorporated many Christian motifs and became one of the strongest heresies of the early church. In Gnostic interpretations, mixed Christian and pagan ideas appealed to divine inspiration or claimed to be revelations of the Resurrected One. The church erected three defenses against the apparently uncontrollable prophetic and visionary efficacy of pneumatic (spiritual) figures as well as against pagan syncretism: (1) the New Testament canon, (2) the apostolic "rules of faith, or creeds," and (3) the apostolic succession of bishops. The common basis of these three defenses is the idea of "apostolicity."

The canon. The early church never forgot that it was the church that created, selected the books, and fixed the canon of the New Testament, especially because of the threat of Gnostic writings. This is one of the primary distinctions between the Orthodox Church vis-à-vis the Reformation churches, which view the Scriptures as the final norm and rule for the church and church teaching. The Orthodox Church, like the Roman Catholic Church, emphasizes the fact that the Christian Church existed prior to the formation of the canon of Scripture—that it is indeed the source and origin of the Scripture itself. Thus, tradition plays a significant role alongside the Holy Scriptures in the Orthodox and Roman churches.

The creed. The apostolic "rule of faith,"—*i.e.*, the creed—issued from the apostolic tradition of the church as a second, shorter form of its solidification, at first oral and then written. It also served as a defense against Gnostic and syncretistic heretical interpretations of the Christian faith.

Apostolic succession. The third defense that the church used against both Gnostic and syncretistic movements and free charismatic movements within the church was the office of bishop, which became legitimized through the concept of apostolic succession. The mandate for missions, the defense against free prophecy, the polemics with Gnosticism and other heresies, the persecution of the church, and, not least of all, management of church discipline—all allowed the monarchical episcopacy to emerge as a strong jurisdictional office in the early centuries. The bishop, in his capacity as leader of the eucharistic worship service, as teacher, and as curer of souls, became the chief shepherd of the church and was considered its representative.

The basic idea of apostolic succession is as follows: Christ appointed the original Apostles and entrusted to them his full spiritual authority; the original Apostles then appointed overseers (bishops) for the churches founded by them and passed on to them, through the sacramental laying on of hands, their authority of office. These men transmitted the office of overseer to their successors also by the laying on of hands. In this manner, apostolic succession guaranteed the legitimacy of episcopal church government, episcopal doctrine, and the validity of the sacraments dispensed by the bishops.

Evolution of the episcopal office. *Evolution of the episcopacy in the East.* The evolution of the episcopal of-

fice followed a different development in the East and in the West. The Orthodox Church accepts the monarchical episcopacy insofar as it involves the entire church, both the visible earthly and the invisible heavenly churches bound together inseparably. The monarchical principle, however, finds no application to the organization of the visible church. The latter is based upon democratic principles that are grounded in the polity of the early church. Just as all Apostles without exception were of equal authority and none of them held a paramount position over against the others, so too their successors, the bishops, are of equal authority without exception.

Thus, the politics of the Eastern Orthodox churches have a decidedly synodal character. Not only the priesthood but also the laity have been able to participate in Orthodox synods. Election to ecclesiastical offices (*i.e.*, pastor, bishop, or patriarch) involves participation by both clergy and laity. The individual polities of modern Orthodox churches (*e.g.*, Greece or Russia) are distinguished according to the amount of state participation in the settlement of ecclesiastical questions.

The ecumenical council, which consists of the assembly of all Orthodox bishops, constitutes the highest authority of Orthodox synodal polity. The bishops gathered at an ecumenical council resolve all questions of Orthodox faith as well as of worship and canon law according to the principle that the majority rules. The councils recognized by the Orthodox Church as ecumenical councils are: Nicaea in 325, Constantinople in 381, Ephesus in 431, Chalcedon in 451, second Council of Constantinople in 553, third Council of Constantinople in 680, and second Council of Nicaea in 787. Since then, no further ecumenical council has taken place.

The division of Orthodoxy into the various old and new types of patriarchal and autocephalous churches and the entanglement of Orthodoxy in the political catastrophes of past and recent centuries have served as a hindrance for a new ecumenical council, which has been demanded by all sides but has not yet taken place.

Evolution of the episcopacy in the Latin West. On the basis of the joint action of special circumstances, in the Roman Church the papacy evolved out of the monarchical episcopate. Rome, as the capital of the Roman Empire, in which a numerically significant Christian community was already formed in the 1st century, occupied a special position. A leading role devolved upon the leading bishop of the Roman community in questions of discipline, doctrine, and ecclesiastical and worship order. This occurred in the Latin provinces of the church in the West (Italy, Gaul, Spain, Africa), whose organization followed the provincial organization of the Roman Empire. A special leadership position devolved upon the Roman bishop after the collapse of the Western Roman Empire. The theological underpinning of this special position was emphasized by Petrine theology, which saw in the words of Jesus, "You are Peter, and on this rock I will build my church" (Matt. 16:18), a spiritual-legal instituting of the papacy by Jesus Christ himself. In the Greek Church of the East (*e.g.*, Origen) and also in Augustine in the West, however, these words were referred to Peter's confession of faith; since the time of the popes Gelasius I (reigned 492–496), Symmachus (reigned 498–514), and Gregory I (reigned 590–604), these words have served as the foundation for the claim of papal primacy over the entire Christian Church.

Authority and dissent. Christianity, from its beginning, tended toward an intolerance that was rooted in its religious self-consciousness. Christianity understands itself as revelation of the divine truth that became man in Jesus Christ himself. "I am the way, and the truth, and the life; no one comes to the Father, but by me" (John 14:6). To be a Christian is to "follow the truth" (III John); the Christian proclamation is "the way of truth" (II Pet. 2:2). He who does not acknowledge the truth is an enemy "of the cross of Christ" (Phil. 3:18); he "exchanged the truth about God for a lie" (Rom. 1:25) and made himself the advocate and confederate of the "adversary, the devil," who "prowls around like a roaring lion" (I Pet. 5:8). Thus, one cannot make a deal with the

---

Marginal notes:

Reasons for the development of the canon, creed, and episcopacy

Democratic principles in the Orthodox Church

The causes of the monarchical episcopate in the West

The tendency of Christianity toward intolerance

devil and his party—and in this lies the basis for intolerance in Christianity.

Christianity consistently practiced an intolerant attitude in its approach to Judaism and paganism as well as heresy in its own ranks. By practicing its intolerance vis-à-vis the Roman emperor cult, it thereby forced the Roman state, for its part, into intolerance. Rome, however, was not adapted to the treatment of a religion that negated its religious foundations, and this inadequacy later influenced the breakdown of paganism.

Early Christianity aimed at the elimination of paganism—the destruction of its institutions, temples, tradition, and the order of life based upon it. After Christianity's victory over Greco-Roman religions, it left only the ruins of paganism still remaining. Christian missions of later centuries constantly aimed at the destruction of indigenous religions, including their cultic places and traditions (as in missions to the Anglo-Saxons, Germans, and Slavs). This objective was not realized in mission areas in which Christian political powers did not succeed in conquests—*e.g.*, China and Japan; but in Indian Goa, for example, the temples and customs of all indigenous religions were eliminated by the Portuguese conquerors.

The furtherance of intolerance in confrontations with Islām The attitude of intolerance was further reinforced when Islām confronted Christianity from the 7th century on. Islām understood itself as the conclusion and fulfillment of the Old and New Testament revelation; from the Christian view, however, Islām was understood eschatologically—*i.e.*, as the religion of the "false prophets," or as the religion of the Antichrist. The aggression of Christianity against Islām—on the Iberian Peninsula, in Palestine, and in the entire eastern Mediterranean area during the Crusades—was carried out under this fundamental attitude of intolerance. Intolerance of indigenous religions was also manifested in Roman Catholic missions in the New World; these missions transferred the methods of the struggle against Islām to the treatment of the American Indians and destroyed Indian cults and cultic places. Against Protestants, the Counter-Reformation displayed the same kind of intolerance and was largely equated with the struggle against the Turks.

The idea of tolerance first arose during a series of historical catastrophes that forced Christianity into self-reflection: the devastating impressions of the military proceedings of the Inquisition troops against the heretical Cathari, Albigenses, and Waldenses during the Middle Ages; the psychological effect of the permanent inquisitional terror; the conquest of Constantinople by the Turks; the fratricidal struggle among the churches that arose during the Reformation; and the battles of the Protestant territorial churches against the sectarian and Free Church groups in their midst.

Thus, for Nicholas of Cusa the conquest of Constantinople became the occasion to demand, for the first time, the mutual toleration of Christianity and Islām as the presupposition for a religious peace. When the Reformation churches asserted the exclusive claim of possessing the Christian truth, they tried to carry it out with the help of the political and military power at their disposal. In the religious wars of the 16th and 17th centuries, Christian intolerance developed into an internal fratricidal struggle in which each side sought to annihilate the other party in the name of truth. Only the fact that such attempts did not succeed led to new reflections upon the justification of one's own exclusive claim to absoluteness.

The intolerance of the Reformation territorial churches found its counterpart in the intolerance of the revolutionary groups of the Reformation period, such as that of the German radical Reformer Thomas Müntzer, which wanted to force the coming of the Kingdom of God through the dominion of the "elect" over the "godless." The legacy of Christian intolerance and the methods it developed (*e.g.*, inquisition, or brainwashing) operates in the intolerance of the ideology and techniques of modern political revolutions.

The initial spokesmen for tolerance were the Baptists and Spiritualists of the Reformation period. Their most important contribution consisted in that they stood up for their constantly reiterated demand for tolerance not only through their preaching but also through their courageous suffering.

The victory of tolerance over intolerance The victory of tolerance contributed especially to the recognition of the evident contradiction between the theological self-conception of Christianity as a religion of love of God and neighbour and the inhumanity practiced by the churches in the persecution of dissenters. Recognition of this contradiction even provoked criticism of the Christian truths of faith themselves.

The Roman Catholic Church in the past has consistently opposed the development of religious toleration. Its claim to absolute power in a state is still practiced in the 20th century in some Catholic countries, such as in Spain and Colombia, in relationships to Protestant minorities. Since Pope John XXIII and the second Vatican Council (1962–65), however, a more tolerant attitude of the Roman Catholic Church has been demanded that is appropriate both to the ecumenical situation of Christendom in the latter part of the 20th century and to the personal character of the Christian faith.

Creeds and confessions. The faith of Christendom is present in the confessions of faith and the creedal writings of the different churches. Three creeds find general ecumenical acknowledgment: the Apostles' Creed, the Nicene–Constantinopolitan Creed (also called the Nicene Creed), and the Athanasian Creed. The Apostles' Creed is the baptismal confession of the Roman community—in its original form a Greek hymn that can be traced back to the apostolic tradition (of the 2nd century). The Nicene–Constantinopolitan Creed is the confession of faith of the ecumenical Council of Nicaea in 325, which was later supplemented at the ecumenical Council of Constantinople in 381. The Athanasian Creed is a Latin creed whose theological content can be traced back to St. Athanasius of Alexandria (4th century) but that probably first originated in the 5th century in Spain or southern Gaul. It contains a detailed formulation of the doctrine of the Trinity and Christology (the two-natures doctrine), which was influenced by Augustine. All three creeds were accepted by the churches of the Reformation. Acceptance of the three ecumenical creeds

Around central confessional statements about Jesus as the Christ in the New Testament—*e.g.*, "Jesus is Lord" (Rom. 10:9); "You are the Christ" (Matt. 16:16)—are concentrated a series of further assertions that laud his significance for salvation and concern his suffering, death by crucifixion, Resurrection, and his exaltation to God. This tradition, through Mark, Luke, and Paul, was called "gospel," or kerygma (proclamation).

The original form of the creed possessed not a didactic but a hymnal character and had its locus in the worship service. Regular use of a creed as a baptismal confession, and, accordingly, in the preparation of candidates for Baptism in catechetical instruction, influenced its fixed formulation. This was also true of its use in the eucharistic worship service as an expression of the congregation's unity in faith before receiving the elements of the Lord's Supper as well as its use as testimony before the world in times of persecution and as norm of faith (*regula fidei*) in the altercation with heresies.

Development of confessions of faith into theological didactic creeds, which began during the Christological controversies of the 5th century, was continued in the Reformation. The relatively short creedal formulas grew into extensive creedal compositions, primarily because the Reformers conducted their battles with the Roman Church as a struggle for "pure doctrine" as well as for a foundation for the unity of the church. In the Diet of Augsburg in 1530, the feuding ecclesiastical parties were induced to deliver a presentation of their faith. Though the Catholics did not accede to this challenge, the Protestants offered the Confessio Augustana (or the Confession of Augsburg). First planned by Philipp Melanchthon, a follower of Luther, as a creed for union, it later became the basic confessional statement of the Lutheran Church. Development of confessions

The formation of various Protestant confessions was achieved in the individual territorial churches and led to the development of diverse *corpora doctrinae* ("bodies of doctrines"). The differences of the traditional creeds and adherence to them are still clearly noticeable in the ecumenical movement of the 20th century.

A similar development of doctrinal confessions occurred in Calvinism. The idea of the completion of confessional writings is missing in the Lutheran churches, but not in Calvinistic churches: the revision of old and the formation of new creedal writings are permitted and in part are provided for in the rules of the church. Thus the Barmen Declaration in 1934, against the "German Christians" and the National Socialist worldview, arose primarily from Reformed circles. The Anglican Church incorporated the Thirty-nine Articles (a confessional statement) and a short catechism into *The Book of Common Prayer* of 1559/1662 (revised in 1928) and thereby emphasized the unity of doctrine and worship.

Of the denominations that arose out of the Reformation churches, most created doctrinal documents that are comparable to the reformational confessional writings (*e.g.*, among Methodists, Baptists, and Congregationalists). Some denominations (*e.g.*, the Quakers), on the other hand, have rejected any form of creed because they believe creeds to be obstacles to the Christian faith, thus conflicting with the freedom of the Holy Spirit.

The shifting of the chief emphasis in church life to "pure doctrine" in the 16th and 17th centuries also obliged the Orthodox and Catholic churches to formulate their teaching in confessional texts. Thus, under the influence of the reformational creedal writings, the Eastern Orthodox Church developed confessional texts. An example is *The Orthodox Confession of Faith* (*Confessio orthodoxa*) of the metropolitan Peter Mogila of Kiev against Cyril Lucaris, a Calvinist-influenced patriarch of Constantinople; it was approved in 1643 by the Greek and Russian patriarchs. At the Council of Trent (1545–63) the Roman Catholic Church countered the Protestant doctrinal creeds with a *Professio fidei Tridentina* ("The Tridentine Profession of Faith"), which at the end of every article of faith respectively anathematizes the dissenting Protestant article of faith.

The development of creedal formulations in the 20th century In modern Christendom, creedal formation is continued in two areas. (1) Within the ecumenical movement attempts have been made to create a uniform confession as the common basis of faith for the Christian churches in the World Council of Churches. These efforts have not yet been concluded. According to its constitution, the World Council of Churches is "a fellowship of Churches which accepts our Lord Jesus Christ as God and Saviour." In 1960 at St. Andrews, Scotland, the World Council's central committee unanimously accepted an expanded draft of the "basis":

> The World Council of Churches is a community of churches which confess the Lord Jesus Christ, according to the Holy Scriptures, as God and Savior and therefore seek to fulfill that to which they are jointly called, to the glory of God the Father, the Son and the Holy Spirit.

This new version ensued mainly at the instigation of the Orthodox churches, for whom the hitherto existing form of the "basis" was not adequate.

(2) Within the so-called younger churches of former mission areas, the doctrinal disputes and confessional battles of Western Christendom have been viewed as imported and often incomprehensible. The union of churches in South India into the Church of South India (1947) occurred only on the basis of the participating churches dismantling their traditional creedal differences. The Church of South India's scheme of union places biblical revelation in the place of a doctrinal formulation. Similarly, the United Church of Christ in Japan (Kyodan) renounced drawing up a new creed and limited itself to a preface to the Apostles' Creed. In the churches of Africa, the inadequacy of the confessions of the 16th century also has been strongly recognized as a result of their own indigenous cultural presuppositions (see also CREED AND CONFESSION; ECUMENISM).

Organization. *The significance of church discipline in the organizational development of churches.* In the early church, discipline—qualified by the ideal of holiness demanded from baptized Christians—concerned

four areas in which there arose violations of the demand for holiness: (1) the relationship to the pagan social milieu and the forms of life and culture connected with it (*e.g.*, idolatry, the emperor's cult, the theatre, and the circus); (2) the relationship of the sexes within the Christian community (*e.g.*, rejection of polygamy, prostitution, pederasty, sodomy, and obscene literature and art); (3) other offenses against the community, especially murder and property crimes of all kinds; and (4) the relationship to teachers of false doctrine, false prophets, and heretics.

Areas in which early Christians sometimes violated ideals of holiness

Employment of church discipline at an early date led to the formation of a casuistry that at first consisted simply of the distinction between "mortal" and "not mortal" sins (I John 5:15 ff.)—*i.e.*, between sins that through their gravity resulted in loss of eternal life and those with which this was not the case. In earliest Christianity, the relapse of a baptized Christian into paganism (*i.e.*, apostasy) was believed to be the most serious offense. In the Letter to the Hebrews one who is baptized irrevocably forfeits his salvation through a relapse into grievous sin. The various difficulties in substantiating the theory and practice of a second repentance were solved by Pope Calixtus (reigned 217/218–222). This question was especially important in Rome because of the great number of offenses against the idea of holiness. Pope Calixtus granted to bishops decisions about definitive exclusion from the congregation or readmission as well as the evaluation of church punishments. Among all the factors that led to the power of the episcopacy, the concentration of penitential discipline in the hands of the bishop probably contributed more to the strengthening of episcopal power and to the achievement of the monarchical episcopate in the church than any other single factor. This development did not take place without fierce opposition (*e.g.*, Montanism).

Attainment of the church's demand of holiness was made more difficult in the large cities, especially in reference to sexual purity. The period of persecution by the pagan emperors and the legal constraint to performance of sacrifice before the altars of the emperor's images brought countless new instances of apostasy. The so-called Lapsi (Lapsedones), who had performed sacrifices before the emperor's image but, after persecution, faded away and then moved back into the churches again, became a serious problem for the church, sometimes causing schisms (*e.g.*, the Donatists).

The execution of church discipline by the clergy was subordinated to the regulations of Canon Law provided for priests. A genuine practice of church discipline was maintained in the monasteries in connection with the public confession of guilt, which was made by every monk before the entire assembly in the weekly gatherings of the chapter. A strong revival of church discipline among the laity also resulted from the church discipline pursued within monasticism.

On the whole, the casuistic regulation of church discipline led to its externalization and devaluation. The medieval sects, therefore, always stressed in their critique of the worldly church the lack of spiritual discipline and endeavoured to realize a voluntary church discipline in terms of a renewed radical demand of holiness based on early Christianity. The radical sects that emerged in the Reformation reproached the territorial churches by claiming that they had restricted themselves to a renovation of doctrine and not to a renewal of the Christian life and a restoration of the "communion of saints." Different groups of Anabaptists (*e.g.*, Swiss Brethren, Mennonites, and Hutterites), especially, attempted to realize the ideal of the purity and holiness of the church through the reintroduction of a strict church discipline.

Results of the externalization of church discipline

The Reformed churches in particular endeavoured to make church discipline a valid concern of the community. In Geneva, church discipline was expressed, at the instigation of Calvin, in the establishment of special overseers, who, in the individual districts assigned to them, had to watch over the moral behaviour of church members. There likewise came about the creation of such social arrangements as ecclesiastically controlled inns and taverns, in which not only the consumption of food and drink but even the topics of conversation were subject to stern regulation. The cooperation of ecclesiastical discipline and state legislation found its characteristic expression in the United States in the Prohibition amendment to the Constitution. Its introduction came most strongly from Free Church circles, above all evangelical and fundamentalist groups, who, through their battle against the misuse of alcohol, wanted to extend their Christian ideal of the church of the saints to the whole of society.

In the 20th century, church discipline, in the original spiritual sense of voluntary self-control, is practiced only in smaller, Free Church communities in which the ideal of holiness of the community is still maintained and in which the mutual, personal bond of the congregational members in the spirit of Christian brotherhood still allows a meaningful realization of a church discipline. It is also practiced in the so-called younger churches. In these churches the practice of church discipline still appears as a vitally necessary centre of the credible self-representation of the Christian community. Characteristically, therefore, the younger churches' main criticism of the old institutional churches has been directed against the cessation of church discipline among their members.

Church polity: episcopal. The development of the episcopacy in the Orthodox and Roman Catholic churches has been covered in the general introduction of this section under evolution of the episcopal office. Occupying a special position is the episcopal polity of the Anglican Communion. Despite the embittered opposition of Puritan and independent groups during the period of the Reformation and Revolution in England, this polity has maintained the theory and practice of the episcopal office of apostolic succession. The Low Church tradition of the Anglican Communion views the episcopal office as a form of ecclesiastical polity that has been tested through the centuries and is therefore commendable for pragmatic reasons; the Broad Church tradition, however, emphatically adheres to the traditional worth of the episcopal office without allowing the faithful to be excessively dependent upon its acknowledgement. The High Church tradition, on the other hand, values episcopal polity as an essential element of the Christian Church that belongs to the church's statements of faith. The episcopal branch of the Methodist Church has also retained in its polity the bishop's office in the sense of the Low Church and Broad Church view.

In the Reformation churches, an episcopal tradition has been maintained in the Swedish state church (Lutheran), whose Reformation was introduced through a resolution of the imperial Diet of Västerås in 1527, with the cooperation of the Swedish bishops. In the German Evangelical (Lutheran and Reformed) territories, the bishops' line of apostolic succession was ruptured by the Reformation. As imperial princes, the Catholic German bishops of the 16th century were rulers of their territories; they did not join the Reformation in order to avoid renouncing the exercise of their sovereign (temporal) rights as demanded by Luther's Reformation. On the basis of a legal construction originally intended as a right of emergency, the Evangelical rulers functioned as the bishops of their territorial churches but only in questions concerning external church order. This development was promoted through the older conception of the divine right of kings and princes, which was especially operative in Germanic lands.

Controversial tendencies originating in the Reformation. In matters of church polity, controversial tendencies that began in the Reformation still work as divisive forces within the ecumenical movement in the 20th century. For Luther and Lutheranism, the polity of the church has no divine-legal characteristics; it is of subordinate significance for the essence of the church, falls under the ordinances of man, and is therefore quite alterable. In Calvinism, on the other hand (*e.g.*, in the *Ecclesiastical Ordinances* [*Ordonnances ecclésiastiques*] of 1541 and in Calvin's *Institutes of the Christian Religion*

[1536]), the Holy Scriptures appear as a codex from which the polity of the congregation can be inferred or certainly derived as a divine law. Thus, on the basis of its spiritual-legal character, church polity would be a component of the essence of the church itself. Both tendencies stand in a constant inner tension with one another in the main branches of the Reformation and within the individual confessions as well.

Even in Lutheranism, however, there has been a demand for a stronger emphasis upon the independent episcopal character of the superintendent's or president's office. Paradoxically, in the Lutheran Church, which came forth with the demand of the universal priesthood of believers, there arose the development of ecclesiastical authorities but not the development of self-contained congregational polities. The latter were, on the other hand, developed in the Reformed churches because the Reformed Church congregation granted greater participation in the life of the congregation to the laity as presbyters and elders. Furthermore, the Reformed Church areas in Germany, France, England, and Scotland, as well as in The Netherlands and Hungary, had to build up their own ecclesiastical structure without dependence upon state authorities.

Among the Protestant Free churches and sects diverse forms of polity have developed. They have all been founded with an appeal to the Holy Scriptures. Their prototypes can, in fact, be identified in the multiformity of congregational polities in the first three centuries before the victory of the monarchical episcopal office.

Church polity: Presbyterian. Presbyterian polity appeals to the model of the original church. The polity of the Scottish Presbyterian Church and the Presbyterian churches of North America is primarily based upon this appeal, which was also found among many English Puritan groups. It proceeds from the basic view that the absolute power of Christ in his church postulates the equality of rights of all members and can find expression only in a single office, that of the presbyter. The calling to this office is through election by church members, formally analogous to the democratic, republican political mode, and, accordingly, in contrast with the monarchy of the papal and the aristocracy of the episcopal church polity. In Presbyterian churches the differences between clergy and laity have been abolished in theory and, to a great extent, in practice. A superstructure of consistories and presbyteries is superposed one upon the other, with increasing disciplinary power and graduated possibilities of appeal. Through their emphases upon the divine-legal character of Presbyterian polity, the Presbyterian churches have represented a Protestant polity that counters the Roman Catholic concept of the church in the area of ecclesiastical polity. In ecumenical discussions in the 20th century, the divine-legal character of this polity is occasionally noticeable in its thesis of an apostolic succession of presbyters as a counterthesis to that of the apostolic succession of bishops.

Church polity: Congregational. Congregationalism stresses the autonomous right of the individual congregation to order its own life in the areas of teaching, worship, polity, and administration. This demand had been raised and practiced by the medieval sects and led to differentiated polities and congregational orders among the Waldenses, the Hussites, and the Bohemian Brethren. Congregationalism was advanced in the Reformation period by the most diverse parties in a renewed and reinforced way not only by the Schwärmer ("fanatics") and Anabaptists, who claimed for themselves the right to shape their congregational life according to the model of the original church, but also by individual representatives of Reformation sovereigns, such as Franz Lambert (François Lambert d'Avignon; at the Homberg Synod of 1526, whose resolutions were not carried out because of a veto by Luther). The beginnings of modern Congregationalism probably lie among the English refugee communities on the European mainland, in which the principle of the established church was first replaced by the concept of a covenant sealed between God or

Jesus Christ and the individual or the individual congregation.

The basic concepts of Congregationalism

The basic concepts of Congregationalism are: the understanding of the congregation as the "holy people" under the regent Jesus Christ; the spiritual priesthood, kingship, and prophethood of every believer and the brotherly exchange of spiritual experiences between them, as well as the introduction of a strict church discipline exercised by the congregation itself; the equal rank of all clergy; the freedom of proclamation of the gospel from every episcopal or official permission; and performance of the sacraments according to the institution of Jesus. By virtue of the freedom of self-determination fundamentally granted every congregation, no dogmatic or constitutional union but rather only county union of the Congregationalist churches developed in England. North America, however, became the classic land of Congregationalism as a result of the great Puritan immigration to New England, beginning with the Pilgrim Fathers on the "Mayflower" (1620). In the 20th century, acknowledgement of the full authority of the individual congregation runs through almost all Protestant denominations in the United States and is even found among the Lutherans. Congregationalism participates in the ecumenical movement, within which it presses for awakening the independent activity of the Christian churches in the entire world in terms of a proto-Christian ideal of the congregation.

Numerous other forms of congregational polity have arisen in the history of Christendom, such as the association idea in the Society of Friends among the Quakers. Even Pentecostal communities have not been able to maintain themselves in a state of unrestrained and constant charismatic impulses but instead have had to develop a legally regulated polity. This was what happened in the early church, which likewise was compelled to restrain the freedom of charisma in a system of rulers and laws. Pentecostal communities either have been constituted in the area of a biblical fundamentalism theologically and on the basis of a congregationalist church polity constitutionally or they have ritualized the outpouring of the Spirit itself. Thus, the characteristic dialectic of the Holy Spirit is confirmed: the Spirit creates law and the Spirit breaks law even in the most recent manifestations of its working.

Liturgy. *The centrality of the Eucharist in the liturgy.* The central focus of the liturgy of the early church was the Eucharist, which the Christian community interpreted as a fellowship meal with the resurrected Christ. Judaism at the time of Christ was dominated by an intense expectation of the Kingdom of God, which would be inaugurated by the Messiah–Son of man. The early Christian Church appropriated this expectation, which revolved around the image of the messianic meal in which the faithful would "sit at table" (Luke 13:29) with the coming Messiah–Son of man. At the centre of Jesus' preaching on the Kingdom of God is the promise that the blessed would "eat bread" with the exalted Messiah–Son of man (Luke 13:29). The Lord himself will serve the chosen community of the Kingdom at the messianic meal (Luke 12:37 ff.), which bears the features of a wedding banquet. The basic mood in the community gathered about him is thus one of nuptial joy over the inauguration of the promised end time, which Jesus emphasized in Matthew, chapter 9, verse 15: "Can the wedding guests mourn as long as the bridegroom is with them?" The supper that Jesus celebrated with his disciples "on the night when he was betrayed" (I Cor. 11: 23) inaugurated the heavenly meal that will be continued in the Kingdom of God. Decisive for understanding the original meaning of the Eucharist are the words of Jesus in Matthew, chapter 26, verse 29: "I shall not drink again of this fruit of the vine until that day when I drink it new with you in my Father's kingdom."

The death of Jesus at first bewildered his community in the face of his promise, but the appearances of the Resurrected One, beginning with Easter morning, confirmed their expectations about the messianic Kingdom. These appearances influenced the expectations about the messianic meal and the continuation of fellowship with the exalted Son of man in the meal. Faith in the Resurrection and an expectation of the continuation of the fellowship meal with the exalted Son of man are two basic elements of the Eucharist that are a part of the liturgy from the beginnings of the church. In meeting the Resurrected One in the eucharistic meal the community sees all the glowing expectations of salvation confirmed.

The basic mood of the community at the eucharistic meal is thereby one of joy. "And breaking bread in their homes, they partook of food with glad and generous hearts, praising God" (Acts 2:46). The Orthodox liturgy has maintained this original Christian mood of joy as at a wedding feast until the present. In Reformation churches, however, a mood of repentance and sorrow over sin often diminished and suppressed the original Christian attitude of joy.

The development of eucharistic and other liturgies. What the Christian community experiences in the eucharistic meal is basically a continuation of the appearances of the Resurrected One in its midst. Thus, many liturgical forms developed, all of which served to enhance the mystery of the eucharistic meal. In the magnificent liturgical creations from the 1st to the 6th century, diversity rather than uniformity was a commanding feature of the development of worship forms. The eucharistic mystery developed from a simple form, as depicted in the 1st-century *Didachē* (*Teaching of the Twelve Apostles*), to the fully developed liturgies of the 5th and 6th centuries in both the East and the West.

This diversity that was demonstrated in the liturgies of the early church is still preserved in the Clementine liturgy (Antioch), the Syrian liturgy, the Liturgy of St. James of the church of Jerusalem, the Nestorian liturgy in Iran, the Liturgy of St. Mark in Egypt, the Roman mass, the Gallic liturgies, and the Ambrosian (Milanese), Mozarabic (Spanish), and Scottish-Irish (Celtic) liturgies.

In the 6th century two types of liturgies were fixed by canon law in the Eastern Orthodox Church: the Liturgy of St. John Chrysostom (originally the liturgy of Constantinople) and the Liturgy of St. Basil (originally the liturgy of the Cappadocian monasteries). The Liturgy of St. Basil, however, is celebrated only 10 times during the year, whereas the Liturgy of St. John Chrysostom is celebrated most other times. In addition to these liturgies is the so-called Liturgy of the Preconsecrated Offerings, attributed to Pope Gregory the Great of the 6th century. In this liturgy no consecration of the eucharistic offering occurs—because the eucharistic offerings used have been consecrated on the previous Sunday—and it is celebrated on weekday mornings during Lent as well as from Monday to Wednesday during Holy Week.

The period of liturgical improvisation apparently was concluded earlier in the Latin West than in the East. The liturgy of the ancient Latin Church is textually available only since the 6th century. Though the Gallic liturgies are essentially closer to the Eastern liturgies, the liturgy of Rome followed a special development. From the middle of the 4th century, the Roman mass was celebrated in Latin rather than in Greek, which had been the earlier practice. The fixing of the Roman mass by canon law corresponds to the Roman tendency toward legalization of the sacred.

Because of the authority inhering in the sacred, every liturgy has the tendency to become fixed in form, and any alteration of the liturgy can thus be regarded as a sacrilege. The spiritual-legal fixation of the liturgy, however, through the process of constant repetition and habit, leads to an externalization that can transfer the liturgy into a lifeless formalism for both the liturgist and the participating community.

Characteristically, all reformation eras in the history of Christianity, in which new charismatic impulses arise in the areas of piety and theology, are also periods of new liturgical creations. Thus in the late-16th-century Reformation a great diversity of new liturgical forms emerged. Luther in Germany restricted himself to a reformatory alteration of the Catholic liturgy of the

Margin notes:
The basic concepts of Congregationalism

The image of the messianic meal

The basic mood of the Eucharist

The tendency of liturgies to become fixed in form

mass, whereas Zwingli in Switzerland attempted to create a completely new evangelical liturgy of the Eucharist based upon a New Testament foundation. The Free churches also showed a strong liturgical productivity; in the Herrnhut Brethren (Moravian) community, Graf von Zinzendorf ushered in the singing worship services. Methodism, influenced by the Moravian spiritual songs and melodies, also produced new liturgical impulses, especially through its creation of new hymns and songs and its joyousness in singing.

The radical sects have been especially productive in this area. The Mormons, for example, developed not only a new type of church song but also a new style of church music in the context of their liturgical new creation (*e.g.,* "sealing"). The mood of charismatic, liturgical new creations has also been preserved in the Baptist Negro churches of the American South, whose spirituals are the most impressive sign of a free and spontaneous liturgical productivity. The Pentecostal churches of the 20th century quite consciously attempt to protect themselves against liturgical formalism. The free, often spontaneously improvised liturgy of the Pentecostal tent missions and their often ecstatic, strongly rhythmized music endeavour to retain certain features of the charismatic spontaneity of the early Christian worship service.

Traditional liturgy fixed by canon law, which could develop into a lifeless formalism, occasionally led to the adoption of a fundamentally anti-liturgical attitude. Zwingli's reformation, for example, exhibited an emphatically anti-liturgical tendency in that it reduced the intricate Roman Catholic order of service to beginning song, prayer, sermon, concluding prayer, and concluding song. In the Reformed churches, anti-liturgical currents developed, which, in art, have been directed against setting up ecclesiastical works of art in the church as well as against the use of the organ in the worship service. The Quakers, the Society of Friends, radically eliminated the liturgy and replaced it with mutual silence, expecting the spontaneous activity of the Holy Spirit.

Forms and variations of the liturgy. Though definite and obligatory liturgies have been established as normative, the forms of the liturgy continue to develop and change. The impulse toward variations in worship services has been especially noticeable in the latter part of the 20th century. In the Eastern Orthodox liturgy, in the Roman mass and the Roman breviary, and in Anglican and Lutheran liturgies, there are both fixed and changing sections. The fixed parts represent the basic structure of the worship service concerned, and the alternating parts emphasize the individual character of a particular service for a certain day or period of the church year. The changing parts consist of special Old and New Testament readings that are appropriate for a particular church festival, as well as of special prayers and particular hymns.

The basic parts of the eucharistic liturgy The eucharistic liturgy consists of two parts: the Liturgy of the Catechumens and the Liturgy of the Faithful. This basic liturgical structure goes back to a time in which the church was a missionary church that grew for the most part through conversion of adults. The latter were first introduced to the Christian mysteries as catechumens through instruction in religious doctrine. They also received permission to take part in the first part of the worship service (which was instructional), but they had to leave the service before the eucharistic mystery was celebrated. The first part of the Orthodox worship service still ends with a threefold exclamation, reminiscent of pre-Christian, Hellenistic mystery formulas: "You catechumens, go forth! None of the catechumens (may remain here)!"

The eucharistic liturgy of the Orthodox Church is a kind of mystery drama in which the advent of the Lord is mystically consummated and the entire history of salvation—the incarnation, death, and resurrection of Christ the Logos, up to the outpouring of the Holy Spirit—is recapitulated. The Orthodox Church also attaches the greatest value to the fact that within the eucharistic mystery an actual transformation of the eucharistic elements in bread and wine takes place. This

is not the same as the Roman Catholic dogma of transubstantiation, which teaches that the substance of the bread and wine is changed into the body and blood of Christ, though the properties of the elements remain the same, when the priest consecrates the bread and wine. According to some Orthodox authorities, the Orthodox view is similar to the Lutheran doctrine of the Real Presence. The essential and central happening in the Orthodox liturgy, however, is the descent of the resurrected Lord himself, who enters the community as "the King of the universe, borne along invisibly above spears by the angelic hosts." The transformation of the elements is, therefore, the immediate emanation of this personal presence. Thus, the Orthodox Church does not preserve and display the consecrated host after and outside the eucharistic liturgy, as in the Roman Catholic Church, because the consecrated offerings are mystically apprehended and actualized only during the eucharistic meal.

In the Roman mass, the sacrificial character of the Eucharist is strongly emphasized, but it is less so in the Orthodox liturgy. This is because in the Orthodox liturgy the Eucharist is not only a representation of the crucifixion sacrifice (as in the Roman mass) but also of the entire history of salvation, in which the entire congregation, priest and laity, participates. Thus, the Orthodox Church has also held fast to the original form of Holy Communion in both kinds.

Liturgical gestures and vestments. The Orthodox Church still preserves the liturgical gestures of the early church. Though in many Protestant churches parishioners sit while praying, the Orthodox worshipper prays while standing (because he stands throughout the service), with arms hanging down, crossing himself at the beginning and ending of the prayer.

Forms of liturgical gestures The prayerful gesture of folded hands among Protestant churches derives from an old Germanic tradition of holding the sword hand with the left hand, which symbolizes one's giving himself over to the protection of God because he is now defenseless. The prayerful gesture of hands pressed flat against one another with the fingertips pointed upward—the symbol of the flame—is practiced among Roman Catholics as well as Hindus and Buddhists. Other liturgical gestures found in many Christian churches are crossing oneself, genuflecting, beating oneself on the chest, and kneeling during prayer or when receiving the eucharistic elements. Among some Holiness or Pentecostal churches spontaneous hand-clapping and rhythmic movements of the body have been stylized gestures in the worship services. These gestures are also practiced among the so-called younger churches of Africa and other mission areas of European and American major churches. Liturgical dancing, widely spread in pagan cults, was not practiced in the early church; vestigial remnants of this ancient practice, however, have been admitted in liturgical processionals. In the latter part of the 20th century, liturgical dances have been reintroduced in some churches but only in a limited fashion. Among the many other gestures of devotion and veneration practiced in the liturgically oriented churches such as the Roman Catholic Church, the High Church Anglican churches, and the Orthodox Church, are kissing the altar, the gospel, the cross, and the holy icons.

Liturgical vestments have developed in a variety of fashions, some of which have become very ornate. The liturgical vestments all have symbolic meaning. In the Orthodox Church the liturgical vestments symbolize the wedding garments that enable the liturgists to share in the heavenly wedding feast, the Eucharist. The *epitrachēlion,* which is worn around the neck and corresponds to the Roman stole, represents the flowing downward of the Holy Spirit. (For a fuller treatment of liturgical vestments, SEE RELIGIOUS DRESS AND VESTMENTS.)

The sacraments. The interpretation and number of the sacraments vary among the Roman Catholic, Orthodox, Eastern independent, and Protestant churches. The Roman Church has fixed the number of sacraments at seven: Baptism, confirmation, the Eucharist, penance, holy orders, matrimony, and anointing of the sick. In the early church the number of sacraments varied, sometimes including as many as 10 or 12. The theology of the Orthodox Church, under the influence of the Roman Catholic Church, fixed the number of sacraments at seven. The classical Protestant churches (*i.e.*, Lutheran, Anglican, and Reformed) have accepted only two sacraments—*i.e.*, Baptism and the Eucharist, though Luther allowed that penance was a valid part of sacramental theology.

The New Testament mentions a series of "holy acts" that are not, strictly speaking, sacraments. Though the Roman Catholic Church recognizes a difference between such "holy acts," which are called sacramentals, and sacraments, the Orthodox Church does not, in principle, make such strict distinctions. Thus, though Baptism and the Eucharist have been established as sacraments of the church, foot washing, which in the Gospel According to John, chapter 13, replaces the Lord's Supper, was not maintained as a sacrament. It is still practiced on special occasions, such as on Holy Thursday in the Roman Church, and as a rite prior to the observance of the Lord's Supper, as in the Church of the Brethren. The "holy acts" of the Orthodox Church are symbolically connected to its most important mysteries. Hence, Baptism consists of a triple immersion that is connected with a triple renunciation of Satan that the candidate says and acts out symbolically prior to the immersions. He first faces west, which is the symbolic direction of the Antichrist, spits three times to symbolize his renunciation of Satan, and then faces east, the symbolic direction of Christ, the sun of righteousness. Immediately following Baptism, chrismation (anointing with consecrated oil) takes place, and the baptized believer receives the "seal of the gift of the Holy Spirit" (see also SACRAMENT).

Tradition. *The development and significance of tradition.* The disposition of Christianity toward tradition has exhibited a characteristic tension from its very beginnings; it has broken tradition and it has created tradition. This tension, which is grounded in its essence, has been continued throughout its entire history. It began with breaking the tradition of Old Testament legalistic piety. In the Sermon on the Mount, Jesus set forth his message as a renunciation of the Old Testament tradition of the Law. Yet, with his coming, new revelation, life, death, and Resurrection, he himself created a new tradition, a "new law," that has been carried on in the church. The dogmatic controversies of the Reformation give the impression that the tradition of the church has to do primarily, if not exclusively, with ecclesiastical doctrinal tradition. Tradition, however, includes all areas of life of the Christian community and its piety, not just the teachings but also the forms of worship service, bodily gestures of prayer and the liturgy, oral and written tradition and the characteristic process of transition of the oral into written tradition, a new church tradition of rules for eating and fasting, and other aspects of the Christian life.

The break with the tradition of Jewish legal piety was not total. The Old Testament was adopted from Jewish tradition, but its interpretation was based upon the concepts of salvation that emerged around the figure of Jesus Christ. The Old Testament book of Psalms, including its musical form, was taken over in Christian worship as the foundation of the liturgy. The new revelation became tradition in the oral transmission of the words of the Lord (the logia) and the reports (kerygma) concerning the events of his life that were important for the early church's faith in him; his Baptism, the story of his Passion, his Resurrection, and his Ascension. The celebration of the Lord's Supper as anticipation of the heavenly meal with the Messiah–Son of man in the coming Kingdom of God, even to the point of preserving in the liturgy the Aramaic exclamation *maranatha* ("O Lord, Come") and its Greek parallel *erche kyrie* ("Come, Lord!") as the supplicant calling for the Parousia—all this became tradition.

In addition to the traditions of the Old Testament

The number of sacraments and forms of sacramentals

The inherent tension regarding tradition in Christianity

synagogal worship service, traditions of the Hellenistic mystery cults also were absorbed and reinterpreted in Christian forms. Among the traditions taken over from the mystery religions were: the arcane discipline—the distinction between the true *mystai* (those initiated into the secrets of the Christian faith), who were permitted to participate in the esoteric worship service (*i.e.*, the Eucharist), and the catechumens (those who attended only the instructional part of the service and were then dismissed); the introduction of hymn singing dependent upon the melodic style of the mystery hymns (in addition to the Jewish Psalms); the retention of the ancient gesture of upraised hands during the epiclesis, the calling down of the Holy Spirit upon bread and wine; and many others.

Of special significance is the oral tradition of doctrinal transmission and its written record. Judaism over the centuries had developed its own unique tradition of the oral transmission of teachings. According to rabbinic doctrine, orally transmitted tradition coexisted on an equal basis with the recorded Law. Both text and tradition were believed to have been entrusted to Moses on Mt. Sinai. Within the unbroken chain of scribes the tradition was passed on from generation to generation and substantiated through scripture and exegesis. The doctrinal contents of the tradition were initially passed on orally and memorized by the students through repetition. Because of the possibilities of error in a purely oral transmission, however, the extensive and growing body of tradition was, by necessity, fixed in written form. The rabbinic tradition of the Pharisees (a Jewish sect that sanctioned the reinterpretation of the Mosaic Law) was established in the Mishnah (commentaries) and later in the Palestinian and Babylonian Talmud (compendiums of Jewish Law, lore, and commentary). Because the essence of tradition is never concluded —*i.e.*, by its very nature is never completely fixed in writing—the learned discussion of tradition by necessity continued in constant exegetical debate with the Holy Scriptures. The written record of tradition, however, never claimed to be equal to the Holy Scriptures in Judaism. A similar process of written fixation also occurred among the sectarians of the commmunity at Qumrān, which in its *Manual of Discipline* and in the *Damascus Document* recorded its interpretation of the Law, developed first orally in the tradition.

In the Christian Church a tradition also was formed proceeding from Jesus himself. The oral doctrinal transmission of the tradition was written down between the end of the 1st and the first half of the 2nd century in the form of various gospels, histories of the Apostles, letters, sermonic literature, and apocalypses. Among Christian Gnostics the tradition also included secret communications of the risen Christ to his disciples.

A new element, however, inhered in the Christian vis-à-vis the Jewish tradition. For Jewish piety the divine revelation encompassed two forms of divine expression: the Law and the Prophets. Nevertheless, this revelation is considered concluded with the last Prophets; its actualization further ensues through interpretation. In the Christian Church the tradition is joined not only to the teachings of Jesus and the story of his life as prophet and teacher that terminated with his death but also to the central event of the history of salvation, which his life, Passion, death, and Resurrection represent—namely, to the resurrected Christ who is henceforth present as the living Lord of the church and guides and increases it through his Holy Spirit. This led to the literary form of church tradition—the Holy Scripture. As the "New Testament," it takes its place next to the Holy Scripture of Judaism, henceforth reinterpreted as the "Old Testament." The tradition of the church itself thereby entered into the characteristic Christian tension between spirit and letter. The spirit creates tradition but also breaks tradition as soon as the latter is solidified into an external written form and thus impedes charismatic life.

Throughout church history, however, the core of this field of tension is formed by the transmission of the Christ event—the kerygma—itself. On the one hand, the kerygma is the bearer and starting point for tradi-

Oral and written tradition

The role of kerygma in tradition

tion; on the other hand, it molds the impetus for ever new impulses toward charismatic, fresh interpretations and, under certain circumstances, suggests or even enforces a conscious elimination of accumulated traditions. Decisive in this respect is the self-understanding of the church. According to the self-understanding of the Roman Catholic and the Eastern Orthodox churches, the church, as the institution of Jesus Christ, is the bearer of the oral and the written tradition. It is the church that created the New Testament canon. The selection of canonical writings undertaken by it already presupposes a dogmatic distinction between "ecclesiastical" teachings—which, in the opinion of its responsible leaders, are "apostolic"—and "heretical" teachings. It thereby already presupposes a far-reaching intellectualization of the tradition and its identification with "doctrine." The oral tradition thus became formalized in fixed creedal formulas.

Accordingly, in the history of the Christian Church a specific, characteristic dialectic has been evidenced between periods of excessive growth and formalistic hardening of tradition that hindered and smothered the charismatic life of the church and periods of a reduction of tradition that follow new reformational movements. The latter occurred, in part, within the church itself, such as in the reforms of Cluny, the Franciscans, and the Dominicans; they also took on the form of revolutionary movements. The Reformation of the 16th century exhibited various degrees of positions toward tradition. All of the Reformers broke with the institution of monasticism, the liturgical and sacramental tradition of the Roman Church, and certain elements of doctrinal tradition. Luther, however, was more conservative in his attitude toward the Roman Church than were Zwingli and Calvin. He was thus especially hated among the representatives of the radical Reformation—e.g., the Anabaptists and Schwärmer ("fanatics"), who demanded and practiced a revolutionary break with the entire Roman Catholic tradition. The new churches that arose from the Reformation, however, soon created for themselves their own new traditions. This was made necessary by the predominance of both the didactic, doctrinaire principle and the founding of one's own church upon one's own "confessional writings." Practical manifestations against the tradition of the Roman Church also had public effects—e.g., the eating of sausage on fast days in Zürich at the start of Zwingli's reformation or the provocative marriages of monks and nuns.

In the 19th century, the period of a progressive revolutionizing of political life in Europe and North and South America, the Roman Church sought to safeguard its tradition—threatened on all sides—through an emphatic program of "antimodernism." It endeavoured to protect tradition both by law and through theology (e.g., in returning to a strict, obligatory neo-Thomism). The representatives of this development were the popes from Pius IX (reigned 1846–78) to Pius XII (reigned 1939–58). With Pope John XXIII (reigned 1958–63), a dismantling (aggiornamento) of antimodernism and a more critical attitude vis-à-vis the "tradition" set in; this extended to traditional dogmatic views as well as to the liturgy and church structure. The second Vatican Council (1962–65) guided this development into moderate channels, but by the 1970s it had not yet come to its conclusion. On the other hand, an opposite development has taken place in the Soviet Union and the east European countries. In these nations the remains of the Orthodox Church, which survived extermination campaigns of the Leninist and Stalinist eras from the 1920s to the 1950s, preserved themselves in a political environment hostile to the church precisely through a retreat to their church tradition and religious functioning in the realm of the liturgy. In the World Council of Churches, the Orthodox Church in the latter part of the 20th century has viewed its task as the bearer of Christian tradition over against the predominant social-ethical tendencies of certain Protestant member churches that have disregarded or de-emphasized the tradition of the church in a wave of antihistorical sentiment.

The Reformation view of tradition

The development of the Scriptures. The most important creation of church tradition is that of the Holy Scriptures themselves and, secondarily, the exegesis (critical interpretations and explanations) of the Scriptures. Exegesis first appeared in Christian circles among Gnostic heretics and the church catechists (teachers)—e.g., in the Christian school systems, such as in Alexandria and Antioch. The heretics, who could not claim the unbroken apostolic tradition maintained by the Orthodox Christian churches, had a necessary interest in claiming the tradition to justify their own movements. Thus, exegesis was directly related to the development of a normative scriptural canon in the Orthodox churches. A similar need for the interpretation of an ecclesiastically fixed scriptural canon resulted in the Christian school system.

The first representatives of early church exegesis were not the bishops but rather the "teachers" (didaskaloi) of the catechetical schools, modelled after the Hellenistic philosophers' schools in which interpretive and philological principles had been developed according to the traditions of the founders of the respective schools. The allegorical interpretation of Greek classical philosophical and poetical texts, which was prevalent at the Library and Museum (the school) of Alexandria, for example, directly influenced the exegetical method of the Christian Catechetical school there. Basing his principles on the methods of Philo of Alexandria and Clement of Alexandria, his teacher, and others, Origen (died c. 254)—the Christian Catechetical school's most significant representative—created the foundation for the type of Christian exegesis (i.e., the typological-allegorical method) that lasted from the patristic period and the Middle Ages up to the time of Luther in the 16th century. Origen based his exegesis upon comprehensive textual-critical work that was common to current Hellenistic practices, such as collecting Hebrew texts and Greek parallel translations of the Old Testament. His main concern, however, was that of ascertaining the spiritual meaning of the Scriptures, the transhistorical divine truth that is hidden in the records of the history of salvation in the Scriptures. He thus developed a system containing four types of interpretation: literal, moral, typological, and allegorical.

The view of "teachers" as charismatic figures (i.e., those gifted by the Holy Spirit with the ability to uncover the hidden spiritual meaning of the letter) long hindered Western theologians in developing their own exegetical works. Exegetical literature was restricted to "chains" (catenae), in which excerpts from commentaries or homilies of the charismatic Fathers were joined together in a "chain" for the individual words and sentences of the Holy Scriptures. This was similar to the way in which early medieval theological works were composed of "sentences"—i.e., individual doctrinal definitions from the writings of authoritative church teachers along with a limited commentary. Typological exegesis attained special significance for medieval Christian mysticism, which was inspired to a great extent by the allegorical interpretation of the Song of Solomon as the wedding between Christ and the soul.

Only with the Reformation, under the leadership of Luther, did there emerge an emphatic turning away from the allegorical exegesis and a turning toward the literal meaning of the Scriptures. This had its beginnings in the early church in the theological school of Antioch. In contrast to the Platonic tradition of the school of Alexandria, the school of Antioch was guided by Aristotelian philosophy. In place of allegorizing, which was consciously rejected, Antiochene exegesis was very much occupied with textual criticism. Both traditions often were included together in the so-called glosses of the Latin Middle Ages, such as in the Glossa ordinaria ("Ordinary Glosses"), edited by Anselm of Laon (died 1117), and the Postillae—the first biblical commentary to be printed (1471–72)—of Nicholas of Lyra (died 1349).

According to his own statement, Luther's reformational breakthrough came about through a fresh exegetical reflection—legendo et docendo ("by perusing and teaching")—in connection with his lectures on the Bible at the

The role of exegesis in scriptural traditions

The exegetical principles of the Reformation

university of Wittenberg in Germany. He used the preliminary work of Humanist philologists for the restoration of the Old and New Testament text (*e.g.*, Erasmus' 1516 edition of the Greek New Testament in the lectures on the Letter of Paul to the Romans). Luther replaced the traditional schema of the fourfold meaning of the Scripture with a spiritual interpretation of the letter—*i.e.*, one based on Christ. Inasmuch as the letter, which speaks historically of the work of Christ, at the same time always means this work as the salvation event that has happened "for us," it always contains the spiritual meaning in itself. In debates with the Spiritualists and Schwärmer ("fanatics"), who made use of the allegorical-tropological (figurative) method, Luther appealed ever more strongly to the unequivocal "clarity" of the letter of the Scriptures, which contains the "clarity" of the "subject" expressed by it. His exegesis is thus also a dogmatic one. The struggle between historical and tropological exegesis was emphasized in the debate between Luther and Zwingli over the understanding of the Lord's Supper.

During the early 18th century, biblical interpretation free of dogmatic interest was achieved among theologians accused of heresy by orthodox colleagues of their confession, such as among the Dutch Arminians (*e.g.*, Hugo Grotius and J.J. Wettstein). Interest in the history of the Old and New Testament period was growing; ancient Near Eastern history, biblical geography and archaeology, and the history of the religions of the ancient East and Hellenism were being included in the interpretation of the Scriptures. Under the influence of the Enlightenment, the historical criticism of the Bible, which was independent of the moral and edifying evaluation of the Holy Scriptures, was established. Soon including criticism of early church dogma, it led directly to the rise of historical criticism of the Bible in the 19th and 20th centuries (see also EXEGESIS AND HERMENEUTICS, BIBLICAL).

**Develop-
ment of
historical
criticism
of the
Bible**

The development of traditions centring on holy times and places. In addition to the tradition of the Holy Scriptures and its interpretation, traditions centring on holy times and holy places also developed. The early church developed its own calendar based upon a specifically Christian understanding of time and history: the church celebrates the repetition of the history of salvation and its most important events in a cycle of days, weeks, months, years, and millennia. In the yearly cycle the entire history of salvation is repeated in a sequence of Christian festivals. The most important point in time for the Christian is the historical event of Jesus Christ's Resurrection; it is decisive for the weekly as well as for the yearly division of time. The Jewish seven-day week viewed the sabbath (the seventh day) as a holiday for Yahweh, interpreted as God's rest at the end of creation (Gen. 2:1–3); the Christian seven-day week accented Sunday (the first day), the day of Jesus Christ's Resurrection.

Originally, the church celebrated Easter on every Sunday, in expectation of the return of the Lord. Later, in linking the Passion and the Resurrection story, Easter was scheduled on Passover, the Jewish feast celebrating the Exodus from Egypt in the 13th century BC. After long and fierce controversies over its date (which is governed by the lunar calendar), the date for Easter set by the Council of Nicaea in 325 is the first Sunday after the full moon that follows the spring equinox. Easter became the centre of a fixed liturgical structure of times and festivals in the church year.

The millennial cycle also played a significant role in Christian historical consciousness until the Copernican world view was accepted in Western thought. This cycle was based on the idea of a world period embracing seven millennia between the creation of the world and the end of the world or the return of Christ. (The creation was, according to the Byzantine calendar, on September 1, 5509 BC; in 3960 BC, according to Luther; in 4713 BC, according to Joseph Scaliger, a 16th–17th-century French scholar; and October 23, 4004 BC, according to James Ussher, a 16th–17th-century Anglican bishop in Ireland.) Various eschatological movements of the Middle Ages

and the modern period have been based upon the calculation of these dates (*e.g.*, Millerites, Seventh-day Adventists, Jehovah's Witnesses).

Christmas, the festival of the birth of Jesus Christ, was established in connection with a fading of the expectation of Christ's imminent return. The Christian festival calendar was thus converted to the Julian solar calendar. The Christmas festival is the Christian revision of the Roman day of the winter solstice—the festival of Dies Invicti Solis (the Day of the Invincible Sun) on December 25. It slowly supplanted Epiphany, which originally was celebrated in the East on January 6 as the birthday of Christ, as the "manifestation" of the heavenly Logos in the flesh. The Fathers of the 2nd and 3rd centuries, such as Clement of Alexandria, Origen, and Epiphanius, contended that Christmas was a copy of a pagan celebration. As the festival of the incarnation of the heavenly Logos, however, Christmas was increasingly entrenched in theology and liturgy under Roman influence during the struggle against Arianism in the 4th century. In Rome the appearance of Christ, the "sun of righteousness" (Mal. 4:2), was celebrated on December 25—in place of the Sol Invictus festival introduced by the emperor Aurelian in the 3rd century—as the festival of victory of Christianity over paganism.

The development of Christmas as the central festival in the West

Thus, the Easter liturgy has been developed more highly in the Eastern Orthodox Church, and the Christmas liturgy more highly in the Roman Catholic Church. Accordingly, the Reformation churches have retained Christmas as their chief festival.

The Christian calendar is the most widely disseminated Christian institution. The seven-day week and the rhythm of the Christian festivals have been accepted even by most of the non-Christian countries. Despite energetic attempts at the introduction of a sliding work week, the seven-day week with work-free Sunday could not be eliminated even in Communist states with an atheist world view. Even in atheistic circles and organizations throughout the world, Christian holidays enjoy an undisputed popularity as work-free days. They have thereby undergone a process of striking desacralization and—especially Christmas—commercialization. The Christological foundation of Christmas was replaced by the myth of Santa Claus (see also CHURCH YEAR; FEAST AND FESTIVAL).

The veneration of holy places is the oldest expression of Christian popular piety. From Judaism the Christian Church adopted the idea and practice of venerating holy places. In post-exilic Judaism (*i.e.*, after the 5th century BC), Jerusalem became the sanctuary and the centre of the Jews in Palestine as well as the goal of the pilgrimages of Jews of the Diaspora. After the destruction in AD 70 of Jerusalem, which was the holy city for the early church, it remained for Christians, too—as the site of the suffering and Resurrection of Jesus Christ and as the place of his return in glory—a holy city and a goal of pilgrimages. Such early bishops as Melito of Sardis and Alexander of Jerusalem and such theologians as Origen embarked on pilgrimages to Jerusalem. When the Christian Church became the state church in the 4th century, pilgrimages to the holy places in Palestine became popular.

The veneration of holy places

The journey of the empress mother Helena to the Holy Land before AD 330 inaugurated the cult of relics through the alleged discovery of the holy cross. Constantine built the Church of the Holy Sepulchre in Jerusalem (335) and the Church of the Nativity over the Grotto of the Nativity in Bethlehem. The numerous other biblical commemorative places of the Old and New Testament history soon followed.

The cult of martyrs and saints led to establishment of shrines outside Palestine that were developed into pilgrimage places. The idea that the martyrs are present at the places of their martyrdom (*e.g.*, Peter's tomb at the Vatican) secured a prominent position for holy places connected with the cult of saints and martyrs. The cult of the martyrs was developed especially in the Roman catacombs, and it contributed to the formation of the Petrine doctrine and the teaching of the primacy of the

Roman bishop. After the 4th century the cult of martyrs spread further and created an abundance of new holy places in the West: thus, Santiago de Compostela in Spain was connected with the tomb of James, to which equal rank with Rome and Jerusalem was later accorded; then Trèves in Germany, with the tomb of Matthew, which exerted a special power of attraction through the relic of the holy robe; and Marburg in Germany, with the shrine of St. Elizabeth. In the Middle Ages, during the development of the Roman Catholic sacrament of penance, holy places became places of grace, the visitation of which was considered a work of penance.

The veneration of relics

The original historical consciousness of the Christian Church is also alive in the cult of relics. In the relics of the body in which the saint suffered martyrdom, the saint himself is believed to be present, or at least something of the power of the Holy Spirit that filled him. The cult of relics began as a result of veneration of a martyr at his or her tomb, over which later was erected an altar of the church built to honour the saint. From the 4th century on in the East, and later also in the West, the remains of the martyrs were distributed in order that as many as possible could share in their miraculous power. Fragments of relics were sewn into a silken cloth (antimension), and the Eucharist could be celebrated only upon an altar that was covered with such an antimension. In times of persecution the Eucharist could be celebrated upon any table, as long as it was covered with the antimension and consecrated through the presence of the martyr. In the Latin Church the relics are enclosed in a cavity (sepulcrum) in the altar top. During the deconsecration of a church, the relic is again removed from the sepulcrum.

In the late Middles Ages the character of the pilgrimage, just like the veneration of relics, underwent a degeneration in connection with the degeneration of the sacrament of penance because of the abuse of the indulgence. Luther's critique of the indulgence began with a criticism of the display of the elector of Saxony Frederick III the Wise's imposing collection of relics in the Schlosskirche of Wittenberg on All Saints' Day (1516). Over against the attacks of Luther, the Council of Trent declared that

the holy bodies of the holy martyrs and others living with Christ, whose bodies were living members of Christ and temples of the Holy Spirit, and will be by him raised to eternal life and glorified, are to be venerated by the faithful, since by them God bestows many benefits upon men.

In order to avoid the development of a holy place at his grave and a reliquary and saintly cult around his person, Calvin arranged by will that his body be buried at an unknown spot. The erection of the giant monument to the Reformer at the supposed place of his burial shows the uselessness of his effort and the strength of the Christian consciousness of tradition.

In the secular sphere the establishment of holy places, the practice of pilgrimages, and the cult of relics have been continued in manifold imitations (e.g., tombs of the Unknown Soldier, the Lenin Mausoleum on Red Square in Moscow).

Forms of the Christian life. *Monasticism.* Monasticism, an institution based on the Christian ideal of perfection, has its roots in New Testament Christianity, in which the baptized were designated as the "perfect ones." In the early church, monasticism equated "perfection" with world-denying asceticism, along with the view that perfect Christianity centred its way of life on the maximum love of God and neighbour.

The roots, ideals, and purposes of monasticism

Monastic discipline, in the course of time, became an external means for the attainment of this ideal of perfect love of God and neighbour. Only a few especially disciplined persons, however, have been able to live according to the path that leads to the ideal of perfection. The masses, on the other hand, are inwardly and outwardly incapable of exercizing ascetic discipline. Therefore, the monastic rules of life were not generally binding "commands" but rather only "counsels" directed to those called to lead an ascetic life. The essential distinction between command and counsel is found in the words of Jesus: he did not command men to "make themselves

eunuchs for the sake of the kingdom of heaven," but rather he recommended this condition only to those who were "able to receive this" (Matt. 19:12). Unmarried ascetics were recognized as a special class in the early church, forming the core of many churches. Later, with its distinction between counsel (suasum) and command (iussum), as in the writings of Tertullian in the late 2nd century, the church found itself in full accord with the oldest Christian view. During the latter part of the 2nd and the beginning of the 3rd century, the combination of asceticism and mysticism, which was to become the spiritual basis of later monasticism in the East and in part also in the West, was emphasized by Clement of Alexandria and Origen.

By the 4th century, monasticism became an established institution in the Christian Church not because of the decadence of the people of late antiquity, as has often been asserted, but rather because it was sustained by the resilient and culturally unexhausted rural populations of Egypt and Syria, who had developed an enthusiasm for asceticism itself. Out of the desire for still further advanced isolation, ascetics moved from a proximity to inhabited places to tombs, abandoned and half-deteriorated human settlements, caves, and, finally, into the wilderness areas of the deserts. The main task of the ascetics— *i.e.*, struggle with the demons—thereby underwent a heightened intensification: the desert was considered the abode of the demons, the place of refuge of the pagan gods falling back before a victorious Christianity. Hence, the expansion of Christianity in the cities of Egypt and the rise of Egyptian desert monasticism in the 4th century occurred both because the masses streamed into the churches as a result of the official imperial toleration and support policies and because ascetics striving for perfection moved into the desert and grew in significant numbers (see also ANGELS AND DEMONS; ASCETICISM).

Certain writings that captured the spirit of monasticism further enhanced the development of this way of life in the church. Athanasius of Alexandria, the 4th century's most significant bishop spiritually and in terms of ecclesiastical politics, wrote the *Life of St. Antony*, which described the eremitic (hermit) life in the desert and the awesome struggle of ascetics with the demons as the model of the life of Christian perfection. This work indicates that the church sanctioned and propagated monasticism.

The influence of the monastic leaders

A former Roman soldier of the 4th century, Pachomius, created the first monastery in the modern sense. He united the monks under one roof in a community living under the leadership of an abbot (father, or leader). In 323 he founded the first true monastic cloister in Tabennisi, north of Thebes, in Egypt, and joined together houses of 30 to 40 monks, each with its own superior. Pachomius also created a monastic rule that, however, served more as a regulation of external monastic life than spiritual guidance. During the remainder of the 4th century, monasticism soon developed in areas outside Egypt. Athanasius brought the monastic rule of Pachomius to the West during his banishment (340–346) to Trèves in Germany—as a result of his opposition to the imperially sanctioned heretical doctrines of Arianism. Mar Awgin, a Syrian monk, introduced the monastic rule in Mesopotamia, and Jerome established a monastic cloister in Bethlehem.

Basil the Great, one of the three Cappadocian Fathers of the 4th century, definitively shaped monastic community life in the Byzantine Church. His ascetic writings furnished the theological and instructional foundation for the "common life" (cenobitism) of monks. He became the creator of a monastic rule that, through constant variations and modifications, became authoritative for later Orthodox monasticism. The Rule of Basil has preserved the Orthodox combination of asceticism and mysticism into the 20th century.

Western monasticism, founded by Benedict of Nursia (Italy) in the 6th century, has gone through a double form of special development vis-à-vis early church monasticism. The first consists of its clericalization. In modern Roman Catholic cloisters, monks are, except for the serv-

The development of Western monasticism

ing brothers (*fratres*), ordained priests and are thereby drawn in a direct way into the ecclesiastical tasks of the Roman Church. Originally, however, monks were laymen. Pachomius had explicitly forbidden monks to become priests on the ground that "it is good not to covet power and glory." Basil the Great, however, by means of a special vow and a special ceremony, enabled monks to cease being just laymen and to attain a position between that of the clergy and the laity. Even in the 20th century, monks of the Orthodox Church are, for the most part, lay monks; only a few fathers (abbots) of each cloister are ordained priests (*hieromonachoi*), who are thus allowed to administer the sacraments.

The second special development in Roman Catholicism consists of the functional characteristics of its many orders. The individual orders aid the church in its various areas of activity—*e.g.*, missions, education, care for the sick and needy, and combating heresy. Developing a wide-ranging diversification in its structure and sociological interests, Roman Catholic monasticism has extended all the way from the knightly orders to orders of mendicant friars, and it has included orders of decided feudal and aristocratic characteristics alongside orders of purely bourgeois characteristics. To the degree that special missionary, pedagogical, scholarly-theological, and ecclesiastically political tasks of the orders increased in the West, the character of ancient monasticism—originally focussed completely on prayer, meditation, and contemplation—receded more and more in importance. Only the Benedictines and the Carmelites, according to some observers, still attempt to preserve the ancient character and purposes of monasticism in Roman Catholicism in the 20th century (see also MONASTICISM).

The saintly life. In Christian popular piety the saint plays a very significant role. Originally a self-designation of all Christians collectively, "the saints," understood in this broad sense, are "sanctified through the name of the Lord Jesus Christ and through the Spirit of our God," according to the First Letter of Paul to the Corinthians, chapter 1, verse 31. On the one hand, the saint may be understood as a Christian who endeavours to fulfill the binding demand of moral holiness in obedience to God and in love of his neighbour (II Cor. 7:1; I Thess. 4:3), or a charismatic figure in whom the gifts of the Holy Spirit operate according to the personal and temporal circumstances of such an individual. Because of certain views on being "called to holiness," members of many radical sects have designated themselves as "the saints"— from Oliver Cromwell's "saints" in 17th-century England to the Mormon "latter-day saints" in the 19th and 20th centuries.

The general meaning of "saint" was transformed during the period of the persecutions of Christians in the Roman Empire. The martyr, the witness in blood to Christ and follower in his suffering, became the prototype of the future ideal of the saint. Veneration of the saints began because of a belief that martyrs were received directly into heaven after their martyrdoms and that their intercession with God was especially effective—in the Revelation to John the martyrs occupy a special position in heaven, immediately under the altar of God (Rev. 6:9). Veneration of confessors (*i.e.*, those who had not denied their belief in Christ but had not been martyred), bishops, popes, early Church Fathers, and ascetics who had led a godlike life was established soon after cessation of the persecutions.

In the Greek church the saints were regarded as charismatic figures in whom the prototype of Christ is reflected in multifarious images. Veneration of the saints in the Orthodox churches was thus based more upon the idea that the saints provided instructional examples of the Christian life of sanctification. In the West, however, cultic veneration of the saints, the concept of patron saints, and the view that saints are helpers in need became predominant. The cult of the saints gradually came under the control of the papacy, which regulated cultic veneration of a saintly personality extolled in popular piety by means of a process of canonization strictly defined by canon law. The saints thus dominated the

church calendar, which notes the names of the ecclesiastically recognized saints of each day of the year. They are venerated on a particular day in the prayer of intercession, and references are made to their deeds, sufferings, and miracles in the liturgy.

Under Pope Paul VI, the Roman Church attempted to reduce the significance of the veneration of saints— and thereby emphasize the idea of their historical exemplariness—by deleting some unhistorical, ostensibly mythological figures from the calendar of saints. The difference between historical and mythological saints, however, is difficult to maintain in details because mythological features from pre-Christian hero myths had often been intermixed, even in the lives of demonstrably historical saints. Thus, deletion of saints from the calendar has had little success in popular piety.

In the early church the veneration of saints at first was restricted to celebrations at their tombs, but the cult of saintly relics soon spread the veneration of particular saints to many areas. The *Martyrdom of Polycarp*, for example, called the remains of the bishop Polycarp of Smyrna, martyred in 156/167, "more precious than costly stones and more excellent than gold." A belief in the need of special protection by saints is the basis of the system of patron saints: most Roman Catholic churches have a saint as their patron, whose presence in the church is represented by a relic of that particular saint. Saints, however, became patrons not only of churches but also of cities, regions, vocational groups, or classes. Saints also won a special significance as patrons of names: in the Roman Catholic and Eastern Orthodox churches a Christian generally received the name of the saint on whose holiday (day of death) he is baptized. The believer is thus joined for life with the patron of his name through the name and the name day, which, as the day of rebirth (*i.e.*, Baptism), is of much greater significance than the natural birthday.

In the Eastern Orthodox Church relics of saints appear less frequently, but icons of saints appear in greater numbers. Though cultic veneration of saints as patrons, tutelary saints, and helpers in need has increased through the centuries, the view that the saints are examples of the Christian life of sanctification has been preserved. The Roman Church, through its use of the canonization of saints, has constantly established new models for practical religiosity and morality to meet contemporary needs —raising to the position of sainthood personages all the way from the holy king to the holy servant girl.

In view of the excess of the veneration of saints, the Reformation not only eliminated the cultic veneration of saints but also images and relics of the saints from churches and homes. Although the Reformation did not theoretically deny the saints their significance as historical witnesses to the power and grace of God, through such radical measures it virtually eliminated the meaning of saints as guiding images and examples of Christian life. Under the influence of Luther's view that all believers are saints, the veneration of the saints and their relics also was either de-emphasized or eliminated. The experience of martyrdom in the times of persecution in the Reformation and Counter-Reformation encouraged the development of a new saintly ideal in the radical Protestant sects in connection with the renewal of a strict demand for sanctification. Such was the case in the Baptists' "Chronicle of the Martyrs" as well as in Spiritualism. The Swedish archbishop Nathan Söderblom's attempt at awakening in Protestantism in the 20th century a new understanding of the saint received notice in Protestant ecumenical circles and led to a rediscovery of saints in the Protestant realm (*e.g.*, through Walter Nigg's book: *Great Saints*). In modern Roman Catholicism, emphasis is increasingly being placed upon the charismatic aspects of the saints and their significance as models of a spiritual, holy Christian life (see also SAINT).

Art and iconography. *Development of art and iconography in the early church.* Christian art constitutes an essential element of the Christian religion. Until the 17th century, the history of Western art was largely identical with the history of Western ecclesiastical and religious

Margin notes:

The veneration of saints, relics, and associated customs

The meaning of "saint"

Reformation and modern views of saints

art. During the first three centuries of the Christian Church, however, there was no Christian art, and the church generally resisted it with all its might. Clement of Alexandria, for example, criticized religious (pagan) art in that it encouraged man to worship that which is created rather than the Creator. About the mid-3rd century an incipient pictorial art began to be used and accepted in the Christian Church but not without fervent opposition in some congregations. Only when the Christian Church became the Roman imperial church under Emperor Constantine in the early 4th century were pictures used in the churches, and they then began to strike roots in Christian popular religiosity.

Later, however, when pictorial art was publicly placed in the service of the church, warnings against this development were voiced by leading theologians. The church historian Eusebius, the most diligent glorifier of Constantine, characterized the use of images of the Apostles Paul and Peter as well as Christ himself as a pagan custom. Asterius, bishop of Amaseia in Pontus during the late 4th and early 5th centuries, similarly stated in a sermon:

Do not picture Christ on your garments. It is enough that he once suffered the humiliation of dwelling in a human body which of his own accord he assumed for our sakes. So, not upon your robes, but upon your soul, carry about his image.

Epiphanius (died 403), bishop of Salamis in Greece, also energetically opposed in word and deed the disposition toward images in the imperial church:

Have God always in your hearts, but not in the community house, for it does not become a Christian to expect the elation of his soul from recourse to his eyes and the roaming about of his senses.

Christian art developed at such a late stage because of its origins in Judaism and its opposition to paganism and the emperor's cult. In addition to a faith in God the Father, Creator of heaven and Earth, and faith in the uniqueness and holiness of God, Christianity also received from its Jewish origins a prohibition against the use of images to depict the sacred or holy, including man, who was created in "the image of God." The early Christian Church was also deeply involved in a struggle against paganism, which, to the Christian observer, was viewed as idolatry in that its many gods were represented in various pictorial and statuary forms. In early Christian missionary preaching, the Old Testament attacks upon pagan veneration of images were transferred directly to pagan image veneration of the first three centuries AD. The struggle against images was conducted as a battle against "idols" with all the intensity of faith in the oneness and exclusiveness of the imageless biblical God.

Abhorrence of images also was furthered because the emperor's cult was so despised by Christians. Christians were compelled, through anti-Christian legislation, to venerate the imperial images by offering sacrifices to them. Refusal to make the sacrifice was the chief cause of martyrdom. Characteristically, thus, the Christian Church's reaction after its public recognition was expressed in the riotous destruction of the pagan divine images.

In spite of these very strong religious and emotional restraints, the church developed a form of art peculiar to its needs. Protestants often have held that the development of ecclesiastical art was a part of the entire process of the inner decay of the Christian Church when it was elevated to the position of the officially favoured religious institution of the Roman Empire. In other words, some groups within Protestantism have claimed that the development of church art was part of the process of the church's inner paganization.

The starting point for the development of Christian pictorial art, however, lies in the basic teaching of the Christian revelation itself—namely, the incarnation, the point at which the Christian proclamation is differentiated from Judaism. The incarnation of the Son of man, the Messiah, in the form of man—who was created in the "image of God"—granted theological approval of a sort to the use of images that symbolized Christian truths.

Clement of Alexandria, at one point, called God "the Great Artist," who formed man according to the image of the Logos, the archetypal light of light. The great theological struggles over the use of images within the church during the period of the so-called Iconoclastic Controversy in the 8th and 9th centuries indicate how a new understanding of images emerged on the basis of Christian doctrine. This new understanding was developed into a theology of icons that still prevails in the Eastern Orthodox Church in the 20th century.

The development of Eastern Christian art and iconography. The great significance of images of the saints for the Orthodox faithful is primarily expressed in the cultic veneration of the images within the worship service. Secondly, it is expressed in the dogmatic fixation of the figures, gestures, and colours in Eastern Church iconic art. In the West, the creative achievement of the individual artist is admired, but Orthodox painting dispenses with the predominance of the individual painter's freely creative imagination. Throughout the centuries the Eastern Church has been content with reproducing certain types of holy images, and only seldom does an individual artist play a predominant role within the history of Orthodox Church painting. Most Orthodox ecclesiastical artists have remained anonymous. Icon painting is viewed as a holy skill that is practiced in cloisters in which definite schools of painting have developed. In the schools, traditional principles prevail so much that different artist-monks generally perform only certain functions in the production of a single icon. Style motifs—*e.g.*, composition, impartation of colour, hair and beard fashions, and gestures of the figures—are fixed in painting books that contain the canons of the different monastic schools of icon painters.

The significance of the image of the saint in the theology, piety, and liturgy of the Eastern Orthodox Church can be judged historically from the fact that the struggle over holy images within Orthodox Church history brought about a movement whose scope and meaning can be compared only with the Reformation of Luther and Calvin. In the 7th century a tendency hostile to images and fostered by both theological and political figures gained ground within the Byzantine Church and upset Orthodox Christendom to its very depths; known as the Iconoclastic Controversy, it was supported by some reform-minded emperors. Although opponents of icons had all the political means of power at their disposal, they were not able to succeed in overthrowing the use of icons. The conclusion of this struggle with the victory of the supporters of the use of icons is celebrated in the entire Orthodox Church on October 13 as the Feast of Orthodoxy.

Orthodox icon painting is not to be separated from its ecclesiastical and liturgical function. The painting of the image is, in fact, a liturgical act in which the artist-monks prepare themselves by fasting, penance, and consecrating the materials necessary for the painting. Before the finished icon is used, it likewise is consecrated. Not viewed as a human work, an icon (according to 8th- and 9th-century literature) was understood instead as a manifestation of a heavenly archetype—*i.e.*, as an object reflecting the true features of the heavenly archetypes. Because an icon is an object that serves as a window between the heavenly and earthly realms, the use of plastic arts within holy art is prohibited. A golden background is used on icons to indicate a heavenly perspective. The icon is always painted two-dimensionally because of the fact that it is viewed as a window through which man can view the heavenly archetype from his earthly position. A figure in the three-dimensionality of the plastic arts would thus be an abandonment of the character of epiphany (appearance).

Ideas of the iconic liturgy dominate the painting manuals of the Orthodox icon painters. The model for icon painters of the Christ figure was found in an apocryphal writing of the early church—the *Letter of Lentulus,* which was a legendary letter supposedly written by a certain Lentulus, who was named consul in the 12th year of the emperor Tiberius. As the superior of Pontius Pilate, the procurator of Judaea, he by chance was staying in Palestine at the time of the trial of Jesus. In an official report to the Emperor about the trial of Jesus, Lentulus included an official warrant for Jesus with a description of the Christ. This apocryphal description furnished the basic model for the Byzantine Christ type.

The Trinity also may not be represented, except in those forms in which, according to the view of Orthodox church doctrine, the Trinity showed itself in the divine Word of the Old and New Testaments. Early church theology interpreted an Old Testament passage (Gen. 18:1 ff.) as an appearance of the divine Trinity—namely, the visit of the three men with the patriarch Abraham at Mamre in Palestine. Also included in icons of the Trinity are the appearance of the three divine Persons—symbolized as a hand, a man, and a dove—at the Baptism of Jesus (Matt. 3:16 ff.) and the Pentecostal scene, in which the Lord, ascended to heaven, sits at the right hand of God and the Comforter (the Holy Spirit) is sent down to the Apostles in the form of fiery tongues (Acts 2). Another Trinitarian iconic scene is the Transfiguration of Jesus at Mt. Tabor (Matt. 17:2).

Icons of Mary were probably first created because of the development of Marian doctrines in the 3rd and 4th centuries. The lack of New Testament descriptions of Mary was compensated by numerous legends of Mary that concerned themselves especially with wondrous appearances of miraculous icons of the mother of God. In Russian and many other Orthodox churches, including the monasteries at Mt. Athos, such miraculous mother of God icons, "not made by hands," have been placed where the appearances of the mother of God took place.

The consecration liturgy of the icons of saints expresses the fact that the saints themselves, for their part, are viewed as likenesses of Christ. In them, the image of God has been renewed again through the working of salvation of the incarnate Son of God.

Varying views on the theology of icons

The foes of images explicitly deny that the New Testament, in relation to the Old Testament, contains any new attitude toward images. Their basic theological outlook is that the divine is beyond all earthly form in its transcendence and spirituality; representation in earthly substances and forms of the divine already indicate its profanation. The relationship to God, who is Spirit, can only be a purely spiritual one; the worship of the individual as well as the community can happen only "in spirit and in truth" (John 4:24). Similarly, the divine archetype can also be realized only spiritually and morally in life. The religious path of the action of God upon man is not the path of external influence upon the senses but rather that of spiritual action upon the mind and the will. Such an effect does not come about through the art of painting. Opponents of icons thus claim that the only way to reach an understanding of the truth is by studying the writings of the Old and New Testaments, which are filled with the Spirit of God.

The decisive contrast between the iconophiles (image lovers) and the iconoclasts (image destroyers) is found in their understanding of Christology. The iconophiles based their theology upon the view of Athanasius—who reflected Alexandrian Christology—that Christ, the God become man, is the visible, earthly, and corporeal icon of the heavenly Father, created by God himself. The iconoclasts, on the other hand, explain, in terms of ancient Antiochene Christology, that the image conflicts with the ecclesiastical dogma of the Person of the Redeemer. It is unseemly, according to their views, to desire to portray a personality such as Christ, who is himself divine, because that would mean pulling the divine down into the materialistic realm.

The theology of the iconoclasts of the Reformation period in the West made use, for the most part, of the same arguments. For the radical Protestants, the realization of God is only in the Word and sacrament.

After iconic theology had overcome opposition in the Byzantine imperial church, there were numerous Christian groups—especially in Asia Minor—in which the old hostility toward church icons was still maintained and which, in part, already had been forced into positions of heresy, such as the Paulicians (members of a 7th–9th-century dualistic sect).

The development of Western Christian art and iconography. The history of iconoclasm began in the early church with an emphatic (and catastrophic) iconoclastic movement that led to the annihilation of nearly all of the sacred art of the pagan religions of the Roman Empire. In Western Christendom, an iconoclastic attitude was again expressed in various medieval lay movements and sects, such as the Cathari and the Waldenses. Iconoclasm underwent a revolutionary outbreak in the 16th-century Reformation in Germany, France, and England. Despite the different historical types of iconoclasm, a surprising uniformity in regard to their affective structure and theological argumentation exists. The Iconoclastic Controversy of the 7th and 8th centuries also became a point of contention in the Western Church. To be sure, the latter had recognized the seventh ecumenical council at Nicaea (787), in which Iconoclasm was condemned. Nevertheless, an entirely different situation existed in the West. The Frankish–Germanic Church was a young church in which images were much more infrequent than in the old Byzantine Church, in which holy icons had accumulated over the centuries. In the West there was still no Christian pictorial art as highly developed as in the East. Also, Christianity there did not have to struggle against a highly developed pagan pictorial art. Donar, a Germanic god, reputedly whispered in a holy oak, and Boniface merely had to fell the Donar oak in order to demonstrate the superiority of Christ over the pagan god. Among the Germanic tribes in the West, there was no guild of sculptors or goldsmiths, as in Ephesus (Acts 19: 24 ff.), who would have been able to protest in the name of their gods against the Christian iconoclasts.

The difference between Eastern and Western views on icons

The Western viewpoint is revealed most clearly in the formulations of the synodal decisions on the question of images, as they were promulgated in the Frankish kingdom in the *Libri Carolini* ("Charles's Books"), Charlemagne's code of laws. In this work it is emphasized that images have only a representative character. Thus, they are understood not as an appearance of the saint but only as a visualization of the holy Persons for the support of recollecting spiritual meanings that have been expounded intellectually through sermons. Hence, this led to an essentially instructional and aesthetic concept of images. The Western Church also viewed images as the Holy Scriptures' substitute for the illiterate—*i.e.*, for the overwhelming majority of church people in this period. Images thus became the Bible for the laity. Pope Adrian I (reigned 772–795), who encouraged Western recognition of the iconophiliac Council of Nicaea, also referred to the perspicuity of the icons. This idea of perspicuity—*i.e.*, the appeal to one's imagination to picture the biblical persons and events to oneself—enabled him to recognize the Greek high esteem for the image without completely accepting the complicated theological foundation for icon veneration. The ideas articulated in the *Libri Carolini* remained decisive for the Western tradition. According to Thomas Aquinas, one of the greatest medieval theologians of the West, images in the church serve a threefold purpose: (1) for the instruction of the uneducated in place of books; (2) for illustrating and remembering the mystery of the incarnation; and (3) for awakening the passion of devotion, which is kindled more effectively on the basis of viewing than through hearing.

In the Western theology of icons, the omnipotence of the two-dimensionality of church art also was abandoned. Alongside church pictorial painting, ecclesiastical plastic arts developed; even painting in the three-dimensional form was introduced through the means of perspective. Art, furthermore, became embedded in the entire life of personal religiosity. The holy image became the devotional image; one placed himself before an image and became engrossed in his meditation of the mysteries of the Christian revelation. As devotional images, the images became the focal points for contemplation and mystical representation. Conversely, the mystical vision itself worked its way back again into pictorial art, in that what was beheld in the vision was re-

Western theology of icons

produced in church art. The burden of ecclesiastical tradition, which weighs heavily upon Byzantine art, has been gradually abolished in the Western Church. In the Eastern Church the art form is just as fixed as ecclesiastical dogma; nothing may be changed in the heavenly prototypes. This idea plays little or no role in the West. There, religious art adjusts itself at any given time to the total religious disposition of the church, to the general religious mental posture, and also to religious needs. Religious art in the West also has been shaped by the imaginative fantasy of the individual artist. Thus, from the outset, a much more individual church art developed in the West. Thus, it became possible to dissociate sacred history from its dogmatic milieu and to transpose it from the past into the actual present, thereby allowing for an adaptable development of ecclesiastical art (see also SYMBOLISM AND ICONOGRAPHY, RELIGIOUS).

Missions. *Eschatological motifs and ascetic ideals.* The missions and expansion of Christianity are among the most unusual of historical occurrences. Other world religions, such as Buddhism and Islām, also have raised a claim to universal validity, but no world religion other than Christianity has succeeded in realizing this claim through missionary expansion over the entire world.

The influence of the concept of the end time

The unique global expansion of Christianity is directly related to the Christian expectation of the end time, in the form of an imminent expectation of the return of Christ. The Christian expectation of the end time never consisted simply of a passive yearning for the coming Kingdom of God. Being grasped by faith in its immediately impending arrival was expressed instead in an incredible activation and acceleration of efforts to prepare the world for the return of Christ and the coming of the Kingdom. This state of being grasped transformed itself into the pressing duty to "prepare the way of the Lord" (Matt. 3:3) and to remove all resistance to the establishment of his Kingdom on Earth.

This eschatological pressure stands behind both the earlier and the later achievements of an ever wider expansion of Christianity. Columbus, in undertaking to cross the ocean in a westerly direction in the 15th century, for example, believed that Satan had settled in India, thus successfully disrupting the extension of the gospel and delaying the return of Christ. According to his eschatological calculations, the time for the return of Christ was nearly at hand; thus, India had to be reached by the shortest way possible so that the last bulwark of Satan might be removed through Christian missions. The same eschatological expectation drove the Spanish Jesuit Francis Xavier to India and Japan in the 16th century. Protestant world missions, commencing a century later, also were influenced by the eschatological expectation of the end time (*e.g.*, the missions of the German Lutherans Bartholomäus Ziegenbalg and Heinrich Plütschau in India in the early 18th century and the missions of the Puritans among the Indians in Massachusetts in the late 17th century). The first seal of Massachusetts displayed an Indian with a beckoning hand and the inscription "Come over and help us"—the words of the Macedonian who appeared to the Apostle Paul in a night vision (Acts 16:9).

Extensive travels of Christian missionaries

The leading missionaries of all times have accomplished great feats of extensive travels. On his numerous missionary journeys, the Apostle Paul showed a greater accomplishment in distances travelled than any known general of the Roman army, official of the Roman Empire, or trader of his time. Francis Xavier also travelled more than any other known person in his times and endured intense physical exertions on land and sea. John R. Mott (died 1955), founder of the World's Student Christian Federation, was the most widely travelled man of the first half of the 20th century. The catchphrase coined by him, "Jesus Christ to the nations in this generation," has been the basic principle of all the great and small missionary impulses that have contributed to the worldwide expansion of Christianity.

This eschatological aspect of Christian missions has continued through the 20th century, especially among Pentecostals and Adventists. The missionary institutions

of these churches come from the tradition of the Christian Free churches, which maintain a strong inclination toward an imminent expectation.

Related to the eschatological motif in missions is the ideal of ascetic homelessness. In imitation of the homeless Christ, who "has nowhere to lay his head" (Matt. 8:20), the early medieval Scottish-Irish monks—as radical Christian ascetics—demanded the renunciation of that which is dearest to man: one's own home. "For the sake of Christ" they assumed ascetic homelessness by leaving their cloisters—often in groups of 12 under the leadership of a 13th—and ventured abroad. They travelled to continental Europe—especially in Celtic areas—as far as Switzerland and over the Alps, and also went to Iceland. Similarly, Russian Orthodox hermits and monks, who often had to flee because of repressive measures by the state and the state church, conducted missions in areas northeast of the Soviet Union, Siberia, the Aleutian Islands, and Alaska. An example of a modern ascetic missionary is the French nobleman Charles-Eugene de Foucauld (died 1916), who became a martyred anchorite missionary among the Bedouin of the Sahara.

The ideal of ascetic homelessness

Missions in Eastern Christianity. Though the missionary expansion of the Eastern Orthodox Church was curtailed by the limitations imposed upon Orthodoxy by the expansion of Islām from the 7th century on, the actual missionary power of the Eastern Orthodox Church continued, especially in the Russian Orthodox Church.

Little missionary activity exists in the 20th century among the remaining Orthodox churches in Syria, Lebanon, Palestine, Egypt, and Ethiopia, nor among the Orthodox Christians of St. Thomas in India and the fragments of the Nestorian Church in Iran. This is because these churches—except for the church in Ethiopia—were constantly exposed to violent persecutions or special fiscal burdens: first by the Muslims of the 7th and 8th centuries, then by the Mongols in the 13th and 14th centuries, and especially by the Turks from the 15th to the first part of the 20th century. Muslim authorities forbade the remaining Orthodox or Independent churches of Eastern Christianity any missionary activity among the Muslims. Under the influence of the Hindu caste system, the Indian Christians of St. Thomas became a caste complete in itself and thereby forfeited possibilities for missionary activities.

These churches were not able to recover from the long periods of legal constraint under the Muslims, even when Roman Catholic and Protestant missions from the 16th century on obtained (because of international agreements) conditions somewhat favourable for their missions. British imperial and colonial policies and French protectorate policies in the Near East, especially, were of some help to the Christian minorities in areas occupied by European powers. Active Roman Catholic and Protestant missions—alongside the surviving Orthodox churches—caused Christians of the West to view the long-persecuted Eastern churches as weak in missionary capabilities.

Prior to the onslaught of Islām, however, Orthodoxy engaged in vigorous missionary activity. Eastern Christianity (especially the Nestorian Church) advanced to the East in the 3rd and 4th centuries to China, Central Asia, and Mongolia. Orthodox missionary activity also advanced westward—where the migrating German tribes experienced their first Christianization in Asia Minor and Byzantium—as well as toward the north, northeast, and northwest—where the various Slavic peoples were missionized from Byzantium. The westward missionary activity of the Orthodox Church was later replaced by Roman Catholic missions. The Germanic and western Slavic tribes were incorporated into the Roman Catholic Church, but the initial missions of Orthodoxy had prepared the way.

The missionary activities of Orthodox and Independent Eastern Christian churches

On the basis of the theological view that the Pentecost experience (Acts 2) elevated popular languages as instruments of proclamation of the divine message of salvation in the whole world among all peoples, Orthodox missionaries have endeavoured to bring to peoples missionized by them the gospel and liturgy in their own languages. From the Orthodox missions in the West and in the East—on Germanic, Slavic, and Central Asian soil as well as on that of Asia Minor—a strong impulse toward linguistic creativity has emanated. Many popular tongues of peoples and tribes missionized by the Orthodox Church in Europe, the Near East, Siberia, and Central Asia were first raised to the rank of literary languages through translations of the Bible and liturgical writings by Orthodox missionaries.

Missions of the Roman Catholic Church. Because missions, civilization, and colonization often have been in direct association with each other, missions proceeding from groups that represented a more advanced level of civilization vis-à-vis the missionized peoples often brought significant changes to the missionized peoples. The Cistercian monks in the Middle Ages, for example, not only introduced higher forms of handicrafts and architecture—from the erection of houses to technical constructions and the building of churches—in their missions among the German and Slavic tribes, but they also spread advanced forms of agriculture, fruit growing, viniculture, and cattle breeding. Above all, they brought noteworthy technical progress through the construction of canals, fishponds, watermills, and windmills.

The elimination of the old cultures by Western missionary activities

The association of missions, civilization, and colonization was continued in the conquest of the New World by the Spaniards and Portuguese. This conquest led to an elimination of the old "Indian" cultures and to a transfer of European, *i.e.*, Spanish, and Portuguese Catholicism, to the newly won colonial areas. This was expressed not only in ecclesiastical organization, in the establishment of universities and other schools, in church construction and church art but also in the entire remolding of the cultural, spiritual, economic, and industrial life of the New World according to the model of the European colonial powers. This character has been preserved, despite the far-reaching changes brought about through Indian nationalism, the European Enlightenment, the influence of North America, and modern Socialism.

In the French colonial sphere of Africa north and south of the Sahara, Catholicism expanded under the leadership of French missionary orders. The great influence of French Catholicism also is to be noted in the Near East, where France exercised the official protectorate over Catholic missions. The strong influence of French missions in Vietnam was clearly noticeable as a political and cultural factor during the early part of the Vietnam war. Belgian Catholicism expanded through its missionary orders in the Belgian Congo, and Portuguese Catholicism in the Portuguese possessions in Africa, South America (Brazil), and India (Goa). The influence of the Spanish church extended beyond South America and over the South Pacific as far as the Philippines.

Problems imposed by changes of colonial powers

As a result of several changes of colonial masters, some colonies have been caught up in the internal conflicts of European churches. The missionary history of Ceylon is typical of this situation. Ceylon, where Buddhism once was the state religion, first became Catholic under Portuguese rule, later Reformed under Dutch colonial control, and finally Anglican under the English. Upon attaining political independence after World War II, a strong Buddhist reaction set in, and many Ceylonese Christians returned to Buddhism.

Missions of Protestant churches. Protestant missions from their beginnings were influenced by the Pietistic motif of illuminating the "darkness" of the pagan world through the "light" of the Christian message. The theology of the Enlightenment, however, recognized the moral and spiritual values of the great Asian religions, especially Confucianism. The German philosopher Gottfried Wilhelm Leibniz drew up a program for bilateral missions. The Chinese were to spread the ideas of natural law and a natural ethic through their Confucian missionaries in Europe, and Christian missionaries in China were to disseminate the teachings of the supernatural, revelatory truths of Christianity and at the same time work as mediators of the Western sciences. This suggestion was not accepted, but for the first time Europe was more than superficially influenced by the ideas of the major Asian religions. In the 19th and 20th centuries the missionary initiative has been carried out by the fundamentalist American Free churches and sects, which were influenced by revival movements. They stressed the missionary commission of every Christian and covered the world with a net of missionary stations in which lay missionaries frequently were active. Among the Reformation territorial churches, Pietistic groups initiated missionary activities. Whereas in the Free churches the missionary task was recognized and realized from the outset as a task of the church, the Reformation territorial churches left foreign missions to private associations of a Pietistic or revivalist character. These missionary associations trained missionaries and sent them to their respective missionary areas.

Missionary societies and the rise of the ecumenical movement. Foreign missions, though often in confessional competition with each other, brought the Christian denominations together and set the ecumenical movement in motion. At the end of the 18th century, cooperation in the area of missions had begun between the Scottish Presbyterian Church and the English Anglican Church, which were divided at home by a deep and traditional religious conflict. The London Missionary Society, without ties to a definite church, was founded in 1795, at a time when Nonconformists from the Established Church of England were merely tolerated and possessed no political rights of any sort. In the British and Foreign Bible Society, founded in 1804, members of the Established Church worked together with the numerous Free churches.

The World Missionary Conference in Edinburgh in 1910 initiated the ecumenical movement. In the 20th century the so-called younger churches, which arose out of European and American missions, have been the strongest promoters of the reunion of the Christian churches. Their interest in the World Council of Churches has been expressed in the fact that conferences of the world churches and world missions in the latter half of the 20th century took place in areas of former missions fields (*e.g.*, New Delhi in 1961; Addis Ababa, Ethiopia, in 1970).

The fact that the missionary churches in the latter part of the 20th century share in so-called foreign aid of secular governments is a result of their familiarity with the indigenous populations of Asia, Africa, and Indonesia and with their special linguistic, religious, cultural, and social conditions. It also results from the fact that the establishment of religious, medical, agricultural, and pedagogical institutions was, until the middle of the 20th century, borne primarily by the missionary churches.

The worldwide influence of the Christian calendar

The Christian calendar, with the seven-day week and the work-free Sunday (or weekend), has been established everywhere in the world. The Western work pattern of regular working hours and regular leisure and vacation time has been introduced everywhere. This development has abrogated the numerous non-Christian festival calendars of Hinduism, Buddhism, and Taoism, with their temple festivals often lasting many nights or, as in Buddhism, with their festival cycles adjusted according to the lunar calendar. The attempt in Ceylon, which was undertaken in conjunction with a national Buddhist reaction, to replace the Christian festival calendar introduced by the Portuguese, Dutch, and English with the Buddhist lunar calendar foundered on the opposition of the Sinhalese themselves. They did not wish to be excluded from the global rhythm of work and freedom in accordance with the Christian seven-day week. In Japan Buddhist sects have changed over to Sunday sermons and the conducting of Sunday schools, although Sunday does not have the slightest thing to do with the order of the Buddhist calendar. Only Jews, Muslims, and the Seventh-day Adventists have held on to their own rhythms of holidays.

LAST THINGS

The "last things" were the first things, in terms of urgency, for the faithful of the early church. The central content of their faith and their hope was the coming

Kingdom of God. They believed that the promises of the Old Testament about the coming bringer of salvation had been fulfilled in Jesus Christ, but that the fulfillment was not yet complete. Thus, they awaited Christ's Second Coming, which they believed was imminent.

Expectations of the Kingdom of God in early Christianity. In early Christianity's expectation of the Kingdom of God, two types were inherited from Judaism. The first was the expectation of a messianic Kingdom in this world, with its centre in Jerusalem, which was to be established by an earthly Messiah from the house of David. The second expectation was that of a heavenly Kingdom, which was to be inaugurated by the heavenly Messiah, Son of man, and in which the elected comrades of the Kingdom from all times would share in the state of the resurrection.

Types of expectations inherited from Judaism

The two types of expectation of salvation did not remain neatly separated in the early church but rather intersected one another in manifold ways. Under the influence of the persecutions of the church, a characteristic combination of the end-time expectations was established. In Paul's letters and in the Revelation to John, the faithful Christians will first reign together with their returning Lord for some time in this world. Those Christians who are still alive at his return will take part in the reign without dying (I Thess. 4:17). Christians who have already died will rise again and, as resurrected ones, share in his Kingdom upon Earth. Only after completion of this first act of the events of the end time will there then follow the general resurrection of all the dead and the Last Judgment, in which the elect will participate as co-judges (I Cor. 6:2).

In the Revelation to John this expectation is condensed into the concept of the 1,000-year (millennial) Kingdom. For 1,000 years the dragon (Satan) is to be chained up and thrown into the abyss. In John's vision, Christians, the first resurrected, "came to life and reigned with Christ a thousand years" (Rev. 20:4). Only later does the resurrection of all the dead take place, as well as the general judgment, creation of the new heaven and the new Earth, and the descent of the new Jerusalem. According to the view of the Revelation to John, this 1,000-year Kingdom is composed of the chosen comrades of the Kingdom, especially the martyrs and all who stood the test in times of persecution; it is a Kingdom of the privileged elect (see also MILLENNIALISM).

Expectations of the millennium

This promise has exerted revolutionary effects in the course of church history. In the early church the expectation of the millennium was viewed as a social and political utopia, a state in which the chosen Christians will rule and judge with their Lord in this world. Such chiliastic (or millennial) expectations provided the impetus for ecclesiastical, political, and social reformations and revolutions in the course of church history. The establishment of a 1,000-year Kingdom in which the elect, with Christ, will reign and receive the administrative and judgeship posts has fascinated religious expectations as well as political and social imagination far more than the second part of the eschatological expectation, the "Last Judgment."

The delay of the Parousia resulted in a weakening of the imminent expectation in the early church. In this process of "de-eschatologizing," the institutional church increasingly replaced the expected Kingdom of God. The formation of the Catholic Church as a hierarchical institution is directly connected with the declining of the imminent expectation. The theology of Augustine constitutes the conclusion of this development in the West. He de-emphasized the original imminent expectation by declaring that the Kingdom of God has already begun in this world with the institution of the church; the church is the historical representative of the Kingdom of God on Earth. The first resurrection, according to Augustine, occurs constantly within the church in the form of the sacrament of Baptism, through which the faithful are introduced into the Kingdom of God. The expectation of the coming Kingdom of God, the resurrection of the faithful, and the Last Judgment have in actuality finally become a doctrine of the "last things" because the gifts of salvation of the coming Kingdom of God are interpreted as being already present in the sacraments of the church.

Expectations of the Kingdom of God in the medieval and Reformation periods. Nevertheless, the original imminent expectation has spontaneously and constantly reemerged in the history of Christianity. In the period before the 16th-century Reformation, heretical groups—such as the 2nd-century Montanists and the medieval Cathari, Waldenses, the followers of Joachim of Fiore, and the Franciscan Spirituals—accused the Roman Church of betraying the original eschatological imminent expectation. These groups revived eschatological expectations. Even within the Catholic Church itself, however, such movements have constantly re-emerged to inspire reform efforts. In the medieval church new outbreaks of an imminent expectation occurred in connection with great historical catastrophes, such as epidemics of the plague, Islāmic invasions, schisms, and wars.

Luther's Reformation also was sustained by an imminent expectation. For all the Reformers, the starting point for their eschatological interpretation of contemporary history was that the "internal Antichrist," the pope, had established himself in the temple at the Holy Place and that through persecution by the "external Antichrist," the Turk, the church had entered into the travails of the end time. The Reformation churches, however, soon became institutional territorial churches, which in turn repressed the end-time expectation, and thus doctrine of the "last things" became an appendix to dogmatics.

Eschatological interpretations of the Reformers

Expectations of the Kingdom of God in the post-Reformation period. In the post-Reformation period, the imminent expectation appeared in individual groups on the margin of the institutional Reformation churches; such groups generally made the imminent expectation itself the object of their sect formation. This has been the result of the fact that, since the Reformation, the Roman Church has been virtually immune to eschatological movements. The Lutheran Church has been less immune; a series of eschatological groups whose activity in the church was determined by their expectation of the imminent return of Christ appeared in Pietism. Among the Anglo-Saxon Free churches and sects, the formation of new eschatological groups has been a frequent occurrence, especially during the period of the English Revolution in the 17th century and during the revival movements in the United States in the 18th–20th centuries. Such groups shared significantly in the renewal and expansion of Christianity in domestic and foreign missions.

The role of imminent expectation in missions and emigrations. The great missionary activities of the Christian Church are in most cases based upon a reawakened imminent expectation, which creates a characteristic tension. The tension between the universal mission of the church and the hitherto omitted missionary duties as well as the idea that the colossal task must be accomplished in the shortest time possible renders comprehensible the astonishing physical and spiritual achievements of the great Christian missionaries. After the inundation of the old Christian areas of Africa and Asia by Islām, Franciscan missionaries in the 13th and 14th centuries, enduring incredible hardships, went by land and by sea to India, China, and Mongolia to preach the gospel. In a similar way, the missionary movement of the 18th and 19th centuries also proceeded from such eschatological groups within Protestantism.

The expectation of the Kingdom of God, in the form of the imminent expectation, plays an especially strong role in emigration movements. In a certain sense, the Crusades could be included among such movements. Great masses of European Christians again and again set out for Palestine with a sense of finding there the land of their salvation and personally being present when Christ returns there to establish his Kingdom. The eschatological strain of the Crusades can be noted in the Crusade sermons of Bernard of Clairvaux in 1147, who kindled enthusiasm to liberate Jerusalem with reference to the pressing terminal dates of the end time.

Influence of eschatological ideas in emigrations to North America and other areas

The emigration movement toward America also was influenced by beliefs in eschatologically fixed dates (*e.g.,* Columbus). Puritans who travelled to America in the 17th century and Quakers, Baptists, and Methodists in the 18th century believed that America was the "wilderness" promised in the Revelation to John. William Penn gave the name Philadelphia to the capital of the woodland areas ceded to him (1681) because he took up the idea of establishing the true church of the end time, represented by the Philadelphian community of the Revelation to John. A great number of the attempts undertaken to found radical Christian communities in North America may be viewed as anticipations of the coming Jerusalem. The same holds true for the emigration of German revivalists of the 18th and early 19th centuries to Russia and Palestine. The "Friends of the Temple"—Swabians who went with Christoph Hoffmann to Palestine in 1866—and the Swabians, Franks, Hessians, and Bavarians, who after the Napoleonic Wars followed the call of Tsar Alexander I to Bessarabia, were all dominated by the idea of living in the end time and preparing themselves for the coming Kingdom of God. In Tsar Alexander I they saw the "eagle . . . as it flew in midheaven" (Rev. 8:13), which prepared the "recovery spot" for them in the East upon which Christ will descend.

Eschatological expectations and secularization. The history of the Christian eschatological expectation has taken place—apart from its treatment as a topic of traditional dogma in theology—as a continuous process of secularization, in the course of which the end-time expectation (Kingdom of God expectation) was transformed into social and societal utopian movements and from there into futurology. Preparation for the time of salvation is an important component of the end-time expectation itself. It includes not only inner personal transformation ("Repent, for the kingdom of heaven is at hand" [Matt. 3:2]), but comprises social penance as well.

In the Gospels the attitude toward the coming Kingdom of God led, over and beyond the expectation of nullifying sin and death, to certain worldly conclusions of an organizational kind. The disciples of Jesus knew that there will be "first ones" in the Kingdom of Heaven; they pressed for the administrative posts in the coming Kingdom of God (*e.g.,* the Apostles James and John). The promise, too, that they are to take part as judges at the Last Judgment (Luke 22:30) sparked definite conceptions of rank. Jesus castigated them in their disputes over rank with the words, "If any one would be first, he must be last of all and servant of all" (Mark 9:35).

Concepts of social utopias and futurology

Despite this warning, the imminent expectation of the coming Kingdom of God awakened concrete, substantial ideas that led ever closer to social utopias. With the 18th-century German Lutheran mystic and Pietist F. C. Oetinger, the end-time expectation generated definite social and political demands—*e.g.,* dissolution of the state, abolition of property, and elimination of class differences. Some of the aspects of the end-time expectation of Pietism were revived in the French Revolution's political and social programs. The transition from the end-time expectation to the social utopia, however, had already been achieved in writings from the 16th and early 17th centuries—*e.g.,* the English Humanist and saint Thomas More's *De optimo reipublicae statu deque nova insula Utopia* (1516; "On the Highest State of a Republic and on the New Island Utopia"), the German theologian Johann Valentin Andreä's *Reipublicae Christianopolitanae Descriptio* (1619; "A Description of the Christian Republic"), the English philosopher Francis Bacon's *New Atlantis* (1627), and the English bishop Francis Godwin's *Man in the Moone* (1638). It is also found in early Socialism of the 19th century—*e.g.,* the French social reformer Henri de Saint-Simon's *Nouveau Christianisme* (1825; "The New Christianity") and the French Socialist Étienne Cabet's *Voyage en Icarie* (1840; "Voyage to Icaria").

What distinguishes the Christian social utopia from the earlier kind of eschatology is the stronger emphasis upon the social responsibility of man for the preparation of the Kingdom of God as well as a considerable preponderance of various techniques in the establishment of the utopian society. (In general, the end-time expectation has also inspired technical fantasy as well as science fiction.) Also characteristic is the basic attitude that man himself has to prepare the future perfect society in a formative and organizing manner and that "hoping" and "awaiting" are replaced by human initiative. A graduated transition from a social utopia still consciously Christian to a purely Socialist one can be observed in the writings and activities of the French Socialists Charles Fourier, Saint-Simon, and Pierre-Joseph Proudhon, the English Socialist Robert Owen, and the German Socialist Wilhelm Weitling. Secularized remnants of a glowing Christian end-time expectation are still found even in the Marxist view of the social utopia.

A state of complete secularization of the end-time expectation is reached in modern futorology. The future is thus manipulated through planning (*i.e.,* "horizontal eschatology") in place of eschatological "hoping" and "waiting for" fulfillment. "Horizontal eschatology" is thus taken out of the sphere of the unexpected and numinous (spiritual); it is made the subject not only of a detailed prognosis based upon statistics but also of a detailed programming undertaken on the basis of this prognosis. An eschatological remainder is found only in an ideological image of man, upon which programming and planning are based.

Concepts of life after death. The Christian end-time expectation is directed not only at the future of the church but also at the future of the individual believer. It includes definite conceptions of the personal continuance of life after death. Many baptized early Christians were convinced they would not die at all but would still experience the advent of Christ in their lifetimes and would go directly into the Kingdom of God without death. Others were convinced they would go through the air to meet Christ returning upon the clouds of the sky: "Then we who are alive, who are left, shall be caught up together with them in the clouds to meet the Lord in the air; and so we shall always be with the Lord" (I Thess. 4:17). In the early imminent expectation, the period between death and the coming of the Kingdom still constituted no object of concern. An expectation that one enters into bliss or perdition immediately after death is also found in the words of Jesus on the cross: "Today you will be with me in Paradise" (Luke 23:43).

In the Nicene Creed the life of the Christian is characterized as "eternal life." In the Gospels and in the apostolic letters, "eternal" is first of all a temporal designation: in contrast to life of this world, eternal life has a deathless duration. In its essence, however, it is life according to God's kind of eternity—*i.e.,* perfect, sharing in his glory and bliss (Rom. 2:7, 10). "Eternal life" in the Christian sense is thus not identical with "immortality of the soul"; rather, it is only to be understood in connection with the expectation of the resurrection. "Continuance" is neutral vis-à-vis the opposition of salvation and disaster, but the raising from the dead leads to judgment, and its decision can also mean eternal punishment (Matt. 25:46). The antithesis to eternal life is not earthly life but eternal death.

Eternal life and eternal death

Eternal life is personal life, and precisely therein is fulfilled the essence of man who is created according to the image of God. Within eternal life there are differences. In the present life there are variations in talent, duty, responsibility, and breadth and height of life, just as there are also distinctions in "wages" according to the measure of the occupation, the sacrifice of suffering, and the trial (I Cor. 3:8). Correspondingly, the resurrected are also distinguished in eternal life according to their "glory":

There is one glory of the sun, and another glory of the moon, and another glory of the stars; for star differs from star in glory. So it is with the resurrection of the dead (I Cor. 15:41–42).

This expectation has had a great influence upon the Christian conception of marriage and friendship. The idea of a continuation of marriage and friendship after death has contributed very much to the deepening of the view of marriage, as is shown by the strong influence of the 17th–18th-century Swedish mystic, philosopher, and scientist Emanuel Swedenborg's ideas upon the romantic philosophy of religion and its interpretation of marriage and friendship in the thought of the German scholars Friedrich Schelling and Friedrich Schleiermacher. The Western concept of personality was thus deepened through the Christian view of its eternal value.

The delay of the imminent expectation brought about the question of the fate of the dead person in the period between the death of the individual Christian and the resurrection. Two basic views were developed. One view is that of an individual judgment, which takes place immediately after death and brings the individual to an interim state, from which he enters into the realm of bliss or that of perdition. The idea of an individual judgment, however, cannot be readily harmonized with the concept of the general Last Judgment on the day of the general resurrection of the dead. It anticipates the decision of the general judgment and thus deprives of its significance the notion of the Last Judgment. A second view, therefore, also prevailed: the sleep of the soul— *i.e.*, the soul of the dead person enters into a sleeping state that continues until the Last Judgment, which will occur after the general resurrection. At the Last Judgment the resurrected will be assigned either to eternal life or eternal damnation. This conception, accepted in many churches, contains many discrepancies, especially the abandonment of the fundamental idea of the continuity of personal life.

Both views contain an inhuman consequence. The first leaves to man no further opportunity to improve the mistakes of his life and to expiate his life's guilt. The second preserves the personality in an intermediate state for an indefinite period so as to later punish it for sins or reward it for good deeds from a time prior to entrance into the sleep of the soul. The belief in purgatory (an interim state in which a correction of a dead person's evil condition is still possible) of the Roman Catholic Church gives the deceased an opportunity for repentance and penance to ameliorate their situation.

The presupposition of the doctrine of purgatory is that there is a special judgment for each individual at once after death. Hence, the logical conclusion is that purgatory ceases with the Last Judgment. The stay in purgatory can be shortened through intercession, alms, indulgences, and benefits of the sacrifice of the mass. The Eastern Orthodox Church has no doctrine of purgatory but does practice an intercession for the dead. It assumes that, on the basis of the connection between the church of the living and that of the dead, an exertion of influence upon the fate of the dead through intercession is possible before the time of the Last Judgment.

The idea of the Last Judgment has often become incomprehensible to modern man. At the most, he apparently is still open to the concept of an individual judgment of the guilt and innocence of the individual man. The idea decisive for the early church's expectation of the Judgment, however, was that the Last Judgment will be a public one. This corresponds to the fundamental Christian idea that human beings—both the living and the dead—are bound together in an indissoluble communion; it presupposes the conception of the church as the body of Christ. All of humanity is as one man. Humans sin with one another, and their evil is connected together in the "realm of sin" in a manifold way, unrecognizable in the individual. Each person is responsible for the other and is guilty with the other. The judgment upon each person, therefore, concerns all. Judgment upon the individual is thus at the same time judgment upon the whole, and vice versa. The Judgment is also public in regard to the positive side—the praise and reward of God for that which is done rightly and practiced in the common life, often without knowing it.

For the most part, the churches of the latter part of the 20th century no longer have the courage to uphold the Christian teaching of life after death. The church has long neglected teachings about the entire area of the last things. The New Testament responses presuppose the imminent expectation and thus leave many questions unanswered that arose because of the delay of the Parousia. The doctrine of the sleep of the soul, on the other hand, contains many absurd consequences that question the fundamental idea of the Christian view of the personality of the *imago Dei* ("image of God"). The beginnings of a further development of the Christian view of life after death, as are found in Swedenborg, have never been recognized positively by the church. For this reason, since the period of Romanticism and Idealism, ideas of the transmigration of souls and reincarnation, taken over from Hinduism and Buddhism, have gained a footing in Christian views of the end-time expectation. Some important impulses toward a new understanding of the view of life after death are found in Christian theosophy, such as the idea of a further development of the human personality upon other celestial bodies after death (see also ESCHATOLOGY).

V. Attitudes concerning the relation of the Christian community and the Christian to the world

THE PROBLEM OF THE KINGDOM OF PEACE AND THE EXECUTION OF JUDGMENT

The relationship of Christians and Christian institutions to forms of the political order has shown an extraordinary diversity in the course of church history; there have been, for example, theocratically founded monarchies, democracies, and communist community orders. In various periods, however, political revolution, based on theological foundations, to eliminate older "Christian" state forms has also belonged to this diversity.

In certain eras of church history a great multiplicity of forms of political and religious institutions were understood respectively as models for shaping the religious and political life of the specific period. An element of power and dominion, which strives for political and social realization, inheres in the Christian idea of the early establishment of the Kingdom of God. From the beginning, however, tendencies toward the realization of theocratic power within the framework of a church institution have entered into a tense rivalry with tendencies toward the transfer of this power to a Christian state. The Christian proclamation of the coming sovereignty of God promised both the establishment of a Kingdom of peace and the execution of judgment—both peace and judgment demand power.

The church, like the Christian state, has been exposed to the temptation of power. The attempt to establish a kingdom of peace resulted in the transformation of the church into an ecclesiastical state. The process took place in the development of the Roman Papal States, but it also occurred to a lesser degree in several theocratic Free churches and was clearly attempted in Calvin's ecclesiastical state in Geneva in the 16th century. In the attempt to execute judgment, the state declares itself a Christian state and the executor of the spiritual, political, and social commission of the church; it understands itself to be the representative of the Kingdom of God. This development took place in both the Byzantine and the Carolingian empires as well as in the medieval Holy Roman Empire (of the German nation). In Hegel's Christian idea of the state the Prussian state became the representative of the Kingdom of God.

The struggle between the church, understanding itself as state, and the state, understanding itself as representative of the church, not only dominated the Middle Ages but continued into the Reformation period. The wars of religion in the era of the Reformation and Counter-Reformation caused the tense theological and ethical idea of the Christian Church and metaphysics of the Christian state to be compromised. In the period of the Enlightenment, this led to the idea of the relationship of church and state as grounded upon ideas of natural law.

DEVELOPMENT OF RELATIONSHIPS BETWEEN THE CHURCH AND THE POLITICAL ORDER

Relationships with the Roman Empire. *Avoidance of the political order*. In the early church, the attitude of the Christian toward the political order was determined by his imminent expectation of the Kingdom of God, whose miraculous power was already beginning to be visibly realized in the figure of the Son of man who had appeared in Jesus Christ. The importance of the existing political order was, thus, negligible, as expressed in the saying of Jesus, "My kingship is not of this world." Orientation toward the coming kingdom of peace placed the Christian in a position of conflict or contrast with the state, which made demands upon Christians that were in direct conflict with their faith.

This contrast was developed most pointedly in the rejection of the emperor cult and in the rejection of certain state offices—above all, that of judge—to which the power over life and death was professionally entrusted. Opposition to fundamental orderings of the ruling state was not found upon any conscious revolutionary program, however, but the expansion of the Christian Church in the Roman Empire probably led to an internal weakening of the empire on the basis of this conscious avoidance of many aspects of public life. When the Western Roman Empire finally collapsed after the conquest of Rome by the Goths in the 5th century, the survivors of the hitherto pagan political leadership were generally convinced that Christians were guilty of the downfall of Rome.

Acceptance and rejection of the political orders. Despite this inner turning toward the coming Kingdom of God, even the Christians of the early generations acknowledged the pagan state as the bearer of order in the old eon, which for the time being continued to exist. Two contrary views thus faced one another within the Christian communities. On the one hand, under the influence of Pauline missions, was the idea that the "ruling body"—*i.e.*, the existing political order of the Roman Empire—is "from God" (Romans, chapter 13) and that Christians should be "subject to the governing authorities." Another similar idea held by Paul (in II Thessalonians) was that the Roman state, through its legal order, "restrains" the downfall of the world that the Antichrist is attempting to bring about.

On the other hand, and existing at the same time, in the Revelation to John was the apocalyptical identification of the imperial city of Rome with the great whore of Babylon (Revelation, chapter 17), "a woman sitting on a scarlet beast, . . . the mother of harlots and of earth's abominations, . . . drunk with the blood of the saints and the blood of the martyrs of Jesus."

The first attitude, formulated by Paul, was decisive in the development of a Christian political consciousness. The second was noticeable especially in the history of radical Christianity and in radical Christian pacifism, which rejects cooperation as much in military service as in public judgeship.

Accommodation to the political order. The demonic interpretation of the state diminished in importance when the Roman state gave up its persecution of Christians as public enemies and Christianity became the basis for the self-establishment of the Roman Empire. The Christian as both a member of the imperial church and a citizen of the Christian empire henceforth appeared under the concept of the "harmony" (*harmonia*) between church and state. This "harmony" at times represented an extraordinarily tense relationship, which, depending upon the position of power, underwent the most diverse kinds of interpretations by both sides.

Relationships with the Byzantine Empire. In the Byzantine Empire the emperor Constantine granted himself, as "bishop of foreign affairs," certain rights to church leadership. These concerned not only the "outward" activity of the church but also encroached upon the inner life of the church—as was shown by the role of the emperor in summoning and leading imperial councils and ratifying their decisions. Thus, the patriarch of Constantinople, as the bishop of the empire, always remained restricted to his spiritual tasks, so that there could never unfold in Byzantium either the tendency toward formation of an ecclesiastical state or one toward development of the bishops into rulers of their territories.

The bishops of the Eastern Orthodox Church were first allotted a political task when, in the period of Turkish rule (after the fall of Constantinople in 1453), an official role devolved upon them as advocates of Christian ethnic groups in the Turkish empire. This political task injected them, at least temporarily, into the political role of popular leaders during the periods of revolution against Turkish dominion by Christian ethnic groups in the Balkans. A recent aspect of this development was represented by the president and archbishop of Cyprus, Makarios III, who became the demarch of the Cypriot people in their liberation struggles against England.

In the Byzantine area there evolved the concept of what has been called caesaropapism, a system in which the *harmonia* between church and state shifted more and more in favour (in terms of power) of the emperor. His ecclesiastical authority was endowed with the idea of the divine right of kings, which was symbolically expressed in the ceremony of crowning and anointing the emperor. This tradition was later also continued in the Russian realms, where the tsardom claimed a growing authority for itself even in the area of the church. Under Peter the Great (reigned 1682–1725) the Russian patriarchate was abolished and a dual system of a synodal church polity and a government procurator as representative of the tsar introduced in its stead; the church was thus rendered completely dependent on the control of the tsar and became an instrument of the state.

Relationships with Western states. Conversely, the theocratic claim to dominion by the church freely developed in the sphere of the Roman Catholic Church after the state and administrative organization of the Roman Empire in the West collapsed in the chaos following the barbarian ethnic migrations. In the political vacuum that arose in the West because of the invasion by the German tribes, the Roman Church was the single institution that still preserved in its episcopal dioceses the Roman provincial arrangement. In its administration of justice the church (and its leader, the pope) largely depended upon the old imperial law and—in a period of legal and administrative chaos—was viewed as the only guarantor of order. The Roman popes used this power, which was in fact allotted to them by circumstances, to develop a specific ecclesiastical state and to base this state upon a new theocratic ideology—the idea that the pope was the representative of Christ and the successor of Peter. From this perspective, the Roman popes detached themselves from the power of the Byzantine emperor, to whom they were indeed subordinate according to prevailing imperial law.

The new relationship with the German kingdoms. Whereas the evolution of the Roman papacy into an ecclesiastical state was not recognized by Byzantium but was instead understood as a political revolt against the empire, the popes did succeed in convincing the rulers of the Frankish (Germanic) kingdom in the 8th century of their leadership role. They also succeeded in winning them as protectors of the papal dominion. These rulers were the first of the German kings to join themselves to the Roman Church. The new relationship opened a new area of tension because the Frankish rulers envisioned a relationship between church and state defined by German ecclesiastical concepts. This view granted the Christian king a leading role vis-à-vis the church similar to that which the Byzantine emperor had claimed for himself.

According to the interpretation of the Frankish emperor Charlemagne, the emperor was the protector of the pope. The emperor convened the imperial synods and bestowed upon their decisions the character of imperial laws. Within the Frankish state church, the pope assumed the position of a state bishop. Moreover, Charlemagne also claimed for himself the right to appoint the bishops of his empire, who were more and more involved in the political affairs of the empire.

In the course of this development, the process of the feudalization of the church—unique in church history—occurred. Ruling political leaders in this system occupied significant positions in the church; by virtue of patron-

Margin notes: The role of the church in weakening the Roman Empire / Harmony between church and state / The break between Rome and Byzantium

The feudalization of the church in the West

age, this development encompassed the whole imperial church. At the conclusion of this development, bishops in the empire were simultaneously the reigning princes of their dioceses; they often were much more interested in the political tasks of their dominion than in the spiritual.

Medieval reform movements in church-state relationships. In the great church-renewal movement, which extended from its beginnings at the monastery at Cluny (France) in the 10th century and lasted until Pope Gregory VII in the 11th century, the papal church rejected both the sacred position of the king and the temporal position of bishops, who were awarded their rights and privileges by the king. This renewal movement proclaimed the freedom of the church from state authority as well as its pre-eminence over worldly powers. This struggle, now remembered as the investiture controversy, was fought out as a dramatic altercation between the papacy and the empire. The church did not, however, gain a complete victory in terms of papal claims of full authority over the spiritual as well as the worldly realms.

With the weakening of the Holy Roman (Germanic) Empire, the European nation-states arose as opponents of the church. The power struggle between state and church thus shifted to the nation-state under the aegis of ideas initiated by Marsilius of Padua in the 14th century. Marsilius demanded that the church, closely restricted to the spiritual area, be subordinated to the state; he thereby opposed papal supremacy.

Contributing to the strengthening of the nation rulers' right of ecclesiastical supervision was the problem of papal schism. Popes and counter-popes reigning simultaneously mutually excommunicated one another, thus demeaning the esteem of the papacy. The schisms spread great uncertainty among the believers of the empire about the validity of the consecration of bishops and the sacraments as administered by the priests they ordained.

Church leadership under the control of the state

Reforms in the 16th century. The 16th-century Reformation forced the church to face its purely spiritual tasks and placed Reformation law as well as the legal powers of church leadership in the hands of the princes. Under King Henry VIII, a revolutionary dissociation of the English Church from papal supremacy took place. In the German territories the reigning princes became, in effect, the legal guardians of the Protestant episcopate—a movement already in the process of consolidation in the late Middle Ages. The development in the Catholic nation-states, such as Spain, Portugal, and France, occurred in a similar way.

During the period of the extreme sharpening of the state church and papal ideal of state and church, demands for the free self-administration of the Christian churches as the free people of God had begun to be heard. The democratic ideas of the freedom and equality of Christians and their representation in a communion of saints by virtue of voluntary membership had been disseminated in various medieval sects (*e.g.*, Cathari, Waldenses, Hussites, and the Bohemian Brethren) and were reinforced during the Reformation by groups such as the radical Free churches, Baptists, Mennonites, Schwenkfeldians, and the Schwärmer (fanatics) followers of Thomas Müntzer. Under the old ideal of an uncompromising realization of Jesus Christ's Sermon on the Mount, there arose anew in these groups a renunciation of certain regulations of the state, such as military service and the acceptance of state offices (judgeship), a radical pacifism, and the attempt to structure their own form of common life in Christian, communist communities. Many of their political ideas—at first bloodily suppressed by the Reformation state and territorial churches—were later prominent in the Dutch wars of independence and in the English Revolution, which led to a new relationship between church and state.

Results of the controversies of the 17th and 18th centuries. In the Thirty Years' War, confessional antitheses were settled in devastating religious wars and the credibility of the highly tense, theological self-interpretations of the feuding ecclesiastical parties was thereby called into question. Subsequently, from the 17th century on,

the tendency toward a new, natural-law conception of the relationship between state and church was begun and continued. Henceforth, in the Protestant countries, state sovereignty was increasingly emphasized vis-à-vis the churches. A revision of state church canon law stipulated the churchly sovereignty of the state. It established the right of the state to regulate educational and marriage concerns as well as all foreign affairs of the church. A similar development also occurred in Roman Catholic areas. In the second half of the 18th century Febronianism demanded a replacement of papal centralism with a national church episcopal system; in the German *Reich*, an enlightened state-church concept was established, under Josephinism (a view advocated by Emperor Joseph I) through the dismantling of numerous ecclesiastical privileges. The Eastern Orthodox Church also was drawn into this development under Peter the Great.

The separation of church and state

The separation of church and state as proclaimed by the French Revolution in the latter part of the 18th century was the result of Reformational strivings toward a guarantee for the freedom of the church and the natural-law ideas of the Enlightenment; it was aggravated by the social revolutionary criticism against the wealthy ecclesiastical hierarchy. The separation of church and state was also achieved during and after the American Revolution. In the United States, Free Church ideas, primarily those resulting from the struggle of the Puritans against the English episcopal system and the English throne, were particularly strong. After the state in France had undertaken the task of creating its own political, revolutionary substitute religion in the form of a "cult of reason," a type of separation of church and state was soon achieved. The French state took over education and the hitherto churchly functions of a civic nature—registration in a recording office and burial in nationalized cemeteries.

Developments in the 19th and 20th centuries. From the late 18th century on, two fundamental attitudes developed in matters relating to the separation of church and state. The first, as inferred in the Constitution of the United States, is supported by a tendency to leave to the church, set free from state supervision, a maximal freedom in the realization of its spiritual, moral, and educational tasks. In the United States, for example, a comprehensive church school and educational system has been created by the churches on the basis of this freedom; numerous universities have been founded by Free churches. The separation of church and state in the Soviet Union and the countries under the Soviet Union's sphere of influence is based upon an opposite tendency. The attempt—begun under Lenin and strengthened under Stalin—at totally exterminating the church in the Soviet Union had far-reaching success. After this attempt, the formal separation of church and state, laid down in the Soviet constitution, was so interpreted as to restrict the remnants of the church to their purely liturgical functions—within the few churches still open. The church, however, was to be excluded from all participation in the social, cultural, and educational tasks of the state.

Hitler's concordat with the Vatican

In contrast to this, in Germany National Socialism during the reign of Hitler showed paradoxical contradictions. On the one hand, National Socialist propaganda pursued a consciously anti-Christian polemic against the church; it proceeded to arrest those clergy opposed to the National Socialist world view and policies. On the other hand, Hitler placed the greatest value upon concluding with the Vatican in 1934 a concordat that granted the Catholic Church more special rights in the German *Reich* than had ever been granted it in any earlier concordat. The concordat with the Vatican represented the first recognition of the Hitler regime by a European government and was viewed by Hitler as a method of entrance into the circle of internationally recognized political powers.

In Germany the old state church traditions had already been eliminated in the revolution of 1918, which, with the abolition of the monarchical system of government, also deprived the territorial churches of their supreme Protestant episcopal heads. In the German Weimar Constitution the revolution had earlier sanctioned the separation of church and state. State-church traditions were maintained in various forms in Germany, not only during the Weimar Republic but also during the Hitler regime and afterward in the Federal Republic of Germany. Thus, through state agreements, definite special rights, primarily in the areas of taxes and education, were granted to both the Catholic Church and the Evangelical (Lutheran-Reformed) churches of the individual states.

Even in the United States, however, the old state-church system, overcome during the American Revolution, still produces aftereffects in the form of tax privileges of the church (exemption from most taxation), the exemption of the clergy from military service, and the financial furtherance of confessional school and educational systems through the state. In the 1960s and 1970s these privileges were questioned and even attacked by certain segments of the American public.

VIEWS OF THE RELATIONSHIP BETWEEN THE CHRISTIAN OR CHRISTIAN INSTITUTIONS AND THE POLITICAL ORDER

The two main forms of the relationship between church and state that have been predominant and decisive through the centuries and in which the structural difference between the Roman Catholic Church and Eastern Orthodoxy becomes most evident can best be explained by comparing the views of two great theologians: Eusebius of Caesarea and Augustine.

The views of Eusebius of Caesarea. Eusebius of Caesarea (died *c.* 340) was the court theologian of Emperor Constantine the Great, who formed the Orthodox understanding of the mutual relationship of church and state.

The mutual relationship of church and state

He saw the empire and the imperial church as sharing a close bond with one another; in the center of the Christian empire stands the figure of the Christian emperor rather than that of the spiritual head of the church. By raising Byzantium to the same status as Rome and by transferring even the state and administrative offices, including the Senate, from Rome to Byzantium, Constantine expressed unequivocally that he wanted to provide the new empire that was founded on the religious basis of Christianity with a new capital separated from pagan traditions. On the one hand, he wanted his new capital to be equal to Rome in splendour; on the other hand, he wanted it to be free of the demonic forces of Rome's past so that it could form a new centre of the Christian empire as well as of the Christian empire church.

Eusebius made this idea the basis of his political theology, in which the Christian emperor appears as God's representative on Earth in whom God himself "lets shine forth the image of his absolute power." He is the "God-loved, three times blessed" servant of the highest ruler, who, "armed with divine armor cleans the world from the horde of the godless, the strong-voiced heralds of undeceiving fear of God," the rays of which "penetrate the world." With these characteristics he is the archetype not only of justice but also of the love of mankind. When it is said about Constantine, "God himself has chosen him to be the lord and leader so that no man can praise himself to have raised him up," the rule of the Orthodox emperor has been based on the immediate grace of God.

The Orthodox interpretation of the Christian emperor

In this religious interpretation of the Christian emperor, the ancient Roman institution of the god-emperor was reinterpreted in the Christian sense: in some of Eusebius' remarks it is possible to recognize the remembrance of the cult of the Unconquered Sun, the Sol Invictus, who was represented by the emperor according to pagan understanding. The emperor—in this respect he also resembles the pagan god-emperor who played the role of the *pontifex maximus* (high priest) in the state cult—took the central position within the church, as well. He summoned the synods of bishops, "as though he had been appointed bishop by God," presided over the synods, and granted judicial power for the empire to their decisions. He was the protector of the church who stood up for the preservation of unity and truth of the Christian faith and who fought not only as a warrior but also as an intercessor, as

a second Moses during the battle against God's enemies, "holy and purely praying to God, sending his prayers up to him." The Christian emperor entered not only the political but also the sacred succession of the Roman god-emperor. Next to such a figure, an independent leadership of the church could hardly develop. The role of the highest bishop of the empire church was, from the beginning, limited to its spiritual functions; *i.e.*, the preservation of the purity of teaching within the church and the preservation of the order of the service.

Orthodox theologians have understood the co-existence of the Christian emperor and the head of the Christian church as *symphōnia*, or "harmony." The church recognized the powers of the emperor as protector of the church and preserver of the unity of faith and limited its own authority to the purely spiritual domain of preserving the Orthodox truth and order in the church. The emperor, on the other hand, was subject to the spiritual leadership of the church as far as he was a son of the church.

The special position of the imperial ruler and the function of the Byzantine patriarch as the spiritual head of the church have been defined in the *Epanagoge*, the judicial ruling establishing this relationship of church and state. The church-judicial affirmation of this relationship in the 6th and 7th centuries made the development of a judicial independence of the Byzantine patriarch in the style of the Roman papacy impossible from the beginning.

The relationship between patriarch and emperor

The *Epanagoge*, however, did not completely subject the patriarch to the supervision of the emperor but rather directed him expressly "to support the truth and to undertake the defense of the holy teachings without fear of the emperor." Therefore, the tension between the imperial reign that misused its absolutism against the spiritual freedom of the church and a church that claims its spiritual freedom against an absolutist emperor or tsar was characteristic for the Byzantine and Slavic political history but not the same as the political tension between the imperial power and the politicized papacy that occurred in the West.

The views of Augustine. Augustine wrote his ideas of the church in the *City of God* during the years AD 413–426. At that time, the empire looked back with admiration to Theodosius I, the Great (reigned AD 379–395), who led the church in the Roman Empire to complete victory in the struggle against paganism and heresy, who raised the ecumenical confession of the councils of Nicaea (AD 325) and Constantinople to prominence in the empire and declared all deviations to be punishable heresy, and in whose empire the emperor and the patriarch of Byzantium, state and church, were united in a visibly existing *symphōnia*.

Augustine's *City of God* attempted to answer the most painful accusation of his century: in AD 410, Rome was destroyed by the Gothic bands of "Alaric, the Barbarian," and survivors from the leading Roman government and administration offices, the majority of whom were still pagan, accused the Christians of destroying the empire with their century-long stubborn resistance to the basic religious view of the Roman Empire embodied in the emperor cult and of undermining the state and judicial authority.

The answers of the City of God

Augustine ignored the myth of Byzantium as the "new Rome" as an answer to this accusation, although it was the answer to be expected from a contemporary of the great flourishing Byzantine Empire. For him, it was not the Christian Byzantium—the seat of the Christian emperor, the patron of the Christian Church, the protector of the Christian faith, the seat of the patriarch, and the teacher of orthodox truth—but the Catholic Church that was the "new Rome." The Christian empire, in fact, did not even exist for Augustine. For him the "new Rome" was the Catholic Church, which is an institution created by Christ as the visible historical image of the Kingdom of God on this earth.

Later developments. Based upon Augustine's views, the historical development of the church in the Latin West took a different course, one away from the Byzantine imperial church. In the West, a new power was formed: the Roman Church, the church of the bishop of Rome. This church understood itself as the successor of the extinct Roman Empire. In the political vacuum of the West that was created by the invasion of the Germans and the destruction of the Roman state and administrative apparatus, the church became great and powerful as the heir to the Roman Empire. Only within this vacuum could the idea of the papacy develop in which the great popes, as bishops of Rome, stepped into the position of the vanished emperors.

The use of the Donation of Constantine

On the ideological basis that was created by Augustine, the judicial pretense of the "gift of the emperor Constantine"—the Donation of Constantine (a forged document that granted the papacy territorial rights to much of the Western world)—became possible, to which the later development of the papacy was connected. The Donation attempted to reconstruct the history of the Roman papacy in retrospect in order to make legitimate the newly gained ecclesiastical and political position of the popes after the extinction of the Western Roman imperial reign. According to the Donation, Constantine transferred his own imperial seat to Byzantium so that the power of the bishop of Rome should not be limited by the presence of an emperor. In this theory, the myth of Byzantium, the "new Rome," was reconstructed by a new myth of the Christian Rome: the Roman bishop, the new lord in the Christian Rome, had taken over all functions of the Roman emperor through a pretended gift of the emperor himself.

For Augustine, this was the point of separation from which the developments in the East and in the West led in two different directions; at this point the development of two different types of a Christian idea of the state and of the church begins, and it subsequently ended in the schism between Rome and Byzantium in 1054.

The basic cause of contention between church and empire

The Roman popes not only based their claim to form and lead their own church state on a spiritual-secular judicial understanding but they also created a theocracy within areas that until then were part of the provinces of the Byzantine emperor. They renounced a number of former imperial rights and claimed them for themselves. They extended the secular claim of government of the church beyond the borders of the church-state and developed the so-called theory of the two swords, stating that Christ gave the pope not only spiritual power over the church but also secular power over the worldly kingdoms. This was the basic cause of contention in the medieval struggle between the Christian emperor and the Roman pope, a struggle that actually began on Christmas Day, 800, when Pope Leo III crowned the ruler of the Franks, Charlemagne, as Holy Roman Emperor. Later conflicts between a Christian charismatic emperor who maintained the supervision of the *corpus Christianum* (the Christian empire and its people) and therefore also of the church of the empire, and the papacy, which understood itself as the office of Peter's successor, the vicar of Christ, and the holder of both powers, the worldly and the spiritual, were all inherent in that initial crowning in 800.

The idea of the church as a state exists not only in the Roman theocracy and in the papal idea of the church, it also appears in a new democratic form and in strict contrast to its absolutist Roman model in the radical sects and Free churches of the post-Reformation period. The sects of the Reformation period renewed the old idea of the Christian congregation as God's people, wandering on this Earth—a people connected with God, like Israel, through a special covenant. This idea of God's people and the special covenant of God with a certain chosen group caused the influx of theocratic ideas, which were expressed in forms of theocratic communities similar to states and led to formations similar to an ecclesiastical state. Such tendencies were exhibited among radical Reformation groups (*e.g.*, the Münster prophets), Puritans in Massachusetts, and various groups of the American Western frontier.

The latest attempt to form a church state by a sect that understood itself as the chosen people distinguished by God through a special new revelation was undertaken by the Mormons, the "Latter-day Saints." Based on the prophetic direction of their leaders, they attempted to found the state Deseret, after their exit into the desert around Great Salt Lake in Utah. The borders of the state were expected to include the largest part of the area of the present states of Utah, California, Arizona, Nevada, and Colorado. The Mormons, however, eventually had to recognize the fact that the comparatively small centre state, Utah, of the originally intended larger Mormon territory, could not exist as a theocracy under a government of Mormon Church leaders. It became a federal state of the United States.

The Mormon attempt to establish a theocratic state

The enlightened absolutist state of the 18th century basically took over the secularized form of the old Christian government that consciously took into account the equality of Christian denominations. A monarch, such as Frederick II the Great of Prussia, exercised his rule over the church according to the concept *Divide et impera* ("divide and rule"). His motto "In my state everybody can be saved according to his own fashion" meant tolerance toward all churches and sects, supported by the conviction that the denominations' urge to rule had to be suppressed and that none of them should be allowed to persecute the others or even rule over them. The state had to take care that coexistence would occur peacefully according to the rules and laws of the state.

THE RELATIONSHIP BETWEEN THE CHRISTIAN OR CHRISTIAN INSTITUTIONS AND THE SOCIO-ECONOMIC ORDER

Early developments. *Concern for the socio-economic order.* Ever since the Reformation, the development of Christianity's influence on the character of society has been twofold. In the realm of state churches and territorial churches, its influence has been a strong element in preserving the status quo of society. Thus, in England, the Anglican Church remained an ally of the throne, as did the Protestant churches of the German states. In Russia the Orthodox Church continued to support the feudal society founded upon the monarchy, and even the monarch himself carried out a leading function within the church as protector.

Preserving or improving the status quo

Though the impulses for transformation of the social order according to the spirit of the Christian ethic came more strongly from the radical Free churches and sects, churches within the established system of state and territorial churches made positive contributions in improving the status quo. In England, Anglican clergymen, such as Frederic Denisen and Charles Kingsley in the 19th century, began a Christian social movement in the throes of the Industrial Revolution. Their movement brought a Christian influence to the conditions of life and work in industry. In Germany, Johann Hinrich Wichern proclaimed his word, "There is a Christian Socialism," at the Kirchentag Church Convention in Wittenberg in 1848, the year of the publication of the *Communist Manifesto*, and created the "Inner Mission" in order to prevent the infiltration of the churches by atheistic Communism. Only in tsarist Russia did the church fail in matters concerning social problems and the Industrial Revolution. There, no strong Christian social movement was formed in the 19th century; and the Bolshevik Revolution, with its basically atheistic orientation, eliminated both the church (for all practical purposes) and the tsar.

The Anglo-Saxon Free churches made the greatest effort to bring the social atmosphere and living conditions into line with a Christian understanding of man. Methodists and Baptists addressed their message mainly to those lower segments of society that were neglected by the established church. They recognized earlier than the churches of Germany, for example, that the distress of the newly formed working class, a consequence of industrialization, could not be removed by the traditional charitable means used by the state churches, and they understood that their concern had to be in helping the new working class that had not been planned for in the growing social order. The fact that in Germany, in particular, the spiritual leaders of the so-called revival movement, such as Friedrich Wilhelm Krummacher (1796–

The consequences of industrialization

1868) and others, denied the right of self-organization to the workers by pointing to the doctrine that all earthly social injustices would receive compensation in heaven, caused Karl Marx and Friedrich Engels to separate themselves completely from the church and its purely charitable attempts at a settlement of social conflicts and to declare religion with its vain promise of a better beyond as the "opiate of the people." This reproach, however, was as little in keeping with the social-ethical activity of the Methodists and Baptists as it was with the selfless courage of the Quakers, who fought against social demoralization, against the catastrophic situation in the prisons, and, most of all, against slavery.

The problem of slavery and persecution. The fight against slavery has passed through many controversial phases in the history of Christianity. Paul recommended to Philemon that he accept back his runaway slave Onesimus since, with regard to the propinquity of the coming Kingdom of God, it was no longer worthwhile to undertake a change of the social structure of this world, of which slavery was a part but which already had been abolished within the fellowship of the members of Christ's body. Medieval society made only slow progress in the abolition of slavery. Even the class of free farmers was deprived of its ancient rights of freedom and converted into a state of serfdom, which was not very different from that of slavery, during the era of the feudal government of the church. One of the special tasks of the orders of knighthood was the liberation of Christian slaves who had fallen captive of the Muslims; and special knightly orders were even founded for the ransom of Christian slaves. Members sworn to these orders were committed to sell themselves, if necessary, in order to ransom an endangered Christian from slavery.

The beginning of the abolition of slavery

With the discovery of the New World, the institution of slavery grew to proportions greater than had been previously conceived, after which only an honest spiritual victory over slavery finally was reached. The widespread conviction of the Spanish conquerors of the New World that its inhabitants were not really human in the full sense of the word and therefore could be made slaves in good conscience because of their low level of humanity added to the problem. The attempt of missionaries, such as Bartholomé de Las Casas in 16th-century Peru, to counter the inhuman system of slavery in the colonial economic systems finally introduced the great basic debate concerning the question of human rights. A decisive part in the elaboration of the general principles of the rights of man was taken, particularly by the Spanish and Portuguese theologians of the 16th and 17th centuries, especially Francisco de Vitoria. Even modern natural law, however, could still be interpreted in a conservative sense that did not make slavery contrary to its provisions. Only Puritanism fought successfully against slavery as an institution. In German Pietism, Count von Zinzendorf, who became acquainted with slavery on the island of Saint Croix in the Virgin Islands, used his influence on the King of Denmark for the human rights of the slaves. In addition to the Methodist and Baptist activities concerning the abolition of slavery in the United States in the decisive years preceding the foundation of the New England Anti-Slavery Society in Boston in 1832 by William Lloyd Garrison, Karl Follen (a Unitarian clergyman and one of German philosopher Johann Gottlieb Fichte's pupils), decisively interceded for freedom of slaves on the basis of Kant's and Fichte's concept of freedom. He started from the fundamental principle that even a slave is created in the image of God and therefore is a free man according to divine right. In regard to the fight against slavery in England and in the Netherlands, which was directed mainly against the participation of Christian trade and shipping companies in the profitable slave trade, the Free churches were very active.

Developments in the 20th century. The fight against slavery is only a model case in the active fight of the Christian churches and fellowships against numerous other attempts at desecration of a Christian understanding of the nature of humanity, which sees in every human being a fellow creature, the neighbour created in God's image and the brother who has also been redeemed by Christ. Similar struggles arose against the persecution of the Jews and the elimination of certain members of society characterized by a certain political or racist ideology as "inferior." In Germany, the members of the Confessing Church fought against the practices of National Socialism, which called for the elimination of the mentally ill and the inmates of mental and nursing institutions, who were considered "unfit to live."

Theological and humanitarian motivations. The modern developments in the fight of Christianity for the realization of a Christian understanding of man in state, society, and family have been characterized by the fact that the specifically Christian theological arguments frequently seem to many to be insignificant in comparison with general humanitarian motivations. Occasionally, the conflict between an understanding of man founded in atheism and a Christian understanding of man becomes obvious even in seemingly common "humanistic" presuppositions; *e.g.*, the many debates concerning euthanasia, capital punishment, contraception, and vivisection. Some churches have adopted purely humanitarian standpoints in order not to seem outdated, though others have emphasized the deep contrast existing in the attitudes toward these decisive problems of society between a Christian understanding of man and secular humanism. On the other hand, professional theologians accused the Alsatian missionary, theologian, and Nobel laureate Albert Schweitzer (whom many saw as the pioneer of a decisively Christian understanding of man) of departing from Christian teaching with his humanistic "liberalism," this despite his ascetic life, his medical care, and his pastoral concern for his African patients.

Decisive impulses for achieving social change

Decisive impulses for achieving changes in the social realm in the sense of a Christian ethic have been and are initiated by men and women in the grasp of a deep personal Christian experience of faith, for whom the message of the coming Kingdom of God forms the foundation for faithful affirmation of social responsibility in the present world. Tendencies since the mid-20th century to reduce the Christian message of the Kingdom of God to its inner-worldly social contents and to deduce from the "Utopia" of the Kingdom of God impulses for a change in society have been more and more absorbed by purely secular theories and practices of revolution.

The transformation of Christianity into a purely transcendental religion in the course of the revival movements has, on the other hand, led to a strong emphasis on the social aspects of Christianity as a counter movement. This movement viewed the Christian message of the Kingdom of God mainly as an impulse for reorganization of the secular conditions of society in the sense of a Kingdom of God ethic. Under the leadership of an American Baptist theologian, Walter Rauschenbusch (died 1918), the movement of the so-called "social gospel" spread in the Anglo-Saxon countries. A corresponding movement was started with the Christian social conferences by German Protestant theologians, such as Martin Wilhelm Rade of Marburg (died 1940). The basic idea of the social gospel—*i.e.*, the emphasis on the social-ethical tasks of the church—gained widespread influence within the ecumenical movement and especially affected Christian world missions. In many respects, modern economic and other forms of aid to developing countries have now succeeded the social gospel.

Changes and problems in the Christian social message

This development has put the Christian message in danger of being reduced to a certain purely secular social-ethical program, which is merely absorbed by political social programs. The result, on the one hand, is a new method of politicizing the church and, on the other hand, a speeding up of an increasing resignation of the church to accept that the religious and transcendental roots of the Christian revelation in matters of social action are insignificant.

Interest in political activities. The interest of the church in the political tasks of the modern world, which began with the Industrial Revolution, led to the formation of a number of new agencies to accomplish the tasks of the church in spite of changes in society. One of the new developments was the founding of Christian political parties, a consequence of the separation of church and state. Because they had lost their traditional direct influence on governments and administrations, the churches had to form their own political institutions within the multiformity of political parties (especially in Europe) in order to be able to carry out their interests in society. The formation of Christian political parties has eventually led to political cooperation of members of different Christian denominations. In Germany, for example, the Zentrum, a Roman Catholic party, was replaced by the interdenominational Christian Democratic Union (CDU) and the Christian Social Union (CSU); in Italy, Spain, France, and some other primarily Roman Catholic countries, the Christian parties have a predominantly Roman Catholic character. In addition to Christian political parties, Christian trade unions were formed on the basis of Christian social and ethical principles—in contrast to the Socialist trade unions that emphasized more or less strongly the ideology of dialectical materialism.

THE RELATIONSHIP BETWEEN THE CHRISTIAN OR
CHRISTIAN INSTITUTIONS AND SCHOLARLY ACTIVITIES
AND EDUCATIONAL INSTITUTIONS

The relationship of the Christian faith to intellectual endeavours. The relationship of the Christian faith to education and to various intellectual endeavours has been marked by two different views—either opposition or acceptance (or accommodation). St. Paul proclaimed: "Has not God made foolish the wisdom of the world?" and: "If any one among you thinks that he is wise in this age, let him become a fool." Tertullian, following this point of view, coined the basic formula for a radically negative attitude toward philosophy and science:

> What do the philosopher and the Christian have in common, Greece's pupil and the pupil of heaven, the falsifier and the restorer of truth, its thief and its keeper? What does Athens have to do with Jerusalem, the academy with the church?

This is a statement of the basic experience of faith: the Christian knowledge of salvation is above all reason.

In contrast to this anti-intellectual attitude, which has been apparent in all eras of church history, an exactly opposite attitude toward intellectual activities has also made itself heard from the beginning of the Christian Church (e.g., Clement of Alexandria). It also has its basis in the nature of Christian faith. Anselm of Canterbury (died 1109) expressed it in the formula: *fides quaerens intellectum* ("faith seeking understanding"), a formula that has become the rallying point for scholastics of all times. Because man has been endowed with reason, he has an urge to express his experience of faith intellectually, to translate the contents of his faith into concepts, and to formulate his beliefs in a systematic understanding of the correlation between God, man, and creation. Christians of the 1st century, who came from the upper levels of society and were acquainted with the philosophy and natural science of their time, refused to give up their intellectual knowledge and concepts when they were baptized. Justin Martyr, a professional philosopher, saw Christian revelation as the fulfillment, not the elimination, of philosophical understanding. The Logos term of the Gospel According to John is the point of departure for the intellectual history of salvation. The light of the Logos had made itself manifest in a number of sparks and seeds in the history of man even before its incarnation in the person of Jesus Christ.

These two contrasting opinions have stood in permanent tension with one another. In medieval Scholasticism the elevation of Christian belief to the status of scientific universal knowledge was dominant. Theology became the instructor of the different sciences, organized according to the traditional classification of trivium (grammar, rhetoric, and dialectic) and quadrivium (music, arithmetic, geometry, and astronomy) and incorporated into the system of education as "servants of theology." This system of education became part of the structure of the universities that were founded in the 13th century. The different sciences only very gradually gained a certain in-

dependence. The universal scientific development in the Christian West, under the predominance of theology, began at first purely in the name of tradition: in theology—the tradition of the Holy Scriptures, the Church Fathers, the councils, the synods, the popes and bishops; in the natural sciences—the tradition of Plato, Aristotle, and their Hellenistic pupils.

The tradition of church laws also contained some contradictory traits in the form of council resolutions, papal decrees, and decisions of the Fathers. The development of a practicable method by which to solve these contradictions was necessary in order to meet the demand to find quick solutions to concrete questions of law. Therefore, the theologian Peter Abelard (1079–probably 1144) developed the so-called *sic-et-non* (yes-and-no) method, which corresponded largely to a judicial method of the church called *concordantia discordantium canonum* (harmonizing contradicting canonical laws).

With the Reformation—in spite of Luther's rejection of Aristotle—another form of Scholasticism (with the tendency toward a universal Christian system of knowledge) developed in a similar way in Protestantism. Open conflict occurred only when the traditional biblical view of the world was seriously questioned, as in the case of the Italian astronomer Galileo (1633). The principles of Galileo's scientific research, however, were themselves the result of a Christian idea of science and truth. Positive tendencies concerning education and science have always been dominant in the history of Christianity, even though the opposite attitude arose occasionally during certain periods.

The attitude that had been hostile toward intellectual endeavours was less frequently heard after the Christian Church had become the church of the Roman Empire and masses of people had streamed into the congregations, but only after a series of disturbances. It passed its first climax as priests and monks who were hostile to education fanatically incited mobs to systematically destroy the temples and sites of ancient pagan civilization. In the course of these events they even made martyrs of members of non-Christian groups (e.g., the philosopher Hypatia in Alexandria in AD 415). The interrelationship between theology and science that had been established by the Fathers of the early church and the scholastics of the Middle Ages was attacked again and again in later centuries. Intellectual activities were attacked when spiritualistic and mystic trends or ascetic trends radically hostile toward culture turned against the dominance of educational theology—emphasizing the "spiritual experience," the "inner light," the "enlightenment through the Holy Spirit," the "Christ in us." This occurred among the radical Franciscans, the German and English lay mystics in the 13th and 14th centuries, and in the *devotio moderna* (i.e., modern devotion, an educational reform movement in Germany and the Netherlands). The relationship between science and theology was also attacked when the understanding of truth that had been developed within theology was withdrawn from the direction of educational theology and turned critically against the dogma of the church itself. This occurred, for instance, after the natural sciences and theology had turned away from total dependence upon tradition and directed their attention toward experience—observation and experiment. A number of fundamental dogmatic principles and understandings were thus questioned and eventually abandoned. The struggle concerning the theory of evolution (e.g., the Scopes Trial in Tennessee in 1925) has been a conspicuous modern symptom of this trend.

The church itself, however, has contributed to the estrangement of theology and natural science. The reformation of Luther, Zwingli, and Calvin produced a great number of denominations, each of which claimed to have the true faith and fought bloody religious wars in order to assert the validity of its position. This seriously harmed the credibility of the dogmatic principles because they had been arrived at through such an obviously non-Christian manner. Scholars withdrew from the decisions of church authorities and were willing

Attitudes of Paul and Tertullian

Theology as the instructor of the various sciences

Hostility toward intellectual endeavours

The church's contribution to the estrangement between theology and science

only to subject themselves to critical reason and experience. The rationalism of the Enlightenment appeared to be the answer of science to the claim of true faith that had been made by the churches, which had become untrustworthy through the religious wars.

Forms of Christian education. The Christian Church created the bases of the Western system of education. Initially, the church separated itself from the basic ideas of pagan education of the late Hellenistic and Roman society but then began to create its own educational institutions. Many important Christian teachers were professional philosophers or rhetors: *e.g.*, Justin Martyr, Tertullian, and Augustine. The first impulse toward education came from the necessity to educate the church's catechumens (learners) in the principles of Christian faith and ethics. In the early Middle Ages, a system of schools was formed at the seats of bishops to educate clergymen and to teach the civil servants of the government and administrative offices. The schools for clergymen adopted the forms of the late Hellenistic and Roman instruction and the arrangement of subjects—trivium and quadrivium—partly with the old instruction books reduced according to Christian standards. The school at the court of Charlemagne, which was conducted by clergymen, the medieval schools of the religious orders, cathedrals, monasteries, convents, and churches, the flourishing schools of the Brethren of the Common Life, and the Roman Catholic school systems that came into existence during the Counter-Reformation under the leadership of the Jesuits and other new teaching orders have contributed as much to the civilization of the West as the foundation of schools and educational reforms that resulted later from the Reformation and were started by the German Reformers Luther, Melanchthon, Johann Bugenhagen, John and August Hermann Francke, and by the Moravian reformers Amos Comenius and Zinzendorf. The church was responsible for the system of schools even after the Reformation. Only since the 18th century, when the idea of general education for the public began to gain support, did the school system start to separate itself from its Christian roots and fall more and more under state control. Until the French Revolution, however, the state viewed itself as a Christian government and understood its responsibility concerning the schools in a Christian sense, using the churches' help.

With the separation of church and state, both institutions have entered into tensely manifold relationships. In some countries, the state has taken over the school system completely and does not allow private church schools except in a few special cases in which constant control is maintained regarding religious instruction as a part of the state's educational task. This has been emphasized in its strongest form by the Roman Catholic Church in Germany since the times of cultural struggle in the 19th century. The Roman Catholic Church demanded that the state institute denominationally separated schools. In a moderate form there has been a demand that all Roman Catholic children receive religious instruction only from the Roman Catholic Church, or under its supervision. Other countries maintain school systems basically free of religion and leave the religious instruction to the private undertakings of the different churches (*e.g.*, France). In the American Revolution the concept of the separation of state and church was a lofty goal that was supposed to free the church from all patronization by the state and to make possible a maximum of free activity, particularly in the area of education. On the other hand, the Soviet Union has used its schools particularly for an anti-religious education based upon the state philosophy of dialectical materialism, practicing the constitutionally guaranteed freedom of anti-religious propaganda in schools, though the churches are forbidden to give any education outside their worship services.

A second problem that results from the separation of church and state is the question of state subsidies to private church schools. These are claimed even in view of the separation of church and state in those countries

Tensions resulting from the separation of church and state

in which the church schools in many places take over part of the functions of the state schools (*e.g.*, in the United States). After the ideological Positivism and the Materialism of the 19th century faded away in many areas, it was realized that religious life had had an important role in the cultural development of the West and the New World and that the practiced exclusion of religious instruction from the curricula of the schools indicated a lack of balance in education. Based on new insights, it has therefore been maintained in the 20th century that religion should be adopted as a subject among the humanities. State universities in the United States, Canada, and Australia, which did not have theological faculties because of the separation of church and state, founded departments of religion of an interdenominational nature and included non-Christians as academic teachers of religion.

The Christian system of education led to the early founding of universities. This highest institution of teaching and learning was a creation of medieval Europe and spread from there to other continents after the 16th century. The autonomy of masters and scholars was fundamental; the designation *universitas magistrorum et scholarium* ("university of masters and scholars") was documented for the first time at the beginning of the 13th century in Paris. The universities that had been formed in the beginning through the unification of schools for monks and schools for regular clergy succeeded in gaining their relative independence by agreements with church and state. The University of Naples was founded in 1224 as a state university by Emperor Frederick II. Based upon the privileges granted by emperor or pope, the following universities were founded: in Spain, Salamanca in 1239 and Seville in 1260; in Portugal, Lisbon in 1290; in France, Toulouse in 1229, Orléans in 1309, and Grenoble in 1339; in Italy, Padua, Rome, Perugia, Modena, Pisa, and Florence. In the middle of the 14th century, foundations of universities in the empire north of the Alps followed in eastern and northern Europe (Prague, Kraków, Vienna, Pécs, Fünfkirchen, Heidelberg, Cologne, Ofen, Erfurt, Leipzig, and Rostock). During the second half of the 16th century, a second wave of universities followed, which were more strongly characterized by Humanism (Greifswald, Fribourg, Basel, Trier, Uppsala, Tübingen, Copenhagen, and Wittenberg). The universities represented the unity of education that was apparent in the common use of the Latin language, the teaching methods of lecture and disputation, the extended communal living in colleges, the periodically changing leadership of an elected dean, the inner structure according to faculties or "nations," and the European recognition of the academic degrees.

The advent of Humanism and the Reformation created a new situation for all systems of education, especially the universities. Humanists demanded plans to provide designated places for free research in academies that were princely or private institutions and, as such, not controlled by the church. On the other hand, the Protestant states of the Reformation created their own new state universities, such as Marburg in 1527, Königsberg in 1544, and Jena in 1558. As a counter-action, the Jesuits took over the leadership in the older universities that had remained Roman Catholic or else founded new ones in Europe and overseas.

An international centre of ecclesiastical education is Rome, where the universities of the large orders such as the Benedictines, the Franciscans, the Dominicans, and the Jesuits, besides the Gregorian University (the papal university), are found.

In overseas areas, Christian education has had a twofold task. Firstly, its function was to lay an educational foundation for evangelization of non-Christian peoples by forming a system of education for all levels from grammar school to university. Secondly, its function was to take care of the education of European settlers. To a large extent, the European colonial powers had left the formation of an educational system in their colonies or dominions to the churches. In the Spanish colonial regions in America, Roman Catholic universities were

The founding of medieval universities

Education in mission areas

founded very early (*e.g.*, Santo Domingo in 1538, Mexico and Lima in 1551, Guatemala in 1562, Bogotá in 1573, and Manila in 1611). In China, Jesuit missionaries acted mainly as agents of European education and culture (*e.g.*, astronomy, mathematics, and technology) in their positions as civil servants of the court.

Since the 18th century, the activities of competing Christian denominations in mission areas has led to an intensification of the Christian system of education in Asia and Africa. Christians in these countries have had, in many instances, a better education and have been much represented in governmental and administrative positions. Many political leaders of African and Asian states were educated in Christian missionary schools. Even where the African and Asian states have their own system of schools and universities, Christian educational institutions have performed a significant function (St. Xavier University in Bombay and Sophia University in Tokyo are Jesuit foundations, Dōshisha University in Kyōto is a Japanese Presbyterian foundation).

In some areas in Africa that have a large number of white people, parallel church-related school systems developed for blacks and whites; *e.g.*, in the Republic of South Africa.

On the continent of North America, however, Christian education took a different course. From the beginning, the churches took over the creation of general educational institutions. In the colonial period the priests and ministers of the churches apparently were considered to be best suited to the task. The various denominations did pioneer work in the field of education; a state school system was established only after the situation had consolidated itself. In the English colonies, later the United States, the denominations founded not only a few theological colleges for the purpose of educating their ministers, but they also established universities dealing with all major disciplines, including theology, often emphasizing a denominational slant. Harvard University was founded in 1636 and Yale University in 1701 as Congregational establishments; and William and Mary College was established in 1693 as an Anglican institution. They were followed during the 19th century by other Protestant universities (*e.g.*, Southern Methodist University, Dallas) and colleges (*e.g.*, Midland Lutheran College, Fremont, Nebraska). In addition, many private universities were based upon a Christian idea of education according to the wishes of their founders.

Christian education has been undertaken in a variety of forms. In countries that do not have religious instruction in schools, the system of Sunday schools in which the different denominations administer the religious education of their members' children has developed more extensively. In Germany, Holland, Switzerland, and Scandinavia the Free churches followed the English-American example. The Protestant churches in Germany practice the children's service instead of Sunday school, which had to take over the role of the Sunday school in the sense of Christian instruction of the young people because of the failure of religious instruction in schools (*e.g.*, during the church's struggle during the Third Reich in Germany).

Confirmation instruction is more specialized, serving different tasks, such as preparation of the children for confirmation, their conscious acknowledgment of the Christian ethic, of the Christian confessions, of the meaning of the sacraments, and of the special forms of congregational life. The Christian system of education differs, furthermore, in innumerable spontaneous personal or group enterprises, which are created in special conflict or crisis situations. Institutions of education based on such new situations are constantly improvised in demonstration of the charismatic productivity and lively spontaneity of Christianity.

THE RELATIONSHIP BETWEEN THE CHRISTIAN OR CHRISTIAN INSTITUTIONS AND THE CARE OF THE SICK AND OTHER AFFLICTED PERSONS

Healing the sick. The Christian Church has administered its concern for the sick in a twofold manner: both by healing the sick and by expressing concern and caring for them. The fact that the practice of healing has retreated into the background in modern times need not discredit the fact that healing played a decisive role and reference to the success of the church and was important in the missionary apologetics of the church. In the Gospels, Jesus appeared as a healer of body and soul. The title "Christ the physician" was the most popular name for the Lord in missionary preaching of the first centuries. Even the Apostles are characterized as healers—the handkerchiefs and aprons of the Apostle Paul are used for miracle healings. The apologetics of the church of the 2nd to 4th century used numerous miraculous healings as arguments for the visible presence of the Holy Spirit in the church. The basis for healings was generally a demonological interpretation of sickness: healing was frequently carried out as an exorcism, that is, a ceremonial liturgical adjuration of the demon that was supposed to cause the illness and its expulsion from the sick person. The Fathers of the first centuries interpreted the entire sphere of charismatic life from the basic concepts that Christ is the physician, the church the hospital, the sacraments the medication, and orthodox theology the medicine chest against heresy. Ignatius of Antioch (*c.* AD 110) called the Eucharist the "medication against death," as "medication that produces immortality."

The history of charismatic healing has hardly been explored. Miracles of healing remain a characteristic attribute of the great Christian charismatics, the saints of the Roman Catholic Church as well as of the Eastern Orthodox. Healing within the church began to retreat only in connection with the transformation of the church into a state church under Constantine and with the replacement of free charismatics by ecclesiastical officials.

The development of exorcisms is characteristic in this respect: the office of the exorcist eventually became one of the lower levels of ordination, which finally led to the priesthood. Traditionally, exorcisms are connected not alone with the rite of Baptism; on the contrary, the *Rituale Romanum* (*Roman Ritual*) contains numerous liturgical formulas for different cases of demoniacal possession. Only the Enlightenment in the 18th century repressed the practice of exorcisms within the Roman Catholic Church.

Remarkably, however, the Enlightenment caused a new growth of exorcistic movements in southern Germany, Austria, and Switzerland, led by Johann Gassner, a Tirolean minister, who carried out tens of thousands of exorcisms in Vorarlberg at Lake Constance and in Upper Swabia during the years 1760–75. The Bavarian Academy of Sciences finally intervened, and Franz Mesmer (died 1815), the discoverer of animal magnetism (hypnotism), refuted Gassner's teachings of demonological sickness. Furthermore, ecclesiastical practice of exorcism was forbidden by the archbishop of Salzburg and eventually by the pope. The liturgical formulas of exorcism, however, were not removed from the *Rituale Romanum*. Because instances of demoniacal possession have been rediscovered in the 20th century by depth psychology, psychoanalysis, and certain secularized forms of therapeutic exorcisms, the church occasionally has returned to the application of exorcism.

In the churches of the Reformation, exorcism never completely vanished; in Pietistic circles several exorcists have appeared; *e.g.*, Johann Christoph Blumhardt the Elder (died 1880). Since the latter part of the 19th century, different groups of the Pentecostal movement have re-accepted the use of exorcistic rituals with great emphasis and—pointing to the power of the Holy Spirit—they claim the charisma of healing as one of the spiritual gifts granted the believing Christian. After the basic connection between healing of the body and healing of the soul and the psychogenic origin of many illnesses was acknowledged theologically and medically, different older churches, such as the Protestant Episcopal Church and even the Roman Catholic Church in the United States, have been influenced by the Pentecostal movement and have re-instituted healing services.

The founding of denominational colleges and universities in the United States

The purpose of confirmation instruction

Jesus and the Apostles as healers

The development of exorcism

Because of the neglect of healing in most institutional churches, mainly since the Enlightenment, during the second half of the 19th century one church has stood out in this respect in North America. Mary Baker Eddy (died 1910), the founder of Christian Science, referred particularly to healing through the Spirit as her special mission. Based on her experience of a successful healing from a serious illness by one of Mesmer's pupils, Phineas Quimby, she wrote her work *Science and Health with Key to the Scriptures* and upon it founded her own church, the Church of Christ, Scientist. According to the instructions of its founder, Christian Science today carries out a practice of "spiritual healing" through its own practitioners throughout the world.

Care for the sick. From the beginning, another concern besides healing was care for the sick, an element of the earliest commandments of Christian ethics. In the Lord's promise to his disciples at his Ascension he said: "In my name they will cast out demons . . .; they will lay their hands on the sick, and they will recover." At the Last Judgment, Christ the Judge says to the chosen ones on his right hand: "I was sick and you visited me," and to the condemned on his left hand: "I was sick and you did not visit me." To the condemneds' surprised questions as to when they saw the Lord sick and visited him, they receive the answer: "As you did it not to one of the least of these, you did it not to me."

The first office that was created by the church in Jerusalem was the diaconate; it spread rapidly throughout the whole church. According to the *Canons of St. Hippolytus*, the care of the sick was carried out by the deacons and widows under the leadership of the bishop. This service was not limited to members of the Christian congregation but was directed toward the larger community, particularly in times of pestilence and plague. Soon ecclesiastical *nosokomeia* (places of care of the sick) were founded. They were mentioned for the first time during the 4th century and were, for example, supported in Cappadocia by the theologian and monastic reformer Basil the Great.

During the Middle Ages the monasteries took over the care of the sick and created a new institution, the hospital. The growing number of pilgrims to the Holy Land and the necessity of care of their numerous sick, who had fallen victim to the unfamiliar conditions of climate and life, led to knightly hospital orders, the most important one of which was the Order of the Hospital of St. John of Jerusalem (later called the Knights of Malta). The service for the sick, which was carried out by the knights besides their military service for the protection of the pilgrims, was not elaborate. The Order of the Knights of the Sword, for example, had taken over the task of caring for the pestilence-stricken; only a knight who had plague spots on his body as a sign of his service could become the master of the order.

In connection with the fight against feudalism within the church, which was initiated by the orders of mendicant friars, especially the Franciscans, bourgeois hospital orders were formed. Even the hospital in Marburg that was founded by St. Elizabeth (died 1231) on the territory of the Knights of the Teutonic Order was influenced by the spirit of St. Francis. Besides these, hospitals were founded as autonomous institutions that were subordinated to the leadership or supervision of a bishop. The meaningful centralization of the different existing institutions became necessary with the growth of the cities and was most frequently undertaken by the city councils. The laity began to take over, but the spiritual and pastoral care of the patients remained a major concern.

In the realm of the Lutheran Reformation, the medieval nursing institutions were continued and adapted to new conditions. The church constitutions in the different territories of Reformed churches not only pointed to the duty of caring for the sick but also gave suggestions for its adequate realization. The office of the deacon was supplemented by that of the deaconess; and these offices of service were considered part of the polity of the church of the New Testament. The Counter-Reformation brought a new impulse for caring for the sick in the

Roman Catholic Church, insofar as special orders for nursing service were founded; *e.g.*, the monk-hospitallers (1572) and nun-hospitallers (1668), by Vincent de Paul, who was himself a notable charismatic healer. According to the example of these two orders, a great number of new orders came into existence and spread the spirit and institutions of ecclesiastical nursing care throughout the whole world as part of Roman Catholic world missions.

In the realm of Protestantism, the Free churches led in the care of the sick. Methodists, Baptists, and Quakers all had a great share in this development, founding numerous hospitals in all parts of the world and supplying them with willing male and female helpers. German Lutheranism was influenced by the development; and Theodor Fliedner founded the first Protestant hospital in Kaiserswerth in 1836, also creating at the same time the female diaconia, an order of nurses that soon found worldwide membership and recognition.

The influence of Christian care for the sick in the secular world. The church hospitals and the ecclesiastical nursing care still maintain a leading and exemplary role in the 20th century, although along with the general political and social development of the 19th century the city or communal hospital was founded and overtook the church hospital. Ecclesiastical nursing care always started with church institutions on church territory and spread from there into the realm of the general communal sphere, which leads to a universal extension of Christian care but also to secularization and lay control. The city councils of the growing cities of the Reformation era, for example, took over the leadership of the ecclesiastical hospitals. Because the separation of church and state was proclaimed during the French Revolution and the trend to assign ecclesiastical welfare tasks to the state grew, a state hospital system was established alongside that of the church. The state institutions, however, preferred to make use of nurses from Roman Catholic orders or deaconess houses.

The most impressive example of the universal spread of care for the sick was the founding of the Red Cross by Henri Dunant. The religious influence of Dunant's pious parental home in Geneva and the shocking impression he received on the battlefield of Solferino in June 1859 led him to work out suggestions that—after difficult negotiations with representatives of numerous states—led to the conclusion of the "Geneva convention regarding the care and treatment in wartime of the wounded military personnel." In the 20th century, the activity of the Red Cross has embraced not only the victims of military actions but also peace activity, which includes aid for the sick, for the handicapped, for old people and children, and for the victims of all types of disasters everywhere in the world.

The danger of secularization is particularly apparent in the area of nursing care. The technical organization of care of the sick, it has been maintained, cannot replace the selfless dedication of voluntary service on which the Christian works of love for the sick are based. It is now commonly asserted that ecclesiastical nursing institutions have relied too much and too long on this spirit of selflessness and sometimes have taken advantage of it. As a result the nursing profession did not keep up with the general social development in the areas of special working hours, adequate living quarters, payment, and Social Security. In the 20th century a crisis arose in the area of nursing care caused, on the one hand, by the fact that illness and need do not pay attention to the general customs of legally determined working hours, and, on the other hand, by the experience that the spirit of serving love cannot be transmitted by mere technical professional training.

Care for the poor, widows, and orphans. The special care of the Christian congregation was directed from the beginning to the poor and sick, widows and orphans, and the dependents of male protectors, though widowers, even after the victory of female emancipation, were never regarded as a group that needed the welfare of the church. Ecclesiastical care for the widows and orphans has been connected to the attitudes of the Old Testament

The command of Jesus and the concern for the Last Judgment

The development of nursing orders and deaconess orders

The founding of the Red Cross

in which Yahweh is the "Father of the fatherless and protector of widows." The Letter of James says: "Religion that is pure and undefiled before God is this: to visit orphans and widows in their affliction." The widows formed a special group in the congregations and were asked to help with nursing care and other diaconic congregational tasks as long as they did not need help and care themselves.

In all eras of church history, widows have played an important role. In the fight of the Roman Catholic Church with the Donatists (an anti-Roman moralistic sect) of North Africa, for example, widows were leading in the Donatist resistance. In Protestant regional churches the widows of ministers played a role in the continuity of the congregation insofar as the young applicant for the ministry had to marry the widow of his predecessor in order to get appointed. This practice was continued in some instances up to the beginning of the 19th century. The most famous widow of the Reformation era was Frau Wibrandis, who was successively married to the Reformers Oecolampadius, Capito, and Bucer, and—a widow for the fourth time after Bucer's death—educated her sons of her three marriages with Reformers in Strassburg to become faithful ministers.

The founding of orphanages and other institutions of mercy

After the church had already founded orphanages, during the 4th century, the monasteries took over this task during the Middle Ages. They also fought against the habit of abandoning unwanted children and established foundling hospitals. In this area, as in others, a secularization of church institutions took place; they were adopted by the city governments during the High Middle Ages in connection with the spreading autonomy of the cities. In the Reformed churches the establishment of orphanages was furthered systematically. In Holland almost every congregation had its own orphanage, which was sustained through the gifts of the members.

Following the great wars of the 17th century the orphanages were reorganized pedagogically, notably by August Hermann Francke, who connected the orphanage in Glaucha (a suburb of Halle), which he had founded, with a modern system of secondary schools. Francke's orphanage became a model that was frequently imitated in England and also in the new English colonies in North America. During the Enlightenment and the revival movement, the traditional orphanages were criticized, and care of orphans in foster families was demanded to replace institutional care. The system of foster care, however, frequently led to exploitation of orphans as cheap labourers, who had insufficient care and accommodation. The discussion of these questions provides a significant contribution to the development of modern youth welfare, which in the 20th century is mainly the responsibility of state, communal, or humanitarian organizations but is still characterized strongly by its Christian roots.

The care of widows and orphans in its original Christian form played a large role in the Christian mission in all parts of the world, mainly in connection with care in refugee camps and for victims of military disputes and political revolutions, such as in Hong Kong, Vietnam, Biafra (which attempted to gain independence from Nigeria, but failed), and Jordan. Christian initiative also played an important part in resistance to the custom of burning widows in India, a practice that was finally forbidden by the English colonial government in 1829 under the pressure of Christian missionary societies. The constitution of the Republic of India adopted the prohibition after independence, in spite of the resistance of some members of conservative religious groups.

The role of pastoral care. Pastoral care has been of special importance among the charismas (spiritual gifts) of the early church. It consists of the ability to penetrate the neighbour to the bottom of his heart and spirit and to recognize whether he is dominated by a good or by an evil spirit and the gift to help him to freedom from his demon. The biographies of the great charismatic ministers, beginning with the Fathers of the Eastern Church and the Western Church, testify to surprising variations of this charisma, which has been institutionalized in the church in connection with the sacrament of penance as

The purpose of pastoral care

confession. First developed in the area of monasticism, the systematic searching of conscience and the private confession in front of a confessor became a daily duty. The private confession then spread from monasticism to the general church practice of the laity, particularly in the Irish-Scottish monastic church.

Two points are decisive in importance in the sacrament of penance. (1) Pastoral care is practiced only by the priest because, according to an interpretation of the Gospel According to Matthew, he has been endowed through ordination with the power to "bind and to loose"; (2) pastoral care of lay people for each other was not appreciated. The priests, who replaced the private philosophers in the educated homes of the early church, played an influential part as private counsellors of prominent personalities, such as kings, emperors and princes, popes, and leading patrician families. Pastoral care, in the course of its institutionalization, led more and more to a judicially founded casuistry of sins. The medieval practice of indulgences, which instituted money as a substitute for satisfactory works—such as prayer, alms, and pilgrimages that had to be fulfilled by the penitent—led to the destruction of the original spiritual purpose of pastoral care.

In the fight against the misuse of the sacrament of penance, Reformed Christianity began to attempt a spiritual renewal of the confession. The Reformers, however, caused severe harm to pastoral care by denying the sacramental character of penance because it was closely connected with personal confession. According to Luther's idea of the priesthood of all believers, every believer has the duty and the power of pastoral care for his neighbour. As a consequence, the institution of confession began to deteriorate in the Lutheran Church. Pastoral care found a new place within the church in the realm of church discipline and was revived particularly in Calvinism, which introduced regular house calls for the control of morals and wakening of conscience. Many Anglo-Saxon Free churches have continued the practice of pastoral care in connection with church discipline. This kind of practice, however, brought about the danger that pastoral care would be converted into an instrument of constant control and supervision of the believers by their appointed spiritual officers. The believers resisted this in particular because the spiritual officers frequently used the means of secular extensions of the state authorities in order to carry through successfully their measures of discipline. For this reason, pastoral care languished in Protestantism and was in practice exercised only occasionally by a charismatically gifted minister who gained the trust of the members of his congregation. Therefore, especially in Protestant countries, pastoral care passed by default from the church into the care of psychiatrists and psychoanalysts, who, on the one hand, claimed to use scientific methods appropriate to modern consciousness and, on the other hand, were bound by law to total confidentiality. The churches so far have not succeeded in regaining the confidence of the people in pastoral care, which they had lost through their own negligence to the psychiatrists and psychoanalysts.

Deterioration of the role of pastoral care in Protestantism

The abolition of confession and official pastoral care in Protestantism led to an intellectual achievement in the area of spiritual literature (*i.e.*, devotional books), whose writers were usually the great leaders of the Reformation and revival movements. An impressive body of devotional literature is oriented toward pastoral care dating from the time of the Reformation, through Pietism, and up to the revival movement. This literature used to be the only reading matter that was read aloud for the whole family in the evenings before mass media, such as newspapers, radio, motion pictures, and television, were invented. Devotional books of ecumenical significance also came out of the English revival movement; *e.g.*, John Bunyan's *Pilgrim's Progress* (1678), a work that has been translated into many languages and influenced Christianity during the 18th and 19th centuries. The new founder of this kind of literature was John Wesley with his *Christian Library*, the first collection of paperbacks of modern times, which contained English translations of classical devotional writings from the times of the early church and the Middle Ages to the Spanish, French, and German mystical writings of his own time. This form of individual pastoral care through Christian devotional literature was only replaced by modern mass media, which turned people's attention to more worldly interests—*e.g.*, entertainment, diversion, education, or information.

The problem of pastoral care in the 20th century

The failure, or the extinction, of pastoral care in the churches of the 20th century left a vacuum that probably cannot be filled by modern psychotherapy and psychiatry and to a great extent is being filled by a multitude of Eastern methods of meditation and practices of Yoga. The Christian pastoral counsellor of former times often has been succeeded in the latter part of the century by a private guru (Hindu teacher). The ecumenical movement of the Christian churches has contributed to a new discovery of pastoral counselling. The liberalization of mixed marriages has freed pastoral care of the totalitarian claim that often had disastrous consequences in counselling to members of a mixed marriage and sometimes led to the withdrawal of persons from the church altogether.

THE RELATIONSHIP BETWEEN THE CHRISTIAN OR CHRISTIAN INSTITUTIONS AND CULTURE

The basic idea that Christian faith creates a new life has led to the fact that Christianity, during the course of its history, has constantly contributed to the creation of new cultural trends and has produced new cultures in its field of influence in the attempt to change its whole environment. Two basic situations must be distinguished when considering this culture-creating influence: (1) Christianity has become a majority of a state or people in some instances, and (2) in other instances a Christian minority has had to resist a non-Christian environment. Both positions have come closer to each other because many Communist countries, which called themselves Christian up to the early part of the 20th century, have adopted an atheistic philosophy as their official ideology and have placed the former Christian state churches in a minority position.

The influence of Christianity on culture in areas in which it is the majority religion. Basically, Christianity urges the development of a Christian culture in all

The creation of a Christian culture

areas of life. Under this kind of imperative, the early church unfolded in the cultural realm of the Christian Roman Empire, starting in Constantinople, and the medieval church in Rome created the culture of the Christian West. Similarly, Protestant culture spread from Germany, Scandinavia, central Europe, and England to North America.

In the Eastern Orthodox Church, orthodox piety penetrated all spheres of intellectual, spiritual, and physical life in the Orthodox community as well as all spheres in the life of the individual believer. The specific forms of Orthodox culture are much more obvious and more easily recognized than the forms of Protestant culture, which have appeared frequently in the shape of "innerworldly" secularized forms, whose Christian origins are difficult to recognize. Three kinds of art are missing in the area of Orthodox culture in the Byzantine Empire and in the ancient schismatic churches of Asia and Africa: sculpture, theatre, and ecclesiastical instrumental music.

Sculpture is missing because of a law against its use in Christian art that is based on the theological understanding of the character of icons. Under the influence of this attitude against sculpture in Byzantine Church art and because of the consequences of iconoclasm, not even a profane art of sculpture developed within the realm of Byzantine culture. Only in the area of miniature art forms was sculpture able to develop (*e.g.*, ivory carving, and working in gold, other metals, and enamel).

Two-dimensional art in Orthodoxy

The restriction of Christian art to two-dimensional pictures led to the growth of mural painting on a larger scale, and most of all to a highly developed mosaic art. The latter was influenced by the feeling for shape and nature of ancient classical times, but it also created an abstract new style of art that dissolved all illusions of

space and live naturalness and was characterized by spiritual-religious composition. In the course of its development, a reverse perspective became dominant, one which did not engender perspective in the eye of the human observer but in a transcendental focal point behind the picture, in the divine eye. For this reason the human beings in the foreground were painted smaller than the central figures of saints, who were closer to God and therefore filled the main space of the icons. Examples of Byzantine mosaic art as well as mural painting are also found in the West, especially in Ravenna and in the Byzantine churches of Sicily. In the East, most of them were destroyed by the Iconoclasts, and another great number was whitewashed by the Muslim Arabs and Turks after their conquest of the Orthodox countries.

Mural paintings have survived the period of the Iconoclasts in hardly accessible cave churches in Cappadocia near Güreme and Ürgüp (9th to 11th centuries). Only very painstaking work of restoration by archaeologists and art experts has re-exposed part of the Byzantine mosaics and mural paintings that were whitewashed during the time of the Turks, especially the mosaics of the Hagia Sophia, the main church of the Byzantine Empire. It had been turned into a mosque after the conquest of Constantinople but was then declared a Turkish national museum. The mosaics of its dome, which had been created after the iconoclastic period, have been restored to their original beauty.

Besides the art of icon and mural painting and mosaics, the art of book illustration was at its zenith. Like the other arts it served not only the theologians and monks who read the richly ornamented and decorated parchment manuscripts of the Church Fathers but also the choir that chanted the liturgy. Book illustration flourished most spectacularly in the entire area of Orthodoxy on Greek, Asian, and African soil because of the numerous commissions of emperors and rich donors. The libraries of the monasteries on Mt. Athos and Sinai, which have only recently been made accessible in the 20th century, contain most impressive testimonies of this miniature art.

The absence of the theatre in the realms of the Orthodox Church is related to the fact that during the early church drama centred mainly on the ancient myths about the gods. Comedy portrayed fornication and immorality in all its forms and theatre itself was considered by Christians to be the retreat of paganism. According to the older church constitutions, the profession of the actor was among those that had to be given up as a condition for Baptism. Therefore, drama never developed in the area of the Byzantine Church. The extinction of ancient drama, however, was compensated for by the extraordinary richness of the liturgy of the church, which actually is a very lively mystery drama with different entrances and processions and responding choirs. A secular dramatic art developed in the Eastern Orthodox countries and in Russia only after the 19th century. The dramatic basic character of the liturgy has constantly led to the creation of new forms, even after the liturgy itself reached a certain uniform shape. In different churches the sermon developed into a dramatized homily, in which the sermon about a certain pericope (specified text) was enlivened by the use of dialogues, scenic passages, monologues, and choirs; and the general mystery drama of the liturgy was interrupted by different biblical scenes. In Byzantium these beginnings of religious drama, however, never have been separated from their liturgical frame.

The development of dramatic forms in the Orthodox liturgy

The absence of ecclesiastical instrumental music in the Orthodox Church likewise has had a dogmatic reason: man is not supposed to use dead metal and dead wood in order to praise God. He should himself be a live instrument of God's praise and glorify God with his own mouth as well as with his whole life. In the pagan cults, mainly in the mystery cults, instrumental music—in particular flutes, drums, and tympani—was used for the enhancement of the dissolute mood; for this reason the Byzantine Church kept its distance from this kind of music as a specific form of pagan worship. Therefore, instrumental music in the Byzantine Empire was reserved solely for secular festivities. Small portable organs were used mainly at court celebrations and in the circus but not in the churches.

The lack of instrumental music led to an unusual development of church choir music and hymnography. The Orthodox worship service contains an extraordinary musical variety that can be mastered—even technically—only by choirs with great musical ability, and a voluminous liturgical repertoire of hymns of all kinds. Even the priests and deacons have to be able to fulfill high musical and vocal requirements.

Up to the second half of the 9th century, the creators of the hymns were at the same time poets and composers, creating the texts of the hymns as well as the melodies belonging to them. Following this period, an epoch of hymnographs began in which new poems were created for the already existing melodies. In the 11th century, a new flourishing Byzantine music developed, which was characterized by extensive coloratura that led directly to a neo-Greek hymn composition. In the Russian Church and in Greece, primarily on the islands that were occupied by the Italians, Byzantine music for one voice was replaced partly or completely by modern western European music with its harmony and its polyphonic choir music, whereas in the monasteries, particularly on Mt. Athos, the unison chant was used, as it still is in the 20th century. In Russia, the older unison chant of Byzantine origin has been retained in the sect of the Starovery (Old-Believers). The Orthodox Church has preserved hymns of older origin from the schools of Kiev, Novgorod, and Moscow. The great Russian composers of the last centuries have contributed to the further development of choir music with modern compositions, which also have influenced the secular works of the Russian composers (*e.g.*, Tchaikovsky).

The influence of Christianity on culture in areas in which it is a minority religion. The tendency to develop an identifiable Christian culture is apparent even where Christian minorities live in a non-Christian environment; *i.e.*, in an environment the life of which has been shaped and is characterized by a non-Christian religion. This is the case with most Christian churches in Asia, Africa, and Indonesia.

For Christian minorities in an environment of non-Christian religion, there are no bodies of non-Christian religions that have preserved a pure culture, except in Muslim states that in their constitutions declare themselves to be Islāmic states (*e.g.*, Pakistan). All areas of former non-Christian religious cultures, such as the Hindu and Buddhist cultures of Southeast and East Asia, have been influenced and changed by Western civilization, which was itself shaped by the Christian culture of the West in its technology, economic system, understanding of time, and idea of possessions and property. The global spreading of Western culture and civilization with its Christian influence during the era of colonialization and the economic expansion of the West, including the United States, has resulted in a global approximation of technical methods in agricultural production, in bank and money matters, in traffic, and in military organization. The encounter of Christianity and the older religions took place in Asia and Africa within this new framework of a unified culture and civilization and is therefore simplified. The constitutions of most countries, even of the new Asian and African states, generally demand the separation of church and state so that a domineering religion cannot be practiced, at least not legally. The principles of the freedom of religion, however, only penetrate gradually. In many newer states of Asia and Africa non-Christian groups exist against the Christian churches based on the fact that during colonial times the former non-Christian indigenous religions were suppressed, disadvantaged, or deprived of their rights, and the Christian churches were privileged. In some countries Christian minorities have had to struggle for their existence and recognition, and there are cases of persecutions of Christians; *e.g.*, the Christian Ibos in Nigeria that in the early 1970s led to the attempt at political secession by Biafra. On the other hand, in some cases the situation of

Christian minorities is ideally suited to demonstrate to outsiders the peculiar style of life of a Christian culture. This is particularly advantageous for the church within a caste state, in which the church itself has developed into a caste, with special extrinsic characteristics in clothing and customs. An example of this phenomenon is the Mar Thoma Church of South India or, in a different form, the messianic Bantu churches of South Africa, which—as a minority—have founded their own settlements where they practice their own Christian style of life in cultural, individual, and congregational life.

A special problem presents itself through the coexistence of racially different Christian cultures in racially mixed states. The influence of the Christian Negro churches, especially of Baptist denominations, has been thoroughly imprinted upon the culture of the North American Negroes. The churches themselves were founded through the missionary work of white Baptist churches but became independent of their mother churches or were established as autonomous churches within the framework of the Baptist denomination. A similar situation exists in South Africa, where white congregations and separate Negro congregations have been established within the white mission churches; independent messianic Negro churches have appeared outside the older organized congregations. In the 20th century, much tension exists in this area.

On the one hand, the Christian Church has from the beginning urged the overcoming of racism. In the early church, racism was unknown; the Jewish synagogues allowed black proselytes. The first Jewish proselyte mentioned in the Acts of the Apostles was a governmental administrator from Ethiopia, who was baptized by the Apostle Philip. The early congregations in Alexandria included many Ethiopians and Negroes. Among the evangelizing churches, the Portuguese Catholic mission in principle did not recognize differences between races—whoever was baptized became a "human being" and became a member not only of the Christian congregation but also of the Christian society and was allowed to marry another Christian of any race. In contrast to this practice, the Catholic mission of the Spaniards introduced the separation of races under the term *casticismo* (purity of the Castilian heritage) in the American mission regions and sometimes restricted marriage between Castilian Spanish immigrants and native Christians. Like the Portuguese in Africa and Brazil, the French Catholic mission in Canada and in the regions around the Great Lakes in North America did not prohibit marriage of whites with Indians but tolerated and and even encouraged it during the 17th and 18th centuries.

Consequently, the Christian churches led in endeavours for racial integration, with the exception of those churches that maintained racial segregation from the beginning, in deference to theological arguments deduced from the "order of the creation" and "predestination." The latter was the case in some Reformed churches of the United States and of South Africa. For a long time the establishment of Negro congregations and Negro churches in the United States was the only chance for Negroes to gain a higher education as Negro ministers, to develop a self-government of the congregations, to gather possessions and property, to be recognized as institutions with judicial privilege, and to practice certain rights. On the other hand, the ideologically and politically founded racial theory has been introduced into the Negro churches in recent times. The demand for a Black Theology with a black Christ in its centre has been made and aggravates the specifically Christian task of racial integration within the church just as much as a theologically and ideologically founded racial theory on the part of the whites.

THE RELATIONSHIP OF THE CHRISTIAN AND OF CHRISTIAN INSTITUTIONS TO THE UNDERSTANDING AND USE OF NATURE

The Christian understanding of nature is in no way theologically unequivocal. In the New Testament nature is on the one hand understood as God's self-revelation insofar as in God's work "ever since the creation of the world his invisible nature, namely, his eternal power and deity, has been clearly perceived in the things that have been made." On the other hand, nature seems to be that which has to be overcome.

Man's relationship to nature. The Christian understanding of nature goes back to God's biblical command for man. In Genesis God introduces the created world and its creatures to man and says: "Fill the earth and subdue it." Since the beginning of Christian theology, this order has not been interpreted as an invitation to exploit nature but to elaborate the fact that man is the only creature that has been created after the image of God and that God has entrusted his creation to him. Therefore, it is directed toward man as God's co-worker, who receives some of the responsibility for maintaining and completing the creation.

Interpretations of man's dominion of the Earth

This command of God, however, was spoken before man's rebellion against God. That expresses the fact—and the Fathers of the early church emphasized this many times—that man's rebellion against God, "the Fall of man," which consists of man's misuse of his God-given freedom, has interrupted not only his relationship with God but also his relationship with creation. The fallen man does not consider and use creation as the garden of God that has been entrusted to his care and responsibility but as an object of selfish exploitation. Exploitation by fallen man is the beginning of the destruction of nature by man, who has always been guilty of this act. The early church was still sensitive to this close relationship between man and creation. It preserved the clear conviction that the destruction of the original relationship of love between God and man destroyed the relationship between man and creation as well. Paul expressed the idea that the whole creation participates in the Fall of man and needs salvation with him: "For the creation waits with eager longing for the revealing of the son of God . . . . We know that the whole creation has been groaning in travail together until now." This idea is supplemented by the corresponding expectation that with the salvation of man, his damaged relationship with nature will be restored, and the whole creation will join with man in salvation "because the creation itself will be set free from its bondage to decay and obtain the glorious liberty of the children of God."

This close connection between man and creation is expressed in an idea that characterized the Christology of early Christianity and of the medieval church as well and that still dominates the understanding of Christ in the Eastern Orthodox Church: Christ is the Creator and Redeemer of the whole universe; the act of salvation is not limited to man but includes the whole creation. This idea is expressed metaphorically in the expectation that the history of salvation will be fulfilled with the creation of a new heaven and a new Earth.

In the tradition of Christian mysticism, the concept that the Fall of man has influenced even his physical structure has grown in importance. According to the German mystic Jakob Böhme (died 1624), only man's rebellion against God has led to a "hardening" of substance. These ideas have not gained recognition in official church theology, but the idea of man's rule over creation has remained dominant.

Attitudes toward animals in Christian theology

This continued emphasis on the importance of man over creation can be seen in the fact that animals have hardly received any attention in Christianity. The basic Christian idea of man as the only creature made in the image of God to whom all other creatures are "subdued" separates man clearly from the animals. In this theory, the concept of brotherly fellowship of man with his fellow creatures is largely lost. In Buddhism, by obvious contrast, man is more clearly viewed as part of the continuing chain of all living creatures, through which he even has to pass upward and, in certain cases, downward in a series of reincarnations. Only in a few single statements of Christian saints is the original concept of solidarity of all creatures before God expressed. Francis of Assisi, for example, in his "Canticle of the Creatures" expressed the brotherhood of man with his "brother Sun" and that brotherhood with all created elements in the

eye of God. He united with all stars and elements in the praising and grateful worship of God. He tried to make the people of his time aware of their responsibility for their fellow creatures and their environment, which is an important part of Christian love of God and love of neighbour. The scarcity of this religious consciousness of the creation toward its Creator is the more conspicuous because it is frequently present in the songs of praise in the Psalms of the Old Testament: "The heavens are telling the glory of God; and the firmament proclaims his handiwork."

Only in Christian eschatology does the animal play a part as companion of man: the coming Kingdom of God appears in prophetic promises as the restoration of the paradise in which the disturbed relationship between man and animal—a consequence of the Fall of man—has been repaired and "the wolf shall dwell with the lamb . . . and the weaned child shall put his hand on the adder's den." This order of paradise is apparent in the surroundings of the saints who live in the solitude of deserts and woods and serve the animals with brotherly love; the wild animal, on the other hand, becomes tame and serves the saints in various ways.

This cosmological aspect of sin and salvation has retreated more and more, particularly since the time of the Reformation. During this period, the main contents of the Christian message have been reduced to the question of man's personal relationship with God. Only in the Roman Catholic theology of Baroque universalism, especially in Jesuit theology, a theological cosmology unfolded once again; in Protestantism, cosmological ideas remained only in the traditions of mysticism and of theosophy. Through the German mystic Jakob Böhme and his English pupils within the circle of the London Philadelphians (a 17th-century esoteric mystical society), the basic ideas of Christian cosmology have influenced the founders of modern natural sciences, particularly Isaac Newton.

The fact that the biblical command "Subdue the earth" was understood and obeyed purely in the sense of exploitation has—in connection with the development of technical possibilities—led to the destruction of the landscape, damage to the Earth by erosion, to pollution of the waters—that is, not only the rivers but also the oceans; to pollution of the atmosphere, and, to a catastrophic degree, to extermination in the animal world and the genetic manipulations of the breeding of animals, purely for profit and gain. Significantly, Christians in particular have vehemently opposed the violation of nature.

The problem of exploitation of the Earth

Man's relationship to the cosmos. Included from the beginning in the concept of man as having been created in the image of God has been the question of man's relationship to the universe. The universe, the cosmos, is the place and the work of God's self-revelation and self-realization as well. Christian anthropology has adopted and reinterpreted the idea of man as microcosm—the small world—from Neoplatonic mysticism, in order to define more closely the relationship of man with the universe. Thus, according to his spiritual-physical nature, man represents a compilation of all forms of life and matter, all elements and powers of the universe. In the entire realm of plants and animals, of the organic and mineral world, all the elements and powers unfold in an experimental or even playful way and find their final form in man. In contrast to the Neoplatonic idea of the microcosm, Christian thinking deduces from man's special position within the universe certain duties of worship, love, service, and responsibility.

Worship. Man is supposed "to use God's creatures to know, praise and glorify God, so that in all things God may be praised through Christ Jesus, our Lord." The creatures that surround man are understood as God's hands and messengers "who shall lead us to God."

Love. A glimpse of the wonderful order of nature reminds man to love God, who has given each single figure of his creation "the sign of his living handwriting and the inscription." To faithful Christians, the universe is to appear as the place of "every perfect gift . . ., com-

The basis
for trust in
God

ing down from the Father of lights" (James) and man is admonished to cling to the unceasing love of God. The world as God's creation is the realm of divine order, the validity of which has its foundation in God's will and is guaranteed by him. This is the basis for a stable inner trust of man in the world as the realm of power and Divine Providence. To Christianity, in the trusting relationship of man and world, the dualism of spirit and matter, soul and body, has been overcome; man and world are both God's creatures, originating from the hands of the almighty Creator. According to this view, man has not fallen or been thrown into a world that is intrinsically evil; he lives in God's world as God's creature, as a God-made microcosm within the God-made macrocosm, which moves according to the same laws and orders and is made of the same elements as the microcosm.

Service. The same order assigns to man his service in the world. Man is "the noblest creature," who has as such the highest responsibility to all other creatures. Though all other creatures have been created to serve man, man has been created to serve God. In the order of creation, man has been created in the image of God, which is the foundation for the unity of mankind. In the light of this foundation, the biological, racial, geographical, and historical differences are only varieties within the realm of one human nature whose significant qualification is that it has been imprinted with the seal of God's image. Therefore, all men are to regard each other "as one man and keep strong unity and peace with one another." In this sense, man stands in the service of a twofold solidarity: on the one hand, in the service of the general brotherhood of man with all other creatures, who—like man—received their nature, their life, and their form from God; on the other hand, in the service of the "closer fellowship" of men among themselves, as they are distinguished from other creatures through the fact that they are created in the image of God.

Responsibility. In the Christian view the responsibility of man has been imposed on him by his position within the whole of creation and the universe; responsibility is above that of dominion. As other creatures have what they have because of man, man has responsibility not only for himself but also for his fellow creatures and for the world that exists before God and for God's sake. Based on this idea of responsibility for fellow creatures, the commission of dominion over the whole hierarchy of creation can be understood. Christian anthropology clearly differs in its understanding of man and the universe from that of non-Christian religions, mainly Buddhism, which understands man as being interwoven into the chain of all living creatures and does not know of a religiously founded claim to power by man. The pioneers of Christian culture and civilization, including modern technology, have particularly referred to God's commission of dominion to man. In its original context this commission to "subdue the earth" was given to man before the Fall and was connected equally with responsible conduct in the world that God had consigned to man.

Responsibility and dominion

The far-reaching changes of the understanding and consciousness of the world since the astronomers Copernicus, Galileo, and Johannes Kepler resulted in a change of the understanding of man. According to the old cosmology, the Earth was the centre of the universe; man was the highest creature of this Earth; and his salvation was the central event in heaven and on Earth. The discovery that the Earth is only one planet among others that rotate around the sun, and that the sun is only an insignificant star among the innumerable galaxies of the cosmos, has shaken the old understanding of man. If the Earth, compared to the huge expanses of the universe, was only a speck of dust in the structure of the macrocosm, Newton and others began to explore the question of how man, the dust of dust, could continue to claim the holy privilege that he and his fame were the goal and culmination of God's actions.

Not only the old understanding of man seemed to be threatened by the new understanding of the world, however, but also the foundation of the Christian faith.

For the theology of the Middle Ages and the Reformation, salvation was a cosmic event; Christ's act of salvation had universal meaning, as well as meaning for rational and dumb creatures. Not only all of humanity but "all of creation groans towards the day of fulfillment" and the blood of the lamb "tinges" the whole world, as Jakob Böhme wrote. According to the new understanding of the world, however, the Earth is nothing more than an inhabited reef in the middle of an ocean that was studded with countless much larger inhabited islands. In view of this fact, the meaning of Christ itself lost some of its impact, and the divine act of salvation appeared merely as a tiny episode within the history of an insignificant little star.

THE RELATIONSHIP BETWEEN THE CHRISTIAN OR CHRISTIAN INSTITUTIONS AND THE FAMILY

The Christian understanding of marriage has been strongly influenced by the Old Testament view of marriage as an institution primarily concerned with the founding and procuring of a family, rather than sustaining the individual happiness of the marriage partners. Until the Reformation, the patriarchal family structure not only had been preserved but also had been defended from all attacks by sectarian groups. In spite of this, a transformation occurred from the early days of Christianity.

Marriage as an institution experienced a growth of individualism and spiritualism, and these eventually led to the demise of traditional patriarchalism. Two basic tendencies, which are in constant tension with one another, can be observed in the Christian understanding of marriage, family, and sex: (1) the tendency to spiritualize and individualize the marriage relationship between man and wife in the light of the Gospel and to realize the basic demands of Christian ethics in marriage and family; and (2) an ascetic tendency that interprets marriage and family as orders of the old world, which have basically been overcome already and have no room in the new eon.

The tendency to spiritualize and individualize marriage. Christianity has contributed to a spiritualization of marriage and family life, to a personal deepening of the relations between marriage partners and between parents and children, as well as between heads of households and domestic servants in large families. In clear contrast to patriarchalism, which characterized Jewish family life, the relationship between man and wife in the Christian family adopts the form of an I-Thou (personalistic) relationship, which has its centre in Christ. Marriage can be called the most intimate form in which the fellowship of believers in Christ is realized. In the early church, children were included in this fellowship. They were baptized when their parents were baptized, took part in the worship life of the congregation, and received Holy Communion with their parents. The Eastern Orthodox Church still practices as part of the eucharistic rite Jesus' teaching, "Let the children come to me, and do not hinder them." During the first decades of the church, congregational meetings took place in the homes of Christian families. The family became the archetype of the church. Paul called the members of his congregation in Ephesus "members of the household of God."

Christian contributions to a deepening of the relations between marriage partners

In the early church, the Christian foundation of marriage—in the participation of Christians in the body of Christ—postulated a generous interpretation of the fellowship between a Christian and a pagan marriage partner: the pagan one is saved with the Christian one "for the unbelieving husband is consecrated through his wife, and the unbelieving wife is consecrated through her husband"; even the children from such a marriage in which at least one partner belongs to the body of Christ "are holy" (I Corinthians). If the pagan partner, however, does not want to sustain the marriage relationship with a Christian partner under any circumstances, the Christian partner should grant him a divorce.

The new understanding of marriage was supported by a mystic-sacramental view. Already in the Old Testament the relationship of Yahweh to his chosen people was described as a marriage, and, accordingly, the revolt against Yahweh was understood as adultery and divorce.

Jesus himself based his parables of the Kingdom of God on the idea of love between a bride and groom and frequently used parables of a wedding that describe the messianic meal as a wedding feast. In Revelation, the glorious finale of salvation history is depicted as the wedding of the Lamb with the bride, as the beginning of the meal of the chosen ones with the Messiah–Son of man (Revelation to John: "Blessed are those who are invited to the marriage supper of the Lamb"). The wedding character of the eucharistic meal is also expressed in the liturgy of the early church. It is deepened through the specifically Christian belief that understands the word of the creation story in Genesis "and they become one flesh" as a secret indication of the oneness of Christ, the head, with the congregation as his body. Only with this in mind does the Christian demand of monogamy become understandable. In contrast to polygamy as a legitimate Jewish institution, Jesus did not demand monogamy in the form of an explicit commandment. Such a command, however, is virtually implied in Mark, chapter 10, in which Jesus deduced the insolubility of marriage from the word in Genesis.

In the so-called ethical lists in the Letter of Paul to the Colossians and in I Peter, Christian marriage is distinguished from the marriage practices of its pagan environment by its stricter ethical demands. The rules concern the mutual relationship of the marriage partners, fidelity, as well as attitudes toward children and slaves of the house.

Christianity did not bring a revolutionary social change to the position of women, but it made possible a new position in the family and congregation. In Judaism of the period of the early church, women were held in very low esteem, and this was the basis for Jewish divorce practices that put women practically at men's complete disposal. With the prohibition of divorce, Jesus himself did away with this low estimation of women. The decisive turning point came in connection with the understanding of Christ and of the Holy Spirit. Even the Jewish view of the patriarchal position of man is substituted by Paul with a new spiritual interpretation of marriage. "There is neither male nor female; for you are all one in Christ Jesus." In fulfillment of the prophecy in Joel, chapter 3, verse 1, the Holy Spirit is poured out over the female disciples of Jesus, as well. This created a complete change in the position of women in the congregation: in the synagogue the women were inactive participants in the worship service and sat veiled on the women's side, usually separated from the rest by an opaque lattice. In the Christian congregation, however, women appeared as members with full rights, who used their charismatic gifts within the congregation. In the letters of Paul, women are mentioned as Christians of full value. Paul addresses Prisca (Priscilla) in Romans, chapter 16, verse 3, as his fellow worker. The four daughters of Philip were active as prophets in the congregation. Peter in a sermon on Pentecost spoke about men and women as recipients of the gifts of the Holy Spirit: "Your sons and your daughters shall prophesy." Pagan critics of the church, such as Porphyry (died *c.* AD 305), maintained that the church was ruled by women. During the periods of Christian persecution, women as well as men showed great courage in their suffering. The fact that they were spontaneously honoured as martyrs demonstrates their well-known active roles in the congregations. In this, representatives of patriarchal, rabbinic, and synagogic traditions within the Christian Church saw a danger to congregational constitutions. Paul, on the one hand, included women in his instruction, "Do not quench the Spirit," but, on the other hand, carried over the rule of the synagogue into the Christian congregation that "women should keep silence in the churches." In the 20th century, this rule is still the basis of the refusal to ordain women as priests in the Roman Catholic Church. Besides the higher status of women in family and congregation, a lower estimation is constantly present in radical asceticism because women carry "the stain of Eve" (*e.g.*, Tertullian and Augustine).

Monogamy and the indissolubility of marriage are not founded pragmatically but religiously in the mysterious character of the heavenly wedding of the Messiah–Son of man with his bride, the church. In contrast to sacrally founded pagan prostitution, the church practices sacrally founded monogamy as part of the fulfillment of the demand to live as saints.

Besides the interpretation of the Song of Solomon referring to the marriage of Christ with the congregation, there is another early interpretation referring to the individual relationship of the soul, as the bride of Christ, to Christ. In the history of the Christian interpretation of the Song of Solomon, which had great influence on the history of Christian mysticism, both interpretations, that of the relationship of Christ with the church and that of the individual soul with Christ, exist next to one another in different variations.

The tendency toward asceticism. The influence of the mystical-sacramental view of marriage grew in two different directions: in very few cases it led to the development of a Christian-spiritual interpretation of the eros (sexual love), such as by Zinzendorf (died 1760), who claimed that the marriage partner is the representative of Christ and that the wife takes the place of the bride of Christ so that sexual intercourse adopts a sacramental character and can be compared to the Eucharist.

The same sacramental interpretation is, on the other hand, used by the representatives of an ascetic theology to demand exclusiveness of devotion by faithful Christians to Christ and to deduce from it the demand of celibacy. This is found in arguments for the monastic life and in the Catholic view of the priesthood. The radical-ascetic interpretation stands in constant tension with the positive understanding of the Christian marriage. This tension has led to seemingly unsolvable conflicts and to numerous compromise solutions in the history of Christianity. Without doubt, from the beginning a strong ascetic tendency dominant in Christianity was emphatically directed against the oversexualization of the Hellenistic culture, against the decay of marital life in the Hellenistic world, against the spreading of pederasty (seduction of young boys) and its social recognition and open institutionalization, against cultic and noncultic prostitution, and against the more or less tolerated sodomy that was excused with pagan mythology. A devaluation of marriage, on the one hand, and a complete demonization of sex, on the other, must be distinguished. Both may occasionally be connected, but they are not identical.

The devaluation of marriage had its basis in the expectation of the near end of time. In the light of the beginning Kingdom of God, marriage was understood as an order of the old passing eon, which would not exist in the approaching new age. The risen ones will "neither marry nor are given in marriage, but are like angels in heaven" (Mark). Because of the coming Kingdom of God (Matthew), marriage could already be renounced; and in the case of an alternative, the renunciation of marriage and family could be demanded (Mark). Similarly, Paul understood marriage in the light of the coming Kingdom of God as an institution that man can belong to only figuratively: "The appointed time has grown very short; from now on, let those who have wives live as though they had none . . . for the form of this world is passing away" (I Corinthians). In view of the propinquity of the Kingdom of God, it was considered not worthwhile anymore to marry; marriage involved man in unnecessary troubles: "I want you to be free from anxieties." Therefore, the unmarried, the widowers, and widows "do better" if they do not marry, if they remain single. In this way, being unmarried becomes a means to accelerate the coming of the Kingdom of God. Paul, who is unmarried himself, states without hesitation: "I wish that all were as I myself am." From this point of view marriage becomes a remedy for fornication. "But because of the temptation to immorality, each man should have his own wife and each woman her own husband" (I Corinthians). Marriage is recommended to those who "cannot exercise self-control . . . for it is better to marry than to be aflame with passion" (I Corinthians). Under this ascetic point of view, marital love is reduced to marital "duty," and the latter finds its only sanction in procreation.

The demonization of sex

This ascetic tendency, which was originally caused by the expectation of the parousia (the Second Coming of Christ), led to a demonization of sex in general under the influence of dualistic Gnostic movements. This was particularly apparent in the ascetic branches of Gnosticism and especially in Manichaeism (an Iranian dualistic religion). Influenced by Manichaeism, Augustine identified original sin with sexual concupiscence. The conscious renunciation by Christians of the customs of their oversexualized pagan environment supported these tendencies. Their motives are apparent in the biographies and letters of the great ascetics, such as Anthony (died AD 355) and Jerome (died AD 420), who report in detail about demonic and sexual temptations in the form of visions in the solitude of the desert. Though in the Pastoral Letters (I Timothy) opponents of marriage are still called heretics, during the middle of the 2nd century radical groups, such as the followers of Marcion and Montanus, radically condemned marriage. This attitude has been continued in church history by later sects up to the Russian Skoptsy (the "castrated") in the 18th century, partly by using self-castration. Within the Roman Catholic Church, the tension between the Christian high esteem and the ascetic devaluation of marriage led to a constantly challenged compromise: celibacy was demanded not only of ascetics and monks but more and more also of members of the clergy as a duty of their office. The ascetic factor is stressed through the idea of the radical divine demand to man, the idea of a "militia of Christ," which demands a complete surrender to Christ and total obedience.

A third tendency has contributed to this ascetical tendency, which is not genuinely Christian but can be found in a number of pre-Christian religions. It is the point of view of cultic cleanness (mainly chastity but also fasting) as conditional for the effectiveness and validity of the sacraments. The charismatic powers of those who bring salvation, mainly the priests, are associated with the idea of a pure life. Chastity gives power; the practice of sexual intercourse means a weakening of the charismatic ability and hinders the execution of the sacraments. The demand of cultic cleanness in the sense of chastity has succeeded in the course of the institutionalization of the Christian priesthood. Every sexual activity makes the performance of the sacraments, particularly the Eucharist, impossible.

This idea of cultic purity has increased the tendency to devaluate marriage and to demonize sex and has led to the demand that priests and monks observe celibacy, which has caused a centuries-long struggle within the church. The early church, and following it the Eastern Orthodox Church, decided on a compromise at the Council of Nicaea (AD 325): the lower clergy, including the archimandrite, would be allowed to enter matrimony before receiving the higher degrees of ordination; of the higher clergy—*i.e.*, bishops—celibacy would be demanded. This solution has saved the Eastern Orthodox from a permanent fight for the demand of celibacy for all clergymen, but it has resulted in a grave separation of the clergy into a white (celibate) and a black (married) clergy, which led to severe disagreements in times of crisis within Orthodoxy.

Problems of overpopulation and birth control

Because the consequences of overpopulation of the Earth have become obvious in connection with the spreading of medical care and social and technological progress, the Christian churches have been confronted with the question of birth control. The question itself has a Christian origin. Thomas Robert Malthus (died 1834), who was the first to demand birth control based on a scientific exploration of the connection between overpopulation and mass poverty, was a minister and founded his demand on Christian responsibility. His suggestions for the practical execution of birth control were taken from the ascetic tradition: he demanded "moral restraint" and late marriage of each marriage partner. Malthus' attitude was basically very close to that of the Roman Church in that he appealed to moral responsibility and abstinence on the part of the individual Christian.

The problem entered a new phase through the invention and mass distribution of technical contraceptive devices on the one hand and through the appearance of a new attitude toward sexual questions on the other. The propagation of modern medical discoveries about the roles of man and woman in procreation removed the myth of the merely passive role of the woman on which the traditional patriarchal dominance of man was based. Psychoanalysis declared the Christian ethic of suppression of sex as "repression," which was determined to be the main cause of severe psychological damage with just as severe emotional and physiological consequences. With the growth of technology and education, the question of birth control became a concern of sociology, statistics, social politics, and development aid. Eros (sexual love) was separated from its connection with procreation with the help of new technical inventions and became an independent act involving little risk. The ascetic aspect of the Christian attitude toward sex was ideologically discredited or ignored, and the Western world was swept by a wave of sexuality that the Communist world thus far has tried to prevent with a hard-line ethic of Socialistic labour and achievement.

In this situation an obvious differentiation of interpretation developed within Christianity: with a few exceptions—*e.g.*, the Mormons—the Protestant churches emphasized birth control, basing their views on their Puritan tradition and responsibility founded on a Christian social ethic. A survey of individually different attitudes has shown a certain common bias insofar as birth control is considered justified only when "an obvious moral obligation to limit or to avoid parenthood exists." In the American Federal Council of Churches the majority of member churches decided in favour of a careful and limited use of contraceptive devices. In the message of the Lambeth Conference of 1930, the Anglican Church "condemned the use of contraceptive methods for reasons of self-protection, craving for pleasure or mere convenience and condemned also abortion." In contrast, the Roman Catholic Church, in the encyclical of Pius XI *Casti Connubii* and in the encyclical of Paul VI *Humanae Vitae* completely rejected any kind of contraception. The struggle over permission for abortion or the further preservation of its prohibition in the latter part of the 20th century is an extension of this argument because the difference between contraceptive means and abortive means has already been blurred by modern assortments of contraception-control pills.

PERSONAL ETHICS

The commandment to love God and neighbour. Christianity has received the main commandment of its ethic from the Old Testament: "You shall love your neighbor as yourself" (Leviticus), but Jesus filled this commandment with a new, twofold meaning. (1) He closely connected the commandment "love your neighbor" with the commandment to love God. In the dispute with the scribes described in Matthew, chapter 22, he quoted the commandment of Deuteronomy 6:5, "You shall love the Lord your God with all your heart, and with all your soul, and with all your might." He spoke of the commandment of love for neighbour, however, as being equal to it. With that he lifted it to the same level as the highest and greatest commandment, the commandment to love God. In the Gospel According to Luke, both commandments have grown together into one single pronouncement with the addition: "Do this, and you will live." (2) The commandment received a new content in view of God and in view of the neighbour through the relationship of the believer with Christ. Love of God and love of the neighbour is only possible because the Son proclaims the gospel of the Father and brings to it reality and credibility through his life, death, and Resurrection. He has brought about the possibility that the neighbour is recognized as a brother in Christ. Only this way does it become possible that the Old Testament ethic of the Law is replaced by the ethic of love. "Therefore love is the fulfilling of the law" (Rom. 13:10). Therefore, Paul considered love the highest gift of the spirit that surmounts all the others, such as prophecy, speaking in tongues, and knowledge. Among the three "abiding" gifts, faith, hope, and love, love is the greatest (I Cor. 13:13). Based on this connection of the Christian commandment of love with the understanding of Christ's person and work, the demand of love for the neighbour appears in John as "a new commandment": "A new commandment I give to you, that you love one another; even as I have loved you, that you also love one another" (John). The love for each other is supposed to characterize the disciples: "By this all men will know that you are my disciples, if you have love for one another."

Love as a new commandment

Here stands forth an ethic that does not base its norms on social, biological, psychological, physiological, intellectual, or educational differences and levels but on an understanding and treatment of man as created in the image of God. Furthermore, the ethic does not deal with man in an abstract sense but with the actual neighbour. The Christian ethic understands the individual person always as a neighbour in Christ.

This is one of its significant differences with the Eastern religions. Hinduism as well as Buddhism in their highest experiences, which can be compared to analogous Christian experiences, aim at the separation of man from his entanglement in suffering and death in order to unite him with his transcendental origin. The religious ethic of Hinduism and Buddhism is finally an individualistic ethic. The new element of the Christian ethic is found in the fact that the individual ethic is founded in a corporate ethic, in the understanding of the fellowship of Christians as the body of Christ. The individual believer does not understand himself as a separate individual who has found a new spiritual and moral relationship with God but as a "living stone" (I Peter), as a living cell in the body of Christ in which the powers of the Kingdom of God are already working. Within this organism of the body of Christ exists a peculiar communication between the separate members. There is intercession but also representative suffering of one for the other; one carries the burden of the other and is able to share his spiritual gifts with him.

The realization of Christian love leads to the peculiar exchange of gifts and suffering, of exaltation and humiliations, of defeat and victory; the individual is able through his sacrifice and suffering to contribute to the development of the whole. In this basic idea of the fellowship of believers as the body of Christ all forms of ecclesiastical, political, and social communities of Christianity are founded. It also has influenced numerous secularized forms of Christian society, even among those that have forgotten or denied their Christian origins.

Tensions inherent in the commandment to love. From the beginning, the commandment contains a certain tension concerning the answer to the question: Does it refer only to "the disciples," that is, fellow Christians, or to "all"; *i.e.*, all fellow men. The practice of love of neighbour within the inner circle of the disciples was a conspicuous characteristic of the young church to the pagan environment. Pagans said: "Look, how they love each other" (Justin). Christian congregations and, above all, small fellowships and sects have stood out throughout the centuries because of the fact that within their communities love of the neighbour was highly developed in the form of personal pastoral care, social welfare, and help in all situations of life.

The question as to who is one's neighbour

The Christian commandment of love, however, has never been limited to fellow Christians. On the contrary, the new factor in Christian ethic was that it crossed all social and religious barriers and saw a brother in every suffering human being. Characteristically, Jesus himself explicated his understanding of the practical implications of the commandment of love in the parable of the Good Samaritan, a non-Jew who followed the commandment of love and helped a person in need whom the believing wanderers—a priest and a Levite—had chosen to ignore (Luke). A demand in the Letter of James, that the "royal law" of neighbourly love has to be fulfilled without "partiality" (James), points to its universal validity. Indeed, the special characteristic of the Christian ethic through the course of the history of Chris-

tianity crossed over all social, political, and racial barriers that formed the framework of different types of conventional ethical norms. In Christian ethics, a new human relationship to one's neighbour was found where the established forms of ethical behaviour only saw an exclusive and basically insurmountable contrast: *e.g.*, Greek or barbarian, Aryan or non-Aryan, Spaniard or Moor, Caucasian or Negro.

The universalism of the Christian command to love is most strongly expressed in its demand to love one's enemies. Jesus himself emphasized this in strong contrast to the ethical demand of Mosaic Law, which is not found in the Scriptures in exactly the same words as he quotes it: "You shall love your neighbor and hate your enemy" (Leviticus), but this quote seems to follow a common oral interpretation of the verse "Love your neighbour as yourself" (Lev. 19:10). In Jewish interpretation, it has been assumed that the "enemy" refers to the national enemy, the idolator, and the personal enemy. Jesus opposed the idea with these words: "Love your enemies and pray for those who persecute you, so that you may be sons of your Father who is in heaven; for he makes his sun rise on the evil and on the good, and sends rain on the just and on the unjust" (Matt. 5:44 ff.). According to this understanding, love of the enemy is the immediate emission of God's love, which includes God's friends and God's enemies. In his explicit inclusion of love of the enemy in the commandment of love, Jesus excluded any limitation by casuistry. In Judaism, the commandment to love had been limited to "brothers" and "the sons of your own people." In Leviticus, it is at least extended to include "the stranger who sojourns with you."

Love to one's enemies

The institutionalization of the commandment to love. The commandment of love as realization of a free spiritual gift led to the inclusion of the Christian ethic into the general crisis of charismatic freedom. No fellowship can live by charismatic inspirations and improvisations over an extended period of time, least of all in the realm of ethics. Firm rules and lists of ethical instructions are necessary. The commandment of love soon turns into a new law, the realization of which makes a certain casuistry necessary. This corresponds with the general process of institutionalization and growth of jurisprudence in Christianity. Already in Paul's letters a limitation of the commandment of love can be found that has been taken from synagogic practice and rabbinic tradition. He comments on the commandment "You shall love your neighbor as yourself" with the words: "Love does no wrong to a neighbor" (Romans). In contrast to Jesus' original demand, this is a casuistic limitation that has been inspired by the fear that love might be "the end of the law." Indeed, a form of Christian love-nihilism does exist that disregards all laws and also all social rules and statutes with the reasoning that Christ is the end of the law. Deeds of a charismatic ethic of love sometimes are necessary, however, in order to break through a stagnant standardized Christian ethic.

The whole history of Christianity is characterized by many attempts to confine the commandment of love to certain categories: the fellow believer, the family member, the fellow tribesman or fellow countryman, or the fellow party member, so that no love is left for "faraway people." Jesus himself excluded any casuistic interpretation from the beginning. "For if you love those who love you, what reward have you? Do not even the tax collectors do the same? And if you salute only your brethren, what more are you doing than others? Do not even the Gentiles do the same?" (Matthew). Similarly, the realization of neighbourly love in "the least of these my brethren" is named as a decisive criterion of the Last Judgment (Matthew). This radical universal realization of the Christian commandment of love has caused revolutions and reformations in the history of Christianity.

Attempts to confine the commandment of love

The Christian Church used a new word for its commandment of love—agape—rather than adopting the familiar concept of eros from the Hellenistic world. Eros did not seem suited for use in church because of its use in pagan teachings about the gods, in sacral prostitution, and in its application to sex in literature and in everyday language—in spite of occasional attempts to spiritualize the term in philosophy.

This linguistic differentiation supported the ascetic understanding of agape and eros as mutually exclusive contrasts and also the demonizing of sex that began already with the Church Fathers. The controversy about eros and agape has continued in modern theological and ethical discussions. The Roman Catholic Church argues that it has preserved the sanctification of sex in the sacrament of marriage, but that the Protestants support the secularization of sex by abolition of the sacrament of marriage. These two standpoints, however, are not very far apart because, according to Roman Catholic teaching, the sacrament of marriage is the only one that is not offered by the priest but by the marriage partners for one another, whereas in the Protestant world church marriage still has a sacramental character according to the view of most members, though this view has been undergoing changes.

Personal and social ethics

Under the influence of Pietism and the revival movement, the personalization (individualistic interpretation) of Christian ethic began. It met, however, with an energetic counterattack from the circles of the Free churches (*e.g.*, Baptists and Methodists) who supported the social task of Christian ethic (mainly through the "social gospel" of the American theologian Walter Rauschenbusch, who attempted to change social institutions and bring about a Kingdom of God), which spread through the whole church, penetrating the area of Christian mission, and which played and continues to play an important role in the 20th century in the struggle between Christianity and Communism and Christianity and Socialism (religious Socialism).

The emphasis on personal ethics or social ethics in the separate denominations has been characterized by different accents. In the Russian Revolution of 1917, this statement was made: Russian Bolshevism has its deepest roots in the piety of Russian Orthodoxy. The Orthodox understanding of church as expressed in the idea of the *sobornost* (the entire ethos, catholicity, and eschatological wholeness of the church) places the idea of collective salvation so much in the centre there is no room for an original Christian consciousness of the individual.

This view, however, is not supported by historical facts. In the entire realm of the development of the Christian Church in East and West, Christian communities have continuously tried to re-form the original Christian community that was described in Acts as the sign of a Christian congregation. The attempts of baptismal, spiritualist, and other radical communities on European and American soil started the development of a Christian Socialism. All of these attempts have been variations of the same endeavour: to realize or at least to prepare for the Kingdom of God on Earth.

There are certain nuances of difference between the Western and the Orthodox understanding of collective and personal consciousness connected with the idea of the Kingdom of God as a fellowship of love. In the West the meaning of the individual personality is emphasized more strongly, presumably under the influence of Roman law, which expressly defended the rights of the individual person. On Russian soil, on the contrary, the community principle has been emphasized over against the special rights of individuality. Even within Orthodoxy, however, the personality keeps its specifically Christian extraordinary meaning through the message of the Resurrection. The Orthodox teaching of *sobornost* contains preventive powers not only against the overemphasis of the personality and individuality and its separation from the community of the mystical body of Christ, as has occasionally happened in the West, but also against an overevaluation of a community that disregards all personal freedom, as has been manifested in Bolshevik social teachings.

MISSIONS

The methods that have been used in Christian missions are extraordinarily manifold and diverse within societies in different epochs and above all have changed greatly during the 1950s and 1960s. A few basic main types can be named, but in practice they mix and overlap in many ways.

The triumphant type. The triumphant method of Christianization came as a consequence of military conquests or voluntary political subordination of a non-Christian territory as a colony, a dominion, or an "associated" country, or a "zone of influence." In such cases, Christianization has been viewed as a function of the government of the ruling Christian occupational power and carried out with the help of state legislation and under governmental supervision. This method involves, for example, a legally founded expropriation of the former ruling pagan religious communities. Frequently, all influence on school and cultural matters was withdrawn from the non-Christian religions, which used to be the established state religions: *e.g.*, in Buddhist countries, such as Ceylon and Burma. The Christian mission, in such cases, was granted judicially and financially privileged work opportunities. The establishment of a Christian school organization and the founding of Christian universities were supported. Institutions of the pagan religions that contradicted Christian ideas were abolished by the Christian government; *e.g.*, the burning of widows in India. Polygamy was denounced by Christian preaching and also made difficult by judicial measures of the colonial government. Baptized "native" Christians frequently received an especially advantageous judicial status and better educational, economic, and political possibilities for advancement than non-Christians.

Subjugation of indigenous traditions

This type of mission was spread by the Roman Catholic Church in the American and Pacific colonial empires, under the Spanish crown; in the areas of the African, Asian, and American colonial empire, under the Portuguese crown; and also in varied forms in the Indonesian colonies of the Protestant Netherlands, in the English colonies and dominions (mainly in India, Ceylon, Burma), and eventually in the zones of influence of the Western powers in China, where gunboats were not infrequently activated when mission stations in the country were attacked.

The heroic type. The "heroic" mission consisted in the courageous single missionary or group of missionaries who ventured into a pagan environment and began a mission project without outward protection, trusting alone in the power of the message. The success of this form of mission was founded upon the fact that the missionaries represented their message credibly through their way of life.

Roman Catholic mission bodies. Mission bodies or personalities can be of different kinds. The Roman Catholic mission is usually supported by an order and the missionaries are usually at the same time ordained priests and therefore qualified to found and to lead their own congregations in the mission field. There are special missionary orders, for example, the White Fathers in Trier. The orders that carry out missionary tasks, such as the Benedictines, the Franciscans, or the Dominicans, have their own training institutions and courses for those fathers and brothers who want to enter missionary work.

Protestant mission bodies. Protestantism utilized lay missions in addition to missionary work of theologically trained personnel. Lay missions are usually supported by pietistic or revivalist lay groups that emphasize the missionary duty of the individual Christian and encourage willing lay Christians to do missionary work.

The significance of Protestant lay missions

The Protestant Free churches have, in most cases, their own boards of missions to supervise the training of missionaries. In the Protestant state and regional churches, private mission societies and alliances were usually founded. Their goal was foreign missions, and they created their own educational institutions (missionary seminaries).

The theological foundation of the Protestant lay mission was in most cases biblically oriented. They considered it their main task to "illuminate" the "darkness" of "paganism" with the "light" of the gospel. As a rule, intellectual arguments with non-Christian religions did not come about until academically trained ministers, familiar with the knowledge and methods of modern history of religions, worked as missionaries. In these cases, a reverse conversion occasionally happened, insofar as outstanding scholars of religion originated in the circle of these missionaries and dedicated their lives to an investigation and study of the sources of the religions that they were supposed to evangelize. In this way these Christian missionaries became communicators and interpreters of the non-Christian higher religions, such as Hinduism, Buddhism, and Taoism (Richard Wilhelm, Hans Haas, Richard Bohner, Wilhelm Hauer, and W. Gundert).

Lay missions sometimes happened when Christian lay groups emigrated. A Christian community would be founded in the new country, often based upon agriculture or trade, which would integrate non-Christian facets of the population into the economic base. Thus, the Christian mission would even become part of the training for an agrarian or trade profession; *e.g.*, the Moravian Brethren, some Mennonites, and other baptismal groups in Asia, Africa, Greenland, Newfoundland, Canada, Central America, and South America.

Educational and medical missions. In a special way, the Christian mission has taken over the spreading of education and medical care in the evangelized countries and peoples. The Roman Catholic Church is responsible for the establishment of a modern educational system in Central and South America and the founding of the oldest universities (*e.g.*, 1538, Santo Domingo; 1551, Mexico and Lima) in the Americas.

The foundation of educational systems

In the same way, the English type of education spread in the areas of the British Empire within the framework of the missionary work of the Christian churches in England—the Anglican Church as well as the English Free churches. The French educational system spread in the areas of the French colonies and protectorates in the Near East, in the Far East (*e.g.*, Vietnam), and in Africa and led to a differentiated school system. Medical missions have been established in connection with missionary societies or as independent creations of Christian doctors, who founded their own missionary centres in the form of Christian mission hospitals (*e.g.*, Albert Schweitzer in Lambaréné, 1927). In the 20th century, Christian missionary work has expanded to include trade and technical training centres, mainly in connection with development aid from the churches. Therefore, the share of the laity as technical and scientific experts has naturally increased even in relation to the position of the monopoly that priests once held in Roman Catholic mission churches.

From the beginning, a special task of the Christian mission has been the training of new generations of priests, ministers, and missionaries in the newly developing mission areas. Many missions, mainly in the South American countries, suffered from a permanent shortage of priests because Christianity was at first forced upon the masses with mass conversions, even though not enough new priests from Europe were available to carry out the inner Christianization of the outwardly Catholic masses of people. Most churches, the Roman Catholic as well as the Protestant mission churches and sects, therefore established their own institutions for ministers and missionaries in order to train a native clergy or native congregational leaders. Just as the mission churches developed into independent churches and grew to spiritual autonomy and self-administration, the missionary seminaries changed into ministers' seminaries and Bible schools.

THE ENCOUNTER WITH NON-CHRISTIAN RELIGIONS

Forms and attitudes of encounter. A spiritual encounter and discussion of Christianity with other world religions has begun only during the 20th century as a consequence of change in the general religious, political, and economic situation of the world. The global spread of Christianity through the activity of the European and American churches in the 18th and 19th centuries led to Christianity's immediate encounter with all other existing religions. Until the beginning of the 19th century, there were still places on Earth where non-Christian religions existed without any contact with Christianity. In the meantime, Christianity entered into a direct contact with all living non-Christian religions in the world. The close connection between Christian world missions and the political, economic, technical, and cultural expansion had, at the same time, been loosened.

Recent Christianity's contacts with non-Christian religions

After World War II, the former mission churches were transformed into independent churches in the newly autonomous Asian and African states. The concern for a responsible cooperation of the members of Christian minority churches and its non-Christian fellow citizens became the more urgent with a surprising renaissance of the old Asian higher religions in numerous Asian states. Hinduism, Buddhism, and Islām since World War II have been trying to regain their former position of leadership in intellectual and spiritual life, mainly in the educational systems of their countries in the Asian states and—in the case of Islām—in some African states.

All Asian higher religions have also turned to activities in world missions in Christian countries in Europe, America, and Australia. Hinduism, for example, has founded numerous Vedānta centres in North America and Europe within the framework of the Ramakrishna and Vivekananda missions. South Asian Theravāda (Way of the Elders) Buddhism and the Mahāyāna (Greater Vehicle) Buddhism of Japan (mainly Zen Buddhism, an intuitive-meditative sect) have begun world missionary activities under the influence of a Buddhist renaissance. This influence has penetrated Europe and America not so much in the form of a directly organized mission as in the form of a spontaneously received flow of religious ideas and methods of meditation through literature, philosophy, psychology, and psychotherapy. As a result, Christianity in the latter part of the 20th century found itself forced to enter into a factual discussion with non-Christian religions, particularly because the constitutional privileges once enjoyed by certain religions had been rescinded in most states.

Modern religious science, on the other hand, has caused a general transformation of the religious conscience in mankind since the middle of the 19th century. Until the beginning of the 20th century, the knowledge of non-Christian higher religions was still the privilege of a few specialists in religious science. In the meantime, in a second wave of enlightenment, a wide range of people have studied the results of research in religious science in the form of translations of source materials from the non-Christian religions. The spreading of the religious art of Tibet, India, and the Far East through touring exhibitions and the possibility of a direct participation in religious ceremonies of non-Christian religions through radio and television has created a new attitude toward the other religions in the broad public of Europe and North America. The knowledge of the plurality of the world religions characterizes the religious consciousness of the 20th century in a way that was unknown in former centuries. In recognition of this fact, numerous Christian institutions for the study of non-Christian religions have been founded in recent years: *e.g.*, in Bangalore, India; in Rangoon, Burma; in Bangkok, Thailand; in Kyōto, Japan; and in Hong Kong.

The increase of knowledge of non-Western religions in the West

The readiness of encounter or even cooperation of Christianity with non-Christian religions is a phenomenon of modern times, with few precedents in the history of the struggle of Christianity and the non-Christian religions. Until the 18th century, Christianity showed little inclination to engage in a serious study of non-Christian religions. Four hundred years after the beginning of the struggle with the Muslims in Spain, almost half a century after the proclamation of the First Crusade against Islām, Peter the Venerable, abbot of Cluny, issued the first translation of the Qur'ān (the Islāmic scriptures) in 1141 in Toledo; but he was not understood by his contemporaries. Bernard of Clairvaux, the propagator of the Second Crusade, even refused to read it.

Four hundred years later, in 1542/43, Theodor Bibliander, a theologian and successor of the Swiss Reformer Zwingli, edited the translation of the Qur'ān by Peter the Venerable again. He was subsequently arrested, and he and his publisher could be freed only by means of the authority of Luther. Knowledge of Hinduism was partially deliberately delayed by the missionaries. August Hermann Francke (died 1727), the supporter of the Lutheran Tranquebar mission in India, prevented the publication of the work of the missionary Bartholomäus Ziegenbalg (died 1719) about the religion of the non-Christian Malabarese of India. The name Buddha is mentioned for the first time in Christian literature—and there only once—by Clement of Alexandria about AD 200; and it vanished after that from Christian literature for a full 1,300 years. Pāli, the language of the Buddhist canon, remained unknown until the beginning of the 19th century, when modern Buddhology was founded. The most important basic source of Buddhism, the *Tripiṭaka* ("Triple Basket"), was discovered by a romantic Hungarian student, Sándor Kőrösi Csoma, in Tibet in 1823.

Reasons for the reticence of contacts with non-Christian religions

The reasons for such reticence toward contact with foreign religions are twofold: (1) The ancient church was significantly influenced by the Jewish attitude toward the pagan religions of its environment. Like Judaism, it viewed the pagan gods as "nothings" next to the true God, the Creator of the world and, in the case of the Christians, the Father of Jesus Christ; they were off-springs of human error that were considered to be identical with their wooden, stone, or bronze images that were made by man. (2) Besides this, there was the tendency to degrade the pagan gods as demons, evil demonic forces engaged in mortal combat with the true God. The conclusion of the history of salvation, according to the Christian understanding, was to be a final struggle between Christ and his church on the one side and the forces, powers, and thrones of the Antichrist on the other, culminating finally with the victory of Christ.

Apologetics. The attempt of Christian apologetics to win the educated class of paganism for Christianity led to an acknowledgment of a certain amount of truth not only in Greek philosophy of religion but in some traditions of pagan mythology as well. The apologetics based this on their teaching of the Logos. They attempted to see the general history of religion, the total religious development of mankind, in a positive relationship to the Christian history of salvation. This universalist understanding of the history of religion was only acceptable, however, as long as the historic situation at least very generally seemed to confirm the correctness of the Logos theory.

The history of religion, however, continued even after Christ. During the 3rd and 4th centuries a new non-Christian world religion appeared in the form of Manichaeism, which countered the Christian Church with new holy books, a new institution, and a new universal claim of validity. The Christian Church never acknowledged Manichaeism as a new religion but considered it a Christian heresy and opposed it as such. When Islām was founded in the 7th century as a new higher religion, it considered revelation as received by the Prophet Muḥammad to be superior to the former levels of Old and New Testament revelation. Christianity also fought Islām as a Christian heresy. This new threat was seen as the fulfillment of the eschatological prophecies of the Apocalypse concerning the coming of the "false prophet" (Revelation to John). When Islām began to spread its rule by means of holy wars in the realm of the oldest Christian mission areas on Arabic, Syrian, Egyptian, and, later, North African soil, spreading even to the Iberian Peninsula, the Christians saw in the different phases of its advance the fulfillment of all the "plagues" mentioned in the Revelation to John, chapter 15, which John had prophesied for the last time of the "sifting" of the church. The relationship of Christianity to Islām, which surrounded it from all sides and separated it from its free access to the continents of Asia and Africa, became a model case of the theoretical and practical attitude of Christianity toward non-Christian religions in general. Even after the collapse of the last phase of Bar-

bary rule on Spanish soil (1492, Granada) and the beginning of the exploration of the New World, the non-Christian empires of Middle and South America were treated in the same way as Islām.

The apocalyptic interpretation of Islām as the religion of the "false prophet" also coined the archetypal struggle of the Christian Church of the Middle Ages against foreign religions, namely, the crusade. The idea of the Crusades has deeply influenced the self-consciousness of Western Christianity even in later centuries. The political idea behind the Crusades was not accepted without opposition. A number of Christian personalities were convinced that the use of military power for the destruction of a heresy was an unacceptable means for Christians to employ. The criticism of the method of crusades, however, became known only when the sword, which Western Christianity had used against Islām, was turned against Eastern Christianity itself and Constantinople fell to the Turks in 1453.

The influence of the crusade ideal

The dialogue of the 15th-century German theologian Nicholas of Cusa on the peace of faith (1453) is the first Christian document that calls for the establishment of an eternal peace among world religions. In spite of this, the idea of the crusade remained the model for the fulfillment of the new missionary task that arose within the Roman Catholic Church with the discovery and exploration of the American continents by Spain and Portugal. Only the penetration of the Islāmic wall that had separated Europe spiritually and economically from the empires of the Asian higher religions and only the encounter with these higher religions in countries such as China and Japan—which could not be subjugated to the rule of Roman Catholic kings by the sword—led to a gradual overcoming of the idea of the crusade. In China and Japan, the missionaries saw themselves forced into an argument with the native higher religions that could be carried on only with intellectual weapons. The old Logos theory prevailed in a new form that was founded on natural law, particularly among the Jesuit theologians who worked at the Chinese emperor's court in Peking.

The philosophy of the Enlightenment in the 18th century spread the acknowledgment of a plurality of higher religions among the educated in Europe, partly—as in the case of the German philosopher Gottfried Wilhelm Leibniz—in immediate connection with the theories of natural law of the Jesuit China missionaries. This insight has pointed to the striking convergence of the non-Christian higher religions with Christianity and in that way prepared the development of a science of comparative religions. Only in the philosophy of the Enlightenment was the demand of tolerance, which thus far in Christian Europe had only been applied as a postulate of behaviour toward the followers of another Christian denomination, extended to include the followers of different religions.

The missions that were carried out in the late 18th and the 19th centuries by pietistically or fundamentally oriented churches ignored this knowledge or consciously fought against it. Simple lay Christianity of revivalist congregations demanded that a missionary denounce all pagan "idolatry." The spiritual and intellectual argument with the non-Christian higher religions simply did not exist for this simplified fundamental theology, and in this view a real encounter of Christianity with the non-Christian higher religions did, on the whole, not occur in the 18th and 19th centuries. In the 20th century the dialectic theology of the Swiss Protestant theologian Karl Barth opposed the thesis of the absolute otherness and "discontinuity" of Christian revelation over against all "religions." Christianity appeared not as a religion but as the "crisis of all religions." This theological theory that was based on the philosophy of religion of the German philosopher Ludwig Feuerbach, however, did not find understanding among the Christians of the "younger churches" of Asia and Africa because they had to live as minorities in the realm of Islāmic or Buddhist populations and had to cooperate with their fellow citizens of different faiths.

Pietistic missionary activities

Developments in the history of religions. In the meantime, religious science, under the influence of the German theologian, Rudolf Otto, and religious sociology, under the influence of a German church historian, Ernst Troeltsch, had led to new insights that prepared the way for a new relationship between religions. According to Otto, there is indeed a common basis for religious experience, a sense of the spiritual within the separate religions that makes a mutual understanding possible, independent of the levels that this religious experience has passed within the different religions. According to Troeltsch, Christianity, as well, is "in all moments of its history a purely historical phenomenon as the other great religions." The argument of the great religions can therefore be acknowledged only in the form of a free competition in the realization of their highest values, which, on their highest level, however, show only comparatively few alternatives.

In the historical argument of religions, the decision lies basically between only two possibilities: on the one hand, salvation through thinking to transcendence, or non-being, as it is understood in the Eastern religions, or salvation through believing trust to share the Personhood of God as it is understood in Christianity. This decision, however, is finally not a decision of scientific argumentation but of religious self-reflection. Troeltsch reflected the idea that an English historian, Arnold Toynbee, has taken up again with the emphasis that possibly "our complete anti-Christian European civilization could be thrown back into barbarism." This would mean the end of Christianity in its present form, but the truth and validity of a personalized idea of salvation would not be finished. The scientific consideration of Christianity overcomes the naïve barriers of the traditional claim of Christianity to be absolute because it teaches Christians not to perceive the uniqueness of their religion compared to other religions as an exclusive contrast but, in a greater context of the history of religion and humanity, as a special kind and a contrast of different levels.

In line with this and similar ideas, as they were deepened by another 20th-century sociologist of religion, Joachim Wach, many international organizations and institutions have been founded that endeavour to establish encounter and cooperation among world religions, such as the World-Brotherhood of Faiths, the Community of Faiths, the Temple of Understanding, Washington, D.C., and corresponding Indian and Buddhist institutions. In the 1960s and 1970s the World Council of Churches in Geneva joined these efforts.

OTHER PROBLEMS CONFRONTING CHRISTIANITY

Esoteric Christianity. A tradition of esoteric Christianity has long existed alongside institutional Christianity. It traces its roots to the New Testament and the early church, which adopted many pre-Christian elements of the arcane disciplines. Jesus' use of parables in Matthew is explained on the basis that it has been given only to the disciples to "know the secrets of the kingdom of heaven," but to the others "it has not been given." The disciples appear as confidants who are trusted with the true hidden meaning of his proclamation. This idea was especially circulated in Gnostic literature.

The mystery traditions of pre-Christian mystery religions as well as the esoteric school tradition of the schools of philosophy of late antiquity, mainly Neoplatonism, have been influential. The Gnostic groups referred particularly to a secret tradition, which the risen Lord entrusted to a few of his disciples. The two sacraments of Baptism and Communion, especially, have an esoteric character. The evangelist John kept secret the institution of Baptism as well as Communion, although he hinted at both. In the church constitution of Hippolytus, a presbyter of Rome, at the end of the orders for Baptism and Communion it is stated: "The unbelievers shall not come to know this." The liturgies of the Byzantine patriarch John Chrysostom and the Cappadocian theologian and bishop Basil of the Eastern Orthodox Church have maintained the esoteric character of their Communion celebrations with a clear distinction between a mass for catechumens and a mass for believers. The creed also had an arcane character and

the catechumens were told its wording sometimes only at their Baptism, after promising "not to disclose the secret to unbelievers." Another esoteric tradition can be traced to visionaries and prophets, who received special revelations that they were not, or not yet, allowed to pass on to everybody. When Paul was "caught up into Paradise . . . he heard things that cannot be told, which man may not utter" (Corinthians).

The institutional church abandoned arcane discipline because it contributed to the defamation of Christians by pagans. To a certain extent, however, an arcane discipline has been continued within the church in the monasticism of the Orthodox Church. Monasticism itself can be called an esoteric movement that separated from the secularized state church and retreated into solitude. Within monasticism special esoteric traditions are found at all times, such as, for example, the so-called Hesychasts (practitioners of a meditative physiological prayer method) of Mt. Athos.

In later centuries, esoteric groups formed spontaneously within the church, to a great extent in deliberate connection with earlier forms. Up to the time of the Enlightenment, however, these groups were always in danger of being declared heretical and excommunicated. True esoteric Christianity since the time of the Gnostics has developed only at the borders of the church.

Consequences of esoteric Christianity. The danger that esoteric Christian groups might be cut off from the church led to three significant consequences: (1) As soon as the church became the established state church, esoteric groups had to share the general fate of all heretics; *i.e.*, persecution by the state. In this way esoteric Christianity was included in the bloody history of persecution of heresies by the state church and the Christian state. The persecution strengthened esotericism and arcane discipline and created esoteric underground churches. (2) Those groups that were pushed to heresy were thus opened up to the influences of other partly heretical Christian groups and also to the influence of non-Christian religions, so that a peculiar syncretism spread among those esoteric groups. The Gnostic groups accepted into their esoteric practices and teachings elements of Zoroastrianism, Hinduism, and Buddhism. (3) In these esoteric sects, a tradition of religious symbols, pictures, and sacred objects was passed on but was lost in the institutional church. Here, as elsewhere, frequent connections can be found between Christian symbols and pictures and those of non-Christian mystery religions.

For these reasons, the history of esoteric Christianity is to a great extent identical with the history of heresy during the Middle Ages. Clear esoteric traits can be found among the Albigenses (a French medieval dualistic sect) as also the Bogomils (a medieval dualistic sect that flourished in the Balkans and Asia Minor). The persecution by the Inquisition strengthened the practice of using secret signs and symbols for recognition of their members and for propagation of their teachings. Their hidden worship services also took on an esoteric character.

Certain traits of esoteric Christianity can be found in the orders of knighthood of the Middle Ages. The most significant of these orders, founded in 1119, was the Knights Templars, which developed its own language of symbols and its own ritual. The Knights Templars were convicted of heresy, and their order dissolved by Pope Clement V in 1312. The fact that within this order a spiritual encounter with the religious traditions of Islām took place, mainly with its esoteric mysticism, was considered a particularly grave offense against established Christianity.

Of all the esoteric movements of the late Middle Ages, the Friends of God deserves special attention. It was started by a small group of lay people who, through mysticism, attempted to lead a general reform of the church. Rulman Merswin (died 1382), a merchant and banker in Strassburg, made the monastery "Zum Grünen Wörth," which he had restored, a centre of this esoteric reform movement. Since the reform plans of this lay movement that was influenced by German mysticism could not be carried out through official channels of the

Recognition of the values of the great religions

The roots of esoteric Christianity

Persecution, influences from other religions, and preservation of symbols

The Friends of God and the Rosicrucians

church, Rulman founded a secret esoteric society of Christian lay people. They appeared as Friends of God who lived hidden in solitude and mainly of the so-called Friend of God from the Highlands, a legendary person who was supposed to influence and transform pietistic life through letters. In the middle of the contemporary corruption of the church, the ideal form of a secret church appeared here, one in which the most significant wishes for reform of the time seemed already fulfilled and one which was considered to be a promising point of departure for a greater future reformation. A historical fact of mysticism is that Christian hermits were partly responsible for the transmission of esoteric traditions and practices.

The persecution of esoteric groups did not end with the Reformation in the 16th century. In addition to the Reformation, various esoteric groups were formed, made up of followers of the Swiss physician and mystical philosopher Paracelsus and the German mystical theologian Kaspar Schwenckfeld. All of these groups met with great resistance from the newly formed Reformed state churches; and most could escape total suppression only by emigrating to America.

New esoteric groups in the Protestant state churches were founded again in the 17th century in connection with the appearance of the Rosicrucians, who can be considered a modern model case of an esoteric Christian group. Johann Valentin Andreae, who became the initiator of a far-reaching reform movement in a way similar to Rulman Merswin in the 14th century, published the *Fama Fraternitatis* (1604), a literary fiction, the subject of which is the appearance of an order that has set for itself the task of renewing religion and science. The intention of *Fama* was to find willing friends of a universal reform and encourage them to join the order of Rosicrucians. Groups soon appeared who called themselves Rosicrucians and claimed to be the fulfillers of this universal reformation. This was the beginning of a widespread expansion of esoteric groups in central Europe, which later on partially merged into the Freemasonry of the 18th and 19th centuries. This esoteric movement was strengthened by the fact that similar hopes of reform were furthered by the mysticism long suppressed by church orthodoxy. Main supporters were the esoteric congregations of Jakob Böhme, which had formed in the Netherlands. In England, as well, a group of Jakob Böhme followers gathered, led by visionaries, the so-called Philadelphians, which soon spread in the Netherlands and in Germany.

In the centuries following the Reformation, the peculiar tendency of the esoteric groups to form a new positive relationship with the religious content of non-Christian higher religions became more obvious. For this reason, Hinduism and Buddhism have penetrated more and more the religious consciousness of the West by way of esoteric groups in the 18th and 19th centuries.

Modern currents of esoteric Christianity

In the 20th century three general currents of an esoteric Christianity exist. (1) One is theosophy, which is represented in different orders, communities, societies, and circles. Its world centre is Adyār, a suburb of Madras, South India. The Theosophical Society, which was founded by Mme Helena Blavatsky in 1875 and afterward led by Mrs. Annie Besant, is characterized mainly by the combination of Christian traditions and teachings of Asian higher religions—the idea of the *karma* (works) and reincarnation. (2) A second current is present in an anthroposophic group, the founder of which is Rudolf Steiner, in whose ideas may be found a number of specifically Christian elements giving his own interpretation based on his understandings and clairvoyance and connected with Eastern ideas. (3) A Christian community that separated from Steiner's anthroposophy undertook the task of superseding Catholicism and Protestantism and building "the third church" under the leadership of a Berlin minister named Friedrich Rittelmeyer.

The esoteric form of teaching and its related form of life, form of community, and liturgical practices represents an original form of religious experience, understanding, and community life that has been present in Christianity from the beginning, that was able to find a connection with certain basic esoteric elements of Christian tradition and that had been suppressed or pushed aside in the course of the development of Christianity into an institutional church. This led esoteric Christianity into a development that was often foreign to its original character. In the 20th century it faced the danger of losing its genuinely Christian substance when it opened up to non-Christian religions. On the other hand, many scholars are convinced that an esoteric Christianity in the 20th century is needed to fulfill a positive task as a countermovement to a loss of spiritual substance of Christianity in a dogmatically, institutionally, and socially static church organization.

VI. Conclusion

SECULARIZATION

Christianity is the spiritual power that has influenced human history more strongly and may have changed it more deeply than any other factor. At the same time it is the spiritual movement that has caused the greatest number of countermovements, which have, in turn, adopted the shape of an aggressive anti-Christianity.

The meaning of secularization

One of the main subjects of 20th-century discussion about the future of Christianity has been covered by the term secularization. The term itself has gone through a significant change of meaning during the course of the centuries. Appearing first as an expression of Roman Catholic Church law, it meant the permission granted to a person of an order to leave the monastery and lead a spiritual life in the world. In this case it was the legitimate return of a clergyman into the world.

During the 17th century, secularization referred to the condition of a thing, a territory, or an institution that had been removed from ecclesiastical administration and placed under worldly supervision. The history of past centuries is the history of secularization of church possessions, up to the largest secularization in the German Empire in 1803.

Only during the 19th century did secularization appear as a term of the arts; *i.e.*, the transformation of originally religious understandings and insights into those of the general human secular intellect that are independent of faith. Eventually, the term came to mean the process of deconsecration and loss of faith. With the sociology of the German social thinkers Max Weber and Ferdinand Tönnies, secularization came to be accepted as a sociological concept referring to "the decrease in meaning of organized religions as a means of social control or as the result of an accepted shrinkage of the range of religious ideas and norms." The term has received a cultural-ideological interpretation in the sense of a slogan of cultural emancipation from the tradition of Christian culture and spirituality, going as far as the proclamation of a "humanity without God."

The term passed through a number of levels from the demand to limit church rule to the statement of the end of its rule and the denial of its right of existence in modern times. In modern criticism of Christianity, the idea is prevalent that the process of secularization, in the sense of a decrease in importance, is irreversible, concerning not only organized religion—that is, the Christian churches—but also concerning religion in general, and that Christianity is aimed irrevocably toward the "end of religion." This thesis has, in part, been supported by certain strata of Christian theology, mainly the philosophy of religion of dialectical theology. The latter understood religion in the sense of the German philosopher Ludwig Feuerbach's philosophy of religion as the self-interpretation of man and, therefore, his self-justification before God by the creation of his own gods. It wanted to save Christianity as nonreligion, however, from the decline of religions and saw in the word of God, as revealed through Christ, "the crisis of all religions." This theology, however, has not prevented the critics of religion from proclaiming the beginning of a post-Christian Era.

The theological attempt of "demythologization" of Christianity has also contributed to secularization in the sense of a shrinking of its religious contents. All of these interpretations, however, are based on its unproved premise, which is deduced from ideologies. Mainly through Feuerbach and Karl Marx, the category of secularization has become a code for an antitheological consciousness.

The church as a contributor to the alarm of seculariza-tion

The church has allowed itself to become alarmed, partly by the unanimous front of its opponents who proclaim the irreversibility of its end, and has adopted an attitude that appears to concede the theory of its attackers. On the one hand, it shifted its emphasis with great eagerness to the area of social ethics and politics in order to show that its influence was not all caught in a process of shrinkage. On the other hand, it retreated from a "triumphant theology" to a theology of the "little flock" (Luke) and refused any claim of power. The positions of the "end of Christianity" theory, on the one hand, and the two above-mentioned attitudes within the church, on the other, would seem to be the historical facts that will be decisive for the future of Christianity. Christianity, which had been proclaimed dead, could not be removed in those areas in which it was persecuted most severely during the 1920s–1970s. Even where it was exposed to a program of destruction, as in the Soviet Union and other Communist states, it survived in contrast to all political predictions and political measures. The Russian Orthodox Church was given back its recognition by the state, and Protestant Free churches of Baptist character have gained an unexpected impetus in the Soviet Union.

The consequence of antichurch politics during the French Revolution, the separation of church and state at that time, and the suppression of the religious orders resulted in a spiritual renewal of Christianity in France that was visible in the foundation of numerous new orders and in a worldwide expansion of the missionary activities of the French orders. In the same way, European Pietism and the English and American Free churches responded to the criticism of Christianity resulting from the Enlightenment with a worldwide expansion of Christian missions supported by the conviction of an evangelistic mission of the laity.

Reactions to "inner seculariza-tion"

Even institutional Christianity has never been completely subject to an inner secularization. Since the 16th and 17th centuries, Free churches, in which the power of the Gospel found free expression, have grown. That power was suppressed in the state churches, which were always most in danger of secularization. After the Free churches began to become secularized and converted into carriers of a bourgeois "cultural Christianity," revivals in the form of the Pentecostal movement appeared, and, in turn, reinfluenced the older churches and the younger Free churches to a kind of reformation. An important basic phenomenon of Christianity came into focus here. Christianity carries in itself two impulses—on the one hand, the urge to identify with the world, to conquer the world, to establish institutions for its realization in the world—that is, in all areas of life of this world; on the other hand, it contains the power, in those cases in which it has been interwoven with the world, to separate itself from the established phase of secularization and to retreat to its spiritual charismatic point of departure. The phenomenon of secularization is by no means as new as the critics of Christianity of modern times have declared it to be. The church has gone through worse periods of secularization than the present one. For example, during the feudalization of the church in the early Middle Ages, which corrupted the entire leadership of the church by making the bishops and abbots feudal landlords of their dioceses and monasteries—a poor mendicant friar, Francis of Assisi, demonstrated credibly the spirit of Protestant Christianity in the secularized feudal church.

AN ANSWER TO SECULARIZATION

The thesis of irreversible secularization, the unavoidability of the end of religion, can be held to be contrary to man's view of himself. In this view, man does not live only in the realm of time and space; he has eternity, the transcendental, as a third dimension. He is a being transcending himself. Part of his human nature is the sense of the divine and the metaphysical, the possibility of experiencing transcendence. It may be that to deny this

sense would be to take humanity away from man, to make him an inhuman creature in the name of a merely rationally understood humanity. Evidence supporting this thesis is the fact that the most intensive, state-supported propaganda in the Communist countries has succeeded only in reducing the activities of organized religious institutions—mainly the Christian churches—to a minimum but has not eliminated religion itself.

It is just as significant that new religions constantly come into existence on all continents. The phenomenon of new religions—which has hardly been studied—disproves the theory of the irreversibility of secularization. That such new religions came into existence, particularly in Japan, where—according to prevalent sociological opinion—it was most strongly exposed to secularization after abolition of the emperor cult and of state Shintō, is most significant. Although nobody could have prevented the Japanese from accepting dialectical materialism, today 20 percent of all Japanese belong to the so-called new religions (there are more than 400 of them). The strongest one, the Sōka-gakkai, originated from Japanese Nichiren Buddhism and has had a great influence on the religious, moral, and political conscience of Japan. Similar developments can be observed in South America and in Africa and in the Near East. Some of these new religions, such as Tenri-kyō, Sōka-gakkai, and Bahā'ī have begun successful world missions.

Besides the new religions, Christian renewal movements spring up all over the world as the result of a new transcendental experience. The rediscovery of liturgy, religious music, meditation, prayer, devotions, pastoral counselling, and the new recognition of charismatic gifts have to be mentioned in this context. Significant in this respect is the great share that the so-called younger churches have had in this development because they possess an inexhaustible life of piety and are frequently closer than their mother churches to the charismatic roots of the gospel. They contribute to the experience of a one-sided type of a theologized, intellectually diluted, demythologized Christianity so that it is filled again with new expressions of ancient spiritual contents.

Renewal movements as a result of new transcen-dental experiences

Christianity has never adopted the idea of progress in its self-understanding and the view of its future. Its historical understanding has always been dramatic. Revelation has remained its model: the Kingdom of Christ is in a permanent struggle with the Kingdom of the Antichrist. These struggles follow in rapid succession, wrestling dramatically; and frequently the existence of the church is at stake. The path to resurrection leads through suffering and death; the sign of victory is the cross. In the Christian understanding of history and of the future, devastating and seemingly total defeat is seen as one step on the path to victory. The only church historian who so far has undertaken a presentation of the complete history of Christianity from its first beginnings up to the present is an American, Kenneth Scott Latourette, who has explored the phenomenon of secularization during the era of revolutions very carefully and has formulated a picture of the future of the church that is distinguished by its expert look at its entirety, both from the practice of complete adaptation as practiced by some churches out of fear and the minimalization of their own importance—the theology of the "little flock"—as others practice it. He has juxtaposed the negative thesis that views Christianity at its end with the thesis that Christianity is standing at its beginning, has just viewed its global realm of activity and taken possession of its geographical field of action, and has yet to begin its great history of penetrating thoroughly the life of individual personalities as well as the life of whole peoples. Afflicted heavily through counterpowers, it has partly activated itself; it is being subjected to a fierce storm, which it has partly called forth itself. In spite of the storm, Christianity is moving forward. He sees important evidence for this in the fact that completely new powers of life spring up in the so-called younger churches. In the 20th century, a historically hardly comprehensible process of a new reception and productive interpretation of Christianity, which can be observed everywhere, consists of the elab-

The view that Christianity is just at its beginning

oration of respective cultural heritages by the separate younger churches of the early mission fields in Japan, India, Africa, and Indonesia. With more or less large differences, the spreading of new churches can be observed, resulting in the establishment of independent churches in all fields of mission, in spite of the manifold evangelical methods that were employed and in spite of the different historical legacies of the different churches of Europe and America that carried out the missions. Because of this situation, an honest ecumenical encounter of churches has become possible in which the old and the young churches cooperate on an equal basis and unite in sharing their ideas about the spiritual, social, and political world mission of Christianity. After the Reformation of the 16th century had led to an unexpected intensification of religious forces in Christianity and these forces unfolded into a confusing number of separate types of churches and mission, church history has obviously entered a new phase of responsible contemplation of common tasks by the various church bodies. In this phase those forces that were so exhausted in the competition between the churches can be developed and utilized more freely in cooperation and supplementation. This may be presented as the Christian antithesis to the thesis of the end of Christianity.

BIBLIOGRAPHY

The essence of Christianity: WILLIAM ADAMS BROWN, *The Essence of Christianity: A Study in the History of Definition* (1902).

Historical background: OWEN CHADWICK, *The History of the Church: A Select Bibliography,* 2nd ed. (1966); KENNETH S. LATOURETTE, *A History of Christianity* (1953); J.H. NICOLS, *History of Christianity, 1650–1950: Secularization of the West* (1956); WILLIAM A. SCOTT, *Historical Protestantism: An Historical Introduction to Protestant Theology* (1971).

Problems of self-definition: SALO W. BARON, *A Social and Religious History of the Jews,* 2nd ed. rev., 8 vol. (1952–58); JOHN C. BENNETT (ed.), *Christian Social Ethics in a Changing World* (1966); MARTIN BUBER, *Two Types of Faith* (1951); HARVEY COX, *The Secular City: Secularization and Urbanization in Theological Perspective,* rev. ed. (1966); JEAN DANIELOU, *Dialogue avec Israël* (1963; Eng. trans., 1968); GEORGE W. FORELL, *The Protestant Faith* (1960); ROBERT M. GRANT, *Augustus to Constantine: The Thrust of the Christian Movement into the Roman World* (1970); ROMANO GUARDINI, *Die Kirche des Herrn* (1965; Eng. trans., *The Church of the Lord,* 1967); ADOLF VON HARNACK, *Die Mission und Ausbreitung des Christentums in den ersten drei Jahrhunderten,* 2 vol. (1902; Eng. trans., *The Mission and Expansion of Christianity in the First Three Centuries,* 1904, reprinted 1962); HANS KUNG, *Die Kirche* (1967; Eng. trans., *The Church,* 1967); A.V. MURRAY, *The State and the Church in a Free Society* (1958); REINHOLD NIEBUHR, *The Structure of Nations and Empires* (1959); PETER RICHARDSON, *Israel in the Apostolic Church* (1969); WOLFGANG S. SEIFERTH, *Synagogue und Kirche im Mittelalter* (1964; Eng. trans., *Synagogue and Church in the Middle Ages: Two Symbols in Art and Literature,* 1970); JAKOB SPEIGL, *Der Römische Staat und die Christen* (1970); ETHELBERT STAUFFER, *Christ and the Caesars* (1955); ERNST TROELTSCH, *Christian Thought: Its History and Applications* (1957).

Major traditional doctrinal issues: (The meaning of dogma): KARL BARTH, *Kirchliche Dogmatik,* 4 vol. (1932–67; Eng. trans., *Church Dogmatics,* 4 vol., 1936–69); EMIL BRUNNER, *The Christian Doctrine of the Church, Faith, and the Consummation* (1962); T.A. BARKILL, *The Evolution of Christian Thought* (1971); YVES M.-J. CONGAR, *A History of Theology* (1968); BRIAN A. GERRISH (ed.), *The Faith of Christendom: A Source Book of Creeds and Confessions* (1963); ADOLF VON HARNACK, *Lehrbuch der Dogmengeschichte,* 3rd ed., 3 vol. (1894–97; Eng. trans., *A History of Dogma,* 7 vol., 1896–99, reprinted 1961); JAROSLAV PELIKAN, *The Christian Tradition: A History of the Development of Doctrine,* vol. 1, *The Emergence of the Catholic Tradition, 100–600* (1971); PAUL TILLICH, *Systematic Theology,* 3 vol. (1951–64); HARRY A. WOLFSON, *The Philosophy of the Church Fathers: Faith, Trinity, Incarnation,* 3rd ed. rev. (1970). (God the Father): GUSTAF AULEN, *Das christliche Gottesbild in Vergangenheit und Gegenwart* (1930); JOHN BAILLIE, *Our Knowledge of God* (1959); PETER A. BERTOCCI, *The Person God Is* (1970); WALTER R. MATTHEWS, *God in Christian Thought and Experience* (1930). (God the Son): GUNTHER BORNKAMM, *Jesus von Nazareth* (1956; Eng. trans., 1960); FREDERICK H. BORSCH, *The Son*

of Man in Myth and History (1967); FRIEDRICH GOGARTEN, *Jesus Christus, Wende der Welt* (1966; Eng. trans., *Christ the Crisis,* 1970); EDWARD R. HARDY (ed.), *Christology of the Later Fathers* (1954); JOHN REUMANN, *Jesus in the Church's Gospels* (1968); EDWARD SCHILLEBEECKX, *Christus, Sacrament van de Godsontmoeting* (1959; Eng. trans., *Christ, the Sacrament,* 2nd ed., 1971); ALBERT SCHWEITZER, *Von Reimarus zu Wrede* (1906; Eng. trans., *The Quest of the Historical Jesus,* 1910, reprinted 1962). (God the Holy Spirit): ERNST BENZ, *Ecclesia Spiritualis,* 2nd ed. (1968), and *Der heilige Geist in Amerika* (1970); FREDERICK DALE BRUNER, *A Theology of the Holy Spirit* (1970); CHARLES WILLIAMS, *The Descent of the Dove: A Short History of the Holy Spirit in the Church* (1950). (The Holy Trinity): H.P. VAN DUSEN, *Spirit, Son and Father: Christian Faith in the Light of the Holy Spirit* (1958); JULES LEBRETON, *Histoire du dogme de la Trinité des origines à saint Augustin,* 2 vol. (1927–28; Eng. trans. of vol. 1, *History of the Dogma of The Trinity, from Its Origins to the Council of Nicaea,* 1939); CLAUDE WELCH, *In This Name: The Doctrine of the Trinity in Contemporary Theology* (1952). (The concept of man): ERNST BENZ, The Concept of Man in Christian Thought," in SARVEPALLI RADHAKRISHNAN and POOLLA T. RAJU (eds.), *The Concept of Man: A Study in Comparative Philosophy,* 2nd ed. (1966); EMIL BRUNNER, *Der Mensch im Widerspruch* (1937; Eng. trans., *Man in Revolt: A Christian Anthropology,* 1947); WERNER G. KUMMEL, *Das Bild des Mensch im Neuen Testament* (1960; Eng. trans., *Man in the New Testament,* 1963); REINHOLD NIEBUHR, *The Nature and Destiny of Man,* 2 vol. (1941–43); WOLFHART PANNENBERG, *Was ist der Mensch?* (1968; Eng. trans., *What Is Man?,* 1970); HENRY W. ROBINSON, *The Christian Doctrine of Man* (1913). (The Church): CARL ANDRESEN, *Einführung in die christliche Archäologie* (1971); JAMES V. BARTLET, *Church-life and Church-order During the First Four Centuries* (1943); ERNST BENZ, *Bischofsamt und apostolische Sukzession im deutschen Protestantismus* (1953); DIETRICH BONHOEFFER, *Sanctorum Communio,* 4th ed. (1969); RUDOLF BULTMANN, *History and Eschatology* (1957); OSCAR CULLMANN, *Christus und die Zeit,* 3rd rev. ed. (1962; Eng. trans., *Christ and Time,* 1964); JOHN G. DAVIES, *The Origin and Development of Early Christian Church Architecture* (1952); FREDERICK W. DILLISTONE (ed.), *Scripture and Tradition* (1955); G.V. FLOROVSKY, "Eschatology in the Patristic Age: An Introduction," *Greek Orthodox Theological Review,* 2: 27–40 (1956); RICHARD GERBER, *Utopian Fantasy* (1955); BRIAN A. GERRISH (ed.), *The Faith of Christendom: A Source Book of Creeds and Confessions* (1963); ADRIAN HASTINGS, *Mission and Ministry* (1971); DANIEL T. JENKINS, *Tradition, Freedom and the Spirit* (1951); GEORGE JOHNSTON, *The Doctrine of the Church in the New Testament* (1943); J.N.D. KELLY, *Early Christian Doctrines,* 4th ed. (1968); HENDRIK KRAEMER, *From Missionfield to Independent Church* (1958); RAJAH B. MANIKAM, *Christianity and the Asian Revolution* (1955); ROMEY P. MARSHALL and MICHAEL J. TAYLOR, *Liturgy and Christian Unity* (1965); PAUL S. MINEAR, *The Christian Hope and the Second Coming* (1954); EINAR MOLLAND, *Konfesjonskunnskap: Kristenhetens trosbekjennelser og Kirkesamfunn* (1953; Eng. trans., *Christendom: The Christian Churches, Their Doctrines, Constitutional Forms and Way of Worship,* 1959); JURGEN MOLTMANN, *Hope and Planning* (1971); LEWIS MUMFORD, *The Story of Utopias* (1922, reprinted 1962); JUERGEN L. NEVE, *Churches and Sects of Christendom,* 3rd ed. (1952); JAMES E.L. NEWBIGIN, *One Body, One Gospel, One World: The Christian Mission Today* (1958); HAROLD H. ROWLEY, *The Relevance of the Bible* (1942); DARRETT B. RUTMAN (ed.), *The Great Awakening: Events and Exegesis* (1970); PHILIP SCHAFF, *The History of the Creeds of Christendom,* 4th ed., 3 vol. (1919); WILLIAM STRAWSON, *Jesus and the Future Life,* rev. ed. (1970); GEOFFREY WAINWRIGHT, *Eucharist and Eschatology* (1971); BARRINGTON R. WHITE, *The English Separatist Tradition* (1971).

Attitudes concerning the relation of the Christian community and the Christian to the world: PAUL LEHMANN, *Ethics in a Christian Context* (1963); REINHOLD NIEBUHR, *An Interpretation of Christian Ethics* (1935); EDWARD SCHILLEBEECKX, *Wereld en Kerk* (1966; Eng. trans., *World and Church,* 1971); HENRY SIDGWICK, *Outlines of the History of Ethics for English Readers,* 6th ed. (1931, reprinted 1960).

The problem of the Kingdom of Peace and the execution of judgment: JOSEPH J. BAIERL, *The Catholic Church and the Modern State* (1955); ROBERT W. and A.J. CARLYLE, *A History of Mediaeval Political Theory in the West,* 6 vol. (1903–36, 1953); SIDNEY Z. EHLER and JOHN B. MORRALL (eds. and trans.), *Church and State Through the Centuries* (1954); NILS EHRENSTROM, *Christian Faith and the Modern State: An Ecumenical Approach* (1937); G.H.C. MacGREGOR, *The New Testament Basis of Pacifism and the Relevance of an Impossible Ideal* (1960).

Views on the relationship between the Christian or Christian institutions and the political order: JOHN C. BENNETT, *Social Salvation* (1935); WALTER G. MUELDER, *Foundations of the Responsible Society* (1959); REINHOLD NIEBUHR, *Moral Man and Immoral Society* (1932); DARRETT B. RUTMAN (ed.), *The Great Awakening: Events and Exegesis* (1970); ERNST TROELTSCH, *Die Soziallehren der christlichen Kirchen und Gruppen*, 2nd ed., 2 vol. (1922; Eng. trans., *The Social Teachings of the Christian Churches*, 2 vol., 1931, reprinted 1960); WILLEM A. VISSER'T HOOFT and J.H. OLDHAM, *The Church and Its Function in Society* (1937); MAX WEBER, *Die protestantische Ethik und der Geist des Kapitalismus* (1920; Eng. trans., *The Protestant Ethic and the Spirit of Capitalism*, 1930; paperback edition, 1958), and *Religionssoziologie* (1922; Eng. trans., *The Sociology of Religion*, 1922; paperback edition, 1964).

The relationship between the Christian or Christian institutions and the socio-economic order: JOHN C. BENNETT (ed.), *Christian Social Ethics in a Changing World* (1966); NORMAN PITTENGER, *The Christian Church as Social Process* (1971); JOACHIM WACH, *Sociology of Religion* (1962).

The relationship between the Christian or Christian institutions and scholarly activities and educational institutions: ALBERT V. MURRAY, *The State and the Church in a Free Society* (1958); WILLIAM R. NIBLETT, *Christian Education in a Secular Society* (1960); ROBERT ULICH, *A History of Religious Education* (1968).

The relationship between the Christian or Christian institutions and the care of the sick and other afflicted persons: ROTHA M. CLAY, *The Mediaeval Hospitals of England*, 2nd ed. (1966); EDGAR E. HUME, *Medical Work of the Knights Hospitallers of Saint John of Jerusalem* (1940); FREDERICK WEISER, *Love's Response: A Story of Lutheran Deaconesses in America* (1962).

The relationship between the Christian or Christian institutions and culture: EMILE BREHIER, *The History of Philosophy*, 7 vol. (1963–69); ERNST H. KANTOROWICZ, *The King's Two Bodies: A Study in Mediaeval Political Theology* (1957); JAMES LIVINGSTON, *Modern Christian Thought: From the Enlightenment to Vatican II* (1971).

The relationship of the Christian and of Christian institutions to the understanding and use of nature: JOSEPH DALBY, *The Catholic Conception of the Law of Nature* (1943); OTTO F. VON GIERKE, *Natural Law and the Theory of Society, 1500 to 1800*, 2 vol. (1934).

The relationship between the Christian or Christian institutions and the family: ERNEST W. BURGESS, HARVEY J. LOCKE, and MARY M. THOMES, *The Family from Institution to Companionship*, 3rd ed. (1963); RICHARD M. FAGLEY, *The Population Explosion and Christian Responsibility* (1960).

Personal ethics: MARTIN BUBER, *Ich und Du* (1966; Eng. trans., *I and Thou*, 1970); KNUD E. LOGSTRUP, *Den etiske fordring*, 8th ed. (1969; Eng. trans., *The Ethical Demand*, 1971); ROBERT C. MORTIMER, *The Elements of Moral Theology* (1947); WILLIAM TEMPLE, *Christian Faith and Life*, rev. ed. (1963); PAUL TILLICH, *The Courage to Be* (1952).

Missions: HENDRIK KRAEMER, *The Christian Message in a Non-Christian World*, 3rd ed. (1966); KENNETH S. LATOURETTE, *A History of the Expansion of Christianity*, 7 vol. (1937–45, reprinted 1971).

The encounter with non-Christian religions: HENDRIK KRAEMER, *Waarom nu juist het Christendom?* (1960; Eng. trans., *Why Christianity of All Religions?*, 1962); RUDOLF OTTO, *West-Östliche Mystik* (1960; Eng. trans., *Mysticism East and West*, 1970); PAUL TILLICH, *Christianity and the Encounter of the World Religions* (1963).

Other problems confronting Christianity: HART M. NELSON et al. (eds.), *The Black Church in America* (1971); JAMES D. ROBERTS, *Liberation and Reconciliation: A Black Theology* (1971); HANS MOL, *Christianity in Chains: A Sociologist's Interpretation of the Churches' Dilemma in a Secular World* (1969).

The present condition and future prospects of the Church: EUGEN ROSENSTOCK-HUESSY, *The Christian Future; or The Modern Mind Outrun* (1946); ARNOLD J. TOYNBEE, *Christianity Among the Religions of the World* (1957); CHARLES W. FORMAN (ed.), *Christianity in the Non-Western World* (1967); W.H. VAN DE POL, *Das Ende des konventionellen Christentums* (1967; Eng. trans., *The End of Conventional Christianity*, 1968).

(E.W.B.)

Christianity Before the Schism of 1054

The history of Christianity from its early beginnings in Judaism to its schism in 1054 (accentuating the split between the Eastern and Western churches) involved a struggle—among competing ideologies and religions—to win acceptance within the Hellenistic world and the environs dominated by the many and various barbarian tribes that were migrating into Europe (the last being the Norsemen and the Magyars).

I. From Jesus to Constantine

THE PRIMITIVE CHURCH

The relation of the early church to late Judaism. Christianity began as a movement within Judaism at a period when the Jews had long been under foreign influence and rule and had found in their religion (rather than in their politics or cultural achievements) the linchpin of their community. From Amos (8th century BC) onward the religion of Israel was marked by tension between the concept of monotheism, with its universal ideal of salvation (for all nations), and the notion of God's special choice of Israel. In the age after Alexander the Great (*i.e.*, the Hellenistic period, 3rd century BC–3rd century AD), the dispersion of the Jews throughout the Hellenistic kingdoms and the Roman Empire gave some impetus to the universalistic tendency. But the attempts of foreign rulers, especially the Syrian king Antiochus Epiphanes (in 168–165 BC), to impose Hellenization (Greek culture) and religious syncretism in Palestine provoked zealous resistance on the part of many Jews. In Palestinian Judaism the predominant note was separation and exclusiveness. Jewish missionaries to other areas were strictly expected to impose the distinctive Jewish customs of circumcision, kosher food, sabbaths, and other festivals.

(margin: Universalistic and particularistic tendencies in Judaism)

The relationship of the primitive (earliest) Christian Church to Judaism turned principally on two questions: (1) the messianic role of Jesus of Nazareth and (2) the permanent validity of the Mosaic Law for all.

The Old Testament faith viewed history as the stage of a providential drama eventually ending in a triumph of God over all present sources of frustration (*e.g.*, foreign domination or the sins of Israel). God's rule would be established by an anointed prince (the Messiah) of the line of David, king of Israel in the 10th century BC. The proper course of action leading to the consummation of the drama, however, was the subject of some disagreement, and various groups gave differing answers. Among the diverse groups were the aristocratic and conservative Sadducees, who accepted only the five books of Moses (the Pentateuch), and the more popular and liberal Pharisees. The Pharisees not only accepted biblical books outside the Pentateuch but also embraced doctrines—such as those on resurrection and the existence of angels—of recent acceptance in Judaism, many of which were derived from apocalyptic expectations that the consummation of history would be heralded by God's intervention in the affairs of men in dramatic, cataclysmic terms. The Sanhedrin (central council) at Jerusalem was made up of both Pharisees and Sadducees. The Zealots were aggressive revolutionaries seeking independence from Rome. Other groups were the Herodians, supporters of the client kingdom of the Herods (a dynasty that supported Rome) and abhorrent to the Zealots, and the Essenes, a quasi-monastic dissident group, probably including the sect that preserved the Dead Sea Scrolls. This latter sect did not participate in the Temple worship at Jerusalem and observed another religious calendar; from their desert retreat they awaited divine intervention and searched prophetic writings for signs indicating the consummation.

(margin: Jewish sectarianism)

What relation the followers of Jesus had to some of these groups is not clear. In the canonical Gospels (those accepted as authentic by the church) the main targets of criticism are the scribes and Pharisees, whose attachment to the tradition of Judaism appears to be legalistic and pettifogging. The Sadducees and Herodians likewise receive an unfriendly portrait. The Essenes are never mentioned. One of Jesus' 12 disciples (Simon) was, or had once been, a Zealot.

Under the social and political conditions of the time, there could be no long future either for the Sadducees or for the Zealots—whose attempts to make apocalyptic dreams effective led to the destruction of Judaea after the

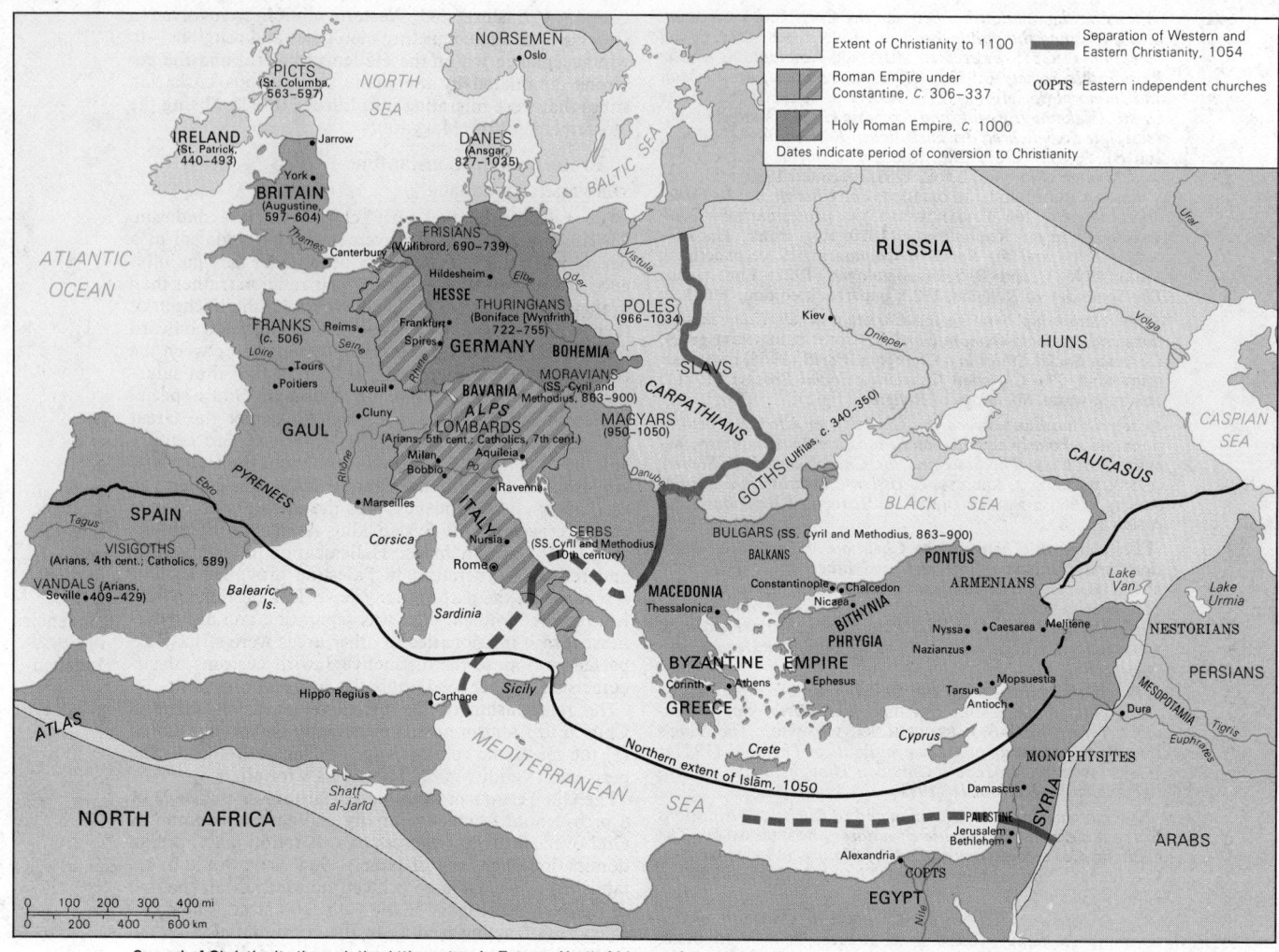

Spread of Christianity through the 11th century in Europe, North Africa, and the Middle East.
Adapted from W. Shepherd, *Historical Atlas*

two major Jewish revolts of 66–70 and 132–135 against the Romans. The choice for many Jews thus lay between the Pharisees and Christianity, the former dedicated to the meticulous preservation of the Mosaic Law and the latter to the universal propagation of the biblical faith as a religion for all mankind. Pharisaism as enshrined in the Mishna (Oral Law) and the Talmud (commentary on and addition to the Oral Law) became normative Judaism. By looking to the Gentile (non-Jewish) world and carefully dissociating itself from the Zealot revolutionaries, Christianity made possible its ideal of a world religion, at the price of sacrificing Jewish particularity and exclusiveness. The fact that Christianity has never succeeded in gaining the open allegiance of more than a minority of Jews is more a mystery to theologians than to historians.

The relation of the early church to the career and intentions of Jesus.   The prime sources for knowledge of Jesus of Nazareth are the four canonical Gospels in the New Testament. Only a few probably authentic sayings of Jesus became preserved in oral tradition independent of these documents, though many sayings came to be put into his mouth. These noncanonical sayings are called Agrapha (without a book). The *Gospel of Thomas,* preserved in a Coptic Gnostic library found about 1945 in Egypt, contains several such sayings, besides some independent versions of canonical sayings. At certain points the Gospel tradition finds independent confirmation in the letters of the Apostle Paul. The allusions in non-Christian sources (the Jewish historian Josephus, the Roman historians Tacitus and Suetonius, and Talmudic texts) are almost negligible, except as refuting the unsubstantiated notion that Jesus might never have existed.

The first three Gospels, Matthew, Mark, and Luke, have a literary relation to one another and are hence called

Synoptic. Mark was probably used by Matthew and Luke. John, differing in both pattern and content, appears richer in theological interpretation but in detail may preserve good historical information. As their titles imply, the Gospels are not detached reports but were written to serve religious needs; they resemble oil paintings rather than photographs. Legendary and apologetic (defensive) motifs, and the various preoccupations of the communities for which they were first produced, can readily be discerned as influences upon their narratives. Historical scholarship at present has insufficient tools to eliminate subjective judgments about the probability of many details (upon which there will always be disagreement), but the most persuasive scholarly consensus accepts the substance of the Gospel tradition as a veracious picture.

A prominent uncertainty is the matter of chronology. Matthew places the birth of Jesus at least two years before Herod the Great's death late in 5 BC or early in 4 BC. Luke connects Jesus' birth with a Roman census that, according to Josephus, occurred in AD 6–7 and caused a revolt against the governor Quirinius. Luke could be right about the census and wrong about the governor. The crucifixion under Pontius Pilate, prefect of Judaea (AD 26–36), was probably about the year 29–30, but again certainty is impossible.

Encounter with John the Baptist, the ascetic in the Judaean Desert who preached repentance and Baptism in view of God's coming Kingdom, marked a decisive moment for Jesus' career. He recognized in John the forerunner of the kingdom that his own ministry was inaugurating. The first preaching of Jesus, in his home region of Galilee, took the form of vivid parables and was accompanied by miraculous healings. The Synoptic writers give a single climactic visit of Jesus to Jerusalem at the end of his career; but John may be right (implicitly supported by Luke 13:7) in representing his visits as more frequent and the period of ministry as lasting more than a single year. Jesus' attitude to the observance of the law generated conflict with the Pharisees, and, though the people protected him, he also aroused the fear and hostility of the ruling Jewish authorities. A triumphal entry to Jerusalem at Passover time (the period celebrating the Exodus of the Hebrews from Egypt in the 13th century BC) was the prelude to a final crisis. After a last supper with his disciples he was betrayed by one of them (Judas). Arrest and trial followed, first before the Sanhedrin and then before Pilate, who condemned him to crucifixion. The accusation before Pilate was sedition, in which the Evangelists saw a framed charge. It was universal Christian belief that three days after his death he was raised from the dead by divine power.

The Kingdom of God and apocalyptic hopes

Jesus preached the imminent presence of God's Kingdom, in some texts as future consummation, in others as already present. The words and acts of Jesus were believed to be the inauguration of a process that was to culminate in a final triumph of God. His disciples recognized him as the Messiah, the Anointed One. He is not recorded to have used the word of himself. The titles Prophet and Rabbi also were applied to Jesus. His own enigmatic self-designation was "Son of man," sometimes in allusion to his suffering, sometimes to his future role as judge. This title is derived from the version of the Book of Daniel (7:13), where "one like a son of man," contrasted with beast figures, represents the humiliated people of God, ascending to be vindicated by the divine Judge. In the developed Gospel tradition the theme of the transcendent judge seems to be most prominent.

Apocalyptic hope could easily merge into messianic zealotry. Moreover, Jesus' teaching was critical of the established order and encouraged the poor and oppressed, even though it contained an implicit rejection of revolution. Violence was viewed as incompatible with the ethic of the Kingdom of God. Whatever contacts there may have been with the Zealot movement (as the narrative of feeding 5,000 men in the desert may hint), the Gospels assume the widest distance between Jesus' understanding of his role and the Zealot revolution.

With this distance from revolutionary idealism goes a sombre estimate of human perfectibility. The gospel of repentance presupposes deep defilement in individuals and in society. The sufferings and pains of humanity under the power of evil spirits calls out for compassion and an urgent mission. All the acts of a disciple must express love and forgiveness, even to enemies, and also detachment from property and worldly wealth. To Jesus, the outcasts of society (prostitutes, the hated and oppressive tax agents, and others) were objects of special care, and censoriousness was no virtue. Though the state is regarded as a distant entity in certain respects, it yet has the right to require taxes and civic obligations: Caesar has rights that must be respected and are not incompatible with the fulfillment of God's demands.

Some of the futurist sayings, if taken by themselves, raise the question whether Jesus intended to found a church. A negative answer emerges only if the authentic Jesus is assumed to have expected an immediate catastrophic intervention by God. There is no doubt that he gathered and intended to gather around him a community of followers. This community continued after his time, regarding itself as the specially called congregation of God's people, possessing as covenant signs the rites of Baptism and Eucharist (Lord's Supper) with which Jesus was particularly associated—Baptism because of his example, Eucharist because the Last Supper on the night before the crucifixion was marked as an anticipation of the messianic feast of the coming age.

Expansion of Christianity to include Gentiles

A closely related question is whether Jesus intended his gospel to be addressed to Jews only or if the Gentiles were also to be included. In the Gospels Gentiles appear as isolated exceptions, and the choice of 12 Apostles has an evident symbolic relation to the 12 tribes of Israel. The fact that the extension of Christian preaching to the Gentiles caused intense debate in the 40s of the 1st century is decisive proof that Jesus had given no unambiguous directive on the matter. Gospel sayings that make the Jews' refusal to recognize Jesus' authority as the ground for extending the Kingdom of God to the Gentiles must, therefore, have been cast by the early community.

The Gentile mission and St. Paul. Saul, or Paul (as he was later called), was a zealous Pharisee who persecuted the primitive church. Born at Tarsus (Asia Minor), he had come to Jerusalem as a student of the famous Rabbi Gamaliel and had harried a Christian group called by Luke the "hellenists," who were led by Stephen (the first Christian martyr) and who regarded Jesus as a spiritual reformer sent to purge the corrupt worship of Jerusalem. Paul was suddenly converted to faith in Christ while on a mission to persecute the followers of Jesus and, simultaneously, to a conviction that the gospel must pass to the non-Jewish world under conditions that dispensed with exclusively and distinctively Jewish ceremonies. Paul was disapproved by Christian Jews who were of conservative opinions and remained throughout his career a controversial figure. He gained recognition for the converts of the Gentile mission by the Christian community in Jerusalem; but his work was considered an affront to Jewish traditionalism, and his program of being "all things to all men" led to bitter charges that he was an unprincipled trimmer. He saw clearly and correctly that the universal mission of the church to all humanity, implicit in the coming of the Messiah, or Christ, meant a radical break with rabbinical conservatism.

Gentile-Jewish debates within Christianity

Due to the preservation of some weighty letters, Paul is the only vivid figure of the apostolic age (1st century AD). Like his elder contemporary Philo of Alexandria, also a Hellenized Jew of the dispersion, he interpreted the Old Testament allegorically (symbolically) and affirmed the primacy of spirit over letter in a manner that was in line with Jesus' freedom with regard to the sabbath. The crucifixion of Jesus he viewed as the supreme redemptive act and also as the means of expiation for the sin of man. Salvation is in Paul's thought, therefore, not found by a conscientious moralism but rather is a gift of grace, a doctrine in which Paul was anticipated by the Jewish philosopher Philo. But Paul linked this doctrine with his theme that the Gospel represents liberation from the Mosaic Law. The latter thesis created difficulties at Jerusalem, where the church was under the presidency of James, the brother of Jesus, and the circle of the intimate disciples of Jesus. James, martyred at Jerusalem in 62, was the primary authority for the Christian Jews, especially those made anxious by Paul; the canonical letter ascribed to James opposes the antinomian (antilaw) interpretations of the doctrine of justification by faith. A middle position seems to have been occupied by Peter. All the Gospels record a special commission of Jesus to Peter as the leader among the 12 Apostles. But Peter's biography can only be dimly constructed; he died in Rome (according to early tradition) in Nero's persecution (64) about the same time as Paul.

Apart from its success, the supremacy of the Gentile mission within the church was ensured by the effects on Jewish Christianity of the fall of Jerusalem (70) and Hadrian's exclusion of all Jews from the city (135). Jewish Christianity declined and became the faith of a very small group without links to either synagogue or Gentile church. Some bore the title Ebionites, "the poor" (cf. Matt. 5:3). Among them some did not accept the tradition that Jesus was born of a virgin.

In the theology of Paul, the human achievement of Jesus was important because his obedient fidelity to his vocation gave moral and redemptive value to his self-sacrifice. A different emphasis appears in the Gospel According to John, written (according to 2nd-century tradition) at Ephesus. John's Gospel partly reflects local disputes, not only between the church and the Hellenized synagogue but also between orthodox Christianity and deviationist Gnostic groups in Asia Minor. John's special individuality lies in his view of the relation between the historical events of the tradition and the Christian community's present experience of redemption. The history is treated symbolically to provide a vehicle for faith. Because it is less attached to the contingent events of a particular man's life, John's conception of the pre-existent divine Word (Logos) becoming incarnate (made flesh) in Jesus made intelligible to the Hellenistic world the universal significance of Jesus. In antiquity, divine presence had to be understood as either inspiration or incarnation. If the Synoptic Gospels suggest inspiration, the Gospel According to John chooses incarnation. The tension between these two types of Christology (doctrines of Christ) first became acute in the debate between the schools of Antioch and Alexandria in the late 4th century.

The contemporary social, religious, and intellectual world. Many Palestinian Jews appreciated the benefits of Roman rule in guaranteeing order and peace. The Roman government could tolerate regional and local religious groups and found it convenient to control Palestine through client kings like the Herods. The demand that divine honours be paid not only to the traditional Roman or similar gods but also to the emperors was not extended to Judaea except under the emperor Caligula (AD 37–41). It was enough that the Jews dedicated temple sacrifices and synagogues in the emperor's honour. The privileges of Roman citizenship were possessed by some Jewish families, including that of the Apostle Paul.

Relationship of early Christianity to various external issues

In his letter to the Romans, Paul affirmed the providential role of government in restraining evil. Christians did not need to be disaffected from the empire, though the deification of the emperor was offensive to them. Moreover, although as an agency of social welfare the church offered much to the downtrodden elements in society, the Christians did not at any stage represent a social and political threat. The ancient world did not possess a working-class movement in the modern sense, and Christianity did not create or foster one. After the example of their master, the Christians encouraged humility and patience before wicked men. Even the institution of slavery was not the subject of fundamental Christian criticism before the 4th century. The church, however, was not lost in pious mysticism. It provided for far more than the cultic (religious) needs of its members. Inheriting a Jewish moral ideal, its activities included food for the poor, orphans, and foundlings; care for prisoners; and a community funeral service.

The church inherited from Judaism also a strong sense of being holy, separate from idolatry and pagan eroticism. As polytheism with its attendant permissiveness permeated ancient society, a moral rigorism severely limited Christian participation in some trades and professions. At Baptism a Christian was expected to renounce his occupation if that necessarily implicated him in public or private compromise with polytheism, superstition, dishonesty, or vice. About military service there was disagreement. The majority held that a soldier, if converted and baptized, was not required to leave the army, but there was hesitation about whether an already baptized Christian might properly enlist. Strict Christians also thought poorly of the teaching profession because it involved instructing the young in literature replete with pagan ideals and what was viewed as indecency. Acting and dancing were similarly suspect occupations. Any involvement in magic was completely forbidden.

The Christian ethic therefore demanded some detachment from society. In some cases this made for economic difficulties. The structure of ancient society was dominated not by class but by the relationship of patron and client. A slave or freedman depended for his livelihood and prospects upon his patron. In antiquity a strong patron was indispensable if one was negotiating with police or tax authorities or lawcourts or if one had ambitions in the imperial service. The authority of the father of the family was considerable. Conversely, a man's power in society depended on the extent of his dependents and supporters. Often, Christianity penetrated the social strata first through women and children, especially in the upper classes. But once the householder was a Christian, his dependents tended to follow. The Christian community itself was close-knit. Third-century evidence portrays Christians banking their money with fellow believers; and widely separated groups helped one another with trade and mutual assistance.

The religious environment of the Gentile mission was a tolerant, syncretistic blend of many cults and myths. Paganism was concerned with success; the gods gave victory in war, good harvests, success in love and marriage, and sons and daughters. Defeat, famine, civil disorder, and infertility were probable signs of cultic pollution and disfavour. Men looked to religion for help in mastering the forces of nature rather than to achieve moral improvement. Individual gods cared either for specific human needs or for specific places and groups. The transcendent God of biblical religion was, therefore, very different from the numerous gods of limited power and local significance. In Asia Minor Paul and his co-worker Barnabas were taken to be gods in mortal form because of their miracles. To offer sacrifice on an altar seemed a natural expression of gratitude to any dead, or even living, benefactor. Popular enthusiasm could bestow divine honours on such heroes as dead pugilists and athletes. In the Roman Empire it seemed natural to offer sacrifice and burn incense to the divine emperor as a symbol of loyalty, much like standing for a national anthem today.

Gentile religious environment

Traditional Roman religion was a public cult, not private mysticism, and was upheld because it was the received way of keeping heaven friendly. To refuse participation appeared to be disloyal. The Jews could gain acceptance for their refusal by virtue of the undoubted fact that their monotheism was an ancestral national tradition. The Christians, however, did everything in their power to dissuade people from following the customs of their fathers, whether Gentiles or Jews, and thereby seemed to threaten the cohesion of society and the principle that each racial group was entitled to follow its national customs in religion.

If ancient religion was tolerant, the philosophical schools were seldom so. Platonists, Aristotelians, Stoics, Epicureans, and Skeptics tended to be very critical of one another. By the 1st century BC, an eclecticism emerged; and by the 2nd century AD, there developed a common stock of philosophy shared by most educated men and by some professional philosophers, which derived metaphysics involving theories on the nature of Being from Plato, ethics from the Stoics, and logic from Aristotle. This eclectic Platonism provided an important background and springboard for early Christian apologetic. Its main outlines appear already in Philo of Alexandria, whose thought influenced not only perhaps the writer of the anonymous letter to the Hebrews in the New Testament but also the great Christian thinkers Clement of Alexandria, Origen, and Ambrose of Milan. Because of this widespread philosophical tendency, the Christian could generally assume some belief in Providence and assent to high moral imperatives. Platonism in particular provided a metaphysical framework within which the Christians could interpret the entire pattern of creation, the Fall of man, the incarnation, redemption, the church, sacraments, and last things.

THE INTERNAL DEVELOPMENT OF THE CHRISTIAN CHURCH

The problem of jurisdictional authority. In the first Christian generation, authority in the church lay either in the kinsmen of Jesus or in those whom he had commissioned as Apostles and missionaries. The Jerusalem church under James, the brother of Jesus, was the mother church. Paul admitted that if they had refused to grant recognition to his Gentile converts he would have laboured in vain. If there was an attempt to establish a hereditary family overlordship in the church, it did not succeed. Among the Gentile congregations, the Apostles sent by Jesus enjoyed supreme authority. As long as the Apostles lived, there existed a living authoritative voice to which appeal could be made. But once they all had died, there was an acute question regarding the locus of authority. The earliest documents of the 3rd and 4th Christian generations are mainly concerned with this issue: what is the authority of the ministerial hierarchy? The apostolic congregations had normally been served by elders (Greek *presbyteroi*, "priests") or overseers (*episkopoi*, "bishops"), assisted by attendants (*diakonoi*, "deacons"). The clergy were responsible for preaching,

Bishops, presbyters, and deacons

for administering Baptism and Eucharist, and for distributing aid to the poor. In each city the president or senior member of the college (assembly) of presbyters naturally had some special authority; he corresponded with other churches and, when they were ordaining a new president, would go as the representative of his own community and as a symbol of the catholicity—the universality and unity—of the church of Christ.

Ignatius, bishop of Antioch early in the 2nd century, wrote seven letters on his way to martyrdom at Rome that indicate how critical the centrifugal forces in the church had made the problem of authority. The bishop, he insisted, is the unique focus of unity without whose authority there is no sacrament and no church. A few years earlier, the letter of Bishop Clement of Rome (c. AD 95) to the church at Corinth based the hierarchy's authority on the concept of a historical succession of duly authorized teachers. Clement understood the clergy and laity to be essentially distinct orders within the one community, just as in the Old Testament there were high priests, priests, Levites (Temple functionaries), and laymen. The principles of Clement and Ignatius became important when the church was faced by people claiming recognition for their special charismatic (spiritual) gifts and especially by Gnostic heretics claiming to possess secret oral traditions whispered by Jesus to his disciples and not contained in publicly accessible records such as the Gospels.

The authority of the duly authorized hierarchy became enhanced by the outcome of another 2nd-century debate, about the possibility of absolution for sins committed after Baptism. The *Shepherd of Hermas*, a book that enjoyed canonical status in some areas of the early church, enforced the point that excessive rigorism produces hypocrisies. By the 3rd century the old notion of the church as a society of holy people was being replaced by the conception that it was a school for frail sinners. In spite of protests, especially that of the schism led by the theologian and schismatic pope Novatian at Rome in 251, the final consensus held that the power to bind and loose (*cf.* Matt. 16:18–19), to excommunicate and absolve, was vested in bishops and presbyters by their ordination.

Expansion of administrative authority

In the East and in North Africa, each township normally had its own bishop. In the Western provinces, bishops were fewer and were responsible for larger areas, which, from the 4th century onward, were called by the (secular) term dioceses (administrative districts). In the 4th century, pressure to bring Western custom into line with Eastern and to multiply bishops was resisted on the ground that it would diminish the bishops' social status. By the end of the 3rd century, the bishop of the provincial capital was acquiring authority over his colleagues: the metropolitan (from the 4th century on, often entitled archbishop) was chief consecrator of his episcopal colleagues. The bishops of Rome, Alexandria, and Antioch in the 3rd century were accorded some authority beyond their own provinces. Along with Jerusalem and Constantinople (founded in 330), these three sees (seats of episcopal authority) became, for the Greeks, the five patriarchates. The title *papa* ("father") was for 600 years an affectionate term applied to any bishop to whom one's relation was intimate; it began to be specially used of bishops of Rome from the 6th century and by the 9th century was almost exclusively applied to them.

From the beginning, the Christians in Rome were aware of special responsibilities for them to lead the church. About AD 165, memorials were erected at Rome to the Apostles Peter and Paul, to Peter in a necropolis on the Vatican Hill, and to Paul on the road to Ostia. The construction reflects a sense of being guardians of an apostolic tradition, a self-consciousness expressed in another form when, c. 190, Bishop Victor of Rome threatened with excommunication Christians in Asia Minor who, following immemorial custom, observed Easter on the day of the Jewish Passover rather than (as at Rome) on the Sunday after the first full moon after the spring equinox. Stephen of Rome (256) is the first known pope to base claims to authority on Jesus' commission to Peter (Matt. 16:18–19).

Bishops were elected by their congregations—*i.e.*, by the clergy and laity assembled together. But the consent of the laity decreased in importance as recognition by other churches increased. The metropolitan and other provincial bishops became just as important as the congregation as a whole; and, though they could never successfully impose a man on a solidly hostile community, they could often prevent the appointment falling under the control of one powerful lay family or faction. From the 4th century on, the emperors occasionally intervened to fill important sees, but such occurrences were not a regular phenomenon (until the 6th century in Merovingian Gaul).

The problem of scriptural authority. After the initial problems regarding the continuity and authority of the hierarchy, the greatest guarantee of true continuity and authenticity was found in the Scriptures. Christians inherited (without debate at first) the Hebrew Bible as the Word of God to the people of God at a now superseded stage of their pilgrimage through history. If St. Paul's Gentile mission was valid, then the Old Testament Law was viewed as no longer God's final word to his people. Thus, the Hebrew Bible began to be called the *old* covenant. There was some hesitation in the church about the exact books included. The Greek version of the Old Testament (Septuagint) included books (such as the Wisdom of Solomon, Ecclesiasticus, and others) that were not accepted in the Hebrew canon. Most, but not all, Gentile Christian communities accepted the Septuagintal canon. The 3rd-century Alexandrian theologian Origen and especially the Latin biblical scholar Jerome (4th–5th century) believed it imprudent to base theological affirmations on books enjoying less than universal recognition. The fact that in many English Bibles the parts of the Old Testament accepted in the Septuagint but not in the Hebrew canon are often printed separately under the (misleading) title Apocrypha is a tribute to these ancient hesitations.

The emergence of a canon of Christian Scripture

The growth of the New Testament is more complex and controversial. First-century Christians used oral tradition more than writing to pass on the story of Jesus' acts and words, often told in the context of preaching and teaching. No one thought they needed to be in writing to bear authority. Mark first conceived the plan of composing a connected narrative. Nevertheless, even after the Gospels were in common circulation, oral tradition was still current and could even be preferred. A carefully copied document, however, provided greater security against contamination of the tradition. The Synoptic Gospels seem to have been used by the Apologist Justin Martyr at Rome c. AD 150 in the form of an early harmony (or synthesis of the Gospels); to this, Justin's Syrian pupil Tatian added the Gospel According to John to make his *Diatessaron* (according to the four), a harmony of all four Gospels so successful that in Mesopotamia (Tatian's homeland) it virtually ousted the separate Gospels for 250 years.

On a second grade of authority stood the apostolic letters, especially those of Paul. The main body of his correspondence was circulating as a corpus (body of writings) well before AD 90.

Paul's antitheses of law and grace, justice and goodness, and the letter and the spirit were extended further than Paul intended by the radical semi-Gnostic heretic Marcion of Pontus (c. 140–150), who taught that the Old Testament came from the inferior vengeful Jewish God of justice and that the New Testament told of the kindly universal Father. As the current texts of Gospels and letters presupposed some divine revelation through the Old Testament, Marcion concluded that they had been corrupted and interpolated by Judaizers. Marcion therefore established a fixed canon of an edited version of Luke's Gospel and some of the Pauline Letters (expurgated), and no Old Testament at all.

Significance of Marcion

The orthodox reaction (by such theologians as Justin, Irenaeus, and Tertullian in the 2nd century) was to insist on the Gospel as the fulfillment of prophecy and on creation as the ground of redemption. Reasons were found for accepting the four already current Gospels, the full corpus of Pauline Letters, Acts, John's Apocalypse (Revelation), and some of the Catholic Letters (these last—*i.e.*, I, II, and III John, James, and Jude—were the subject of hesitations). On the authorship of the Letter to the Hebrews there were doubts: Rome rejected it as non-Pauline and Alexandria accepted it as Pauline. The list once established was a criterion (the meaning of "canon") for the authentic Gospel of the new covenant and soon (by transference from the old) became entitled the New Testament. (The Greek word *diathēkē* means both covenant and testament.) The formation of the canon meant that special revelation ended with the death of the Apostles and that no authority could be attached to the apocryphal gospels, acts, and apocalypses proliferating in the 2nd century.

The problem of theological authority. Third, a check was found in the creed. At Baptism, after renouncing "the devil and his pomps," the initiate declared his faith in response to three questions of the form:

Do you believe in God the Father almighty? Do you believe in Jesus Christ his Son our Lord . . .? Do you believe in the Holy Spirit in the church and in the Resurrection?

In time, these interrogations became the basis of declaratory creeds, adapted for use by the clergy who felt themselves required to reassure colleagues who were not especially confident of their orthodoxy. The so-called Apostles' Creed is a direct descendant of the baptismal creed used at Rome by AD 200. Each church (or region) might have its own variant form. But all had the threefold structure.

The internal coherence given by creed, canon, and hierarchy was necessary both in the defense of authentic Christianity against Gnostic theosophical speculations and also in confronting pagan society. The strong coherence of the scattered congregations was remarkable to pagan observers.

Early heretical movements. Gnosticism was the greatest threat to Christianity before 150 and somewhat thereafter. Gnostics taught that there is total opposition between this evil world and God. Redemption was viewed as liberation from the chaos of a creation derived from either incompetent or malevolent powers, a world in which the elect are alien prisoners. The method of salvation was to discover the Kingdom of God within one's elect soul and to learn how to pass the hostile powers barring the soul's ascent to bliss. Gnosticism destroyed the notion of a historical disclosure of God. Its pessimism and dualism (in which matter was viewed as evil and spirit good) had disturbing moral consequences, involving both asceticism and libertinism. Its claims to a totally transcendent revelation were antirational, allowed for no natural goodness in the created order, and eliminated individual responsibility. Both the orthodox theologians and the pagan 3rd-century philosopher Plotinus dismissed Gnosticism as a pretentious but dangerous mumbo jumbo for misleading the half-educated.

The orthodox stressed the need to adhere to tradition, which was attested by the churches of apostolic foundation. A more hazardous reply was to appeal to ecstatic prophecy. About AD 172 a quasi-pentecostal movement in Phrygia was led by Montanus with two prophetesses, reasserting the imminence of the end of the world. He taught that there was an age of the Father (Old Testament), an age of the Son (New Testament), and an age of the Spirit (heralded by the prophet Montanus). Montanism won its chief convert in the Latin theologian Tertullian of Carthage (North Africa). Its claim to supplement the New Testament was generally rejected.

THE RELATIONSHIP BETWEEN CHRISTIANITY AND THE ROMAN GOVERNMENT AND THE HELLENISTIC CULTURE

Church–state relations. The Christians were not respectful toward ancestral pagan customs. Their preaching of a new king sounded like revolution. The opposition of the Jews to them led to breaches of the peace. Thus the Christians could very well be unpopular, and they often were. Paul's success at Ephesus provoked a riot to defend the cult of the goddess Artemis. In AD 64 a fire destroyed much of Rome; the emperor Nero killed a "vast

multitude" of Christians as scapegoats. For the first time, Rome was conscious that Christians were distinct from Jews. But there probably was no formal senatorial enactment proscribing Christianity at this time. Nero's persecution was local and short. Soon thereafter, however, the profession of Christianity was defined as a capital crime, though of a special kind because one gained pardon by apostasy (rejection of a faith once confessed) demonstrated by offering sacrifice to the pagan gods or the emperor. Popular gossip soon accused the Christians of secret vices, such as eating murdered infants (due to the secrecy surrounding the Lord's Supper and the use of the words "body" and "blood") and sexual promiscuity (due to the practice of Christians calling each other "brother" or "sister" while living as husband and wife). The governor of Bithynia in AD 111, the younger Pliny, told the emperor Trajan that to his surprise he discovered the Christians to be guilty of no vice, only of obstinacy and superstition. Nevertheless, he executed without a qualm those who refused to apostatize.

Early persecutions were sporadic, caused by local conditions and depending on the attitude of the governor. The fundamental cause of persecution was that the Christians conscientiously rejected the gods whose favour was believed to have brought success to the empire. But distrust was increased by Christian detachment and reluctance to serve in the imperial service and in the army. At any time in the 2nd or 3rd centuries, Christians could find themselves the object of unpleasant attention. A pogrom could be precipitated by a bad harvest, a barbarian attack, or a public festival of the emperor cult. Yet, long periods of peace occurred. In 248–250, when Germanic tribes threatened the empire, popular hostility culminated in the persecution under the emperor Decius (reigned 249–251): by edict all citizens were required to offer sacrifice and to obtain from commissioners a certificate witnessing to the act. Many of these certificates have survived. The requirement created an issue of conscience, especially because certificates could be bought by bribes. Under renewed attack (257–259), the great bishop-theologian Cyprian of Carthage was martyred. The persecuting emperor Valerian, however, became a Persian prisoner of war, and his son Gallienus issued an edict of toleration restoring confiscated churches and cemeteries. The church prospered from 261 to 303, but the empire suffered external attack, internal sedition, and rampant inflation. In February 303 the worst of all persecutions erupted under the co-emperors Diocletian and Galerius. The persecutions ended, and peace was reached with the Edict of Milan, a manifesto of toleration issued in 313 by the joint emperors Licinius and his Christian colleague Constantine. Disagreements about the point at which the state must be resisted led to long lasting schisms in Egypt (Melitianism) and North Africa (Donatism).

Christianity and classical culture. St. Paul could quote such pagan poets as Aratus, Menander, and Epimenides. Clement of Rome cited the dramatists Sophocles and Euripides. Educated Christians shared this literary tradition with educated pagans. The defenders of Christianity against pagan attack (especially Justin Martyr and Clement of Alexandria in the 2nd century) welcomed classical philosophy and literature; they wished only to reject all polytheistic myth and cult and all metaphysical and ethical doctrines irreconcilable with Christian belief (*e.g.*, Stoic materialism, Platonic doctrines of the transmigration of souls and the eternity of the world). Clement of Alexandria, second known head of the Catechetical school at Alexandria, possessed a wide erudition in the main classics and knew the works of Plato and Homer intimately. His successor at Alexandria, Origen, showed less interest in literary and aesthetic matters but was a greater scholar and thinker; he first applied the methods of Alexandrian philology to the text of the Bible.

Nevertheless, both pagans and Christians instinctively assumed the unity of ancient culture and pagan religion; it was hard for Christians to attack paganism without seeming negative toward the totality of classical culture as well as disaffected toward the imperial government.

Gnosticism and Montanism

Causes of persecutions

The urgent eschatological hope of the earliest church had built into its ethic a deep detachment from this world's goods, however beautiful they might be regarded. This detachment emerged in one form in the evaluation of celibacy as superior over marriage, in another in a conscious renunciation of pretensions to high culture (in the manner of the not always popular or socially accepted pre-Christian Cynic philosophers with whom pagans found it natural to compare the Christians). The passionate urgency of the Christian mission stamped any serious interest in science, history, or belles lettres with the stigma of worldliness.

Attitude of Christians toward other religions The attitude of the Christians toward other religions (except Judaism) was generally very negative. All forms of paganism—the Oriental mystery (salvational) religions of Isis, Attis, Adonis, and Mithra as well as the ancient cults of classical Greece and Rome—were regarded as the cults of evil spirits. Like the Jews, the Christians (unless Gnostic), were opposed to syncretism. With the exception of the notion of Baptism as a rebirth, Christians generally and significantly avoided the characteristic vocabularies of the mystery religions. The mysteries of Isis, Attis, Adonis, and (to some extent, perhaps) Mithra were basically fertility rites to ensure good crops. They answered to needs different from those addressed by the Christian gospel. A Mithraic rite with bread and water was noted by Justin Martyr as a counterpart of the bread and wine of the Christian Eucharist. The spring rites mourning Attis' death and then celebrating his revival at the festival known as the Hilaria offered a parallel to the ceremonies of Holy Week and Easter as developed in the 4th century. The point where parallel can be treated as influence, however, is a delicate matter to determine. Between Christianity and the pagan cults the most prominent difference consisted in the syncretistic tolerance of the latter; initiation into the mysteries of Isis did not mean renouncing allegiance to Apollo or Attis, whereas the Christian Baptism required exclusive devotion.

Many converts naturally brought old attitudes with them into the church. Amulets and peasant superstitions were long the object of critical attention by the clergy. The Christians tried to provide counterattractions by placing Christian festivals on the same days of the year as pagan feasts. Solar monotheism was popular in late-3rd-century paganism, and soon the Western churches were keeping the winter solstice (December 25) as Christ's nativity—the East kept January 6. Midsummer Day was replaced by the feast of John the Baptist. The church fought hard against the heathen celebration of January 1, but with little success. Only Easter (celebrating Christ's Resurrection) and Pentecost (celebrating the advent of the Holy Spirit) were feasts owing nothing to Gentile analogies for their origin; they both were derived from Jewish feasts. From the 5th century AD on, great pagan temples, such as the Parthenon in Athens (Greece), were gradually transformed into churches.

Apologetics. The Christian Apologists of the 2nd century sought to drive a wedge between the pagan religion that they abhorred and the Greek philosophy that, with occasional reservations, they welcomed. Second-century Platonism found it easy to think of Mind (*nous*) or Reason (*logos*) as divine power immanent within the world. Philo of Alexandria had spoken of the *logos* as mediating between the transcendent God and this created order. The *logos* theology was developed by Justin Martyr both to make a positive evaluation of the best elements in the Greek philosophical tradition and to make the incarnation of Christ intelligible to the Greek mind. But the Apologists upset some of their fellow Christians by talking of the divine *logos* as virtually a second God beside the Father and thus compromising the monotheism that the orthodox were defending against Gnostic dualism. The critics of the *logos* theology, labelled Monarchians, affirmed that Father, Son, and Spirit were one God; the three names were epithets, not substantives. In the 3rd century a Roman presbyter, Sabellius, was excommunicated for this opinion, and the defenders of the *logos* theology ousted the opponents of

speculative Apologetics. Clement of Alexandria and Origen provided the Greek churches with a Platonizing theology that was strongly opposed to the Monarchian position.

LITURGY, THE CALENDAR, MUSIC, ART, AND LITERATURE

Christian worship and practices Paul's letters mention worship on the first day of the week. In John's Apocalypse, Sunday is called "the Lord's day." The weekly commemoration of the Resurrection replaced for Christians the synagogue meetings on Saturdays; the practice of circumcision was dropped, and initiation was by Baptism; continuing membership of the church was signified by weekly participation in the Eucharist. Baptism in water in the name of Father, Son, and Holy Spirit was preceded by instruction (catechesis) and fasting. The person about to be baptized renounced evil and, as he made his declaration of faith, was dipped in water; he then received by anointing and by the laying on of hands (confirmation) the gift of the Holy Spirit and incorporation within the body of Christ, thus concluding the entire rite. Only the baptized were allowed to be admitted to the Eucharist, when the words of Jesus at the Last Supper were recalled; the Holy Spirit was invoked upon the people of God making the offering, and the consecrated bread and wine were distributed to the faithful. Accounts of these rites are given in the works of Justin (*c.* 150) and especially in the *Apostolic Tradition* of Hippolytus of Rome (*c.* 220).

To fall into a grave fault after Baptism entailed exclusion. The excommunicated person would continue to attend for the first part of the service, which included psalms, readings, and a sermon. Montanists, such as Tertullian, and the Roman schismatic Novatian denied the church's power to grant absolution. Even Cyprian of Carthage found Novatian easier to criticize for schism than for rigorism. But in the 3rd century a system of public penance emerged; it was allowed once a lifetime under condition of ascetic discipline. Penitents were restored to fellowship with church members by the laying on of hands. In time, less arduous and less public severities came to be required.

Before the 4th century, worship was in private houses. A house church of 232 AD has been excavated at Dura on the Euphrates. Whereas pagan temples were intended as the residence of the god, churches were designed for the community. The rectangular basilica with an apse (semicircular projection to house the altar) was found specially suitable. The Dura church has Gospel scenes on the walls. But many Old Testament heroes also appear in the earliest Christian art; Jewish models probably were followed. The artists also adapted conventional pagan forms (good shepherd; praying persons with hands uplifted). Fishing scenes, doves, and lyres also were popular. In themselves neutral, they carried special meaning to the Christians.

The words of several pre-Constantinian hymns survive (*e.g.,* "Shepherd of tender youth," by Clement of Alexandria), but only one with musical notation (Oxyrhynchus papyrus 1786 of the 3rd century).

The earliest Christians wrote to convert or to edify, not to please. Their literature was not produced with aesthetic intentions. Nevertheless, the pulpit offered scope for oratory (as in Melito of Sardis' *Homily on the Pascha, c.* 170). Desire for romance and adventure was satisfied by apocryphal Acts of the Apostles, recounting their travels, with continence replacing love. Justin and Irenaeus did not write for high style but simply to convey information. Apologists hoping for well-educated readers, however, could not be indifferent to literary tastes. By AD 200 the most graceful living writer of Greek literature was Clement of Alexandria, the liveliest writer of Latin, Tertullian. Wholly different in temperament (Clement urbane and allusive, Tertullian vigorous and vulgar), both men wrote distinguished prose with regard to form and rhetorical convention.

By the 3rd century the Bible needed explanation. Origen of Alexandria set out to provide commentaries and undertook for the Old Testament a collation of the various Greek versions with the original Hebrew. Many of

The Good Shepherd (centre), Orantes with uplifted hands, and (in the four quarters) the story of Jonah with figures derived from Greek mythological prototypes. Ceiling painting in the catacombs of SS. Peter and Marcellinus, Rome, 3rd century.

Vincenzo Biolghini

his sermons and commentaries were translated into Latin by Rufinus and Jerome (*c.* 385–400) and by their learning and passionate mystical aspiration deeply influenced Western medieval exegesis (critical interpretive methods).

II. From Constantine to Gregory the Great

THE PROBLEMS OF THE ALLIANCE
BETWEEN CHURCH AND EMPIRE

Constantine the Great, declared emperor at York, Britain (306), was converted to Christianity (312), became sole emperor (324), virtually presided over the ecumenical Council of Nicaea (325), founded the city of Constantinople (330), and died in 337. Fourth-century men regarded him as the great revolutionary, especially in religion. He did not make Christianity the religion of the empire, but his foundation of Constantinople (conceived to be the new Rome) as a Christian city profoundly affected the future political and ecclesiastical structure. Relations with old Rome were not to be cordial either in matters of church or state. Despite massive legislation (some attempting to express Christian ideals—*e.g.*, making Sunday a rest day), he failed to check the drastic inflation (that began *c.* 250), which soon created deep unrest and weakened the empire before the barbarian invasions of the 5th century.

Constantine brought the church out of its withdrawal from the world to accept social responsibility and helped pagan society to be won for the church. On both sides, the alliance of the church and emperor evoked opposition, which among the Christians emerged in the monks' retirement to the desert. Except for the brief reign of Julian the Apostate (361–363), pagans relapsed into passive resistance. The quietly mounting pressure against paganism in the 4th century culminated in the decrees of Emperor Theodosius I (reigned 379–395), who made orthodox Christianity an ingredient of good citizenship. Under Theodosius many pagan temples were closed or even destroyed (*e.g.*, the Alexandrian Serapeum). But until the time of Justinian (reigned 527–565), pagans were largely unmolested by the government. Heretics were more harshly treated. Ecclesiastical censures (from 314 on) were often enforced by the civil penalty of exile. One heretic, Priscillian, was even executed for witchcraft (385), but in the face of vehement church protests. The link between church and state was expressed in the

Marginal note: Constantinople as the new Rome

civil dignity and insignia granted to bishops, who also began to be entrusted with ambassadorial roles. By 400 the patriarch of Constantinople (to his avowed embarrassment) enjoyed precedence at court before all civil officials. In the writings of Ambrose (bishop of Milan, 374–397), "Roman" and "Christian" are almost synonyms. The Arian controversy (involving a denial of the divinity of Jesus) developed into a conflict between church and state when the emperor Constantius was supporting Arianism; and Ambrose enforced upon Theodosius submission to the church as its son, not its master. With an orthodox emperor, however, most Christians thought of church and empire as virtually coterminous.

The church was significantly slow to undertake missionary work beyond the frontiers of the empire. The Goth Ulfilas converted the Goths to Arianism (*c.* 340–350) and translated the Bible, omitting, as unsuitable, warlike passages of the Old Testament. The Goths passed their Arian faith on to other Germanic tribes, such as the Vandals. (The first tribe to become Catholic was the Franks, *c.* 506, soon to be followed by the Visigoths.) In the 5th century the Western provinces were overrun by the barbarian Goths, Vandals, and Huns. The Roman Army had long drawn its recruits from the barbarian tribesmen and was itself now under barbarian generals. Theodosius I's will placed his two sons under the guardianship of the barbarian general Stilicho, who effectively ruled until they were able to assume responsibility. In the 5th century, Western emperors exercised less power than generals, and the imperial succession ended when a German leader, Odoacer, decided (476) to rule without an emperor. The end of the line of Western emperors made little difference to either church or state. In the West the position of the papacy was enhanced by its decline, and this prepared the way for the popes' temporal sovereignty over parts of Italy (which they retained from the 7th to the 19th centuries).

The barbarian invasions destroyed Western schools. Specifically church schools were first created in late antiquity. The main preservers and transmitters of ancient culture, however, were the monks. Monasticism had begun in the Egyptian desert in the 4th century with Anthony the Hermit and with Pachomius, the first organizer of an ascetic community under a rule of obedience. Basil, bishop of Cappadocian Caesarea (370–379), rejected the hermit ideal and insisted on communities with a rule safeguarding the bishop's authority and with concrete acts of service to perform (*e.g.*, hospital work and teaching). The monastic ideal quickly spread to the West but owed its decisive shape there to John Cassian of Marseilles (*c.* 360–435) and Benedict of Nursia (*c.* 480–*c.* 550). The manual work of monks often was the copying of manuscripts. Benedict's contemporary Cassiodorus (*c.* 485–582) had the works of classical authors copied (*e.g.*, Cicero and Quintilian) as well as Bibles and the works of the early Church Fathers.

THEOLOGICAL CONTROVERSIES
OF THE 4TH AND 5TH CENTURIES

Western controversies. Until about 250 most Western Christian leaders were Greek, not Latin, speakers (*e.g.*, Irenaeus and Hippolytus). The main Latin theology came not from Rome but from North Africa (*e.g.*, Tertullian and Cyprian). Tertullian wrote *Against Praxeas*, in which he discussed the doctrines of the Trinity and the Person of Christ. But in 251 Novatian's schism at Rome diverted interest away from speculative theology to juridical questions about the membership of the church and the validity of sacraments. These questions dominated not only the career of Cyprian (bishop of Carthage, 248–258) but all North African church life as a result of a schism at Carthage led (from 313) by the schismatic Donatus. The Donatist issue turned on whether the validity of the sacraments depended on the worthiness of the minister. Cyprian and the Donatists said that the validity of the sacraments involved the worthiness of the minister; Rome and North African Christians in communion with Rome said that it did not because the sacraments were Christ's, not man's. Thus, even if in-

Marginal notes: Relationships with the barbarians

Donatism, Pelagianism, Arianism, and Monophysitism

efficacious, Baptism could be validly administered by a schismatic. Much of the great theologian Augustine's energies as bishop of Hippo (from 395 to 430) went into trying to settle the Donatist issue, in which he finally despaired of rational argument and came to justify the use of coercion.

The other major controversy of the Western Church was a more confused issue, viz., whether faith is caused by divine grace or human freedom. Augustine ascribed all credit to God. The British monk Pelagius protested that Augustine was destroying responsibility and denying the capacity of man to do what God commands. Both men applied inappropriate, impersonal categories of thought to the problem; and though Pelagianism was condemned, several of the extreme positions of Augustine (especially on predestination and the transmission of original sin) failed to receive the church's cordial endorsement.

Eastern controversies. In the Greek East, the 4th century was dominated by controversy about the propositions of Arius, an Alexandrian presbyter (died c. 335), that the incarnate Lord who was born, wept, suffered, and died could not be one with the transcendent first cause of creation who is beyond all suffering. The Council of Nicaea (325) condemned Arianism and affirmed the Son of God to be identical in essence with the Father. As this formula included no safeguard against Monarchianism, a long controversy followed, especially after Constantine's death (337). Athanasius, bishop of Alexandria (328–373), fought zealously against Arianism in the East and owed much to Rome's support, which made the controversy add to the tensions between East and West. These tensions survived the settlement of the Arian quarrel when the Council of Constantinople (381) eliminated Arianism in the East but also asserted Constantinople to be the second see of Christendom, as the new Rome. This assertion was unwelcome to Alexandria, traditionally second city of the empire, and to Rome because it implied that the dignity of a bishop depended on the secular standing of his city. Rivalry between Alexandria and Constantinople led to the fall of John Chrysostom, patriarch of Constantinople (398–404), when he appeared to support Egyptian monks who admired the controversial theology of Origen. It became a major feature of the emerging Christological debate (the controversy over the nature of Christ).

The Christological controversy stemmed from the rival doctrines of Apollinaris of Laodicea (flourished 360–380) and Theodore of Mopsuestia (c. 350–428), representatives of the rival schools of Alexandria and Antioch, respectively. At the Council of Ephesus (431), led by Cyril, patriarch of Alexandria (412–444), an extreme Antiochene Christology—taught by Nestorius, patriarch of Constantinople—was condemned for saying that the man Jesus is an independent person beside the divine Word and that therefore Mary, the mother of Jesus, may not properly be called mother of God (Greek *theotokos*, or "God bearer"). Cyril's formula was "one nature of the Word incarnate." A reaction led by Pope Leo I (died 461) against this one-nature (Monophysite) doctrine culminated in the Council of Chalcedon (451), which affirmed Christ to be two natures in one person (hypostasis). Thus, the Council of Chalcedon alienated Monophysite believers in Egypt and Syria.

During the next 250 years the Byzantine emperors and patriarchs desperately sought to reconcile the Monophysites. Three successive attempts failed: (1) under the emperor Zeno (482) the *Henotikon* (union formula) offended Rome by suggesting that Monophysite criticism of Chalcedon might be justified; (2) under the emperor Justinian (reigned 527–565) the Chalcedonian definition was glossed by condemning the "Three Chapters," which includes the writings of Theodore of Mopsuestia, Theodoret, and Ibas, all strong critics of Cyril of Alexandria's theology and of Monophysitism; and the Syrian Monophysite Jacob Baradaeus reacted to this by creating a rival Monophysite episcopate and permanent schism; (3) under the emperor Heraclius (610–641) the Chalcedonians invited the Monophysites to reunite under the formula that Christ had two natures but only one will (Monotheletism), but this reconciled almost no Monophysites and created divisions among the Chalcedonians themselves.

POPULAR CHRISTIANITY IN THE LATE EMPIRE

The continuity of pre-Christian antiquity and Christian society is nowhere more apparent than in popular religious practice. Pagans were normally devoted to local shrines of particular gods. The church tried to meet this psychological need by establishing shrines of martyrs. The martyr cult, a matter of private devotion from 150 until 250, became so popular after the Decian persecution that official control was required. Invocation of Mary as "mother of God" is first attested in a 3rd-century papyrus. At Rome the shrines of Peter and Paul, where Constantine built basilicas, attracted many pilgrims. The holy places in Jerusalem and Bethlehem, however, were pre-eminent. Preachers might warn that pilgrimage did not necessarily bring one nearer to God and that one must not worship the martyrs being venerated, but that at the popular level such exhortations seemed sophisticated. The bones of martyrs and holy men were so treasured that a traffic in bogus relics was created. By 400, particular saints were being invoked for particular needs (one for health, another for fertility, travel, prediction, or the detection of perjury). When the barbarian leader Alaric's Goths sacked Rome (410), citizens asked why Peter and Paul had failed to protect their city.

Pagan critics said that the old gods, true givers of success and miracle, were offended by neglect. To meet such criticisms the churches found it necessary to provide similar assurances of success, miraculous cures, and patron saints. By the 6th century, wonder-working shrines, cloths that had touched holy relics, and pictures (icons) were invested with numinous (spiritual) power. Because of the anti-elitist ideology of the Christian tradition, even highly educated figures such as Augustine and Pope Gregory the Great (died 604) were sympathetic to this popular movement. It became a means of winning the barbarian tribesmen.

LITURGY, MUSIC, ARCHITECTURE, AND LITERATURE

The veneration of martyrs and the growth of pilgrimages stimulated liturgical elaboration. Great centres (Jerusalem and Rome, in particular) became models for others, which encouraged regional standardization and cross-fertilization. Though the pattern of the eucharistic liturgy was settled by the 4th century, there were many variant forms, especially of the central prayer called by the Greeks *anaphora* ("offering") and by the Latins *canon* ("prescribed form"). Liturgical prayers of Basil of Caesarea became widely influential in the East. Later, liturgies were ascribed to local saints and heroes: Jerusalem's to St. James, Alexandria's to St. Mark, and Constantinople's to John Chrysostom. The spirit of Greek liturgies encouraged rich and imaginative prose. Latin style was restrained, with epigrammatical antitheses; and the Roman Church changed from Greek to Latin about 370 AD. The Canon of the Latin mass as used in the 6th century was already close to the form it has since retained.

Music also became elaborate, with antiphonal psalm chanting. Some reaction came from those who believed that the music was obscuring the words. Both Athanasius of Alexandria and Augustine defended music on the condition that the sense of the words remained primary in importance. The Latin theologians Ambrose of Milan, Prudentius, and Venantius Fortunatus provided Latin hymns of distinction. The ascription of the Roman chants (Gregorian) to Pope Gregory the Great was first made in the 9th century. In the Greek East in the time of Justinian, Romanos created the kontakion, a long poetic homily.

Architecture was stimulated by Constantine's great buildings at Jerusalem and Rome. The exteriors of these churches remained simple, but inside they were richly ornamented with marble and mosaic, the decoration being arranged on a coherent plan to represent the angels

Emergence of the cult of martyrs and saints

Development of new forms of worship

Christ as Ruler, with the Apostles and Evangelists (represented by the beasts). The female figures are believed to be either Santa Pudenziana and Santa Praxedes or symbols of the Jewish and Gentile churches. Mosaic in the apse of Sta. Pudenziana, Rome, AD 401–417.
De Antonis

and saints in heaven with whom the church on earth was joining for worship. An enormous number of churches built in and after the 4th century have been excavated. The outstanding buildings that survive largely intact belong to the age of Justinian (6th century) and are at Constantinople and Ravenna (Italy).

The veneration of saints led to the production of a specific category of literature known as hagiography. If available, authentic tradition would be used; but if there was none, the writers felt quite free to create a biography from conventional materials and elements of folklore. The lives of saints belong to the poetry of the Middle Ages but are important to the historian as documents of social history.

Historical and polemical writings

The first known church historian was Eusebius, bishop of Caesarea (died c. 340), who carefully collected records up to the advent of Constantine. His work was translated and continued in Latin by Rufinus of Aquileia. The history of the church from Constantine to about 430 was continued by three Greek historians: Socrates, Sozomen, and Theodoret (whose works were adapted for the Latin world by Cassiodorus). The Eastern Church from 428 to 594 was chronicled by Evagrius of Antioch. The consequences of Chalcedon as interpreted by Monophysite historians were recorded by Timothy Aelurus, Zacharias of Mitylene, and John of Nikiu.

The monastic movement produced its own special literature, especially the classic *Life of Anthony* by Athanasius, the collections of sayings of the Desert Fathers, John Climacus' *Heavenly Ladder*, and Moschus' *Spiritual Meadow*.

The Arian and Christological controversies produced important polemical writers—Athanasius, the three Cappadocian Fathers (Basil, Gregory of Nazianzus, and Gregory of Nyssa), Cyril of Alexandria, and Theodoret. After 500, Monophysite theology had eminent figures—Severus of Antioch and the Alexandrian grammarian John Philoponus, who was also a commentator on Aristotle and a scientist. But much theology was nonpolemical—*e.g.*, catechesis and biblical commentaries. The quantity of exegesis became so great that, in the 6th century, "chains" (*catenae*) began to be produced in which the reader was given a summary of the exegesis of a succession of commentators on each verse.

In the West, Hilary of Poitiers, Ambrose of Milan, and,

above all, the incomparable scholar Jerome gave Latin theology confidence and so made possible the massive achievement of Augustine—the exquisite prose of his Confessions and his majestic treatises *On the Trinity* and *The City of God*.

III. East and West

POLITICAL RELATIONS

The old tensions between East and West were sharpened by the quarrels about Chalcedon. In Rome every concession made by Constantinople toward the Monophysites increased the distrust. Justinian's condemnation of the Three Chapters (Fifth Council, Constantinople, 553) was forced on a reluctant West, where it created temporary schisms but was eventually accepted. From the time of Pope Gregory I (reigned 590–604) the papacy—encouraged by the successful mission to the Anglo-Saxons—was looking as much to the Western barbarian kingdoms as to Byzantium.

Reciprocal influences between theology and political thought and action

In the 7th century the Eastern Empire was fighting for its life, first against the Persians and then the Arabs, and the Balkans were occupied by the Slavs. The submergence of Alexandria, Antioch, and Jerusalem under Muslim rule left the patriarch of Constantinople with enhanced authority, whereas the Slav invasions drove a wedge between East and West that encouraged separate developments. The attempts of the Byzantine emperors to force the papacy to accept the Monothelite (one-will) compromise produced a martyr pope, Martin (649–655); the story of his tortures did nothing to make Rome love the Byzantines. When the Monothelite heresy was finally rejected at the Sixth Council (Constantinople, 680–681), the imprudent pope Honorius (625–638), who had supported Monothelitism, was expressly condemned, which distressed Roman defenders of papal prerogatives. Greek hostility to the West became explicit in the canons of a council held at Constantinople (Quinisext, 692) that claimed to have ecumenical status but was not recognized in Rome.

From 726 on, Byzantium was absorbed in the iconoclastic (destruction of images) debate, which became a struggle not only to keep icons but also to combat the subjection of the church to the will of the emperor. The imperial attack on images was severely criticized in the West. Yet, after the Greek iconoclasts were condemned at the Seventh Council (Nicaea, 787), the bishops of the

Frankish king Charlemagne at the synod of Frankfurt in Germany (794)—with the reluctant consent of Pope Adrian I (reigned 772–795)—censured the decision. A renewed upsurge of iconoclasm in the East (815–843) produced a counterreaction in the West, and ultimately the West accepted the decisions of the Seventh Council. Icons were differently evaluated in the Western churches, where holy pictures were viewed as devotional aids, not, as was the case in the East, virtually sacramental media of salvation.

The greatest protagonist of icons was John of Damascus, an Arab monk in Muslim Palestine, who was the author of an encyclopaedic compendium of logic and theology. Within the empire, Theodore, abbot of the Studium (monastery) at Constantinople, vigorously attacked iconoclasm; he also led a revival of monasticism and stressed the importance of copying manuscripts. His ideals passed to the monastic houses that began to appear on Mount Athos from 963 onward.

The hostility between the iconoclast emperors and the popes encouraged the 8th-century popes to seek a protector. This was provided by the rise of Charles Martel (719–741) and the Franks. The Frankish kings guarded Western Church interests, and the papal–Frankish alliance reached its climax in the papal coronation of Charlemagne as the first Holy Roman emperor at Rome on Christmas Day, 800—the Holy Roman Empire lasted until 1806. Charlemagne exercised immense authority over the Western Church, and the Carolingian revival of church life produced theological controversies about predestination (Gottschalk, Erigena, Hincmar of Reims) and about the Eucharist (Paschasius Radbertus, Ratramnus, Rabanus Maurus). The Christological controversy had a late revival with a Spanish dispute as to whether Christ was adopted to be Son of God.

In the chaos of the rapid Frankish decline, the papacy was glad to look again to Constantinople for protection. The emperor Basil I (867–886), founder of the Macedonian dynasty, could not prevent the Arabs from taking Sicily, but he was able to re-establish Byzantine control in south Italy.

In the 10th century, however, the West passed under the control of the Ottonian dynasty in Germany. The Ottos, accustomed to the system where great landowners built and owned the churches on their estates as private property, treated Rome and all important sees in this spirit. Bishops were appointed on royal nomination and forbidden to appeal to Rome.

The rise of Islām and the Arab campaign to subjugate unbelievers by military conquest broke upon the Byzantine Empire in 634, just as it was exhausted after defeating Persia. The will to resist was wholly absent. Moreover, the provinces initially overrun, Syria (636) and Egypt (641), were already alienated from the Byzantine government that was persecuting Monophysites in those areas. In 678 and again in 718, the Arabs were at the walls of Constantinople. In the West, their defeat by Charles Martel at Poitiers, France (732), limited their advance to the Pyrenees. The Monophysite Copts in Egypt and Syrian Jacobites (followers of Jacob Baradaeus) soon found that they enjoyed greater toleration under Muslim Arabs than under Chalcedonian Byzantines, just as in later times the Greeks were to discover more religious freedom under Turkish than under Latin rule. In the 8th century the Muslims were more a military than a theological threat, and a considerable time passed before Christian and Muslim theologians engaged in serious dialogue.

LITERATURE AND ART

The Monothelite and iconoclastic controversies produced herculean theological endeavours: the criticism of Monothelitism by the monk Maximus the Confessor (580–662) was based upon subtle and very careful considerations of the implications of Chalcedon. The great opponents of iconoclasm, John of Damascus and Theodore of Studium, also composed hymns and other theological treatises. Greek mystical theology had an outstanding representative in Symeon the New Theologian (949–1022),

abbot of St. Menas at Constantinople, whose doctrines about light visions anticipated the hesychasm (quietistic prayer methods) of Gregory Palamas in the 14th century. But the most learned theologian of the age was beyond doubt the patriarch Photius (see below *The Photian schism*).

Iconoclasm was not an anti-intellectual, anti-art movement. The iconoclasts everywhere replaced figures with the cross or with exquisite patterns. The ending of iconoclasm in 843 (the restoration of orthodoxy), however, liberated the artists adept in mosaic and fresco to portray figures once again, and this created a new revival of decoration. Music also became more elaborate; the kontakion was replaced by the *kanon*, a cycle of nine odes, each of six to nine stanzas and with a different melody. The *kanon* gave more scope to the musicians by providing greater variety (nine melodies where the kontakion had only one). Byzantine hymns were classified according to their mode, and the mode changed each week. Besides John of Damascus, the great hymn writers of this period were Cosmas of Jerusalem, Theodore of Studium, and Joseph of Studium.

The so-called Dark Ages in the West produced virtually no sculpture or painting—other than illuminated manuscripts, of which marvellous specimens were made (*e.g.*, the Book of Kells and the Lindisfarne Gospels). The Irish and Anglo-Saxon monks did not construct noble buildings but knew how to write and to illuminate a book. In the age of Charlemagne exquisite calligraphy was continued (*e.g.*, the Utrecht Psalter), with intricate ivory and metalwork of superb finesse. Great buildings also began to emerge, partly based on Byzantine models, such as the churches at Ravenna, Italy. The Ottonian renaissance in Germany encouraged even more confidently the erection of church buildings, producing such masterpieces as the surviving cathedrals at Hildesheim and Spires and setting out a characteristically German style of architecture.

The barbarian kingdoms soon produced their own Christian literature: Gregory of Tours wrote the history of the Franks, Isidore of Seville (560–636) that of the Visigoths, Cassiodorus that of the Ostrogoths. Isidore, utilizing his vast reading, compiled encyclopaedias on everything from liturgical ceremonies to the natural sciences. The outstanding figure of this incipient "nationalist" movement was the English monk Bede, whose *Ecclesiastical History of the English People* was completed in 731 and whose exegetical works came to stand beside Augustine and Gregory the Great as indispensable for the medieval student.

MISSIONS AND MONASTICISM

The Arian barbarians soon became Catholics, including, by 700, even the Lombards in north Italy. There remained immense areas of Europe, however, to which the Gospel had not yet been brought. Gregory the Great evangelized the Anglo-Saxons, who in turn sent missionaries to northwestern Europe—Wilfrid and Willibrord to what is now The Netherlands, and Boniface to Hesse, Thuringia, and Bavaria. In consequence of Boniface's work in Germany, a mission to Scandinavia was initiated by Ansgar (801–865) and the mission reached Iceland by 996. In the 10th century the mission from Germany moved eastward to Bohemia, to the Magyars, and (from 966) to the Poles. By 1050 most of Europe was under Christian influence with the exception of Muslim Spain.

In the Byzantine sphere, early missions went to the Hunnish tribesmen north of the Caucasus. The Nestorians, entrenched in Persia, carried the Gospel to the Turkmen and across Central Asia to China. In the 9th century the mission to the Slavs began with the work of Cyril and Methodius, who created a Slavonic alphabet and translated the Bible into the Slavonic language. Although their labours in Moravia were undermined by Frankish clergy, it was their achievement that made possible the faith and medieval culture of both Russia and Serbia.

The Benedictine Rule—initiated by Benedict of Nursia

The Holy Roman Empire

The Dark Ages in the West and the influence of missions

Conversion of northern and eastern tribes and peoples

Virgin Mary with (left) Justinian, holding a model of Hagia Sophia, and (right) Constantine,
holding a model of the city of Constantinople. Mosaic from Hagia Sophia, 9th century.
By courtesy of the Dumbarton Oaks Center for Byzantine Studies, Washington, D.C.

(died *c.* 547)—succeeded in the West because of its simplicity and restraint; more formidable alternatives were available in the 6th century. By 800, abbeys existed throughout western Europe, and the observance of Benedict's Rule was fostered by Charlemagne and his son Lewis the Pious. These houses, such as Bede's monastery at Jarrow (England) or the foundations of Columban (540–615) at Luxeuil (France) and Bobbio (Italy), became centres of study and made possible the Carolingian renaissance of learning. In this renaissance the 8th-century English scholar Alcuin and his monastery at Tours occupy the chief place. Around monasteries and cathedrals, schools were created to teach acceptable Latin, to write careful manuscripts, and to study not only the Bible and Fathers but also science. Scribes developed the beautiful script that was known as Carolingian minuscule. The Carolingian renaissance was short-lived, however, and decay began to set in (850–950) and was not checked until the foundation of the monastery at Cluny (France) in 909.

Monasticism in 9th-century Byzantium was centred upon the Studites, who came to be a faction against the court. A more remote and otherworldly asceticism developed with the foundation of monasteries on Mount Athos (Greece) from 963 onward. A distinctive feature of Athonite monasticism was that nothing female was to be allowed on the peninsula.

THE PHOTIAN SCHISM AND THE GREAT EAST–WEST SCHISM

The Photian schism. The end of iconoclasm (843) left a legacy of faction. Ignatius, patriarch of Constantinople intermittently from 847 to 877, was exiled by the government in 858 and replaced by Photius, a scholarly layman who was head of the imperial chancery—he was elected patriarch and ordained within six days. Ignatius' supporters dissuaded Pope Nicholas I (reigned 858–867) from recognizing Photius. Nicholas was angered by Byzantine missions among the Bulgars, whom he regarded as belonging to his sphere. When Nicholas wrote to the Bulgars attacking Greek practices, Photius replied by accusing the West of heretically altering the creed in saying that the Holy Spirit proceeds from the Father *and the Son* (Filioque). He declared Pope Nicholas deposed (867), but his position was not strong enough for such imprudence.

A new emperor, Basil the Macedonian, reinstated Ignatius; and in 869 Nicholas' successor, Adrian II (reigned 867–872), condemned Photius and sent legates to Constantinople to extort submission to papal supremacy from the Greeks. The Greeks resented the papal demands, and when Ignatius died (877) Photius quietly became patriarch again. Rome (at that moment needing Byzantine military support against Muslims in Sicily and southern Italy) reluctantly agreed to recognize Photius, but on the condition of an apology and of the withdrawal of Greek missions to the Bulgars. Photius acknowledged Rome as the first see of Christendom, discreetly said nothing explicitly against the Filioque clause, and agreed to the provision that the Bulgars could be put under Roman jurisdiction providing that Greek missions were allowed to continue.

The main issue in the Photian schism was whether Rome possessed monarchical power of jurisdiction over all churches (as Nicholas and Adrian held), or whether Rome was the senior of five semi-independent patriarchates (as Photius and the Greeks thought) and therefore could not canonically interfere with the internal affairs of another patriarchate.

The great East–West schism. The mutual distrust shown in the time of Photius erupted again in the middle of the 11th century after papal enforcement of Latin customs upon Greeks in southern Italy. The patriarch of Constantinople, Michael Cerularius, closed Latin churches in Constantinople as a reprisal. Cardinal Humbert came from Italy to protest, was accorded an icy reception, and left a bull of excommunication (July 16, 1054) on the altar of the great church Hagia Sophia. The bull anathematized (condemned) Michael Cerularius, the Greek doctrine of the Holy Spirit, the marriage of Greek priests, and the Greek use of leavened bread for the Eucharist.

At the time, the breach was treated as a minor storm in

The significance of the date 1054

which both sides had behaved with some arrogance. As Greeks and Latins became more estranged, however, people looked back on the events of 1054 as the moment of the final breach between East and West. (Not until December 7, 1965, were the mutual excommunications of 1054 abolished, by Pope Paul VI and the ecumenical patriarch Athenagoras I.)

BIBLIOGRAPHY. The best guides to the first four or five centuries of Christianity are L.M.O. DUCHESNE, *Early History of the Christian Church*, 3 vol. (1909–24); H. LIETZMANN, *Geschichte der alten Kirche*, 4 vol. (1932–44; Eng. trans., *A History of the Early Church*, 1950–52); H. VON CAMPEN-HAUSEN, *Die Griechischen Kirchenväter*, 2nd ed. (1956; Eng. trans., *The Fathers of the Greek Church*, 1959), and *Latein-ische Kirchenväter* (1960; Eng. trans., *The Fathers of the Latin Church*, 1964); a short outline in H. CHADWICK, *The Early Church* (1967); and R.W. SOUTHERN, *Western Society and the Church in the Middle Ages* (1970). Full bibliographies of the Church Fathers may be found in B. ALTANER, *Patrologie*, 6th ed. (1960; Eng. trans., 1960); and J. QUASTEN, *Patrology* (1950–   ). On the relation of the early church to state and society, see R.M. GRANT, *Augustus to Constantine* (1970); W.H.C. FREND, *Martyrdom and Persecution in the Early Church* (1956). On the pagan background, see A.D. NOCK, *Conversion* (1933), and *Early Gentile Christianity and Its Hellenistic Background* (1964).

For discussions on more specialized topics, see V. TCHERI-KOVER, *Hellenistic Civilization and the Jews* (Eng. trans., 1959); P. FEINE and J. BEHM, *Einleitung in das Neue Testament*, 14th rev. ed. by W.G. KUMMEL (1965; Eng. trans., *Introduction to the New Testament*, 1966); F.F. BRUCE, *New Testament History* (1969); A.N. SHERWIN-WHITE, *Roman Society and Roman Law in the New Testament* (1963); M. BLACK, *The Scrolls and Christian Origins* (1961); R.M. GRANT, *Gnosticism and Early Christianity*, 2nd ed. (1966); H. JONAS, *The Gnostic Religion* (1958); W. TELFER, *The Office of a Bishop* (1962); A. VON HARNACK, *Die Mission und Ausbreitung des Christentums in den ersten drei Jahrhunderten*, 2 vol. (1902; Eng. trans., *The Mission and Expansion of Christianity in the First Three Centuries*, 2nd rev. and enl. ed., 1908, reprinted 1962). On Christian apologetic, see C. BIGG, *The Christian Platonists of Alexandria* (1913, reprinted 1969); H. CHADWICK, *Early Christian Thought and the Classical Tradition* (1966); T.D. BARNES, *Tertullian* (1972); G.S.M. WALKER, *The Churchmanship of St. Cyprian* (1968).

For the 4th century, see R. MACMULLEN, *Constantine* (1969); A.H.M. JONES, *Constantine and the Conversion of Europe* (1948); S.L. GREENSLADE, *Schism in the Early Church* (1953); W.H.C. FREND, *The Donatist Church*, 2nd ed. (1971); A. MOMIGLIANO (ed.), *The Conflict Between Paganism and Christianity in the Fourth Century* (1963); K.M. SETTON, *Christian Attitude Towards the Emperor in the Fourth Century* (1941); J.N.D. KELLY, *Early Christian Creeds* (1950). On monks, see O. CHADWICK, *John Cassian*, 2nd ed. (1968); K.E. KIRK, *The Vision of God* (1931); D.J. CHITTY, *The Desert a City* (1966).

For the 5th century, see G. BONNER, *St. Augustine of Hippo* (1964); P. BROWN, *Augustine of Hippo* (1967); F. VAN DER MEER, *Augustine the Bishop* (1962); S. DILL, *Roman Society in the Last Century of the Western Empire*, 2nd ed. (1899). On theological controversies, see A. GRILLMEIER, *Die theologische und sprachliche Vorbereitung der christologischen Formel von Chalkedon* (1954; Eng. trans., *Christ in Christian Tradition*, 1965); J.N.D. KELLY, *Early Christian Doctrines*, 4th ed. (1958).

For after the 5th century, see H. ST. L.B. MOSS, *The Birth of the Middle Ages* (1935); M.L.W. LAISTNER, *Thought and Letters in Western Europe A.D. 500 to 900*, rev. ed. (1957); E.C. BUTLER, *Benedictine Monachism*, 2nd ed. (1924); D. KNOWLES, *Christian Monasticism* (1969); and with D. OBO-LENSKY, *The Christian Centuries*, vol. 2, *The Middle Ages* (1968), for a masterly general survey.

For the East, see J.M. HUSSEY, *The Byzantine World* (1957); G. OSTROGORSKY, *History of the Byzantine State* (1956; Eng. trans. from Russian, 1947), the best outline; N.H. BAYNES, *Byzantine Studies and Other Essays* (1955); J.M. HUSSEY (ed.), *The Cambridge Mediaeval History*, vol. 4, 2 pts. (1966–67); F. DVORNIK, *The Photian Schism* (1948); S. RUN-CIMAN, *The Eastern Schism* (1955). On music, see E. WEL-LESZ, *A History of Byzantine Music and Hymnography*, rev. ed. (1971).

On liturgy, see J.A. JUNGMANN, *The Early Liturgy to the Time of Gregory the Great* (1961); T. KLAUSER, *The Western Liturgy and Its History* (Eng. trans., 1952), and *Kleine abendländische Liturgiegeschichte*, 5th ed. (1965; Eng. trans., *A Short History of the Western Liturgy*, 1969).

On art, see W.F. VOLBACH, *Frühchristliche Kunst* (1958; Eng. trans., *Early Christian Art*, 1962); F. VAN DER MEER and C. MOHRMANN, *Atlas van de oudchristelijke wereld* (1958; Eng. trans., *Atlas of the Early Christian World*, 1958); JEAN LAS-SUS, *The Early Christian and Byzantine World* (1967); G. BOVINI, *Mosaici di Ravenna* (1956; Eng. trans., *Ravenna Mosaics*, 1956); D. TALBOT RICE, *Art of the Byzantine Era* (1963); R. KRAUTHEIMER, *Early Christian and Byzantine Architecture* (1965).

(H.Cha.)

Christian Mysticism

Christian mysticism here refers to the human soul's direct experience of oneness with ultimate Reality, or God, in the context of the Christian faith. This article deals with the history, phases, and forms of mysticism in Christianity.

NATURE AND SIGNIFICANCE

The essence of mysticism is the sense of contact with the Divine or Transcendent, involving in its higher forms the experience of union with divine Reality. Whatever may be one's judgment of its value, there can be no doubt that mysticism has played an important role in the history of the Christian religion. In the religion of Paul and John "Christ-mysticism" is fundamental; in the life of the Eastern Church mystical aims and methods have been pursued from an early period; in the West, mysticism was of vital importance during the Middle Ages; it was a significant factor in the 16th and 17th centuries; and it has once again become a noticeably living influence in recent times.

Mysticism underlies some of the greatest cultural achievements of Christianity—from the writings of Paul and John through the *Confessions* of St. Augustine, the work of Dante Alighieri, *Imitatio Christi* (*Imitation of Christ;* often attributed to Thomas à Kempis), the sermons of St. Bernard of Clairvaux, of Meister Eckehart, and Johannes Tauler to the inspired prose of William Law and Thomas Traherne and the poems of Henry Vaughan, of William Blake, of William Wordsworth, of T.S. Eliot, and many others.

Mysticism extends far outside the sphere of Christianity. It is a dominant tendency in such other forms of religion as the higher religion of India, Mahāyāna Buddhism, Islāmic Ṣūfīsm, in the Jewish Kabbala and Ḥasidism. Among mystics everywhere there is a common element in the consciousness of the Transcendent and in the more developed phases of mystical experience of union with the divine.

Yet, while there is an underlying identity of experience among the mystics, there are important differences in the interpretation placed upon it. Like the mystics of Islām, Judaism, and certain varieties of Hinduism, Christian mystics are theistic (concerned with a personal or suprapersonal God) in their outlook.

The philosopher Henri Bergson has suggested, in his *Two Sources of Religion and Morality*, that in the identification of the human will with the divine, the distinguishing mark of Christian mysticism is to be found. With other forms of mysticism, he says, the tendency is to regard the attainment of an inner state of consciousness ("ecstasy" or "contemplation") as the goal of the inner life, whereas with Christian mystics the goal is action; *i.e.*, a state of being wherein God acts in and through the soul.

Henri Bergson's view

The Hindu or Buddhist mystic seeks (in Bergson's view) to escape from life; the Christian seeks rather to be a channel of the divine Love. But whereas the Hindu or the Buddhist seeks to be delivered from the round of rebirth, the Christian looks to heavenly bliss in the world beyond. Bergson, moreover, overlooks the variety of attitudes among Eastern mystics. Among Hindus, the sacred text known as the *Bhagavadgītā* emphasizes the necessity of action, and for the *bhakti* (or devotional) school as a whole, which was inspired by the Gītā, the great motive-force is love. Among Christian mystics love constitutes a truly dynamic power. The same thing is basically true among Mahāyāna Buddhists and Hindu *bhakti* saints. This is also true in the case of both Islāmic and Jewish mystics.

HISTORY OF CHRISTIAN MYSTICISM

Origins and early development. If the essence of mysticism is the sense of contact with the Transcendent, then mystical experience played a vital part in the religion of the early church. The religion of the early church was a religion of the spirit, which expressed itself in the heightening and enlargement of human consciousness. It is clear from the gospels that there was a numinous (spiritual) dimension in the life of Jesus, in whom the experience of the Hebrew prophets was renewed. In the primitive church an active part was played by "prophets," who were believed to be recipients of a revelation coming directly from the Spirit.

The mystical aspect of primitive Christianity finds its fullest expression in the letters of Paul and the Fourth Gospel (John). The classical mysticism of the Christian Church centres in the knowledge of God and in union with him. For Paul and John, however, the centre of mystical experience and aspiration is union with Christ. It is Paul's supreme desire to know Christ and to be united with him. The recurring phrase, "in Christ," implies personal union, a participation in Christ's suffering, resurrection, and destiny. The Christ with whom Paul is united is not the man Jesus who is known "after the flesh." He has been exalted and glorified, so that he is one with the Spirit.

Christ-mysticism

Christ-mysticism finds renewed embodiment in the Gospel according to St. John, particularly in the farewell discourse (chapters 14–16), where Jesus speaks of his impending death (which is his "glorification") and of his return in the Spirit to unite himself with his followers. In the prayer of Jesus in chapter 17 there is found the vision of an interpenetrating union of souls. In this vision all who are one with Christ share his perfect union with the Father.

In the early Christian centuries the mystical trend found expression not only in the stream of Pauline and Johannine Christianity but also in the Gnostics (early Christian heretics who viewed matter as evil and the spirit as good), to whom it was opposed. Gnosticism appears to have originated through the penetration of mystical Judaism with Zoroastrian and other Oriental influences. The mysticism of the Gnostics is seen at its best in the religion of Valentinus (excommunicated *c.* AD 150), who was probably the author of the *Gospel of Truth* (discovered in 1945).

The central feature of his religion was mystical contemplation. Men are alienated from God because of their spiritual ignorance; Christ brings them into the gnosis (esoteric revelatory knowledge) that is union with God. All men come from God, and all will in the end return to him. Some Gnostics held that there were three types of men—"spiritual," "psychic," and "material"— and only the first two can be saved. The *Pistis Sophia* (3rd century) is preoccupied with the question of who finally will be saved. Those who are saved must renounce the world completely and follow the pure ethic of love and compassion. They will then be identified with Jesus and become rays of the divine Light.

In the 3rd century Gnosticism found a new expression in the rise of Manichaeism, founded by Mani in Persia. Mani is said to have received a spiritual illumination in his early manhood. He claimed to be a manifestation of the Paraclete (Holy Spirit) and the last of the prophets, who completed the work of Jesus, Buddha, and Zoroaster, the great founders of religion. It was Mani's aim to establish a universal religion. Like the Gnostics, he saw the two principles of Light and Darkness as in perpetual conflict; but he recognized the supreme Deity as the source of all things. In the end the Light will be victorious, and all souls subject to matter and the forces of Darkness will be redeemed.

Eastern Christianity. Mystical experience sometimes occurs spontaneously and unsought. So it was apparently with the Christ-mysticism of the early church. But it is characteristic of mystical religion generally that the experience of God, whereby men are lifted into union with him, occurs as the outcome of conscious preparation and practice. It was through the contact of Christianity with Platonism that this type of aspiration and endeavour was developed in the church. In the growth of mysticism a contributory factor is found in the lives of the desert saints, who, under the stress of persecution, and in anticipation of becoming the vanguard of God's army against the spiritual forces that were contacted in the waterless wastes, fled from the inhabited world and devoted themselves to meditation and prayer in the 3rd and 4th centuries.

Early desert saints

In the 5th century John Cassian, who lived for a time among the ascetics of the Egyptian desert, gave a systematic exposition of the "degrees of prayer" in his *Conferences.* He observed: "by constant meditation on things divine, and spiritual contemplation . . . the soul is caught up into . . . an ecstasy" (iii.7). According to him the soul enters at length into a union with God so close and continuous that "whatever we breathe or think, or speak is God. . . ." (x.7.) Cassian was a pioneer of monasticism in western Europe, but his affinities are Eastern rather than Western.

Among Eastern teachers who followed the mystic way were Gregory of Nyssa (4th century), St. Ephraem Syrus, John of Lycopolis, Macarius (4th century), Isaac of Nineveh, and Maximus Confessor (7th century). John of Lycopolis uses the analogy, so often employed by medieval mystics, of iron and fire, for the union of the soul with God. But incomparably the most influential of all Eastern Christian mystics was the man who wrote in the 5th or 6th century in the name of Dionysius the Areopagite, Paul's convert at Athens. He was probably a Syrian monk. His chief works are *De mystica theologia* (*Concerning Mystical Theology*) and *De divinis nominibus* (*Concerning the Names of God*). His main emphasis was on the ineffability of God ("the Divine Dark") and hence on the "apophatic" or "negative" approach to God (see below, *The Divine Dark and the via negativa: God and the Godhead*). Through an unknowing attitude (*i.e.,* placing "a cloud of forgetting" between the self and the realm of "things") men rise "towards union with Him who transcends all being and all knowledge" (*De mystica theologia,* ch. 1).

Eastern mystics distinguish between the essence of God and his attributes, which they regard as energies that penetrate the universe. Creation is a process of emanation, whereby the divine Being is "transported outside of Himself . . . to dwell within the heart of all things . . ." (Dionysius the Areopagite, *De divinis nominibus,* iv.13). The divinization of man is fundamental to Eastern mysticism.

Divinization comes through contemplative prayer, and especially through the method of Hesychasm (from *hesychia,* "stillness") adopted widely in the church through the influence of St. Symeon the New Theologian (died 1022). The method consisted in the concentration of the mind on the divine Presence, induced by the repetition of the "Jesus-prayer" ("O Lord Jesus Christ, Son of God, have mercy on me a sinner"), which culminated in the ecstatic vision of the divine Light and was held to penetrate and divinize the soul through the divine energy implicit in the name of Jesus.

Divinization of man

Eastern mystics were in general rigidly ascetic, but they laid utmost stress on the positive power of love. To them love is a divine power which perfects human nature and unites men with God.

In the Eastern as in the Western Church mystical religion received at times heretical expression. The main influence in this direction was the teaching of the Manichaeans, which led to the rise of the Paulicians and later of the Bogomils (both dualistic sects). For these sects the church was a purely spiritual body, each member of which could become a Christ. This type of doctrine was taught in Russia soon after the introduction of Christianity in the 11th century. Other mystic sects grew up in Russia. The Khlysti ("flagellants"), founded in 1645, stood for complete surrender to the influence of the Holy Spirit; they practiced a dervish-like dance, in which they prophesied. The Molokani and the Dukhobors, who originated in the 18th century among the peasants, resemble the Quakers in their indifference to outer forms. The Dukhobors also stand for the final authority of the Inner Light; they hold that every man is essentially divine through the indwelling presence of the Spirit. They were severely persecuted in Russia and migrated to Canada early in the 20th century.

Mysticism in the Western Catholic Church. The main influence shaping the thought of the mystics in Western as in Eastern mysticism was Neoplatonism. Until the 12th century, when the translation of the works of Dionysius made by John Scotus Erigena in the 9th century first became widely known, this influence was exerted through the work of St. Augustine (died 430). Augustine's experience, as related in the *Confessions*, was the vision of the divine Light as the inmost fact and the transforming power of his being. Similarly, in the view of Pope Gregory the Great (6th and 7th centuries) God is the boundless Light, and contemplation is the endeavour to fix the eye of the heart on its ray. After the period known as the Dark Ages (7th to 10th centuries) the mystical life was revived in the 12th century.

For St. Hildegard von Bingen, a visionary and a prophetess who denounced political corruption, God is the "Living Light." St. Bernard (1090–1153) was a contemporary who exercised a profound influence on medieval piety. The central fact for him, as for later mystics, was the union of the soul with God. Great influence was exerted by Richard of Saint-Victor (died 1173), who taught in Paris. In his works *Benjamin minor* and *Benjamin major* he made a systematic study of the contemplative life. Influence of another type was exercised by St. Francis of Assisi (died 1226). St. Francis was a contemplative who emphasized the practical following of Christ as the way that leads to divine union. The same emphasis is typical of *Imitatio Christi*, which reflects the spirit of the Brotherhood of the Common Life founded by Gerhard Groote in Holland in the 14th century. The biographer of St. Francis, St. Bonaventure, was himself a mystic influenced by Dionysius. Other Italian mystics were Dante and Àngela da Foligno, who tells of her own mystical experience in *The Book of Divine Consolation of the Blessed Angela of Foligno*.

Meister Eckehart and the Rhineland school Perhaps the greatest of all Christian mystics in profundity of thought was Meister Eckehart (died 1329), the founder of the Rhineland school, which included Heinrich Suso, Johann Tauler, Jan van Ruysbroeck, and the authors of the *Theologia Germanica* and *The Book of the Poor in Spirit* (known also as *The Following of Christ*). The Rhineland mystics emphasized the reality of the ideal world, in which all things are eternally present as elements in the being of God. In their totality, Eckehart taught, they are the Son of God eternally begotten by the Father. Man himself has his inmost being there. Eckehart was condemned for saying that "there is something in the soul that is uncreated or uncreatable"; although he denied having said that, in substance it was his teaching. After Eckehart's death the adherents of the school formed a loose association known as the Friends of God.

The 14th century was "the flowering time of mysticism." In England there was a popular cult of the Holy Name of Jesus, which originated probably in the 12th century and was marked by intense Christocentric fervour. This movement provided the emotional preparation for the growth of English mysticism. It affected the work notably of two mystics—Richard Rolle, a layman who wrote *The Fire of Love*, and Julian of Norwich, author of *Revelations of Divine Love*. Other notable English mystics were Walter Hilton, who wrote a guide to the contemplative life, *The Scale [Ladder] of Perfection*, and the author of *The Cloud of Unknowing*, who probably is also the author of *Dionise Hid Divinite*, a translation of *De mystica theologia* of Dionysius, a work which greatly influenced his work.

Among the greatest of the medieval mystics were St. Catherine of Siena (died 1380), proclaimed a doctor of the church in 1970, and St. Catherine of Genoa (died 1510). The former was an ecstatic and visionary who played an active part in the ecclesiastical politics of her day, seeking to restore the broken unity of the church. She exerted an immense spiritual influence on the common people of Italy. The other Catherine is notable for her experience of the "Spiritual Marriage" as well as for her compassion for animals and for her work among the sick and poor.

Spanish mysticism flourished at the time of the Catholic Counter-Reformation in the 16th century. Its leading exponents were St. Teresa of Avila, proclaimed a doctor of the church in 1970, and St. John of the Cross. Both are notable for the heights of contemplation that they attained and for their writings in which the secrets of the contemplative life are expounded.

Medieval mystical heresies The Middle Ages were noteworthy for the growth of mystical heresies. In the 10th century the Gnostic trend spread, through the Bogomils and Paulicians, into Italy and France, where its adherents were known as Cathari, or Albigenses. The movement was destroyed by the Albigensian Crusade in the 13th century. Another type of heresy became widespread in Europe under the name of "The Free Spirit." Its philosophical basis was Neoplatonism as taught by Amalric in Paris. His followers looked to the coming of a new age based on the consciousness of God. (The idea of three ages—the Age of the Father, the Son, and the Spirit—was taught in the 12th century by Joachim of Fiore.) In spite of severe persecution, the same essential outlook arose among the new lay orders of Beghards and Beguines (male and female members of communal orders not living under vows) and among the Friends of God. A leader of the movement was Nicholas of Basel, burned in 1397. The "Spirituals" of the Franciscan order cherished the same ideal of a new era of the Spirit, inaugurated, as they believed, by St. Francis. Their movement also was crushed by persecution.

The conflict between mystical religion and ecclesiastical authority was renewed in the 17th century with the Quietists, whose leaders were Miguel de Molinos, Mme Guyon, and Fénelon, archbishop of Cambrai, all of whom received official condemnation. Molinos was the author of *The Spiritual Guide* (1675), which enjoyed immense popularity in Italy and France. He taught the doctrine of the "One Act": the will once fixed on God in contemplative prayer constitutes a permanent attitude. Self-action must be replaced by the divine activity. Antoinette Bourignon (died 1680) rejected all ecclesiastical authority and all set forms of worship; and it was doubtless the fear of this tendency that lay behind official hostility to the movement. The reaction against mysticism went so far among the Jesuits that in the 17th and 18th centuries they sometimes denied the very possibility of mystical experience.

Protestant mysticism. The chief representatives of Protestant mysticism are the Continental "Spirituals," among whom Sebastian Franck (died 1542), Valentin Weigel (died 1588), and Jakob Böhme (died 1624) are especially noteworthy; the Anglican divines known as the "Cambridge Platonists"; and the Quakers, headed by George Fox (died 1691). For a time the followers of Böhme formed groups of their own; they were eventually absorbed in England by the Quakers. In Holland a mystical group known as Collegiants, similar in principle and practice to the Quakers, broke away from the Remonstrant (Calvinist) Church. (The philosopher Spinoza was for a time a member of the group.) Other mystical bodies were the Schwenckfeldians, founded by Kaspar Schwenckfeld, and the Family of Love, founded in Holland by Hendrik Niclaes early in the 16th century and brought to England about 1550. The religion of the Ranters (17th century) in England had a mystical aspect.

The cardinal feature of Protestant mysticism is the emphasis laid on the divine element in man variously known as the "spark" or "centre" or "ground" of the soul, the "divine image" or "holy self," the "Inner Light," the "principle of God in man," the "Christ within." For Böhme and the Spirituals, essential reality lies in the ideal world, which Böhme described as "the uncreated Heaven." Recent study has served to emphasize the influence on Böhme of Paracelsus, the mystical nature philosopher and alchemist, whose thought was deeply affected by the Kabbala and the teaching of the Gnostics. Böhme took over the Gnostic belief that the physical world arose from a primeval fall, renewed with the historic fall of Adam. His teaching was the main formative influence on the developed outlook of William Law (died 1761) and William Blake (died 1827).

The mystical view of sin

For Protestant as well as for Catholic mystics, sin is essentially the assertion of the self in its separation from God. The divine Life is embodied in "the true holy self that lies within the other" (Jakob Böhme, *First Epistle*). When that self is manifested, there is a birth of God (or of Christ) in the soul. Protestant mystics rejected the Lutheran and Calvinist doctrine of the total corruption of human nature. William Law remarked: "the eternal Word of God lies hid in thee, as a spark of the divine nature. . . ." (*The Spirit of Prayer*, I.2.) "The eternal Word of God" is the inner Christ, incarnate whenever men rise into union with God: "the Son of God . . . must become man and be born in you, if you will know God" (Jakob Böhme, *The Threefold Life*, III.31). By the Spirituals Christ is viewed as the ideal Humanity born in God from all eternity. This conception received its greatest emphasis with Kaspar Schwenckfeld, who, unlike Protestant mystics generally, taught that man as a created being is totally corrupt; salvation means deliverance from our creaturely nature and union with the heavenly Christ.

Protestant mystics explicitly recognize—what is implied in Catholic teaching—that the divine Light or Spark is a universal principle. Hans Denck in the early 16th century speaks of the witness of the Spirit in "heathens and Jews." Sebastian Franck, like the Cambridge Platonists, finds divine revelation in the work of sages like the Greek philosopher Plato and the Roman sage Seneca. George Fox appealed to the conscience of the American Indians as a proof of the universality of the Inner Light. William Law described non-Christian saints as "apostles of a Christ within." Protestant mystics saw too and stated plainly that, for the mystic, supreme authority lies of necessity not in the written word of Scripture but in the Word of God in himself. Fox said: "I saw, in that Light and Spirit that was before the Scriptures were given forth, . . ." (*Journal*, chapter 2). It was especially on this ground that the mystics were brought into conflict with the established church, whether Catholic or Protestant.

The teaching of the Ranters in the 17th century closely resembles that of the Brethren of the Free Spirit. They revived the idea of three stages of revelation, the stage then beginning being that of the Spirit, which rules men from within. They held, in common with Fox, that perfection is possible in this life. The same thing was taught by Hendrik Niclaes, the founder of the Family of Love, who emphasized the idea of deification as a present experience. The Ranters were denounced by the Puritan leaders under the Commonwealth for their "blasphemous and execrable opinions." There was, no doubt, an antinomian tendency among them which rejected the principle of moral law. Some of them, indeed, rejected the very notion of sin. In essence their outlook was Neoplatonic. Jacob Bauthumley said: "as all things had their subsistence and being in God, before they were ever manifested in the world of Creatures: so in the end, . . . they shall all be rapt up into God againe."

PHASES AND FORMS OF CHRISTIAN MYSTICISM

Phases. *Mystical discipline: introversion and purgation.* The practice of meditation and contemplative prayer, leading to ecstasy, is typical of Christian, as of other varieties of theistic mysticism. As Dionysius emphasized, the exercise of discursive thought must be transcended, all images and memories of outer things must be set aside, so that the eye of inner vision may be opened and may look upon God within. Such ideas are presented in the 14th-century tract *De adhaerendo Deo*, translated in 1947 as *Of Cleaving to God*. Introversion leads to ecstasy, in which "the mind of man is ravished into the abyss

of divine Light" (Richard of Saint-Victor, in *De quattuor gradibus violentae caritatis*).

The goal of the mystic is not simply a transient ecstasy; it is a permanent state of being in which his nature is transformed. If this state of being ("deification" or "the spiritual marriage") is to be attained, it is necessary to follow the way of "purgation"; the soul must be purified of all those feelings and desires and attitudes that separate it from God. Christian mystics constantly emphasize the need of walking in the way of Christ, who was for them a deified man in whom God dwelt fully. According to the *Theologia Germanica*, "Christ's human nature was so utterly bereft of self, and apart from all creatures, as no man's ever was, and was nothing but 'a house and habitation of God' " (chapter 15). The following of Christ involves fundamentally a dying to self, a giving up of ourselves wholly to God, that the divine Love may possess us. Love, according to Böhme, devours "all *Egoity* or that which thou callest *I* and *Me* as standing in a separate root, and divided from the Deity, the Fountain of thy being" (*Dialogues on the Supersensual Life*, second dialogue). In that sense self must be annihilated, so that the Will of God may become our will. The *Theologia Germanica* states that the "humble and enlightened man . . ." is desirous "to become as nought in himself, having no will, and that the eternal Will may live in him and have full possession of him" (chapter 51).

Goals of mysticism

The mystics agree upon the necessity of dying to the self. Man must learn detachment from the self and from the things of this world, which tend to dominate him. Such detachment was sometimes taken to involve an entire renunciation of all human ties. "The more you strip yourself of earthly thoughts and of exterior, worldly and sensible entanglements, the more your soul will regain its inner strength and power of knowing and tasting the things of heaven" (*Of Cleaving to God*, chapter 6). It is often assumed that the mystical life must be one of thoroughgoing asceticism. According to Meister Eckehart, "The more a man flees from the created, the more the Creator hastens to him" (sermon on "Sanctification"). Yet Eckehart repudiates the necessity of "worldflight." What is necessary, he says, is to "get a strong impression of God firmly fixed in one's mind" (*Talks of Instruction*, chapter 6). Protestant mystics are even more emphatic in this regard. In the words of William Law: "The one true way of dying to self wants no cells, monasteries or pilgrimages. It is the way of patience, humility and resignation to God" (*The Spirit of Love*, Part the First).

Illumination: visions and voices. In the state of ecstasy as described by Christian mystics the sense of self and the world disappears; the soul is wholly absorbed in the consciousness of God. But there are other phases of mystical experience in which the sense of self and the world remains along with the consciousness of God. "In the state known as 'illumination' individual self-consciousness remains . . . ," and along with the consciousness of selfhood there is the awareness of the world. In this state the consciousness of God may be mediated through the objects and forces of nature. Friedrich Schleiermacher in his *Addresses* held that it is only through such mediation that the mystic consciousness arises; there is no direct or immediate consciousness of God. The experience of the mystics shows conclusively that Schleiermacher's negation was unjustified. But experience also shows that R.C. Zaehner is probably mistaken in supposing that in religious mysticism there must be "a total and absolute detachment from Nature. . . ." Joseph Estlin Carpenter, a pioneer in the study of comparative religion, described in a letter an experience that once came to him in the countryside: "I had as direct perception of the being of God all round about me as I have of you when we are together," and he added, "I remember the wonderful transfiguration of the far-off woods and hills as they seemed to blend in the infinite being with which I was thus brought into relation." The experience of Böhme was similar: "my spirit suddenly saw through all, and *in* . . all creatures, even in herbs and grass it knew God, . . ." (*The Aurora*, xix, 13).

Mysticism and nature

It is in terms of vision or illumination that the mystics constantly speak of the knowledge or intuition of God. Of this Àngela da Foligno remarked: "the eyes of my soul were opened and I beheld the plenitude of God. . . ." Illumination may express itself in actual radiance. St. Symeon speaks of a young man who saw "a brilliant Divine radiance . . ." filling the room where he was.

St. Teresa classifies visions as "intellectual," "imaginary," and "corporeal." For all mystics, the height of vision is the vision of God. Among the mystics, however, many have experienced visions of other types. They have also heard voices. But in general they lay no great emphasis on such things. For example, St. John of the Cross says deprecatingly, "we must never rely upon them or accept them. . . ." (*Ascent of Mount Carmel* 2.11.) St. Teresa had many such experiences. She had visions of her father and mother in heaven, of St. Clare, of the Virgin Mary, and also of Satan and hell. In her autobiography St. Teresa reports that she heard many "locutions," which sometimes came outwardly, sometimes inwardly. Their content was often wholly unexpected: they interfered with her plans and warned her of coming events. Mystics (such as St. Catherine of Siena, Böhme, Mme Guyon) have recorded teachings that came to them automatically. Mme Guyon reported: "I was given light to perceive that I had in me treasures of knowledge and understanding which I did not know that I possessed." Such experiences Evelyn Underhill says represent "invasions from beyond the threshold" of consciousness, "revelations mediated by the deeper mind"; they "established a communion between two planes of existence."

Deification, the spiritual marriage, and the dark night of the soul. Christian mystics claim that the soul may be lifted into a union with God so close and so complete that it is merged in the being of God and loses the sense of any separate existence. Jan van Ruysbroeck says that in the experience of union "we can nevermore find any distinction between ourselves and God. . . ."; "we are one being and one life and one blessedness with God" (*The Sparkling Stone*, chapters 10 and 12). Eckehart speaks of this identification with the divine as "the birth of the Son" in us: "He makes me His only-begotten Son without any difference." St. John of the Cross and some other Spanish mystics say essentially the same thing: "the soul seems to be God rather than a soul, and is indeed God by participation. . . ." (*Ascent of Mount Carmel*, ii, 5:7.)

Spiritual marriage and the unitive life

In one aspect, therefore, deification is an experience of identity attained in the consciousness of ecstatic union. But deification is also a permanent state of being into which the soul enters progressively—the "unitive life" or "spiritual marriage." "In this union," observed Walter Hilton, "a true marriage is made between God and the soul which shall never be broken" (*The Ladder of Perfection*, 1.8). It is the power of love transforming the soul that brings about this state of being; "Love is a unitive and transforming power that changes the lover into what he loves. . . ." (*Of Cleaving to God*, chapter 12.) For Eastern mystics love is a divine energy flowing forth from God to deify the soul. "Love, the divine gift, perfects human nature until it makes it appear in unity and identity by grace with the divine nature" (Maximus Confessor). Böhme states: "[Love] brings thee to be as high as God himself is, by being united with God. . . ." (*Dialogues on the Supersensual Life*, First Dialogue.)

The unitive life has two main aspects. In the first place, while the consciousness of self and the world remains in it, that consciousness is accompanied by a continuous sense of union with God. St. Catherine of Genoa lived an active life for 22 years in an almost unbroken consciousness of the divine presence. Brother Lawrence said that while he was at work in his kitchen he possessed God " 'in as great tranquility as if I were upon my knees at the blessed sacrament . . .' " (*The Practice of the Presence of God*, chapter 4). Second, the spiritual marriage is a "theopathic" state: the soul is felt to be in all things the organ or instrument of God. In the unitive life, Mme

Guyon says, the soul "no longer lives or works of herself: but God lives, acts and works in her. . . ." In the deified life, according to the text of the *Theologia Germanica*, the Incarnation is renewed: "in me, too, God must be made man; . . . so that he alone may do all things in me. . . ." (chapter 3.)

A phase of the dying to self that this implies is the "dark night of the soul," experienced by many Christian mystics. The primary fact in that experience is the temporary cessation of the divine union, which gives rise to emotional lethargy, followed by a state of desolation and despair sometimes lasting for months or years. The soul that accepts its trials with patience attains to the utmost transcendence of self, through its willingness to be deprived of the greatest of all blessings.

Forms of Christian mysticism. *Christ-mysticism.* The earliest form of Christian mysticism was the Christ-mysticism of Paul and John. For Christian mysticism in its traditional and classical expression the centre of experience and aspiration is union with God. Yet Christ-mysticism has from time to time been renewed in the church. In the Eastern Church emphasis was placed especially on the divine Light that appeared to the disciples at the Transfiguration; men sought to identify themselves with Christ in his divine glory. St. Symeon says of a certain mystic that "he possessed Christ whoily. . . . He was, in fact, entirely Christ." For Western Catholic mystics Jesus was himself the perfect mystic. "Christ," according to *The Book of the Poor in Spirit*, "is one with God and hence it is necessary that he who desires to be one spirit with God should first unite himself with Christ." Luis de León speaks of the theopathic life in terms of Christ-mysticism: "the very Spirit of Christ comes and is united with the soul—nay, is infused throughout its being, as though he were soul of its soul indeed." According to St. Teresa devotion to Christ led to the sense of his living presence: "I was in prayer one day . . . when I saw Christ close by me, or, to speak more correctly, felt him. . . ."

Mysticism of Paul and John

With Protestants, the attempt to return to primitive Christianity has led to a certain renewal of Christ-mysticism. One expression of this is the thought of the birth of Christ in the soul. "The Son of God," according to Böhme, "must become man and be born in you, if you will know God" (*The Threefold Life*, iii.31). The early Quaker George Keith says that Christ is born spiritually in us when "his life and spirit are united unto the soul." Gerrard Winstanley, the founder of the Digger movement in England, identifies the Inner Light with "the mighty man Christ Jesus." "Your body is his body, and now his spirit is your spirit, and so you are become one with him and with the Father."

The chief representative of Christ-mysticism among the early Protestants was Kaspar Schwenckfeld. For him Christ was from all eternity the God-man, and as such he possessed a body of spiritual flesh, in which he lived on earth, and which he now possesses in heaven. As a created being man is totally corrupt, but he may receive a divine and spiritual life from Christ. In his exalted life Christ unites himself inwardly with the souls of men and imparts to them his own divinity. In the 18th century William Law speaks constantly of the "Inner Christ" as the divine Life in the soul, the Word or Wisdom of God, revealed wherever men are moved by the spirit of prayer, which is the desire for union with God.

The Divine Dark and the via negativa: God and the Godhead. An important aspect of Christian mysticism is the doctrine of the ineffability of God and the negative way to which that doctrine gave rise. The main exponent of this teaching in early centuries was the pseudo-Dionysius. Dionysius distinguishes "the super-essential Godhead," who is the origin and the goal of all, and the "Deity," whose being arises from it by an eternal process of emanation. (Like Eckehart, he sometimes uses the term "God" for the Godhead.) He recognizes the partial validity of the positive approach (*via affirmativa*): it gives men knowledge not of the divine essence but of the divine attributes—the names applied to God in Scripture (Life,

Via affirmativa and *via negativa*

Light, Love, Power)—which are the divine energies whereby God communicates his being. "If we call the super-essential Mystery by the name of 'God' or 'Life' or 'Being' or 'Light' or 'Word,' we conceive of nothing else than the powers that stream therefrom to us" (*De divinis nominibus*, ii.7). But the negative way (*via negativa*) is the higher way, because no positive ideas can truly express the divine Reality, and because the negative way is the way of the inner stillness that brings illumination. It "lifts the soul above all things cognate with its finite nature, . . . and there joins us unto God Himself. . . ."

In the West the influence of Dionysius may be seen especially in the Rhineland school. As Eckehart shows, it is because of the very fullness and perfection of his being that God transcends intellectual knowledge. Even being and goodness are "garments" or "veils" under which he is hidden, and in mystical contemplation he may be seen unveiled. "What God is in himself no man can tell except he be ravished into the light that God is himself." In that vision the soul rises beyond the thought of "God" in the ordinary sense to the Godhead. "God" as Eckehart sometimes employs the term is the triune, the creative God of theology—God conceived as an active power. In that sense "God and the Godhead are as different as heaven and earth." What Eckehart calls "intellect"—*i.e.*, the power of spiritual vision—"is truly as little satisfied with God as with a stone or a tree. . . . she breaks into the ground out of which goodness and truth break forth. . . ."

The thought of the Godhead was renewed in the teaching of Böhme, who speaks of it as the *Ungrund*—"the great Mystery," "the Abyss," "the eternal Stillness." Böhme's emphasis, however, is strikingly different. He stresses the fact of divine becoming (in a nontemporal sense): God is eternally the dark Mystery of which nothing can be said, but eternally he puts on the nature of Light, Love, and Goodness wherein he is revealed to man.

VALUE AND CONTRIBUTION

The study of Christian mysticism presents both the unity of mysticism as a phase of human experience and the diversity of the expression that it has received in the sphere of Christian faith. The mystic claims everywhere that he is in contact with an order of reality that transcends the world of the physical senses; he claims that he has entered into an immediate knowledge of the divine. The Christian mystic shares a secret that unites him with a great cloud of witnesses. The secret has been renewed amid an immense diversity of changing thought and circumstance. The claim is all the more significant in that Roman Catholics, Protestants, and Orthodox are here at one. The identity between them is an identity not of dogma but of experience. The mystic has been likened to an explorer—a discoverer in the hidden realm of divine Reality. The discovery that he brings is of incalculable importance, since it affects the very nature of the universe and of the human self. In an age when the claims of authoritarian religion are so widely questioned or denied, the mystic's discovery is supremely significant.

The Christian mystic takes his stand with the mystics of other religions in pointing to "the Beyond that is within." Their discovery may contain the key to the pressing problem of religious unity. The great question that confronts the present age is the relation of Christianity to other world religions—whether Christianity can enter into relations of real unity and cooperation with other religions. It may be contended that Christianity, if it is to embark upon such relations, must be deeply imbued with the insight and experience of the mystics.

BIBLIOGRAPHY. General works include: SIDNEY SPENCER, *Mysticism in World Religion* (1963), a comprehensive survey; EVELYN UNDERHILL, *Mysticism*, 12th ed. (1930), a full account and discussion of mystical experience in its psychological and theological aspects; R.C. ZAEHNER, *Mysticism, Sacred and Profane* (1957), on the fundamental contrast between theistic and monistic mysticism. Collections of extracts from the writings of mystics may be found in F.C. HAP-POLD, *Mysticism: A Study and an Anthology* (1963), especially of Christian mystics; and W.T. STACE, *The Teachings of the Mystics* (1960), with commentary. For a comparison of Śaṅkara and Eckehart, see RUDOLF OTTO, *West–Östliche Mystik* (1926; Eng. trans., *Mysticism East and West*, 1932, reprinted 1970). Philosophical works include: W.T. STACE, *Mysticism and Philosophy* (1960); and HENRI BERGSON, *Les Deux Sources de la morale et de la religion* (1932; Eng. trans., *The Two Sources of Morality and Religion*, 1935), with an important chapter on this subject.

Four works specifically on Christian mysticism are: E. HERMAN, *The Meaning and Value of Mysticism* (1915); W.R. INGE, *Christian Mysticism*, 7th ed. (1932), a valuable survey covering Christian mystics of all types; R.M. JONES, *Studies in Mystical Religion* (1909), especially valuable for the study of the medieval period; and EVELYN UNDERHILL, *The Mystics of the Church* (1925), for the history of Christian mysticism in the West. On Eastern Christian mysticism, see VLADIMIR LOSSKY, *Essai sur la théologie mystique de l'Église d'Orient* (1944; Eng. trans. *The Mystical Theology of the Eastern Church*, 1957); and MARGARET SMITH, *Studies in Early Mysticism in the Near and Middle East* (1931).

(S.Sp.)

Christian Myth and Legend

The myths and legends of Christianity—based upon enhancing, and in some respects refining, earlier Jewish and Greek myths and legends as well as those of people who later interacted with or were dominated by Christians—have exerted a significant influence in Western civilization in the areas of political theory, economic thought, the visual arts, music, popular piety, and science.

Nature and significance. *Interpretations of Christian myth.* Myth, whether Christian or other, is an exposition of truth expressed in the form of a story. The meaning given to "myth" in the 19th century—*i.e.*, that myth is fiction—continues to exert a pervasive influence in popular and journalistic literature. It is this 19th-century view of myth as fiction that has caused many Christians in the 20th century to reject the notion that Christianity contains within its Scriptures, theology, and practices various mythological elements. Mythological themes taken over from the Greeks and the Jews (*e.g.*, the origin of the world, the Fall of man, the divine in human form, and other themes) have been transformed by Christian concepts of history and the development of Christian doctrine.

In the 20th century three interpretations of Christian myth have prevailed among scholars: the history of religions (for want of a better term), the psychoanalytical, and the Existential interpretations. According to the history of religions interpretation, myth is a sacred story. Mircea Eliade, an eminent Romanian–American historian of religions, has defined myth as sacred history—*i.e.*, as a description of "the various and sometimes dramatic break-throughs of the sacred (or the 'supernatural') into the World." Knowing the sacred story and participating in its ritual re-enactment at a sacred time (*e.g.*, the Lord's Supper, especially on Holy Thursday) enables the believer to understand his origins and his place in the world.

The psychoanalytical interpretation views myth in symbolic terms. The Swiss psychoanalyst Carl Jung defined myth as a depiction of the unconscious archetypes—*i.e.*, of the innate tendencies to form symbolic images. Thus, myths are viewed as stories of significance for an individual (and culture) based on primary mental forms (basic symbols, often geometric) that help one to understand his human condition.

The Existential interpretation has gained wide acceptance among Christian scholars. Rudolf Bultmann, a German theologian of the 20th century, views myth as a form of expression by which man understands himself. The imagery of myth, according to Bultmann, is taken from this world, which is qualitatively different from the sacred realm; thus, there is a basic contradiction between this world of space, time, and cause-and-effect and the transcendent realm of God. Bultmann notes that God is thus conceived of in spatial terms (*e.g.*, a Being up in the sky), whereas the spiritual realm is by definition beyond the space-time world. Because of the discontinu-

Major interpretations of Christian myth

ity between the transcendent (sacred) and the spatial-temporal realms, Bultmann argues for a "demythologization" of New Testament mythological themes. This simply refers to a reinterpretation of Christian myths in terms of man's existence. The cross, for example, is a symbol of a historical event that is described in mythical terms as the primary sacrifice for the sins of the world. Through the sacrament of the Lord's Supper, the crucifixion-resurrection of Christ is re-enacted and the believer understands his existence as one of freedom from sin. The virgin birth of Christ, interpreted from this point of view, is a mythological expression of the fact that God acts in the world of men, and that ·God's action is of significance for the individual who is attempting to live an authentic existence—*i.e.*, to take responsibility for himself. The fact that an event is described in mythical terms neither denies nor affirms its historicity.

The function and role of Christian myth in Western civilization. The function of Christian myth is to express in imaginative and often dramatic terms answers to the most significant questions asked by man: Who am I? Where did I come from? Where am I going? Though these questions are universal, in Western civilization they have been answered, for the most part, by those cognitive and imaginative elements influenced by Christian myth. Concerned with the nature, origin, and destiny of man, his society, and his world, Christian myth seeks to elucidate and describe the truth of the human condition (for those affected by Western civilization) in a manner that goes beyond the mere apprehension and comprehension of facts that can be empirically verified—*i.e.*, substantiated by the senses.

Employing the imagination to communicate concepts, Christian myth is concerned with the realm of the spirit —*i.e.*, the sphere of meaning and value. That area—involving man's understanding of himself and his relationship to his society and world and to the sacred or holy—may also be defined and described in nonmythical forms; namely, as doctrine, history, and philosophy. Doctrine employs reason and logic based upon axioms or presuppositions either the same as or similar to those expressed in myth. History interprets meaning and value within the framework of events that are judged significant by a community. Philosophy attempts to describe, through a rational and coherent system, meaning and value as they are accepted or as they ought to be—according to the presuppositions of the philosopher. Christianity has utilized all of these modes of expression to communicate what it conceives is of qualitative significance (*i.e.*, truth); but myth, using the imagination, has retained its primary importance as a basis for Christian faith for nearly 2,000 years, whereas doctrinal debate, historical interpretations, and philosophical thought have undergone periods of acceptance and periods of questioning. During the modern period, in which the sciences are concerned with the quantitative (measurable) aspects of the human condition, the mythological elements of Christianity continue to emphasize the qualitative aspects.

Christian legend. Legends, the edifying stories of saints, martyrs, or heroes, are similar to myths in that they employ the imaginative faculty of man. They are to be distinguished from myths in terms of origin and function. Legends are based upon historical (or reputedly historical) events and persons—with generous embellishments from imaginative popular piety—and have often included elements (*e.g.*, the Holy Grail) taken over from myths of previously pagan peoples. The term legend (from Latin *legendum*, "something to be read") came from the practice of reading accounts of saints, martyrs, and monks to those who were expected to be edified thereby. Rivalries between those who espoused the cause of a particular local or area saint often led to distortions of historical facts and deliberate embellishments in order to portray the particular personage's exceptional holiness and favour from God. Such distortions and embellishments—along with a primary interest in the Scriptures—led the Protestant Reformers of the 16th century to reject or de-emphasize the role of saints. For these same rea-

sons modern scholars—from the Rationalists of the 18th century (*e.g.*, Voltaire) to historical critics in the 20th century—have looked askance at the legends of Christianity and other religions, and thus in modern popular usage legend has become (like myth) a synonym for fiction.

Myth and legend from the 1st to the early 2nd centuries. Christianity arose during the middle of the Hellenistic period (*c.* 300 BC–*c.* AD 300) in Palestine, and thus was influenced by the contemporary Greek and Near Eastern cultures, including their mythological themes and modes of expression. Appropriated from its Jewish Near Eastern background were mythological subjects such as the creation of the world and man, the Fall of man, the saved saviour, the Eschaton (consummation of history), and the Last Judgment. Not only the Old Testament but also Jewish apocalyptic writings (a type of literature depicting the intervention of God in history to the accompaniment of sudden, dramatic, and cataclysmic events and written in symbolic or cryptographic terms) influenced the interpretation of myth and mythological themes in the early church. From its Hellenistic (Greek) background Christianity appropriated a concept of myth that influenced it to reject myths as false or fictional. Since the 5th and 4th century BC—as exemplified in the writings of the Greek philosopher Plato—myth had shifted in meaning among the Greeks from that of a true account of the state of human and divine affairs to that of fiction. The New Testament, illustrating this Hellenistic view of myth, on the one hand rejects myths—*e.g.*, I Tim. 4:7, "Have nothing to do with godless and silly myths"—but on the other hand is replete with mythological themes —*e.g.*, Christ as the second Adam (Rom. 5:12–14), the heavenly spheres (II Cor. 12:2–4), and the celestial battle between angels and demons.

The ages of the world. One of the most pervading and dominant mythological themes to be noted in the New Testament and the writings of the subapostolic church (late 1st–early 2nd centuries) was that of the ages of the world. Derived from Indo-Iranian (or Indo-European) sources and transformed through Jewish concepts of history, the theme of the ages of the world that most influenced Christianity came from the apocalyptic speculation that flourished during the period of the rise of Christianity.

Found all the way from the Indus River to the Mediterranean Sea, the theme of the ages of the world has exerted considerable influence on the thinking and ways of life (*e.g.*, economic, political, and social) not only of ancient man but, to a great extent, on modern Western man, whose roots lie in a Christian world view. In the 8th century BC in Greece, the poet Hesiod described the ages of the world; they were four in number and symbolized by gold, silver, bronze, and iron, with each age successively declining in morality. Though he bemoaned the injustice of men during his age (the Iron Age), Hesiod believed that the god Zeus had ordained justice and the punishment of the unjust. Because the Greeks viewed time as cyclical and man's existence in history as tragic, their concept of the ages of the world influenced Christianity only superficially. In India, among the Hindus, who likewise viewed time as cyclical, the four *yuga*s (Sanskrit: "world ages"), symbolized by the four throws of an Indian dice game (Kṛta, or four; Tretā, or three; Dvāpara, or two; and Kali, or "strife"), also are viewed as descending—though in repetitive cycles—from perfection to moral chaos. In Indian thought the number four signifies totality and perfection (*e.g.*, "four square"); three signifies the beginning of imperfection; two signifies the balance between perfection and imperfection; and one signifies imperfection, "strife," and the worst of anything. Though some Indian thought had reached the Mediterranean area by the time of the rise of early Christianity, because of its views of time, as well as other religious views, it had little or no effect on the milieu of mythological thought that most influenced Christianity.

It was Iranian mythological concepts of the ages of the world, translated through Jewish apocalyptic views, that most influenced Christian views of time, history, and

Relation of myth to meaning and value

Influence of the ages of the world theme

man's ultimate destiny. The prophet Zoroaster (c. 7th century BC) and his followers in Iran had taught a doctrine of the four ages of the world in which each age of 3,000 years' length was divided into three millennia. Ahura Mazdā (the Wise Lord), symbolized by light and later called Ormazd, dwelt in infinite time with Ahriman, symbolized by darkness. Ahriman, like Satan in Christianity, went against the Wise Lord. The four ages of the world created after the fall of Ahriman depict the successive stages of the struggle in finite time between the lords of good and evil for the allegiance and the souls of men. In the last millennium of the fourth age a saviour (Saoshyans) will come and inaugurate the last judgment and the new world in which truth, immortality, and righteousness will prevail and finite time will merge with infinite time (see also ZOROASTRIANISM AND PARSIISM).

The theme of the ages of the world and its attendant subthemes that came primarily from Iranian mythology were transformed by apocalyptic literature—which flourished in Judaism and then Christianity from about the 2nd century BC to about the 2nd century AD—into a historical context, though Zoroastrianism had done this in reference to the last age. Indo-Iranian myth was thus historicized through the Judeo-Christian view of historical time as the arena of struggle between good and evil. The four ages of the world in Christianity are: (1) from creation of the world and man to the Fall of man; (2) from the Fall of man to the first advent of Christ; (3) from the first to the second advent of Christ, which includes the 1,000-year reign of Christ and his saints and the Last Judgment; and (4) the creation of a new heaven and a new earth in which those who have chosen the good (i.e., Christ) will live in eternity.

The two apocalyptic biblical books that most clearly depict the theme of the four ages of the world, concentrating on the period before the Final Judgment, are the Old Testament Book of Daniel and the New Testament Book of Revelation (the Apocalypse). Daniel, written perhaps about 165 BC, utilized this theme by applying it to the kingdoms of the ancient Near East prior to the inauguration of the Hasmonean kingdom (i.e., the Maccabean dynasty) in Judah, 165–163 BC. An image composed of gold, silver, bronze, and iron (mixed with clay) symbolizes four kingdoms of the ancient Near East— i.e., Babylonia, Media, Persia, and the Greek kingdoms of the Seleucid dynasty of Syria and the Ptolemaic dynasty of Egypt. The image will be destroyed because the fourth kingdom has feet of clay, and after this is accomplished, the Kingdom of God will be inaugurated. In another apocalyptic vision in Daniel, the four kingdoms are described according to the imagery of four beasts. The fourth beast will be destroyed, and "one like a son of man," as well as the "saints of the Most High," will be given dominion over all of the nations. Before the reception of the dominion by the saints, however, there will be a time of tribulation in which the last king of the fourth kingdom will try to "change the time and the law."

Apocalyptic imagery depicting the last times, influenced by Daniel and other similar Jewish apocalyptic writings, is found throughout the Revelation to John in the New Testament, especially the theme of the Son of man (Christ) and the great tribulation prior to the judgment of the world. The battle between Christ and the Antichrist is similar thematically to the struggle between Ormazd and Ahriman in Iranian religion. The Antichrist, under the symbol of a beast (Rev. 19:19–20), will inaugurate a period of chaos in which he will attempt to overthrow the religious, moral, and social values that have enabled men to live in relative peace. The Antichrist is viewed as a false messiah (the anointed redeemer), as "the liar" who denies that Jesus is the Christ (I John 2:18–22). He will come just before the 1,000-year period in which Satan, symbolized as a dragon, will not be able to deceive the nations of the world.

Because the Judeo-Christian view of history is linear— i.e., nonrepetitive or noncyclical—the mythological theme of the four ages of the world has influenced various concepts of progress toward a better state of existence. These views of progress can be noted all the way from Montanus, a heretical Christian prophet of the early 2nd century, to Karl Marx, a prophet of Communism from the 19th century who has influenced vast numbers of people in the 20th century. Montanus claimed that history progressed from an age of the Father, to an age of the Son, to an age of the Holy Spirit, of whom Montanus was the manifestation. A rigid moralism accompanied his views. Marx taught a theory of history in which there are stages (i.e., ages), a final battle, and a final classless society in which the "evils" of private property that is used to produce capital will be eliminated and man will live in peace.

Other mythological themes. Early Christianity also appropriated various other mythological themes from the Hellenistic world of thought. Among them was the theme of a miraculous birth of a deity. That the virgin birth of a god or goddess was a theme common in the mythology of the Hellenistic world does not disprove the historicity of the virgin birth of Christ. On the other hand, it does nothing to prove its historicity. Births of deities often were described in miraculous terms. Aphrodite (Venus), the goddess of sexual love, is depicted as springing from a seashell, a miraculous birth difficult to supersede. Mithra, the Iranian god of light and sacred contracts, is described as being born from a rock, the birth being witnessed by shepherds on a day (December 25) that was later claimed by Christians as the nativity of Christ. Luke, the Gospel writer who narrated the virgin birth of Christ, was more interested in emphasizing the humanity of Christ, which is just the opposite of the emphasis of many modern Christians, who view the story of the virgin birth as a proof of Christ's divinity. The story of the virgin birth of Alexander the Great (4th century BC) from his mother Olympias, whose reputation was not that of a virgin, was used to prove Alexander's divinity. Thus, many modern Christians, in their attempt to prove the divinity of Christ by means of the story of the virgin birth, use this mythological theme in a manner very similar to that of persons living in the Hellenistic world. The Gospel writers, however, were more interested in emphasizing Christ's humanity—e.g., the philosophical description of the same event by the writer of the Fourth Gospel (John) in the phrase "the Logos (Word) became flesh."

Myth and legend from the 2nd through the 5th centuries. *The writings of the Apologists and polemicists.* Christians of the early church, especially in the 2nd and 3rd centuries, either accepted Hellenistic mythological themes by reinterpreting them as useful aids in making Christian concepts intelligible to Greek-speaking converts from paganism or by totally rejecting such themes. The former, the Apologists, were represented by such thinkers as Clement of Alexandria, often called the last and greatest of the Apologists, and Justin Martyr. The latter, the polemicists, were represented by thinkers such as Tertullian, a Latin-speaking philosopher-theologian trained in law from North Africa who is famous for his question "What has Athens to do with Jerusalem?" That question indicated a definite rejection of Hellenism as an influence on religious thought.

In his attempt to bring about a rapprochement between Hellenism and Christian theology, Clement often utilized motifs from Greek mythology, though he also severely criticized the acceptance of Greek myths as being true. His book *Protrepticus* ("Exhortation") is replete with both utilizations and castigations of Greek myths. Clement's use of the Homeric story of Odysseus at the mast is an example of how he attempted to make the Christian Gospel intelligible to Greek-speaking converts. In the *Odyssey* by Homer, a Greek poet of the 8th century BC, the hero Odysseus, on his way home to Ithaca, sails past the island of the Sirens. The Sirens are divine-human women who, by their seductive singing, lure sailors to destruction on the rocky shores. Odysseus instructs his companions to fill their ears with wax so that they will not hear the fatal songs. He does not fill his own ears with wax, however, because he wants to sail past the island "having full knowledge" of the sensual appeal of

Margin notes:

Apocalyptic imagery in Daniel and Revelation

The theme of miraculous birth of a deity

The theme of Odysseus at the mast

Greek and Christian treatment of the Homeric story of Odysseus at the mast.
(Left) Ship of Odysseus passing the Sirens, detail from an Attic vase, *c.* 490–480 BC. In the British Museum. (Right) Odysseus bound to the mast of his ship while passing the Sirens, 3rd-century mosaic from Dougga, Tunisia. In the Musée National du Bardo, Tunis, Tunisia.
By courtesy of (left) the trustees of the British Museum, (right) the Musée National du Bardo, Tunis, Tunisia

the Sirens' songs. He ties himself to the mast so that he will not be able to succumb to the temptation to go closer to the rocky shores and thus risk destruction of both himself and his companions. Clement reinterprets this motif by stating that the mature Christian may "sail" through all of the enticements of the world of the senses and pagan philosophical thought, "having full knowledge," if he, like Odysseus, ties himself to the cross, which is the "mast" of the church. In another book, the *Paedagogus* ("Instructor"), Clement relates that Christians often wore a signet ring engraved with a ship homeward bound to heaven.

The Christian who is able to understand mythological and philosophical thought Clement calls a Gnostic—*i.e.*, one who knows. He contrasted this Christian Gnostic to the heretical Gnostics who reinterpreted the events of Christian history in a mythological framework.

The writings of the Gnostics. The heretical Gnostics of the 2nd and 3rd centuries were religious dualists who believed that there were two worlds or realms: the world of matter created by an evil god (of the Old Testament), and the realm of the spirit created by the good God revealed in the New Testament. They also claimed they had secret esoteric knowledge (*gnosis*), the revelation of which to an individual would bring salvation. The many Gnostic sects (*e.g.*, the Valentinians, Basilidians, Ophites, and Simonians) developed a variety of myths. The Valentinians (named for their founder Valentinus, who flourished in the mid-2nd century in Alexandria and Rome) developed an elaborate myth: in the beginning there was a spiritual realm (*plērōma*); then a fall within the spiritual realm; an expulsion from the *plērōma*; a creation of the material world by the aborted demiurge (the Creator-God of the Old Testament) who attempted to keep from the Gnostics—in whom were imprisoned the divine sparks that had left the *plērōma* during the expulsion—a knowledge of who they were, where they had come from, and what their destinies were; the sending of Christ from the *plērōma* to the created world in order to teach Gnostics the saving knowledge of their true identities; and the coming of the Holy Spirit, after Christ returned to the *plērōma* because the demiurge had discovered that Christ was in Jesus and thus crucified the man Jesus. The Valentinians, in this way of viewing the events of the New Testament, mythologized history.

The Ophites (from the Greek word *ophis*, "serpent") reinterpreted the mythological theme of the Fall of man in Genesis. According to the Ophite view, the serpent of the Garden of Eden wanted Adam and Eve, the first man and woman, to eat from the tree of knowledge (*gnosis*) so that they would know their true identities and "be like God" (Gen. 3:5). The serpent, thus, is interpreted as a messenger of the spiritual god, and the one who wanted

to prevent Adam and Eve from eating the fruit of the tree of knowledge is viewed as the demiurge. In their rejection of the God of the Old Testament, who gave the Ten Commandments, the Ophites flaunted their freedom from the law and conventionality by extreme sexual license.

The Gnostics separated the spiritual and material aspects of man, and by doing so enforced a heretical view of man that persists to the 20th century within Christianity. The attempt to "save souls" by Christians who display little interest in the material well-being of man is an example of the persistence of Gnostic mythological themes (see also GNOSTICISM).

The development of legends. Legends developed in Christianity because of a need to answer questions posed by the less intellectual Christians, the need for stories of exemplary Christians, and the transference of the deeds of pagan gods and goddesses in popular piety to those of saints and martyrs.

Many Christians were not satisfied with the gaps in the narration of Christ's life in the canonical Gospels. There thus developed several apocrypha (late, noncanonical works), often influenced by Gnosticism, that provided legendary accounts of Christ's life, as well as those of the Apostles. Among them are the infancy gospels and the *Acts of Paul and Thecla.* In *The First Gospel of the Infancy of Jesus Christ* (Arabic infancy gospel), for example, Jesus and his playmates were playing on a rooftop and one fell down and died. The other playmates ran away, leaving Jesus to be accused of pushing the dead boy. Jesus, however, went to the dead boy and asked, "Zeinunus, Zeinunus, who threw you down from the housetop?" The dead boy answered that Jesus had not done it and named another (*I Infancy* 19:4–11). This and other such stories were narrated to demonstrate the power of Jesus even as a boy. The *Acts of Paul and Thecla* narrates the story of a lady friend of St. Paul who was thrown to the lions—one of which defended her in a manner similar to that of the lion in the story of Androcles, a well-known legend—and who later in life defended her virginity. Thecla was an example to Christian ascetics (those who denied bodily needs and pleasures). Other exemplary legends were recounted in the Acts of the Martyrs and various histories. Some saints were not martyrs, such as St. Nicholas (a 4th-century bishop of Myra, in Asia Minor), the patron of schoolchildren and sailors (who was dropped from the Roman liturgical calendar in 1969), and legends concerning their deeds and miracles multiplied according to the needs of popular piety.

The development and growth of legends in the Middle Ages. As Christianity expanded from the cultural milieu of the Mediterranean area to the north and east, the

Gnostic reinterpretation of the Garden of Eden

Legends of
saints and
other
personages

various converted tribes and peoples did not, understandably, forget their own religious heritages. Just as attributes of the Roman god of war, Mars, had been transferred to Michael, the archangel who is the leader of the heavenly hosts, in the early centuries of the church, so also the attributes of the gods of the Germanic, Baltic, Slavic, and other peoples were transferred to angels and saints during the Middle Ages. Legends of saints—such as St. George, who rescued a maiden after slaying a dragon—were often overlaid with details from pagan myths and legends. St. George became the patron saint of England and one of the most popular saints among the Balts (among whom St. George replaced the god Kalvis, the heavenly smith and dragon slayer), though he has been reduced (1961) by the Roman Catholic Church to mere commemoration (from veneration) and dropped from the calendar of saints (1969) whose days are to be universally celebrated.

"St. George and the Dragon," oil on canvas by Paolo Uccello (1397–1475). In the National Gallery, London.

Legends of personages other than saints, as well as folktales, had a prolific growth in the Middle Ages. The legend of Prester John, for example, was so well received that Pope Alexander III dispatched a letter to him in 1177. Prester (Presbyter) John was believed to be a Christian priest-king of the Orient (India) who might be able to help Christians against the Muslims. The search for his legendary kingdom set the stage for later voyages of discovery to the East. The legend of the Wandering Jew, who was doomed to live forever because he had taunted Jesus on his way to be crucified, was popular in the 13th century. From the 17th century on, the story of Ahasuerus, the Wandering Jew, became popular in Western literature. The legend of Perceval, a hero of the knights of King Arthur and the winner of the Holy Grail (the chalice used by Jesus in the Last Supper), was popular among the chivalric-minded knights of the Crusades and later. Perceval became the subject of the opera *Parsifal* by Richard Wagner, the 19th-century German composer who attempted to revive legendary themes of Germany's past. Perceval was superseded by Galahad as the winner of the Holy Grail in later variations of the legend, Galahad being viewed as a descendant of Joseph of Arimathea (the member of the Jerusalem council in whose tomb the body of Jesus was laid), who was believed to have gone to Glastonbury, England, with the Holy Grail. Another legend that received wide circulation in the Middle Ages was that of the true cross, the relic reputed to be the cross on which Jesus was crucified. According to the legend, Helena, the mother of the first Christian Roman emperor, Constantine, discovered the true cross in 326. Reliquaries (containers) of pieces of the true cross proliferated throughout Europe and Asia Minor, many of them being well executed artistically. Among the many other sources of legends in the Middle

Ages are the bestiaries, collections of stories of mythical and real animals, plants, and natural objects that were used for teaching moral and religious precepts.

Modern developments. Since the Reformation (16th century), because of a de-emphasis of allegory (symbolization) and an emphasis on biblical doctrinal themes by the Protestant Reformers, legend and myth have been relegated to the background of much Christian teaching. In the 20th century, however, there has been a recovery of an appreciation of the nature and function of myth. Certain Christian mythological themes are now viewed by scholars as being presuppositions—often unrecognized among the general public—of various Western concepts that are considered secular. The American concept of the separation of church and state, for example, can be traced to the following Christian sources that are thematically mythical: Clement of Alexandria's concept of the city of heaven and the city of the earth; Augustine's theory of the City of God and the City of the World; and Luther's doctrines of the visible and the invisible church and the two realms of authority. These in turn can be traced back ultimately to the statement of Jesus: "Render therefore to Caesar the things that are Caesar's, and to God the things that are God's" (Matt. 22:21). Judeo-Christian mythological concepts that the world is good and real and, therefore, worth studying (or having dominion over the world) are presuppositions that lie behind Western science. It is no accident that modern science developed in the West with its Jewish and Christian concepts of nature, rather than in the East where, in Hinduism, for example, nature is often viewed as relatively unreal or as an illusion. Evolutionary thought, as regards both biological and human social development, likewise owes much to the Jewish and Christian mythological theme of the linear progress of time.

In the late 19th and 20th centuries there has been a resurgence of Christian mythological themes, especially those of the apocalyptic variety. The short story of the Antichrist in *Tri razgovora o voyne progresse i kontse vsemirnoy istorii* (1900; *War, Progress, and the End of History*, 1915) by Vladimir Solovyov, a Russian philosopher of the 19th century, is one of the best examples of modern apocalyptic literature. In this story, Solovyov anticipates the coming world wars, the ecumenical movement, and an eventual salvation of the faithful remnant. Apocalyptic themes are also to be noted in secularized versions of Christian mythology—*i.e.*, science-fiction literature, in which there is usually a cataclysm of crisis proportions and the salvation of a remnant who have been faithful to certain values and principles.

BIBLIOGRAPHY. ALBAN BUTLER, *The Lives of the Saints*, 12 vol. (1902), legends of the saints of the Roman Catholic Church arranged according to their feast days; RUDOLF BULTMANN, *Das Urchristentum im Rahmen der antiken Religionen* (1949; Eng. trans., *Primitive Christianity in Its Contemporary Setting*, 1956), an interpretation of early Christianity from the standpoint of demythologization; CLEMENT OF ALEXANDRIA, *Exhortation to the Greeks, the Rich Man's Salvation, and the Fragment of an Address Entitled: To the Newly-Baptized* (1919), contains a translation by G.W. BUTTERWORTH of the *Protreptikos*, an early Christian attack on belief in Greek myths, though utilizing Greek mythological themes; MIRCEA ELIADE, *Myth and Reality* (1963), an interpretation of myth from the "history of religions" viewpoint; GEORGE EVERY, *Christian Mythology* (1970), well illustrated, with bibliography; S.L. FRANK (ed.), *A Solovyov Anthology* (1950), contains the short story of the Antichrist; ROBERT M. GRANT, *Gnosticism and Early Christianity*, 2nd ed. (1966), useful in describing and interpreting Gnostic myths; CARL JUNG et al. (eds.), *Man and His Symbols* (1964), a psychoanalytical interpretation of myths and symbols, see especially pp. 95–156; WILHELM SCHNEEMELCHER (ed.), *New Testament Apocrypha*, 2 vol. (1963–66), contains many legendary accounts of Christ and his disciples; H.G. MAY and B.M. METZGER (eds.), *The Oxford Annotated Bible* (1962), notes helpful in interpreting apocalyptic works; HUGO RAHNER, *Griechische Mythen in christlicher Deutung* (1945; Eng. trans., *Greek Myths and Christian Mystery*, 1963), especially useful for the story of Odysseus; HELEN J. WADDELL (trans.), *The Desert Fathers* (1957), contains legends of 4th-century monks in the Egyptian desert.

(L.F.)

Christian Philosophy

Christian philosophy was regarded by some early church writers as synonymous with Christian theology. The Scholastics, however, dominant philosophers of the Middle Ages, gradually came to distinguish philosophy (including natural theology, which is concerned with the existence and nature of God), with its universally accessible truths, from revealed theology derived from the Bible. Consequently, while, in later times, numerous Christians continued to become philosophers (among them René Descartes, John Locke, Gottfried Leibniz, George Berkeley, and Thomas Reid), they sought universal truths rather than the distinctive characteristics of the Christian revelation. In 1931, however, Émile Bréhier, a French Rationalist and historian of philosophy, contended that such a thing as Christian philosophy never has been nor can be.

THE 20TH-CENTURY DEBATE ON CHRISTIAN PHILOSOPHY

Early
arguments
that
Christianity and
philosophy
are incompatible

Bréhier argued that early church writers, as well as St. Augustine in the 4th century and St. Thomas Aquinas in the 13th century, appropriated unchanged pagan ideas and thus created incompatible unions of Christianity with Platonism and with Aristotelianism. Similarly, in modern times, philosophy has either been impressed into a nonphilosophical role as the servant of theology or treated as a wholly autonomous enterprise. The former result, Bréhier concluded, may be Christian, but it is not philosophy; and the latter may be philosophy, but it is not Christian.

Some Christian thinkers immediately agreed, among them certain followers of Thomas Aquinas, at the University of Louvain, in Belgium. Three principal reasons are offered for denying that there is a Christian philosophy: first, if the distinctives of Christianity are known to man through the biblical revelation and if theology is the systematic study of that revelation, then whatever is distinctively Christian will appear in theology. Second, whereas philosophy requires the autonomous exercise of human reason seeking universally accessible truth and pursues this goal by logical means, independently of religious presuppositions or special revelation, Christian philosophy, on the other hand, requires commitment to revealed truth; for philosophy, however, this is a self-contradiction. Third, philosophy discusses problems on which the biblical revelation is silent. One can ask, for instance, what Christianity has to say about sense perception or the foundations of mathematics that cannot be said equally well from other points of view. On such questions there is no distinctively Christian philosophical position.

This point of view does not mean, however, that there are no Christian philosophers: there are obviously many of them, and they are often especially interested in philosophical matters bearing on their faith and in the influence of Christianity on the history of philosophy. The French theologian Roger Mehl holds that there can be a "Christian intention" to bear witness in the field of philosophy to the reality of the religiously renewed mind. The Christian witnesses not by developing new philosophical concepts from Christian doctrines but by placing his philosophy, like all of life, under the judgment and promise of God. As he participates personally in a living dialectic between time and eternity and between sin and salvation, he finds the courage to break with pagan ideas.

Others disagree with Bréhier's contention and argue that Christian philosophy is possible without losing the autonomy proper to either theology or philosophy and without confusing the two disciplines. Three arguments may be noted:

Étienne Gilson, a historian of medieval philosophy, maintains that, both during the Middle Ages and subsequently, the spirit of Christianity penetrated the Greek tradition and drew out of it a specifically Christian world view. Perspectives previously undreamed of were thus opened up to human reason, perspectives that revelation proposed but that reason explored and established by purely philosophical means. Thus, philosophy and theology represent two distinct orders, each with questions and methods peculiarly its own, yet with mutual influences that are of value to both.

Whereas Gilson's argument is largely historical, a second attempt, pursued differently by such 20th-century writers as Leonard Hodgson, in England, Claude Tresmontant, in France, and Herman Dooyeweerd, in The Netherlands, stresses the world view that is implicit in biblical revelation. Christian philosophy, they hold, consciously develops the theoretical consequences of belief in God and creation, of man's condition in sin and grace, and of other distinctively Christian orientations. Proceeding from such starting points, Christian philosophy lays its credentials before the human mind as the only acceptable alternative to naturalistic, nihilistic, and other philosophies. Hodgson, for example, claims that a Christian philosophy that takes God's self-revelation in Christ as its clue to the understanding of the universe can properly embrace more empirical evidence than any other known system. It is not theology but philosophy that addresses the perennial problems by considering both scientific evidence and ordinary human experience.

A third argument contends that Christian philosophy is made possible by the impact of the faith in the life of the philosopher. The French philosopher Maurice Nédoncelle repudiates, as inhuman and outdated, Bréhier's Rationalist claim that philosophy is an impersonal and neutral undertaking and argues that the personality of the philosopher inevitably affects his work. The particular interests that a man pursues and the colouring that his own life gives to his universe all affect his thought. Moreover, the Christian philosopher cannot escape the light of Jesus Christ, which he feels gradually enriches and transforms the natural mind. Yet he cannot disentangle what he owes to grace from what he owes to nature. Consequently, the tradition of Christian philosophy is woven inextricably into the fabric of Western thought, addressing distinctively philosophical questions under the influence of both nature and grace. It is therefore at the same time both philosophy and Christian.

MEANING OF CHRISTIAN PHILOSOPHY

No one understanding of what is meant by Christian philosophy has yet gained general acceptance. Differences follow both theological and methodological lines.

Views based on theological differences. The Thomistic doctrine that nature and grace are distinguishable but mutually complementary realms suggests that Christian philosophy shares with other species of philosophy a common subject matter and method but that it is enriched and purified by its peculiar relationship to divine grace. The Catholic philosopher Jacques Maritain delineates the nature from the state of philosophy. Its nature, he holds, is defined by its end: natural knowledge of the essential and universal nature of things attained by rational means. Its state is defined by the concrete conditions under which human agents operate historically, including the limitations imposed by the weakness of human nature and the difficulty of the task. Whether a man speaks of a philosophy as Greek, as Cartesian, or as Christian, his adjectives refer to the historical state of philosophy rather than to the nature of the undertaking as such. Christian philosophy, according to Maritain, shares a common nature with other historical philosophies but is distinguished from them by its peculiar state.

Thomistic
and
Reformed
viewpoints

Divine grace changes the philosopher's condition both objectively and subjectively. Objectively, God reveals truths beyond what unaided reason can discover: the far-reaching ideas of creation, of God as Being-itself, of human reason validated by the Creator, and of the incarnation of Jesus Christ (being in the flesh) as the central clue to man's full self-understanding. Subjectively, God's grace lends new energy and strength to the philosophical mind, helping it toward the truth that is accessible in principle to the unaided intellect but that finite men may not otherwise grasp. It is the help of divine grace that marks the state of Christian philosophy.

Reformed theology (of the Protestant tradition from John Calvin) is dissatisfied with the Thomistic doctrine of nature and grace and stresses instead the sovereignty of God over every operation of human nature and the equally pervasive influence of sin. The problem with natural reason, in this view, is not only man's finiteness but —just as profoundly—his sin. It is a sin to assert the autonomy of philosophical reason and thus to presume that man can think effectively in independence of God; and this sin perverts philosophical understanding. Dooyeweerd, accordingly, draws a sharp line between Christian philosophy, which stems from the regenerate heart in obedience to sovereign God, and all of the other philosophies. The difference affects the very nature of philosophy: Christian philosophy is unique, according to Dooyeweerd, in its goal of obedience to sovereign God and to his law in every sphere of life and thought. The inquirer who asserts the neutrality of philosophical inquiry rejects this motive, reveals the apostate heart from which non-Christian philosophy springs, and so generates certain fatal antinomies (contradictions) that Dooyeweerd finds throughout the history of philosophy.

Existential theology exhibits the influence of contemporary Existentialism, a philosophy that stresses concrete human existence, in its view both of philosophy and of Christianity. Philosophy, in this view, is no longer a theoretical quest for the universal and essential nature of things but the desperate attempt of historical men to understand their life world and, in the face of dehumanizing forces, to affirm some ground for being. The Christian revelation uncovers the divine ground of Being in relation to the situation of man as a human being; and the Bible is a human witness to the Existential discovery of meaning rather than an authoritative record of revealed doctrine.

According to the Existential thought of John Wild, philosophy explores the universal characteristics of the human life world in order to uncover the values and "global meanings" that guide human existence and elicit a world view. For lack of complete and perfect knowledge, every philosopher elaborates his world view under the influence of some guiding image; and the Christian philosopher chooses to do so with the guiding image of the Christian faith. This image is not a set of doctrines about God and man but a variety of attitudes and values concerning life. Wild therefore rejects the role of Christian theology as a guide in formulating philosophical doctrines and speaks instead of the role of the Christian faith in lending meaning to human experience and, therefore, in shaping a philosophical world view.

Christian philosophy may be defined according to differences that Christianity makes either to (1) the person of the philosopher, (2) to the content of his thought, (3) to philosophical method, or (4) to some combination of these elements. References have already been made to the first and second; and the distinctive content of Christian philosophy will be elaborated subsequently. At this juncture, some comments on method remain.

Views based on methodological differences. Christian philosophy employs various common methods: speculative, Analytic, or Phenomenological. Christian philosophers tend, however, to oppose reductionist methods that eliminate metaphysics (which probes the ultimate nature of Being) or normative value judgments or that are narrowly empirical, acknowledging only scientifically observable fact. The Christian belief in God as Creator of all is a metaphysical belief implying an evaluation of man and nature; thus, any philosophical methods that place this belief or its consequences beyond meaningful discussion are naturally likely to be criticized by the Christian. And, finally, Christian philosophers cultivate methods that are specially developed to subserve their peculiar concerns, such as the use of analogy in understanding the transcendent God or the use of symbol and paradox in drawing implications from his historically unique acts.

The Frenchman Maurice Blondel, known for his philosophy of action, is especially significant because it was his work that provoked Bréhier's classic attack and because he was one of the first to respond to it in print. Blondel had proposed a so-called method of immanence, which, starting within human thought rather than within the Christian revelation, compels philosophy to see its own limitations and discover its need for grace. Unlike theology, this method does not treat the supernatural as a historical reality; neither does Blondel, in using this method, treat the supernatural as an arbitrary hypothesis or an optional addition to man's understanding, nor as the natural culmination of human evolution, nor as a totally ineffable object. The method of immanence works from within human thought, he explains, showing that the supernatural is indispensable but at the same time inaccessible by natural means. By thus entering wholly into human reason, Christian philosophy is fully philosophical; but it is not yet fully Christian because it is still to be completed by the development of a philosophy adequate to man's supernatural destiny.

On the other hand, Dooyeweerd criticizes Blondel because the objectivity of an immanentist method contradicts the biblical view that every human activity and thought proceeds "out of the heart." He proposes, instead, what he calls a "transcendental method" to penetrate the religious preconditions of theoretical thought in the heart of man. His criticism of "erroneous" historical philosophies therefore presses beyond the antinomies that he underscores and uncovers the faulty religious attitude that lies at the source of the error; and his constructive philosophy starts from the biblical themes of God as sovereign lawgiver and of man as involved in sin and redemption and works out the effects of these motives in each branch of philosophy. Dooyeweerd moves philosophy closer to theology than does Blondel and therefore sees in Christian philosophy a distinctive content as well as a distinctive method.

In general, it may be concluded that the term Christian philosophy indicates not so much a specific position or concept as a historical tradition, parallel to such other philosophical traditions as naturalistic philosophy or Islāmic philosophy but distinguished by the influence of Christian perspectives. It is a pluralistic tradition, however, varying with philosophical as well as theological differences, rather than a uniform phenomenon. It explores philosophical questions in the light of the Christian faith and enriches the Christian mind with philosophical inquiry, rather than offering a ready-made system of fully revealed answers to the problems of man.

DISTINCTIVE THEMES IN CHRISTIAN PHILOSOPHY

The simplest way to understand Christian philosophy is to isolate the root ideas that are clearly of philosophical consequence, ideas that distinguish the biblical perspective on man and the world from other ancient roots of Western thought.

God and creation. At the outset, the Christian's world is the creation of God. This simple assertion, basic to every other concept, is unique in ancient thought. It is true that some Near Eastern peoples other than the Hebrews had religious creation myths. The Babylonians, for instance, spoke of the god Marduk as having killed the monster Tiamat and having formed the cosmos from her dismembered body. Despite its rich religious and cultural symbolism, however, the Babylonian myth speaks of the construction of the universe out of existing materials rather than of an absolute *ex nihilo* ("out of nothing") creation, and it sees the world as born out of conflict rather than from a free act.

In the 4th century BC, Plato, in his *Timaeus*, developed a typically Greek outlook, speaking of the Demiurge, a subordinate deity who brought eternal forms and recalcitrant matter together, like the two halves of some mythical creature, to fashion a changing and imperfect temporal world. Despite the metaphysical ramifications of this view, however, Plato—like the Babylonians—speaks of construction out of existing ingredients rather than of absolute creation.

Ancient thought tended either to dualism, which posits two basic principles, or to emanationism, which views the world as an efflux from the One, or to some combination of the two. For example, according to Manichaeism, a Parthian religion of the 3rd century AD, on the one hand, there is a dualism of matter and spirit (or reason), the former being evil and the latter good. The universe is then an arena for conflict between these two eternal forces. In contrast to the Hebrew–Christian Scriptures, which suggest that, even though men abuse the good, life is yet essentially good, Manichaean dualism asserts a necessary and unavoidable tension between Good and Evil.

According to the emanationism of Plotinus, the principal representative of Neoplatonism, on the other hand—not unlike parallels in Indian religion, in Benedict de Spinoza, and in German Idealism—particular things emerge out of the One as light emanates from the sun, made of the being of the One and without independent status. They exist by negating the One and the Good and Being itself, so that individual existence is a negative rather than a positive thing, and the world of particulars is an inferior realm of necessarily semi-evil part-beings.

Hebrew creationism

By contrast, the Hebrews saw the creation of the world neither as a necessary emanation nor as the outcome of cosmic conflict. Instead, in the Hebrew view:

Creation is a free and personal activity expressing the wisdom and power of the Creator. The idea of a Fall in which the good is perverted by evil is separate from that of creation.

Creation continues; *i.e.*, God continues to act creatively not only in nature and in history but also in works of grace. In the Old Testament the verb *bara* ("to create") embraces both God's original creative work and his subsequent creative activity.

Time and history are therefore not a purposeless cycle making life meaningless but the arena of creative action for God and of sacred responsibility for man. According to the Logos concept of the Apostle John, the eternal Creator-God who illumines all of life is now incarnate in history, making a new creation among men.

Eternity is conceived not in Greek terms, as static timelessness, but as purposeful activity that goes on "from everlasting to everlasting."

Everything is dependent on God, but God is independent: the relation is asymmetrical. No other being is eternal; thus, there is no ultimate dualism here. Irenaeus, a 2nd-century Church Father, apparently introduced the phrase "creation *ex nihilo*" in opposition to Gnostic dualism, to indicate that God created out of nothing and therefore transcends his creation.

The transcendence of God means that he is absolutely free to create and to create what he will: he is not compelled to create, nor limited by existing materials or available forms. His freedom and transcendence produce an aura of mystery—not the perplexing mystery about nature that scientific analysis dispels but the mystery connected with a person whose dignity and character can never be exhaustively revealed by his activities and who therefore elicits religious awe and devotion.

The biblical assertion that the world is created by God is presented in dramatically historical and personal form rather than in theoretical abstractions, as in Greek philosophy. What makes the world and history what they are is the creative activity of God and not the relentless necessities of impersonal reason or arbitrary fate. This view, unique in ancient thought, is the root idea from which springs a distinctively Christian approach to man and history, to good and evil, to freedom and morality.

God and man. In the Christian view, men are creatures of God; thus, what is true of creation is true of man. Nothing in man has emanated from God or becomes divine; nor is human reason a seed of the divine, as Stoic philosophy supposed.

Body–soul unity; sanctity of the body

Doctrine of the human self. Man is not a composite of two ultimately incompatible parts that struggle together in this life while awaiting separation at death. The biblical view allows no Gnostic dualism of body and spirit, the one evil and the other good, but stresses rather the unity of the human self. The terms flesh and spirit are moral, not metaphysical, designations; they indicate the kind of person a man is, whether dominated by selfish desire or guided by godly interests, rather than representing two distinguishable parts of a man. Similarly, the Platonic dualism of body and soul is absent, along with the 17th-century Cartesian dualism of mind and body. In the Bible, "soul" (Hebrew *nefesh;* Greek *psychē*) is roughly synonymous with "self" or "life" and often refers to the whole person. The soul is not eternal, pre-existing and later reincarnated, but is created by God. While man's soul survives death and so is capable of immateriality, his destiny involves not a disembodied immortality but the resurrection of the body.

The Hebrew examines his own concrete self-awareness rather than considering one part of his being in theoretical abstraction from the whole. He confesses himself to be a creature of God made in the image of God, a free agent who finitely reflects the Creator in his own personal activities. Because he images the Creator in his physical work and in the bodily delights that God has created, the Hebrew gains a higher evaluation of the body than that which either dualism or emanationism allowed.

This view of man is reiterated in the incarnation and Resurrection of Jesus Christ: he "became flesh," and, after the crucifixion, his bodily life was renewed. The church early repudiated the idea that Jesus only seemed to have a body—as the Gnostic Docetists proposed, who regarded the body as evil and therefore unworthy of God—because then the whole of a man created by God could not be redeemed by Christ. The early church also repudiated the idea that Jesus Christ assumed only a human body and not human nature wholly because the whole man whom God created has sinned and needs redemption. The body is thus sacred, and there is something sacramental about man's activities in the physical world. Both physical work and bodily delights are the gifts of God, to be "received with thanksgiving" by those who remember the responsibilities that life brings. This emphasis in the poetic literature of the Old Testament and especially in Ecclesiastes and the Song of Solomon becomes the basis for the New Testament concept of life's stewardship. As God's creature in God's creation, a man lives under the law of God, which orders his relationship to God, to other men, and to nature. The law of God embodies what is right or just in creation and is summarized by love both for God and for men.

The moral view of man. The biblical ethic accordingly contrasts with Greek ethics in the value it places on the body and on all men as creatures in the image of God. Whereas the Greeks tend to make human reason the key to morality—so that evil arises either from ignorance or from a lack of rational harmony in the soul or in society—the biblical ethic neither blames reason nor places its hope in it. To the Christian, knowing the good is not sufficient for doing the good, and the rule of reason is no sure path either to virtue in a man or to justice in society. Good and evil are produced by the moral disposition of the heart; that is to say, by what a man loves most. Evil is therefore voluntary rather than a matter of ignorance, and its cure requires that God's grace convert a man's disposition toward God and his law. Grace, rather than the rational nature alone, is needful.

Human freedom

The contrast with Greek thought also appears in regard to human freedom. The Greek tradition, like that of the modern Enlightenment, speaks of freedom in metaphysical terms: man, being rational, is by nature free; for the rational will is free from physical and emotional determinism. The more concrete biblical view sees freedom, on the other hand, in moral terms: men have forfeited the freedom they enjoyed in loving and obeying God from the heart and have fallen into bondage to sinful desires. St. Augustine, at the turn of the 5th century, insisted, in the Pelagian Controversy over this very issue, that man is no longer free not to sin and that the rational will cannot reassert its freedom, for it too is enslaved by lesser loves than the love of God. Moral freedom stems from love for God, and its restoration accordingly depends on the work of God's grace in a man's life.

This moral view of man extends to the concept of truth. The Hebrew term *emet* ("truth"), employed in the Old Testament, speaks of stability and reliability and thus of moral trustworthiness rather than of the truth of propositions. What God or a trustworthy man says can also be trusted and is thus *emet,* but the concept of propositional truth remains derivative from the moral idea. The New Testament term aletheia suggests trustworthy disclosures rather than theoretical knowledge, and "the truth" frequently refers simply to the Christian Gospel. Underlying this usage is the idea, inherent in a belief in God as Creator, that in him "are hid all the treasures of wisdom and knowledge." As the early-Christian writer, Clement of Alexandria, saw around AD 200, all truth is God's truth —known fully to him alone (as the omniscient Creator) but made known in part to his creatures as well. The Christian therefore adopts a creaturely modesty in epistemology (the theory of knowledge). Man owes his knowledge to what God reveals, whether to men in general, through what is created, or to Israel and the church in particular, through his redeeming activity in their history and through the account of that activity given by the prophets and Apostles.

The biblical view of man as a moral creature gives rise to a moral interpretation of history, in contrast to the more metaphysical accounts attempted by the Greeks. Men live in responsibility to the law of God, and the creative activity of God expresses itself in the retributive justice that he exercises in human history. The Creator is the King of kings, active in the course of human affairs, drawing history to its destiny.

The biblical view of man and the world thus stands apart from the more abstract and speculative tendencies of the Greek tradition. Whether the two approaches are incompatible, complementary, or even fundamentally alike is a basic question for any Christian philosophy. But, directly or indirectly, the Judeo-Christian view will significantly affect the philosophical work of the Christian thinker.

HISTORICAL DEVELOPMENTS IN CHRISTIAN PHILOSOPHY

Underlying any philosophical use of biblical ideas is the fundamental question of the relation of revelation to reason and, more specifically, of the Christian revelation to philosophy. This relation has been variously perceived throughout history depending on the type of philosophy that prevailed from time to time, and, especially since about 1800, it has varied with the concept of revelation. Examples of the process may be supplied in each major period of the history of philosophy.

Platonic-Christian philosophy

In patristic and medieval philosophy. In patristic and medieval times, Christianity experienced a confrontation with Greek philosophy. The initial reaction to Platonism varied from the negative responses of the Church Father Tertullian and the Assyrian Apologist Tatian, based on their belief that its lack of any adequate doctrine of creation also threatened belief in the incarnation and Resurrection, to the positive use that the Church Fathers Clement of Alexandria and Origen made of Platonic doctrines. Philosophy was to the Greeks what the law was to the Jews, a preparation for Christ, and Plato possessed a fragment torn from the eternal truth of the living Logos (Word). Justin Martyr was so impressed by the work of Plato that he ascribed his insights to an acquaintance with the teaching of Moses. But, whatever the vehicle, truth in philosophy comes from God and is to be prized for its part in the divine Logos, whereas the Christian revelation provides a fuller disclosure that makes philosophy complete.

Augustine picked up the suggestion that Jesus Christ fulfills Plato's philosophical hopes by converting Plato to the doctrine of creation: Plato's ideal forms became archetypal ideas in the mind of God, who, at creation, implanted seminal forms in nature, thus making the physical world an orderly intelligible revelation of his wisdom and goodness. Augustine then countered Manichaean dualism with the claim that evil is due not to the existence of physical things but to the privation of their forms, which are good—a privation that, in nature and in contingent things, operates by deterioration and in morality, by concupiscence.

Though Augustine gave more value to the physical world and to sense perception than Plato did, eternal truths are still innate in the mind, as in Plato, and universally accessible by recollection. By appealing to innate ideas, he countered the Skeptic claim that no knowledge is possible at all. All men possess truth, he insisted, and this proposition in itself argues for the reality of an eternal Truth in which their fragments of truth participate. There is, however, a mode of cognition other than Plato's innate knowledge and sense opinion, viz., belief in the Christian revelation proclaimed by the church and attested by persuasive evidence. The revelation of eternal truth as the incarnate Logos makes Plato's quest complete.

Augustine, accordingly, capitalized on three patristic beliefs: (1) that both Plato and Neoplatonism lack any adequate doctrine of creation to explain the participation of particulars in eternal forms; (2) that, if God is Creator of all, then all truth is God's truth, and no conflict is inherently necessary between the Christian revelation and philosophical thinking; and (3) that, in consequence, Platonism's valuable insights are completed and corrected by the revelation of the Creator as the incarnate Logos.

Aristotelian-Christian philosophy

The same beliefs guided St. Thomas Aquinas in his conversion of Aristotelianism into a Christian philosophy. Aristotle, too, according to Aquinas, lacks an adequate doctrine of creation, for the unmoved mover (Aristotle's God) is pure form controlling the forms of things rather than giving existence.

If God is regarded as one whose essence is to exist and who freely gives things existence, then the existence of the natural order—as Aristotle described it, with material and efficient as well as formal and final causes— argues for the existence of God.

But philosophy is at best preparatory and incomplete. It may demonstrate the existence of God and the immortality of the soul; but the fuller truth on these issues is given in revealed doctrines concerning the divine Trinity and the saving grace of Christ. Reason helps man to understand revealed doctrines, but it cannot demonstrate them.

In the 13th and 14th centuries, as in patristic times, disagreement intensified over this threefold relation of Christianity to philosophy. Duns Scotus and William of Ockham agreed that the basic hiatus in Greek philosophy is its lack of the doctrine of creation.

But, even when converted to that doctrine, neither Plato's nor Aristotle's theory of Forms is adequate to it, for they subordinate the creative act to the restraints of a universal necessity and leave individuality either to a privation of form or to material causes. Scotus therefore introduced a separate individuating principle (haecceitas, "thisness") that allowed God to choose the forms that he uses for each particular, whereas Ockham abandoned forms altogether. Creation, they both argued, is a free act of the divine will that both fashions individuals and gives them existence, rather than a gift of existence to what is rationally determined by eternally fixed universals.

Ockham pushed the doctrine furthest. Whatever values may accrue from philosophical logic and language, the truth about God and man, he urged, must be learned from the Christian revelation. No Christian philosophy exists—either preparatory to theology or otherwise. The patristic belief that philosophy grasps truth independently and is fulfilled by Christianity is gone, and with it is gone the idea of Christian philosophy.

Influence of mechanistic science

In 17th- and 18th-century philosophy. Renaissance and Enlightenment philosophers continued, in theory, to separate philosophy from theology and to engage in philosophical argument that purported to be universally valid apart from religious presuppositions. In practice, however, they did not escape Christian influences. Their philosophy was shaped by the new science of Newton and Galileo, which propounded both conceptions and methods that Christian philosophers were forced to reckon with.

The mechanistic concept of material particles moved by the forces operating under the laws of motion seemed to the French philosopher René Descartes to be an appropriate account of how God has ordered his creation. Yet the image of the universe as a self-operating machine was equally compatible with a Deism according to which

God originated the natural order but does not act in revelation or in grace. Attempts to argue the existence of God from such a creation, however, could not adjudicate between a deistic and a theistic understanding of the Creator without appealing to the further evidence of miracles and revelation.

The mechanistic concept of nature also posed problems concerning man. Descartes avoided these difficulties by arguing first the existence of the rational soul and the existence of God as a perfect Creator who guarantees the trustworthiness of reason; on that basis, he then went on to establish the reality of the material world and its laws of motion. Consequently, man is, in his view, an interacting combination of soul and body, the former equipped with a reason and a will that can act independently of bodily causes. But more empirical thinkers, such as Thomas Hobbes, were unconvinced by his a priori arguments and saw no evidence for any other reality in man than matter in motion. Although he affirmed the existence of the Creator, Hobbes relegated religious considerations to theology and confined his philosophy to its scientific sources.

Other Christian philosophers, however, refused to take mechanistic science as an adequate description of reality. The Dutch occasionalist Arnold Geulincx attributed physical effects directly to the causal power of the Creator, so that physical antecedents are simply occasions for divine creativity. The Rationalist Gottfried Leibniz developed a theory of monads (centres of psychic force), each in constant dependence on God, viewing these as more ultimate realities than matter and the laws of motion. George Berkeley, a British phenomenalist, held that Isaac Newton's concepts of matter and of absolute space and time lack reference either to experience or to reality; he thus developed the Idealist claim that only God and other minds exist and that these alone create the experience that scientists describe. Adaptations of this sort served two purposes: they made it possible to conceive creation in nonmechanistic and, therefore, non-deistic terms, and they made it possible to conceive man in either more than or other than materialistic terms.

Philosophy meantime modelled its methods on those of the new science. The Rationalism of Descartes and of Leibniz, on the one hand, was modelled on the mathematical procedures that had proved successful in science. But the justification that they offered invoked the Christian doctrine of creation: reason is trustworthy, they argued, because its Creator is perfectly trustworthy, and there are universal truths to be known because all truth is objective, being known perfectly to God the Creator.

On the other hand, the Empiricism of John Locke and of Berkeley was modelled on the observational and inductive methods of the new science. But the beginnings of empirical science were nurtured by the Christian theology of late medieval times. Creation is contingent on God: its orderliness reveals his wisdom, and its intelligibility to men reflects his purpose, which, as Francis Bacon had noted, is that men should exercise dominion over nature. Consistent with this tradition, Locke talked of the rule of reason over nature, and Berkeley ascribed the content and orderliness of human experience to the creative mind of God. The doctrine of creation, in other words, provided Christian philosophers with a rational justification for their empirical methods. The philosophical development of both Rationalism and Empiricism was thus encouraged by Christian perspectives. What revelation provides, Locke asserted, is additional propositions beyond those that can be known by reason alone. But the doctrine of creation is nonetheless the foundation of reason.

Three generalizations may be made concerning this period in history, not unlike those regarding patristic and medieval times: (1) Mechanistic science itself cannot justify its own methods or establish a Christian conception either of God as Creator or of man as a rational and free being. (2) If God is regarded in Christian fashion as Creator of all, then reason and science are God's gifts, and all truth is God's truth. (3) For truth to be whole, the scientific account must be enlarged by other philosophical means, and philosophy itself must be enlarged by revelation.

In recent and contemporary philosophy. In the 19th and 20th centuries, philosophical thought reacted against Enlightenment concepts of reason and revelation modelled on scientific knowledge and toward the kind of self-consciousness that finds expression in the humanities. Not nature but the human spirit now provides the avenue to knowledge.

Late in the 18th century, Immanuel Kant had found in the moral will a basis both for arguing for the freedom and immortality of the soul and the existence of God and for interpreting Christian theology in purely ethical terms. Because the incarnation, in Kant's view, is a symbol of the sense of duty embedded in human conscience, the Christian revelation republishes what is already known rather than proclaiming additional truths (as Locke had supposed). In Kant's opinion, there is no Christian philosophy that has distinctive perspectives to develop; the particular symbols of theology can rather be translated into universal concepts.

Kant's Idealist successors likewise assumed that God is revealed in human self-consciousness. The Romanticist Friedrich Schleiermacher focussed on man's feelings of finiteness and of absolute dependence on the ground of Being, whereas Hegel traced the growth of religious consciousness in the historical evolution of the human spirit. For both of these men, Christian theology is a symbolic rendering of universal concepts; thus, there are no distinctively Christian perspectives to influence Christian philosophers. Special Christian revelation is merged into the universal revelation of God in human consciousness.

Underlying this change is their conscious rejection of the duality of God and creation (which they associated with Enlightenment thought) in favour of Benedict de Spinoza's monism. History is a mode of the divine being, they held, and human consciousness is an expression of God's self-consciousness. God is not the transcendent Creator acting freely in revelation and grace but the immanent ground of all Being. Some 20th-century Christian philosophers, notably Archbishop William Temple and the French Jesuit Teilhard de Chardin, a paleoanthropologist, have developed this kind of Idealism while trying to preserve sufficient divine transcendence to avoid the problems that ancient theories of emanation posed.

Existential philosophers object that such Idealistic immanentism strips God of his mysterious transcendence and obscures the historical predicament within which each man must live. Søren Kierkegaard, the Danish precursor of Existentialism, for example, dramatically reaffirmed the otherness of the Eternal: God is not revealed in the universal concepts of a human genius but confronts men with a particular fact—his incarnation. The genius can build a logical system, but, in Kierkegaard's view, logic can never embrace either the paradox of the eternal uniquely incarnated in time or the all-absorbing passion of a man's faith in God. If philosophy requires the logical systematization of universal and necessary truths, then no philosophy of existence is possible, not even a Christian philosophy.

Christian philosophy is also unlikely to exist in an Existentialist setting if revelation is confined to existential confrontation without the doctrinal content that gives normative direction to thought. Kierkegaard, however, did not limit revelation in that fashion; and his argument about philosophical systems allows, nonetheless, a philosophy of existence of a sort that does not claim completeness as a logical system of all truth. Kierkegaard anticipated the work of such contemporary Christian philosophers as the French scholars Gabriel Marcel and Paul Ricoeur, whose phenomenology of human existence shows the openness of man's experience to the activity of a transcendent God. But, because Phenomenology concerns itself with concrete experience rather than with theoretical concepts, this type of Christian philosophy does not develop the philosophical implications of the doctrine of creation that concerned patristic and medieval thinkers. Christian faith is more likely to affect the philosopher himself, as Roger Mehl and others declare, than to pro-

Kant and 19th-century Idealism

Recent Existentialism and Analytic philosophy

vide presuppositions or directions for metaphysical inquiry.

Analytic philosophy also, being less concerned with world views than with particular problems, is unlikely to produce a systematic Christian philosophy. Yet the tradition of Christian philosophy persists among Analysts. Like the medievals, first, they have given attention to arguments for the existence of God and to the use of analogy and other logical devices in religious discourse. Second, they have used philosophical methods to clarify such theological conceptions as creation and revelation and to analyze the problems of freedom and evil. Third, and most directly significant, they have discussed the prospects for metaphysics within an Analytic context and have explored the integrative role that is played by the concept of God as Creator in unifying metaphysical understanding.

PROBLEMS CONFRONTING CHRISTIAN PHILOSOPHY

Problems regarding creationist metaphysics. The doctrine of creation, which has proved to be foundational to Christian philosophy, is a metaphysical belief. The possibility of any Christian philosophy therefore appears to be tied to that of metaphysics, and the justification of belief in God as Creator seems logically akin to the justification procedures for metaphysical beliefs. Three kinds of apologetic approaches may thus be distinguished among Christian philosophers, reflecting three more general views of metaphysics.

> Different approaches to metaphysics

Some Christian philosophers hold that metaphysics is a science, a rigorous theoretical discipline, in which the truth of its statements is logically demonstrable. This kind of view characterized the medieval Aristotelians for whom metaphysics is the science of first principles; it characterized Renaissance and Enlightenment Rationalists, such as Descartes and Leibniz, in their quest for universal and necessary truths; and it characterizes certain contemporary Logical Analysts.

From these points of view, the possibility of Christian philosophy is tied to the possibility of natural theology—that branch of metaphysics that is concerned with the existence and nature of God. (It should be remembered, however, that not all of the natural theologians admit that a distinctively Christian philosophy influenced by the Christian revelation is possible.) In natural theology, meaningful discourse about God is possible because some analogy exists between God's creatures, through whom he is known, and God himself; and this analogy facilitates intelligible predication. The classic arguments for the existence of God still interest philosophers, viz., the a priori ontological argument of Anselm and Descartes (based on the very nature of the God concept) and the five empirically based proofs of Thomas Aquinas that anticipated later cosmological and teleological arguments (based upon the contingency and purposiveness of nature, respectively). If metaphysical science can establish the existence of God and the possibility of intelligible discourse about him, then the root idea of Christian philosophy is also justified.

A second kind of approach, stressing the transcendence of God and the necessity of his self-revelation, rejects the metaphysical approach to understanding and justifying belief in God as Creator. Blaise Pascal, a 17th-century apologist, and Karl Barth, a 20th-century Neo-orthodox theologian, represent this tradition. Metaphysical arguments, they maintain, are ineffective; the abstract God of the philosophers is a far cry from the personal God of Scripture; Christian belief therefore depends on the self-validating character of God's revelation rather than on metaphysical speculation. One recent variant of this non-metaphysical approach is that of the British philosopher John Hick, who suggests that because the truth claims of Christianity are not empirically confirmed in this life, the believer anticipates what he calls an "eschatological (or 'last times') verification."

A third kind of approach, stemming from Kant, sees metaphysics as the systematic development of a world view from postulates demanded by man's attempt to understand life. This approach appears variously in the root-metaphor theory of the aesthetician Stephen Pepper, as a provisional scheme of interpretive categories in the process philosopher A.N. Whitehead, or as a conceptual map-work in the philosopher of religion I.T. Ramsey, bishop of Durham.

When Christian philosophy is viewed in this fashion, then its root idea that God is Creator serves either as a model to be developed, as an integrator concept around which the system of Christian philosophy is organized, or as a presupposition from which the system is derived. In any case, the meaning of such discourse is relative to the system in which it functions, and belief in God is justified not as an isolated proposition but through its systematic role. Granted this presupposition, a logically coherent world view is possible, covering adequately every kind of empirical consideration and opening up the meaning that Christianity ascribes to life. The case for a Christian philosophy therefore lies in its systematic appeal rather than in the scientific demonstrability of its first principles.

Though the root idea of creation *ex nihilo* arises in philosophical debates on a variety of topics, its effect seems to be indecisive. Reference was made above, for instance, to the status of universals as archetypal ideas in the mind of God and to the participation of particulars in those universals by a creative act rather than by emanation or imitation. Yet Christian philosophers disagree about how to account for individuality, whether by natural process or by direct creation, and about how to account for universal order, whether by inherent forms or by direct creation. In both instances, an appeal to the processes and inherent forms of nature indicates adherence to Greek ideas and to the primacy of intellect over will in the Creator. Likewise, an appeal to direct creation indicates a break with Greek ideas in favour of the primacy of God's will. Despite their disagreement, however, Christian philosophers insist that God creates both individuality and order in nature and that creation is therefore the key to the problem.

> Creationist impact on universals; on teleology

Mechanism and teleology afford different accounts of the order of nature, the one ascribing it to imposed forces and the other to inherent purposes. Greek and modern philosophy alike are divided on this issue, and divine creation does not immediately resolve it. That God orders his creation for good ends Christian philosophers agree, but they differ on whether he does so by externally imposed forces or by inherent ends that nature unconsciously pursues. In the early days of mechanistic science, René Descartes and Francis Bacon assigned the discussion of ends and purposes to theology, and, by confining philosophy to more mechanical processes, they adopted the mechanistic view. Aquinas and Leibniz and such 20th-century philosophers as William Temple and Teilhard de Chardin, on the other hand, find philosophical reasons for the teleological view. In either case, however, the Christian philosopher disagrees with the mechanistic Materialist who explains the natural order by chance rather than by purpose.

Substance and process represent two aspects of nature, each of which has at times been taken as basic to the other. The insistence of substance philosophy on the order of nature, the indestructibility of soul substance, and the immutability of God understandably appeal to such Christian thinkers as Aquinas and Descartes. Process philosophy, on the other hand, points to the flux of consciousness, to evolutionary and individual development, and to relativity theory; and in some cases it extends its categories of change to God. To a varying extent, it has appealed to such philosophers as Hegel, Temple, and Teilhard de Chardin. The issue hinges largely on whether process philosophy can give sufficient meaning to the unchanging nature of God and, if not, whether process categories can be confined to the philosophy of nature and of man. In any case, the Christian idea of creation grants the contingency and mutability of created things.

> On substance and process philosophies

Problems regarding man in the world. The Christian affirmation that creation is good implies a positive evaluation of the natural order. The effect of this affirmation on asceticism has been noted (see above *God and man*) and on the problem of evil: if creation is good, then evil is a privation of that good either by destruction or by perversion of the creature. Even when evil is present, the creature remains good to the extent that it is unperverted. Creation retains a potentiality for good that can yet be actualized, for God who permits evil also makes evil serve the good. Evil is not absolute, not an ultimate lack of teleology, because God alone is absolute as Creator of all.

These classic assertions, developed by such philosophers as Augustine, Aquinas, and Leibniz, also affect certain other philosophical matters:

They underscore the meaningfulness of existence. An ultimate pessimism—such as that presented by atheistic Existentialism and the Theatre of the Absurd—is alien to Christianity because it rests on the postulate that God is dead and anything is possible. Because God is actively Creator and because creation is good, the Christian philosopher denies that existence is meaningless. He may, of course, appeal to the theory of universals to reunite existence with essence; or he may, like Gabriel Marcel, call attention to the faith, hope, and love that save fragile man from despair. But, if God creates individuals, value extends to each individual in creation.

The assertion that creation is good affirms a relation between fact and value that affects ethical theory. The Thomistic doctrine of natural law, for instance, derives moral and political obligation from the created order. Other Christian philosophers, whose Empiricist epistemology precludes any logical derivation of value from fact, have developed an intuitionist ethic. Yet intuitionists, from Joseph Butler to the present, make their judgments in the light either of the facts in a particular case or of a logical analysis of meta-ethical concepts. Moral intuition, in contrast to Positivist explanations of morality, is a rational act that requires the objectivity of value.

The objectivity of truth as well as that of goodness (some have added beauty) is implied by belief in God as Creator. Medieval philosophers distinguished three senses of truth: eternal truths (*rationes aeternae*) in the mind of God, the ontological truth of beings that conforms to their eternal archetypes, and the truth of propositions about such beings. When philosophers abandoned the Platonic theory of forms, only propositional truth survived; but for Christian philosophers such propositions still retained objective reference to the natural order and to the mind of God.

This situation does not mean that Christian philosophers have always been committed to the theory that defines truth in terms of the correspondence between a proposition and a state of affairs. Idealists have preferred the coherence theory, which defines it in terms of the unified nature of a system of thought, on the grounds that such correspondence cannot be verified and that truth in the mind of God is coherent in itself whether or not he has created independent beings. In either case, Christian philosophers who affirm the omniscience of God have in him a point of objective reference when they declare that "X is true."

The objectivity of truth stands in opposition to any relativism that defines truth in terms of individual preference rather than of its universally normative status. Human knowledge is often relative, and decisions may at times depend on individual preference; but truth to the Christian philosopher is still the normative quality of God's knowledge by which human knowledge is judged. Human knowledge may involve subjectivity in the sense of personal concern, selectivity, or the use of presuppositions; but these do not always preclude knowledge of "God's truth." Kierkegaard regarded subjectivity as essential to the truth; a Christian concept of truth precludes only that form of subjectivity that views all truth as private and relative (so that objective truth does not exist). If truth is not objective, God is not the omniscient Creator of all.

Yet Christian philosophy is divided on the extent of subjectivity in human knowledge. Until about 1800, most philosophers assumed that knowledge is by definition neutral, objective, and certain; but recent Christian philosophers, influenced by Existentialist thought and by Analytical philosophy, now grant that subjectivity is ingredient to scientific and metaphysical, as well as to religious, knowledge. To the extent that this is so, they part company with Scholastic, Empirical, and Rationalist epistemologies, which seek objective certainty for human knowledge.

The concept that man is created in God's image affects both philosophical anthropology and ethics. From early Christian times, for instance, it was recognized that God has created not souls to be planted in bodies but unitary human individuals; and the early church accordingly rejected the pre-existence of the human soul. Christian philosophy is concerned not only with individuality but also with the unity of the individual, something that even Descartes admitted, despite his difficulties in explaining it. His problem stems from the mechanistic conception of body. The unity of mind and body is more readily conceivable when the individual is regarded as a teleological unity (as with Aquinas and modern Idealists) rather than as an interacting conjunction of two substances.

In Descartes's view of the soul, which was indeterministic, freedom is ascribed to the will. On the teleological view, however, freedom belongs to the individual: it is an expression of inner purpose, a kind of self-determination rather than an indeterminism; and it finds expression in a variety of ways in addition to voluntary choice. To make values and goals heartily one's own, to rest one's faith in God, to love and trust other people, to transcend past experience in creative imagination, art, and speculative thinking—this is to be free. A man is not free who is driven by emotion or habit. Freedom consists of being an individual, a subject who initiates action that is genuinely his own rather than of being merely a bandied object.

Christian philosophers have welcomed recent Phenomenological accounts of freedom couched in terms of the difference between personal and impersonal experience. An I–Thou experience frees both individuals by aiding their self-fulfillment, whereas an I–It experience objectifies and dehumanizes. It is noteworthy that the Bible speaks of revelation in I–Thou language and that the divine–human encounter enhances the freedom of man.

Christian ethics has historically stressed both the concept of law and the concept of love: in natural law ethics, for instance, love is recognized as the highest virtue; and in the Bible it is love for God that produces hearty obedience to his law. Recent emphasis on the I–Thou character of religious and interpersonal experience has given new prominence to love, producing a so-called agapistic ethic (Greek *agapē*, "spiritual love"), which admits no other moral obligation than the prudent maximization of love, defined in Existentialist terms as personal fulfillment through an I–Thou relationship. The result is that, instead of focussing on ethical duties (deontology), Christian morality consists of acts determined by their consequences ("act-Utilitarianism"). Traditionally, Christian ethics has traced man's duties back to God the Creator and held man responsible to God for the consequences of his acts. Agapistic ethics, however, does not consistently develop this relationship.

A Christian philosophy of history is shaped by the belief that creation is good and that man is created in the image of God to fulfill his Creator's purposes on earth. Augustine, taking these purposes to be primarily ethical, the practice of righteousness on earth through love for both God and men, produced an ethical interpretation of history in his *City of God*, using the prophetic theme of retributive justice to explain human history from Adam to the fall of Rome and to show the reasonableness of a Final Judgment. For Augustine, time is not Plato's moving shadow determined by an impersonal eternity, and history is no meaninglessly recurrent cycle of futile human attempts at justice. Time is ruled by the freedom of an eternal Creator who achieves his just and loving purpose in history: history is purpose achieving.

The rise of evolutionary theory in the 19th century generated among Christian thinkers the hope of a historical utopia through the growth of the Kingdom of God on earth. Writers of the 20th century, however, such as the theologian Reinhold Niebuhr, are less optimistic. But the ethical interpretation of history continues, along with widespread emphasis on the social and cultural responsibilities that accompany membership in the Kingdom of God.

SUMMARY AND EVALUATION

As a historical tradition adjusting to philosophical changes and contributing to philosophical inquiry, Christian philosophy has proved to be a persistent and creative force in the West. As a set of biblical ideas with far-reaching implications for a philosophically developed world view, it is an enduring reality. But one will be disappointed if he looks for a definitive position to which all of the Christian philosophers adhere on the major problems of Western thought. That no such unanimity exists is due to historical, theological, and personal variables that intrude into theoretical thought, as well as to the philosophical complexities concerned. Pluralism within Christian philosophy, however, is an advantage, if it can prevent premature dogmatism and contribute to the vigour, the competence, and the biblical perceptivity of philosophers who are Christians.

BIBLIOGRAPHY. The classic article that triggered the debate of the 1930s was by E. BREHIER, "Y a-t-il une philosophie chrétienne?" *Revue de Metaphysique et de Moralle*, 38:133–162 (1931). For the English-speaking reader, that debate is discussed by M. NEDONCELLE in *Existe-t-il une philosophie chrétienne?* (1956; Eng. trans., *Is There a Christian Philosophy*, 1960); ETIENNE GILSON expresses his position in *Christianisme et philosophie* (1936; Eng. trans., *Christianity and Philosophy*, 1939); and H. DOOYEWEERD, *In the Twilight of Western Thought* (1960), consisting of lectures he gave in America, affords the best introduction to his thought. An overview of recent Catholic and Protestant discussion in the light of the history of Christian philosophy is provided by A.F. HOLMES in *Christian Philosophy in the Twentieth Century* (1969).

CLAUDE TRESMONTANT has made outstanding contributions on biblical distinctives in *Essai sur la pensée hébraïque*, 2nd ed. (1956; Eng. trans., *A Study of Hebrew Thought*, 1960) and *Les Origines de la philosophie chrétienne* (1962; Eng. trans., *The Origins of Christian Philosophy*, 1963). The classic works on the history of Christian philosophy are by ETIENNE GILSON, notably his *Reason and Revelation in the Middle Ages* (1938) and *The Spirit of Medieval Philosophy* (1936). J.V.L. CASSERLEY, *The Christian in Philosophy* (1949), moves from a historical account to highlight the significance of subjectivity and of revelatory events for philosophy. A good account of one historical period is A.H. ARMSTRONG and R.A. MARKUS, *Christian Faith and Greek Philosophy* (1960).

Some contributions of Christianity to various particular philosophical problems may be seen in L. HODGSON, *Towards a Christian Philosophy* (1942); more systematically in WILLIAM TEMPLE, *Nature, Man and God* (1934); and on epistemology in A.F. HOLMES, *Faith Seeks Understanding* (1971). Writers of varying points of view have contributed to R.M. MCINERNY, *New Themes in Christian Philosophy* (1968).

In addition to bibliographical materials in these works, two reference volumes by G.F. MCLEAN should be noted: *An Annotated Bibliography of Philosophy in Catholic Thought, 1900–1964* (1967) and *A Bibliography of Christian Philosophy and Contemporary Issues* (1967).

(A.F.Ho.)

Christian Science

Christian Science is a religious system of therapy and metaphysics that was established as a church in Boston in 1879. Though the great majority of its adherents are Americans, the movement is found in all countries with large Protestant populations. In this article the movement's history, organization, teachings, therapeutic practices, and contemporary strength are described.

NATURE AND SIGNIFICANCE

Mary Baker Eddy (1821–1910) gave the name Christian Science to the system of thought that she developed between 1862 and 1875, the first published statement of which, *Science and Health*, appeared in 1875. Mrs. Eddy claimed to have discovered the principles by which Jesus

healed the sick and raised the dead, and to have successfully demonstrated them, first in recovering from what was thought to be a fatal accident, and then in healing others. She began teaching metaphysical healing in the late 1860s and later set up a college. As a philosophy, Christian Science approximates subjective idealism in that it declares matter to be unreal, and God or Mind, to be infinite. By affirming propositions such as these, Christian Scientists believe they bring the condition of the unreal material body into harmony with the real spiritual estate of man, who, as the image of God, should manifest perfection. Thus, it is true knowledge alone that heals the sick. Mental affirmation of these propositions is prayer, and this "mental work" may be undertaken for oneself or by a Christian Science practitioner.

In 1879, Mrs. Eddy established the Church of Christ, Scientist, in Boston, as the Mother Church, thus instituting a dual structure in her movement—a system of therapeutics with accredited practitioners, and an ecclesiastical organization, the Mother Church and its branches. The two elements are structurally only loosely articulated. Although all practitioners must be members of the Mother Church, they do not necessarily, or usually, play prominent parts in local church life. Control of the movement is vested in the Christian Science Board of Directors of the Mother Church. Subsidiary boards regulate all public presentations of Christian Science and the instruction given to those seeking to become teachers (who themselves give private instruction indispensable to those who wish to become practitioners). **Establishment of the Mother Church**

Although Christian Scientists dissociate their movement from the New Thought teachings that arose in the late 19th century, its origins and its optimistic, expansive, and positive orientation to the world are similar to theirs. In somewhat dilute form, the idea that affirmative thinking is necessary for the attainment of bodily health, worldly wealth, and social success passed into the popular presentations of many major American denominations. This development is partly attributable to Christian Science and New Thought. Their growth also stimulated spasmodic interest in spiritual healing.

Unlike many sects, Christian Scientists have never withdrawn from worldly involvements, and in 1908 the movement endorsed ideals of responsibility in public life by establishing a newspaper, *The Christian Science Monitor*, dedicated to the presentation of wholesome news and the avoidance of sensationalism. In its news coverage, the *Monitor* applies the Christian Science theory that the mere discussion of evil invests evil with seeming power: its policy is to concentrate on the good in the world. Today, the *Monitor* may be a better known representative of Christian Science than metaphysical healing, although it is through its therapeutic practice that Christian Science has chiefly recruited its following.

HISTORY AND ORGANIZATION

Controversy surrounds Mrs. Eddy's discovery of Christian Science. Between 1862 and 1866, Mrs. Eddy was the patient and pupil of the mental healer Phineas P. Quimby, who had originally practiced hypnotism, but who had, by this time, concluded that cures were effected by correcting the thought of his patients. Although she later likened their relationship to that of Jesus and John the Baptist, with herself in the role of Jesus, when Quimby died in 1866, Mrs. Eddy described him as healing "with the Truth that Christ taught." By the early 1870s, Mrs. Eddy asserted that her healing system was her own discovery, and, in a spiritualist journal, she advertised for fee-paying pupils who wished to learn a lucrative profession. Unlike Quimby, she gathered her students together for religious meetings, though this was some years before she organized a church. Many early students quarrelled with Mrs. Eddy, and it was only after her removal to Boston from Lynn, Massachusetts, that she began to attract a stable following. The basic concepts of mental healing in *Science and Health* were derived from Quimby (most evidently in the subsequently withdrawn first edition), but Mrs. Eddy discarded some of Quimby's ideas from the outset, and she used theological language much more extensively than he had done. There are stronger similarities with idealist philosophy in her book than in Quimby's manuscripts, but whether Mrs. Eddy acquired these notions from one Hiram Crafts, in whose home she lived while writing her book, remains an open question. Though verbatim passages—from Emanuel Swedenborg, Thomas Carlyle, and John Ruskin among others—appear without attribution in Mrs. Eddy's writings, the fragments are neither extensive nor of fundamental importance to her thought.

The Massachusetts Metaphysical College

In 1879, she and her students founded the church, and in 1881 she opened the Massachusetts Metaphysical College, which had power to confer degrees. Students paid $300 for a course lasting about three weeks and were then eligible to set up as practitioners, or, following a further course, as teachers of Christian Science. Metaphysical Obstetrics was also taught.

Graduates disseminated the new cult throughout America and set up healing institutes as well as churches. Teachers sometimes embellished Mrs. Eddy's ideas, however, and outright defectors established rival movements. In 1889–90, Mrs. Eddy, in a series of reforms, asserted her control. She dissolved existing national associations, closed her college, opened the Mother Church to all Christian Scientists and made membership in it obligatory for practitioners, and defined all local churches as branches of the Mother Church. In 1895, she replaced the pastors of individual branch churches by readers, and since then all sermons have comprised set readings from the Bible and *Science and Health*. She published a governing instrument, the *Manual of The Mother Church*, adopted by all branch churches, which defined the obligations of Christian Scientists, including that of complete loyalty to Mrs. Eddy. From a healing cult, Christian Science became a highly centralized organization, and its implicit dualism as a system of therapy and a church was at least partially coordinated and brought under the firm control of the directors of the Mother Church.

Mrs. Eddy left control to the five directors in the later years of her life, and after her death they became a self-perpetuating body in which the majority acquired the right—in a protracted and sordid lawsuit—to remove any individual director. The ambiguities of the *Manual* led to a further dispute about power between the trustees of the Christian Science Publishing Society and the directors, and this, too, was settled in favour of the directors after long and bitter litigation. Two would-be successors to Mrs. Eddy led schismatic movements in the two decades following her death. In London, Mrs. Annie C. Bill (later joined by a dissident ex-director) established the Christian Science Parent Church. Mrs. A.E. Stetson, a successful New York teacher of Christian Science, who had been excommunicated before Mrs. Eddy's death, might have been a more serious challenge, had she not, having affirmed that her ideas were inspired by Mrs. Eddy, refused to set up a "material organization" that would necessarily "corrupt" the spirituality of Christian Science. Over the years a considerable number of prominent practitioners and teachers have disagreed with the way in which the directors have governed the movement and have often sought freedom to expand and develop Christian Science ideas. Many of these have withdrawn or have been expelled but have continued to practice metaphysical healing.

BELIEF AND PRACTICES

Science and Health

Science and Health with Key to the Scriptures (1891; the 56th edition of *Science and Health*) is the only official exposition of Christian Science. It is a repetitive book, and its lack of system is evident from the fact that Mrs. Eddy, in her many revisions, more than once changed the order of chapters. Mrs. Eddy's other writings have incidental historical interest but add little of substance to her doctrines. Her autobiographical sketch is uninformative, and her poetry is not well regarded except by Christian Scientists. Since her death her work has not been revised in

any way, and loyal Christian Scientists regard it as perfect and complete.

Christian Science teaches that God is divine Principle, Mind, Soul, Spirit, Life, Truth, and Love. The "real" man reflects God and is spiritual; the material body and the mortal mind are unreal counterfeits. Realization of this proposition destroys disharmony, sin, sickness, and death. Men suffer because they entertain a false sense of themselves. At an absolute level, Christian Science denies the evidence of the senses, but there is also a human level at which evidence of physical improvement is taken as confirmation of the truth of spiritual thinking. Christian Science claims to produce health by correcting man's delusions that he sins, suffers, or may die.

The movement's unitarian theology teaches that the Holy Ghost, or Comforter, is Christian Science itself, by which Jesus, the exemplar, healed the sick. Mrs. Eddy did not openly claim equality with Jesus, but some followers regard her as ". . . a woman clothed with the sun, . . ." (Rev. 12). In the section "Key to the Scriptures" of her textbook, the prophetic texts of Revelation are treated to the exclusion of any other part of the New Testament. Like other mental healing cults, Christian Science has little teaching about the afterlife, although there is a suggestion that men must all, sooner or later, accept Christian Science, and that "mental work" here will reduce suffering in life hereafter. A distinctive teaching concerns *malicious animal magnetism*, evil thought that appears to be powerful because men believe in it. All advanced Christian Scientists learn how to undertake defensive mental work to neutralize the effect of animal magnetism.

Healing is accomplished by "an application of the distinction between absolute and real being and the human mortal concept of man." Practitioners treat patients—usually *in absentia*—by affirming truth and by denying error and animal magnetism. Mrs. Eddy denied that healing was ever accomplished by drugs and medicines; when they appeared to heal, they did so by altering the patient's thoughts.

Church services

Except for hymns and incidentals, the Sunday services, which are conducted by readers, are uniform in all churches on any given day. Sermons cover 26 subjects, taken in succession twice a year. The readings are chosen by a special committee in Boston. Good Christian Scientists read these texts every day in the week before they are publicly read in church. Churches are austere but comfortable, and services are unemotional. Christmas and Easter are not commemorated. There is no baptism or other sacrament. Twice in the year the congregation kneels to commemorate, not the Last Supper, but the joyous morning meal beside the lake of Galilee, attended by the risen Christ. All churches maintain a reading room and most of them a Sunday school. A local meeting is granted the status of church only if there are at least 16 members, 4 of whom must be members of the Mother Church and one of whom must be a practitioner.

Many advanced members undergo a week's instruction from a teacher, and those who then cease other gainful employment may register as approved practitioners and take fee-paying patients. Teaching is from a particular chapter of *Science and Health*, and special attention is given to animal magnetism. A practitioner may become a teacher after three years of healing and a course organized by the Christian Science Board of Education. Most higher officials of the movement are teachers.

The movement is primarily an association of the likeminded. It lacks a shared community life. Its style is impersonal, somewhat austere, but not particularly ascetic. Adherents participate freely in social, political, and business life, and believe that their religion promotes their worldly success. Recreation and entertainment are not disapproved, and the strongly solicited abstinence from tobacco and alcohol is dictated less by asceticism than because these things are seen as drugs. There is no hostility to education (except in medicine) and there are some private Christian Science schools. Mrs. Eddy may have taught an ascetic sex ethic to some women followers, and she affirmed that when the truth was fully understood childbirth would cease to be physical, but such ideas are not emphasized today. Christian Science adherents often seek dental and optical treatment. They submit, when necessary, to vaccination and inoculation, affirming that it can neither harm nor help the real man.

CHRISTIAN SCIENCE TODAY

A high proportion of members are middle-aged and elderly women from the middle and upper middle classes. The movement's strength is in metropolitan centres, spas and resorts, and prosperous residential areas. About 85 percent of its officially listed practitioners are women, although about 50 percent of its teachers (who are far fewer) are men. No figures of membership have been published since 1936, when there were about 269,000 Christian Scientists in the United States in about 2,000 churches and societies. In 1968, there were about 2,380 churches and societies in the United States. Rate of growth has slowed considerably since 1950, and—in America—only in California, Florida, and Texas have the number of organizations significantly increased. The number of listed practitioners fell by almost one-third between 1953 and 1968 in the United States, to a total of less than 5,400. This trend has been reflected in the United Kingdom (from 898 to 543), Canada, Australia, New Zealand, South Africa, and Switzerland in the same 15-year period. In the Federal Republic of Germany the decline has been less severe. The movement has about 500 churches and societies in western Europe, of which 315 are in the United Kingdom and 110 in the Federal Republic of Germany.

BIBLIOGRAPHY. The controversy about the origins of Christian Science, the obscurity of periods of Mrs. Eddy's life, and the inaccessibility of the archival materials of the Mother Church are together responsible for the absence of completely reliable standard works on the movement.

Mary Baker Eddy: E.S. BATES and J.V. DITTEMORE, *Mary Baker Eddy: The Truth and the Tradition* (1932); NORMAN BEASLEY, *Mary Baker Eddy* (1963); E.F. DAKIN, *Mrs. Eddy: Biography of a Virginal Mind* (1929); A.H. DICKEY, *Memoirs of Mary Baker Eddy* (1927); H.A.S. KENNEDY, *Mrs. Eddy* (1947); GEORGINA MILMINE, *The Life of Mary Baker Eddy and the History of Christian Science* (1909); S. WILBUR, *The Life of Mary Baker Eddy* (1908).

History of Christian Science: NORMAN BEASLEY, *The Cross and the Crown* (1952); C.S. BRADEN, *Christian Science Today: Power, Policy, Practice* (1958), an objective study; H.A.S. KENNEDY, *Christian Science and Organized Religion* (1930); ROBERT PEEL, *Christian Science: Its Encounter with American Culture* (1958).

Origins of Christian Science: H.W. DRESSER (ed.), *The Quimby Manuscripts* (1921), contains the correspondence of Mrs. Eddy with Quimby; H.S. FICKE, "The Source of *Science and Health,*" *Bibliotheca Sacra,* 85:417–423 (1928); C.H. MOEHLMAN, *Ordeal by Concordance* (1955); B.R. WILSON, "The Origins of Christian Science: A Survey," *Hibbert Journal,* 57:161–170 (1959).

Christian Science teachings: MARY BAKER EDDY, *Science and Health with Key to the Scriptures* (1891), *Manual of The Mother Church* (1895).

(B.R.W.)

Christina of Sweden

One of the wittiest and most learned women of her age, Queen Christina of Sweden astonished the Christian world by abdicating her throne in order to become a Roman Catholic. An inveterate politician, she attempted at various times after her abdication to become queen of Naples and of Poland, but she is best remembered for her lavish patronage of the arts and her influence on European culture.

The daughter of King Gustavus II Adolphus and Maria Eleonora of Brandenburg, she was born in Stockholm on Dec. 8, 1626. After her father died in the Battle of Lützen, Christina, his only heir, became queen-elect before the age of six. By his orders she was educated as a prince, with the learned theologian Johannes Matthiae as her tutor. Five regents headed by the chancellor Axel Oxen-

Christina, engraving by Cornelis Visscher published by P. Soutman, 1650.
By courtesy of the Svenska Portrattarkivet, Stockholm

stierna governed the country. Her brilliance and strong will were evident even in her childhood. Oxenstierna himself instructed her in politics and first admitted her to council meetings when she was 14.

When Christina came of age and was crowned queen in 1644, she opposed Oxenstierna; and there was constant friction between them thereafter, particularly concerning the Thirty Years' War (*q.v.*). In spite of his opposition, she was a prime mover in concluding the Peace of Westphalia and ending the war. An assiduous politician, Christina was able to keep the bitter class rivalries that broke out after the war from lapsing into civil war but was unable to solve the desperate financial problems caused by the long years of fighting. In the end, she had to recall Oxenstierna. Highly cultured and passionately interested in learning, she rose at five in the morning to read and invited eminent foreign writers, musicians, and scholars to her court. Descartes himself taught her philosophy and died at her court. For her wit and learning, all Europe called her the Minerva of the North; she was, however, extravagant, too free in giving away crown lands, and intent on a luxurious court in a country that could not support it and did not want it. Her reign was nevertheless beneficent: it saw the first Swedish newspaper (1645) and the first countrywide school ordinance; science and literature were encouraged, and new privileges were given to the towns; trade, manufactures, and mining also made great strides.

Christina's abdication after ten years of rule shocked and confused the Christian world. She pleaded that she was ill and that the burden of ruling was too heavy for a woman. The real reasons, however, were her aversion to marriage and her secret conversion to Roman Catholicism, which was proscribed in Sweden. She chose her cousin Charles X Gustav as her successor, and when he was crowned on June 6, 1654, the day of her abdication, Christina left Sweden immediately.

In December 1655 Pope Alexander VII received Christina in splendour at Rome. He was, however, soon disillusioned with his famous convert, who opposed public displays of piety. Although she was far from beautiful (short and pockmarked, with a humped right shoulder), Christina, by her manners and personality, created a sensation in Rome. Missing the activity of ruling, she entered into negotiations with the French chief minister, Cardinal Mazarin, and with the Duke of Modena to seize Naples (then under the Spanish crown), intending to become queen of Naples and to leave the throne to a French prince at her death. This scheme collapsed in 1657, during a visit by Christina to France. When staying at Fontainebleau, she ordered the summary execution of her equerry, the Marchese Gian Rinaldo Monaldeschi, alleging that he had betrayed her plans to the Holy See. Her refusal to give reasons for this action, beyond insist-

Abdication and conversion to Catholicism

ing on her royal authority, shocked the French court, nor did the pope welcome her return to Rome.

In spite of this scandal, Christina lived to become one of the most influential figures of her time, the friend of four popes, and a magnificent patroness of the arts. Always extravagant, she had financial difficulties most of her life: the revenues due from Sweden came slowly or not at all. She visited Sweden in 1660 and in 1667. On the second journey, while staying in Hamburg, she had Pope Clement IX's support in an attempt to gain another crown, that of her second cousin John Casimir, who had abdicated the throne of Poland; but her failure seemed to please her since this meant that she could return to her beloved Rome. There she had formed a strong friendship with Cardinal Decio Azzolino, a clever, charming, prudent man, leader of a group of cardinals active in church politics. It was generally believed in Rome that he was her lover, a view sustained by her letters, which were decoded in the 19th century. With him, she, too, became active in church politics, insisting for years on the pursuance of the Christian war against the Turks. Pope Innocent XI, who pushed this war to its victorious conclusion, stopped her pension at her own urgent request in order to add it to the war treasury. In 1681, having secured a trustworthy administrator for her lands in Sweden, Christina at last became financially secure.

Patronage of the arts

Christina's extraordinary taste in the arts has influenced European culture since her time. Her palace, the Riario (now the Corsini, on the Lungara in Rome), contained the greatest collection of paintings of the Venetian school ever assembled as well as other notable paintings, sculpture, and medallions. It became the meeting place of men of letters and musicians. The Accademia dell' Arcadia for philosophy and literature, which she founded, still exists in Rome. It was at her instigation that the Tordinona, the first public opera house in Rome, was opened, and it was she who recognized the genius of and sponsored the composer Alessandro Scarlatti, who became her choirmaster, and Arcangelo Corelli, who directed her orchestra. The sculptor and architect Giovanni Bernini, her friend, considered her his saviour when she commissioned the art historian Filippo Baldinucci to write his biography while he was being discredited in 1680. Her enormous collection of books and manuscripts is now in the Vatican library. She was renowned, too, for her militant protection of personal freedoms, for her charities, and as protectress of the Jews in Rome.

Christina died in the Riario palace on April 19, 1689. She made Cardinal Azzolino her heir, but he died two months after her. Her tomb is in St. Peter's in Rome.

BIBLIOGRAPHY. The definitive source containing all the documents on Christina known up to the time of its publication, including the beginning of her own autobiography, is J. ARCKENHOLTZ, *Mémoires concernant Christine*, 4 vol. (1751–60). Christina's *Maxims* and her *Reflections on Alexander the Great*, her best known original writing, are in *Pensées de Christine, reine de Suède* (1825). Among various collections of her letters to important personages, the most valuable are *Lettres choisies de Christine, reine de Suède* (1760); and LE BARON DE BILDT, *Christine de Suède et le Cardinal Azzolino* (1899), in which were published the previously uncoded letters that changed many historians' viewpoints. In contemporary English, the most complete account is in RUTH STEPHAN, *The Flight* (1956), on Christina's years in Sweden; and *My Crown, My Love* (1960), on the Queen's years in Rome—both fictional memoirs based on fact and further research. Important works of Swedish historians are: CURT WEIBULL, *Drottning Kristina*, 3rd ed. (1961; Eng. trans., *Christina of Sweden*, 1966), her history until 1657; SVEN STOLPE, *Königin Christine von Schweden* (1962; Eng. trans., *Christina of Sweden*, ed. by SIR ALEC RANDALL, 1966), tracing her career from Stoicism to mysticism; and SVEN INGEMAR OLOFSSON, *Drottning Christinas, tronavsägelse och trosförändring* (1953), on her abdication and change of faith.

(Ru.S.)

Chromatography

Chromatography is a technique for separating chemical substances on the basis of relative rates of adsorption from a moving liquid or gaseous stream. It is widely used in biochemical research for the separation and identification of chemical compounds of biological origin. In the chemical industry the technique is employed to separate and analyze complex mixtures, such as petroleum. Because certain forms of chromatography are capable of detecting extremely small amounts of materials, they are used to identify trace contaminants, such as chlorinated insecticides, in biological materials.

Advantages as a separation method

As a separation method, chromatography has a number of advantages over older techniques—crystallization and distillation, for example (see CHEMICAL SEPARATIONS AND PURIFICATIONS). It is capable of separating a multicomponent chemical mixture without requiring an extensive foreknowledge of the identity, number, or relative amounts of the substances present. It is versatile in that it can deal with molecular species ranging in size from viruses composed of millions of atoms to the smallest of all molecules—hydrogen—which contains only two; furthermore, it can be used with large or small amounts of material. Some forms of chromatography detect substances present at the picogram (10^{-12} gram) level, thus making the method a superb analytical technique. It is also effective as a large-scale preparative method. Its resolving power is unequalled among separation methods; more than 100 constituents can be isolated from complex mixtures such as gasoline.

Chromatography is carried out by utilizing a gas or liquid (the mobile phase) flowing over or through an adsorbing material (the stationary phase) of high surface area. The components of the mixture to be separated are introduced into this system and allowed to migrate in the direction of the flow at different rates, which are determined by their relative distributions between the mobile and stationary phases. Chromatography is thus a differential migration technique, along with electrophoresis (separation in an electrical field) and sedimentation (separation in a gravitational field). It depends for its separating ability on differential retardation, or retention, caused by the unequal degree of adsorption of the solutes washed along by the fluid stream.

HISTORY

The first purely pragmatic applications of chromatography can be traced to the early dye chemists, who tested their dye mixtures by dipping strings or pieces of cloth or filter paper into the dye vat. The dye solution migrated up the inserted material by capillary action, and the dye components separated into bands of different colour. In the 19th century, several German chemists carried out deliberate experiments to explore the phenomenon. They observed, for example, the development of concentric, coloured rings by dropping solutions of inorganic compounds onto the centre of a piece of filter paper; a treatise was published in 1861 describing the method and giving it the name "capillary analysis." For the following 50 years, the technique was used for the analytical separation of a large variety of materials, including biological samples.

Discovery of chromatography

The discovery of chromatography, however, is generally attributed to the Russian botanist Mikhail S. Tsvet (also spelled Tswett) because he recognized the physicochemical basis of the separation and applied it in a rational and organized way to the separation of plant pigments, particularly the carotenoids and the chlorophylls. Tsvet's book, published in 1910, described a technique that is used today in essentially the same form. A vertical glass column is packed with an adsorptive material, such as alumina or powdered sugar; a solution of the plant pigments is added to the top of the column, and the pigments are washed through the column with an organic solvent. The pigments separate into a series of discrete coloured bands on the column, divided by regions entirely free of pigments. After the column of adsorptive material is extruded carefully from the tube, the different zones of pigments are isolated by cutting the material into sections. Pigment is then washed off each section with a solvent. Because Tsvet worked with coloured substances, he called the method chromatography (from

Greek words meaning colour writing). About 1900 an American chemist separated the components of crude oil by passing the sample through a column of fuller's earth; he was well aware of the analytical importance of this process, but his work was not widely followed outside the petroleum field. Tsvet's development of chromatographic procedures also was generally unknown to chemists in the Western world because he published either in German botanical journals or in Russian works. In 1931 chromatography emerged from its relative obscurity when the German chemist Richard Kuhn (who later received the Nobel Prize for Chemistry) and co-workers reported the use of this method in the resolution of a number of biologically important materials. Ten years later, two British chemists, A.J.P. Martin and R.L.M. Synge, began a study of the amino-acid composition of wool. Their initial efforts, in which they used a technique called liquid–liquid countercurrent distribution, failed to give them adequate separation; they conceived, therefore, of an alternate method, in which one liquid was firmly bound to a finely granulated solid packed in a glass tube and a second liquid, immiscible with the first, was percolated through it. Silica gel served as the granular solid, and Martin and Synge pictured the gel as composed of water tightly bonded to the crystals of silica; the mobile phase was chloroform. Their work with this technique was remarkably successful. Although their method was mechanically identical with the method of Tsvet, it was innovative in that it involved the concept of a stationary liquid (water) supported on an inert solid (silica), with the result that the solute molecules partitioned between the stationary liquid and a separate mobile liquid phase (chloroform). The new technique was called partition chromatography, and in 1952 Martin and Synge were awarded the Nobel Prize for their work.

The initial partition-chromatography system presented difficulties because of lack of reproducibility in the properties of the silica gel and lack of uniformity in the packing of columns. Partly for this reason, Martin, Synge, and their co-workers worked out a new procedure in which the stationary medium consisted of a sheet of filter paper. The paper was thought of as consisting of water bonded to cellulose, giving another partition method. The technique gave the desired reproducibility, and beginning in the 1940s paper chromatography found wide application in the analysis of biologically important compounds, such as amino acids, steroids, carbohydrates, and bile pigments. In this field it has replaced, to a large extent, the column technique initiated by Tsvet.

Motivated probably by the same drawbacks to column chromatography, two Russian pharmacists developed a technique for distributing the support material as a thin film on a glass plate. The plate and support material could then be manipulated in a fashion similar to that of paper chromatography. The results of the Russian studies were reported in 1938, but the potential of the method was not widely realized until 1956, when intensive research on its application was begun. The new chromatographic system became known as thin-layer chromatography.

Still another chromatographic technique, gas chromatography, was first carried out in Austria, but the first extensive exploitation of the method was made by Martin and A.T. James in 1952, when they reported the elution gas chromatography of organic acids and amines. In this work, small particles of support material were coated with a nonvolatile liquid and packed into a heated glass tube. Mixtures injected into the inlet of the tube and driven through by compressed gas appeared in well-separated zones. This development was immediately recognized by petroleum chemists as a simple and rapid method of analysis of the complex hydrocarbon mixtures encountered in petroleum products. A major advance came with the elimination of the support material and the coating of the liquid on the wall of a long capillary tube. With this development, it has become possible to carry out such extraordinary separations as the identification of 350 different components of coffee flavour in a single chromatographic "run."

Discovery of gas chromatography

In the years since the rediscovery of chromatography by Kuhn, chromatographic separations have contributed greatly to many fields and possibly have been the greatest single cause of the dramatic acceleration that occurred in biochemical research during this period. Discovery of the structure of insulin, for example, was made possible when the British biochemist Frederick Sanger rationally and methodically applied chromatography to the fragments of the ruptured insulin molecule. He received the 1958 Nobel Prize for Chemistry for his work.

METHODS

Classification. Classification of the various chromatographic techniques is somewhat confusing because the descriptive terms used may refer to the state of the adsorptive material, the nature of the adsorptive force, the nature of the mobile phase, the method of termination, the method of solute introduction, and the presence or absence of gradients. In column chromatography, the adsorptive material is placed in a column of glass or metal, generally long and narrow in form. The adsorbent may be granular and fill the column (packed column), or it may be a liquid coating the inside column wall (capillary column). The mobile phase is drawn through the column by gravity or forced through by pumps. In paper and thin-layer chromatography, the adsorptive material consists, respectively, of a sheet or a thin film. In either case, liquid is drawn over the initially dry film by capillary action.

If the adsorptive force is provided by molecules attaching to the surface of a solid that is packed in a column, spread as a thin film on a glass or plastic sheet, or coated on the inside walls of a tube, the method is termed adsorption chromatography. If the solid is a polymeric material containing attached ions that can be exchanged for ions in the solution mixture, the method is termed ion-exchange chromatography (see ION-EXCHANGE REACTIONS). If the sorptive force is provided by the molecules dissolving in a liquid coated on a granular solid or on the walls of a column, the method is termed partition chromatography (meaning that the solute is partitioned between two liquid phases; in this case the term "adsorption" might be considered something of a misnomer). If the molecules diffuse into narrow pores within a solid, the process is termed molecular sieving, gel filtration, or gel-permeation chromatography. (Again, in these cases, it is questionable whether true adsorption is involved.) Regardless of the mechanism involved, in all types of chromatography the material that takes up the solute remains fixed and is called the stationary phase.

Adsorption chromatography

The method is further classified by the nature of the mobile phase. When this is a gas, the method is called "gas chromatography"; when it is a liquid, "liquid chromatography." Adsorption chromatography, then, can be either gas–solid chromatography or liquid–solid chromatography, depending upon whether the mobile phase is a gas or a liquid. Similarly, partition chromatography can be gas–liquid or liquid–liquid chromatography.

Chromatographic methods also can be classified according to the method used to terminate a single chromatographic procedure, or "run." In development chromatography, the flow of the mobile phase simply is halted after a certain time interval. Because the average velocities of the solutes differ, depending upon their retardation, each is displaced a different distance. The distance moved by a solute relative to the distance moved by the solvent is a measure of the retention and is called the R_f value. Slightly retained solutes move a large distance (that is, have a large R_f value), whereas strongly retained solutes remain close to the site of sample introduction (that is, have a small R_f value). In elution chromatography all of the solutes migrate through the entire adsorptive bed and appear at its terminus at different times. Solutes that are slightly retained by the stationary phase have small retention times, whereas those more tenaciously retained have large retention times. (Retention times can be converted to retention volumes by multiplying the times by the volumetric flow rate of the mobile phase.)

In zonal chromatography, the most common form, the

mixture of solutes to be separated is introduced as a narrow zone, or spot, either added to the incoming mobile phase or applied directly to the adsorptive material. In the method called frontal analysis, by contrast, the mixture to be resolved is introduced as a continuous stream or "train." If the letters A, B, and C represent the solutes in order of increasing affinity for the stationary phase, then the first zone to appear is the front of the A solute train, the second zone consists of part of the A train and the front of the B train, and the final zone contains the remainder of all three solute trains. The zones are contiguous.

When A, B, and C are strongly retained, and a large, but discrete, sample of the mixture is placed at the top of an adsorptive bed, the solutes come to occupy contiguous bands. The top band is almost exclusively C because it has the greatest affinity for the adsorptive sites and is concentrated enough to displace the more weakly adsorbed A and B from these sites. The next band consists almost exclusively of B, for the same reasons. The lowest band consists of A. If a fourth substance, D, which is the most strongly adsorbed of all, then is introduced continuously into the column, it displaces C, which in turn displaces B, which displaces A. The zones then migrate through the medium in this order. This procedure is called displacement chromatography. It is not widely used because there is no space between zones and it is, therefore, difficult to achieve separations.

Quite often, gradients—smooth changes in temperature or in composition of the mobile phase—are used in elution chromatography to speed up sluggish zones. If temperature is varied steadily during the run, the process is called programmed temperature chromatography. If mobile-phase composition is changed, it is gradient elution chromatography.

Technique. *Gas chromatography.* In gas chromatography, helium, hydrogen, nitrogen, or some other inert gas is employed as the mobile phase. With gas–solid chromatography, a stationary phase of an adsorptive solid, such as carbon, alumina, or silica, either is packed in the column as small particles or is coated on the inside wall as a film. Retention, in either case, is by weak adsorptive forces between the solute molecules and adsorptive sites on the solid material. The solid support also can be a porous, relatively nonadsorptive material, as is the case with the so-called molecular sieves, and the molecules then are separated on the basis of molecular size rather than degree of adsorption. Small molecules diffuse preferentially into the small regular pores of the sieve and thus are retarded relative to larger molecules, which are not so trapped. In gas–liquid chromatography, a nonvolatile liquid is coated on a finely divided solid, the support, and these particles are packed in the column, or the liquid may be coated on the inside wall of a small diameter tube. The stationary liquids include high-molecular-weight hydrocarbons and complex polymers, such as the polyesters.

An important consideration in gas chromatography is detection of the material as it comes off the column in the carrier gas. Thermal-conductivity detectors compare the heat-conducting ability of the exit gas stream to that of a "reference" stream of pure carrier gas. To accomplish this, the gas streams are passed over heated filaments in thermal-conductivity cells. Measured changes in filament resistance of the cells reflect temperature changes caused by increments in thermal conductivity. This resistance change is monitored and registered continuously on a recorder. An alternate type of detector is the flame-ionization detector, in which the gas stream is mixed with hydrogen and burned. Positive ions and electrons are produced in the flame when organic substances are present. The ions are collected at electrodes and produce a small, measurable current. The flame-ionization detector is highly sensitive to hydrocarbons, but it will not detect carrier gases, such as nitrogen and oxygen, or highly oxidized materials, such as carbon dioxide, carbon monoxide, sulfur dioxide, and water. In another device, the electron-capture detector, a stream of electrons from a radioactive source is produced in a potential field. Materials in

the gas stream containing atoms of certain types capture electrons from the stream and measurably reduce the current. Most important of the capturing atoms are the halogens—fluorine, chlorine, bromine, and iodine. This type of detector, therefore, is particularly useful with chlorinated pesticides. Other important detector systems are: the helium-ionization detector, the flame-photometric detector, and the microcoulometric detector. The effluent gas from the gas chromatograph also can be led directly to the inlet port of a mass spectrometer, a device that separates materials on the basis of their masses. This procedure not only tells when materials come off the column, but also identifies them.

Liquid–solid chromatography. Liquid–solid chromatography is carried out with a liquid mobile phase and a solid stationary phase. In liquid–solid chromatography, as it is generally practiced, the solid is packed into a vertical tube, the sample is introduced onto the top of the packing bed, and a solvent is added continuously to the top of the column to wash the mixture through by gravity flow. Results from gas chromatography suggested that separation could be improved in liquid chromatography if the diameter of the tube and the sizes of the solid particles were reduced and if the pressure driving the liquid through were increased. A number of instances of improved separations using long, narrow columns and high inlet pressures, in fact, have been reported. The capacity of such columns is reduced, however, and sensitive detectors must be employed to locate the small amounts of material in the effluent.

If the solute components are coloured, their position on the column, or their appearance in the effluent, is easily determined. In early work employing development chromatography with colourless solutes, the column packing was extruded to yield a long cylinder; a colour-developing reagent was then streaked along the column to indicate the presence of a solute band. In elution chromatography, successive samples of the effluent are collected in tubes held in a mechanically driven rotating tray, called a "fraction collector." Reagents are added to the sequential fractions to determine the presence of a solute, perhaps by producing a coloured product or a precipitate; or the fractions can be examined by a spectrophotometer, which detects substances by their light-absorption properties. This time-consuming process has now been automated. With solutes that respond to the chemical reagent ninhydrin (especially, amino acids) the effluent is automatically mixed with the colour-developing reagent, and the solution continuously passed through a spectrophotometer cell. The absorption of light is recorded on a photoelectric tube connected to a recorder. A tracing then records the solutes as they pass off the column. Solutes absorbing light in the ultraviolet region can be similarly monitored. In another detection method, dissolved solutes produce a change in the refractive index of the effluent, another light effect that can be continuously monitored. Other detecting devices, called moving-wire and chain detectors, also can be used.

Popular adsorbents for liquid chromatography are alumina and silica. Ion exchange columns employ both positively charged (cationic) and negatively charged (anionic) exchangers. The column may be packed with a porous polymer, a porous glass, or a gel (modified cellulose or agarose) for molecular-sieve chromatography.

Thin-layer chromatography. In thin-layer chromatography, the adsorbent is mixed with a binder, such as calcium sulfate, and a slurry of adsorbent, binder, and water is coated on a glass plate. As the plate dries, the binder and adsorbent particles together form a thin film. The thin-layer plate is then heated to drive off water and activate the adsorbent. The sample mixture is placed on one edge of the plate as a spot, a row of spots, or a continuous streak. The plate is clamped vertically between two other glass plates with the lower edge of the adsorbent exposed in a trough of solvent. The solvent rises up through the adsorbent by capillary action to produce the mobile-phase flow. Alternatively, the loaded edge can be placed in the upper position and solvent can be fed to the plate by wick systems, with the result that flow is downward by gravity, as well as by capillary action. In any case, flow is normally halted before the solvent progresses to the other edge. For uncoloured solutes the plate is sprayed with a colour-developing reagent, or the presence of solutes is detected by ultraviolet absorption or fluorescence. No matter which method is used, the result is a series of spots or bands arranged in the direction of flow.

Liquid–liquid chromatography. In liquid–liquid chromatography, both the stationary and mobile phases are liquid. When hydrated silica gel and powdered cellulose are used in columns, the stationary phase, in both cases, is presumed to be water bonded to the solid support. The mobile phase is normally a liquid immiscible with water. Sheets of filter paper are used in the same manner as that described for thin-layer chromatography, but, in this case, the stationary material is the liquid (water) bonded to the cellulose support. This is paper chromatography. Reversed-phase paper chromatography involves impregnation of the paper with an organic fluid, which adheres firmly to the paper. The mobile phase is then water or a water-miscible liquid. Paper also can be chemically modified so that it acts as an ion exchanger, or it can be impregnated with a liquid exchanger. Another technique sometimes used consists of passing a solution of two liquids through a column packed with a solid. One of the liquids shows preferential adsorption to the solid, with the result that there are effectively two liquid phases, the adsorbed liquid and the equilibrium solution that remains unadsorbed.

THEORETICAL CONSIDERATIONS

Retention. The rates of migration of substances in chromatographic procedures depend on the relative affinity of the substances for the stationary and the mobile phases. Those solutes attracted more strongly to the stationary phase are held back relative to those solutes attracted more strongly to the mobile phase. The forces of attraction are usually selective; that is, stronger for one solute than another. At least one of the two phases must exert a selective effect, and very often both phases are selective. In gas chromatography, the mobile phase is ordinarily a gas that exerts essentially no attractive force on the solutes at all. In this case the mobile phase is entirely nonselective.

The forces attracting solutes to the two phases are the normal forces existing between molecules—intermolecular forces. There are five major classes of these: (1) the universal, but weak, interaction between all electrons in neighbouring atoms and molecules, called dispersion forces; (2) the induction effect, by which polar molecules (those having an asymmetrical distribution of electrons) bring about a charge asymmetry in other molecules; (3) an orientation effect, caused by the mutual attraction of polar molecules resulting from alignment of dipoles (positive charges separated from negative charges); (4) hydrogen bonding between dipolar molecules bearing positive hydrogen ions; and (5) acid–base interactions in the Lewis acid–base sense; that is, the affinity of electron-accepting species (Lewis acids) to electron donors (Lewis bases). In the special case of ions—charged molecules and atoms—a strong electrostatic force exists, in addition to the other forces; this electrostatic force attracts each ion to ions of opposite charge. This is an important element of ion-exchange chromatography.

In studies of chromatographic behaviour, the retention ratio, the relative speed of solute and mobile phase, is a quantity of major significance. It is approximately equal to the experimentally determined R_f value described above. Its value never exceeds one, because the solute can never move faster than the mobile phase that carries it along. The retention ratio is inversely related to the distribution coefficient, a factor that describes the relative distribution of solute between the mobile and the stationary phases. The precise relationship of the retention ratio and the distribution coefficient is expressed in the following equation: $R = (1 + K V_s/V_m)^{-1}$, in which R is the retention ratio, K is the distribution coefficient,

and V_s/V_m is the ratio of the amount of stationary phase present (V_s) to the amount of mobile phase (V_m).

The versatile operation of chromatography requires that solute velocity, and thus the retention ratio, be subject to control. As the above equation suggests, partial control can be gained by altering the ratio of stationary phase to mobile phase (V_s/V_m). Greater control can be gained by manipulating the distribution coefficient (K), because there are many factors that affect it. Changes in the chemical nature of the stationary and mobile phases, for example, alter the distribution coefficients of different solutes in the solvent system. This provides selectivity control; that is, it makes it possible to separate solutes by changing solvent systems. Changes in the chemical nature of the phases also cause gross shifts in individual distribution coefficient, because the intermolecular forces involved are altered. Increased temperature generally decreases the distribution coefficient, drastically so in gas chromatography, in which a 20° C rise in temperature may halve the distribution coefficient and, as a consequence, double the retention ratio. Variations in mean pressure affect the distribution coefficient if they are high enough—tens and hundreds of atmospheres of pressure are necessary to influence gas and liquid chromatography, respectively.

Local changes in distribution coefficient may occur as "pulses" of solute in high concentration appear. Very low solute concentrations do not affect the distribution coefficient, but at high concentrations solute molecules interact with one another as well as with the constant background presented by the mobile and stationary phases. In adsorption chromatography, the interaction takes the form of a competition for adsorption sites on the stationary phase. The limited sites available accommodate only limited amounts of solute and, as these sites are filled, the amount adsorbed finally becomes independent of the amount present. For all such interactions, the distribution coefficient changes with concentration in a nonlinear fashion. In modern chromatographic practice, nonlinear distribution is avoided wherever possible, because it distorts and broadens chromatographic zones, making separations less sharp.

Resolution. Chromatography separates complex mixtures into individual solute zones; a written, or traced, record of a chromatographic procedure is a chromatogram. For development chromatography, as in paper chromatography, the final chromatogram consists of a series of spots or zones arranged along the migration coordinate. In elution chromatography, when a detector is used, the chromatogram is a trace on a recorder chart of the solute concentration plotted against the time. This yields a concentration profile, exhibiting discrete peaks at points where zones of solute appear. A similar profile can be produced from a development chromatogram by recording the concentration of the solute along the migration path, using a radioactive detector or an optical densitometer (a device that is used for detecting solutes optically).

There are two features of the concentration profile important in the separation or resolution of solute zones. Peak position, the first, refers to the location of the maximum concentration of a peak. To achieve satisfactory resolution, the maxima of two adjacent peaks must be disengaged. Such disengagement depends upon the identity of the solute and the selectivity of the stationary and mobile phases.

The second feature important to resolution is the width of the peak. Peaks in which the maxima are widely disengaged still may be so broad that the solutes are incompletely resolved. For this reason, peak width is of major concern in chromatography. It is infrequently measured as such, however, but rather is reflected in a quantity called the plate height, or the height equivalent to a theoretical plate. (These phrases are borrowed from the separation procedure called fractional distillation, in which separation is achieved by distillation and condensation on obstructions called "plates.")

Chromatographic peaks ordinarily are bell-shaped. Mathematically, they present the profile shown in Figure

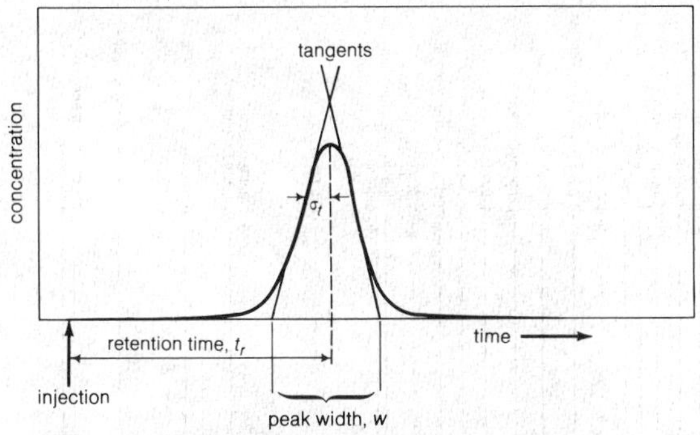

Figure 1: Peak shape, peak width, and plate height parameters in elution chromatography.

1. The so-called standard deviation (represented by sigma, σ) is one-quarter of the baseline width (w) between lines drawn tangent to the points of inflection of the peak. Either the standard deviation or the baseline width may be taken as a measure of peak width in comparing peaks for various purposes.

In chromatography, peak width increases in proportion to the square root of the distance that the peak has migrated. Mathematically, this is equivalent to saying that the square of the standard deviation is equal to a constant times the distance travelled. The height equivalent to a theoretical plate is defined as the proportionality constant relating the standard deviation and the distance travelled. Thus, the defining equation of the height equivalent to a theoretical plate is as follows: HETP $= \sigma^2/L$, in which HETP is the height equivalent to a theoretical plate, σ is the standard deviation, and L the distance travelled. The use of the plate height is superior to the use of peak width in evaluating various chromatographic systems, because it is constant for the chromatographic run, and it is nearly constant from solute to solute.

In elution chromatography, in which the peak develops on a time scale, an equivalent form of the above equation is: HETP $= L\ \sigma_t^2/t_r^2$, in which L is now the column length, t_r the time of retention of the peak by the column, and σ_t is the standard deviation of the peak in time units. (Several other equivalent equations exist, some of them using the baseline width rather than the standard deviation of the peak.)

Processes contrib-
uting to plate heights Three basic processes contribute to plate height (HETP): (1) Molecular diffusion, in which solute molecules diffuse outward from the centre of the zone. This effect is inversely proportional to the flow velocity, because rapid flow reduces the time for diffusion. Mathematically, the contribution to plate height of this factor is expressed B/v, in which B is a constant. (2) Eddy diffusion, in which solute is carried at unequal rates through the tortuous pathways of the granular bed. The contribution to plate height is a constant factor, A, independent of velocity. (3) Nonequilibrium or mass transfer, in which the slowness of diffusion in and out of the stationary and mobile phases causes fluctuations in the times of residence of the solute in the two phases and a consequent peak broadening. The effect is proportional to velocity and is expressed as $C_s v$ and $C_m v$, in which C_s and C_m are constants relating to the stationary and mobile phases, respectively.

The function of chromatographic theory has been twofold: (1) to evaluate B, A, C_m and C_s, in terms of underlying diffusivity and flow processes, and (2) to assemble them into a total plate height equation.

The general equation used is HETP $= A + B/v + C_s v$. This is inadequate at high velocities, however, and is replaced by the equation

$$\text{HETP} = (1/A + 1/C_m v)^{-1} + B/v + C_s v.$$

Knowledge of the component terms in such equations allows one to optimize chromatographic operating conditions.

Chromatographic columns are often characterized by the total number of theoretical plates, N, often also called column efficiency. This is defined as $N = L/\text{HETP}$.

Typically, the total number of theoretical plates (N) is about 10^2, but it ranges from 10 to 10^6.

APPLICATIONS

Chemical separation problems are enormous in scope. More than 1,000,000 known chemical compounds exist and are found primarily in the form of mixtures; these must be separated if the individual components are to be either characterized or utilized. In biological systems alone, thousands of known compounds, and undoubtedly thousands more that are unknown, require separation if they are to be detected and isolated in a pure state for characterization. Chromatography bears the main burden of such separations. The multitude of possible chromatographic techniques, and the variations possible within each technique, provide the flexibility needed to meet extreme demands. A few general principles govern the strengths and weaknesses of the various techniques and determine their suitability for different applications.

Gas chromatography is faster than liquid chromatography, separation times usually being seconds or minutes with the former and minutes or hours with the latter. Detection sensitivity also is superior with gas chromatography. The fundamental limitation of the method, however, is that solutes must be reasonably volatile, so that a finite fraction of solute is distributed in the gaseous phase. For organic substances, volatility is rarely adequate if the molecular weight of the compound exceeds 500. High temperatures, often up to 300° C, enhance volatility, but decomposition of the substance can result. High pressures, ranging from 50 to 1,000 atmospheres, also enhance volatility, but this technique is not widely used. Nonvolatile compounds often are converted to volatile derivations so that they can be separated by gas chromatographic techniques. Fatty acids, for example, are converted to their volatile methyl esters for gas chromatography. These considerations generally make gas chromatography the method of choice for most organic substances used and produced in industry and research. Common solvents, petroleum products, flavours, pollutants, and insecticides are examples (see Figure 2 for an example of a practical separation achieved with this technique). Gas chromatography also has invaded biochemistry, serving ideally for small- and medium-sized molecules, such as amino acids, fatty acids, essential oils, simple sugars, steroids, and alkaloids. For larger molecules (many steroids and some alkaloids), and particularly for natural and synthetic macromolecules (polymers), gas chromatography is entirely inappropriate. In these fields, liquid chromatography comes into widest use.

In gas chromatography, the partition method (gas–liquid chromatography) is generally chosen over the adsorption method (gas–solid chromatography). A bigger sample capacity, an improved reproducibility, and a wider range in solute type and molecular weight are possible with the former method. Gas–solid chromatography, however, often is more selective in separating molecules with only slight geometrical differences. Analysis of complex samples of natural products with a wide range of molecular weights is generally carried out using programmed-temperature gas–liquid chromatography in order to hasten the elution of retarded components.

Molecules of moderately large size can be treated conveniently by either liquid–liquid chromatography or liquid–solid chromatography. Ion-exchange chromatography is generally applied to substances with ionic groups. As molecular size increases, retention becomes more difficult to regulate by the partition and adsorption methods. Gel-permeation and gel-filtration methods are then preferred. Macromolecules, such as synthetic polymers and proteins, are separated mainly by these techniques.

Column chromatography has a better inherent resolution than does thin-layer or paper chromatography. Nonetheless, the latter methods are widely used for biochemical applications because of their speed, convenience, and low cost.

Advantages of gas chromatography

BIBLIOGRAPHY. E. HEFTMANN (ed.), *Chromatography*, 2nd ed. (1967); H.G. CASSIDY, *Fundamentals of Chromatography* (1957).

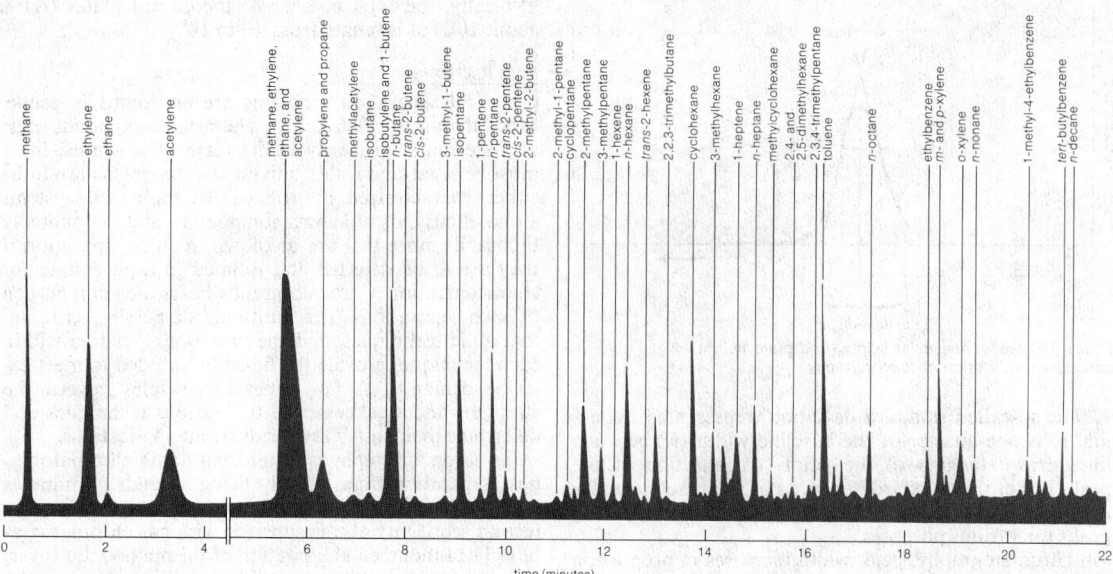

Figure 2: Gas chromatogram of hydrocarbon auto-exhaust pollutants.
From J. Giddings and R. Keller (eds.), *Advances in Chromatography*, vol. 8, p. 338; Marcel Dekker, Inc., N.Y. (1969)

Theory: J.C. GIDDINGS, *Dynamics of Chromatography* (1965).

Thin-layer chromatography: J.G. KIRCHNER, *Thin-Layer Chromatography* (1967); E. STAHL (ed.), *Thin-Layer Chromatography: A Laboratory Handbook* (1965).

Paper chromatography: R.J. BLOCK, E.L. DURRUM, and G. ZWEIG, *A Manual of Paper Chromatography and Paper Electrophoresis*, 2nd ed. rev. (1958); I.M. HAIS and K. MACEK, *Paper Chromatography: A Comprehensive Treatise*, 3rd ed. (1963).

Gas chromatography: A.B. LITTLEWOOD, *Gas Chromatography: Principles, Techniques, and Applications*, 2nd ed. (1970); O.E. SCHUPP, *Gas Chromatography* (1968).

Gel chromatography: L. FISCHER, *An Introduction to Gel Chromatography* (1969); H. DETERMANN, *Gel Chromatography*, 2nd ed. (1969).

(J.C.Gi/Ro.A.K.)

Chromium Products and Production

Chromium is unusual among metals in that its ores were used extensively long before the pure metal was prepared. As early as 1800, they were used to make pigments and chemicals for leather tanning. In 1879 they were successfully used as refractories. In 1893 Henri Moissan obtained pure chromium through reduction of chromic oxide by coal in an electric furnace, and in 1898 Hans Goldschmidt obtained carbon-free chromium through the reduction of this oxide by aluminum. By 1910 the importance of chromium ores in metallurgy was established. For the chemical and physical properties, see TRANSITION ELEMENTS AND THEIR COMPOUNDS.

Ores. Chromium is never found in nature in the free state. Its chief ores are made up of the mineral chromite, $FeO \cdot Cr_2O_3$. The actual composition of high grade ores varies between 42%–56% Cr_2O_3 and 10%–26% FeO, together with varying amounts of MgO, Al_2O_3, and SiO_2. For the properties of the mineral, see ORE DEPOSITS.

The majority of chromium ores can be concentrated with only hand sorting. This process can yield a concentrate containing about 50% Cr_2O_3, but the chromium to iron ratio is often not affected.

Chromium ores are divided into three groups: metallurgical, refractory, and chemical, depending on their end use. The metallurgical ore must be hard and lumpy, contain a minimum of 48% Cr_2O_3, and have a chromium to iron ratio of 3 to 1 for maximum usefulness. The ores used for refractories must be high in Cr_2O_3 plus Al_2O_3 and low in iron. Magnesium oxide is added in excess to these ores to form magnesium silicates on firing. For chemical purposes, ores should be high in Cr_2O_3 and low in Al_2O_3 and SiO_2; the specifications for this type are determined by price, availability, and experience.

Two classes of metallic chromium are available to industry: chromium metal and ferrochromium.

Chromium metal. Pure chromium metal may be arc cast by consumable or nonconsumable electrode techniques or formed by powder metallurgy methods. The product possesses a certain degree of hot workability.

Chromium surfaces are produced on other metals by electroplating and chromizing. There are two types of electroplating: decorative and "hard." Decorative plate varies between 0.00001 and 0.00002 inch in thickness and is usually deposited over nickel. "Hard" plating is used because of its wear resistance and low coefficient of friction. For these types of plating, solutions of CrO_3 are used (see also ELECTROPLATING).

In one method of chromizing, chromium is condensed on the surface from the vapour and is diffused into the metal by heating. In another method a chromium layer is fused on the surface and diffused in. Electron beam deposition of chromium onto the surface followed by diffusion into the metal has also been used. Salt bath chromizing using $CrCl_2$ has been tried.

Ferrochromium. Ferrochromium is an alloy added to steel to increase corrosion and oxidation resistance and strength (see also STEEL PRODUCTION).

High-carbon ferrochromium (4%–6% C, about 68% Cr) is used to produce steels in which chromium and carbon must be present. The chromite ore used for ferrochromium production contains a minimum of 48% chromic oxide and has, preferably, a ratio of chromium to iron of three to one. To produce high-carbon ferrochromium, ore and coke are fed into the top of an open-top, submerged arc furnace, and the alloy is tapped from the furnace into chill molds. After cooling, it is broken into lumps and graded.

For steels in which carbon is detrimental, low-carbon ferrochromium is produced. A silicon reduction of chromite is accomplished in a two-step process. In the first stage, a high-silicon ferrochromium, substantially carbon-free, is produced in a submerged arc furnace. This product is treated in an open arc furnace with a synthetic slag containing chromic oxide. The alloy produced ranges in carbon from 0.03% to 0.25%.

A ferrochromium of very low carbon content is made by heating high-carbon ferrochromium with ground quartzite or oxidized ferrochromium in a vacuum. Carbon is removed as carbon monoxide. This ferrochromium has a carbon content of about 0.01%.

Other chromium alloys. Up to 3% chromium is added to steel to improve the physical properties and increase the heat treatability. Steels containing chromium in combination with other elements, such as molybdenum, nickel, manganese, and vanadium are used for springs, roller and ball bearings, dies, rails, and high-strength structures. Steels containing 5%–6% chromium have increased corrosion and oxidation resistance and are used in the form of tubes in the oil industry. Stainless steels, **Stainless steels** which have a high resistance to oxidation and atmospheric corrosion, contain between 10% and 18% chromium. The low-carbon varieties (0.1% carbon or lower) cannot be heat-treated if the chromium is more than 13%. The higher chromium (17%–18% Cr) steels are used as automobile trim and for equipment to handle nitric acid. Steels with about 13% chromium and 0.3% carbon are used for cutlery. High-carbon (1%–2%) steels of this type are used when hardeners and abrasion resistance are desired. Steels containing 25%–30% chromium have excellent oxidation resistance and are used for products subjected to high temperatures such as furnace parts, burner nozzles, and kiln linings.

Nickel and manganese can be added to high-chromium steels to form the austenitic types, of which the 18%-chromium–8%-nickel variety is probably the best known. In addition to their resistance to oxidation and corrosion, austenitic steels maintain their strength at high temperatures better than do the plain chromium steels. Sometimes molybdenum, tungsten, columbium, or titanium are added to improve strength and corrosion resistance or to stabilize the carbides present.

Chromium is also added to cast iron to increase its tensile strength and resistance to wear and heat.

Chromium is added to cobalt alloys in amounts up to 25% to obtain corrosion resistance and hardness. Cobalt-chromium-tungsten alloys are used for cutting tools and hard facings.

Nickel base alloys with up to 20% chromium and sometimes a little iron are used for high-temperature electric resistance applications.

Chromium is added to niobium base alloys to improve their strength and their oxidation resistance. It is also used in the so-called superalloys for high-temperature applications.

Refractory applications. The use of chromite as a refractory is next in importance to the metallurgical applications of chromium. A typical analysis of a chromite suitable for refractory purposes is 38% to 48% Cr_2O_3, 12% to 24% Al_2O_3, 14% to 24% Fe_2O_3, 14% to 18% MgO, and less than 10% SiO_2. The usefulness of chromite as a refractory is based on its high melting point, moderate thermal expansion, the stability of its crystalline form at elevated temperatures, and its neutral chemical behaviour.

The melting point frequently given for chromite is 2,180° C. Chromite refractories are among the heaviest produced; the specific gravity varies between 4 and 4.6. Thermal stability is one of their most valuable properties; there are no polymorphous forms to cause sudden volume changes on heating. As a result of the silicates present, chromite exhibits some shrinkage on heating. Cuban ore at 1,500° C shows a linear shrinkage of 1.5%.

Chrome refractories are available in the form of molded bricks and shapes, plastic mixtures consisting of moistened aggregates that are rammed in place, castables composed of dry aggregates and a binder that after mixing with water can be poured like concrete, and mortars and cements for laying brickwork. Crushed raw ore is also sold for patching or filling holes.

Bricks of 100% chrome ore have been largely replaced by bricks composed of mixtures of chrome ore and magnesia for greater refractoriness, volume stability, and resistance to spalling. One of the refractories used in the fused-cast condition is composed of 80% alumina and 20% chromite. This product is highly resistant to the corrosive action of a variety of fluxes, slags, and glasses.

Chemical applications. The third major area of chromite applications is the production of chrome chemicals. For this purpose the ore should contain a minimum of 45% Cr_2O_3. The iron content may be higher than for the other applications. The production of sodium dichromate is usually the first step in making chemicals. This reagent is produced by heating the ore with soda ash and then leaching out soluble chromate, which is then converted to the dichromate by treatment with sulfuric acid.

Pigments account for about one-third of the primary production of chromium chemicals. Chrome oxide green, which is nearly pure Cr_2O_3, is the most stable green pigment known. It is used for colouring roofing granules, cements, and plasters. It is also employed as a fine powder for polishing. Chromium yellow varies greatly in the shades available and is essentially lead chromate. This pigment makes an excellent paint for both wood and metal. Zinc yellow, a basic zinc chromate, is used as a corrosion-inhibiting primer on aircraft parts fabricated from aluminum or magnesium. Molybdate orange is a combination of lead chromate with molybdenum salts. Chrome green is a mixture of lead chromate with iron blue. This pigment has excellent covering and hiding power and is widely used in paints.

The textile industry accounts for about 10% of the primary production of chromium chemicals. They are used in mordanting, in textile-printing compounds, and in aftertreatments. Reagents employed include basic chromic acetate, basic chromic chloride, chromic fluorides, bisulfites, lactates, bromates, oxalates, and thiocyanates.

About 25% of the chromium chemicals produced go into chrome tanning of leather. This process uses chrome **Chrome tanning** reagents in the form of basic chromic sulfates that, in turn, are produced from the dichromate.

The insolubilizing action of chromium chemicals makes them useful in hardening photographic films and in photoengraving.

More than one-fourth of the production of primary chromium chemicals is used in metal-surface treatments and corrosion control. Such applications include chromium plating, chromizing, anodizing of aluminum, and treatment of zinc and magnesium. Chromium chemicals are used in dips for iron, steel, brass, and tin and also as inhibitors for brines and for recirculating water systems.

These chemicals also find important application in organic oxidations such as the production of synthetic dyes, saccharin, benzoic acid, anthraquinone, camphor, and synthetic fibres. They are used for bleaching, for the purification of chemicals, as analytical reagents, for inorganic and electrochemical oxidations, and in the manufacture of sponge rubber. They also have applications in electric dry cells, slushing compounds, phosphate coatings and catalysts,

Production. The chief chromite-producing countries are listed in the Table below.

World Production of Chromite (thousands of short tons)			
country	1978	1979*	1980†
South Africa	3,466,000	3,634,000	3,764,000
Soviet Union†	2,550,000	2,650,000	2,700,000
Albania	1,090,000	1,120,000	1,190,000
Turkey	700,000	900,000	800,000
Philippines	592,000	618,000	631,000
Others	1,565,000	1,589,000	1,640,000

*Preliminary.   †Estimate.
Source: U.S. Department of the Interior, Bureau of Mines, *Minerals Yearbook 1980*.

Although the United States has reserves of 11,000,000 tons of low-grade ore, there is no U.S. production. About 57% of the ore used in the United States is metallurgical, 18% refractory, and 25% chemical grade.

Production of chromium metal. Chromium metal is produced commercially by two methods: by electrolysis, or by the reduction of purified chromium compounds, usually Cr_2O_3.

Reduction processes. Aluminum has been used to reduce Cr_2O_3 to produce large amounts of chromium metal by the reaction

$$Cr_2O_3 + 2Al = 2Cr + Al_2O_3.$$

This reaction is self-sustaining and is carried out by igniting a mixture of oxide and aluminum powder in a refractory-lined container. A 97%–99% chromium metal is thus obtained, with aluminum, iron, and silicon the chief impurities. Such a metal also contains about 0.03% carbon, 0.02% sulfur, and 0.045% nitrogen.

Silicon is also used to reduce Cr_2O_3 and produce chromium metal:

$$2Cr_2O_3 + 3Si = 4Cr + 3SiO_2.$$

This reaction is carried out in an electric furnace since it is not self-sustaining. The resulting metal may contain up to 0.8% silicon.

Carbon may also be used as a reducing agent for Cr_2O_3 to produce chromium metal:

$$Cr_2O_3 + 3C = 2Cr + 3CO.$$

This reaction is carried out by briquetting a mixture of finely divided oxide and carbon and heating the briquettes to 1,200°–1,400° C in a refractory vessel at a reduced pressure of 280 to 315 microns of mercury (1 micron = 0.001 millimetre) for reduction at 1,400° C. Low pressure causes some chromium volatilization. The product contains 0.015% C, 0.001% N_2, 0.04% O_2, about 0.02% Si, and under 0.03% Fe.

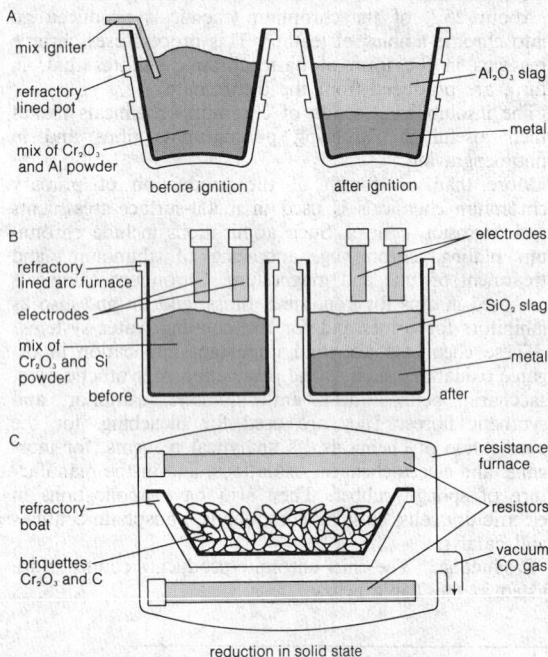

Stages in the production of chromium metal by reduction processes.
(A) Aluminothermic, **(B)** silicothermic, **(C)** carbothermic.

Electrolytic processes. There are two commercial processes for the electrolytic recovery of chromium metal. One uses a chrome–alum electrolyte and the other a chromic acid electrolyte. Although the chrome–alum electrolyte may be prepared from chrome ore, the difficulties encountered in preparing a pure solution make this process uneconomical. A commercially available product, high-carbon ferrochromium, is used as a starting material.

Crushed ferrochromium is slowly fed to a brick-lined steel tank in which it is leached (treated with a solvent) by a mixture of reduced anolyte (anode electrolyte), chrome–alum mother liquor, and sulfuric acid. A heating coil in the tank keeps the temperature near the boiling point, and a condenser controls the resulting spray. Leaching and digestion time is 48 hours. The slurry (liquid mixture) is then transferred to a holding tank and cooled to 80° C by the addition of cold mother liquor. The silica and undissolved solids are filtered from the solution. By heating at elevated temperature for a few hours, the chromium in the filtrate is converted to the non-alum-forming condition. The temperature is then lowered to about 5° C, and crude iron-sulfate crystals are formed that are removed from the mother liquor by a vacuum drum filter. The crude iron sulfate is dissolved by the liquor that results from washing the leach residue. Ammonium sulfate is added, and the solution is conditioned at elevated temperatures for several hours. The ferrous ammonium sulfate formed is recovered and sold for fertilizer or other purposes.

The mother liquor, free from the crude iron sulfate, is clarified in a filter press and aged at about 30° C. About 80% of the chromium is stripped as ammonium chrome-alum. The slurry is then filtered and washed, and the filtrate is sent to the leach circuit while the chromium-alum crystals are dissolved in hot water to produce cell feed.

To obtain good cell operation, close pH (hydrogen ion concentration) control of the catholyte (cathode electrolyte) is essential, as is the presence of divalent chromium at the cathode. A diaphragm cell is used to prevent the chromic and sulfuric acids formed at the anodes from mixing with the catholyte.

The flow of the catholyte through the diaphragm into the anolyte compartment controls the pH. The sulfuric acid in the anolyte is held at 250–300 g/l (grams per litre) by the addition of water.

In 72-hour cycles the cathodes are removed from the cells, the adhering salts removed by hot water, and the brittle chromium deposit (⅛–½ inch thick) is stripped by hand. This material is crushed by rolls and washed with hot water. It is then sealed in stainless-steel cans and heated to remove water and hydrogen.

An overall current efficiency of 45% can be obtained, which includes the low efficiencies prevailing during cell start-up. A pH of 2.1–2.4 contributes to lower efficiencies but gives a safe operating latitude.

The process results in a metal that contains 99.8% Cr, 0.14% Fe, 0.01% C, 0.001% Cu, 0.002% Pb, 0.5% O_2, 0.004% H_2, ≤ 0.01% N_2, and no Si, P, Al, or Mn.

The second way of producing electrolytic chromium is from a chromic acid bath operating at an efficiency of about 6.7%. Current efficiency is inherently low because six electrons are necessary to reduce the hexavalent ions to chromium metal and is further reduced by hydrogen evolution at the cathode. This metal has a lower oxygen content than that from the chrome-alum process. It contains 0.02% oxygen, 0.0025% nitrogen, and 0.009% hydrogen.

BIBLIOGRAPHY. Two works covering all aspects of this subject are A.H. SULLY, *Chromium*, 2nd ed. (1967); and M.J. UDY (ed.), *Chromium*, 2 vol. (1956–57). Information may also be found in C.A. HAMPEL (ed.), *The Encyclopedia of the Chemical Elements* (1968), dealing with ores, thermal and electrolytic production, chemical and physical properties, alloys, and chemical and refractory uses; and *The Encyclopedia of Electrochemistry* (1964), a description of electrolytic production; R.E. KIRK and D.F. OTHMER (eds.), *Encyclopedia of Chemical Technology*, 2nd ed., vol. 5 (1964), a comprehensive treatment, including economics; and W.J. MEAD (ed.), *The Encyclopedia of Chemical Process Equipment* (1964), a description of electrolytic cells.

(F.E.B.)

Chronology

Chronology, in the broadest sense, is a time scale, a method of ordering time. This article, however, deals mainly with systems of chronology used by different peoples in recording their history.

Scientific chronology, which seeks to place all happenings in the order in which they occurred and at correctly proportioned intervals on a fixed scale, is used in many disciplines and can be utilized to cover vast epochs. Astronomy, for example, measures the sequence of cosmic phenomena in thousands of millions of years; geology and paleontology, when tracing the evolution of the Earth and of life, use similar epochs of hundreds or thousands of millions of years. Geochronology reckons the more distant periods with which it deals on a similar scale; but it descends as far as human prehistoric and even historic times, and its shorter subdivisions consist only of thousands of years. Shortest of all are the chronological scales used in the recording of human events in a more or less systematic and permanent manner. These vary in scope, accuracy, and method according to the purpose, degree of sophistication, and skill of the peoples using them, as do the calendrical systems with which they are inextricably bound up; throughout this article, frequent reference, therefore, will be made to the article CALENDAR.

It is difficult to fix ancient historical chronologies in relation to scientific chronology. The terms of reference of ancient peoples were vague and inconsistent when judged by modern standards, and many of their inscriptions and writings have inevitably disappeared. The gaps in their records are increasingly filled in and their inconsistencies removed by the results of archaeological excavation. Guided by these findings, scholars can confirm, refute, or amend chronological reconstructions already tentatively made (see ARCHAEOLOGY). Astronomical calculation and dating by radioactive-carbon content are also helpful in the work of fixing ancient chronologies.

CHINESE

Chinese legendary history can be traced back to 2697 BC, the first year of Huang Ti (Chinese: Yellow Emperor), who was followed by many successors and by the three dynasties, the Hsia (c. 2205–c. 1766 BC), the Shang (c. 1766–c. 1122 BC), and the Chou (c. 1122–221 BC). Recent archaeological findings, however, have established an authentic chronology beginning with the Shang dynasty, though the exact date of its end remains a controversial topic among experts. The so-called oracle-bone inscriptions of the last nine Shang kings (1324–1122 BC) record the number of months up to the 12th, with periodical additions of a 13th month, and regular religious services on the summer and winter solstice days, all of which indicates the adjustment of the length of the lunar year by means of calculations based on the solar year. Individual days in the inscriptions are named according to the designations in the sexagenary cycle formed by the combination of the ten celestial stems and 12 terrestrial branches (see CALENDAR: *The Chinese Calendar*). Every set of 60 days is divided into six ten-day "weeks." Also recorded are numerous eclipses that can be used to verify the accuracy of the Shang chronology. In the oracular sentences of the last Shang king, Chou Hsin, the year of his reign is referred to as "the King's *n*th annual sacrifice."

From the beginning of the following (Chou) dynasty, the word year was etymologically identical with "harvest." Thus, "King X's *n*th harvest" meant the *n*th year of his reign. The lunar month was then divided into four quarters—Ch'u-chi, Tsai-sheng pa, Chi-sheng pa and Chi-szu pa—and the practice of using the 60 cyclical names for the days was continued. Thus, in the inscription on a Chou bronze vessel, a typical date would read: "In the King's *n*th harvest, in the *n*th quarter of the *n*th month, on the day X-*y*, etc."

The nien-hao system

The tradition of recording events by referring to the king's regnal year continued until 163 BC, when a new system, *nien-hao* ("reign-period title"), was introduced by Emperor Han Wen Ti of the Former Han dynasty (206 BC–AD 8). Thereafter, every emperor proclaimed a new *nien-hao* for his reign at the beginning of the year following his accession (sometimes an emperor redesignated his *nien-hao* on special occasions during his reign). A typical date in the *nien-hao* system might read, "the third year of the Wan-li reign period" (Wan-li san nien). In order to date any event in Chinese history, it is necessary to convert the year in the period of the designated *nien-hao* into the Western calendar.

During the Chou dynasty the civil year began with the new moon, which occurred before or on the day of the winter solstice. This "first month" of the Chou year (Chou *cheng*) was equivalent to the 11th month of the Hsia year (Hsia *cheng*) or to the 12th month of the Shang year. The first emperor, Shih Huang Ti, of the short-lived Ch'in dynasty (221–206 BC) made the year begin one month earlier—*i.e.*, with the lunation (the period of time between one new moon and the next) before the one in which the winter solstice occurred. The Ch'in year was continuously used until 104 BC, when Emperor Han Wu Ti promulgated the T'ai-ch'u calendar by reverting to the Hsia *cheng*—*i.e.*, by taking the third month of the Chou

year, or the second lunation after the winter solstice, as the first month of the civil year. This lunar year (or Hsia *cheng*) was used till the last day of the Ch'ing, or Manchu, dynasty (1644–1911). When in 1911 the first republic was founded, the solar year was officially adopted, but successive governments kept the *nien-hao* tradition by referring any date to the number of years since the establishment of the republic—*e.g.*, 1948 was chronicled "the 37th year of the republic." In 1949, when the People's Republic of China was proclaimed, the old system was replaced by the Gregorian calendar.   (W.S.-cg.)

JAPANESE

The principal chronicles describing the origins of Japanese history are the *Nihon shoki* ("Chronicle of Japan") and the *Koji-ki* ("Record of Ancient Matters"). The *Nihon shoki* (compiled in AD 720) assembled information in a chronological order of days, months, and years starting several years before 660 BC, which was the year of the enthronement of the first Japanese emperor, who was posthumously named Jimmu. The *Koji-ki* (compiled in AD 712) related events under the reign of each emperor without a strict chronological order. Sometimes the *Koji-ki* gave the years of emperors' deaths and their ages at death. This information is different from that recorded in the *Nihon shoki*.

Native Japanese scholars since Fujiwara Teikan in the 18th century have realized that the *Nihon shoki* was historically inadequate and different from the *Koji-ki*, at least insofar as the chronological information is concerned. They have suggested that the foundation year of Japan was 600 years later than stated in the *Nihon shoki*. Naka Michiyo (late 19th century) argued with minute detail about the question of Japanese chronology. His ideas were supplemented by those of other Japanese scholars, who pointed out that: (1) the reigns of the earlier Japanese emperors as stated in the *Nihon shoki* are unnaturally long; (2) the date of the enthronement of the emperor Jimmu should be reconsidered; (3) a chronological gap exists between the *Nihon shoki* and contemporary Chinese and Korean chronicles. In comparison with Korean chronicles, they argued, the *Nihon shoki* has created an intentional expansion of chronology—*i.e.*, the entries about the empress Jingō and the emperor Ōjin can be identified with historical facts relating to the Korea of the 4th and 5th centuries and therefore must be placed 120 years later than mentioned in the *Nihon shoki*. When comparing the *Nihon shoki* with Chinese chronicles, one finds the chronological gap somewhat reduced. The Chinese chronicles provide information about the tributes sent individually by five Japanese "kings" to Liu-Sung and Southern Ch'i during the 5th century. There are still questions about the identification of these kings, but it is generally accepted that the "king" written in Chinese character as Wu must be the Japanese emperor Yūryaku. By the late 5th century the gap between Japanese and Korean records, on the one hand, and Japanese and Chinese, on the other hand, disappears.

Reforms of Naka Michiyo

The intentional expansion of the chronology of the *Nihon shoki* was adopted by its compilers, who identified Queen Himiko (Pimihu) of Yamatai of the chronicle of Wei China with the Empress Jingō of Japanese legend.

The method of designating a year by the *kan-shi* (sexagenary cycle) appears to have begun about the reign of Emperor Yūryaku, when, as mentioned above, the gap between the continental and Japanese chronologies was bridged. The inscription on remarkable copper images of Buddha cast just after the period of Prince Shōtoku's regency (AD 593–621) bear a *nengō* (*nien-hao*, or reign-year title), although not a strictly authorized one. It was at this time that the Chinese luni-solar calendar system was adopted. The first official *nengō* was Taika, which was adopted by the imperial court in 645. Since 701, when the second title, Taihō, was adopted, the reign-year system has been continuously used in relation to the emperors' reigns up to the present day. In medieval times Japanese chronology underwent a remarkable evolution: (1) when the Imperial dynasty split into two courts (1336–92), two series of *nengō* began to be used; (2) during the

Ashikaga period some private *nengō* again appeared; (3) some dates of the authorized "central" calendars did not correspond with those of locally compiled calendars. Moreover, military leaders would not accept some of the new *nengō*. Minamoto Yoritomo, for example, did not use the *nengō* that was adopted by the emperor Antoku and the Taira regime, and Ashikaga Mochiuji and Ashikaga Shigeuji did not use the official, respectively Eikyō and Kōshō, *nengō*.

In the Tokugawa period (1603–1867), gaps between central and provincial calendars disappeared, especially after the establishment of the Jōkyō calendar, the first native calendar compiled in Japan, instead of the Chinese-based one that was in use until this period. On January 1, 1873, Emperor Meiji adopted the Gregorian calendar in use in the West and at the same time adopted the "Japanese Era," with Emperor Jimmu as its founder, in addition to the *nengō* system. (Hi.Mo.)

HINDU

Two kinds of chronological systems have been used in India by the Hindus from antiquity. The first requires the years to be reckoned from some historical event. The second starts the reckoning from the position of some heavenly body. The historical system, the more common in modern times, exists side-by-side with Muslim and international systems successively introduced.

Reckonings dated from a historical event. The inscriptions of the Buddhist king Aśoka (c. 265–238 BC) give the first epigraphical evidence of the mode of reckoning from a king's consecration (*abhiṣeka*). In these inscriptions (Middle Indian language in India or Greek and Aramaean in what is now Qandahār, Afghanistan) the dates are indicated by the number of complete years elapsed since the king's consecration. But the earlier existence of a reckoning of duration of reigns and dynasties is evidenced by the testimony of the Greek historian Megasthenes, who in 302 BC was the ambassador of Seleucus I Nicator, founder of the Seleucid Empire, to the court of Candragupta Maurya, Aśoka's grandfather. According to Megasthenes, the people of the Magadha kingdom, with its capital Pāṭaliputra (Patna), kept very long dynastic lists, preserved in the later Sanskrit Purāṇas (legends of the gods and heroes) and later Buddhist and Jain chronicles. They generally indicate, in years or parts of years, the duration of each reign.

Similar records of other periods and regions exist, and a relative chronology may be established. Unfortunately, it is not always possible to connect them with any absolute chronology, the precise dates of the reigns given being still unsettled. For example, in the Scythian period of the history of northern India, several inscriptions are dated from the beginning of the reign of Kaniṣka, the greatest king of the Asian (Kuṣāṇa) invaders, but his dates are still uncertain (AD 78, 128–129, 144, etc., have been suggested for the beginning of a Kaniṣka era).

Other records give regnal years that can be linked with absolute chronology through other data—*e.g.*, those of several rulers of the Rāṣṭrakūṭa of the Deccan.

Hindu dynastic eras

The dynastic eras, founded by several rulers and kept up or adopted by others, are also numerous. The most important were the Licchavi era (AD 110), used in ancient Nepal; the Kalacuri era (AD 248), founded by the Abhūrī king Īśvarasena and first used in Gujarāt and Mahārāshtra and later (until the 13th century) in Madhya Pradesh and as far north as Uttar Pradesh; the Valabhī era (AD 318, employed in Saurāṣṭra) and the Gupta era (AD 320), used throughout the Gupta Empire and preserved in Nepal until the 13th century. Later came the era of the Thakuri dynasty of Nepal (AD 395), founded by Aṃśuvarman; the Harṣa era (AD 606), founded by Harṣa (Harṣavardhana), long preserved also in Nepal; the western Cālukya era (AD 1075), founded by Vikramāditya VI and fallen into disuse after 1162; the Lakṣmaṇa era (AD 1119), wrongly said to have been founded by the king Lakṣmaṇasena of Bengal and still used throughout Bengal in the 16th century and preserved until modern times in Mithilā; the Rājyabhīṣekaska or Marāthā era (1674), founded by Śivajī but ephemeral.

Later, instead of the beginning of a reign or of a dynasty, the death of a religious founder was adopted as the starting point of an era. Among Buddhists the death of the Buddha and among the Jains the death of the Jina were taken as the beginning of eras. The Jain era (*vīrasaṃvat*) began in 528 BC. Several Buddhist sects (no longer existing in India) adopted different dates for the death (Nirvāṇa) of the Buddha. The Buddhist era prevailing in Ceylon and Buddhist Southeast Asia begins in 544 BC.

Historical events, now obscure, were the basis of the two most popular Indian eras: the Vikrama and the Śaka.

The Vikrama era (58 BC) is said in the Jain book *Kālakācāryakathā* to have been founded after a victory of King Vikramāditya over the Śaka. But some scholars credit the Scytho-Parthian ruler Azes with the foundation of this era. It is sometimes called the Mālava era because Vikramāditya ruled over the Mālava country, but it was not confined to this region, being widespread throughout India. The years reckoned in this era are generally indicated with the word *vikramasaṃvat*, or simply *saṃvat*. They are elapsed years. In the north the custom is to begin each year with Caitra (March–April) and each month with the full moon. But in the south and in Gujarāt the years begin with Kārttika (October–November) and the months with the new moon; in part of Gujarāt, the new moon of Āṣāḍha (June–July) is taken as the beginning of the year. To reduce Vikrama dates to dates AD, 57 must be subtracted from the former for dates before January 1 and 56 for dates after.

The Śaka era

The Śaka, or Salivāhana, era (AD 78), now used throughout India, is the most important of all. It has been used not only in many Indian inscriptions but also in ancient Sanskrit inscriptions in Indochina and Indonesia. The reformed calendar promulgated by the Indian government from 1957 is reckoned by this era. It is variously alleged to have been founded by King Kaniṣka or by the Hindu king Salivāhana or by the satrap Nahapāna. According to different practices, the reckoning used to refer to elapsed years in the north or current years in the south and was either solar or luni-solar. The luni-solar months begin with full moon in the north and with new moon in the south. To reduce Śaka dates (elapsed years) to dates AD, 78 must be added for a date within the period ending with the day equivalent to December 31 and 79 for a later date. For Śaka current years the numbers to be added are 77 and 78. The official Śaka year is the elapsed year, starting from the day following that of the vernal equinox. A normal year consists of 365 days, while the leap year has 366. The first month is Chaitra, with 30 days in a normal year and 31 in a leap year; the five following months have 31 days, the others 30.

A Nepalese era (AD 878) of obscure origin was commonly used in Nepal until modern times. The years were elapsed, starting from Kārttika, with months beginning at new moon. Another era, the use of which is limited to the Malabar Coast (Malayalam-speaking area) and to the Tirunelveli district of the Tamil-speaking area, is connected with the legend of the hero Paraśurāma, an avatar (incarnation) of the god Viṣṇu. It is called the Kollam era (AD 825). Its years are current and solar; they start when the Sun enters into the zodiacal sign of Virgo in north Malabar and when it enters into Leo in south Malabar. It is sometimes divided into cycles of 1,000 years reckoned from 1176 BC. Thus, AD 825 would have been the first year of the era's third millennium.

Cosmic cycles

Eras based on astronomical speculation. During the period of elaboration of the classical Hindu astronomy, which was definitively expounded in the treatises called *siddhānta*s and by authors such as Āryabhaṭa I (born AD 476), Varāhamihira, Brahmagupta (7th century AD), etc., were developed the ancient Vedic notions on the cycle of years, embracing round numbers of solar and lunar years together. On the one hand, greater cycles were calculated in order to include the revolutions of planets, and the theory was elaborated of a general conjunction of heavenly bodies at 0° longitude after the completion of each cycle. On the other hand, cosmologists speculated as to the existence of several successive cycles constituting successive periods of evolution and involution of the universe. The period calculated as the basis of the chronology of the universe was the *mahāyuga*, consisting of 4,320,000 sidereal years. It was divided into four *yuga*s, or stages, on the hypothesis of an original "order" (*dharma*) established in the first stage, the Kṛta *yuga*, gradually decaying in the three others, the Tretā, Dvāpara, and Kali *yuga*s. The respective durations of these four *yuga*s were 1,728,000, 1,296,000, 864,000, and 432,000 years. According to the astronomer Āryabhaṭa, however, the duration of each of the four *yuga*s was the same—*i.e.*, 1,080,000 years. The basic figures in these calculations were derived from the Brahmanical reckoning of a year of 10,800 *muhūrta* (see CALENDAR: *The Hindu calendar*), together with combinations of other basic numbers, such as four phases, 27 *nakṣatra*s, etc. The movement of the equinoxes was at the same time interpreted not as a circular precession but as a libration (periodic oscillation) at the rate of 54 seconds of arc per year. It is in accordance with these principles that the calculation of the beginning of the Kali *yuga* was done in order to fix for this chronology a point starting at the beginning of the agreed world cycle. Such a beginning could not be observed, since it was purely theoretical, consisting of a general conjunction of planets at longitude 0°, the last point of the *nakṣatra* Revati (Pisces). It has been calculated as corresponding to February 18, 3102 BC (old style), 0 hour, and taken as the beginning of the Kali era. In this era, the years are mostly reckoned as elapsed and solar or luni-solar.

In Hindu tradition the beginning of this era was connected with (1) events of the Mahābhārata war; (2) King Yudhiṣṭhira's accession to the throne; (3) 36 years later, King Parikṣit's consecration; (4) Lord Kṛṣṇa's death. Its years are still regularly given in Hindu almanacs.

An era resting upon a fictitious assumption of a complete 100-year revolution of the Ursa Major, the Great Bear (*saptarṣi*), around the northern pole was the Saptarṣi, or Laukika, era (3076 BC), formerly used in Kashmir and the Punjab. The alleged movement of this constellation has been used in Purāṇa compilations and even by astronomers for indicating the centuries.

Two chronological cycles were worked out on a basis of the planet Jupiter's revolutions, one corresponding to a single year of Jupiter consisting of 12 solar years and the other to five of Jupiter's years. The second, the *bṛhaspaticakra*, starts, according to different traditions, from AD 427 or from 3116 BC. Before AD 907 one year was periodically omitted in order to keep the cycle in concordance with the solar years. Since 907 the special names by which every year of the cycle is designated are simply given to present years of the almanac.

Side-by-side with Hindu and foreign eras adopted in India, several eras were created in the country under foreign influence, chiefly of the Mughal emperor Akbar: Bengali San (AD 593), Amli of Orissa and Vilayati (AD 592), Faṣlī (AD 590, 592 or 593 according to the district), and Sursan of Mahārāshtra (599).   (J.L.A.F.)

EGYPTIAN

At the end of the 4th millennium BC, when King Menes, the first king of a united Egypt, started his reign, the ancient Egyptians began to name each year by its main events, presumably to facilitate the dating of documents. These names were entered into an official register together with the height of the Nile during its annual inundation. Short notes at first, the year names developed into lengthy records of historical and religious events, especially of royal grants to the gods. These lists grew into annals, which were kept during the entire history of Egypt so that later kings could, after important events, consult the annals and ascertain whether a comparable occurrence had happened before. Unfortunately, these annals are lost. Only fragments from the 1st to the 5th dynasty (*c.* 3100–*c.* 2345 BC) are preserved, copied on stone. These fragments, however, are in such poor condition that they raise more chronological problems than they solve.

The Egyptian priests of the Ramessid period (*c.* 1300 BC; see below) copied the names and reigns of the kings from Menes down to their time from the annals, omitting all references to events. Even this king list would have given a safe foundation of an Egyptian chronology, but the only extant copy, on a papyrus now kept at the Museo Egizio in Turin, has survived only in shreds, entire sections having been lost. Extracts from this king list, which name only the more important kings, are preserved in the temples of the kings Seti I and Ramses II at Abydos and on the wall of a private tomb at Ṣaqqārah (now in the Egyptian Museum), but they give little help in chronological matters.

The Turin Papyrus

When the Greeks began to rule Egypt after the conquest of Alexander the Great, King Ptolemy II Philadelphus, hoping to acquaint the new ruling class with the history of the conquered country, commissioned Manetho, an Egyptian priest from Sebennytos, to write a history of Egypt in the Greek language. As Manetho had access to the ancient annals, he added some of their entries to his list of kings and reigns, especially during the first dynasties. The more he progressed in time, the more he added semihistorical traditions and stories as they were composed by the Egyptian priests to discuss moral problems in the disguise of a historical "novel." There had been, undoubtedly, fewer historical facts in Manetho's history than one might expect. But Manetho's work, too, is lost except for some excerpts used by Sextus Julius Africanus and Eusebius in writing their chronicles. These, in turn, represented the material used in part by George Syncellus in the 8th century AD. During copying and recopying, Manetho's text clearly suffered many changes, unintentionally or by purpose. The figures of the reigns, especially of the older dynasties, for instance, were enlarged when some of the early Christian historians tried to equate King Menes with Adam. In addition, the excerpts were done carelessly. Therefore, Manetho's work, as handed down to us, is short of useless. Nevertheless, together with the fragments of the annals and of the king list of Turin, they create a framework of Egyptian chronology; so the division into dynasties was taken over from Manetho. But to achieve a continuous history of Egypt and to bridge the gaps left by the fragmentary state of the extant chronological material, scholars must turn to other means, particularly astronomical references found in dated texts. These are related principally to the rising of Sothis and to the new moon.

Theoretically, the Egyptian civil year began when the Dog Star, Sirius (Egyptian Sothis), could first be seen on the eastern horizon just before the rising of the Sun (*i.e.*, 19/20 of July). As the civil calendar of the ancient Egyptians consisted of 12 months (each of 30 days) and five odd days (called epagomenal days), the civil year was a quarter of a day too long in relation to the rising of Sothis, so that the new year advanced by one day every four years. New Year's Day and the rising of Sothis coincided again only after approximately 1,460 years, the so-called Sothic cycle. Dated documents mentioning the rising of Sothis can be translated into the present calendar by multiplying the number of days elapsed since the first day of the year by four and subtracting this sum from the date of the beginning of the particular Sothic cycle. The dates for the start of each Sothic cycle are fortunately known because the Roman historian Censorinus fixed the coincidence of New Year's Day and heliacal rising of Sothis in AD 139. Taking into account a slight difference between a Sothic year and a year of the fixed stars, the years 1322, 2782, and 4242 BC are taken as starting points of a Sothic cycle.

The Sothic cycle

There are six ancient Egyptian documents extant giving Sothis dates, but only three of these are of value. The oldest is a letter from the town of Kahun warning a priest that the heliacal rising of Sothis will take place on the 16th day of the 8th month of year 7 of a king who, according to internal evidence, is Sesostris III of the 12th dynasty. This date corresponds to 1866 BC, according to the corrected Sothic cycle. The next date is given by a medical papyrus written at the beginning of the 18th dynasty, to which a calendar is added, possibly to ensure a correct conversion of dates used in the receipts to the actual timetable. Here it is said that the 9th day of the

11th month of year 9 of King Amenhotep I was the day of the heliacal rising of Sothis—i.e., 1538 BC. This date, however, is only accurate provided that the astronomical observations were taken at the old residence of Memphis; if observed at Thebes in Upper Egypt, the residence of the 18th dynasty, the date must be lowered by 20 years—i.e., 1518 BC. The third Sothis date shows that Sirius rose heliacally sometime during the reign of Thutmose III, which lasted for 54 years, on the 28th day of the 11th month; so year 1458 BC (point of observation at Memphis) or 1438 BC (point of observation at Thebes) must have belonged to the reign of this king. From these dates it is possible to calculate the absolute dates for the reigns of the 12th dynasty, as the durations of most of the reigns of the kings belonging to this dynasty are preserved on the king list of the Turin Papyrus. On the other hand, chronologists are able to compute the reigns of the kings of the 18th dynasty by utilizing the highest dates of their documents and the figures preserved by Manetho. Historians are also helped by the fact that the Egyptians sometimes identified a certain day as "exactly new moon"; they reckoned new moon from the morning after the last crescent of the waning moon had become invisible in the east just before sunrise. As there is a 25-year lunar cycle, such ancient Egyptian moon dates could be calculated with a fair amount of certainty but of course only if the ancient Egyptians themselves observed this celestial phenomenon accurately. There is some doubt, however, as it is shown by the attempts of very competent scholars to convert these moon dates. Sometimes even moon dates given by the same papyrus contradict themselves; in another case, the date given by a document had to be amended to achieve a reasonable result. These and other examples show that ancient Egyptian statements on celestial phenomena, especially on new moons, tend to be inaccurate because of faulty or inexact observations. Therefore, every date given for a fixed reign should be used with caution as the astronomical observation on which it is based may be inexact. Sometimes they are controlled by synchronism with Babylonian, Assyrian, or Hittite king lists or, later on, by the close interconnections between Greek and Egyptian history. Sometimes even biographical data are helpful. The statements found on small stelae inside the burial ground of the holy bulls of Memphis (Apis) register the dates of birth, enthronement, and death of these animals accurately. But the more time recedes, the more the chronology of the Egyptian history becomes uncertain, even when astronomical data are available. Up till now even carbon-14 data are of no great help, as uncertainties are mostly not greater than the standard deviations to be expected in a carbon-14 calculation.

Nevertheless, Egyptologists believe themselves to be on fairly firm ground when dating the beginning of the Ancient Kingdom (1st and 2nd dynasty) about 3090 BC, the beginning of the 11th dynasty at 2133 BC, and of the Middle Kingdom (12th dynasty) at 1991 BC. The New Kingdom started at 1567 or 1552 BC, depending on a choice for the first year of Ramses II of either 1290 BC or 1304 BC—one lunar cycle earlier. The following centuries still pose many chronological questions down to 664 BC, when Greek historiography took over.   (W.H.)

BABYLONIAN AND ASSYRIAN

Mesopotamian chronology, 747 to 539 BC. The source from which the exploration of Mesopotamian chronology started is a text called Ptolemy's Canon. This king list covers a period of about 1,000 years, beginning with the kings of Babylon after the accession of Nabonassar in 747 BC. The text itself belongs to the period of the Roman Empire and was written by a Greek astronomer resident in Egypt. Proof of the fundamental correctness of Ptolemy's Canon has come from the ancient cuneiform tablets excavated in Mesopotamia, including some that refer to astronomical events, chiefly eclipses of the Moon. Thus, by the time excavations began, a fairly detailed picture of Babylonian chronology was already available for the period after 747 BC. Ptolemy's Canon covers the Persian and Seleucid periods of Mesopotamian history,

but this section will deal only with the period up to the Persian conquest (539 BC).

The chief problem in the early years of Assyriology was to reconstruct a sequence for Assyria for the period after 747 BC. This was done chiefly by means of *limmu*, or eponym, lists, several of which were found by early excavators. These texts are lists of officials who held the office of *limmu* for one year only and whom historians also call by the Greek name of eponym. Annals of the Assyrian kings were being found at the same time as eponym lists, and a number of these annals, or the campaigns mentioned in them, were dated by eponyms who figured in the eponym lists. Moreover, some of the Assyrian kings in the annals were also kings of Babylonia and as such were included in Ptolemy's Canon.

The limmu lists

Good progress was therefore being made when, soon after 1880, two chronological texts of outstanding importance were discovered. One of these, now known as King List A, is damaged in parts, but the end of it, which is well preserved, coincides with the first part of Ptolemy's Canon down to 626 BC. The other text, *The Babylonian Chronicle*, also coincides with the beginning of the canon, though it breaks off earlier than King List A. With the publication of these texts, the first phase in the reconstruction of Mesopotamian chronology was over. For the period after 747 BC, there remained only one serious lacuna—i.e., the lack of the eponym sequence for the last 40 years or so of Assyrian history. This had not been established by the early 1970s.

Assyrian chronology before 747 BC. German excavations at Ashur, ancient capital of Assyria, yielded further eponym lists. By World War I the full sequence of eponyms was known from about 900 to 650 BC. A further fragmentary list carried the record back to about 1100 BC, and on this basis Assyrian chronology was reconstructed, with little error, back to the first full regnal year of Tiglath-pileser I in 1115 BC. Without another eponym list, a king list was needed for substantial further progress. King lists found at Ashur proved disappointing. Those fairly well preserved did not include figures for the reigns, and those with figures were very badly damaged.

In 1933, however, an expedition from the University of Chicago discovered at Khorsabad, site of ancient Dur Sharrukin, an Assyrian king list going back to about 1700 BC. But for the period before 1700 BC the list is damaged and otherwise deficient, and Assyrian chronology prior to this date is still far from clear.

Before 747 BC it was the custom of the Assyrian kings to hold eponym office in their first or second regnal year. Thus, in an eponym list, the number of names between the names of two successive kings usually equals the number of years in the reign of the first of the two kings. It would have been easy to compile a king list from an eponym list, and there is evidence that this Assyrian king list was compiled from an eponym list probably in the middle of the 11th century BC. As an eponym list is a reliable chronological source, since omission of a name entails an error of only one year, the king list, if based on one, will have preserved much of the structure of older eponym lists now lost. (Except for one fragment, no known eponym list goes back further than the beginning of the 11th century BC.)

Eponym lists

Babylonian chronology before 747 BC. In the long interval between the fall of the last Sumerian dynasty *c.* 2000 BC and 747 BC there are two substantial gaps in chronology, each about two centuries long. The earlier gap is in the 2nd millennium, from approximately 1600–1400 BC, the later gap in the 1st millennium, from *c.* 943–747 BC. During these gaps the names of most of the kings are known, as well as the order, but usually not the length of their reigns.

A means of checking the reliability of the Babylonian king list is provided by the chronicles, annals, and other historical texts that show that a given Assyrian king was contemporaneous with a given Babylonian king. There are no fewer than 15 such synchronisms between 1350 and 1050 BC, and, when the Babylonian and Assyrian king lists are compared, they all fit in easily. Only one of them, however, provides a close approximate date in

Babylonian chronology. This synchronism shows that the two-year reign of the Assyrian king Ashared-apil-Ekur (c. 1076–c. 1075 BC) is entirely comprised within the 13-year reign of the Babylonian king Marduk-shapik-zeri. The Assyrian's dates are probably correct to within one year. Thus, if Marduk-shapik-zeri is dated so that equal proportions of his reign fall before and after that of Ashared-apil-Ekur, a date is obtained for the former that should not be in error more than six years. This synchronism constitutes a key to the structure of Babylonian chronology by providing the base date for all the reigns in the interval c. 1400–943 BC for which the Babylonian king list gives figures. All the dates thus obtained are subject to the six-year margin of error.

These synchronisms between Assyrian and Babylonian kings continue throughout the period that corresponds to the second gap in the Babylonian king list—from c. 943–747 BC. Since the Assyrian chronology in that period is firmly established, these synchronisms provide a useful framework for the structure of Babylonian chronology in that period.

The gap in the 2nd millennium BC, however, is not as easy to fill. The fact that the magnitude of the gap is uncertain constitutes the main problem in the chronology of the 2nd millennium BC and also affects the chronology of the preceding Sumerian period. The problem is not yet solved. Observations of the planet Venus made during the reign of King Ammisaduqa, less than 50 years before the end of the 1st dynasty of Babylon, permit only certain possible dates for his reign. Translated into dates for the end of the dynasty, the three most likely possibilities are 1651, 1595, and 1587 BC. The evidence is not yet conclusive and leaves uncertain what choice should be made among the three. The chronology adopted here is based on the second of these dates for the end of the 1st Babylonian dynasty—i.e., 1595 BC.

Prior to this gap in the 2nd millennium BC, there is a period of five centuries with a well-established chronological structure. All the kings in the major city-states are known, as well as their sequence and the length of their reigns. Which sets of dates should be assigned to these reigns, however, depends on the date adopted for the 1st dynasty of Babylon. This period of five centuries extends from the beginning of the 3rd dynasty of Ur to the end of the 1st dynasty of Babylon—i.e., on the chronology adopted here, 2113–1595 BC. During this period the Babylonians dated their history not by regnal years but by the names of the years. Each year had an individual name, usually from an important event that had taken place in the preceding year. The lists of these names, called year lists or date lists, constitute as reliable a source in Babylonian chronology as the eponym lists do in Assyrian chronology. One of the events which almost invariably gave a name to the following year was the accession of a new king. Hence, the first full regnal year of a king was called "the year (after) NN became king." In Assyria the number of personal names in an eponym list between the names of two successive kings normally equalled the number of years in the reign of the first king, and, similarly, in Babylonia the number of year names between two year names of the above kind nearly always equalled the number of years in the reign of the first king. Just as in Assyria, the eponym lists are almost certainly the source of the king lists, so in Babylonia the king lists are based on the year lists. Several of these king lists, compiled at a time when the year lists were still in use, survive. One gives the 3rd dynasty of Ur and the dynasty of Isin, another gives the dynasty of Larsa. Both may be school texts.

The 3rd dynasty of Ur and the dynasty of Isin also figure in the Sumerian king list, which reaches far back into the Sumerian period. The original version probably ended before the 3rd dynasty of Ur, but later scribes brought it up to date by adding that dynasty as well as the dynasty of Isin. (M.B.R.)

Babylonian year lists

JEWISH

The era at present in vogue among the Jews, counted from the creation of the world (*anno mundi;* abbrevi-ated to AM), came into popular use about the 9th century AD. Traceable in dates recorded much earlier, this era has five styles conventionally indicated by Hebrew letters used as numerals and combined into mnemonics, which state the times of occurrence of the epochal mean conjunctions of *moladim* (see CALENDAR: *Middle Eastern calendar systems: The Jewish calendar*) or the orders of intercalation in the 19-year cycle or both. The respective epochs of these styles fall in the years 3762–3758 BC, inclusive. By about the 12th century AD the second of the mentioned styles, that which is in use at present, superseded the other styles of the era *anno mundi.*

The styles of this era arise from variations in the conventional rabbinical computation of the era of the creation. This computation, like hundreds of other calculations even more variable and no less arbitrary, is founded on synchronisms of chronological elements expressed in the terms of biblical and early postbiblical Jewish eras.

The biblical era *anno mundi* underlies the dating of events (mainly in the book of Genesis) prior to the Exodus from Egypt. This period of biblical chronology abounds in intractable problems caused by discrepancies between the Jewish and Samaritan Hebrew texts and the Greek version known as the Septuagint, by apparent inconsistencies in some of the synchronisms, and by uncertainties about the method of reckoning.

Discrepancies in biblical texts

During the period from the Exodus to the founding of Solomon's Temple, the only continuous biblical era (chiefly in the remaining books of the Pentateuch) is the era of the Exodus. With regard to a crucial date expressed in this era—"In the four hundred and eightieth year after the people of Israel came out of the land of Egypt, in the fourth year of Solomon's reign over Israel, in the month of Ziv, which is the second month, he began to build the house of the Lord" (I Kings 6:1)—there is again a discrepancy between the Hebrew text and the Septuagint. Other problems to be met with during this period are due to the obscurity of chronological data in the book of Judges and in I and II Samuel.

During the following period, the Bible uses the eras of the regnal years of monarchs (the kings of Judah, Israel, and Babylon) and of the Babylonian Exile. This period of biblical chronology likewise poses numerous problems, also the result of apparent inconsistencies of the synchronisms—e.g., in the period from the accession of Rehoboam of Judah and of Jeroboam of Israel to the fall of Samaria "in the sixth year of Hezekiah [of Judah], which was the ninth year of Hoshea king of Israel" (II Kings 18:10) the reigns of the southern kingdom exceed those of the northern kingdom by 25 years.

Dating by the kings of Israel

The biblical data might be easier to harmonize if the occurrence of coregencies were assumed. Yet, as an ever-variable factor, these evidently would not lead to the determination of the true chronology of this period. Scholars therefore seek additional information from sources outside the Bible—e.g., inscriptions on Assyrian monuments, which are dated by the so-called eponym lists. Substantial use also has been made of the data in the king list known as Ptolemy's Canon (compiled in the 2nd Christian century) commencing in 747 BC with the reigns of the Babylonian kings (see above *Babylonian and Assyrian*). Scholars differ widely, however, in their interpretation of details, and numerous chronological problems remain unsolved. Only a few dates in this period can be fixed with any degree of confidence.

After the Babylonian Exile, as evidenced by the data in the Bible and the Aswān papyri, the Jews reckoned by the years of the Persian kings. The chronological problems of this period are caused by the apparent disorder in the sequence of events related in the biblical books of Ezra and Nehemiah and by the difficulty of identifying some of the Persian kings in question. For example, the King Artaxerxes of these books may stand for Artaxerxes I Longimanus (465–425 BC), for Artaxerxes II Mnemon (404–359/358 BC), or in the case of Ezra at any rate, for Artaxerxes III Ochus (359/358–338/337 BC).

Reckoning by Persian kings

From the Grecian period onward, Jews used the Seleucid era (especially in dating deeds; hence its name Minyan

Shetarot, or "Era of Contracts"). In vogue in the East until the 16th century, this was the only popular Jewish era of antiquity to survive. The others soon became extinct. These included, among others, national eras dating (1) from the accession of the Hasmonean princes (*e.g.,* Simon the Hasmonean in 143/142 BC) and (2) from the anti-Roman risings ("era of the Redemption of Zion") in the years 66 and 131 of the Common (Christian) Era. Dates have also been reckoned from the destruction of the Second Temple (*le-ḥurban ha-Bayit*). The various styles of the latter, as also of the Seleucid era and of the era *anno mundi,* have often led to erroneous conversions of dates. The respective general styles of these eras correlate as follows: 3830 AM = year 381 of the Seleucid era = year 1 of the Era of the Destruction = year 69/70 of the Common (Christian) Era.

Earlier
Jewish
chronol-
ogies

The earliest Jewish chronologies have not survived. Of the work of the Alexandrian Jew Demetrius (3rd century BC), which deduced Jewish historical dates from the Scriptures, only a few fragments are extant. In the *Book of Jubilees,* events from the creation to the Exodus are dated in jubilee and sabbatical cycles of 49 and 7 years, respectively. Scholars differ as to the date and origin of this book. The era of the creation therein is unlikely to have been other than hypothetical.

The earliest and most important of all Jewish chronologies extant is the *Seder ʿOlam Rabba* ("Order of the World"), transmitted, according to Talmudic tradition, by Rabbi Yosi ben Halafta in the 2nd century AD. The author was possibly the first to use the rabbinic Era of the Creation. His chronology extends from the creation to Bar Kokhba in the days of the Roman emperor Hadrian (2nd century AD); but the period from Nehemiah to Bar Kokhba (*i.e.,* from Artaxerxes I or II to Hadrian) is compressed into one single chapter. The Persian phase shrinks to a mere 54 years. The smaller work *Seder ʿOlam Zuṭa* completes the *Rabba*. It aims to show the Babylonian exilarchs as lineal descendants of David.

Megillat Taʿanit ("Scroll of Fasting"), although recording only the days and months of the year without the dates of the years, is nevertheless an important source for Jewish chronology. It lists events on 35 days of the year that have been identified with events in five chronological periods: (1) pre-Hasmonean, (2) Hasmonean, (3) Roman (up to AD 65), (4) the war against Rome (65–66), and (5) miscellaneous. The authors, or rather the last revisers, are identified with Zealots guided by Hananiah ben Hezekiah ben Gurion and his son Eliezer. (E.J.Wi.)

GREEK

As the cities of ancient Greece progressed to their classical maturity, the need arose among them for a chronological system on a universally understood basis. In the archaic period, genealogies of local monarchs or aristocrats sufficed for the historical tradition of a given area, and events were associated with the lifetimes of well-known ancestors or "heroes." The *synoikismos* (founding of the united city) of Athens took place "in the time of Theseus"; the Spartan ephorate (chief magistracy) was established "in the reign of King Theopompus." When the city-states adopted annual magistracies, the years were designated by the eponymous officials—"in the archonship of Glaucippus" or "when Pleistolas was ephor." This was the local usage throughout classical and Hellenistic Greece, the title of the magistrate varying in different cities. Sometimes tenure of a priesthood provided the chronological basis, as at Argos, where years were dated as the *n*th of the (named) priestess of Hera. The correctness of the series was a matter first of memory and later of careful record. The list of annual archons at Athens was known back to 683 BC (in modern terms). Lists of dynasties also amounted to recorded folk memory, and in all genealogical reckoning there is a point, for modern critics, at which acceptable tradition shades into myth. Corruption of the records was introduced through error or political design, and traditions often conflicted.

Chronology became subject to systematization when cities felt a national need for accurate clarification of their past. In literature the growth of historiography in-

Dating by
local
records

itiated a search for a method of dating that could be universally applied and acknowledged. In the 5th and 4th centuries, local historians used local magistracies as their framework; research was devoted to rationalization of conflicting traditions and production of definitive lists. Charon of Lampsacus, perhaps in the early 5th century, compiled a record of Spartan magistrates; Hellanicus of Lesbos, author of the earliest history of Athens, wrote on the priestesses of Argos. Lists of victors in the great Olympic games were valid for all Greece, pointing the way to the widely accepted reckoning by Olympiads (see below). The Athenian Philochorus was the latest (early 3rd century BC) of compilers of Olympionikai.

The 5th-century historian Herodotus relied for his chronology principally upon the reckoning by generations used by his informants, conventionally accepted as showing three generations to a century. In some cases a 40-year, or other, reckoning was used, and varying traditions sometimes produced difficulty of synchronism. Thucydides, writing "contemporary" history, recognized the chronological problems involved. He dated the beginning of the Peloponnesian War by the Athenian, Spartan, and Argive systems and thenceforward marked the passage of time by seasonal indications. Synchronization was not helped by the fact that the official year began at different times in different cities. In later historical writing the impossibility of accurately coordinating the Athenian and Roman years resulted in serious chronological difficulties.

The system of dating by Athenian archons came to be recognized outside Attica as of wider value, but, in the Hellenistic period, Alexandrian scholarship, represented especially by Eratosthenes of Cyrene, the "father of chronology," was instrumental in promoting the use of the Olympiads as an acceptable system, reckoning a four-year period from each celebration of the Olympic Games. Timaeus of Tauromenium (*c.* 356–260 BC) was the first historian to employ it, but it was little used outside historical writing. Aristotle had been concerned to identify the generation of the first Olympiad, accepted as 776 BC on modern reckoning. For convenience, the beginning of the Olympic year was equated with the summer solstice, when the Athenian year also began. This makes it generally necessary for a Greek year to receive a double date in modern terms (*e.g.,* the death of the philosopher Epicurus in 271/270 BC). Eratosthenes' system produced tables of dates, from which, for example, the fall of Troy could be dated to 1184/83 BC. The "Parian Marble" of 264/263 BC is an inscribed record of events from the time of Cecrops, first king of Athens, reckoning years between the date of the inscription, fixed by the Athenian archon, and each event concerned. Some cities inscribed lists of their eponymous magistrates; the Athenians were the first to do so *c.* 425 BC. A list from Sicilian Tauromenium originally spanned some 300 years. The regnal years of the Hellenistic monarchs or the count from a fixed event (a city foundation or refoundation) also provided acceptable chronological reckoning often useful for more than contemporary or local purposes.

Dating
by the
Olympiads

The use of these chronological possibilities is best seen in historians using the annalistic method, of whom Diodorus Siculus is most notable. In the Christian period, Eusebius, followed by St. Jerome, began the work of reconciling all these indications to the Judaic tradition and produced the foundation of chronology in terms of the Julian calendar upon which modern historians have constructed their framework.

For modern scholarship the problem, in E.J. Bickerman's words, is "how we know Caesar was assassinated on March 15, 44 BC." Before 480 BC, no date can be precise in terms of the Julian calendar unless confirmed by astronomical phenomena. Archaic chronology relies upon the typology of Corinthian pottery in relation to the foundation dates for Greek colonies in Sicily implicit in Thucydides, book vi. Julian dates given for this period (*e.g.,* for the tyranny of Peisistratus in Athens) stem from a complex combination of ancient chronographic tradition with modern archaeology, acceptable only with appropriate reserve. Literary tradition gives the succession of Athenian archons from 480 to 294 BC. The regnal, era, and Olympiad years also provide dates within a twelve-month period. Closer dating is seldom possible unless the sources give precise information in calendric terms, as occasionally in literature and regularly in Athenian and Egyptian public documents. Even these are not translatable into Julian months and days unless coordinated with knowledge of contemporary solar or lunar phenomena and of possible official interference with the calendar. (A.G.W.)

ROMAN

The establishment of a sound chronology for Roman history, as for Greek, depends on the assessment of the evidence available, which falls into two categories—literary and archaeological.

Literary evidence. Although by the late 3rd century BC the Greek mathematician Eratosthenes was working on the systematization of chronography and a series of learned historians had used the documentary method— *e.g.*, for Roman history, Timaeus of Tauromenium, to whom are probably due many of the synchronizations of Roman history with the Greek Olympiads—unfortunately this tradition of documentation and concern for chronology did not immediately pass over into Roman historiography. According to Cicero in *De oratore*, the earliest Roman historians did no more than "compile yearbooks"—for example, Fabius Pictor in the late 3rd century BC, Lucius Calpurnius Piso in the 2nd, and the so-called Sullan annalists in the 1st. Of these authors it is possible to judge only at second hand, and only those of the 1st century were much used directly by the historians whose work survives in any quantity, notably Livy, Dionysius of Halicarnassus, and Diodorus Siculus. In these authors, as in other 1st-century historians such as Sallust, there is little concept of documentation or research other than comparison of literary sources; for none was chronology a direct concern, and in many cases dramatic effectiveness took priority over fidelity to truth. Apart from the Greek Polybius, who treated the rise of Roman power in the Mediterranean from 264 to 146 BC, it was not until Cicero's time that the conception of historical scholarship developed in Rome. Cicero's friend Atticus not only was concerned to draw up a chronological table in his *Liber annalis* but had undertaken research to that end, and the great scholar Marcus Terentius Varro and a little later the learned Marcus Verrius Flaccus produced a vast body of erudite work, nearly all lost. To this source must probably be ascribed the *Fasti Capitolini*, a list of magistrates from the earliest republic to the contemporary period, set up near the *regia* (the office and archive of the *pontifices*, or high priests), perhaps on the adjacent Arch of Augustus, at the end of the 1st century BC. This work, since it is based on inscriptions, is sometimes given precedence over literary evidence, but, since it is a compilation, it is still subject to serious error.

> Magistrate lists

Sources used by Roman historians. The traditionally early extant bodies of law, such as the Twelve Tables from the early republic, were of little chronological value, and juristic *commentarii* were liable to mislead through their zeal for precedent, while Cicero, in spite of Polybius' claim to have inspected early treaties preserved in the Capitol definitely states that there were no public records of early laws. A source frequently referred to is the *Annales maximi*, a collection made about 130 BC of the annual notices displayed on a white board by the *pontifices* and containing notes of food prices, eclipses, etc. Dionysius of Halicarnassus implied that they gave a date for the foundation of the city but was reluctant to accept their authority; and one of the eclipses is referred to by Cicero as being mentioned also by Ennius, but unfortunately the number of the year "from the foundation of the city" is corrupt in the text. Although it is possible to calculate the dates of eclipses astronomically in terms of the modern era, it is difficult to link these to Roman chronology because of the uncertainty of the figures and because of the confused state of the Roman calendar before the Julian reform (see CALENDAR: *Early calendar systems: The early Roman calendar*). Another

difficulty is that the early records may have been burned in 390 BC when Celtic tribes sacked the city; also they would probably have been largely unintelligible if authentic.

Livy quoted the 1st-century annalist Gaius Licinius Macer as having found in the temple of Juno Moneta "linen rolls" giving lists of magistrates; but he also said that Macer and Quintus Aelius Tubero both cited the rolls for the consuls of 434 but gave different names. In any case, it is unlikely that the list could have been older than the temple, which dates from 344 BC. It is clear that the chief sources for the lists were the pedigrees of prominent Roman families, such as the Claudii Marcelli, Fabii, and Aemilii, drawn up by Atticus; but Cicero and Livy agree that tendentious falsifications had in many cases corrupted the records, and other suspicious facts are the appearance of obviously later or invented *cognomina*, or third names, and of plebeian gentile names for the earliest period, when only patricians bore them. Many scholars, however, accept the general authenticity of the lists—one reason being the appearance in them of extinct patrician families—but prefer Livy's version to that of the Capitoline lists, which show signs of late revision, often give names in incorrect order, and contain other anomalies.

The question, therefore, remains whether Roman chronography was dependent on the lists of magistrates or whether these were adapted to fit other known datings. The apparent advantages of the existence of a terminal date, the "foundation of the city," is illusory for Roman chronology, since it depended on back reckoning and was not agreed even in antiquity. Various ancient scholars each assumed a different date. Each computed his date by adding a different number of years of kingly rule from the foundation of the city to his estimate of the date of the foundation of the republic. This, in turn, was presumably computed by counting back over the yearly lists of magistrates. There may have been traditions about the intervals between certain events in early Roman history, but the frequently accepted reckoning of 244 years of kingly rule seems to be a calculation based only on the conventional 35-year generation for the rule of the seven legendary kings. Polybius claimed that the dating of the first republican consulship to 508/507 BC could be substantiated by an extant copy of a contemporary treaty. Combined with the traditional kingly period, this would give a foundation date of 751–750, reckoned inclusively, and 752–751, exclusively (Cato's date). The chronological scheme worked out by Varro added two years of nonconsular rule, thus the foundation of Rome was put in 754/753 and the beginning of the republic in 510/509. Varro's dates became standard for later Romans and are sometimes also used by modern scholars in a purely conventional sense. But it remains uncertain whether the dating depended on the magistrate lists or whether these were "doctored" to synchronize with given dates or intervals, whether these were traditional or calculated in some other way. Anomalies such as Livy's five-year anarchy 15 years after the Gallic invasion, Diodorus' repetition of magistrates' names, and the "dictator years" in the lists are perhaps attempts to synchronize the various pedigrees.

> Fixing the terminal date

Contribution of archaeology. Archaeology can provide many dates useful to the detailed study of Roman history, especially from coins and inscriptions, but, for the general scheme of early chronology, its value is largely negative. It shows, for example, that Rome evolved over a lengthy period and was not really "founded," though a "foundation" date might perhaps refer to the first common celebration of the Septimontium, or festival of the seven hills; again, if that dating is dependent on the seven kings, archaeology shows that the tradition about them, though it may preserve genuine names and events, is largely legendary.

Datings after the 1st century BC. In this better documented period, datings to consul years, or later to the years of tribunician power of the emperors, are normally intelligible, despite a few notorious cruxes, although up to the Julian reform the state of the calendar has always to be taken into account. In parts of the empire, however, different eras were used—*e.g.*, that of the Seleucids —and from the 4th century AD dates were often calculated in terms of the years of the indiction, a 15-year cycle connected with the levying of taxes (every 15 years starting afresh, counting 1, 2, 3 . . . 15), a method that continued in use for many centuries in spite of difficulties, such as lack of synchronization among the various provinces. (Ed.)

CHRISTIAN

The Christian Era

The Christian Era is the era now in general use throughout the world. Its epoch, or commencement, is January 1, 754 AUC (*ab urbe condita*—"from the foundation of the city [of Rome]"—or *anno urbis conditae*—"in the year of the foundation of the city"). Christ's birth was at first believed to have occurred on the December 25 immediately preceding. Years are reckoned as before or after the Nativity, those before being denoted BC (before Christ) and those after by AD (*anno Domini*, "in the year of the Lord"). Chronologers admit no year zero between 1 BC and AD 1. The precise date of commencing the annual cycle was widely disputed almost until modern times, December 25, January 1, March 25, and Easter day each being favoured in different parts of Europe at different periods.

The Christian Era was invented by Dionysius Exiguus (*c.* AD 500–after 525), a monk of Scythian birth resident in Italy; it was a by-product of the dispute that had long vexed the churches as to the correct method of calculating Easter. Many churches, including those in close contact with Rome, followed 95-year tables evolved by Theophilus, bishop of Alexandria, and by his successor, St. Cyril; but some Western churches followed other systems, notably a 532-year cycle prepared for Pope Hilarius (461–468) by Victorius of Aquitaine. In 525, at the request of Pope St. John I, Dionysius Exiguus prepared a modified Alexandrian computation based on Victorius' cycle. He discarded the Alexandrian era of Diocletian, reckoned from AD 284, on the ground that he "did not wish to perpetuate the name of the Great Persecutor, but rather to number the years from the Incarnation of Our Lord Jesus Christ."

Somehow Dionysius reckoned the birth of Christ to have occurred in 753 AUC; but the Gospels state that Christ was born under Herod the Great—*i.e.*, at the latest in 750 AUC. Dionysius' dating was questioned by the English saint Bede in the 8th century and rejected outright by the German monk Regino of Prüm at the end of the 9th. Nevertheless, it has continued in use to the present day, and, as a result, the Nativity is reckoned to have taken place in or shortly before the year 4 BC, when Herod died.

The new chronology was not regarded as a major discovery by its author; Dionysius' own letters are all dated by the indiction (see below). The use of the Christian Era spread through the employment of his new Easter tables. In England the era was adopted with the tables at the Synod of Whitby in 664. But it was the use, above all by Bede, of the margins of the tables for preserving annalistic notices and the consequent juxtaposition of historical writing with calendrical computations that popularized the new era. Outside Italy it is first found in England (in a charter of 676) and shortly after in Spain and Gaul. It was not quickly adopted in royal diplomas and other solemn documents, however, and in the papal chancery it did not replace the indiction until the time of John XIII (965–972). The era did not become general in Europe until the 11th century; in most of Spain it was not adopted until the 14th and in the Greek world not until the 15th.

Of the alternative chronologies used by Christians, the most important were: (1) the indiction, (2) the Era of Spain, and (3) the Era of the Passion. The indiction was a cycle of 15 years originally based on the interval between imperial tax assessments but during the Middle Ages always reckoned from the accession of Constantine, in 312. Years were given according to their place in the cycle of 15, the number of the indiction itself being ignored. This chronology was the most widespread in the early Middle Ages, but its use diminished rapidly in the 13th century,

although public notaries continued to use it until the 16th. The Era of Spain was based on an Easter cycle that began on January 1, 716 AUC (38 BC), marking the completion of the Roman conquest of Spain. First recorded in the 5th century, it was in general use in Visigothic Spain of the 6th and 7th centuries and, after the Arab invasions, in the unconquered Christian kingdoms in the north of the Iberian Peninsula. It was abolished, in favour of the Era of the Incarnation, in Catalonia in 1180, in Aragon in 1350, in Castile in 1383, and in Portugal in 1422. The Era of the Passion, commencing 33 years after that of the Incarnation, enjoyed a short vogue, mainly in 11th-century France. (Ed.)

MUSLIM

Unlike earlier chronological systems in use before Islām, Islāmic chronology was instituted so soon after the event that was to be the beginning of the Muslim era that no serious problems were encountered in its application. According to the most reliable authorities, it was 'Umar I, the second caliph (reigned 634–644), who introduced the era used by the Muslim world. When his attention was drawn by Abū Mūsā al-Ash'arī to the fact that his letters were not dated, 'Umar consulted with men at Medina and then ordered that the year of the *hijrah* (hegira), the Prophet's flight from Mecca to Medina, be taken as the beginning of an era for the Muslim state and community. According to the Muslim calendar, the *hijrah* took place on 8 Rabī' I, which corresponds to September 20, 622 (AD), in the Julian calendar (see CALENDAR: *Middle Eastern calendar systems: The Muslim calendar*). But, as Muḥarram had been already accepted as the first month of the lunar year, 'Umar ordered that (Friday) 1 Muḥarram (July 16, 622) be the beginning of the reckoning. It is generally accepted that this was done in AH 17 (*anno Hegirae*, "in the year of the Hegira").

The era of the *hijrah*

There are a few points in connection with this that deserve mention: first, there is no real agreement on the exact date of the *hijrah*—other dates given include 2 and 12 Rabī' I; second, the year in which 'Umar issued the order is a point of contention—the years 16 and 17 are sometimes given; third, some people have ascribed the use of the chronology to the Prophet himself. According to some sources, the *hijrah* date was first used by Ya'lā ibn Umayyah, Abū Bakr's governor in Yemen. This sounds somewhat plausible because Yemenis were probably used to affixing dates to their documents. There is, however, a consensus among workers in the field that 8 Rabī' I was the day of the *hijrah*, that 'Umar instituted the use of the date for the new era, and that this was done in AH 17. The choice of the *hijrah* as the beginning of the epoch has two reasons. On the one hand, its date had been fixed; on the other, 'Umar and his advisers must have recognized the importance of the migration—Islām had become, as a result, a religion and a state.

Before the introduction of the new epoch, the Arabs had been acquainted with chronologies used by their neighbours, the Seleucids and the Persians. In Yemen the practice of dating had been perfected to the extent that inscriptions show the day, the month, and the year. In Mecca the "year of the Elephant," supposedly coinciding with the birth of the Prophet, had been in use. For the period between the migration and the institution of the new epoch, the Muslims of Medina resorted to naming the year after local events—"the year of the order of fighting" and "the year of the earthquake," etc.

The lunar year was adopted by the Muslims (see CALENDAR: *The Muslim Calendar*) for the new chronology. In this there was hardly any innovation insofar as Arabia was concerned.

The chronology introduced by 'Umar was adopted throughout the Muslim world, although earlier epochs continued in use in outlying provinces. Muslim historians, annalists, and chroniclers met with difficulties when writing their books on pre-Islāmic history. No practice had as yet developed for pre-*hijrah* dating; therefore, when writing about the history of various lands in pre-Islāmic times, authors resorted to the use of chronologies previously in existence there (*e.g.*, Persian, Indian, Seleucid, Alexandrian). For the histories of the area under Islām, writers used only Muslim chronology, while non-Muslim authors (*e.g.*, Bar Hebraeus) used the Seleucid and the *hijrah* dates when discussing events pertaining to provinces that had been Byzantine and therefore still had fairly large groups of Christians.

The era of the *hijrah* is in official use in Saudi Arabia, the two Yemens, and in the Persian Gulf area. Egypt, Syria, Jordan, Morocco, Algeria, Libya, and Tunisia use both the Muslim and the Christian eras. Many Muslim countries, such as Turkey, Nigeria, and Pakistan, use the Christian Era.

Variants of the *hijrah* era

Within the general uniformity of applying the *hijrah* era proper, there existed differences, some of which were the result of earlier pre-Islāmic practices; others were the result of continuous contacts of Muslim countries with their European neighbours, with whom they had economic as well as political relations. An example of the former was the work of the ʿAbbāsid caliph al-Muʿtaḍid, who brought the Nowrūz (Persian New Year's Day) back to date in keeping with the agricultural activities of the community. Ghāzān Maḥmūd introduced the Khānian era in Persia in AH 701, which was a reversion to the regnal chronologies of antiquity. It continued in use for some generations, then the ordinary *hijrah* era was reintroduced. A similar step was taken by Akbar when he established the Ilāhī era, which began on Rabīʿ II 963 (February 13, 1556), the date of his accession; the years were solar.

Two Muslim countries, Turkey and Iran, introduced more drastic changes into their chronology because of European influences.

In Turkey the Julian calendar was adopted in AH 1088 (AD 1676–77) and used solar months with *hijrah* dating. The year was officially called the Ottoman fiscal year but was popularly known as the *marti* year, after *mart* (Turkish for March), which was the beginning of the year. Under Mustafa Kemal Atatürk, the Gregorian calendar and the Christian Era were officially adopted in Turkey (1929). Iran also adopted a solar year; the names of the months in its calendar are Persian, and the era is still that of the *hijrah*. (N.A.Z.)

PRE-COLUMBIAN AMERICAN

Maya and Mexican. *Lowland Maya.* The lowland Maya had a 365-day year formed of 18 "months." Each month consisted of 20 days, plus five "nameless" days, which the Maya considered an extremely dangerous and unlucky period and during which activities were kept to a minimum. Leap days were not intercalated (see CALENDAR: *Calendar systems of the Americas: The Maya calendar system*).

Reckoning was not by those years, but by *tuns* (360 days) and their multiples of 20: *katuns* (20 *tuns*), *baktuns* (400 *tuns*), *pictuns* (8,000 *tuns*), *calabtuns* (160,000 *tuns*), and *kinchiltuns* (3,200,000). In practice, the last three were seldom used. The *tun* comprised 18 *uinals*, each of 20 *kins* (days), but these did not coincide with the equivalent divisions of the 365-day year. The Maya normally carved or wrote these in descending order; students transcribe them in Arabic numerals—*e.g.*, 9.10.6.5.9 represents nine *baktuns*, ten *katuns*, six *tuns*, five *uinals*, nine *kins*.

With this system, current dates were related to the start of the Maya era, which, because of the Maya system of re-entering cycles marked both the end of 13 *baktuns* (written 13.0.0.0.0) and the start of another cycle of *baktuns*, and perhaps commemorated a re-creation of the world, the *baktun* about to enter being numbered 1, not 14. Because of the construction of the calendar, this start of the era happened to be day 4 Ahau falling on the eighth day of the month Cumku.

Such reckonings are called Initial Series, or Long Counts, the former because they usually stand at the start of an inscription (see CALENDAR). For example, the combination day 8 Muluc, falling on second of Zip (third month), recurs every 52 years, but the Initial Series (here 9.10.6.5.9 8 Muluc 2 Zip) pinpoints its position. The next occurrence, 52 years later, would be 9.12.19.0.9 8 Muluc

2 Zip. Each unit had its own glyph (or symbolic character), with appropriate number (normally a dot for 1 and bar for 5) attached.

A shorter dating system was by "Period Endings"—that is, by recording the ending of the current *baktun*, *katun*, or *tun*. Thus, day 13 Ahau and month position 13 Muan with 13 *tuns* added is an abbreviation of 9.17.13.0.0 13 Ahau 13 Muan, a combination that will not repeat for over 900 years (949 *tuns*). A still shorter but less precise method was to give the day and its number ending the current *katun*.

Several Maya dates were commonly linked to Initial Series or Period Endings by series of additions or subtractions—a glyph signifying count indicated forward or backward by secondary attachments.

Dates were normally reckoned from the 4 Ahau 8 Cumku base, nearly 4,000 years before most inscriptions, but some calculations ranged far into the past and a few into the distant future. One reaches backward nearly 1,250,000 years, but the deepest probings of eternity are embodied in texts that seemingly record positions respectively 90 and 400 million years ago. Although the interpretation of these last computations is disputable, the Maya certainly thought in millions of years a millennium before Europe discarded the view that the world was only some 6,000 years old.

Maya conception of time

The Maya conceived of time as a journey through eternity in which each deified number—all time periods and their numbers were gods—carried his period on his back supported by a tump line. Each evening the procession rested. Next morning, carriers whose period was completed were replaced. For instance, if the *uinal* and *kin* numbers were 15 and 19 respectively, the new carriers would be the deified 16 and 0 (the latter because *kin* numbers go no higher than 19). Other period numbers would journey on until it came time to change the *tun* carrier. Much ritual and imagery grew out of this concept of the march of time; sculpture illustrates bearers lowering their burdens at journey's end.

Correlation of the Maya calendar with ours depends on several factors. First, the 260-day almanac still functions in some Maya villages in the Guatemalan highlands. As there is excellent evidence it has neither gained nor lost a day since the Spanish conquest, despite strong Spanish efforts to suppress it, one may reasonably assume no break under the more favourable pre-Columbian conditions. Lunar and other data support such a view. Second, month positions in Yucatán and southern Petén at the Spanish conquest also are reliably correlated to the day with the present Western calendar. Third, the combined day and month parts of the Maya calendar are in day-for-day agreement with the present Western calendar within a 52-year span (after that given day and month positions repeat). The *katun* (specifically, 13 Ahau) current at the Spanish conquest is, however, known, thereby fixing any day and month position in a longer range of 260 years because a named *katun* repeats only after 260 *tuns*. Those conditions produce a correlation of the two calendars that is either correct to the day or is 260 or even 520 years wrong, since historical evidence does not specify which particular *katun* 13 Ahau coincided with the Spaniards arrival. Fourth, such factors as astronomy (Maya records of heliacal risings of Venus and of many dates with moon age stated), pottery sequences, architectural changes (less reliable), and data from neighbouring areas govern choice of the applicable *katun* 13 Ahau. Weight of evidence led to wide acceptance of the Goodman–Martínez–Thompson correlation that equates 13.0.0.0.0 4 Ahau 8 Cumku, start of the Maya era, with August 10, 3113 BC, and the Classic period with AD 300 to 900. Fifth, when the carbon-14 dating technique was first applied to the problem, various difficulties attendant on the use of new techniques and failure to take into account that a tree dies year by year from its centre outward (so that a sample from the core might give a date well over a century before felling) distorted readings, producing results favourable to the correlation making Maya dates 260 years earlier. Now, with better technique and averaging of many "runs" of samples of latest growth from beams at Tikal with secure Maya dates, carbon-14 readings overwhelmingly support the Goodman–Martínez–Thompson correlation.

Highland Maya. The only other Middle American calendar with a known era is that of the Cakchiquel of highland Guatemala. The system was vigesimal: *kih*, day; *uinak*, 20 days; *a*, 400 days; and *may*, 8,000 days. The 400-day "year" ran concurrently with the 260-day almanac, which, in turn, synchronized with all other Maya almanacs. Like the 360-day *tun* of the lowlands, the 400-day *a* was the counting unit, for reckoning was always in multiples of the *a*, never by days, as in our Julian calendar. *May* signifies twenty, and is so named because it comprised 20*a*. At the arrival of the Spaniards, reckoning was from a revolt in AD 1493. Earlier eras may be postulated, but inscribed calendrical texts are lacking in Cakchiquel territory.

Aztec. The Aztec and related peoples of central Mexico employed the cycle of 52 years, constructed, like its Maya equivalent, of concurrent 365-day years and 260-day cycles, any position of the former coinciding with a given position of the latter only at 52-year intervals. Again leap days were not used. At completion of the 52 years, known as "binding of the years," elaborate ceremonies were held to avert destruction of the world expected on that occasion. The last occurrence before the Spanish conquest was in AD 1507. Although the last creation of the world was designated by a day name, neither that nor any other was in general use in central Mexico as the start of an era. Aztec reckoning is normally from their arrival in the Valley of Mexico, supposedly the year 1 Flint (AD 1168).

There is much confusion in placing events in Mexican history because no system of distinguishing one 52-year cycle from another was employed except by writing every year glyph throughout the period covered, a clumsy arrangement. Each year was named for either its last day (omitting the five-day unlucky period) or for the last day of the fifth month (both choices have distinguished supporters). In either case, only four day names (House, Rabbit, Cane, and Flint), each with its accompanying numeral, could designate a year. The Spanish conqueror Hernán Cortés seized the Aztec capital in 1521, year 3 House, but some past event, also assigned to a year 3 House but unlocated in a full sequence of years, might refer to AD 1261, 1313, or 1365, etc. Month positions were rarely given in chronological statements.

Peoples of Oaxaca and the Isthmus of Tehuantepec. Pictorial books of the Mixtec of Oaxaca record events in the lives of ruling families covering seven centuries, but, again, happenings are fixed only by the day on which each occurred and the year in which the day fell. Sequence is usually clear, but at times there is doubt as to which 52-year period is meant when parenthetical material, such as life histories of secondary characters, is inserted.

No era is recognizable. A clouded entry concerning the descent to Earth of the Sun and Venus, perhaps assignable to AD 794, is a logical starting point, but other entries are earlier.

Little is known of the calendar of the Zapotec, neighbours of the Mixtec. Years began on a different set of days, and glyphs differ from those of Mixtec and Aztec. Months are not recorded on monuments, which are numerous, and no chronological system has survived. Most Zapotec texts are early.

Rare inscriptions in western Chiapas, southern Veracruz, and the Guatemalan Pacific coast resemble the abbreviated lowland Maya Initial Series used in script and on a single sculpture in that numerical bars and dots are in a vertical column with period glyphs and month signs suppressed, clearly place numeration, that is, the value of each unit was shown by its position in the column. The linguistic affiliation of their sculptors is unknown.

All texts are either fragmentary or damaged; the two complete ones, unlike Maya Initial Series, open with days signs (and different ones at that). If, as one may reasonably assume, the series of bars and dots departed from those day signs, a fixed era is questionable. Nevertheless,

some scholars postulate use of the Maya era (13.0.0.0.0 4 Ahau 8 Cumku). This little understood system may have been ancestral to the Maya Initial Series, the Maya perhaps developing a fixed era, for they alone seem to have been interested in an exact chronological system.

(J.E.S.T.)

BIBLIOGRAPHY

General works: JAMES C. MacDONALD, *Chronologies and Calendars* (1897); ALFRED E. STAMP, *Methods of Chronology* (1933); R.L. POOLE, *Studies in Chronology and History*, collected and ed. by A.L. POOLE (1934, reprinted 1969).

Chinese: On the astronomical basis of Chinese calendrical systems, see JOSEPH NEEDHAM, *Science and Civilisation in China*, vol. 3, pp. 390–408 (1959). A standard reference for conversion between Chinese and Western calendars is MATHIAS TCHANG, *Synchronismes chinois* (1905).

Hindu: ROBERT SEWELL and S.B. DIKSHITA, *The Indian Calendar* (1896), describes the various systems of calendars in India, with tables of concordance and a useful index; ROBERT SEWELL, *The Siddhantas and the Indian Calendar* (1924), a study of the Hindu astronomical system as a basis for the traditional calendar; SWAMIKANNU PILLAI, *An Indian Ephemeris*, 6 vol. (1922), tables of concordance of Hindu, Muslim, and modern calendars; JEAN FILLIOZAT, "Notions de chronologie," in LOUIS RENOU and JEAN FILLIOZAT, *Inde classique*, vol. 2 (1953), a general summary and list of different eras used in India.

Egyptian: RICHARD A. PARKER, *The Calendars of Ancient Egypt* (1950), a basic work providing valid solutions to most of the problems of Egyptian chronology; "Lunar Dates of Thutmose III and Ramesses II," *J. Near Eastern Stud.*, 16: 39–43 (1957), an analysis of the more important lunar dates of the New Kingdom; M.B. ROWTON, "Manetho's Date for Ramesses II," *J. Egyptian Archaeol.*, 34:57–74 (1948), and "Comparative Chronology at the Time of Dynasty XIX," *J. Near Eastern Stud.*, 19:15–22 (1960), two articles that deal with the date for the accession of Ramses II (1290 or 1304 BC); ERIK HORNUNG, *Untersuchungen zur Chronologie und Geschichte des Neuen Reiches* (1964), the most up-to-date synthesis of the chronological problems of the New Kingdom; I.E.S. EDWARDS, "Absolute Dating from Egyptian Records and Comparison with Carbon-14 Dating," *Phil. Trans. R. Soc.*, Series A, 269:11–18 (1970), includes a complete list of all radiocarbon dates taken from Egyptian samples.

Babylonian and Assyrian: The most complete general work on the chronology of Western Asia, including Mesopotamia, is P.E. VAN DER MEER, *The Chronology of Ancient Western Asia and Egypt*, 2nd rev. ed. (1955); however, it should be used with caution. For the general chronology of ancient Western Asia, with special reference to Mesopotamia, see M.B. ROWTON in *The Cambridge Ancient History*, 3rd ed., vol. 1, pp. 193–237 (1970), and the extensive literature quoted there (up to 1959). For a discussion of the gap in the 2nd millennium BC, see A. GOETZE, "The Kassites and Near Eastern Chronology," *J. Cuneiform Stud.*, 18:97–101 (1964); and B.L. VAN DER WAERDEN, *Die Anfänge der Astronomie*, pp. 28–49 (1966). For the chronology of the late 2nd millennium BC and the chronological gap in the 1st millennium BC, see J.A. BRINKMAN, *A Political History of Post-Kassite Babylonia, 1158–722 B.C.*, pp. 37–85 (1968).

Jewish: B. RATNER, *Seder Olam Rabba: Die grosse Weltchronik* (1897), the authoritative edition, carefully annotated and with a detailed introduction, of the oldest rabbinic chronology extending from the earliest records to the first century of the current era; E. MAHLER, *Handbuch der jüdischen Chronologie* (1916), the only comprehensive work on Jewish chronology, covering all aspects and summarizing most previous works on the subject; S. ZEITLIN, *Megillat Taanit As a Source for Jewish Chronology and History in the Hellenistic and Roman Periods* (1922), removes all discrepancy in I and II Maccabees' and Josephus' chronological data in the Hasmonean phase of Jewish history, thus reinvesting their statements with historical significance and authority.

Greek: ALAN E. SAMUEL, *Greek and Roman Chronology: Calendars and Years in Classical Antiquity* (1972), a fundamental work; HENRY FYNES CLINTON, *Fasti Hellenici*, 3 vol. (1834), still useful in providing the sources for the framework of Greek chronology; J.W. KUBITSCHEK, *Grundriss der antiken Zeitrechnung* (1928), the standard handbook but unreliable; A.E. SAMUEL, *Ptolemaic Chronology* (1962); E.J. BICKERMAN, *Chronology of the Ancient World* (1968), a summary survey to be used judiciously; W. DEN BOER, *Laconian Studies*, p. 1, "The Struggle for the Chronological Pattern" (1954), on ancient attempts to systematize archaic chronology; A.G. WOODHEAD, *The Greeks in the West*, pp. 69–72 (1962), on dates in the archaic period.

Roman: E.J. BICKERMAN, *Chronology of the Ancient World* (1968), an excellent short manual, unfortunately marred by a number of factual errors; AGNES KIRSOPP MICHELS, *The Calendar of the Roman Republic* (1967), contains much valuable information on chronology as well as the calendar—probably the best book ever written on the Roman calendar; F.K. GINZEL, *Handbuch der mathematischen und technischen Chronologie das Zeitrechnungswesen der Völker*, 3 vol. (1906–14), the standard work of reference on its subject.

Christian: F.K. GINZEL, *Handbuch der mathematischen und technischen Chronologie das Zeitrechnungswesen der Völker*, 3 vol. (1906–14), still the fundamental work; JACK FINEGAN, *Handbook of Bible Chronology* (1964), the best for its subject; E.J. BICKERMAN, *Chronology of the Ancient World* (1968), very thorough and complete.

Muslim: AL-BIRUNI, *The Chronology of Ancient Nations*, Eng. trans. by C. EDWARD SACHAU (1879), useful source material on the Muslim knowledge of chronology down to the 10th century AD; see especially pp. 16–82. For actual tables of Muslim chronological information and comments, the following may be consulted: E. LACOINE, *Tables de concordance des dates des calendriers . . .* (1891); C.L. IDELER, *Handbuch der mathematischen und technischen chronologie*, 2 vol. (1825–26); S. LANE-POOLE, *The Mohammedan Dynasties* (1894); and C.E. BOSWORTH, *The Islamic Dynasties* (1967). See also articles on calendar, chronology, and "Hidjra" in the *Encyclopaedia of Islam*.

Pre-Columbian American: S.G. MORLEY, "An Introduction to the study of the Maya Hieroglyphs," *Bull. U.S. Bur. Am. Ethnol.*, no. 57 (1915, reprinted 1968), a clear exposition of Maya chronology; J. ERIC S. THOMPSON, *Maya Chronology: The Correlation Question* (1935) and *Maya Hieroglyphic Writing: Introduction* (1950, reprinted 1971); H.J. SPINDEN, *The Reduction of Maya Dates* (1924), a presentation of earlier correlation; L. SATTERTHWAITE and E.K. RALPH, "New Radiocarbon Dates and the Maya Correlation Problem," *Am. Antiq.*, 26:165–184 (1960).

(W.S.-cg./J.L.A.F./W.H./M.B.R./
E.J.Wi./A.G.W./N.A.Z./J.E.S.T.)

Chrysostom, Saint John

St. John Chrysostom was a Christian teacher, a scriptural exegete, an archbishop of Constantinople, and a Church Father. His fame, during his lifetime and for posterity, rests on his preaching and his exposition of the Bible, whence his surname Chrysostom, "golden-mouthed." He was a leading exponent of the method of scriptural exegesis (the Antiochan school) that emphasized the literal or natural sense of the text, as opposed to the allegorical sense, and throughout the ages he has been revered as one of the four greatest Eastern doctors, or teachers, of the whole church.

John was born at Antioch in Syria about the year AD 347, the son of a high-ranking military officer. He was brought up as a Christian by his widowed mother and was intended for the law, to which end he studied under a distinguished pagan rhetorician, Libanius. But John also studied theology, and before long he gave up his profession to become a hermit-monk. This life was not for him, either. His health gave way, and he returned to Antioch, becoming an ordained deacon and priest there. For 12 years (from 386) he established himself as a great preacher, his homilies (sermons) including some on the first and fourth gospels and on eight of St. Paul's letters. A sensational episode of this period was a riot in 387, during which the citizens of Antioch treated the images of the sacred emperors with disrespect and were threatened with reprisals; in a famous course of sermons, "On the Statues," Chrysostom set himself to bring his hearers to a frame of mind suitable both to the season, Lent, and to the dangerous situation in which they stood. His reputation as a preacher was now assured. He was unfailing in the practical application of his scriptural learning to everyday life, and he did it with understanding and sympathy and without compromise. His brilliant exposition and moral teaching have the note of universality; his words strike the reader today as forcefully as ever, and his humorous sallies are as pungent as when they provoked laughter in the congregations of Antioch and Constantinople. He was concerned, above all, for the spiritual and temporal welfare of the needy and op-

St. John Chrysostom, detail of a mosaic by an unknown artist, 12th century. In the Palatine Chapel, Palermo, Italy.
Anderson—Alinari

pressed. He was not alone among the early Fathers in speaking out against the abuse of wealth, teaching that personal property is not strictly private but a trust, and declaring that what was superfluous to one's reasonable needs ought to be given away. But none surpassed John Chrysostom in eloquent, moving, and repeated insistence on almsgiving, and in no narrow sense.

In 398 Chrysostom was called to Constantinople to be its archbishop, much against his will. The imperial city afforded yet more scope for his reforming zeal, but his vigour and thoroughness were not balanced by temperateness and discretion; he gained a large following among the people, but his castigation of the misuse of riches angered the wealthy and influential. An unscrupulous alliance against John was made by Eudoxia, the wife of the Eastern Roman emperor Arcadius, and the archbishop of the rival see of Alexandria, the powerful Theophilus. In 403 Theophilus convened a synod of disaffected or subservient Syrian and Egyptian bishops at The Oak, across the Bosporus. This gathering indicted John on a large number of charges, many of which were purely frivolous or vexatious; the most important of them were that he had protected the Tall Brothers, a group of Egyptian monks who had incurred the wrath of their archbishop, Theophilus; and that John was guilty of treason, in that he had publicly used reproachful language about the character of the empress Eudoxia. Chrysostom refused to appear before the synod, whereupon it condemned him and professed to depose him from his see. The emperor Arcadius therefore banished Chrysostom from the city, recalled him at once, and finally banished him again in the following year. He was kept in confinement at Cucusus in Armenia.

Chrysostom appealed to the bishop of Rome, Pope Innocent I; he, with the help of the Western emperor Honorius, tried to intervene, but his efforts were brought to nothing by Chrysostom's enemies. But John, in exile, was able to keep up a lively correspondence with his supporters, and many details about his enforced sojourn at Cucusus are recorded in his letters to the deaconess Olympias and others. These letters are marked, too, by a deep concern for his friends, his flock, and the missions he had established in Syria and among the Goths. He suffered much from ill health in the bitter winters, but from Cucusus he was still able to exert influence in his cause, and word came from Constantinople that he was to be removed to a more remote place at the eastern end of

Archbishop of Constantinople

the Black Sea. Chrysostom did not survive the journey, dying of exhaustion at Comana in Pontus on September 14, 407. The official rehabilitation of John Chrysostom came about 31 years later, when his relics were brought from Comana to Constantinople and were solemnly received by the then archbishop Proclus and the emperor Theodosius II, son of Arcadius and Eudoxia.

Signifi-
cance and
works Chrysostom was not an outstanding theologian or theological writer; it has been said that a detailed history of Christian theology could be written without mentioning his name. His works consist of a very large number of scriptural homilies and other sermons, together with some treatises and letters. The first collected edition of the texts of Chrysostom's works were edited, simultaneously and separately but not without mutual consultation, by the Jesuit Fronton du Duc (Latin, Ducaeus) in France (published 1609–33) and by Sir Henry Savile in England (1610–13). The edition now most easily available for consultation is that in J.-P. Migne's *Patrologiae Cursus Completus* (Series Graeca), volumes 47–64; the text of this is substantially that of Bernard de Montfaucon (1718–38).

The most frequently used of the three eucharistic services of the Eastern Orthodox Church is called the Liturgy of St. John Chrysostom, but the evidence that he had anything to do with its composition is unconvincing. The Prayer of St. John Chrysostom in *The Book of Common Prayer* of the Church of England is taken from this liturgy, hence the attribution of the prayer. Chrysostom's feast day is kept, in the new general calendar of the Roman Church (1969), on September 13; the Orthodox Church commemorates him on January 30 and other dates.

BIBLIOGRAPHY. The chief source for Chrysostom's life is a *Dialogue* on that subject, attributed to PALLADIUS, bishop of Heliopolis, a personal friend of the saint; Eng. trans. by H. MOORE (1921); Greek text ed. by P.R. COLEMAN-NORTON (1928). The standard modern biography is by C. BAUR, *Der heilige Johannes Chrysostomus und Seine Zeit* (1929–30; Eng. trans. *John Chrysostom and His Time*, 2 vol., 1959–60). A. MOULARD, *Saint Jean Chrysostome: sa vie, son oeuvre* (1949), is a study of his pastoral method as well as a biography. For a more popular treatment, see D. ATTWATER, *Saint John Chrysostom: Pastor and Preacher* (1959). There are 16 volumes of English translations of scriptural homilies, the sermons on the Statues, and other material in the "Library of the Fathers" (1839–52); see also "Select Library of Nicene and Post-Nicene Fathers of the Christian Church," 1st series, vol. 9–14 (1888–93).

(D.At.)

Chuang-tzu

Taoism has had many interpreters in Chinese history, but none has been more significant than Chuang-tzu (Pinyin romanization Juang-zu). Among the basic Taoist texts, the book that bears his name, the *Chuang-tzu*, is more comprehensive and definitive even than the famous *Tao-te Ching* ("Classic of the Way of Power"), attributed to Lao-tzu, Taoism's first major patriarch. Kuo Hsiang (died AD 312), the first and, many scholars think, best commentator on Chuang-tzu, secured the sage's position as a primary source for Taoist thought. Buddhist scholars, especially those of the Ch'an (Zen) school, also drew heavily from Chuang-tzu's works. His particular interpretation of the Tao (the Way) provided a touchstone for the development of Buddhist philosophy within the traditional framework of Chinese thought. In addition to the role he played in both Taoism and Buddhism, the themes and interests of Chuang-tzu were frequent subjects of subsequent Chinese landscape paintings and poetry.

Reported
facts about
Chuang-
tzu's life In spite of his importance, details of Chuang-tzu's life are unknown. The "Grand Historian" of the Han dynasty, Ssu-ma Ch'ien (died *c.* 85 BC), incorporated in his biographical sketch of Chuang-tzu only the most meagre information. It indicates that Chuang-tzu was a native of the state of Meng, that his personal name was Chou, and that he was a minor official at Ch'i-yüan in his home state. He lived during the reign of Prince Wei of Ch'u (died 327 BC) and was therefore a contemporary of Mencius, an eminent Confucian scholar known as China's Second

Chuang-tzu, ink on silk by an unknown artist. In the National Palace Museum, Taipei, Taiwan.
By courtesy of the National Palace Museum, Taiwan, Republic of China

Sage. According to Ssu-ma Ch'ien, Chuang-tzu's teachings were drawn primarily from the sayings of Lao-tzu; but his perspective was much broader. His literary and philosophical skills were used to refute the Confucianists and Moists (followers of Mo-tzu, who advocated universal love). In addition, he is reported to have written "The Old Fisherman," "Robber Chi," and "Opening Trunks," all devoted to attacks on Confucianism, and *Wei lei hsü* and *Keng san tzu*, which are imaginative fictions.

Chuang-tzu is best known through the book that bears his name, the *Chuang-tzu*, also known as *Nan-hua chen-ching* ("The Pure Classic of Nan-hua"). It is composed of 33 chapters, and evidence suggests that there may have been as many as 53 chapters in copies of the book circulated in the 4th century AD. Numerous editions of the text have appeared since then, and variant readings have obscured the original content. It is generally agreed that the first seven chapters, the "inner books," are, for the most part, genuine, whereas the "outer books" (chapters 8–22) and the miscellany (chapters 23–33) are largely spurious, even though some passages reflect Chuang-tzu's own hand. The more vivid descriptions of Chuang-tzu's character come from the anecdotes about him in the later chapters of the book, which are reputedly apocryphal.

Chuang-tzu appears in these passages as an unpredictable eccentric sage, who seems careless about personal comforts or public esteem. His clothing is shoddy and patched, and his shoes have to be tied to his feet with string in order to keep them from falling apart. Nevertheless, he does not consider himself to be miserable, only poor. When his good friend Hui Shih comes to console him upon the death of his wife, he finds the sage sitting on a mat, singing and beating on a basin. Hui Shih reprimands him, pointing out that such behaviour is improper at the death of someone who has lived and grown old with him and has borne him children. Character
according
to
anecdotal
accounts

When she died, how could I help being affected? But as I think the matter over, I realize that originally she had no life; and not only no life, she had no form; not only no form, she had no material force (*ch'i*). In the limbo of existence and non-existence, there was transformation and the material force was evolved. The material force was transformed to be form, form was transformed to become life, and now birth has transformed to become death. This is like the rotation of the four seasons, spring, summer, fall, and winter. Now she lies asleep in the great house (the universe). For me to go about weeping and wailing would be to show my ignorance of destiny. Therefore I desist.

When Chuang-tzu himself was at the point of death, his disciples began to talk about an elaborate burial for him. Chuang-tzu immediately stopped the discussion by declaring that he did not need the paraphernalia of a great funeral, that nature would be his inner and outer coffin, and the sun and the moon his jade rings, the stars and the planets his jewelry. All creation would make offerings and escort him. He needed no more. Somewhat taken aback, his disciples declared that they were afraid that the crows and the buzzards might eat him. To this Chuang-tzu replied,

> Above the ground it's the crows and the kites who will eat me; below the ground it's the worms and the ants. What prejudice is this, that you wish to take from the one to give to the other?

Chuang-tzu's eccentricities stem directly from his enlightened fatalism. Enlightenment for Chuang-tzu comes with the realization that everything in life is One, the Tao.

View of the Tao

Chuang-tzu taught that what can be known or said of the Tao is not the Tao. It has no beginning or end, no limitations or demarcations. Life is subject to the eternal transformation of the Tao, in which there is no better or worse, no good or evil. Things should be allowed to follow their own course, and men should not value one situation over another. A truly virtuous man is free from the bondage of circumstance, personal attachments, tradition, and the need to reform his world. Chuang-tzu declined an offer to be prime minister of the state of Ch'u because he did not want the entanglements of a court career. It was better to be a free pigling wallowing in the mire than to be a sacrificial cow adorned for the kill.

The complete relativity of his perspective is forcefully expressed in one of the better known passages of the *Chuang-tzu*.

> Once I, Chuang Chou, dreamed that I was a butterfly and was happy as a butterfly. I was conscious that I was quite pleased with myself, but I did not know that I was Chou. Suddenly I awoke, and there I was, visibly Chou. I do not know whether it was Chou dreaming that he was a butterfly or the butterfly dreaming that it was Chou. Between Chou and the butterfly there must be some distinction. This is called the transformation of things.

The relativity of all experience is in constant tension in the *Chuang-tzu* with the unity of all things. When asked where the Tao was, Chuang-tzu replied that it was everywhere. When pushed to be more specific, he declared that it was in ants and, still lower, in weeds and potsherds; furthermore, it was also in excrement and urine. This forceful statement of the omnipresence of the Tao had its parallels in later Chinese Buddhism, in which a similar figure of speech was used to describe the ever present Buddha. Chuang-tzu was *par excellence* the philosopher of the unattached man who is at one with the Tao.

BIBLIOGRAPHY. WING-TSIT CHAN (comp. and trans.), *A Source Book in Chinese Philosophy* (1963; paperback, 1969); selections, excellent translation; YU-LAN FUNG, *Chuang-Tzu*, 2nd ed. (1964), "Inner Books," with commentary of KUO HSIANG; HERBERT A. GILES, *Chuang Tzu*, 2nd ed. (1926), an older translation with commentary (technical terms are inaccurate); JAMES R. WARE, *The Sayings of Chuang Chou* (1963), a readable though sometimes questionable translation; BARTON WATSON (trans.), *Chuang Tzu: Basic Writings* (1964), good introduction, bibliography, and translation of selections.

(J.H.Wa.)

Chu Hsi

Chu Hsi (in Pin-yin romanization, Chu Xi) was the most influential philosopher to arise in China during the last thousand years. Though his ideas never went unchallenged, his Neo-Confucianism long dominated Chinese intellectual life and even won a following and political patronage in Korea and Japan. His commentaries on the Classics were required reading for all who hoped to pass the civil service examinations.

Early life. Chu Hsi was born on October 18, 1130, in Yu-hsi, Fukien Province, where his father was a local official. Though tales of childhood precocity are standard in traditional accounts of admired men, they may well be true of Chu Hsi, who passed the highest civil service examination at the age of 18, when the average age was 35. He owed his early education to his father and, after the latter's death in 1143, to three of his father's friends.

Chu Hsi's first official position was as a registrar in

Chu Hsi, ink on paper, by an unknown artist. In the National Palace Museum, Taipei, Taiwan.
By courtesy of the National Palace Museum, Taiwan, Republic of China

T'ung-an (1151–58), where he not only was responsible for local records but also became involved in a wide range of administrative tasks. His efforts to keep the records honest, his notable contributions to education, and his concern for public morality distinguished him as a good Confucian official. His intellectual development during the 1150s, under the influence of his teacher Li T'ung, was marked by a turn away from Ch'an Buddhism (Japanese, Zen) to his lifelong commitment to Confucianism.

Involvement in public affairs

After the T'ung-an post, Chu Hsi did not accept another official appointment until 1179. But he did express his political views, as in the memorial that he submitted in 1162 to the newly ascended emperor of the Sung dynasty, Hsiao-tsung, which led to his being called to the capital. Here, in 1163, he was received by the Emperor and given the opportunity to repeat his moral admonitions and to argue for a strong, militant policy toward the "barbarian" Chin state then in control of the ancient heartland of Chinese civilization in the north. Though Chu Hsi was involved in public affairs, establishing, for example, a communal granary as a form of famine insurance, his persistent refusal to accept a substantive public office reflects his dissatisfaction with the men in power and their policies, his spurning of factional politics, and his preference for the life of a teacher and scholar made possible by a series of government sinecures.

These years were productive in thought and scholarship, as indicated both by his formal writings and by his correspondence with Chang Shih and other friends; for Chu Hsi always welcomed the stimulus of discourse, in person or by letter, with scholars of diverse views. Most famous is his encounter with the Idealist (Hsin Hsüeh) philosopher Lu Chiu-yüan (Lu Hsiang-shan), at which neither man was able to win over the other. A major disagreement concerned the value of book learning, which was stressed by Chu Hsi, who himself added considerably to the corpus of Neo-Confucian writing. In a number of books, including a compilation of the works of Ch'eng I and Ch'eng Hao, brother-philosophers of the preceding century, and studies on Chang Tsai and Chou Tun-i, Chu Hsi expressed his esteem for these four philosophers, whose ideas he incorporated into his own philosophy. Passages from their writings were also selected by Chu Hsi and his co-compiler, Lü Tsu-ch'ien, for their famous anthology, *Chin-ssu Lu* (*Reflections on Things at Hand*).

The philosophical ideas of Chu Hsi were also reflected in his enormously influential commentaries on the *Lun Yü* (*Analects*) and *Mencius*. In addition to his wide-ranging philosophical interests and his studies of the Classics, Chu Hsi was also a student of history and directed a reworking and condensation of Ssu-ma Kuang's history, the *Tzu-chih t'ung-chien*, to illustrate moral principles.

Devotion to teaching

In or out of office, Chu Hsi was always devoted to teaching. When prevailed upon to become prefect in Nan-k'ang, Kiangsi Province (1179–81), he used the opportunity to rehabilitate the White Deer Grotto Academy, where he tended the moral development of the students as well as their intellectual training and gave regular lectures himself. He did not allow the academy, however, to interfere with his other duties, including famine fighting, which involved numerous requests for such things as tax relief, the distribution of grain, and the construction of dikes.

Later life. In 1180 he submitted a memorial to the throne strongly criticizing government corruption and suggesting that the Emperor himself was in the hands of unscrupulous favorites. His next government service was rendered in eastern Liang-che (Chekiang) as Intendant for Ever-normal Granaries, Tea, and Salt, a post that he assumed in 1182, after using the occasion of an Imperial audience to repeat his criticism of the government. His tour as an intendant was noteworthy for his administration of famine relief and for a number of indictments of corrupt officials. This led to a political attack on Chu Hsi himself, which enabled him once more to withdraw from active political life.

In 1188, after an Imperial audience, Chu was appointed to a position in the Ministry of War. Chu declined this post, providing the occasion for a sharp attack on his attitude toward government service and on his work as a scholar. Before obtaining yet another sinecure, Chu Hsi wrote an important memorial in 1188, in which he restated his conviction that the Emperor's character is fundamental for the well-being of the realm and went on to discuss specific policy issues ranging from the education of the heir apparent to military reform.

In 1189 Chu completed commentaries on *Ta hsüeh* ("The Great Learning") and *Chung Yung* ("The Doctrine of the Mean"), which, together with *Lun Yü* (*Analects*) and *Mencius*, became the *Ssu shu* (*The Four Books*) of Neo-Confucianism. When, also in 1189, the emperor of the Sung dynasty, Kuang-tsung, came to the throne, Chu Hsi was again drawn into government service and, as prefect of Chang-chou, Fukien Province (1190–91), tried unsuccessfully to institute a land survey in order to reform tax collection.

After a crisis at court was resolved in 1194 with the accession of Kuang-tsung's son, Ning-tsung, Chu Hsi became a Lecturer-in-Waiting for the new emperor but was removed as part of the campaign of the ambitious Han T'o-chou to oust his political opponents. Further, to silence the opposition, Han and his associates then organized an attack on what they termed spurious learning, singling out Chu Hsi for especially vigorous denunciation, but allowing him to withdraw to his teaching and writing. He was still under a political cloud when he died on April 23, 1200.

Chu Hsi's philosophy

Chu Hsi's philosophy (Li Hsüeh), as it developed over the years, is contained in his voluminous writings and conversations recorded by some of his numerous disciples. His metaphysics was based on the dualism, originated by Ch'eng I, between *li* (principle or a network of principles) and *ch'i* (energy that when it condenses becomes matter) through which they (or it) run. One of Chu Hsi's major contributions was to identify these principles with the Supreme Ultimate (T'ai Chi) as developed in the cosmology of Chou Tun-i. Because these principles are normative as well as descriptive, they constitute the key to self-cultivation, a major occupation of Sung Confucians intent on building a personal faith as well as a metaphysics to supplant Buddhism and an important ingredient in their advice to emperors through whose self-cultivation order might be restored in the world. In contrast to Lu Chiu-yüan's intuitionism, which focussed on the principles within oneself, Chu Hsi and his followers stressed the "investigation of things," by which they meant primarily ethical conduct and the revered Classics, although Chu Hsi's own intellectual interests encompassed the physical world around him as well as a wide

range of traditional Chinese learning and the personal and theoretical implications of commitment to traditional moral values, the hallmark of a Confucian.

Because he was the author of the philosophy that became China's official orthodoxy, the evaluation of his life and work has been deeply influenced by assessments of the political and social system that Neo-Confucianism helped to sustain. After being admired for centuries, he came to be regarded by contemporary Chinese scholars as a benighted Idealist; others, however, still find in him a source of intellectual stimulation and insight.

BIBLIOGRAPHY. Chu Hsi's philosophy is discussed in FUNG YU-LAN, *A History of Chinese Philosophy*, 2nd ed., vol. 2 (Eng. trans. 1953); and there are excerpts from his writings in WING-TSIT CHAN (comp. and trans.), *A Source Book in Chinese Philosophy* (1963; paperback, 1969). WING-TSIT CHAN has also translated CHU HSI and LU TSU-CH'IEN, *Chin-ssu lu* (Eng. trans., *Reflections on Things at Hand*, 1967), and is the author of *An Outline and Annotated Bibliography of Chinese Philosophy*, rev. ed. (1969). J.P. BRUCE, *Chu Hsi and His Masters* (1923), though it should be used with care, includes quite an extensive discussion of Chu Hsi's life. For his political career, see CONRAD M. SCHIROKAUER, "Chu Hsi's Political Career: A Study in Ambivalence," in ARTHUR F. WRIGHT and DENIS C. TWITCHETT (eds.), *Confucian Personalities* (1962).

(C.M.S.)

Chungking

Chungking (Ch'ung-ch'ing in Wade-Giles romanization; Qong-qing in Pin-yin romanization), the largest city in Szechwan Province and the leading river port and industrial centre in southwest China, is 1,400 miles from the sea, at the confluence of the Yangtze and Chia-ling rivers. During World War II it was the capital of Nationalist China. The city was named Ch'ung-ch'ing (literally Double-Blessed) in 1188 under the Southern Sung dynasty (AD 1126–1279) because it occupied a commanding position between the cities of Shun-ch'ing (modern Nan-ch'ung) to the north and Shao-ch'ing (modern P'eng-shui) to the south. The Ch'ung-ch'ing Shih (Chungking Municipality) covers an area of about 4,000 square miles (1971).

HISTORY

Early history. According to ancient accounts, Chungking was the birthplace of the consort of Emperor Yü of the legendary Hsia dynasty, about 4,000 years ago. In the 11th century BC, under the Western Chou dynasty, the region surrounding Chungking became a feudal state known as Pa. In the 5th century BC, Pa established relations with the mid-Yangtze kingdom of Ch'u. In 316 BC it was incorporated into the Ch'in empire, with Chiang-chou, the present site of Chungking, as its capital. By the mid-3rd century BC the region became part of the kingdom of Shu and was totally independent of North and central China.

The swing of the historical pendulum—in which the city's status varied between being ruled by an empire in North China, forming part of an empire in central China, and detaching itself to become independent of both North and central China—continued throughout subsequent centuries. It finally became an integral part of the unified empire under the Ming (1368–1644) and the Ch'ing (1644–1911) dynasties.

The city walls

The first city wall of any permanence was constructed around 250 BC. It was repaired and expanded during the 3rd century AD and rebuilt with solid stone in 1370, at the beginning of the Ming dynasty. In the 1630s, at the end of the Ming, the rebellion of Chang Hsien-chung subjected Chungking to plunder, slaughter, and incredible destruction. The city wall was restored in 1663. Some five miles in circumference, it had a total of 17 gates: eight gates remained closed on the advice of geomancers (practitioners of divination by means of figures or lines), while nine were open to traffic. Additional work was done to strengthen the city wall in 1760.

The 20th century. Chungking was opened to British trade in 1890, but navigational difficulties on the Yangtze delayed steamer traffic for a decade. Meanwhile, the

Chungking, built on a promontory at the confluence of the Chia-ling (left) and Yangtze (upper right) rivers.
Eastfoto

Treaty of Shimonoseki (1895) gave Japan the right to establish a concession. Accordingly, in 1901, when British trade opened, a Japanese concession was established at Wang-chia-to, on the south shore of the Yangtze. This concession lasted until 1937, when it was abandoned by Japan on the outbreak of war.

On the eve of the revolution of 1911 Chungking, along with the provincial capital, Ch'eng-tu, played a major role in bringing about the overthrow of the Manchus; many patriots of the region joined the revolutionary party of the Chinese Nationalist leader Sun Yat-sen (*q.v.*). Yet, despite such progressive trends and a nominal allegiance to the central government, Chungking remained true to its tradition; the city was unable to break away from the grip of regional separatism.

This state of affairs ended when war broke out with Japan. In 1938 Chungking became the capital of the Nationalist government. Hundreds of government offices were moved to the city from Nanking, along with the diplomatic missions of foreign powers; and tens of thousands of people came from coastal provinces, bringing with them arsenals, factories, and schools. Friendly powers, too, rushed supplies to Chungking to bolster its war effort. Despite the bombings by the enemy, the morale of its population—more than a million strong—ran high. Chiang Kai-shek's failure to control inflation and corruption, however, caused the war effort to falter from 1942 onward. In 1946, on the eve of the renewed civil war against the Communists, the Nationalist capital returned to Nanking. Three years later, in April, 1949, Nanking fell. The Nationalist government fled to Canton and then once again—for less than two months—to Chungking (October to December 1949). When the Nationalists fled to Taiwan in December, the victory of the people's republic on the mainland was complete.

Margin note: Capital of the Nationalist government

THE CONTEMPORARY CITY

Physical environment. Chungking lies within Pa Hsien (Pa County), although the municipality as now constituted embraces two additional counties—Ch'i-chiang to the south and Ch'ang-shou to the north. Also included under its jurisdiction is the adjacent city of Chiang-pei.

Location. Located at the confluence of the Yangtze and Chia-ling rivers, Chungking is the gateway city to Szechwan Province. To the east, some 1,400 miles of the Yangtze form a mighty waterway linking it with such major Chinese cities as Wan-hsien, I-ch'ang, Wu-han, Chiu-chiang, Nanking, and Shanghai. To the west it occupies a commanding position on the route to a vast hinterland. The trade and transport of the Ch'eng-tu Plain, of Yunnan and Kweichow provinces, and of eastern Tibet flow into Chungking via Lu-chou and I-pin on the Yangtze;

and those of southern Shensi and eastern Szechwan likewise converge there, via Nan-ch'ung and Ho-ch'uan on the Chia-ling.

Climate. Chungking is noted for its mild climate. Shielded from the cold northern winds by the Tsinling Mountains, it has little frost or ice in winter; the mean temperatures in January and February, the only two cool months, are 47° F (8° C) and 50° F (10° C), respectively. Summer, from May through September, is hot and humid, the August mean temperature being 84° F (29° C). The remaining months are warm, with mean temperatures ranging between 58° and 67° F (about 14° and 19° C). The bulk of rain falls in the period from April through October, the average annual total being about 43 inches. Owing to high humidity, fog and mist are particularly heavy. During the months from October to April the city is perpetually blanketed by fog—a phenomenon that gave its population welcome protection against Japanese air raids during World War II.

Layout of the city. Chungking is built on the Chin-pi Shan, a rocky promontory of red sandstone bounded on the north by the Chia-ling Chiang (with the city of Chiang-pei on its north bank) and on the east and south by the Yangtze. The Old City (formerly surrounded by the city wall and gates, of which only the names now remain) occupies the entire promontory below T'ung-yüan Men. The south and east slopes facing the waterfront form the "lower city," while the remainder is the "upper city." A major east–west avenue runs through the middle of each of these districts, and a third runs atop the spine of the ridge. Cross streets are narrower and often winding: following the topography of the hill, they go up and down in long flights of hundreds of steps.

The new sections of the city lie to the west of T'ung-yüan Men. The districts of Ts'eng-chia-yen, Shang-ch'ing-shih, Ta-ch'i-kou, and Ts'ai-yüan-pa spread far along the banks of the two rivers, covering an area considerably larger than the Old City. During World War II these were the districts in which most of the offices of the Nationalist government were located, and they are now the sites of modern government office buildings and of spacious residences. The growth of the city has been so great that beyond these new sections numerous industrial towns and suburban communities have extended the city limits to Pei-p'ei in the north (including Hsiao-lung-k'an, Sha-p'ing-pa, Tz'u-ch'i-k'ou, Ko-lo-shan, and Ch'ing-mu-kuan) and to Pai-shih-i in the southwest (including Hsin-chiao and Shan-tung).

Equally important are the suburban districts on the south shore of the Yangtze, notably Wang-chia-to, Tan-tzu-shih, Yüan-tan-miao, Lung-men-hao, Hai-t'ang-ch'i, and Huang-kuo-to. In former times, crossings were made

Margin note: New districts and suburbs

by ferries; travel across the river is now possible by bridge. These districts are free from the smoke and dust of the Old City; with spacious gardens and beautiful residences, they contribute much to relieving the crowded conditions of the downtown areas. The south shore is also the gateway to Kweichow Province, as the Chungking–Kuei-yang highway has its terminus at Hai-t'ang-ch'i.

Transportation.   Since 1949, chairs on bamboo poles and rickshas have been replaced as the principal means of transport in Chungking by pedicabs, bicycles, and buses. Cable tramways provide cheap and convenient transport over the steep hills.

River transport.   Served by two great rivers, the Yangtze and the Chia-ling, Chungking is the leading port of southwestern China. As a result of extensive dredging work, clearing of shoals, and installation of buoys and signals in the 1950s, navigation through the Yangtze Gorges has been rendered easy and safe. Steamers now make a round trip between Hankow and Chungking in less than a week. Above Chungking smaller steamers sail up to I-pin on the Yangtze (and beyond to Chia-ting on the Min) and up to Nan-ch'ung on the Chia-ling. Above these points, navigation is possible by junks that go beyond Ch'eng-tu to Kuan-hsien and Mao-hsien on the Min and to Lüeh-yang in southern Shensi on the Chia-ling. The city's wharves are well equipped with chutes, hoists, conveyor belts, and cable cars.

Railroads.   Chungking has experienced a rapid development of railroads since 1949. The Chungking–Ch'eng-tu railroad, completed in 1952, is the vital link between the Ch'eng-tu Plain and the Yangtze. The Ch'eng-tu–Pao-chi line, completed four years later, connects the city with the Lunghai Railroad and the entire Northwest. The Chungking–Kuei-yang railroad not only connects Chungking with the province of Kweichow to the south but also joins other lines in Yunnan and Kwangsi running to the North Vietnamese border.

Road and air transport.   The first roads for wheeled traffic in the city were built only in 1933. As a result of work begun during World War II, Chungking is now the hub of an extensive network of highways. Major arterials lead south to Kuei-yang (303 miles), northeast to Wan-hsien (258 miles), and northwest to Ch'eng-tu (275 miles). As an air terminal, Chungking is served by regular flights to Ch'eng-tu; to Sian, T'ai-yüan, and Peking; to Wu-han, Nanking, and Shanghai; and to Kuei-yang and K'un-ming.

Demography.   The municipality of Chungking (including the counties of Pa, Ch'i-chiang, and Ch'ang-shou) has a population of 4,400,000 (1970 estimate). Before the war with Japan, Chungking had less than 250,000 people. From 1938 onward, people from the coastal provinces flocked to the wartime capital at an astonishing rate. By 1942 the population was some 1,000,000 and in 1945, 1,500,000. In the early 1970s the population was believed to be well over 4,500,000—an increase accounted for by the expansion of the municipal area to embrace Ch'i-chiang and Ch'ang-shou. The bulk of Chungking's population increase since 1938 has consisted of government workers, factory personnel, and refugees from other provinces. As a result of the mingling of the local inhabitants and people from downriver, Chungking has lost much of its parochialism and has become a cosmopolitan city. The Szechwan dialect is quite intelligible to speakers of Mandarin, but it is characterized by a heavy, vulgarized accent and many regional slang words.

City plan, housing, and landmarks.   Before 1938 Chungking was a city of narrow streets and crowded housing. Built to fit the contours of the hills, the streets and lanes followed no rational pattern. The houses were constructed of bamboo, wood, or thatch in poorer districts and of brick in wealthier districts. In all districts there was a high degree of congestion. A vigorous modernization program was introduced when the city became the seat of the Nationalist government. Part of the city wall was demolished to make way for new streets, and existing streets were graded and widened. The tremendous demand for housing created by the government

Population changes

workers and refugees led to the rapid expansion of the new sections west of the Old City.

Bombing, rebuilding, and modernization.   From 1938 to 1942 Chungking suffered heavy aerial bombardment by the Japanese. The destruction that resulted, however, permitted the erection of new and better buildings.

After the transformation effected during the war years, the present regime has experienced little difficulty in carrying forward the tasks of modernization and expansion. By the early 1970s new buildings, following modern architectural designs, stood in the central districts in the downtown area and on the tip of the promontory overlooking the confluence of the two rivers. In Sha-p'ing-pa, Tzu'u-ch'i-k'ou, and adjacent areas, large buildings providing living quarters for workers and accommodations for factories and workshops were added at an astonishing rate. The large brick apartments, generally four to six stories high, were surrounded by trees and vegetable gardens. Yet, Chungking remained a city of striking contrasts. Houses of traditional design, blackened by weather or wartime camouflage, were still to be found on steep hills and along the highways to the suburbs. Bamboo structures still lined the river bluffs. Much of the new housing was shoddy in appearance and poorly finished inside. Furthermore, new apartments were available to only a small percentage of the population.

Outlying suburbs.   In contrast to the congested living conditions in the city and the industrial districts, the outlying suburbs have a number of delightful resorts and spas. Among the scenic spots on the south shore are the temple in honour of Empress Yü, consort of the Hsia dynasty emperor of the same name, on Tu Shan; the wooded summer resorts of Ch'ing-shui-ch'i (Clear Water Creek) and Yang-t'ien-wo (Sky-gazing Hollow) on Huang Shan; and Nan-wen-ch'üan (South Warm Springs), which has delightful retreats at Hua-ch'i (Flower Creek) and Hu-hsiao-k'ou (Tiger Roar Gap). A short distance north of the city are the flowers and springs of Ko-lo-shan. Farther up the Chia-ling Chiang at Pei-p'ei are located the Chin-yün Shih Temple, the celebrated retreat of the Sung dynasty savant Feng Chin-yün, and Pei-wen-ch'üan (North Warm Springs), reputedly superior to the South Warm Springs because its water is warmer in winter and cooler in summer.

Resorts and spas

Economic life.   The foundations of Chungking's modern industry were laid between 1938 and 1945, when factories transplanted from the coastal provinces began production under the aegis of the Nationalist government. Because of the proximity of coal, iron, and other resources, rapid expansion subsequently followed under the present government. In the early 1970s Chungking was the largest and fastest growing industrial centre in southwest China. Its complex of integrated iron and steel plants draws upon ore from Ch'i-chiang (the southern county in the municipality) and Wei-yüan (a short distance west of Nei-chiang). Coal is mined at Chiang-pei, Pei-p'ei, Pa-hsien, Pi-shan, and Ho-ch'uan (either in the municipality or on its periphery). Electric-power-generating capacity has been greatly enlarged since the completion of the Shih-tze-t'an hydroelectric station on the Lung-ch'i Ho (Lung-ch'i River), northeast of the city. Other important heavy industries include machine, farm tool, and munitions factories; truck and motor-coach manufacturing plants; and chemical and fertilizer plants (manufacturing soap and candles, acid and soda, fertilizers and plastics). The city also has a copper refinery, alcohol plants (making gasoline substitutes), and rubber reconditioning plants. In light industries Chungking leads the entire Southwest of the nation. Noteworthy are cotton, silk, paper, and flour mills, dyeing factories, and vegetable-oil and food-processing plants. Chungking is also famous for its handicrafts, especially lacquer ware.

As noted above, Chungking is the focal point of trade and transport not only of Szechwan but of the hinterland provinces of Shensi, Yunnan, and Kweichow and of the autonomous region of Tibet. Exports to downriver provinces and abroad include silk, goatskin, wool, hides, hog bristles, salt, sugar, tobacco, tung oil, jute, wax, medicinal herbs, rhubarb, and musk. Before World War II, Chung-

Industrial growth

king imported large quantities of consumer goods from downriver or from abroad. This trade pattern changed, however, as rapid industrialization brought self-sufficiency in consumer goods to Szechwan and the interior provinces. The city's imports now consist primarily of industrial equipment for installing new plants.

Political institutions. The Chungking Municipal People's Council, elected by the Municipal People's Congress, is the executive organ of government. Composed of the mayor, deputy mayors, and some 40 council members, it formulates policies, issues administrative orders, collects taxes, determines the budget, carries out economic plans, maintains order, and safeguards the rights of citizens. Serving under the council's direction are bureaus and commissions in charge of civil affairs, public security, justice, planning, finance, food, taxation, industry, commerce, labour, culture, education, public health, physical culture and sports, projects of municipal construction, and public services.

Administratively, the city is divided into districts (*ch'u*), each under a district mayoralty. At the next lower level are police substations and street mayoralties that handle civil affairs in the same subareas. Neighbourhood street committees perform the auxiliary functions of mediating disputes and promoting literacy campaigns, sanitation, welfare, and the "weeding out of bourgeois elements." These committees are quasi-official administrations, consolidated under Communist Party leadership and covering blocks of streets of varying sizes. The Chungking Municipality, as presently constituted, represents a deliberate policy to extend the territorial limits of the municipal area so as to include a series of integrated urban-rural units surrounding the city proper. Chungking is located in a rapidly developing area where urban management personnel and urban workers are expected to associate themselves with the life of the countryside as well as of the city itself. This policy is designed to reduce the tension inherent in an urban-rural dichotomy.

Policy of urban-rural integration

Public utilities, health, and safety. *Public utilities and hygiene.* In the late 1920s and early 1930s a modernization drive was launched by local leaders in Chungking to improve living conditions. Along with the widening of the streets, a piped water system, an electric-light plant, and a telephone exchange were introduced. Even during the 1940s, however, sanitation and public hygiene were poor. The city had the largest per capita rat population in the world. Opium smoking in homes and inns was widespread. Lice-ridden waifs and beggars were a familiar sight. Because of energetic measures carried out since 1949, these conditions belong to the past. Chungking is now noted for its cleanliness. Opium traffic and smoking have been stamped out, and beggars and waifs have been given productive work. In addition, the installation of 250 miles of sewers, coupled with the extermination work of sanitary squads in every block, has dethroned the rats.

Health. Chungking has a considerable number of hospitals. The major share of medical care, however, is provided by clinics and health stations operated by neighbourhood street committees. The clinics are equipped with a limited number of beds and are manned by graduate physicians. Combined use is made of Western-style medicine, traditional herb medicine, and acupuncture (the practice of puncturing the body with special needles to cure disease). Midwives preside over 80 percent of childbirths. Contraceptives are available at nominal cost. That there still is a shortage of medical facilities is recognized by the government. For this reason, great emphasis is placed on the drive for physical fitness. In the early 1970s "health defense clubs" and associations for the promotion of physical culture reported rapid increases in membership.

Safety. The city has a large and efficient police department, which has branch departments and substations in all districts; there is also a large fire-fighting force with modern equipment. The difficulties of fire control and prevention in the past have been considerably alleviated as a result of the widening of streets, the creation of open squares and vacant lots, the installation of adequate hydrants, and the use of fireproof materials in new buildings.

Education and cultural life. Since the present government came to power, the number of schools at all levels —the kindergartens, primary schools, middle schools, and colleges—has undergone marked expansion. The growth of kindergartens, which were poorly developed in prewar years, has enabled many women to take up productive work. The present regime attaches great importance to the establishment of teacher-training schools, vocational-technical schools, and part-time agricultural middle schools. These are maintained by factories, street committees, or specific agencies of the government. A number of special normal schools offer intensive instruction to meet particular needs, such as two-year courses in Russian, in mathematics, or in applied physics. In accordance with the government's policy of integrating theory and practice, students in all middle schools are required to spend a substantial part of their time working in the factories or the communes.

The Chungking University, with 13 departments, offers a comprehensive range of studies. Other institutions of higher learning include the Southwestern Institute of Law; the Chungking Medical College; the Chungking Technical University; the Chungking Institute of Architectural Engineering; the Southwestern Institute of Agriculture; the Southwestern Institute of Fine Arts; and the Laboratory of Pedology (a subdivision of the department of geography and geology of the Academy of Sciences). The Chungking Library (with 1,850,000 volumes) and the Chungking Municipal Museum are among the leading cultural centres in the city.

Institutions of higher learning

The media. Chungking's principal newspaper is the *Ch'ung-ch'ing jih-pao* (*Chungking Daily*), the official organ of the Municipal Party Committee. The source of news for all papers is the state-controlled New China News Agency. Since the start of the Cultural Revolution in 1966, *ta-tzu-pao*, or large-character wall posters, have become a familiar sight in streets, public squares, and parks, as well as in front of large buildings. Television in the early 1970s was a relatively young medium of communication. Radio broadcasting was thoroughly developed, with loudspeakers installed at all street corners and rebroadcasting stations established in all factories, offices, and schools.

Recreation. In Chungking, as in other cities in China, great emphasis is placed on recreation and sports for improving the quality of living. Among notable parks and playgrounds are the Chung-shan Park in the Old City; the Nan-ch'u Park in the new district overlooking Shan-hu-pa Island in the Yangtze; the Chiang-pei Park in Chiang-pei; the Pei-p'ei Park, the North Warm Springs, and Chin-yün-shih Park in Pei-p'ei; the National Forest at Ko-lo-shan; and the Nan-shan Park, the South Warm Springs, and the sunbathing facilities at Clear Water Creek on the south shore. Enthusiasm for sports is widespread. The municipal gymnasium has a capacity of 50,000. According to one report, there were 20,000 basketball teams in Chungking in the 1960s. Next to basketball, the popular sports in the city include soccer, tennis, volleyball, and track and field events. Lists of qualified athletes (ranked in four grades) are regularly maintained by athletic directors, who are eager to locate potential champions to enter in provincial and national tournaments.

BIBLIOGRAPHY. *Nagel's Encyclopaedia-Guide to China* (1968) is excellent for general reference. Chungking during the war years is vividly portrayed in THEODORE H. WHITE and ANNALEE JACOBY, *Thunder Out of China* (1946). EDGAR SNOW, *The Other Side of the River, Red China Today*, pp. 578–586 (1962), contains one of the best descriptions of the contemporary scene. Those interested in the city's streets and architecture will find interesting reading in J.E. SPENCER, "Changing Chungking," *Geogrl. Rev.*, 29:46–60 (1939). For geography and economic developments, see, respectively, GEORGE B. CRESSEY, *China's Geographic Foundations* (1934); and T.R. TREGEAR, *An Economic Geography of China* (1970). Articles in *China Reconstructs* and *Far Eastern Economic Review* contain useful information on current developments.

(P.-c.K.)

Church and State

The subject of church and state refers to the existence among the same people of two institutions, religious and secular, both claiming the people's loyalty. Theoretically, the loyalty is clearly divided: "Render therefore to Caesar the things that are Caesar's, and to God the things that are God's" (Matt. 22:21); but, in fact, the areas in which the ecclesiastical and temporal powers claim loyalty tend to overlap, offering the possibility of frictions.

Unity of the religious and the temporal in primitive society

In primitive human society it is impossible to distinguish between the religious and secular aspects of community life in the way customary today. Not only are practically all activities of the tribe—hunting, agriculture, legislation, and justice, for example—permeated by concepts and rites that one would call religious but the community as a whole also worships its gods or venerates impersonal supernatural forces. Because kingship and priesthood are closely linked, the ruler is normally the representative of his people to the gods or spirits and is indeed often himself regarded as divine. The same is broadly true of all early civilizations and can be observed in China, Egypt, Babylonia, Assyria, and Persia, for example, and is a recognized feature of the life of the classical world of Greece and Rome. Down to the adoption of Christianity by the Roman Empire the emperor held the title of *pontifex maximus* and controlled the state religion, and he himself was the object of worship as a god on earth. Relics of this practice persisted long into the Christian Era, especially in Byzantium, as is shown in the continued use of such epithets as "divine" in reference to the person and court of the emperor. The concept of church and state as used by historians and sociologists today had no place in the ancient world and could become meaningful only when a distinction was drawn between the secular human community on the one hand and the religious community or communities within a political entity on the other.

EARLY RELATIONS BETWEEN CHURCH AND STATE

Judaism and the beginnings of Christianity. It would not be strictly accurate to say that the distinction between church and state was created by Christianity, even though it was largely responsible. The process began in Judaism, with the fall of Jerusalem in 586 BC, after which the Jews ceased to exist as an independent political community (except briefly under the Maccabees). Both in Palestine itself and in the Diaspora, they were under alien rule, a religious minority in non-Jewish states, and they therefore had to think of their religious fellowship and their secular citizenship as two distinct things—the essence of the distinction between church and state. From the beginning, Christianity, itself a schism from official Judaism, found itself in a position that, because of its claim to a unique revelation, prevented it from joining in the cults of non-Christian states and compelled it to think of itself as a religious brotherhood submitting to non-Christian rulers in political matters but having its own organization, deriving from the original Apostolic Church. This attitude in religious matters cut the Christians off from their fellow citizens and became the basic cause of their persecution by the Romans, who could not conceive of the compatibility of political loyalty with a refusal to worship the official gods. (The Christian use of the term ecclesia to express this primary loyalty is noteworthy here. Originally, the Greeks used the term to denote the legislative meetings of citizens; then they also used the term to translate the Hebrew *qahal*, the technical word for the congregation of Israel, the religious fellowship of the chosen people. Because the notion of any religious community distinct from the state was foreign to the Greco-Roman world, there was no term in Greek, other than a political one, which could express it.)

Differing Roman and Christian views of loyalty

With the end of the period of persecution and the introduction of toleration by the emperor Constantine the Great in the fourth century, Christianity was faced with an entirely new aspect of the relations of church and state. What were to be the relations between the Christian ecclesiastical community and the political state in an empire of which the rulers themselves were Christians? It was a novel position with no precedents except those that could be found in the Old Testament, when there had been a Jewish monarchy. Moreover, there was a period of transition during which the state paganism of Rome remained an established religion that the emperors did not dare to disfranchise, while at the same time the Christian Church, to which the emperor personally belonged and which was now not only tolerated but privileged, had equally the official recognition of the state. It is clear that the early Christian emperors regarded themselves as holding a position in the church in some ways equivalent to that which, as *pontifices maximi*, they had held in Roman state paganism—that is, they were not only the protectors of the church but in some sense its rulers. This becomes very obvious when one considers their actions in the doctrinal disputes that broke out within Christianity during the 4th and 5th centuries, beginning with the Arian controversy (see CHRISTIANITY BEFORE THE SCHISM OF 1054). They summoned councils of bishops and were far from remaining neutral in the ensuing debates, while they enforced conciliar decisions by means of their political authority. The bishops' attitudes toward this exercise of imperial authority varied. Some were primarily courtiers, ready to lend their support, sometimes unthinkingly, to the theology favoured by the emperor; others, especially in the West, claimed that it was for the church to decide its doctrines for itself and for the secular power, itself part of the lay element in the church, to accept the decisions of the episcopate, the chief depositary of Christian revelation and tradition.

The problem was not made easier when, from the time of Theodosius I the Great at the end of the 4th century, Christianity became the sole official religion of the Roman Empire, and both paganism and Christian heterodoxy were proscribed. For now the process began by which church and state came to be seen as two aspects of one Christian society, the *res publica Christiana*. Now freedom of conscience—which Christianity had early claimed as a right and which it largely continued to preach theoretically, in the sense that it normally frowned upon forcible conversion—would obviously be in jeopardy, if only because the state considered it its duty to suppress the practice of any beliefs or cults opposed to orthodox Christianity. In the case of paganism, which it considered to be not merely an error but a positive worship of demonic powers, the church fairly readily agreed to, and indeed incited, the emperors' efforts to close temples and prohibit pagan rites. With a little more reluctance, but finally with positive approval, it accepted the policy of proscribing heresy, which it saw as a danger to the Christian faith and harmful to souls. By the 5th century the state's enforcement of orthodoxy was an accepted principle, even if practical difficulties often made it impossible to implement fully.

The *res publica Christiana*

At this point, enforced state orthodoxy came up against major political problems and added to their intractability. The conquest of the West by Teutonic barbarians who professed Arian Christianity resulted in Catholicism's becoming a subject religion in the Visigothic and Ostrogothic states in Spain and Italy and actually suffering acute persecution in Vandal Africa. This situation was altered only after the conquest of Gaul by the Franks, who had been converted directly from paganism to Catholic Christianity, and after Emperor Justinian I's reconquest of North Africa and Italy during the 6th century. In the East the rejection of the teachings of the Coptic and Syrian churches by the Council of Chalcedon in 451 led many Egyptians and Syrians to acts of resistance; they were the more ready to oppose the emperors' religion because of their resentment against oppressive political rule and their nationalistic desire to revert to their old Coptic and Syriac cultures that had lain so long submerged under Hellenic and Roman civilization. Attempts by the Eastern emperors to reach doctrinal compromises with the Egyptians and Syrians for the sake of political unity failed because of the papacy's refusal to agree and the strong opposition of hard liners in the Eastern Church. All this further exacerbated the tensions inevitably involved in the very notion of a *res publica Christiana*.

Islām. It was upon a Christendom vexed in this way that the storm of militant Islām fell in the 7th century; indeed, the dramatic and rapid Muslim conquests were facilitated by the readiness of dissident Egyptians and Syrians to accept Muslim rule, knowing as they did that Islām believed in the toleration, albeit as second-class citizens, of non-Muslims who were monotheists, whether Jew or Christian. This is the place to consider the policy of Islām, which, in its own way, was faced by a problem akin to that of church and state in Christendom. Because Muhammad, unlike Christ, became the secular as well as the religious leader of his followers, Islām was a far more unified community than Christendom; and this remained true even when the Islāmic armies, after effecting their conquests, separated off into different Islāmic states. To this day Islāmic countries, except insofar as secularism has affected them, know no distinction between the political society and the religious such as is expressed in the Christian phrase church and state. The caliphs, the successors of the Prophet as Commanders of the Faithful, held absolute sway, limited only by their obligation to obey the rule in accordance with the doctrines of Islām and the *sharīʿah*, or sacred law, which regulated social as well as religious life. Because Islām has never had a priesthood like that of Christendom claiming spiritual authority deriving from the Apostles, there has been no room for an organized church of the Christian form, distinct from the state. Nevertheless, the *ʿulamāʾ*, the learned expounders of Islāmic religion and law, have, in virtue of their function, been able to exercise a considerable influence not only over the ordinary believers but also over Muslim rulers; and to this extent one can speak of a "spiritual power" akin to the medieval Christian use of that phrase standing over against the temporal power of secular rulers.

Christianity in the early Middle Ages. Although Islām was a serious rival to Christianity in the early Middle Ages and offered a military threat that did not end until the decline of the Ottoman Empire after the 16th century, it played no part in molding the pattern of church and state in Christendom. One can trace a polarization of two different notions of church-state relations as the Middle Ages developed, and this polarization corresponded to the differences between the Eastern and Western churches that by the 11th century escalated into open schism. East and West had different conceptions of imperial power and differing political evolutions. None of the emperors of Constantinople was able to maintain direct authority in the West or to break the pattern of independent kingdoms established there after the barbarian invasions. Emperor Charlemagne did temporarily coalesce these kingdoms along the lines of the old Roman Empire, but his empire did not long survive his death in 814. All this gave the papacy in Rome the opportunity to become an international power, claiming, and normally receiving, spiritual obedience from the whole Western Church and often wielding considerable authority over the Christian sovereigns of the West. In the Eastern Empire, though its territories diminished steadily until the final fall of Constantinople to the Turks in 1453, Christian emperors ruled over all the orthodox Christian lands and maintained control over the church.

The Eastern Orthodox Church. The Byzantine or Eastern system may be considered first. This system has

been described, not altogether accurately, as caesaropapism, conventionally defined in *The Oxford English Dictionary* as "the supremacy of the civil power in the control of ecclesiastical affairs." If this term is understood to mean that Byzantine emperors occupied a position akin to that of the pope of Rome, it is certainly not true. There was no suggestion that the emperor possessed sacerdotal status; he was a layman, albeit a privileged one. But it is true that Eastern emperors regarded themselves as divinely appointed protectors and guardians of the church, with a responsibility for its good order; that they could and did legislate about ecclesiastical disci-

pline; and that their ecclesiastical decrees were regarded as part of the canon law of the church. They influenced the choice of bishops and claimed a right to confirm their elections, and they never hesitated to depose prelates who displeased them. They formally invested the patriarch of Constantinople before consecration. They summoned councils and watched their proceedings either in person or through a delegate. Moreover, various emperors issued dogmatic decrees professing to lay down the orthodox interpretation of the church's faith. But, on the other hand, it should be noted that on every occasion on which the imperial decision proved to be contrary to the general mind of the church (as in the Iconoclastic controversy over the veneration of images), they ultimately failed. Nor was it impossible for the Byzantine patriarchs to excommunicate emperors who had transgressed the church's moral code. As in the West, the balance between civil and episcopal power varied according to the strength or weakness of individual monarchs and ecclesiastics. It has been noted by a distinguished Byzantinist, Louis Bréhier, that in the last centuries of the Eastern Empire ecclesiastical opposition to unpopular imperial policies grew stronger; therefore, "the Church ended by detaching itself completely from the imperial power." The same author defines the Byzantine system as not caesaropapism but rather "a theocracy, in which the Emperor holds a preponderant position, but not an exclusive one"; and this is perhaps the best description of the facts. (From L. Bréhier, *Le Monde byzantin*, II, *Les institutions de l'empire byzantin* [Paris, 1949], pp. 440, 442.)

The Roman Catholic Church. In the West down to the 11th century, the relations of church and state were not wholly different, even though the papacy, which claimed spiritual authority even over the whole of Christendom, possessed an aura never attained by the patriarchs of Constantinople. Its position, nevertheless, did not free it from some degree of control by the secular powers—then or ever. Official doctrine on the matter was laid down in 494 by Pope Gelasius I in a letter to the emperor Anastasius I (a time when the papacy still recognized the emperors of Constantinople): there were, he said, two principles by which the world was ruled, "the sacred authority of pontiffs and the royal power," of which the pontifical authority was weightier because bishops had to render account to God even for secular rulers. The emperor, though taking precedence over the human race in dignity and, by divine appointment, having a right to the obedience even of bishops in matters of public order, nonetheless had to "bow his neck" to prelates in spiritual matters and especially to the pope, the head of the episcopate. Obviously this theory, which was not wholly different from that current at Byzantium, left scope for a great deal of dispute as to what matters were spiritual and what temporal; and indeed the subsequent history of Western Christendom is studded with disagreements about the limits between secular and ecclesiastical power.

In fact, for some centuries after 494 the balance swung in favour of the state as, after the disappearance of direct imperial authority in the West, the new barbarian monarchies established themselves and claimed power over the church. The most noteworthy swing came with the consolidation of the Carolingian Empire, which controlled virtually all the land area of western Europe, a phenomenon canonized by the Pope's coronation of Charlemagne as "Emperor and Augustus" in AD 800. Although Charlemagne did not necessarily regard himself as sole Roman emperor (there were many precedents for the coexistence of two or more emperors in the Roman world) and seems to have thought of himself as a colleague rather than a rival of the Byzantine emperors, his power was supreme in the West, and his conception of the rights that his position gave him in the church was no different from those claimed by the Eastern emperors and indeed virtually surpassed them. As king of the Franks he had already regarded himself as divinely authorized to rule the church, and his new title added nothing to his practical ecclesiastical power. Thus, in his edicts he legislated on church affairs as well as on secular ones. In 794 he presided over the Council of Frankfurt, which he had summoned, and manoeuvred it into accepting certain of his recommendations that ran counter to those approved by the pope. Charlemagne usually appointed bishops by his own authority and, when appointed, required them, in addition to their ecclesiastical functions, to undertake many of the duties incumbent upon secular vassals. Byzantium could go no further, if as far.

CHURCH AND STATE IN THE LATE
MIDDLE AGES AND THE REFORMATION

The antithesis to the Carolingian system developed in the 11th century. With the decay of the Carolingian state and its territorial division, centralized secular institutions were largely replaced by feudalism at a local level. This event increased the hold of the laity over ecclesiastical institutions, for landowners maintained almost complete control over the churches that they built and endowed upon their land, and over the clergy who served them. In parallel fashion, kings and great vassals regarded bishoprics and abbeys as private churches on a larger scale and treated them as fiefs, appointing the bishops and abbots. This led to simony, the buying and selling of church offices; also, because of the laxity regarding clerical celibacy, some of these clerical fiefs became almost hereditary. It was against such developments that church reformers of the early 11th century set their face, at first quite happy to work with monarchs willing to use their power in church to effect reform. But, after the middle of the century, the great pope Gregory VII adopted a policy of demanding freedom, as he understood it, for the church, insisting on the right of free election of bishops and abbots and striving by every means to bring lay control of ecclesiastical offices to an end. This almost necessarily involved a claim that the spiritual power was superior to the temporal; and it developed into a doctrine that, in the last resort, the papacy could coerce secular authorities. The papacy, it was held, could excommunicate recalcitrant rulers; it could proclaim their deposition and absolve their subjects from the duty of obedience; it could even promote armed rebellion.

Struggles between popes and monarchs. From the 11th to the 13th centuries the theory, implied or stated, that the ecclesiastical power was naturally superior to the secular and in the last resort could control it was never universally held, even by the clergy; but it had great influence and lay at the root of the great disputes between the papacy and the Holy Roman Empire, which were such striking features of the age, as well as of quarrels between popes and national monarchs, such as King John of England. The theory was usually defended on the ground that when a ruler violated the Christian moral law in exercising his power, he was, like any other Christian, subject to the censures of the church and could be coerced physically by those laymen loyal to the church. (This is what is known technically as the *ratione peccati* argument for indirect papal power in temporal affairs.) A more extreme thesis, delivered formally by Pope Boniface VIII in his bull *Unam Sanctam* in 1302 (though adumbrated earlier), was that the powers over the church given by Christ to St. Peter, the Apostle, and his successors, the popes, included ultimate temporal supremacy simply because the spiritual power was by its nature superior to the temporal. Upon St. Peter and his successors Christ had bestowed "two swords" (Luke 22:38), symbolizing spiritual and temporal power; the spiritual sword the popes wielded themselves, delegating the temporal sword to lay rulers, but the latter must nevertheless use the temporal sword according to papal directions.

It is significant that Boniface, who issued this declaration in his quarrel with Philip IV the Fair, of France, failed to enforce it and died after being temporarily kidnapped by agents of the French monarch. The papacy was to find the rapidly developing national states less tractable than the old Holy Roman Empire. By the end of the Middle Ages it was becoming more and more apparent that once again the lay powers were gaining

The idea of the natural superiority of the church

dominance over the church in the national states, in the almost independent principalities within the Holy Roman Empire, and even in city-states within and without the empire. The papacy was also weakened by the 15th-century Conciliar movement, which tried to make the papacy subject to general councils of the whole church. The papacy was therefore in no position to assert power over the states of western Europe and instead had to make ecclesiastical treaties (concordats) with them that granted their rulers considerable rights over the church in their domains. A good example was the informal arrangement whereby the kings of England nominated their candidates for bishoprics, and the popes thereupon almost automatically accepted the nominees and "provided" them their sees. More than a century before Henry VIII broke with Rome and had Parliament give him the right to appoint bishops without reference to the pope, his predecessors had in fact been choosing their own bishops with only a nod to the popes.

The Protestant reformers. The Reformation in one sense began with Martin Luther's denial of any real distinction between the spiritual and temporal powers. He naturally tended to support the idea of state control of the church and contended that since the laity, no less than the clergy, were baptized Christians, the lay power had both the right and the duty to reform the church, which the clergy, left to themselves, would never do. This view was enhanced by his doctrine that every Christian possessed priestly powers, the clergy being merely a body of men chosen to fulfill duties that could be performed by any layman; they were not a sacramentally ordained group possessing an indelible character that gave them supernatural powers. Huldrych Zwingli, the Swiss reformer, believed rather similarly that the state should decide how its religion should be organized and what doctrines should be taught, according to its assessment of the arguments of such reformers as himself, whose function he equated with that of Old Testament prophets sent by God to declare his will to rulers.

John Calvin's conception of the relationship of church and state was rather different. He believed that even though the personnel of church government and state government were virtually identical, the two organizations should be distinct in their functions. It was the function of the church community to decide upon doctrine and to maintain moral discipline by spiritual censures; it was the function of the state to enforce this discipline upon recalcitrants. It will be noticed that this system is in fact almost identical with the medieval system that held that the duty of the secular arm was to enforce the doctrinal and disciplinary judgments of the church by burning obdurate heretics and imprisoning excommunicates who refused to seek absolution and make amends. (One of the most significant differences between Calvin's view and the medieval view, however, was that Calvin invited lay participation in church government, whereas the medieval church strictly excluded laymen from its government.) Under this circumstance, one can understand the epigram of the French scholar Georges de Lagarde that whereas Luther had secularized the church, Calvin clericalized the state. Neither remark is entirely accurate, but the broad distinction is true. In this respect, Calvinism, as was often maintained in the 17th century, stood closer to Roman Catholicism than it did to Lutheranism.

Effects of the religious wars. In the outcome, Lutheranism, Calvinism, and Roman Catholicism alike had to accept a greater measure of state control of the church than any of them would have ideally liked. The fundamental cause of this was that in a world torn by religious dissension and wars, all three religions were compelled to rely for survival upon state support. Lutheranism would have been suppressed in Germany but for the armed aid of those secular princes who accepted it, and Luther was driven more and more to attribute ecclesiastical authority to the godly prince. As Calvinism outside Geneva—in such countries as the Netherlands and France—met with opposition and persecution, it was increasingly dependent upon the armed support of its laity. This brought about a diminution in the influence of the

The Lutheran view

The Calvinist view

Church dependence on the state

Calvinist clergy in secular affairs and a greater authority of the laity—although, relatively speaking, the Calvinist tradition remained less tolerant of state control than did the Lutheran, as can be seen in England and Scotland, where Calvinism was critical of state-ordered religion and proved at times a revolutionary force. Roman Catholicism, strive as it might to maintain the independence of the church under the authority of the pope, ultimately relied upon state support for the Counter-Reformation and thus had to accept a very considerable measure of state control. In Spain, the Inquisition itself was controlled by the crown; papal bulls could be put into effect only with the state's consent; and the crown nominated to all bishoprics. In the New World, Spanish control of the church was even more absolute, and it was only through the crown that the clergy could communicate with Rome. In France, the Gallican doctrine that papal authority was limited by the traditional rights of the Gallican Church came to mean in practice that the church was subject to the king in large areas of its activity. In the Catholic states of the Holy Roman Empire, the princely governments kept tight control of ecclesiastical matters.

All these tendencies were reinforced by the principle adopted in the Peace of Augsburg of 1555, which ended the wars between Catholic and Lutheran princes; the principle of *cujus regio, ejus religio* ("whose kingdom, his religion") held that it was for the local prince to decide which religion should be maintained in his territories. Adherence to this principle was felt to be the only way of curbing religious wars, as in fact it did until the outbreak of the Thirty Years' War in the next century. It is significant that the Peace of Westphalia (1648) ending this latter war endorsed and extended the principle, adding Calvinism to the other two religions that princes could maintain exclusively in their lands. Indeed, down to the French Revolution, the idea of religion as an affair of state remained the norm in Europe; church and nation were regarded as inseparable.

THE EVOLUTION OF TOLERATION

The claims of the individual conscience nevertheless could not be wholly ignored. Minority groups of Protestants in Catholic countries, as well as of Catholics in Protestant countries, could not be exterminated, even though they were often fiercely persecuted. Smaller sects that often regarded state establishment of religion as false in principle managed to maintain themselves despite state attempts at repression. Though the number of thinkers who regarded toleration as right in principle were few, politicians increasingly came to see that the endeavour to maintain strict religious uniformity defeated its own political purpose, namely that of preserving the unity of the nation. This was earliest seen in France, where, during the course of religious wars, certain people known as Politiques argued for toleration on the ground that religious differences should be subordinated to nationalist ends. Such a principle was adopted by Henry IV, who became a Catholic in 1593 in order to win acceptance as king of France and then by the Edict of Nantes in 1598 secured for his erstwhile Protestant or Huguenot supporters not only freedom of worship in their own districts but also political and military safeguards for their continuing freedom. Although these latter safeguards were drastically limited by Cardinal de Richelieu in the Peace of Alais in 1629, after the Huguenots had risen in rebellion, the Edict of Nantes itself was not repealed until 1685, by Louis XIV. Even then the more steadfast Huguenots resisted conversion; and although many emigrated, many remained to survive the suppressions and severe disabilities until the French Revolution won them freedom. These Protestants remain a relatively small but important element in the French nation to this day.

The English compromise. The advance of toleration was irregular both in time and place, chiefly because the pressures toward or against it varied according to the political circumstances of each nation and state. In this connection, it is particularly instructive to turn one's eyes to the British Isles, where the Reformation and its after-

Role of religious minorities

math took a peculiar and virtually unique course. In the first instance, the English Reformation was political rather than doctrinal. As is well known, it began with the quarrel between Henry VIII and Pope Clement VII over the Pope's refusal to grant Henry's request to nullify his marriage to Catherine of Aragon in order that he might wed Anne Boleyn and hopefully secure a male heir to the throne. It is conceivable that a breach with Rome would have come about anyway as an outcome of the dissatisfaction felt by a powerful dynasty like the Tudors with the medieval system under which, as Henry put it, the clergy were "but half his subjects and scarce his subjects," their spiritual allegiance being to the pope and not to him. But this is no more than speculative; the actual immediate reason why in 1533–34 the King renounced obedience to the Pope and established royal ecclesiastical supremacy in place of papal was the necessity, as he saw it, of carrying through the divorce, now urgently necessary because of the imminence of the birth of Anne's first child in 1533. The only alternative to a papal nullity decree was to secure one through the new archbishop of Canterbury, Thomas Cranmer; and that in turn meant bringing the English ecclesiastical courts under royal authority. As royal supremacy was rapidly extended to make the king supreme in various ecclesiastical matters, the advantages in securing unitary sovereignty for the monarchy became more and more apparent. Thus, after 1534 Henry took the title of supreme head of the Church of England, though he claimed no sacerdotal powers, and exercised all the jurisdiction in England hitherto claimed by the pope. The title and powers passed to his son, Edward VI, in whose reign Protestant doctrines were furthered by the government, resulting in radical doctrinal and liturgical changes. When Catholic Mary I succeeded her brother in 1553, she was able to reverse these trends and even restore papal authority. But on Mary's death in 1558, Elizabeth I, Anne's daughter, restored the royal supremacy and adopted a religious compromise. The alteration in the royal title, by which Elizabeth claimed to be supreme governor rather than head of the English Church, may have been designed to placate Catholics and some Protestants who found her father's title offensive, especially when attributed to a woman; but the change made no practical difference to the powers over the church wielded by the Queen.

Doctrine of royal supremacy

What was hoped to be a final settlement of religion met opposition from the first, both from Roman Catholics who refused to abandon the pope or accept the changes in worship and also from extreme Protestants who regarded these changes as insufficiently radical. Throughout the reign, the government was occupied with trying to force Roman Catholics to conform and to compel Puritan clergymen to carry out the Anglican ceremonies. Both tasks were made more difficult by the relations of both parties with continental developments. Some Puritans who admired the Calvinist polity of Geneva tried by parliamentary means to set up similar presbyterianism in England and, when that failed, set about establishing at the local level private shadow presbyteries designed in due time to supplant the medieval structure of dioceses continued in the Elizabethan Church. Some Roman Catholics, after failing to replace Elizabeth with her Catholic cousin Mary, queen of Scots, turned increasingly to Philip II of Spain, the former husband of Mary I and for a brief time king of England, as champion of the Catholic cause. The Elizabethan government naturally regarded one movement as seditious and the other as treasonable and persecuted them with greater rigour than ordinary refusal to conform. The whole story illustrates vividly the inevitable links between religious and political disputes in the circumstances of the day and the difficulties faced by any idea of toleration, a policy that, in any case, had few supporters in an age when uniformity of religion was assumed to be called for both by the demands of truth and by the need for national unity. The situation was complicated first by the problem of Ireland, where the vast majority of the population, always restive under English rule, remained firmly Roman Catholic

Links between religious and political disputes

and resisted conversion by force, and second by the problem of Scotland, where a radically Protestant Reformation had succeeded in setting up a Calvinist Church, though the Scottish king James VI, destined to succeed Elizabeth on the English throne as James I in 1603, disliked the Calvinist policy. These events caused the Elizabethan policy, at once antipapal and anti-Puritan, to be continued in the next century, and the situation became even more acute when, under James's son Charles I, the monarchy increasingly identified itself with the anti-Puritans and appeared, at least to the Puritans, to be moving in the direction of Rome. This was one of the causes of the English Civil War (1642–51), which brought about the defeat and execution of Charles and the temporary overthrow of the Anglican system. When Anglicanism was restored, together with the monarchy, in 1660, the new king, Charles II, inclined carefully toward toleration and secretly allied with Catholic France; but his avowedly Roman Catholic brother, James II, succeeding to the throne in 1685, pursued open policies leading to rebellion against him in 1688, whereupon he was driven into exile. Under succeeding Protestant monarchs, William and Mary, and Anne, Protestantism was secured in England.

It is perhaps surprising that the maelstrom of the 17th century did not do away with the Anglican pattern of church settlement established by Elizabeth I. Its survival can be explained only on the supposition that, though without many positive defenders at first, it came gradually to commend itself to the majority of Englishmen as a *via media* between Roman Catholicism and Protestantism of the continental types. Whatever the reason, it has continued into the 20th century, and the relations between church and state in England today are, at least theoretically, those established in 1558. The royal supremacy is acknowledged, and no changes of moment can be made in the Anglican Church without the consent of the monarch in Parliament. Since the Enabling Act of 1919, however, the church has gained the right to initiate legislation in its National Assembly (succeeded in 1970 by the General Synod), legislation that, if not challenged in Parliament, receives the royal assent and goes into effect. The Anglican Church, though the nation's established church, has, of course, ceased for a long time to be a body to which citizens are compelled to belong. After the Restoration of 1660 the nonconformist groups, though placed under severe disabilities, were allowed to exist and by the 19th century had gained complete toleration. The penal laws against Roman Catholics became less and less rigorously enforced during the 18th century and were abolished by the Catholic Emancipation Act of 1829.

Effects of the French Revolution **The continental solution.** The situation in the British Isles described above is in many ways almost unique in the modern world. On the continent of Europe the French Revolution ended almost everywhere the old concept of church and state as two aspects of a national society. The Revolution was anticlerical and secularist, influenced as it was by the ideas of the 18th-century Enlightenment, which had undermined faith in the Christian religion and had attempted to propagate, if not atheism, a natural religion derived from philosophy. In France itself, after an attempt to set up a democratically organized and state-controlled church had failed, Napoleon concluded the Concordat of 1801 with Pope Pius VII, which established a system whereby the church accepted the confiscation of its landed property carried out by the Revolution, and the state, in return, paid the stipends of the Catholic bishops and clergy (as well as those of Protestant ministers and Jewish rabbis) and retained the right to nominate bishops. By the Organic Articles added unilaterally to the concordat, Napoleon gave himself the power to restrict papal jurisdiction in France and to influence the curricula in the seminaries. Despite the successive revolutions and changes of regime that characterized 19th-century French history, this system was maintained until 1905, when the Third Republic, in the anticlerical crisis created by the Dreyfus affair, denounced the concordat and broke off diplomatic relations with the Vatican. Since then the French Catholic Church has been a self-supporting body, allowed by the state to use the churches, which are legally state property, but paying its clergy from the offerings of the faithful.

CHURCH AND STATE IN THE MODERN WORLD

It is impossible to describe in detail the varying types of church-state relationships in the modern world because they vary greatly from country to country. In most Roman Catholic countries there are concordats between the state and the Vatican that define the legal position of the church and the precise degree of self-government allowed it. (In some cases the state is given some control over episcopal appointments.) Establishment, in the historic sense, implying a union of church and state, scarcely exists, though sometimes, as in the case of the Irish republic, the state formally recognizes the Roman Church as the religion of the majority of its people. In the Eastern Orthodox world, the church of Greece preserves the old Byzantine tradition of church-state unity, and the state has a large measure of control over the church. Because almost everywhere else the Orthodox Church lives under either Muslim or Communist regimes, its position is regulated by states that are to a greater or lesser degree antipathetic to it; in the Soviet Union, of course, the state is determinedly antireligious. Thus, in such areas, though the church is allowed to exist, it is kept under strict surveillance and control.

In the United States, the First Amendment of the ten original amendments to the Constitution forbids Congress to make any law "respecting an establishment of religion, or prohibiting the free exercise thereof," thus establishing the principle that all religious bodies shall be voluntary organizations within the state, enjoying the privileges of such organizations and subject only to the general laws governing them. This may be said to be today the general pattern of church-state relations in democratic states (with the exceptions already noted), even where freedom of religion, subject only to the requirements of public order, is not explicitly written into the constitution. Separation of church and state

This does not mean, of course, that states escape having to deal with religious matters in law courts or legislatures. In the United States, for example, the migration of the 1840s brought in thousands of people whose tradition was Roman Catholic. Fears that the new immigrants would receive public funds for their separate educational facilities resulted in many states' adopting restrictive clauses in their constitutions against such a practice. The 20th century saw the First and Fourteenth amendments to the Constitution applied with considerable strictness by the courts in the field of education. These judicial decisions prohibited aid to private education or the introduction of any form of religious belief or teaching (including prayers) in public schools.

In many countries the very fact that religious bodies are incorporated causes them to make appeals to the state or to be somehow supervised by the state. On occasion they may have to resort to state courts for adjudication of their own internal affairs or to request legislation to enable them to amend their organization or rules (as happens in the case of other incorporated associations). One of the most celebrated instances of this occurred in Scotland in 1900, when the Free Church united with the United Presbyterian Church to form the United Free Church. Some members of the old Free Church, claiming that the union violated certain doctrinal standards hitherto held, refused to enter the union. A lawsuit, taken on appeal from the Scottish courts to the House of Lords, the supreme appeal court for the British Isles, resulted in the contention of the dissidents being upheld and all the property of the Free Church adjudged to the small dissident body. Because this was considered inequitable, even if legal, a special act of Parliament of 1905 divided the property in dispute, allocating most of it to the new United Free Church. These events are a good illustration of how impossible it is even for voluntary religious bodies, if they are incorporated, to be free from all connection with the political state.

Nevertheless, it can be said that in the modern world, in which the idea of conterminous religious and political human communities has to all intents and purposes disappeared, the problems of church and state relations that have played such a large and often divisive part in Christian history have assimilated themselves to the general problems presented by the relationship of sovereign states to human associations within them.

BIBLIOGRAPHY. Detailed accounts of the varying relations of church and state must of course be sought in general historical works or in histories of the regions or periods concerned. The following books will be found of value for general study of the problem. LUIGI STURZO, *Chiesa e Stato*, rev. ed., 2 vol. (1958–59; Eng. trans., *Church and State*, 1939; 2-vol. paperback, 1962), surveys the whole subject. T.M. PARKER, *Christianity and the State in the Light of History* (1955), attempts an outline history of church-state relations from earliest times to the 16th century. A full treatment of the medieval period may be found in R.W. and A.J. CARLYLE, *A History of Mediaeval Political Theory in the West*, 3rd ed., 6 vol. (1928–36). A very valuable survey of the same period is C.H. MCILWAIN, *The Growth of Political Thought in the West, from the Greeks to the End of the Middle Ages* (1932). Other books of unusual insight are WALTER ULLMANN, *The Growth of Papal Government in the Middle Ages*, 3rd ed. (1970), and the same author's *Principles of Government and Politics in the Middle Ages* (1961). For Byzantium, see LOUIS BREHIER, *Le Monde byzantin*, vol. 2, *Les Institutions de l'empire byzantin* (1948). J.N. FIGGIS, *Studies of Political Thought from Gerson to Grotius, 1414–1625*, 2nd ed. (1916, reprinted 1956), surveys brilliantly the transition from medieval to modern times. For the vital period of the Reformation, see J.W. ALLEN, *A History of Political Thought in the Sixteenth Century*, 2nd ed. (1941; reprinted with revised bibliographical notes, 1957); and PIERRE MESNARD, *L'Essor de la philosophie politique au XVIe siècle*, 2nd ed. (1951). For church-state developments in Russia, JAMES CRACRAFT, *The Church Reform of Peter the Great* (1971), is important. A penetrating examination of the ideas underlying modern relations of church and state is J.N. FIGGIS, *Churches in the Modern State* (1913).

(T.M.P.)

Churchill, Sir Winston

Winston Churchill, author, orator, and statesman, led Britain from the brink of defeat to victory as wartime prime minister from 1940 to 1945. After a sensational rise to prominence in national politics before World War I, he acquired a reputation for erratic judgment in the war itself and in the decade that followed. Politically suspect in consequence, he was a lonely figure in the 1930s, until his response to Adolph Hitler's challenge brought him to leadership of a national coalition in 1940. In combination with Franklin D. Roosevelt and Joseph Stalin he shaped the Allied strategy in World War II, and after the breakdown of the alliance he alerted the West to the expansionist threats of the Soviet Union. He led the Conservative Party back to office in 1951 and remained prime minister until 1955, when ill health forced his resignation.

Churchill was born on November 30, 1874, prematurely, at Blenheim Palace, Oxfordshire. In his veins ran the blood of both of the English-speaking peoples whose unity, in peace and war, it was to be a constant purpose of his to promote. Through his father, Lord Randolph Churchill, the meteoric Tory politician, he was directly descended from John Churchill, 1st duke of Marlborough, the hero of the wars against Louis XIV of France in the early 18th century. His mother, Jennie Jerome, was the daughter of a New York financier and horse racing enthusiast, Leonard W. Jerome.

The young Churchill passed an unhappy and sadly neglected childhood, redeemed only by the affection of Mrs. Everest, his devoted nurse. After indifferent preparatory schooling he entered Harrow, where his conspicuous lack of success at his studies seemingly justified his father's decision to enter him on an army career. It was only at the third attempt that he managed to pass the entrance examination to the Royal Military College, now Academy, Sandhurst, but, once there, he applied himself seriously and passed out (graduated) 20th in a class of 130. In 1895, the year of his father's tragic death,

Churchill, photographed by Yousuf Karsh.
© Karsh

he entered the 4th Hussars. The young subaltern craved action and an opportunity to make his mark. Initially the only prospect of action was in Cuba, where he spent a couple of months of leave reporting the Cuban war of independence from Spain for the *Daily Graphic* (London). In 1896 his regiment went to India, where he saw service as both soldier and journalist on the North–West Frontier (1897). Expanded as *The Story of the Malakand Field Force* (1898), his dispatches attracted such wide attention as to launch him on a career of authorship, which he intermittently pursued throughout his life. In 1898 he wrote *Savrola* (1900), a Ruritanian romance, and got himself attached to Lord Kitchener's Nile expeditionary force in the same dual role of soldier and correspondent. *The River War* (1899) brilliantly describes the campaign. *Early career as a soldier and journalist*

POLITICAL CAREER BEFORE 1939

The five years after Sandhurst saw Churchill's interests expand and mature. Routine army life in India bored him, but he put its enforced leisure to good use by a program of reading designed to repair the deficiencies of Harrow and Sandhurst. In 1899 he resigned his commission to make a living by his pen and to enter politics. Immediately on his return to England he fought a by-election at Oldham as a Conservative. He lost by a narrow margin but found quick solace in reporting the South African War for *The Morning Post* (London). Within a month after his arrival in South Africa he had won fame for his part in rescuing an armoured train ambushed by Boers, though at the price of himself being taken prisoner. But this fame was redoubled when less than a month later he escaped from military prison. Returning to Britain a military hero, he laid siege again to Oldham in the "Khaki" election of 1900, so called because the Conservatives appealed to their recent victories in the South African War. Churchill this time succeeded in winning by a margin as narrow as that of his previous failure. But he was now in Parliament and, fortified by the £10,-000 his writings and lecture tours had earned for him, was now in a position to make his own way in politics.

A self-assurance redeemed from arrogance only by a kind of boyish charm made Churchill from the first a notable House of Commons figure, but a speech defect, which he never wholly lost, combined with a certain psychological inhibition to prevent him from immediately becoming a master of debate. He excelled in the set speech, on which he always spent enormous pains, rather than in the impromptu; Lord Balfour, the Conservative leader, said of him that he carried "heavy but not very mobile guns." In matter as in style he modelled himself on his father, as his admirable biography, *Lord Randolph Churchill* (1906; revised edition 1952), makes evident, and from the first he wore his Toryism with a difference.

advocating a fair, negotiated peace for the Boers and deploring military mismanagement and extravagance.

As Liberal minister. In 1904 the Conservative government found itself impaled on a dilemma by Colonial Secretary Joseph Chamberlain's open advocacy of a tariff. Churchill, a convinced free trader, helped to found the "Free Food League." He was disavowed by his constituents and became increasingly alienated from both the tariff zealots and the ambivalent leadership of the party. In 1904 he crossed the floor of the House to take his seat with the Liberals, where he won renown for the audacity of his attacks on Chamberlain and Balfour. The radical elements in his political makeup came to the surface, under the influence of two colleagues in particular, John Morley, a political legatee of W.E. Gladstone, and David Lloyd George, the rising Welsh orator and firebrand. In the ensuing general election in 1906 he secured a notable victory in Manchester and began his ministerial career in the new Liberal government as undersecretary of state for the colonies. He soon gained credit for his able defense of the policy of conciliation and self-government in South Africa. When the ministry was reconstructed under Prime Minister Herbert H. Asquith in 1908, Churchill was promoted to president of the Board of Trade, with a seat in the Cabinet. He failed to hold the fickle affections of the electors at Manchester and secured instead election as member for Dundee. In the same year he married the beautiful Clementine Hozier; it was a marriage of unbroken affection that provided a secure and happy background for his turbulent career.

At the Board of Trade, Churchill emerged as a leader in the movement of Liberalism away from laissez-faire toward social reform. He completed the work begun by his predecessor, Lloyd George, on the bill imposing an eight-hour maximum day for miners. He himself was responsible for attacking the evils of "sweated" labour by setting up trade boards with power to fix minimum wages and for combatting unemployment by instituting state-run labour exchanges. Valuable in themselves, the exchanges were also a necessary precondition for that first installment of the modern welfare state, the system of unemployment insurance, which Churchill also elaborated at the Board of Trade, though it was left to his successor to introduce the legislation.

When this Liberal program necessitated high taxation, which in turn provoked the House of Lords to the revolutionary step of rejecting the budget of 1909, Churchill was Lloyd George's closest ally in developing the provocative strategy designed to clip the wings of the upper chamber. Churchill became president of the Budget League, and his oratorical broadsides at the House of Lords were as lively and devastating as Lloyd George's own. Indeed Churchill, as an alleged traitor to his class, earned the lion's share of Tory animosity. His campaigning in the two general elections of 1910 and in the House of Commons during the passage of the Parliament Act of 1911, which curbed the House of Lords' powers, won him wide popular acclaim. In the Cabinet his reward was promotion to the office of home secretary. Here, despite substantial achievements in prison reform, he had to devote himself principally to coping with a sweeping wave of industrial unrest and violent strikes. Upon occasion his relish for dramatic action led him beyond the limits of his proper role as the guarantor of public order. For this he paid a heavy price in incurring the long-standing suspicion of organized labour.

In 1911 the provocative German action in sending a gunboat to Agadir, the Moroccan port to which France had claims, convinced Churchill that in any major Franco-German conflict Britain would have to be at France's side. When transferred to the Admiralty in October 1911, he went to work with a conviction of the need to bring the navy to a pitch of instant readiness. His first task was the creation of a naval war staff, a task in which he was assisted by Adm. Sir John Fisher, the inventor of the "Dreadnought," whom he enticed back from retirement. To help Britain's lead over steadily mounting German naval power, Churchill successfully campaigned in the Cabinet for the largest naval expenditure in British history. Nor did he shirk his share of responsibility for the government's other policies in the troubled years before World War I. Despite his inherited views on Ireland, he wholeheartedly embraced the Liberal policy of home rule, moving the second reading of the Irish home rule Bill in 1912 and campaigning for it in the teeth of Unionist opposition. Although, through his friendship with F.E. Smith (later 1st earl of Birkenhead) and Austen Chamberlain, he did much to arrange the compromise by which Ulster was to be excluded from the immediate effect of the bill, no member of the government was more bitterly abused—by Tories as a renegade and by extreme home rulers as a defector.

During World War I. War came as no surprise to Churchill. He had already held a test naval mobilization. Of all the Cabinet ministers he was the most insistent on the need to resist Germany. On August 2, 1914, on his own responsibility, he ordered the naval mobilization that guaranteed complete readiness when war was declared. The war called out all of Churchill's energies. In October 1914, when Antwerp was falling, he characteristically rushed in person to organize its defense. When it fell the public saw only a disillusioning defeat, but in fact the prolongation of its resistance for almost a week enabled the Belgian Army to escape and the crucial Channel ports to be saved. At the Admiralty, Churchill's partnership with Fisher, the first sea lord, was productive both of dynamism and of dissension. In 1915, when Churchill became an enthusiast for the Dardanelles expedition as a way out of the costly stalemate on the Western Front, he had to proceed against Fisher's disapproval. The campaign aimed at forcing the straits and opening up direct communications with Russia. When the naval attack failed and was called off by Adm. J.M. de Robeck on the spot, the Admiralty war group and Asquith both supported de Robeck rather than Churchill. Churchill came under heavy political attack, which intensified when Fisher resigned. Preoccupied with departmental affairs, Churchill was quite unprepared for the storm that broke about his ears. He had no part at all in the manoeuvres that produced the first coalition government and was powerless when the Conservatives, with the sole exception of Sir William Maxwell Aitken (soon Lord Beaverbrook), insisted on his being demoted from the Admiralty to the duchy of Lancaster. Here he was given special responsibility for the Gallipoli campaign (a land assault at the straits) without, however, any powers of direction. Reinforcements were too few and too late; the campaign failed and casualties were heavy; evacuation was ordered in the autumn.

In November 1915 Churchill resigned from the government and returned to soldiering, seeing active service in France as lieutenant colonel of the 6th Royal Scots Fusiliers. Although he entered the service with zest, army life did not give full scope for his talents. In 1916, when his battalion was merged, he did not seek another command but instead returned to Parliament as a private member. He was not involved in the intrigues that led to the formation of a coalition government under Lloyd George, and it was not until 1917 that the Conservatives would consider his inclusion in the government. In March 1917 the publication of the Dardanelles commission report demonstrated that he was at least no more to blame for the fiasco than his colleagues.

Even so, Churchill's appointment as minister of munitions in July 1917 was made in the face of a storm of Tory protest. Excluded from the Cabinet, Churchill's role was almost entirely administrative, but his dynamic energies thrown behind the development and production of the tank (which he had initiated at the Admiralty) greatly speeded up the use of the weapon that broke through the deadlock on the Western Front. Paradoxically, it was not until the war was over that Churchill returned to a service department. In January 1919 he became secretary of war, charged also with responsibility for the Royal Air Force. Here he presided with surprising zeal over the cutting back of military expenditure, working to the "ten-year rule"—that Britain would not be engaged in any major war during the next ten years. The

Attacks on Conservatives

Home secretary

The Dardanelles campaign

major preoccupation of his tenure of the War Office was, however, the Allied intervention in Russia. Churchill, passionately anti-Bolshevist, secured from a divided and loosely organized Cabinet an intensification and prolongation of the British involvement beyond the wishes of any major group in Parliament or the nation—and in the face of the bitter hostility of labour. And in 1920, after the last British forces had been withdrawn, Churchill was instrumental in having arms sent to the Poles when they invaded the Ukraine.

Appointment to the Colonial Office

In 1921 Churchill moved to the Colonial Office, where his principal concern was with the mandated territories in the Middle East. For the costly British forces in the area he substituted a reliance on the air force and the establishment of rulers congenial to British interests; for this settlement of Arab affairs he relied heavily on the advice of T.E. Lawrence. For Palestine, where he inherited conflicting pledges to Jews and Arabs, he produced in 1922 the White Paper that confirmed Palestine as a Jewish national home while recognizing continuing Arab rights. For a solution of the persistent problems of Ireland, Churchill never had departmental responsibility, but he progressed from an initial belief in firm, even ruthless, maintenance of British rule to an active role in the negotiations that led to the Irish treaty of 1921. Subsequently, he gave full support to the new Irish government; "Tell Winston," said the Irish leader Michael Collins, "we could never have done without him."

In the autumn of 1922 the insurgent Turks appeared to be moving toward a forcible reoccupation of the Dardanelles neutral zone, which was protected by a small British force at Chanak (now Canakkale). Churchill was foremost in urging a firm stand against them, but the handling of the issue by the Cabinet gave the public impression that a major war was being risked for an inadequate cause and on insufficient consideration. A political debacle ensued that brought the shaky coalition government down in ruins, with Churchill as one of the worst casualties. Gripped by a sudden attack of appendicitis, he was not able to appear in public until two days before the election, and then only in a wheelchair. He was defeated humiliatingly by over 10,000 votes. He thus found himself, as he said, all at once "without an office, without a seat, without a party, and even without an appendix."

In and out of office, 1922–29. In convalescence and political impotence Churchill turned to his brush and his pen. His painting never rose above the level of a gifted amateur's, but his writing once again provided him with the financial base his independent brand of politics required. His autobiographical history of the war, *The World Crisis*, netted him the £20,000 with which he purchased Chartwell, henceforth his country home in Kent. When he returned to politics it was as a crusading anti-Socialist, but in 1923, when Stanley Baldwin was leading the Conservatives on a protectionist program, Churchill stood, at Leicester, as a Liberal free trader. He lost by 4,000 votes. Asquith's decision in 1924 to support a minority Labour government moved Churchill farther to the right. He stood as an "Independent Anti-Socialist" in a by-election in the Abbey division of Westminster. Although opposed by an official Conservative candidate—who defeated him by a hairbreadth of 43 votes—Churchill managed to avoid alienating the Conservative leadership and indeed won conspicuous support from many prominent figures in the party. His fighting power, however volatile, was obviously too valuable an asset for the party to ignore. Archibald Salvidge, the potent Conservative manager from Liverpool, promoted his cause. In the general election in November 1924 he won an easy victory at Epping under the thinly disguised Conservative label of "Constitutionalist." Baldwin, free of his flirtation with protectionism, offered Churchill, the "constitutionalist free trader," the post of chancellor of the exchequer. Surprised, Churchill accepted; dumbfounded, the country interpreted it as a move to absorb into the party all the right-of-centre elements of the former coalition.

Chancellor of the exchequer under Baldwin

In the five years that followed, Churchill's early liberal-

ism survived only in the form of advocacy of rigid laissez-faire economics; for the rest he appeared, repeatedly, as the leader of the diehards. He had no natural gift for financial administration, and though the noted economist John Maynard Keynes criticized him unsparingly, most of the advice he received was orthodox and harmful. His first move was to restore the gold standard, a disastrous measure, from which flowed deflation, unemployment, and the miners' strike that led to the general strike of 1926. Churchill offered no remedy except the cultivation of strict economy, extending even to the armed services. Churchill viewed the general strike as a quasi-revolutionary measure and was foremost in resisting a negotiated settlement. He leaped at the opportunity of editing the *British Gazette*, an emergency official newspaper, which he filled with bombastic and frequently inflammatory propaganda. The one relic of his earlier radicalism was his partnership with Neville Chamberlain as minister of health in the cautious expansion of social services, mainly in the provision of widows' pensions.

In 1929, when the government fell, Churchill would have liked a Tory–Liberal reunion and deplored Baldwin's decision to accept a minority Labour government. Next year an open rift developed between the two men. On Baldwin's endorsement of a Round Table Conference with Indian leaders, Churchill resigned from the shadow cabinet and threw himself into a passionate, at times almost hysterical, campaign against the Government of India bill (1935) designed to give India dominion status.

Exclusion from office, 1929–39. Thus, when in 1931 the National Government was formed, Churchill, though a supporter, had no hand in its establishment or place in its councils. He had arrived at a point where, for all his abilities, he was distrusted by every party. He was thought to lack judgment and stability and was regarded as a guerrilla fighter impatient of discipline. He was considered a clever man who associated too much with clever men—Birkenhead, Beaverbrook, Lloyd George—and who despised the necessary humdrum associations and compromises of practical politics.

In this situation he found relief, as well as profit, in his pen, writing, in *Marlborough: His Life and Times*, a massive rehabilitation of his ancestor against the criticisms of the 19th-century historian Thomas Babington Macaulay. But overriding the past and transcending his worries about India was a mounting anxiety about the growing menace of Hitler's Germany. Before a supine government and a doubting opposition, Churchill persistently argued the case for taking the German threat seriously and for the need to prevent the Luftwaffe from securing parity with the Royal Air Force. In this he was supported by a small but devoted personal following, in particular the gifted, curmudgeonly Oxford physics professor Frederick A. Lindemann (later Lord Cherwell), who enabled him to build up at Chartwell a private intelligence centre the information of which was often superior to that of the government. When Baldwin became prime minister in 1935, he persisted in excluding Churchill from office but gave him the exceptional privilege of membership in the secret committee on air-defense research, thus enabling him to work on some vital national problems. But Churchill had little success in his efforts to impart urgency to Baldwin's administration. The crisis that developed when Italy invaded Ethiopia in 1935 found Churchill ill prepared, divided between a desire to build up the League of Nations around the concept of collective security and fearful of driving Benito Mussolini into the arms of Hitler. The Spanish Civil War (1936–39) found him convinced of the virtues of nonintervention, first as a supporter and later as a critic of Francisco Franco. Such vagaries of judgment in fact reflected the overwhelming priority he accorded to one issue—the containment of German aggressiveness. At home there was one grievous, characteristic, romantic misreading of the political and public mood, when, in Edward VIII's abdication crisis of 1936, he vainly opposed Baldwin by a public championing of the King's cause.

When Neville Chamberlain succeeded Baldwin, the gulf

The biography of Marlborough

between the Cassandra-like Churchill and the Conservative leaders widened. Repeatedly the accuracy of Churchill's information on Germany's aggressive plans and progress was confirmed by events; repeatedly his warnings were ignored. Yet his handful of followers remained small; politically, Chamberlain felt secure in ignoring them. As German pressure mounted on Czechoslovakia, Churchill without success urged the government to effect a joint declaration of purpose by Great Britain, France, and the Soviet Union. When the Munich Agreement with Hitler was made in September 1938, sacrificing Czechoslovakia to the Nazis, Churchill laid bare its implications, insisting that it represented "a total and unmitigated defeat." In March 1939 Churchill and his group pressed for a truly national coalition, and at last sentiment in the country, recognizing him as the nation's spokesman, began to agitate for his return to office. As long as peace lasted, Chamberlain ignored all such persuasions.

LEADERSHIP DURING WORLD WAR II

In a sense, the whole of Churchill's previous career had been a preparation for wartime leadership. An intense patriot; a romantic believer in his country's greatness and its historic role in Europe, the empire, and the world; a devotee of action who thrived on challenge and crisis; a student, historian, and veteran of war; a statesman who was master of the arts of politics, despite or because of long political exile; a man of iron constitution, inexhaustible energy, and total concentration, he seemed to have been nursing all his faculties so that when the moment came he could lavish them on the salvation of Britain and the values he believed Britain stood for in the world.

On September 3, 1939, the day Britain declared war on Germany, Chamberlain appointed Churchill to his old post in charge of the Admiralty. The signal went out to the fleet: "Winston is back." On September 11 Churchill received a congratulatory note from Pres. Franklin D. Roosevelt and replied over the signature "Naval Person"; a memorable correspondence had begun. At once Churchill's restless energy began to be felt throughout the administration, as his ministerial colleagues as well as his own department received the first of those pungent minutes that kept the remotest corners of British wartime government aware that their shortcomings were liable to detection and penalty. All his efforts, however, failed to energize the torpid Anglo-French entente during the so-called "phony war," the period of stagnation in the European war before the German seizure of Norway in April 1940. The failure of the Narvik and Trondheim expeditions, dependent as they were on naval support, could not but evoke some memories of the Dardanelles and Gallipoli, so fateful for Churchill's reputation in World War I. This time, however, it was Chamberlain who was blamed, and it was Churchill who endeavoured to defend him.

As prime minister. The German invasion of the Low Countries, on May 10, 1940, came like a hammer blow on top of the Norwegian fiasco. Chamberlain resigned. He wanted Lord Halifax, the foreign secretary, to succeed him, but Halifax wisely declined. It was obvious that Churchill alone could unite and lead the nation, since the Labour Party, for all its old distrust of Churchill's anti-Socialism, recognized the depth of his commitment to the defeat of Hitler. A coalition government was formed that included all elements save the far left and right. It was headed by a war Cabinet of five, which included at first both Chamberlain and Halifax—a wise but also magnanimous recognition of the numerical strength of Chamberlainite conservatism—and two Labour leaders, Clement Attlee and Arthur Greenwood. The appointment of Ernest Bevin, a tough trade-union leader, as minister of labour guaranteed cooperation on this vital front. Offers were made to Lloyd George, but he declined them. Churchill himself took, in addition to the leadership of the House of Commons, the Ministry of Defence. The pattern thus set was maintained through the war despite many changes of personnel. The Cabinet became an agency of swift decision, and the government

that it controlled remained representative of all groups and parties. The Prime Minister concentrated on the actual conduct of the war. He delegated freely but also probed and interfered continuously, regarding nothing as too large or too small for his attention. The main function of the chiefs of the armed services became that of containing his great dynamism, as a governor regulates a powerful machine; but though he prodded and pressed them continuously, he never went against their collective judgment. In all this Parliament played a vital part. If World War II was strikingly free from the domestic political intrigues of World War I, it was in part because Churchill, while he always dominated Parliament, never neglected it or took it for granted. For him, Parliament was an instrument of public persuasion on which he played like a master and from which he drew strength and comfort.

On May 13 Churchill faced the House of Commons for the first time as prime minister. He warned members of the hard road ahead—"I have nothing to offer but blood, toil, tears and sweat"—and committed himself and the nation to all-out war until victory was achieved. Behind this simplicity of aim lay an elaborate strategy to which he adhered with remarkable consistency throughout the war. Hitler's Germany was the enemy; nothing should distract the entire British people from the task of effecting its defeat. Anyone who shared this goal, even a Communist, was an acceptable ally. The indispensable ally in this endeavour, whether formally at war or no, was the United States. The cultivation and maintenance of its support was a central principle of Churchill's thought. Yet whether the United States became a belligerent partner or no, the war must be won without a repetition for Britain of the catastrophic bloodlettings of World War I; and Europe at the conflict's end must be re-established as a viable, self-determining entity, while the Commonwealth should remain as a continuing, if changing, expression of Britain's world role. Provided these essentials were preserved, Churchill, for all his sense of history, was surprisingly willing to sacrifice any national shibboleths—of orthodox economics, of social convention, of military etiquette or tradition—on the altar of victory. Thus, within a couple of weeks of this crusading anti-Socialist's assuming power, Parliament passed legislation placing all "persons, their services and their property at the disposal of the Crown"—granting the government in effect the most sweeping emergency powers in modern British history.

The effort was designed to match the gravity of the hour. After the Allied defeat and the evacuation of the battered British forces from Dunkirk, Churchill warned Parliament that invasion was a real risk to be met with total and confident defiance. Faced with the swift collapse of France, Churchill made repeated personal visits to the French government in an attempt to keep France in the war, culminating in the celebrated offer of Anglo-French union on June 16, 1940. When all this failed, the Battle of Britain began. Here Churchill was in his element, in the firing line—at fighter headquarters, inspecting coast defenses or anti-aircraft batteries, visiting scenes of bomb damage or victims of the "blitz," smoking his cigar, giving his V sign, or broadcasting frank reports to the nation, laced with touches of grim Churchillian humour and splashed with Churchillian rhetoric. The nation took him to its heart; he and they were one in "their finest hour."

Other painful and more debatable decisions fell to Churchill. The French fleet was attacked to prevent its surrender intact to Hitler. A heavy commitment was made to the concentrated bombing of Germany. At the height of the invasion threat, a decision was made to reinforce British strength in the eastern Mediterranean. Forces were also sent to Greece, a costly sacrifice; the evacuation of Crete looked like another Gallipoli, and Churchill came under heavy fire in Parliament.

In these hard days the exchange of U.S. overage destroyers for British Caribbean bases and the response, by way of lend-lease, to Churchill's boast "Give us the tools and we'll finish the job" were especially heartening to one who believed in a "mixing-up" of the English-speaking democracies. The unspoken alliance was further cemented in August 1941 by the dramatic meeting between Churchill and Roosevelt in Placentia Bay, Newfoundland, which produced the Atlantic Charter, a statement of common principles between the United States and Britain.

Formation of the "grand alliance." When Hitler launched his sudden attack on the Soviet Union, Churchill's response was swift and unequivocal. In a broadcast on June 22, 1941, while refusing to "unsay" any of his earlier criticisms of Communism, he insisted that "the Russian danger . . . is our danger" and pledged aid to the Russian people. Henceforth, it was his policy to construct a "grand alliance" incorporating the Soviet Union and the United States. But it took until May 1942 to negotiate a 20-year Anglo-Soviet pact of mutual assistance.

The
accord
with
Roosevelt

The Japanese attack on Pearl Harbor (December 7, 1941) altered, in Churchill's eyes, the whole prospect of the war. He went at once to Washington, D.C., and, with Roosevelt, hammered out a set of Anglo-American accords: the pooling of both countries' military and economic resources under combined boards and a combined chiefs of staff; the establishment of unity of command in all theatres of war; and agreement on the basic strategy that the defeat of Germany should have priority over the defeat of Japan. The grand alliance was now in being. Churchill could claim to be its principal architect. Safeguarding it was the principal concern of his next three and one-half years.

In this, the respect and affection between him and Roosevelt were of crucial importance. They alone enabled Churchill, in the face of relentless pressure from Stalin and ardent advocacy by the U.S. chiefs of staff, to secure the rejection of the "second front" in 1942, a project he regarded as premature and costly. In August 1942 Churchill himself flew to Moscow to advise Stalin of the decision and to bear the brunt of his displeasure. At home, too, he came under fire in 1942: first in January after the reverses in Malaya and the Far East and later in June when Tobruk in North Africa fell to the Germans during his second visit to Washington, but on neither occasion did his critics muster serious support. The year 1942 saw some reconstruction of the Cabinet in a "leftward" direction, which was reflected in the adoption in 1943 of Lord Beveridge's plan for comprehensive social insurance, endorsed by Churchill as a logical extension of the Liberal reforms of 1911.

Military successes and political problems. The Allied landings in North Africa necessitated a fresh meeting between Churchill and Roosevelt, this time in Casablanca in January 1943. There Churchill argued for an early, full-scale attack on "the under-belly of the Axis" but won only a grudging acquiescence from the Americans. There too was evolved the "unconditional surrender" formula of debatable wisdom. Churchill paid the price for his intensive travel (including Tripoli, Turkey, and Algeria) by an attack of pneumonia, for which, however, he allowed only the briefest of respites. In May he was in Washington again, arguing against persistent American aversion to his "under-belly" strategy; in August he was at Quebec, working out the plans for "Overlord," the cross-Channel assault. When he learned that the Americans were planning a large-scale invasion of Burma in 1944, his fears that their joint resources would not be adequate for a successful "Overlord" revived. In November 1943 at Cairo, he urged on Roosevelt priority for further Mediterranean offensives, but at Teheran, in the first "Big Three" meeting, he failed to retain Roosevelt's adherence to a completely united Anglo-American front. Roosevelt, though he consulted in private with Stalin, refused to see Churchill alone; for all their friendship there was also an element of rivalry between the two Western leaders that Stalin skillfully exploited. On the issue of Allied offensive drives into southern Europe, Churchill was outvoted. Throughout the meetings Churchill had been unwell, and on his way home he came down again with pneumonia. Though recovery was rapid, it was mid-January 1944 before convalescence was complete. By

Project
"Overlord"

May he was proposing to watch the D-Day assaults from a battle cruiser; only the King's personal plea dissuaded him.

Insistence on military success did not, for Churchill, mean indifference to its political implications. After the Quebec conference in September 1944, he flew to Moscow to try to conciliate the Russians and the Poles and to get an agreed division of spheres of influence in the Balkans that would protect as much of them as possible from Communism. In Greece he used British forces to thwart a Communist take-over and at Christmas flew to Athens to effect a settlement. Much of what passed at the Yalta Conference in February 1945, including the Far East settlement, concerned only Roosevelt and Stalin, and Churchill did not interfere. He fought to save the Poles but saw clearly enough that there was no way to force the Soviets to keep their promises. Realizing this, he urged the United States to allow the Allied forces to thrust as far into eastern Europe as possible before the Russian armies should fill the vacuum left by German power, but he could not win over Roosevelt, Truman, or their generals to his views. He went to Potsdam in July in a worried mood. But in the final decisions of the conference he had no part; halfway through, his government was defeated in parliamentary elections; he had to return to England and tender his resignation.

Electoral defeat. Already in 1944, with victory in prospect, party politics had revived, and by May 1945 all parties in the wartime coalition wanted an early election. But whereas Churchill wanted the coalition to continue at least until Japan was defeated, Labour wished to resume its independence. Churchill as the popular architect of victory seemed unbeatable, but as an election campaigner he proved to be his own worst enemy, indulging, seemingly at Beaverbrook's urging, in extravagant prophecies of the appalling consequences of a Labour victory and identifying himself wholly with the Conservative cause. His campaign tours were a triumphal progress, but it was the war leader, not the party leader, whom the crowds cheered. Labour's careful but sweeping program of economic and social reform was a better match for the nation's mood than Churchill's flamboyance. Though personally victorious at his Essex constituency of Woodford, Churchill saw his party reduced to 213 seats in a Parliament of 640.

POSTWAR POLITICAL CAREER

As opposition leader and world statesman. The shock of rejection by the nation fell heavily on Churchill. Indeed, though he accepted the role of leader of the parliamentary opposition, he was never wholly at home in it. The economic and social questions that dominated domestic politics were not at the centre of his interests. Nor, with his imperial vision, could he approve of what he called Labour's policy of "scuttle," as evidenced in the granting of independence to India and Burma (though he did not vote against the necessary legislation). But in foreign policy a broad identity of view persisted between the front benches, and this was the area to which Churchill primarily devoted himself. On March 5, 1946, at Fulton, Missouri, he enunciated, in the presence of President Truman, the two central themes of his postwar view of the world: The need for Britain and the United States to unite as guardians of the peace against the menace of Soviet Communism, which had brought down an "iron curtain" across the face of Europe. With equal fervour he emerged as an advocate of European union. At Zürich, Switzerland, on September 19, 1946, he urged the formation of "a council of Europe" and himself attended the first assembly of the council at Strasbourg in 1949. Meanwhile, in private he busied himself with his great history, *The Second World War*, six volumes (1948–54).

The "iron
curtain"
speech

The general election of February 1950 afforded Churchill his long-awaited opportunity to seek again for a personal mandate. He abstained from the extravagances of 1945 and campaigned with his party rather than above it; even so, his personality, his zest in the knockabout of campaigning, and, above all, his oratory dominated the election.

The electoral onslaught shook Labour but left them still in office. It took what Churchill called "one more heave" to defeat them in a second election, in October 1951. Churchill again took a vigorous lead in the campaign. He pressed the government particularly hard on its handling of the crisis caused by Iran's nationalization of British oil companies and in return had to withstand charges of warmongering. The Conservatives were returned with a narrow majority of 26, and Churchill became prime minister for the second time. He formed a government in which the more liberal Conservatives predominated, though the Liberal Party itself declined Churchill's suggestion of office. A prominent figure in the government was R.A. Butler, the progressive-minded chancellor of the exchequer. Anthony Eden was foreign secretary. Some notable Churchillians were included, among them Lord Cherwell, who, as paymaster general, was principal scientific adviser with special responsibilities for atomic research and development.

As prime minister again. The domestic labours and battles of his administration were far from Churchill's main concerns. Derationing, decontrolling, rehousing, safeguarding the precarious balance of payments—these were relatively noncontroversial policies; only the return of nationalized steel and road transport to private hands aroused excitement. Critics sometimes complained of a lack of prime ministerial direction in these areas and indeed of a certain slackness in the reins of government. Undoubtedly Churchill was getting older and reserving more and more of his energies for what he regarded as the supreme issues of foreign affairs, peace and war. He was convinced that Labour had allowed the transatlantic relationship to sag, and one of his first acts was to visit Washington (and also Ottawa) in January 1952 to repair the damage he felt had been done. The visit helped to check United States fears that the British would desert the Korean War, harmonized attitudes toward German rearmament and, distasteful though it was to Churchill, resulted in the acceptance of a United States naval commander in chief of the eastern Atlantic. It did not produce that sharing of secrets of atom bomb manufacture that Churchill felt had unfairly lapsed after the war. To the disappointment of many, Churchill's advocacy of European union did not result in active British participation; his government confined itself to endorsement from the sidelines, though in 1954, faced with the collapse of the European Defense Community, Churchill and Eden came forward with a pledge to maintain British troops on the Continent for as long as necessary.

The year 1953 was in many respects a gratifying one for Churchill. It brought the coronation of Queen Elizabeth II, which drew out all his love of the historic and symbolic. He personally received two notable distinctions, the Order of the Garter and the Nobel Prize for Literature. He rejoiced in having his old comrade-in-arms Dwight D. Eisenhower in the White House and lost no time in establishing personal contact by a meeting in New York en route to a January holiday in Jamaica. Soon plans were set afoot for a meeting at Bermuda in July, when Churchill hoped to secure Eisenhower's agreement to "summit talks" with the Russians, following on the death of Stalin. But Churchill had been carrying too heavy a load, even taking on the foreign secretaryship when Eden fell ill in April. On July 27 he collapsed with a sudden stroke that brought on partial paralysis. The Bermuda meeting had to be postponed. Churchill, however, made a recovery that even for a younger man would have been remarkable, and by October he was back at work again. The postponed meeting, at which the French were also represented, was held at Bermuda in December. Outwardly, it recaptured the flavour of the wartime conferences. In fact it was not an instrument for decision making but for consultation and exchange of views. Easy intimacy was established, but two obstacles prevented the full re-establishment of the "special relationship" between Britain and the United States that Churchill cherished; first, their changed positions in world politics and, second, the failure of the two principal subordinates, Eden and John Foster Dulles, to see

Heart attack

eye to eye. The year 1954 brought the problems of the Indo-China War to an acute pitch; Churchill and Eden visited Washington in June in hopes of securing a more wholehearted United States acceptance of the Geneva Accords than, in fact, was forthcoming. Over Egypt, however, Churchill's conversion to an agreement permitting a phased withdrawal of British troops from the Suez base won Eisenhower's endorsement and encouraged hopes, illusory as it subsequently appeared, of good Anglo-American cooperation in this area. In 1955, "arming to parley," Churchill authorized the manufacture of a British hydrogen bomb while still striving for a summit conference. Age, however, robbed him of this last triumph. His powers were too visibly failing. His 80th birthday, on November 30, 1954, had been the occasion of a unique all-party ceremony of tribute and affection in Westminster Hall. But the tribute implied a pervasive assumption that he would soon retire. On April 5, 1955, his resignation took place, only a few weeks before his chosen successor, Sir Anthony Eden, announced plans for a four-power conference at Geneva.

Retirement and death. Although Churchill laid down the burdens of office amid the plaudits of the nation and the world, he remained in the House of Commons (declining a peerage) to become "father of the house" and even, in 1959, to fight and win yet another election. He also published another major work, *A History of the English-Speaking Peoples*, four volumes (1956–58). But his health declined, and his public appearances became rare. On April 9, 1963, he was accorded the unique distinction of having an honorary United States citizenship conferred on him by an act of Congress. His death at his London home on January 24, 1965, was followed by a state funeral at which almost the whole world paid tribute. He was buried in the family grave in Bladon churchyard, Oxfordshire.

MAJOR WORKS

HISTORY: *The Story of the Malakand Field Force* (1898); *The River War* (1899); *The World Crisis* (1923–29); *The Eastern Front* (1931); *The Second World War* (1948–54); *A History of the English-Speaking Peoples* (1956–58).

BIOGRAPHY AND AUTOBIOGRAPHY: *Lord Randolph Churchill* (1906); *My African Journey* (1908); *My Early Life* (1930); *Marlborough: His Life and Times* (1933–38).

SPEECHES: *Into Battle* (1941); *The Unrelenting Struggle* (1942); *The End of the Beginning* (1943); *Onwards to Victory* (1944); *The Dawn of Liberation* (1945); *Victory* (1946); *Secret Session Speeches* (1946); *The Sinews of Peace* (1948); *Europe Unite* (1950); *In the Balance* (1951); *Stemming the Tide* (1953); *The Unwritten Alliance* (1961).

OTHER WORKS: *Savrola* (1900); *Thoughts and Adventures* (1932); *Painting As a Pastime* (1948).

BIBLIOGRAPHY. The official biography, *Winston S. Churchill* (1966–   ), was begun by his son, RANDOLPH S. CHURCHILL, and is being continued by MARTIN GILBERT. Churchill's own writings are an indispensable autobiographical source. See *While England Slept: A Survey of World Affairs, 1932–1938*, with preface and notes by RANDOLPH S. CHURCHILL (1938). LADY VIOLET BONHAM-CARTER, *Winston Churchill As I Knew Him* (1965), is a vivid memoir. The diaries of LORD ALAN-BROOKE, *Triumph in the West*, 2 vol., ed. by ARTHUR BRYANT (1957–59), illuminate the war years. *Churchill: The Struggle for Survival, 1940–1965* (1966), written by his physician LORD MORAN, gives intimate glimpses of his late years.

(H.G.N.)

Church Year

The Christian church year is an annual cycle of seasons and days observed in the Christian churches in commemoration of the life, death, and resurrection of Jesus Christ and of his virtues as exhibited in the lives of his saints. This article surveys the origin and meaning, development, and current revisions of this cycle.

ORIGINS

Religious times and seasons. The church year has deep roots in primitive man's impulse to mark certain times with sacral significance and ritual observance. These are times when he gives conscious attention to the mysterious forces that surround and involve him and all living creatures in the natural and inexorable cycles of light and darkness; labour and rest; and birth, growth, decay, and death.

Two interrelated cycles have had primary importance in the shaping of religious calendars. One is cosmic: the phases of the moon and the solar equinoxes. The other is the periodic succession of the seasons of nature that determine times of sowing and reaping. Both cycles speak to man of the mystery of birth, death, and rebirth and of his dependence upon the fecundity of life given to him in the natural creation.

Jewish background. The Jewish religious year, grounded in the divinely revealed Law of the Old Testament, was the foundation for the church year of Christians. Historically, it was a lunar-month calendar stemming from the primitive nomadic life of the Hebrews, with its chief festival at the first full moon of spring, known later as the Passover. Grafted into this calendar after the settlement of the Hebrew tribes in Palestine were the agricultural festivals—dependent upon "the early and later rains"—the firstfruits at Passover, the first harvest at the Feast of Weeks or Pentecost, and the final harvest at the Feast of Tabernacles or Booths.

Of uncertain origin, but prior to the monarchical period (11th to 6th centuries BC), the Hebrews observed a seven-day week, of which the last day, or sabbath, was a

The sabbath

holiday and day of rest. Whatever its original purpose, it became transformed into a sacral day, consecrated to Yahweh, the one God of the Hebrews, and increasingly surrounded with restrictions upon all activity other than worship. In the time of Jesus (1st century AD), "keeping holy the sabbath day" was a principal hallmark of adherence to Judaism.

The remarkable aspect of the Jewish religious year was its transformation, in successive codifications of the Old Testament Law, into a series of historical commemorations associated with God's deed in creation and in the redemption of his people. At first, the sabbath was related to the Exodus, the deliverance of the Hebrews from Egypt in the 13th century BC (Deut. 5:15), and, later, to the rest of God at the completion of his creation (Ex. 20:8–11; Gen. 2:2–3). The three agricultural feasts became a sequence of remembrances of the Exodus from Egypt and the pilgrimage through the wilderness to the promised land (Ex. 12:1–20; Lev. 23; Deut. 16:1–17). Through these annual celebrations the devout Jew relived the saving events of the past and anticipated the final deliverance of the people of God in the age to come. Rabban Gamaliel, a contemporary of Jesus, said, "In every generation a man must so regard himself as if he came forth himself out of Egypt. . . ." (From Mishna, *Pesaḥim* 10:5; see also JEWISH RELIGIOUS YEAR.)

Formation of the church year. In his earthly life Jesus was subject to the law of sabbath, feast, and fast prescribed in the Old Testament; but his ministry and teaching pointed to a new age, the coming kingdom of God, when the Law would be fulfilled. He was, therefore, not so much concerned with outward conformity to legal regulations as he was with the spirit in which they were observed. "The sabbath was made for man, and not man for the sabbath" (Mark 2:27). It was in the context of a celebration of the Passover feast with his disciples that he was arrested, tried, and put to death.

Early Christians believed that the new age promised by Jesus had dawned with his Resurrection, on "the first day of the week" (Matt. 28:1; Mark 16:2; Luke 24:1; John 20:1). By this event the Law was fulfilled. Now every day and time were viewed as holy for the celebration and remembrance of Jesus' triumph over sin and death. Though many of his disciples continued to observe the special times and seasons of the Jewish Law, new converts broke with the custom because they regarded it as no longer needful or necessary. St. Paul, himself a dutiful observant of the Law, considered the keeping of holy days a matter of indifference, provided the devotion be "in honor of the Lord" (Rom. 14:5–9). He warned his converts not to judge one another with regard "to a festival or a new moon or a sabbath" (Col. 2:16).

From the beginning, the church took over from Judaism the seven-day week. Before the end of the apostolic age (1st century AD), as the church became predominantly Gentile in membership, the first day of the week, or Sunday, had become the normative time when Christians assembled for their distinctive acts of worship, in commemoration of the Lord's Resurrection (Acts 20:7; I Cor. 16:2). During the first two centuries AD, the Greco-Roman world in general adopted the planetary seven-day week of the astrologers.

Christian writers of the 2nd century came to view Sunday, "the Lord's day," as a symbol of Christianity in distinction from Judaism. Most of the churches decided to observe the Lord's Passover (Easter) always on a Sunday, after the Jewish feast was over. In addition, local churches began to celebrate annually the anniversaries of the death of their martyrs, called "birthdays in eternity," for these also were regarded as witnesses to the resurrection triumph of Christ in his followers. The weekly Sunday and the annual Paschal (Passover) observance of 50 days from Easter to Pentecost (the Jewish harvest festival that also commemorated the revelation of the Law to Moses) were thus the principal framework of the church year until the 4th century—reminders of the new age to be brought by Christ at his coming again in glory at the end of time, when the true believers would enter their inheritance of perpetual joy and feasting with their Redeemer and Lord.

Sunday

The establishment of Christianity as a state religion, following the conversion of the emperor Constantine (AD 312), brought new developments. The Paschal season was matched by a longer season of preparation (Lent) for the many new candidates for baptism at the Easter ceremonies, and the discipline and penance of those who for grievous sins had been cut off from the Communion of the church.

A new focus of celebration, to commemorate the birthday of Christ, the world Redeemer, was instituted at the ancient winter solstices (December 25 and January 6) to rival the pagan feasts in honour of the birth of a new age brought by the Unconquered Sun. Later, the Western churches created a preparatory season for this festival, known as Advent. Many new days were gradually added to the roster of martyr anniversaries to commemorate distinguished leaders, the dedication of buildings and shrines in honour of the saints, and the transferral of their relics.

Agreements and differences of the churches. Unlike the cycle of feasts and fasts of the Jewish Law, the Christian year has never been based upon a divine revelation. It is rather a tradition that is always subject to change by ecclesiastical law. Each self-governing church maintains the right to order the church year according to pastoral needs of edification. The pattern of the year therefore varies in the several churches of the East and of the West. The subtle adjustments of a lunar-month calendar, with its movable date of Easter, and a solar calendar of fixed dates require many rules to avoid conflict of observances.

In the Western churches periodic reforms of the church year occur, notably in the Reformation era and again at the present time. The Protestant Reformers of the 16th century took differing attitudes toward such reforms. With their strong sense of the prime authority of Scripture and of the freedom of the gospel from all legalisms in liturgical matters, they revised the church year with varying degrees of radicalism. Lutherans and Anglicans took a conservative position, retaining the traditional seasons but eliminating commemorations that had no connection with the biblical record.

Reforms in the church year

The Reformed churches, on the other hand, allowed only those feasts with a clear basis in the New Testament: Sundays, Holy Week and Easter, Pentecost, and in some cases, Christmas. The Church of Scotland and Anabaptist and Puritan groups abolished the church year entirely, except for Sundays. In recent years this attitude has been very much modified. Their protest has been a reminder to the church that all days are regarded as belonging to Christ in the freedom of his Spirit, who cannot be controlled by rigid systems of special observances.

THE MAJOR SYSTEMS IN THE CHURCHES

The church year consists of two concurrent cycles: (1) the Proper of Time (Temporale), or seasons and Sundays that revolve about the movable date of Easter and the fixed date of Christmas, and (2) the Proper of Saints (Sanctorale), other commemorations on fixed dates of the year. A popular division of the year into two halves—Advent to Pentecost and Pentecost to Advent—as recalling Christ's life and his teaching, respectively—has no basis in liturgical tradition. Every season and holy day is a celebration, albeit with different emphases, of the total revelation and redemption of Christ, which are "made present at all times" or proclaim "the paschal mystery as achieved in the saints who have suffered and been glorified with Christ" (second Vatican Council, "Constitution of the Sacred Liturgy," Chapter V, paragraphs 102–105). The church year is an epitome in time of the history of salvation in Christ.

Orthodox calendar

Eastern churches. The Orthodox churches of the Byzantine tradition recall the Resurrection of Christ every Sunday. Many Sundays take their title from the Gospel lesson for the day. In addition to Easter, "the feast of feasts," there are 12 other major feasts: Christmas, Epiphany, Hypapante (Meeting of Christ with Simeon, February 2), Palm Sunday, Ascension, Pentecost, Transfiguration (August 6), Exaltation of the Holy Cross (September 14), and four feasts of the Blessed Virgin Mary—her Nativity (September 8), Presentation in the Temple (November 21), Annunciation (March 25), and Falling Asleep (August 15).

The principal cycle consists of (1) ten weeks before Easter, contained in the *Triōdion* (pre-Easter liturgical service book); the first four of these Sundays prepare for the Great Fast, or Lent (*i.e.*, the Sunday of the Pharisee and Publican; the Sunday of the Prodigal Son; Meat-Fast Sunday, after which abstinence from meat is enjoined; and Cheese-Fast Sunday, after which the fast includes cheese, eggs, butter, and milk), and (2) eight weeks after Easter, contained in the *Pentēkostarion* (post-Easter liturgical service book), including the Feast of Ascension, 40 days after Easter, and concluding with the Festival of All Saints on the Sunday after Pentecost. Other special commemorations of the period are Orthodoxy Sunday, on the first Sunday in Lent, recalling the end of the Iconoclastic Controversy (concerning the destruction of Christian icons) in 843; and the feast of the Fathers of the first Ecumenical Council of Nicaea in 325 on the sixth Sunday after Easter.

The schedule of fixed holy days in the *Mēnologion* (liturgical service book for each month) begins on September 1, the New Year's or Indiction Day of the Byzantine Empire. It is notable for the inclusion of many Old Testament saints. Since the Iconoclastic Controversy no saints have been added except St. Gregory Palamas (died 1359), the mystic theologian of Hesychasm (monastic spiritual system involving prayer and meditation through quietude), who is commemorated on the second Sunday in Lent.

Calendar of the Eastern independent churches

The separated churches of the East (those not accepting the jurisdiction of Orthodox patriarchs or bishops) have calendars basically similar to the Byzantine. West Syrians (Jacobites) and East Syrians (Nestorians) begin the year with a series of Sundays devoted to themes of the Dedication of the Church (consecration by a bishop) and the Annunciation (of the angel Gabriel to Mary that she would bear the Son of God)—the West Syrian sequence starting on November 1, the East Syrian on December 1. There are few saints' days in the Nestorian calendar. The Copts (Egyptians) and Ethiopians date their year from August 29, considered the beginning of the Christian Era in the persecution of the emperor Diocletian (AD 303–311). They have some 32 feasts of the Virgin Mary and many feasts of angels. The Armenian Church follows the Byzantine in beginning the year with the

preparatory Sundays before Lent, but it commonly observes fixed holy days on the nearest Sunday. It is the only ancient church that never adopted the feast of Christmas on December 25 but celebrates the incarnation only on Epiphany, January 6.

The Roman Catholic Church. The church year begins on the first Sunday in Advent, which is the fourth Sunday before Christmas Day. After Advent and Christmas, there follow the seasons of Epiphany, Pre-Lent, Lent, Easter, Ascension, and Pentecost. The first day of Lent is Ash Wednesday, being the 40th day (exclusive of Sundays) before Easter. A special festival of the Holy Trinity occurs on the first Sunday after Pentecost, after which the Sundays are named numerically "after Pentecost." Corpus Christi, a feast celebrating the Real Presence of Christ in the bread and wine of the Eucharist (Communion meal, or the Lord's Supper), was instituted in 1264 by Pope Urban IV and is observed on the Thursday after Trinity Sunday. In 1925 Pope Pius XI created the Feast of Christ the King, assigned to the last Sunday in October.

Fixed holy days

The fixed holy days begin with St. Andrew (November 30), the nearest to the beginning of Advent. The three days before Ascension Day, called Minor Rogation Days ("Days of Asking"), are devoted to special prayers for fruitful harvests. Found primarily in the Roman Church are the fasts of the four seasons (*quatuor tempora*), known as Ember Days, and especially associated with ordinations to the ministry. They occur on the Wednesdays, Fridays, and Saturdays after the third Sunday in Advent and the first Sunday in Lent, in the week of Pentecost and the week after Holy Cross Day (September 14).

Regulations regarding holy days and processes leading to the canonization of saints are controlled by the Sacred Congregation for Divine Worship (formerly the Congregation of Rites). Certain feasts, in addition to all Sundays, are designated "holy days of obligation," when all the faithful must attend Mass. In the United States these are: Christmas Day (December 25), the Octave of Christmas (New Year's Day), Ascension Day, the Assumption of the Blessed Virgin Mary (August 15), All Saints' Day (November 1), and the Immaculate Conception of the Blessed Virgin Mary (December 8). In addition to these, "days of obligation" observed elsewhere include: St. Joseph's Day (March 19), the Annunciation (March 25), SS. Peter and Paul Day (June 29), and the Feast of Corpus Christi.

Protestant churches. Lutheran and Anglican churches preserve in their liturgies the seasons of the Roman Catholic calendar; but they have reduced the fixed holy days to primary feasts of Christ, the Apostles and evangelists, Michaelmas Day (September 29), and All Saints' Day (November 1). In the second half of the year, Sundays are named "after Trinity" rather than "after Pentecost." Lutherans celebrate a festival of the Reformation on October 31, or the Sunday preceding that date. Many recent Anglican calendars have restored for optional use a number of nonbiblical saints.

In other Protestant churches only Sunday observance remains obligatory, including Easter and Pentecost. Holy Week is frequently observed, and Christmas is more commonly celebrated liturgically on the Sunday preceding December 25. A revived interest in the traditional seasons is taking place, and contemporary Protestant service books now provide suitable formularies for their observance. The American Methodists have adopted a season known as Kingdomtide, which begins on the last Sunday in August—first promoted in a pamphlet of the Federal Council of the Churches of Christ in America (*The Christian Year*, 1937). Protestant churches devote many Sundays to special themes of a religious, charitable, or civic nature, such as Race Relations, Rural Life, Christian Home, and Labour Sundays.

Revived interest in traditional seasons

Harvest festivals, common in the Western churches since the Middle Ages, have a distinctive American tradition in Thanksgiving Day, on the fourth Thursday in November. Originating in the Plymouth (Massachusetts) colony in 1621, it was first proclaimed a national holiday by Pres. Abraham Lincoln in 1863. Ecumenical services, now worldwide, are observed during the Octave or Week of Prayer for Christian Unity, January 18–25—a custom started by Paul James Wattson (died 1940) of the Franciscan Friars of the Atonement and developed by Abbé Paul Couturier (died 1953). The week is now jointly sponsored by the World Council of Churches and the Vatican Secretariat for Promoting Christian Unity.

HISTORY OF THE CHURCH YEAR

Sunday. Regular Christian corporate worship on Sundays goes back to the apostolic age, but New Testament writings do not explain how the practice began. Jewish Christians probably kept the sabbath at the synagogue, then joined their Gentile fellow believers for Christian worship after the close of the sabbath at sundown, either in the evening or early Sunday morning. When the church became predominantly Gentile, Sunday remained as the customary day of worship. Assemblies for the Eucharist were common on Saturday, however, as well as on Sunday in the Eastern churches on into the 5th century, and Eastern canons forbade the practice, customary in the Roman Church, of fasting on the sabbath.

The term Lord's Day, signifying the triumph of Christ in his resurrection and the beginning of a new creation, was in use by the end of the 1st century (Rev. 1:10; *Didachē* 14; Ignatius of Antioch, *Magnesians* 9:1). Some writers referred to the sabbath as the rest promised to the people of God at the end of time, and Sunday as "the eighth day," or beginning of a new world (Heb. 4:4–11; *Letter of Barnabas* 15).

Sunday as a legal holiday

In 321 the Roman emperor Constantine decreed Sunday to be a legal holiday and forbade all trade and work other than necessary agricultural labour. Later emperors extended the prohibition to include public amusements in the theatre and circus. Church councils of the period were more concerned to enforce the obligation of Sunday worship, the earliest being the Spanish Council of Elvira (*c.* 300); but a synod of Laodicea (*c.* 381) enjoined Christians not to "judaize" but to work on the sabbath and rest, if possible, on the Lord's Day. The Old Testament commandment of sabbath rest received a spiritual interpretation from the Church Fathers when they applied it to Sunday; *e.g.*, St. Augustine of Hippo held that the sabbath rest from servile work meant abstention from sin (*cf. Tract. in Joannis*, Book III, chapter 19; Book XX, chapter 2).

A literal application of the sabbath law to Sunday became evident in conciliar canons and civil laws of the Frankish kingdoms in the 6th century, climaxed by Charlemagne's capitulary adopted by the Council of Aachen, 789 (canon 80). Medieval legislation thereafter repeatedly sought to enforce the "holiday" of Sunday, as also of many other holy days, for the benefit of serfs and labourers. Even today, Roman Catholic canon law forbids "servile work" on Sunday, unless necessary for public safety, communications, and health (*Codex Juris Canonici*, canon 1247–49).

Sabbatarian laws applied to Sunday were also continued by the Protestant Reformers. The Acts of Uniformity of Edward VI in 1552 and of Elizabeth I in 1559 required all persons to attend worship on Sunday, the latter imposing a fine for neglect to do so. The Church of England's Canons of 1604 (number 13) make similar provision. The Puritans were strongly sabbatarian in sentiment. Many of them referred to Sunday as "the sabbath."

Blue Laws

In the Puritan colonies of New England, the so-called Blue Laws of Sunday observance were especially severe. Today most states and cities in the United States have statutes restricting certain trades and amusements on Sunday. Church laws continue to insist upon the moral obligation to attend worship every Lord's Day.

Advent. The Advent (from Latin *adventus*, "coming") season is peculiar to the Western churches, though its original impulse probably came from the East, where it was common, after the ecumenical Council of Ephesus in 431, to devote sermons on Sundays before Christmas to the theme of the Annunciation. In Ravenna, Italy—a channel of Eastern influences upon the Western Church—St. Peter Chrysologus (died *c.* 450) delivered such homilies (sermons). The earliest reference to a season of Advent is the institution by Bishop Perpetuus of Tours (461–490) of a fast before Christmas, beginning from St. Martin's Day on November 11. Known as St. Martin's Lent, the custom was extended to other Frankish churches by the Council of Mâcon in 581.

The six-week season was adopted by the church of Milan and the churches of Spain. At Rome, there is no indication of Advent before the latter half of the 6th century, when it was reduced—probably by Pope Gregory the Great (reigned 590–604)—to four weeks before Christmas. The longer Gallican season left traces in medieval service books, notably the Use of Sarum (Salisbury), extensively followed in England, with its Sunday before Advent. The coming of Christ in his nativity was overlaid with a second theme, also stemming from Gallican churches, namely, his Second Coming at the end of time. This interweaving of the themes of two advents of Christ gives the season a peculiar tension both of penitence and of joy in expectation of the Lord who is "at hand."

Popular piety in Advent is chiefly devoted to musical and dramatic performances based upon biblical prophecies and stories of the nativity of Christ. In many homes and churches simple devotions are associated with an Advent evergreen wreath, in which four candles are inserted and lighted, one by one, each week, as a symbol of the coming of the "Light" of the world.

Christmas. The word Christmas is derived from the Old English *Cristes maesse*, "Christ's Mass." There is no certain tradition of the date of Christ's birth. Christian chronographers of the 3rd century assumed that the creation of the world took place at the spring equinox, then reckoned as March 25; hence the new creation in the birth and death of Christ must have occurred on the same day. The first notice of a feast of the nativity of Christ occurs in a Roman almanac (the Chronographer of 354, or Philocalian Calendar), which indicates that the festival was observed by the church in Rome by the year 336.

Influence of solar cults

It is commonly supposed that the emperor Constantine was influential in the institution of a Christian feast of "the birthday of the Sun of Righteousness" (Mal. 4:2) as a rival to the popular pagan festival of the Unconquered Sun (Sol Invictus) at the winter solstice. This cult of Oriental origin, syncretistic (fusing the beliefs of many cults) but leaning toward monotheism, had received official recognition by the emperor Aurelian in 274. It was popular in the armies of the Illyrian (Balkan) emperors of Rome of the late 3rd century, and to it Constantine himself had adhered before his conversion to Christianity in 312. But the exact circumstances of the beginning of Christmas Day at Rome remain obscure.

From Rome the feast spread to other churches of the West and East, the last to adopt it being the Church of Jerusalem in the time of Bishop Juvenal (424–458). Coordinated with Epiphany, a feast of Eastern origin commemorating the manifestation of Christ to the world, the celebration of the incarnation of Christ as Redeemer and Light of the world was favoured by the intense concern of the church of the 4th and 5th centuries in formulating creeds and dogmatic definitions relating to Christ's divine and human natures.

Christmas is the most popular of all festivals among Christians and many non-Christians alike, and its observance combines many strands of tradition. From the ancient Roman pagan festivals of Saturnalia (December 17) and New Year's come the merrymaking and exchange of presents. Old Germanic midwinter customs have contributed the lighting of the Yule log and decorations with evergreens. The Christmas tree comes from medieval German mystery plays centred in representations of the Tree of Paradise (Gen. 2:9). St. Francis of Assisi popularized the Christmas crib, or crèche, in his celebration at Greccio, Italy, in 1223.

Another popular medieval feast was that of St. Nicholas of Myra (c. 340) on December 6, when the saint was believed to visit children with admonitions and gifts, in preparation for the gift of the Christ child at Christmas. Through the Dutch, the tradition of St. Nicholas (Sinter Klaas, hence "Santa Claus") was brought to America in their colony of New Amsterdam, now New York. The sending of greeting cards at Christmas began in Britain in the 1840s and was introduced to the United States in the 1870s.

Epiphany. In Hellenistic times an epiphany (from the Greek *epiphania*, "manifestation") or appearance of divine power in a person or event was a common religious concept. The New Testament uses the word to denote the final appearing of Christ at the end of time; but in II Tim. 1:10 it refers to his coming as Saviour on earth. In this latter sense, a festival of Christ's epiphany is first attested among heretical Gnostic Christians (those who believed that man was saved by secret knowledge, not faith, and that matter was evil and the spiritual world good) in Egypt in the late 2nd century (Clement of Alexandria, *Stromata*, Book I, chapter 21), on January 6, when he was manifested as Son of God at his baptism. The date is that of an ancient Egyptian solstice, celebrated by pagans as a time of overflow of the waters of the Nile, and in certain mystery cults as the occasion of the birth of a new aeon, or age, from the virgin goddess Kore, daughter of the earth-mother goddess Demeter. In other places of the Middle East, the time was associated with miraculous fountains from which wine flowed in place of water.

Origin of Epiphany celebrations

Nothing more is known of an Epiphany feast until the 4th century, when it appears in the Eastern churches as a festival second in rank only to Easter. It commemorated three "manifestations": the birth, the Baptism, and the first miracle of the Lord at Cana (John 2:1 ff.). In the latter half of the century Eastern and Western churches adopted each other's incarnation festival, thus establishing the 12-day celebration from Christmas to Epiphany. The particular emphasis in the Eastern feast upon the Baptism of Christ led to special liturgical ceremonies of the blessing of waters and the ministration of Baptism at this time. In the West, where Christmas was the primary festival, the Epiphany was associated particularly with the Adoration of the Magi to the infant Jesus (Matt. 2:1–12), as anticipation of the universal redemption of Christ in his "Manifestation to the Gentiles."

The 12 days of Christmas

Pre-Lent. The season of Pre-Lent is peculiar to the Western churches. It developed in the 6th century as a time of special supplication for God's protection and defense in a period of great suffering in Italy from war, pestilence, and famine. It is marked by three Sundays before the beginning of Lent, called, respectively, Septuagesima, Sexagesima, and Quinquagesima—roughly 70, 60, and 50 days before Easter. Though not included in the discipline of Lenten penitence and fast, the season is related by some authorities to influences from the East, especially upon Roman monastic customs, for a longer Lent of eight weeks.

Shrove Tuesday, the day before Ash Wednesday (the initial day of Lent), is in many places a day of carnival, though its name derives from the custom of going to confession for absolution and penance before Lent (from the Middle English word *shriven*, "to shrive"). A famous carnival is that of Mardi Gras (French "fat Tuesday") in New Orleans.

Lent. The Lenten (from Middle English *lenten*, "spring") season is rooted in the preparation of candidates for Baptism at the Paschal vigil. For several weeks they received intensive instruction, each session followed by prayer and exorcism. The earliest detailed account of these ceremonies is in the *Apostolic Tradition* of Hippolytus, c. 200. At the conclusion of this period all the faithful joined the catechumens (inquirers for instruction) in a strict fast on the Friday and Saturday before Easter. These were the days "when the Bridegroom was taken away" (cf. Mark 2:20).

As a 40-day period (six weeks) Lent is mentioned in

canon 5 of the first ecumenical Council of Nicaea in 325. In the 4th century instruction of the baptismal candidates was normally given by the bishop. Several such "catechetical lectures" on the creed and sacraments have come down to us, notably those of Cyril of Jerusalem (died 386?) and Theodore of Mopsuestia (died 428). St. Augustine's treatise *De catechizandis rudibus* (c. 400) gave a less dogmatic and more biblical and historical approach. The Roman Church organized its instruction around three (later seven) "scrutinies," at which the catechumens were introduced to the Gospels, the Apostles' Creed, and the Lord's Prayer.

Since Sunday was never a fast day, piety sought to conform the Lenten fast exactly to 40 days, after the examples of the 40 days in the wilderness of Moses, Elijah, and Christ. In the Eastern churches, where Saturdays were also excluded from fasting, this developed into an eight-week Lent. At Rome, from the late 5th century, the fast began on Wednesday before the first Sunday in Lent. During Lent also, grievous sinners were excluded from Communion and prepared for their restoration. As a sign of their penitence, they wore sackcloth and were sprinkled with ashes (Tertullian, *De paenitentia* 11; cf. the biblical precedents: Jer. 6:26; Jonah 3:6; Matt. 11:21). This form of public penance began to die out in the 9th century. At the same time it became customary for all the faithful to be reminded of the need for penitence, by receiving an imposition of ashes on their foreheads on the first day of Lent—hence the name Ash Wednesday.

Ash Wednesday and Holy Week

The last week of Lent was one of special devotion in remembrance of the Lord's Passion. St. Athanasius (c. 295–373) in his *Festal Letter* of 330 called it "holy Paschal week." The Church of Jerusalem in particular organized dramatic ceremonies during the week at appropriate holy sites of its neighbourhood. A detailed description is contained in the account of a Spanish nun (c. 395), *Peregrinatio ad loca sancta* (Sections 30–38). From Jerusalem many of these ceremonies, such as the Palm Sunday procession and the Good Friday veneration of the cross, spread to other churches.

The Roman liturgy of Holy Week begins with the blessing of palms and a procession on Sunday, with a solemn rendition of St. Matthew's Passion narrative at the mass. On Thursday the bishop blesses the sacred oils for the catechumens and sick and the chrism (oil) for confirmation, and, in ancient times, penitents were reconciled for their Easter Communion. After a festal mass commemorating the institution of the Eucharist, the altars are stripped and washed. An additional ceremony, of medieval origin, has given its name to this day—the washing of feet, in imitation of the Lord's action at the Last Supper (John 13:2–15). It is popularly called the Maundy, from the anthem sung during the ceremony (Mandatum, "a new commandment," John 13:34).

Maundy Thursday

Another medieval custom, which has had a popular revival today, is the service of Tenebrae, held on Wednesday, Thursday, and Friday, in the evening. It is the old choir office of Matins and Lauds, originally sung before dawn and marked by the gradual extinguishing of candles before the breaking of the light of day.

On Good Friday (the day commemorating the crucifixion of Christ), the Mass of the Presanctified is observed, its name being derived from the fact that there is no consecration of the sacred elements of bread and wine but with Communion ministered from the Reserved Sacrament (consecrated elements retained from previous celebrations). Other features are the singing of the Passion according to John, the impressive series of intercessions, and the adoration of the cross with singing of the Reproaches and the hymn "Pange lingua" ("Sing, my tongue, the glorious battle"). Following the Communion and dismissal of the people, there are no further liturgical rites other than the daily choir offices until the vigil of Easter.

Easter. The term Easter, commemorating the resurrection of Christ, comes from the Old English *ēaster* or *ēastre*, a festival of spring; the Greek and Latin Pascha, from the Hebrew Pesaḥ, "Passover." The earliest Christians celebrated the Lord's Passover at the same time as the Jews, during the night of the first full moon of the first month of spring (Nisan 14–15). By the middle of the 2nd century, most churches had transferred this celebration to the Sunday after the Jewish feast. But certain churches of Asia Minor clung to the older custom, for which they were denounced as "judaizing" (Eusebius, *Ecclesiastical History*, Book V, chapters 23–25). The first ecumenical Council of Nicaea in 325 decreed that all churches should observe the feast together on a Sunday. Yet many disparities remained in the way the several churches calculated the date of Easter. Today the Eastern churches follow the Julian calendar, the Western churches its correction by Pope Gregory XIII in 1582, so that in some years there may be a month's difference in the time of celebration.

Differences in the celebration of Easter

The Easter celebration continues for 50 days, to and including the Feast of Pentecost. In the early church, as on all Sundays, there was no fasting or kneeling in prayer during the period.

The liturgy began with a solemn vigil on Saturday evening. A new fire was lit for the blessing of the Paschal candle (the Exultet)—symbol of the driving away of the powers of darkness and death by the Passover of the Lord. There followed a series of lessons from the Old Testament, with a homily based upon the narrative of Exodus 12. Then, toward midnight, while the faithful were engaged in prayers, candidates for Baptism were taken to the baptistery for their initiation. Returning to the assembly, they were confirmed by the bishop with chrism and the laying on of hands, and toward dawn the Easter Eucharist was completed. A similar celebration was repeated on the eve of Pentecost for those who were hindered from receiving Baptism at Easter.

As at Christmas, so also at Easter, popular customs reflect many ancient pagan survivals—in this instance, connected with spring fertility rites, such as the symbols of the Easter egg and the Easter hare or rabbit. The Easter lamb, however, comes from the Jewish Passover ritual, as applied to Christ, "the Lamb of God" (*cf.* John 1:29, 36; I Cor. 5:7).

Ascension. At first, the church commemorated the Ascension (from the Latin *ascensio*, "ascent") of Christ into heaven, after his Resurrection (Luke 24:50–51; Acts 1:1–11), as part of the total victory of Christ celebrated from Easter to Pentecost. A special feast of the Ascension is not mentioned before the 4th century. The Spanish Council of Elvira, *c.* 300, appears to have rejected it as an unwarranted innovation. But by the end of the 4th century the feast had become universal in the church, on the 40th day after Easter.

The old English popular name for the feast is Holy Thursday, but there is no liturgical tradition to support the idea of an "Ascensiontide" as a season distinct from Easter. From the 10th century there developed an "octave" of Ascension, which was adopted at Rome in the 12th century but suppressed in 1955. The three days before Ascension Day, known as Minor Rogation Days, were instituted by Bishop Mamertus of Vienne (Gaul) in 470 and extended to all the Frankish churches at the Council of Orléans in 511. Pope Leo III (reigned 795–816) adopted them at Rome. They are observed by processional litanies and fasting as a supplication for clement weather for the crops and deliverance from pestilence and famine.

Pentecost. The Jews had an early harvest festival seven weeks after the firstfruit offerings of Passover, called the Feast of Weeks. The Priestly Code (Lev. 23:15–16) assigned it to "the morrow after the seventh sabbath" —which would be a Sunday. Early rabbinic tradition (Babylonian Talmud, *Pesaḥim* 68b) associated the festival with the giving of the Law at Sinai, on the basis of Ex. 19:1.

New Testament origins of Pentecost

The Christian festival of Pentecost (from the Greek *pentecoste*, "50th day"), unlike Easter, is not rooted in Judaism but is based upon the narrative of Acts 2, recording the gift of the Holy Spirit to the disciples and the launching of the church's mission to all peoples on the Pentecost that followed the Lord's Resurrection. The outpouring of the Spirit was the final seal upon Christ's redemptive work, a sign of the inauguration of the new age when the Law was fulfilled and the way to salvation opened to the Gentile peoples. For this reason the early Christians considered Pentecost to be included in, but climactic of, the great "50 days" of Easter. Pentecost was in fact the name commonly given by the early Fathers to the whole season.

As early as the 5th century, baptisms were administered at Pentecost to those unable to be initiated at Easter, and a vigil rite was developed comparable to that of the Pascha (Leo the Great, *Letters* 16; Leonine and Gelasian sacramentaries). The Anglo-Saxons called the feast White Sunday (Whitsunday), from the white garments bestowed upon the newly baptized (*cf.* Bede, *Ecclesiastical History*, Book II, chapter 9; *Penitential* of Archbishop Theodore of Tarsus, 668–690). The term Whitsunday has been customary in the Anglican churches since the First Prayer Book of Edward VI (1549).

Pentecost or Trinity Season. The Sundays after Pentecost mark the season of the life of the church between the two advents of Christ as it fulfills its mission to the world under the guidance of the Spirit.

Bishop Stephen of Liège (902–920) instituted a Feast of the Holy Trinity on the first Sunday after Pentecost, which spread to many religious orders and churches of northern Europe. It was taken up in the Use of Sarum and was accepted at Rome in 1334 by Pope John XXII. It became common to date the Sundays after this feast, instead of after Pentecost, as in the Roman liturgy, and this practice is still followed by the Carthusians and the Dominicans and in the Lutheran and Anglican churches.

Saints' days and other holy days. The celebration of days in honour of the saints or "heroes of the faith" is an extension of the devotion paid to Christ, since they are commemorated for the virtues in life and death that derive from his grace and holiness. Originally each local church had its own calendar. Standardization came with the fixation of the rites of the great patriarchal sees, which began in the 4th century and was completed for the Byzantine churches in the 9th century. The Roman calendar of the Gregorian Sacramentary became the basis of the Western Church's observances with the liturgical reform of Charlemagne (*c.* 800), but it was constantly supplemented throughout the Middle Ages by new additions from diocesan or provincial areas. It was not until 1634 that the Roman see gained complete control over the veneration and canonization of saints in the Roman Catholic Church subject to its jurisdiction.

Before the toleration of the Christian Church under Constantine (AD 312), the several churches commemorated only their martyrs, on the anniversaries of their deaths, commonly called their *natale*, or birthday, with rites similar to those of Easter. By giving up life for his faith, often after cruel tortures, the martyr was the supreme example of the imitation of Christ. The earliest attested institution of such an anniversary is recorded in the *Martyrdom of Polycarp* of Smyrna (*c.* 155). The oldest Roman calendar of the martyrs reaches only to the beginning of the 3rd century and includes the joint martyrdom of its apostolic founders SS. Peter and Paul (June 29), a feast apparently instituted in the year 258.

Veneration of martyrs and the relics of saints

After the age of the martyrs, the calendars continued to be enriched by entries of eminent bishops, teachers, ascetics, and missionaries. Other new feasts were associated with the transfer of the relics of saints to sumptuous shrines or churches dedicated in their honour. A precedent of great influence was the feast of dedication of the Church of the Holy Sepulchre (or Anastasis, "resurrection") at Jerusalem, on September 14, 335, where the discovered tomb and cross of Christ were enshrined on the supposed site of his victory over death. The feast is popularly called Holy Cross Day. From the 4th to the 6th centuries many "inventions" or discoveries of relics were produced and fictitious "Acts" written to promote the cultus of apostles, evangelists, and hitherto unknown martyrs of earlier times.

In the late 4th century, a feast of All Martyrs was observed by the East Syrians on May 13 and by the West Syrians and Byzantines on the Sunday after Pentecost. Pope Boniface IV received from the emperor Phocas (died 610) the Pantheon at Rome, which he dedicated on May 13 to St. Mary and All Martyrs. The Feast of All Saints at Rome on November 1 was promulgated by Pope Gregory IV in 835, in place of the May festival. Some authorities believe this festival to be of Irish origin; others relate it to a chapel of All Saints in St. Peter's Basilica established by Pope Gregory III (reigned 731–741).

Venera-
tion of
Mary

Liturgical feasts in honour of St. Mary—related to the incarnation cycle—developed in the East after the third ecumenical Council of Ephesus in 431, where she was declared to be Theotokos ("God-bearer"). At Rome the earliest special commemoration was on the Octave of Christmas, but Pope Sergius I (reigned 687–701), an Easterner, introduced to Rome her four major feasts: her Nativity (September 8); Purification of the Blessed Virgin Mary (February 2, with its procession of candles—hence "Candlemas"); Annunciation (March 25); and Assumption (August 15).

LITURGICAL COLOURS

The early Christians had no system of colours associated with the seasons, nor do the Eastern Churches to this day have any rules or traditions in this matter. The Roman emperor Constantine gave Bishop Macarius of Jerusalem (died between 331 and 335) a "sacred robe . . . fashioned with golden threads" for use at baptisms (Theodoret, *Ecclesiastical History*, Book II, chapter 23). Toward the end of the 4th century, references are made to shining white garments worn by celebrants at the Eucharist (*Apostolic Constitutions*, Book VIII, chapter 12; Jerome, *Dialogi contra Pelagianos*, Book I, chapter 29). Inventories of Frankish churches in the 9th century reveal a variety of colours used for vestments, but without any particular sequence for their use; but the *Ordo* of St. Amand of the same period refers specifically to dark vestments at the major litanies and black ones at the Feast of Purification (February 2).

The modern colour sequence of the Roman Catholic Church is first outlined in Pope Innocent III's treatise *De sacro altaris mysterio* (Book I, chapter 65, written before his election as pope in 1198), though some variations are admitted. White, as a symbol of purity, is used on all feasts of the Lord (including Maundy Thursday and All Saints') and feasts of confessors and virgins. Red is used at Pentecost, recalling the fiery tongues that descended upon the Apostles when they received the Holy Spirit, and also at feasts of the Holy Cross, Apostles, and martyrs, as symbol of their bloody passions (sufferings and deaths). Black is used as a symbol of mourning on days of fasting and penitence and at commemorations of the departed—but violet, symbolizing the mitigation of black, is allowed during Advent, Pre-Lent, and Lent. Green is used on other days, without special significance, as a compromise colour distinguished from white, red, and black. Innocent's symbolism is based upon allegorical (symbolic) interpretations of colours and flowers mentioned in Scripture, especially in the Song of Solomon.

In the later Middle Ages other colours were used in various churches, such as blue for certain feasts of the Virgin Mary, and rose (a mitigation of violet) on the third Sunday in Advent and the fourth Sunday in Lent. The missal of Pope Pius V in 1570 prescribed the sequence of Innocent III, with rose on the two Sundays mentioned. In 1868 the Congregation of Rites allowed the use of gold vestments in place of white, red, and green. Medieval English uses showed much variation, but the predominant principle was use of the finest vestments, of whatever colour, on great feasts, and others on lesser days of importance. In the Sarum Use, white, red, and blue were the primary colours; but in Lent an unbleached cloth was customary, changing to deep red during the two weeks before Easter.

Anglican and Lutheran churches have in recent times generally followed the Roman sequence, although some Anglican churches have restored the colours of the Sarum Use. In the liturgical experiments of the present time, the sequences and symbolism inherited from the Middle Ages are being abandoned, and a greater freedom is evident in paraments (vestments and hangings), with increasing variety and combinations of colours, especially on festal occasions.

CURRENT REVISIONS

At the present time in the Western churches the church year is undergoing an overall revision comparable in scope only to that of the 16th century. This is due to a number of currents of interest that are converging; *i.e.,* advances in historical and liturgical studies, changes in theological perspectives, and ecumenical encounters.

Roman Catholic Church. The first stage was the revised calendar issued by Pope John XXIII in 1960. The "Constitution on the Sacred Liturgy" of the second Vatican Council called for further reforms. These have been completed in the new calendar and lectionary promulgated by Pope Paul VI in 1969.

The most important feature of the new calendar is the restoration of all Sundays as feasts of Christ. No saints' days, even of the Virgin Mary, may take precedence of a Sunday. In the Proper of Time, the season of Pre-Lent has been eliminated, and two cycles are provided: (1) the principal seasons, Sundays, and holy days from Advent to Pentecost and (2) a schedule of 33 Sundays per annum to be observed in sequence for the Sundays after Epiphany and after Pentecost. The ancient Roman Feast of St. Mary has been restored to the octave of Christmas (January 1); a new Feast of the Baptism of Christ has been assigned to the first Sunday after Epiphany; and the Feast of Christ the King has been shifted to the last Sunday after Pentecost. All octaves have been eliminated.

The
revised
Roman
Catholic
calendar

A considerable simplification, reclassification, and in many cases shifting of dates have been made in the Proper of Saints. Except for 13 "solemnities" (including major feasts of Christ) and 25 "feasts," all other saints' days and holy days have been reduced to "memorials," either obligatory or optional—with the right of national and regional episcopal conferences to alter their rank. Ember and Rogation Days have been assigned as votive masses to be observed according to regional directives.

Protestant churches. The revisions of Lutheran and Anglican service books, currently in progress, are influenced by the new designs of the Roman calendar, notably proposals to eliminate Pre-Lent and to name Sundays after Pentecost instead of after Trinity. Anglican calendars are also enriching their entries with many nonbiblical saints and holy days, but for optional observance. Among the traditionally nonliturgical Protestant churches, new service books and hymnals exhibit interest in recovering the major seasons of the Proper of Time, from Advent to Pentecost, and in some cases the Feast of All Saints. Especially significant is the restoration of the seasons in the Presbyterian churches of Scotland and America, evident in the *Book of Common Order of the Church of Scotland* (Church of Scotland, 1940), *The Directory for the Worship of God* (United Presbyterian Church in the U.S.A.), and *The Book of Church Order of the Presbyterian Church in the United States* (Presbyterian Church in the U.S., 1964).

Fixed date of Easter. Since 1900 various religious, business, and professional groups have promoted the concept of a fixed world calendar, which would include a fixed date for Easter. Proposals have been placed before the League of Nations and its successor, the United Nations.

The second Vatican Council in its "Constitution on the Sacred Liturgy" (1963) accepted the principle of a fixed date for Easter, subject to approval by other churches, provided that no world calendar impaired the regular succession of a seven-day week. The World Council of Churches in the early 1970s was canvassing its member bodies to this end, and a large majority had replied in favour of such a change. An Easter message of Athenagoras I, the Orthodox Patriarch of Constantinople, in 1969, called for a resolution of the differences between the Eastern and Western churches and a search for a common date. Among those preferring a fixed date for the observance of Easter—regardless of the issue respecting a common world calendar—the second Sunday in April is widely proposed.

BIBLIOGRAPHY. L. DUCHESNE, *Christian Worship*, ch. 8 (1919), is fundamental, but should be supplemented by later handbooks, such as J.A. JUNGMANN, *Public Worship*, ch. 9 (1957; orig. pub. in German, 1955); and J.H. MILLER, *Fundamentals of the Liturgy*, ch. 8 (1960). Good summary accounts are those of N.M. DENIS-BOULET, *The Christian Calendar* (1960; orig. pub. in French, 1959); and A.A. MCARTHUR, *Evolution of the Christian Year* (1953). More popular treatments, valuable for their detail of popular observance, are the works of F.X. WEISER, *The Christmas Book* (1952); *The Easter Book* (1954); *The Holyday Book* (1956); and *Handbook of Christian Feasts and Customs* (1958). Insights into primitive and non-Christian backgrounds of the church year are contained in MIRCEA ELIADE, *The Myth of the Eternal Return* (1955; orig. pub. in French, 1949); E.O. JAMES, *Seasonal Feasts and Festivals* (1961); and especially for the incarnation cycle. H. RAHNER, *Greek Myths and Christian Mystery* (1963). A standard monograph on the origin of the seven-day week is F.H. COLSON, *The Week* (1926); more exhaustive and detailed is W. RORDORF, *Sunday* (1968; orig. pub. in German, 1962). For the first three centuries, see M.H. SHEPHERD, *The Paschal Liturgy and the Apocalypse* (1960). Medieval developments of a special character are outlined in J.W. TYRER, *Historical Survey of Holy Week* (1932). C.A. SEIDENSPINNER, *Great Protestant Festivals* (1952), defends nontraditional observances in modern Protestant churches.

(M.H.S.)

Cicero

Cicero, a Roman statesman, lawyer, scholar, and writer, who in vain upheld republican principles in the civil struggles that destroyed the Republic of Rome, is best remembered as the greatest Roman orator and innovator of what became known as Ciceronian rhetoric.

Cicero, marble bust. In the Capitoline Museum, Rome.
By courtesy of the Musei Capitolini, Rome; photograph, Oscar Savio

He was born Marcus Tullius Cicero in 106 BC in Arpinum (Arpino), of a wealthy local family. Admirably educated in Rome and in Greece, he did military service in 89 under Pompeius Strabo (the father of Pompey) and made his first appearance in the courts defending Quinctius in 81.

His brilliant defense, in 80 or early 79, of Sextus Roscius on a fabricated charge of parricide established his reputation at the bar, and he started his public career as quaestor (an office of financial administration) in western Sicily in 75. His skill as a lawyer was confirmed in 70 by his unorthodox prosecution of Gaius Verres (governor of Sicily, 73–71 BC) for extortion; restricting himself to a short speech, he relied on the evidence of witnesses to secure a condemnation.

Prosecution of Verres

As praetor, a judicial office of great power at this time, in 66 he made his first important political speech, when, against Catulus and leading Optimates (the conservative element in the Senate), he spoke in favour of conferring on Pompey command of the campaign against Mithridates, king of Pontus. His relationship with Pompey, whose hatred of Marcus Licinius Crassus he shared, was to be the focal point of his career in politics. His election as consul for 63 was achieved through Optimates who feared the revolutionary ideas of his rival, Catiline.

Consulship. In the first of his consular speeches, he opposed the agrarian bill of Servilius Rullus, in the interest of the absent Pompey; but his chief concern was to discover and make public the seditious intentions of Catiline, who, defeated in 64, appeared again at the consular elections in 63 (over which Cicero presided, wearing armour beneath his toga). Catiline lost and now planned to carry out armed uprisings in Italy and arson in Rome. Cicero had difficulty in persuading the Senate of the danger, but the "last decree" (*Senatus consultum ultimum*), something like a proclamation of martial law, was passed on October 22. On November 8, after escaping an attempt on his life, Cicero delivered the first speech against Catiline in the Senate, and Catiline left Rome that night. Evidence incriminating the conspirators was secured on the night of December 2–3 through Gallic envoys who were arrested leaving Rome, and on December 5, after a senatorial debate in which Cato spoke for execution and Caesar against, they were executed on Cicero's responsibility. Cicero, announcing their death to the crowd with the single word *vixerunt* ("they are dead"), received a tremendous ovation from all classes, which inspired his subsequent appeal in politics to *concordia ordinum*, "concord between the classes." He was hailed by Catulus as "father of his country." This was the climax of his career.

Execution of Catiline

In his exposure of the conspiracy he acted admirably, as even his critics agreed (*e.g.*, Marcus Junius Brutus, who called him *optimus consul*, and the historian Sallust in the *Conspiracy of Catiline*), but, though he never regretted the execution of the conspirators, its legality was doubtful. Its authority was the "last decree" passed by the Senate, but this administrative enactment, first employed in 121, which denied the fundamental right of a Roman citizen to trial before execution, had never been approved by the Populares, the opponents of senatorial domination in government, and had indeed been challenged with Caesar's encouragement during the course of a murder trial in the summer of 63.

Exile. At the end of 60, Cicero declined Caesar's invitation to join the political alliance of Caesar, Crassus, and Pompey, which he considered unconstitutional, and also Caesar's offer in 59 of a place on his staff in Gaul. When Publius Clodius, whom Cicero had antagonized by speaking and giving evidence against him when he was tried for profanity early in 61, became tribune in 58, Cicero was in danger, and in March, disappointed by Pompey's refusal to help him, fled Rome. On the following day Clodius carried a bill forbidding the execution of a Roman citizen without trial. Clodius then carried through a second law, of doubtful legality, declaring Cicero an exile. Through his gangsters, Clodius destroyed Cicero's house on the Palatine Hill, which he had bought in 62, and his villas at Tusculum and Formiae.

Cicero went first to Thessalonica, in Macedonia, and then to Illyricum. In 57, thanks to the activity of Pompey and particularly the tribune Milo, he was recalled on August 4. Cicero landed at Brundisium (Brindisi) on that day and was warmly acclaimed all along his route to Rome, where he arrived a month later. His precipitate departure from Rome, which he had previously deplored, he now viewed and represented to the Romans as an act of altruistic heroism.

Alignment with Pompey, Caesar, and Crassus. In winter 57–56 Cicero attempted unsuccessfully to estrange Pompey from Caesar. Pompey disregarded Cicero's advice and renewed his compact with Caesar and Crassus at Luca in April 56. Cicero now agreed, under pressure from Pompey, to align himself with the three in politics, and he committed himself in writing to this effect (the "palinode"). The speech *De provinciis consularibus* marked his new alliance. He was obliged to accept a number of distasteful defenses (in particular that of Publius Vatinius, Caesarian tribune of 59, and Aulus Gabinius, the unfriendly consul of 58 who helped to exile him), and he abandoned public life. In the next few years he completed the *De oratore* (55) and *De republica* (started in 54, finished in 52) and began the *De legibus* (52). In 52 he was delighted when Milo killed Clodius but failed disastrously in his defense of Milo (later written for publication, the *Pro Milone*).

De oratore and De republica

In 51 he was persuaded to leave Rome to govern the province of Cilicia, in south Asia Minor, for a year, with a strong subordinate staff, which included his brother, Quintus, and Gaius Pomptinus, both former praetors and experienced soldiers. The province had been expecting a Parthian invasion, but it never materialized, although Cicero did suppress some brigands on Mt. Amanus. The Senate granted a *supplicatio* (a period of public thanksgiving), although Cicero had hoped for a triumph, a processional return through the city, on his return to Rome. All admitted that he governed Cilicia with integrity.

Return to Rome. By the time Cicero returned to Rome, Pompey and Caesar were struggling for complete power. He was in the outskirts of Rome when Caesar crossed the Rubicon and invaded Italy in January 49. Cicero met Pompey outside Rome on January 17 and accepted a commission to supervise recruiting in Campania. He did not leave Italy with Pompey on March 17, however. His indecision was not discreditable, though his criticism of Pompey's strategy was inexpert. In an interview with Caesar on March 28, Cicero showed great courage in stating his own terms—his intention of proposing in the Senate that Caesar should not pursue the war against Pompey any further—though they were terms that Caesar could not possibly accept. He sailed from Gaeta to join Pompey on June 7; in 48 he left Pompey's camp for Dyrrhachium because of illness, refused the command of the republican forces after Pompey's defeat at Pharsalus, and returned to Italy in October 48, after receiving a guarantee of safety from Caesar. He disapproved of Caesar's dictatorship; yet he realized that in the succession of battles (which continued until 45) he would have been one of the first victims of Caesar's enemies, had they triumphed. This was his second period of intensive literary production, works of this period including the *Brutus, Paradoxa, Orator* in 46; *De finibus* in 45; and *Tusculanae disputationes, De natura deorum,* and *De officiis,* finished after Caesar's murder, in 44.

Cicero was not involved in the conspiracy to kill Caesar on March 15, 44, and was not present in the Senate when he was murdered. On March 17 he spoke in the Senate in favour of a general amnesty, but then he returned to his philosophical writing and contemplated visiting his son, who was studying in Athens. But instead he returned to Rome at the end of August, and his 14 Philippic orations (so called in imitation of Demosthenes' speeches against Philip II of Macedonia), the first delivered on September 2, 44, the last on April 21, 43, mark his vigorous re-entry into politics. His policy was to make every possible use of Caesar's adopted son Octavian, whose mature intelligence he seriously underestimated, and to drive the Senate, against its own powerful inclination toward compromise, to declare war on Antony, who had controlled events immediately following Caesar's death and who now was pursuing one of the assassins in Cisalpine Gaul. No letters survive to show how Octavian deceived Cicero in the interval between the defeat of Antony in Cisalpine Gaul on April 14 and Octavian's march on Rome to secure the consulship in August. It was in May that Octavian learned of Cicero's unfortunate remark that "the young man should be given praise, distinctions—and then be disposed of." The triumvirate of Octavian, Antony, and Lepidus was formed at the end of October, and Cicero was soon being sought for execution. He was captured and killed near Caieta on December 7. His head and hands were displayed on the *rostra,* the speakers' platform at the Forum, at Rome.

Death of Caesar

Political judgment. In politics Cicero constantly denigrated his opponents and exaggerated the virtues of his friends. As a "new man," a man without noble ancestry, he was never accepted by the dominant circle of Optimates, and he attributed his own political misfortunes after 63 partly to the jealousy, partly to the spineless unconcern, of the complacent Optimates. The close political association with Pompey for which he longed was never achieved. He was more ready than some men to compromise ideals in order to preserve the republic, but, though he came to admit in the *De republica* that republican government required the presence of a powerful individual—an idealized Pompey perhaps—to ensure its stability, he showed little appreciation of the intrinsic weaknesses of Roman republican administration (the failure of legislation to check bribery, the absence of machinery for enforcing law and order in Rome, the powerlessness of the government to control the armies). His appeal in 63 to the concept of *concordia ordinum* and his eloquent but unconvincing demonstration in the *Pro Sestio* in 56 that there was no fundamental incompatibility between Optimates and Populares did not touch the fringe of the real problems.

Cicero's marriage to Terentia, a woman of wealth and breeding, in 80, produced, probably in 79, a daughter, Tullia, and, in 65, a son, Marcus. He divorced Terentia in late 47 or early 46 and married Publilia, a girl of 15, for her money. Tullia, to whom he was devoted, married three times and died in February 45. Soon afterward Cicero divorced his second wife. His brother and nephew were killed in the proscriptions of 43 after the triumvirate had been formed; his unattractive son, Marcus, escaped, fought at Philippi, was reconciled to Octavian, and became consul in 30. Though barristers were forbidden by law to receive more than a token fee, Cicero's money was made at the bar (often through legacies of grateful clients). He was extravagant, especially in the number of his villas, and continually in difficulty over money.

Marriage and children

Letters. From Cicero's correspondence between 67 and July 43 BC over 900 letters survive, and, of the 835 written by Cicero himself, 416 were to his friend, financial adviser, and publisher, the knight Titus Pomponius Atticus, and 419 to one or other of some 94 different friends, acquaintances, and relatives. The number obviously constitutes only a small portion of the letters that Cicero wrote and received. Many letters that were current in antiquity have not survived; for instance, the account of the suppression of Catiline's conspiracy, mentioned in the *Pro Sulla* and *Pro Plancio,* which Cicero sent to Pompey at the end of 63; Pompey hardly as much as acknowledged it, and Cicero was mocked about it in public later. Many letters were evidently suppressed for political reasons after Cicero's death. Therefore nothing survives of the letters written by Atticus, of Cicero's correspondence with Octavian in 44–43, or of his letters to Atticus later than November 44.

There are four collections of the letters: to Atticus (*Ad Atticum*) in 16 books; to his friends (*Ad familiares*) in 16 books; to Brutus; and, in three books, to his brother (*Ad Quintum fratrem*). His most unguarded and self-revelatory letters were to Atticus and Quintus. In his letters to Atticus, he constantly resorted to Greek quotations and sayings for the *mot juste.*

The idea of publishing some of his letters was entertained by Cicero in 45, and in July 44 his freedman Tiro had collected about 70 that were to form the basis of the publication. These doubtless included specimens of elaborate, fine writing, such as the invitation to L. Lucceius in 56 to write a monograph on Cicero's consulship, which Cicero himself thought a particularly good letter. But the publication did not take place in Cicero's lifetime, and, when the letters were published, many were trivial; for instance, the 81 letters of personal recommendation, mostly to provincial governors on behalf of friends, which constitute *Ad familiares* (book 13).

The letters constitute a primary historical source such as exists for no other part of the ancient world. They often enable events to be dated with a precision that would not otherwise be possible, and they have been

Impor-
tance of
the letters

used, though with no very great success, to discredit the accuracy of Caesar's commentaries on the civil war. Cicero's personal character has been assailed most unfairly on the basis of his letters describing his extravagant despair in exile and his (understandable) indecision in the early months of 49. On the other hand, his reporting of events, naturally enough, is not objective, and he was capable of misremembering or misrepresenting past events so as to enhance his own credit.

Cicero as a poet. Cicero is a minor but by no means negligible figure in the history of Latin poetry. His best known poems (which survive only in fragments) were the epics *De consulatu suo* (*On His Consulship*) and *De temporibus suis* (*On His Life and Times*), which were criticized in antiquity for their self-praise. Cicero's verse is technically important; he refined the hexameter, using words of two or three syllables at the end of a line, so that the natural word accent would coincide with the beat of the metre, and applying rhetorical devices to poetry; he is one of those who made possible the achievement of Virgil. He was unsympathetic to contemporary trends in poetry. Fragments of his translations from Homer and the Greek dramatists also survive.

Cicero as an orator. Cicero made his reputation as an orator in politics and in the law courts, where he preferred appearing for the defense (though his prosecution of Verres is perhaps his most famous case) and generally spoke last because of his emotive powers. Unfortunately, not all his cases were as morally sound as the attack on Verres. In his day Roman orators were divided between "Asians," with a rich, florid, grandiose style, of which Quintus Hortensius was the chief exponent, and the direct simplicity of the "Atticists," such as Caesar and Brutus. Cicero refused to attach himself to any school. He was trained by Molon of Rhodes, whose own tendencies were eclectic, and he believed that an orator should command and blend a variety of styles. He made a close study of the rhythms that were likely to appeal to an audience, especially in the closing cadences of a sentence or phrase. Cicero's rhetoric was a complex art form, and the ears of the audience were keenly attuned to these effects. Of the speeches, 58 have survived, some in an incomplete form; it is estimated that about 48 have been lost. Some of the speeches were revised for publication; the most notable is *Pro Milone*. Cicero's original speech was unsuccessful, and he rewrote it and sent it to Milo, in exile at Massilia (Marseilles), who had the wit and grace to say that if the revised version had been given he would never have sampled the excellent local fish. It is, in any event, unlikely that procedure in a Roman court permitted the sort of continuous address that the published speeches represent, and it is known that Cicero relied to some extent on improvisation. Nonetheless, it need not be supposed that the versions extant are radically altered from the originals.

The
equipment
of an
orator

Cicero in *Brutus* implicitly gives his own description of his equipment as an orator—a thorough knowledge of literature, a grounding in philosophy, legal expertise, a storehouse of history, the capacity to tie up an opponent and reduce the jury to laughter, the ability to lay down general principles applicable to the particular case, entertaining digressions, the power of rousing the emotions of anger or pity, the faculty of directing his intellect to the point immediately essential. This is not an unjust picture. It is the *humanitas* of the speeches that turns them from an ephemeral tour de force into a lasting possession. This may be seen supremely in *Pro Archia*—

> Studies of this kind [literature and philosophy] are the food of the young, the diversion of the old, an adornment to success, a refuge for consolation in adversity, a private delight without being a public disadvantage, our constant companions at night, abroad or in the country.

His humour is at its best in his bantering of the Stoics in *Pro Murena* in order to discredit Cato, who was among the prosecutors, and at its most biting when he is attacking Clodia in *Pro Caelio*. His capacity for arousing anger may be seen in the opening sentences of the first speech against Catiline and, for arousing pity, in the last page of *Pro Milone*. His technique in winning a case

against the evidence is exemplified by *Pro Cluentio*, a speech in an inordinately complex murder trial; Cicero later boasted of "throwing dust in the jurymen's eyes."

Ancient critics stressed his forcefulness and fullness. These qualities are described by the anonymous work, formerly attributed to Longinus, *On the Sublime*, contrasting his diffuseness with the terseness of Demosthenes: "Cicero, like a spreading conflagration, ranges and rolls far and wide; his inner fire is abundant and unextinguishable; he applies it in varying intensity at different points, and keeps it fed with relays of fuel." His fullness revolutionized the writing of Latin; he is the real creator of the "periodic" style, in which phrase is balanced against phrase, with subordinate clauses woven into a complex but seldom obscure whole. His style, in truth, formed the style of Renaissance Europe. Quintilian, an ardent Ciceronian, declared that his name was synonymous with oratory, and the historian Livy that a second Cicero would be needed to praise him adequately.

Cicero's
contri-
bution to
literary
theory

Cicero made a significant contribution to literary theory. His early *De inventione* is slight, but between 55 and 46 BC he made an important survey of oratorical principle and practice, notably in *De oratore*, *Brutus*, and *Orator*. In his broad, spacious, artistic treatment, he invokes classical principles. The aim of oratory is threefold: it must be instructive, attractive, and emotive. For the first the orator needs a well-stored mind; for the second a sense of balance between the exoticism of the Asians and the starkness of the Atticists; for the third a sound understanding of psychology. Great oratory comes from a combination of natural capacity, training, and a sound liberal education.

Cicero as a philosopher. Cicero studied under the Epicurean Phaedrus (c. 140–70 BC), the Stoic Diodotus (d. c. 60 BC), and the Academic Philo of Larissa (c. 160–80 BC), and thus he had a thorough grounding in three of the four main schools of philosophy. Epicureanism he rejected, though his friend Atticus remained an adherent. During his travels in the east in 79–77 he developed an admiration for Antiochus of Ascalon, an Academic with leanings to Stoicism, and for the great Stoic Poseidonius. Cicero called himself an Academic, but this applied chiefly to his theory of knowledge, in which he preferred to be guided by probability rather than to allege certainty; in this way, he justified contradictions in his own works. In ethics he was more inclined to dogmatism and was attracted by the Stoics, but for his authority he looked behind the Stoics to Socrates. In religion he was an agnostic most of his life, but he had religious experiences of some profundity during an early visit to Eleusis and at the death of his daughter in 45. He usually writes as a theist, but the only religious exaltation in his writings is to be found in the "Somnium Scipionis" ("Scipio's dream"), at the end of *De republica*, with its sublime vision of a future life.

Philo-
sophical
writings

Cicero did not write seriously on philosophy before about 54, a period of uneasy political truce, when he seems to have begun *De republica*, following it with *De legibus* (begun in 52). These writings were an attempt to interpret Roman history in terms of Greek political theory. Cicero rejected democracy, oligarchy, and monarchy (which he considered the best of the three) in favour of a mixed constitution, such as he imagined Rome to possess. An interesting feature of his theory is the presence of a *moderator* or *rector*, a philosophical autocrat; this concept was used by later Romans to buttress the position of the emperor.

The bulk of his philosophical writings belong to the period between February 45 and November 44. His output and range of subjects were astonishing: the lost *De consolatione*, prompted by his daughter's death; *Hortensius*, an exhortation to the study of philosophy, which proved instrumental in St. Augustine's conversion; the difficult *Academica* (*Academic Philosophy*), which defends suspension of judgment; *De finibus*, or *The Supreme Good* (Is it pleasure, virtue, or something more complex?); *Tusculanae Disputationes*, or *Tabletalks at Tusculum* (Is death an evil? Is pain an evil? Can a wise man suffer distress? Mental perturbation? Is virtue sufficient for blessedness?); *De natura deorum* (*On the Nature of the Gods*); and *De officiis* (*Moral Obligation*). Except in the last book of *De officiis*, Cicero lays no claim to originality in these works. Writing to Atticus, he says of them "They are transcripts; I simply supply words, and I've plenty of those." His aim was to provide Rome with a kind of philosophic encyclopaedia. He derived his material from Stoic, Academic, Epicurean, and Peripatetic sources. The form he used was the dialogue, but his models were Aristotle and the scholar Heracleides Ponticus rather than Plato. His general method may be seen in *De finibus*, in which first the Epicurean view and next the Stoic view are expounded and criticized, the last book providing an account of the views held in common by Academics and Peripatetics.

Cicero's importance in the history of philosophy is as a transmitter of Greek thought. In the course of this role, he gave Rome and, therefore, Europe its philosophical vocabulary. We owe to Cicero words such as quality, individual, vacuum, moral, property, induction, element, definition, difference, notion, comprehension, infinity, appetite, and many others. In this way he has molded contemporary ways of thinking, and, in a century when philosophy has increasingly concentrated on language-problems, he should not be underestimated. He was once valued, and is still worth reading, for his content. Petrarch said: "You could sometimes fancy that it is not a pagan philosopher but a Christian apostle who is speaking." Today one is more inclined to echo Voltaire's "We honour Cicero, who taught us how to think." The highest tribute came from his great adversary Julius Caesar: "It is better to have extended the frontiers of the mind than to have pushed back the boundaries of empire."

MAJOR WORKS

SPEECHES: *Pro Quinctio* (81), *Pro Roscio Amerino* (80 or early 79), *Pro Roscio Comoedo* (77?), *In Caecilium divinatio, In Verrem actio* I, *actio* II, 1–5 (70) *Pro Tullio, Pro Fonteio, Pro Caecina* (69), *Pro Lege Manilia, Pro Cluentio* (66), *Contra Rullum* I–III, *Pro Rabirio, In Catilinam,* I–IV, *Pro Murena* (63), *Pro Sulla, Pro Archia* (62), *Pro Flacco* (59), *Post reditum ad Quirites* and *Post reditum in Senatu, De domo sua* (57), *De haruspicum responso, Pro Sestio, In Vatinium, Pro Caelio, De provinciis consularibus, Pro Balbo* (56), *In Pisonem* (55), *Pro Plancio, Pro Rabirio Postumo* (54), *Pro Milone* (52), *Pro Marcello, Pro Ligario* (46), *Pro rege Deiotaro* (45), *Philippicae* I–XIV (44–43).

CRITICAL: *De inventione* (84), *De oratore* I–III (55), *Oratoriae partitiones* (54?), *De optimo genere oratorum* (52), *De republica* I–VI (51; completed 52), *Brutus, Paradoxa Stoicorum, Orator* (46), *Academica* I–II, *De finibus* I–V, *Tusculanae disputationes* I–V, *De natura deorum* I–III, *De divinatione* I–II, *De fato, De senectute, De amicitia, De officiis* I–III, *Topica* (45–44), *De legibus* (begun in 52 but published posthumously).

LETTERS: *Ad Atticum* I–XVI, *Ad familiares* I–XVI, *Ad Quintum fratrem* I–III, *Ad Brutum* I–II.

TRANSLATIONS: A translation of most of Cicero's works is available in the "Loeb Series" (1912–58). Other recommended translations are: *Selected Works* by M. Grant (1965); *Nine Orations and the Dream of Scipio* by P. Bovie (1967); *Letters* by L.P. Wilkinson (1949); *On the Commonwealth* by G.H. Sabine and S.B. Smith (1929); *On Moral Obligation* by J. Higginbotham (1967); and *On the Art of Growing Old* by H.N. Couch (1959).

BIBLIOGRAPHY

Editions with notes: R.Y. TYRRELL and L.C. PURSER, *The Correspondence of M. Tullius Cicero,* 7 vol. (1899–1918); D.R. SHACKLETON-BAILEY, *Cicero's Letters to Atticus,* 7 vol. (1965–70); W.W. EWBANK, *Poems of Cicero* (1933); R.G. AUSTIN, *Pro M. Caelio,* 3rd ed. (1960); J.D. DENNISTON, *Philippics I–II* (1939); L.G. POCOCK, *In Vatinium* (1926); R.G. NISBET, *De Domo Sua* (1939); R.G.M. NISBET, *In Pisonem* (1961); W. KROLL, *Orator* (1913); A.E. DOUGLAS, *Brutus* (1966); A.S. PEASE, *De Natura Deorum,* 2 vol. (1955–58).

Modern works: On Cicero's style, the best works are in French and German: J. LEBRETON, *Études sur la langue et la grammaire de Cicéron* (1901); T. ZIELINSKI, *Das Clauselgesetz in Ciceros Reden* (1904); L. LAURAND, *De M. Tulli Ciceronis studiis rhetoricis* (1907); *Études sur le style des discours de Cicéron,* 3 vol. (1938–40); J. HUMBERT, *Les Plaidoyers écrits et les plaidoiries réelles de Cicéron* (1925).

Zielinski's was the pioneering work on the rhythm of Cicero's cadences; Laurand's is the most comprehensive. On Cicero as a lawyer, see A.H.J. GREENIDGE, *The Legal Procedure of Cicero's Time* (1901, reprinted 1971); and R.N. WILKIN, *Eternal Lawyer* (1947). On Cicero's thought, H.A.K. HUNT, *The Humanism of Cicero* (1954), a good general work. M. VAN DEN BRUWAENE, *La Théologie de Cicéron* (1937), is comprehensive on its subject with a systematic study of sources. Other studies include: JEROME CARCOPINO, *Les Secrets de la correspondance de Cicéron,* 2 vol. (1947; Eng. trans., *Cicero: The Secrets of His Correspondence,* 1951), an unsuccessful attempt to discredit Cicero; F.R. COWELL, *Cicero and the Roman Republic* (1948), lively and readable; T.A. DOREY (ed.), *Cicero* (1965), essays by seven Ciceronian scholars; H. FRISCH, *Cicero's Fight for the Republic* (1946), an excellent account of Cicero in politics after Caesar's murder; MATTHIAS GELZER, *Cicero: Ein biographischer Versuch* (1969), the most detailed and authoritative book on Cicero that exists; H.J. HASKELL, *This Was Cicero* (1942), a lively account; D.R. SHACKLETON-BAILEY, *Cicero* (1971), by a scholar with unrivalled knowledge of the *Letters;* R.E. SMITH, *Cicero the Statesman* (1966), a flattering, somewhat uncritical appraisal of Cicero; DAVID STOCKTON, *Cicero: A Political Biography* (1971), a lively account of the man and his career; and H. STASBURGER, *Concordia Ordinum: Eine Untersuchung zur Politik Ciceros* (1931), a very important examination of Cicero's political ideal.

(J.Fe./J.P.V.D.B.)

Ciconiiformes

The Ciconiiformes constitute an order of five or six families of storklike birds: herons and bitterns (Ardeidae), the shoebill (sole species of the Balaenicipitidae), the hammerhead (sole species of the Scopidae), typical storks and wood storks (Ciconiidae), ibis and spoonbills (Threskiornithidae), and, according to some authorities, flamingos (Phoenicopteridae). Most are of substantial size, long-legged and long-necked, and adapted for wading. They are widely distributed, often abundant, and apt to be conspicuous in their open habitats or in the air. Many are notably graceful in form and movement, and some have spectacular powers of flight.

GENERAL FEATURES

Size range and diversity of structure. Some storks are very large, standing over 1.2 metres (4 feet) high and having wingspans of up to 2.6 metres (8.5 feet). The larger herons are about as tall when standing erect. Flamingos are also tall, with great length of neck and legs. Species of medium size usually stand 60–90 centimetres (2–3 feet) high and some of the smaller ones as little as 30 centimetres (12 inches). Exceptionally small are the little bitterns of the widespread genus *Ixobrychus,* weighing less than 100 grams (a few ounces).

With the partial exception of the flamingos, the structural characteristics of the order are well-marked, and the same is true of the families. The storks, even including the wood storks, form a recognizable group of birds of from medium to large size. The ibis form an even more homogeneous group, birds of medium size with markedly down-curved bills, except for the spoonbills. The herons are more diverse, with a greater size range, the bitterns standing a little apart in behaviour more than in structure. Each of the remaining two families contains a single species with some peculiar characteristics.

Distribution, habitat, and abundance. Ciconiiforms are found throughout the world, except in the polar regions, but the largest number of species is found in the warmer parts. Some of those breeding in the North Temperate Zone perform long migrations. The herons are the most cosmopolitan family, some being found even on remote oceanic islands. The shoebill (*Balaeniceps rex*) has a limited distribution in tropical Africa, and the hammerhead (*Scopus umbretta*) is almost confined to that continent. The typical storks (subfamily Ciconiinae) are not represented in North America and have only one species in the Australasian Region; the wood storks (subfamily Mycteriinae) are represented by one species in the New World and three in the Old World. The ibis are widely distributed, but are not found in New Zealand. The flamingos are found throughout the tropics, but are not represented in the Australasian Region.

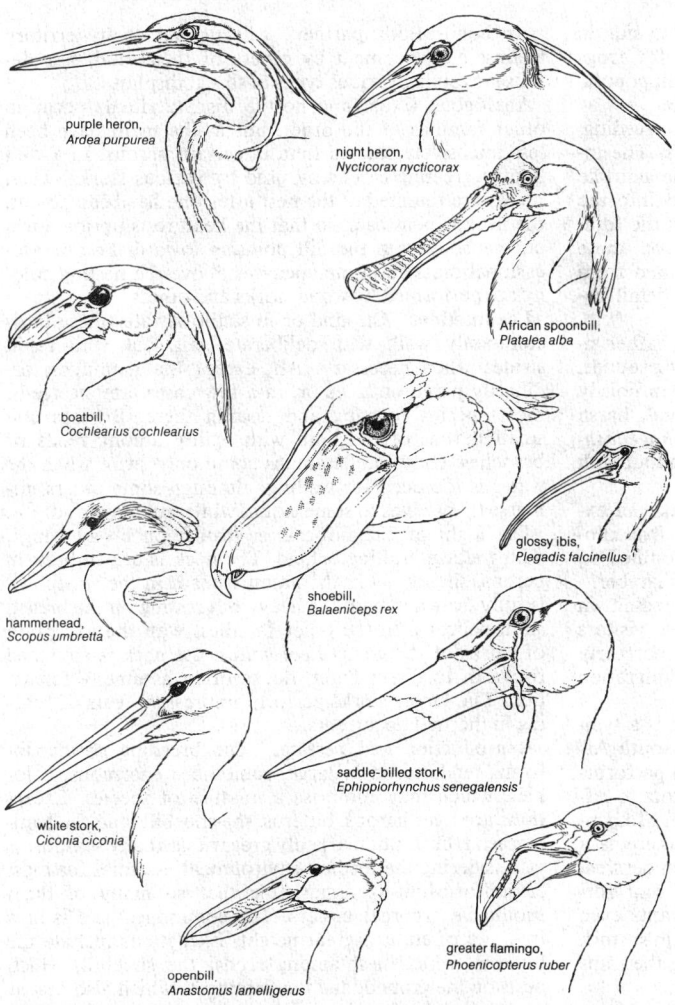

purple heron,
Ardea purpurea

night heron,
Nycticorax nycticorax

African spoonbill,
Platalea alba

boatbill,
Cochlearius cochlearius

glossy ibis,
Plegadis falcinellus

hammerhead,
Scopus umbretta

shoebill,
Balaeniceps rex

saddle-billed stork,
Ephippiorhynchus senegalensis

white stork,
Ciconia ciconia

openbill,
Anastomus lamelligerus

greater flamingo,
Phoenicopterus ruber

Figure 1: Variation in beak structure among ciconiiform birds.
Drawing by R. Keane

The usual habitat of ciconiiforms is near water, chiefly fresh, and only a few species, such as the white stork (*Ciconia ciconia*), live largely on dry ground. The flamingos require brackish or alkaline water, and two species inhabit Andean lakes at elevations of up to about 4,000 metres (14,000 feet).

Many of the species in the order are very abundant, with world populations running into millions, and some assemblages, such as those of the lesser flamingo (*Phoeniconaias minor*) in Africa, are enormous. At the other extreme, the Japanese ibis (*Nipponia nippon*) is on the verge of extinction, only one small colony being known.

Relations with man. Although some freshwater fishing interests may regard herons as undesirable competitors, on the whole the members of this order are considered to be either beneficial or neutral in respect to the human economy. They are not sought by man, and many are protected. At one time a number of species of little egrets were persecuted at their breeding places for the sake of their nuptial plumes—aigrettes (or ospreys)—but such killing has now largely been stopped.

The association of the white stork with mankind in its preference for nesting on buildings is further mentioned below, but it is not the only species thus involved. Abdim's stork (*Sphenorhynchus abdimii*), for instance, will nest on native huts in a treeless area. And many of the arboreal colonies of heron and stork species in Africa are in or near villages. The cattle egret's dependence on domestic stock to flush insects, as an alternative to wild herbivores, brings it into a familiar relationship with human beings.

NATURAL HISTORY

Feeding habits. Most ciconiiforms subsist wholly or mainly on animal food, which is usually swallowed whole, indigestible matter being regurgitated later as pellets. Fish are the prey of many species such as the larger herons, but small mammals, birds, reptiles, and amphibians are also taken, as well as invertebrates, including mollusks, crustaceans, insects, and worms.

The flamingos, on the other hand, live chiefly on minute algae.

The methods of fishing are varied. Some of the larger herons stand solitary and motionless until a fish comes within reach and the long neck suddenly shoots out. Certain herons employ a hunting method known as "canopy feeding," in which one or both wings are held forward, forming a canopy over the head and creating a patch of shaded water. It is thought that fish mistake the shaded area for a safe refuge; another interpretation is that the canopy aids the bird's vision by reducing surface reflections. Other herons go actively in pursuit, stirring up the bottom with their feet or wading rapidly about. The night herons are largely nocturnal in their fishing. Some members of the heron family are not fish eaters. The cattle egret (*Ardeola ibis*) lives on insects caught when disturbed by the large mammals with which the bird associates.

The food of storks is also varied and may be sought on dry land, in marshy ground, or in shallow water. White storks wintering in Africa take large numbers of locusts when the latter are swarming. Wood storks fish by plowing the water, with mandibles open and partly submerged, as they wade in the shallows. The marabou (*Leptoptilos crumeniferus*) and other members of the same genus are partly predatory but largely scavengers and carrion eaters, and they may often be seen with vultures at a carcass.

Ibis use their long bills for probing the ground or mud. The spoonbills catch small organisms by moving their

Specialized feeding of herons

bills, with mandibles slightly open, from side to side in shallow water. The hammerhead often hunts for frogs and will use the back of an almost submerged hippopotamus as a vantage point. The shoebill is a fish eater.

Flamingos have a highly specialized method of feeding, which has its closest parallel in certain whales. The inside of the mandibles carries a series of fine hairlike plates that act as filters when water is sucked into the mouth and then expelled. The head is held with the forehead downward. The food particles caught on these plates are ultimately worked on to the tongue and from there are swallowed. There are differences of detail between the species.

Vocalization. Many of the ciconiiforms are rather silent, making at most various croaking or grunting sounds. Some storks utter scarcely any sounds, but often noisily clatter their mandibles. Some herons have loud, harsh cries. Among the ibis, the hadada (*Hagedashia hagedash*) of Africa is exceptional in being noisy—flying about with yelping cries.

In spring, the males of the large bitterns make an extraordinary booming sound audible at up to five kilometres; for this purpose, the esophagus is modified so that it can be inflated and serve as a resonating chamber.

Migration. The relatively few species breeding in northern areas with hard winters are summer visitors there. In some herons there is a tendency to a northerly postbreeding dispersal before the time of true migration southward.

The white stork of Europe and northern Asia is a typical long-distance migrant, travelling as far as South Africa and India. The black stork (*Ciconia nigra*) performs a similar migration, but it is doubtful that visitors to Africa now penetrate beyond the Zambezi River in Mozambique. In South Africa, on the other hand, there is a sparse resident population believed to have been derived, within the twentieth century, from migrants that formerly made a longer journey. There are migrants even among species confined to the tropics; Abdim's stork breeds in the northern tropics of Africa during the rains and migrates across the Equator.

Apart from regular movements, recent years have seen a notable range expansion by the cattle egret from Africa and Asia to the Americas and to Australia.

Behaviour. An outstanding feature in ciconiiform behaviour is gregariousness. Even where the mode of obtaining food necessitates solitude and therefore dispersal, the tendency is for reassembly at the end of the day and then flight in formation to a communal roost. Breeding is mostly colonial. Species able to feed in flocks are gregarious at all times. Some of the assemblies are enormous; for example, over 1,000,000 lesser flamingos occur on a single African lake. There may be a seasonal element, as when white storks, dispersed in the breeding season, form flocks for migration.

There are some exceptions. Bitterns and tiger herons, relying on concealment for protection, are not markedly gregarious, nor is the hammerhead. The shoebill is usually seen singly or in pairs. It is rather silent, partly nocturnal, and has even been credited with a morose disposition.

Courtship behaviour of herons

Behaviour related to mating and the pair bond is well marked and has been described in detail for several species, notably of herons. Among these, the first signs of breeding may be the assembly of birds on a gathering ground adjacent to the colony and the performance there of various strutting and dancing rituals. A male may then take off on a "circle flight" ending at the site which he has chosen for the future nest. There he may adopt a series of stereotyped display postures, such as the "stretch," in which he first extends the head and neck vertically and after a moment bends them rearward until the head is almost touching the back. There may also be a "snap" display, in which the head and neck are extended forward and downward, the feathers of the neck, face, and crest are erected, and the mandibles are brought together with a loud clap. After the male heron has attracted a mate, various mutual displays during building, or at nest relief during incubation, apparently help to maintain the pair bond. Both partners will defend their territory against encroachment by others of their kind, this defense involving various types of threat display.

Analogous sexual and hostile display rituals occur in other families of the order, but in the main have been less intensively studied than in certain herons. In a well known greeting ceremony used by various storks, when mates are reunited at the nest after one has been absent, the neck is bent back so that the head rests upside down on the body with the bill pointing toward the tail. Occasional mass aerial manoeuvres above the nesting colony are performed by wood storks and others.

Locomotion. On land or in shallow water these birds commonly walk with deliberate gait, but with rapid strides when necessary. All, except the flamingos, ordinarily perch on trees or, in a few cases, among reeds, most species roosting and nesting there. Bitterns and small herons often climb with agility among reeds or branches. Only the flamingos commonly swim when the water is too deep for wading, although some others immerse themselves to some extent while catching food.

The flight of ciconiiforms is strong, on broad wings, with the legs trailing behind. The neck is drawn back in herons, slightly so in the hammerhead; in the shoebill it is fully drawn in with the heavy bill resting on the breast, as in pelicans. In the other families, with the exception of storks of the genus *Leptoptilos*, the neck is stretched forward. In direct flight, flocks often assume V-formation. The larger storks perform impressive feats of soaring in thermal upcurrents.

Reproduction and nesting. The breeding of ciconiiforms tends to be in large, sometimes enormous, colonies, which may comprise a mixture of species. Exceptions are tiger herons, bitterns, the shoebill, and the hammerhead, birds not markedly gregarious at any season.

Considering the feeding environment essential for most ciconiiforms, it is remarkable that so many of them should be arboreal nesters. The commonest site is in a tree and often at a great height. Exceptions include the bitterns, which nest among reeds; the shoebill, which nests on the ground; and the flamingos, which also nest at ground level, often in shallow water. Among the storks the choice is more varied. Most species nest in tall trees, but some use cliffs or buildings. In parts of Europe, as an alternative to buildings, the white stork often uses artificial platforms erected for its benefit, commonly a cartwheel lying horizontally on top of a high pole, or a similar structure. The site is variable in night herons, ibis, and spoonbills, whose nests may be in trees, in low bushes, among reeds, or even on the ground (ibis and spoonbills), or on cliffs (some species of night herons).

Nest structure

The nest itself is usually a loose platform of sticks and stems. Rushes are much used in marshy situations. The nest of the hammerhead, placed in a tree and often at no great height, is an enormous structure of sticks and other vegetation, forming a closed chamber sometimes a metre or more in diameter with an entrance tunnel at one side. The cavity is lined with mud or dung. The shoebill, in contrast, does no more than flatten a patch of long grass on dry ground. Flamingos build cones of mud on the lakeshore, 15–35 centimetres (6–14 inches) high, with a shallow depression scooped out of the top of each. The incubating bird sits on top of this nest, with its long legs folded beneath its body. Sometimes, as on small rocky islands, other materials are used in the absence of mud.

As a rule, flamingos lay only a single egg and the shoebill one or two. The usual clutch is three or four in ibis and spoonbills, three to six in storks and the hammerhead, three to seven in herons, and four to six in bitterns. There is a tendency for the eggs to be ovoid (*i.e.*, with the ends equally rounded) and to have a white chalky outer layer, underneath which there may be a coloured shell. The colours range from white to pale blue, green, or buff in most groups, to olive brown in the bitterns, and to dark greenish-blue in some ibis. The ground colour of ibis eggs may be spotted or blotched with brown, but the eggs of most others are plain. There are faint or scanty markings in a few.

The chicks are downy when hatched, or quickly be-

Figure 2: Common egrets, *Egretta alba* (top left and right), with snowy egrets, *Egretta thula* (centre), in a typical colonial nesting situation.

Allan D. Cruickshank—National Audubon Society

come so, but, except for those of flamingos, they remain in the nest, dependent on their parents for food until full-grown. In the herons there is only one down plumage, but in storks and ibis there are two in succession. The downy young of flamingos are gray, with bills and legs that are red at first, but become black within a few days. After the first two or three days, the flamingo chicks leave the nest and move freely about the adjacent part of the colony. As they grow older they are herded in groups by a few adults, but each apparently continues to be fed by its own parents. The bill acquires its specialized form only as the young flamingo grows. Among some other members of the order, there is a tendency for the bill to be shorter and of a more generalized type during the early stage of postnatal development.

So far as information is available for different species, ciconiiform birds first breed when from two to four years old. Parental care is usually shared between the sexes, both taking part in building the nest, incubating the eggs, and feeding the chicks. Bitterns of the genus *Botaurus* seem to be exceptional in that only the female incubates the eggs and tends the young. Feeding is usually by regurgitation. In herons, for example, the parent's bill is seized crosswise by the young bird, and the food is passed sideways to its mouth from between the adult's mandibles. In flamingos, the regurgitated food is of fluid consistency, and the young must continue to be fed in this way until their own filtering apparatus is adequately developed at the age of some two months.

Feeding of nestlings

FORM AND FUNCTION

General characteristics. The carriage of the body is markedly upright in many species, but more horizontal in others. Length of neck and length of legs tend to be correlated; but the chestnut-bellied heron (*Agamia agami*) of tropical America combines short legs with a long neck. In herons, particularly, the neck is curled back on itself at rest but can be instantly straightened on alert or to seize prey.

Long legs and toes are often an adaptation for wading. The toes of herons are long and flexible, with just a hint of webbing for walking or standing on soft ground, the functional hind toe aiding in perching. The hind toe of storks and ibis is reduced and elevated, an adaptation for more walking and less perching. The relatively short front toes of the flamingos are completely webbed and the hind toe small or absent; these birds walk extensively on soft bottom mud. In the herons, and also in the hammerhead, the claw on the middle toes is serrated (pectinate) on its inner border, an aid to preening.

Bill shape. The bill shows various adaptations to methods of feeding (Figure 1). In herons it is typically long, straight, and pointed; although spearlike in appearance, it is used for grasping rather than impaling. In the boat-billed heron (*Cochlearius cochlearius*) the bill is flattened into a broad scoop and is used as such in feeding. In bitterns, both mandibles are finely serrated

near the tip. The bill of the hammerhead is relatively short and slightly hooked. The shoebill has a large head with a heavy, bulging, hooked bill; this may be an adaptation to digging lungfish out of the mud, but is used also for catching other fish.

In storks, the bill is usually long and strong, as in herons, but not always straight; it may be decurved as in the wood storks, or slightly upturned as in the jabiru (*Jabiru mycteria*) of tropical America. In the two open-bills of the genus *Anastomus*, when the mandibles are closed a wide gap remains between their outer portions, except at the tips, probably in adaptation to holding large water snails. The ibis have long, thin, and markedly decurved bills; and in the spoonbills the tip of the long straight bill is flattened and broadened, thus forming a thin spatula.

In the flamingos the bill is bent downward in the middle of its length and has the filtering mechanism already described.

Plumage and coloration. Among the herons, plumages in patterns of blues, grays, and white are common; some, such as various egrets, are all white. In storks, contrasting areas of black and white are characteristic. Some of the ibis are notable for the metallic sheen on the feathers. The hammerhead is of a sombre brown hue. The large bitterns and the tiger herons have cryptic coloration, which is associated with their habit of standing motionless among the reeds with their bills pointing toward the sky.

Touches of bright red on the plumage or on bare parts are not infrequent. A few species have brightly coloured plumage, such as the scarlet ibis (*Eudocimus ruber*) and the roseate spoonbill (*Ajaia ajaja*), both of tropical America, and, in varying degree, the flamingos.

Orna- mental coloration

The sexes are usually alike in plumage, or nearly so, exceptions being the little bitterns. The immature may be like the adult or quite different; in the scarlet ibis it is dull brown. Some herons have, in both sexes, long plumes descending from the head, neck, breast, or back, in most only during the breeding season. Some species (*e.g.*, certain ibis, the boat-billed heron, and many typical herons) have crests on the crown or nape. The hammerhead gets its name because the bill appears balanced by an erectile tuft of feathers projecting backward. Patches (two or more pairs) of powder-down feathers are especially characteristic of the herons. These feathers break down to produce a fine powder, which is distributed to the plumage with the bill in preening.

The head and neck are partly or wholly bare of feathers in some species, and the exposed skin may be black, as in the sacred ibis (*Threskiornis aethiopica*), or brightly coloured red in the hermit ibis (*Geronticus eremita*) and others. In the marabou, the head and neck are almost naked and from the front of the neck extends a distensible pouch of pink skin.

Seasonal change in plumage is seen mainly in the shedding of the ornamental breeding plumes of some herons, but there are some changes in the colour of the bill, irises of the eyes, legs, and bare patches of skin during the season of sexual display. The colours then become brighter, commonly redder, and there may even be an intensification of the hue in moments of excitement.

Another characteristic of the herons, notably the egrets, is a tendency to dimorphism, resulting in a population containing both white and slate blue individuals.

EVOLUTION AND PALEONTOLOGY

The Ciconiiformes are generally accepted as being a primitive group. Apart from the equivocal position of the Phoenicopteri, and with possible reservations about *Balaeniceps*, there seems to be little doubt that the order evolved through a single phyletic line. The two main branches produced the herons and the storks, with the remaining forms probably nearer the latter.

In the fossil record, the first heron, *Proherodius*, dates from the lower Eocene of England (about 54,000,000 years ago), and other herons from later in the Eocene of North America. The first ibis (*Ibidopsis*) is from the upper Eocene of England and the first stork from the late Eocene or very early Oligocene of France. From the Pliocene of North America (about 7,000,000 to 2,500,000 years ago) there are fossil forms of modern heron genera (*Ardea* and *Nycticorax*) and a modern ibis genus (*Eudocimus*).

The flamingos and their extinct allies have a long record, beginning with *Scaniornis* from the lower Paleocene (about 65,000,000 years ago) in Sweden. The first true flamingo (*Elornis*) is from the late Eocene of England, and another flamingo-like form, *Agnopterus*, from the same level; *Paloelodus* dates from the lower Miocene in France (about 26,000,000 years ago). Fossil families have been named for each of these three extinct genera.

CLASSIFICATION

Distinguishing taxonomic features. The members of the order possess in common, but not exclusively, a number of anatomical characters that are considered to be conservative (*i.e.*, changing only slowly in evolution), indicative of kinship in descent, rather than convergent evolution. These features include the arrangement of the palatine bones, the presence of diastataxy (*i.e.*, the wing apparently lacks a secondary feather associated with the fifth secondary covert, which is present), the presence of intestinal ceca (blind pouches), nearly always minute, the possession of 16–20 cervical (neck) vertebrae, and the presence of only a single pair of sternotracheal muscles in the syrinx (voicebox).

Annotated classification. The following taxonomic arrangement is widely accepted by students of this order. Groups marked with a dagger (†) are known only from fossils.

ORDER CICONIIFORMES

Suborder Ardeae

Family Ardeidae (herons, egrets, and bitterns)

Lower Eocene to Recent. Loose-plumaged wading birds of moderate to large size, most with slim body and long neck; bill usually long, straight and sharp; legs medium to long, lower tibiae bare; partial web between outer and middle (sometimes also between middle and inner) toes, and hind toes at same level as front toes; claw on middle toe pectinate (*i.e.*, with comblike inner edge). Many with ornamental plumes in breeding season. Adult length 28–142 cm (11–56 in.). About 75 species (and 17 fossil species) usually divided into 2 subfamilies: Ardeinae (typical herons, egrets, tiger herons, night herons) and Botaurinae (bitterns). Worldwide, except in polar regions.

Suborder Balaenicipites

Family Balaenicipitidae (shoebill or whale-headed stork)

A large wading bird, stoutly built, with moderately long neck and short tail. Bill large, broad, and flattened, with hooked tip on upper mandible. Legs long, hind toe on same level as others, claw on middle toe slightly pectinate. Plumage sombre; short bushy crest. Length 117 cm (46 in.). One species, confined to tropical east central Africa.

Suborder Ciconiae

Family Scopidae (hammerhead, hamerkop, or hammerheaded stork)

A moderate-size bird with large head, short neck, rather long wings, and moderate length tail. Bill medium length and laterally compressed, straight, and slightly hooked at the tip. Legs long; toes slender, with partial web connecting front three; hind toe at same level. Plumage brown, substantial crest projecting horizontally from back of head. Length 50 cm (20 in.). Africa, southwestern Asia, Madagascar.

Family Ciconiidae (storks)

Upper Eocene to present. Medium to large wading or walking birds, stoutly built, with long necks. Bill long and massive, straight or curved up or down (or with gap between closed mandibles); legs long, with partial web between middle and outer toes, hind toe smaller and raised. Plumage often boldly patterned in black and white; parts or whole of head bare in some species. Length 76–152 cm (30–60 in.); 21 fossil and 17 Recent species, divided in to 2 subfamilies. Ciconiinae (typical storks) and Mycteriinae (wood storks). Worldwide in warm regions but most species in the Old World.

Family Threskiornithidae (ibis and spoonbills)

Upper Eocene to present. Medium to large wading or walking birds, with long neck and short tail; bill long, slender, curved downward (ibis), or straight and spatulate at the tip (spoonbills). Legs long; front toes slightly webbed at base, hind toe small and elevated. Many with crests; some ibis with whole or part of head and neck bare. Length 48–107 cm (19–42 in.). Seven fossil and about 28 Recent species, in 2 subfamilies. Threskiornithinae (ibis) and Plataleinae (spoonbills). Virtually worldwide in tropics and subtropics, a few species in temperate regions.

†*Family Plegadornithidae*

Fossil only; 1 species; Upper Cretaceous of Alabama.

Suborder Phoenicopteri

†*Family Torotigidae*

Fossil only; 3 monotypic genera; Cretaceous of western Europe and western North America.

†*Family Scaniornithidae*

Fossil only; 1 species; lower Paleocene of Sweden.

†*Family Telmabatidae*

Fossil only; 1 species; lower Eocene of Argentina.

†*Family Agnopteridae*

Fossil only; 3 species; upper Eocene of England and France, and upper Oligocene of Kazakhstan, U.S.S.R.

Family Phoenicopteridae (flamingos)

Upper Eocene to present. Very tall wading (and swimming) birds, with slender bodies, long thin necks, large wings, and short tails. Bill stout, bent sharply down at midpoint, and furnished with lamellar filtering apparatus. Legs very long; front toes relatively short and fully webbed, hind toe small or absent. Plumage mainly white, tinged pink, or light vermilion; face bare. Length 91–122 cm (36–48 in.). Nine fossil and 4 Recent species; shallow lakes and lagoons in tropics; worldwide, except Australasia.

†*Family Palaelodidae*

Fossil only; 8 species, lower Miocene to lower Pliocene; France, Germany, and western United States.

Critical appraisal. There is little controversy about the limits of the order Ciconiiformes apart from the question of whether the flamingos (Phoenicopteri) should be given separate ordinal rank (Phoenicopteriformes) as some authorities hold (see BIRD). The flamingos have affinities with the Anseriformes (*q.v.*) as well as with the Ciconiiformes. Neither is there much difference of view about the division into families, except that some authorities place the boat-billed heron (*Cochlearius*) in its own family, Cochleariidae. Apart from the specialized shape of the bill and associated modifications in the skull, which are clearly adaptive features, the characters seem to be mainly those of the Ardeidae. Superfamilies have been erected from the three families of the Ciconiae; but with only one family in each, the device merely emphasizes their distinctiveness. On the other hand, some do not place the Balaenicipitidae in a separate suborder, but with the Ciconiidae as the superfamily Ciconioidea.

The precise position of the two species in monotypic families has been much debated. The strongest affinities of *Scopus* appear to be with the suborder Ciconiae, in which its family is here placed, but it also shows resemblances to the Ardeae and the Balaenicipites. *Balaeniceps* was at one time even placed in another order, the Pelecaniformes, and further osteological evidence tending in this direction has recently been adduced; others attribute the resemblances to convergence. Within the

Ciconiiformes, the shoebill has affinities with both the Ciconiae and the Ardeae.

BIBLIOGRAPHY. R.P. ALLEN, *The Flamingos: Their Life History and Survival* (1956), a survey of the family; W.J. BOCK, "A Generic Review of the Family Ardeidae (Aves)," *Am. Mus. Novit.*, no. 1779 (1956), a discussion of the taxonomy of the herons; L.H. BROWN, *Mystery of the Flamingos* (1959), a description of the natural history of the East African species; F.A. LOWE, *The Heron* (1954), a discussion of the natural history of the European grey heron (*Ardea cinerea*); A.J. MEYERREICKS, *Comparative Breeding Behaviour of Four Species of North American Herons* (1960), a valuable contribution to knowledge of behaviour in the group; R.S. PALMER (ed.), *Handbook of North American Birds*, vol. 1 (1962), detailed accounts of 22 species of the order; A.L. THOMSON (ed.), *A New Dictionary of Birds* (1964), short articles on individual ciconiiforms.

(A.L.T.)

Cid, El

El Cid (from Spanish Arabic *as-sīd*, "lord") is the popular name, dating from his lifetime, of Rodrigo Díaz de Vivar, the most prestigious military leader produced by 11th-century Christian Spain. His biography presents special problems for the historian because he was speedily elevated to the status of national hero of Castile, and a complex heroic biography of him, in which legend played a dominant role, then came into existence. For authentic information historians have to rely mainly on a few contemporary documents, on the *Historia Roderici* (a reliable, private 12th-century Latin chronicle of the Cid's life), and on a detailed eyewitness account of his conquest of Valencia by the Arab historian Ibn 'Alqāmah. Rodrigo Díaz became the hero of the 12th-century epic poem of Castile, *El cantar de mío Cid* ("The Song of the Cid").

Rodrigo Díaz was born *c.* 1043 at Vivar, near Burgos. His father, Diego Laínez, was a member of the minor nobility (*infanzones*) of Castile. But the Cid's social background was less unprivileged than later popular tradition liked to suppose, for he was directly connected on his mother's side with the great landed aristocracy, and he was brought up at the court of Ferdinand I in the household of that king's eldest son, the future Sancho II of Castile. When Sancho succeeded to the Castilian throne (1065), he nominated the 22-year-old Cid as his standard-bearer (*armiger regis*), or commander of the royal troops. This early promotion to important office suggests that the young Cid had already won a reputation for exceptional military prowess. In 1067 he accompanied Sancho on a campaign against the important Moorish kingdom of Saragossa (Zaragoza) and played a leading role in the negotiations that led to its king, al-Muqtadir, becoming a tributary of the Castilian crown.

The king's standard-bearer

Ferdinand I, on his death, had partitioned his kingdoms among his various children, leaving Leon to his second son, Alfonso VI. Sancho began (1067) to make war on the latter with the aim of annexing Leon. Later legend was to make the Cid a reluctant supporter of Sancho's aggression, but it is unlikely that the real Cid had any such scruples. He played a prominent part in Sancho's successful campaigns against Alfonso and so found himself in an awkward situation in 1072, when the childless Sancho was killed while besieging Zamora, leaving the dethroned Alfonso as his only possible heir. The new king appears to have done his best to win the allegiance of Sancho's most powerful supporter. Though the Cid now lost his post as *armiger regis* to a great magnate, Count García Ordóñez (whose bitter enemy he became), and his former influence at court naturally declined, he was allowed to remain there; and, in July 1074, probably at Alfonso's instigation, he married the King's niece Jimena, daughter of the Count of Oviedo. He thus became allied by marriage to the ancient royal dynasty of Leon. Very little is known about Jimena. The couple had one son and two daughters. The son, Diego Rodríguez, was killed in battle against the Muslim Almoravid invaders from North Africa, at Consuegra (1097).

The Cid's position at court was, despite his marriage, precarious. He seems to have been thought of as the natural leader of those Castilians who were unreconciled

to being ruled by a king of Leon. He certainly resented the influence exercised by the great landed nobles over Alfonso VI. Though his heroic biographers would later present the Cid as the blameless victim of unscrupulous noble enemies and of Alfonso's willingness to listen to unfounded slanders, it seems likely that the Cid's penchant for publicly humiliating powerful men may have largely contributed to his downfall. Though he was later to show himself astute and calculating both as a soldier and politician, his conduct vis-à-vis the court suggests that resentment at his loss of influence as a result of Sancho's death may temporarily have undermined his capacity for self-control. In 1079, while on a mission to the Moorish king of Seville, he became embroiled with Alfonso's close counsellor, Count García Ordóñez, who was aiding the King of Granada in an invasion of the kingdom of Seville. The Cid defeated the markedly superior Granadine army at Cabra, near Seville, capturing García Ordóñez. This victory prepared the way for his downfall; and when, in 1081, he led an unauthorized military raid into the Moorish kingdom of Toledo, which was under Alfonso's VI's protection, the King exiled the Cid from his kingdoms. Several subsequent attempts at reconciliation produced no lasting results, and after 1081 the Cid never again was able to live for long in Alfonso's dominions.

Break with Alfonso VI

The exile offered his services to the Muslim dynasty that ruled Saragossa and with which he had first made contact in 1065. The king of Saragossa, in northeast Spain, al-Mu'tamin, welcomed the chance of having his vulnerable kingdom defended by so prestigious a Christian warrior. The Cid now loyally served al-Mu'tamin and his successor, al-Musta'īn II, for nearly a decade. As a result of his experience he gained that understanding of the complexities of Hispano-Arabic politics and of Islāmic law and custom that would later help him to conquer and hold Valencia. Meanwhile, he steadily added to his reputation as a general who had never been defeated in battle. In 1082, on behalf of al-Mu'tamin, he inflicted a crushing defeat on the Moorish King of Lérida and the latter's Christian allies, among them the Count of Barcelona. In 1084 he defeated a large Christian army under King Sancho Ramírez of Aragon. He was richly rewarded for these victories by his grateful Moorish masters.

In 1086 there began the great Almoravid invasion of Spain from North Africa. Alfonso VI, crushingly defeated by the invaders at Sagrajas (October 23, 1086) suppressed his antagonism to the Cid and recalled from exile the Christians' best general. The Cid's presence at Alfonso's court in July 1087 is documented. But shortly afterward, he was back in Saragossa, and he was not a participant in the subsequent desperate battles against the Almoravids in the strategic regions where their attacks threatened the whole existence of Christian Spain. The Cid, for his part, now embarked on the lengthy and immensely complicated political manoeuvring that was aimed at making him master of the rich Moorish kingdom of Valencia.

His first step was to eliminate the influence of the counts of Barcelona in that area. This was done when Berenguer Ramón II was humiliatingly defeated at Tébar, near Teruel (May 1090). During the next years the Cid gradually tightened his control over Valencia and its ruler, al-Qādir, now his tributary. His moment of destiny came in October 1092 when the *qāḍī* (chief magistrate), Ibn Jaḥḥāf, with Almoravid political support rebelled and killed al-Qādir. The Cid responded by closely besieging the rebel city. The siege lasted for many months; an Almoravid attempt to break it failed miserably (December 1093). In May 1094 Ibn Jaḥḥāf at last surrendered and the Cid finally entered Valencia as its conqueror. To facilitate his takeover he characteristically first made a pact with Ibn Jaḥḥāf that led the latter to believe that his acts of rebellion and regicide were forgiven; but when the pact had served its purpose, the Cid arrested the former *qāḍī* and ordered him to be burnt alive. The Cid now ruled Valencia directly, himself acting as chief magistrate of the Muslims as well as the

Conquest of Valencia

Christians. Nominally he held Valencia for Alfonso VI, but in fact he was its independent ruler in all but name. The city's chief mosque was Christianized in 1096; a French bishop, Jerome, was appointed to the new see; and there was a considerable influx of Christian colonists. The Cid's princely status was emphasized when his daughter Cristina married a prince of Aragon, Ramiro, lord of Monzón, and his other daughter, María, married Ramón Berenguer III, count of Barcelona. The Cid died in Valencia on July 10, 1099, aged 56.

Historical assessment

The great enterprise to which the Cid had devoted so much of his energies was to prove totally ephemeral. Soon after his death Valencia was besieged by the Almoravids, and Alfonso VI had to intervene in person to save it. But the King rightly judged the place indefensible unless he diverted there permanently large numbers of troops urgently needed to defend the Christian heartlands against the invaders. He evacuated the city and then ordered it to be burned. On May 5, 1102, the Almoravids occupied Valencia, which was to remain in Muslim hands until 1238. The Cid's body was taken to Castile and reburied in the monastery of San Pedro de Cardeña, near Burgos, where it became the centre of a lively death cult.

That the Cid was a brilliant and much-feared general and an iron-willed but crafty political leader is beyond doubt. On the long view, however, his historical role is plainly open to serious criticism. His unwillingness to come to terms with Alfonso VI and his determination to carve out a private state for himself in the eastern zone of the peninsula meant that the King was left to carry out his critical fight against the Almoravids largely without the Cid's support. It was not surprising, therefore, that, when turning him into the exemplary embodiment of the national ethos of medieval Castile, poets, monks, and chroniclers found it necessary to restructure substantially the facts of his historical biography.

BIBLIOGRAPHY. RAMON MENENDEZ PIDAL, *La España del Cid*, 5th ed., 2 vol. (1956), is the major though now rather out of date scholarly biography on the subject. There is an abridged English translation of the first edition of this work by H. SUNDERLAND, *The Cid and His Spain* (1934). The text of the *Historia Roderici Campidoctori* is printed in Menéndez Pidal, *op. cit.*, vol. 2. For Ibn 'Alqāmah's account of the conquest of Valencia, see E. LEVI-PROVENCAL, "La toma de Valencia por el Cid," *Al-Andalus*, 13:97–157 (1948).

(P.E.R.)

Cimabue

The art of Cimabue, created at the close of the 13th century, represents the culmination of the Byzantine style that had dominated Italian painting in the early Middle Ages. Cimabue's style provided the firm foundation upon which rested the art of Giotto and Duccio in the 14th century, although he was superseded in his own lifetime by these artists, both of whom he had influenced and perhaps trained. His great contemporary, Dante, recognized the importance of Cimabue and placed him at the forefront of Italian painters. Giorgio Vasari, in his *Lives of the Most Eminent Italian Painters, Sculptors and Architects . . .* (1550), begins his collection of biographies with the life of Cimabue. Art historiographers from the 14th century to the present have recognized the art and career of Cimabue as the dividing line between the old and the new traditions in western European painting.

The earliest biography of Cimabue, by Vasari, states that he was born in 1240 and died in 1300. The dates can only be approximations, for it is documented that Cimabue was alive and working in Pisa in 1302. The only other document relative to his life identifies him as a master painter and witness to a document signed in Rome in 1272. From this it can be concluded that he was born prior to 1251. Other documents indicate that he was christened Bencivieni di Pepo, or Benvenuto di Giuseppe in modern Italian. Cimabue was a nickname that through an error later became a family name.

Nothing is known of his early training. Vasari's assertion that he was apprenticed to Greek Byzantine painters living in Italy is probably an attempt to explain both the style and the sudden emergence of this genius. He was

"Sta. Trinita Madonna," painted wood panel by Cimabue, c. 1290. In the Uffizi, Florence. 3.85 m x 2.23 m.
Alinari

certainly influenced by the Italo-Byzantine painter Giunta Pisano and by Coppo di Marcovaldo and may have been an apprentice to Coppo.

Cimabue's character may be reflected in his name, which can perhaps best be translated as "bullheaded." An anonymous commentator in a work on Dante written in 1333–34 said that Cimabue was so proud and demanding that if others found fault with his work, or if he found something displeasing in it himself, he would destroy the work no matter how valuable. It is perhaps significant that in the *Divine Comedy* Dante places Cimabue among the proud in Purgatory. And the poet refers to him to illustrate the transience of earthly fame: "Cimabue thought to hold the field in painting, and now Giotto hath the cry." But pride in his own accomplishments and a high personal standard of excellence separated Cimabue from the anonymous artists of the Middle Ages; indeed, these factors declared him a "modern" man.

Personality and character

Only Cimabue's last work, the mosaic of "St. John the Evangelist," in the Duomo of Pisa, is dated (1301–02). The large "Crucifix," in S. Domenico, Arezzo, is generally accepted as his earliest work and datable before 1272. The frescoes in the Upper Church of S. Francesco, Assisi, were probably done between 1288 and 1290. The period 1290–95 includes the large "Crucifix" for Sta. Croce in Florence—about 70 percent destroyed in the floods of 1966, though restoration is being attempted; the "Sta. Trinita Madonna," an altarpiece now in Florence's Uffizi; and the "Madonna Enthroned with St. Francis," in the Lower Church of S. Francesco at Assisi.

Despite the small number of Cimabue's works that have survived, they fully support the reputation that the artist has acquired. In certain formal or more "official" commissions, such as crucifixes and large altarpieces, Cimabue adhered closely to the formal vocabulary of the Byzantine tradition. And yet he breathes new emotive content into the abstract or stylized forms. In the fresco cycle at Assisi, Cimabue found an especially receptive patron, for the art commissioned by the Franciscans from Cimabue's time on is generally characterized by a dramatic and emotive narrative.

Along with the traditional stylization of the human form, Cimabue seems to have been among the first to return to a close observation of nature. In a highly formal altarpiece such as the "Sta. Trinita Madonna," he introduces at the base of the throne four prophets who are modelled through light and dark in a highly sculptural manner that seems far in advance of its date. Cimabue seems also to have been one of the first to recognize the potentialities of painted architecture, which he introduced into his scenes to give an indication of place and a heightened sense of three-dimensionality. The fresco "The Four Evangelists," in the vault of the crossing of the Upper Church at Assisi, is sculpturally conceived, but its solidity and bulk is heightened by the crystalline city views that accompany each of the figures. The view of Rome that accompanies St. Mark, for example, is not only one of the earliest recognizable views of the city but is also one of the first in which the buildings seem solid and separated one from the other by a clearly defined space. This concern with the illusion of space and with a three-dimensional form occupying that space is rarely met with in medieval painting prior to Cimabue, but it is highly characteristic of Cimabue's leading student and rival, Giotto.

In Cimabue's more formal works he follows tradition closely, but he brings to that tradition a heightened sense of drama. After him the Byzantine tradition in Italy died out, partly because it had been superseded by a new style but also because he had exhausted all the possibilities inherent in the tradition. In his less formal works he was able to exploit a growing interest in narrative that had been inherent in the Byzantine tradition but never fully developed. Finally, he brought to Italian painting a new awareness of space and of sculptural form. By his own personality and by his contributions to painting he merits Vasari's characterization of him as the first Florentine painter and the first painter of "modern" times.

MAJOR WORKS

"Crucifix" (S. Domenico, Arezzo); frescoes of the Upper Church (S. Francesco, Assisi), including four Evangelists in the vaults, "Great Crucifixion" in the left (or south) transept, scenes from the Apocalypse in the lunettes and wall area of the left transept, scenes from the life of the Virgin in the apse, and "St. Peter Healing the Lame" and "St. Peter Healing the Sick" in the right transept—all the frescoes except the four Evangelists are in poor condition). "Crucifix" for Sta. Croce (Museo di Sta. Croce, Florence); "Sta. Trinita Madonna" (an altarpiece of Madonna and Christ Child enthroned with angels and four prophets; Uffizi); "Madonna Enthroned with St. Francis" (fresco, Lower Church of S. Francesco, Assisi); "St. John the Evangelist" (mosaic; Cathedral, Pisa). The following works have been attributed to Cimabue, but opinion is not as unanimous as it is with the above. "Joseph Sold into Egypt" (mosaic; Baptistery, Florence); "Madonna and Child Enthroned with Angels" (from Pisa; Louvre, Paris); "Madonna and Child Enthroned with Two Angels," known as "The Servi Madonna" (Sta. Maria dei Servi, Bologna).

BIBLIOGRAPHY. The earliest literary reference to Cimabue is to be found in DANTE's *Divine Comedy*, "Purgatorio," canto XI, verses 94–96 The earliest biography, although somewhat fanciful in details, is that by GIORGIO VASARI in *Vite . . .*, vol. 1 (1550?; Eng. trans., *Lives of the Most Eminent Painters, Sculptors, and Architects*, 1852–59 and later). All subsequent biographies rely upon Vasari, with the addition of a few documentary references. The earliest author to consider Cimabue seriously was JOSEPH STRZYGOWSKI, *Cimabue und Rom* (1888). ALFRED NICHOLSON, *Cimabue* (1932), is the first American monograph of importance on the artist. Among recent works ROBERTO SALVINI's article in the *Encyclopedia of World Art*, vol. 3, col. 614–619 (1960), sums up recent opinion and summarizes Salvini's own Italian monograph on the artist of 1946. EDWARD B. GARRISON, *Italian Romanesque Panel Painting* (1949), provides a means of comparing Cimabue with his contemporaries. EVE BORSOOK, *The Mural Painters of Tuscany, from Cimabue to Andrea del Sarto* (1960), places Cimabue in the context of the fresco tradition in Italy. EUGENIO BATTISTI, *Cimabue* (1963; Eng. trans., 1967), refers to the standard literature on the artist but is more concerned with the social and religious environment in which Cimabue worked.

(J.R.Sp.)

Cimon

Cimon, an Athenian statesman and general, was remembered chiefly for his leadership of the conservative faction, his policy of friendship with Sparta, his consolidation of the Delian League (an alliance of Greek states), and his vigorous and successful prosecution of its object, war against Persia.

Born about 510 BC, Cimon was the son of Miltiades, of an aristocratic Athenian family, and a Thracian princess. Miltiades, who defeated the Persians in the Battle of Marathon (490), died in disgrace the next year, unable to pay a large fine imposed on him for allegedly misconducting a subsequent operation; but Cimon, after arranging the marriage of his sister to the richest man in Athens, was able to discharge the debt. His conspicuous valour in the victorious sea fight with the Persians at Salamis (480) led soon to his election as strategus—one of Athens' ten annual war ministers and generals—and he was apparently re-elected every year until his ostracism in 461. In 478 he helped the Athenian statesman and general Aristides to secure the transference from Sparta to Athens of the leadership of the Greek maritime states, which had been recently liberated from Persia, and he became the principal commander of the Delian League thus formed.

Valour against the Persians

He first expelled from Byzantium the Spartan general Pausanias, who had been dismissed on suspicion of treasonable dealings with Persia, and he drove the Persians from most of their strongholds on the Thracian coast. Next he subdued the pirates of the island of Scyros and replaced them with Athenian settlers and transported back to Athens in triumph the supposed remains of Theseus, the ancient king of Athens, who was said to have been buried there. Cimon gained his greatest victory (c. 467) when, as leader of an allied fleet of 200 ships, he routed the much larger Phoenician fleet near the mouth of the River Eurymedon in Pamphylia and subsequently defeated the King's forces on land, thus gravely weakening Persian control over the eastern Mediterranean.

Cimon now returned to the Aegean and drove the Persians out of the Thracian Chersonese (Gallipoli). When the rich island of Thasos seceded from the Delian League, Cimon defeated the Thasians at sea, and after a blockade of two years, they surrendered to him (463). Back in Athens, however, he was charged by Pericles and other democratic politicians with having been bribed not to attack the King of Macedonia (who may have been suspected of covertly helping the Thasian rebels).

Though Cimon was acquitted, his star was no longer in the ascendant. The aristocratic faction, which he led, was losing influence; its support rested on the well-to-do citizens who fought as hoplites (heavy armed infantry) and who admired the conservative land power of Sparta. Cimon was personally popular because of his victories and because he spent the wealth those victories brought him on the adornment of the city and the entertainment of the citizens. But the victories were achieved mainly by the fleet, which was manned by the poorer Athenians, who were less well disposed toward Sparta. Elated by their successes and beginning to feel their power, the sailors looked to other leaders, Ephialtes and Pericles, who shared their distrust of Sparta and promised them a larger share in the government.

Those new leaders soon came into their own. When, in 462, the Spartans were vainly endeavouring to reduce the mountain stronghold of Mt. Ithome in Messenia, where a large force of rebellious helots (state-owned serfs) had taken refuge, they asked all their erstwhile allies of the Persian wars, including the Athenians, to help. Cimon urged compliance, comparing Athens and Sparta to a yoke of oxen working together for the good of Greece. Although Ephialtes maintained that Sparta was Athens' rival for power and should be left to fend for herself, Cimon's view prevailed, and he himself led 4,000 hoplites to Mt. Ithome. But after an attempt to storm the place had failed, the Spartans began to wonder if they could trust the Athenians not to take the helot side and, retaining their other allies, sent Cimon and his men home. This insulting rebuff caused the immediate collapse of Cimon's popularity at Athens: at the next opportunity an ostracism, or vote for the exile of the most unpopular citizen, was held; Cimon headed the poll and had to leave Athens for ten years (461).

Cimon's fall from popularity and ostracism

The end of his ascendancy was marked by democratic reforms and the renunciation of the alliance with Sparta. Soon the two states were at war. In 457 their land armies met at Tanagra in Boeotia. Cimon presented himself to the Athenian generals and begged leave to fight in the ranks but was refused. He adjured his personal followers, suspected like him of favouring the Spartans, to fight bravely, and they all perished in the battle.

Perhaps this caused a revulsion of feeling. At any event, Pericles himself proposed and obtained an abbreviation of Cimon's exile. On his return he worked for peace with Sparta. When, eventually, peace came (451), he was allowed to lead a big, new naval expedition against Persia, despite the disastrous failure of the previous Greek enterprise in Egypt (459–454). He took 200 ships to Cyprus, detaching 60 to help the Egyptian nationalists, but during the siege of the Phoenician city of Citium, he died of sickness or a wound.

Cimon was tall and handsome, open and affable in manner, and straightforward in action, a natural leader and perhaps the best general Athens ever had. He married twice, a woman from Arcadia and Isodice, of the noble Athenian family of the Alcmaeonids. Of his six sons, three were named after the peoples of Sparta, Elis, and Thessaly, whose interests he represented at Athens. He was no less determined than Pericles to maintain Athenian naval supremacy in the Aegean but differed from him in upholding the leadership of Sparta on the Greek mainland.

BIBLIOGRAPHY. The ancient evidence for the life of Cimon consists of the biography in Greek by PLUTARCH (early 2nd century AD) and a small amount of earlier material. There are English translations of Plutarch's *Cimon* in the Everyman edition of the *Lives*, vol. 2, pp. 181–200 (1910); and by B. PERRIN in the Loeb edition, vol. 2, pp. 405–467 (1914, reprinted 1959). The main facts are certain, though there are a number of problems, ably discussed by E. MEYER in *Forschungen zur alten Geschichte*, vol. 2, pp. 1–87 (1899). There is no separate modern biography, but the short articles by A.H. CLOUGH in W. SMITH, *Dictionary of Greek and Roman Biography and Mythology*, vol. 1, pp. 749–751 (1844); and by J.M. MUNRO in the *Encyclopædia Britannica*, 11th ed., vol. 6 (1911), are useful. Cimon receives lively personal treatment in the accounts of the period by E.M. WALKER in the *Cambridge Ancient History*, vol. 5, pp. 33–97 (1927); and A.R. BURN, *Pericles and Athens*, pp. 32–96 (1948).

(T.J.C.)

Circulation and Circulatory Systems

Circulation, which means "to pass round," is used in biology in two ways. The more usual is to describe those processes by which metabolic materials are conveyed about in an organism in an orderly manner. The other use of "circulation" is in relation to the passage of certain substances into organisms from the environment and the subsequent release of substances into the environment from the organism or its dead remains. Substances released into the environment may be conserved by passing in turn into another organism and so circulate in the organic world, or biosphere. To this form of circulation the term cycle is usually applied; hence "nitrogen cycle" and "carbon cycle" (see BIOSPHERE).

This article is divided into the following sections:

I. General features

The unique feature of an organism is that it preserves its integrity while taking from its environment materials that it converts to its own substance and releasing byproducts. Within the organism the materials move, or are moved, according to the complexity of the organism, in such a manner that they reach those places in which they are required or from which they can be expelled. In many organisms of microscopic size, diffusion alone may be sufficient to allow for the transportation of the respiratory gases (oxygen and carbon dioxide), while very slow movement of the fluid portions of the protoplasm is sufficient to distribute the larger molecules of sugars, fats, and proteins as they take part in the basic biochemical activities. In organisms of larger size, materials are conveyed in internal fluid in such a way that it can be said to circulate; and in more complex animals the circulating fluid is moved around in special channels, often called blood vessels, by some form of propelling structure that, if restricted in position, is usually called a heart.

The simplest form of circulation, streaming movement of fluid cytoplasm (cyclosis), can be seen in single-celled organisms and in cells of multicellular organisms. Fluids that circulate in cells are taken up in two ways. The first is physicochemical: the concentration of salts within the cell results in osmotic forces drawing water into cells from the surrounding medium. The second is biological: water in the surrounding environment is enclosed in vacuoles by the activities of the surface membrane of the cell, and the completed vacuole passes into the interior of the cell (see CELL AND CELL DIVISION). The physicochemical method of osmotic intake of water is typical of the protist and plant kingdoms. Nutrient salts enter by a process of selective absorption through the cell membrane; the water together with the dissolved nutrients is passed to those parts that need it by methods appropriate to the anatomical complexity of the organism (see PLANT INTERNAL TRANSPORT).

Fluid uptake

The mechanisms by which the fluid contents and their chemical constitution are regulated and maintained at optima for the correct functioning of an organism are termed homeostatic (literally the "same state"). Thus the circulating fluids of multicellular animals play an essential part in maintaining the homeostasis of the whole animal by distributing materials to parts of the body when they are required and removing others from sites in which they must not accumulate (see HOMEOSTASIS).

Circulation, therefore, has to do with all the fluids of the body. In the cells and tissues are the tissue fluids; in the sites exposed to a fluid external medium, some fluid may pass in from the environment by osmosis; this is obvious in such instances as Protozoa, but it also occurs where animals have some permeable surface although the greater part of the surface is impermeable. In land-living animals fluid reaches the cells from water that is drunk and is absorbed by the wall of the alimentary canal; from there it passes to the bloodstream and then to the tissues. In some instances, water from the exterior is not truly absorbed but passed through water channels; in echinoderms, for example, water from the sea is circulated through a special water-vascular system. Typically, however, water absorbed from the exterior through the alimentary canal is passed into the blood. When it leaves the blood to become tissue fluid, it is accompanied by other constituents of the blood, notably food in solution. When this portion of the blood passes back again from the tissues it is in the form of lymph. Its return to the blood is often, as in vertebrates, through special pathways called lymphatic vessels, which thus provide for a lymphatic circulation (see BLOOD AND LYMPH; TISSUES AND FLUIDS, ANIMAL).

The circulation of blood in animals can be compared with the movement of fluids through the tissues of higher plants only in the most general terms. Water and nutrient salts enter plant roots by physicochemical means and are then transferred into the special conducting, or vascular, tissues that extend from the roots through the stem and into the leaves. There are two specialized types of tissue involved in transport of materials, xylem (or wood) and phloem (or bast). The xylem and phloem remain in neighbouring columns throughout the plant and are frequently bound together in association with unspecialized tissue. These associations, called vascular bundles, and their distribution, architecture, and functions are dealt with in the article PLANT INTERNAL TRANSPORT. The vascular tissues of plants convey a fluid consisting basically of water in which are dissolved gases, nutrient salts, elaborated foodstuffs, the products of metabolism, and plant hormones.

II. Circulation and transport patterns

Before an account of circulatory systems of the phyla is given, it is necessary to consider the general aspects common to all circulatory systems and to define terms of general application.

CIRCULATION IN SINGLE CELLS

Cyclosis

As mentioned earlier, circulation in single cells is accomplished by cyclosis, streaming movements within the protoplasm. These movements transport materials intracellularly and supply general metabolic needs. In motile cells cyclosis may also serve the function of locomotion. Amoeboid protozoans can glide over solid surfaces via pseudopodia, projections of the cell boundary as a result of localized and transient flow of protoplasm. Slime molds and white blood cells (leukocytes) exhibit similar streaming movements that serve locomotion (see LOCOMOTION).

In ciliated protozoans, in which the body has a definite shape and limiting layer (*e.g.*, *Paramecium*), internal streaming is associated with feeding. Small particles are taken in at the base of a tubular gullet and enclosed in a food vacuole and then pass through the organism in a definite pathway. In some cells of the pond-weed *Chara* circulation can clearly be seen, and similar streaming movements may be responsible for the transport of sugars and other materials in the phloem of vascular plants (see PLANT INTERNAL TRANSPORT). In many cells of multicellular animals, streaming movements are important; this is particularly clear in the case of neurons (nerve cells), in which the distances the materials have to diffuse may be several centimetres or more.

CIRCULATION IN MULTICELLULAR ANIMALS

Major roles of circulation. Animals that live in water obtain their oxygen from atmospheric oxygen dissolved in it. Volume for volume, water contains about one-thirtieth of the amount of oxygen as does air at the same temperature and pressure. Thus an animal living in water must pass a large volume of water over its respiratory surface (which may be localized as a gill) to obtain access to the same amount of oxygen an air-breathing animal could obtain from contact with a much smaller volume of air. Water is much more dense than air so that aquatic animals, which "breathe" water by muscular action, must expend considerably more energy in this process than would an air-breathing animal. Once obtained, the supply of oxygen must be transported to the internal parts of the body via the circulatory system.

Another function of circulation is to convey digested foodstuffs around the body to places where they are needed. But in many aquatic animals feeding and respiration are connected in another way. This is in the process of filter feeding, which is met with in many sedentary animals. In the current of water that the animal causes to pass over its gills, where gaseous exchange can take place, are large quantities of organic particulate matter suitable for food. These particles are strained out of the water and passed to the alimentary canal for ingestion at the same time that the gills are extracting oxygen from the same current of water.

Modes of circulation. Although examples will be given below of instances in which the external water of the surroundings is actually circulated through the body of an animal for respiratory and, in the case of coelenterates, nutritive purposes, this condition is unusual in the animal kingdom as a whole, and an independent fluid, blood, is circulated within the organism.

External versus internal circulation

The development of a blood system can, to a certain extent, be correlated with the degree of complexity of the organism. Multicellular animals above the sponge level can be conveniently divided into two groups: those in which the body is made of two cell layers (diploblastic) and those that consist of three cell layers (triploblastic). The diploblastic animals comprise the phylum Coelenterata (jellyfish, sea anemones, corals, etc.); their two cell layers are the ectoderm (on the outside) and the endoderm (on the inside) lining a blind tube that suffices for alimentary and other needs. Between these two layers is a structureless gelatinous substance (mesoglea), which may attain considerable thickness, as in jellyfish. The triploblastic animals have a third cellular layer between the ectoderm and endoderm: namely, the mesoderm. In its simplest form the mesoderm looks like a meshwork of cells in which the various organs are packed; a good example is the condition met with in Platyhelminthes (flatworms). This is the acoelomate condition.

An important further advance is the development in the mesoderm itself of a fluid-filled cavity; this is the coelom and the fluid is the coelomic fluid.

Coelomates, animals that possess a coelom, or body cavity, show complexity of structure far surpassing that of noncoelomates. The presence of a coelom results in the separation of the ectoderm, together with the outer layer of mesoderm, from the endoderm (and inner layer of mesoderm) by the coelomic fluid. Diffusion of gases and metabolites through this fluid would be so inefficient a means of transport as to be useless except in very special circumstances, such as in animals of minute size. Thus, a system of communication across the coelom is necessary. This function is served by the blood system. As will be seen below, the coelom and blood system are not always separate; mixed hemocoeles are found. Further, the development of a blood system and the existence of a coelomic cavity does not mean that in aquatic animals external water is never circulated through the body: in echinoderms (starfish, sea urchins, etc.) a very elaborate water-vascular-system occurs in addition to other blood hemal systems as will be described.

Circulating fluids. In the great majority of multicellular animals the following fluids are present: tissue fluid; coelomic fluid: and blood. These fluids are all related in that their vehicle is water derived from the environment. They differ, sometimes remarkably, as to the nature of the materials added to the water in various ways. This regulation is to a large extent a property of the living membranes that separate these fluids and so allow them to vary both chemically and biologically.

Water as the basis of all circulating fluids

Blood differs from coelomic fluid in that it occupies its own channels, blood vessels, through which it is circulated so that it provides a means of communication by which materials in solution can be passed around the body. Where hemocoeles are found, blood, instead of coelomic fluid, occupies the body cavity. Blood can vary in composition from a fluid, which in some aquatic animals is basically the surrounding water (modified only slightly by the addition of foodstuffs and metabolites undergoing transportation), to, in others, a highly complex tissue containing many millions of cells of several different types and functions.

Lymph is derived from blood plasma modified in its passage through the tissues. This fluid is called lymph generally if its return to the bloodstream is in a pathway clearly defined and separate from blood vessels and the coelomic space.

Blood systems. Unlike coelomic fluid, which is moved in an apparently random manner in response to the alterations of the body that contains it, blood is circulated through the vessels that make up the blood vascular system. Circulation of blood is brought about by contraction of the muscular elements of the vessels. Such vessels, or portions of the system showing this propulsive action are known as "hearts." Vessels contractile over a considerable length are often referred to as tubular hearts; sometimes the muscular region is restricted to a special part of the system and is called a chambered heart. Although most animals possess one heart, this condition is by no means universal.

The characteristic feature of a heart is its continued pulsation throughout life. A heart receives blood under low pressure and forces it outward into the circulation once again at higher pressure. The blood is directed by valves, which usually take the form of flaps of tissue arranged around the circumference of the tube. These allow the blood to flow forward but prevent backflow.

A chambered heart consists of a series of chambers separated by such valves. The early chambers act as reservoirs from which blood passes to the main pumping chamber, or ventricle. The expansion of a chamber is known as diastole and the contraction, systole. As one chamber undergoes systole the next in sequence undergoes diastole, and the blood passes onward. This sequence of events, during which blood in the first chamber is moved through all the other chambers, is called a cardiac cycle.

The muscular ventricle propels the blood through the vessels. This force is the blood pressure. As pressure rises in the ventricle, at some point it becomes sufficiently great to open the valves, which had been closed by the attempted reversed flow of blood in the previous cycle. At this point ventricular pressure is suddenly transmitted to the blood in the arterial system and travels as a wave through the column of fluid at high speed; this pressure wave is the pulse. The amount of blood discharged by the ventricle at each contraction is known as the stroke volume and normally depends on the activity of the animal.

On leaving the heart the blood is conveyed by vessels that branch repeatedly, the diameter of the branches becoming smaller at each division. The smallest branches reached are usually only a few microns in diameter; these are the capillaries. Capillaries have very thin walls through which the fluid part of the blood passes and bathes the tissue cells. The capillaries pick up wastes and then rejoin into larger collecting vessels, which ultimately return the blood to the heart.

In vertebrate animals there are structural differences between the vessels called arteries, which carry blood away from the heart under considerable pressure, and the vessels called veins, which return the blood to the heart at a reduced pressure. In other groups of animals it is not always possible to distinguish between arteries and veins, and such vessels are referred to simply as blood vessels.

In two large phyla of animals, namely the Mollusca and the Arthropoda, there are "open" blood systems in which the blood leaves the heart through vessels that, instead of dividing into smaller vessels, open into the body cavity so that all the organs are directly bathed in blood, forming a hemocoele. This name indicates that the blood system and the body cavity (coelom), distinct in other phyla, are here fused together.

Initiation of the heartbeat The contraction of the heart itself may be initiated in either of two ways. First the periodic contraction may be an intrinsic property of the heart muscle itself; this condition, termed myogenic, is universal in vertebrates. In some arthropods, the beat is initiated by a nerve impulse arriving from outside the heart muscle, a condition called neurogenic.

III. Invertebrate circulatory systems

CIRCULATION IN SPONGES AND COELENTERATES

Sponges are made up of cellular masses pierced by a system of ramifying water channels. These channels, lined by flagellated collar cells (choanocytes), open on the sides of the sponge at inhalant apertures. The channels join together in the center to form one or more larger exhalant channels; these open by a common channel often at the top of the sponge (Figure 1A). The beating

From (B,F) R. Buchsbaum, *Animals Without Backbones* (1948); University of Chicago Press, (C) T.J. Parker and W.A. Haswell, *Textbook of Zoology*; St. Martin's Press, Inc., Macmillan & Co., Ltd., (E,G) Biological Sciences Curriculum Study, *Biological Science: An Inquiry Into Life*, second edition, 1968, Harcourt Brace Jovanovich

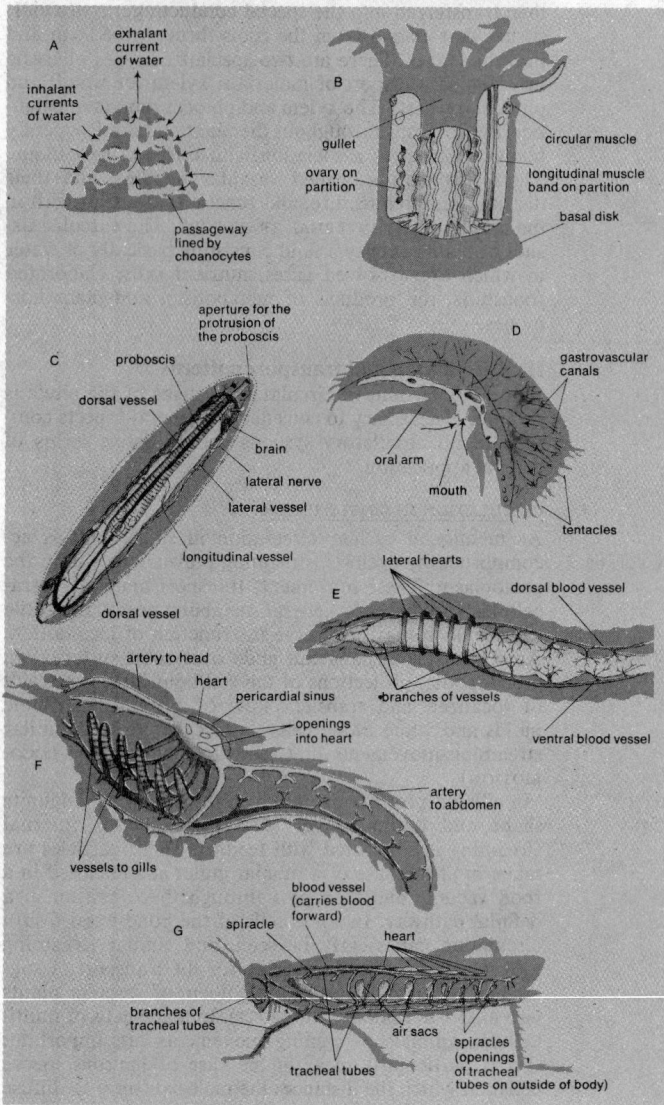

Figure 1: Vertical section through (A) sponge and (B) sea anemone, with water circulation indicated by arrows; (C) circulation in nemertean worm; (D) internal arrangement of ciliated endodermal canals in jellyfish; arrows show the direction of water currents; (E) circulation in earthworm; (F) circulation in decapod crustacean; (G) circulation in insect (grasshopper).

of flagella draws water into the channels through the inhalant apertures and ejects it through the exhalant ones. This current has two functions, respiratory exchange and feeding. Food particles in the water adhere to the choanocytes and are subsequently ingested. Transport of nutrients and respiratory exchange within the cell mass is effected largely by diffusion.

The coelenterates rely on diffusion for transport of materials within the cell layers. Circulation of water occurs inside the body cavity, or coelenteron (Figure 1B). In the scyphozoan jellyfishes, the body cavity consists of a series of complex branching channels that ramifies within the jellylike bell of the organism (Figure 1D). These channels are lined with ciliated cells that create water currents in the interior of the bell, thus promoting the exchange of oxygen and carbon dioxide between the water and the organism and conveying food particles to the digestive regions of the coelenteron. The movement of water in these ducts is assisted by the muscular activity of the bell. In hydroids and sea anemones, water currents are circulated from the outside through the coelenteron by means of cilia arranged in tracts on its surface.

CIRCULATION IN TRIPLOBLASTS

Acoelomates. In this varied assembly of triploblastic animals, a blood system is present in only one major group, the marine nemertean worms. The blood is contained in special vessels, of mesodermal origin, that form a closed circulatory system (Figure 1C). The pattern of these vessels is somewhat variable; in many species there is a median dorsal longitudinal vessel and two lateral ones. Blood is pumped through these by pulsatile regions of the vessels and is passed through lateral branches into capillaries in the tissues. The blood in some nemerteans contains hemoglobin, either dissolved in the plasma or contained inside special cells, and has a respiratory transport function. This is the most primitive true blood system found among invertebrates.

Unusual "circulation" in flatworms Flatworms (platyhelminths) are generally regarded as having no recognizable circulation of fluids, since there are no large internal cavities or vessels. There are, however, spaces between the loosely packed cells of the mesoderm through which tissue fluid can flow by the action of the body muscles. In the roundworms (nematodes) there is an extensive body cavity, the pseudocoel, which is not regarded as a true coelom since it forms by the breakdown of part of the mesoderm late in embryonic development. It is not lined by a special layer of cells (mesothelium) as in true coelomates. This cavity is filled by tissue fluid set in motion by the general movement of the body muscles; this assists diffusion between the internal and external body layers. In some roundworms (*e.g.*, *Ascaris*) hemoglobin is found in the pseudocoel and can form an oxygen reserve.

In rotifers, small aquatic filter-feeding animals of microscopic size, there is another type of pseudocoel (of different embryological origin), containing the internal organs; tissue fluid lies in this cavity and is moved as in nematodes. In other acoelomate groups that lack a large body cavity, such as the wormlike entoprocts, kinorhynchans, acanthocephalans, and gordiaceans, tissue fluid fills intercellular spaces as in the flatworms, but the body size is generally so small that diffusion is probably the chief means of internal transport. Where a body cavity is present it also acts as a hydrostatic skeleton and makes possible various movements of the body.

Coelomates. *Annelids.* The phylum Annelida comprises all segmented coelomate worms and includes marine bristleworms (Polychaeta), earthworms (Oligochaeta), and leeches (Hirudinea). A blood system may be lacking in some very small annelids, diffusion assisted by body muscle movements sufficing for internal transport. In the majority, however, the blood system is well developed, consisting of a series of narrow vessels and sometimes wider blood spaces (sinuses) through which blood is pumped by tubular hearts or pulsatile vessels. The blood system is therefore usually of the closed type; partly open systems are found in some forms having large sinuses.

In the bristleworms and earthworms the usual circulatory pattern is as follows (Figure 1E). Blood flows forward along a dorsal median vessel to the anterior end of the worm, where it passes through a number of connecting vessels around the gut to a ventral median blood vessel. This takes blood backward and distributes it by side channels to the various organs and tissues where the vessels become capillaries or blood sinuses. Blood is then collected into larger vessels and returned to the median dorsal vessel. All vessels except the median longitudinal ones are arranged on a segmental basis corresponding generally to the body segmentation. Pulsatile blood vessels may be distributed widely in the body and may, as in the bristleworm *Nereis* and the earthworm *Lumbricus*, have specialized enlarged regions, or hearts, in the more anterior lateral vessels. The larger blood vessels are provided with pocket valves that ensure unidirectional flow of blood. The hearts in most annelids are neurogenic, the nerve cells usually being situated in or on the walls of the heart.

In most leeches the blood system is open. The coelom contains special packing tissue that fills most of the body cavity. Spaces around the dorsal and longitudinal collecting vessels, and in many parts of the body, form sinuses. The walls of the midline vessels allow blood to enter the coelomic sinuses. In addition, a pair of lateral longitudinal vessels pump the blood forward and then through the sinuses, from which it is returned to the lateral vessels. These vessels pulsate alternately.

The blood in annelids, as well as carrying nutrients from the gut to other parts of the body, is a carrier of respiratory gases, particularly oxygen. The capillaries of the body wall are often very close to the body surface and oxygen diffuses rapidly into the blood from the outside water or air. Many bristleworms have gills provided with a rich supply of blood; in others the tentacles used in filter feeding may act as an important surface for respiratory exchange. Some waste carbon dioxide is also carried in the blood, but direct diffusion from the tissues to the exterior (partly by way of the coelom) is also important.

Respiratory pigments in annelids Annelid blood consists of plasma and nonpigmented phagocytic cells (leukocytes). Oxygen-carrying pigments are found in many species; hemoglobin is present in solution in the plasma of bristleworms such as *Arenicola*, earthworms such as *Lumbricus*, and leeches such as *Hirudo*. In some bristleworms chlorocruorin is present (*e.g.*, *Sabella*); both chlorocruorin and hemoglobin are found together in *Serpula*. Hemerythrin is present in corpuscles in *Magelona*.

The respiratory pigments of these worms play an important part in acting as an oxygen reservoir, particularly in species that burrow in sand or mud. Many aquatic annelids circulate water externally by means of cilia, in some instances over gills, or by muscular action to create feeding and respiratory currents. The coelom also acts as an important hydrostatic skeleton enabling annelids to achieve a high level of motility.

Arthropods. The phylum Arthropoda includes the crustaceans, arachnids, centipedes, millipedes, and insects. All possess a rigid exoskeleton and jointed appendages. In many features, particularly the external division of the body and in the nervous system, they show a segmental organization, but this does not extend to the coelom.

The circulation is open, and the coelom has large blood spaces with a cellular lining (endothelium) like that of blood vessels. This true hemocoel occupies most of the coelom, extends inside the jointed appendages and other structures, and lies in close proximity to all organs in the body. The heart is tubular and usually consists of a longitudinal blood vessel lying in the midline dorsally. It is suspended by strips of muscle or ligaments in a blood sinus, the pericardium, and on both sides a row of small apertures (ostia), segmentally arranged and guarded by flap valves, allows the passage of blood from the pericardium to the heart. Blood, pumped forward in the heart, is conveyed anteriorly by an aorta to a series of tubular vessels, which supply the hemocoel. In decapod crustaceans such as the crabs the heart is shortened and lies more anteriorly in the body (Figure 1F). Blood may pass posteriorly from this structure to the abdomen. Longitudinally running septa in the hemocoel may divert the blood along regular circulatory pathways. The blood finally returns by sinuses or narrower blood vessels to the pericardium.

Accessory hearts in arthropods In very small arthropods such as mites, the blood system may be reduced or absent. In some crustaceans such as the fairy shrimp *Chirocephalus*, the jointed appendages are in constant activity for respiratory and feeding purposes; blood may be pumped mainly by the internal pressure changes these movements cause in the sinuses of the appendages. Where appendages are very long or broad, accessory hearts situated at their bases may boost the supply of blood; *e.g.*, accessory hearts are found at the bases of the antennae and of the wings in insects (Figure 1G).

Many crustaceans have gills situated at the base of jointed appendages, and through them blood is pumped to promote respiratory exchange. The movements of the associated appendages are often used to ventilate these gills with a current of water. In crabs and lobsters the blood from all parts of the body returns to the heart by way of the gill sinuses so that all blood gains oxygen and loses carbon dioxide each time it is circulated. In the horseshoe crab the gills hang in a series of plates ventrally to form gill books, and in scorpions and spiders similar plates, called lung books, are found in special cavities that protect against dehydration.

In onychophorans, millipedes, centipedes, and insects, oxygen reaches the tissues through a network of air passageways, the tracheal system, the ultimate branches of which penetrate the cells; in these cases oxygen transport is not an important function of blood. Carbon dioxide transport may still be carried out by blood.

The blood of arthropods consists of plasma in which lie several types of white cells called hemocytes. Some of these are chiefly phagocytic in activity, whereas others are able to adhere to each other to form a clot when the lining of the blood system is damaged and so prevent leakage. In many arthropods there are also explosive cells that initiate clot formation by precipitating protein fibres from the plasma.

In many arthropods where oxygen transport is a function of the blood, respiratory pigments are found. Hemoglobin is present in a few crustaceans (*e.g.*, *Daphnia*) and in some insects (*e.g.*, the larvae of chironomid midges). Hemocyanin is common in crustaceans and is also the pigment of the horseshoe crab.

The heartbeat is neurogenic in many arthropods. Special nerve cells, called pacemaker neurons, situated in or on the heart muscle initiate the contraction wave, which starts at the posterior end and spreads anteriorly. Other neurons may have an inhibitory action. In some less advanced crustaceans and in insect larvae the heartbeat is myogenic and probably without nervous regulation.

Since the blood fills a large hemocoel, its pressure serves as a hydrostatic skeleton. In barnacles the appendages, and in spiders the legs, are extended and relaxed by alteration of blood pressure within them, brought about by muscular action. In insects that pass through a pupal stage, the wings are extended after emergence by the pressure of blood being pumped into their veins.

Mollusks. In the phylum Mollusca the true coelom is much reduced and in the adult mollusk is represented by restricted cavities around the heart (pericardium), kidneys, and reproductive organs. Circulation is usually open, with large hemocoels as well as narrower blood vessels (Figure 2A). The hemocoels develop as spaces in the body tissues, being the remains of the primary embryonic cavity, or blastocoel. They do not appear to be lined with endothelium, so tissue fluid and blood are not separated.

Unlike other mollusks, cephalopods (squids and octopods) have closed circulation (Figure 2B), and blood flows through a series of relatively narrow vessels with thick walls, enabling a high pressure and high rate of flow to be maintained, correlated with the greater metabolic needs of these highly active animals.

Molluscan blood flow Blood flow in all mollusks is unidirectional. The heart, which is of the chambered type, usually consists of a single median ventricle to which blood is pumped by one or two auricles, or atria. Blood is forced by the ventricle along an aorta, which branches in various directions to supply the different parts of the body. Venous return from the tissues is by way of a varied number of blood sinuses, among them the pericardium, where phagocytic cells remove solid contaminants from the blood. Another sinus surrounds the kidney, where excretory materials are eliminated. One of the routes back to the heart passes through the gills, where gases are exchanged. Blood from each gill passes directly into an atrium of the heart; thus there is a correspondence between the number of gills and the number of atria. Bivalve mollusks and some gastropods (*e.g.*, limpets and whelks) have two gills and two atria; most gastropods have one gill and one atrium; some cephalopods have two gills, and some four, with corresponding numbers of atria. The primitive mollusk *Neo-*

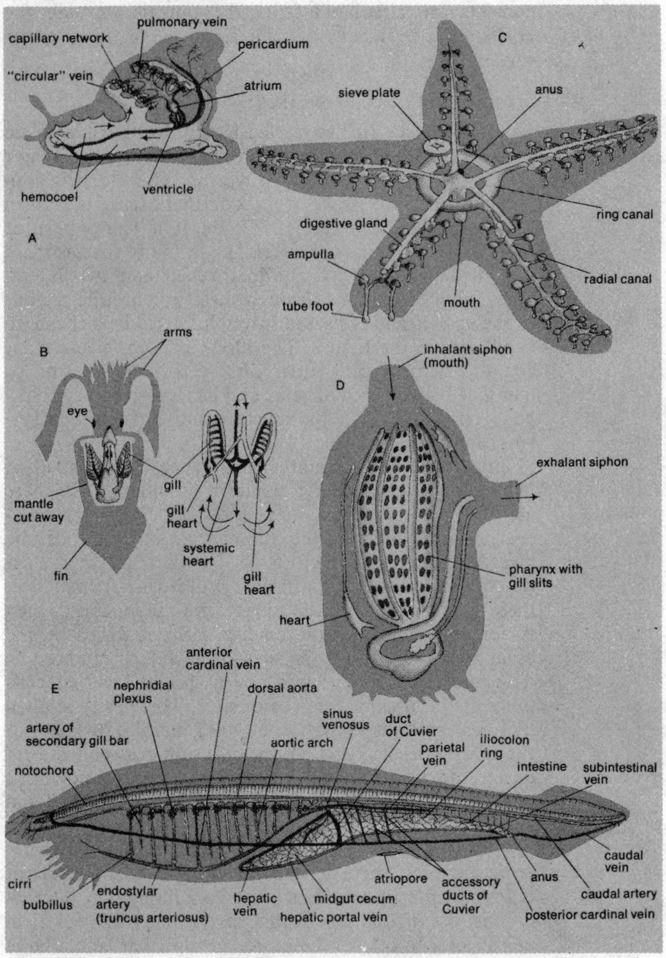

Figure 2: Circulatory system of (A) snail, (B) cephalopod, (C) starfish, (D) tunicate, (E) amphioxus.

From (A,C) *Life: An Introduction to Biology*, 2nd ed., by George Gaylord Simpson and William S. Beck, © 1957, 1965 by Harcourt Brace Jovanovich, Inc., and reproduced with their permission; (B,D) H. Curtis, *Biology*, Worth Publishers, New York, 1968, pages 275, 297; (E) L. Hyman, *Comparative Vertebrate Anatomy* (1942), University of Chicago Press

pilina possesses five pairs of gills, four auricles, and two ventricles; this condition may be a vestige of a segmental organization of ancestral mollusks.

The molluscan heart is myogenic, usually with neural control of acceleration and deceleration. In cephalopods there are, in addition to the main heart, branchial hearts at the bases of the gills. In most other mollusks only a fraction of the blood leaving the main heart at any one time passes through the gills on its way to the tissues; the blood reaching the tissues is therefore a mixture of oxygenated and deoxygenated blood. In cephalopods, however, the supply of oxygen to the tissues is enhanced because blood is pumped by the main heart through the body tissues and is conveyed back by way of the gills and is therefore oxygenated when recirculated. The extra branchial hearts act as booster pumps in passing the blood across the gill capillaries and so back to the main heart. Such hearts are termed ampullar hearts.

In mollusks the blood transports nutrients, respiratory gases, and waste materials. Although gaseous exchange can occur at all parts of the exposed body surface, it does so particularly at the gills, over which water is passed by ciliary or muscular action. In bivalves the large folded gills are used in both respiration and filter feeding; another membranous fold of the body surface, the mantle, lines the inside of the shell and acts as an important additional respiratory surface. In the land and freshwater snails (class Pulmonata), part of the body surface is turned into an internal sac that forms a respiratory cavity, or lung, supplied with many blood vessels.

Respiratory pigments are found in the blood of many mollusks. Hemocyanin dissolved in the plasma is the most common (*e.g.*, as in cephalopods). In the freshwater snail *Planorbis*, hemoglobin in the plasma acts as an oxygen store; hemoglobin is also present in the blood corpuscles of some bivalves.

Blood pumped at high pressure into blood sinuses in the foot of bivalves aids in burrowing movements.

Echinoderms. The phylum Echinodermata includes starfish, brittle stars, sea urchins, sea cucumbers, and sea lilies. Most adult echinoderms have a five-rayed pattern (pentamerous arrangement) of the organ systems.

The larvae, however, are bilaterally symmetrical; during development three pairs of coelomic cavities are formed between the ectoderm and endoderm. The hindmost pair form the perivisceral coelom and the middle pair the water-vascular system; the left anterior cavity forms the axial sinus and the right anterior cavity disappears. During development, cells that break off from the developing endoderm wander into the blastocoele cavity as mesenchyme and form mesoderm in addition to that which surrounds the various coelomic cavities. The blood system forms as channels in the mesenchyme. It is much reduced in importance compared with the animals so far considered because circulation is accomplished by the water-vascular system and the perivisceral coelom.

The perivisceral coelom is the general body cavity, in which the branches of the alimentary canal lie. It contains a fluid very like seawater in chemical composition but includes some proteins and unpigmented coelomic cells. This fluid is moved by the cilia of the cells lining the cavity. Diffusion of gases between the surrounding water and the coelomic fluid takes place across the body wall. In some starfishes (Figure 2C) hollow fingerlike projections of the coelom (papulae) project through the upper surface so that the coelomic fluid is separated from the seawater by a very thin layer of mesoderm and ectoderm. In sea urchins branched gills may be present round the mouth; in sea cucumbers the posterior part of the gut is infolded to form a "respiratory tree" of highly branched blind-ending tubes that project into the coelom. Seawater can be taken into the gut through the anus and forced by muscular action into the respiratory tree. The tube feet of echinoderms also provide a high surface area for respiratory exchange (see below).

The "respiratory tree" in sea cucumbers

The cells of the coelomic fluid are mostly wandering phagocytes, but other cell types are also present. Some species, such as the sea cucumber *Cucumaria*, possess hemoglobin in coelomic cells; this may act as an oxygen reservoir when the external oxygen concentration is low.

The blood system consists of a series of vessels associated chiefly with the gut wall and with the ventral surfaces of the arms (or corresponding structures). A circumoral hemal ring lies ventrally, and from this a hemal strand runs along each arm. A vertical axial strand lies to one side of the stone canal (see below) and near the gut, ventrally, it joins the circumoral ring. At the dorsal tip of the axial strand is a nodular expansion, the axial organ; other similar enlargements are found elsewhere in the hemal system. These may produce new coelomic cells and also have a phagocytic action on foreign particles. The vessels of the hemal system are not lined by special cells, but appear rather to be gaps in the body tissues, which communicate freely with the coelom. Pulsations occur in various parts of the system, but the flow of fluid can reverse from time to time. The vessels do not form capillaries but end blindly in the tissues; the importance of the system probably lies in promoting the penetration of coelomic fluid into the internal organs, particularly the gut wall, and its subsequent passage back to the coelom for nutritional and respiratory purposes. In sea cucumbers branches of the hemal vessels form an elaborate network, the rete mirabile, over the surface of the respiratory tree. The hemal vessels are generally enclosed throughout their course in a special portion of coelom called the perihemal system.

The water-vascular system of echinoderms

That the hemal system is so poorly developed may be accounted for largely by the existence of the water-vascular system, which originates from the coelom (hydrocoele) in the manner described. The water-vascular system usually acquires an opening to the outside through a perforated calcareous plate, the madreporite. In sea cucumbers, however, this opens internally into the coelom, so the system is filled with coelomic fluid.

From the madreporite, a vertical canal (the stone canal) runs down the axis of the body and joins a circumoral ring vessel ventrally. The water-vascular system is kept filled with fluid drawn in through the madreporite by the cilia of the stone canal. Blind-ending sacs called polian vesicles and Tiedemann's bodies open onto the stone canal. From the circumoral ring, radial canals extend along each arm, from which open the blind-ending sacs that form the tube feet. In many groups there is a hollow reservoir or ampulla at the base of each tube foot. Contracting the muscles of the ampulla and the circular muscles of the tube foot extends the foot; contracting the longitudinal muscles of the foot shortens the tube foot. This forms the basis of locomotion in most echinoderms (see LOCOMOTION).

Crinoids, or sea lilies, also use changes in fluid pressure in the radial canals to move their arms in a swimming motion.

Minor coelomate phyla. The Echiurida, Sipuncula, and Priapulida are wormlike marine burrowers that possess coeloms but lack the segmentation typical of the annelids. Of these phyla only some echiuroids possess a blood system. Coelomic fluid circulation brought about by movements of the body muscles transports nutrients and respiratory gases. In those echiuroids that possess a closed blood system there are dorsal and ventral median longitudinal vessels with side branches, and blood apparently circulates much as in annelids. Hemoglobin is present in special coelomic cells. Hemerythrin is the respiratory pigment of sipunculids and priapulids. The coelomic cavity also forms an important hydrostatic skeleton allowing burrowing movements in these animals.

The phoronid worms and the beardworms, unrelated filter feeders, possess a simple closed circulatory system consisting, respectively, of median and lateral, and dorsal and ventral blood vessels through which blood is circulated by a tubular heart. The anterior crown of ciliated tentacles possesses a rich supply of blood and forms a respiratory surface as well as a filter-feeding apparatus. Hemoglobin is present in some blood cells of *Phoronis*.

In the bryozoans (ectoprocts), small sedentary filter feeders, and in the arrowworms, carnivorous planktonic animals, a blood system is lacking. Fluid may circulate in the coelom by ciliary or muscular action, as it does in the brachiopods (lamp shells), some of which possess the pigment hemerythrin in coelomic cells. In the brachiopods there is also a poorly developed closed blood system with a saclike heart.

Chordates. The phylum Chordata includes all those animals that at some stage, at least, of their life history possess a notochord, a dorsal tubular nerve cord, and a series of paired visceral clefts connecting the cavity of the pharynx with the exterior. Although these features are shown by all vertebrates (including man), some are also displayed by three other groups of chordates: the Hemichordata, Urochordata, and Cephalochordata. In the vertebrates the relationship between the blood vessels and the visceral clefts is of paramount importance in understanding the comparative morphology of the arterial system.

The hemichordates, or acorn worms, have a circulatory system somewhat like that of annelids. Blood is pumped by pulsatile vessels forward along the dorsal midline and backward along the ventral one. The blood is distributed to the tissue by paired segmental vessels. In addition there is a pulsatile heart at the anterior end situated dorsally at the base of the proboscis. The blood is devoid of pigment. In other species the blood system is similar but reduced.

The hemichordate circulatory plan

The urochordates, or tunicates (Figure 2D), have a blood system partly of the open type: the heart is a tube that pumps blood into small vessels opening into peripheral blood sinuses. The direction of blood flow alternates, since the heart forces the blood one way for a few beats and then reverses its direction. The blood is colourless but in many species contains the vanadium-rich pigment hemovanadin inside corpuscles.

In the cephalochordates, represented by amphioxus (Figure 2E), the blood flow is of the vertebrate pattern: backward along a median dorsal distributing vessel (dorsal aorta) into capillaries and sinuses of the tissues, from which it is collected by a number of ventral veins to be returned forward to a pulsatile vessel in the midventral line. From here the blood is pumped forward through a midventral vessel, which branches on both sides to give off a further series of vessels that lie in the bars of tissue separating slitlike apertures in the wall of the pharynx. These bars are called visceral arches. The vessels run in arches to join together dorsally into a simple vessel on each side (lateral aortae), which in turn fuse more posteriorly to form the single median dorsal aorta.

Many of the vessels of amphioxus are pulsatile and assist in promoting circulation; small accessory "hearts" (bulbils) are present at the bases of the visceral arches.

IV. The vertebrate circulatory system
THE BASIC VERTEBRATE PATTERN

The plan. The vertebrate heart is situated below the alimentary canal close to the midventral line and is enclosed in its own portion of the body cavity, the pericardial coelom. In fishes and in embryos of higher vertebrates, the heart is found below the posterior region of the pharynx. In adults of the higher groups, notably reptiles, birds, and mammals, the heart shifts posteriorly during embryonic development and may be far removed from its original position.

The study of the early stages of the development of the heart and circulation is important from the evolutionary point of view, for all the patterns of circulation seen in vertebrates can be related to a common "ancestral" pattern (Figure 3A).

In so far as the soft tissues of the heart and blood vessels are not preserved in fossils, the evolution of the heart cannot be demonstrated in the same way as can the evolution of the skeleton, but comparative studies show a pattern of increasing complexity related to adaptation to life on land.

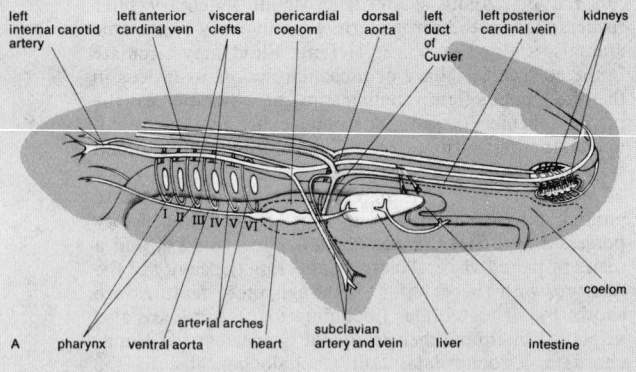

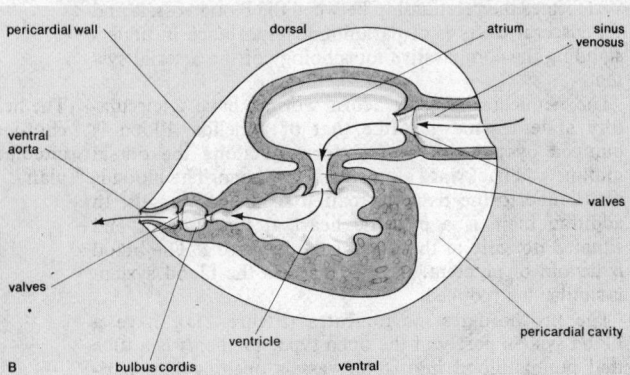

Figure 3: (A) Lateral view of a hypothetical primitive vertebrate showing arterial and venous systems in relation to each other and to alimentary canal. (B) Left side longitudinal section of basic form of vertebrate heart; arrow represents direction of blood flow.

The venous system. It is convenient to start a comparative survey by considering the venous system as it is seen in all vertebrate embryos and with only minor modifications in the adults of sharks and sharklike fishes (elasmobranchs). In the venous system, blood in the capillaries is gathered up into veins, most prominent of which are the paired anterior and posterior cardinal veins (left and right), which return blood from the front and hind ends of the body, respectively. The cardinal veins drain into the ducts of Cuvier, which, running deep in the animal on either side of the alimentary canal, transfer the blood from a position dorsal to the alimentary canal to one ventral to it; the duct on either side traverses the pericardial wall and enters the heart, delivering the blood into the most posterior chamber, the sinus venosus. Other tributary veins enter the anterior and posterior cardinal veins. The inferior jugular veins, returning blood from the lower part of the head, enter the ducts of Cuvier directly.

Lower vertebrates possess two portal systems, portions of the venous system that begin in capillaries in tissues and join together to form veins that then break down to form another capillary network on their way to the heart. The two systems are the hepatic portal and renal portal; they appear to have important functions in transportation of materials that do not pass directly into the general circulation. *The portal systems*

The hepatic portal system begins in the capillaries of the intestinal region of the alimentary canal and carries blood to the sinusoids of the liver; here food materials absorbed in the wall of the intestine can be transferred to the liver cells, which by differential absorption exercise control over substances circulating in the blood. The renal portal system arises from the caudal vein, which reaches the level of the kidneys and branches into two veins that convey blood to capillary networks in the kidneys.

The function of the renal portal system is not so obvious as is that of the hepatic portal system, for there is no evidence that the blood entering the kidney by these vessels is modified in chemical composition as it passes through the kidney. The physiological action of the kidney in excretion is apparently reserved for blood that reaches the kidney directly from the arterial system; only after such modification has taken place do the two kinds of blood, arterial and portal, mix to return through the renal veins to the heart.

The heart. The myogenic heart beats continuously throughout life, being composed of automatically rhythmical contractile muscle (cardiac muscle) not found elsewhere in the body. The ducts of Cuvier, mentioned above, conduct the blood into the sinus venosus, the most posterior chamber of the heart (Figure 3B). From the sinus venosus the blood is passed to the atrium, thence to the ventricle, and finally to the bulbus cordis, through which it leaves the heart and is discharged into the arterial system. The passage of the blood through the heart is brought about by the sequential contraction of the chambers, commencing with the sinus venosus. Each complete sequence of contraction and subsequent relaxation is known as a cardiac cycle. From an early stage in development, the length of the cardiac tube becomes considerably greater than the corresponding dimension of the pericardial cavity, with the result that the heart tube twists upon itself in such a way that the chambers take on an S-shaped bend; thus, the atrium, which comes to lie anteriorly to the sinus venosus, passes blood posteriorly into the ventricular part of the tube. The ventricular loop then leads forward again into the bulbar region. During development the passages between the chambers become guarded by valves, which permit the blood to flow in one direction only. In the bulbus cordis, valves prevent the backflow of blood from the arterial system.

The arterial system. From the bulbus cordis the blood is forced into the ventral aorta of the arterial system. Blood leaves the heart through the ventral aorta, which in the midventral line divides anteriorly into two external, or ventral, carotid arteries, which supply blood to the lower part of the head. In the earliest embryos, branches from the ventral aorta on either side penetrate the tissues between the developing skeletal and muscular tissues of the visceral arches between which gill clefts are formed and give rise to vessels that, making loops around the alimentary canal, join the developing dorsal aortae; these lie dorsal to the alimentary canal and just ventral to the incipient vertebral column. These dorsal aortae are at first separate but later coalesce to a greater or lesser degree; therefore, the term dorsal aorta is often restricted to the part unpaired in the adult. In the gill region of fishes the lateral dorsal aortae are recognizable, and their anterior prolongations convey blood into the anterior part of the animal dorsal to the alimentary canal. These anterior vessels are the dorsal carotid arteries or, as they enter the skull (and supply blood to the brain), the internal carotid arteries. It is significant that, although there are a few species of fishes with more than six visceral clefts (*e.g.*, *Hexanchus*, a shark with six gill clefts and one spiracular cleft, and *Heptranchias* with seven), all other fishes and all higher vertebrates have arterial arches demonstrably related to the basic number of six clefts (including the hyoid, which becomes part of the ear).

The evolutionary trends. The division between jawless (*Agnatha*) and jawed vertebrates (*Gnathostomata*) is deep in spite of the superficial resemblance of cyclostomes to fish. Not only do cyclostomes lack jaws but they also lack paired fins and scales. Their blood system is the more primitive and differs markedly from that of the typical jawed vertebrate.

Condition in jawless vertebrates. In the venous system there are no renal portal vessels, the blood from the posterior part of the body being returned through paired posterior cardinal veins. From the anterior part of the body and the head, blood is returned by paired anterior cardinal veins and a median inferior jugular vein, which during development replaces paired jugular veins. In lampreys the cardinal veins open into the right duct of Cuvier (the left duct disappears during development). In myxinoids the blood returns through the left duct and the right disappears. It should be noted that although in adult cyclostomes the arrangement of the vessels is asymmetrical, it can nevertheless be related to the primitive plan of the venous system.

The lamprey heart is enclosed in a pericardium that, being strengthened for the greater part by cartilage, encloses the organ in a cartilaginous "shell." The atrium and ventricle lie side by side, with the atrium on the animal's right. The sinus venosus, which receives blood from the single duct of Cuvier, opens laterally into the atrium. At the base of the ventral aorta, and within the pericardium, is the bulbus arteriosus. Its wall contains elastic fibres, but no cardiac muscle, and longitudinal ridges that presumably act as valves.

Backflow of blood between the ventricle and atrium, and between bulbus and ventricle, is prevented by nonmuscular paired valves. The heart receives its supply of oxygen and food from the blood passing through it; there is no supply from a separate coronary system.

The ventral aorta gives rise to paired afferent vessels that convey the blood to the gill filaments. In lampreys there are eight afferent vessels to supply seven gill clefts; the second to seventh afferent vessel of each side supplies a complete gill (*i.e.*, the hemibranchs on the posterior and anterior faces of adjacent gill clefts successively), but the first afferent vessel supplies only the hemibranch on the anterior surface of the first gill cleft and the eighth vessel only the most posterior hemibranch.

In the myxinoids the arrangement is different, each afferent vessel supplying the hemibranchs on the anterior and posterior surfaces of one gill cleft; thus the afferent vessels run toward the clefts and divide around them.

The oxygenated blood is collected into efferent vessels, which join to form the dorsal aorta, single for the greater part of its length. The blood supply to the head is primarily by internal carotid arteries originating at the extreme anterior end of the dorsal aorta and, secondarily, from vessels originating from the ventral ends of some anterior efferent branchial vessels.

The main part of the body is supplied with blood through the dorsal aorta. The arteries to many parts of the body, but not those to the kidneys, have valves that appear capable of reducing blood flow to parts of the body while permitting a copious flow to the kidneys.

Condition in jawed vertebrates. The blood system of a species, although related to its mode of life, clearly reflects evolutionary history. From the fish of Devonian times arose amphibians capable of living on land for some part, at least, of the life cycle. These animals, in turn, gave rise to reptiles, dominant vertebrates of the later Mesozoic periods. Reptiles, by laying heavily yolked eggs, became free from the aquatic medium for any part of the life history. From the reptiles arose, by quite separate lines, the birds and the mammals. The change from completely aquatic to completely aerial respiration was accompanied by considerable changes of blood systems and the heart.

The greatest advance, correlated with the change to lung breathing, is the modification of the air bladder, or swim bladder, of fishes into an organ of respiratory exchange and the development of the pulmonary vein, which carries oxygenated blood to the left side of a divided heart—two physiologically separate pumps lying side by side, the so-called double circulation (Figure 4).

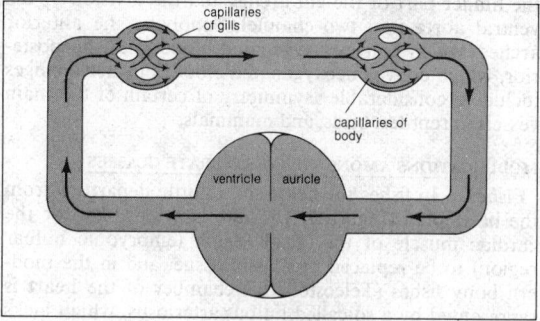

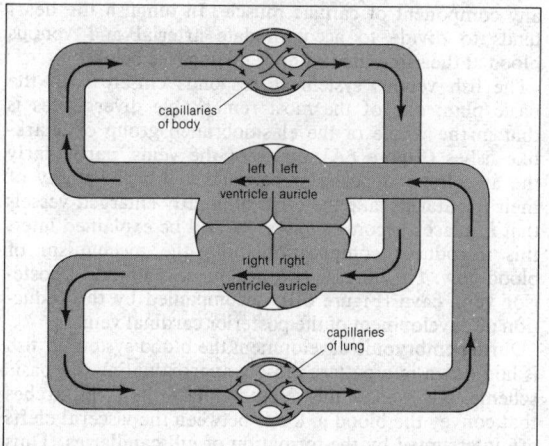

Figure 4: (Top) Single circulation of a fish; (bottom) double circulation of birds and mammals.

Other modifications are the replacement of the posterior cardinal veins by a median posterior vena cava, the elimination of the renal portal system, and the prolongation of a posterior vena cava into the caudal vein.

In fishes the four chambers of the heart are all well developed. The blood is passed from the sinus venosus to the atrium and from the atrium to the ventricle, each of these chambers being filled in sequence; thus when expanded they can accommodate equal volumes of blood. The ventricle is the main pumping chamber. The bulbus cordis of the embryo undergoes much modification in the various vertebrate groups. If represented in the adult by a contractile chamber of cardiac muscle, it is called a conus arteriosus, which may modify the action of the ventricle, perhaps by absorbing a sudden increase in pressure that might otherwise be transmitted to delicate gills.

In higher vertebrates the bulbus region tends to be absorbed during development into the ventricle and also into the valves at the base of the aortae. Some authorities refer to the part from which the valves are formed as the truncus arteriosus or trunco-conal region. Similarly, the sinus venosus is absorbed into the atrial region, being represented in birds and mammals by the sinuauricular node. The atrium itself, in mammals, ceases to be a complete reservoir for the ventricle and is divided into two auricles.

Apart from these general trends the chief modifications of the heart have to do with replacement of gill breathing of fish by the aerial breathing of terrestrial quadrupeds. It is self-evident that blood returning from the lungs through the pulmonary vein in a highly oxygenated condition would mix in the heart with venous blood if it were not kept separate during its passage through the heart. In birds and in mammals, complete separation has been achieved by the continuous partitioning of the heart; this is the complete double circulation.

The main modifications of the basic arterial pattern are those concerned with ensuring, in fishes, that the blood supplied to the head region through the ventral or external carotid vessels is oxygenated. In land-living vertebrates (tetrapods) the arterial modifications are concerned with the development of pulmonary arteries from the hinder part of the gill arches and the division of the ventral aorta into two channels supplying the anterior arches, which convey oxygenated blood, and the posterior, which convey deoxygenated blood. Further changes include a considerable asymmetry of certain of the main vessels in reptiles, birds, and mammals.

MODIFICATIONS AMONG THE VERTEBRATE CLASSES

Fishes. In fishes the heart shows little departure from the basic plan (Figure 5A). There is a tendency for the cardiac muscle of the conal region (embryonic bulbar region) to be replaced by elastic tissue, and in the modern bony fishes (Teleostei) this chamber of the heart is represented by a so-called bulbus arteriosus, which lacks any component of cardiac muscle. In lungfish the heart tends to divide to accommodate arterial and venous blood at the same time without mixing (see below).

The fish venous system corresponds closely with the basic plan; one of the most remarkable divergences is that in the whole of the elasmobranch group of shark-like fishes (Figure 6A), many of the veins, particularly the anterior and posterior cardinal veins, and many of their tributaries take the form of greatly enlarged vessels that in places become sinuses. As will be explained later, this introduces complications into the mechanism of blood flow. The lungfish (Dipnoi) possess a median posterior vena cava (Figure 6B), accompanied by the reduction of development of the posterior cardinal veins.

During embryonic development the blood system of fish is laid down in a pattern closely approximating the basic scheme, but even as this is taking place the atrial arches that convey the blood in loops between the visceral clefts are interrupted by the formation of gill capillaries. Thus each arterial arch of the embryo comes to consist of a ventral afferent portion, bringing blood to the gill, and a dorsal efferent portion, which conveys blood from the gills to the dorsal aorta. During this process secondary shifts of connection sometimes take place, so that in the adult fish the afferent and efferent portions of the original arches may, in some instances, no longer be strictly referred to each other.

An important departure from the primitive scheme is seen at the forward end of the series of gill clefts. In fishes (other than lung breathers, to be considered below) the blood passing through the heart is devoid of oxygen; it is pumped into the ventral aorta for passage to the gill filaments, where it is oxygenated. From the ventral aorta, the blood passes through the symmetrical afferent branchial arteries to the gill filaments. In adult fishes the ventral aorta does not continue beyond the second of the original series of six visceral clefts, for the first cleft loses its respiratory function and becomes the spiracle (in higher animals it will become part of the ear apparatus);

Extent of the ventral aorta among fishes

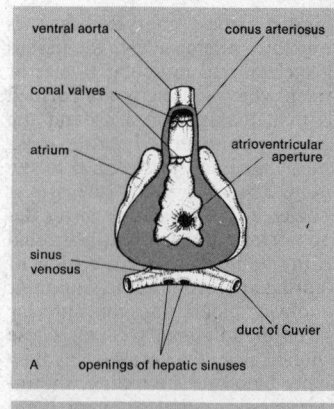
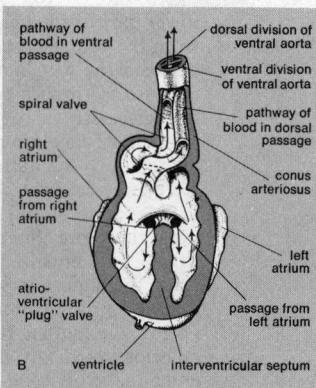
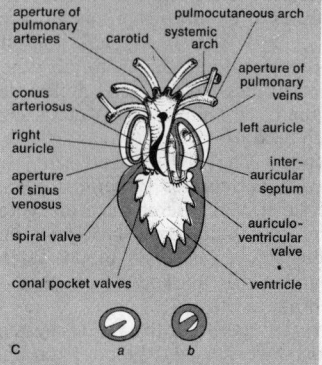
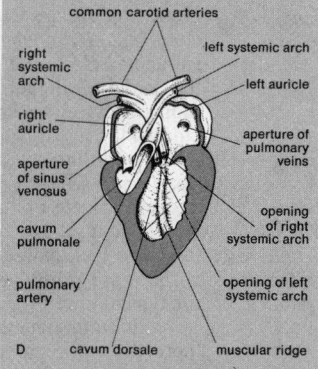
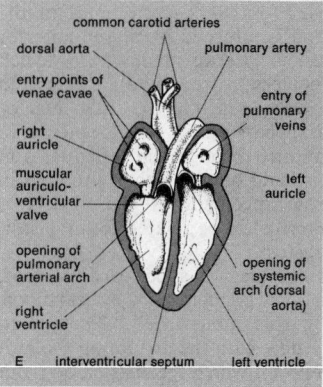
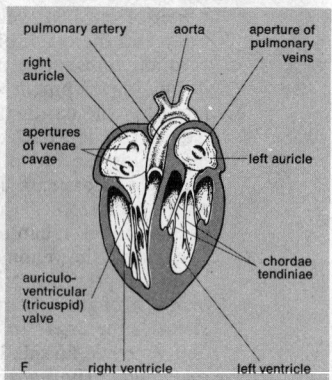

Figure 5: *Vertebrate hearts.*
(A) Dogfish (a shark); (B) lungfish; (C) frog (inset shows transverse sections of conus arteriosus in diastole [a] and systole [b]); (D) lizard; (E) bird; (F) mammal.

thus there are at most five pairs of afferent vessels. The external carotid arteries lose their original connection with the anterior end of the ventral aorta and become connected with the efferent vessels of the first of the five remaining gill clefts (second of the original series). This arrangement ensures that oxygenated blood passes through the external carotid arteries to the lower part of the head.

Further variations in blood systems of fishes. Many fishes live in poorly oxygenated water and develop accessory organs of aerial respiration. In many bony fishes the accessory respiratory organs often take the form of chambers in the gill region crowded with capillaries, which while bathed with water retain quantities of moist air so that physiologically they are lunglike in their action. A well-known example is *Anabas*, the so-called climbing perch, of tropical and subtropical Asia and Africa. A similar modification is found in the snakeheads (Ophiocephaloidea). Some catfish, notably *Clarias*, have extensive gill chambers modified for air breathing that enable them to stay out of water for several hours. A peculiar modification is found in the loach *Haplosternum*, in which air is taken into the vascularized intestine, where blood is oxygenated and returned to the heart unimpeded.

In fishes other than elasmobranchs an air bladder usually develops (unless, as in some individual genera and species, it is secondarily suppressed); this is a median diverticulum of the esophageal region of the alimentary canal. Some people refer to this bladder in fishes as the swim bladder—the name swim bladder describes its flotation function in many species. In some species the developmental connection with the esophagus is lost and gas is secreted into the bladder through a network of blood vessels called a rete mirabile, or gas gland. This gas often contains a much higher concentration of oxygen than the atmosphere and can be used as an oxygen reserve. When the connection with the esophagus remains open, there is always the possibility of the fish rising to the surface and swallowing air to be passed to the air bladder; this stored air can be used for adjustment of buoyancy in water or, in a few instances, for respiration. In most fishes, blood is supplied to the air bladder by vessels that originate from the dorsal aorta and is returned through the hepatic portal system and posterior cardinal veins.

A small number of archaic fish species, survivors of groups dominant in late Palaeozoic times, are of evolutionary interest in that they show some of the modifications of the circulatory system that have taken place in connection with the evolution of land vertebrates. It must

not be supposed, however, that any of these extant fish can be considered as ancestors. What is indicated is that some anatomical arrangements typical and universal in amphibians and reptiles were foreshadowed by similar but perhaps more elementary arrangements in a wide variety of early fishes and that the emergence of life on land was but one step in the evolution of the history of these fish.

In the African fish *Polypterus* the air bladder can be used for respiration, and the veins from it (pulmonary veins) enter the posterior cardinal veins; thus the blood from the air bladder enters the venous system very near the heart. This may represent a stage in the evolution of a "pulmonary vein" proper that enters the left side of the atrium. A fully developed pulmonary vein taking blood direct to the heart is seen in dipnoans and lungfishes.

There are three genera of recent dipnoans: *Neoceratodus* (Australia), with one lung, and *Protopterus* (Africa) and *Lepidosiren* (S. America), each with two. In all three genera the atrial region of the heart is nearly completely divided into left and right sides by a central partition. Into the right cavity opens the sinus venosus, which collects the blood returning from the systemic veins, and into the left cavity opens the pulmonary vein.

The least divided state of the ventricle is seen in *Neo-*

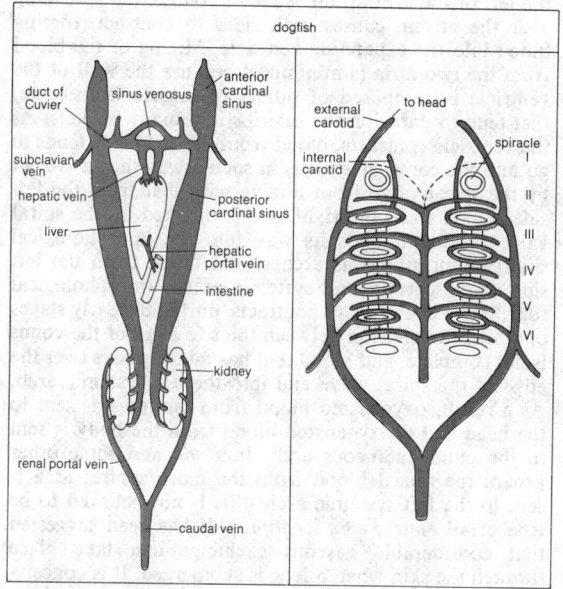

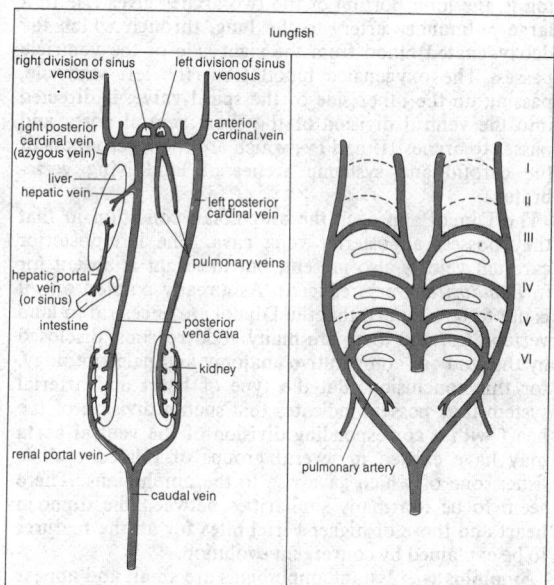

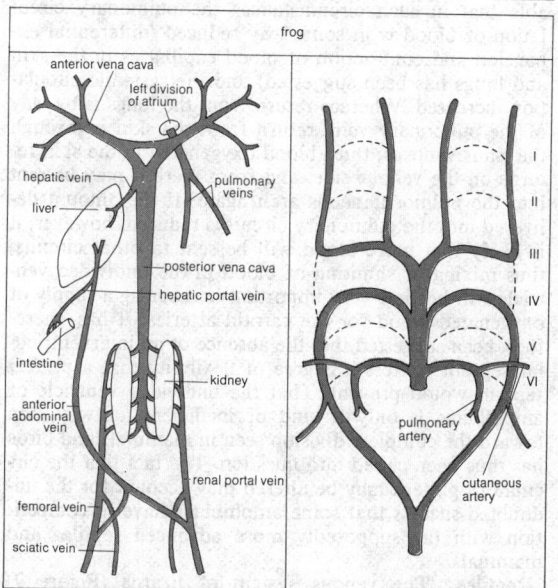

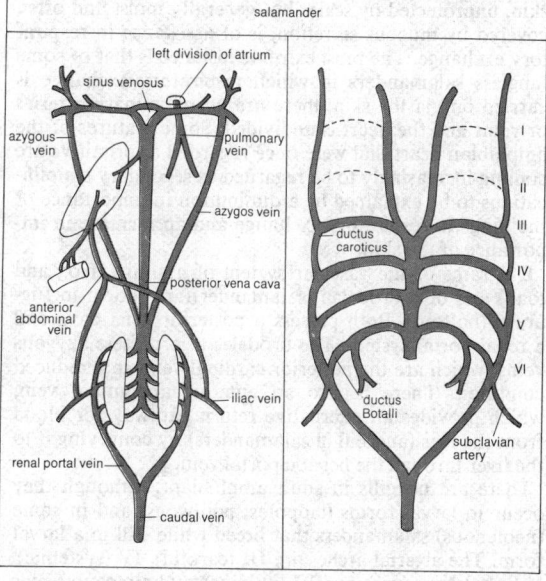

Figure 6: Vascular systems of representative vertebrates, showing venous system on the left and arterial system on the right.

ceratodus, and the most divided in *Lepidosiren* (Figure 5B). In all three genera there is a large conus arteriosus, divided more or less completely into two passages by compound valves. At the ventricular end of the conus these passages are left and right, corresponding with the ventricular division; but if they are traced anteriorly to where they meet the short ventral aorta, they are seen to have spiralled to the left through three right angles (270°) so that the original right and left divisions are replaced by a dorsal and a ventral division, respectively. By means of this compound partition, the spiral valve, the blood on the left in the ventricle (*i.e.*, the arterial blood that has returned from the lungs) is passed into the ventral division of the ventral aorta, which connects with the more anterior of the arterial arches; the blood on the right in the ventricle takes a spiral path first ventrally and then dorsally around to the dorsal division of the ventral aorta, which is connected to the two most posterior arches conveying it mainly to the lungs. In *Lepidosiren* (Figure 6), which, of all lungfishes, seems most dependent on aerial respiration, there are four pairs of arches joining the ventral and dorsal aortas. These are arches III to VI of the basic series of six as described above. Although they bear some gill filaments, these are short and do not form a true capillary network, the arch being continuous throughout. On each side, arches V and VI join together to enter the dorsal aorta as one; but before joining it, the joint portion of the two arches gives rise to a large pulmonary artery to the lung, through which the deoxygenated blood from the right side of the ventricle passes. The oxygenated blood from the left ventricle, passing up the other side of the spiral valve, is directed into the ventral division of the short ventral aorta and passes to arches III and IV, which are the forerunners of the carotid and systemic arches of land-living vertebrates.

The Dipnoi approach the amphibian condition in that they possess a posterior vena cava. The left posterior cardinal vein is also present, but the right is absent (or in *Lepidosiren* very reduced). As already pointed out, it is not to be assumed that the Dipnoi are ancestral to land vertebrates, and there are many good reasons, disclosed by the study of comparative anatomy and palaeontology, for this conclusion. But the type of heart and arterial system they possess indicates that such a division of the heart with a corresponding division of the ventral aorta may have existed in several groups of related archaic fishes, one of which gave rise to the amphibians. There seem to be too many similarities between the dipnoan heart and those of higher vertebrates for all the features to be explained by convergent evolution.

Amphibians. Extant amphibians are small and appear to be specialized for existence in habitats where their skin, unprotected by scales but generally moist and often covered by mucous secretion, is of assistance in respiratory exchange. The most extreme instance is that of some lungless salamanders in which respiratory exchange is carried on via the skin; there are no pulmonary arteries or veins and the heart is undivided. Some features of the amphibian heart that were once regarded as primitive are coming increasingly to be regarded as secondary simplifications to be explained by a diminution in importance of the lungs in respiratory exchange and an increase in importance of the skin.

Diagrams of the vascular system of anurans (frog and toad) and of a urodelan (salamander) are shown in Figure 6 (bottom). Both possess a posterior vena cava and a renal portal system. The urodeles also possess azygous veins, which are the posterior cardinal veins in a reduced condition. There is also an anterior abdominal vein, which provides an alternative return pathway for blood from the legs (and tail in salamanders) by conveying it to the liver through the hepatic portal vein.

There are no gills in adult amphibians, although they occur in larval forms (tadpoles; polliwogs) and in some (neotenous) salamanders that breed while still in a larval form. The arterial arches are III (carotid), IV (systemic), V (in salamanders), and VI (pulmonary; pulmocutaneous in frogs) of the basic series of six. They spring directly

from the truncal region of the conus arteriosus, there being no ventral aorta. A distinct advance over the dipnoan condition is that the pulmonary supply is from arch VI, which has no connection with the dorsal aorta. In frogs and toads the heart is more compact than in fishes, the pulmonary vein opening into the left division of the atrium and the sinus venosus into the right (Figure 5C). Among certain salamanders that spend their whole life in water, the interatrial septum is not complete, and in the lungless salamander, as already remarked, it has disappeared entirely.

In none of these amphibians is a ventricular septum found. Yet the conus arteriosus, which is more compact than in fishes, typically has a spiral valve, which on contraction of the conus creates channels that connect with different arterial arches. This absence of a ventricular septum was long thought to be a primitive character, a view based on the study of anurans and urodeles. A third group of extant amphibians, the Apoda, present some evidence of incipient septum formation, which has cast doubt on the dictum that an undivided ventricle is primitive in Amphibia.

The cardiac cycle of a frog (*Rana* species) is as follows. Blood flows through and into the sinus venosus and on into the right division of the atrium; the sinus venosus then contracts and drives the blood into the atrium; at the same time blood from the lungs has been flowing into the left of the atrium; the wave of contraction spreading over the atrium causes both sides to contract, forcing blood into the expanding ventricle. Mixing of the blood from the two atria is minimized because the wall of the ventricle is composed of pillars of muscle (trabeculae) that tend to partition the interior into many pockets. As the ventricle contracts, blood from the right side tends to go into the conus arteriosus in such a way that it is kept by the spiral valve from mixing with that from the left side. Blood from the right side is directed by the spiral valve so that it finds its way into the (morphological sixth) pulmocutaneous arches, and blood from the left side to the carotid and systemic arches (morphological fourth). Next, the conus contracts, during the early stages of which the division between the two sides of the conus is not complete, and blood that has mixed passes over the edge of the spiral valve and into the left systemic arch. As a result, oxygenated blood from the lungs is sent to the head and deoxygenated blood from the body is sent to the pulmocutaneous arch. In *Rana* and some other genera the mixed blood from the more central area is sent to the left systemic arch (this is not believed to be true of all anura; *e.g.*, *Xenopus*). It has been suggested that considerable gaseous exchange can take place through the skin when a frog is submerged. It is conceivable that in such circumstances the pulmonary circulation of blood is in some way reduced (differential expansion and contraction of blood capillaries in the skin and lungs has been suggested) and the systemic circulation increased. Whereas return from the lungs is by way of the pulmonary vein, return from the skin is through the sinus venosus; thus, blood oxygenated in the skin returns on the venous side, and from there it may be sent into the pulmocutaneous arch again. If the amount delivered into the pulmonary circuit is reduced, however, it is likely that more blood will be sent to other circuits; thus mixing or shunting of blood in the undivided ventricle will become very important in securing a supply of oxygenated blood for the carotid arteries. It has, therefore, been suggested that the absence of an interventricular septum confers a degree of flexibility that a perfect septum would prevent. That the undivided ventricle of amphibians is only a kind of inefficient halfway step toward the complete division seen in mammals and birds has thus been called into question. The fact that the circulatory pattern may be altered may account for the undoubted success that some amphibians have in competition with the supposedly more advanced reptiles and mammals.

Reptiles. The venous system of lizards (Figure 7) shows marked similarities to that of anuran amphibians. The caudal vein divides to form renal portal veins. Before the renal portal veins enter the kidney, each gives rise to a pelvic vein into which the veins from the legs enter. These pelvic veins, having received the blood from the legs, then join to form a median abdominal vein, which runs forward to join the hepatic portal vein and to enter the liver. Thus blood from the legs is conveyed directly to the liver, just as some of the blood from the legs of a frog is carried through the anterior abdominal vein.

The arterial system shows a feature that has not been met with before, namely, the tendency for the heart, during development, to take up a position far removed from the pharyngeal region, as in crocodiles, and also for the anatomical relationships of various structures anterior to the heart to be disturbed by the development of the neck, a phenomenon observable in crocodiles and lizards. The elongated body of snakes also produces special relationships. These matters, however, are not considered in the diagrammatic presentation of the modification of the six primary arches in Figure 7A. A portion of the original lateral dorsal aorta persists between the third and fourth arches and is called the ductus caroticus. The fifth arch of the series is missing and the sixth becomes the pulmonary artery.

Complete separation of the atria in reptiles

Apart from the crocodiles (see below), the atria, which are completely separated, are of different capacities, the left being smaller than the right (Figure 5D). The sinus venosus is present but comparatively small. The ventricle is incompletely divided in a manner that varies somewhat in different reptilian groups. In lizards and turtles the ventricle has an almost complete oblique septum, which cuts off a right ventral portion called the cavum pulmonale. On atrial contraction some of the blood from the larger right atrium enters the cavum pulmonale; the rest remains in the larger dorsal portion of the ventricle (cavum dorsale). Here it is joined by the blood from the left atrium. The mixing is not very complete since the cavum dorsale has a muscular ridge that tends to divide it into right and left parts; the blood from the left atrium (oxygenated) tends to remain in this left portion.

Three large vessels, the pulmonary artery and the right and left systemic trunks, take their origin from the ventricle. When the ventricle contracts, the free edge of the cavum pulmonale is forced against the base of the pulmonary artery; temporarily, division of the heart is complete, and ventricular blood is forced into the pulmonary arteries. The blood from the right of the cavum dorsale is forced into the base of the next vessel, which leads only to the left systemic arch; the blood from the left of the ventricle is forced into the most leftwardly placed vessel, which gives rise to the right systemic artery and the carotid arteries associated with it.

The lizard-like tuatara (*Sphenodon*) appears to be the only extant reptile possessing a conus arteriosus. This animal, from coastal islands of New Zealand, is classified with some extinct species, separately from any other recent species of reptile. It has a swelling at the base of the arterial vessels where they leave the ventricle, which is held to be the remains of the conus arteriosus.

The crocodilians are of special interest in that the ventricular septum is complete, forming two chambers of equal dimensions. The sinus venosus leads to the right atrium, and the pulmonary vein enters the left atrium. The blood is thus kept unmixed during its passage through the heart. The right ventricle gives rise not only to the pulmonary artery but also to the left systemic arch. Where the left and right systemic arches cross, however, is an opening known as the foramen of Panizza, which, in the spectacled cayman, permits much blood to pass through so that the left systemic arch carries blood almost entirely derived from the left ventricle.

The crocodiles also show a good example of arterial rearrangement correlated with the posterior position of the heart. The subclavian arteries, which supply the forelimbs, originate in most vertebrates from the lateral dorsal aorta at the level of the fourth arch. Its origin has shifted in crocodiles so that it appears on a branch of the carotid artery as a secondary subclavian artery.

Birds. The avian venous system (Figure 7B) is notable for a marked reduction of the renal portal vessels.

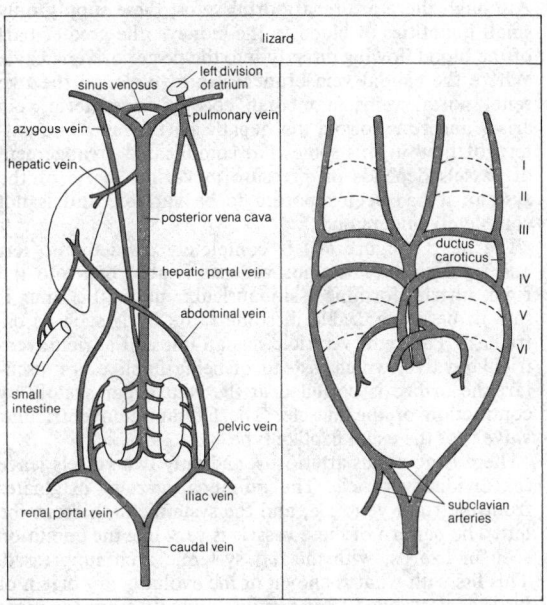

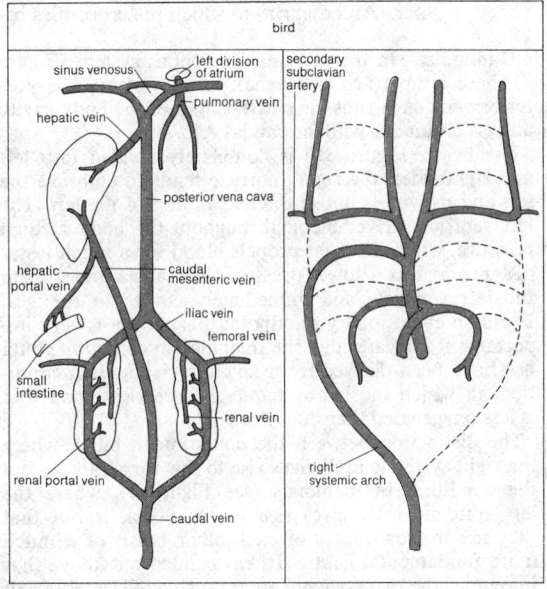

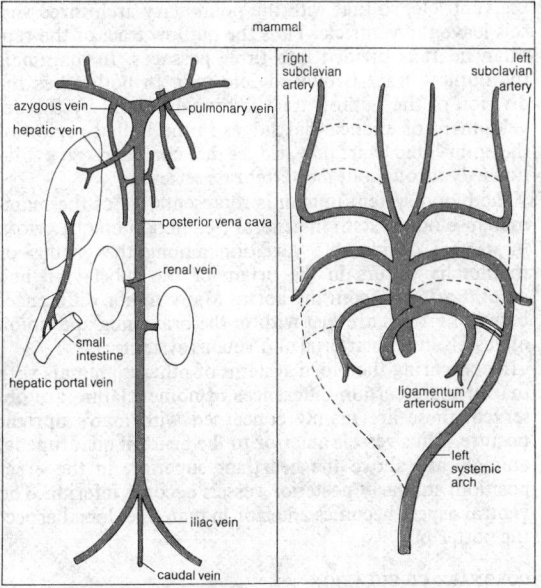

Figure 7: Vascular systems of representative vertebrates, including a lizard, bird, and mammal. The venous system is shown on the left and the arterial system on the right.

Although there are renal portal veins, these supply only small quantities of blood to the kidneys, the greater part of the blood flowing directly into the posterior vena cava. Where the caudal vein branches to give rise to the two renal portal veins, a median coccygeomesenteric vein arises and runs to join the hepatic portal vein. The pattern of flow in this somewhat complicated arrangement of vessels depends on pressure in various parts of the system; it has been reported to be variable and is not completely understood.

The heart (Figure 5E) is completely divided into left and right sides. The sinus venosus is absorbed into the right auricle, forming a sinuauricular node (the sinus is said to be recognizable in some ratite birds such as ostriches). The right ventricle has an unusual auriculoventricular valve, which instead of being flaplike is muscular; the orifice is occluded at the ventricular systole by contraction of the muscle. The left auriculoventricular valve is of the usual flaplike type.

There is no conus arteriosus, and only two vessels leave the divided ventricle. The pulmonary artery originates from the right ventricle, and the systemic arch from the left. The pattern of these vessels is very like the condition seen in lizards, with the left systemic arch suppressed. This fits with what is known of the evolutionary origin of birds as descended from reptiles, actually from the same ancestral stock (Archosauria) to which the crocodiles belong.

Support for reptilian origin of birds

Mammals. In the mammalian venous system (Figure 7) there is no trace of a renal portal system. The posterior vena cava runs the entire length of the body cavity and is continuous with the caudal vein.

The heart (Figure 5F) is completely divided into left and right sides; the right ventricle tends to embrace the left and its wall is not so thick as in that of the left. The left ventricle drives blood throughout the body at high pressure, while the right propels blood for a much lesser distance and at a lower pressure. The aorta arises from the left ventricle and immediately curves to the left. From an evolutionary standpoint this pattern is very important: it indicates that the mammalian condition could not have been derived from any known reptilian condition, in which the left systemic arch carries blood that is less oxygenated than does the right.

The distinction between the condition in birds, where the right systemic arch gives rise to the dorsal aorta, and the condition in mammals (see Figure 7), where the left systemic arch gives rise to the aorta, is not that they are mirror images of each other but is of a much more fundamental nature. It was pointed out above that in reptiles the two systemic arches spring separately from the ventricle, so that with the pulmonary arch three vessels leave the ventricle. Thus the outflow tract of the reptilian heart is divided into three passages. In mammals the outflow tract is divided into two. In both cases the division of the outflow tract is brought about by the development of endocardial ridges in the bulbar region of the embryonic heart tube, ridges that can be traced evolutionarily throughout the vertebrate series.

The blood system in man is representative of the mammalian blood system in general (see BLOOD CIRCULATION, HUMAN). Considerable variation among the groups of mammalia occurs in the origin of the subclavian and carotid arteries from the aorta. Many minor differences between groups are met with in the branching and union of vessels in both arterial and venous systems.

In comparing the blood systems of other mammals with that of man, certain differences of nomenclature are observed; these are mainly concerned with man's upright posture. Thus vessels anterior to the heart in quadrupedal animals are above the heart, or superior, in the erect position; similarly posterior vessels become inferior. The ventral aspect becomes anterior in man, the dorsal aspect the posterior.

CORONARY CIRCULATION

Throughout this article the respiratory importance of blood has been stressed. The contraction of the heart muscle starts at an early stage in correlation with the necessity of moving the blood in the developing circulatory system. The cardiac muscle itself therefore needs an oxygen supply from the earliest stages until the death of the animal; this is the function of the coronary system. In all mammals, including man, the coronary arteries arise from the root of the aorta just beyond the valves that prevent backflow into the left ventricle; the disastrous results of occlusion of the coronary supply are so well known as to need no emphasis (see CARDIOVASCULAR SYSTEM DISEASES AND DISORDERS).

In lampreys and other cyclostomes the blood passing through the heart suffices for all needs, including that of the heart muscle itself. The blood passing through the heart, therefore, must contain sufficient oxygen for the heart's metabolic activities, and the tissue of the heart must be loose enough to allow exchange of gases and nutrients.

A similar situation is met with in Amphibia. Although blood vessels run in the outer surface of the amphibian heart, they do not convey arterial blood to the muscular wall of the ventricle. The blood oxygenated in the skin is returned to the right auricle mixed with blood from other parts of the body; thus the difference in oxygen content between blood returning from the lungs and from other regions is not as great as is usual in divided hearts. The musculature of the ventricle is spongelike, allowing blood to penetrate deeply between the cells (it has been estimated that no cell of the ventricle of a European common frog is more than 10 μ from a blood-containing space).

In fishes there is a well-developed coronary supply. Arteries associated with those that bring arterial blood from the efferent branchial vessels supply the musculature of the lower part of the pharyngeal region, which is in constant movement pumping the water from the mouth out of the gill clefts and over the gill filaments. This system of blood vessels is the hypobranchial arterial system. The hypobranchial arteries give rise to the coronary arteries (paired, one on each side). In the dogfish *Squalus* there is no connection between the hypobranchial and subclavian arteries, the blood of the hypobranchial vessels being derived from the second and third efferent loops. In the ray (*Raja*) the heart receives blood from the forward region of the second and third gill clefts and from the subclavian artery as well. In the lungfishes there is no supply to the heart from the subclavian route, but the blood is derived from those anterior branchial vessels that (particularly in *Protopterus* and *Lepidosiren*) carry oxygenated blood. Thus the condition met with in many reptiles, where corresponding arteries arise from the systemic arches and then run back along them to supply the heart wall, has been foreshadowed in the lungfish. Into this picture the rather curious and apparently functionless arrangements seen in amphibians fit as vestiges no longer required, as the blood passing through the heart contains all the oxygen and nutriment necessary.

Curious vestiges in amphibians

In reptiles the point at which the coronary arteries take their origin from the systemic arches (usually the right) varies with the species. From this point the arteries run back along the systemic arch and over the heart. In some reptiles this point is very close to the heart, leading directly to the condition found in birds and in mammals where the coronary arteries originate just outside the valves at the base of the aorta.

The return of the coronary blood is by veins that, in general, run beside corresponding arteries. They diverge from the arteries to enter the main venous return in the neighbourhood of the heart itself. In mammals the veins open by way of the coronary sinus into the base of the left precaval vein, close to the right atrium. In fishes the coronary veins of the two sides open separately into the sinus venosus. In the frog the few capillaries that branch over the conus, but do not supply the heart muscle, rejoin to form a vein that opens into the anterior abdominal vein, which joins the hepatic portal vein.

DEVELOPMENT OF THE CIRCULATORY SYSTEM

The blood system. In the earliest stages of embryonic development diffusion alone suffices for the movements of the gases and metabolites, but in a very short time some system of active circulation becomes necessary. In many animals the circulatory system becomes functional at a time when other organs and organ systems are still in rudimentary form.

The heart is formed from mesodermal tissue ventral to the anterior region of the alimentary canal (foregut), in front of the developing liver. In the development of the trunk region the mesoderm inserts itself between the outer covering (ectoderm) of the body wall and the inner lining (endoderm) of the foregut by downgrowth on each side of the body; eventually the downgrowths of the two sides meet in the midventral line. The downward-growing mesoderm on each side soon comes to contain a cavity, the coelom. The outer layer of cells, next to the ectoderm, is the somatic layer of mesoderm, and that next to the alimentary canal the splanchnic layer. When the downgrowths meet, except in the position of the heart, they fuse in the midventral line, and the coelom becomes continuous from side to side. But in the heart region matters are more complex.

As the splanchnic mesoderm of the two sides approach each other below the foregut, some cells, apparently derived from this layer, detach and form a thin-walled tube, which joins headward and tailward with blood vessels also forming in the mesoderm. This tube is the endocardium of the heart (in the embryo chick it is, at first, two parallel tubes). After giving rise to the endocardial cells, the splanchnic layers meet below the endocardial tube and form the ventral mesocardium. Later, mesoderm also unites above the endocardium, forming the dorsal mesocardium. The mesodermal coat that surrounds the endocardial tube is the myocardium, and it will form the muscular wall of the heart. Although the ventral mesocardium soon disappears, the dorsal mesocardium persists for some time. The outermost layer of cells of the myocardium takes on an epithelial nature and is sometimes called the epicardium, but as it is not always separable from the underlying heart muscle, the term epimyocardium is often used. Unequal thickening of the endocardium forms ridges and protrusions that will give rise to the heart valves.

The coelomic cavity in which the heart lies is called the **Pericardial coelom** pericardial coelom, and by the development of secondary partitions it is cut off from the remainder of the coelom, the perivisceral coelom.

The pericardial wall in fishes tends to be firm and surrounds a distinct cavity that maintains its proportions, but in amphibians and higher vertebrates the wall is pliable and follows every movement of the heart, a serous fluid between the pericardial wall and the epicardium serving for lubrication.

As the heart grows it appears to outstrip the space available to it, so that it bends on itself within the pericardial cavity. Correlated with this bending, the dorsal mesocardium virtually disappears. Throughout the vertebrate series the heart bends in the same way. The sinus venosus is dorsal and leads forward (sometimes slightly left); the atrium is also dorsal and forward of the sinus. The atrium loops around and leads back into the following ventricular loop; thus in the atrial region the direction of flow is changed. The ventricular loop lies ventral and posterior to the atrium. In the ventricular loop the direction of flow is again changed, and the blood flowing posteriorly from the atrium is directed once more toward the head; it now enters the fourth chamber, the bulbus cordis, which conveys it to the ventral aorta.

As has been explained, the development of pulmonary respiration has brought about the necessity of the division of the heart tube throughout its length; this is accomplished by a series of partitions, or septa. These develop independently in the different heart chambers. To some extent the actual flow of blood through the heart in early stages may assist in the formation of septa. It has been suggested that in the areas of slow movement the septa develop more readily.

The ultimate stages in the development of the heart in higher vertebrates (birds and mammals) are concerned with proper alignment of the septa, dividing the heart into arterial and venous sides. Many congenital heart malformations in man are due to the failure of the septa to align correctly or to develop to normal size. The only example of an adult vertebrate heart with no bends or loops is that of the coelacanth *Latimeria*, which has its chambers in a straight line. It would be of great interest to know whether this straight heart tube is also found in the embryo, but this is as yet undescribed.

In the adult mammal, arterial and venous blood is precisely divided, but in the embryo, where blood is oxygenated in the placenta, other arrangements are found. In the fetus, blood oxygenated in the placenta is returned with blood from the rest of the body to the right atrium via the umbilical vein. It enters the right atrium through the posterior vena cava and mixes only minimally with the blood being returned through the anterior venae cavae. The oxygenated blood from the placenta then passes through an opening, the foramen ovale, into the left atrium and then into the left ventricle. Meanwhile the less oxygenated blood from the anterior venae cavae fills the right ventricle and then leaves through the root of the pulmonary artery. The bulk of this blood passes through the ductus arteriosus (which is part of the sixth embryonic arterial arch of the left side) and is conveyed into the dorsal aorta by this short cut and then to the placenta for oxygenation. Only a minimal quantity of blood passes to the lungs.

At birth the ductus arteriosus closes, and the pulmonary vessels then receive a full supply of blood. The rapid rise in oxygen content of the blood passing through the ductus, consequent on inflating the lungs and breathing air, stimulates its closure, and the foramen ovale, which has a flaplike valve, closes as the pressure difference between arterial and venous circuits is established.

The condition in birds is quite different: a special yolk-sac circulation provides food; circulation in other compartments provides for oxygen needs and storage of nitrogenous wastes. Blood is short-circuited from the pulmonary to the systemic circulation by a ductus arteriosus on each side (compare with mammalian and reptilian patterns). In the bird a large part of the so-called left ductus arteriosus is, in reality, a persisting part of the left lateral dorsal aorta.

The extreme precocity of development of the avian **Early** blood system is noteworthy. In the much studied chick **development** embryo, mesodermal cells at an early stage start to form **ment of** a flat plate (blastoderm) over the yolk; these differentiate **bird blood** into red blood cells and form "blood islands." From **system** these islands small vessels grow out to join each other and form larger veins leading into the embryo. Two large vessels, the vitelline veins, lead into the embryo and join the endothelial tubes where the heart will develop; at this stage the myocardium comes to lie around the tubes and form the heart. From the anterior end of the developing heart the first pair of arterial arches develops, and soon the myocardium begins to contract, propelling the blood.

In the developmental stages the modifications of the basic vertebrate arterial pattern can be seen to be taking place. The evolutionary stages, of course, are not recapitulated in any detail. For example, only in frog tadpoles do some of the gill clefts bear gill filaments. Not all of the six arterial arches of the basic pattern appear in the chick; the fifth seems quite variable. How far the blood system as a whole, including the heart, gives clues to the evolutionary pathways by which the recent vertebrates obtained their present forms is a subject much debated.

The lymphatic system. The return of tissue fluid, or lymph, takes place in vertebrates through a series of channels, called lymphatic vessels, that drain into the venous system. Tracing a lymphatic vessel backward toward its origin is much the same as tracing a river system from its mouth to the source. Many lymphatic tributaries subdivide over and over again until the smallest of them end blindly like the fingers of a glove between the cells of the tissues in all parts of the body (Figure 8A). In general, the main lymphatic vessels in all vertebrates follow the paths of the veins of the embryo, and the main points of entry of the vessels into the venous system are

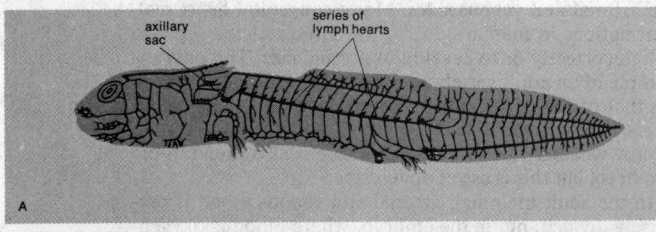

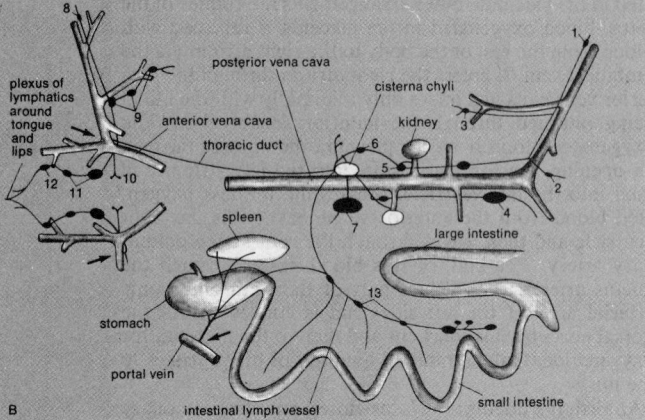

Figure 8: (A) Lateral view of salamander showing superficial lymph vessels. (B) Deep vessels of lymphatic system of the rat, anterior end at left. Lymphatics are shown in solid black. Nodes are numbered according to region in which they lie: 1, knee; 2, tail; 3, inguinal; 4, lumbar; 5, kidney; 6, nodes about the cisterna chyli; 7, intestinal node; 8, elbow; 9, axilla; 10, thoracic; 11, cervical; 12, submaxillary; 13, mesenteric nodes. Arrows indicate point of entrance of lymph into veins near junction of jugular and subclavian and into portal vein.

From A.S. Romer, *The Vertebrate Body*, 4th ed. (1970); W.B. Saunders Company, Philadelphia

in the region of the cardinal veins close to their entrance to the Cuverian ducts. In mammals (Figure 8B), in which the lymphatic system is best known, the vessels of the posterior part of the body combine to open into the left subclavian vein through the thoracic duct; the vessels from the left side of the head also join this duct. The right anterior part of the body has a right thoracic duct.

In lower vertebrates the main lymphatic vessels foreshadow the arrangements in mammals and open into the venous system in a corresponding position, but there are also other connections. In fishes, for example, lymphatic vessels make connections with the caudal vein. Movement of the lymph in the vessels, the larger of which are provided with valves to ensure unidirectional flow, is, in mammals, brought about by some degree of pressure from the tissue fluid (ultimately due to arterial pressure and physicochemical forces of cell contents) and, much more importantly, by the massaging effect of muscular action on the vessels themselves. In a healthy mammal the normal muscular activities of the body suffice to bring about this movement, but in lower vertebrates muscular swellings of the vessels, called "lymph hearts," pump the lymph.

In fishes lymph hearts are especially prominent in the tail region, where they pump lymph into the caudal vein. Lymph hearts are best known in frogs, where two pairs may be seen beating under the skin. The anterior pair, in the region of the shoulder girdle, returns lymph to the vertebral veins; the posterior pair, in the region of the urostyle, returns lymph to the iliac veins. Some urodele amphibians (salamanders, etc.) have a considerable number of lymph hearts (Figure 8A). In reptiles lymph hearts, corresponding to the posterior lymph hearts of frogs, are found. In birds posterior lymph hearts occur transitorily during developmental stages, persisting into the adult stage only in ostriches and other ratite birds. Lymph hearts do not occur in mammals.

Lymph, as mentioned, is derived from the cells; and as the cells may produce various substances in different parts of the body, the constituents of lymph may vary

considerably from one anatomical site to another and in accordance with the physiological state of the animal (see BLOOD AND LYMPH).

Lymphoid tissue occurs in various parts of the body, but especially associated with the lymphatic vessels. Lymphoid tissue consists of two groups of cells concerned with the defense reactions of the body: lymphocytes and macrophages. Lymphocytes produce antibodies involved in the chemical neutralization of foreign materials (antigens) that get into the body. Macrophages ingest unwanted solid materials. Some macrophages are fixed in their location, but others can wander about the body, leaving the bloodstream for the tissues and later re-entering it. Such phagocytic cells are considered to belong to the reticuloendothelial system.

Lymphoid tissue also acts as a local defense in regions particularly liable to infection. It is found in small amounts in the lining of the alimentary canal and in the respiratory tract. Larger accumulations, well-known in man, are the paired tonsils and the median tonsil (adenoids). Other large masses of lymphoid tissue act as filters for the lymph as it flows through the vessels; these are the lymph nodes. Further concentrations of lymphoid tissue act as filters for blood; these form hemal nodes and a specialized lymphoid organ, the spleen. Another large aggregation of lymphoid tissue in mammals is the thymus gland.

Signifi-
cance of
lymphoid
tissue

V. Biodynamics of vertebrate circulation

BLOOD PRESSURE AND BLOOD FLOW

Hemodynamics, the study of blood flow, is based partly on conventional hydrodynamics but is much more complicated. Water flows through pipes and conduits of fixed dimensions, but blood vessels, having elastic walls, change in shape as blood, under pressure, passes through them. The physical problems associated with the study of blood flow can be best illustrated by an account of these matters in relation to vertebrates.

The bulk of the blood is attributable to blood cells: in man cells occupy approximately 45 percent of the blood volume; in fish and amphibians about 30 percent or less. Red cells (erythrocytes) may be small and numerous or larger and fewer: the common frog of Europe (*Rana temporaria*), with red cells 22 μ across, has about 400,000 cells per cubic millimetre, whereas the mud puppy (*Necturus*), a salamander of North America, with red cells 58 μ across, has about 51,000 cells per cubic millimetre.

Blood, like water, is virtually incompressible, so that flow in large vessels may well be governed by the same factors that apply to water flowing through pipes. But other factors must be considered in the case of smaller vessels and of capillaries, the diameter of which is barely sufficient for the passage of a single cell without deformation of its shape. One such factor is viscosity. Where the liquid is in contact with the walls of the vessels, flow is impeded by viscous drag developed against the wall itself and perhaps against a monomolecular stationary layer of liquid coating the wall. In large vessels the stationary and the slower moving layers immediately adjacent to the wall are of negligible dimensions compared with the total volume of blood flowing through the vessel, but in capillaries the proportions will be quite different. Furthermore, in capillary networks blood cells are often forced through passages so narrow that the cells are severely distorted.

The heart moves the blood by exerting a positive pressure, which, however, is unevenly felt throughout the circulatory system, making deductions on patterns of flow extremely difficult. Before the heart can exert any pressure on the blood within it, its most anterior chamber, at least, must be filled. There are two ways in which this filling might come about: by positive pressure of the venous blood, forcing itself into the expanding chamber; or by negative pressure formed in the expanding first chamber, drawing blood in by suction. Both mechanisms occur in varying importance in different vertebrate groups. Negative pressure is dominant in the elasmobranch fish (sharks, etc.), in which the heart is contained in a cavity of constant size; as one part of the heart contracts to force blood outward to the gills a negative pressure is created, drawing blood to the heart from the large sinuses of the venous system. A similar negative pressure dominates in the lungfish system.

In bony fishes the muscular movements of swimming massage the veins and help propel the blood forward to the heart. The pericardial wall is not so stiff as in elasmobranchs, and negative pressure is not so great. In amphibians the pericardial wall is extremely thin and follows every movement of the heart wall itself; thus differences of pressure are negligible. In mammals, however, the heart and its closely applied pericardial wall are contained, along with the lungs, in the thorax, an air-tight box. At each beat of the heart a volume of blood leaves **Importance** the thorax and an equal volume is drawn into it to re-**of** place it. Muscular activity of the body plays a consider-**muscular** able part in the return of the blood to the heart, espe-**activity to** cially from limbs and most especially when gravity is a **blood flow** strong force, as in man, with his upright posture.

Blood returning to the heart enters the expanding sino-atrial region. In fish and amphibians it appears that pressure in the sinus venosus assists the blood on its way into the atrium and, more certainly, that the atrium pumps the blood into the ventricle. The volume of blood that can be contained by the atrium and by the ventricle is, therefore, approximately equal. In mammals and birds, however, the blood is returned to the heart with considerable residual pressure and passes through the atrial region (divided into two auricles) into the ventricles as they expand. The auricles undergo contraction shortly before the ventricles, but they appear to force only a minimal quantity of blood into the already distended ventricles. The stepwise passage of blood from chamber to chamber, typical of fish and amphibians, has thus been replaced by a more efficient mechanism, from which the sinus venosus and conus arteriosus are excluded and in which the atrium plays a subsidiary part.

In the completely divided heart of birds and mammals, the pressures achieved in the aorta and the pulmonary arteries may be quite different, based on the different nature of the circuits. The shorter and lesser pulmonary circulation does not require the same force to circulate the blood as does the longer and greater aortic circulation. In man and dogs pressure in the pulmonary artery at its peak is generally regarded as being about one-sixth of the level in the aortic circulation. In fish the capillary network of the gills offers resistance to flow; however, these gill capillaries have much greater diameters than other capillaries, and the drop in pressure brought about by passage through the gill is not as great as might be supposed. Furthermore, there is some correlation between the rate of heartbeat and the water-breathing movements of some fishes. The muscles of the gill region surround the blood vessels in such a way that their contraction assists in the movement of blood through the vessels, creating a secondary "heart" mechanism in the gill region.

The main pumping chamber of the heart is the ventricle. In general, when the ventricle starts to fill, the outflow valves are kept closed by back pressure from the arteries (and the conus arteriosus where it is present). The filled ventricle is stimulated to contract by the arrival of the excitation wave (see below). Contraction brings about an immediate increase in pressure, but no blood can leave the heart until this pressure rises above that holding the valves of the outflow tract closed. This period of isometric contraction is short, and blood is soon forced out of the ventricle. As this happens, full ventricular pressure is applied to the blood in the arterial system as a pressure wave, called the "pulse pressure." Though transmission of the pulse is instantaneous, the column of blood behaving like a solid rod, the flow it brings about is not. Flow is rapidly accelerated, then more slowly decelerated. How far and how fast a given blood cell travels at each heartbeat depends upon many factors, including the position of the cell in relation to the wall of the vessel (in midstream or near the wall) and the type of flow (turbulent or streamlined).

As contraction of the ventricle comes to an end, ventricular pressure falls. At this stage the blood in the arteries nearest the heart tends to back up and close the semilunar valves of the outflow tract (including those of the conus arteriosus, when present). Meanwhile the blood just sent from the heart on ventricular contraction expands the arteries, but as the outflow ceases and pressure is reduced, the elastic walls of the arteries contract, forcing blood onward through the arterial vessels. The forward flow of arterial blood is occasionally disturbed by back-ups, which appear not to be very significant. When the blood has reached vessels of capillary size, flow is usually continuous.

ELECTRICAL ACTIVITY OF THE HEART

The beating of all hearts is accompanied by alterations of electrical charges carried on the membranes of the cardiac cells involved (see MEMBRANES, BIOLOGICAL).

The vertebrate heart is myogenic; its rhythmic contraction is an intrinsic property of cardiac muscle. Each chamber of a heart has its own rate of contraction. In the frog's heart the sinus venosus has the fastest rate, the atrium somewhat slower, the ventricle slower still, and the conus arteriosus slowest of all. The sinus venosus acts as the pacemaker in establishing the rate of the heart as a **The pace-** whole. In birds and mammals the pacemaker resides in **making** the sinuauricular node of the right auricle. **function**

Each contraction of the frog's heart begins with a localized negative charge that spreads rapidly over the sinus venosus. Since the speed of the contraction is much slower than that of the excitation wave, delays are provided at the junctions between the chambers. In fishes and amphibians such delays appear to be related to the arrangement of the muscle cells of the heart. In lower vertebrates conduction appears to be a property of the general heart muscle. In mammals and birds special conducting fibres (Purkinje fibres) provide the pathway for contraction stimulus. Although similar conducting tissue has been reported in reptiles (see below BIBLIOGRAPHY, *J.S. Robb*), it is generally accepted that specialized conducting tissue is restricted to birds and mammals.

The passage of these changes of potential over the heart can be recorded by placing electrodes on the heart itself or much more conveniently on the skin (which registers the internal changes). In this way the changes of potential may be turned into a visible record called the electrocardiogram. All electrocardiograms show peaks of activity corresponding to the spread of the excitation wave over each heart chamber. Each peak is followed by a return to equilibrium as repolarization of the chamber takes place.

CONTROL OF THE HEART AND CIRCULATION

The control of the heart and circulation in both vertebrates and invertebrates varies from time to time depending on the immediate needs of the organism for food, for oxygen, for escape, etc. In general, the degree of development of the blood system and its control mechanism are closely connected. The most perfect control mechanisms are found in the homeothermic ("warm-blooded") vertebrates with their double circulation.

Basically there are two ways in which the circulation may be controlled, and usually they work in conjunction: (1) the character of the heartbeat (rate and amplitude or stroke volume) and (2) the state of the peripheral vessels, whether constricted or dilated. In poikilothermic ("cold-blooded") animals the heart rate varies with the temperature of the surrounding medium, increase in temperature resulting in an increased heart rate. In homeothermic animals the temperature of the internal medium is constant; thus the heart rate is constant in the resting animal so long as the homeothermic controls are functioning correctly. Rise in temperature (as in fever **Tempera-** or inflammation in man) results in an increase in the **ture and** heart rate. **heart rate**

Myogenic hearts with nervous control show marked changes in rate brought about by nervous stimulation. Throughout the vertebrates a branch of the vagus nerve (cranial nerve X) that supplies the heart is known as the cardiac depressor; stimulation of this nerve mediated by the release of the substance acetylcholine from the nerve endings, slows the heart rate.

Increase of the heart rate by nervous stimulation is brought about in a less direct way. Nervous impulses arriving at the suprarenal bodies, in fishes, or the medulla of the adrenal body, in mammals, bring about the secretion into the blood stream of adrenalin and noradrenalin, which stimulate the heart muscle to beat faster. These substances, usually secreted into the blood under conditions of nervous excitement, also cause the walls of the blood vessels of the alimentary canal and skin to contract, diverting blood into the muscles. At the same time, glycogen in the liver is converted into sugar and released into the blood; these combined changes provide the animal with the requisites for extreme physical exertion, as might be required in escape or battle.

The stroke volume of the heart is capable of variation. Within limits, as more blood flows into the heart, the heart exerts greater power at each stroke to discharge the greater volume; in vertebrates this causes a rise in blood pressure in the arteries leaving the heart. Pressure receptors in the walls of these vessels (in mammals they are situated in the carotid sinus) detect such changes of pressure and call homeostatic mechanisms of blood pressure control (both nervous and chemical) into play to prevent too great a rise.

In invertebrates with myogenic hearts with nervous regulation, the principles are the same but the details differ. Adrenalin, noradrenalin, and acetylcholine have the same effects as on vertebrate heart muscle, the hearts usually being extremely sensitive to these substances when applied artificially. Myogenic hearts lacking nervous control, such as those of vertebrate embryos before nervous control is established, insect larvae, and tunicates, are insensitive to these substances.

Neurogenic hearts respond differently, for in them contraction is believed often to be initiated by the liberation of acetylcholine or some similar substance from nerve endings in the muscle. Thus acetylcholine may speed neurogenic hearts when applied artificially. Adrenalin, however, may have little effect.

Many substances both inorganic and organic affect the functioning of hearts, either directly or indirectly. Salts of calcium, sodium, and potassium must be present in definite proportions for the proper action of the heart muscle. In many marine invertebrates the required proportions are similar to those in which the salts are found in seawater. That land-living animals require the same salts for their hearts to work properly is evidence of a general nature for the widely held belief that life began in the sea.

Organic substances affecting the heart include numerous compounds, some of natural occurrence, such as atropine and digitalis, which have remarkable effects on the heart and are well-known heart drugs. Atropine counteracts the retarding effects of acetylcholine, and ergotamine counteracts the stimulating effects of adrenalin. Nicotine and acetylcholine are also retardants.

When all the controls are functioning correctly, the actual pressures developed in a blood system depend to some extent on the size of the organism, but to a much greater degree on the efficiency of the blood system. In general, invertebrate blood pressure is very low, but in the closed system of cephalopod mollusks it may reach figures close to those in the higher vertebrates. In frogs a systolic pressure measured in the systemic arch just outside the heart itself is usually between 20 and 30 millimetres of mercury (able to support a column of mercury 20 to 30 millimetres high) in active animals in good physiological condition; during colder times of the year, when these animals are relatively inactive, pressures of 12 millimetres or less may be found. In mammals and birds pressures are generally considerably higher: in small mammals pressures from about 70 millimetres upward have been found, and in the horse 183 millimetres has been recorded.

BIBLIOGRAPHY. General accounts of the circulation of materials in nature and elementary descriptions of circulatory systems are found in many biology textbooks, including the following: G.J. HARDIN, *Biology: Its Principles and Implications*, 2nd ed. (1966); C.A. VILLEE, *Biology*, 5th ed. (1967); and P.B. WEISZ, *Science of Biology*, 3rd ed. (1967). Among textbooks dealing with animal structure at a more advanced level the following are recommended to supplement this article: R.M. BUCHSBAUM, *Animals Without Backbones*, 2nd ed. (1948); L.A. BORRADAILE and F.A. POTTS, *The Invertebrata*, 4th ed. rev. by G.A. KERKUT (1961); and T.J. PARKER and W.A. HASWELL, *A Text-Book of Zoology*, vol. 2, *Vertebrates*, 7th ed. rev. by A.J. MARSHALL (1962); A.S. ROMER, *The Vertebrate Body*, 3rd ed. (1962); and C.K. WEICHERT, *Anatomy of the Chordates*, 3rd ed. (1965). The following are more specialized books and articles: F. DAVIES and E.T.B. FRANCIS, "The Conducting System of the Vertebrate Heart," *Biol. Rev.*, 21:173–188 (Oct. 1946); G.E.H. FOXON, "Problems of the Double Circulation in Vertebrates," *Biol. Rev.* 30:196–228 (May 1955); E.S. GOODRICH, *A Treatise on Zoology*, pt. 9, *Vertebrata Craniata: Cyclostomes and Fishes*, ed. by E.R. LANKESTER (1909), and *Studies on the Structure and Development of Vertebrates* (1930); K.J. JOHANSEN, "Air-Breathing Fishes," *Sci. Am.*, 219:102–111 (Oct. 1968); O.F. KAMPMEIER, *Evolution and Comparative Morphology of the Lymphatic System* (1969), a comprehensive work on the vertebrate lymphatic system and a succinct and well-illustrated review of circulatory systems of invertebrates; J.G. KERR, *Text-Book of Embryology*, vol. 2, *Vertebrata (With the Exception of the Mammalia)* (1919); D.A. MCDONALD, *Blood Flow in Arteries* (1960); A.W. MARTIN and K.J. JOHANSEN, "Adaptations of the Circulation in Invertebrate Animals," in *Handbook of Physiology*, sect. 2, *Circulation* (1965); J.A.C. NICOL, *Biology of Marine Animals* (1960); C.L. PROSSER and F.A. BROWN (eds.), *Comparative Animal Physiology*, 2nd ed. (1961); and J.S. ROBB, *Comparative Basic Cardiology* (1965), a valuable source book, with extracts of many important original papers in this field.

(G.E.H.F./L.H.Ba.)

Circus

In its modern sense, the word circus refers to an entertainment, usually with a spectacular appeal, composed primarily of a variety of trained animal acts and exhibitions of human skill and daring. The word has the same root as "circle," "circumference," and, more directly, "Circus Maximus," the huge hippodrome in ancient Rome in which a wide variety of public attractions were presented. Thus, the term circus may also denote an oval or circular structure, ringed with tiers of seats, in which such spectacular entertainments are offered.

Any further definition of the term would reduce its application to a particular nationality, generation, or proprietorship. A circus may travel by horse, railroad, or motor vehicle; it may use one or several rings; it may be housed in a building or tent, or in the open air; it may offer a street parade, menagerie, or side show; it may exist for a few days under temporary sponsorship or for more than a hundred years under a world-famous name. In any of these circumstances it is still what the public identifies as a circus.

ORIGINS OF THE CIRCUS

Roman origins. Although some may argue that the recognizable beginnings of the circus may be found as far back as the ancient Greek hippodrome, its origin is usually traced to the circuses and amphitheatres of ancient Rome. Both the Roman circuses and amphitheatres, however, were designed for horse racing or spectacles intended to end fatally for either man or beast—the antithesis of the displays of cooperation that were the essence of the circus in the second half of the 20th century.

The Roman circus was built on the model of the Greek hippodrome. The first and largest was the Circus Maximus in Rome, which was rebuilt in the time of Julius Caesar in the 1st century BC and held perhaps as many as 150,000 seats, situated on three sides of the course. It was enlarged by succeeding emperors, and at its greatest, under Constantine in the 4th century AD, it must have measured about 2,000 by 600 feet.

The arena (Latin *arena*, "sand," "beach") was divided longitudinally by a wall (*spina*) decorated with obelisks and shrines and set obliquely to give more room at the beginning of the race. Horses and chariots lined up in the stalls, which were arranged at a slight angle along one end to ensure a fair start. At the other end, the barrier

The
Roman
circus

flanking the track made a semicircular turn, the whole forming a U-shaped course. Chariots were drawn by two, three, four, or sometimes more, highly trained horses. The drivers, who were often slaves, wore helmets and were wrapped in lengths of reins. They carried knives to cut themselves free if the chariots collided or overturned. The competing teams bore different colours: red and white at first, later green, blue, purple, and gold. Four, six, eight, or even twelve chariots raced at a time, and the course consisted of seven laps, the distance travelled and the progress of the competitors being signalled from each end of the *spina*. Admission was free, though the wine merchants and pastry cooks plied their wares inside the circus, and bookmakers and prostitutes solicited there.

Spectacles other than chariot racing were sometimes produced. During Augustus' reign (27 BC–AD 14) 3,500 beasts are said to have been killed, and under Nero in the 1st century AD the torture of Christians was an added attraction at the Circus Caligulas. Most exhibitions of this sort, however, were presented in the amphitheatres.

The Roman amphithe-atre

The amphitheatre was purely Roman. The largest was the Colosseum, which was dedicated in AD 79, and is estimated to have held between 45,000 and 50,000 persons. There the public paid for admission, and, although the arena was sometimes flooded for nautical pageants, the dominant theme was the slaughter of animals and men. Gladiators, who had first appeared in 264 BC and were outlawed in AD 404, were among the most popular performers: 2,000 gladiators and about 230 wild animals were billed to die in one celebration. Until Constantine repealed the law in AD 326, a man could be condemned to the wild beasts in the arena. The "hunting" of wild animals in the Colosseum continued until AD 523.

Other Roman amphitheatres were built at Pompeii (*c.* 80 BC), Verona (AD 290), Pozzuoli, Capua, and Pola in Italy; Syracuse in Sicily; at Arles and Nîmes in France; at el-Djem, near Carthage in North Africa; and at Dorchester and Caerleon in England.

Modern origins. There were no organized circuses during the Middle Ages, but tumblers, jugglers, acrobats, actors, and dancers wandered individually or in groups through Europe, Asia, and Africa. They appeared wherever groups of people gathered, in nobles' halls, at community celebrations, and at market places. King Alfred of England (848 or 849–899) was entertained by a wild beast show; William the Conqueror (king of England 1066–87) brought performing troupes of rope-dancers, tumblers, and contortionists from France to England. Itinerant players trained bears, monkeys, horses, dogs, and other animals and brought them to fairs. Fairs played an important role in developing trade throughout Europe from the 7th century onward. By the late medieval period, however, as more regular channels of marketing were standardized, fairs tended to become less a place for trading than for entertainment, with many of the performers, animals, and other characteristics associated with the circus.

The modern circus came into being in England, in 1768, when Philip Astley (1742–1814), a former sergeant major turned trick rider, found that if he galloped in a circle while standing on his horse's back, centrifugal force helped him to keep his balance. In doing so he traced the first ring. The name circus was first used in 1782 when the Royal Circus was set up near Astley's by Charles Hughes, one of Astley's horsemen.

Circumstances were favourable for the development of the circus. During the second half of the 18th century a number of trick riders were appearing in London and elsewhere, but none thought of riding in a circle until Astley led the way. At this same time the fairs were going into decline. The run of many of the most famous fairs was curtailed and some of the main attractions were banned. Many showmen, looking for a new outlet, found it in the circus, as did ropedancers, acrobats, jugglers, and others whose performances were based on dexterity, agility, and strength, and who discovered that their performances were better appreciated in the ring, where it could be seen clearly that nothing was faked.

In 1772 Astley went to France to present his "daring feats of horsemanship" before the king and the French court, and he found that there, too, many showmen were ready to forsake the fairgrounds. Ten years later he returned to Paris and opened the amphitheatre. When hostilities between Britain and France developed after the outbreak of the French Revolution, he leased it to Antonio Franconi (1738–1836), a member of a noble Venetian family, who had been forced into exile after a fatal duel. He became first a showman and later a trick rider, but it was as a director that he excelled. He joined forces with Astley and, in Astley's absence, continued on his own. His sons, Laurent and Henri, continued in his footsteps and the Franconi family became the founders of the French circus. They are reputed to have standardized the diameter of the ring at 13 metres (or 42 feet approximately), a size that is still recognized.

Spread of the circus to Europe and America

In 1782 Astley travelled as far as Belgrade, visiting Brussels and Vienna on the way, and during his life he built 19 permanent circuses. It was Hughes, however, who first introduced the circus to Russia. He added a company of trick riders to the stud of horses he had been commissioned to deliver to Catherine the Great in 1793, and he was rewarded with a private circus in the royal palace in St. Petersburg. The Russian circus was later developed by a Frenchman, Jacques Tourniaire (1772–1829).

In 1793 John Bill Ricketts opened circuses in Philadelphia, Pa., and New York City, the first seen in the New World. At the same time Benito Guerre was presenting his feats of horsemanship in Spain, and a cut on a contemporary handbill shows a rider leaping through a paper hoop—a scene that still epitomizes this form of entertainment. By the turn of the century the circus had spread throughout Europe and was firmly established in America. Performances were given mostly in permanent or semipermanent buildings. The greatest hazard was fire, from which Astley and Ricketts suffered particularly: Astley's amphitheatre burned down three times in the first 62 years of its history, and Ricketts lost his circuses in both New York City and Philadelphia as a result of fires.

In the permanent circus buildings in Europe the true circus had become adulterated through a misalliance with the theatre. The tiers of encircling seats were broken to accommodate a proscenium arch and stage behind the ring. Equestrian drama, with plots based on battles and sieges, became the rage. The French public, who had generally shown a deep appreciation of the true circus spectacle, soon tired of the intrusion and applauded horsemanship without histrionics, but in England this hybrid form of entertainment continued. *Richard III* and even *Il trovatore* were performed on horseback at Astley's, where the theatrical influence could still be seen at the end of the 19th century. Astley's, however, never became as fashionable as the permanent circuses on the Continent. At the Cirque d'Été the most exclusive club in Paris kept its own private box, and in St. Petersburg the stables were regularly scented for the benefit of aristocratic visitors.

The misalliance with theatre

Circus families became prominent during the 19th century. From one generation to another, members of a family would be trained from earliest childhood in the skills and discipline necessary to achieve perfection either in one specialty or in a group of related specialties. For example, the Cristiani family of Italy was known chiefly for its expert riders, but some members excelled in the skills of tumbling, ballet, and acrobatics. Circus families often intermarried. The Cooke family, which moved from Scotland to New York City in the early 1800s, was an equestrian group that intermarried with the Coles and the Ortons, both well known circus families. As a circus family expanded, branches were established in numerous areas and members often went from one branch to another. The Cristiani family established branches in the United States and elsewhere in Europe, as well as Italy. Toward the end of the 19th century, the Russian circus was dominated by an Italian circus family, which, like many others, made its name outside its own country.

Circus families

At the beginning of the 20th century the circus was still spreading to many other countries. The British circus family of Harmston settled in east Asia, and for years their only rival was the Russian circus, Isako. The Boswells forsook England for South Africa, where, from time to time, they met competition from Pagel, who was of German origin. Frank Brown, whose father had been a clown at Astley's, toured South America for many seasons. In Australia the circus prospered under the Wirths. The Lobes, from Budapest, made Persia their tenting ground and the Sidolis settled in Romania.

Keystone

D. Kossmeyer, in Bertram Mills Circus, London, performing an equestrian act reminiscent of trick-riding feats originated by Andrew Ducrow.

CIRCUS ATTRACTIONS

Horses and riders. From its modern origin, the circus has retained performing horses and riders as a fundamental feature. Most great riders have been champions of the art of bareback riding, performing acrobatic and gymnastic feats on the bare backs of loping horses. Horses that perform free of rider, reins, or harness, directed solely by visual or oral command, are called liberty horses. The Barnum & Bailey Circus, the most famous name in the U.S. circus, in 1897 presented the largest troupe of liberty horses, 70 performing simultaneously in one ring. The traditional finale of the larger tent shows was the Great Roman Hippodrome Races, composed of novelty races, steeplechase, and the ancient arts of chariot racing and Roman standing riding. James Robinson, a mid-19th-century American, was one of the greatest riders. He was billed as "the One Great and Only Hero and Bareback Horseman and Gold Champion-Belted Emperor of All Equestrians."

A great exponent of trick riding was the Englishman Andrew Ducrow (1793–1842), who, after achieving notable success on the Continent, ran Astley's amphitheatre from 1824 until his death. One of his acts, "The Courier of St. Petersburg," was still seen in the circus in the latter half of the 20th century. In this act, a rider straddles two cantering horses while other horses, bearing the flags of those countries that a courier would traverse on his journey to Russia, pass between his legs.

Voltige, trick riding, and high-school Equestrian acts of the 20th century could be divided into three main groups: voltige, in which a rider vaults on and off a horse's back; trick riding, in which the rider spends more time turning somersaults, dancing pirouettes, and balancing on a horse's back; and high-school, a

spectacular form of dressage, in which a horse performs complex manoeuvres in response to its rider's imperceptible commands. The Schumann family, directors of the permanent circus in Copenhagen and excellent high-school riders, became leading horse trainers of the world.

Jungle acts. The introducton of wild animals to circuses was an American innovation. I.A. Van Amburgh (1801–65) is generally cited as the first to enter a cage of jungle beasts in a public exhibition. The date is reported variously as 1820 and as 1833. Some credit Antonio Franconi with accomplishing this feat before Van Amburgh, but he appears to have done it only once, while Van Amburgh initiated the practice as a profession. He first appeared in New York at the Zoological Institute, a name that was the forerunner of the high-sounding American circus titles of the mid-19th century, for example the Equescurriculum, the Hippolymiad, and the Cirqzooladon. Van Amburgh is also reputed to have been the first man to put his head in a lion's mouth. Animal trainers had been seen on the fairgrounds of Europe for centuries, and the first great trainer to appear in the circus was Henri Martin (1793–1882), a Frenchman. Both he and Van Amburgh appeared in theatrical productions such as *The Lions of Mysore* and *The Brute Tamer of Pompeii*, as well as at the circus.

There is a marked difference in European and American styles of jungle act. In the American style, the trainer, with his gun blazing and whip cracking, is pitted against roaring animals, apparently on the attack, with the final outcome seemingly in doubt. By an apparent hair's breadth margin, the disciplined routine imposed by the trainer triumphs over jungle fury. The master of this style was the American Clyde Beatty (1903–65), who subjugated as many as 40 "black-maned African lions and Royal Bengal tigers" at one time.

By courtesy of Circus World Museum, Baraboo, Wisconsin, and Ringling Bros. and Barnum & Bailey Circus

Clyde Beatty, animal trainer, rehearsing lions, c. 1932.

In the European style, the trainer endeavours to prove his mastery and skill by presenting his jungle charges in the role of obedient, even playful, pets. The wild character of the animals, however, is revealed just often enough to remind the spectator that what he sees is indeed the result of masterful training.

Elephants are the very hallmark of circuses. The awesome size of the elephant makes its adaptability to man a curious paradox. The first recorded presentation of several elephants performing together in one ring occurred in 1874 in Howes' Great London Circus and Sanger's Royal British Menagerie. The largest herd ever employed by a single circus was the 50 elephants of the Ringling Bros. and Barnum & Bailey Circus in 1955. Countless other species of animal have performed in a circus ring, although few are more often associated with circus tradition than elephants. The hallmark of circuses

Acts of skill. In 1859 the invention of the flying trapeze by the French acrobat J. Léotard (1838–70), and Charles Blondin's crossings of Niagara Falls on a tightrope in the same year, rekindled the public interest in the work of the aerial gymnast and acrobat. Although the trapeze had never been seen before, ropedancing can be

Elephants in three-ring performance from Ringling Bros. and Barnum & Bailey Circus, 1970.
By courtesy of Circus World Museum, Baraboo, Wisconsin, and Ringling Bros. and Barnum & Bailey Circus

traced back to ancient Greece. By the turn of the century, acrobats had had an extensive influence, although they never usurped the supreme position of the horse.

The human performer offers not the mystery of the exotic circus animals but the realization that a fellow man, of the same substance as the spectators, can achieve astonishing discipline and mastery. The circus audience identifies itself with the performer as he attempts a feat of daring or skill. Completion of such feats as a double somersault to a four-high human pyramid fills the crowd with satisfaction and relief. A misstep on the tightwire seems to elicit greater distress in the spectators than in the performer himself. And the circus performance is not on film or tape but alive: there can be no retake to erase an error. With evidence of man's weaknesses and failures so prevalent everywhere, the circus is unusual in showing man at his best in physical achievement and skilled coordination. This realization comes to mind, for example, at the sight of the Wallendas, a family of high wire artists originally from Germany, balancing three-high on bicycles on the high wire. For Americans, after World War

Novosti Press Agency

The Bubnovs, aerial gymnasts from the Moscow Circus.

II, it may have come from witnessing the mastery of Unus, who balanced himself on his forefinger. It may have come from seeing petite Lillian Leitzel, born in Bohemia of a German circus family, who could pivot a hundred times on her shoulder socket in a manoeuvre called the "plange"; she spun from a rope like a pinwheel. Again, its source may have been the skill of Australian-born Con Colleano, "the Toreador of the Tight Wire," whose dance on the wire to a Spanish cadence thrilled American audiences for decades. The example could have been any of a great number of other performers of like skill.

Traditionally, certain nationalities tend to dominate specific areas of circus performance. Just as bareback riding long remained an English specialty and wild animal training a specialty of Germans and Americans, acrobatics and tumbling remain the realm of Eastern Europeans. Asians excel in juggling and balancing acts. Although there are frequent exceptions to these tendencies, especially in recent years, these and other traits are identifiable. These traditions may be related to the existence of circus families, whose specialties are passed on for several generations. To many people, such a life would appear to be a nomadic existence, without either the comforts of a permanent residence or the security of permanent employment. On the other hand, to experience circus life is to see seeming disadvantages become sources of strength. The appeal of a travelling life is strong to many persons, as is the bond that is built between show people in overcoming common hardships.

Clowns. When the human capacity for amazement, thrill, and suspense approaches its limits, the circus unleashes its clowns to freshen the atmosphere, lighten the emotional load, and recondition the spectator's mind for the next turn. One of the great clowns of the modern era, Oleg Popov, of the Moscow Circus, became well known not only in the U.S.S.R. but also in Europe and America. His style differed from that of the conventional circus clown. Wearing a minimum of makeup, he appeared in the ring with little to set him apart from the others except a wardrobe that was slightly unorthodox. Like other great comedians of the world, his mere appearance brought anticipatory laughter from the audience. Popov impersonated a rube character who is forever trying to mimic the legitimate performers. Frequently he almost succeeded, but only after sufficient bungling to make his performance a comedy. Actually, in areas such as rope walking and juggling, he demonstrated professional abilities.

Supporting attractions. *Band music.* Behind it all is the circus band, setting the pace and mood, cuing the acts,

National traditions

and substituting for scenery. The composition of circus music has, over the years, become an art of its own. Playing its characteristic forms, such as the march, the gallop, the fox trot, the tango, or various national airs, the circus band maintains the tempo of each event. It signals the change of emphasis among the simultaneous presentations as one event after another is highlighted, maintaining the seemingly perpetual flow of music.

The menagerie. About 1815 Hackaliah Bailey, of Somers, N.Y., toured New England with his elephant "Old Bet," thereby introducing the menagerie. Its success resulted in imitators, expansion, and mergers. In a very short time, there were noteworthy travelling collections of wild animals, such as the Zoological Institute of June, Titus & Angevine and Van Amburgh's Menagerie, both in America, and Wombwell's Menagerie in England. Subsequently, circuses and menageries were combined. By the time American circuses achieved their massive character in the 1870s, the menagerie was a major feature. It remained so through the 1940s. The circus menagerie was exhibited in a separate tent through which the public passed on its way to the main performance. The beautifully carved wagons that held the wild animal cages lined the perimeter of the tent. The elephants were chained in position, and the "lead stock," including uncaged exotic animals such as camels, llamas, bison, oxen, and zebras, were picketed together. The larger circuses had extensive collections, including rhinoceroses and giraffes in their own portable corrals.

The side show. In 1871, after he had already achieved success through his famous New York museum, P.T. Barnum entered into a partnership with two men from Wisconsin, who organized "P.T. Barnum's Great Traveling Museum, Menagerie, Caravan, and Hippodrome." It offered several strange and curious attractions, borrowed from his museum, from which evolved another major feature of circuses—the side show, or annex. Its characteristic attractions included the giant, the fat lady, the thin man, the midget, the three-legged boy, and the armless wonder, as well as such other curiosities as the fire eater, the sword swallower, the snake enchantress, and the magician. Housed in its own tent, the side show typically was fronted by giant banners or panels illustrating the marvels offered inside. A unique and vital element of the side show was the barker, whose fog-horn voice and unceasing patter attracted the public to the show.

The big top. The origin of the circus big top—the huge main tent of the circus—is generally believed to have originated in the circuses of Aaron Turner and Seth B. Howes in the 1820s. Portable seats for the patrons were also introduced at that time. At first circus tents were very small, housing one ring and a few hundred seats. In their heyday, however, the great American tented circuses played under what could be called canvas coliseums. The big top of the Ringling Bros. and Barnum & Bailey Circus covered the equivalent of a hectare, or more than two acres; supported by several centre poles that rose 65 feet (nearly 20 metres), it sheltered from 10,000 to 12,000 people. From their portable stands, these crowds could watch as many as seven rings and stages at one time. A typical big top of standard American circuses such as Hagenbeck–Wallace or Cole Bros. would be somewhat smaller, housing about 5,000 seats. The European and British circuses generally retained the one-ring format. The term "one-ring circus" may sound derogatory to Americans, but not to Europeans. Such one-ring circuses as Knie of Switzerland, Krone of Germany, or Bertram Mills, Sanger's, or Fossett's of England, to list a few, meet the highest standards. The one-ring pattern was dictated by European tastes, not by any lack of growth. In order to maintain the one-ring design while expanding the area, the European tent is designed with the four centre poles forming a square instead of a single file line as with American big tops.

One or three rings

COMMERCIAL AND TECHNICAL ASPECTS

From 1840 onward, circus combines and amalgamations became widespread in the United States, and partnerships were made and broken with bewildering frequency. This practice culminated in 1907 when the Ringling brothers bought Barnum & Bailey Ltd. and its extensive holdings. The separate Barnum & Bailey and Ringling Bros. circuses were combined into one in 1919. The last competing syndicate, the American Circus Corp., which comprised five circuses, was bought in 1929 to remove the last serious challenge to Ringling supremacy. This was never the case in Europe, where families tended to split up rather than combine, so that more than one circus may bear the name Pinder, Fossett, Ginnett, or Sanger.

The mid-19th century was a period of great technical development in the United States. Spencer Q. Stokes invented the derrick-like apparatus for training trick riders, which still goes by the name of the American Riding Machine. At one time his circus travelled by river boat, though he did not give performances on a showboat as did "Dr." Gilbert Spaulding (1811–80). This former chemist from Albany, New York, is said to have invented quarter poles (which support the canvas roof of the big top between the central king poles and the side poles) and was also one of the first circus proprietors to experiment with railroad transport.

The circus train. Before 1872 all travelling circuses were designed to be moved from town to town by horse and wagon. This form of transport necessarily limited the size of the shows. But in that year Barnum, Coup, and Castello were able to expand their circus significantly by acquiring 65 railroad cars that were designed to meet the needs of their continually moving show. The age of the giant railroad circuses had dawned. The largest of them all, the Ringling Bros. and Barnum & Bailey Combined Circus, "The Greatest Show on Earth," was transported on four trains comprising as many as 107 seventy-foot railroad cars (1941).

Railroads were more frequently used in the U.S. than in any other country. In Europe rail transport for circuses was never very popular, and, although a few attempts at travelling by rail were made, it was not until the second quarter of the 20th century that rail travel came into regular use by any European show. In Latin America and East Asia it was used, when available, after 1900. The American W.C. Coup (1837–95) introduced the end loading of circus trains, in which the gaps between flatcars were bridged and each wagon, fully loaded, was pushed down the length of the train. A model of logistical efficiency, circus methods led the way to the creation of the modern system of rail-truck freight handling.

The parade. The free circus street parade originated in America as a triumphal entry into town by each overland circus caravan. By the 1840s it was recognizable as a parade with bandwagons and trappings. It was the English, however, who created the finest and most ornately carved circus parade wagons. In 1865 Seth. B. Howes imported to America several English wagons, which prompted an upsurge of interest in circus parades. These processions, which wound their way through the town back to the circus field ("lot" in the U.S., "tober" in the U.K.), were a great feature of British tenting circuses, particularly that of "Lord" George Sanger (1827–1911), who also owned Astley's amphitheatre from 1871 until it was demolished in 1893. (Once he even tacked his parade onto the end of a military escort accompanying Queen Victoria across London.)

In the United States the circus parade became the climax of a highly developed mass publicity campaign to arouse maximum interest in the circus during its brief appearance at any one place.

The first steps were taken by the general agent of the circus, who made arrangements for a city license, showgrounds, railroad routing, and other details. The impact of organized publicity hit the community when the first advance car arrived in town two or three weeks before show day. In larger shows as many as four advance advertising cars involving 60 to 80 men were used. A concentrated mass publicity campaign then unfolded. Billposters, lithographers, and bannermen plastered the town and its environs with tens of thousands of square feet of "paper." The programmer recruited youngsters to scatter

A 16-camel team in a 1911 Ringling Bros. Circus parade.
By courtesy of Circus World Museum, Baraboo, Wisconsin, and Ringling Bros. and Barnum & Bailey Circus

Heralds, handbills, and "rat sheets"

thousands of printed heralds, multi-paged couriers, hand bills, and "rat sheets" (used to disparage other circuses when they happened to be in same vicinity at the same time). Press agents turned the power of the press to the purposes of the circus. Other agents attended to such matters as water, food, fuel, feed, and preparations for showgrounds and railroad crossing.

On circus day itself the train arrived with its stock cars, perhaps with animals probing outside openings, and a long line of flatcars loaded with red baggage wagons, pole wagons, bandwagons, tableaus, chariots, the steam boiler wagon, and canvas-covered wild animal cages. In a large circus there would be several trains. The initial train would be the "flying squadron" bearing the cook house, horse tents, menagerie, and steam calliope, having departed while the crowds were still watching the last performance in the previous town. At intervals would follow the "canvas train" and "lumber train" bearing construction materials in the order they would be needed. Wagons were pulled by baggage horse teams to the showgrounds, directed by arrows chalked on posts and trees by an advance man.

The showgrounds became a scene of organized confusion: acres of canvas and a forest of poles were assembled before swarms of curious people—affectionately called "lot lice" by showmen. Then "parade call" was trumpeted and performers, musicians, animal attendants, wardrobe crews, drivers, and brakemen assembled for the grand free street parade that was usually scheduled for 11 AM. Following the bugle brigade heralding the grand event, there was a procession, up to a mile and a half long, of horses, flag bearers, bands on magnificent wagons, allegorical tableaus, clowns, teams of exotic animals, knights in armour, beautiful ladies on steeds, Roman chariots, chimes, bells, a band organ, cage after cage of wild animals (some open to view, and others closed to prompt curiosity), cowboys, Indians, and a long line of highly caparisoned elephants shuffling along trunk-to-tail. The traditional finale to the circus parade was the

The calliope

pied piper of the circus, the steam calliope: 32 steam whistles, keyboard operated, powered by coal fire and boiler, hissing steam and smoke, and blasting out such favorites as "Go Tell Aunt Rhodie" and "The Sidewalks of New York." Under steam pressure of from 80 to 100 pounds, its tones carried four miles against a breeze. After two shows daily and the teardown, which took place at night, the wagons and teams followed flares to

the train, where they rolled back onto the flatcars to disappear into the night.

Winter quarters. In the United States and to some extent in Europe, circuses annually retired to winter quarters to endure the winter's elements and refurbish for another season. Among the cities that became identified with the circus heritage as winter-quarters towns were Peru, Indiana, which sheltered Hagenbeck–Wallace and other shows, and Baraboo, Wisconsin, the winter home for the circus of the Ringling Bros. and their cousins the Gollmar Bros. Ringling Bros. and Barnum & Bailey Circus established its winter quarters in Sarasota-Venice, Florida, from 1927 onward.

VARIATIONS ON THE CIRCUS THEME

Wild West shows. Wild West shows, which were similar to circuses in many respects, emphasized displays and events of America's old West instead of wild animals or acrobats. A Wild West show usually presented its exhibition not in a tent but in a large open field surrounded by circus-type seats covered by a canvas canopy to protect the patrons from the elements. These shows featured such historic events as the Indian attack on the stagecoach or wagon train, with a rescue by the U.S. Cavalry, bronco busting, roughriding, roping, Indian ceremonials, and sharpshooting. William F. ("Buffalo Bill") Cody organized the first and greatest Wild West show in 1883. Buffalo Bill's Wild West & Congress of Rough Riders of the World continued in operation until 1913. Pawnee Bill's Wild West and Miller Bros. 101 Ranch Real Wild West were prominent competitors of Buffalo Bill over the years. The famous riflewoman Annie Oakley, "Little Miss Sure-Shot," gained her fame as a star of the Wild West shows. Many film stars were associated with the old Wild West shows, among them Tom Mix and Will Rogers. The last Wild West show was Col. Tim McCoy's Wild West of 1938.

Carnivals. The public sometimes confuses circuses with carnivals, but they are quite different, even though both are travelling amusements. Instead of presenting a performance in one large enclosure, a carnival presents a midway lined with many tented side shows, musical and dancing reviews, concessions, special attractions, and rides or thrill events in which the patrons are participants, not spectators. Carnivals usually stay a full week or longer in any one location. In their modern American form, carnivals originated around the end of the 19th century when such rides as the Ferris wheel and steam-operated merry-go-round (carousel) became popular. Many other rides were later introduced to the carnival midway. Carnivals became standard features of state and county fairs, and more than 175 carnival companies prospered in the United States.

"Shrine" circuses. In the mid-20th century the so-called "Shrine" circuses became both popular and numerous. A Shrine circus is a specially contracted group of circus acts brought together by a promoter or booking agent, usually to appear in an arena-type building. Sometimes the group will be contracted for a full season to play a series of cities, in the manner of the tent shows. Frequently, however, the acts and performers are assembled only for one city's exhibition; these shows are usually known by the names of the local organizations that sponsor them, often Shrine clubs. When referring to any specific show, showpeople are likely to call it by the name of the sponsor, but when referring to the entire field of such exhibitions, they usually call them "Shrine Shows." County fairs, community celebrations, and shopping centre promotions also include many circus-like acts.

THE STATE OF THE ART

Circuses in Europe began to encounter economic difficulties in the period after World War I, when foreign travel was inhibited by the passport formalities, customs duties, quarantine restrictions, and currency regulations. For large companies with much equipment the difficulties were particularly acute. In order to evade inflation and crisis at home, a European circus toured South America in 1923 and 1934.

In the 1920s the circus in Britain declined. It was revived by Bertram Mills, a coachbuilder, who introduced the greatest international circus stars to the British public at Olympia, London, and ran the only tenting circus to travel by rail in England.

After World War II the circus flourished in Europe. A large number of small family tenting shows sprang up and, in London, the Christmas circus flourished.

In the U.S. the combines and amalgamations led to bigger shows. In order to make these pay, tents that held up to 10,000 spectators would be erected for one day in each town on the circus schedule. The ring had to be flanked by other rings and intervening stages to suit the new and larger tents. This altered the type of show, which could no longer be confined to single acts but had to include spectacular processions and aerial ballets for mass effect. Travelling became more and more difficult, and in 1956 increased freight rates and other problems arising from inflation induced "The Greatest Show on Earth" to give up tenting and appear only in permanent buildings such as exhibition halls. The circuses that still toured the United States were smaller, and most travelled by road instead of rail.

Moving by truck

The era of the truck show or motorized circus had dawned in the United States in 1918 with the short-lived Great United States Motorized Circus. Motor transport proved successful in the 1920s for Downie Bros. Circus, Seils-Sterling Circus, and some others. At first there was a tendency within the profession to belittle truck transported circuses, but the 1930s produced several outstanding travelling shows that moved by motor transport, including a show owned by the famous cowboy actor Tom Mix. Motorization enabled the canvas-tent circus to survive.

It should be emphasized that circuses had never entirely discontinued the use of indoor facilities for their exhibitions. European circuses continued to perform in buildings throughout the heyday of the canvas shows. Even the greatest tent shows opened their seasons in metropolitan buildings, enabling them to expand their seasons into weather periods not conducive to canvas operations. Such was the case with the annual opening of Bertram Mills Circus at the Olympia in London, Ringling Bros. Circus at Chicago's Coliseum, and Barnum & Bailey at Madison Square Garden in New York City. In fact, the first Madison Square Garden was built and opened in 1874 by P.T. Barnum and W.C. Coup for their circus.

In the Soviet Union, the circus became one of the most popular forms of entertainment and in the 1960s boasted of more than 100 permanent and tenting shows. Each year, approximately 22,000,000 people watched acrobats, riders, trainers, and clowns trained in the state circus school. Soviet circus companies appeared in the European capitals and audiences saw remarkably high standards achieved. The distinguishing features were the originality of the apparatus, the costumes, and the presentation. In the high-wire act of the Voljankis, for example, the wire changed from being horizontal to an oblique angle, while the tension was maintained; the Koch sisters performed on a giant semaphore arm that revolved slowly as they balanced on the outside edge. Brilliantly designed circular carpets covered the sawdust, and drapes were used to decorate the ring fence. Safety lunges were used for all acts that involved risk to human life.

The Soviet circus

Preservation of the past. From the early part of the 20th century there was a growing interest in preserving the circus's colourful past. Pursuing this end were collectors and historians throughout the world, as well as associations, including the Circus Fans Association (England and America), the Société du Club du Cirque (France), Gesellschaft der Circusfreunde (Germany and Austria), and the Circus Historical Society and Circus Model Builders Association (America). Schools at Peru, Indiana; Sarasota, Florida; and Wenatchee, Washington, developed highly successful programs in the performing arts of circuses within their physical education departments. Sarasota also developed two circus museums, the Circus Hall of Fame and the Ringling Museum of the Circus. At Baraboo, Wisconsin, where Ringling Bros. Circus maintained its winter quarters from 1884 to 1918, the extensive Circus World Museum, including a Circus Library and Research Center, is operated by the State Historical Society of Wisconsin. Each July 4, a train of 24 circus railroad cars transports more than 70 restored circus parade wagons from the Circus World Museum to Milwaukee, where they are joined by hundreds of privately owned baggage horses for a parade through the streets of the city.

Contemporary challenges. American circuses experienced financial difficulties in the 1950s, when inflation increased expenses more rapidly than income. They successfully adjusted to these problems largely by appearing in fewer places for longer runs, by modernizing business practices, by automation, and by increasing income from other sources. In the 1960s European circuses experienced similar tribulations and such stalwarts as Bertram Mills's circus closed. While there was a widespread impression that the circus was on the wane, it would be more correct to say that it was changing. In 1969, under the management of the Feld brothers, a second complete unit of the Ringling Bros. circus was created, a demonstration of the continuing vigour of the industry.

It has been said that the circus is ever changing, yet never changing. It is possible to delineate some of the unchanging characteristics of the circus. It is free from obscenity and has never had to be censored; it must be fit for children of all ages. The circus must be unbiassed and nonpolitical. It must remain an entertainment for everybody, never an editorial outlet that sides with some at the expense of others. Dramatizing real life may be appropriate in the movies or television, but the circus must remain a fantasy, forever unreal and divorced from life's routine. The circus must be ageless, bridging all gaps of time and generations. To maintain public appeal it must be fresh, unusual, and unique wherever it appears—never commonplace, never overexposed, always a curious fascination. As for the circus acts themselves, variety and flexibility are healthy; but innovation must not be practiced at the expense of tradition. The expectation of seeing elephants, clowns, performing horses, aerialists, and acrobats should not be disappointed. Above all, the circus must be alive. Film, record disc, and electronic tube may serve to advertise the live circus but never to replace it.

BIBLIOGRAPHY. E.C. MAY, *The Circus from Rome to Ringling* (1932), the standard comprehensive history of circuses;

Ferris wheels and carousels

C.P. FOX and T. PARKINSON (eds.), *The Circus in America* (1969), expansive coverage of the American circus detailing aspects not heretofore recorded, with many good illustrations; FRED BRADNA, *The Big Top: My Forty Years with the Greatest Show on Earth* (1952), a personal, colourful account by a man who became a circus legend; C.P. FOX, *Circus Parades* (1953), a thoroughly illustrated documentary of circus street parades, *A Pictorial History of Performing Horses* (1960), a good primer on the subject of circus performing horses; R.H. GOLLMAR, *My Father Owned a Circus* (1965), a revealing, detailed insight into the realities of life around a typical American circus; HENRY RINGLING NORTH and ALDEN HATCH, *The Circus Kings* (1960), the story of the Ringling family; D. RUSSELL, *The Wild West* (1970), the best treatment of the American Wild West shows.

(R.L.P./A.D.H.C.)

Cirripedia

Barnacles and their allies are sedentary marine crustaceans constituting the class Cirripedia. Authorities who treat the Crustacea as a class (see CRUSTACEA) consider the Cirripedia a subclass. The Cirripedia are divided into four principal orders. The most important are the shell-bearing Thoracica, consisting of the pedunculate (stalked) barnacles and the sessile (directly attached) barnacles, the latter being divided into asymmetrical and symmetrical suborders. The other three orders are the Acrothoracica, a group of burrowers in carbonate materials; the Rhizocephala, all parasites, primarily on decapod crustaceans (crabs and lobsters); and Ascothoracica, parasitic on echinoderms and some corals. Barnacles range in size from one millimetre (about 0.04 inch) to more than ten centimetres (four inches) and in weight from less than one to more than 500 grams (about 0.04 to 18 ounces). Individuals remain attached to some surface during adult life. Most feed upon plankton (drifting plant and animal life) captured by extending legs (cirri) into the water, but others exhibit varying degrees of symbiosis (living with other organisms). Although many species have separate sexes, common forms are cross-fertilizing hemaphrodites—*i.e.*, each individual possesses both male and female sex organs and is capable of exchanging sperm with another individual. Eggs are brooded and hatch as planktonic (weakly-swimming) larvae.

General features. *Distribution.* Barnacles occur in virtually all marine environments, from the tropics to polar regions. Benthic (bottom) forms live from the highest reaches of the tides to the depths of the oceans. Others float at the sea surface or travel on pelagic (open-sea-dwelling) animals. A few species live in estuaries, but none completes its life cycle in freshwater. Habitat diversity is concomitant with a great diversity in form, and many species found below the reach of the tide bear little resemblance to those found along the shore.

Biological significance. Barnacles have a good fossil record and are, therefore, of interest to students of evolution, biogeography, and paleontology. It is not generally known that before publishing his famous theory of evolution, Charles Darwin wrote four volumes (1851–54) concerning the systematics and evolution of living and fossil cirripeds, in which he formulated such principles as neoteny (the retention of larval characteristics into adulthood) and specialization through simplification. Today, because of their abundance and intricate associations, many species are of concern in ecological studies, and a number are of economic significance.

Importance to man. About 12 species of pedunculate and acorn barnacles foul marine structures, several of them constituting a serious economic problem. They usually occur with other fouling organisms and can greatly reduce the progress of a ship through the water. Antifouling paints, which contain poisons but tend to slough off, have helped with this problem; ultrasonics may eventually be of some use. Acorn barnacles also foul the submerged portions of marine installations, pilings, floats, buoys, and mooring cables, causing drag and increasing their weight. They tend to increase corrosion of metals, even stainless steel. Ships and shore installations that circulate seawater for various purposes may also have problems with the clogging of lines by barnacles. Various methods, such as flushing with chemicals or freshwater, have been used with success.

Barnacles are consumed as food in some countries. In Spain the pedunculate barnacle *Pollicipes* is served with drinks, much as pretzels are in other countries, and in Chile *Balanus* is sold fresh or canned. In Japan stakes are put out in shallow water, and the encrustations of accumulated barnacles are used as fertilizer.

In recent years certain species of *Balanus* have provided useful laboratory preparations for physiological studies on the fundamental properties of both photoreceptors and membrane phenomena in muscle. The "glue" by which the animals attach themselves to submerged objects (even to plastics with low surface tensions) is of interest in dental research.

Fouling of marine structures by barnacles

After (*Ascothorax*) Wagin, *Acta Zool.* (1946), and (*Berndtia*) H. Utinomi, both in A. Kaestner, *Invertebrate Zoology* (1970), John Wiley & Sons, Inc.; from (*Lepas fascicularis*) The National Audubon Society; (*Lepas anatifera*) L.A. Borradaile and F.A. Potts, *Invertebrata*, 4th ed. (1967), Cambridge University Press; (*Verruca*) P.P.C. Hoek, *The Cirripedia of the Siboga-Expedition: Siboga-Expeditie XXXI;* (others) *Invertebrate Zoology* by Paul A. Meglitsch, Copyright © 1967 by Oxford University Press, Inc., reprinted by permission

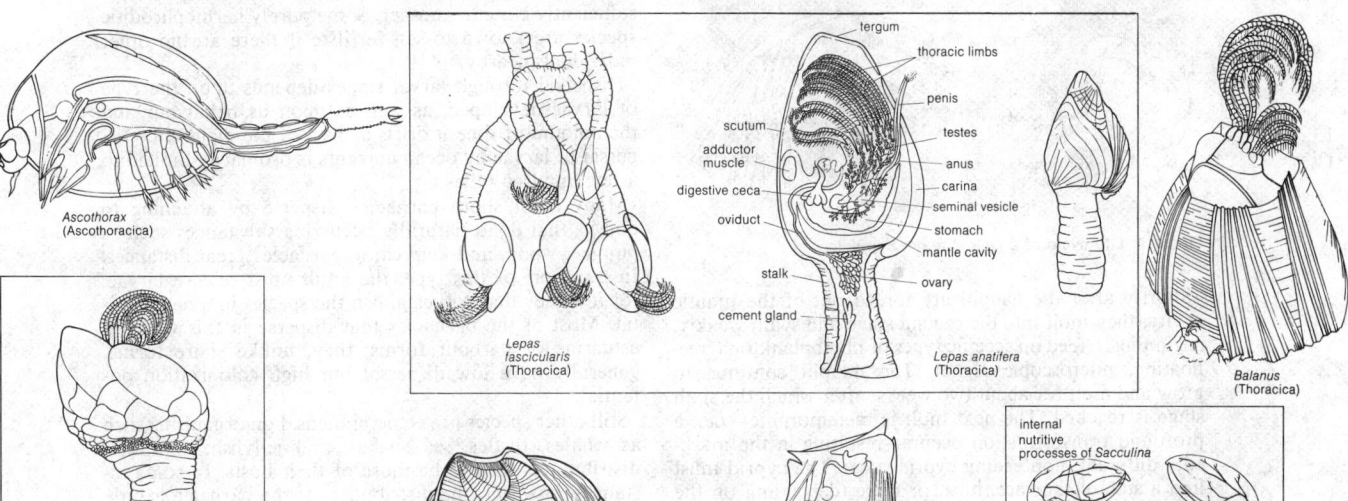
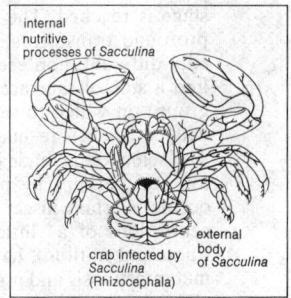

Ascothorax (Ascothoracica)

Lepas fascicularis (Thoracica)

tergum
thoracic limbs
penis
scutum
adductor muscle
testes
digestive ceca
anus
oviduct
carina
seminal vesicle
stomach
mantle cavity
stalk
ovary
cement gland

Lepas anatifera (Thoracica)

Balanus (Thoracica)

Pollicipes (Thoracica)

Verruca (Thoracica)

Berndtia (Acrothoracica)

internal nutritive processes of *Sacculina*

external body of *Sacculina*

crab infected by *Sacculina* (Rhizocephala)

Figure 1: Representative cirripeds.

Barnacles have always been important in marine ecology because of their abundance along shores in temperate regions. Different species tend to occupy distinctive bands along the shore, thereby illustrating certain physiological and ecological principles related to drying out, competition, and predation.

The myth of geese from barnacles

Near the close of the Middle Ages, in northern Europe generally but particularly in the western British Isles, there was a prevalent myth that barnacles, especially *Lepas*, grew out of wood steeped in sea water or even on trees along the shore and that these were actually embryonic geese of species not known to breed at those latitudes. Geese could thus be eaten on fasting days, because they came from shellfish rather than flesh. Linnaeus was aware of the myth, for he named one species of *Lepas* (shellfish) *L. anatifera* (duck-bearing) and another *L. anserifera* (goose-bearing).

Natural history. Mating usually occurs shortly after the female has molted. Weak organic acids induce mating behaviour in some species in the laboratory, suggesting that a pheromone (chemical substance involved in communication) may play a role in nature. Hundreds of eggs are generally fertilized at one time, and usually several batches are laid each year by adults that may live as long as 30 years. The offspring are retained in the adult's mantle cavity until near the end of the first larval stage. Shortly after fertilization eggs undergo spiral cleavage. Development progresses rapidly until the first stage nauplius larvae appear within the egg membranes. Nauplii of crustaceans have three pairs of multipurposed appendages. Cirriped nauplii (except Ascothoracica) differ from those of other crustaceans in having the anterior margin of the dorsal shield drawn out into a pair of laterally projecting horns.

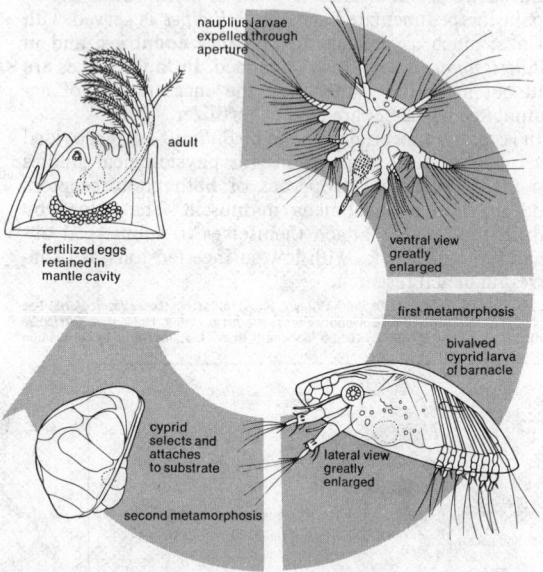

Figure 2: Life cycle of a typical acorn barnacle.

Shortly after the nauplii are forced out of the mantle cavity, they molt into the second stage and swim weakly, beginning to feed on specific types of phytoplankton (free-floating, microscopic algae). The nauplii continue to grow and molt for about two weeks, after which the sixth stage is reached. The next molt is metamorphic—*i.e.*, a profound transformation occurs—resulting in the markedly different, nonfeeding cyprid stage. The cyprid must find a suitable surface, host, or mate (depending on the group) on which to settle in a relatively short time or it will perish before undergoing the final metamorphosis. The selection is made by light, chemical and tactile stimuli, and perhaps by pheromones when sexual selection occurs. Certain insect juvenile hormone mimics, in concentrations of as little as one to two parts per billion (thousand million), have recently been shown to disrupt metamorphosis and prevent settling.

The cyprid swims with six pairs of thoracic appendages

(the cirri of the adult) and locates the settling site, be it an inanimate object or another organism. The great number of cyprids may turn water dark brown as they appear along the shore to settle. Gregarious forms are attracted to established members or to their remains, apparently by proteinaceous substances in the shells called "arthropodins." Commensal (those that coexist with other animals without deriving nourishment from them) and parasitic species, many of which are host specific, also detect the host chemically. When an appropriate place is found, a glue, secreted by glands in the antennae, attaches the larva permanently, before it undergoes metamorphosis into the adult form.

Unusual life cycle of parasitic forms

Metamorphosis of a cyprid into a young barnacle adult is complicated, but most basic structural characteristics of the cyprid are retained. In the Rhizocephala, for the most part parasitic on decapod crustaceans, however, a remarkable sequence of events takes place. The cyprid seeks out a host, such as a crab, attaching to it by antennae at the base of a seta (bristle). Undifferentiated tissue at the anterior end of the body is then extruded through a hypodermic-like structure (kentrogon) into the host at the point of attachment. The tissue migrates into the host's body and sends out a system of rootlike nutritive projections to virtually all the tissues of the host. This internal phase (called the interna) produces a mushroomlike reproductive body (externa) that appears on the surface in the position normally occupied by the eggs (in crablike hosts) at the time of the host's next molt. The externa is usually female and receives one or more male cyprid larvae, which attach at the aperture of the externa and undergo a metamorphosis comparable to that undergone by the cyprid that initially infected the host. The undifferentiated male cells pass out through one of the antennae and migrate into the female cavity. They come to reside in male cell receptacles, where they redifferentiate into functional spermatozoa ready to fertilize the eggs. This recently discovered sequence may be generally the case in Rhizocephala, but some species are still thought to be self-fertilized hermaphrodites.

Sexuality in ordinary barnacles

Sexuality in ordinary barnacles also is sometimes remarkable. Most species are cross-fertilizing hermaphrodites. In others with separate sexes, one or more male cyprids seek out the female and settle upon her, sometimes in a special pocket. Settling is followed by metamorphosis into a degenerated dwarf male. Males sometimes accompany hermaphrodites; these males, termed "complemental" by Darwin, would seem to exist to ensure cross-fertilization, should one hermaphrodite not be sufficiently close to another. Some purely hermaphroditic species are known to self-fertilize if there are no other individuals nearby.

Dispersal through larval stages depends upon the type of larvae developed, as well as upon its behaviour and the amount of time it drifts as part of the plankton. Dispersal of larvae by ocean currents is ordinarily limited to a few hundred miles.

Many adult shore barnacles disperse by attaching to objects that float; naturally occurring substances such as pumice, wood, and kelp carry barnacles great distances. In transport of this type, the adult must release larvae, for it is they that will establish the species in a new habitat. Most of the barnacles that disperse in this way are estuarine or harbour forms; they, unlike shore forms, generally have low dispersal but high colonization potential.

Still other species are ectocommensal on organisms such as whales, turtles, sea snakes, and jellyfish, and their distributions tend to be those of their hosts. In some instances, however, the distribution of the barnacle is only a restricted portion of the range of the host, suggesting that other factors may limit the barnacle's range.

In the open ocean, the larvae of most species of the pedunculate (stalked) barnacle *Lepas* seek out objects (*e.g.*, ships, logs, coconuts) large enough to support the weight of numerous fully developed adults, but one species commonly settles on small objects (feathers, bits of tar) that would sink if required to support even one mature individual. After metamorphosis, they secrete a multichambered gas-filled float; in this way they avoid dependency on floating objects in the adult stage and, consequently, competition with species that require them. The floating clusters tend to attract other organisms, such as copepods and small fishes on which the barnacles feed. Since virtually any floating object is apparently suitable for settlement, primarily the availability of such objects presently limits the abundance of *Lepas* species in the sea.

Although a number of comprehensive studies have been made on numerical abundance, distribution, breeding cycles, prey–predatory relationships, selection of attachment sites, and tolerances of temperature and salinity, especially along temperate shores, the biology of barnacles is only beginning to be well-known.

Form and function. The shells of most species of sessile barnacles are composed of six vertical wall plates that form a truncate cone, with a membranous or calcareous foundation or basis for attachment. In addition, there are two pairs of movable valves on the free ends of the shell, opposite the basis, forming the operculum. In some of the stalked barnacles, the body is well covered with hard calcareous plates; in others the shell may be only partly calcified or almost absent, being represented by tiny vestiges. The calcareous plates are connected at their interfaces by chitin (a polysaccharide compound related to sugars) and are lined internally by the fleshy mantle.

The body is contained within the shell and carries out the function of feeding, digestion, respiration, and reproduction. The body more closely resembles the typical crustacean than might be expected from external appearances, having jointed appendages (cirri) and a soft, chitinous covering (exoskeleton) that also lines the foregut and hindgut.

Evolution and classification. *Evolution.* Morphological evidence indicates that the cirripeds are more closely related to the Copepoda (copepods) and their allies than to the Branchiopoda or the Malacostraca (the group that includes lobsters, crabs, and shrimps). The most generalized order, the Ascothoracica, is represented by semiparasitic to wholly parasitic forms, but there are no fossils recognizable as their free-living ancestors. From some such inferred ancestor, however, the remainder of the Cirripedia must have evolved.

The fossil record for the planktotrophic (plankton-eating) Thoracica begins in the Silurian (more than 400,000,000 years ago), but the order is not well represented until the Mesozoic, when in the Cretaceous Period (about 65,000,000 to 136,000,000 years ago) various pedunculate groups start giving rise to sessile forms. Sessile barnacles diversified throughout the Cenozoic (the last 65,000,000 years), and, as Darwin noted, the present epoch may well go down in the fossil record as the age of barnacles.

The wholly parasitic Rhizocephala and the planktotrophic Acrothoracica are both considered specialized offshoots of the Thoracica because of larval similarities. There are thoracicans that have given up filter feeding and extend rootlike nutritive structures into their hosts; they illustrate the intermediate stages that must have occurred in the evolution of the Rhizocephala.

Annotated classification.

CLASS (OR SUBCLASS) CIRRIPEDIA
Distinguished from all other crustaceans in having cyprid larvae with prehensile (adapted for grasping) first antennae and the female genital aperture on the first thoracic segment. Related to the Copepoda and other Maxillopoda that otherwise have a similar body plan. Principal characteristics used in classification include armature of the outer covering, form of appendages, and larval stages. Approximately 1,000 species known.

Order Ascothoracica
Cretaceous to Recent. A relatively obscure semiparasitic to wholly parasitic group having the most generalized morphology found in the Cirripedia. Up to a few millimetres in length.

Order Thoracica (barnacles)
Silurian to Recent. Exterior usually strengthened by calcareous plates.

Suborder Lepadomorpha (pedunculate or stalked barnacles)
Body divided into capitulum (that part of the body enclosed in mantle, which is an extension of the body wall homologous with the carapace of other Crustacea) and peduncle.
Family Scalpellidae (leaf barnacles). Upper Triassic to Recent. Capitulum protected by more than 5 plates, peduncle with calcareous plates. Size moderate, up to 10 cm (4 in.).
Family Lepadidae (goose barnacles). Middle Eocene to Recent. Capitulum typically with 5 calcareous plates. Size moderate, from 1 to as much as 75 cm in length.
Suborder Brachylepadomorpha
Upper Jurassic to upper Miocene. Symmetrical sessile barnacles, but little modified over the lepadomorphan grade of construction.
Suborder Verrucomorpha (wart or asymmetrical sessile barnacles)
Upper Cretaceous to Recent. Size ranges from 1 mm to more than 1 cm in height.
Suborder Balanomorpha (rock, acorn, or symmetrical sessile barnacles)
Upper Cretaceous to Recent. Size ranges from a few millimetres to as much as 10 cm in diameter and to 23 cm in length.
Family Chthamalidae. Upper Cretaceous to Recent. Distinguished from balanids (following) by the rostrum being overlapped, rather than overlapping, adjacent plates and usually occurring higher intertidally. Size from a few millimetres to 4 cm in diameter.
Family Balanidae (rock, turtle, and whale barnacles). Lower Eocene to Recent. Size range from a few millimetres to more than 20 cm in length. Rock barnacles to 10 cm but usually 1–2 cm in diameter.

Order Acrothoracica (burrowing barnacles)
Carboniferous to Recent. Size usually small, a few millimetres in length; burrow in calcareous substrates.

Order Rhizocephala
Recent. Wholly parasitic on crustaceans, primarily decapod malacostracans. Size of externa (reproductive body) from a few millimetres to 5 cm in length.

Order Apoda
A parasite having but two pairs of appendages, including biting mouthparts. Affinities with Cirripedia uncertain.

Critical appraisal. The category Maxillopoda, as first proposed in 1956, included the cirripeds, copepods, mystacocarids, branchiurans, and possibly the ostracods. The Maxillopoda is becoming increasingly recognized by crustacean specialists as a class, equalling the rank of the Malacostraca, Cephalocarida, and Branchiopoda. The fundamental body plan, exemplified by the Cirripedia and Copepoda, includes five cephalic and six thoracic appendage-bearing segments and five abdominal segments, the last bearing a furca. From this fundamental plan, the remaining categories can be derived.

BIBLIOGRAPHY. CHARLES DARWIN, *A Monograph on the Sub-Class Cirripedia*, 2 vol. (1851–54, reprinted 1964), is the first and most comprehensive monograph on the Thoracica, still an important source to workers in the field. PAUL KRUGER, *Cirripedia*, in *Bronns Klassen und Ordnungen des Teirreichs*, vol. 5, div. 1, fasc. 3, pt. 3 (1940), provides an authoritative compilation of knowledge of all cirriped orders (in German). A. GRUVEL, *Monographie des Cirrhipèdes ou Thécostracés* (1905, reprinted 1965), is a comprehensive monograph of all orders, but systematics of thoracicans is not accepted today (in French). W.A. NEWMAN, V.A. ZULLO, and T.H. WITHERS, "Cirripedia," in R.C. MOORE (ed.), *Treatise on Invertebrate Paleontology*, pt. R, *Arthropoda 4*, vol. 1, pp. R206–R295 (1969), provides a synoptic monograph of all orders, with sections on natural history and evolution. R.D. BARNES, *Invertebrate Zoology*, 2nd ed. (1968), is a textbook including general biology and morphology of barnacles. R.C. NEWELL, *Biology of Intertidal Animals* (1970), is a textbook on the biology and physiology of intertidal organisms, including barnacles. EDWARD HERON-ALLEN, *Barnacles in Nature and in Myth* (1928), includes a scholarly treatment of the goose barnacle myth. H.A. PILSBRY, "The Barnacles (*Cirripedia*) Contained in the Collections of the U.S. National Museum," *Bull. U.S. Natn. Mus.*, vol. 60 (1907), and "The Sessile Barnacles (*Cirripedia*) Contained in the Collections of the U.S. National Museum," *ibid.*, vol. 93 (1916), are the principal systematic monographs of North American thoracican barnacles. T.H. WITHERS, *Catalogue of Fossil Cirripedia in the Department of Geology* (of the British Museum), 3 vol. (1928–53), the most comprehensive monographs on the systematics of fossil barnacles.

(W.A.N.)

Secretion of gas-filled float by a *Lepas* species

City Government

A city cannot operate without a government of some kind. There are, indeed, no known examples of a city without government, however far back one goes in history. In some European countries cities were for centuries virtually independent political entities in themselves. Although the city-states of ancient Greece are the most famous illustration of this phenomenon, local government even in such countries as England, France, Italy, Spain, and Germany is much older than national government. In the modern world, however, cities are contained within the boundaries of national states, and city government forms part of a much larger and more complex constitutional regime.

City government as a reflection of national government

City government invariably reflects the general characteristics of this national regime. When political democracy exists at the national level, as in most of the Western world and Japan today, cities will enjoy a substantial degree of local autonomy and will have democratic systems of government. When the regime is authoritarian, central control is likely to diminish or extinguish local self-government and to suppress democratic forms. This was demonstrated by the suppression of democratic local government in Fascist Italy and Nazi Germany. Similarly, a country that prefers to concentrate power and responsibility in a single individual—or, conversely, in a committee—is likely to display this preference in its cities no less than in its central government. Thus, in the United States there is a president at the federal level, a governor in each state, and an elected mayor or city manager in the municipalities. In England there is a cabinet at the centre and a committee system in the municipalities.

In the modern world, cities can no longer hope to have complete autonomy or even the same degree of independence that existed, for example, in the United States in the 19th century. Several factors have drawn city, regional, and national governments into a close and continuing partnership. There is, for example, the recognition that some locally administered services—such as those relating to health or crime prevention—are of wider importance; there is also belief that local authorities must resort to national governments for aid in the form of subsidies or general grants to supplement municipal revenue. The terms of the partnership vary greatly in different systems of government, and so do the results, but the general trends are similar in all developed countries and in many developing ones. Because greater importance is now given to national planning, the development of backward regions, the construction of new towns, highways, and airports, and similar matters, the links between the levels of government are likely to increase.

Hitherto, the jurisdiction of city governments has been limited to the built-up urban area although there are exceptions to this in Brazil, South Africa, and Yugoslavia. A clear distinction between the city and the surrounding countryside no longer exists. The built-up and often congested central area extends without any sharp dividing line to the suburbs, then to the farther fringe composed of housing estates and villages for commuters, interspersed with small produce farms, golf clubs, recreational areas, industrial estates, and so forth, all of which may form a single area of interrelated activities. An army of commuters daily invades the main city, in which the workers earn their living, and at the close of the day they retreat to their homes in the suburbs or beyond. They and their families use the great city for such purposes as recreation, trade, shopping, professional services, and higher or technical education. The city depends for its economic health on their services and their purchasing power. But commuters also have to be provided with costly daytime services such as police and fire protection, water supply, sewage, public health, highways, and public transport, although those who live outside the city limits usually contribute little or nothing to the municipal revenue.

Urban technology and the patterns of behaviour of contemporary life have made it difficult or impossible for municipalities to cope with the mounting problems of the city region, and particularly those of the metropolitan areas, unless drastic changes of structure and scope are carried out. So far this has occurred in fewer than half a dozen of the great cities.

Services rendered by city government. Certain functions must be performed in every city. Law and order must be maintained, and this requires a police force, courts of justice for civil and criminal trials, and prisons for the punishment of offenders. There must be some regulation of building to ensure a minimum of safety and to ensure that houses or workshops are not constructed on public land or in improper places. There must be regular methods of preventing, controlling, and extinguishing fires. There must be regulations and executive action to protect the health of the citizens. For centuries, however, cities have regulated the life of the community in many other ways. Manchester, England, prior to 1838, for example, had Inspectors of Weights and Measures, Market Lookers for the Assize of Bread, Officers for Tasting Wholesome Ale and Beer, Officers for Muzzling Mastiff Dogs, and a Pounder (a dogcatcher). These were all very ancient offices, and Manchester also had a borough reeve and constables, surveyors of highways, police and improvement commissioners, and churchwardens and overseers who had care of the church and the poor and responsibility for assessing and collecting the poor rate. Thus, in the course of the centuries, the most elementary regulation of town life had by various devices been expanded to include a considerable number of additional functions.

The primary functions of law, order, safety, and health

The services now provided by city governments are different in nature and wider in scope than in the past. Generalization is impossible, but the most widespread functions today are the environmental and personal health services, including clinics and hospitals; primary, secondary, and further education; water supply, sewage, refuse collection and disposal; construction, maintenance, and lighting of streets; public housing; welfare services for the old, destitute, physically and mentally handicapped, orphans and abandoned children, unemployed and disabled workers, and other categories needing help; cemeteries and crematoriums; markets and abattoirs. The traditional services have been transformed beyond recognition.

Contemporary expansion of services

Many cities have had museums and art galleries for a century or more. Today such institutions are often part of extensive programs for recreation sponsored by the municipality. Such programs include support for concerts, theatres, opera, films, ballet, festivals, exhibitions of painting and sculpture, lectures, and libraries. Public parks and playgrounds are not a new feature of city life, but they too have become part of the comprehensive programs of outdoor recreation organized by the municipality.

A group of public-utility services comprising the supply of gas, electricity, water, and public transport are frequently provided by the city government itself, by a public corporation closely connected with it, or by a commercial company operating under a concession granted by the municipality. In some countries, municipal enterprise in the public utility field has been supplanted by larger regional or national schemes.

A city council inevitably takes an interest in the economic well-being of the city that it governs. Every city government wishes to do what it can to assist industry and promote trade, but there are great differences in the role assigned to local authorities in this respect in different countries. In the Communist regimes of eastern Europe, nearly the whole of local trade and much local industry is directly or indirectly under the control of the city government. On the other hand, in the United States a city government can control local industry only by means of zoning regulations, restrictions imposed under public health legislation, and so forth. In any case, municipal governments can do much to assist industry and commerce by good planning and physical development, by providing for trade fairs and exhibition centres, and by designing and developing roads, public housing, schools, and other municipal services to meet the needs of employers and employees. The attraction of tourists also has become an almost universal goal of every city that has the slightest pretension to be of interest to visitors, and here too the municipality can do much to attract tourists by providing not only publicity and information but also convenient and agreeable facilities. German towns have long been well known for their municipal hotels, restaurants, cafes, and beer halls. The towns of Switzerland have done much to uphold the high standard of hotel and restaurant management by their strict licensing requirements.

City planning

The most significant contemporary function is city planning. The finest cities always have been planned: no one can suppose that Paris, Washington, D.C., Leningrad, or Venice came to be what they are by chance. The finest features of London and Stockholm bear the imprint of the master planner. The planning of cities has now outgrown the limits of the jurisdiction of nearly all municipal authorities, and the need for planning on a metropolitan or regional scale is now generally acknowledged.

Types of city government. There are today four principal types of municipal systems of government: (1) the decentralized system found in federal constitutions; (2) the decentralized system found in unitary constitutions; (3) the supervisory system found under the "Napoleonic," or French-type, administration; and (4) the integrated system found in eastern Europe. (Although it is possible to classify municipal institutions under these headings, it should be acknowledged that some systems of local government blend the characteristics of more than one of these four principal types.)

DECENTRALIZED CITY GOVERNMENT IN FEDERAL SYSTEMS

In federal constitutions, local government is usually a matter lying within the jurisdiction of the state or provincial government rather than that of the national government. This is the position in the United States, and it accounts for the great diversity of municipal organization existing in that country.

Evolution of municipal government in the United States. Local government in the United States is based on English foundations. The early colonists introduced primary units of administration such as the township, the parish, and the manor similar to those that had existed for centuries in rural England. They appointed justices of the peace with functions similar to those of the same officer left behind in the motherland. The sheriff, the constable, the mayor, the controller, the coroner, and other officials in American cities and counties are derived from English officers of great antiquity, some of which originated in continental European countries.

In the colonial period, the more important cities, such as New York and Philadelphia, were granted charters that gave them the status of municipal corporations similar to that enjoyed by English towns at the end of the 17th century. They had a mayor, a recorder, aldermen, and a number of common councilmen who were all members of the city council. They were elected by a relatively restricted body of freemen. Their functions were mainly concerned with the regulation of trade and industry, such as markets, docks, and ferries, or the regulation of bakeries. A distinctive feature of the early American scene was the New England unincorporated town, which contained certain features of the parish and the manor. In such places, an annual town meeting of all the citizens was called to elect officers, adopt bylaws, levy taxes, and discuss the affairs of the town. The executive body chosen by the meeting was known as the selectmen.

In the American colonies, the mayor possessed few powers, and his position compared unfavourably in this respect with his counterpart in England. In the course of time, however, their relative positions have been reversed. The English mayor has lost all his powers and become little more than a ceremonial head of the city government, whereas in the United States the mayor has become a highly important figure. After the American Revolution (1775–1783), the American mayor's position was enhanced by the application to city government of the belief in democracy, the separation of powers, and the doctrine of checks and balances. The first signs of change appeared in Baltimore, where the mayor was given the power to veto the decisions of the council in 1797, and in Boston, where the mayor was elected by direct election in 1822, an innovation that became the accepted practice in all cities by the middle of the 19th century. In 1830 the mayor of New York City was given the right of an absolute veto.

Types of city government in the United States. The mayor-and-council form is the traditional type of city government in the United States. It prevails in a majority of American cities whether large or small. The relations between the mayor and the council are by no means uniform, but in general the borough or city council, which was the dominant partner in colonial days, has lost power as the role of the mayor has expanded. Bicameral councils have disappeared.

Mayor and council

In the weak-mayor form, the council retains a good deal of administrative power that it exercises through committees. The mayor has few administrative powers but possesses a number of legislative and judicial functions. Many of the municipal officers in such cities are directly elected. The so-called long ballot emerged when the citizens were asked to cast their votes for the fire chief, the treasurer, the solicitor, the marshal, the engineer, the tax collector, the assessor, the constable, the auditor, and other city officials. This was one of the consequences of Jacksonian democracy. The result was a lack of organized leadership because power and responsibility were too widely diffused. This diffusion tended to increase when the committee system broke down with the growth of cities and when it was then replaced by elective officials and boards that took over some of the council's functions. The only person able to coordinate the fragmented authority of these several parts of the city government was the party boss. It has been truly remarked that the price paid for his services was high (in graft) even though his product was of low quality.

It is against this background that the rise of the strong-mayor system is to be seen—a system that now exists in most of the larger American cities and many of the smaller ones. In this type, the mayor presides over the council and usually has the right to veto its ordinary legislative acts. The veto may be absolute, or it may be a suspensory veto that can be overcome if the measure in question is again passed by the council by a specified majority. The mayor usually prepares the budget for submission to the council. He can convene special sessions of the council to consider particular questions. He generally appoints and dismisses heads of departments and can give them instructions or directions. He appoints the chairmen and members of boards or commissions. He may decide or participate in the appointment of other city employees, such as policemen, firemen, and clerks, though patronage of this kind may be restricted by a civil service commission.

The strong-mayor form has several advantages over the weak-mayor type because it focusses power and responsibility in the mayor as the centre of public leadership. But its arrival happened to coincide with a period of municipal corruption and degradation that was described by Lincoln Steffens under the title *The Shame of the Cities* and has been referred to by more scholarly writers as the dark ages of American municipal history. It lasted from the end of the Civil War (1865) until the close of the 19th century.

The "commission" form, devised partly as a remedy for the corruption and inefficiency that afflicted the city governments, was introduced in Galveston, Texas, after a disastrous flood in 1900. A body of five commissioners was elected to serve the city as full-time officials. Individually they acted as heads of departments; collectively

"Commission" government

they formed the city council. The innovation proved a great success in Galveston, and the commission form was adopted in numerous other cities in Texas, Idaho, Iowa, Kansas, North Dakota, and South Dakota.

The commission form takes its name from the fact that the council is replaced by a small body of elected commissioners who decide general policies of municipal administration in addition to performing the usual functions of a council. Each of the commissioners also serves as head of one or more departments. The commission may also appoint various boards and committees to work with it in such spheres as health, libraries, and recreation. A member of the commission is chosen to be mayor either by the citizens or by his fellow commissioners. He is not the chief executive but only *primus inter pares* (first among equals). He seldom has a veto power and is distinguished from the other commissioners only on ceremonial occasions.

The commission pattern of city government has never made great inroads on the mayor and council form. It exists in fewer than 10 percent of American municipalities at the present time and is now on the decline. Its lack of success is due to the divided authority among the elected commissioners and its inability to concentrate responsibility in a single officer.

City manager

A more serious challenge to the traditional form of city government came from the city-manager system. The most recently developed and the most rapidly spreading, it is derived from the method of organizing business corporations that was in favour in the first quarter of the 20th century; a general manager was entrusted with operating activities by a board of directors to whom he was responsible. When the concept was applied to city government, there emerged a small council numbering from three to nine members, all elected at large. The council passes ordinances, adopts the budget, decides rates of taxation, and engages the manager. The mayor (if there is one) has a role that is chiefly ceremonial. The city manager is the real chief executive. He appoints and dismisses heads of departments and coordinates departmental activity. He advises and reports to the council, prepares the budget, presents an annual report to the citizens, and carries out any general policies laid down by the council. The position of the manager is generally set out in the city charter, which states that the council shall not interfere with his administrative functions. He has a duty to provide the council with whatever information they need to determine matters of policy.

A by-product of the manager system has been the recognition that, although strong mayors are usually good politicians, they frequently lack the experience and knowledge of managerial skills required of a chief executive. In consequence, a number of cities have appointed a director of administration to assist the mayor in this task. His function is to coordinate the work of the administrative departments, to supervise the municipal administration as a whole, and to advise and assist the mayor. The appointment of such an officer in no way derogates from the position of mayor as the centre of public leadership and responsibility.

Independent boards and commissions

In addition to these principal forms of municipal government, there are in most American cities a considerable number of ad hoc boards and commissions possessing varying degrees of independence. The school board is invariably separate from the rest of the city administration, and there are usually many other independent boards. Some of them can appoint and dismiss their own staff. The mayor may have the power to appoint the chairmen and members, but thereafter his power to direct or influence may become slight or even negligible. A widespread characteristic of all forms of American city government is the fragmentation of authority caused by such devices.

The relation of city government to state and national government. State governments in the U.S. exercise many different kinds of supervision and control over the cities within their jurisdiction. The structure of local government is determined by state law, and every municipality owes its corporate status and machinery of self-gov-

ernment to the state. Although a "home rule" movement, which began in Missouri in 1875, seeks to ensure that local communities shall be granted the right to self-government without interference by the state, such independence is a utopian dream that is incapable of realization under contemporary conditions. What it means in practice is that certain classes of local units (usually those over a specified size) are authorized to draft a charter for the government of the local community.

State-granted city charters and "home rule"

Although the adoption of a charter establishes the framework for city government, the ultimate supremacy of the state is unimpaired and is exercised in many different ways. A high proportion of the laws enacted by state legislatures deal with local matters of various kinds, and various state bureaus regularly intervene in local affairs by supplying city officials with technical assistance or advice, by obtaining information and statistics, and by exercising specific controls. State supervision takes many forms and varies not only among states but also between functions within each state. It is most extensive in education; the state superintendent of education can often impose uniform practices or minimum standards on local school boards, determine the choice of textbooks, the courses of study, school building plans, and many other matters. Highways represent another area in which a large share of the responsibility has been taken over by the states. In recent decades, federal, state, and local governments have cooperated in developing the highway system. A third sphere in which state governments have close relations with the cities is finance. One aspect of this is that states give substantial financial aid to municipalities, which may be as much as 20 to 40 percent of the state budget. The aid is given partly by direct grants and partly in the form of shared taxes. States also are involved in auditing municipal accounts, approving city budgets, scrutinizing municipal indebtedness, and so forth.

The field in which least has been done and in which most needs to be done is the reorganization of municipal areas and authorities. The growth of metropolitan areas is the most significant urban development in the United States during the past 40 years, yet no serious attempt has been made by any state to reorganize local government units so that their boundaries and powers would correspond to the facts of modern life. The case of the New York metropolitan area, with its 1,400 governments, is well known, but in none of the great metropolitan centres is there a metropolitan authority possessing power to plan the metropolis as a whole or to administer the services that require large-scale organization. The obstacles to reform are in part the indifference of state governments, in part the opposition of small suburban councils to being absorbed by or in any way subordinated to a metropolitan authority, and in part a belief that local government units must not be merged or otherwise tampered with unless a referendum has been held and a majority obtained in favour of the proposal.

Constitutional theory excludes any direct relation between the federal government and municipal authorities. In practice, however, there are important connections. For example, even though many federal grants for such services as the care of disabled persons, maternity and child welfare, and aid to dependent children are made to the state governments, the states later may pass all or some of the money on to the city governments to carry out the work. Slum clearance, urban renewal, low-rent public housing, airport and air terminal construction, disaster relief, the reduction and control of water pollution, and certain aspects of education are among the many areas in which the initiative for progress and the resources necessary to achieve it have come directly to the cities from the federal government.

Evolution of municipal government in Germany. German cities have had a long and checkered history of both freedom and subordination. In the 12th and 13th centuries, they bought rights of self-government from their rulers or overlords, and the halcyon days of municipal life took place in the later Middle Ages. North of the

Rhine were many fortified towns or boroughs, the largest of them enjoying a remarkable degree of autonomy and being known as "free cities." They formed the Hanseatic League, to which in its heyday nearly a hundred cities belonged, including the leaders Hamburg, Bremen, Lübeck, Danzig, and Frankfurt. There were other leagues of towns elsewhere in Germany, such as the Swabian League in the South.

The Hanse cities were generally governed by a burgomaster, a senate, and a city council elected by the merchants. The rest of the citizens had little part in this system because the councillors appointed the senators and the burgomaster (*Bürgermeister*). This was the era of the guilds, which made the cities closed plutocratic corporations. After the Peace of Westphalia (1648), which ended the Thirty Years' War, municipal power was usurped by small groups of men with far less right to speak or act for the community than the members of the merchant guilds who had previously wielded power. Even the pretense of an election was often abandoned, and a period of arbitrary rule ensued. In the 17th and 18th centuries, the princes reasserted their claims over the cities and revived and extended their former prerogatives. Absolutism gained ground, and local autonomy declined under the weight of state control. The Thirty Years' War had ruined many towns, and their desperate plight made state intervention inevitable. By the middle of the 18th century, municipal autonomy had ceased to exist. The cities were deprived of their powers and subordinated to the prince, who often ruled through his appointed officers.

Autocracy was especially marked in Prussia, which became a kingdom in 1701. The Prussian monarchy under Frederick I, Frederick William I, and Frederick II the Great resulted in the decline of the towns as independent entities. At the beginning of the 19th century, Berlin was governed by a semimilitary autocracy. The citizens had no voice in choosing either the burgomaster or the executive. In any case, the city's executive exercised only unimportant powers, and the principal services such as education, public health, and poor relief were administered by organs appointed by and responsible to the crown. Local initiative and responsibility had everywhere been reduced to a shadow.

After the collapse of Prussia at the Battle of Jena in 1806, Napoleon entered Berlin, abolished the military and monarchical government, and appointed an administrative committee elected by 60 delegates chosen by 2,000 of the leading citizens. A mayor appointed by the crown was placed in charge of local affairs.

Revival
of limited
local
autonomy
under the
Stein
reforms

Municipal reform began in 1808 when Freiherr vom Stein persuaded Frederick William III that in order to rehabilitate the country it was necessary to establish free towns in a free state, a policy he linked with the emancipation of the peasants and the abolition of the remaining relics of feudalism. The outcome was the Municipal Ordinance of Nov. 19, 1808, which applied to all the towns in Prussia. Under this law, every town was to have a mayor, an executive, and a popular assembly, all directly or indirectly elected. Everyone was to pay taxes and to use the municipal services, although not everyone was to have the right to vote. The cities would henceforth perform all municipal functions, whereas the state would have a supervisory role to ensure legality and a due regard for state policy. Other states such as Bavaria and Württemberg followed the Prussian example and introduced similar reforms, sometimes of a more liberal character.

Each state determined the system of local government within its boundaries. There was much diversity, but certain national trends could be detected. After the Stein reforms, the separation of executive and legislative organs was everywhere applied. Except with regard to finance, the city councils occupied a role subsidiary to that of the burgomaster and other executive bodies. Just as the imperial and state parliaments lacked supremacy and effective control over the executive and bureaucracy, so in the cities a similar situation existed before 1945. The Prussian Municipal Ordinance of 1853 required that the

appointment of municipal officials be confirmed by the crown or its agents.

The Stein reforms sought to introduce citizen participation in local government and to remove or reduce state tutelage. In the course of the 19th century, these aims were furthered in many of the German states, although the fact that the state was the police authority, combined with the theory that all local government is a devolution of state functions, set clear limits to municipal autonomy. In the sphere of education, state control was particularly severe. (Later, during the Weimar Republic of the 1920s, municipalities relied to an increasing extent on central government grants and were subjected to ever greater control by the higher authorities.)

Meanwhile, in the 19th century, three main forms of city government emerged in Germany. One was the magisterial system (*Magistratsverfassung*), in which executive power lay in the hands of an administrative board containing both lay and professional members appointed by the council. The lay members were not required to be councillors. A second form was the strong burgomaster system (*Bürgermeisterverfassung*), in which an indirectly elected burgomaster (or mayor) presided over the council and controlled the entire municipal administration. He appointed and dismissed all city employees other than chief officers within the limits of the civil service laws. The third form was the town-council system (*Stadtratsverfassung*), in which the council was composed not only of the elected members but also of the chief administrative or professional officers. In all three systems, the mayor was appointed by the council. In the larger towns he served for a twelve-year term in the first instance and thereafter for life.

In 1935 the National Socialist (Nazi) government of Adolf Hitler introduced a national system of supervision and suppression of local self-government. The Local Government Act of that year concentrated entire responsibility in the executive head of each commune and simultaneously deprived the council of effective power. Election was abolished, and the councillors were selected by a Nazi delegate in agreement with the appointed mayor. An agent of the Nazi Party was appointed to watch each local authority, and he was authorized to intervene on specified occasions. The appointment and recall of the mayor and chief officers were strictly controlled by the Nazi Party. By this means, the political reliability of every burgomaster and chief officer was scrutinized with the utmost care by the Nazi Party leaders. The idea of official neutrality was repugnant to Hitler's totalitarian creed, and Wilhelm Frick, his minister of the interior, declared that every local government officer had a legal obligation "to take at all times a stand for the principles and aims pursued by the Nazi Party."

Types of present-day municipal government in West Germany. The primary unit of local government in the Federal Republic of Germany is the commune or municipality (*Gemeinde*). It may be either rural (*Landgemeinde*) or urban (*Stadt*). Above the municipality is the *Kreis*, which corresponds to a district or county containing villages, hamlets, and small towns; it is an upper tier of local self-government that exercises supervisory powers and also provides services. Some 140 towns, most of them with more than 100,000 population, however, are independent of this *Kreis* (*Kreisfreie Städte*, or "Kreis-free towns"). Above the *Kreis* is the province or administrative district (*Regierungsbezirk*) of the state (*Land*), though the *Regierungsbezirk* does not exist in the small states of the Saarland and Schleswig-Holstein. The three great cities of Bremen, Hamburg, and West Berlin rank as states as well as municipalities within the federation of West Germany.

Several fundamental changes were introduced when the republic was constituted after World War II. As in the past, municipalities are the creatures of their respective states (*Länder*); but the Bonn constitution requires that the representative organs of the municipalities shall be elected by universal, direct, free, equal, and secret ballot. Furthermore, the elected council is declared to be the supreme organ in the municipality, and chief executives must be chosen by either the citizens or the council.

The structure of local government varies among the different states. In Bavaria and Baden-Württemberg, the burgomaster and deputy burgomasters, who form the executive organ, are directly elected by the citizens. In Nordrhein-Westphalia and Lower Saxony, the burgomaster retains only political functions, his former administrative functions having been transferred to a city director (*Stadtdirektor*) or chief executive officer. The *Bürgermeisterverfassung* prevails in the Rhineland-Palatinate and the Saarland and entails a functional distinction between the respective powers of the council and the mayor. The *Magistratsverfassung* obtains in Hesse, Schleswig-Holstein, and Bremen. The council elects its own chairman and also appoints a board consisting of 6 to 12 members to act as the executive organ of the municipality. The council designates one of the members of this board to serve as its chairman and as burgomaster. Whatever the form of the executive organ, it must prepare and carry out the resolutions, policies, and administrative decisions of the council. Only in urgent matters or emergencies can the executive decide in place of the council. The distribution of power in West German municipalities is now far more democratic than it has ever been.

The relation of city government to higher authorities. The smaller towns are subject to supervision by the *Kreis*, whereas the larger cities come directly under the authority of the provincial authority (*Regierungsbezirken*), headed by the *Regierungspräsident*, who is a state-appointed official. In Schleswig-Holstein and Saarland, there are no provincial organs, and their functions are assumed by the state minister of the interior.

Each *Kreis* has a directly elected council and an executive committee appointed by the council from outside its members. The council president (*Landrat*) is chosen by various methods: in Bavaria he is directly elected locally; in the Rhineland-Palatinate he is a state official; elsewhere he is a kind of prefect, with allegiances to both the *Kreis* and the state. He is subordinate to the president of the provincial authority (*Regierungspräsident*), who is a state functionary and who can supervise the legality, but not the merits, of decisions or activities of the towns or cities within his jurisdiction.

Federal supervision of city governments in regard to the exercise of their own powers is limited to questions of legality, but where functions are delegated to a city by the federal government, it must carry out any instructions or directions that may be given to it.

DECENTRALIZED CITY GOVERNMENT IN UNITARY SYSTEMS

Municipal government in Great Britain. The evolution of municipal government in Great Britain is the prime example of another kind of development of decentralized systems. First, it should be noted that town government in Britain evolved apart from the parish and the county. William the Conqueror granted a new charter and gave special protection to the City of London in 1066. Other boroughs sought charters from the king, and by the middle of the 12th century, many had obtained them. The effect of a charter was to confer an independent status by giving the borough the right to choose its own officers, to operate markets, and to govern itself in other ways. Many towns had to purchase their independent status also from the person who was currently lord of the manor. In feudal society, the lord of the manor administered justice, and the fines imposed were a source of revenue to him. He was also entitled to charge rents for stalls and impose tolls for permission to trade in the town markets. The money value of these privileges was the basis of the annual rent that the town had to pay for the right to govern itself. The purchase of manorial rights was not inconsistent with obtaining a royal charter, which was, indeed, an additional safeguard for the town's independence. A charter granted by one monarch, however, did not bind his successor, and it became necessary to seek the renewal or replacement of the charter whenever a new king succeeded to the throne.

Medieval boroughs

The eventual enfranchisement of the towns usually led to the domination of the merchant guilds in the conduct of municipal affairs because they alone had the wealth to purchase rights from an overlord, but whether the town government originated from a merchant guild or from a group of free citizens, oligarchy tended to prevail. The general body of citizens had no control over the city government, and the door was opened wide to abuse of office, corruption, patronage, and extravagant use of municipal property, which had come to be regarded as belonging personally to the members of the closed corporation.

The first comprehensive inquiry into town government was carried out by the Royal Commission on Municipal Corporations reporting in 1835. There were at that time 246 boroughs, and no attempt previously had been made to impose a uniform system of government; in consequence, they displayed an immense diversity of forms, procedures, attitudes, and standards of behaviour. The royal commission issued a highly coloured report criticizing all the boroughs for the defects and abuses of only a few of them and ignoring some other serious drawbacks. The report served the political purpose of its authors, and within a short time there was enacted the Municipal Corporations Act (1835), which applied initially to 179 boroughs and established a uniform system of city government that has survived in a greatly developed form to the present day. In brief, the act transformed the closed corporations into public authorities. The ratepaying citizens elected the council, which was made responsible for policy, finance, and execution. The revenues and property of the corporation were to be applied in future only to authorized public purposes. Although initially the franchise was narrowly based and the functions of the municipal corporations were restricted, as the century wore on, the franchise was extended, and more and more powers were given to the municipal corporations. The mayor has remained a ceremonial officer—the first citizen of the borough, but without significant executive power. Municipal authority resides in the council and in the numerous functional committees into which it is divided. There is no separate executive.

Reforms of 1835

County government was not reformed until 1888, when the Local Government Act introduced elected county councils for certain major functions, leaving the more local functions to the borough councils. Eventually, though, 61 municipal corporations in Great Britain were given the status of both counties and boroughs; as "county boroughs," they are excluded wholly, for local government purposes, from the administrative county in which they are geographically situated. Towns with growing populations eagerly sought county borough status.

"County boroughs" and noncounty boroughs

By 1970, 83 cities in England had attained it. Moreover, as urban development spread into the suburbs, the county boroughs endeavoured to extend their boundaries in order to include the homes in which an increasing number of city workers lived. Both types of expansion have met with fierce resistance from the county councils.

Noncounty boroughs—that is, those boroughs that share government with the counties—have fared badly in recent decades. Power and responsibility have shifted to county councils with respect to education, police forces, fire brigades, town and country planning, and health services. Moreover, both county boroughs and noncounty boroughs have lost control and ownership of the major public utilities, which have been nationalized and transferred to public corporations; municipal hospitals have become part of the National Health Service, and public assistance has become the responsibility of the central government. Valuation of property for local taxation has been transferred from local authorities to the Inland Revenue. Municipal omnibus services have been nationalized. The list of lost functions is a long one. It is due partly to the obsolete structure of local government and partly to a tendency toward centralization that can be seen in many countries.

The government of Greater London has been the object of considerable reorganization in recent years, beginning with the London Government Act of 1963, which swept

Government of Greater London

away about 100 local authorities of various kinds and established in their place a new two-tier system for an area covering 610 square miles and containing a population of almost 8,000,000. The Greater London Council is a directly elected organ entrusted with functions relating to the metropolis as a whole, such as the preparation of master plans and major schemes of comprehensive development and the governance of traffic, public transport, fire protection, ambulances, the sewage system, building regulation, refuse disposal, parks and open spaces of regional importance, entertainment, concerts, and museums of more than purely local interest. A second tier consists of 32 London borough councils and the corporation of the ancient City of London. The London boroughs are responsible for refuse collection, personal health and welfare services, housing within their own areas, local roads, public libraries, local parks and playgrounds, local art galleries and museums, cemeteries and crematoriums, and so forth. The London boroughs also are required to make detailed plans for their areas in conformity with the master plans. Although the Greater London Council and the London borough councils are independent within their respective spheres, they share responsibility and power for highways, housing, and planning and thus must seek close cooperation.

In Britain, as elsewhere, central control has grown during the 20th century. Each department of the national government uses its own methods, but typical among them are the approval (or rejection) of schemes submitted by local authorities for town planning, education, and highways; approval of the appointment or qualifications of chief officers; and approval of slum clearance schemes and purchases of land. They also hear appeals by citizens dissatisfied with certain decisions of local authorities, and they inspect the police forces and the schools administered by local authorities. The overriding feature of central–local relations is the fact that local authorities have become increasingly dependent on central grants for their revenue. Their only source of tax revenue consists of rates levied on real property (leaving aside rents and fees for services). The result is that central grants are now larger than income from rates. Unless local authorities are given additional sources of fiscal revenue, they are unlikely to achieve a position of greater independence —despite strong movements for the reform of local controls and for a reduction in central control.

Local government structure

Municipal government in Japan. The modernization of local government in Japan began in 1888 with the establishment of municipal authorities in cities, towns, and villages. This was followed in 1890 by the introduction of prefectures and counties as a higher tier of authorities. The counties were abolished in 1922, and since then the structure has consisted of an upper tier of prefectures and a lower tier of cities, towns, and villages.

The pattern of local government was originally based on the Prussian model and was highly bureaucratic and centralized. The powers of local authorities were narrow and circumscribed, but they gradually broadened until the outbreak of World War II, when once again bureaucracy and centralization became the dominant features.

After the war, a radical reform of local government took place directed toward the creation of political democracy in Japan. The new constitution provided that local authorities should be organized and operated in accordance with the principle of local autonomy, that both the chief executives and the local assemblies should be directly elected by popular vote, and that local authorities should have the right to manage their property and affairs and to make their own regulations within the law. A Local Autonomy Law passed in 1947 prescribed in detail the organization and functions of local government. Legislation followed on finance and the public service.

The municipalities consist of cities (*shi*), towns (*machi*), and villages (*mura*). All have the same structure and legal status but differ in powers. A city must have a population of not less than 50,000 (formerly 30,000), of which at least 60 percent must engage in commerce and industry; and it must possess civic halls, a sewage system, libraries,

and other public amenities. In 1953 a compulsory amalgamation of local government units reduced the number of towns and villages from 9,610 to 2,915, while the number of cities was increased to 556. These figures have changed only slightly since.

There are 44 prefectures, or 45 if Okinawa is included. Tokyo has a special structure because of its vast size and its position as the national capital. For nearly a decade after 1888, the duties normally performed by a mayor were carried out by the governor of Tokyo prefecture, who was appointed by the central government. In 1898 the City Council was permitted to elect a mayor, although Tokyo remained under the supervision of both the prefectural governor and the minister of home affairs.

In 1943 the prefecture of Tokyo was merged with the city, which then became the metropolis, combining the powers of a prefecture with those of a city. The Tokyo Metropolitan Government is directly responsible for municipal administration in the special ward area, in which there are 23 subordinate bodies known as ward councils performing minor functions. Outside the ward area, the Tokyo Metropolitan Government has the powers of a prefecture over 17 cities and 24 towns and villages; nine of the towns and villages are on certain islands in the Pacific Ocean.

The separation of powers is applied in municipalities of all types. The mayor is directly elected by the voters and so too is the assembly of which he is not a member; the only exceptions are the special wards in which the mayors are appointed by the ward council with the concurrence of the metropolitan governor. The assembly passes the budget, enacts bylaws, approves the accounts, decides the local taxes, disposes of property, and can demand reports or carry out investigations. The mayor (or governor of Tokyo) controls the entire administration, except certain functions that have been entrusted to separate administrative boards. These include education boards, election administrative commissions to manage both national and local elections, audit and inspection commissions, civil service commissions, and police boards.

The mayor, or the governor of Tokyo, has the right to convene the council and to place bylaws before it. He is the ceremonial head of the city as well as its chief executive. He is also entrusted with certain duties on behalf of the central government, such as the maintenance of national roads and the census.

Relations with higher authorities

The prefectures act in a dual capacity to a greater extent than the municipalities. They serve as local agencies of the state in directing and supervising the activities performed by the municipalities on behalf of the central government. They also administer services requiring a larger area of administration than that of a municipality. These include development planning; land conservation projects such as flood control; and the construction, improvement, and control of roads, bridges, rivers, canals, and so forth. The prefectural governments are entrusted with some highly specialized services that municipalities might not have sufficient resources to provide, such as art museums, hospitals, schools for the physically and mentally handicapped, laboratories, experimental stations, and other establishments concerned with health and social welfare. In some spheres the prefectures and the municipalities have concurrent powers—*e.g.*, the establishment of museums. In other spheres a service may be shared between the two levels. An example is education, in which municipalities run elementary and junior high schools while the prefectures provide the senior high schools. The six largest cities aside from Tokyo (Osaka, Nagoya, Yokohama, Kyōto, Kōbe, and Kitakyūshū) are empowered to perform functions concerning social welfare, public health, city planning, and other services that elsewhere are entrusted to a prefecture.

The control over the cities exercised by the central government is considerable. The Ministry of Autonomy is the department mainly concerned with local government, but the ministries of Finance, Education, Construction and Transport exercise varying degrees of control over local authorities. One of the unresolved problems in Japan is the reluctance of central departments to coordinate their activities, and this often leads to serious inconsistencies and conflicts of policy.

The central ministries give information and technical advice to the municipalities. If the central government suspects unlawful or improper action on the part of a municipality, it may direct the local authority to take whatever measures are considered necessary to remedy the defect.

The chief instrument of central control is finance. City government can levy taxes on inhabitants and on fixed assets, light vehicles, tobacco, electricity and gas, mineral products and timber, but the revenue from local taxes provides only about one-third of local expenditures. Taxes allocated or transferred by the central government and subsidies and other payments by the central government amount to about 42 percent of local revenues. The general position is shown by the fact that the central government levies about 70 percent of the nation's taxes, while local authorities spend about a similar proportion of the total tax revenue. The dependence of local authorities on central finance is similar in Japan to that in many other developed countries. Central grants and subsidies involve supervision by the prefectural governor as well as by the competent minister who can inspect and direct the service or project for which the money is given. Borrowing is regulated by the minister of finance with great severity—which has seriously retarded social investment in Tokyo.

The tradition of bureaucratic domination is not infrequently found in the departments of the central government, but this tradition is now confronted, particularly in the great cities, by a spirit of independence and a determination to uphold and strengthen the autonomy guaranteed to the municipalities by the constitution and the laws. Each side has its strength and weakness.

THE NAPOLEONIC SUPERVISORY SYSTEM

The evolution of French municipal government. The present system of local government in France derives mainly from the French Revolution and the Napoleonic era (although the close relation between central and local government and the subordination of the local government did have roots in the *ancien régime*). It was Napoleon who laid down the basic organization of a highly centralized administrative state in which the communes were local units of the central government. And historically this French pattern of government has had far-reaching influence in Europe, Africa, and Asia.

The mayor and the prefect

The French system today has two tiers of authorities. In each of the 38,000 *communes* (which comprise municipal units of all sizes, from tiny villages to large cities), there is an elected council and a mayor (*maire*), appointed by the councillors from among their own members. In each of the 94 regional *départements* into which France is divided, there is a prefect (*préfet*) who is appointed by and responsible to the central government and who is assisted by an elected departmental council. The separation of powers has been applied at both levels, and the mayor and the prefect are executive officers, whereas the councils are deliberative and legislative bodies.

The mayor is the responsible head of the municipality. He represents the local community. He presides at council meetings and carries out its decisions. He prepares the budget and submits it to the council for its consideration. He initiates proposals for new measures or policies and must approve all expenditures. In the large towns, the mayor will have the help of several assistant mayors; he can delegate particular tasks to one or more of them, and he can also delegate functions to a councillor. In the larger municipalities, the mayor appoints a secretary general who is answerable to him for the day-to-day administration, thus leaving the mayor free to devote himself to political leadership and policy making. Mayors are not infrequently among the leading national figures in French politics.

The mayor acts in a dual capacity, since he is both the head of the municipality and also a representative of the central government for certain purposes. Thus he is required to perform certain functions in the *commune* on behalf of the state, such as collecting statistical and other information; registering births, deaths, and marriages; officiating at civil marriages; compiling lists of men liable for military service; promulgating laws; and controlling the municipal police force, which is part of the national police.

Powers of the commune or city

A city government is legally authorized to deal with all matters of local interest, but the extent to which it does so depends on the attitude of the council and its mayor, the resources at its disposal, and the degree of control exercised by higher authority. The prefect is the supervisory agent who possesses the authority of all the national ministries, including even those that have their own specialists working in the field. When the mayor is carrying out his duties as an agent of the state, the prefect is his hierarchical superior and can amend or set aside his decisions. When the mayor acts as head of the municipality, the relation is one of tutelage. This contains both negative and positive elements. On the one hand, the prefect's approval, explicit or implicit, is required for important matters such as the budget, the purchase or sale of public property, loans, bylaws, the starting of new municipal services, and staff appointments. On the other hand, if a municipality has failed to provide an obligatory service or failed to raise the necessary revenue by taxation, the prefect can act to remedy the default; when a commune fails to balance its budget, for instance, the prefect can do so by levying the necessary taxes. The extent of the tutelage is shown by the fact that all decisions of the municipal council must be referred to the prefect or subprefect, and its minutes must have his signature in order to be valid.

The ultimate sanction for this tutelage is the power of the prefect to suspend the mayor, who can be dismissed by the minister of the interior. The council also can be suspended or dissolved. The city council can appeal to the prefect if it considers that the mayor has neglected his duties or has exceeded his powers. Alternatively, the council may ask an administrative court to annul mayoral decisions that are thought to be in conflict with the intention of the laws.

Powers of the *département*

Apart from the supervisory duties of the prefect, the *département* is also a unit of local government, although the fact that the prefect is appointed by and responsible to the central government precludes it from being an organ of local self-government. The elected council is a relatively weak body and meets only twice a year for about six weeks in all. It is far less powerful than the prefect. Nevertheless, the fact that the *département* has a representative council prevents it from being regarded merely as a unit of central administration. In fact, all the councillors of all *départements* acting together elect the members of the national senate.

The competence of this council includes powers similar to those of a municipal council in regard to finance, property, and highways. *Départements* are also authorized to provide any services considered necessary or useful for the welfare of the community. Under these general powers, they administer numerous services, either exclusively or in cooperation with the municipalities or the state. Hospitals, for example, are either communal, intercommunal, or departmental; the regional director of the Ministry of Public Health and the prefect decide on the area to be served by a particular hospital. Education is organized regionally under the direction of the minister of education; the *départements* are responsible for providing part of the cost. Numerous other health and welfare services are administered by *départements* and regulated by the departmental councils. The *département*, like the municipality, is also the unit for the administration of national services. These relate to such matters as the armed forces, the judiciary, and the postal and telegraph services. Partly to administer these services, partly to advise and assist the municipalities, and partly to help the prefect and the departmental council, the central ministries have many of their own officers stationed in the *dé-*

partements, either in the capital town or in the subprefectures within a *département*. Legally and constitutionally, these officials are subordinate to the prefect, who alone represents all the ministries.

More than 80 percent of the *communes* have a population of less than 1,000. Because units of this size cannot hope to provide the services demanded by advanced nations today, they are permitted under French law to form joint associations for common tasks, or to merge and constitute a new municipality, or to establish a *syndicat*, or corporate body, with its own budget to carry out particular functions. Although these devices have been used in cities of medium size, they have not solved the problems of the metropolitan areas. Under a law enacted in 1966, metropolitan authorities must be established in the great urban concentrations of Lyon, Lille-Roubaix Tourcoing, Bordeaux, and Strasbourg; similar action is permitted in any other concentrated area of 50,000 or more inhabitants. Under this law, each constituent municipality continues to be responsible for administering and developing a wide range of services concerning its own area; but the metropolitan authority undertakes a number of functions of interest to the metropolis as a whole. These relate to such matters as town planning and the public services involving roads, water, sanitation, housing, industrial estates, transport, secondary schools, and the like. Also included are public investments for assisting the arts, sports, hospitals, and other social and educational facilities. The governing body of the metropolitan authority is a council of between 50 and 90 members, who are representatives of the local authorities.

Government of Paris

Paris has always had a system of government different from that of the rest of France. It has not had a mayor but has been governed by the prefect of police (*préfet de police*) and the prefect of the Seine (*préfet de la Seine*), with a weak elected council. The object of this differentiation was to keep control of the capital firmly in the hands of the central government. Beginning in 1964, a new approach to the problems confronting the metropolis was taken—first, by the establishment of the District of the Region of Paris, an area containing over 9,000,-000 people. The three *départements* that had previously existed were replaced by eight *départements*, one of them being the ancient Ville de Paris, the core city within the walls, which became a *département* with its own *préfet de Paris*. The 1,100-odd *communes* in the region continue to operate. At the metropolitan level, there is a regional prefect known as the *délégué général*, appointed by the government and directly responsible to the premier's office. There is an administrative council to assist him, consisting of 28 members who are elected representatives of the *départements* and municipalities; half of them are elected to the council by the mayors of the *communes* and the departmental councils; the other half are appointed by the government. Overall, this new regional authority has restricted functions and limited funds at its disposal; its essential function is to provide for the strategic planning and large-scale development of the metropolitan area.

The evolution of Italian municipal government. After Italian national unity had been achieved in 1870, the state consolidated its authority over municipalities and provinces by passing legislation based on the model introduced by Napoleon Bonaparte. Although there were subsequent efforts to decentralize the system by giving increased powers once again to the local authorities, the consolidation of the Fascist regime in 1926 destroyed all traces of local autonomy. The election of local councils was abolished, and the functions of the council were transferred to the mayor, who became an agent of the central government.

The Italian mayor and prefect

After World War II, local self-government acquired a new significance with the restoration of democratic institutions. The Italian constitution of 1948 guaranteed the autonomy of all regions, provinces, and local authorities. But despite differences of structure, the organization remained patterned after the French supervisory system. Every city and town (*comune*) has a local elected council (*consiglio communale*), which elects a mayor (*sindaco*) and also a number of deputy mayors or "assessors" (*assessori*) who together form the executive committee (*giunta municipale*). The mayor represents the city, presides over the council, draws up its agenda, and is the chief executive of the municipality; as in France, however, he also performs certain functions on behalf of the state. The *giunta*, of which he is chairman, directs day-to-day administration, makes recommendations to the council, and acts in its place when it is not in session. Each member is usually assigned general oversight over one or more bureaus or departments. The chief administrative officer, appointed by the central government, is the "secretary" (*segretario*), who advises the city government on legal or technical questions.

The Italian province is the counterpart of the French *département*, and its *prefetto* corresponds to the French prefect. There is, however, a dual organization in the province. One, consisting of an elected council, an executive committee, and a chairman who presides over both bodies, is concerned with such matters as roads, bridges, and dikes; certain health measures; secondary schools; and agricultural improvements. The other consists of the *prefetto* (sometimes aided by an administrative commission), who is responsible for law and order, enforcing national laws, and scrutinizing the bylaws.

Latin American variations of the supervisory system. The tendency in Latin American countries is to adopt the basic principles of the supervisory system. This involves appointing central government officers of the prefectoral type who exercise control over local authorities.

Despite this general trend, there are large differences in the degree of local autonomy existing in the various countries of Latin America. In Argentina, for example, where there have been no elections since a military government assumed power in 1966, the former elected city councils have been supplanted by advisory committees appointed from above. There is at present no local self-government in Argentina. A similar absence exists in Peru.

In Ecuador the municipalities have elected councils and indirectly elected mayors who undertake local government functions. They are supervised by the centrally appointed "political chief" of the municipality (*jefe político*); his immediate superior is the provincial governor, who is appointed by the president of the republic. The *jefe político* supervises the city council and reports any illegal or irregular acts to the provincial governor; he also performs a number of state functions in the municipality. The provincial governor is charged with maintaining public order and upholding the law and constitution and is also responsible for developing the education, health, welfare, and cultural services and the public works projects.

Chile generally has elected municipal councils that appoint their own mayors, but in the large cities of Santiago, Valparaíso, Viña del Mar, and Concepción, the mayors are appointed and removable by the president. At each level of administration—provincial, departmental, municipal, and district—there is a representative of the president assisted by a small elected council. This follows the essential principle of the French system. El Salvador, Costa Rica, Guatemala, Panama, and Honduras have also adopted the prefectoral model. Even more subordinate to the central government are the cities in countries where the mayor is appointed by either the president or the prefect on his behalf. This occurs in Bolivia, Colombia, Nicaragua, and the Dominican Republic. The municipalities have elected councils, but their functions are mainly advisory. A high degree of local autonomy exists in Uruguay, where the voters elect not only the municipal council but also local executive organs in place of a mayor. In Mexico, too, both mayors and councils are elected.

THE INTEGRATED SYSTEM

The evolution of municipal government in the Soviet Union. Local self-government in Russia began in the 18th century, when Catherine II granted to almost the whole male population the right to take part in municipal affairs. This measure was not properly carried out and became obsolete. In 1870 a municipal act was passed modelled on Prussian legislation, whereby the municipal council was supposed to be in charge, but in practice a governor assisted by a special board appointed by the tsar controlled the city. Between 1870 and 1917 central government control increased. The suffrage was restricted to property owners, who numbered about 1 percent of the population. Mayors and councillors were classed as imperial officials and treated as civil servants. The appointed governors were given increased powers and were authorized to impose an absolute veto on municipal activities. There was no serious attempt at local self-government in the cities until the short-lived Kerensky regime of 1917, when for a period of five months various democratic municipal practices were introduced.

The "soviets" under Communism

The U.S.S.R. was from the beginning based on local "soviets" (elected councils) set up by the Communist Party in every province, district, city, town, or village throughout the land. These soviets were responsible not only for managing the affairs of their own areas but also for electing the soviet of the next higher level of government. Thus, the entire hierarchy of councils except those at the lowest level was based on indirect election. For this reason, the U.S.S.R. was originally described as a state of soviets. When direct election was introduced at all levels in 1936 this ceased to be a correct description, but the local soviets remained organs of local government. The regime has, however, retained a feature of great importance known as "democratic centralism." This means that each local authority is responsible to and must carry out the directions of the corresponding organ at the next higher level of government. Thus a local soviet is subordinate to the soviet of the district, and the executive committee of a municipality is answerable both to the soviet at its own level and to the executive committee of the next higher level of government. Although some policies may originate locally, they have to be submitted to the next higher soviet for approval or, if of sufficient importance, to even soviets up the line. This hierarchical and integrated structure explains why every soviet is considered a local organ of the state.

The U.S.S.R. today is divided into republics, provinces, towns, districts, villages, and settlements. At the 1967 elections, there were almost 50,000 soviets covering an immense variety of areas, ranging from Moscow, with a population of nearly 7,000,000, to a small village with a few hundreds. Municipal soviets may range from a minimum of 50 deputies to several hundreds. The Moscow city soviet had 2,100 deputies before the 1939 election, but the numbers were reduced to 1,500 in 1953 and 813 in 1955. A similar tendency to reduce their size is evident in other large cities, but the municipal councils of soviet cities continue to be far larger than those in Western countries.

The local soviets meet infrequently; the Russian republic, for instance, requires only four sessions a year for cities divided into districts and six for others, and each session seldom lasts for more than one day. Candidates for election can be nominated by the Communist Party, trade unions, youth organizations, or any other group of activists; but the nominating process is controlled by the party, and usually only one candidate is nominated for each vacancy.

The executive committee and the presidium

A city soviet elects an executive committee (*ispolkom*), which in turn appoints a presidium, the principal executive organ. The presidium of Leningrad consists of a president, six vice-presidents, and the secretary of the executive committee. It formulates operational and financial policies and directs the conduct of the city's services, whereas the full executive committee confines itself mainly to confirming the actions of the presidium. The executive committee is also responsible for preparing the agenda for the soviet, seeing that its decisions are carried out, ensuring that directions from above are obeyed, and giving advice or help to deputies and their committees.

The president is the most important public figure in the municipality; he supervises personnel policy, convenes meetings of the executive committee, sees that complaints and petitions from citizens come to the executive committee, allocates functions to the administrative departments, and generally supervises the work of the city government. He is likely to be held personally responsible if things go wrong or if plans are not fulfilled.

The city soviet wields comparatively little power. Its short sessions, large membership, and crowded agenda preclude detailed discussion of problems. The deputies nevertheless do form a vital link between the citizens and the city government; and, moreover, the city soviets do have standing commissions called activists who are prepared to take an interest in a particular service such as housing or public health. In a large city, there may be as many as 15 of these commissions inspecting and reporting grievances or defects to the soviet, including alleged improper or criminal actions on the part of officials. About 2,500,000 activists are engaged in this work of the commissions. This attempt to achieve mass participation in the conduct of local government is a special feature of the soviet system. It exists side by side with a high degree of central control.

Functions of soviet city governments

A city government in the Soviet Union has in theory an almost unlimited jurisdiction. It administers the services for which municipal authorities are responsible in most developed countries, but in addition it is engaged in retail distribution, local industry of many kinds, public utilities, and many other kinds of municipal enterprises. It controls the entire construction industry and employs all of the architects. A city soviet will even control many aspects of industrial enterprises that are not directly subordinate to it; thus, for example, the soviet will verify whether or not factories are fulfilling the plans for housing and communal facilities to meet the needs of their workers and whether or not safety regulations, hygiene, and fire precautions are being observed. The city government must also see that enterprises keep within their budgets and that their staffs do not exceed authorized complements. It owns all the land and allocates it for factories, housing, and other types of development. If there is horticulture, forestry, or agriculture within its area, the city government must try to increase its productivity. This extensive range of functions is liable to restriction, expansion, or direction by the soviet organs at the next higher level of government or by the Communist Party apparatus. With increasing knowledge, professional skill, and experience, however, the governments of the larger cities have been accorded a greater degree of discretion than formerly in dealing with municipal affairs.

About 90 large cities are responsible directly to the governments of their respective republics. They include Moscow, Leningrad, Kiev, Sevastopol, and other capital cities, as well as some other important cities in the smaller republics. The great majority of cities is subordinate to intermediate authorities such as the *oblast* (provincial) soviets or the *krai* (area) soviets. The smallest towns are supervised by the district soviets.

Cities with a population exceeding 100,000 may have a lower tier of wards or *rayon* soviets. Moscow has 24 of these, Leningrad, 14. They are, in most respects, replicas of the main city government except that their executive committees do not appoint presidia; they also have fewer administrative departments. A *rayon* soviet shares many functions with the main city government. It may run the local shops, schools, clinics, and even hospitals. It has its own planning organ and its own budget, but its plans must be approved by the city government, and the expenditure and revenues of the *rayon* are embodied in the budget of the main city. This embodiment of the budget of a local soviet in the budget of a higher authority is a common practice in the Soviet Union. It applies equally to the budgets of even large cities, which are embodied in the budgets of the republican government.

The problem of reorganizing local government in metropolitan areas to adjust it to changes in the distribution of population, the location of employment, and patterns of commuting has been solved more easily in the U.S.S.R. than in Western countries. One reason is that the big city government exercises a much greater degree of control over the surrounding area. The Leningrad city government, for example, has under its jurisdiction five suburban *rayons* as well as its 14 urban *rayons* and thus is able to plan and control the development of the metropolitan area in a comprehensive and rational manner. Another advantage is the ease with which changes in the arrangement or boundaries of areas and authorities are carried out; such matters, under the direction of republican ministries, are effected with little difficulty or opposition.

Variation on the soviet system: Poland. Poland has adopted the soviet model with certain modifications. All levels of government are completely integrated, and the various people's councils are regarded as links in a unified system of state power. For the realization of its policies, the central government relies entirely on the people's councils in the provinces, districts, towns, and so on, and the principle of democratic centralism applies throughout.

The country is divided into 17 provinces and 5 major cities enjoying provincial status. Below the provinces are 317 districts and 74 cities having the status of districts. The districts are further divided into rural municipalities and the smaller towns. In Warsaw and the seven other largest cities, a two-tier structure has been established, consisting of a people's council for the entire city and a number of local councils for the separate wards or boroughs. Poland has also developed small neighbourhood units in the form of committees that play a significant part in such matters as the development of housing, the care of gardens, and the improvement of amenities, and generally in securing widespread participation by the citizens in the city government. The soviet concept of mass participation in municipal affairs has been vigorously applied in Poland. The people's council of Warsaw has over 700 delegates.

Each people's council elects from its members an executive board and also sets up numerous committees, which include nonelected persons, to carry out functions similar to those undertaken by the standing commissions in Soviet cities. They do not have the right to make decisions or to lay down rules or regulations, but they can supervise the activities of the city government and give advice or submit reports to the people's council.

The city government has extensive functions: it operates the shops, schools, hospitals, transport, gas and electricity supply, local industries, theatres, museums, and other forms of indoor and outdoor recreation. It may undertake, alone or jointly with neighbouring local authorities, the building of roads, bridges, and other public works. Although the main industries are administered by separate agencies that are not controlled by the city government, these agencies must keep the city informed of any policy decisions or activities that would affect the inhabitants of the city, and they must obtain the city's approval of such changes.

CONCLUSION

One or the other of the four types of city government described in this article forms the basis of nearly every system of local self-government in the civilized world. The British system was transplanted to the United States, Canada, Australia, New Zealand, Ireland, and South Africa, although in each of those countries significant divergences appeared. The most important was the emergence in the United States of a strong, directly elected mayor as the chief executive responsible for the administration of the city, subject to certain overriding controls by the city council. The British system also was established in the former British colonies in Africa and Asia under the tutelage of British appointed officers resembling prefects. (In the largest Indian cities, such as Calcutta

and Bombay, however, the state government appoints a municipal commissioner who controls the administration.) The directly elected mayor and council has been transplanted from the United States to parts of West Germany, Japan, the Philippines, and to one or two Latin American states. The French system was established in all of the former French colonies, but it has also been widely imitated in Latin America and elsewhere. The soviet system has been adopted in all of the Communist regimes of eastern Europe except Yugoslavia.

The principal problems confronting city governments are broadly similar irrespective of the constitutional type. They concern the planning and development of large cities, particularly those classed as metropolitan areas; the continual erosion of local autonomy by the increase of central governmental control; the municipal dependence on grants and subsidies from the central government; and the immense difficulty of providing adequate traffic and transport facilities, housing, education, and welfare services at an acceptable standard. Finally, the deterioration of the environment has become a matter of serious concern that is likely to persist for many years.

BIBLIOGRAPHY. The most useful general description of city government in many countries is S. HUMES and E.M. MARTIN, *The Structure of Local Government: A Comparative Survey of 81 Countries* (1969). A much more detailed study of a selected group of large cities may be found in W.A. ROBSON and D.E. REGAN (eds.), *Great Cities of the World: Their Government, Politics and Planning*, 3rd rev. ed. (1971). A reference volume (in English, French, German, and Italian) containing information about local government in western European countries is W. HAUS and A. KREBSBACH, *Gemeindeordnungen in Europa* (1967). A short handbook on the legal status, constitutions, and finances of local authorities in Germany, England, Switzerland, Austria, France, Belgium, The Netherlands, and Sweden is the INSTITUT EUROPÉEN D'ETUDES ET DE RELATIONS INTERCOMMUNALES, *Pouvoirs locaux en Europe* (1964). W. ANDERSON (ed.), *Local Government in Europe* (1939), gives a good account of local government in England, France, Germany, Italy, and the Soviet Union on the eve of the Second World War. H.F. ALDERFER, *American Local Government and Administration* (1956), provides an excellent general description, including the historical background; supplemented by H. ZINK, *Government of Cities in the United States* (1939); and E.C. BANFIELD and J.Q. WILSON, *City Politics* (1963). The history of English city government may be studied at length for the period 1688–1835 in SIDNEY and BEATRICE WEBB, *The Manor and the Borough*, 2 vol. (1908, reprinted 1963); or more briefly in J. REDLICH and F.W. HIRST, *The History of Local Government in England* (1903, reprinted 1958). J.H. THOMAS, *Town Government in the Sixteenth Century* (1933), depicts municipal life in several ancient English cities. Modern history is covered in H.J. LASKI, W.I. JENNINGS, and W.A. ROBSON (eds.), *A Century of Municipal Progress 1835–1935* (1935); and briefly in J.H. WARRNEN, *The English Local Government System* (1968). The reform of London government is described in G. RHODES, *The Government of London: The Struggle for Reform* (1970); the need for the reform of local government in the rest of Britain is forcefully explained in W.A. ROBSON, *Local Government in Crisis*, 2nd ed. (1968). The best historical work dealing with Germany is W.H. DAWSON, *Municipal Life and Government in Germany* (1914). R.H. WELLS, *German Cities* (1932), carries the story up to the collapse of democracy in face of the Nazi regime. For a recent statement, see W. BOCKELMANN, W. HAUS, and H. VON HERZFELD (eds.), *Kommunalwissenschaftliche Forschung* (1966). The best and only books on French city government other than legal treatises are B. CHAPMAN, *Introduction to French Local Government* (1953), and *Prefects and Provincial France* (1955). There is a good chapter on local government in F. RIDLEY and J. BLONDEL, *Public Administration in France* (1964). For Italy the only relevant work is R.C. FRIED, *The Italian Prefects* (1963). On Latin America there is very little of value, but some information may be found in J. LAMBERT, *Latin America: Social Structure and Political Institutions* (Eng. trans. 1967). Local government in the Soviet Union may be briefly studied in some of the following books describing the system of government as a whole: L.G. CHURCHWARD, *Contemporary Soviet Government* (1968); L. SCHAPIRO, *The Government and Politics of the Soviet Union*, 2nd ed. (1967); H. MCCLOSKY and J.E. TURNER, *The Soviet Dictatorship* (1960); and D.J.R. SCOTT, *Russian Political Institutions*, 4th ed. (1969). See also E. SIMON *et al., Moscow in the Mak-*

ing (1937); and L.G. CHURCHWARD, "Soviet Local Government Today," *Soviet Studies*, 17:431–452 (1966). The special problems of metropolitan areas are analyzed in R.E. DICKINSON, *City Region and Regionalism* (1947); and in the reports of the WORLD CONFERENCE OF LOCAL GOVERNMENT, *Local Government Structure and Organization: Problems of Metropolitan Areas* (1962).

(W.A.R.)

Civil Engineering

The definition of civil engineering embodied in 1828 in the royal charter of the Institution of Civil Engineers, London, remains valid: "Civil engineering is the art of directing the Great Sources of Power in Nature for the use and convenience of man. . . ."

The term civil was used in the 19th century to distinguish the new profession from military engineering, until then pre-eminent. From earliest times, however, engineers have engaged in peaceful, as well as warlike, activities, and many of the civil engineering works of ancient and medieval times—such as the Roman public baths, roads, bridges, and aqueducts; the Flemish canals; the Dutch sea defenses; the French Gothic cathedrals; and numerous other monuments—reveal a continuing history of inventive genius and persistent experimentation in this type of construction.

The beginnings of civil engineering as a separate discipline may be found in the foundation in France in 1716 of the Corps des Ponts et Chaussées ("Bridges and Highways Corps") out of which, in 1747, grew the École des Ponts et Chaussées ("Bridges and Highways School"). Its teachers wrote books that became standard works on the mechanics of materials, machines, and hydraulics, and leading British engineers learned French to read them. As design and calculation displaced rule of thumb and empirical formulas and expert knowledge—hitherto the accumulated experience of the military engineer—was codified and formulated, the nonmilitary engineer moved to the front of the stage. Talented, if often self-taught, craftsmen, stonemasons, millwrights, toolmakers, and instrument makers became civil engineers. In Britain, James Brindley began as a millwright and became the foremost canal builder of the century; John Rennie was a millwright's apprentice who eventually built the new London Bridge; Thomas Telford was a stonemason who became Britain's leading road builder and the first president of the Institution of Civil Engineers.

Smeaton's work

John Smeaton, the first man to call himself a civil engineer, was originally an instrument maker. His design of Eddystone Lighthouse with its interlocking masonry, was based on a craftsman's experience and intuition, and in the same year (1759) he described to the Royal Society his own experiments with scale models of watermills and windmills to determine their efficiencies. Smeaton's works were backed by thorough research and his services were much in demand. In 1771 Smeaton founded the Society of Civil Engineers (now known as the "Smeatonian Society"). Its object was to bring together experienced engineers, entrepreneurs, and lawyers to promote the building of large public works, such as canals (and later, railways), and to secure the parliamentary powers necessary to execute their schemes. Their meetings were held during parliamentary sessions; the society follows this custom to this day.

The École Polytechnique was founded in Paris in 1794 and the Bauakademie was started in Berlin in 1799, but no such schools existed in Great Britain for another two decades. It was this lack of opportunity for scientific study and for the exchange of experiences that led a group of young men, in 1818, to found the Institution of Civil Engineers, "a Society for the General Advancement of Mechanical Science and more particularly for promoting the acquisition of that species of knowledge which constitutes the profession of a Civil Engineer," to quote from the institution's royal charter.

The founders were young men keen to learn from each other's experiences and from their elders, and in 1820 they invited Thomas Telford, by then the dean of British civil engineers, to be their first president.

There were similar developments elsewhere. The Civil Engineers Society of Ireland was founded in 1835 and was renamed the Institution of Civil Engineers of Ireland in 1844. It became the Institution of Engineers of Ireland in 1969 after merging with the Cumann n nInnealtoiti.

In 1837 the Société Suisse des Ingénieurs et des Architectes was formed, followed by the Koninklijk Instituut van Ingenieurs (Royal Institute of Engineers) in The Netherlands in 1847.

The Société des Ingénieurs Civils de France, founded in 1848, and the Österreichischer Ingenieur und Architektenverein (Association of Austrian Engineers and Architects), founded in Austria in the same year continued the pattern of societies covering all branches of engineering, in several cases including architecture.

The American Society of Civil Engineers was founded in 1852; it grew out of the Boston Society of Civil Engineers, which had been founded in 1848. James Laurie (1811–75), first president of the "Boston Society," became the first president of the "American Society."

In Germany the Verein Deutscher Ingenieure was founded in 1856 by members of the academic association Hütte, itself founded ten years earlier at the Royal Prussian College of Technology, Berlin. The following century produced similar institutions in almost every country in the world.

Engineering education

Meantime, formal education in engineering science became widely available as other countries followed the lead of France and Germany. In Great Britain the universities, traditionally seats of classical learning, were reluctant to embrace the new disciplines. University College, London, founded in 1826, provided a broad range of academic studies and offered a course in mechanical philosophy. King's College, London, first taught civil engineering in 1838, and in 1840 Queen Victoria founded the first chair of civil engineering and mechanics, at the University of Glasgow. In the U.S., Rensselaer Polytechnic Institute, founded in 1824, offered the first courses in civil engineering in that country. The number of universities throughout the world with engineering faculties, including civil engineering, increased rapidly in the 19th and early 20th centuries, with Russia, Japan, and the Latin American countries joining in. Civil engineering today is taught in universities on every continent.

CIVIL ENGINEERING FUNCTIONS

The functions of the civil engineer can be divided into three categories—those he performs before construction (feasibility studies, site investigations, and design); those performed during construction (dealing with clients, consulting engineers, and contractors); and those performed after construction (maintenance and research).

Feasibility studies. No major project today is started without an extensive, and sometimes lengthy, study of the objective and the factors affecting the attainment of the objective and without preliminary studies of possible plans leading to a recommended scheme, perhaps with alternatives. Feasibility studies may cover alternative methods—*e.g.*, bridge versus tunnel, in the case of a water crossing—or, once the method is decided, the choice of route. The economic, as well as the engineering, problems must be considered.

Site investigations. A preliminary site investigation is part of the feasibility study, but once a plan has been adopted a more extensive investigation is usually imperative. Money spent in a rigorous study of ground and substructure may well save large sums later—in remedial works or in changes made necessary in constructional methods.

Soil mechanics

Since the load-bearing qualities and stability of the ground are such important factors in any large-scale construction, it is surprising that a serious study of soil mechanics did not develop until the mid-1930s. Karl von Terzaghi, the chief founder of the science, gives the date of its birth as 1936, when the First International Conference on Soil Mechanics and Foundation Engineering was held at Harvard University, Cambridge, Massachusetts, and an international society was formed. Today, there are specialist societies and journals in many countries, and most universities that have a civil engineering faculty have courses in soil mechanics.

Design. The results of research in structural analysis and the technology of materials have opened the way for more rational designs, new design concepts, and greater economy of materials.

The theory of structures and the study of materials have advanced together as more and more refined stress analysis of structures and systematic testing has been done.

The modern designer not only has advanced theories to assist him and design data easily and readily available, but his structural designs can now be rigorously analyzed by computers.

Although most works have a structural content, civil engineering is not confined to structural design.

The design of engineering works may require the application of design theory from many fields—*e.g.*, hydraulics, thermodynamics, or nuclear physics.

Construction. The promotion of civil-engineering works may be initiated by a private client, but the bulk of work nowadays is undertaken for large corporations, central or local government authorities, or for public boards and authorities. Many of these have their own engineering staffs, but where large specialized projects are concerned it is usual to employ consulting engineers.

The role of the consulting engineer

The consulting engineer may be required first to undertake feasibility studies; he then recommends a scheme and quotes an approximate cost. He is responsible for the design of the works, supplying specifications, drawings, and legal documents in sufficient detail to seek competitive tender prices. He must compare quotations and recommend acceptance of one of them. Although he is not a party to the contract, his duties are defined in it; his staff must supervise the construction throughout and he must certify completion of the work. His actions must be consistent with his duty to his client; the professional organizations exercise disciplinary control over professional conduct. The consulting engineer's senior representative on the site is the resident engineer.

A phenomenon of recent years has been the use of the "turnkey" or "package" contract, in which the contractor undertakes to finance, design, specify, construct, and commission a project in its entirety. In this case, the consulting engineer is engaged by the contractor for specialist advice, rather than by the client.

The contractor is usually an incorporated company, which secures the contract on the basis of the consulting engineer's specification and general drawings. The consulting engineer must agree to any variations introduced and must approve the detailed drawings.

Maintenance. The contractor maintains the works to the satisfaction of the consulting engineer. Responsibility for maintenance extends to ancillary works and temporary works, where these form part of the overall construction.

Following construction, a period of maintenance is undertaken by the contractor, and the payment of the final installment of the contract price is held back until released by the consulting engineer.

Central and local government engineering and public works departments are primarily concerned with maintenance for which they employ direct labour.

Research. Development, no less than invention, needs the support of research. Research in the civil-engineering field is undertaken by government agencies, industrial foundations, the universities, and other institutions. Most countries have government-controlled agencies, such as the United States Bureau of Standards and the National Physical Laboratory of Great Britain, involved in a broad spectrum of research and establishments in building research, roads and highways, hydraulic research, water pollution, and other areas. Many are government-aided but depend partly on income from research work promoted by industry.

BRANCHES OF CIVIL ENGINEERING

In an 1828 description of the functions of the civil engineer, Thomas Tredgold of England wrote:

The most important object of Civil Engineering is to improve the means of production and of traffic in states, both for external and internal trade. It is applied in the construction and management of roads, bridges, railroads, aqueducts, canals, river navigation, docks and storehouses, for the convenience of internal intercourse and exchange; and in the construction of ports, harbours, moles, breakwaters and lighthouses; and in the navigation by artificial power for the purposes of commerce.

It is applied to the protection of property where natural powers are the sources of injury, as by embankments for the defence of tracts of country from the encroachments of the sea, or the overflowing of rivers; it also directs the means of applying streams and rivers to use, either as powers to work machines, or as supplies for the use of cities and towns, or for irrigation; as well as the means of removing noxious accumulations, as by the drainage of towns and districts to . . . secure the public health.

Aspects of civil engineering

A modern description would include the production and distribution of energy in the form of gas and electricity; the development of aircraft and airports; the construction of chemical process plants; the development of nuclear power stations; and water desalination. These various aspects of civil engineering may conveniently be considered under the following headings: construction, transportation, maritime and hydraulic engineering, power, and public health.

Construction. Practically all civil engineering contracts include some element of construction work. The development of steel and concrete, including reinforced and prestressed concrete, as building materials had the effect of placing design more in the hands of the civil engineer than the architect. The engineer's analysis of a building problem, based on function and economics, determines the building's structural design.

Transportation. Roman roads and bridges were products of military engineering, but the pavements of McAdam and the bridges of Perronet were the work of the civil engineer. So were the canals of the 18th century and the railways of the 19th, which, by providing bulk transport with speed and economy, lent a powerful impetus to the Industrial Revolution. The civil engineer today is concerned with an even larger transportation field —*e.g.*, traffic studies, design of systems for road, rail, and air, and construction including pavements, embankments, bridges, and tunnels.

Maritime and hydraulic engineering. Harbour construction and shipbuilding are ancient arts. For many developing countries today the establishment of a large, efficient harbour is an early imperative, to serve as the inlet for industrial plant and needed raw materials and the outlet for finished goods.

In the developed countries the expansion of world trade, the use of larger ships, and the increase in total tonnage call for more rapid and efficient handling. Deeper berths and alongside-handling equipment (for example, for ore) and navigation improvements are the responsibility of the civil engineer.

The development of water supplies was a feature of the earliest civilizations and the demand for water continues to rise today. In developed countries, the demand is for industrial and domestic consumption, but in many parts of the world—*e.g.*, the Indus Basin—vast schemes are under construction, mainly for irrigation to help satisfy the food demand, and are often combined with hydroelectric power generation to promote industrial development.

Dam engineering

Dams today are among the largest construction works, and design development is promoted by bodies like the International Commission on Large Dams. The design of large impounding dams in places with population centres close by requires the utmost in safety engineering, with emphasis on soil mechanics and stress analysis. Most governments exercise statutory control of engineers qualified to design and inspect dams.

Power. The Industrial Revolution was based on the availability of iron ore and coal. Civil engineers have always played an important part in mining for coal and metals; the driving of tunnels is a task common to many branches of civil engineering. In the 20th century, the design and construction of power stations has advanced with the rapid rise in demand for electric power, and nuclear power stations have added a whole new field of design and construction, involving prestressed concrete pressure vessels for the reactor.

The exploitation of oilfields and the discoveries of natural gas in significant quantities have initiated a radical change in gas production. Shipment in liquid form from the Sahara, or piping from the bed of the North Sea have been among the novel developments.

Civil engineers also cooperate with chemical engineers in the design of the new, large chemical plants, which play so significant a role in modern life.

Public Health.   Drainage and liquid-waste disposal are closely associated with antipollution measures and the re-use of water.

The urban development of parts of water catchment areas can alter the nature of "runoff," and the training and regulation of rivers produce changes in the pattern of events, resulting in floods and the need for flood prevention and control.

Modern civilization has created new problems of solid-waste disposal, from the large-volume manufacture of durable goods, such as automobiles and refrigerators, produced in large numbers with a limited life, to the small package—previously disposable, now often indestructible.

The civil engineer plays an important role in the conservation and preservation of the environment, principally through design of works to enhance, rather than to damage or pollute.

CIVIL ENGINEERING EDUCATION

Undergraduate training.   The professional engineer must have a university degree or a recognized qualification at degree level. Entrance to a university or college course of studies requires a demonstrated proficiency in basic mathematics and science. The first year is usually devoted to general engineering studies common to all disciplines; in the second year specialization is begun in a specific branch of engineering. Within civil engineering, subspecialist subjects are taught, but the trend in the 1970s in most countries is away from specialization. In addition to his academic studies, the student must have practical training, and there are several schemes for providing this.

In Great Britain the university graduate follows a recognized course of practical training for at least three years following his degree course. Alternatively, "sandwich" courses are available in which the student has alternate periods between college and industry throughout the length of his course. The training that is given in industry is specified and supervised by the Institution of Civil Engineers.

When the graduate has completed his training and has acquired some experience in employment, he is examined by the Institution of Civil Engineers before being granted the status of a Chartered Civil Engineer.

In continental Europe the length of a degree course is usually longer than in Great Britain, but within its span practical training is provided. The Soviet Union follows the European pattern.

The professional civil engineer is usually supported by a staff of technicians with specialized practical training and experience. In some countries, such as Great Britain, technicians are formally qualified by certification.

Postgraduate and midcareer training.   The university graduate in civil engineering may remain at the university to obtain a higher degree or to undertake research. More attention is now being given to continuing education throughout the career of the engineer. To further such midcareer training, many governments in the 1970s are entering into arrangements with universities and industry.

Registration.   In many countries registration is a legal requirement in certain levels of responsibility for engineering work. In Canada, registration is by provincial associations of professional engineers. In the U.S., registration is a state government matter. In most countries in which it is compulsory, it takes the form of a license to practice, and more and more governments are imposing

"Sand-
wich"
courses

this type of control. In Great Britain and in Europe, registration, where it exists, is voluntary. Recently, arrangements have been made to set up a European register under the auspices of the Fédération Européenne d'Associations Nationales des Ingénieurs. Engineers' names are entered in the register by nomination through their appropriate national qualifying body.

PROFESSIONAL SOCIETIES

When the Institution of Civil Engineers was founded in 1818, it had as its sole object "the advancement of Mechanical Science." This object is achieved by the promotion of research, the publication and discussion of technical papers, and the study and discussion of engineering design and practical work. This "learned society" function is the primary aim of most engineering societies today. But it has been supplemented by a second function.

In 1896 the Charter of the Institution of Civil Engineers was extended to permit the holding of examinations and to limit membership to those who reached an adequate standard of qualification, both academically and in practical training and experience. Here again other societies followed the institution's lead, conducting examinations and conferring qualification. Not all national societies, however, have assumed this role.

Another society function stems from the increasingly large size of civil-engineering undertakings, which tend to place the majority of engineers in the position of employee. But as a minority among employees, their special position as professional men is not always recognized. This has led to the formation of a number of societies to provide this protective function—for example, in Great Britain, the Engineers' Guild was founded in 1939 primarily for this reason.

In some countries, on the other hand, the older professional societies give personal service to members concerning their conditions of employment, though few adopt trade-union practices.

A feature of the professional institutions that are qualifying bodies is their insistence on a high ethical standard and the adoption of rules of professional conduct with the sanction of a disciplinary code.

The basis of these professional conduct rules is the special position of the engineer in giving to the public advice derived from professional knowledge he alone possesses; his duty is to see that his advice is impartial, is the best available advice, and is untainted by any personal considerations whatever.

Within the developed countries there promises to continue a steady demand for orthodox structures from tall buildings to tunnels, from maritime works to airfields, but unorthodox solutions are not infrequently applied. In developing countries with rapidly expanding populations, tall buildings for housing, rapid-transit systems for commuter traffic, and improved highways are also needed; improved drainage and public-health schemes are essential. Large-scale irrigation schemes with vast reservoirs and river regulation are needed to expand food production in parts of the world faced with the threat of famine.

Many underdeveloped countries have facilities for training engineers at home or abroad, but a lack of capital to invest in major works limits development. Aid programs that include the import of more highly developed technology make more efficient use of capital investment. This problem has been actively pursued by the International Bank for Reconstruction and Development (the World Bank).

BIBLIOGRAPHY

HISTORY: H. HARTLEY and W.G. BOWMAN, *Engineering Societies in the Life of a Country* (1968); J.P.M. PANNELL, *An Illustrated History of Civil Engineering* (1964); C.M. NORRIE, *Bridging the Years: A Short History of British Civil Engineering* (1956); H. STRAUB, *A History of Civil Engineering* (Eng. trans. 1953); J.K. FINCH, *Engineering and Western Civilisation* (1951); R.S. KIRBY and P.G. LAURSON, *Early Years of Modern Civil Engineering* (1932); S. SMILES, *Lives of the Engineers*, 5 vol. (1874–99); A.K. BISWAS, *A Short History of Hydrology* (1969).

Practice: K.L. NASH, *Civil Engineering*, 4th ed. (1967); R. HAMMOND (ed.), *Modern Civil Engineering Practice* (1961); E.E. MANN, *An Introduction to the Practice of Civil Engineering*, 2nd ed. (1949).

Societies: Conference reports of the Commonwealth Engineering Conferences (1946–69); *Conference reports of the Engineering Societies of Western Europe and USA* (EUSEC) (1961, 1965); *Transactions*, Institution of Civil Engineers of Ireland (1889–1966); *Revue*, Ecole Nationale des Ponts et Chaussées (1961).

(J.G.W.)

Civilization and Cultural Evolution

Definitions of culture and civilization

The term culture in anthropology has been defined variously by different writers, but two broad classes of definitions are useful for this article. The first is a "universalistic" definition, equating culture with the total social heredity of mankind; the classic definition was offered by the English anthropologist E.B. Tylor in 1871:

Culture or Civilization, taken in its wide ethnographic sense, is that complex whole which includes knowledge, belief, art, morals, law, custom, and any other capabilities and habits acquired by man as a member of society. (From *Primitive Culture*.)

The second broad class of definitions offers a "pluralistic" or relativistic conception of culture. It confines culture to a single people or group; in the words of American anthropologists Clyde Kluckhohn and W.H. Kelly,

A culture is an historically derived system of . . . designs for living, which tends to be shared by . . . members of a group. (From "The Concept of Culture," in R. Linton, ed., *The Science of Man in the World Crisis*, Columbia University Press, 1945.)

It encompasses the group's language, traditions, customs, and institutions, including the motivating ideas, beliefs, and values, and their embodiment in material instruments and artifacts (see HUMAN CULTURE for an extended discussion of definitions of culture).

The word civilization was used early in the 19th century in its now familiar sense, referring to the aggregate of characteristics displayed in the collective life of an advanced people or an historic period—as, for instance, in "Greek civilization at the time of Pericles." But the term civilization could be used, as it was by Tylor, to refer to the total achievements of the most "advanced" people to date, as if civilization were a unilinear development out of the past, with "lesser" peoples at different stages of that development.

This article deals with theories regarding the evolution of culture—or cultures—and with theories intended to explain the rise and fall of individual civilizations.

THE 17TH AND 18TH CENTURIES

Theories of progress and perfectibility

The Age of Discovery following the voyages of Columbus, an age that introduced Europeans to primitive peoples around the world, witnessed the beginnings of modern anthropology, as intellectuals sought to explain the existence of these primitives and to theorize on the evolution of European society from people assumed to be very much like them. When the 17th-century English philosopher Thomas Hobbes described primeval man as "solitary, poor, nasty, brutish, and short," with "no arts, no letters, no society," he was very much proclaiming a popular conception of the "savage." Everything that was good and civilized resulted from the slow development *out* of this lowly state. Eventually there formed the idea of human progress or perfectibility. The 18th-century German theologian Johann Gottfried von Herder would plead that man, as a divine creation, must naturally have a purpose on earth, namely, his own progressive perfection. But even more rationalist Philosophes like Voltaire implicitly assumed that enlightenment gradually resulted in the upward progress of mankind. As a fellow Frenchman, the economist A.R.J. Turgot, would declare,

In the history of the world manners are gradually softened, the human mind takes enlightenment, separate nations draw nearer to each other, commerce and policy connect at last all parts of the globe, and the total mass of the human race, by the alternations of calm and agitation, of good conditions and of bad, marches always, although slowly, towards still

higher perfection (*Réflexions sur la formation et la distribution des richesses*, 1766; *Reflections on the Formation and Distribution of Wealth*, 1793).

Together with the idea of progress there grew the notion of fixed "stages" through which man progresses, usually numbering three—savagery, barbarism, and civilization—but sometimes many more. The marquis de Condorcet listed ten stages or "epochs," the final one having started with the French Revolution, which was destined, in his eyes, to usher in the rights of man and the perfection of the human race. Indeed, the French Revolution with its ideals of freedom and equality was one of the forces that helped to instill the idea of progress firmly into the mainstream of thought in the 19th century.

The 18th and early 19th centuries, it should be noted, also briefly gave recognition to a completely different picture of man's history. Man in the "state of nature," according to Jean-Jacques Rousseau, had been "free, healthy, honest, and happy" but had been corrupted and enslaved by the growth of social institutions (*Discours sur l'origine et les fondements de l'inégalité parmi les hommes*, 1755; *A Discourse upon the Origin and Foundation of the Inequality Among Mankind*, 1761). This was essentially the theory of progress turned upside down. It engendered a whole Romantic literature on the "noble savage," best known perhaps in the early 19th-century novels of the vicomte de Chateaubriand, who, as an émigré from the French Revolution, developed a skeptical, cynical view of human nature and destiny: man does not progress, he decays.

THE 19TH AND EARLY 20TH CENTURIES

The unilinear theorists. *Comte's positivism.* Auguste Comte (1798–1857), the French philosopher who gave the social science of sociology its name and its first basic principles, was strongly influenced by the earlier conceptions of human progress and by those tenets of the French Revolution that had repudiated Christianity and installed the worship of reason. From such sources he derived his idea that the history of man's intellectual development had consisted of three stages—theological, metaphysical, and scientific, with the scientific (or positivist) being the ultimate achievement.

Comte's theological metaphysical, and scientific stages

In the theological stage, according to Comte, all cosmic phenomena are thought to be governed by "wills" much like man's. First there is fetishism, in which men regard all things as if they were animate, living, intelligent. Then men become polytheistic, conceiving invisible beings to govern events. Finally, in the monotheistic phase of the theological stage, these beings merge into one god who created the world and governs it directly or through supernatural agents. Next, in the metaphysical stage, events are no longer governed by supernatural forces but rather by fundamental abstract ideas, essences, or energies. Nature—virtually personified—contains certain governing tendencies. Finally, in the positive or scientific stage, phenomena are explained by principles of cause and effect, which are discovered by observation, hypotheses, and experimentation. In his way, of course, Comte shared the basic ideas and convictions of those intellectuals of his day who regarded the new scientific philosophy and the applications of science to society as "the mission of the century." Thus could Comte propose the three stages of intellectual development, the need for a new and secularized spiritual order to supplant supernaturalism and metaphysics, and the belief that social phenomena could be reduced to laws, that the purpose of the new social sciences should be ameliorative, and that the ultimate outcome of all this innovation and systematization should be the guidance of social planning.

Evolutionary anthropologists. The anthropologists E.B. Tylor (1832–1917) in England and Lewis H. Morgan (1818–81) in the United States were the chief exponents of cultural stages in the evolution of mankind. (Morgan, though, used the term ethnical periods rather than stages itself.) Theirs was often a concern with culture in general, not individual cultures, except as they might be fitted in as illustrations of their theories, including their theories of the overall evolution of man and civilization.

Although Tylor is perhaps the better known anthropologist and the more influential, the work of Morgan sums up the stages approach quite well. Morgan was an upstate New York lawyer who first became interested in the Iroquois Indians, a study that eventually led him to investigations of cultures around the world, particularly in terms of their kinship systems. In studying these systems, he became convinced that he had found what he called survivals in modern society—customs and practices belonging to an earlier age of man but surviving in some residual form even in the most modern societies. Thus, for him, social man seemed to progress in evolutionary stages—seven of them, from "lower savagery" to civilization—and Morgan gave his "proof" by citing contemporary societies characteristic of each stage (except the very lowest). In *Ancient Society* (1877) he epitomized his view:

Since mankind were one in origin, their career has been essentially one, running in different but uniform channels upon all continents, and very similarly in all the tribes and nations of mankind down to the same status of advancement. It follows that the history and experience of the American Indian tribes represent, more or less nearly, the history and experience of our own remote ancestors when in corresponding conditions.

Such a historical thesis, of course, is rejected by most modern anthropologists.

Social Darwinists. The development of concepts of progress and cultural evolution was enormously influenced in the mid-19th century by the wider acceptance of theories of organic or biological evolution and particularly by the publication of Charles Darwin's theories centring (to use the title of his 1859 work) *On the Origin of Species by Means of Natural Selection, or the Preservation of Favoured Races in the Struggle for Life.* The world of social science took the ideas of biological evolution as an attractive solution to similar questions regarding the origins and development of social behaviour. Indeed, the idea of a society as an evolving organism was a biological analogy taken up by many anthropologists and sociologists and persists in some quarters even today.

Darwin, of course, did not invent the idea of organic evolution; many of his contemporaries had arrived more or less independently at similar conclusions, including the English philosopher Herbert Spencer (1820–1903). Spencer had originally conceived that evolution was caused by the inheritance of acquired abilities, and not until after Darwinism became popular did he himself accept the theory that natural selection was at least one of the causes of biological evolution; in fact, he coined the phrase survival of the fittest. He eventually worked out a general evolutionary scheme that included human society. He held that an unknown and unknowable absolute force was continuously operating on the material world and producing variety, coherence, integration, specialization, and individuation. Gases concentrated to form planets; the earth became more variegated and gave birth to such simple animals as the amoeba; man evolved from less complex species and at first lived in undifferentiated hordes; various social functions were developed so that there were priests, kings, scholars, workers, and so forth; and knowledge was differentiated into the various sciences. In short, along with all other changing things, human societies evolved from undifferentiated hordes, by means of increasing division of labour, into complex civilizations.

In the hands of some writers, social Darwinism (or social evolution) was used as a defense of contemporary social and economic philosophies. The American William Graham Sumner (1840–1910), for example, expounded his firm belief in laissez-faire, individual liberty, and the innate inequalities among men. As a social Darwinist he viewed competition for property and social status as resulting in a beneficial elimination of the ill-adapted and the preservation of racial "soundness" and cultural vigour. Governmental attempts to alter this situation through welfare measures would, he felt, impede progress.

Marxism. Karl Marx (1818–83) and his followers possessed a philosophy of history that was significantly tied to the idea of progress. But, in their view, straight-line, gradual progress never led to worthwhile results; piecemeal reforms represented progress only if they operated as a foreign body within the existing system and thus accelerated its death. True reform was complete revolution, and the suffering and sacrifice of this violent change was the price that mankind had to pay to have any essential progress at all. Revolution, furthermore, was born out of class conflict: in the course of history Marx saw each principle of economic organization represented by a social class—slavery by a patrician class, feudalism by a landed nobility, capitalism by the entrepreneurs, Socialism by the workers. In each era the victory of a new class was followed by repression of the former ruling class until the last vestiges of the old order were extinguished. In the struggle of the workers against the capitalists, this repression would result in the "dictatorship of the proletariat," as the political form of society in the period of transition from capitalism to full Communism, which was the ultimate goal of mankind.

In short, Marx looked upon the whole history of mankind as a class struggle between possessors and dispossessed, exploiters and toilers, masters and slaves. Capitalism was fighting today, as feudalism had fought in its own day, to preserve itself, but the end was inevitable. Dying institutions, like dying individuals, in the Marxist view, could do nothing to stop the irresistible march of time (see also MARXISM; COMMUNISM).

Anarchism. In a sense, anarchism was an echo of Rousseau's philosophy of degenerationism or regression. Anarchists, who were most active in the 19th and early 20th centuries, insisted that human nature was inherently good but was warped and depraved by authority and complex social institutions. They envisioned a stateless society in which harmony would be maintained by voluntary agreements among individuals and groups. Without governments and other machinery of force, they expected that unjust social arrangements would quickly disappear and be replaced by fair and equitable agreements freely accepted and maintained (see also ANARCHISM).

The theorists of rationalized progress. *Theories of telic progress.* The first quarter of the 20th century was marked by a clash between social Darwinists like William Graham Sumner, who argued laissez-faire and the futility of reform, and a group of sociologists, including the Americans Lester F. Ward (1841–1913) and Albion W. Small (1854–1926), who took up the Darwinian thesis and gave it a completely different social interpretation. In their view, evolution by natural selection, which governed changes in animals, was replaced in social man by "telic" or planned, purposive change, which only man was capable of accomplishing. Man had a mental faculty that enabled him to pursue ends that he foresaw and estimated to be profitable. In other words, man could plan and institute his own progress; he did not have to depend upon the slow, wasteful, and bloody processes of evolution to assure the development of society. Such views were used in support of social planning and progressive reforms and legislation.

Theory of bureaucratization. The German sociologist Max Weber (1864–1920) saw historical development as progress toward "rationalization" of the means of leadership and administration of society, as society became larger and larger. Broadly, there were three means of leadership. The first was what he called charismatic—the leadership of men who possessed charisma, literally (from the Greek) "divine grace" but referring generally to some kind of extraordinary, magnetic personality. The second type of leadership was traditional and was based on legitimacy and inheritance. The leader's power was circumscribed by custom, as was the king's in feudal society; but, because his dominion did not depend merely on his own personality, his administration could extend over wider areas, not limited to a few immediate disciples. Finally, the relations between ruler and ruled evolved into something more "legalized," with the ruler achieving his position by means of rationalized political processes hedged in by many rules rather than by means

Weber's
charis-
matic,
traditional,
and
bureau-
cratic
administra-
tion

of inheritance or charisma alone. Bureaucracy was this ruler's means of administration, consisting of a hierarchy of specialized officials proceeding according to systematic, standardized rules. Weber considered that bureaucracy was indispensable to large-scale modern society and that indeed this regularized administration would pervade all areas of life—political, economic, religious, military, educational, and social. Unlike the anarchists and some Communists, Weber never considered any "withering away of the state" (see also BUREAUCRACY).

Theories of the growth of modern mass society. Like Weber, a number of writers, particularly in the late 19th and early 20th centuries, were concerned with the apparent trend of Western civilization toward ever greater division of labour, specialization, impersonality in human relations, and the like. The German sociologist Ferdinand Tönnies (1855–1936) conceived of two types of society. *Gemeinschaft* ("communal society") was the society of familial and kinship groups, clans, and peasant communities, in which the social bonds among the members were natural, spontaneous, instinctive, intimate, and personal. Blood ties, neighbourhood, and friendship maintained the unity and solidarity of the group. Personal and occupational roles were blended and indistinguishable; that is, one's role was "naturally" determined by one's sex, place of birth, and parentage. Other writers—with, of course, different emphases—would call this folk or traditional society. Some would call such face-to-face relations primary relations. In Tönnies' *Gesellschaft* ("associational society"), on the other hand, the social bonds were largely contractual, impersonal, voluntary, artificial. Individuals entered relations or roles not because they had to or because it was "natural" but because it was a way of rationally and efficiently getting things done. Other writers—again with different emphases—would call this sensate, or mass, society, and the relations secondary relations.

Tönnies' *Gemeinschaft* and *Gesellschaft*

In the formulations of the French sociologist Émile Durkheim (1858–1917), division of labour became the important element of historical development. In primitive societies he found little division of labour but a great deal of "mechanical solidarity" (mutual dependence) or like-minded solidarity in which the individual is subordinate to the group. As a society developed, a division of functions and corresponding activities took place; mechanical solidarity gave way to a considerable degree to an "organic solidarity"; and individuals became objectively aware of social values (which were no longer all so ingrained as to pass unnoticed). Under organic solidarity, conflicts of interest occurred, and constraint, in the form of laws and governmental force, became necessary. To the two forms of solidarity, Durkheim tied the concept of "collective conscience." In primitive societies all individuals had very similar values and outlooks; like molecules in inert bodies, all consciences were part of a collective conscious. In modern societies, on the other hand, individuals were dissimilar though organically related, like limbs and organs of a body. The collective conscience did not coincide with all the particular consciences. There was left far more margin for individual differentiation.

Durkheim's mechanical and organic solidarity

The grand diffusionists. Among the chief challengers of the unilinear evolutionary theories proposed by Tylor, Morgan, the social Darwinists, and others, were a number of German anthropologists led by Fritz Graebner (1877–1934) and Wilhelm Schmidt (1868–1954). Their theory of the world's historical development centred on "diffusion"; that is, the spread of cultural traits through migration, trade, and other contacts between different peoples. In their view, all cultures past and present developed out of the intermingling of bits of cultural traits that had originated in a limited series of places and times in the early world; that is, the early history of man was the scene of a certain number of "cultural spheres" (*Kulturkreise;* singular, *Kulturkreis*), and all cultures today, whether primitive or modern, stemmed from these single archaic types.

A somewhat parallel school of diffusionists consisted of the English anthropologists George Smith (1840–76) and W.J. Perry (1868–1949), who also believed that the spreading of culture was the elemental force of human development and that diffusion explained almost all the cultural similarities throughout the world. This English school, in contrast to the Austrian *Kulturkreis* school, however, made Egypt the font of all subsequent cultural development.

RECENT 20TH CENTURY

As early as the turn of the century in the United States, and somewhat later in Europe, there began what was eventually to become a widespread reaction against sweeping generalizations about cultural evolution. Theories regarding "stages" of evolution were especially criticized as illusions. All cultures were to be regarded as unique in time and place. In the United States this movement was led by the German-born anthropologist Franz Boas (1858–1942), who, along with a generation of students, turned completely away from broad interpretations and concentrated on fieldwork among primitive peoples, harvesting all variety of facts and artifacts as empirical evidence of cultural processes of the living. This "culture history" approach dominated American anthropology for the first half of the 20th century and so influenced anthropology elsewhere that high-level generalization and "systems building" became far less common than in the past.

Reactions against evolutionism

If there was a diminution of grand theories, there was never a disappearance. Two areas of concern were pursued with special vigour by some writers from the 1920s to the 1950s: the concern for the "life cycle" of civilizations and the concern for how civilizations were born. From the 1950s on, too, there developed a revival of evolutionary theory among a few scholars.

The theorists of cyclical history. Two men, the German philosopher Oswald Spengler (1880–1936) and the English historian Arnold Toynbee (1889–), are notably associated with concepts attempting to explain the rise and fall of civilizations. By comparing classical antiquity with its modern Western descendant, Spengler claimed to be able to discern the outline of a life cycle (birth, youth, maturity, senescence, death) through which all civilizations pass. His own view of the prospects of Western civilization was pessimistic. Because the West, he believed, had already passed through the mature creative stage of culture into the stage of reflection and material comfort, the future could only be a period of decline; nor was there any prospect of reversing the process, for civilizations blossomed and decayed like natural organisms, and true rejuvenation was as impossible in the one case as in the other.

For Toynbee, the decline of civilization was a process of exhaustion, but he was interested less in their fall than in their rise, which he conceived to be not as the result of such factors as superior racial qualities or geographical environment but rather as a people's response to a challenge in a situation of special difficulty that rouses them to make an unprecedented effort. His explanation of the rise of civilizations rested on the theory that difficult rather than easy conditions prompted men to cultural achievement.

Theories of challenge and response

A variation on the theme of challenge was put forward by the Canadian-born American historian William H. McNeill (1917–). In his view, a people rise to civilization as a response to the threat of force from alien peoples. The mobilization in face of threat is often accompanied or followed by an absorption of the aliens' technology, institutions, and ideas. NcNeill's is obviously, in part, a diffusionist theory (though it bears, of course, no relation to the grand theories of Graebner, Schmidt, Smith, and Perry).

Theory of urban revolution. The birth of civilization as a process in the cultural development of a people has been discussed by several archaeologists. Their attention has been especially directed toward the Near East, particularly what is now Iraq (Mesopotamia), where the hunting and food-gathering way of life was rather quickly transformed, about 6000 BC, into a food-producing way with settled agricultural villages. This manner of living was in turn changed, about 3000 BC, into a civilized cul-

Conceptions of the origin of civilization

ture with urban centres and a literate tradition. The question pursued has been how did this "spontaneous" civilization (one without antecedent civilizations to imitate or build on) come about? Perhaps no one has satisfactorily answered the question, but the Australian V. Gordon Childe (1892–1957) did show the significance of certain technological–economic advances—the urban revolution, in his terms—that marked the advent of civilization wherever it has appeared on earth, though particularly in the Near East.

In the view of Childe and others in his tradition, the urban revolution was characterized by a remarkable increase in the scale and complexity of society. It depended on the prior development of agriculture, which could provide storable food surpluses (chiefly grain) and thus permit a larger percentage of the population to engage in nonagricultural pursuits in commerce, religion, and the arts. But more than the invention of agriculture per se—that is, a food-producing revolution—is necessary; many cultures have developed horticulture without transforming further. There must be an unprecedented social, as well as technological, condition. In the Near East, this social condition is alleged to have been dictated by the nature of the lowland agriculture along the Tigris and Euphrates rivers, where the scant rainfall and alluvial conditions demanded irrigation and other techniques of collective control. Also in these plains, with collective effort, agricultural yields—and thus surpluses—could be greater. Overall, it may be said that—according to urban revolution theory—the combined social and technological changes served to produce food surpluses, to increase the size of populations, to promote property in both slaves and land, to develop ever-greater division and specialization of labour, to inspire the invention of writing as a means of keeping accounts, and to call for more complex political and commercial administration and more decided social stratification.

It should be noted that theories of the origin of civilization have come in for considerable criticism. The Dutch-born American archaeologist Henri Frankfort (1897–1954), for instance, argued that the forces behind the origins of civilization and cultures may never be known. Searching out these forces, he said, "can but lead [a scholar] astray in the direction of quasi-philosophical speculations, or tempt him to give pseudo-scientific answers." (From *The Birth of Civilization in the Near East,* 1951.)

Recent varieties of evolutionary theory. After mid-century there developed a revival of evolutionary theory among a very few scholars, almost all of them American anthropologists. Although they have sometimes, somewhat misleadingly, been labelled neo-evolutionists, the fact is that there has been no restoration of the old evolutionism of either Darwin or Spencer—and cannot be. Philosophy, history, and science have been infused by new knowledge and thus by new attitudes and methods for viewing matter, life, and society.

The new evolutionists

One thing absent in the new evolutionary theories of such anthropologists as Leslie A. White, Julian H. Steward, Marshall D. Sahlins, and Elman R. Service is the notion of a single evolutionary process or pattern. There is, for instance, no attempt to define progress or evolution in terms of laissez-faire, survival-of-the-fittest doctrine, or some invisible hand of fate. Nor, conversely, is there any attempt to fasten on so-called telic, rational, conscious change as the single motive of evolution. The modern evolutionists would contend that the processes are mixed. In various societies at various times, planning and accident have been ingredients of varying proportions. Evolution is the result of invention and discovery, historical accident, cultural borrowing or diffusion—that is, the result of various combinations of changes from any source.

The new evolutionists reject universal stages outright. Evolution is multilinear, consisting of a number of forward paths of different styles and lengths. Some scholars, nevertheless, would still distinguish between "specific" and "general" evolution. There may be a specific process of evolution for specific peoples, but mankind does generally evolve or progress, with specific peoples providing breakthroughs making all mankind more adaptable to and dominant over the environment and socially more complexly organized. Only in this sense can the whole of world civilization be viewed as the product of a unitary process.

BIBLIOGRAPHY. ALEXANDER GOLDENWEISER, *Anthropology: An Introduction to Primitive Culture* (Eng. trans. 1937), contains an interesting study on animal, man, race, culture, primitive life and thought, and the ways of culture. MELVILLE JACOBS and BERNHARD J. STERN, *Outline of Anthropology* (1947), is a well-known textbook on anthropology for beginning students and laymen who wish a broad and contemporary view of the science. See also V.F. CALVERTON (ed.), *The Making of Man: An Outline of Anthropology* (1931), a compilation of ideas on prehistoric man, social organization, evolution, and culture; and *Man in Contemporary Society* (1962), a source book prepared under the direction of the Contemporary Civilization Staff of Columbia College, Columbia University. ARNOLD J. TOYNBEE, *A Study of History*, vol. 1 (1946), offers an interpretation of the genesis of civilization. A reinterpretation of the theory of evolution in the light of modern physics is presented in LECOMTE DU NOUY, *Human Destiny* (Eng. trans. 1947). HENRI FRANKFORT, *The Birth of Civilization in the Near East* (1951), is a study of social and political innovations in which the great change became manifest. L.A. WHITE, *The Evolution of Culture* (1959); J.H. STEWARD, *Theory of Culture Change: The Methodology of Multilinear Evolution* (1955); and M.D. SAHLINS and E.R. SERVICE (eds.), *Evolution and Culture* (1960), offer new points of view on cultural evolution.

(B.M.P.)

Civil Law

The group of laws that has grown up on the continent of Europe as a combination of Germanic traditions, with Roman, ecclesiastical, feudal, commercial, and modern social influences, is known generally as the civil law. In this sense, the civil law, the common law or Anglo-American law, and the socialist law constitute the three great law families of Western civilization.

In ancient Rome, the term *jus civile* ("civil law") was used to distinguish the proper or ancient law of the city or state of Rome from the *jus gentium,* or the law thought to be common to all the peoples comprising the Roman world, as developed and incorporated with the former through the praetors (magistrates) and jurists (see ROMAN LAW). The phrase has also been used to distinguish private law, or the law governing the relationships between citizens, from public law and criminal law. Again, the national law of a state is sometimes described as civil law, in contrast to international law. This article does not discuss civil law in these senses.

Global distribution of civil and common law

The common law is, essentially, the law of England and the law of those countries in which the law of England has been received or implanted and, though often transformed in certain respects or supplemented by local or religious traditions, has been preserved in its principal features. Besides England, common-law countries in the strict sense are thus Canada, Australia, New Zealand, the Republic of Ireland, and the present and former British areas of the West Indies. A new type of common law that in many respects differs from the English type is that of the United States. Common law also prevails in India, Pakistan, Burma, Malaysia, and Singapore, where it is supplemented in matters of personal status by religious laws, as well as in Liberia and in most of those parts of Africa and Oceania that were, or still are, British colonies, protectorates, or trust territories, and where the common law is supplemented in many respects by native customs (see COMMON LAW).

Most of the laws of the legal systems of continental Europe are traditionally classified as civil law. From there the type spread to Latin America and later to those countries of Asia and Africa that found it necessary to westernize their laws—for example, Japan (in which common law has also had some influence), Thailand, Turkey, and Ethiopia. It also prevails, supplemented by religious laws or native customs, by and large in those regions that were, or still are, colonies, protectorates, or trust territories of France, Belgium, The Netherlands, Spain,

Portugal, and Italy, including Morocco, Algeria, Zaire, Indonesia, and Somalia, as well as those that still are dependencies or outlying parts of European countries, for example, Martinique and Curaçao in the West Indies and Angola and Mozambique in Africa. Civil law, supplemented by Islāmic law, has come to prevail in the countries of the Near East, but not in Israel, Libya, and Iraq, where common law has been influential.

Another group may be said to be constituted by the laws of the Scandinavian countries (Sweden, Finland, Denmark, Norway, and Iceland), which are closer to the civil law, however, than to the common law. In the Soviet Union and the other Socialist countries of eastern Europe, all law is permeated with the collectivist spirit, and new beginnings have been made in numerous respects. But civil-law concepts are still used in legal thinking.

In a few parts of the world, civil law and common law have come to interpenetrate each other—for example, in Scotland, in Quebec (Canada), in the U.S. state of Louisiana, in Puerto Rico, the Philippines, South Africa, Rhodesia, Sri Lanka (Ceylon), and Mauritius. While in most of these places the common law seemed to be the prevailing influence, an opposite trend set in after the 1920s, so that in most of these areas the private law can be regarded as still being close to the civil-law pattern.

HISTORICAL DEVELOPMENT OF CIVIL LAW

The features characteristic of each of the two systems have been shaped by history. In the 5th and 6th centuries western and central Europe was dominated by Germanic peoples, especially those who had overrun the Roman Empire. Among them were the Anglo-Saxons of England, the Franks of western Germany and northern France, the Burgundians, the Visigoths of southern France and Spain, and the Langobards of Italy. Although Roman law traditions lingered on for some time, the Germanic customs came to prevail in most regions. In the Middle Ages these customs underwent vigorous growth to satisfy the complex needs of a society of changing feudalism, chivalry, growing cities, Eastern colonization, increasing trade, and a constantly refined culture. Among the many strands that went into the weaving of the complex pattern of medieval law, the customs of the merchants and the canon law of the Roman Catholic Church were of special significance. It was through the canon law that the concepts and ideas of ancient Rome continued to make their presence felt, even when, as a whole, Roman law had been forgotten. In the late 11th century Roman law was rediscovered and made the subject matter of learned study and teaching by scholars in northern Italy, especially at Bologna. With the increasing demand for trained judges and administrators, first by the Italian city-republics, then by princes in other localities, students flocked to Bologna from all over Europe, until the learning and teaching were gradually taken over by local universities. As a result of this process, Roman law penetrated into the administration of justice north of the Alps, especially in Germany and The Netherlands, where the Roman-law influence finally became so strong that one came to speak in these countries of a reception of the Roman law.

In the Holy Roman Empire of German nations the reception was facilitated because its emperors cherished the idea of being the direct successors of the Roman Caesars; the Roman law, collected in the Corpus juris civilis by the emperor Justinian I between 527 and 565, could be regarded as still being in effect simply because it was the imperial law. Decisive for the reception, however, was the superiority of the specialized training of Roman-law jurists over the empirical activities of the lay judges and practitioners of the local laws; equally decisive was the superiority of the Roman-canonical type of procedure, with its rational rules of evidence, over the forms of local procedure involving proof by ordeal, battle, and other irrational methods. Nowhere, however, did the Roman law completely supplant the local laws. So far as the content of the law was concerned, there developed various amalgams. Roman law strongly influenced the law of contracts and torts; canon law achieved supremacy in the field of marriage; and combinations of Ger-

Revival of Roman law

manic, feudal, and Roman traditions developed in matters of property and succession. The conceptual formulations in which the norms and principles of the law were expressed, as well as the procedural forms in which justice was administered, were also strongly Roman. The system that thus emerged was called the *jus civile*. In actual practice it varied from place to place, but it was nevertheless a unit that was held together by a common tradition and a common stock of learning. The law of the Corpus juris civilis, especially its main part, the Digest, the writings of the jurists, was, as such, in effect nowhere but constituted the basis of study, training, and discourse everywhere. In spite of all variety, the civil-law world experienced a sense of unity that corresponded to the strongly felt unity of European civilization.

This unity was undermined by the religious split of the Reformation and Counter-Reformation and by the rise of nationalism that accompanied the unification and stabilization of the European nations and their struggle for hegemony. In the field of law the split found expression in the national codifications, through each of which the law was unified within a particular nation but simultaneously set apart from that of all others. In Denmark codification occurred in 1683, in Norway in 1687, in Sweden-Finland in 1734, and in Prussia in 1791. Because of the personality of their backer and the novel technique applied, great fame and influence were achieved by the Napoleonic codifications of the private and criminal law of France, especially their central piece, the Civil Code (Code Civil or Code Napoléon) of 1804.

National codifications

Codification continued after the Napoleonic era. In Belgium and Luxembourg, which had been incorporated into France under Napoleon, his codes were simply left in effect. The Netherlands, Italy, Spain, and numerous countries of Latin America followed the French model not only in the undertaking of national codification but also in the techniques and arrangements of their codes. Naturally, their courts and legal scholars were, at least in the earlier decades of the 19th century, inclined to pay great attention to French legal learning.

In Germany national codification came considerably later than in France. Only a commercial code had been uniformly created by the independent German states shortly after the revolution of 1848. The unification of the criminal law came almost simultaneously with the political unification of the country, which occurred in 1871. Codification of the organization of the courts and of civil and criminal procedure came in 1879. But the Civil Code (Bürgerliches Gesetzbuch für das deutsche Reich) was not completed until 1896, and it did not take effect until January 1, 1900. But all through the 19th century the vigorous German science of law exercised much influence in Austria (which as early as 1811 had codified its law in a technique different from that of France), in Switzerland, in the Scandinavian countries, and, later on, in most of eastern Europe. When Swiss law was codified in 1907–12, it became the model for the Turkish codification of 1926 and strongly influenced that of China, which is still in effect in Taiwan.

Due to the different dates of codification and the different style and attitude of legal learning, the civil-law family of laws is thus divided into the French, or Romance, branch and the German, or Germanic, branch. Their main features are determined by those of their prototypes. The legal system of Japan belongs essentially to the German branch, but it presents important features of its own.

THE FRENCH SYSTEM

In France the revolutionary period was one of extensive legislative activity: long-desired changes were enthusiastically introduced. A new conception of law appeared in France: statute was deemed the basic source of law. Customs remained only as long as they could not be replaced by a statute, and the *parlements*, the major courts of the nation, were dismissed. They were replaced by a unified system of courts that were merely supposed to apply the law and never to lay down general rules.

The main ideas embodied in the revolutionary legisla-

Changes induced by the French Revolution

tion are to be found in the Revolution's motto (which is still that of the French republic), "*Liberté, Égalité, Fraternité*." The passionate desire for liberty and equality aroused by the 18th-century philosophers inspired the changes that took place.

The system that has come to be called feudal, although it had little to do with the feudalism of the High Middle Ages, was hated by the peasants and the bourgeoisie for the privileges it accorded—especially those exempting the nobles and clergy from taxation. These privileges were abolished early in the Revolution. The revolutionaries detested organized groups of any kind, for it was thought that only one authority should exist over the citizens—that of the state. As a result, the guilds which demanded compulsory membership and regulated every profession, were suppressed, and freedom of commerce was established. The old-style universities were dissolved, and in the same spirit the property of the Roman Catholic Church was secularized, and the priests and bishops were made state employees, a situation that most of them did not accept.

Family relations were deeply transformed according to the principles of liberty and equality. Marriage was organized as a merely civil act; divorce was permitted; paternal authority was limited; and parents' consent was not required for marriages of children over 21 years of age. A short experiment was made with "family courts" that were to overrule paternal decisions, and the wife was declared equal to her husband. As regards successions, equal parts were given to all children. A testator's right to dispose of his property by will was limited in order to prevent the re-establishment of inequalities by this device.

Throughout the revolutionary period, successive governments were committed to consolidate the legal changes in a set of codes. Drafts were made, but time and authority were lacking, and none was enacted until society was restabilized under Napoleon.

The concept of codification. From a practical point of view, the Code Civil achieved unification of French civil law. This was not, however, the only concern of its drafters. They shared with most of their contemporaries and with most modern French lawyers the belief that the law should be written, in clear language, so that it might be accessible to every citizen. In such a view a code must be complete in its field, setting forth general rules and arranging them logically. Finally it must not unnecessarily break with tradition.

The Code Civil is made up of short articles on the assumption, first, that the legislator cannot pretend to foresee all circumstances that may arise in life and, second, that only conciseness can make the code flexible enough to adapt old principles to new circumstances. The general rules contained in the code have been applied to concrete circumstances without much difficulty. When interpretation is required, it is the responsibility of the courts to give it, taking into consideration the "spirit" of the code in order to apply to each case the solution that would have been desired by the legislator.

Logic and experience in the codification

The drafters of the code strove toward inner consistency in their work, so that reliance on logic might ensure satisfactory application of it. They saw no contradiction between logic and experience. Since the 17th-century beginnings of the Age of Reason, logic had been inherent in the French approach to law as to life in general. For this reason articles of the code are not regarded as narrow rulings. If no one article is found to apply exactly to a given situation, it is proper to consider several and to draw from them a more general rule that can be either itself applied to the case or combined with others to reach a solution.

Although the code is a work of logic, it relies mainly on experience. Its drafters were exceptionally well qualified in this respect: they had lived the first half of their lives under the laws of ancient France and then had known the Revolution. Their purpose was not so much to create new law as to restate existing law, subject to choice when revolutionary enactments varied from previous ones and when previous ones differed from one another. They

were ready to adopt any rules that they might deem best suited to the French people on the basis of experience; they recognized that laws could not be inflexible "but must be adapted to the character, the habits, and the situation of the people for whom they are drafted."

Later changes and adaptations. No important changes were made in the Code Civil from 1804 to 1880, except the repeal of divorce in 1816, when a Catholic monarchy was restored. The political and legislative power was held by the bourgeoisie, and they were entirely satisfied with the basic principles of the code, which favoured individualism and free will. In fact, from 1804 until the enactment of the constitution of the Third Republic in 1875 the Code Civil remained the law of France, whatever the changes of political regime. Jurisprudence was centred upon it; in both teaching and writing, scholars used to discuss it article by article. The courts fulfilled the role that the drafters had stressed for them; imbued with the spirit of the code, they applied its general rules to particular cases.

Changes during the Third Republic

The social atmosphere changed during the Third Republic, when universal suffrage gave the labouring class influence on legislation. Faith in liberalism was shaken, and the idea grew that the state should intervene to protect the weak. Statutes increased in number. This movement was accentuated by World Wars I and II, when a mass of emergency regulations had to be passed, and the power of the state to encroach on private interests for the sake of the community was increased.

Subsequent amendments to the code reveal two trends: first, greater individualism in family law; second, qualification of individual rights for the sake of social interests —what has been called "socialization" of the law.

Adaptation of the law to new social needs was not made only by statute. The courts to a certain extent adjusted the law to modern circumstances. They did this, however, in the consciousness of their subordinate position. They recognized that, as a general rule, basic changes were the province of the legislature and not of the judge, though this did not prevent them from gradually adapting the law to modern conditions of life.

Legal learning also had a role. A number of important statutes were drafted by commissions including judges, professors, and lawyers; and authors often suggested to the courts new developments in the application of rules of law. Most of the statutes passed during the 19th and 20th centuries, however, were left outside the code but have been published along with editions of the code.

By the middle of the 20th century, it had become apparent that the code should be revised. This task was entrusted to a commission, which by the early 1970s had made much headway. Further changes were expected, although an effort to replace the old code by a complete new one was halted when Charles de Gaulle returned to power in 1958. But the continuing development of multinational institutions such as the European Economic Community seems likely to require readjustments on a broad scale, especially in the field of commercial law and perhaps even in that of contract law.

The main parts of French private law. The French Civil Code uses many of the categories that were developed in ancient Rome, but its law is that of its own time.

Marriage and family. The drafters of the French Civil Code regarded marriage as the basic institution of a civilized society. Taking into account the variety of religious attitudes in France, they decided that only marriage ceremonies celebrated before secular officials should be legally valid. This did not deprive ministers of the various faiths of the right to celebrate religious marriage ceremonies, but these were held to be void of any legal effect and had to take place after the secular ceremony in order to avoid any risk of confusion. Parental control over children's marriages was partially restored; consent was required for sons under 25, daughters under 21. After 1900 the formalities of marriage were made easier and parental control over it curtailed. Twentieth-century statutes gradually re-established the revolutionary rule that when the parties are over 21, consent of the parents is no longer necessary.

Marriage viewed as basic to civilized society

In France under the *ancien régime*, the family had been centred upon the husband, whose strong authority and powers were inherited from the Roman paterfamilias (head of family). Although the Revolution proclaimed women to be equal in rights with men, it did little to implement this view in law. The drafters of the code saw no reason to modify the traditional situation, and Napoleon himself favoured subordination of the wife to the husband. The code expressly stated that she owed him obedience. With very few exceptions, she had no legal capacity to act. Without the written consent of her husband, the wife could not sell, give, mortgage, buy, or even receive property through donation or succession. Statutes of 1938, 1942, and 1965 severely diminished the authority of the husband over his wife. The law still stipulates that the husband is the head of the family, but he must exercise his authority in the interest of his family. If he is for any reason unable to make the necessary decisions, his wife is empowered to replace him. Moreover, the principle of her incapacity has been abandoned.

Rights of husband and wife

In recent years matrimonial regimes for the control of marital property have been revised in numerous countries, the tendency being toward a partnership in property acquired after the marriage, with each party retaining control over the property he or she had before the marriage. Although the Napoleonic Code provided for a statutory regime (if no particular marriage contract had been made), under which all chattels and earnings of the spouses would fall into a community property to be shared equally between them or their heirs at the dissolution of the marriage, the husband was vested with all active powers, even over his wife's property. It has only been with the acquisition of legal capacity that the French wife has been free to manage her own property and to dispose of it. In 1965 movables owned by either spouse before marriage were excluded from the community fund, which now consists only of the fruits of the spouses' work or frugality during marriage. Management of the community fund is still with the husband—with the exception of the part acquired through the wife's work and subject to the requirement of the wife's consent for major transactions.

Divorce. Divorce was first introduced into France by the Revolution. It was made very easy and was even allowed by mutual agreement.

The drafters of the code decided that since many persons were not prevented by religious conviction from seeking divorce, it was not for the legislator to oblige unhappy spouses to live together for life or even, if parted, to live alone, unable to contract a more fortunate union. Divorce, therefore, was allowed, but within strict limits, so that "the most sacred of contracts should not become the toy of caprice." The only grounds for divorce were adultery, punishments for the most serious crimes, excesses such as gambling habits and expenditures, cruel treatment, or serious insult. Mutual agreement was added under the personal pressure of Napoleon, already intent on divorcing his first wife, by whom he had no child. But the procedure of divorce by mutual agreement was extremely long, complicated, and costly, and no second marriage could take place within six years thereafter.

Divorce was repealed in 1816 after Napoleon's fall and the restoration of the monarchy, but it was reintroduced in 1884, when much of the original legislation of 1804 was utilized. Divorce by mutual agreement, however, was not reinstated.

Succession and gifts. The Napoleonic Code adopted many of the ideas of the Revolution toward succession. But its formulators tempered them with exceptions and combined them with ideas from the *ancien régime*.

The revolutionary law on intestate succession (sucession without a valid will) relied upon two basic principles: (1) that no distinctions be made within the estate of the deceased; land and chattels were treated in the same way, and no account was taken of the origin of landed property; and (2) that equal parts be given to all heirs of the same degree of kindred; the advantages accruing through some customs to the firstborn or to male children were abolished.

The code took over these two principles and provided that an estate should devolve first of all upon the children and other descendants. If certain heirs of one degree predeceased others of the same degree and left children, representation (the principle that the children of a deceased heir inherit his share) applied. In other cases distribution was made per capita, an equal share to those of equal degree. Illegitimate children might inherit from their parents but received less than legitimate children and could not cut out either the deceased's own parents or his brothers and sisters. Since then, the rights of illegitimate children to succeed to their parents have been increased.

Rights of heirs and surviving spouse

According to the code, the spouse could succeed only if there were no persons who are related to the deceased up to a degree specified by law. A surviving wife was, thus, in a bad position if no gift or legacy had been made to her, though under the statutory matrimonial regime she received half of the community property into which all chattels of both spouses fell. The rights of the surviving spouse have been increased at various times during the 20th century. By midcentury the surviving spouse was entitled to at least the usufruct (similar to a life interest) of one-quarter of the property left by the deceased. The survivor also inherits half of the estate if there are no children and if there are relatives on only one side of the deceased's family.

Wills may be formal or informal. Unwitnessed wills are valid, provided that they are written throughout, and dated and signed, by the testator's own hand. Wills are self-effective, and do not need to be probated. Freedom to dispose of property by will or by gift is limited, in order to protect children and other descendants as well as parents and grandparents, who have to be allowed a certain proportion.

Property. The intricate system of obligations and rights inherited by the *ancien régime* from feudalism had been rejected by the Revolution, which restored a system patterned on that of Roman law.

The only classification of goods is the basic one of immovables (which are defined as having a fixed place in space) and movables (which include all goods that are not immovables). In contrast to the "feudalist" complexities in the common law, the normal relationship between persons and things is ownership, which is defined as a complete, absolute, free, and simple right. But as in other modern nations, the use of property is subject to many kinds of restrictions imposed in the public interest. Usufructs or servitudes are possible, but rights in an estate never require the person in whom they are vested to do anything. The code states that a servitude "is a charge laid on an estate for the use and utility of another estate belonging to another owner," and it emphasizes that "servitudes do not establish any pre-eminence of one estate over another." Title in land may be acquired within 10 or 20 years if the possessor believed in good faith that he was the real owner. Furthermore, the bona fide purchaser of movable property immediately becomes its owner, and nobody can prove a better title against him unless the property has been lost or stolen.

Concept of movables and immovables

The section on mortgages in the Civil Code was weak. An excellent statute of the Revolution (1798) had set up a system of registration for all transfers of land titles and real estate mortgages. A buyer of land could ascertain whether he was buying from a regular owner and whether the land was mortgaged, and if it were, he could clear his title by offering the price to the mortgagee.

The drafters of the code maintained compulsory registration, but only for gifts and for contractual mortgages. Sales of real estate and a number of legal mortgages were not subject to registration. This gap left prospective creditors or buyers with insufficient information. It was only after reforms were made in 1855, 1935, and 1955 that there was a comprehensive, but still not fully reliable, system of publicity for mortgages and conveyances of immovable property.

Contracts and torts. The French Revolution brought no changes into the law in this nonpolitical field. The drafters of the code merely restated the law that had developed in the course of centuries and that authors already had analyzed. The basic principles of contract law are informality and freedom, which is limited, however, when demanded by public policy. The code states that "agreements legally entered into have the effect of laws on those who make them." The whole matter of torts is dealt with in five short articles. The general basis for liability is this: "If anybody causes a damage by his own fault, there is a legal obligation upon him to repair it." The subsequent articles regulate liability for damages caused by things, animals, children, and employees. It was left to the courts to work out a complete system based on these few articles.

Informality and freedom of contract

THE GERMAN SYSTEM

In Germany, Roman law as embodied in the Corpus juris civilis was "received" from the 15th century onward, and with this "reception" came a legal profession and a system of law developed by professionals (*Juristenrecht*). Roman law provided the theoretical basis for legal progress, culminating in the work of the scholars of the 19th century. Under this tradition, the legal process has been viewed in Germany as the application of more or less generally formulated rules to the individual cases; the courts have not been as dominant in developing the law as they have been in the common-law countries, such as England. Roman law provided tools to strengthen sovereignty, as well as the correlative ideas that the legislative function is a state monopoly and that the responsibility for the development of law rests with a legally trained, state-controlled bureaucracy rather than—as in 18th- and 19th-century England—with a combination of gentry and leaders of the bar. German judges have been university-trained experts under the authority of the state and anonymity of the court.

Contrasts between the German and French codes

The German Civil Code. Because the German Civil Code of 1896 came almost 100 years later than the code of France, its draftsmen profited from the intensive efforts at systematization, clarification, and modernization of the law that had been carried on by German scholars during that century. As a result, the German code is markedly different from its French predecessor. Its arrangement is more orderly, its language more precise, and its use more exacting.

The appeal of the German code is from lawyers to lawyers; the matter-of-fact, neutral tone contrasts with the livelier mood in which the French Civil Code was written. It does not try to teach men in a broad sense, but it emphasizes ethical imperatives. Good faith and fair dealing are to be observed in all affairs. Breaches of good morals, abuse of rights, and underhanded legal transactions are defeated. The code was meant to fit the society of the turn of the century, but through general clauses that leave the making of specific norms to the judges, it could be adapted to new economic, cultural, and sociopolitical postulates.

Modern law in West Germany assumes that the proper form of society is that of a social democracy, not merely conferring individual rights but also involving the responsibility of the state for social welfare and the duty of individuals to behave in a socially responsible way. The former concern of German law with abstract concepts has given place to a more pragmatic approach with the aim of applying the scale of values of a pluralistic society containing strong elements of the welfare state and emphasizing civil liberties.

The main parts of German private law. The German civil code starts out with the proposition that upon the completion of his birth every person acquires the capacity to exercise rights and to fulfill duties. A minor's interests are guarded by a representative who acts in his name, and although certain legal transactions may be entered into at age seven, full legal capacity is not acquired until age 21. Every person possesses the right, protected by an action in court, to freedom from personal injury and from attacks on individual dignity.

Marriage and family. Since 1875 marriage has required civil celebration by a registrar, who cannot be a priest. Celebration in church may follow the civil ceremony. Marriage can be declared null and void on application of one of the spouses or by the public prosecutor on various grounds, such as lack of form or affinity, but the consequences of such nullity are approximate to those of divorce: the children are not necessarily illegitimate. The grounds for divorce, which have been relaxed, include adultery, violation of any matrimonial duty leading to disruption of the marriage, some adverse physical or mental condition of a spouse, or a deep-rooted disruption of the marital relation without expectation of restoration of common life. The last must be preceded by a separation of at least three years. Custody of children on divorce is decided on the basis of their own welfare.

Rights of husband and wife

The provisions of the German Civil Code concerning rights of women in marriage were less restrictive than those of the French. After World War II all rules contradicting the principle of equality of men and women were repealed. The ordinary statutory regime, with the husband administering and using the wife's estate, has been replaced by the regime of separation of assets and equal shares of the spouses in acquisitions made during marriage. Upon death of one spouse the surviving spouse is entitled to a generous share in the estate. Care for the person and property of the children belongs to both spouses. The court, for the protection of wards, may take steps to prevent dangers to children threatened by parental neglect or discord.

Succession. In contrast to Anglo-American law, the assets of the decedent pass directly to the heirs, who may be determined by the rules of intestacy or by testamentary disposition. As a general rule, the estate does not pass through a stage of administration by an administrator or executor. The heirs are liable for the debts of the decedent with their own property but by taking appropriate steps may limit their liability to the assets of the estate. A testator may appoint an executor to perform certain functions in the settlement. A will may be unwitnessed, but then it must be entirely in the testator's handwriting. Public wills are either made orally before a public official, who records them, or set down in a document that the testator hands to the official with a declaration that it is his last will. Descendants and other close relatives cannot be deprived of more than one-half of their intestate shares.

Property. Property is declared to entail obligations to serve the community. This is particularly important in terms of farmland, which may be pooled and redistributed to make better use of machinery and to increase production. Every creation, transfer, encumbrance, or cancellation of a right in an immovable requires, in addition to the agreement of the parties, registration with the district court. A person who acquires an interest in land in good faith from the person registered is protected. In order to obtain title to a chattel from a person who does not have it, the transferor must have had possession, the transferee must have been in good faith, and the owner must not have lost possession involuntarily. But neither in the case of land nor in that of chattels is it required that the transfer to the transferee has been for value. Even if the transferee acquires title he may be required to surrender the asset or to pay its value if the acquisition appears to be a legally unjustified enrichment.

Contract and delict. Parties are free to regulate their relations by contract, within limits set by express statutory prohibitions and by good morals. Strict limits are set against overreaching of one contracting party by the other. In the case of a valid contract, the parties must observe the requirements of good faith, with ordinary usage taken into consideration. The determination of "ordinary usage" is left to the courts. This has been particularly advantageous with the rapidly changing conditions of the 20th century.

Compensations for breach of contract and injury

Unless the promisor can prove that a breach of contract has been caused in a way entirely outside his sphere of risk, he is liable in damages. But if the promisee chooses to do so, he may have the promisor ordered to render specific performance as long as it is not shown that performance is not actually impossible. The principle that "anyone who through an act performed by another or in any other way acquires something at the expense of that other without legal justification is bound to return it to him" is stated in broad terms, but is cautiously applied by the courts.

In terms of delict, the German code provides that any person who intentionally or negligently injures unlawfully the life, body, health, property, or any other absolute right of another person is bound to compensate him for any damage arising therefrom. Damages are due also for harm caused by the violation of a statute meant to protect others and for harm caused intentionally and immorally. If a public officer violates his statutory duty, court remedies are readily available against the government.

OTHER SIGNIFICANT CODIFICATIONS

Swiss and Italian codes

Codification in Germany was followed by that of Switzerland, which issued a Civil Code in 1907 and a separate Code of Obligations in 1910. This new Swiss federal code superseded the earlier codes of the separate cantons (which had generally been patterned after the Austrian or the French model), and its draftsmen took advantage of earlier experiences with respect to codification technique —drawing especially upon both the *Code Napoléon* and the German code. The Swiss code, which exists in German, French, and Italian versions of equal authority, represents one of the most masterly attempts to summarize and systematize civil law and has influenced codification in countries as diverse as Brazil and Turkey.

The French code was introduced into parts of Italy with the Napoleonic conquests. Even after the collapse of Napoleon's empire, when French law was abrogated, the *Code Napoléon* still served as the model for the new codes of several Italian states. While the peninsula was being politically united in the 1860s, the new Civil Code (1865) for the Kingdom of Italy was enacted, reproducing in structure and content the French Civil Code. Significantly, however, this code has since been revised. Unlike France and Germany, which have occasionally tried to draft new codes but still have not replaced their original ones, Italy in 1942, during the Fascist era, succeeded in introducing a reformed code. This code remains, with amendments due mainly only to the change in political regime. Set against the Civil Code of 1865, Italy's code of 1942 appears inspired by less individualist views—for instance, in property law, in which the social aspects are stressed, and in labour legislation.

The Japanese code

After the Meiji Restoration of 1868, which restored effective political power to the emperor, Japan sought to construct an economic, political, and legal structure capable of commanding respect internationally. The introduction of Western law was one element in a wholesale importation of things Western. In legal matters, the Japanese took for models the systems of continental Europe, especially the German. The drafters of the Japanese Civil Code of 1898 surveyed many legal systems, including the French, Swiss, and common laws, taking something from each. Their final product is, however, best characterized as following the first draft of the German Civil Code. In its subsequent development, the Japanese legal system remained true to these sources. The 1947 revisions of the code provisions dealing with family law and succession, which had reflected traditional Japanese attitudes, completed the transition of Japanese civil law to the continental European family of laws.

On a few points, however, Japanese law is closer to that of the United States than to European models. This is largely a result of the post-World War II occupation and of subsequent contacts with U.S. legal thinking and education. The examination of witnesses in civil cases, for instance, is now (at least theoretically) modelled after U.S. procedure. From the perspective of rules and institutions, the Japanese legal system is admittedly closer to the civil law of Europe than to the common law. In many ways, nevertheless, the Japanese legal order differs markedly from all Western legal orders.

The fact that Japanese law is not the product of organic evolution suggests a significant point—that the role of law in modern Japanese society differs markedly from its role in Western societies. In Japan, law plays a far less pervasive role in the resolution of disputes and the creation and adjusting of rules regulating conduct. There are few Japanese decisions involving automobile accidents or manufacturer's liability for defective products and nuisance. The size of the Japanese bar is small, and extralegal methods of resolving disputes continue in large measure. For many purposes a family transcending man, wife, and dependent children still exists. The notion that a business is analogous to a family unit persists and colours all labour relations, especially in small and middle-sized firms. In the relatively homogeneous Japanese society, social status carries heavy obligations, and community pressure is extremely powerful.

Thus, although Japan early adopted a version of the German Civil Code, it did not adopt the Germans' strong consciousness of legal rights. In large areas of Japanese life it is still difficult to predict whether a dispute will be settled under legal standards, and it is often impossible to know whether a person will enforce those rights available to him. The concepts, pervasive in Western law, that the legal consequences of particular conduct should be predictable before the conduct has occurred or any dispute arisen, that the courts should give full effect to claims, a plaintiff receiving all or nothing, and that individual disputes should be resolved without considering the parties' social and economic background have not yet penetrated deeply into Japanese law. In contrast, facilities for conciliation are used to promote adjustment in terms of nonlegal considerations: local police stations provide conciliation rooms; elders act as go-betweens. Compromise based on legally irrelevant considerations is encouraged, utilizing techniques outside formal law for resolving disputes.

As Japan's westernization continues, however, law may come to play in Japan a role fully comparable to its role in the West; the sociological supports essential to the continued vitality of the Japanese conception of law are clearly being undercut by Japan's shift to a highly urban, mechanized society.

COMPARISON OF CIVIL LAW AND COMMON LAW

Between the 11th and 15th centuries the law of England was strongly influenced by Roman-law learning, and, in the 16th century, experts trained in Roman law were welcomed as administrators as much by the kings of England as by continental rulers. In contrast to the countries of the Continent, however, where justice was administered locally, it had, as a result of the Norman Conquest, been centralized in England. There had grown up at the courts of Westminster a profession of practitioners expert in the law and procedure of the centralized court system, strongly organized and unwilling to yield its position, power, and income to a new group of specialists of Romanist learning. In its resistance to royal innovation, the organized bar allied itself with the parliamentary party in the great constitutional struggle of the 17th century. Thus, a reception of Roman law of continental style was prevented in England. The connection between the principles of constitutionalism and individual freedom on the one side and the common law on the other, which has created the image of the common law as the legal system of freedom, in contrast to the civil law as the system in which the state is exalted over the individual, was therefore established. This view seems to obtain support from the fact that free political institutions were developed earlier and have been maintained more firmly in countries of the common law than in countries of the civil law.

Political institutions are one thing, however, and techniques of dealing with civil litigation and criminal prosecution are another. Intimate connections exist, of course, between the two; a society is not free if civil cases are not handled impartially and if persons accused of crime are not safeguarded against injustice. In both of these respects, however, neither of the two great legal systems lags behind the other. The ways of argumentation and procedure differ, but in its own way each of the two systems has developed its own guarantees and safeguards, and neither can be shown to be superior to the other. The view frequently found in England and the United States, that in civil-law criminal procedure the accused is presumed guilty until he has proved his innocence, is as unfounded as the view widely held on the Continent that trial by jury is tantamount to lawless appeal to passion and emotion.

If one compares countries having firmly established institutions of constitutional government, such as, on the one hand, the United Kingdom and the United States and, on the other, Belgium, The Netherlands, Switzerland, the Federal Republic of Germany, or France, it appears that in the civil-law countries the protection of the individual against illegal actions by executive agencies is generally about the same and in some respects even more elaborate than in the United States and the United Kingdom. Again, the United States has not yet fully caught up with Germany as regards compensating an individual out of public funds for harm caused to him by wrongful acts of public servants. In general, it may also be said that it is less expensive on the Continent for the citizen to seek legal protection of his private rights than it is in the common-law countries.

It is difficult to define what constitutes the real difference between common law and civil law. It would be erroneous simply to identify civil law with codified or even statutory law and common law with judge-made or case law. For one thing, the contrasts between the two systems existed long before the civil-law countries began to enact their codes. In addition, large parts of Anglo-American law are also contained in statutes or even codes, while in France, Germany, and other civil-law countries parts of the law have never been reduced to statute at all but have been developed by the courts; and many of the statutes and code provisions have come to be overlaid by judicial opinions and interpretations to such an extent that, in effect, they are dominated by judge-made law.

Role of judicial precedent
No essential difference can be found, either, in the role of judicial precedent. In theory, it is true, common-law courts are bound by precedent in the sense that once a legal question has been decided a certain way by a court, it must always be decided in the same way by all other courts of inferior or equal rank until the legislature sees fit to change the rule. In civil-law countries, on the other hand, courts are, in official theory, free to consider anew any legal question irrespective of how often it may have been determined before by other courts or even by the one before which it is pending. In practice, however, common-law courts, especially those in the United States, have developed techniques for distinguishing new cases from older ones that have reduced the need to appeal to judicial precedent to the measure suitable for maintaining the stability of social life; and civil-law courts, on their part, have been inclined to follow precedent, not only for the sake of continuity and social stability but also in accord with the inclination of courts everywhere to save time and effort by avoiding rethinking every problem each time it arises for judicial determination.

Role of the professors
The main difference between the systems consists of the ways in which the norms of the law are articulated and in which new rules are derived from older ones in novel cases. Though law cannot remain static, the change must be orderly and gradual so as not to interrupt the continuity and stability of life. In the common law, this role of adapting the law to changing conditions has traditionally been the task of the judges. In civil-law countries, the task had generally been performed by university professors, since the multiplicity of courts prevented the leading role from being assumed by the judges, who could well assume it in England, where the administration of justice was centralized. Judges must proceed from case to case, and cases present themselves in isolation and without prearrangement. Professors deal with hypothetical cases rather than actual ones. They can develop comprehensive ideas and principles, and they are impelled toward systematization and conceptualization by the didactic necessities of instruction. The civil law, as a

professorial law, has thus tended to be more systematic and more comprehensive and consistent in its propositions and terminology than the judge-made common law, which may have tended, on its part, to be closer to life and perhaps more detailed.

These traditional differences may diminish, however, for in the civil-law countries judicial power has increased with the national centralization of the administration of justice, while in the common-law part of the world the courts of Westminster have lost their supremacy to the multiplicity of supreme courts in the United States and in the commonwealth. The role of maintaining the unity of the law is thus passing to that group of professionals —the professors—by which it was once exercised in the civil-law world. Gradual assimilation of the techniques of the two great systems of law may thus well be expected.

What is likely to continue, however, is the marked difference between the two great families of legal systems that exists in the field of procedure and, to some extent, in the personnel by whom justice is administered. All civil-law countries have adopted the adversary type of procedure that for centuries was peculiar to the common law, and they have abandoned the canonical procedure in which proceedings were dominated by the judge, to whom the evidence was presented in the form of a written record made up by a public officer and mostly in the absence of the parties. In the adversary procedure of the common law, arguments are addressed orally to the court, and the evidence is directly presented to it or to the jury. In the 19th century, jury trial was widely adopted in civil-law countries, but only for criminal cases. In the 20th century it was largely abandoned, mostly in favour of the system of the mixed bench, on which professional, legally trained judges sit together with laymen and decide together with them not only, as the common-law jury does, questions of fact but also those of law. In civil cases concerning matters of business or of labour relations, the lay members of the court are picked from among business people or from the circles of management and labour.

Role of the adversary system

In common-law countries the mode of adversary procedure is still followed rather consistently in both civil and criminal cases. In civil-law countries witnesses are generally examined by the presiding judge, who has also the power to expedite the conduct of a case and, when he regards it as necessary, to influence the parties' conduct of the case. Although it is conceivable that a judge having such powers may be swayed from strict impartiality, the scales can be balanced in favour of the party represented by counsel less able or less ruthless than that of his adversary.

BIBLIOGRAPHY. The world's legal systems are comparatively presented in KONRAD ZWEIGERT and HEIN KOTZ, *Einführung in die Rechtsvergleichung auf dem Gebiete des Privatrechts*, 2 vol. (1969–71); and in RENE DAVID and JOHN E.C. BRIERLEY, *Major Legal Systems in the World Today: An Introduction to the Comparative Study of Law* (1968). The German work contains in its second volume models of comparative study of selected topics of the law of contracts, torts, and restitution. Both works contain extensive bibliographies. ERNST RABEL, *Private Law of Western Civilization* (1950), is a series of lectures by a great scholar of comparative law. JOHN P. DAWSON, *The Oracles of the Law* (1968), is a penetrating analysis of the methods of legal thought in the Anglo-American law and the French and German systems, as developed through the different roles played in them by judges and scholars. ARTHUR TAYLOR VON MEHREN, *The Civil Law System* (1957), is a rich collection of cases and other source materials from France and Germany. Helpful guides to the study of the legal systems of particular countries are: MAURICE SHELDON AMOS and FREDERICK PARKER WALTON, *Introduction to French Law*, 3rd ed. by F.H. LAWSON, A.E. ANTON, and N. BROWN (1967); RENE DAVID and H.D. DE VRIES, *The French Legal System* (1957), a concise introduction; FREDERICK HENRY LAWSON, *A Common Lawyer Looks at the Civil Law* (1955), primarily concerned with French law; ERNST JOSEPH COHN, *Manual of German Law*, 2nd rev. ed. (1968), a book written for lawyers; MAURO CAPPELLETTI, JOHN HENRY MERRYMAN, and JOSEPH M. PERILLO, *The Italian Legal System* (1967); LESTER B. ORFIELD, *The Growth of Scandinavian Law* (1953); PHANOR JAMES EDER, *A Comparative Survey of*

Anglo-American and Latin-American Law (1950); JOHN N. HAZARD, ISAAC SHAPIRO, and PETER B. MAGGS, The Soviet Legal System: Contemporary Documentation and Historical Commentary, rev. ed. (1969); JOHN N. HAZARD, Communists and Their Law (1969); ARTHUR TAYLOR VON MEHREN (ed.), Law in Japan: The Legal Order in a Changing Society (1963); KENNETH ROBERT REDDEN, The Legal System of Ethiopia (1968). Current materials and articles are published in the American Journal of Comparative Law (quarterly); and the International and Comparative Law Quarterly. All books and articles published in English since 1790 on the subject of civil law are listed in CHARLES SZLADITS (comp.), A Bibliography on Foreign and Comparative Law, 3 vol. (1955–68; suppl. 1966–67, 1970), and annual supplements in the American Journal of Comparative Law.

(M.Y.R./Ed.)

Civil Service

The civil service is a body of professional, full-time officials employed in the civil affairs of a state in a nonpolitical capacity. Traditionally this body is contrasted with other bodies serving the state in a full-time capacity, such as the military service, the judicial service, and the police service. In modern times there have also developed specialized services sometimes referred to as scientific or professional civil services, but these are distinguishable from the civil services proper in that they provide technical rather than general administrative services. Traditionally, in most countries, a distinction is also made between the home civil service and those persons engaged abroad on diplomatic duties. A civil servant, therefore, is one of a body of persons who are directly employed in the administration of the internal affairs of the state and whose role and status are not political, ministerial, military, or constabulary.

In most countries the civil service does not include local government employees nor the staffs of public corporations, such as, in the United Kingdom, the National Coal Board. In some other countries, however—particularly those unitary states in which provincial administration forms part of the central government—some provincial staffs are civil servants. In the United States, all levels of government have their own civil services, federal, state, and local, and a civil service is specifically that part of governmental service entered by examination and offering permanent tenure.

Common characteristics   Certain characteristics are common to all civil services. Most civil servants become skilled professionals in a branch of public administration, some of them with specialized skills in such technical fields as accounting, economics, engineering, and medicine. They are regarded as the professional advisors to those who formulate state policy—professional in the sense that their experience of public affairs is thought to provide them with the knowledge of the limits within which state policy can be made effective and of the probable administrative results of different courses of action. To this extent every country expects its civil servants to be impartial and neutral; their role is to advise, warn, and assist those responsible for state policy and, when decided, to provide the organization for its implementation. The responsibility for policy decisions lies with the political members of the executive, and, customarily, civil servants are protected from public blame or censure for their advice. The acts of their administration may, however, be subject to special judicial controls from which no member of the executive can defend them.

Civil services are organized upon standard bureaucratic lines (using "bureaucratic" in a purely neutral, non-pejorative sense), in which a chain of command stretches in pyramid fashion from the lowest offices to the highest. This command implies obedience to the lawful orders of a superior, and in order to maintain this system, the hierarchy of offices is marked by fixed positions, with well-defined duties, specific powers, and salaries and privileges objectively assessed. The civil services of some countries allow for the direct appointment to higher office of persons not previously employed by the service, but even in such countries a recognized system of internal promotion emphasizes the nature of the hierarchical pyramid (see also BUREAUCRACY).

HISTORY

Ancient systems. Bureaucracy (the pyramidal system) and civil service (the staffing of this system) date back to earliest times. Their origin may be found in the needs of the great Asian river civilizations, when irrigation required orderly, predictable, and comprehensive social control by means of organized structures of clerks, secretaries, and royal advisers. The Egyptians and the Greeks organized public affairs by office, and the principal officers under the sovereign were regarded as being principally responsible for administering justice, maintaining law and order, and providing plenty. With the Romans a more sophisticated administrative structure began to appear, and the affairs of state were distinguished into the administration of justice, military affairs, finance and taxation, foreign affairs, and the internal affairs of the state. Each administration had its own hierarchy and its own principal officers of state. An elaborate administrative structure, later imitated by the Roman Catholic Church, covered the entire empire, with a hierarchy of officers reporting back through their superiors to the emperor. This sophisticated structure disappeared after the fall of the Roman Empire in western Europe, but many of its practices continued to flourish in the Eastern Empire at Constantinople, where civil service rule was reflected in the pejorative use of the word Byzantinism.

The civil service in China was undoubtedly the longest lasting; it was first organized, along with a centralized administration, during the T'ang dynasty (618–907) and further perfected during the Sung dynasty (960–1279). The administration was organized so well that the pattern stood, with few changes, until 1912. During the Sung dynasty there developed the full use of civil service examinations. Candidates were subjected to successive elimination through written tests on three levels—more than a hundred persons beginning the ordeal for each one who emerged successful. Although there was strong emphasis on the Chinese classics (because knowledge of the classics was thought to form the virtues of a good citizen), there was also an effort to devise objective and meaningful tests for practical qualities, and there were always long contentions over subject matter and testing methods. To preserve the anonymity of the candidate and to ensure fairness in grading, examination papers were copied by clerks, examinees were identified by number only, and three examiners read each paper. Higher officials were privileged to nominate junior relatives for admission to the bureaucracy, but the great stress on examination grades in promotion, the use of annual merit ratings, and the practice of recruiting many lower officials from the ranks of the clerical service ensured a considerable freedom of opportunity.   **Chinese civil service**

Modern developments. Prussia. The foundations of the modern civil service in Europe were laid in Prussia in the late 17th and 18th centuries. The electors of Brandenburg, later the kings of Prussia, determined on a policy of strength, saw in the formation of a powerful army and a rigidly centralized system of government the best means for ensuring stability and furthering dynastic objectives. Their principal effort was devoted in the first instance to the suppression of the autonomy of the cities and the elimination of the feudal privileges of the aristocracy. This centralization was effected by the appointment of civil servants to the provinces, where the administration of crown lands and the organization of the military system were combined in a Kriegs- und Domänen-Kammer (Office of War and Crown Lands). Subordinate to these offices were the Steuerräte (tax councillors), who controlled the administration of the municipalities and communes. These officials were all appointed by the central government and were responsible to it. At the apex of the new machinery of government was the elector.   **The Prussian bureaucracy**

This centralized system was strengthened by creating a special corps of civil servants. In the beginning these civil servants—in a real sense servants of the crown—were sent out from Berlin to deal with such purely military matters as recruiting, billeting, and victualling the troops, but in the course of time they absorbed civil matters as well as military affairs. By 1713 there were clearly recognizable administrative units dealing in civil affairs and staffed by crown civil servants.

Special ordinances in 1722 and 1748 regulated recruitment to the civil service. Senior officials were required to propose to the king the names of candidates suitable for appointment to the higher posts, while the adjutant general proposed noncommissioned officers suitable for subordinate administrative posts. Further steps were taken throughout the 18th century to regularize the system of recruitment, promotion, and internal organization. All of these matters were brought together in a single General Code promulgated in 1794. The merit system of appointment covered all types of posts, and the general principle laid down was that "special laws and instructions determine the appointing authority to different civil service ranks, their qualifications, and the preliminary examinations required from different branches and different ranks." Entry to the higher civil service required a university degree in cameralistics, which, though strictly speaking the science of public finance, included also the study of administrative law, police administration, estate management, and agricultural economies. After the degree course, candidates for the higher civil service spent a further period of supervised practical training in different branches of the administration, at the end of which they underwent a further oral and written examination, which, if passed, made them eligible for appointment to office. The basic principles of modern civil services are to be found in this General Code.

France. A fundamental change in the status of the civil servant came about as a result of the French Revolution of 1789. The abolition of the monarchy and the creation of a republic meant that the civil servant was the servant no longer of the crown but rather of the state. The civil servant became an instrument of public power, not the agent of a person. This depersonalization of the state encouraged a rapid growth in the field of public law concerned with the organization, duties, and rights of "the public power," of which civil servants were the principal component. To the ordered structure of the Prussian bureaucracy there began to be added the logical development of administrative law.

Napoleonic system

This bureaucratization was greatly fostered by Napoleon I, who built up a new civil service marked not only by some of the features of military organization but also by the principles of rationality, logic, and universality that were the inheritance of the Enlightenment. There was a clear chain of command and a firmly established hierarchy of officials, with duties clearly apportioned between authorities. Authority was depersonalized and went to the office and not the official—although Napoleon insisted that each official should be responsible for action taken in the name of his office. France was divided into new territorial units: *départements, arrondissements,* and *communes.* In each of these, state civil servants had a general responsibility for maintaining public order, health, and morality. They were all linked in a chain to the national Ministry of the Interior. A special school, the École Polytechnique, was set up to provide the state with technical specialists in both the military and the civil fields—particularly in general administration. In the field of general administration, the Conseil d'État (Council of State), descended from the old Conseil du Roi (Council of the King), thus imposed an intellectual as well as a judicial authority over the rest of the civil service; and as the first major European administrative court, it became the creator of a new type of administrative jurisprudence. The prestige of the new French administrative organization and the logical arrangement of its internal structure prompted many other European countries to copy its principal features. And the expansion of the French Empire spread many of its features across the world.

In France under the Third Republic (1870–1940) there developed, however, considerable political interference in some branches of the civil service; and much of its vitality was diminished as its bureaucratic practices tended to become unwieldy and its personnel lethargic. Not un-

til 1946 was the system reformed—which involved overhauling the administrative structure of the central government, centralizing personnel selection, creating a special ministry for civil service affairs, and setting up a special school, the École National d'Administration, for the training of senior civil servants. This school in particular has attracted worldwide attention for its ability to instill in its graduates both specialist and generalist skills.

The British Empire. The first attempts by Great Britain to create efficient administrative machinery arose from its commitment to govern India and to avoid in that country the periodic scandals that marked some of the rule of the East India Company. Robert Clive, appointed governor for the second time in 1765, introduced a civil service that forbade servants of the company from accepting bribes or gifts from native traders or from engaging in personal trade. Subsequent governors strengthened the ban, compensating for the loss of benefits by substantially increasing salaries, introducing promotion by seniority, and re-organizing the higher echelons of administration. Recruitment was carried on by the company in London, and after 1813 entrants to the civil service had to study the history, language, and laws of India for a period of four terms at Haileybury College, England, and to obtain a certificate of good conduct before taking up their posts. After 1833 recruitment was organized on the basis of new rules stipulating that four candidates had to be nominated for each vacancy and that they were to compete with each other in "an examination in such branches of knowledge and by such examinations as the Board of the Company shall direct."

British civil service in India

Further criticisms of the administration of the government of India, however, led to the appointment of a parliamentary committee in 1835, under the chairmanship of Lord Thomas Macaulay, to report on recruitment to the Indian Civil Service. The work of this committee led indirectly to the foundation of the modern civil service in the United Kingdom: a report published in 1854 on the organization of the Permanent Civil Service in Britain drew much of its inspiration from the work of the Indian committee. The report of 1854 recommended the abolition of patronage and recruitment by open competitive examination. It further recommended (1) the establishment of an autonomous semijudicial body of Civil Service Commissioners to ensure the proper administration of recruitment to official posts; (2) the division of the work of the civil service into intellectual and routine work, the two sets of offices to have separate forms of recruitment; and (3) the selection of higher civil servants more decidedly on the basis of general intellectual attainment rather than specialized knowledge. The Civil Service Commission was established in 1855, and during the next 30 years patronage was gradually eliminated. The two original classes were increased to four, and some specialized branches were amalgamated to become the Scientific Civil Service. The new civil service began to attract a direct entry of candidates from the older universities, highly capable, discreet, and self-effacing.

The United States. In the United States patronage remained the norm for considerably longer than in Britain. This slow development had good democratic roots. From the early days of the federation two principles were firmly held. First, there was antipathy to the notion of a cadre of permanent civil servants; President Jackson clearly dismissed this elitist concept of a civil service when he said, in 1829, that "the duties of all public officers are . . . so plain and simple that men of intelligence may readily qualify themselves for their performance." As a consequence "I can not but believe that more is lost by the long continuance of men in office than is generally to be gained by their experience. No one man has any more intrinsic right to official station than another." The second principle followed more or less automatically—namely, that as far as possible public office should be elective. But because this principle could not be made wholly effective at the subordinate levels of administration, there developed the "spoils system," in which public office became a perquisite of political victory and was

Establishment of U.S. Civil Service Commission

widely used to reward political support. This system, however, led to persistent, blatant, and ultimately unacceptable degrees of inefficiency, corruption, and partisanship. These particular faults were strongly felt after the Civil War (1861–65), during the period of rapid economic and social development. Under considerable pressure, the federal government accepted a restricted principle of entry by competitive open examination, and in 1883 the U.S. Civil Service Commission was established to control entry to office in the federal service. The work of the commission was mainly restricted to the lower grades of employment, and it was not until the first 20 years of the 20th century that the merit system of recruitment expanded to cover half the posts in the federal service. Since that period the commission's control has gradually been further extended, but mainly to cover the lower, middle, and managerial offices in the federal service. The principal policy making offices, numbering some 2,000 offices in all, remain outside its jurisdiction and are filled by presidential nomination.

The development of civil service in U.S. local governments was as varied as the states, counties, and cities themselves. The adoption of a merit system can usually be dated from the early 1900s, during the reform period called the "muckraking era," when alleged corruption in states and municipalities was a special target of social reformers. But the record was spotty. In some states in which the merit system made significant inroads, a central personnel office, which included a civil service commission or board similar to the federal model, was established. At the other extreme there simply developed a central personnel office headed by a single personnel director unassociated with any advisory board. At the municipal level, by the mid-20th century, most large cities in the United States had developed some sort of merit system; as city size decreased, however, so did the extent of merit system coverage. In the counties, the majority of which were rural and had relatively few public employees, formally established merit systems were hard to find.

Communist nations. The revolutionary turmoil of the 20th century led to extensive changes in traditional forms of government. The deliberate destruction of regimes and their replacement by new systems dedicated to the pursuit of revolutionary ideals posed unprecedented problems of administrative organization. In Russia the Revolution of 1917 swept away the structures of the old tsarist government and deliberately destroyed the existing civil service, which had been based on the system. The Communist Party was strongly infused with the belief that a strong administrative organization was in itself anti-revolutionary and bound to damage the ethos of the revolution by dampening spontaneity and other revolutionary virtues. But it soon became clear that a regime dedicated to social engineering, economic planning, and world revolution could not begin to achieve its purposes without the support of trained and competent administrators. The pressure of events was too great, and the threat of total collapse too close, so that the regime fell back, albeit reluctantly, upon the expertise of the more reliable of the former tsarist civil servants to establish working administrative machinery. In deference to the expressed fears of disloyalty and a possible return to "bureaucratic tyranny," the party did, however, surround the new civil service with elaborate controls in an attempt to ensure that its members remained loyal to party directives and did not re-create a state within a state.

The old revolutionary suspicions gradually weakened, however, as the Communist Party itself became bureaucratized and as the more enthusiastic revolutionary leaders were eliminated. Special industrial academies were set up for party members who had shown some talent for administration. The working of the First Five-Year Plan (1928–32) confirmed the importance of an enlarged, competent civil service; the status of civil servants was improved, and their conditions of service were made less rigid, even though the party never relaxed its tight system of control over all branches of the state apparatus. In 1935 the State Commission on the Civil Service was created and attached to the Commissariat of Finance with

responsibility for ensuring general control of personnel practice. This commission laid down formal patterns of administrative structure, reformed existing bureaucratic practices, fixed levels of staffing, standardized systems of job classification, and eliminated unnecessary functions and staff. The inspectorate of the Ministry of Finance ensured that the commission's general policies were carried out in the ministries. The commission itself remained under the close supervision of the Council of People's Commissars to ensure that it complied with party directives, and the commission's members were appointed directly by the council.

Creation of Soviet commission

The Soviet commission, unlike those in such countries as Great Britain and the United States, was given no jurisdiction over the recruitment of civil servants, which remained the function of the ministries and agencies. The highest administrative and technical staff members were recruited by each ministry. Each branch of industry and administration had its own training schools, from which it selected qualified students with satisfactory records. On appointment, the student was bonded for a minimum of three years and liable to criminal proceedings if he refused or voluntarily relinquished his assignment. At the lower levels of administration, recruitment and job placement were the responsibility of the Commissariat of Labour Reserves, which had an overall responsibility for conscripting young people and for establishing annual quotas for industrial or clerical training.

As the civil service became more accepted and of proven competence, the Communist Party made determined attempts to recruit the elite of civil servants as party members. These drives, which followed periodically after the 1930s, went a long way toward transforming the party itself into an administrative and managerial elite and uniting the party and the state administration. It is now generally believed that the highest levels of the civil service represent an influential apparatus and power centre in its own right. The internal structure of the civil service, moreover, has been fashioned along the classic lines of the French and German models; and titles, ranks, insignia, and uniforms have officially appeared in various parts of the public services.

Communist China also illustrates the conflict between revolutionary suspicions of bureaucracy and the need to construct strong administrative machinery in order to attain revolutionary goals. As noted earlier, China had the longest continuous administrative service in the world; for centuries the country was ruled by a highly organized bureaucracy. This tradition left an indelible mark on the country despite the most strenuous efforts of the Communist Party leadership to maintain revolutionary fervour and to establish some identity of interest and purpose between the governors and the governed. Within a decade after the party came to power in 1949, the weight of the administration had already led, according to party dicta, to a gap between the elite and the masses and also to excessive stratification among the ruling bureaucrats themselves, or cadres. Not only was there a distinction between "old cadres" and "new cadres," a classification that referred simply to the date of an official's entry into the revolutionary movement, but there was also a complex system of job evaluation that divided the civil service into 24 grades, each with its own rank, salary scales, and distinctions. These ratings disguised very considerable differences of power, prestige, and prerogatives and erected psychological barriers between the highest and lowest grades at least as great and as conspicuous as between the cadres and the masses. These distinctions and discrepancies were widely attacked during the social upheavals of the 1960s, but they remained deeply ingrained in the administrative structure.

Communist Chinese system

Japan. The difficulty of changing the ethos of a long and strongly established civil service is also illustrated by events in post-World War II Japan. After 1945 the Allied occupation authorities, headed by U.S. General Douglas MacArthur, directed the passage of a Japanese law that guaranteed that all public officials should clearly be servants of the people rather than of the emperor. The National Public Service Law of 1947 set up an independent

National Personnel Authority to administer the detailed provisions on recruitment, promotion, conditions of employment, standards of performance, and job classification for the new civil service. Technically in law the emperor himself became a civil servant, and detailed regulations brought within the scope of the law all civil servants from labourers to the prime minister. Civil servants were classified into two groups, the regular service and a special service. Civil servants in the former category entered the service by competitive examination on a standard contract with tenure. The special service included elected officials and political appointees and covered such officials as members of the Diet, judges, members of the audit boards, and ambassadors.

Although in theory the sovereign people had an inalienable right to choose and dismiss all public officials who were constitutionally described as "servants of the whole community," both tradition and political practice have allowed the civil service in Japan to retain and consolidate its old position in government. The idealization of the scholar-bureaucrat of the Confucian tradition borrowed from China has been little affected by the growth of a more democratic style of government, and the public prestige of the civil service largely reinforces its position as an independent power centre. Political struggles in the Diet have led to constantly changing ministries, and individual ministers rarely stay in one office long enough to establish firm control of their administration. This tendency, widely marked in democratic countries with volatile political systems, leads to administrative control passing into the hands of the senior civil service, a trend reinforced in many countries by the great growth of national services requiring a high level of administrative and technical competence.

Developing nations. Less developed countries have had to face the opposite problem with their civil services. The disintegration of the great colonial empires after World War II resulted in many countries acquiring political independence before reaching administrative maturity. Few of the colonial powers had laid sufficiently long-term educational plans to allow for the rapid substitution of their own civil servants by properly trained indigenous administrators. The British left a viable administrative structure in India and a partly Indianized Indian Civil Service, but when the country was partitioned, the overwhelming majority of its members opted to serve in India, leaving the newly independent Pakistan virtually bereft of experienced civil servants. The Belgians left the Congo without any trained administrative or technical staff, and for some years the entire system of government collapsed into conditions of lawlessness and near anarchy.

Even when the old colonial powers had shown foresight, the political aspirations of the new independence movements conflicted with administrative expediency. Power was frequently transferred without the preliminary formation of a trained indigenous civil service. On the one hand, new governments wished to assert their authority rapidly and fulfill the promises made before independence in order to meet their supporters' expectations. On the other hand, expatriate civil servants feared the domination of new political masters whose political and administrative ideas might vary widely from their own. Where there were real political difficulties at the time of independence, the exodus of expatriate civil servants only worsened the situation. The serious revolt in the southern Sudan in 1955 had as one of its causes the withdrawal of British civil servants and their hasty replacement by indigenous civil servants from the north who knew neither the area nor its language. In many other countries the enrollment of an indigenous civil service led to a sharp decline in efficiency.

The lack of qualified personnel in some cases led to not only a reduction in efficiency but also to a decline in administrative morality. Nepotism, tribalism, and corruption in the civil service were difficulties often added to the other trials of independence. In many countries the incapacity of the civil service had as much to do with the introduction of military rule as had the political failings of the elected leaders. Military regimes have frequently been the last resort of a country where the civil power has failed to cope with the problems of independence. In the face of these difficulties, the United Nations (UN), in conjunction with the governments of advanced countries, began to develop training programs in public administration training and to set up special training establishments for civil servants from underdeveloped countries. The first demand came from Latin America, which led to the founding of a school of public administration in Brazil, followed in 1953 by an Advanced School of Public Administration for Central America. Similar institutions were set up with assistance in Turkey, Egypt, Ethiopia, and Tangier (Morocco). The UN and the advanced nations have set up their own training programs for overseas officials—programs frequently involving a prominent local national university —and they have also made facilities available for training in their own specialized national institutions. In addition, assistance also has been given in the form of detachment of technical experts and civil servants for temporary duty at the request of developing countries to organize or re-establish a ministry or public service. This arrangement normally requires the civil servant so transferred to train his successor in office.

Influence of Confucian tradition on Japan

UN training programs for civil servants

ORGANIZATION OF CIVIL SERVICE

Appointment. In earlier times, when civil servants were part of the king's household, they were literally the monarch's personal servants. As the powers of monarchs and princes declined and as, in some countries, their sovereignty was denied them, appointment became a matter of personal choice by ministers and heads of departments.

In all countries senior posts in the bureaucracy are regarded as having no security of tenure. The influence they may wield over policy and the need for them to work in harmony as the closest advisers of ministers means that all governments feel it necessary to have complete freedom of choice in the matter of appointment, even when, as in Great Britain, the use of this right is rare. In some countries, of which the most notable is the United States, there are extensive changes in the senior advisers whenever a new government takes office.

In Europe in the 19th century, appointment was frequently a matter of personality or political favour, but permanency and security of tenure was common in the lower and middle ranks once an appointment had been made. The favour of the minister or head of department remained necessary, however, for obtaining promotion.

This feeling of dependency on a superior's favour led the civil servants to ally themselves with liberal public opinion, which was critical of the waste and corruption involved in political patronage. The combined pressure for reform led to official formulations of basic qualifications for different posts; appointments and promotions boards were established within each department to prevent or obstruct overt political favouritism and nepotism; salary scales were introduced for different grades to provide a civil servant with increments for good service while still holding the same post. In many countries civil service commissions were set up to ensure the objectivity of entry procedures and to lay down broad principles for personnel management in the civil service. General service entries in many European countries were linked with the national educational systems so that there was a natural outlet into the civil service at each level of secondary and higher education: the highest class of civil servants entered service after graduation from a university; the executive class entered after full completion of secondary school; the clerical class entered after the intermediate school examination. The manual workers in the service were mainly recruited from among those persons of mature age who had left school after primary education or, in such countries as France and Germany, from among military veterans of long service. As public administration became more complex in the 20th century, specialized categories of civil servants were created to bring into the service specialists and professional ex-

Status of "senior servants"

Varieties of entry procedures

perts such as doctors, scientists, architects, naval constructors, statisticians, lawyers, and so on. In several countries the establishment of these special classes caused some internal difficulties in the service because their salary scales had to be linked with those of competing professional groups outside the service rather than with the scales of the administrative and executive civil servants. With only very rare exceptions, countries have always regarded their diplomatic and consular officials as forming a class apart. This distinction has been the cause of certain difficulties because there has consequently been inadequate liaison between the overseas representatives and the foreign policy makers at home. In the United States, the Rogers Act of 1924 unified the overseas service itself, but the civil servants of the State Department in Washington continued to be regarded as part of the federal civil service. There have been recommendations that the overseas and home staffs be brought under one system, but so far this has not been accomplished.

The posts that fall under the rules of the U.S. Civil Service Commission are not grouped into a small number of general classes but are minutely specified by job specifications with entry qualifications geared to them. Although designed to select entrants with special knowledge or skills for individual posts, this system has been criticized for failing to make the best use of the talent available to the government; and in 1966 the Civil Service Commission introduced the executive assignment system, the main purpose of which is to allow early identification of talent and to allow for promotion within the government service across departmental boundaries.

Competitive examinations

In all countries the nature of appointment is also linked to some kind of competitive arrangement between candidates for office. In some countries great emphasis is placed upon formal written examinations supplemented by interviews. Such is the situation in France, where entry into the higher civil service is channelled through the École Nationale d'Administration. In Great Britain, traditionally one of the great advocates of entry by formal examination, the Civil Service Commission relies more on informal tests and a series of interviews and observations and tends to measure the candidate's intellectual competence by the quality of his university degree. The written examination is dispensed with also in such European countries as Sweden, Finland, Switzerland, The Netherlands, Portugal, Denmark, and the West German *Länder*, or states, where selections for posts are made first by comparing the qualifications and references of all the candidates and then by having the most eligible interviewed by a departmental board. In the German *Länder*, for instance, the procedure is as follows: after having completed a lengthy program of academic work for professional qualification and a period of subsequent training in a variety of public institutions under official supervision, candidates are interviewed by the personnel department of each ministry and are then recommended to the minister, who makes appointments to higher grade posts, or to the heads of department, who handle the middle and lower categories. On the face of it, this method offers fewer guarantees of impartiality than does the traditional method of formal written examination, but the attractions of a civil service career are less apparent today than in the past; and the civil service has to compete, usually at lower salaries, with business and the professions for the best available talent. Civil services have therefore turned to following normal business recruiting practices. In Sweden a constitutional provision requires that all public documents be open for public inspection (except, of course, those clearly involving national security or foreign affairs), and this publicity extends to the proceedings of appointing authorities, thus providing a salutary check upon informal corruption or favouritism.

Most federal and culturally diverse countries try to ensure an equitable distribution of posts among the different parts of the country. In Switzerland the federal authorities try to maintain a balance of posts not only between the cantons but also between the political parties, religions, and languages. The federal civil service in Western Germany draws on the public service officers in the *Länder*, and some degree of proportional representation is attempted. There was an increasing pressure in Canada in the 1970s to ensure a more equitable distribution of federal civil service posts between the English- and French-speaking populations. It is also clear that many African states are compelled to recognize regional and tribal origins in their appointments to the civil service.

Conditions of service. In early times, when civil servants were members of the royal household, they had duties but no rights. The first attempts to formalize methods of appointment and conditions of service were made in Prussia in the 18th century. Elsewhere these attempts were frustrated by political and public objections. The increase in the formal regulation of conditions of service came about sometimes only when civil servants organized themselves into professional groups, in some countries barely distinguishable from trade unions. The difficulty that the countries faced was that civil servants are agents of the public power, operating in a context unique in society and providing some services on which public law, order, and health depend. Thus, it has always been a matter of controversy as to whether or not civil service organizations should be permitted to strike; if they could not lawfully strike, of course, they were deprived of the main weapon in pressing for reforms in their conditions of service. Thus, as an alternative, there developed special arrangements within the civil service to review conditions of service periodically and to mediate contentious issues—all in order to avoid situations comparable to industrial conflicts. In particular, it has been necessary to have a properly recognized system for regulating conduct and discipline. In the United Kingdom, traditional standards are supplemented or revised to accord with recommendations from periodic commissions of enquiry, which pay special attention to official conduct in relation to political activities and business dealings. In France and Germany these codes of conduct have been based mainly upon the rules of administrative law and the jurisprudence of administrative courts, although certain civil service rights and duties are specified in constitutional law. In other countries, particularly in the United States and India, conduct and discipline are regulated by administrative rules and codes promulgated after discussion and enquiry by executive order.

Codes of conduct

The restrictions upon a civil servant's conduct are partly those to be expected from any loyal, competent, and obedient employee and partly those enjoined upon him by his unique role as an agent of the public power. Ideally, he should be above any suspicion of partiality, and he should not let his personal sympathies, loyalties, or interests affect him in the performance of his duties; for example, because of the dangers to society inherent in corrupt economic practices, a civil servant is obliged to be circumspect in his private financial dealings. As a general rule, a civil servant is not allowed to engage directly or indirectly in any trade or business and is allowed to engage in social or charitable organizations only if these have no connection with his official duties. There are always strict limits on a civil servant's right to engage in speculative trades or to lend or borrow money. There is a universal rule—not always observed, however—prohibiting civil servants from accepting gifts.

There are different attitudes about the extent to which civil servants may engage in political activities. One view is that a civil servant has the same constitutional rights as other citizens and that it is therefore unconstitutional to attempt to limit these rights other than by the common law. The opposing view is that since civil servants are engaged in the unique function of national government, their integrity and loyalty to their political masters might be affected by active participation in political affairs, and public confidence in their impartiality could be shaken by too close an involvement in contentious matters. Broadly speaking, those countries that traditionally expect a civil servant to behave with complete impartiality and to conform to ministerial policy with energy and good will, whether he agrees with the policy or not, expect all civil

Political involvements of civil servants

servants to behave with circumspection in political affairs. The United Kingdom has a total ban on its senior civil servants engaging in any form of political activity. The prohibition becomes progressively less strict, however, for the medium and lower grades of the service.

Another group of countries, such as France and Germany, have deemed policy and administration to be so intimately connected that all of the most senior posts are filled at the discretion of the government of the day; thus, civil servants are allowed greater scope in political activities. They are nevertheless expected to act with greater discretion and public decorum than is necessarily the rule for a private citizen, and an excess of power or an abuse of office by a civil servant for political purposes renders him instantly liable both to statutory regulations and to severe internal disciplinary proceedings.

Traditionally, governments have been hostile toward civil service unions, and in the past repressive laws made strike action unlawful. Strikes nevertheless occurred, and governments' attitudes changed from open hostility to tolerance and from tolerance, with experience, to open encouragement. Most governments accept, in theory at least, that the state as a matter of principle should attempt to be a model employer. It follows that if it genuinely pursues a policy of discussion and negotiation with representatives of the civil service and attempts properly to fulfill all its agreements with them, it should as a counterpart be freed from the threat of strike action. Governments have also been mindful that the withdrawal of civil servants from some public services would lead to the breakdown of public security. Consequently, many governments have found it prudent to establish permanent constitutional and administrative channels through which civil service representatives can negotiate about conditions of service, salaries, discipline, promotion procedures, and job evaluation. These countries have recognized civil service organizations empowered to represent the interests of civil service staffs and have created a "management" side of senior officials to represent the state so that the negotiations can be conducted on lines similar to the employer–employee confrontation of private industry. The United Kingdom has the longest established structure of consultation and negotiation. Following a report in 1917, so-called Whitley Councils were set up, consisting of equal numbers of medium and lower staff on the one hand and directing and supervisory staffs on the other. These councils operate within the ministries, and a National Whitley Council performs central advisory functions for the government. These councils have no powers of decision, only of recommendation, because governments are never prepared to surrender their ultimate responsibility for determining the public interest. The councils have provided an invaluable source of contact, however, and they have done a good deal to provide a sense of common purpose and joint responsibility within the civil service as a whole.

In France each department has a comparable consultative body, but its work is broader in scope in that it not only acts as an advisory body but also has powers to scrutinize matters of recruitment, personnel records, promotions, and disciplinary procedures. There is also a national council that is presided over by a premier or a specially nominated minister for civil service affairs, and that is concerned with all matters of personnel policy, conditions of service, and coordination of the work of the departmental committees.

Until after World War II, the commonly accepted view in the United States was that expressed succinctly, if extremely, by Calvin Coolidge: "There is no right to strike against the public safety by anybody, anywhere, at any time." Although he was referring to striking Boston policemen, the dictum generally applied to all government employees. This opposition to any organized means of consultation, however, has lessened, and in many federal departments appeals committees comprising departmental heads and one or more members of the Civil Service Commission may now hear appeals from civil servants against decisions adversely affecting their careers. These committees also are consulted on general matters of de-

partmental interest, such as job classifications, pension schemes, promotion policies, and office procedures.

Patterns of control. Fears have arisen that civil services have become autonomous powers in their own right, no longer subject to the traditional forms of control. On the one hand, the vast increase in the powers exercised by governments has led civil servants to intrude into social, economic, and legal fields quite unimagined when present systems were first created. On the other hand, the complexity of government and the need to formulate long-term policies has greatly increased the informal power of senior civil servants acting as advisers to ministers—a particularly crucial issue in countries where ministries change hands frequently.

In the 19th century a civil service normally was restricted to a law and order and regulatory role. The subordination of civil servants to their political masters and their political masters' responsibility to the courts and the legislatures seemed to provide an adequate safeguard against arbitrary administrative actions. But in some countries, notably Germany, France, and Austria, the administrative leaders endowed their civil services with extensive social and economic powers, operated as part of the police power. These extensive powers of control caused concern because civil servants were exempt from normal legal processes when performing their official functions. For this reason special administrative courts were set up to which private citizens or corporations could appeal against administrative acts both on grounds of equity and of law. There were, however, several limitations, and redress was frequently slow. The courts themselves remained specialized institutions of the executive rather than normal parts of the judiciary.

Sweden provided a marked contrast. Not only was the absolutism of executive power swept away by the constitution of 1809 but also the legislature's control of executive action was reinforced by the creation of a special post, the ombudsman, who was an officer of the legislature, independent of both executive and judiciary, with absolute powers to inquire into the detail of any administrative or executive act and into some judicial activities reported to him by individuals as an abuse of rights. He had effective authority to prosecute civil servants and other public officers, including, on occasion, ministers themselves.

The vast increase in government activities during and after World War I raised these important issues even in countries that previously had been content to rely upon the traditional notions of control through ministerial responsibility and the normal legal processes. The range of administrative discretion greatly increased; civil servants became as much adjudicators between different social groups as they were administrators; and their influence upon economic life increased. By the beginning of World War II the state had become, even in the most conservative countries, an economic regulator, an industrial producer of overwhelming importance, and a social conciliator between competing interests. In all of these matters civil servants were the effective agents of the state.

In the United States the threatened increase in civil service power was countered by a new institution created by Congress. As early as the late 19th century, when legislating for new areas of government, Congress assigned the new powers to specialized agencies or commissions, specifying their powers, competence, and composition in the empowering and specifically freeing them from direct presidential control. In this way large areas of government escaped the control of the executive branch of government, including the federal civil service. These independent regulatory commissions covering major fields of economic importance included, for example, the Interstate Commerce Commission, the Federal Communications Commissions, the Tennessee Valley Authority, and the Atomic Energy Commission. This policy laid Congress open to the charge that it had created a headless fourth branch of government, but the move has successfully prevented the emergence of a monolithic federal civil service.

To counter charges that the U.S. civil service was en-

Unions of civil servants

Ombudsman

Regulatory agencies

croaching on the powers of the judiciary, the Administrative Procedure Act of 1946 laid down detailed provisions to safeguard the citizen's rights in matters in which the administration had powers of adjudication. These rights included the right to ample previous notice of proceedings, the right to submit evidence, the right to have independent hearing officers (to the exclusion of investigating or prosecuting officers), and the right to a decision based solely on testimony and papers actually entered in the proceedings.

Other democratic countries have been concerned about the growing powers of the civil service and about whether or not traditional forms of judicial control and ministerial control are adequate to cope with these new powers. Many European countries have modelled their forms of administrative jurisdiction and administrative jurisprudence on the structure and precedents of the French Conseil d'État (Council of State), regarded as the leading administrative court in Europe. In the United Kingdom the creation of a special administrative jurisdiction of this kind was opposed by both parliamentary and judicial opinion, but in the face of mounting criticism against the immunity of the civil service from detailed control, Parliament created the special office of parliamentary commissioner to inquire into allegations of maladministration. This new office was modelled largely on that of the Swedish ombudsman, but with lesser powers. Public access to his office is by way of a member of Parliament, and the commissioner is excluded from inquiring into matters of policy and the affairs of local government authorities or the operations of lower judicial bodies. Offices similar to that of the Swedish ombudsman have been created in the other Scandinavian countries, in Western Germany (where the office is primarily concerned with military affairs), in New Zealand, and in a growing number of newly independent states.

Communist controls over the civil service Special problems of control have arisen in Communist countries. In the U.S.S.R. the government's main preoccupation has been to ensure the civil service's continual loyalty to the regime and to the party leadership. It has had much less concern with ensuring its impartiality and objectivity in its dealings with the public. A body of administrative procedure has been built up, but this has always been subordinated to the political directives of the party leadership. The U.S.S.R., as well as other Communist countries, has also had to contend with establishing criteria of performance in conditions of total state monopoly when traditional incentives have been largely discounted.

Countries modelled on the Soviet system of government have tended to create elaborate series of controls. In the U.S.S.R. all ministries have a special section staffed by, and responsible to, the Ministry of Internal Affairs. This section provides security control over civil servants and the work of the ministry, and its personnel are not part of the ministry's official structure. The Communist Party maintains further control through its own network of party members and the internal party apparatus, and it maintains close supervision over senior appointments and promotions.

The Soviet system of government has planning, financial, and personnel controls of a technical kind comparable to those in democratic countries, but in addition there are two special supervisory agencies. The Commission of State Control is responsible for maintaining strict control of state property and administration. The ministry provides the Communist Party with an important check on the honesty and efficiency of civil servants and other public officials. Its internal departments parallel the different branches of state administration and maintain audits of their work. Its officers have the right of access to all administrative records and can issue directives to other institutions. They have powers to prosecute civil servants before the courts for criminal offences, and they can apply a formidable range of disciplinary measures on civil servants, either by direct action or through the responsible minister.

A second type of special control arose because of the difficulty of reconciling industrial differences between production units and their controlling ministries in an economy that lacks the traditional forms of market discipline and cannot rely upon an enforceable law of contract. A special system of compulsory arbitration, therefore, came into being, operated under the general planning directorate known as Gosarbitrazh, and it is required to deal with all disputes concerning the contracts, the quality of goods, and other property disputes between various state enterprises. The system is operated by civil servants charged with enforcing "contractual and plan discipline," but it is supported by technical experts qualified in economic and industrial matters. (B.Ch.)

INTERNATIONAL CIVIL SERVICE

The elements of an international civil service were first found in the Universal Postal Union (established 1874–75). The League of Nations and the International Labour Organization (ILO) required a staff of almost 600 experts and subordinate personnel that took the form of a true international civil service. It drew mainly on British, French, and Swiss sources, but more than 40 states contributed members in response to the requirement that the staff should be recruited on as wide a geographical basis as possible. There were no formal methods of selection for the higher personnel; the secretary general of the League depended on personal acquaintanceship and trustworthy recommendations. The staff fell into three divisions: administrative, supervisory and clerical, and custodial. The main point of interest in an international civil service lies perhaps in the steps it takes to free itself from national loyalties. The League existed during a period of rampant nationalism and irreconcilable conflict, but its experience showed that a broad measure of international loyalty could be achieved, even under difficult conditions. The staff of the League was dispersed after 1939, but that of the ILO was maintained.

A much larger international civil service was required for the United Nations and the specialized agencies. In the United Nations Charter, each member state undertook to respect the international character of the duties of the staff and to refrain from influencing them in their work. The staff of the UN Secretariat is recruited on a merit basis, with regard, however, to equitable geographical distribution. Members of the organization are required to take an oath of loyalty to the United Nations and are not permitted to receive instructions from member governments.

International secretariats are also provided for such other organizations as the Organization for Economic Co-operation and Development. Officials and employees of such organizations are paid from the funds of each of these organizations and are assigned duties by its head. They are subject to its discipline and owe it full responsibility. (E.B.)

BIBLIOGRAPHY. There are few general comparative studies on civil services. The important comparative works in the prewar period are H. FINER, *Theory and Practice of Modern Government*, rev. ed. (1949); ERNEST BARKER, *The Development of Public Services in Western Europe, 1660–1930* (1944); L.D. WHITE (ed.), *The Civil Service in the Modern State* (1930), and *The Civil Service Abroad* (1935). Two postwar comparative studies are P. MEYER, *The Administrative State* (1958); and BRIAN CHAPMAN, *The Profession of Government* (1959). The two classic works that established the modern theory of the relations between civil servants and the state are R. GNEIST, *Der Rechtsstaat* (1872); and L. DUGUIT, *Les transformations du droit public* (1913).

European countries with long traditions of civil service government have very considerable bibliographies on various aspects of public administration. For general surveys of the civil service in individual countries the following are of the greatest general interest: F. WALTER, *Die oesterreichische Zentralverwaltung* (1950); H. PETERS, *Lehrbuch der Verwaltung* (1949); R. GREGOIRE, *La fonction publique* (1954); G. HESSLEN, *Public Administration in Sweden*, rev. ed. (1965); and W.J.M. MACKENZIE and J.W. GROVE, *Central Administration in Britain* (1957). The special aspect of control of the civil service is best understood through the two most interesting institutions, and these are dealt with by D.C. ROWAT (ed.), *The Ombudsman: Citizen's Defender* (1965); and M. MARTIN, *Le Conseil d'État* (1945). The political background to the struggle for civil servants' rights may be traced through P.D. HUGUES, *La guerre des fonctionnaires* (1912); and O. RANELLETTI, *Il sindicalismo nella Pubblica Amministrazione* (1927).

The overall pattern of the federal civil service and administration in the United States is dealt with in E.S. CORWIN, *The President: Office and Powers, 1787–1957*, 4th rev. ed. (1957); and M.H. BERNSTEIN, *The Role of the Federal Executive* (1958). The special problem of the United States diplomatic service was the subject of a special enquiry by the COMMITTEE ON FOREIGN AFFAIRS PERSONNEL in a report *Personnel for the New Diplomacy* (1962); the relations between the civil service and Congress are studied in depth in JOSEPH HARRIS, *Congressional Control of Administration* (1964).

General studies on the organization of executive power in communist countries are H.G. SKILLING, *The Governments of Communist Eastern Europe* (1966); and G. IONESCU, *The Politics of the European Communist States* (1967). A detailed study of the organization of authority in the U.S.S.R. may be found in M. TATU, *Power in the Kremlin* (Eng. trans. 1969); this is contrasted with Chinese theory and practice in D.W. TREADGOLD (ed.), *Soviet and Chinese Communism: Similarities and Differences* (1967). The internal organization and structure of government in China itself may be found in H.F. SCHURMANN, *Ideology and Organization in Communist China* (1966); and A.D. BARNETT, *Cadres, Bureaucracy, and Political Power in Communist China* (1967).

The special problems of civil services in new states were outlined in K.G. YOUNGER, *The Public Service in New States* (1960); and in A.L. ADU, *The Civil Service in New African States* (1965). Interesting comparative, theoretical, and institutional studies on a broad front are found in R.J.D. BRAIBANTI (ed.), *Asian Bureaucratic Systems Emergent from the British Imperial Tradition* (1966); J.D. MONTGOMERY and W.J. SIFFIN (eds.), *Approaches to Development: Politics, Administration and Change* (1966); and G. LA PALOMBARA (ed.), *Bureaucracy and Political Development* (1963).

(B.Ch.)

Civil War, U.S.

The American Civil War was a fratricidal four-year conflict between the United States federal government and the Confederate States of America, 11 Southern states that claimed their right to leave the Union.

The flash and dull roar of a ten-inch mortar on April 12, 1861, announced to a startled world the opening of the American Civil War. After a 34-hour bloodless bombardment, Robert Anderson, in command of a Federal garrison of about 85 soldiers, surrendered Ft. Sumter in the harbour of Charleston, South Carolina, to some 5,500 besieging Confederate troops under P.G.T. Beauregard.

Surrender of Ft. Sumter

With war upon the land, Union president Abraham Lincoln called for 75,000 three-month militiamen. He proclaimed a naval blockade of the Confederate States of America, directed the Secretary of the Treasury to advance $2,000,000 to assist in raising troops, and suspended the right of habeas corpus. The Confederate government had previously authorized a call for 100,000 soldiers for at least six months' service, and this figure was soon increased to 400,000.

This article deals with the military aspects of the United States Civil War. For a discussion of the issues that underlay the war, see UNITED STATES, HISTORY OF THE.

THE BACKGROUND OF THE WAR AND GENERAL CONSIDERATIONS

Comparison of North and South. At first glance it seemed that the 23 states of the Union were more than a match for the 11 seceding Southern states—South Carolina, Mississippi, Florida, Alabama, Georgia, Louisiana, Texas, Virginia, Arkansas, Tennessee, and North Carolina. There were approximately 21,000,000 people in the North compared with some 9,000,000 in the South (of whom about 3,500,000 were Negro slaves). In addition, the Federals possessed over 100,000 manufacturing plants as against 18,000 south of the Potomac River, and more than 70 percent of the railroads were in the North. Furthermore, the Union had at its command a 30-to-1 superiority in arms production, a 2-to-1 edge in available manpower, and a great preponderance in commercial and financial resources. It had a functioning government and a small but efficient regular army and navy.

But the Confederacy was not predestined to defeat. The Southern armies had the advantage of fighting on interior lines, and their military tradition had bulked large in the history of the United States before 1860. Moreover, the long Confederate coastline of 3,500 miles (5,600 kilometres) seemed to defy blockade; and the Confederate president, Jefferson Davis, hoped to receive decisive foreign aid and intervention. Finally, the gray-clad Southern soldiers were fighting for the intangible but strong objectives of home and white supremacy. So the Southern cause was not a lost one; indeed, other nations had won independence against equally heavy odds.

The high commands. Command problems plagued both sides. Of the two rival commanders in chief, most people in 1861 thought Davis to be abler than Lincoln. Davis was a West Point graduate, a hero of the Mexican War, a capable secretary of war under Pres. Franklin Pierce, and a United States senator from Mississippi; whereas Lincoln—who had served in the Illinois state legislature and as an undistinguished one-term member of the U.S. House of Representatives—could boast of only a brief period of military service in the Black Hawk War, in which he did not do well.

Performances of Davis and Lincoln

As president and commander in chief of the Confederate forces, Davis revealed many fine qualities, including patience, courage, dignity, restraint, firmness, energy, determination, and honesty; but he was flawed by his excessive pride, hypersensitivity to criticism, and his inability to delegate minor details to his subordinates. To a large extent Davis was his own secretary of war, although five different men served in that post during the lifetime of the Confederacy. Davis himself also filled the position of general in chief of the Confederate armies until he named Robert E. Lee to that position on February 6, 1865, when the Confederacy was near collapse. In naval affairs—an area about which he knew little—the Confederate president seldom intervened directly, allowing the competent secretary of the navy, Stephen Mallory, to handle the Southern naval buildup and operations on the water. Although his position was onerous and perhaps could not have been filled so well by any other Southern political leader, Davis' overall performance in office left something to be desired.

To the astonishment of many, Lincoln grew in stature with time and experience, and by 1864 he had become a consummate war director. But he had much to learn at first, especially in strategic and tactical matters and in his choices of army commanders. With an ineffective first secretary of war—Simon Cameron—Lincoln unhesitatingly insinuated himself directly into the planning of military movements. Edwin M. Stanton, appointed to the secretaryship on January 20, 1862, was equally untutored in military affairs, and he was fully as active a participant as his superior.

Winfield Scott was the Federal general in chief when Lincoln took office. The 75-year-old Scott—a hero of the War of 1812 and of the Mexican War—was a magnificent and distinguished soldier whose mind was still keen in 1861. But he was physically incapacitated and had to be retired from the service on November 1, 1861. Scott was replaced by young George B. McClellan, an able and imaginative general in chief but one who had difficulty in establishing harmonious and effective relations with Lincoln. Because of this and because he had to campaign with his own Army of the Potomac, McClellan was relieved as general in chief on March 11, 1862. He was eventually succeeded on July 11 by the inept Henry W. Halleck, who held the position until replaced by Ulysses S. Grant on March 9, 1864. Halleck then became chief of staff under Grant in a long-needed streamlining of the Federal high command. Grant served efficaciously as general in chief throughout the remainder of the war.

After the initial call by Lincoln and Davis for troops and as the war lengthened indeterminately, both sides turned to raising massive armies of volunteers. Local citizens of prominence and means would organize regiments that were uniformed and accoutred at first under the aegis of the states and then mustered into the service of the Union and Confederate governments. As the war

Recruitment of troops

dragged on, the two governments had to resort to conscription to fill the ranks being so swiftly thinned by battle casualties.

Strategic plans. In the area of grand strategy, Davis persistently adhered to the defensive, permitting only occasional "spoiling" forays into Northern territory. Yet perhaps the Confederates' best chance of winning would have been an early grand offensive into the Union states before the Lincoln administration could find its ablest generals and bring the preponderant resources of the North to bear against the South.

Lincoln, on the other hand, in order to crush the rebellion and re-establish the authority of the Federal government, had to direct his blue-clad armies to invade, capture, and hold most of the vital areas of the Confederacy. His grand strategy was based on Scott's so-called Anaconda plan, a design that evolved from strategic ideas discussed in messages between Scott and McClellan on April 27, May 3, and May 21, 1861. It called for a Union blockade of the Confederacy's littoral as well as a decisive thrust down the Mississippi River and an ensuing strangulation of the South by Federal land and naval forces. But it was to take four years of grim, unrelenting warfare and enormous casualties and devastation before the Confederates could be defeated and the Union preserved.

THE LAND WAR

The war in 1861. The first military operations took place in northwestern Virginia, where non-slaveholding pro-Unionists sought to secede from the Confederacy. McClellan, in command of Federal forces in southern Ohio, advanced on his own initiative in the early summer of 1861 into western Virginia with about 20,000 men. He encountered smaller forces sent there by Lee, then in Richmond in command of all Virginia troops. Although showing signs of occasional hesitation, McClellan quickly won three small but significant battles: at Philippi on June 3, at Rich Mountain on July 11 (where some 553 Confederates were captured), and at Carrick's Ford on July 13. McClellan's casualties were light, and his victories went far toward eliminating Confederate resistance in northwestern Virginia and paving the way for the admittance into the Union of the new state of West Virginia in 1863.

Meanwhile, sizable armies were gathering around the Federal capital of Washington, D.C., and the Confederate capital of Richmond, Virginia. Federal forces abandoned Harpers Ferry on April 18, and it was quickly occupied by Southern forces, who held it for a time. The Federal naval base at Norfolk fell into enemy hands on April 20. On May 6 Lee ordered a Confederate force— soon to be commanded by Beauregard—northward to hold the rail hub of Manassas Junction, some 26 miles (42 kilometres) southwest of Washington. With Lincoln's approval, Scott appointed Irvin McDowell to command the main Federal army, being hastily collected near Washington. But political pressure and Northern public opinion impelled Lincoln, against Scott's advice, to order McDowell's still-untrained army forward to push the enemy back from Manassas. Meanwhile, Federal forces were to hold Confederate soldiers under Joseph E. Johnston in the Shenandoah Valley near Winchester, thus preventing them from reinforcing Beauregard along the Bull Run near Manassas.

McDowell advanced from Washington on July 16 with nearly 35,000 men and moved slowly toward Bull Run. Two days were spent in reconnaissances, and when McDowell finally attacked on July 21 in the First Battle of Bull Run (or Manassas), he discovered that Johnston had escaped the Federals in the Valley and had joined Beauregard near Manassas just in time, bringing the total Confederate force to around 32,000. McDowell's sharp attacks with green troops forced the equally untrained Southerners back a bit, but a strong defensive stand by Jackson (who thereby gained the nickname "Stonewall") enabled the Confederates to check and finally throw back the Federals that afternoon. The Federal retreat to Washington soon became a rout. McDowell lost 2,708

First Bull Run (margin)

men—killed, wounded, and missing (including prisoners) —against a Southern loss of 1,981. Both sides now settled down to a long war and began to make elaborate preparations.

The war in the East in 1862. Fresh from his victories in western Virginia, McClellan was called to Washington to replace Scott. There he began to mold the Army of the Potomac into a resolute, effective shield and sword of the Union. But personality clashes and unrelenting opposition to McClellan from the Radical Republicans in Congress hampered the sometimes tactless, conservative, Democratic general. It took time to drill, discipline, and equip this force of considerably more than 100,000 men, but as fall blended into winter loud demands arose that McClellan advance against Johnston's Confederate forces at Centreville and Manassas. McClellan, however, fell seriously ill with typhoid fever in December, and when he had recovered weeks later he found that Lincoln, desperately eager for action, had ordered him to advance on February 22, 1862. Long debates ensued between President and Commander. When in March McClellan finally began his Peninsular Campaign, he discovered that Lincoln and Stanton had withheld large numbers of his command in front of Washington for the defense of the capital—forces that were actually not needed there. Upon taking command of the army in the field, McClellan was relieved of the duties of general in chief.

The Peninsular Campaign. Advancing up the historic peninsula between the York and James rivers, McClellan began a month-long siege of Yorktown and captured that stronghold on May 4, 1862. A Confederate rearguard action at Williamsburg the next day delayed the blue-clads, who then slowly moved up through heavy rain to within four miles of Richmond. Striving to seize the initiative, Johnston attacked McClellan's left wing at Seven Pines (Fair Oaks) on May 31 and, after scoring initial gains, was checked; Johnston was severely wounded, and Lee, who had been serving as Davis' military adviser, succeeded Johnston in command of the Army of Northern Virginia. McClellan counterattacked on June 1 and forced the Southerners back into the environs of Richmond. The Federals suffered a total of 5,031 casualties out of a force of nearly 100,000, while the Confederates lost 6,134 of 74,000 men.

Federal threat to Richmond (margin)

As McClellan inched forward toward Richmond in June, Lee prepared a counterstroke. He recalled from the Shenandoah Valley Jackson's forces—which had threatened Harpers Ferry and had brilliantly defeated several scattered Federal armies—and, with about 90,000 soldiers, attacked McClellan on June 26 to begin the fighting of the Seven Days' Battles (usually dated June 25–July 1). In the ensuing days at Mechanicsville, Gaines's Mill, Savage's Station, Frayser's Farm (Glendale), and Malvern Hill, Lee tried unsuccessfully to crush the Army of the Potomac, which McClellan was moving to another base on the James River; but the Confederate chieftain had at least saved Richmond. McClellan inflicted 20,614 casualties on Lee while suffering 15,849 himself. McClellan felt he could not move upon Richmond without considerable reinforcement, and against his protests his army was withdrawn from the peninsula to Washington by Lincoln and the new general in chief, Halleck. Many of McClellan's units were given to a new Federal Army commander, John Pope, who was directed to move overland against Richmond.

Second Battle of Bull Run (Manassas) and Antietam. Pope advanced confidently toward the Rappahannock River, while Lee, once McClellan had been pulled back from near Richmond, moved northward to confront Pope before the latter could be joined by all of McClellan's troops. Daringly splitting his army, Lee sent Jackson to destroy Pope's base at Manassas, while he himself advanced via another route with James Longstreet's half of the army. Pope opened the Second Battle of Bull Run on August 29 with heavy but futile attacks on Jackson. The next day Lee arrived and crushed the Federal left with a massive flank assault by Longstreet, which, combined with Jackson's counterattacks, drove the Northerners back in rout upon Washington. Pope lost 16,054 men out of a force of more than 70,000, while Lee lost 9,197 out of some 55,000. With the Federal soldiers now lacking confidence in Pope, Lincoln courageously reinstated McClellan to the command of the Army of the Potomac.

Lee's first invasion of the North

Lee followed up his advantage with his first invasion of the North, pushing as far as Frederick, Maryland. McClellan had to reorganize on the march, a task that he performed capably. But he was beset by contradictory orders: Lincoln urged him to pursue Lee more swiftly; Halleck directed him to slow down and to stay closer to Washington. Biding his time, McClellan pressed forward and wrested the initiative from Lee by attacking and defeating a Confederate force at three gaps of the South Mountain between Frederick and Hagerstown on September 14. Lee fell back into a cramped position along the Antietam Creek, near Sharpsburg, Maryland. After a delay, McClellan struck the Confederates on September 17 in the bloodiest single-day's battle of the war. Although gaining some ground, the Federals were unable to drive the Confederate Army into the Potomac; but Lee was compelled to retreat back into Virginia. At Antietam, McClellan lost 12,410 of some 69,000 engaged, while Lee lost 13,724 of 52,000 effectives. When McClellan was unable to pursue Lee as quickly as Lincoln and Halleck thought he should, he was replaced in command by Ambrose E. Burnside, who had been an ineffective corps commander at Antietam.

Fredericksburg. Burnside delayed for a number of weeks before marching his reinforced army of 120,281 men to a point across the Rappahannock River from Fredericksburg, Virginia. On December 13 he ordered a series of 16 hopeless, piecemeal, frontal assaults across open ground against Lee's army of 78,513 troops, drawn up in an impregnable position atop high ground and behind a stone wall; the Federals were repelled with staggering losses. Burnside had lost 12,653 men, compared to Lee's 5,309. The plunging Federal morale was reflected in an increasing number of desertions. Therefore, on January 25, 1863, Lincoln replaced Burnside with a proficient corps commander, Joseph ("Fighting Joe") Hooker, who was a harsh critic of other generals and even of the President. Both armies went into winter quarters near Fredericksburg.

The war in the West in 1862. Military events, meanwhile, were transpiring in other arenas.

Trans-Mississippi theatre and Missouri. In the Trans-Mississippi theatre covetous Confederate eyes were cast on California, where ports for privateers could be seized, as could gold and silver to buttress a sagging treasury. Led by Henry Sibley, a Confederate force of some 2,600 invaded the Union's Department of New Mexico, where the Federal commander, Edward Canby, had but 3,810 men to defend the entire vast territory. Although plagued by pneumonia and smallpox, Sibley bettered a Federal force on February 21, 1862, at Valverde and captured Albuquerque and Sante Fe on March 23. But at the crucial engagement of La Glorieta Pass (known also as Apache Canyon, Johnson's Ranch, or Pigeon's Ranch) a few days later, Sibley was checked and lost most of his wagon train. He had to retreat into Texas, where he reached safety in April but with only 900 men and seven of 337 supply wagons left.

Fighting in New Mexico

Farther eastward, in the more vital Mississippi Valley, operations were unfolding as large and as important as those on the Atlantic seaboard. Commanders there—especially on the Federal side—had greater autonomy than those in Virginia. Missouri and Kentucky were key border states that Lincoln had to retain within the Union orbit. Affairs began inauspiciously for the Federals in Missouri when Federal general Nathaniel Lyon's 5,000 troops were defeated at Wilson's Creek on August 10, 1861, by a Confederate force of more than 10,000 under Sterling Price and Benjamin McCulloch, each side losing some 1,200 men. But the Federals under Samuel Curtis decisively set back a gray-clad army under Earl Van Dorn at Pea Ridge (Elkhorn Tavern), Arkansas, on March 7–8, 1862, saving Missouri for the Union and threatening Arkansas.

SEVEN DAY'S BATTLES (1862)
1. Mechanicsville, June 26
2. Gaines's Mill, June 27
3. Savage's Station, June 29
4. Frayser's Farm (Glendale), June 30
5. Malvern Hill, July 1

† Federal victories
× Confederate victories
✕ Indecisive battles

The main area of the eastern campaigns, 1861–65.

Operations in Kentucky and Tennessee. The Confederates to the east of Missouri had established a unified command under Albert Sidney Johnston, who manned, with only 40,000 men, a long line running in Kentucky from near Cumberland Gap on the east through Bowling Green, to Columbus on the Mississippi. Numerically superior Federal forces cracked this line in early 1862. First, George H. Thomas smashed Johnston's right flank at Mill Springs (Somerset), Kentucky, on January 19. Then, in February, Grant, assisted by Federal gunboats commanded by Andrew H. Foote and acting under Halleck's orders, ruptured the centre of the Southern line in Kentucky by capturing Ft. Henry on the Tennessee River and Fort Donelson, 11 miles (18 kilometres) to the east on the Cumberland River. The Confederates suffered more than 16,000 casualties at the latter stronghold—most of them taken prisoner—as against Federal losses of less than 3,000. Johnston's left anchor fell when Pope seized New Madrid and Island Number Ten in the Mississippi in March and April. This forced Johnston to withdraw his remnants quickly from Kentucky through Tennessee and to reorganize them for a counterstroke. This seemingly impossible task he performed splendidly.

The Confederate onslaught came at Shiloh, Tennessee, near Pittsburg Landing, to which point on the west bank of the Tennessee River Grant and William T. Sherman had incautiously advanced. In a herculean effort, Johnston had pulled his forces together and, with 40,000 men, suddenly struck a like number of unsuspecting Federals on April 6. Johnston hoped to crush Grant before the arrival of Don Carlos Buell's 20,000 Federal troops, approaching from Nashville. A desperate combat ensued, with Confederate assaults driving the Unionists perilously close to the river. But at the height of success, Johnston was mortally wounded; the Southern attack then lost momentum, and Grant held on until reinforced by Buell. On the following day the Federals counterattacked and drove the Confederates, now under Beauregard, steadily from the field, forcing them to fall back to Corinth, in northern Mississippi. Grant's victory cost him 13,047 casualties, compared to Southern losses of 10,694. Halleck then assumed personal command of the combined forces of Grant, Buell, and Pope and inched forward to Corinth, which the Confederates evacuated on May 30.

Beauregard, never popular with Davis, was superseded by Braxton Bragg, one of the President's favourites. Bragg was an effective drillmaster and organizer; but he was also a martinet who was disliked by a number of his principal subordinates. Leaving 22,000 men in Mississippi under Price and Van Dorn, Bragg moved through Chattanooga with 30,000, hoping to reconquer Tennessee and carry the war into Kentucky. Some 18,000 other Confederate soldiers under Edmund Kirby Smith were at Knoxville. Buell led his Federal force northward to save Louisville and force Bragg to fight. Occupying Frankfort, Bragg failed to move promptly against Louisville. In the ensuing Battle of Perryville on October 8, Bragg, after an early advantage, was halted by Buell and impelled to fall back to a point south of Nashville. Meanwhile, the Federal general William S. Rosecrans had checked Price and Van Dorn at Iuka on September 19 and had repelled their attack on Corinth on October 3–4.

Buell—like McClellan a cautious, conservative, Democratic general—was, despite his success at Perryville, relieved of his command by Lincoln on October 24. His successor, Rosecrans, had to safeguard Nashville and to move southeastward against Bragg's army at Murfreesboro. He did so, with partial success, bringing on the bloody Battle of Stones River (or Murfreesboro, December 31, 1862–January 2, 1863). Again, after first having the better of the combat, Bragg was finally contained and forced to retreat. Of some 41,400 men, Rosecrans lost 12,906, while Bragg suffered 11,739 casualties out of about 34,700 effectives. Although it was a strategic victory for Rosecrans, his army was so shaken that he felt unable to advance again for five months, despite the urgings of Lincoln and Halleck.

The war in the East in 1863. In the East, after both armies had spent the winter in camp, the arrival of the active 1863 campaign season was eagerly awaited—especially by Hooker. "Fighting Joe" had capably reorganized and refitted his army, the morale of which was high once again. This massive host numbered around 132,000—the largest formed during the war—and was termed by Hooker "the finest army on the planet." It was opposed by Lee with about 62,000. Hooker decided to move most of his army up the Rappahannock, cross, and come in upon the Confederate rear at Fredericksburg, while John Sedgwick's smaller force would press Lee in front.

Chancellorsville. Beginning his turning movement on April 27, 1863, Hooker masterfully swung around toward the west of the Confederate Army; thus far he had apparently outmanoeuvred Lee. But Hooker was astonished on May 1 when the Confederate commander suddenly moved the bulk of his army directly against him. "Fighting Joe" lost his nerve and pulled back to Chancellorsville in the Wilderness, where the superior Federal artillery could not be used effectively.

Lee followed up on May 2 by sending Jackson on a brilliant flanking movement against Hooker's exposed right flank. Bursting like a thunderbolt upon Oliver O. Howard's 11th Corps late in the afternoon, Jackson crushed this wing; while continuing his advance, Jackson was accidentally and fatally wounded by his own men. This helped stall the Confederate advance. Lee then resumed the attack on the morning of May 3 and slowly pushed Hooker back; the latter was wounded by Southern artillery fire. That afternoon Sedgwick drove Jubal Early's Southerners from Marye's Heights at Fredericksburg, but Lee countermarched his weary troops, fell upon Sedgwick at Salem Church, and forced him back to the north bank of the Rappahannock. Lee then returned to Chancellorsville to resume the main engagement; but Hooker, though he had 37,000 fresh troops available, gave up the contest on May 5 and retreated across the river to his old position opposite Fredericksburg. The Federals suffered 17,278 casualties at Chancellorsville, while the Confederates lost 12,764.

Gettysburg. While both armies were licking their wounds and reorganizing, Hooker, Lincoln, and Halleck debated Union strategy. They were thus engaged when Lee launched his second invasion of the North on June 5, 1863. His advance elements moved down the Shenandoah Valley toward Harpers Ferry, brushing aside small Federal forces near Winchester. Marching through Maryland into Pennsylvania, the Confederates reached Chambersburg and turned eastward. They occupied York and menaced Carlisle and Harrisburg. Meanwhile, the dashing Confederate cavalryman, J.E.B. ("Jeb") Stuart, set off on a questionable ride around the Federal Army and was unable to join Lee's main army until the second day at Gettysburg.

Hooker—on unfriendly terms with Lincoln and especially Halleck—ably moved the Federal forces northward, keeping between Lee's army and Washington. Reaching Frederick, Hooker requested that the nearly 10,000-man Federal garrison at Harpers Ferry be added to his field army. When Halleck refused, Hooker resigned his command and was succeeded by George Gordon Meade, the commander of the Fifth Corps. Meade was granted a greater degree of freedom of movement than Hooker had enjoyed, and he carefully felt his way northward, looking for the enemy.

Learning to his surprise on June 28 that the Federal Army was north of the Potomac, Lee hastened to concentrate his far-flung legions. Hostile forces came together unexpectedly at the important crossroads town of Gettysburg, in southern Pennsylvania, bringing on the greatest battle ever fought in the Western Hemisphere. Attacking on July 1 from the west and north with 28,000 men, Confederate forces finally prevailed after nine hours of desperate fighting against 18,000 Federal soldiers under John F. Reynolds. When Reynolds was killed, Abner Doubleday ably handled the outnumbered Federal troops, and only the sheer weight of Confederate numbers forced him back through the streets of Gettysburg to strategic Cemetery Ridge south of town, where Meade assembled the rest of the army that night.

Margin notes:

The Battle of Shiloh

The largest army of the war

Lee's second invasion of the North

On the second day of battle Meade's 88,289 troops were ensconced in a strong, fishhook-shaped defensive position, running northward from the Round Tops hills along Cemetery Ridge and thence eastward to Culp's Hill. Lee, with 75,000 troops, ordered Longstreet to attack the Federals diagonally from Little Round Top northward and Richard S. Ewell to assail Cemetery Hill and Culp's Hill. The Confederate attack, coming in the late afternoon and evening, saw Longstreet capture the positions known as the Peach Orchard, Wheat Field, and Devil's Den on the Federal left in furious fighting but fail to seize the vital Little Round Top. Ewell's later assaults on Cemetery Hill failed, and he could capture only a part of Culp's Hill.

On the morning of the third day, Meade's right wing drove the Confederates from the lower slopes of Culp's Hill and checked Stuart's cavalry sweep to the east of Gettysburg in midafternoon. Then, in what has been called the greatest infantry charge of history, Lee—against Longstreet's advice—hurled 15,000 soldiers, under the immediate command of George E. Pickett, against the centre of Meade's lines on Cemetery Ridge, following a fearful artillery duel of two hours. Despite heroic efforts, only several hundred Southerners temporarily cracked the Federal centre at the so-called High-Water Mark; the rest were shot down by Federal cannoneers and musketrymen, captured, or thrown back, suffering casualties of almost 60 percent. Meade felt unable to counterattack, and Lee conducted an adroit retreat into Virginia. The Confederates had lost 28,063 men at Gettysburg, the Federals, 23,049. After indecisive manoeuvring and light actions in northern Virginia in the fall of 1863, the two armies went into winter quarters. Never again was Lee able to mount a full-scale invasion of the North with his entire army.

The war in the West in 1863. *Arkansas and Vicksburg.* In Arkansas, Federal troops under Frederick Steele moved upon the Confederates and defeated them at Prairie Grove, near Fayetteville, on December 7, 1862—a victory that paved the way for Steele's eventual capture of Little Rock the next September.

More importantly, Grant, back in good graces following his undistinguished performance at Shiloh, was authorized to move against the Confederate "Gibraltar of the West"—Vicksburg, Mississippi. This bastion was difficult to approach; Adm. David G. Farragut, Grant, and Sherman had failed to capture it in 1862. In the early months of 1863, in the so-called Bayou Expeditions, Grant was again frustrated in his efforts to get at Vicksburg from the north. Finally, escorted by Adm. David Dixon Porter's gunboats, which ran the Confederate batteries at Vicksburg, Grant landed his army to the south at Bruinsburg on April 30, 1863, and pressed northeastward. He won small but sharp actions at Port Gibson, Raymond, and Jackson, while the Confederate defender of Vicksburg, John C. Pemberton, was unable to link up with a smaller Southern force under Joseph E. Johnston near Jackson.

Turning due westward toward the rear of Vicksburg's defenses, Grant smashed Pemberton's army at Champion's Hill and the Big Black River and invested the fortress. During his 47-day siege, Grant eventually had an army of 71,000; Pemberton's command numbered 31,000, of whom 18,500 were effectives. After a courageous stand, the outnumbered Confederates were forced to capitulate on July 4. Five days later, 6,000 Confederates yielded to Nathaniel P. Banks at Port Hudson, Louisiana, to the south of Vicksburg, and Lincoln could say, in relief, "The Father of Waters again goes unvexed to the sea."

Chickamauga and Chattanooga. Meanwhile, 60,000 Federal soldiers under Rosecrans sought to move out from central Tennessee against the important Confederate rail and industrial centre of Chattanooga in the southeastern corner of the state, then held by Bragg with some 43,000 troops. In a series of brilliantly conceived movements, Rosecrans manoeuvred Bragg out of Chattanooga without having to fight a battle. Bragg was then bolstered by Longstreet's veteran corps, sent swiftly by rail from

Lee's army in Virginia. With this reinforcement, Bragg turned on Rosecrans and, in a vicious two-day battle (September 19–20) at Chickamauga Creek, Georgia, just southeast of Chattanooga, gained one of the few Confederate victories in the West. Bragg lost 18,454 of his 66,326 men; Rosecrans, 16,170 out of 53,919 engaged. Rosecrans fell back into Chattanooga, where he was almost encircled by Bragg.

But the Southern success was short-lived. Instead of pressing the siege of Chattanooga, Bragg sent Longstreet off in a futile attempt to capture Knoxville, then being held by Burnside. When Rosecrans showed signs of disintegration, Lincoln replaced him with Grant and strengthened the hard-pressed Federal Army at Chattanooga by sending, by rail, the remnants of the Army of the Potomac's 11th and 12th Corps, under Hooker's command. Outnumbering Bragg now 56,359 to 46,165, Grant attacked on November 23–25, capturing Lookout Mountain and Missionary Ridge, defeating Bragg's army and driving it southward toward Dalton, Georgia. Grant sustained 5,824 casualties at Chattanooga and Bragg, 6,667. Confidence having been lost in Bragg by most of his top generals, Davis replaced him with Joseph E. Johnston. Both armies remained quiescent until the following spring.

The war in 1864–65. Finally dissatisfied with Halleck as general in chief and impressed with Grant's victories, Lincoln appointed Grant to supersede Halleck and to assume the rank of lieutenant general, which Congress had re-created. Leaving Sherman in command in the West, Grant arrived in Washington on March 8, 1864. He was given largely a free hand in developing his grand strategy. He retained Meade in technical command of the Army of the Potomac but in effect assumed direct control of it by establishing his own headquarters with it. He sought to move this army against Lee in northern Virginia while Sherman marched against Johnston and Atlanta. Several lesser Federal armies were also to advance in May.

Grant's overland campaign. Grant surged across the Rapidan and Rappahannock rivers on May 4, hoping to get through the tangled Wilderness before Lee could move. But the Confederate leader reacted instantly and, on May 5, attacked Grant from the west in the Battle of the Wilderness. Two days of bitter, indecisive combat ensued. Although Grant had 115,000 men available against Lee's 62,000, he found both Federal flanks endangered. Moreover, Grant lost 17,666 soldiers compared to a probable Southern loss of about 8,000. Pulling away from the Wilderness battlefield, Grant tried to hasten southeastward to the crossroads point of Spotsylvania Courthouse, only to have the Confederates get there first. In savage action (May 8–19), including hand-to-hand fighting at the famous "Bloody Angle," Grant, although gaining a little ground, was essentially thrown back. He had lost 18,399 men at Spotsylvania. Lee's combined losses at the Wilderness and Spotsylvania were an estimated 17,250.

Again Grant withdrew, only to move forward in another series of attempts to get past Lee's right flank; again, at the North Anna River and at the Tototomoy Creek, he found Lee confronting him. Finally at Cold Harbor, just northeast of Richmond, Grant launched several heavy attacks, including a frontal, near-suicidal one on June 3, only to be repelled with grievous total losses of 12,737. Lee's casualties are unknown but were much lighter.

Grant, with the vital rail centre of Petersburg—the southern key to Richmond—as his objective, made one final effort to swing around Lee's right and finally outguessed his opponent and stole a march on him. But several blunders by Federal officers, plus swift action by Beauregard and Lee's belated though rapid reaction, barely enabled the Confederates to hold Petersburg. Grant attacked on June 15 and 18, hoping to break through before Lee could consolidate the Confederate lines east of the city, but he was contained with 8,150 losses.

Unable to admit defeat but having failed to destroy

Pickett's charge

Grant's siege of Vicksburg

Grant's appointment as Federal general in chief

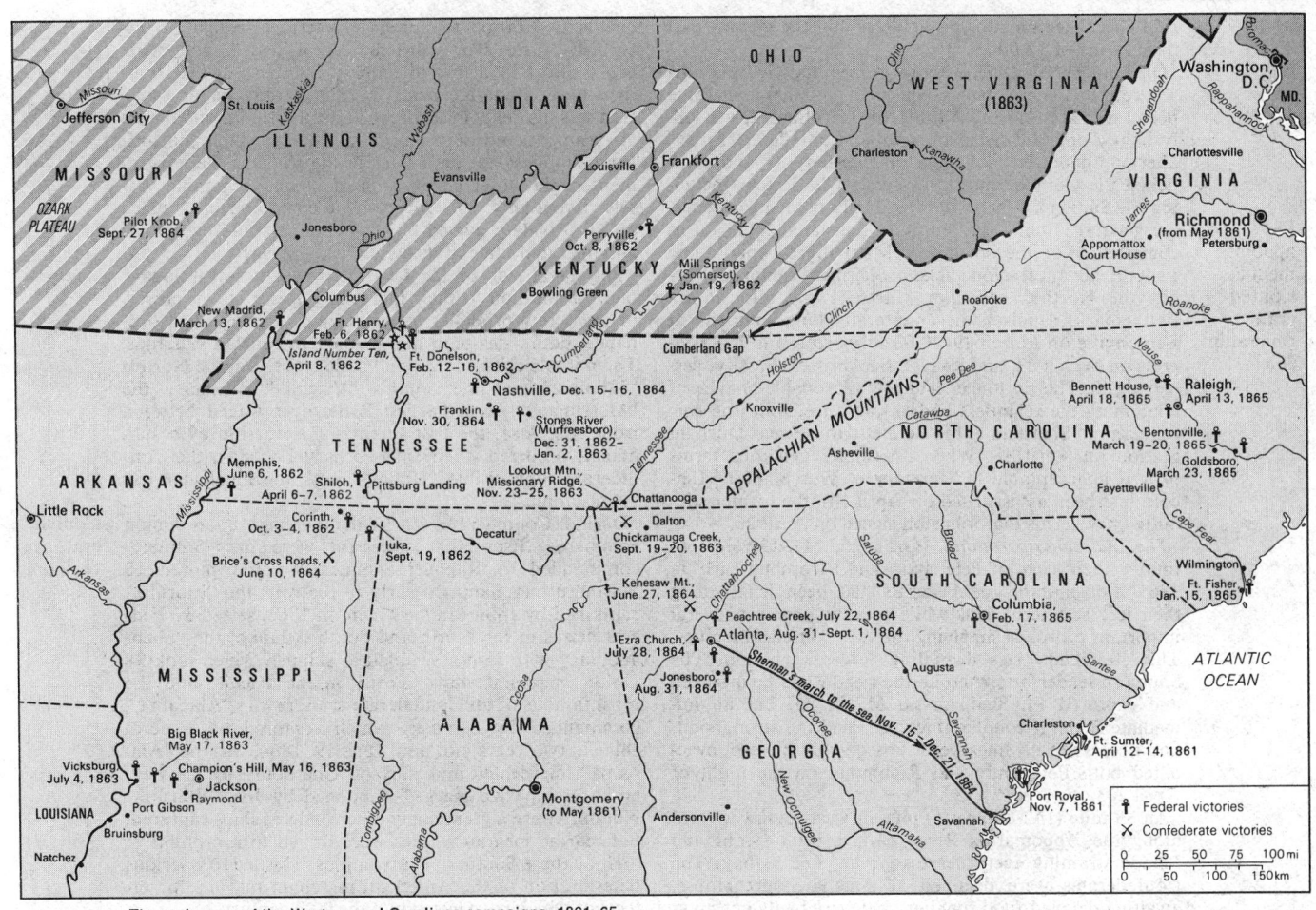

The main area of the Western and Carolinas campaigns, 1861–65.

Lee's army and capture Richmond, Grant settled down to a nine-month active siege of Petersburg. The summer and fall of 1864 were highlighted by the Federal failure with a mine explosion under the gray lines at Petersburg on July 30, and the near capture of Washington by the Confederate Jubal Early in July and his later setbacks in the Shenandoah Valley at the hands of Philip H. Sheridan.

Sherman's campaigns. Meanwhile, Sherman was pushing off toward Atlanta from Dalton, Georgia, on May 7, 1864, with 110,123 men against Johnston's 55,000. This masterly campaign comprised a series of cat-and-mouse moves by the rival commanders. Nine successive defensive positions were taken up by Johnston. Trying to outguess his opponent, Sherman attempted to swing around the Confederate right flank twice and around the left flank the other times, but each time Johnston divined which way Sherman was moving and each time pulled back in time to thwart him. At one point Sherman's patience snapped and he frontally assaulted the Southerners at Kennesaw Mountain on June 27; Johnston threw him back with heavy losses. Also, Sherman's lines of communication in his rear were being menaced by audacious Confederate raids conducted by Nathan Bedford Forrest and Joseph Wheeler. Forrest administered a crushing defeat to Federal troops under Samuel D. Sturgis at Brice's Cross Roads, Mississippi, on June 10. But these Confederate forays were more annoying than decisive, and Sherman pressed forward.

When Johnston finally informed Davis that he could not realistically hope to annihilate Sherman's mighty army, the Confederate president replaced him with John B. Hood, who had already lost two limbs in the war. Hood inaugurated a series of premature offensive battles at Peachtree Creek, Atlanta, Ezra Church, and Jonesboro but was repulsed in each of them. With his communications threatened, Hood evacuated Atlanta on the night of August 31–September 1. Sherman pursued only

at first. Then, on November 15, he commenced his great march to the sea with more than 60,000 men, laying waste to the economic resources of Georgia in a 50-mile-wide swath of destruction. He took Savannah on December 21.

Hood had sought unsuccessfully to lure Sherman out of Georgia and back into Tennessee by marching northwestward with nearly 40,000 men toward the key city of Nashville, the defense of which had been entrusted by Sherman to George H. Thomas. At Franklin, Hood was checked for a day with severe casualties by a Federal holding force under John M. Schofield. This helped Thomas to retain Nashville, where, on December 15–16, he delivered a crushing counterstroke against Hood's besieging army, cutting it up so badly that it was of little use thereafter.

Sherman's force might have been larger and his Atlanta–Savannah Campaign consummated much sooner had not Lincoln approved the Red River Campaign of Banks in the spring of 1864, aimed as much at capturing cotton as at defeating Southern forces under Kirby Smith and Richard Taylor. Accompanied by Porter's warships, Banks moved up the Red River with some 40,000 men. Not only did he fail to net much cotton but he was also checked with loss on April 8 at Sabine Cross Roads and forced to retreat. Porter lost several gunboats, and the campaign amounted to a costly debacle.

That fall Kirby Smith ordered the reconquest of Missouri. Sterling Price's Confederate army advanced on a broad front into Missouri but was set back temporarily by Thomas Ewing at Pilot Knob on September 27. Resuming the advance toward St. Louis, Price was forced westward along the south bank of the Missouri River by pursuing Federal troops under A.J. Smith, Alfred Pleasonton, and Samuel Curtis. Finally, on October 23, at Westport, near Kansas City, Price was decisively defeated and forced to retreat along a circuitous route, arriving back in Arkansas on December 2. This ill-fated

Sherman's march to the sea

raid cost Price most of his artillery and the greater part of his army of 12,000.

On January 10, 1865, with Tennessee and Georgia now securely in Federal hands, Sherman's 60,000-man force began to march northward into the Carolinas. It was only lightly opposed by much smaller Confederate forces. Sherman captured Columbia on February 17 and compelled the Confederates to evacuate Charleston (including Ft. Sumter). When Lee was finally named Confederate general in chief, he promptly reinstated Johnston as commander of the small forces striving to oppose the Federal advance. Nonetheless, Sherman captured Fayetteville, North Carolina, on March 11 and, after an initial setback, repulsed the counterattacking Johnston at Bentonville on March 19–20. Goldsboro fell to the Federals on March 23, and Raleigh on April 13. Finally, perceiving that he no longer had any reasonable chance of containing the relentless Federal advance, Johnston surrendered to Sherman at the Bennett House near Durham Station on April 18. When Sherman's generous terms proved unacceptable to Secretary of War Stanton (Lincoln had been assassinated on April 14), the former submitted new terms that Johnston signed on April 26.

The final land operations. Grant and Meade were continuing their siege of Petersburg and Richmond early in 1865. For months the Federals had been lengthening their left (southern) flank while operating against several important railroads supplying the two Confederate cities. This stretched Lee's dwindling forces very thin. The Southern leader briefly broke the siege when he attacked and captured Ft. Stedman on March 25. But an immediate Federal counterattack regained the strongpoint, and Lee, when his lines were subsequently pierced, evacuated both Petersburg and Richmond on the night of April 2–3.

An 88-mile (142-kilometre) pursuit west-southwestward along the Appomattox River ensued, with Grant and Meade straining every nerve to bring Lee to bay. The Confederates were detained at Amelia Court House, awaiting delayed food supplies, and were badly cut up at Sayler's Creek and Five Forks, with their only avenue of escape now cut off by Sheridan and George A. Custer. When Lee's final attempt to break out failed, he surrendered the remnants of his gallant Army of Northern Virginia at the McLean house at Appomattox Court House on April 9. The lamp of magnanimity was reflected in Grant's unselfish terms.

On the periphery of the Confederacy, 43,000 gray-clad soldiers in Louisiana under Kirby Smith surrendered to Canby on May 26. The port of Galveston, Texas, yielded to the Federals on June 2, and the greatest war in history on American soil was over.

THE NAVAL WAR

While the Federal armies actually stamped out Confederate land resistance, the increasingly effective Federal naval effort must not be overlooked. If Union sea power did not win the war, it enabled the war to be won. When hostilities opened, the United States Navy numbered 90 warships, of which only 42 were in commission, and many of these were on foreign station. Fortunately for the Federals, Lincoln had, in the person of Gideon Welles, a wise secretary of the navy and one of the President's most competent Cabinet members. Welles was ably seconded by his assistant, Gustavus Vasa Fox.

By the time of Lee's surrender, Lincoln's navy numbered 626 warships, of which 65 were ironclads. From a tiny beginning force of 9,000 seamen, the Union Navy increased by war's end to some 59,000 sailors, whereas naval appropriations per year leaped from $12,000,000 to $123,000,000. The blockade of 3,500 miles of Confederate coastline was a factor of incalculable value in the final defeat of the Davis government, although the blockade did not become effective before the end of 1863.

The Confederates, on the other hand, had to start from almost nothing in building a navy. That they did so well was largely because of untiring efforts by the capable secretary of the navy, Stephen Mallory. He dispatched

agents to Europe to purchase warships, sought to refurbish captured or scuttled Federal vessels, and made every effort to arm and employ Southern-owned ships then in Confederate ports. Mallory's only major omission was his delay in seeing the advantage of Confederate government control of blockade runners bringing in strategic supplies; not until later in the war did the government begin closer supervision of blockade-running vessels. Eventually, the government commandeered space on all privately owned blockade runners and even built and operated some of its own late in the war.

The naval side of the Civil War was a revolutionary one. In addition to their increasing use of steam power, of the screw propeller, of shell guns, and of rifled ordnance, both sides built and employed ironclad warships. The notable clash on March 9, 1862, between the North's "Monitor" and the South's "Virginia" (formerly the "Merrimack") was the first battle ever waged between ironclads. Also, the first sinking of a warship by a submarine occurred when, on February 17, 1864, the Confederate submersible "Hunley" sank the blockader USS "Housatonic."

Daring Confederate sea raiders preyed upon Union commerce. Especially successful were the "Sumter," commanded by Raphael Semmes, which captured 18 Northern merchantmen early in the war; the "Florida," captained by John Maffit, which, in 1863, seized 37 Federal prizes in the North and South Atlantic; the "Shenandoah," with James Waddell as skipper, which took 38 Union merchant ships, mostly in the Pacific; and the most famous of all Confederate cruisers, the "Alabama," commanded by Semmes, which captured 69 Federal ships in two years; not until June 19, 1864, was the "Alabama" intercepted and sunk off Cherbourg by the Federal warship "Kearsarge," captained by John Winslow. Not only were a great many other Federal ships captured, but marine insurance rates were driven to a prohibitive high by these Southern depredations. This led to a serious deterioration of the American merchant marine, the effects of which have lasted into the 20th century.

Besides fighting efficaciously with ironclads on the inland rivers, Lincoln's navy also played an important role in a series of coastal and amphibious operations, some in conjunction with the Federal Army. As early as November 7, 1861, a Federal flotilla under Samuel F. Du Pont seized Port Royal, South Carolina, and another squadron under Louis M. Goldsborough assisted Burnside's army in capturing Roanoke Island and New Berne on the North Carolina littoral in February–March 1862. One month later, Savannah was closed to Confederate blockade runners when the Federal Navy reduced Ft. Pulaski guarding the city; and on April 25 Farragut, running the forts near the mouth of the Mississippi, took New Orleans, which was subsequently occupied by Benjamin F. Butler's army.

But in April 1863, and again in July and August, Federal warships were repelled at Ft. Sumter when they descended upon Charleston, and a Federal army under Quincy A. Gillmore fared little better when it tried to assist. Farragut had better luck, however, when he rendered Mobile, Alabama, useless by reducing Ft. Morgan and destroying several defending Confederate ships on August 5, 1864, in the hardest fought naval action of the war. The last open Atlantic port, Wilmington, North Carolina, successfully withstood a Federal naval attack by Porter on defending Ft. Fisher when Butler's army failed to coordinate its attack properly in December 1864, but it fell one month later to Porter and an ably conducted army assault led by Alfred H. Terry. Only Galveston remained open to the Confederates in the last months of the war. In short, "Uncle Sam's web feet," as Lincoln termed them, played a decisive role in helping crush the Confederacy.

FOREIGN AFFAIRS

Davis and many Confederates expected recognition of their independence and direct intervention in the war on their behalf by Great Britain and possibly France. But they were cruelly disappointed, in part through the skill-

---

Lee's appointment as Confederate general in chief

Lee's surrender at Appomattox Court House

Confederate sea raiders

ful diplomacy of Lincoln, Secretary of State William H. Seward, and the Union ambassador to England, Charles Francis Adams, and in part through Confederate military failure at a crucial stage of the war.

The Union's first trouble with Britain came when Capt. Charles Wilkes halted the British steamer, "Trent," on November 8, 1861, and forcibly removed two Confederate envoys, James M. Mason and John Slidell, bound for Europe. Only the release of the two men prevented a diplomatic rupture with Palmerston's government in London. Another crisis erupted between the Union and England when the "Alabama," built in the British Isles, was permitted upon completion to sail and join the Confederate Navy, despite Adams' protestations. And when word reached the Lincoln government that two powerful ironclad rams were being constructed in Britain for the Confederacy, Adams sent his famous "this is war" note to Palmerston and the rams were seized by the British government at the last moment.

The diplomatic crisis of the Civil War came after Lee's striking victory at Second Manassas in late August 1862 and subsequent invasion of Maryland. The British government was set to offer mediation of the war and, if this were refused by the Lincoln administration (as it would have been), forceful intervention on behalf of the Confederacy. Only a victory by Lee on Northern soil was needed, but he was stopped by McClellan in September at Antietam, the Union's most needed success. The Confederate defeats at Gettysburg and Vicksburg the following summer ensured the continuing neutrality of England and France, especially when Russia seemed inclined to favour the Northern cause. Even the growing English shortage of cotton from the Southern states did not force Palmerston's government into Davis' camp, particularly when British consuls in the Confederacy were more closely restricted toward the close of the war. In the final act, even the Confederate offer to abolish slavery in early 1865 in return for British recognition fell on deaf ears.

The diplomatic crisis of the war

THE COST AND SIGNIFICANCE OF THE CIVIL WAR

On the positive side, the triumph of the North, above and beyond its superior naval forces, numbers, and industrial and financial resources, was due in part to the statesmanship of Lincoln, who by 1864 had become a masterful war leader; to the pervading valour of Federal soldiers; and to the increasing skill of their officers. On the negative side, the victory was due in part to failures of Confederate transportation, matériel, and political leadership. Only praise can be extended to the continuing bravery of Confederate soldiers and to the strategic and tactical dexterity of such generals as Lee and Joseph E. Johnston.

While there were some desertions on both sides, the personal valour and the enormous casualties—both in absolute numbers and in percentage of numbers engaged—have not yet ceased to astound scholars and military historians everywhere. Based on the three-year standard of enlistment, some 1,556,000 soldiers served in the Federal armies, which suffered a total of 634,703 casualties (359,528 dead and 275,175 wounded). There were probably some 800,000 men serving in the Confederate forces, which sustained approximately 483,000 casualties (about 258,000 deaths and perhaps 225,000 wounded).

War casualties

The cost in treasure was, of course, staggering for the embattled sections. Both governments, after strenuous attempts to finance the prosecution of the war by increasing taxes and floating loans, were obliged to resort to the printing press to make fiat money. While separate Confederate figures are lacking, the war finally cost the United States over $15,000,000,000. In sum, although the Union was preserved and restored, the cost in physical and moral suffering was incalculable, and some spiritual wounds caused by the holocaust still have not yet been healed.

The American Civil War has been called by some the last of the old-fashioned wars; others have termed it the first of the modern wars of history. Actually it was a transitional war, and it had a profound impact, technologically, on the development of modern weapons and techniques. There were many innovations. It was the first war in history in which ironclad warships clashed; the first in which the telegraph and railroad played significant roles; the first to use, extensively, rifled ordnance and shell guns and to introduce a machine gun; the first to have widespread newspaper coverage, voting by servicemen in national elections, and photographic recordings; the first to organize medical care of troops systematically; and the first to use land and water mines and to employ a submarine that could sink a warship. It was also the first war in which armies widely employed aerial reconnaissance (by means of balloons).

The Civil War has been written about as has no other war in history. More than 60,000 books and articles give eloquent testimony to the accuracy of Walt Whitman's prediction that "a great literature will . . . arise out of the era of those four years." The events of the war left a rich heritage for future generations, and that legacy was summed up by the martyred Lincoln as showing that the reunited sections of the United States comprised "the last best hope of earth."

BIBLIOGRAPHY. The most recent scholarly, comprehensive study of the Civil War is ALLAN NEVINS, *The War for the Union,* 4 vol. (1959–71), although the older volumes by JAMES FORD RHODES, *History of the United States from the Compromise of 1850,* vol. 3–5 (1895–1904), are still useful for military operations, politics, and wartime diplomacy. For the war in the East on the Federal side, see the documented work by WARREN W. HASSLER, JR., *Commanders of the Army of the Potomac* (1962); and for an excellent study of the top Confederate generals in the East, consult DOUGLAS SOUTHALL FREEMAN, *Lee's Lieutenants,* 3 vol. (1942–44). Less has been written about the war in the Western theatre. An older but still useful introduction is JOHN FISKE, *The Mississippi Valley in the Civil War* (1900); STANLEY F. HORN, *The Army of Tennessee* (1941), is a satisfactory account of the main Confederate army west of the Appalachians. For the naval war, see the full and readable account by VIRGIL CARRINGTON JONES, *The Civil War at Sea,* 3 vol. (1960–62). The enormous historical literature of the war is selectively assessed in ALLAN NEVINS, JAMES I. ROBERTSON, JR., and BELL I. WILEY (eds.), *Civil War Books: A Critical Bibliography,* 2 vol. (1967–69). Easily the best collection of articles written by principal participants is ROBERT U. JOHNSON and CLARENCE C. BUEL (eds.), *Battles and Leaders of the Civil War,* 4 vol. (1887–88). For statistics, the most reliable study remains that by THOMAS L. LIVERMORE, *Numbers and Losses in the Civil War in America, 1861–1865,* 2nd ed. (1901).

(W.W.H.)

Clair, René

One of the outstanding figures of the international cinema in the years between the two world wars, René Clair gained recognition as a creative artist long before screenwriters and directors generally were accorded serious critical attention. Each of his films revived and enriched his own wonderfully diverse view of the world. This poetic universe often centred on Paris, and Clair has been called the most French of film makers. His penchant for invention, research, and experimentation allied him to the pioneers of the film art; for him, to create a motion picture was not merely to express but to invent cinematically. Far from limiting his work to the avant-garde, however, he applied his techniques to comedies that poked fun at everyday life and were appreciated by vast audiences of moviegoers. His art, the refined and sentient art of an intellectual, was also a popular art.

Combining the avant-garde and the popular

Clair was born René Chomette on November 11, 1898, in Paris and was raised in the market quarter of the city, the memory of which inspired some of his films. During World War I he served with the French ambulance corps, and afterward he worked as a journalist, critic, and songwriter before entering motion pictures as an actor in 1920, when he adopted the name of Clair. He also wrote film criticism and worked as an assistant director. In 1923 he wrote and directed his first film, *Paris qui dort* (1923), also shown under the title *The Crazy Ray.* His next film, *Entr'acte* (1924), which was created to be shown between acts of a ballet by the modernist French

Clair, photography by Yousuf Karsh.
© Karsh–Rapho Guillumette

composer Erik Satie, featured in its cast some of the most innovative artists of the day, including Satie and the Dadaist painters Marcel Duchamp, Francis Picabia, and Man Ray. These two films established Clair as a leader of the avant-garde. The great Russian writer Vladimir Mayakovsky wrote a scenario especially for him, though it was never produced. Subsequently, in such films as *The Italian Straw Hat* (1927), based on the farce by Eugène Labiche, he combined the avant-garde and the popular, modernity and tradition, in an original way. During this time he also published a novel, *Adams* (1926), written in a cerebral and an elliptical style.

The advent of sound in motion pictures in the late '20s disoriented Clair until he recognized that sound need not kill the art of the film, as he had predicted it would. He learned to use sound not as a duplicate or substitute for visual representation but, rather, as a counterpoint to it. His *Sous les toits de Paris* (1930), *Le Million* (1931), and *À nous la liberté!* (1931) constituted a homage to the art of silent films and a manifesto for a new cinema. Clair rigorously constructed comical situations using either images or sounds independently, and his skillful use of music to further the narrative—rather than for production numbers in the manner of stage musicals—introduced a new form of musical film. The satirical edge of these films and his *Le Dernier Milliardaire* (1934), an anti-Fascist film banned in Germany and elsewhere, resulted in political and financial difficulties for Clair. He went to England to make *The Ghost Goes West* (1935), an effective merging of English humour with French verve that became an international triumph. He returned to France but soon left again in 1940, when the Germans overran the country in World War II. He spent the war years in Hollywood, where he made *The Flame of New Orleans* (1940), which was not at all successful. His *I Married a Witch* (1942), however, was well received, as were *It Happened Tomorrow* (1944), the most striking of his fantastic comedies, and *And Then There Were None* (1945), an adaptation of a mystery by Agatha Christie. After the war, he returned to France, where he made *Le Silence est d'or* (1947), a masterful renewal of his Parisian past and his youth, which was to be his artistic testament. Though Clair's subsequent films, such as *La Beauté du diable* (1949), which propounded the Faust theme, and *Les Grandes Manoeuvres* (1955), a seriocomedy in a 1914 setting, were noteworthy, they were not equal to his earlier French films. In 1960 he was elected to the French Academy. Clair died on March 15, 1981, in Neuilly-sur-Seine, a suburb of Paris.

Years in England and Hollywood

MAJOR WORKS
Paris qui dort (1923); *Entr'acte* (1924); *Le Fantôme du Moulin Rouge* (1924); *Le Voyage imaginaire* (1925); *La Proie du vent*

(1926); *The Italian Straw Hat* (1927); *Les Deux Timides, La Tour* (1928); *Sous les toits de Paris* (1930, *Under the Roofs of Paris*); *Le Million* (1931); *À nous la liberté!* (1931); *Quatorze Juillet* (1932); *Le Dernier Milliardaire* (1934); *The Ghost Goes West* (1935); *Break the News* (1937); *The Flame of New Orleans* (1940); *I Married a Witch, Forever and a Day* (1942), an episode; *It Happened Tomorrow* (1943); *And Then There Were None* (1945); *Le Silence est d'or* (1947); *La Beauté du diable* (1949, *Beauty and the Devil*); *Les Belles de nuit* (1952, *Beauties of the Night*); *Les Grandes Manoeuvres* (1955); *Porte de lilas* (1957, *Gates of Paris*); *La Française et l'amour* (1960, *Love and the Frenchwoman*), episode "Le Mariage"; *Tout l'or du monde* (1961); *Les Quatre Vérités* (1962), episode "Les Deux Pigeons"; *Les Fêtes galantes* (1965).

BIBLIOGRAPHY. GEORGES CHARENSOL and ROGER REGENT, *50 ans de cinéma avec René Clair* (1979), an excellent study of Clair, written by two of his close friends, both excellent critics; RENÉ CLAIR, *Réflexion faite* (1951; Eng. trans., *Reflections on the Cinema*, 1953), the author's recollections of his career and reflections on the history of the cinema through his own experiences; BARTHÉLEMY AMENGUAL, *René Clair* (1963), a critical essay (in French) on the man and his work, followed by remarks of René Clair, critical views, statements, songs from films, filmography, and bibliography; CELIA MCGERR, *René Clair* (1980), a survey (in English) of Clair's work.

(B.Am.)

Clarendon, Edward Hyde, 1st Earl of

The English statesman and historian Lord Clarendon made a profound contribution to the course of English politics as a participant and interpreter. A farsighted minister of Charles I and Charles II, he presided over the Restoration of 1660 and left an invaluable account of the English Civil War.

Edward Hyde was born on February 18, 1609, the eldest surviving son of Henry Hyde of Dinton, Wiltshire. He was educated at Magdalen Hall, Oxford, and was trained in the law in London's Middle Temple. His first wife, Anne Ayliffe, died in 1632, within six months of their marriage. Two years later he married Frances, daughter of Sir Thomas Aylesbury, who held a high legal office and through whom he was able to pursue a successful career at the bar and become keeper of the writs and rolls of common pleas. He also established himself in literary and philosophical circles and counted the dramatist Ben Jonson, the jurist and scholar John Selden, and the statesman Lord Falkland among his friends.

In 1640 he was drawn into politics as a member in the Short Parliament (April–May 1640), called to finance Charles I's war against Scotland, and in the Long Parliament, which opposed Charles during the Civil War. Emerging as a critic of Ship Money (a tax levied for defense) and other new policies of the crown, he joined the attack on the misuse of the royal prerogative and helped to abolish oppressive courts and commissions. But he resisted measures that might permanently damage the balanced relations among king, House of Lords, and the Commons and opposed efforts to dictate the king's choice of ministers. From the first, he championed the Anglican establishment, for which he was commended by Charles I. It was as a parliamentarian, however, that he opposed the execution of the Earl of Strafford, one of the King's chief advisers, and resisted the Root and Branch Bill, which would have abolished the episcopacy.

Early career and relation to king

With the Commons' adoption of the Grand Remonstrance of November 1641, which demanded a voice for Parliament in the appointment of the king's ministers and in the reform of the church, accommodation between Charles I and Parliament became more difficult. Henceforth, Hyde chose to work behind the scenes as an adviser of the crown. He recommended moderate measures, which if consistently pursued might have undermined support for John Pym's radical leadership in the Commons. But Charles's attempt to seize five members of Parliament in January 1642 brought Hyde nearly to despair. After that, although civil war was not yet inevitable, few men were able to trust the King. For a while, Hyde's constructive moderation prevailed.

Joining the King at York about the end of May 1642, Hyde was proscribed by Parliament as an "evil counselor." Though he became a member of the Royalist council of war, Hyde was never a combatant in the ensuing conflict. From 1643, as a privy councillor and as chancellor of the Exchequer, he tried to moderate the influence of the military leaders. He advised Charles to summon a parliament at Oxford in December 1643. Its success was limited, however, and a year later Hyde agreed to recognize Westminster's claim to be the true Parliament. In January 1645, he vainly tried to temper parliamentary demands for control of the militia and for a Presbyterian type of church government. By then there was little room left for Hyde's scrupulous constitutionalism, and his appointment as guardian to the Prince of Wales was a convenient means of disposing of him.

Hyde left Charles I in March 1645 and accompanied the Prince to the island of Jersey in April 1646. Later, the Queen ordered the Prince to move to Paris, a step that he had advised against. Unable to influence events, Hyde began a draft of his *History of the Rebellion and Civil Wars in England* in the hope that his interpretation of recent errors might instruct the King for the future.

Although he rejoined the Queen and Prince in Paris in 1648, Hyde remained a powerless spectator of Charles I's last efforts to save his throne and his life. He was no less helpless in seeking to guide the new King. Disapproving strongly of Charles II's policies, he was glad to escape from the quarrelsome court by accompanying a mission to Madrid, one, however, that proved unsuccessful in securing assistance from Spain.

After Charles II's escape to France from his unsuccessful invasion of England in the fall of 1651, Hyde rejoined him in Paris and followed him to Cologne in 1654 and Bruges in 1656. His object was to keep Charles from renouncing his Anglican faith, a step that would prejudice reconciliation with his subjects. Although he encouraged internal opposition to Oliver Cromwell, who as lord protector had by then become de facto ruler of England, Hyde held out against schemes for reconquest that would simply reunite the republican factions. Meanwhile, he closely followed events in England. After Cromwell's death in 1658, the overtures of the Presbyterians for a restoration of the monarchy were received. Hyde, who was appointed lord chancellor that same year, answered them. The Declaration of Breda (1660) embodied Hyde's belief that only a free parliament, matching the king's intentions with its own good will, could bring about a reconciliation. The final settlement, however, diverged from his own plans in several respects.

Lord chancellor

As lord chancellor, Hyde pressed for a generous Act of Oblivion, which spared most republicans from royalist vengeance, and for speedy provision of royal revenue. He hastened the disbanding of the army and strove to create a spirit of accommodation among religious leaders. He was not successful, however; for the Parliament elected in 1661 at the height of the reaction initiated statutory persecution of Nonconformists far exceeding anything desired by the easygoing Charles II or even by the impeccably Anglican lord chancellor.

Although he denied being a "premier minister," Hyde, who was created earl of Clarendon in 1661, dominated most aspects of the administration. By the marriage of his daughter Anne to James, duke of York, in 1660 he became related to the royal family and, ultimately, grandfather to two English sovereigns, Queen Mary II and Queen Anne. But he took little pleasure in his distinctions, knowing himself to be hated by those impoverished royalists for whom the Restoration had brought little reward. Clarendon also was held responsible for unpopular decisions, such as the sale of Dunkirk to France. The Anglo-Dutch War of 1665, which he had opposed, proved his final downfall.

Fall from power

There were personal factors in his disgrace. Never a man to suffer fools gladly, his temper was shortened by attacks of gout that also incapacitated him for business. When he became openly critical of the King's immorality, the old friendship between them disappeared, and Clarendon became the butt of a young and frivolous court. The death of allies left him exposed, and Parliament was determined to find in him the scapegoat for the disasters of the war. Thus, in August 1667 Clarendon was dismissed from the chancellorship, and in October the House of Commons began his impeachment. The charges lacked foundation, and the House of Lords refused to accept them; but by November, under threat of trial by a special court, Clarendon was forced to flee.

For the rest of his life, Clarendon remained an exile in France, cut off by an act of banishment that made correspondence with him treasonable. Determined to vindicate himself, he began writing an autobiography that narrated his political life from the 1630s to the 1660s. It lacked documentation, but in 1671 his son Lawrence was allowed to visit him, bringing manuscripts that included the unfinished *History* of the 1640s. This Clarendon now completed, inserting into it sections of the recently written autobiography. Consequently, the accuracy of the finished *History of the Rebellion and Civil Wars in England* varies considerably according to the date of its composition. The deficiencies of the *History* and the *Life*, which was later published from the remaining fragments of autobiography, do not always derive from inadequate documentation. For all his judicious moderation and the magisterial dignity of his prose, Clarendon was not always an objective historian. His accounts of opponents are sometimes unfair, and his analysis of events in which he participated diverge from the judgments guiding him at the time. They are the inevitable blemishes of a work of vindication written in the bitterness of exile.

With his hopes of pardon unfulfilled, Clarendon died at Rouen on December 9, 1674. He was buried in Westminster Abbey a month later.

BIBLIOGRAPHY. A detailed, scholarly biography of Clarendon has yet to be written, but one of the earliest attempts, T.H. LISTER, *The Life and Administration of Edward, First Earl of Clarendon*, 3 vol. (1837–38), is still valuable for its use of Clarendon's vast correspondence, selections from which are printed in volume 3. SIR HENRY CRAIK, *The Life of Edward, Earl of Clarendon, Lord High Chancellor of England*, 2 vol. (1911), is a conscientious study, also based on the manuscript sources, but its judgments are not uniformly reliable. By far the most acute and sensitive appraisal of Clarendon's early political career is B.H.G. WORMWALD, *Clarendon: Politics, History and Religion, 1640–1660* (1951). It is a remarkable study in historiography that skilfully disentangles the motives of Hyde's actions in the 1640s from his subsequent explanation of them in the 1670s. An earlier reconstruction of Clarendon's historical methods is C.H. FIRTH, "Clarendon's 'History of the Rebellion,'" *English Historical Review*, 19:26–54, 246–262, 464–483 (1904); and Firth's general appreciation of Clarendon as an author was published in his *Essays, Historical and Literary*, ed. by GODFREY DAVIES (1938). The most recent discussion of Clarendon's position in the English literary tradition is H.R. TREVOR-ROPER, "Clarendon and the Practice of History," in *Milton and Clarendon: Papers on 17th Century English Historiography* (1965).

Classification, Biological

Everyone classifies, grouping sense impressions into categories—*e.g.*, heavy, triangular, wide, quick. The most frequently encountered combinations of objects are rapidly recognized, grouped, and arranged. For ease of reference, the groups are given names, and in order to avoid mistakes, each group is given some sort of description or definition. This is true for all things that can be recognized, whether sharply defined and easily sorted, sharing some characters, or intergrading in many characters. The classification of living things, which change during their lifetimes and of which there are so many varied kinds, is an especially difficult problem.

Informal classifications of living organisms arise according to need and are often superficial. Anglo-Saxon terms such as worm and fish have been used to refer, respectively, to any creeping thing—snake, earthworm, intestinal parasite, or dragon—and to any swimming or aquatic thing. Although the term fish is common to the names shellfish, crayfish, and starfish, there are more anatomical differences between a shellfish and a starfish than there are between a bony fish and a man. Vernacular names vary widely. The American robin (*Turdus migratorius*), for example, is not the English robin (*Erithacus rubecula*), and the mountain ash (*Sorbus*) has only a superficial resemblance to a true ash.

Biologists, however, have attempted to view all living organisms with equal thoroughness and thus have devised a formal classification. A formal classification provides the basis for a relatively uniform and internationally understood nomenclature, thereby simplifying cross-referencing and retrieval of information.

The usage of the terms taxonomy and systematics with regard to biological classification varies greatly. American evolutionist Ernst Mayr has stated that "taxonomy is the theory and practice of classifying organisms" and "systematics is the science of the diversity of organisms"; the latter, therefore, has considerable interrelations with evolution, ecology, genetics, behaviour, and comparative physiology that taxonomy need not have.

THE OBJECTIVES OF BIOLOGICAL CLASSIFICATION

A classification or arrangement of any sort cannot be handled without reference to the purpose or purposes for which it is being made. An arrangement based on everything known about a particular class of objects is likely to be the most useful for many particular purposes. One in which objects are grouped according to easily observed and described characteristics allows easy identification of the objects. If the purpose of a classification is to provide information unknown to or not remembered by the user but relating to something the name of which is known, an alphabetical arrangement may be best. Specialists may want a classification relating only to one aspect of a subject. A chemist analyzing the essential oils of plants, for instance, is interested only in the oil content of plants and probably requires such information in far greater detail than would anyone else.

Keys and characters in biological classification

Classification is used in biology for two totally different purposes, often in combination, namely, identifying and making natural groups. The specimen or a group of similar specimens must be compared with descriptions of what is already known. This type of classification, called a key, provides as briefly and as reliably as possible the most obvious characteristics useful in identification. Very often they are set out as a dichotomous key with opposing pairs of characters. The butterflies of a region, for example, might first be separated into those with a lot of white on the wings and those with very little; then each group could be subdivided on the basis of other characters. One disadvantage of such classifications, which are useful for well-known groups, is that a mistake may produce a ridiculous answer, since the groups under each division need have nothing in common but the chosen character (*e.g.*, white on the butterfly wings). In addition, if the group being keyed is large or given to great variation, the key may be extremely complex and may rely on characters difficult to evaluate. Moreover, if the form in question is a new one or one that is not in the key (being, perhaps, unrecorded from the region to which the key applies), it may be identified incorrectly. Many unrelated butterflies have a lot of white on the wings—a few swallowtails, the well-known cabbage whites, some of the South American dismorphiines, and a few satyrids. Should identification of an undescribed form of fritillary butterfly containing much white on the wings be desired, the use of a key could result in an incorrect identification of the butterfly. In order to avoid such mistakes, it is necessary to consider many characters of the organism: not merely one aspect of the wings but their anatomy and the features of the various stages in the life cycle.

Unfortunately, little is known about many of the vast variety of living things. In poorly known groups—and most living things are poorly known—the first objective is identification. There are, for example, about 250,000 species of beetles; many are known only from a single specimen of the adult. In such groups the tendency is to produce classifications which, although purporting to be natural ones, are actually dichotomous keys. Although most common earthworms have on each body segment four pairs of special bristles (chaetae) that are used in locomotion, some species have many chaetae arranged in a complete ring around the body on each segment (perichaetine condition). Because the chaetae are an easily observed character, the latter species were once placed together as a natural group, the family Perichaetidae; knowledge of other aspects of earthworm anatomy, however, made it obvious that several different groups had independently evolved the perichaetine condition. Many current so-called natural groups, especially those at the lower levels of classification, are probably not natural at all but are based on some easily observed characters.

A natural classification is advantageous in that it groups together forms that seem fundamentally to be related. Information utilized in the definition of a group thus need not be repeated for each constituent. This provides concision and efficient information storage. A certain amount of prediction is also possible—a new form with a few ascertained characters similar to those of a natural group probably has other similar characters. As long as no difficult intermediary forms are found, all of the different types can be classified into definite discrete categories. Biological classification has progressed from artificial or key classifications to a natural classification; it has also been realized that division into sharply separated groups often is not possible. Formal classification thus sometimes obscures actual relationships.

HISTORY OF BIOLOGICAL CLASSIFICATION

People who live close to nature usually have an excellent working knowledge of the elements of the local fauna and flora important to them and also often recognize many of the larger groups of living things (*e.g.*, fishes, birds, and mammals). Their knowledge, however, is according to need, and such people generalize only rarely.

From the Greeks to the Renaissance. The first great generalizer in classification appears to have been the Greek philosopher Aristotle, who virtually invented the science of logic, of which for 2,000 years classification was a part. Greeks had constant contact with the sea and marine life, and Aristotle seems to have studied it intensively during his stay on the island of Lesbos. In his writings, he described a large number of natural groups, and, although he ranked them from simple to complex, his order was not an evolutionary one. He was far ahead of his time, however, in separating invertebrate animals into different groups and was aware that whales, dolphins, and porpoises had mammalian characters and were not fish. Lacking the microscope, he could not, of course, deal with the minute forms of life.

Aristotle's classification into natural groups

The Aristotelian method dominated classification until the 19th century. His scheme was, in effect, that the classification of a living thing by its nature—*i.e.*, what it really is, as against superficial resemblances—requires the examination of many specimens, the discarding of variable characters (since they must be accidental, not essential), and the establishment of constant characters. These can then be used to develop a definition that states the essence of the living thing—what makes it what it is and thus cannot be altered; the essence is, of course, immutable. The model for this procedure is to be seen in mathematics, especially geometry, which fascinated the Greeks. Mathematics seemed to them the type and exemplar of perfect knowledge, since its deductions from axioms were certain and its definitions perfect, irrespective of whether a perfect geometrical figure could ever be drawn. But the Aristotelian procedure applied to living things is not by deduction from stated and known axioms; rather, it is by induction from observed examples and thus does not lead to the immutable essence but to a lexical definition. Although it provided for centuries a procedure for attempting to define living things by careful analysis, it neglected the variation of living things. It is of interest that the few people who understood Charles Darwin's *Origin of Species* in the mid-19th century were empiricists who did not believe in an essence of each form.

Aristotle and his pupil in botany, Theophrastus, had no notable successors for 1,400 years. In about the 12th century AD, botanical works necessary to medicine began to contain accurate illustrations of plants, and a few began to arrange similar plants together. Encyclopaedists

Botany
and
zoology of
the Renais-
sance

also began to bring together classical wisdom and some contemporary observations. The first flowering of the Renaissance in biology produced, in 1543, a treatise on human anatomy by the Flemish physician Andreas Vesalius and, in 1545, the first university botanic garden, founded in Padua, Italy. After this time, work in botany and zoology flourished. An English naturalist, John Ray, summarized in the late 17th century the available systematic knowledge, with useful classifications. He distinguished the monocotyledonous plants from the dicotyledonous ones in 1703, recognized the true affinities of the whales, and gave a workable definition of the species concept, which had already become the basic unit of biological classification. He tempered the Aristotelian logic of classification with empirical observation.

The Linnaean system. Carolus Linnaeus, the Swedish botanist who is usually regarded as the founder of modern taxonomy and whose books are considered the beginning of modern botanical and zoological nomenclature, drew up rules for assigning names to plants and animals and was the first to use binomial nomenclature consistently (1758). Although he introduced the standard hierarchy of class, order, genus, and species, his main success in his own day was providing workable keys, making it possible to identify plants and animals from his books.

For plants he made use of the hitherto neglected smaller parts of the flower.

Linnaeus attempted a natural classification but did not get far. His concept of a natural classification was Aristotelian; *i.e.*, it was based on Aristotle's idea of the essential features of living things and on his logic. He was less accurate than Aristotle in his classification of animals, breaking them up into mammals, birds, reptiles, fishes, insects, and worms. The first four, as he defined them, are obvious groups and generally recognized; the last two incorporate about seven of Aristotle's groups.

The standard Aristotelian definition of a form was by genus and differentia. The genus defined the general kind of thing being described; the differentia gave its special character. A genus, for example, might be "Bird" and the species "Feeding in water," or the genus might be "Animal" and the species "Bird." The two together made up the definition, which could be used as a name. Unfortunately, when many species of a genus became known, the differentia became longer and longer. In some of his books Linnaeus printed in the margin a catch name, the name of the genus and one word from the differentia or from some former name; in this way he created the binomial, or binary, nomenclature. Thus, modern man is *Homo sapiens,* Neanderthal man *Homo neanderthalensis,* the gorilla *Gorilla gorilla,* and so on.

Creation
of binary
nomen-
clature

Classification since Linnaeus. *The importance of natural relationships.* Classification since Linnaeus has incorporated newly discovered information and more closely approaches a natural system. When the life history of barnacles was discovered, for example, they could no longer be associated with mollusks because it became clear that they were arthropods (jointed-legged animals such as crabs and insects). The French naturalist Jean-Baptiste Lamarck, an excellent taxonomist despite his misconceptions about evolution, first separated spiders and crustaceans from insects as separate classes; he also introduced the distinction, no longer accepted by all workers as wholly valid, between vertebrates—*i.e.*, those with backbones, such as fishes, amphibians, reptiles, birds, and mammals—and invertebrates, which have no backbones. The invertebrates, defined by a feature they lack rather than by those they have, constitute in fact about 90 percent of the diversity of all animals. The mixed group "Infusoria," which included all the microscopic forms that would appear when hay was let stand in water, was broken up into empirically recognized groups by the French biologist Felix Dujardin. The German biologist Ernst Haeckel proposed the term Protista in 1866 to include chiefly the unicellular plants and animals because he realized that, at the one-celled level, there could no longer be a clear distinction between plants and animals.

The process of clarifying relationships continues—only

in 1898 were agents of disease discovered (viruses) that would pass through the finest filters, and it was not until 1935 that the first completely purified virus was obtained. Primitive spore-bearing land plants (Psilophyta) from the Cambrian Period, which dates from 570,000,000 years ago, were discovered in Canada in 1859. The German botanist Wilhelm Hofmeister in 1851 gave the first good account of the alterations of generations in various nonflowering (cryptogamous) plants, on which many major divisions of higher plants are based. The phylum Pogonophora (beardworms) was recognized only in the 20th century.

The impact of Darwin. The immediate impact of Darwinian evolution on classification was negligible for many groups of organisms, and unfortunate for others. As taxonomists began to accept evolution, they recognized that what had been described as natural affinity—*i.e.*, the more or less close similarity of forms with many of the same characters—could be explained as relationship by evolutionary descent. In groups with little or no fossil record, a change in interpretation rather than alteration of classifications was the result. Unfortunately, some authorities, believing that they could derive the group from some evolutionary principle, would proceed to reclassify it. The classification of earthworms and their allies (Oligochaeta), for example, which had been studied by using the most complex organism easily obtainable and by then arranging progressively simple forms below it, was changed after the theory of evolution appeared. The most simple oligochaete, the tiny freshwater worm *Aeolosoma,* was considered to be most primitive, and classifiers arranged progressively complex forms above it. Later, when it was realized that *Aeolosoma* might well have been secondarily simplified (*i.e.*, evolved from a more complex form), the tendency was to start in the middle of the series, and work in both directions. Biassed names for the major subgroups (Archioligochaeta, Neoligochaeta) were widely accepted, when in fact there was no evidence for the actual course of evolution of this and other animal groups. Groups with good fossil records suffered less from this type of reclassification because good fossil material allowed the placing of forms according to natural affinities; knowledge of the strata in which they were found allowed the formulation of a phylogenetic tree (*i.e.*, one based on evolutionary relationships), or dendrite (also called a dendrogram), irrespective of theory.

The
formula-
tion of
phyloge-
netic trees

The long-term impact of Darwinian evolution has been different and very important. It indicates that the basic arrangement of living things, if enough information were available, would be a phylogenetic tree rather than a set of discrete classes. Many groups are so poorly known, however, that the arrangement of organisms into a dendrite is impossible. Extensive and detailed fossil sequences —the laying out of actual specimens—must be broken up arbitrarily. Many groups, especially at the species level, show great geographical variation, so that a simple definition of species is impossible. Difficulties of classification at the species level are considerable. Many plants show reticulate (chain) evolution, in which species form, then subsequently hybridize, resulting in the formation of new species. And because many plants and animals have abandoned sexual reproduction, the usual criteria for the species—interbreeding within a pool of individuals—cannot be applied. Nothing about the viruses, moreover, seems to correspond to the species of higher organisms.

THE TAXONOMIC PROCESS

Basically, no special theory lies behind modern taxonomic methods. In effect, taxonomic methods depend on: (1) obtaining a suitable specimen (collecting, preserving and, when necessary, making special preparations); (2) comparing the specimen with the known range of variation of living things; (3) correctly identifying the specimen if it has been described, or preparing a description showing similarities to and differences from known forms, or, if the specimen is new, naming it according to internationally recognized codes of nomenclature; (4) determining the best position for the specimen in existing classifications and determining what revision the classification may require as a consequence of the new discovery; and (5) using available evidence to suggest the course of the specimen's evolution. Prerequisite to these activities is a recognized system of ranks in classifying; recognized rules for nomenclature; and a procedure for verification, irrespective of the group being examined. A group of related organisms to which a taxonomic name is given is called a taxon (plural taxa).

Ranks. The goal of classifying is to place an organism into an already existing group or to create a new group for it, based on its resemblances to and differences from known forms. To this end, a hierarchy of categories is recognized; for example, an ordinary flowering plant, on the basis of gross structure, is clearly one of the higher green plants, not a fungus, bacterium, or animal, it can easily be placed in the Kingdom Plantae (or Metaphyta). If the body of the plant has distinct leaves, roots, a stem, and flowers, it is placed with the other true flowering plants in the division Magnoliophyta (or Angiospermae), one subcategory of the Plantae. If it is a lily, with sword-like leaves, with the parts of the flowers in multiples of three, and with one cotyledon (the incipient leaf) in the embryo, it belongs with other lilies, tulips, palms, orchids, grasses, and sedges in a subgroup of the Magnoliophyta, which is called the class Liliatae (or Monocotyledones).

In this class, it is placed, rather than with orchids or grasses, in a subgroup of the Liliatae, the order Liliales; this procedure is continued to the species level. Should the plant be different from any lily yet known, a new species is named, as well as higher taxa, if necessary. If the plant is a new species within a well-known genus, a new species name is simply added to the appropriate genus. If the plant is very different from any known monocot it might require, even if only a single new species, the naming of a new genus, family, order, or higher taxon; there is no restriction on the number of forms in any particular group. The number of ranks recognized in a hierarchy is a matter of opinion. Shown in Table 1 are seven ranks accepted as obligatory by zoologists and botanists. In botany, the term division is often used as an equivalent to the term phylum of zoology. The number of ranks is expanded as necessary by using the prefixes sub-, super-, and infra- (*e.g.*, subclass, superorder) and by adding other intermediate ranks, such as brigade, cohort, section, or tribe. Given in full, the zoological hierarchy for the timber wolf of the Canadian subarctic would be as follows:

Kingdom Animalia
  Subkingdom Metazoa
    Phylum Chordata
      Subphylum Vertebrata
        Superclass Tetrapoda
          Class Mammalia
            Subclass Theria
              Infraclass Eutheria
                Cohort Ferungulata
                  Superorder Ferae
                    Order Carnivora
                      Suborder Fissipeda
                        Superfamily Canoidea
                          Family Canidae
                            Subfamily Caninae
                              Tribe (none described
                              for this group)
                              Genus *Canis*
                                Subgenus (none
                                described for this
                                group)
                                  Species *Canis lupus* (wolf)
                                  Subspecies *Canis lupus occidentalis* (northern timber wolf)

Although the name of the species is binomial (*e.g.*, *Canis lupus*) and that of the subspecies trinomial (*C. lupus occidentalis* for the northern timber wolf; *C. lupus lupus* for the northern European wolf), all other names are single words. In zoology, convention dictates that the names of superfamilies end in *-oidea*, and the code dictates that the names of families end in *-idae*, those of subfamilies in *-inae*, and those of tribes in *-ini*. Unfortunately, there are no widely accepted rules for other major divisions of living things because each major group of animals and plants has its own taxonomic history, and old names tend to be preserved. Apart from a few accepted endings, the names of groups of high rank are not standardized and must be memorized.

Name endings

Table 1: Obligatory Hierarchy of Ranks		
	animals	plants
Kingdom	Animalia	Plantae
Phylum	Chordata	Tracheophyta
Class	Mammalia	Pteropsida
Order	Primates	Coniferales
Family	Hominidae	Pinaceae
Genus	*Homo*	*Pinus*
Species	*Homo sapiens* (man)	*Pinus strobus* (white pine)

The discovery of the only living coelacanth fish *Latimeria*, in 1938, caused virtually no disturbance of the accepted classification, since the suborder Coelacanthi was already well-known from fossils. When certain unusual worms were discovered in the depths of the oceans about ten years later, however, it was necessary to create a new phylum, Pogonophora, for them since they showed no close affinities to any other known animals. The phylum Pogonophora, as usually classified, has one class—the animals in the phylum are relatively similar—but there are two orders, several families and genera, and more than 100 species. Both of these examples have been widely accepted by authorities in their respective areas of taxonomy and may be considered stable taxa.

It cannot be too strongly emphasized that there are no explicit taxonomic characters that define a phylum, class, order, or other rank. A feature characteristic of one phylum may vary in another phylum among closely related members of a class, order, or some lower group. The complex carbohydrate cellulose is characteristic of two kingdoms of plants; among animals, however, cellulose occurs only in one subphylum of one phylum. It would simplify the work of the taxonomist if characters diagnostic of phylum rank in animals were always taken from one feature, the skeleton, for example; those of class rank, from the respiratory organs; and so on down the taxonomic hierarchy. Such a system, however, would produce an unnatural classification.

The taxonomist must first recognize natural groups and then decide on the rank that should be assigned them. Are seasquirts, for instance, so clearly linked by the structure of the extraordinary immature form (larva) to the phylum Chordata, which includes all the vertebrates, that they should be called a subphylum; or should their extremely modified adult organization be deemed more important, with the result that seasquirts might be recognized as a separate phylum, albeit clearly related to the Chordata? At present, this sort of question has no precise answer.

Some biologists believe that "numerical taxonomy," a system of quantifying characteristics of taxa and subjecting the results to multivariate analysis, may eventually produce quantitative measures of overall differences among groups, and that agreement can be achieved so as to establish the maximal difference allowed each taxonomic level. Although such agreement may be possible, many difficulties exist. An order in one authority's classification may be a superorder or class in another. Most of the established classifications of the better known groups result from a general consensus among practicing taxonomists. It follows that no complete definition of a group can be made until the group itself has been recognized, after which its common (or most usual) characters can be formally stated. As further information is obtained about the group, it is subject to taxonomic revision.

"Numerical taxonomy" as a system of quantifying characteristics

Nomenclature. Communication among biologists requires a recognized nomenclature, especially for the units in most common use. The internationally accepted taxonomic nomenclature is the Linnaean system, which, although founded on Linnaeus' rules and procedures, has been greatly modified. There are separate international codes of nomenclature in botany, (first published in 1901), in zoology (1906), and in microbiology (bacteria and viruses, 1948). The Linnaean binomial system is not employed for viruses. There is also a code, established in 1953, for the nomenclature of cultivated plants, many of which are artificially produced and are unknown in the wild.

The codes, the authority for each of which stems from a corresponding international congress, differ in various details, but all include the following: the naming of species by two words treated as Latin; a law of priority that the first validly published and validly binomial name for a given taxon is the correct one and that any others must become synonyms; recognition that a valid binomen can apply to only one taxon, so that a name may be used both in botany and in zoology but for only one plant taxon and one animal taxon; that if taxonomic opinion about the status of a taxon is changed, the valid name can change also; and, lastly, that the exact sense in which a name is used be determined by reference to a type. Rules are also given for the obligate categories of the hierarchy and for what constitutes valid publication of a name. Finally, recommendations are given on how to derive names.

Linnaeus believed that there were not more than a few thousand genera of living things, each with some clearly marked character, and that the good taxonomist could memorize them all, especially if their names were well chosen. Thus, although the naming of the species might often involve much research, the genus at least could be easily found.

Ability to interbreed as a criterion of species

At the present time, in many taxa, the species has a definite biological meaning—it is defined as a group of individuals that can breed among themselves but do not normally breed with other forms. Among micro-organisms and other groups in which sexual reproduction need not occur, this criterion fails.

In botanical practice, matters more usually resemble the Linnean situation. Many sorts of chromosomal variants (individuals with different arrangements of chromosomes, or hereditary material, which prevent interbreeding) and marked ecotypes (individuals whose external form is affected by the conditions of soil, moisture, and other environmental factors), as well as other forms, that would clearly be classified as separate species by the zoologist may be lumped together unrecognized or considered subspecies by the botanist. Botanists commonly use the terms variety and form to designate genetically controlled variants within plant populations below the subspecies level.

The use of a strictly biological species definition would enormously increase rather than reduce the number of names in use in botany. A recognized species of flowering plant may consist of several "chromosomal races"—*i.e.*, identical in external appearance but genetically incompatible and, thus, effectively separate species. Such various forms are often identifiable only by cytological examination, which requires fresh material and extensive laboratory work. Many botanists have said that there has been so little stability in the accepted nomenclature that further upheavals would be intolerable and render identification impossible for many applied botanists who may not need to go into such refinements. To postpone recognition of such forms, however, will probably cause upheaval in the future.

Some species of birds are widespread over the archipelagos of the Southwest Pacific, where nearly every island may have a form sufficiently distinct to be given some kind of taxonomic recognition. For example, 73 races are currently recognized for the golden whistler (*Pachycephala pectoralis*). Before the realization that species could vary geographically, each island form was named as a separate species (as many of the races of *P. pectoralis* actually were). It is often believed—and often it is only belief rather than fact—however, that all of these now genetically isolated populations arose as local differentiations of a single stock; thus, they are now usually classed in zoological usage as subspecies of one polytypic species. The term polytypic indicates that a separate description (and type specimen) is needed for each of the distinct populations, instead of one for the entire species. The use of a trinomial designation for each subspecies (*e.g.*, *Pachycephala pectoralis bougainvillei*) indicates that it is regarded as simply a local representative (in this case, on Bougainville Island in the Solomons) of a more widely distributed species. The decision on whether to consider such island forms as representatives of one species depends partly on whether, in the judgment of the taxonomist, populations from adjacent islands are sufficiently similar to allow free interbreeding. For further discussion of species concepts, see SPECIES AND SPECIATION.

Polytypic species

Verification and validation by type specimens. The determination of the exact organism designated by a particular name usually requires more than the mere reading of the description or the definition of the taxon to which the name applies. New forms, which may have become known since the description was written, may differ in characteristics not originally considered; or later workers may discover, by inspection of the original material, that the original author inadvertently confused two or more forms. No description can be guaranteed to be exhaustive for all time. Validation of the use of a name requires examination of the original specimen. It must, therefore, be unambiguously designated.

At one time an author might have taken his description from a series of specimens, or partly (or even wholly) from other authors' descriptions or figures, as Linnaeus often did. Much of the controversy over the validity of certain names in current use, especially those dating from the late 18th century, stems from the difficulty in determining the identity of the material used by the original authors. In modern practice, a single type specimen must be designated for a new species or subspecies name. The type should always be placed in a reliable public institution, where it can be properly cared for and made available to taxonomists. For many micro-organisms, type cultures are maintained in qualified institutions. Because of the short generation time of micro-organisms, however, they may actually evolve during storage.

A complex nomenclature is applied to the different sorts of type specimens. The holotype is a single specimen designated by the original describer of the form (a species or subspecies only) and available to those who want to verify the status of other specimens. When no holotype exists, as is frequently the case, a neotype is selected and so designated by someone who subsequently revises the taxon; the neotype occupies a position equivalent to that of the holotype. The first type validly designated has priority over all other type specimens. Paratypes are specimens used, along with the holotype, in the original designation of a new form; they must be part of the same series (*i.e.*, collected at the same immediate locality and at the same time) as the holotype. For a taxon above the species level, the type is a taxon of the next lower rank (for a genus, for instance, it is a species); from the level of the genus to that of the superfamily there are rules regarding the formation of a group name from the name of the type group. The genus *Homo* (man) is the type genus of the family Hominidae, for example, and the code forbids its removal from the family Hominidae as long as the Hominidae is treated as a valid family and the name *Homo* is taxonomically valid. Whatever the remainder of its contents, the family that contains the genus *Homo* must be the Hominidae.

Nomenclature associated with type specimens

Indiscriminate collecting is of little use today, but huge areas of the Earth still are poorly known biologically, at least as far as many groups are concerned, and there remain many groups for which the small number of properly collected and prepared specimens precludes any thorough taxonomic analysis. Even in well-studied groups, such as the higher vertebrates, new methods of analyzing material often necessitate special collecting. The determination of variation within species or populations may necessitate the study of more specimens than are available, even when (as is usual) the specialist can utilize material from many institutions. Usually, collecting is done to fill gaps (in geographical range, geological formations, or taxonomic categories) already brought to light by specialists reviewing the available material. The well-informed collector of living things knows where to go, what to look for, and how to spot anything especially valuable or extraordinary.

The actual techniques of collecting and preserving vary greatly from one group of organisms to another—soil protozoa, fungi, or pines are neither collected nor preserved in the same manner as birds. Some animals can be preserved only in weak alcohol; others macerate (decompose) in it. Certain earthworms "preserved" in weak alcohol simply flow out of their own skins when lifted out. Special methods are used after long experience to preserve characters of special value in taxonomy. Some methods make specimens difficult to observe; this is especially true of material that has to be sectioned or otherwise made into preparations suitable for microscopic observation.

After taxonomic material has been collected and preserved, its value can be lost unless it is accurately and completely labelled. Only rarely is unlabelled or insufficiently labelled material of any use. The taxonomist normally must know the locality of collection of each specimen (or lot of specimens), often the habitat (*e.g.*, type of forest, marsh, type of seawater), the date, the name of the collector, and the original field number given to the specimen or lot. To this information is added the catalog number of the collection and the sex (if not already determined in the field and if relevant). The scientific identity of the specimen, as determined by an acknowledged specialist, is usually added to the label at the museum. Also included is the name of the specialist who identified the specimen. Later revisions of the classification and additional knowledge of the organism may result in later alterations of the scientific name, but the original labels must still be kept unaltered.

Labelling the specimens

Other information may also be required; for example, the males and females of some insect groups are extremely different in appearance, and males and females of the same species may have to be identified. The capture of a pair in the wild actually in copulation gives a strong (but, surprisingly, not absolute) indication that the male and female belong to the same species; the labels of each specimen (if they are separated) indicate the specimen with which it was mating.

Taxonomic characters. Comparison of material depends to some extent on the purposes of the comparison. For mere identification, a suitable key, with attention given only to the characters in it, may be enough in well-known groups. If the form is likely to be a new one, its general position is determined by observing as many characters as possible and by comparing them with the definitions and descriptions in a natural classification. The new specimen is compared with its nearest known relatives, usually with reference to type material. Any character may be of taxonomic use. In general, taxonomists tend to work from preserved material, so that their findings can be checked. For extinct forms, of course, only preserved material (fossils) is available.

Many biochemical, physiological, or behavioral characters may be at least as good as anatomical characters for discriminating between closely related species or for suggesting relationships. There has been a tendency in recent years rather to discount anatomical characters, but when they are obtainable in quantity (as for most plants and animals), they probably represent as large a sample of the effects of the organism's heredity as can be got, short of complete genetic analysis. Enthusiasts in genetics often stress that the only real basis for classification is the actual genotype of each organism—*i.e.*, the hereditary information by which the organism is formed. It is impossible to obtain such information for extinct forms, and the time required to obtain it for most existing ones would be enormous, even if the techniques were available. An important development, however, has been the hybridization technique employing deoxyribonucleic acid (DNA), the substance by which hereditary information is coded. With this technique, it has been possible to determine similarities in parts of DNA molecules from different organisms but not the nature of their differences.

In making comparisons, resemblances resulting from convergence must be considered. Whales and bony fishes, for example, have similar body shapes for the same function—progression through water; their internal features, however, are widely different. In this case, the convergence is evident because of the large number of characters that link whales to other mammals and not to the fishes and because the fossil record for the vertebrates provides a fair indication of the actual evolutionary sequence from primitive fishes through primitive amphibians to primitive reptiles, mammal-like reptiles, and mammals. In the absence of a good fossil record it may be difficult or impossible to identify positively a case of convergence; yet it has been asserted that the occurrence of convergence must not be stated unless it has been "proved." To obey this assertion would be to make the method of analysis dictate in part the results achieved.

The role of convergent resemblances

In some forms, especially internal parasites, great modification has occurred in adapting to a parasitic way of life. The "root system" of the "tumour" (in reality a parasite) found under the abdomen ("tail") of some crabs, for example, penetrates through the crab's body; the parasite is unrecognizable as a close relative of the barnacles (crustaceans not far removed from the crabs themselves) without the free-swimming larval stage, which shows its affinities. Transient or inconspicuous characters may be of great importance in indicating affinities; the complete life cycle of a specimen may have to be observed before its affinities can be determined. Although such characters may be useless for identification and for definition of a natural group if only a few forms in a group show them, they may be of the utmost importance in understanding relationships. Characters are therefore weighted to some extent by the taxonomist according to their utility for different purposes. Any characters intrinsic to the organism can be used in classification. Extrinsic characters, including the position of fossils in a geological sequence and geographical distribution of fossil and recent forms, may force the taxonomist to look more closely at the intrinsic characters.

Weighting of characters

Weighting or nonweighting (*i.e.*, by the degree of importance) of characters has been a subject of great dispute. On the one hand it has been pointed out that weighting is often demonstrably arbitrary and always imprecise. On the other, it has been said that if characters were actually examined without weighting, some obvious cases of extreme convergence would have to be classed with each other instead of in their proper place. A classification based on unweighted characters is called a phenetic one (based on appearances) as opposed to a phyletic one, in which characters are weighted by their presumed importance in indicating lines of descent. The quarrel results in part from a misunderstanding of aims.

At present, the classification of living things is a rough, non-quantitative sketch of their diversity. A properly surveyed map of this diversity would advance classification enormously. If, on such a map, the diving petrels (*Pelecanoides*) of the Southern Hemisphere and the little auk (*Plautus*) of the Northern Hemisphere were closer to each other than to their phylogenetic relatives (the other petrels, fulmars, and albatrosses; and the guillemots, terns, gulls, and shorebirds, respectively), this would show the extent of their convergence, which is certainly great, but it would not be a reason for combining them in a separate group. In recent years numerical techniques have been developed for estimating overall resemblance or phenetic distance. For these methods, it is necessary to use large numbers of characters taken from each form and, as far as possible, at random; this involves enormous labour. The mathematical techniques are not as yet wholly satisfactory, some having been borrowed from statistical analysis and applied to taxonomic problems without any consideration of whether they were designed to answer the questions asked by the taxonomist.

It is worth noting that if there were a complete fossil record for any group, then simply placing any form nearest to those most like it (which must be its immediate ancestors or descendants) would produce an arrangement in which all cases of parallelism and convergence would be revealed. Since evolution occurs by descent with modification, this arrangement would presumably reflect the greatest use of the information available about the group and thus would also be the most useful general arrangement. For such groups, the phenetic arrangement is the phyletic one also.

Making a classification. When some idea has been obtained of the constituent forms in a group and of the similarity and dissimilarity that they bear to each other, it is necessary to fit a hierarchical system to them. As already indicated, for groups with good fossil records, a dendritic, or branching, arrangement is desired, and classification must be partly arbitrary because of lack of knowledge. If the taxonomist has two compact groups of species, those within each group agreeing closely with each other in many characters and differing sharply from members of the other group in others, there is no difficulty in classification except in ranking. If each group contains a scattering of forms, any one close to another but the most divergent members in each group less like each other than they are like certain of the other group, breaking up the groups into definite classes becomes arbitrary.

A particularly difficult case arises when these forms also occur in time series: the present-day dogs, cats, hyenas, and other carnivores differ greatly from each other, but at one time their ancestors were much alike; presumably, therefore, they came from one ancestral stock. Paleontologists trace back each taxonomic line and are inclined to carry their separations of taxonomic groups as far backward in time as possible, until the earliest members of related groups are far more like each other than each is to the rest of the later members of the group to which it is assigned. This separation of groups is extreme phyletic splitting, but cutting off a large basal group containing all the primitive members may require arbitrary breaks in the many lines of descent and will obscure the evolutionary relationships. There is no answer to this dilemma except to avoid extremes.

A similar difficulty arises when the same character complex has arisen independently in related lines. American paleontologist George Gaylord Simpson, for example, has pointed out that mammalian characters such as the single jawbone (dentary) have arisen several times in groups of the extinct mammal-like reptiles. To use Sir Julian Huxley's useful terminology, the definition of the Mammalia expresses a grade of organization (the attainment of a particular level of advancement), not a clade (a single phyletic group or line). Some taxonomists insist that in an evolutionary classification every group must be truly monophyletic—that is, spring from a single ancestral stock. Usually, this cannot be ascertained; the fossil material is insufficient or, as with many soft-bodied forms, nonexistent. Definite convergence must not be overlooked if it can be detected.

How far groups should be split to show phyletic lines and what rank should be given each group and subgroup thus are matters for reasonable compromise. The resulting classification, if fossils are unknown, may be frankly "natural" or phenetic, as is often explicitly the case with the flowering plants and is actually the case with many animal groups. If sufficient fossils are available, the resulting classification may be consonant with what is known about the evolution of the group or with what is merely conjectured. In reality, many classifications are conjectural or tendentious, and simpler and more natural ones might be closer to the available facts.

Even when only mere fragments are dealt with, a classification of some sort may still be necessary. Large numbers of leaves, some stems, trunks or roots, many seeds, and few flowers are known as fossils and may be of interest to the evolutionist. It may be many decades before a particular sort of fossilized leaf can be associated with a particular sort of branch, let alone trunk, flower, or seed. It is customary to construct form groups (*i.e.*, a genus or species name is assigned to the fossilized material based on its structure) in order to classify fossilized remains and to give them valid binomial names. When (if ever)

two or more bits of fossil material are identified as belonging to one organism, one name only is retained. This procedure is best known for plants, but one phylum of animals (the Conodonta) is made up of enigmatic structures that are obviously some part of something animal.

CURRENT SYSTEMS OF CLASSIFICATION

Division of organisms into kingdoms. As long as the only known plants were those that grew fixed in one place and all known animals moved about and took in food, the greater groups of organisms were obvious. Linnaeus, like his predecessors, recognized three kingdoms in the empire of nature: animal, vegetable, and mineral; even in the time of Linnaeus, many biologists wondered about such animal groups as corals and sponges, which were fixed in position and in some ways even flowerlike. Were they zoophytes—animal–plants—intermediate between the two kingdoms? When these problems were solved by the recognition of corals and sponges as animal, a more serious one arose over how to classify microscopic forms. An example is *Euglena*, a single cell with the characteristic green coloration of a plant, yet with animal features such as an eyespot and locomotion by means of a flagellum. Some related micro-organisms can either photosynthesize like a plant or become parasitic inside animals and ingest complicated materials as food. The true slime molds (Myxomycetes) at one stage of their life history form great composite amoeboid (changeable in shape) sheets that can move about and ingest food; yet, when they arrive at the reproductive stage, they produce spore-bearing bodies remarkably like those of fungi. It has often been proposed that the unicellular forms—which include some obvious animals, such as *Plasmodium* (the parasite that causes malaria) and the well-known *Amoeba*, and some obvious plants (such as diatoms and desmids), as well as some forms that could be called either animals or plants—all should be placed in a separate kingdom, the Protista. This is not a happy solution, as some of the "unicellular" plants occur in "colonies" of various numbers of cells and even may have specialized reproductive cells. There is no satisfactory clear break between them and multicellular algae; and it seems unsatisfactory to put them in a kingdom different from that of their nearest relatives. Among the animal-like forms are some that live in colonies, which seem to behave in some respects like a single individual. The difficulty of producing good, simple, clear-cut classes is evident. Although complex definitions can be formulated that define most known forms, they sharply separate rather closely related groups. And although a formal classification is of great practical use, the taxonomic biologist is uncomfortably aware of its shortcomings.

With the development of techniques for examining the smallest living things, an even greater difficulty arose. All higher plants (Metaphyta or Plantae) and the higher animals (Metazoa or Animalia) are composed of thousands or millions of cells (each one a blob of cytoplasm containing a nucleus and various other components), modified cells, and cell products. Bacteria, however, although usually regarded as allied to plants, do not have a definite nucleus (*i.e.*, one bounded by a membrane) containing the hereditary material; they do, however, usually have not only a membrane covering the surface of the body but also a rather rigid wall outside it and, outside this, a definite capsule. They show something like sexual activity, moreover, exchanging genetic material. Many bacteria do not use oxygen in their energy-releasing life processes; rather, unlike other living things, they utilize iron or sulfur compounds. Some are motile, using a flagellum (a whiplike structure); others move with a curious gliding motion. They divide by fission, as do many protists. Some produce highly resistant bodies called spores.

Viruses, however, are far more difficult to classify. They are only known as parasites; no free-living forms have been found. They have a far simpler structure than bacteria and reproduce by injecting their hereditary material, which is either deoxyribonucleic acid (DNA) or ribonucleic acid (RNA) but not both (as in all other living

Compact and scattered groups of species

Form group classification of fossil remains

Problem of relationships of bacteria and viruses

things), into cells of other organisms. In effect, viruses utilize the host's protein synthesizing mechanism to reproduce. The individual virus particle (virion), therefore, does not grow and divide by fission as do bacteria. Some biologists have speculated that viruses are genes that have got out of control and become parasitic; others have denied that viruses can be considered living at all. Some forms of virus, when purified, can be obtained as true crystals while retaining their infectious abilities. Many are highly important disease producers in plants, animals, and bacteria.

The principal characteristic shared by bacteria and viruses is that the hereditary material is not contained within a special nuclear membrane. Such a condition, which might be postulated by evolutionists as primitive when compared with forms with a complex nucleus, is called procaryotic—as opposed to eucaryotic, with a true nucleus—and bacteria and viruses together are usually referred to as the Procaryota. All other living things (with the exception of the procaryotic blue-green algae) are described as eucaryote. Viruses, as they now exist, may be the simplest of living things, but it is not known how much they are modified from ancestral forms that are assumed not to have been parasitic and that were evidently on the main line of evolution; nor is their relation to bacteria known. Some authors have used the term Monera for viruses and bacteria and have set them off as a separate kingdom; but the term Monera was originally introduced for a postulated early stage in evolution with which neither bacteria nor viruses need have any connection; on the other hand, the term Procaryota describes their condition without any undesirable theoretical overtones.

There are further complications. Some entities, often referred to as pseudoviruses, resemble true viruses in a few characters but, like bacteria, have both DNA and RNA. These include the rickettsias and the entities causing diseases such as psittacosis and lymphogranuloma. Most authorities regard them as odd types of bacteria and not as truly intermediate forms. Another procaryotic group, the blue-green algae, is traditionally placed with the other algae (*e.g.,* seaweeds) and studied more by botanists than by microbiologists. Blue-green algae may be either unicellular or filamentous, and they behave like true plants, photosynthesizing in a way that resembles green plants rather than bacteria. Many move by gliding, as do some bacteria and some true unicellular algae. They are often extremely abundant around hot springs or at the edges of muddy ponds, and, although they are resistant to harsh environments, blue-green algae are killed by many drugs (*e.g.,* antibiotics) used against bacteria. Perhaps they are best regarded as representing a group close to the main evolutionary line that gave rise to the eucaryotic plants.

The preceding considerations exemplify the difficulties of producing a hard-and-fast classification, even at the highest levels. Another problem relates to the position of the fungi, a large group including not only familiar forms, such as mushrooms, toadstools, molds, and yeasts, but also, according to some authorities, the true slime molds (Myxomycetes). The majority of fungi are eucaryotic, lack chlorophyll (and therefore cannot photosynthesize as do green plants), and have rigid walls to the "cells," or filaments (hyphae) that sometimes contain cellulose, as do green plants. Some fungi walls or filaments are made of chitin, the major constituent of the external skeleton of insects and other arthropods, or even of other structural compounds. A fungal cell usually contains many nuclei. Asexual and sexual spores are usually produced; some produce motile spores with flagella, like the spores of some algae. The sexual cycle is often very complex. Because fungi in general grow and produce "fruit" like ordinary plants, they have traditionally been included with them; but the differences between the fungi and the metaphyta seem considerable, and it has been suggested that they should be placed in a separate kingdom.

The most elaborate modern classification (a five-kingdom scheme) is that shown on Table 2. Such a scheme may be useful, but the relations are complex and cannot

The
blue-green
algae

be represented by any sort of linear arrangement of groups. Many protophyta, for example, are extremely close to true algae and to some protozoa.

Table 2: The Five-Kingdom Scheme of Classification

kingdom	members
Procaryota	viruses, bacteria (and rickettsiae, etc.), Cyanophyta (blue-green algae)
Protista	Protophyta, several phyla: unicellular algae and their close relatives
	Protozoa: unicellular animals—amoeba, some flagellates, ciliates, parasitic protozoa
Fungi	
Metaphyta (Plantae)	all other plants—true algae, mosses, liverworts, ferns and related forms, conifers and allies, flowering plants
Metazoa (Animalia)	all other animals—sponges, corals, flatworms, flukes, tapeworms, wheel animalcules, roundworms, mollusks, arthropods (joint-legged animals), sea mats, arrowworms, lamp shells, seasquirts, lancelets, and all the vertebrates from lampreys to man

A classification of living organisms. An alternative scheme is the four-kingdom classification presented below. In it the fungi are considered a division (Mycota or Fungi) of the kingdom Protista. This classification is that used in the major biological articles in the *Macropaedia.* The use of "division" by botanists and "phylum" by zoologists for equivalent categories leads to a rather awkward situation in the Protista, a group of interest to both botanists and zoologists. As used below, the terms follow prevailing usage: phylum for the primarily animal-like protozoa and division for all other protistan groups, which are more plantlike and of interest primarily to botanists.

The discussion above shows the difficulty involved in classification; major classificatory systems should perhaps be thought of as indexes to chapters in systematic treatises.

KINGDOM MONERA (bacteria and blue-green algae)
Division Schizophyta (bacteria)
Photosynthetic and chemosynthetic bacteria, true bacteria, sheathed bacteria, budding bacteria, filamentous bacteria, branching bacteria, gliding bacteria, slime bacteria, spiral bacteria, and mycoplasms or pleuropneumonia organisms (see BACTERIA).
Division Cyanophyta (blue-green algae; see ALGAE).

KINGDOM PROTISTA (protists)
Algae other than the blue-greens, protozoa, slime molds, and fungi.

Subkingdom Protophyta (algae, slime molds, lichens, water molds, sac fungi (yeasts, many bread molds, powdery mildews, morels, cup fungi, truffles, most lichen fungi, and others), club fungi (jelly fungi, smuts, rusts, mushrooms, puffballs, stinkhorns, earth stars, bird's-nest fungi and others; see ALGAE; MYCOTA; SLIME MOLD; LICHEN).

Subkingdom Protozoa (protozoa)
Phylum Protozoa; see PROTOZOA.

KINGDOM PLANTAE (METAPHYTA OR EMBRYOPHYTA) (bryophytes and vascular plants)
Includes mosses, liverworts, hornworts, whisk ferns, club mosses, horsetails, ferns, cycads, conifers, and flowering plants.
Division Bryophyta (mosses, liverworts, and hornworts); see BRYOPSIDA).
Division Psilotophyta (whisk ferns or psilopsids; see PSILOPSIDA).
Division Lycopodiophyta (club mosses and quill worts; see LYCOPSIDA).
Division Equisetophyta (horsetails; see SPHENOPSIDA).
Division Polypodiophyta (ferns; see FERN).
Division Pinophyta (or *Gymnospermae*) (gymnosperms)
Includes conifers (pines, yews, spruces, firs, junipers, redwoods, and others), cycads, ginkgos, joint firs, and others: see CONIFER; see also GYMNOSPERM.
Division Magnoliophyta (or *Angiospermae*) (flowering plants)
Includes monocots (grasses, rushes, sedges, cattails and pondweeds, palms, pineapple and other bromeliads, lilies, bananas, ginger, orchids, and others) and dicots or broad-

leaved plants (most trees, buttercups, poppies, roses, violets, cacti, mints, squashes, sunflowers, and many others; see ANGIOSPERM). Major angiosperm orders are covered in individual articles under the ordinal names.

KINGDOM METAZOA (higher animals)

Subkingdom Parazoa (sponges)

Phylum Porifera (sponges; see PORIFERA).

Subkingdom Metazoa

Phylum Mesozoa (mesozoans; see MESOZOA).

Phylum Cnidaria (or *Coelenterata*) (cnidarians; see CNIDARIA).

Phylum Ctenophora (ctenophores; see CTENOPHORA).

Phylum Platyhelminthes (flatworms; see PLATYHELMINTHES).

Phylum Nemertea (or *Rhynchocoela*) (ribbonworms; see NEMERTEA).

Phylum Acanthocephala (spiny-headed worms; see ACANTHOCEPHALA).

Phylum Rotifera (rotifers or wheel animalcules; see ASCHELMINTHES).

Phylum Gastrotricha (gastrotrichs; see ASCHELMINTHES).

Phylum Kinorhyncha (or *Echinoderida*) (no common name; see ASCHELMINTHES).

Phylum Priapulida (priapulids; see ASCHELMINTHES).

Phylum Nematoda (roundworms; see ASCHELMINTHES).

Phylum Nematomorpha (horsehair worms; see ASCHELMINTHES).

Phylum Conodonta (conodonts; see CONODONTA).

Phylum Entoprocta (or *Kamptozoa*) (entoprocts; see ENTOPROCTA).

Phylum Annelida (annelid worms; see ANNELIDA).

Phylum Arthropoda (arthropods; see ARTHROPODA).

Phylum Mollusca (mollusks; see MOLLUSCA).

Phylum Bryozoa (or *Ectoprocta*) (bryozoans; see BRYOZOA).

Phylum Phoronida (phoronid worms; see PHORONIDA).

Phylum Brachiopoda (brachiopods; see BRACHIOPODA).

Phylum Sipunculoidea (or *Sipuncula*) (sipunculid worms; see SIPUNCULA).

Phylum Chaetognatha (arrowworms; see CHAETOGNATHA).

Phylum Echinodermata (echinoderms; see ECHINODERMATA).

Phylum Hemichordata (hemichordates; see HEMICHORDATA).

Phylum Pogonophora (breadworms; see POGONOPHORA).

Phylum Graptolites (graptolites).

Phylum Chordata (chordates; see CHORDATA).

For a more detailed treatment of chordate groups, see FISH; AMPHIBIA; REPTILIA; BIRD; MAMMALIA.

BIBLIOGRAPHY. GEOFFREY C. AINSWORTH and P.H.A. SNEATH (eds.), *Microbial Classification* (1962), a symposium of the Society of General Microbiology, with discussion of the principles of classification and their application to microbial groups; GUY R. BISBY, *An Introduction to the Taxonomy and Nomenclature of Fungi*, 2nd ed. (1953); ARTHUR J. CAIN (ed.), *Function and Taxonomic Importance* (1959), a symposium of the Systematics Association on the relevance of function to classification, especially to convergence; OLOV HEDBERG (ed.), *Systematics of Today* (1958), symposium held at the University of Uppsala to commemorate the 250th anniversary of Linnaeus's birth; JOHN G. HAWKES (ed.), *Symposium on Chemotaxonomy and Serotaxonomy* (1968); WILLI HENNIG, *Phylogenetic Systematics* (1966), a statement of phylogenetic "principles"; VERNON H. HEYWOOD and J. MCNEILL (eds.), *Phenetic and Phylogenetic Classification* (1964); ROBERT R. SOKAL and P.H.A. SNEATH, *Principles of Numerical Taxonomy* (1963), an important introduction to numerical taxonomy.

General texts: RICHARD E. BLACKWELDER, *Taxonomy* (1967); VERNON H. HEYWOOD and PETER H. DAVIS, *Principles of Angiosperm Taxonomy* (1963); JULIAN S. HUXLEY (ed.), *The New Systematics* (1940); ERNST MAYR, *Principles of Systematic Zoology* (1969); GEORGE G. SIMPSON, *Principles of Animal Taxonomy* (1961).

Codes: INTERNATIONAL ASSOCIATION OF MICROBIOLOGICAL SOCIETIES, *International Code of Nomenclature of Bacteria and Viruses* (1958); JOSEPH LANJOUW (ed.), *International Code of Botanical Nomenclature* (1966); INTERNATIONAL COMMISSION ON ZOOLOGICAL NOMENCLATURE, *International Code of Zoological Nomenclature* (1961).

(A.J.Ca.)

Classification Theory

In apprehending the world, men constantly employ three methods of organization, which pervade all of their thinking: (1) the differentiation of experience into particular objects and their attributes—*e.g.*, when they distinguish between a tree and its size or its spatial relations to other objects; (2) the distinction between whole objects and their component parts—*e.g.*, when they contrast a tree with its component branches; and (3) the formation of and the distinction between different classes of objects—*e.g.*, when they form the class of all trees and the class of all stones and distinguish between them. Of these methods, the differentiation of objects and attributes is obviously presupposed by the other two. Though the whole–part and the class–member relationships are quite different, the work of developmental psychologists has indicated that children below the age of five cannot distinguish between them. This article, however, deals only with the third method.

Most practical activities, whether on an individual or social level, involve classification. The buying and selling of commodities (such as carloads of melons), for example, often concerns objects considered as members of a class (melons) rather than as concrete particulars. Classification is no less involved in any attempt at a theoretical understanding of the whole of reality or of some aspects of it. Ancient and recent metaphysicians, in their efforts to determine the structure of reality, have put forward classificatory schemes that allegedly reflect this structure. Formulation of scientific laws presupposes classifications, because to formulate a law of nature is to state relations between the members of different classes.

Uses of classification

THE PRINCIPLES OF CLASSIFICATION

Logical principles. From the purely logical point of view, a classification of a domain of things does not depend on the nature of the criteria for class membership. It coincides with what, in the mathematical theory of sets, is called a "partition": a division of a set of objects into subsets is a partition if and only if

1. no two subsets have any element in common and
2. all of the subsets together contain all of the members of the partitioned set;

i.e., they are mutually exclusive and jointly exhaustive. A classification or partition may be refined by classifying or partitioning the subsets and their subsets until (if ever) a class of only one member is reached. If a set is manageably finite, its partition can proceed without employing any criteria for class membership by simply forming collections that satisfy the two conditions for a partition; *e.g.*, when the set {a, b, c, d} is subdivided into the subsets {a, b} and {c, d}. If a set is infinite or finite but unmanageably large, then its partition requires the use of criteria; *e.g.*, when the set of integers {1, 2, 3, . . .} is partitioned into the subsets of even and of odd integers. A criterion for class membership may be either a simple characteristic (*e.g.*, being an even integer) or a compound characteristic (*e.g.*, being divisible by 2 and by 3 or being divisible by 2 or by 3) so that possession of the characteristic is a necessary and sufficient condition for an object's membership in the class.

The mathematical theory of sets, however (see SET THEORY), makes the unrealistic assumption that every set is exact or extensionally definite. It disregards the frequent occurrence of borderline cases; *i.e.*, of objects that can with equal correctness be accepted or rejected as members of a class. Such borderline cases, common to two otherwise exclusive classes, are relevant in biological classification. A logical theory that allows for inexact classes has been developed for analyzing the relation between mathematical and perceptual propositions.

Material principles. Though governed by the same formal principles, classifications may differ widely in their classificatory criteria and in the principles determining their choice. It is usual to distinguish between natural and artificial, between essential and empirical, and between pragmatic and otherwise-justified classifications.

1. The distinction between natural and artificial classifi-

cations is hardly an absolute one: it is relative with respect not only to different cultures but also to different phases in the history of one culture; and this relativity applies even if a natural classification is defined by classes the members of which share the maximal number of attributes. To a contemporary Westerner, for example, the classifications employed by the members of some primitive tribe—of days into auspicious and inauspicious, for example—may seem wholly artificial. Again, those of St. Thomas Aquinas, which contain a class of angels, may seem equally unnatural to him.

2. The distinction between essential and empirical classification is based on the assumption that the former rests on a priori ideas as to what is important, whereas the latter rests on observation alone. Yet no scientific classification is independent of theoretical assumptions as opposed to uninterpreted observations, if, indeed, there are such things (see SCIENCE, PHILOSOPHY OF). To regard, for example, zoological classifications that are not genetic as wholly nonempirical and those that are genetic as wholly empirical is to mistake a change of theory for a discovery of an error.

3. Pragmatic classifications in the sense of philosophical Pragmatism (q.v.) must be distinguished from pragmatic classification meant to be merely provisional, heuristic (aiding discovery), auxiliary, or made independently of scientific theorizing.

THE DOMAINS OF CLASSIFICATION

General problems. In every attempt at classifying a domain of objects, the extent to which the choice of classificatory principles depends upon the nature of the objects must be considered. More specifically, the choice of the principles may depend, as in acoustics, on the extent to which the objects of the domain are given in perception; as in paleontology, on the extent to which they are subject to change or development; as in petrology, on the extent to which their differences are differences in degree rather than in kind; or, as in fluid dynamics, on the extent to which their differences are differences in quantity rather than quality.

Classification of perceptual and nonperceptual objects. In forming classes of perceptual objects—*e.g.,* the class of green things, of elephants, or of motorcars—the perceptual resemblances and dissimilarities between their members play an important role. Whatever definition of such a resemblance class may be adopted, it must always satisfy the following requirements: (1) the qualifications and disqualifications for membership must include a method for exhibiting standard members and nonmembers of the class, such that (2) an object qualifies for membership only if it is sufficiently similar to the standard members and sufficiently dissimilar to the standard nonmembers. Although the latitude allowed by these conditions can be restricted by various means, it cannot

be wholly eliminated; thus, resemblance classes are inexact; *i.e.,* they admit of borderline cases. Their existence, far from impairing the classificatory scheme, may be a logical consequence or a postulate of a scientific theory employing the scheme. After all, if, say, the development of living organisms implies gradual change, their classification would be unrealistic if it did not allow for cases on the borderline between species. On the other hand, many scientific theories, such as those of theoretical physics, do not refer directly to perceptual phenomena but do so indirectly by relating a perceptual domain to a domain of abstract or ideal objects; *e.g.,* of Newtonian particles or Maxwellian fields. Such objects are described and classified by means of nonperceptual, structural properties and relations and expressed in the language of a mathematical theory—especially algebra, the theory of functions, and topology.

Classification by morphological and genetic criteria. A domain of objects that are unchanging or the history of which is regarded as negligible is classified only in terms of form or structure; *i.e.,* morphologically. Thus, Christian biologists of the 18th century would hold that animal species are constant, having been created constant; and some contemporary anthropologists would hold that

the history of a primitive tribe does not affect its basic social structure. If, on the other hand, the domain of classification consists of developing populations of plants, animals, or stars, then the criteria of classification are likely to be genetic; *i.e.,* to refer to what are regarded as crucial developmental stages. Whereas a morphological classification need not be genetic, any genetic classification must be to some extent morphological.

Classification by differences of kind and of degree. Sometimes the objects of a classificatory domain differ from each other not so much in their characteristics as in the degree to which they possess them. Thus, minerals may be classified according to their increasing hardness and commodities by the increasing preference shown for them by the buying public. A classification of this type is or is based on a so-called partial ordering. More precisely, a domain of objects is partially ordered by a relation —say, $\leq$ ("smaller than or equal to")—if and only if, for any objects x, y, z of the domain, (1) $x \leq x$, (2) $x \leq y$ and $y \leq x$ implies that $x = y$, and (3) $x \leq y$ and $y \leq z$ implies that $x \leq z$. In technical language, the relation must be reflexive (holding between an object and itself), antisymmetrical (the applicability of both the relation and its converse implying the identity of the terms), and transitive (as in descendance, which implies that the descendant of the descendant of some forebear is *ipso facto* a descendant of this forebear). That a partial ordering involves a classification is especially clear where a larger number of objects are equal with respect to the ordering relation; *e.g.,* belong to a fairly large class of minerals of equal hardness or to a class of commodities none of which the buying public prefers to any other. A partial ordering is total if and only if the ordering relation is dichotomous; *i.e.,* if, for all x and y, $x \leq y$ or $y \leq x$.

Classification by differences of quantity and of quality. Quantitative measurement, as opposed to mere ordering, establishes equalities and inequalities of order or rank not only between different single members of a domain but also between different pairs of them. It allows a scientist, for example, not only to order objects by their temperature but also to order the differences in temperature between any two of them. (For details see MEASUREMENT, THEORY OF.) Just as the ordering of a domain establishes classes of objects equal in rank, so also its measurement establishes classes of objects equal in quantity. Though many sciences have tended to develop from mere qualitative comparison and classification toward ordering and measurement, the adage that science is measurement is an exaggeration.

Classification in particular domains. Principles of classification depend to some degree upon the domain involved.

Classification in the natural sciences. The greater the role played by purely quantitative methods, the smaller that played by merely qualitative classifications. Hence, comparatively less attention is given to classification in the physical than in the biological sciences. In the more descriptive parts of physics, however, classification is still of utmost importance. In astronomy, for example, difficulty is experienced not only in determining characteristic features (as in the case of the galaxies) but also in making sure that their observability is not lost as increasingly distant objects are studied. In moving from physics through chemistry to biology, the role of classification becomes more dominant; and, in biology, taxonomy, or the ordering of organisms into species, genera, families, and so on, constitutes a central part of the theory.

Classification in the social sciences. Classification in the social sciences was and still is to some extent concerned with so-called ideal types, such as the "typical bureaucrat," limiting concepts, which, though not exemplified in reality, serve nevertheless to explain the social behaviour of real people by concentrating on and even exaggerating certain features of people while ignoring others. Though the predominance of ideal types in the social sciences may simply mark an early stage in their development, whether they are now dispensable is controversial. From the logical point of view, a classification into ideal types is a classification of real people only insofar as real people can be ordered by the degree to which they approximate the type. And, more generally, a classification into ideal phenomena requires for its application an ordering of real phenomena.

Classification in the applied sciences and medicine. Although the distinction between pure and applied sciences —say, between zoology and animal husbandry—is not sharp, the latter are more concerned with practical than with theoretical ends. Thus, a rough classification of a domain—say, of different building materials or of different strains of a virus—may be preferable to a finer classification if their practical utility—say, for the building of bridges or the curing of diseases—is the same; or if, relative to their respective utility, the cost of the rough classification is very much lower than that of the fine.

Classification of information. When the purpose of classification is simply to make information available, the predominance of purely practical ends over theoretical is even more marked. Thus, the purpose of library classification is not so much to exhibit the fundamental relations among the things classified as it is to exhibit relations that are helpful in locating the information being sought. It would seem futile to argue, for example, whether "coal mining" should be a subdivision of "mining" or of "coal" (there are actual systems that do it each way). Similar problems arise for the classification schemas underlying encyclopaedias such as the present work, which aims at treating every existing subject. When information is stored by computers, the usual principles of classification are modified by those governing the technology of computers.

THE PLACE AND ROLE OF CLASSIFICATION IN SCIENTIFIC METHOD

Classification: its relation to and dependence on theory. Though purely classificatory sciences are sometimes contrasted with explanatory sciences, it must be emphasized that the formulation of scientific laws presupposes classification. This is true not only of universal laws of nature but also of probabilistic laws. As R.B. Braithwaite, a British philosopher of science, has emphasized, every deterministic scientific generalization may be (at least partly) analyzed as a concomitance generalization to the effect that everything that is *A* is *B*—provided that *A* and *B* are sufficiently complex properties—and, clearly, the principles for setting up the classes *A* and *B* in the first place must serve as a basis for the generalization.

Probabilistic or statistical laws of nature also presuppose classification, because any such law has the form of a statement that a certain proportion of things belonging to class *A* belongs to class *B* or that there is a certain probability that a thing that belongs to *A* also belongs to *B*. Universal laws that can be formulated within one classificatory scheme may not be amenable to formulation within another. And the same holds for statistical laws. Here the proper choice of the related classes is important: the mortality, for example, of people of ages 40 to 50 suffering from a certain disease is of interest but not that of people so aged whose Christian name consists of two syllables.

While every theory presupposes a classificatory scheme, this scheme is in turn influenced by the content of the theory. This influence is perhaps most obvious in biology, in which the transition from the pre-evolutionary to the evolutionary point of view has influenced taxonomy in several ways. First, the hypothesis that species are not fixed units but are entities that change and grade into each other has made it necessary to regard the extension of species as variable and as necessitating borderline cases. Second, the hypothesis that one species may descend from another as a result of organic reproduction has made it necessary to base the classification into species on the notion of a population of animals exhibiting a frequency distribution of certain characters (see POPULATION, BIOLOGICAL).

The tendency to base classifications on frequency and probability distributions of variable characters within populations (or ensembles) rather than on homogeneous classes has been manifest also in theoretical physics ever

(margin: Priority of classification)

(margin: The statistical approach)

since quantum mechanics was developed as an irreducibly statistical theory. Whereas before the advent of quantum mechanics statistical hypotheses were regarded as compatible with and, at least in principle, reducible to universal laws, the opposite point of view is now dominant. Thus, the physical and biological sciences reinforce each other in implying that the theoretically most basic scientific classifications depend on statistical distributions of variable characteristics rather than on constant criteria.

A similar shift toward classification in terms of statistical distributions can also be noticed in the social sciences, in which, as Paul Lazarsfeld, a communications sociologist, has emphasized, the investigator will frequently have to develop his own classificatory scheme rather than to take one over from a developed, explicit theory. The place of the theory is taken by a provisional model or scheme of the whole situation in which the inquiry has taken place. Use of such a model suggests that a classificatory scheme is required that, when modified as a result of the inquiry, will in turn suggest modifications of the model. The distinction between classifications based on explicit theories and classifications suggested by structural models is, of course, not sharp. And, again, the latter kind of classification cannot be sharply distinguished from those based on a more or less implicit sense of proportion or reasonableness.

Classification and scientific nomenclature. The more complex a classificatory scheme, the more difficult is its application and the more important the choice of a suitable terminology and nomenclature. These problems are particularly pressing in biology, in which, as the leading evolutionist G.G. Simpson points out, the existence of millions of species is acknowledged, each of which must be named—quite apart from more general and less general classes. The subjective and arbitrary element in the choice of a system of nomenclature is recognized by the organization of international congresses to arrive at agreements on conventional names. Objectively, the taxonomically most important features must also be emphasized in the system of nomenclature. Thus, according to Darwin, those characters that, in the course of evolution, have suffered the least modification are taxonomically most important and should be given a central place in any system of nomenclature. The history of the transition from Linnaean to Darwinian and post-Darwinian theory illustrates the dependence of nomenclature on taxonomy and of taxonomy on theory. At the same time it also shows how an established nomenclature tends to preserve established taxonomical principles and thus indirectly to perpetuate the theory on which they are based.

Philosophical issues regarding classification. From the rise of philosophical reflection, some classifications have been viewed as adequate to reality and others as erroneous. Plato's theory of Forms, the earliest metaphysical theory of classification, is still the paradigm of all typological classifications. The Platonic Forms are unchanging ideal objects—in particular, mathematical objects—by reference to which the fluctuating objects of sense experience are classified and ordered. Perceptual objects and the relations between them are not instances of Forms or of relations between Forms but only participate in or approximate them. In asserting that one apple and one apple make two apples, one asserts that perishable perceptual objects approximate eternal mathematical units and that a physical operation involving perishable objects approximates a mathematical relationship (see PLATO).

Aristotle rejects the Platonic Forms and the relationship of participation in favour of the relationship between attributes and their instances. The Aristotelian theory of classification and of definition by classification has both an uncontroversial logical aspect and a controversial metaphysical aspect. A definition formulated by classification of kinds of things consists, according to Aristotle, in indicating a simple or compound attribute that the defined kind shares with other kinds and by indicating another such attribute that it does not share with the other kinds. A definition by classification is also called a defini-

(margin: Platonic Forms and Aristotle's theory of classification)

tion by *genus proximum* ("next-higher genus") and *differentia specifica* ("specific difference")—a nomenclature especially apt if one assumes, with Aristotle, that the correct choice of *genus* and *differentia* is not dependent on convention or convenience but on the nature of reality. It is held by some theorists that there is one and only one adequate classificatory hierarchy such that each kind of thing, unless it is a lowest kind (*infima species*), is divided into two or more lower kinds (*species*) and that each kind of thing, unless it is a highest kind (*summum genus*), falls under one higher kind—a view that is sometimes called essentialism, because it bases the classification of things on their alleged essences. Some form of the essentialist doctrine that there must be one essentially natural system of classification is held by most metaphysicians, who thus assume that whatever exists falls into one or more natural kinds (*e.g.*, minds, bodies, or minds and bodies).

Jevons' anti-essentialism

The essentialist doctrine is clearly rejected by W.S. Jevons, one of the founders of modern symbolic logic and philosophy of science. He devotes a whole chapter to classification, the value of which he regards as "coextensive with the value of science and general reasoning." His careful investigation into the employment of classification in the different branches of science, which is as modern today as in 1874, convinces him that there is no unique, essential, natural, or a priori system of classification that is alone adequate to the nature of reality.

This conclusion is compatible with the possibility and, indeed, the historical fact that at some period of time a certain classificatory scheme or part of one that is actually employed may appear to its users to be more adequate than any alternatives and thus to be incorrigible.

BIBLIOGRAPHY. K. KURATOWSKI and A. MOSTOWSKI, *Teoria mnogości*, 2nd ed. (1966; Eng. trans., *Set Theory*, 1967), one of many excellent books on set theory; S. KORNER, *Experience and Theory* (1966), contains elaborate discussions of inexact classes and empirical continuity; CLAUDE LEVI STRAUSS, *La Pensée sauvage* (1962; Eng. trans., *The Savage Mind*, 1966), contains an anthropological theory of the nature and function of classification; G.G. SIMPSON, C.S. PITTENDRIGH, and L.H. TIFFANY, *Life* (1957), an excellent survey; C.G. HEMPEL, *Aspects of Scientific Explanation, and Other Essays in the Philosophy of Science* (1965), contains one of the best discussions of typological classification; E.P. HUBBLE, *The Realm of the Nebulae* (1936, reprinted 1958), a standard book; J. MILLS, *A Modern Outline of Library Classification* (1960), an informative survey; R.B. BRAITHWAITE, *Scientific Explanation* (1953), a clear discussion of most problems in the philosophy of science; P.A.M. DIRAC, *The Principles of Quantum Mechanics* (1930), a fundamental work; P.F. LAZARSFELD and M. ROSENBERG (eds.), *The Language of Social Research: A Reader in the Methodology of Social Research* (1955), contains informative methodological papers; A.J. CAIN (ed.), *Function and Taxonomic Importance* (1959), a modern discussion of classification theory; W.S. JEVONS, *The Principles of Science*, esp. pp. 305–315 (1874), a classic; J.H. WOODGER, *Biology and Language* (1952), mainly concerned with logical questions.

(S.Kö.)

Claude Lorrain

The French artist Claude Lorrain is the best known and one of the greatest masters of ideal-landscape painting, an art form that seeks to present a view of nature more beautiful and harmonious than nature itself. The quality of that beauty is governed by classical concepts, and the landscape often contains classical ruins and pastoral figures in classical dress. The source of inspiration is the countryside around Rome—the Roman Campagna—a countryside haunted with remains and associations of antiquity. The practitioners of ideal landscape during the 17th century, the key period of its development, were artists of many nationalities congregated in Rome. Later, the form spread to other countries. Claude, whose special contribution was the poetic rendering of light, was particularly influential, not only during his lifetime but, especially in England, from the mid-18th to the mid-19th century.

Life and works. Claude Lorrain, properly Claude Gellée (also spelled Gelée, Gille, etc.), is usually called simply Claude in English. He was born in 1600 of poor par-

"Landscape: The Marriage of Isaac and Rebekah," oil on canvas by Claude Lorrain, 1648. In the National Gallery, London. 1.49 m × 1.97 m.
By courtesy of the trustees of the National Gallery, London

ents at Chamagne, a village in the then independent duchy of Lorraine. He received little schooling, and, according to his first biographer, Joachim von Sandrart, was brought up to be a pastrycook. His parents seem to have died when he was 12 years old, and, within the next few years, he travelled south to Rome.

Early training in Rome

In Rome he was trained as an artist by Agostino Tassi, a landscapist and the leading Italian painter of illusionistic architectural frescoes. At what stage and for how long he was apprenticed is uncertain, and, either before or during this period, Claude probably spent two years in Naples with Goffredo Wals, another pupil of Tassi. Tassi taught Claude the basic vocabulary of his art—landscapes and coast scenes with buildings and little figures—and gave him a lasting interest in perspective and, thus, in landscape painting.

In 1625, according to his second biographer, Filippo Baldinucci, Claude left Tassi and went back to Nancy, the capital of Lorraine, where he worked for a year as assistant to Claude Deruet on some frescoes (since destroyed) in the Carmelite church. But, in the winter of 1626–27, Claude returned to Rome and settled there permanently. He never married, but he had a daughter, Agnese (1653–*c*. 1713), who lived in his house; also staying with him were a pupil, Giovanni Domenico Desiderii, from 1633–*c*. 1656, and two nephews, Jean from *c*. 1663 and Joseph from *c*. 1680. In 1633, to further his career, Claude joined the painters' Academy of St. Luke.

Little is known of his personality. He took no part in public events and lived essentially for his work. In his early period he mixed with other artists, especially those who were of north European origin like himself, but in his 40s he apparently became more solitary. He remained on good terms with the painter Nicolas Poussin, another French master of the ideal landscape, yet there was hardly any artistic contact between them. Although ill-educated in the formal sense (both his spelling and counting were eccentric, and he wrote haltingly in French and Italian), Claude was not the ignorant peasant of legend. The subjects of his paintings show that he had an adequate knowledge of the Bible, Ovid's *Metamorphoses*, and the *Aeneid*. He had a special feeling for the country but his mode of life was that of a bourgeois. Industrious, amiable, and shrewd, surrounded by his modest household, and keenly sought after as an artist, he pursued a successful career into old age and amassed a comfortable fortune.

No work by Claude survives from before 1627, and he probably did not take up landscape until after that date. His first dated work is a "Landscape with Cattle and Peasants." Painted in 1629, it hangs in the Philadelphia Museum of Art. Soon after, in the early 1630s, he rose to fame. He did this partly on the basis of two or three series of landscape frescoes (all but one, a small frieze in the Crescenzi palace at Rome, are now lost), but, according to Baldinucci, he achieved renown chiefly because of his skill in representing "those conditions of nature which produce views of the sun, particularly on seawater and over rivers at dawn and evening." By about 1637—with commissions from Pope Urban VIII, several cardinals, and Philip IV of Spain—Claude had become the leading landscape painter in Italy.

In 1635–36 he began the *Liber Veritatis* (British Museum, London), or "Book of Truth," a remarkable volume containing 195 drawings carefully copied by Claude after his own paintings, with particulars noted on the backs of the drawings indicating the patron for whom, or the place for which, the picture was destined, and, in the second half of the book, the date. Although most paintings executed before 1635 and a few executed afterward are not included, the *Liber Veritatis* was compiled throughout in chronological order and thus forms an invaluable record of Claude's artistic development, as well as revealing his circle of patrons. Undertaken, as he told Baldinucci, as a safeguard against forgery of his paintings, the book gradually became Claude's most precious possession and a work of art in itself; he may also have used it as a stock of motifs for new compositions.

Claude's patrons were international and predominantly aristocratic, the majority being French or Italian noblemen. He was a fastidious worker and an expensive artist. He always worked on commission, at first sometimes selling his paintings through agents, but later he negotiated directly with patrons, with whom he would agree as to the size, price, and subject. Initially a fast painter, his rate of production subsequently slowed down. His late works are often individually larger and were still more carefully executed. About 250 paintings by Claude, out of a total of perhaps 300, and more than 1,000 drawings have survived. He also produced 44 etchings.

Stylistic development. Although they are basically consistent in method and aim, Claude's paintings show a gradual stylistic evolution, and it is possible to distinguish the phases of his development. His early works, showing the influence of Tassi and of Dutch and Flemish artists, are busy, animated, and picturesque. They are full of charm and effects of surprise. His smaller pictures, painted on copper, reflect the spirit of the German artist Adam Elsheimer, who had died in Rome in 1610. Occasionally Claude painted directly from nature during this period, although no examples have been certainly identified; his normal method of nature study was by means of drawings. A pattern common in the early paintings is a dark mass of foliage on one side in the foreground contrasted with a misty sunlit distance on the other. Herdsmen tending cattle or goats move out from beneath the trees or sit beside a stream (scarcely any of Claude's paintings at any time are without figures and animals). Simultaneously Claude developed the traditional subject of a coastal scene with boats into a new type of picture: the seaport. This is an idealized harbour scene flanked on one or both sides with palaces, the latter often being adapted from actual ancient and contemporary buildings. Tall ships ride at anchor, recently arrived or preparing to depart. Light, however, is the key feature of the seaport pictures. Its source is often a visible sun just above the horizon, which Claude first introduced in 1634 in "Harbour Scene" and, in so doing, used the sun as the means of illuminating a whole picture for the first time in art. This use of light from the sky above the horizon, whether emanating directly from the sun or not, enforces another characteristic of Claude's paintings: recession in depth. Recession is further emphasized by subtle atmospheric perspective achieved through a gradual diminishing of the distinctness of outline and colour from the foreground to the background. The light is nearly always that of dawn or evening, which imparts a poetic mood to the painting.

Beginning around 1640 Claude began to make his compositions more classical and monumental. The influence of contemporary Bolognese landscape painting, particu-

Characteristics of early works

larly the works of Domenichino, replaces that of Tassi and the northerners. During this decade something like a formula establishes itself: tall trees on one side of the picture balanced by a classical ruin and smaller trees further back on the other; a foreground "stage" with figures; a winding river conducting the eye by stages through an open landscape to the horizon; and distant hills, often with a glimpse of the sea. The figures are not, as often before, in contemporary dress but are always represented in classical or biblical costume. Contrary to popular belief, virtually all of Claude's figures were painted by himself. Sometimes they are merely shepherds, but frequently they embody a subject from classical mythology or sacred history. The light is clearer than in paintings of the early or late periods. Spacious, tranquil compositions are drenched in an even light, as can be seen in "Landscape: The Marriage of Isaac and Rebekah" (also called "The Mill"), dated 1648.

The 1650s witness some still larger and more heroic paintings, including "The Sermon on the Mount." In the middle of the following decade, Claude's style moved into its last phase, when some of his greatest masterpieces were produced. The colour range is restricted, and the tones become cool and silvery. The figures are strangely elongated and by conventional standards ill drawn. At the same time, the subjects define the mood and sometimes determine the composition of the landscape. The paintings of this period are solemn and mysterious and radiate a sublime poetic feeling. It was in this spirit that Claude painted his famous work "The Enchanted Castle."

Achievement as a draftsman. Claude's drawings are as remarkable an achievement as his paintings. About half are studies from nature. Executed freely in chalk or pen and wash, they are much more spontaneous than his paintings or studio drawings and represent informal motifs—trees, ruins, waterfalls, parts of a riverbank, fields in sunlight—that Claude saw on his sketching expeditions in the Campagna. Many were executed in bound books, which have since been broken up. The studio drawings consist partly of preparatory designs for paintings—Claude prepared his work more carefully than any previous landscape artist—and partly of compositions created as ends in themselves. Some are copies of paintings, comparable to the drawings in the *Liber Veritatis*. He kept almost all of his drawings in his studio until his death.

Claude died on November 23, 1682, and was buried in SS. Trinità dei Monti at Rome. Apart from Desiderii, by whom only a few drawings are known, he had one pupil, Angeluccio (active c. 1640–50). But his paintings had influenced a group of Dutchmen in Rome in the later 1630s and 1640s, including Herman van Swanevelt, Jan Both, and Claes Berchem. He also influenced the 17th-century French artist Pierre Patel. Claude's later work was less popular with artists during his lifetime. The revival of his art began about 1750, with English painters, such as John Wootton, George Lambert, and Richard Wilson, but in the wider sense, his art penetrated the styles of a century of English landscape painters, down to J.M.W. Turner and Samuel Palmer. Englishmen of the 18th and early 19th centuries were also the most avid collectors of Claude. Even now, more great paintings by Claude are in English public and private collections than anywhere else, and half his drawings are in the British Museum.

Claude's reputation declined in the later 19th century in the face of Ruskin's art criticism. Ruskin thought Claude's work insipid and inaccurate when judged by reference to scientific truth. The zenith of his fame was reached about 1800, but he is scarcely less highly regarded in the 20th century. The serene, enchanted art of Claude still offers aesthetic refreshment and visual repose.

MAJOR WORKS

"Landscape with River" (1631; Museum of Fine Arts, Boston); "Harbour Scene" (1634; Hermitage, Leningrad); "View of the Campo Vaccino" (1636; Louvre, Paris); "Landscape with a Country Dance" (1637; Earl of Yarborough, Habrough, Lincolnshire); "Seaport with the Villa Medici"

(1637; Uffizi, Florence); "Landscape: The Finding of Moses" (c. 1640; Prado, Madrid); "Landscape: The Burial of St. Serapia" (c. 1640; Prado); "Landscape near Rome with a View of the Ponte Molle" (1645; City Museum and Art Gallery, Birmingham, England); "Seaport: The Embarkation of Ulysses" (1646; Louvre); "Landscape: Hagar and the Angel" (1646; National Gallery, London); "Landscape: The Marriage of Isaac and Rebekah," also called "The Mill" (1648; National Gallery, London; autograph replica of the same date, Galleria Doria-Pamphili, Rome); "Seaport: The Embarkation of the Queen of Sheba" (1648; National Gallery, London); "Pastoral Landscape with the Arch of Constantine" (1648–51; Trustees of the Grosvenor Estate, London); "Sacrifice at Delphi" (1650; Galleria Doria-Pamphili); "Pastoral Landscape" (1651; Trustees of the Grosvenor Estate); "Landscape with the Adoration of the Golden Calf" (1653; Staatliche Kunsthalle, Karlsruhe); "The Sermon on the Mount" (1656; Frick Collection, New York City); "Landscape: David at the Cave of Adullam" (1658; National Gallery, London); "Landscape: The Rest on the Flight to Egypt" (1661; Hermitage); "Landscape: The Father of Psyche Sacrificing to Apollo" (1662; National Trust, Fairhaven Collection, Anglesey Abbey, Cambridgeshire); "Landscape: Tobias and the Angel" (1663; Hermitage); "Landscape with Psyche at the Palace of Cupid," also called "The Enchanted Castle" (1664; Loyd Collection, Wantage, Berkshire); "Coast Scene: The Rape of Europa" (1667; Buckingham Palace, London); "Landscape With the Nymph Egeria Mourning over Numa" (1669; Museo e Gallerie Nazionali di Capodimonte, Naples); "Coast Scene with Perseus: The Origin of Coral" (1674; Earl of Leicester, Holkham, Norfolk); "Landscape: The Arrival of Aeneas at Pallanteum" (1675; National Trust, Fairhaven Collection, Anglesey Abbey, Cambridgeshire); "Landscape with Ascanius Shooting the Stag of Sylvia" (1682; Ashmolean Museum, Oxford).

BIBLIOGRAPHY. M. ROTHLISBERGER, Claude Lorrain: The Paintings, 2 vol. (1961), and Claude Lorrain: The Drawings, 2 vol. (1968), two fully illustrated, complete catalogs, with introductions and notes, are the standard works. They include in English translation all the early material on the artist, i.e., the annotations to the Liber Veritatis, his will of 1663 (codicils 1670 and 1682), the inventory of his possessions at his death, and the biographies of him by JOACHIM VON SANDRART (1675), FILIPPO BALDINUCCI (1728), and LIONE PASCOLI (1730). Only the etchings are not adequately covered by Röthlisberger: see A. BLUM, Les Eaux-fortes de Claude Gellée (1923). Other recent works include: M. ROTHLISBERGER, "Additions to Claude," Burlington Magazine, 110:114–119 (1968); M. CHIARINI, Claude Lorrain: Selected Drawings (1968), with superb plates; and M. KITSON, The Art of Claude Lorrain (1969), an exhibition catalog, Arts Council, London.

(M.W.L.K.)

Claudius I

Claudius I (Tiberius Claudius Drusus Nero Germanicus) was the Roman emperor and historian who extended Roman rule in North Africa and made Britain a Roman province. A member of the patrician branch of the clan (gens) of the Claudii, he was born in Lugdunum (modern Lyon) on August 1, 10 BC. The son of Nero Claudius Drusus, a popular and successful Roman general, and the younger Antonia, he was the nephew of the emperor Tiberius and a grandson of Livia Drusilla, the wife of the emperor Augustus. Ill health, unattractive appearance, clumsiness of manner, and coarseness of taste did not recommend him for a public life. The imperial family seems to have considered him something of an embarrassment, and he was long left to his own private studies and amusements. It was the historian Livy who recognized and encouraged his inclination for historical studies. Claudius wrote a pamphlet defending the republican politician and orator Cicero, who was executed by the triumvirs; and, having discovered that it was difficult to speak freely on the civil wars toward the end of the Roman Republic, he began a history of Rome with the principate of Augustus. He composed 20 books of Etruscan and 8 books of Carthaginian history, all in Greek; an autobiography; and a historical treatise on the Roman alphabet with suggestions for orthographical reform—which as emperor he later tried not very successfully to implement. He also wrote on dice playing, of which he was fond. All his works are lost, and their importance cannot be measured. The Etruscan history may have had original material: his first wife, Plautia Urgul-

anilla, had Etruscan blood, and her family was probably able to put Claudius in touch with authentic Etruscan traditions. After divorcing Urgulanilla, he in turn married Aelia Paetina, Valeria Messalina, who was his wife at his accession, and, finally, Agrippina the Younger. By his first three wives he had five children, of whom Drusus and Claudia died before he became emperor. As a young man Claudius was made a member of various religious colleges, but he became consul only under the reign of his older brother's son Gaius (Caligula) in 37. There was, however, little cordiality between the two.

Alinari

Claudius I, bust found near Priverno. In the Vatican Museum.

Power came to Claudius unexpectedly after Gaius' murder on January 24, 41, when he was discovered trembling in the palace by a soldier. The Praetorian Guards, the imperial household troops, made him emperor on January 25. By family tradition and antiquarian inclinations, Claudius was in sympathy with the senatorial aristocracy; but soldiers and courtiers were his real supporters, while freedmen and foreigners had been his friends in the days of neglect. Initially, the attitude of the Senate was at best ambiguous. In 42 many senators supported the ill-fated rebellion of the governor of Dalmatia. Even later, several attempts on Claudius' life involved senators and knights. Though paying homage to the dignity of the Senate (to whose administration he returned the provinces of Macedonia and Achaea) and giving new opportunities to the knights, Claudius was ruthless and occasionally cruel in his dealings with individual members of both orders. From the very beginning he emphasized his friendship with the army and paid cash for his proclamation as emperor.

Claudius' decision to invade Britain (43) and his personal appearance at the climax of the expedition, the crossing of the Thames and the capture of Camulodunum (Colchester), were prompted by his need of popularity and glory. But concern with the anti-Roman influence of the Druid priesthood, which he tried to suppress in Gaul, and a general inclination toward expanding the frontiers were other reasons. Claudius planted a colony of veterans at Camulodunum and established client-kingdoms to protect the frontiers of the province; these were afterward a source of trouble, such as the revolt in 47 of Prasutagus, client-king of the Iceni, and later the general revolt instigated by his wife Boudicca (also called Boadicea). He also annexed Mauretania (41–42) in North Africa, of which he made two provinces (Caesariensis in the east and Tingitana in the west), Lycia in Asia Minor (43), and Thrace (46). Though he enlarged the kingdom of Herod Agrippa I, he later made Judaea a province on Agrippa's death in 44. In 49 he annexed Iturea (northeastern Palestine) to the province of Syria. He was careful not to involve the empire in major wars with the Ger-

Emperor and colonizer

mans and the Parthians. Claudius supported Roman control of Armenia, but in 52 he preferred the collapse of the pro-Roman government to a war with Parthia, leaving a difficult situation to his successor.

In the civil administration, many measures demonstrate Claudius' enlightened policy. He improved in detail the judicial system, and, in his dealings with the provinces, he favoured a moderate extension of Roman citizenship by individual and collective grants: in Noricum, a district south of the Danube comprising what is now central Austria and parts of Bavaria, for instance, five communities became Roman municipalities. He encouraged urbanization and planted several colonies, for example at Camulodunum and at Colonia Agrippinensis (modern Cologne) in Germany in 51. In his religious policy Claudius respected tradition; he revived old religious ceremonies, celebrated the festival of the Secular Games in 47 (three days and nights of games and sacrifice commemorating the 800th birthday of Rome), made himself a censor in 47, and extended in 49 the *pomerium* of Rome (*i.e.*, the boundary of the area in which only Roman gods could be worshipped and magistrates ruled with civil, not military, powers). He protected the haruspices (diviners) and probably romanized the cult of the Phrygian deity Attis. According to the biographer Suetonius in *Claudius* (25), during a period of troubles Claudius expelled the Jews from Rome for a short time; Christians may have been involved. Elsewhere he confirmed existing Jewish rights and privileges, and in Alexandria he tried to protect the Jews without provoking Egyptian nationalism. In a surviving letter addressed to the city of Alexandria, he asked Jews and non-Jews "to stop this destructive and obstinate mutual enmity." Although personally disinclined to accept divine honours, he did not seriously oppose the current trend and had a temple erected to himself in Camulodunum. His public works include the reorganization of the corn supply of Rome and a new harbour at Ostia, which was later improved by the emperor Trajan.

Claudius' general policy increased the control of the emperor over the treasury and the provincial administration and apparently gave jurisdiction in fiscal matters to his own governors in the senatorial provinces. He created a kind of cabinet of freedmen, on whom he bestowed honours, to superintend various branches of the administration. An impressive series of documents, such as a speech for the admission of Gauls to the Senate recorded on a partly defective inscription at Lugdunum (Lyons), the edict for the Anauni (an Alpine population who had usurped the rights of Roman citizenship and whom Claudius confirmed in these rights), and the above-mentioned letter to the city of Alexandria (AD 41), survive as evidence of his personal style of government: pedantic, uninhibited, alternately humane and wrathful, and ultimately despotic. The inscription from Lugdunum is an interesting comparison with the version of the historian Tacitus in his *Annals*, which gives an account of the same speech. The speech as recorded in the inscription, in spite of irrelevance, inconsequence, and fondness for digression (much of which is absent in the version of Tacitus), shows that Claudius knew what he wanted and that he appreciated the latent forces of Roman tradition.

His marriage with Messalina ended mysteriously in 48 when she apparently conspired against him and married one Gaius Silius. Messalina and Silius were killed on Claudius' order, and he married his niece Agrippina, an act contrary to Roman law, which he therefore changed. To satisfy Agrippina's lust for power, Claudius had to adopt her son Lucius Domitius Ahenobarbus (later the emperor Nero) to the disadvantage of his own son Britannicus. In addition, the new commander of the guards, Afranius Burrus, was protected by Agrippina. Roman tradition is unanimous in stating that Claudius was poisoned by Agrippina on October 13, AD 54, though the details differ. A version of poisoning by mushrooms prevailed. Lucius Annaeus Seneca, the politician and satirist, who had been exiled by Claudius at his accession but had been recalled at Agrippina's urging to educate Nero, derided the dead emperor and his apotheosis (duly decreed

by the Senate) in the satire *Apocolocyntosis divi Claudii* ("The Pumpkinification of Claudius the god"; the title and its exact meaning are both subject to dispute).

The picture of Claudius that appears in this work has much in common with that of later Roman historians who give details of the unpopular side of Claudius' administration. The *Apocolocyntosis* ridicules his uncouth physical appearance and attacks his habit of giving legal judgments without a hearing and the executions of relatives, senators, and knights. Tacitus, Suetonius, and the later historian Dio Cassius attribute Claudius' mistakes to infirmity of character and the influence of his wives and freedmen. They echo the hostility of the upper classes of Rome against an emperor who, in spite of his own words, had been unfavourable to them. That this tradition is one-sided is shown by the surviving documents of the reign and the energy with which Claudius carried out the practical affairs of government.

BIBLIOGRAPHY. The main sources are TACITUS, *Annals* xi–xii (for the years 47–54); DIO CASSIUS, book 60; SUETONIUS, *Divus Claudius* (a good Latin commentary by HENRICUS SMILDA, 1896); JOSEPHUS, *Antiquities of the Jews*, book 19. These writers have common sources: probably historians contemporary with Claudius, such as Pliny the Elder and Cluvius Rufus. On this see RONALD SYME, *Tacitus*, 2 vol. (1958); and *Ten Studies in Tacitus* (1970). Inscriptions and papyri have been collected by E.M. SMALLWOOD in *Documents Illustrating the Principates of Gaius, Claudius and Nero* (1967); papyri also in *Corpus papyrorum judaicarum*, vol. 2 with commentary (1960). Standard modern monographs include ARNALDO MOMIGLIANO, *L'opera dell'imperatore Claudio* (1932; Eng. trans., *Claudius: The Emperor and His Achievement*, 1934, reprinted with up-to-date bibliography, 1962); M.P. CHARLESWORTH and A.D. NOCK in *The Cambridge Ancient History*, vol. 10 (1934); VINCENT M. SCRAMUZZA, *The Emperor Claudius* (1940); and ALBINO GARZETTI, *L'Impero da Tiberio agli Antonini* (1960). The novels of ROBERT GRAVES, *I, Claudius* and *Claudius, the God, and His Wife, Messalina* (1934), draw from the traditions of the ancient historians.

(A.D.Mo.)

Clausewitz, Carl von

One of the most important of all writers on military strategy, whose theories have had wide influence on military practitioners in the 19th and 20th centuries, Carl von Clausewitz was born at Burg, near Magdeburg, Germany, on June 1, 1780.

By courtesy of the Staatsbibliothek Berlin

Clausewitz, lithograph by Franz Michelis after an oil painting by Wilhelm Wach, 1830.

Born to a poor but middle class family of professional background, Clausewitz entered the Prussian Army in 1792. He was commissioned during the Rhine campaign of 1793–94 against the French Revolutionary army and spent the next several years on garrison duty, a circumstance that enabled him to devote a large amount of time to educating himself. His efforts eventually enabled him to gain admission to the War College in Berlin in 1801.

During his formative years in Berlin, Clausewitz learned military science under the guidance of his mentor, Gerhard von Scharnhorst; studied philosophy and literature; and developed his basic strategic concepts. Scharnhorst

Administrative innovations (left margin)

Early military experience (right margin)

introduced him at court—where he met his future wife, the Countess Marie von Brühl—and obtained for him an appointment as aide to Prince August. He served in this capacity in the campaign of Jena (1806), was captured by the French at Prenzlau, and returned to Prussia in 1808. Clausewitz became one of the leaders of Prussian Army reform under Scharnhorst but resigned his commission on the eve of Napoleon's invasion of Russia (1812) and, like other German patriots, entered Russian service.

In the campaign of 1812, Clausewitz distinguished himself as a Russian staff officer. He was partially responsible for the Russians' successful strategic retreat and for negotiating the Convention of Tauroggen, which marked the beginning of Prussia's abandonment of the French cause.

After having served in various capacities during the campaigns of 1813–14, he returned to Prussian service and served as chief of staff of an army corps during the Waterloo campaign. In 1818 he became a general and was appointed administrative head of the War College. During the next 12 years, Clausewitz used much of the leisure that this position provided in writing his historical studies and his major work on strategy, *On War* (*Vom Kriege*). It is on these that his fame rests. Drawing on the experiences of Frederick the Great and Napoleon, Clausewitz tried to analyze the workings of military genius by isolating the factors that decide success in war. His conclusions have remained generally applicable, and since his work contains a minimum of technical discussion, it has retained a wide appeal. Clausewitz produced no system of strategy, thus breaking with the more rigid and mechanistic concepts of his predecessors. Instead, he emphasized the importance of psychological and accidental factors that elude exact calculation and the necessity of a critical approach to strategic problems. By means of a lengthy discussion of a variety of situations likely to confront the military leader, Clausewitz tried to develop in his reader a theoretically founded military judgment, capable of weighing all pertinent factors in a given situation. He stated that strategy should aim at three main targets: the enemy's forces, his resources, and his will to fight. Defensive warfare, he argued, is both militarily and politically the stronger position.

Essence of Clausewitz' approach

Before he completed *On War*, Clausewitz was transferred to Breslau and then assigned to Prussian forces deployed to observe the Polish revolution of 1830. He contracted cholera and died on November 16, 1831, shortly after his return to Breslau. His papers were edited and published by his devoted widow.

Clausewitz' personality reflected not only his relatively humble origins but also the strong influence of contemporary German literature and philosophy. Shy and sensitive by nature, he often kept his ideas to himself. He never had a command of his own but served mostly in a staff capacity, distinguishing himself through his sound advice and bravery in combat. His background and career identified him more closely with the broader movements for national German revival than with the aristocratic Prussian military tradition.

Influence on military thought

While Clausewitz' extensive histories of the various Napoleonic campaigns are only of technical interest, *On War* has had a profound influence on modern strategic concepts. Its most significant single contribution is the doctrine of political direction in military matters. In maintaining that "war is nothing but a continuation of political intercourse with the admixture of different means," he denied that war is an end in itself.

Clausewitz was studied closely by his countrymen and left his imprint on German military thought, but his influence on actual German strategy has been overrated. Beginning with the 1853 edition of *On War*, a crucial passage calling for cabinet control of strategy was altered to prescribe the reverse, and German military planning became increasingly devoid of political purpose. There was, however, a considerable revival of interest in Clausewitz during the interwar period.

Clausewitz was read extensively outside of Germany. Swedish, Dutch, Swiss, and Austrian officers took an early interest in his doctrines, and most of his works were translated into French. An English translation of *On War* appeared in 1873, and other editions exist in Russian, Italian, Hebrew, Hungarian, Serbian, and Spanish. By 1900 his doctrines were known in the United States and Japan. The first American translations appeared during World War II. Marx and Engels discussed Clausewitz' work, and Lenin studied his political doctrines during his exile in Switzerland. Communist theory on the nature of war, including such concepts as that of "imperialistic war," was largely derived from Clausewitz, whose authority has been recognized in the Communist world. By the middle of the 20th century, when new long-range weapons systems had appeared, the significance of Clausewitz' strategic concepts relating exclusively to land warfare declined, although many of his basic ideas remained as valid as ever.

BIBLIOGRAPHY. English translations of *Vom Kriege* (*On War*) include those by J.J. GRAHAM, 4th ed. (1940); and O.J. JOLLES (1943). HANS ROTHFELS, "Clausewitz," in E.M. EARLE, *Makers of Modern Strategy* (1943), provides a balanced appraisal by a leading historian. ROGER PARKINSON, *Clausewitz* (1971), is informative and has a bibliography.

(A.H.P.)

Clay, Henry

Patriot and politician, Henry Clay was one of the most influential leaders in the United States in the decades before the Civil War. He was a founder and leader of the Whig Party and led the more conservative minded of the nation in their struggle with Jacksonian democracy. Because of his services in forging the Compromises of 1820, 1833, and 1850, his admirers called him "the great pacificator."

Clay, by Frederick and William Langenheim, 1850.
By courtesy of the Library of Congress, Washington, D.C.

Born in Hanover County, Virginia, on April 12, 1777, of moderately well-to-do parents, young Clay studied law under Chancellor George Wythe and was admitted to the Virginia bar in November 1797. He then moved to Lexington, Kentucky, a rising western community and a paradise for lawyers because of interminable lawsuits over land titles that were contested there. Endowed with great vitality, a ready but not profound intellect, and a gift for eloquent oratory, he was quick-witted and self-confident. Sociable, charming, and high-spirited, he loved to drink and gamble, qualities not distasteful to most of his contemporaries in Kentucky society. He was also hot-tempered, sensitive, and extremely ambitious.

Kentucky background

Clay was spectacularly successful at the Kentucky bar in both civil and criminal cases, and he never lacked for clients. He acted as counsel for Aaron Burr (1806) in a Kentucky grand jury investigation of Burr's plan to establish an empire in the Southwest. Kentucky Republicans believed that Burr had been a victim of a Federalist conspiracy, and Clay's reputation did not suffer when his client's designs were later exposed.

Clay established his social position in 1799 by marrying Lucretia Hart, daughter of a wealthy Lexington businessman. By 1812 he possessed a 600-acre estate known as "Ashland," where he bred livestock and raised hemp, corn, and rye. He and Lucretia had 11 children, six daughters and five sons.

Clay entered politics shortly after arriving in Kentucky by championing liberalization of the state's constitution. A Jeffersonian Republican, he shared that leader's distaste for slavery and was an advocate of gradual emancipation in Kentucky, but he abandoned this idea when it proved a losing cause. Like Jefferson, he learned to accept slavery, though, unlike him, he provided for the freeing of his slaves in his will. His eloquent opposition to the Alien and Sedition Acts of 1798, a series of repressive measures designed to curb the pro-French activities of the Jeffersonian Republicans, made Clay popular with Kentucky voters, and (1803–09) they elected him to seven terms in the state legislature. In 1809 he fought a duel with a Federalist Party legislator, Humphrey Marshall, in which both men were wounded.

Clay advocated the establishment of banks, internal improvements, and manufacturing, thus foreshadowing his future national career. Twice he went to Washington to fill out unexpired terms in the United States Senate, and in 1811 he was elected to the U.S. House of Representatives. There, as speaker (1811–14), he was one of the leaders who pushed the country into the War of 1812. He also served as a member of the commission at Ghent that drew up the terms of peace with Britain in 1814.

During the next ten years, Clay was Kentucky's outstanding representative in the United States Congress, usually serving as speaker of the House. Experience and a broadening outlook made him a neo-Jeffersonian Republican; he espoused internal improvements at national expense, a protective tariff, a national bank, and distribution of land-sale revenues to the states. Already he was developing a project of joining the industrial East and the agricultural West in a political alliance under the banner of his American System. He coveted appointment as secretary of state as a step toward the White House and was furious when Pres. James Monroe gave that post to John Adams. In 1819 he attacked Andrew Jackson for his invasion of Florida, thus earning Old Hickory's lasting enmity. In 1820 he promoted the passage of the Missouri Compromise—which maintained the balance between the slave states and free states within the Union—and his followers began to call him "the great pacificator." Then came one of the fateful crises in his career.

Clay was an unsuccessful candidate for the presidency in the election of 1824. But the decision in that election between the front-running candidates John Quincy Adams and Andrew Jackson was thrown into the House of Representatives. As speaker of the House, Clay was in an influential position. He had decided to vote for Adams before leaving Kentucky. Conferences with Adams satisfied him that he could have any position in the government that he desired if Adams won. He threw his support to Adams, who was elected and who made Henry Clay his secretary of state. Clay never lived down the resultant cry of "bargain and sale."

His four years in the state department were frustrating, largely because of the political machinations of the Jacksonians. Clay was thwarted in his effort to send delegates to a Pan American Congress at Panama, nor did he reach an accord with Great Britain on West Indian trade. Sneers at the "bargain" were hard to bear; a bitter attack on Clay by Congressman John Randolph led to a duel, in which neither man was wounded.

Adams was inept at political infighting, and Jackson won the election of 1828 decisively. The National Republican Party, the opposition party that had arisen in opposition to the Jacksonians, began to go to pieces and in 1834 was absorbed by the Whig Party. After Jackson's victory Clay retired for a time to Ashland, but in 1831 he returned to the Senate where he headed the opposition to the Jacksonian democracy and championed the renewal of the charter of the second Bank of the

United States, which he had helped to found in 1816. Nominated for the presidency by the National Republicans in 1832, he was defeated by Andrew Jackson, largely on the bank issue. The following year he successfully piloted through Congress the compromise tariff of 1833, thus ending the so-called Nullification crisis, in which South Carolina threatened to secede from the Union.

Clay remained in the Senate, leading an uphill fight against the policies of the Jacksonians and becoming a leader of the Whig Party, which gradually emerged in the middle 1830s. He refused to run for the presidency in 1836, when the Whigs put up sectional candidates, and it was with a heavy heart that he accepted re-election to the Senate in 1837. His mood changed with the panic of 1837 and the consequent rise of Whig fortunes. He confidently expected the party's nomination in 1840, but, to his bitter disappointment, the Whig politicians turned to a military hero, Gen. William Henry Harrison, who, with John Tyler of Virginia as his running mate, was easily elected.

Clay's hopes and plans had been thwarted, and his temper had not been improved by years of political frustration. He was now bent upon dictating his party's policies from his post in the Senate. He tried to dominate Harrison, who lived only a month after his inauguration, and was determined to do the same with Tyler. The latter, a stubborn man, vetoed two bank bills that had Clay's approval, and, when other items in the Kentuckian's program of legislation were challenged from both Congress and the White House, he resigned from the Senate in 1842.

Confronted by a choice between Tyler and Clay as leader of the party, the Whigs rallied to Clay, nominating him for president in 1844 with a great display of enthusiasm for the "Old Prince," but once again fate proved unkind. Texas desired annexation to the Union. Clay came out against immediate annexation on the ground that it would stir up the already rising controversy over slavery and certainly involve the United States in war with Mexico, but the Democrats nominated James K. Polk, an ardent annexationist. Faced by a swelling tide of Manifest Destiny sentiment, Clay tried to explain his position in such a way as to satisfy pro-annexation, pro-slavery voters in the South without offending anti-slavery voters in the North. The effort was vain, and once again his greatest ambition was unsatisfied.

Frustration continued to be Clay's lot. He opposed war with Mexico but supported its prosecution after the guns went off. He hoped for the Whig nomination in 1848, but the Whigs turned from their 71-year-old leader (even Kentucky refused to support him) and nominated a Mexican War hero, Gen. Zachary Taylor. Nevertheless, one last act of service to the nation remained for "the great pacificator."

The annexation of territory in the Southwest heightened the strife between North and South over the extension of slavery, and Clay came back to the Senate in 1849 resolved to confront the growing threat of disunion. There in a great speech (February 5–6, 1850) he outlined the principal features of what became the Compromise of 1850 and put the weight of his reputation and influence behind its passage. The compromise again kept the numerical balance between slave and free states and perhaps delayed the Civil War by a decade. This was his last act of statesmanship. His health failed, and he died of tuberculosis in the National Hotel at Washington, D.C., June 29, 1852.

Clay was a man whose charm and nationalist fervour, coupled with the appeal of his ideas to the more conservative minded, made him a national leader loved and honoured by many thousands of Americans. Mistakes of judgment, together with the skill and good fortune of his political opponents, kept him from reaching the White House, and the passage of the years has somewhat dimmed the aura that surrounded him while he lived. During the Civil War, President Lincoln and Secretary of State William H. Seward, discussing the political past, agreed that Clay's selfishness had injured the Whig Party, and historical scholarship has shown that the importance

Clay's
American
System

Failure
to get
presidential
nomination

The
Compromise of
1850

of his influence on the passage of the Compromise of 1850 was less than had been thought. But he was a staunch defender of the Union, a man who spent his life in public service and in that service helped to guide his country through some of the most difficult crises in its history.

BIBLIOGRAPHY. GLYNDON G. VAN DEUSEN, *The Life of Henry Clay* (1937, reprinted 1967), is the standard life of Clay, superseding CARL SCHURZ, *Life of Henry Clay*, 2 vol. (1887, reissued in 1915 as *Henry Clay*, reprinted 1968), which is a 19th-century work reflecting passions engendered by the Civil War. CLEMENT EATON, *Henry Clay and the Art of American Politics* (1957), is an admirable, brief study of Clay as an antebellum political leader, with some attention to his personal life. GEORGE R. POAGE, *Henry Clay and the Whig Party* (1936, reprinted 1965), is an intensive examination of Clay's party leadership from 1840 to 1852. BERNARD MAYO, *Henry Clay* (1937, reprinted 1966), is a detailed and delightfully written study of Clay's early career, covering the period from his birth down to the War of 1812.

(G.G.V.D.)

Clay Minerals

Clay may be defined as a natural, earthy, fine-grained material that develops plasticity when mixed with a limited amount of water. The term is also used to designate the smallest particles in sedimentary rocks and soils (*q.v.*), etc. The maximum size of particles in the clay size grade is commonly considered to be two microns (0.002 millimetre). Clays are composed essentially of silica, alumina, and water, and appreciable quantities of iron, alkalies, and alkaline earths are frequently present. Until recently there were no analytical techniques by which to determine the precise nature of the components of these elements in clays and soils. X-ray diffraction techniques developed in the 1920s, followed a few years later by improved microscopic and thermal procedures, established that clays are composed of a few groups of crystalline minerals that have come to be called the clay minerals. Small amounts of amorphous material occur in some clays and varying amounts of such minerals as quartz, feldspar, mica, and iron oxides may also be present. The clay mineral components provide the essential characteristics and properties of clay, however.

Clay minerals occur in flake-shaped, lath-shaped, and needle-shaped units. The individual units are measured in angstroms (Å = 10^{-4} microns) but they occur in clays in booklike particles, aggregates of flakes, or bundles of laths and needles that are of the order of microns in diameter. Kaolin-type clay, for example, is essentially an aggregation of book-shaped units of sheets of the clay mineral kaolinite.

Clay minerals occur in nature in sedimentary rocks of all ages and in continental and marine sediments accumulating at the present time. They are formed as a result of weathering processes and, as a consequence, are found as the essential components of most soils. Clay minerals are also formed as a result of hydrothermal activity and are associated with volcanic activity and some metallic ore deposits.

Clays have a wide variety of physical characteristics, such as plasticity, refractoriness, colour, and colloidal properties that make them suitable for a wide variety of industrial purposes. They are used, for example, in the ceramic industry for the manufacture of whiteware, porcelain, refractories, and other clay products. Some types of clay are extensively used for filling and coating paper and as fillers, extenders, and reinforcing agents in plastics, paint, adhesive, and rubber manufacturing. Their colloidal properties in water systems make them suitable for use as drilling muds, which is of great importance to the oil industry.

Uses of clay

COMPOSITION AND STRUCTURE OF CLAY MINERALS

Numerous classifications that vary in detail have been suggested for the clay minerals. It is generally agreed, however, that they can be classified on the basis of variations of atomic structure and chemical composition into the following groups: (1) allophane; (2) kaolinite; (3) halloysite; (4) smectite; (5) illite; (6) chlorite; (7) vermiculite;

(8) sepiolite, attapulgite, and palygorskite; (9) mixed-layer clay minerals. Information on and structural diagrams for these groups are given below.

The composition and structure of the clay minerals has been determined largely by X-ray diffraction methods. Diffraction data for the clay minerals, as well as data on their infrared spectra, which can be related to chemical composition, are available in the clay-mineral literature.

The atomic lattices of most of the clay minerals consist of two structural units. In the first, two sheets of closely packed oxygen atoms or hydroxyls have aluminum, iron, or magnesium atoms sandwiched between them. Each metal atom is in the centre of, and equidistant from, six oxygens arranged in an octahedron (Figure 1). This

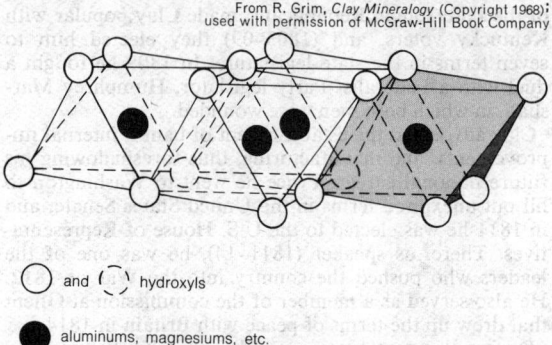

From R. Grim, *Clay Mineralogy* (Copyright 1968); used with permission of McGraw-Hill Book Company

○ and ◌ hydroxyls

● aluminums, magnesiums, etc.

Figure 1: Single octahedral unit (shaded) and the sheet structure of octahedral units.

structure is called the gibbsite structure when aluminum predominates; only two-thirds of the possible central positions are filled in this case, and the structure has the formula $Al_2(OH)_6$. The structure is called the brucite structure when magnesium predominates; in this case all of the central positions are filled, and the structure has the formula $Mg_3(OH)_6$.

In the second unit, a silicon atom is at the centre of and equidistant from four oxygens or hydroxyls arranged to form a tetrahedron (Figure 2). These are joined at their bases into a hexagonal network that is repeated indefinitely. The tips of all of the tetrahedrons point in the same direction, and the bases of all tetrahedrons are in the same plane; the sheet formed has the formula $Si_4O_6(OH)_4$.

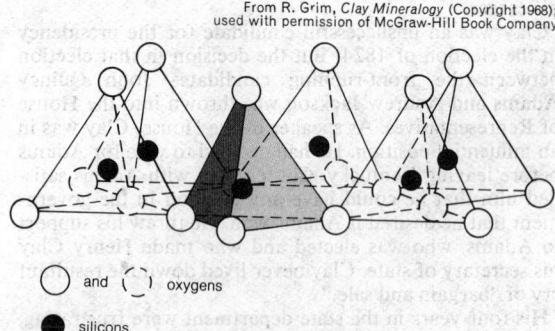

From R. Grim, *Clay Mineralogy* (Copyright 1968); used with permission of McGraw-Hill Book Company

○ and ◌ oxygens

● silicons

Figure 2: Single silica tetrahedron (shaded) and the sheet structure of silica tetrahedra arranged in hexagonal network.

Recent detailed structural investigations have shown that consideration must be given to the substantial distortion of the clay mineral structural units to allow them to fit into determined unit cell dimensions of the minerals. Thus opposing rotation (from a few degrees to a theoretical maximum of 30°) of alternate tetrahedrons distorts the ideally hexagonal network of silica tetrahedrons and produces a ditrigonal (literally, doubly triangular) surface symmetry. Departure from geometrical regularity frequently occurs in the octahedral layer when the upper and lower equilateral triads of anions rotate around one central metal atom. In experiments with kaolinite it has been observed that rotation around alu-

Distortion of structural units

minum sites in the upper triads is $+6.5°$ and in the lower triads is $-4°$.

Sepiolite, attapulgite, and palygorskite are fibrous clay minerals and are composed of different structural units. Their configurations will be discussed later.

Allophane. Allophane is the name given to an amorphous inorganic compound found in some clays. Such material may be considered as composed of tetrahedral and octahedral units that are arranged in too irregular a fashion or on too small a scale to provide X-ray diffraction effects. In some cases such material has sufficient order to diffract electrons, although not X-rays.

The chemical composition of allophane is variable. It has been observed that some specimens resemble halloysites, whereas others have a composition more like smectites. Also, some allophane samples contain notable amounts of sulfate and phosphate compounds.

Kaolinite. The kaolinite structural unit (Figure 3) consists of a tetrahedral and octahedral sheet, so arranged that a common layer is formed by one of the anionic layers of the octahedral sheet and the tips of the silica

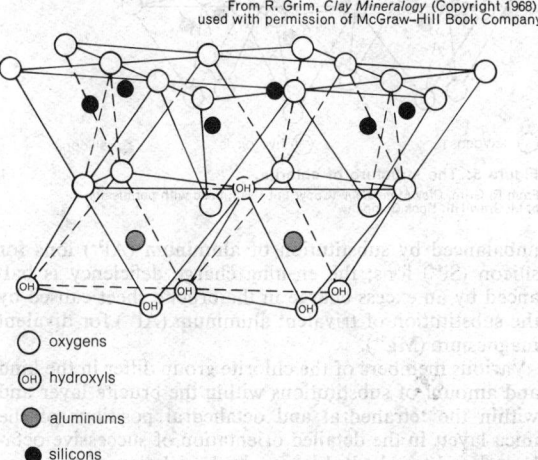

○ oxygens
(OH) hydroxyls
● aluminums
● silicons

Figure 3: Structure of the kaolinite layer (see text).

tetrahedra. In this common layer silicon and aluminum atoms share two-thirds of the anions, which then become O instead of OH. Out of all the possible positions for aluminum in the octahedral sheet only two-thirds are filled and charges are balanced within the structural unit. The structure has the formula $(OH)_8Si_4Al_4O_{10}$, and its theoretical composition, as oxides, is SiO_2, 46.54 percent; Al_2O_2, 39.50 percent; H_2O, 13.96 percent. Analysis shows very little substitution occurring within the lattice.

Kaolinite minerals consist of such sheet units continuous in two directions (along the a and b axes) and stacked one above the other in the third direction (along the c axis). Variation between members exists in the stacking pattern of the unit layers or perhaps in positions of the octahedral layer's sites filled by aluminum atoms. Kaolinite has triclinic symmetry; the anions (oxygens or hydroxyls) of successive unit sheets are paired, which suggests hydrogen- or hydroxyl-type bonds between the layers.

Kaolinite minerals of lower crystallinity than that of the well-crystallized material just noted are quite common. This is usually a matter of random layer displacements parallel to the b axis. Also, in poorly crystallized kaolinite, it is quite conceivable that the vacancy in octahedral positions may occur in different sites of each layer.

Halloysite. One of the two forms of halloysite has the composition $(OH)_8Si_4Al_4O_{10}$ and the other has the composition $(OH)_8Si_4Al_4O_{10} \cdot 4H_2O$; the latter form irreversibly dehydrates (loses the four water molecules) to the former at relatively low temperatures (60° C). The dehydrated form has a basal spacing about the thickness of a kaolinite layer or about 7.2Å, and the hydrated form has a basal spacing of about 10.1Å; the difference between them, 2.9Å, is about the thickness of a sheet of water one

molecule thick. Consequently, the layers of kaolinite in the hydrated form are separated by monomolecular water layers. These are lost during the transition from the hydrated to the dehydrated form. X-ray diffraction shows the absence of sharp hkl (faces perpendicular to the a, b, and c axes, respectively) reflections in the dehydrated form, which is explained by displacement parallel to both the a and b directions in a highly random manner.

Electron micrographs have shown the tubular nature of much halloysite. Recent studies have indicated that the tubes are commonly prismatic rather than round in cross section.

Smectite. The structural units (Figure 4) of smectite consist of two silica tetrahedral sheets with a central alumina octahedral sheet. The tips of each tetrahedral sheet all point in toward the centre of the unit, and combine with one octahedral sheet to form a common layer; atoms common to both layers become O instead of OH. The units are continuous in two directions and are stacked one above the other.

In the stacking of the silica-alumina-silica units, a weak bond is formed and an excellent cleavage results between the outside (oxygen) layers of each unit because they are adjacent to similar layers of neighbouring units. The particular distinction of the smectite structure from the other types is that water and other polar molecules (as certain organic substances) can, by entering between the unit layers, cause the lattice to expand in the direction of stacking (along the c axis). Thus this dimension may vary from about 9.6Å, when there are no polar molecules between the unit layers, to nearly complete separation of the individual layers.

Without considering lattice substitutions, the theoretical formula of the smectite structural unit is $(OH)_4 Si_8Al_4O_{20} \cdot nH_2O$ (interlayer); without considering the interlayer material the theoretical composition, as oxides, is SiO_2, 66.7 percent; Al_2O_3, 28.3 percent; and H_2O, 5 percent.

In actuality, smectite always differs from this theoretical formula because substitution occurs within the lattice. Aluminum or phosphorus may substitute for silicon in the tetrahedral sheets, and magnesium, iron, zinc, nickel, lithium, and others may substitute for aluminum in the octahedral sheet. Substitution of aluminum (Al^{3+}) for silicon (Si^{4+}) in the tetrahedral sheets seems to be limited to less than 15 percent. In the above formula, only two

Substitutions for silicon

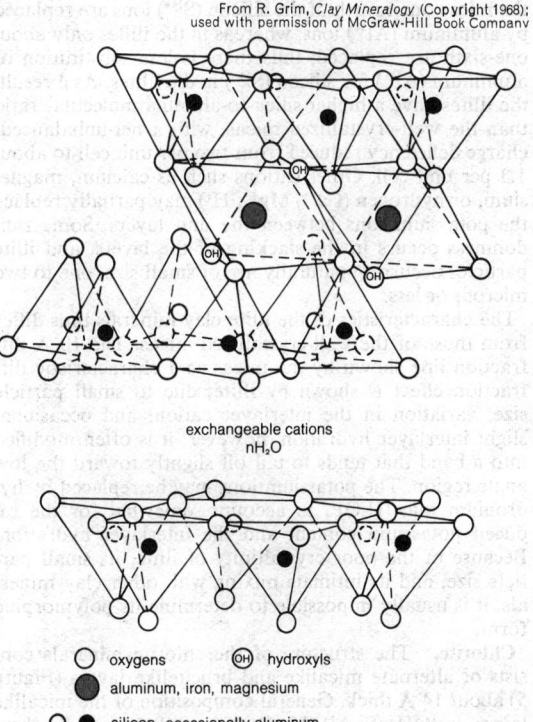

exchangeable cations
nH_2O

○ oxygens   (OH) hydroxyls
● aluminum, iron, magnesium
○ ● silicon, occasionally aluminum

Figure 4: The structure of smectite.

thirds of the possible positions in the octahedral sheet are filled; one magnesium (Mg^{++}) ion may substitute for one aluminum (Al^{3+}) ion, which continues to leave the structure with only two-thirds of the octahedral sites filled; or three magnesium (Mg^{++}) ions may substitute for two aluminum (Al^{3+}) ions, in which case all possible octahedral positions are filled. These substitutions vary from few to complete within the octahedral sheet. Total replacement of aluminum by magnesium yields saponite; replacement by iron yields nontronite; by chromium, volkhonskoite; and by zinc, sauconite.

Smectite also differs from the theoretical formula because the lattice charge is always unbalanced by the substitution of ions of different valence (as Mg^{++} for Al^{3+}; or Al^{3+} for Si^{4+}); the imbalance may occur in the tetrahedral or octahedral sheet or in both, and that in one sheet may be partly compensated by substitution in the other sheets of the unit layer. Thus, compensation for the substitutions of aluminum (Al^{3+}) for silicon (Si^{4+}) may result from filling slightly more than two-thirds of the octahedral positions, or from the substitution of hydroxyl ions for oxygen in the octahedral layer. In the smectite lattice, substitutions, including the internal compensating substitutions, always result in about the same net charge on the lattice, about two-thirds unit per unit cell. Exchangeable cations adsorbed between the unit layers and around their edges balances this net-charge deficiency; the deficiency would require the substitution of one magnesium (Mg^{2+}) ion for every sixth aluminum (Al^{3+}) ion, for example, or about one aluminum (Al^{3+}) ion for every sixth silicon (Si^{4+}) ion.

Illite. Micas have a basic structural unit the same as that of smectite (two silica tetrahedral sheets sandwiching an octahedral sheet), but some of the silicons are always replaced by aluminums. This results in a charge deficiency that is balanced by potassium ions between the unit layers. The sheet thickness (c-axis dimension) is fixed at about 10 Å. Some of the micas, such as muscovite, are dioctahedral and only two-thirds of the possible octahedral positions are filled with aluminum atoms. Other micas are trioctahedral and all of the octahedral positions are filled with magnesium (Mg^{2+}) or iron (Fe^{2+}, Fe^{3+}) ions. Various polymorphic forms of the micas occur, depending on the stacking arrangement of the unit layers.

The several ways in which the illite clay minerals, sometimes called the hydrous micas, differ from the well-crystallized micas may be exhibited by any single sample. In the micas one-fourth of the silicon (Si^{4+}) ions are replaced by aluminum (Al^{3+}) ions, whereas in the illites only about one-sixth are replaced; thus there is less substitution of aluminum (Al^{3+}) for silicon (Si^{4+}) in the illites. As a result, the illites have a higher silica-to-alumina molecular ratio than the well-crystallized micas, with a net-unbalanced-charge deficiency reduced from two per unit cell to about 1.3 per unit cell. Other cations such as calcium, magnesium, or hydrogen (Ca^{++}, Mg^{++}, H^+) may partially replace the potassium ions between the unit layers. Some randomness occurs in the stacking of the layers, and illite particles occurring naturally are of small size, one to two microns or less.

Characteristics of illite clay

The characteristics of the illite clay minerals thus differ from those of the well-crystallized micas. The 10 Å diffraction line shown by the micas as a characteristic diffraction effect is shown by illite; due to small particle size, variation in the interlayer cation, and occasional slight interlayer hydration, however, it is often modified into a band that tends to tail off slightly toward the low angle region. The potassium ions may be replaced by hydronium ion, ($H_3O)^+$, to account somewhat for the reduced potassium content and the interlayer hydration. Because of the poor crystallinity of illite, its small particle size, and its intimate mixing with other clay minerals, it is usually impossible to determine its polymorphic form.

Chlorite. The structure of the chlorite minerals consists of alternate micalike and brucitelike layers (Figure 5) about 14 Å thick. General composition of the micalike layers is $(OH)_4(Si,Al)_8(Mg,Fe)_6O_{20}$, and that of the brucitelike layers is $(Mg,Al)_6(OH)_{12}$. The micalike layer is

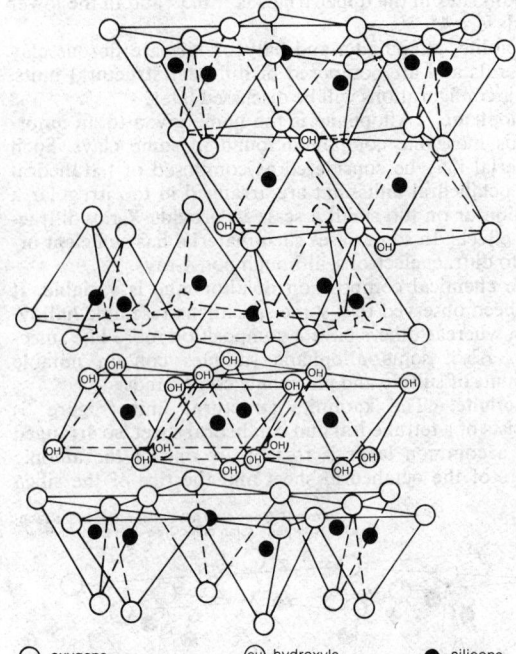

○ oxygens   ⊕ hydroxyls   ● silicons

Figure 5: The structure of chlorite.
From R. Grim, *Clay Mineralogy* (Copyright 1968); used with permission of McGraw-Hill Book Company

unbalanced by substitution of aluminum (Al^{3+}) ions for silicon (Si^{4+}) ions; the ensuing charge deficiency is balanced by an excess charge in the brucite sheet caused by the substitution of trivalent aluminum (Al^{3+}) for divalent magnesium (Mg^{2+}).

Various members of the chlorite group differ in the kind and amount of substitutions within the brucite layer and within the tetrahedral and octahedral positions of the mica layer, in the detailed orientation of successive octahedral and tetrahedral layers, in the relation of the mica to brucite layers, and in the stacking of successive chlorite units. The symmetry of specimens also is variable. The range of polymorphic forms of chlorite in clay minerals has not been established. Available evidence suggests that clay-mineral chlorites differ from well-crystallized material in the random stacking of layers and in hydration. Because chlorite in clay generally occurs mixed with other clay minerals, diffraction data permit only the identification of a mineral with a fixed thickness of 14 Å and not the polymorphic form.

Vermiculite. The vermiculite unit structure consists of sheets of trioctahedral mica or talc separated by layers of water molecules and occupying a space about two water molecules thick (4.98 Å). Substitutions of aluminum (Al^{3+}) for silicon (Si^{4+}) constitute the chief imbalance but the net-charge deficiency may be partially balanced by other substitutions within the mica lattice; there is always a residual net-charge deficiency of 1 to 1.4 per unit cell, however. Exchangeable cations occur chiefly between the mica layers to satisfy the charge deficiency: in the natural mineral, the balancing cation is magnesium (Mg^{++}), sometimes with a small amount of calcium (Ca^{++}) also present; the cation-exchange capacity is the same as smectite, or somewhat higher.

Heating vermiculite to temperatures as high as 500° C (900° F) drives the water out from between the mica layers, but the mineral quickly rehydrates at room temperature. The vermiculite lattice, therefore, can expand, but the expansion is restricted to about 4.98 Å, or the thickness of two water layers.

Sepiolite, attapulgite, and palygorskite. The important structural element in the fibrous clay minerals is the amphibole double silica chain, which is oriented parallel to the c axis. There are two distinct fibrous clay minerals, one type called attapulgite or palygorskite, and the second type similar to sepiolite. The attapulgite structure consists of double silica chains with oxygen linking the chains together at their longitudinal edges. The apexes of the tetrahedrons in successive chains point in opposite directions, and the linked chains, thus, form a kind of double-ribbed sheet of two rows of tetrahedral apexes that alternate between the top and bottom of the sheets. The apexes of successive sheets point together and aluminum or magnesium or both in octahedral coordination link the apex oxygens. Similarity exists between this octahedral layer and that in the layer clay minerals, but it is continuous in only one direction. It is completed by hydroxyl groups in the centres and at the open sides. A weak link through the oxygen of the silica chains in the ribbed layer causes the mineral to have a good cleavage parallel to the c axis. The interstices between the amphibole chains are filled by chains of water molecules running parallel to the chains. The cavities accommodate four molecules of water per unit cell, which would account for the dehydration loss at low temperatures. The names attapulgite and palygorskite are used interchangeably for a clay mineral with this structure.

The structure of sepiolite is similar to that of attapulgite, except that three pyroxene chains (see PYROXENES) are linked to form two continuous amphibole-type chains. The b dimension of sepiolite therefore is about one-third greater than that of attapulgite. Substantially all of the octahedral positions in the sepiolite structure are populated with magnesiums, whereas there is some replacement by aluminum and iron in attapulgite.

Mixed-layer minerals. Many clay materials are mixtures of more than one clay mineral. One kind of mixture consists of discrete clay-mineral particles in which there is no preferred geometric orientation of one particle with respect to the surrounding clay-mineral particles. Another kind is the interstratification of the layer clay minerals where the individual layers are composed of only a single or a few alumino-silicate sheets. These mixed layer structures result from the strong similarity that exists between the layers of the different clay minerals, all of which are composed of silica tetrahedral-hexagonal layers and closely packed octahedral layers of oxygens and hydroxyl groups. Therefore, mixed-layer structures occur as stable as those composed of a single kind of layer.

These structures of mixed-layer clay minerals are of two different types. The interstratification may be regular, with the different layers regularly repeated in the stacking sequence. In such cases distinctive characteristics result; the unit cell is equivalent to the sum of the component layers and regular reflections are obtained. Chlorite composed of a regular alternation of mica and brucite layers is an example of a regular mixed-layer mineral.

Random, irregular interstratifications of layers also exists, with no uniform repetition of layers. The mineral glauconite frequently exhibits this structure, with a random interstratification of smectite and illite. Mixed-layer structures are very common in clays and soils. The precise identification of the components of such structures requires detailed X-ray diffraction analyses.

PROPERTIES OF THE CLAY MINERALS

Ion exchange. Clay minerals are able to adsorb certain positively and negatively charged particles (cations and anions) and retain them around the outside of the structural unit in an exchangeable state. The exchange reaction differs from simple sorption because it is stoichiometric (involving equal amounts), and it generally does not affect the silica-alumina structure. The range of the cation and anion exchange capacities of the clay minerals is given in the Table.

Exchange capacities vary with particle size, perfection of crystallinity, and nature of the adsorbed ion; hence, a range of values exists for a given mineral rather than a single specific capacity. Cation-exchange capacity results from broken bonds around the edges of the structural units, which give rise to unsatisfied charges. Substitutions within the lattice structure (for example, trivalent aluminum for quadrivalent silicon) and possibly the hydrogen of exposed hydroxyls, also provide cation exchange ca-

Exchange Capacities of Clay Minerals (milliequivalents per 100 g)			
cation-exchange capacity		anion-exchange capacity (approximate)	
Kaolinite	3–15	Smectite	23
Halloysite (2H$_2$O)	5–10	Nontronite	20
Halloysite (4H$_2$O)	40–50	Saponite	21
Smectite	80–150	Vermiculite	4
Illite	10–40	Kaolinite	13, 3
Vermiculite	100–150		
Chlorite	10–40		
Sepiolite-attapulgite-palygorskite	3–15		

pacity. Anion-exchange capacity may be due to (1) the replacement of hydroxl ions at the edges of the lattice structures, (2) adsorption because of the geometry of the anion in relation to the geometry of the clay-mineral structural units (the adsorption of phosphate at the edges of silica tetrahedrons, for example, and (3) possibly because of unbalanced charges within the lattice, such as that which would result from an excess of aluminum in octahedral positions.

The rate of ion exchange varies with clay mineral type and the nature and concentration of the ions. In general, the reaction for kaolinite is most rapid, being almost instantaneous. It is slower for smectite and for attapulgite, and requires even longer time, perhaps hours or days, to reach completion for illites. Under a given set of conditions the various cations are not equally replaceable and do not have the same replacing power. Calcium, for example, will replace sodium more easily than sodium will replace calcium.

The ion exchange properties of the clay minerals are extremely important because these properties determine their physical characteristics and economic use. The availability and retention of fertilizers in soils, plasticity, and other clay properties, depend to a great extent on ion exchange in general and on the identity of the exchange cation.

Clay-water relations. Clay materials contain water in several forms. The water may be held in pores and may be removed by drying under ambient conditions. Water also may be adsorbed on the surface of the clay mineral structures and in smectites, vermiculites, and attapulgites; this water may occur in interlayer positions or within structural channels. Finally, the clay mineral structures contain hydroxyls that are lost as water at elevated temperatures.

Adsorbed water may be removed by heating to temperatures of the order of 100–200° C (212–392° F) and in most cases is regained readily at ordinary temperatures. It is generally agreed that this adsorbed water, directly adjacent to the clay mineral surfaces, has a structure other than that of liquid water. As the thickness of the adsorbed water increases outward from the surface, the nature of the water changes abruptly or gradually to liquid water. Ions and molecules adsorbed on the clay mineral surface tend to exert a major influence on the thickness of the adsorbed water layers and on the nature of this water. The nonliquid water may extend out from the clay mineral surfaces as much as 60–100 Å.

Hydroxyl ions are driven off by heating clay minerals to temperatures of 400°–700° C (752–1292° F). The rate of loss of the hydroxyls and the energy required for their removal is, in general, a specific characteristic of the various clay minerals. The reaction for dioctahedral minerals (in which only two-thirds of the possible octahedral positions of aluminum are occupied by other cations) such as kaolinite is abrupt, whereas the loss takes place rather gradually in trioctahedral minerals (in which all possible octahedral positions of aluminum are occupied by other cations) such as the micas.

Differential thermal analysis is a procedure for measuring the temperatures at which thermal reactions take place, and the intensities of these reactions, when materials are heated to elevated temperatures. The reactions for the loss of hydroxyls are endothermic (involve heat

Causes of anion exchange

Differential thermal analysis procedures

absorption), and reactions for the development of new crystalline phases at elevated temperatures are endothermic or exothermic (generate heat). Characteristic differential thermal curves can be used as diagnostic criteria for identifying the various clay minerals.

High-temperature reactions. When hydroxyls are lost by heating, the lattice structure may be destroyed or simply modified, depending on the composition and structure of the clay minerals. In the presence of fluxes, such as iron or potassium, fusion may follow dehydration very quickly. In the absence of such components, particularly for aluminous dioctahedral minerals, a succession of new phases may be formed at increasing temperatures prior to fusion. Thus, in the case of kaolinite, the first high-temperature phase formed is a spinel that is followed at a higher temperature by the development of mullite and cristoballite prior to fusion. In general terms, the first high-temperature phases are a consequence of the original structure of the clay mineral, whereas the later phases are more in accord with the chemical composition. Recent studies have been accomplished with a small furnace mounted in an X-ray diffraction unit; these studies have provided diffraction data gathered while the sample is at an elevated temperature. Such information has thrown much light on high-temperature-phase formation of the clay minerals.

Organic reactions. Organic material occurs in clays in discrete particles and as reaction compounds with the clay minerals. Ionic organic compounds, such as the amines, may replace inorganic ions on the surfaces of the clay minerals. They may be held in interlayer positions within the expandable clay minerals.

Polar organic molecules may replace adsorbed water on exterior surfaces and in interlayer positions. As organic molecules coat the clay mineral surfaces, the material's affinity for oil increases, so that it can react with additional organic molecules. The organic molecules may be one or several molecular layers thick on the clay mineral surfaces.

Some of the clay minerals possess catalytic properties towards various organic substances. Also, some clay mineral organic reactions develop particular colours and these may be of diagnostic value in identifying specific clay minerals. Organically clad clay minerals are used extensively in paint, ink, and plastics.

Optical properties. Clay mineral particles are commonly too small for the measurement of optical properties. Oriented aggregates that are large enough for optical measurements can, however, be prepared by allowing the flake-shaped clay mineral particles to settle from a clay water suspension on a horizontal surface. The particles settle with one flake on top of another so that their basal plane surfaces are essentially parallel. Though optical properties can be measured in oils, optical characteristics will change because some of the clay minerals will adsorb such oils. Moreover, optical data from interlayered structures can easily be mistaken for that of a single mineral.

Size and shape. The size and shape of clay minerals have been determined by electron micrographs (Figure 6). Allophane, the amorphous clay mineral, shows no definite morphology. Kaolinite occurs as well-formed six-sided flakes, frequently with a prominent elongation in one direction. Particles with maximum surface dimensions of 0.3 to about 4 microns, and thicknesses of 0.05 to about 2 microns are common. The flakes of disordered kaolinite have poorly developed hexagonal outlines. Halloysite commonly occurs as tubular units with an outside diameter ranging from 0.04 to 0.19 micrometres.

Electron micrographs of smectite frequently show broad undulating mosaic sheets. In some cases, the flake-shaped units are discernible but frequently they are too small to be seen individually.

Illite occurs in poorly defined flakes commonly grouped together in irregular aggregates. Many of the flakes have a diameter of 0.1 to 0.3 microns, and the thinnest flakes are approximately 30 Å thick. Little information is available regarding the vermiculite and chlorite minerals, but based on structural considerations they probably are similar in character to the illites.

Electron micrographs show that attapulgite occurs in single and bundles of elongated laths. Frequently the individual laths are many microns in length and 50 to 100 Å in width. Sepiolite occurs in similar lath-shaped units but the laths are somewhat thicker and shorter than in attapulgite.

Surface-area measurements indicate that the value for kaolinite is about 15–20 square metres per gram, whereas illite is 80–90 square metres per gram and halloysite is about 40 square metres per gram. The theoretical surface area of smectites, when dispersed to nearly unit cell dimensions, is 8×10^6 square centimetres per gram. However, values similar to those of illite are frequently obtained because the nitrogen does not penetrate between the layers.

Solubility of the clay minerals. Solubility of the clay minerals in acids varies with the nature of the acid, the acid concentration, the acid to clay ratio, the temperature, and the duration of treatment. It also varies as a function of heating of the clay minerals and the firing temperatures prior to the acid attack. In general the acid first attacks the adsorbed cations and then the components of the octahedral part of the clay mineral structure. Frequently the silica sheets are not attacked and the morphology of the clay minerals may be retained after solution of all components except silica.

In alkaline solutions a cation exchange reaction first takes place and then the silica part of the structure is attacked. The reaction depends upon the same variables as those stated for acid reactions.

By courtesy of the Smithsonian Institution, Washington, D.C.; photographs, Kenneth M. Towe

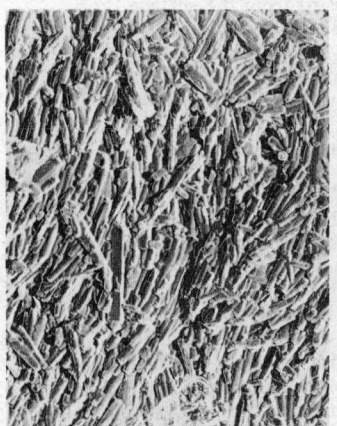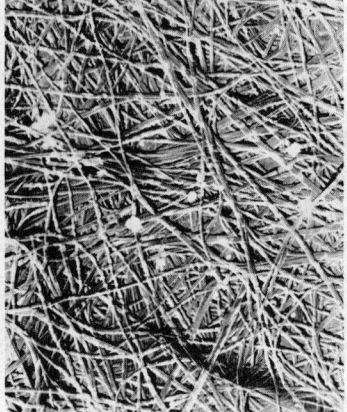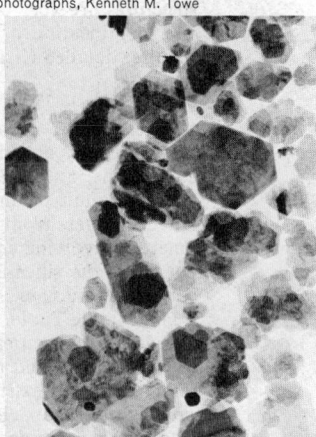

Figure 6: *Electron micrographs of clay minerals.*
(Left) Tubular units of halloysite (magnified about 8,400 ×). (Centre left) Broad, undulating mosaic sheets of smectite (magnified about 3,750 ×). (Centre right) Elongated, lath-shaped units of attapulgite (magnified about 9,475 ×). (Right) Six-sided kaolinite flakes (magnified about 22,000 ×).

OCCURRENCE OF THE CLAY MINERALS

Soils and recent sediments. All types of clay minerals have been reported in soils (*q.v.*). Kaolinite is the dominant component and in some instances the only component in podsols (soils rich in ash and organic matter). Varying amounts of illite and smectite are also usually present.

Illite and smectite, with occasional small amounts of kaolinite, occur in prairie soils and smectite and illite predominate in soils of arid regions and in chernozems (black, fertile soils). Attapulgite has been reported in a few desert soils and kaolinite is the dominant component in laterites (residual soils).

Soil composed of illite and chlorite is better suited for agriculture than kaolinitic soils because of their relatively high ion-exchange properties and, hence, their capacity to hold plant nutrients. Moderate amounts of smectite in soils are advantageous for the same reason but when present in large amounts (50 percent ±), smectite is detrimental because it is impervious and has too great a water-holding capacity.

Illite and chlorite are the dominant clay minerals in marine sediments (*q.v.*) that are accumulating in the seas today. Smectite also may be present and in some areas, such as the Gulf of Mexico, it is relatively abundant. Kaolinite also is common but is usually in small amounts.

Sediment accumulating under nonmarine conditions may have any clay mineral composition. Under highly saline conditions in desert areas, however, illite, chlorite, or attapulgite or both are likely to develop, depending on the nature of the cation present.

Ancient sediments. Analyses of many ancient sediments in many parts of the world indicate that smectite is much less abundant in sediments older than the Mesozoic Era than in younger sediments. The available data also suggest that kaolinite is less abundant in very ancient sediments than in those deposited after the Devonian Period. Stated another way, the very old argillaceous (clay-rich) sediments are largely composed of illite and chlorite. Attapulgite and sepiolite have not been reported in sediments older than the Tertiary Period.

Material classed as clay may have any clay mineral composition. In some instances, the component is a single clay mineral, but more often there is a mixture of clay minerals. Materials that are described as shales (*q.v.*) because they are relatively hard and have a laminated character frequently are composed of illite and chlorite. Smectite is a common component of many shales of Mesozoic and younger ages. Kaolinite is a common component of some shales but it usually occurs in minor amounts. Sepiolite-attapulgite minerals frequently occur in argillaceous sediments associated with ancient saline deposits. Smectite, illite, and chlorite also are common components of such sediments.

Slates appear to be composed primarily of illites and chlorites. These clay minerals generally have a relatively higher degree of crystallinity in slates than when found in clays. Kaolinite has been reported in some slates, particularly those that have relatively low schistosity (subparallel arrangement of mineral components due to metamorphic pressures).

The clay minerals found in carbonate rocks are chiefly illite and chlorite. Kaolinite and smectite are sometimes present in small amounts; however, smectite and attapulgite may be an important constituent in the younger carbonate rocks.

Kaolinite and illite have been reported in various coals (*q.v.*). The data are insufficient, however, to indicate whether there is any general relationship between the nature of the clay mineral component and the character and age of the coals.

Bentonite generally is defined as a clay composed largely of smectite, which has high colloidal, plastic, and adsorption properties. Much bentonite has formed by the devitrification of volcanic ash *in situ*. Other clays that have been called bentonite have formed by hydrothermal processes and, possibly, by weathering.

Hydrothermal deposits. All of the clay minerals, except attapulgite, have been found as alteration products associated with hot springs and geysers and as aureoles around metaliferous deposits. Frequently there is a zonal arrangement of the clay minerals around the source of the alteration; mica and kaolinite are close to the source whereas chlorite and smectite are more distant.

ORIGIN OF THE CLAY MINERALS

All of the clay minerals, with the possible exception of halloysite, have been synthesized from mixtures of oxides or hydroxides at moderately low temperatures and pressures. Kaolinite tends to form in alumina-silica systems without alkalies or alkaline earths. Illite is formed when potassium is added to such systems, and smectite or chlorite is formed when magnesium is added depending on the concentration of the magnesium. The clay minerals can be synthesized at ordinary temperatures and pressures if the oxides are mixed together very slowly and in great dilution.

Weathering processes. The formation of the clay minerals by weathering (*q.v.*) processes is determined by the nature of the parent rock, climate, topography, vegetation, and the time period during which these factors have operated. Climate, topography, and vegetation influence weathering processes by their control of the character and direction of movement of water through the weathering zone.

When the dominant movement of water is downward through the alteration zone, any alkalies or alkaline earths tend to be leached and primary minerals containing these components are first degraded and then broken down. If the leaching is intense, then after the removal of the alkalies and alkaline earths the aluminum or silica may be removed from the alteration zone. This will depend on the pH (index of acidity–alkalinity) of the downward-seeping waters. The pH of such water is determined, in turn, by the climate and cover of vegetation. Under warm and humid conditions, with long wet and dry periods, the surface organic material tends to be completely oxidized. The downward-seeping waters therefore are neutral or perhaps slightly alkaline and silica will be removed, whereas alumina and iron will be left behind and concentrated. The result is a lateritic type of soil. Under more temperate conditions, the surface organic material is not completely oxidized and the downward-seeping water contains organic acids. In this case, alumina and iron oxides are leached and the silica is left behind; podsolic types of soils will develop.

In dry areas the dominant movement of water is not downward and leaching does not take place. The alkalies and alkaline earths remain close to the surface and chernozem soils containing illite, chlorite, and smectite, will develop. In extremely dry desert areas where the concentration of magnesium is particularly high, the formation of attapulgite has been reported.

Other changes. As the clay minerals are transported from freshwater to a marine environment a definite regrading of the micas takes place. Illite and chlorite tend to develop from smectites by the respective adsorption of potassium and magnesium from sea water. Diagenetic changes tend to occur during sedimentation and compaction and similar changes take place when metamorphic processes are involved.

In the development of clay minerals by natural hydrothermal processes, the presence of alkalies and alkaline earths influence the resulting products in the same manner as shown by synthesis experiments.

INDUSTRIAL USES OF THE CLAY MINERALS

Ceramics. Clays composed of kaolinite are required for the manufacture of porcelain, whiteware, and refractories. The absence of iron in this clay mineral gives it a white burning colour, and the absence of alkalies and alkaline earths gives it a very high fusion temperature that makes it refractory. Whiteware bodies frequently contain talc, feldspar, and quartz, in addition to the kaolinite clay, in order to develop desirable shrinkage and burning properties. If the kaolinite is poorly crystalline the clay will have higher plastic and bonding properties.

Clays composed of a mixture of clay minerals, in which

Kaolinite in shales

illite is most abundant, are used in the manufacture of brick, tile, stoneware, and glazed products. Small proportions of smectite in such clays provide good plastic properties, but in large amounts smectite is undesirable because it causes too great a degree of shrinkage.

Oil industry. Bentonite clays composed of smectite are used primarily in the preparation of muds for drilling oil wells. This type of clay, which swells to several times its original volume in water, provides desirable colloidal and wall-building properties. Attapulgite clays also are used because of their resistance to flocculation (grouping or clustering of individual grains or flakes) under high salinity conditions.

Certain clay minerals, notably attapulgite and some smectites, possess substantial ability to remove colour bodies from oil. These so-called fuller's earths are used in processing many mineral and vegetable oils. Acid treatment of some smectite clays increases their decolourizing ability.

Fuller's earth

Much gasoline is manufactured by using catalysts prepared from either smectite, kaolinite, or halloysite types of clay minerals. The preparation may be by acid treatment to modify the structure, or by the use of kaolinite and halloysite as a source of alumina and silica for the synthesis of new zeolite-type structures.

Paper. Large tonnages of kaolinite clays are used to fill and coat paper. The coating clays are washed to free them from grit and then are processed by physical and chemical techniques to improve their whiteness and viscosity. In general, well crystallized kaolinite that cleaves easily into thin flakes is desired. Attapulgite clays are used in the preparation of no-carbon-required paper because of the colour they develop during reactions with certain colourless organic compounds.

Metallurgical industries. Large tonnages of bentonite are used as bonding agents in foundry sands for casting metals. Some poorly crystallized illites and kaolinites are also used for this purpose. Bentonite is combined with lime and coke to pelletize finely ground iron ore; this renders it suitable for use in blast furnaces.

Because many clay minerals have aluminum oxide contents of the order of 30 to 40 percent, they are potential ores of aluminum. A variety of processes have been developed to extract this metal from clays but clays are not yet competitive with bauxite as a source of aluminum. Extremely large tonnages of reasonably pure clay, preferably of the kaolinite type, would be required for this purpose.

Other uses. Clays have a tremendous number of miscellaneous uses and for each use a particular type of clay with particular properties is important. For example, attapulgite and smectite clays are used as carriers for insecticides and pesticides. Smectite clays are used as plasticizing agents, and kaolinite clays are used as extenders and fillers in a large number of organic and inorganic bodies. Kaolinite and smectite clays also are used in a variety of pharmaceutical and medicinal preparations.

Smectite and kaolinite clay minerals can be coated with organic molecules for use in many organic systems. Often such organic-clad clays are tailor-made to fit a particular organic system, and thus become an integral part of the system rather than a simple diluent.

CLAY MINERALS AND TECHNOLOGY

Information on the composition and properties of the various clay minerals is important for various technologies. The plasticity, consolidation, and stability properties of soils that the construction engineer encounters depend on the clay mineral composition. Knowledge of the structure and properties of the clay minerals is therefore extremely important in the evaluation of sites on which a structure is to be built. Such knowledge better permits the engineer to predict how the soil will act under load, in a fill, or under changed drainage conditions. It is now common practice for the construction engineer to obtain clay mineral analyses of soil materials in order to guide his design and construction activities.

Site evaluation

The clay mineral composition of a sediment may indicate the conditions under which it has been formed in the geologic past and, consequently, may be important in the search for petroleum by suggesting that a given area or a sequence of formations may or may not be favourable for the occurrence of petroleum (*q.v.*). Moreover, the clay mineral composition of a particular formation may be unique, which will aid in stratigraphic correlation and, hence, determination of favourable structures for oil accumulation.

In the secondary recovery of petroleum, water or some other fluid is forced through an oil-producing formation to flush oil into open wells when it will not flow freely into such wells. The clay mineral composition of the formation largely determines the porosity and permeability and the likelihood of the formation being clogged in the course of recovery operations. Smectite, because of its dispersability and ion-exchange properties, is much more likely to cause difficulties than kaolinite or illite.

Clay minerals also are relevant to atomic-energy technology. In the development of energy from atomic reactions, and in laboratories devoted to atomic research, large quantities of isotopes that have high potency and a long half-life are produced in dilute solutions. The adsorptive properties of certain clay minerals, notably illite, permits the fixation of isotopes such as cesium when disposal is required.

BIBLIOGRAPHY. G. BROWN (ed.), *X-Ray Identification and Crystal Structures of Clay Minerals*, 2nd ed. (1961), a comprehensive consideration of the atomic structure and X-ray diffraction characteristics of the mineral components of clays; R.E. GRIM, *Applied Clay Mineralogy* (1962), a discussion of the application of clay mineralogy in the ceramic, petroleum, paper, foundry, and other industries as well as in engineering practice; *Clay Mineralogy*, 2nd ed. (1968), a discussion of the structure, properties, origin, and mode of occurrence of the clay minerals; P.F. LOW, "Physical Chemistry of Clay-Water Interaction," *Advan. Agron.*, vol. 13 (1961), a fundamental and theoretical discussion of the structural characteristics of water adsorbed by the clay minerals; R.C. MACKENZIE (ed.), *The Differential Thermal Investigation of Clays* (1957), information on differential thermal analytical techniques and their application to clay mineralogy; C.E. MARSHALL, *Physical Chemistry and Mineralogy of Soils* (1964), a general discussion of the mineralogy of soils from the point of view of physical chemistry; H. RIES, *Clays: Their Occurrence, Properties, and Uses*, 3rd ed. (1927), a general discussion of the occurrence, properties, and uses of clays prior to the development of the clay mineral concept; H. VAN OLPHEN, *An Introduction to Clay Colloid Chemistry* (1963), an analysis of the properties of the clay minerals from the point of view of colloid chemistry; B.B. ZVYAGIN, *Electron-Diffraction Analysis of Clay Mineral Structures* (1967; orig. pub. in Russian, 1964), a presentation of electron diffraction techniques as applied to clay mineral analysis and resulting structural data.

(R.E.G.)

Cleisthenes of Athens

Cleisthenes, an Athenian statesman of the late 6th century BC, deserves to be regarded as the founder of Athenian democracy. He belonged to the Alcmaeonid family, which had played a leading part in Athenian public life since the early Archaic period, and was born, *c.* 570, the son of Megacles. At the time, the family was still affected by a public curse incurred by his great-grandfather, also named Megacles. The latter had been chief archon when an Athenian noble Cylon had made an unsuccessful bid to seize the Acropolis and make himself tyrant (*c.* 632). Some of his followers had taken refuge at an altar and did not abandon their sanctuary until they had been promised that their lives would be spared. They were, however, put to death, and Megacles was held responsible. On the advice of Apollo's oracle at Delphi, a curse was pronounced on the Alcmaeonids, who had to go into exile, but they were back in Athens when the lawgiver Solon was called on to avert civil war in 594. The Alcmaeonids were strong supporters of Solon, and Megacles' son Alcmaeon led an Athenian contingent that fought with Thessaly and Cleisthenes, the powerful tyrant of Sicyon, in a so-called Sacred War for the protection of Delphi. It is not surprising that, when the tyrant of Sicyon was looking for a husband for his daughter Agariste (*c.* 574), he should have chosen Megacles, son of

Curse of the Alcmaeonids

Alcmaeon. The first son of the marriage was named Cleisthenes after his grandfather.

In the period following Solon's reforms, Attica was unsettled. The old nobility thought that Solon had gone too far and were anxious to reverse the trend; the common people thought that he had not gone far enough. The Alcmaeonids, whom the curse had alienated from the nobility, championed a middle way based on Solon's reforms; but both these parties were outmanoeuvred by Peisistratus, a noble with a good military reputation who appealed to the poorer classes and, with their support, seized power in 560. After an unsuccessful attempt to share power with the tyrant, the Alcmaeonids joined the opposition; but, when Peisistratus, having built up his resources during a ten-year exile, defeated his enemies, the Alcmaeonids again had to leave Attica (546). Cleisthenes was now about 25 years old, and for nearly 20 years he could not return. Nothing more is heard of his father, who probably died before Peisistratus. The Alcmaeonids'

Restoration of Delphi's favour

part in the Sacred War ensured the favour of Delphi; this support was further strengthened by the part played by the family in the rebuilding of Apollo's temple, which had burned down around 548. The Alcmaeonids had won the contract for building a new temple for 300 talents, but, in a well-calculated act of piety, they used the more expensive Parian marble for the facade in place of the limestone specified by the contract.

The fragment of an archon list found in the excavation of the Athenian Agora has shown that Cleisthenes was chief archon in 525–524. It seems that when Peisistratus died in 527, his son and successor, Hippias, tried to win back those nobles who had been most hostile to the tyranny. But the reconciliation did not last. In 512, at a time when Hippias, frightened by the murder of his brother in 514, had become increasingly repressive, the Alcmaeonids tried unsuccessfully with other nobles to fight their way back. They were more successful when they enlisted the help of Delphi. The Spartans were repeatedly urged by Delphi to set Athens free, and it was finally a Spartan army that forced Hippias and his family to leave Attica.

In the struggle for power that followed the fall of the tyranny, Cleisthenes failed to impose his leadership, and in 508 Isagoras, the leader of the more reactionary nobles, was elected chief archon. It was at this point, according to later tradition, that Cleisthenes took the people into partnership and transformed the situation. Before the year 508–507 was over, the main principles of a complete reform of the system of government had been approved by the popular Assembly, a relative of the Alcmaeonids had been elected chief archon for the following year, Isagoras had left Athens to invoke Spartan intervention, and Sparta had declared for Isagoras. The Spartan king demanded the expulsion of "those under the curse," and Cleisthenes and his relatives were again exiles. The Spartans had no wish to see a democratic Athens, but they misjudged the mood of the people. The attempt to impose Isagoras as the leader of a narrow oligarchy was strongly resisted, and the Spartans had to withdraw. The Athenians now recalled the exiles and sent an embassy to seek alliance with the Persians; for Sparta was now an open enemy, and all Athens' neighbours were hostile to the new democracy. But events took a quite unexpected turn. An invading army led by Sparta disintegrated because the two Spartan kings quarrelled and because Corinth, at this stage, did not want to see Athens humiliated. Athens was thus able to defeat in separate battles both the Boeotians and Chalcidians, who had planned to join Sparta against Athens. The Athenians could now, in full confidence, carry into effect the decisions that the Assembly had taken in 508.

Cleisthenes had seen that though the tyranny had improved the economic condition of the common people and temporarily at least broken the political power of the noble houses, most of the old families were still looking to the past rather than the future and that the full promise of the Solonian reforms could not be realized unless the principle of hereditary privilege was attacked at the roots. He therefore persuaded the people to change the basis of

political organization from the family, clan, and phratry (kinship group) to the locality. Public rights and duties should henceforward depend on membership of a deme, or township, which kept its own register of citizens and elected its own officials. The citizen would no longer be known only by his father's name but also or alone by the name of his deme. Ten new local tribes were formed to take the place of the four Ionic blood tribes, and, to make faction building more difficult, Attica was divided into three areas—the city itself and its suburbs, the coastal area, and the inland area; and townships from each of the three areas were included in each tribe, ten counties, *trittyes*, being formed in each area for this purpose. And in this grouping steps were probably taken to diminish the local influence of some of the main priestly families. The mixed local tribe became the basis of representation in public office, and the Solonian Council of Four Hundred was increased to 500 (50 from each tribe, with members selected from demes according to their numbers). *Isonomia*, the principle of equality of rights for all, was one of the proudest boasts of the reformers, and there is no doubt that Cleisthenes' work led to a much wider and more active participation in public life. The people would soon be moving still further toward their control of the executive, but already Cleisthenes gave them the opportunity, by his introduction of ostracism, to exile for ten years, by their votes, any citizen who seemed dangerously powerful.

Reorganization of the state

When Athens sent envoys to make alliance with Persia, it was probably known that the price of alliance would be a token submission. This the envoys made, but, when Athens was no longer in acute danger, the giving of earth and water was repudiated. It is widely held that Cleisthenes had been responsible for the approach to Persia and fell into disgrace because of it, but for this there is no firm evidence. The late story of his ostracism is clearly invented. He may have died in full honour shortly after his reforms; he had passed his 60th year.

BIBLIOGRAPHY. The reforms of Cleisthenes are interestingly discussed in W.G. FORREST, *The Emergence of Greek Democracy, 800–400 B.C.*, pp. 191–203 (1966); and in more detail by CHARLES HIGNETT, *A History of the Athenian Constitution to the End of the Fifth Century B.C.*, pp. 124–158 (1952). *Clisthène l'Athénien*, by PIERRE LEVEQUE and PIERRE VIDAL-NAQUET (1964), is a stimulating study of Cleisthene's intellectual background.

(Ru.M.)

Clemenceau, Georges

Physician, journalist, author, statesman, upholder of the French Third Republic, Georges Clemenceau was a pioneer for democracy. Chief of state at the age of 76, he made a powerful contribution to the victory of the Allies in World War I and was called the "Father of Victory" by the combatants. He was renowned as a man of action with a character of steel, an uncompromising patriot, and a republican of physical courage and unshakable morale.

Youth and education. Clemenceau was born on September 28, 1841, one of six children of an unassuming family in Mouilleron-en-Pareds, in Vendée, a coastal *département* of western France. He remained strongly marked by his native province: he was strong willed, impulsive, proud, and savagely independent. His youth was spent among peasants, but it was his father Benjamin, a Voltairean, positivist, and admirer of the Revolution of 1789, who shaped him and remained his model.

At the age of 12, he entered the lycée in Nantes. Through his father he met men who were plotting to overthrow the emperor Napoleon III and came to know the historian Jules Michelet, who was being hunted by the imperial police. Benjamin was arrested briefly in 1858. Three years later (November 1861), he took Georges to Paris to study medicine. In the Latin Quarter, Clemenceau associated with young men of the republican opposition, who created an avant-garde association named Agis comme tu penses ("Act as you think"). Clemenceau, with some friends, founded a journal, *Le Travail* ("Work"), which set forth the views that were to

Early journalism

Clemenceau.
EB Inc.

characterize his future political action. It was seized by the police and, because of an advertisement inviting the workers of Paris to commemorate the 14th anniversary of the Revolution of 1848, Clemenceau was imprisoned for 73 days. Upon his release, he started a new paper, *Le Matin* ("Morning"), which was in turn seized by the authorities. Having completed his studies, Clemenceau left for the United States, where he was to spend most of the next four years (1865–69). He reached New York at the height of the Civil War and spent much time in libraries and in clubs where he might meet writers and journalists for his own political enrichment. He was struck by the freedom of discussion and expression, unknown in France at the time, and he had great admiration for the politicians who were forging American democracy. When his father refused to continue financial aid, he taught French and horseback riding in a girls' school in Stamford, Connecticut; in due course, despite the opposition of her guardian, he married one of his pupils, Mary Plummer, in 1869. Three children were born of this union, but the couple separated after seven years.

Early political career. Five days after his marriage, Clemenceau returned to France and set himself up as a doctor in Vendée. But politics soon took him back to Paris. In July 1870, Napoleon III declared war on Germany. Less than two months later, the French were defeated at Sedan and the empire collapsed. Clemenceau was among the crowd that invaded the Palais-Bourbon on September 4 and hailed the radical leader Léon Gambetta, who was proclaiming the republic. Soon afterward, Clemenceau was named mayor of the 18th *arrondissement* (district) of Paris (Montmartre) and, on February 8, 1871, was elected as a Radical Republican deputy to represent the Seine *département* in the National Assembly held in Bordeaux. He voted against the preliminaries of the harsh peace terms demanded by Germany and left Bordeaux determined to avenge France's "shameful humiliation."

Back in Paris, he became involved in the insurrection known as the Paris Commune and tried to mediate between its leaders and the National Assembly, then meeting at Versailles. He was not successful and, therefore, resigned as mayor and deputy (March 27, 1871). In 1876 he stood again for the Chamber of Deputies and was elected for the 18th *arrondissement*. He joined the extreme left, and his energy and mordant eloquence speedily made him the leader of the Radical bloc.

Toppler of ministries. In 1877, in the constitutional crisis precipitated on *le seize mai* (May 16), when President Patrice MacMahon attempted to make the government responsible to him rather than to the National Assembly, Clemenceau took a leading part in resisting such antirepublican policy. In 1880 he started his newspaper, *La Justice*, which became the principal organ of the Radicals in Paris; and from that time onward, throughout

Le seize mai

the presidency (1879–87) of Jules Grévy, he rapidly built up his reputation as a political critic of republicans and radicals as well as of conservatives and as a destroyer of ministries who would not, however, take office himself. Hostile to the colonial expansion that was dispersing the resources of a weakened France, he mercilessly attacked its promoters, and in 1885 his use of a minor reverse in Tongking (Indochina; now North Vietnam) was the principal factor in the fall of Jules Ferry's cabinet. At the elections of 1885, he was returned both for his old seat in Paris and for the *département* of Var, for which he chose to sit. Refusing to form a ministry himself, because he could not command a majority in the Senate, he supported the government of Charles de Freycinet in 1886 and was responsible for the inclusion in the cabinet of General Georges Boulanger as minister of war. Clemenceau had mistakenly imagined Boulanger to be a republican, but when he showed himself an irresponsible demagogue and nationalist, a focus for both Bonapartist and monarchist support, Clemenceau became a vigorous opponent of the Boulangist movement and helped to form the League of the Rights of Man to press for radical reforms.

By his share in the exposure of President Grévy's son-in-law for trafficking in honours, Clemenceau caused the resignation of another prime minister, Maurice Rouvier, in 1887. Yet, he refused Grévy's request that he himself should form a ministry and intrigued to keep various other leaders out of office. His destructive political power won him an ever-increasing number of enemies, and his implication in the scandal of 1892, caused by the failure of the Panama Canal Company, gave them all—especially the Boulangists—an unrivalled opportunity for revenge. Clemenceau's associations with the Jewish financier Cornélius Herz, who was deeply involved in the affair, inevitably threw suspicion on him; later he was accused of being in the pay of the British Foreign Office. The attack on Clemenceau was mounted in the powerful daily newspaper, *Le Petit Journal;* it took a dramatic turn when, in the Chamber of Deputies on December 20, 1892, the author and Boulangist Paul Déroulède denounced him as the protégé and supporter of Herz. Clemenceau claimed that Déroulède was lying and challenged him to a duel, in which neither was hurt. More effectively, Clemenceau brought a successful lawsuit against his detractors. Their condemnation forced some of them to resign as deputies, but in the end they took Clemenceau with them. All the accumulated venom he had aroused was concentrated in the election of 1893 when, standing again for the Var *département*, Clemenceau was attacked on all sides. Despite conducting an exhaustive and brilliant campaign, he was defeated. His failure induced a mood of savage despair, and shortly afterward he wrote to a friend,

> I have been misunderstood by my own family, betrayed by my friends, abandoned by my party, ignored by the voters, suspected by my country. . . . I have nothing left, nothing, nothing, nothing.

Journalistic interlude. But Clemenceau was too much of a fighter to give in to discouragement. He started upon a serious career in journalism and, after a difficult beginning, came to be classed among the foremost political writers of his time. A new Clemenceau was revealed: a man of reflection, of vast culture, a friend of the best known writers and artists of the period. His forceful personality was an inspiration to artists. Jean-François Raffaëlli and Claude Monet painted his portrait, Auguste Rodin did a bust of him. An ardent supporter of the Impressionists, he especially favoured the work of Monet: after World War I he arranged for a series of Monet's paintings to be exhibited in the Orangerie in the Tuileries Gardens.

At the same time, Clemenceau was writing books, mainly political and sociological, but his *Au pied du Sinaï* (Eng. trans., *At the Foot of Mount Sinai*, 1922), illustrated by Henri de Toulouse-Lautrec, was a volume of sketches on the history of the Jewish people. He also tried his hand at writing a play.

He was, however, essentially a journalist and inevitably

wrote much about the Dreyfus case, which agitated France from 1894 to 1906. At first Clemenceau had assumed that the young Jewish officer Alfred Dreyfus had, indeed, been guilty of selling secrets to Germany. But, once convinced of his innocence, Clemenceau carried on an eight-year battle (1897–1905) in his newspapers *La Justice* and *L'Aurore* (founded in 1897). Gradually the case assumed increasing political overtones, and Clemenceau's support for Dreyfus brought him back into favour with his fellow republicans and, moreover, showed to good advantage his qualities of leadership and tenacity. He was prevailed upon to accept election as senator for Var in April 1902.

Ministerial office, 1906–09. This election was of vital importance in the political career of Clemenceau. He remained a senator from Var until 1920, the year in which he voluntarily ended his political activity. It was as senator that he was to show his greatest qualities as a statesman. He became a member of the cabinet in 1906 as interior minister and was premier from 1906 to 1909. Finally, in 1917, after three years of World War I, when France's morale and resources were at their lowest ebb, he accepted President Raymond Poincaré's invitation to head the war government (1917–20). His steadfast and ruthless pursuit of war brought him the title "Father of Victory."

From the time of his first speech in the senate (October 30, 1902), on the question of restricting the formation of religious congregations, Clemenceau defended freedom of thought, belief, conscience, and education. He opposed any interference by the temporal power of the Vatican in French affairs and also resisted the monopoly of education demanded by the Socialists.

As minister of the interior, Clemenceau faced difficult problems, notably the enforcement of the new law (1905) separating church and state, as well as serious labour problems. When a strike of miners in the Pas-de-Calais led to a threat of disorder in 1906, he resolved to employ the military. His attitude in this matter alienated the Socialist Party, from which he definitely broke in a notable speech. It marked him, however, as the "strong man" of the day in French politics; and, when the ministry of Ferdinand Sarrien resigned in October 1906, Clemenceau became premier. During 1907 and 1908 the new entente with England was cemented. In Morocco, a dispute between France and Germany over the harbouring in the German consulate of German deserters from the French Foreign Legion brought renewed tension between the two countries. Austria-Hungary urged calmness on the Germans, and in February 1909 a joint agreement was signed, recognizing the economic interests of Germany and the special political interests of France in Morocco. The Clemenceau government fell on July 20, 1909, Clemenceau resigning after a violent and unexpected argument with the influential statesman Théophile Delcassé.

Freed from the responsibilities of power, Clemenceau travelled abroad. He took advantage of this opportunity to make speeches in Argentina, Uruguay, and Brazil on the subject of democracy. "I am a soldier of democracy," he said. "It is the only form of government which can establish equality for all, and which can bring closer the ultimate goals: freedom and justice."

Leadership during World War I. Back in the Senate (1911), Clemenceau became a member of its commissions for foreign affairs and the army. He was convinced that Germany intended war, and, haunted by the fear that France might again be caught unprepared, he enquired diligently into the state of France's armaments. In order to publicize his views on rearmament, he founded in May 1913 a new daily paper, *L'Homme Libre*, with himself as editor.

Clemenceau stood against anything that could undermine France's moral strength. When World War I broke out in July 1914, the partisan in him gave way to the patriot, who called upon every Frenchman to join the fray. *L'Homme Libre* suffered at the hands of the censors for Clemenceau's plain speaking and, in September 1914, was suppressed. Two days later, however, it reappeared entitled *L'Homme Enchaîné*, and, although at first it was

subjected to much cutting, later excisions became rare. Meanwhile, in the Senate Clemenceau agitated for more and more guns, munitions, and soldiers, for judicious use of the available manpower, and for a better organized and equipped medical service. Deeply concerned about the attitude of the United States to the war, he sent urgent appeals to the American public and to President Woodrow Wilson and was overjoyed at the United States' entry into the war in April 1917.

Above all, Clemenceau strove to create an indomitable "will to victory." As the war dragged on, weariness, slackness, and pacifism began to appear. He was the first to draw public attention to such insidious perils. In these difficult conditions, President Poincaré, in November 1917, called upon Clemenceau to form a government. Clemenceau knew that his task meant victory or death: morale at the front was bad and at home even worse; resources were nearly at an end. Though he was 76 years of age, he formed his cabinet with himself as minister of war as well as premier. He proceeded at once to translate his words into action, defining, in his first pronouncement as prime minister, the meaning of action for him: "To be entirely in unity with the soldier, to live, to suffer, to fight with him; to renounce all that does not directly further our country's interest." For traitors and defeatists he had no clemency. Clemenceau's single purpose was to win the war, and to this aim all other interests were subordinated. The hope of victory urged him on. Yet he was obsessed with the need for a unified military command and was able ultimately to convert to his viewpoint the allied governments and military leaders. In March 1918, Ferdinand Foch was designated sole commander. Despite disasters in May 1918, Clemenceau's resolve remained unshaken, and he declared that he would wage war "to the last quarter hour, for the last quarter hour will be ours."

Negotiation of the peace. The armistice signed by the defeated Germans on November 11, 1918, proved him right and brought him, the last survivor of those who had protested at Bordeaux in 1871 against the harsh terms imposed on France, the satisfaction of seeing Alsace-Lorraine returned to France. Clemenceau found that building the peace was a more arduous task than winning the war. He wanted the wartime alliance to be followed by an indefectible peacetime alliance. He presided with authority over the difficult sessions of the Paris Peace Conference (1919). Robert Lansing, the United States secretary of state, who attended the conference, described him at its sessions:

head held high, tilted backward, between broad shoulders, bony hands in gray gloves resting on the table before him, dark eyes almost hidden behind bushy eyebrows, yet sparkling brightly when he addressed a delegate.

The Treaty of Versailles was in preparation, and this necessitated strenuous days of work and delicate negotiations. Clemenceau made it his task to reconcile the interests of France with those of Great Britain and the United States. He defended the French cause with enthusiasm and conviction, forcing his view alternately on the British prime minister David Lloyd George and the United States president Woodrow Wilson. He also took care to see that Germany was disarmed. With his desire for poetic justice, he insisted that the Treaty of Versailles was signed (June 28, 1919) in the Hall of Mirrors of the Versailles palace where, in 1871, William I had had himself proclaimed German emperor.

Meanwhile, the French Assembly began to grow restless, for it saw itself put to one side in the peace negotiations. It no longer regarded Clemenceau as indispensable. A new Chamber of Deputies was elected on November 16, 1919, and Clemenceau imagined that he would have its support, since many of its members were former servicemen. But the politicians could not forgive him for having excluded them not only from the conduct of the war but from the negotiation of the peace. He also had to face hostility from the clerical party on the extreme right and from the pacifist element on the extreme left. Defeated in the presidential election of January 17, 1920, he then, as was customary on the election of a new president, resigned the premiership. He also gave up all other political activities. "This time," said Lloyd George ironically, "it is the French who have burnt Joan of Arc."

Retirement and death. Clemenceau was nearly 80 years old when he retired to Vendée, to Bel-Ebat, a modest cottage on a dune overlooking the Atlantic. He spent a few days in Corsica with his friend Nicolas Piétri, whom he named as executor of his will and whom he persuaded to accompany him on a long sea voyage to India, from September 1920 to May 1921. In Singapore, he dedicated a street bearing his name. He went tiger hunting and amazed his hosts with the spryness of his wit and with his insatiable intellectual curiosity. Everywhere he was warmly welcomed as "the statesman who has deserved his world-wide reputation and who has done so much for the cause of the Allies."

Visit to the United States

When it appeared that the United States was seeking to dissociate itself from European affairs, Clemenceau, now 81 years old, visited the United States (November 1922) in an attempt to arouse its citizens from isolationism. He was welcomed triumphantly and in three weeks delivered about 30 speeches, admonishing his audiences that if they forgot that there had been a war, another would break out. Woodrow Wilson, whom he visited, thanked him with great feeling for this peace crusade. Before returning to France, Clemenceau undertook a pilgrimage to the places where French soldiers had fought in the battle for American independence. His friendship for the Americans was very real. When asked the reason, he would reply good-humouredly, "Because you are so young, so much fun!" Then he would add, "And because we were a hair's breadth from disaster when you came over, and you saved my grey hair from defeat and shame."

He retired finally to Bel-Ebat, although he still made short trips to Paris. He loved the sea and walks on the dunes. And he loved his garden, a jumble of plants and flowers with here and there a rosebush, which, contrary to all advice, he had planted in the sandy soil, exposed to the salt spray. Of these he was particularly fond, "because these roses show so much courage."

At last he had found serenity. "It is fitting that the end of my life should be so completely different from what I have been, from the whole nature of my character. I owe it to my work." He read a great deal and particularly enjoyed rereading Greek and Latin works in the original. He wrote *Démosthène* (1926; Eng. trans., *Demosthenes*, 1926), a study of Demosthenes and the fate of Greece, whose political instability had compromised its independence. He also wrote *Au soir de la pensée* (1927; Eng. trans., *In the Evening of My Thought*, 1929), a sort of philosophic testament. He remained interested in political events and was grieved by them. In 1926 he sent a virulent letter to the United States president Calvin Coolidge, calling for solidarity among the Allies in the face of German demands.

The years went by, bringing bereavements. The death of Foch saddened him, for he had admired him. But the posthumous publication of the Marshal's *Mémorial* aroused in him bitterness and indignation. With sadness but with pride, he answered it in his own unfinished memoirs, *Grandeurs et misères d'une victoire* (1930; Eng. trans., *Grandeur and Misery of Victory*, 1930).

On March 28, 1929, he wrote down his last wishes: to be buried near his father at Colombier, a spot of wild natural beauty in his native Vendée. He wanted no funeral procession, no official or religious ceremony. Around his tomb there was to be a very simple iron railing, with no inscription. He died on November 24, 1929, in his rue Franklin apartment in Paris.

BIBLIOGRAPHY. The great abundance of written material that has been published on Clemenceau necessitates listing only a few of the principal works devoted to him.

Definitive biographies: GASTON MONNERVILLE, *Clemenceau* (1968), an impartial study (in French) that presents a forceful picture of Clemenceau the man; GEORGES WORMSER, *La République de Clemenceau* (1961), an important, well-documented work written by one of the last survivors among the political collaborators of Clemenceau, with an interesting bibliography.

Other works: GUSTAVE GEFFROY, *Georges Clemenceau, sa vie, son oeuvre*, new ed. (1932), by one of the men who knew Clemenceau best; ROBERT LANSING, *Mémoires* (1925; Eng. trans., *War Memoirs*, 1935), includes a description of the important role of Clemenceau during the Versailles Peace Conference; JEAN MARTET, *M. Clemenceau peint par lui-même* (1929) and *Le silence de M. Clemenceau* (1929), two works by a former collaborator of Clemenceau to whom he entrusted the task of editing his papers (both full of intimate details and of Clemenceau's opinions of the men of his time); JOHN HAMPDEN JACKSON, *Clemenceau and the Third Republic* (1946); GEOFFREY BRUUN, *Clemenceau* (1943, reprinted 1968).

(G.Mo.)

Clement of Alexandria, Saint

Clement of Alexandria, the last and greatest of the Christian Apologists of the 2nd century (*i.e.*, those who attempted to explain and defend Christian beliefs to the Greco-Roman intelligentsia and political authorities), brought about, with much success, a rapprochement between Greek philosophy and the Mosaic tradition of the Jews under the aegis of the Christian faith. He thus laid the groundwork for the great doctrinal developments in the next three centuries. As a transitional missionary theologian to the Hellenistic (Greek cultural) world, Clement addressed his apologetics and polemics to the cultural despisers from without, and the uncultured critics and heretics from within, the church.

St. Clement of Alexandria, detail of a stained-glass window, 1954. In Boe Memorial Chapel, St. Olaf College, Northfield, Minnesota.

Early life and education. Born about 150 in Athens Clement was named Titus Flavius Clemens by his parents, who were pagans according to Epiphanius, a 4th-century bishop. Other than this meagre information, there is no significant information about his early life. As a student he travelled to various centres of learning in Italy and in the eastern Mediterranean area. Converted to Christianity by his last teacher, Pantaenus—reputedly a former Stoic philosopher and the first recorded president of the Christian catechetical school at Alexandria —Clement succeeded his mentor as head of the school in about 180.

Leadership of the catechetical school of Alexandria. During the next two decades Clement was one of the major intellectual leaders of the Alexandrian Christian community: he wrote several ethical and theological works and biblical commentaries; he combatted heretical Gnostics (religious dualists who believed in salvation through esoteric knowledge that revealed to men their spiritual origins, identities, and destinies); he engaged in polemics with Christians who were suspicious of an intellectualized Christianity; and he educated persons who later became theological leaders (*e.g.*, Origen) and ecclesiastical leaders (*e.g.*, Alexander, bishop of Jerusalem).

Among his ethical and theological works is a famed trilogy: the *Protreptikos* ("Exhortation"), the *Paidagōgos* ("The Instructor"), and the *Strōmateis* ("Miscellanies").

Ethical and theological works

The last of these contained seven complete books. The eighth book of the *Strōmateis* is in the form of notes.

In the *Paidagōgos* Clement referred to the order in which the Logos (the Word, or Christ) leads men to salvation. The Logos is successively the Protreptikos, who persuades men to be saved, the Paidagōgos, who trains men in the direction of moral improvement, and the Didaskalos (the Teacher), who instructs men in intellectual and spiritual goals so that they might comprehend and apprehend the revelation of the Word. Because the titles of the first two works of the trilogy and the terms Clement used for the first two modes of operation of the Logos were identical, scholars once thought that there must be another work, *Didaskalos*, no longer extant; however, this view is no longer held. Other extant works include a tract on the use of wealth, *A Discourse Concerning the Salvation of Rich Men;* a moral tract, *Exhortation to Patience or Address to the Newly Baptized;* a collection of sayings by Theodotus, a follower of Valentinus (a leading Alexandrian Gnostic), with commentary by Clement, *Excerpta ex Theodoto;* the *Eclogae Propheticae* (or Extracts), in the form of notes; and a few fragments of his biblical commentary *Hypotyposeis* (Outlines). Other works (of which some survive only in fragments, others not at all) to which early Christians referred are *On the Resurrection, On Prophesy, On the Soul, On Genesis, On Continence, First Principles, On Easter, Ecclesiastical Canon or Against the Judaizers, Homilies on Fasting and Calumny, On the Prophet Amos,* and *On Providence.*

Clement presented a functional program of witnessing in thought and action to Hellenistic inquirers and Christian believers a program that he hoped would bring about an understanding of the role of Greek philosophy and the Mosaic tradition within the Christian faith. According to Clement, philosophy was to the Greeks, as the Law of Moses was to the Jews, a preparatory discipline leading to the truth, which was personified in the Logos. His goal was to make Christian beliefs intelligible to those trained within the context of the Greek *paideia* (educational curriculum) so that those who accepted the Christian faith might be able to witness effectively within Hellenistic culture. He also was a social critic deeply rooted in the 2nd-century cultural milieu.

Clement's view, "One, therefore, is the way of truth, but into it, just as into an everlasting river, flow streams but from another place" (*Strōmateis*), prepared the way for the curriculum of the catechetical school under Origen that became the basis of the medieval quadrivium and trivium (*i.e.*, the liberal arts). This view, however, did not find ready acceptance by the uneducated orthodox Christians of Alexandria, who looked askance at intellectuals, especially at the heretical Gnostics who claimed a special knowledge (*gnōsis*) and spirituality. Led by Demetrius, the ecclesiastical reformer and bishop of Alexandria who was elevated to the episcopacy in 189, they taught a legalistic doctrine of salvation and preached that the Christian was saved by faith (*pistis*). Clement attempted to mediate between the heretical Gnostics and the legalistic orthodox Christians by appropriating the term gnostic from the heretical groups and reinterpreting it to meet the needs of both the uneducated orthodox stalwarts and the growing numbers of those educated in the Greek *paideia* who were enlisting in the Christian Church. *Gnōsis* became, in Clement's theology, a knowledge and aspect of faith; he viewed it as a personal service that "loves and teaches the ignorant and instructs the whole creation to honor God the Almighty" (*Strōmateis*). Thus, Clement's Christian Gnostic—as opposed to the heretical Gnostic—witnessed to nonbelievers, to heretics, and to fellow believers, the educated and uneducated alike, by teaching new insights and by setting a lofty example in moral living. Like the pistic Christians (those who claimed that man was saved by faith, which was to be demonstrated in legalistic and moral terms), Clement held that faith was the basis of salvation; but, unlike them, he claimed that faith was also the basis of *gnōsis*, a spiritual and mystical knowledge. By distinguishing between two levels of believers—

i.e., the pistic Christian, who responds through discipline and lives on the level of the law, and the Christian Gnostic, who responds through discipline and love and lives on the level of the gospel—Clement set the stage for the efflorescence of monasticism that began in Egypt about a half century after his death.

Though much of Clement's attention was focussed upon the reorientation of men's personal lives in accordance with the Christian gospel, his interest in the social witnessing of Christians also involved him in the political and economic forces that affected man's status and dignity. In keeping with the *logos–nomos* (word–law, or, sometimes, gospel–law) theme ·that pervades his works, Clement alluded to the theory of the two cities, the city of heaven and the city of the earth. Like Augustine, the great theologian who utilized the same theme two centuries later in *De civitate Dei* (*The City of God*), Clement did not equate the city of heaven with the institutional church. According to Clement, the Christian was to live under the Logos as befitting a citizen of heaven and then, in an order of priorities, under the law (*nomos*) as a citizen of the earth. If a conflict should arise between God and Caesar (*i.e.*, the state), the Christian was to appeal to the "higher law" of the Logos. At one point Clement advocated the theory of the just cause for open rebellion against a government that enslaves people against their wills, as in the case of the Hebrews in Egypt. In this view he also anticipated Augustine's theory of the just war, a theory that has been dominant in Western civilization since the early Middle Ages. He also struck at racism when it is considered a basis for slavery.

In Egypt during the late 2nd century the rising inflation, high cost of living, and increased taxes placed extreme burdens not only on the poor but also on the relatively wealthy middle class, which was eventually ruined. From the tenor of the *Paidagōgos*, one can conclude that the majority of Clement's audience came from the ranks of Alexandrian middle and upper classes, with a few intelligent poorer members coming from the Alexandrian masses. The problem of wealth was disturbing to the pistic Christians, who interpreted literally the command of Christ to the rich young man who wanted to be saved, "sell what you have and give to the poor." In response to the literal interpretation, Clement wrote *The Discourse Concerning the Salvation of Rich Men*, in which he stated that wealth is a neutral factor in the problem. Possessions are to be regarded as instruments to be used either for good or for evil. "The Word does not command us to renounce property but to manage property without inordinate affection" (*Eclogae Propheticae*). In the matter of welfare (almsgiving), Clement's views are not consistent. On the one hand, he advised that the Christian should not judge who is worthy or unworthy of receiving alms by being niggardly and pretending to test whether or not a person is deserving. On the other hand, he stated that alms should be dispensed with discernment to the deserving, for freeloaders, who are lazy and have some possessions, take what can be given to the needy.

Later career. Because of the persecution of Christians in Alexandria under the Roman emperor Severus in 201–202, Clement was obliged to leave his position as head of the catechetical school and to seek sanctuary elsewhere. His position at the school was assumed by his young and gifted student Origen, who became one of the greatest theologians of the Christian Church. Clement found safety and employment in Palestine under another of his former students, Alexander, bishop of Jerusalem. He remained with Alexander until he died, sometime between 211 and 215.

Significance. In his various roles, as missionary theologian, Apologist, and polemicist, Clement developed or touched upon ideas that were to influence the Christian world in the areas of monasticism, political and economic thought, and theology. In this last area, the Greek Church regarded his views as too close to Origen's, some of which were considered heretical. In the Latin Church, however, he was regarded as a saint, and his feast day was celebrated on December 4. In 1586, however, be-

Clement's
views on
wealth

Clement's
view of
the roles
of faith
and
knowledge

cause some of his views were questioned in regard to their orthodoxy, Sixtus V deleted his name from the Roman martyrology.

BIBLIOGRAPHY
Works: O. STAHLIN, *Die griechischen christlichen Schrift-steller der ersten drei Jahrhunderte,* vol. 12, 15, 17, 39 (1905–36), the only critical edition of the Greek text; J.P. MIGNE, *Patrologia Graeca,* vol. 8–9 (1890–91), Latin and Greek texts.
Translations: W. WILSON, "Clement of Alexandria," in *The Ante-Nicene Fathers,* vol. 2 (1956); S.P. WOOD (trans.), *Clement of Alexandria, Christ the Educator* (1954); J.E.L. OULTON and H. CHADWICK, *Alexandrian Christianity* (1954). For various aspects of Clement's thought, see also C. BIGG, *The Christian Platonists of Alexandria* (1886, reprinted 1968); E.F. OSBORN, *The Philosophy of Clement of Alexandria* (1957); R.B. TOLLINTON, *Clement of Alexandria: A Study in Christian Liberalism* (1914); W. JAEGER, *Early Christianity and Greek Paideia* (1961); E. MOLLAND, *The Conception of the Gospel in the Alexandrian Theology* (1938); and H. CHADWICK, *Early Christian Thought and the Classical Tradition* (1966).

(L.F.)

Cleopatra

Cleopatra VII, famous in history and drama as, simply, Cleopatra, is thrice renowned: she was the only human being except Hannibal who struck fear into Rome; second, her ambition no less than her charm as focussed on Julius Caesar and Mark Antony actively influenced Roman politics at a crucial period; and third, although she was the most practical of women, she has come to represent, as no other woman of antiquity has, the prototype of the romantic *femme fatale,* an evolution all the more remarkable in that the ancient sources for her life are uniformly hostile. This bias makes it hard to form a just estimate of her.

Cleopatra, detail of a bas relief, *c.* 69–30 BC. In the Temple of Hathor, Dandarah, Egypt.

Life and career. Cleopatra was born in 69 BC, the second daughter of King Ptolemy XII, and was destined to become the last sovereign of the Macedonian dynasty that ruled Egypt between the death of Alexander the Great in 323 and its annexation by Rome in 31. The line had been founded by Alexander's marshal Ptolemy. Cleopatra was of Macedonian descent and had no Egyptian blood, although she alone of her house took the trouble to learn Egyptian, and for political reasons regarded herself as the daughter of Re, the sun god. Coin portraits of her show a countenance alive rather than beautiful, with a sensitive mouth, firm chin, liquid eyes, broad forehead, and prominent nose. Her voice, says the Greek biographer Plutarch, "was like an instrument of

many strings." He adds that "Plato admits four sorts of flattery, but she had a thousand." When Ptolemy XII died in 51, the throne passed to his 15-year-old son, Ptolemy XIII, and that king's sister–bride, Cleopatra. They soon fell out, and civil war ensued. Ptolemy XII had been expelled from Egypt in 58 and had been restored three years later only by means of Roman arms. Rome now felt that it had a right to interfere in the affairs of this independent, exceedingly rich kingdom, over which it had in fact exercised a sort of protectorate since 168. No one realized more clearly than Cleopatra that Rome was now the arbiter and that to carry out her ambition she must remain on good terms with Rome and its rulers. Thus when Caesar, the victor in the civil war, arrived in Egypt in October 48, in pursuit of Pompey (who, a fugitive from his defeat at Pharasalus in Thessaly, had been murdered as he landed four days before), Cleopatra set out to captivate him. She succeeded. Each was determined to use the other. Caesar sought money— he claimed he was owed it for the expenses of her father's restoration. Cleopatra's target was power: she was determined to restore the glories of the first Ptolemies and to recover as much as possible of their dominions, which had included southern Syria and Palestine. She realized that Caesar was the strong man, the dictator, of Rome and it was therefore on him that she relied. In the ensuing civil war in Egypt Caesar was hard-pressed by the anti-Cleopatra party, led by her brother, Ptolemy XIII, but Caesar eventually defeated them and re-established the joint rule of brother and sister–wife. Caesar, having won his victory on March 27, 47, left Egypt after a fortnight's amorous respite. Whether Caesar was in fact the father of Cleopatra's son whom she called Caesarion cannot now be known.

The meeting with Caesar

It took Caesar two years to extinguish the last flames of Pompeian opposition. As soon as he returned to Rome, in 46, he celebrated a four-day triumph—the ceremonial in honour of a general after his victory over a foreign enemy—in which Arsinoe, Cleopatra's younger and hostile sister, was paraded. Munda, in 45, was the *coup de grace.* Cleopatra was now in Rome, and a golden statue of her had by Caesar's orders been placed in the temple of Venus Genetrix, the ancestress of the Julian family to which Caesar belonged. Cleopatra herself was installed by Caesar in a villa that he owned beyond the Tiber. She was accompanied by her husband–brother and was still in Rome when Caesar was murdered in 44. She behaved with a discretion that she was later to discard, and her presence seems to have occasioned little comment; officially she was negotiating a treaty of alliance. Cicero, the politician and writer, mentions her in none of his contemporary letters, though his later references to her show that he regarded her, as most Romans did, with rancour.

Caesar's assassination put an end to Cleopatra's first campaign for power, and she retired to Egypt to await the outcome of the next round in the Roman political struggle. When, at the Battle of Philippi in 42, Caesar's assassins were routed, Mark Antony became the heir-general of Caesar's authority—or so it seemed, for his great nephew and personal heir, Octavian, was but a sickly boy. When Antony, bent on pursuing the eternal mirage of Roman rulers, an invasion of Persia, sent for Cleopatra, she was delighted. Here was a second chance of achieving her aim. She had known Antony when he had been in Egypt as a young staff officer and she had been 14. She was now 28 or 29 and completely confident of her powers. She set out for Tarsus in Asia Minor, loaded with gifts, having delayed her departure to heighten Antony's expectation. She entered the city by sailing up the Cydnus River in the famous barge that Shakespeare immortalized in *Antony and Cleopatra.* Antony was captivated, and Cleopatra subtly exploited his raffish and unstable character. Forgetting his wife, Fulvia, who in Italy was doing her best to maintain her husband's interests against the growing menace of young Octavian, Antony put off his Persian campaign and returned as Cleopatra's slave to Alexandria, where he treated her not as a "protected" sovereign but as an

Captivation of Antony

independent monarch. "Her design of attacking Rome by means of Romans," as one historian put it, "was one of such stupendous audacity that we must suppose that she saw no other way." Her first effort had been frustrated by Caesar's death; she felt now that she could win all by using the far more pliant and apparently equally powerful Antony. In Alexandria Cleopatra did all she could to pander to his weaknesses. They formed a society of "inimitable livers," whose members in fact lived a life of debauchery and folly. Cleopatra, however, knew how to handle her catch. Yet the final struggle for the dominion of Rome was to last for ten years and was to end in disaster for Cleopatra (no less than for Antony), largely promoted by Cleopatra herself.

In 40 BC, Antony left Alexandria to return to Italy, where he was forced to conclude a temporary settlement with Octavian, whose sister Octavia (Fulvia having died) he married. Three years later Antony was convinced that he and Octavian could never come to terms. He went east again and again met Cleopatra; he needed her money for his postponed Parthian campaign. He then took the fatal step of marrying her. The union was not only utterly insulting to Octavia and her brother but in Roman law it was also invalid. Henceforward all Rome was united against him.

Antagonism of Herod

Meanwhile, during Antony's absence, Cleopatra had committed another act of disastrous folly. She had antagonized Herod of Judaea, by far the ablest, richest, and most powerful of the "protected" sovereigns, or "client kings," of Rome. Herod and Antony were old friends; but in the year 40, after Antony's departure, Cleopatra unsuccessfully tried to seduce Herod on his way through Egypt. Cleopatra never forgave him for the rebuff. She went much further: when she and Antony were reunited, she persuaded him to give her large portions of Syria and Lebanon and even the rich balsam groves of Jericho in Herod's own kingdom. But Antony refused to sacrifice Herod wholly to Cleopatra's greed, whereupon she hated Herod more than ever, and even interfered in his unhappy family affairs by intriguing against him with the women of his household. She made a tour of her new acquisitions, on which Herod received her with simulated delight; but she remained as jealous and hostile as ever, bitterly resentful that anyone other than herself should influence Antony. The fruit of her folly was soon to be gathered.

Cleopatra had merely acquiesced in the Parthian campaign: she sought other ways of spending her money. The campaign itself was a costly failure, as was the temporary conquest of Armenia. Nevertheless, in 34 Antony celebrated a fantastic triumph in Alexandria. Crowds beheld Antony and Cleopatra seated on golden thrones, with their own three children and little Caesarion, whom Antony proclaimed to be Caesar's son, thus relegating Octavian, who had been adopted by Caesar as his son and heir, to legal bastardy. Cleopatra was hailed as queen of kings, Caesarion as king of kings. Alexander Helios was awarded Armenia and the territory beyond the Euphrates, his brother Ptolemy the lands to the west of it. The boys' sister, Selene, was to be ruler of Cyrene. Octavian, now lord of the ascendant in Italy, seized Antony's will from the temple of the Vestal Virgins, to whom it had been entrusted, and revealed to the Roman people that not only had Antony bestowed Roman possessions on this foreign woman but had intended to transfer the capital from Rome to Alexandria, there to found a new dynasty.

Antony and Cleopatra spent the winter of 32–31 in Greece amid revels and dissipation. The Roman Senate deprived Antony of his prospective consulate for the following year. When it finally declared war against Cleopatra the unwisdom of her policy against Herod was revealed, for she had contrived to embroil him with the King of Petra just when his ability and resources would have been of the utmost value to Antony. At the naval Battle of Actium, in which Octavian faced the combined forces of Antony and Cleopatra on September 2, 31, Cleopatra suddenly broke off the engagement and set course for Egypt. Inevitable defeat followed. Antony went on board her flagship and for three days refused to see her; but they were reconciled before they reached Alexandria, styling themselves no longer "inimitable livers" but "diers together."

Cleopatra with all her subtlety, all her political foresight, had backed two losers, first Caesar and then Antony, to whose downfall she had notably contributed. Octavian now became the magnet. Cleopatra realized that she could neither kill Antony nor exile him. But she believed that if he could be induced to kill himself for love of her, they would both win undying renown. She retired to her mausoleum, then sent messengers to Antony to say she was dead. He fell on his sword, but in a last excess of devotion had himself carried to Cleopatra's retreat, and there died, after bidding her to make her peace with Octavian.

Death of Antony and Cleopatra

Death and assessment. When Octavian visited her, Cleopatra tried yet once again to captivate the leading Roman. She used all her arts: she failed. She knew, then, that Octavian intended that she and her children should adorn his triumph. Rather than be dragged through the city in which she had been borne as a queen, she killed herself, in August 30, possibly by means of an asp, symbol of divine royalty. Octavian, on receiving her letter asking that she might be buried with Antony, sent messengers posthaste. "The messengers," Plutarch says, "came at full speed, and found the guards apprehensive of nothing; but on opening the doors they saw her stonedead, lying upon a bed of gold, set out in all her royal ornaments." She was 39 and had been a queen for 22 years and Antony's partner for 11. They were buried together, as both of them had wished, and with them was buried the Roman Republic.

In retrospect, Cleopatra's political career ended in utter failure. Had she been less ambitious she might have preserved her kingdom as a client, as her rival Herod did with complete success. In overreaching herself she ruined all. And yet it was this political failure that was to be transmuted into the grand original of the great lover, consecrated by the art of Shakespeare himself. The best epitaph on Cleopatra is that of the historian Dio Cassius: "She captivated the two greatest Romans of her day, and because of the third she destroyed herself."

BIBLIOGRAPHY. All the authorities, ancient and modern, including papyri, inscriptions, and coins, are exhaustively set out in the appendix to HANS VOLKMANN, *Kleopatra* (1953; Eng. trans., 1958), the standard work on the subject. They are in brief, and chiefly, as follows. (*Ancient sources*): These are copious and hostile. PLUTARCH's *Life of Antony* is one of his longest and most vivid. His grandfather remembered contemporary Alexandrian gossip; but Plutarch cites other contemporaries as well. Despite his bias against both Antony and Cleopatra, he does not deny them greatness of soul, especially in their last hours. JOSEPHUS, a Jewish historian writing under Roman supervision a little before Plutarch, is uniformly hostile to Cleopatra, especially in regard to her intrigues against Herod. DIO CASSIUS, a Bithynian who wrote a history of Rome in Greek at the end of the 2nd century AD, gives a fair and straightforward narrative of events. He holds that Cleopatra betrayed Antony. From VIRGIL onward, Roman poets treat Cleopatra with disdain and abuse. (*Modern sources*): SHAKESPEARE was the first to present Cleopatra as the *grande amoureuse*. She is the "lass unparallel'd," the "Egyptian dish," the "serpent of old Nile," and Antony the "doting mallard." This characterization, one of the most splendid in all literature, was the received version until modern times. GEORGE BERNARD SHAW's version in his *Caesar and Cleopatra* has no historical basis. The first to restore Cleopatra to her predominantly political role was JOHN BUCHAN, Lord Tweedsmuir, himself a statesman of distinction, in his *Augustus* (1937). The most recent scholarly view, in accord with Buchan, is that of J.P.V.D. BALSDON in his *Julius Caesar and Rome* (1967; U.S. title, *Julius Caesar: A Political Biography*, 1967). In vol. 10, pp. 35–111, of the *Cambridge Ancient History*, WILLIAM W. TARN and M.P. CHARLESWORTH cover the main events of Cleopatra's life and her part in them. THEODORE JOHN CADOUX's article in the *Oxford Classical Dictionary*, 2nd ed., pp. 251–252 (1970), is a good compendium. Narrative references to Cleopatra may be found in *The Life and Times of Herod the Great* (1956), and *The Death of the Roman Republic* (1969), both by STEWART PEROWNE.

(S.H.P.)

Climate

From the ancient Greek origins of the word (*Klíma*, "an inclination or slope"—*e.g.*, of the sun's rays; a latitude zone of the Earth; a clime), and from its earliest usage in English, climate has been understood to mean the atmospheric conditions that prevail in a given region or zone. In the older form, "clime," it was sometimes taken to include all aspects of the environment, including the natural vegetation. The best modern definitions of climate regard it as comprising the total experience of weather and atmospheric behaviour over a number of years in a given region. It is not just the "average weather" (an obsolete, and always inadequate, definition). A satisfactory specification of climate should include average values of the various climatic elements, such as temperature, humidity, rainfall, and wind, that prevail at different times of the day or year, as well as their extreme ranges, variability, and frequency of various occurrences. Just as one year differs from another, the values for one decade or one century are found to differ from one another by a smaller but sometimes significant amount: climate is, therefore, time dependent, and climatic values or indices should not be quoted without specifying what years they refer to.

Climatic history, forecasts, and statistics

As these considerations imply, climate has a history of its own and this clearly has had an impact on human history and on the distribution of animals and plants through time. In connection with modern long-term planning and decision making in agriculture, industry, and trade, the information required is a climatic forecast. There is as yet, however, no scientific method of general applicability whereby this demand can be met. A few apparently well-reasoned forecasts have been made in recent years of the general character or trend of climate (especially of specific items, such as temperature or sea ice) in cases where the relevant data and knowledge of the governing circumstances have seemed sufficient. Reservations are inevitable, however, even in these cases, because of the effects that might arise from certain unforeseeable external influences, such as the incidence of great volcanic dust veils in the atmosphere or the increasing scale and variety of man's pollution of the terrestrial environment.

In the absence of a satisfactory forecasting method, climatic statistics of observations made over some former period of time have to be used as the main guide to the future. Here it is important to know which years of observation were consulted and to consider how far the character of those years is likely to be relevant to the planning period. Studies of the climatic figures obtained in the years since the network of well-instrumented observing stations was established indicate that assumptions about the immediate future (one to five years ahead), at any time, are subject to least error when the values of the immediate past (ten to 20 years) are used. For longer term future planning, the average values, frequencies, and "return periods" (intervals between recurrences of rare phenomena) derived from 100 years or more of past data are desirable, except where urban or industrial growth is known to have altered the situation.

Climatology and meteorology

Climatology is the scientific study of climate. It was formerly regarded as purely descriptive, as much a branch of geography as of meteorology. Modern climatology is concerned with the causes and prediction of the processes that generate the observed climates and their continual variations. The elements of climate are the same ones (solar and terrestrial radiation, temperature, humidity, cloudiness, rainfall, wind, and atmospheric pressure) that meteorology deals with. Climatology may therefore be regarded as the long-range branch of meteorology. It treats the same atmospheric processes but also seeks to identify the slower acting influences and longer term changes that are important. These considerations include, for example, the circulation of the oceans, floating sea ice, and the impact of small, observable variations in the intensity of the Sun's radiation.

The factors that determine climate are: (1) the balance of incoming and outgoing radiation at any place, (2) the temperatures of the surface and of the atmosphere that result partly from the radiation balance and partly from the heat transported into and out of the area by winds and ocean currents, (3) the horizontal and vertical motion of the air (from quite small-scale circulations up to the large-scale circulation of the winds over the globe), and (4) the moisture cycle—evaporation from sea and land surfaces, the transport of this moisture over great distances and to great heights by the winds, and its ultimate precipitation as rain, hail, or snow.

This article treats the processes that generate climate and cause its variation, the distribution and classification of climates, and the effects of climate upon plants, animals, and human endeavour. Further information on climatic variability, prediction, and the relation of climate to atmospheric conditions is discussed more fully under CLIMATIC CHANGE; WEATHER FORECASTING; and WINDS AND STORMS. The special climatic conditions near the ground and in urban areas are covered in the articles MICROCLIMATES; and URBAN CLIMATES. The discussion of atmospheric–oceanic interaction is covered in OCEANS AND SEAS; and the article HYDROLOGIC CYCLE carries relevant data on the influence of the oceans and of atmospheric moisture on climate. The disciplines of climatology and meteorology are covered in ATMOSPHERIC SCIENCES. This article is divided into the following sections:

I. Factors that generate climate
   Solar radiation
   Temperature
   Atmospheric pressure
   The world's oceans
   The moisture cycle
II. Climatic variation
   Seasonal changes
   Local effects
III. Climatic types
   Köppen classification system
   World climates and their distribution
IV. Climate and life
   Marine and terrestrial organisms
   Vegetation and crops
   Climate and man

I. Factors that generate climate

SOLAR RADIATION

Variability of incident radiation. The heating of the Earth and the energy available to drive the winds and ocean currents come from the Sun. At the average distance of the Earth from the Sun, the mean intensity or strength of the solar beam was estimated from the latest measurements in the 1960s to be about 1.94 gram calories per minute, per square centimetre of a plane surface presented at right angles to the beam outside the atmosphere. This is called the solar constant: it would be the amount of energy available to heat the Earth's surface if the atmosphere were perfectly transparent and if the Sun were vertically overhead. Wherever the Sun is at a lower angle of elevation, its energy is spread by the slanting rays over a greater area of the Earth's surface, and the heating of each square centimetre is correspondingly weaker (Figure 1). Hence, the intensity of the solar radia-

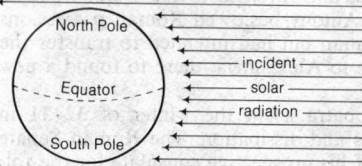

Figure 1: Variation of the angle of incident solar radiation with latitude.

tion depends upon latitude and the time of year (Figure 2). But the total amount of energy received in 24 hours depends also on the length of the day between sunrise and sunset. Because of this factor, the daily totals of available solar radiation are actually greatest at the poles in midsummer—although the total over the year is about two

Seasonal and other variations

and a half times as great at the Equator as at the poles. Because the Earth's orbit is somewhat elliptical, and the distance from the Sun currently is shortest in December–January, the greatest daily totals occur in the Antarctic summer; the daily totals at the Equator likewise are greater in December than in June.

From H.H. Lamb, *Climate: Present, Past and Future;* Methuen & Co. Ltd

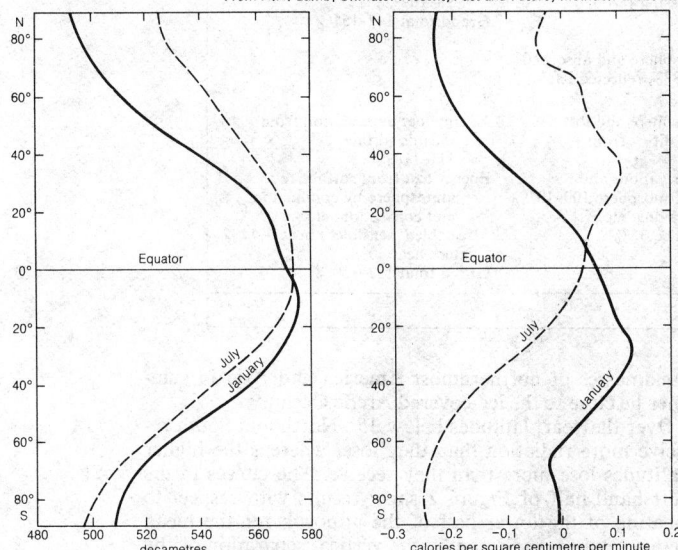

Figure 2: *Seasonal variation of radiation and of heating of the atmosphere with latitude.*
(Left) Mean 500 to 1,000 millibar thickness in the atmosphere. (Right) Intensity of net radiation received.

Because of cyclic changes in the ellipticity of the Earth's orbit, its seasonal position within the orbit, and the tilt of the axis of rotation, which affects the latitudes of the tropical and polar circles, the daily and seasonal totals of solar radiation undergo slow, cyclic changes over tens of thousands of years. It is argued by some authorities that these factors could weaken summer radiation and thus start an ice age on the lands in high northern latitudes through failure to melt the winter's snow.

There is some evidence that the strength of the solar beam reaching the Earth also undergoes fluctuations of about one-half of 1 percent twice within each (roughly 11-year) sunspot cycle, and that it possibly varies by a few percent over periods of about two centuries or more, because of longer period fluctuations in the output of the Sun itself. The former fluctuations seem to be correlated with some variations of the prevailing wind and weather patterns from year to year, but the latter seem liable to trigger greater and longer lasting climatic deviations. The question of solar variability and its possible influences on weather has been fraught with difficulties and controversy, partly because of the margins of error and the short length of record of solar-beam strength outside the atmosphere. Research is creating a firmer basis of knowledge, but the matter remains unresolved.

Effects of the atmosphere. The energy in the solar beam is mainly in the form of shortwave radiation, about half of it within the spectrum of wavelengths that are visible to the human eye as light (0.40 to 0.74 microns). The distribution of wavelengths indicates that the Sun's surface temperature is about 6000° C (11,000° F). The outgoing radiation from the Earth is so feeble by comparison that it just balances the strength of the solar beam at the mean distance of 150,000,000 kilometres (93,000,000 miles) from its source, and so the Earth remains at a nearly constant temperature. (Despite ice ages and warm, ice-free eras of geological time, the world average temperature has remained within the fairly narrow range required to support the development of life for hundreds of millions of years.) Corresponding to the low temperature of the Earth, the radiation sent out to space is mainly in much longer wavelengths (99 percent of it between three and 100 microns) than those of the strongest energy in the solar beam.

The oxygen, ozone, water vapour, and clouds (see Figure 6) in the atmosphere absorb the solar radiation of certain wavelengths; but the water vapour, clouds, and the carbon dioxide present in the atmosphere are most effective in absorbing energy in the long wavelengths of the outgoing terrestrial radiation. This energy warms the air at the levels where it is absorbed; and the air reradiates the energy in all directions, so that some of it returns to the Earth and much of it is involved in further radiation exchanges within the atmosphere. As a result, the average temperature near the surface of the Earth is kept at a level (about 15° C or 59° F) that is higher by about 40° C (72° F) than it would be in the absence of the atmosphere. From this reasoning it seems that the 10 percent increase in the amount of carbon dioxide in the atmosphere from the 1890s to the 1960s should tend to maintain a somewhat warmer climate (on average, the effect should be about 0.3° C or 0.5° F) than that of the last century.

The clouds, dust, and other particulate matter suspended in the atmosphere tend to reflect back, scatter, and absorb some of the radiation falling upon them. Hence, the solar radiation reaching the Earth's surface near the Equator, in the belt of equatorial rains, where dense clouds prevail and the sunshine averages only about five hours a day, is less than in the subtropical desert zones on either side. Over the Bay of Bengal in the summer monsoon there is actually a net loss of radiation. The variations of cloudiness and its distribution, the occurrence of dust veils in the atmosphere after great volcanic eruptions, and, possibly, industrial pollution by smoke, dust, and other substances, seem capable of producing years that are colder than usual or even longer lasting climatic fluctuations.

Heating of the Earth's surface. After passing through the atmosphere the radiation that reaches the Earth's surface is by no means all used in heating the surface. Some is reflected away and wasted: 80 to 90 percent goes in this way from a surface of new-fallen snow, 30 to 35 percent from deserts, from 5 to 40 percent from forests (depending on the colour of the leaves), from 8 to 25 percent from grasses and crops, and as little as 2 to 5 percent from a water surface when the Sun is high (but nearly 80 percent is reflected when the Sun is near the horizon). These figures, which measure the reflective property, are called the albedo of the respective surfaces. For comparison, the albedo of the upper surface of dense clouds is from 50 to 70 percent, for thin, high clouds, about 21 percent.

Water surfaces register the least rise in temperature for a given quantity of radiant energy falling upon them. The specific heat of water is greater than that of any other commonly occurring substance: thus, one calorie is required to raise the temperature of a gram of water by 1° C (2° F), and only about 0.2 calories for most types of rocks. Moreover, the incoming radiation penetrates to some depth in water, about 10 percent of it to a depth of ten metres (33 feet) in the ocean (0.5 to 1 percent to this depth in turbid coastal waters). Stirring of the water by wave action distributes the heat fairly evenly through this depth in rough seas. By contrast, the land area—particularly dry sands and soils that contain air spaces—heats and cools rapidly in response to radiation gain or loss. The heat absorption or loss is concentrated at the surface itself, as the thermal conductivity of sand and rock (and of the trapped air) is small. The sand surface of the Sahara commonly changes temperature by 40° to 50° C (about 70° to 90° F) from night to day, and an extreme diurnal range of 84° C (151° F) has been observed. The temperature of a fresh-snow surface (with air trapped in the layer blanketing the ground) in middle latitudes in winter may drop 10° to 20° C (about 20° to 40° F) under a clear sky at night. These figures compare with a normal diurnal range of rather less than 1° C (2° F) for the ocean surface in the tropics and only a few degrees for wet ground in clear weather.

Dry ground normally reaches its highest temperature within about three hours after midday and, in continental interior regions, the warmest time is within one

The radiation balance (marginal note, left)

Effects of clouds, dust, and volcanic eruptions (marginal note, right)

Table 1: Earth's Mean Radiation Budget*

Incoming energy	absorbed	ozone in stratosphere 2%; oxygen 2%; water vapour in lower atmosphere 7%; clouds 10%; Earth's surface (direct from Sun) 22%	Total radiation received at Earth's surface: shortwave radiation from Sun 44–55%
	passed on after scattering or absorption and reradiation by the atmosphere	scattered by the blue sky and absorbed at Earth's surface 5–6%; absorbed at Earth's surface after passing through clouds 17%	long-wave radiation from atmosphere 98–109% Grand total 142–154%
	Earth radiation returned by the atmosphere	reradiated from the atmosphere and absorbed at Earth's surface 90–98%; reflected back to Earth 8–11%	
Outgoing energy	Earth radiation lost to space	reradiated from the atmosphere and lost to space 54%; to space direct from Earth's surface 11%	Energy lost by radiation from Earth's surface 111–118%
	Earth radiation from surface to atmosphere returned solar radiation	absorbed, largely by water vapour and carbon dioxide, in the atmosphere 100–107% reflected from atmospheric dust etc., clouds and Earth's surface 35%	Energy lost from surface to atmosphere by conduction and convection, etc. feelable ("sensible") heat 6–12% latent heat 20% Grand total 137–150%

*Percentages are of the solar beam strength.

month after the summer solstice; its lowest temperatures occur close to dawn and within about one month of the winter solstice. The warmest and coldest months in the oceans in middle and higher latitudes are generally August and February, and the seasonal range of temperature is much smaller than for land areas in the same latitude.

The average energy budget represented by these processes is summarized in Table 1 as closely as present estimates permit. The grand totals of incoming and outgoing radiation balance each other within the margin of uncertainty of the global all-seasons estimates. It is probable, however, that the budget is not perfectly balanced every year and that some accumulations or deficiencies of heating are left over to be dispersed or made good in the years that follow. Such tabulations make it easier to see where variations of one or another item could have a greater or lesser effect on surface climate or the distribution of heat at different levels in the atmosphere.

TEMPERATURE

Variation with latitude. The steepest temperature gradients are in middle latitudes, and especially where heated landmasses of northernmost America and Asia in summer lie close to the ice-covered Arctic Ocean.

Over the year, latitudes below 35° North and South receive more radiation than they lose, whereas the higher latitudes lose more than they receive. The curves in the left hand half of Figure 2 show results with respect to heating of the lower half of the atmosphere: the mean temperature is indicated by the vertical separation of the levels where the pressure of the atmosphere is 1,000 millibars (29.53 inches of mercury) and where it is 500 millibars. Air under constant pressure—like most other substances—expands when it is heated, and contracts when it is cooled, so the depth, or thickness, of the lower layer of the atmosphere can be used as a measure of its temperature. In the strict sense, it increases or decreases as the air's density decreases or increases; the density is reduced a little by the water vapour in the air, so the thickness of the 1,000–500 millibar layer really varies with the "virtual temperature" of the air—*i.e.*, the corresponding temperature of dry air with the same density as the actual air. Hence, the maximum thickness is displaced towards the Equator by the great moisture content of the air in those latitudes. The distribution of

The energy budget

From H.H. Lamb, *Climate: Present, Past and Future;* Methuen & Co. Ltd

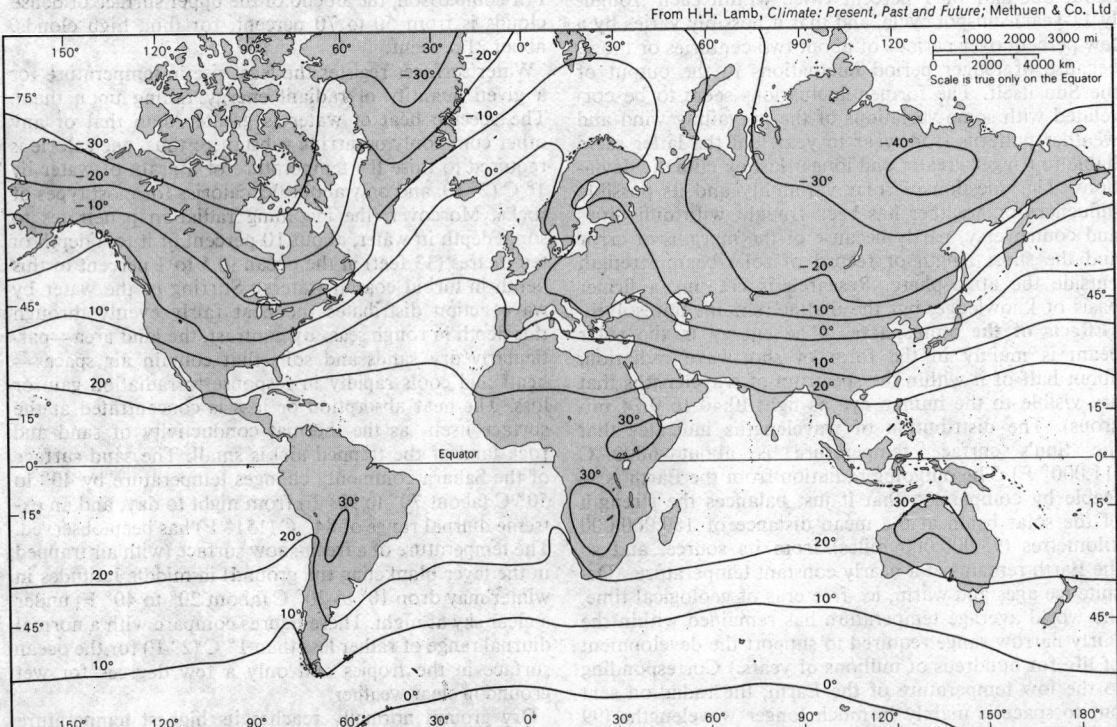

Figure 3: Average surface air temperatures (°C) reduced to sea level (January).

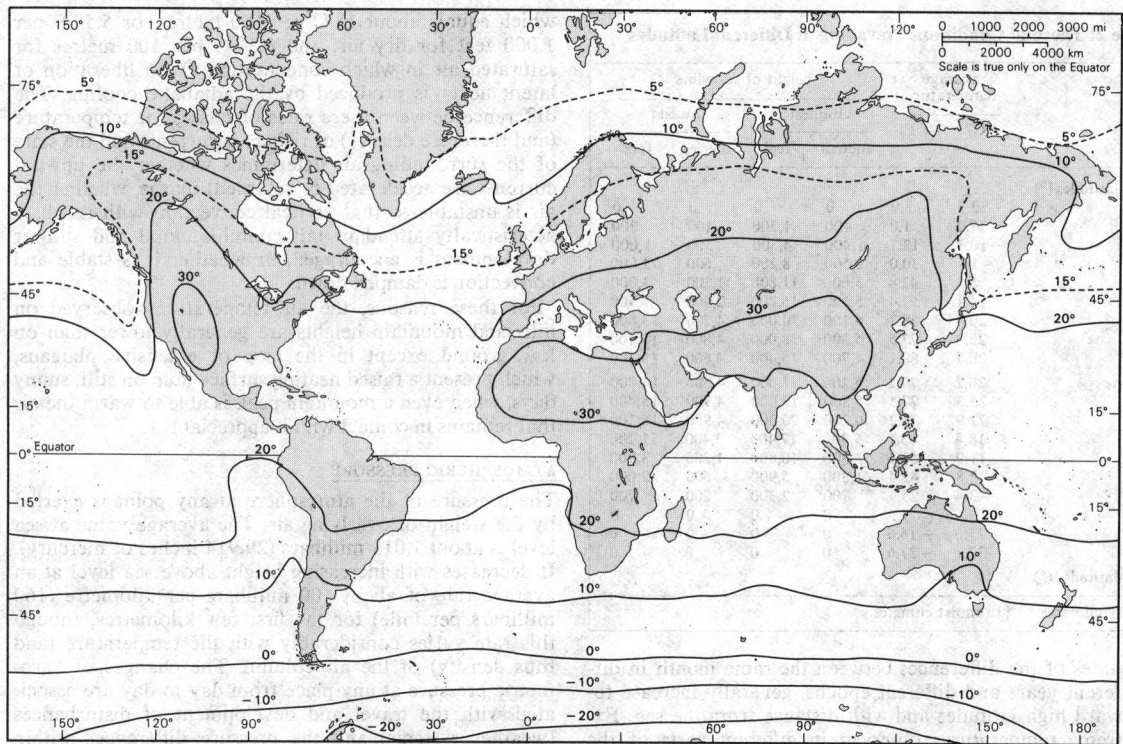

Figure 4: Average surface air temperatures (°C) reduced to sea level (July).
From H.H. Lamb, *Climate: Present, Past and Future;* Methuen & Co. Ltd.

Effects of wind flow

warm and cold air is also affected by the circulation of the atmosphere, including its vertical motion. Despite all these provisos, there is a definite relationship between the thickness of the 1,000–500 millibar layer in the atmosphere and the net radiation receipt at the Earth's surface.

These last points are important because the lifting of much of the upper layers of the atmosphere, as the lower layers expand, creates the differences of pressure that set the winds in motion. The expansion is great over the warm regions of the Earth, and indeed over all the lower latitudes, whereas the lower air layers contract over the cold regions and all the higher latitudes. This establishes a very simple mean pressure distribution in the atmosphere at heights between about two and 20 kilometres (one and 12 miles) above the Earth's surface, with high pressure generally over low latitudes and low pressure generally near the poles. The wind flow which is set up by these pressure differences and the effect of the rotation of the Earth is correspondingly simple: one great circumpolar vortex of upper westerly winds over each hemisphere. The flow of these winds swings poleward to round the edge of warm regions that project toward high latitudes and swings equatorward around cold regions that extend toward low latitudes: these regional, tonguelike extensions of the regimes of warm and cold latitudes, respectively, constitute (warm) ridges and (cold) troughs in the upper-level pressure distribution and huge wavelike meanderings of the upper westerly windstreams (see WINDS AND STORMS; JET STREAMS). This deep current of the upper winds carries most of the momentum of the atmosphere. Disequilibrium with the forces acting upon the great upper windstream at points of curvature, or acceleration (where the pressure gradient changes), causes the development of cyclones and anticyclones (*q.v.*) near the surface, and these systems, which bring the surface weather and its changes, are steered along by the upper wind flow. Moreover, the dynamics of this upper flow determine the wavelength, or spacing between the great ridges and troughs, described above. Some of these ridges and troughs are induced by the flow around, and over, barriers such as the Rocky Mountains and Andes; but downstream ridge and trough positions, due to the favoured wavelength, determine regions that are also respectively warmer and colder than the average of their latitude.

The average distribution of air temperature at the surface, near sea level, is illustrated by world maps for January and July (Figures 3 and 4). The general gradient is poleward and strongest in middle latitudes, particularly near the limits of ice and snow surface. The difference of response to seasonal heating and cooling between land and sea also accounts for some strong gradients near the margins of the continents. In the Northern Hemisphere, the cold regions in winter extend over the northeastern sectors of the great continents and in central and eastern Europe; in summer, they are over the northwestern sectors of the oceans as well as off northwest Europe and the Pacific seaboard of America. These locations correspond to common positions of cold troughs in the upper westerly wind flow.

The distribution of mean temperature for the whole year, reduced to sea level, and the height above sea level of the limit of permanent snow, by latitudes is given in Table 2. A noticeable feature is the lower temperatures in the Southern Hemisphere, attributable to the lower proportion of land in the latitudes where there is a net radiation gain and the occupation of the polar regions by a continent.

Diurnal, seasonal, and extreme temperatures. The diurnal range of temperature generally increases with distance from the sea and toward those places where the solar radiation is strongest, in dry tropical climates and on high mountain plateaus (owing to the reduced thickness of the atmosphere to be traversed by the Sun's rays). The average difference between the day's highest and lowest temperatures in January is 3° C (about 5° F; in July it is 5° C [9° F]) in those parts of the British Isles nearest the Atlantic. It is 4.5° C (8° F) in January and 6.5° C (11.5° F) in July on the small island of Malta in the Mediterranean Sea. At Tashkent it is 9° C (16° F) in January and 15.5° C (28° F) in July, and at Khartoum the corresponding figures are 17.0° C (30.5° F) and 13.5° C (24.5° F). At Qandahār, over 1,000 metres (3,300 feet) above sea level in Afghanistan, it is 14.0° C (25° F) in January, 20° C (36° F) in July, and exceeds 23° C (41° F) in September and October when the cloudiness is less than in July. Near the ocean at Colombo, Ceylon, the figures are 8° C (14° F) in January and 4.5° C (8° F) in July.

The seasonal variation of temperature and the magni-

Table 2: Thermal Conditions Prevailing at Different Latitudes

| | average temperature | | height of snowline | | | |
| | | | highest* | | lowest† | |
	(°C)	(°F)	metres	feet	metres	feet
North latitudes (°)						
90	−22.7	−8.9	0	0	0	0
80	−17.2	1.0	400	1,300	100	300
70	−10.7	12.7	1,300	4,300	300	1,000
60	−1.1	30.0	2,500	8,200	600	2,000
50	5.8	42.4	3,600	11,800	1,200	3,900
40	14.1	57.4	5,100	16,700	2,400	7,900
30	20.4	68.7	6,100	20,000	4,200	13,800
20	25.3	77.5	5,500	18,000	4,800	15,700
10	26.7	80.1	4,700	15,400	4,600	15,100
Equator	26.2	79.2	5,200	17,000	4,500	14,800
10	25.3	77.5	5,800	19,000	4,700	15,400
20	22.9	73.2	6,200	20,300	4,900	16,100
30	18.4	65.1	5,300	17,400	3,400	11,200
40	11.9	53.4	3,300	10,800	1,200	3,900
50	5.8	42.4	1,800	5,900	600	2,000
60	−3.4	25.9	700	2,300	200	700
70	−13.6	7.5	0	0	0	0
80	−27.0	−16.6	0	0	0	0
90	−33.1	−27.6	0	0	0	0
South latitudes (°)						

*In dry climates.   †In moist climates.

tudes of the differences between the same month in different years and different epochs, generally increase toward high latitudes and with distance from the sea. Extreme temperatures observed in different parts of the world are listed in Table 3.

Variation with height. There are two chief levels where the atmosphere is heated, namely at the Earth's surface and at the top of the ozone layer (about 50 kilometres or 30 miles up) in the stratosphere, these being where the radiation balance most generally shows a net gain. Prevailing temperatures tend to decrease with distance from these heating surfaces (apart from the ionosphere and outer atmospheric layers where other processes are at work). The world's average lapse rate of temperature (change with altitude) in the lower atmosphere is 0.6 to 0.7° C per 100 metres, or between 3 and 4° F per 1,000 feet. Lower temperatures prevail with increasing height above sea level because of the less favourable radiation balance in the free air, and because rising air (whether lifted by convection currents above a relatively warm surface or forced up over mountains) undergoes a reduction of temperature associated with its expansion as the pressure of the overlying atmosphere declines. This is the adiabatic lapse rate of temperature

Temperature lapse rate

which equals about 1° C per 100 metres, or 5.5° F per 1,000 feet for dry air, and 0.5° C per 100 metres for saturated air in which condensation (with liberation of latent heat) is produced by the adiabatic cooling. The difference between these rates of change of temperature (and therefore density) of rising air currents and the state of the surrounding air determines whether the upward currents are accelerated or retarded; that is, whether the air is unstable so that vertical convection with its characteristically attendant tall cumulus cloud and shower development is encouraged, or whether it is stable and convection is damped down.

For these reasons, the air temperatures observed on hills and mountain heights are generally lower than on low ground except in the case of extensive plateaus, which present a raised heating surface (and on still, sunny days, when even a mountain peak is able to warm the air that remains in contact with it appreciably).

ATMOSPHERIC PRESSURE

The pressure of the atmosphere at any point is exerted by the weight of overlying air. The average value at sea level is about 1,013 millibars (29.914 inches of mercury). It decreases with increasing height above sea level at an average rate of about 100 millibars per kilometre (160 millibars per mile) for the first few kilometres, though this rate varies considerably with the temperature (and thus density) of the air column. The changes of barometric pressure at any place from day to day are associated with the travel and development of disturbances (weather systems) and the pressure differences within them. Horizontal differences of atmospheric pressure are brought about by imbalance within the massive flow of the deep current of the circumpolar vortex, particularly near the level of strongest winds in the jet stream (ten to 14 kilometres or six to nine miles above sea level). This imbalance causes deviations of the flow, convergence, and piling up of the air in the levels concerned over some areas, and divergence with abstraction of air from other areas. The strongest effects of this kind are related to points of marked curvature and change of pressure gradient in the upper wind flow; but there is a general tendency to produce increased atmospheric pressure along the warm, low-latitude flank of the strongest upper winds —hence the subtropical anticyclone belts in either hemisphere—and a tendency also to cause a reduction of pressure along the cold, high-latitude flank of the upper flow—hence the belts of low pressure near the Arctic and Antarctic circles. Atmospheric pressure over the polar regions, and over the great continents in winter, is increased by the density of the very cold surface air.

Pressure variation with height

Table 3: World Temperature Extremes

| continent or region | highest recorded air temperature | | | lowest recorded air temperature | | |
| | place | temperature | | place | temperature | |
		(°F)	(°C)		(°F)	(°C)
Africa	al-'Azīzīyah, Libya (112 m or 367 ft asl.*)	136	57.7	Ifrane, Morocco (1,635 m or 5,363 ft asl.)	−11	−23.9
Antarctica	Bahía Esperanza (Hope Bay) 63°23′ S, 57°00′ W (7 m or 23 ft asl.)	58	14.6	Vostok II 78°27′ S, 106°52′ E (3,420 m or 11,218 ft asl.)	−127	−88.3
Asia	Jacobābād, W. Pakistan (57 m or 187 ft asl.)	127	52.8	Verkhoyansk, NE Siberia, U.S.S.R. (137 m or 449 ft asl.)	−94	−69.8
Australia	Cloncurry, Queensland (193 m or 633 ft asl.)	127.5	53.1	Charlotte Pass, New South Wales	−8	−22.2
Europe	Seville, Spain (39 m or 128 ft asl.)	122	50.0	Ust-Shchugor, U.S.S.R. (85 m or 279 ft asl.)	−74	−59.0
N. America	Death Valley (Greenland Ranch), California (−54 m or −177 ft asl.)	134	56.7	Snag, Yukon (646 m or 2,119 ft asl.)	−81	−62.8
S. America	Rivadavia, Argentina (205 m or 672 ft asl.)	120	48.9	Colonia, Sarmiento, Argentina (268 m or 879 ft asl.)	−27	−33.0
Tropical Pacific islands	Echague, Luzon, Republic of the Philippines (78 m or 257 ft asl.)	105	40.5	Haleakala, Hawaii (2,972 m or 9,748 ft asl.)	18	−7.8

*asl.—above sea level.

Pressure systems and winds. The distribution of atmospheric pressure determines the winds except where local effects, such as a deep valley channel, are very strong. The winds blow clockwise around regions of high pressure and counterclockwise around regions of low pressure in the Northern Hemisphere. The rules about direction of flow around high and low pressure are reversed in the Southern Hemisphere. At the surface, there is usually also a component of motion from high toward low pressure.

A purely zonal arrangement of high pressure over subtropical latitudes and near the poles, with low pressure near the polar circles and also near the Equator, and the belts of prevailing east and west winds determined by this regime, would not transport heat from low latitudes (where the incoming radiation is in excess) to the high latitudes (where the radiation received is less than that sent out to space). The individual travelling cyclones and anticyclones can be considered as eddies in the wind flow that perform an important role in transporting heat poleward. Nevertheless, longer lasting breakdowns of the mean zonal pressure distribution and wind circulation also occur when anticyclones are established in one or more sectors in subpolar latitudes and reverse the usual flow of the winds in middle latitudes. These are called blocking anticyclones because they appear to block the westerly and southwesterly winds that usually prevail in the Northern Hemisphere temperate zone. This phenomenon is common in the Northern Hemisphere and obviously owes something to the geography of land and sea, which introduces great temperature differences within the same latitude zone at times, distorting the upper wind flow into stationary waves of large amplitude. The occurrences of blocking contribute to the variability of temperature in middle and high latitudes. Similar developments occur on a more modest scale in the Southern Hemisphere, chiefly in two or three longitude sectors where the geography evidently provides a little support for a stationary wave pattern.

At any one time the atmospheric pressure at sea level commonly ranges within one hemisphere over 50 to 100 millibars (corresponding to 5–10 percent of the atmosphere's mass), and commonly it is between about 970 and 1,030 millibars. The extreme values of record are 877 millibars in a typhoon in the western Pacific in September 1958 and 1084 millibars in northwest Siberia in December 1968.

World storm belts and their distribution. The geographical distribution of anticyclones over the Northern and Southern Hemispheres can be indicated by the frequency of occurrence of centres of high pressure in different areas in winter. The subtropical anticyclone belt is prominent in both cases, but the positions frequented by centres of blocking anticyclones also make their mark, and these constitute an eccentric ring in the Northern Hemisphere, centred away from the pole and with a separate maximum of occurrences near its centre in the Greenland–Iceland area. There may be traces of a similar ring in the Southern Hemisphere centred near 70° S about the Tasmanian sector, but the most noticeable feature of the distribution is the extreme rarity of anticyclones over the Southern Ocean, particularly between 90 and 180° E.

The highest values of monthly mean atmospheric pressure departures occur along arcs that follow roughly the same paths as the zones of relatively high anticyclone frequency. They also are close to the belts of maximum frequency of the auroras (q.v.), a yet unexplained association. The high values of monthly mean pressure departures that are liable to occur within these belts bear witness to the occurrence of some long spells with blocking anticyclones centred in the areas concerned. In an extreme case, northeasterly winds replaced the usual southwesterlies over most of Europe in January 1963, producing the coldest month in more than 200 years in England.

A worldwide pattern of correlations of atmospheric pressure variation has been called the Southern Oscillation because its strongest feature is the opposite variation of pressure in the South Pacific anticyclone area and

the equatorial regions of the Indian Ocean. Other aspects of this linkage suggest that it is also related to the prevalence or the lack of blocking anticyclones in different years near the Arctic and Antarctic circles and may be associated with extensive anomalies of the surface temperature of the oceans near the Equator. The latter would certainly affect the energy and pattern of the atmospheric circulation.

The climatology of wind strengths, like that of wind directions, is determined by the global distribution of atmospheric pressure and, particularly, by where strong pressure gradients lie. The distribution is briefly illustrated here by the listing in Table 4 of the locations of the strongest observed winds.

Table 4: World Extremes of Wind and Precipitation

Wind	maximum observed gust speeds near sea level 303 km/hr (188 mph) at Jan Mayen Island 71° N, 8½° W 250–280 km/hr (155–175 mph) in a number of tropical hurricanes and typhoons* maximum observed gust speed on a mountain 372 km/hr (231 mph) on Mt. Washington, New Hampshire, 1,909 m (6,262 ft) above sea level† maximum observed winds at jet stream levels 630 km/hr (392 mph) over the Sea of Japan 500 km/hr (310 mph) at 6 to 8 km height (20,000–26,000 ft) over Korea in February 1953 555 km/hr (345 mph) at 11 km (36,000 ft) over Amsterdam Island (38° S) in September 1956
Rainfall	greatest amount in one year 22,990 mm (905 in.) at Cherrapunji, Assam, India, 1,313 m (4,307 ft) above sea level in 1861 greatest amount in one month 9,300 mm (366 in.) at Cherrapunji greatest falls in one day 1,870 mm (73.6 in.) at Cilaos, on Réunion Island (27° S, 55½° E), 1,200 m (3,900 ft) above sea level on March 16, 1952 1,166 mm (45.9 in.) at Baguio, Luzon, Republic of the Philippines, 1,482 m (4,861 ft) above sea level on July 15, 1911 greatest fall in one hour 305 mm (12.0 in.) at Holt, Missouri, on June 22, 1907 greatest fall in five minutes 63 mm (2.48 in.) at Portobelillo, Panama, on Nov. 29, 1911 greatest fall in one minute 31 mm (1.22 in.) at Unionville, Maryland, on July 4, 1956
Snow	deepest falls in one day 193 cm (76 in.) at Silver Lake, Colorado, 3,050 m (10,000 ft.) above sea level on April 14–15, 1921 183 cm (72 in.) on Dartmoor, England, on Feb. 16, 1929 greatest known total fall in one season 25.4 m (83 ft.) on the southern slope of Mt. Rainier, Washington, about 1,680 m (5,510 ft) above sea level in 1955–56 quickest known melting of consolidated snow cover 65 cm (26 in.) in ten days in the Harz Mountains, E. and W. Germany, in April 1952

*It is estimated that extreme speeds of over 400 km/hr (250 mph) sometimes occur, in narrow rings sometimes only a foot or two (under one metre) across, in tornadoes.   †It is probable that even stronger winds occasionally blow on the peaks of the Himalayas and Andes when these are affected by the jet stream.

THE WORLD'S OCEANS

Circulation, currents, and ocean–atmosphere interaction. The circulation of the oceans is part of the apparatus that produces the observed climates. Ocean currents (q.v.) that have a northward or southward component, like the warm Gulf Stream in the North Atlantic, or the cold Humboldt Current off South America, effectively exchange heat between low and high latitudes. In tropical latitudes the oceans account for a third or more of the poleward heat transport; at latitude 50° N the ocean's share is about one-seventh. In the particular sectors where the currents are located their importance is, of course, much greater than these figures, which represent hemispheric averages. Because warm water of Gulf Stream origin enters and occupies the eastern part of the Norwegian Sea, warmth is imparted to the winds blowing over the water, and the average air temperature over the year at Tromsø, Norway (69° 40′ N), is above the aver-

Margin notes (left): Variation of pressure in the Northern and Southern Hemisphere

The Southern Oscillation

Margin notes (right): Effects of currents on air temperature

age for its latitude by a margin of 14° C (about 25° F); in winter the excess is even greater, 24° C (43° F) in January. The mean annual temperature at Quito (Ecuador), on the Equator, is nearly 14° C below the average for the latitude. (This is an extreme departure found only close to the almost perpetually cloudy coast, where the drift of the current westward into the ocean causes water even colder than the Peru [Humboldt] Current surface waters to well up from below.)

The oceans, particularly in areas where the surface is warm, also supply moisture to the atmosphere. This, in turn, contributes to the heat budget of those areas in which the water vapour is condensed into clouds, liberating latent heat in the process, often in high latitudes and in places remote from the oceans where the moisture was taken up.

The great ocean currents are themselves wind-driven—set in motion by the drag of the winds over vast areas of the sea surface, especially where waves increase the friction. At the limits of the warm currents, especially where they abut directly upon a cold current, as at the left flank of the Gulf Stream in the neighbourhood of the Newfoundland Banks and at the Subtropical and Antarctic convergences in the Southern Hemisphere oceans, the strong thermal gradients in the sea surface result in marked differences in the heating of the atmosphere on either side of the boundary. These tend to position and guide the strongest flow of the jet stream in the atmosphere above and thereby influence the development and steering of weather systems.

Interactions between ocean and atmosphere proceed in both directions. They also operate at different rates. Some interesting lag effects, which are of value in long-range weather forecasting, arise through the much slower circulation of the oceans. Thus, enhanced strength of the easterly Trade Winds over low latitudes of the Atlantic, north and south of the Equator, impels more water toward the Caribbean and Gulf of Mexico, producing a stronger flow and greater warmth in the Gulf Stream some six months later. Anomalies in the position of the Gulf Stream–Labrador Current boundary, producing a greater or lesser extent of warm water near the Newfoundland Banks, so affect the energy supply to the atmosphere and the development and steering of weather systems from that region that they are associated with rather persistent anomalies of weather pattern over the British Isles and northern Europe. Anomalies in the equatorial Pacific and in the northern limit of the Kuroshio Current seem to have effects on a similar scale. Indeed, through their influence on the latitude of the jet stream and the wavelength (spacing of cold trough and warm ridge regions) in the upper westerlies, these ocean anomalies exercise an influence over the atmospheric circulation that spreads to all parts of the hemisphere. In the case of sea-temperature anomalies in the equatorial Pacific—anomalies that are traceable, at least in part, to variations in the South Pacific Trade Winds and the upwelling they produce at the coast of Peru and Ecuador—the character of the atmospheric circulation over both hemispheres is affected.

Certain regions of the world's oceans may, therefore, be identified as peculiarly sensitive climatically because variation of the prevailing conditions is likely to have wide-ranging, or in some cases global, effects. The neighbourhood of the nose, or oceanward projection, of Brazil, near Pernambuco (7–8° S), is one such region. If for some time, through a southward displacement of the pattern of prevailing winds, the westward-moving South Equatorial Current in the South Atlantic Ocean is similarly displaced, the proportions going into the two branches into which it splits at this point will be altered and the supply of warm water to the Caribbean, and ultimately to the Gulf Stream, will be reduced. This seems to be a case where the resulting oceanic temperature difference should tend to coincide with and reinforce the initial atmospheric temperature differences. A southward displacement of the ocean-current pattern in this sense seems certain to have occurred in the ice ages and can be traced in more recent periods of cold climate. Recovery

Sea temperature anomalies

from this situation may require a period of unusual warmth over wide areas of the tropical Atlantic.

Surface salinities and surface ice. Another sensitive point appears to be the surface layer, only 100–200 metres thick (330 to 660 feet), of relatively low salinity on the surface of the Arctic Ocean, in which the pack ice forms that largely covers that ocean today. Salinities observed in this layer are between 20 and 30 parts per thousand, as against 34 to 37 in most of the world's oceans and in the deeper levels of the Arctic Ocean itself. Salt ocean water increases in density as its temperature falls, right down to its freezing point (about −2° C or 28° F); hence, cooling by the atmosphere and by the radiation regime in high latitudes normally causes the cold water to sink and to be replaced by other water from below the surface. Convective overturning would have to cool the whole depth of the ocean before its surface could freeze. This convection is presumably the reason why the Norwegian Sea and the saltwater regions of the Barents Sea, as far north as 75° N, never freeze. Similarly, deep convection presumably also goes on in the central Arctic under the ice. In the regions of variable ice cover around Greenland and Labrador, and elsewhere, advances and retreats of a surface layer of fresher water and consequently lower density can be traced. Fresh water has its greatest density at 4° C (about 39° F): it expands as it is cooled below this temperature, and so the coldest water tends to stay at the surface. Hence, the extent of the Arctic sea ice can be expected to vary with any variation in the supply of fresh water to that ocean from the rivers draining the surrounding continents, from such glaciers as flow into the Arctic Basin, and from precipitation over the ocean itself.

The surface of an ice-free Arctic Ocean would be approximately 10° to 15° C (about 20° to 30° F) warmer than now, averaged over the year as a whole and 20° to 30° C (about 35° to 55° F) warmer than now in winter. The strength of the existing thermal gradients—and, hence, the intensity and the pattern of atmospheric circulation development and the steering of surface weather systems—would all be affected. Through the greater input of moisture into the air in high latitudes, precipitation over the polar regions should be increased, whereas it seems probable that the altered pattern of the atmospheric circulation would yield less rain and snow than now over a zone in middle latitudes.

It has been found from studies in the North Atlantic–European sector that, in years when the pack-ice limit is unusually far south, the eastward-travelling, rain-giving cyclonic depressions in summer and autumn generally pass several degrees of latitude farther south and extend their influence toward central Europe; in years when the ice limit is far north the depressions travel on more northern tracks and much of Europe is likely to escape their influence.

It seems probable that the great ice sheet covering Antarctica will occasionally be subject to forward surges, like most glaciers. Such an event must produce an extension of the surface layer of low salinity on the surrounding ocean and tend to bring about a widening of the pack-ice belt for some time.

The extreme positions at which stray icebergs have been recorded depend on the original size of the berg when it calved (or broke) off the front of a glacier or floating ice shelf, but they also bear witness to the vagaries of wind-driven ocean currents and to the occasionally very great spread of denser cold water beneath the warmer portions of the ocean surface. Thus, bergs or smaller pieces of floating ice have been reported about 60–61° N 0–10° W, in the vicinity of the Shetland and Orkney islands, about three times in 100 years and have occasionally reached 35–37° N in the central and western Atlantic. In the middle part of the South Atlantic one berg was sighted at 26.5° S in the last century, and others reached 36° S, off the mouth of the Río de la Plata (River Plate), and 34–35° S near the Cape of Good Hope. Around 1900 the Antarctic pack ice is believed to have reached within 100 miles of Cape Horn, and in 1968 (as in 1888) Iceland was for a time half surrounded by the Arctic pack ice, al-

Influence of the Arctic Ocean

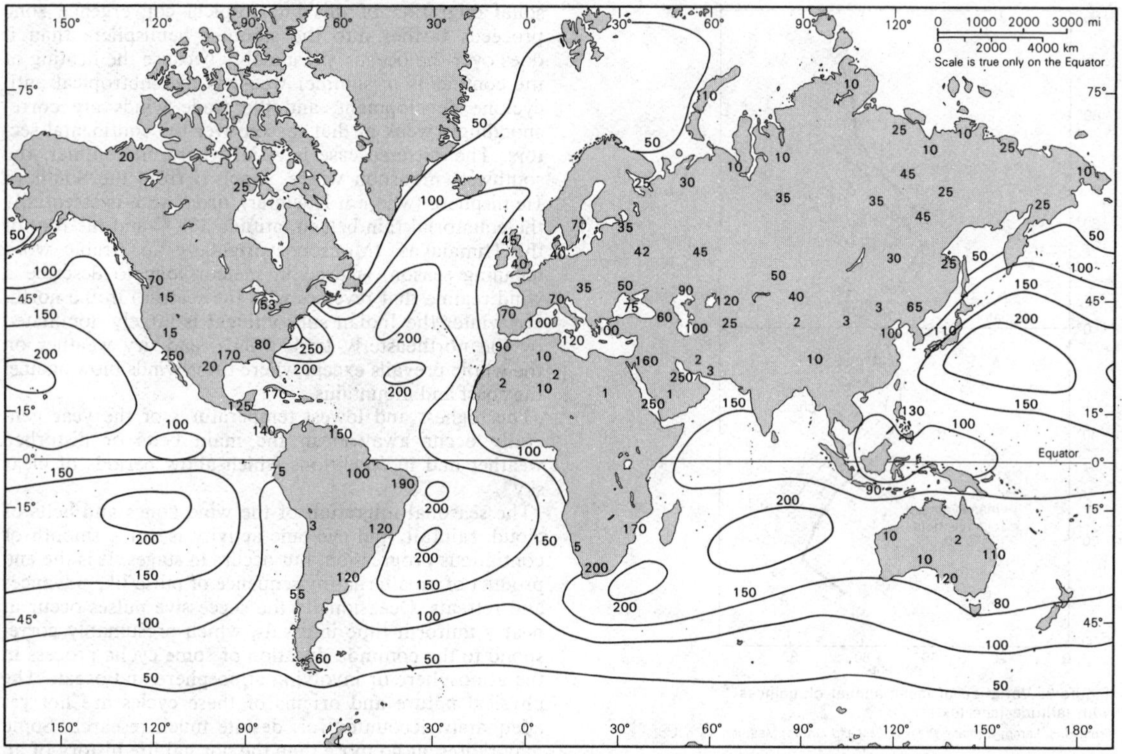

Figure 5: Average annual evaporation in centimetres.
From H.H. Lamb, *Climate: Present, Past and Future;* Methuen & Co. Ltd.

though the usual limits of ice are well short of these positions (see further ICEBERGS AND PACK ICE).

THE MOISTURE CYCLE

Evaporation and condensation. Water vapour is taken up by the air from the seas, lakes, rivers, soils, vegetation, and animal life over which it passes. The amount evaporated depends upon the degree of unsaturation of the air (the saturation deficit) and the vertical gradient of moisture within it; evaporation also increases with the temperature and wind speed. The amount of water vapour needed to saturate air at 27° C (81° F) is six times, at 16° C (61° F) three times, and at 10° C (50° F) twice, the amount required at the freezing point.

The average yearly total of water evaporated in different parts of the world is shown in Figure 5. The low values over desert areas are due to lack of available surface water.

Transit time of a water molecule

On the average, a water molecule is thought to spend about 10 days in the atmosphere and travel 5,000 to 10,000 kilometres (3,000 to 6,000 miles) before being deposited once more as rain, snow, or hail. Some have a much briefer sojourn than this, perhaps being evaporated from a wet surface after a thunderstorm and redeposited again in the same area within the hour; at the other extreme, the small quantity of water vapour that enters the stratosphere from the tops of the highest thunderclouds in the tropics may stay in the stratosphere for years.

Condensation into a mist, fog, or cloud of minute water droplets (or ice crystals) depends on chilling of the air to its dew point, the temperature at which the vapour it contains is enough to saturate it. This chilling may occur through contact with cold surfaces, as when mild air comes over the notoriously fogbound cold waters on the Newfoundland Banks or through radiation cooling of land surfaces at night. Fog (defined by visibility less than 1,000 metres or 1,100 yards) is observed on more than 80 days of the year over the Newfoundland Banks and the cold waters off parts of west Greenland and the Siberian Arctic coast, as well as off southern Chile and the southwest Africa. The foggiest land areas appear to be the European plains and the lowlands about the lower St. Lawrence River in Canada.

World cloudiness and sunshine. Clouds are formed wherever expansion of air rising into regions of ever

lower atmospheric pressure reduces its temperature to the dew point. This occurs: (1) in convective upcurrents; (2) in the general horizontal convergence and uplift, particularly upgliding over the sloping upper (frontal) surface of another, colder airstream, in cyclonic situations; (3) where the wind is forced up over the slopes of mountains; and (4) in eddies induced by the presence of obstacles and by shear layers at the boundary surfaces between different airstreams. The cloud forms developed in each case are characteristically different and betray the form of the air motions producing the cloud. The world distribution of cloudiness by latitude, as derived from the average of many years of conventional observations and from a sample year of photography from artificial satellites, is shown in Figure 6. The main features are the high percentages of cloud cover in the regions of prevailing low pressure and cyclonic weather near latitudes 60° North and South of the Equator and in the equatorial zone itself, and also over the cold surface of the Arctic Ocean.

Sunshine, of course, is most abundant where cloudiness is least, particularly in the subtropical desert zones—where most places have more than 3,000 hours in an average year—and on the central parts of the great ice caps in northern Greenland and Antarctica. Yearly totals are less than 1,000 hours in various parts of the subpolar cyclonic belts—particularly over the oceans and mountainous coasts exposed to the prevailing winds—and probably less than 500 hours in some places of this kind. Because of the prevailing levels at which low clouds and fogs are formed, their upward growth being often checked by the gently descending motion of the upper air in anticyclones, such upland places as the Alpine summits and other high ground in central Europe receive much more sunshine than the low ground in winter.

Rain and snow. Growth of cloud particles into raindrops and snowflakes is facilitated by the introduction of ice crystals into the clouds, when their tops grow to high levels, and by the collisions and coalescences that occur with vigorous vertical motion in warm clouds where the moisture content is great. Precipitation may be classified, according to the processes producing it, as either convective, frontal or cyclonic, and orographic (associated with uplift over the windward slopes of mountains). The intensity and magnitude of rainfall or snowfall depend

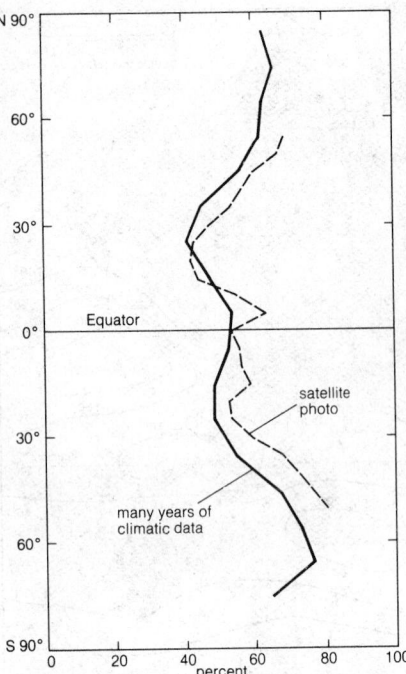

Figure 6: Variation of mean annual cloudiness with latitude (see text).
From H.H. Lamb, *Climate: Present, Past and Future;* Methuen & Co. Ltd.

upon the abundance of moisture in the clouds (therefore tending to increase with the temperature) and upon the vigour of the vertical motions of the air. The average yearly total rainfall, including its equivalent in melted snow, in different parts of the world is shown in Figure 7. The greatest falls (see extreme values in Table 4) are associated with convection in warm countries and over islands, where the moisture content of the air is great, and particularly over mountain slopes, as in the equatorial rain zone and where the Asian southwest monsoon is forced up against the slopes of the Himalayas and their foothills. Other regions of very great rainfall occur in the subpolar zones of cyclonic activity, particularly where prevailing winds from the ocean blow up against mountains, as in parts of Britain, Iceland, and southern Chile.

II. Climatic variation

SEASONAL CHANGES

Each year the Earth experiences changes in its radiation budget, and in the distribution of heat input into the atmosphere, in the course of the seasonal migration of the zenith Sun between 23° N and 23° S. These are far greater than any changes associated with the differences of one year from another and also are greater than the differences between different climatic epochs, except those resulting from the presence of extensive ice sheets during the ice ages. The seasonal changes are accompanied by a general northward and southward movement of the subtropical anticyclone belts and other main features of the atmospheric circulation, including expansion of the circumpolar vortex of upper winds over the hemisphere where it is winter and contraction of the vortex over the summer hemisphere. But the seasonal migration of these circulation features is on average no more than 10° of latitude (and generally less than this in the Southern Hemisphere); *i.e.*, much less than that of the zenith Sun.

As a result of the seasonal migration north and south of the respective belts of cyclonic activity over the middle and high latitudes of each hemisphere, and of the equatorial rain zone, many places quite regularly experience a wet season and a dry season each year. Near the Equator there are two wet seasons, as the rain belt associated with the zone of convergence between the surface winds from the two hemispheres moves north and south between its extreme positions. Over the continents the sea-

sonal migration of this intertropical convergence zone proceeds farther into the summer hemisphere than it does over the oceans, presumably because the heating of the continents in summer weakens the subtropical anticyclone development, and the trade winds are correspondingly weak at that season over the continental sectors. The extreme case is Asia, where, in summer, the southwest monsoon winds, supplied from the Southern Hemisphere (where it is winter), drive what is essentially the equatorial rain belt to latitude 30° N and the foot of the Himalayas. (Monsoon, originally an Arabic word meaning season, is used in meteorology to describe a wind regime that reverses with the season.) In the northern winter the Indian subcontinent is largely dominated by the northeasterly trade winds, and dry weather on the whole prevails except where these winds blow against the coast and mountains.

The highest and lowest temperatures of the year generally occur away from the main belts of disturbed weather and in conditions which allow periods of clear sky.

The seasonal migration of the wind zones and belts of cloud, rainfall, and cyclonic activity is not a smooth or continuous progression, but occurs in stages. It is the end product of an alternating sequence of pulse-like advances and retreats. Occasionally the successive pulses occur at nearly uniform time intervals, which presumably correspond to the common duration of some cyclic process in the atmosphere or involving atmosphere and ocean. The physical nature and origins of these cycles are not yet adequately accounted for, despite much research. Some may represent no more than the normal life history of an individual anticyclone cell from its first appearance to its decay or rejuvenation. Others seem to correspond to a repeating cycle affecting much of one hemisphere, with intense development of the middle latitudes westerlies, at one phase, followed by breakdown and the appearance of blocking or extended meridional (north–south) circulation cells. It is unusual for any of these sequences, however, to recur more than a few times before their regularity is lost. Their occurrence is prominent enough, however, to produce many statistical traces of preferred periods of around five, seven, and (especially) 30 days.

The 30-day oscillation is often expressed in a recurrent tendency toward periods of low barometric pressure, cyclonic influence, and stormy weather spreading in over Europe from the Atlantic about the end of each month, particularly from October to March, and toward anticyclonic influence culminating about the 15th to the 20th of each month. Calendars that are based on weather phenomena related to such cyclic oscillations have been produced through the years. The tendency for precision (or regularity) of the dates of these phenomena seems greatest in high latitudes in the sectors of the Earth affected and may indicate an origin associated with the onset of the polar winter darkness.

One other period length, the very curious one of about 26 months, is strongly marked in a monsoonal alternation between prevailing west and east winds in the equatorial stratosphere, and traces of it are found in the statistics of so many surface weather conditions in both low and high latitudes, that it must be accepted as affecting also the lower atmosphere over the whole Earth. This also appears to be the time scale of the so-called Southern Oscillation. Like the other circulation cycles here mentioned, it is not altogether regular in its performance. The cycle length varies at least from 22 to 35 months, and as every third or fourth cycle is more prominent than the others, it also gives rise to an appearance of some roughly seven-year repetitions. At other times, it may cease to be discernible at all. Its occurrences presumably bear witness to an incomplete return of the oceanic and atmospheric heat economy to its initial condition in certain individual years.

LOCAL EFFECTS

The climate of any place is likely to be considerably modified by the effect of the terrain on the local radiation budget and on the flow of the winds. The presence of wa-

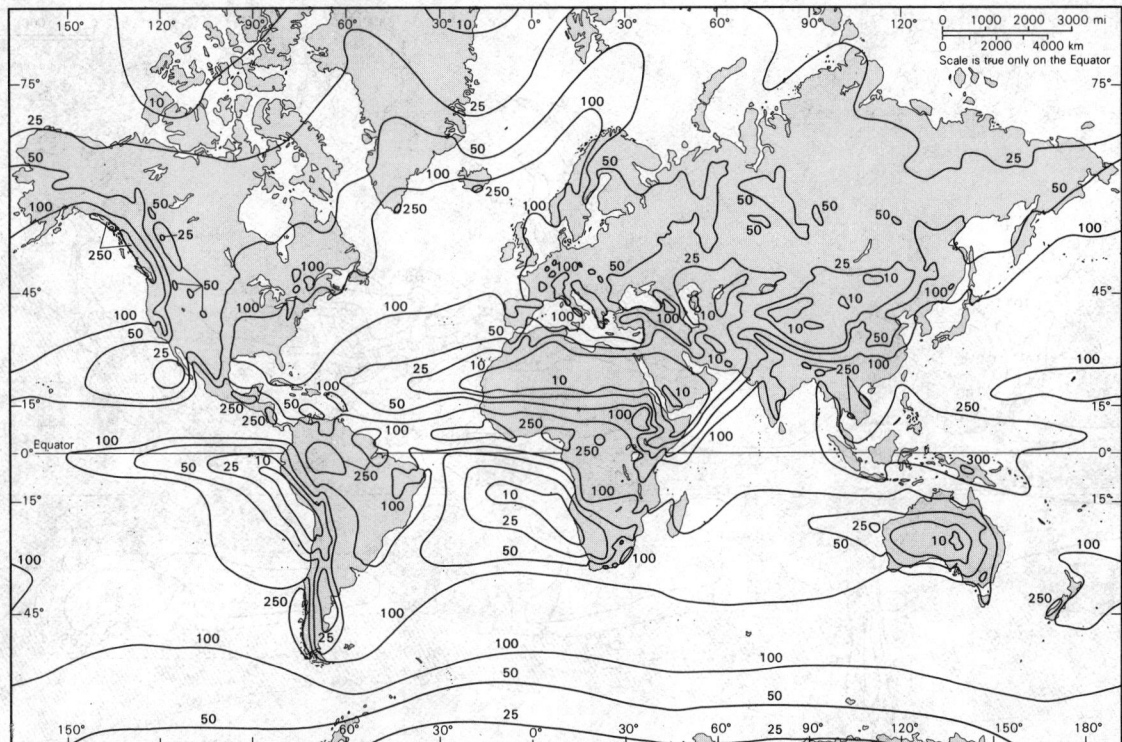

Figure 7: Distribution of mean annual rainfall (including snowmelt) in centimetres.
From H.H. Lamb, *Climate: Present, Past and Future;* Methuen & Co. Ltd.

**Topo-
graphic
influences**

ter bodies or vegetation and the nature of the soil, also affect the local storage of heat and supply of moisture.

A slope tilted toward the midday Sun receives the intensity of radiation appropriate to a lower latitude, though the length of day is not similarly affected. The heating and cooling of mountains gives rise to a system of local winds blowing upslope (anabatic winds) by day and downslope (katabatic winds) by night: the latter flow converges in the main valleys and in suitably shaped valleys sometimes causes cold katabatic night winds of fearsome strength.

The different heating of land and water produces alternating day and night breezes near coasts. The sea breeze that blows in from the sea by day cools and freshens the climate of the land near the coast, and may produce clear skies there as well as over the sea, though the moisture it brings tends to build up clouds some distance inland. At night a gentle breeze tends to drift off the land out to sea. The development of all these diurnal breezes is caused by a local convection in which air that is warmer (and lighter) than its environment tends to rise, whereas cooler (and denser) air sinks, flows downhill, and spreads out horizontally beneath the rising warm air.

Mountains are important as barriers to the wind flow. Strong winds occur where the flow is diverted around or over the tops of a massif and where it is funnelled into narrow valleys and fjords. Rainfall is increased by the uplift, cooling, and condensation of moisture where the wind is forced to rise over mountains; it is decreased on the lee side. These effects are called orographic precipitation and rain shadow, respectively.

Wind speeds are usually greater over open country than in forested or built-up areas. Clearings and avenues in a forest, open spaces and street corners in a town, may, however, provide local concentrations of strong wind, whereas sheltered points, at which cold air drainage collects and stagnates, produce frost pockets.

III. Climatic types

Different types of climate may be recognized and defined in accord with their mode of generation or their effects, particularly in the way the ranges of conditions which they provide affect life forms and habitats. A genetic classification is concerned with the radiation regime, especially the altitude of the midday Sun and the length

of day (both of which depend on latitude), and is closely linked with the general atmospheric circulation. The winds that prevail in each zone acquire their characteristic temperature and humidity values, and a vertical structure marked either by convection or a temperature inversion (*i.e.,* by heating or cooling and by picking up moisture from the surfaces over which they pass). To these influences must be added the local effects of the region itself: the tendency of the local surfaces to attain strong or weak changes of temperature in response to radiation gain and loss; the development of diurnal breezes; forced uplift of the wind or the effects of valleys, hills, and smaller obstacles which channel, guide, or reduce the wind flow. Because the end result of all these processes produces the prevailing amounts of sunshine and cloudiness, temperatures, rainfall, and wind values observed, a genetic classification of climate is by no means unrelated to a system of classification that is based on the effects of climate.

KOPPEN CLASSIFICATION SYSTEM

Climates may be classified on the basis of temperature, precipitation, vegetation, or air-mass meteorology (as discussed above). With regard to the first three parameters, some advantages and disadvantages are readily apparent. If temperature serves as the basis of classification then the world's climates may be classified as tropical, midlatitude, and polar, but because precipitation is omitted no discrimination between arid and humid regions is possible. If precipitation is used to classify world climates then six to ten principal rainfall regions may be delineated, depending upon the class intervals chosen, but areas of intermediate or seasonal rainfall are poorly described and omission of temperature is an obvious drawback. Vegetation has been used by a number of scientists to provide such regionally descriptive terms as steppe, desert shrub, tundra, and others, but despite the fact that vegetation reflects temperature, precipitation, evaporation, soil conditions, and other variables of considerable interest, it is an effect rather than a cause of climate and thus cannot serve alone as an ideal classification base.

The best known and most widely used classification of climates according to their effects is that developed by W. Köppen, a German meteorologist and climatologist.

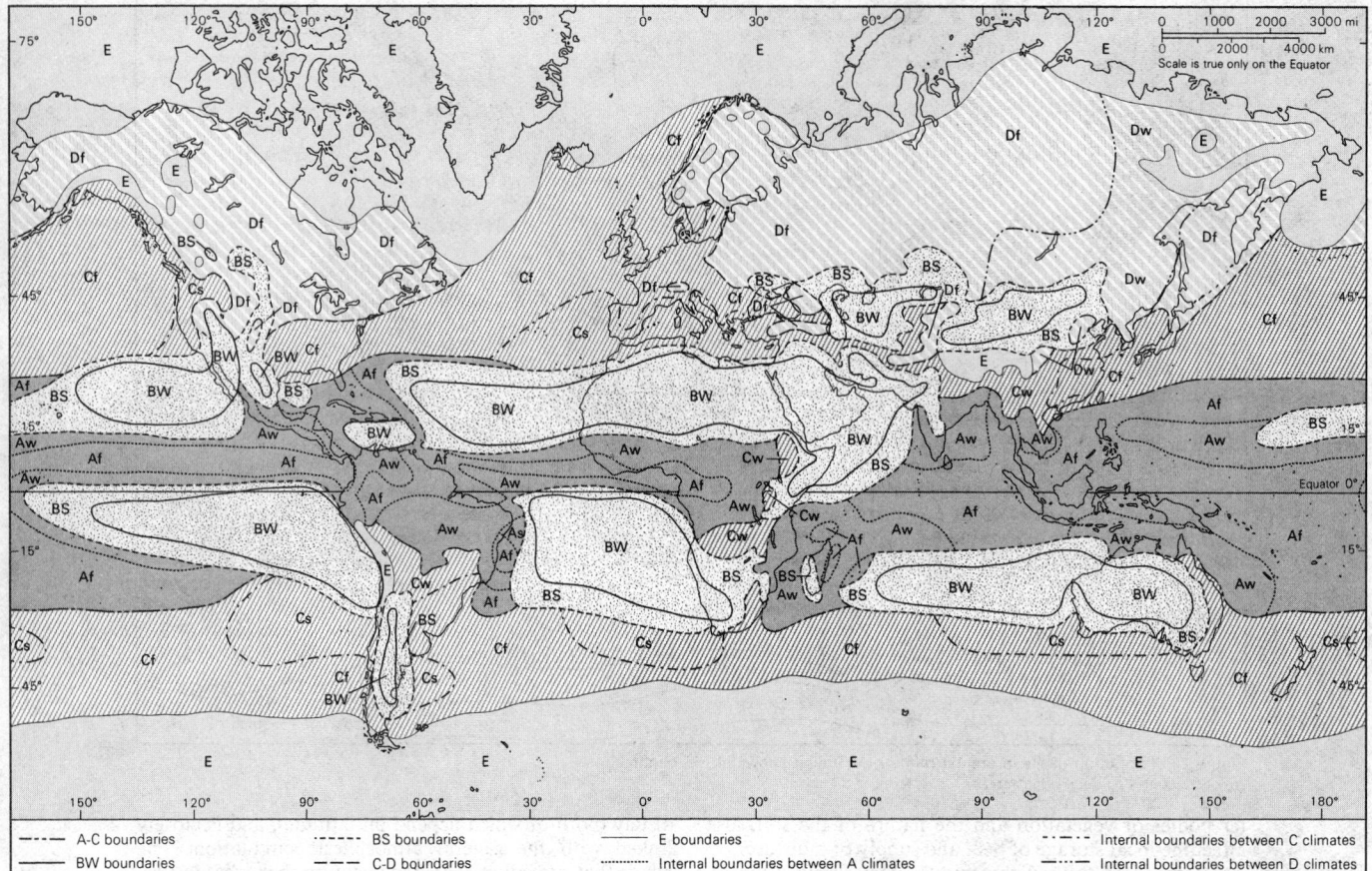

----- A-C boundaries	······· BS boundaries	——— E boundaries	—··—··— Internal boundaries between C climates
——— BW boundaries	——— C-D boundaries	·········· Internal boundaries between A climates	—···—··· Internal boundaries between D climates

Figure 8: World distribution of climatic types according to the Köppen system (see text).
From H.H. Lamb, *Climate: Present, Past and Future;* Methuen & Co. Ltd.

Symbology of the Köppen system

The distribution of Köppen's climatic types is here shown in Figure 8. In this system, A stands for equatorial and tropical rain climates, B for the dry climates of the arid zone, C for temperate climates of the mainly broad-leafed forest zone, D for the colder temperate forest climates, and E for treeless polar climates. The boundaries and subdivisions have been defined by climate values that appear to limit the characteristic species of vegetation. The notation is as follows:

A average temperature of every month above 18° C (64° F).

B average rainfall for the year (R) is
(a) less than $2T + 28$ where summer is the rainiest season
(b) less than $2T + 14$ where the rainfall is fairly uniform throughout the year
(c) less than $2T$ where winter is the rainiest season.
In these formulas T is the average temperature over the year in ° C.

C average temperature of the coldest month in the range 18° C (64° F) to −3° C (27° F); warmest month in no case below 10° C (50° F).

D average temperature of the coldest month below −3° C (27° F); warmest month in no case below 10° C (50° F).

E average temperature of every month below 10° C (50° F).

s dry season in summer.
w dry season in winter.
f all seasons moist.

Köppen's classification system has been criticized because it does not express the prevailing rates of evaporation as directly as the temperatures or rainfall. Other classifications have been invented to do this, though with some loss of simplicity. Köppen's boundary values were arrived at after working with experimental proposals for more than half a century and successively refining the definitions. More rainfall is known to be required to establish moist conditions in warm climates than in cold ones because of the different rates of evaporation, and this fact is built into the system. Additional points of

definition concern climatic types shown on the world distribution map (Figure 8) and they elucidate the indirect ways in which evaporation is incorporated into the classification.

Af—the driest month must have 60 millimetres (2.4 inches) or more of rain.

Aw—the driest month has less than 60 millimetres rain and the year's total rainfall fails to make up for the deficiency.

(**Af** produces rain forest; **Aw** produces savanna, a vegetation that is largely grassland with a few trees.)

BS—the average yearly rainfall (R) exceeds $T + 14$ in areas with summer rainfall, is between this figure and $T + 7$ where the rains are spread over the year, and is between this value and $R = T$ in areas with mainly winter rainfall.

(The **S** stands for steppe or savanna; these climates produce grassland or bush.)

BW—in these climates R is less than $T + 14$ where summer is the rain season, under $T + 7$ where the rains are spread over the year, and less than T where winter is the rain season.

(The **W** stands for desert wastes.)

Cs—in these climates the wettest month comes in winter and has over three times the rainfall of the driest (summer) month.

Cw—in these climates the wettest month comes in summer and has more than ten times the rainfall of the driest (winter) month.

Cs climates produce broad-leafed evergreen forest; **Cw** produces the evergreen forests of the mountain heights in the **Aw** zone and hardly occurs anywhere else.

Dw—the wettest month comes in summer and provides more than ten times the water equivalent of the total downput of rain and snow in the driest (winter) month. The milder **D** climates go with deciduous, broad-leafed forest, the colder **D** climates with needle-tree forest. **D** climates are only found in the great continents of the northern hemisphere.

WORLD CLIMATES AND THEIR DISTRIBUTION

Reverting to genetically derived climates, the following types are recognized. The statistical figures quoted in the examples relate as nearly as possible to the last hundred years.

Equatorial rain climates. These climates are found in a latitude belt near the Equator over which the zone of convergence between the (surface level) trade winds from the Northern and Southern Hemispheres migrates north and south seasonally, roughly accompanying the zenith Sun. The convergence is marked by intense uplift of air and by cloud and rain development. Wetter and drier seasons occur as the axis of this development passes over any area and then moves farther away, north or south; but normally no month is dry, and all are warm and moist. A typical example is Belém, near the mouth of the Amazon in Brazil, with the mean temperature of every month near 26° C (79° F), and average monthly rainfalls ranging from 94 to 436 millimetres (four to 17 inches). Sunshine averages about five and one-half to six hours a day over the year. This is the zone of jungles, hard-wood forests, and swamps (see further JUNGLES AND RAIN FORESTS).

Deserts near the Equator

The desert islands, near the Equator, in the central and eastern Pacific represent one of the most extraordinary climates in the world. They owe their dryness to the fact that the intertropical convergence of the hemispheric wind systems is almost always north of the Equator in that sector and a cool sea surface is maintained by the ocean circulation, partly derived from the Peru (Humboldt) Current. In occasional years this regime fails, probably owing to a weaker drive of the South Pacific trade winds; the wind convergence and the associated equatorial rain clouds then reach these islands and a warmer than usual sea intensifies the convective ascent of air into these clouds. The result is an extraordinary variability of rainfall: average yearly totals of 500 to 750 millimetres (20 to 30 inches) are quoted for many of the islands, but in some years only 50 to 150 millimetres (two to six inches) fall and in the few wet years there may be up to 2,500 millimetres (100 inches).

Monsoon climates. These climates are experienced in regions where the equatorial rain system occurs only at one season of the year, the summer of the hemisphere concerned. In most cases the prevailing winds of the wet and dry seasons are from nearly opposite directions. The latitudes affected range up to 30° N in Asia (perhaps to 40° N near the China Sea). There is a considerable range of the prevailing temperatures in the seasons when the sky is least clouded. Delhi (latitude 29° N) provides an example: monthly mean temperature ranges from 14° C (57° F) in January to 34.5° C (94° F) in June just before the monsoon, average rainfall from one millimetre (0.04 inch) in November and seven millimetres (0.3 inches) in April to 211 millimetres (8.3 inches) in July. The yearly total sunshine is about 2,500 to 3,000 hours, equivalent to seven to eight hours a day over all, but very unequally divided seasonally. The extreme example with regard to rainfall is Cherrapunji in the uplands of Assam, with average monthly rainfall ten to 15 millimetres (0.4 to 0.6 in) in December and January and 2,600 to 2,700 millimetres (100 to 105 inches) in June and July. The Himalayas mark a sharp climatic frontier between the monsoon climate to the south and the continental interior temperate climates farther north.

Tropical grassland climates. In Africa, both north and south of the Equator and in parts of the other continents, there is a steady transition from the rain forest climates of the equatorial zone through the zone of summer monsoon rains to the desert. The desert is fringed by areas with enough rain to support grassland, in places only seasonally, but towards the wetter margin isolated trees are supported. The grasslands are known as savanna or, in South America, llanos and campos.

Tropical highland climates. These climates have the same type of seasonal rainfall as places at lower levels in the same latitudes, though the rainfall amount decreases with increasing distance from the oceans, especially where the winds have crossed mountain ranges. Temperatures become lower, the greater the altitude; but their seasonal variation, or lack of it, is the same as other places at the same latitude.

Trade-wind climates. The trade winds are only well developed over and near the oceans in latitudes 10 to 30° North and South of the Equator. The climate they bring is generally sunny, typically with small cumulus clouds, except over lee coasts, where clear skies and drought prevail and over windward slopes of mountains, where there may be almost perpetual cloudiness and frequent drizzle or light rains. The Canary Islands and Madeira, and St. Helena in the South Atlantic, provide examples. Monthly average temperatures range, according to latitude, from 15° to 20° C (59° to 68° F) in the coldest month to 22° to 25° C (72° to 77° F) in the warmest months. The average rainfalls are almost nothing in summer to 25 to 50 millimetres (one to two inches) in the wettest winter months (80 to 100 millimetres [three to four inches] at Madeira, where the trade wind regime is disturbed by intrusions of the middle latitudes westerlies). Sunshine averages about six hours a day over the year (seven hours at the Canary Islands, and up to eight hours where the trade wind blows from land to ocean at the coasts of the continents). Parts of the trade wind zones are liable to occasional violent disturbance of the usually pleasant regime by tropical hurricanes and typhoons (*q.v.*), though it is rare for any one place to experience more than one to three of these storms in any one year, even in the worst-affected areas.

Climates of the Atlantic islands

Desert climates. The world's great deserts lie in the zones of subtropical anticyclones, especially on their equatorward side between latitudes 15 and 30° north and south of the equator, but reach 40° N in parts of Asia and North America. The air is not without moisture; but at the high temperatures prevailing, the amount of water vapour required to produce saturation is considerable (about 24 grams per cubic metre at 30° C and normal atmospheric pressure at sea level, against three grams at the freezing point). The descending motion of the upper air in the anticyclonic situation generally checks convective up-currents rising from the hot ground surface before the condensation level is reached. Hence, the skies remain largely cloudless. Sunshine averages over the year are about 10 hours a day and even exceed this in some areas. Surface temperatures become very high, but night cooling is also strong. Ground frosts are by no means unknown in winter. The range of air temperature commonly is about 40° C (70° F) or more from night to day. In the hot afternoons, evaporation proceeds until all soil moisture near the surface is evaporated. Monthly mean air temperature ranges seasonally from about 23° C (73° F) to 34° C (93° F) at Timbuktu and Khartoum and from 11° C (52° F) to 29° C (84° F) at Alice Springs in the heart of the Australian desert. Rainfall in many parts of the world's deserts occurs largely as occasional, torrential, thunderstorm downpours, followed by flooding, perhaps once in several years; trivial amounts that are quickly evaporated are not so rare, and there is dependable rainfall on some mountainous areas where convective clouds and storms are formed more easily. Average annual rainfall becomes a nearly meaningless concept in the deserts, but is less than 150 millimetres (six inches) over most of the North African and Arabian deserts and only 30 millimetres (one inch) near Cairo.

Characteristics of arid climates

There are other desert areas, notably in central Asia and parts of Chile and Argentina, where the dryness is due to mountain ranges which the prevailing winds (where one direction is strongly dominant) must cross before reaching there. The average annual rainfall at a number of places in southern Argentina, protected by the Andes from the moisture brought by the prevailing westerly winds from the Pacific, is no more than 120 to 150 millimetres (five to six inches). Despite low temperatures, averaging about 10° C (50° F) over the year at latitude 45° S, the climate is windy, evaporation is considerable, and the ground supports little vegetation.

Subtropical ocean and island climates. The ocean areas that are commonly occupied by anticyclones between latitudes 20 and 40° enjoy mainly light winds, moist air, varying amounts of cloud and sunshine, and equable temperatures. Sunshine averages fall with increasing latitude from about seven to four hours a day (2,500 to 1,500 hours a year). Average temperatures range from 22° C (72° F) in the coldest month to 26° C (79° F) in the warmest month at Honolulu (21° N) and from 14° C (57° F) to 22° C (72° F) in the Azores (38° N). The average yearly rainfalls range from about 500 to 1,000 millimetres (20 to 40 inches), fairly evenly distributed over the year, though least in summer; but there are considerable variations and much more rain falls at times when the anticyclonic regime is replaced by blocking patterns—so much so that the average rainfall in the Azores between 1940 and 1960 was 30 percent more than for the previous 40 years.

Mediterranean climates. The warm temperate climate of the Mediterranean, with its dry summers, wet and sometimes stormy winters, is a type characteristic of latitudes affected by the anticyclones of the desert zone in summer and invaded by the travelling cyclonic disturbances of middle latitudes in winter. The type is recognized by the same name wherever it occurs; *e.g.*, California, Cape Province in South Africa, and much of southern Australia. An example is the Mediterranean island of Malta, where the three summer months of June to August are usually rainless, and occasionally the rainless season lasts six months; the winter months each have about 100 millimetres (four inches) of rain. The temperatures are quite similar to those of the Azores. More continental places in the region, particularly those near the fringe of the desert, have much higher maximum temperatures in summer and are colder in winter; Tripoli (Libya), for example, has air temperature extremes of 47° C (117° F) and 1° C (34° F). Rainfall is heavier on the mountains, and inland from the African coast the transition to the full desert climate is rapid. Al-ʿAzīzīyah, barely 40 kilometres (about 25 miles) south of Tripoli, has an average rainfall of 224 millimetres (8.8 inches) compared with Tripoli's 381 millimetres (15 in.) and has had extreme air temperatures of 57.7° C (136° F) and −3.3° C (26° F). Both places, as might be expected, experience their highest temperatures from air that has crossed the Sahara, and the air tends to be hottest toward the end of its passage across the hot desert surface. Death Valley, California, where temperatures almost as high (56.6° C or 134° F) as at al-ʿAzīzīyah have been observed, is about 200 kilometres (120–130 miles) from the Pacific coast.

Middle latitudes climates. This zone is characterized by changeable weather, with precipitation in all seasons. The variability of temperature from day to day and month to month and the differences between the same month in different years or epochs tend to increase with the latitude and from the oceans towards the continental interiors. Variability of rainfall, as a percentage of the norm, is greatest in regions nearest the subtropical arid zone, and in those parts of the high latitude fringe where the prevailing westerly winds are oftenest interrupted by spells with blocking anticyclones (notably, northwest Europe and Alaska). Temperatures generally decrease poleward; mean annual temperature at any latitude decreases towards the continental interiors owing to the coldness of the winters, especially where snow surfaces are established.

Maritime and continental climates. The differences between oceanic (or maritime) and continental climates, though operative in all latitudes, are most apparent in middle latitudes. The most obvious features are the windiness, relatively small temperature variations, and even distribution of rainfall (though with some tendency for an autumn or winter maximum) in oceanic climates. By contrast, the continental areas have their heaviest rainfall in summer, frequently in the form of thunderstorms, great extremes of temperature, and few strong winds except for the fierce gusts and squalls, and occasional tornadoes, that feed the upcurrents in convective clouds and accompany thunderstorms. These differences are illustrated in Table 5.

Because westerly winds prevail in middle latitudes, oceanic climate characteristics spread farther into the continents from the western than from the eastern coasts, except where a mountain barrier stands in the way. It is toward the eastern (or downwind) limits of the land

Table 5: Climatic Averages for Representative Oceanic and Continental Stations

	temperature				rainfall			
	January		July		January		July	
	(°F)	(°C)	(°F)	(°C)	(in.)	(mm)	(in.)	(mm)
Oceanic stations								
Valentia, Ireland 52° N, 10° W (1870–1950)	45.0	7.2	58.8	14.9	6.5	165	4.0	102
Vancouver, British Columbia 49° N, 123° W (1941–60)	36.1	2.3	63.7	17.6	5.5	139	1.0	26
Continental stations								
Irkutsk, U.S.S.R. 52° N, 104° E (1830–1915)	−5.3	−20.7	64.4	18.0	0.7	18	3.0	75
Winnipeg, Manitoba 50° N, 97° W (1931–60)	+0.1	−17.7	68.4	20.2	1.0	26	2.7	69

areas that the most extreme continental conditions are observed. And even at the eastern seaboards the climates are more continental, and in winter much more severe, than at the western limits of the continents. This is illustrated by the averages in Table 6, which compares places at similar latitudes.

Over and near the oceans the frequent strong winds and gales are the most severe element of the climate, hampering the activities of man, limiting the growth of trees, and imposing a seaward limit to the forest. Gales (defined by a Beaufort wind force of eight or more) blow on about 70 days a year over the wide Southern Ocean, near Cape Horn, and also near the coasts of Greenland; the figures are 30 to 60 days a year over the North Atlantic and the coasts bordering it between Nova Scotia, Scotland, and Iceland. The frequency in inland areas of England, Germany, and Sweden is generally under ten days a year; in most parts of southern United States gales blow on about five to 15 days a year and 15 to 30 days near the Great Lakes and Canadian border.

Coastal climates. The climate of coastal regions and islands differs from that of the open sea chiefly through the frequent development of diurnal land and sea breezes. These are caused by the convective overturning of air due to the unequal heating of land and sea surfaces, and this results in a marked tendency to develop a belt of clear sky along, or parallel with, the coast where the descending air motion suppresses cloud development. There is, therefore, more sunshine on the coastal area than out at sea, and generally more sunshine than inland, where convective cloud development by day and fogs and haze caused by ground radiation cooling overnight, restrict the hours of sunshine. Similar tendencies affect the shores of lakes and inland seas. There is also, however, generally more rainfall than over the open sea because of the forced uplift of air over the coast, particularly (but not only) over mountainous coasts.

Mountainous coasts and fjords are also liable to stronger winds than the open sea owing to convergence effects where the windstream is constrained, or channelled, by the mountain walls.

Mountain climates. These climates are generally cooler than the surrounding lowlands, except in the quiet winter weather that favours the development of inversions of temperature. They are also generally windier; convergence effects may produce extra high wind velocities on summits and ridges and where valleys channel the general windstream or the katabatic drainage of cold night air off the slopes. Development of diurnal upslope and (nighttime) downslope breezes is characteristic and tends to promote, and intensify, convection cloud development over the ridges and peaks by day. Rainfall generally increases with height and steepness of the slopes facing the prevailing wind, partly owing to the forced uplift and partly because of the frequency of convective clouds. On very high mountains, however, precipitation decreases above a certain height about 1,500–2,000 me-

Table 6: Climatic Averages at Western and Eastern Seaboards												
	temperature						rainfall					
	January		July		year		January		July		year	
	(°F)	(°C)	(°F)	(°C)	(°F)	(°C)	(in.)	(mm)	(in.)	(mm)	(in.)	(mm)
New York City 41° N, 74° W (1869–1949)	30.6	−0.8	73.9	23.3	52.7	11.5	3.7	94	4.2	107	42.8	1,086
Lisbon 39° N, 9° W (1856–1950)	50.7	10.4	70.3	21.3	60.6	15.9	3.5	89	0.2	5	27.6	701

tres (5,000–7,000 feet) because of the low temperatures and consequently small amounts of water vapour usually present, except when rapidly transported up from lower levels.

Steppe and prairie climates. The natural vegetation of the lands in the temperate zone is forest except in the drier regions. In continental interiors, which are remote or screened by mountains from the moisture brought by the prevailing winds, especially between latitudes 35 and 50° where evaporation is considerable, the natural vegetation is grassland. Grain crops also thrive, and these areas were the sources of the wild grasses from which most modern cultivated grains have been developed. In the drier years, however, the crops and grasses are liable to fail unless maintained by irrigation. The summers are hot and the winters cold or very cold. Precipitation comes largely in the form of thunderstorms, sometimes giving damaging hail, in summer; in winter it comes mainly as snow. Deficiency at either season may cause drought and crop failures. These lands have also been the age-old home of nomadic peoples, and periods of drought seem to have forced them to depart and migrate, sometimes over great distances, seeking other pastures at the cost of the peoples previously settled there. Such migrations can be traced in the history and prehistory both of Asia and North America. Examples of this climate are: Barnaul, U.S.S.R. (53° N, 84° E) with mean temperatures of the summer months 17 to 20° C (63 to 68° F) and of the winter −16 to −18° C (3 to 0° F), and average annual precipitation 280 to 300 millimetres (11 to 12 inches) in the period 1838 to 1890 and about 480 millimetres (19 inches) in the period 1890 to 1950; Sarmiento, Argentina (46° S, 69° W) with average monthly temperatures from 17° C to 4° C (63° F to 39° F), and average annual precipitation 164 millimetres (6.5 inches) in the period 1931 to 1950 and 128 millimetres (5 inches) in the period 1951 to 1960.

Tundra, polar seas, and ice sheets

Cold climates. Over land areas north of the Arctic forest limit, where the surface becomes free of snow and ice in summer, a special climate occurs; this is the tundra. The winters experience temperatures approaching the extreme low levels of the central and eastern parts of the great continents but are more liable to periods of cyclonic disturbance with higher temperatures, wind and snow. The summer months June, July, and sometimes August are the quiet season, when strong winds are rare. Average temperatures remain below 10° C (50° F) in summer. In the moister regions with permanently frozen subsoil (permafrost or tjaele) the seasonal snowmelt is followed by a period of widespread flooding, and overcast skies, and occasional fogs, which sometimes recur all summer. In the drier regions, the summers bring some days with really high temperatures (up to 25 to 30° C, 77 to 86° F) with the 24-hour sunshine. Despite the somewhat different latitude and generally windier climate, a tendency to similar conditions can be recognized in the drier parts of southernmost South America.

Strong winds occur over polar seas at times, particularly in the eight or nine months of the colder seasons, but are much less frequent over the pack ice than over the open ocean. There is frequent, but never heavy precipitation; the average yearly total rain equivalent in areas north of 75 to 80° N is about 100 millimetres (four inches). This may actually fall as rain in the season when there are areas of open water among the ice, and rain is not unknown at the North Pole. Summer is a season of fogs and skies commonly overcast with low stratus cloud, with very uniform surface air temperatures varying only a few degrees above or below the freezing point. Once the cooling season sets in, the open-water areas begin to freeze over and clear skies become more common. Temperatures then fall more rapidly and within two months after the onset of darkness (*i.e.*, after the equinox) are near their winter minimum. The liability to occasional intrusions of milder air from other latitudes, owing to the stronger atmospheric circulation in winter, makes the attainment of still greater extremes of temperature as the winter goes on improbable—hence the nearly uniform level of the average temperatures of the four or five winter months (despite sometimes great changes from one day to the next), the *kernlose Winter* (coreless winter) of the polar regions.

The climates on the great ice sheets covering Greenland and Antarctica are more continental; clear skies are frequent in summer and winter, greater extremes of temperature occur, and, at least in the interior, less precipitation falls than over the neighbouring oceans. The overall average cloud cover is about 50 percent or less in the interior, compared with about 80 percent over the northernmost Atlantic and the Southern Ocean between 60° S and the Antarctic Circle. The air temperature is kept below the freezing point, even in summer, by the extent and great mass of the ice: the average for the warmest month of the year is −12° C (10° F) in central Greenland and around −30° C (−22° F) on the high ice plateau of Antarctica. The severest element of the climate, however, is the wind, particularly the katabatic gales blowing down the slope near the margin of the ice sheet, always accompanied by blowing snow drifted up from the surface.

IV. Climate and life

MARINE AND TERRESTRIAL ORGANISMS

The simplest one-celled forms of life, algae and Protozoa, are at the mercy of the climate of the water (its temperature, salinity, pollution, and the amount of sunlight penetrating it) in which they live. Similarly, the bacteria that float in the air, as well as in water, and are found in the soil, only grow and multiply within a range of temperatures that suits each species: some demand ice-cold water, others prefer high temperatures. The larger and higher forms of animal life—fish, birds, and land mammals—are also limited in their ranges by the prevailing temperatures, but they enjoy the ability to move at will and can migrate in search of their accustomed foods and the comforts of a favourable climatic environment. Indeed, changes of the weather seem to play a part in the inception of the seasonal migrations of birds and probably of other animals also, good weather being chosen for the start of the journey.

The so-called cold-blooded species—all fishes, reptiles, and amphibians, as well as insects—have a body temperature that always approximates to the temperature of their surroundings (except where heated or cooled directly by radiation): when the blood temperature falls low, the organism becomes lethargic, and prolonged freezing or excessive heat and drought cause death. Locusts, for example, become lethargic at temperatures below about 15° C (59° F), though individuals in flight have from time to time survived while borne by a southerly wind to various parts of northern Europe, including England. The desert locust seems to require a body temperature

Locust migration and temperature

between 25 and 35° C (77–95° F) for sustained flight, though sunshine and its own metabolic heat may give it a temperature as much as 10° C (18° F) above that of the surrounding air. Long distances can only be covered, therefore, with air temperatures over 15° C (59° F) and then only if the insect has sufficient reserves of fat. Short flights have been observed at temperatures down to 9° C (48° F) in Morocco. Temperatures over about 50° C (122° F) appear to be fatal; locusts are not killed by such overnight frosts as occur in Africa, but do succumb when they sink into snow and are frozen in. The malarial parasite fails to mature within the lifetime of the mosquito that carries it at temperatures below about 20° C (68° F), and the (*Anopheles*) mosquito itself cannot breed at temperatures below 16° C (61° F) or at relative humidities under 63 percent. The life cycle of the bubonic-plague-bearing flea is speeded up the more the temperature rises above 20° C (68° F), but death also comes sooner and with temperatures of 32° C (90° F) and humidities below 30 percent the life of the flea is cut to one quarter of what it is with humidity near 100 percent: under such dry, hot conditions the plague bacillus therefore has little chance to develop.

Warm-bloodedness is found only in birds and mammals: it means that the organism maintains a nearly constant body temperature (and level of activity when not sleeping), and when it feels cold it takes appropriate action to correct this. Nevertheless, warm-blooded species may be killed by the onset of temperatures which impose too great a strain—*i.e.*, are beyond their limits of tolerance—or by drought or drowning, as well as by the attacks of other animals or disease-bearing insects and bacteria which thrive in the given conditions.

Climatic limitations of animal species

Thus, all animal life has definable climatic limits for each species; though the actual limits of their distribution are determined only partly by the direct influence of weather and climate. Much depends on availability of food, and on the food chain itself (including the vegetation that climate and habitat provide), as well as on how the organism fares in competition with other species. Underlying these seemingly independent controls are, however, the climatic limitations of all the animal and plant life involved. Thus, each climate tends over a long period of time to bring into being a certain "climax community," which represents the ultimate ecological development, a community whose makeup remains stable—in equilibrium with the environment—as long as the physical conditions remain essentially unchanged.

The existence of such communities in ages long past can be recognized by the finding of remains of the life forms concerned and may provide evidence of changes of climate and shifts of the limits of warm and cold ocean currents. Care is needed in the interpretation of such evidence, however, since the disappearance of the mammoth from Eurasia and of many wild animals, now limited to a few hot climates, from much of Europe and Asia, appears to be attributable to the depredations of man rather than to climatic change. Because of their wide climatic range, their ability to migrate over great distances, and a certain capability of acclimatization within a single lifetime, the strict climatic limits of the larger animals, and of man, are less clear than those of smaller species, especially insects and plants.

The differentiation of species in animals, as to some extent in man, gives innumerable examples of the emergence of dominant types with characteristics specially suited to the climates of the regions in which they live. One of the most remarkable instances is the prevalence, in the northern snow climates, of types of unrelated animals and birds that change the colour of their fur or plumage to white in winter.

VEGETATION AND CROPS

As with the fauna, the distribution of plants also has distinct climatic limits. And in this case, too, any species may fail to reach the limit of its climatic tolerance through being ousted in the competition with more successful species. The continuance of any climatic regime over a sufficiently long period tends to produce a distinctive climax vegetation that is perhaps the main part of the climax community of life forms. Thus, birch trees (*Betula*) and pines (*Pinus*), with the most northerly habitats of any trees, seem to be limited by climates where the average temperature of the warmest month fails to exceed about 10° C (50° F). Near this limit they only produce successful seedlings in a minority of years; but they will also grow and thrive in much warmer climes. Where the average temperatures of the summer months are generally above 13–15° C (55–59° F), however, the seedlings of broad-leafed bushes and trees, hawthorn (*Crataegus*), hazel (*Corylus*), oak (*Quercus*), and similar types soon gain the mastery.

Many species are unable to survive in climates where the winter temperatures are too low. The limiting conditions have been closely studied for a few species: it is clear, for example, that holly (*Ilex*) demands a temperate, oceanic climate with the average temperature of the coldest month not normally below 0° to −1° C (32° to 30° F). In exceptionally severe weather many oak trees have been split and killed by frost, even in western Europe; the extreme limits of the oak in the climates of today are in south Sweden and western European Russia.

Plant survival requirements

Discussion of the climatic limits of species in terms of temperature alone gives an oversimplified picture. The conditions of humidity, rainfall, and soil moisture, cloudiness, sunshine, and wind must also be within the plant's tolerance. Near the ocean not only may the winds be often too strong for seedlings to grow into an upright tree but the leaves of young trees and old may be "burnt" by the salt spray carried by storm winds.

Fruit trees, flowers, grasses, and cultivated grains each have their own climatic requirements. The northern limit of successful cultivation of the vine is close to the mean July isotherm of 19° C (66° F), though the length of the summer is also important; for citrus fruits the limit is about the July isotherm of 22° C (72° F). These crops also require sufficient soil moisture supplied by rainfall or irrigation. Both vine and orange-growing near their northern limits have at various times suffered disasters caused by late frosts when the fruit was forming. Modern agriculture has been improved by artificial selection and development of seed varieties that are hardier against climatic vicissitudes and diseases, as well as giving a heavier yield, than the primitive varieties that had often been taken far from ther natural habitats. Nevertheless, each plant demands temperatures within a certain range, enough sunshine, and the right amount of soil moisture. Most grains are vulnerable to wind and rain in the ripening stages. Though their natural habitat is the steppe, the crop fails in some years in dry climates through drought. Crop failures occur in wet climates through excessive rain and lack of sunshine in poor summers. Wheat is seldom grown where the annual rainfall exceeds 1,000 millimetres (40 inches).

Root crops such as potatoes are a staple in areas with wet summers, but certain combinations of warmth and humidity produce fungus diseases; the potato blight commonly breaks out in Europe in summer after 48-hour periods in which temperature never falls below 10° C (50° F) and relative humidity exceeds 90 percent for 11 hours or more. In dry summers these crops are more liable to suffer from insect pests.

CLIMATE AND MAN

Climate exercises its influence on man and his way of life both directly and indirectly, through the types of vegetation and animal life which it encourages or permits. The development of the different races of man seems itself to have been a process of selection and adaptation to climate and the environment that goes with it. This is particularly expressed in terms of body size, shape, and pigmentation. The white- or pink-skinned peoples who are descended from the earlier inhabitants of northwest Europe fare best in, and are perhaps the race best adapted to, cool, cloudy climates without much sunshine. Their skin type burns easily when exposed to strong radiation (particularly ultraviolet) from Sun and sky. The brown and black races possess a skin that is not

Climatic influence on body size, shape, and pigmentation

at all vulnerable to this type of damage; their characteristics were presumably developed originally by peoples who lived between the tropical desert margin and the equatorial rain forest in Africa and Asia and also were well suited to life in Australia. The third skin type has many shades that range from a sallow or olive white to yellow and brown in different individuals; it readily tans, or darkens, when exposed to the sun and becomes pale again in indoors living or in a cloudy season. As with other warm-blooded animals, persons living in the colder climates of their range tend to be bigger than those living in the warmer areas. Because the volume of an object increases in proportion to the cube of its radius, whereas the surface area varies with the square of the radius, this arrangement ensures a smaller ratio of cooling surface to body bulk in the inhabitants of the cold regions. The average weight of the peoples of northern Europe is 70 to 80 kilograms (150 to 175 pounds) in contrast to 50 to 60 kilograms (110 to 130 pounds) for the native peoples in the Middle East and in southern Asia. The build of the native inhabitants of cold countries tends to be large or stocky, whereas natives of hot countries tend to be lean or lanky and even to have longer fingers. There is evidence that the Old Norse colony in Greenland, when cut off from Europe and dying out in the 15th century because of increased ice on the seas and the onset of colder climate, suffered a marked decrease of body size and stature, but this also can doubtless be attributed to undernourishment.

Prolonged genetic selection seems to have developed further functional differences. Negroes are more vulnerable to frostbite in cold climates than are whites, but tolerate humid heat better than the latter because their body temperature does not require so much sweating and evaporation from the skin to keep it from rising. Man's powers of acclimatization over time, however, have confused these issues. Among the most remarkable abilities acquired by acclimatization are those of the Arctic fishermen who manipulate wet lines and nets in near-freezing weather without distress; the ability of the native inhabitants of Tierra del Fuego and of the Australian desert to sit comfortably and even to sleep in the frost; and the adaptation of mountaineers to the reduced oxygen pressure at heights above 2,500 to 3,000 metres (8,000 to 10,000 feet), which can produce mountain sickness in tourists who have been carried quickly upward by cable car. Acclimatization to central-heated indoor environments may increase the vulnerability of whites to exposure to cold.

The wind-chill factor

Human comfort in the open air depends not only on air temperature but also on wind, humidity, and radiation conditions. Various formulas have been developed to express the cooling power of the air, commonly known as wind chill; the one most generally used was derived from experiments in Antarctica. In this formula the cooling effect of the wind on the human body is measured by the heat K (in kilogram calories) lost by one square metre of skin in one hour:

$$K = (10.45 + 10 \sqrt{v} - v)(33 - T)$$

in which v is the wind speed in metres per second and T is the air temperature in degrees Centigrade. The right-hand bracket represents the dependence of cooling power on the difference between the temperature of the air and the normal skin temperature of 33° C (91.4° F). The formula is most satisfactory for low temperatures, in which sweating does not play an important part; humidity is not considered. The evaporation of sweat increases the cooling power, but solar radiation decreases it; in bright sunshine, for example, the cooling rate may be reduced by 200 kilogram calories. Driving open vehicles, skiing downhill, and other similar movement may effectively increase the wind speed so as to expose a person to the equivalent of very low temperatures. A wind felt at 30 miles per hour (13.4 metres per second) in air at −5° C (23° F), for example, produces the same cooling as a temperature of −25° C (−13° F) in calm conditions. At high air temperatures the body depends on the evaporation of sweat from the skin, which is facilitated by air movement, to keep the

skin temperatures at an acceptable level. Heat produced by the body's metabolism and by exertion must be dissipated if body temperature is not to rise.

The basic purpose of man's clothing and the buildings he erects is to provide shelter from the adverse effects of weather and climate, from wind, rain, and snow, and from excessive exposure to radiation. In cold climates clothing reduces the wind speed and so allows a film of air remaining in contact with the skin to acquire the body's own temperature. An artificial climate is thus created between the clothing and the skin. The climate inside buildings, and to some extent in the streets and even the parks of towns and cities, is also artificial, but it is not always well designed for comfort. In most parts of the world traditional forms of architecture have been evolved through long experience to provide the basic necessities. In low latitudes thick walls of stone or mud and small windows provide an interior in which the strong solar heating is moderated and there is rest from the bright light outside. Elsewhere in hot climates wide overhanging eaves provide shade in the streets outside. In the humid tropics an overhanging roof carries off the rain, while flimsy walls made of leaves and similar materials allow ventilation. In higher latitudes larger windows provide more light, where it is needed, but they have traditionally not been so large as to cool the interior excessively or allow a psychologically chilling view of bleak weather outside; steeper roofs help dispose of rain and winter snow. The revolution in architecture and building techniques in the 20th century has tended to create the same styles everywhere, a development that often fails to provide basic comforts and conveniences without resort to expensive heating and cooling systems.

The climates in which men are able to do most physical work are cooler than those that are most comfortable when resting or in a sedentary occupation. Man's mental capacity appears to be stimulated by living in a changeable climate and by colder weather outside than in the workroom. One study has shown that, despite different achievements associated with different types of social and industrial organization in different countries, those nations and peoples living in climates where the mean temperature of the warmest month does not exceed about 24° C (75° F) and that of the coldest month is not below 0° C (32° F) display the most energy. Maintenance of high energy output in the colder parts of these regions in winter, of course, depends on satisfactory control of the climate in the buildings and clothing in which the people spend most of their time. Indeed, meeting this problem is one of the challenges that seems to have been necessary for all the world's leading civilizations of every age. Provided that not too much effort is wasted in dealing with the fogs and ice and snow of the cold season, it seems that the greatest productive energy of all may be shown by the peoples living in the coldest parts of the regions marked out by the above summer and winter temperatures. Clearly, the effects could be important if modern technology succeeded in extending the region of optimum climate to include areas where the temperatures of the coldest month are somewhat lower, say between 0° and −5° or −10° C (32° and 23° or 14° F). A moderate climate seems beneficial to man, but too severe a climate is crippling.

BIBLIOGRAPHY. Fundamental references in theoretical and observational climatology include: B.P. ALISSOW, O.A. DROSDOW, and E.S. RUBINSTEIN, *Lehrbuch der Klimatologie* (1956); E.C. BARRETT, *Climatology from Satellites* (1974); F. BAUR, *Physikalisch-statistische Regeln als Grundlagen für Wetter- und Witterungsvorhersagen*, 2 vol. (1956–58); J. BLUTHGEN, *Allgemeine Klimageographie*, 2nd ed. (1966); C.E.P. BROOKS and N. CARRUTHERS, *Handbook of Statistical Methods in Meteorology* (1953); V. CONRAD and L.W. POLLAK, *Methods in Climatology*, 2nd rev. ed. (1950); R. GEIGER, *Das Klima der bodennahen Luftschicht*, 4th ed. (1961; Eng. trans., *Climate Near the Ground*, 4th ed., 1965); W.G. KENDREW, *Climatology*, 2nd ed. (1957); W. KOPPEN and R. GEIGER (eds.), *Handbuch der Klimatologie*, 5 vol. (1930–39, reprinted 1972); H.H. LAMB, *Climate: Present, Past and Future*, 2 vol. (1972–77); H.E. LANDSBERG, *Physical Climatology*, 2nd ed. (1958), and *et al.*, *World Survey of Climatology*, 15 vol. (1969–); JOHN R.

MATHER, *Climatology: Fundamentals and Applications* (1974); R.C. SUTCLIFFE, *Weather and Climate* (1966); and U.S. DEPART- MENT OF AGRICULTURE, "Climate and Man," *1941 Yearbook of Agriculture* (1941, reprinted 1974).

Three descriptive works are: J. GENTILLI, *A Geography of Climate*, 2nd rev. ed. (1958); I.R. TANNEHILL, *Weather Around the World*, 2nd ed. (1952); and G.T. TREWARTHA, *The Earth's Problem Climates*, 2nd ed. (1981).

Works concerned with the effects of climate on human life include: J.E. ARONIN, *Climate and Architecture* (1953); C.E.P. BROOKS, *Climate in Everyday Life* (1950, reprinted 1976); E. HUNTINGTON, *Civilization and Climate*, 3rd ed. rev. (1924, reissued 1971); S.F. MARKHAM, *Climate and the Energy of Nations*, rev. ed. (1947); R.I. ROTBERG and T.K. RABB (eds.), *Climate and History* (1981); L.P. SMITH, *Weather and Food* (1962); S.W. TROMP, *Biometeorology* (1980); L. WEICKMANN *et al.*, *Klima, Wetter, Mensch*, 2nd ed. (1952); and WORLD METEO- ROLOGICAL ORGANIZATION, *Proceedings of the World Climate Conference: A Conference of Experts on Climate and Mankind* (1979).

(H.H.L.)

Climatic Change

The meteorologist's concept of climate is a dynamic one, including day-to-day changes of weather, the seasonal cycle, and small-scale variations of atmospheric conditions measurable over periods of 2 to 25 years. Long series of observations show something like a "beat" phenomenon, with an unevenly varying wavelength. This built-in vari- ability of the atmosphere results from the varying time lag between any single cause and effect, from the interaction of multiple factors, and from mechanisms set in progress by one or more variables operating over different time scales. Climate is never stable but is subject to continuing oscillations, such as the waxing and waning of many atmospheric components over a variable period of 23 to 29 months. For these reasons it is necessary to define climatic variations of different wavelength and amplitude and to decide which qualify as short- or long-term fluctu- ations and which are part of the built-in, year-to-year variability and thus deserving of the rank of oscillations. Only when a series of fluctuations moves in one direc- tion—sufficiently long and effectively to modify other environmental parameters—is it justified to speak of cli-

Table 1: Orders of Climatic Variation

Minor fluctuations within the instrumental record (10 years)	fluctuations operating over regular intervals of 30–100 years
Postglacial and historical (100 years)	variations over intervals on the order of 300–1,000 years; *e.g.*, the Little Ice Age and others affecting glaciers and vegetation
Glacial (10,000 years)	the phases within an Ice Age; *e.g.*, the du- ration of the Würm–Wisconsin glacial episode on the order of 65,000 years
Minor geological (1,000,000 years)	duration of Ice Ages as a whole; *e.g.*, the duration of the Pleistocene Epoch that is on the order of 3,000,000 years
Major geological (100,000,000 years)	Ice Ages at intervals of 280,000,000 years

Source: Modified after Gordon Manley.

matic change. Table 1 outlines five orders of climatic vari- ation beyond the level of minor oscillations: the first-or- der variations include true fluctuations that can be observed within a lifetime; the second-order variations are best considered as a minimum threshhold to qualify as a climatic change.

This definition of climatic fluctuation or change obvious- ly differs sharply from the subjective evaluation of the layman, who is puzzled by the vagaries of the weather, or of the "old-timer," who remembers how climate differed when he was a boy. The constant flux of natural phenom- ena is almost impossible for man to recognize without the help of a long series of observations that are susceptible to statistical analysis. Real and significant changes of climate take place over millennia or millions of years, and the scale of climatic history is astronomical.

In the last 600,000,000 years the Earth's climate, on a planetary scale, generally has been much warmer than it is today. At such times there are no ice caps near the poles, the polar seas are open, and there are no glaciers on even the highest mountain ranges. Instead, temperate conditions prevail beyond the Arctic Circle. This picture of a relatively warm, ice-free planet applies for perhaps 95 percent of the geological past. Ice caps are anomalous in this framework of reference, and their presence has indi- cated past and present ice ages. There were several of these fourth-order, cold aberrations during the history of the Earth; the first two occurred about 570,000,000 and 280,000,000 years ago. The third began about 3,000,000 years ago, bringing on a sequence of cold and relatively warm spasms known as the Pleistocene Ice Age. Several of the glacial intervals produced ice sheets on the North American and European continents; the relatively warm phases, or interglacials, were comparable to present con- ditions, and there is every reason to believe that the first- and second-order climatic fluctuations of the historical era are really no more than minor variations within the second half of an interglacial period. In other words, modern climates are still referable to the Pleistocene Ep- och today.

Matters of perspective aside, even small-scale variations are of great practical importance to man in his depen- dence on Earth resources. Year-to-year climatic oscilla- tions control agricultural yields, bringing famine or plen- ty; abnormal snowfalls snarl communications systems, and the melting snows may contribute to record floods at a later date; wet summers influence vacation activities and may have severe repercussions on resort industries. First-order fluctuations over several decades lead to ad- vance or recession of mountain glaciers, to changes in stream discharge or lake levels, and to slight shifts in storm tracks or ocean currents—with possible repercus- sions ranging from widespread desiccation to faunal shifts. East Africa was drier between 1898 and 1961, for exam- ple, than it had been for at least several centuries; rainfall was, perhaps, 15–30 percent lower than it was before or has been since. Similarly, the warming of the waters off Greenland since the early 1900s has led to a change from a sealing-whaling economy to herring fishing as the Arctic mammals retreated and great shoals of fish moved in. Climatic oscillations and fluctuations have at least as great an impact on worldwide economic productivity as any of the sociopolitical factors reflected by stock-market indexes. Yet, people have always accepted the inevitability of good years and bad years, despite occasional vocifer- ous discontent. Whether climate has influenced the course of history is controversial, however. Certainly climatic variation can have severe economic repercussions and as one of several economic variables can contribute to social or political crises. Whether, however, the rise or decline of civilizations should be interpreted by resort to climatic history is quite another matter.

This article treats the evidence for the several orders of climatic change through geological time and the charac- teristics of each change. For related information on mete- orological aspects, see CLIMATE; WINDS AND STORMS; and WEATHER FORECASTING. The effects of climatic change are cited in many related articles. See, particularly, PLEISTO- CENE EPOCH; HOLOCENE EPOCH; RIVERS AND RIVER SYSTEMS; PALEOGEOGRAPHY; and LANDFORM EVOLUTION.

EVIDENCE OF PRE-PLEISTOCENE CLIMATIC CHANGES

General framework of reference. The unravelling of the geological eras during the 19th century raised many ques- tions about the climate and environment of the distant past. Today inferences are still made largely on the basis of organic and inorganic materials in the geological rec- ord, presuming that meaningful analogies can be drawn from an understanding of contemporary formations and related living organisms. At best such evidence can only be evaluated qualitatively and within a conceptual frame- work different from that of present Earth conditions. The atmosphere and oceans at the dawn of history, for exam- ple, differed considerably from those of today (see OCEANS, DEVELOPMENT OF; ATMOSPHERE, DEVELOPMENT OF). Terrestrial plants represent another changing factor. They developed during the Silurian Period (395,000,000 to 430,000,000 years ago) and remained few and sparse

Effects of short-term climatic oscillation

until Carboniferous time (about 345,000,000 years ago). A closed vegetation mat, efficient in retarding runoff and inhibiting erosion, did not develop until Late Cretaceous time (about 70,000,000 years ago), when the rapidly evolving angiosperms preceded an equally rapid evolution of mammalian grazers. Consequently the hydrological cycle, complicated by a chemically different ocean and atmosphere, remains enigmatic before the Late Paleozoic if not the Early Tertiary (about 60,000,000 years ago).

The configuration of land and sea has been subject to continuous change in the wake of crustal deformation. Today the seas comprise 71 percent of the Earth's surface, and the average elevation of the land is 880 metres (2,900 feet). These two values have been highly variable in the geological past, because continental masses have fused or rifted apart in the course of continental drift (*q.v.*).

Geophysical and astronomical variables also have changed through time. The position and magnetic field of the magnetic poles has changed frequently, with as yet poorly understood implications. The length of the day has increased as the Earth's rotational velocity has decreased through tidal friction, cutting the number of days in a year from about 425 during the Cambrian to 365 today. Accordingly, the diurnal radiation budget has changed, favouring greater daily temperature amplitudes as time has passed. Completely speculative as yet is the constancy of the Sun's energy and particle emission over 10^6 to 10^9 years.

Coral reefs and other carbonate rocks. Tropical seas are delineated by the limits of reef coral formation (see CORAL ISLANDS, CORAL REEFS, AND ATOLLS). Some modern corals, mainly of the solitary kind, grow in temperate or cool waters (Japan 35° N, winter water temperatures of 12° C [54° F]; Norway 69° N, 6–7° C [43–44° F]; however, most of the colonial forms thrive only at temperatures of 25–30° C (77–86° F) and do not tolerate temperatures under 18° C (64° F). In addition, corals are found exclusively in waters with a salinity of 2.7–4.0 percent, free of suspended sediment and preferably agitated by wave action. Light is required for photosynthesis, so that coral growth is limited at depths of 25 m (85 ft) and impossible below about 60 m (200 ft). If reef corals that evolved during the Cambrian and Ordovician had similar limitations, then coralline limestones provide a useful index of warm waters. The absence of coral also may reflect salinity or depth factors, however.

The organic record of coral is complemented by the distribution of carbonate rocks such as limestone and dolomite. Carbonates are scarce in the marine oozes of cool and temperate seas today but abundant in the subtropics and tropics, because carbon dioxide (CO_2) is most soluble in cold water and thus more calcium carbonate ($CaCO_3$) can be held in solution. Marine carbonates in the record generally suggest comparatively warm waters. Paleotemperatures have been inferred from variations of the O^{18} : O^{16} isotope ratio of planktonic foraminifera in deep-sea oozes; however, recent work indicates that changes of salinity and water density are primarily responsible for latitudinal or vertical shifts of marine planktonic habitats.

When occurrences of coralline limestones are plotted for the different geological epochs, they fall into a distinct zonal arrangement that probably reconstructs the position of the equatorial seas. This coral belt shifts with time, reflecting continental drift, and varies in width, possibly indicative of world temperature distributions. If the latter assumption applies, then the Jurassic, Cretaceous, and Tertiary periods were relatively warm and the Permian and Triassic cool.

Glacial deposits. Glacial phenomena provide unmistakable evidence of cold climate in the pre-Pleistocene record. These include undifferentiated moraines cemented into tillites, ice-rafted blocks and boulders bedded within marine strata, and striated or ice-gouged pavements under tillites. Recognition of true glacial, or glaciomarine, features poses serious problems, however (see GLACIA-

TION, LANDFORMS PRODUCED BY). Morainic materials are normally unstratified, unsorted as to size, and unclassified as to lithology or origin; the matrix is commonly clayey, the coarse material ranging in size from a few millimetres to boulders, mostly subangular in shape but with rounded edges and frequent facets or striations. Unfortunately, comparable deposits can be produced by a host of other marine and subaerial processes in various climatic zones. The result has been a profusion of claims of tillites that have not survived the scrutiny of careful study.

Extensive Late Paleozoic glaciation is irrefutably documented by massive, extensive, and widespread tillites and well-defined glacial pavements in Australia and South Africa. Comparable tillites are known from South America, the Falkland Islands, Madagascar, and India. This Permo-Carboniferous Ice Age remains unique between the close of the Proterozoic about 570,000,000 years ago and the onset of the Pleistocene Epoch about 3,000,000 years ago. Some seven or eight major glacial phases can be recognized in Argentina and eastern Australia beginning in mid-Carboniferous times; more general glaciation was limited to a time span of perhaps 10,000,000 years during the Early Permian (about 280,000,000 years ago), when ice sheets covered much of Gondwanaland, the land mass in the Southern Hemisphere prior to continental drift. A final record of glaciation in Australia, perhaps local in nature, comes from the mid-Permian.

Recognition of Proterozoic glaciations is far more difficult because outcrops are fragmented and greatly deformed. Most authors accept an Infra-Cambrian Ice Age (about 570,000,000 years ago) recorded in what are now Australia, southern Africa, China, northwestern Europe, and Greenland.

Evaporite deposits. The desert belt of lower midlatitudes and the continental interiors is today characterized by widespread saline deposition in nonoutlet lakes and pans, coastal lagoons, and in massive soil horizons. Sediments include sodium chloride, sodium bicarbonate, gypsum, borax, saltpetre, anhydrite, and potash salts (see EVAPORITES). Saline precipitates elsewhere are few and restricted in development, and salt deposits in the geological record therefore are used as potential indices of an arid and relatively warm climate, at least when they are widespread and well developed.

By plotting the distribution of sodium-chloride beds and other evaporites for each geological epoch, it has been possible to reconstruct the probable former arid zones. Extensive warm, arid climates can be deduced for the early Cambrian, the Late Silurian, the Late Devonian, the Permian, the Late Triassic, the Late Jurassic and Early Cretaceous, the Eocene–Oligocene transition, and the Miocene. At other times the intensity and distribution of evaporites was restricted, suggesting a more limited distribution of dry climates. In some instances, particularly in the Permian of Germany, evaporites show distinct cyclical banding, probably reflecting annual alternations of a seasonal nature; successive increments of these varved deposits (*q.v.*) do not display any convincing periodicities.

Eolian sandstones and red beds. Wind-driven sand is today found wherever loose sand is available and where vegetation is inadequate to bind sand or impede its movement. Contemporary sand dunes and sand sheets therefore are found primarily in desert environments, in some polar environments, along sandy beaches, and adjacent to some sandy riverbeds. Considering the paucity of continental vegetation before the Late Devonian and the imperfect nature of the vegetation cover before the Late Cretaceous, eolian sandstones can be expected to be common within continental deposits of Paleozoic and Mesozoic age. Only when found in regional association with evaporites are they convincingly related to arid climates (see DESERTS).

Eolian sandstones in the geological record consist mainly of quartz and are primarily recognized on the basis of specific angles of cross-bedding (bedding is inclined to the horizontal in alternating and intersecting beds) and

Inferences from coral growth

Tillites and former glacial episodes

Saline precipitates and aridity

Climatic
implica-
tions of
Eolian
sandstones

broad but flat ripple patterns. Most eolian sands are well sorted into finer size grades; shape varies from subangular to well-rounded, and frosting (by micropitting) is common although not diagnostic. Faceted pebbles (ventifacts) may be found on deflated surfaces or interfaces, preserving a lag of coarser particles. Prevailing wind directions can be identified from the dominant direction of bedding. Deposits fitting these specifications are widespread in the Late Carboniferous to Jurassic record of the western United States, in the Permian and Triassic of western Europe, and in the Triassic and Jurassic of southern Brazil. Arid coastal plains or interior deserts are inferred, with persistant prevailing winds ("northerly" in the western United States, "easterly" in western Europe, "westerly" or "easterly" depending on latitude in South America) that can be related to the former climatic belts.

Deposits of reddish colour also have been widely interpreted as evidence of dry conditions. These range from sandstones to shales with matrices of reddish-brown mud or ferric oxides. Such red beds have had different origins. Many of Permian and Triassic age interfinger with eolian sandstones and evaporites, and are marked by dehydration cracks, rain-pitted surfaces, and silicified wood; these suggest warm, dry climates with a rainy season to permit sufficient oxidation and to account for the massive fanglomerates interbedded in some areas. Other red beds that are rich in hematite and kaolinite (or certain other clay minerals) suggest derivation from humid tropical soils; they may grade into laterites or bauxite deposits and provide evidence for warm and moist environments. Still other red beds may be the result of semiarid weathering after deposition.

Coal measures. Coal deposits, found as organic seams or measures interbedded with mineral lenses (see COALS), form the primary botanical record of the Late Paleozoic and Mesozoic. Best known are the widespread coal measures of the Carboniferous Period. These were deposited in lowland or delta swamps where a luxuriant, semiaquatic vegetation of extinct arborescent families (scale trees, ancestral conifers, seed ferns) flourished. Analogies have been suggested with tropical mangrove swamps, but many coal swamps appear to have developed in subtropical or warm-temperate conditions, judging by their distribution. Some beds accumulated with submerged root zones and peat accumulation under anaerobic conditions; this would require abundant freshwater and a permanently high-water level. Other coal beds suggest emergent roots with acid soil environments; in this case the vegetation was probably maintained by a constant, high atmospheric humidity. Both varieties suppose a humid climate without a dry season.

Coal swamps of Mesozoic age were initially dominated by conifers, later by broad-leaved trees, many of them deciduous; this suggests that the paleoclimatic implications of the Late Paleozoic coal measures cannot be extended to more recent periods of time.

Fossil flora and fauna. Ecological interpretation of the extinct families of Paleozoic and Mesozoic plants and animals in the fossil record (q.v.) is highly precarious, since they have few surviving relatives and new adaptive traits may have developed in the meanwhile. Although fascinating insights have been obtained into the possible ecology of some earlier forms, little systematic information is available before the Early Tertiary, when floras and faunas become sufficiently "modern" to evaluate as assemblages. The evidence, preserved sporadically, ranges from plant macrofossils (leaves, fruits, seeds, stems) and microfossils (pollen, spores) to various phyla of invertebrates (such as arthropods, brachiopods, mollusca) and the various classes of marine and terrestrial vertebrates.

Fossil floras and faunas provide the bulk of the paleoclimatic data for the Cenozoic, indicating remarkably warm conditions for the Early Tertiary and a general cooling trend in middle and high latitudes during the Late Tertiary, as a prelude to the Pleistocene Ice Age. Initially, a warm-temperate Arcto-Tertiary forest, with

Swamps
of the
Carbon-
iferous

Tertiary
plant
assem-
blages

sequoia, pine, fir, spruce, willow, birch, and elm dominated the planetary belt 50 to 70° N, while a subtropical, evergreen forest with palms and numerous tropical oaks was found between 25 and 50° N, with coral reefs at the same latitudes. Molluskan assemblages from the west coast of North America indicate Eocene winter water temperatures as much as 15° C (27° F) warmer than today, floras from the western United States suggest mean temperatures 20° C (36° F) and from western Europe, 12° C (22° F) warmer than now (see Figure 2A). Semiarid floras are evident along the western littorals of lower middle latitudes, and increasing continentality with drier conditions is evident in the lee of mountain ranges developing during the Alpine orogeny. Temperatures trended downward in higher latitudes beginning in mid-Oligocene times, increasingly so by the Late Miocene.

Synopsis of pre-Pleistocene climates. Few inferences can be made for geological climates before the nebulous ice age that heralded the beginning of the Paleozoic. Thereafter the record is discernible in its basic outlines, despite countless controversial details and general difficulties in overall interpretation.

The Infra-Cambrian (c. 570,000,000 years ago), Permocarboniferous (c. 280,000,000 years ago), and Pleistocene (c. 3,000,000 years ago to the present) ice ages are exceptional in the geological history of the Earth. There is no evidence of any glacial phenomena between the mid-Permian and Late Miocene (a span of 250,000,000 years), when mountain glaciers are first indicated in Alaska; similarly, glaciation was rare or absent from Early Cambrian to mid-Carboniferous times (again, about 250,000,000 years). Glaciers are anomalous on Earth, even in polar latitudes.

The "normal climate" of geological times was comparatively warm, with few extremes of temperature. Polar latitudes were cool–temperate, with open seas, and a reduced albedo (index of reflection of radiation from the Earth's surface) in the absence of snow or ice. Midlatitudes were subtropical or warm–temperate, although the tropics do not appear to have been warmer than the modern equatorial zone.

Despite the complications of continental drift and the wanderings of the magnetic poles, a distinct zonation of climates can be recognized since mid-Paleozoic times, including a belt of equatorial seas, a zone of warm deserts reaching to the continental west coasts, and extensive higher latitude regions with warm or temperate humid climate. Latitudinal temperature gradients were much reduced, however, and the winter gradient between 0° and 90° N was probably comparable to that between 0° and 40° N today. In fact, during eras of "normal climate" a (modern) summer-type circulation pattern must have applied all year: winter airmass contrasts would have been small, and westerly depressions were probably shallow and slow moving.

Subdued variations of nonglacial climate from one era to the next are evident—e.g., the mid-Paleozoic was comparatively cool; the Permian and Triassic cool and relatively dry; the Jurassic, Cretaceous, and Tertiary distinctly warmer, with fluctuating moisture anomalies. It is probable that much of this variation reflects episodes of mountain building and increased continentality on the one hand and long periods of low continental masses with minimal relief differentiation on the other.

The apparent periodicity of ice ages at intervals of about 275,000,000 years remains unexplained, although the Pleistocene was clearly announced by falling temperatures in higher latitudes during the Late Tertiary (see Figure 2A).

EVIDENCE OF PLEISTOCENE CLIMATIC CHANGES

Glaciers and ice sheets. Although the criteria for and the isotopic age of the Pliocene–Pleistocene boundary (see PLEISTOCENE EPOCH; STRATIGRAPHIC BOUNDARIES) is a matter of lively disagreement, extensive mountain glaciation or ice caps are first recorded from the Sierra Nevada of California, from Iceland, from the Andes of Argentina, from the New Zealand Alps, and from interior

Antarctica between 3.2 and 2.5 × 10⁶ years ago. Absolute age dating generally indicates that higher latitudes were quite cold by 3,000,000 years ago and that latitudinal temperature gradients were approaching those of today.

Glacial–interglacial oscillation

The formation of major ice sheets—comparable in size to those of modern Antarctica—over North America and northern Europe began at a later, as yet uncertain date. In North America there were at least four major glaciations, in northern Europe at least five, in the Alps six or seven. The suite of glacial periods was interrupted by temperate or warm interglacials. The "last (Wisconsin–Würm) glacial" began c. 75,000 BP ("before present," which means before 1950 by convention) and terminated c. 10,300 BP (depending upon latitude), interrupted by a long interstadial with partial deglaciation and repeated climatic oscillations intermediate between those of the glacial and interglacial norm. Other datable glacial episodes in the mid-Pleistocene record of Europe lasted only 40,000 or 50,000 years. The "last (Sangamon–Eem) interglacial" can be dated c. 125,000 to 75,000 BP, and earlier interglacials were of comparable or slightly briefer duration. It is a major paleoclimatic problem to explain the rapid and violent oscillations between glacials and interglacials. The regional and planetary temperature anomalies are best inferred from other lines of evidence because growth and wastage of glaciers provide no quantitative data on the magnitude of climatic changes. Crude estimates can be obtained from the Pleistocene depression of the climatic snow line in mountain regions, but such values are as strongly influenced by differences in precipitation frequency and amounts as by temperature changes.

Sea-level fluctuations. The growth of the Pleistocene glaciers was made possible by the withdrawal of water from the interconnected world oceans. If the residual glaciers of Antarctica, Greenland, and other polar or mountain regions melted today, the ice would return to the oceans and thus raise world sea level by about 66 m (220 ft). Estimates of the volume of ice held in the Pleistocene glaciers and physical evidence of submerged shorelines (see CONTINENTAL SHELF AND SLOPE) indicates that world sea level was 100 to 150 m (350–500 ft) lower during the last glacial interval than it is today. These glacial–eustatic fluctuations allow for variations of sea level in a range of about 220 m (730 ft).

The significance of these sea-level fluctuations is entirely indirect; they provide a worldwide record of glacial and interglacial episodes that can be used to correlate geomorphologic records (wind action, fluvial processes, soils) of climatic change by means of marine terraces and other coastal features. The removal or return of vast volumes of water affected density and salinity of ocean waters and thereby left a succinct record of glacial–interglacial oscillations in the foraminiferal composition of deep-sea sediment increments. Also, the record of interglacial beaches at or above modern sea level provides excellent opportunities for isotopic dating of the interglacial intervals. The lowering of glacial-age sea levels by 150 m (500 ft) presumably reduced mean continental temperatures by about 1° C (1.8° F).

Distribution of permafrost. Active permafrost (q.v.), permanently frozen subsoil, is not found today in regions with mean annual temperatures above −2° C (29° F), and fossil indicators of permafrost therefore provide an index of former temperature conditions that can be obtained from no other criteria. Relevant here are a number of kinds of patterned ground and other soil-frost phenomena, the only conclusive one of which is ice wedges.

At the maximum of the Würm glacial episode ice wedges were actively forming in Europe as far south as latitude 46° N; from this it can be inferred that mean annual temperatures were *at least* 10 to 12° C (18–22° F) lower than at present in the climatic belt ahead of the Pleistocene glaciers in European midlatitudes. In North America, where the Wisconsin-age glacier advanced southward as far as 39°30′ N (compared with 52°30′ N for the Würm glacier in Europe), the permafrost belt was

very narrow and possibly discontinuous; its equatorward margin apparently coincided with the modern 24° C (76° F) July isotherm; mean annual temperatures in the northern United States were at very least 12° C (22° F) colder. No systematic data on fossil ice wedges are available from either Asia or the Southern Hemisphere.

Fluctuation of stream discharge. The unstable patterns of Pleistocene climate affected the hydrological balance of streams during the course of both glacial and interglacial stages. In midlatitude areas of severe cold the glacials accelerated frost activity, and this added greater sediment loads to streams. Runoff was concentrated immediately after the snow-melt and during the summer months, as in polar regions today; this circumstance produced torrential discharge capable of transporting large masses of comparatively coarse material on floodplains much broader than those existing today. Other midlatitude streams were potent because of augmentation by glacial meltwaters. In semiarid environments of midlatitudes, however, reduced evaporation during the glacials improved the vegetation mat. This reduced runoff rates as well as the seasonal concentration of discharge of streams not emanating from mountains or glaciated regions; here the alluvial record consists of fine silts, deposited by muddy waters with little sand or gravel. In desert regions there were repeated increases of rainfall that promoted greater erosion and redeposition of coarse sediments by short-lived but torrential streams over broad alluvial surfaces. In tropical environments the alluvial terraces of stream systems are far more difficult to interpret because of the complex interrelationships between rainfall amount and seasonality, evaporation, vegetation mat, and discharge.

Patterns of stream discharge

Alluvial terraces provide a complementary record of Pleistocene climatic changes, but, unfortunately, they are not amenable to realistic quantification of former hydrological conditions.

Lake-level fluctuations. A number of nonoutlet lakes expanded considerably during the Pleistocene as a result of climatic changes within their immediate catchments.

In the Great Basin of the United States there were many small and two large lakes, with records that go back over 400,000 years. Lake Bonneville, a predecessor of the Great Salt Lake, was 10 times larger and up to 335 m (1,130 ft) deep, overflowing into the Snake River drainage. Lake Lahontan, in what is now northwestern Nevada, had a maximum depth of 213 m (720 ft). Both of these lakes were high during the glacials, responding to every cold oscillation with rises of lake level, falling off during interstadials: the last major maxima were attained about 15,000–12,000 BP, a final high stand about 10,500 BP. The hydrological budget of these lakes traditionally has been reconstructed by assuming a 5° C (9° F) drop in annual temperature and a corresponding 25 to 30% decrease in evaporation; this would suggest a precipitation increase of 65 to 80%. An alternative budget has been suggested, however, and a 10 to 12° C (18–22° F) drop of temperature with a 10 to 20% decrease in precipitation could produce similar "pluvial" lakes. A comparable problem of interpretation exists for the now nonoutlet Caspian Sea at similar latitudes. The level was as much as 77 m (260 ft) higher than at present, with an overflow to the Black Sea, during the first part of the Würm glacial; a part of the influx was derived from glacial meltwaters. European authors now generally assume that glacial-age precipitation was less than that of today in their interpretation of high lake levels and greater stream discharge in middle latitudes.

The tropics are another matter. Well-dated nonoutlet lake sequences exist in Africa, where Lake Chad in the southern Sahara was greatly expanded before 20,000 BP and again 9250–7000 BP and 5500–3100 BP. The deepest lake, with shorelines at +50 m (165 ft) was attained c. 9000 BP following a long, dry interval. In East Africa, Lake Rudolf was 80 m (265 ft) higher than today a little before 35,000 BP, and again from 9700–7500 BP, 6200–4400 and c. 3250 BP; at these times the lake overflowed into the Nile system. At the maximum of the Würm gla-

Evidence from African lakes

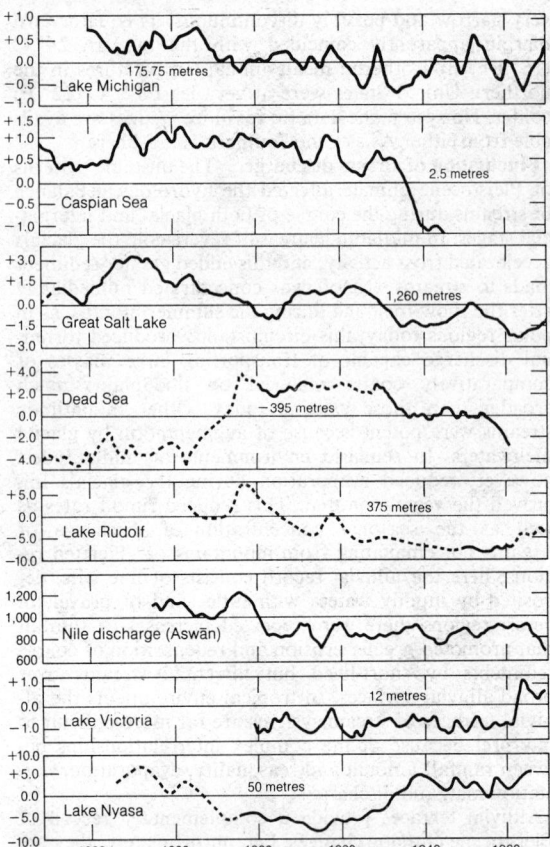

Figure 1: Annual fluctuations of lake levels (in metres) and five-year running means for Nile discharge (in cubic metres × 10⁸). Heavy lines are gauge readings; dotted lines, reconstructed.

cial (c. 35,000–10,000 BP), however, the level was no higher than today. Smaller lakes (Nakuru, Naivasha) in the Kenya Rift Valley had a similar history; minimal depths occurred for some time prior to 12,500 BP, and high levels c. 12,200–3400 BP. Lake Victoria was without an outlet from somewhat before 14,500 until about 12,-000 BP and again for a short period about 10,000 BP; several high levels can be dated c. 9500–6500 BP, and an outlet has been maintained since. These data indicate that there is no correlation between relatively moist "pluvial" intervals and glacials but that parts of both the Würm interstadial and the Holocene were moist—in contradistinction to the lake evidence from middle latitudes.

Inactive eolian sands. In some areas of the world immobile dunes and sand sheets that are now fixed by vegetation testify to significantly drier periods of climate than presently occur.

Widespread eolian silts (including loess) and restricted dune sands, with some areas of wind-excavated blowouts, are found across the Great Plains of North America and in parts of midlatitude Europe. In both areas the loess sheets relate to open, polar vegetation and to geomorphic processes that are associated with the cold glacials. The European dunes still fall within this former periglacial environment, but those of the semiarid United States do not: on the basis of lake deposits and dated pollen records the latter correlate with shrinking "pluvial" lakes during warmer, interstadial oscillations.

The situation is different in low-latitude dry lands where eolian phenomena can be correlated with the glacial maxima. In Nigeria, dunes advanced so far into the present savanna that annual precipitation probably was 150 millimetres (6 inches) in areas where 750 millimetres (30 inches) of rain fall today; the pattern is similar all along the southern margins of Sahara and on the northern margins of the Kalahari, with a major dry interval of dune advance or activation dating from the Würm-glacial maximum.

Migrations of flora and fauna. The floral record of the Pleistocene, based partly upon macrofossils but to an increasing extent on pollen stratigraphy, provides an invaluable climatic record for certain periods in some areas.

The first half of the Pleistocene was marked by a gradual elimination of tropical and most subtropical genera from temperate Europe; each successive cool phase eliminated additional elements, until the first verified continental glaciations promoted continent-wide shifts of vegetation belts at a fairly rapid rate. The botanical and pollen data permit reconstruction of the broad patterns of vegetation for large parts of Eurasia during the terminal Pliocene, the last two interglacials, and the last two glacials. These data indicate that parts of the interglacials were a little warmer than the present and, at times, moister, too. The glacials saw elimination of forests from most of midlatitude Europe and much of the northern Mediterranean Basin, partly as a result of the cold and partly due to aridity. Changes in moisture are further attested to by variable composition of the nontree floras—maximum aridity coincided with the last maximum of the Würm glacial, whereas earlier phases were moister. From the position of the polar tree line in midlatitude Europe, mean July temperatures at the height of the glaciations were probably 7 to 9° C (13–16 ° F) colder than today, if modern approximations are relevant. This suggests winter temperature depressions of almost 20° C (36° F) to account for mean annual temperatures at least 10 to 12° C (18–22° F) lower than today. The Wisconsin glacial saw widespread coniferous forests throughout the eastern United States, but little or no open tundra, even close to the ice front. Parklands or woodlands of pine were widespread in arid or semiarid parts of the western United States, probably reflecting reduced evaporation. No temperature estimates are possible.

In lower latitudes the pollen record of East Africa locally corroborates the geomorphic record; in addition, greater cold is indicated in the high mountains, with a depression of the vertical vegetation belts by 1,000 to 1,-100 m about 27,000–14,000 BP; this suggests a temperature reduction on the order of 5 to 6° C (9–11° F). Similar evidence, for a 1,000-m (3,300-ft) lowering of vegetation belts during the last glacial, is available from Costa Rica and Colombia.

By comparison, faunal changes and migrations are of limited paleoclimatic value. Strong environmental adaptations are not apparent among the Pliocene and early Pleistocene megafauna, and specific cold-tolerant forms such as the woolly mammoth and woolly rhino only evolved during the successive continental glaciations. The most characteristic "cold" faunas are, therefore, those of the last glacial; in Europe they include an extinct steppe bison, musk-ox, reindeer, wild horse, a cold-steppe antelope, and countless steppe rodents. Paleontologists now feel that this faunal assemblage was more adapted to dry than to cold conditions and thrived on open, grassy vegetation that palynologists have shown to be more comparable with that of cold midlatitude grasslands than with polar tundra. The North American faunas were less specialized as an assemblage, although woolly mammoth and musk-ox were most abundant between the Great Lakes and the Ohio River.

Synopsis of Pleistocene climatic changes. The large body of available information on Pleistocene environments permits a far more realistic assessment of climatic change than can be made for any of the earlier geological periods.

The first part of the Pleistocene (c. 3,000,000 to 1,-000,000 years ago) saw a series of cool and warm oscillations that ultimately climaxed in successive spasms of continental glaciation in North America and Europe. These early cool episodes saw the onset of glaciation in suitable high mountain and high latitude localities, with repercussions among midlatitude floras.

The last part of the Pleistocene (beginning before 400,-000 years ago) witnessed a series of major glacial episodes, synchronous on all continents, and with a mean duration of 50,000 years. At their maximum, these gla-

Floral data for Eurasia, North America, and Africa

Pleistocene megafauna

cials were associated with mean annual temperatures 10–12° C (18–22° F) colder than today on those continents affected by major glaciation and perhaps 5–6° C (9–11° F) colder on the low-latitude landmasses. Winter temperature anomalies were probably greater than summer fluctuations. Because ocean-bottom waters are near the freezing point today, oceanic temperatures were probably not much lower, but an overall reduction of planetary temperatures is suggested. Latitudinal temperature gradients were greater, with mean summer gradients on the glaciated Northern Hemisphere continents almost comparable to those of the winter season today; land–sea gradients must have been correspondingly exaggerated, with unusual air-mass contrasts.

The Pleistocene glacials were only relatively moist in midlatitudes, with an inverse correlation between temperature and precipitation; in lower latitudes the glacial maxima were dry, the interstadials moist. Initially, the onset of the Pleistocene may have been wet at most latitudes. The aridity of the glacial maxima may be due to reduced evaporation over cooler ocean surface waters and more extensive seasonal or permanent pack ice.

The Pleistocene interglacials were in part comparable to those of the Holocene, in part moister in lower latitudes or warmer in higher latitudes. Their mean duration was a little less than that of the glacials.

EVIDENCE OF HOLOCENE CLIMATIC CHANGES

The pollen record. Pollen stratigraphy provides the primary evidence for climatic change during the terminal millennia of the Pleistocene and for the Holocene Epoch. Excellent records, with fairly good isotopic dating, are available for temperate Europe, North America, southern Chile, Japan, and New Zealand. Unfortunately, the record of vegetation change that can be inferred from pollen records provides at best an indirect index of climate, because forest successions require long periods of time that are conditioned by soil properties and rates of floral migration. In addition, man has influenced the record, increasingly so during recent millennia. Most sensitive to climate are marginal environments, such as the late glacial forest–tundra transition belt in midlatitudes or the postglacial, subalpine belt in mountain environments. Equally good are specific warm-climate indicator plants, such as hazel in the boreal woodlands of Scandinavia or holly, ivy, and mistletoe in the mixed forests of central Europe.

The earliest worldwide oscillation in the pollen record (compare Figure 2B) is the warm Allerød interval, c.

Palynology and climatic indices (margin note)

10,200–9400 BC, which saw a first major forest readvance at the tree line and temperatures averaging only 1–2° C (2–3° F) colder than the present. Equally striking is the partial return to open vegetation in marginal environments during the cold relapse of the Younger Dryas interval, c. 9400–8300 BC, with mean annual temperatures about 5° C (9° F) colder than today. Thereafter conditions warmed up very rapidly, and following a cold oscillation before c. 7100 BC, attained a thermal maximum in higher midlatitudes c. 6200–3300 BC, with mean temperatures 1–2° C (2–3° F) warmer than today (Hypsithermal interval). After a major cold oscillation (1–2° C colder than today), c. 3300–2500 BC, higher midlatitudes were relatively warm until after 1000 BC.

Post-Pleistocene precipitation changes in higher midlatitudes are subjects of disagreement. In semi-arid environments, however, there is increasing evidence of moisture oscillations in the pollen record. In North America there was a relatively dry period (the Xerothermal) on the Columbia Plateau, in the Great Basin, and across the Great Plains c. 6000–2000 BC, although the summer-rainfall belt in Arizona and New Mexico was comparatively moist c. 4000–2000. Fragmentary pollen records from tropical Africa suggest one or more warm, moist episodes dated at c. 7500–1500 BC, with Mediterranean-type vegetation widespread in the highlands of the central and southern Sahara; but there is no evidence for greater rainfall in the winter-rainfall belts of the Mediterranean Basin or South Africa. These discrepancies appear to indicate differences of climatic trends in tropical and extratropical dry lands (see Table 2).

Discharge fluctuations of major rivers. Fluvial geomorphology provides useful evidence for changes of the hydrological balance in semiarid or arid regions. Specifically, well-dated, fine-grained alluvial fills in semiarid Arizona and New Mexico suggest that runoff was inhibited by an effective vegetation mat except for brief periods of relative aridity c. 8500–8000 BC, c. 6500–3800 BC, and again c. AD 500–1000. In addition, falling water tables are indicated c. 8500–5000 BC, rising water tables c. 2500–1500 BC. Comparable deposits may exist in central India and South Africa. In the arid axis of the Sahara, increased stream activity is indicated c. 7500–6500 BC and c. 3500–2500 BC, coincident with periods of significantly higher Nile floods. Alluvial deposits of comparable age elsewhere are either unstudied, undated, poorly developed, or uninformative. Still enigmatic are alluvial deposits of post-Roman to late medieval age found throughout the Mediterranean Basin, temperate Europe, and western Asia: in part they relate to man-influenced soil erosion, in part they may also reflect climatic variations of uncertain character.

Fragmentary records of Nile flood levels, providing an index of total flood volume and of rainfall in eastern Africa, exist back to 3100 BC, but few systematic data are preserved before AD 622. Of particular interest is the downward trend of flood levels after 3000 BC, culminating in abnormally low floods between 2180–1950 BC that led to severe famines and allowed sand dunes to invade parts of the former floodplain. A number of surviving records indicate exceptionally high floods c. 1840–1780 BC and again in the 8th and 7th centuries BC. On the basis of the gauge readings, Nile floods were abnormally low AD 756–1089, 1192–1382, and 1452–1506; they were unusually high c. 1610, 1727–1776, and 1846–1892; total discharge has been measured regularly since 1870 and shows a sharp decrease since 1899 (see Figure 1).

The Nile floods (margin note)

Fluctuation of lake levels. The most conspicuous fluctuations of lake level during early to mid-Holocene times come from tropical Africa, where major high levels of Lakes Chad, Rudolf, Naivasha, Nakuru, Victoria, Rukwa, and others can be dated c. 7700–5500 and 4000–2400 BC; several lake levels rose again c. 1500–400 BC. Together with evidence of stream discharge fluctuations, this shows that at least tropical Africa was moister during most of Holocene time than it has been during the last 2,500 years. The residual Lake Chad and most East African lakes fell rapidly in level after AD 1899.

Relative moisture during Holocene time (margin note)

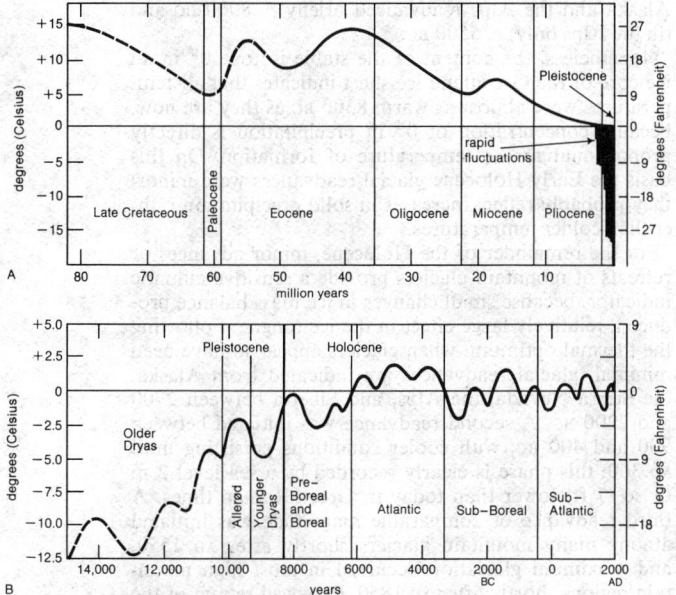

Figure 2: *Variations of average temperature from that of the present.* (A) In the middle latitudes from Late Mesozoic to Pleistocene. (B) In Europe and temperate North America since 15,000 BC.

Table 2: Chronology of Climatic Change During the Holocene Epoch

pollen zone	North America and Europe	tropical Africa
Subatlantic (400 BC to present)	warmer with glacier retreats since c. 1900 (the "recent climatic change")	abrupt decline of stream discharge and lake levels c. 1900
	colder (−1° or 2° C) with minor glacier readvances c. 1550–1900 (latest phase of Little Ice Age) in high and middle latitudes	high Nile floods c. 1610, 1727–76, 1846–92; lake levels generally intermediate
	cooler winters and wetter summers in Europe c. 1300–1550; frequent droughts in American Southwest	Nile floods high 1383–1451, low 1452–1506
	warmer (+0.5 to 1.5° C) with drier summers in Europe c. 1000–1300, and Iceland–Greenland c. 1000–1200 (the "little optimum")	Nile floods high 1090–1191, low 1192–1382
	frequent droughts in American Southwest c. AD 500–1050	Nile floods low AD 756–1089
	readvance of mountain glaciers and generally cooler −1° to 2° C) c. 400 BC–AD 300 (second phase of Little Ice Age)	
Subboreal (400 to 3300 BC)	warm (+1° C) in higher latitudes c. 2000–900 BC (last phase of "thermal optimum" = "hypsithermal"); summers relatively dry in humid zones	last high ("pluvial") lake levels c. 1500–400 BC, with unusually high Nile floods c. 800–600 BC
	cooler (−1° or 2° C) with minor glacier readvances c. 3300–2000 BC (first phase of Little Ice Age); dry ("xerothermal") in most of semiarid America, but moister in Arizona–New Mexico	Nile floods initially high but declining after 3000 BC to a low c. 2180–1950 BC; lake levels relatively low
Atlantic (3300 to 6200 BC)	warm (+1° to 2° C) in higher latitudes c. 6200–3300 BC, interrupted by cool interval c. 5500–4500 BC; summers relatively moist in humid zones; dry ("xerothermal") throughout semiarid North America	high ("pluvial") lake levels and Nile floods c. 4500–3300 BC and c. 7700–5500 BC
Boreal and Preboreal (6200 to 8300 BC)	warming in higher latitudes c. 7700–6200 BC	
	warming rapidly, with cold oscillation c. 8000 BC in higher latitudes; recolonization of high-latitude tundra–steppe by forests; rapid drop of lake levels and a decrease of arboreal vegetation in semiarid North America	lake levels low

By contrast, the "pluvial" lakes of the Great Basin have been at low levels since the Early Holocene, essentially disappearing c. 6000 BC; they were recreated about 1000 BC, with only minor fluctuations since. The Great Salt Lake was relatively high during 1865–1880 and 1910–1927, with major lows around 1860, 1905 and 1940 (Figure 1). The Caspian Sea provides some relevant although controversial data for the period since the 5th century AD: levels were low from the 5th to the 8th and during the 12th century; high lake levels are indicated in the 10th, 13th, and 17th to 19th centuries, when the mean level was at least 3 m (10 ft) higher than that of the last three decades. Gauge readings extend back to 1839, and they suggest a relationship of high lake levels with cool, rainy summers over the Volga drainage basin in central Russia; the lake level fell almost steadily 1929–1945, in part due to the removal or retention of Volga waters for irrigation and hydroelectric projects. Many of the patterns recall the fluctuations of Lake Michigan since 1860 (Figure 1). The levels of the Dead Sea can be reconstructed from 1807 to 1930, when level readings were begun. After a major low of 5 m below the 1960 level (397 m below sea level) in 1820, the level fluctuated at −0.5 to −1.5 m from 1835–1885. A marked rise to +4 to +6 m occurred from 1895–1932, and levels have fallen again since then.

Fluctuations of tree-ring width. Tree-ring widths in areas of marginal tree growth can provide evidence of summer warmth in cold environments or evidence of available moisture in dry environments. Long records with sufficient control are only available from the intermontane basins of the western United States; these go back to AD 435. A period of unusually small radial tree growth suggests a "Great Drought" between AD 1273–1285; serious droughts also are indicated during 1573–1593 for the Colorado Plateau, 1571–1597 for southern California, and 1565–1580 and 1594–1599 in eastern Oregon; this suggests another widespread anomaly of some persistence. Other severe droughts on the Colorado Plateau have central dates of AD 517, 565, 614, 844, 884, 1170, 1402, 1525, and 1670; humid spells are recorded around central dates of AD 494, 688, 858, 1126, 1329, 1708, and 1905.

More limited tree-ring series from Alaska and Finland indicate relatively warm summers during most of the 16th century AD, with less favourable growing seasons in Finland after about 1590, and in Alaska since the mid-17th century. The period of coolest summers in Finland (1600–1650) preceded that of Alaska by about a century.

Glacier fluctuations. Near the beginning of the Holocene Epoch, around 8300 BC, the continental glaciers had not yet disappeared: Finland, Norway, and most of Scandinavia were still under ice in Europe, while almost all of Canada remained glaciated. In fact, world sea level was still at least 40 m (135 ft) lower than today. Deglaciation, involving a general thinning and retreat of the ice margins, proceeded slowly. The residual ice caps of Scandinavia melted off after 6000 BC, whereas the ice remnants in northern Canada persisted until 3000 BC; sea level approached its present level at this time. Deglaciation did not proceed without interruptions; a major halt or regrowth of the North American glacier is recorded c. 6500 BC (Cochrane stade), whereas mountain glaciers in Alaska and the Alps readvanced briefly c. 8000 BC and (in the Alps only) c. 5500 BC.

Nonetheless, the content of the stable isotope O^{18} in an ice core of the Greenland ice sheet indicates that air temperatures were almost as warm 8300 BC as they are now, because concentration of O^{18} in precipitation is directly proportional to the temperature of formation. On this basis the Early Holocene glacial readvances were minor; they probably reflect increases in solid precipitation rather than colder temperatures.

For the remainder of the Holocene, minor advances or retreats of mountain glaciers provide a sensitive climatic indicator, because small changes in ice mass balance produce a relatively large effect in the ice tongue. Following the thermal optimum, when glaciers appear to have been minimal, glacial readvances are indicated from Alaska, the Sierra Nevada, the Alps, and Siberia between 2700 and 2200 BC. A second readvance was initiated between 900 and 400 BC, with cooler conditions persisting until AD 300; this phase is clearly recorded by a sea level 2 m or so (7 ft) lower than today in Greco-Roman times. A third readvance of comparable magnitude was initiated among many mountain glaciers shortly after AD 1550, and maximum glaciation occurred in most high mountain regions shortly after AD 1850. Renewed retreat of the glaciers began in the 1890s and, after a positive oscillation in the 1920s, became almost universal. Glacier trends since the 1950s are mixed and uncertain, with most

Deglaciation and its interruptions

readvances linked to local or regional increases in precipitation. The total of minor glacial stades since 2700 BC are commonly grouped as the "Little Ice Age" or Neo-glacial; they mark the passing of the Holocene thermal optimum.

Archaeological and historical data.   Before the instrumental record, historical documentation of droughts, floods, great heat or cold, exceptional ice conditions, and times of crop harvest provide an indirect source of information on year-to-year fluctuations of climate. Grouped in decades or centuries, such data can, under optimal conditions, be used for semiquantitative assessments.

In the Mediterranean world occasional commentaries related to weather go back to Grecian times, but no systematic trends can be observed, even though some long drought spells can be inferred (*e.g.*, AD 591–640) in the eastern Mediterranean Basin. The recession of agriculture along the desert margins of Syria, Palestine, and Libya in late Roman (Byzantine) times has frequently been cited in favour of a declining rainfall; the evidence, however, points to unstable political conditions as the major reason for land abandonment, with both the disappearance of irrigation works and severe soil erosion reducing land potential in the wake of nomadic settlement. Other historical events, such as the Mycenaean decline (after *c.* 1200 BC), also have been (incorrectly) linked to climatic events; but pollen records in southeastern Europe, Anatolia, Italy, and Spain do not reveal climatic trends during the last 3,000 years.

In temperate Europe trends are clear and often more dramatic. The period *c.* AD 1000–1300 was 0.5–1.5° C (1–2.5° F) warmer than the present century, judging by a host of agricultural records, which include the distribution of vineyards, the average dates of the grape harvest, and the altitudinal limits of various crops in mountain country. Winter sea ice was minimal off Iceland, where the years 1010–1030 and 1080–1170 were unusually benign. Summers in western Europe were relatively dry from AD 1000–1200, but the subsequent centuries were comparatively wet, and unusually wet autumns are notable in 1300–1350 and again in 1650–1700. Marked cooling is apparent in 1420–1500 and again in 1560–1700, which in the North Atlantic was reflected by unfavourable ice conditions after 1590 that persisted until the close of the 19th century. Ice blocked the coast of Iceland for an average of 5–6 months a year, compared with 1–3 weeks today. European temperature means were at least 1° C (2° F) cooler at the climax of these cold centuries.

Comparable historical records from China and Japan remain to be fully evaluated. Of particular interest from Japan are average dates for the first cherry blossoms and the freezing dates of lakes. These dates suggest a higher frequency of late springs during the 11th to 14th and the 16th centuries AD and of mild winters during the 19th century.

Synopsis of Holocene climatic trends.   The preceding materials are collated and summarized in Table 2. It is apparent that the African lakes and the Nile flood levels do not correspond exactly with anomalies in higher latitudes. The high (pluvial) lake levels in tropical Africa all coincided with glacial recessions; the same applies to the significantly higher Nile discharge recorded by floodplain aggradation prior to 3000 BC. During the last century or two, however, minor fluctuations of moisture in tropical Africa appear to show a positive correlation with cooler anomalies in higher latitudes. Moisture fluctuations in the semiarid tropics and midlatitudes trend in opposite directions; this is an important realization that has been gained from recent isotopic dating of lake levels, alluvial formations, and pollen spectra.

MODERN CLIMATIC TRENDS AND METEOROLOGICAL RECORDS

Early meteorological records.   The instrumental record is disappointingly short. Tantalizing references suggest regular recordings of some sort in Alexandria during the mid-2nd century AD; after the rain gauge was invented in Korea, sporadic measurements began in 1442. Practical

thermometers and instruments for recording atmospheric pressure were first developed in the 16th century, and systematic documentation of day-to-day parameters began with the Florentine Accademia del Cimento (1652) and the Royal Society of London (1660). Uninterrupted temperature readings are available from England since 1670, and precipitation and air pressure records from the Netherlands since 1715 and 1740, respectively. Scientifically comparable observations were assured in 1781–95 when the Societas Meteorologica Palatina of Mannheim organized a network of stations in Europe, Greenland, and the United States with standardized equipment, recording hours, exposure, and elevation above ground.

About a century ago, in 1870, the network of stations was still very uneven, with over 100 stations in Europe, 33 in North America (the earliest records going back to Charleston, S.C., with interruptions since 1738, and New Haven, Conn., since 1780), 22 in South America (beginning with Cayenne, French Guyana, in 1845), 47 in Asia (beginning with Seoul, Korea, in 1772), 20 in Oceania (beginning with Adelaide, South Australia, in 1839), and only 4 in Africa (Capetown, since 1841). In effect, Alaska, boreal Canada, tropical South America, Africa, most of Asia, and all but southeastern Australia were almost complete voids. As late as the 1930s there still were very few stations in desert regions and in the humid tropics, so that basic climatic data—apart from long-term records— remain inadequate for many continental areas. It is even more difficult to establish climatic trends for the world's oceans. Finally, measurement of essential data such as wind speed, wind directions, rainfall frequency and intensity, snowfall, and various upper air phenomena have no time depth whatsoever.

Evaluation of long meteorological records.   One of the most difficult problems with long-term meteorological records is establishing their consistency. Instruments break and are replaced, sometimes by different equipment; instruments also go awry, and observations often continue for months or years before the defect becomes evident. Observers come and go, and their exactitude varies, particularly in exigencies when individuals are away or ill. Even if the instrumentation and recording techniques remain consistent, exposures change as trees grow, houses are built, and urban environments are created. Over a 50-year span ventilation can change from an open field to a walled-in garden, where reduced wind speeds will affect precipitation measurements, especially during rain or snow storms. Cities create heat of their own, and many urban stations tend to record the steadily increasing temperatures associated with industrialization and artificial climate control (see URBAN CLIMATES). Finally, stations frequently have been moved to new locations, and the new records often are not comparable to the old. For these reasons, records are studied in many ways to determine their consistency and reliability; techniques range from historiography to statistical tests that are intended to reveal discontinuities.

Given a scattering of good, long-term records, it is still difficult to infer climatic trends beyond the local level. Changes in long-term stream discharge in lake levels, glaciers, or vegetation reflect real and composite trends over broad areas—information that is often more meaningful than an isolated record of temperature and rainfall. Climatic fluctuations involve multivariate phenomena that are only crudely and inadequately abstracted by simple measurements of pressure, temperature, and precipitation. Consequently, large, dense networks of station records are necessary before climatological parameters can replace the indirect indicators of true change provided by other natural phenomena. And such data are unavailable on a worldwide scale before the 1870s.

A last problem raised by meteorological records is the definition of a standard. Because climatic parameters vary from year to year and from one nonrandom oscillation to the next, a basic period of observation is necessary to define the "normal," from which deviations through time can be measured. To assure that regional data are comparable, most meteorological services strive

Agri-
cultural
records

Meteoro-
logical
station
networks

The
definition
of
normal
climate

for a 30-year mean for an identical period (*e.g.*, 1910–1940 or 1940–1970). Other organizations feel that a 100-year period of observation is necessary before the full range of mean and extreme values can be properly understood. A common technique to smooth minor variations and establish trends is to utilize running or overlapping means. For all practical purposes, 30-year running means do express first-order climatic fluctuations, but, unfortunately, records are seldom long enough to provide more than a regional perspective.

Temperature fluctuations since the 1870s. Most short-term climatic oscillations are of a regional nature, and temperature or precipitation anomalies in one area are compensated for by excess or deficit in another. At the scale of first-order fluctuations, however, trends become more universal and often can be rationally linked to patterns of the general atmospheric circulation. This is the case for temperatures since the 1870s. Figure 3 shows

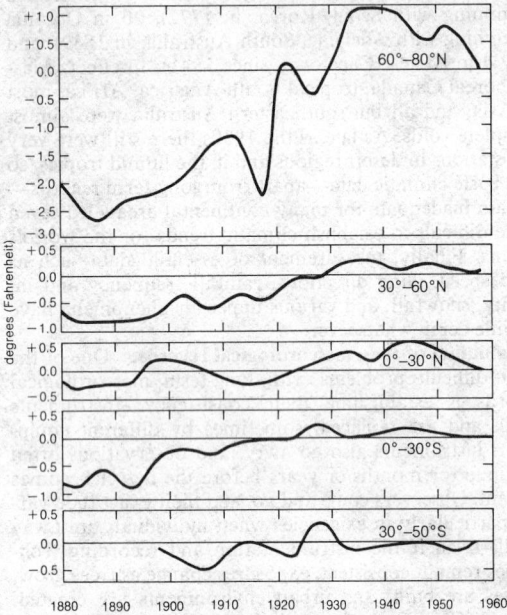

Figure 3: Trend of five-year mean values of temperatures for various latitudinal bands from 1880 to 1960.

the trends of mean temperatures averaged out over various latitudinal bands from 1880–1960. The data are drawn from a large percentage of coastal and island stations, so that they are essentially representative of the circumplanetary picture. Temperatures fell markedly in each latitudinal band during the 1960s, just as they did during the late 1870s. Consequently, the temperature deviations since 1880 have been given with respect to the 1955–1959 mean.

Temperatures during the 1880s were generally low: as much as 2.7° F (1.5° C) colder in the Arctic (60–80° N latitude), 0.8° F (0.4° C) in midlatitudes of the Northern Hemisphere (30–60° N), 0.3° F (0.2° C) in the northern tropics (0–30° N), and 0.9° F (0.5° C) in the southern tropics (0–30° S). With various regional anomalies and superimposed oscillations, the trend was upward until about 1940, when temperatures were 1° F warmer (than 1955–59) at 60–80° N and 0.2–0.5° F warmer between latitudes 30° S and 60° N. Only in midlatitudes of the Southern Hemisphere, where landmasses and station members are limited, has the trend been indistinct. The total picture is that of a first-order temperature fluctuation from a low about 1885 to a high in 1940, followed by a slight but accelerating reversal since that date. This trend from 1885 to 1940 is known as the "recent climatic fluctuation."

The warm-up of 1885–1940 was most pronounced in high latitudes of the Northern Hemisphere, particularly poleward of 50° N, where temperature deviations were in the order of three or four times greater than in any other zonal belt. Winter temperatures were more con-

spicuously affected than annual means, and the continental interiors warmed up considerably more than coastal regions. Thus the recent warm-up was primarily a matter of decreased continentality, milder winters, and reduced latitudinal temperature gradients (at least on the Northern Hemisphere). In other words, winter circulation patterns were a little less marked and tended more toward their summer counterparts.

Recent warm trend and subsequent reversal

The recent warm-up was not restricted to the land surfaces; it also can be identified from both ocean air temperatures (recently compiled from millions of ship observations over the past century) and water temperatures. It is estimated that mean surface water temperatures rose 1.3° F (0.8° C) (1880–1940). This was most dramatic in high latitudes, where the Arctic pack ice retreated several hundred miles. Temperatures are now dropping once again as the pack ice readvances. Glaciers have behaved accordingly. The minor glacial advance of *c.* 1890 was preceded by a decade of falling temperatures and unusually high precipitation; the subsequent retreat and thinning of ice sheets produced a ten centimetre (four inch) rise in world sea level. Glacier trends of the 1960s are uncertain; considering the time lag of previous advances, more universal glacier growth can be expected by the late 1970s.

In summary, the 75-year warm-up (1885–1940) was a planetary phenomenon that raised temperatures of the lower atmosphere by at least 1° F (0.6° C). The amplitude and duration of the negative trend developing since the 1940s suggests that a reversed first-order fluctuation is currently under way. It is therefore unsurprising that the winter of 1962–63 in many parts of the Northern Hemisphere was one of the coldest in a century.

Precipitation fluctuations since the 1870s. Unlike the temperature trends of the past hundred years, there were no worldwide precipitation fluctuations. On a regional scale, some climatic provinces show long-term anomalies, but others do not.

Precipitation variability in middle and high latitudes and in the Indian monsoon province has been limited to short- and long-term oscillations. On the basis of precipitation, stream-discharge, and lake-level records (Figure 1), there are no defined moisture trends in Europe and North America. The 1870s were relatively wet, the 1910s dry, and the 1930s often moist in western and central Europe. The pattern in continental eastern Europe and central North America differs in that the 1930s were dry, while in northern Europe the early 20th century was moist. Falling lake levels and groundwater tables are commonplace since about 1940, primarily because of increased use or overexploitation of water resources. In India the Madras record (since 1813) shows no trends whatsoever, whereas that of Seoul (since 1772) indicates a single, major dry spell in Korea centred *c.* 1900.

Patterns in arid and semiarid environments are highly complex, with significant changes in seasonal precipitation and the frequency of rain often masked by little or no change in annual values. In Arizona and New Mexico, for example, both winter and summer rains occur. The winter rains (and snows) are generally light, but they are protracted and highly efficient in terms of available moisture for vegetation. The summer rains are intensive and showery, with a high ratio of runoff to precipitation and rapid evaporation. Whereas the summer rains tended to increase in New Mexico and Arizona (1897–1930) due to a strengthening of the onshore trade winds from the Gulf of Mexico, winter rains declined, favouring a change from grassy vegetation to semidesert shrub. This seems to explain much of the gully cutting initiated in the southwestern United States between the 1880s and 1910s; a comparable change of seasonality can be postulated for interior South Africa. In the Great Basin, with a predominance of winter precipitation, rainfall was generally below average in 1915–1935, although lake levels only began to fall in the late 1920s concomitant with a rise in temperature. Yet at similar latitudes the dry belt of Central Asia enjoyed more rain in the 30-year period after 1910 than that preceding 1910. In the Mediterra-

Precipitation in arid and semiarid regions

nean Basin the period 1880–1900 was relatively moist, that of 1920–1940 dry; Capetown, in a comparable climate, enjoyed a high rainfall from 1875 to 1905 and a lower rainfall from 1905 to 1930, with a subsequent rise.

In the tropics of Africa and Australia there is a clearly defined trend with higher rainfalls and high lake levels from before 1870 until the late 1890s, when rainfall decreased sharply. The subsequent dry anomaly remained in effect until the early 1960s, when conditions abruptly reverted to their late 19th-century patterns. But here as elsewhere the geographical complexity of annual or five-year anomalies cautions against generalization from one area to the next.

Of particular interest are the droughty Dust Bowl years of the 1930s in the U.S. These provide an example of how an unusual succession of severe droughts can drastically affect large areas such as the Great Plains, where rainfall averages for the decade 1931–1940 were 10–20 percent lower and temperatures were 1.4° F (0.8° C) higher. Similar droughts occurred in the Near East and parts of the Mediterranean Basin at this time, although the 1930s were moist in the Mediterranean climates of the Southern Hemisphere. A similar succession of arid years with persistent summer and winter droughts is apparent a century earlier (in the 1830s) in the Mediterranean climate zones of Europe, as well as those of the Cape province, southern Australia, and Chile. Wet years seldom provide economic hardships of equal severity because marginal crop yields in cool–wet environments primarily reflect a lack of summer warmth, whereas catastrophic floods are seldom linked with wet years but rather to isolated rainstorms of exceptional proportions or to sudden thaws in mid- or late winter.

Synopsis of modern climatic fluctuations. Instrumental records supplement other observations during the 200-year period 1670–1870, after which meteorological records become the primary criterion of climatic variation. During the past 100 years a worldwide first-order fluctuation has been discernible. A warm-up began in the mid-1880s and reached its climax about 1940; by 1955 temperature trends had generally been reversed, and during the 1960s there was a distinct cooling trend. The half-wavelength of this "recent climatic fluctuation" has been just over 75 years, and its amplitude amounts to at least 1° F (0.6° C) for planetary air and surface-water temperatures. The recent climatic fluctuation was not accompanied by any consistent or significant trend of precipitation, except in many semiarid tropical regions, where the period c. 1898–1961 was decidedly dry. Short-term cold or dry oscillations were apparent during 1870–1970, but they were only of a regional or latitudinal nature.

To a large extent the recent climatic fluctuation can be understood in terms of trends of the general circulation, shifts in the position and intensity of pressure cells and wind belts, and in the changing frequency of large-scale pressure patterns. Most of these changes must be considered as symptoms of the adjustment of the general circulation to changes of the planetary heat balance, although many of the superimposed oscillations can be attributed to the built-in variability of the atmosphere. Countless unsuccessful attempts have been made to recognize strict periodicities in the progression of atmospheric parameters, and it is now clear that such periodicities do not exist. On the other hand, there are observable oscillations of varying order but with constantly changing wavelengths and amplitudes. These reflect upon the interacting, multivariate components of the atmosphere that build up repeatedly until reversed by a complex system of balances. Unfortunately, the science of meteorology has not yet been able to properly explain the rationale of the general circulation, and some decades may elapse before these mechanics will be understood. (See CLIMATE; WINDS AND STORMS.)

THEORIES OF THE CAUSES OF CLIMATIC VARIATION

Variations of solar radiation through time. The most probable cause of climatic variation would seem to be the Sun, which regulates the basic heat budget of Earth. Measurements of the solar constant and of certain variants within the solar spectrum have become available only in recent decades, and for total incoming radiation the apparent variability is only about as great as the possible margin of error. Orbiting satellites and rockets have begun to provide new data, essentially uninfluenced by the problems of reflection, scattering, and absorption that plague measurements from the Earth's surface. Total change in radiation flux probably does not exceed 1 percent and may be as little as 0.2 percent during the course of an 11-year sunspot cycle, although ultraviolet and cosmic radiation show far more appreciable changes: the X-rays of cosmic radiation have varied by factors ranging from 7 to 600 since 1953, for example, whereas ultraviolet varied on the order of a factor of two from sunspot minimum to maximum. Ultraviolet flux in recent times can be inferred from the progression of sunspot cycles that is numerically documented since AD 1749 and can be estimated with a certain amount of confidence since about AD 300.

The sunspot cycle is the shortest observable variation, ranging from 8 to 16 years but averaging 11.1 years (22.2 years for a complete cycle); some authors claim to see higher order, superimposed periodicities, mainly in multiples of 11, but these have not been satisfactorily established. There are, however, longer term fluctuations, not demonstrably periodic. The basic cycle is closely related to fluctuations of ultraviolet, electromagnetic, and high-energy particle radiation. Although the solar cycle is significant on the basis of various statistical tests (harmonic and power spectrum analyses, etc.), similar rigorous tests have *not* been able to demonstrate correlations with precipitation amounts, tree-ring widths, lake-level fluctuations, seasonal temperatures, or pressure anomalies, despite the visual appeal of superficial similarities between many long data series. Nonetheless, long-range weather forecasting continues to use sunspot activity and periodicities to predict weather patterns, and a large number of meteorologists do believe that there is a real but complex relationship between this solar factor and latitudinal heat exchange, as well as the intensity and patterns of the general circulation.

For climatic fluctuations in the geological record there is little information beyond the hypothesis that the Sun may be a variable star, with fluctuations of luminosity and energy generation over periods of about 250,000,000 years, possibly accompanied by several minor reactory cycles. A 10 percent change in the solar constant could theoretically change temperatures in the tropics by about 5.5° F (3.4° C) and by 18° F (11° C) or more in high latitudes.

Variations of atmospheric transparency through time. Fluctuations of solar radiation provide fascinating but inconclusive possibilities for climatic change. Other possibilities for modification of radiation lie within the Earth's atmosphere, where carbon dioxide (CO_2), water vapour, ozone (O_3), and pollutants such as volcanic dust operate as selective screens for short-wave (incoming) and long-wave (outgoing) energy. Each tends to absorb solar radiation, converting it to energy that is released to the lower atmosphere; at the same time cooling of the atmosphere is retarded. An increase of these components therefore favours higher planetary temperatures.

The CO_2 level of the atmosphere is decreased when CO_2 is absorbed by the oceans, precipitated from seawaters in the form of carbonates, or becomes bound up in organic deposits such as coal measures. On the other hand, atmospheric CO_2 is increased as rocks weather or plant materials decay, as fossil fuels are burned, or when released by the oceans (as temperatures increase or water volume decreases). The affect of decreasing ocean volume would be offset by decreasing water temperatures during the course of a glacial cycle, however. The key to CO_2 as a factor in climatic change lies in the complex atmosphere–ocean equilibrium, which probably has neutralized any major change in atmospheric CO_2 concentration since the Late Paleozoic or Mesozoic, when the present

The solar constant and sunspot cycles

Atmospheric CO_2 and water vapour

atmospheric ratios of nitrogen, oxygen, and carbon dioxide were established. In addition, recent recalculations have shown that doubling or halving of the atmospheric CO_2 would have only a small quantitative affect on planetary temperature.

Water vapour in the atmosphere can vary according to ocean surface area, atmospheric and surface-water temperatures, and wind speeds. This would limit any change of mean water-vapour content to a secondary role but one of potential significance. Cooling and contraction of the oceans during a glacial episode would reduce evaporation and thereby increase the loss of terrestrial heat. This effect would probably be offset by reduced precipitation over the ice sheets, and the reduced cloud cover would increase radiation; both factors favour ice wastage.

The ozone of the upper atmosphere fluctuates in proportion to the ultraviolet radiation received, but it is also influenced by stratospheric mixing. Although strongly influenced by sunspot activity, ozone largely absorbs the ultraviolet radiation that is responsible for increasing the ozone concentration. Ozone absorption of terrestrial reradiation is too small to affect planetary temperatures appreciably.

Volcanic dust is injected into the stratosphere following the rare, violent eruptions that occur every generation or two. The dust veil can reduce direct solar radiation by 5 to 10 percent, but careful observations following an eruption in 1963 indicated a corresponding increase in diffuse sky radiation, with little overall change in total or global radiation. Observations of worldwide temperature anomalies following similar cataclysmic eruptions in 1883 and 1912 appeared to be considerable (-2 or $3°$ F) (-1 or $2°$ C) but have since proved to be fortuitous and exaggerated: both took place during cool oscillations that began months before the eruptions, and the cold anomalies were neither universal nor in proportion to the volcanic dust in various latitudinal bands. Considering the questionable magnitude of change and the short time required for the dust to fall out of the stratosphere (about three years), volcanic dust seems an unlikely contender for a significant role in climatic change. Finally, there is no evidence in the geological record for the frequency of violent eruptions that would be necessary to produce a long-term effect on climate.

Variations of Earth orbit through time. Perhaps one of the most controversial theories of climatic change is that invoking periodicities of the Earth's orbital geometry. Three variables are involved. (1) *The angle of the ecliptic:* Earth's axis to its orbital plane is oblique, varying from $65° 24'$ to $68° 21'$ over a period of between 38,000 and 45,000 years. When the obliquity is increased, seasonal contrasts are magnified, and vice versa. (2) *The precession of the equinoxes:* the date of perihelion, the day when the Sun and Earth are closest (approximately January 2), shifts around the calender with a period varying from 16,000 to 26,000 years. About AD 1200 perihelion was on December 21 (reducing winter cold on the Northern Hemisphere), whereas about 9300 BC that date was June 21 (increasing summer warmth on the Northern Hemisphere). As a result this precession alternatingly increases or decreases seasonal contrasts, in opposite directions in each hemisphere. (3) *The eccentricity of the orbit:* Earth's orbit deviates from a true circle to an ellipsoid, with a variable eccentricity in a poorly known periodicity of perhaps 92,000 years. This again influences seasonal contrasts. Altogether these periodicities of orbital geometry do not affect total radiation received from the Sun, but they do affect the degree of continentality, the latitudinal distribution of incoming radiation, and hemispheric contrasts.

Since 1920 these variables have been computed and recomputed into various "radiation curves" that span the last 600,000 years, and the most significant of which is that for summer at $65°$ N latitude. The assumption is made that cool summers will favour glaciation with a time lag of several millennia; eventually the growing glaciers will increase the albedo of higher latitudes, provid-

ing a powerful feedback mechanism to increase the heat deficit of the glaciated continents. Because Antarctica has remained glaciated since the Late Tertiary and because there is little or no land in higher midlatitudes of the Southern Hemisphere, the opposing hemispheric trends are felt by some to be unimportant; the alternation of glacial and interglacial phases essentially is controlled by changes on the Northern Hemisphere. Recent computer analysis, using thermodynamic models of the general circulation, show that the surface temperature changes due to these variations are very small (less than 2 or $3°$ F), although the slight changes in differential heating of various latitudinal belts may well have been sufficient to affect upon air pressure and wind patterns. Consequently, the chronological similarity of inferred and observed glacial phases, allowing a 5,000-year time lag, may in fact be real, and the 41,000-year periodicity computed for semiannual insolation in middle and high latitudes does appear to correspond to the approximate duration of glacials and interglacials through much of the Pleistocene.

Although further, rigorous study is required, these orbital variations may help explain the third-order variations (10^4 years) of climate evident in the Pleistocene record. They cannot, however, explain either the fourth- or second-order variations—*i.e.*, the occurrence of ice ages or the sudden and dramatic changes superimposed upon glacial–interglacial cycles (*e.g.*, the Upper Dryas cold relapse).

Polar wandering and continental drift. The Permo-Carboniferous Ice Age can only be understood in the context of continental drift (*q.v.*) and polar wandering (SEE ROCK MAGNETISM), despite several ingenious attempts to explain the widespread tillites in now tropical environments by great elevations (3,000–4,500 m, 10,-000–15,000 ft) and rearranged oceanic currents. Paleomagnetic, tectonic, and floristic data can only be reconciled when South America, Africa, Arabia, India, Australia, and Antarctica are placed in close proximity; the magnetic South Pole was coincident with the African landmass. In other words, glaciation was restricted to high latitudes. If, as is indicated, planetary climate was cooling during the Late Carboniferous times, the total absence of verified tillites from North America and Eurasia only makes sense in the context of continental drift, particularly when the local floras suggest warm–temperate or tropical conditions.

For the Pleistocene, the location of an almost-land-locked ocean in the Arctic and of a continental landmass in the Antarctic was fortuitous and favoured high-latitude glaciation. Paleomagnetic (and paleobotanical) data suggest that the North Pole was near $78°$ N and $153°$ E by early Tertiary times, however, and thereafter remained essentially constant in its present position over the last 20,000,000 years. The first record of glaciation in Alaska is dated at 13,000,000 years and the first in Antarctica shortly thereafter; but extensive ice caps only developed between 3,200,000 and 2,500,000 years, so that polar "continentality" is a necessary but not a sufficient condition for continental glaciation.

An ice-free Arctic Ocean. At present the heat balance of the Arctic ice pack is very sensitive and close to zero. A relatively slight but continuous increase (by 3 or $4°$ F) in one of the heat fluxes (*e.g.*, that contributed by the oceans) could theoretically remove the ice cover. In that eventuality, winter air temperatures in the central Arctic would rise strongly to about $40°$ F ($4°$ C), summer temperatures to $50°$ F ($10°$ C). Surface-water temperatures would be in approximate equilibrium with air temperatures, and winter heat loss from the Arctic Ocean would be retarded by a band of coastal pack ice. The net effects would decrease surface albedo from 61 to 10 percent, with much greater absorption of radiation and reduced loss by reradiation—in view of greater atmospheric moisture and cloud cover. Under these circumstances the Arctic would not be a source of extremely cold air masses in winter but, instead, would provide large amounts of precipitation at all seasons.

Periodicities of orbital variables

The Arctic
Ocean and
glacier
growth

One theory of Pleistocene glaciation attributes initial glacier growth to an open Arctic Ocean, which would have provided winter snowfall on the adjacent continents in excess of summer ablation. Once large peripheral ice sheets had formed, a new moisture source would be provided by maritime air masses from lower latitudes, while the Arctic Ocean froze over again, with no further contribution to the continental glaciers. Eventually the lower surface-water temperatures of the oceans would starve the ice sheets, leading to their dissipation and inaugurating a new interglacial. Opening of the Arctic Ocean, possibly coupled with isostatic rebound of the peripheral continents, would eventually set the stage for renewed glaciation.

This theory is somewhat satisfying because the alternation of ice-covered and ice-free conditions would provide the desired mechanism for major glaciations. More recent studies of Arctic deep-sea sediments, however, fail to provide support; there is no indication that pack ice was absent in the Arctic Ocean prior to about 700,000 years ago.

Topographic variations through time. Mountain building (orogeny) and continental uplift (epeirogeny) may have been the most significant factors in preparing the Earth for the glacial-interglacial fluctuations that marked the Pleistocene and possibly also the Permo-Carboniferous ice ages. In particular, if the planet approached a threshold of climatic sensitivity, with incipient polar glaciation, then relatively minor changes of solar or orbital origin could have initiated spasms of glaciation over North America, Europe, or the other continents located in the higher mid-latitudes.

The geological record indicates many periods of orogeny, with distinct concentrations through much of the Paleozoic and during the Late Tertiary (see EARTH, GEOLOGICAL HISTORY OF). There also were periods of epeirogeny, with crustal upwarping, rising continents, and contracting oceans, during which time the epicontinental seas emerged with interruption or inhibition of free oceanic circulation patterns. Whenever accelerated orogenic activity coincided with worldwide epeirogeny, continental relief and roughness was strongly increased. Such was the case during the Late Paleozoic and again during the Late Tertiary and Pleistocene. Today, the mean elevation of the continents is 880 m (2,950 ft), whereas this value may have been as little as 200 m (650 ft) for Late Mesozoic times. A difference of about 700 m (2,300 ft) in elevation implies a mean temperature difference of 8° F (4.5° C). The cumulative effect would be even greater, with increased continentality in the lee of meridional mountain ranges (such as the American cordilleran belts) and cooling of fractionated water bodies in higher latitudes. In addition, glacial regressions of sea level, coupled with the thickness of the growing mid-latitude ice sheets, would periodically raise the mean elevation of continents another 350 m (1,200 ft), with further cooling of 4° F (25° C).

Most geologists concur that the land–sea distributions, major mountain lineaments, increased continentality, and overall continental relief of the Late Carboniferous, on the one hand, and of the Pliocene, on the other, were prerequisite to the subsequent Pleistocene ice ages. As well supported as these factors are, they can only help explain fourth- and fifth-order climatic variations in the order of 10^6 to 10^8 years. It is precisely this inadequacy of any one or even two hypotheses to explain all orders of variation that dictates the conclusion that climatic change is a complex, multivariate process.

FUTURE CLIMATES

Because the underlying mechanisms of climatic variation are so imperfectly understood, it is difficult to predict future climatic trends other than on the basis of empirical experience. When seen from an immediate perspective, the cool-moist trend of the 1960s was of sufficient magnitude and universality to suggest that the next few decades would continue to be on the cool side in the higher latitudes and on the moist side in the areas of the tropics. Winters would more often than not be colder and snowier than the average, and more summers would be either cool

or wet. The minor readvance of mountain glaciers that this could be expected to produce should actually be beneficial because summer meltwaters help maintain stream flow in semiarid environments. When viewed on a broad time scale, the Holocene Epoch is but another interglacial of the Pleistocene Ice Age. This can be inferred from the persistence of ice sheets on Antarctica and Greenland and of a frozen Arctic Ocean. Previous interglacials have been approximately 40,000 years long, so there is no reason to believe that another glacial is imminent, at least not for another 20,000 years or so. One thermal maximum was passed some 6,000 years ago, but there is no reason why there should not be at least another hypsithermal or two before glaciers re-form over the areas of northern Canada and Scandinavia.

BIBLIOGRAPHY. H.H. LAMB, Climate: Present, Past and Future, 2 vol. (1972–77), a comprehensive work; G. MANLEY, "Climatic Variation," Q. Jl. R. Meteor. Soc., 79: 185–209 (1953), a valuable introduction to the subject; M. SCHWARZBACH, Climates of the Past (1963), a comprehensive study of the evidence of climatic change through geological time; K.W. BUTZER, Environment and Archeology: An Ecological Approach to Prehistory, 2nd ed. (1971), an introduction to the study of Pleistocene environments and their significance for early man; B. FRENZEL, Die Klimaschwankungen des Eiszeitalters (1967; Eng. trans., Climate Fluctuations of the Ice Age, 1973), a presentation of paleobotanical evidence of changing climate in Eurasia during the Pleistocene; H.C. FRITTS, Tree Rings and Climate (1976), a comprehensive account of the information provided by tree rings; E. LE ROY LADURIE, Histoire du climat depuis l'an mil (1967; Eng. trans., rev. and updated, Times of Feast, Times of Famine: A History of Climate Since the Year 1000, 1971), an unusual documentation of climatic anomalies in Europe during the past millennium; P.S. MARTIN, The Last 10,000 Years (1963), a work that exemplifies environmental changes in the American Southwest on the basis of pollen evidence; A.B. PITTOCK et al., Climatic Change and Variability: A Southern Perspective (1978), the history of climate with emphasis on Australia and the Antarctic Ocean; J.S. SAWYER (ed.), World Climate from 8000 to 0 B.C. (1966), a representative set of background papers to a professional symposium; H.H. LAMB and A.I. JOHNSON, Secular Variations of the Atmospheric Circulation Since 1750 (1966), interesting reconstructions of pressure patterns for the Atlantic hemisphere; J.M. MITCHELL, "On the Worldwide Pattern of Secular Temperature Change," in Changes of Climate: Arid Zone Research, vol. 20, pp. 161–181 (1963), an authoritative analysis of climatic trends since the mid-19th century, and (ed.), Cause of Climatic Change (1968), a useful series of symposium papers; R.P. BECKINSALE, "Climatic Change," in J.B. WHITTOW and P.D. WOOD, Essays in Geography for Austin Miller, pp. 1–38 (1965), a discussion of the major ice-age theories; Climate Change to the Year 2000: A Survey of Expert Opinion (1978), a study conducted by the RESEARCH DIRECTORATE OF THE NATIONAL DEFENSE UNIVERSITY.

(K.W.B.)

Clive, Robert

Robert Clive, the conqueror and first British administrator of Bengal, laid the foundations for Britain's rule over India. He was born on September 29, 1725, at Styche, his family's estate, in the parish of Moreton Say, Shropshire. His father for many years represented Montgomeryshire in Parliament. Young Clive was a difficult boy and was sent to several schools, including the Merchant Taylors' School in London, without much visible profit. In 1743, when 18, he was sent to Madras in the service of the English East India Company.

At Madras, Clive was moody and quarrelsome, attempted suicide, and once fought a duel. He found solace in the governor's library where he virtually educated himself. Hostilities between the English and French East India companies and their competitive support of rival Indian princes drew Clive into military service and gave him a chance to demonstrate his ability. In 1751 Chanda Sahib, an ally of the French, was besieging his British-connected rival, Muḥammad ʿAlī, in the fortress of Trichinopoly. Clive offered to lead a diversion against Chanda's base at Arcot. With a force of 200 Europeans and 300 Indians, he seized Arcot on August 31 and then successfully withstood a 53-day siege (September 23–November 14) by Chanda's son. Clive's feat proved to be the turning point in a contest with the French commander, Joseph-Fran-

First years
in India

Clive, replica of an oil painting by N. Dance (1735–1811). In the National Portrait Gallery, London.

By courtesy of the National Portrait Gallery, London

çois Dupleix. In the next months Clive established himself as a brilliant exponent of guerrilla tactics. In March 1753 he left Madras with his bride, Margaret Maskelyne, and something of a fortune, having been appointed in 1749 a commissary for the supply of provisions to the troops.

In 1755, after unsuccessfully standing for Parliament, he was sent out again to India as governor of Ft. St. David and with a lieutenant colonel's commission in the Royal Army. With him went troops intended to expel the French from India. On the way, at the request of the Bombay government, he stormed the pirate stronghold at Gheriah on the western coast.

Reaching Madras in June 1756, Clive immediately became involved in the affairs of Bengal, with which, henceforward, his fate was to be linked. Hitherto Bengal had been ruled by viceroys of the figurehead Mughal emperor, and it was under their protection that the English East India Company carried on its trade. The principal city, Calcutta, had come to rival Madras as a trading centre, and its commerce was the most valuable in India. In 1756 a dispute with the British about fortifying the city caused the new nawab (Mughal viceroy) of Bengal, Sirāj-ud-Dawlah, to attack and capture the fort there.

News of the fall of Calcutta reached Madras in August 1756. After some delay Clive was given command of the relief expedition and set out on October 16, 1756, with 900 Europeans and 1,500 Indians. Clive retook Calcutta on January 2, 1757, and forced the Nawab to restore the company's privileges, pay compensation, and allow the British to fortify Calcutta. Determined to take advantage of discontent with the Nawab's regime, he sponsored a new ruler in order to ensure conditions agreeable to the company's trade. His candidate was Mīr Ja'far, an elderly general secretly hostile to Sirāj-ud-Dawlah. Clive broke with Sirāj-ud-Dawlah and overthrew him at the battle of Plassey on June 23. The conflict was more of a cannonade than a battle, and only 23 of Clive's men were killed. Clive was the virtual master of Bengal.

The Battle of Plassey

Clive's first government lasted until February 1760. He was confirmed as governor by the company and went about the business of strengthening Mīr Ja'far's authority, though at the same time keeping him under control. A challenge from the Mughal crown prince was repulsed at Patna in 1759. The Dutch, who sought to play on the Nawab's discontent at Clive's restraints, sent a force to their settlement at Chinsura, but through a series of adroit moves Clive destroyed this force even though England was at peace with the Netherlands. By 1760 Mīr Ja'far's authority was unchallenged throughout Bengal and Bihar, and his subservience to the company was complete. In addition, by the dispatch of a force under Col. Francis Forde in 1758, Clive secured the Northern Sarkārs from the French garrison.

His settlement of the company's affairs was less skillful. First, he accepted not only full compensation for loss to the East India Company and the Calcutta citizens but also large payments to himself and the council. He himself received in all £234,000 in cash, a Mughal title of nobility, and an estate, or *jāgīr*, with an annual rental of about £30,000. This example opened the way to a flood of corruption that nearly ruined both Bengal and the company and which Clive himself later struggled to control. Second, he obtained from the Nawab the practical exemption from internal duties, not only of the company's goods but also of the private trade of the company's servants as well. Since the company possessed paramount force and its servants believed in working on their own behalf, this had a most harmful effect on the economy of Bengal.

Though stained by corruption and duplicity, Clive's first government was a tour de force of generalship and statecraft. He had snatched the richest province of India out of the hands of his political superiors and with the authority of the Mughal regime. Returning to England in February 1760, he was given an Irish peerage as Baron Clive of Plassey in 1762 and was knighted in 1764. He was described by William Pitt (afterward 1st earl of Chatham) as "a heaven-born general." He became member of Parliament for Shrewsbury, purchased an estate, and tried to use his Indian wealth to carve out an English political career. But he had to reckon with the current jealousy toward any upstart, however brilliant, the unpopularity of returned Indian "nabobs" and suspicions within the East India Company resulting from his suggestion to Pitt that the state should take over its territories. His critics, led by a former friend who was then chairman of the company, tried to cut off the income from his Indian estates. Though they failed to ruin him, they did prevent him from becoming a national statesman.

In 1764 opinion within the company turned in Clive's favour because of the news from India. Clive's protégé Mīr Ja'far had been deposed in favour of Mīr Qāsim, who in turn had been deposed in 1763. Shāh 'Ālam II, the Mughal emperor, attacked again, and the company seemed to be on the brink of disaster. Clive was appointed governor and commander in chief of Bengal with power to override the council. Arriving in Calcutta for the second time on May 3, 1765, he found that the decisive Battle of Baksar (Buxar) had already been won; Shujā'-ud-Dawlah, the Nawab of Oudh, was in flight and the Emperor had joined the British camp. But there was a political and military vacuum between Bengal and Delhi (the Mughal capital), and the whole Bengal administration was in confusion.

Clive's chief claim to fame as a statesman rests upon the achievements of his second governorship. His work falls into three parts: external policy, the settlement of Bengal and the reform of the company's service. In his external policy Clive had to face one of the most difficult tests of statesmanship: that of knowing where to stop. Though there was nothing to prevent him from restoring Shāh 'Ālam II to Delhi and ruling north India in his name, he wisely decided to limit the company's commitments to Bengal and Bihar. Oudh was returned to Shujā'-ud-Dawlah as a buffer state between Bengal and the turbulent northwest. The Emperor was solaced with an annual tribute, and in return he conferred the revenue administration (dewanee) of Bengal on the East India Company. This grant formed the key to Clive's second achievement, the settlement of Bengal. It gave legal authority to the company to collect the revenues of Bengal and Bihar, sending the Emperor only his annual tribute. The administration of the dewanee was organized through a deputy nawab appointed by the company. The police and magisterial power was still exercised by the Nawab of Bengal as the Emperor's deputy, but he in turn nominated the company's deputy to act for him. This was Clive's so-called dual system, which made the company the virtual ruler of India's two richest provinces.

Clive's third task was the reform of the company's service. Within two days of landing he superseded the Cal-

Clive's administrative achievements

cutta council, which defied his predecessor, Henry Vansittart. He re-established discipline by accepting all resignations, enforcing others, and bringing replacements from Madras. All company servants were required to sign covenants not to receive presents worth more than 1,000 rupees without the consent of the governor. Private trade, the abuse of which had caused the war, was forbidden. This was the least successful measure because the company's officials were not adequately paid and had no other means of livelihood. Clive tried to meet the difficulty by forming a trading company that administered the salt monopoly and in which the servants received shares according to their rank. These two measures, only partially successful, marked the end of nearly ten years' reckless plunder in Bengal. Finally Clive dealt with the army with equal rigour. He cut down swollen allowances and faced with dauntless courage the White Mutiny of discontented officers, when for a time he stood almost alone in Bengal.

Clive left Calcutta in January 1767. His second government was his crowning achievement, but he had made many enemies. An active group, supported by Lord Chatham, feared the corrupting influence of Indian wealth on English public life. In 1772, when the company appealed to the government to save it from bankruptcy, it appeared that Clive's system of government in Bengal had not been as successful as had been hoped. Two parliamentary committees uncovered the facts of corruption among the company's servants, and this set off an attack on Clive as the instigator of the whole process. He defended himself in Parliament (1773) with characteristic vigour and conviction, complaining of being treated like a sheep stealer and declaring "I stand astonished at my own moderation." In 1773 Parliament declared that he did "render great and meritorious services to his country." This triumph was his last. With his already shaken health, the strain on his melancholic temperament was *His suicide* too great: on November 22, 1774, he died by his own hand at his house in London. Clive's talents were outstanding, his character no more unscrupulous than that of many men of his day, and his work marked the real beginning of the British Empire in India.

BIBLIOGRAPHY. For Clive's Indian career, the best book is H.H. DODWELL, *Dupleix and Clive* (1920, reprinted 1968); and for his relations with the East India Company in Britain, see LUCY SUTHERLAND, *The East India Company in 18th Century Politics* (1952). Both works are of outstanding merit. A detailed but uncritical biography is G.W. FORREST, *The Life of Lord Clive*, 2 vol. (1918); the best personal study is A.M. DAVIES, *Clive of Plassey* (1939).

(T.G.P.S.)

Clocks, Watches, and Sundials

Clocks, watches, and sundials are devices used to record or indicate the time of day. Sundials or shadow clocks, earliest of the three types of timekeeping devices, indicate the time of day by the position of the shadow of some object on which the sun's rays fall. As the day progresses, the sun moves across the sky, causing the shadow of the object to move. Clocks are machines in which a device that performs regular movements in equal intervals of time is linked to a counting mechanism that records the number of movements. All clocks, of whatever form, are made on this principle. A watch is a portable timepiece. The general term horology, used to describe the art of measuring time or making clocks, is derived from the Greek *hōra* ("time") and *logos* ("telling").

PRIMITIVE TIMEKEEPERS

Shadow clocks or sundials. The first device for indicating the time of day was probably the gnomon, dating from about 3500 BC. It consisted of a vertical stick or pillar; the length of the shadow that it cast gave an indication of the time of day. By the 8th century BC, more precise devices were in use; the earliest known sundial still preserved is an Egyptian shadow clock of green schist dating at least from this period. It consists of a straight base with a raised crosspiece at one end. The base, on which is inscribed a scale of six time divisions,

is placed in an east–west direction with the crosspiece at the east end in the morning and the west end in the afternoon. The shadow of the crosspiece on this base indicates the time. Clocks of this kind are still in use in primitive parts of Egypt.

Another early device was the hemispherical sundial or hemicycle, attributed to the Babylonian astronomer Berosus, about 300 BC. Made of stone or wood, the instrument consisted of a cubical block into which was cut a hemispherical opening; to this was fixed a pointer or style, the end of the style lying at the centre of the hemispherical space. The path travelled by the shadow of the style was, approximately, a circular arc. The length and position of the arc varied according to the seasons, so an appropriate number of arcs was inscribed on the internal surface of the hemisphere.

Temporary hours Each arc was divided into 12 equal divisions, and each ray, reckoned from sunrise to sunset, had, therefore, 12 equal intervals or hours. Because the length of the day varied according to the season, these hours, likewise, varied in length from season to season and even from day to day and were consequently known as temporary hours. The dial of Berosus was widely used for many centuries, and, according to the Arab astronomer al-Battānī (Albategnius, *c.* AD 858–929), was still in use in Muslim countries during the 10th century.

The Greeks, with their geometrical prowess, developed and constructed sundials of considerable complexity. Apollonius of Perga (*c.* 250 BC) developed the hemicyclium by using a surface of conic section upon which the hour lines were inscribed; this arrangement gave greater accuracy. Ptolemy used the analemma, a device that enabled shadows to be projected geometrically onto flat surfaces inclined at various angles to the horizontal. In general, it appears that the Greeks constructed instruments with either vertical, horizontal, or inclined dials, indicating time in temporary hours. The Tower of the Winds in Athens, octagonal in shape, and dating from about 100 BC, contains eight sundials. It is, therefore, clear that dials facing various cardinal points were in use for a long time.

The Romans also used sundials with temporary hours. The first dial set up in Rome in 290 BC had been captured from the Samnites, but it was not until almost 164 BC that a sundial was actually constructed for the city. In his great work *De architectura*, the Roman architect and engineer Marcus Vitruvius Pollio (1st century BC) mentions many types of sundials, some of which were portable.

Arab sundials The Arabs attached much importance to the study of sundials, the principles and design of which they derived from the Greeks. They increased the variety of designs available and, at the same time, simplified the processes of design and construction by using the principles of trigonometry. Abū al-Ḥasan, at the beginning of the 13th century AD, wrote on the construction of hour lines on cyclindrical, conical, and other surfaces and is credited also with introducing equal hours, at least for astronomical purposes. With the advent of mechanical clocks in the early 14th century, sundials with equal hours gradually came into general use.

Water clocks and clepsydras. Simple water clocks were used in Egypt to record time at night or when the sun was obscured; examples from about 1400 BC survive. These were bucket-shaped vessels from which water was allowed to escape by a small hole at the base. Uniform scales of time, one for each month to allow for the different seasonal length of Egyptian hours, were marked on the inside. By the end of the first hour, water filled to the brim would have fallen to the first mark of the scale of the month in question. The difficulty of regulating the pressure of outflow of these clocks, only partly achieved by the sloping sides of the vessel, and the variations in viscosity of water, according to the temperature, rendered them inaccurate.

From Egypt, water clocks were introduced into the classical world and called clepsydras (Greek *kleptein*, "to steal," and *hydōr*, "water"). By adjusting the outflow, Greeks and Romans were able to make such clocks record regular temporal hours. The Roman clepsydra took the form of a cylinder into which water dripped from a reservoir. Readings were taken against a scale with a float in the cylinder. With a full reservoir, irregularity of flow was minimized. Vitruvius describes a water clock with a wheel and ratchet mechanism. A shaft attached to the float had teeth that engaged a cogwheel fixed to a pointer moving over a dial. Such dial clocks were perfected by the Chinese and Arabs and used in Europe until the 16th century.

Sand glasses. Along with the development of water clocks during the 1st century AD, sand glasses, which measured time by means of sand running from one glass vessel to another through a narrow passage, were introduced. Some of these devices were quite large, running for up to an hour. During the 16th and 17th centuries, sand glasses were made to run for periods of fifteen and thirty minutes; some were used in churches to time the length of sermons. At a later period a long narrow sand glass was used in pulpits; similar in appearance to a test tube with a pinched center, this device was slotted into a board with markings indicating periods of up to twenty minutes. The sand glass was pivoted in the center so that it could be swivelled to start the sand pouring. There exists a leather case with four sand glasses fitted so that all are visible and made to run for a quarter, half, three-quarters, and one full hour; this device was made sometime during the 16th century.

Lamps and candle clocks. Lamp clocks appeared about the same time as hour glasses. These devices looked much like a candlestick with a glass bottle at their top and a horizontal projection at the side to hold the wick. Oil would drain from the glass bottle into a small tube into which a small wick was inserted; as the oil burnt away, the level of oil in the glass reservoir would lower. Numbers inscribed on the side of the bottle would indicate the hour. During the 17th century, lamp clocks of various forms were made and used in the countries of the Middle East, and in Europe, especially Germany.

King Alfred the Great of Wessex (849–899) is said to have used candles to measure the passage of time. Each candle, placed in a lantern with horn-shaped sides to protect the flame from drafts, was made long enough to burn away in four hours.

MECHANICAL AND ELECTRICAL CLOCKS

Weight-driven clocks of the 14th century. The origin of the all-mechanical escapement clocks (see below) is still unknown, although it is possible that the first such devices were invented and used in monasteries to sound an alarm and so alert the sacristan to toll a bell that called the monks to prayers. The first mechanical clocks to which clear references exist were large, weight-driven machines, fitted into towers, and known as turret clocks. These early devices were timepieces only; they did not strike the hour, nor did they have hands and a dial. They simply contained an alarm which would alert the keeper to toll a bell for the benefit of the public.

Public striking clocks

The first public striking clock (*i.e.*, that struck the hour) was made and erected in Milan, Italy in 1335. During the next decades, public striking clocks made their appearance in the principal cities of the Continent. The oldest surviving clock in England is that at Salisbury Cathedral, which dates from 1386. A clock erected at Rouen, France, in 1389 is still extant, and one built for Wells Cathedral, England, is preserved in the Science Museum, London. The Salisbury clock strikes the hours, and those of Rouen and Wells also have mechanisms for ringing chimes at the quarter hour. Other English clocks of somewhat later date were large, iron-framed structures driven by falling weights attached to a cord wrapped around a drum and regulated by a mechanism known as a verge (or crown wheel) escapement. The escapement, so called because it allows the power of the falling weight to escape at regular intervals.

Figure 1 shows the verge escapement. A crossbar or foliot carries two regulating weights and is mounted on a vertical spindle, carrying two projections or pallets. As the foliot swings to and fro, the teeth of the weight-driven escape wheel are released one by one. As each tooth is released, it gives an impulse to the pallet and thus keeps the foliot swinging. The time of a swing depends on the driving weight and upon the position of the weights on the foliot. Their errors probably were as large as a half hour per day. The first domestic clocks were smaller versions of these large public clocks. They appeared late in the 14th century and few examples have survived; most of them, extremely austere in design, had no cases or means of protection from dust. These clocks stood on a pedestal with an aperture to accommodate the weights. Eventually the foliot gave way to the balance, a circular wheel without teeth, in domestic clocks. The foliot and the balance preceded the pendulum by more than 300 years.

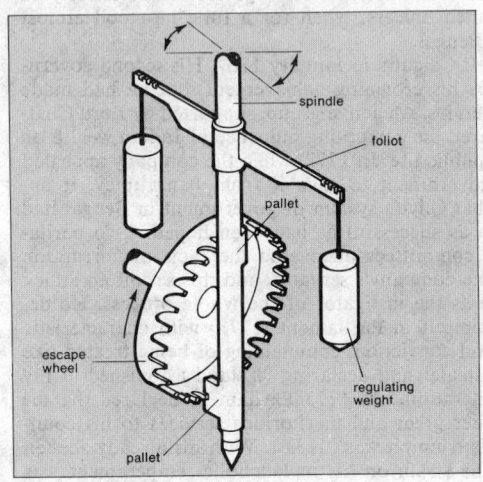

Figure 1: Verge escapement mechanism.

Spring-driven clocks. About 1500 Peter Henlein, a German locksmith, began to make small clocks driven by a spring. These were the first portable timepieces, representing one of the great strides in horology; from this period to the end of the century, progress was great. The dials of these clocks, placed on the top, and possessing an hour hand only (minute hands did not appear until 1670), was exposed to the air; there was no form of cover such as a glass until the first quarter of the 17th century (see *The watch* below).

From the end of the 16th century, clocks were made in the upright form, but still with the balance as controller. They were similar to the domestic weight-driven clocks described above, but were not portable. During the early part of the 17th century, the mechanism was enclosed; the cases were made of brass and a style developed known as lantern clocks.

Pendulum clocks. About 1582 Galileo (1564–1642) noticed the characteristic timekeeping property of the pendulum, which, in the form of a weight attached to a cord of predetermined length, was used by members of the medical profession to count the pulse of a patient. It was the Dutch astronomer and physicist Christiaan Huygens (1629–95) who was responsible for the general application of the pendulum as a time controller in clocks from 1656 onward. Huygens' invention brought about a great increase in the importance and extent of clockmaking. Clocks, weight driven, with short pendulums, were encased in wood and made to hang on the wall. In 1670 the long, or seconds, pendulum was introduced by William Clement, an English clockmaker. The next step was to enclose the pendulum and weights, and the long case or grandfather clock was born.

Application of the pendulum

The great virtue of the pendulum as a time measurer lies in the fact that, for small arcs, the time required for a complete swing (period) depends only on the length of the pendulum and is almost independent of the extent of the arc. The length of a pendulum beating seconds with a bob (weight) and a light rod is about 39 inches (990 millimetres), and an increase in length of 0.001 inch

(0.025 millimetres) will make the clock lose about one second per day. Altering the length of a pendulum is, therefore, a sensitive means of regulation. The alteration is usually carried out by allowing the bob to rest upon a nut that can be screwed up or down the pendulum rod.

Any expansion or contraction of the rod caused by changes of temperature will affect the timekeeping of a pendulum; *e.g.*, a pendulum clock with a steel rod will lose one second a day for a rise in temperature of 4° F (2.2° C), and will gain one second per day for a similar fall in temperature. If accurate timekeeping is required, the pendulum must be compensated by some device which will keep its length as constant as possible. This may be done in several ways, some of which use the differing coefficients of expansion (the amount of expansion per degree change in temperature) of different metals to obtain a cancelling-out effect. In one popular compensation method, the bob consists of a glass or metal jar containing a suitable amount of mercury. The gridiron pendulum employs rods of brass and steel, while in the zinc-iron tube, the pendulum rod is made up of concentric tubes of zinc and iron. A less expensive method, however, is to make the pendulum rod from a special alloy called Invar. This material has such a small coefficient of expansion that small changes of temperature have a negligible effect.

Invar alloy pendulums

The escapement of a pendulum clock usually consists of two parts: an escape wheel of special shape geared to the clock's main train of wheels, and an oscillating system linked with the pendulum and carrying two projections or pallets that engage alternately with the teeth of the escape wheel. The wheel is allowed to escape through the pitch of one tooth for each swing of the pendulum, and in escaping it transmits an impulse through the pallets to the pendulum to keep it swinging. An ideal escapement would perform both functions without interfering with the free swing; the more closely an actual escapement approaches this standard, the better it is.

Improved escapements. When first introduced, the pendulum was used with the verge escapement (Figure 1), but eventually adapted to pendulum control. In a short time the verge was replaced by the anchor or recoil escapement, invented in England about 1660 by Robert Hooke. This was a great improvement and is still used for many domestic clocks.

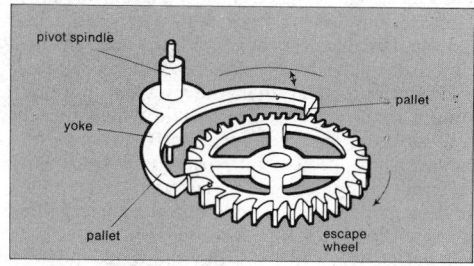

Figure 2: Recoil escapement.

Recoil escapement

The recoil escapement (Figure 2) has two pallets mounted on the ends of a curved bar or yoke that spans a part of the circumference of the escape wheel. At a point approximately equidistant from both pallets, the yoke is attached to a pivoted spindle linked to the pendulum by a light bar, or crutch. As the pendulum swings it causes the pallet spindle to oscillate, and this in turn engages and disengages the pallets with the teeth of the escape wheel, so permitting the wheel to advance in a step-by-step motion. The inclined acting faces of the pallets not only arrest and release the teeth of the escape wheel but also transmit to the pendulum, in the form of impulses, some of the energy used to drive the clock. Because of the construction of the pallets, however, any additional swing made by the pendulum after a tooth has engaged with them causes the escape wheel to recoil. This defect was modified by a device known as the deadbeat escapement (Figure 3) invented in 1715 by the British inventor George Graham (1675–1751), who also devised mer-

curial compensation for pendulums. The deadbeat escapement is used in precision clocks.

In the deadbeat escapement the acting surfaces of the pallets have two distinct parts, known as the dead and impulse faces. The teeth of the escape wheel fall first upon the dead faces and rest upon them before the movement of the pallets allows them to reach the impulse faces and finally to escape.

The dead faces of the pallets are made in the shape of arcs of a circle whose centre is the arbor carrying the pallets, so that as the pallet system moves with an escape wheel tooth resting upon a dead face, the escape wheel remains at rest; there is no recoil. The wheel is then neither pushing the pallet nor recoiling from it, the only interaction being a slight friction. To minimize interference still further by reducing friction, the pallets of very precise clocks have pieces of jewel inserted in their acting faces.

One of the defects of both the recoil and deadbeat escapements is that the impulse they transmit to the pendulum can vary because of variations in the power transmitted by the wheelwork. Such changes arise from thickening of the oil, from dust, wear or, in the case of tower clocks, wind pressure and snow or ice on the hands. To overcome this, a number of inventors designed escape-

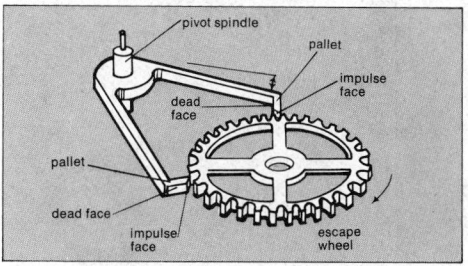

Figure 3: Deadbeat escapement.

ments in which weighted arms are raised by the escape wheel and then delivered the impulse of the pendulum as they descended to their original position. The first really successful escapement of this kind was invented about 1853 by J.M. Bloxam, a barrister. A much better form, the double three-legged gravity escapement, was invented by Edmund Beckett, afterward Lord Grimthorpe (1816–1905), and used by him for the great clock at Westminster, now generally known as Big Ben, which was installed in 1859. It has since become standard for all really accurate tower clocks.

The mechanism of a modern mechanical clock. The wheelwork or train of a clock is the series of moving machine parts (gears) that transmits motion from a weight or spring to the minute and hour hands. With all but the gravity escapement, it is most important that the energy transmitted by the wheelwork be as constant as possible. The wheels and pinions must be made accurately, and the tooth form designed so that the transference of power takes place as steadily as possible. Advances in gear design and manufacture have made present-day clocks far better than older ones in this respect.

Constant motion from weight to hands

In a weight-driven or spring-driven clock, the power of the weight or spring is first transmitted by the great or main wheel. This engages with the first pinion (a gear with a small number of teeth designed to mesh with a larger wheel), whose spindle (a turning rod to which gears are attached) is attached to the second wheel that, in its turn, engages with the second pinion, and so on, down through the train to the escapement. The gear ratios are such that one spindle, usually the second or third, rotates once an hour and can be used to carry the minute hand. A simple 12-to-1 gearing, known as the motion work, gives the necessary step-down ratio to drive the hour hand. The spring or weight is fitted with a mechanism so it can be rewound when necessary, and the spindle carrying the minute hand is provided with a simple slipping clutch that allows the hands to be set to the correct time.

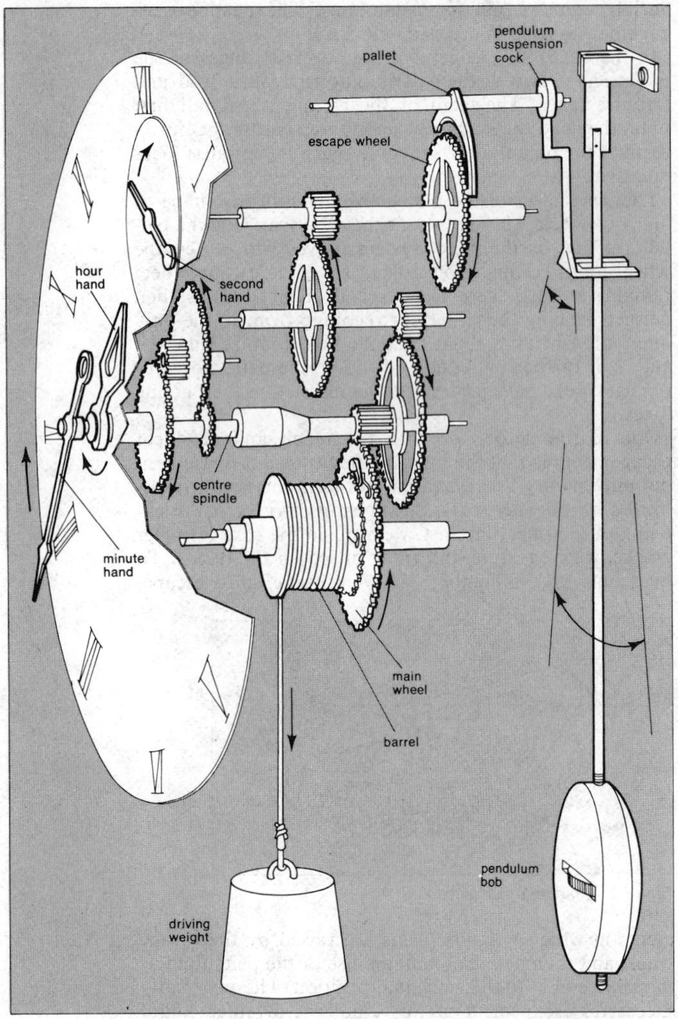

Figure 4: Weight-driven clock.

The timekeeping part of all clocks, including large tower clocks, is substantially the same. Figure 4 shows the mechanism of a simple weight-driven timepiece with a pendulum. The frame is made up of two plates that carry the pivots of the various wheels and other moving parts and that are united and spaced by four pillars. The driving weight hangs from a line coiled around the drum and is wound by means of the winding square. The main wheel engages with the centre pinion on the spindle of which is also mounted the centre wheel. The front pivot of this wheel and pinion is lengthened to the left of the illustration, and carries the minute hand and part of the gearing necessary to drive the hour hand.

The centre wheel is also coupled through a suitable gear train to the escape wheel, which engages with the pallets, that are fixed to the spindle and pivot between the front plate and the pendulum suspension cock. Also fixed to the pallet spindle is the crutch, which terminates at its lower end in a fork that embraces the pendulum rod. This pendulum is suspended by a thin flat suspension spring.

Driving the hour hands

The motion work used for driving the hands at their relative speeds is mounted between the dial and the front plate of the frame. The wheel driving the hour hand rotates once an hour; it is coupled to the centre spindle by a flat spring that acts as a clutch and permits the hands to be set.

Electrical clocks. Electrical currents are used in two different ways in clocks: to replace the weight or spring as a source of power, and as a means of signalling time indications from a central master clock to a wide range of distant indicating dials. Invented in 1840, the first battery electric clock was driven by a spring and pendulum, and employed an electrical impulse to operate a number of dials. Considerable experimental work followed, and it was not until 1906 that the first self-contained battery-driven clock was invented.

Master clock system

In a master clock system electricity is used to give direct impulses to the pendulum that in turn causes the clock's gear train to move, or to lift a lever after it has imparted an impulse to the pendulum. In various modern master clocks the pendulum operates a light count wheel that turns through the pitch of one tooth every double swing and is arranged to release a lever every half-minute. This lever gives an impulse to the pendulum and is then restored to its original position by an electromagnet. The pulse of current that operates the electromagnet can also be transmitted to a series of distant dials, advancing the hands of each through the space of a half-minute. Thus a master clock can control scores of dials in a large group of buildings, as well as such other apparatus as time recorders and sirens.

Electrical master clocks of this type are good timekeepers, since the impulse can be given symmetrically as the pendulum passes through its middle position and the interference with its motion is small.

Synchronous electric clocks. With the application of the synchronous electric motor to clocks in 1918, domestic electric clocks became popular. A synchronous electric motor runs in step with the frequency of the electric power source, which in most countries alternates at 60 hertz (cycles per second). The electric motor is coupled to a reduction gearing that drives the clock hands at the correct rate.

The synchronous electric clock has no timekeeping properties in itself, and is wholly dependent upon the frequency stability of the alternating current supplied by the power station. If this frequency is changed for some reason, the electric clock will not keep correct time. Power stations are under no obligation to maintain a constant frequency, but it is usually so carefully controlled that the time shown on a synchronous electric clock is normally correct to within a few seconds.

Shortt pendulum clock. The most accurate mechanical timekeeper is the Shortt pendulum clock; it makes use of the movement described above for electric master clock systems. The Shortt pendulum clock consists of two separate clocks, one of which synchronizes the other. The timekeeping element is a pendulum that swings freely, except that once every half-minute it receives an impulse from a gently falling lever. This lever is released by an electrical signal transmitted from its slave clock. After the impulse has been sent, a synchronizing signal is transmitted back to the slave clock that ensures that the impulse to the free pendulum will be released exactly a half-minute later than the previous impulse. The pendulum swings in a sealed box in which the air is kept at a constant, low pressure. Shortt clocks in observatories are kept in a room, usually a basement, where the temperature remains as constant as possible, and under these conditions can maintain the correct time to within a few thousandths of a second per day.

Quartz-crystal clocks. In 1929 the quartz crystal was first applied to timekeeping; this invention was probably the single greatest contribution to precision time measurement. Quartz crystals oscillating at frequencies of 100,000 hertz (cycles per second) can be compared and frequency differences determined to an accuracy of one part in 10^{10}.

Quartz clock time-keeping element

The timekeeping element of a quartz clock consists of a ring of quartz about two-and-one-half inches (64 millimetres) in diameter, suspended by threads and enclosed in a heat-insulated chamber. Electrodes are attached to the surfaces of the ring and connected to an electrical circuit in such a manner as to sustain oscillations (see also PIEZOELECTRIC DEVICES). Since the frequency of vibration, 100,000 hertz, is too high for convenient time measurement, it is reduced by a process known as frequency division or demultiplication, and applied to a synchronous motor connected to a clock dial through mechanical gearing. If a 100,000 hertz frequency, for example, is subjected to a combined electrical and mechanical gearing reduction of 6,000,000 to one, then the second hand of the synchronous clock will make exactly one rotation in 60 seconds. The vibrations are so constant that the maximum error of an observatory quartz-crystal clock is only a few ten-thousandths of a second per day, equivalent to an error of one second every ten years.

Originally, quartz-crystal clocks were fairly large, but size has been reduced; a quartz-crystal clock operating from the power line and measuring ten inches (250 millimetres) high by four inches (100 millimetres) wide and four inches deep, has been produced in Switzerland. Rechargeable batteries contained within the clock will keep it working for five days should the power fail. Maximum error is in the order of one second per day.

Light clock. Invented and manufactured in Switzerland, the light clock contains a conventional watch movement and tiny storage batteries kept charged by photoelectric cells exposed to light. The batteries drive a tiny electric motor, which in turn winds the mainspring of the watch movement. Fully charged, the batteries can operate the clock for at least 12 months without being recharged.

THE WATCH

The word watch is derived from the Old English *wæcce*, which designated those who kept observation; that is, the watchmen of the night who called the hours. When watches were first made is uncertain, but there can be little doubt that the first appeared shortly after the invention of the mainspring (see below) about 1500, by Peter Henlein, a locksmith, in Nuremberg, Germany. Clocks had originally been weight driven, but after the invention of the mainspring, they could be made truly portable. The escapement used in the early watches was the same as that used in the early clocks, the verge escapement shown in Figure 1. Early watches were made in Germany, and at Blois in France. These early timepieces were large, measuring some four to five inches (100 to 125 millimetres) in diameter, and about three inches (75 millimetres) deep. They were carried about in the hand, and some old engravings illustrate a servant carrying a clock while following his master.

First watches

The mainspring. A mainspring consists of a flat spring steel band stressed in bending or coiling; when the watch, clock, or any spring-driven mechanism, is wound, the curvature of the spring is increased, and energy thus stored. In a watch, this energy is transmitted to the oscillating section of the watch (called the balance) by the wheel train and escapement, the motion of the balance itself controlling the release of the escapement and consequently the timing of the maintaining impulse. A friction drive to the hands is provided from a wheel rotating at a convenient rate, usually once per hour. The friction drive permits the hands to be set.

In the first spring-driven timekeepers the mainspring was hooked to an arbor (small shaft) at its centre or "eye," while its outer end was attached to the frame. A ratchet and click allowed the arbor to be rotated during winding without disturbing the first wheel or "great wheel" of the train.

Improvements in early watches. One of the main defects of the early watches was the variation in the torque output of the mainspring; that is, the force of the mainspring was greater when fully wound than when it was almost run down. Since the timekeeping of a watch fitted with a verge escapement is greatly influenced by the force driving it, this problem was quite serious. An attempted remedy was the stackfreed, a device that acted against the pull of the mainspring when fully wound, exerting less restraint as the mainspring ran down. The stackfreed was, in effect, little more than a crude auxiliary spring. Solution of the problem was advanced between 1515 and 1540 by the invention, by Jacob the Czech of Prague, of the fusee, a cone-shaped grooved pulley used together with a barrel containing the mainspring. With this arrangement, the mainspring is made to rotate a barrel in which it is housed; a length of catgut, later replaced by a chain, is wound on it, the other end being coiled around the fusee. When the mainspring is fully wound, the gut or chain pulls on the smallest radius of the cone-shaped fusee; as the mainspring runs down,

The fusee

the leverage is progressively increased as the gut or chain pulls on a larger radius. With correct proportioning of mainspring and fusee radii, an almost constant torque is maintained as the mainspring unwinds. A later invention, the going barrel, a device to keep the watch going during winding, is fitted to all modern watches and has superseded the fusee. By carefully proportioning the barrel arbor (the shaft of the barrel) and barrel diameters to the thickness of the mainspring, torque variations have been reduced to a minimum. Because the average length of run of the modern watch is over 30 hours, the centre part of the mainspring is used.

Up to about 1580, the mechanisms of watches were made wholly of iron; at about this time, brass was introduced. It was not until about 1625, however, that brass was used for some parts of the watch, and steel for the more delicate pieces.

In the earliest timekeepers, a weighted crossbar (foliot) or a wheel with a heavy rim known as the balance was used to control the rate of going of the mechanism. It was subjected to no systematic constraint, and it was not possible to define its period of oscillation mathematically. Consequently, its period of oscillation, and, hence, the rate of the timekeeper, were dependent on the driving force; this explains the great importance of the fusee.

Robert Hooke claimed to be the first to control the oscillations of a balance by a hairspring or balance spring, c. 1660; it was applied to watches for him by Thomas Tompion. The balance spring is a delicate ribbon of steel or other suitable spring material, generally wound into a spiral form. The inner end is pinned into a collet (a small collar), which fits friction-tight on the balance staff, while the outer end is held in a stud fixed to the movement. This spring acts on the balance as gravity does on the pendulum. If the balance is displaced to one side the spring is wound and energy stored in it; this energy is then restored to the balance, causing it to swing nearly the same distance to the other side, if the balance is released.

Use of the balance spring

If there were no frictional losses (*e.g.*, air friction, internal friction in the spring material, and friction at the pivots), the balance would swing precisely the same distance to the other side and continue to oscillate indefinitely; because of these losses, however, the oscillations in practice die away. It is the energy stored in the mainspring and fed to the balance through the wheel train and escapement that maintains the oscillations. The frequency of the balance is generally one-fifth of a second or 18,000 vibrations per hour.

The mechanism of a modern watch. *Balance wheel and hairspring.* A watch's performance depends on the uniformity of the period of oscillation of the balance; *i.e.*, the regularity of its movement. The balance takes the form of a wheel with a heavy rim, while the spring coupled to it provides the restoring torque (see Figure 5A). The balance possesses inertia, dependent on its mass and configuration. The spring should ideally provide a restoring force directly proportional to the displacement from its unstressed or zero position.

The balance is mounted on a staff or spindle with pivots and, in watches of good quality, these run in jewels. Two jewels are used at each end of the balance staff (item 15 in Figure 5A), one pierced to provide a bearing, the other a flat end stone providing axial location by bearing against the domed end of the pivot. Frictional effects at the pivots influence the performance of the watch in various positions; for example, lying and hanging.

The balance and spring can be brought to time or "regulated" by varying either the restoring couple provided by the spring or the inertia of the balance. In the first case (by far the more common), this is generally effected by providing a pair of curb pins mounted on a movable regulator index which lengthen or shorten the hairspring as needed.

In the second instance, screws are provided at one of two pairs of opposite points on the rim of the balance wheel: these screws are friction-tight in their holes and thus can be moved in or out so as to adjust the inertia of the balance. In "free-sprung" watches no regulator index

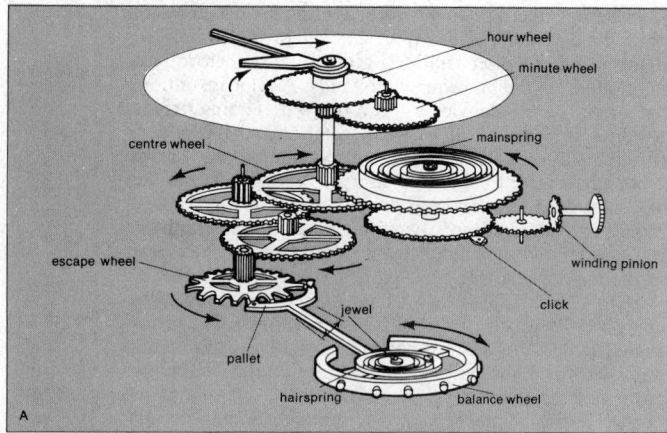

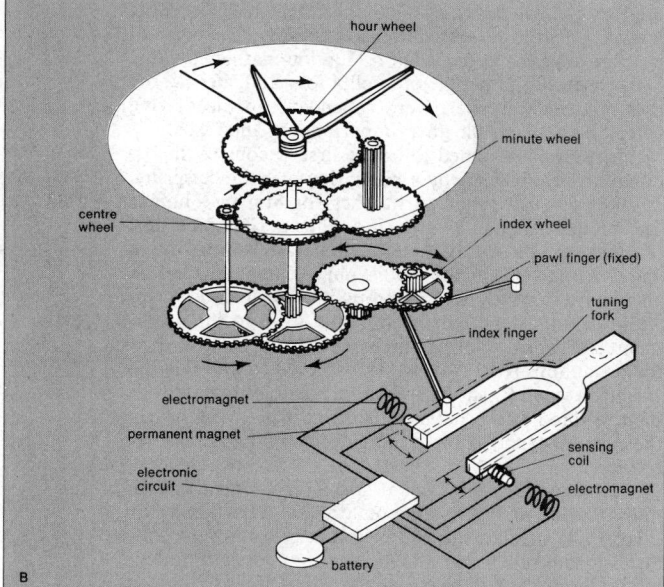

Figure 5: Components of (A) mechanical watch and (B) electrical watch.

In good quality watches, the club-toothed wheel is made of hardened steel, with the acting surfaces ground and polished; its geometry reduces loss of motion between wheel and pallets. The lever escapement is also characterized by double-roller safety action in which the intersection between the guard pin and roller, which takes place underneath the roller, is much deeper than in early single rollers; thus, any friction caused by jolts encountered in wear causes less constraint on the balance and endangers the timekeeping properties of the watch less. By far the most important watch escapement today, the lever escapement is used in its jeweled form in watches of moderate to excellent quality and with steel pallet pins and a simplified fork and roller action in cheap watches (known as pin pallet watches).

Gear train. In the wheel train of a modern watch, it is necessary to achieve a step-up ratio of approximately one to 4,000 between barrel and escape wheel. This involves four pairs of gears, the ratio per pair commonly being between six to one and ten to one. Because of space considerations, the pinions must have a low number of leaves (projections), commonly six to twelve. This entails a number of special gearing problems, aggravated by the fineness of their pitch. Any error in centre distance, form, or concentricity is therefore proportionately more important than in larger types of gearing.

Jewels. The first patent covering the application of jewels in watches was taken out in 1704; diamonds and sapphires were used. The sapphires were pierced with diamond splints and steel wires charged with diamond powder; this was practised only in England until about 1790. Synthetic jewels are now commonly used; they are made from fused powdered alumina (aluminum oxide).

Watch jewels are prepared from the raw jewel to exceedingly close limits and are given a very high polish. A uniform outside diameter for the jewel bearings is highly important, since they are fitted by the friction jewelling method, being pressed into accurately sized holes smaller than the jewels themselves and held there by friction. The hole diameter of a typical balance jewel is about 0.1 millimetre.

Preparing watch jewels

Special purpose watches. A chronometer is a timekeeping device of great accuracy, particularly one used for determining longitude at sea. The word was originally employed to denote any time-measuring instrument. Early weight- and pendulum-driven clocks were highly inaccurate at sea due to temperature changes and the ship's motion. It was not until the 18th century when John Harrison, a self-taught English carpenter, invented and constructed four practical marine timekeepers, the fourth of which won him the reward of 20,000 pounds offered in 1714 by the British government for any means of determining a ship's longitude within 30 nautical miles (34 miles) at the end of a six week's voyage. A timekeeper fulfilling this condition would have to keep time within three seconds per day, a standard that, at the date the reward was offered, had not been attained by the best pendulum clocks on shore. Though Harrison's original invention was complicated, delicate, and costly, his success led to further investigations by others and eventually to the modern marine chronometer.

The first chronometer

The modern chronometer. The modern chronometer is, broadly speaking, a large, well-made watch, suspended in gimbals (a set of two rings connected by bearings) so poised as to remain horizontal whatever the inclination of the ship. It is thus safeguarded from those alterations of position which slightly affect the timekeeping of even the best watches. In addition, it differs somewhat in its mechanism from the ordinary watch, the spiral balance spring and lever escapement of the latter being replaced by a helical balance spring and a spring detent or "chronometer" escapement. This form of escapement is mechanically superior to any other, and requires no oiling other than at the pivots, but is not suitable for use in pocket watches, because if given a more or less circular twist, it will "trip," causing a rapid gain. For the purpose of equalizing the force of the mainspring, almost all chronometers are fitted with a fusee (no longer used in watches) and chronometer compensation balances, by

is provided, and the only adjustment available is the screws on the balance rim.

Timing errors

There are several other types of errors in timekeeping that may result from minor maladjustments in the mechanism of the watch. Curb pin errors, for example, occur when the regulator curb pins are not correctly adjusted. The pins must not grip the spring for this will cause the spring to buckle when the index is moved. Escapement error results when the escapement, whose function is to supply the balance and spring with energy obtained from the mainspring via the wheel train to keep the balance in oscillation, does not give impulses at the proper time. As a result, the balance may receive a forward impulse when they are approaching zero position, and the watch will run too fast. Alternatively, if the balance receives a backward impulse while approaching zero position, the watch will run slow. Changes in temperature may also affect the performance of the watch by causing the spring to lose its elasticity, thus changing the period of oscillation of the balance. Several approaches to this problem, including the use of special alloys such as Invar, have been used.

Escapement. Of the great number of escapements invented, some have already been discussed. Many modern mechanical watches use a lever escapement (Figure 5A). Originally invented in 1765 by Thomas Mudge, this escapement leaves the balance free to turn, coupling to it only while receiving the impulse from the mainspring via the wheel train and while unlocking. It was developed into its modern form with the club-toothed escape wheel at the beginning of the 19th century but was not universally adopted until the early 20th century.

Lever escapement

which the effects of heat and cold upon their timekeeping are practically nullified. Chronometers are also larger and heavier than ordinary watches.

The chronograph. Developed in 1855 to measure time intervals in addition to the time of day (in sports events, for example), the chronograph contains an additional second hand that is engaged with the wheel train by pressing the pendant or stem of the watch, disengaged by a second pressure, and returned to zero by a third. Split-second chronographs have two chronograph second hands; these begin to move together, and one can be stopped to take a reading and then made to catch up with the other. It is thus possible to clock the times of more than one competitor in a race.

The stopwatch. The stopwatch is made for purposes that do not warrant the more expensive chronograph. In a stopwatch, the balance is actually started and stopped, whereas in the chronograph it oscillates continually. Minute and sometimes hour recorders are added to chronographs and to stopwatches. All the hands are returned to zero when required by the action of strikers pressing against heart-shaped cams. In certain cases, the balance vibrates more rapidly than the usual 18,000 half-cycles per hour; it is thus possible to record tenths or hundredths of a second.

Self-winding watch. The first patent on the self-winding pocket watch was taken out in London in 1780. An English invention patented in 1924, the self-winding wrist watch contains a swinging weight pivoted at the centre of the movement, coupled to the barrel arbor through reduction wheels and gears. The modern self-winding watch is fitted with a weight or rotor that swings and winds 360 degrees in both directions. Though considerable development and refinement has followed the invention, self-winding watches still operate on the original principle.

There exist innumerable other special-purpose watches such as those used by the blind that strike a gong or other signal on the quarter hour and minutes, or that have a dial with braille-type numerals. Other watches maintain a perpetual calendar, show the phases of the moon, and the rising and setting of the sun.

Electrical and electronic watches. Electric powered watches use one of three drive systems: (1) the galvanometer drive, consisting of the conventional balance-hairspring oscillator, kept in motion by the magnetic interaction of a coil and a permanent magnet; (2) the induction drive, in which an electromagnet attracts a balance containing soft magnetic material; or (3) the resonance drive (illustrated in Figure 5B), in which a tiny tuning fork (about one inch or 25 millimetres in length) driven electrically, provides the motive power. Both types (1) and (2) use a mechanical contact, actuated by the balance motion, to provide properly timed electric drive pulses. Each oscillation of the balance operates a time-indicating gear train by advancing a toothed wheel one tooth. First produced in 1953, type (3), properly called an electronic watch, is inherently more accurate since it operates at a frequency higher than that customarily used with balance-type watches, and the tuning fork is a fairly stable source of frequency. The higher frequency requires the replacement of a mechanical contact by a transistor. The minute and rapid motion of the tuning fork moves forward an extremely fine-toothed ratchet wheel. There is very little friction in the electronic watch; only tiny amounts of oil are needed. When the battery is too weak to operate the tuning fork, the watch simply stops, without deterioration. Miniature high-energy-density batteries are used as power sources in all three types; these last for about twelve months.

(margin note: Tuning fork drive)

THE ATOMIC CLOCK

Accuracy exceeding even that of quartz-crystal clocks can be attained by atomic clocks that utilize and register oscillations taking place in individual atoms. These small electrical and magnetic vibrations are almost wholly independent of normal external conditions and, as their frequencies are a property of the atoms themselves, they are identical for all atoms of the same kind.

The ammonia maser or ammonia clock. A maser (acronym for microwave amplification by stimulated emission of radiation) is a device that can generate microwaves (high-frequency radio waves) of precise frequency or can amplify such waves. Developed in 1954, the ammonia maser utilizes the ammonia (NH_3) molecule that can exist in two different energy levels. In the ammonia maser, these two types of molecule are separated and those in the higher energy state enter a cavity. Some of the molecules fall to the lower energy state and in so doing, emit electromagnetic radiations of high and constant frequency. These oscillations can be employed for the precise determination of time.

The cesium clock. In one of the most commonly used types of atomic clocks, first investigated in the United States in 1952, the atoms used are those of cesium. In a magnetic field, each cesium atom behaves like a small magnet. The polarization of the atoms can be made to change direction if they are placed in an alternating magnetic field where the frequency of the alternations is equal to the natural frequency of the cesium atoms.

In practice, the frequency of the alternating field is varied slowly until the maximum response is obtained at the detector, and the frequency is then known to be exactly equal to that of the cesium atoms. The tuning is so precise that the frequency can be measured to 1 part in 30,000,000,000—equivalent to a discrepancy of one second in 1,000 years. This is the accuracy of the second cesium atomic clock installed at the National Physical Laboratory at Teddington, near London.

Other types of atomic clocks include those that employ the element rubidium instead of cesium and those employing hydrogen or rubidium.

THE WATCH AND CLOCK INDUSTRY

Production techniques. The earliest watchmakers and clockmakers were hand craftsmen, many of whom had formerly been locksmiths or blacksmiths. Watches and clocks were made in Germany, Italy, France, and England.

Up to about 1850, England led in watch manufacture, with the trade centred in London, Liverpool, and Coventry. The watchmaker was really an assembler who procured the various parts from specialists (escapement makers, dial makers, hand makers, and case makers). He would fit the balance spring and time the watch, making it ready for sale. Either the name of the maker, or the vendor for whom the watch was made, was engraved on the movement and marked on the dial. This form of production continued until about 1914; the watches produced were almost all pocket watches.

In the market square at Le Locle, Switzerland, there stands a statue of a boy in a blacksmith's apron; his name is Daniel Jean-Richard (1672–1741). It is said that an English horse dealer passing through town showed his broken watch to Daniel's father, and that Daniel implored the Englishman to let him repair it. He was so intrigued with this extraordinary piece of mechanism that he determined to make one himself and after eighteen months succeeded. The five sons of Jean-Richard ended by devoting themselves to this new industry.

(margin note: Origin of the Swiss watch industry)

The Swiss were a community of farmers and the opportunity to work indoors during the long winter months was welcome. By about 1800 whole families were engaged in making parts of watches. The master maker would then assemble and market the watches.

By 1850 the Swiss began to invest in watchmaking machinery. The English meanwhile were content to continue in the old hand-production methods; as time passed, Swiss watch production equalled, then surpassed that of Britain. By 1900 the takeover was almost complete. The English struggled on, still making high quality watches (mainly pocket watches for men) by hand, and producing a few pocket and wrist watches by machine methods. Wrist and bracelet watches began to become popular about 1900 and were firmly established by 1914. Scorned by the English watchmakers as absurd, they were made in Switzerland and France. By the 1920s, watch manufacturing had become one of Switzerland's most important industries. Japan entered the field about this time, but the Soviet Union did not begin large-scale production until the 1960s. Also significant producers of watches, the Americans are credited with introduction of mass-production techniques to Switzerland.

Highly and efficiently organized, the watch trade in Switzerland today has assumed almost governmental status. The Fédération Suisse des Associations de Fabricants d'Horlogerie (the Swiss Federation of the Associations of Watch Manufacturers) controls the industry, dictating product quality and prices charged. The master watchmaker, known as the *établisseur*, takes financial responsibility for the finished watches. The rough unfinished movement, known as the *ébauche*, is made in special factories, under strict conditions of quality control for the different component parts. For example, there are three qualities of jewels, six qualities of mainsprings, nine qualities of escapement, and four qualities of balance spring.

The master maker begins by procuring rough movements from an *ébauche* maker, then finishes them in his own factory or sends them to a finisher. The movements then go to the jewelling manufacturer and to the escapement maker. Finally the master maker procures dials, hands, winding buttons, and cases, completes assembly, and times the watches.

In assembly, some parts of the movement are oiled and assembled automatically. Next, the partly assembled movement is placed in a circular plastic container that is covered with a transparent plastic lid with an opening. When the operator presses a foot pedal the lower part of the container rotates and a movement is automatically pushed up through the opening. The operator then assembles some parts to the movement. When the whole container has been completed, it is removed and passed on to another operator who adds more parts and so on until each movement is fully assembled. Where it is necessary to make some finer assembly and adjustment, a special form of binocular glass is employed and, by depressing a button on the side, a puff of air is blown on to the movement to ensure freedom from dust.

Electronic timing test

When completely assembled, each watch is submitted to an electronic timing test. The first test ensures that the watch is in a fit condition and will respond to regulation. Next, each watch is timed while it is automatically placed in different positions. Results of the timing test are recorded on a band of paper, and the proper adjustments made to correct any errors.

It is possible for a watch to be made using the same *ébauche*, with either the best, or inferior components; the mechanism will appear precisely the same. *Ébauche* manufacturers stamp their products with an identification mark, and the parts comprising the movement are numbered so that a watch repairer can obtain spare parts with ease.

Finally, to ensure that the reputation of the Swiss watch-manufacturing industry is maintained, a spot check is made at the point of export. A sample of watches is removed from a parcel and submitted to timing tests to ascertain that the timing is in accordance with the standard set for the production of the manufacturer dispatching the watches. If the samples selected are not up to standard, all the watches are tested and then returned to the manufacturer with the report. Roughly similar systems of manufacture prevail in the United States, Germany, and elsewhere.

World production. Worldwide watch and clock production amounts to approximately 152,000,000 units per year with Switzerland accounting for 69,500,000 units, mostly watches; the Soviet Union producing 36,000,000, mainly watches; Japan and the United States both producing 31,750,000 units—but with Japanese production mostly watches, and United States about equally divided between watches and clocks. The leading clock producer is Germany with 28,000,000 units, followed by France (9,000,000), the United Kingdom (5,100,000), and Italy (2,500,000).

BIBLIOGRAPHY. PAUL M. CHAMBERLAIN, *It's About Time* (1941), treats practically every form of escapement, with a short history of notable persons in the history of horology and many superb line drawings; DONALD DE CARLE, *Watch and Clock Encyclopedia*, 3rd ed. (1971), treats practically every part of clocks and watches, with sections devoted to antique clocks of Europe and the United States and nearly 1,500 line drawings; *Horology* (1965), a small and concise history from the early 14th century up to the Quartz Crystal Clock and Tuning Fork Watch of today; J. DRUMMOND ROBERTSON, *The Evolution of Clockwork* (1931), an important work on the development of clocks in general with a special section devoted to clocks of Japan; R.N. and M.L. MAYALL, *Sundials* (1938), an excellent book treating the history, use, and making of sundials; R.T. GOULD, *The Marine Chronometer* (1923), devoted entirely to the development of the marine chronometer, its history and construction; S.F. PHILPOTT, *Modern Electric Clocks*, 4th ed. (1949), deals with all forms of electric clock, including turret clocks and the Shortt Free Pendulum Clock.

(D.de C.)

Clothing and Footwear Industry

The clothing and footwear industries, sometimes called the apparel and allied industries, the soft-goods industries, or the garment industries, include factories and mills producing outerwear, underwear, headwear, footwear, belts, purses, luggage, gloves, scarfs, ties, and household soft goods such as drapes, linens, and slipcovers. The same raw materials and equipment are used to fashion these different end products.

HISTORY

In the late Stone Age northern Europeans made garments of animal skins sewn together with leather thongs. Holes were made in the skin and a thong drawn through with a hooked instrument something like a crochet hook. In southern Europe fine bone needles from the same period indicate that woven garments were already worn. Weaving and embroidery were developed in the ancient civilizations of the Middle East. The equipment used in the fabrication of clothes remained simple and has, in fact, always lagged behind the development of techniques for spinning and weaving. An important advance took place in the Middle Ages, when iron needles were introduced in Europe.

All operations continued to be performed by hand until factory production of cloth was made possible by the invention of foot and water-powered machinery for spinning and weaving in the 18th century. This development in turn stimulated the invention of the sewing machine. After several attempts a practical machine was patented in 1830 by Barthélemy Thimonnier, of Paris, who produced 80 machines to manufacture army uniforms. But Thimonnier's machines were destroyed by a mob of tailors who feared unemployment. Thimonnier's design used one thread; an American, Elias Howe, improved on it significantly with a lock-stitch machine that used two threads, a needle, and a shuttle. Though patented, it was not accepted in the United States; Howe took it to England where he sold part of his patent rights. The objections of the American tailors and seamstresses were finally overcome by a machine designed in 1851 by Isaac M. Singer of Pittstown, N.Y. When the sewing machine was first introduced, it was used only for simple seams; the more complex sewing operations were still done with a hand needle. The machines before Singer's were hand powered, but Singer quickly popularized foot-power machines.

Invention of the sewing machine

Before the second half of the 19th century, the fabric or leather sections of clothing and footwear were cut by shears or by a short knife with a handle about 5 inches (13.5 centimetres) long and a 3-inch (7-centimetre) tapered blade. All pressing, whether the finished press or underpressing (between sewing operations), continued to be done with the stove-heated hand flatiron. The flatiron and the iron (later steel) needle were for a long time the only major advances in making clothing and footwear since caveman days. Tailors and dressmakers used hand needles, shears, short knives, and flatirons. Footwear was made using hand needles, curved awls, curved needles, pincers, lap stone, and hammers.

For many years the sewing machine was the only machine used by the clothing industry. The next major development was the introduction in England in 1860 of the band-knife machine that cut several thicknesses of cloth at one time. It was invented by John Barran of Leeds, the founder of the Leeds clothing industry, who substituted a knife edge for the saw edge of a woodworking machine. The resulting increased cutting productivity motivated the development of spreading machines to spread fabric from long bolts in lays composed of hundreds of plies of fabrics. The height and count of the lay depended on the thickness and density of the fabric as well as the blade-cutting height and power of the cutting machine.

The first spreading machines in the late 1890s, often built of wood, carried fabrics in either bolt or book-fold form as the workers propelled the spreading machines manually and aligned the superposed plies vertically on the cutting table, thus making the cutting lay. Although most of the early machines operated with their supporting wheels rotating on the cutting table, on some machines the wheels rode on the floor.

The Reece Machinery Company of the United States pioneered buttonhole machines at the end of the 19th century; later the Singer Company developed its own buttonhole machines and machines for sewing on buttons. The introduction of the Hoffman press enabled pressing to be done more quickly than by hand, although hand pressing is still used at various stages for high-grade garments. All of these developments made the factory production of clothing economic in industrialized countries. Though the first manufactured garments were shoddy in both make and materials, they were welcomed by poorer people, who previously had to make their own. As the industry developed it improved the quality of production and materials and catered more and more to the well-to-do.

Social aspects. Until the second half of the 19th century, nearly all clothes and shoes were produced by individual tailors and cobblers working either alone or with one or two apprentices or journeymen. The goal of every apprentice tailor was to learn to make an entire garment as soon as possible. The output of a tailor or seamstress was usually limited to specific women's, men's, or children's garments; the journeyman sought to learn as much as possible from a specialized master craftsman. The same apprentice–journeyman system prevailed in the footwear industry, in which all cobbler craftsmen were male.

The advent of the sewing machine enlarged craftsmen's shops and converted them to factories. In many factories workers owned their machines and carried them from factory to factory whenever they changed jobs. Needleworkers lugging their machines on their backs were a common sight on the downtown East side streets of New York City, the garment-manufacturing capital of the world at the turn of the 20th century. Taking advantage of the low capital investment per worker, many clothing entrepreneurs began to farm out their cut garments to be sewn at home. The bundle brigades—men, women, and children trudging through the streets lugging bundles of cut or finished garments to and from their flats in the East side tenements—replaced the sewing-machine carriers of previous years.

Most apparel factories at this time were as crowded, poorly lit, airless, and unsanitary as the home workshops. The term sweatshop was coined for such factories and home workshops at the beginning of the 20th century, when workers in the apparel industries began forming unions to get better pay and working conditions. The International Ladies' Garment Workers' Union, organized in 1900, and the Amalgamated Clothing Workers of America, formed in 1914, became pioneer unions in mass-production industries in the United States as well as the largest garment unions in the world.

Modern developments. Throughout the first half of the 20th century the apparel industry remained largely concentrated in the United States and the United Kingdom, especially in the United States, where the industry received an enormous impetus from World War II. In most other countries, garment making remained a home or cottage industry. The U.S. industry was divided among six types of firms: contractors, who produced apparel from raw material for a jobber or manufacturer; jobbers, who purchased raw materials they supplied to contractors to make into garments; manufacturers, who bought materials and designed, made, and sold the products wholesale; manufacturer-distributors, who sold their products through their own retail outlets; vertical mills, which performed all operations from yarn to finished garment under one corporate roof, and usually one plant roof; and vertical-mill distributors, who marketed their products through their own retail outlets.

By the 1950s other countries were beginning to develop and expand their apparel industries. Besides the United Kingdom, which continued to specialize in high-quality goods, the Scandinavian countries, Belgium, The Netherlands, Canada, South Africa, Japan, and Australia expanded ready-made clothing manufacture. Another development of the 1950s was the expansion of many firms inside the industry into other areas (for example, men's clothing manufacturers entering the women's-wear field).

During the 1960s the garment industry of the world underwent rapid expansion, with many of the newer producing countries showing spectacular increases. Most of the industrialized countries of Europe, North and South America, Australia, New Zealand, South Africa, and Israel had clothing and footwear industries capable of meeting virtually all of their own needs. The United Kingdom, France, Italy, Spain, Sweden, West Germany, South Korea, Japan, Taiwan, and Hong Kong all expanded their export trade throughout the decade. Great Britain, which more than doubled its exports, continued to concentrate largely on men's fashion items in clothing and footwear. France exported principally high-fashion women's wear, especially in the form of selected original designs sold to manufacturers abroad to be copied and mass-produced locally. Italy became a major producer of knitted outerwear and of footwear; Israel exported knitted outerwear and all types of women's wear, especially pantyhose; Spain produced leather goods, knitwear, and high-fashion clothes; while Sweden and West Germany concentrated on sport and spectator wear.

During the 1970s the growth of the world garment industry continued at a rapid pace. The exports of Italy, Hong Kong, Taiwan, West Germany, France, and the United Kingdom increased by 400 to 500 percent, while those of South Korea increased by 1,200 percent. One important international trend was the expansion of U.S. and European firms into places with relatively low labour costs, such as Hong Kong, South Korea, Taiwan, and Japan. In addition to outright ownership and partnership, many U.S. and European firms expand their operations by franchise. Several high-fashion French, British, and Italian firms, for example, sold franchises to U.S. manufacturers to produce their European name brands, while U.S. firms sold franchises to Australian, Canadian, New Zealand, and other manufacturers to produce their name brands.

The greatest volume of export trade in the 1970s originated in Europe. It was shared principally among four producers: Italy, West Germany, France, and the United Kingdom. In 1979 Italy, with the largest share of world trade, exported clothing and footwear valued at around $8,100,000,000; West Germany exported $2,900,000,000 worth of goods, France about $2,500,000,000, and the United Kingdom about $1,800,000,000.

During the 1970s, however, the European countries' share of export trade decreased steadily, while the share of Far East countries increased. The principal exporters there were Hong Kong, South Korea, Taiwan, and Japan. In 1979 Hong Kong exported clothing and footwear valued at $4,200,000,000. South Korea's exports were $3,500,000,000, Taiwan's $1,900,000,000, and Japan's $400,000,000.

The tremendous increase in productivity and exports of clothing and footwear from the Orient resulted from well-engineered factories established there during the 1960s and 1970s. These plants are not sweatshops like the crowded, ill-lighted factory lofts in which garment workers of the United States, the United Kingdom, and western European countries once worked 12 and 14 hours a day. Many Asian factory workers have better working and living conditions than obtained in U.S. and European plants in the 1920s and '30s, and in some cases Asian plant facilities are superior in working conditions and productivity to contemporary U.S. and European factories.

There has been, however, a distinct difference between Asia and the West in working hours and pay, though pay and hours have been upgraded in Japan, Hong Kong, and Taiwan. Beginning in 1968, for example, legislation in Hong Kong progressively reduced the factory work week to 48 hours, which was the average work week in clothing factories in the United States in the 1930s. By 1979 the average week in U.S. apparel plants was 35 hours; in the United Kingdom and western Europe the average week ranged from 28 to 45 hours. Wage rates in Hong Kong also have been increased, but daily rates there are still only slightly more than hourly rates in the United States. Radical differences in living costs and various fringe benefits to Hong Kong workers (*e.g.*, subsidized meals or food allowances) have reduced this differential.

None of the Communist countries of eastern Europe or Asia is a major exporter of clothing, but many, notably the Soviet Union, have developed large-scale manufacturing. In several countries, especially the Soviet Union and East Germany, highly developed production methods are widely used.

THE MODERN INDUSTRY: MATERIALS AND DESIGN CONSIDERATIONS

Raw materials. Raw materials for apparel and allied products may be classified according to construction. Strand construction converts yarns into woven, knitted, and braided fabrics. Matted construction converts fibres into felts, paper, and padding yardage. Molecular-mass construction produces plastic film, metal foil, and rubber sheetings, while cellular construction is the building block for skins, furs, hides, and synthetic foam.

All four constructions are used for all types of apparel, though only minute quantities of molecular-mass and cellular construction are used for underwear. Most outerwear is made from woven and knitted fabrics, with some use of hides, skins, furs, plastics, rubber, foams, and metallics. Footwear that was originally made exclusively from leather (treated hides) may now be made from fabrics, plastics, rubber, foams, and metallics.

Textile fabrics. Woven fabrics are constructed by interlacing two or more yarns perpendicularly to each other. Braiding is an interlacing in which two or more yarns are interlaced diagonally to each other. In knitting, yarns are interlooped. Yarns are strands spun either from natural fibre such as cotton, linen, or wool or from synthetic fibres such as rayon and nylon. Practically all synthetic fibres are made originally in filament form and then cut into staples, or fibre lengths. A textile filament is a single hairlike strand of indeterminate length. The only natural filament is silk.

Weave construction

Basic weave constructions are plain, twill, satin, basket, jacquard, lappet, leno, and pile. The two basic knit constructions are warp, or flat, and weft, or circular, knitting. Types of weft knitting are jersey, rib, purl, run resist, tuck stitch, and interlock. Types of warp knitting are tricot, milanese, and raschel simplex. The classifying is based on principles of linking the yarns in structuring the fabric. (See also TEXTILE INDUSTRY.)

Leathers and synthetics. Most leathers are made from skins of sheep, goats, kids, calves, pigs, horses, and cattle; the skins of lizards, snakes, alligators, elk, buffalo, ostrich, kangaroo, chamois, walrus, elephant, and seal are used to a lesser degree for exotic leathers (see also LEATHER AND HIDES). Suede and patent leather are types of finishes. Plastics, foams, felts, paper, rubber, and metallics are used in thicknesses ranging from gossamer, cobweb thinness to the thickest of hides.

Quality in apparel and allied products. Quality is measured by three characteristics—durability, utility, and emotional appeal, with respect to the raw materials used, the product design, and the construction of the product.

Durability factors are tensile strength, tear strength, abrasion resistance, colourfastness, and cracking and bursting strength. Utility factors are air permeability, water permeability, thermal conductivity, crease retention, wrinkle resistance, shrinkage, and soil resistance. Appeal factors are eye appeal of fabric face, tactile response to fabric surface, fabric hand (reaction to hand manipulation of the fabric), and eye appeal of the garment's face, silhouette, design, and drape. The principles involved are the same whether the garment is made of leather, plastic, foam, or textiles such as woven, knit, or felt fabric.

The quality of textiles and apparel is usually governed by standards set by the industry or the government or the two acting together, along with textile associations, testing societies, retail associations, consumer organizations, and service associations such as laundering and cleaning groups. Standards cover performance in cleaning and wearability for tailored clothing, outerwear and rainwear, work clothes, slacks, shirts and blouses, men's underwear, women's underwear, sleepwear, and accessories.

Design in clothing and footwear. Clothing, headwear, footwear, and accessories businesses are the fashion industries par excellence. As such their goal is to give the wearer a sense of well-being based on being attractive to oneself and others. At the same time, an inescapable function of fashion in most countries is to serve as a status symbol, a consideration leading to the wardrobe concept in designing; that is, separate business attire, evening wear, casual clothes, spectator-sportswear, active-sportswear, and other prescribed attire that clothing entrepreneurs and designers promote.

Five elements of design

Designers use five elements to create a design that will stimulate the potential consumer to buy: (1) colour, (2) silhouette, (3) drape, (4) texture, and (5) line balance on the product's surface. Design ideas are derived from configurations or colour combinations or both in historical, ethnic, national, natural, geographic, and modern themes that can be advertised and promoted to boost sales. Besides choosing textiles and other raw materials with specific properties and characteristics of colour, drape, hand, and texture, the designer selects findings—buttons, zippers, snaps, grommets, thread, lace, tapes, braids, medallions, sequins, and a variety of ornaments and closures—as decorative devices to impart the desired design effect. Line balance is generally achieved by the sectional patterns of raw materials such as textiles and leather that the designer shapes to form the finished product. Fashion in clothing and footwear operates in cycles, but, with respect to design construction, clothing and footwear may be lined, interlined, or unlined regardless of the cycle.

Designers use a variety of fitting forms for clothing, shoe lasts for footwear, and hat blocks for headwear to approximate human anatomical dimensions. The basic patterns that fit the form, last, or block with minimal seams and skintight precision form the foundation pattern. In the drafting method of designing style patterns, the designer manipulates the foundation pattern to develop the style pattern, which is used to cut the raw materials into the sections required for the garment. The drapery method is used by designers who prefer to drape the actual material for the garment on the form, block, or last; cutting patterns for cutting the raw materials are traced from the draped sections. Cutting patterns may be made of rigid or semirigid paper or plastics.

Pattern grading

Pattern grading, making sets of patterns to fit a range of sizes, is the next step in the design process. Anthropometric tables for sizing apparel have been compiled by various government agencies and other sources. Formerly pattern grading was a completely manual drafting process, but in the 1950s pattern-grade machines were invented to increase the speed of grade-drafting patterns.

These machines were manually paced; that is, they followed the lead of a draftsman. In 1967 the computerized grader machine was invented to grade and cut patterns directly from an original set, performing automatically without manual contact with the drafting and cutting process. By 1970 various U.S., British, and Japanese computerized graders were available, which automatically take measurements from a set of style patterns, then grade, draft, and cut sets of patterns in the sizes desired. These computerized graders contain memory banks of the anthropometric specifications required. Some computerized grading machines can provide graded patterns in any of three media: acetate patterns for making photo markers; rigid plastic patterns for conventional chalk, crayon, pen, pencil, or spray manual marking methods; or stack drafts, which put the entire desired size range from smallest to largest, concentrically, on one sheet. In conjunction with any of these, the computer can issue data sheets with costing and material usage per size or range. The actual processing of the raw material begins after the patterns are graded.

MODERN MANUFACTURING PROCESSES AND EQUIPMENT

Many different sequences of the three major processes, cutting, sewing, and pressing, are used. The exact sequence depends on the raw materials for the garment, the processing equipment, the garment's design, and quality specifications. Five other processes are used to assemble, decorate, and finish the components into the finished garment: baking or curing, cementing, fusing, molding, and riveting, including grommetting and nailing.

Cutting processes. Cutting involves three basic operations: making the marker, spreading the fabric, and chopping the spread fabric into the marked sections. The marker, or cutting lay, is the arrangement of patterns on the spread fabrics. When hides are cut the lay length is the hide size; many hides are cut in single plies. Short lengths are spread by hand, but large lays, made from large bolts of material with lengths of more than 100 feet (30 metres) and heights containing hundreds of plies, must be spread with travelling spreading machines. Stationary spreaders are used for small sample lots. Manual and semiautomatic spreading machines are propelled manually over the lay length as the machine feeds the fabric ply onto the cutting table. Some machines book-fold the successive plies as the fabric is spread; others have turntable devices permitting one-way spreads. Lays may be spread with all plies of fabric facing one way or with successive plies facing each other in face-to-face spreads. Turntable spreaders were introduced in 1920, face-to-face spreaders in 1938, and in 1946, electric-powered spreading machines that spread a full bolt automatically without manual attention. The electronic program machine, a later development, carries out the spreading in a programmed sequence. In 1950 cutting blades were invented to cut the ply at each end of the lay as it is spread. These cutoff spreaders are automatic. Electric-eye edge controls for precise superposing of plies were available on automatic machines in 1962. In 1969 piggyback automatic spreaders were introduced, which carry a second bolt that is spread as soon as the first bolt is on the lay.

The marker is superposed on the completed lay. Markers are made of one of three materials: the fabric being cut, an inexpensive felt of muslin type cloth, or one of a variety of papers. When paper with a low coefficient of friction is used, the marker is fastened to the lay by stapling or two-sided adhesive stripping. Papers with an adhesive on one side can be heat-sealed to a fabric and are commonly used with woollens or soft fabrics. Photomarking machines are used for duplicating often-used paper markers. Many markers are first made in miniature, with precise, scaled-down patterns to determine the optimum layout for minimal yardage; the optimal miniature marker is then used as the guide for making the full-scale cutting marker. Some automated equipment is capable of both making the graded pattern and laying it out on the fabric to minimize waste. A sprayer machine, which sprays the entire length of the lay around the pattern, eliminates the need for manual marking-in.

Six types of machines are available to chop or cut a lay into the component parts of the marker: rotary-blade (round-knife) machines; vertical reciprocal-blade machines; band knives, similar to band saws; die clickers, or beam presses; automatic computerized cutting systems with straight blades; and automated computerized laserbeam cutting machines.

Round-knife machines rotate a circular blade down into the lay, whereas straight-knife machines oscillate a

Spreading

Making the marker and cutting

straight blade in and out of the lay in jigsaw fashion. Both machines are portable, manual-paced machines; that is, the machine is manually pushed through the lay as the blade cuts. Some models have dual speed controls and automatic blade sharpeners. In band-knife cutting, blocks of fabric cut from the lay with round- or straight-knife machines are trimmed precisely to pattern specifications as the blocks are manipulated against the band-knife rotating in a fixed orbit. Some band-knife machines are mounted on travelling platforms that carry machine and operator along the entire length of the cutting table, permitting band-knife cutting at any point of the lay.

Round-knife machines vary in blade diameter, blade perimeter, and revolutions per minute of the blade. Band blades operate in broad oval or large cam-shaped perimeter patterns. Vertical blade edges may be straight, waved, notched, serrated, or striated; band blade edges may be straight, waved, or saw toothed. Straight-edge blades, including the circular perimeter of rotary blades, are used most often; the others are special-purpose blades.

Die clickers cut by pressing dies, superposed on the lay, through the depth of the lay. The cutting dies outline the patterns to be cut. Die presses may be stationary or travelling; travelling die presses cover the entire width of the lay and move throughout the lay length and press dies into the fabric with intermittent strokes across the lay width until the entire lay is cut. In stationary clickers, the lay or section of the lay is pulled under the pressure beam for each die cutting stroke. Machine cutting of footwear, bags, pocketbooks, and similar items is done with die presses.

In automatic computerized cutting systems, introduced in 1967, the lay is covered with a thin plastic film drawn firmly to the lay by a vacuum operating through a porous cutting table and the porous fabric of the lay. The vacuum pulls the impermeable film firmly onto the lay preventing any movement during the cutting action. There are two types of cutting actions: the lay may be stationary and the knife move or the lay may move forward and the knife move horizontally.

A cutting system introduced in 1971 employed a computer-controlled laser beam to burn, or vaporize, the fabric rather than cut it. Unlike other methods requiring the accumulation of large orders before it becomes efficient to cut a specific style, the laser system, which provided for storage of programmed cutting instructions, allowed one complete garment to be cut at a time from a single layer of material (see photograph). Among the advantages claimed for the system are the elimination of variations within a specific size, improved cloth utilization, efficient production of smaller orders, lower inventory requirements, and faster delivery.

Two types of auxiliary cutting equipment are used: cutting drills to drill holes through the superposed plies in a lay, and notches to notch the perimeters of the cut sections. These holes and notches guide the sewing operations. Cut sections are ticketed to insure proper sizing and shading during the assembly of the garment.

Sewing production. Clothing, footwear, and allied industries have been known as the needle trades because sewing is the major assembly and decorative process used. Some items such as plastic raincoats and footwear are assembled and decorated by fusing, but the number of garments produced completely by fusing, cementing, and mold casting are infinitesimal compared to those produced by sewing.

More than 10,000 different models of industrial sewing machines have been made. Most are produced by Great Britain, West Germany, Italy, Japan, and the United States. Sewing machines are classified according to stitch type and bed type (the shape of the machine's frame). The seven basic beds, or frames, are flatbed, raised-bed, post, cylinder, off-the-arm, closed-vertical, and open-vertical. The bed type is determined by the manner in which fabric passes through the machine as it sews. There are four categories with regard to operational control, all electrically powered: manual-paced, automatic cycle with manual loading and extraction, fully automatic, and automated.

Sewing machines

Pattern cutting.
(Left) Traditional manual operation: working with multiple plies of fabric, patterns are laid out and chalked (foreground), then cut with an electrically powered tool (background).
(Right) Laser beam apparel cutter: single ply fabric is unrolled in five-foot sections onto a conveyer belt (background); the laser beam, which cuts the pattern (centre), is programmed by a separately housed computer for pattern specifications and is directed by a pentaprism arrangement of mirrors; excess material is then removed and pieces are rolled by conveyer belt (foreground).
By courtesy of (left) Hart Schaffner & Marx, (right) Genesco, Inc.

The prime characteristic of a sewing machine is the stitch it makes. Until 1926 stitches were classified willynilly with trade terms that often varied from one place to another and even from shop to shop. In 1926 the U.S. government became the first government to issue a seam and stitch classification to specify its requirements. During the 1960s other countries began to adopt the latest versions of these specifications for sewing equipment and sewn products, and these specifications have been adopted throughout the world for industrial sewing.

The first hand-powered sewing machines in the 19th century sewed 20 stitches per minute. At the turn of the 20th century some electrically powered machines sewed 200 stitches, and by the mid-20th century machine speeds reached 4,500. Most machines now sew 7,000, and some can sew 8,000 stitches per minute. The first integrated sewing machine was introduced in 1969 by Singer Company. Before that, manual-paced sewing machines had a separate clutch motor with start, speed, and braking controlled by foot treadle action; a belt drive ran the machine via treadle action to the motor's clutch, which actuated or stopped the belt drive while the motor ran continuously. The integrated sewing machine eliminated the separate motor, its clutch, and the belt drive. The integrated machine frame contains the motor module, which is actuated, controlled, and stopped by a four-speed switch operated by a device resembling the former foot treadle. The motor in this machine rotates only when the treadle is actuated, and so electricity is used only when the machine is sewing.

Special-purpose machines sew automatic cycles for operations such as buttonholing, button sewing, contour seaming, profile stitching, seaming for patch pockets, dart stitching, tacking, welt pocketing, and padding cycles such as blindstitching interlinings to the outer shell. In semiautomatic special-purpose machines, reloading per product unit sewed is done manually, whereas in automatic machines reloading and extraction are both done by the machine. Contour seamers are sewing machines that sew curved seams automatically; most machines are semiautomatic. Profile seamers and stitchers seam or stitch angular or curved designs in which a backtrack path, such as a U seam or angled seam (a square U), is sewed. These machines are also semiautomatic.

A sequential sewing machine introduced in the 1960s repeatedly sews an automatic cycle on the same garment with predetermined spacing between the operations. A sequential buttonhole machine, for example, sews five buttonholes on a shirt front automatically, one after the other, with predetermined spacing. Sequential sewing machine modules are synchronized automatic systems consisting of two or more sewing machines that sew the operation in series; the first machine completes its operation and then the garment or section is fed into the second machine for the next operation. The first machine sews the centre front placket of a shirt front; the second machine sews a series of buttonholes on the placket. In tandem-machine arrangements two machines sew simultaneously on the same unit. Gang-machine operation is an arrangement of three or more machines operating automatically under the care of one operator. The introduction in 1930 of stop-motion devices for stopping a sewing machine when the thread broke or ran out made gang-machine operation possible in the 1930s, tandem machines in the 1940s, and sequential machines and modules in the 1960s.

Before 1950 most industrial sewing machines had only the basic mechanical-linkage system of shafts, cams, gears, rods, belts, chains, and pulleys, with manual lubricating systems. Higher speeds, fully automatic cycling, and automatic sequential systems were developed later and were made possible by automatic lubrication systems with pumps and reservoirs, fluidic controls, and electronic controls.

The quality of manual-paced sewing depends on the integration of six variables: the needle, its size, shape, and finish; the type of feed system; the coordination of needle and feed; thread tension adjustments; the thread; and operator handling. Seam slippage, yard severance, puckering, elongation, gathering, and feed mark off are some of the quality areas affected. Machine manufacturers make needles in a variety of diameters, point shapes, and finishes as well as different types, shapes, and sizes of feeds and presser feet to improve quality and output.

Sewing machine attachments are jigs and fixtures used with sewing machines to decrease downtime (the time a machine is inoperative) and thus increase productivity by getting the fabric to the needle, aligning and repositioning fabric under the needle, or extracting and disposing of the sewed materials sooner. Trade terms for some of these sewing aids are needle positioners, stackers, programmers,

Sewing machine attachments

guides, hemmers, binders, thread trimmers, stitching templets, seam folders, pipers, and shirrers. Needle positioners automatically set the needle in or out of the sewn materials as desired when the machine stops. Stackers extract and dispose of the sewed sections with one of five actions: flipping, sliding, lifting, shuttle-drop, or conveyor cycle. Programmed sewing is an automatic sewing cycle controlled by a module that sets the time sequence of initial positioning, sewing, repositioning if needed, thread trimming, extraction, and disposal. The times and sequence of these elements in the sewing operation may be changed for different sewing cycles. Automated sewing is a self-correcting system that operates when the section being sewed varies beyond given tolerance limits.

Fusing and cementing are two major processes for stitchless or decorative seaming in apparel and allied production. In fusing, the seam bond or decoration is formed by melting some fibre or finish content in the material in a manner that joins sections or decorates the desired area. In cementing, the bond, or decoration, is made by an adhesive, such as cement, glue, or plastic, applied to the materials during or preceding the cementing process. Fusing is either by direct heat using hot-head fusing presses, in which pressure surfaces are heated by electric heating grids or steam, or by electronic high-frequency or infrared systems. Cementing processes use mechanical-pressure systems with or without heat application, depending on the adhesive and materials used. Fusing, introduced in the 1950s, has replaced sewing in some operations such as joining interlining to collars, cuffs, and coat fronts as well as seaming clothing and footwear made from certain synthetic yarns or plastic films.

Pressing and molding processes. Molding is any process that changes the surface characteristics or topography of a garment or shoe or one of its sections by the application of heat, moisture, or pressure. Pressing, pleating, blocking, mangling, steaming, creasing, curing, and casting are trade terms for various molding processes in producing clothing and footwear.

Pressing has two major divisions: buck pressing and iron pressing. A buck press is a machine for pressing a garment or section between two contoured, heated, pressure surfaces that may have steam and vacuum systems in either or both surfaces. Before 1905 all garment pressing was done by hand irons heated by gas flame, stove plate heat, or electricity; introduction of the steam buck press changed most press operations. The first pressing machines had no pressure, heat, or steam controls such as those built after 1940. Modern buck presses are made to fit certain garment sections, such as a jacket front, pant leg, pant top, or shoulder area for a specific style and size. These improved presses have gauges to measure and control steam pressure and temperature, mechanical pressure, vacuum pressure, and the press cycle time. Cycle-time controls permit one operator to work a series of machines. A presser, for example, handles four presses doing the same or different operations; by the time a worker finishes extracting and loading the fourth machine, the first machine is ready for extraction and reloading. Cycle-time controls apply and shut off steam and vacuum action and open the pressing machine automatically in the desired sequence. Conveyor buck presses, which may move intermittently or continuously, are buck-pressing systems in which sections or garments to be pressed are fed into a buck press and extracted from it by a conveyor belt.

In iron pressing, a hand iron functions as the top pressure surface. The two major types of hand irons are steam ejectors and dry irons. Electric hand irons are equipped with thermostats that regulate temperature. Steam-heated irons, whether ejection or dry, have fixed temperatures depending on the steam pressure servicing the iron. Many hand irons are equipped with lift devices and gear drives to control stroke rate and minimize operator fatigue. Hand irons are made in a variety of sizes, weights, shapes, and surfaces; the specific usage determines the combination.

Pleating. Pleating is the process of putting a design of creases into fabric. Accordion, side, box, inverted, sun-

burst, air-tuck, Van Dyke, and crystal are trade terms for some pleat designs. Pleating is accomplished by machine or by the use of interlocking paper pleat patterns. Pleating machines have blades or rotary gearlike surfaces that crease the fabric as it passes between two heated rotary mangles, setting the creases. Machines may be used for pleating either specific cut garment sections or lengths of fabric that are then cut after pleating into garment sections. In pattern pleating, the garment section or fabric length is sandwiched between two complementarily creased plies of paper that shape the fabric into the desired pleat design. This creased trio is inserted in a steam chamber, or autoclave, for a given length of time, depending on fabric characteristics and pleat durability desired.

Creasing. Creasing machines differ from pleating machines in that they fold the edges of garment sections and set the fold crease as an aid for such operations as sewing the edges of collars, cuffs, and patch pockets. Creasing diminishes the time for positioning the creased section during sewing.

Mangling. Mangling is the process of pressing a garment or section between two heated rotary circular pressure surfaces.

Blocking. Blocking involves encompassing a form, block, or die with the garment with skintight precision. The item is blocked or pressed by superposing a complementary pressing form that sandwiches the shaped garment or section between the interlocked blocks. This process is used for such items as hats, collars, cuffs, and sleeves.

Curing. Curing consists of baking a garment or garment section in a heated chamber to either set creases in the fabric permanently or to decompose auxiliary media used as a sewing aid. Curing, for example, permanently sets previously pressed creases in certain permanent press, durable press, and wash and wear garments. Curing decomposes the backing material that facilitates the embroidering in garments.

Casting. Casting, largely experimental, consists of making a garment or garment section by pouring a fluid or powder into a mold that forms the garment or section when the fluid or powder evaporates or solidifies.

Special footwear processes. Footwear may be classified according to the section of the foot it covers and how it is held on: sandals, slip-ons, oxfords, ankle-support shoes, and boots. The term shoe refers to footwear exclusive of sandals and boots. Sandals cover only the sole and are held onto the foot by strapping. Slip-ons cover the sole and instep and may or may not cover the entire heel; styles include pumps and moccasins. Oxfords cover the sole, instep, and heel and have closures such as laces, straps, buckles, buttons, or elastic to secure the shoe to the foot. Ankle-support shoes cover sole, instep, heel, and ankle and secure the shoe to the foot with a closure device; the chukka is an ankle-support style. Boots cover the foot from the sole to various heights above the ankle: shin height, calf length, knee length, and hip length. Closures may or may not be used, depending on the degree of snugness desired.

Most footwear factories that produce dress, play, and work footwear in slip-on, oxford, ankle-support, and boot categories from leather or synthetics simulating leather have eight processing departments: (1) cutting; (2) stitching, which sews the upper section above the sole; (3) stock fitting, which prepares the sole section; (4) lasting, which attaches the upper and its lining to a wooden foot shape, the last, in order to assemble the sole section to the upper; (5) bottoming, which attaches the sole to the upper; (6) heeling, which attaches and shapes the heel bottom into its final form; (7) finishing, which includes polishing, extracting the lasts, stamping the shoe brand and name on the sole, inserting heel and sole pads, and inspection of the inner shoe; and (8) treeing, which includes attaching laces, bows, and buckles, and final cleaning and inspection.

There are three basic methods of attaching soles to uppers. The bottoming may be done by sewing, cementing, nailing, or a combination of these three joining

Buck pressing and iron pressing

Types of footwear

techniques. Nailing may be with nails, screws, staples, or pegs. Sewing may be with or without the use of welt, insole, middle sole and filler sections; the same applies to cementing soles to uppers. Sole sections vary in ply count; a three-ply sole has a middle sole sandwiched between outer sole and inner sole; the two-ply sole consists of outer and inner sole; the single sole has only one ply.

PRODUCTION CONTROL AND PLANT CONSIDERATIONS

Sectionalization. In the first clothing and footwear factories, one worker assembled and finished an entire garment or shoe. This whole-garment system, however, rarely existed after 1940 for ready-to-wear apparel. Sectionalization came into being for three reasons: (1) to increase productivity per man-hour, (2) to improve product quality, and (3) to reduce inventory-in-process time. The main function of production control is to schedule the operations required to produce the garment or shoe in such a manner as to hold the total processing time, or calendar time, to a minimum. This scheduling is accomplished by determining the operations required per garment to yield the desired quality with minimal processing costs (labour, overhead, capitalization) and by arranging these operations so that most of them may be done simultaneously in the least number of successive steps, or time units. If 24 operations are required to make a given garment, a schedule in which these 24 operations are performed in six time units, with four operations made simultaneously in each unit, is superior to a schedule requiring seven or more successive time units with four or fewer simultaneous operations in each time unit.

Unit flow and multiple flow. There are two basic section systems in assembly-line production: unit flow and multiple flow. The unit-flow system is continuous; the unit moves to the next operation as soon as it is processed by the previous operation. The multiple-flow system is intermittent; a given group of units moves to the next operation simultaneously as a bundle, or batch, after the last unit in the batch is processed in the previous operation. Regardless of which flow is used, efficient production control depends on synchronized movement of the garment sections in the least time units required for minimal inventory-in-process time.

Assembly-line systems

Plant layout and materials handling. To minimize the cost of transporting and storing processed garment sections while they move through the prescribed production sequence, two factors are considered: the arrangement of processing equipment to minimize distances between operations, and the utilization of labour, transport equipment, and utilities to minimize total cost per product moved.

Transportation equipment such as chutes, conveyor systems, and carts are used to transport the work through the successive operations. Some conveyor systems, such as Eton of Dalsjöfårs of Sweden, incorporate a stationary synchronized extractor on the conveyor that extracts and disposes a sewed section to a mobile conveyor hanger.

The two types of plant layout are process layout and product layout. In process layout, equivalent processing equipment is grouped in the same area regardless of whether the product can be passed through successive operations without backtracking. In production layout, processing equipment is arranged in the succession required for making the garment in the prescribed sequence without backtrack and with minimal transport between successive operations. Most apparel and allied production is with product layout, but in a few instances the process layout is more economical.

Research and development. All research and development in apparel manufacture is based on increasing productivity per man-hour, an emphasis that tends to increase capitalization for equipment. Research is under way to develop a process to produce some apparel items in one step. These items would be cast in one process, such as is used to produce plastic items. The finished product would be as pliable, soft, and porous as desired. Acceptance of such products depends not only on their utility and durability but also on the extent to which fashion habits and preferences change. Until one-step clothing and footwear are produced for business, sport, and formal

One-step manufacturing

wear, productivity of conventional operations such as cutting, sewing, pressing, lasting, fusing, cementing, and curing, is likely to be increased, both through better worker–machine combinations and through automation and computer devices designed to eliminate manual contact with the garment processed and to speed up the processing of a garment from the first to the last operation.

BIBLIOGRAPHY. J. SOLINGER, *Apparel Manufacturing Analysis* (1961), and *Apparel Manufacturing Handbook* (1980), detailed analyses of all subjects in the manufacture of apparel and allied items; H.C. CARR (ed.), *The Clothing Factory* (1972), provides information and analysis on garment technology and garment production management; J. KORN (ed.), *Boot and Shoe Production* (1953); and W.E. COHN, *Modern Footwear Materials and Processes* (1969), detailed technology of footwear production; UNITED SHOE MACHINERY CORP., *How Modern Shoes are Made* (1936), a concise booklet outlining the elements in constructing basic shoe styles; M.D. DANISH and L. STEIN (eds.), *ILGWU News History, 1900–1950* (1950), a history of the first 50 years of the ILGWU; SINGER SEWING MACHINE CO., *Invention of the Sewing Machine* (1955), a pamphlet that gives a brief history of the invention of the sewing machine; *Manufacturing Clothier* (1946–), a monthly magazine that reports changes and innovations in the design, production, and marketing of women's wear in Europe, with particular emphasis on the British Isles; *FemmeLines* (1956–), a bimonthly magazine dealing with trends and innovation in the design, production, and marketing of women's wear in the United States; *MascuLines* (1956–), a bimonthly magazine dealing with trends and innovation in the design, production, and marketing of men's wear in the United States; *Daily News Record* (1892–), a daily paper reporting trends and innovations in design, production, and marketing of men's and boys' wear; *Women's Wear Daily* (1910–), a daily paper that reports trends and innovations in the design, production, and marketing of women's and children's wear; *The Bobbin* (1958–), a monthly magazine for management in the needle trades.

(J.So.)

Clouds

A cloud is a mass of condensed water above the ground, in the form of a visible aggregation of tiny water droplets, ice crystals, or a mixture of both. A shallow layer of cloud in contact with the ground is termed a fog.

Though at first glance a cloudy sky may appear chaotic, to a perceptive observer there is some semblance of order. The recognizable patterns and distinctive cloud types—in their infinite variety of shape and form—are themselves expressions of the way in which the air has risen to fashion them. Clouds formed in an extensive sheet hundreds of miles across, for example, indicate a steady ascent of air over large areas; clouds scattered over the sky in isolated puffs or heaps with clear spaces in between reveal the presence of irregular, local upcurrents. These formations are, respectively, the stratiform, or layer, clouds, and the cumuliform, or heap, clouds. The prolonged ascent of air leads to deeper and denser clouds, and finally to precipitation (*q.v.*); widespread, persistent rain or snow is produced by layer clouds, and rain showers or hail are produced by cumuliform clouds.

With the exception of certain rare types, such as nacreous and noctilucent clouds (clouds visible only at night), clouds are generally confined to the troposphere, where they may appear at any level (*e.g.*, from near the ground up to heights of about 11 kilometres [37,000 feet] in temperate latitudes, and at about 16 kilometres [53,000 feet] near the Equator). Clouds rarely form in the lower stratosphere because of its extreme dryness.

The forecasting of the formation, persistence, and dispersal of low clouds and fog, and of their horizontal extent, height, thickness, and opacity, are of great importance to the operation and safety of aircraft and most forms of surface transportation. The formation of clouds and their release of precipitation constitute a vital phase of the natural hydrologic cycle (*q.v.*), by which water from the oceans is evaporated, condensed, and returned as rain or snow to the Earth.

CLOUD FORMATION

Clouds are formed when air containing water vapour rises, expands when under the lower pressures prevailing at higher levels in the atmosphere (*q.v.*), and thereby cools adiabatically (without heat exchange with the surrounding air) until the temperature falls below the dew point and the air becomes saturated with water vapour (see HUMIDITY, ATMOSPHERIC). The excess vapour then condenses on to some of the wide variety of airborne particles present, which exist in concentrations ranging from fewer than 100 particles per cubic centimetre in clean maritime air to as much as 10^6 per cubic centimetre in the highly polluted air of an industrial city (see URBAN CLIMATES). A fraction of these particles are hygroscopic (readily absorb or retain moisture) and promote condensation at relative humidities below 100 percent, but for continued condensation leading to the formation of cloud droplets, the air must be slightly supersaturated (containing moisture in excess of normal capacity). Among the most efficient condensation nuclei are salt particles, produced by the bursting of air bubbles from breaking wave crests (these particles have masses ranging from about 10^{-15} grams to 10^{-9} grams); particles produced by natural or man-made fires and by the raising of dust clouds also are important. Condensation about the nuclei continues as rapidly as water vapour is made available by cooling of the air; this gives rise to droplets on the order of 0.01 millimetre or 10 microns in diameter. These droplets, usually present in concentrations of a few hundreds per cubic centimetre, constitute a nonprecipitating water cloud. In the cold, upper parts of clouds, cloud droplets may exist in the supercooled liquid state even though the temperature is well below 0° C, the normal freezing point of water in bulk. Layer clouds may consist almost entirely of supercooled droplets if their summit temperatures (at cloud tops) are above −10° C, whereas, cumuliform clouds often remain mainly liquid at temperatures down to −25° C. At temperatures between these approximate limits and −40° C, below which all droplets quickly freeze, clouds generally consist of a mixture of droplets and ice crystals with crystals predominating in the lower part of the temperature range.

Condensation nuclei

Because growing clouds are sustained by upward air currents ranging in velocity from a few centimetres per second to several metres per second, some cloud droplets, whose average falling speeds are only about one centimetre per second, must grow considerably if they are to fall through the cloud, survive evaporation in the unsaturated air beneath, and reach the ground as drizzle or rain. Within the normal life time of a cloud, water droplets cannot grow to even drizzle-drop size (radius greater than 0.1 millimetre) by condensation alone. There are, however, two other recognized ways in which a few relatively large cloud particles may be produced from a large population of smaller ones and may become incipient raindrops. In the first of these, the larger sized cloud droplets, falling faster than the smaller ones, will overtake, collide, and fuse (coalesce) with some of those lying in its fall path. This process goes very slowly until the droplet achieves a radius of about 30 micrometres after which it will occur at an ever-increasing rate and may eventually achieve raindrop size.

Growth of droplets and clouds

Alternatively, in the cold, upper regions of a cloud, an appreciable fraction of the supercooled droplets may freeze and later grow into ice crystals by the sublimation (direct transition from vapour to solid phase) of water vapour into ice. Because air that is saturated with liquid water will usually be strongly supersaturated with ice, the ice crystals grow much more rapidly than would water droplets under the same conditions, and crystals several millimetres across can grow in about ten minutes. An aggregation of several such crystals produces a snowflake which, if it melts during fall, may reach the ground as a raindrop.

DESCRIPTION AND CLASSIFICATION OF CLOUDS

The meteorologist classifies clouds mainly by their appearance, according to an international system essentially similar to a classification originally proposed in 1803. But because the dimensions, shape, structure, and texture of clouds are all influenced by the kind of air movements that result in their formation and growth, and by the properties of the cloud particles, much of what was originally a purely visual classification can now be justified on physical grounds.

The first *International Cloud Atlas* was published in 1896. Developments in aviation during the First World War stimulated increased interest in cloud formations and in their importance as an aid in short-range weather forecasting. This in turn led to the publication of a more extensive atlas, the *International Atlas of Clouds and States of Sky,* in 1932, and to a revised edition in 1939. After the Second World War, the World Meteorological Organization published a new *International Cloud Atlas* (1956), in two volumes. It contained 224 plates, describing ten main cloud genera (families) subdivided into 14 species based on cloud shape and structure. Nine general varieties, based on transparency and geometrical arrangement, also are described. The genera, listed according to their height are as follows:

I. High: mean heights from 16,500 to 45,000 feet (5 to 13 kilometres)
    A. Cirrus
    B. Cirrocumulus
    C. Cirrostratus

II. Middle: mean heights 6,500 to 23,000 feet (2 to 7 kilometres)
    A. Altocumulus
    B. Altostratus
    C. Nimbostratus

III. Low: mean heights 0 to 6,500 feet (0 to 2 kilometres)
    A. Stratocumulus
    B. Stratus
    C. Cumulus
    D. Cumulonimbus

Heights given are approximate averages for temperate latitudes. Clouds of each genus are generally lower in the polar regions and higher in the tropics. The definitions and descriptions of the cloud genera used in the *International Cloud Atlas* are given in the accompanying Figures 1–3, which illustrate some of their characteristic forms.

Four principal classes are recognized when clouds are classified according to the kind of air motions that produce them: (1) layer clouds formed by the widespread regular ascent of air; (2) layer clouds formed by widespread irregular stirring or turbulence; (3) cumuliform clouds formed by penetrative convection; and (4) orographic clouds formed by ascent of air over hills and mountains.

The widespread layer clouds associated with cyclonic depressions (see CYCLONES AND ANTICYCLONES), near fronts and other bad-weather systems, frequently are composed of several layers that may extend up to 30,000 feet (9 kilometres) or more, separated by clear zones that become filled in as rain or snow develops. These clouds are formed by the slow, prolonged ascent of a deep layer of air, in which a rise of only a few centimetres per second is maintained for several hours. In the neighbourhood of fronts, vertical velocities become more pronounced and may reach about 10 centimetres per second.

Layer clouds formed by widespread regular ascent

Most of the high cirrus clouds visible from the ground lie on the fringes of cyclonic cloud systems, and, though due primarily to regular ascent, their pattern is often determined by local wave disturbances that finally trigger their formation after the air has been brought near its saturation point by the large-scale lifting.

On a cloudless night, the ground cools by radiating heat into space without heating the air adjacent to the ground. If the air were quite still, only a very thin layer would be chilled by contact with the ground. More usually, however, the lower layers of the air are stirred by motion over the rough ground, so that the cooling is distributed through a much greater depth. Consequently, when the air is damp or the cooling is great, a fog several hundred feet deep may form, rather than a dew produced by condensation on the ground.

Layer clouds caused by irregular stirring motions

In moderate or strong winds the irregular stirring near the surface distributes the cooling upward, and the fog may lift from the surface to become a stratus cloud,

Figure 1: *High clouds.*
(Top left) Cirrostratus nebulosus, producing halo phenomenon. (Top centre) Cirrus fibratus, nearly straight or irregularly curved fine white filaments, generally distinct from one another. (Top right) Cirrus uncinus, detached clouds of delicate white filaments, often comma-shaped and ending at the top in a hook or tuft. (Bottom left) Cirrus spissatus, detached fibrous clouds of sufficient optical thickness to appear grayish when viewed against the Sun. (Bottom centre) Cirrocumulus, a thin white cloud patch composed of small elements in the form of ripples. (Bottom right) Cirrostratus fibratus, a thin whitish veil of nearly straight filaments.

Top left, top right, bottom left, bottom centre) Louis D. Rubin, Richmond, Virginia, (top centre, bottom right) Photo Researchers, (top centre) Nick Impenna, (bottom right) John G. Ross

which is not often more than 2,000 feet (600 metres) thick.

Radiational cooling from the upper surfaces of fogs and stratus clouds promotes an irregular convection within the cloud layer and causes the surfaces to have a waved or humped appearance. When the cloud layer is shallow, billows and clear spaces may develop so that it is described as stratocumulus instead of stratus.

Convective clouds Usually cumuliform clouds appearing over land are formed by the rise of discrete masses of air from near the Sun-warmed surface. These rising lumps of air, or thermals, may vary in diameter from a few tens to hundreds of metres as they ascend and mix with the cooler, drier air above them. Above the level of the cloud base the release of latent heat of condensation tends to increase the buoyancy of the rising masses, which tower upward and emerge at the top of the cloud with rounded upper surfaces.

At any moment a large cloud may contain a number of active thermals, and the residues of earlier ones. A new thermal rising into a residual cloud will be partially protected from having to mix with the cool, dry environment and therefore may rise farther than its predecessor. Once a thermal emerges as a cloud turret at the summit or the flanks of the cloud, rapid evaporation of the droplets chills the cloud borders, destroys the buoyancy, and produces sinking. A cumulus, therefore, has a characteristic pyramidal shape and viewed from a distance appears to have an unfolding motion, with fresh cloud masses continually emerging from the interior to form the summit and then sinking aside and evaporating.

In settled weather, cumulus clouds are well scattered and small; horizontal and vertical dimensions are only a kilometre or two. In disturbed weather they cover a large part of the sky, and individual clouds may tower as high as ten kilometres or more, often ceasing their growth only upon reaching the very stable stratosphere. These are the clouds that produce heavy showers, hail, and thunderstorms (*q.v.*).

At the level of the cloud base the speed of the rising air masses is usually about one metre per second, but may reach 5 metres per second, and similar values are measured inside the smaller clouds. The upcurrents in thunderclouds, however, often exceed 5 metres per second and may reach 30 metres per second or more.

The rather special orographic clouds are produced by the ascent of air over hills and mountains. The air stream is set into oscillation when it is forced over the hill and the clouds form in the crests of the (almost) stationary waves. There may therefore be a succession of such clouds stretching downwind of the mountain, which remain stationary relative to the ground despite strong winds that may be blowing through the clouds. The clouds have very smooth outlines and are called lenticular (lens-shaped) or wave clouds. Thin wave clouds may form at great heights (up to 10 kilometres, even over hills only a few hundred metres high) and occasionally are observed in the stratosphere (at 20 to 30 kilometres) over the mountains of Norway, Scotland, Iceland, and Alaska. These atmospheric wave clouds are known as nacreous or "mother-of-pearl" clouds because of their brilliant irridescent colours.

Clouds produced by orographic disturbances

CLOUDS AND WEATHER

A depression or cyclone (low-pressure system) in temperate latitudes usually brings several hours of continuous rain followed by showers and brighter intervals. It is heralded by the appearance, at heights of more than 20,000 feet (6 kilometres) above the ground, of thin, high cirrus clouds either in the form of trails or streaks composed of delicate white filaments, or as tenuous white patches and narrow bands. After approaching steadily for two or three hours, the leading cirrus arrive overhead and the barometer begins to fall. Gradually, the clouds thicken, and the bands merge to form a great veil of silken cirrostratus cloud covering the whole sky. At first this veil is translucent and the Sun shines palely through it. Centred on the Sun but at an angular distance of 22° from it, there occasionally is a halo, a bright ring of light tinged with orange red on the inside. This and other optical phenomena are caused by the refraction of sunlight through the ice crystals formed at these levels, where the

Figure 2: *Middle clouds.*
(Top left) Altocumulus undulatus, a layer of shaded, regularly arranged rolls. (Top right)
Altocumulus perlucidus, a white and gray layer in which there are spaces between the
elements. (Bottom left) Altostratus translucidus, showing the Sun as if seen through
ground glass. (Bottom right) Altocumulus radiatus, a layer with laminae arranged in parallel
bands.
Photo Researchers, (top left) Richard Jepperson, (top right) H. von Meiss-Teuffen,
(bottom left) Russ Kinne, (bottom right) Lawrence Smith

temperature is usually below −25° C. The cirrostratus shield usually has an irregular texture so that only fragments of the halo are seen, but sometimes the cloud is very thin and diffuse, perhaps only a milky film over the blue sky; then the halo may appear very bright and may have other rings and arcs around it, some with rainbow colours.

Four or five hours after the appearance of the first cirrus, the clouds overhead will have thickened and darkened so much that the halo will be extinguished and the Sun seen only as a brighter patch, with smudged edges. At this stage, the cloud is called altostratus; it continues to thicken, becomes lower, and patches of cloud form beneath it, making dark wavy patterns. With the closer approach of the storm centre, the wind freshens, the barometer falls rapidly, and within an hour or two the first raindrops fall. The rain soon becomes heavier and the cloud base lowers closer to the ground. It is difficult to discern any real structure in this grey nimbostratus or rain cloud, but beneath it tattered fragments of scud (fractostratus) are driven along in the wind.

After some hours the steady rain ends and the barometer ceases to fall; the sky lightens as much of the upper cloud becomes thin and broken, or clears away, but the lower overcast of ragged stratus clouds persists and gives rise to intermittent drizzle.

Sometime later the wind freshens again, the sky darkens, and there is heavy rain for a short while, quickly followed by a sudden improvement in the weather. The wind veers sharply, becomes gusty and cool, the barometer begins to rise, and the low clouds lift and break. Above them the dappled high clouds and cirrus recede to leave a clear sky.

The widely scattered low clouds are now cumulus, the heap clouds, with fairly level bases and rounded tops like cauliflowers. Some of these clouds grow larger and taller and, within about 15 minutes, tower up to 20,000 feet (6 kilometres) or more. Before long the largest clouds produce descending trails of rain; they have become cumulonimbus, or shower, clouds. Usually there is a striking change in the appearance of the cloud tops as the shower develops. The sharp, clear outlines of the cauliflower become smudged, ragged, and soft; the bulges flatten, the cracks become filled in, and the upper part of the cloud takes on the fibrous texture of cirrus. Often this is drawn sideways by the stronger winds aloft, projecting beyond the cloud base in the shape of an anvil. Eventually, the upper section may separate from the lower part of the cloud (which usually subsides and dissolves with the development of the shower), drifting away as a slowly evaporating mass of anvil cirrus.

An individual shower cloud may decay within half an hour of its inception, but as one tower releases its rain and evaporates, another springs up on its flanks, and the cloud mass may travel as a recognizable whole for several hours.

After some hours, convection declines; the larger clouds appear even more rarely, the showers cease, and the wind moderates. The barometer continues to rise, but more slowly, and finally even the small cumulus disappear. The whole cloud system of the storm has passed away.

On the fringes of the large storm-cloud systems and in weaker storms, the layer clouds are usually thinner and broken up into dapples or parallel rolls (billows). The top of a cloud layer tends to cool by radiating heat into space, while the interception of the Earth's radiation at

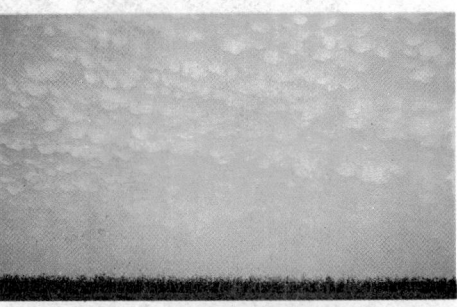

Figure 3: *Low clouds.*
(Left) Cumulonimbus calvus, a dense, heavy cloud with a considerable vertical extent, the upper portion of which has already lost its sharp outline. (Top centre) Cumulonimbus capillatus, showing the characteristic anvil-shaped upper portion, or thunderhead. (Top right) Cumulonimbus mamma, a light-coloured cloud sheet that has hanging protuberances on the undersurface. (Centre) Stratocumulus opacus, an extensive gray sheet with rounded masses, the greater part of which is sufficiently opaque to mask completely the Sun or Moon. (Bottom centre) Cumulus humilis, characterized by only a small vertical extent and appearing flattened. (Bottom right) Stratocumulus cumulogenitus (shown here with bright crepuscular rays), a gray layer with dark parts composed of elongated nonfibrous masses. These clouds represent a late stage of daytime development of cumulus.

(Left) William Belknap, Jr.—Rapho Guillumette, (top centre, top right, centre, bottom centre) Photo Researchers, (top centre and centre) Russ Kinne, (top right) Irvin L. Oakes, (bottom centre) John G. Ross, (bottom right) Louis D. Rubin, Richmond, Virginia

the base of the layer tends to warm it. After some time, slow convective motions are produced in the layer giving it a dappled structure. All shallow-layer clouds soon assume this structure unless they are shielded by a higher cloud layer. The dapple clouds are conventionally classified as cirrocumulus, altocumulus, or stratocumulus, according to their height (see Figures 1–3).

In stratocumulus layers, which may be quite thick, the rolls are often so close together that their edges join, giving the undersurface an undulating appearance without any clear chinks (Figure 3). Such clouds sometimes cover the sky for days on end in spells of quiet winter weather.

FOG

Definition and formation of fog

The term fog usually is applied to a cloud of small water droplets near ground level and sufficiently dense to reduce horizontal visibility below 1,000 metres. It also may refer to clouds of smoke particles, ice particles, or to mixtures of these components. Under similar conditions, but with visibility greater than 1,000 metres, the phenomenon is termed a mist or haze, depending on whether the obscurity is due to water drops or solid particles. The term smog is sometimes used to describe the thick, persistent fogs that occur in industrial areas, which are composed of both smoke and water particles.

Fog is formed by the condensation of water vapour on the condensation nuclei that are always present in natural air. This results as soon as the relative humidity of the air exceeds saturation by a fraction of 1 percent. In highly polluted air the nuclei may grow sufficiently to cause fog at humidities of 95 percent or less. Growth of the drops may be helped by the absorption of certain

soluble gases, notably sulfur dioxide to form dilute sulfuric acid. The relative humidity of the air can be increased by three processes: cooling of the air by adiabatic expansion; mixing two humid air streams having different temperatures; and direct cooling of the air by radiation.

The first process, adiabatic expansion, is responsible for the formation of clouds and plays a part in the formation of upslope fogs that are formed by the forced ascent of humid air up the sides of hills and mountains.

The mixing process is manifest when air that has been in contact with a wet ground or water surface having a different temperature from that of the air above is mixed with this air.

The most stable fogs occur when the surface is colder than the air above; that is, in the presence of a temperature inversion. Fogs also can occur when cold air moves over a warm, wet surface and becomes saturated by the evaporation of moisture from the underlying surface. Convection currents, however, tend to carry the fog upward as if forms, and it appears to rise as steam or smoke from the wet surface. This is the explanation of steam fogs that are produced when cold arctic air moves over lakes, streams, inlets of the sea, or newly formed openings in the pack ice; hence, the term, arctic sea smoke.

Fog types

Advection fog is formed by the slow passage of relatively warm, moist, stable air over a colder wet surface. Common at sea whenever cold and warm ocean currents (*q.v.*) are in close proximity, it may affect adjacent coasts. A good example is provided by the frequent dense fogs formed off the Grand Banks of Newfoundland in summer, when winds from the warm Gulf Stream blow over the cold Labrador Current. It also may occur over land, especially in winter when warm air blows over frozen or snow-covered ground (Figure 4). Advection fogs occur most readily with winds of about five metres

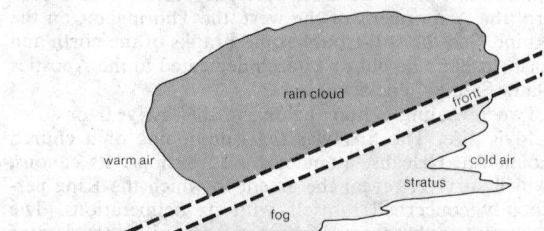

Figure 4: Formation of stratus cloud and fog beneath a frontal surface.

per second (ten miles per hour), sufficiently light to maintain a temperature contrast between air and surface and not strong enough to produce turbulent mixing through a considerable depth of the atmosphere. Typical advection fogs extend up to heights of a few hundred metres and sometimes also occur in conjunction with radiation fogs.

Radiation fog forms over land on calm, clear nights when loss of heat by radiation cools the ground and chills the air in the lowest few metres to below the dew-point temperature. Once dense fog has formed, the top of the fog replaces the ground as the effective surface cooled by radiation and the fog increases progressively in depth as long as there is sufficiently moist air above it. The development of a strong temperature inversion tends to stabilize the fog and suppress air motions but slow, turbulent stirring motions are usually present and probably are important in maintaining the fog. They do so by replacing the air in the lowest layers, which is losing moisture by deposition on the ground, with moister air from above. Typical inland radiation fogs reach to heights of 100–200 metres (328–656 feet).

Inversion fogs are formed as a result of a downward extension of a layer of stratus cloud, situated under the base of a low-level temperature inversion. They are particularly prevalent off western coasts in tropical regions in the summer, when the prevailing winds blow toward the Equator and cause the upwelling of cold water along the coast. Air that passes over the cold water becomes chilled, its relative humidity rises, and it becomes trapped under the inversion. Subsequent nocturnal cooling may then cause a stratus layer to form and build down to the ground to form an inversion fog as demonstrated in Figure 5 shown below.

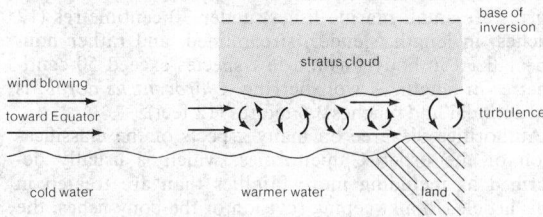

Figure 5: Formation of inversion fog.

Frontal fog forms near a front when raindrops, falling from relatively warm air above a frontal surface, evaporate into cooler air close to the Earth's surface and cause it to become saturated.

When the air temperature falls below 0° C the fog droplets become supercooled. At temperatures between 0° and −10° C, only a small proportion of the droplets freeze and the fog is composed mainly or entirely of liquid water. However, at lower temperatures, more and more droplets freeze so that below about −35° C and certainly below −40° C, the fog is composed entirely of ice crystals. The visibility in an ice fog is often considerably worse than that in a water fog containing the same concentration of condensed water.

Although it is convenient to classify fogs according to the physical processes that produce saturation of the air,

it is difficult to apply such a clear-cut classification in practice. Usually, more than one of the processes acts at the same time, and their relative importance varies from case to case and with time. Probably no two fogs are controlled by exactly the same combination of factors, a fact which makes forecasting the formation and dispersal of fog difficult (see WEATHER FORECASTING).

Advection fog at sea persists until there are changes in the general conditions of wind, temperature, and humidity that cause it. Over land it may disperse by the advection of warmer air or by solar heating. Radiative fog often disperses within a few hours of dawn, as the ground is warmed by the Sun's rays. A thick fog, however, may reflect so much solar radiation that little heat penetrates to the ground and the fog will then persist until a freshening wind removes it.

In most geographical locations subject to fog, frequency and persistence of the fogs show a marked seasonal dependence. Conditions favourable to the formation of radiation fog, namely, clear skies and light winds, often occur in the central regions of anticyclones and ridges of high pressure so that the advantages of dry settled weather are often nullified by the occurrence of fog, especially in autumn and winter. Advection fog may occur in any season of the year and at any time of day or night and is not restricted to conditions of light winds and clear skies. Over land it is especially liable to occur in winter with the incursion of mild damp air over a frozen or snow-covered surface. Over the coastal waters of the British Isles, it occurs chiefly in late spring and early summer when the sea is still cold.

Dense fog presents one of the greatest hazards to aviation and to nearly all forms of surface transportation. Modern aircraft generally are not allowed to take off or land if the visibility along the runway is less than 600 metres. In many countries, especially those in temperate latitudes, fog causes widespread dislocation and delay in transportation systems on several days each year.

Dense smogs, which may last for several days, and which often are associated with rather low temperatures and high concentrations of pollution, cause widespread illness and sometimes deaths among people suffering from bronchitis and other respiratory complaints.

BIBLIOGRAPHY. B.J. MASON, *The Physics of Clouds*, 2nd ed. (1970), is a comprehensive, detailed treatment of all the microphysical processes involved in the growth of particles in clouds, the development of precipitation, artificial modification of rainfall, radar studies of clouds, and thunderstorm electrification. It is an advanced monograph intended mainly for graduate students and research workers. B.J. MASON, *Clouds, Rain and Rainmaking* (1962), discusses the same material as the previously cited work, but at a level more suitable for high school and college students and is well-illustrated. N.H. FLETCHER, *The Physics of Rainclouds* (1962), is intermediate in level between the two books by Mason and is concerned mainly with the physics of rain-forming processes.

(B.J.M.)

Clovis

Founder of the Frankish kingdom that dominated much of western Europe in the early Middle Ages, Clovis (*c.* 466–511) was the son, and probably the only son, of Childeric I, king of the Salian Franks of Tournai.

To judge from the remains of Childeric's burial at Tournai, he seems to have been a federate chieftain (within the Roman Empire) of some standing and certainly a pagan. Under the same pagan gods, his son Clovis, who succeeded him in 481, advanced south to conquer northern Gaul. There survives a letter to him written by Bishop Remigius of Reims, congratulating him on taking over the administration of Belgica Secunda and advising him to listen to the bishops. At Soissons, in 486, Clovis defeated Syagrius, the last Roman ruler in Gaul. This opened to him the whole area of the Somme and the Seine and in particular brought him the extensive properties of the Roman *fiscus* (treasury) in that area. Clovis appears to have met with some resistance from the cities, and Franks not of his following seem to have been slow in coming to his aid. But he established

Fogs in relation to weather and climate

his power at least as far south as Paris between the years 487 and 494. The Armoricans of western Gaul and the Germanic peoples of the Rhineland offered more serious opposition; and at the Loire he made contact with the Visigoths, protégés of Theodoric, the formidable ruler of Ostrogothic Italy. Of the history of these early years, virtually nothing is known that is not recorded by Bishop Gregory of Tours, who wrote toward the end of the 6th century. Gregory's aim was to depict a heroic warrior who owed his success to conversion to Catholicism. The outlines of his story are acceptable as historical fact, being based partly on the epic traditions of the Merovingian (from Merovech, father of Childeric) family itself and partly on annalistic records kept by the church.

Character of Clovis

The king Gregory portrays is primarily a warrior—bold, subtle, and unscrupulous in dealing with possible rivals among the Frankish chieftains of the northeast. A famous story told of him by Gregory best illustrates his qualities. A splendid vase was seized by Clovis' followers from a church (perhaps Reims), and the Bishop begged for its return. At the next division of booty, which took place at Soissons, the King asked for the vase in addition to his agreed share of booty. One Frank objected and smashed the vase with his axe. The King restored it, broken as it was, to the Bishop and said nothing. But a year later, at a military assembly, he recognized the offending warrior and took occasion to rebuke him for his ill-kept weapons, flinging his axe to the ground. As the man bent to pick it up, the King split his skull with his own axe, remarking, "Thus you treated the vase at Soissons." Gregory entirely approved: the church was avenged and so was the King; and the rest of Clovis' following was terrified.

But Clovis was also pious and credulous, as befitted a warrior whose gods had brought him great success. Though master of a Roman province effectively controlled by dynasties of able Gallo-Roman bishops, he showed no disposition to seek conversion till after his marriage to a Catholic princess, the Burgundian Chrotechildis, in about 493. Three years later he undertook a campaign against the Alamanni of the Middle Rhine, and at Zülpich (Tolbiac) his forces faced defeat. Only at this point did he think of invoking the help of his wife's god; and defeat was turned to victory. Even then a period of some two years elapsed before the combined efforts of Chrotechildis and Bishop Remigius persuaded him to seek Baptism. This took place at Reims, after a visit to Tours and due consultation with his warriors, 3,000 of whom were baptized with him. The Frankish settlers of the countryside remained pagan, and their conversion was a slow and spasmodic business. Their grave goods were to betray a rustic paganism at least until the 7th century.

It was to Catholicism, not to Arianism, that Clovis had turned. This may have affected his abortive intervention in the political affairs of Burgundy shortly afterward, for the Burgundians were mostly Arians. Some Burgundian detachments followed him on his subsequent campaigns; but he cannot be said to have conquered Burgundy or annexed it to Francia. A letter to him from Avitus, bishop of Burgundian Vienne, fully recognizes the risk to his barbarian charisma that the King ran in denying the pagan gods of his ancestors. In place of pagan *fortuna*, the Bishop urges, the King has acquired Christian *sanctitas*, which will equally see him to victory.

In 506 Clovis was still active in the Rhineland against both the Alamanni and the Thuringians. In 507 he finally turned against the powerful Visigoths of Gaul south of the Loire. But first he sought the patronage of St. Martin of Tours, greatest of the Gallo-Roman saints. His subsequent victory over the Arian Visigoths at Vouillé, near Poitiers, was attributed by him to that patronage. His family had acquired a spiritual patron revered by all his Gallo-Roman subjects. Though he penetrated as far south as Bordeaux and sent his son to capture the Visigoth capital of Toulouse, he did not expel the Goths from Septimania or turn southern Gaul into a settlement area for his people. He contented himself with returning to Tours, where he gave thanks to St. Martin for victory

and received the insignia of an honorary consulate from the Eastern emperor, Anastasius. He abandoned the Gallo-Roman south to its own devices and established himself at Paris, a good forward post from which to control the Armoricans of the west, the Thuringians on the Rhine, and the still-troublesome Franks of the north and east. In Paris he built a church dedicated to the Apostles (later Sainte-Geneviève).

Two revealing actions belong to the last year or so of Clovis' life. The first was the summoning of a church council at Orléans, attended by 32 bishops. Its canons, which survive, reveal the extent to which the King personally concerned himself with its deliberations. The second was the promulgation of Lex Salica, the law of the Salian Franks who accepted his authority. This constitutes 65 clauses regulating the life of the countryside. Uninfluenced by Christianity, they are a political manifesto rather than a precise legal statement of how the Franks ordered their lives. What they certainly reveal is the enhanced authority of the King and his willingness to make use of Gallo-Roman skills in ruling his own barbarians. Clovis died at Paris late in 511, at the age of 45, and was buried in his Church of the Apostles. His Christian grave has never been found.

Assessment of Clovis' achievements

Making every allowance for Gregory of Tours's intention to represent him as a second Constantine, Clovis still stands out as a barbarian of heroic stature. Starting from small beginnings, he had been accepted as ruler by the Gallo-Romans; with imperial approval he had made the first serious attack on the Arian-Gothic confederation of western Europe; he had taken for his people the momentous decision that they were ultimately to be converted to Catholicism, not Arianism; and, perhaps most difficult of all, he had made one political people of the various Frankish tribes of modern Belgium and the Rhineland. Henceforward, Frankish power was to penetrate and colonize east of the Rhine. His family was secure in an unrivalled dominance that was to last until the 8th century.

BIBLIOGRAPHY. The chief source for the life of Clovis is the *History of the Franks* by Gregory of Tours, Eng. trans. by O.M. DALTON, 2 vol. (1927). Among modern works, see G. TESSIER, *Le Baptême de Clovis* (1964); E. ZOLLNER, *Geschichte der Franken* (1970); and J.M. WALLACE-HADRILL, *The Long-Haired Kings* (1962).

(J.M.W.-H.)

Clupeiformes

The order Clupeiformes, containing some of the world's most numerous and economically important fishes, includes more than 400 species, about 20 of which provide more than one third of the world fish catch. Most clupeiforms are small marine fishes, under 30 centimetres (12 inches) in length, slender, streamlined, and rather nonspecialized in body form; a few species exceed 50 centimetres in length. A wolf herring, *Chirocentrus dorab*, is exceptional and reaches 3.6 metres (12 feet).

Authorities disagree on many aspects of the classification of the order Clupeiformes, which is usually described as including more families than are treated in this article. In a sweeping revision of the bony fishes, the ichthyologists P.H. Greenwood of Great Britain and Donn E. Rosen, Stanley H. Weitzman, and George S. Myers of the United States have restricted the order to the families Clupeidae (herrings, sardines, and allies), Engraulidae (anchovies), Chirocentridae (wolf herrings), and Denticipitidae, a single, little known African species. The last two families are of purely scientific interest; the dominant members of the order, in abundance and therefore in economic importance, are the herrings, sardines, pilchards, menhadens, sprats, anchovies, and anchovetas. Other fish groups formerly included in the Clupeiformes are the tarpons and bonefishes (see ELOPIFORMES); salmons, trouts, and pikes (see SALMONIFORMES); and bony tongues and mormyrs (see OSTEOGLOSSOMORPHA).

GENERAL FEATURES

Importance to man. The Clupeiformes are by far the most heavily exploited of all fish groups, and the world

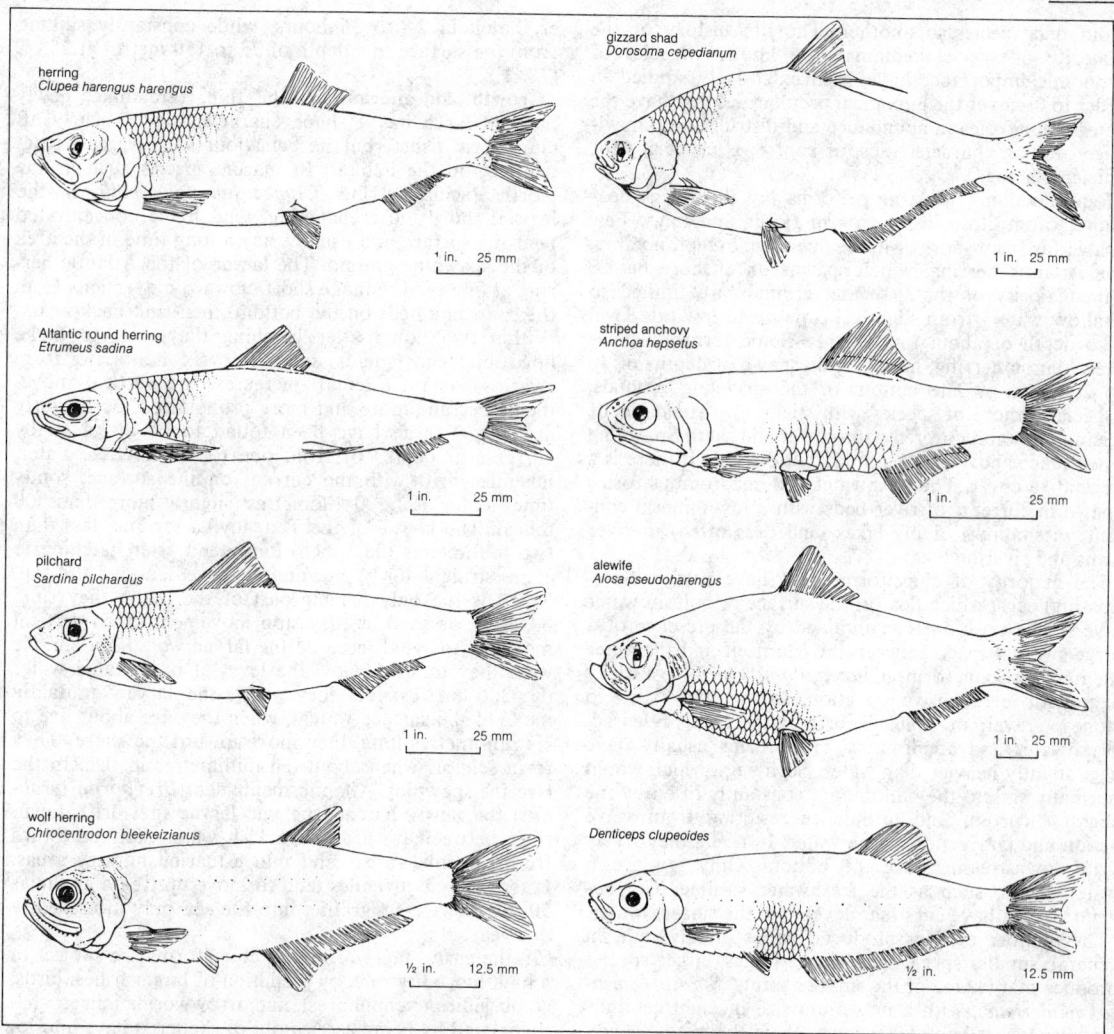

Figure 1: Body plans of representative clupeiform fishes.

Drawing by A. Murawski based on (*Clupea harengus, Etrumeus sadina, Anchoa hepsetus, Alosa pseudoharengus*)
A.H. Leim and W.B. Scott, *Fishes of the Atlantic Coast of Canada* (1966); Fisheries Research Board of Canada;
reproduced by permission of Information Canada; (*Denticeps clupeoides, Chirocentrodon bleekeizianus*) *Bulletin of
the American Museum of Natural History* (1966); (*Dorosoma cepedianum*) D.S. Jordan, *A Guide to the Study of Fishes*

catch increases yearly. Of the 1968 world fish catch of 66,000,000 tons, 23,000,000 tons, or 36 percent, were clupeiforms. This represented a substantial increase over 1958, when clupeiforms constituted 8,400,000 tons (26 percent) of the world total of 33,000,000 tons. Most of the increase in the intervening decade resulted from the exploitation of previously unfished resources of the South Pacific anchoveta (*Cetengraulis mysticetus*), 12,-425,000 tons of which were taken in 1968 by Chile and Peru; and of the South African pilchard (*Sardinops sagax ocellatus*), 1,750,000 tons of which were taken by southern African nations. By comparison, the total catch of the herring (*Clupea harengus*) in the Atlantic Ocean by many Northern Hemisphere countries was 3,614,000 tons.

Distribution. Most clupeiforms inhabit more or less offshore open waters in abundant schools. Although usually considered pelagic (inhabiting the open ocean), in relation to distribution and life history, they are closer to the neritic (coastal) fauna because they do not usually occur in the really open parts of the oceans; rather, they stay close to shore and in bays. Even the truly pelagic and migratory species spawn close to shore. The geographical distribution of the order is limited mainly by temperature and salinity. About 70 percent of the species occurs in tropical waters, only few visiting subtropical regions. More than 20 species are limited to purely boreal and sub-Arctic distribution. Remarkably few species are found in the Southern Hemisphere. In relation to salinity clupeiform fishes represent a fairly mixed group: most of them, approximately half of the living species, are wholly marine; a smaller part are anadromous (living

in the sea but entering freshwater to breed); and nearly the same number are wholly freshwater fishes. The order includes some marine genera with large numbers of species, such as *Sardinella* and *Harengula*, which together comprise more than 60 genera and nearly 220 species. There are fewer anadromous clupeids, about 10 genera with 40 species, distributed mostly in temperate regions, but some in subtropical areas. Freshwater clupeiform fishes include 31 species in 16 genera, most of them limited to the tropics. Nine genera with 15 species inhabit the rivers and lakes of Central and West Africa; six species are distributed in freshwaters of the Indo-Malayan Archipelago and Australia; two genera with four species occur in freshwaters of India; some species of the genera *Sigualosa* and *Dorosoma* occur in Central America; and single species of otherwise marine genera are found in the Amazon River (*Rhinosardinia amazonica*), in the rivers of Borneo (*Ilisha macrogaster*), and in freshwater lakes of the Philippines (*Harengula tawilis*). A few other species occasionally occur in freshwater.

Of the families and subfamilies of the Clupeiformes, the subfamilies Dussumieriinae (round herrings), Clupeinae (typical herrings), and Pristigasterinae, and the family Chirocentridae are purely marine; the Denticipitidae and Pellonulinae are limited to freshwater; the Alosinae (shads and alewives) and Dorosomatinae (gizzard shads) are anadromous, freshwater, brackish, or marine; and the Engraulidae are brackish or marine.

NATURAL HISTORY

It is impossible to make a general statement about the biology of clupeiform fishes, except that it varies greatly

Spawning
habitats

from one species to another. The life history of the majority of species remains little known. Species of economic importance have been extensively studied in order to discover the biological peculiarities that have the determining roles in abundance and distribution; knowledge of such characteristics, of course, is necessary for efficient fishing.

Reproduction. Most clupeiforms lay their eggs near shore, often close inshore or in fjords and bays. Few spawn far from shore or in the open sea, except, notably, the Atlantic herring, which spawns on offshore banks. The majority of the spawning grounds are limited to shallow waters from slightly below mean low-tide level to a depth of about four metres. Some forms, such as the Atlantic herring, however, do spawn at depths of 40 to 200 metres. The bottom of the spawning grounds, especially those of species with sticky eggs, tends to be clean, hard, and covered with gravel and sand. Spawning takes place above a soft, muddy bottom only if there is a vegetative cover. The freshwater and anadromous forms spawn in currents of river beds with a low mineral content, in shallows of big lakes, and (less often) in river arms and riverine lakes.

The majority of clupeiform fishes have pelagic (free-floating) eggs, which float in the surface or bottom water layers. Egg position is maintained by the presence of a large swollen space between the egg itself and the outer membrane. Some forms (*Clupea, Pomolobus*) have sticky eggs with an adhesive secretion, so that they stick to stones, gravel, or plants shortly after being released. Freshwater and anadromous clupeiforms usually have eggs slightly heavier than water. Such eggs, which would normally sink to the bottom, are constantly lifted by the slightest current and turbulence resulting from wave action and convection of the water. In rivers they freely drift downstream above the bottom. Only few freshwater forms, such as the freshwater sardine (*Clupeonella abrau*), have eggs that develop in the surface water.

The number of eggs produced varies greatly, but, in general, smaller species produce few eggs, larger species produce many. One of the smaller sprats (*Sprattus sprattus phalericus*), with a maximum size of eight centimetres, produces about 2,000 eggs; one of the biggest shads, *Alosa kessleri kessleri*, can produce more than 300,000 eggs; and menhaden (several species of *Brevoortia*) produce more than 500,000. Freshwater species usually have more eggs than marine species of comparable size, evidently an adaptation against the higher mortality in riverine conditions. Clupeiforms with adhesive eggs produce more eggs than do those with free-floating eggs; apparently, eggs that develop sticking to the bottom are exposed to a much higher mortality from predators than are pelagic eggs. Of great importance in reducing mortality rates is "repeated portion" spawning: in the majority, if not in all, clupeiform fishes, the eggs in the gonads do not become ripe all at once but in two or more portions, allowing more eggs in the limited space of the body cavity and enhancing the chances of some surviving if the first are destroyed. The many causes of spawn mortality range from those of a physical character, such as wave action and sudden temperature drops, to biological ones, such as predation by gulls and ducks. An important protective mechanism against destruction of the abundant schools is the remarkably early age at which they first breed; females begin frequently to spawn only a few months after hatching. This, coupled with high fecundity, gives the order a high reproductive potential.

Variation
in hatching
times

The duration of egg development varies from a few hours to nearly two months. An important factor in the rate of development is the temperature of the surrounding water; the cold-water herrings have the longest developmental period. The egg development of the Atlantic herring takes as long as 47 to 50 days at a temperature of 0.1° C (just above 32° F), but only eight days at 19° C (66° F). Some shad eggs develop in about 75 hours at 17° C (63° F) but require only 49 hours at 19° C. The eggs of the Tanganyika sardine (*Stolothrissa tanganicae*), an open-water, freshwater, surface spawn-

er, hatch in 24 to 36 hours, while constantly sinking from the surface to a depth of 75 to 150 metres at 25° C (77° F).

Growth and mortality. The thin, threadlike, newly hatched larva has a shape characteristic of nearly all clupeiform fishes, but its behaviour varies greatly, depending on the habitat. In marine species such as the North Pacific herring (*Clupea harengus pallasii*), the larvae, shortly after hatching, tend to be concentrated near the surface and usually stay a long time in the area of the spawning ground. The larvae of the Atlantic herring at first tend to make short, upward movements from the spawning beds on the bottom, then sink back again. Within two hours after hatching they start to make horizontal movements and, after six hours, to form swarms. As their length increases, the vertical movements become more and more pronounced, particularly at night. Larvae have been found to be dispersed by currents at depths of from one to 600 metres. Later, juveniles drift with the current on the surface, sometimes as far as 1,300 kilometres (slightly more than 800 miles). The larvae of the Tanganyika sardine, less than two millimetres (0.08 inch) long, tend after hatching to come straight up by swimming movements of the tail, which is the only flexible part of the body; they sink, however, as soon as they stop movement. Such vertical movement is vital, because the larvae would not survive were they to sink below the level of oxygenated water (80–200 metres). As they grow, the larvae gradually move to the surface waters; when they are about five to six millimetres long, they move toward the shore. They form schools when about ten millimetres in size. In the riverine-spawning Atlantic menhaden (*Brevoortia tyrannus*) the newly hatched pelagic larvae first drift downriver between fresh and brackish water and shoreward from spawning areas and into estuarine nursery areas. Later, pelagic juveniles tend to move upstream as far as 50 kilometres, emigrating into the sea only after nearly one year.

Causes of
larval
mortality

In the early stages of life all clupeiforms are subject to a high mortality rate, by predation of larger fishes, birds, comb jellies (ctenophores), and arrowworms (chaetognathans) and by being carried out of sheltered bays into localities in which the proper food is lacking. Mortality has been estimated at well over 99 percent, but because of the extremely high fecundity, the distribution, and the early maturity, the recruitment of new breeding individuals remains high. The age of first sexual maturity is seldom more than three years, and the length at maturity rarely exceeds more than 15 centimetres. Late-spawning species are usually larger and move over long distances. The age at first breeding is broadly correlated with rate of growth of the individual and with maximum length attained by the species, but there are other determining factors, some of which are unknown. The Siberian shad (*Alosa saposhnikovi*), Baltic sprat (*Sprattus sprattus balticus*), and the *Clupeonella engrauliformis* all mature at two to three years of age, but at lengths of 160 to 200 millimetres, 120 to 130 millimetres, and 85 to 100 millimetres, respectively. Different populations of a species may vary in their growth rates; the races of the Atlantic herring vary from two to seven years in age at maturity and from 100 to 185 millimetres in length at maturity. Members of anadromous populations of the alewife (*Alosa pseudoharengus*) reach maturity at three to four years of age and 150 to 170 millimetres in length, but those of landlocked populations breed at one to two years of age and 95 to 100 millimetres.

Migration. During their life cycle some clupeiforms undertake very long migrations of several thousand kilometres; others live in a more or less circumscribed area. Such differences occur, however, even within a species; some races of the herring, for example, spend their entire lives in more or less limited areas; others undertake some of the longest known migrations. Some forms of the Caspian shad (*Alosa caspia*) remain all year round in the southern region of the Caspian Sea, but others move long distances from winter habitats in southern parts to spawning grounds in the northern region of the Caspian.

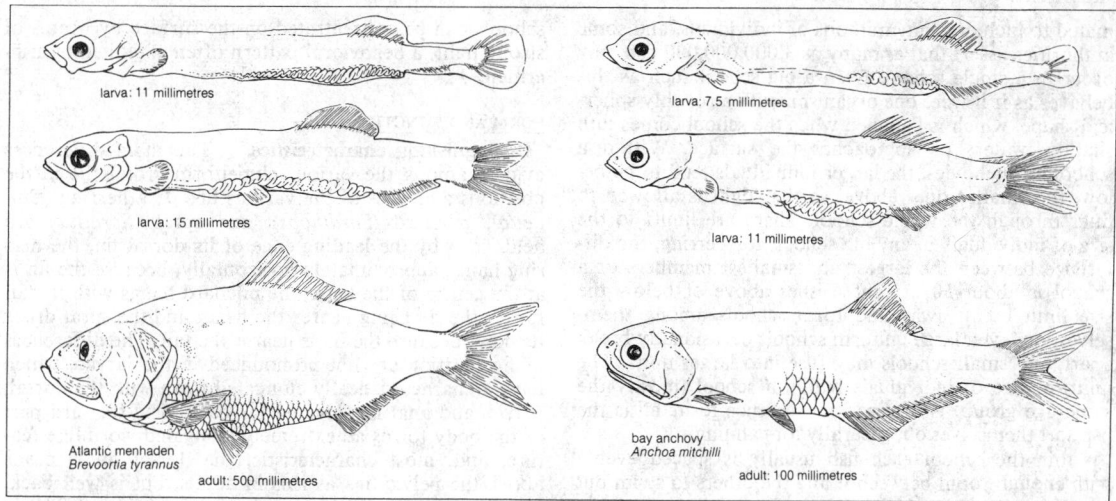

Figure 2: Changes in body proportions and fin position between larvae and adult in two clupeiform fishes.

From (adult Atlantic menhaden) A.H. Leim and W.B. Scott, *Fishes of the Atlantic Coast of Canada* (1966), Fisheries Research Board of Canada, reproduced by permission of Information Canada; and (adult *Anchoa mitchilli*) A.J. Mansueti and J.D. Hardy, *Development of Fishes of the Chesapeake Bay Region: An Atlas of Egg, Larval, and Juvenile Stages*, by the Natural Resources Institute, University of Maryland

In addition to spawning migrations, some species travel long distances for feeding. Japanese pilchards (*Sardinella sagax melanosticta*) winter and spawn in the southern part of the Sea of Japan and on the Pacific side of the southern islands of Japan, then, in early summer, move to the northern end of the Tatar Strait and, in warm years, even to the eastern shore of the Kamchatka Peninsula. Similar or even longer migrations are made by the Californian pilchard or Spanish sardine (*Sardinella anchovia*) and others. Most of these spawning and feeding migrations are from south to north and occur along the coast with the aid of some of the larger ocean currents. As the fish move fairly close to shore, they become the object of intensive fishing.

Long-distance movements of herring Some of the longest migrations extend over several years and start in the larval stages. The majority of the young North Pacific herring spend part or the whole of their first year in shallow coastal waters. Larvae of the Murman race of North Pacific herring and Norwegian race (or spring race) of North Atlantic herring usually hatch on offshore spawning grounds and start their long journey drifting with the currents. Those of the Murman race drift with the North Atlantic Current along the coast of northern Norway, north and east, and later, as juveniles, spread actively into the Barents Sea and even into the White Sea. After their first spawning, the Murman herrings move north to the waters around Spitsbergen. The movements of the Norwegian spring herring are similar to those of the Murman race. The young herrings move into deeper water and, as they grow bigger, move farther and farther from the coast. While still immature, they are taken by fisheries in Norway, Denmark, and Scotland and are processed for oil and into meal. As a rule, migrations are oriented by the sea currents near the spawning grounds, but the fish go as well with or against the current direction; four forms of the Caspian shad are known to move against currents.

Food ecology. Intensity of movement and feeding habits determine the relative abundance of various species of clupeiform fishes; these same factors determine economic importance. All of the abundant (and economically important) species feed on plankton—pelagic protozoans (diatoms and flagellates), copepods, metazoan larvae, euphausids, and amphipods. Some apparently feed all the year round, as long as food is available, but most change their feeding habits seasonally. It is known that all forms of the herring and most members of the genera *Alosa* and *Clupeonella* do not feed during the spawning season; feeding is most intensive in the summer after spawning and less so in spring before spawning.

Predatory clupeids seem to be relatively scarce and usually have a much smaller commercial value than do the plankton feeders. The fish-eating race of Russian shad *Alosa kessleri kessleri*, for instance, is far less abundant and is caught less often than is the plankton-feeding race *A. k. volgensis*.

Some evidence suggests that even among plankton-feeding clupeiform fishes, while some species are as a rule abundant, many others are more or less rare. This variation is apparently primarily determined by the size of the inhabited area and the size of spawning grounds; of secondary importance are the time and distance of migrations preceding the age of first reproduction. The Pacific sardine (*Sardinops sagax*)—which inhabits vast areas on both sides of the North Pacific, the South Pacific coasts of South America and Australia, and the Indian Ocean coasts of Australia and Africa—is a good example of a widespread, highly migratory, and economically important species; the herring *Clupea harengus* provides a similar example. Most of the Pacific races of herring, on the other hand, are local and nonmigratory, and their role in commercial catches is far below the value of the Atlantic races. The Japanese pilchard is known to feed in southern as well as in northern regions, and from the ecological point of view this whole area of the Pacific is fully utilized. The high abundance of anchovies is determined more by their early age of sexual maturity than by their movements; similarly, the relatively high abundance in a restricted habitat of the Tanganyika sardines appears to stem from precocious breeding.

The size of the inhabited area is reflected in the presence of more progressive adaptive morphological characteristics. All of the clupeiforms with more primitive features (*e.g.*, *Denticeps*, *Dorosoma*, *Clupeonella*) are less abundant and are limited to small areas. Tropical genera have more different species; subtropical and temperate genera are more often monotypic (comprising a single species) but far more abundant.

Schooling behaviour. With few exceptions, the important behavioral characteristics of clupeiforms are schooling and diurnal (daily) vertical movements. Schools are formed with larvae or young juveniles. A fish less than ten millimetres long approaches the tail of another; both vibrate their bodies in a series of rapid motions, after which they swim together. Occasionally, they are joined by others, and as the fish grow a few more millimetres in length, the first small schools increase in size and begin to show a steady schooling pattern. Opinions differ on whether the school keeps together through visual contact—it sometimes tends to break up at night—or through sensations received by the lateral-line system, a series of sensory endings extending along the side of the fish. When the schools do persist after nightfall, the lateral-line system may also play a significant role in preventing one animal from straying.

Single schools of herring or anchoveta have been esti-

Factors affecting abundance

Size,
shape, and
arrange-
ment of
schools

mated to include many millions of individuals, and some authorities assert that as many as 3,000,000,000 fish may occur in a single school. Even a big school such as this behaves as if it were one organism, with a roughly spherical shape, which is flattened when the school comes into shallow waters or approaches the surface. Within a school of anchovies, the larger individuals tend to be below, the smaller ones above, so that light is allowed to filter through the whole school. There are limits to the size of individuals in any big school; for herring, the difference between the largest and smallest members of a school is about 50 percent. Fishes above or below the size limit break away and form schools among themselves, but even large uniform schools occasionally break apart, and small schools may fuse into larger units. The uniform size of individuals within a school (mostly the same age group) is of great convenience to man, as the fish sort themselves out naturally for canning.

Within the school each fish usually is spaced evenly with enough room between it and the others to swim but not to turn around. In all schools of some species, and in some schools of others, the fish swim with their heads side by side; in other species (e.g., herring) the head of each fish lies next to the middle of its neighbour's body. The schools may spread out or become very tight, depending on the occasion.

The
adaptive
value of
schooling

The primary advantage of the schooling habit seems to lie in the safety of the individual fish. Sardines react to attacks by predators by swimming closer together and milling around in tight, compact balls; herring form a close school with any approach of danger. The reaction of anchovies to predators is even more intense; a school that may be spread over several hundred metres contracts at the approach of a predator to a moving, writhing sphere of thousands of fishes only a few metres across. In such a situation the predator cannot concentrate on a single individual and may be frustrated in its attempt to catch any fish. The adaptive value of schooling behaviour is poorly understood, but several logical explanations have been advanced. Schooling evidently provides a better chance for small fish to survive many environmental hazards than if they live solitarily. The instinctive tendency of the tiny larva to associate, even though hatched from scattered eggs, ensures the formation of the school, with its protection from predation. Certain hydrodynamic interactions between members of the school are thought to facilitate feeding movements; and the aggregation of so many fish simplifies the finding of mates.

Although anchovy schools progress steadily through the water, they do not seem to have any leader or leader groups. Observers from the air have noted that

fish travelling in the vanguard often drop back and are replaced by others from the flanks and this is repeated in due course. When the school changes course, the fish from the flank find themselves on the leading edge and the previous leading edge becomes a flank. These manoeuvres are carried out with such precision that one has the impression of watching a single creature moving through the water.

The behaviour of the school is determined most probably by the order of feeding. If a school were to swim straight forward, the fish in front would capture most of the food organisms, and those in the rear would starve. Instead, the leading individuals turn back to either flank and, step by step, return to the rear of the school; in this way, each fish gets its turn to feed.

The depth at which the schools swim depends on the movements of plankton, light intensity, temperature, and the maturation cycle of gonads (i.e., whether or not the fish are in breeding condition). There are diurnal vertical movements of schools, related mainly to the corresponding movements of plankton. Most clupeiform schools are believed to stay near the bottom or in deep water during the day and to move toward the surface during the night. Herring often make a vertical migration from a depth of 300 to 400 metres in the day toward the surface water at night; they therefore move from deep cold waters of about 3° C (37° F) to somewhat warmer surface waters of 5° to 7° C (41° to 45° F). On moonless nights clupeid

schools can be concentrated on the surface by beams of strong light, a behavioral pattern often exploited by fishermen.

FORM AND FUNCTION

Distinguishing characteristics.   The main differences evident among the various clupeiform groups lie in the positions and sizes of the various fins. If a herring (*Clupetta*), pilchard (*Sardinops*), and sprat (*Sprattus*) are held, each by the leading edge of its dorsal fin, the herring hangs approximately horizontally, because the fin is at the centre of the back; the pilchard hangs with its tail lower, the fin being nearer the head; and the sprat drops its nose, because the fin is nearer the tail. The differences of fin position are not pronounced in the larvae, which have a characteristically elongated form with the dorsal, pelvic, and anal fins located far back. The forward part of the body forms an extremely elongated wormlike feature, and, most characteristic, the dorsal fin is never above the pelvic fins as it is in adults, but is well back, usually somewhere between the pelvic and anal fins; in larval anchovies it is even above the anal fin. During the larval transformation the elongated anterior part of the body becomes progressively shorter, as the fins shift forward by a complicated morphological process. The dorsal fin is shifted forward above the lateral body muscles (myomeres); the pelvic fins move backward to their adult position; and the anal fin moves forward simultaneously. In adults of the families Denticipitidae and Chirocentridae, the dorsal fin stays above the anal fin, far back on the body; in the Engraulidae it usually stops a little farther back than the pelvic fins; and in the Clupeidae it generally reaches a position directly above the pelvic fins. As a rule, however, even within families and genera the relative positions of the dorsal, anal, and pelvic fins are somewhat variable and are often used in classification. The position of the dorsal fin becomes stable at the time the larvae transform into juveniles. The positions of the anal and pelvic fins, however, often change later in life, probably because of the swelling of the body cavity with gonad development.

With only a few exceptions, fishes with more forwardly positioned dorsal fins have fewer rays in their anal fin but more rays in the dorsal. The lateral line canals on the head are most developed in fishes with the dorsal fin located anteriorly. The lateral line system serves as an orientation device. As it is sensitive to disturbances in the surrounding water, it is most important in fishes that school densely. Not surprisingly, the species with the most progressively developed morphological features (i.e., the greatest changes from the "primitive" condition of the larval stage), such as the anteriorly located dorsal fin, a smaller number of rays in the anal fin, and a strong lateral-line system on the head, are the best swimmers and undertake the longest migrations.

The development of denticles (toothlike skin projections) and teeth represents another specialization of evolutionary importance. The most primitive clupeiform fishes have an enormous number of dermal denticles (on the head and in the mouth), which have been replaced in evolutionarily more advanced forms by teeth, which are larger and fewer in number. In *Denticeps*, for example, the whole head and part of the body are covered by numerous small dermal denticles. Different species of the Clupeidae have small denticles or teeth limited to the bones of the mouth cavity, and anchovies have rows of tiny teeth in the jaws. Finally, *Chirocentrus* has straight sharp teeth on the upper jaw, the tongue, and in a few other places in the mouth, and has large "canine" teeth on the lower jaw.

The ventral part of the body in the majority of clupeiform fishes forms a keel, the function of which is widely considered to be an adaptation for removing the sharp shadow that would be created below the central part of the body by top lighting, were the fish cylindrical. Prevention of such a shadow is important to an open-water fish often living close to the surface and unprotected from all sides. Seen from below, the keel and the glossy silver sides of the body cause the fish to disappear in the

Distinctive
differences
in fin
position

Relative
numbers of
denticles
and teeth

The value
of the
ventral
keel

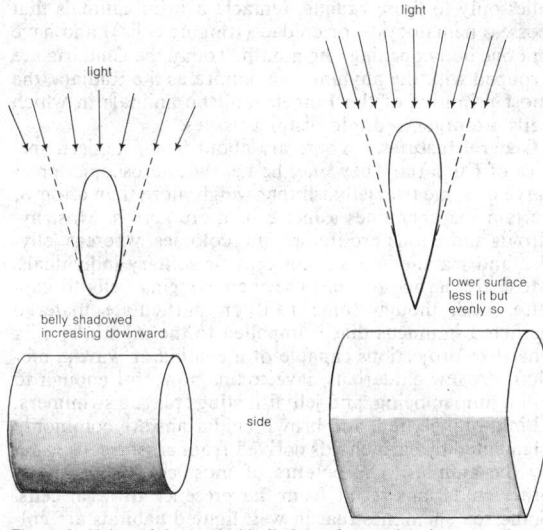

Figure 3: Value of the keeled belly in surface-swimming fishes (see text).

mirror-like reflection of the water surface. Viewed from above, the fish is protected by the dark cryptic colouring of the dorsal part, which simulates the colour of the deep water. The predator who encounters and sees the whole school is also deceived by the resemblance of the tight school to a larger organism. Against man's nets and electronic devices, however, such coloration and schooling behaviour afford little protection.

Physiology. The movement of anadromous clupeiforms from the salt ocean into freshwater rivers and lakes requires special physiological adaptations to regulate the blood's osmotic pressure (basically, the pressure of a water solution of salts exerted in either direction against a semipermeable membrane caused by differences between the concentrations of dissolved salts within the body and those outside, in the sea). When a fish enters water of salinity lower than seawater, slight increases in osmotic pressure cause the kidneys to excrete larger amounts of water. The conversion from saltwater to freshwater physiology requires some time, however, so the fish usually remains in brackish waters to avoid a sudden physiological shock. During the periods when anadromous fishes are migrating into or out of freshwater, they form large aggregations in estuaries, awaiting the changeover in their osmotic regulating systems.

CLASSIFICATION

Distinguishing taxonomic features. Three main character complexes have recently been recognized and accepted as distinguishing the clupeiform fishes: (1) the presence of an internal connection between the swim bladder and the inner ear, usually forming two large vesicles (cavities) within the skull bones; (2) certain peculiarities of the skull, involving the relation of the lateral line canals to each other and to the ear; (3) certain complex features in the caudal (tail) fin skeleton.

Annotated classification. A recent and widely accepted classification of the order Clupeiformes by P.H. Greenwood *et al.* is presented below. These authors consider the Clupeiformes as the only order in the superorder Clupeomorpha, which formerly included other major fish groups (see above).

ORDER CLUPEIFORMES
Silvery, laterally compressed fishes; mainly marine, but many anadromous or wholly freshwater; mostly pelagic and schooling fishes. Lateral-line canal on head usually extending over operculum (gill cover). About 400 living species.

Suborder Denticipitoidei
Caudal skeleton of extremely primitive type; small arches present on 2 centra (bodies of vertebrae) to carry the first 3 hypural bones (fused spines of the vertebrae) of the tail fin. One family.

Family Denticipitidae
The most primitive living clupeiform. Numerous dermal denticles present on head, on the dorsal part of the secondary pectoral girdle, and on the scales around the anterior end of the lateral line. Lateral line completely developed on the trunk. A single living species, *Denticeps clupeoides*, in fast-running clear water in medium-sized streams of West African Nigeria; and a single fossil species, *Palaeodenticeps tanganikae*, from the Tertiary lacustrine sediments in East African Tanzania.

Suborder Clupeoidei
Characteristic caudal skeleton: the second hypural bone lacks any connection with the urostyle (tail support) and is separated from it by a distinct gap. Lateral line pores completely lacking on trunk. Keeled scutes (projecting scales) usually present along the ventral midline of the abdomen.

Family Clupeidae (herrings, sardines, pilchards, shads, menhadens, and allies)
Teeth usually absent in mouth or very weakly developed; minute in jaw. Keel scales well developed, except in round herrings (subfamily Dussumieriinae), in which they are absent, and the ventral part of body rounded. About 50 genera and 190 species, virtually worldwide in marine waters and in many bodies of freshwater.

Family Engraulidae (anchovies)
Mostly smaller fishes than clupeids, with the snout projecting beyond the very wide mouth. Upper and lower jaws usually armed with rows of minute teeth that sometimes become larger in the posterior end of the jaws. About 200 species; primarily marine with a few anadromous; found in very large schools.

Family Chirocentridae (wolf herrings)
Body laterally compressed and elongated, with sharp, keeled ventral margin; scales small. Lower jaw strongly projecting; large fanglike teeth in both jaws. Two species, *Chirocentrus dorab* and *C. nudus*; widely but sparsely distributed in the Sea of Japan, the Pacific Ocean off Australia and in Melanesia, the Red Sea, and along the east coast of Africa. Used for food in some areas but not very palatable. Larger than other clupeiforms, reaching at least 3.6 metres (12 feet) in length.

Critical appraisal. Until the revision of the bony fishes by Greenwood and his colleagues in 1966, the most widely accepted classifications were those by an American, C.T. Regan, in 1929, a Soviet ichthyologist, L.S. Berg, in 1940, and two from France, L. Bertin and Camille Arambourg, in 1958. The three earlier systems differ widely from one another in the scope of the order Clupeiformes, in the subdivisions of the order, and in the order of families, but they have in common the inclusion of many more groups than were considered related to the clupeid fishes by Greenwood *et al.* The earlier classifications grouped together in one order, Clupeiformes or Isospondyli, a large number of fishes characterized by having soft, as opposed to spiny, fin rays.

Greenwood *et al.* postulated, on the basis of a number of other features in both modern and fossil fishes, that this similarity is overridden by more fundamental differences that indicate a long history of phyletic separation. These authors separated the families Denticipitidae, Clupeidae, Engraulidae, and Chirocentridae in a distinct superorder Clupeomorpha, placed in Division I, one of the three subgroups of the bony fishes. The bony tongues, mormyrs and relatives, treated by Bertin and Arambourg as suborders of the Clupeiformes, were placed by Greenwood *et al.* in the superorder Osteoglossomorpha, sole group in their Division II. The remaining fishes formerly included in the Clupeiformes, consisting mainly of the salmons, trouts, pikes, and a number of deepsea forms, were placed in a large order Salmoniformes, part of Division III.

BIBLIOGRAPHY. P.H. GREENWOOD *et al.*, "Phyletic Studies of Teleostean Fishes with a Provisional Classification of Living Forms," *Bull. Am. Mus. Nat. Hist.*, 131:339–455 (1966), contains the latest classification, which is used also in this article. Some different classifications and arrangements are in: L.S. BERG, "Classification of Fishes, Both Recent and Fossil," *Trav. Inst. Zool. Acad. Sci. U.S.S.R.*, vol. 5, no. 2 (1940; reprinted in book-form, 1947), Russian and English texts; LEON BERTIN and CAMILLE ARAMBOURG, "Super-ordre des téléostéens (Teleostei)," in P.P. GRASSE (ed.), *Traité de zoologie*, vol. 13, fasc. 3, pp. 2204–2500 (1958); P.J.P. WHITEHEAD, "A Contribution to the Classification of Clupeoid Fishes," *Ann. Mag. Nat. Hist.*, Series 13, 5:737–750 (1962); H.S. CLAUSEN, "Denticipitidae, a New Family of Primitive Isospondylous Teleosts from West African Freshwater," *Vidensk. Meddr. Dansk Naturh. Foren.*, 121:141–151 (1959), the first scientific description of an unknown and evolutionary important Clupeiformes family; M.B. SCHAEFER, "Men, Birds and Anchovies in the Peru Current: Dynamic Interactions," *Trans. Am. Fish. Soc.*, 99:461–467 (1970), a modern evaluation of the most abundant species resources; A.J. MANSUETI and J.D. HARDY, *Development of Fishes of the Chesapeake Bay Region: An Atlas of Egg, Larval, and Juvenile Stages* (1967); E.K. BALON, "First Catches of Lake Tanganyika Clupeids (kapenta—*Limothrissa miodon*) in Lake Kariba," *Bull. Fish. Res. Zambia*, 5:175–186 (1971), an account of successful artificial introduction into a new area; and A.N. SVETOVIDOV, "Fauna of the U.S.S.R.," *Fishes*, vol. 2, no. 1, *Clupeidae* (1963; orig. pub. in Russian, 1952), a good source of biological and morphological data with extensive bibliography.

(E.K.B.)

Cnidaria

The phylum Cnidaria consists of a group of primitive aquatic animals including the hydroids, hydrocorals, hydromedusae, true jellyfish (scyphomedusae), sea anemones, soft corals, sea pens, sea fans, and true corals. The variety and exquisite symmetry of the body forms, the varied coloration, and the sometimes complex life histories of cnidarians fascinate the layman and scientist alike. Inhabiting all marine environments, these animals —particularly the corals, soft corals, and sea fans— are most abundant and diverse in tropical waters. No other animal can compare to the corals in its effect on the surface features of the Earth. The skeletons of corals constitute the atolls distributed throughout the Indo-Pacific region and the Great Barrier Reef that extends more than 1,000 miles along the northeast coast of Australia.

The phylum has been known as the Coelenterata, a name derived from their simple organization around a central gut or coelenteron. As first defined the Coelenterata included not only the animals now designated cnidarians, but also the sponges (Porifera; *q.v.*) and comb jellies (Ctenophora; *q.v.*). The name Cnidaria ap-

plies only to those radiate, tentacle-bearing animals that possess nematocysts, or cnidae (stinging cells), and have but one body opening, the mouth. Today the Cnidaria are grouped with the phylum Ctenophora as the Radiata, the most primitive of the Eumetazoa, the animals in which cells are organized into distinct tissues.

General features. There are about 9,000 modern species of Cnidaria. They may be nearly microscopic, or as large as some true jellyfish that weigh more than a ton or certain sea anemones a metre or more across. Most hydroids and corals proliferate into colonies, whereas jellyfish and sea anemones occur only as solitary individuals. Most are carnivores and use their stinging cells to capture food, though some feed on particulate material gathered in mucus that is impelled to the mouth by cilia (hairlike projections capable of a beating or waving motion). A few cnidarians have toxins powerful enough to kill a human being, and jellyfish stings plague swimmers.

Pink, orange, red, and brown cnidarians are commonly pigmented by carotenoids derived from crustaceans eaten by the animals. The colours of most corals and many other cnidarians result from the presence of algal cells. Some sea anemones that in well lighted habitats are coloured green by algae are white and translucent in caves too dark for the algal symbionts.

Cnidarians occur in two forms, polyp and medusa, both of which may be present in a single colony or, in some species, as parts of a single life history (see Figure 1). A polyp usually has an elongated cylindrical body enclosing the gut or coelenteron. It is sessile—that is, its base is firmly attached to some object—with the free end elaborated into tentacles radially arranged around the central mouth. The medusa (jellyfish), a slow-swimming, planktonic animal, usually has the form of a bell or an umbrella with tentacles at the margin. The mouth is at the end of a tube, the manubrium, that hangs under the bell and communicates with the gut. The sexes are commonly separate, though hermaphroditism is not unknown. The larval form, known as a planula, is elongated and usually possesses a ciliated (sensory?) tuft at the end directed forward in locomotion. The planula may be free-swimming and planktonic or crawling and benthic.

Polyps and medusae (margin note)

NATURAL HISTORY

Life Cycles. The phylum Cnidaria is divided into three classes, and the life histories of each class will be treated separately. One class, the Anthozoa (sea anemones, corals, and sea pens), consists solely of polyps, whereas the other classes, the Scyphozoa (true jellyfish) and Hydrozoa (hydroids and hydromedusae), commonly pass through both polypoid and medusoid stages.

Anthozoa. The sea anemone, a typical anthozoan, has a simple life history. Adult anemones usually have the gonads in the lining of the gut. The eggs or sperm are extruded from the coelenteron through the mouth into the water, where fertilization takes place. Cleavage of the fertilized egg results in a ciliated ball of cells that elongates, develops a tuft of cilia at one end, and becomes the planula. After a period of free life as either a planktonic or a benthic form, the planula attaches by its forward end to some solid object, develops tentacles around its posterior end, and takes up life as a polyp. Further development consists of the growth of more tentacles, elaboration of a multicompartmented gut, and an overall increase in size. Later, gonads develop, and at maturity spawning occurs.

Planula (margin note)

Scyphozoa. The life history of the Scyphozoa (see Figure 2) involves the alternation of an asexual and a sexual generation. The sexes are usually separate, and most spawn into the water. The larval stage is followed by a polypoid stage that by asexual reproduction gives rise to the sexually mature jellyfish. The planula is usually planktonic and attaches to a solid object. The polyp that grows from the planula has four compartments in its gut and bears tentacles around its mouth. In some species the polyp, called a scyphistoma, remains solitary, but in others it produces colonies of scyphistomae by budding off new individuals. A scyphistoma, by an asexual fission called strobilization, can cut off the free oral end, and

Figure 1: *Structure of cnidarians.*
(A) Hydroid polyp; (B) unexploded nematocyst; (C) exploded nematocyst; (D) cross section of polyp; (E) hydrozoan medusa; (F) cross section of medusa; (G) anthozoan (anemone) showing hexamerous biradial symmetry; (H) anthozoan (alcyonarian) showing octomerous radiobilateral symmetry.
From L.H. Hyman, *The Invertebrates*, vol. 1 (1940); reproduced by permission of McGraw-Hill Book Co.

mouth
gastrovascular cavity
radial canals
manubrium
epidermis
mesoglea
ring canal
tentacles
tentacular bulb with eyespot
manubrium
stem
velum
mesoglea
pedal disk
gastrodermis
tentacles

exumbrellar epidermis
subumbrellar epidermis
mesoglea
gastrodermal radial canal
epidermis of manubrium
subumbrellar cavity
gastrodermis of manubrium
gastrodermal lamella

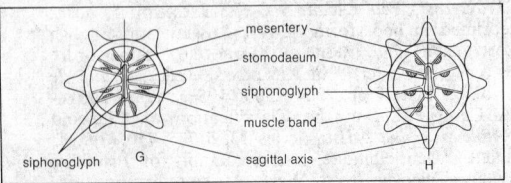

mesentery
stomodaeum
siphonoglyph
muscle band
siphonoglyph
sagittal axis

called gonozooids, develop reproductive structures called gonophores. One group of free-floating colonial hydrozoans, the Siphonophora, displays an even greater variety of polymorphs. These may include gas-filled floats, or pneumatophores; pulsating, locomotory medusoid structures called nectophores; and flattened, protective individuals called bracts or phyllozooids.

Growth and habitats. New individuals of most cnidarian species can develop from small pieces of living individuals. Some hydroids bud off bits of tissue at the ends of stolons; these bits then develop into new polyps. Colonies grow by asexual formation of new polyps, which remain interconnected and share a continuous coelenteron, through which food captured by any polyp is distributed to all members of the colony.

Most polyps require solid substrates, though a few burrow in soft materials, extending only their tentacular crowns above the surface (see Figure 3). Medusae swim freely but weakly, mostly to maintain a favoured depth in the water, and they are carried about by currents. Most hydromedusae and scyphomedusae occur in surface waters, most commonly in bays and along coasts. Hydrozoan and anthozoan polyps are most abundant in shallow waters. Most sea anemones, because of their attachment to fixed objects, cannot escape the attacks of certain starfishes and sea slugs. A few species, however, can elude those predators by releasing themselves from their substrate and swimming away.

Behaviour. *Associations.* Cnidarians enter into complex associations with a variety of other organisms, notably unicellular algae, fishes, and hermit crabs.

Algae live in the cells lining the coelenteron, particularly in the reef-forming corals and sea anemones, many of which harbour brownish or golden-green algae. Though cnidarians cannot digest the algal cells in their bodies, they do derive a variety of nourishing substances, including glucose and oxygen, from them. Carbon dioxide produced by the respiration of the animal may be directly utilized in photosynthesis by the algal cell. Many corals are so highly dependent on algae that they cannot live in the dark, and coral reefs develop only in shallow, well-illuminated water.

Fishes associate with large jellyfishes and with several sorts of large tropical sea anemones. If a predator threatens these fishes they find protection by hiding among the tentacles. The immunity of the symbiotic fish results from a thin layer of mucus that the fish acquires by repetitive contacts with the tentacles of the anemone. If such a fish is captured, wiped free of the covering mucus, and returned, it usually is stung to death and eaten by the anemone. Anemone fishes, as they are called, serve their hosts by attacking and driving away fishes and certain sea turtles that prey on anemones.

Many sea anemones live on gastropod shells occupied by hermit crabs. These anemones, when removed from these shells, remount themselves on new ones. Certain

Sipho-nophora

Anemone fishes

Figure 2: Life cycle of the scyphozoan jellyfish *Aurelia*.

this piece becomes an eight-armed, free-swimming form, known as an ephyra, from which the medusa develops. The typical adult jellyfish has a central mouth at the end of the manubrium, which hangs below the bell. The mouth opens into a compartmented gut that in turn gives rise to a series of canals joining a ring canal at the margin of the bell. As adulthood is reached, gonads develop, mature in the gut, and spawning produces a new generation.

Hydrozoa. In the Hydrozoa the medusa is usually the adult. The sexes are separate in hydromedusae, and the gonads develop in the epidermis. In most species the planula attaches to a solid substrate and by asexual reproduction grows to form prostrate, bushy, or feathery colonies, called hydroids, of many interconnected polyps. The polyp of hydrozoans has an undivided gut. Medusae are budded from ordinary or specialized polyps in colonial species. The newly released medusae usually have four tentacles and four radial canals running to the ring canal. The adult medusae may possess additional tentacles and develop their gonads on the sides of the manubrium or below the four radial canals.

Polymorphism. A striking feature of the colonial Hydrozoa, less common in the Anthozoa, is the variation, called polymorphism, of polyps within a colony. Each zooid, or different type of polyp, is specialized for some specific function. For example, certain polyps, called gastrozooids, bear tentacles and are specialized for feeding. Some colonies also possess tentacleless polyps heavily armed with nematocysts that may assist in feeding, but seem primarily concerned with defense. Some zooids,

Specialized polyps

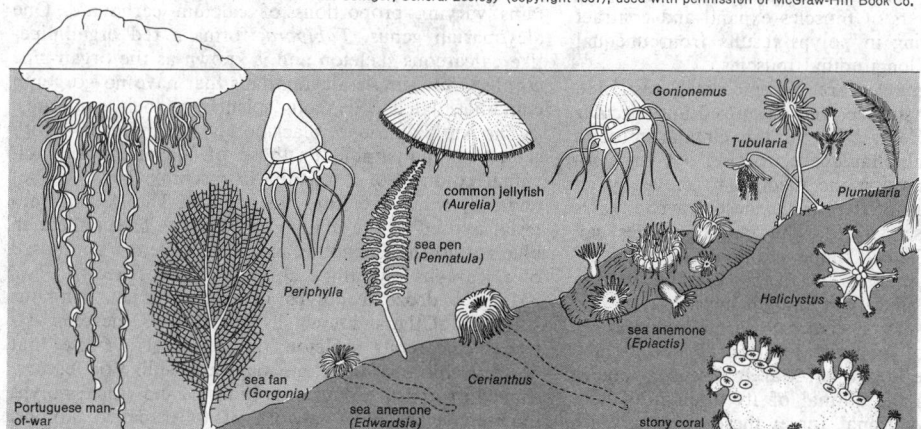

Figure 3: Marine cnidarians in characteristic habitats. (*Physalia, Gonionemus, Tubularia, Plumularia*) Hydrozoa; (*Gorgonia, Edwardsia, Pennatula, Cerianthus, Astrangia, Epiactis*) Anthozoa; (*Periphylla, Aurelia, Haliclystus*) Scyphozoa.

species of hermit crabs deliberately acquire sea anemones, even assisting the anemones in attaching themselves. Certain true crabs also collect anemones that they carry about on their backs and legs or even in their claws. These associations may benefit the anemone by providing it with a means of locomotion, and sometimes the anemone is able to steal food that the crab or hermit crab has found. In turn, the sea anemone protects its host from predators such as octopuses and other crabs.

Feeding. Cnidarians feed in a variety of fashions. Hydromedusae alternately swim upward and sink: as the medusa swims upward its tentacles trail behind and are not apt to encounter food organisms, but as it sinks, the extended tentacles "fish" through the water and capture food. In many scyphomedusae the edges of the mouth have become elaborated into mouth arms that trail behind the slowly swimming jellyfish. These arms present huge surfaces for food gathering. In a few scyphomedusae, notably the rhizostomes, the mouth is subdivided into thousands of minute pores that lead by tubes to the coelenteron. Each external pore is associated with an external ciliated gutter, and as these medusae rest mouth upwards on the sea bottom, the ciliated gutters collect minute organisms and detrital materials that settle on the mouth apparatus.

Sessile polyps depend for food on organisms that come into contact with their tentacles. Some colonial corals have minute polyps and depend more on the collection of detrital material than on the capture of living organisms. In colonies of hydroids, the extended tentacles form an effective trap for small organisms in the water.

FORM AND FUNCTION

Tissues. Cnidarians consist of two tissue layers, an outer epidermis and an inner gastrodermis, lining the coelenteron; they do not possess organs. Between the two tissue layers is sandwiched a largely non-cellular layer that may be microscopically thin or very thick. This layer, the mesoglea, consists of a jelly-like material permeated by a complex network of supporting fibres. The fibres and jelly are elastic; in medusae they make up the bulk of the animal and act as a resilient skeleton. In polyps, the water-filled coelenteron acts as a hydroskeleton and in concert with the thin, elastic mesoglea maintains the varying forms of these animals.

Muscles. Muscles in cnidarians occur only as extensions of the bases of the epidermal and gastrodermal cells. Individual muscle cells are relatively long and may occur in dense tracts in jellyfish or sea anemones. Most muscles in cnidarians, however, occur only as thin sheets at the base of the epidermal or gastrodermal layers. Typically in polyps the layer under the epidermis is oriented along the cylindrical body and the tentacles; the layer under the gastrodermis is usually circular. Contraction of the circular muscles against the fluid in the coelenteron causes the body of the polyp to elongate; contraction of the longitudinal muscles causes it to shorten. Similar layers of muscles expand and contract the tentacles. Bending in polyps results from unequal contractions of the longitudinal muscles.

In medusae the muscles are all epidermal, restricted to the subumbrellar surface, and organized into circular and radial tracts. Contraction of the circular muscles squeezes the subumbrellar space, forcing out the contained water and causing the medusa to move by jet propulsion. Recovery of the elastic mesoglea re-extends the contracted muscle fibres. The radial muscles can contract to distort the bell shape and direct the water jet at angles to the longitudinal axis of the bell, allowing the medusa to swim in other than straight lines.

Nervous and sensory system. Swimming and other body movements of medusae are coordinated by the nervous system (see Figure 4). Marginal sensory bodies (statocysts) inform the animal of its orientation with respect to the gravitational force; these structures are closely associated with a nerve ring that is in turn in contact with one or more nerve nets. No ganglia or other accumulations of nerve cell bodies occur in the Cnidaria. In hydrozoan polyps, the only elements of

the nervous system known are those of the epidermal nerve network, which interconnects all members of the colony. Scyphozoans and anthozoans have both epidermal and gastrodermal nerve nets, though the manner in which these are interconnected is not clear. Nerve cells are not present in the mesoglea.

Nematocysts. Undifferentiated interstitial cells, within the epidermis and the gastrodermis, presumably replace older cells of these tissues as needed and appear to be the source of the cnidoblasts, cells that produce nematocysts. Nematocysts contain an evertible, usually armed, thread. When the tissue carrying nematocysts contacts foreign objects, the capsule opens, or "explodes," and ejects the thread. The thread may be adhesive, or may be thrown into a coil that entangles the object. Both types serve to hold food items, which may then be transferred to the mouth. Another type of thread is armed with spines that penetrate the food objects. These threads are hollow and open ended, and toxins contained in the capsule are introduced through the thread into the prey, soon killing it.

Digestion, respiration, and excretion. Once a polyp has captured a food item, its tentacles move toward the mouth. The mouth opens, the lips grasp the food, and muscular actions complete the swallowing. Once food is in the coelenteron, it is broken into small particles by enzymes and engulfed by the gastrodermal cells wherein digestion is completed. Respiration and excretion in Cnidaria are carried on by individual cells, which obtain their oxygen directly from the environment and return metabolic wastes to it.

Skeletons. Skeletons of several sorts occur in the Cnidaria. Most hydroids have a horny, chitinous external skeleton that is flexible and bends with water movements but also protects the delicate stolons, stems, branches, and individual polyps in the colony. A few scyphozoan polyps have comparable chitinous skeletons.

The Anthozoa develop a variety of skeletons, perhaps the most spectacular being the massive calcareous structures that form coral reefs. The skeleton of an individual coral is a cup-shaped structure, into which the animal can nearly completely retract. The skeletons of hydrocorals and true corals build up by fusion of individual crystals of calcium carbonate. Skeleton formation is essentially continuous in those polyps that produce them; in corals the skeleton is laid down at a rate of about one centimetre per year.

Sea anemones do not produce skeletal structures, though their close relatives, the Zoanthidea, incorporate foreign objects (sand grains, sponge spicules) into their body walls. These objects give the animals rigidity and a toughness not found in other anthozoans.

One group of Anthozoa has developed internal skeletons. This group, the Alcyonaria, includes the sea fans, the sea pens, and the branched upright gorgonians. The colonial animal covers the skeletal structure, which consists largely of a horny protein, gorgonin, that contains varying proportions of calcium carbonate. One alcyonarian genus, *Tubipora,* forms a red organ-pipe-like calcareous skeleton and is known as the organ-pipe coral. A few simple alcyonarians that have no gorgonin contain isolated calcareous spicules in their epidermis.

The Antipatharia, or black corals, are anthozoans with skeletons comparable to those of alcyonarions. Individual colonies of Antipatharia resemble black bushes and may stand over three metres tall. The skeletal material is used in the making of jewelry. The anthozoan blue corals, the Coenothecalia, have skeletons composed of calcareous crystalline fibres fused into sheets.

Many hydrozoan polyps develop external chitinous skeletons. Others, known as hydrocorals, develop external calcareous skeletons as do corals. Those that develop chitinous skeletons may be bushlike or feather-shaped or appear as fuzzy growths of individual polyps interconnected by a network of tubes called stolons. Those with calcareous skeletons may occur as encrusting masses with the interconnected polyps regularly dispersed over the skeleton or as upright, massive branching hydrocorals. The hydrocorals include the millepores,

Marginal notes:

Stinging cells

Coral reefs

Loco-motion

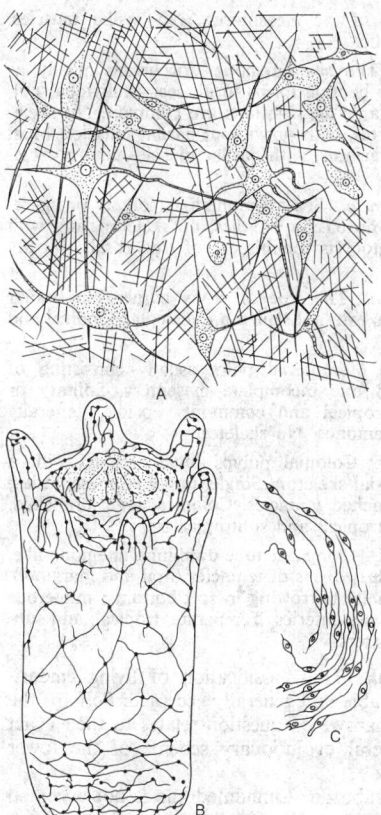

Figure 4: *Cnidarian nervous systems (enlarged).*
(A) Nervous tissue of an anemone, showing the epidermal ganglion-cell layer from the oral disk as seen from the inner surface of the epidermis; (B) nervous system of hydra; (C) ring arrangement of epidermal nerve cells in the pedal disk of hydra.
From The Zoologischen Instituten der Universität Wien and The Zoologischen Station in Triest

commonly called the stinging corals, and the precious red coral used in making jewelry.

EVOLUTION AND PALEONTOLOGY

Origin. Among the theories proposed on the evolution of the Cnidaria, most treat the radial symmetry and simple tissue level of organization as evidence that the group is truly primitive. One theory, however, suggests that the Cnidaria have evolved from bilateral flatworms and views the Anthozoa as the stem of the phylum. The evidence cited to support this theory is the presence in the Anthozoa of a symmetry usually described as biradial. Many scientists have argued that either the polyp or the medusa is the primitive body form and have concluded that the Hydrozoa are the most ancient of the three classes of the phylum. Others have suggested that the original cnidarian was a planula-like organism that evolved into a polyp or a medusa.

Fossil record. The fossil record of the cnidarians is very spotty: although they are an ancient group, Cnidaria are soft-bodied, and preservable skeletal structures may have developed late in their evolution. The earliest fossil cnidarians, assigned to the class Protomedusae, appeared in the Precambrian and are represented in Cambrian and Ordovician deposits. Their form, known from impressions in sedimentary rocks, is sometimes reminiscent of certain scyphozoans. There are Cambrian records of three other groups of cnidarians; namely, the Conulariida, the Hydroida, and the Stromatoporoidea. The fossil record of conulates, presumed to be the skeletal remains of scyphozoan polyps, extends from the Cambrian to the Triassic. There are no accepted modern derivatives of this group.

The Stromatoporoidea, treated as a fossil order of the Hydrozoa, have a record extending from the mid-Cambrian to the Cretaceous. Their colonies produced massive skeletons, some of which are now fossil reefs.

The Siphonophorida and the Hydroida have fossil records extending from the Ordovician to the present. Modern corals, the Scleractinia, have records from the Triassic into the Recent. The blue corals, gorgonians, millepores, hydrocorals, and some scyphozoans have records from the Jurassic or Cretaceous to the present. Most other cnidarians are known only from the Recent.

Annotated classification. The following classification, limited to living cnidarians, generally follows that used by L.H. Hyman in her treatise *The Invertebrates*.

PHYLUM CNIDARIA (COELENTERATES)

Nematocyst-bearing, radial metazoans possessing no organs. Body composed of an inner and an outer tissue layer separated by a noncellular layer, the mesoglea. Two body forms, polyp and medusa; both may be present in a single life history. Most polyps have tentacles surrounding the mouth; the tentacles of medusae occur at the margin of the bell. A single internal cavity, the gut or coelenteron, with one primary opening to the exterior, the mouth. About 9,000 species.

Class Hydrozoa (hydroids)

Nearly exclusively marine polypoid forms and medusae called craspedote because of the presence of a tissue, the velum, which reduces the diameter of the subumbrellar aperture. Tetramerous or polymerous radial symmetry. Colonial forms commonly polymorphic; most life histories involve both polypoid and medusoid stages. Simple gastrovascular cavity, without intrinsic nematocysts or stomodaeum. Gonads epidermal. About 3,000 species.

Order Hydroida. The hydroids. Usually colonial and polymorphic and release free medusae or retain modified medusoid reproductive structures on the colony. Usually a chitinous exoskeleton. This order includes the naked, solitary freshwater polyps (Hydra).

Suborder Anthomedusae. Medusae bell-shaped, with gonads on the sides of the manubrium and sensory structures consisting of pigmented eye spots. No skeleton or, if present, no cup or hydrotheca into which the polyp may withdraw (gymnoblastic hydroids). Most abundant in bays and shallow coastal waters.

Suborder Leptomedusae. Medusae saucer-shaped; gonads below the radial canals. Sensory structures usually are statocysts. Hydroids with hydrothecae (calyptoblastic hydroids). Many species do not release free medusae. Occur in all shallow marine waters.

Suborder Limnomedusae. Small medusae with gonads on both the manubrium and below the radial canals. Polyps commonly with few (2 or 1) tentacles and no skeleton. Eyespots on medusae.

Order Chondrophora. Floating oceanic hydroid colonies supported by chitinous skeleton. Free medusae are produced.

Order Milleporina. Tropical colonial forms producing massive calcareous skeletons. Reduced, non-feeding medusae are released. Gastrozooids and dactylozooids project through pores in the surface of the skeleton.

Order Stylasterina. Hydrocorals resembling millepores, forming erect branching colonies or occurring as simple adherent prostrate forms. Commonly blue, red, or pink. Cup, in which the gastrozooid occurs, has a central spine. No free medusae, but reduced medusae develop and produce gametes in special cavities in the skeleton. Mostly tropical and subtropical; includes the precious red coral, *Corallium*.

Order Trachylina. Oceanic; reduced or no hydroid stage. Statocysts and special sensory structures (tentaculocysts). Differ from other hydromedusae by having tentacles inserted above the umbrellar margin.

Suborder Narcomedusae. Scalloped margin; gonads in the floor of the stomach.

Suborder Trachymedusae. Smooth bell margin; gonads below the radial canals.

Order Pteromedusae. Bipyramidal, medusa-like, oceanic organism with four swimming arms. Statocysts in the arms. Gonads epidermal at the midline.

Order Siphonophora. Complex polymorphic swimming or floating colonies that contain both polypoid and medusoid individuals. Polyps of three sorts: gastrozooids, dactylozooids, and gonozooids. Some medusoids are purely locomotory; others protective or reproductive. Oceanic, worldwide in distribution. Genera include Portuguese man-of-war (*Physalia*).

Class Scyphozoa

Acraspedote medusae (without a velum) or sessile polyps with the gut divided into four compartments. Distinctive gastrodermal tentacles borne on the four septa of the gut. Intrinsic epidermal and gastrodermal nematocysts; gonads develop in lining of the gut. Marginal sensory structures (rhopalia) occur. Tetramerous radial symmetry marks both medusae and polyps. Life histories commonly involve an alternation of a polyp, the scyphistoma, which produces free ephyrae that develop into the adult medusae. Most abundant in coastal waters, but there are some oceanic species. About 200 species.

Order Stauromedusae (Lucernarida). Polypoid scyphozoans with a four-compartmented gut. Vase-, goblet- or trumpet-shaped polyps, usually bearing eight groups of tentacles. Usually 2–3 cm long or less. Temperate and cold temperate waters of all oceans.

Order Cubomedusae (Carybdeida). Tropical, cuboidal medusae with four flattened sides to the bell. Margin simple and square with single or grouped tentacles arising above the four corners. Most species do not have a known polypoid stage. Fiercely stinging members (sea wasps) can cause human fatalities.

Order Coronatae. Medusae conical, dome-shaped, or flattened with a coronal furrow around the bell above the scalloped margin. Ocelli may or may not be present. Some species have a scyphistoma stage with an external chitinous skeleton. Oceanic, some species living at great depths.

Order Semaeostomeae. Commonest and best known scyphozoans. Bell may be domed or flattened, marginally scalloped into eight or more areas. Mouth edges drawn out into four long arms. Most species live in warm, coastal waters, a few in frigid waters; some oceanic. Full alternation of polyp and medusa. The group includes the giant *Cyanea arctica*, which may be more than 2 m in diameter.

Order Rhizostomeae. Medusae shaped like those of Semaeostomeae but with mouth subdivided into minute pores that connect with the gut. Life history includes scyphistoma and ephyra stages. Mostly tropical.

Class Anthozoa

Exclusively polypoid with radial or radiobilateral symmetry. Oral end expanded into a disk with a central mouth. Hollow tentacles at the margin or surface of the oral disk. The mouth leads to the coelenteron via the stomodaeum. Ciliated troughs (siphonoglyphs) for water transport, along the stomodaeum. Coelenteron divided into compartments by mesenteries arranged like the tentacles. Gonads on the mesenteries. About 6,000 species.

Subclass Alcyonaria

Polyps with eight pinnately branched tentacles, eight mesenteries, and a single siphonoglyph in the stomodaeum. Nearly all colonial with "internal" skeletons.

Order Stolonifera. Colonies of individual polyps connected by stolons or a basal mat with stolons. Some colonies with skeletons of spicules, or spicules may fuse into tubes. Shallow tropical and temperate seas.

Order Telestacea. Tropical, colonial; long axial polyps bear lateral polyps. Skeleton of spicules fused with a horny material.

Order Alcyonacea. Small to massive colonial forms (soft corals); lower parts of the polyps fused into a fleshy mass; the oral ends protrude from the colony. Isolated calcareous spicules. Primarily tropical.

Order Coenothecalia. A single representative, the tropical blue coral *Heliopora*. Massive lobed calcareous skeleton.

Order Gorgonacea. A large, diverse order, commonly arborescent; includes the sea fans, sea feathers, and sea whips. The axial skeleton contains gorgonin or may consist solely of calcareous spicules, or both. Polyps are rarely dimorphic. Found in tropical and subtropical waters, especially in the Caribbean.

Order Pennatulacea. Fleshy, always dimorphic, unbranched colonies, with one axial polyp and many lateral polyps. Body divided into a polyp-free area (peduncle) and a polyp-bearing area (rachis). On soft sea bottoms, the peduncle burrows into the substrate. Central skeleton a calcified axial rod; polyps and rachis have isolated calcareous spicules.

Subclass Zoantharia (Hexacorallia)

Simple, rarely branched tentacles. Mesenteries commonly arranged hexamerously, but never as in the Alcyonaria. Solitary or colonial polyps. Without skeletons or with calcareous or horny, non-spicular skeletons. Usually two siphonoglyphs.

Order Ptychodactiaria. Sea anemone-like, but no ciliated tract on the edge of the mesenteries. No basilar muscles. Arctic and Antarctic.

Order Actiniaria. The sea anemones, occurring mostly as attached littoral or benthic forms in all seas. Individual polyps only, though large aggregations are common. No skeleton. Burrowing forms, with or without basilar muscles. Most attached to solid surfaces, with basilar muscles, and possessing a pedal disk.

Order Corallimorpharia. Sea anemone-like, solitary or aggregated polyps with no basilar muscles, no skeleton, and with muscles and nematocysts reminiscent of true corals. Mostly tropical.

Order Madreporaria. The true or stony corals. No basilar muscles; calcareous external skeleton and septa. Tropical and subtropical.

Order Zoanthidea. Mesenterial pairs usually consisting of one complete and one incomplete mesentery. Solitary or colonial, mostly tropical and commonly epizoic, generally resembling sea anemones. No skeleton.

Order Antipatharia. Colonial polyps (black corals) with a thorny, hornlike axial skeleton. Single, unpaired mesenteries; 6 simple or 8 branched tentacles. Colonies large, branched, and bushy. Deep tropical and subtropical seas.

Order Ceriantharia. Elongate, tube-dwelling, anemone-like, solitary polyps with two sets of tentacles (oral and marginal). No pedal disk, usually burrowing in soft bottoms; numerous unpaired complete mesenteries. Temperate, tropical, and subtropical shallow waters.

Critical appraisal. The classification of living cnidarians is relatively stable and generally accepted. Perhaps the most profound unanswered question relates to their exact place in the general evolutionary scheme of the lower Metazoa.

The hydrozoan suborder Limnomedusae is not accepted by some workers, and the groups assigned to it are treated as members of the other suborders. In substantial ways, many of the Limnomedusae possess characters that bridge the differences between the Anthomedusae and the Leptomedusae. The hydrozoan order Chondrophora has morphological characteristics suggesting that the group might better be treated as part of Anthomedusae, rather than as a discrete order. It appears that their unusual pelagic habit is the primary basis for the separation of this order.

A more fundamental disagreement concerns the class assignment of the Pteromedusae. They were treated here as hydrozoans, but some students of this group have assigned them to the Scyphozoa. It has been suggested that the swimming plates of pteromedusans are homologues of the arms of ephyrae, rather than modified velar and bell-margin structures derived from hydrozoan ancestors.

There is little debate about the class Scyphozoa, though it has been suggested that the Cubomedusae represent a discrete fourth class of cnidarians. The Anthozoa, too, are a well-defined, coherent group. The orders Ptychodactiaria, Corallimorpharia, Actiniaria, Madreporaria, and Zoanthidea are so similar that treatment of them as suborders of a single order would better express their relationships. More divergent are the Antipatharia and Ceriantharia. The Antipatharia have been treated by some students as near relatives of the Alcyonaria and, indeed, their morphology is more suggestive of that group than of the Zoantharia. The Ceriantharia, too, sit uncomfortably in the Zoantharia, though they bear no special relationship to the Alcyonaria. They generally are viewed as early offshoots of the Anthozoan line that have diverged notably from the hexacorallian pattern. Treatment of both the Antipatharia and Ceriantharia as subclasses of Anthozoa might better express their position in the class.

(C.H.Ha.)

BIBLIOGRAPHY. The standard advanced technical treatment of the Cnidaria is L.H. HYMAN, *The Invertebrates*, vol. 1, *Protozoa through Ctenophora* (1940); the history of the phylum as deduced from the fossil record is covered in R.C. MOORE (ed.), *Treatise on Invertebrate Paleontology*, part F, *Coelenterata* (1956) and W.J. REES (ed.), *The Cnidaria and Their Evolution* (1966); a recent technical survey is L. MUSCATINE and H.M. LENHOFF (eds.), *Coelenterate Biology: Reviews and New Perspectives* (1974).

Coal Mining

Coal mining is a worldwide basic industry. More than sixty countries produce annually some 3,300,000,000 metric tons, most of which is burned to produce heat used to generate electric power. Though the industry has operated on a huge scale for decades, the existence of vast coal reserves in many parts of the world guarantees its future, at least until coal has been superseded as a source of energy and of many chemical compounds. The use of coal in power generation is treated in the articles ELECTRIC POWER and STEAM POWER. The article COAL PROCESSING covers the conversion of substantial amounts of coal into other products, principally coke (used in metallurgy and as a fuel) and gases (used mostly as fuels). Coal itself is the subject of the article COALS.

Few industries operate under so many different conditions. The endless variability of coal mining, together with competition inside the industry and from other fuels, has encouraged innovation and technological improvement.

HISTORY OF COAL MINING

Ancient use of coal

There is archaeological evidence that coal was burned in funeral pyres during the Bronze Age, 3,000 to 4,000 years ago, in Wales. Aristotle mentions coal ("combustible bodies") in his *Meteorologica,* and his pupil Theophrastus also records its use. The Romans in Britain burned coal before AD 400; cinders have been found among the ruins of Roman villas and towns and along the Roman wall, especially in Northumberland, near the outcrop of coal seams. The Hopi Indians of the present southwestern United States mined coal by picking and scraping and used it for heating, cooking, and in ceremonial chambers as early as the 12th century AD; in the 14th century they used it industrially, in pottery making. Marco Polo reports its use as widespread in 13th-century China. The Domesday Book (1086), which recorded everything of economic value in England, does not mention coal. London's first coal arrived by sea in 1228, from the area of Fife and Northumberland, where lumps broken from submarine outcroppings and washed ashore by wave action were gathered by women and children. Thereafter, the name sea coal was applied to all bituminous coal in England. Later in the century, monks began to mine outcroppings in the north of England.

Early mining technology. Except for the Chinese, who may have mined coal underground, all the early coal seams were worked from the surface, in fully exposed outcroppings. In the later Middle Ages, however, exhaustion of outcrop coal in many places forced a change from surface to underground, or shaft, mining. Early shaft mines were little more than wells widened as much as miners dared in the face of danger of collapse. Shafts were sunk on high ground, with adits—near-horizontal tunnels—for drainage driven into the side of the hill. In England, some shallow mine shafts were exhausted as early as the 14th century, making it necessary to go deeper and expand mining at the shaft bottoms. These remained small operations; a record of 1684 shows 70 mines near Bristol, employing 123 workers.

Greater depth created many problems. First, water could no longer simply be drained away. Crude methods were devised to lift it to the surface. A bucket and chain device was first powered by men and later by horses; a continuous belt of circular plates was drawn up through a pipe. Windmills were used for pumps. But shafts had to be restricted to depths of 300 to 350 feet (90 to 105 metres) and a mining radius of 600 feet (180 metres). It was not until 1710 that the water problem was eased by Thomas Newcomen's steam atmospheric engine, which supplied a cheap and reliable power source for a vertical reciprocating lift pump.

Raising the coal itself was another problem. Manpower, operating a windlass, was replaced by horsepower; and as the shafts went deeper, more horses were added. At Whitehaven in 1801, coal was hoisted 600 feet (180 metres) by four horses at the rate of 42–44 metric tons in nine hours. The introduction of the steam engine to hoist coal was a major turning point for the industry. Small steam-powered windlasses were successfully tried out about 1770. About 1840, the first cage was used to hoist the loaded car; and from 1840 onward, advances in coal-mining techniques were rapid.

Early mining methods

Early European miners wedged coal out of the seam or broke it loose with a pick. After explosives were introduced, it was still necessary to undercut the coal seam with hand tools. The advent of steam, compressed air, and electricity brought relief from this hard, dangerous work. In 1868, after almost 100 years of trial and error, a commercially successful revolving-wheel cutter for undercutting the coal seam was introduced in England. This first powered cutting tool was soon improved by introduction of compressed air as a power source in place of steam. Later, electricity was used. The longwall cutter was introduced in 1891. Originally driven by compressed air, and later electrified, it could begin at one end of a long face (the vertical, exposed cross section of a seam of coal) and cut continuously to the other.

Early transportation methods. In the first shaft mines, coal was loaded into baskets that were carried on the backs of men or women, or loaded on wooden sledges or trams that were pushed or hauled through the main haulage roadway to the shaft bottom to be hung on hoisting ropes or chains. In drift and slope mines, the coal was brought directly to the surface by these and similar methods. Sledges were pulled first by men and later by animals, including mules, horses, oxen, and even dogs and goats.

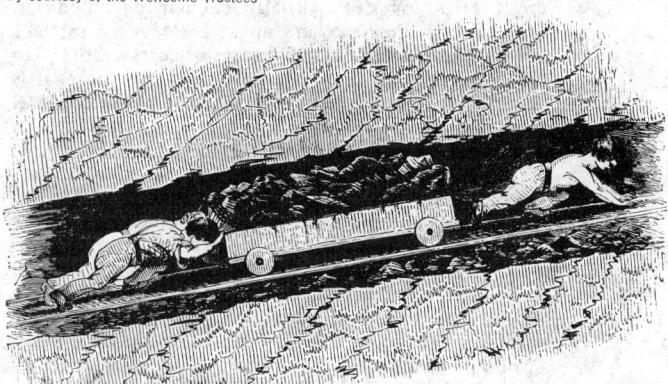

Figure 1: Children propelling a tram loaded with coal from an early 19th-century mine in England.

Steam locomotives designed by Richard Trevithick were used in the fields of South Wales and Tyne, and later in Pennsylvania and West Virginia, but they created too much smoke. Compressed-air locomotives, which appeared in the 1880s, proved expensive to operate. Electric locomotives, introduced in 1887, rapidly became popular; but mules and horses were still working in some mines as late as the 1940s.

UNDERGROUND MINING

Methods of gaining access to coal. Three methods, drift, slope, and shaft (or various combinations thereof), are used to gain access to coal located too deep underground for surface mining.

Drift

A drift is a horizontal, or nearly horizontal, tunnel driven, or dug, from a place at which a level or only slightly inclined seam crops out at the surface. The drift usually follows the seam and provides the cheapest method of access, permitting continuous transportation from the coal face to the surface by any conventional means.

A slope is an inclined opening driven to work a seam that is not horizontal or to reach from the surface to a seam or between seams. Men and supplies frequently are moved on a track in the same slope opening in which a belt conveyor for the coal is located.

A shaft is a vertical opening driven from the surface to provide access to a seam or seams. Such an opening

Figure 2: Longwall face with powered roof supports and segmented conveyor in a coal mine in Nottinghamshire, England.
By courtesy of Dowty Mining Equipment Limited, Gloucestershire, England

driven from one seam down to another is called a blind shaft.

Early shafts were small, multipurpose openings, lined at first with wood and later with brick. Modern shafts from the surface are normally lined with reinforced concrete, brick, or steel. Usually circular or oblong in cross section, they measure up to 22 feet (6.6 metres) across. If shafts are the only means of access, more than one is required at a mine. Inside the mine, the coal is dumped into a bin at the side of the shaft, below the level of the seam, and fed into a skip (a large, rectangular, cagelike container), which then is hoisted from the mine. At the Prosper Colliery in the Ruhr district of West Germany, a fully automatic system hoists more than 1,000 metric tons per hour from a depth of 3,300 feet (1,000 metres).

The shaft is used almost exclusively today to reach a deep seam. In the past, belt conveyors were used on slopes, but now, with automatic, high-speed hoisting machinery available, shafts are replacing the long slopes.

Mining techniques. *Room-and-pillar and longwall mining.* Two basic methods of underground mining, room-and-pillar and longwall, are employed.

The room-and-pillar method, the older of the two, grew naturally out of the need to recover more coal as mining operations became deeper and more expensive. In this system, galleries, or tunnels, are driven into the coal seam with wider openings driven from them. Thick pillars of coal are left to support the overhead strata of earth and rock (overburden).

In the modern longwall method, two widely spaced tunnels are driven into the seam from the main haulage tunnel and are linked by a fourth tunnel. The fourth tunnel may be near the main haulage tunnel (the advancing longwall method) or may be at the ends of the widely spaced tunnels (the retreating longwall method). Coal is removed by widening the fourth tunnel. The need for support posts limits the amount of open working space next to the coal face to such an extent that cars cannot be used; conveyors must be employed, and for the first half of the 20th century longwall mining was less productive than room-and-pillar mining. The productivity of longwall mining was significantly increased by the British in the 1950s, however, when they introduced powered roof supports that can be quickly advanced as mining progresses (Figure 2).

In choosing between the two methods, a very important consideration is pressure. Because internal stresses increase with depth and density of rock, underground workings become progressively more hazardous as they go deeper. The zones of depth may be grouped into three areas of rock pressure.

In the first zone (the exact depth of which varies because

of different types of overlying strata), rock pressure presents no problem if mining dimensions are kept within established limits. Most of the coalfields in the U.S., New South Wales, South Africa, and the Lorraine region of France lie within this zone. Room-and-pillar mining is practicable, and many strata permit use of the longwall method; the choice is a matter of economics.

In the second zone, pressures are greater; regardless of precautions, collapses occur, though damage can be limited by providing adequate support. Most of the coalfields of the United Kingdom and the Soviet Union now being worked (almost entirely by the longwall method) lie in this zone.

In the third zone of depth are coalfields in the Ruhr Valley, The Netherlands, and Belgium. At these depths, only the longwall method is employed.

Mining plans. The idea of planning a mining operation developed quite early. The panel system, in which the mine was divided to isolate problems, was in use in England by 1795. Multiple entries replaced the single entry for improved ventilation and safety. Planned backfilling became a practice in the anthracite mines toward the end of the 19th century. At the beginning of the 20th century, the replacement of man and animal power by mechanization, followed by a trend toward concentration, further modified mining plans, particularly in the United States, where conditions are more adaptable to variation.

Submarine mining. Both room-and-pillar and longwall methods are used under the ocean, with certain restrictions based on the enormous weight of the water over the mine. In Canada, for example, for total (longwall) undersea extraction, a minimum of 100 feet of cover (distance between the sea floor and the top of the seam) per foot of thickness of seam is required by law. In practice, however, longwall extraction is not conducted under less than 1,000 feet (300 metres) of cover. This is considered safe, even if parallel seams have already been worked.

In the United Kingdom, 197 feet (60 metres) of cover is required for undersea room-and-pillar extraction, but pillar size and roadway width are restricted according to depth and thickness of seam.

Mechanization and automation. The two principal methods of underground mechanized mining are conventional, also called "cyclic," mining and continuous mining.

Conventional (cyclic) mining. Conventional mechanized mining involves the following sequence of operations: supporting the roof, cutting, drilling, blasting, and loading. After the roof above the seam has been made secure by timbering or rock bolting, normally one horizontal—and sometimes a second, vertical—slot, 6 inches

Pressure considerations

Cover requirements

(15 centimetres) wide and up to 15 feet (4.5 metres) deep, is cut into the coal seam. The slots, which make room for expansion of the coal upon blasting, are cut with a mobile cutting machine, which is essentially a large chain saw. The holes for the explosive charges are bored by power drills. The coal is broken down by special explosives that produce less heat and fewer unpleasant fumes than ordinary high explosives do.

After breakage, the coal is loaded into rubber-tired electric trucks, called shuttle cars, or onto chain or belt conveyors. Several types of hand-loaded conveyors developed in the first three decades of the 20th century were made obsolete by the development of the more productive mobile loader and of surface mining.

Mobile loaders are most adaptable to the room-and-pillar method of mining. The Stanley Header, the first coal-loading machine used in the U.S., was developed in England and tested in Colorado in 1888. Others were developed, but few progressed beyond the prototype stage until the Joy machine was introduced (1914), employing the gathering-arm principle and providing the pattern for future successful mobile loaders. Upon the introduction of rubber-tired shuttle cars in 1938 and, in the late 1940s, rock bolting for roof support, which provided an unobstructed working area, mobile loading rapidly supplanted track loading.

Continuous mining. Introduced during the late 1940s, continuous mining began to replace the cyclic operations used in the room-and-pillar method. A single machine, the continuous miner, broke off the coal from the seam and transferred it back to the haulage system. The Joy Ripper (1948) was the first continuous miner applicable in the room-and-pillar method. In 1950 the Jeffrey Colmol, a boring machine adaptable to thin seams, was placed on the market. Many such machines were installed underground, some producing more than 10 metric tons per minute. Their use reduced the number of men required in a mining crew and eliminated the expense of explosives and machines for cutting and drilling the coal.

One continuous longwall mining system involved the "plow," developed near the end of World War II by Wilhelm Loebbe of Germany. Pulled across the face of the coal, guided by a pipe on the face side of a segmented conveyor, it carved a gash two to six inches (50 to 150 millimetres) wide along the bottom of the seam. The hardness of the coal determined the depth of the cut. The plow was forced against the coal face by the conveyor, which in turn was under uniform pressure from equally spaced compressed-air rams. The conveyor snaked against the face behind the advancing plow to catch the coal that chipped off from above the gash. Substantially reducing the labour required at the coal face except that needed to install roof support, the Loebbe system quickly became popular in Germany, France, and the Low Countries. U.S. installations met with varying degrees of success. Competition from other, more productive continuous mining devices and from strip mining temporarily made the plow outmoded in the United States toward the end of the 1950s, but development of powered roof supports reinstated the system by drastically reducing the need for roof control crews. Improvements in the design of the plow increased the range of applications of the system. In 1968 a new drive design increased the plow and conveyor speed, resulting in record production capacity.

Though the Loebbe plow had limited application in British mines, the power-advanced segmented conveyor became a fundamental part of equipment used at the coal face in continuous mining. In 1952 a simple continuous loader, called a shearer, was introduced (Figure 3). The shearer is a longwall cutting machine that is pulled along the face astride the conveyor, bearing a series of disks with picks on their perimeters, on a shaft perpendicular to the face. These revolving disks cut a slice from the coal face as the machine is pulled along. A plow behind the machine cleans up any coal dropped between the face and the conveyor.

Shearer installations increased rapidly in the United Kingdom, in step with the adoption of powered roof sup-

Loebbe's plow system

Shearer

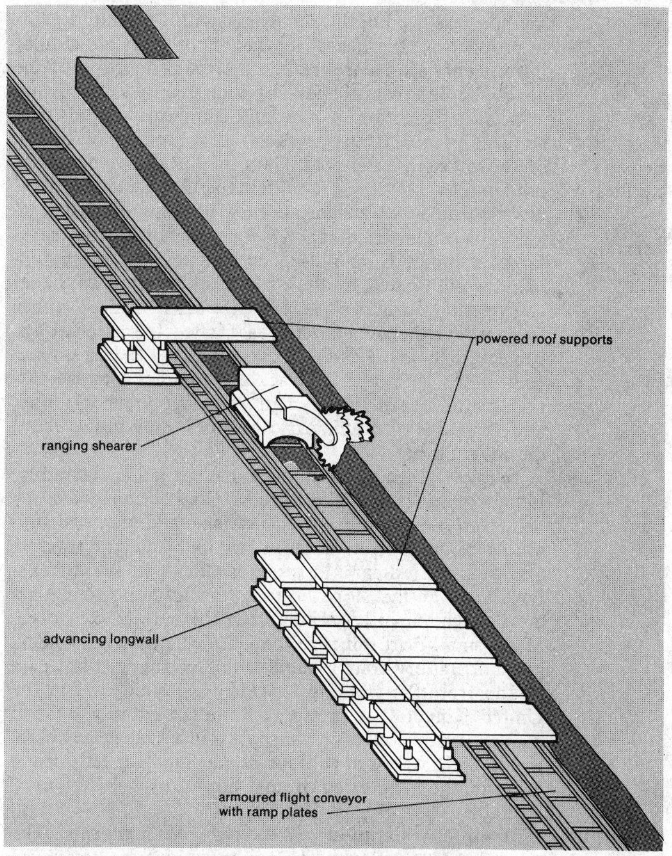

Figure 3: Section of longwall mining as practiced in the U.K., showing the ranging shearer cutting a horizontal seam and loading broken coal on a conveyor.

ports. More than 300 were in use in 1958, when a novel combination boring-and-cutting machine called a trepanner was introduced. Though the trepanner was slower and harder to control, it produced a greater proportion of lump rather than fine coal, desirable in the U.K. The basic flexibility of the shearer design permitted modification, however, and in 1961 installation of shearers resumed. Later, hybrid machines called trepan shearers were introduced.

Underground haulage. Shuttle cars or conveyors transfer the coal from the production area to the main haulage system. A conveyor belt was successfully used in an anthracite mine in central Pennsylvania in 1924 to carry coal from a group of room conveyors to a string of cars at the mine entry. In the early 1930s, such a relay system, with a continuous car feeder, provided uninterrupted coal transportation. The use of these moving belts gained acceptance gradually, and the first mine completely equipped with conveyors began operating in the anthracite field in 1933. During the 1950s and 1960s, relay belts almost completely replaced rail cars for intermediate transportation in the mines.

Battery-powered, rubber-tired cars, designed to carry coal from the loading machine to the elevator, were first used successfully in northern West Virginia in 1938. Later, shuttle cars were designed to permit direct discharge of coal onto a belt conveyor or into a quick-discharge belt feeder.

With shuttle cars came complete off-track face equipment, supplied with electric power by trailing cables. Shuttle cars also were gradually changed over to electric cables in place of batteries, reducing manoeuvrability but increasing payloads. In the late 1960s, convertible battery-cable cars appeared.

The trend continued toward larger capacity to make loading more nearly continuous, until car size had to be balanced against awkwardness. In thin seams, the limitation on car size led to direct loading onto the relay belt conveyor by way of a bridge conveyor or conveyors, with excellent results. Beginning in the late 1960s, this

Use of the conveyor belt

Moving men and supplies

method was tried in thicker seams, with substantial gains in production. In Australia, where conditions are similar but the coal seams are thicker, a large proportion of the coal is hauled from the face by shuttle cars.

The transportation of men and supplies must be independent of coal transportation, to prevent interruption of movement of the coal. Cars on tracks are normally used in most countries, though in the U.S. there is a trend toward trackless transportation by battery-powered tractors and rubber-tired cars. In some instances, the transfer of supplies from rail-borne cars to trackless equipment is eliminated by the use of rubber-tired cars that can operate on as well as off the tracks. In deep mines the floor of the mined-out area (called the gateway) is subject to heaving, and tracks usually are laid to the face; if the gateways are trackless, supplies may be carried by monorail, while men walk. In the horizontal, thicker seams of South African mines, men move about the mine on bicycles.

Completely trackless mining has expanded steadily, mostly in mines with slope access. Coal is transported by belt from the seam face to the surface, and men and supplies are hauled from the slope bottom by electric tractors and rubber-tired cars. In some instances, to avoid transfer delays at the slope bottom, the tractor-pulled cars are brought directly to and from the surface by hoists. Many small drift mines in the U.S. have no track underground. Battery tractors haul trains of rubber-tired cars to and from the working face. Underground coal in the United Kingdom is transported almost entirely by belt conveyor, and conveyor transport is increasing elsewhere. In the U.S., where conditions permit high-capacity track haulage, the proportion of coal moved by belt conveyor is smaller.

Special considerations. *Powered roof supports.* The necessity of laborious and slow operations of shoring up the roof of the mine prevented longwall mining from realizing its potential until the 1950s. The powered, self-advancing roof supports introduced by the British provide a prop-free area—between the coal face and the first row of jacks—for equipment and a canopied pathway between the first and second rows of jacks. Individually or in groups, these supports, attached to the conveyor, are hydraulically lowered, advanced, and reset against the roof.

The introduction of powered supports was followed by rapid adaptation of their design to the many mining conditions in the United Kingdom and continental Europe. The large number of designs made it possible for

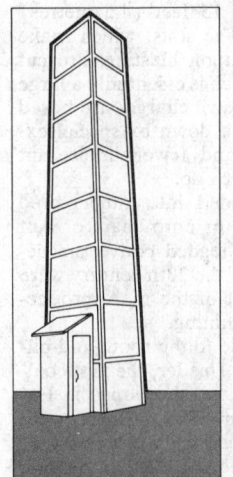 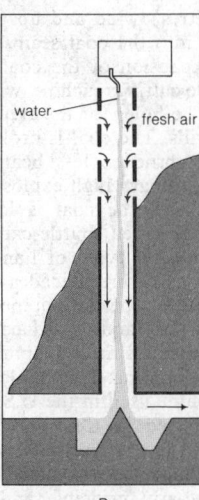 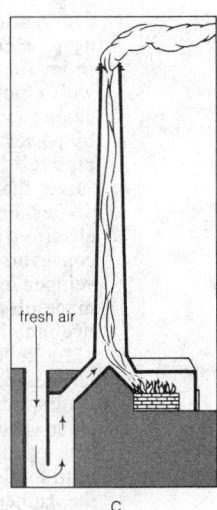

Figure 5: *Methods of ventilation.*
(A) Ventilation stack. (B) Water trompe; air is drawn into the mine shaft by falling water. (C) Furnace ventilation.
From *Coal Age Magazine* (October, 1936); McGraw-Hill

the United Kingdom, in the short period of 15 years, to equip 760 faces with powered supports.

Rock bolting. The origin of rock bolting (or roof bolting) to support and reinforce the roof and ribs, or walls, of coal-mine openings is obscure, but the technique was in limited use in Europe and the U.S. before World War I. In this technique, steel rods are installed in holes drilled into exposed strata and anchored under tension (Figure 4).

Rock bolting is intended (1) to tie weak strata to overlying strong strata; (2) to reinforce horizontal strata; or (3) to combine suspension and reinforcement. To make the system effective, bolts must be installed as soon as possible after the roof and ribs have been exposed.

Ventilation. The presence of noxious and flammable gases caused miners to recognize the critical importance of ventilation in coal mines from the earliest days (Figure 5). Natural ventilation was afforded by level drainage tunnels driven from the sloping surface to connect with the shaft. Surface stacks above the shaft increased the efficiency of ventilation; their use continued in small mines until the early 20th century. The most reliable method, before the introduction of fans, was the use of

Natural ventilation

Figure 4: Rotary roof bolter installing bolts that support the roof.

a furnace at the shaft bottom or on the surface. Despite the hazard of fire and explosion, there were still a large number of furnaces operating, at least in nongassy mines, in the early 20th century. Open-flame illumination, however, was a much commoner cause of explosions until the introduction of the Davy safety lamp (about 1815), in which the flame is enclosed in a double layer of wire gauze that prevents ignition of flammable gases in the air of the mine. Presence of strong air currents, however, made even the Davy lamp unsafe.

Rotary ventilating fans were introduced in mines in the 18th century. Originally of wood and powered by steam, they were improved throughout the 19th and 20th centuries by the introduction of steel blades, electric power, and aerodynamically efficient shapes for the blades. The practice of making highly accurate airflow measurements was initiated to evaluate the effectiveness of ventilating systems. The quality of the atmospheric environment in coal mines is now ensured by supplementing ventilation with automatic controls of the temperature and the humidity.

Intro-
duction
of fans

In small mines, in the past, methane that accumulated near the roof was often cleared, before the working shift, by burning with lighted candles mounted on poles. Portable electrical instruments for detecting gas were developed before the middle of the 20th century. More recently, methane detectors, which give a flashing signal or sound an alarm when the methane content of the mine atmosphere reaches a certain value (0.25–3 percent), have been introduced. Monitoring systems now can keep a constant check on fan operation and the condition of the mine atmosphere.

The rapid advances in longwall mining made since the mid-1950s have drawn attention to more effective use of "bleeder systems," which drain methane from large mined and caved-in areas, and other advanced ventilation techniques. In the United Kingdom, gas removed from the mines is often collected and sold.

Research. Continuous mining, especially by the longwall method, has created many problems that have led to intensive research by government, the coal industry, and machinery manufacturers. Subjects of research include instrumentation, controls, environmental conditions, suitable fluids and metals, communications, improvement of machinery, coal-sensing and steering of machines, ventilation control, and development of supports.

Mining research by use of models has been carried on extensively in West Germany and the Soviet Union since the late 1950s. Australia has had model equipment similar to that used in West Germany since 1966. The United Kingdom, Canada, and the United States are participating in similar investigations.

SURFACE MINING

Surface mining has a long history. Modern earth-moving equipment has made it a major technique and one that has aroused much debate because of the damage it does to the land. The size of the property, the thickness and slope of the coal seam, and the type of overburden greatly influence the size and type of surface operation. The basic determinant of economic feasibility is the ratio of depth of overburden to thickness of coal. This varies from 1:8 in thick brown coal deposits of Australia to 30:1 in some U.S. strip mines.

Open-pit mining. Open-pit (also called opencut, or opencast) mining is used to remove coal from thick veins covered by little overburden. When open-pit operations begin, the valuable topsoil is carefully scraped away; after mining and backfilling, it is redistributed over the surface for resumption of agriculture. Two specific operations under entirely different conditions illustrate the open-pit method.

The Yallourn Mine, Australia. The largest single brown-coal deposit in the world, containing 12,820,000,-000 tons (11,630,000,000 metric tons) of coal recoverable by present methods, lies in the Latrobe Valley, east of Melbourne, Australia. The coal seams are approximately horizontal and from 100 to more than 300 feet (30 to 90 metres) thick. In some places several

superimposed seams, up to 880 feet (264 metres) in thickness, are broken only by thin layers of waste. A clay and gravel overburden varies from 40 to 90 feet (12 to 27 metres) in depth. Overburden and coal are excavated by large, mobile, continuous bucket-wheel excavators that operate on benches within the coal seam at levels depending upon the capacity of the machine. These remove the material from the working faces with large, toothed buckets mounted on a wheel. The bucket-wheel excavator cuts 70 feet (21 metres) above and 25 feet (7.5 metres) below the crawler tracks that transport the machine. Similar machines with buckets mounted on an endless chain are called bucket-chain excavators. They reach 80 feet (24 metres) above and 87 feet (26 metres) below the crawlers. To prevent fires, water is sprayed on the coal faces during summer months.

Bucket-
wheel
excavators

The Garsdorf Mine, West Germany. The Garsdorf property, located in the Rhineland deposit in the state of Nordrhein-Westfalen, contains a 1,000,000,000-ton reserve of lignite of Miocene age. Broken by faulting into offset blocks, the 50- to 200-foot (15- to 60-metre)-thick seam dips northward to a cover depth of 800 feet (240 metres). The overburden consists of water-bearing strata of gravels, sands, and clays. The open-pit technique was chosen after efforts, made before 1950, to deep-mine the deposit were defeated by water and other problems. It is estimated that the Garsdorf pit will reach a depth of 1,000 feet (300 metres), with ratio of five overburden to one coal. Though this ratio is not exceptional, most of the overburden must be transported to a distant point, which makes disposal a serious problem. Large-capacity equipment is employed to keep down costs. Because the seam is faulted and because it is not horizontal, lignite and waste must be handled alternately as the machinery travels along a level path.

In open-pit work, the slope of the walls must be carefully considered; the slopes at the bottom of a deep pit cannot be as steep as those near the surface, because the forces causing collapse increase with depth. Mined-out areas must be promptly backfilled; water is drained from the next lower level to assure slope stability. At Garsdorf, draining is accomplished with submersible pumps.

Area strip mining. Area strip mining is applicable to relatively flat terrain and a nearly horizontal seam. A trench, or box cut, is made from one end of the area to the other, and the coal is removed. The overburden from each succeeding parallel cut is placed in the previous cut. In this manner, the final cut before grading is the only excavated area; the remainder of the property is shaped into a series of rounded ridges.

Area strip mining is practiced widely in the United States (Figure 6). The first U.S. strip mining was carried out near Danville, Illinois, in 1866. Overburden, removed by horse-drawn plows and scrapers, was hauled away in carts and wheelbarrows. Steam-powered shovels first proved successful in the Mission field of Illinois in 1911. Capacity of strip-mining equipment has continuously increased since then.

First U.S.
strip
mining

Shovels or draglines are normally used for strip mining in the United States because the earth strata are usually consolidated, requiring drilling and blasting. It would be prohibitively costly to blast consolidated strata fine enough for handling by a wheel excavator. When unconsolidated glacial deposits are found above the normal strata, however, as in Indiana, Illinois, and northern Missouri, the efficient wheel excavator is used in combination with the shovel and dragline. The determining factor in the purchase of such large equipment is productivity. An all-purpose dragline is more versatile than a shovel. On the other hand, a shovel for the same boom and carrying unit works faster.

A large operation in eastern Ohio exemplifies the equipment used in strip mining. The property had two overburden conditions, an average 80-foot (24-metre) and 104-foot (31-metre) cover of consolidated strata and topsoil. Basically, the machines chosen are the same; for the first, a 170-foot (51-metre) boom with a 130-cubic-yard (99-cubic-metre) capacity; for the second, a

Figure 6: Strip mining near Freeburg, Illinois.
By courtesy of the National Coal Association, Washington, D.C.

200-foot (60-metre) boom with a 100-cubic-yard (76-cubic-metre) capacity.

The width of coal uncovered is determined by the angle of repose, or natural slope, of the loose material; for the 80-foot cover area, a width of 130 feet (39 metres) is used. The large shovel is followed by a 9½-cubic-yard (7.2-cubic-metre) coal-loading shovel. The operating cycle consists of: (1) drilling and blasting, (2) excavation, (3) coal loading, and (4) restoration. Allied equipment for each uncovering unit includes a bulldozer on the highwall (the ledge above the mined area) to cut a road for the drilling rig; a blast-hole drill; a bulldozer in the pit to push loose debris into heaps for the shovel; a road grader or small bulldozer (and, if necessary to meet ash requirements of the mined coal, a powered-type street sweeper) to remove loose soil and rock from the exposed surface of the coal; a 9½-cubic-yard (7.2-cubic-metre) shovel to load coal; power-cable handling equipment with a hydraulically operated reel for a 7,200-volt cable for the large shovel and 4,100-volt cable for the small shovel; and 50- and 120-ton trucks.

The first requirement of preparation is thorough fragmentation of rock overburden by blasting to allow steady operation of the shovel with the bucket filled to capacity. The trend is toward larger drills and blasting holes of larger diameter. The drilling pattern is staggered, and hole spacing depends upon the size of the hole, as uniform fragmentation requires the same blasting ratio (the volume of explosive needed to fragment a given volume of rock).

An indication of the trend in equipment is illustrated by the change since 1940, when a six-cubic-yard (4.6-cubic-metre) shovel having a capacity of 300 cubic yards (228 cubic metres) of fragmented material per hour was used in starting the Ohio operation: the present 130-cubic-yard (99-cubic-metre) shovel has a capacity of 7,000 cubic yards (5,320 cubic metres) per hour. By the late 1970s, bucket-wheel excavators capable of moving 10,900 cubic yards (8,300 cubic metres) per hour were available.

In response to serious abuses in the past by some mining firms, most U.S. state laws require bonding to ensure complete compliance with regulations concerned with restoring a strip-mined area. After backfilling, limestone is deposited next to the top with sufficient select topsoil on the surface to promote prompt growth of vegetation. Piles of overburden are graded to a gentle, rolling contour and planted with grasses and trees to prevent erosion.

Contour strip mining. Contour strip mining is practiced where deposits occur in high, rolling, or mountainous terrain and the overburden ratio is high. About one-half of the U.S. surface mining has been accomplished by this method. Removal of overburden starts at the outcrop, following along the hillside, creating a shelf with a slope on the side below at the angle of repose of the material. The uphill side of the cut is an almost vertical highwall. As succeeding cuts are made, the overburden is piled on the previous cut area until the economical overburden height is reached.

Generally, the operating procedure is similar to that of area strip mining, except that equipment is normally smaller because of the need for adaptability to varying conditions and because it must frequently be moved from one site to another as the deposits are exhausted. In the Appalachian area, where conditions normally require contour strip mining, several coal seams that occur close together may be mined simultaneously.

Restoration is more difficult and more expensive in rolling terrain. No single set of procedures is applicable to all conditions. The ideal is total backfill, which is practical in some of the rolling hills of Pennsylvania. When restoration is completed, no signs of mining are evident. Restoration in the steep hills of West Virginia has created slightly sloping benches now useful for grazing and agriculture in places where previously only difficult-to-recover timber could be grown.

Regardless of the restoration plan used, it is necessary to cover the remaining coal and other toxic material, establish noneroding gradients on the benches, control the movement of water to prevent saturation of the soil and erosion of the spoil banks, and provide a good vegetation cover. These steps can be taken most effectively when they are planned as part of the whole mining operation.

Auger mining. Recovering coal by boring into a seam located at the base of a highwall is normally one of the cheapest mining systems, but it is limited to horizontal

Operating cycle (margin)

Restoration of mined areas (margin)

or lightly pitching seams that have been exposed by geologic erosion, such as the coalfields of the Appalachian area. Recovery is approximately 50 percent. Very little coal is produced in this manner.

Augering is usually associated with contour strip mining, recovering coal for a limited depth beyond the point at which the overburden ratio has reached its economical limit for stripping. It is also used to recover coal between the outcrop and the depth needed for safe underground mining.

The only preparation required for auger mining is establishment of a well-drained pit or bench of sufficient width for the operation and a highwall clear of loose material. Where the operation closely follows stripping, and care is taken on the final highwall blasting, little or no additional work is necessary. Only a bulldozer is needed in addition to the auger equipment and trucks. Where auger mining is conducted independently of stripping, a small shovel may be needed to prepare the bench and highwall.

Power-driven auger heads range from 16 to 84 inches (40 to 210 centimetres) in diameter and are used singly or in groups of two, three, four, or five. Multiple units can be mounted side by side or, where two are used, one above the other for selective mining above and below a band of impurity. Multiple augers may overlap to leave no coal between them. With these, production is increased, and holes can be held straighter. Production varies with so many factors that generalizing has little meaning. For example, one triple-head auger in West Virginia averages 225 tons per shift, while the same type of device in Ohio averages 324 tons.

Multiple augers

TRANSPORTATION OF COAL

Because coal is inexpensive, the cost of transportation from the mine to the consumer is an important part of the total cost; when exported, it is often a major portion (Table 1). Coal-conveying facilities are competitive;

Table 1: Comparative Costs of Various Coal Transportation Methods

method	cost per ton-mile ($)
Heavy truck (one-way haul)	.050 –.080
Bulk rail (standard rate)	.009 –.014
Unit train	.004 –.009
Tug and barge	.002 –.030
Cargo-liner vessel	.001 –.004
Bulk carrier vessel	.0003–.0006
EHV transmission (electricity)	.0067–.012
Slurry pipeline	.0035–.011

there is a continuous effort to stabilize delivered costs. Current trends are toward larger unit capacities, more automation, and new techniques.

By vehicle. *Railroads.* Coal and railways, among other things, were the base for industrialization of Europe and

Table 2: Methods of Shipment of Coal from the Mine

(percentage of total)

country	year	rail	water	motor vehicle	pit mouth use
Belgium*	1965	46	34	20	
The Netherlands*	1965	39	17	44	
U.S.	1968	72	12	12	4
Soviet Union	1968	97			
Canada	1968	53			
Australia	1968	38	1	16	45†
U.K.‡	1966	74	1	25	excl.
West Germany‡	1966	69	21	10	excl.
Poland‡	1966	91	1	1	7

*Does not include anthracite. †One percent direct to ship. ‡Brown coal excluded.

the U.S. Furthermore, coal has been the railroads' most important cargo since the middle of the 19th century.

Figure 7: Unit train arriving at a loading plant in southern Illinois. In 2½ hours, each of 70 hopper cars will be filled with 105 tons of coal to be carried to an electric generating station.

By courtesy of the National Coal Association, Washington, D.C.

Thus the coal-mining industry and the railways have found themselves sharing common problems.

Rail transportation techniques improved with growing tonnage, but by the 1950s the coal industry was looking to alternative means of transportation for further cost savings (Table 2).

In the 1950s a plan originated in France for assembling whole trainloads of coal destined for a single major customer. Unit train operations, with rapid, continuous loading and unloading, are now common in Europe and North America (Figure 7). Trains with large loads can be hauled by several locomotives scattered through the train. On a western Canadian line, 13 locomotives, controlled by radio, pulled 105 cars holding 11,000 tons. A U.S. line assembled a 500-car train, more than four miles (six kilometres) long, to carry 25,000 tons (22,700 metric tons) of coal over a distance of 157 miles (251 kilo-

Unit train operations

Table 3: Coal Rail and Export Statistics

country	coal as percentage of total rail-borne freight (1975)	percentage of rail-borne coal shipped by unit train (1967)	million tons exported (1976)
U.S.*	25.5	27	55.7
Soviet Union	19.8	mainly	30.4
Canada	8.4	...	12.2
Australia	38.1	3	31.4
U.K.	55.1	...	2.6
West Germany	25.6	32	21.0
Poland	36.5	53†	45.1
Czechoslovakia	33.8	53†	7.6

*1974. †1966.

metres). In Europe, where distances are shorter and interruptions for passenger train traffic more frequent, shorter, faster trains have been favoured.

A number of trains operate continuously, without ever uncoupling, moving even during loading and unloading. In the United Kingdom, this practice is called "merry-go-round." One U.S. short haul of 15 miles (24 kilometres) is completely automatic, handled from a control centre. In Europe, many unit trains operate on the "block system," in which coal is carried from several mines for

Integrated rail-and-water routes

a single customer or from a single mine for several consumers in a single region.

Water carriers. New approaches are also evident in transportation of coal by means of inland waterways. For example, conveyors are employed to carry coal from mines to the rivers or canals. Transportation over integrated rail-and-water routes is increasing; *e.g.,* coal is moved by rail to docks on the Great Lakes and in the Tidewater region of Virginia. On the Great Lakes, coal is conveyed by belts to the ships, at rates up to 6,000 tons per hour. At piers accommodating larger vessels, the loading rate is even higher.

Motor vehicles. Shipment of coal by truck, while substantial in volume, is generally more expensive than shipment by rail or barge; restrictions on weight also contribute to making highway movement of coal less significant than movement by rail or water in most places.

Trucks are most useful in off-the-highway haulage and in delivery to small consumers. Coal for power stations, however, may be trucked substantial distances if a return load of fly ash is available.

By wire. Extra-high voltage (EHV) transmission of electric power (sometimes in excess of 500,000 volts) from generating stations located at or near the mine mouth is rapidly increasing as a means of transporting energy to distant cities. "Coal by wire" is low in cost, is unimpeded by difficult terrain, allows location of power plants away from populated areas, and can be interconnected with other power lines. Disadvantages of the system include power-line losses and the need for purchasing costly rights-of-way for transmission lines in populated areas. Transport of coal by wire over short distances, however, has been accepted practice in some countries for years. The Yallourn Mine in Australia began power transmission in 1925. Frimmersdorf, West Germany, has a very large mine-mouth generating station and steam power plant.

Mine-mouth generating stations have developed into huge complexes in the U.S., both in established coal-producing areas in the Appalachians and in newer fields in western states. Plants in the Chestnut Ridge generating area of western Pennsylvania, completed in 1971, use more than 16,000,000 tons of bituminous coal per year. In the western U.S., extensive reserves, isolated because of terrain and distance from markets, are being exploited by utilizing the coal-by-wire method to transmit energy from coalfields in New Mexico, Arizona, and Wyoming to serve the expanding population of the West, particularly Southern California.

It is possible also to burn, or heat, the coal in the ground, collect the resulting gases, burn the gas to generate electricity, and transmit the electrical energy by wire.

By pipeline. The long-distance coal-slurry pipeline was the outcome of a research evaluation of alternative transportation methods in an effort to reduce the cost of taking coal to the consumer. After five years of research, including pilot-plant operation, a pipeline, 10 inches (25 centimetres) in diameter, buried 3½ feet (1.05 metres) underground, was placed in service in 1957 in Ohio, carrying pulverized coal, mixed with water, a distance of 108 miles from Cadiz to a power plant on Lake Erie. During approximately six years of operation, it transported more than 7,000,000 tons of coal. The project was a complete success, technically and commercially, even though it was closed down when unit-train freight rates between the two points were established, reducing the cost per ton from $3.47 to $1.88.

In the same year a 72-mile, six-inch (115-kilometre, 15-centimetre) line for transporting gilsonite (a black, lustrous asphalt) entered service in Utah. For this project, a boiler for the use of coal in liquid form was designed and demonstrated.

These two successes proved that the technology required for the construction of cross-country coal pipelines was

Mine-mouth generating stations

Table 4: Comparative Data of Coal Mining in Selected Countries, 1968

item	Australia	Canada	U.S.	West Germany	U.K.	South Africa	Soviet Union	Japan	India
Geologic age*									
Anthracite	P	Cr	Pa–Te	none	C	C–Tr	C	none	Pa–C
Bituminous	Tr or P	Cr–C–Te	C–Te	C–Cr–Te	C	C–Tr	C–Ju	Tr–Ju–Te	P–C–Te
Lignite or brown	Te	Cr–Te	Cr–Te	Te–Pl	none	none	Te–Me	Te	Te
Tectonic movement									
Folding (pitch)	90% < 10°, 1% > 20°	heavy in areas	limited areas	22% > 20°	heavy in areas	<5°	heavy in areas	heavy	heavy†
Faulting	limited	in the west	limited areas	extensive	extensive	none	prevalent	prevalent	prevalent
Igneous intrusion	extensive	...	very limited areas	limited	limited	heavy in areas	...	heavy in areas	heavy in areas
Depth of overburden									
Average (ft)	520	1,700	<500‡	2,400	1,468	<300	1,130	1,510	490
Maximum (ft)	1,200	2,500	...	10% > 3,300	3,765	1,430	3,600	3,025	1,970
Seam thickness									
Average (in.)	102	96	63.6§	62.6	51.2	...	60	71.6	118
Minimum (in.)	36	60	24§	19.7	18	24	20	...	31
Maximum (in.)	216	...	7.1% > 86§	197	150	240	1,180	...	827
Underground methods									
Longwall	3.3%	32%	1.34%	99%	96.5%	2 faces	85%	87.5%	1.3%
Longwall, with powered roof supports	100%	...	100%	27.5%	760 faces	100%	549 faces	14.7%	—
Room-and-pillar (%)	96.7	68	98.65	0	3.5	>98‡	1.7, 8 incl. slicing, 3.2 shield, 2.1 other	7.1	98.7
Hand loading (%)	0.5	0	4.55	8.7	8.0‖	60	...	...	97
Mechanical loading (%)	99.5	100	95.45	90.3	92	40	2 hydraulic	...	3
Conventional (%)	23.3	0	51	0	9	96	48	...	99.63
Continuous	75.7	100	49	100	91	4	50	67	0.37
Productivity¶									
Underground	10.06	6.14	15.07♀	3.89	3.42	2.83	2.19	2.44	—
Surface	52.4	43.4	36.1♀	...	...	none	13.33	—	—
Total average	30.9	27.4	19.17♀ 18.8♂	3.44	...	2.83	2.78	2.44	0.65
Largest operation (000,000 tons)	12.0 opencut	...	5.8 strip	20.0 opencut	...	4.27 underground	5.5 opencut	...	1.19 opencut

*P–Permian; Tr–Triassic; Te–Tertiary; Cr–Cretaceous; Pa–Pennsylvanian; C–Carboniferous; Ju–Jurassic; Pl–Pleistocene; Me–Mesozoic. †Mining mostly 6–12 degrees pitch seams—access 59% shaft. ‡Estimated. §1965. ‖1969. ¶Based on tons per day for all employees to point of shipment. ♀Bituminous and lignite, 1967. ♂Bituminous, lignite, and anthracite, 1967.

Sources: U.S. Department of the Interior, Bureau of Mines, IC 8345 (August 1967); *Coal—Bituminous, Lignite and Anthracite*, Bureau of Mines Yearbook (1968 preprints); National Coal Association, *World Coal Trade* (1969); *Mining Congress Journal* (December 1969).

Table 5: World Coal Production and Reserves

key: A—anthracite; B—bituminous; L—lignite or brown

country	type of coal	production (000 metric tons) av. 1964–67	production 1976 (prelim.)	reserves and resources (000,000 metric tons) year	total	total of economic value*
North America						
Canada	(B)	8,516	20,796	1973	97,040	13,488
	(L)	1,847	4,680	1970	5,080	4,361
Greenland	(A,B)	27	...	1967	2	1
Honduras	(B)	—	—	1913	1	—
	(L)	—	—	1913	4	—
Mexico	(A,B)	2,158	5,500	1975	12,000	698
United States	(A)	12,983}	607,152	1975	21,099	3,349
	(B)	469,746}		1975	2,782,218	182,065
	(L)	3,258	22,980	1975	794,992	12,637
Total North America		498,535	661,108		3,712,436	
South America						
Argentina†	(B,L)	367	612	1974	645	100
Brazil	(B)	2,102	3,132	1974	3,256	1,790
Chile	(B)	1,666	1,200	1972	3,945	58
Colombia	(B,L)	3,425	3,300	1971	5,330	109
Peru	(A)	151	85	1973	281	77
Venezuela	(B)	34	86	1975	15,260	4,128
Total South America		7,745	8,415		28,717	
Europe						
Albania	(L)	362	445		—	—
Austria	(B)	49	—	1975	10	—
	(L)	5,275	3,180	1975	378	104
Belgium	(A,B)	18,756	7,236	1973	253	131
Bulgaria	(B)	529	288	1972	34	29
	(L)	24,901	25,176	1972	5,198	4,358
Czechoslovakia	(A,B)	27,125	28,272	1966	11,573	2,493
	(L)	73,572	89,472	1966	9,857	3,870
Denmark†	(L)	1,926	399	1970	561	—
France	(A,B)	50,588	22,008	1975	1,547	478
	(L)	2,607	3,132	1967	94	—
East Germany	(B)	2,082	456	1956	50	100
	(L)	249,705	246,888	1966	30,000	25,200
West Germany	(A,B)	128,822	89,268	1971	230,303	30,000
	(L)†	101,925	134,532	1975	56,751	10,471
Greece	(L)	4,941	22,236	1961	1,575	680
Hungary	(B)	4,225	2,940	1966	714	225
	(L)	6,092	22,320	1966	5,679	1,450
Ireland	(A,B)	193	48	1974	55	12
Italy	(A,B)	422	529	1967	1	—
	(L)	1,370	1,224	1972	110	30
The Netherlands	(A,B)	10,260	756	1972	3,705	1,840
Norway (Spitsbergen)	(B)	432	515	1975	180	24
Poland	(A,B)	120,515	179,304	1967	45,741	17,800
	(L)	22,834	39,300	1967	14,862	4,840
Portugal	(A)	434	192	1972	15	8
	(L)	70	8	1972	27	25
Romania	(A,B)	6,239	7,248	1966	590	50
	(L)	6,863	18,816	1966	1,367	1,100
Spain	(A,B)	12,589	10,488	1970	2,370	907
	(L)	2,679	4,140	1970	1,192	736
Sweden	(B)	48	10	1975	60	200
Switzerland	(B)	—	—		‡	—
United Kingdom	(B)	184,878	123,804	1975	163,576	3,887
Yugoslavia	(B)	1,122	588	1971	104	70
	(L)	27,688	35,700	1971	21,647	16,800
Total Europe		1,122,333	1,120,918		610,179	
Europe-Asia						
Turkey	(A,B)	4,693	4,644	1974	6,619	134
	(L)	4,320	7,116§	1974	5,328	—
Soviet Union	(A,B)	431,823	474,000	1971	3,993,300	82,900
	(L)	146,305	150,000	1971	1,720,300	53,700
Total Europe-Asia		587,141	635,760		5,725,547	
Asia						
Afghanistan	(A,B)	136	200	1965	85	—
Bangladesh†	(B)	—	—	1963	1,606	519
Burma	(B)	15	16	1960	21	7
	(L)	—	—	1951	265	—
China	(A)	285,000‖}	490,000	1913	1,000,000	80,000
	(B,L)}			1956	700	—
India	(A,B)	66,445	100,992	1972	80,952	10,683
	(L)	2,342	3,900	1972	2,025	897
Indonesia	(B)	341	204	1974	661	80
	(L)			1974	1,960	...
Iran	(A,B)	284	1,200	1972	385	193
Japan	(A,B)	49,713	...	1973	7,443	933
	(L)	520	48	1973	1,185	93
North Korea	(A)	18,300‖	43,000	1962	1,190	—
South Korea	(A)	10,979	16,428	1975	1,434	327
Malaysia	(B)	—	—		...	—
Mongolia	(B)	941	1,075	—		...
Pakistan	(B)	1,362	1,344	1972	410	402
	(L)	—	—	1972	243	243
Philippines	(B)	88	158	1966	...	—
	(L)	—	—	1973	...	91
Taiwan	(B)	5,044	4,473	1965	660	261
Thailand	(L)	184	408§	1967	235¶	118
Vietnam	(A)	3,300}	5,500	1952	1,000	...
	(L)	20}				
Total Asia		445,014	668,946		1,102,460	
Africa						
Algeria	(A,B)	48	3	1957	20	5
Botswana	(A,B)	—	228	1961	506¶	506
Egypt	(A,B)	10	—	1965	25	13
Lesotho	(B,L)	—	—	1947		‡
Malagasy Republic	(B)	2	—	1963	60¶	30
	(L)	—	—	1963	32	9
Malawi	(A,B)	—	—	1960	38	...
Morocco	(A)	438	708	1960	96	15
Mozambique	(L)	265	372	1969	400	80
Nigeria	(B)	570	250	1963	359	180
	(L)	—	—	1975	135	45
Rhodesia	(B)	3,083	3,550	1975	5,000	734
Sierra Leone	(L)	—	—	1967	...	—
South Africa	(A,B)	47,654	75,732	1974	82,018	13,060
Swaziland	(A,B)	45	...	1961	5,022	1,820
Tanzania	(A,B)	2	1	1967	370	180
Zaire	(B)	116	108	1956	73	—
Zambia	(B)	127	792	1974	228	34
Total Africa		52,360	81,744		94,382	
Oceania						
Australia	(B)	32,230	74,856	1975	227,620	17,834
	(L)	21,557	30,936	1975	122,202	30,400
New Caledonia	(B)	—	—	1952	15	3
New Zealand	(B)	2,503	456	1974	599	177
	(L)	164	1,992	1974	153	34
Total Oceania		56,454	108,240		350,589	
World total		2,769,582	3,285,131		11,624,310	

Reserves are known, or measured, deposits of coal, brown coal, or lignite for which reliable data exist on thickness and extent, reported on a standard basis of minimum seam thickness of 30 centimetres for all grades and a maximum deposit depth of 1,200 metres for coal and 500 metres for brown coal and lignite; resources are additional deposits of the same fuels, which are indicated, or reasonably inferred, to exist within the same limits of seam thickness and depth but for which investigations are incomplete.

*Economically recoverable reserves include the portion of the known reserves considered recoverable under current technology and economic conditions.

†Includes peat. ‡Negligible. §1975. ‖Estimated. ¶Incomplete.

Sources: Direct correspondence; World Energy Conference, *Survey of Energy Resources* (1968, 1974, and 1976 [supplement]); U.S. Bureau of Mines, *International Coal Trade*, vol. 38, no. 8 (August 1969); *Coal Resources of the United States*, Geological Survey Bulletin 1275 (January 1, 1967); *Minerals Yearbook*, vol. III, U.S. Department of the Interior (1967); *Minerals Yearbook 1974*, vol. I and III, U.S. Department of the Interior (1976).

available. Included were the discovery of a "stabilized" coal slurry that solved the problem of solids settling out during a shutdown; the proving in of an automatic remote-control system; and developments that made obsolete the original terminals—that is the slurry preparation, the dewatering, and the drying.

Black mesa pipeline Early in 1971, the Black Mesa pipeline for coal slurry was put into operation. This is an 18-inch, 275-mile (45-centimetre, 440-kilometre) system designed to carry 5,000,000 tons of coal per year from the Kayenta Mine in Arizona to the Mohave steam-generating plant near Davis Dam, Nevada.

Coal may also be transported by pipeline in the form of gas, after underground gasification at the mine.

PRODUCTIVITY AND WORLD PRODUCTION

Productivity. Stimulated by competition, the coal industry throughout the world has made continuous improvement in productivity (output per man-hour) through ingenuity and technological innovation. In the U.S., productivity tripled during the 20 years from 1948 to 1968, actually reducing the average cost of a ton of coal at the mine. During the same 20 years, the average hourly earnings of the miners doubled; the costs of supplies and equipment also increased rapidly.

Other countries have also made tremendous strides in productivity of underground mining, though their gains do not equal those of the U.S. Difficult geologic conditions impose restrictions in some areas, increasing the expenditure of work in moving the coal from the working face to the surface. Some geologic phenomena that have a marked effect on productivity are (1) great depth of overburden, which, through excessive pressure, increases roof and floor maintenance problems at the face and in the roadways out from the face; (2) faults that displace the seam, restricting the direction and extent of mining and sometimes requiring excavation through the rock strata to reach the continuation of an interrupted seam; (3) igneous intrusions (molten materials forced from within the Earth's crust through fissures or weak planes in the strata) that isolate coal areas or limit continuity of operation by making the seam nonuniform; (4) structural deformations of the Earth's crust that when light can be responsible for clay veins and when heavy can be responsible for steep, pitching seams that may require a series of tunnels through the rock to reach different levels.

Geologic effects on productivity

The influence of various factors on productivity is indicated in Table 4. The table reflects conditions in selected countries that for the most part have excellent mining research and development programs but that vary widely in mining conditions. The listing is in order of overall productivity, reflecting more difficult mining conditions in the same order.

WORLD PRODUCTION

The latter half of the 1960s and the first half of the '70s saw a growth in total output, despite cutbacks by a number of the world's leading producers. The member countries of the European Economic Community and Japan have all experienced shutdowns of higher cost operations in the face of competition from other energy sources. These losses have been outweighed, however, by increases in Australia, China, Korea, Poland, the Soviet Union, and the U.S.

To show trends, the production figures in Table 5 list the average output for each country for the four years ending in 1967 in order to smooth out yearly fluctuations for comparisons with the 1976 preliminary figures.

WORLD RESOURCES

It is the opinion of those who have devoted much time in geologic surveys of coal that actual resources exceed those published because of insufficient exploration in some areas of the world. It is known that uncharted coal deposits exist in the Antarctic and Greenland. Large areas of Africa, Australia, China, India, and other countries have not been sufficiently explored to provide reliable data. In late 1969, for example, a large deposit of anthracite, 100 feet (30 metres) below the surface, was unexpectedly discovered in South Africa.

Uncharted deposits

Some countries, including the U.S., list recoverable reserves at 50 percent of the total. Many methods have been devised to increase the percentage of coal actually recovered, and it is reasonable to assume that this figure will be exceeded.

BIBLIOGRAPHY. H.N. EAVENSON, *The First Century and a Quarter of American Coal Industry* (1942), is the most complete history of the American coal industry assembled to date. His earlier *Coal Thru the Ages* (1935) might be termed an introduction to the story of America's entrance into coal mining. E.S. MOORE, *Coal*, 2nd ed. (1940), is a concise treatise on the physical properties, geology, and geographic distribution of coal. *The Coal Mine Mechanization Year Books*, ed. by G.B. SOUTHWARD (1928–29), include reports and analyses of early underground studies on coal-mining operations. J.D.A. MARROW presented a paper in 1962 to the Illinois Min-

ing Institute entitled "History of Development of Mining Machines," containing not only his own experiences but also very substantial research; this article was published in the *Proc. Ill. Mining Inst.*, pp. 62–81 (1962). H.L. HARTMAN (ed.), *Case Studies of Surface Mining* (1969), includes papers concerning unique mining conditions throughout the world, together with procedures in arriving at final solutions to the various problems. It is a companion piece to *Surface Mining*, ed. by E.P. PFLEIDER (1968), the authoritative reference in this field. A biennial report of the NATIONAL COAL ASSOCIATION to keep the industry apprised of progress is *Bituminous Coal Facts. Surface Mining and Our Environment*, issued by the UNITED STATES DEPARTMENT OF INTERIOR (1967), is a beautifully illustrated text describing the degradation of the environment in the recovery of some resources, showing what has been done and what can be done to correct the abuse.

(M.A.E.)

Coal Processing

Coal processing is the conversion of coal into useful solid, gaseous, and liquid products. Most of them are used as fuels, but others are important in the chemical, building, and road-making industries.

This article does not deal with the mining of coal or with coal combustion (see COALS; COAL MINING).

The general objectives of coal processing may be classified as follows: (1) to render coal suitable for various processes or purposes (*e.g.*, to make metallurgical coke or smokeless domestic fuel); (2) to convert coal into more valuable fuels (*e.g.*, briquetting of small coals, complete gasification to make fuel gas, or conversion into gasoline and fuel oil); and (3) to enlarge markets by using coal as a chemical raw material.

Although such carbonization by-products as benzol and tar have been very important in the development of the chemical industry, carbonization has rarely been carried out for the sake of these by-products alone. The manufacture of the main products, coke, smokeless fuel, and town gas, has been the main end.

HISTORY

Coal processing probably originated in the 16th century, when it became necessary to find a source of carbon to supplement wood charcoal for making iron in blast furnaces. Consequently, processes of carbonization were devised, leading to the manufacture of coke. By 1709 coke was regularly used by Abraham Darby in his blast furnaces in Coalbrookdale, Shropshire. The original primitive carbonization processes were progressively replaced by more complicated methods in larger plants as technology advanced. In 1968, the world consumption of metallurgical coke required the use of over 400,000,-000 metric tons of coal. (The metric ton [or tonne] is equal to 1,000 kilograms and is very nearly equal to the U.S. long ton, 1,016 kilograms; the U.S. short ton is 907.18 kilograms, or 2,000 pounds.) Although alternative methods for making iron have been developed, the main method throughout the world still requires use of the blast furnace, and the manufacture of metallurgical coke seems likely to remain as the major example of coal processing.

The carbonization of coal with the prime object of making town gas, with coke as a by-product, began commercially about 1800, after William Murdock had first used gas lighting in England in 1792. The practice spread rapidly in many countries until practically every town had its own gasworks; a visit to such a gasworks, often the only "chemical" plant in the neighbourhood, played a considerable part in arousing the interest of schoolchildren in chemistry. Other methods of making town gas from petroleum products and the use of natural gas, however, eliminated the need for the classic gasworks. The change was completed in most parts of the U.S. by 1950; in the U.K., where 24,000,000 metric tons of coal were treated in gasworks in 1955, the change began around 1960. Very little coal was carbonized in gasworks after 1970.

Town gas

The by-products of coal carbonization are tar, benzol, and ammonia. Tar was first recovered from gasworks soon after 1800, but by-product coke ovens were not successfully operated until after 1850. The recovery of tar, and later of benzol, grew rapidly because of the requirements of the chemical industry, particularly for dyestuffs and explosives. Ammonia formed the basis of the only manufactured nitrogenous fertilizers until it was made synthetically after 1913. Later, the importance of these by-products decreased as the chemical industry more frequently turned to petroleum sources for its raw materials. Nevertheless, since the late 19th century, coal tar and benzol have provided the livelihood for three generations of chemists and have formed the basis for the growth of organic chemistry on a commercial scale.

In addition to high-quality town gas, the need for a lower grade industrial fuel gas led to "complete gasification" processes, producing no coke as a by-product. Processes for making "producer gas" from coal or coke were in use from the mid-19th century, reaching their peak in the U.K. in the period from 1930 to 1950, when several million metric tons per annum of coal were used in this way. Producer gas from coal was particularly valued in steelworks because of its high flame luminosity and good heating qualities. The high price of coal relative to oil and high labour costs, however, had closed practically all such plants by 1970. From about 1880 to 1920, the economics of the Mond producer-gas process, which used a large excess of steam, was helped materially by the exceptionally high yield of ammonia obtained from it.

In the 1930s, the Lurgi Company in Germany produced a complete gasification process that was particularly successful with noncoking coals. Plants were built in several countries, but they too suffered from natural gas and petroleum product competition and many had already closed by 1970. The Lurgi plant in South Africa, based on very cheap coal, makes "synthesis gas" (see below).

Much work continued in the U.S. to make town gas of high caloric value from coal, against the day when natural gas and oil become scarce and the relatively large reserves of coal have to be employed. Technically, the problem is solved, and the time is almost ripe for an economic application. In the U.K. coal is too expensive for any chance of economic success.

"Synthesis gas"
From 1920 to 1960, much effort was devoted throughout the world to devise processes for making "synthesis gas" from coal. Such gas can be used to make ammonia, methanol, and gasoline. Germany has been prominent with several processes, particularly with the more reactive brown coal and lignite. Another approach to "oil-from-coal," also pioneered in Germany in the 1930s, was hydrogenation of coal under pressure. The process, using bituminous coals, was technically very successful. It seems likely indeed that Germany could not have entered World War II without the support of such processes. Germany depended on them to supply not only ammonia (and hence explosives and fertilizers) but also most of her motor and aviation fuel. At the peak (May 1944), oil was being produced in Germany's oil-from-coal plants at the rate of 6,000,000 metric tons per annum. The only oil-from-coal plants to survive after 1945, however, were in East Germany, particularly those using brown coal. The only other plant operating on bituminous coal by 1970 was in South Africa. But the U.S. is also developing oil-from-coal processes against the day when oil becomes scarce and expensive.

Work on coal processing has had profound effects on the chemical industry, both in technological developments and on the structure of the industry. The Winkler process, introduced in Germany in 1926 for the gasification of brown coal, was the first large-scale use of the technique of fluidization and later became widely used in the petroleum industry. Experience gained from the new processes and technologies has greatly influenced the direction of company growth and the spread of ideas.

Solid smokeless fuels
The development of solid smokeless fuels from coal has been an objective in many countries for centuries. Methods of cooking and house heating evolved from the use of wood and charcoal. When wood grew scarce, people searched for a substitute that they could use in their existing appliances. As coke was developed for metallurgical processes, the smaller sizes naturally became available for domestic use. With the manufacture of town gas by the carbonization of coal, large quantities of gas coke also were applied to domestic use. In the period 1920–40, much work was carried out on low-temperature carbonization processes, especially in the U.K., to make solid smokeless fuel together with oils suitable for use as gasoline and diesel oil. Not until the passing of the Clean Air Act in 1956, however, did the demand for smokeless fuels in the U.K. become great enough to warrant much expansion in production. In 1969, the production of manufactured smokeless fuels by the National Coal Board and private industry used 5,000,000 metric tons of coal; this was in addition to anthracite and gas coke. No other country has produced manufactured smokeless fuel on this scale.

The conversion of small coal and dust into larger lumps by briquetting has been of considerable importance since the early 19th century. While still important, later emphasis was on adding a further stage to make the briquettes smokeless.

Employing coal directly as a chemical raw material is of fairly recent origin, since the chemistry, like the coal itself, is complicated. But throughout the 20th century, workers in many countries have attacked coal with various chemicals, trying to convert it to a material that could then be used for a variety of purposes. They have also tried to convert it to active carbon. Although this research has uncovered some commercial applications, the quantities of coal consumed in this way have been small. Nevertheless, the work goes on, and outlets for modest quantities of coal are likely to be found in these directions.

Summing up, the processing of coal represents an important outlet for coal, in many countries exceeding 20 to 30 percent of the total market. The manufacture of metallurgical coke represents the biggest use in most countries and is likely to continue. In the U.K. and to a lesser extent in other countries, the manufacture of solid smokeless fuels is also important and likely to remain so. The amount of coal converted to town gas and industrial gases has declined rapidly in most countries, but coal may be used extensively again for making gas as natural gas and oil products become scarce and expensive. There are other minor uses for processed coal, and some new ones are being developed in the chemical, building, and road-making fields, but the quantities of coal involved are likely to remain fairly modest.

GENERAL CONSIDERATIONS

Classification and evaluation of coals. The types and ranks of coal are described in the article COALS. Any of these coals may be processed in one or many ways, but not all coals can be used in a particular process. Economic considerations are as important as technical considerations in selecting the coal to be used.

Clearly, coals with a high ash content are undesirable for making solid products of low ash content unless the coal can be cleaned first. The behaviour of the coal on heating (in particular, whether it becomes plastic and can make a good coke) determines its suitability for carbonization and the type of oven or retort that can be used. In general, coals with a volatile content of 15 to 35 percent, often as blends, are used to make metallurgical coke, while coals with 30 to 45 percent volatile content are used to make town gas. Coals of medium rank are used for low-temperature carbonization because they yield reactive cokes. Coals of very low or very high volatile-matter content will not form strong coke merely by heating. When such coal is not in lump form, briquetting at some stage is necessary if satisfactory metallurgical fuels and smokeless fuels are to be made from, for example, small anthracite, low-rank bituminous coal fines, or brown coal.

Any coal may be totally gasified by the appropriate process; the ash content is then a minor consideration. Any tarry material evolved during the gasification process has to be separated or gasified as well.

Large and graded coal is usually best suited for processing, because it usually is more easily cleaned and dried. Crushing is economical, but briquetting is expensive. Nevertheless, a large proportion of coal is mined as small pieces. Most commercial processes have been developed to use small coal because it is available at lower prices and overall is cheaper, even with the disadvantages noted.

Cleaning and other preparatory steps.   Mined coal contains a varying proportion of noncoal substances; for example, shales and rocks from roof and floor and shales embedded in the coal seams. Coal and other material may vary in size from 300 mm (12 in.) or more to dust. Modern mechanical mining methods yield a high proportion of small coal; *i.e.*, below 50 mm. The coal and other material with it is frequently wet. Since more than one seam is often worked at the same time, a varying mixture reaches the surface.

The function of coal preparation is to separate this mixture and prepare from the cleaned coal fractions of consistent size and quality for various markets. For example, clean large coal may be separated for domestic use, clean graded coal (25 to 75 mm) for domestic and industrial use, clean small coal for carbonization, or a partially cleaned coal for steam raising in central power stations. Waste is discarded by being stowed underground or tipped at the surface. Separation into wanted and unwanted fractions must be conducted with maximum efficiency not only to obtain clean products but to avoid undue loss of coal to the waste. Inevitably, in practice, compromises have to be made to achieve optimum economic working.

The largest material brought up from the mine is often first crushed, sometimes after large rock is removed by hand. Subsequently, coal is separated from other materials by taking advantage of the difference in density between coal (sp gr—specific gravity—1.3 to 1.6) and other material (sp gr 1.8 to 2.4). The actual separation takes place in special washers. The upward velocity of the water can lift the coal but not the heavier material, as in the Baum jig, where a pulsating motion of the water assists the separation. Alternatively, the coal may be floated in a "dense medium"; *i.e.*, water containing fine solids of high specific gravity such as magnetite, which can be easily recovered magnetically. The smallest sizes may be treated by froth flotation. Air is blown through a suspension of the fines in water, and the coal (but not the shale particles) attach themselves to the air bubbles. A reagent may be added to help the separation, and the clean coal froth that accumulates is floated off. Water is removed from the washed products by drainage, filtration, centrifuging, or by heat drying.

It is not always economic to clean coal for central power stations. It is also desirable to avoid adding water to the coal by trying to wash it. If the ash content is sufficiently low, the run-of-mine material is merely screened and the oversize is washed, crushed, and mixed back with the unwashed undersize.

When seams of low inherent ash content were mined by hand methods, the coal did not need washing. Such coal is still being worked, and the large sizes at least are not washed. Some of the brown coal and lignite in Germany and Australia are also clean enough, after briquetting and carbonization, for domestic and industrial use; the dirtier coals are generally not washed; they are used for power generation or gasification.

Rocks and shales, the waste products of coal preparation plants, sometimes find low-grade uses. Some of them go into road making, while certain shales may be treated in kilns to make light-weight aggregates for building construction, a process that takes advantage of the small amount of combustible material (coal and carbonaceous shales) present.

PYROLYSIS

When coals are heated in the absence of air (pyrolysis), changes occur as illustrated in Table 1.

Coals differ greatly in their behaviour on heating.

Table 1: General Effects of Pyrolysis	
temperature (°C)	changes
Above 100°	free water evaporates
Above 200°	combined water and carbon dioxide evolved
Above 350°	bituminous coals soften and melt to some extent: decomposition begins; tar and gas evolved
400° to 500°	most of the tar is evolved
450° to 550°	decomposition continues and residue turns solid
Above 550°	solid becomes coke; only gas now evolved
By 900°	no more gas evolved; coke only remains
Above 900°	small physical changes occur

Anthracite does not soften and evolves only a little gas. Low-rank coals yield much gas, carbon dioxide, and water, and give a coke of low mechanical strength. Medium-rank coals are intermediate in behaviour and yield strong cokes.

Low-temperature carbonization.   Low-temperature carbonization usually describes the pyrolysis of coal to a final temperature of up to 700° C. The final solid product is a rather weak coke. Compared with high-temperature carbonization, this process yields more oil and tar but less gas. Between 1920 and 1940, low-temperature carbonization was applied extensively. The objective then was partly to obtain the high yield of tar and oils. After 1945, low-temperature carbonization was carried out commercially only to obtain the solid residue for use as a domestic, smokeless fuel. Nevertheless, the tar and oils formed simultaneously are processed further and sometimes add significantly to the economics of the process.

Processes.   Over 100 processes have been developed but only a few have operated successfuly. Some examples follow: (1) noncaking lump coal or briquettes are heated in internally-heated retorts (*e.g.*, the Lurgi-Spülgas and Rexco processes); (2) small caking coal is heated in externally-heated tubes, from which the agglomerate of coke is eventually discharged (*e.g.*, the Coalite process); (3) small caking coal is heated in a rotary kiln, the plastic char so formed balling up to form lumps of coke (*e.g.*, the Disco process); (4) small coal is heated in a fluidized bed to form a smokeless char that is compacted, while still hot and plastic, in a press with or without the addition of a binder (*e.g.*, the Char Briquetting process of the National Coal Board [U.K.]); (5) low-volatile coal is briquetted with some substance such as pitch and then carbonized (*e.g.*, the Phurnacite and Syntraciet processes).

The Rexco process uses a simple plant of low capital cost, but suitable lump coal is more expensive than others and not always available. The Lurgi-Spülgas process is more complicated but upgrades cheap brown coal. The Char Briquetting process leaves over 20 percent volatile matter in the smokeless fuel, providing a free-burning fuel in high yield. In the Coalite process, the by-products are particularly valuable; typical yields appear in Table 2.

Table 2: Yields of By-products from the Coalite Process	
	kg per 1,000 kg coal (9% moisture)
Coalite (large)	700
Coalite (other sizes)	50
Gas	83 (700 × 10⁶ cals)
Tar	75
Light oil	12

In processes for carbonizing briquettes, the starting material is usually lignite or small coal. Briquetting and carbonizing are expensive, but the final product is dense and uniform, commanding a premium price. One process for rendering pitch-bound briquettes smokeless treats them at 350° to 400° C in an atmosphere containing oxygen (*e.g.*, the Anthracine process in France, the Inichar process in Belgium, and the Multiheat process in the U.K.).

The Disco process, formerly operated in Pittsburgh, has been abandoned. All the other processes mentioned

Density separation

Rocks and shales

Comparison of processes

operate in Europe, often in competition with one another. No one process predominates because it is necessary to use the variety of coals that are naturally available and because some of the final fuels suit some appliances and not others. The prices of the final products delivered to the householder also tend to differentiate the market. Processes based on lignite are commercially important in Europe and elsewhere, but in the U.S. are still under development.

Products. Low-temperature cokes and other smokeless fuels burn readily; they contain 5 to 20 percent volatile matter but nevertheless burn without smoke. The properties of low-temperature tars and light oils are described below.

High-temperature carbonization. In high-temperature carbonization, coal is heated to temperatures of 900° C to 1,200° C. The lower temperatures are used for the manufacture of town gas, with coke as a by-product, and the higher temperatures for the manufacture of metallurgical coke, with gas as a by-product. High-temperature coke may also be made especially for domestic use, with gas as a by-product.

For producing town gas, the type of coal and the carbonizing conditions are selected to give the maximum yield of gas. The gas coke is weak and small but satisfactory as a domestic fuel. For making metallurgical coke, a blend of coals and the carbonizing conditions are selected to give hard strong coke.

Processes. For a high-temperature carbonizing process to be commercially satisfactory, it is necessary to (1) pass large quantities of heat into a mass of coal at temperatures up to 900° C or more; (2) extract readily the completed coke from the vessel in which it is carbonized; (3) avoid atmospheric pollution and arduous working conditions for the operators; and (4) carry out the whole operation on a large scale and at a low cost.

Metallurgical coke and coke ovens. Carbonization on a tiny scale was probably first employed by the smiths, who gave coal a preliminary heating on the hearth to leave a residue of coke. Then followed processes akin to charcoal burning. Beehive ovens, developed earlier for the carbonization of wood, were used with coal in the 18th century in Durham, England. These were roughly hemispherical furnaces, containing a coal layer about 750 mm (2½ ft) thick. The gas and tar evolved were burned in the upper part of the furnace, and the heat so developed was reflected back to the coal. The operation could easily take three days. These ovens were small, required much labour, and led to atmospheric pollution. The last beehive ovens in the U.K. closed in 1954, but an improved form persisted in the U.S. in the 1970s. Because of their simplicity and low capital cost, they are useful in meeting peak demands for coke.

Successful ovens that recovered by-products followed the use of narrow side-heated or slot ovens, operating in Belgium in 1850–60. Constructed with a good grade of firebrick, each oven held about four metric tons of coal. Increasingly larger ovens for higher temperatures and faster carbonization followed. Fuel gas (usually coke oven gas but sometimes blast furnace or producer gas) was burned in flues outside the oven walls. Silica, first used in the U.S. before 1900, introduced the refractory most widely used with flue temperatures up to 1,450° C. Modern coke ovens can be as large as 6.5 m (21 ft) high, 15.5m long, and 0.46m wide, each oven holding up to 33 metric tons of coal. The coking time, *i.e.*, between charging and discharging, is about 15 hours. Such ovens are arranged in batteries, containing up to 100 ovens each. A coking plant may consist of several such batteries. The largest coking plants in the U.S. and in the U.S.S.R. carbonize annually 5,000,000 to 10,000,000 metric tons of coal each, but older coking plants are still operating throughout the world with quite small ovens and annual throughputs of only 100,000 to 300,000 metric tons. Figure 1 illustrates the sections of a coking plant. Modern coke ovens are highly mechanized, thus minimizing atmospheric pollution and lessening the

Beehive ovens (margin note)

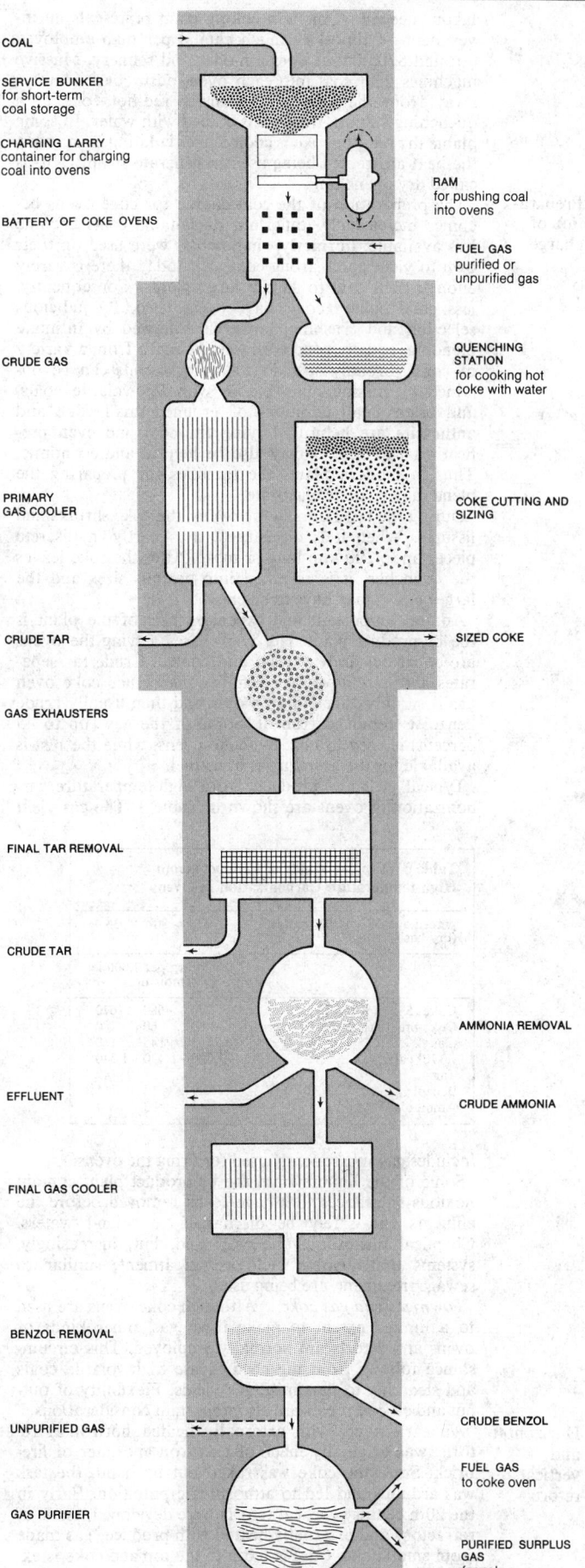

Figure 1: The processing of coal in a coking plant.

labour needed. A modern coking plant represents an investment of almost as much capital per man employed (around $70,000) as does a modern oil refinery. Massive machines load coal into each oven, push coke sideways away from the oven, and transfer red-hot coke to a quenching station, where it is cooled with water. In some plants the red-hot coke is cooled in circulating inert gases, the heat abstracted being used to generate steam. This is called dry quenching.

The preparation of the coal charge for coke ovens becomes increasingly important as suitable coals become less available. Formerly, single coals were used on their own to yield good strong coke, but today there is rarely enough such coal to supply large plants. Consequently, less good coking coals have to be used. By judicious selection and crushing, however, followed by intimate blending, equally good cokes can be made from a variety of coals. Broadly speaking, suitable blends can be obtained by mixing high-volatile with low-volatile coals, and often small additions of ground, small coke and anthracite are helpful. Drying the coal and even preheating it to 200° C may also be helpful and economic. Thus in modern plants the facilities for preparing the blend may be quite elaborate.

During the last hours in the ovens, the coke shrinks and fissures. When it is discharged, it is partly in discrete pieces up to 200 mm long or more. After the coke leaves the quencher, it is screened into various sizes and the larger pieces may have to be cut.

Another important and expensive part of the plant is the by-product plant. Hot tarry gases leaving the ovens are collected, drawn away, and cooled. Crude tar separates and is removed for refining. The crude coke oven gas is scrubbed free of ammonia and then usually crude benzol is removed from it. Some of the gas (up to 45 percent) is used to heat the coke ovens, while the rest is available for use as town gas or as fuel.

Typical yields of products from high-temperature carbonization in ovens are shown in Table 3. The gas yield

Table 3: Typical Yields of Products from High-temperature Carbonization in Ovens

percentage of volatile matter (dry basis)	23	30	35
	Yields kg per 1,000 kg (9% moisture)		
Coke (5% moisture)	750	680	620
Coke breeze (less than 12 mm)	40	60	80
Gas	135	148	160
(10⁶ cal)	1,300	1,430	1,540
Tar	27	38	42
Benzol	9	12	15
Ammonia	2	3	4

includes gas subsequently used for firing the ovens.

Some of the liquors from the by-product plant contain noxious substances that have to be removed before the effluents can safely be discharged to inland waters. Chemical means may be employed, but, increasingly, systems that involve biological treatment, similar to sewage treatment, are being used.

Town gas and gas coke. Although coke ovens are used to a limited extent to make town gas, other kinds of ovens and retorts are normally employed. This circumstance follows from the need to use high-volatile coals and steaming to maximize gas yields. Flexibility of output and ease of repair are also important considerations.

An early type, with externally heated horizontal retorts, was originally made of cast iron and later of firebrick. Since the coke was raked out by hand, the task was arduous and led to atmospheric pollution. Early in the 20th century vertical retorts were developed, made of refractory and externally heated with producer gas made from small coke. Coal is fed into the top and coke is extracted from the bottom, with the operation continuous or intermittent. Steam is usually introduced into the bottom of the vertical retorts, serving both to cool the coke

and to convert some of it into gas. Several such retorts were normally grouped together in a retort house, sharing certain services and facilities. Gasworks of this kind were often quite small. Even in large towns, there rarely was more than one million metric tons per annum of coal carbonized in one gasworks. In many countries, gasworks that make gas from coal are being rapidly replaced by natural gas and town gas made from petroleum products.

The by-products plant at a gasworks is similar to that described for coking plants. The gas is cooled, and tar, ammonia, benzol, and hydrogen sulfide removed. Pressure boosters then send the gas through distribution mains.

Coke discharged from the retort is cooled with water and prepared for market by cutting and screening. Noxious effluents from the by-product plant are usually treated in domestic sewage plants after preliminary treatment.

Typical yields of products from vertical retorts with steaming are shown in Table 4.

Table 4: Typical Yields of Products from Vertical Retorts with Steaming

	per 1,000 kg coal (3% moisture)
Town gas	458 cubic metres (1,930 × 10⁶ cal)
Coke and breeze*	635 kg
Tar	63 kg
Benzol (recovered)	10 kg
Ammonia	3 kg

*Of which 140 kg is used to fire the retorts.

Products and their uses. *Coke.* The bulk of oven coke (sized about 40 to 100 mm) is used throughout the world in blast furnaces to make iron. Much smaller quantities are employed in other metallurgical processes, such as the manufacture of ferroalloys, lead, and zinc, and in kilns to make lime and magnesia. Exceptionally large strong coke, known as foundry coke, is used in foundry cupolas to melt iron. The smaller sizes, (15 mm to 50 mm) of both oven and gas coke are suitable for heating houses, hospitals, schools, and commercial buildings. Coke in 10 mm to 25 mm sizes is much used in the manufacture of phosphorus and calcium carbide; from the latter acetylene, mainly for chemical purposes, is made. Large quantities of the smallest sizes (less than 12 mm), known as coke breeze, are suited for sintering small iron ore prior to use in blast furnaces. Any surplus breeze serves as an industrial boiler fuel. There are a number of small uses for coke where a cheap source of impure carbon is required.

Until 1940 coke was much used in water-gas generators, in which it reacted with steam and air to make a mixture of nitrogen and hydrogen for the manufacture of practically all synthetic ammonia. But by 1969 hardly any ammonia was made from coke, since cheaper sources of hydrogen could be obtained from natural gas and petroleum.

Coal tar. Crude tar is refined; *i.e.*, separated into its various constituents by distillation and chemical processing. Typical analyses of tar are shown in Table 5, although the recovery of the pure chemicals as such is not complete in practice.

Table 5: Typical Analyses of Tars (percent by weight)

	coke oven tar	gasworks tar	low-temperature tar
Pitch	59.0	44.0	26.0
Creosote	31.0	42.0	55.0
Light oils	2.5	5.4	6.7
Heavy oils	5.4	6.5	9.4
In the oils and creosote occur:			
Tar acids (*e.g.*, phenol, cresols)	3.1	16.0	29.3
Tar bases (*e.g.*, pyridine)	1.8	2.1	2.1
Naphthalene	8.8	3.0	0.7
Anthracene	1.0	0.26	0.06

Either pot stills or more usually pipe stills with a fractionating column are employed. Pitch is run off the bottom of the column, while all other fractions, boiling (up to 400° C), are distilled overhead, being separated into several fractions according to boiling range. Each fraction is then further worked up for the recovery of any desired chemical component. Tar acids are recovered from aqueous liquors by solvents and from certain oil and creosote fractions with caustic soda, while tar bases are recovered by extraction with sulfuric acid. Naphthalene is recovered by distillation or crystallization, and anthracene by crystallization of appropriate fractions. The crude chemicals so recovered from several tar refineries are processed into pure chemicals in secondary plants.

Pitch products

Pitch is a valuable binder for briquetting and in making electrodes. The aluminum industry of the world depends heavily on electrodes made from petroleum coke, pitch coke, and pitch. Pitch and mixtures of pitch and creosote in various proportions constitute road tar and fuels. Creosote is valuable for timber preservation. Because of its valuable waterproofing properties, pitch is employed in a number of formulations for treating walls, roofs, and floors. Digesting coal in pitch and heavy oils produces pipe-coating enamels that protect gas and oil mains buried under land and water. The heavy oils are also used for making carbon black.

Of the simpler chemical substances that appear in some of the fractions, the light oils are processed further into benzene, toluene, and xylene for chemical use or as solvents. Naphthalene is processed into mothballs but more importantly is used in dyestuffs and to make phthalic anhydride, in turn used to make plasticizers, resins, and paints; while anthracene is used mainly by the dyestuffs industry. Tar acids and bases enter into a wide range of chemicals, such as plastics, explosives, dyestuffs, agrochemicals, and pharmaceuticals.

Historically, coal tar is important because it has supported the chemical industry with such chemicals as benzene, toluene, phenol, cresol, naphthalene, and anthracene. In the 1930s, however, such substances began to evolve from petrochemical sources, which took over the major supply of the requirements of the chemical industry. Only anthracene and some of the higher tar acids and bases are still obtained more from coal tar than from petrochemicals.

Light oil. After tar has been removed, coal gas still contains some hydrocarbons that can be removed and recovered as a light, oily liquid often referred to as benzol, which can be refined and separated into fractions. Typical analyses of light oil are given in Table 6.

Table 6: Typical Analyses of Light Oil
(percent by weight)

	coke ovens (benzol)	gasworks (benzol)	low-temperature (light oil)
aromatics			
Benzene	65	45	
Toluene	15	8	15–20
Xylene	5	4	
Naphtha	12	20	30–35
paraffins	2	20	40–45

The light oils from tar distillation are somewhat similar to, and sometimes are refined together with, the benzol. Benzene and toluene are used as chemicals, along with larger quantities of these substances made from petrochemical sources. During both world wars, large quantities of toluene were employed to make the explosive trinitrotoluene, but the uses of toluene later became more modest and various. The light naphtha contains coumarone and indene, which are extracted and converted to resins. All fractions are to some extent used as solvents over a wide field. The benzol from gasworks and low-temperature carbonization is usually too paraffinic, containing too few aromatic hydrocarbons to justify recovering benzene from it. After fractionation and treat-

ment, such benzol is often used as gasoline and diesel fuel, though these are now low-value outlets and often such benzols are left in the gas or otherwise used as fuel.

Gaseous products. Coke oven gas is employed as fuel and town gas. Unpurified or partly purified gas is used in steelworks. Purification (removal of sulfur compounds) is effected by passing the gas through beds of iron oxide mixtures or by scrubbing it with chemical solutions. In Germany, coke oven gas is sent through a pressure grid over long distances, a practice that justifies operating the by-product plant, after cooling and tar removal, at elevated pressure. Coke oven gas from large plants formerly was used as a source of hydrogen to make synthetic ammonia, but this practice is fast disappearing, except in the U.S.S.R., since it is much cheaper to make hydrogen from natural gas or petroleum naphtha.

The coal gas from a gasworks is employed as town gas. Sulfur removal by the method described is then required by law. Most gasworks carbonize coal at atmospheric pressure, thus permitting limited quantities of gas to be stored economically in gasholders, a prominent feature of such plants. Some of these hold as much as 350,000 cubic metres of gas. Newer gasworks, operating at pressure on petroleum feedstocks, cannot economically employ this method of storage.

Typical analyses are shown in Table 7.

Table 7: Typical Analyses of Coal Gas
(percent by volume)

	H_2	CH_4	CO	CO_2	N_2	O_2	other hydrocarbons
Coke oven gas	54	28	7	2	6	0.4	2.6
Town gas*	49	20	18	4	6	0.4	2.0

*From continuous vertical retorts with steaming.

OTHER PROCESSING TECHNIQUES AND PRODUCTS

Briquetting. In mining it is economically necessary to utilize small coals to the best purpose. If lump fuel is required for any purpose, it is necessary to convert the small coal into strong coherent lumps, which can be done by briquetting: mixing the coal with a binder and then pressing the mixture together to form shapes of the required size.

With brown coal, no binder is needed since the coal, after drying, can be extruded or otherwise pressed into shapes. With bituminous coal it is necessary to use pitch, bitumen, or other materials. The production of briquettes from cheap brown coal is still popular in Germany, where they find ready use as domestic fuel. Since they are not smokeless, however, such briquettes are increasingly carbonized before sale. Bituminous coal briquettes also are not smokeless and their use has declined rapidly. By contrast, the use of briquettes rendered smokeless by carbonization or other means has increased steadily in many countries, notably in the U.K. and northwestern Europe.

Smokeless binders such as starch, synthetic resin, and sulfite lye have been used to make smokeless briquettes, but these are costly or have other drawbacks. Nevertheless, it is likely that processes utilizing such binders will grow.

Coal, if heated to about 400° C, can be briquetted hot without a binder. The property is utilized in the Char Briquetting process of the National Coal Board (U.K.).

Metallurgical fuels

Metallurgical fuels, sometimes known as formed coke, can also be made by carbonizing briquettes produced from coal, char, or coke. These can be made from noncoking coal (incapable of being formed into coke in ovens). They have uniform size and other properties, from piece to piece. Successful processes of this kind have been developed in Poland (to make foundry fuel), in the U.S. (the National Fuels Corporation process), and in Germany (the Steinkohlenbergbauverein and Lurgi processes).

In the German processes, part of the coal is converted into char in a fluidized bed at about 700° C. The remainder of the coal is added prior to briquetting hot at about 400° C, and the briquettes are subsequently carbonized. It seems likely that formed-coke plants for making metallurgical fuels will be built in those countries that have noncoking coals but insufficient coking coal.

Gasification. Here the objective is to convert most of the coal substance into gas, leaving behind only ash and a little carbon as a solid residue.

Carbon reacts with steam chemically to form hydrogen and carbon oxides; thus

$$C + H_2O \rightarrow H_2 + CO$$
$$C + 2H_2O \rightarrow 2H_2 + CO_2$$

This process is endothermic (absorbs heat), and heat therefore must be added to the vessel in which coal and steam are reacting. The various ways of doing this and the varying nature of the fuel used and the gas obtained have led to the large number of gasification systems, dozens of which have reached commercial importance.

The simplest process is to add air with the steam to form producer gas; some of the coal is burnt to provide heat for the gasification of the remainder. This producer gas contains up to 55 percent nitrogen. Since it has a low caloric value, it can be used only as fuel gas. In this form, however, it can be used where coal itself cannot. The presence of nitrogen may be avoided by using oxygen instead of air or a mixture of oxygen and air if some nitrogen can be tolerated. Such gas was once widely used as synthesis gas for making ammonia. By operating under pressure, the gas produced contains some methane, which much improves the calorific value. One such process, developed by Lurgi (see Figure 2) in Germany, has been employed both to make town gas in Germany, the U.K., and Australia, and synthesis gas in the Sasol synthetic oil plant in South Africa.

Continuous and cyclical gasification When using air or oxygen with steam, coal may be gasified in the following ways: in lump form in fixed beds (as in gas producers or in the Lurgi process); small coal in fluidized beds (the Winkler process); or in total suspension (the Koppers-Totzek and Texaco processes). The coal is sometimes carbonized first and the resultant coke used advantageously in the gasifier. It is necessary to avoid clinker forming from the ash: either the gasifier must be run below clinkering temperatures (about 1,200° C) using plenty of steam or above 1,300° C with the minimum of steam so that the ash is melted to form a slag. The Texaco process is a slagging process in which coal and oxygen and a little steam react at elevated pressure and at temperatures exceeding 1,300° C. The Leuna fixed-bed process can be worked under either nonslagging or slagging conditions according to the amount of steam used.

The preceding are continuous processes. Gasification may also be carried out cyclically. Some fuel is burned with air and the heat stored in a regenerator. Steam is then preheated in the regenerator before passing through a fuel bed with some air or oxygen. In a coke water-gas generator, air and steam are passed alternately; heat evolved when air is passed is stored in the coke bed and made available when steam is passed. Oil can also be injected into the hot gases to be cracked and to provide additional caloric value. Carburetted water gas made in this way was once much used to meet peak demands for town gas.

In theory, a reactor could be designed to preheat steam sufficiently to satisfy the heat requirements of the steam–coal reaction. Existing materials of construction so far have prevented an economic solution. Some work is commencing in the use of nuclear heat for this purpose. It would perhaps be easier to do this with lignite, which is reactive, than with bituminous coal, which requires higher temperatures.

Finally, gasifiers have been designed in which coal is held in metal or ceramic retorts and heated externally while steam is passed through the coal. This process is used in vertical retorts to increase the yield of town gas, but it is not normally economic to gasify coal completely in this way.

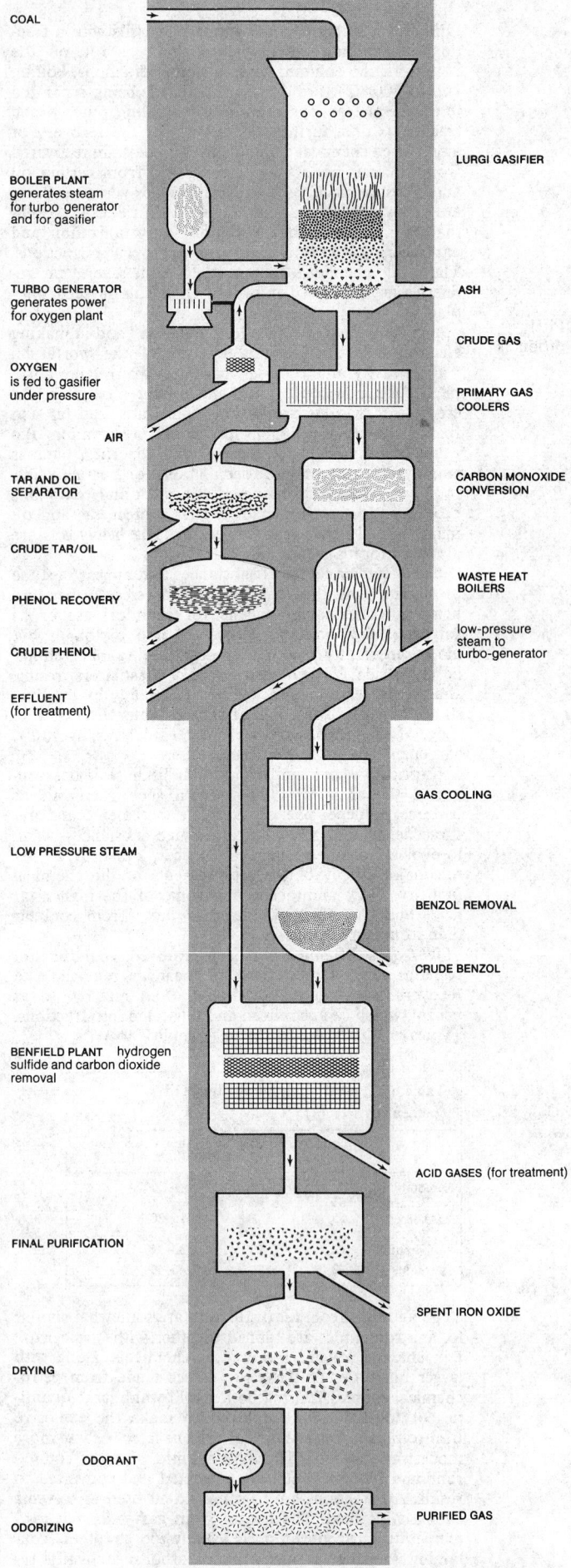

Figure 2: The processing of coal at the Lurgi gasification plant.

Typical analyses of some manufactured gases are contained in Table 8. In addition, the gases contain various amounts of sulfur compounds.

Table 8: Typical Analyses of Some Manufactured Gases (percent by volume [crude gas])

Fuel	Gas	H$_2$	CH$_4$	CO	CO$_2$	N$_2$	other hydrocarbons
Coal	Producer	12	3	29	4	51.6	0.4
Coke	Producer	11	0.5	29	5	54.5	0
Coke	Water gas	49	0.5	41	5	4.5	0
Coal	Lurgi	39.8	11	16	32	1	0.2
Coal	Koppers-Totzek	33.9	0.1	51	13	2	0

Hydrogenation. Coal can be converted substantially into oil and gas by reaction with hydrogen at pressures of 250 atmospheres or more. Such oils may be fractioned and purified to make excellent gasoline. In the Bergius process, developed in Germany in the 1930s, clean coal was slurried with recycled oil, and tin compounds were added as catalysts. The mixture was passed through large forgings that constituted the reactors. Compressed hydrogen was passed through the mixture to provide the hydrogen required chemically and to control the resultant rise in temperature. The final mixture was cooled and the pressure reduced. After the unconverted coal and ash were separated, the clean heavy oils were distilled. The heaviest fraction was recycled with fresh coal to the first stage, and the lighter fractions were passed forward to the next stage, where they were further hydrogenated, again at high pressure but now in the vapour phase, over a catalyst (tungsten sulfide). The products from this stage were fractionated and worked up to gasoline.

The difficult stage was the first: quantities of expensive hydrogen were required, and corrosion and erosion caused much trouble. In practice this stage was often bypassed by starting with tar or creosote.

Nevertheless, Germany produced about 75 percent of its synthetic oil in this way in 1941 to 1944. The economics of hydrogenation, however, are unattractive under normal conditions. The most advantageous conditions are to use cheap lignite in circumstances where natural petroleum is expensive. The possibility of such a plant in the U.S. has been envisaged for the future, working on the scale of several million tons of oil annually. The lignite would be carbonized, the resultant tar being hydrogenated and the residual char being used as boiler fuel or for making hydrogen.

In the 1950s, a U.S. firm studied hydrogenation of coal for the production of aromatic hydrocarbons, phenol, and other products. Although these were obtained in good yield, the costs, including those of separating the mixtures of products, were too high for the process to be economic at that time.

Underground gasification. In underground mining, men work under conditions that are often unpleasant and sometimes dangerous. A method of obtaining energy from coal without actually mining it therefore has attractions. One possibility is to pass air and steam through a burning seam of coal underground, recovering the producer gas so formed and using it as a source of energy to generate steam and electricity. Much effort was devoted to this method in the period from 1940 to 1960 in the U.S.S.R., in Western Europe, the U.K., and the U.S. In practice, two boreholes, spaced up to 60 m apart, were sunk from the surface into the seam. Sometimes a length of seam was prepared in some way; e.g., by forcing hot air through it at pressure. Air and steam were then alternately blown through.

The U.S.S.R. claimed some commercial success, particularly in a steeply sloping seam gasified from the bottom. Little had been heard from there in the late 1960s and no other country claimed commercial success. The major difficulty seems to be in keeping control of the

Energy from unmined coal

system. Often the gasification zone would bypass large areas, leaving them untouched, and the caloric value of the gas would vary widely. No significant effort was being devoted to the idea in the 1970s.

Desulfurization and other processes. In most of its uses, the sulfur content of coal is objectionable in varying degrees. Part of the sulfur is associated with ash, and coal washing removes some sulfur along with the ash. Much sulfur, however, is more intimately associated with the coal substance itself and cannot be removed by washing. Since carbonization removes some sulfur, coke usually contains a lower percentage of sulfur than did the coal from which it was made. During total gasification most of the sulfur is converted into hydrogen sulfide, in which form it can be readily separated from the gas. Extraction of coal with solvents produces an extract of relatively low sulfur content. Despite the use of these methods and considerable effort, no effective method has been devised to reduce the sulfur content substantially, particularly the portion closely associated with the coal substance.

Sulfur content

Active carbons, akin to charcoal, are produced when coal is subjected to rapid heating followed by steaming. They can be used for the same purposes as active charcoal. One process in commercial operation in the U.K. and in the U.S.S.R. starts from granular anthracite with no briquetting stage involved.

Particularly after calcining, small anthracite is useful as a source of carbon in certain metallurgical processes in which it acts chemically to form carbon electrodes for certain electrochemical and electrometallurgical processes. Granular anthracite, after sizing and drying, is useful as a filter material, particularly in the treatment of water for domestic use and for process water, because it is chemically inert in water.

COAL AS A CHEMICAL

Coal has a complicated chemical structure based on carbon and hydrogen, with a certain amount of oxygen, nitrogen, sulfur, and other elements. One way to use coal as a source of chemical compounds is to break it down by heating or by reaction with steam and oxygen or with hydrogen. It then forms relatively simple compounds such as carbon, carbon oxides, benzene, naphthalene, and phenol. This process of degradation is expensive, however, particularly if chemicals subsequently have to be synthesized again from these simple compounds. Attempts therefore have been made to use coal as a macromolecule without breaking it down unduly.

Coal reacts readily with a wide range of chemicals. The effects of mild oxidation and treatment with nitric acid and caustic soda have been well explored. With low-rank coals particularly, this yields complex organic acids, called humic acids. Unfortunately, these acids have still not found a useful outlet of any size. Ammonia also reacts with coal to form substances containing up to 16 percent nitrogen which could be used as a fertilizer, providing both nitrogen and humus-forming material, but so far production appears to be uneconomic. Coal reacts readily with phenol in the presence of catalysts to form products that are soluble in solvents and of potential value to the plastics industry.

In another approach, coal is digested with solvents. Particularly effective are tetralin, phenanthrene, and tetrahydroquinoline. Over 80 percent of bituminous coal can be dissolved by digestion at 300° C for a few hours. Such digests still contain undissolved coal and ash that can be separated only with some difficulty. The extract so obtained is essentially coal in solution. The solvent itself can be separated and recycled, leaving behind solid coal extract. Chemically this is rather similar to coal but has a lower molecular weight, is free from ash, and is low in sulfur. The extract, after hydrogenation, can be used to make synthetic oil or even power-station fuel where sulfur is particularly objectionable, but the practicability of the application depends upon the price of coal. More attractive is the use of coal extract as a source of carbon or graphite for electrodes or artifacts. Furthermore, the ability of coal extracts to mix with and react with simple polymers, such as polyvinyl chloride, may open the way to less expensive plastics for building and civil engineering. Coal digests, before the separation of ash and undissolved coal, may find uses in road surfacing to supplement road tar and as a binder to supplement pitch in briquetting.

Despite the successful new chemical uses for coal developed, it seems clear that the amount of coal employed in this way will always be small relative to the amounts used as fuel and for the manufacture of coke.

BIBLIOGRAPHY. H.H. LOWRY (ed.), *Chemistry of Coal Utilization*, 2 vol. (1945, suppl. vol. 1963), a text dealing with all aspects of coal utilization, including an extensive bibliography; D.W. VAN KREVELIN, *Coal: Typology, Chemistry, Physics, and Constitution* (1961), an authoritative survey of scientific aspects of coal; W. FRANCIS, *Coal: Its Formation and Composition* (1954), a useful account of scientific aspects of coal; H.M. SPIERS (ed.), *Technical Data on Fuel*, 6th ed. (1961), basic data on all kinds of fuel; J.W. LEONARD and D.R. MITCHELL (eds.), *Coal Preparation*, 3rd ed. (1968), a modern text dealing with all aspects of coal preparation; R.A. MOTT (ed.), *The History of Coke Making* (1936), a brief historical account of coke making, *The Triumphs of Coke* (1965), a brief account of some processes for making and using coke; O. GROSSKINSKY (ed.), *Handbuch des Kokereiwesens*, 2 vol. (1955–58), a German text dealing with all aspects of coke manufacture; D. MCNEIL, *Coal Carbonization Products* (1966), a brief text with emphasis on the refining of tar and benzole; G. CLAYTON (ed.), *Benzole: Production and Uses* (1961), an authoritative and comprehensive survey.

(R.J.M.)

Coals

Coal is a general designation for a great number of solid, organic minerals with very different compositions and properties; all of them are rather rich in carbon and have a dark colour, generally black. They are found in stratified deposits, sometimes at great depths. All coals owe their origin to slow decomposition and chemical conversion of immense masses of organic material.

There exists a genetic relationship among peats, brown coals, lignites, bituminous coals, and anthracites. This does not mean that brown coal necessarily is an intermediate stage in coal formation; there are indications that brown coals and some lignites are end products of a special genesis. As a whole, however, the process of coal formation, or coalification, proceeds as a continuous transformation of plant material, each phase being characterized by a degree of coalification, or rank. As a measure of this rank the carbon content or some related parameter can be used.

Next to mineral oil and kerogen, coal is the most important reservoir of carbon in the world. Although the carbon content of the Earth's crust does not exceed 0.1 percent by weight, carbon may be called the most important element. It is an indispensable necessity of life and also is the main source of energy; many manufactured products consist of carbon compounds.

Coal resources located at workable depths are enormous; they are on the order of 10^{12} tons. The present yearly production and consumption of coal is approximately 2,000,000,000 tons, exclusive of lignite (about 800,000 additional tons).

This article treats the classification, properties, occurrence and distribution, and origin of coals. For further information on the environments of coal formation, see articles CARBONIFEROUS PERIOD, UPPER; CARBONIFEROUS PERIOD, LOWER; and SWAMPS, MARSHES, AND BOGS. See also FOSSIL RECORD and the articles on related fossil fuels, namely, PETROLEUM and OIL SHALES. The mining and production of coal are covered in COAL MINING.

CLASSIFICATION OF COALS

There are several different ways to classify coals; most common is the classification by rank, or degree, of coalification. This classification is suitable for practical as well as scientific purposes because such properties as the potential amount of volatile (gaseous) products, the heat of combustion, and the coking properties are determined by rank. Another important mode of classification is according to rock type, based on the petrological components of coal. This classification is genetic because it includes the materials from which the coal was formed and the subsequent transformation processes that occurred.

Rank and properties. The oldest classification system, drawn up by French chemist Henri-Victor Regnault (1837), was based on chemical composition. This approach found its final perfection in later years when a classification system utilizing the carbon and hydrogen content of coal was developed. Scientifically, this system is the most valuable. Because the relationship between chemical composition and technological properties is a complicated one, this system has never been accepted for practical uses. Attempts have been made, however, to use the technological properties themselves as classification parameters.

In all countries the classification systems used are based primarily on the content of volatile matter, namely, the loss of weight by heating to about 950° C (1,750° F). Broadly speaking, the classes distinguished in the several national systems are alike. Coals with less than about 8 percent of volatile matter are called anthracites. A very special type with volatile-matter content of less than 2 percent is called meta-anthracite, or graphitoid coal. The next class, containing about 8 to 14 percent of volatile matter, is called semi-anthracite, or lean (dry-steam), coal. Next is a transition class that contains from 14 to about 20 percent of volatile matter, its name differing from country to country (low-volatile bituminous in the United States; low-volatile coking steam coal in Great Britain; *Esskohle* in Germany; and *demi-gras* in France). The group with about 20 to 30 percent volatile matter is called medium-volatile bituminous, or real, coking coal (*Fettkohle* in Germany, *gras* in France). When the volatile-matter content is greater than 30 percent it becomes difficult to classify coals on the basis of volatile matter alone, and a second parameter usually is applied. In the United States, the calorific value is used for further subdivision into different classes of high-volatile bituminous, sub-bituminous, and lignitic coals. The calorific value is based on mineral-matter-free coal with a moisture content corresponding to natural conditions (96 percent relative humidity at 30° C or 86° F). In Great Britain, the coking value is used as a classification parameter, and in most of the other countries the "swelling index," or crucible-swelling number, defining the appearance of the coke button after removal of the volatiles, has been accepted as a second parameter.

After World War II the United Nations stimulated the development of an international coal-classification system. This system involves four parameters: volatile-matter content, calorific value, caking properties (crucible-swelling number), and coking (swelling) properties.

Petrologic components. Coal is an organic rock. Just as an inorganic rock is composed of petrologic components known as minerals, coal consists of petrological components called macerals. Coal components can only be identified microscopically, by either of two techniques. The first is the thin-section, or transmitted-light, technique, mainly developed in the United States and Great Britain; the second is the polished-section, or reflected-light, technique, mainly developed in Europe. The thin-section technique is advantageous for morphological investigations, whereas the reflection technique is suitable for quantitative measurements. The differences in the two techniques of investigation have led to two different nomenclatures in coal petrology (see Table).

It has been found that woody tissue is capable of two extreme ways of coalification without loss of morphological structure: to telinite or anthraxylon on the one hand and to fusinite on the other. Although the woody structure has been preserved in both extreme modifications, telinite is transparent (orange or red) in thin section (except in coal of the highest rank), whereas fusinite is always opaque (see Figure 1). The structures in telinite are always filled with colloidal, humic matter, or resin, whereas those in fusinite are either empty or filled with mineral constituents. Telinite has a vitreous lustre; fusinite is dull or silky in appearance and is very friable. The

Volatile-matter content

Preservation of woody tissue

Petrologic Components (Macerals) in Coal and Their Groupings

maceral grouping in Europe	macerals or components		maceral grouping (constituents) in the U.S.
	name in Europe*	name in the U.S.†	
Vitrinite	telinite	megascopic anthraxylon	anthraxylon
		attrital anthraxylon	
	collinite	subanthraxylon	translucent attritus
		humic matter	
		light-brown matter	
Exinite	resinite	red resins	
		yellow resins	
	cerinite	amorphous wax	
	sporinite (exinite)	spore coats	
	cutinite	cuticles	
	suberinite	suberin	
	alginite	algal bodies	
Inertinite	massive micrinite	dark-brown matter	opaque attritus
		amorphous opaque matter	
	granular micrinite	granular opaque matter	
	sclerotinite	fusinized fungal matter	petrologic fusain
	semifusinite	dark semifusain	
	fusinite	attrital fusain	
		megascopic fusain	

*The majority of these names originated with M.C. Stopes (1935) and were adopted by the International Stratigraphical Congresses (1935 and 1951) at Heerlen. †These names are mainly from R. Thiessen.

transition between the two modifications is called semifusinite.

In the course of the coalification process woody tissue may, however, completely lose its structure. The col-

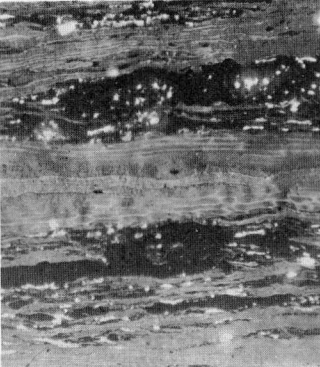

Figure 1: Polished thin section from Pond Creek Seam, Kentucky, with a blend of vitrinite or anthraxylon (gray) and fusinite in reflected light (left) and in transmitted light (right); magnified about 127 X.

loidal modification, which is translucent in thin sections, is called collinite. This term corresponds with the term humic matter (partly with brown matter) in the American nomenclature.

The other form, completely opaque under transmitted light, is known by the name micrinite (granular or massive), which is identical with opaque matter in the American nomenclature. As to the other plant constituents, the resins and waxes (resinite and cerinite), spore coats (sporinite), cuticles (cutinite), fungal sclerotia (sclerotinite), and algal bodies (alginite) can be clearly distinguished. The macerals and components have been compiled in the accompanying Table, in which the maceral groupings used in Europe and the United States are given.

In Europe, the macerals are classified according to their technological properties: vitrinite includes the technologically identical substances telinite and collinite. On heating, these macerals normally leave a fused coke button as their main product; exinite includes the remainders of waxy and corky products that, on heating, are largely transformed into gas and tar; inertinite includes all chemical, practically inert, macerals that do not soften or cake on heating and cannot be hydrogenated. In the United States, the macerals (except anthraxylon) are classified mainly according to their morphological and optical properties into the following categories: translucent attritus, opaque attritus, and fusain.

On the basis of the components or macerals (see Figure

2), coal is classified into various rock types. Coal with more than 95 percent vitrinite is called vitrain; coal containing both vitrinite and exinite is known as clarain. Vitrain and clarain form the group of the bright coals. If the coal contains micrinite and exinite (besides smaller additions of other constituents), it is called durain or dull coal. Finally, coal composed mainly of a mixture of fusinite and semifusinite is called fusain. This nomenclature is based on the original macroscopic (appearance in hand specimen) classification of coals.

The above list of normal coal types may be extended. Others, formed under special conditions, include cannel coal (micrinite with many microspores), pseudocannel coal (mainly composed of micrinite and mineral matter), and boghead coal, or torbanite (alginite and micrinite).

PHYSICAL AND CHEMICAL CHARACTERISTICS

All properties of coal and its components vary with its elemental composition and hence with rank. The rank can best be expressed in terms of the carbon content of the pure vitrinite that occurs, among other macerals, in the coal sample or in the coal seam.

Density and porosity. The true density of coal increases with increasing rank. Exinites have a lower density and micrinites a higher density than vitrinites of the same rank; the differences gradually decrease with increasing rank and disappear when the carbon content reaches 92 percent. Coals contain two pore systems, one with a mean-pore diameter of 500 Å (one angstrom unit equals 10^{-6} millimetre) and a second system of pores measuring five to 15 Å in diameter. The latter pores have a small volume but a large internal surface (about 200 m^2/g). The coarser pores of 500 Å have an internal surface of no more than about one m^2/g. In the early phases of coalification, coal possesses many polar groups and an extended, coarse-pore system. Hence the absorptive capacity for moisture is high. With increasing coalification the polar groups and the coarse pores disappear gradually. During the final stages of coalification a new pore system is formed; on its surface methane (CH_4), which is formed during coalification, can be absorbed. Low-volatile bituminous coals have a high sorption capacity for methane and a low rate of diffusion in the undamaged coal. This is associated with the frequent occurrence of outbursts of methane in low-volatile coal mines when cracks are formed that allow rapid desorption.

Optical, electrical, and magnetic properties. The reflecting power of coal surfaces is one of its principal optical properties. Reflectance increases sharply with increasing rank, and a measuring technique of rank is based on this property. Electrical properties are of interest because coal becomes a semiconductor with increasing rank. The magnetic properties are even more interesting. Measurements show that free radicals (molecules in which one of the atoms exhibits a valence one unit less than normal—e.g., C^{3+} rather than C^{4+}) are present in coal. Their maximum concentration occurs at a carbon content of 92 percent (one free radical per 1,000 carbon atoms).

Hardness. Hardness increases with rank, passes through a maximum at 84 percent carbon, decreases again, passes through a minimum at 90 percent carbon, and increases again. The reverse is true with respect to the grindability of coals.

Hydrogen, oxygen, and carbon content. The hydrogen (H) and oxygen (O) contents of the macerals are generally plotted as functions of the carbon (C) content, and points of equal rank are connected by broken lines. At equal rank, exinites are always richer and micrinites (and semifusinites) are always poorer in hydrogen than vitrinites; the reverse applies for oxygen. Differences between the macerals disappear progressively with increasing rank, so that in anthracite all macerals have become chemically identical. The same conclusion can be drawn from Figure 3, which shows the development lines of the macerals in terms of the atomic ratio H/C, which is plotted against O/C.

Other chemical constituents. All coals contain mineral matter or inorganic constituents that partly originate

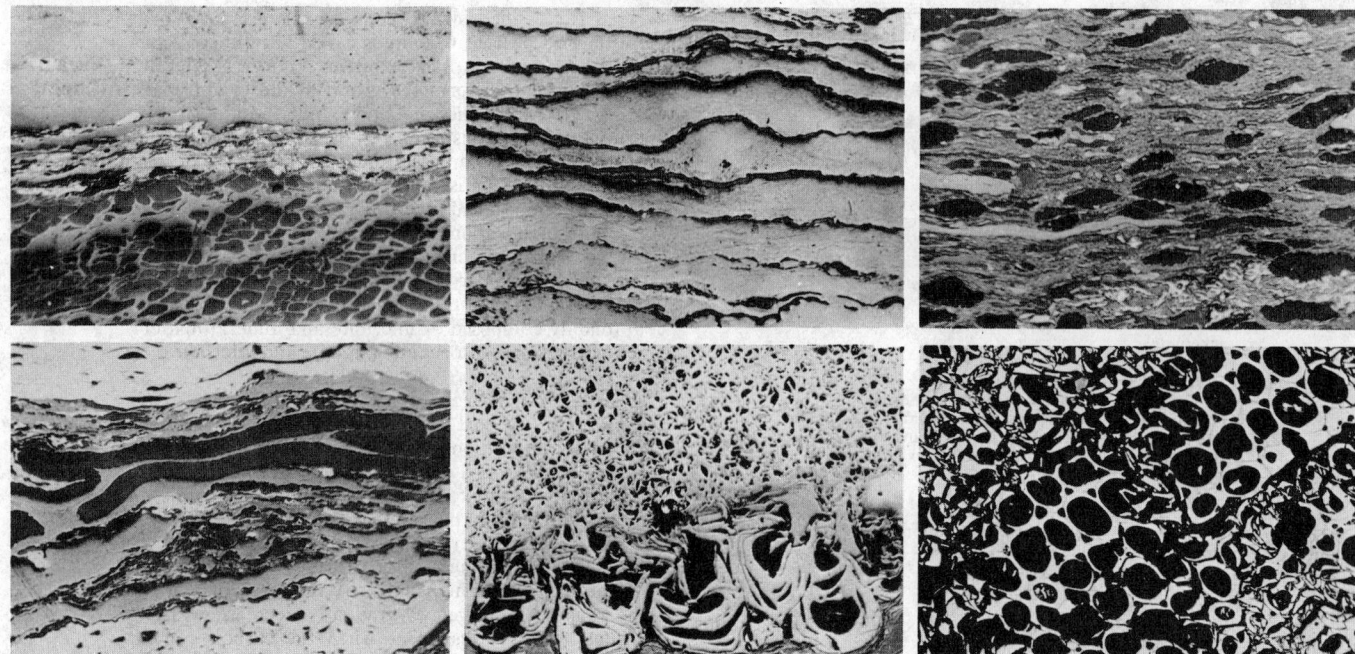

Figure 2: *Typical macerals.*
(Top left) Collinite (upper part) and telinite (lower) with resinite inclusions. (Top centre) Cutinite embedded in collinite. (Top right) Boghead-cannel coal with alginite. (Bottom left) Sporinite (macrospores and microspores) embedded in collinite (gray) and surrounded by micrinite (white). (Bottom centre) Semifusinite (upper part) and sclerotinite (lower). (Bottom right) Fusinite. Photomicrographs in reflected light (oil-immersion); magnified about 144 X.
By courtesy of M.Th. Mackowsky, Bergbauforschung, Essen, Germany

Trace elements

from coal-forming plants and partly are added to the deposits after the death of the plants. Nearly all the inorganic matter of the mineral coals consists of clays, sulfides, and chlorides. Selected vitrains may contain less than 1 percent of mineral matter; for an arbitrary coal sample the ash content is much higher. Many investigations have been made of the occurrence of minor elements in coal and coal ash. The common trace elements in parts per million in coal are arsenic (100), lead (100), manganese (100), and titanium (700). The development of transistors by the electronic industry has promoted an intensive search for germanium. Although certain coalified logs contain unusually high concentrations (up to 9 percent germanium in the ash), the normal average con-

tent of coals is only ten parts per million. Appreciable quantities of uranium are present in certain low-rank coals and lignites (up to 0.1 percent), but high-rank coals are practically nonradioactive.

Coal structure. The structural aspect of the coal matrix (vitrinite) may briefly be summarized as follows: Coal possesses a composition that is similar in some respects to that of such substances as pitch and bitumen. It is made up of a large number of chemical units that are identical in type but very different in molecular fine structure and molecular weight. All these units, however, have one feature in common; namely, a more or less flat lamellar shape. The dimensions of the condensed (aromatic) nuclei of the lamellae, as well as the number and character of the functional groups in the molecular periphery, can be derived by means of modern structural analysis.

When coalification starts, the aromatic clusters are still relatively small and probably are connected by nonaromatic bridges. This explains why the lowest rank coals possess a pronounced polymeric (*i.e.*, chainlike) character and more or less open structure. From a chemical point of view, coalification must be considered as a process in which the degree of condensation of the material increases continuously; the bridge structures become unstable as the interaction forces between the aromatic nuclei grow stronger. On continued coalification, the structure is modified into what has become known as the liquid, or glassy, structure revealed in X-ray studies. This structure is typical of coking coal. Subsequently, the structure stiffens again (anthracitization), and the lamellae display a growing tendency for orientation parallel to the bedding plane. The tendency of the flat lamellae to coalesce into small stacks can be observed in all terms of the coalification series; and this phenomenon becomes more marked as coalification advances. The interlamellar (and intralamellar) holes constitute the ultramicropore system. In a qualitative respect this explanation also holds for the other macerals, with the understanding that as far as ring condensation and cluster dimensions are concerned, exinites always lag behind vitrinites of the same rank and that micrinites have advanced further. The physical and chemical properties of coal can be interpreted in the light of this structural picture.

Coal rank and structural change

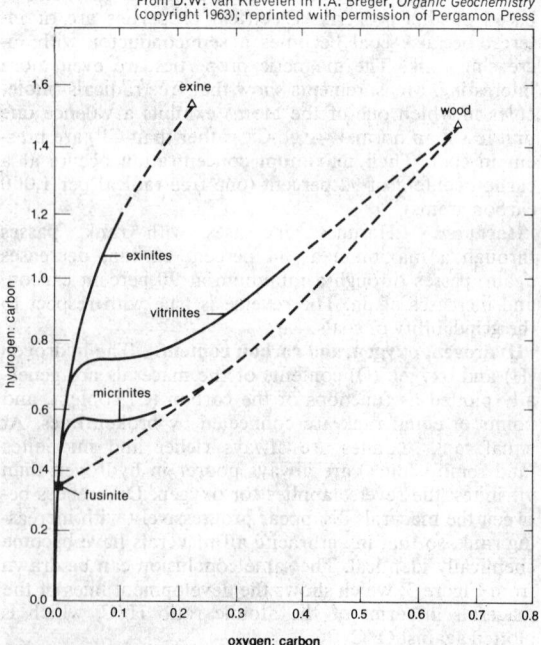

From D.W. van Krevelen in I.A. Breger, *Organic Geochemistry* (copyright 1963); reprinted with permission of Pergamon Press

Figure 3: Development lines of macerals in terms of their carbon, hydrogen, and oxygen content.

ORIGIN OF COALS

General occurrence and distribution. Two great eras of coal formation are known in geological history. The older era, which extends from the Lower Carboniferous to the Permian Period, or from 225,000,000 to 345,000,-000 years ago, is usually called the Anthracolithicum. The great coal resources of North America and Europe are a result of the extensive development of the coal deposits of this era, especially those of the Carboniferous. Carboniferous rocks were laid down in a wide belt mainly within the Northern Hemisphere. The accumulated thickness of these formations was enormous; it must have exceeded three miles during Upper Carboniferous time alone. It is most likely, therefore, that during this period, uninterrupted, widespread swamps must have gone through a process of steady subsidence, which was largely balanced by sedimentation. One example of such an extensive sunken area, known as a geosyncline, is in the eastern part of the United States, from which the Pittsburgh Seam can be mined over an area of 8,000 square miles (21,000 square kilometres). Earth movements have caused the loss of much of the productive Upper Carboniferous strata in many places. As a result, considerable differences exist in coal deposits through the Carboniferous belt. The total volume of coal deposits does not exceed about 2 percent of the Carboniferous sediments, so that coal is rare even within Carboniferous strata. The process of coal formation generally started in the Northwest (North America) and gradually spread toward the Southeast. This trend is based on the observation that the coal strata in Siberia, eastern Asia, and Australia were laid down during Permian time (from 190,-000,000 to 225,000,000 years ago). The second era of coal formation, which is qualitatively less important than the Carboniferous, commenced in the Late Cretaceous (about 70,000,000 years ago) and reached its peak during the Tertiary Period (from 2,500,000 to 65,000,000 years ago). From this era come nearly all lignites and brown coals. This coal-forming process also began in the northwestern part of the Northern Hemisphere. In the western part of North America, tremendous coal fields that accumulated during the Cretaceous extend from Utah into Alaska. In Europe, lignite fields developed in southern France and in central Europe during the Late Cretaceous and Early Tertiary. The majority of the lignite formations, in addition to the Tertiary coals of Japan, Indonesia, and Patagonia, were laid down in the Miocene Epoch (7,000,000 to 26,000,000 years ago).

Coal-forming plants. For the most part, no macroscopically recognizable plant remains are found in coal; on the other hand, well-preserved remains and indications of ancient plant life are found in the underlying and sometimes the overlying deposits (Figure 4).

There are four main divisions of Carboniferous flora: the Sphenopsids (horsetails), the Lycopsids (club mosses), and the Pteropsid groups of Pteridophyllae (ferns and their allies) and Cordaitales (Gymnosperms). In the Sphenopsid group, only the *Calamites* grew in tree forms. These trees, which grew in swamps, had a long, transversely ribbed and jointed stem, with tiny leaves or whorls of sparse foliage growing from the nodes. In the Lycopsid group the most important members were the Lepidodendrons and the *Sigillaria*, which were also high trees that grew in a somewhat drier habitat than the *Calamites*. Their bark showed regular patterns of large scars, caused by the loss of leaves during secondary thickening of the bark. Included in the Pteridophyllae are both the ferns proper (Filicinae) and the extinct seed ferns (Pteridospermae). These ferns were the finest plant species existing during Carboniferous time. They grew in a profuse variety of types in a relatively dry environment. The final group, the Cordaitales, had a high stem with leaves that somewhat resembled long and narrow palm leaves. Like the ferns, these plants did not favour wet environments and probably did not occur in swampy grounds but grew on the slopes of the hinterland. These examples show that the type of vegetation may indicate the conditions under which humification—the initial stage of coalification—must have occurred. Plant spores often constitute an important component of coal and occur in practically all coal seams. They therefore are of particular importance to the study and identification of coal strata (see further POLLEN STRATIGRAPHY).

Carboniferous forests occurred in areas that were almost completely flat and where forest vegetation did not vary to much extent. This idea is supported by the existence of plant banks that, over areas of several square miles, have only a small number of plant types and nearly exclude all other forms of vegetable life. These forests must have had a monotonous appearance because mixed forests rarely occurred. Fern fields were predominant over vast areas in other regions. In the case of fern fields, peat swamp, rather than forest swamp, might be a more correctly used term. The climate during the Carboniferous was very rainy and the temperature was rather constant, as indicated by the absence of annual rings in the tree trunks. This climate, therefore, probably had a subtropical character.

Processes of coal formation. To explain the formation of the vast and thick peat beds that later were transformed into coal it must be assumed that the geosyncline did not sink at a constant rate but that there occurred periods of slower subsidence alternating with periods of more rapid sinking. Obviously, when the rate of subsidence slackens, the basin tends to fill by sedimentation. The lagoons, therefore, become shallow, and extensive swamps, marshes, and bogs form from the growth of aquatic plants. Except for a few rivers traversing the swamp, the water is almost stagnant and the accumulation of plant debris continues. Later, trees the roots of which (*Stigmaria*) are found in nearly all coal seams develop on this weak, boggy soil; this may be regarded as a clear proof that the coal generally has been formed *in situ* (autochthonous formation). The origin of most coal deposits goes back to a living peat bog, which may still be found in several places. The growth of this vegetation continues for many generations; the plant material settles on the bottom of the swamp and microbiological attack converts it into peat. Peat accumulation continues until the rate of subsidence of the basin increases again. In spite of the altered conditions, the swamp vegetation persists for some time, especially those plant types that are capable of deepwater growth. The swamp finally is submerged, however, and sedimentary deposits cover it so that a future coal seam has formed. The cycle may later be repeated, and this sequence accounts for the formation of all the numerous coal seams in the course of hundreds and thousands of years (see CYCLOTHEMS).

The process outlined above, with the peat formation beginning under relatively dry conditions and ending with the flooding of the area, may be considered to have been the usual way in which coal was formed. This has not been true everywhere, however, and in some cases peat formation started under very moist conditions be-

Nature of Carboniferous flora

Role of subsidence

By courtesy of Rijks Geologische Dienst, Geologisch Bureau, Heerlen, The Netherlands

Figure 4: *Pecopteris plumosa* from Oranje Nassau I Seam B, Heerlen, The Netherlands.

Post-
deposi-
tional
changes

cause of the silting up of deeper waters. In almost every case the cessation of the peat-forming process was a result of submergence of an entire region (geosynclinal subsidence). An important part is also played by the settling of the older underlying strata. Extensive settling can be noted, particularly in the case of buried peat beds. This might explain the variety of differences observed in the individual development of sedimentary layers and coal strata.

After peat formation, a period of far-reaching diagenesis (compositional change) and tectonism (movements of the Earth's crust) influenced the strata. In the following review of the changes thus brought about, discussion is restricted to Carboniferous coal strata because of the greater variation in their history compared to that of Tertiary coals. The Late Carboniferous buried, peat-bearing strata initially lay in a horizontal plane. Shortly after their formation, the deeply buried strata were exposed in many places to a process of folding and faulting (orogenesis). Tectonic forces that afterward acted upon the Earth's crust were no longer capable of refolding the stiffened Carboniferous strata. Consequently, great and long faults developed in this period, along which sections of the crust were raised or depressed in a movement similar to that of ice floes. The chemical composition of the peat beds began to change from the time the beds first became buried under sedimentary accumulations and gradually sank more and more deeply into the Earth's crust. When waterlogged peat is covered by an impervious sediment the peat is slowly altered under waterlogged conditions by chemical reactions (metamorphosis). As the carbon content of the fossil plant material gradually increases, the chemical change that occurs is called coalification. Information derived from available data suggests that a genetic relationship must exist in the peat-lignite-bituminous-anthracite series, known as the coalification series.

Biochemical factors are important in the very first stage of the coalification process. Only as long as fungi and bacteria are capable of participating in the attack on the material can microbiological decomposition continue. Fungi are not found at a depth below about 40 centimetres (16 inches), and the formation of lignite, therefore, cannot have been influenced by the action of these organisms. Depth also decreases the effect of bacterial action, so that extensive bacterial conversion is impossible at great depth. It can be concluded from this that geophysical factors must have been effective in coalification beyond the lignite stage.

Not all investigators have agreed with this view. Some authorities believed bacterial decomposition to have been the controlling agency in the formation of various coal types. Decomposition by bacteria was considered to depend on the pH (measure of acidity) and the degree of oxidation of the environment. It was postulated that the latter depends almost completely upon how deep the material is submerged, and that it is stabilized by the action of micro-organisms.

Beyond the lignite stage, time seems to have scarcely any influence on coalification. The brown coal of the Moscow Basin has not been coalified to a higher rank, although it was deposited during Lower Carboniferous time; evidence exists to show that this coal was never buried to a great depth. To attribute overburden (the weight of the rock strata overlying the coal seam) alone as the cause of coalification would not be consistent with thermodynamics. Pressure, however, has an influence upon compactness and porosity and therefore on the moisture content of the soil. Coalification has not been significantly affected by tectonic pressure, as is indicated by the lack of correlation between the coal rank and the intensity of the crustal movements. From investigations in the Ruhr and South Limburg basins it is evident that coalification was relatively completed before tectonism began.

According to the majority of the investigators, only the influence of temperature is a possible explanation of metamorphosis. As previously mentioned, a very thick sedimentary cover must have overlain the Carboniferous strata. The temperature gradient determines the temperature to which the strata were exposed, which is usually about 1° C per 30 metres (1° F per 55 feet). Temperatures lower than about 200° C (400° F), therefore, would have been effective for anthracite formation. The geothermal gradient, however, is not constant, and local magma pockets under the Earth's crust may have exerted a strong regional influence that led to higher temperatures. There seems to have been no appreciable effect on coalification by contact metamorphism resulting from igneous activity because of its localized character.

Genesis of the macerals and rock types. Evidence shows that woody tissue may be transformed into at least four macerals (telinite, collinite, fusinite, and semifusinite) and that, in addition, micrinite probably originates in lignified material. It is obvious that the differences among the end products resulting from the coalification of similar plant materials have been mainly a result of the differences in the conditions under which humification occurred.

Effect of
relatively
dry
conditions

The assumption must be made that fusain was formed in very dry sites. Because of the strong similarity between fusain and charcoal, it is believed by many investigators that forest fires, caused by lightning storms, have been responsible for the formation of fusain. It is also plausible that fusain may have been produced by a special exothermal microbiological process resembling the spontaneous combustion of hay. An obvious fact in considering the origin of vitrain is that the lumina are filled with collinite (occasionally with resinite), in contrast to fusain, where the lumina are hollow or filled with mineral matter. The fact that vitrinite was probably also formed under fairly dry conditions, perhaps in a swamp where the ground level was only slightly below the surface, is suggested by the frequent concurrence of fusinite and vitrinite and the existence of transitory gradations between these macerals (semifusinite). The entire structure of vitrain reveals that the woody tissue has gone through a mummification process. The dead plant material must have sunk rapidly into the weak humus soil and become bedded in an almost stagnant water medium. There is so little oxygen present in such a medium that even the growth of anaerobic bacteria is inhibited. The material in this toxic environment is kept away from the influence of the micro-organisms and is essentially mummified.

The coalification process proceeds along different lines in a true wet swamp. When the groundwater present is sufficient to cover the surface of the soil, a certain amount of drift may occur so that the oxygen supply is constantly replenished and the water is prevented from becoming acidified. Decomposition of plant debris under these conditions occurs to a far greater degree, so that just the more resistant parts are left. This explains the difference between vitrain and durain, the latter partly consisting of highly resistant exinite. It must be concluded, therefore, that the formation of durain took place in much wetter sites. Another reason for this conclusion is that durain is rich in spores formed by the Sphenopsids, a flora growing in very swampy soils. There is less woody tissue in this vegetation than that responsible for the formation of vitrain. Durain also contains more mineral matter than vitrain. The wettest conditions were responsible for the production of the extreme variety of durain, classified as a pseudocannel.

Cannel
coal and
boghead

Cannel coal shows a strong resemblance to pseudocannel in its outward appearance but contains less mineral matter and far more microspores. Although the parent material of cannel coal had a quantitatively differing composition to that of pseudocannel, their genesis conditions must have been identical. Cannel is probably also produced in lakes and pools but, contrary to pseudocannel, originates from accumulations of floating spores transported by wind and water and deposited in the vegetable mud. Tasmanite, an extreme variety of cannel, is a light-brown rock found in North Tasmania. It is almost exclusively composed of spores, the dark groundmass being absent.

Boghead, too, is almost identical to cannel coal in its outward appearance, but their parent materials are different. A microscopic examination by transmitted light reveals that boghead consists of numerous white globules embedded in a dark groundmass. The algal-origin view of boghead has long been held. Algal formations of recent age have been discovered in Balkash Lake (Balkashite), Kazakh S.S.R., and in Australia (Coorongite). These algae, which are included in the Botryococcacea group, are especially rich in proteins and fats and are found in rather deep and clear freshwater pools or open lakes. It must be realized that these conditions were rather rare in a Carboniferous swampy region, which explains the sporadic occurrence of boghead coal. Boghead coal has been considered to be a transition stage between true coal and mineral oil.

BIBLIOGRAPHY. Classic works on coals that are written in English include the following: D. WHITE and R. THIESSEN, "The Origin of Coal," *Bull. U.S. Bur. Mines 38* (1913); M.C.C. STOPES and R.V. WHEELER, *Monograph on the Constitution of Coal* (HMSO, 1918); E.S. MOORE, *Coal: Its Properties, Analysis, Classification, Geology, Extraction, Uses and Distribution*, 2nd ed. (1940); and H.H. LOWRY (ed.), *Chemistry of Coal Utilization*, 2 vol. (1945).

Modern standard books include W. FRANCIS, *Coal: Its Formation and Composition*, 2nd ed. (1961); D.W. VAN KREVELEN, *Coal: Typology, Chemistry, Physics and Constitution* (1961); and H.H. LOWRY (ed.), *Chemistry of Coal Utilization, Supplementary Volume* (1963). These three books contain additional information on all the subjects treated in this article and refer to the original literature on coals.

(D.W.v.K.)

Coastal Features

Seacoasts localized many of man's activities when he acquired hominid physical characteristics several million years ago. Food available in shallow water was easily gathered and highly nutritious. The shores of lakes provided fish and, along with banks of streams, were places where game could be stalked or trapped.

Some millions of years later, man acquired most of the attributes of civilization, developed agriculture, domesticated animals, adapted himself to a great variety of habitats, and became less dependent on the sea. Those individuals remaining on coasts developed new skills. Primitive ways of capturing fish, such as placing rows of stones between tidal limits, were replaced by the building of weirs, placing of traps, use of poison for stunning, and the perfecting of hooks, lines, nets, and harpoons.

Importance to man

Today, the most concentrated populations occupy coasts or lowlands leading to them. Few major cities have locations other than along coasts or navigable rivers. Natural harbour sites are particularly favoured, but in their absence artificial ones are created. Deep rivers, estuaries, and gulfs and bays are highly desirable because they shelter ships and provide easy access to valleys. Around the Mediterranean, however, the flow of rivers is highly erratic and navigation is impossible during violent floods or extremely low stages of flow. Alexandria, Barcelona, and Marseilles are examples of ports that serve valleys but are located away from river mouths. Excessive tidal range is unfavourable, but this does not prevent port development. Liverpool's floating docks, connected to the shore by roads that resemble huge gangplanks, rise and fall with ships attached. Minor ports, as in Alaska and on the Bay of Fundy, are reached at high tide, and lines from wharves to ships are lengthened as the tide ebbs. In many places hulls rest on the bottom before the tide is completely out. At Port Hedland, on the northern coast of Western Australia, where the tidal range approaches 12 metres, before 1968, ships could enter only at high tide and had little more than an hour in port if they wished to leave on the same tide. Subsequently, a large turning basin and a deep channel through offshore reefs were dredged. Many irregular coastlines appear to offer more port locations than actually exist. Along the coast of Norway, for example, fjords extend many tens of miles inland but are not useful because their ice-scoured floors are too smooth to hold the flukes of anchors, and their hinterlands have little commercial potential. In the United States, three-quarters of the population resides in states bordering seas or the Great Lakes. All continents display similar im-

balance. In Asia, over half the world's population is concentrated in 10 percent of its land area, along the southern and eastern coasts or on lowlands leading to them. Maritime activities and commerce are partially responsible for these conditions of population imbalance, but of greater significance is the production of many of the world's most valuable crops on river floodplains.

Although commercial factors contribute to dense populations near modern ports, the attraction of seacoasts also depends on such variables as climates that are favourable to physical well-being and aesthetic values. The price of these amenities at times is high because serious hazards exist.

The most catastrophic events are tsunamis, which are waves that result from volcanic explosions, dislocations of the Earth's crust by faulting, or immense rockfalls. The waves may be several hundred miles long and move up to 10,000 miles per day. Their passage is imperceptible to ships on the open ocean, but on reaching shallow bottoms around islands or continental shores, the waves slow down and pile up to tremendous heights.

Hazards of sea coasts

High seas during intense winds and storms or prolonged periods of high-sea stand create havoc on many coasts. Although they may result in considerable loss of life and property, they are ordinarily taken in stride by coastal inhabitants, who in many cases rebuild without adequate protection against repetitions or actually invite even more serious trouble by removing protective dunes or by building too close to shorelines. Prolonged gales raise water levels along the sandy east coast of the United States between Long Island and Cape Hatteras, especially during winter and early spring. With wind from easterly quadrants the waves created may be highly destructive, as in March 1962, when 34 lives were lost and property damage amounted to $190,000,000. The shallow North Sea is particularly vulnerable when low barometric pressure, high tide, and strong winds coincide. Under such conditions in 1953, waves broke dikes, and widespread flooding of Dutch polders drowned 2,000 people.

The most intense tropical storms, hurricanes and typhoons, are concentrated along east coasts of continents. They originate well within the tropics and increase in intensity while moving westward and poleward to a latitude of about 30°, where they are likely to recurve eastward and speed up rates of advance. Extremely low barometric pressure toward their central eyes raises water level and attracts a swirl of winds with velocities up to 150 miles per hour or more. Seas may become extremely high (waves well above six, and in some cases more than nine, metres high), but the hurricane wave under the central eye remains low in deep ocean and increases in height across shallow bottoms. On islands surrounded by deep bottoms the damage from a hurricane results from excessive wind velocities and to a lesser extent from destructive waves. An Indian Ocean tropical storm in 1960 brought 150-mile-per-hour gusts to Mauritius, across which its 35-mile-wide eye passed, but tide gages indicated a rise in sea surface (still-water level, excluding waves) of less than one metre. In contrast, a similar hurricane crossing up to 100 miles of shallow continental shelf in 1957 flooded the marshes of western Louisiana as much as four metres, drowning 430 people.

Normal tides are hardly a hazard. They occur regularly along most coasts, and, even though in extreme cases flood and ebb levels differ more than 15 metres, everyone adjusts his activities to the change. Incoming tides create bores in some estuaries. These steep walls of water rush inland with heights of about three metres in parts of the Bay of Fundy, 7.5 metres in the Ban Ch'ien Tang at the head of Hangchou Bay south of Shanghai, and six metres in channels near the Amazon and Pará rivers (Brazil). Less predictable and more damaging are seiche waves that occur in some lakes and occasionally on seacoasts. Without warning the water may suddenly rise 1.5 metres or so. A seiche is a result of oscillations, with resonance determined by basin size and bottom configuration. Unexpected seiche waves swamp small craft, damage docks, and cause temporary changes along beaches.

Classifica-
tion of
coastal
features

Coastal landforms, in broadest terms, may be classified as initial—or present for reasons other than coastal location—erosional, or depositional. Initial landforms include such obvious examples as volcanoes rising to the sea surface, such as Surtsey Island (Iceland), formed in 1963, and Anak Krakatoa (Java), created in 1929. Even these forms are dependent upon the balance of lava supply and wave erosion. Most landforms are composite rather than members of a single group in all respects.

The classical classification of shorelines originated in the 1890s with William Morris Davis and his student E.P. Gulliver; it was later elaborated by Douglas Johnson. Popularity of the system declined because its major distinction was whether coastal lands were rising (emergent) or sinking (submergent), which is now known to be very rarely a factor. Many recent classifications have appeared, notably by André Guilcher, H. Valentin, and Francis P. Shepard. But a definitive solution to the problem probably awaits accumulation of more factual knowledge than is now available.

Davis is best known for essays of a general nature, not specifically on seacoasts. An acceptable coastal classification, however, will probably incorporate one of his most fundamental concepts, namely that structure acted upon by processes through time results in sequential groups of landforms.

Coastal landforms and features are varied, and examples must be selected either because of known interest or capability of stimulating intellectual curiosity. Although less scenic than erosional landforms, depositional features attract more visitors and for that reason will be described first.

COASTAL FEATURES RESULTING FROM DEPOSITIONAL PROCESSES

Beach
charac-
teristics

Generally defined, a beach is an area extending upward and inland from the lowest surface commonly exposed to view to limits reached by wave uprush during high seas. The inner boundary may be a sea cliff, a row of sand dunes, or other topographic break (see BEACHES). More precisely defined, a beach is a deposit surfaced by the area just described, called the upper beach, and divided into a sloping foreshore and flat or irregular backshore. Below is the lower beach, which extends across the surf (or breaker) zone into water shallow enough to permit entrainment and transport of sand during ordinary high seas. This depth, the surf base, is likely to be between nine and 11 metres. During extremely high seas, however, the entrainment–transport zone may extend several times deeper. In many cases the boundary between upper and lower beach is marked by a locally steepened slope (the step) where sediment is coarser than that either above or below. This is noted by swimmers who must wade across coarse sand, shell, or gravel before reaching a flatter and smoother bottom a few feet away.

Winter and summer beaches. Large shells and flotsam may be scattered on the backshore, carried there by high waves. But high, steep-fronted waves entrain and carry away sand and shingle, eroding beaches to wide flats at relatively low level. These are called winter beaches. As soon as wave energy begins to decrease, coarse and heavy sediments are deposited across these low surfaces as far as the backshore. With further energy decrease, the deposits become finer and lighter. After a period of calm a beach becomes more voluminous, its front attains maximum steepness, and the earlier deposits of heavy materials become buried under finer sand. A person may dig holes or trenches in which it is possible to trace the heavier materials down to the step, where they ordinarily emerge.

The expression winter beach arose because in most developed countries winter is the season of storms, high seas, and low beaches. But winter beaches may develop during any month, whenever a beach is eroded by high, steep-fronted waves. Summer beaches also appear at any season, the requisite being a significant period during which low-energy, relatively flat waves are present. As a matter of fact, winter and summer beach conditions al-

ternate so frequently that vertical sections in a beach ordinarily reveal many contrasting layers of coarser and finer, or darker and lighter coloured, sediment, in many instances including shell or gravel layers. On the smallest of scales, there is a tendency for beaches to erode during each rising tide and to receive deposits as soon as the tide ebbs. Most people are more familiar with summer than with winter beaches because summer beaches are more suitable for recreational activities. Their surfaces are agreeable to lie upon, and seasonally warmer water may add to the attraction.

Beach materials. Although the generalizations above are true, the point must be stressed that any current may entrain and transport only such materials as it acts upon. Little or no erosion or depositional activity is possible behind a broad flat of bedrock, such as is present along some coasts. Materials must be available on the lower beach if they are present on upper beaches. Around much of the coast of England, sand is rare in comparison with shingle (coarse gravel and even boulders), so the Englishman develops devotion to beaches that residents of the United States, who often have fine-grained sand beaches available to them, might shun. Some beaches consist of such large boulders that they have almost no popular recreational value.

By courtesy of the Coastal Studies Institute, Louisiana State University, Baton Rouge; photograph, R.J. Russell

Beach of shingle and large boulders, Baillif, Basse-Terre, Guadeloupe, French West Indies.

Quartz is one of the most abundant, hardest, and chemically most resistant minerals in continental rocks. When broken into sand-sized particles or grains, it usually constitutes the most common deposit along stream banks and shores of seas and lakes. Mainland dwellers find that most sand consists of quartz. Not so on oceanic islands, where quartz is ordinarily absent in rocks, and greenish or black beaches consist of rock or mineral fragments, and pinkish or white beaches of coral or shell fragments. In many places these organic particles are large and sharp enough to be unpleasant to lie upon and to cut bare feet. Some black-sand beaches, when dry, emit sounds when walked across, an effect present in the barking sands of Kauai and other Hawaiian islands. Black sands, in rare cases containing sufficient zirconium, titanium, or other metals to be worth mining, also occur on many continental beaches, as in Australia. Parts of some Florida beaches include huge numbers of glass shards that have drifted from volcanoes in the West Indies or Central America. These buoyant shards are spherical shells around air-filled central voids. Calcareous beaches are common in all parts of the world. If shells or corals have been ground to extremely small size, they cling to the skin tenaciously.

Black sand
and
"singing"
sand

Beach cusps. Beach cusps are minor topographic forms that invariably attract attention. These are more or less triangular deposits that point seaward and are separated by rounded embayments spaced from a few to more than 46 metres apart. They are composed of coarser material than the beach upon which they form. When waves approach with crests parallel to the shoreline, their uprush is concentrated toward cusp points (apices), where the flow is divided to return in the embayments on either side. Transported load is deposited on apices and sides of cusps, but much returns down the embayments in currents that may gradually gain enough momentum to jet into or across the surf, developing rotating eddies on either side. Cusps form while wave energy is declining. Their coarse composition results from deposition of material eroded from the step. In many cases cusps form at several levels and are more widely spaced upward in the sequence. At first the deposits may be spaced irregularly, but in a short time regularity develops at intervals determined by frequency of wave arrivals, wave heights, and volumes of water in uprush and backwash. If the direction of wave approach becomes somewhat oblique, cusps are eroded promptly.

Beach rock. Another minor topographic form, beach rock, may be noted along parts of beaches in warm climates. Beach rock consists of cemented beach material of any kind: ordinarily, sand, gravel, or shells, but also exotic material such as the refuse of city dumps. It crops out at sea level or that of high neap tide if the tidal range is considerable. Outcrops appear on eroding beaches, in many cases as distinct bands (pavements) parallel to the shoreline. Each band marks a new episode of coastal recession. The outer band is oldest and most covered by algae and other organic growths. When first exposed the cemented layer is readily broken. Later, after exposure to rain, spray, and overwash, the cement hardens, and the mass becomes as durable as concrete. Boats have been wrecked by sudden collisions against beach rock, particularly when the rock is unnoticed and landings by nosing the boat into soft sand are contemplated. The cementation present initially extends back along the upper limit of groundwater and characterizes some hardpans in inland positions. Around Puerto Rico, beach rock is most common along the north coast, where the hinterland contains a great amount of limestone. But on Oahu, Hawaii, and in many other places where limestone bedrock does not exist, the cementing lime is derived from shells and other organic materials within the beach. Cementation occurs only if groundwater temperature never drops lower than 68° F. Unlike most other substances, calcium carbonate dissolves more rapidly as temperature lowers. When the groundwater is cold, lime remains in solution and is flushed away in the water's seaward flow. Beach rock is cemented rapidly, as shown by the artifacts it contains—toys used by children playing in sand, bottles, cartridges from World War II, etc.—but its durability is indicated by artifacts dating from Roman times on Rhodes and by Indian pottery in the West Indies. Some beach rock exists in Florida; it is abundant in the West Indies and around shores of the Mediterranean, on islands south of Japan, and on tropical beaches generally.

Berms. Beaches commonly display more than a single backshore summer beach surface. Each is called a berm and lies at a height determined by wave uprush when it was created. Following periods of high seas, when large volumes of beach material are eroded, the amount available for building a summer beach is large, and a conspicuous berm is deposited. Some berms last for years, particularly in tropical climates, where they are soon covered by vegetation. The highest berm is the most permanent and is commonly called a storm beach, but in the Seychelles, where it is planted to coconuts, it is called a plateau. In climates where the sand remains dry and vegetation is sparse, small hummocks of sand accumulate in the lee of obstacles such as small shrubs. With extremely high uprush, the hummocks and considerable additional sand are swept inland to accumulate as a beach ridge. Such ridges may be formed on the inner side of a widening or prograding beach if the sand supply is abundant. In many cases they are most numerous near mouths of rivers that transport considerable sand. They attain heights of three metres or more and may be fixed by vegetation or by internal cementation.

Role of vegetation

Sand and sand dunes. Sand dunes form on and behind many beaches. They range in size from small hummocks to ridges well over 46 metres high. Low frontal dunes on the backshore are subject to removal by wave uprush, but larger dunes may extend inland for many miles. Dune shapes vary, but generally windward slopes are gentle and firm, whereas leeward slopes are steep and soft. Transverse dunes parallel many shorelines, aligned at right angles to the effective wind direction. Linear dunes directed inland occur behind some wide beaches and indicate surplus sand. The most photogenic dunes, barchans, indicate deficient sand supply. In shape they are crescents, with horns pointing downwind on either side of a concave, steep front. Overwhelming surpluses of sand result in dunes of irregular shapes within large sand areas.

Most dunes migrate, particularly during early stages of development. Later, they may attain fixed positions. Fixation may be hastened by the planting of marram or other grasses on dune surfaces. Marram is most commonly used because it thrives in salt air and where sand accumulates around its stems. As stems are covered, new roots develop at higher levels and thicken the zone in which sand is retained. If dissipation of barren dunes is desired, it may be accomplished by scattering large stones or placing widely spaced posts on the surface. These obstacles increase turbulence in wind, promoting rates of sand entrainment. In warmer climates, dunes consisting mainly of shell fragments experience some solution of calcium carbonate during each rain. The lime is translocated a short distance downward, where it precipitates as cement that binds sand grains together. In this way dune rock (eolianite) develops and dunes become firmly fixed.

On many coasts two groups of dunes are present: older, higher, and more firmly fixed dunes, which may be covered by shrubs or trees, behind younger, smaller, migrating, and much whiter dunes. The sand of the older dunes is yellowish or reddish from oxidation, and its upper surface may exhibit soil-profile development. The old dunes accumulated more than 3,000 years ago, when there was more sand on beaches than is the general case today (see below *Depositional barriers and beach nourishment*). The young dunes originated during times of decreasing sand supply. This contrast does not occur back of beaches that have surplus sand at the present time.

Action of waves and currents

For many years swimmers have feared currents that carry them rapidly across the surf zone, regarding the danger as being a result of undertow. Now it is known that rip currents most commonly are to blame. These become active when fairly vigorous waves or swells pile water to irregular levels along the shore. Heads of water at higher levels are relieved by swift, suddenly appearing flows in restricted currents that jet into the surf, after which they widen and lose velocity. When caught in a rip current, an experienced swimmer will relax, knowing that in a very short time he will reach water from which he may return without difficulty, possibly drifting most of the way. Novices become panicky and sometimes lose their lives trying to fight rip currents (see WATER WAVES).

Waves striking the shore at oblique angles create alongshore currents. These hug the shoreline, commonly with velocities sufficient to entrain and transport sand, with effects that are unpleasant to bathers, who do well to seek relief from drifting and skin-peppering by swimming across the surf.

Alongshore and rip currents, when sufficiently vigorous, change beaches rapidly but temporarily. Sand eroded by rips is soon deposited to form transverse bars, pointing in directions determined by sets of currents. These may be spaced at distances of up to 60 metres. A beach exhibiting these bars is said to display rhythmic topography. If wave crests parallel the shoreline, alongshore currents fail to develop and parallel bars may form at increasing depths on the lower beach. While people may wade on crests of the first or second bar, nonswimmers often lose their lives by stepping into a trough between bars.

If crests of waves or swell move against a shore with directions within 20° of its trend, the alongshore current flows parallel to the coast as a mach wave, with velocity and elevation that increase with additional water supplied by each contributing wave. High swells from the Southern Ocean strike the coasts of southwestern Australia and South Africa with terrific force, raising surfaces of mach waves to 12 metres or more. On both coasts these are known as king waves, and rocky areas are conspicuously posted with warning signs because fishermen and visitors who fail to recognize their approach, by the increasing rumble caused by impacts of boulders they transport, may be swept to eternity when the wave front appears at high speed.

Spits, antidunes, and bars

At places where a shoreline trend changes so that the distance increases between an alongshore current and the land, the current sets straight ahead as a result of its momentum. As it diverges from the coast, the flow broadens, loses velocity, and decreases in transport ability. The sediment it deposits forms a spit. As the end·of the spit reaches deeper water, it encounters waves with greater energy. These ordinarily transport part of the current's load toward the shore with changed trend. The visible end of the spit commonly "recurves" shoreward under such conditions. Alternations in wave energy may result in more than a single recurving, producing complex spit topography such as may be seen along shores of many lakes and in some cases on seacoasts.

If the tidal range is considerable, the parallel bars of some shorelines extend into the upper beach, where they are known as ridges (or balls) and are separated by runnels (or lows). Crests of ridges rise up to several feet higher than the troughs of runnels. When the tide ebbs, many of the runnels contain pools, most of which cut outlet channels into the next runnel below. If flow is vigorous, sand beaches may develop a fascinating phenomenon, the appearance of antidunes on channel beds. Ripple marks suddenly appear on a smooth bed. They grow rapidly and increase turbulence enough to cause erosion on the upcurrent sides of growing ripple marks and deposition on their downcurrent slopes. With sediment loss on one side and gain on the other, crests of greatly enlarged ripple marks or dunes migrate upstream against the current and direction of sediment transport. At this stage the channel-floor irregularities are called antidunes. Their upstream advance increases turbulence so sharply that the entire train of antidunes washes away, and the channel bed returns to a smooth condition, after which a new cycle of antidune development begins. Each cycle may last two or three minutes, and they occur one after another until the pool in the runnel above is drained to the point where rapid outlet flow ceases.

Bars across mouths of river channels or other shoreline interruptions differ from spits only in being attached to land at both ends. They may build above tidal levels and dam channels, creating lagoons with more or less brackish water. During high river stage or times of severe marine attack, outlets may be eroded across bars. Some bars of coarse sand or gravel permit such rapid percolation that outlets are formed infrequently or not at all.

Depositional barriers and beach nourishment

The largest depositional features paralleling a coast are offshore barriers, some of which are well over 200 miles long. These offshore beaches resemble those along straight coasts and in many cases lead into them. The Outer Banks, north of Cape Hatteras, continue as an ordinary beach north of the Virginia state line. Most offshore barriers originated toward the end of the last major rise of sea level (about 3,000 years ago). From some 137 metres below today's sea level, water rose at rates of up to one metre per century, converting coastal plains into continental shelves. During the rise, waves encountered large volumes of sand, which they pushed ahead to form migrating beaches. About 6,000 years ago the rate of rise dropped appreciably, and 3,000 years ago became so insignificant that relative stillstand (stability of sea level) appeared. The coastal plains no longer provided large volumes of sand for beach nourishment when submergence rates were reduced, and very little is con-

tributed by erosion of sea cliffs or river transport. Instead of growing, many beaches now lose sand because when erosion is severe some sand is transported to depths too low for entrainment. Reduction in beach volume was first regarded as acute on areas used for recreation. It has intensified because a terrific demand for concrete has arisen. This has resulted in strict regulation or even prohibition of mining of beach sand by most seaboard nations.

Beaches and coastal sand dunes were most voluminous about 6,000 years ago, when sea level was some six metres lower than at present. With diminishing nourishment, many beaches were unable to grow at a rate necessary to advance shoreward and became barriers separated from land because the rise of sea level, although diminished in rate, continued to "drown" lowlands; lagoons, as along the coasts of southern Texas and adjacent Mexico, and shallow sounds, as on the coast of North Carolina, were created. The barriers are excellent areas for recreation. Offshore barriers of still earlier times originated during halts in rising sea level and became completely submerged during periods of rapid rise, so that today they remain as linear sand deposits on continental shelves. Many of these are excellent fishing banks.

Coastal barriers commonly are anchored against points of land or masses of slightly submerged bedrock or durable material such as compact clay. The Outer Banks are anchored at Capes Hatteras and Lookout. Barrier trends change abruptly at each point, and in a minor way at Wimble Shoal to the north. Along Onslow Bay, west of Cape Lookout, the barrier becomes a shoreline beach. From there to southern Florida it forms the mainland shoreline much of the way, but for considerable stretches it fronts a narrow lagoon. South of Miami to beyond Key West are barriers that have a similar appearance on maps, but which are composed of old coral rock.

Some offshore barriers tie islands to the mainland. If they rise above sea level, these beaches are called tombolos. In some cases tombolos reach both sides of an island and may enclose a somewhat triangular lagoon. In some places very complex tombolo patterns arise from more than double ties.

River deltas. River deltas (*q.v.*) are depositional areas localized at river mouths if loads of fluvial sediment exceed the transport capabilities of alongshore currents or other marine processes. The framework of a delta consists of one or more natural levees along the sides of channels. If a river has more than one outlet, each distributary builds its own natural levees. These are present not only on land but also as submarine ridges extending from channel mouths. The most turbulent flow in a channel is located toward the bottom and near each bank. Deposition is most rapid in places where turbulence drops sharply, in locations near maximum threads of turbulence. If the channel is narrow, the strips most rapidly alluviated are the natural levees and their submarine extensions. In wider channels less turbulent water also occurs centrally, localizing midchannel bars or shoals. These shoals commonly grow into islands that divide distributary channels, establishing a tendency for them to multiply in geometric progression (2, 4, 8, etc.). But some distributaries wax while others wane, and marine processes also oppose realization of the progression. A delta ordinarily attains maximum complexity if river deposition dominates marine processes, as on the shore of a small lake or estuary. The bird-foot pattern of the Mississippi Delta is the best example of a large, complex delta. The arcuate pattern of the Nile and Niger deltas indicates dominance of alongshore currents. The single-outlet cuspate deltas of the Tiber (Italy) and the Sakarya (Turkey) indicate comparatively little sediment supply from rivers.

Delta patterns and depositional processes

Arctic deltas are extremely complex. Many remain frozen, together with channels upstream, for much of the year. Floods resulting from ice melting cut new channels and distribute sediment broadly, commonly in patterns differing from year to year (see ICE IN RIVERS AND LAKES). Rivers leading to the Arctic Ocean transport huge floating loads, mainly trees that become driftwood along shores. During storms this driftwood is carried inland and deposited in rows that may block stream channels, causing rivers to create entirely new distributaries. The delta of Blow River, near the mouth of the Mackenzie, is an excellent example.

Relatively broad basins between active natural levees of a complex delta contain lakes, swamps, marshes, and natural levees along abandoned river courses. The basins are wide and low in comparison with higher, narrow, natural levees along active channels, so for the most part deltas are low, wet areas. If natural levees jut out from a coast, as on sides of the "passes" of the Mississippi, V-shaped bays, with points directed inland, lie between them. During floods, when levee crests are overtopped, sediment accumulates in the bays, so that in time they become mudflats (slikke) or marshes that attain the level of high tide. Bars ordinarily form at the open ends of bays because marine turbulence drops sharply.

A river builds a new delta if it is diverted into a new channel. Most diversions occur well inland. An excellent example is provided by the Huang Ho, which has diverted many times at a place some 250 miles inland to established outlets on either side of Shantung Peninsula, resulting in deltas on both the Yellow Sea and the Gulf of Po-Hai, some 150 miles to the north. Locations of Mississippi River deltas have varied about 200 miles during the last 6,000 years. Most of the major diversions occurred 200 miles or more inland. As several of the deltas were large, an extensive area was added to the Gulf Coast deltaic plain. If the area is added to contributions of rivers on either side of Louisiana, the total plain is up to several tens of miles wide and extends from Alabama to Túxpan, Mexico. In some places the deposits are sandy, but silt, clay, shells, and peat prevail.

The weight of a large delta deposit causes local subsidence that is shared by marginal land, as shown by conspicuous bays and water-covered areas at the sides of the Ganges-Brahmaputra, Mekong, Rhine, Mississippi, and other deltas that press against the rock they lie upon. This condition is relieved by a rise in land elevation (isostatic compensation). Immediately north of the latest deltas of the Mississippi, the land uplift attains a maximum elevation of about 137 metres. The submarine delta of the Amazon imposes a load that has uplifted an extensive land area in the vicinity of Belém and northward. A minor but interesting result of this uplift is the inclusion of an area that had eroded into hills during times of low sea level. The summits of the hills have become islands close to the river mouth. On looking at a map a person almost certainly would conclude that these are alluvial islands of recent Amazon origin, but this is not the case. They rise well above river level, are surrounded by receding sea cliffs, were originally forested, have well-developed soils, and in part are cleared for agricultural use. Recent deltaic islands, such as occur farther upstream, are low, flanked by willows growing on natural levees, have wet interior basins, and provide only narrow strips for field crops along levee crests.

Coral reefs. Organic deposits form important coastal features (see CORAL ISLANDS, CORAL REEFS, AND ATOLLS; here the discussion is limited to large physical features).

The active face of a coral reef is characterized by plants and animals in growth positions. As the face builds out, organic remains retain these positions in the reef. Of greater extent, as a rule, is the shoreward reef flat, which consists of clastic debris derived from the active face and lodged with random orientation, to which are added the remains of organisms that grow on its surface, mainly in pools. The largest pool is likely to be a moat close to the beach. Habits of coral colonies vary according to environments. A species that forms thin incrustations on reef flats or crests commonly assumes a colonial tabular habit down the reef face, because the polyps best supplied with oxygen, and their associated algae with nu-

trients, are located on the outer fronts of tables, where water flow is most vigorous. The tabular growths are highly vulnerable to breakage when seas are unusually high. The resulting debris is carried over the crest and lodged on the reef flat, where it soon disintegrates into smaller fragments.

Nearshore fringing reefs approach or reach coasts of headlands, toward which waves converge, and bottoms are firm. In embayments, reefs stand farther out and their flats are usually wider. The upward limit of most reef crests is set by the level of low tides because dry coral polyps die in a short time. In some places, especially in the Pacific, algae more tolerant of desiccation form ridges along reef crests, adding a few feet to their heights. Nature lovers are rewarded by walks across reef flats, and professional shell collectors, their hands heavily gloved, reap rich harvests by turning over detrital blocks in order to find living specimens with natural colours. A person who stands near a reef crest is soon impressed by the fact that the many irregularities on the active face are the most effective of all means for dampening wave energy. It is a thrill to watch the approach of a wave more than three metres high and not much more than 30 metres away, confident that its surge will be little more than ankle deep after passing over the crest. Terrifying, however, are surge channels leading into the reef flat, in which violent flow develops during each wave surge and ebb into wave troughs. Often, people tempted by the prospect of fishing fall into surge channels, losing their lives when bashed against the irregular walls of these channels.

Barrier reefs stand well offshore. Some were fringing reefs a few thousand years ago, managing to hold their positions as the sea level rose. Others are anchored on shoals. The Great Barrier Reef, Queensland, is recognized as being over 1,000 miles long but is not continuous. It is a complex combination of reefs and reef flats, many of which are tied to "high islands" of bedrock.

A kaleidoscopic pattern of colours visible from the air above the Bahama Islands, Java Sea, some atoll lagoons, and places such as the margins of the Coral Sea is due mainly to numerous patch reefs that rise to or toward the surface. On some reef flats are found small, intensely blue or black "ocean holes" (or wells). These were formed by solution of coralline limestone during times of low sea level. They have many counterparts along the western mainland of peninsular Florida and in other limestone regions.

Atolls have provoked more scientific controversy than have other reefs. In the ideal development they are round, have central lagoons or mangrove swamps with entrances to leeward, and dunes behind reef flats. But ideal shapes are uncommon; many are complex, and some string out in linear chains. What they have in common is absence of bedrock; they are "low islands" composed wholly of organic debris. High seas have breached their dunes and left beach or reef flat debris that extends as tongues toward central lagoons.

Among other significant organic deposits in tropical regions is mangrove peat. In northern Borneo and elsewhere it builds into broad mounds up to nine metres high. Where rainfall is heavy, the peat remains saturated and at times breaks through somewhat drier walls to flow rapidly, in some cases burying villages and killing their inhabitants. A small-scale equivalent is the "bursting" of bogs in England.

Marshes. Marshes extend inland from many low shores as grassy flats (see SWAMPS, MARSHES, AND BOGS). Grass roots may accumulate to form peat, of considerable thickness if the region is subsiding. Where clay is dominant, marsh surfaces are soft, but shells, sand, and silt render them firm. Bordering beach deposits wash inland during storms, so saline marsh near shores is ordinarily firmer than brackish or fresh varieties inland. The surface attains a level about equal to that of high tide back of beaches and ordinarily rises slowly inland. In flat areas "flotant" may be present. These surfaces of interlaced plant roots are buoyant enough to overlie

Fringing reefs

Atolls

ooze or even water. Flotant quakes when walked upon. Crossing a flotant requires skill, because if not firm, floating marsh must be crossed rapidly by a person able to make instantaneous estimates of footings that will sustain his weight and to switch to other choices if the appraisal is faulty. Winding tidal channels develop low natural levees that ordinarily are the firmest strips of land present. If the tidal range is considerable, the channels cut deeply, providing access by small boats at high tide. Channel floors become bands of soft mud when the tide is out. Drainage of groundwater during low tide firms marshes near deep channels. Wind "tides" may be very significant in regions where the range of lunar tides is small. Landward winds may keep marshes flooded for several successive days. Seaward wind depresses water levels. Small basins in marshes may accumulate salt after seawater evaporates. Larger than these natural salt pans on many coasts are artificial ponds that yield salt commercially.

Tree-covered swamps are rare along seacoasts. They occur in the tropics where mangroves are abundant or nipa palms thrive, but are more characteristic of sides of river channels and estuaries (*q.v.*) than of shorelines.

COASTAL FEATURES RESULTING
FROM EROSIONAL PROCESSES

Destructive processes create the most scenic coastal features. Although these may not hold vacationers as long as beaches or provide biologists with the variety of life present in coral deposits, deltas, or marshes, destructional landforms are photogenic, and some become "musts" on tourist itineraries. Many destructive processes are uniquely marine, such as the pounding of waves or atmospheric phenomena characteristic of marine environments. Lake shores are similar in many regards but lack features resulting from major fluctuations of sea level and have less biological diversity.

Sea cliffs · Sea cliffs fringe many, but not all, rocky coasts. Some are essentially initial landforms, but most were created by gravitational processes (see EARTH MOVEMENTS ON SLOPES) following erosional steepening of their lower parts. While exposure to the full fury of ocean waves and swell (waves from distant storms) does little to change walls of durable rock that plunge well below sea level, there are few places where that condition is pres-

By courtesy of the Coastal Studies Institute, Louisiana State University, Baton Rouge; photograph, R.J. Russell

Plunging sea cliff, Cape Saint Vincent, southwest Portugal.

ent. In most places parts of cliffs near sea level are highly vulnerable to attack. Alternate drying and wetting speeds weathering. If rocks contain open cracks, each

wave arrival results in increasing water pressure and compressing air, causing fluctuations that widen cracks and reduce rock stability. If sand or coarse solids are hurled against cliffs, they have abrasive effects, in many cases cutting notches. Snails, sea urchins, and other animals are capable of rasping even the hardest rock, while clams, sponges, worms, algae, and other organisms weaken it by boring or secreting chemically active solvents. These attacks are concentrated within tidal limits and assist in deepening notches. Notches below overhanging visors result from solution along many limestone coasts.

Rubble supplied by retreating cliffs or brought by alongshore currents provides cutting tools that etch rocks. If rubble is transported away about as rapidly as it arrives, notches do not develop. If surplus rubble is

By courtesy of the Coastal Studies Institute, Louisiana State University, Baton Rouge; photograph, R.J. Russell

Bench swept clean of rubble and unnotched sea cliff, Muriwai, North Island, New Zealand.

present, it dissipates wave energy, and notches are deepened only when waves are extraordinarily high or not at all. Wide beaches also are effective in protecting coasts. Although they experience almost continuous short-term changes, the bedrock behind them is shielded because practically all wave energy is consumed in the shifting of sand or shingle. Wide, shallow bedrock benches are also protective because they reduce wave energy through friction and intensification of turbulent motions in the water.

Erosion of cliff bases reduces support for overlying rock, providing conditions favouring cliff collapse or internal dislocations that weaken rock. Heavy rains increase overburden weight and lubricate clay or internal-fracture surfaces. Cliffs recede most rapidly during wet seasons. Basal steepening, however, fails to develop in materials such as loose sand or gravel. Wave attack may be minimized by the presence of aprons of debris, or at best results in landward retreat of comparatively gentle slopes. Along some coasts, clay cracks easily when dried and shrinks into small blocks that are readily transported downslope by water currents during rains or when doused by spray. The resulting coastal badlands have rounded crests if the clay is homogeneous but exhibit pinnacles, perched rocks, or ledges if layers of cemented sandstone are present. The resulting landforms resemble those providing the scenic attraction of Bryce Canyon, Utah.

Steep slopes along coasts are commonly compound features consisting of an active sea cliff below an inactive false (or dead) cliff of earlier origin. The false cliff may be an inheritance from older topography or the result of intermittent uplift along an active fault zone, as in the case of the steep-fronted Santa Lucia Range (California), which has risen some 183 metres since midden-building Indians began to gather clams along the shore, probably less than 10,000 years ago.

Bedrock platforms between surf-base and wave-uprush limits have many causes. A belief that a platform fronts · Bedrock platforms every sea cliff is not strictly true. Wave erosion drives cliffs back and forms platforms only where suitable lithology exists. In many cases this depends on the presence of rock that has been weakened by oxidation, leaching, and various physicochemical processes and that overlies more durable rock below the water table. These platforms slope gently toward the level of high neap tide. The localization of temporary "perched" water tables within the leached zone promotes rapid cliff recession and formation of small benches above ordinary platform levels. In high latitudes frost shattering reduces rock durability above about 51 centimetres from sea level, with a result that wide, "half-metre benches" characterize the coast of Norway and others with similar climate. In warmer climates bedrock is attacked by organisms that thrive between tidal limits, and flats also are created by solution and chemical processes resulting from frequent changes in water composition. On most coasts, however, the extent of depositional flats is much greater than that of flats of erosional origin.

Rates of coastal recession

Rates of coastal recession may be measured directly or estimated on evidence such as the disappearance of landmarks or habitations known to have been present at various dates. In the volcanic ash of Krakatoa, the recession averaged nearly 46 metres per year between 1883 and 1928. This excessive rate in part depended on direct exposure to high swell from the Southern Ocean. Brittenburg, a Roman fort at a former mouth of the Rhine, occupied a position in the North Sea about a mile north of The Hague. Withernsea, north of the River Humber (England), experienced 305 metres of coastal recession between 1847 and 1908. In 1953, during the storm that so damaged The Netherlands, Covehithe, on the English coast, experienced coastal recession up to 27.5 metres in places, and during 24 hours an estimated 300,000 tons of rock slid down nearby cliffs. At Seaton, on Lyme Bay (Devon), on Christmas Day 1839, 8,000,-000 tons of sea cliff collapsed to form a staircase of faulted blocks because a thick section of firm chalk lost the support of underlying clay that had been wetted by heavy rain. Spectacular as these values may be, a widespread belief that Great Britain is being consumed by the sea was negated by a study published in 1911 by the Royal Commission on Coastal Erosion, which found that the 6,640 acres lost during the preceding 35 years were more than balanced by 48,000 gained by accretion. The exchange was a poor one, however, because land lost had considerable agricultural value, whereas that gained consisted largely of shingle or rather useless marsh deposits. Presumably there has been no comparative study of losses and gains along the world's 278,000 miles of (smoothed) shoreline, but it seems likely that during the existing stillstand of sea level the area added by accretion is considerably larger than that lost to erosion.

COASTAL FEATURES DEPENDENT ON LITHOLOGY STRUCTURE OR INHERITED TOPOGRAPHY

Lithology determines appearances of sea cliffs and other coastal features. Volcanic rocks are likely to form steep cliffs and in many cases arcuate coasts. Excellent examples include the northern end of Martinique (French West Indies), where recent extrusives from Mt. Pelée produce a bulge with a four-mile radius; the northern end of St. Vincent (West Indies), where a similar outline fringes flows of lava and deposits of ash from Soufrière; and, on a much larger scale, the eastern part of Maui (Hawaii), which is centred on the cone of Haleakala. The spectacular Giants Causeway of Northern Ireland is an eroded accumulation of columnar basalt, with pillars arranged like the cells of a honeycomb. Fingals Cave, on the Island of Staffa, north of the Firth of Lorne (Scotland), exhibits similar columns, as do the Palisades of the Hudson.

Massive crystalline rock, such as granite, commonly erodes into rounded domes. The destructional process involved is called exfoliation or spheroidal weathering and may be observed on all scales down to the rounding of small blocks. The weathering results in isolating thin, convex scales that spall off, most rapidly at angularities. Domed surfaces characterize granitic coasts in all climates: on the Kola Peninsula (U.S.S.R.) north of the White Sea, along shores of the Gulf of Bothnia, near Albany (Western Australia), and in the vicinity of Rio de Janeiro. Another characteristic of crystalline rock is the presence of plane surfaces developed along joints. As the joints occur in two or more sets, commonly at about 90°, their planes intersect at sharp angles. In some cases joint-plane surfaces may be large, as on the walls of Yosemite Valley (California) or Norwegian fjords, but ordinarily they are evident only as small-scale angularities.

Benches

Massive limestone may form nearly vertical cliffs, but in some cases the rock is bedded and individual layers differ in solubility. The effect of destructive processes is to produce steplike surfaces in which the less soluble layers form treads and the more soluble become risers that may be vertical or concave. Similar benches occur in stratified rocks, in some cases forming wide platforms separated by steep cliffs such as are exhibited on the sides of the Grand Canyon of the Colorado River (Arizona). Benches are developed on layers of durable sandstone that alternate with beds of readily eroded shale. Small shells and thin opercula of snails that live along the coast are found on benches as high as 18 metres. These are transported with spray. The specimens remain in scattered locations in spite of the fact that water returning downslope flows with a force sufficient to remove rock fragments and to sweep clean most of the bench surfaces.

Massive sedimentary rock commonly forms steep cliffs, something true even of clay and silt layers because they possess considerable internal cohesion. The characteristic durability of sandstone results from cementation. Benching ordinarily develops if the rock is stratified.

Karstic features characterize many limestone and occasionally other coasts. The name refers to Karst, a portion of Dalmatia (Yugoslavia) north of the Adriatic Sea. The characteristics of karst are numerous sinkholes, abandoned surface valleys, underground drainage, caves and grottoes, and roughened bedrock surfaces exhibiting small pinnacles (lapiés), small rills (rillen, gutters), and pools with overhanging sides. Within, the spray zone surfaces are roughened, the scale becoming more impressive downslope and gross within the limits of wave uprush.

Erosional benches are about horizontal if rock bedding is nearly flat, but are inclined if layers dip. Some form ramps that can be followed to positions below sea level. If the stratification of sedimentary rocks or the internal structure (schistosity, gneissic banding, etc.) of metamorphic rocks approaches the vertical, the rocks are described as "standing on edge," and they erode into complex forms, such as the needles responsible for the naming of Africa's southernmost tip, Cape Agulhas. The jagged needles are not only exposed within tidal limits but also extend far seaward across a relatively shallow platform, where they have caused many shipwrecks.

Bedrock structures

Fault and joint structures in bedrock localize zones that yield readily to destructive marine agents of erosion. Tabular dikes of igneous rock that intrude bedrock about vertically in many cases are highly susceptible to attack. Weakened rock localizes such fascinating features as sea caves, spouting (or blow) holes, arches, and deep coastal indentations. In some places a person may note gaps in the continuity of breakers above scoured troughs localized along zones where readily eroded rock occurs. Resistant rock structures determine positions of capes, headlands, seaward-jutting peninsulas, and islands. Many interesting scenic features result from etching of highly deformed, intensely folded sedimentary rock.

Craters at summits of volcanic mountains may be created explosively or by sinking of lava in a volcano's throat. Larger examples are called calderas and in some cases extend below sea level. The island of Thera (Santorin) in the Aegean, about 150 miles southeast of

Needles eroded in conspicuously jointed Cape System Sandstone, Cape Agulhas, South Africa.
By courtesy of the Coastal Studies Institute, Louisiana State University, Baton Rouge; photograph, R.J. Russell

Athens, is part of a caldera rim on a depression that provides an excellent harbor. Deep and well-sheltered Castries Harbour, on St. Lucia (West Indies), is a smaller caldera.

Low coasts develop relatively few scenic features. Cliffs along higher coasts reveal the topography of land under destruction. Heights are uniform in front of tablelands, but are varied if the topography is irregular. Most valleys erode to a base set by sea level, but in some cases cliff recession is more than a match for deepening, leaving the ends of truncated valleys hanging. Many examples occur in the chalk cliffs of England and France, and some are found along the coast of Mauritius. But coastal recession does not explain the most spectacular hanging valleys. Streams plunge over waterfalls along the Santa Lucia coast of California because the mountains are being uplifted so rapidly. The most scenic falls and cascades issue from the sides of fjords. These main valleys, now deepened by glacial scour, are flanked by tributary valleys that have been left hanging at high levels.

In viewing a rocky coast, a person should bear in mind that, while coastal recession creates new surfaces, most of the physical landscape developed on bedrock originated during the last 2,000,000 years or more, when the average sea level was considerably lower than at present (see PLEISTOCENE EPOCH). Seaward ends of valleys excavated during that time are now drowned and have become estuaries or are in various stages of alluvial filling, dating from not more than a few thousand years ago. On many coasts a sharp topographic break occurs between bedrock topography and adjacent, relatively flat surfaces of water or alluvium. The bedrock valleys bottom some 122 metres below fill that surfaces close to present sea level. During the last major rise of sea level, many old hilltops became islands, such as those in San Francisco Bay. Some rise above new alluvial surfaces, as in the case of El Cerrito, near Berkeley. Most small islands near coasts were isolated from mainlands by rising sea level, but some originated because retreating sea cliffs cut through land behind them, and still others are initial landforms faulted up to their present positions or left by volcanic activity. If their areas are tiny and they rise precipitously, they are called sea stacks. These are most numerous near the cliffs from which they were detached. Many are picturesque.

Topography, lithology, or structure may account for peninsulas or islands that parallel coasts or that diverge at various angles. The Dalmatian Coast is famous for its many bedrock islands that, for lithologic reasons, parallel the shore. The largest examples of parallel trends result from seismic activities and include Baja California, many islands off British Columbia, the Aleutians, Kuriles, Japan, and others toward New Zealand, also island arcs (*q.v.*) extending between eastern Indonesia and south-western Burma. Transverse trends are less conspicuous, but lithology explains why peninsular Florida points southward, Brittany protrudes from France, and Cornwall juts southwestward from Great Britain, as well as many minor irregularities along other coasts. All such structural features are reflected topographically.

Quaternary glaciation brought continental ice that covered large parts of North America, northwestern Europe, and other high-latitude areas. The ice was water that had been subtracted from the oceans, causing their levels to drop 137 metres or so at four or five widely separated times. There is now enough ice above sea level on Antarctica and Greenland to raise sea level more than 61 metres were it all to melt. The ice volume is about one third that of any glacial stage at its maximum development. Returning meltwater during each declining glacial stage raised sea level to approximately its present stand. Possibly at no other time in earth history have estuaries and coastal indentations been so numerous. Western Europe and North America are highly favoured by having very irregular coastlines.

The erosional results of glaciation include deepened valleys with steepened sides that became scenic fjords when sea level rose. The best examples are in Norway, British Columbia and Alaska, Chile, New Zealand, and on Arctic islands. Less deep are the fjords of Sweden and Finland, which lie between low, rounded hills. Abrasion by rocks carried deep in the ice left scratches (striae) that are evident on Vancouver Island, in Scandinavia, and elsewhere. Continental ice scoured irregular surfaces on bedrock, leaving basins now occupied by lakes or bogs. The eroded rock was carried to ice margins, where it was deposited as moraines, and much debris was left on deglaciated surfaces when ice melted. These deposits account for highly complex shorelines in New England and other places. Most of the world's lakes occupy depressions of glacial origin, owing both to scour and to deposition, and hence are most numerous in mountains or high latitudes, as in Finland, Minnesota, and over much of Canada. (R.J.R.)

LIFE ALONG SEA COASTS

Coasts as habitats. A great variety of plant and animal life, of numbers not found in other marine habitats, is compressed into a narrow strip along the rim of the sea, stretching from the highest level wetted by waves at the highest tides down through low tide to a level where seaweeds cease to grow. This zone of coastal life can be as much as 100 metres in vertical extent, but is usually much less. The upper limit of the zone depends on how high the waves can reach; cliffs exposed to frequent ocean storms may be wetted 30 metres or more above nominal high tide. The lower edge of coastal life may be the edge of the seaweed "forest," the seaward slope of a

Quaternary glaciation

Life-zone limits

coral reef, or it may merge imperceptibly with the benthic life of the sea bed, as on many sand beaches. The lower limit of coastal life depends on extent of light penetration, and varies from a few metres in muddy waters of temperate and Arctic regions to 100 metres in clear tropical seas.

A factor common to all coastal life is the continuous water movement: the daily or twice daily rise and fall of the tide, the perpetual to and fro of alongshore currents, and the crash and wash of wind-formed waves. By these means the supply of oxygen and nutrients in the water is continuously renewed.

In most parts of the world, the tide is the most obvious environmental influence on the shore. The period of the tide and the extent of the rise vary greatly, and the part of the shore directly influenced—the intertidal zone— also varies greatly in extent and type.

Wave action along the shore also varies, but much more irregularly than the tide. Its influence is difficult to relate to the distribution of coastal life, and almost impossible to separate completely from purely tidal factors.

It is obvious that physical forces mold coastal communities. Not so obvious, but just as certain, is that the organisms themselves affect the habitat. Gastropod mollusks such as winkles, limpets, and top-shells (turban shells) contribute significantly to erosion of the rock while grazing on attached seaweeds. Erosion from such sources is uneven, resulting in the formation of pits and hollows that encourage other erosive forces. Along the open ocean coasts of Portugal, Spain, France, west Ireland, and the northwestern U.S., sea urchins honeycomb the lower rocks. A group of bivalves, found on most shores, can tunnel into all but the hardest rock.

The animals living on sandy and muddy shores vary widely in response to the predominant particle size (*e.g.*, whether coarse sand, fine sand, silt, or mud). Many of the animals continually burrow in the deposit and turn it over much in the same way as earthworms do on land. Where the deposit is sheltered from wave action, complex burrows and hollows may build up.

Many worms and some mollusks secrete tubes of limestone or of sand grains cemented together. In some parts of the world, aggregations of these tube-building creatures build up large reef structures near low tide. The greatest reef builders, of course, are the corals and other organisms associated with them in tropical seas.

Habitat zonation The ecologist divides up the shore and shallow sea into a series of horizontal belts, or zones, according to the dominant plants or animals found in each. The widely used scheme of T.A. and Anne Stephenson recognizes three main zones and two fringing zones, as follows: The supralittoral zone, subject to salt air and some spray but not normally wetted by the highest tides, is inhabited by salt-tolerant lichens and maritime land plants, insects,

and coastal birds. On sandy shores this is the seaward side of the dune formation, and in mangrove swamps the upper edge of the buttonwoods. On tropical shores there are animals of marine origin, including robber and ghost crabs. The supralittoral fringe extends from the highest level washed by the waves at high tide down to the upper limit of barnacles. The organisms in this fringing zone are wetted only by the higher tides each month and may thus remain dry for several days at a time. On a rocky shore the typical inhabitants are small winkles and the dark, encrusting marine lichens that form a black band on the rocks. Some grapsid crabs and isopods may be found, though these all take refuge in crevices when disturbed. The red alga *Porphyra* and, in the North Atlantic region, two brown algae, *Pelvetia* and *Fucus spiralis*, occur at the lower end of the zone. The midlittoral, or eulittoral, zone can be divided into three subzones on most rocky shores. The uppermost part is usually dominated by barnacles (*Chthamalus, Balanus*) and by more of the winkles. In shelter, algae may take over from the barnacles; for example, in the North Atlantic and North Pacific, various species of brown seaweeds (fucoids) and the green alga *Enteromorpha*. The middle region of the midlittoral is often barnacle-dominated like the upper part, but limpets, mussels, and stalked barnacles (*Pollicipes*) may be present; in shelter from wave action, the barnacles tend to be overshadowed or replaced by algal growths. The lowest part of the midlittoral is the easiest to distinguish; it often lacks barnacles and may be dominated by a red algal turf or by an association of limpets and encrusting calcareous algae or by large brown seaweeds. Locally it may show reefs formed from the tubes of marine worms or mollusks or sheets of anemones. The lowest part of the intertidal zone is called the infralittoral fringe and is often regarded as an upward extension of the infralittoral (sublittoral) zone. The fringe may be continuously submerged for days and is often characterized by growths of large brown seaweeds. Where the laminarian seaweeds are not present, the infralittoral fringe may take the form of a turf of small red seaweeds of many genera, without large limpets and with masses of encrusting calcareous algae, or in tropical regions it is part of the coral-reef formation. Other more local forms of the infralittoral fringe occur: groups of sea urchins, associations of anemones and starfish, and beds of marine grasses, which can mingle with the laminarian seaweeds. In the Southern Hemisphere a fringe of sea squirts can dominate this part of the shore.

As already noted, the infralittoral or sublittoral zone itself is not unlike the infralittoral fringe, and many organisms are common to both. In temperate and cold climates it is pre-eminently the home of the large seaweeds (laminarians and giant kelps) that can reach up from as much as 30 metres depth to float part of their fronds at

Adapted from *Ecology and Field Biology* by Robert Leo Smith, illustrated by Ned Smith (Harper & Row, 1966)

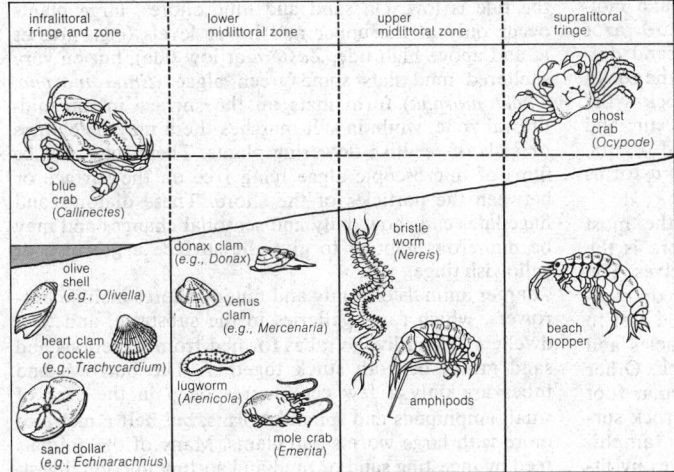

Coastal life on the sandy shores of the North American Atlantic coast.

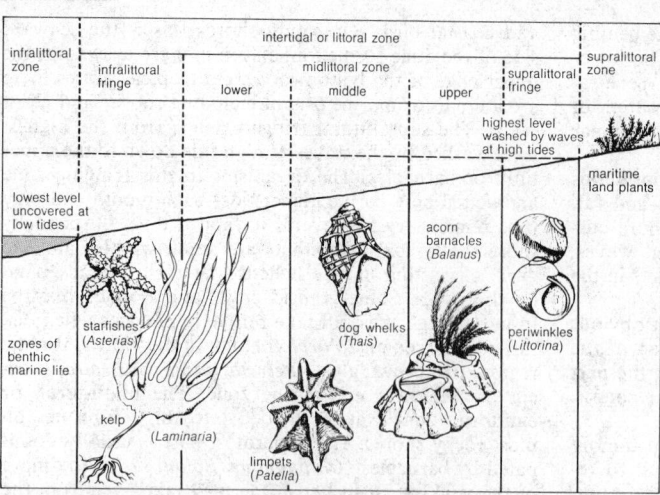

Typical life-forms of a partly wave-beaten rocky shore of the North Atlantic.
Adapted from *Ecology and Field Biology* by Robert Leo Smith, illustrated by Ned Smith (Harper & Row, 1966)

the surface. In warmer waters the corresponding algae are much smaller. As the influence of exposure to air and strong light decreases, the hardy forms typical of the intertidal zone become less abundant and their place is taken by more delicate forms; *e.g.*, smaller limpets, gastropod mollusks, sponges, long-spined sea urchins, starfish, and the finer red algae. In the tropics the infralittoral zone is often part of the coral reef formation.

Sand and mud shores

On sand and mud shores the same basic zones can be recognized, though the organisms are very different from those described for rocky shores. The supralittoral fringe of a sandy shore is the semiarid region of loose sand near the high-water mark, with varying amounts of dried seaweed fragments and other detritus left by the tide; it is inhabited by sand hoppers, which live in burrows in the damp sand. The corresponding part of a mud shore may carry a typical salt marsh association (see below) or may be a shingle (pebbly) bank with sand hoppers among lines of rotting seaweed. The midlittoral of sand and mud shores is usually inhabited by several types of polychaete worm, the most typical being lugworms. Other worms, such as species of *Nereis* and spionids, may be commonest near the upper edge, corresponding to the barnacle zone of rocky shores, while other species of *Nereis* and *Nephtys* may predominate lower down. On wave-beaten shores, the worms are fewer, but are accompanied by a large transient population of crustaceans, amphipods, isopods (which swim about in the sea at high tide), and the mole crab. The fiddler crab occurs widely on sand and mud shores. With increasing shelter from wave action, a beach becomes more muddy and is inhabited by the smaller mollusks, common in the lower half of the midlittoral, and in full shelter the larger clams may be found. The infralittoral fringe of a sandy shore is usually inhabited by the same worms and mollusks found higher up, but in addition there are razor clams, cockles, burrowing heart urchins, and sand dollars. The infralittoral fringe is less marked than the rocky shores, and many of these organisms continue below the level of low tide. Where a few loose stones occur, and where water movement is slight, brown seaweed occurs, while in muddy places the marine grass *Zostera* forms dense beds.

Character of coastal populations. One of the most characteristic features of life on the rocky shore is the tenacity with which the organisms attach themselves. The large brown seaweeds have strong disk-shaped or rootlike extensions of the thallus by which they hold fast to the rock. Many of the animals (*e.g.*, the barnacles and tube worms) are permanently cemented to rock. Other animals, such as the limpets, have a large muscular foot capable of strong temporary attachment to the rock surface. Some shore animals, such as small crabs, amphipods, and isopods, resist detachment by the waves by fitting themselves into crevices, using some of their legs as

anchors. Small crustaceans and mollusks take refuge among the fronds of seaweeds. Perhaps the most highly adapted clinging organ is found in the sucker fish, which has pelvic fins modified as vacuum cups.

Many inhabitants of severely wave-beaten rocky shores also show adaptations that reduce the effects of waves; *e.g.*, the depressed conic shape of limpets and barnacles, the short, relatively unbranched yet flexible and mucus-coated thallus of the seaweeds.

Feeding habits of shore animals

The animals of the shore are ultimately dependent on seaweed and larger plants for food, supplemented by plankton from the ocean and by organic debris from the land. The main herbivores of the shore—the limpets, winkles, and top shells—are all grazers. They feed on the mature, large algae directly or on the smaller recently settled plants and other simple algae on rock surfaces. Pieces of seaweed that accumulate after rough seas also are eaten by winkles and top shells, which can thus act as scavengers.

Most of the crustaceans of rocky shores feed on a wider variety of organisms, and also are scavengers. The barnacles that sweep the water passing over them with a net formed from six of their appendages can eat anything from microscopic algae up to crustaceans a few millimetres long. Other crustaceans stir up and sort over the silt often found in crevices. Bivalve and vermetid mollusks, and some tube worms and sea squirts, feed on floating particles they remove from the water by filtering.

The predators of rocky shores include dog whelks (*Thais*), phyllodocid worms, crabs, and shore fishes. Many of these predators, especially fishes and starfishes, lurk in pools and crevices or below low-tide mark and come up to feed only at high tide. In contrast, rodents and seabirds feed on mollusks and crustaceans when the tide is low. On sand and mud shores, large plants occur only at the upper and lower levels (*e.g.*, grasses at and above high tide, *Zostera* at low tide), but on very sheltered mud flats some green algae (*Enteromorpha*, *Chaetomorpha*) form mats on the surface in the midlittoral zone, while in salt marshes there may be clumps or beds of reedlike flowering plants. There may also be films of microscopic algae lying free on the surface or between the particles of the shore. These diatoms and flagellates can show daily and seasonal changes and may be numerous enough to give the surface a greenish or yellowish tinge.

Larger animals of sandy and muddy shores include burrowers, which form galleries in the substrate, and tube dwellers, which live in tubes formed from secretions and sand grains or both stuck together. The burrows and tubes are only a few centimetres deep in the case of small amphipods and spionid worms, but half a metre or more with large worms and clams. Many of the animals feed by ingesting sand or mud and sorting out and digesting the organic fraction inside their gut. Some carry out more complex sorting operations to explore the surface of the ooze and suck in lighter particles. A large proportion of the mollusks of beaches are plankton feeders, who lie in the substrate with extensible siphons raised above the surface of the bottom. The sabellid worms found at low-tide levels feed in much the same way.

On the whole, predators are less common in sandy or muddy beaches or are less easy to recognize. There may be predatory gastropods and various small crabs, but much of the predation occurs at high tide, when crustaceans and fishes move in and attack exposed siphons and tentacles of partly buried plankton feeders. At low tide wading birds probe wet places with their beaks or puddle shallow pools with their feet to get at crustaceans and other small animals buried shallowly. Some animals of muddy shores are more or less sedentary (*e.g.*, tube-living worms such as the clymenids and sabellids), but others, like the small clams, are mobile and search for food. Generally, plankton feeders are evenly spread out, while deposit feeders aggregate where the organic content is highest or the particle size easiest to sort.

Several specialized habitats of coastal life form distinct associations, which are discussed briefly below.

Coral reefs are among the best known and probably the most specialized of these coastal communities. A typical reef consists of the interlocking and encrusted calcareous skeletons of reef corals and hydrocorals (both colonial coelenterates) and calcareous algae. Reefs are particularly well developed in the Indo-Pacific area and in the Caribbean, but are much scarcer in most of the Atlantic. Reefs occur where the mean sea temperature is as high as 24° C, and where temperatures below 18° C are rare and of short duration. Reefs flourish best where water movement prevents deposition of silt, and where the water is clear enough to allow maximum penetration of sunlight. Reef growth stops at 50-metre depth, though a few coral species can survive down to 150 metres. The leeward side of a coral reef, most often the landward side, tends to form a reef flat of shallow pools and tortuous channels where a variety of organisms abound (see also CORAL ISLANDS, CORAL REEFS, AND ATOLLS).

Mangrove swamps, restricted to the warmer parts of the world, are often found in estuaries and sandy marine inlets. There is a general succession of species from low tide to high tide. The outer edge usually consists of red mangroves (*Rhizophora*), regarded as the primary colonizers, whose stiltlike, exposed roots afford shelter to a variety of animals, particularly barnacles, small oysters, the hermit crab *Clibanarius*, the mudskipper fish (*Periophthalmus*), and many gastropod mollusks. Farther inland, the red mangroves are replaced by a belt of black mangroves (*Avicennia*), which usually continues to the top of the intertidal zone, forming a salt-marsh community but lacking the strictly marine animals associated with the red mangroves. In the supralittoral fringe, black mangroves are replaced by transition forms such as the buttonwoods, which themselves give way to a full swamp formation, including palms, in the supralittoral zone.

Tide pools can be found at any level on the coast, from extreme high-tide level in the supralittoral fringe down to low water. They can be regarded as extensions of the infralittoral zone, since the organisms living in them are not exposed to air, but most pools show a wide variation in other environmental factors (*e.g.*, temperature, pH, and salinity) compared with the sea, and hence the number of species is often less than the infralittoral.

Lagoons may be regarded as very large tidal pools often cut off from the sea for very long periods or connected through narrow channels. Under these conditions some parts of the lagoon may become two or three times saltier than the sea. The fauna is often that of brackish water; *e.g.*, *Nereis*, certain small clams, the barnacle *Balanus eburneus*, mullets, sand smelts, and cyprinodont fishes. Lagoons with a flow of freshwater that more than balances evaporation may be much less salty than the sea, and have a fauna with more freshwater tolerant, but related, species (see also LAGOONS).

Salt marshes border creeks and sheltered inlets, where the shore is mainly mud or sand. The low-tide level, equivalent to the infralittoral fringe, may consist of a typical sandy beach with few plants or may be dominated by marine grasses. The middle region of a salt marsh is subject to stronger erosive forces than at higher and lower levels and may show little plant growth other than diatoms, but when suitably sheltered from wave action, it may carry extensive mats of blue-green algae. The fauna is often estuarine in character, with amphipods such as *Corophium* and the hardier polychaete worms, sometimes with cockles and more often clams. The most conspicuous part of a salt marsh is the upper edge of the shore, corresponding to the supralittoral fringe, with rushes (*Juncus*), sea lavender (*Limonium*), sea plantain (*Plantago*), and species of *Spartina*. This extensive salt-flat region gradually transforms into salt meadow or rough scrub above the reach of the tides (see also SWAMPS, MARSHES, AND BOGS).

Adaptations to coastal living. The animals and plants of the intertidal zone are subjected to daily or twice daily tidal flow, with concomitant changes in humidity, temperature, illumination, and other factors.

Physical factors. Algae high up on the shore are remarkably tolerant of water loss, much of the water being lost from the thick cell walls and not from the cell contents. Simple seaweeds such as *Porphyra* can dry out to an almost paperlike consistency and revive when wet again. Many of the animals resist water loss by withdrawing inside an impervious shell that can be tightly closed (barnacles and mussels), sealed off by a membrane (littorinids), or kept closely pressed to the rock (limpets). Other animals with thinner shells or skins seek crevices when the tide falls (*e.g.*, many crabs, worms, and shore fishes), but a few soft-bodied forms secrete copious mucus and thus resist drying.

In the cool temperate regions, the relative humidity of the air rarely falls below 45 percent and may be as high as 90 percent on moist autumn days. With high humidities, particularly at night, many of the animals remain active, continuing to feed and move about. In dry tropical climates there is real danger of desiccation, and intertidal gastropods (littorinids and top shells) show a graded resistance to drying according to how high up the shore they live. The animals of sandy and muddy shores withdraw deeper into the bottom as the surface dries.

Greater extremes of temperature occur on shore compared with the sea. Animals with thick shells gain some protection from the worst extremes. Some can withstand changes from below freezing in winter to 40° C in summer. Certain tropical mollusks can cool themselves by leaking water to evaporate outside the shell, but this risks desiccation. Cold weather on shore is less severe than inland because of the heat capacity of the sea; nevertheless, organisms in boreal and Arctic regions must resist freezing or migrate below the intertidal zone in winter. Some (*e.g.*, *Balanus*) survive frozen deeply into shore ice, which offers protection against excessive cold and abrasion by floating ice. (The latter factor is responsible for producing the bare intertidal zone of many Arctic and sub-Arctic shores.) Animals living in sand and mud are less subject to extremes of temperature.

Physiological needs. Many intertidal animals have delicate surfaces that must be kept moist for breathing (gills, branchiae, or tentacles). Such surfaces are often drawn into a compartment of the shell cavity when the animal is exposed to air. Quite often the animal remains quiescent during low tide, and any oxygen debt run up by anaerobic respiration is removed by vigorously ventilating the shell cavity or burrow when the tide rises. The polychaete worms *Sabella* and *Nephtys* are good examples of this type; the respiratory pigment in their blood is of use only at high oxygen tensions. More specialized burrowers such as *Arenicola* show greater adaptation: the burrow may remain open during low tide, and partly filled with water containing small amounts of oxygen; the respiratory pigment is able to take up oxygen at low concentrations, and the animal can continue aerobic respiration. Some of the less specialized animals of the

Specialized coastal communities

Resistance to drying

Gas exchange

seashore (*e.g.*, anemones and starfish), including those normally found in pools, may cease activity completely at low oxygen levels.

The animals of a rocky shore show a progressive tendency toward aerial respiration the higher up they live on shore. In some littorinids, which are often out of the water much longer than barnacles and limpets, the number of gills is reduced and the shell cavity is well supplied with blood vessels and acts like a lung. A further reduction in gills is found in tropical hermit crabs and ghost crabs, which spend much of their lives out of water; some have an arrangement for pumping air in and out.

Most shore animals can feed only when covered by the tide, and the whole alimentary system may be governed by tidal rhythms, particularly in ooze and plankton feeders such as bivalves. Grazing animals, such as limpets and littorinids, feed at any time, moving about without danger of desication. It appears, however, that many high-level littorinids feed only in wet weather. Limpets likewise may feed mainly at low tide at night or under other damp conditions. Barnacles are well adapted to take advantage of wave wash and splash as well as tide; they open very quickly when wetted by seawater, and will feed even under a thin film of water.

Most shore animals readily dispose of their waste products when covered by the tide, and there are few obvious adaptations. Fecal pellets, which may be held in the shell cavity for some hours, are often of firm consistency (*e.g.*, limpets) or enclosed in membranes (barnacles). In the littorinid mollusks that stay a long time out of water, the urine is higher in uric acid content, a well-known water-saving mechanism further developed in land animals.

Reproduction and dispersal. Many marine animals shed their eggs and sperm in the sea, where fertilization occurs and where the egg develops into a planktonic larval stage that has to feed and grow before assuming the adult form. Many, but not all, animals living on the shore, and also many in the immediate coastal areas of the shallow sea in colder climates, have modified this pattern. Some worms have large eggs that fall to the bottom after fertilization or that are enclosed in gelatinous capsules; in both types there is usually direct development, without further feeding, of a tiny replica of the adult. Most species of limpets have external fertilization, and a short planktonic larval stage, but other gastropods have cross-fertilization and lay eggs in gelatinous masses or incubate them inside the shell. In barnacles and oysters, fertilization is internal, and the eggs undergo some development before being liberated as free-swimming larvae. Among echinoderms, which are generally restricted to pools or low levels on the shore, a few species incubate their larvae in brood pouches (*e.g.*, *Leptasterias mulleri*). Some intertidal sea anemones brood the eggs and produce live young (*e.g.*, *Actinia*), while many of the hydroids that show alternation of generations omit the planktonic medusa stage and produce a crawling planula larva directly.

Many coastal animals with motile larvae show remarkable adaptations for settling in a suitable place to grow. Animals that are permanently attached as adults, of course, must select the correct place at once or they will fail to survive: in most of them the free-swimming larva possesses special tactile and chemical senses for recognizing suitable habitats. There is generally an exploratory phase at the end of the larval life, lasting from a few hours (as in serpulid worms) to some days (as in barnacles), during which larvae can settle almost instantly once they find the right spot.

Rhythmic activities. The commonest rhythm of the shore is connected with the twice daily tidal flow, with maximum activity occurring when the tide is in. Many anemones, crabs, and mollusks respond to these semidiurnal floodings by quickening their activities generally. Certain crabs and prawns change colour, darkening in the daytime. Other animals show a peak of activity at low tide during the night.

A more prolonged type of rhythm, with periods of 14 or 28 days, corresponds to the phase of the moon. The

Patterns of fertilization

14-day cycle is obviously keyed to the period of the highest tides. The best known example of such a cycle is that of the grunion, a Pacific fish that comes ashore along California and lays its eggs: spawning occurs on the highest tides, and the eggs are deposited in the sand at the extreme upper limit, where they develop and await washing out on the next high tide 14 days later before hatching into young fish. If these tides are not high enough to reach the eggs, hatching can be delayed for another 14 days until the next set of high tides. Periods of 28 days are found in the breeding behaviour of the palolo worm. The response is again to a tidal factor, since the rhythm is synchronized with the very highest tides of the month, which occur at 28-day intervals. Daily and longer rhythms appear to occur in the growth of many coastal animals, such as corals and bivalve mollusks.

Associations. Shallow-water and shore habitats are very rich in associations between different species. Some are casual and purely protective. Small fishes live among the tentacles of tropical sea anemones or among the long spines of sea urchins, blind gobies live in the burrows of the mud shrimp *Callianassa*, and arrow gobies take shelter in the tubes of echiuroids. In a more closely related form of association, one of the partners is more or less dependent on the other for food.

The classic example of commensalism is provided by the hermit crab *Eupagurus*, which shares its shell with the worm *Nereis* (inside) and the sea anemone *Calliactis* (on the outside). The worm clearly benefits by protection and by taking food from the host, and the anemone confers some protection to the crab in return for food and mobility. Full parasitism is common in coastal life, and the gaining organism is often highly modified for life within the tissues of the host. The isopod *Portunion* and the cirripede *Sacculina*, both of which live on the shore crab *Carcinus*, are quite nondescript sacs of breeding tissue as adults. Copepod parasites infest a wide variety of shore animals: in some the larval stage is parasitic, and the adult stage is free-living but does not feed; in others the larval stage is free and later becomes modified. The typical parasitic worms, the trematodes and cestodes, infest shallow water and intertidal animals no more than they do animals of nonmarine habitats, but the various complications of their life histories are interesting.

Perhaps the most abundant parasites in typical shore animals are representatives of the protozoan group Sporozoa. Many of these infest the whole population of the host animals (*e.g.*, in *Arenicola*) to which they presumably do little damage.

On the shore and in shallow water, true mutual associations, or symbiosis, in which each partner is to some extent dependent on the other, are mostly between animals on the one hand and unicellular algae (zooxanthellae) on the other. Examples of this symbiosis are found in coelenterates, turbellarians, and mollusks, but the best known are those in which zooxanthellae are found in the reef-building corals and in the giant clams (*Tridacna*). The coral animals receive as much benefit as the plants; the latter take up the animal's excretory products, which the plant uses in order to grow; in return the plant excretes glucose and other organic compounds needed by the animal. The corals themselves are not especially changed by this association, though it clearly limits the level in the sea at which they can grow. The giant clams are highly modified, however, having on either side of the shell opening large flaps of tissue displaying an algal "garden."

Productivity of coastal communities. The large seaweeds are the most obvious primary producers of energy-containing matter. In the northern, cool temperate regions, the fresh weight of brown seaweeds such as *Ascophyllum* can reach 32 kilograms per square metre of shore, and one kilometre of shoreline may hold up to 40 metric tons of one species of laminarian. The annual production of new organic matter from these plants averages about 10 to 20 metric tons per hectare per year. This production on rocky shores may be compared with

Commensalism

Mutualism

values of 20 to 30 metric tons per hectare per year from the best cultivated crops on land, and 30 to 75 metric tons per hectare per year from salt marshes and tropical swamps.

The algal symbionts in animal tissue are a special case. Primary production in coral may be as high as 30 to 40 metric tons per hectare per year, though the algal biomass may be no more than 0.7 kilograms dry weight per square metre. Of this, the larger proportion belongs to filamentous algae growing within the reef structure below the animal tissue, and not to the symbiotic algae. The total animal tissues in a coral reef may reach 0.2 kg/m^2, and it appears that the primary production just about balances the needs of this animal tissue.

The phytoplankton in the sea is the least productive in terms of unit area and is generally found to be about one to five metric tons per hectare per year. The relatively greater production of coastal communities is a matter of greater actual utilization of energy in the shallow-water habitat and a better supply of nutrients circulated by vigorous water movements.

The production of animal organic matter, the so-called secondary production, is always less than the primary production on which it is based. On rocky shores the animal biomass may include 0.2 to 0.3 kilograms dry organic matter per square metre of barnacles, 0.2 to 2 kg/m^2 of mussels, but only 60–100 g/m^2 of littorinids. The barnacle zone of the midlittoral zone of a Pacific shore has been shown to contain 315 g/m^2 algal tissue, 2.2 kg/m^2 of barnacles and other filter feeders, and 130 g/m^2 of limpets, winkles, top shells, and other herbivores. In limpet-dominated communities, there may be only from 20 to 50 g/m^2 of these herbivores, and since many of them live a long time and grow slowly, the annual production will be very much less.

In sand and mud communities the biomass can be even smaller. For example, high values of the order of 20 to 80 g/m^2 of clams and 4 to 12 g/m^2 of lugworms (*Arenicola*) have been noted in favourable places, but average shores of muddy sand show a total biomass of only 1 to 15 g/m^2, of which the largest component is *Arenicola*. There are as yet no estimates of production of animal matter in the whole community of a sand or mud shore, but in warm waters the small clams may grow fast enough to show an annual production of two to three times the biomass, which is, however, very small (0.2 g/m^2).

It seems that of the high primary production of shore communities, only a small proportion, less than one-tenth, is turned into animal matter, even less if allowance is made for the contribution of organic matter from the land and the ocean. The shore is less efficient overall than the ocean in spite of having higher primary production, and much of the organic matter of the shore is lost to other communities—*e.g.*, to coastal plankton; to benthic life below the level at which seaweeds grow; and to land animals. (A.J.So.)

MANMADE COASTAL FEATURES

Heroic attempts to halt coastal recession involve covering bases of sea cliffs by concrete, masonry, or heavy riprap. In many parts of the world, low coasts have not been permitted to remain in their natural condition. Harbour works, man-made land, and excavation of complex marinas come to mind. Piers and moles are built for commercial or recreational reasons, and some are protected by breakwaters. Coastal engineering dates from at least the 2nd century BC, when an unsuccessful groin was constructed to preserve the harbour of Ephesus (Turkey). The coast there has now returned to its natural condition, except that it lies more than four miles seaward of the abandoned port. Breakwaters, sea walls, and other defenses against the sea line thousands of miles of coast. Some jetties have succeeded in increasing flow velocities enough to deepen bars across river channels, permitting larger ships to enter. Striking examples include the Sulina mouth of the Danube and the South Pass jetties of the Mississippi.

Breakwaters and groins protect many large, and countless numbers of small, harbours. Massive, solid structures of concrete or heavy riprap are being superseded by irregularly shaped metal or concrete solids that admit some flow and create complex turbulence, somewhat imitating faces of coral reefs. An important factor contributing to the success of these structures is their effectiveness in creating foam, because a wave consisting of admixed water and air exerts less impact pressure than one composed only of water. In some structures, through-flow is prevented by covering central cores of structures with sheets of durable plastic, a practice gaining popularity in Japan.

Groins jut out from thousands of miles of coasts; they are placed to deflect waves or to accumulate sand on their upcurrent sides. Groins have successfully preserved beaches of Belgium because they diminish transport of sand toward the coast of The Netherlands. Accumulation of sand on one side of a groin, however, accelerates erosion beyond the side opposite. Protection of a harbour at Santa Barbara, California, resulted in disastrous erosion of valuable property downcurrent. The Malibu Beach, near Los Angeles, now has a sawtooth outline, with teeth spaced at distances determined by groins. Private individuals often construct groins to protect their property, with a result that neighbours may experience severe losses.

Expensive efforts are made to preserve or nourish beaches used for recreation. Groins are built and sand may be brought in from distant sources. A fairly adequate beach is maintained west from Biloxi, Mississippi, by offshore dredging, sand being replenished after severe storms. Natural alongshore transport is aided in some places by pumping of sand across inlets.

Although there has been notable improvement in the design of defenses against the sea, engineers commonly lack adequate scientific information concerning the problems they face. In many cases it is uneconomic to design against storms of extreme severity because they occur so infrequently. (R.J.R.)

BIBLIOGRAPHY. A. GUILCHER, *Morphologie littorale et sousmarine* (1954; Eng. trans., *Coastal and Submarine Morphology*, 1958), the most authoritative modern book on seacoasts; D.W. JOHNSON, *Shore Processes and Shoreline Development* (1919, reprinted 1965), an influential classical treatment, although no longer considered completely authoritative; G.H. LAUFF (ed.), *Estuaries* (1967), a symposium volume containing contributions of scientists throughout the world on practically all processes that occur within estuaries; R.J. RUSSELL, *River Plains and Sea Coasts* (1967), a brief, copiously illustrated treatment of processes involved in creating alluvial and coastal features in many parts of the world; F.P. SHEPARD, *The Earth Beneath the Sea* (1959), a book containing a considerable amount of coastal information and material of popular interest, although the emphasis is geological; and *Submarine Geology*, 2nd ed. (1963), an authoritative work including technical discussions of the processes acting upon shores and a classification of seacoasts; J.A. STEERS, *The Coastline of England and Wales*, 2nd ed. (1964), an authoritative work including detailed descriptions and discussions of processes and matters of general interest; H. VALENTINE, *Die Küsten der Erde* (1952), an interesting work containing a popular classification scheme; V.P. ZENKOVITCH, *Processes of Coastal Development* (1967; orig. pub. in Russian, 1962), an important monograph on the results of coastal investigations in the U.S.S.R.

Life along seacoasts: J.H. BARRETT and C.M. YONGE, *Collins Pocket Guide to the Sea Shore* (1958), the best general book on northern European shores (many of these animals and plants also found in New England and eastern Canada); I. BENNETT, *The Fringe of the Sea* (1967), a splendidly illustrated introduction to coastal life of the Southern Hemisphere; N.A. HOLME and A.D. MCINTYRE (eds.), *Methods for the Study of Marine Benthos* (1971), a biological handbook with a section on coastal life and on primary production of coastal communities; J.R. LEWIS, *The Ecology of Rocky Shores* (1964), a detailed, well-illustrated treatment of zonation on rocky shores in the British Isles; G.E. and N. MacGINITE, *The Natural History of Marine Animals*, 2nd ed. (1968), extensive information on the behaviour of Pacific coast animals, including commensalism and other associations; J.A.C. NICOL, *The Biology of Marine Animals*, 2nd ed. (1967), an account of how marine animals live, eat, respire, excrete, and behave; A.J. SOUTH-WARD, "The Zonation of Plants and Animals on Rocky Sea Shores," *Biol. Rev.*, 33:137–177 (1958), brief descriptions of shores in all parts of the world and a discussion on the causes of zonation; T.A. and A. STEPHENSON, *World Between Tide-marks* (1971), a summary of the Stephensons' investigations of sea shore life and zonation in both hemispheres, together with a review of other investigations in places not visited by the Stephensons; L.A. ZENKEVITCH, *Biology of the Seas of the U.S.S.R.* (1963), a translation providing valuable insight into Russian work on coastal communities and their production, including data on North Atlantic and North Pacific coasts.

(R.J.R./A.J.So.)

Cobalt Products and Production

Cobalt, a chemical element long known in impure compounds as a source of beautiful blue colours, has contemporary importance in many branches of science and industry. In both its pure and combined states, cobalt closely resembles iron and nickel, metals with which it is associated in the periodic table of elements.

The chemical and physical properties of the element and its occurrence are dealt with in the articles TRANSITION ELEMENTS AND THEIR COMPOUNDS; ORE DEPOSITS.

History. Ores containing cobalt have been used since antiquity as pigments to impart a blue colour to porcelain and glass. It was not until 1742, however, that a Swedish chemist, Georg Brandt, showed that the blue colour was due to a previously unidentified metal, cobalt.

In 1874 the output of cobalt from European deposits was surpassed by production in New Caledonia; in about 1905, Canadian ores assumed the leadership. Since 1920 the dominant world producer has been the Belgian Congo, now Zaire. Other important producers are the Soviet Union, Zambia, Australia, Morocco, Finland, Cuba, and West Germany.

Trends in consumption

Prior to World War I, most of the world's production of cobalt was consumed in the ceramic and glass industries. The cobalt, in the form of cobalt oxide, served as a colouring agent. Since that war, increasing amounts have been used in magnetic and high-temperature alloys and in other metallurgical uses; about 80 percent of the output is now employed in the metallic state.

Mining, refining, and recovery. Because nearly all cobalt is derived from ores of copper, copper–nickel, or nickel, conventional underground or open-pit-mining techniques are employed.

In the copper–cobalt ore bodies of Central Africa and the Soviet Union, cobalt occurs as sulfides (carrollite, linnaeite, or siegenite) and as the oxidized minerals heterogenite (hydrated cobalt oxide), asbolite (mixture of manganese and cobalt oxides), and the carbonate sphaerocobaltite. In the copper–nickel–iron sulfide mines of Canada, Australia, the Soviet Union, and other regions, cobalt is present as a substitute for nickel in many minerals.

Cobalt arsenides, such as smaltite, safflorite, and skutterudite, with the sulfoarsenide cobaltite and the arsenate erythrite, are mined in Morocco and on a much smaller scale in many other countries.

Huge nickel-containing deposits found in New Caledonia, Cuba, Celebes, and other countries contain a small quantity of cobalt in the form of oxidized minerals, such as asbolite.

A few pyrite (iron disulfide) deposits mined for their sulfur content contain enough cobalt to warrant the extraction of the latter from the roasted residue. Cobalt sulfides occasionally occur in lead–zinc deposits in quantities sufficient to justify their recovery.

Cobalt ores, like those of most metals, usually require concentration (beneficiation) before production of a refined product. Such concentrating processes may include hand sorting, separation by gravity or magnetic means, and a variety of techniques based on heating and leaching.

In copper–nickel–iron sulfide ores, cobalt accompanies nickel to the refinery. In an electrolytic nickel refinery, the cobalt is precipitated out of the impure solution surrounding the anode, is purified, and finally electrolyzed. In the purification processes, the impure cobalt solution is treated with sodium hypochlorite, precipitating the cobalt as cobaltic hydroxide and leaving nickel in solution. If nickel is being refined by the carbonyl process (see NICKEL PRODUCTS AND PRODUCTION), the residues are roasted and then leached, a process in which a liquid is allowed to percolate through the roasted residue. Copper and iron are removed from the solution, and cobalt is separated by sodium hypochlorite. Another refining process for nickel sulfide concentrates consists of leaching with acid or ammonia solutions at high temperature and pressure, followed by successive precipitation of nickel and cobalt from the solution by adding hydrogen.

For copper–cobalt ores, a sulfide concentrate is roasted under controlled conditions to transform most of the cobalt sulfide to sulfate while minimizing the change of copper and iron to their water-soluble states. The product is leached, and the resulting solution is treated to remove copper and iron, and the cobalt is finally recovered by electrolysis. If the copper and cobalt ores are in the oxidized state, copper can be removed by electrolysis in sulfuric acid solution, and the cobalt precipitated from the spent electrolyte by adjustment of the acidity of the solution. Cobalt is again eventually obtained in the metallic state by electrolysis.

Concentrates of cobalt arsenides are smelted with coke and limestone in a blast furnace. After several specialized treatments of the impure mass, cobalt is precipitated by sodium hypochlorite. Arsenical ores can also be treated by leaching and precipitating the cobalt with hydrogen as with nickel sulfide concentrates.

Recovery from production of sulfuric acid

In several countries, cobalt is recovered from the residues that remain after the roasting of pyrite for the production of sulfuric acid. The roasting operation may be controlled to yield a maximum amount of cobalt sulfate with a minimum quantity of iron sulfate; subsequent treatment gives a hydrated cobalt oxide.

Some cobalt is still obtained from high-grade oxide ores and slags of copper–cobalt smelting operations by reduction with coke and limestone in an electric furnace to produce a copper–cobalt–iron alloy. The latter is dissolved with sulfuric acid, the copper remaining insoluble. Iron is precipitated by sodium chlorate and soda ash, and cobalt finally precipitated as hydroxide by sodium hypochlorite (see also METALLURGY).

Uses of cobalt and cobalt alloys. *Cemented carbides.* In the production of a so-called cemented carbide, such as tungsten carbide, a briquetted mixture of tungsten carbide and cobalt powder is heated at a temperature above the melting point of cobalt. The latter melts and binds the hard carbides, giving them the toughness and resistance to shock needed to make carbides of practical value for machine tools, drill bits, dies, and saws. Cobalt is the most satisfactory matrix metal for this purpose and may be present in amounts from 3 to 25 percent by weight.

Cobalt-60. A radioactive form of cobalt, cobalt-60, prepared by exposing cobalt to the radiations of an atomic pile, is useful in industry and medical science. Cobalt-60 is used in place of X-rays or radium in the inspection of materials to reveal internal structure, flaws, or foreign objects. It is used in cancer therapy and as a radioactive tracer in biology and industry. The advantages of cobalt-60 over radium lie in lower cost, more homogeneous gamma radiation and softer beta radiation, which can be easily filtered out, in the absence of contamination, and in its ability to be machined or shaped in any form before irradiation to fit special requirements.

Magnetic alloys. About 25 percent of the world's cobalt output goes into magnets. Cobalt is one of three elements that exhibits magnetic properties at room temperature. (The others are iron and nickel.) It has the highest Curie point (the temperature at which the magnetic properties disappear) of any metal or alloy. For the past 50 years, the best permanent magnets have always contained a substantial quantity of cobalt.

Cobalt steels, containing 2–40 percent cobalt, are used extensively as magnets. Iron–cobalt–vanadium alloys, such as the so-called Vicalloys, are employed for ductile permanent magnets, as are the Cunicos—*i.e.*, alloys of copper, nickel, and cobalt. Another magnet alloy is iron–cobalt–molybdenum, typified by Remalloy or Comol.

Since 1930 it has been known that a series of alloys, the Alnicos, containing 6–12 percent aluminum, 14–30 percent nickel, 5–35 percent cobalt, and the balance largely iron, with small quantities of copper and titanium, make the best permanent magnets. Cobalt is also used in some soft magnetic alloys such as the Perminvar alloys of nickel–iron–cobalt, the Permendur alloys of iron–cobalt, and the cobalt ferrites. Nearly all magnetic alloys are used in electrical equipment and electronic devices (see also MAGNETS AND ELECTROMAGNETS).

High-temperature alloys. An important use for cobalt, accounting for about 25 percent of the world's output, is in the field of high-temperature steel alloys. Required in gas turbines, jet engines, and similar applications, such alloys retain their strength above 1,200° F (650° C); these alloys contain from 5 to 65 percent cobalt.

Cutting and wear-resistant alloys. The addition of 2–12 percent cobalt to tool steels enables them to be used more effectively on hard materials for which deep cuts and high speeds are required.

Cobalt improves the wear resistance of many alloys. Hard-facing materials contain 10–65 percent cobalt, and abrasion-resistant die steels usually have 0.4–4 percent cobalt (see also MACHINE TOOLS).

Glass-to-metal sealing alloys. Alloys, such as Kovar and Fernico, containing 15–25 percent cobalt, are used extensively in glass-to-metal seals because they have expansion characteristics similar to those of certain glasses.

Dental and surgical alloys. Materials containing 28–68 percent cobalt, with chromium, nickel, and molybdenum, are used in dentistry and bone surgery. They have excellent resistance to tarnish and abrasion, compatibility with mouth tissues and body fluids, high strength and stiffness, good casting properties, and low cost in comparison with precious metals.

Electroplating. For certain applications requiring smooth, bright films that are hard but relatively ductile, an alloy of cobalt–nickel is deposited instead of the conventional nickel-plating. The plating alloy may contain 1–18 percent cobalt, and the electrolyte contains both cobalt and nickel salts.

Other alloys. Cobalt-base alloys having 40–50 percent cobalt are often used as springs. Beryllium copper, used for a multitude of applications besides springs, generally contains 0.1–2 percent cobalt.

An alloy of 54 percent cobalt, 9.5 percent chromium, and 36.5 percent iron changes dimensions very little with changes in temperature. Cobalt-base alloys of 56–63 percent cobalt, with iron and chromium or vanadium, have the advantage in certain applications of very little variation in elasticity regardless of temperature.

Another alloy, a stainless steel containing 18 percent nickel and 8 percent cobalt, also has some industrial applications.

Important cobalt compounds. *Cobalt oxide.* This substance, usually prepared by heating the cobaltic hydroxide that is precipitated from cobalt-containing solutions by sodium hypochlorite, has a number of important uses in the glass and ceramics industries.

Cobalt oxide additions of from five ounces to ten pounds (140 to 4,500 grams) per ton of glass are made to impart a blue colour to structural glass, bottles, and optical filter glasses. To neutralize the yellow tint of iron in plate and window glass, small quantities of cobalt oxide, 1–45 grams (0.04–1.6 ounces) per ton of glass, are added. In the proportion of about one pound (454 grams) per ton of dry clay, cobalt oxide is also employed to neutralize the iron colour in pottery, sanitary ware, and tiles, and in larger quantities to add blue colour. A rich blue is obtained by adding 5 percent cobalt oxide to a glaze of high lead content. Thenard's blue, a turquoise, is characteristic of cobalt aluminate, whereas cobalt silicate gives a unique violet-blue shade. Cobalt oxide in white enamels neutralizes yellow caused by iron; larger amounts give a blue or black colour. In quantities of 0.2–2 percent, used in enamel coats on steel, it promotes adherence of the enamel to the metal.

Cobalt salts. Cobalt salts are usually made by the action of the appropriate acid on cobalt metal or oxide. A number of cobalt salts, particularly organic compounds, are excellent driers of paints, varnishes, and inks. Cobalt linoleates, resinates, oleates, stearates, tallates, and naphthenates, containing 4–12 percent cobalt, are used (see also PAINTS, VARNISHES, AND ALLIED PRODUCTS).

Cobalt, usually in the form of a cobalt–thoria–kieselguhr catalyst, is used in the synthesis of liquid hydrocarbons. Many other cobalt catalysts have been used for a wide variety of chemical reactions.

In many parts of the world, the content of cobalt in the soil and herbage is too low to maintain the health of cattle and sheep. The addition of a small quantity of a cobalt compound to the ration, water, salt lick, or fertilizer has become a well-established practice.

Vitamin B_{12} contains 4.3 percent cobalt; it is the only vitamin known to contain a heavy metal.

Annual world production of cobalt in the early 1970s reached about 22,000 tons. Prices of cobalt have varied little since 1930, ranging from $1.50 to $2.50 per pound. In 1971 the price for most grades was about $2 per pound, compared with that of nickel of $1.30 and of iron about $0.07.

BIBLIOGRAPHY. J.W. MELLOR, *A Comprehensive Treatise on Inorganic and Theoretical Chemistry*, vol. 14 (1935); and N.V. SIDGWICK, *The Chemical Elements and Their Compounds*, vol. 2 (1950), give a full description of the physical and chemical properties of cobalt and its compounds. The production and uses of cobalt, together with general information on the element in all its important forms, are detailed in ROLAND S. YOUNG (ed.), *Cobalt: Its Chemistry, Metallurgy, and Uses* (1961), and his *Analytical Chemistry of Cobalt* (1966), which discuss all aspects of the analytical chemistry of this metal. Statistics and notes of current interest on cobalt may be found in the *United States Bureau of Mines Mineral Yearbook* (annual). The Centre d'Information du Cobalt, Brussels, Belgium, issues *Cobalt* (quarterly), containing papers and abstracts and a variety of other technical literature.

(R.S.Y.)

Cobbett, William

The greatest English popular journalist and one of the most mettlesome figures on the political scene in the early 19th century, William Cobbett was born in Farnham, Surrey, on March 9, 1763. His father was a small farmer and innkeeper. Cobbett's memories of his early life were pleasant, and, although he moved to London when he was 19, his experiences on the land left their impressions on his life. Cobbett's careers as a journalist and, for the last three years of his life, as a member of the House of Commons were devoted to restoring his ideal of rural England in a country rapidly being transformed by the Industrial Revolution into the world's foremost manufacturing nation.

Although he embraced advanced political ideas, Cobbett was at heart not a radical but instead deeply conservative, even reactionary. His object was to use radical means to break the power of what he regarded as a selfish oligarchy and thus establish the earlier England of his imagination. In his England, political parties, the national debt, and the factory system would not exist. Instead, all classes would live in harmony on the land. Despite this seemingly backward-looking viewpoint, Cobbett's writings were widely read, in part because of his lucid, racy style but mainly because he struck a powerful chord of nostalgia at a time when rapid economic changes and war with France had produced widespread anxiety.

At the age of 21, Cobbett joined the army, in which he eventually rose to the rank of sergeant major. He taught himself English grammar and thus laid the foundation of his future career as a journalist. After serving in Canada, he returned to England in 1791 and charged certain of his former officers with corruption. Although venality was all but general in the army, indeed in the whole of public life, his charges boomeranged when the officers sought to bring countercharges against him. Rather than appear at a court-martial, Cobbett fled to France. Quickly realizing that France in the throes of revolution was

Use in Alnico magnets

Applications in glass industry

Cobbett's ideal of a bygone rural England

Cobbett, painting by an unknown artist. In the National Portrait Gallery, London.
By courtesy of the National Portrait Gallery, London

no place for an Englishman, he sailed for America, settling in Philadelphia, where he supported himself and his family by teaching English to French émigrés.

An effusive welcome accorded Joseph Priestley by radical republican groups in the United States after the radical scientist had left England in 1794 drew Cobbett into controversy. Convinced that Priestley was a traitor, Cobbett wrote a pamphlet, *Observations on the Emigration of Joseph Priestley*. It launched his career as a journalist. For the next six years he published enough writings against the spirit and practice of American democracy to fill 12 volumes. His violent journalism won him many enemies and the nickname "Peter Porcupine." After paying a heavy fine in a libel judgment, Cobbett returned to England in 1800.

The Tory government of William Pitt welcomed Cobbett and offered to subsidize his powerful pen in further publishing ventures. But Cobbett, whose journalism was entirely personal and always incorruptible, rejected the offer and in 1802 started a weekly, *Political Register*, which he published until his death in 1835. Though the *Register* at first supported the government, the Treaty of Amiens (1802) with France disgusted him, and he promptly called for a renewal of the war. Cobbett believed that commercial interests were dictating English foreign policy and were responsible for all that was wrong with the country. In 1805 he announced that England was the victim of a "System," which debauched liberty, undermined the aristocracy and the Church of England, and almost extinguished the gentry. His conviction grew in the following year after he witnessed the widely accepted corruption in parliamentary elections. Cobbett's career as an orthodox Tory was over. Advocacy of radical measures brought him into an uneasy association with reformers. Cobbett and the radicals could never be close, however, since his goals were so different from theirs.

Cobbett was at his best when condemning specific abuses. He spent two years in jail (1810–12) and paid a fine of £1,000 after denouncing the flogging of militiamen who had protested against unfair deductions from their pay. He also recognized that unrest among the poor was caused by unemployment and hunger and not, as the government had alleged, by a desire to overthrow English society. Cobbett could see no solution to economic distress without a reform of Parliament and reduction of interest on the national debt. In 1816, at the height of his influence, he was able to reach the common man by putting out the *Political Register* (denounced as Cobbett's "two-penny trash") in a cheap edition that avoided the heavy taxes on ordinary newspapers. The government, seeing sedition in even the most moderate proposals for change, repressed dissent; and the following year Cobbett was forced to flee to the United States to avoid arrest.

Founding of the *Political Register*

Renting a farm on Long Island, New York, Cobbett continued to edit and write for the *Political Register*, which was published by his agents in England. When he returned to England at the end of 1819, his influence had waned and he was insolvent. During the 1820s he supported many causes in an attempt to regain his standing and in the hope that they would lead to the changes in England's political and economic system that he desired. He unsuccessfully tried to be elected to the House of Commons in 1820 from Coventry and in 1826 from Preston. His famous tours of the countryside began in 1821 and were to lead to his greatest book, *Rural Rides*, which was an unrivalled picture of the land.

Although he had no love for the Whigs, Cobbett supported the parliamentary Reform Bill of 1832, which, despite its limited nature, he sensed was the best that could be had. In 1830 agricultural labourers in his beloved southern England had rioted in protest against their low wages. Cobbett defended them and as a result was prosecuted in 1831 by a Whig government that was anxious to prove its zeal in moving against "sedition." Acting as his own counsel, Cobbett confounded his opponents and was set free. Yet, despite this threat of another jail term, he supported his persecutors on the issue of parliamentary reform.

In 1832 Cobbett was elected to Parliament as a member from Oldham. At 69 years of age he found the nocturnal schedule of Parliament an unpleasant contrast to his lifelong preference for early rising and working in the morning. Essentially an individualist and a man of action, he chafed at parliamentary routine. Most members of the House of Commons did not respect him, and Cobbett's parliamentary career was a failure. The unnatural hours hastened his death, from influenza, on June 18, 1835.

Passionate and prejudiced, Cobbett's prose, full of telling phrases and inspired ridicule, was completely personal. He had no theoretical understanding of the complicated issues about which he wrote. While his views of the ideal society were retrograde, no one could excel him in specific criticisms of corruption and extravagance, harsh laws, low wages, absentee clergymen—indeed, nearly everything that was wrong with England.

BIBLIOGRAPHY. G.D.H. COLE, *The Life of William Cobbett*, 3rd ed. (1947), still the best biography, but should be read with JOHN W. OSBORNE, *William Cobbett: His Thought and His Times* (1966), an up-to-date reassessment of Cobbett's career in topical form; M. PEARL, *William Cobbett* (1953), an attempt at a complete bibliography; L. MELVILLE, *The Life and Letters of William Cobbett in England and America* (1913), valuable only for the correspondence of Cobbett that it contains.

(J.W.O.)

Cobden, Richard

An English politician of the early 19th century and the great apostle of international free trade, Richard Cobden was the chief public spokesman for the repeal of the Corn Laws, which taxed imported grain and thus raised the domestic price of food.

He was born on June 3, 1804, near Midhurst, Sussex, the fourth of 11 children of a poor farmer. Raised by relatives, Cobden attended a second-rate boarding school and then entered his uncle's warehouse in London. In 1828 he and two other young men set up a calico wholesale business and in 1831 opened a calico-printing mill in industrial Lancashire. He made enough money to enable him to travel abroad, and, between 1833 and 1839, he visited France, Germany, Switzerland, the United States, and the Middle East. During that period he wrote two influential pamphlets—*England, Ireland, and America* (1835) and *Russia* (1836)—in which he demanded a new approach to foreign policy, based not on attempts to maintain a balance of power but on the recognition of the prime necessity of promoting international economic expansion through the free movement of men and materials. He continued to advance similar free-trade arguments throughout his life.

Between 1839 and 1846 he became a prominent figure in British politics, devoting most of his energies to the

Cobden, pencil sketch by V. Manzano. In the West Sussex Record Office (Cobden Papers 762).
By courtesy of the Governors of Dunford and the County Archivist of West Sussex

Campaign to repeal the Corn Laws

repeal of the British Corn Laws, which he maintained were both economically disastrous and morally wrong. In his view, the only class that benefitted from protection were the landlords, and they were enriched at the expense of the middle classes and working classes alike. He proved himself a brilliant organizer, building up the Anti-Corn Law League, which became a national organization in 1839 and the most efficient and successful of all 19th-century British pressure groups. He entered Parliament in 1841, one year after he had married a Welsh girl, Catherine Williams. Thereafter, he could conduct his political campaign not only by mobilizing public opinion but also by directly confronting Sir Robert Peel, the prime minister, in debate. Cobden played a considerable part in converting Peel to take the momentous and controversial decision to repeal the Corn Laws in 1846. Peel then paid a remarkable tribute to Cobden as the man whose name, above all others, ought to be associated with the measure.

The seven-year struggle established Cobden's reputation but left him financially ruined. A public subscription was raised for him in 1847, and, with part of the proceeds, he bought the house in Sussex where he had been born and continued to live there for the rest of his life with his wife and five daughters (his only son died suddenly in 1856). Unlike most of the radicals who shared his views, Cobden came from the south of England. Nor was he—as most of them were—a religious dissenter but rather was a member of the Church of England. Yet he and the Quaker John Bright were the acknowledged leaders of what came to be called the Manchester school, which espoused free trade and an economic system free of government interference. He sat in Parliament for the West Riding of Yorkshire from 1847 to 1857 and for Rochdale, Bright's hometown, from 1859 to his death.

His association with Bright was close. They were at one in believing that free trade would result in the reduction of armaments and the promotion of international peace. They were at one also in demanding a reduction of taxation and a check on imperial expansion. One of Cobden's most powerful pamphlets, *1793 and 1853, in Three Letters* (1853), was a plea to his contemporaries to avoid "past errors" and keep out of war with France. During the next three years, he argued eloquently that Britain should be friendly with Russia, even after the Crimean War had begun. He was bitterly attacked for his opinions during the war, when he and Bright often seemed to be standing alone in face of belligerent public opinion. In 1857 he was successful in rallying members from all sides of the House of Commons to support a motion criticizing the aggressive China policy of Lord Palmerston, the prime minister. At the general election that followed, however, Palmerston won overwhelming national support, and Cobden lost his seat.

Position on imperialism

The attacks and his defeat strengthened his radicalism on domestic issues, and he was openly scornful of Palmerston's middle class supporters. He was ill at ease during the political lull of the early 1860s, when there seemed to be little interest in political reform. Indeed, he asked the working classes in 1861 why they did not have a leader among them who could lead a revolt against their political tormentors. He demanded a system of universal education and, after some initial hesitation, was a staunch supporter of the North during the American Civil War. There was no 19th-century Englishman who had a more confident belief in the future of America than Cobden. His correspondence with Charles Sumner, an American statesman who supported the abolition of slavery, provided an important unofficial contact between Britain and the United States.

The most important activity of the last years of his life was his successful attempt to improve relations between Britain and France. Despite the differences in their political views, Palmerston had invited Cobden to join his broad-based ministry in 1859 as president of the Board of Trade. Cobden declined, but he worked indefatigably for a commercial treaty with France in 1860. The "most favoured nation clause" incorporated in the treaty, which stipulated that neither party could enforce against the other any prohibition on imports or exports that did not also apply to other nations, was to be duplicated in many later agreements with other nations. Cobden did not live long enough to see the eclipse of his free-trade hopes, which continued to be shared by the Cobden Club, founded to perpetuate his principles. The strain of the protracted Anglo-French negotiations undermined his health, and he had to spend many months outside London. He died on April 2, 1865, having made a last effort to leave his sickbed and attend Parliament to vote against new expenditures on national fortifications.

BIBLIOGRAPHY. The standard edition of Cobden's speeches was edited by J. BRIGHT and J.E. THOROLD ROGERS, *Speeches on Questions of Public Policy*, 2 vol. (1870). The classic biography is J. MORLEY, *The Life of Richard Cobden* (1881), but it can be usefully supplemented by J.A. HOBSON, *Richard Cobden* (1918), which examines his life in world perspectives. D. READ, *Cobden and Bright* (1967), is the chronicle of their close political friendship, but it makes no use of original manuscripts.

(As.B.)

Cocoa Production

Cacao, a tropical plant indigenous to the equatorial regions of the Americas, produces the cocoa bean from which cocoa powder and chocolate are made. The plant was cultivated more than 3,000 years ago by the Mayas, Toltecs, and Aztecs, who prepared a beverage from the bean (sometimes using it as a ceremonial drink) and also used the bean as a currency.

Columbus brought cocoa beans to Spain after his fourth voyage in 1502, and the Spanish conquistadores, arriving in Mexico in 1519, were introduced to a chocolate beverage by the Aztecs.

Early uses of cocoa

The Aztec beverage was made from sun-dried shelled beans, probably fermented in their pods. The broken kernels, or nibs, were roasted in earthen pots, then ground to paste in a concave stone, called a *metate*, over a small fire. Vanilla and various spices and herbs were added, and maize (corn) was sometimes used to produce milder flavour. The paste, formed into small cakes, was cooled and hardened on shiny leaves placed under a tree. The cakes were broken up, mixed with hot water, and beaten to foamy consistency with a small wooden beater, a molinet, producing the beverage called *xocoatl* (from Nahuatl words meaning "bitter water").

Too bitter for European taste, the mixture was sweetened with sugar when introduced to the Spanish court. Although Spain guarded the secret of its *xocoatl* beverage for almost 100 years, it reached Italy in 1606 and became popular in France with the marriage of the Spanish princess Maria Theresa to Louis XIV in 1660. In 1657 a Frenchman opened a London shop, selling solid chocolate to be made into the beverage, and chocolate

Illustrative Cocoa Crops*

	1901		1940		1980	
	tons (000)	percent of world production	tons (000)	percent of world production	tons (000)	percent of world production
Africa	20	17.4	452	66.3	1,021	59.4
Cameroon	1	0.9	27	4.0	121	7.0
Ghana	1	0.9	242	35.5	281	16.4
Guinea	1	0.9	16	2.4	9	0.5
Ivory Coast	...	...	45	6.6	358	20.8
Nigeria	...	...	107	15.7	193	11.2
São Tomé e Príncipe	17	14.7	7	1.0	9	0.5
Togo	...	...	5	0.7	20	1.2
Other Africa	...	...	3	0.4	30	1.7
America	59	51.3	173	25.4	568	33.1
Brazil	18	15.7	118	17.3	324	18.9
Ecuador	23	20.0	11	1.6	105	6.1
Mexico	1	0.9	1	0.2	40	2.3
Venezuela	9	7.8	15	2.2	19	1.1
Other America	8	6.9	28	4.1	80	4.7
West Indies	31	27.0	46	6.8	40	2.3
Dominican Republic	7	6.2	24	3.6	35	2.0
Trinidad and Tobago	12	10.4	11	1.6	2	0.1
Other West Indies	12	10.4	11	1.6	2	0.1
Asia and Oceania	5	4.3	10	1.5	89	5.2
Malaysia	...	...	...	...	36	2.1
Papua New Guinea	...	...	...	...	33	1.9
Philippines	1	0.9	1	0.2	4	0.2
Other Asia and Oceania	4	3.4	9	1.3	16	0.9
World total	115	100.0	681	100.0	1,717	100.0

* Figures may not add to totals given because of rounding.
Sources: *World Agricultural Production and Trade, Statistical Report*, 1971; *Monthly Bulletin of Statistics*, September 1981.

houses, selling the hot beverage, soon appeared throughout Europe. By 1765 chocolate manufacture had begun in the American colonies at Dorchester, Massachusetts, using cocoa beans from the West Indies.

In 1828 C.J. van Houten of The Netherlands patented a process for obtaining "chocolate powder" by pressing much of the cocoa butter from the ground and roasted cocoa beans. In 1847 the English firm of Fry and Sons combined cocoa butter, a by-product of the pressing, with chocolate liquor and sugar to produce eating chocolate, and in 1876 Daniel Peter of Switzerland added dried milk to make milk chocolate. The proliferation of flavoured, solid, and coated chocolate foods rapidly followed.

Starting in the Americas, in an area from southern Mexico to northern South America, commercial cacao cultivation spread around the world to areas within 20° of the Equator where rainfall, temperatures, and soil conditions were suitable for its growth. Consumption approximately equals production, which increased from 115,000 tons in 1901 to 1,485,000 tons in 1965 and 1,717,000 tons in 1980. In the late 1970s, West Africa was producing about 60 percent of the world's cocoa crops.

CULTIVATION

Cacao tree: description, pests, and diseases. The cacao tree (*Theobroma cacao*), an evergreen, is a lower canopy forest tree that matures at a height of between 20 and 40 feet (6 to 12 metres) and usually reaching only to the lower end of this height range. It thrives usually at altitudes of from 100 to 1,000 feet above sea level, in areas where the temperature range does not fall below 65° F (18° C) or rise to much above 85° to 90° F (29° to 32° C). Rainfall requirements depend upon both the frequency and distribution of rain and the degree of water retention by the soil; the minimum rainfall is 40 inches (1,000 millimetres) per year with good distribution and may be, under some circumstances, as much as 200 inches per year. Successful cultivation also requires deep, well-drained soil, porous and rich in humus; protection against strong winds, because of the shallow root system; and insect and disease control.

The flowers, which can be present at all times, appear in abundance twice a year. Growing from "flower cushions" on the trunk and limbs and reaching about ¼ inch in height and breadth, they have no aroma and, depending on the species, can be white, rosy coloured, pink, yellow, or bright red (see Figure 1).

The fruit develops into small elliptical pods, or cherelles, maturing within four to six months to a length of 6–10 inches and a width of 3–4 inches at the centre. Each pod yields 20 to 40 seeds, or cocoa beans, arranged around a longitudinal axis; the seeds are covered with a sweet-sour-tasting, white mucilaginous pulp. The beans are dicotyledonous (two seed leaves), oval shaped, and about 1–1½

Production and consumption

By courtesy of (left) OAS, (centre) Cia. Shell de Venezuela; photograph, (right) Richard Harrington—Three Lions Inc.

Figure 1: (Left) Buds and flowers sprouting from the bark of a cacao tree. (Centre) Cocoa pods that have formed on the trunk of the tree. (Right) A cocoa pod severed lengthwise to show the beans covered with white pulp before fermentation.

inches long. After fermentation and drying, 20 to 30 cocoa beans of most species will weigh one ounce (28 grams).

The most commonly destructive diseases of the cacao tree are black pod and swollen shoot. Black pod is caused by a fungus (*Phytophthora*) spreading rapidly on the pods under conditions of excessive rain and humidity, insufficient sunshine, and temperatures below 70° F (21° C). Control requires timely treatment with sprays of copper salts and constant removal of infected pods. Swollen shoot is caused by viruses, which have eluded permanent identification through mutation of sufficient scope. A plant immune to a specific form is vulnerable to the mutation, and the only useful measure is to cut out and destroy diseased trees.

Other fungus diseases harmful to the cacao tree are witches' broom, monilia, and ceratocystis, found in the Americas and West Indies. Such common diseases as cherelle (young pod) wilt, cushion galls, and dieback are not yet thoroughly understood and may result from a combination of physiological, viral, nutritional, and fungal conditions. Many different insects cause vegetative and crop damage to cacao, but the most important commercially is the capsid family, to be found primarily in West Africa, where the major portion of the world crop is grown. Capsids attack the tree canopy, quickly destroying major portions of a developing crop if not controlled by diligent spraying with insecticides. Mass control of capsids contributed to the increase in African crops between 1958 and 1963.

Commercial plantings. Most of the world's cacao is grown on small farms, two to five acres (from less than one to 2.5 hectares) in size. Plantings, from seeds, seedlings, or cuttings, are spaced at intervals that range anywhere from five to 15 feet. The tree begins bearing satisfactory fruit between its third and eighth years, depending on the strain. Commercial cocoa-bean crop yields may vary from as little as 100 to as much as 1,400 pounds per acre (110 to 1,600 kilograms per hectare), with the world average probably ranging between 200 and 300 pounds per acre.

Although cultivation in a few isolated areas is as highly sophisticated as modern orchard care anywhere, most of the world's cacao crop is grown on small peasant farms with cultivation limited to provision for shade from higher tree canopies, weeding, a small amount of pruning, and spraying against fungus and insects. It is estimated that, with modest application of proven cultivation practices, the same acreage could yield crops two to four times greater than those that have been produced.

Harvesting. Harvesting can proceed all year, but the bulk of the crop is gathered in the two flush periods occurring from October to February and from May to August. The ripe pods are cut from the trees and split open with machetes. The beans, removed from the pods with their surrounding pulp, are accumulated in leaf-covered heaps, in leaf-lined holes dug in the ground, or in large shallow boxes that have perforated bottoms to provide for drainage.

Fermentation. The pulp of common grades (Forastero) is allowed to ferment for five to seven days, and the pulp of the more distinctively flavoured grades (Criollo) for one to three days. Frequent turnings dissipate excess heat and provide uniformity. During fermentation, the juicy sweatings of the pulp are drained away, the germ in the seed is killed by the increased heat, and flavour development begins. The beans become plump and full of moisture, and the interior develops a reddish-brown colour and a heavy, sharp fragrance. The fermented beans are sun-dried or kiln-dried to reduce moisture content to 6–7 percent and are bagged for shipment.

COCOA PROCESSING AND PRODUCTS

Figure 2 shows the steps involved in processing.

Cleaning and grinding. Cocoa beans are subjected to various cleaning processes to remove such contaminants as twigs, stones, and dust. Roasting develops flavour, reduces acidity and astringency, lowers moisture content, deepens colour, and facilitates shell removal. In the crack-

Black pod and swollen shoot diseases

ing and fanning (winnowing) process, machines crack the shells, then separate them from the heavier nibs by means of blowers. The cell walls of the nibs are in turn broken by grinding, releasing the fat, or cocoa butter, which forms a paste called chocolate liquor, or cocoa mass. In the production of alkalized (Dutched) chocolate liquor, the raw cocoa beans may be winnowed and the raw nibs alkalized and then roasted prior to grinding.

Conching. Conching, a flavour-developing, aerating, and emulsifying procedure, performed by conche machines, requires from four to 72 hours, depending upon the results desired and the machine type. Temperatures used in this process range from 130° F (54° C) to 190° F (88° C) and are closely controlled to obtain the desired flavour and uniformity.

Molding. In molding, the chocolate is cast in small consumer-size bars or in blocks weighing about 10 pounds for use by confectioners and then subjected to cold air to produce hardening.

Cocoa powders. Cocoa powders are produced by pulverizing cocoa cakes, made by subjecting the chocolate liquor, with about 53 to 56 percent cocoa butter content, to hydraulic pressing to remove a predetermined amount of cocoa butter. The cocoa butter content remaining in the powder may range from 8 to 36 percent, with the most common commercial grades in the United States containing 11, 17, or 22 percent cocoa butter. In Great Britain, cocoa sold for beverage use must contain a minimum of 20 percent.

Cocoa butter content

Natural process. Natural process cocoa powders and chocolate liquors receive no alkali treatment. Cocoa beans are normally slightly acid, with a pH of 5.2–5.8. When the pH remains unchanged, the beans produce pleasantly sharp flavours blending well in many foods and confections.

Dutch process. Dutch process cocoa powders and chocolate liquors are treated at either the nib, liquor, or powder stage. The treatment is frequently referred to as "Dutching" because the process, first applied by C.J. van Houten in The Netherlands, was introduced as "Dutch cocoa." In this alkalizing process, a food-grade alkali solution may be applied to partially neutralize the natural cocoa acids, composed primarily of acetic acid, like that found in vinegar, or it may be used to produce a strictly alkaline product, with a pH as high as 8.0. Potassium carbonate is most commonly used as an alkalizer, although other alkalies, such as sodium carbonate, may be used. In addition to altering the pH of the cocoa powder, the process darkens colour, mellows flavour, and alters taste characteristics.

Chocolate products. Chocolate products usually require the addition of more cocoa butter to that already existing in the chocolate liquor.

Baking chocolate. Baking (bitter) chocolate, popular for household baking, is pure chocolate liquor made from finely ground nibs, the broken pieces of roasted, shelled cocoa beans. This chocolate, bitter because it contains no sugar, can be either the natural or alkalized type.

Sweet chocolate. Sweet chocolate, usually dark in colour, is made with chocolate liquor, sugar, added cocoa butter, and such flavourings as vanilla beans, vanillin, salt, spices, and essential oils. Sweet chocolate usually contains at least 15 percent chocolate liquor content, the average being between 25 and 35 percent. The ingredients are blended, refined (ground to a smooth mass), and conched. Viscosity is then adjusted by the addition of more cocoa butter or lecithin (an emulsifier), or by a combination of the two.

Milk chocolate. Milk chocolate is formulated by substituting whole milk solids for a portion of the chocolate liquor used in producing sweet chocolate. It usually contains at least 10 percent chocolate liquor and 12 percent whole milk solids. Manufacturers usually exceed these values, frequently using 12–15 percent chocolate liquor and 15–20 percent whole milk solids. Milk chocolate, which is usually lighter in colour than sweet chocolate, is sweeter or milder in taste because of its lower content of bitter chocolate liquor. Processing is similar to that of sweet chocolate. "Bitter chocolate" refers to either bak-

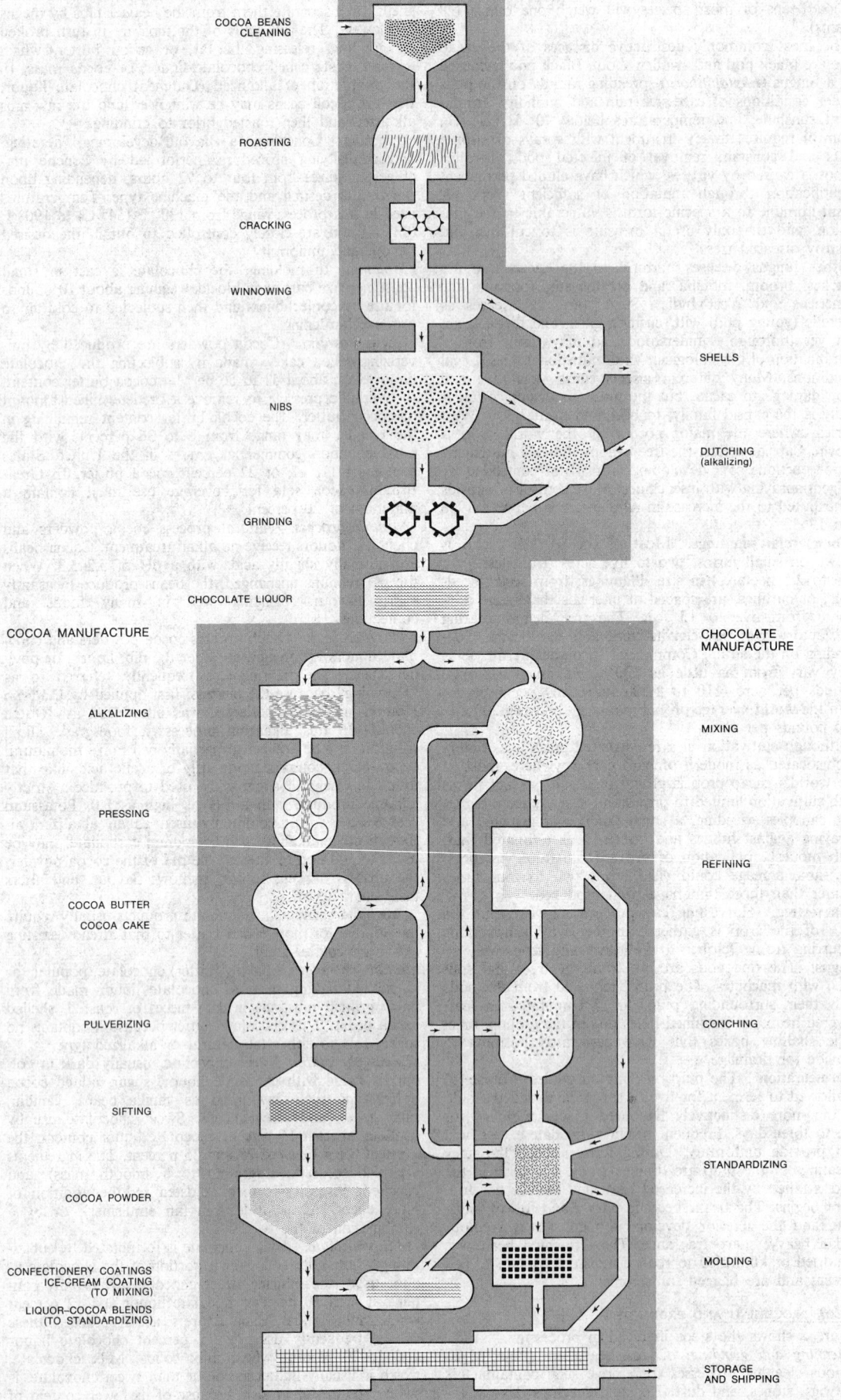

COCOA BEANS
CLEANING

ROASTING

CRACKING

WINNOWING

SHELLS

NIBS

DUTCHING
(alkalizing)

GRINDING

CHOCOLATE LIQUOR

COCOA MANUFACTURE

CHOCOLATE
MANUFACTURE

ALKALIZING

MIXING

PRESSING

REFINING

COCOA BUTTER
COCOA CAKE

PULVERIZING

CONCHING

SIFTING

STANDARDIZING

COCOA POWDER

MOLDING

CONFECTIONERY COATINGS
ICE-CREAM COATING
(TO MIXING)
LIQUOR–COCOA BLENDS
(TO STANDARDIZING)

STORAGE
AND SHIPPING

Figure 2: Stages in the manufacture of cocoa and chocolate.

ing chocolate or bittersweet chocolate. Bittersweet is similar to sweet chocolate but contains less sugar and more chocolate liquor. Minimum percentages of chocolate liquor are fixed by law in some countries, such as the United States.

Chocolate-type coatings. Confectionery coatings are made in the same manner as similar chocolate types, but some or all of the chocolate liquor is replaced with equivalent amounts of cocoa powder, and instead of adding cocoa butter, with a melting point of about 90°–92° F (32°–33° C), other vegetable fats of equal or higher melting points are used. In the United States the legal name of this coating is "sweet cocoa and vegetable fat (other than cocoa fat) coatings." In the "chocolate" coating usually applied to ice cream and other frozen novelties, legally known as "sweet chocolate and vegetable fat (other than cocoa fat) coatings," the cocoa butter usually added to chocolate is replaced by lower melting point vegetable fats, such as coconut oil.

The various forms of chocolate are available for home use in consumer-size packages and in larger bulk sizes for use by food manufacturers and confectioners. Most European confectioners make their own chocolate; other confectioners buy chocolate from chocolate-manufacturing specialists. For large commercial orders, chocolate is shipped, warm and in liquid form, in heated sanitary tank trucks or tank cars.

Cocoa production by-products. Shells, the major by-product of cocoa and chocolate manufacturing, represent 8–10 percent of raw cocoa bean weight, and they are blown off in the cracking and fanning operation. They are used for fertilizer, mulch, and fuel.

Chocolate and cocoa grades. In chocolate and cocoa products, there is no sharp difference from one grade or quality to the next. Chocolate quality depends on such factors as the blend of beans used, with about 20 commercial grades from which to choose; the kind and amount of milk or other ingredients included; and the kind and degree of roasting, refining, conching, or other type of processing employed. Chocolate and cocoa products are only roughly classified; there are hundreds of variations on the market, alone or in combination with other foods or confections.

Care and storage. Chocolate and cocoa require storage at 65°–68° F (18°–20° C), with relative humidity below 50 percent. High (80°–90° F, or 27°–32° C) or widely fluctuating temperatures cause fat bloom, a condition in which cocoa butter infiltrates the surface, turning products gray or white as it recrystallizes.

Fat bloom and mustiness

High humidity causes mustiness in cocoa powder and can lead to mold formation in cocoa powder or on chocolate. Excessive moisture can also dissolve sugar out of chocolate, redepositing it on the surface as sugar bloom, distinguished from fat bloom by its sandy texture.

Use in industry. Chocolate is used in industry by confectioners, as coating for candy bars and boxed or bulk chocolates; by bakery product manufacturers and bakers, as coating for many types of cookies and cakes; and by ice-cream companies, as coating for frozen novelties (see also CONFECTIONERY AND CANDY PRODUCTION).

Cocoa powders, chocolate liquor, and blends of the two are used in bulk to flavour various food products and provide the flavours in such "chocolate" products as syrups, toppings, chocolate milk, prepared cake mixes, and pharmaceuticals.

Nutritive value. Cocoa, a highly concentrated food containing approximately 2,214 calories per pound (1,005 calories per kilogram), provides carbohydrates, fat, protein, and minerals. Its theobromine and caffeine content produce a mildly stimulating effect. The carbohydrates and easily digested fats in chocolate make it an excellent high-energy food.

BIBLIOGRAPHY. A review of the literature on this subject may be found in W.T. CLARKE, "Early Literature on Cacao Technology," *Canad. Food Indus.*, vol. 30, no. 3, pp. 57–59 (1959), and vol. 30, no. 4, pp. 41–43 (1959). Early histories include HISTORICUS, *Cocoa: All About It* (1896); and FERNANDO COLOMBO, *Historia del almirante Don Cristóbal Colón,* 2 vol. (1892), a history of cocoa in the West Indies prior to 1892. A

text covering the cocoa and chocolate industry from the growing of cocoa beans to the finished cocoa and chocolate products is L. RUSSELL COOK, *Chocolate Production and Use* (1963, reprinted 1972). Two technical reports, proceedings of the seventh and eighth Inter-American cacao conferences, are T.A. JONES and G.K. MALIPHANT, *High Yields in Cacao Field Experiments and Their Significance in Future Cacao Research* (1958); and D.B. MURRAY, *A Ton of Cacao per Acre?* (1960), a report on research developments directed toward increasing the per-acre yield of cocoa beans. JOHN SIMMONS (ed.), *Cocoa Production: Economic and Botanical Perspectives* (1976), is a source of basic information, including a worldwide survey of research. A bibliographic source is UNITED NATIONS INDUSTRIAL DEVELOPMENT ORGANIZATION, *Information Sources on the Coffee, Cocoa, Tea, and Spices Industry* (1977).

(L.R.C.)

Cocteau, Jean

Probably the most versatile artist of the 20th century, Jean Cocteau achieved distinction as a poet, novelist, dramatist, filmmaker, essayist, ballet designer, and painter. Yet, because of the eccentricity of his behaviour and the obscurity of much of his work, his importance was continually questioned and reassessed during his lifetime. Ultimately it became clear that his long career had been motivated not by an ambition to shock or to amuse but by his profound conviction in a supernatural force that directs the natural forces of the artist. In the poetic universe in which he believed, the arts could not be separated.

Gisele Freund

Cocteau, 1939.

Jean Cocteau was born on July 5, 1889, in Maisons-Laffitte, near Paris, but grew up in Paris and always considered himself Parisian by speech, education, ideas, and habits. His family was of the solid Parisian bourgeoisie—cultivated, wealthy, and interested in music, painting, and literature.

Heritage and youth

Cocteau's earliest memories had to do with the theatre, in popular forms, such as the circus and the ice palace, as well as serious theatre, such as the tragedies performed at the Comédie-Française. At 19, he published his first volume of poems, *La Lampe d'Aladin.* Cocteau was the product of the years immediately preceding World War I; years of refined artistic taste that were devoid of political turmoil. His real exploration of the world of the theatre began when he encountered the Ballets Russes, then under the direction of Sergey Diaghilev. When Cocteau expressed a desire to create ballets, Diaghilev challenged him to "Étonne-moi" ("Surprise me"). This famous remark seems to have guided the poet not only in his ballets, such as *Parade* (1917), with music by Erik Satie, and *Le Boeuf sur le toit* (1920), with music by Darius Milhaud, but also in his other works; and it is sometimes quoted in his plays and films.

During World War I, Cocteau served as an ambulance driver on the Belgian front. The landscape he observed there was later used in his novel *Thomas l'imposteur* (1923). He became a friend of the aviator Roland Garros and dedicated to him the early poems inspired by aviation, *Le Cap de Bonne-Espérance* (1919). At intervals during the years 1916 and 1917, Cocteau entered the world of modern art, then being born in Paris; in the bohemian Montparnasse section of the city, he met painters such as Picasso and Modigliani, and writers such as Max Jacob and Guillaume Apollinaire.

Influence of Radiguet

Soon after the war, Max Jacob introduced Cocteau to the future poet and novelist Raymond Radiguet. Then a boy of 16, he appeared to all of Picasso's group to be a young prodigy, advocating an aesthetic of simplicity, of classical clarity, qualities that would become characteristic of Cocteau's work. The example of Radiguet counted tremendously for Cocteau; and when Radiguet died in 1923, at the age of 21, the older man felt bereft of a friendship based upon a constant interchange of ideas, encouragement, and enthusiasms.

An addiction to opium, brought on by Cocteau's grief over Radiguet's death, necessitated a period of cure. Jacques Maritain, a French Thomist philosopher, paid his first visit to Cocteau in the sanatorium. Through Maritain, Cocteau returned briefly to religious practice. These complex experiences initiated a new period in his life, during which he produced some of his most important works. In the long poem *L'Ange Heurtebise* (1925) the poet engages in a violent combat with an angel that was to reappear continually in his works. His play *Orphée*, first performed in 1926, was destined to play a part in the resurrection of tragedy in contemporary theatre; in it, Cocteau deepened his interpretation of the nature of the poet. The novel *Les Enfants terribles*, written in the space of three weeks in March 1929, is the study of the inviolability of the character of two adolescents, the brother and sister Paul and Elisabeth. In 1950 Cocteau prepared the screenplay for a film of this work, and he spoke the commentary.

Cocteau had enlarged the scope of his work by the creation of his first film, *Le Sang d'un poète* (1932), a commentary on his own private mythology; the themes that then seemed obscure or shocking today seem less private and more universal because they have appeared in other works. Also in the early 1930s, Cocteau wrote what is usually thought to be his greatest play, *La Machine infernale* (1934), a treatment of the Oedipus theme that is very much his own. In these two works he moved into closer contact with the great myths of humanity.

Film making in the 1940s

In the 1940s, Cocteau returned to film making, first as a screenwriter and then also as a director in *La Belle et la bête* (1945), a fantasy based on the children's tale, and *Orphée* (1950), a re-creation of the themes of poetry and death that he had dealt with in his play.

Also a visual artist of significance, Cocteau in 1950 decorated the Villa Santo Sospir in Saint-Jean-Cap-Ferrat, and began a series of important graphic works: frescoes on the City Hall in Menton, the Chapel of Saint-Pierre in Villefranche-sur-Mer, the Church of Saint-Blaise-des-Simples in Milly-la-Forêt. His adopted son, the painter Édouard Dermit, who also appears in his later films, continued the decoration of the chapel at Fréjus, a work Cocteau had not completed at his death at Milly-la-Forêt, on October 11, 1963, at the age of 74.

Cocteau's death gave a new dimension to his work and to the legends that had grown up around his name. The judgments during his lifetime had been varied. He was variously called the restorer of Greek tragedy, as in *La Machine infernale*; the author of bourgeois drama, as in *Les Parents terribles* (1938); a classicist, as in his novel *Les Enfants terribles*; a surrealist, as in some of his poetry. Some critics thought him the type of artist given to over-repeated, over-facile emblems, such as statues, angels, roses, snow, while others regarded him as the artist who had articulated the deepest drama of his time. Nonetheless, the highest and most solemn honours came to him: an honorary degree at Oxford (1956) and membership in the Académie Royale de Langue et de Littérature Française de Belgique (1955) and the Académie Française (1955). To love and to feel himself loved were

indivisible needs of his temperament, and they lay at the basis of the artist's impulse to create and to justify his life in the eyes of friends and of all those he did not know but looked upon as friends.

MAJOR WORKS

BALLET SCENARIOS: *Parade*, to music by Erik Satie, Picasso did the backdrop (1917); *Le Boeuf sur le toit*, music by Darius Milhaud, decor by Dufy (1920); *Le Gendarme incompris*, collaboration with Raymond Radiguet, music by Poulenc (1921); *Les Mariés de la Tour Eiffel*, music by Les Six—i.e., Durey, Honegger, Milhaud, Germaine Tailleferre, Auric, and Poulenc (1921); *Les Biches*, music by Poulenc (1924); and *Les Fâcheux*, music by Auric (1924); *Le Jeune Homme et la mort*, music by Bach (1946); *Phèdre*, music by Auric (1950).

FILMS: *Le Sang d'un poète* (1932, scenario, dialogue, and direction; scenario trans. 1949); *Le Baron fantôme* (1943, dialogue only); *L'Éternel retour* (1944, scenario and dialogue); *La Belle et la bête* (1945; adaptation, direction, and dialogue); *Ruy Blas* (1947), co-directed with Pierre Billon, also dialogue; *La Voix humaine* (1947), co-directed with Rossellini; *Les Parents terribles* (1948; direction, scenario, and dialogue); *Orphée* (1950; direction, scenario, and dialogue); and *Les Enfants terribles* (1950; direction, scenario, and dialogue).

NOVELS: *Le Potomak* (1919); *Le Grand Écart* (1923; *The Grand Écart*, 1925; *The Miscreant 1913–1914*, 1958); *Thomas l'imposteur* (1923; Eng. trans. 1925 and 1957); *Le Livre blanc* (1928; *The White Paper*, 1957); *Les Enfants terribles* (1929; *Enfants Terribles*, 1930; *Children of the Game*, 1955); *Le Fantôme de Marseille* (1933); *La Fin du Potomak* (1939).

POETRY: *Le Cap de Bonne-Espérance* (1919); *L'Ode à Picasso* (1919); *Vocabulaire* (1922); *Plain-Chant* (1923); *L'Ange Heurtebise* (1925); *Opéra* (1927), a collection; *Morceaux choisis* (1932), a collection; *Allégories* (1941), a collection; *Léone* (1945); *La Crucifixion* (1946); *Le Chiffre sept* (1952); *Appogiatures* (1953); *Clair-obscur* (1954).

OTHER WRITINGS: *Opium* (1930; Eng. trans., 1932); *La Belle et la bête: Journal d'un film* (1946; Eng. trans., 1950).

PLAYS: *Romeo et Juliette* (produced and adapted 1924); *Orphée* (1926; Eng. trans., 1933); *Oedipe-roi* (produced and adapted 1937, published 1962); *La Voix humaine* (1930; Eng. trans., 1951); *La Machine infernale* (1934; Eng. trans., 1936); *L'École des veuves* (1936); *Les Chevaliers de la table ronde* (1937; Eng. trans. and production, 1955); *Les Parents terribles* (1938; Eng. trans., 1956; produced as *Intimate Relations*, 1952); *Les Monstres sacrés* (1940; Eng. trans., 1962; produced as *The Holy Terrors*, 1953); *La Machine à écrire* (1941; Eng. trans., 1962; produced as *The Typewriter*, 1948); *Renaud et Armide*, in verse (1943); *L'Aigle à deux têtes* (1946; Eng. trans., 1948); *Bacchus* (1952; Eng. trans. and production, 1955).

OTHER DRAMATIC WORKS: *Oedipus-Rex*, opera-oratorio, text to music by Stravinsky (1927; first performed in English, 1961); *Antigone*, lyric tragedy to music by Honegger (1927; performed London, 1963; published 1962).

ART: *Poésie plastique-objets-dessins* (1928); *Soixante Dessins pour Les Enfants terribles* (1934).

BIBLIOGRAPHY. *The Journals of Jean Cocteau*, ed. and trans. by WALLACE FOWLIE (1964), contains a long introduction to the writings and films of Cocteau and passages from seven of his books. These passages deal with such subjects as morality, aesthetics, and Cocteau's relationship with Apollinaire, Picasso, Proust, and other figures in art and literature. WALLACE FOWLIE, *Jean Cocteau: The History of a Poet's Age* (1966), is a study of the various genres used by Cocteau in his writings. It attempts to analyze the success or lack of success of the various works in terms of the historical moment at which they appeared. NEAL OXENHANDLER, *Scandal and Parade: The Theater of Jean Cocteau* (1957), is an analysis of the plays of Cocteau based largely on the myths behind the plays and the personal myths or legends of Cocteau himself. FRANCIS STEEGMULLER, *Cocteau: A Biography* (1970), is the most fully documented study of Cocteau's life that has yet appeared.

(W.F.)

Coen, Jan Pieterszoon

One of the outstanding figures in imperial history, Jan Pieterszoon Coen laid the foundation for the powerful 17th-century Dutch commercial empire in the East Indies (see also LOW COUNTRIES, HISTORY OF). As the fourth governor general of the Dutch East Indies, he established a chain of fortified posts in the Indonesian Archipelago, displacing the Portuguese and preventing penetration by the English. From the native chieftains he secured spice monopolies, which he ruthlessly enforced, and aimed at controlling the great volume of inter-Asian trade, hitherto ignored by European merchants. His dream of a vast maritime empire stretching from Japan to India never came to fruition, but his energetic administration established Dutch rule in Indonesia, where it remained for four centuries.

By courtesy of the Rijksmuseum, Amsterdam

Coen, oil painting by an anonymous artist, first half of the 17th century. In the Rijksmuseum, Amsterdam.

Coen, born at Hoorn, in the Dutch province of North Holland on January 8, 1587, was raised in a strict Calvinist atmosphere. He received his merchant's training from a Flemish company in Rome and in 1607 he sailed to Indonesia with the fleet of Admiral Pieter Verhoeff as assistant merchant of the Vereenigde Oostindische Compagnie, or VOC (Dutch East India Company), which had received from the Dutch government exclusive shipping and trading rights in the area from the Cape of Good Hope east to South America. While on this journey, Verhoeff and 50 of his men were killed during negotiations with the chiefs of the Banda Islands. Upon his return to Holland in 1610, Coen submitted to the Company's directors an important report on trade possibilities in Southeast Asia. As a result of this report, he was again sent overseas in 1612 with the rank of chief merchant. In August of 1613, after a trip to the Spice Islands, he was appointed head of the company's post at Bantam, in Java, and, in November of 1614, he also became director general of the company's commerce in Asia.

As a merchant and Calvinist, Coen was convinced of the necessity of strict enforcement of contracts entered into with Asian rulers. He often aided Indonesian princes against their indigenous rivals or against other European powers and was given commercial monopolies for the Company in return. In this way the Dutch, at the cost of heavy military and naval investment, gradually gained control of the area's rich spice trade. Between 1614 and 1618, Coen secured a clove monopoly in the Moluccas and a nutmeg monopoly in the Banda Islands. When the sultan of Bantam resisted his attempts to control the pepper trade, Coen transferred his headquarters to Jacatra (present Djakarta), so as to be freer to pursue his aims. In October 1617, he received news of his appointment as governor general.

In the meantime, relations had deteriorated with the English, who threatened the Dutch monopoly in the Indies. At the end of 1618 an English force, with a fleet commanded by Sir Thomas Dale, arrived at Jacatra and tried to establish a fort there. An inconclusive naval battle followed in which Coen had only a few ships at his disposal, and these loaded with precious merchandise. He gave orders to defend the Dutch fort as well as possible against the English and the Jacatrans and left for Amboina (Ambon, in the Moluccas) to reorganize his fleet.

Career as merchant

Returning to Jacatra at the end of May, he found the situation completely changed: in February, the sultan of Bantam had suddenly overpowered his Jacatran vassal, had forced the English to withdraw, and had placed the Dutch fort under siege. Coen forced the Bantams out of Jacatra on May 30th, burned the city, and on its ruins founded the Dutch city of Batavia. He later gave orders to pursue the English fleet, which had scattered over the archipelago. Coen now had available to him a fortified city in the western part of the archipelago, which soon became the centre of Dutch power in Asia.

Founding of Batavia

Word came to him, however, in March 1620 that the Dutch and English trading companies had reached an agreement in London: each would let the other engage in trading activities in the existing settlements, without interference, and a joint fleet would be outfitted against common enemies. Coen, seeing part of his work destroyed, reacted by defining the Company's "Jacatra Kingdom" as far as the sea south of Java, making it impossible for the English to claim jurisdiction over any Javanese territory whatsoever.

In January 1621, after inviting the English to participate, Coen headed an all-Dutch fleet to the Banda Islands on a campaign of conquest, on the pretext of punishing the Bandanese for disregarding previous commercial agreements. His wholesale slaughter and enslavement of the natives shocked contemporaries as unusually severe and even drew a reprimand from the Company's directors. In 1622, he sent a large expedition to the coast of China but overestimated his strength; from this, however, a Dutch settlement was established on Formosa, resulting in the foundation of a firmer base for profitable trade with Japan and China.

The VOC now maintained settlements—mostly outside their own territory—from Japan to Surat on the west coast of India and, in addition, enjoyed trade relations with Arabia and Persia. Coen thought that the time had come to attract Dutch settlers. Batavia, he hoped, would become an eastern replica of Amsterdam, with colonists handling the inter-Asian trade along the coasts of southern and eastern Asia, while the company took care of the long-haul traffic with Europe. In order to urge his plans on the directors, he left for the Netherlands in February of 1623; at first he appeared to be successful, but his plans were cut short by the so-called Amboina massacre. Shortly after his departure from Batavia, a few Englishmen in Amboina, suspected of complicity in a plot to take over the Dutch settlement, were questioned, tortured, and sentenced to death by the Dutch factors. This was considered murder in England and Coen was held morally responsible. Since, in Europe, the English and the Dutch were on friendly terms, Coen was temporarily forbidden to return to the Indies. He went back for the last time in 1627, travelling incognito and accompanied by his wife and a party of other women of good social standing, in an effort to attract Dutch settlers to Batavia. But Coen's third visit to Asia had less significance than his previous ones; after many years in the tropics he apparently no longer possessed his old energy. Moreover, his hopes for attracting free Dutch settlers were undermined by the directors' decision not to grant the colonists free-trade privileges. And, in addition, in Batavia Coen had his hands full with the attacks by the Sultan of Mataram, the most powerful ruler on Java. In August 1628 and again in August 1629 a Javanese army besieged the city. During this last siege, on Sept. 21, 1629, Coen died suddenly, probably of dysentery.

Amboina "massacre"

BIBLIOGRAPHY. The definitive work on Coen with a full bibliography of source material is H.T. COLENBRANDER and W.P. COOLHAAS, *Jan Pieterszoon Coen: Bescheiden omtrent zijn Bedrijf in Indië*, 8 vol. (1919–53). A defense of Coen's generalship is given by C. GERRETSON in *Coen's Eerherstel* (1944).

(W.Ph.C.)

Coeur, Jacques

The career of the immensely wealthy and powerful French merchant Jacques Coeur, who became councillor to King Charles VII, remains a major example of the spirit of enterprise and the social progress among the merchant classes during the early period of the rise of France after the Hundred Years' War.

Coeur was born *c.* 1395 in Bourges, a cloth-producing, commercial town in central France. The son of a furrier, he provided his own training through experience in financial operations and during a commercial trip to the Near East. After Paris was recovered from the English by Charles VII, Coeur won the confidence of the King and became an *argentier* (steward of the royal expenditure and banker of the court) and then a member of the King's council. He was put in charge of the collection of taxes, as *commissaire* in the estates' assemblies of the Languedoc region and as inspector general of the salt tax. He also was entrusted with diplomatic missions to Spain and Italy.

Coeur was ennobled in 1441, and, after arranging for the marriage of his daughter to a nobleman, he obtained the archbishopric of Bourges for his son Jean and the bishopric of Luçon for his brother. He also was able to acquire about 40 *seigneuries*, or manors, and he built a palace in Bourges, a structure that remains one of the finest lay monuments of Gothic architecture from the end of the Middle Ages.

Because of his flair for business opportunities, Jacques Coeur was able to make use of every occasion and every means to increase his wealth. Without being a real statesman, he was able to serve the state as much as he served his own interest. His position as *argentier* was the basis for all his activity. It not only gave him access to the King and to the clientele of the court but also access to merchandise from every source; his stores, located in Tours, stocked cloth, silks, jewels, armour, and spices. Coeur also augmented his fortune by dealing in salt on the Loire and the Rhône rivers, in wheat in Aquitaine, and in wool in Scotland. Montpellier, where he built a *loge*, a kind of stock exchange for the merchants, was the first centre of his Mediterranean trade. In Florence, where he was registered in the Arte della Seta (Silk Makers' Guild), he owned a workshop for the manufacture of silks.

A staff of travelling salesmen, drivers, and especially shipowners supplied his communications and transportation needs, and Coeur himself owned at least seven ships in the Mediterranean. Like the Italians, he set up individual companies for each branch of trade. He financed his businesses with credit (bills of exchange) that he obtained at fairs in Geneva, Avignon, Florence, and Rome, and by using *recettes fiscales* (fiscal receipts) from the King. He had the political support of Alfonso V, king of Aragon, and the cities of Genoa, Florence, and Barcelona, as well as the popes, who authorized his trade with the Muslims in Alexandria.

Although his wealth in real estate and personal property, his luxurious style of life, his titles, influence, and personal dynamism were impressive, Coeur's prosperity was fragile. He had few efficient associates, the risks of maritime commerce at that time were great, and his competitors, especially in Montpellier, were ruthless. He loaned a great deal of money, and the accumulated credits represented large, collateral-based loans. Either through purchase or repossession of his debtors' goods, Jacques Coeur had frozen a large part of his capital in nonproductive goods (jewelry, furniture, tapestries) or in rural properties, which yielded a low return of about 5 percent, despite careful administration. Though he always appeared to be short of money, he was rich enough to be able to lend the King funds necessary for the reconquest of Normandy in 1450 and to become creditor for a large part of the aristocracy. Coeur thus became to many people an object of envy and jealousy.

He was falsely accused of having arranged the poisoning of Agnès Sorel, mistress of Charles VII, and of having engaged in dishonest speculation. As a result of these changes, he was arrested in 1451 and condemned to remain in prison until an enormous fine was paid. With the help of friends, he escaped from prison and took refuge, first in Florence and in 1455 in Rome. On November 25 of the following year he died, probably on the Aegean island of Chios, where he had gone in command of a naval expedition organized by Pope Calixtus III against the Turks. His experience, although tragically interrupted by his death, was not without its effects. Louis XI made amends for Coeur's treatment by his father, Charles VII, by returning some of Coeur's property to his sons and by reviving enterprises that the former *argentier* had initiated: the silk workshop in Lyons and the first attempts to set up a company in the Middle East.

Jacques Coeur was representative of his generation; his ambitions for honours, noble rank, and land were traditional. His banking methods were simple and empirical, though his accounting seems to have been rudimentary. He differed from his more mediocre contemporaries by the sheer volume and extent of his trade, his audaciousness and tenacity, his self-confidence, his talent for making himself loved or hated, and especially by his flair for seizing opportunities. He understood business opportunities for his generation but was not prophetic. He was the incarnation of the rise of the merchant middle class, imitated in succeeding generations in Lyons and Tours with the same success.

The legend of Jacques Coeur remains many-faceted, and history has preserved conflicting images of him. For a long time he was seen as an adventurer, exploiting for his own profit the revenue of the kingdom and deceiving his master. The crowd, hostile to a *nouveau riche*, brought him down; he was accused of magic. By the 18th century, the century of the Enlightenment, he was regarded as a victim of despotism. An eminent 19th-century historian, Jules Michelet, however, was the first to look upon Coeur as the model for a whole generation and as a precursor of the powerful bourgeois class that developed in succeeding centuries.

BIBLIOGRAPHY. The basic biography is P. CLEMENT, *Jacques Coeur et Charles VII*, 2nd ed., 2 vol. (1866), upon which almost all later works are based: H. PRUTZ, *Jacques Coeur von Bourges: Geschichte eines patriotischen Kauffmanns aus dem 15. Jahrhundert* (1911); A.B. KERR, *Jacques Coeur: Merchant Prince of the Middle Ages* (1927); R. BOUVIER, *Jacques Coeur, un financier colonial au XVe siècle* (1952); and C.M. CHENU, *Jacques Coeur* (1962). The main source and the most coherent is the report of the sequestration of his property, M. MOLLAT (ed.), *Les Affaires de Jacques Coeur: Journal du Procureur Dauvet*, 2 vol. (1952).

(M.J.Mo.)

Coffee Production

The coffee plant, a tropical evergreen shrub or small tree of African origin (genus *Coffea*, family Rubiaceae), is cultivated for its seeds, or beans, which are roasted, ground, and sold for brewing coffee. The beverage is consumed either hot or cold by about one-third of the people in the world, in amounts larger than those of any other drink. Its popularity can be attributed to its invigorating effect, which is produced by caffeine, an alkaloid present in green coffee in amounts between 0.8 and 1.5 percent for the Arabica species, and 1.6 to 2.5 percent for the Robusta species.

Because of its caffeine and other alkaloids, coffee has physiological effects, particularly on the nervous and circulatory systems. It stimulates cerebral and cardiac activity and functions as a diuretic. Coffee or caffeine may be prescribed in the treatment of a number of cases of heart disease, dropsy, migraine, chronic asthma, and barbiturate poisoning. Excessive amounts may produce excessive gastric acidity, nervousness, and heightened cardiac action. Fatal results from overdoses of coffee or caffeine have never been reported in humans but can be demonstrated in laboratory animals.

HISTORY

Wild coffee plants, probably from Kefa, (Kaffa), Ethiopia, were taken to southern Arabia and placed under cultivation in the 15th century. One of many legends about the discovery of coffee is that of Kaldi, an Arab goatherd, who was puzzled by the queer antics of his flock. About AD 850 Kaldi supposedly sampled the berries of the evergreen bush on which the goats were feeding and, on experiencing a sense of exhilaration, proclaimed his discovery to the world.

Whatever its historical origin, the stimulating effect of coffee undoubtedly made it popular, especially in connection with the long religious service of the Muslims. The orthodox priesthood pronounced it intoxicating and therefore prohibited by the Qur'ān, but despite the threat of severe penalties, coffee drinking spread rapidly among Arabs and their neighbours.

Introduction into Europe During the 16th and 17th centuries coffee was introduced into one European country after another; many accounts are recorded of its prohibition or approval as a religious, political, and medical potion. Coffee gained popularity as a beverage in the coffeehouses of London, which became centres of political, social, literary, and eventually business influence. The first London coffeehouse was established about 1652. In Europe, too, the coffeehouse flourished later in the 17th century. In such North American cities as Boston, New York City, and Philadelphia, coffeehouses became popular starting about 1689.

Until the close of the 17th century the world's limited supply of coffee was obtained almost entirely from the province of Yemen in southern Arabia. But, with the increasing popularity of the beverage, the propagation of the plant spread rapidly to other parts of the world, including Ceylon (now Sri Lanka) in 1658, Java and other islands of the Indonesian archipelago starting about 1696, Haiti and Santo Domingo 1715, Surinam (now Suriname) 1718, Martinique 1723, Brazil 1727, Jamaica 1730, Cuba 1748, Puerto Rico 1755, Costa Rica 1779, Venezuela 1784, Mexico 1790, Colombia late 18th century, and El Salvador 1840. Coffee cultivation was started in the Hawaiian Islands in 1825.

By the 20th century coffee had become responsible for much of the income of many countries lying between the Tropic of Capricorn and the Tropic of Cancer. Although practically every country within this area produces some coffee, the greatest concentration of production has come to be centred in the Western Hemisphere. This situation changed somewhat, however, toward the mid-20th century as the production of coffee in Africa began to assume greater importance.

COFFEE PRODUCTION

Cultivation and harvesting. The Arabica species of coffee is cultivated mostly in Latin America, while the Robusta species predominates in Africa. Both coffee species are grown in India, Indonesia, and other Asian countries. There are many varieties, forms, and types of each. The effects of environment and cultivation further increase this diversity.

Climatic factors most important for coffee growth are temperature and rainfall. No variety can withstand a temperature in the vicinity of 32° F (0° C). Temperatures between 73° and 82° F (23° and 28° C) are the most favourable. Rainfall of 60 to 80 inches (1,500 to 2,000 millimetres) per year is required with a dry period lasting from two to three months for the Arabica species. Irrigation is required where annual rainfall is less than 40 inches. Plantations are usually established in cleared forestland.

Figure 2: Coffee cherries spread out on a patio in Brazil to be raked and turned several times a day for even drying.
By courtesy of the Pan-American Coffee Bureau, New York

The young shrubs are planted in rows spaced so that the density varies between 500 and 750 plants per acre (1,200 and 1,800 per hectare). Seedlings or cuttings raised in nurseries are carefully planted at the beginning of the rainy season; until they start producing fruit three to four years later, their care is limited largely to the trimming required to give them a robust, balanced framework and to stimulate fruiting.

Cultivation without shade For a long time coffee was cultivated in the shade. This is still done in many areas but is losing popularity because better results can be obtained without shade or with very light shade if other practices, such as trimming, weeding, and fertilization, are followed. Yields as high as 2,000 to 3,000 pounds (2,300 to 3,460 kilograms per hectare) can be grown, compared with 450 to 900 pounds per acre by traditional methods. With modern mechanical cultivation, the average yields range from 700 to 1,100 pounds per acre for the Arabica coffee, and 2,200 to 4,000 pounds per acre for the Robusta coffee.

Among the diseases of the coffee shrub are leaf rust caused by the fungus *Hemileia vastatrix*, which does considerable damage in the plantations of Arabica, and the coffee berry disease caused by the fungus *Colletotrichum coffeanum*, which also attacks the Arabica. Robusta appears to be resistant, or only slightly susceptible, to these scourges. Among the numerous parasites that attack the coffee shrub is the berry borer (*Stephanoderes hamjei*), which damages the seeds of both the Arabica and Robusta species.

The time between blooming and maturing of the fruit varies appreciably with the variety and the climate; for the Arabica this time is about seven months, and for the Robusta it is about nine months. The fruit is gathered by hand when it is red-purple in colour, the sign that it is fully ripe.

Processing. The ripened fruits of the coffee shrubs are processed by disengaging the coffee seeds from their coverings and from the pulp. Two different techniques are used: a wet process and a dry process.

The wet process. First the fresh fruit is pulped by a pulping machine. Some pulp still clings to the coffee, however, and this residue, a mucilaginous substance, is eliminated by fermentation in tanks, which brings about a decomposition of pectic substances in 18 to 36 hours. Washing clears all remaining traces of pulp from the coffee seeds, which are then dried to a moisture content of about 12 percent either by exposure to the sun (see Figure 2) or by hot-air driers. The mechanical operation that follows removes the seed parchment, the endocarp, and also the pellicle more or less completely, sometimes with polishing.

The dry process. In the dry process the fruits are immediately placed to dry either in the sun or in hot-air driers. More time and equipment are required for drying than in

By courtesy of (left) the OAS; photograph, (right) John H. Gerard—National Audubon Society

Figure 1: (Left) Coffee flowers. (Right) Coffee cherries, each containing two beans.

the wet process. When the fruits have been dried to a water content of 12 percent, they are mechanically hulled to free the seeds from their coverings.

Grading and storage. The practice of grading coffee gives sellers and buyers a guarantee concerning the origin, nature, and quality of the product to aid their negotiations. Each country has a certain number of defined types and grades, but there are no international standards outside the contract market.

The prolonged storage of coffee in the producing countries may present problems, especially in the warm and humid coastal regions, where molds and parasites may develop and cause damage; for this reason coffee from these areas is exported as quickly as possible. In moderate climates the conservation of dry lots does not pose a problem as long as they are stocked in well-ventilated places.

MANUFACTURE OF COFFEE PRODUCTS

Roasting. The aromatic and gustatory qualities of coffee only appear and are developed by the high temperatures to which they are subjected during the course of a process called either roasting or broiling.

Temperatures are raised progressively to about 430–440° F (220–230° C). This releases steam, carbon dioxide, carbon monoxide, and other volatiles from the beans, resulting in a loss of weight between 14 and 23 percent. Internal pressure of gas expands the coffee seeds volumetrically from 30 to 100 percent. The seeds become deep, rich brown in colour; their texture becomes porous and crumbly under pressure. But the most important phenomenon of roasting is the appearance of the characteristic aroma of coffee, which arises from very complex chemical transformations within the bean.

In the most common method for roasting, hot air is propelled by a blower into a metal cylinder containing the coffee. In another technique, called singeing, the seed is submitted to the direct action of a flame. In the latter method, which is older, a metal cylinder, or sphere, containing the coffee is rotated above a source of heat such as charcoal, gas, or electricity.

Regardless of the method used, the coffee, after leaving the industrial roasters, is rapidly cooled in a vat, where it is stirred and subjected to cold air propelled by a blower. Good-quality coffees are then sorted by electronic sorters in order to eliminate those seeds, either too light or too dark, that roasted badly, and whose presence depreciates the quality.

Grinding. Some coffees are left as whole beans to be ground at the time of purchase or by the consumer at home. But a large part of the coffee is ground, or milled, by the manufacturer immediately after roasting. There are special types of mills for the dripolator, percolator, espresso, and other methods of brewing. The degree of fineness of the grind is important; if a coffee is too coarse, water filters through too fast to pick up enough aroma; if a coffee is too fine, water filters through too slowly and retains small particles that deposit at the bottom of the cup.

Packaging. Effective packaging prevents air from reaching the coffee. Ground coffee alters rapidly and loses its aromatic qualities if it is not put into hermetically sealed containers immediately.

The air, especially in humid atmospheres, causes rancidity through oxidation of fatty components. Modern packaging materials, plastic films like polyethylene and complexes of aluminum and cellulose, are capable of conserving the quality of coffee for a time. But the most satisfactory solution to the problem is packing under vacuum or in an inert gas, in rigorously impervious containers.

Types of coffee. *Soluble coffee.* In the manufacture of soluble coffee, a liquid concentration of coffee prepared with hot water is dehydrated. This can be done by spray drying the coffee in hot air, by drying it under vacuum, or by lyophilization (freeze drying). The operations are complex, and the methods vary among manufacturers. The resulting soluble powder, on the addition of hot water, forms reconstituted coffee. The average yield is 25 to 30 percent by weight of the ground coffee. Because it picks up moisture readily, soluble coffee needs special vacuum packages.

Decaffeinated coffee. Caffeine may be freed from its combinations in green coffee by the action of acids, alkalis, hot water, or steam; it may be extracted using a chlorinated solvent such as dichloroethylene or trichloroethylene. The coffee is then roasted. The caffeine content of decaffeinated coffees is often regulated by law. In France, for example, caffeine content must be less than 0.1 percent by weight.

Coffee substitutes. Of the many substitutes for coffee, the most popular is the roasted and ground root of the chicory plant, *Cichorium intybus,* used mainly in Belgium, The Netherlands, Germany, and India. Chicory is also used in some areas in order to flavour or to adulterate coffee.

Certain cereal grains, particularly barley, and leguminous seeds, such as lupin and soya, are sometimes roasted and used as a coffee substitute.

World trade, production, and consumption. At the beginning of the 20th century world imports totalled about 1,000,000 tons; they had doubled by the middle of the century, and had risen to more than 4,100,000 tons by 1980, firmly establishing coffee as a leading commodity in international commerce.

In spite of steadily rising world demand, serious disturbances have affected the international coffee market: the excess harvests from 1925 to 1940 depressed prices and caused a grave crisis, particularly in Brazil, which then produced two-thirds of the world's coffee. After World War II new plantings in the United States and Africa caused another excess supply and depressed prices again. In 1962 producers and consumers reacted by creating the International Coffee Organization, whose purpose is to stabilize the coffee market and maintain prices at a relatively satisfactory level for both producers and consumers by restricting exports.

The geographic pattern of coffee production has changed significantly since 1900. Africa hardly figured in coffee production at the start of the century; by 1980 it accounted for more than 1,100,000 tons, about one-fourth of world exports. Brazil still ranks first among the coffee producing countries, but its share has fallen from 66 percent in 1900 to about 20 percent in 1980. Colombia ranks second in world production, and the Ivory Coast, in West Africa, is third.

Coffee consumption in Europe has declined slightly, from 1,800,000 tons in 1970 to 1,450,000 by 1980. Europeans consume about one-fourth as much coffee as do Americans, the largest consumers. Approximately 1,180,000 tons, about one-third of world imports, are consumed in the United States.

BIBLIOGRAPHY. A. CHEVALIER, *Les Caféiers du globe,* 3 vol. (1929–47), a historical work on the worldwide use of coffee, including botanical descriptions; R. COSTE, *Les Caféiers et les cafés dans le monde,* 2 vol. (1955–61), a scholarly study of coffee-tree culture, production, and consumption, and *Le Caféier* (1968), a study of the agricultural problems and the production conditions of the principal markets of the world; A.E. HAARER, *Modern Coffee Production,* 2nd ed. (1962), a discussion of coffee production in East Africa (Tanganyika [now Tanzania], Kenya, and Uganda); INSTITUT FRANÇAIS DU CAFE ET DU CACAO, *Protection des cultures de caféiers, cacaoyers et autres plantes pérennes tropicales* (1961), an illustrated review of the more common plant diseases and parasites of coffee trees; M. SIVETZ and NORMAN W. DESROSIER, *Coffee Technology* (1979), a comprehensive survey of roasted, soluble, and extracted coffees; W.H. UKERS, *All About Coffee,* 2nd ed. (1935, reissued 1976), an excellent retrospective view of coffee technology and production. Statistical data may be found in U.S. FOREIGN AGRICULTURAL SERVICE, *Foreign Agriculture Circular: Coffee,* issued monthly with an annual summary.

(R.C.)

Cohn, Ferdinand Julius

Ferdinand Cohn, a botanist who contributed to many fields, but mainly to the study of algae and of fungi, is remembered as one of the founders of bacteriology.

Cohn was born on January 24, 1828, in the ghetto of Breslau, Silesia (now the Polish city of Wrocław), the first of three sons of a Jewish merchant. His father spared no effort in the education of his precocious oldest child. Ferdinand retained a melancholy recollection of his studious childhood. He had a weak body, and games with children his own age were considered incompatible with his scholarly growth. He was also awkward at making friends, a difficulty further accentuated by poor hearing. But, except for a brief adolescent lapse, he was successful in his studies even though a part of what was discussed at lectures escaped him because of his poor hearing.

Cohn.

Cohn started university studies at Breslau where, as a Jew, he could not be admitted to the candidacy for the doctor's degree. He received his Ph.D. from the more liberal University of Berlin when he was only 19. The year was 1847; in Paris, Louis Pasteur was also receiving his doctorate, but at the more conventional age of 25. Both men, who in different ways were to lay the foundations of microbiology, finished their studies in a troubled political atmosphere. Many universities, including that of Berlin, were centres of political liberalism. In February 1848, a revolution in Paris put an end to Louis-Philippe's reign and kindled revolutionary embers in other European capitals. Riots took place in Berlin, and the liberal-minded Cohn barely escaped arrest.

In his studies Cohn was briefly exposed to the teachings of such eminent scientists as Eilhardt Mitscherlich, the chemist whose observations on tartrates were the starting point of Pasteur's life work; Johannes Müller, the authority on animal physiology; and Christian Gottfried Ehrenberg, remembered for his work with protozoa.

In 1850 Cohn was named lecturer at the University of Breslau. This appointment did not receive warm endorsement from the Minister of Education, who told Cohn that as long as he was in office, a professorship in Silesia would be out of the question. Cohn got his professorship in 1857, but he had to wait 20 years before receiving the laboratory space he needed. The range of his studies was very wide. Among the subjects that he brilliantly investigated were rotifers, luminous worms, the physiology of seeds, and the proteins of potato.

Although Cohn was a shy man, his public lectures were popular because of his poetic and learned approach. Among those who came was a young woman he had known as a schoolgirl and whom he married in 1867.

Around 1868 Cohn started to study bacteria. For the rest of his life he was the leading general bacteriologist of his time. He complained of contemporary microscopes that they put him "in the situation of a traveller who wanders in an unknown country at twilight when he can no longer clearly distinguish objects," but he lived to see them improved.

In 1870 he was made editor of a new journal entitled *Beiträge zur Biologie der Pflanzen* ("Contributions to the Biology of Plants"), in which he played such a large part

that it came to be known as "Cohn's *Beiträge*." It was there, in 1872, that he published the first installment of his *Untersuchungen über Bacterien* ("Researches on Bacteria"), which may be considered the starting point of bacteriology. The same year he published a small book on bacteria, *Über Bacterien, die kleinsten lebenden Wessen* (Eng. trans., *Bacteria, the Smallest of Living Organisms*, 1881). In 1875, after Louis Pasteur's discovery that bacteria formed shiny corpuscles, Cohn described the formation of endospores by *Bacillus subtilis*. Two years later, studying the effect of heat on the sterilization of hay infusion, he demonstrated their resistance to heat and their presence in so-called spontaneous generation.

In 1876, Robert Koch, who was then unknown but was later to become the founder of medical bacteriology, turned to Cohn for a prepublication appraisal of his work on the cause of anthrax, a disease of cattle, sheep, and, sometimes, of men. Cohn was accustomed to receiving letters from people who wanted to show him their discoveries. He generously agreed to see the unknown country physician without expecting the meeting to be anything but a loss of time. He quickly recognized Koch as "an unsurpassed master of scientific research." It was in Cohn's *Beiträge* that Koch published his paper demonstrating that *Bacillus anthracis* was the causative agent of anthrax, and Cohn remained his faithful supporter.

Cohn travelled widely in Europe, visiting many of the leading scientists of the time. He was an expansive, likable person in conversation, always trustful and optimistic. At Breslau he became a close friend of the algologist Nathanael Pringsheim. Cohn's letters to Pringsheim show a whimsical and amiable side of his nature that he did not manifest to everyone. As he grew older he became increasingly nearsighted and deaf. More and more he turned to reading the classics and to writing poetry, being the sort of man who could involve himself intelligently in almost any field of human endeavour. Along with the numerous honours that came his way as he grew older, he derived great satisfaction from the spread of his teachings and from the growing influence of his Institute of Plant Physiology. He died in his native Breslau at the age of 61, on June 25, 1898.

Two of Cohn's contributions to science were equally important. One of these was his formulation of the concept that bacteria can be classified into species on the basis of their morphology and physiological characteristics. The other was his discovery of the bacterial endospore, an advance that played an important part in the development of techniques of sterilization and in the rejection of the doctrine of spontaneous generation.

BIBLIOGRAPHY. For Ferdinand Cohn's place in science, see WILLIAM BULLOCH, *The History of Bacteriology* (1938); and H.A. LECHEVALIER and M. SOLOTOROVSKY, *Three Centuries of Microbiology* (1965). A second edition of the English translation of Cohn's book, *Bacteria: The Smallest of Living Organisms* (1939), contains a bibliography of his publications. His wife PAULINE COHN wrote his biography, *Ferdinand Cohn: Blätter der Erinnerung* (1901).

(H.A.L.)

Coins and Coinage

The use of cast-metal pieces as a medium of exchange is very ancient and probably developed out of the use in commerce of ordinary ingots of bronze and other metals that possessed an intrinsic value. Until the development of bills of exchange in medieval Europe and paper currency in medieval China, metal coins were the only such medium. Despite their diminished use in most commercial transactions, coins are still indispensable to civilized economics; in fact, their importance is growing due to the widespread use of coin-operated machines.

HISTORY

Early cast-bronze animal shapes of known and readily identifiable weight, provided for the beam-balance scales of the Middle Eastern civilizations of the 7th millennium BC, are evidence of the first attempts to provide a medium of exchange. More convenient than cattle or other commodities, and readily acceptable because of their easy convertibility into tools, implements, or articles of decoration, such cast shapes demonstrated their exchange value sufficiently so that the animal forms were discarded in favour of easily cast wedges. The word coin derives from the Latin *cuneus*, or wedge.

Gold and silver were more valuable than bronze because of their beauty, malleability, and relative scarcity; consequently an ingot or coin of gold or silver represented a value many times its weight in bronze and hence provided a better coin. The first true coins, that is, cast disks of standard weight and value specifically designed as a medium of exchange, were probably produced by the Lydians of Anatolia in about 640 BC from a natural alloy of gold containing 20 to 35 percent silver. The cast disks of this natural alloy, known as electrum, were placed on an anvil that had been roughened by striations cut into it, and each disk was coined by hammering an upper die, or punch, made of bronze, onto it. The punch bore in relief the figure of a lion, signifying value; later a lower bronze die replaced the anvil surface. The electrum alloy, however, varied in composition from sample to sample, impairing its trade value. The purification of gold and silver was accomplished by Egyptian King Croesus of Lydia, who created the first official government coinage during his reign (560–546 BC), with the purity and weight of gold certified by the government.

The art of minting spread among the Greeks and was carried by them to Italy and other countries around the Mediterranean.

Hand striking. For many centuries few changes occurred in the hand-coining technique. The earliest Greek coins were made by melting electrum in a clay crucible and casting it into molds, leaving cavities to produce a comparatively round button. This button, or coinage blank, was reheated red-hot, removed from the fire by tongs, and placed on the anvil over the lower die. The striker, holding the cold upper die with one hand or by tongs centred on the planchet or coinage blank, produced the coin by a heavy hammer blow on the upper die. Coins could be struck from cold blanks; in that case the bronze dies deformed rapidly. There is some evidence that the same technique was used for the preparation of the dies themselves from a cold "master hub."

One of the great improvements introduced by the Romans later was the use of iron dies, which were sufficiently hard and durable to permit the blanks to be coined while cold. Such dies continued to be used until the development of modern tool steels.

A further development, not widely adopted, involved the invention of a hinged pair of coining dies, consisting of two dies mounted on long arms, connected by a peg-in-hole hinge, so that the dies could be opened and closed in reasonably perfect alignment; then a heavy hammer blow squeezed the dies against the blank with sufficient pressure to form the coin.

The major objective in coinage remained the provision of a known weight and composition, and therefore value, of a precious metal in convenient form. Casting procedures, involving the use of clay or stone two-part molds, producing 10 or 12 round cavities with interconnecting gates, proved too crude. The next step was to cast strip-shaped bars of the desired thickness. With heavy shears, square pieces were cut from these bars, hammered round, resoftened by annealing, and rehammered into approximately round shape. The smaller, thinner blanks were later made from metal cast into thin plate, hammered into sheet metal, and then cut approximately round with shears.

During a span covering the Greek and Roman developments, it is notable that the Chinese never adopted any of the procedures involved in the striking of coins. Up until the 20th century, Chinese coins were cast in much the same fashion as that used for casting round blanks by the early Greeks. The square-holed Chinese bronze coins were issued in essentially the same size and shape for almost 2,500 years.

Medieval coinage. The selection of two commodities —gold and silver—as the basis for measuring all other goods and services has provided serious problems since antiquity. The increase in supply of either metal depended upon factors such as ease of location of deposits; the amount of labour required to mine, mill, smelt, and transport; and political factors such as conquest and pillage of other states. In view of the varying demand for the two metals in terms of ounces of each, the original concept of coinage was abandoned. The citizen wished the sovereign to bear the cost of coinage entirely, of course, and to provide him, for example, with one ounce of gold in the form of a coin with the crown stamp thereon for the bullion value of one ounce. On the other hand, the sovereign insisted that in exchange for protection and warranty of the contents of a coin, the face value should represent bullion value plus the cost of minting and seigniorage, or profit. The growth of the sovereign prerogative led to the widespread debasement of coins. The percentage composition of gold in the coin was artfully reduced from legitimate compositions provided to extend wear, such as $\frac{11}{12}$ gold, $\frac{1}{12}$ copper, to alloys or composites containing only token quantities of gold. As such token compositions came into disrepute, while the need for precious metals in trade steadily increased, new sources for silver and gold were providentially discovered in the New World.

The debasement of coinage alloys by sovereigns multiplied counterfeiting a hundredfold. Because coins were of irregular shape, the citizen was unable to determine by inspection or even by weighing whether a gold or silver coin contained the amount of metal represented or only a fraction of that amount. For this reason, at the close of the Renaissance precious metal coins fell into widespread disrepute.

The development of equipment capable of providing coins of reliable weight and size had its beginning in Italy in the late 15th century, spreading to Germany, France, and England. By the middle of the 17th century, a rolling mill was used to reduce the thickness of cast bars to the gauge required.

To insure that the finished rolled strip was of uniform thickness throughout, each strip was subjected to a "draw bench" operation. The leading end of the strip was swaged or pounded to such a thickness that it could be threaded through a sizing die and tightly clamped. The strip was then pulled through the die in the procedure employed in modern times for the production of copper wire.

A blanking press, incorporating a punch and a hollow die capable of cutting accurately round blanks from the rolled strip, provided for the first time a planchet, or blank, of proper weight and constant diameter. The planchet was placed in a ring collar, on top of the lower die, in a screw press. The upper die was driven down on the planchet by means of the screw. The collar, in the case of precious-metal coins, was reeded to produce a characteristic milled edge, designed to foil the coin clipping prevalent in the Middle Ages.

During the 18th and 19th centuries, developments moved in the direction of improving and perfecting the coinage processes; an acceptable quality of product had been achieved. The major breakthrough was the introduction of the lever coining press. In this case, the top die is raised and lowered by a knuckle-joint action; mechanical fingers convey the blank onto the collar and the struck coin away and provide for the automatic extrusion of the struck coin from the collar by the action of a cam raising the lower die after the coin is struck.

In the preparation of dies, the development of steels capable of successive softening by annealing and later hardening and the employment of matrices, or "hubs," of high quality provided for successive manufacture of exact replicas of the original master die.

To extend the life of dies, equipment capable of "upsetting," or rolling up the edge of blanks prior to coining, was adopted. This equipment was also used to provide a "security inscription" on the edge of coins, prior to stamping, to assist in the suppression of counterfeiting.

When, in the 19th century, automatic balances for weighing single coins were devised, the major objectives

Early cast disks

Chinese coins

The lever coining press

of a good coinage system, from the standpoint of governments at least, had been achieved: accuracy of dimension, reproduction of design, and weight of a known value of a precious-metal alloy. Thereafter, the unique colour and patina of gold and silver coinage alloys permitted anyone quickly to establish, by a simple weighing operation, whether a coin was genuine.

National coinage systems have always been forced to respond, however, to world political, economic, and monetary pressures. World attempts to establish a fixed value relationship between gold and silver encountered insuperable problems, and, during the 20th century, a single gold standard for international payments evolved, leading to a free market for silver. Financial exhaustion of many governments forced reduction in the precious-metal content of coins, and even complete withdrawal of precious metals from coinage systems. Certain governments resorted to gradual reduction, especially in the case of silver coins; the effect of such debasement was a substantial increase in counterfeiting.

COIN MANUFACTURE

The modern mint is designed to manufacture coins from those metals that, by reason of colour and physical properties, are amenable to the coinage operation. Nonferrous metals, such as pure nickel, cupronickel, brass, bronze, German silver, aluminum bronze, and aluminum, fall in that category. Most modern coinage systems employ such alloys. The maintenance of a sound coinage system requires that changes in design and size be minimal in order to provide the least disturbance to automatic merchandising and other coin-handling equipment. The design and execution of higher value coins made from low-cost materials requires, in order to suppress counterfeiting, a degree of sophistication readily apparent to the ordinary citizen and easily checked by banks and government authorities. Most coin-operated vending machines contain devices designed to reject counterfeits or slugs, on the basis of physical measurements including weight, diameter, edge thickness, and electrical properties such as resistivity. For example, in the case of the U.S. transition from silver to nonsilver coins (1965–69) it was necessary to develop a material that would (1) be accepted in coin-operated equipment side-by-side with the 90 percent silver, 10 percent copper coins, (2) be capable of being processed by mint equipment, (3) be sufficiently sophisticated in makeup as to make the production of slugs or counterfeits difficult, (4) permit the use of resulting scrap for the production of coins, and (5) be available at reasonable cost. The material selected for the U.S. 25-cent and 10-cent coins was a composite metal, consisting of a top and bottom layer of homogeneous 75 percent copper–25 percent nickel alloy, metallurgically bonded to a central core of pure copper.

The material chosen for the U.S. half-dollar was a different composite metal, the two outside layers consisting of homogeneous 80 percent silver–20 percent copper alloy, metallurgically bonded to a core consisting of homogeneous 21 percent silver–79 percent copper alloy. This coin had an average composition of 40 percent silver–60 percent copper. The above compositions were established by the U.S. Coinage Act of 1965. By the Coinage Act of December 1970, the 40 percent silver, 60 percent copper-clad metal combination was established for a silver dollar coin for limited issue to coin collectors; that silver-clad combination was discontinued for half-dollars. Further, that act provided for one-dollar, 50-cent, 25-cent, and 10-cent coins for regular issue, all of them to be of the cupronickel-on-copper composition.

For virtually identical reasons, particularly the existence of a flourishing automatic vending-machine industry, several other governments have taken the same approach. The Swedish mint, for example, produces a three-layer, clad-metal-composite "one krona" coin that is acceptable in automatic equipment alongside its former 40% silver, 50% copper, 5% nickel, 5% zinc homogeneous alloy.

As a result of the growing pressure for development of more sophisticated coinage materials, and a need for a worldwide rational approach to the possible use by different governments of the same material for coins of the same size and weight but widely different value, the European Mint Masters have established a Central Information Agency. The information collected there will serve as a guide to governments planning changes in their coinages. By reason of the continuing increase in the world price of copper and nickel (the basic materials traditionally used in the makeup of coins of lowest denominations) and coupled with successive devaluations of the currencies of various nations, the metal value of former cupronickel and bronze coins issued by several nations now exceeds the face value. This situation inevitably results in the hoarding and illicit subsequent melting down of such coins. To prevent this, many governments have resorted to clad-metal combinations such as pure nickel or cupronickel thinly clad on ordinary steel, for "white" coins, and to copper, brass, or bronze, thinly clad on steel for "red" or "yellow" coins. Other nations have resorted to the use of white aluminum coins as a replacement or to the abandonment of low denominations.

Formerly, mints were designed for the security protection of a precious-metal-processing operation. Metal in process was handled in very small batches and carefully weighed and accounted for between makeup, melting, rolling, and blanking processes. Metallurgically, silver alloys segregate in casting; in order to hold the fineness of coins within legal limits of composition, the ingots processed were very small (e.g., 6 pounds, or 2.5 kilograms) and narrow. Until recently, it was impossible to control the gauge of strip during rolling across a width much greater than a few inches, and therefore to control the weight of individual blanks cut from wider strip. For this reason, the size of equipment used, and the size of ingot processed, was very small. The major processes involved in coinage were, and are, as follows: (1) receipt, weighing, and analysis of purchased coinage metals; (2) batch weighing to prepare the metals required to make an alloy of proper proportion; (3) melting the metals and casting the molten metal into molds to produce a bar or ingot; (4) rolling out the bar in a rolling mill by successive passes to reduce its thickness to the proper gauge by extending it lengthwise; (5) cutting disks or blanks from the strips; (6) softening the blanks by annealing; (7) upsetting or raising the edge of each blank by means of a side rolling operation; (8) striking each blank in a collar between a top die and a bottom die; (9) weighing, examining, counting, and bagging (see chart).

In connection with plans for replacement or modernization of world mints, governments necessarily have taken into account the changes in coinage materials that have been made or are under consideration, the total projected annual requirements, the economics of total "in house" operations as opposed to coinage via procurement of blanks furnished by others, and the extent to which the projected volume justifies automation. The production activities performed in a "total in-house" such as the new U.S. mint at Philadelphia, include the following major segments, with related quality-control techniques:

1. Brass-mill operations: receipt and handling of virgin metals and "in-house" coinage scrap; preparation of furnace charges; melting and casting of ingots or bars for rolling; rolling of bars to proper gauge for blanking

2. Mint coining operations: production of cut blanks from strip; annealing, cleaning, and upsetting of blanks; coining, counting, bagging, delivering, or storing

3. Die-making operations: preparation of designs by artist-sculptor; preparation of master dies by engraver; manufacture of working dies, collars, and other unique coinage paraphernalia.

The new mint at Philadelphia, designed to produce 8,000,000 coins each 8-hour shift and operating on a two-shift basis to produce 4,000,000,000 coins each 250-working-day year, may be used to illustrate the operation of the most modern coinage technology, automated to the maximum extent feasible. Of the total coins produced, 70 percent are of the 95 percent copper–5 percent zinc alloy U.S. cent; 15 percent are of the homogeneous

Rejecting counterfeit coins

Major coinage processes

Initial
handling

75 percent copper–25 percent nickel alloy five-cent coin;
the remaining 15 percent are of the cupronickel-clad-on
copper U.S. dimes and quarters.

Incoming metal, in the form of refinery cathodes piled
on skids, is delivered to a shear line that cuts each cathode into smaller pieces, approximately 5 × 5 inches. The
cut pieces are delivered by belt conveyor to the charge-
weight makeup section of the melting division and deposited in appropriate overhead bins. The coinage scrap
resulting from rolling and blanking operations is simultaneously delivered by conveyor to the makeup section
and deposited in its appropriate overhead bin. Computer-
controlled weighing equipment discharges into a charging bucket the metal of each type required to produce a
charge of the proper average composition. The metal is
moved by overhead crane and dumped into the entry-
charging container, whence it is advanced by vibrator
feed chute and discharged downward into a 15,000-
pound-capacity electric-induction melting furnace. The
charge is melted and skimmed, and metallurgical additions required for de-oxidation are made. The furnace is
then tilted forward to pour the molten metal into a water-cooled, semicontinuous casting-machine mold. As
casting proceeds, the movable bottom plate of the mold
is lowered by hydraulic cylinder, producing an ingot 16
inches (40 centimetres) wide, 6 inches (15 centimetres)
thick, and 18 feet (6 metres) long, weighing approximately 6,600 pounds (3,000 kilograms). The vertical ingot is
deposited by roller conveyor in a horizontal position on
a transfer roller table, with its end in line for entry into
the rolling mill straight-line conveyor system. The ingot
is cross-cut by rotary saw into two 9-feet lengths, each
weighing 3,300 pounds (1,500 kilograms). The length,
now described as the rolling mill bar, is conveyed flat to
the entry side of a bar preheater, upended so that it
stands on one edge, and in that position is raised into a
high-frequency, electric-induction coil. In approximately
15 minutes, the temperature of the bar is high enough
for hot rolling. In the case of the "95–5" copper–zinc alloy, this temperature is approximately 1,500° F (815° C).
The bar is lowered out of the furnace, shifted to a horizontal position, and conveyed through the hot rolling
mill for the breakdown operation. The mill is designed
for either computer or manual operation. In nine passes
back and forth in three minutes, the bar's thickness is
reduced to less than a half-inch, and its length extended
from nine feet to over 110 feet. The red-hot strip travels
forward by roller conveyor through a water-quench
shower shed. Reduced to room temperature, it travels
through surface-milling equipment and the oxidized layer
top and bottom is removed. The new, shiny strip is then
coiled. The coil is carried by overhead crane to the cold-
rolling mill, where it is deposited on a "run-around"
conveyor. Rolling is on a batch basis, with about 15
coils in a batch. For the successive passes, each coil is
unwound into the rolls, recoiled on the exit side of the
mill, and redeposited on the run-around conveyor for
subsequent passes. After the strip's gauge has been reduced to $\frac{1}{10}$ inch, the coil moves by roller conveyor to
the entry side of a welding and trimming line. Here the
successive coils are uncoiled, trimmed on ends and edges,
electrically welded, and recoiled into one big coil weighing 10,000 pounds (4,545 kilograms).

This coil is then transferred to the entry side of a four-
high "back and forth" finishing rolling mill, where it is
rolled under tension. At this point the gauge or thickness
of the strip is controlled either by X-ray or contact
thickness-measuring equipment that regulates roller pressure and tension to produce the desired thickness.

Later steps

The coil is now fed through a slitting line, which either
(1) slits the 15-inch (38-centimetre) wide coil into two
rings, each 7½ inches in width, for subsequent use in
certain small blanking presses, or (2) delivers the full-
width coil direct to the larger blanking presses. These
high-speed presses cut as many as 21 blanks per stroke,
using carbide blanking-die punches and thimbles. The
remaining skeleton, or scissel, is chopped into small
pieces and delivered by conveyor back to the melting
room. In the case of cent coinage, blanks are automati-

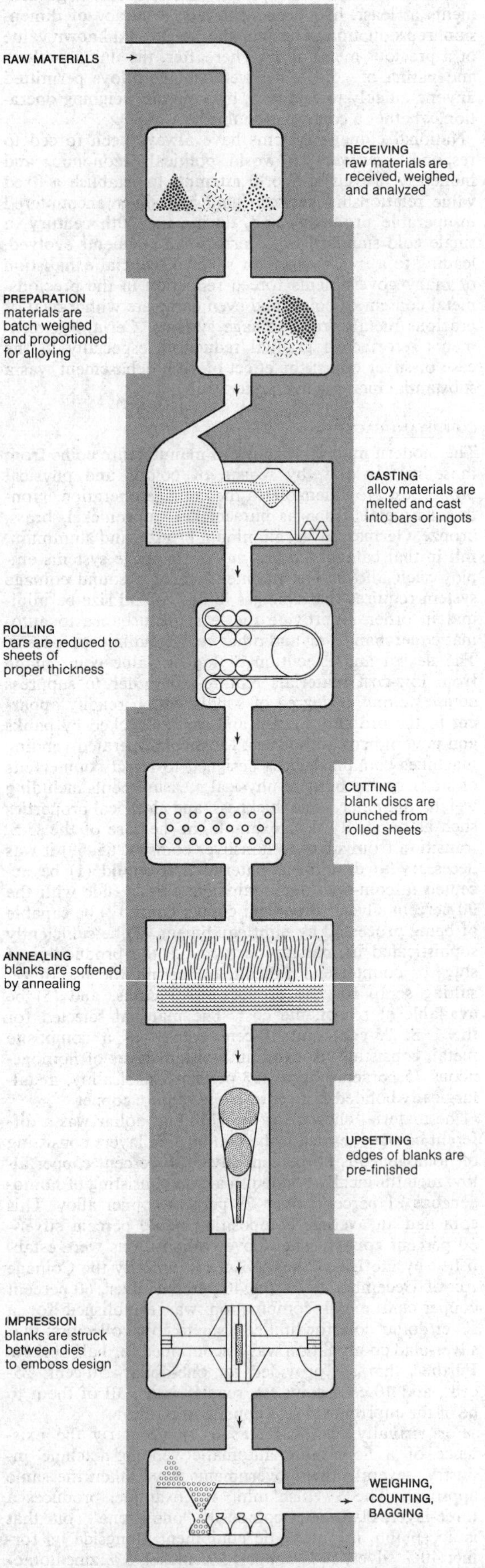

RAW MATERIALS

RECEIVING
raw materials are
received, weighed,
and analyzed

PREPARATION
materials are
batch weighed
and proportioned
for alloying

CASTING
alloy materials are
melted and cast
into bars or ingots

ROLLING
bars are reduced to
sheets of
proper thickness

CUTTING
blank discs are
punched from
rolled sheets

ANNEALING
blanks are softened
by annealing

UPSETTING
edges of blanks are
pre-finished

IMPRESSION
blanks are struck
between dies
to emboss design

WEIGHING,
COUNTING,
BAGGING

Diagrammatic illustration of the basic processes involved in
coin making, showing the several sequential stages required
to convert raw materials to the final product.
Drawing by D. Meighan

cally conveyed into rotary "Archimedes' screw" annealing furnaces, softened, quenched in water, and conveyed into a cleaning unit that cleans, polishes, and dries the blanks. A conveyor carries the blanks through the upsetting or edge-rolling machine, by which each blank is thickened at the edge to facilitate the later coining operation and to provide a rim that will protect the coin from wear.

The process by which coin blanks are converted into coins by receiving an impression from engraved dies has already been described. The upper die is brought down forcibly, the pressure causing the soft metal to flow like a viscous solid, its lateral escape prevented by the collar. The lower die then pushes the coin out of the collar, and the mechanical fingers carry it to its delivery chute.

Cent coin presses are equipped for the striking of four coins at each stroke of the press. Two sets of dual fingers constitute a transfer mechanism to carry the four blanks across the press with each stroke, and deposit each blank in proper juxtaposition to its pair of dies and collar.

Blanks are delivered to hoppers on each coining press by overhead bucket conveyors. Struck coins are delivered from each press into its "trap," or temporary retention container. If inspection shows the coins to be of acceptable quality, the contents of the trap are discharged into a conveyor for delivery.

Coins flow from the chute on elevated containers or tanks into a double-counting machine operation, and thence into coin bags. Each bag is stitched closed, and the bags are placed on skids for delivery to banks.

QUALITY CONTROL

For reasons explained, coins are necessarily precise objects. Those of each denomination must meet the basic legal requirements as to weight, diameter, composition, and design; further, such coins must, by reason of physical state, exhibit the required electrical properties to provide for acceptance in vending machines, pay telephones, and other automatic coin-handling equipment. All purchased metals, and certain classes of mill scrap, are carefully analyzed. Certain coinage alloys, notably cupronickel, require very careful chemical and metallurgical control immediately before casting into ingots to produce an ingot of proper composition and physical condition for subsequent successful processing.

The quality-control division is equipped with modern analytical and metallurgical testing units capable of providing the needed information in a few minutes in order to be in a position to correct the composition by making additions to the molten metal in the melting furnace before pouring it. Each ingot cast represents about 5 percent of the shift's production; the importance of quality control at these initial stages cannot be overemphasized. Before preheating for hot rolling, and after the ingot has been sawed into two pieces to make two rolling-mill bars, a thin slice is taken for examination as to physical state. If within the limits of acceptability, the bars are released to the rolling operations. Quality control thereafter is designed to ensure that the output of each process is in proper physical condition as to weight, dimensions, hardness, and appearance for the succeeding operation.

BIBLIOGRAPHY. PERCY GARDNER, *A History of Ancient Coinage* (1918, reprinted 1974), an exhaustive study of the development of early measures of value, the origin of coin standards, and the mutual relationship of precious metals; J.G. MILNE, *Greek Coinage* (1931, reprinted 1979), an excellent description of early coining tools, dies, and metallurgical procedures; HAROLD MATTINGLY, *Roman Coins from the Earliest Times to the Fall of the Western Empire*, 2nd ed. rev. (1960, reprinted 1977), a thorough treatise on the development of coinage in the early Roman Empire, based on the Grecian pattern, with emphasis on the political, administrative, and technical activities of evolving mints; MARTIN J. PRICE (ed.), *Coins, an Illustrated Survey: 650 B.C. to the Present Day* (1980), a collection of essays, profusely illustrated.

(P.B.N.)

Coke, Sir Edward

English common law won its supremacy over the prerogative power of the crown and the encroachments of ecclesiastical jurisdiction largely through the efforts of Sir Edward Coke. A prominent jurist and politician during the reign of three monarchs, Coke was initially a vigorous supporter of the crown, but in the course of his career he became a progressively more forceful upholder of the common law.

By courtesy of the Inner Temple, London; photograph, Courtauld Institute of Art

Coke, oil painting by Paul van Somer (1576–1621). In the Inner Temple, London.

Edward Coke was born at Mileham in Norfolk on February 1, 1552. He was educated at Norwich Grammar School and Trinity College, Cambridge, and entered the Inner Temple, one of the four inns of court that constituted "colleges in the university of law," in 1572. Called to the bar in 1578, he soon acquired a reputation; his early cases included the Cromwell libel case for words uttered by Edward Denny, a Norfolk vicar, imputing sedition to Henry, Lord Cromwell, and Shelley's case, a seminal decision in the history of English land law. Under the patronage of William Cecil, Lord Burghley, Elizabeth I's first minister, Coke entered the public service and rose rapidly, becoming member of Parliament for Aldeburgh in 1589, and solicitor general and recorder of London in 1592. A year later he was elected speaker of the House of Commons, showing considerable skill in carrying out Queen Elizabeth's policy of curbing the Commons' passion for discussing ecclesiastical matters. In 1593 he first crossed the path of Francis Bacon. The attorney generalship fell vacant, and Bacon, supported by the Earl of Essex, became Coke's rival for the post. Coke won the appointment in 1594 and then kept Bacon from becoming solicitor general as well, or so Bacon thought. Coke's first wife, Bridget Paston, died in 1598 and four months later Bacon was again his unsuccessful rival when Coke married Lady Elizabeth Hatton.

As attorney general, Coke was the champion of the crown and its prerogative powers. He started a series of state prosecutions for libel and conducted several great treason trials of the day, prosecuting the Earls of Essex and Southampton in 1600–01, Sir Walter Raleigh in 1603, and the Gunpowder Plot conspirators in 1605. His methods in these trials, especially in that of Raleigh, were brutal even by the standards of his age.

In 1606 Coke was made chief justice of the court of common pleas, and there began the series of conflicts that eventually broke his judicial career. At the time of Coke's appointment Archbishop Richard Bancroft had already started his attempt to shake off the control that the common-law courts exercised over the jurisdiction of ec-

Career as a chief justice

clesiastical courts. This matter came to a head in Fuller's case (1607–08) when Coke, summoned to a disputation on the king's power to withdraw a case from the courts, earned James I's fury by asserting that the common law was the supreme law and that "the king in his own person cannot adjudge any case. . . ." In 1610 Coke again crossed the King when he gave a celebrated opinion on proclamations before the royal council, in which he stated that the king cannot change any part of the common law nor create any offense by proclamation that was not an offense before. The same year he disputed the claim of the court of high commission to imprison for adultery and when, in 1611, James attempted to put him on the commission he refused.

Coke's position was strong. Incorruptible and respected, he was the embodiment of the common law. A last attempt was made to "buy" him in August 1613 when James, on Bacon's advice, appointed him chief justice of the king's bench where it was hoped he would look after the royal interests. He was also made a privy councillor and as such was to be called lord chief justice of England. At the king's bench he retained his predominance and continued to maintain the supremacy of the common law over all persons and institutions except Parliament. In Peacham's case he protested against the practice of consulting the judges individually and separately, which James, abetted by Bacon, was more or less driven to follow when the whole bench, if consulted together, merely echoed Coke. In 1615, however, he overreached himself when the court of king's bench started, and failed to win, a dispute with Lord Chancellor Ellesmere of the court of chancery over that court's right to interfere with, and indirectly nullify, a common-law decision. Coke was also believed to be at the bottom of the abortive attempt to make some suitors who had attempted to invoke the court of chancery's assistance in defiance of a king's bench decree liable to the penalties of a praemunire (an offense against the king and his government). Meanwhile, he had further endangered his position by throwing out from the bench in the Overbury murder trials dark hints of scandal in high places ("God knows what became of that sweet babe, Prince Henry, but I know somewhat"). Finally he came into collision with James I over the king's right to grant permission to hold several ecclesiastical benefices at the same time. Coke and the other judges ignored a royal injunction that they should take no action on a case involving this right until the King's pleasure was known. They were called before the King and council and ordered to obey the injunction. The other judges submitted, but Coke merely said that he would do what an honest and just judge ought to do.

In June 1616 the privy council, with Bacon behind it, formulated three charges against him. One was a trivial matter, never proved, about a bond that had passed through his hands. The other two were charges of interference with the court of chancery and of disrespect to the king in the matter of plural benefices. Coke was forbidden to go on circuit, ordered to revise the "errors" in his *Reports*, and on Nov. 14, 1616, he was dismissed. Thereupon, presumably in search of an influential friend, he offered his daughter in marriage to Sir John Villiers, brother of the Duke of Buckingham. His wife, supported by Bacon, objected and hid the child, who was then only 14. Coke abducted her violently and had her married, strongly against her will, to Villiers. Coke then made a gradual return to public life, and by 1617 was back in the privy council and in the Star Chamber.

In 1620 Coke entered Parliament again as member for a Cornish borough, in theory as a supporter of the king. Yet for the rest of his career he was a leading member of the popular party. He opposed Prince Charles's proposed Spanish marriage, took a part in drawing up the bribery charges against Bacon, and spoke in 1621 in major debates on the liberties of Parliament. He spent nine months in prison as a result, but nothing was found that could incriminate him. In 1628 it was his bill of liberties that ultimately took the form of the Petition of Right.

This was his greatest parliamentary hour. Admitting his changed views, Coke, at the age of 76, molded the ancient precedents, including Magna Carta, into a charter of liberty limiting the royal prerogative. He retired at the end of the session and died at Stoke Poges, Buckinghamshire, on Sept. 3, 1634. His papers were instantly seized and some, including his will, were never recovered.

It is true that Coke was inclined to be overbearing and impatient both at the bar and on the bench, that he was undoubtedly rather narrow, and that he was not always logical. His knowledge of law, however, was unequalled, though he "read the *Year Books* [the old *Law Reports*] as a Tudor, not as a medieval lawyer." Coke manipulated medieval "precedents" and used them to support his 17th-century view of the common law. He successfully upheld this common law in the courts and in Parliament, against the church, the admiralty, and the dangerous claims of the royal prerogative. He only failed in trying to uphold it against the chancery (the High Court of Equity), which was too strong for him. While he was issuing his *Reports*, in which he systematized the principles of English law as he related and commented on decisions, no other jurists published theirs. They are not so much reports in the modern sense as compendiums of the law bearing on a particular case, with personal comments on points raised or general remarks. A balanced estimate of his importance as a legal authority is that of Chief Justice William Best in 1824:

> The fact is, Lord Coke had [often] no authority for what he states, but I am afraid we should get rid of a great deal of what is considered law in Westminster hall, if what Lord Coke says without authority is not law. He was one of the most eminent lawyers that ever presided as a judge in any court of justice . . . .

Among his other publications are four volumes of *Institutes of the Lawes of England*, of which volume 1 is known as *Coke Upon Littleton* (1628).

As a man, he evokes admiration more readily than sympathy. More learned a lawyer than Bacon but without his philosophical genius, proud, ambitious, and domineering, a just judge but a savage prosecutor, obstinate in his opposition to illegal exercise of authority, resolute in his faith in the supremacy of the common law even to the extent of challenging the equity of the chancellor, he could cringe before the king even in the act of defying the crown.

BIBLIOGRAPHY. There is no adequate biography of Coke. The best accounts are in the *Dictionary of National Biography*, vol. 11, pp. 229–244 (1917); W.S. HOLDSWORTH, *A History of English Law*, 2nd ed., vol. 5, pp. 423–493 (1937); and S.E. THORNE, *Sir Edward Coke, 1552–1952* (1957).

(G.H.J.)

Colbert, Jean-Baptiste

Jean-Baptiste Colbert, the French statesman and minister of finance to Louis XIV, is remembered for his efforts to make France the dominant commercial and military power of Europe. His financial and industrial reforms contributed greatly to the splendour of the Sun King's reign. To subsequent generations of Frenchmen, his name came to represent the mercantilist view of economic affairs, namely, that a country can prosper in international commerce only at the expense of other countries.

Colbert was born on August 29, 1619, at Reims, of a merchant family. After holding various administrative posts, his great opportunity came in 1651, when Cardinal Mazarin, the dominant political figure in France, was forced to leave Paris and take refuge in a provincial city —an episode in the Fronde, a period (1648–53) of struggle between the crown and the French *parlement* (see FRANCE, HISTORY OF). Colbert became Mazarin's agent in Paris, keeping him abreast of the news and looking after his personal affairs. When Mazarin returned to power, he made Colbert his personal assistant and helped him purchase profitable appointments for both himself and his family. Colbert became wealthy; he also acquired the barony of Seignelay. On his deathbed, Mazarin recommended him to Louis XIV, who soon gave Colbert his

Colbert, bust by A. Coysevox, 1677. In the
Louvre, Paris.
Giraudon

confidence. Thenceforth Colbert dedicated his enormous
capacity for work to serving the King both in his private
affairs and in the general administration of the kingdom.

The struggle with Fouquet. For 25 years Colbert was
to be concerned with the economic reconstruction of
France. The first necessity was to bring order into the
chaotic methods of financial administration that were
then under the direction of Nicolas Fouquet, the immensely powerful *surintendant des finances.* Colbert destroyed Fouquet's reputation with the King, revealing
irregularities in his accounts and denouncing the financial
operations by which Fouquet had enriched himself. The
latter's fate was sealed when he made the mistake of receiving the King at his magnificent chateau at Vaux-le-
Vicomte; the Lucullan festivities, displaying how much
wealth Fouquet had amassed at the expense of the state,
infuriated Louis. The King subsequently had him arrested. The criminal proceedings against him lasted three
years and excited great public interest. Colbert, without
any rightful standing in the case, interfered in the trial
and made it his personal affair because he wanted to succeed Fouquet as finance minister. The trial itself was a
parody of justice. Fouquet was sent to prison, where he
spent the remaining 15 years of his life. The *surinten-
dance* was replaced by a council of finance, of which Colbert became the dominant member with the title of intendant until, in 1665, he became controller general.

Financiers and tax farmers had made enormous profits
from loans and advances to the state treasury, and Colbert established tribunals to make them give back some
of their gains. This was well received by public opinion,
which held the financiers responsible for all difficulties;
it also helped to lighten the public debt, which was further reduced by the repudiation of some government
bonds and the repayment of others without interest.
Many private fortunes suffered, but no disturbances ensued, and the King's credit was restored.

Financial and economic affairs. Colbert's next efforts
were directed to reforming the chaotic system of taxation, a heritage of medieval times. The King derived the
major part of his revenue from a tax called the taille,
levied in some districts on individuals and in other districts on land and businesses. In some districts the taille
was apportioned and collected by royal officials; in others
it was voted by the representatives of the province. Many
persons, including clergy and nobles, were exempt from
it altogether. Colbert undertook to levy the taille on all
who were properly liable for it and so initiated a review
of titles of nobility in order to expose those who were
claiming exemption falsely; he also tried to make the tax
less oppressive by a fairer distribution. He reduced the
total amount of it but insisted on payment in full over a
reasonable period of time. He took care to suppress many
abuses of collection (confiscation of defaulters' property,

seizure of peasants' livestock or bedding, imprisonment
of collectors who had not been able to produce the due
sums in time). These reforms and the close supervision of
the officials concerned brought large sums into the treasury. Other taxes were increased, and the tariff system
was revised in 1664 as part of a system of protection. The
special dues that existed in the various provinces could
not be swept away, but a measure of uniformity was obtained in central France.

Colbert devoted endless energy to the reorganization of
industry and commerce. He believed that in order to increase French power it would be essential to increase
France's share of international trade and in particular to
reduce the commercial hegemony of the Dutch. This necessitated not only the production of high-quality goods
that could compete with foreign products abroad but
also the building up of a merchant fleet to carry them.
Colbert encouraged foreign workers to bring their trade
skills to France. He gave privileges to a number of private
industries and founded state manufactures. To guarantee
the standard of workmanship, he made regulations for
every sort of manufacture and imposed severe punishments (fines and the pillory) for counterfeiting and shortcomings. He encouraged the formation of companies to
build ships and tried to obtain monopolies for French
commerce abroad through the formation of trading companies. The French East India and West India companies, founded in 1664, were followed by others for trade
with the eastern Mediterranean and with northern Europe; but Colbert's propaganda for them, though cleverly
conducted, failed to attract sufficient capital, and their
existence was precarious. The protection of national industry demanded tariffs against foreign produce, and
other countries replied with tariffs against French goods.
This tariff warfare was one of the chief causes of the
Dutch War of 1672–78.

Colbert's system of control was resented by traders and
contractors, who wanted to preserve their freedom of action and to be responsible to themselves alone. Cautious
and thrifty people, moreover, still preferred the old outlets for their money (land, annuities, moneylending) to
investing in industry. The period, too, was one of generally falling prices throughout the world. Colbert's success, therefore, fell short of his expectation, but what he
did achieve seems all the greater in view of the obstacles
in his way: he raised the output of manufactures, expanded trade, set up new permanent industries, and developed communications by road and water across
France (Canal du Midi, 1666–81).

Colbert and the navy. The controller general's sphere
of activity continually expanded. He busied himself with
everything, from questions of finance to the naming of
Louis' illegitimate children. As secretary of state for the
navy from 1668, he undertook to make France a great
power at sea. This meant forming a fighting fleet, building and equipping the king's ships, fortifying ports, and
encouraging the merchant navy. The Atlantic fleet was
composed of sailing ships; the Mediterranean fleet, of
galleys. To man the Atlantic fleet, professional sailors
were required to sign on for the king's service. For the
galleys, Colbert encouraged magistrates to sentence common criminals to serve in them and had no scruple about
making use of other sources of manpower: political offenders, Protestants, and slaves seized from Africa and
Canada.

Colbert reconstructed the works and arsenal of Toulon
and founded the port and arsenal of Rochefort and naval
schools at Rochefort, Dieppe, and St.-Malo. Calais, Dunkerque, Brest, and Le Havre were fortified. The need for
naval construction goes far to explain Colbert's vigilance
over the forests (*Ordonnance des eaux et forêts*, 1669),
one of the most corruptly administered sectors of the
royal domain. As he also wanted the French ships of the
line to have a handsome appearance, in order to impress
foreigners, he engaged excellent artists, such as Pierre
Puget, to decorate them. Encouragement was given to the
building of ships for the merchant navy by allowing a
premium on those built at home and imposing a duty on
those built abroad; and as French workmen were for-

Efforts at
financial
reform

Reorgani-
zation of
industry

The
strengthen-
ing of the
French
navy

bidden to emigrate, so French seamen were forbidden to serve foreigners on pain of death.

The arts. In 1669 the King added still further to Colbert's dignities by making him responsible for the intellectual and artistic life of the country, as secretary of state for the king's household. He applied to the arts the same principle that had guided him previously: the enhancement of the power and prestige of France.

Colbert, himself a member of the Académie Francaise, founded the Académie des Inscriptions et Belles-Lettres (1663) to choose inscriptions for medals and monuments celebrating the king's victories; the Académie des Sciences (1666) to study how the sciences could be exploited to the kingdom's advantage; and the Académie Royale d'Architecture (1671) to lay down rules and refine the taste of French work. He also founded schools, such as the Académie de France in Rome, in which artists could be trained under some of the great masters of the time; and schools for practical purposes, such as the École des Jeunes de Langues, for the study of oriental languages. The Observatoire de Paris, of which the Italian astronomer Giovanni Cassini was put in charge, was founded by Louis XIV at Colbert's instigation. The Italian architect G. L. Bernini was invited to submit a design for the Louvre, but its execution proved too expensive, and plans by French architects eventually were adopted.

Other spheres of activity. Colbert encouraged emigration to Canada to form the colony of New France. He promoted legislation on many matters, such as the *Ordonnance criminelle* of 1670, commercial laws, and the so-called Code Noir on slave labour. In agriculture he tried to protect the peasants so far as was consistent with his general economic system, to improve the breed of horses and sheep, and to promote new crops. His concern for economic progress made him hostile to measures against the Protestants (many of whom were in business) and mistrustful of monks and even of the secular clergy (on the ground that too many men who should have been in commerce took holy orders). He himself remained a faithful Catholic.

Last years · At the end of his life, however, Colbert was a disappointed man. For the carrying out of his far-reaching reforms, the country needed peace; but Louis XIV had been drawn into a series of wars that imposed a heavy drain on the national revenues. Even so, by energetically applying the authoritarian methods of the times, without distinction of persons or heed to public opinion, Colbert had made the monarchy stronger and the nation better equipped. The order that he had introduced into public administration was to have a lasting effect.

Colbert died in Paris on September 6, 1683, a very rich man. His eldest son, Jean-Baptiste, marquis de Seignelay, had been granted the right to succeed his father as secretary of state for the navy; the second son, Jacques-Nicolas, was archbishop of Rouen; the fourth son, Jules-Armand, marquis d'Ormoy, was *surintendant des bâtiments* (minister of construction); and three of his daughters were married to dukes.

BIBLIOGRAPHY

Writings of Colbert: Colbert left among his papers *Mémoires sur les affaires de finance de France* (written *c.* 1663); a fragment entitled *Particularités secrètes de la vie du Roy;* and other accounts of the earlier part of Louis XIV's reign. There is an edition of the *Lettres, instructions et mémoires de Colbert*, by P. CLEMENT, 9 pt. (1861–82).

Works about Colbert: An English-language study of Colbert's life and work is C.W. COLE, *Colbert and a Century of French Mercantilism*, 2 vol. (1939). Authoritative works in French are: P. CLEMENT, *Histoire de la vie et de l'administration de Colbert* (1846) and *Histoire de Colbert et de son administration*, 3rd ed., 2 vol. (1892); C. DE LA RONCIERE, *Un Grand ministre de la marine: Colbert* (1923) and *Historie de la marine française*, vol. 5 (1935); C.J. GIGNOUX, *Monsieur Colbert* (1942); and G. MONGREDIEN, *Colbert, 1619–1683* (1963).

(V.L.T.)

Coleoptera

The members of the Coleoptera—beetles and weevils—comprise the largest order of insects, about 40 percent of the known species. Among the approximately 250,000 species of Coleoptera are many of the largest and most conspicuous insects, some of which also have brilliant metallic colours, showy patterns, or striking form. Beetles can usually be recognized by their two pairs of wings; the front pair is modified into horny covers (elytra) that hide the rear pair and most of the abdomen and usually meet down the back in a straight line. Coleoptera occur in nearly all climates. They may be divided into four groups: the Archostemata, the Adephaga, and the Myxophaga contain relatively few families; the majority of beetles are placed in the Polyphaga.

Beetles attract attention for many different reasons—economic importance, size, abundance, appearance, and remarkable habits. Several groups of beetles (*e.g.*, Lampyridae) are among the few terrestrial animals capable of producing light; members of several other families (*e.g.*, Anobiidae) can produce sound (stridulate). Most large beetles make a loud noise during flight, and many species, both large and small, are attracted to light at night. Some beetles (*e.g.*, burying beetles of the family Silphidae and whirligig beetles of the family Gyrinidae) attract attention by their bizarre habits; others do so by their grotesque forms (*e.g.*, Scarabaeidae). Many beetles have become adapted to an aquatic environment (*e.g.*, Hydrophilidae); others (*e.g.*, Thorictidae) live in association with ants and termites.

GENERAL FEATURES

Distribution and abundance. Beetles are found in nearly all climates and latitudes, except in such extreme environments as those in Antarctica and at the highest altitudes. They are found on sub-Antarctic islands, close to the northern extremes in the Arctic, and on many mountain tops. Although many species occur in temperate environments, the number of species is greatest in the tropics; in general, individuals of a species are most abundant in temperate areas, and fewer individuals of more species are found in the tropics.

Some species are solitary, others occur in aggregations. Predators like the ground beetles (Carabidae) are more apt to be found alone, as are many long-horned wood-boring beetles (Cerambycidae) and weevils (Curculionidae). Ladybugs (Coccinellidae), leaf beetles (Chrysomelidae), pleasing fungus beetles (Erotylidae), darkling beetles (Tenebrionidae), checkered beetles (Cleridae), bess beetles (Passalidae), sap beetles (Nitidulidae), and some species of scarab beetles (Scarabaeoidea) are often found in aggregations of one or several different species.

Solitary and gregarious beetles ·

Most families contain both widely distributed species and some with very limited ranges. Wide distribution in this sense refers to a zoogeographical or faunal region, limited distribution to a single valley, plain, island, altitude zone, or vegetation type on a mountain.

Size range and diversity of structure. Coleoptera vary greatly in size, from a fraction of a millimetre to more than 200 millimetres (almost 8 inches) in length (*e.g.*, rhinoceros beetle, *Xyloryctes satyrus*) and up to 75 millimetres in width (*e.g.*, goliath beetle, *Goliathus goliathus*).

Diversity of structure among adult beetles is as great as range of size. The ground beetles (Carabidae) have a rather generalized (primitive) form—the flattened, oval body has a relatively even surface, with regular ridges or grooves; antennae and legs are of moderate length and slender. The underside of most water beetles (Hydrophilidae) is oval, smooth, and flattened, the antennae either short or very slender, and the forelegs short, the hindlegs long and fringed with hairs that are used as paddles. Rove beetles (Staphylinidae) have very short elytra and a slender abdomen. Staphylinid larvae have a form similar to that of the adults. Soldier beetles (Cantharidae), fireflies (Lampyridae), and net-winged beetles (Lycidae) have an un-beetle-like appearance; *e.g.*, soft elytra.

Click beetles (Elateridae) have a hingelike joint in the body region called the thorax that enables them to snap their bodies and jump high in the air; their relatives, the Buprestidae (metallic wood borers), cannot jump but take flight very quickly. Cleridae (checkered beetles) are usually oblong or cylindrical, fairly active, and often brightly

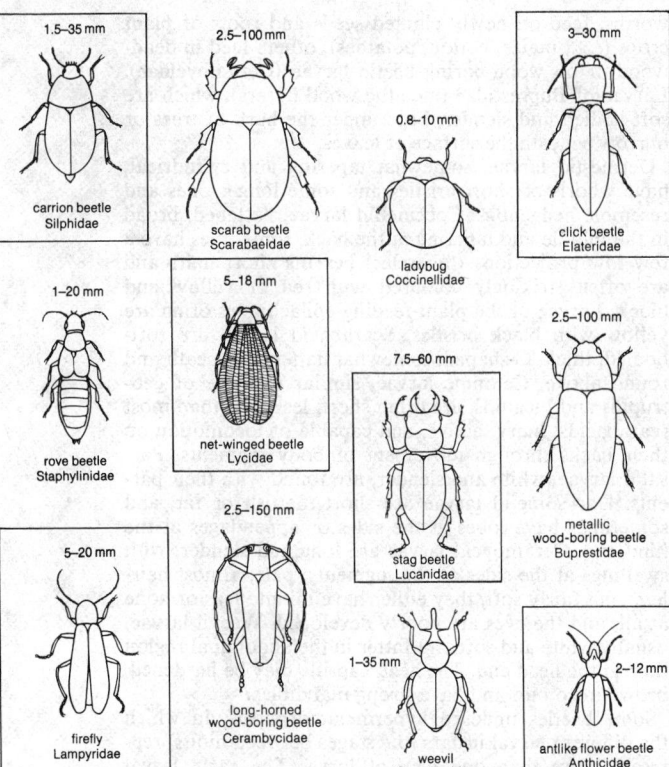

1.5–35 mm

carrion beetle
Silphidae

2.5–100 mm

scarab beetle
Scarabaeidae

0.8–10 mm

ladybug
Coccinellidae

3–30 mm

click beetle
Elateridae

1–20 mm

rove beetle
Staphylinidae

5–18 mm

net-winged beetle
Lycidae

7.5–60 mm

stag beetle
Lucanidae

2.5–100 mm

metallic
wood-boring beetle
Buprestidae

5–20 mm

firefly
Lampyridae

2.5–150 mm

long-horned
wood-boring beetle
Cerambycidae

1–35 mm

weevil
Curculionidae

2–12 mm

antlike flower beetle
Anthicidae

Figure 1: Representative beetles.
From R.A. Pimentel, *Invertebrate Identification Manual*, ©1967 by Litton Educational Publishing, Inc.; reprinted by permission of Van Nostrand Reinhold Company

rounded projections (tubercles), those of others may be smooth or grooved. The mouth is located on the end of a snoutlike projection, which varies in shape from short and stout to long and slender and sometimes exceeds the length of the rest of the body. Some Anthribidae (fungus weevils), usually cylindrical in shape, have slender antennae that may be longer than the rest of the body; they are easily confused with the cerambycids. Brenthidae (primitive weevils) usually are long and slender with antennae projecting from the sides of the snout. Scolytidae (bark beetles, ambrosia beetles) do not have a distinct snout and are usually cylindrical in shape, as are Platypodidae.

IMPORTANCE

As predators. The Coleoptera are of great economic importance; many species harm plant crops, others are beneficial to man. Predators such as Carabidae (ground beetles) and Staphylinidae (rove beetles) help to control the populations of many insects by feeding on caterpillars and other immature insects (larvae), many soft-bodied adult insects, and insect eggs. Most of the Coccinellidae (ladybugs, ladybird beetles) are highly beneficial to man; both larvae and adults feed on plant-sucking insects (Homoptera) such as aphids and scale insects. Only a few coccinellids (*e.g.*, *Epilachna*) feed on plants.

As plant feeders. Most of the beetles and weevils harmful to man are phytophagous (plant feeders). Of primary importance are the leaf beetles (Chrysomelidae) and the weevils and their relatives (Curculionoidea). Leaf-beetle larvae feed on leaves, stems, or roots of plants; and most adults chew leaves. Weevil larvae or adults feed on almost every plant part; especially numerous are species that bore into trunks, stems, and seeds. Both larval and adult forms of Scolytidae (bark beetles) are serious pests; they feed beneath tree bark, harming vital areas of living trees (*e.g.*, cambium, pine needles, leaf stalks). The Platypodidae have similar habits, but the tropical Brenthidae usually attack deadwood.

The long-horned beetles (Cerambycidae) bore into stems, trunks, roots, and cones of living and dead trees and large semiwoody herbs; adults often feed on tender, new bark. Most pea-weevil larvae (Bruchidae) develop in dried seeds of leguminous plants (peas, beans). Buprestidae (metallic wood borers) have habits similar to those of cerambycids, and many kill trees or branches by boring in the cambium. The scarab beetles (Scarabaeidae) include many important pests of plant crops, lawns, and pastures. The larvae of many Melolonthinae (June beetles, chafers), for example, feed on grass roots. The Dynastinae (rhinoceros, unicorn, and elephant beetles) are often pests of palms, killing them by destroying the growing points. Lumber, furniture, and other items made from wood are often severely damaged by several groups of beetles that bore in dry wood; *e.g.*, powder-post beetles (Lyctidae), deathwatch beetles (Anobiidae), and branch borers (Bostrychidae). Some anobiids also feed on various types of dried products; *e.g.*, the cigarette beetle, *Lasioderma serricorne*, feeds on tobacco, various dried foods, and drugs.

As scavengers. Many groups of beetles function as scavengers, breaking down materials such as dead logs, lumber used in houses (in which case they are pests), dead plant and animal matter, excrement, and other waste products. Coleopterans that function as scavengers include Scarabaeidae, Tenebrionidae (darkling beetles), Silphidae (carrion and burying beetles), and Dermestidae (dermestid or hide beetles). Some dermestid species cause serious damage in museums by feeding on dried animal materials. The larvae of several species of small dermestids damage carpets, upholstery, and clothing. However, some dermestids are valuable as scavengers; some of the carrion-feeding species (*e.g.*, *Dermestes caninus*) are used by zoologists to clean skeletons of animals.

In transmitting plant diseases. Little is known concerning the role of beetles in transmitting plant diseases. Since beetles do not suck plant juices as do plant-sucking insects (Homoptera), there is less likelihood of disease transmission. Transmission of diseases may occur, however, if beetles carry fungal spores on external parts; *e.g.*,

coloured. Nitidulidae (sap beetles) are short, flattened, and have slightly shortened elytra. Coccinellidae (ladybugs, ladybird beetles) are rounded, with a smooth, raised upper surface and a flat underside. The Endomychidae (handsome fungus beetles) often have enlarged, rounded elytra. The Erotylidae (pleasing fungus beetles) are usually slender, smooth, and shiny, as are the Languriidae.

Among the stout or cylindrical lamellicorns (Scarabaeoidea) are a number of bizarre forms. The male rhinoceros beetles (Dynastinae) have one or more horns on the head and sometimes on part of the thorax. Many of the true scarabs (Scarabaeinae) and other dung-feeding groups of the lamellicorns also have horns, including some of the goliath beetles (Cetoniinae). Male stag beetles (Lucanidae) have greatly enlarged mandibles (jaws); some are as long as the rest of the body.

The Chrysomelidae (leaf beetles) vary from simple egg-shaped forms to slender, flat, or wedge-shaped ones, with wide elytra in the tortoise beetles (Cassidinae) and often numerous spines or tubercles in the leaf-mining leaf beetles (Hispinae). The Bruchidae (pea weevils) are short and stumpy, with short stout legs. The head, slightly elongated in front, is similar to that of the curculionid weevils. The Cerambycidae (long-horned wood-boring beetles), diverse in form and structure, usually have antennae that are longer than the body. Cerambycids may be slender and medium to large in size or very small.

The extremely diverse Tenebrionidae (darkling beetles) are not always recognized as members of one family. Most arboreal (tree-dwelling) forms in the tropics or subtropics are slender and long legged. Some slender and egg-shaped forms have a metallic sheen; most of the ground-dwelling forms are black and robust. The large, tropical Trictenotomidae resemble some cerambycids (Prioninae) but are not related to them. The Alleculidae (comb-clawed beetles) resemble some of the slender tenebrionids but are usually more active. Lagriidae (lagriids) have a characteristic shape, usually widened behind, and sometimes a metallic sheen. Colydiidae (cylindrical bark beetles), hard-bodied and shiny or roughened, may be cylindrical and somewhat flattened.

Weevils   The weevils range from slender to stout, elongated to egg-shaped; the bodies of some species contain many

the fungus that causes Dutch elm disease is transmitted by the European elm bark beetle, *Scolytus multistriatus*.

NATURAL HISTORY

Reproduction and life cycle. *General features.* Reproduction is almost always bisexual in beetles, although some species consist of females only, and parthenogenesis (reproduction without fertilization) sometimes occurs. The male reproductive organ is a hardened tubelike structure called the aedeagus. The aedeagus enters a structure in the tip of the abdomen of the female (bursa copulatrix), and the sperm are stored in a saclike structure in the female (spermatheca) until they are needed to fertilize eggs. The females of most species lay eggs. After the larva has hatched, it feeds until its skin (cuticle) becomes too small and splits; the larva crawls out of the old skin (exuviae), and a new skin forms and hardens. The process, called molting, is repeated, usually from three to five times, until the larva is mature. During a nonfeeding period (prepupal stage) the insect enters the pupal stage. The pupa, which forms beneath the final larval skin and emerges when it splits, resembles the adult, except that it is soft and pale; in addition, the appendages are curled or loosely attached to the body, and the small wings are in flat bags called wing pads. The adult emerges when the thin skin of the pupa is shed; the wings stretch out to full size, and the new outer skeleton hardens and becomes coloured. No further growth of the hardened skeleton occurs; the abdomen of the gravid (pregnant) female may enlarge, however, by stretching of membranes between the abdominal segments. The four developmental stages of Coleoptera—egg, larva, pupa, adult—constitute complete metamorphosis. The length of each stage in the life cycle depends on several factors; *e.g.*, climate, nature of habitat, available food.

Eggs. Eggs vary in form, may be laid singly or in groups, and usually are laid at a site that allows proper development of the larva—on a leaf of a host plant (leaf-eating species), in bark, or in tree trunks (woodborers). Eggs also may be laid near roots, in flowers, in fruits, in tree injuries, on water plants, or under rocks.

Larvae. There are several types of coleopteran larvae (see Figure 2). Carabid larvae have a tapering, flattened, smooth body, as do those of staphylinids (rove beetles) and silphids (carrion beetles); larvae of the Dytiscidae (diving beetles), although somewhat similar to those of carabids, have a lobed air-float at the end. Larvae of click beetles (Elateridae) are cylindrical or flat and slender and have a hard surface; some click beetle larvae, called wire-

worms, feed on newly planted seeds and roots of plant crops (*e.g.*, maize, cotton, potatoes); others feed in dead-wood or on wood-boring beetle larvae (Cerambycidae). Larvae of Buprestidae (metallic wood borers), which are soft-bodied and slender, bore under the bark of trees or burrow beneath the surface of leaves.

Dermestid larvae, somewhat tapering and cylindrical, have whorls of short bristles and some longer ones and resemble hedgehogs. Coccinellid larvae, flattened, broad in the middle and tapering at the back, sometimes have a few low projections (tubercles) bearing short hairs and are often strikingly coloured with red or yellow and black. Larvae of the plant-feeding epilachnines often are yellow with black bristles. Scarabaeid larvae are soft-bodied, thick, C-shaped, somewhat flattened beneath and round above. Cetonine larvae, similar to those of geotrupids and lucanids, are often short, less bent than most scarabaeids, hairy, active, and capable of locomotion on their backs through movement of body segments. Passalid larvae, white and slender, are found with their parents. Chrysomelid larvae are short, flattish or fat, and sometimes have lobes at the sides or appendages at the hind end. Cerambycid larvae are long and slender, with swellings at the sides of the segments; pale, almost hairless, and fairly soft, they either have minute legs or none at all, and the eyes are poorly developed. Weevil larvae, usually white and soft, are fatter in the abdominal region than at the head end. The head capsule may be hardened, brown in colour, and have strong mandibles.

Some beetles undergo hypermetamorphosis, in which the different larval instars (the stages between molts) represent more than one type of larva. The early larval stages usually are active, and the later stages are parasitic on other organisms. The active, young larvae of most Meloidae (blister beetles), called triungulins, for example, hatch from eggs laid on flowers, become attached to bees visiting the flowers, and thus are carried to a bee nest, where they become parasitic on bee larvae.

Pupae. Pupae of beetles usually have the form of the adult, except that the elytra are represented by pads on the sides; the colour, generally white, is sometimes pale brown or patterned. As the time for emergence of the adult approaches, the pupa may darken, especially on the mandibles and eyes. After emerging from the pupal skin, the adult rapidly assumes its final adult form and coloration, although metallic colours may take some days to develop their final appearance.

Larvae that bore in wood, cones, or seeds and those that live in the ground or in excrement chew or dig a cavity, or pupal cell. In some cases, the pupa lies on a cushion of frass (chewed or torn wood fibres) or other material; in others, it is enclosed in a cocoon of frass or other material (*e.g.*, a smooth, white, hard covering similar to the shell of a bird's egg). Sometimes material is used only to seal off the open end of the tube, gallery, or cell for protection from ants and other predators. After the body of the adult has hardened, the adult breaks or dissolves the barrier and emerges. Many wood borer adults must chew through solid wood, although the larva usually chews close to the surface of the tree, or to the bark, before pupating.

Typical life cycle. The adult *Aspidomorpha furcata*, a tortoise beetle of South China, feeds on the leaves of the host plant *Ipomoea* (sweet potato), where the entire life cycle takes place. Eggs, laid in small groups, are cemented together in a thin paperlike egg capsule whose thin brown layers separate and camouflage them. The larva, which hatches in four to six days, burrows directly through the egg capsule and feeds on the leaf epidermis for about three days before it molts. Later it eats through the entire leaf. When the fifth instar larva is fully grown, it goes through a resting period, the prepupal period, before pupation occurs. During each molt, the old larval skin is pushed back and attached to new processes, which form at the hind end. The dried and shrunken skins plus extruded feces combine to camouflage the larva. When pupation takes place, the combination of exuviae (molted skins) and feces becomes attached to a paired process at the hind end of the pupa, thus camouflaging and shielding

Egg-laying sites (margin note)

Egg capsule (margin note)

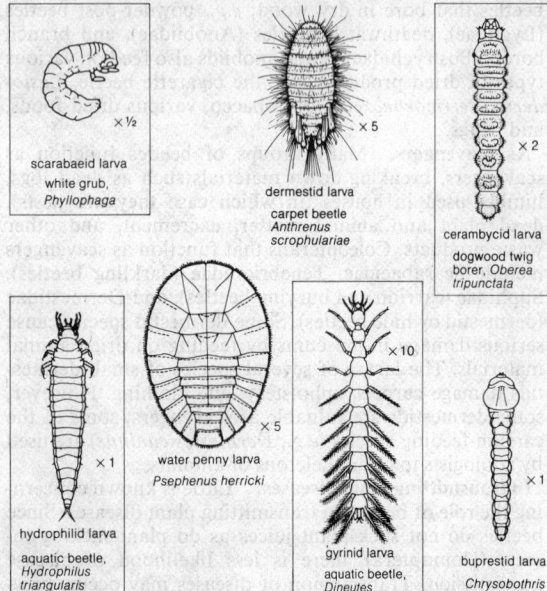

By courtesy of (*Phyllophaga*) Ohio Agricultural Research and Development Center, Wooster, Ohio; (*Anthrenus scrophulariae*) Cornell University Agricultural Experiment Station, Ithaca, New York; (*Chrysobothris trinerva*) the U.S. Department of Agriculture; (*Oberea tripunctata, Hydrophilus triangularis, Psephenus herricki, Dineutes*) from A. Peterson, *Larvae of Insects*

scarabaeid larva
white grub,
Phyllophaga
× ½

dermestid larva
carpet beetle
Anthrenus scrophulariae
× 5

cerambycid larva
dogwood twig
borer, *Oberea tripunctata*
× 2

hydrophilid larva
aquatic beetle,
Hydrophilus triangularis
× 1

water penny larva
Psephenus herricki
× 5

gyrinid larva
aquatic beetle,
Dineutes
× 10

buprestid larva
Chrysobothris trinerva
× 1

Figure 2: Diversity of beetle larvae.

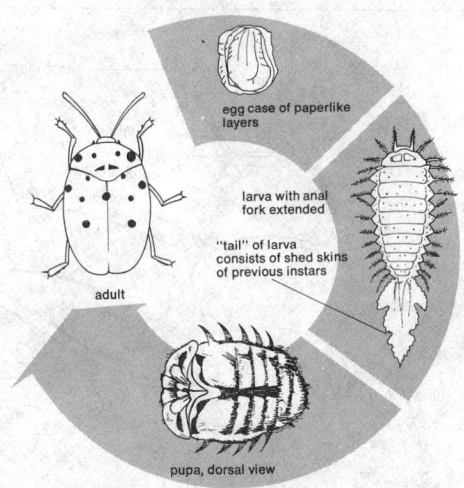

egg case of paperlike layers

larva with anal fork extended

"tail" of larva consists of shed skins of previous instars

adult

pupa, dorsal view

Figure 3: Life cycle of a tortoise beetle.
By courtesy of the U.S. Department of Agriculture

it. The last larval skin is used to attach the end of the abdomen of the pupa to the leaf surface. The pupa usually rests with its camouflage flat over its back, although it may erect the camouflage and turn it back to discourage an enemy.

The pupal stage lasts four days or longer. The life cycle from egg to adult requires 21 to 27 days in mild weather, longer in winter; adults may live more than 230 days. Females lay from 63 to 228 egg cases, with an average of about 3 eggs per case. There may be several generations per year. (See Figure 3 for the stages in the life cycle of a tortoise beetle.)

In cooler temperate areas life cycles may occupy much longer periods, even up to four years or more. In general, wood-boring beetles and root feeders have longer life cycles, leaf-feeding species have short ones, with several generations per year possible with subtropical and tropical species.

Ecology. Ecology, the relationship of organisms to each other and to their environment, represents fundamental interactions in nature. The habits of some of the small families of beetles have not yet been established.

Beetles as prey. In general, beetles are very well armoured insects and thus are reasonably protected against enemies; most, however, have parasites. Some tachinid flies, for example, lay their eggs on adult beetles, and the larvae feed inside their bodies. Beetle larvae also often have hymenopterous parasites; *e.g.*, wasps. Wood-boring long-horned beetle larvae (Cerambycidae) are parasitized by wasps that lay their eggs directly on or in beetle larvae. Beetles are probably attacked by fewer predators than are many other insects; birds that often feed on various kinds of insects may not eat some kinds of beetles. Swifts and other birds, insectivorous mammals including bats, reptiles, frogs, and other insects may act as beetle predators. Some beetle predators feed particularly on beetle larvae, although many beetle larvae that feed on plants and in the ground probably are distasteful to birds and other predators.

Feeding habits and habitats. Beetles are found in almost any habitat occupied by insects and feed on a variety of plant and animal materials. Many are predatory, some are scavengers, many are plant feeders (phytophagous), others feed on fungi, and a few are parasitic on other organisms. Beetles may live beneath the ground, in water, or as commensals in the nests of social insects such as ants and termites. Plant-feeding species may eat foliage, bore in wood or fruit, and attack roots or blossoms; any part of a plant may be a food source for some type of beetle. Many beetles eat stored plant or animal products, including various types of foods and clothing.

Adult carabids are nocturnal hunting predators whose prey ranges from miscellaneous small insects to fairly large caterpillars and land snails. Many small carabids live in moss on tree trunks and feed on small insects hidden in the moss. The predatory larvae remain more hid-

den than the adults. Both larval and adult dytiscids (diving beetles) feed on various water insects, small frogs, and small fish. Gyrinids (whirligig beetles) feed both on water insects and on other insects that fall into the water. Staphylinids (rove beetles) are usually predatory, both as larvae and as adults. Hydrophilids are water scavenger beetles and eat various dead organisms and live algae in freshwater. Silphids, which dig under small dead animals so that they settle into the ground, lay their eggs on the carrion, on which the larvae feed. Dermestids feed on dead animal skins, dead insects, birds' nests, other animal nests, and accumulations of debris. Ptinidae (spider beetles) feed on dead insects and animal skins, as do certain Anobiidae (*e.g.*, the cigarette beetle, which also feeds on tobacco and other dried products). Heterocerids and histerids prey on fly larvae or those of beetles living in excrement or in carrion. Some Elateridae (click beetles) are predatory as larvae, feeding on the larvae of wood-boring insects; others feed on roots of various crops. Most larvae of Cantharidae (soldier beetles), which prey on worms and larvae of other insects, occur under bark, in rotting wood, or in soil; the adults are usually found on flowers. The lampyrids (fireflies), which are often luminous both as larvae and as adults, are primarily predators upon snails. Clerid larvae are largely predators of wood-boring beetle larvae, although some of the adults are flower feeders.

Among the lamellicorns, the true scarabs (Scarabaeinae) and several related groups (*e.g.*, Aphodiinae, Geotrupinae) are dung feeders. Some make balls of animal excrement (*e.g.*, of cattle) and roll them to protected spots for burying. Eggs are laid on the buried balls, and the larvae feed on the excrement.

Dung feeders

The Melolonthinae (June beetles, chafers) are phytophagous, the larvae usually feeding on roots of grasses or other plants, the adults feeding on leaves. The larvae of Rutelinae (shining leaf chafers), which have similar habits, sometimes feed in humus or in rotten wood. The adults of Cetoniinae feed on pollen and tree juices; the larvae, often called white grubs, feed on organic matter in the soil and may damage plant roots. The Dynastinae (rhinoceros, unicorn, and elephant beetles) feed in rotting wood, decaying vegetation, or humus. Buprestidae bore into living and dead trees, generally feeding on the cambium layer. Some of the small buprestids are leaf miners; that is, they feed on leaf cells between the upper and lower surfaces of a leaf. Moderate numbers of larvae and adults of Passalidae (bess beetles), which feed on rotting logs, generally are found together; apparently the adults protect and feed their young, an unusual habit among beetles. The lucanids feed in logs and stumps as larvae; the adults often feed on juices from damaged trees, particularly at openings of larval tunnels of Cerambycidae (long-horned wood-boring beetles).

Tenebrionidae (darkling beetles) live in various habitats as scavengers or predators. Those in rotten wood and under bark may be predatory on other larvae; those in damp places may feed on rodent excrement, on other wastes, or on fungi; and those in stored products feed on grain, meal, and other staples. Lagriidae (lagriids) and Cistellidae (comb-clawed beetles) feed in rotten logs. Melandryidae (false darkling beetles) usually feed on fungi or in old wood. Pythids usually are scavengers in burrows of other beetles, including weevils. Rhipiphoridae (wedge-shaped beetles), which usually are parasites in wasps' nests and undergo hypermetamorphosis, are related to another group of insects, the Strepsiptera, which are mostly parasitic in the bodies of wasps, leafhoppers, grasshoppers, and other insects. Some larvae of Mordellidae (tumbling flower beetles) may live in dead or dying deciduous wood or attack the heartwood of weak trees; others may be found in pith or herbaceous weeds. The adults frequent flowers and are good fliers. Meloidae (blister beetles) undergo hypermetamorphosis and usually live in bee nests, feeding on eggs and stored food. The larvae of Pyrochroidae (fire-coloured beetles) live under bark and in rotting wood. Most cerambycid larvae are wood borers; a few live in large herbs or in cones, and many feed in roots. The adults, which chew new bark or other plant parts, at times cut rings in branches, killing them so that the larvae can bore in. Some chrysomelid larvae eat leaves; many others are root feeders. Members of one group of chrysomelid larvae (Sagrinae) bore in stems of leguminous vines, causing gall-like swellings; others (Donacinnae) feed on and in the stems of freshwater plants, often below the water level, or hide (Hispinae) in unopened parts of monocot plants such as palms, grasses, bamboos, and gingers; still others (Alticinae) may feed on both roots and leaves or act as leaf miners. Bruchidae live primarily in the seeds of legumes; hence, their common name, seed beetles.

Weevils also are diverse in habits. Many larvae bore into solid wood of living or dead trees and stumps; some feed on or in roots or in stems of semiwoody plants; and others feed in seeds, pods, grain, meal, fruits, nuts, and other parts of plants; some are hidden inside the plants. Most adults are able to fly; nonflying forms, however, are more abundant on small oceanic islands than are flying forms. Some species, which develop in rotting stumps, soil, or palm trunks, make a rough cocoon from frass. Brenthids develop in dead trunks and stumps; anthribids live in various parts of plants, often in seeds; and scolytids feed largely under the bark of living trees, although some bore in other parts of plants, seeds, cones, and needles.

Special ecological relationships. Certain beetles have special ecological relationships. Beetles that live in nests of ants and in nests of termites have become modified in form because certain structures no longer needed have degenerated (*e.g.,* wings, wing covers); some have almost lost the power of locomotion. Some species have evolved glands that produce secretions attractive to the host ants or termites.

An association of a different type is known involving beetles in the mountains of New Guinea; called epizoic symbiosis, the association occurs on the backs of large leaf-feeding weevils found on *Nothofagus* and other trees in the moss forests. Various kinds of algae, fungi, lichens, liverworts, mosses, and ferns develop on the backs of the weevils. Among them live protozoans, rotifers, nematodes, phytophagous mites, and parasitic mites. The phytophagous mites, known only from this association, feed primarily in the fungal growth on the backs of the beetles. Plant spores, which may be carried from one weevil to another either by the mites during mating of the weevils or by air dispersal, are trapped with a sticky fluid that may be produced by the weevils for this purpose.

Ambrosia beetles (Scolytidae) associate with fungi in the host tree. Certain adult scolytids and platypodids have specialized structures called mycetangia, which are used to carry the fungi when the beetles seek out new host trees.

FORM AND FUNCTION

Adult features. Many structural modifications are found among the beetles. So varied is the structure that it is difficult to make general statements; for example, a few beetles have no elytra, and some have no wings.

As in all adult insects, the segmented body consists of three primary body regions: head, thorax, and abdomen (see Figure 4). In beetles, however, two of the three thoracic segments (mesothorax and metathorax) are attached to the abdomen; the third (prothorax), isolated as the region between the head and trunk, is covered by a dorsal plate, the pronotum. The body covering (exoskeleton) varies from very horny and rigid to soft and flexible, but it usually consists of hard plates (sclerites) separated by flexible membranes.

The antennae are usually 11-segmented but vary widely in form. The jaws (mandibles) may be relatively large, as long as the rest of the body, or almost completely absent; usually they are triangular in shape and suitable for biting or chewing. The paired maxillary and labial palps are usually small and are used for feeding or handling food, but in some beetles one or the other may be greatly enlarged. The compound eyes are usually prominent, sometimes reduced or absent, and occasionally divided. Simple eyes (ocelli) are rarely present. A neck is

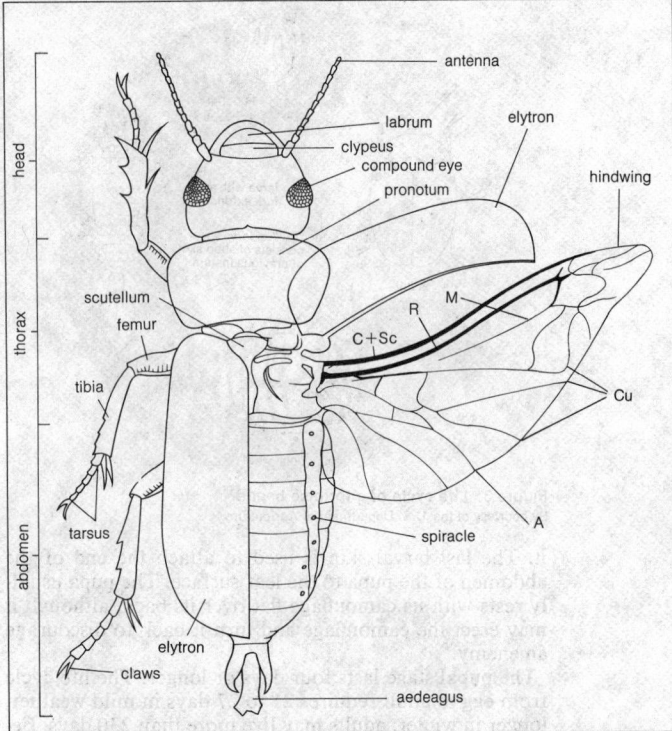

Figure 4: *Coleopteran body plan.*
The wing veins shown (with their abbreviations in parentheses) are anal (A), cubitus (Cu), media (M), radius (R), and costa + subcosta (C + Sc).
From H. Weber, *Grundriss der Insektenkunde,* 4th ed. (1966); Gustav Fischer Verlag

sometimes evident, but in many beetles the head is recessed into the prothorax or under the pronotum.

The prothorax is generally very distinct; the mesothorax and metathorax are hidden under the elytra along with most of the abdomen. The pronotum may be four-sided very wide or very long, and sculptured with lateral spines or grooves and pits. The front legs emerge from cavities in the underside that may be confluent or separated by other parts. The mesothoracic spiracle (respiratory opening) is often visible just behind the base of the front legs. The mesothorax bears the elytra (wing covers) and the second pair of legs. The metathorax bears the flying wings (hindwings) and the third pair of legs.

The legs are modified in various ways, for running, swimming, jumping, digging, or clasping. In some beetles, wings are not capable of producing flight, but in many others, they are powerful and sustain strong flight.

The abdomen is composed of nine or ten segments, but often some of these are not externally visible. From five to eight segments can usually be seen, with short apical appendages evident in some beetles. Each abdominal segment has a pair of spiracles, the openings into the airtube (tracheal) system. Predatory beetles generally have short digestive tracts. Differences in salivary glands occur, depending on the food source.

Larval features. Coleoptera larvae differ in appearance from adults. This is characteristic of insects with complete metamorphosis (Endopterygota), in which the wings develop internally until they become apparent in the pupal stage. The differences in body form of the larvae are closely associated with larval habitats and modes of feeding. The numerous predatory types, for example, have slender or gradually tapered bodies, with large, slender, mandibles, and relatively long legs; thus, these larvae are adapted to be rapid runners that capture and hold prey with their mandibles. A mouthpart structure (epipharynx) may be adapted for imbibing body fluids that exude from wounds caused by the mandibles. Typical predatory larvae are found in the dytiscids (predacious water beetles) and carabids (ground beetles). The larvae of tiger beetles (Cicindelidae), although similar to the dytiscid type, live in holes in the ground or in branches and capture passing insects. The enlarged head of the tiger beetle larva fills the burrow opening, and its legs are modified for attachment and leverage. Haliplid, staphylinid, and gyrinid larvae, are also similar to those of dytiscids, except that the gyrinids have a gill on the side of each abdominal segment, rather than at the tip of the abdomen, as do most of the others. Some predatory larvae are generally less tapered, sometimes less armoured, and have shorter appendages than do the dytiscids; *e.g.*, larvae predatory on other larvae in deadwood or in the ground. Larvae such as those of the Histeridae (hister beetles), which usually live in special environments such as dung and tunnels in wood, have short appendages but slender mandibles.

Another larval type includes many of the scavengers; *e.g.*, silphids, hydrophilids. These larvae have short legs and mandibles.

Wood-feeding borer larvae (cerambycid and buprestid type) have soft white bodies that may be cylindrical or flattened. The thoracic region of buprestids is flat and broad, the head is dark and retracted in the thorax, and the mandibles are short and stout. Larvae of wood-boring beetles usually have yeast associated with the digestive tract; they help to convert wood to digestible compounds.

Larvae that feed on leaves, stems, and roots (chrysomelid type) are short and oval shaped. Coccinellid larvae, similar in form except for longer legs, however, prey on soft-bodied insects like aphids.

The lamellicorn larval type is C-shaped, has a soft body, and a hard, dark, nonretractile head. These larvae usually are found in protected habitats, where they feed on roots, rotten wood, or excrement. Weevil larvae have a similar form, although the head may be a little smaller, the body less arched. Another larval type is that of the elaterids and many tenebrionids, which have very slender usually brown bodies, with a hard outer skeleton.

Adaptations. *Protection.* Coleoptera protect themselves against enemies in various ways. Some closely resemble their surroundings; the upper surface of one African species (*Petrognatha gigas*), for example, resembles dead velvety moss, and its irregular antennae are very much like dried tendrils or twigs. Many weevils fall and feign death at the least alarm and, folding their limbs closely around the body, look like seeds or particles of soil, thus escaping observation.

Certain beetles, especially those living in ants' nests, resemble ants, and the common wasp beetle of Europe, *Clytus arietis*, both in its movements and coloration, closely resembles a wasp.

Some beetles obtain some measure of protection possibly from their repellent appearance or from their evil-smelling or distasteful secretions, either in the form of exudations of blood from definite parts of the body or as the product of special fetid glands. The so-called bombardier beetles of the Carabidae have the property of secreting an evil-smelling defensive fluid from the anal end of the body. In some cases, this fluid volatilizes explosively into a gas at high temperature when it comes into contact with the air; it acts as a repellent to other insects or enemies. A number of beetles secure protection by virtue of their agility; many ground beetles and tiger beetles run rapidly, and the latter also take to wing with great readiness. The flea beetles (a group of the Chrysomelidae) have remarkable powers of leaping.

Sound production. Many beetles produce sound, usually by rubbing one part of the body (a scraper) against another part (the file). These stridulating organs are generally present in both sexes and probably serve for mutual sex calling. Some beetles have a filelike area on the head that is rasped by the front margin of the prothorax. Among the cerambycids, sound is produced either by rubbing the rear margin of the prothorax over a grooved area on the mesothorax or by rubbing the femurs of the hindlegs against the margins of the elytra.

Stridulation, however, is not confined to adult beetles; it occurs also in certain larvae. Some larvae of the Scarabaeoidea, for example, have a series of ridges, or tubercles, on the coxal segment of the middle pair of legs, and the hindlegs are modified in various ways as rasping organs. In the larvae of some chafers (Melolonthinae), a

Marginal note (left): Stridulation in larvae

ridged area on the mandible is rasped by a series of teeth on the maxillae. Stridulation in larvae is independent of sex and may be used to warn neighbouring larvae to avoid getting in each other's way.

Light production. Some beetles emit a bright light, whose source is in special luminous organs that consist of an outer, light-producing layer and an inner reflector layer. The outer layer is supplied with oxygen by means of air tubes (tracheae), and the reflector layer contains crystals that apparently act as a background, scattering the light and preventing its dispersion internally. The light is produced during a reaction involving a compound (luciferin) and an enzyme-like substance (luciferase) in the outer layer of the luminous organ (see also BIOLUMINESCENCE). Luminous beetles include the Lampyridae (fireflies), Phengodidae, Drilidae, and certain Elateridae (click beetles). A familiar example of a firefly is the common European glowworm (*Lampyris noctiluca*), whose wingless female emits a bright light near the hind end of the body; the winged male emits a much feebler light. Both sexes of the elaterid genera *Pyrophorus* and *Photophorus* are winged and luminous.

EVOLUTION AND PALEONTOLOGY

Coleopterans are very ancient insects; they date from the Permian Period (about 225,000,000–280,000,000 years ago), after the appearance of gymnosperm plants. Although the beetles have a number of similarities to another ancient group of insects, the cockroaches (Blattaria), they probably evolved from ancestors of the present-day Neuroptera. This theory is based largely on the nature of the life cycle of beetles and on their larval structure. Although many beetle fossils are known, they consist mostly of isolated elytra, which reveal little about the history of the order. Complete fossil specimens are closely related to living forms. The evolution of elytra may have been associated with the habit of living under bark of trees, where protection for flying wings is required. Most of the insects that live under bark are beetles.

CLASSIFICATION

Distinguishing taxonomic features. One distinctive feature of coleopterans is wing structure. Most beetles have two pairs of wings. The front pair, which may be thickened, leathery, or hard and brittle, are called elytra and usually serve only as protective covers. A few beetles have greatly reduced wings. Variations in the structure of the first abdominal segment is one criterion used to separate the various suborders of Coleoptera; the hindcoxal leg segments (by which the legs are attached to the body) may divide the abdominal segment partially or completely. Sometimes the abdominal segments are fused to form sutures.

Variation in length, texture, and appearance of elytra, as well as the number of abdominal segments exposed by short elytra, are used to distinguish superfamilies. Characters associated with the size and shape of the coxae also are used. Structure of antennae and legs are important taxonomic criteria, as are larval structure, head structure (including mandibles, or jaws), pattern of veins in wings (see Figure 4), habitats, and behaviour.

Annotated classification. About 135 families of beetles are known, of which 120 occur in the Western Hemisphere.

There have been a number of different classifications of Coleoptera. Many were based on the suborders Adephaga and Polyphaga; the latter, which contains about 90 percent of the beetles, included a number of divisions (*e.g.*, clavicorns, serricorns, lamellicorns, phytophagous beetles, and weevils). Sometimes these divisions are considered as superfamilies or series, and sometimes (particularly weevils and relatives) as suborders. The classification below is based on that of R.A. Crowson (1955); it includes four suborders.

ORDER COLEOPTERA (beetles, weevils)

Largest insect order; more than 250,000 species; size range from less than 1 mm to more than 12 cm (5 in.); modified front wings, called elytra, usually meet in a straight line down the middle of the back, covering membranous hindwings; hindwings usually longer than front wings, folded under front wings when at rest; mouthparts adapted for chewing; form of antennae variable; large compound eyes; hard outer skeleton; complete metamorphosis; found in almost all types of habitats; many plant feeders; many species of economic importance, either cause damage or benefit man; worldwide distribution.

Suborder Archostemata

Hindcoxae rarely fused to metasternum; distinct notopleural suture between notum and pleural sclerites.

Family Cupesidae (*Cupedidae*; reticulated beetles). Small and little-known; found under bark; about 20 species widely distributed.

Family Micromalthidae. Rare; 1 to 2 species; most complex life cycle among coleopterans.

Suborder Adephaga

Larval structure primitive; legs specialized for predatory life; hindcoxae of legs immovable fixed to metasternum; distinct notopleural suture between notum and pleural sclerites; wing with base of (radial sector) Rs vein distinct.

Family Cicindelidae (tiger beetles). Voracious and fierce, especially larvae; *Cicindela; active;* often brightly coloured; about 2,000 species; mostly tropical and subtropical.

Family Rhysodidae (wrinkled bark beetles). Small, slender, brownish beetles; about 100 species, mostly tropical.

Family Paussidae. Sometimes a subfamily of Carabidae; about 400 species; tropical or subtropical; associated with ants.

Family Carabidae (ground beetles). Usually dark, shiny, flattened; larvae and adults predatory; *Calosoma* feed on caterpillars; *Brachinus*, bombardier beetles, eject fluid from anus; about 20,000 species; worldwide distribution.

Family Trachypachidae. A few species in Europe and North America.

Family Haliplidae (crawling water beetles). About 200 small aquatic species; wide geographical range.

Family Amphizoidae (trout-stream beetles). About 5 species (*Amphizoa*) in Tibet, North America; feed on drowned insects.

Family Hygrobiidae. A few species (*Hygrobia*) widely distributed; aquatic; produce sound.

Family Gyrinidae (whirligig beetles). About 700 species; surface swimmers; sometimes gregarious.

Family Noteridae (burrowing water beetles). Similar to Dytiscidae; small; larvae burrow.

Family Dytiscidae (true water beetles). Worldwide distribution; about 4,000 species; found in flowing and still water; *Siettitia* eyeless; *Dytiscus* best known.

Suborder Myxophaga

Wing with base of Rs vein absent; prothorax usually with distinct notopleural suture.

Family Calyptomeridae. Sometimes placed in Clambidae.

Family Lepiceridae. A few Central American species.

Family Sphaeriidae (minute bog beetles). Less than 1 mm in length; 1 genus; a few widespread species; sometimes placed in Staphylinoidea.

Family Hydroscaphidae (skiff beetles). Size about 1.5 mm; found in algae on rocks in streams; sometimes placed in Staphylinoidea; generic example: *Hydroscapha;* widely distributed.

Suborder Polyphaga

Includes the majority of beetles; wing with base of Rs vein absent; prothorax never with distinct notopleural suture.

Superfamily Hydrophiloidea

Head usually with Y-shaped line on front; antennae short, hairy and club-shaped at end; habits mostly aquatic; maxillary palp usually longer than antennae.

Family Hydrophilidae (water scavenger beetles). About 2,000 species, numerous in tropics; aquatic and terrestrial; most live on decomposing vegetable matter; *Hydrophilus* is predatory; other examples: *Cercyon, Helophorus.*

Superfamily Histeroidea

Antennae geniculate (elbow-shaped) with last 3 segments club-shaped; wing with medio-cubital loop reduced; elytron truncate leaving 1 or 2 segments of abdomen exposed.

Family Sphaeritidae. One genus, about 4 species.

Family Synteliidae. One genus, a few species in Mexico and the Orient.

Family Histeridae (hister beetles). Small, dark, shiny; found in decaying organic matter; predatory on small insects; about 2,500 species; wide distribution; examples: *Hister, Niponius.*

Superfamily Staphylinoidea

Very large group; antennae with last 3 segments rarely club-shaped; outer skeleton rarely very hard, shiny; wing veins M

(media) and Cu (cubitus) not connected; elytron truncate, usually more than 2 abdominal segments exposed.

Family Limulodidae (horseshoe crab beetles). One mm or less; in United States and Australia; ride on ants; 5 genera, about 30 species.

Family Ptiliidae (feather-winged beetles). Among the smallest beetles; live in dung, rotting wood, fungi; about 350 species; temperate and neotropical regions.

Family Leptinidae (mammal-nest beetles). Feed on eggs and young of small anthropods in small-mammal nests; wingless; widely distributed.

Family Anisotomidae (*Leiodidae*; round fungus beetles). Small, shiny; habitats vary—caves, fungi, mammal nests; about 1,000 species.

Family Dasyceridae. About 10 species; Holarctic.

Family Silphidae (carrion beetles, burying beetles). Relatively large, bright-coloured; usually feed on carrion; some predatory, some plant feeders; examples: *Silpha, Nicrophorus;* about 230 species; widely distributed.

Family Scydmaenidae (antlike stone beetles). Under stones, logs; in ant nests; very small, hairy; widely distributed; about 1,200 species; example: *Scydmaenus.*

Family Scaphidiidae (shining fungus beetles). In fungi, dead leaves, rotting wood; small, very shiny; about 250 species; example: *Scaphidium.*

Family Staphylinidae (rove beetles). Short elytra; size variable; active; strong mandibles; in ant nests, predatory on other insects in decaying matter; about 20,000 species; widely distributed; examples: *Stenus, Dinarda.*

Family Pselaphidae (short-winged mold beetles). Very small; diverse in form; live in ant nests; about 3,500 species; worldwide distribution but most abundant in tropics; example: *Claviger.*

Superfamily Scarabaeoidea (Lamellicornia)

Antennae 10-segmented with last 3 to 7 segments forming a lamellate (platelike) club; body stout; larvae without cerci (appendages at end of abdomen); males and females often differ in appearance; outgrowths on head and thorax produce bizarre forms; produce sound (stridulate).

Family Lucanidae (stag beetles, pinching bugs). Large; variable in size; males with enormous mandibles (jaws); about 900 species; widely distributed; example: *Lucanus.*

Family Passalidae (bess beetles). Large, dark, flattened; about 800 species, mostly in moist, warm forests; live in decaying wood.

Family Trogidae (skin beetles). About 150 widely distributed species; example: *Trox;* dung or carrion feeders.

Family Acanthoceridae. About 100 tropical species; associated with rotten wood.

Family Geotrupidae ("dor" beetles). Large; about 300 species; widely distributed; habits variable; examples: *Lethrus, Geotrupes.*

Family Scarabaeidae (scarab beetles, June beetles, tumblebugs, leaf-chafers). Variable in colour, size, habits; most feed on dung, carrion, other decaying matter; about 20,000 species; widely distributed; examples: *Cetonia, Melolontha.*

Superfamily Dascilloidea

Forecoxae projecting; abdomen with 5 visible segments; wing with radial cell short; anal cell of wing, if present, with 1 apical vein.

Family Clambidae (fringed-wing beetles). Small, hairy; in decaying plant material; about 30 species; worldwide distribution; sometimes placed in Staphylinoidea.

Family Eucinetidae. About 25 widely distributed species; in rotten wood; example: *Eucinetus.*

Family Helodidae (marsh beetles). Small, oval; on vegetation in swampy places; aquatic larvae; about 350 species; widely distributed; example: *Scirtes.*

Family Dascillidae. About 200 moderate-sized species; found on vegetation in moist places.

Superfamily Byrrhoidea

Forecoxae large; antennae more or less thickened at tip; body short, with legs and antennae retractable into grooves on under surface.

Family Byrrhidae (pill beetles). Small, oval; found under debris, in sand, at grass roots; about 270 species; widely distributed; example: *Byrrhus.*

Superfamily Dryopoidea

Forecoxae sometimes slightly projecting; antennae usually filiform (threadlike) or short and broad; head with distinct labrum (upper lip); last tarsal segment of leg often as long as preceding 3 or 4 together.

Family Psephenidae (water-penny beetles). Larvae flat, almost circular; a few species, mostly in India, North America.

Family Eurypogonidae. A few species in Northern Asia, North America.

Family Ptilodactylidae. About 200 tropical species; aquatic or in rotten wood.

Family Chelonariidae. About 50 species in tropics of Asia and America.

Family Heteroceridae (variegated mud-loving beetles). About 500 widely distributed species; example: *Heterocerus.*

Family Limnichidae (minute marsh-loving beetles). Similar to Dryopidae; a few widely distributed species.

Family Dryopidae (long-toed water beetles). Small; downy; crawl on stream bottoms; few species; widely distributed.

Family Elmidae (riffle beetles). Varied habitat; several hundred widely distributed species.

Superfamily Rhipiceroidea

Antennae flabellate (fanlike); noselike projection between mandibles; about 180 species; widely distributed; 2 families, Rhipiceridae (cedar beetles), Callirhipidae; example: *Sandalus.*

Superfamily Buprestoidea

Antenna short, serrate; abdomen weakly hardened.

Family Buprestidae (metallic wood-boring beetles). Brightly coloured, metallic sheen; inhabit various hot, moist forests; about 15,000 species, mostly tropical; examples: *Agrilus, Sphenoptera, Chrysobothris.*

Superfamily Elateroidea

Forecoxae small; metasternum without transverse suture; larvae with no free labrum.

Family Cerophytidae. About 12 species in Europe and America; in hollow trees.

Family Cebrionidae. About 200 species; in mild regions; female often wingless.

Family Elateridae (click beetles). About 7,000 species; widely distributed; can leap when lying on back; adults, plant feeders; larvae sometimes damage plants; examples: *Pyrophorus, Agriotes, Athous.*

Family Trixagidae (*Throscidae;* throscid beetles). Small, oblong; about 200 species; widely distributed.

Family Perothopidae. Medium-sized; on trunks or branches of old beech trees.

Family Eucnemidae (false click beetles). Closely related to Elateridae; about 1,000 species, mostly in warm climates; example: *Melasis.*

Superfamily Cantharoidea

Larvae with grooved or channelled mandibles; front coxae large, projecting; 6 or 7 visible abdominal segments.

Family Brachypsectridae. A few species in Asia and California.

Family Homalisidae. A few species in Mediterranean region.

Family Karumiidae. A few species in Iran, South America.

Family Drilidae. About 80 species, mainly in Europe; larvae prey on snails.

Family Phengodidae. About 50 species in America; produce light.

Family Lampyridae (lightning bugs, fireflies). Produce light in species—characteristic flashing rhythm; wingless females and most larvae called glowworms; about 1,000 species; widely distributed; examples: *Lampyris, Photinus.*

Family Cantharidae (soldier beetles). Soft-bodied, predatory; about 3,500 species; widely distributed; examples: *Cantharis, Rhagonycha.*

Family Lycidae (net-winged beetles). About 2,800 species, mostly tropical; often bright-coloured; distasteful to birds; example: *Dulitocola.*

Superfamily Dermestoidea

Last 3 antennal segments forming a club; tarsi of legs all 5 segmented, simple.

Family Derodontidae. About 12 widely distributed species.

Family Nosodendridae. About 30 widely distributed species; found under bark.

Family Dermestidae (skin beetles, dermestid beetles). Many economically important species; mostly scavengers on plant and animal products; small to moderate-sized; hairy or with scales; examples: *Dermestes, Anthrenus;* widely distributed.

Family Thorictidae. About 80 species, commonly in Mediterranean region; associate with ants.

Superfamily Bostrychoidea

Larvae soft-bodied, lack specialized setae (hairs), maintain a C-shaped position; adult hard, head region hoodlike; members often associated with timber, destructive.

Family Anobiidae (drugstore and death-watch beetles). Live in dry vegetable materials; some species destructive pests; examples: *Xestobium, Stegobium, Lasioderma;* about 1,100 widely distributed species.

Family Ptinidae (spider beetles). Long legs; spiderlike appearance; sometimes infest stored products; about 500 widely distributed species.

Family Bostrychidae (branch and twig borers). Attack living and deadwood; about 550 species; worldwide distribution; examples: *Sinoxylon, Dinoderus.*

Family Lyctidae (powder-post beetles). Related to Bostrychidae; damage timber and furniture; about 90 widely distributed species.

Family Psoidae (psoid branch and twig beetles). Medium-sized; sometimes cause extensive orchard damage; examples: *Psoa, Polycaon.*

Superfamily Cleroidea

Tarsi of legs always 5-segmented; forecoxae projecting or transverse; abdomen with 5 or 6 visible segments.

Family Trogositidae (bark-gnawing beetles). About 500 species, mostly tropical; vary in shape and habits; sometimes in stored products; example: *Tenebroides.*

Family Chaetosomatidae. Three genera in New Zealand.

Family Cleridae (checkered beetles). Small; many brightly coloured; downy; most adults and larvae predatory on other insects; some adults pollen feeders; about 3,000 species, mainly tropical; examples: *Corynetes, Necrobia.*

Family Melyridae (soft-winged flower beetles). About 4,000 species widely distributed; diverse; example: *Malachius.*

Family Phloiophilidae. Rare; 1 species in Britain.

Superfamily Lymexyloidea

Antennae short, more or less serrate; abdomen with 6 or 7 visible segments.

Family Lymexylidae (ship-timber beetles). About 50 species; worldwide distribution; damage wood; examples: *Lymexylon, Hylecoetus.*

Superfamily Cucujoidea

Usually 5 visible abdominal segments; antennae filiform or clubbed, rarely serrate.

Section Clavicornia. All visible abdominal segments usually movable; sometimes less than 7 pairs of abdominal spiracles (respiratory holes).

Family Passandridae. Few species; mostly in warm climates.

Family Smicripidae. Sometimes placed in Nitidulidae; a few species in tropical America; example: *Smicrips.*

Family Nitidulidae (sap beetles). Variable size, shape, habits; usually found around fermenting plant fluids or moldy plant materials; about 2,200 species; examples: *Meligethes, Cybocephalus.*

Family Byturidae (fruitworm beetles). Small, hairy; few genera; damage raspberry blossoms and fruit; example: *Byturus.*

Family Biphyllidae (silken fungus beetle). About 200 species; mostly tropical; example: *Biphyllus.*

Family Rhizophagidae (root-eating beetles). Usually occur under bark; few species; sometimes placed in Nitidulidae.

Family Cisidae (minute tree-fungus beetles). Occur under bark, in wood, or in dry woody fungi; about 360 species; widely distributed.

Family Protocucujidae. Two species; Chile and Australia; similar to Sphindidae.

Family Sphindidae (dry-fungus beetles). Small, dark; occur in dry fungi; about 30 species; widely distributed.

Family Cucujidae (flat bark beetles). Flat, medium-sized; predatory on mites and other insects; some species hypermetamorphic; example: *Catogenus.*

Family Silvanidae (flat grain beetles). Closely related to Cucujidae; some feed on grain (*Oryzaephilus*); another genus, *Silvanus.*

Family Hypocopridae. Little known; few species.

Family Helotidae. About 80 species in warm parts of Asia.

Family Phycosedidae. Few species; examples: *Phycosecis, Alfieriella;* in Australia, Asia, Africa.

Family Propalticidae. About 20 species in warm regions of Old World.

Family Cryptophagidae (silken fungus beetles). Mostly fungus feeders; sometimes in nests of bees and wasps; about 800 species; examples: *Cryptophagus, Antherophagus.*

Family Phalacridae (shining flower beetles). Larvae develop in certain flower heads (*e.g.,* goldenrod), about 500 species; widely distributed; example: *Olibrus.*

Family Languriidae. Feed on plant leaves and stems; example: *Languria;* about 400 species mostly in Asia and North America.

Family Erotylidae (pleasing fungus beetles). Shiny; found with fungi; about 1,600 species; many in South America.

Family Cerylonidae. Often placed in Colydiidae; few species.

Family Coccinellidae (ladybird beetles, ladybugs). Many

predatory on aphids and coccids, a few serious plant pests (*Epilachna*); mostly beneficial; about 5,000 species, usually bright-coloured, spotted; widely distributed; another genus, *Rodolia*.

Family Corylophidae. About 300 species; widely distributed; minute in size.

Family Endomychidae (handsome fungus beetles). Shiny, usually brightly coloured; feed on fungi (mold); about 600 species; mostly in tropical forests; examples: *Endomychus*, *Mycetaea*.

Family Discolomidae. About 30 tropical species; many wingless.

Family Merophysiidae. Few species, sometimes placed in Lathridiidae.

Family Lathridiidae (minute brown scavenger beetles). Found in fungi, debris, flowers; about 600 widely distributed species.

Section Heteromera. Abdomen with 7 pairs of spiracles; forecoxae usually projecting.

Family Merycidae. A few Australasian species; example: *Meryx;* affinities uncertain.

Family Mycetophagidae (hairy fungus beetles). Mostly associated with fungi; often brightly marked; about 200 species.

Family Colydiidae (cylindrical bark beetles). More than 1,400 species; especially in tropics, but many in New Zealand; diverse; example: *Bothrideres*.

Family Pterogeniidae. Two Indo-Malayan genera of uncertain affinities.

Family Nilionidae. About 40 species, mostly in tropics; associate with fungi on trees.

Family Lagriidae. Medium-sized with metallic sheen; found in foliage, on bark.

Family Tenebrionidae (darkling beetles). Varied group; mostly plant scavengers; examples: *Eleodes, Tenebrio;* about 10,000 species; widely distributed.

Family Alleculidae (*Cistelidae;* comb-clawed beetles). Found on flowers, foliage, fungi, under dead bark; 100 species; worldwide distribution; example: *Omophlus*.

Family Monommidae. Adults occur in leaf litter; larvae in rotten wood; about 100 species in warm regions; example: *Monomma*.

Family Zopheridae. Few species, mostly in America.

Family Elacatidae (false tiger beetles). Widely distributed; numerous species; examples: *Othnius, Eurystethus*.

Family Boridae. Widely distributed small group; sometimes placed in Tenebrionidae.

Family Inopeplidae. One genus, *Inopeplus;* related to Salpingidae.

Family Salpingidae (narrow-waisted bark beetles). Superficial resemblance to Carabidae (ground beetles); adults and larvae predatory; adults occur under rocks, or bark, in leaf litter, on vegetation; few species but widely distributed; examples: *Salpingus, Lissodema*.

Family Cononotidae. Similar to Salpingidae; several genera.

Family Mycteridae. Resemble Salpingidae.

Family Hemipeplidae. Few species in warm regions; live beneath palm leaves.

Family Trictenotomidae. About 12 species in forests of Oriental region.

Family Pythidae. Few species widely distributed in Eurasia and America; example: *Pytho*.

Family Pyrochroidae (fire-coloured beetles). Adults large, found on foliage or flowers, under bark; about 100 species in north temperate region; example: *Pyrochroa*.

Family Tetratomidae. Similar to Melandryidae.

Family Melandryidae (false darkling beetles). Usually found under bark or logs; examples: *Penthe, Osphya;* about 400 species in woodlands of temperate regions.

Family Scraptiidae. About 200 species widely distributed; associated with rotten wood, fungi; example: *Scraptia*.

Family Mordellidae (tumbling flower beetles). Wedge-shaped, hump-backed; common on flowers; active; about 650 species.

Family Rhipiphoridae (wedge-shaped beetles). About 400 species, many with specialized parasitic habits on other insects; complicated life cycle; examples: *Pelecotoma, Metoecus*.

Family Cephaloidae (false longhorn beetles). About 11 species in east Asia, North America.

Family Meloidae (blister beetles, oil beetles). Body fluids contain cantharadin, sometimes used as a drug (*Lytta*); several important plant pests (*Epicauta*); many larvae beneficial, feed on grasshopper eggs; hypermetamorphic; complicated life cycle; about 2,000 species; widely distributed.

Family Oedemeridae (false tiger beetles). Adults usually on flowers or foliage; larvae in moist decaying wood; about 600 species; widely distributed, but especially abundant in temperate regions; example: *Nacerdes*.

Family Aderidae (antlike leaf beetles). About 350 species; usually found in deadwood or vegetable refuse; example: *Aderus*.

Family Anthicidae (antlike flower beetles). Many occur in vegetable refuse; about 1,000 species; sometimes placed in Pedilidae; examples: *Anthicus, Notoxus*.

Superfamily Chrysomeloidea

Mostly wood or plant feeders; body shape very variable; antennae not clubbed.

Family Cerambycidae (long-horned, wood-boring beetles). Some large in size; plant feeders; many brightly coloured; larval stage usually wood-boring, sometimes cause tree damage; about 25,000 species; worldwide distribution; examples: *Macrotoma, Titanus, Clytus, Monochamus*.

Family Chrysomelidae (leaf beetles). Closely related to Cerambycidae; larvae usually plant feeders; many serious pest species; overwinter as adults; more than 26,000 species; widely distributed.

Family Bruchidae (seed beetles, pea weevils). Most larvae live in leguminous seeds; examples: *Acanthoscelides, Bruchus;* damage stored seeds; about 900 species; widely distributed.

Superfamily Curculionoidea (snout beetles)

One of the largest and most highly evolved groups of coleopterans; head prolonged into beak or snout; mouthparts small; antennae usually clubbed and geniculate; larvae C-shaped; mostly plant feeders; of economic importance as pests.

Family Anthribidae (fungus weevils). Found in dead wood and fungi; about 2,400 species, mostly in tropics; *Brachytarsus* predatory on scale insects.

Family Nemonychidae (pine-flower snout beetles). Small group sometimes placed in Curculionidae or Attelabidae.

Family Belidae. Small group found in Australia, New Zealand, South America attached to a variety of plants.

Family Oxycorynidae. Small group; found in South America (*Oxycorynus*), East Indies (*Metrioxena*), tropical America (*Allocorynus*).

Family Aglycyderidae (*Proterhinidae*). About 200 species; *Proterhinus* found in Pacific region; one *Aglycyderes* species in Canary Islands.

Family Attelabidae (leaf-rolling weevils). Form leaf rolls on various trees; moderate number of species; widely distributed.

Family Brenthidae. About 1,700 species, mostly in wooded tropical countries; variable size range; males unlike females in structure.

Family Apionidae. Moderate number of species; *Apion, Cylas;* several species injure leguminous crops.

Family Curculionidae (weevils). About 30,000 species, many with scales; many injurious species; worldwide distribution; *Anthonomus*, (cotton boll weevil, apple blossom weevil); *Calandra* (granary weevil, rice weevil); *Sitona* species pests of leguminous crops.

Family Scolytidae (bark beetles). Numerous species; damage trees; *Scolytus* (elm bark beetle); other genera: *Ips; Dendroctonus; Hylastinus*.

Family Platypodidae (pin-hole borers or flat-footed ambrosia beetles). Seldom attack healthy trees; example: *Platypus;* fungus food called ambrosia.

Critical appraisal. There are many different opinions among coleopterists concerning the relationships of the various groups of beetles; the groups that should be given family status; and the placement of families in superfamilies and suborders. Little information is available about many coleopteran groups, so that their taxonomic affinities are uncertain. Although Crowson includes Strepsiptera (twisted-wing parasites) as a superfamily of Coleoptera, opinion is divided concerning their status, and they have not been included here (see INSECTA). Some classifications of Coleoptera recognize three suborders, Archostemmata, Adephaga, and Polyphaga, rather than the four used by Crowson.

BIBLIOGRAPHY

General: In addition to information given in textbooks of entomology, the following works should be consulted: J.R. DIBB, *Field Book of Beetles* (1948); R.H. HARNETT, JR. *The Beetles of the United States* (1968); H.E. JAQUES, *How to Know the Beetles* (1951); G. TAYLOR, *Some British Beetles* (1948); UNITED STATES DEPARTMENT OF AGRICULTURE, "Insects," *1952 Yearbook of Agriculture* (1952), many chapters of this work are devoted to pestiferous beetles—their ravages and control; A.G. BØVING and F.C. CRAIGHEAD, "An Illustrated

Synopsis of the Principal Larval Forms of the Order Cole-optera," *Ent. Amer.*, vol. 11 (1930–31); J.H. FABRE, *Souvenirs entomologiques*, 10 vol. (1879–1907). Many of these detailed popular accounts of natural history are available in English. A standard anatomical and biological work, based upon a study of the water beetle *Dytiscus*, is E. KORSCHELT, *Der Gel-brand Dytiscus marginalis*, 2 vol. (1923–24).

Advanced: R.A. CROWSON, *The Natural Classification of the Families of Coleoptera* (1955, reprinted 1967), a descriptive synopsis of all families of beetles, with illustrated key, and many new arrangements; W.W. FOWLER, *Coleoptera: General Introduction and Cicindelidae and Paussidae* (1912), a general treatment of morphology, including the internal anatomy of beetles, with a general discussion of organs, biology, and classification; J.T. LACORDAIRE, "Histoire naturelle des insectes: Genera des coléoptères, ou exposé méthodique et critique de tous les genres proposés jusqui'ici dans cet ordre d'insectes," 12 vol. (1854–76, reprinted 1954–72), the standard work on all the families and genera of beetles known at the time, still extremely useful, with keys to all categories (in French).

Catalogues of the species of Coleoptera include the *Cata-logus Coleopterorum Europeae*, 2nd ed. (1906) by L. HEYDEN, E. REITTER, and J. WEISE; C.W. LENG, *Catalogue of the Coleoptera of America, North of Mexico* (1920), with five supplements (1927–48); W. JUNK, *Coleopterorum Catalogus* (1910–39); R.E. BLACKWELDER (comp.), *Checklist of the Coleopterous Insects of Mexico, Central America, the West Indies, and South America*, 6 pt. (1944–57).

(J.L.G.)

Coleridge, Samuel Taylor

Samuel Taylor Coleridge was one of the most influential English poets and thinkers of the early 19th century.

Besides writing two of the greatest poems in English literature, he perfected a mode of sensuous lyricism that is often echoed by later poets; his speculative and inquiring mind was a constant intellectual stimulus to his contemporaries; and the religious thinking of his old age influenced many theologians, notably those of the Broad Church movement, in which liberal theology was matched by social concern.

Coleridge, oil painting by Washington Allston, 1814. In the National Portrait Gallery, London.

Early life and works. He was born at Ottery St. Mary, in Devonshire, on October 21, 1772, his father being vicar of Ottery and headmaster of the local grammar school. As a child he was already a prodigious reader and immersed himself to the point of morbid fascination in romances and Eastern tales such as *The Arabian Nights' Entertainments*, which were then fashionable. In 1781 his father died suddenly. In 1782 Coleridge entered Christ's Hospital in London, where he completed his secondary education. In 1791 he entered Jesus College, Cambridge. At both school and university he continued to read voraciously, particularly in works of imagination and visionary philosophy and was remembered by his contemporaries for his eloquence and prodigious memory. At

Cambridge, however, his career suffered the first of many setbacks. In his third year, oppressed by financial difficulties, he went to London and enlisted as a dragoon under the assumed name of Silas Tomkyn Comberbache. Despite his unfitness for the life, he remained enlisted until discovered by his friends; he was then bought out by his brothers and restored to Cambridge.

On his return, he was restless. The intellectual and political turmoil surrounding the French Revolution had set in motion intense and urgent discussion concerning the nature of society. The trial in 1793 of William Frend, a radical fellow of his own college, for publishing a seditious pamphlet, had been a celebrated case in the university. Coleridge, who had been a leader of undergraduate opinion in Frend's favour, now conceived the design of circumventing the disastrous violence that had destroyed the idealism of the French Revolution by establishing a small society that should organize itself and educate its children according to better principles than those obtaining in the society around them. A chance meeting with the poet Robert Southey led the two men to plan this scheme of "pantisocracy" in which 12 men and 12 women would set up a community by the Susquehanna River in Pennsylvania. To this end Coleridge left Cambridge for good and set up with Southey as public lecturer in Bristol. In October 1795 he married Sara Fricker, daughter of a local schoolmistress, swayed partly by Southey's suggestion that he was under an obligation to her since she had been refusing the advances of other men.

Shortly afterward, Southey defected from the pantisocratic scheme, leaving Coleridge married to a woman whom he did not really love. In a sense his career never fully recovered from this blow: if there is a makeshift quality about many of its later events, one explanation can be found in his constant need to reconcile his intellectual aspirations with the financial needs of his family. For a time he continued to pursue his social and political interests by publishing a journal, *The Watchman*, devoted to expressing a liberal spirit both in its political reports and more generally through poems and essays. This ran for ten issues (March–May 1796). Coleridge also preached in Unitarian chapels and undertook occasional journalism and tutorage. By July 1797, however, he was writing to J.P. Estlin: "I am wearied with politics even to soreness. I never knew a passion for politics exist for a long time without swallowing up, or absolutely excluding a passion for Religion. . . ." And, in March of the following year, he could write to his brother that he had withdrawn himself almost totally from the consideration of "immediate causes" (that is, current political arguments) and proclaim his ambitions as follows:

in poetry, to elevate the imagination and set the affections in right tune by the beauty of the inanimate impregnated, as with a living soul, by the presence of Life—in prose, to the seeking with patience and a slow, very slow mind . . . what our faculties are and what they are capable of becoming.

Collaboration with Wordsworth and major poems. During the intervening period, Coleridge's intellect had been flowering in an extraordinary manner, as he embarked on his investigation of the nature of the human mind, joined by William Wordsworth, with whom he had become acquainted in 1795. Together they entered upon one of the most influential creative periods of English literature. Coleridge's intellectual ebullience and his belief in the existence of a powerful "life consciousness" in all individuals rescued Wordsworth from depression, into which recent events had cast him, and made possible the new approach to nature that characterized his contributions to *Lyrical Ballads* (which was to be published in 1798). Coleridge, meanwhile, was developing a new, informal mode of poetry in which, following the tradition of poets such as William Cowper, he could use a conversational tone and rhythm to give unity to a poem. Of these poems, the most successful is "Frost at Midnight," which begins with the description of a silent frosty night in Somerset and proceeds through a meditation on the relationship between the quiet work of frost and the quiet breathing of the sleeping baby at the poet's side, to conclude in a resolve that his child shall be

Meeting with Robert Southey

Coleridge's new, informal mode of poetry

brought up as a "child of nature," so that the sympathies that the poet has come to detect may be reinforced throughout the child's education.

At the climax of the poem, he touches another theme, which lies at the root of his philosophical attitude:

> . . . so shalt thou see and hear
> The lovely shapes and sounds intelligible
> Of that eternal language, which thy God
> Utters, who from eternity doth teach
> Himself in all, and all things in himself.

Coleridge's attempts to learn this "language" and trace it through the ancient traditions of mankind also led him during this period to return to the visionary interests of his schooldays: as he ransacked works of comparative religion and mythology, he was exploring the possibility that all religions and mythical traditions, with their general agreement on the unity of God and the immortality of the soul, sprang from a universal life consciousness, which was expressed particularly through the phenomena of human genius. While these speculations were at their most intense, he retired to a lonely farmhouse near Culbone, Somersetshire (probably during a walking tour with Wordsworth and his sister Dorothy in the autumn of 1797) and, according to his own account, composed under the influence of laudanum the mysterious poetic fragment known as "Kubla Khan." The exotic imagery and rhythmic chant of this poem have led many critics to conclude that it should be read as a "meaningless reverie" and enjoyed for its vivid and sensuous qualities. An examination of the poem in the light of Coleridge's psychological and mythological interests, however, suggests that it has, after all, a complex structure of meaning and is basically a poem about the nature of human genius. The first two stanzas show the two sides of what Coleridge elsewhere calls "commanding genius," its creative aspirations in time of peace imaged in the projected pleasure dome and gardens of the first stanza, its destructive power in time of turbulence imaged in the wailing woman, the destructive fountain, and the voices prophesying war of the second stanza. In the final stanza the poet writes of a state of "absolute genius" in which, if inspired by a visionary "Abyssinian maid," he would become endowed with the creative, divine power of a sun god—an Apollo or Osiris subduing all around him to harmony by the fascination of his spell.

Coleridge's reticence on the subject of this poem and his eventual description of it as a "psychological curiosity" is probably due to the extravagant claims of the last stanza; he was enabled to explore the same range of themes less egotistically in "The Rime of the Ancient Mariner," composed during the autumn and winter of 1797–98. For this, his most famous poem, he drew upon the ballad form. The main narrative tells how a sailor who has committed a crime against the life principle by slaying an albatross, suffers from torments, physical and mental, in which the nature of his crime is made known to him. The underlying life power against which he has transgressed is envisaged as a power corresponding to the influx of the sun's energy into all living creatures, thereby binding them together in a joyful communion. By killing the bird that hovered near the ship, the mariner has destroyed one of the links in this process. His own consciousness is consequently affected: the sun, previously glorious, is seen as a bloody sun, and the energies of the deep are seen as corrupt.

Com-
position of
"The Rime
of the
Ancient
Mariner"

> All in a hot and copper sky,
> The bloody Sun, at noon,
> Right up above the mast did stand,
> No bigger than the Moon.
> . . . .
> The very deep did rot; O Christ!
> That ever this should be!
> Yea, slimy things did crawl with legs
> Upon the slimy sea.

Only at night do these energies display a sinister beauty.

> About, about, in reel and rout
> The death-fires danced at night;
> The water, like a witch's oils,
> Burnt green, and blue and white.

After the death of his shipmates, alone and becalmed, devoid of sense of movement or even of time passing, he is in a hell created by the absence of any link with life. Eventually, however, a chance sight of water snakes flashing like golden fire in the darkness and an answering gush of love from his heart reinitiates the creative process: he is even given a brief vision of the inner unity of the universe, in which all living things hymn their source in an interchange of harmonies. Restored to his native land, he remains haunted by what he has experienced but is at least delivered from nightmare, able to see the ordinary processes of human life with a new sense of their wonder and mercifulness.

These last qualities are reflected in the poem's attractive combination of vividness and sensitivity. The placing of it at the beginning of *Lyrical Ballads* was evidently intended to provide a context for the sense of wonder in common life that marks many of Wordsworth's contributions. While this volume was going through the press, Coleridge began a complementary poem, a Gothic ballad entitled "Christabel," in which he aimed to show how naked energy (as imaged in the mariner's act or in the figure of the serpent) might be redeemed through contact with a spirit of innocent love. Christabel, a gentle maiden living in a castle that has been, since the loss of her mother, a place of death, goes out into the surrounding forest to pray for her lover; she there encounters a beautiful maiden who appeals to her for help and takes her into the castle. Once inside, however, it becomes clear that deeper forces are involved: Geraldine is a figure not only of romance but also of a pure energy that threatens to subdue Christabel's identity. At the end of the first part, nevertheless, Christabel has survived the spiritual struggle of the night and is sleeping peacefully.

The
theme of
"Christ-
abel"

Troubled years. Early in 1798, while still writing his great poems, Coleridge had again found himself preoccupied with political issues. The states of the Swiss Confederation had been suppressed by the French. The event was of considerable importance ideologically, for it was the first occasion on which the French government could be said to have acted deliberately in a way that ran counter to the principles of the Revolution. Coleridge's bitterness was expressed in a poem entitled "France: An Ode."

He had also passed through a crisis in his own affairs, during which he had been on the point of becoming a full-time Unitarian minister at Shrewsbury. From this decision he was diverted by the munificence of the brothers Josiah and Thomas Wedgwood, who, impressed by his intelligence and promise, offered him in 1798 an annuity of £150 as a means of subsistence while he pursued his intellectual concerns. He decided to make use of this new independence to visit Germany, where many of the most exciting literary and intellectual activities of the day were taking place. Having set off with the Wordsworths, he left them at Goslar for the winter while he attended lectures on physiology and biblical criticism at Göttingen. As a result of this and his subsequent reading, he became aware of developments in German scholarship that were little known in England until many years later. He always maintained, nevertheless, that the distinctive patterns of his own thinking were laid down before the German visit.

On his return to England, new troubles awaited him. His devotion to the Wordsworths had long been a source of irritation to his wife, and the tensions of their marriage were exacerbated when he fell in love with Sara Hutchinson, sister of Wordsworth's future wife, at the end of 1799. The removal of Coleridge's family to Keswick, Cumberland, so that he could be nearer to the Wordsworths (now settling at Grasmere) did little to help matters, and for some years afterward Coleridge was troubled by domestic strife, accompanied by worsening of his health and an increasing dependence on opium. Meanwhile, he supplemented his income by political journalism and by translating two plays of the German dramatist Friedrich von Schiller, while devoting much of his time to further psychological investigations and

Domestic
strife

speculations in the hope of presenting a new view of human knowledge. His main literary achievements during the period included another section of "Christabel," devoted to a further exploration of the relationship between Geraldine's snakelike energy and Christabel's dovelike innocence. The second part is largely devoted to the misunderstanding of their relationship by Christabel's death-haunted father; only the bard, still in touch with the life principle, sees the true situation and resolves to cleanse the forest with songs and harmony. In 1802, Coleridge's domestic unhappiness gave rise to "Dejection: An Ode," originally a longer verse letter sent to Sara Hutchinson in which he lamented the corrosive effect of his intellectual activities when undertaken as a refuge from the lovelessness of his family life. The poem employs the technique of his conversational poems; the sensitive rhythms and phrasing that he had learned to use in them are here masterfully deployed to represent his own depressed state of mind.

Although Coleridge hoped to combine a platonic love for Sara with fidelity to his wife and children and to draw sustenance from the Wordsworth household after Wordsworth's marriage to Sara's sister Mary, his hopes were not realized, and his health deteriorated further. He therefore resolved to spend some time in a warmer climate and, late in 1804, accepted a post in Malta, first as private, later as public, secretary to the acting governor, **Diplomatic** Sir Alexander Ball. Later he spent a long time journeying **post in** across Italy, where, according to his own account, he was **Malta** at one time pursued by Napoleon's agents, in consequence of articles against Bonaparte that he had written earlier. In Rome he encountered a number of well-known intellectuals including Washington Allston, Ludwig Tieck, and Wilhelm von Humboldt.

Despite his hopes, his health did not improve during his time abroad—on the contrary, his friends were alarmed by the change in his appearance when he returned. The time spent in Malta had also been a time of personal reappraisal. Brought into direct contact with men accustomed to handling affairs of state, he had found himself lacking an equal forcefulness and felt that in consequence he often forfeited the respect of others. On his return to England he resolved to become more manly and decisive. Within a few months he had finally decided to separate from his wife (who continued to live at Greta Hall, Keswick, where Southey and his family were now installed) and to live for the time being with the Wordsworths. Southey atoned for his youthful advice by exercising a general oversight of Coleridge's family for the rest of his days, while Coleridge gave financial assistance whenever he could and continued to interest himself in his children's education.

His time in Malta had also made him aware of the vacillation of contemporary British foreign policy. Molding himself to Wordsworth's growing sense of political responsibility, he decided to start a periodical, to be known as *The Friend*, where he hoped to offer, in a series of essays on all aspects of human life, a set of principles to which politicians and others could refer in ordering human affairs. In spite of many financial setbacks, the periodical was published from June 1809 to March 1810 and ceased only when Sara Hutchinson, who had been acting as amanuensis, found the strain of the relationship too much for her and retired to her brother's farm in Wales. Coleridge, resentful that Wordsworth, who already had both wife and sister to minister to him, should apparently have encouraged the withdrawal, resolved shortly afterward to settle in London again.

The period immediately following was the darkest of his life. His disappointment with Wordsworth was followed by anguish when a wounding remark of Wordsworth's was carelessly reported to him. For some time he remained in London, nursing his grievances and producing little. Opium retained its powerful hold, and the writings that survive from this period are redolent of a general unhappiness, with self-dramatization veering toward self-pity.

In spite of this, however, there also appear signs of a slow revival. This was aided by a new spirit in the London of the day. From 1811 onward the Regency stimulated a new interest in the arts, which was to flourish still more strongly when the Napoleonic Wars ended. For the first time, Coleridge knew what it was to be a fashionable figure. A course of lectures delivered during the winter of 1811–12 attracted a large audience, including the poets Samuel Rogers and Lord Byron. For many years Coleridge had been fascinated by Shakespeare's achievement, and his psychological interpretations of the chief characters (which were in line with and sometimes drawn from the work of contemporary German critics and in turn became a basis for much 19th-century criticism, culminating in the work of A.C. Bradley) were new and exciting to his contemporaries. During this period, Coleridge's play *Osorio*, written many years before, was accepted by the proprietors of the Drury Lane and produced, with the title *Remorse*, in January 1813.

The encouragement from these successes could not, however, touch the deeper sources of his malaise. The breach with Wordsworth had been a particularly bitter blow, since he had earlier felt his ill health and unhappiness to be compensated by the sense of working with William and Dorothy Wordsworth toward the establishment of a new view of human life, based on love and imagination. With the cutting of these ties, he found himself intellectually abandoned, forced to look for new bearings.

Late life and works. In the end, consolation came from an unexpected source. In dejection, unable to produce extended work or break the opium habit, he spent a long period with friends in Wiltshire, where he was introduced to Archbishop Robert Leighton's commentary on the First Letter of Peter. In the writings of this 17th-century divine, he found a combination of tenderness and sanctity that appealed deeply to him and seemed to offer an attitude to life that he himself could fall back on. The discovery marks an important shift of balance **Shift** in his intellectual attitudes. Christianity, hitherto one **in his** point of reference for him, now became his "official" **intellectual** creed. By aligning himself with the Anglican Church of **attitudes** the 17th century at its best, he hoped to find a firm point of reference that would both keep him in communication with orthodox Christians of his time (thus giving him the social approval he always needed, even if only from a small group of friends) and enable him to pursue his former intellectual explorations in the hope of reaching a Christian synthesis that might help to revitalize the English Church both intellectually and emotionally.

One effect of the adoption of this basis for his intellectual and emotional life was a sense of liberation and an ability to produce large works again. He drew together a collection of his poems (published in 1817 as *Sibylline Leaves*) and wrote *Biographia Literaria*, in which he outlined the evolution of his thought and developed an extended critique of Wordsworth's poems. For the general reader it is a misleading volume, since it moves bewilderingly between entertaining autobiography, abstruse philosophical discussion, and literary criticism. It has, however, an internal coherence of its own that is partly obscured by a gap in the middle of the volume. Coleridge had intended to end his first volume with a long essay on the nature of human imagination, which would make clear the grounds from which he was criticizing Wordsworth. In the end, however, he gave up the attempt, offering instead one or two pregnant paragraphs on imagination and fancy. To this extent, therefore, the work is broken-backed; but the individual components— first an entertaining account of Coleridge's early life, then an account of the ways in which he became dissatisfied with the associationist theories of David Hartley and other 18th-century philosophers, then a reasoned critique of Wordsworth's poems (including some excellent detailed criticism)—are fascinating. Over the whole work hovers the ghost of Coleridge's veneration for the power of imagination: biographically as his one constant guide in life, intellectually as the power that was a necessary complement to associationism in explaining the workings of the human mind, and critically as the criterion by which he finally praised Wordsworth or found him wanting. Once this key is grasped, the unity of the work becomes evident.

The *Biographia* and some of his other writings have created a problem for later critics by their incorporation without acknowledgment of some passages translated from the works of German contemporaries. It is not always clear whether these plagiarisms were due to a genuine belief on his part that passages previously translated or lodged in his memory were original or whether he drew on them in desperation when pressed to complete a piece of writing. What is perhaps more important is to establish the exact nature of his debt to German thought, a question that, in spite of some good studies, still awaits full and authoritative treatment.

Role in the *Encyclopaedia Metropolitana*

A new dramatic piece, *Zapolya*, though not accepted for the stage, was published in 1817. In the same year Coleridge became associated for a time with the new *Encyclopaedia Metropolitana*, for which he planned a novel system of organization, outlined in his *Prospectus*. His preliminary treatise "On Method" appeared as the General Introduction to all the early editions, but on first publication (1818) he immediately withdrew, claiming that alterations had been made without his consent, and revised the essay for his new edition of *The Friend*. Turning his attention to politics again, he produced two "Lay Sermons," in the first of which he reverted to the theme of *The Friend* but showed the new cast of his thinking by focussing his argument on particular passages of the Bible. In the second, directed to the public generally, he attacked contemporary willingness to allow the commercial spirit to flourish unchecked; in the following year the practical side of his social concern was shown by his pamphlets in favour of Sir Robert Peel's bill against the exploitation of child labour.

Despite these activities (undertaken partly to supplement his income) Coleridge always shrank from permanent employment or from projects that could not be related to his projected great work, in which he hoped to prove that the *logos*, the creative "word" of God, was an ultimate key to knowledge of the universe. Although manuscript drafts for this work exist, they have not hitherto been shown to justify these larger hopes and claims; his best thinking seems to have resisted attempts to develop it into a large system.

While he was trying to put together this larger work, Coleridge was pressed to offer more immediate help to those who were troubled by the skepticism of the age, particularly in theology. In 1822 he began his "Thursday evening classes," which in succeeding years were attended by various young men and some distinguished visitors. He also projected an anthology of extracts from Archbishop Leighton's writings accompanied by comments of his own. Some of his own ideas proliferated, however, so that the final volume, *Aids to Reflection*, though beginning as Coleridge originally proposed, moves into long theological discussions. The liberal attitude that he invoked was admired by some of his contemporaries, particularly in the United States, as offering a necessary complement to the dry rationalism of much contemporary theology. Several well-known U.S. writers, including James Fenimore Cooper and Ralph Waldo Emerson, later called on him in London.

These were more settled years for him. Since 1816, he had lived in the house of James Gillman, a surgeon at Highgate, north of London. His election as a fellow of the Royal Society of Literature in 1824 had brought an annuity of £105 and a sense of recognition. In 1830 he joined the controversy that had arisen around the issue of Catholic Emancipation by writing *On the Constitution of the Church and State*, in which he argued that they were as necessary to one another as the vine and the elm, each ministering to the other's life. Another work, the *Confessions of an Inquiring Spirit*, in which he maintained that it was not necessary to believe every part of the Scriptures to be equally inspired, was published after his death. Its arguments, if accepted, would have rendered some bitter Victorian disputes unnecessary.

During his later years, Coleridge's nephew and son-in-law, Henry Nelson Coleridge, helped with the later collections of his poetry and recorded his table talk. He died at Highgate on July 25, 1834.

Evaluation. Although not a handsome man, Coleridge was attractive to those who fell under the spell of his personality. His own self-description gives as vivid a sense of his appearance as any:

Personal traits

> My face, unless when animated with immediate eloquence, expresses great sloth, and great, indeed almost idiotic, good nature. 'Tis a mere carcase of a face: fat, flabby, and expressive chiefly of inexpression. Yet I am told that my eyes, eyebrows and forehead are physiognomically good; but of this the Deponent knoweth not. As to my gait it is awkward, and the walk of the whole man indicates *indolence capable of energies*.

His capacity for talk was his most noticeable characteristic: he could monopolize a conversation for hours on end. Some people found this offensive or boring, but, to those who had attuned themselves to his eloquence, he was irresistible, particularly in his earlier years. "He talked on forever," said the essayist William Hazlitt, "and you wished him to talk on forever." Although Wordsworth declared that there was always a binding train of thought running through his discourse, Thomas Carlyle, who heard him in his later years, gave a memorable and biting description of his tendency toward digression; yet he, too, acknowledged the power of his eloquence at its best.

Coleridge's influence on his literary contemporaries ran deep. Charles Lamb, Hazlitt, and Thomas De Quincey, all of whom knew him, acknowledged a lasting debt. The poets were more subtly influenced. Byron responded most to his sense of energy and charm, veiled in "Christabel," openly expressed in "Kubla Khan." John Keats, who heard him discourse on the song of the nightingale in a lane near Highgate in 1819, wrote his own "Ode to a Nightingale" shortly afterward; long before that his poetic style had been exploring modes opened up by Coleridge's conversational poems. Percy Bysshe Shelley, who never met him, read his work voraciously and pursued a vein of visionary metaphysics that can be related to many of Coleridge's favourite themes.

In the next generation Coleridge's reputation as a poet suffered by comparison with the firmer achievements of his successors and by reason of a growing taste for naturalism. At the end of the century, however, the enthusiasm of writers such as Walter Pater and Algernon Charles Swinburne led to an "aesthetic" reading of his poetry for its sensuous and musical qualities. When fashion turned against aestheticism, his reputation declined again. The most influential study of this century, John Livingston Lowes's *Road to Xanadu* (1927), reading the great poems against a tradition of imagist criticism, dwelt on the sources of his imagery in travel books that he had read and showed how such images acquired vividness in passing through his imagination. More recently, however, some critics, feeling that such a reading ignores other important qualities in the poems, have explored the symbolism of the poems more sympathetically.

Coleridge's Victorian successors were particularly interested in his later prose writings. His argument that the Bible and Christianity were their own best evidence when searched for the truths that "find" a man appealed to a generation bemused by the so-called evidences of earlier theologians. Similarly, to those who found their beliefs unsettled by contemporary criticism of the Bible, he offered a view of Christianity as a set of beliefs that remained symbolically true, whatever the status of the historical traditions that enshrined them. His call for a group of intellectual luminaries, a "clerisy" consisting of professional men who should act as a leaven in society, mediating between the established church and the people, was influential in the establishment of groups such as the Cambridge Apostles. More generally, his theology was a prime force in the Broad Church movement, which numbered among its adherents John Sterling, Julius Hare, F.D. Maurice, and Charles Kingsley.

Influence of later prose writings on his Victorian successors

Despite his influence, however, Coleridge's ideas remained in the next period without an advocate powerful enough to give them an acceptable intellectual setting.

The most acute of Victorian thinkers found their admiration for him tempered by important reservations. The poet Arthur Hugh Clough, though attracted by the idea that commitment to Christianity would bring belief in its train, was probably speaking for himself when he made one of his characters exclaim, "Action will furnish belief, but will that belief be the true one?" John Henry Newman, a theologian seriously disturbed by the idea of resting Christian faith on a set of symbols, threw himself into the battle for a more "real" religion, which he could discover only in the Roman Catholic Church.

These thinkers had not known Coleridge personally; they simply examined his writings and tested them by their own internal coherence. The true spell of Coleridge had always been exerted more in personal contact. Indeed, he could talk well only when he was conscious of a sympathetic rapport with his audience, his desire for a sympathetic hearing being at one with his belief that affectionate love was one of the ultimate values at the heart of the creation. This idea appealed to many of his Victorian successors, but, when taken in isolation, it easily degenerated into sentimentalism; it was this danger that was sensed by thinkers such as Clough and Newman. Coleridge's equally important belief in the power of the imagination, on the other hand, had been undermined by his own unhappiness, illness, and opium addiction. These, working together, had sapped his "shaping spirit" and sometimes turned imagination to nightmare. He expressed the dilemma well when, finally publishing "Kubla Khan" after nearly 20 years, he juxtaposed this great celebration of imaginative genius with "The Pains of Sleep," in which he wrote of the horrific effects of the same powers when turned against him in nightmare.

Yet, although Coleridge remained doubtful of the status of poetic imagination and tended in his later years to subordinate it, his exploration of its potentialities is the basis of his most original work—his attempt to establish a new status for all phenomena associated with "romance" as providing an alternative way of knowing the universe of human experience. In the end this exploration was undermined less, perhaps, by personal distresses than by his attempts to link it with a belief in affectionate love and in Christian values; this led to the bitterness of his domestic life and to a general overstraining of his sensibility. The quality for which he remains valuable is his sense that the mind works in two separate ways, the one reaching out to assess the world and to store information about it, the other imposing patterns, unifying experience, and making human identity possible.

Ability to think at two levels

The accompanying ability to think at two levels characterizes many of Coleridge's best achievements. In his poetry it appears most openly in his highly developed sense of metre, which enables him to handle rhythmic shifts with great subtlety while also expressing his ideas more precisely through symbolic images or overt verbal statement. This method is particularly successful in the conversational poems, in which it is suited to the reflective argument being carried on; in the greater poems, where rhythm, imagery, and ideas are not so closely synchronized, a more sophisticated reading is necessary.

In Coleridge's early notebooks, the same phenomena are subjected to a subtle investigation. His sensitive handling of rhythm assists the delicacy of the analysis. He is at his best in examining the nature of mental processes: some of his best insights, such as his phrase "willing suspension of disbelief" to describe the effect of dramatic illusion, spring directly from his sense of the two levels in mental process. Although his later writings have many attractive features, their achievement is best appraised in the light of these speculations, which affect their shape in important ways. If the "shaping spirit" is less evident in them, Coleridge's other phrase for himself, "inquiring spirit," remains apposite to the end. John Stuart Mill expressed this side of his general achievement when, describing Coleridge, along with the philosopher Jeremy Bentham, as one of the "two great seminal minds of England of their age," he characterized the difference between them by the two types of intellectual inquiry they prompted: "By Bentham . . . men have been led to ask themselves, in regard to any ancient or received opinion, Is it true? and by Coleridge, What is the meaning of it?"

MAJOR WORKS

POETRY AND DRAMA: *Poems on Various Subjects* (1796; 2nd ed., substantially altered, 1797); *Lyrical Ballads* (1798, with William Wordsworth; Coleridge's contributions included "The Rime of the Ancient Mariner" and "The Nightingale"); "Fears in Solitude," "France, an Ode," and "Frost at Midnight" (all 1798); *The Piccolomini* and *The Death of Wallenstein* (translations from a dramatic trilogy by Friedrich Schiller, 1800); *Remorse* (a tragedy, 1813; two fragments had appeared in *Lyrical Ballads*); "Christabel," "Kubla Khan," and "The Pains of Sleep" (all 1816); *Sibylline Leaves* (1817).

LITERARY CRITICISM: *Biographia Literaria; or, Biographical Sketches of My Literary Life and Opinions*, 2 vol. (1817); *The Literary Remains of Samuel Taylor Coleridge* (published posthumously by H.N. Coleridge, 1836–39), notes and reports of lectures given 1805–18; *Specimens of the Table Talk of the Late Samuel Taylor Coleridge* (published 1835), a record of Coleridge's conversation kept by his nephew H.N. Coleridge; *Anima Poetae* (published 1895), title adopted by E.H. Coleridge, the poet's grandson, for a collection of aphorisms, reflections, collections, and soliloquies collected from Coleridge's notebooks and pocketbooks.

PHILOSOPHICAL WRITINGS: Contributions to *The Friend* (weekly paper conducted by Coleridge between 1809–10); *Biographia Literaria* (see above); "On Method" (1818); *Aids to Reflection* . . . (1825); *On the Constitution of the Church and State, According to the Idea of each* . . . (1830); *Confessions of an Inquiring Spirit* (published posthumously by H.N. Coleridge, 1840); *Hints Towards the Formation of a More Comprehensive Theory of Life* (ed. by S.B. Watson, 1848).

BIBLIOGRAPHY. *The New Cambridge Bibliography of English Literature*, vol. 3 (1969), contains an extensive listing of works by and about Coleridge. Important manuscript collections are held in the British Museum and at Victoria College, Toronto.

Major editions: The Collected Works of Coleridge (1969–)—Lectures, 1795, on Politics and Religion, The Watchman, The Friend, and Lay Sermons issued so far; Poems, ed. by E.H. COLERIDGE (1912, reprinted 1949); Poems, ed. by JOHN B. BEER (1963); Collected Letters, ed. by E.L. GRIGGS, 6 vol. (1956–71); Notebooks, ed. by KATHLEEN COBURN (1957–).

Biography and criticism: There is no definitive biography. E.K. CHAMBERS, Samuel Taylor Coleridge (1938), which gives the fullest account of the events of the life, is unsympathetic and partly out of date; W.J. BATE, Coleridge (1968), provides the best brief account. Other biographical studies include: WILLIAM HAZLITT, "My First Acquaintance with Poets," in The Liberal (April 1823), and "Mr. Coleridge," in The Spirit of the Age (1825); THOMAS DE QUINCEY, Reminiscences of the English Lake Poets (1834–40; rev. ed., 1961); THOMAS CARLYLE, Life of John Sterling, ch. 8 (1851); LAWRENCE HANSON, The Life of S.T. Coleridge: The Early Years (1938, reprinted 1962); DAVID BERES, "A Dream, a Vision and a Poem: A Psycho-analytic Study of the Origins of the Rime of the Ancient Mariner," International Journal of Psycho-analysis, 32:97–203 (1951); ELISABETH SCHNEIDER, Coleridge, Opium, and Kubla Khan (1953); GEORGE WHALLEY, Coleridge and Sara Hutchinson, and the Asra Poems (1955); DONALD SULTANA, Samuel Taylor Coleridge in Malta and Italy (1969); NORMAN FRUMAN, Coleridge, the Damaged Archangel (1971); JOHN CORNWELL, Coleridge, Poet and Revolutionary, 1772–1804: A Critical Biography (1973).

Nineteenth-century studies of Coleridge's poetry: A.C. SWINBURNE, Essays and Studies (1875); LESLIE STEPHEN, Hours in a Library (1879); WALTER PATER, Appreciations (1889).

Modern studies of Coleridge's poetry: JOHN L. LOWES, The Road to Xanadu, rev. ed. (1964); STEPHEN POTTER, Coleridge and S.T.C. (1935, reprinted, 1965); G. WILSON KNIGHT, The Starlit Dome (1941, reprinted 1971); ROBERT PENN WARREN, "A Poem of Pure Imagination," in Selected Essays (1958); ARTHUR HUMPHRY HOUSE, Coleridge: The Clark Lectures (1953); JOHN B. BEER, Coleridge, the Visionary (1959); EDWARD E. BOSTETTER, The Romantic Ventriloquists (1963); GEORGE WATSON, Coleridge the Poet (1966); STEPHEN PRICKETT, Coleridge and Wordsworth: The Poetry of Growth (1970).

Coleridge's ideas: J.H. MUIRHEAD, Coleridge As Philosopher (1930); I.A. RICHARDS, Coleridge on Imagination (1934, reprinted 1960); KATHLEEN COBURN (ed.), Coleridge's Philosophical Lectures, 1818–1819 (1949) and Inquiring Spirit: A New Presentation of Coleridge from His Published and Unpublished Prose Writings (1951); PAUL DESCHAMPS, La Formation de la pensée de Coleridge, 1772–1804 (1964); J.A. AP-

PLEYARD, *Coleridge's Philosophy of Literature* (1965); THOMAS MCFARLAND, *Coleridge and the Pantheist Tradition* (1969); OWEN BARFIELD, *What Coleridge Thought* (1971).

Coleridge as literary critic: THOMAS M. RAYSOR (ed.), *Coleridge's Shakespearean Criticism*, 2 vol. (1931), and *Coleridge's Miscellaneous Criticism* (1936); JAMES V. BAKER, *The Sacred River: Coleridge's Theory of the Imagination* (1957); RICHARD H. FOGLE, *The Idea of Coleridge's Criticism* (1962).

Coleridge as political thinker: ALFRED COBBAN, *Edmund Burke and the Revolt Against the Eighteenth Century*, 2nd ed. (1960); JOHN COLMER, *Coleridge: Critic of Society* (1959); CARL R. WOODRING, *Politics in the Poetry of Coleridge* (1961); DAVID P. CALLEO, *Coleridge and the Idea of the Modern State* (1966).

Coleridge as religious thinker: FREDERICK D. MAURICE, *The Kingdom of Christ*, new ed., 2 vol. (1958); C.R. SANDERS, *Coleridge and the Broad Church Movement* (1942); JAMES D. BOULGER, *Coleridge as Religious Thinker* (1961); J.R. BARTH, JR., *Coleridge and Christian Doctrine* (1969).

General and introductory: F.J.A. HORT, "Coleridge," in *Cambridge Essays*, vol. 2 (1856); JOHN STUART MILL, "Coleridge," in *Dissertations and Discussions*, vol. 1 (1859); R.W. ARMOUR and R.F. HOWES (eds.), *Coleridge the Talker* (1940); BASIL WILLEY, *Nineteenth Century Studies* (1949); CLARENCE D. THORPE, CARLOS BAKER, and BENNETT WEAVER (eds.), *The Major English Romantic Poets: A Symposium in Reappraisal* (1957); KATHLEEN COBURN (ed.), *Coleridge: A Collection of Critical Essays* (1967); R.L. BRETT (ed.), *S.T. Coleridge* (1971), essays.

(J.B.B.)

Collective Behaviour

Collective behaviour is a sociological term referring to the ways in which people behave together in crowds, panics, fads, fashions, crazes, publics, cults, followings, reform and revolutionary social movements, and other similar groupings. Common sociological usage limits the term to groups that are fairly large, relatively unorganized, and somewhat ephemeral. Because it emphasizes group patterns, the study of collective behaviour is different from the study of individual behaviour, though psychological inquiries into the motivations and attitudes of individuals in these groupings are often required. Collective behaviour resembles group behaviour and organizational behaviour in that it consists of people acting together; but it is more spontaneous—and consequently more volatile and less predictable—than is behaviour in groups that have well-established rules and traditions specifying the groups' purposes, membership, leadership, and mode of operation.

Robert E. Park, who coined the term, defined collective behaviour as "the behavior of individuals under the influence of an impulse that is common and collective, an impulse, in other words, that is the result of social interaction." By defining it in this way, he emphasized that participants in crowds, fads, or in other forms of collective behaviour share a common attitude or behave similarly, not because of an established rule or the force of authority, and not because they happen as individuals to have the same attitudes at the start, but because of something that occurred during their interaction.

Absence of formal or established rules
The absence of formally or traditionally established rules by which to distinguish between members and outsiders, to identify the legitimate leaders, to establish the aims of the collectivity, to set the limits of acceptable behaviour for members, and to specify how collective decisions are to be reached accounts for the often-noted volatility of collective behaviour. The leader of a mob can become the object of the mob's hatred in a matter of minutes; a fashion leader can become suddenly passé.

Though agreeing that collective behaviour exhibits great license with respect to everyday rules, some investigators emphasize the emergence of rules and patterns within the collectivity that have understandable relationship to the surrounding social structure. Ralph Turner and Lewis Killian define collective behaviour on the basis of "the spontaneous development of norms and organization which contradict or reinterpret the norms and organization of society." Somewhat similar is Neil Smelser's definition: "mobilization on the basis of a belief which redefines social action." The distinctive belief—which is a generalized conception of events and of the members' relationships to them—supplies the basis for the development of a distinctive and somewhat stable organization within the collectivity. But Smelser's definition points attention, in a way that other definitions do not, toward the unique manner in which members perceive reality—without such a distinctive view a group of people would not be engaged in collective behaviour.

Another slightly different emphasis is incorporated in Herbert Blumer's definition: "a collective enterprise to establish a new order of life." This definition excludes many of the temporary escapes from conventional life through revelry and orgies, punitive actions such as lynchings, and panics. Although it is useful to call attention to the fact that riots, fads, cults, and other collective phenomena that often seem pointless and purely impulsive to outsiders are frequently guided by a vision of a different kind of society, most students would not restrict the field in this way. Likewise, most scholars hesitate to include so difficult a criterion to assess as the beliefs held by members in defining collective behaviour.

I. Elementary collective behaviour

Regardless of the situation in which collective behaviour develops, people cannot act together without some preparation. In organized groups there are rituals, such as personal introductions, ice-breaking games, the toastmaster's humour, and group singing, to facilitate the transition from individual action to group collaboration. People may act together very quickly if they have been well drilled in a pattern of behaviour such as the fire drill, but the result is less collective behaviour than it is organized behaviour. Lacking a standard pattern, people must first become sensitized to one another so that obstacles to expressing or recognizing intimate feelings are overcome. An early piece of research showed that groups of young men who knew each other well were quicker to develop fear and to break down a laboratory door to escape what they thought was fire danger than were similar groups whose members did not know each other beforehand. The basic processes of sensitization and communication are essential to all forms of collective behaviour and have been called elementary collective behaviour. Three important forms, milling, rumour, and social unrest, merit discussion.

MILLING

Prior to most instances of developed collective behaviour there is a period during which people seem to move about in a somewhat agitated but aimless way. Early students of crowd behaviour, struck by the resemblance to the milling of cattle before a stampede, called this form of collective behaviour milling. This kind of physical restlessness can be seen in an audience waiting for a late-starting program to begin or among citizens who have just received word of an assassination attempt. In the former case people scuffle their feet, leave their seats and walk about, and sometimes join spontaneously in coordinated rhythmic behaviour such as foot stamping. In the latter case people discontinue routine activities and talk with neighbours, friends, and even strangers. In most situations milling also means looking for such clues to others' feelings as sweating, nervous motions, and changes in tone of voice.

Effects of milling
Human milling has at least four important effects. First, it sensitizes people to each other and orients them toward the emerging collectivity. In this sense the milling of less inhibited individuals distracts others from their own concerns and focusses their attention on the collectivity and on the subject or problem. Second, milling tends to produce a common mood among the interacting individuals. Where some might react with sorrow, others with anger, and still others with partisan delight or indifference, milling helps to diffuse a single mood among a majority of the people in a group. Third, milling commences development of a common image or interpretation of the situation. The milling throng decides whether

the Western tourist taking pictures of a marketplace in the native quarter of an Oriental city is harmless or an affront to native dignity; whether the police in an American city are simply performing their duty in arresting a drunken driver or engaging in unprovoked brutality against an oppressed minority. Finally, milling sets in motion the process of redefining the rules that govern behaviour. The milling of an audience is usually the signal that customary rules of courtesy toward performers and speakers are no longer applicable. New rules take effect, in keeping with the mood and the image that are diffusing the collectivity.

In some cases milling is intensified into what Blumer calls collective excitement. The attractive power of excitement monopolizes attention, diminishing awareness of diverting or contradictory stimulation. Excitement speeds up the process of action and response, so that exploration of alternative images and courses of action is unlikely.

RUMOUR

Tamotsu Shibutani defines rumour as "a recurrent form of communication through which men caught together in an ambiguous situation attempt to construct a meaningful interpretation of it by pooling their intellectual resources." A rumour need not be false. What makes it rumour rather than news is that the accepted means for authenticating an account are not available. News is sometimes false and rumour the corrective: biased newspaper reports and official government deceptions are often countered by a rumour grapevine that reveals what official sources are suppressing. But the attitude of participants in the rumour process is distinctive because of the lack of authentication. Rumours are different from other beliefs and accounts but are like news in that they deal only with what is just happening or impending.

There are times when rumour abounds and times when there is little rumour to be heard. Gordon Allport and Leo Postman offer the generalization that rumour intensity is high when both the *interest* in an event and its *ambiguity* are great. Shibutani makes a similar point by saying that rumour abounds when the demand for news is greater than the supply made available through institutional channels. Attitudes toward an event often cause people to regard news of it ambiguously. For example, at the close of World War II it was widely believed among Hawaiian Japanese that Japan had actually won the war and that the American government was concealing the fact from the American people. The news was complete and unambiguous in the usual sense, but it ran too strongly against expectations held by many older generation Japanese to be creditable.

Situations inspiring rumour. The occasion for rumour is a profound concern for the common fate of a group of people. The interest is not idle curiosity but a need to understand conditions that determine how people are to continue their lives in common. In even the most trivial form of rumour—gossip—the group pursues agreement in characterizing a common friend or acquaintance, thereby fixing the group position he is to occupy. Hence two conditions must be added to interest and ambiguity as rumour prerequisites. First, rumour abounds when a group of people share the motivation or necessity to act, but are reluctant to do so until the situation can be better defined. Second, rumour abounds only when the situation requires that in some essential respect the members of the group act in concert rather than individually.

There are three kinds of situations in which these four conditions are commonly met and rumour is rampant. *Conditions encouraging rumour* First, in a social order in which the information that identifies the common fate of its members is believed to be strictly controlled by authorities, rumour will be intense. When control over news is a continuing (rather than temporary) condition, rumour process becomes regularized as an essential aspect of daily life. Grapevines of this sort are regular features of totalitarian national regimes, military organizations, and subordinated ethnic groups, races, and social classes.

Second, rumour abounds whenever events threaten the common understandings upon which the normal round of life is based. A major disaster or a scandal of large proportions presents such a challenge. Daily sacrifices and the investment of effort and resources all rest on the assumption that group goals will be realized in the future. The prospect that events over which the group has no control might wipe out the fruits of group dedication forces people to wonder whether they should live merely for the present. Any change in the regular accommodations between potentially conflicting or competing groups in society similarly calls into question the usual patterns of conduct. The suggestion that management may start enforcing factory rules more strictly, or the suggestion that a college faculty is considering either stiffening or relaxing degree requirements, immediately provokes intense rumour.

Third, rumour springs up when a strong, shared incentive to act is blocked in some way, even by merely the lack of an occasion for action. During states of boredom rumour capitalizes on minor events, magnifying them into occasions for exciting collective action. More often the blockage comes from established rules that prohibit the behaviour in question. Rumour advances a view of events that enables people to consider the rules inapplicable or to justify their violation. In Tikopia, in the Solomon Islands, anthropologist Raymond Firth observed that a recurrent rumour that a ship had been sighted justified the natives in their habit of dropping their routine work responsibilities to gather in a festive mood at the place from which the ship was supposed to have been seen.

Persons involved in the transmission of rumour. Prior social position and personal characteristics affect the extent to which anyone will be "in" on the rumour process. *Social status and education* The part each person plays in the rumour process also affects his subsequent position in the group or community. Rumour spreads most rapidly along preexisting social networks: among friends, associates, and peers rather than among persons of unequal standing. The messenger who first relates a rumour earns prestige by doing so. Moreover, any specific rumour tends to spread most rapidly when it first enters a group, and to reach persons faster who have responsibilities and interests connected with the event.

Because of the status-seeking aspect of rumour transmission, and because of the unverified and often unsettling effects of rumour, it is frequently supposed that rumours are most often transmitted by the least educated and least responsible individuals. But empirical investigations fail to confirm this belief. In a study of a 1954 incident in Seattle, Wash., when the community was swamped with subsequently unverified reports that automobile windshields were being mysteriously pitted, it was found that persons of considerable education and community responsibility were more likely than others to have reported pitting to authorities. If we think of rumour not as a tale being passed about the community without adequate verification, but as the process whereby members of the community try to reach a dependable understanding of confusing or unsettling events, it is to be expected that persons accustomed to assuming responsibility for community welfare will play a more active part in rumour process than will other people. The hypothesis that well-educated persons are more likely than others to make efforts to verify a rumour before passing it on has likewise not been confirmed by empirical research.

Moreover, it is frequently assumed—incorrectly—that people transmit rumours only when they believe them, and that discrediting a rumour will stop its spread. Other evidence suggests that people pass on rumours in appropriate situations whether they believe them or not, and that the likelihood of belief increases with repeated hearing of the same account. Again this pattern is understandable when rumour is seen as a seeking, rather than a believing, process, in which every idea, no matter how invalid, becomes a perspective from which to essay a new comprehension of a troublesome event. But since the group finds it urgent to reach some common understanding, pressure toward universal acceptance of some favoured version grows as the rumour process matures. Eventually, there is often a sorting out of accounts and an intolerant insistence that everyone agree to the "consensual" account, which then serves as the agreed upon basis for collective action.

Stages of transmission. There is evidence that rumour follows a typical course, leading either toward a true account of events or an account that is distorted in systematic ways. Evidence suggests that the rumour process eliminates the most improbable and unreliable accounts and achieves a high degree of veracity when (1) there is considerable recirculation of rumour and (2) there is a fairly well-routinized grapevine. When rumour is recirculated the opportunity to compare versions with different groups of people acts as a brake on exaggeration and rubs off the idiosyncratic aspects of the story. With an established grapevine, the source of rumours can often be checked, and individuals who are known to have inside information are regularly consulted for verification.

In both early and late stages, rumour content changes with successive retelling in the direction of the understandable and familiar and in the direction of supporting the actions that the group is starting to take. The former is called assimilation by Allport and Postman, and is illustrated by the tendency to make rumour details consistent with prejudice. The latter tendency means that a group is inclined to support those beliefs that supply justification for the course of action toward which they are already predisposed.

SOCIAL UNREST

The general condition of the community in which milling is both frequent and widespread and in which rumour is recurrent is the crucible in which the more highly developed forms of collective behaviour mature. This condition is known as social unrest. The American urban black uprisings of the 1960s were preceded and accompanied by a rise in tensions in black communities all over the nation; the Russian Revolution was preceded by several years of constant turmoil, involving random assassinations, strikes, and riots.

There are several distinguishing characteristics to social unrest. First, there is a general impairment of collective life routines. People find it difficult to concentrate on their work or even to adhere to rules in playing games. Any occasion to abandon routines is welcomed. Second, people are hyperreactive. The magnitude of the response is out of proportion to the usual meaning of any stimulating incident. A small police provocation elicits a major outcry of police brutality; a trivial success is the occasion for large-scale celebration. Milling and rumour abound because incidents that would normally pass with little notice become occasions for both. Third, social unrest is marked by contagiousness. When restlessness is strictly individual, one person's restlessness merely annoys another. But when restlessness becomes a shared experience, people are highly suggestible to each other. Questioning and exploring alternative courses of action are reduced to a minimum. Fourth, social unrest is unspecific with respect to grievances or activities. When there is social unrest in a school, students complain of both restrictions on their behaviour and the lack of clearly defined rules; they find fault both with school administrators and with their fellow students. Finally, social unrest is perhaps the most volatile of collective states. Unlike rumour or milling, it does not remain focussed on an issue or problem. Unlike crowd behaviour or crazes and fads, it has not yet been channelled into one main direction. Although social unrest may eventually die down without any serious aftermath, it is a condition in which people can be easily aroused.

II. Major forms of collective behaviour

RESPONSES TO DISASTER

A disaster-stricken community affords a prototypical situation for collective behaviour. The lives of persons are disrupted indiscriminately by a tornado, flood, or earthquake, and coping with the resulting destruction and disorder is beyond the capacity of conventional institutions. Of perhaps greatest importance, the assumption of a reasonably stable and predictable reality, upon which all human planning and investment are based, is undermined.

Two different patterns of collective behaviour are stimulated by disasters, one among the victims and near victims and another among persons who are either concerned or curious about the event. The first pattern stems from a vital sense of shared tragedy. Members' attention is turned inward upon the community. Their chief concern is with the fate of those close to them; they seek a reassuring kind of ingroup solidarity that lessens barriers among fellow victims and near victims but frequently augments barriers against outsiders. The second pattern mobilizes a mixed group, including many people who send assistance or come in person to help, and many others who have no particular concern for the victims. Convergence behaviour, as it is called, becomes a major problem to people in the disaster area. Telephone service, postal facilities, and highways are clogged so that essential communications are delayed. Goods that are often unneeded or inappropriate arrive by the truckload, and someone's effort must be diverted from more pressing tasks to accept and dispose of them. Even persons offering to help generally arrive after the most urgent rescue work is completed and inadvertently create new demands upon the disaster community. Hostility generally develops between the disaster community and the convergers.

Common misconceptions. A number of common assumptions about behaviour under stress have been dispelled by research on responses to disaster. First, panic is rare. The quite specific conditions under which panic occurs will be described later, but stoic, unbelieving, or even resigned reactions are more common than panic. Second, scapegoating is not the rule. Some investigations have suggested an almost unnatural avoidance of singling out villains and placing blame. Within the disaster community the establishment of solidarity is a concern that dampens scapegoating, at least until the immediate emergency is past. Third, there is much less looting and vandalism than is popularly supposed. Even among persons who converge from outside the community there is more petty pilfering for souvenirs than serious self-aggrandizement and destructiveness. Fourth, initially an altruistic selflessness is more prevalent than self-pity and self-serving activity. Frequently noted are dramatic instances of persons who have suffered injury or property damage themselves devoting their time to helping others in no greater need. Fifth, the disruption of established organizations and customary behaviour does not lead primarily to innovation and the exercise of freedom from old restraints. Instead, people more frequently cling to the familiar and seek reinstatement of the old.

The disaster cycle. Collective behaviour in disaster follows a characteristic cycle, from first warning to community rehabilitation.

Warning period. Although individuals read widely different meanings into disaster warnings, the striking feature of this initial stage is the slowness to believe and the reluctance to act upon warnings. People often remain in their houses in spite of imminent flooding, and remain on familiar low ground in the face of tidal wave warnings. The surface calm that each person seeks to maintain in the presence of others can lead to collective self-deception and the inhibition of tendencies toward flight.

Impact and stock-taking period. In disasters such as floods and some hurricanes there is a distinctly long period of impact, which can be separated from a subsequent period of stock taking or "immobility." In earthquakes and explosions, on the other hand, the impact is so brief that the periods can hardly be separated. The combined period of impact and stock taking is marked initially by a fragmentation of human relations, as each individual is separated from others and from his customary moorings; it is then marked by a resurgence of interpersonal warmth that transcends customary social barriers within the disaster community. Perhaps because of the initial fragmentation, the emotional breakdowns and panicky reactions of a few are not contagious. The magnitude of the event requires some time and personal reorientation for comprehension; hence the immobility at this stage. The unusual warmth and fellow feeling among survivors at the end of this period facilitate the collaborative efforts that commence in earnest in the rescue stage.

Rescue period. Just as initial fragmentation is followed by unnatural solidarity, stunned immobility gives way to a frenzy of activity in the rescue stage. Although activity is often inefficient, the task of rescuing persons who are trapped and of getting the injured to first-aid facilities is usually accomplished fairly expeditiously, often before outside help arrives. This is the period in which altruism becomes the norm, and old rivalries and conflicts are suspended. Many business concerns adopt an uneconomic generosity, and some individuals disregard their personal welfare. The imperious demand to "do something" at once creates an urgent demand for leadership. People turn first to established community leaders, and, when they are equal to the demands, such figures as police and fire officials, school principals, and mass-media personages are quickly accepted as leaders. Frequently these public figures are as bewildered and distracted as everyone else in the community and are soon abandoned in the restless search for leadership. The leaders then are found among persons who have the specific skills and tools required for the rescue efforts of the moment. Often these are people who do not normally exercise community leadership.

Although all the rescue activity is focussed and generally rational from the limited perspective of each separate rescue enterprise, the total rescue operation often is badly disorganized. Efforts are duplicated and groups work at cross-purposes; resources are in surplus at one location and deficient at another. There is rigid adherence to customary procedures in many situations calling for innovation. Medical personnel, for example, are often unwilling to delay treatment of minor injuries in order to concentrate on emergency cases. Finally, the strongest ties in time of disaster are family ties. Preoccupation with the safety and welfare of immediate family members often prevents officials charged with general rescue work from performing their tasks efficiently.

Rebuilding or "brickbat" period. The buoyed-up state of the disaster community can last only a short time. Tasks that call for intense effort within a brief time span are completed, and the slow and discouraging work of rebuilding confronts the community. Because the old community cleavages begin to reappear, and because tensions created and repressed during the rescue phase are now released, this period has been called the brickbat stage. The most notable characteristic of this period is the tendency to reinstitute the old community—to rebuild homes on old foundations, to reinstate old forms of organization. In spite of criticism against the ineptitude of established authorities, and in spite of evidence that building locations and methods are vulnerable to the elements, it requires strong leadership to guide the community toward innovation that makes use of what can be learned from the disaster experience.

COLLECTIVE OBSESSIONS

Common characteristics of collective obsessions

The various kinds of collective obsession—fads, crazes, and the like—have several features in common. (1) The most conspicuous sign is a remarkable increase in the frequency and intensity with which people engage in a specific kind of behaviour or assert a belief. There was an "epidemic" of flying-saucer sightings; children in every residential neighbourhood in the United States played on skateboards; there was a sudden rush to buy Florida land. (2) The behaviour—or the abandon with which it is indulged—is ridiculous, irrational, or evil in the eyes of persons who are not themselves caught up in the obsession. In the case of recreational fads such as

skateboarding, nonfaddists are amazed at the tendency to drop all other activities in order to concentrate on the fad; the hundreds of incidents in which swastikas were daubed on synagogues during a few weeks in 1959 and 1960 in the United States, West Germany, and 32 other countries, shocked the sensibilities of a world that remembered the Nazi persecution of the Jews. (3) After it has reached a peak, the behaviour drops off abruptly and is followed by a counterobsession. To engage in the fad behaviour after the fad is over is to be subjected to ridicule; after the speculative land boom declines, there is a mad rush to sell property at whatever price it will bring.

Fads. It is tempting to explain fads on the basis of a single motive such as prestige. Prestige is gained by being among the first and most adept at a skill that everyone else covets. That the skill fails as a source of prestige when it is no longer scarce is an important explanation for the abrupt end of a fad. But motives are complex and varied. The exhilaration of joining a band of devotees in an intense preoccupation and the joy of mastering the novel are not to be discounted.

An examination of fads in such enterprises as scientific research and recreation sheds light on the fundamental dynamics of all kinds of fads. First, the scientific fad begins with a new idea or a rediscovered idea—though not just any new idea will set off a fad. The new idea must be a "key invention," one that opens up the possibility for a wide range of minor innovations. Discovery of a potent new drug, for example, is followed by a rush to test the drug in all kinds of situations. Similarly, recreation and style faddists do not merely copy a pattern; they try out a variety of novel uses and variations on the basic pattern. The Hula-Hoop was an ideal fad because each child could develop his own particular variation in spinning the hoop. The central characteristic of the fad is the opportunity for individual variation on a basic theme in which there is intense interest.

Second, the termination of fads is largely explained by the exhaustion of innovative possibilities. The drug has been tested in all of the apparently relevant settings; children have run out of new ways to twirl the Hula-Hoop. The duration of a fad is determined by the time it takes to exhaust these possibilities.

Third, the faddish preoccupation means holding in abeyance many routine activities as well as awareness of drawbacks to the fads. So long as the fad is in full force, a sharp ingroup-outgroup sense insulates faddists against these concerns. But once the faddists run out of new variations they begin to be aware of the extent of their neglect of other activities and to consider possible dangers in the fad.

Hysterical contagion. Occasionally waves of fear find expression in a rash of false perceptions and symptoms of physical illness. Girls in an English school fainted in great numbers; women in Mattoon, Illinois, reported being anesthetized and assaulted by a mysterious prowler. The best documented case is that of a clothing factory that had to be closed down and fumigated because of reports of toxic insect bites—reports that could not subsequently be substantiated. Alan Kerckhoff and Kurt Back found that the crisis came after a period during which the women employees had performed unusual amounts of overtime work. The women who became ill from the mysterious insect bites had generally worked more overtime than others and had serious family responsibilities that they could not fulfill because of job demands. Afraid to refuse overtime work lest their job prospects be damaged, yet increasingly upset over neglect of family responsibilities, they found themselves in a conflict from which they could not extricate themselves. Illness from an insect bite provided an excuse to leave work for a day or two. The epidemic continued for about 11 days. It began immediately after a large shipment of foreign cloth had arrived, rendering plausible the assumption that some strange new insect had been introduced to the plant. The first women "bitten" were social isolates, lacking normal social defenses and controls. A rapid spread then took place among women who belonged to intimate cliques, in accord with the theory that social diffusion occurs most readily along well-established lines of social interaction. In the final stage the illness spread to others, irrespective of friendship ties or isolation.

Crazes.   Financial booms or crazes are occasions when the value of land, stock, or other merchandise is driven well above its intrinsic value by speculation. Crazes are peculiarly a modern phenomenon, since they require that there be surplus wealth and a flexible and storable medium of exchange. They represent the escalation of a buoyant confidence in the economic future that goes far beyond realistic limits. Crazes normally occur after a period of economic expansion and are associated with what seems to be the sudden emergence of a new area of opportunity. The post-war opening up of Spanish New World colonies to British trade was the occasion for the famous 18th-century South Sea Bubble. Combined with this optimism in a craze is the fear of lost opportunity— that is, that the supply of land (or whatever) is not inexhaustible and that only those who buy early will benefit from the initial low prices. The famous crazes have generally received the stamp of authenticity from respected figures who themselves invested and endorsed the enterprise. No less a person than the king of England lost money when the South Sea Bubble burst. Indeed, the largest and most disastrous of these "bubbles" were organized as schemes to pay off a national debt.

Thus crazes are like fads in representing the discovery of what seems to be a vast realm of opportunity. Like faddists, the investors set aside normal caution, relying on optimism and prestigious leadership to justify them. Like hysterical contagion, the craze requires that a distorted perception of the situation be maintained.

Deviant epidemics.   Faddish behaviour also is observed within deviant groups in society. After Edward G. Robinson starred in the motion picture *Little Caesar* (1932), a rash of undersized juvenile delinquents aped his manner. In 1959 and 1960 there was a rash of incidents in which synagogues were desecrated, usually by painting Nazi swastikas on them, and anti-Semitic slogans were painted in public places. In the United States the epidemic began the day after Christmas and continued for nine weeks, encompassing 600 reported incidents. Incidents reached a peak in the third week, with the cycle in small communities lagging a little behind the large cities. In the early and late weeks Jewish synagogues, houses, and other specifically Jewish properties were the main targets. During the middle three weeks anti-Semitic symbols were often placed elsewhere, leading investigators to infer that during the peak of the epidemic many participants were drawn in who were less preoccupied with anti-Semitism than those who initiated the incidents. Only a minority of the perpetrators were identified and arrested, but these were principally adolescent boys who worked together in small unorganized and heterogeneous groups. Some were strongly anti-Semitic in their attitudes, while others were no more hostile toward Jews than they were toward many other groups or aspects of society.

In this kind of episode socially disapproved feelings are given vent in a rash of incidents following an initial dramatic and well-publicized incident that keynotes the epidemic. Beginning with persons who have been holding back a specific feeling for some time and now find the encouragement to express it, the epidemic builds up until persons with other types of suppressed feelings join in. As the epidemic recedes, these secondary participants drop out first.

Fashion.   Fashion is much like fads and other collective obsessions, except that it is institutionalized and regularized, becoming continuous rather than sporadic, and partially predictable. Whereas fads often challenge the established class structure of a society by popularizing modes of behaviour deriving from lower echelons, fashion flows predictably from the higher levels to the lower levels, providing a continuous verification of class differences. Continuous change is essential if the higher

classes are to maintain their distinctiveness after copies of their clothing styles appear at lower levels. Fashions tend to change cyclically within limits set by the more stable culture.

CROWDS

There is a thin line separating the activities of crowds from collective obsessions. The crowd is, first, more concentrated in time and space. Thus a race riot, a lynching, or an orgy is limited to a few days or hours, and occurs chiefly within an area ranging from a city square or a stadium to a section of a metropolitan area. Second, the overriding concern of the crowd (overriding because every crowd includes many individuals who participate but do not share the concern) is a collaborative goal rather than parallel individual goals. The "june bug obsession" cited earlier, in which dozens of women went home from work because of imaginary insect bites, could have turned into a crowd action if the women had banded together to demand a change in working conditions or to conduct a ceremony to exorcise the evil. Third, because the goal is collaborative, there is more division of labour and cooperative activity in a crowd than in collective obsessions. Finally, the overriding concern is with some large-scale transformation expected as a result of the crowd's activity. Labour rioters expect management to be more compliant after the riot; participants in a massive religious revival expect life in the community to be somehow better as a result.

Crowd behaviour, like other collective behaviour, is spontaneous, but the occasion for the crowd is not always spontaneous. Any audience or public gathering can be transformed into a crowd. The crowd develops out of a period of elementary collective behaviour. Either an exciting event brings people together and provides the occasion for milling, or the relatively aimless milling of a mass of spectators is suddenly given focus and direction by an exciting event. Occasionally a single event is sufficient to instigate full development of a crowd, but usually the initial event merely focusses attention and provides the occasion for milling, and further crowd development depends upon subsequent incidents occurring as collective readiness to act is heightened. Precipitating incidents need not be of sufficient intrinsic importance to account for the reaction; it is more important that they symbolize an intense and widely shared concern of a group of people. Indeed, such extreme incidents as assassinations often provoke a mood of dread and mobilize defenses *against* the prospect of more killing and destruction, so that full-scale crowd behaviour is forestalled.

The crucial step in developing crowd behaviour is the formation of a common mood directed toward a recognized object of attention. In a typical riot situation a routine police arrest or a fist fight between individuals from opposing groups focusses attention. Milling and rumour then establish a mood of indignation and hostility toward a broad spectrum of enemies. In a collective religious experience there is usually some amazing event that rivets attention. Through elementary collective behaviour the mood is defined as religious awe and gratitude toward the supernatural and its agents.

As the mood and object become established, either an "active" crowd or an "expressive" crowd is formed. The active crowd is usually aggressive, such as a violent mob, though occasionally it acts to propel members into heroic accomplishments. The expressive crowd has also been called the dancing crowd because its manifestations are dancing, singing, and other forms of emotional expression.

Active crowds.   The active crowd identifies some object or group of objects outside itself and proceeds to act directly upon it or them. It will brook no delay or interference, no discussion of the desirability of acting, and no dissent from its course of action. Because of the high pitch of crowd interaction, subtle and indirect courses of action cannot win crowd support, though members are highly suggestible to all proposals and examples for

Cause of crazes

Fashion as a show of class differences

Precipitating incidents for crowd behaviour

action in keeping with the mood and the object. The stage of transformation from shared mood to shared action constitutes the beginning of the true crowd or mob.

The crucial feature of this stage is overcoming the barriers to such behaviour as the destruction of property or violence toward persons—actions against which most people have strongly ingrained inhibitions. Four aspects of the way crowd members feel about the situation make this possible. First, there is a sense of an exceptional situation in which a special moral code applies. The crowd merely carries further the justification for a special code of ethics incorporated in the slogan "You have to fight fire with fire!" Second, there is a sense of power in the crowd, with its apparent determination and uniform will, that overcomes the individual's doubts concerning his own ability to carry out a momentous task successfully. Third, there is a sense of impunity, of safety from personal injury and punishment so long as the individual is on the side of the crowd. And finally, there is a sense of inevitability, that the crowd aim will be accomplished regardless of the doubts and opposition of individuals.

The recruits who make up the crowd are a heterogeneous collection of people with diverse motivations and attitudes. Some are persons with a burning concern for the cause for which the crowd is mobilized. But others are persons looking for fun and excitement, or idle spectators, or persons opposed to the crowd's main thrust. If the sense of an omnipotent and righteous community is to dominate the crowd, many of the initially more casual participants must be brought into full participation and others must be effectively silenced.

One means of arousing crowd support is the process of keynote and response. A keynote is a concise declaration or proposal that is made by someone in the crowd and that is picked up and repeated throughout the crowd because it captures the spirit of the occasion and the inclination of the more aroused members. A constant process of creating leadership operates in the crowd. Any individual who makes a dramatic move or seems to be taking steps in the direction indicated by the mood attracts an instant following. By exhibiting their insistent expectation that he lead them, members of the following often precipitate the leader into initiating actions for the crowd to follow. The initiating example sets in motion another important process. Individuals are hesitant to throw rocks at police but, under conditions of heightened readiness to act, the example of one person throwing a rock is often enough to overcome the barrier for others to do likewise. Justification through authoritative support is frequently an important process. Many mobs have burst into full operation after police officers or other representatives of authority were seen to ignore scattered acts of violence or destruction. In more extreme instances, a recognized public personage has fired one of the first shots or led the lynching party in person. Justification is also achieved in an opposite manner, by confrontations creating indignation. In race riots in the United States in the first half of the 20th century, justification through authoritative support was almost always observed. In the race riots of the 1960s, and in typical wildcat strikes, the justification is through confrontation. Police efforts to control the emerging crowd lead to incidents that are interpreted as outrageous police brutality. Or efforts by labour union officials to discourage the unauthorized strike lead to an impasse that is seen as betrayal and repudiation of the workers by their leaders. The crowd also inspires fear among its uncommitted members. Just the physical pressure and jostling among crowd members constitute a frightening experience for persons who are not caught up in the crowd élan. And members of the crowd quickly vent their hatred on anyone who seems to express dissent or to stand in their way. Some individuals trade this fear for the crowd élan, and others either flee the crowd or remain silent.

Once the crowd breaks through the barrier of conventional restraints there is typically a "Roman holiday" period during which all restraint appears to be dropped. To the outsider, people seem to have gone mad. Rage is entirely uninhibited. But at the same time an atmosphere of intense enjoyment and release is evident. There is laughing and cheering as the violence and destruction become part of a tremendous carnival.

Collapse of conventional restraints

Under cover of the Roman holiday people pursue many different interests. Looting for personal gain is infrequent in the early stages of rioting. The leading agents in bringing the mob into being are too preoccupied with their indignation for this. But once the general attack is under way, looting for gain, vandalism for fun, and attacks on specific objects to pay off old grudges become prevalent. In Russian and Polish pogroms of the 19th and early 20th centuries, peasants came with their carts to loot Jewish property after they heard that the pogrom was under way. Southern U.S. lynchings in the early part of the 20th century were frequently followed by general forays on black neighbourhoods.

Once crowd action has been instigated by recognized leaders, these leaders often lose their control. Often the instigators have a restricted objective in mind and wish to avoid excesses that discredit the whole effort. Once the crowd gets demonstrably out of their control, instigators are in a less favourable position for bargaining with authorities over reforms or personal gain.

The limits of crowd development and action during this peak stage have been much debated. One view stresses the mutual breakdown of inhibitions and the stimulation to even more extreme actions, until fatigue, a rainstorm, exhaustion of suitable objects, catharsis, satiation, or superior force brings the crowd to a stop. Another view sees the crowd as governed by a general sense of grievance and a fairly well defined sense of object. According to this view, crowd activity normally stays within identifiable limits and objects are attacked selectively. The small number of persons killed or seriously injured by rioters in spite of the magnitude of the riots in the United States in the late 1960s, as well as the immunity of such establishments as gasoline stations in many instances, lend support to the latter view. Nevertheless, scattered excesses always occur, and no one has yet devised a way to predict the limits of crowd action.

The acting crowd normally ends with a tapering-off period, which is sometimes preceded by a stage of siege. In riots of limited scale in which no massive police or military forces are used, the peak day is followed by a few more days of successively smaller numbers of widely scattered encounters. Often the last incidents are in areas not previously hit by rioting, as if persons in the hinterlands were belatedly trying to join the bandwagon. There seems to be some internal mechanism limiting the duration of crowd behaviour, though whether it is fatigue, catharsis, or reassertion of ingrained standards of behaviour is uncertain. In serious riots, however, the police and other armed forces are brought into action long before the riot can decline naturally. When police power is applied with only enough force to insure a standoff between rioters and authorities, there is a period—usually ranging from one to three or four days—of siege. The mood of buoyancy gives way to a mood of dogged persistence. Rioters are more cautious and deliberate in what they do. The desire to have the riot over grows among the participants and in the community, but there is reluctance to give up the fight until concessions have been won.

A crowd develops only when a necessary sequence of events occurs and when conditions conducive to crowd development are present. There are at least six such conditions of importance. First is a deep frustration that is shared by an important segment of the population and that has been festering for a considerable period of time. The frustration is especially poignant when widening intergroup contacts make the frustrated segment more vitally aware of its disadvantages, when its members have been encouraged by education or a public policy statement to aspire to relatively unattainable objectives, and when a period of steadily improving conditions is sud-

Development of active crowds

denly interrupted. Second is the presence of deep intergroup cleavages in society. A crowd must have not only a grievance but an oppressor whom it can blame for its condition. Clearly observable periods of mounting intergroup tensions precede crowd eruptions. Third is some contradiction in the value system of society, so that there is support both for the social arrangements that the group finds frustrating and for its demands for change. Fourth is a failure of communication, so that grievances can no longer be presented to the appropriate authorities with confidence that they will be given some consideration. Fifth is some failure in the system of control. Mobs often catch police unprepared. In many instances the police, by virtue of their class or ethnic identity, are in sympathy with mobs and unwilling to enforce order. Sixth, there are experiences leading people to hope that conditions will be improved as a result of violent or disruptive action. Many riots have the support of a well-developed ideology, or they follow occasions when demonstrations and other less extreme tactics have won gains. There may be crowd actions stemming from sheer desperation, but they appear to be rare. Among the reasons that mob actions do not soon recur in a given location are that the forces of order are usually strengthened, the hope of great gain is dampened, and channels of communication are usually improved after a mob action.

Expressive crowds. Not all crowds act. In some crowds the participants are largely preoccupied with themselves or with one another, and with participation in a common experience. Beginning as early as the 7th century in Europe, and continuing throughout the Middle Ages, there were reported epidemics in which groups of people were caught up in a frenzy of dancing that continued until they dropped. Later a collective frenzy of dancing, singing, and shouting became a regular feature of frontier revivals in 19th-century America. Crowds that exceeded conventional limits of revelry have been common in many historical eras. In San Francisco in 1945, license for public violation of sexual mores characterized the day of celebration at the end of the war with Japan.

Expressive crowds may be secular or religious. What distinguishes them is that the production of a shared subjective experience is the crowd's measure of its accomplishment, rather than any action upon objects outside the crowd. One interpretation is that the same determinants of social unrest and frustration give rise to both the expressive crowd and to the active crowd, but the expressive crowd fails to identify an object toward which to act; hence members must release accumulated tension through motions and gestures expressing emotion. According to this view an expressive crowd can fairly quickly metamorphose into an active crowd if an object becomes apparent to them. Another interpretation sees the expressive crowd as equally equipped with an object, but with an object that must be acted upon symbolically rather than directly. Thus one crowd engages in a wild dance to exorcise evil spirits, whereas another seeks to destroy buildings associated with the "establishment" that it blames for many ills.

The similarity of mechanisms and processes in active and expressive crowds, and the similar social unrest that leads to both, suggest that differences should not be unduly emphasized. But the expressive crowd may serve best those types of frustrations requiring revitalization of the individual and group rather than direct modification of external circumstances. Expressive crowds may be especially frequent in periods of frustration and boredom over the predictability and routinization of life, from lack of a sense of meaning and importance in the daily round of life, and from a sense of interpersonal isolation in spite of the physical closeness of others.

PANIC

The term panic is often applied to a strictly individual, maladaptive reaction of flight, immobility, or disorganization stemming from intense fear. For example, a student "panics" during an examination and is unable to

call upon his knowledge in answering questions, or a disaster victim in a situation of mild danger panics and flees into much greater danger. Individual panic frequently occurs as a unique individual response without triggering a similar reaction in others.

Panic as collective behaviour, however, is shared behaviour. When an entire military unit breaks into disorderly flight, a group pattern of orderly behaviour is replaced by a group pattern of panic.

There are four distinguishing features to collective panic. First, several persons in social contact with one another simultaneously exhibit intense fear and either flee (or demonstrate disorganization leading toward flight) or remain immobile. Second, each individual's fear and his evaluation of the danger are augmented by the signals he receives from others. Third, flight is indicated as the only conceivable course of action by the signals each is receiving from others. Fourth, the usual rules according to which individuals adjust their behaviour so as not to work at cross-purposes are nullified. In the more dramatic instances of collective panic, people trample one another in vain efforts to reach safety.

Four types of causes for collective panic are recognized. First, collective panic usually occurs in the kind of situation arousing fear in any individual. Hence the psychological causes for individual panic are also fundamental causes for collective panic. Some students de-emphasize the collective behavioural aspects, assuming that collective panic is merely the simultaneous panic of individuals confronted with the same situation. Other students, however, find it less easy to dismiss the interaction among participants as an important cause.

A second cause of panic is the special character of the situation in which people find themselves. Students of responses to disaster observe that collective panic occurs only when people perceive a danger that is both immediate and severe, when they know of only a very limited number of escape routes from the danger, and when they believe those routes are being closed off so that the time for escape is extremely limited. The requirement that all three conditions be present underlines the observation that intense fear in situations from which there is apparently *no* escape elicits no collective panic and very little individual panic.

Psychologists have suggested that terror has been over-emphasized in understanding collective panic, and that the breakdown of rules for orderly departure and mutual considerateness can be created in a laboratory without any intense emotion. This feature of panic can occur whenever the individuals see that taking turns or following the rules is likely to prevent their successful completion of a task to which they are committed. Following a similar line of thought, Turner and Killian suggested that collective panic be viewed as part of a broad class of individualistic crowds. Individualistic crowds include such phenomena as the crush and breakdown of order that sometimes occur at a bargain sale, or the transformation of an orderly ticket-window queue into a shoving and pushing crowd. All the usual mechanisms of crowd behaviour are in operation, but in contrast to the lynch mob or race riot, the situation encourages the intensified pursuit of individual rather than collective goals.

The situational explanation is not complete by itself, however, as indicated by such occasions as the sinking of the ocean liner "Titanic" with great loss of life but without panic. The ship was visibly sinking, and there were known to be too few lifeboats for all the passengers, and yet men were frequently reluctant to board the boats until all women and children had first been rescued. Hence the third set of causes is the interstimulation of elementary crowd behaviour, the milling, rumour, and social unrest, through which the group forms a collective view of the situation and of the appropriate behaviour. It is difficult to find any explanation for the difference in behaviour between the "Titanic" passengers and passengers who have panicked in other maritime disasters, except that a norm of gentility and heroism came to dominate the collective definition through these elementary pro-

Characteristics of panic

Behaviour of passengers during the "Titanic" disaster

cesses. Elementary collective behaviour also is required to explain instances of collective panic in the absence of real danger, or to explain ticket-window crushes when there are actually plenty of good seats for all. In these cases a rumour of danger or shortage becomes the accepted collective definition, usually because it is not convincingly negated by persons in a position to speak authoritatively. The concept of elementary collective behaviour is also necessary to explain the diversion of attention away from alternate escape routes in cases such as a stampede toward one exit to the neglect of others. Here the attention of individuals is so rivetted on the crowd that the possibility of conceiving other courses of action is drastically reduced.

Since the most dramatic feature of panic behaviour is every individual's disregard for his fellows' lives, many students believe that the fourth set of causes lies in the *quality* of every individual's relations with his fellows. Sigmund Freud proposed that panic expresses the exceptional terror of the child who suddenly feels that he has lost the love of his parents. Without the love of the group leader, the entire foundation for group life is undermined. Translating Freud's interpretation into more sociological terms, Kurt Lang and Gladys Lang view panic as the end point in a process of demoralization in which behaviour becomes privatized and there is a general retreat from the pursuit of group goals. Thus the essential characteristic of demoralization is the emergence of isolated individuals fearfully pursuing strictly private goals, and released from all sense of group loyalty. When panic is viewed this way the investigator looks for circumstances that have undermined group morale, that have destroyed the individual's trust in his fellows and eliminated the sense of common interest. This approach helps to explain why one group dissolves quickly into collective panic while another maintains its solidarity in the face of a similar threat. The strongest defense against collective panic is a well-developed sense of common purpose and an attitude of mutual trust among group members.

PUBLICS AND MASSES

Crowd behaviour, and such related forms as crazes, fads, and panics, are often contrasted with "publics," in which more of an attitude of deliberation prevails. Crowds and publics were first distinguished according to proximity, the public consisting of dispersed individuals communicating indirectly. Interaction in the public sometimes has been termed rational in contrast to the emotional or irrational behaviour of crowds, but neither distinction is crucial. The most important distinction is that people in the public recognize that there is a division of opinion about an issue and are prepared to interact with a recognition and tolerance of difference. Herbert Blumer defines the public as "a group of people who (a) are confronted by an issue, (b) are divided in their ideas as to how to meet the issue, and (c) engage in discussion over the issue." Another important difference is that the product of interaction in the public is public opinion, rather than the collective action or experience of collective ecstasy that eventuates from active and expressive crowds.

Publics are common in societies where public officials and institutional leaders are thought to be responsive to indications of public opinion. When this condition does not prevail, collective behaviour does not usually crystallize beyond the elementary forms, stopping with the establishment of a rumour grapevine. When disillusionment over official response to public opinion reaches a high pitch, publics either do not form or turn quickly into crowds that take direct action.

Compari-
son of
crowds,
publics,
and masses

The public and crowd should be distinguished from the "mass." Members of a mass exhibit similar behaviour, simultaneously, but with a minimum of interaction. Masses include a wide range of groups. They include, for instance, women simultaneously reading the newspaper advertisement for a department store sale and simultaneously converging on the store with similar objects in mind; but masses also involve people converging in a disaster or a gold rush or a mass migration. In the public

and the crowd, social interaction plays a large part in accounting for common definitions of an issue and similar views about how to deal with a problem. But in a mass a great many people react similarly to a common stimulus just because they have common attitudes and motivations. Election behaviour is often closer to the mass than to the public, when taboos on discussing controversial topics lead each person to make up his mind privately on the basis of what he gleans from the mass media of communication.

SOCIAL MOVEMENTS

Collective behaviour in crowds, crazes, panics, and elementary forms (milling, etc.) are of brief duration or episodic, and guided largely by impulse. When short-lived impulses give way to long-term aims, and when sustained association takes the place of situational groupings of people, the result is a social movement. Stanley Milgram and Hans Toch define a social movement as "a spontaneous large group constituted in support of a set of purposes or beliefs that are 'shared' by the members." Placing more emphasis on the duration of the group and its relation to change in society. Turner and Killian define a social movement as a "collectivity acting with some continuity to promote a change or resist a change in the society or group of which it is a part."

A movement is not merely a perpetuated crowd, since a crowd does not possess organizational and motivational mechanisms capable of sustaining membership through periods of inaction and waiting. Furthermore, crowd mechanisms cannot be used to achieve communication and coordination of activity over a wide area, such as a nation or continent. A movement is a mixture of organization and spontaneity. There is usually one or more organizations that give identity, leadership, and coordination to the movement, but the boundaries of the movement are never coterminous with the organizations. For example, although organizations such as California's Sierra Club are influential in the movement to preserve the natural environment, anyone who works for the cause and interacts with other workers for this purpose is a member of the conservationist movement. The famous John Brown was not a member of any major abolitionist organization, but his martyrdom made him a leader and symbol for the movement, even though organizational leaders were reluctant to recognize him.

Followings and cults. Two forms of collective behaviour that meet the Milgram-Toch criteria for social movements, but not the Turner-Killian criteria, are "followings" and "cults." A following is a collectivity made up of people whose collaboration is limited to expressing their love and admiration for a chosen public figure, without attempting to make changes in society. A cult is a group of people who withdraw among themselves and carry on a unique style of common life without concerning themselves about the course of events in the outside world.

Primitive and millenarian movements. Movements that resemble crowds most closely have sometimes been called primitive movements or protest movements. These are movements that consist of a series of activities to register a continuing grievance, but have no plan for reform to promote. Often these movements involve a series of planned crowd actions to harass groups in authority or to punish hated groups. The first stirrings of tribal and nationalist sentiment, the first expressions of resentment from depressed classes, and protest from any group whose members lack understanding of how their society functions are likely to take this form. Whether they are the Luddites of 19th-century England destroying machinery, or the earlier peasants protesting their lot at the close of the feudal era, their gratification comes from retaliating against their supposed oppressors rather than from amelioration of their condition. These movements usually are reactionary in the sense that participants would like to see history turned back to an earlier period that they imagine to have been idyllic compared with the present.

The advent
of a
messiah

The stronger and more sustained movements of this kind are typically oriented to a millenarian or chiliastic theme. Originally referring to a second coming of Christ to rule the earth for a thousand years, these terms are applied more broadly to any doctrine that prophesies the advent of a messiah who will destroy the world as it exists and establish an ideal society in which the chosen people will occupy the place of privilege. A succession of such movements commanded support from large numbers of the dispossessed in Europe during the later Middle Ages. During the 20th century, movements of this sort have sprung up in most underdeveloped areas of the world, notably Africa, the East Indies, and Latin America. Recruits to these movements largely detach themselves from the world in which they live, often destroying their material wealth, giving up their employment, and systematically violating many established customs and mores while adhering puritanically to the distinctive code of the movement. By thus purifying and ingratiating themselves with the messiah, they are prepared to be among the chosen at the time of his imminent arrival on earth. There is always a moment of reckoning for these movements when the prophecy fails. But the movement often has served as a rehearsal for independence, preparing the members for later participation in movements for the more active reform of society.

Movements of the spirit. Throughout history proponents of special beliefs, codes of behaviour, and methods of worship have organized to protect their way of life from erosion or repression from outside and to proselyte others to the true faith. Most of these movements have been dependent upon a charismatic leader whose faith was then perpetuated through an organization formed by his disciples. A charismatic leader is one to whom his followers often attribute superhuman power and wisdom. Most religious movements began as stirrings of discontent within an established religious organization. When satisfaction was not received and discontent grew, divisive or separatist movements flourished. During the Middle Ages these movements in the Christian Church were known as heresies, and some were accommodated by the establishment of separate orders within the church or toleration of saintly cults. In recent times the Protestant churches, unable to make accommodations, spawned a large number of sectarian movements that became competing churches.

Sectarian
and
secular
move-
ments

H. Richard Niebuhr developed the thesis that sectarian religious movements represent the interest of socioeconomic classes whose denial of equal status in the larger community is paralleled by second-class church citizenship. Once they have a sect whose form of worship is attuned to their disposition, the poor are motivated toward diligence and dependability by their religious training. Within a few generations their socioeconomic status becomes securely middle class, they acquire middle class tastes, and the sect is transformed into a denomination that adjusts comfortably to the world about it and creates its own class of excluded poor. Many students regard sectarian movements as forerunners of modern political movements, developed before classes became sophisticated about the possibilities for reforming the economic and social order.

The 19th century witnessed many movements that either mixed religious and secular themes or employed a wholly secular doctrine, promising the key to personal happiness, business success, physical or mental health, or other personal rewards to those who diligently adhered to their precepts. From Christian Science, with its predominantly religious emphasis, to scientology, with its secular appeal, these movements drew upon the magical perspective with which modern science is popularly endowed.

Humanitarian and reform movements. Once a group of people dedicated to a particular way of life has achieved some success in proselyting, it is easily tempted to seek ways of imposing its standards upon the whole community. A great many movements of humanitarian concern for the underprivileged, for reform of corrupt and entrenched political machines, and for the improve-

ment of public morals have emanated from religious sources. When such movements, like the American movement for the abolition of slavery, persist in the face of great opposition, it is usually because their aim is related to a major struggle for power in the community. The abolition movement became increasingly an aspect of the struggle by the industrial Northeast to wrest control from the plantation South. Similarly, movements against corruption in local government are most enthusiastically supported when they serve the interests of an ethnic group or a political party'. Humanitarian movements have a notable tendency to place the people whose welfare they serve in a subordinated status within the movement and to demand gratitude and conformity as conditions for their wholehearted effort. Hence humanitarian movements often help to educate a depressed group to the possibility of demanding better conditions, only to be repudiated later by the group they serve. Early movements to improve the labourer's lot and movements for Negro rights in the United States were largely dominated by middle class whites. Eventually both the labour movement and the civil rights movement became interest-group movements and either forced middle class whites out of the movement or required that they assume a subordinated status.

Interest-group movements. The most relentless movements for change are the movements of social classes, ethnic groups, regional populations, age groups, sex groups, and other population segments who organize to promote their own interests. The modern state, with its enlarging powers and monopoly of legitimate force, has become the main target for interest-group movements that seek to alter the objective conditions of society through political means. These movements bring about radical reforms, however, only when the group's own power somehow increases or when the group is able to form a coalition with another relatively powerful group. The liberal reforms of governments in western Europe in the late 18th and the 19th centuries were spearheaded by middle class interest-group movements, who already had potential power and were belatedly brushing aside the archaic political forms left over from a period when economic power was concentrated in the hands of hereditary landowners. In the United States, the recognition of labour's right to organize and bargain collectively with management came during the 1930s, when labour and the Democratic Party formed a mutually profitable coalition.

Politically
oriented
interest-
groups

Revolutionary movements. Although most movements work within the confines of the state and prevailing folkways, some movements threaten a total transformation of society. Some students distinguish the "reform movement," which seeks change within the accepted value system, from the "revolutionary movement," which rejects society's main value system. Other students, however, believe that a movement either operates within the system or challenges the whole system, largely depending on whether the movement is accepted as a legitimate vehicle of dissent or repressed as threatening by agents of the community. Once a movement takes on a thoroughly revolutionary cast, it requires a dedicated and highly disciplined core of workers, and it must obstruct efforts to ameliorate conditions when amelioration might lessen discontent and potential support for the revolutionary aims.

Nationalist movements. Nationalist movements are among the most vital agencies fostering change in the contemporary world. Nationalism became important in 19th-century Europe with the self-rediscovery of historic entities such as the Slavs, whose populations were divided among several states, and with the union of fractionated principalities, such as the German states, into a single nation. Subsequently it became the principal force in underdeveloped countries seeking to throw off both political and economic control by more developed nations. Most recently nationalism has been expressed as the tie between national minorities and the country of their origin, as in French-Canadian and Mexican-American nationalisms. Between World Wars I and II, nationalisms in Europe were largely conservative movements to resist the advance of international Socialist movements, as in Germany and Spain. In underdeveloped countries, nationalist movements are confronted with the dilemma that they must glorify traditional culture and values against the inroads of colonial powers; but they must promote modernization if they are to raise living standards, and they must combat the divisiveness of the archaic tribal or folk basis of organization.

III. Theories of collective behaviour

Because much collective behaviour is dramatic, unpredictable, and frightening, the early theories and many currently popular views are more evaluative than analytic. Gustave Le Bon identified the crowd and revolutionary movements with the excesses of the French Revolution; Boris Sidis was impressed with resemblance of crowd behaviour to mental disorder. Many of these early theories depicted collective behaviour as an atavism, in which the evolutionary accomplishments of civilization were stripped away and man's behaviour returned to an earlier stage of development. Sigmund Freud retained this emphasis in viewing crowd behaviour and many other forms of collective behaviour as regressions to more elementary or instinctual forms of behaviour.

Social and revolutionary theories

More sophisticated recent efforts to treat collective behaviour as a pathological manifestation employ *social disorganization* as an explanatory approach. From this point of view collective behaviour erupts as an unpleasant symptom of frustration and malaise stemming from cultural conflict, organizational failure, and other societal malfunctions. The distinctive feature of this approach is a reluctance to take seriously the manifest content of collective behaviour. Neither the search for enjoyment in a recreational fad, the search for spiritual meaning in a religious sect, nor the demand for equal opportunity in an interest-group movement is accepted at face value.

An opposite evaluation of many forms of collective behaviour has become part of the analytic perspective in revolutionary approaches to society. From the revolutionist's point of view, much collective behaviour is a release of creative impulses from the repressive effects of established social orders. Revolutionary theorists such as Frantz Fanon depict traditional social arrangements as destructive of human spontaneity, and various forms of crowd and revolutionary movements as man's creative self-assertion bursting its social shackles.

INDIVIDUAL MOTIVATION THEORIES

Psychiatric and sociological traditions

Among the analytic theories that seek to eschew evaluation, the most popular stress *individual motivation* in accounting for collective behaviour. Frustration and lack of firm social anchorage are the two most widely used explanations for individual participation in collective behaviour of all kinds. In the psychiatric tradition, frustration heightens suggestibility, generates fantasy, brings about regressions and fixations, and intensifies drives toward wish fulfillment so that normal inhibitions are overcome. Since most forms of collective behaviour promote thoughts that are not otherwise taken seriously, and that breech behavioural inhibitions, this is often a fruitful source of explanation.

In the sociological tradition of Émile Durkheim, absence of firm integration into social groups leaves the individual open to deviant ideas and susceptible to the vital sense of solidarity that comes from participation in spontaneous groupings. Drawing upon both the psychiatric and the sociological traditions, Erich Fromm attributes the appeal of mass movements and crowds to the gratifying escape they offer from the sense of personal isolation and powerlessness that men experience in the vast bureaucracies of modern life. Extending Karl Marx's theory of modern man's alienation from his work, many contemporary students attribute faddism, crazes, crowds, movements of the spirit, and interest-group and revolutionary movements to a wide-ranging alienation from family, community, and nation, as well as from work.

According to an approach suggested by Hadley Cantril, participation in vital collectivities supplies a sense of meaning through group affirmation and action, and raises the member's estimate of his social status, both of which are important needs often frustrated in modern society. Eric Hoffer attributes a leading role in collective behaviour to "true believers," who overcome their own personal doubts and conflicts by the creation of intolerant and unanimous groups about them.

INTERACTION THEORIES

Sociologists and social psychologists, without denying the place of individual motivation in any complete explanation for collective behaviour, have more often stressed a distinctive quality or intensity of *social interaction*. The American sociologists Robert E. Park and Ernest Burgess associated collective behaviour with "circular reaction," a type of interaction in which each person reacts by repeating the action or mirroring the sentiment of another person, thereby intensifying the action or sentiment in the originator. Herbert Blumer added a subtlety to this theory by sharply distinguishing circular reaction from "interpretative interaction," in which the individual first interprets another's action and then makes a response usually different from the stimulus action. Another stream of thought has stressed difference of intensity rather than kind of interaction. Following Gabriel Tarde and Alfred Binet, many investigators have looked for clues that normal imitative tendencies and suggestibility may be intensified in collective behaviour. An important approach is based on social psychologist Floyd H. Allport's criticism of Gustave Le Bon and William McDougall for their concept of "group mind," and for their apparent assumption that collective behaviour makes people do things to which they are not predisposed. Allport insisted instead that collective behaviour involves merely a group of people doing what they had previously wanted to do, but for which they lacked the occasion and the support of like-minded associates.

Contagion, convergence, and emergent norm

These interaction theories have been labelled *contagion* and *convergence* theories, respectively—the former stressing the contagious spread of mood and behaviour; the latter stressing the convergence of a large number of people with similar predispositions. Both have sought to explain why a group of people feel and act (1) unanimously, (2) intensely, and (3) differently from the manner in which they customarily act. Other interaction theorists have challenged the assumption of unanimity, proposing that in most kinds of collective behaviour a single mood and course of action is established with such force and intolerance that the many who privately dissent are silenced, creating an illusion of unanimity. Rather than contagion, it is an emergent norm or rule that governs external appearances and, to a lesser extent, internal convictions in collective behaviour.

Freud, too, stressed a distinctive pattern of interaction in collective behaviour. The key to these groupings is the desire to possess a beloved leader. Because the leader is unattainable, and because his attentions must be shared among many followers, a relation of identification is expressed in the demand for uniformity that the followers insistently impose on each other, according to the example of the leader.

SOCIAL CHANGE

A final set of theories stresses characteristics of social organization that generate collective behaviour. Collective behaviour is commonly seen by sociologists as a normal accompaniment and medium for social change, relatively absent in periods of social stability. With the more or less continuous shifts of values in any society, emerging values are first given group expression in collective behaviour; efforts to revitalize declining values also bring forth collective behaviour. Again, the constant readjustments in the power of different population segments are implemented and resisted through collective behaviour. Because it is a means of communication, and because it is always characterized by novel or intensified control over individuals, collective behaviour also arises to bypass communication blockages and to install an emergent order when formal or informal regulation of behaviour is inadequate.

The most comprehensive theory specifying necessary conditions for the development of most major forms of collective behaviour is advanced by Neil Smelser. Six conditions must all be present: (1) the social structure must be peculiarly conducive to the collective behaviour in question; (2) a group of people must experience strain; (3) a distinctive type of belief must be present to interpret the situation; (4) there must be a precipitating event; (5) the group of people must be mobilized for action on the basis of the belief; and (6) there must be an appropriate interaction between the mobilized group and agencies of social control. The detail for each condition varies with the type of collective behaviour.

IV. The results of collective behaviour

THE VARIETY OF EFFECTS

Short-term effects. The most notable immediate effect of all kinds of collective behaviour is to alter the salience of various problems, issues, and groups in public awareness. Popular concern about disarmament grew large as "Ban-the-Bomb" demonstrations proliferated during the late 1950s and early 1960s; then public interest waned as demonstrations became infrequent or ceased. A fad or craze calls attention to recreational needs or the workings of financial institutions; the circumstances surrounding a panic monopolize public attention. Second, all forms of collective behaviour contribute to polarizations, forcing people to take sides on issues and eliminating the middle ground. If polarization seems intense enough, there is also a counterreaction directed toward protecting the solidarity of the community against the divisiveness of polarization. The result is often a three-sided conflict among the two polarized groups and mediators who wish to de-emphasize divisive issues altogether. Third, every instance of collective behaviour either alters or strengthens the makeup of group and community leadership. The swings of fashion discredit some clothes designers and boost others to prominence. A riot or a wildcat strike usually reveals the inability of established leaders to control their members and produces emergent leaders from among the spokesmen acceptable to members.

Contingencies. How the immediate effects of collective behaviour are translated into long-term consequences depends upon several contingencies, of which four merit attention. First, the nature of the response by authorities affects the immediate course of the collective behaviour. Some evidence suggests that alarmed and repressive reactions strengthen polarization, that moderate reactions strengthen the mediation viewpoint, and that inaction or ineffectual action facilitates efforts toward usurpation of authority.

Second, the response of authorities will affect public definitions of the meaning of the collective behaviour. Publics have variously defined particular fads as harmless diversions, threats to authority and order, threats to health and well-being, visitations of the Holy Spirit, and possession by the devil, treating them quite differently in consequence. Lynchings are vigilante actions, or they are criminal subversions of justice. Riots can be viewed as mass criminality or as social protest. Social movements are defined as respectable, or as peculiar but harmless, or as dangerous and revolutionary, evoking polite support, embarrassed avoidance, or active repression respectively.

A third contingency affecting the aftermath of collective behaviour concerns the nature and strategy of the countermovements or counterfads that arise. When the countermovement arises, acquires a bitter and reactionary tone, and becomes a "backlash," polarization and heightened disorder often lead to demands for order at any cost, at the expense of any amelioration that might otherwise have occurred. But backlash is often self-discrediting as "extremism," and over the long run some-

times pushes many people onto the side of amelioration. Countermovements that avoid the backlash pattern typically try to undermine the group they oppose by taking some of the latter's aims as their own, thereby helping to effect reforms sought in the initial protest.

Finally, the effect of collective behaviour depends upon the ubiquitous process of conventionalization. In a spontaneous fad or mob action, participants usually copy the pattern of earlier incidents with which they are familiar, so that separate incidents in a wave of collective behaviour exhibit a similarity indicating the development of customary ways of rioting, or playing at a fad, and possibly even of panicking. When incidents are repeated, a gradual accommodation between participants in collective behaviour and the authorities becomes routinized. Once the behaviour is conventionalized in this fashion, there are increasing efforts to create and use the conventionalized form of collective behaviour for private and public aims. Much advertising seeks to create fads in conventionalized ways. Political rallies, sports rallies, and some of the ceremonies of established religious organizations seek to conventionalize the enthusiasm and sense of solidarity of expressive crowds. Social movements rapidly acquire stable organizations, sects become denominations, political movements become political parties or are absorbed into parties, and humanitarian movements become stabilized as associations to promote some form of human betterment. Conventionalization extends the influence of orienting ideas and gives them a fairly permanent place in the community. But it also insures compromise and abandonment of the most disruptive and controversial features of the initial behaviour.

Long-term effects. In the long run it is difficult to be sure whether collective behaviour actually makes a difference or whether it is merely a shadow cast by passing events. Scattered collective behaviour is endemic in every society. But when there is widespread discontent, collective behaviour soon becomes a prominent feature of group life. When there are no exciting new ideas—such as the liberal humanitarian vision of the 18th and 19th centuries, the Socialist idea of the 19th and 20th centuries, and the nationalist mystique of the 20th century— collective behaviour consists principally of expressive behaviour, panics, and unfocussed disruption or intergroup vengeance such as pogroms. This kind of collective behaviour probably contributes little to change. But when there is a new perspective to give meaning to discontent, many forms of collective behaviour appear to become agents of change. Even a recreational fad becomes a form of self-assertion for a rising class or age group. Gustave Le Bon suggested that in a period of widespread discontent crowd action serves to destroy an old order in preparation for a new one. Social movements help to build the new order.

One view holds that collective behaviour supplies a testing ground on which new ideas are tried out for general acceptability and on which groups test their strength against forces of resistance. The outcome of this testing is sometimes change and sometimes public demonstration that the old order is still viable. This view suggests that collective behaviour has as great a function to play in stability as in change, disposing of challenges to a vital social order by catharsis or by discrediting the challenge in a public test.

ATTEMPTS AT CONTROL

Advocates of change seek to control countermovements and backlash crowds, as well as those expressive crowds and fads that anesthetize people to their grievances, whereas advocates of stability seek to control crowds and movements that undermine public order or threaten revolution. Advocates of both change and stability likewise make use of collective behaviour in achieving their aims. The volatile and unpredictable nature of all collective behaviour renders manipulation and control highly problematic, however, and such masters as Robespierre have often been victims of the followers they once manipulated.

"Conventionalization" of collective behaviour

The most sensitive and difficult control problem occurs at the moment of the first precipitating incident and during the stage of transformation in an active crowd. A show of weakness—or maybe even unnecessary repression—will escalate the crowd into the Roman-holiday stage. It is essential to identify spokesmen who command a hearing with the crowd—often not the established group leaders—and open serious negotiations with them. Poorly arranged negotiating sessions before television cameras are easily turned into occasions for incitement of the crowd. If the provocations of excessive policing are avoided and one or two dramatic concessions of great symbolic importance made, a cooling-off period may be secured in which more comprehensive measures to relieve tensions in the situation can be undertaken.

Once collective behaviour is fully escalated there is seldom any technique available except massive suppression, and some experts believe that crowd behaviour will spring up again if crushed before it has substantially run its course. Interference with an expressive crowd, and even with many fads, crazes, and instances of hysterical contagion, often turns it into a hostile, active one. As the intensity of feeling begins to decline, the time is then ripe to quicken the end of crowd behaviour by intensifying negotiations with spokesmen respected by the crowd.

BIBLIOGRAPHY. The following works are the major general treatments of the subject: H. BLUMER, "Collective Behavior," in A.M. LEE (ed.), *New Outline of the Principles of Sociology*, 2nd rev. ed. (1951), a classic sociological statement of a widely used approach; R.W. BROWN, "Mass Phenomena," in G. LINDZEY (ed.), *Handbook of Social Psychology*, vol. 2, pp. 833–876 (1954); and S. MILGRAM and H. TOCH, "Collective Behavior: Crowds and Social Movements," in G. LINDZEY and E. ARONSON (eds.), *Handbook of Social Psychology*, 2nd ed., vol. 4, pp. 507–610 (1968), comprehensive reviews presented by psychologists; R.R. EVANS (ed.), *Readings in Collective Behavior* (1969), a collection of classic journal articles; K. and G.E. LANG, *Collective Dynamics* (1961), a standard textbook; N.J. SMELSER, *Theory of Collective Behavior* (1963), a classic theoretical treatise and text; R.H. TURNER, "Collective Behavior," in R.E.L. FARIS (ed.), *Handbook of Modern Sociology*, pp. 382–425 (1964), an analytic statement of the field for the advanced student in sociology; and R.H. TURNER and L.M. KILLIAN, *Collective Behavior* 2nd ed. (1972), a standard textbook.
The following are more specialized references arranged by topic.
Elementary collective behaviour: G.W. ALLPORT and L. POSTMAN, *The Psychology of Rumor* (1947, reprinted 1965); T. SHIBUTANI, *Improvised News: A Sociological Study of Rumor* (1966).

Responses to Disaster: G.W. BAKER and D.W. CHAPMAN (eds.), *Man and Society in Disaster* (1962); W. LORD, *A Night to Remember* (1955); H.E. MOORE, *Tornadoes Over Texas: A Study of Waco and San Angelo in Disaster* (1958).

Collective obsessions: D. CAPLOVITZ and C. ROGERS, *Swastika 1960: The Epidemic of Anti-Semitic Vandalism in America* (1961); J. CARSWELL, *The South Sea Bubble* (1960); A.C. KERCKHOFF and K.W. BACK, *The June Bug: A Study of Hysterical Contagion* (1968); C. MACKAY, *Memoirs of Extraordinary Popular Delusions,* 3 vol. (1841).

Crowds: E.L. BACKMAN, *Religious Dances in the Christian Church and in Popular Medicine* (1952); H.D. GRAHAM and T.R. GURR (eds.), *The History of Violence in America: Historical and Comparative Perspectives* (1969); G. LE BON, *The Crowd: A Study of the Popular Mind* (1896); *Report of the National Advisory Commission on Civil Disorders* (1968); A.F. RAPER, *The Tragedy of Lynching* (1933); G.F.E. RUDE, *The Crowd in History: A Study of Popular Disturbances in France and England, 1730–1848* (1964); F. STAGG, E.G. HINSON, and W.E. OATES, *Glossolalia: Tongue Speaking in Biblical, Historical and Psychological Perspective* (1967).

Social movements: N.R.C. COHN, *The Pursuit of the Millenium*, 2nd ed. (1961); E.J. HOBSBAWM, *Social Bandits and Primitive Rebels: Studies in Archaic Forms of Social Movement in the 19th and 20th Centuries* (1960); P. WORSLEY, *The Trumpet Shall Sound: A Study of Cargo Cults in Melanesia* (1957).

Theories of collective behaviour: H. CANTRIL, *The Psychology of Social Movements* (1941); SIGMUND FREUD, *Group Psychology and the Analysis of the Ego* (1922); W.A. GAMSON, *Power and Discontent* (1968); E. HOFFER, *The True Believer:*

Thoughts on the Nature of Mass Movements (1951); R.T. LA PIERE, *Collective Behavior* (1938).

(R.H.T.)

Colloids

A colloid is any substance composed of fine particles whose dimensions are much larger than those of atoms or ordinary molecules but much smaller than those of particles visible to the unaided eye; colloids cannot be detected by optical microscopes in transmitted light. Usually colloidal particles exist as a dispersion in some medium, but they may exist purely—*i.e.*, without a medium. Some colloids are vital to everyday life—cheese, dough, paints, silk, rubber, proteins, plastics, clay, foam, smoke, and gelatin, for example. The presence or absence of colloids may be harmful or useful. They can be generated and also eliminated by nature as well as by industrial or technological processes. Because colloidal systems have certain properties in common and because their existence is limited by a range of factors, such as temperature, they were once classified as another state of matter (liquid, solids, and gas being the three classical states, or phases). This classification is no longer adequate. A classification according to the particular states of matter involved—*e.g.*, solid in liquid, liquid in liquid, solid in gas—although not exhaustive is still useful.

To understand the behaviour of colloids, a knowledge of molecular structure is necessary, but only a brief generalization can be given here (for a full account, see CHEMISTRY; ATOMIC STRUCTURE; MOLECULAR STRUCTURE; CHEMICAL BONDING). Every atom, the smallest particle of an element, consists of a positively charged nucleus surrounded by negative electrons (equal in number to the positive charges) arranged in a characteristic structure for each element. These electron structures tend to be unstable, and the neutral atoms either gain or lose electrons to become charged negatively or positively; or atoms share electrons in order to achieve stable configurations. Charged atoms are called ions. Oppositely charged particles attract one another, and ions may thus bond to form compounds that are termed electrovalent, or ionic. Shared electrons, on the other hand, do not produce ions but directly bond the sharing atoms into molecules, or other kinds of aggregates, and such bonds and compounds are called covalent. Other kinds of bonding between molecules and atoms result in the various states of matter and in special kinds of association, especially among organic molecules. Organic compounds all have in common the fact that they are built around open or closed chains of covalently bonded carbon atoms and that these structures can be classified and named according to their characteristics. Furthermore, types of organic compounds can be linked together in various ways, a fact of primary importance in the study of colloids. Various groups of atoms, called functional groups, which are not compounds and cannot exist free, may also be linked in endless variation to the carbon chains and cycles; functional groups always give the parent molecule their own characteristic properties, and therefore an organic molecule may have many properties that react to the environment in recognizable ways, no matter how complex it may be. Chemical reactions always involve changes in the electron structures of atoms and, therefore, in the bonds between atoms or the molecules involved.

Colloidal particles consist of aggregates of molecules, sometimes only of atoms, linked or bonded together in a variety of ways. The production of colloidal particles or their elimination, either by further clotting or by breaking them up into molecules, is based on standard principles of chemical and physical bonding, but still contains elements of empiricism, especially in obtaining the desired size range (between 10^{-7} and 10^{-3} cm). It is safe to say that the colloids prepared in living organisms by biological processes are absolutely vital to the existence of the organism and that the colloids generated with inorganic compounds in the earth, waters, atmosphere, and in technological processes, though not nearly so important at first examination, are just as vital to the existence of life-forms.

The general structure of matter

This article is divided into the following sections and subsections:

HISTORY OF COLLOID STUDIES

The art of preparing and processing colloidal materials goes back as far as civilization itself. The scientific study of colloids, however, dates only from the beginning of the 19th century, one of the first important experiments being with a lump of clay in a U-tube filled with water. When an electric potential difference was applied to the two ends of the tube, the water was seen to move toward the negative electrode, while particles of clay moved toward the positive electrode. Such a movement to either positive or negative electrode of suspended, now called colloidal, particles under an applied electrical field is termed electrophoresis. Another early discovery was that particles in suspension when viewed under a microscope are in ceaseless, irregular, or random motion, called Brownian movement in honour of a British botanist, Robert Brown, who in 1827 first recorded the phenomenon using aqueous suspensions of pollen. Brownian movement is now known to result from the irregular bombardment of colloidal particles by molecules of the surrounding liquid.

Francesco Selmi, an Italian chemist, published (1845–50) the first systematic study of inorganic colloids, in particular silver chloride, Prussian blue, and sulfur. Selmi showed that these colloidal bodies would coagulate (group together into large aggregates that separated from the liquid, a process similar to the precipitation of a substance from solution into solid particles that then settle out) if salts were added to the system and that the salts differed in their coagulating or precipitating power. From the absence of temperature changes upon coagulation, or upon another process called peptization (see below), he concluded that the particles were not simple molecules distributed as molecules throughout the medium but some kind of combination of molecules.

Graham's
definitions Thomas Graham, a Scottish chemist, is usually regarded as the founder of modern colloid science. During the 1860s, Graham clearly recognized those properties regarded as characteristic of the colloidal state, such as absence of crystallinity and of ordinary chemical relations and an exceedingly low rate of diffusion, which arises from the large size of colloidal particles (about 10^{-7} to about 10^{-5} centimetre). He also recognized the biological significance of colloids.

The term colloid (from the Greek word for "glue") was coined by Graham in 1861 and applied by him to such substances as gelatin, albumin, and gums, which are retained by membranes such as parchment paper when subjected to dialysis (a technique of separating substances by their different rates of diffusion through semipermeable membranes). Such substances as salts and sugars, which readily pass through the membrane, he termed crystalloids, because of the comparative ease with which they could be obtained in crystalline form from their solutions. Of Graham's other contributions to the nomenclature of colloids, those still in use are the terms sol, gel, peptization, and syneresis. A sol is a dispersion of a solid in discrete units (*i.e.*, a solid broken up into independent particles and distributed through a liquid or gaseous medium), the type of dispersion medium being shown by a prefix—*e.g.*, hydrosol (for dispersions in water), aerosol (for dispersions in air). A gel is a dispersion of the solid particles linked together to form a structure with some mechanical strength. Peptization, from analogy with peptic digestion, referred to the spontaneous dispersion

of a precipitate to form a colloid as, for example, the dispersion of a precipitate of Prussian blue when an attempt is made to wash it. The term syneresis (from a Greek word meaning "to contract") was suggested by the study of silicic acid (obtained from water glass and dilute acids) for the phenomenon of spontaneous shrinkage of a gel with the exudation of the dispersion medium.

An interesting example is provided by gold sols, colloids that are prepared by reducing (freeing the elemental metal from its compound) dilute solutions of gold chloride and that are usually strikingly coloured (ruby red, blue, green, and other colours). Although gold sols had been known to the alchemists of the 17th century, the English physicist and chemist Michael Faraday, in 1857, was the first to make a scientific study of their preparation and properties. He showed that addition of salts turned the ruby-red sols blue and then coagulated them and that these effects could be prevented by the addition of gelatin and other hydrophilic (easily dissolved in water as compared with hydrophobic, difficult to dissolve in water) colloids. The ruby sols, which had all the appearances of solutions, were shown by him to contain particles of gold because, unlike true solutions, a cone of light passing through them became visible to an observer situated at right angles to the beam. This phenomenon, later studied in more detail by John Tyndall, a British physicist, is usually referred to as the Tyndall effect. Of the other metal sols, those of silver were much studied, particularly in the United States, in connection with the photographic process. The preparation and purification of sols were facilitated by electrodialysis (separation by applying an electrical field, and allowing the dissolved impurities to diffuse through a membrane) and by ultrafiltration—*i.e.*, filtration through filters of very fine pore size.

Stability
of sols The stability of hydrophobic sols to salts that were added to the system was quantitatively examined after electrophoresis had shown that all colloids carry an electric charge, the same kind of charge on each particle in the system, and that it is to this charge that hydrophobic colloids owe their stability; because like charges repel one another, the particles cannot come into collision and, therefore, cannot coagulate and group together into larger than colloidal size. Coagulation is brought about, however, by the addition of an ion carrying the charge opposite to that on the colloidal particle, and the coagulating power of an ion increases rapidly with its charge (*e.g.*, to coagulate negatively charged sols such as gold or arsenic sulfide, the requisite concentration of sodium, calcium, and aluminum ions, with single, double, and triple positive charges, respectively, are approximately in the ratio 1:1/70:1/900). Addition of a hydrophilic colloid to a hydrophobic one protects the latter from the coagulating action of salts, a phenomenon termed protection. Hydrophilic colloids such as the proteins, the condensation products of amino acids that are the essential constituents of all living cells, are only precipitated by high concentrations of a salt. For a series of salts, the comparative efficacy runs approximately parallel to their solubility in water, indicating that precipitation of the colloid is caused by dehydration, or removal of water molecules, from the colloid particle.

In 1903 the invention of the ultramicroscope brought a notable advance in techniques for examining colloidal systems. The chief difference from the usual method of microscopic examination was the mounting of the microscope at right angles to the incident light beam, which strikes the object to be examined; the colloidal particles, because of the light they scatter laterally, then stand out as bright points of light on a dark ground. This apparatus can detect particles down to about 100 angstroms (Å) in size (one angstrom is 10^{-8} centimetre, or 3.9370079×10^{-9} inch), compared with about 2000 Å for the ordinary microscope.

In 1905 the terms hydrophilic and hydrophobic were introduced to differentiate aqueous suspensions of markedly differing properties, as typified by gelatin and the colloidal dispersion of metals, respectively. These types differ in many ways, the most striking being in their stability to salts added to their systems and their reversibility after precipitation. A gelatin solution, for example, is only precipitated by high concentrations of salts and, after drying, will readily take up water again. It "likes" water; it is hydrophilic. A sol of a metal, or of an insoluble salt, is precipitated readily by traces of salts and does not return to the colloidal state, even if the salts are eliminated by washing the precipitate. It "abhors" water: it is hydrophobic. These phenomena reveal the reversible property of hydrophilic systems and the irreversible property of hydrophobic ones. For dispersion media other than water, the parallel terms lyophilic and lyophobic (*lyo-* from a Greek word meaning "to loosen, to dissolve") were proposed.

Many striking developments in physics and chemistry in the early years of the 20th century were relevant to colloids, including, for example, the increase in knowledge of the electronic structure of the atom, of molecular size and shape, and of the nature of solutions. In addition, powerful new methods for studying the size and shape of colloidal particles were developed, such as ultracentrifugation, electrophoresis, diffusion, and the scattering of light and of X-rays. The study of interfaces (surfaces of discontinuity between substances or states of matter), clearly of great relevance to colloids, developed as a major field, surface chemistry. The investigation of colloids in industry and biology also led to major developments in the knowledge of detergents, dyes, proteins, polymers, and other substances.

IRREVERSIBLE SYSTEMS

The main classification of colloids is into reversible and irreversible systems. (Any system is irreversible if, after its components have been induced to interact, the products of their reaction are so stable, or are removed so effectively from the system, that no manipulation of the system will bring about a reaction to reproduce the original components. In a reversible system the products of a reaction may be induced to react in a way that will reproduce the original components. The reactions may be physical or chemical.) In the irreversible systems, to which belong sols (dilute suspensions), emulsions, foams, pastes (concentrated suspensions), and certain types of gels, the size of the particles is greatly dependent upon the method of preparation. In the reversible systems particle size is either determined by the molecular size of the colloidal material, as in polymers, polyelectrolytes, and proteins, or the particles are formed from small molecules by a reversible association, as in soaps, detergents, and certain dyes. The most important aspects of these diverse systems are outlined below.

Lyophobic sols (dilute suspensions). Lyophobic sols are dilute systems, some typical examples of which are colloidal metals, silver chloride, and Prussian blue, which already have been mentioned. Of suspensions in gaseous media (aerosols), some, such as fogs, mists, and smokes, are well-known; others, such as airborne suspensions of bacteria, viruses, and molds, are less obvious but of equal importance. Various kinds of smoke have found considerable use in war for camouflage and antipersonnel purposes, and peacetime uses of aerosols include insecticidal sprays and frost prevention in orchards by means of smudge pots. The removal of smokes still presents a major industrial problem. In an electrostatic precipitator, the smoke passes between oppositely charged wires (charged to a high potential difference); because of the charges that smoke particles carry or that are induced upon them by the electrical field, the particles are attracted to one or other of the wires, which then neutralizes them and thereby enables the particles to cluster into aggregates too large to be carried upward by the rising gases; these larger masses can then be collected by mechanical means from the precipitators.

Dilute suspensions are known in all three dispersion media, gas, liquid, and solid. Only those in air and in aqueous solutions will be considered here. The dispersed particles are almost invariably composed of a large number of atoms or molecules and are usually visible in the ordinary microscopes or ultramicroscopes (about

$\frac{1}{1,000,000}$ to about $\frac{1}{1,000}$ centimetre). The amount of particles in the dispersed phase is always small, usually much less than 1 percent. Suspensions can be prepared by breaking down particles of macroscopic (large-scale) dimensions, a process called dispersion, or by growth from molecular or atomic units, a process called aggregation, until particles of the requisite colloidal dimensions are obtained.

Dispersion is usually carried out in the laboratory by grinding the substance in an agate mortar and, commercially, by means of a colloid mill in which the mixture of coarse particles and dispersion medium is subjected to intense shearing forces; a protective colloid is frequently added to prevent the colloidal particles produced by the mill from reaggregating. Metals can be dispersed in liquids by striking an electric arc between them, usually in the presence of a trace of sodium hydroxide to stabilize (*i.e.*, prevent from forming agglomerates) the sol formed. In some cases dispersion can be brought about by adding a small amount of a third substance called a peptizing agent; clays, for example, are peptized by alkalies, and many finely divided precipitates are peptized by soaps or other hydrophilic colloids.

In aggregation processes the first step is to form a supersaturated solution (in which more solute is dissolved than the solvent can contain normally, and any disturbance of the system will force the excess of dissolved solute out of solution) by chemical or physical means. This supersaturation leads to formation of solute nuclei that grow to colloidal size and then have to be stabilized in order to prevent flocculation—*i.e.*, coagulation of the particles into large flakes. An example of such a chemical process is the reaction between arsenic oxide and hydrogen sulfide in very dilute solution; in this reaction the insoluble arsenic sulfide appears in the form of minute particles dispersed in the aqueous solution. A common physical method is typified by the formation of sulfur sols by pouring a solution of sulfur in alcohol into water. Mist, fog, and clouds are aerosols formed by physical means in the atmosphere—the rapid cooling of air that is saturated with water vapour to a temperature at which the vapour condenses into minute droplets of water.

The size of the particles formed in aggregation processes is determined by the rates of nucleation (formation of nuclei) and by the growth of the nuclei into crystals or crystal-like growths. A high rate of nucleation is imperative for the formation of small particles, because the fewer the nuclei are, the larger they will grow, the total mass of substance precipitating being the same whatever the number of nuclei.

Liesegang rings. Another phenomenon in which nucleation plays an important role, the Liesegang rings (named after the German physicist and chemist R.E. Liesegang), is observed if an insoluble precipitate is formed during the diffusion of one reactant into the other. If, for example, a thin layer of dilute potassium dichromate in a gelatin gel is placed on a glass plate and a crystal of silver nitrate is placed at the centre, a precipitate of insoluble silver chromate is eventually produced in the form of concentric rings as shown in Figure 1. Each band is formed when a certain supersaturation has been reached locally, so that nucleation occurs. By subsequent growth of the nuclei, the concentration is lowered in the neighbourhood of the bands, and the diffusion of silver nitrate can proceed a certain distance before a sufficient degree of supersaturation is again reached and the next band precipitates. These bands are very similar to the banding in some minerals, such as agate, and are believed to explain such formations.

Stability. The stability of sols arises chiefly from the electrical charges carried by the particles (all being negative or all being positive), thus preventing contact under conditions such that without charges collisions would occur. The charges are usually obtained by the preferential adsorption of one type of ion, often a negative ion, because most sols are negatively charged. When the sol particles are close together, however, attractive forces (of the same nature as those between gas molecules, which cause gases to condense into liquids) make themselves

Marginal notes:

Hydrophilic and hydrophobic suspensions

Classes of colloids

Electrostatic precipitators

Importance of large numbers of nuclei

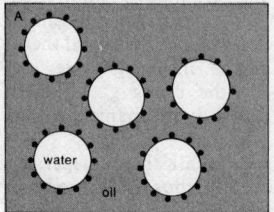

Figure 1: Liesegang rings of silver chromate. These resemble the banding in many minerals and are believed to explain the mineral formation (see text).

felt. The addition of inorganic salts, which effectively screen the charges on the colloidal particles, leads to a reduction of the range of the electrical repulsive forces, so that the attraction becomes predominant and coagulation follows.

Emulsions. The term emulsion is used to denote any colloidal dispersion of one liquid in another, but in practice only oil and water (aqueous) solutions need to be considered, because biological emulsions, as well as those of most domestic and industrial importance, contain an oil and an aqueous solution as the two immiscible phases. In order to attain the requisite degree of stability, a third component, called the emulsifying agent, is necessary and is usually present in amounts of about 1 to 5 percent. Emulsions can exist in two types, oil-in-water (indicated by O/W) and water-in-oil (W/O), depending upon whether the aqueous or the oil phase is the continuous one (*i.e.*, one in which the other exists in dispersed form). Two fundamental problems arise: the origin of the stability induced by the emulsifying agent and the reason some agents promote oil-in-water and others water-in-oil.

Impor-
tance of
emulsions

The technical and biological aspects of emulsions are vast. The principal technical uses are in pharmacy and cosmetics (creams and ointments are usually emulsions), in food preparations (*e.g.*, salad dressings, mayonnaise, margarine), and in many industries, particularly leather, textiles, and paper. Margarine, for example, is a water-in-oil emulsion stabilized by about 1 percent of oxidized soybean oil; mayonnaise and other salad dressings are emulsions of edible vegetable oils in aqueous solutions of edible acids stabilized by egg yolk.

Commercially, oils are often emulsified with water to achieve three main goals: dilution of the oil, increase in area of interface or overall surface contact between the components, and modification of physical properties. Dilution effects economy by spreading the oil over a larger surface, as, for example, in polishes and oil-soluble insecticides. An increase in area of interface may accelerate some chemical reactions (*e.g.*, polymerization of vinyl compounds, hydrolysis of fats in soap manufacture). The modification of physical properties includes the removal of objectionable characteristics, as, for example, emulsification diminishes the taste or smell of pharmaceutical preparations such as cod-liver oil and increases the fluidity of heavy oils such as tar. On the other hand, crude petroleum is frequently produced as a water-in-oil emulsion. Breaking up this emulsion is often difficult, but it is a necessary step before further processing of the petroleum can take place.

In evaluating the stability of emulsions, creaming, coagulation, and coalescence should be distinguished. Cream-

ing is the accumulation of the droplets, usually at the top of the emulsion, under the influence of gravity. Small drops cream much more slowly than large ones. In coagulation the droplets come together to form aggregates in which the original drops are still separated. Coagulation enhances creaming. Coalescence means that the drops unite to form a continuous phase; fresh milk creams markedly in a few hours, and by acidification it can be made to coagulate, after which coalescence is strongly increased by churning.

Creaming,
coagula-
tion, and
coales-
cence

Emulsification is achieved by intense agitation of the mixture. On a small scale this can sometimes be achieved merely by shaking the mixture by hand, but it is more usual to force the coarse emulsion under pressure through some type of valve, as in the farmer's "cream machine." Industrially, various types of colloid mills are used in which the emulsion is subjected to intense shearing forces, finally passing through a homogenizer. These treatments decrease the particle size and so increase the stability. (Milk is frequently homogenized in order to diminish creaming.)

The principal emulsifying agents for oil-in-water emulsions are: proteins, gums, carbohydrates, natural and synthetic soaps, clays, and certain hydrated oxides, particularly of silicon or aluminum; for water-in-oil emulsions: heavy metal salts of the fatty acids (*e.g.*, zinc stearate, nickel oleate), long-chain alcohols such as cetyl alcohol, long-chain esters such as glyceryl monooleate, oxidized oils, soot, lampblack, graphite, and other substances.

Various theories have been advanced to explain emulsifiers, the most simple being that originally suggested for solid powders. As Figure 2 shows, for idealized spherical particles, if the solid is preferentially wetted by one component or phase, then more particles can be accommodated if the interface between the two components is convex to the wetting phase; and, in an encounter between two droplets, actual contact between the liquid in the droplets is prevented by the particles clinging to them, so that coalescence of the droplets cannot occur. In other words, preferential wetting by water should tend to give oil-in-water emulsions as in Figure 2B, while preferential wetting by oil should give the inverse type, as in Figure 2A. This difference is in agreement with the above list of emulsifiers, those promoting oil-in-water emulsions being all hydrophilic, whereas those that favour water-in-oil are more oleophilic (readily soluble in oil). Other conditions are also involved, however, in particular the relative amounts of oil and water and even the order in which the phases are mixed.

Natural and synthetic soaps soluble in water are among the most widely used oil-in-water emulsifying agents. Certain synthetic soaps (see below *Association colloids*) are often preferable to ordinary (fatty acid) soaps, because they are not precipitated by calcium ions (which do form a precipitate with ordinary soaps), and so the synthetic soaps can be used with hard water (high in calcium ion). The electrical charge acquired by the oil drops when they adsorb the soap ions is one factor in stability; the mechanical properties of the adsorbed film seem to be another one. The strong reduction of the interfacial tension facilitates emulsification greatly.

As mentioned before, the salts of divalent and trivalent metals with fatty acids (*e.g.*, nickel oleate) are efficient emulsifiers for the water-in-oil type. In these systems, the

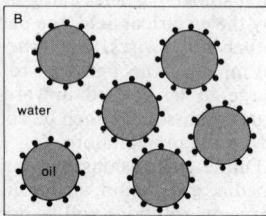

Figure 2: Solid powder at an oil–water interface, showing (A) how preferential wetting by oil tends to give water–oil emulsions and (B) how preferential wetting by water tends to give oil–water emulsions.

interfacial film consists of solid particles or of a polymolecular skin rather than a film one molecule deep, a monolayer. A simple experiment to illustrate phase inversion (reversal of the roles components play in a system) is to prepare an oil-in-water emulsion stabilized by sodium oleate (soluble in water) and to add a few drops of saturated magnesium chloride; on being shaken, the system inverts to the water-in-oil type because of the magnesium oleate that is formed. Proteins and gums as emulsifiers normally promote only the oil-in-water type of emulsion. A great variety of proteins are used commercially, such as egg albumin, dried blood, casein (from milk); and proteins are wholly or partly responsible for the stability of many natural emulsions such as milk and rubber latex. Food emulsions are frequently stabilized by proteins, gelatin, and other substances. The stabilizing action of these arises from the mechanical protection given by the protein monolayers, or films, that form spontaneously and that are relatively impenetrable for oil.

Foams. A foam is a gaseous dispersion, usually of air, in a liquid. Pure liquids do not give stable foams, and, for any reasonable stability, a third component, the foaming agent, is essential. Of the great variety of substances that act as foam promoters, the best known are the natural and synthetic soaps, proteins including gelatin and other compounds obtained from proteins, certain finely divided solid powders, certain polymers (large molecules formed from smaller ones), and the saponins (naturally occurring substances that produce a soapy lather).

Household soap, which consists chiefly of a mixture of sodium stearate and sodium palmitate, is well-known for its bubble-blowing capacity. This property is greatly improved by the addition of glycerol, which probably acts by increasing the viscosity of the film. Many synthetic soaps, sodium cetyl sulfate, for example, are equally effective and have an added advantage in that their lathering power is not readily diminished by hard water (see below *Association colloids*).

Stabilization of foams arises mainly from the same factors that govern the stability of emulsions. Indeed, a suspension of air bubbles in water (a foam) is very similar to a suspension of oil droplets in water. In both cases the same types of stabilizers are used. Proteins as in whipped cream, marshmallow (made from gelatin and sugar), and meringue (from egg white) find a wide use as foaming agents in foodstuffs, because of their edible or nontoxic nature. The fire foam used to combat oil fires consists of bubbles of carbon dioxide (liberated from sodium bicarbonate and aluminum sulfate) stabilized by dried blood, glue, or any other cheap protein-containing materials. Beer froth is believed to be stabilized by the colloidal constituents in the brew, which include proteins and carbohydrates. Saponins, noted for their foaming capacity, are obtained commercially from various plants and are complex mixtures. They form rather solid surface films with a mechanical strength to which their foams owe their stability, just as in the case of proteins. Of the polymers with foaming power for aqueous solutions, the most important are methyl cellulose (water-soluble type) and polyvinyl alcohol (see below *Polymers*). Certain finely divided solids, particularly if they have a waxy or hydrophobic (not soluble in water) surface, such as aluminum stearate or heavy metal soaps insoluble in water, remain at the air–water interface on agitation and stabilize the foam so formed. By suitable treatment many other materials can be made to behave similarly, and this behaviour forms the basis of what is called the froth-flotation method for separating minerals. The structure of a single bubble in a foam stabilized by a fine powder is quite similar to that of the emulsion droplet represented in Figure 2B.

Foaming may often be an undesirable property, as in lubricating oils, and its prevention is not always easy. Aqueous foams can usually be broken by spraying with small amounts of certain alcohols (*e.g.*, amyl, octyl) or fatty acids.

Pastes (concentrated suspensions). Pastes are concentrated dispersions of fine solid particles in a liquid continuum. From the practical point of view they are of extreme importance, covering such diverse materials as paints, putty, clays, dough, drilling muds, toothpaste, and others. These materials are all noted for their peculiar and characteristic mechanical properties, as is indicated by such terms applied to them as plasticity, ductility, and moldability. The study of the flow and deformation properties of pastes, which are so vital in their practical uses, belongs to the science called rheology.

The flow behaviour of a paste is determined not only by the volume concentration of the solid particles but also by their size and shape, by their size distribution, and by the colloidal stability of the suspended particles. At a given solid concentration, a flocculated paste (one in which particles are held together loosely in amorphous, cloudy flakes) may be stiff and plastic, whereas a stable, or deflocculated, one may be easily pourable. Examples of flocculated systems are very polar compounds (in a polar molecule the distribution of electrons is not symmetrical and causes the molecule to behave as though it had a positive end and a negative end, or pole) in organic media (*e.g.*, silica, calcium carbonate, and other inorganic salts in such oils as benzene) or nonpolar substances such as carbon black in polar media such as water. Such systems can be rendered deflocculated by suitable additives, a practical example being the addition of aluminum stearate to the oil vehicle of inorganic paints. By such means a higher concentration of the disperse phase can be obtained without increasing the consistency of the material; or, alternatively, an increase in pourability can be obtained at the same solid concentration. It is for higher concentration that materials such as sodium silicate are added to potter's clay, because the water present, which ultimately will have to be removed, should be kept to a minimum. Putty, another example of a paste, consists of finely ground whiting (natural calcium carbonate) in a medium of linseed oil.

Pastes, particularly those with the higher concentrations of disperse phase, usually show some sort of yield value (give) upon deformation (alteration of form). This property is clearly essential if the material is to exhibit plastic properties (*e.g.*, potter's clay), because it has to retain its shape against the forces of gravity. Certain pastes exhibit the phenomenon known as thixotropy; *i.e.*, after stirring or shaking they become much thinner in consistency, returning to their original state on being allowed to stand. A well-known example is quicksand, which consists of a paste of sand and water made thixotropic by the presence of certain clays. Paint should be thixotropic in order to flow easily under the brush and to allow the brush streaks to disappear. After a short time the applied paint should solidify to prevent the paint from flowing away from vertical planes. The reverse phenomenon, termed dilatancy, in which a suspension that flows freely under a small force turns rigid when larger forces are applied, is shown by very concentrated, highly stabilized suspensions —*e.g.*, by pastes of pure silica in water.

Gel structures. A flocculated paste, or suspension of very fine particles, often behaves as a gel—*i.e.*, a quasi-homogeneous solid-like system, but rich in liquid. During the flocculation a scaffolding structure is formed by the molecules, preventing sedimentation of the floc in the structure and enmeshing the dispersion medium. Such structures are preferentially formed by long or flat particles. The systems are often thixotropic; the bonds between the particles can be broken by mechanical action. They show syneresis; *i.e.*, in the long run the scaffolding retracts by further flocculation, and liquid is exuded. Examples of gels are: certain clays, particularly bentonite (flat particles), iron hydroxide (flat), and vanadium pentoxide (needles). Those gels formed from ferric hydroxide are reddish brown and become more transparent when liquefied. Fatty-acid salts such as aluminum, calcium, and zinc oleates are the thickening agents in many greases, which are examples of gels with a nonaqueous liquid phase.

In some cases gels are formed directly by chemical reaction. Substances that tend to separate as amorphous precipitates frequently give colloids that are gels when first formed, the hydroxides of aluminum, chromium, and silicon being good examples. Of these, the formation of silica gel by reaction between sodium silicate (water glass) and acids or between silicon tetrachloride and water has been much studied. The colloid, a sol, first formed slowly transforms spontaneously into another type of colloid, a translucent gel, that shows bluish opalescence, and this gel may later shrink, exuding the aqueous medium (syneresis). The changes are believed to arise from polymerization (the process of linking together small molecules, called monomers, into chains to form large molecules—the polymer—consisting of as many as hundreds of thousands of monomers) of the monosilicic acid first formed. The process can be repeated in one, two, or three dimensions, leading to a colloid composed of silicic acids with high molecular weight that form a rather rigid three-dimensional gel.

Ion-exchange in clays A property of clays of great agricultural importance is called base exchange or, more correctly, ion or cation exchange (ions are atoms or groups of atoms with electric charges; cations have positive, anions have negative charge). If, for example, a salt solution such as potassium sulfate percolates through a soil, the potassium ions (with a single positive charge) are removed and replaced by an equivalent amount of calcium ions (with two positive charges) originally present in the clay. The percentages and types of clay in soil determine its physical structure as well as its chemistry, both of which are of primary importance to the growth and health of plants. Such ion-exchange processes form the basis of the zeolite process and of similar processes. In the above case, calcium ions in the water are replaced by sodium ions, which have one less positive charge, and the water is thus softened because sodium salts are soluble whereas calcium salts are not.

Clays, the finest mineral constituents of the soil, consist of layer structures of aluminosilicates (compounds of aluminum, silicon, and an alkali or alkaline-earth metal) in which some cations are easily accessible and exchangeable. The nature of these ions is not critical for maintaining the clay structure; only their total electric charge is important.

Zeolites are essentially infinite three-dimensional frameworks, potentially infinite in size, as in the various forms of silica (silicon dioxide), except that some of the silicon atoms (often about one-half) are replaced by aluminum atoms. This replacement makes the framework of the colloid negative (silicon has four positive while aluminum has three positive charges), and equivalent cations are taken up in the interstices to maintain electrical neutrality. Synthetic zeolites have been manufactured in various ways, such as by fusing a mixture of sodium carbonate, china clay or alumina, and silica (sand, quartz, etc.), the resulting glassy (vitreous) mass being then washed out (leached) with water.

REVERSIBLE SYSTEMS

Reversible colloids are characterized by the fact that colloidal solutions or gels can be formed spontaneously when the dry colloid and the dispersion medium are brought together. The size of the particles in reversible colloids is determined by the molecular weight of the colloidal material in the case of polymers or by reversible association (as explained below) in the case of detergents, certain dyes, and a few other substances.

Polymers. Polymers are high-molecular-weight substances built up of a large number of identical (or practically identical) repeating units (generally, simple molecules), the single conglomerate molecule being of colloidal dimensions. Familiar polymeric materials that are colloids are cellulose in wood and plants and proteins in horn, hair, and wool. In nature, three different functions of polymers can be distinguished: they serve as building materials (cellulose, proteins of skin and muscle); they are storage substances (starch, glycogen); and they play a fundamental role in biochemical reactions (enzymes, nucleic acids, genes). These functions are related to the high molecular weight of the substances. The bonds between atoms holding them together in organic molecules

(called primary bonds) are quite strong, not inferior to the bond strength between atoms in inorganic molecules. The bonds, however, between organic molecules (called secondary bonds) are weak and can be easily disrupted. Crystals of organic substances of low molecular weight, as a rule, are soft, indicating weak intermolecular bonds. Consequently, a structure built of organic materials in order to be strong should contain a high proportion of primary bonds, a condition that can be achieved by building the structure with polymers. Another important property of organic materials is that they can be processed at much lower temperatures than are needed to process inorganic materials, such as metals or ceramics. The intricate functions necessary to regulate biochemical reactions including reproduction can, of course, be more easily incorporated in large than in small molecules, because the large molecules allow more diversification. The commercial synthesis of polymers—broadly speaking, of plastics—seeks to mimic nature in many respects. Strong, tough, and insoluble materials are manufactured at much lower temperatures than metals or glass for an almost endless list of purposes.

Polymer chains Most polymers, both natural and synthetic, are linearly built; i.e., they are long chains. In solution, and often even in the dry state, the colloid composed of this long chain is folded or coiled. In proteins and nucleic acids the coiling is regular. In synthetic polymers and in many natural ones such as rubber and gums, the coiling is irregular and determined by chance rather than by some building principle, so that the term statistical coils is used. The large extension in solution of polymer molecules is the cause of a high viscosity (sluggish flow), which can be used for determining the molecular weight of the polymer. When linear polymers are interconnected locally, a cross-linked polymer network is obtained. Such a network, when deformed, tends to return to its original shape because that was the situation of most probable coiling. A network, therefore, cannot flow at all but behaves as a gel. The behaviour of coils cross-linked in such networks also explains both the elasticity of rubber and the swelling of dried polymer gels.

Polymers are usually subdivided, according to their origin, into natural and synthetic, although an intermediate class, man-made derivatives from natural polymers, is also a convenient classification. Some of the more important members of these three subgroups are as follows:

1. Natural polymers: cellulose, starch, rubber, proteins, nucleic acids, and the products from linseed and other drying oils.

2. Derivatives from natural polymers: nitrocellulose, cellulose acetate, regenerated cellulose (viscose, cellophane), and vulcanized rubber.

3. Purely synthetic polymers: nylon, polystyrene, polythene, synthetic rubbers, silicones, phenol–formaldehyde and urea–formaldehyde resins.

Natural polymers. Cellulose is a colloid that is the principal building constituent of the plant kingdom. Paper is derived from wood pulp. Cotton and flax, widely used in the textile industries, are almost wholly cellulose. The cellulose molecule consists of a linear array of many thousands of molecules of glucose, linked end to end in a process that eliminates one water molecule (a reaction called condensation) at each link. The chain length, or degree of polymerization, depends upon the source and the method of extraction of the cellulose.

Starch is another colloid of great importance in the plant world, not as a building material but as a convenient means of storing glucose and, hence, energy and food; wheat, maize (corn), and other grains consist largely of it. It resembles cellulose in being a product of glucose but differs in having a branched-chain structure rather than a straight-chain one. Starch can be dispersed in hot water and is then used for various purposes.

Structure of rubber Natural rubber is a linear polymer built up from units of the compound isoprene and is a colloid with characteristic properties. The rubber is obtained in the form of a milky suspension called latex from a wide variety of plants and trees. After the latex has been coagulated by adding acetic acid, or in other ways, the resulting so-called crepe rubber is usually compounded with other materials to make it suitable for industrial use. For example, in the manufacture of tires it is compounded with carbon black and certain inorganic fillers such as zinc oxide and sulfur, and then subjected to heat treatment. The action of sulfur leads to vulcanization, as it is termed, which is the formation of cross-links between the chains through one or more sulfur atoms. Vulcanization makes the product colloid more resilient and less liable to plastic flow.

Paints usually consist of a colloidal dispersion of an inorganic coloured powder (*e.g.*, lead chromate, zinc oxide) in an oily medium containing unsaturated compounds, such as linseed oil, which, when exposed as a thin film to the action of air, rapidly oxidize and polymerize, forming a protective skin for the underlying material and the pigment. In modern paints the linseed oil is often replaced by rubber or synthetic polymers.

Derivatives from natural polymers. Cellulose forms the basis from which several important colloidal substances are derived. A group of compounds called nitrocellulose, or cellulose nitrate, made by treating cotton or other cellulose materials with a mixture of nitric acid and sulfuric acid, have properties that vary considerably, the members with high nitrate content being used as propellants (*e.g.*, cordite), the ones with less nitrate as lacquers, etc. Celluloid, the oldest commercially made plastic, consists of a mixture of cellulose nitrate with camphor. Cellulose acetate, obtained from cellulose and acetic acid, is manufactured for artificial silk, for lacquers, for safety film, and for water-desalting membranes. Cellulose can also be dissolved and reprecipitated to form the colloids cellophane and rayon.

Purely synthetic polymers. The science and the production of purely synthetic polymers were greatly developed during World War II. Synthetic rubber was and is still made on a large scale by copolymerizing a mixture of butadiene and styrene, both of synthetic origin, to give a linear polymer resembling in many ways natural rubber. Nylon is made by condensing diamines with dibasic acids, the resulting structure having a close resemblance to that of natural silks and other fibrous proteins.

Many other types of colloidal polymers are made by polymerization of vinyl compounds, for example, polythene, polyvinyl chloride, polymethyl methacrylate (Perspex or Plexiglas), and polyacrylonitrile (Orlon).

The silicones are more recently developed polymers based upon a silicon–oxygen chain. They are much more stable to heat, organic solvents, and chemical reaction than are the older plastics and thus find many uses.

Bakelite

Another well-known type of colloid, the polymer Bakelite, is made by heating phenols with formaldehyde. These are cross-linked polymers, termed thermosetting, because once formed they do not soften when warmed, in contrast with the linear polymers noted above that are thermoplastic; *i.e.*, they soften upon warming and harden again upon cooling.

Polyelectrolytes. Polymers carrying a large number of ionizable groups deserve special attention. An example of these so-called polyelectrolytes is polyacrylic acid, a long-chain polymer with a carboxylic acid group on every other carbon atom of the chain. Many natural polymers, such as gum arabic, agar, proteins, and nucleic acids, are also polyelectrolytes. Because of the mutual repulsion between the ionized groups linked to the polymer chain, the form of the coil of a linear polyelectrolyte depends greatly upon its degree of ionization. Viscosity and swelling increase strongly with ionization.

Proteins and nucleic acids. The most important classes of hydrophilic colloids in living organisms are the proteins and the nucleic acids. The complete genetic information of the cell is laid down in the molecular structure of the nucleic acids, in particular that of deoxyribonucleic acid (DNA). This information is transported from the cell nucleus to the rest of the cell in the form of ribonucleic acid (RNA), which in its turn directs the synthesis of the proteins. Simple viruses are nucleoproteins (combinations of nucleic acids and proteins) that have the ability to reproduce themselves when injected into an uninfected host organism. Enzymes are proteins that regulate and catalyze all of the complex chemical reactions that occur in the cell and are essential for life. Nature uses proteins also as protective colloids, for example for fat particles in milk or rubber particles in latex, and as a means of building rigid structures in which mechanical strength is required. Materials such as horn, hair, skin, cuticle, connective tissue, and muscle are largely protein in nature. Gelatin and glue are breakdown products from proteins such as collagen. Biological membranes are colloidal and consist of lipids (fatty material) associated with proteins and nucleic acids.

The nucleic acid molecules are very long chains, consisting of alternating phosphate and sugar groups, each sugar group carrying one of four organic bases as a side group. The sugar in RNA is ribose, in DNA it is deoxyribose, containing one oxygen atom less than ribose. The great variety necessary for carrying all the genetic information is obtained by variations in the order in which the four different bases are arranged along the chain. The molecular weight of the DNAs is in the many millions, that of the RNAs varies with their specific role in the cell and ranges from about 25,000 to a few millions.

Protein molecules are chains called polypeptides, built up by condensing a long series of α-amino acids, the simplest of which are glycine and alanine.

Proteins can be classified in various ways—for example, according to their degree of complexity, their size and shape, their solubility, their origin, and in other ways. Classified on the basis of complexity, proteins are divided into those that contain only α-amino acids (*e.g.*, egg albumin, the chief constituent of egg white) and those that contain additional groups (*e.g.*, hemoglobin, the red pigment of blood responsible for oxygen transport, in which the protein part of the molecule is linked to a substance called heme, which is one of a group of compounds called the porphyrins). On the basis of shape, proteins are frequently classed as globular or fibrous, the former having a corpuscular shape (*e.g.*, hemoglobin, egg albumin), sometimes approximately spherical, the latter being very much more elongated (*e.g.*, myosin, an important constituent of muscle). Two other important fibrous proteins—both insoluble—are keratin, of which hair and wool are largely composed, and fibroin, the chief constituent of natural silk. Under some conditions (*e.g.*, strong urea solutions), globular proteins can be unrolled, or denatured, forming fibrous proteins that are much less soluble than the native proteins.

In the early days, proteins were largely separated by means of repeated (fractional) precipitation with salts—those precipitated by half-saturated ammonium sulfate being termed globulins, and those that required fully saturated ammonium sulfate being called albumins. Alcohol can also precipitate proteins; added in less than precipitating amounts, it renders them more readily coagulated by salts. In all cases precipitation occurs most readily at the isoelectric point (see below).

The size and shape of soluble proteins (and of other polymers in solution) have been found chiefly by measuring rates of diffusion and their rates of movement in very strong centrifugal fields. In the ultracentrifuge, the protein molecules are subjected to intense forces up to 1,000,000 times that of gravity. By such means it has been determined that the molecular weight of many proteins lies in the range from about 10,000 to several million. The single molecules are thus of sufficient size to bring them into the colloidal range. For example, hemoglobin has a molecular weight of about 68,000; hemocyanin, the respiratory pigment of certain snails, has a molecular weight of about 5×10^6. In both these cases, the molecules are approximately spherical in shape, showing that in the colloidal particle the polypeptide chain must be folded in some way, whereas others, such as myosin, are quite elongated, with the polypeptide chain more or less fully extended.

Because of the presence of ionizable groups, protein molecules in solution normally carry a charge. In very acid solutions they are positively charged; in very alkaline ones, negatively charged. At some value of acidity the

Classification of proteins

Size and shape of proteins

net charge is zero. This value is termed the isoelectric point and is of considerable importance. It can be determined in various ways, usually by applying the process of electrophoresis.

Gels. Several lyophilic colloids can form gels, which can be considered as network structures with enmeshed liquid. The jelling component may be gelatin, agar, starch, pectin, or some other substance, which is usually present in concentrations of less than 10 percent. Table jellies are usually made from gelatin, a protein; jams are jelled by pectin, a carbohydrate derivative. Agar plates, widely employed in bacteriological work, consist of a suitable nutrient medium jelled by the addition of 1–2 percent agar, a polymer of carbohydrate prepared from certain seaweeds. Some materials such as gelatin and agar set to a gel on cooling, whereas in other cases gelation is brought about by heating as in egg white and blancmange. In both cases, however, gelation arises from a process akin to a diminution of the solubility of the jelling agent leading to the formation of interconnections between the individual molecules.

Association colloids. Soaps and other detergents and a number of dyes constitute by far the most important substances classed as association colloids—*i.e.*, substances of relatively small molecular weight that associate spontaneously to form particles of a type called micelle (defined below) of colloidal size in certain concentration ranges.

Soaps. Soaps were originally limited to colloidal substances of natural occurrence, but a great number of compounds have been prepared synthetically in view of their importance as wetting agents, emulsifiers, and detergents. A few typical soaps, classified as anionic (negative), cationic (positive), and neutral according to the charge carried by the organic part of the molecule, are: sodium palmitate, anionic; sodium dodecyl sulfate, anionic; cetyltrimethylammonium bromide, cationic; polyethylene oxide derivatives, neutral. In addition, there are naturally occurring colloids that act as soaps, such as the bile salts and lecithin, substances of great biological importance.

All these colloids, as well as the colloids that are dyes, despite their diverse chemical types, have as common features a large hydrocarbon portion (also called paraffin or alkane) and a small polar (charge-carrying) group. These two parts of the molecule differ radically in their affinity for water, and it is this two-sided contradictory, or amphipathic, nature that leads to the formation of colloidal aggregates.

With aqueous solutions of the sodium and potassium salts of the long chain fatty acids, certain physical properties such as a high electrical conductivity suggest that the ions on the paraffin chain are aggregated, forming a **Micelles** colloidal particle—*i.e.*, an ionic micelle (defined below), as shown in Figure 3. In the case of sodium palmitate,

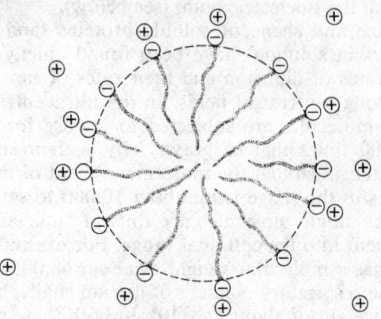

Figure 3: Structure of a micelle formed by the aggregation of paraffin-chain ions in a soap solution.

for example, the diameter of the micelle, as determined from diffusion measurements, is about 40 angstroms and thus contains about 50 molecules, the molecular weight being about 14,000. In relatively dilute solutions the shape of micelles is spherical or slightly elongated. In concentrated solutions they may be spherical, elongated rods or threads, or flat structures.

Aggregation to micelles is caused by the tendency of the water to squeeze out the paraffin chains, the same factor that is largely responsible for the marked surface activity of soap solutions. The characteristic features of soap solutions arise from the combination of surface activity and the peculiar properties of micelles in solution. The power of soap solutions to dissolve organic compounds that are insoluble or only slightly soluble in water arises directly from the presence of micelles. Micelles, as shown in Figure 3, have an interior closely resembling a droplet of liquid hydrocarbon, in which hydrocarbons and other compounds can dissolve. One important application of this phenomenon is in connection with synthetic polymers, for it enables polymerization of relatively insoluble monomers such as styrene (see above *Polymers*) to be carried out in aqueous solution or emulsion.

The characteristic and most widely used colloidal property of soap solutions is, of course, their detergent action. What is generally called dirt consists either of greasy materials or of particles with a greasy surface. Its removal involves three separate stages—access of the detergent to the dirty surface, the loosening or peptizing of the dirt, and finally its removal into the bulk of the solution. Because of its greasy surface, dirt is hydrophobic and not wetted by water, but adsorption of the surface-active soap molecules makes its outer surface hydrophilic and therefore greatly increases its affinity for water. In addition, the detergent, because of its powerful tendency to adsorb on, or cling to, all surfaces, will tend to displace the grease from the surface. The dirt thus loosened is detached by mechanical agitation and carried away into the solution as an emulsion or suspension, or solubilized in the interior of the micelles.

The chief drawback of fatty-acid soaps (ordinary household soaps) arises from their property of having insoluble calcium or magnesium salts. This characteristic explains the impossibility of getting a lather in seawater with ordinary soap and the necessity to soften hard water; *i.e.*, the calcium and magnesium ions must be removed in order to keep the soap in solution. Many of the synthetic detergents do not suffer from this disadvantage and thus are used in seawater soaps.

Ordinary household soap is prepared by boiling natural fats (compounds that are glycerides of the higher fatty acids) with strong caustic soda solution. After hydrolysis is complete, the soap is salted out by addition of common salt. The potassium salts, which make soft soap, are preferable to sodium salts for some purposes, because the potassium soaps have a higher solubility in cold water.

Dyes. Dye molecules, although resembling the soaps in possessing a hydrophobic part and one or more polar groups, lack their comparative uniformity as regards the relative disposition of these constituent parts. This situation results in the aggregation being much more specific and hence in a more varied colloidal behaviour. Dyestuffs are usually classed as acidic or basic (corresponding to anionic or cationic soaps) according to whether the organic ion carries a negative or a positive charge. The question of aggregation is of considerable importance in connection with the colloidal aspect of the dyeing process. The size of the aggregates, or micelles can be determined by the same methods as for soaps, diffusion being regarded as the best. The degree of association is increased by increasing salt content, which explains the influence of salts in dyeing.

The dyeing process has naturally excited considerable interest throughout history, although it is by no means fully understood. The materials to be dyed are usually colloids of a fibrous nature, consisting of macromolecules of vegetable, animal, or purely synthetic origin. Most vegetable fibres, such as linen and cotton, have the colloidal structure of cellulose as the fundamental constituent; wool and silk are the principal animal fibres, and, of the purely synthetic materials, nylon is without doubt the best known. In dyeing a fibre, the coloured molecules have to diffuse into the interior, in which they are held in position by precipitation or by some other reaction.

The soaping process

The dyeing process

The behaviour of wool and silk is probably the simplest, for the major factor in bringing about combination is believed to be salt formation between the dye anions on the fibre. With cellulose (cotton and rayon) the affinity of the dye for the fibre is probably caused by van der Waals forces and hydrogen bonding.

Dyes also find an important use in the identification of biological materials (*e.g.*, bacteria) by staining methods. These depend upon the different affinities of the enveloping constituents for various dyes, the principles involved being closely related to those in ordinary dyeing. Dyestuffs of the basic type (*e.g.*, Gentian Violet) find use as antiseptics, resembling the cationic soaps in their bactericidal powers.

BIBLIOGRAPHY. DUNCAN J. SHAW, *Introduction to Colloid and Surface Chemistry*, 2nd ed. (1970), modern and fairly elementary, not containing much on hydrophilic colloids; KAROL J. MYSELS, *Introduction to Colloid Chemistry* (1959), modern and more advanced than Shaw's book but still elementary; HUGO R. KRUYT (ed.), *Colloid Science*, vol. 1, *Irreversible Systems* and vol. 2, *Reversible Systems*, Eng. trans. by L.C. JACKSON (1952, 1949; reprinted 1969), advanced texts, slightly outdated, especially vol. 2, but more modern books at this level are not available; ALBERT E. ALEXANDER and PALEY JOHNSON, *Colloid Science*, 2 vol. (1949; reissued in one vol., 1952), an advanced text, also somewhat outdated but containing more on proteins than Kruyt's work; *High Polymers* (1940–), a continuing classic series on polymers; CHARLES TANFORD, *Physical Chemistry of Macromolecules* (1961), contains much on polyelectrolytes and biopolymers; J.T.G. OVERBEEK, *Colloid and Surface Chemistry* (1971–72), a videotaped self-study course in 4 vol. (55 lessons), with printed studyguides, advanced level, and many demonstrations.

(J.T.G.O.)

Cologne

A river port on the Rhine, Cologne (German Köln) is the fourth largest city in the Federal Republic of Germany, or West Germany, the largest city in the *Land* (state) of Nordrhein-Westfalen (North Rhine-Westphalia), and the historic, cultural, and economic capital of the Rhineland. Cologne's historic importance is due to its location at the crossing of the route from England, France, Belgium, and The Netherlands to eastern Europe with that route between Italy and northwestern Europe, a great traffic artery of the Rhine. The medieval commercial centre that grew up there was also a centre of learning and the arts.

Despite the destruction of 90 percent of the central city during World War II, Cologne's appearance still reflects its history; religious and secular buildings and monuments of all periods remain standing. It is the see of a Roman Catholic archbishop, and its cathedral is the largest Gothic church in northern Europe. It is an important banking and insurance centre, and its manufactures include the famous eau de Cologne toilet water.

History. After Julius Caesar destroyed the Eburones in 53 BC, the Roman general Agrippa colonized the area with the Ubii, who came from the right (east) bank of the Rhine. In AD 50, at the request of Agrippina the Younger, the wife of the emperor Claudius, the title of Roman colony was conferred upon the town that was her birthplace. It was named Colonia Claudia Ara Agrippinensium, which was shortened to Colonia; later it was made the headquarters of the governor of Lower Germany. The excavated remnants of the Praetorium, the governor's residence, are located beneath the present city hall. After AD 258, Postumus ruled as emperor from Cologne a separate empire comprising Gaul, Britain, and Spain. The emperor Constantine the Great built a castle (310) and a permanent bridge to it across the Rhine. Ceramics and glass were manufactured in Cologne in Roman times. About 456 it was conquered by the Franks, and it soon became the residence of the kings of the Ripuarian part of the Frankish kingdom.

A Christian community existed in the town probably as early as the 2nd century, the first-known mention of a bishop having been in 313. Charlemagne made it an archbishopric, and, by the 10th century, the archbishop dominated the city, receiving a wide range of tolls, customs duties, and other payments. The city's industry and trade grew during the Middle Ages, especially from about the 10th century, and increasingly bitter conflicts developed between the wealthy merchants and the archbishop. The former sought commercial and political freedom, the latter the preservation of his temporal power, which was augmented from the 13th century when the archbishop became one of the electors privileged to choose the German king. It was not until the battle of Worringen, in 1288, that the Archbishop was finally defeated, and the city of Cologne secured full self-government. From that time, Cologne was, in fact, a free imperial city, although it was only officially recognized as such in 1475.

Until the end of the 14th century, the government of the city of Cologne was in the hands of the wealthy patricians, but, in 1396, after a bloodless revolution, a new municipal constitution was established under which the 22 branches of the guilds became the basis of the government, for they elected a council that had power over all internal and external affairs.

This medieval period was a splendid one for Cologne. It was a prominent member of the mercantile Hanseatic League, and its merchants had probably the widest connections and the most varied trade of all the German towns. Crafts included the manufacture of textiles and books and leather, enamel, and metalworking, the work of Cologne's goldsmiths being particularly fine. The wine industry was well established, the arts flourished, and the city had many beautiful churches. The three greatest of the later Catholic scholars and theologians known as the Scholastics—Albertus Magnus, St. Thomas Aquinas, and John Duns Scotus—all taught in its schools. After the Thirty Years' War (1618–48), involving all western Europe in a struggle for balance of power, the city declined. As late as 1794, when the French occupied Cologne, public Protestant services were still banned, and the city has remained predominantly Roman Catholic ever since. The Jewish community, which had existed from the time of Constantine the Great, was expelled in 1424, and until 1794 no Jew was allowed to remain overnight in the city.

In 1798 Cologne was taken by France, and, when the Archbishop Elector died in 1801, the see was left vacant and was to be so for 20 years until the archbishopric was

Prosperity in the Middle Ages

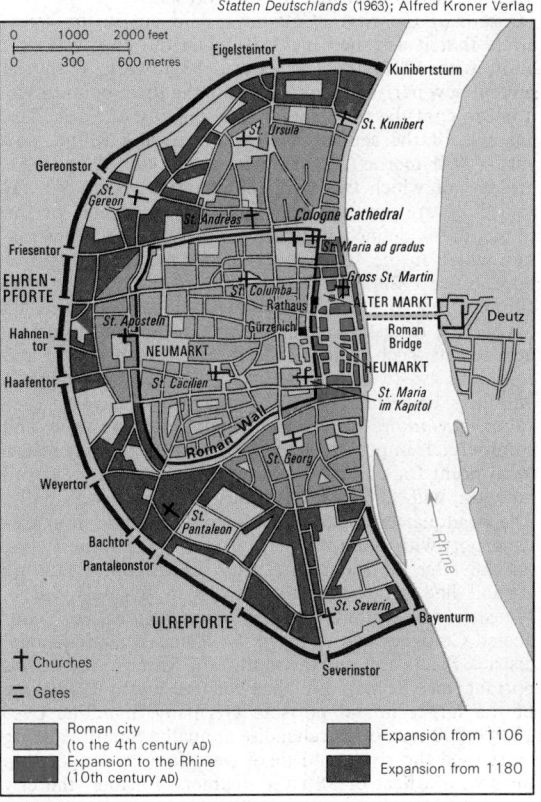

Adapted from J. von Reinhardt, *Handbuch der historischen Statten Deutschlands* (1963); Alfred Kroner Verlag

Cologne in 1752.

restored in 1821. In 1815 Cologne passed to Prussia, and from that time a new era of prosperity began. Its industry showed as wide a variety as in medieval days, and, when railways were introduced, its geographical position made it a great railway centre. The interest in organization, shown in the days of the guilds, contributed in 1797 and 1803 to the formation of a chamber of commerce, the oldest of its kind in Germany. The arrest of the Archbishop in 1837 created a sensation that became known as the Cologne Incident. Liberal points of view were represented in the 19th century by the *Rheinische Zeitung*, edited (1842–43) by Karl Marx and Moses Hess, while the *Neue Rheinische Zeitung*, edited (1848–49) by Marx, Friedrich Engels, and Ferdinand Freiligrath, was a Socialist newspaper. After German defeat in World War I, Cologne was garrisoned by the British army until 1926. The population grew from 41,685 in 1801 to 372,529 in 1900 and reached 768,352 in 1939.

World War II damage In World War II, Cologne sustained 262 air raids, there were 20,000 casualties, and the city was left in ruins, with nearly all the dwellings in the old town damaged and 91 out of 150 churches destroyed. In March 1945, the war's end for Cologne, the population had sunk to 40,000. By December, however, there were 447,000 in the city, and the population continued to rise rapidly while a vast work of clearance and reconstruction was undertaken. Most new industries located in new business districts, and much of the growing population settled in satellite suburbs.

The modern city. *Location and boundaries.* Cologne, which is situated about 44 miles northeast of Aachen, 21 miles northwest of Bonn, and 25 miles southeast of Düsseldorf, lies 210 feet above sea level. Most of the city is on the left bank of the Rhine in a fertile lowland plain. The area of the modern city region is about 97 square miles (251 square kilometres), the greatest distance west to east being about 13 miles and, north to south, 15 miles. Cologne has 52 suburbs administered in eight city areas. The heavily industrialized districts of Rodenkirchen, Hürth, Frechen, and Dormagen and the rural residential areas of Lövenich, Widdersdorf, Pulheim, Sinnersdorf, and Stommeln surround the city on the left bank of the Rhine. On the right bank are the districts of Deutz, Mülheim, and Kalk and the adjacent towns of Porz, Bensberg, Bergisch Gladbach, and Leverkusen.

Layout of the city. Cologne is laid out in the semicircle that it assumed in 1180, when the city wall was built, with 12 fortified gates and 83 towers. With the several new parishes brought within the town boundaries, it became, at the time, larger than the city of Paris. The flat side of the semicircle lies athwart the Rhine, 440 yards (400 metres) across, which is spanned by eight bridges, of which five were rebuilt after World War II and three are new constructions. The perimeter of the semicircle is defined by great ring roads, the Ringstrassen, which in the 1880s replaced the medieval fortifications. Since 1920, greenbelts have been laid out along the 19th-century fortifications. Modern suburbs have grown beyond the Ringstrassen, but the main shopping and business streets, such as the Hohe Strasse (north–south) and Schildergasse (west–east), as well as the city's historic buildings, lie within it.

Transportation. Cologne's geographical position and commercial importance have combined to make it a focal point for communications. The city is a great rail junction, with 800 to 1,000 trains passing through daily. The headquarters of the West German airline, it shares its airport with Bonn, to the southeast, in the 1970s, on the edge of the central city, a helicopter landing ground had services to fly patrons to Brussels, Liège, Maastricht, and Bonn. The *Autobahn* "expressway" connected Cologne with Aachen, the Rhine–Ruhr industrial district, Frankfurt, and the south. The Rhine harbour, important since Roman days, had become, by the 1970s, one of the larger inland ports in Germany, handling over 10,000,000 tons of merchandise annually. Small seagoing craft used the river, and there were four passenger-ship lines with a fleet of 38 river steamers. Further, the city was served by 15 streetcar and 30 bus routes.

Population. Of the population of more than 862,000 in 1970, 63 percent were Roman Catholic, 28 percent were Protestant, 17 percent were refugees from the lost eastern territories and the German Democratic Republic (East Germany) after 1961 or from elsewhere in eastern Europe, and about 7 percent were foreigners. The population density was about 8,800 per square mile.

Architectural features. The Cologne Cathedral (Dom) dominates all other historic buildings in the city. It stands on the site of a church completed in 873. After a fire in 1248, rebuilding was begun: the choir was completed in 1322, and work on the cathedral went on until 1510, when Renaissance contempt for the Gothic style is said to have brought building to a halt. Work was resumed in 1842, and the building was completed according to the original design in 1880. It was badly damaged during air raids in 1944, but by 1948 the choir was again in regular use, as was the rest of the interior by 1956. Recent excavations supplied proof that the bishop's church was located on this site during the Merovingian period, and it is probable that the Roman bishop's seat was located here also. **Cologne Cathedral's history and art**

The cathedral, 470 feet long and 175 feet wide, is impressive in its vastness. Its great twin towers rise 515 feet above the centre of the city. The 14th-century stained-glass windows in the choir are considered especially beautiful, and the cathedral is also notable for its other art treasures. On the high altar are relics attributed to the Magi, sent to Cologne from Mailand (1164) and preserved in a gold shrine (begun by Nikolaus von Verdun in the 1180s) that is one of the finest medieval examples of the goldsmith's art. The painting above a secondary altar is a triptych by Stefan Lochner, the outstanding painter of the Cologne school of the early 15th century. In clear, bright colours it depicts the adoration of the kings. A reminder of Cologne's more ancient past lies at the south side of the cathedral—a mosaic floor of a banquet hall of a great Roman villa discovered during excavations near the cathedral in 1941. Other Roman remains in Cologne are a 1st-century tower of the earliest city wall, Roman–Frankish catacombs, and a Roman mausoleum in Weiden, on the outskirts. The Ubier Monument, discovered in the 1960s, dates from the period of Ubii occupation of the area. Remains of the medieval walls may still be seen, and there are three surviving gates, the Eigelsteintor, Hahnentor, and Severinstor. The Bayenturm, a medieval tower, stands near the Rhine.

The cathedral itself is ringed with noble churches, largely built in the prosperous Middle Ages. St. Gereon, St. Severin, and St. Ursula are of late Roman origin, although the buildings are 11th–13th century. The Romanesque St. Maria im Kapitol and St. Kunibert were severely damaged in World War II. Both date from the 7th century, although the actual buildings are 11th and 13th century, respectively. Famous also are the Romanesque churches of St. Pantaleon, St. Aposteln, and Gross St. Martin. Numerous other churches date from as early as the 11th century. The 14th-century Antoniterkirche, a secularized monastery church, was made over to the Protestants in 1802 and became the first public Lutheran church in Cologne. It contains a war memorial, the "Angel of Death," by the contemporary sculptor Ernst Barlach. **Medieval churches**

Among Cologne's secular medieval buildings that suffered in World War II and have undergone reconstruction are the Overstolzenhaus and the Gothic Rathaus (Town Hall), with its 16th-century porch. The Gürzenich, or Festhaus (banqueting hall), of the merchants of the city (1441–47), reconstructed as a concert and festival hall, and the 16th-century Zeughaus, or arsenal, which contains a historical museum, were only outwardly restored in medieval form.

These ancient buildings share the crowded city centre with modern banking and insurance houses, shops and offices, a new theatre and opera house (opened 1957), and, immediately north of the cathedral, the great railway station. Near the perimeter of the city is the new town hall.

The centre of Cologne as seen from the Rhine. The Cologne Cathedral is in the centre with St. Martin's Church and the Rathaus on the left.
Theo Felten

Economic life. The city remains a banking centre, as it was in the Middle Ages, and the wine trade and textile manufacturing are still prominent. In modern times, however, insurance became of great importance, and engineering and electro-engineering, metals and chemicals, and a pharmaceutical industry came to the fore. After Nikolaus Otto invented the gas engine in 1867 and the four-stroke internal-combustion engine in 1876, the city became the centre of the motor industry. After World War II, a number of petrochemical plants were developed in the Cologne area, with pipelines to the seaports of Rotterdam and Wilhelmshaven. Other manufactures include chocolate and eau de Cologne, which was first produced industrially at the beginning of the 18th century. The lignite (low-grade coal) industry, the largest in Germany, is the basis of an electricity plant that supplies large parts of West Germany.

Education. The University of Cologne, founded in 1388, was dissolved in 1798 during the French Revolution and refounded in 1919. In the early 1970s there were some 20,000 students. Teacher-training colleges, a school of sports, and colleges for the study of music, engineering, administration, and other professions and trades are also located in the city, as are 32 *Gymnasien* and 24 *Realschulen* specializing in science.

Cultural life. Cologne's museums include the Wallraf-Richartz-Museum, the largest art gallery in the Rhineland, with an exceptionally comprehensive collection ranging from paintings of the medieval Cologne school to the Pop and Op art of the 1960s; the Schnütgen Museum of medieval ecclesiastical art; the Museum für Ostasiatische Kunst, with the art of China and Japan; and the Rautenstrauch-Joest Museum, with ethnological collections. There is also a Motor Museum and a museum showing the history of the production of eau de Cologne. Special exhibitions are held in the new exhibition-centre art gallery (1967) on the Neumarkt. Cologne's municipal archives are the largest such collection in Germany.

Throughout most of the year, Cologne provides a variety of musical programs. Particularly notable are the Gürzenich concerts and those held in the concert hall of the Westdeutscher Rundfunk (WDR; West German Radio), the high reputation of the latter being largely due to the WDR's encouragement of contemporary music. A full repertoire is offered in theatre and opera as well, and the municipal theatre has its own ballet ensemble.

An annual festival, part of the Rhenisch pre-Lenten carnival, is celebrated with great ceremony. A folk festival, the Kölscher Fasteleer, is peculiar to the city.

Recreation. A large proportion of Cologne's area consists of parkland, woods, lakes, sports grounds, and open spaces. Among the several parks are the zoological and botanical gardens to the north, the Stadtgarten and the Volksgarten, while on the right bank is the Rhine Park, with the Tanzbrunnen (Dancing Fountain) and halls where many fairs and exhibitions are held.

To the west of the city boundary stretching for more than 16 miles is the Äusserer Grüngürtel (Outer Greenbelt), created under the administration of Konrad Adenauer, the federal chancellor who was *Oberbürgermeister*, or chief mayor, of Cologne from 1917 to 1933. A wooded area, it contains extensive recreation grounds and the Müngersdorf sports stadium.

BIBLIOGRAPHY

General: K. KAYSER and T. KRAUS (eds.), *Köln und die Rheinlande* (1961); J. KLERSCH, *Volkstum und Volksleben in Köln*, 3 vol. (1965–68), a sociological study; P. FUCHS, *Köln: Wesen, Werden, Wirken* (1968), mostly photos; R.G. HEMDAHL, *Cologne and Stockholm: Urban Planning and Land-Use Controls* (1971).

History: HERMANN SCHMITZ, *Colonia Claudia Ara Agrippinensium* (1956); LEONHARD ENNEN, *Quellen zur Geschichte der Stadt Köln* . . ., 6 vol. (1860–79); HERMANN KEUSSEN, *Topographie der Stadt Köln im Mittelalter*, 2 vol. (1910), on the topography of Cologne in the Middle Ages; HUGO STEHKAEMPER (ed.), *Köln, das Reich und Europa* (1971), essays on Cologne's involvement in politics, law, and business during the Middle Ages; ARNOLD STELZMANN, *Illustrierte Geschichte der Stadt Köln* (1962), an illustrated history; KARL MARX and FRIEDRICH ENGELS, *The Cologne Communist Trial*, comp. by RODNEY LIVINGSTONE (1971).

Art and architecture: P. CLEMEN, *Die Kunstdenkmäler der Stadt Köln*, 11 vol. (1897–1937), on art monuments; HANS VOGTS, *Köln im Spiegel seiner Kunst* (1950); ALBERT VERBEEK, *Kölner Kirchen*, 2nd rev. ed. (1969), on the churches of Cologne; W.D. ROBSON-SCOTT, *The Literary Background of the Gothic Revival in Germany* (1965), on aspects of the cathedral.

(Ma.Ko./H.Sr.)

Colombia

The Republic of Colombia (República de Colombia) occupies the northwestern corner of the South American continent. Its 1,000 miles of coast to the north are bathed by the waters of the Caribbean Sea, and its 800 miles of coast to the west are washed by the Pacific Ocean. The country is bordered by Panama, which divides the two bodies of water on the northwest; Venezuela and Brazil on the east; and Peru and Ecuador on the south. Its area of 439,737 square miles (1,138,914 square kilometres) includes the Archipiélago de San Andrés y Providencia, located in the Caribbean off the coast of Nicaragua, and the islands of Rosario and San Bernardo, in the Caribbean, and Gorgona and Malpelo, in the Pacific. Bogotá, the national capital, occupies a valley high in the Andes mountains, which contained most of the country's 21,785,700 people in 1971.

Colombia strongly reflects its history as a colony of Spain. It is often referred to as the most Roman Catholic of the South American countries, and its people are proud of the relative purity of their Spanish language. Although its population is largely mestizo (of mixed European and Indian descent), Spanish culture has predominated over indigenous Indian forms. The economy is also descendant from that of the former colony. The nation is overly dependent upon the production of coffee, an agricultural product highly sensitive to fluctuations in the international market. Most of the population is engaged in agriculture. Industry is largely undeveloped and related to the processing of raw materials. Political instability is closely tied to the unequal distribution of wealth, which, again, has strong historic precedent.

(For related physical features see AMAZON RAIN FOREST; AMAZON RIVER; ANDES MOUNTAIN RANGES; LLANOS; and ORINOCO RIVER. For a detailed description of the national capital see BOGOTA. For history see COLOMBIA, HISTORY OF.)

THE LANDSCAPE

The natural environment. *Relief features.* A country of varied surface configuration, Colombia is comprised of cordilleras (mountain chains), isolated mountains, *mesetas* (plateaus) and intermontane basins, river valleys and gorges, lowlands, and hilly areas. There is also a multiplicity of lesser forms created by erosion and the deposition of alluvial soil; these include terraces, alluvial fans (alluvial deposits of streams where they issue from gorges upon a plain or join another stream), river deltas, and glacial moraines (accumulations of earth and stones deposited by glaciers) and cirques (deep, steep-walled montane basins).

The Colombian Andes

The cordilleras belong to the northern portion of the great Andean mountain system that extends along the Pacific coast of South America. The Andes enter Colombia across the Ecuador border. At the Nudo de los Pastos (Pastos mountain knot), near the border, the mountains bifurcate into the Cordillera Occidental (Western Range), which runs parallel to the Pacific coast, and the Cordillera Central (Central Range), which, with its numerous volcanoes, its igneous rocks (formed by solidification from the molten state), and metamorphic rocks (formed under heat and pressure), forms the backbone of the system and runs in a generally southwest to northeast direction. At the Gran Macizo Colombiano (Great Colombian Massif) of the Cordillera Central, the Cordillera Oriental (Eastern Range) branches off in a more decidedly northeastern direction.

The Cordillera Central is the highest of the Andes mountains in Colombia, rising to an average height of 10,000 feet (3,000 metres). The Cordillera Oriental, branching into Venezuela, is the longest of the three ranges, running a total length of about 750 miles (1,200 kilometres), and has the broadest base, of about 120 miles (200 kilometres).

There are several lesser cordilleras on the periphery of the central system. They include the Serranía de Baudó along the northern Pacific coast, the Serranía del Darién along the Panamanian border, and the ranges of Abibe–Las Palomas, San Jerónimo–Montes de María, Ayapel, and San Lucas, which extend as spurs from the northern edges of the western and central ranges into the Atlantic lowlands. In the northeast the Cordillera Oriental slowly

becomes transformed into the Serranía de los Motilones, Valledupar, and Montes de Oca as it nears the Península de la Guajira.

There are also isolated mountain formations that are not of Andean origin. The Sierra Nevada de Santa Marta in the north rises from a triangular-shaped base to the peaks of Colón and Bolívar, which attain altitudes of 18,947 and 16,411 feet, respectively, making them the highest mountains in the country. On its northern side, the mountain massif thrusts directly into the Caribbean, while its other two sides come into almost abrupt contact with the surrounding Atlantic plain. The Serranía de la Macarena, located southeast of Bogotá and of the Cordillera Oriental, is composed of an old base overlain with newer material.

The *mesetas* are of two types. Those of volcanic origin include the plateaus of Nariño and Cauca in the southwest. Others, such as the plateaus in the northern extent of the western and central ranges, have been formed by the action of erosion on batholithic (subsurface igneous rock) intrusions. In the Cordillera Oriental a number of plateaus were formed by the deposition of sediment in depressions created during the Tertiary Period (from 65,000,000 to 2,500,000 years ago) and the Quaternary Period (within the past 2,500,000 years). The most important of these high valleys is the Sabana de Bogotá, site of the national capital and the vital centre of Colombia.

The *mesetas* and plains

These abrupt formations offer marked contrast to the plains that extend along the Atlantic and Pacific coasts and the interior. From the shore of the Caribbean to the spurs of the western and central ranges extends a slightly undulating plain generally known as the Llanura Atlántica (Atlantic Plain). Dotted by hills and grading off in certain areas into a floodplain, it surrounds the inland portion of the Sierra Nevada de Santa Marta. In the southwest another coastal plain, alternating with fringes of hills, extends along the Pacific shoreline; its lower portion is periodically inundated by the sea.

Extending eastward from the Andes to the Orinoco River is a great plain that includes both the Llanos to the north of the Río Guaviare and the Amazonia region of Colombia, between the Guaviare and the Putumayo and Amazon rivers. The area is divided into three physical regions—the central portion between the Guaviare and Caquetá rivers, over the eroded surface of which rivers form torrents and rapids, and the two sedimentary basins of the Río Meta to the north and the Putumayo to the south. Lesser features include the eddies and small currents of the rivers north of the Guaviare and island-mountains, tablelands, and bluffs in the Amazon region.

Along Colombia's extensive coasts are numerous physical features formed by the sea, rivers, wind erosion, or tectonic (deformation of the Earth's crust) activity. Steep and articulated coastal areas marked by bays, inlets, capes, and promontories occur on the Pacific coast north of Cabo Corrientes or along the Caribbean, where the sea beats against the base of the Sierra Nevada de Santa Marta.

In other areas, the coastal plain slopes gently toward sandy beaches and shoals that were formed by marine currents and wind such as the "island" of Salamanca in the north, or is marked by river deltas such as those of the Atrato, Sinú, and Magdalena rivers on the Caribbean coast and of the San Juan and Patía rivers along the Pacific.

Drainage. In general, the character of Colombia's relief and the trend of its mountain ranges cause its rivers to be distributed in four watersheds—the Caribbean, the Amazon, the Pacific, and Lake Maracaibo, in Venezuela. The orientation of the Andes causes several large rivers to run toward the Caribbean Sea, including the Atrato, the Sinú, the Magdalena and its tributary the Cauca, and the Ranchería.

Four drainage systems

The great eastern watershed, the waters of which are carried by the Orinoco and Amazon rivers to the Atlantic Ocean, is subdivided into two sections. The Arauca and Meta, the lower reaches of which cross into Venezuela, and the Vichada, Inírida, and Guaviare rivers flow into the Orinoco. The Vaupés, Caquetá and Putumayo, all of the lower reaches of which lie in Brazilian territory, flow into the Amazon.

The third watershed contains those rivers that flow toward the Pacific. Unlike the rivers already mentioned, which are of enormous size, the rivers of the Pacific are short; they descend rapidly from the Cordillera Occidental before reaching the sea. They carry a large volume of water, however, because they flow through a region that receives heavy rainfall. Among the rivers belonging to the Pacific watershed are the Baudó, San Juan, Dagua, Naya, Micay, Sanquianga, Patía, and Mira, the source of which is in Ecuador.

The rivers that rise in Colombia and empty into Lake Maracaibo may be considered as belonging to a fourth, smaller watershed. The principal river of this group is the Catatumbo.

High in the Andes are several lakes, known as *lagunas* (lagoons). The three largest lakes are Tota, which is the source of the Río Upía; Fúquene, which is drying up and which contains the single island of Santuario in its centre; and La Cocha, from which rises a high tributary, the Guamués. The floodplains of many Colombian rivers contain numerous permanent or seasonal *ciénagas* (marshes).

A great variety of soils is encountered, reflecting climatic, topographic, and geological variations. The soils best suited for agriculture are found in the Cauca, Sinú, Magdalena, César, and Ariguaní valleys; also productive are the soils of the Bogotá savanna region, the Túquerres *meseta*, the Quindío region, the plains of the Llanos, and the Sibundoy, Ubaté, and Chiquinquirá valleys.

Climate. Because of the country's geographical position, its climate is generally tropical and isothermal (without any real change of seasons). The only genuinely variable climatic element is the amount of annual precipitation. Climatic differences are related to altitude and the displacement of the Intertropical Convergence Zone between the two major air masses from which the Northeast Trade Winds and the Southeast Trade Winds originate.

The climate of the tropical rain forest in the Amazon region, the northern Pacific coast, and the central Magdalena Valley is marked by an annual rainfall of more than 100 inches (2,500 millimetres) and annual average temperatures above 74° F (23° C). The tropical monsoon climate is similar to that of the rain forest but is marked by a dry season, which occurs—at various times according to the area—along the southern Pacific coast, on the Caribbean coast near Panama, and in the interior in the Quindío department area of the Cordillera Occidental and the eastern foothills of the Cordillera Oriental near Villavicencio.

The tropical savanna conditions of alternately wet and dry seasons comprise the predominant climate of the Llanura Atlántica; the dry season occurs from November to April, and the wet season (broken by dry periods) from May to November. This climate is found also in the Llanos region and in part of the Upper Magdalena Valley. It is characterized by an annual rainfall of less than 70 inches (1,800 millimetres) and annual temperatures usually above 74° F (23° C). The dry season, accompanied by dust and wind, coincides with the true winter of the Northern Hemisphere.

The dry savanna climate prevails on the Caribbean littoral from the Golfo de Morrosquillo (Morrosquillo Gulf) to the Península de la Guajira in the northeast. The rains occur in two wet seasons (in April and in October to November, respectively), but rarely exceed 30 inches (800 millimetres) annually. The temperature is hot— more than 81° F (27° C)—with daily variations corresponding to the degree of aridity; at Guajira the daily range is more than 36° F (20° C). This type of climate also occurs in the deep gorges of such rivers as the Patía, Cauca, Chicamocha, and Zulia, and in parts of the Upper Magdalena Valley.

The climate of the mountain regions is greatly affected by altitude. On the mountain slopes and Andean heights above 5,900 feet, temperatures are usually below 64° F (18° C), and the annual precipitation of 70 to 110 inches (1,800 to 2,000 millimetres) occurs in a succession of more or less rainy periods. Between 8,200 and 10,000 feet, temperatures range between 57° and 52° F (14° and 11° C). Formerly, the Andes in this climatic zone were shrouded in fog, but settlement has resulted in the elimination of most of the "fog forest."

The climate of the high mountain regions—the paramos —between 10,000 and 15,000 feet above sea level is characterized by temperatures lower than 50° F (10° C), fog, overcast skies, frequent winds, light rain, or drizzle. The paramos are habitable up to an altitude of 12,000 feet and are most extensive in the Cordillera Oriental. At altitudes above 15,000 feet there is perpetual snow and ice, the temperatures average around 32° F (0° C), winds and light rain are frequent, and solar radiation is strong.

Vegetation and animal life. The varied combinations of climate, soil, and topography have produced some 23 plant communities that are distributed in horizontal and vertical bands. They include the mangrove swamps of the maritime coasts, the thistle clumps of the Guajira region, the forests of the Llanos, the palm groves of the Llanura Atlántica, the rain forests of the Amazon and Chocó regions, and the Andean forests.

Centuries ago the natural vegetation of the Andean region and the Caribbean plains was replaced by cultivated lands. Even in less populated areas, large expanses of land have been cut down to obtain wood, and remnants of the primitive forests occur only in a few patches of trees.

The rich animal life of the Amazon region includes opossums, anteaters, sloths, several monkeys, tapirs, peccary, the spectacled bear, deer, and large tropical rodents, such as the agouti and paca. Carnivores include pumas, jaguars, and raccoons.

Animal life

There are more than 1,500 species of birds, including toucans, hummingbirds, and those that migrate from North America. Turtles, lizards, snakes, caimans, and crocodiles abound. Freshwater fish include catfish and characin (small, brightly coloured tropical fish), and there are electric eels. Abundant insects include wood borers and mosquitoes.

Traditional regions and settlement patterns. Colombia can be divided into five traditional geographic regions: the Caribbean lowlands, the Pacific coastal region, the Andean region, the eastern Llanos (or Orinoquia), and the Amazonian rain forest. Of early colonial importance, the Caribbean lowlands contain about 17 percent of the population, which is concentrated in Barranquilla and the country's first permanent cities of Cartagena and Santa Marta. Stock raising and mixed agriculture are traditional economic activities, and large-scale commercial agriculture has been successful. The Pacific coastal region, with its lush rain forest and infertile soils, is little inhabited. Most of its people are descendants of liberated African slaves who settled in agricultural clearings along the rivers.

The Andean region is the centre of national political and economic power. It contains almost 80 percent of the population and the three largest cities, Bogotá, Medellín, and Cali. The enormous area may be broken into numerous sectors and subregions, the three largest of which perhaps are the Cordillera Oriental, the Magdalena Valley, and the Cordilleras Central and Occidental.

Although the Llanos and the Amazonian rain forest together comprise two-thirds of the country, they contain less than 2 percent of the population. Orinoquia has long been used as a vast cattle range, and most of its towns are strung out along the Andean foothills. The remote Amazon region is sparsely inhabited by small groups of Indians.

PEOPLE AND POPULATION

Population groups. In Colombia, great care is taken to preserve the linguistic purity of the official language, Castilian Spanish, and there are close ties between the Spanish and Colombian language academies. Spanish as spoken in Colombia is, however, undoubtedly marked by the presence of Colombianisms, many of which have

Languages

been analyzed and accepted by both academies. In addition to Spanish, there are more than 180 indigenous languages and dialects belonging to five major linguistic groups; they include Aymara, Arawak, Chibcha, Carib, Quechua, Tupí-Guaraní, and Yurumanguí.

In general, the Colombian population has its ethnic origins in the early groups of Indians, Spaniards, and Africans. Later immigrants from the Near East, non-Iberian Europe, and the Far East have also been absorbed. In the 1970s, the mestizos (persons of mixed European and Amerindian descent) probably represented almost 50 percent of the population. Mulattos comprised almost 25 percent of the total. Twenty percent were Europeans, or whites, 4 percent were blacks, and 1 percent were Indians.

Religious liberty is guaranteed by the constitution, although Roman Catholicism is the official religion and the faith of more than 95 percent of Colombians. Protestants number over 100,000 and the Jewish community about 25,000. Some Indians continue to follow their traditional religious beliefs.

Demography. The annual birth rate of 38 per 1,000 population is one of the highest in Latin America and is responsible for Colombia's position as one of the countries of largest population growth. During 1970–75 the rate of natural increase was 31 per 1,000 population. The death rate of almost 8 per 1,000 population is expected to decline as living conditions are improved throughout the country.

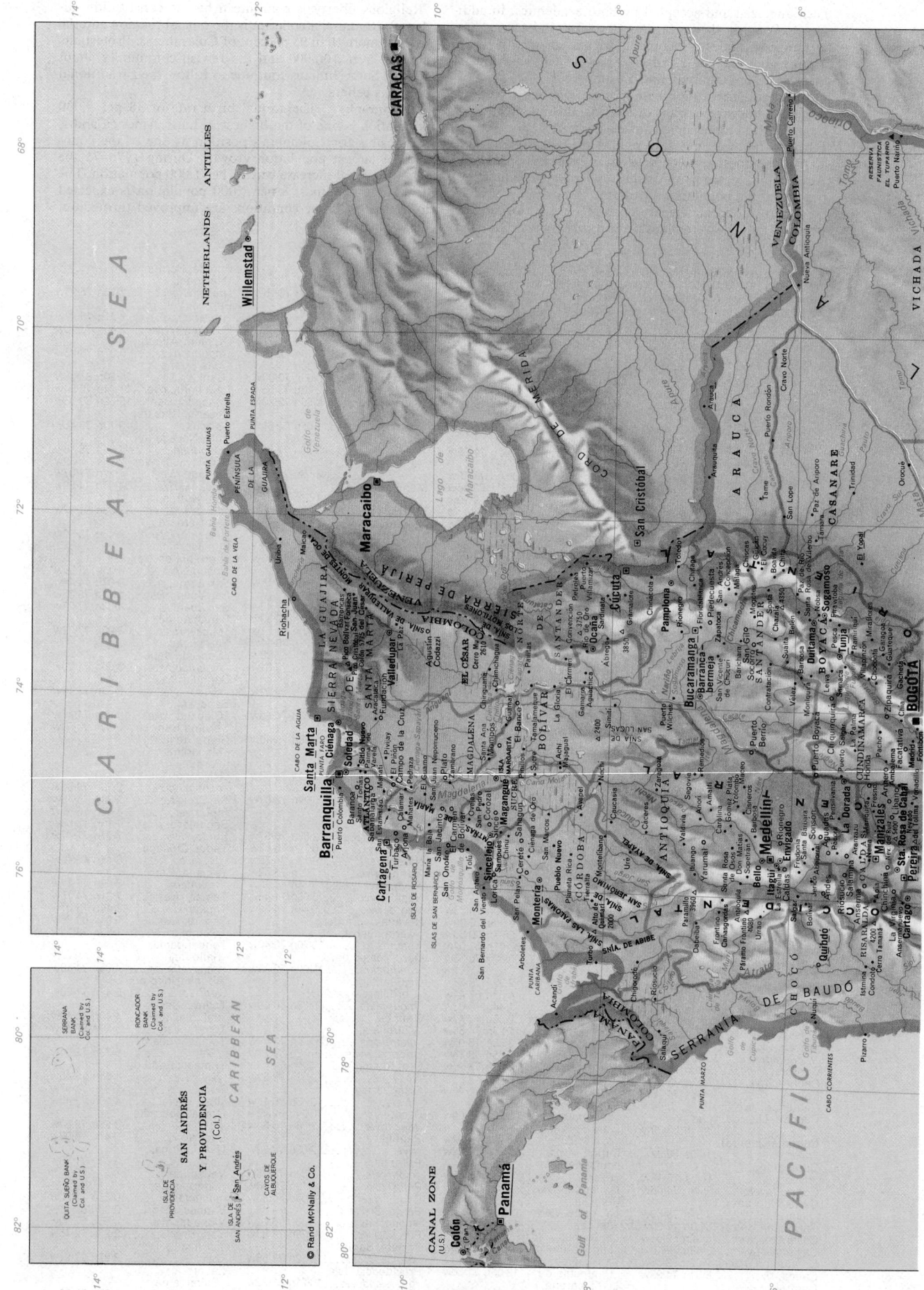

CARIBBEAN SEA

NETHERLANDS ANTILLES

Willemstad

CARACAS

VENEZUELA

COLOMBIA

Barranquilla
Cartagena
Santa Marta
Cienaga
Soledad

Riohacha

Valledupar

Maracaibo

Lago de Maracaibo

Gulfo de Venezuela

PUNTA GALINAS
Puerto Estrella
PUNTA ESPADA

PENINSULA DE LA GUAJIRA

LA GUAJIRA

SIERRA NEVADA DE SANTA MARTA

EL CESAR

MAGDALENA

ATLANTICO

BOLIVAR

CORDOBA

ANTIOQUIA

Montería
Sincelejo

Quibdó

Medellín
Bello
Itagüí
Envigado

Manizales
Pereira
Cartago
Armenia

Bogotá

CUNDINAMARCA

BOYACÁ

SANTANDER

Bucaramanga
Barrancabermeja

NORTE DE SANTANDER

Cúcuta
Pamplona

San Cristóbal

ARAUCA

Arauca

CASANARE

VICHADA

MERIDA

CORDILLERA

ORIENTAL

SERRANÍA DE BAUDÓ

SERRANÍA DEL DARIÉN

PANAMA
COLOMBIA

CANAL ZONE
(U.S.)

Colón
(Pan.)

Panamá

Gulf of Panama

PACIFIC

© Rand McNally & Co.

QUITA SUEÑO BANK
(Claimed by
Col. and U.S.)

SERRANA BANK
(Claimed by
Col. and U.S.)

RONCADOR BANK
(Claimed by
Col. and U.S.)

ISLA DE
PROVIDENCIA

SAN ANDRÉS
Y PROVIDENCIA
(Col.)

ISLA DE
SAN ANDRÉS · San Andrés

CAYOS DE
ALBURQUERQUE

CARIBBEAN

SEA

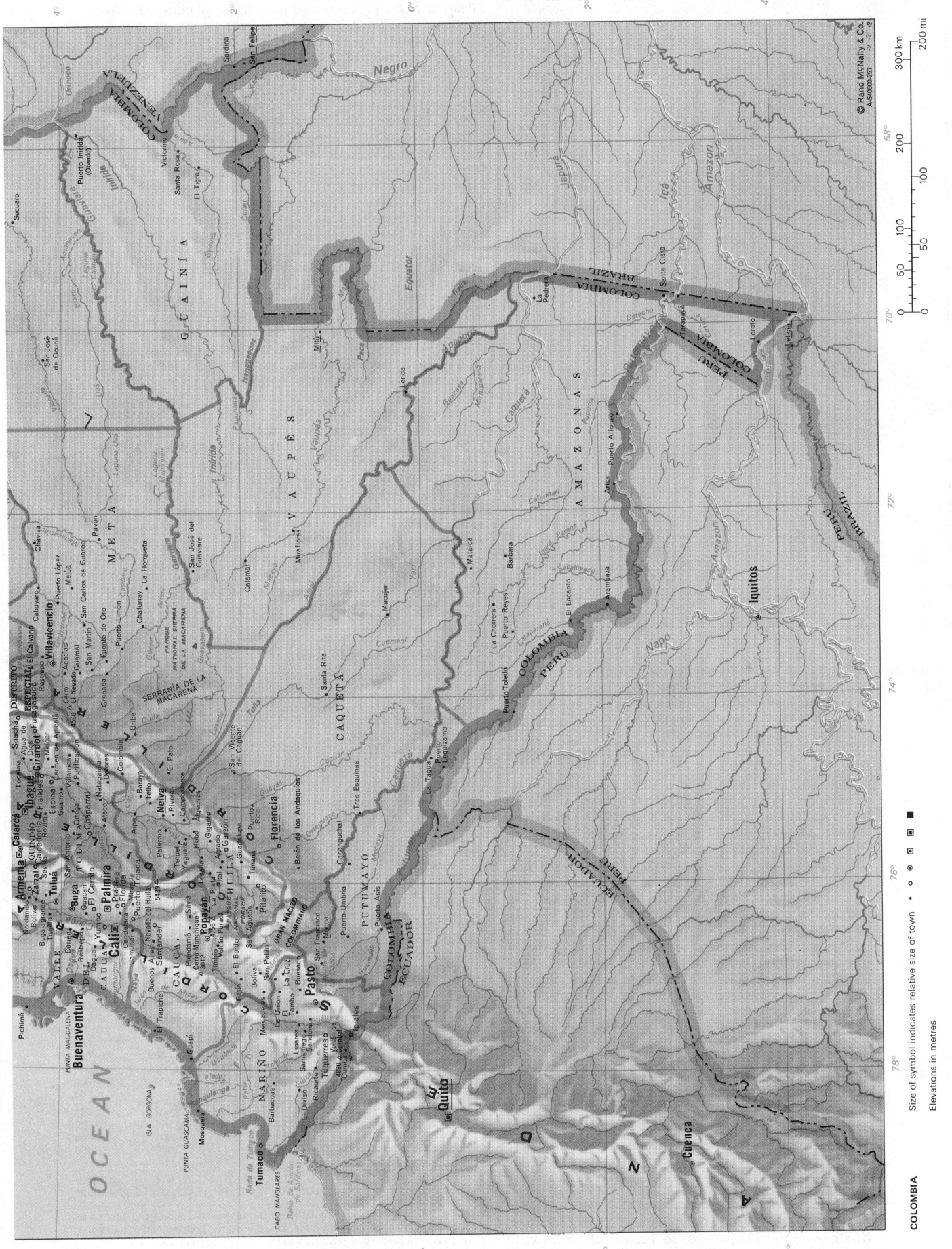

COLOMBIA

Size of symbol indicates relative size of town

Elevations in metres

© Rand McNally & Co.
A-540000.557 -2 -2 -2

Population density of Colombia.

because of the prevalence of poor soils and unfavourable climatic conditions. The eastern plains are almost entirely uninhabited, the region closest to the Pacific Ocean is largely undeveloped because of high humidity and heavy rainfall, and large areas in the middle and Upper Magdalena Valley remain untouched.

Natural resources. Colombia's mineral wealth is incalculable. The entire Pacific slope of the Cordillera Occidental contains a seemingly inexhaustible stratum of gold and alluvial platinum deposits. The Cordillera Central is rich in gold and silver and the industrial minerals iron ore, lead, zinc, mercury, and coal. Although not as rich in precious metals, the Cordillera Oriental contains promising deposits of coal, iron ore, copper, silver, lead, marble, limestone, and zinc. Coal reserves are about as large as those of all the other Latin American countries combined. The eastern mountains also yield rock salt and the most highly prized emeralds in the world. Other minerals that occur in smaller quantities include mercury, sulfur, barite (barium sulfate), uranium, antimony, feldspar, gypsum, talc, mica, asbestos, and bauxite.

Petroleum is the most valuable natural resource; it is an important element in economic development and a source of foreign exchange. Deposits occur in the Central Magdalena Valley, in the basin of the Río Catatumbo, in the Caribbean region, on the Pacific coast, and in both the Llanos and Amazon regions of the east.

Biological resources include the vast expanses of rainforest and grasslands, which offer valuable timber (mahogany, lignum vitae, brazilwood, walnut, cedar, oak, and virola [which yields a reddish-brown wood]), and grazing land. The oceans, rivers, and lakes are important sources of fish.

Electrical energy in the northern coastal region is primarily generated by thermal means. In the Andean region, however, hydroelectric plants are in operation. The unused hydroelectric potential is considerable and in the early 1970s was to be partially developed to meet

Marginal note: Mineral wealth

Migration to the cities

There is an observable emigration from the rural areas to the cities, partially determined by the search for higher wages and better living conditions. In the period from 1946 to 1958, the rural population comprised more than 60 percent of the national whole; in the early 1970s, however, 60 percent of the nation's population inhabited urban areas.

Colombia has not received a large number of immigrants, and its population growth is related almost entirely to natural increase. In the early 1970s, immigrants comprised only a small percentage of the population. There is no substantial rate of emigration.

The population, estimated at 22,491,000 in 1972, is unequally distributed over the country. Over 2,800,000 live in the Bogotá Distrito Especial (Bogotá Special District), which comprises 613 square miles (1,587 square kilometres) in the area of the capital city. The remaining population is divided between the high Andean regions and the Caribbean and Pacific lowlands. Most people prefer the cold and temperate regions, although the warm, dry areas are also significantly settled. The hot, humid regions of the east, together with the high paramos of the Andes, have the lowest population density.

Demographic trends

Rapid population growth, together with industrialization and the excessive growth of the cities, offers a serious challenge to economic planning and development. There is a need to undertake programs of family planning, and increasing air and water pollution offer serious problems for the future.

THE ECONOMY

Agriculture is the basis of the Colombian economy, although industrial development since the 1940s has been truly remarkable. In 1968 the country had a work force of almost 6,500,000 persons, 35 percent of whom were engaged in agriculture, forestry, hunting, and fishing. A proportion of Colombian land is uncultivated, however,

Colombia, Area and Population

	area		population	
	sq mi	sq km	1964 census	1972 estimate
Commissariats (*comisarías*)				
Amazonas	46,811	121,240	13,000	18,000
Guainía	30,141	78,065	4,000	5,000
Vaupés	34,990	90,625	13,000	19,000
Vichada	38,213	98,970	10,000	10,000
Departments (*departamentos*)				
Antioquia	24,274	62,870	2,477,000	3,221,000
Atlántico	1,263	3,270	717,000	964,000
Bolívar	10,190	26,392	694,000	902,000
Boyacá	26,158	67,750	1,058,000	1,252,000
Caldas	2,812	7,283	713,000	852,000
Cauca	11,774	30,495	607,000	732,000
Chocó	18,226	47,205	182,000	221,000
Córdoba	9,720	25,175	586,000	819,000
Cundinamarca*	8,638	22,373	1,122,000	1,285,000
El Cesar	9,186	23,792	261,000	510,000
Huila	7,718	19,990	416,000	511,000
La Guajira	7,792	20,180	147,000	273,000
Magdalena	8,843	22,903	528,000	650,000
Meta	33,116	85,770	166,000	281,000
Nariño	11,987	31,045	706,000	825,000
Norte de Santander	8,037	20,815	534,000	647,000
Quindío	705	1,825	306,000	363,000
Risaralda	1,530	3,962	437,000	537,000
Santander	11,950	30,950	1,001,000	1,194,000
Sucre	4,063	10,523	313,000	380,000
Tolima	9,006	23,325	841,000	940,000
Valle del Cauca	8,203	21,245	1,733,000	2,244,000
Intendancies (*intendencias*)				
Arauca	9,070	23,490	24,000	34,000
Caquetá	34,821	90,185	104,000	168,000
Putumayo	9,873	25,570	56,000	93,000
San Andrés y Providencia	17	44	17,000	32,000
Special district (*Distrito Especial*)*	613	1,587	1,697,000	2,818,000
Total Colombia	439,737†	1,138,914	17,485,000†	22,491,000

*The *Distrito Especial* of Bogotá is part of the *departamento* of Cundinamarca; however, it is an autonomous administrative entity. The area and population of both have been listed separately in the table.   †Figures do not add to total given because of rounding.
Source: Official government figures.

rising needs. Coal and gas resources also constitute a large reserve available for generating thermal power.

Sources of national income. *Agriculture, forestry, and fishing.* The mountainous character of much of Colombia's territory allows for the production of a variety of crops ranging from those that require warm temperatures for growth to those that can be grown only in a cold climate.

Modern agricultural techniques are employed chiefly in those areas in which the topography makes their use possible. Chemical fertilizers are widely used, and large tracts of land have been redeemed for agricultural purposes through irrigation. Many small farmers, however, cling to traditional methods of agriculture because of their reluctance to adopt new and more technical modes of operation.

The importance of coffee

Colombia's chief agricultural product is coffee. Almost 2,000,000 acres (900,000 hectares) are given over to coffee plantations, whose yearly production of approximately 510,000 tons makes Colombia the second largest producer of coffee after Brazil. Coffee represents the backbone of the Colombian economy and comprises almost 60 percent of total exports.

Coffee grows best at an elevation of between 4,300 and 6,600 feet (1,300 and 2,000 metres). The greater number of plantations are found in four zones in the three Andean ranges and the Sierra Nevada de Santa Marta.

Bananas and plantains (a type of banana) are also important. Most of the bananas grown are exported from the plantations located on the Caribbean coast. The plantain is a basic part of the Colombian diet.

The production of sugarcane has notably increased in recent years as a result of the export quotas established in the international market. Sugarcane is grown in almost all the hot and temperate zones of the country; the Valle de Cauca department, on the central Pacific coast, is the major producer. About 80 percent of the cane is used in the manufacture of unrefined brown sugar; refined sugar, honey, molasses, and alcohol are also produced.

Corn (maize) is grown everywhere except in the paramo and is an important food staple, especially for the poor. The production of rice is constantly increasing; it is grown in almost all of the hot and humid areas.

Other agricultural products are important to the national economy either because of the large areas given over to their production or because of the volume of such production. They include cotton, potatoes, yuca (manioc), wheat, barley, tobacco, cacao, and beans. Less important crops include hemp, tomatoes, coconuts, soybeans, aniseed, rubber, sesame seeds, peanuts, African palms, Indian figs, grapes, legumes, green leafy vegetables, and citrus and other kinds of fruits.

Stock raising is another reliable source of national wealth. There are almost 20,000,000 beef and dairy cattle, as well as many horses, mules, donkeys, pigs, sheep, and goats. The Sinú and San Jorge river valleys, the savannas of the Llanura Atlántica, and the eastern Llanos are the regions in which most of the stock is raised. Animals of exceptionally fine calibre are found on the savanna of Bogotá and in the valleys of the Cauca and Sinú rivers. Poultry raising, producing about 26,000,000 fowl, has shown the greatest rate of expansion, principally as a result of the application of modern techniques.

The rich resource of the forests has not been exploited because access roads to them are few. The lumber industry is in the process of development, however, and in the early 1970s there were numerous factories for the manufacture of different types of plywood for domestic use and export.

The fishing industry is a potential source of wealth because of the country's two ocean coasts and its numerous lakes, rivers, and marshes. Because of lack of financing, it remained little developed in the early 1970s.

Mining of precious metals

Mining and quarrying. Colombia is the largest producer of gold in South America and the tenth largest in the world. Platinum, which occasionally occurs together with gold, is mined intensively on the Pacific mountain slopes. Silver is mined together with gold in the central

and eastern cordilleras. There are no important iron deposits, but coal is mined mainly in the Andean region.

The Empresa Colombiana de Petróleos (Colombian Petroleum Company) and several foreign companies are in charge of the extraction of petroleum. There are 16 pipelines that carry petroleum and seven others for derivative products. The natural gases, such as methane, butane, and propane, are also drawn off and used in various ways. This distillation of petroleum is used to manufacture a number of by-products, such as gasoline, naphtha, kerosene, diesel oil, lubricating oils, vaseline, paraffin, and asphalt.

Manufacturing. Throughout the nation in the early 1970s there were some 12,000 manufacturing establishments, employing about 350,000 persons. The textile industry employed the largest number of workers and (after agriculture) was second with respect to the monetary value of its production. Having experienced remarkable growth since World War II, the industry manufactures products of excellent quality that not only supply the national demand but also compete favourably in the international market.

Industrial development programs

The Instituto de Fomento Industrial (Institute of Industrial Development) has supplied the necessary capital for enterprises too large to be financed by private investment. These include industries that produce goods that were previously imported, those that employ a large number of highly trained personnel, and those that use a high percentage of national raw materials. The institute has invested large sums to strengthen the metalworking industry, to set up automotive assembly plants, to stimulate the construction of railroad cars and fishing vessels, and to encourage the manufacture of paper, vegetable oils, and petroleum derivatives.

Despite all that has been accomplished, however, the greater part of Colombian industrial activity is carried on by small enterprises that produce various types of consumer goods. These include breweries and factories that manufacture clothing, cigarettes, soap, shoes, cement, drugs, chemical products, fertilizers, rubber and leather articles, and home appliances.

Energy. One of the obstacles to industrial development has been an inadequate supply of electricity, despite the increase of power production since 1960. The total national generation capacity was 670,000 kilowatts in 1960, almost 1,245,000 kilowatts in 1965, and more than 2,000,000 kilowatts in 1970.

Though Colombia has more than 800 generation plants, only eight of them have a capacity of more than 25,000 kilowatts. About 76 percent of this power is produced by hydroelectric plants located mainly in the Andean areas and the remainder by thermoelectric stations (using coal, gas, or diesel oil) located mainly in northern Colombia.

Studies of the country's hydrographic system foresee the installation by the 1980s of an additional 40,000,000 kilowatts of hydroelectric power. The departments that had the best supply of electricity in the early 1970s were Cundinamarca, Antioquia, and Valle del Cauca, which together used 65 percent of the total national supply.

Financial services. The banking system in the early 1970s was composed of a central bank, the Banco de la República, and over 30 general banking institutions, six of which were foreign owned. The Monetary Commission, created by the government in 1963, is the highest authority in matters involving the extension of credit. Such credit was extended through the central bank, which also issues currency, acts as banker for the government and other banks, serves as a guardian and administrator of the country's international reserves, and acts as a clearing house.

The national banks

Among the national banks, the Banco Central Hipotecario (Central Mortgage Bank) grants loans for construction on the basis of guaranteed mortgages. The Caja de Crédito Agrario, Industrial, y Minero (Bank of Agrarian, Industrial, and Mining Credit) and the Banco Ganadero (Cattleman's Bank) are concerned with specialized forms of credit, mostly for agriculture. The banks operate according to a system of branch banks and agencies that are located throughout the country and are inspected by the Superintendencia Bancaria (Bank Examiners' Office). About 50 local and 20 foreign insurance companies were in operation in the early 1970s. Both Bogotá and Medellín have stock exchanges.

Foreign trade. Foreign trade is concerned principally with the exportation of raw materials and the importation of machinery and manufactured goods. The chief purchasing countries are the United States—which buys about 40 percent of Colombia's exports—West Germany, The Netherlands, Spain, Sweden, Peru, and the United Kingdom. Exports to the United States include coffee, crude petroleum, bananas, cotton, fuel oil, sugar, cardboard cartons, textiles, tobacco, and cement.

Almost 50 percent of all imports are obtained from the United States; other sources are West Germany, Spain, Japan, the United Kingdom, Mexico, Sweden, Canada, and Italy. Imports consist of machinery and transportation equipment, chemical products, manufactured articles, noncombustible raw materials, and foodstuffs and live animals.

Management of the economy. Colombia's economy is dominated by private enterprise, and direct government participation is limited to such enterprises as the ownership of the railways. The government has attempted to foster economic stability and encourage private enterprise through indirect measures, such as a favourable system of taxation and the extension of credit to new industries.

Trade unions and employer associations. In addition to several independent unions, there are two trade union associations. The Unión de Trabajadores de Colombia (UTC; National Union of Colombian Workers) has about 600 affiliates, including national, regional, and local organizations. The smaller Confederación de Trabajadores de Colombia (CTC; Colombian Confederation of Workers) includes about 400 affiliates. Salaried rural workers are organized into guilds. Other organizations include rural credit unions and urban cooperatives that attempt to raise productivity, increase income, and improve the standard of living.

There are numerous employers' and producers' associations. They include the Asociación Colombiana Popular de Industriales (ACOPI), the Asociación Nacional de Industriales (ANI), and organizations of producers of sugarcane, cattle, cacao, and coffee.

Economic policies and prospects. The government has bent its efforts toward the development of an economy of abundance. Accordingly, it has attacked the problem of scarcity by furthering the rapid expansion of production in order to meet growing demand. It has aided such expansion by the extension of short-term financing to improve methods of production. An indirect outcome of this policy has been to increase competition by providing greater flexibility within the economy. As the problems of productivity are resolved, costs should be reduced and markets expanded to reap the benefits of large-scale production.

Monetary policies in effect in the early 1970s were being revised in order to reduce inflation; the accumulation of savings was encouraged and controls over interest rates were being exercised.

TRANSPORTATION

In the western Andean region, where over 80 percent of the population is concentrated, transportation is carried on by sea, river, land, and air. In the eastern regions of the Orinoco and Amazon, however, transportation is limited to aircraft and riverboats.

Water transport. Cargo ships ply the waters of both the Caribbean and the Pacific, which are joined to the north by the Panama Canal (*q.v.*). The Caribbean ports of Cartagena, Barranquilla, and Santa Marta have relatively deep water and are equipped with modern services and port facilities. On the Pacific coast, the port of Buenaventura is of easy access and has a good lighthouse and modernized installations, while Tumaco was in need of further development in the early 1970s.

The most important river from the standpoint of transportation is the Magdalena. Other rivers expected to play a larger role in transportation include the Atrato, the Orinoco, and the Meta.

Consideration has been given to the possibility of uniting the Caribbean with the Pacific by the construction of a canal between the Atrato and San Juan rivers. There is also the possibility of constructing a canal between the Caquetá and Putumayo rivers across the narrow strip of land between La Tagua and Puerto Leguízamo.

Railways. The more than 2,000 miles of standard-gauge railroad lines are owned by the government. The main line is the Ferrocarril del Atlántico, which runs north for 600 miles (1,000 kilometres) between Bogotá and the seaport of Santa Marta. At Puerto Berrío, in the Magdalena Valley, the mainline connects with the railway that passes south through Medellín and Cali and then turns northwest to the seaport of Buenaventura. Other less important lines extend to the regional capitals of Bucaramanga, Tunja, Ibagué, Neiva, and Popayán.

Roads. There are some 29,000 miles of roads; over 3,700 miles are paved and 20,000 miles covered with gravel and crushed stone. Two parallel trunk roads traverse the country from north to south. The road runs along the Cordillera Oriental to Bogotá, where it bifurcates; one branch runs northeastward to the Venezuela border at Puerto Carreño and the other continues north to Santa Marta. The western road runs along the Cordillera Occidental from the Ecuador border to Barranquilla. In the early 1970s construction continued on Colombia's section of the Pan-American Highway, which includes the western trunk road. In the early 1970s, studies for a highway along the eastern foothills of the Cordillera Oriental were being made.

Several roads run from east to west and serve to connect the two trunk roads. In the north, the Caribbean road runs between Cartagena, Barranquilla, Santa Marta, Riohacha, and Maicao, near the Venezuelan border.

Air services. Because the construction of mountain roads is difficult, much attention has been paid since 1919 to the development of the airways. Air services now join the regional capitals and other important cities with the national capital. The principal international airport is that of the city of Bogotá, and there are other international airports at Cali, Medellín, Cartagena, and Barranquilla, and over 100 domestic airports. Furthermore, international and domestic services are supplied by three national airlines, and there are also several national domestic airlines.

ADMINISTRATION AND SOCIAL CONDITIONS

Government structure. *Constitutional framework.* Under the constitution of 1886 Colombia is a republic the public powers of which are divided between the executive, legislative, and judicial branches of government. The president, who may not succeed himself, is elected to a four-year term by universal suffrage. The executive also includes a Cabinet of 13 ministers who are appointed by the president. The seven-member Council of State acts in consultative capacity to the president.

The bicameral legislature is composed of a senate and a house of representatives, both of whose members are elected by universal suffrage to four-year terms. The senate is composed of three or more representatives from each department (one for each 190,000 persons), and the house contains three or more representatives from each department, or one for each 90,000 persons. Legislation may be passed upon a simple majority vote.

Local government. The country is divided for administrative purposes into 22 *departamentos* (departments), four *intendencias* (intendancies), four *comisarías* (commissariats), and one *distrito especial* (special district, of Bogotá). The departments are headed by governors, appointed by the president, and each has an elected legislature. The departments are subdivided into *municipios* (municipalities), which are headed by mayors appointed by the governors. The intendancies of Arauca, Caquetá, Putumayo, and San Andrés y Providencia—as well as the commissariats of Amazonas, Guainía, Vaupés, and Vichada—are governed directly by representatives of the central government. The special district of Bogotá is an

Possible canal systems

The legislature

autonomous administrative entity within the Cundinamarca department.

The political process. The Colombian political process had its origins during the formation of the republic. For more than 100 years, the two largest political parties—the Liberals and the Conservatives—maintained a struggle for power. In 1958, in order to overthrow the dictatorship of Rojas Pinilla, the parties agreed upon a truce that was to continue for 16 years. According to the agreement, the two major parties—together known as the National Front—were to govern alternately for four-year periods and maintain political equality throughout the entire administration.

The National Front

Rule by the National Front was scheduled to end in 1974, at which time the country was expected to return to its traditional system of competition between political parties. Organizations outside the National Front included, in the early 1970s, the Communist, Socialist, Christian–Democratic, and National Popular Alliance parties.

The political participation of the citizens is exercised by means of free and democratic elections. All Colombians over 21 years of age may vote.

Justice. There are two court systems. The regular courts have jurisdiction over civil, penal, labour, customs, and court-martial matters. The administrative courts deal with cases involving private individuals and government agencies.

The Supreme Court of Justice is the highest tribunal and is endowed by the constitution with supreme power in jurisdictional matters. It is divided into various *salas*, or lesser courts, formed by several judges who interpret the law. The president of the Supreme Court is elected annually by and from the members of the court.

Local judicial districts

The country is divided into judicial districts, each containing a regular and an administrative court. The magistrates of the regular courts are named by the Supreme Court, and those of the administrative court are appointed by the Council of State.

The armed forces. Military service is compulsory for one year for all men between the ages of 18 and 30. The standing army consists of about 50,000 men stationed throughout the country in nine operational units. The navy consists of more than 8,000 men and a unit of 800 marines. The 6,000-man air force maintains nine scattered bases. There are also about 35,000 national police.

The social milieu. *Education, health, and welfare.* The educational system includes more than 3,000 kindergartens (preschool facilities) and about 30,000 primary schools; primary education is free but not compulsory. There are almost 3,000 secondary schools and other educational facilities that offer training in industry, domestic science, veterinary science, business, nursing, theology, and art. There are almost 300 teacher-training schools on the secondary level and about 200 night schools that offer courses in adult education. In the early 1970s, about 78 percent of the population was literate.

Institutions of higher learning

The majority of the country's 40 universities are located in the capital city. Public institutions of higher learning include the Universidad Nacional de Colombia, the Universidad Distrital "Francisco José de Caldas," the Fundación Universidad Central, and the Universidad Pedagógica Nacional Femenina—all of which are in Bogotá—as well as universities in such other major cities as Medellín, Barranquilla, Cartagena, Popayán, and Cali. Private universities in Bogotá include the Fundación Universidad de Bogotá, the Pontificia Universidad Javeriana, and the Universidad de los Andes.

The Ministry of Public Health seeks to arouse the interest of individual communities in seeking solutions to health problems through independent efforts. Projects include the construction of systems to supply drinking water; public education in the matters of basic sanitation, home maintenance, balanced diet, and personal cleanliness; and the control of industries and organizations the mode of operation of which might be hazardous to community health.

Health facilities

In the late 1960s, there was one hospital bed for every 420 persons and one doctor for every 2,194 persons. Almost three-fourths of the country's practicing physicians were concentrated in the capital cities of the various departments, serving less than one-third of the total population.

Working through the Ministry of Public Health, the government strives to maintain good health through the promotion of campaigns to prevent illness. Activities include maternal and infant hygiene programs; cleanup campaigns; programs against venereal disease, tuberculosis, and leprosy; and instruction in proper care of the teeth.

Welfare services date back to the 1930s. Social security programs include health and maternity benefits, workmen's compensation, and allowances for those unable to work.

The Housing Institute was established to direct the construction of adequate housing for the low-income population in both rural and urban areas.

Social conditions. The cost of living in Colombia has risen sharply since the mid-1950s. Between 1953 and 1960 it had jumped by 69 percent, and the rise continued into the 1970s. In 1970 the gross national product per capita was computed to equal U.S. $300.

Except for local areas such as the cities of Barranquilla, Cartagena, and Santa Marta, the coasts and lower river valleys are unhealthy and plagued by malaria and dysentery. The swamps of the Magdalena Valley provide vast breeding grounds for mosquitoes, and hookworm is common. The ports are generally free of yellow fever and similar diseases. Health conditions in general are poor; many health problems are caused by malnutrition.

Because of the country's geographic composition, local isolation is an important factor in Colombian life, and cultural particularism is highly developed. People are often known by the department in which they live, and Antioqueños, Santandereanos, Tolimenses, Nariñenses, Bogotanos, and Boyacanses are recognized by their dress, diet, and speech. The most important social group is that of the Antioqueños, who migrated from Antioquia southward along the Cordilleras Central and Occidental during the 19th century. Numbering almost 5,000,000, the Antioqueños grow about three-fourths of the nation's coffee crop and control much of Colombia's trade, banking, and industry.

CULTURAL LIFE AND INSTITUTIONS

Cultural origins. Before the time of the discovery of the New World in the 15th century, the various native Indian tribes of Colombia had achieved different levels of cultural development. Although all groups had some form of social organization and employed various techniques in pottery making, weaving, planting corn, and fishing, only such Andean tribes as the Chibchas, Quimbayas, Taironas, and Tumacos had made any progress in goldsmithing, sculpture, and ceramics. While groups of Caribbean origin were warlike and practiced ritual cannibalism, others from the interior possessed a rich mythology and a religion that upheld certain ethical standards and norms that were applied to questions of private ownership and the prevention of crime.

No group left any large architectural monuments—such as those erected by the Aztecs, Mayas, or Incas—because the population lived in widely dispersed, small settlements and had no important "urban" centres of either a civil or religious nature.

Heritage of the Andean Indians

The Andean Indians, particularly the Chibchas, practiced sedentary agriculture and were able to offer but small resistance to the Spanish invader. Instead, they became the great biological and cultural contributors to the process of racial amalgamation, or *mestizaje*. The low demographic density of the pre-Hispanic population, its swift destruction, and the relatively limited African immigration to Colombia led to the formation of a rather open society and to the substitution of Hispanic forms of culture for the indigenous. Since the 17th century the most widely used native language, Chibcha, has virtually disappeared, and the tribal religions have been almost completely replaced by Roman Catholicism.

Throughout its existence as a republic, Colombia has

continued to follow the educational policies established by Spain during the colonial period. It has attempted to raise the cultural level of the population and to enrich it with all the scientific and technical knowledge to be found in the most highly developed countries. Since colonial times, Bogotá—the Athens of South America— has been the nation's cultural centre, and most cultural institutions are located within the metropolitan area. Other cities of cultural importance include Cali, Medellín, and Manizales.

Cultural institutions. The history and culture of Colombia's indigenous peoples are revealed in several museums of outstanding reputation. The Museo del Oro of Bogotá contains a famous collection of goldwork, while the Museo de Arte Colonial de Bogotá has a rich collection of criollo (*e.g.*, by Spanish persons born in Colombia) religious sculpture and painting. The Museo Nacional displays treasures and relics dating from prehistoric times to the present and possesses various collections of Colombian painting and sculpture. The Museo 20 de Julio contains precious documents of the period of independence, and the National Mint displays a complete collection of national coins.

No less important vehicles for the diffusion of culture are the Biblioteca Nacional de Colombia (National Library), with 350,000 volumes, and the Biblioteca "Luis Angel Arango" del Banco de la República, which contains a vast amount of reading material, exposition and music halls, and a concert theatre.

Outside Bogotá there are other institutions of this kind, including the Museo Zea, in Medellín, and the Casa de Don Juan de Vargas (the House of Don Juan de Vargas), in Tunja.

The arts. The arts are fostered and developed by conservatories and schools that function in several cities either in connection with the universities or independently and by the growing number of concert halls and galleries. Persons of middle income levels display considerable curiosity and the desire to be informed about contemporary artistic developments, and this same eclectic spirit is found among the artists themselves. There is no distinct national school of art because of the cultural osmosis promoted by the speed of international communications.

Handicrafts suffered a decline during the colonial period as well as during the early years of the republic, but since the early 1930s have experienced a revival, especially in the production of textiles. There was also a revival in the manufacture of ceramics and pottery, chiefly in the municipalities of Ráquira, El Espinal, and Malambo. Basket weaving, harness making, passementerie (fancy edging or trimming on clothing or upholstery), and toy making are also popular crafts.

Popular traditions concerning manners and customs, music, legends, and food preparation continue in somewhat attenuated form in their places of origin. Perhaps the most deeply rooted folkloric form of expression is that of music. The tunes and melodies of the indigenous tribes are sung only in limited geographical areas. The music of the mestizo can be divided into that of the Andes, the plains, and the Llanura Atlántica and the Pacific coast. Some music forms of the colonial period also have survived.

Fairs. Since the 1960s regional fairs have been held in various parts of the country to celebrate occurrences of local importance. They are government subsidized and, with the additional stimulus afforded by modern means of communication, have done a great deal to promote and preserve popular tunes and dances and the costumes worn while they are being performed.

The mass media. The Colombian defends vigorously all the means of expression, particularly that of the written word. Since the early days of the republic, the national press has been known for its honesty, its zealous defense of civil rights, and its correct and elegant style of writing. The nation's leading daily newspaper is *El Tiempo*, published in Bogotá. Other important dailies from the capital include *El Espectador*, *El Siglo*, and *La República*. Regional dailies of importance are *El Colom-*

biano, of Medellín; *El País*, of Cali; and *El Heraldo*, of Barranquilla.

Radio and television exert a powerful cultural influence throughout the nation. Several of the 300 Colombian radio stations are well-known for their consistent efforts to raise the cultural level of their listeners. Radio Sutatenza in Boyacá department is internationally known for its programs aimed at the eradication of illiteracy among the rural population. The network of Radio Cadena Nacional supplies its affiliates with documentaries and newscasts. Other stations in towns throughout the country include La Voz del Río Cauca, La Voz del Tolima, and La Voz de Antioquia.

Television channels are government owned but are generally leased to private individuals who direct their programming. The government reserves a certain amount of time for its programs dealing with its projects and accomplishments. There is also a channel devoted to a program of adult education that complements the educational programs of Radio Sutatenza.

PROSPECTS FOR THE FUTURE

In an economy like that of Colombia, necessary social change cannot be effected solely by the redistribution of national income. It can only be achieved by correcting the causes of low productivity, such as poor health and generally inadequate technical preparation. The introduction of profit sharing and the provision of new sources of capital are other means that the government intends to use in the abolition of great economic inequalities.

It is impossible to speak of equality of opportunity while a considerable number of the people are still not reached by preventive medicine and have no access at reasonable cost to medical and hospital services. In the early 1970s the government was actively involved in effecting plans to remedy this situation. Much must be done, however, before such plans can operate efficiently. More doctors must be educated and more auxiliary personnel trained; more hospitals must be built and equipped; and health clinics must be set up in the rural areas.

The new forms of social capitalization that the country wished to create in the early 1970s were to be based on the accumulation of capital by cooperatives, savings and loan associations, and savings banks as well as labour unions and special foundations.

BIBLIOGRAPHY. WILLIAM F. JENKS (ed.), *Handbook of South American Geology* (1956), technical information on the physical features of the continent, including those in Colombia; FRED A. CARLSON, *Geography of Latin America*, 3rd ed. (1952), a general guide to the South American countries; PRESTON E. JAMES, *Latin America*, 4th ed. (1969), standard geographic textbook; ERNESTO GUHL, *Colombia* (1967); MANUEL JOSE FORERO, *Reseña histórica de la geografía de Colombia* (1969); and INSTITUTO GEOGRAFICO AGUSTIN CODAZZI, *Atlas de Colombia*, 2nd ed. (1969), three general texts (in Spanish); ROBERT C. WEST, *The Pacific Lowlands of Colombia* (1957), a physical, historical, and human geography of northwestern Colombia; ORLANDO FALS-BORDA, *Peasant Society in the Colombian Andes* (1955), a highly recommended work on social organization, culture, and ecology; BURTON L. GORDON, *Human Geography and Ecology in the Sinú Country of Colombia* (1957), a regional study of northern Colombia; JAMES J. PARSONS, *Antioqueño Colonization in Western Colombia*, rev. ed. (1968), a regional analysis; INTERNATIONAL BANK FOR RECONSTRUCTION AND DEVELOPMENT, *The Basis of a Development Program for Colombia* (1950), a dated but basically sound treatment of Colombia's economy; WILLIAM M. GIBSON (ed.), *The Constitutions of Colombia* (1948), a general account of the country's government; JOHN J. JOHNSON, *Political Change in Latin America* (1958), a major work on the economic, political, and social changes in some countries, including Colombia; JORGE ARANGO and CARLOS MARTINEZ, *Arquitectura en Colombia* (1951), a fine text in Spanish, English, and French; see also the publications of the Departamento Administrativo Nacional de Estadística, the Banco de la República, and the Sociedad Geográfica de Colombia.

(C.Ga.)

Colombia, History of

The national history of what is now Colombia began in 1819, when the area was liberated after more than 300

Major museums and libraries

Colombian handicrafts

years of Spanish rule. Before independence, Colombia had been part of the *audiencia* of Santa Fe de Bogotá from 1550 to 1740, and then of the viceroyalty of New Granada; for that period see LATIN AMERICA AND THE CARIBBEAN, COLONIAL.

Colombia to 1930. The independence of Colombia was established at the Battle of Boyacá (Aug. 7, 1819) shortly after the South American liberator Simón Bolívar completed his successful march across the Andes and into the eastern highlands north of Bogotá, where his 3,000 insurgents defeated a larger force of Spanish regulars. The fighting continued in the South, however, until the final defeat of the Spaniards at the Battle of Ayacucho in 1824.

The establishment of the nation. The first decade of independence saw the political breakdown of Gran Colombia—a union of what became the now-individual nations of Ecuador, Colombia, Panama, and Venezuela. Venezuela withdrew from the union in 1829, and Ecuador in 1830. Nueva Granada, as Colombia was then called, a country of 1,500,000 inhabitants in 1835, was left on its own (Colombia continued to exercise control over Panama until 1903).

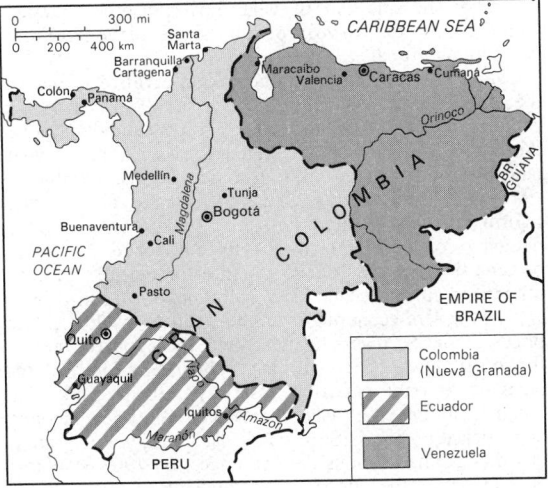

Adapted from D. Worcester and W. Schaeffer; *The Growth and Culture of Latin America*, vol. 1, 2nd ed.; Oxford University Press, Inc.; New York (1970)

The division of Gran Colombia (1830).

Revolution and violence, 1840–1903

Francisco de Paula Santander, who was a general, vice president under Bolívar, and then leader of the opposition to Bolívar's imperial ambitions in 1828, held the presidency from 1832 until 1837 and was the dominant political figure of that era. The 1830s brought some prosperity to the new nation, but a civil war that broke out in 1840 ended a nascent industrial development, disrupted trade, and discouraged local enterprise. The seeds of political rivalry between liberals and conservatives had already been sown, and they bore fruit in the bloody revolution and costly violence that ravaged the country in the years between 1840 and 1903. It has been estimated that more than 130,000 deaths can be attributed to the civil wars of that period.

Conservative–Liberal struggle (1840–80). Colombia's modern political history began in the late 1840s with the delineation of the Liberal and Conservative parties. Gen. Tomás Cipriano de Mosquera, a Conservative, during his first term as president (1845–49), replaced the government monopoly on tobacco sales with a private monopoly and expanded international trade. These changes increased the production and export of tobacco but reduced the tax income of the national government, which had received more than a third of its revenue from the tobacco monopoly.

In 1849 Gen. José Hilario López, of the radical faction of the Liberal Party, became president. It later became his task to implement the reforms passed in 1850, which were to galvanize political sentiment and divide the country politically and economically for half a century. The guiding principle of the radical Liberals under General López was greater liberty for the people of Colombia. His government ended slavery, ended communal ownership of Indian lands in favour of simple tenure for individual members of Indian communities, diverted tax resources from the central to local governments, and eliminated a number of specific taxes and monopolies held exclusively by the central government.

Rather than eliminating the institutional barriers to self-fulfillment by the people, however, the reforms of 1850 tended to eliminate the traditional proscriptions that had stood as safeguards against the exploitation of the poor by the rich. The reforms, despite the liberal rhetoric that accompanied them, legalized, indeed encouraged, a redistribution of landed property and tended to strengthen the position of the wealthy landowners, merchants, and professionals against the mass of poor Indians, peasants, and artisans. Since there were only 25,000 slaves (in a country of 2,000,000 in 1851), the effects of manumission were small compared to those of the breakdown of the Indian communal system, which affected a third of the population. The Indians were induced to give up their little plots of land and the small amount of independence they enjoyed. Within a few years the ownership of Indian lands was concentrated in a few hands; the Indian had become a tenant, his land used for grazing cattle.

But while class conflict seethed under the surface in Colombian society, the struggle between members and groups within the elite was more open. Two issues in particular divided the upper class: first, whether a centralist or federalist political system would be the best arrangement for Colombia, and second, what role was appropriate for the Roman Catholic Church and particularly for its clerics in Colombian society. Adherents of federalism were strongest in the years between 1863 and 1880, during which years the country was called the United States of Colombia. Subsequent government publications were to refer to that period as the "Epoch of Civil Wars." In 51 of the 240 months that passed in the 1860s and '70s, there was some form of civil conflict taking place within the country. The size of the Colombian army was fixed at a figure that was so low that public order could not be maintained by the central government.

The power of the anticlerical faction reached a peak in the early 1860s. A revolutionary government headed by Mosquera expropriated church lands in 1861, and a constitution adopted in 1863 guaranteed freedom of religious practice, thus bringing to an end the traditional intimate relationship between church and state in Colombia.

The return of the Conservatives (1880–1930). Both actions were reversed during the period of Regeneration (1880–95) under Rafael Núñez, and the Conservatives who followed him. After further civil conflict in the 1880s Núñez was able to promulgate a new constitution in 1886 (which still remained in force in the 1970s), to re-establish relations with the Vatican via the Concordat of 1887, and to promote some internal improvements and industrial development.

But the political struggle between Liberals and Conservatives was far from over. Armed conflict reached its peak in the War of a Thousand Days (1899–1903). The estimates of the number of deaths in that struggle range from 60,000 to 130,000.

The tragedy of civil war was followed by the loss of Panama. The Colombian Congress vacillated too long in considering a United States offer to build a canal across the isthmus and in 1903 the Panamanians revolted against the government in Bogotá and arranged for a treaty agreement providing for United States sovereignty in the ten-mile-wide Canal Zone in exchange for United States agreement to build the canal and to provide a regular annual payment to Panama. Although the United States government later agreed to pay $25,000,000 to Colombia, it never admitted any direct United States role in the Panamanian secession. The episode embittered Colombian–United States relations for many years (see further CENTRAL AMERICAN STATES, HISTORY OF; PANAMA CANAL).

Colombia's
internal
develop-
ment

Colombia's internal development quickened after 1905, with coffee exports expanding by nearly 10 percent per year between 1909 and 1928. At the beginning of the 20th century Colombia supplied about 3 percent of world coffee exports; by 1923 its share had risen to nearly 10 percent. In the late 1920s coffee accounted for some 18 percent of the gross domestic product—a larger amount than manufacturing, government services, or transportation.

Colombia since 1930. The new dependence on exports was not without its pitfalls. In the late 1920s coffee, petroleum, and bananas accounted, respectively, for 69, 17, and 6 percent of total Colombian exports, and all three dropped precipitously in value during the Great Depression. This economic collapse had an immediate political result; the Conservatives were ousted from the presidency by Enrique Olaya Herrera (who served 1930–34).

The era of the Liberals (1930–46). During the presidency of Alfonso López, from 1934 to 1938, a series of reforms, called the "Revolution on the March," was instituted. The most important social act of the López regime established effective occupancy as the legal basis for tenure (1936), thus upholding the rights of thousands of peasant squatters against the claims of landowners who had been holding land without using it in any productive way. In the coffee growing zone of Cundinamarca, west of Bogotá, thousands of landless families obtained recognition of their ownership by occupation. Subsequent governments took a more conservative stance toward the question of land rights of the poor, but in 1961 continuing social pressure finally resulted in passage of legislation to create the Instituto Colombiano de Reforma Agraria (Colombian Institute of Agrarian Reform). By the mid-1970s, more than 135,000 land titles had been distributed by the Institute in programs that foresaw the eventual distribution of almost 19,000,000 acres.

Rapid industrial development started in the 1930s. Medellín became the principal producer of cotton textiles and other fabrics. The limited availability of imports because of the Depression enabled local manufacturing to get its start. The tendency toward substitution of home products for imports continued into the 1950s and 1960s, until Colombia became practically self-sufficient in production of consumer nondurables. By the late 1970s, however, manufacturing still accounted for the same one-fifth of the gross domestic product that it had in the early 1960s, although this was being achieved by a smaller proportion (only about 11 percent) of the labour force.

Civil unrest, dictatorship, and democratic restoration (1946–70). Liberal hegemony continued through the 1930s and the World War II era. In the elections of 1946, however, two Liberal candidates, Gabriel Turbay and Jorge Eliécer Gaitán, stood for election and thus split the Liberal vote. A Conservative, Mariano Ospina Pérez, took office, and Conservatives instituted crude reprisals against Liberals. On April 9, 1948, Jorge Eliécer Gaitán, leader of the left wing of the Liberal Party, was assassinated in broad daylight in downtown Bogotá. The resulting riot and property damage (estimated at $171,000,000 in Bogotá alone and at a total of $570,000,000 for the country as a whole) has come to be called the *bogotazo.*

There is disagreement on whether the acts of violence began in 1930 when the Liberals came to power, in 1946 with the Conservatives, or in 1948 with the death of Gaitán. There is agreement that they sprang from a political feud between Liberals and Conservatives that had little to do with class conflict, foreign ideologies, or other matters extraneous to the Colombian scene. Authoritative sources estimate that some 200,000 persons lost their lives in the *violencia* between 1948 and 1962; in 1955 financial losses equalled the government budget for the entire year. The most spectacular aspect of the violence, however, was the extremes of cruelty perpetrated on the victims. The rage and aggressive force unleashed by that political conflict has been a continuing problem of study for Colombians.

The *violencia* intensified under the regime of Laureano

The
bogotazo

Gómez (1950–53), who attempted to introduce a fascist state. His excesses brought his downfall by military coup —Colombia's first in the 20th century. Gen. Gustavo Rojas Pinilla assumed the presidency in 1953 and, aided by his daughter, María Eugenia Rojas, began an effort to end the *violencia* and to stimulate the economy. Rojas was a populist leader who appealed to the masses and supported their call for the redress of grievances against the elite. Support for Rojas began to collapse when it appeared that he would not be able to fulfill his promises and when the economy faltered as a result of a disastrous fall in coffee prices in 1957. Rojas was driven from office in 1957 by a military junta that guaranteed free elections the following year.

The arrangement for the National Front (Frente Nacional) government—a coalition of Conservatives and Liberals—was made by Alberto Lleras Camargo, representing the Liberals, and Laureano Gómez, leader of the Conservative Party, in the Declaration of Sitges (1957). The unique agreement provided for alternation of Conservatives and Liberals in the presidency, an equitable sharing of ministerial and other governmental posts, and equal representation on all executive and legislative bodies. The agreement was to remain in force for 16 years—equivalent to four presidential terms, two each for Conservatives and Liberals. The question of what governmental structure would follow the 16-year period of the National Front was left unsettled.

The
National
Front

It had been contemplated that a Conservative would be the first to occupy the presidency in 1958. When the Conservative Party could not agree on a candidate, however, the National Front selected Lleras Camargo, who had previously served in that office for 12 months in 1945–46. During Lleras Camargo's tenure an agrarian reform law was brought into effect, national economic planning for development got its start, and Colombia became the showcase of the Alliance for Progress (a U.S. attempt to further economic development in Latin America). But severe economic difficulties caused by low coffee prices, domestic unemployment, and the apparent end of the possibilities of substituting industrialization for imports were only partially offset by Alliance aid. The Alliance, in any case, only increased Colombia's economic dependence on the U.S., a condition that some Colombians thought had serious disadvantages. By 1962 economic growth had come almost to a standstill.

The precarious state of the economy and the degree of social tension were revealed when only about half of those eligible to vote did so in the 1962 presidential elections, which brought Guillermo León Valencia, a Conservative, to the presidency. During Valencia's first year in office internal political pressures led to devaluation of the peso, wage increases among unionized workers of some 40 percent, and the most rampant inflation since 1905. Extreme deflationary policies were applied in the next three years, raising the unemployment rates above 10 percent in the major cities and turning even more Colombians against the National Front. Less than 40 percent of the voters went to the polls in the 1964 congressional elections.

Carlos Lleras Restrepo was the third National Front president (1966–70). He was able to return the economy to a sound footing, to improve government planning for economic development, and to push through political reforms essential to an orderly end to the National Front (which seemed increasingly to constitute a monopoly of power by the Liberal–Conservative oligarchy). Semiautonomous government corporations expanded their services to the private sector: the capital and reserves of the Instituto de Fomento Industrial (Institute of Industrial Development), for example, were increased from 6,600,000 pesos in 1967 to some 77,000,000 pesos in 1969. Colombia achieved its best rate of economic growth near the end of the Lleras administration, when the real gross domestic product increased by some 6.9 percent. These successes were in part due to the fortuitous circumstance of high coffee prices, but effective government policy was of undeniable importance.

Govern-
ment of
Lleras
Restrepo

The 1970s. In the 1970 presidential election, Misael

Pastrana Borrero, the Conservative candidate backed by the National Front, nearly lost to former dictator Gustavo Rojas Pinilla because the urban vote went strongly against the Front. (The 1964 census had shown that Colombia for the first time had a population that was more than 50 percent urban. A rapid migration from country to city created in the late 1950s, '60s, and '70s new urban interest groups—particularly in the lower middle and working classes—that felt unrepresented by the traditional parties.) The large turnout for Rojas represented a vote against the National Front. Nonetheless, the traditional parties prevailed and were not again successfully challenged in the 1970s.

The process of change brought with it new political, economic, and social problems in the 1970s. In all three areas of national concern, the problems stemmed from uneven development, unequal gains, and a growing perception that the benefits of higher income on average were not widely shared. The transition from National Front to moderate political competition between Liberals and Conservatives in 1974 was reasonably smooth. Alfonso López Michelsen of the Liberal Party served his four-year term as president (1974–78) and handed power to Julio César Turbay Ayala, a centrist Liberal. Low rates of voter participation continued, keeping alive fears that military alternatives to democratic elections might be sought from the right or the left.

Return to political competition

The revolution in commodity prices and worldwide inflation had their effect on Colombia. After another severe Brazilian frost in 1975 destroyed that nation's coffee crop, Colombian exporters earned the highest prices ever for their coffee, and a new and endemic inflation, at rates above 20 percent per annum, occurred during three of the following four years. The real per capita national product grew between 3 and 4 percent annually, and the gradual shift from a rural, agricultural economy to an urban, industrial one continued. Manufactured exports in 1976 were almost 23 times greater in value than those of 1963, much of that growth attributable to opportunities for trade within the Andean Pact trade group of Bolivia, Chile, Colombia, Ecuador, and Peru. Colombia continued to receive foreign economic assistance throughout the 1970s, but the economy was insufficiently vigorous to draw a significant increase in private investment.

Demographic changes

Perhaps the most impressive social phenomenon of the 1970s was the rapid decline in the rate of population growth, unmatched by many other countries of a comparable level of development. The number of births per thousand population declined from 46 in 1960 to 30 in 1977. The population continued to grow, however, reaching more than 26,000,000 in 1979.

Migration out of the rural areas continued to fuel the rapid growth of large cities. The share of total population in urban areas grew from 48 percent in 1960 to 66 percent by 1975. The Special District of Bogotá was home to 17 percent of all Colombians in 1960 and to more than 25 percent of them in 1980. Educational attainment also expanded: the percentage of students enrolled in higher education quadrupled between 1960 and 1975.

The sum of two decades of change after the disturbances of the *violencia* was a more modern, urbanized, and educated populace than Colombia had previously experienced. The remaining problem of dualism—the perpetuation of absolute poverty for a quarter of the population in the midst of economic growth—was brought into relief by the title of the government's 1975–78 development plan, *Para cerrar la brecha* ("To Close the Gap"). An elaborate plan for food production and child nutrition was also addressed to that problem. Many, perhaps too many, however, were still left behind in the long process of economic and social change.

BIBLIOGRAPHY. ACADEMIA COLOMBIANA DE HISTORIA, *Historia extensa de Colombia* (1964–   ), a multivolume work covering all facets of Colombian history from precolonial to contemporary times—useful to the specialist; ALBERT BERRY and MIGUEL URRUTIA, *Income Distribution in Colombia* (1976), a survey of economic and social change; A. BERRY, R.G. HELLMAN, and M. SOLAUN, ed., *Politics of Compromise: Coalition Government in Colombia* (1979), reviews political, economic, and social aspects of the National Front (1958–74); GABRIEL GARCIA MARQUEZ, *Cien años de soledad* (1967; *One Hundred Years of Solitude*, 1970), provides a fictionalized account of Colombian history in the 20th century that makes excellent reading; CHARLES W. BERGQUIST, *Coffee and Conflict in Colombia, 1886–1910* (1978), covers the critical period from the end of the Regeneration to the start of the coffee boom; W.P. MCGREEVEY, *An Economic History of Colombia, 1845–1930* (1971), surveys economic development and foreign trade; MARCO PALACIOS, *El Cafe en Colombia (1850–1970)* (1979; *Coffee in Colombia: Eighteen Fifty to Nineteen Seventy*, 1980), reviews the role of coffee production and export; J.J. PARSONS, *Antioqueño Colonization in Western Colombia*, rev. ed. (1968), an excellent study of the most progressive region of Colombia to 1968.

(W.P.McG.)

Colombo

Colombo, the capital of Sri Lanka (formerly Ceylon), is the centre of the largest urban concentration in the island republic. It is the seat of government and the country's main financial and commercial centre. With one of the largest artificial harbours in the world, it is a principal port of the Indian Ocean, in which it occupies a central position. The city had a population of more than 600,000 in the late 1970s and the larger urban area had about 1,000,000 inhabitants.

Colombo is situated on the west coast of the island. The Kelani River, which has its source in the Adams Peak area of mountains less than 50 miles inland, forms the city's northern boundary. In earlier times, Arab, Persian, and Chinese sailing ships, finding that the area offered a fairly safe anchorage because of a bend in the coast just south of the river's mouth in the vicinity of the cinnamon-producing district, used it as a seaport. The modern city, which covers an area of about 14.4 square miles (37.3 square kilometres), has a seafront about ten miles (16 kilometres) long, the greater part of which is served by a railroad running to the south. An old Dutch canal forms the southern boundary, but it has not interrupted development along the coastal road and railroad to the south, which now links a series of suburban towns. Marshes and swamps on the eastern (landward) side formerly hindered expansion in that direction. In the last few decades, however, much of this swampy land has been reclaimed for building purposes.

Colombo appears to have been founded as a permanent settlement some time during the 8th century AD, when Arab traders settled near the site of the modern port and, with the permission of the Sinhalese king of the region, built themselves warehouses and dwellings. From the 16th century onward, the port was developed by the Portuguese, Dutch, and British, who, each in turn, established themselves on the island. Although Western influence has sharply diminished since Sri Lanka gained political independence in 1948, the contemporary city is largely the product of the 150 years of British occupation, bearing only a few traces of the earlier Portuguese and Dutch periods.

Founding in the 8th century

The Portuguese were the first Western power to call the city Colombo, though they did not coin the name. The earliest written mention of the port may be that of Fa-hsien, a Chinese traveller of the 5th century AD, who referred to the port as Kao-lan-pu. Another Chinese writer, Wang Ta-yuan, in 1330 described Kao-lan-pu as "a deep, low-lying land, the soil poor, rice and corn very dear, and the climate hot." Ibn Baṭṭūṭah, the renowned Arab traveller, described how, in 1344, he "took the route for the town of Calembou, one of the largest and most beautiful in the island of Serendib." The Sinhalese called the port Kolamba. The Portuguese thought the name was derived from the Sinhalese word for mango trees (*kola*, "leaves"; *amba*, "mango"). A more likely explanation is that *kolamba* was an old Sinhalese word meaning "port" or "ferry." Whatever the derivation may have been, the Portuguese were not displeased that, by coincidence, the name of their new possession resembled that of Cristoforo Colombo (Columbus), the discoverer of the New World.

History. The first Portuguese commander to put into Colombo was Dom Lourenço de Almeida, son of the viceroy of Goa. He had set out from the Portuguese-held port of Cochin on the Indian coast hoping to intercept Muslim ships bound for Mecca, but his fleet was caught in a storm and driven to the coast of Ceylon. As Colombo came into view, the Portuguese saw fishing craft as well as sailing ships loading cinnamon and elephants. They anchored outside the small port on November 15, 1505, causing, according to the Portuguese writer De Queroz (1688), "As much astonishment to the natives as grief to the Moors [Arabs]." Dom Lourenço set up a stone marker, carved with the arms of Portugal, which has been preserved.

The Arabs until then had enjoyed a virtual monopoly of the foreign trade of Ceylon. When negotiations began between the Sinhalese king and the Portuguese, the Arabs became alarmed and warned the King that the arrival of the Portuguese constituted a threat to the national religion. The Portuguese, nevertheless, sent emissaries to the ruler, whose capital was at Kotte, a few miles away, and obtained permission to build a "factory" (trading post) on the narrow end of the harbour point that now forms the foot of the breakwater. The Portuguese were under constant attack during the ensuing years by the Arabs, the Sinhalese, and, on occasion, by rival claimants to the throne.

The Portuguese period

In 1551 a young prince named Dharmapala was acclaimed king of Kotte. When the Portuguese viceroy in Goa, the principal Portuguese base in the Indian Ocean, heard of this, he hastened to Colombo and, taking advantage of disunity among the Sinhalese, attacked Kotte and made a vassal of Dharmapala, who was then baptized a Christian and given the name Don Juan. His capital was moved from Kotte to Colombo. Don Juan lived for another 46 years, during which time the real ruler in Colombo was the Portuguese captain general. Don Juan was childless and bequeathed his dominions and the overlordship of Ceylon to the King of Portugal. "Colombo, from being a small stockade of wood, grew to be a gallant city," wrote the Portuguese historian Captain João Ribeiro. The Dutch, however, laid siege to Colombo, which they captured with the help of the king of the central part of the island.

They then ruled Colombo and other parts of maritime Ceylon from 1658 to 1796, in which year all the Dutch settlements passed to the British with little resistance. It was not, however, until 1815, when the Sinhalese chiefs deposed the King of Kandy in the heart of Ceylon and ceded his territory to the British, that Colombo became the capital of the island.

The oldest districts of the city, which are nearest to the harbour, are known as the Fort and the Pettah (a name deriving from the Tamil word *pettai*, meaning the town outside the fort). In the early years of British rule the Fort was occupied chiefly by government officials and the garrison. The European and Eurasian survivors of the Dutch and Portuguese periods lived in the Pettah, then a residential area. The Fort is still a focal point of government and commerce, although less so than in the past. The Pettah has long since ceased to be a residential area, having become a district of small shops, markets, and pavement stalls, with all the characteristic features of an oriental bazaar.

The contemporary city. The modern city covers an area of more than 9,200 acres (37 square kilometres), including a built-up area of about 6,000 acres (24 square kilometres), a lake of about 200 acres (0.8 square kilometre), about 200 acres (0.8 square kilometre) of public parks, and marshy and open land of about 1,000 acres (4 square kilometres). Most of the surface is between 10 and 40 feet (3 and 12 metres) above sea level, with less than 150 acres (0.6 square kilometre) above 50 feet (15 metres). The lake, popularly known as the Beira, was created by the Portuguese, who dammed a rivulet that flowed through the marshes. It is now primarily a commercial annex to the port.

The earliest street planning began with the clearly defined gridiron or checkerboard system used in the street plans of the Fort and Pettah districts. The residential areas, such as Cinnamon Gardens, where cinnamon was grown during the Dutch period, were laid out on generous lines. Lack of control over building has, however, robbed Colombo of its former reputation as a garden city. Many of the larger houses have gardens, but these are becoming fewer and smaller. Such houses have a great variety of flowers, including roses, bougainvillea, jasmine, frangipanni, and multicoloured creepers. On the sides of the roads are many flowering trees, while the spreading branches of the banyan, peepul (a tree resembling the banyan), and rain trees offer shade from the tropical sun. Many home gardens have some fruit trees, including the mango, papaya, sapodilla plum, and golden king-coconut trees.

Gardens and streets

The basic street plan consists of a framework of main roads radiating from the central business district and connecting it to the major provincial towns. These roads are intercepted by a series of lateral roads along which the residential areas have grown, stretching out to the suburbs. Only a few of the substantially built villas, with gardens dating from the early British period, are left. Many gardens are giving way to smaller building lots. Multistoried apartment buildings, although seldom of more than three floors, are appearing in the more expensive residential areas.

The average height of buildings in the Fort is about 60 or 70 feet (18 or 21 metres). Among the more conspicuous are the bank buildings, Ceylinco House, the new Secretariat, the General Post Office, and the Hotel Taprobane. Elsewhere a low profile may be seen, but the Houses of Parliament, the old Secretariat, the Town Hall, the offices of the British High Commission, the dome of St. Lucia's Cathedral, the Supreme Court with its doric columns on a hill, and the Galle Face Hotel contribute to the skyline. Other distinctive buildings in the city are the Wolvendahl Church, built by the Dutch in 1749; the complex of hospitals; the university; several Buddhist and Hindu temples; and the residences of the head of state and of the prime minister.

The climate is warm and humid for the greater part of the year. The mean temperature is 80° F (27° C) and the mean rainfall 91 inches (2,300 millimetres). Toward the end of the year, temperatures in the 60s are not unusual. With most of the amenities of a modern city, such as an adequate water supply and drainage, Colombo has a good health record. It is free from cholera, smallpox, yellow fever, and the plague; malaria is rare nowadays, and filaria (a parasitic disease) is under control. The Colombo Municipal Council maintains 21 free dispensaries, a dental clinic, and an eye clinic. There are also 21 dispensaries of the Ayurvedic (ancient Hindu) system of medicine. There is also a comprehensive hospital system. Colombo General Hospital, for example, has in its wards an average of 3,000 patients a day. There are several specialized hospitals and nursing homes.

Population. There are reliable records of the population of Colombo since early British times. The rate of growth may be judged from the following figures: 26,000 in 1816; 96,000 in 1871; 155,000 in 1901; 244,000 in 1921; 362,000 in 1946; 426,000 in 1953; 512,000 in 1963; 562,000 in 1971. The density of population is about 37,500 per square mile. In recent years the population of the suburbs has grown at a much faster rate than that of the city. The Colombo district, which has a radius of about 20 miles (32 kilometres) on the land side of the city and which includes several small towns, has a population of over 2,600,000. The Sinhalese, who form nearly three-fourths of the population of Sri Lanka, comprise a little more than half of the resident population of Colombo. The Ceylon Tamils are next with 18.3 percent, followed by the Ceylon Moors with 18.2 percent. Indians of various communities make up about 7 percent. Less in number are the Burghers and the Eurasians (who are in part descendants of the European residents of the colonial period), Malays, and the European community (now numbering barely a thousand). Among the religious groups, the Buddhists number over 240,000, the Muslims over 120,000, the Christians about 90,000, and the Hindus over 90,000.

The Sinhalese majority

Administration. Colombo has a municipal council of 47 members, each representing a ward, and a mayor elected by the council from among its members. The mayor is assisted in his executive functions by a commissioner appointed by a Local Government Services Commission. The main divisions of the administration are those of the secretary, treasurer, chief medical officer of health, municipal engineer, waterworks engineer, chief veterinary surgeon, charity commissioner, municipal assessor, and chief officer of the fire brigade and ambulance department.

Economy. Historically, the economy of Colombo has been formed of industries and services concerned with the operation of the port, which became the gateway to the island's commerce after the opening of the Suez Canal in the 19th century. Today manufacturing industries deal with the processing of raw materials exported through the port; general engineering industries are connected with public utilities and with the sales, service, repair, and assembly of motor vehicles and other machinery; and light manufacturing industries process food, drinks, and tobacco. The present trend is for manufacturing industries to move out of the city. Factories for the manufacture of textiles, shoes, shirts, biscuits, confectionery, pharmaceuticals, radios, sewing machines, soap, asbestos products, desiccated coconut and coconut oil, plastic goods, hardware, and ceramics have sprung up on the city's periphery. Meanwhile, Colombo's position as the commercial centre of the island has not changed since independence. The head offices of local and foreign banks, the Insurance Corporation (which has a monopoly of insurance), the brokerage houses, and the government corporations are all to be found here.

The suburbs. The high price of land in the city, together with the shortage of housing, has given an impetus to the development of the suburbs, both for industrial and residential purposes. A blight caused by the erection of shanties and hovels, as well as of insanitary tenements and slums, however, has accompanied this development. Suburban expansion is due not only to the growth of population, but also to a continuous influx from outside. Middle class families find it advantageous to move out to more open country where small gardens are still to be had and where electricity and running water are increasingly available. Development is taking place along the main roads, such as the Galle Road, the Negombo Road, the Kandy Road, and the High Level Road. The oldest of the suburbs is Mount Lavinia, seven and a half miles from the Fort, which has an excellent bathing beach, a hotel first built as a governor's residence, a railway station, and good schools. Kotte, six miles from the Fort, the original capital of the Sinhalese king of the region, is now almost part of Colombo, although it has its own municipal council. Negombo in the north is fast developing as a tourist centre, with modern hotels. On a fork from the Kandy Road is Kelani Buddhist Temple, on the banks of the Kelani River. One of the most famous temples in Sri Lanka, it was rebuilt in 1310.

Transport. Train services connect Colombo with the nine provinces of the island. There are bus services within the city as well as with all parts of the island. Motor traffic on the roads is relatively heavy, and at peak hours the public transport system is heavily strained. Trucks and vans have largely displaced bullock carts for the transport of goods. Horse-drawn carriages have disappeared from the roads, and the rickshaw—a familiar mode of locomotion in the past—is as rare as the horse.

Colombo is served by two airports—the modern international airport at Katunayaka, 23 miles (37 kilometres) from Colombo and 3 miles (5 kilometres) from Negombo, and the Ratmalana Airport, 9 miles (14 kilometres) from Colombo and 2 miles (3 kilometres) from Mount Lavinia. There are internal air services from Ratmalana.

Education and culture. Colombo University offers courses in the arts and sciences, medicine, law, and architecture. In the academic year 1970–71 there were 3,600 students. Its medical school, which was founded long before the university, recently celebrated its centenary. A few of the secondary schools in Colombo were started early in the last century, using English as the medium of instruction. The state, which provides free education from kindergarten to university, has absorbed most private schools. With a few exceptions, teaching in school is in Sinhalese and Tamil.

The daily press and the radio use Sinhalese, Tamil, and English. All newspapers of any importance are published in Colombo and are distributed throughout the island. Two of the English language newspapers are over 100 years old.

Recreation. Colombo is well served with parks and playing fields, although their geographical distribution is somewhat uneven. Among them are the Galle Face Green by the sea, Vihara Maha Devi Park, and the Golf Links. There are also various cricket and football grounds scattered through the city and various semipublic or private open spaces. Horse racing was abolished some years ago. A large stadium has been constructed in north Colombo for track events. The popular field sports are football (soccer and rugby), cricket, tennis, and track and field. Sea bathing and surf-riding can be enjoyed at Mount Lavinia Beach. Near the southern boundary of the city is the Dehiwala Zoo, with about 40 acres of landscaped ground.

BIBLIOGRAPHY

History: H.W. CODRINGTON, *A Short History of Ceylon* (1939); DONALD FERGUSON, "The Discovery of Ceylon by the Portuguese," *J. R. Asiat. Soc. (Ceylon),* 19:284–385 (1907); J. RIBEIRO, *Ceilão,* Eng. trans. by SIR PAUL PIERIS, *Ceylon: The Portuguese Era,* 2 vol. (1913); PHILLIPUS BALDAEUS, *Ceylon,* first pub. in 1672, trans. by PETER BROHIER (1959); *Travels of Ibn Batuta,* trans. by SIR ALBERT GRAY in *J. R. Asiat. Soc. (Ceylon),* special vol. (1883); SIR JAMES EMERSON TENNENT, *Ceylon,* 2 vol. (1860); C.M. FERNANDO, "History of Ceylon," in *Twentieth Century Impressions of Ceylon* (1907).

Geography: B.L. PANDITARATNA, "The Colombo Townscape: Some Aspects of its Morphology," *Univ. Ceylon Rev.,* vol. 19 (April 1961), "The Functional Zones of the Colombo City," *ibid.* (Oct. 1961); E.K. COOK, *A Geography of Ceylon* (1931).

Statistics: Statistical Pocket Book of Ceylon (1969), pub. by the DEPARTMENT OF CENSUS AND STATISTICS, COLOMBO; and the Administration Reports of the Mayor of Colombo.

(H.A.J.H.)

Colonialism

The age of modern colonialism began about 1500, following the European discoveries of a sea route around Africa's southern coast (1488) and of America (1492). With these events sea power shifted from the Mediterranean to the Atlantic and to the emerging nation-states of Portugal, Spain, the Low Countries, France, and England. By discovery, conquest, and settlement, these nations expanded and colonized throughout the world, spreading European institutions and culture.

This article is divided into the following sections:

I. European expansion, 1450–1763

ANTECEDENTS OF EUROPEAN EXPANSION

Early communications with the Near East

Medieval Europe was largely self-contained until the First Crusade (1096–99), which opened new political and commercial communications with the Muslim Near East. Although Christian crusading states founded in Palestine and Syria proved ephemeral, commercial relations continued, and the European end of this trade fell largely into the hands of Italian cities.

Early European trade with Asia. The Oriental land and sea routes terminated at ports in the Crimea, until 1461 at Trebizond (now Trabzon, Turkey), Constantinople (now Istanbul), Asiatic Tripoli (in modern Lebanon), Antioch (in modern Turkey), Beirut (in modern Lebanon), and Alexandria (Egypt), where Italian galleys exchanged European for Eastern products.

Competition for Mediterranean control of Asiatic commerce gradually narrowed to a contest between Venice and Genoa, with the former winning when it severely defeated its rival city in 1380; thereafter, in partnership with Egypt, Venice principally dominated the oriental trade coming via the Indian Ocean and Red Sea to Alexandria.

Overland routes were not wholly closed, but the conquests of the central Asian warrior Timur Lenk (Tamerlane)—whose empire broke into warring fragments after his death in 1405—and the advantages of a nearly continuous sea voyage from the Middle and Far East to the Mediterranean gave Venice a virtual monopoly of some oriental products, principally spices. The word spices then had a loose application and extended to many oriental luxuries, but the most valuable European imports were pepper, nutmeg, cloves, and cinnamon.

The Venetians distributed these expensive condiments throughout the Mediterranean region and northern Europe; they were shipped to the latter first by pack trains up the Rhône Valley and, after 1314, by Flanders' galleys to the Low Countries, western Germany, France, and England. The fall of Constantinople to the Ottoman Turks in 1453 did not seriously affect Venetian control. Though other Europeans resented this dominance of the trade, even the Portuguese discovery and exploitation of the Cape of Good Hope route could not altogether break it.

Early Renaissance Europe was short of cash money, though it had substantial banks in northern Italy and southern Germany. Florence possessed aggregations of capital, and its Bardi bank in the 14th century and the Medici successor in the 15th financed much of the eastern Mediterranean trade.

Later, during the great discoveries, the Augsburg houses of Fugger and Welser furnished capital for voyages and New World enterprises.

Gold came from central Africa by Saharan caravan from Upper Volta near the Niger, and interested persons in Portugal knew something of this. When Prince Henry the Navigator undertook sponsorship of Portuguese discovery voyages down the western coast of Africa, a principal motive was to find the mouth of a river to be ascended to these mines.

Geographical knowledge and technological improvements. By the 15th century, the more knowledgeable western Europeans believed the Earth a sphere, as had a few even in the Dark Ages. Two English scholars, John Holywood (also known as John Halifax and Johan-

nes de Sacro Bosco) and Roger Bacon, had lent powerful support to the idea in the 13th century. The most quoted geographic authority, however, was the 2nd-century Alexandrian astronomer and geographer Ptolemy, whose works had become available in Latin. Ptolemy was more a compiler of earlier knowledge than an original thinker, and his serious errors had great influence; he underestimated the Earth's circumference and exaggerated the eastward extent of Asia, and both mistakes affected the thinking of Columbus.

Ptolemy's underestimation of the Earth's circumference

The existence, under Genghis Khan's successors, of the Mongol Empire, embracing most of Asia and fomenting trade, made possible visits to the East by missionaries and merchants in the 13th and 14th centuries. Two Franciscan friars, Giovanni da Pian del Carpine and William of Rubruquis, reached Mongolia on religious missions and wrote of their travels even before the Venetian Polos had visited the Mongol court at Peking. Marco, most famous of the Polos, spent 17 years in the Far East in the service of Kublai Khan, the grandson of Genghis.

Several years after returning to Venice in 1295, he dictated his famous travel book in which he described Asia and many adjacent islands, including Japan, which he described inaccurately from hearsay. His was nonetheless the best description of the Far East that Europe would have for centuries.

Though somewhat disdained by the learned at first, Marco Polo's book became very popular and was translated into several languages before the invention of printing. Christopher Columbus acted partly on the strength of Polo's account, unaware that it described a political situation long vanished.

Europe had made some progress in discovery before the main age of exploration. Genoese seamen had rediscovered the Madeira Islands and probably the Azores in the 14th century. A Catalan voyager appears to have ventured southward past Cape Bojador, the formidable promontory in the present Western Sahara. These early Atlantic discoveries could not be followed up immediately, however, because they had been made in galleys built for the Mediterranean and ill suited to ocean travel; the numerous rowers they required and their lack of substantial holds left only limited room for provisions and cargo. In the early 15th century all-sails vessels, the caravels, largely superseded galleys for Atlantic travel; these were light ships, having usually two but sometimes three masts, ordinarily equipped with lateen sails but occasionally square-rigged. When longer voyages began, the *nao*, or carrack, proved better than the caravel; it had three masts and square rigging and was a rounder, heavier ship, more fitted to cope with ocean winds.

Navigational instruments improved. The compass, probably imported in primitive form from the Orient, was gradually developed until, by the 15th century, European pilots were using an iron pin that pivoted in a round box. They realized that it did not point to the true north, and no one then knew of the magnetic pole, but they learned approximately how to correct. The astrolabe, used for determining latitude by the altitude of stars, had been known since Roman times, but its employment by seafarers was rare as late as 1300; it became more common during the next 50 years, though most pilots probably did not possess it and often did not need it because most voyages took place in the narrow waters of the Mediterranean or Baltic or along western European coasts. For longitude, then and much later, dead reckoning had to be employed, but this could be reasonably accurate when done by experts.

The typical medieval map had been the planisphere, or *mappemonde*, which arranged the three known continents in circular form on a disk surface and illustrated a concept more theological than geographical. The earliest surviving specimens of the portolanic, or harbour-finding, charts date from shortly before 1300 and are of Pisan and Genoese origin. Portolanic maps aided voyagers by showing Mediterranean coastlines with remarkable accuracy, but they gave no attention to hinterlands. As Atlantic sailings increased, the coasts of west-

Medieval maps

ern Europe and Africa south of the Strait of Gibraltar were shown somewhat correctly, though less so than for the Mediterranean.

VOYAGES OF DISCOVERY AND THE SPANISH AND PORTUGUESE EMPIRES (16TH CENTURY)

Portuguese discoveries and conquests. Aided by geographical factors, Portugal became the leader in overseas expansion. It had a long ocean frontage, a narrow hinterland, and a merchant marine whose seamen stood no chance of entering the coveted Mediterranean trade. Portugal hoped to spread Christianity and carry further the anti-Muslim crusade that, in Prince Henry the Navigator's time, had nearly expelled the Moors from the Iberian Peninsula. The search for wealth in the form of gold, ivory, spices, and slaves spurred the Portuguese and may have been the strongest motivating force.

Prince Henry died in 1460 after a career that had brought the colonization of the Madeira Islands and Azores, the discovery of Cape Verde Islands, and the traversal of the African coast to Sierra Leone. A generation after Henry's death, John II of Portugal resumed discovery work in earnest. Whatever Henry's ultimate objectives had been—and they are uncertain—John meant his seamen to round Africa and reach India. His captain, Diogo Cam, discovered the Congo River in 1482; six years later Bartolomeu Dias rounded the Cape of Good Hope and beheld the Indian Ocean.

John died in 1495, but his successor, Manuel I, vigorously continued the effort. Vasco da Gama reached India in 1498 and returned to Portugal with a cargo of spice. Pedro Álvares Cabral, the next Portuguese commander, struck the Brazilian coast in 1500 while proceeding to India; after rounding the Cape he discovered Madagascar. Voyages to India became annual events, even though the Portuguese found that the European products they brought for exchange had small value to Asiatics.

In 1505 Manuel's government, in part, gave up a policy of pure trade for one that included conquest. It had, however, no wish to build a large land empire and meant only to capture and hold key ports to provide safety for Portuguese traders. This new policy was carried out principally by two viceroys, Francisco de Almeida in 1505–09 and Afonso de Albuquerque in 1509–15. Almeida seized several eastern African and Indian points and defeated a Muslim naval coalition off Diu (now in Gujarat, India). Albuquerque endeavoured to gain a monopoly of European spice trade for his country by sealing off all entrances and exits of the Indian Ocean competing with the Portuguese Cape route. In 1510 he took Goa, in western India, which became the capital and stronghold of the Portuguese East, and in 1511 he captured Malacca, Malaya (now part of Malaysia), at the farther end of the ocean. Later he subdued Hormuz (now in Iran), commanding the Persian Gulf. Albuquerque failed in an effort to take Aden at the Red Sea entrance, and thus the trade through Alexandria with Venice continued almost as vigorously as before the Portuguese intrusion.

Manuel's subjects pressed beyond the Strait of Malacca to the East Indies, Siam (now Thailand), and Canton in Ming-dynasty China. Trade with the celestial empire, difficult at first because of China's exclusionist policies, at length grew, especially after Portugal in 1557 leased Macau, through which for the next 300 years passed much of the Occidental trade with China. Individual Portuguese reached Japan in 1542, followed by traders and Francis Xavier (later made a saint), a renowned Jesuit missionary who laboured with small success to make converts. In the next century, the Japanese adopted a rigorous exclusionist policy, although they allowed Portugal's successors, the Dutch, to conduct a limited trade from the small island of Deshima, near Nagasaki.

Though awarded the coast of Brazil by the Treaty of Tordesillas (see below), the Portuguese government neglected it for three decades. It proved nearly useless as a way station to the Cape; its Indian population was savage; and its products, consisting chiefly of *pau brasil*

Manuel's policy of conquest

(Brazilian dyewood), yielded much less revenue than those of India.

Spanish discoveries and conquests. In 1492, six years before Vasco da Gama reached India, Christopher Columbus of Genoa had discovered, and claimed, the Bahama Islands, Cuba, and Hispaniola for Ferdinand II and Isabella I of Spain. Columbus returned from the voyage convinced that Cuba was the Asiatic mainland and that Hispaniola was Japan, the latter unvisited but described by Marco Polo. Columbus made four voyages to America, in which he discovered the Greater Antilles, many of the lesser islands, and the mainland coasts of modern Venezuela, Central America, and modern Panama. He died in Spain, unshaken in the belief that he had discovered continental Asia and its offshore islands.

By then others had already undertaken several explorations. A succession of Spanish voyagers had traced the South American main from the Brazilian shoulder to the Isthmus of Panama. Amerigo Vespucci of Florence, sailing under the Portuguese flag, had followed the continent southward to Patagonia (modern Argentina) and called it a New World, a world soon to bear his name.

Following Columbus' first voyage, the rulers of Portugal and Spain, by the Treaty of Tordesillas (1494), partitioned the non-Christian world between them by an imaginary line in the Atlantic, 370 leagues (about 1,300 miles) west of the Cape Verde Islands. Portugal could claim and occupy everything to the east of the line and Spain everything to the west, though no one then knew where the demarcation would bisect the other side of the globe. In 1517, five years after Vespucci's death, Ferdinand Magellan, a Portuguese who had served in the East, appeared in Spain to ask for command of a fleet. He declared that the clove-growing Moluccas (now part of Indonesia) lay in the part reserved to Spain by the Tordesillas agreement and promised to sail westward to those islands. He obtained the fleet and departed in 1519; three years later a single ship returned to Spain with 18 survivors, having circumnavigated the Earth. Magellan himself had found the strait bearing his name, near the southern tip of South America, had conducted the fleet across the Pacific, and had died while recklessly taking part in a skirmish between Filipino chieftains. The voyage removed any remaining doubts of the Earth's sphericity and furnished an approximate idea of its circumference by revealing the width of the Pacific. The Moluccas lay in the Portuguese half of the Earth; but Magellan's expedition had not clearly established this, and Spain sent several more fleets across the Pacific until the futility of claiming the islands became apparent. A later result of the Magellan voyage was the Spanish occupation of the Philippines from New Spain (Mexico), beginning in 1565.

Only gradually did Spaniards realize the possibilities of America. They had completed the occupation of the larger West Indian islands by 1512, though they largely ignored the smaller ones, to their ultimate regret. Thus far they had found lands nearly empty of treasure, populated by naked primitives who died off rapidly on contact with Europeans. In 1508 an expedition did leave Hispaniola to colonize the mainland, and, after hardship and decimation, the remnant settled at Darién on the Isthmus of Panama, from which in 1513 Vasco Núñez de Balboa made his famous march to the Pacific. On the Isthmus the Spaniards heard garbled reports of the wealth and splendour of Inca Peru. Balboa was succeeded (and judicially murdered) by Pedrarias Dávila, who turned his attention to Central America and founded Nicaragua.

Expeditions sent by Diego Velázquez, governor of Cuba, made contact with the decayed Maya civilization of Yucatán and brought news of the cities and precious metals of Aztec Mexico. Hernán Cortés entered Mexico from Cuba in 1519 and spent two years overthrowing the Aztec confederation, which dominated Mexico's semi-civilized heartland. The Spaniards used firearms effectively but did most of their fighting with pikes and blades, aided by numerous Indian allies who hated the dominant Aztecs. The conquest of Aztec Mexico led

Columbus' voyages

Beginnings of the Spanish conquest in America

directly to that of Guatemala and about half of Yucatán, whose geography and warlike inhabitants slowed Spanish progress.

Mexico yielded much gold and silver, and the conquerors imagined still greater wealth and wonders to the north. None of this existed, but it seemed real when a northern wanderer, Alvar Núñez Cabeza de Vaca, brought an exciting but fanciful report of the fabulous lands to Mexico in 1536. Expeditions explored northern Mexico and the southern part of what is now the United States, notably that of Juan Rodríguez Cabrillo by sea along what are now the California and Oregon coasts and those of Hernando de Soto and Francisco Vázquez Coronado through the southeastern and southwestern U.S. regions. These brought geographical knowledge but nothing of value to the Spaniards, who for years thereafter ignored the northern regions.

Meanwhile the Pizarro brothers entered the Inca Empire from Panama in 1531 and proceeded with its conquest. Finding the huge realm divided by a recent civil war over the throne, they captured and executed the incumbent usurper, Atahualpa. But the conquest took years to complete; the Pizarros had to crush a formidable native rising and to defeat their erstwhile associate, Diego de Almagro, who felt cheated of his fair share of the spoils. The Pizarros and their followers took and divided a great amount of gold and silver, with prospects of more from the mines of Peru and Bolivia. By-products of the Inca conquest were the seizure of northern Chile by Pedro de Valdivia and the descent of the entire Amazon by Francisco de Orellana.

The cities of the semicivilized Chibcha Indians lay in the Andean Plateau around Bacata (Bogota). Their conquest was undertaken in 1536 from Caribbean Santa Marta (now in northern Colombia) by Gonzalo Jiménez de Quesada, whose chief problem arose when two other conquistadors arrived—Sebastián de Belalcázar, a Spaniard who came there from Popayán (now in southern Colombia), and Nikolaus Federmann, a German Welser employee from Venezuela, which the Holy Roman emperor Charles V (Charles I of Spain) had leased to the Augsburg bankers. The three leaders finally decided to leave disposition of the conquered land to the ruler, and Charles awarded the governorship of the region, named New Granada, to a fourth party in Spain.

The Spanish Empire in America was thus basically formed by 1550, though such areas as the Río de la Plata, Venezuela, northern Mexico, and Yucatán were not yet under control. Generations of missionaries and minor conquerors later brought these and other regions into subjection.

Portugal's seaborne empire. Portuguese rule in the East and in Brazil rested on discovery, on the Treaty of Tordesillas, and on papal sanction (Pope Leo X, by a bull of 1514, forbade others to interfere with Portugal's possessions). Except for such minor incursions as those of Magellan's surviving ship in 1522 and the Englishman Sir Francis Drake's voyage around the world in 1577–80, the Portuguese operated in the East for nearly a century without European competition. They faced occasional Oriental enemies but weathered these dangers with their superior ships, gunnery, and seamanship.

Territorially, theirs was scarcely an empire; it was a commercial operation based on possession of fortifications and posts strategically situated for trade. The viceroy and his staff resided at Goa, with subordinate officials at coastal points from eastern Africa to Chinese Macau. Limited numbers of warships, based mostly on Goa, patrolled the seas to keep commercial routes open. They brought soldiers from the home country in limited numbers; but the Portuguese also relied on alliances with native states and enlisted sepoy troops, a policy later followed by the French and English.

Portugal never fully dominated the Indian Ocean because it lacked warships necessary to control the vast water expanse. Albuquerque's failure to capture Aden allowed the old traffic through Egypt to Venice to resume following an initial dislocation, and this continued after the Ottoman Turks conquered Egypt in 1517. Much of the Indian Ocean trade was local and, until the Portuguese incursion, had been conducted by Arabs or at least by Muslims. The Portuguese, who at first had intended to oust the Arabs entirely, found it impossible to manage without them. The Hindus, whom they hoped to use for local trade purposes, proved unenterprising and had caste restrictions regarding sea voyages. Muslims were soon trafficking again vigorously, with Portuguese sanction.

Partial domination of the Indian Ocean and much of its valuable trade did not, finally, bring Portugal's crown as much profit as had been anticipated. The intention had been to make Oriental trade a royal monopoly; but Portuguese, from viceroys to humble soldiers and seamen, became private merchants and lined their own pockets to the deprivation of the royal treasury. The Eastern footholds were expensive to maintain, and frequent mishaps to vessels of the Indian fleets, from shipwreck or enemies, reduced gains. The lack of a true monopoly prevented the Portuguese from charging the prices they wished in European markets. Moreover, Lisbon, while an ideal starting point for voyages around the Cape, proved poorly situated as a distribution centre for spice to northern and central Europe. Antwerp, on the Scheldt, was far superior, and for a time Portugal maintained a trading house there; but Portuguese agents found spice sales taken out of their hands by more experienced Italian, German, and Flemish merchants, and the Antwerp establishment was closed in 1549.

It has been asserted that the Portuguese had no racial prejudice, but their record proves the opposite. In the 16th and 17th centuries, they could not be expected to be tolerant of Oriental religions, although they soon realized that wholesale conversion to Catholicism was impossible. Some Africans and Asiatics became Christians and even entered the clergy; but seldom if ever did they rise above the status of parish priests. In other affairs the Portuguese generally treated the dark-skinned peoples as inferiors.

The eastern coast of Brazil belonged to Portugal by the Tordesillas pact. The government of Manuel I and his successor, John III (ruled 1521–57), paid it small attention for 30 years, although individual Portuguese meanwhile traded and even settled there. Threats of French and Spanish intrusion caused John III, in 1530, to send Martim Afonso de Sousa to make a careful survey of the Brazilian coast and to suggest sites for colonization. Next, the littoral was partitioned into strips called *capitanias*, each colonized and governed under feudal terms by a proprietor, or *donatário*. Some limited settlement followed, and in 1549 the *capitanias* were united under a governor general residing at Bahia (now Salvador, Brazil).

In 1580 Philip II of Spain seized the Portuguese throne, which had fallen vacant and to which he had some blood claim. Portugal remained theoretically independent, bound only by a personal union to its neighbour; but succeeding Spanish monarchs steadily encroached on its liberties until the small kingdom became, in effect, a conquered province. Spain's European enemies meanwhile descended on the Portuguese Empire and ended its Eastern supremacy before the restoration of Portugal's independence in 1640.

Spain's American empire. A colonial period of nearly three centuries followed the major Spanish conquests. Spain had gained experience by governing the subjected peninsular Moors and the recently conquered Canary Island natives, and the Spaniards used some familiar methods and institutions in their new American possessions. The empire was created in a time of rising European absolutism, which flourished in both Spain and Spanish America, and reached its height in the 18th century. The overseas colonies became and remained the king's private estate.

Shortly before the death of Queen Isabella I in 1504, the Spanish sovereigns created the House of Trade (Casa de Contratación) to regulate commerce between Spain and the New World. Their purpose was to make the trade monopolistic and thus pour the maximum amount

Portuguese colonization of Brazil

Portuguese dominance of Eastern commerce

of bullion into the royal treasury. This policy, seemingly successful at first, fell short later because Spain failed to provide necessary manufactured goods for its colonies, foreign competitors appeared, and smuggling grew.

In 1524 Charles V created the Council of the Indies as a lawmaking body for the colonies. During the three centuries of its existence, this council enacted a massive amount of legislation, though much grew obsolete and became a dead letter. The industrious Philip II died in 1598, and his indolent or incompetent successors left American affairs to the Casa and Council; both proved generally conscientious and hard-working bodies, though, for a time in the 17th century, appointments to the legislating council could be purchased.

The viceregal system dated from 1535, when Antonio de Mendoza was sent to govern New Spain, or Mexico, bypassing the still-vigorous Cortés. A second viceroy was named for Peru in 1542, and the viceroyalties of New Granada and Río de la Plata were formed in 1739 and 1776, respectively. By the 18th century, viceroys served average terms of five years, and under them functioned a hierarchy of bureaucrats, nearly all sent from Spain to occupy frequently lucrative posts. American-born Spaniards resented this favouritism shown the peninsular Spaniards, and their jealousy accounted in part for their later separation from Spain. Lower socially and economically than either white class were the mestizo offspring of white and Indian matings, and still lower were the humble Indians and Negro slaves.

Though a belief to the contrary exists, Spain sent many colonists to America. One indication of this is the number of new cities founded, distinct from the old Indian culture centres. A partial list of such cities, besides the early island ones, includes Vera Cruz, New Spain; Panama, Cartagena, and Guayaquil, in New Granada (in modern Panama, Colombia, and Ecuador, respectively); Lima, Peru; and all those of what are now Chile, Paraguay, Argentina, and Uruguay.

A problem early faced and never truly solved by Spain was that of the Indians. The home government was generally benevolent in legislating for their welfare but could not altogether enforce its humane policies in distant America. The foremost controversy in early decades involved the *encomienda*, by which Indian groups were entrusted to Spanish proprietors, who in theory cared for them physically and spiritually in return for rights to tribute and labour but who in practice often abused and enslaved them.

Spanish Dominican friars were the first to condemn the *encomienda* and work for its abolition; the outstanding reformer was a missionary, Bartolomé de Las Casas, who devoted most of his long life to the Indian cause. He secured passage of laws in 1542 ordering the early abolition of the *encomienda*, but efforts to enforce these brought noncompliance in New Spain and armed rebellion in Peru. A belief held by some Spanish theologians that Indians were inferior beings and natural slaves, to be subdued and forcibly converted, generally prevailed over the opposition of Las Casas and fellow Dominicans. The *encomienda* or its equivalent endured, although this feudal institution declined as royal absolutism grew.

The Indians became real or nominal Christians, but their numbers shrank, less from slaughter and exploitation than from Old World diseases, frequently smallpox, for which they had no inherited immunity. The aboriginal West Indian population virtually disappeared in a few generations, to be replaced by Negro slaves. Indian numbers shrank in all mainland areas: at the beginning of Spanish settlement there were perhaps 50,000,000 aborigines; the figure had decreased to an estimated 4,000,000 in the 17th century, after which it slowly rose again. Meanwhile the hybrid mestizo element grew and somewhat replaced the Indians.

The Leyenda Negra (Black Legend) propagated by critics of Spanish policy still contributes to the general belief that Spain exceeded other nations in cruelty to subject populations; on the other hand, a review of Spain's record suggests that it was no worse than other nations and, in fact, produced a greater number of humanitarian reform-

ers. When Dominican zeal declined, the new and powerful Jesuit order became the major Indian protector and led in missionary activity until its expulsion from the Spanish Empire in 1767; the Jesuits took charge of large converted native communities, notably in the area of the viceroyalty of Río de la Plata that is now Paraguay, in their paternalism often imposing stern discipline.

Effects of the discoveries and empires. Before the discovery of America and the sea route to Asia, the Mediterranean had been the trading and naval focus of Europe and the Near East. Italian seamen were rightly considered best, and they commanded the first royally sponsored transatlantic expeditions—Columbus for Spain, John Cabot for England, and Giovanni da Verrazano for France.

Europe's shift to the Atlantic. Until then the Western countries had lain on the fringe of civilization, with nothing apparently beyond them but Iceland and small islands. With the discovery of the Cape route and America, nations formerly peripheral found themselves central, with geographical forces impelling them to leadership.

The Mediterranean did not become a backwater, and the Venetian republic remained a major commercial power in the 16th century. Venice's decline came in the 17th, though the Venetians were still formidable against the Turks. As the more powerful Dutch, French, and English replaced the Eastern pioneers of little Portugal, however, the burden of competition became more than the venerable republic could bear. The last decisive naval battle fought by Mediterranean seamen was Lepanto (Náupaktos, Greece), where Don John of Austria, in 1571, commanding Spanish and Italian galleys, defeated an Ottoman fleet. Though Atlantic powers thereafter often fought in the Mediterranean, they mainly fought each other, while the Italian cities became pawns in international politics. The nation-state was superseding the small principality and city-state, a trend that had begun before the discoveries. The new nations lay on the Atlantic; and though Spain and France had Mediterranean frontages, the advantage went to those seaports belonging to substantial countries with ready access to the outer world.

Changes in Europe. The opening of old lands in Asia and new ones in America changed Europe forever, and the Iberian countries understandably felt the changes first. The Portuguese government, for a time, made large profits from its Eastern trade, and individuals prospered; but Oriental luxuries were costly compared with the European goods Portugal offered, and the balance had to be made up in specie. This eastward drain of gold and silver had gone on long before Portuguese imperial times, but it was now intensified. Much of the bullion reaching the Orient did not circulate but was hoarded or made into ornaments; consequently, there was no inflation in Asia, and prices there did not rise enough to create a demand for Western goods, which would have reversed the flow of bullion from the West. The Portuguese obtained most of the precious metal for this trade from spice sales through Antwerp and from Africa. The drain proved critical, and, by the reign of John III, the government found itself hard pressed economically and forced to abandon overseas posts that were a financial burden. Later, beginning in the 17th century, Portugal drew its own supply of jewels and gold from Brazil.

Spain's case was the reverse; although the first American lands discovered yielded little mineral wealth, the mines of Mexico by the 1520s and those of Potosí (in modern Bolivia) by the 1540s were shipping to Spain large quantities of bullion, much of it crown revenue. This did not furnish Charles V and Philip II their largest income; Spanish taxation still exceeded wealth from the New World, yet American silver and gold proved sufficient to cause a price revolution in Spain, where costs, depending on the region, were multiplied by three and five during the 16th century. The Spanish government wished to keep bullion from leaving the kingdom, but high prices in Spain made it a good market for outside products. Spanish industry declined in the 16th century,

(marginal notes)
The viceregal system

Diminution of the Indians

Eastward drain of Portuguese gold and silver

in part because of the sales taxes imposed by the crown, which necessitated more buying of foreign merchandise. Great quantities of bullion had to be poured out to finance the expensive Spanish European empire and the costly wars and diplomacy of Charles V and Philip II, both of whom were constantly in debt.

Price rise followed in other countries, largely from the influx of Spanish bullion. In England, where some statistics are available, costs by 1650 had risen by 250 percent over those of 1500.

The European commercial revolution, which brought increased industry, more trade, and larger banks, had begun before the discoveries, but it received stimulus from them. Bullion from America helped create a money economy, replacing the older and largely barter exchange —a trend accentuated by greater European mineral production in the early 16th century. The trade emporiums of Italy and the Baltic Hanseatic League declined and were largely replaced by those of the Low Countries, England, and France. Joint-stock companies made an impressive appearance, notably the East India Companies of the Low Countries, England, and France in the 17th century. The mercantile theory that precious metals are the true wealth, though it had been always somewhat present, now came into full vogue and continued, even to the present day in many minds, to dominate economic thinking.

New products for Europe

Discovery introduced Europe to new foods and beverages. Coffee, from Ethiopia, had been consumed in Arabia and Egypt before its wide European use began in the 17th century. Tobacco, an American plant smoked by Indians, won an Old World market despite many individual objectors; the same proved true of chocolate from Mexico and tea from Asia. The South American potato became a staple food in such places as Ireland and central Europe. Cotton, from the Old World, took firm root in the New, from which Europe received an enormously increased supply. Sugar, introduced to the American

tropics, along with its molasses and rum derivatives, in time became the principal exports of those regions. Spice was certainly more plentiful than before the discoveries, though the Dutch, when they controlled the East Indies, were able to limit production and thus to keep the price of cloves and nutmegs high.

The influence of the discoveries permeated literature. Sir Thomas More's *Utopia*, printed in 1516 and dealing with an imaginary island, was suggested by South America. The Portuguese poet Luís de Camões recounted the voyage of Vasco da Gama, though fancifully, in epic verse. Michel de Montaigne discoursed upon American savages, some of whom he had seen in France. Christopher Marlowe's drama *Tamburlaine* (1587), though based on the life of the Asiatic conqueror, was an exhortation to his fellow Englishmen to penetrate the New World.

Historiography acquired a broader base by taking the newly discovered lands into account. Astronomy was revolutionized by European penetration of the Southern Hemisphere and discovery of constellations unknown before. Mapmakers, typified by the Fleming Gerardus Mercator and the Dutchman Abraham Ortelius, portrayed the world in terms recognizable today.

COLONIES FROM NORTHERN EUROPE AND MERCANTILISM (17TH CENTURY)

The northern Atlantic powers, for understandable reasons, acquired no overseas possessions before 1600. The Low Countries spent the final decades of the 16th century winning independence from Spain; France had constant European involvements and wars of religion; England, matrimonially allied with Spain as late as 1558, experienced its Protestant Reformation and long felt unwilling to challenge predominant Spain openly in any manner.

The Dutch.   Although England's defeat of Philip II's Armada in 1588 helped to lessen Spanish sea power, it

European expansion, 1600–1700.

was the Dutch who early in the next century really broke that power and became the world's foremost naval and commercial nation, with science and skills commensurate with their prowess. Only late in the 17th century did they decline, because of their limited size and the inferiority of their geographical position to England's. The Dutch, meanwhile, penetrated all the known oceans, including the Arctic, and waged unrelenting war against the Iberian kingdoms.

The Dutch coveted the Portuguese commercial empire more than the Spanish continental one. They took much of the Portuguese East and invaded Brazil (1624–54), the richer half of which they controlled for a time. They also penetrated Portuguese Angola, which they desired because the slaves it exported were beginning to work the Brazilian plantations. They ultimately failed in the South Atlantic, though they gained Dutch Guiana (now Surinam), Curaçao, and what later became British Guiana (Guyana). Meanwhile, Willem Schouten, one of their free-lance voyagers, had made the discovery of Cape Horn in 1616.

Eastern pursuits.   The Dutch States General, in 1602, chartered the Dutch East India Company, a joint-stock enterprise with investment open to all. In control was a board of 17 directors, the so-called Heeren XVII, who received a monopoly of navigational rights eastward around the Cape of Good Hope and westward through the Strait of Magellan. They could make treaties with native princes on behalf of the States General (from which they were scarcely separable), establish garrisoned forts, and appoint governors and justices. The company had no interest in extending Protestantism, and there was no mention of religious conversion, though Calvinist ministers later gained converts in the East, mostly in communities previously made Catholic by Portuguese Jesuits.

The company established headquarters first at Bantam in Java in 1607, later moving them to Djakarta, renamed

Formation of the Dutch East India Company

Batavia, in the same island. Its two main objectives were the ouster of European competitors—Portuguese, English, and Spanish—and dominance of local trade, previously in native hands. Portuguese vigour had somewhat declined, and the Dutch were victorious in most armed encounters. They also squeezed out the English, whose own East India Company thereafter concentrated efforts in the Indian peninsula.

The principal builder of the Dutch Oriental empire was Jan Pieterszoon Coen, company governor general from 1618 to 1623 and again from 1627 until his death in 1629. Financially, local trade monopoly was even more important than the expulsion of white competitors. The extension of Dutch control to islands beyond Java had started before the governorship of Coen, who accentuated the process. He and other company officials behaved ruthlessly; for example, when the inhabitants of the nutmeg-growing island of Great Banda (modern Pulau Banda Besar in Indonesia) resisted the Dutch in 1621, Coen had 2,500 of the inhabitants massacred and 800 more transported to Batavia. Company policy was to restrict clove production to Amboina and a few neighbouring islands firmly under Dutch control. To insure this, about 65,000 clove trees were destroyed in the Moluccas, and Dutch subjection of Macassar made the monopoly virtually complete. In 1656 the famous Moluccas were described as a wilderness. Besides being a conqueror, Coen was an able businessman and, by his own lights, an economist. When he died he was engaged in gaining a monopoly of the pepper of interior Sumatra, which was later sealed off securely by the fall of Portuguese Malacca in 1641.

Batavia became the focal point of the Dutch East, and through it passed the commerce of China, Japan, India, Ceylon, and Persia, bound for Europe or other Oriental ports. The Dutch never monopolized the China trade because the Portuguese held Macau, the Spaniards held Manila, and the Japanese, for a time, engaged in this

Batavia as the focal point of the Dutch East

From W. Shepherd, *Historical Atlas*, Harper & Row, Publishers (Barnes & Noble Books), New York; revision copyright © 1964 by Barnes & Noble, Inc.

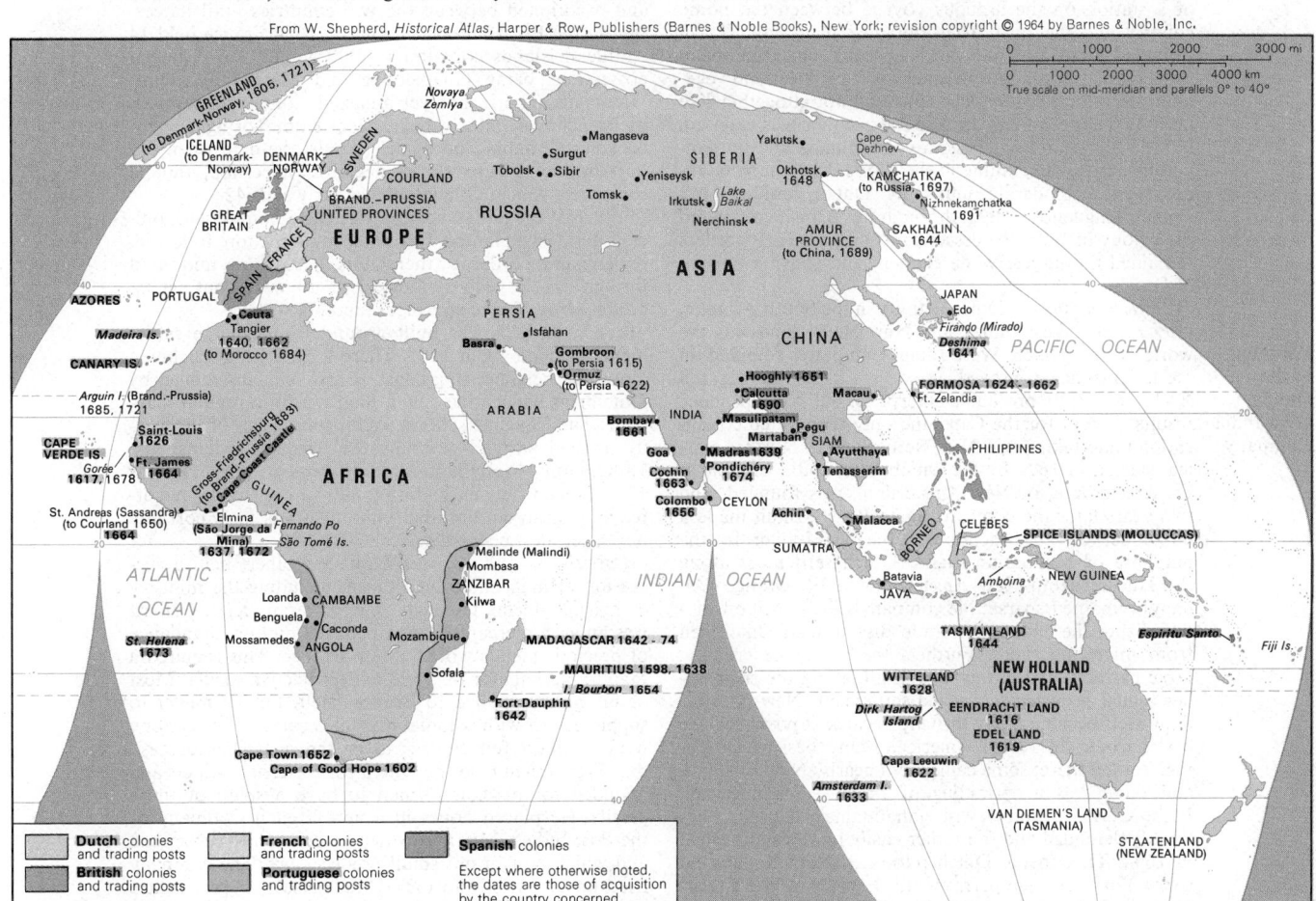

commerce. The Dutch gained a foothold in Formosa in 1624 but lost it to a Chinese pirate in 1662. After Japan became exclusionist in 1641, a trickle of Dutch trade continued to enter it through the small island of Deshima (now part of Nagasaki, Japan), even after the dissolution of the East India Company in 1799.

The economy of Java changed somewhat after the importation of the coffee plant in 1696. Coffee, often simply called java, rapidly became a major island crop and was exported from there to Dutch America. The company had earlier brought coffee to Ceylon, but that experiment had failed when a blight attacked its leaves. The company ousted the Portuguese from Ceylon and dominated the island until it was itself dispossessed by the British in 1796. Under its jurisdiction, as earlier, the major Ceylonese export was cinnamon, though the Dutch also dealt in jewels and pepper and carried on a trade in elephants.

In their constant search for commercial outlets, the company's officials sponsored new exploration. Coen's ablest successor, Antonio van Diemen, governor general in 1636–45, sent Abel Tasman to investigate the great land (Australia) previously sighted by Spanish, Portuguese, and Dutch seamen. Tasman sailed around the continent and discovered Van Diemen's Land (Tasmania), Staatenland (New Zealand), and the Tonga and Fiji Islands, but their commercial possibilities seemed insufficient to warrant further attention.

Dutch penetration of the East was not colonization; small farmers and artisans neither could nor would compete with the abundant, cheap native labour. Those Dutchmen going eastward were company officials, seamen and soldiers, overseers of plantations and commerce, and a few scientists and Calvinist clergymen; there was no place for others.

The Dutch moved into uninhabited Mauritius, which they later abandoned and saw pass first to France and finally to Great Britain. The Heeren XVII felt the need of a station on the arduous voyage between the home country and the East. They obtained it at Cape Town (founded in 1652 by Jan van Riebeeck), which company ships thereafter regularly visited for fresh meat and vegetables to reduce scurvy. The town did not altogether live up to first expectations because the harbour was exposed, but the hinterland possessed a good climate and no dangerous natives. Beginning in the 1680s, the company encouraged a moderate influx by Dutch families and French Huguenot exiles. Although the British conquered the colony in 1806, the descendants of these early settlers remained the largest white element and spoke a variant of Dutch.

Western pursuits.   Dutch activity in the South Atlantic, Guyana, the West Indies, and New Netherland was the work of the Dutch West India Company, founded in 1621. This never proved as successful as the Heeren XVII's generally profitable enterprise, but it did produce results. Except for the Cape, the only real Dutch colonization undertaking was New Netherland in North America, started in 1624 by the Dutch West India Company. Ft. Amsterdam, or New Amsterdam, was founded, and two years later the company agent Peter Minuit made a 60-guilder ($24) transaction with the local Indians for the purchase of Manhattan island. Dutch settlement along the Hudson from New Amsterdam to Ft. Orange (Albany) remained sparse; the company's insistence on monopolizing the Indian fur trade discouraged Dutchmen from migrating there. Further, the policy of creating large patroon land grants, five in all, along the river under feudal proprietors, limited settlement. New Amsterdam itself became fairly thriving because it possessed the best harbour in North America. Many besides Dutchmen settled there; some came from nearby New England, and there was a sprinkling of French, Scandinavian, Irish, German, and Jewish inhabitants. The city was weakly defended and fell rather easily to an English fleet in 1664. Though the Dutch retook it, New Netherland (New York) became permanently English by the Treaty of Westminster in 1674. The Dutch West India Company was then dissolved, to be reconstituted for exploitation

Founding of the Dutch West India Company

of the Caribbean holdings but to attempt no further territorial expansion.

The French.   France could probably have become the leading European colonial power in the 17th and 18th centuries. It had the largest population and wealth, the best army while Louis XIV ruled, and, for a time in his reign, the strongest navy. But France pursued a spasmodic overseas policy because of an intense preoccupation with European affairs; England, France's ultimately successful rival, was freer of such entanglements.

Early settlements in the New World.   Verrazano reconnoitered the North American coast for France in 1524, and in the next decade Jacques Cartier explored the St. Lawrence River and planned a colony that came to nothing. During most of the rest of the 16th century, French colonization efforts were confined to short-lived settlements at Guanabara Bay (Rio de Janeiro) and Florida; both met sad ends. France meanwhile was troubled by home religious strife and, for a time, was dominated by Philip II of Spain. But at the turn of the century, with Spanish power declining and domestic religious peace restored by King Henry IV's Edict of Nantes (1598), granting religious liberty to the Huguenots, the King chartered a West India Company. This led to further exploration and to a small Acadian (Nova Scotian) settlement, and in 1603 Samuel de Champlain went to Canada, called New France. Champlain became Canada's outstanding leader, founding Quebec in 1608, defeating the Iroquois of New York, stimulating fur trade, and exploring westward to Lake Huron in 1615. He introduced Recollet (Franciscan) friars for Indian conversion, but the Jesuit order soon became the principal missionary body in Canada.

Under the ministership of Cardinal Richelieu (served 1624–42), a Council of Marine was created, with responsibility for colonial affairs. French West Indian settlement, following the activities of pirates and filibusters, began in 1625 with the admission of French settlers to St. Christopher (already settled by the British in 1623 and partitioned between the two countries until its cession to the British in 1713), and by 1664 France held 14 Antillean islands containing 7,000 whites, the principal possessions being Guadeloupe and Martinique. Saint-Domingue (Haiti), not yet annexed, contained numbers of Frenchmen, mostly buccaneers from Tortuga. Sugar became the main crop of the islands; the date when importation of Negro slaves began is uncertain, though some were sold at Guadeloupe as early as 1642.

French West Indian settlement

French West Indian society was caste bound, with officials and large planters (*gros blancs*) at the top, followed, in descending order, by merchants, buccaneers, and small farmers (*petits blancs*). Lowest of all were contract labourers from France (*engagés*) and black slaves.

French Guiana was built around the Cayenne settlement, founded about 1637. There were other Frenchmen along the neighbouring coast at first, but, threatened by Dutchmen and natives, they finally took refuge at Cayenne. The Cayenne settlers, lacking any basis of prosperity, existed partly by raiding the Amazon Indians. The 18th century brought some improvement, but as late as 1743 French Guiana had only 600 whites, living by coffee and cacao culture and without means to import any but the crudest necessities.

Activities in India.   Jean-Baptiste Colbert held a succession of high offices in France, including the ministry of marine, during the early reign of Louis XIV. Colbert was an arch mercantilist and believed that an abundance of precious metals would enrich France. This required a favourable balance of trade and protective tariffs. Most of his policy applied to France itself, but he meant to supplement it with colonial markets protected by a strong navy. Colbert felt concern over the quantities of cash that Frenchmen paid the Dutch for Eastern products and intended for his countrymen to have a share of those profits. He placed hopes in a new French Company of the East Indies (1664), to which he personally subscribed and which bought out small predecessors. The company tried unsuccessfully to make Madagascar a great centre of trade, and the huge island became a stronghold of piracy, though the French acquired nearby Mauritius.

French
and
English
rivalry

In the Indian peninsula, where the English East India Company had holdings, French progress was slow in Colbert's time and after, partly because the last great Mughal emperor, Aurangzeb, reigned and dominated India. The company did acquire Pondichéry and several other posts, however, and an affiliate opened a limited trade with China. When Aurangzeb died in 1707, his empire declined rapidly. Thereafter, the question of future control of India lay chiefly between the French and English companies, which backed or opposed warring native rulers and exacted a price for financial support and for arming and drilling the native sepoy troops in the European manner. By the 1740s the French had gained the upper hand, and in the War of the Austrian Succession (1740–48) the French governor general of India, Joseph-François Dupleix, captured Madras, the centre of British power. But in the ensuing Treaty of Aix-la-Chapelle the British, who had made gains in North America, recovered Madras. Never again did the French come so near success, and their fortunes soon declined. Their company had not made large profits because expensive wars and the costs of subsidizing native princes had consumed revenue. The home government seldom cooperated, and French investors on the whole declined to speculate in overseas ventures.

Colonization of New France. New France became a royal province in 1663, with both good and bad results. The arrival of troops in 1665 lessened the danger from the hostile Iroquois. Jean Talon, the powerful intendant sent by Colbert in the same year, strove to make Canada a self-sustaining economic structure, but his plan was finally thwarted by his home government's failure to supply financial means chiefly because of the King's extravagance and costly European wars.

Colbert gave some stimulus to colonization of New France. Grants of land, called *seigneuries*, with frontages on the St. Lawrence, were apportioned to proprietors, who then allotted holdings to small farmers, or habitants. More land came under cultivation, and the white population grew, though immigration from France declined sharply after 1681 because the home authorities were reluctant to spare manpower for empty Canada. After 1700 most French Canadians were North American born, a factor that weakened loyalty to the mother country.

North American exploration proceeded rapidly in Colbert's time. Fur traders had earlier reached Lake Superior; Louis Jolliet and Jacques Marquette now travelled the Fox and Wisconsin rivers to the Mississippi in 1673 and descended it to the Arkansas. Robert Cavelier, sieur de La Salle, followed the Mississippi to the Gulf of Mexico in 1682 and claimed the entire Mississippi River Basin, or Louisiana, for France; a later consequence was the founding of New Orleans in 1718 by Jean-Baptiste Lemoyne, sieur de Bienville, the governor of Louisiana. French traders ultimately reached Santa Fe in Spanish New Mexico, and the sons of explorer Pierre Gaultier de Varennes, sieur de la Vérendrye, Louis-Joseph and François, visited the Black Hills of South Dakota and may have seen the Rocky Mountains.

Jesuit
mission
work

The Roman Catholic Church became firmly rooted in Canada, without the intellectual opposition and anticlericalism that developed in 18th-century France. Jesuit mission work among the Indians, extending to the Middle West, saw more devotion and bravery by the priests than substantial results. Christianity made small appeal to most Indians, who could accept a supreme being but rejected the Christian ethic. Several zealous Jesuits became martyrs to the faith; genuine conversions were few and backslidings frequent.

In the 18th century, with the pioneering period over, life in New France became easygoing and even pleasant, despite governmental absolutism. But the fur trade in the west drew vigorous young men from the seigneurial estates to become *coureurs de bois* (fur traders), and their loss crippled agriculture. Civil and religious authorities tried to hold settlers to farming because furs paid neither tithes nor seigneurial dues. This drainage of manpower partly explains the slow growth of New France, which, by a census of 1754, had only 55,000 whites.

The English. There is evidence that Bristol seamen reached Newfoundland before 1497, but John Cabot's Atlantic crossing in that year is the first recorded English exploration. After the death of King Henry VII in 1509, England largely lost interest in discovery and did not resume it until 1553 and the formation of the Muscovy Company, which tried to find a Northeast Passage to Asia, discovered the island of Novaya Zemlya (in modern U.S.S.R.), and opened a small trade with Russia. The English then turned to a search for a Northwest Passage, and Martin Frobisher sailed to Greenland, Baffin Island, and the adjacent mainland.

English ascendancy in India. Francis Drake and others raided the Spanish Main, and Drake and Thomas Cavendish sailed around the world. The defeat of Philip II's Armada in 1588, though less disastrous to Spain's seapower than commonly assumed, somewhat opened the way for English colonization of America. Interest in the Orient at first proved greater, however, and, in 1600, London merchants formed an East India Company. It could not compete with the rival Dutch company in the region of largest profits—the East Indies—so it shifted its emphasis to the Indian peninsula. The English acquired Masulipatam in 1611 and Madras in 1639, having meanwhile destroyed Portuguese Ormuz in 1622. Charles II obtained Bombay in 1661, as part of his Portuguese queen's marriage dowry, and awarded it to the company.

Collapse of the Mughal Empire after 1707 led ultimately to armed conflict between the British and French companies for increased trade and influence. Dupleix had won the upper hand for France by 1748; but in the ensuing Seven Years' War (1756–63), fought between the major European powers in various parts of the world, the British company gained ascendancy in India, thanks largely to the ability of Robert Clive, and held it thereafter. Pondichéry surrendered, and though France recovered this post by the ensuing Treaty of Paris (1763), French power in India had shrunk almost to nothing, while the British company's was now rivalled only by that of the native Marāthā confederacy.

Company profits from India came first from the familiar spices, but after 1660, Indian textiles outstripped these in importance. Cheap cloths, mainly cottons, found a mass market among the English poorer classes, though dainty fabrics for the wealthy also paid well. Imports of calicoes (inexpensive cotton fabrics from Calicut) to England grew so large that in 1721 Parliament passed the Calico Act to protect English manufacturers, forbidding the use of calico in England for apparel or for domestic purposes (repeal of the act in 1774 coincided with inventions of mechanical devices that made possible English cloth production in successful competition with Eastern fabrics).

England's American colonies. The English West Indies for many years exceeded North America in economic importance. The Lesser Antilles, earlier passed over by Spain in favour of the larger islands, lay open to any colonizer, although their ferocious Carib inhabitants sometimes gave trouble. The Leeward Islands of Antigua, St. Kitts, Nevis, and Barbados, as well as the Bermudas, were settled by Englishmen between 1609 and 1632. Barbados, at first the most important, owed its prosperity to the introduction of sugar culture about 1637. The size of landholdings increased in all the islands, and the white populations accordingly diminished as slavery came to furnish most of the raw labour. When an expedition sent by Oliver Cromwell took Spanish Jamaica in 1655, that island became the English West Indian centre. Settlement of Belize (later British Honduras) by buccaneers and log cutters began in 1636, although more than a century elapsed before Spain recognized the English right to be there.

Settle-
ments
in the West
Indies

The English islanders, to the envy of their Dutch and French neighbours, enjoyed such constitutional privileges as the right to elect semipopular assemblies. Barbados once hoped to have two representatives in Parliament, and some Barbadians, during the English (Glorious) Revolution (1688–89), thought of making their island an independent state, but nothing came of this.

The original English mainland colonies—Virginia

(founded 1607), Plymouth (1620), and Massachusetts Bay (1630)—were founded by joint-stock companies. The later New England settlements—New Hampshire, New Haven, Connecticut, and Rhode Island—began as off-shoots of Massachusetts, which acquired jurisdiction over the Maine territory. The New England colonies were first peopled partly by religious dissenters, but except for the separatist Plymouth Pilgrims they did not formally secede from the Church of England for the time being.

Proprietary colonies, under individual entrepreneurs, began with Maryland, founded in 1634 under the Catholic direction of Cecilius and Leonard Calvert. Also proprietary was Pennsylvania, which originally included Delaware, founded by the Quaker William Penn, in 1682. Maryland and Pennsylvania, except for a brief royal interlude in Maryland, continued under Calvert and Penn heirs until the American Revolution; all other colonies except Connecticut and Rhode Island ultimately had royal governments. The Carolinas, after abortive attempts at colonization, were effectively founded in 1670 and became first proprietary and, later, royal colonies. Georgia, last of the 13, began in 1732, partly as a philanthropic enterprise headed by James Oglethorpe to furnish a rehabilitation home for debtors and other underprivileged Englishmen. All the mainland colonies eventually had representative assemblies, chosen by the propertied classes, to aid and often handicap their English governors.

The original settlers, predominantly English, were later supplemented by French Huguenots, Germans, and Scots-Irish, especially in western New York, Pennsylvania, and the southern colonies. New York, acquired from the United Provinces of the Netherlands and including New Jersey, continued to have some Dutch flavour long after the Dutch had become a small minority. By the French and Indian War (1754–63, the American portion of the Seven Years' War), the total population of the mainland colonies was estimated as 1,296,000 whites and 300,000 Negroes, enormously in excess of the 55,000 whites inhabiting French Canada.

The only bond of union among the British colonies was their allegiance to the king, and in the wars with France (c. 1689–1763) it proved hard to unite them against the common enemy. All the colonies were agricultural, with New England being a region of small farms, the Middle Atlantic colonies having a larger scaled and more diversified farming, and the southern ones tending to plantations on which tobacco, rice, and indigo were raised by slaves (although slavery was legal throughout all the colonies). There was much colonial shipping, especially from New England, whose merchants and seamen traded with England, Africa, and the West Indies; Massachusetts shipbuilders had built more than 700 ships by 1675. By 1763 several towns had grown into cities, including Boston, New York, Philadelphia, Baltimore, and Charleston, South Carolina.

Mercantilism. By the time the term mercantile system was coined in 1776 by the Scottish philosopher Adam Smith, European states had been trying for two centuries to put mercantile theory into practice. The basis of mercantilism was the notion that national wealth is measured by the amount of gold and silver a nation possesses. This seemed proven by the fact that Spain's most powerful years had occurred when it was first reaping a bullion harvest from its overseas possessions.

The mercantile theory held that colonies exist for the economic benefit of the mother country and are useless unless they help to achieve profit. The mother nation should draw raw materials from its possessions and sell them finished goods, with the balance favouring the European country. This trade should be monopolistic, with foreign intruders barred.

The Spanish fleet system. Spain acted upon the as yet undefined mercantile theory when, in 1565, it perfected the fleet (*flota*) system, by which all legal trade with its American colonies was restricted to two annual fleets between Seville and designated ports on the Gulf of Mexico and Caribbean. The outgoing ships bore manufactured articles; returning, their cargoes consisted partly of gold

and silver bars. Though the system continued for nearly two centuries, Spain was a poor country by 1700.

French mercantilist activities. Ignoring this lesson, other European states adopted the mercantilist policy; the France of Louis XIV and Colbert is the outstanding example. Colbert, who dominated French policy for 20 years, strictly regulated the economy. He instituted protective tariffs and sponsored a monopolistic merchant marine. He regarded what few overseas possessions France then had as ultimate sources of liquid wealth, which they were poorly situated to furnish because they lacked such supplies of bullion as Spain controlled in Mexico and Peru.

The English navigation acts. England adhered to mercantilism for two centuries and, possessing a more lucrative empire than France, strove to implement the policy by a series of navigation acts. The first, passed by Cromwell's government in 1651, attempted chiefly to exclude the Dutch from England's carrying trade—goods imported from Africa, Asia, or America could be brought only in English ships, which included colonial vessels, thus giving the English North American merchant marine a substantial stimulus. After the royal Restoration in 1660, Parliament renewed and strengthened the Cromwellian measures. By then colonial American maritime competition with England had grown so severe that laws of 1663 required colonial ships carrying European goods to America to route them through English ports, where a duty had to be paid, but from lack of enforcement these soon became inoperative. In the early 18th century the English lost some of their enthusiasm for bullion alone and placed chief emphasis on commerce and industry. The Molasses Act of 1733 was in the interest of the British West Indian sugar growers, who complained of the amount of French island molasses imported by the mainland colonies; the French planters had been buying fish, livestock, and lumber brought by North American ships and gladly exchanging their sugar products for them at low prices. Prohibition of colonial purchases of French molasses, though decreed, went largely unenforced, and New England, home of most of the carrying trade, continued prosperous.

THE OLD COLONIAL SYSTEM
AND THE COMPETITION FOR EMPIRE (18TH CENTURY)

Faith in mercantilism waned during the 18th century, first because of the influence of French Physiocrats, who advocated the rule of nature, whereby trade and industry would be left to follow a natural course. François Quesnay, a physician at the court of Louis XV of France, led this school of thought, fundamentally advocating an agricultural economy and holding that productive land was the only genuine wealth, with trade and industry existing for the transfer of agricultural products.

Adam Smith adopted some physiocratic ideas, but he considered labour very important and did not altogether accept land as the sole wealth. Smith's *Inquiry Into the Nature and Causes of the Wealth of Nations* (1776), appearing just as Britain was about to lose much of its older empire, established the basis of new economic thought—classical economics. This denigrated mercantilism and advocated free, or at least freer, trade and state noninterference with private enterprise. *Laisser-faire et laisser-aller* ("to let it alone and let it flow") became the slogan of this British economic school. Smith thought that regulation only reduced wealth, a view in part adopted by the British government 56 years after his death.

Slave trade. Slavery, though abundantly practiced in Africa itself, had a limited existence in the ancient Mediterranean world and nearly died out in the Middle Ages. It was revived by the Portuguese in Prince Henry's time, beginning with the enslavement of Berbers in 1442. Portugal populated Cape Verde, Fernando Po, and São Tomé largely with black slaves and took many to the home country, especially to the regions south of the Tagus River.

New World black slavery began in 1502, when Gov. Nicolás de Ovando of Hispaniola imported a few evi-

Economic activities in the English colonies

Publication of *Wealth of Nations*

dently Spanish-born Negroes from Spain. Rapid decimation of the Indian population of the Spanish West Indies created a labour shortage, ultimately remedied from Africa. The great reformer, Las Casas, advocated importation of Negroes to replace the vanishing Indians, and he lived to regret having done so. The population of the Greater Antilles became largely Negro and mulatto; on the mainland, at least in the more populated parts, the Indians, supplemented by a growing mestizo caste that clung more tenaciously to life and seemed more suited to labour, kept African slavery somewhat confined to limited areas.

The Portuguese at first practiced Indian slavery in Brazil and continued to employ it partially until 1755. It was gradually replaced by the African variety, beginning prominently in the 17th century and coinciding with the rapid rise of Brazilian sugar culture.

As the English, French, Dutch, and, to a lesser extent, the Danes colonized the smaller West Indian islands, these became plantation settlements, largely cultivated by Negroes. Before the latter arrived in great numbers, the bulk of manual labour, especially in the English islands, was performed by poor whites. Some were indentured, or contract, servants; some were redemptioners who agreed to pay ship captains their passage fees within a stated time or be sold to bidders; others were convicts. Some were kidnapped, with the tacit approval of the English authorities, in keeping with the mercantilist policy that advocated getting rid of the unemployed and vagrants. Black slavery eventually surpassed white servitude in the West Indies.

John Hawkins commanded the first English slave-trading expedition in 1562 and sold his cargo in the Spanish Indies. English slaving, nevertheless, remained minor until the establishment of the English island colonies in the reign of James I (ruled 1603–25). A Dutch captain sailed the first Negro cargo to Virginia in 1619, the year in which the colony exported 20,000 pounds (9,000 kilograms) of tobacco. The restored Stuart king, Charles II, gave English slave trade to a monopolistic company, the Royal Adventurers Trading to Africa, in 1663, but the Adventurers accomplished little because of the early outbreak of war with Holland (1665). Their successor, the Royal African Company, was founded in 1672 and held the English monopoly until 1698, when all Englishmen received the right to trade in slaves. The Royal Africans continued slaving until 1731, when they abandoned it in favour of traffic in ivory and gold dust. A new slaving company, the Merchants Trading to Africa (founded 1750), had directors in London, Liverpool, and Bristol, with Bristol furnishing the largest quota of ships, estimated at 237 in 1755. Jamaica offered the greatest single market for slaves and is believed to have received 610,000 between 1700 and 1786. The slave trade still flourished in 1763, when about 150 ships sailed yearly from British ports to Africa with capacity for nearly 40,000 slaves.

There was no well-organized opposition to the slave trade before 1800, although some individuals and ephemeral societies condemned it. The Spanish church saw the importation of Negroes as an opportunity for converting them. The English religionist George Fox, founder of Quakerism (founded in the 1650s), accepted the fact that his followers had bought slaves in Barbados, but he urged kind treatment. The English novelist and political pamphleteer Daniel Defoe later denounced the traffic but seemingly regarded slavery itself as inevitable. The English and Pennsylvania Quakers passed resolutions forbidding their members to engage in the trade, but their wording suggests that some were doing so; in fact, 84 of them were members of the Merchants Trading to Africa.

Those opposing the slave trade often objected on other than humanitarian grounds. Some colonials feared any further growth of the Negro percentage of the population. Others, who justified English slave sales to the Spanish colonies because payment was in cash, condemned the same traffic with French islanders, who paid in molasses and thus competed with nearby English sugar planters.

Colonial wars of the 18th century. From 1689 to 1763, the British and French fought four wars that were mainly European in origin but which determined the colonial situation, in some cases for two centuries. Spain entered all four, first in alliance with England and later in partnership with France, though it played a secondary role.

King William's War (War of the League of Augsburg). The war known in Europe as that of the Palatinate, League of Augsburg, or Grand Alliance, and in America as King William's War, ended indecisively, after eight years, with the Treaty of Rijswijk in 1697. No territorial changes occurred in America, and because the great Mughal emperor Aurangzeb reigned in India, very little of the conflict penetrated there.

Queen Anne's War (War of the Spanish Succession). Queen Anne's War, the American phase of the War of the Spanish Succession (1701–14), began in 1702. Childless king Charles II of Spain, dying in 1700, willed his entire possessions to Philip, grandson of Louis XIV of France. England, the United Provinces, and Austria intervened, fearing a virtual union between powerful Louis and Spain detrimental to the balance of power, and Queen Anne's War lasted until terminated by the Treaty of Utrecht in 1713. England (Great Britain after 1707) gained Gibraltar and Minorca and, in North America, acquired Newfoundland and French Acadia (renamed Nova Scotia). It also received clear title to the northern area being exploited by the Hudson's Bay Company. Bourbon prince Philip was recognized as king of Spain, but the British secured the important *asiento*, or right to supply Spanish America with slaves, for 30 years.

King George's War (War of the Austrian Succession). There followed a peace almost unbroken until 1739, when, with the *asiento* about to expire and Spain unwilling to renew it, Great Britain and Spain went to war. The recent amputation of an English seaman's ear by a Spanish Caribbean coast guard caused the conflict to be named the War of Jenkins' Ear. This merged in 1740 with the War of the Austrian Succession (called King George's War in America), between Frederick II the Great of Prussia and Maria Theresa of Austria over Silesia. France joined Spain and Prussia against Great Britain and Austria, and the war, which was terminated in 1748 by the Treaty of Aix-la-Chapelle, proved indecisive. New England colonials captured Louisbourg, the fortified French island commanding the St. Lawrence entrance, but France's progress in India counterbalanced this conquest. With the Mughal Empire now virtually extinct, the British and French East India Companies fought each other, the advantage going to the French under Dupleix, who captured Madras and nearly expelled the British. The peace treaty restored all conquests; France recovered Louisbourg, and the British regained Madras and with it another chance to become paramount in India.

The French and Indian War (the Seven Years' War). Until 1754, when the two powers resumed their conflict in the French and Indian War in America, the overseas possessions maintained a show of peace. During this prewar period the French attempted to increase their hold on the Ohio Valley and in 1754 built Fort-Duquesne at the future site of Pittsburgh. Lt. Col. George Washington with colonial forces, in 1754, and Gen. Edward Braddock with British regulars, in 1755, were defeated in attempts to dislodge them. Dupleix and his successor, Charles-Joseph Patissier, marquis de Bussy-Castelnau, increased their influence in India; but the recall of Dupleix in 1754 damaged French prospects there.

The Seven Years' War, fought in Europe by Frederick the Great of Prussia against Austria, France, and Russia, ended with his survival against overwhelming odds. His one ally, Great Britain, helped financially but could render small military assistance. Overseas, the British triumphed completely over France, aided by Spain in the last years of the war. The French at first had the upper hand in both India and America, but the turning point came after William Pitt the Elder, later earl of Chatham, assumed direction of the British war effort. In 1757

First
Negroes in
English
North
America

British
gains in
North
America

Britain's
overseas
triumph
over
France

Clive won victory at Plassey over the Nawab of Bengal, an enemy of the British company; Sir Eyre Coote's victory at Wandewash in 1760, over the French governor Thomas Lally, was followed by the capture of Pondichéry.

In America, thanks largely to the vigorous policy of Pitt, the British won repeated victories. The French forts Frontenac, Duquesne, and Carillon fell in 1758 and 1759. British generals Sir Jeffrey Amherst and James Wolfe took Louisbourg in 1758, Quebec in 1759, and Montreal in 1760, and the surrender of Montreal included that of the entire French colony. Meanwhile, Adm. Edward Hawke destroyed or immobilized the principal French line fleet at Quiberon Bay in 1759. Spanish intervention in the war in 1761 merely enabled the British to seize Havana and Manila.

The Treaty of Paris in 1763 gave Britain all North America east of the Mississippi, including Spanish Florida. France ceded the western Mississippi Valley to Spain as compensation for the loss of Florida. Besides having a clear path to domination of India in the Old World, Great Britain also gained African Senegal. In the West Indies, it returned Martinique and Guadeloupe to France for the sake of peace but remained easily second to Spain there in importance.

The first great era of colonial conflict had ended, and the British Empire, a century and a half old, had become the world's foremost overseas domain. Though exceeded in size by that of Spain, it was the wealthiest, backed by the overwhelming naval power of Great Britain. British prestige had reached a new height, greater perhaps than it would ever attain again.   (C.E.No.)

II. European expansion since 1763

The global expansion of western Europe between the 1760s and the 1870s differed in several important ways from the expansionism and colonialism of previous centuries. Along with the rise of the Industrial Revolution, which economic historians generally trace to the 1760s, and the continuing spread of industrialization in the empire-building countries came a shift in the strategy of trade with the colonial world. Instead of being primarily buyers of colonial products (and frequently under strain to offer sufficient salable goods to balance the exchange), as in the past, the industrializing nations increasingly became sellers in search of markets for the growing volume of their machine-produced goods. Furthermore, over the years there occurred a decided shift in the composition of demand for goods produced in the colonial areas. Spices, sugar, and slaves became relatively less important with the advance of industrialization, concomitant with a rising demand for raw materials for industry (*e.g.*, cotton, wool, vegetable oils, jute, dyestuffs) and food for the swelling industrial areas (wheat, tea, coffee, cocoa, meat, butter).

This shift in trading patterns entailed in the long run changes in colonial policy and practice as well as in the nature of colonial acquisitions. The urgency to create markets and the incessant pressure for new materials and food were eventually reflected in colonial practices, which sought to adapt the colonial areas to the new priorities of the industrializing nations. Such adaptation involved major disruptions of existing social systems over wide areas of the globe. Before the impact of the Industrial Revolution, the changes forced upon the non-European world were largely confined to: (1) occupying areas that supplied precious metals, slaves, and tropical products then in large demand; (2) establishing white-settler colonies along the coast of North America; and (3) setting up trading posts and forts and applying superior military strength to achieve the transfer to European merchants of as much existing world trade as was feasible. However disruptive these changes may have been to the societies of Africa, South America, and the isolated plantation and white-settler colonies, the social systems over most of the Earth outside Europe nevertheless remained much the same as they had been for centuries (in some places for millennia). These societies, with their largely self-sufficient small communities based on subsistence agri-

culture and home industry, provided poor markets for the mass-produced goods flowing from the factories of the technologically advancing countries; nor were the existing social systems flexible enough to introduce and rapidly expand the commercial agriculture (and, later, mineral extraction) required to supply the food and raw material needs of the empire builders.

The adaptation of the nonindustrialized parts of the world to become more profitable adjuncts of the industrializing nations embraced, among other things: (1) overhaul of existing land and property arrangements, including the introduction of private property in land where it did not previously exist, as well as the expropriation of land for use by white settlers or for plantation agriculture; (2) creation of a labour supply for commercial agriculture and mining by means of direct forced labour and indirect measures aimed at generating a body of wage-seeking labourers; (3) spread of the use of money and exchange of commodities by imposing money payments for taxes and land rent and by inducing a decline of home industry; and (4) where the precolonial society already had a developed industry, curtailment of production and exports by native producers.

The classic illustration of this last policy is found in India. For centuries India had been an exporter of cotton goods, to such an extent that Great Britain for a long period imposed stiff tariff duties to protect its domestic manufacturers from Indian competition. Yet, by the middle of the 19th century, India was receiving one-fourth of all British exports of cotton piece goods and had lost its own export markets.

Clearly, such significant transformations could not get very far in the absence of appropriate political changes, such as the development of a sufficiently cooperative local elite, effective administrative techniques, and peace-keeping instruments that would assure social stability and environments conducive to the radical social changes imposed by a foreign power. Consistent with these purposes was the installation of new, or amendments of old, legal systems that would facilitate the operation of a money, business, and private land economy. And tying it all together was the imposition of the culture and language of the dominant power.

The changing nature of the relations between centres of empire and their colonies, under the impact of the unfolding Industrial Revolution, was also reflected in new trends in colonial acquisitions. While in preceding centuries colonies, trading posts, and settlements were in the main, except for South America, located along the coastline or on smaller islands, the expansions of the late 18th century and especially of the 19th century were distinguished by the spread of the colonizing powers, or of their emigrants, into the interior of continents. Such continental extensions, in general, took one of two forms, or some combination of the two: (1) the removal of the indigenous peoples by killing them off or forcing them into specially reserved areas, thus providing room for settlers from western Europe who then developed the agriculture and industry of these lands under the social system imported from the mother countries, or (2) the conquest of the indigenous peoples and the transformation of their existing societies to suit the changing needs of the more powerful militarily and technically advanced nations.

At the heart of Western expansionism was the growing disparity in technologies between those of the leading European nations and those of the rest of the world. Differences between the level of technology in Europe and some of the regions on other continents were not especially great in the early part of the 18th century. In fact, some of the crucial technical knowledge used in Europe at that time came originally from Asia. During the 18th century, however, and at an accelerating pace in the 19th and 20th centuries, the gap between the technologically advanced countries and technologically backward regions kept on increasing despite the diffusion of modern technology by the colonial powers. The most important aspect of this disparity was the technical superiority of Western armaments, for this superiority enabled the West

Shift in colonial trade strategy

Adaptation of nonindustrialized regions

New trends in colonial acquisitions

to impose its will on the much larger colonial populations. Advances in communication and transportation, notably railroads, also became important tools for consolidating foreign rule over extensive territories. And along with the enormous technical superiority and the colonizing experience itself came important psychological instruments of minority rule by foreigners: racism and arrogance on the part of the colonizers and a resulting spirit of inferiority among the colonized.

Naturally, the above description and summary telescope events that transpired over many decades and the incidence of the changes varied from territory to territory and from time to time, influenced by the special conditions in each area, by what took place in the process of conquest, by the circumstances at the time when economic exploitation of the possessions became desirable and feasible, and by the varying political considerations of the several occupying powers. Moreover, it should be emphasized that expansion policies and practices, while far from haphazard, were rarely the result of long-range and integrated planning. The drive for expansion was persistent, as were the pressures to get the greatest advantage possible out of the resulting opportunities. But the expansions arose in the midst of intense rivalry among major powers that were concerned with the distribution of power on the continent of Europe itself as well as with ownership of overseas territories. Thus, the issues of national power, national wealth, and military strength shifted more and more to the world stage as commerce and territorial acquisitions spread over larger segments of the globe. In fact, colonies were themselves often levers of military power—sources of military supplies and of military manpower and bases for navies and merchant marines. What appears, then, in tracing the concrete course of empire is an intertwining of the struggle for hegemony between competing national powers, the manoeuvring for preponderance of military strength, and the search for greatest advantage practically obtainable from the world's resources.

Influences behind expansion policies

EUROPEAN COLONIAL ACTIVITY (1763–c. 1875)

Stages of history rarely, if ever, come in neat packages: the roots of new historical periods begin to form in earlier eras, while many aspects of an older phase linger on and help shape the new. Nonetheless, there was a convergence of developments in the early 1760s, which, despite many qualifications, delineates a new stage in European expansionism and especially in that of the most successful empire builder, Great Britain. It is not only the Industrial Revolution in Great Britain that can be traced to this period but also the consequences of England's decisive victory over France in the Seven Years' War and the beginnings of what turned out to be the second British Empire. As a result of the Treaty of Paris, France lost nearly the whole of its colonial empire, while Britain became, except for Spain, the largest colonial power in the world.

The second British Empire. The removal of threat from the strongest competing foreign power set the stage for Britain's conquest of India and for operations against the North American Indians to extend British settlement in Canada and westerly areas of the North American continent. In addition, the new commanding position on the seas provided an opportunity for Great Britain to probe for additional markets in Asia and Africa and to try to break the Spanish trade monopoly in South America. During this period, the scope of British world interests broadened dramatically to cover the South Pacific, the Far East, the South Atlantic, and the coast of Africa.

The initial aim of this outburst of maritime activity was not so much the acquisition of extensive fresh territory as the attainment of a far-flung network of trading posts and maritime bases. The latter, it was hoped, would serve the interdependent aims of widening foreign commerce and controlling ocean shipping routes. But in the long run many of these initial bases turned out to be stepping-stones to future territorial conquests. Because the indigenous populations did not always take kindly to foreign incursions into their homelands, even when the foreigners

British naval superiority

limited themselves to small enclaves, penetration of interiors was often necessary to secure base areas against attack.

Loss of the American colonies. The path of conquest and territorial growth was far from orderly. It was frequently diverted by the renewal or intensification of rivalry between, notably, England, France, Spain, and the Low Countries in colonial areas and on the European continent. The most severe blow to Great Britain's 18th-century dreams of empire, however, came from the revolt of the 13 American colonies. These contiguous colonies were at the heart of the old, or what is often referred to as the first, British Empire, which consisted primarily of Ireland, the North American colonies, and the plantation colonies of the West Indies. Ironically, the elimination of this core of the first British Empire was to a large extent influenced by the upsurge of empire building after the Seven Years' War. Great Britain harvested from its victory in that war a new expanse of territory about equal to its prewar possessions on the North American continent: French Canada, the Floridas, and the territory between the Alleghenies and the Mississippi River. The assimilation of the French Canadians, control of the Indians and settlement of the trans-Allegheny region, and the opening of new trade channels created a host of problems for the British government. Not the least of these were the burdensome costs to carry out this program on top of a huge national debt accumulated during the war. To cope with these problems, new imperial policies were adopted by the mother country: raising (for the first time) revenue from the colonies; tightening mercantile restrictions, imposing firm measures against smuggling (an important source of income for colonial merchants), and putting obstacles in the way of New England's substantial trade with the West Indies. The strains generated by these policies created or intensified the hardships of large sections of the colonial population and, in addition, disrupted the relative harmony of interests that had been built up between the mother country and important elite groups in the colonies. Two additional factors, not unrelated to the enlargement of the British Empire, fed the onset and success of the American War of Independence (1775–83): first, a lessening need for military support from the mother country once the menacing French were removed from the continent and, second, support for the American Revolutionary forces from the French and Spanish, who had much to fear from the enhanced sea power and expansionism of the British.

Imperial policies in the late 18th century

The shock of defeat in North America was not the only problem confronting British society. Ireland—in effect, a colonial dependency—also experienced a revolutionary upsurge, giving added significance to attacks by leading British free traders against existing colonial policies and even at times against colonialism itself. But such criticism had little effect except as it may have hastened colonial administrative reforms to counteract real and potential independence movements in dependencies such as Canada and Ireland.

Conquest of India. Apart from reforms of this nature, the aftermath of American independence was a diversion of British imperial interests to other areas—the beginning of the settlement of Australia being a case in point. In terms of amount of effort and significance of results, however, the pursuit of conquest in India took first place. Starting with the assumption of control over the province of Bengal (after the Battle of Plassey, 1757) and especially after the virtual removal of French influence from the Indian Ocean, the British waged more or less continuous warfare against the Indian people and took over more and more of the interior. The Marāthās, the main source of resistance to foreign intrusion, were decisively defeated in 1803, but military resistance of one sort or another continued until the middle of the 19th century. The financing and even the military manpower for this prolonged undertaking came mainly from India itself. As British sovereignty spread, new land-revenue devices were soon instituted, which resulted in raising the revenue to finance the consolidation of power in India and the

Defeat of the Marāthās

conquest of other regions, breaking up the old system of self-sufficient and self-perpetuating villages and supporting an elite whose self-interests would harmonize with British rule.

Global expansion. Except for the acquisition of additional territory in India and colonies in Sierra Leone and New South Wales, the important additions to British overseas possessions between the Seven Years' War and the end of the Napoleonic era came as prizes of victory in wars with rival European colonial powers. In 1763 the first British Empire was primarily focussed on North America. By 1815, despite the loss of the 13 colonies, Britain had a second empire, one that straddled the globe from Canada and the Caribbean in the Western Hemisphere around the Cape of Good Hope to India and Australia. This empire was sustained by and in turn was supported by maritime power that far exceeded that of any of Britain's European rivals.

Policy changes. The half century of global expansion is only one aspect of the transition to the second British Empire. The operations of the new empire in the longer run also reflected decisive changes in British society. The replacement of mercantile by industrial enterprise as the main source of national wealth entailed changes to make national and colonial policy more consistent with the new hierarchy of interests. The restrictive trade practices and monopolistic privileges that sustained the commercial explosion of the 16th and most of the 17th centuries— built around the slave trade, colonial plantations, and monopolistic trading companies—did not provide the most effective environment for a nation on its way to becoming the workshop of the world.

The desired restructuring of policies occurred over decades of intense political conflict: the issues were not always clearly delineated, interest groups frequently overlapped, and the balance of power between competing vested interests shifted from time to time. The issues were clearly drawn in some cases, as for example over the continuation of the British East India Company's trade monopoly. The company's export of Indian silk, muslins, and other cotton goods was seen to be an obstacle to the development of markets for competing British manufactures. Political opposition to this monopoly was strong at the end of the 18th century, but the giant step on the road to free trade was not taken until the early decades of the 19th century (termination of the Indian trade monopoly, 1813; of the Chinese trade monopoly, 1833).

Contro-
versy over
the slave
trade

In contrast, the issues surrounding the strategic slave trade were much more complicated. The West Indies plantations relied on a steady flow of slaves from Africa. British merchants and ships profited not only from supplying these slaves but also from the slave trade with other colonies in the Western Hemisphere. In fact, the British were the leading slave traders, controlling at least half of the transatlantic slave trade by the end of the 18th century. But the influential planter and slave-trade interests had come under vigorous and unrelenting attack by religious and humanitarian leaders and organizations, who propelled the issue of abolition to the forefront of British politics around the turn of the 19th century. Historians are still unravelling the threads of conflicting arguments about the priority of causes in the final abolition of the slave trade and, later, of slavery itself, because economic as well as political issues were at play: glutted sugar markets (to which low-cost producers in competing colonies contributed) stimulated thoughts about controlling future output by limiting the supply of fresh slaves; the compensation paid to plantation owners by the British government at the time of the abolition of slavery rescued many planters from bankruptcy during a sugar crisis, with a substantial part of the compensation money being used to pay off planters' debts to London bankers. Moreover, the battle between pro-slavery and anti-slavery forces was fought in an environment in which free-trade interests were challenging established mercantilist practices and the West Indies sugar economy was in a secular decline.

The British were not the first to abolish the slave trade. Denmark had ended it earlier, and the United States

Constitution, written in 1787, had already provided for its termination in 1808. But the British Act of 1807 formally forbidding the slave trade was followed up by diplomatic and naval pressure to suppress the trade. By the 1820s Holland, Sweden, and France had also passed anti-slave-trade laws. Such laws and attempts to enforce them by no means stopped the trade, so long as there was buoyant demand for this commodity and good profit from dealing in it. Some decline in the demand for slaves did follow the final emancipation in 1833 of slaves in British possessions. On the other hand, the demand for slaves elsewhere in the Americas took on new life—*e.g.*, to work the virgin soils of Cuba and Brazil and to pick the rapidly expanding U.S. cotton crops to feed the voracious appetite of the British textile industry. Accordingly, the number of slaves shipped across the Atlantic accelerated at the same time Britain and other maritime powers outlawed this form of commerce.

Involvement in Africa. Although Britain's energetic activity to suppress the slave trade was far from effective, its diplomatic and military operations for this end led it to much greater involvement in African affairs. Additional colonies were acquired (Sierra Leone, 1808; Gambia, 1816; Gold Coast, 1821) to serve as bases for suppressing the slave trade and for stimulating substitute commerce. British naval squadrons touring the coast of Africa, stopping and inspecting suspected slavers of other nations, and forcing African tribal chiefs to sign anti-slavery treaties did not halt the expansion of the slave trade, but they did help Britain attain a commanding position along the western coast of Africa, which in turn contributed to the expansion of both its commercial and colonial empire.

The growth of informal empire. The transformation of the old colonial and mercantilist commercial system was completed when, in addition to the abolition of slavery and the slave trade, the Corn Laws and the Navigation Acts were repealed in the late 1840s. The repeal of the Navigation Acts acknowledged the new reality: the primacy of Britain's navy and merchant shipping. The repeal of the Corn Laws (which had protected agricultural interests) signalled the maturation of the Industrial Revolution. In the light of Britain's manufacturing supremacy, exclusivity and monopolistic trade restraints were less important than, and often detrimental to, the need for ever-expanding world markets and sources of inexpensive raw materials and food.

Repeal of
the
Navigation
Acts and
Corn Laws

With the new trade strategy, under the impetus of freer trade and technical progress, came a broadening of the concept of empire. It was found that the commercial and financial advantages of formal empire could often be derived by informal means. The development of a worldwide trade network, the growth of overseas banking, the export of capital to less advanced regions, the leading position of London's money markets—all under the shield of a powerful and mobile navy—led to Great Britain's economic pre-eminence and influence in many parts of the world, even in the absence of political control.

Anti-colonial sentiment. The growing importance of informal empire went hand in hand with increased expressions of dissatisfaction with the formal colonial empire. The critical approach to empire came from leading statesmen, government officials in charge of colonial policy, the free traders, and the philosophic Radicals (the latter, a broad spectrum of opinion makers often labelled the Little Englanders, whose voices of dissent were most prominent in the years between 1840 and 1870). Taking the long view, however, some historians question just how much of this current of political thought was really concerned with the transformation of the British Empire into a Little England. Those who seriously considered colonial separation were for the most part thinking of the more recent white-settler colonies, such as Canada, Australia, and New Zealand, and definitely not of independence for India nor, for that matter, for Ireland. Differences of opinion among the various political factions naturally existed over the best use of limited government finance, colonial administrative tactics, how much foreign territory could in practice be controlled, and such issues as the costs of friction with the United States over Canada. Yet, while there were important differences of opinion on the choice between formal and informal empire, no important conflict arose over the desirability of continued expansion of Britain's world influence and foreign commercial activity. Indeed, during the most active period of what has been presumed to be anti-colonialism, both the formal and informal empires grew substantially: new colonies were added, the territory of existing colonies was enlarged, and military campaigns were conducted to widen Britain's trading and investment area, as in the Opium wars of the mid-19th century (see below *Penetration of the West in Asia*).

Continued imperial growth

Decline of colonial rivalry. An outstanding development in colonial and empire affairs during the period between the Napoleonic Wars and the 1870s was an evident lessening in conflict between European powers. Not that conflict disappeared entirely, but the period as a whole was one of relative calm compared with either the almost continuous wars for colonial possessions in the 18th century or the revival of intense rivalries during the latter part of the 19th and early 20th centuries. Instead of wars among colonial powers, the period witnessed wars against colonized peoples and their societies, incident either to initial conquest or to the extension of territorial possessions farther into the interior. Examples are Great Britain in India, Burma, South Africa (Kaffir Wars), New Zealand (Maori Wars); France in Algeria and Indochina; the Low Countries in Indonesia; Russia in Central Asia; and the United States against the North American Indians.

Contributing to the abatement of intercolonial rivalries was the undisputable supremacy of the British Navy during these years. The increased use of steamships in the 19th century helped reinforce this supremacy: Great Britain's ample domestic coal supply and its numerous bases around the globe (already owned or newly obtained for this purpose) combined to make available needed coaling stations. Over several decades of the 19th century and until new developments toward the end of the century opened up a new age of naval rivalry, no country was in a position to challenge Britain's dominance of the seas. This may have temporarily weakened Britain's acquisitive drive: the motive of preclusive occupation of foreign territory still occurred, but it was not as pressing as at other times.

On the whole, despite the relative tranquillity and the rise of anti-colonial sentiment in Britain, the era was marked by a notable wave of European expansionism. Thus, in 1800 Europe and its possessions, including former colonies, claimed title to about 55 percent of the Earth's land surface: Europe, North and South America, most of India, the Russian part of Asia, parts of the East Indies, and small sections along the coast of Africa. But much of this was merely claimed; effective control existed over a little less than 35 percent, most of which consisted of Europe itself. By 1878—that is, before the next major wave of European acquisitions began—an additional 6,500,000 square miles (16,800,000 square kilometres) were claimed; during this period, control was consolidated over the new claims and over all the territory claimed in 1800. Hence, from 1800 to 1878, actual European rule (including former colonies in North and South America) increased from 35 to 67 percent of the Earth's land surface.

Consolidation of European colonial rule

Decline of the Spanish and Portuguese empires. The early 19th century, however, did witness a conspicuous exception to the trend of colonial growth, and that was the decline of the Portuguese and Spanish empires in the Western Hemisphere. The occasion for the decolonization was provided by the Napoleonic Wars. The French occupation of the Iberian Peninsula in 1807, combined with the ensuing years of intense warfare until 1814 on that peninsula between the British and French and their respective allies, effectively isolated the colonies from their mother countries. During this isolation the long-smouldering discontents in the colonies erupted in influential nationalist movements, revolutions of independence, and civil wars. The stricken mother countries

could hardly interfere with events on the South American continent, nor did they have the resources, even after the Peninsular War was over, to bring enough soldiers and armaments across the Atlantic to suppress the independence forces.

Great Britain could have intervened on behalf of Spain and Portugal, but it declined. British commerce with South America had blossomed during the Napoleonic Wars. New vistas of potentially profitable opportunities opened up in those years, in contrast with preceding decades when British penetration of Spanish colonial markets consisted largely of smuggling to get past Spain's mercantile restrictions. The British therefore now favoured independence for these colonies and had little interest in helping to reimpose colonial rule, with its accompanying limitations on British trade and investment. Support for colonial independence by the British came in several ways: merchants and financiers provided loans and supplies needed by insurrectionary governments; the Royal Navy protected the shipment of those supplies and the returning specie; and the British government made it clear to other nations that it considered South American countries independent. The British forthright position on independence, as well as the availability of the Royal Navy to support this policy, gave substance to the U.S. Monroe Doctrine (1823), which the United States had insufficient strength at that time to really enforce.

After some 15 years of uprisings and wars, Spain by 1825 no longer had any colonies in South America itself, retaining only the islands of Cuba and Puerto Rico. During the same period Brazil achieved its independence from Portugal. The advantages to the British economy made possible by the consequent opening up of the Latin American ports were eagerly pursued, facilitated by commercial treaties signed with these young nations. The reluctance of France to recognize their new status delayed French penetration of their markets and gave an advantage to the British. In one liberated area after another, brokers and commercial agents arrived from England to ferret out business opportunities. Soon the continent was flooded with British goods, often competing with much weaker native industries. Actually, Latin America provided the largest single export market for British cotton textiles in the first half of the 19th century.

South American independence

Despite the absence of formal empire, the British were able to attain economic pre-eminence in South America. Spanish and Portuguese colonialism had left a heritage of disunity and conflict within regions of new nations and between nations, along with conditions that led to unstable alliances of ruling elite groups. While this combination of weaknesses militated against successful self-development, it was fertile ground for energetic foreign entrepreneurs, especially those who had technically advanced manufacturing capacities, capital resources, international money markets, insurance and shipping facilities, plus supportive foreign policies. The early orgy of speculative loans and investments soon ended. But before long, British economic penetration entered into more lasting and self-perpetuating activities, such as promoting Latin American exports, providing railroad equipment, constructing public works, and supplying banking networks. Thus, while the collapse of the Spanish and Portuguese empires led to the decline of colonialism in the Western Hemisphere, it also paved the way for a significant expansion of Britain's informal empire of trade, investment, and finance during the 19th century.

The emigration of European peoples. European influence around the globe increased with each new wave of emigration from Europe. Tides of settlers brought with them the Old World culture and, often, useful agricultural and industrial skills. An estimated 55,000,000 Europeans left their native lands in the 100 years after 1820, the product chiefly of two forces: (1) the push to emigrate as a result of difficulties arising from economic dislocations at home and (2) the pull of land, jobs, and recruitment activities of passenger shipping lines and agents of labour-hungry entrepreneurs in the New World. Other factors were clearly also at work, such as the search for religious freedom, escape from tyrannical gov-

Spread of European culture and technology

ernments, avoidance of military conscription, and the desire for greater upward social and economic mobility. Such motives had existed throughout the centuries, however, and they are insufficient to explain the massive population movements that characterized the 19th century. Unemployment induced by rapid technological changes in agriculture and industry was an important incentive for English emigration in the mid-1800s. The surge of German emigration at roughly the same time is largely attributable to an agricultural revolution in Germany, which nearly ruined many farmers on small holdings in southwest Germany. Under English rule, the Irish were prevented from industrial development and were directed to an economy based on export of cereals grown on small holdings. A potato blight, followed by famine and eviction of farm tenants by landlords, gave large numbers of Irish no alternative other than emigration or starvation. These three nationalities—English, German, and Irish—composed the largest group of migrants in the 1850s. In later years Italians and Slavs contributed substantially to the population spillover. The emigrants spread throughout the world, but the bulk of the population transfer went to the Americas, Siberia, and Australasia. The population outflow, greatly facilitated by European supremacy outside Europe, helped ease the social pressures and probably abated the dangers of social upheaval in Europe itself.

Advance of the U.S. frontier. The outward movement of European peoples in any substantial numbers naturally was tied in with conquest and, to a greater or lesser degree, with the displacement of indigenous populations. In the United States, where by far the largest number of European emigrants went, acquisition of space for development by white immigrants entailed activity on two fronts: competition with rival European nations and disposition of the Indians. During a large part of the 19th century, the United States remained alert to the danger of encirclement by Europeans, but in addition the search for more fertile land, pursuit of the fur trade, and desire for ports to serve commerce in the Atlantic and Pacific oceans nourished the drive to penetrate the American continent. The most pressing points of tension with European nations were eliminated during the first half of the century: purchase of the Louisiana Territory from France in 1803 gave the United States control over the heartland of the continent; settlement of the War of 1812 ended British claims south of the 49th parallel up to the Rocky Mountains; Spain's cession of the Floridas in 1819 rounded out the Atlantic coastal frontier; and Russia's (1824) and Great Britain's (1846) relinquishment of claims to the Oregon territory gave the United States its window on the Pacific. The expansion of the United States, however, was not confined to liquidating rival claims of overseas empires; it also involved taking territory from neighbouring Mexico. United States settlers wrested Texas from Mexico (1836), and war against Mexico (1846–48) led to the U.S. annexation of the Southwest region between New Mexico and Utah to the Pacific Ocean.

Diplomatic and military victories over the European nations and Mexico were but one precondition for the transcontinental expansion of the United States. In addition, the Indian tribes sooner or later had to be rooted out to clear the new territory. At times, treaties were arranged with Indian tribes, by which vast areas were opened up for white settlement. But even where peaceful agreements had been reached, the persistent pressure of the search for land and commerce created recurrent wars with Indian tribes that were seeking to retain their homes and their land. On the whole, room for the new settlers was obtained by forced removal of natives to as yet non-white-settled land—a process that was repeated as white settlers occupied ever more territory. Massacres during wars, susceptibility to infectious European diseases, and hardships endured during forced migrations all contributed to the decline in the Indian population and the weakening of its resistance. Nevertheless, Indian wars occupied the United States Army's attention during most of the 19th century, ending with the eventual isolation of

the surviving Indians on reservations set aside by the U.S. government.

THE NEW IMPERIALISM (c. 1875–1914)

Re-emergence of colonial rivalries. Although there are sharp differences of opinion over the reasons for, and the significance of, the "new imperialism," there is little dispute that at least two developments in the late 19th and in the beginning of the 20th century signify a new departure: (1) notable speedup in colonial acquisitions; (2) an increase in the number of colonial powers.

New acquisitions. The annexations during this new phase of imperial growth differed significantly from the expansionism earlier in the 19th century. While the latter was substantial in magnitude, it was primarily devoted to the consolidation of claimed territory (by penetration of continental interiors and more effective rule over indigenous populations) and only secondarily to new acquisitions. On the other hand, the new imperialism witnessed a burst of activity in carving up as yet independent areas: taking over almost all Africa, a good part of Asia, and many Pacific islands. This new vigour in the pursuit of colonies is reflected in the fact that the rate of new territorial acquisitions of the new imperialism was almost three times that of the earlier period. Thus, the increase in new territories claimed in the first 75 years of the 19th century averaged about 83,000 square miles (210,000 square kilometres) a year. As against this, the colonial powers added an average of about 240,000 square miles (620,000 square kilometres) a year between the late 1870s and World War I (1914–18). By the beginning of that war, the new territory claimed was for the most part fully conquered, and the main military resistance of the indigenous populations had been suppressed. Hence, in 1914, as a consequence of this new expansion and conquest on top of that of preceding centuries, the colonial powers, their colonies, and their former colonies extended over approximately 85 percent of the Earth's surface. Economic and political control by leading powers reached almost the entire globe, for, in addition to colonial rule, other means of domination were exercised in the form of spheres of influence, special commercial treaties, and the subordination that lenders often impose on debtor nations.

New colonial powers. This intensification of the drive for colonies reflected much more than a new wave of overseas activities by traditional colonial powers, including Russia. The new imperialism was distinguished particularly by the emergence of additional nations seeking slices of the colonial pie: Germany, the United States, Belgium, Italy, and, for the first time, a non-European power, Japan. Indeed, this very multiplication of colonial powers, occurring in a relatively short period, accelerated the tempo of colonial growth. Unoccupied space that could potentially be colonized was limited. Therefore, the more nations there were seeking additional colonies at about the same time, the greater was the premium on speed. Thus, the rivalry among the colonizing nations reached new heights, which in turn strengthened the motivation for preclusive occupation of territory and for attempts to control territory useful for the military defense of existing empires against rivals.

The impact of the new upsurge of rivalry is well illustrated in the case of Great Britain. Relying on its economic pre-eminence in manufacturing, trade, and international finance as well as on its undisputed mastery of the seas during most of the 19th century, Great Britain could afford to relax in the search for new colonies, while concentrating on consolidation of the empire in hand and on building up an informal empire. But the challenge of new empire builders, backed up by increasing naval power, put a new priority on Britain's desire to extend its colonial empire. On the other hand, the more that potential colonial space shrank, the greater became the urge of lesser powers to remedy disparities in size of empires by redivision of the colonial world. The struggle over contested space and for redivision of empire generated an increase in wars among the colonial powers and an intensification of diplomatic manoeuvring.

Marginal notes:

Penetration of the American continent

Increase in new territories in Africa and Asia

Struggle over redivision of empire

Rise of new industrialized nations. Parallel with the emergence of new powers seeking a place in the colonial sun and the increasing rivalry among existing colonial powers was the rise of industrialized nations able and willing to challenge Great Britain's lead in industry, finance, and world trade. In the mid-19th century Britain's economy outdistanced by far its potential rivals. But, by the last quarter of that century, Britain was confronted by restless competitors seeking a greater share of world trade and finance; the Industrial Revolution had gained a strong foothold in these nations, which were spurred on to increasing industrialization with the spread of railroad lines and the maturation of integrated national markets.

Moreover, the major technological innovations of the late 19th and early 20th centuries improved the competitive potential of the newer industrial nations. Great Britain's advantage as the progenitor of the first Industrial Revolution diminished substantially as the newer products and sources of energy of what has been called a second Industrial Revolution began to dominate industrial activity. The late starters, having digested the first Industrial Revolution, now had a more equal footing with Great Britain: they were all starting out more or less from the same base to exploit the second Industrial Revolution. This new industrialism, notably featuring mass-produced steel, electric power and oil as sources of energy, industrial chemistry, and the internal-combustion engine, spread over western Europe, the United States, and eventually Japan.

A world economy. To operate efficiently, the new industries required heavy capital investment in large-scale units. Accordingly, they encouraged the development of capital markets and banking institutions that were large and flexible enough to finance the new enterprises. The larger capital markets and industrial enterprises, in turn, helped push forward the geographic scale of operations of the industrialized nations: more capital could now be mobilized for foreign loans and investment, and the bigger businesses had the resources for the worldwide search for and development of the raw materials essential to the success and security of their investments. Not only did the new industrialism generate a voracious appetite for raw materials, but food for the swelling urban populations was now also sought in the far corners of the world. Advances in ship construction (steamships using steel hulls, twin screws, and compound engines) made feasible the inexpensive movement of bulk raw materials and food over long ocean distances. Under the pressures and opportunities of the later decades of the 19th century, more and more of the world was drawn upon as primary producers for the industrialized nations. Self-contained economic regions dissolved into a world economy, involving an international division of labour whereby the leading industrial nations made and sold manufactured products and the rest of the world supplied them with raw materials and food.

New militarism. The complex of social, political, and economic changes that accompanied the new industrialism and the vastly expanded and integrated world commerce also provided a setting for intensified commercial rivalry, the rebuilding of high tariff walls, and a revival of militarism. Of special importance militarily was the race in naval construction, which was propelled by the successful introduction and steady improvement of radically new warships that were steam driven, armourplated, and equipped with weapons able to penetrate the new armour. Before the development of these new technologies, Britain's naval superiority was overwhelming and unchallengeable. But because Britain was now obliged in effect to build a completely new navy, other nations with adequate industrial capacities and the will to devote their resources to this purpose could challenge Britain's supremacy at sea.

The new militarism and the intensification of colonial rivalry signalled the end of the relatively peaceful conditions of the mid-19th century. The conflict over the partition of Africa, the South African War (the Boer War), the Sino-Japanese War, the Spanish–American War, and

the Russo-Japanese War were among the indications that the new imperialism had opened a new era that was anything but peaceful.

The new imperialism also represented an intensification of tendencies that had originated in earlier periods. Thus, for example, the decision by the United States to go to war with Spain cannot be isolated from the long-standing interest of the United States in the Caribbean and the Pacific. The defeat of Spain and the suppression of the independence revolutions in Cuba and the Philippines finally gave substance to the Monroe Doctrine: the United States now became the dominant power in the Caribbean, and the door was opened for acquisition of greater influence in all of Latin America. Possession of the Philippines was consistent with the historic interest of the United States in the commerce of the Pacific, as it had already manifested by its long interest in Hawaii (annexed in 1898) and by an expedition by Commo. Matthew Perry to Japan (1853).

Historiographical debate. The new imperialism marked the end of vacillation over the choice of imperialist military and political policies; similar decisions to push imperialist programs to the forefront were arrived at by the leading industrial nations over a relatively short period. This historical conjuncture requires explanation and still remains the subject of debate among historians and social scientists. The pivot of the controversy is the degree to which the new imperialism was the product of primarily economic forces and in particular whether it was a necessary attribute of the capitalist system.

Serious analysts on both sides of the argument recognize that there is a multitude of factors involved: the main protagonists of economic imperialism recognize that political, military, and ideological influences were also at work; similarly, many who dispute the economic imperialism thesis acknowledge that economic interests played a significant role. The problem, however, is one of assigning priority to causes.

Economic imperialism. The father of the economic interpretation of the new imperialism was the British liberal economist John Atkinson Hobson. In his seminal study, *Imperialism, a Study* (first published in 1902), he pointed to the role of such drives as patriotism, philanthropy, and the spirit of adventure in advancing the imperialist cause. As he saw it, however, the critical question was why the energy of these active agents takes the particular form of imperialist expansion. Hobson located the answer in the financial interests of the capitalist class as "the governor of the imperial engine." Imperialist policy had to be considered irrational if viewed from the vantage point of the nation as a whole: the economic benefits derived were far less than the costs of wars and armaments; and needed social reforms were shunted aside in the excitement of imperial adventure. But it was rational, indeed, in the eyes of the minority of financial interest groups. And the reason for this, in Hobson's view, was the persistent congestion of capital in manufacturing. The pressure of capital needing investment outlets arose in part from a maldistribution of income: low mass consuming power blocks the absorption of goods and capital inside the country. Moreover, the practices of the larger firms, especially those operating in trusts and combines, foster restrictions on output, thus avoiding the risks and waste of overproduction. Because of this, the large firms are faced with limited opportunities to invest in expanding domestic production. The result of both the maldistribution of income and monopolistic behaviour is a need to open up new markets and new investment opportunities in foreign countries.

Hobson's study covered a broader spectrum than the analysis of what he called its economic taproot. It also examined the associated features of the new imperialism, such as political changes, racial attitudes, and nationalism. The book as a whole made a strong impression on, and greatly influenced, Marxist thinkers who were becoming more involved with the struggle against imperialism. The most influential of the Marxist studies was a small book published by Lenin in 1917, *Imperialism, the Highest Stage of Capitalism.* Despite many similarities,

Need for heavy capital investment

Hobson's interpretation of the new imperialism

Marxist interpretation

at bottom there is a wide gulf between Hobson's and Lenin's frameworks of analysis and also between their respective conclusions. While Hobson saw the new imperialism serving the interests of certain capitalist groups, he believed that imperialism could be eliminated by social reforms while maintaining the capitalist system. This would require restricting the profits of those classes whose interests were closely tied to imperialism and attaining a more equitable distribution of income so that consumers would be able to buy up a nation's production. Lenin, on the other hand, saw imperialism as being so closely integrated with the structure and normal functioning of an advanced capitalism that he believed that only the revolutionary overthrow of capitalism, with the substitution of Socialism, would rid the world of imperialism.

Lenin placed the issues of imperialism in a context broader than the interests of a special sector of the capitalist class. According to Lenin, capitalism itself changed in the late 19th century; moreover, because this happened at pretty much the same time in several leading capitalist nations, it explains why the new phase of capitalist development came when it did. This new phase, Lenin believed, involves political and social as well as economic changes; but its economic essence is the replacement of competitive capitalism by monopoly capitalism, a more advanced stage in which finance capital, an alliance between large industrial and banking firms, dominates the economic and political life of society. Competition continues, but among a relatively small number of giants who are able to control large sectors of the national and international economy. It is this monopoly capitalism and the resulting rivalry generated among monopoly capitalist nations that foster imperialism; in turn, the processes of imperialism stimulate the further development of monopoly capital and its influence over the whole society.

The difference between Lenin's more complex paradigm and Hobson's shows up clearly in the treatment of capital export. Like Hobson, Lenin maintained that the increasing importance of capital exports is a key figure of imperialism, but he attributed the phenomenon to much more than pressure from an overabundance of capital. He also saw the acceleration of capital migration arising from the desire to obtain exclusive control over raw material sources and to get a tighter grip on foreign markets. He thus shifted the emphasis from the general problem of surplus capital, inherent in capitalism in all its stages, to the imperatives of control over raw materials and markets in the monopoly stage. With this perspective, Lenin also broadened the concept of imperialism. Because the thrust is to divide the world among monopoly interest groups, the ensuing rivalry extends to a struggle over markets in the leading capitalist nations as well as in the less advanced capitalist and colonial countries. This rivalry is intensified because of the uneven development of different capitalist nations: the latecomers aggressively seek a share of the markets and colonies controlled by those who got there first, who naturally resist such a redivision. Other forces—political, military, and ideological—are at play in shaping the contours of imperialist policy, but Lenin insisted that these influences germinate in the seedbed of monopoly capitalism.

Noneconomic imperialism. Perhaps the most systematic alternative theory of imperialism was proposed by Joseph Alois Schumpeter, one of the best known economists of the first half of the 20th century. His essay "Zur Soziologie des Imperialismus" ("The Sociology of Imperialism") was first published in Germany in the form of two articles in 1919. Although Schumpeter was probably not familiar with Lenin's *Imperialism* at the time he wrote his essay, his arguments were directed against the Marxist currents of thought of the early 20th century and in particular against the idea that imperialism grows naturally out of capitalism. Unlike other critics, however, Schumpeter accepted some of the components of the Marxist thesis, and to a certain extent he followed the Marxist tradition of looking for the influence of class

Schumpeter's interpretation

forces and class interests as major levers of social change. In doing so, he in effect used the weapons of Marxist thought to rebut the essence of Marxist theory.

A survey of empires, beginning with the earliest days of written history, led Schumpeter to conclude that there are three generic characteristics of imperialism: (1) At root is a persistent tendency to war and conquest, often producing nonrational expansions that have no sound utilitarian aim. (2) These urges are not innate in man. They evolved from critical experiences when peoples and classes were molded into warriors to avoid extinction; the warrior mentality and the interests of warrior classes live on, however, and influence events even after the vital need for wars and conquests disappears. (3) The drift to war and conquest is sustained and conditioned by the domestic interests of ruling classes, often under the leadership of those individuals who have most to gain economically and socially from war. But for these factors, Schumpeter believed, imperialism would have been swept away into the dustbin of history as capitalist society ripened; for capitalism in its purest form is antithetical to imperialism: it thrives best with peace and free trade. Yet despite the innate peaceful nature of capitalism, interest groups do emerge that benefit from aggressive foreign conquests. Under monopoly capitalism the fusion of big banks and cartels creates a powerful and influential social group that pressures for exclusive control in colonies and protectorates, for the sake of higher profits.

Notwithstanding the resemblance between Schumpeter's discussion of monopoly and that of Lenin and other Marxists, a crucial difference does remain. Monopoly capitalism in Lenin's frame of reference is a natural outgrowth of the previous stage of competitive capitalism. But according to Schumpeter, it is an artificial graft on the more natural competitive capitalism, made possible by the catalytic effect of the residue from the preceding feudal society. Schumpeter argued that monopoly capitalism can only grow and prosper under the protection of high tariff walls; without that shield there would be large-scale industry but no cartels or other monopolistic arrangements. Because tariff walls are erected by political decisions, it is the state and not a natural economic process that promotes monopoly. Therefore, it is in the nature of the state—and especially those features that blend the heritage of the previous autocratic state, the old war machine, and feudal interests and ideas along with capitalist interests—that the cause of imperialism will be discovered. The particular form of imperialism in modern times is affected by capitalism, and capitalism itself is modified by the imperialist experience. In Schumpeter's analysis, however, imperialism is neither a necessary nor inevitable product of capitalism.

The state as the progenitor of imperialism

Quest for a general theory of imperialism. The main trend of academic thought in the Western world is to follow Schumpeter's conclusion—that modern imperialism is not a product of capitalism—without paying close attention to Schumpeter's sophisticated sociological analysis. Specialized studies have produced a variety of interpretations of the origin or reawakening of the new imperialism: for France, bolstering of national prestige after its defeat in the Franco-Prussian War (1870–71); for Germany, Bismarck's design to stay in power when threatened by political rivals; for England, the desire for greater military security in the Mediterranean and India. These reasons—along with other frequently mentioned contributing causes, such as the spirit of national and racial superiority and the drive for power—are still matters of controversy with respect to specific cases and to the problem of fitting them into a general theory of imperialism. For example, if it is found that a new colony was acquired for better military defense of existing colonies, the questions still remain as to why the existing colonies were acquired in the first place and why it was considered necessary to defend them rather than to give them up. Similarly, explanations in terms of the search for power still have to account for the close relationship between power and wealth, because in the real world adequate economic resources are needed for a nation to hold on to its power, let alone to increase it. Conversely, increasing a nation's wealth often requires power. As is characteristic of historical phenomena, imperialist expansion is conditioned by a nation's previous history and the particular situation preceding each expansionist move. Moreover, it is carried forth in the midst of a complex of political, military, economic, and psychological impulses. It would seem, therefore, that the attempt to arrive at a theory that explains each and every imperialist action—ranging from a semi-feudal Russia to a relatively undeveloped Italy to an industrially powerful Germany—is a vain pursuit. But this does not eliminate the more important challenge of constructing a theory that will provide a meaningful interpretation of the almost simultaneous eruption of the new imperialism in a whole group of leading powers.

PENETRATION OF THE WEST IN ASIA

Russia's eastward expansion. European nations and Japan at the end of the 19th century spread their influence and control throughout the continent of Asia. Russia, because of its geographic position, was the only occupying power whose Asian conquests were overland. In that respect there is some similarity between Russia and the United States in the forcible outward push of their continental frontiers. But there is a significant difference: the United States advance displaced the indigenous population, with the remaining Indians becoming wards of the state. On the other hand, the Russian march across Asia resulted in the incorporation of alien cultures and societies as virtual colonies of the Russian Empire, while providing room for the absorption of Russian settlers.

Although the conquest of Siberia and the drive to the Pacific had been periodically absorbing Russia's military energies since the 16th century, the acquisition of additional Asian territory and the economic integration of previously acquired territory took a new turn in the 19th century. Previously, Russian influence in its occupied territory was quite limited, without marked alteration of the social and economic structure of the conquered peoples. Aside from looting and exacting tribute from subject tribes, the major objects of interest were the fur trade, increased commerce with China and in the Pacific, and land. But changes in 19th-century Russian society, especially those coming after the Crimean War (1853–56), signalled a new departure. First, Russia's resounding defeat in that war temporarily frustrated its aspirations in the Balkans and the Near East; but, because its dynastic and military ambitions were in no way diminished, its expansionist energies turned with increased vigour to its Asian frontiers. Second, the emancipation of the serfs (1861), which eased the feudal restrictions on the landless peasants, led to large waves of migration by Russians and Ukrainians—first to Siberia and later to Central Asia. Third, the surge of industrialization, foreign trade, and railway building in the post-Crimean War decades paved the way for the integration of Russian Asia, which formerly, for all practical purposes, had been composed of separate dependencies, and for a new type of subjugation for many of these areas, especially in Central Asia, in which the conquered societies were "colonized" to suit the political and economic needs of the conqueror.

This process of acquisition and consolidation in Asia spread out in four directions: Siberia, the Far East, the Caucasus, and Central Asia. This pursuit of tsarist ambitions for empire and for warm-water ports involved numerous clashes and conflicts along the way. Russian expansion was ultimately limited not by the fierce opposition of the native population, which was at times a stumbling block, but by the counterpressure of competitive empire builders, such as Great Britain and Japan. Great Britain and Russia were mutually alarmed as the distances between the expanding frontiers of Russia and India shortened. One point of conflict was finally resolved when both powers agreed on the delimitation of the northern border of Afghanistan. A second major area of conflict in Central Asia was settled by an Anglo-Russian treaty (1907) to divide Persia into two separate

spheres of influence, leaving a nominally independent Persian nation.

As in the case of Afghanistan and Persia, penetration of Chinese territory produced clashes with both the native government and other imperialist powers. At times China's preoccupation with its struggle against other invading powers eased the way for Russia's penetration. Thus, in 1860, when Anglo-French soldiers had entered Peking, Russia was able to wrest from China the Amur Province and special privileges in Manchuria (Northeast Provinces) south of the Amur River. With this as a stepping-stone, Russia took over the seacoast north of Korea and founded the town of Vladivostok. But, because the Vladivostok harbour is icebound for some four months of the year, the Russians began to pay more attention to getting control of the Korean coastline, where many good year-round harbours could be found. Attempts to acquire a share of Korea, as well as all of Manchuria, met with the resistance of Britain and Japan. Further thrusts into China beyond the Amur and maritime provinces were finally thwarted by defeat in 1905 in the Russo-Japanese War.

The partitioning of China. The evolution of the penetration of Asia was naturally influenced by a multiplicity of factors—economic and political conditions in the expanding nations, the strategy of the military officials of the latter nations, the problems facing colonial rulers in each locality, pressures arising from white settlers and businessmen in the colonies, as well as the constraints imposed by the always limited economic and military resources of the imperialist powers. All these elements were present to a greater or lesser extent at each stage of the forward push of the colonial frontiers by the Dutch in Indonesia, the French in Indochina (Vietnam, Laos, Cambodia), and the British in Malaya, Burma, and Borneo.

Yet, despite the variety of influences at work, three general types of penetration stand out. One of these is expansion designed to overcome resistance to foreign rule. Resistance, which assumed many forms ranging from outright rebellion to sabotage of colonial political and economic domination, was often strongest in the border areas farthest removed from the centres of colonial power. The consequent extension of military control to the border regions tended to arouse the fears and opposition of neighbouring states or tribal societies and thus led to the further extension of control. Hence, attempts to achieve military security prompted the addition of border areas and neighbouring nations to the original colony.

A second type of expansion was a response to the economic opportunities offered by exploitation of the colonial interiors. Traditional trade and the free play of market forces in Asia did not produce huge supplies of raw materials and food or the enlarged export markets sought by the industrializing colonial powers. For this, entrepreneurs and capital from abroad were needed, mines and plantations had to be organized, labour supplies mobilized, and money economies created. All these alien intrusions functioned best under the firm security of an accommodating alien law and order.

The third type of expansion was the result of rivalry among colonial powers. When possible, new territory was acquired or old possessions extended in order either to preclude occupation by rivals or to serve as buffers for military security against the expansions of nearby colonial powers. Where the crosscurrents of these rivalries prevented any one power from obtaining exclusive control, various substitute arrangements were arrived at: parts of a country were chipped off and occupied by one or more of the powers; spheres of influence were partitioned; unequal commercial treaties were imposed—while the countries subjected to such treatment remained nominally independent.

The penetration of China is the outstanding example of this type of expansion. In the early 19th century the middle part of eastern Asia (Japan, Korea, and China), containing about half the Asian population, was still little affected by Western penetration. By the end of the century, Korea was on the way to becoming annexed by

Overland conquests

Penetration of China

Rivalry
over
China

Japan, which had itself become a leading imperialist power. China remained independent politically, though it was already extensively dominated by outside powers. Undoubtedly, the intense rivalry of the foreign powers helped save China from being taken over outright (as India had been). China was pressed on all sides by competing powers anxious for its trade and territory: Russia from the north, Great Britain (via India and Burma) from the south and west, France (via Indochina) from the south, and Japan and the United States (in part, via the Philippines) from the east.

The Opium wars. The first phase of the forceful penetration of China by western Europe came in the two Opium wars. Great Britain had been buying increasing quantities of tea from China, but it had few products that China was interested in buying by way of exchange. A resulting steady drain of British silver to pay for the tea was eventually stopped by Great Britain's ascendancy in India. With British merchants in control of India's foreign trade and with the financing of this trade centred in London, a three-way exchange developed: the tea Britain bought in China was paid for by India's exports of opium and cotton to China. And because of a rapidly increasing demand for tea in England, British merchants actively fostered the profitable exports of opium and cotton from India.

An increasing Chinese addiction to opium fed a boom in imports of the drug and led to an unfavourable trade balance paid for by a steady loss of China's silver reserves. In light of the economic effect of the opium trade plus the physical and mental deterioration of opium users, Chinese authorities banned the opium trade. At first this posed few obstacles to British merchants, who resorted to smuggling. But enforcement of the ban became stringent toward the end of the 1830s; stores of opium were confiscated, and warehouses were closed down. British merchants had an additional and longstanding grievance because the Chinese limited all trade by foreigners to the port of Canton.

In June 1840 the British fleet arrived at the mouth of the Canton River to begin the Opium War. The Chinese capitulated in 1842 after the fleet reached the Yangtze, Shanghai fell, and Nanking was under British guns. The resulting Treaty of Nanking—the first in a series of commercial treaties China was forced to sign over the years—provided for: (1) cession of Hong Kong to the British crown; (2) the opening of five treaty ports, where the British would have residence and trade rights; (3) the right of British nationals in China who were accused of criminal acts to be tried in British courts; and (4) the limitation of duties on imports and exports to a modest rate. Other countries soon took advantage of this forcible opening of China; in a few years similar treaties were signed by China with the United States, France, and Russia.

Opening
of China

The Chinese, however, tried to retain some independence by preventing foreigners from entering the interior of China. With the country's economic and social institutions still intact, markets for Western goods, such as cotton textiles and machinery, remained disappointing: the self-sufficient communities of China were not disrupted as those in India had been under direct British rule, and opium smuggling by British merchants continued as a major component of China's foreign trade. Western merchants sought further concessions to improve markets. But meanwhile China's weakness, along with the stresses induced by foreign intervention, was further intensified by an upsurge of peasant rebellions, especially the massive 14-year Taiping Rebellion (1850–64).

The Western powers took advantage of the increasing difficulties by pressing for even more favourable trade treaties, culminating in a second war against China (1856–60), this time by France and England. Characteristically, the Western powers invading China played a double role: in addition to forcing a new trade treaty, they also helped to sustain the Chinese ruling establishment by participating in the suppression of the Taiping Rebellion; they believed that a Taiping victory would result in a reformed and centralized China, more resistant to Western penetration. China's defeat in the second war with the West produced a series of treaties, signed at Tientsin with Britain, France, Russia, and the United States, which brought the Western world deeper into China's affairs. The Tientsin treaties provided, among other things, for the right of foreign nationals to travel in the interior, the right of foreign ships to trade and patrol on the Yangtze River, the opening up of more treaty ports, and additional exclusive legal jurisdiction by foreign powers over their nationals residing in China.

Foreign privileges in China. Treaties of this general nature were extended over the years to grant further privileges to foreigners. Furthermore, more and more Western nations—including Germany, Italy, Denmark, The Netherlands, Spain, Belgium, and Austria-Hungary —took advantage of the new opportunities by signing such treaties. By the beginning of the 20th century, some 90 Chinese ports had been opened to foreign control. While the Chinese government retained nominal sovereignty in these ports, de facto rule was exercised by one or more of the powers: in Shanghai, for example, Great Britain and the United States coalesced their interests to form the Shanghai International Settlement. In most of the treaty ports, China leased substantial areas of land at low rates to foreign governments. The consulates in these concessions exercised legal jurisdiction over their nationals, who thereby escaped China's laws and tax collections. The foreign settlements had their own police forces and tax systems and ran their own affairs independently of nominally sovereign China.

These settlements were not the only intrusion on China's sovereignty. In addition, the opium trade was finally legalized, customs duties were forced downward to facilitate competition of imported Western goods, foreign gunboats patrolled China's rivers, and aliens were placed on customs-collection staffs to ensure that China would pay the indemnities imposed by various treaties. In response to these indignities and amid growing anti-foreign sentiment, the Chinese government attempted reforms to modernize and develop sufficient strength to resist foreign intrusions. Steps were taken to master Western science and technology, erect shipyards and arsenals, and build a more effective army and navy. The reforms, however, did not get very far: they did not tackle the roots of China's vulnerability, its social and political structure; and they were undertaken quite late, after foreign nations had already established a strong foothold. Also, it is likely that the reforms were not wholehearted because two opposing tendencies were at play: on the one hand, a wish to seek independence and, on the other hand, a basic reliance on foreign support by a weak Manchu government beset with rebellion and internal opposition.

Chinese
attempts
at mod-
ernization

The Open Door Policy. In any event, preliminary attempts to Westernize Chinese society from within did not deter further foreign penetration; nor did the subsequent revolution (1911) succeed in freeing China from Western domination. Toward the end of the 19th century, under the impact of the new imperialism, the spread of foreign penetration accelerated. Germany entered a vigorous bid for its sphere of influence; Japan and Russia pushed forward their territorial claims; and United States commercial and financial penetration of the Pacific, with naval vessels patrolling Chinese rivers, was growing rapidly. But at the same time this mounting foreign interest also inhibited the outright partition of China. Any step by one of the powers toward outright partition or sizable enlargement of its sphere of influence met with strong opposition from other powers. This led eventually to the Open Door Policy, advocated by the United States, which limited or restricted exclusive privileges of any one power vis-à-vis the others. It became generally accepted after the anti-foreign Boxer Rebellion (1900) in China. With the foreign armies that had been brought in to suppress the rebellion now stationed in North China, the danger to the continued existence of the Chinese government and the danger of war among the imperialist powers for their share of the country seemed greater than ever. Agreement on the Open Door Policy helped to retain both a compliant native government and equal opportunity for commerce, finance, and investment by the more advanced nations.

Japan's rise as a colonial power. Japan was the only Asian country to escape colonization from the West. European nations and the United States tried to "open the door," and to some extent they succeeded; but Japan was able to shake off the kind of subjugation, informal or formal, to which the rest of Asia succumbed. Even more important, it moved onto the same road of industrialization as did Europe and the United States. And instead of being colonized it became one of the colonial powers.

Japan had traditionally sought to avoid foreign intrusion. For many years, only the Dutch and the Chinese were allowed trading depots, each having access to only one port. No other foreigners were permitted to land in Japan, though Russia, France, and England tried, but with little success. The first significant crack in Japan's trade and travel barriers was forced by the United States in an effort to guarantee and strengthen its shipping interests in the Far East. Japan's guns and ships were no match for those of Commodore Perry in his two U.S. naval expeditions to Japan (1853, 1854).

The Japanese, well aware of the implications of foreign penetration through observing what was happening to China, tried to limit Western trade to two ports. In 1858, however, Japan agreed to a full commercial treaty with the United States, followed by similar treaties with the Low Countries, Russia, France, and Britain. The treaty pattern was familiar: more ports were opened; resident foreigners were granted extraterritorial rights, as in China; import and export duties were predetermined, thus removing control that Japan might otherwise exercise over its foreign trade.

Many attempts have been made to explain why a weak Japan was not taken over as a colony or, at least, did not follow in China's footsteps. Despite the absence of a commonly accepted theory, two factors were undoubtedly crucial. On the one hand, the Western nations did not pursue their attempts to control Japan as aggressively as they did elsewhere. In Asia the interests of the more aggressively expanding powers had centred on India, China, and the immediately surrounding areas. When greater interest developed in a possible breakthrough in Japan in the 1850s and 1860s, the leading powers were occupied with other pressing affairs, such as the 1857 Indian mutiny, the Taiping Rebellion, the Crimean War, French intervention in Mexico, and the United States Civil War. International jealousy may also have played a role in deterring any one power from trying to gain exclusive control over the country. On the other hand, in Japan itself, the danger of foreign military intervention, a crisis in its traditional feudal society, the rise of commerce, and a disaffected peasantry led to an intense internal power struggle and finally to a revolutionary change in the country's society and a thoroughgoing modernization program, one that brought Japan the economic and military strength to resist foreign nations.

The opposing forces in Japan's civil war were lined up between the supporters of the ruling Tokugawa family, which headed a rigid hierarchical feudal society, and the supporters of the emperor Meiji, whose court had been isolated from any significant government role. The civil war culminated in 1868 in the overthrow of the Tokugawa government and the restoration of the rule of the Emperor. The Meiji Restoration also brought new interest groups to the centre of political power and instigated a radical redirection of Japan's economic development. The nub of the changeover was the destruction of the traditional feudal social system and the building of a political, social, and economic framework conducive to capitalist industrialization. The new state actively participated in the turnabout by various forms of grants and guarantees to enterprising industrialists and by direct investment in basic industries such as railways, shipbuilding, communications, and machinery. The concentration of resources in the industrial sector was matched by social reforms that eliminated feudal restrictions, accelerated mass education, and encouraged acquisition of skills in the use of Western technology. The ensuing industrialized economy provided the means for Japan to hold its own in modern warfare and to withstand foreign economic competition.

Soon Japan not only followed the Western path of internal industrialization, but it also began an outward aggression resembling that of the European nations. First came the acquisition and colonization of neighbouring islands: Ryukyu Islands (including Okinawa), the Kuril Islands, Bonin Islands, and Hokkaido. Next in Japan's expansion program was Korea, but the opposition of other powers postponed the transformation of Korea into a Japanese colony. The pursuit of influence in Korea involved Japan in war with China (1894–95), at the end of which China recognized Japan's interest in Korea and ceded to Japan Taiwan, the Pescadores, and southern Manchuria. At this point rival powers interceded to force Japan to forgo taking over the southern Manchuria peninsula. While France, Britain, and Germany were involved in seeking to frustrate Japan's imperial ambitions, the most direct clash was with Russia over Korea and Manchuria. Japan's defeat of Russia in the war of 1904–05 procured for Japan the lease of the Liaotung Peninsula, the southern part of the island of Sakhalin, and recognition of its "paramount interest" in Korea. Still, pressure by Britain and the United States kept Japan from fulfillment of its plan to possess Manchuria outright. By the early 20th century, however, Japan had, by means of economic and political penetration, attained a privileged position in that part of China, as well as colonies in Korea and Taiwan and neighbouring islands.

PARTITION OF AFRICA

By the turn of the 20th century, the map of Africa looked like a huge jigsaw puzzle, with most of the boundary lines having been drawn in a sort of game of give-and-take played in the foreign offices of the leading European powers. The division of Africa, the last continent to be so carved up, was essentially a product of the new imperialism, vividly highlighting its essential features. In this respect, the timing and the pace of the scramble for Africa are especially noteworthy. Before 1880 colonial possessions in Africa were relatively few and limited to coastal areas, with large sections of the coastline and almost all the interior still independent. By 1900 Africa was almost entirely divided into separate territories controlled by European nations. The only exceptions were Liberia, generally regarded as being under the special protection of the U.S.; Morocco, conquered by France a few years later; Libya, later taken over by Italy; and Ethiopia.

The second feature of the new imperialism was also strongly evident. It was in Africa that Germany made its first major bid for membership in the club of colonial powers: between May 1884 and February 1885, Germany announced its claims to territory in Southwest Africa, Togoland, Cameroon, and part of the East African coast opposite Zanzibar. Two smaller nations, Belgium and Italy, also entered the ranks, and even Portugal and Spain once again became active in bidding for African territory. The increasing number of participants in itself sped up the race for conquest. And with the heightened rivalry came more intense concern for preclusive occupation, increased attention to military arguments for additional buffer zones, and, in a period when free trade was giving way to protective tariffs and discriminatory practices in colonies as well as at home, a growing urgency for protected overseas markets. Not only the wish but also the means were at hand for this carving up of the African pie. Repeating rifles, machine guns, and other advances in weaponry gave the small armies of the conquering nations the effective power to defeat the much larger armies of both the advanced and the technically backward peoples of Africa. Rapid railroad construction provided the means for military, political, and economic consolidation of continental interiors. With the new steamships, men and materials could be moved to Africa with greater dispatch, and bulk shipments of raw materials and food from Africa, prohibitively costly for some products in the days of the sailing ship, became economically feasible and profitable.

(Marginal notes:)

Japanese resistance to colonization

The Meiji Restoration

French penetration of North Africa

Penetration of Islāmic North Africa was complicated, on the one hand, by the struggle among European powers for control of the Mediterranean Sea and, on the other hand, by the suzerainty that the Ottoman Empire exercised to a greater or lesser extent over large sections of the region. Developments in both respects contributed to the wave of partition toward the end of the 19th century. First, Ottoman power was perceptibly waning: the military balance had tipped decisively in favour of the European nations, and Turkey was becoming increasingly dependent on loans from European centres of capital (in the late 1870s Turkey needed half of its government income just to service its foreign debt). Second, the importance of domination of the Mediterranean increased significantly after the Suez Canal was opened in 1869.

France was the one European nation that had established a major beachhead in Islāmic North Africa before the 1880s. At a time when Great Britain was too preoccupied to interfere, the French captured the fortress of Algiers in 1830. Frequent revolts kept the French Army busy in the Algerian interior for another 50 years before all Algeria was under full French rule. While Tunisia and Egypt had been areas of great interest to European powers during the long period of France's Algerian take-over, the penetration of these countries had been informal, confined to diplomatic and financial manoeuvres. Italy, as well as France and England, had loaned large sums to the ruling *beys* of Tunisia to help loosen that country's ties with Turkey. The inability of the *beys* to service the foreign debt in the 1870s led to the installation of debt commissioners by the lenders. Tunisia's revenues were pledged to pay the interest due on outstanding bonds; in fact, the debt charges had first call on the government's income. With this came increased pressure on the people for larger tax payments and a growing popular dissatisfaction with a government that had "sold out" to foreigners. The weakness of the ruling group, intensified by the danger of popular revolt or a military coup, opened the door further for formal occupation by one of the interested foreign powers. When Italy's actions showed that it might be preparing for outright possession, France jumped the gun by invading Tunisia in 1881 and then completed its conquest by defeating the rebellions precipitated by this occupation.

The Europeans in North Africa. The course of Egypt's loss of sovereignty resembled somewhat the same process in Tunisia: easy credit extended by Europeans, bankruptcy, increasing control by foreign-debt commissioners, mulcting of the peasants to raise revenue for servicing the debt, growing independence movements, and finally military conquest by a foreign power. In Egypt, inter-imperialist rivalry, mainly between Great Britain and France, reached back to the early 19th century but was intensified under the circumstances of the new imperialism and the construction of the Suez Canal. By building the Suez Canal and financing Egypt's ruling group, France had gained a prominent position in Egypt. But Britain's interests were perhaps even more pressing because the Suez Canal was a strategic link to its empire and its other Eastern trade and colonial interests. The successful nationalist revolt headed by the Egyptian army imminently threatened in the 1880s the interests of both powers. France, occupied with war in Tunisia and with internal political problems, did not participate in the military intervention to suppress the revolt. Great Britain bombarded Alexandria in 1882, landed troops, and thus obtained control of Egypt. Unable to find a stable collaborationist government that would also pay Egypt's debts and concerned with suppressing not only the rebellion but also a powerful anti-Egyptian Mahdist revolt in the Sudan, Britain completely took over the reins of government in Egypt.

The rest of North Africa was carved up in the early 20th century. France, manoeuvring for possession of Morocco, which bordered on her Algerian colony, tried to obtain the acquiescence of the other powers by both secret and open treaties granting Italy a free hand in Libya, allotting to Spain a sphere of influence, and acknowledging Britain's paramountcy in Egypt. France had,

however, overlooked Germany's ambitions, now backed by an increasingly effective army and navy. The tension created by Germany led to an international conference at Algeciras (1906), which produced a short-lived compromise, including recognition of France's paramount interest, Spanish participation in policing Morocco, and an open door for the country's economic penetration by other nations. But France's vigorous pursuit of her claims, reinforced by the occupation of Casablanca and surrounding territory, precipitated critical confrontations, which reached their peak in 1911 when French troops were suppressing a Moroccan revolt and a German cruiser appeared before Agadir in a show of force. The resulting settlements completed the European partition of North Africa: France obtained the lion's share of Morocco; in return, Germany received a large part of the French Congo; Italy was given the green light for her war with Turkey over control of Tripoli, the first step in her eventual acquisition of Libya; and Spain was enabled to extend her Río de Oro protectorate to the southern frontier of Morocco. The more or less peaceful trade offs by the occupying powers differed sharply from the long, bitter, and expensive wars they waged against the indigenous peoples and rulers of Islāmic North Africa to solidify European rule.

The race for colonies in sub-Saharan Africa. The partition of Africa below the Sahara took place at two levels: (1) on paper—in deals made among colonial powers who were seeking colonies partly for the sake of the colonies themselves and partly as pawns in the power play of European nations struggling for world dominance —and (2) in the field—in battles of conquest against African states and tribes and in military confrontations among the rival powers themselves. This process produced, over and above the ravages of colonialism, a wasp's nest of problems that was to plague African nations long after they achieved independence. Boundary lines between colonies were often drawn arbitrarily, with little or no attention to ethnic unity, regional economic ties, tribal migratory patterns, or even natural boundaries.

Before the race for partition, only three European powers—France, Portugal, and Britain—had territory in tropical Africa, located mainly in West Africa. Only France had moved into the interior along the Sénégal River. The other French colonies or spheres of influence were located along the Ivory Coast and in Dahomey and Gabon. Portugal held on to some coastal points in Angola, Mozambique (Moçambique), and Portuguese Guinea. While Great Britain had a virtual protectorate over Zanzibar in East Africa, her actual possessions were on the west coast in the Gambia, the Gold Coast, the Sierra Leone, all of them surrounded by African states that had enough organization and military strength to make the British hesitate about further expansion. Meanwhile, the ground for eventual occupation of the interior of tropical Africa was being prepared by explorers, missionaries, and traders. But such penetration remained tenuous until the construction of railroads and the arrival of steamships on navigable waterways made it feasible for European merchants to dominate the trade of the interior and for European governments to consolidate conquests.

Colonies in West Africa

Once conditions were ripe for the introduction of railroads and steamships in West Africa, tensions between the English and French increased as each country tried to extend its sphere of influence. As customs duties, the prime source of colonial revenue, could be evaded in uncontrolled ports, both powers began to stretch their coastal frontiers, and overlapping claims and disputes soon arose. The commercial penetration of the interior created additional rivalry and set off a chain reaction. The drive for exclusive control over interior areas intensified in response to both economic competition and the need for protection from African states resisting foreign intrusion. This drive for African possessions was intensified by the new entrants to the colonial race who felt menaced by the possibility of being completely locked out.

Perhaps the most important stimulants to the scramble

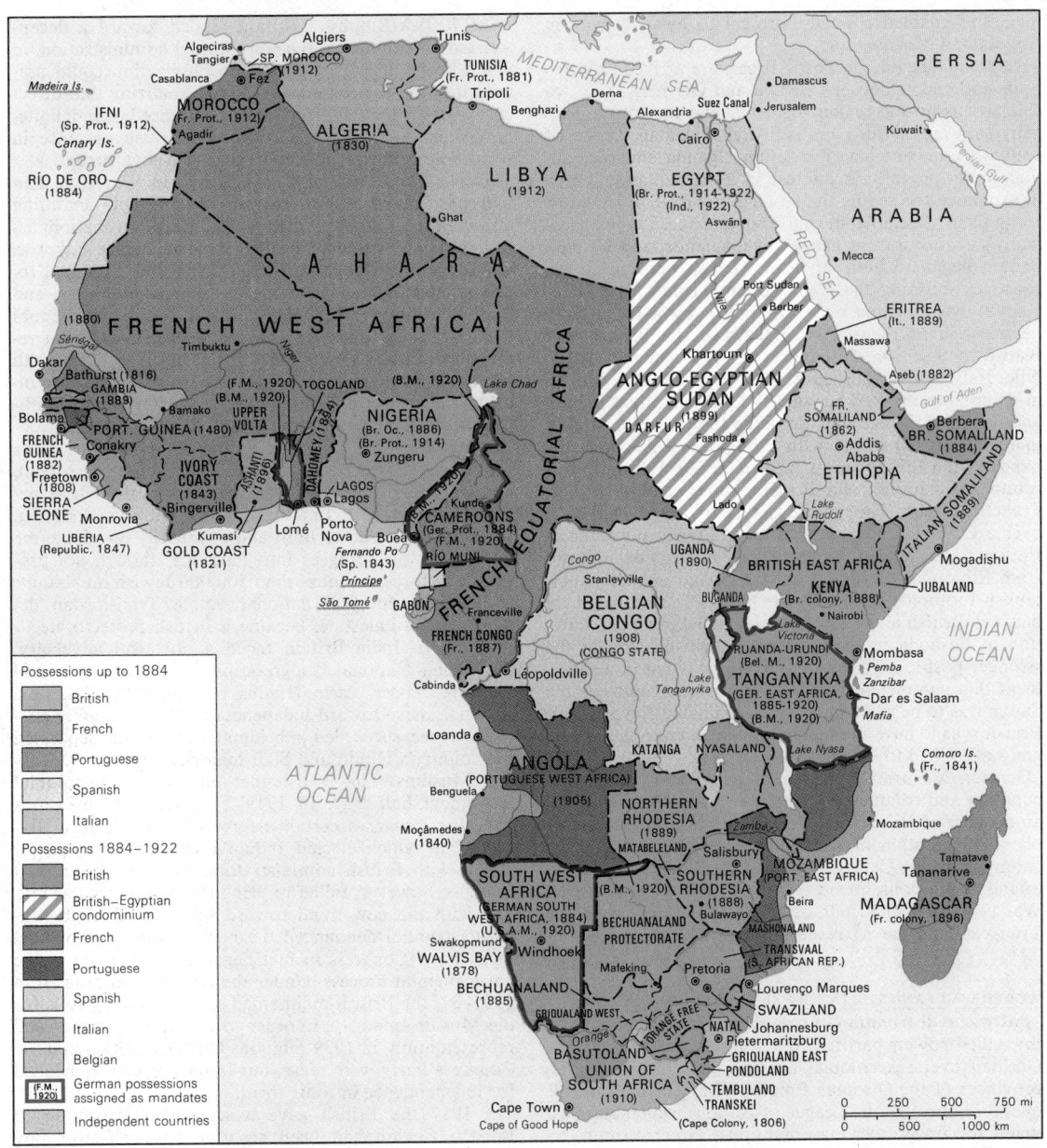

The European partition of Africa.

From W. Shepherd, *Historical Atlas*, Harper & Row, Publishers (Barnes & Noble Books), New York; revision
Copyright © 1964 by Barnes & Noble, Inc.

for colonies south of the Sahara were the opening up of
the Congo Basin by Belgium's king Leopold II and Germany's energetic annexationist activities on both the east
and west coasts. As the dash for territory began to accelerate, 15 nations convened in Berlin in 1884 for the
West African Conference, which, however, merely set
ground rules for the ensuing intensified scramble for
colonies. It also recognized the Congo Free State ruled
by King Leopold, while insisting that the rivers in the
Congo Basin be open to free trade. From his base in the
Congo, the King subsequently took over mineral-rich
Katanga, transferring both territories to Belgium in 1908.

In West Africa, Germany concentrated on consolidating
her possessions of Togoland and Cameroon (Kamerun),
while England and France pushed northward and eastward from their bases: England concentrated on the
Niger region, the centre of its commercial activity, while
France aimed at joining its possessions at Lake Chad
within a grand design for an empire of contiguous territories from Algeria to the Congo. Final boundaries were
arrived at after the British had defeated, among others,
the Ashantis, the Fanti Confederation, the Opobo kingdom, and the Fulani; and the French won wars against
the Fon kingdom, the Tuaregs, the Mandingos, and other
resisting tribes. The boundaries determined by conquest

and agreement between the conquerors gave France the
lion's share: in addition to the extension of its former
coastal possessions, France acquired French West Africa
and French Equatorial Africa, while Britain carved out
its Nigerian colony.

In Central Africa, the inter-colonial rivalries chiefly involved the British, the Portuguese, the South African Republic of the Transvaal, the British-backed Cape Colony,
and the Germans. The acquisitive drive was enormously
stimulated by dreams of wealth generated by the discovery of diamonds in Griqualand West and gold in
Matabeleland. Encouraged by these discoveries, Cecil
Rhodes (heading the British South Africa Company) and
other entrepreneurs expected to find gold, copper, and
diamonds in the regions surrounding the Transvaal,
among them Bechuanaland, Matabeleland, Mashonaland,
and Trans-Zambezia. In the ensuing struggle, which involved the conquest of the Nbele and Shona peoples,
Britain obtained control over Bechuanaland and, through
the British South Africa Company, over the areas later
designated as the Rhodesias and Nyasaland. At the same
time, Portugal moved inland to seize control over the
colony of Mozambique. It was clearly the rivalries of
stronger powers, especially the concern of Germany and
France over the extension of British rule in Central Af-

rica, that enabled a weak Portugal to have its way in Angola and Mozambique.

The boundary lines in East Africa were arrived at largely in settlements between Britain and Germany, the two chief rivals in that region. Zanzibar and the future Tanganyika were divided in the Anglo-German treaty of 1890: Britain obtained the future Uganda and recognition of its paramount interest in Zanzibar and Pemba in exchange for ceding the strategic North Sea island of Heligoland (Helgoland) and noninterference in Germany's acquisitions in Tanganyika, Ruanda, and Urundi. Britain began to build an East African railroad to the coast, establishing the East African Protectorate (later Kenya) over the area where the railroad was to be built.

Rivalry in northeast Africa between the French and British focussed on domination of the upper end of the Nile. Italy had established itself at two ends of Ethiopia, in an area on the Red Sea that the Italians called Eritrea and in Italian Somaliland along the Indian Ocean. Italy's inland thrust led to war with Ethiopia and defeat at the hands of the Ethiopians at Adowa (1896). Ethiopia, surrounded by Italian and British armies, had turned to French advisers. The unique victory by an African state over a European army strengthened French influence in Ethiopia and enabled France to stage military expeditions from Ethiopia as well as from the Congo in order to establish footholds on the Upper Nile. The resulting race between British and French armies ended in a confrontation at Fashoda in 1898, with the British army in the stronger position. War was narrowly avoided in a settlement that completed the partition of the region: eastern Sudan was to be ruled jointly by Britain and Egypt, while France was to have the remaining Sudan from the Congo and Lake Chad to Darfur.

Germany's entrance into southern Africa through occupation and conquest of South West Africa touched off an upsurge of British colonial activity in that area, notably the separation of Basutoland (Lesotho) as a crown colony from the Cape Colony and the annexation of Zululand. As a consequence of the South African (Boer) War (1899–1902) Britain obtained sovereignty over the Transvaal and the Afrikaner Orange Free State.

(Ha.Ma.)

WORLD WAR I AND THE INTERWAR PERIOD (1914–39)

Postwar redistribution of colonies. After World War I the Allied powers partitioned among themselves both the German overseas colonial holdings and the vast Arab provinces of the Ottoman Empire. They carried out this operation through the League of Nations, which awarded

mandates under varying conditions. Great Britain received as mandates Iraq and Palestine (which it promptly split into Transjordan and Palestine proper); the Palestine mandate obligated Britain to respect its contradictory wartime commitments to both Jews and Arabs. France assumed a mandate over both Syria and Lebanon. In Africa the two powers divided Togo and Cameroon between them, Britain acquired Tanganyika (with a few thousand German settlers), Belgium took Ruanda-Urundi, and South Africa received German South West Africa (Namibia). Italy, as compensation for not sharing in the award of mandates, obtained from Britain the Juba (Giuba) Valley on the Kenya–Somali frontier, and France eventually ceded to Italy a desert area that rounded out Libya's southern frontiers.

The interwar years mark the apex of colonial empires throughout the world, and indirect forms of colonial penetration grew with the development of the petroleum industry. Nevertheless, most colonial systems began to show clear signs of strain and even revolt. The Russian Revolution, the Nationalist and Communist successes in China during the 1920s and '30s, the radical nationalism of Kemal Atatürk, all contributed to the rise of political movements opposed to colonialism. The very process of economic modernization, however—with the rise of factories, coordination with the world market, and mass urbanization—did more than any political or cultural factor, taken in itself, to undermine the paternal-militaristic forms of direct colonial domination.

The British Empire. Britain tended toward a decentralized and empirical type of colonial administration, in which some degree of partial decolonization could prepare the way for eventual self-rule. Realizing that direct rule over ancient civilized lands could not last indefinitely, Britain worked for a continued British presence in areas where the empire conferred self-government.

Middle East. At the outset of World War I, Britain had proclaimed a protectorate over Egypt, annulling Ottoman sovereignty; afterward, Egyptian nationalist leaders finally brought the British to recognize Egypt as an independent kingdom in 1922. In 1936–37 Egypt received control over its own economic development, and British military forces were confined to the Suez Canal area. Britain granted Iraq independence in 1932 but retained a military power base in the new kingdom. Both the world strategic balance and the British petroleum industry ruled out any possibility of a real British withdrawal from either of these Middle Eastern states.

In Palestine the political claims of Arabs and Jews proved to be irreconcilable, and insurrection, terrorism, and occasional guerrilla warfare marked the whole period of British rule. Finally, in 1939, with war looming, the British decided to limit and eventually terminate the flow of Jewish refugees into Palestine, though not proposing to force the more than 500,000 Jewish inhabitants to live under an Arab national regime. Transjordan, detached from Palestine, became a British protectorate.

India. In India Britain faced a powerful adversary, the Indian National Congress, uniting businessmen and working classes, caste Hindus and untouchables, in a common drive toward independence. The Congress never, however, succeeded in bridging the gap that separated the country's Hindu and Sikh majority from its 90,000,-000 Muslims. The British met the Indian anticolonial movement half way. In 1919–23 a series of measures gave the Indians a certain degree of self-rule in a "dyarchy" in which elected Indian ministers governed together with British administrators. These constitutional reforms, however, failed to bring the princely states into line with the new trend toward self-rule. Though Mahatma Gandhi denounced the new system as a "whited sepulchre," Congress in fact began to participate in the governmental process. Under the constitution granted in 1935–37, the British maintained separate voting rolls for the Muslim minority, in order to ensure its proportional representation; in 1939 relations between Britain and the Congress Party were tense, but India was clearly headed for independence in some form.

In 1937 the British gave a separate constitution to Burma. Ceylon had been separate and self-governing since 1931.

Africa. In British Africa decolonization progressed more slowly, but London began to accept it as an ultimate outcome. In Kenya, for example, the British government refused to grant the 20,000 European settlers in the "white highlands" any kind of direct political power over the mass of tribal blacks who constituted the colony's overwhelming majority. In British West Africa the passage from direct colonial government to self-rule by a black elite had started by 1939, there being no white settlers or Indian merchants (as there were in East Africa) to complicate matters. Only in the mining areas of Northern Rhodesia (the Copperbelt) and in Southern Rhodesia, where white farmer settlers enjoyed self-government and caste privileges over a disenfranchised black majority, did decolonization make no headway at all.

Overseas France. France, in contrast to Britain, preferred centralized and assimilative methods in an effort to integrate its colonies into a greater Overseas France. It made no progress in colonial devolution and refused even to grant independence to Syria and Lebanon. In North Africa the French energetically implanted large agrarian capitalist enterprises as well as some industries connected with the area's mineral wealth. These modern production centres and infrastructures were directed and financed by metropolitan French business and were staffed and operated by a large, politically aggressive European settler population. The Muslim majority was subordinate both politically and economically; North African peasants struggled to subsist on the margins. Overt resistance was strongest in Morocco, where a rural Muslim rebellion endangered both the French and the Spanish protectorates. Abd el-Krim, a Berber Moroccan leader who combined tradition with modern nationalism, waged a brilliant five-year campaign till a combined French and Spanish force finally defeated him in 1926. After 1934, resistance to France revived in Morocco, this time in the cities. In Tunisia resistance was centred in Habib Bourguiba's constitutional party; in Algeria the urban Muslim middle classes merely asked for true civil rights and integration. The French Communist Party did not move to mobilize the peasant masses in an anticolonial struggle, and, in consequence, future rebellion in the Maghrib was to be Arab nationalist and not Marxist in its leadership and doctrines.

Matters were different in French Indochina, where the growth of a modern, French-directed agricultural economy had thrown masses of peasants into debt slavery. The circumstances favoured the formation of an independence movement much influenced by both the Chinese Kuomintang and the Chinese Communist Party; the movement in the 1930s took the form of a Communist party under the leadership of Ho Chi Minh.

French sub-Saharan Africa attracted no European settler population. The French colonial authorities promoted a shift from subsistence to market economies, and their methods, including labour conscription for public works, led to protest and questions in the French parliament. The results, guaranteed by a protective tariff linking the colonies to France, were solid but unspectacular.

Axis Powers. The 1930s saw the rise of an aggressive new colonialism on the part of the Axis Powers, which developed a new colonial doctrine ("living space" in German geopolitics, the "empire" in Italian Fascist ideology, the "co-prosperity sphere" in Japan) aiming at the repartition of the world's colonial areas, justified by the supposed racial superiority, higher birth rates, and greater productivity that the Axis Powers enjoyed as against the "decadent" West. To this the Japanese added a slogan of their own, "Asia for the Asians." In fact, the three powers aimed at carving out for themselves vast, self-sufficient empires. Though intent on a new colonialism of their own, they had to use anticolonialism as a political instrument before and during World War II; in doing so, they helped in the process of world decolonization.

Fascist Italy's first colonial war was a long, bloody campaign in Cyrenaica that lasted until the early 1930s, when Italy began developing Libya as a place of settlement for Italian peasants. Then a dispute over the border between Italian Somaliland and Ethiopia (1934) gave the Italian dictator, Benito Mussolini, the opportunity to move against the African power that had routed Italian armies at Adowa. In October 1935 Italian troops from Eritrea moved into the Tigre province of northern Ethiopia, although war was never declared. Ethiopia, under-equipped and feudal, could not long hold out in open combat, especially against Italian air attacks. In May 1936 Italian motorized columns reached Addis Ababa, and the Emperor went into exile. Mussolini proclaimed the Italian "empire" in East Africa. In reality, however, Ethiopian feudal chiefs continued violent resistance, even in the environs of the capital, while the Italians massacred hundreds of nobles, clergy, and commoners in an effort to repress Ethiopia by terror. In this their success was limited. The Italians built roads and kept control over all principal communication lines, but they never subdued the mountainous hinterland.

The Greater East Asia Co-prosperity Sphere, Japan's new order, amounted to a self-contained empire from Manchuria to the Dutch East Indies, including China, Indochina, Thailand, and Malaya as satellite states. Japan intended to exclude both European imperialism and Communist influence from the entire Far East, while ensuring Japanese political and industrial hegemony.

The United States and the Soviet Union. During World War I the United States purchased the Virgin Islands from Denmark (1917), but it acquired no new col-

onies thereafter. In the 1920s the United States agreed to leave unfortified its possessions beyond Hawaii, in exchange for Japan's accepting naval limitations. The Philippines, by the Tydings–McDuffie Act of 1934, were to become independent on July 4, 1946. Until U.S.–Japanese relations began to worsen, in 1939, United States possessions in the Pacific counted for little in world affairs. On the other hand, the United States established or continued virtual protectorates in Cuba, Haiti, the Dominican Republic, Nicaragua, and Panama during the Harding and Coolidge administrations (1921–29), a trend reversed under Hoover and Roosevelt, particularly under the latter's Good Neighbor Policy toward Latin America.

The new Soviet Russian regime succeeded, after years of civil and foreign war, in regaining the Asian possessions of its tsarist predecessor. The Caucasus was repossessed step by step between 1919 and 1921; after the mountain areas and Azerbaijan were brought back under Soviet control, Armenia was partitioned between Russia and Turkey. Then Georgia, an independent parliamentary republic, was overrun by the Red Army. Russian Turkistan was subdued by 1922, and the khanates of Khiva and Bukhara were suppressed. By 1922, Outer Mongolia was also solidly linked to the Soviet state. Nevertheless, the Russian revolutionary government was ideologically opposed to colonialism, especially where it had no colonial interests that it cared to defend. In general, the Soviet authorities hesitated during the whole interwar period between the alternatives of backing liberation movements of "national bourgeoisies" and supporting peasant revolutionary parties.

In Central Asia the Soviet authorities followed a moderate line up to 1928, but with the advent of Stalin a new policy, consisting in purges of national leaders, increasing industrialization, and forced settlement of nomad populations, led to a great increase in the proportion of European settlers, mostly Russians and Ukrainians, to native Muslims. During the 1930s the Kazakhs declined sharply in absolute numbers as well as in ratio to the Europeans in their areas. Other Muslim nationalities, especially the Uzbeks, stemmed the Slavic tide of settlement only by virtue of their birth rates, which greatly exceeded those of the Russians and Ukrainians.

WORLD WAR II (1939–45)

Although the Axis Powers failed in their global strategy, they crippled European colonial rule in Asia.

Asia. Japan conquered its Greater East Asia Co-prosperity Sphere and arrived at the gates of India, displacing British, Dutch, and French colonial rulers as well as the Americans in Guam and the Philippines. The Japanese had to allow some margin of freedom to their satellite regimes in Burma and Indonesia in both of which preexisting local parties proved capable of creating sovereign states after the war. On August 17, 1945, Sukarno declared Indonesia independent. Indonesia had had a long history of Muslim, nationalist, and Communist agitation against the Dutch; with captured Japanese arms, Indonesia could resist reimposition of Dutch authority.

In India the Congress Party, though totally unsympathetic to the Axis, tried to take advantage of Britain's wartime extremity in order to secure immediate independence. The Muslim League supported the British administration during the war but demanded a sovereign Muslim homeland (Pakistan) as a postwar objective. By 1945 direct British rule in India was coming to an end, but the contest between Britain, the Congress Party, and the Muslim League clouded any final settlement.

Middle East. In the Middle East, Britain returned to forms of direct colonial control as Axis forces drew near, and in June–July 1941 it occupied Syria and Lebanon, under the guise of Free French administration. With Beirut and Damascus secured, the British supported Syrian and Lebanese independence from France; in fact, the two states were incorporated into the sterling area. Only U.S. and Soviet support guaranteed the independence of the two republics (1944) and their subsequent admission to the UN.

In Egypt, when Axis forces in 1941 and 1942 came with-

Abd el-Krim

Italy in Ethiopia

Roosevelt's Good Neighbor Policy

Indonesian independence

in striking distance of Alexandria, both the king, Farouk, and groups of dissident army officers were ready to welcome them and turn against the British. In February 1942 the British minister forced the King to appoint a government willing to cooperate with the Anglo-Americans; the defeat of the Germans in the Egyptian desert later that year put Egypt firmly in the Allied camp. Nevertheless much anti-British and anticolonial bitterness remained in Egypt, with postwar consequences.

At the outset of World War II Iran was pro-German, and in August 1941 the Soviet Union and Britain jointly occupied the country, which then became the main supply line connecting the Soviet Union with the Western Allies. In 1942, in a three-power treaty, both Britain and Russia promised to leave Iran six months after the end of the war. Notwithstanding such commitments, the Soviet Union began to build spheres of influence in northern Iran; in 1944 the Soviet Union brought pressure to bear on Iran for an oil concession.

During the final years of World War II the United States became vitally interested in the Middle East because of U.S. petroleum ventures in Saudi Arabia and because of strategic considerations. By the end of the war it was clear to both the Soviet Union and Britain that the U.S., as a world power, would support no imposition of direct colonial controls in the postwar Middle East.

Africa.   During World War II Italy lost its entire colonial domain. Ethiopia was restored as an independent empire, and the other colonies eventually came under United Nations jurisdiction, in the first step toward decolonization in the African continent.

DECOLONIZATION FROM 1945

In the first postwar years there were some prospects that (except in the case of the Indian subcontinent) decolonization might come gradually and on terms favourable to the continued world power positions of the western European colonial nations. After the French defeat at Dien Bien Phu (in Indochina) in 1954 and the abortive Anglo-French Suez expedition of 1956, however, decolonization took on an irresistible momentum, so that by the mid-1970s only scattered vestiges of Europe's colonial territories remained.

The reasons for this accelerated decolonization were threefold. First, the two postwar superpowers, the United States and the Soviet Union, preferred to exert their might by indirect means of penetration—ideological, economic, and military—often supplanting previous colonial rulers; both the U.S. and the Soviet Union took up positions opposed to colonialism. Second, the mass revolutionary movements of the colonial world fought colonial wars that were expensive and bloody. Finally, the war-weary public of western Europe eventually refused any further sacrifices to maintain overseas colonies.

In general, those colonies that offered neither concentrated resources nor strategic advantages and that harboured no European settlers won easy separation from their overlords. Armed struggle against colonialism centred in a few areas, which mark the real milestones in the history of postwar decolonization.

British decolonization, 1945–56.   General elections in India in 1946 strengthened the Muslim League. In subsequent negotiations, punctuated by mass violence, the Congress leaders finally accepted partition as preferable to civil war, and in 1947 the British evacuated the subcontinent, leaving India and a territorially divided Pakistan to contend with problems of communal strife.

Far more damaging to Britain's world position as a great power was the end of the Palestine mandate. The British would have favoured an Arab state in Palestine, tied to the British system in the Middle East, with Jews as a permanent minority. The Jewish national movement, however, succeeded in making this policy both costly and unpopular; in particular, the U.S. and Soviet governments began to see a Jewish state in Palestine as a necessary solution to the problem of Europe's surviving Jewry. All Arab spokesmen expressed intransigent opposition to any two-nation solution. Britain, isolated internationally, threw the problem into the lap of the United

Nations; in November 1947 the General Assembly voted for partition. Britain, exhausted both politically and financially, decided to leave by May 15, 1948. The Jewish national movement's military branch succeeded in defeating the Palestine Arab terrorist and guerrilla bands step by step, and after British evacuation, and the declaration of Israel's independence, the Arab states in turn suffered a series of military defeats. The new Jewish state, recognized by the U.S., the Soviet Union, and France, reached an uneasy armistice with the Arabs in 1949, and Britain's position in the Middle East began to crumble.

The Arab chain reaction against Britain started in Egypt, where in July 1952 a group of army officers seized power. By the end of 1954, Gamal Abdel Nasser had induced Britain to accept total withdrawal by June 1956 and set to work to undermine Britain's position in Iraq and Jordan. In June 1956 the British troops quit Suez on schedule. At that point Britain's whole Middle Eastern position, which depended on a chain of bases and friendly governments, was imperilled. Iran had moved close to the United States, warding off Soviet penetration and expropriating British oil holdings. Now Cyprus and the Persian Gulf oil ports remained the last outposts under British control in the Middle East. Nasser's next move was to cut the link between them. On July 26, 1956, he nationalized the Suez Canal Company, ending the last vestiges of European authority over that vital waterway and precipitating the most serious international crisis of the postwar era (see below).

Wars in overseas France, 1945–56.   The constitution of the French Fourth Republic provided for token decentralization of colonial rule, and cycles of revolt and repression marked French history for 15 years after the end of World War II. The first focus of colonial war was Indochina, where a power vacuum, caused by Japan's removal after wartime occupation, gave a unique opportunity to the Communist Viet Minh. When in 1946 the French Army tried to regain the colony, the Communists, proclaiming a republic, resorted to the political and military strategies of Mao Tse-tung to wear down and eventually defeat France. All chances for maintaining a semicolonial administration in Indochina ended when the Communists won the civil war in China (1949). Eventually, in 1954, when the French engaged the Communist armies in a pitched battle at Dien Bien Phu, the Communists won with the help of new heavy guns supplied by the Chinese. The Fourth Republic left Indochina under the terms of the Geneva Accords (1954), which set up two independent regimes.

By 1954 French North Africa was beginning to stir; guerrilla warfare occurred in both Morocco (where the French had deposed and exiled Sultan Muhammad V) and Tunisia. On November 1, 1954, Algerian rebels began a revolt against France in which for the first time urban Muslims and Muslim peasants joined forces. In March 1956 France accorded complete independence to Morocco and Tunisia, while the army concentrated on a "revolutionary" counterinsurgent war in order to hold Algeria, where French rule had solid local support from about a million European settlers. The Muslim rebels depended on help from the Arab world, especially Egypt. Hence the French took the initiative, in October 1956, in forming an alliance with Nasser's principal adversaries, Britain and Israel, to reclaim the Suez Canal for the West and overthrow the pan-Arab regime in Cairo.

The Sinai–Suez campaign (October–November 1956).   On October 29, 1956, Israel's army attacked Egypt in the Sinai Peninsula, and within 48 hours the British and French were fighting Egypt for control of the Suez area. But the Western allies found Egyptian resistance more determined than they had anticipated. Before they could turn their invasion into a real occupation, U.S. and Soviet pressure forced them to desist (November 7). The Suez campaign was thus a political disaster for the two colonial powers. In the decline of western European colonialism, November 1956 marks the point of no return.

Algeria and French decolonization, from 1956.   Between 1956 and 1958 French army commanders in Algeria, politically radicalized, tried to promote a new

Franco-Muslim society in preparation for Algeria's total integration into France. Hundreds of thousands of rural Muslims were resettled under French military control, Algiers was successfully cleared of all guerrilla cells, French investments in Saharan petroleum grew, and, in a dramatic climax, a coalition consisting of European settlers, colonial troops, and armed forces commanders in May 1958 refused any further obedience to the Fourth Republic.

De Gaulle and decolonization

Charles de Gaulle, first president of the Fifth Republic, thought that the effort of fighting colonial wars had prevented France from developing nuclear weapons and also came to realize that Algerian Muslims could not be converted to a French identity. He began to negotiate with the rebels; the negotiations culminated in a plebiscite, French evacuation, and the declaration of an independent Muslim Algeria (July 1962). De Gaulle then proceeded to develop a nuclear striking force as the new foundation of France's status as a great power. The Fifth Republic moved rapidly toward freeing the colonies of sub-Saharan Africa, and France's colonial realm became vestigial and insular.

British decolonization after 1956. During the 15 years after the Suez disaster, Britain divested itself of most colonial holdings and abandoned most power positions in the Afro-Asian world. In 1958 the pro-British monarchy in Iraq fell; during the 1960s Cyprus and Malta became independent; and in 1971 Britain left the Persian Gulf. Of the imperial lifelines, only Gibraltar remains. After 1956 Britain moved rapidly to grant independence to its black African colonies. One British colony, Southern Rhodesia, broke away unilaterally in 1965.

In Malaya the British were able to fight a successful counterinsurgency action against what was predominantly a Chinese guerrilla movement and then turned over sovereignty to a federal Malaysian government (1957). In 1971 the Royal Navy left Singapore (an independent state since 1965), thus formally ending the British presence in the Far East.

Britain's world position shrank, in effect, to membership in the North Atlantic Treaty Organization and the European Economic Community, with the postcolonial Commonwealth decreasing in importance.

Dutch, Belgian, and Portuguese decolonization. After World War II the Dutch attempted to regain some of their lost control in Indonesia. The Sukarno regime held fast through three years of intermittent warfare, but the Dutch found no allies and no international support. In 1950 Indonesia became a centralized, independent republic.

The Belgian Congo

The Belgian administration in the Congo had never trained even a small number of Africans much beyond the grade-school level. When Britain and France began to divest themselves of their colonies, Belgium was in no position to impose on the Congo a schedule of its own for gradual withdrawal. The abrupt granting of independence to the Belgian Congo in the summer of 1960 led to a series of civil wars, with intervention by the UN, European business interests employing white mercenaries, and other outside forces. In 1965, Joseph Mobutu (later Mobutu Sese Seko) gained control over the central government and created an independent African state, renamed Zaire in 1971.

Portugal, in the 20th century the poorest and least developed of the western European powers, was the first nation (with Spain) to establish itself as a colonial power and the last to give up its colonial possessions. In Portuguese Africa during the authoritarian regime of António de Oliveira Salazar, the settler population had grown to about 400,000. After 1961 pan-African pressures grew, and Portugal found itself mired in a series of colonial wars, while the development of mining in Angola and Mozambique revealed hitherto unknown economic assets. In 1974 the armed forces overthrew the successors to Salazar, and in the unstable political situation it became clear that Portugal would cut its colonial ties to Africa. Portuguese Guinea (Guinea-Bissau) became independent in 1974. In June 1975 Mozambique achieved independence as a people's republic; in November 1975 Angola, in-

volved in a civil war between three rival liberation movements, also received sovereignty.

Conclusion. Historians will long debate the heritage of economic development, mass bitterness, and cultural cleavage that colonialism has left to the world, but the political problems of decolonization are grave and immediate. The international community is laden with minute states unable to secure either sovereignty or solvency and with large states erected without a common ethnic base. The world's postcolonial areas often are scenes of protracted and violent conflicts: ethnic, as in Nigeria's Biafran war; national–religious, as in the conflicts between Arabs and Israelis, the civil wars in Cyprus, and the continual clashes between India and Pakistan; or purely political, as in the confrontation between Communist and Nationalist regimes in the divided Korean Peninsula. Most ominously, the fading away of colonialism has created power vacuums, notably in the Indian Ocean area, into which the two superpowers have rushed. The end of colonialism has not brought with it the spread of new, neatly divided nation-states throughout the world, nor has it abated or eased the continuing rivalry between the great powers.

Postcolonial conflict

(R.A.We.)

BIBLIOGRAPHY

European expansion, c. 1450–1763: OTTO BERKELBACH VAN DER SPRENKEL, *Die überseeische Welt und ihre Erschliessung* (1959), is a collaborative work by specialists covering all areas and subjects included here. ROMOLA and ROGER C. ANDERSON, *The Sailing-Ship*, 2nd ed. (1980), offers a concise account of sailing until the advent of steam. WILBUR CORTEZ ABBOTT, *The Expansion of Europe*, 2nd rev. ed., 2 vol. (1938), covers colonialism to 1815, with a great deal of attention given to European backgrounds. JOHN H. PARRY, *The Age of Reconnaissance*, 2nd ed. (1966), is a history of discovery and conquest to 1650, offering a good scientific and maritime survey. EDGAR PRESTAGE, *The Portuguese Pioneers* (1933, reprinted 1967), is the best work in English on Portuguese voyages. CHARLES R. BOXER, *The Portuguese Seaborne Empire, 1415–1825* (1969), covers the older Portuguese empire by topics. ROGER B. MERRIMAN, *The Rise of the Spanish Empire in the Old World and the New*, 4 vol. (1918–34, reprinted 1962), follows Spain in the Americas to the death of Philip II; LOUIS A. HARTZ (ed.), *The Founding of New Societies* (1964), presents a highly original series of essays on the colonization of Spanish America, Canada, South Africa, and the 13 colonies. *The Cambridge Economic History of Europe*, 2nd ed., vol. 4 (1967), covers the economies of the early Dutch, French, and English empires. SHEPARD B. CLOUGH and RICHARD T. RAPP, *European Economic History*, 3rd ed. (1975), are especially good for the effects of the discoveries on Europe. GEORGE MASSELMAN, *The Cradle of Colonialism* (1963), describes the Dutch early activities in the East, providing a good European background. CHARLES R. BOXER, *The Dutch Seaborne Empire, 1600–1800* (1965), is a major work on the great age of Dutch imperialism. HERBERT I. PRIESTLEY, *France Overseas* (1938, reprinted 1966), presents a fairly good, if somewhat disjointed, account of early French overseas activity. ELI HECKSCHER, *Der Merkantilismus*, 2 vol. (1932; Eng. trans., *Mercantilism*, 2nd ed., 2 vol., 1955), is the acknowledged standard work on theoretical and historical mercantilism. ERIC WILLIAMS, *Capitalism and Slavery* (1944, reprinted 1966); and FRANK J. KLINGBERG, *The Anti-Slavery Movement in England* (1926, reprinted 1968), have chapters on the early years of the slave trade. ALFRED T. MAHAN, *The Influence of Sea Power upon History, 1660–1783* (1890, many later editions); and LAWRENCE H. GIPSON, *The British Empire Before the American Revolution*, 15 vol. (1936–70; rev. ed., 1958–), describe the colonial wars in some detail.

European expansion since 1763: DAVID K. FIELDHOUSE, *The Colonial Empires* (1966), and *Colonialism, 1870–1945* (1980), are useful general surveys of the growth and decline of empires from the 18th and 19th centuries. On the British Empire the best source is *The Cambridge History of the British Empire*, especially vol. 2, *The Growth of the New Empire, 1783–1870*, 2nd ed. (1963) and vol. 3, *The Empire Commonwealth, 1870–1919*, 2nd ed. (1967). HENRI BRUNSCHWIG, *Mythes et réalités de l'impérialisme colonial français (1871–1914)* (1960; Eng. trans., *French Colonialism, 1871–1914*, 1966), presents the case against the economic interpretation of French colonialism. A sociological study of how French colonialism operated will be found in JEAN SURET-CANALE, *L'Afrique noire: occidentale et centrale*, vol. 2, *L'Ère coloniale, 1900–1945* (1964; Eng. trans., *French Colonialism in Tropical Africa, 1900–1945*, 1971).

PROSSER GIFFORD and WILLIAM R. LOUIS (eds.), *Britain and Germany in Africa* (1967), and *France and Britain in Africa* (1971), contain useful collections of essays on British, German, and French colonialism. The scramble for Africa viewed as part of Britain's striving for security in the Mediterranean and the East is forcefully argued in RONALD ROBINSON and JOHN GALLAGHER with ALICE DENNY, *Africa and the Victorians* (1961). On the growth of empire in the Far East, MICHAEL EDWARDES, *Asia in the European Age, 1498–1955* (1962), should be consulted; but see also this history as examined by an Asian in K.M. PANIKKAR, *Asia and Western Dominance*, new ed. (1959, reprinted 1969). An illuminating comparative study of colonial policies is contained in JOHN S. FURNIVALL, *Colonial Policy and Practice: A Comparative Study of Burma and Netherlands India* (1956). For a Marxist view of the impact of colonialism as related to the problems of economic development of the former colonies, see PAUL A. BARAN, *The Political Economy of Growth*, 2nd ed. (1962). U.S. expansion from the Civil War to the Spanish–American War is explored by WALTER LAFEBER in *The New Empire* (1963); and the economic aspects of U.S. expansionism are discussed by HARRY MAGDOFF in *The Age of Imperialism* (1969), and *Imperialism: From the Colonial Age to the Present* (1978). HERBERT FEIS, *Europe, the World's Banker, 1870–1914* (1930, reprinted 1964), is a useful reference work on the connection between world finance and diplomacy before World War I. A standard and detailed diplomatic history of the new imperialism is found in WILLIAM L. LANGER, *The Diplomacy of Imperialism, 1890–1902*, 2nd ed. (1950, reprinted 1965). The psychological impact of colonialism, viewed from an African perspective, is explored in FRANTZ FANON, *Les Damnés de la terre* (1961; Eng. trans., *The Wretched of the Earth*, also as *The Damned*, 1963). The case against the continuation of Western domination in the period of decolonization is found in KWAME NKRUMAH, *Neo-Colonialism: The Last Stage of Imperialism* (1965, reprinted 1981). Theories of imperialism are discussed in JOHN A. HOBSON, *Imperialism*, rev. ed. (1938, reprinted 1975); LENIN, *Imperialism, the Highest Stage of Capitalism* (1939; orig. pub. in Russian, 1917); JOSEPH SCHUMPETER, *Imperialism and Social Classes*, ed. by PAUL M. SWEEZY (1951); ARCHIBALD P. THORNTON, *Imperialism in the Twentieth Century* (1978); and WOLFGANG J. MOMMSEN, *Imperialismustheorien*, 2nd ed. (1979; Eng. trans., *Theories of Imperialism*, 1980).

(C.E.No./Ha.Ma.)

Colorado

Colorado is classified as one of the Mountain States of the United States, although only about one-half of its approximately 104,247 square miles (269,998 square kilometres) lies in the Rocky Mountains. It borders Wyoming and Nebraska on the north, Nebraska and Kansas on the east, Oklahoma and New Mexico on the south, and Utah on the west.

Like the geological past that is revealed on its surface, Colorado's human history is written in the names of its cities, towns, mountain ranges, and passes. Indian and Spanish names alternate with those of American frontiersmen, and many ghost towns are mute reminders of the thousands of prospectors who streamed into the territory in the mid-19th century to pursue their dreams of gold bonanzas. The vast cattle ranges and agricultural acreage fed by huge irrigation projects are more characteristic of modern Colorado, however, as are the diversified industries and the educational and research facilities in its urban centres. (For information on related topics, see UNITED STATES OF AMERICA; UNITED STATES, HISTORY OF THE; NORTH AMERICA; and ROCKY MOUNTAINS.)

THE HISTORY OF COLORADO

The earliest inhabitants. The influence of Indian culture on Colorado's development and culture has been strong. Not only have Indian place-names enriched the English vocabulary, but also Indian folktales, music, and dances have been assimilated into American culture. Of more practical value, Indian food and artwork has made valuable and unique contributions to the Colorado economy. The cliff dwellings in Mesa Verde National Park are among the physical remains of early Indian communities.

The Plains Indians, mainly Arapaho and Cheyenne, helped the explorers, traders, and trappers to find their way across the plains. The Indians knew the streams, the natural routes, the sources of fresh water and firewood, the areas of natural protection, and the feeding grounds

Indian and Spanish heritages

of the buffalo. The Great Basin Indians, mainly the Utes, made similar contributions to knowledge of the Rocky Mountains.

The Indians, however, were displaced by Spanish explorers from Mexico in search of cities of gold and silver. Fearing attacks by the United States, they strengthened the Spanish frontier in the 1840s with huge land grants reaching as far north as the Arkansas River. On these grants were established the first permanent white settlements in Colorado and, in 1851, the first recorded irrigation. The Spanish language is imprinted on Colorado geography. The state was named from the Spanish *colorado* ("red," or "ruddy"). Twenty large streams in Colorado are called *ríos*, and numerous cities, villages, and mountain ranges and peaks have such Spanish names as the Sangre de Cristo (Blood of Christ) Mountains.

The U.S. territory. Immediately after the purchase of the Louisiana Territory by the United States in 1804, American exploration began. Dispatched to map, to explore, and to record scientific data about the new land were Zebulon Pike in 1806, Stephen Long in 1820, and John C. Frémont in 1842. As knowledge of the area spread, fur traders and trappers followed. Permanently stamped on the land are the names of such frontier scouts as Kit Carson and Jim Bridger. Ft. Bent and Ft. St. Vrain served as collection points for furs, places for food and supplies, and shelter and protection from Indians.

In 1859 gold was discovered. A sudden great influx of people took place to the cry of "Pikes Peak or bust," and the bustling gold-dust towns of Central City, Black Hawk, Gold Hill, and Cripple Creek made mining history. The first gold was panned from the stream beds, after which came the search for the mother lode in the mountains.

The Colorado gold rush

In these frontier mining districts civil and criminal codes were drawn up, and penalties for crimes were established. Of the thousands of seekers for gold, only a few found their bonanza. By 1890 the mountains were empty except for a few permanent mining towns.

Contemporaneous with the mining rushes was Colorado's period of territorial government. In 1861 congressional legislation provided for administrative officials to be appointed by the president. Seven governors were appointed in 15 years, and none served a full four-year term, a fact suggesting the social instability of the Colorado Territory. In 1875 a constitution was drawn up and ratified by the territorial assembly, and on August 1, 1876, Colorado became a member of the Union.

Economic and social growth. It was not possible to bring enough food by wagon train to feed the thousands of miners in Colorado. Shortages of food during the gold rush led enterprising pioneers to initiate a new and significant component to the regional economy. Water was taken from the streams and put onto the land in what has been called the single most significant event in Colorado history. There evolved an entirely new social code and economy and a western water law. The industries and inhabitants of cities and towns came to depend upon irrigation agriculture. Sugar factories, which extracted the juice from the sugar beet, sprang up across the landscape.

By 1881 the buffalo herds on Colorado's high plains had been massacred, and the buffalo were replaced by cattle and sheep. From its mountain valleys, plains, and feed lots, Colorado became a major producer of meat. Automobiles, railroads, and a tunnel through the mountainous backbone united the mountains and high plateaus of western Colorado with the flat eastern half of the state, and the flow of resources set the pace for industrial development. In 1892 the Colorado Fuel and Iron Company, based on local deposits of iron ore and coal, was established in Pueblo, and it became a major steel producer. By 1930, 16 sugar factories were in operation. During World War II the need for metals, especially molybdenum, led to new industry. In the 20th century Colorado became a tourist state because of its climate, majestic scenery, and national parks and monuments. Since 1955 it has been not only the leading ski area in the United States but also a base for sophisticated scientific research and development.

THE LANDSCAPE

Colorado's natural landscape is too varied to be encompassed within a single profile. The land ranges from the flat, grass-covered high plains, through the rolling, hilly Colorado Piedmont paralleling the Rocky Mountain front, to the high and numerous mountain ranges and plateaus that make up the southern Rocky Mountains and the Colorado Plateau. Within these areas the state rises from about 3,500 feet (1,100 metres) in the east to more than 14,000 feet in the Rockies.

The high plains. Lack of water is the dominant characteristic of Colorado's eastern high plains region. The average annual precipitation of 16 inches (406 millimetres) is erratic. Approximately 70 percent of it falls during summer, and hail is frequent. The Arkansas and South Platte are the major rivers, but both rise in the mountains to the west. Many other rivers are dry during much of the year, and the land is flat. Underlain by layered rocks, sandstones, shales, and limestones covered by a short grass vegetation, the natural environment is inhabited by prairie dogs, jackrabbits, coyotes, rattlesnakes, antelope, and such birds as the meadowlark and lark bunting.

The barren stretches

Summer temperatures on the high plains average 75° F (24° C) for July and August, with extremes above 100° F (38° C). In the summer daily temperatures may vary as much as 40° to 50° F (22° to 28° C), although the general variation is about 25° F (14° C). Winters are dry, cold, windy, and generally harsh. The high plains form a playground for the wind, and, though snowfall is light, the winter blizzard becomes a dread element for both humans and animals. Average winter nighttime low temperatures range from 10° to 30° F (−12° to −1° C), with daily highs from 40° to 60° F (4° to 16° C). From October through February the precipitation, usually snow, rarely exceeds two inches.

The climate, flatness, and layered rocks have produced very fertile soils that lack only moisture. Nearly all of the high plains are covered by brown soils, which support a strong mat of buffalo and grama grass, a valued resource for cattle grazing.

The Colorado Piedmont. About 50 miles (80 kilometres) wide and 275 miles long, the Colorado Piedmont is a picturesque, hilly to mountainous landscape sandwiched between the high plains and the southern Rocky Mountains. It encompasses all of the large urban complexes, the major transport arteries, most of the industry, a majority of the major colleges and universities, and four-fifths of the state's people. The layered rocks have been uptilted and dissected into prominent stream divides and deep valleys by the major rivers and numerous smaller streams that debouch onto the piedmont from the mountains. Terrain, ground cover, and climatic conditions provide suitable habitats for rabbits, waterfowl, pheasants, coyotes, deer, raccoon, and, on the arid foothills and unirrigated uplands, rattlesnakes. Many species of birds prevail, of which the meadowlark, crow, dove, and western magpie are most numerous.

The more habitable climes

There is less precipitation annually than on the high plains, though about 70 percent of it falls in summer also, mostly in thunderstorms. July temperatures in Denver, the state capital, average 73° F (23° C); and January temperatures, 29° F (−2° C). Short hot and cold spells of above 90° F (32° C) and below 10° F (−12° C) are not uncommon. The chinook wind—a very dry, descending airstream from the high mountains that is warmed by compression as it descends—often raises temperatures 30° to 40° F (16° to 22° C) in less than an hour, melts the snow cover, and can produce violent winds that have been recorded in excess of 100 miles per hour (161 kilometres per hour). The soils of the Colorado Piedmont are alluvial, or water transported.

The climate and land of the Colorado Piedmont are strong attractions for tourists, homeseekers, and farmers. Multicoloured ridges, or hogbacks, and parallel, or strike, valleys make fine homesites. The major cities and the wealthy farm areas lie where the streams have broadened the valleys. Among the attractive features of the landscape is the high, grotesque, and multicoloured agglomeration of sandstones northwest of Colorado Springs known

as the Garden of the Gods. In the foothills southwest of Denver is one of the world's largest and most beautiful outdoor amphitheatres, Red Rocks Park. Since 1880, more than 400 reservoirs have been built in the piedmont to store water for irrigation. These sites are meccas for water sports, hunting, and house building.

The Rocky Mountains. The western half of Colorado is the huge mountain upthrust, comprising most of the southern Rocky Mountains. High plateaus, mesas, and mountain ranges alternate with broad, intervening valleys and deep, narrow canyons. This mountain land provides water for six states and Mexico. Snow and rain, almost equally divided, fall copiously on the mountains in amounts ranging from 20 to 50 inches annually. The drainage pattern from the Rockies is oriented by the mountains themselves, which form the Continental Divide, the main watershed of the continent.

The mountainous west

The mountainous half of Colorado comprises a great number of individual mountain ranges. In the north and northwest the Front, Medicine Bow, Park, and Rabbit Ears ranges are major uplifts, and Rocky Mountain National Park (established 1915) is a major attraction. The western and southwestern extremity of the state comprises the tilted and acutely uplifted layered rock of the Colorado Plateau. The Grand Mesa and the White River Plateau, both above 10,000 feet, are major attractions. The region also contains several national monuments and parks, some of them primarily scenic, others the remnants of Indian settlements.

The San Juan Mountains, a large, heavily ice-dissected volcanic plateau above 13,000 feet, rise in the southwest. The Sangre de Cristo Range is a prominent linear range in the south central region of the state. At the western base of this range are some of the largest sand dunes in the interior of the North American continent, an area of 61 square miles set aside in 1932 as the Great Sand Dunes National Monument.

The Sawatch, Colorado's highest range and the central core of the Colorado Rockies, consists of Mt. Elbert—at 14,433 feet the highest point in the state—and many other elevations above 14,000 feet. The Colorado Rockies contain a significant share of the U.S. public domain in the form of 12 national forests, which total almost 13,800,000 acres (5,585,000 hectares) of land. There are 53 peaks more than 14,000 feet in elevation and 831 peaks between 11,000 and 14,000 feet.

Natural plant and animal life. Ecologically, there are six life zones from the high plains to the high mountain peaks. In the foothills zone, from 5,500 to 7,000 feet, oak, mountain mahogany, juniper, and piñon pine are the dominant vegetation. Higher zones, from 7,000 to 12,000 feet, feature a coniferous forest in which the ponderosa pine, Douglas fir, and blue and Engelmann spruce are dominant, interspersed with some deciduous, broad-leaved species. The alpine tundra zone, from 12,000 to 14,000 feet, has sparse vegetation, mainly mosses and sedges.

Most species of the animal kingdom have no permanent habitat in the Colorado Rockies. They move to high elevations where food and cover are plentiful during summer and return to the warmer lower elevations during winter. Deer, elk, and mountain sheep are the most common game animals. Among the furbearers, the coyote, wildcat, badger, marten, muskrat, and beaver are prevalent.

THE PEOPLE OF COLORADO

The first Colorado territorial census, in 1860, showed a population of 34,277, 86 percent of it rural. This pattern continued until 1910, when 50.3 percent of the nearly 800,000 inhabitants were urban. After 1950 the urban percentage rose sharply, reaching 81 percent of the population of more than 2,300,000 in 1980. The number of blacks is small, but more than 340,000 Coloradans are of predominantly Mexican descent. As in most of the nation, minority groups are hampered by inadequacies in education, housing, and economic opportunity. The conditions of seasonal migratory labour have been of increasing concern at all levels of government. An overall consideration of Colorado's population, like that of its physical environment, is most meaningful in a regional context.

Population statistics

High-plains population. The demography of Colorado's high plains is much affected by the region's rigorous physical geography: its dryness, bareness, wind, and capricious precipitation. The seven high-plains counties comprise 14 percent of Colorado's land area but have a dwindling population, the density of which rarely exceeds five persons per square mile. The towns of the high plains, all located on highways and railroads, serve vast rural hinterlands where livestock raising is important and where wheat and sorghum are major products. Limon, Burlington, Cheyenne Wells, and Yuma, each with fewer than 4,000 people, are the largest towns.

Piedmont population. Ready availability of water, a climate conducive to outdoor work and recreation, and proximity to the mountain front are mainly responsible for the large population growth of the Colorado Piedmont. The 22 counties occupy 35 percent of the land area, and more than 70 percent of the state's people live in the metropolitan areas of Denver–Boulder, Colorado Springs, and Pueblo.

Denver's industry employs 40 percent of Colorado's industrial labour force; Colorado Springs, 8 percent; and Pueblo, 4 percent, figures comparable to the percentages of the state's population in these urbanized areas. Contributing further to the density of the piedmont are more than 12 other cities with more than 10,000 population. Intensive irrigation agriculture contributes substantially to the local and national economies. The number of farms and the rural population are declining, but farm size is increasing.

Mountain population. In population density and distribution Colorado's mountain counties mirror the rigours of the environment. Terrain, isolation, severe winters, and separation from the piedmont counties by the mountainous Continental Divide are major limiting factors. The 34 mountain counties occupy 51 percent of the state's land area, but six have fewer than two people per square mile, 10 have a density of from two to five per square mile, 15 counties have five to 20, and three about 20 to 25. Unlike the high plains, however, the population is increasing slowly. The rural population is settled mainly in restricted mountain valleys, where ranching and irrigation farming support the family unit.

THE STATE'S ECONOMY

Location, soil, minerals, water, space for expansion, and physical beauty are positive resources in Colorado's growth. Among the Rocky Mountain states Colorado accounts for two-fifths of the population but about one-half of all manufacturing employment.

Manufacturing. Employment in manufacturing, the strongest segment of Colorado's economy, increased 47 percent during 1967–77 compared with the U.S. average of 1.4 percent. Major industries in the early 1980s included printing and publishing, machinery production, food and food products, metal production, lumber and wood products, and military ordnance and accessories. The total nonagricultural employment was 1,217,000 in 1979, more than five times the 1940 figure.

Agriculture. From the outset, agriculture has been the most basic asset of Colorado's economy. Colorado was the first state to abrogate the riparian doctrine of water use, based on English common law, which gave prior water rights to owners of adjoining lands. It evolved instead a totally new concept for use of water resources based on the rights of the larger public. This Colorado doctrine has been adopted and adapted by most of the 17 Western states. The state ranks fifth, behind California, Texas, Nebraska, and Idaho, in the amount of land under irrigation. During the 1970s, gross farm income more than doubled, from $1,182,000,000 to $3,181,000,000. Corn (maize), wheat, hay, and sugar beets are the major crops.

Animals and animal products are significant aspects of the agricultural economy. Colorado is an important cattle producer and also raises large numbers of hogs and lambs. Weld, Morgan, Larimer, and Boulder counties are the national centre for the production of cattle fattened in feedlots rather than on the open range. A spectacular sight of the piedmont landscape is the acres of fat cattle

Cattle production

feeding on corn, alfalfa (lucerne), and sugar beets near Greeley. There is much corporate farming, and generally it is highly mechanized.

Tourism and sports. Although manufacturing, agriculture, and summer tourism are the mainstays of Colorado's economy, winter sports have grown at an almost alarming rate. Transport, housing, and lift facilities are inadequate for the annual ski invasion. Whereas in 1955–56, approximately 30,000 out-of-state skiers spent $3,000,000, the figure had risen by 1968–69 to 986,020 persons spending almost $34,000,000. The total number of ski visits to Colorado winter-sports areas in 1960–61 was about 462,000; in 1978–79 the 29 ski areas of Colorado issued 7,215,316 lift tickets.

Mining. Although it is by no means the leader that it was in the mining bonanzas of a century ago, the minerals industry continues to make substantial contributions to the economy. Among the principal minerals are coal, petroleum, molybdenum, and sand and gravel. In 1971, 14,400 employees worked in mineral resources, but by 1980 this figure had risen to 35,300. Northwestern Colorado has some of the largest and most valuable coal deposits in the United States, but the industry is relatively dormant because of decreasing national demands. In 1979 petroleum and gas reserves, much of them in the form of oil shales, were estimated to have a value of about $700,000,000. Production of metals increased during the 1970s and accounts for a substantial part of the total value of mining extraction.

Power. Basic to all aspects of Colorado's life and economy are the state's power resources. Power generation is based on coal, hydropower, petroleum, and natural gas. Consumption is immense, and demands are difficult to meet. Capacity and production increased more than three-fold during the 1960s and 1970s. About two-fifths of the total capacity and production is privately owned.

Transportation. Colorado ranks first among the Mountain States in road mileage, with more than 82,000 miles of highways and rural roads. There is no set road pattern, although main highways tend to be east–west, circumvent high mountain masses, and follow valleys and canyons to their heads in the 32 mountain passes over the Continental Divide. The highest of the passes, at 12,183 feet, is Trail Ridge Road in Rocky Mountain National Park. Seventeen other passes exceed 10,000 feet in elevation. Several portions of the Interstate Highway System run through the state and radiate to neighbouring states in all directions. In 1962 work started on twin vehicular tunnels under the Continental Divide. The first bore was opened to traffic in 1973, and the second in 1979.

Denver's Stapleton International Airport is a major centre in the nation's air-traffic pattern. It is served by several major airlines, and carriers also link Denver with other Colorado cities and with neighbouring states. Several large air-freight depots adjoin Stapleton Airport. Railroad lines in Colorado are mainly bulk-freight carriers using multilevel railcars and flatcars for containerized freight. There are more than 3,450 miles of track, which connect the major urban areas in the state.

ADMINISTRATION AND SOCIAL CONDITIONS

Governmental structure. In 1875 a convention drew up the constitution for the prospective state, and in 1876 Colorado was admitted to the Union as the 38th state. From its admission 100 years after the signing of the Declaration of Independence, it became known as the Centennial State.

Executive power. The executive branch of government has six offices: governor, lieutenant governor, secretary of state, attorney general, treasurer, and auditor. All offices were created by the Colorado constitution, and the elected officials serve four-year terms. Numerous commissions, boards, and examiners are appointed to discharge the executive functions of state government. At the county level, the constitution provides for several kinds of officers.

Legislature. The Colorado General Assembly, which meets annually, comprises a Senate of 35 members elected to four-year terms and a house of representatives of 65 members elected to two-year terms. The Legislative

Council, created by statute in 1953, is a 13-member fact-finding agency of the General Assembly, and the Joint Budget Committee, established in 1959, is the permanent agency for fiscal and budgetary review. Under the Administrative Organization Act of 1968, the Commission on Uniform State Laws was created; and the Commission on Interstate Cooperation dates from 1937.

Judicial system. The Colorado judiciary is composed of courts at various levels. The highest is the state Supreme Court, with seven justices. Below it are district courts, which encompass one or more counties, and a county court in each county. In addition, such special bodies as juvenile and probate courts are set forth in the constitution, as are the municipal courts, which provide the grass-roots core of the judicial system.

Municipal government. More local, but of increasing importance, are the municipal governments. In 1959 there were 246 municipalities; by 1977 there were 262. Their government includes mayor–council and council–city manager forms.

Political balance
Politics. Since World War II each state political campaign has involved the issue of extension of federal activities, with Democrats generally committed to extension, and Republicans opposed. Since the 1920s each of the two parties has won control of the legislature in about one-half of the elections, indicating a fairly even balance within the state.

Welfare and health. Colorado's per capita income is higher than the national average, and its expenditure on public assistance is also higher. The requisite age of old-age pensioners is 65, and they must have resided in Colorado in five of the previous nine years. Average monthly benefits for retired workers are lower than the national average, but benefits for disabled workers and Medicare payments are higher. The monthly payments provided by federally administered public-aid programs for families with dependent children and for the aged and disabled increased substantially during the 1970s.

Education. The people of the Colorado Territory, despite being on the edge of the frontier, were concerned with education, and they created the University of Colorado in 1861. The school did not open until 1877, but publicly supported primary education began in 1862, with secondary schools opening in the following decade. The great population increases since the end of World War II have produced severe problems in funding, in instructional space, and in busing to achieve improved instructional programs. Curriculum and instructional revision has been undertaken in all areas, although foreign languages and mathematics have been particularly stressed.

In addition to the University of Colorado, at Boulder, the University of Denver (1864), the Colorado School of Mines, at Golden (1869), and Colorado State University, at Fort Collins (1870), were founded before statehood. By 1979 Colorado had 41 colleges, junior colleges, and universities, 23 of them publicly supported. Attendance at those institutions increased substantially during the 1960s and 1970s, and in 1978 there were almost 152,000 students enrolled. Of special note is the U.S. Air Force Academy, authorized by Congress in 1954. In 1958 it moved into its campus near Colorado Springs.

CULTURAL LIFE

The arts. Red Rocks Park, a large natural amphitheatre in the foothills west of Denver, is Colorado's best known theatre; it hosts frequent musical events. The Central City Opera House, dating from 1878, has a summer season of opera and drama. Summer fare is available as well at Elitch Gardens Theatre, opened in Denver in 1890, and at festivals in Aspen and Boulder. The Fine Arts Center in Colorado Springs is a regional art centre. In 1971 additions to the Denver Art Museum were completed to house collections of Renaissance and Peruvian paintings.

Libraries. Libraries have an important function in Colorado's cultural milieu. There has been a continuing trend to organize regional libraries to provide adequate service to every community. The Bibliographical Center for Research, Rocky Mountain region, is one of three such centres in the United States and has a catalogue of 5,000,000 cards. The Colorado State Library is responsible for furnishing all Colorado institutions with research, reference, and general reading services.

Research centres. Because of its location and altitude, Colorado has three important observatories. The High Altitude Laboratory, with high-altitude-research facilities at Mount Evans, and the Chamberlain Observatory are operated by the University of Denver. The National Center for Atmospheric Research is a cooperative project of more than 30 U.S. universities, sponsored by the National Science Foundation. It has ties also to the Department of Astrophysics and Atmospheric Physics of the University of Colorado.

Historic sites. The State Historical Society maintains nine historic properties. These include the Colorado State Museum in Denver, several houses and forts dating from the early days of the state, and the Ute Indian Museum in Montrose and the El Pueblo Museum in Pueblo. On the western and southwestern plateaus, the Black Canyon (established 1933), Colorado (1911), and Dinosaur (1915) national monuments are preserved as scenic attractions. Because of their cultural and historic value, Mesa Verde National Park (1906) and Hovenweep (1923) and Yucca House (1919) national monuments in the southwest—all relics of former Indian civilizations—are preserved for public use and for archaeological study and exploration.

Communications. Colorado has 152 daily, Sunday, and weekly newspapers, 123 radio stations, and 12 television stations with commercial and national educational television affiliations. In addition, 15 radio stations devote air time to foreign-language broadcasts, in Spanish, Navajo and Ute, and Slovenian.

PROSPECTS

Generally, Colorado has not been hit as hard as other states by economic reversals, due to its varied economic pattern, nor has it achieved the pinnacles of economic expansion attained elsewhere. During the 1970s and early 1980s this trend was reversed somewhat, as the development of Colorado's energy resources precipitated an economic boom comparable to that of the mid-19th-century gold rush. By 1982, however, economic expansion began to slow, after it was decided to abandon a synthetic-fuel project that was to utilize Colorado's vast shale-oil reserves. With expansion has come a growing population, in the mountain counties as well as in the urban areas; continued pressure on, and development of, the state's vast recreation potential; an increasing strain on the state's water supply; and continued encroachment on irrigated land by land developers.

BIBLIOGRAPHY

General works: CARL UBBELOHDE, *A Colorado History*, 5th ed. (1982), concise history articulating major developments since territorial days; L.R. HAFEN (ed.), *Colorado and Its People*, 4 vol. (1948), discussion of its history from simple cultures to industrial society, transportation, culture and the arts, with biographical sketches; MARSHALL SPRAGUE, *Colorado* (1976), a readable one-volume history; M.E. GARNSEY, *America's New Frontier, the Mountain West* (1950), comprehensive book dealing with the economic and geographic development of the Rocky Mountain states; T.K. KELLEY, *Living in Colorado* (1964), geographic analysis of how the resources of Colorado are used with the land, and how they affect population growth and distribution; M.S. WOLLE, *Stampede to Timberline*, 2nd ed. (1974), analysis of the miners' surge into the mountains, with drawings of ghost towns and descriptions of life in mining camps; *Colorado Magazine* (quarterly), a historical journal that portrays Colorado's history in its special and general aspects.

Specialized works: FRANCIS RAMALEY, *Colorado Plant Life* (1927), classic book dealing with plants as they are affected by environmental changes; T.D.A. COCKERELL, *Zoology of Colorado* (1927), full account of the animal life ranging from its genesis to description, and to geographic distribution; PUBLIC LAND LAW REVIEW COMMISSION, *One Third of the Nation's Land* (1970), description of the entire life ladder in Colorado, from mammals to birds, fishes, mollusks, insects, crustaceans, and protozoans; M.J. LOEFFLER, *The Population Syndromes on the Colorado Piedmont* (1965), analysis of the population geography of the Piedmont corridor.

(M.J.Lo.)

Colorado River

Fed by thick blankets of melting snow where it rises in the high Rocky Mountains of north central Colorado, western United States, the Colorado River cuts a winding path for 1,440 miles (2,320 kilometres) southwestward to the Gulf of California. Its drainage basin covers 244,000 square miles (632,000 square kilometres) and includes parts of seven states—Wyoming, Colorado, Utah, New Mexico, Nevada, Arizona, and California. For 17 miles it forms the international boundary between Arizona and Mexico before flowing 80 miles through Mexico to the gulf. The Colorado River is a unique river system. No other stream in the world has cut such a remarkable number of extremely deep trenches, of which the Grand Canyon (q.v.) is the largest and most spectacular. The river drains the largest, most arid sector of the North American continent; and because of its intensive development it is called the "Lifeline of the Southwest."

Course and natural environment. For more than 1,000 miles of its course, the Colorado has cut a deep gorge. Where lateral streams join the river system—the Virgin, Kanab, Paria, Escalante, Fremont, San Rafael, Price, Duchesne, and Green rivers from the west, the Little Colorado, San Juan, Dolores, and Gunnison from the east— a transverse system of narrow, winding deep canyons has been cut. Each entering river and each lateral creek has cut another canyon, and thus the upper and middle parts of the Colorado Basin are traversed by a labyrinth of deep gorges. The longest of these unbroken trunk canyons through which the Colorado flows is the Grand Canyon, extending from the mouth of the Paria to the Grand Wash.

On the California (western) side of the Lower Colorado is the Salton Basin, a large desert extending northwestward from the head of the Gulf of California, a distance of 150 miles. At one time the gulf extended a greater distance farther to the northwest, above the point at which the Colorado now enters. As the river brought its load from the mountains and hills above to the gulf, however, it gradually erected a vast natural dam, and the waters on the north were separated from those on the south. The Colorado then cut a channel into the lower gulf. The upper waters, cut off from the sea, gradually evaporated, forming a large area of desert land about 235 feet below sea level. On the Arizona side are similar but discontinuous desert plains interrupted by mountains.

In 1905 there occurred, about three miles below the California–Mexico line, a break that diverted all the waters of the Colorado into the Salton Sink, creating the Salton Sea, about 70 feet deep, 50 miles long, and 10 to 15 miles wide, with a total water area of 300 square miles. The break threatened to inundate the agriculturally rich Imperial Valley and to block permanently a major railroad route. Because of imminent danger, the railroad repaired the break and, in 1907, completed a line of protective levees.

Development of the river. The Colorado River system was the first drainage basin in which the concept of multiple use of water was attempted: *e.g.*, power development, irrigation, recreation, flood control, and navigation.

In 1922 the Colorado River Compact was agreed upon by the seven states that comprise its drainage area. In the compact the river was divided at Lees Ferry, Arizona, into the lower compact states—Arizona, Nevada, and California—and the upper compact states—Wyoming, Utah, Colorado, and New Mexico; the total flow of the Colorado River was established as 17,000,000 acre-feet (an acre of area covered to a depth of 12 inches) at Lees Ferry, of which 15,000,000 acre-feet were equally divided between the lower and the upper compact states. A water reserve was maintained for Mexico, which was agreed upon by treaty in 1944.

The first major developments of the Colorado began in 1928, when Congress passed the Boulder Canyon Project Act. The act authorized the construction of Boulder (now Hoover) Dam, a multipurpose water-storage project that was a major engineering feat of its time; since its completion in 1936, the dam and Lake Mead, which it created with its impounded waters, have become major tourist attractions.

Many additional projects have since been approved and completed. Although Hoover Dam was the engineering marvel of its time, in the mid-1960s Glen Canyon Dam was completed, impounding Lake Powell; both dam and lake are almost identical in size and storage capacity to the older dam and lake. In addition to these two large control units, three key multiple-storage projects upstream have been completed on major tributaries. Flaming Gorge on the Green River in Wyoming and Utah, Curecanti on the Gunnison River in Colorado, and the Navajo on the San Juan River in New Mexico and Colorado are fully operational.

Shortly after the completion of Hoover Dam, the people of southern California voted to build Parker Dam downstream; from Havasu Lake, 1,000,000,000 gallons of water are taken daily 250 miles across California to supply a part of the water needs for Los Angeles and all of the water supply for San Diego.

This does not complete the demands for water from the Colorado. In 1945 the Colorado-Big Thompson Project, the first federal interbasin water-diversion project in the United States, was completed. Water was diverted by tunnel beneath the Continental Divide in Rocky Mountain National Park to help irrigate 700,000 acres of cropland in northern Colorado. Under construction in the early 1970s was another large water-diversion project, the Fryingpan-Arkansas Project. Water is taken from the Fryingpan Creek, a Colorado tributary, diverted under the Sawatch Mountains of the Colorado Rockies, into the Arkansas River to supply water for the rapidly growing municipal areas of Pueblo and Colorado Springs. On the Blue River, another tributary, Denver has built Dillon Reservoir, the water of which is diverted beneath the Continental Divide to supply additional water for over 1,000,000 people in the Denver Basin.

In the mid-1960s, a United States Supreme Court decision reduced the quantity of water previously awarded to California by the Boulder Canyon Project Act of 1928, and an amount roughly equal to the amount of water transferred to Los Angeles and San Diego from Havasu Lake was decreed to Arizona. The additional water awarded to Arizona was a focal point of strife and controversy. To capture the water and to transfer it to Phoenix, Arizona, which had no Colorado River water, the Central Arizona Project (CAP) was proposed for the lower reaches of the Grand Canyon.

Laced with innumerable dams, both large and small, that impound the total flow of the Colorado and by increasingly severe competition for whatever small quantities of water might remain, the basin remains fraught with litigation and controversy. Although previously approved, water projects must now undergo thorough environmental-impact studies in accordance with the federal National Environment Policy Act of 1969. In addition, controversy continued between the United States and Mexico over the high salt content of the Colorado's water by the time it reaches Mexico. But these problems are overshadowed by the sobering fact that because the Colorado drains one of the most arid regions of the world, water evaporation rates are extremely high, and the quantity of water that evaporates from the man-made lakes exceeds any further quantity that can be stored.

BIBLIOGRAPHY. R. KAY GRESSWELL and ANTHONY HUXLEY (eds.), *Standard Encyclopedia of the World's Rivers and Lakes* (1965), a descriptive and factual analysis of the Colorado River, its many tributaries from source to mouth, the use of its water, the major urban centres along its course, and the early civilizations and explorations of the basin; JOHN A. SHIMER, *This Sculptured Earth* (1959), a brief, easily understandable description and analysis of the Colorado River, its course to the sea, and its work in cutting the Grand Canyon; UNITED STATES GEOLOGICAL SURVEY, *John Wesley Powell* (1969), a brief historical account of the exploration of the Grand Canyon and Powell's contribution to science—includes information on the stratified rocks of the canyon and on the course and history of the Colorado River, with detailed descriptions of its major rapids and pools.

(M.J.Lo.)

Coloration, Biological

Coloration is the general appearance of an object in terms of the quality and quantity of light that is reflected or emitted from its surfaces. It depends upon several factors: the colour and distribution of the object's pigments, particularly the relative location of differently coloured areas; the shape, posture, position, and movement of the object; and the quality and quantity of light impinging on its surfaces. The perceived coloration depends also on the visual capabilities of the organism viewing the object. Coloration is a dynamic and complex characteristic and must be clearly distinguished from the concept of "colour," which refers only to the spectral qualities of emitted or reflected light. Coloration serves many vital functions in the lives of plants and animals. An organism with an easily noticed pattern draws the attention of other organisms, with some sort of adaptive interaction the frequent result. Such "advertising" colorations may attract animals such as insects that carry pollen to brightly coloured flowers. Advertisement may also repel animals; a tide pool blenny drives other fish from its territory by displaying its brightly coloured chin. This sort of coloration frequently serves the broadly interpreted function of communication or transfer of information.

There are also various means by which coloration may help to conceal the location or identity of an organism. Coloration of this type serves to lessen detrimental or maladaptive interactions with other organisms. Cryptic coloration, or general background resemblance, is the most frequently encountered type of concealing, or protective, coloration and may be employed by both predatory and prey species in order to avoid detection. But bright coloration may also conceal an organism, as in the case of many tropical reef fishes, which show contrasting bars of colour that disrupt their outlines and help to conceal their identity as a possible predator or prey. Organisms may also mimic specific objects in their environment and thus convey false information as to their identities.

Coloration may also affect an organism in ways other than its interaction with other organisms. "White" light is composed of rays of a variety of wavelengths. Most coloration depends primarily upon the reflected wavelengths of light, those not absorbed by the organism. The absorbed light serves as an energy source to the organism and may either be utilized in biochemical reactions, such as occur in photosynthesis, or merely contribute to the thermal balance of the organism. A dull black surface absorbs nearly all wavelengths of light and is quickly warmed by bright sunlight. Excess light absorption may upset the thermal balance of the organism, however, and must be dissipated as heat energy. Shiny, white surfaces reflect the most light and can maintain a cooler temperature when illuminated.

Emitted light, resulting from bioluminescent activity, forms a portion of the coloration of some organisms. Although it may reveal an organism to nearby animals, it may also serve as a light source in animals such as the pinecone fishes (*Monocentris*). These fishes feed at night and have bright photophores, or bioluminescent organs, at the tips of their lower jaws; they appear to use these organs much like tiny search lights as they feed on planktonic (minute floating) organisms.

Because many pigments are natural or only slightly modified by products of some metabolic process, it seems logical that some coloration might be without evident function. It is highly unlikely, however, that any apparently fortuitous coloration could long escape the processes of natural selection and remain thus totally without function. Examples of seemingly functionless coloration might be cited from areas such as dark caves or abyssal depths where light is almost totally absent and vision is of little or no importance. In the absence of light or of organisms capable of perceiving light, such examples are best considered as lacking in coloration, rather than having coloration without function.

It is natural that man, a visually oriented animal, should be interested in biological coloration. Much of his life is devoted either to the appreciation of naturally occurring coloration or to the alteration of the environment to provide more pleasant or varied colorations. Human attention to coloration ranges from purely aesthetic endeavours to the applied use of coloration. Soft, pastel colorations aid in increasing work efficiency and contribute to tranquil moods; bright, strongly contrasting colours seem to contribute to excitement and enthusiasm. It is tempting to speculate that these phenomena are extensions of man's basic response to the soft blue, green, and brown background colorations of the environments as opposed to sharply contrasting advertising or warning colorations found on many dangerous organisms. It is possible that much of the aesthetic value that is attached to coloration is closely related to its broad biological functions.

Man's interest in coloration has also aided in biological studies. The classical work by the Moravian abbott Gregor Mendel on inherited characteristics, based largely on plant coloration, formed the foundation for modern genetics, and coloration remains an important tool in the study of genetics. Features such as eye coloration are easily sampled and located on chromosomes.

Coloration also aids man, as it does other visually dependent animals, in the identification of organisms. It is an easily perceived, described, and compared characteristic. Related species living in different habitats, however, frequently have strikingly different colorations. Since coloration is susceptible to alteration in various functional contexts, it usually lacks value as a conservative characteristic for determining systematic relationships between all but the most closely related species.

(G.S.Lo.)

This article is divided into the following sections:

Related articles of interest include COMMUNICATION, ANIMAL; MIMICRY.

I. The expression of colour

Plants and animals commonly possess characteristic colorations. They range in plants from the brilliant hues of many fungi through various browns, reds, and greens for species that can synthesize their food from inorganic substances (autotrophs) to the colourful floral displays of seed plants. The pigments of animals are located in nonliving skin derivatives such as hair in mammals, feathers in birds, scales in turtles and tortoises, and cuticles and shells in many invertebrates. Pigments also occur within living cells of the skin. The outermost skin cells may be pigmented, as in man, or special pigment-containing cells, chromatophores, may occur in the deeper layers of the skin. Depending on the colour of their pigment, chromatophores are termed melanophores (black), erythrophores (red), xanthophores (yellow), or leucophores (white).

CONTROL OF COLORATION

Genetic influences. Coloration is often sufficiently definable and species specific to serve as a moderately dependable basis for species recognition, as in birds, and hence in large measure it is determined genetically. The inheritance of colour in garden peas, which provided part of the basis of the pioneering studies of heredity by Mendel, led to the postulation of unit hereditary characters and their independent segregation into reproductive cells and to the discovery of the phenomenon of dominance. The unit genetic determiners are now termed alleles. An individual usually possesses a pair of such alleles for any hereditary character; they are situated at corresponding

---

The importance of coloration in plants and animals

The importance of natural coloration to man

loci on the paired chromosomes found in diploid cells—*i.e.*, cells containing two similar sets of complementary chromosomes. Segregation of the alleles occurs during formation of reproductive cells, with the result that only one of the pairs enters each cell, which is called a haploid cell.

Red-flowered peas (*Pisum*) have both alleles—*i.e.*, they are homozygous for the dominant character red, usually written *RR;* plants homozygous for the recessive white are designated *rr*. When Mendel crossed *RR* peas with *rr* ones, he obtained a first filial (F₁) generation with a heterozygous genetic composition, written *Rr;* all of the flowers were red, however, because the allele *R* completely dominates its mate, *r*, and thus is expressed in the red colour of the flowers. Dominance is often incomplete, however; a crossing between homozygous red Japanese four-o'clocks (*Mirabilis*) and homozygous white ones yields heterozygous *Rr* offspring, which are all pink. A cross of the heterozygous pink generation of four-o'clocks with each other yields a second generation with the colour ratio of 25 percent red (*RR*), 50 percent pink (*Rr*), and 25 percent white (*rr*). This is because each of the parent (F₁) plants produces equal numbers of *R*- and *r*-containing reproductive cells through segregation, and there is a random chance of either type of male haploid cell (gamete) fertilizing either of the two female types. For peas, on the other hand, the ratio resulting from a cross of parent (F₁) plants is three red (one *RR* and two *Rr*) to one white (*rr*) because of the dominance of *R*.

Although the principle of inheritance of colour and coloration patterns in all organisms is like that for the two plants described above, it is usually far more complex. Within the species population, a particular chromosome site may have multiple alleles instead of two; thus numerous combinations within any individual may be possible; in addition, the coloration may depend upon genes at several sites. In this case either all pairs may segregate simultaneously and more or less independently into the gametes or the genes may be linked in their inheritance by location on the same chromosome. Such possibilities, together with different degrees of dominance, result in tremendously complex hereditary bases for the genetic control of colour and colour patterns within many species.

Physiological control. The development of coloration often depends upon regulatory substances (hormones) secreted by endocrine glands. In birds the level of the hormone thyroxine may determine the coloration of feathers and bill; sex hormones and even lutenizing hormone from the pituitary gland attached to the base of the brain may also play roles. The variability in control among bird species is so great, however, that generalizations are impossible. Even sexual differences in plumage range from almost complete genetic control (*e.g.*, the house sparrow, *Passer domesticus*) in some species to a high degree of endocrine control in other species. The species specificity of coloration patterns, however, always depends upon a genetically determined responsiveness of various target tissues to certain hormones.

Chromatophores, which provide for relatively rapid colour changes, are found in a number of lizards, amphibians, fishes, crustaceans, insects, and mollusks. Chromatophores either allow conspicuous display of a given pigment by dispersing it in the chromatophore-bearing surface or conceal the pigment by concentrating it into small areas. The colour repertoire of an animal is limited, of course, by the colours of the pigments it has.

The most rapid colour changes occur in the octopus, squid, and cuttlefish, in which extensive changes in skin colour may be effected in seconds; in some cases, waves of colour change progress rapidly over the body. The rapid change is possible because of a unique type of chromatophore, one consisting of an elastic sac filled with pigment; a ring of radiating muscle fibres, upon contraction, stretches the sac into a thin disk. The muscles are regulated by nerve fibres.

A chromatophore role in the walkingstick insect (Phasmida) is played by the epidermal cells over the whole body, under hormonal control. The outer portion of these cells contains a nonmobile yellow-green pigment. Within this layer is a red pigment that can be either clumped into small dots or dispersed broadly. Also present is a mobile black pigment, which may migrate to a superficial location in the cells, darkening the skin, or move below the yellow-green layer, permitting lightening.

The chromatophores of crustaceans and vertebrates are stellate (star-shaped) cells, usually with many branches; the pigment is conspicuously displayed when it disperses from a central condensed ball to fill the whole cell. One animal may contain pigments of several colours, commonly red, yellow, black, and reflecting white; prawns also have a blue pigment. By appropriate migrations of their pigments, the animals achieve substantial alterations

From (A, B) *Proceedings of the Royal Society* (1923)

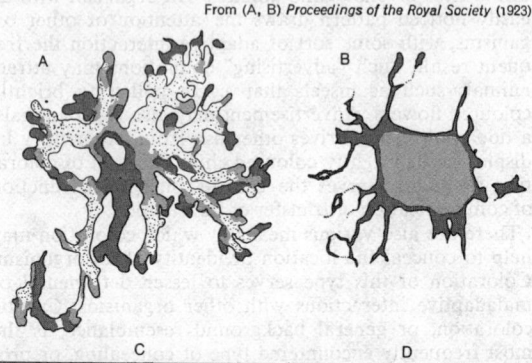

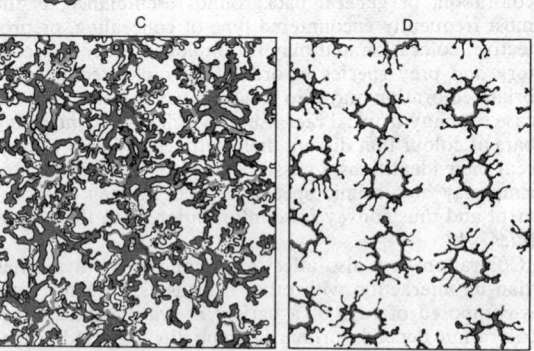

Figure 1: *Colour change in frog skin by expanded and contracted melanophores.*
(A) Melanophore expanded; (B) melanophore contracted;
(C) section of skin with melanophores expanded; (D) section of skin with melanophores contracted.

in their colours or shades for varying periods of time—*e.g.*, minutes in some bony fishes to hours in some amphibians. In prawns, dispersion of blue and yellow yields green; unequal dispersion of pigments over parts of the body yields colour patterns. The chromatophores of bony fishes are regulated chiefly by nerves; those of amphibians and crustaceans are usually under hormonal control. In elasmobranch fishes (sharks and rays) and lizards, nerves and hormones collaborate.

Rapid physiological colour changes are supplemented by morphological ones, the animal either gradually synthesizing or destroying pigments, usually in an adaptive manner.

Other factors influencing colour. Many environmental factors influence animal coloration. In many animals, coloration reflects the brightness of illumination and the colour, shade, or pattern of the background. The depth of colour of butterfly pupae may vary with temperature. Tactile (touch) stimuli may affect coloration; the crustacean *Hyperia*, a parasite of jellyfishes, is dark in colour when free-swimming but becomes pale upon reaching its highly transparent host. The walkingstick insect darkens with increases in humidity. Emotional state plays a role in some cephalopods (octopuses and squid), fishes, and horned lizards (*Phrynosoma*). When excited, some fishes and horned lizards undergo a transient blanching termed excitement pallor, which probably results from the secretion of adrenaline, a hormone known to concentrate the dark pigment of vertebrates. Excited squid and cuttlefish exhibit spectacular displays of colour. Among animals with chromatophores, rhythmic long-term colour changes generally occur and are independent of the natural daily changes of factors such as light and temperature.

LONG-TERM COLORATION CHANGES

Seasonal changes of colour

Seasonal changes in coloration of fields and forests include the annual colour changes involving foliage, flowers, fruits, and seeds of plants. Numerous songbirds adopt attractive nuptial plumage for the breeding season, reverting to drab, so-called eclipse plumage in the fall. Comparable special breeding colorations also occur in other animals, including some fishes. Several northern animals, such as the varying hares (*Lepus*), some weasels (*Mustela*), and ptarmigans (*Lagopus*), turn white in winter. Such seasonal changes are commonly regulated by the changing relative lengths of daylight and darkness, which alter the output of certain hormones (see PERIODICITY, BIOLOGICAL).

Colour changes during the life of an individual are common. Graying hair is a familiar badge of the elderly, both in man and, to varying degrees, in other mammals. Young birds of many species have a juvenile plumage that later gives way to an adult one. Most gulls, for example, deep gray or brown during the first year, become increasingly white thereafter. (F.A.B.)

II. The structural and biochemical bases for colour

Colour is manifested in organisms through two entirely different means: (1) chemically, by natural pigments (biochromes)—*i.e.*, coloured molecules that reflect or transmit (or both) certain fractions of visible light; and (2) physically, by colourless, submicroscopic structures (schemochromes), including ridges, striations, facets, successive layers; multiple fine, randomly dispersed, light-scattering bodies, which fractionate incident light into its component colours. Pigmentary colours are not substantially altered by physical means, such as crushing or grinding; schemochromes, or structurally produced colours, however, are altered and sometimes destroyed. If, for example, an area of a feather from a blue jay (*Cyanocitta cristata*) is struck with a hammer, it turns black. The blue colour is structural; it arises from the differential scattering of ordinary light by the delicate organization of a colourless, horny, subsurface layer of alveolar spaces—*i.e.*, spaces filled with submicroscopic air chambers. Black melanin pigment, lying beneath the light-scattering layer, absorbs the longer wavelengths of light, such as red, orange, and yellow; the very fine microbubbles of air above the melanin deposit reflect the blue light component back to the viewer's eye. A blue feather, viewed by transmitted light (*i.e.*, with the light source behind it) appears dark because the blue rays are reflected back toward the light and the other rays are absorbed. When the alveolar (air-filled) spaces are flattened by a hammer blow, a clear window into the dark melanin layer below results. The hammered feather is permanently damaged and remains blackened in the parts struck. A feather blackened by filling the small air spaces with a foreign fluid such as phenol, however, may readily be rendered blue once more by merely removing the phenol and drying the feather.

The changeable spectral effects generated by very thin, alternating layers of material—*e.g.*, as in iridescent feathers or in some beetles' wing covers—are modified by either compressing them together or causing them to thicken and spread.

STRUCTURAL COLOURS (SCHEMOCHROMES)

Although biochromy, being of molecular origin, may be expressed quite independently of any special minute, optically effective structural sources of colour, the reverse is not always true, for the schemochromic colours are greatly reinforced by the presence of pigment, whether in underlying or in superimposed strata or within the colour-producing structures themselves.

The physical principles of total reflection, spectral interference, scattering, and, to some extent, polychromatic diffraction, all of which are familiar among inanimate objects, are also encountered among tissues and tissue products of living forms. They are encountered only in animals, however, except for the total reflection of white light by some fungi and bacteria, and by the petals of some flowers and barks, and by some spectral interference in certain sea plants.

Reflection. Total reflection of light, which imparts whiteness to certain blossoms and to various animal structures, often arises from the separation of finely divided materials by minute air spaces. Examples of this are seen in certain cells of white petals (aerenchymous cells); in white feathers, fur, and hair; and in the white wings of certain butterflies. Secretions or deposits in tissues may also contribute to the whiteness—*e.g.*, the white, sticky fluid secreted by some plants; the fat and protein in mammalian milk; the calcium carbonate in the shells of mollusks, crustaceans, certain echinoderms, corals, and protozoans; the silica in sponges; the proteinaceous matter in various serous membranes; the white pterin pigments in the wings of pierid and other butterflies; and white or silvery aggregates of guanine and related compounds (see below) in the covering of numerous invertebrates, the scales of fishes, and the specular tapetum lucidum (the effective layer of the retina) of the eyes of fishes and reptiles.

Iridescent colours

Interference. Fractionation of white light into its components occurs in organisms (chiefly animals) through interference: the incident light penetrates the animal structure and is reflected back through successive ultra-thinly layered films, giving striking iridescence, even in diffuse light, as a result of the asynchrony between the wavelengths of visible light that enter and those that return. In 1704 Sir Isaac Newton stated this principle, as it applies to soap bubbles and other thin films, in his book *Opticks*, and the British physicists the elder and younger lords Rayleigh, between 1919 and 1923, applied Newton's interference principle in a discussion of the rich colours of various structures in many beetles and other animals.

Brilliant interference colours may display variety or be predominantly of one kind, depending upon the relative thicknesses of layers and interlaminar spaces giving rise to the colours. Such colours also are changeable with the angle of vision of the viewer.

Iridescent interference colours are common in many animal structures, including the wing scales of *Morpho* and other butterflies; the feathers of hummingbirds, peafowl (*Pavo*), pheasants, and many other birds; the wing covers of many beetles; the outer skin of some snakes (before or after it is shed, or molted); the nacreous (mother-of-pearl) surfaces of pearls and the inner lining of abalone and some other mollusks; the surfaces of some seaweeds under water (*e.g.*, *Iridophycus*); and, among land plants, the upper leaf surfaces of a club moss (*Selaginella* species) from rain forests of Costa Rica.

The lustre and iridescent appearance in sunlight of human and other mammalian hair results from the same phenomenon—the light is reflected in its components by minute transparent scales surrounding each hair. The coarse, brilliantly coloured setae (bristles) of the sea mouse *Aphrodite*, a large marine polychaete worm, furnish an outstanding instance of interference. Purely prismatic refraction of light (sometimes confused with interference iridescence) is probably rare in animals and is limited to instances in which direct beams of light impinge upon certain microcrystalline deposits. Polychromatic diffraction—*e.g.*, by natural, fine gratings or regular fine striations—may be observed among certain insects, but, like prismatic refraction, it is conspicuous only when a direct beam of light strikes such structures and they are viewed at an angle.

Origin of Tyndall effect in animals

Scattering. A special instance of diffraction, often referred to as the Tyndall effect (after its discoverer, the 19th-century British physicist John Tyndall), is common among animals. It results in blue colours quite distinct in origin from blue anthocyanin pigments common in many flowers. The Tyndall effect arises from the reflection of the shorter (blue) waves of incident light by finely dispersed particles situated above the dark layers of pigment, commonly melanin deposits; it results in the display of blue colours. Examples of Tyndall blue schemochromes are numerous—*e.g.*, blue eyes, in which the iris tissues overlie the dark membrane, or uvea. The blue colour of the skin about the head and neck of turkeys, guinea-fowl, cassowaries, and some other birds and upon the face, buttocks, and genital areas of certain primates is derived from the scattered reflection of the blue and violet fractions of light by particles dispersed within epidermal tissues that overlie a dark, absorbing screen of melanin in the dermis. The blue colours of many feathers are generated by the reflection of blue light by very tiny air vesicles that lie above melanin deposits. Similarly, the blues of many fishes and reptiles arise by the reflection of short light rays by microcrystals of guanine (see below *Pigments [biochromes]: Purines and pterins*) or by fine aggregates of certain proteins.

In these blue-scattering systems, the reflecting entities—whether very small globules of protein or lipid, semisolid substances in aqueous mediums, or very small vesicles of air—are of such small size as to approximate the wavelength of light (about 0.4 micron). The longer waves, such as red, orange, and yellow, pass through such mediums and are absorbed by the dark melanin below; short waves, violet and blue, because they encounter bodies of approximately their own dimensions, are reflected back.

Two types of coloration may act in combination; in some instances, for example, structurally coloured and pigmented layers may be superimposed. Most of the greens found in the skin of fishes, amphibians, and reptiles do not arise from the presence of green pigments (although exceptions occur); rather, they result from the emergence of scattered blue light through an overlying layer of yellow pigment. Similarly, the purple hues seen between the red and blue areas in the naked skin of cassowaries and those of certain baboons and other primates are derived from the complementary colour effects of blue scattering and superimposed red resulting from the pigment hemoglobin. A red pigment overlying the Tyndall-blue-scattering elements of a feather can render it purple; a yellow gives an otherwise blue feather a green colour. Extraction of the yellow pigment from the overlying cuticle of a green feather or of a reptilian skin leaves the object blue.

PIGMENTS (BIOCHROMES)

Chemical and biochemical features. The dimensions of molecules are far smaller than are those of particles dispersed in a medium (*i.e.*, colloids). The visible range of light is selectively affected by reflection from or transmission through molecules whose size or vibrational wavelengths or both lie between 3000 and 7000 angstroms (one angstrom equals 10^{-7} millimetre).

It will be recalled that the physical structures in living things that fractionate white light include very thin, finely spaced laminations, ridges, or striations, which give spectral colours of interference, or colloidally dispersed particles, which manifest Tyndall blues of scattering. The colour of a chemical compound, however, depends upon the selective absorption of light fractions lying within definite wavelengths; the absorbed light energy is converted into heat, and the residual, unabsorbed rays are reflected or transmitted to the eye. The capacity to absorb visible light selectively results from sites of special molecular activity in the colour-carrying groups (chromophores) within the molecule. These sites of activity arise from retardation in the relative speed or vibrational frequency of the many rapidly vibrating electron pairs found in a compound. Sufficient modification in the frequency of vibration imparts to the whole molecule a special motion, or chemical resonance, that absorbs entering light rays of matching frequency with the evolution of heat; the residual, unabsorbed light is transmitted.

If the molecular resonance involves short, rapid waves, the shorter visible light waves are absorbed (*i.e.*, violet and blue) and the compound appears yellow or orange; red-appearing substances, having slightly longer resonance values, absorb light from the blue and green regions;

Selective absorption of light rays

and blue and green compounds result from cancellation of light in the red or orange realms. Black substances absorb all light equally and completely; white compounds absorb no light in the visible spectrum, only in the ultraviolet regions.

The colour reflected by a pigment usually includes all of the wavelengths of visible light except the absorbed fraction; the commonly observed colour of a compound thus depends upon the dominant wavelength reflected or transmitted.

A number of biochromes are well-known biocatalysts (substances that facilitate chemical reactions without contributing to the end products); these include chlorophylls, cytochromes, and other porphyrins; riboflavin (also called lactoflavin, a member of the vitamin B_2 complex); xanthopterin; certain quinones and some carotenoids, some of which are involved in the synthesis of vitamin A, a compound important in vision, growth, and mucus secretion; and other molecules containing 40 carbon atoms, which function in photosynthesis in certain seaweeds or exercise other photokinetic roles, such as light screens or phototactic effectors.

The more important natural pigments may be grouped arbitrarily into (1) classes whose molecules lack nitrogen and (2) those that contain nitrogen. Of the non-nitrogenous pigments, by far the most important, conspicuous, and widely distributed in both plants and animals are the carotenoids, or polyenes. Chromolipids, naphthoquinones, anthraquinones, and flavonoids are other nitrogenfree pigments that occur in animals, all but the first being synthesized originally in plants, as are the carotenoids. But unlike the carotenoids, the others have a limited distribution in animals, and little is known of their physiological attributes in either kingdom.

In the nitrogenous group are several diverse pigment classes. Tetrapyrrolic pigments include both the porphyrin class (*i.e.*, the heme compounds in the red and some green blood of many animals and the green chlorophylls of many plants) and the bile pigments, which occur in many secretions and excretory products of animals and in plant cells. Melanins are dark pigments found in skin, hair, feathers, scales, and some internal membranes; they represent end products from the breakdown of tyrosine and related amino acids. Several purine compounds, although characteristically white or silvery in natural deposits, are included with true pigments because they often contribute to the overall colour or colour patterns of animals such as insects, coelenterates, fishes, reptiles, and amphibians. Similarly, the pterins, which are derived from pyrimidine, often are white but may also frequently be yellow, orange, or red. The flavins, or lyochromes, detectable in the tissues of all living organisms, are identified with certain important biocatalysts. The indigoids, which are somewhat limited in distribution, are end products of metabolism, as are purines, pterins, and melanins. A number of miscellaneous pigments are of incompletely known constitution; the great majority are nitrogenous in character, and several are chromoproteins.

Below are outlined the basic chemical configuration, colours, sources, and metabolic features of some representative biological pigments.

Carotenoids. The carotenoids constitute a group of yellow, orange, or red pigments of almost universal distribution in living things. The number of known representatives steadily increases. Carotenoids generally are insoluble in water but dissolve readily in fat solvents such as alcohol, ether, and chloroform. They can be crystallized and in solution exhibit usually two or three, but sometimes only one, light absorption peaks, characteristically in the violet to blue region of the spectrum and sometimes extending into the green region. They are readily bleached by light and by exposure to atmospheric oxygen and are also unstable in acids such as sulfuric acid.

Carotenoids are synthesized by bacteria, fungi, algae, and other plants to highly evolved flowering forms, in which they are most conspicuous in petals, pollen, fruit, and some roots—*e.g.*, carrots, sweet potatoes, tomatoes, and citrus fruits. All animals and protozoans contain

Distinction between nitrogenous and non-nitrogenous pigments

β-carotene

carotenoids, although the blood plasma of a number of mammals (*e.g.*, swine, sheep, goats, some carnivores) is almost entirely free of these pigments. The livers of animals often yield carotenoids; all animals depend upon a nutritional supply of vitamin A or one of its precursors, such as carotene, for maintenance of normal metabolism and growth. Carotenoids are relatively more concentrated in such structures as ovaries, eggs, testes (some animals), the liver (or the liver-like analogue of invertebrates), adrenal glands, skin, and eyes. In birds, carotenoid pigmentation may be conspicuous in the yellow tarsal (lower leg) skin, external ear, body fat, and egg yolk (especially in poultry) and in red-coloured feathers. Carotenoids are also found in the wings or wing covers of many insects and in the milk fat of cattle.

Two basic types of carotenoids
Carotenoids occur as two major types: the hydrocarbon class, or carotenes, and the oxygenated (alcoholic) class, or xanthophylls. Some animals exhibit a high degree of selectivity for the assimilation of members of one or the other class. The horse (*Equus caballus*), for instance, absorbs through its intestine only the carotenes, even though its green food contains both classes (and indeed mostly xanthophylls); the domestic hen (*Gallus domesticus*), on the other hand, stores only members of the xanthophyll class, as do many fishes and invertebrates. Other animals, including certain frogs, an *Octopus* species, and man, have been found to assimilate and store both classes in the liver and in fat deposits; swine, carnivores (dogs, cats, bears), and several other animals assimilate no carotenoids.

Some interesting exceptions have been found to the storage of plant carotenoids. Flamingos, for example, display in their bright red feathers and tarsal skin oxygenated carotenoids derived through the metabolism of yellow carotenes in their diet. Indeed, the most brilliantly red or pink species, the American flamingo (*Phoenicopterus ruber*), and probably the other five species as well, convert beta-carotene from the diet into the unusual red compound canthaxanthin (diketo-beta-carotene) and other even more heavily oxygenated derivatives, storing them, but not beta-carotene, in the feathers and leg skin. In this regard, such birds as flamingos, the roseate spoonbill (*Ajaia ajaja*), and the scarlet ibis (*Guara rubra*) exhibit features of carotenoid metabolism more characteristic of some coelenterates, crustaceans, and other invertebrates, as well as certain fishes. Captive birds, unless fed generous supplies of carotenoids in their diet, lose, through fading, the pink pigmentation from the tarsal skin and, through the seasonal molt, that from the feathers.

Striking displays of carotenoid pigmentation are found in the skins of many fishes, amphibians, and marine invertebrates, including sea stars, brittle stars, mollusks, sea squirts, crustaceans, anemones, corals, and many marine worms. The blue, green, gray, chocolate, violet, and near-black pigmentations of certain crustaceans, shell-less mollusks, and sea stars result in most instances from the presence of a carotenoid, astaxanthin, that is linked to a protein through conjugation. Immersion in boiling water or alcohol of an animal so coloured frees the carotenoid, unmasking its red or orange colour; hence the familiar red colour of boiled lobsters and the leaching away of red pigment from brightly coloured blue or green specimens preserved in alcohol.

Aquatic animals commonly derive their rich supplies of carotenoids directly or indirectly from algae and other plants. Even carnivorous fishes and flesh- or mud-eating invertebrates from the unlighted depths of the ocean frequently exhibit rich pigmentation derived indirectly from

supplies of carotenoids generated earlier in illuminated waters above them by the phytoplankton (minute plants), which represent one of the richest depots of such compounds.

Carotenoids in coral
Certain brightly coloured corals store carotenoids, quite apart from those in their soft parts, within their skeletons of aragonite (a form of calcium carbonate); the chromogenic molecules apparently are firmly joined in some fashion with the calcium carbonate. This joining occurs in the gorgonian fan-coral *Eugorgia ampla*, within whose yellow-orange microspicules (spines) a carotenoid is tightly chelated to the calcium carbonate. Two even more spectacular instances are found in the hard skeletons of the hydrocorals *Allopora californica*, the so-called purple coral from waters off southern California, and *Distichopora violacea*, of bright vermilion hue, found on Eniwetok Atoll, in the Marshall Islands. These corals owe the pigmentation of their skeletons to the presence of astaxanthin, a red diketo-dihydroxy-beta-carotene, firmly chelated to the calcium carbonate.

A yellow condition of otherwise pale human skin—known as xanthosis, carotenemia, or artificial jaundice—may follow the excessive consumption of carotenoid-rich foods such as oranges, carrots, or certain cucurbits. The condition, less common in adults than in children, involves no pathological symptoms and gradually disappears when excessive carotenoids are withheld from the diet. The body carotenoids of many birds and fishes are utilized in their eggs during the reproductive season, often with visible loss of the yellow pigment from the skin of the females.

Quinones. The bichrome class of quinones is best divided into the benzoquinones, naphthoquinones, anthraquinones, and polycyclic quinones.

Benzoquinones. Benzoquinones are represented by compounds that occur in certain fungi and in roots, berries, or galls (abnormal growths) of higher plants, from which they can be recovered as yellow, orange, red, violet, or darker coloured crystals or solids. Small quantities of pale-yellow crystals of one member, coenzyme Q, have been obtained; apparently this pigment, or one or more closely related to it, is almost universally distributed in plants and animals. The various members of the coenzyme Q series are often called ubiquinones, connoting their nearly universal occurrence. The ubiquinones impart no recognizable coloration to an organism because of their very small concentrations; their role as respiratory enzymes in catalyzing cellular oxidations is an important one, however.

[ubiquinone (50)] or coenzyme Q_{10}

Naphthoquinones. Naphthoquinones are encountered in many parts of higher plants—*e.g.*, leaves, bark, seeds, roots, and other woody parts. They also occur in some bacteria, from which they can be recovered as yellow, orange, red, or purple crystals. They are soluble in organic solvents and have been used extensively as dyes for fabrics.

K vitamins
Among the naphthoquinones of biochemical and physiological importance are the K vitamins. Vitamin K_1 (a phylloquinone), a yellow, viscous oil recoverable from green plants such as alfalfa and tomatoes and from cer-

tain bacteria, is employed medically to treat hypoprothrombinemia (deficiency of a blood-clotting factor, prothrombin); vitamin K_2, the antihemorrhagic compound, is recovered as pale-yellow crystals from several bacterial species and from putrefied fish meal.

vitamin K_2

Another series within this class of biochromes manifests conspicuous red, purple, or sometimes green colours in a few animal types. The echinochromes and spinochromes are so named because they are conspicuous in tissues and in the calcareous tests (shells) of echinoids, or sea urchins. Some pigments of this group also occur in a few red crinoids, or sea lilies. The skull, teeth, and other bony parts of sea otters (*Enhydra lutris*) often exhibit pink to purple coloration as a consequence of their having consumed large numbers of urchins. Similarly, the teeth and the dorsal spine of the horned shark (*Heterodontus francisci*) often exhibit bright-pink coloration for the same reason. In the above instances, the echinochrome material is sufficiently acidic to form a coloured calcium salt, which then is incorporated into the skeletal material of the consumer.

No definite physiological function has been recognized for the echinochromes in skeletal parts and soft tissues, but their naphthoquinone structure is reminiscent of the K vitamins. These naphthoquinones originate in plants, whence the echinoids derive them.

echinochrome A

Anthraquinones. The anthraquinones occur widely in plants but in only a few animals. These brilliantly coloured compounds have found wide application as dyes and as chemical indicators of acidity or alkalinity.

Cochineal is the potassium salt of carminic acid, a red

carminic acid

Dyes obtained from scale insects

pigment occurring in fat-body cells of female cochineal scale insects (*Dactylopius*) that feed upon certain cactus plants of Mexico and Central America. Other scale insects store the same or closely allied pigments. The dye is not confined to the fat body but is also present in the eggs and in cells of the larvae. It may account for a considerable proportion of the adult female's weight but is present in lesser amounts in males. Carminic acid, extracted chemically from powdered insects, imparts a permanent red colour to wool that has been mordanted—*i.e.*, pretreated with a chemical fixer. Cochineal has been largely replaced by synthetic aniline dyes, but it still is used to colour certain fabrics, inks, and confections.

Kermesic acid, a red dye popular in ancient Greece and Rome, is extracted from the female kermes scale insect (*Kermes ilicis*), which thrives upon certain species of oak in Spain, Portugal, and Morocco. Yellow-red in water and violet-red in acidic solutions, kermesic acid is chemically allied with carminic acid.

Laccaic acid, isolated from lac dye, is the solid resinous secretion covering the female bodies of some lac insects of Southeast Asia.

The conspicuous anthraquinones described above doubtless are acquired by the insects from their plant hosts, but no information is yet available as to the manner in which the compounds are metabolized or their possible significance in either the plant or the insect. Anthraquinones have been discovered in red crinoids, notably *Comatula pectinata*.

Polycyclic quinones. The polycyclic quinones occur in some bacteria, fungi, and parts of higher plants. One of the more interesting representatives is the aphin group, so called because of their initial recovery from the hemolymph (circulating fluid) of several coloured species of aphids; aphids parasitize plants, as do the other quinone-assimilating insects. *Aphis fabae*, for example, feeds upon the broad bean plant *Vicia faba*. Insects placed in hot water yield protoaphin, which, when crystallized, forms pale-yellow needles. The protoaphin in freshly crushed insects not treated with hot water is converted to another yellow compound, xanthoaphin, which can be modified to yield chrysoaphin; this, in turn, can be further converted to a red compound, erythroaphin. Each of the aphins exhibits characteristic properties regarding appearance of crystals, colour, flourescence, and absorption spectrum.

erythroaphin

The aphins do not melt; rather, they decompose with charring at temperatures above 300° C (600° F). Readily soluble in pyridine, but less so in other organic solvents, aphins contain no nitrogen or sulfur; their colours are evoked by their quinone groupings, and their acidic properties arise from the phenolic hydroxyl groups. No physiological function has yet been recognized for the aphins and the compounds related to them.

Flavonoids. The biochromes in the class of flavonoids, another instance of compounds lacking nitrogen, are extensively represented in plants but are of relatively minor and limited occurrence in animals, which rely on plants as sources of these pigments. Flavonoids consist of a 15-carbon skeleton compound called flavone (2-phenylbenzopyrone), in which one or more hydrogen atoms (H) is replaced either by hydroxyl groups (−OH) or by methoxyl groups (−OCH₃). Flavonoids occur in living tissue mainly in combination with sugar molecules, forming glycosides. Many members of this group, notably the anthoxanthins, which include the flavones and flavonals, impart yellow colours, often to flower petals; the class also includes the anthocyans, which are water-soluble plant pigments exhibiting orange reds, crimson, blue, or other colours.

Anthoxanthins. A prominent flavonoid is the pale-yellow flavonal quercitin, first isolated from an oak Quercitin

quercitin

(*Quercus*) but widely distributed in nature. A weak acid, it combines with strong acids to form orange salts, which are not very stable and readily dissociate in water. Salt formation results from a structural peculiarity common to both the anthoxanthins and anthocyanins. Quercitin is a strong polygenetic dyestuff; *i.e.*, it yields more than one colour, depending on the mordant used. A yellow pigment isolated from the wings of the butterfly *Melanargia galatea* possesses chemical properties closely allied to those of this flavonoid. Derivatives of quercitin have been obtained from capers (*Capparis*), buckwheat (*Fagopyrum*), clover flowers (*Trifolium*), onion skins (*Allium*), tea leaves (*Camellia* or *Thea*), apple-tree bark (*Malus*), and many other sources. Although there may be some significance to such a wide distribution, the variety of anthoxanthins is greater than that of anthocyanins, and new anthoxanthins are continuously being discovered. Among the better known anthoxanthins are the following (in all cases, except possibly chrysin, they occur in plants, in combination with sugars): chrysin in the leaf buds of the poplar (*Populus*); apigenin in the leaves, stem, and seeds of parsley (*Petroselinum*) and the flowers of the camomile (*Anthemis*); galangin in the galanga root (*Alpinia*); and luteolin in weld (*Reseda luteola*).

Anthocyanins. The anthocyanins are largely responsible for the red colouring of buds and young shoots and the purple and purple-red colours of autumn leaves. The red colour becomes apparent when the green chlorophyll decomposes with the approach of winter. Intense light and low temperatures favour the development of anthocyanin pigments. Some leaves and flowers lose anthocyanins on reaching maturity; others gain in pigment content during development. Often an excess of sugars exists in leaves when anthocyanins are abundant. Injury to individual leaves may be instrumental in causing the sugar excess in such cases. Anthocyanins also occur in blossoms, fruits, and even roots (*e.g.*, beets) and occasionally in larval and adult flies and in true bugs (Heteroptera).

Anthocyanins as indicators of nutritional deficiencies in plants

The development of characteristic colorations in parts of plants is often useful in the diagnosis of mineral deficiencies in the plant nutrient supply. This is particularly true for phosphorus, potassium, magnesium, and boron deficiencies. Insufficient phosphorus induces a pronounced development of purple coloration in the leaves and stalks of some strains of corn. Development of brown, bronze, red, or purple areas in leaves is often characteristic of potassium deficiencies in potato, cotton, cabbage, apple, and orange plants. Boron deficiency causes development of a red coloration in alsike clover and alfalfa leaves. Magnesium deficiency in cotton results in the formation of leaves that are coloured a beautiful purplish-red between the dark-green veins. These changes are caused by the production of large quantities of anthocyanin pigments, probably followed by destruction of chlorophyll. Anthocyanin formation in such deficiency diseases can take place only in plants that possess the specific genetic factors necessary to produce this pigment.

One interesting property of the anthocyanins is the change of colour they exhibit when treated with acids or alkalis. The exposure of a red flower petal to fumes of ammonia (alkaline) cause it to turn blue or green; a blue flower turns red when touched with vinegar or a mineral acid.

A green colour results from the combined effect of yellow and blue pigments: the bright-yellow colour is produced by the action of the alkali on an almost colourless anthoxanthin in solution; the blue colour is produced by the anthocyanin. Many white flowers (*e.g.*, jasmine and *Antirrhinum*) develop bright-yellow colorations in ammonia. A typical anthocyanin is red in acid, violet in neutral, and blue in alkaline solution. Thus, the blue cornflower, the bordeaux-red cornflower, the deep-red dahlia, and the red rose contain the same anthocyanin, the variation in colour resulting from the different degrees of acidity and alkalinity of the cell sap. More than one anthocyanin may be present in a flower or blossom, and the colours of many flowers are caused by the presence of both anthocyanins and plastid pigments in the tissues. Yellow wallflowers contain a plastid pigment and an anthoxanthin that contribute little to the total tinctorial effect, the different shades of red wallflowers resulting from varying proportions of anthocyanin and plastid colouring matter. Moreover, small genet-

ic changes in varieties or species may be associated with the development of different anthocyanins.

The principal chemical factors affecting the colours in cell sap are (1) the nature and concentration of anthocyanins; (2) the state of aggregation of the anthocyanins, which is affected by the acid–base condition (pH) and by colloids such as pentosans; (3) the presence of co-pigments; and (4) possibly the presence of alkaloids and metallic complexes.

The colouring matter cyanin exists in the blue cornflower as its blue potassium salt, but the substance can also react with acids to form red salts, and advantage may be taken of this property in the isolation of the pure substance as cyanin chloride. Cyanin chloride ($C_{27}H_{31}O_{16}Cl$), like all anthocyanins, contains sugar (glucose) in a combined form. This is readily detached by the action of boiling 20 percent hydrochloric acid, leaving a salt, termed cyanidin chloride, that in many properties closely resembles cyanin chloride. Each molecule of cyanin chloride gives rise to one of cyanidin chloride and two of glucose. Cyanin chloride is thus a diglycoside of cyanidin chloride.

cyanidin chloride   apigenin

Mecocyanin chloride from the poppy (*Papaver rhoeas*, purple-scarlet variety) has the same composition as cyanin chloride and, like it, is degraded to cyanidin chloride and glucose. There are, however, differences among them—a solution of cyanin in aqueous sodium carbonate is blue, whereas that of mecocyanin is violet. The explanation for these divergencies lies in the different mode of the molecular attachment of the cyanidin and glucose in the two substances.

Chrysanthemin, the pigment of the deep-red garden chrysanthemum, resembles mecocyanin, but it gives rise to only one molecule of glucose for each molecule of a cyanidin salt; *i.e.*, it is monoglycosidic. Careful treatment of mecocyanin with hydrochloric acid causes loss of one of the glucose molecules; the result is chrysanthemin chloride. Other anthocyanins derived from cyanidin are known; their differences may be traced to the varying nature of the sugars, to the number of sugar molecules attached to cyanidin, and to the position of such attachment. In the magenta snapdragon the pigment is a cyanidin glycoside containing one molecule of glucose and one of rhamnose.

It is a curious fact that, despite the existence in nature of a range of colour unrivalled by art, the number of fundamental sugar-free pigments of the cyanidin chloride type, termed anthocyanidins, is very limited. There are but three fundamental anthocyanidins: cyanidin, pelargonidin, and delphinidin. These in turn are built upon the same molecular plan.

Three fundamental anthocyanidins

The chemistry of anthocyanin pigments is important to the canning industry. Anthocyanins of fruits form insoluble salts of tin and iron after these metals are made available by corrosion of the cans initiated by fruit acids. Thus, high anthocyanin content may greatly increase the corrosion over that which could be attributed to the acid alone. Fruit quality is thereby lowered.

Of the class of natural substances called leucoanthocyanidins, some give rise, upon treatment with strong acids, to anthocyanidins that do not occur naturally. The leucoanthocyanins and leucoanthocyanidins that give perlagonidin, cyanidin, and delphinidin are known to occur in plants, but none of the leucoanthocyanins has yet been isolated as a pure substance.

The larva of the beetle *Cionus olens* reportedly carries, associated with the inclusions of certain cells, an anthocyan of blue, red, or intermediate violet or purple colour, depending on the pH. An aphid, *Tritogenaphis rudbeckiae*, yields a vermilion pigment, insoluble in ordinary fat solvents but readily soluble in aqueous mediums or in cold methanol, that shows reversible colour changes when treated with ammonia and a green colour on exposure to ferric chloride. These chemical properties resemble those of anthocyanins, many of which are acid-base sensitive. No physiological functions seem to have been definitely established for the flavonoids in animals and plants. It has been pointed out, however, that flower colour is valuable in attracting bees, butterflies, and other pollen-transporting visitors that implement fertilization in plants; brightly coloured fruits have improved seed dispersal by animals attracted to them as food.

Tetrapyrroles, porphyrins, and their derivatives. A biologically important class of water-soluble, nitrogenous 16-membered ring, or cyclic, compounds is referred to as porphyrins. Porphyrins combine with metals (metal-

porphin

loporphyrins) and protein. They are represented by the green, photosynthetic chlorophylls of higher plants and by the hemoglobins in the blood of many animals.

Some porphyrins are chemically identified as hemoproteins: cytochrome, a red enzyme, occurs in minute concentrations in most cells and is involved in oxidative processes; catalase, also a widely distributed enzyme, accelerates the breakdown of hydrogen peroxide; pinnaglobin, a brown compound, may serve as a respiratory aid in the bivalve mollusk *Pinna squamosa;* chlorocruorin, which is green, plays a similar role in the blood of tube-building sabellid worms; the erythrocruorins, possessing the same heme moiety (*i.e.*, the iron-porphyrin moiety) as do hemoglobins but with a much larger protein component, serve in the respiration of many red-blooded invertebrates; helicorubin, a red compound, is encountered in the gut of some snails; and actiniohematin is responsible for some of the red colours in certain sea anemones. The physiological function, if any, of the last two pigments has not been established.

Porphyrins. Many invertebrates display in their skins or shells porphyrin pigments (or salts of them), some showing fluorescence (*i.e.*, the emission of visible light during exposure to outside radiation). The worm *Thalassema lankestri* and its relative *Bonellia* possess a bluish-green porphyrin in the skin and mucus. In certain solutions the pigment is green, and it fluoresces under ultraviolet light. A pigment called protoporphyrin IX is present in solid aggregates within the cells of the red-orange freckles on the siphon of the wood-boring bivalve *Bankia setacea*. It has also been detected in red sea pens, such as *Pennatula*, and renders the soft parts of these coelenterates highly photosensitive.

Like the bug *Rhodnius*, certain parasitic worms presumably derive their characteristic porphyrin pigments from the heme of their vertebrate hosts; some parasites believed to store porphyrins are *Tetrathrydium*, a tapeworm of the hedgehog (*Erinaceus*); *Eustrongylus*, a red nematode found in the dog; and the tapeworm *Taenia solium*, one stage of which infests the pig.

The substances uroporphyrin III and coproporphyrin III have been recovered from the calcareous (calcium-containing) shells of many mollusks; and coloured oyster pearls yield traces of porphyrins and metalloporphyrins. Higher proportions of metalloporphyrins, apparently involving lead or zinc, seem to occur in green pearls; pink pearls have been reported to possess less total porphyrin and thus less is available to combine with metals.

Various porphyrins occur in secretory and excretory products of animals, and some kinds, predominantly the phorbides, which result from the breakdown of chlorophyll, have been recovered from ancient natural deposits such as coal and petroleum and from muds of long-buried marine and lacustrine strata. Ooporphyrin is responsible for the red flecks on the eggshells of some plovers and many other birds. Greenish porphyrin derivatives have been recovered from the hepatopancreas, or digestive gland, of a cephalopod, *Octopus bimaculatus*. The African turacos (Musophagidae) secrete a copper salt of uroporphyrin III into their wing feathers. This deep-red pigment, turacin, is readily leached from the feathers by water containing even traces of alkali. The green plumes of these birds owe their colour to the presence of turacoverdin, a derivative of turacin.

Evidence indicates that, in various animals, certain porphyrins may be involved in activating hormones from the pituitary gland, including those concerned with the period of sexual heat in certain female animals. Porphyrins in the integument (skin) of some mollusks and coelenterates are regarded as being photosensitive receptors of light.

Hemoglobins. Hemoglobins are present in the red blood cells of all vertebrate animals and in the circulatory fluids of many invertebrates, notably annelid worms, some arthropods, echinoderms, and a few mollusks. The hemoglobin molecule consists of a heme fraction and a globin fraction; the former consists of four pyrrole moieties (porphin) with a ferrous iron (Fe^{2+}) atom in the centre. The globin fraction is a protein that may constitute more than 90 percent of the total molecular weight of hemoglobin. Hemoglobins have the capacity to combine with atmospheric oxygen in lungs, gills, or other respiratory surfaces of the body and to release it to tissues. They are responsible for the pink to red colours observed in combs and wattles of birds and in the skin of man and other primates. Particularly prominent are portions of the face, buttocks, and genital areas of baboons. Hemoglobins are conspicuous also in the blood and muscles of many polychaete worms; they impart pink colours to the buccal (mouth-and-throat cavity) gland and the musculature involved in moving the radula, a file-like, rasping tongue of many marine snails; they similarly colour the foot, adductor muscle, brain, and gills of at least one bivalve mollusk, the edible Pismo clam (*Tivela stultorum*) of the Pacific Coast. Myoglobin, the name given to hemoglobin in muscles, is present in the posterior adductor muscle and in the heart of the "pileworm," or wood-boring teredinid bivalve (*Bankia setacea*). The sea cucumbers *Cucumaria miniata* and *Molpadia intermedia* carry hemoglobin in their red blood cells. The presence of hemoglobin has been recorded in water fleas (*Daphnia*) and other freshwater crustaceans, in certain aquatic insects, notably the midge *Chironomus riparius*, in the pond snail *Planorbis corneus*, and in the echiurid worm *Thalassema neptuni*. In *Daphnia* the blood pigment level varies, depending partly on the aeration of the habitat, fading somewhat in well-aerated waters but increasing conspicuously in oxygen-poor waters; similar conditions apply to the brine shrimp (*Artemia salina*). The ability to synthesize hemoglobin when necessary is an important adaptation toward survival; similarly, humans synthesize red blood cells, which contain hemoglobin, when exposed to high altitudes or to environments in which considerable quantities of carbon monoxide are generated.

Some parasitic animals seem to derive their hemoglobin directly from the host. This is true of some copepod crustaceans that invade the gills of fishes; the nematode worms that infest the tissues of swine and horses; the larva of the botfly *Gastrophilus*, which is parasitic in the stomach of the horse; and the bloodsucking bug *Rhodnius prolixus*.

An interesting discovery of the 1940s was the occurrence of hemoglobin in green plants—in the root nodules of peas, beans, and other leguminous plants harbouring the symbiotic bacterium *Rhizobium*. Evidence indicates that hemoglobin may, in this instance, serve as a catalyst during the process by which atmospheric nitrogen is con-

Porphyrins in secretory and excretory products

verted to inorganic substances (nitrogen fixation), a process that is known to take place in root nodules.

Chlorophylls. Chlorophyll, one of the most important pigments in nature, is capable of channelling the radiant energy of sunlight into chemical energy usable in the reactions of the cell through the process of photosynthesis. A pigment very much like chlorophyll was probably the first step in the evolution of self-sustaining life. Chlorophyll exists in several forms. Chlorophylls *a* and *b* are the chief forms in higher plants and green algae; combinations of *a* with *c* or *d* occur in different algae; bacteriochlorophyll is found in certain photosynthetic bacteria. Chlorophyll *e* is a rare pigment first demonstrated in one of the golden algae. Protochlorophyll, a presumed precursor of chlorophyll, is found in seedlings grown in darkness and plants grown in inadequate light. Protochlorophylls have been found that are converted into chlorophylls on exposure to light. *Chlorobium* chlorophyll (bacterioviridin) is found in green bacteria.

The chlorophylls are magnesium porphyrin compounds in which four linked pyrroles are attached to a single central magnesium atom. The various forms differ in minor modifications of side groups attached to the pyrrole groups. Basically, the chlorophyll molecule consists of two portions: a flattened square, the tetrapyrrole configuration, and a long tail formed of phytyl, which is also found in vitamins K and E. Phytyl is derived from the alcohol phytol, $C_{20}H_{39}OH$. In higher plants, chlorophyll is bound to proteins and lipids as chloroplastin in definite and specific laminations in bodies called chloroplasts.

The combination of chlorophyll with protein in chloroplastin is of special significance, because only as a result of the combination is chlorophyll able to remain resistant to light. Chloroplastins from different plants are not identical. A characteristic of chloroplastin is its great tendency toward agglomeration; and even the lowest molecular weights run into several millions.

The pure chlorophylls are usually obtained as dark-green waxes. Both chlorophylls *a* and *b* may be characterized by their absorption spectra and be crystallized, component *a* being obtained in green hexagonal plates and component *b* in dark-green needles.

The chlorophylls contain two hydrogen atoms more than the other porphyrins. Magnesium forms an essential component of the molecules of the natural chlorophylls. It may be that the magnesium shares the role played by chlorophyll in the assimilation process. The magnesium atom also constitutes a characteristic difference between the chlorophylls and the blood pigment hemin, which contains iron. When the chlorophylls are treated with acids, the magnesium atom is easily split off, the colour changing from pure to brownish green. The magnesium can be replaced by copper, zinc, or other metals. The corresponding copper complexes are stable and are used as industrial pigments—*e.g.*, in the soap and cosmetic industries.

Chlorophyll *b* differs from chlorophyll *a* only in having an aldehyde group (—CHO) in place of a methyl group in one ring; *i.e.*, it has an oxygen atom in place of two

chlorophyll *a*

hydrogen atoms. The complete chemical synthesis of chlorophyll was accomplished in 1960.

Bacteriochlorophyll can be derived from chlorophyll *a* by the addition of two hydrogen atoms to the double bond in one ring and by replacement of the vinyl group (CH₂ = CH —) in the molecule by acetyl (CH₃CO —).

The function of chlorophyll in photosynthesis has been defined as that of an energy transformer. The path of the assimilated carbon, from carbon dioxide to the final products, especially in the case of sucrose, has been traced using radioactive carbon (see PHOTOSYNTHESIS).

Bilins. Among the metabolic products of certain porphyrins, including the heme portion of hemoglobin, is a series of yellow, green, red, or brown nonmetallic compounds arranged as linear, or chain, structures rather than in the cyclic configuration of porphyrins. These so-called bilins, or bilichromes, are typified by the most simple member, a colourless synthetic substance called

bilane

bilane. Small quantities of the red waste compound, bilirubin ($C_{33}H_{36}O_6N_4$); a green product formed from it by the removal of two hydrogen atoms, biliverdin ($C_{33}H_{34}O_6N_4$); and various other chemically similar compounds occur in normal tissues and may be conspicuous in excretory or secretory materials under normal circumstances and certain pathological conditions. The bile pigments, although first identified in mammalian tissues or products (*e.g.*, in the bile of the gall bladder), are by no means confined thereto. Various members of the bilichrome series are encountered in invertebrates, lower vertebrates, and in red algae and green plants.

Pterobilin is a blue pigment found in the wings of many pierid butterflies and other insects; the larvae contain or excrete allied compounds. Certain leeches, nourished by the blood of their vertebrate hosts, contain blue-green, red, or brown bilichromes in their blood, probably as a consequence of the degradation of ingested hemoglobin. A violet bilichrome, haliotiviolin, has been recovered from the shell of the black abalone (*Haliotis cracherodii*), and a purple one, aplysioviolin, occurs in the conspicuous ink secreted by the sea slug *Aplysia californica*. The blue alcyonarian coral *Heliopora caerulea* carries a blue compound, helioporobilin (biliverdin IXα), firmly bound to its calcareous skeleton.

Many fishes, notably among the needlefishes (Belonidae) and sculpins (Cottidae), have strikingly blue-green skeletons, reflecting the presence of bilichromes. Thus the green pigment in bones and scales of the needlefish *Belone belone* is closely related to or identical with biliverdin. The California needlefish (*Strongylura exilis*) likewise owes its green skeletal pigmentation to a very similar bilichrome, and, among the mackerels and tunas (Scombridae), commercial catches of the skipjack *Katsuwonus pelamis* yield rare individuals whose endoskeletons, particularly the skulls and vertebrae, are green or blue-green because of the presence of an insoluble salt of a pigment closely resembling biliverdin. Contrary to the impression of some fishermen, commercial dealers, and consumers, the green colours persistent in the bones, and even in the flesh of some fish species, do not reflect the presence of copper or other poisonous substances, but of a green bilichrome that disappears on cooking.

Oöcyan, a pigment responsible for blue or blue-green colours in eggshells of gulls and some other wild birds, is believed to be biliverdin. Indeed, the dark-green pigment of the emu's egg has been proved to involve biliverdin and minor amounts of bilirubin. Another green pigment identified with biliverdin was once called uteroverdin because it originates outside of the liver and is observed in hemorrhagic placental areas in dogs. The conspicuous yellow colour of horses' blood plasma arises in considerable part from relatively high concentrations of bilirubin, which increases when the animals fast but returns to normal levels after a full diet has been restored.

Although the bile pigments of animals arise in all probability from the catabolism of heme precursors, there is evidence that bilirubin, accompanied by iron salts, promotes the synthesis of new hemoglobin when injected into humans, dogs, or rabbits suffering from secondary anemia.

In addition to the chlorophylls, plants also contain linear bilichromes, which have especially important roles in green plants. Among them are the blue phycocyanins and the red phycoerythrins, which serve, in red algae, as accessory pigments in photosynthesis. Another example is phytochrome, a bilichrome pigment of blue colour, which, although present in very minute quantities in green plants, is indispensable in various photoperiodic processes.

Types of phytochrome Phytochrome exists in two alternative forms: P_{660} and P_{730}, sometimes designated as P_r and P_{fr}, respectively. The two phases of phytochrome appear to involve a kind of balanced positioning of a pair of hydrogen atoms, each of which migrates reversibly to its respective position. The paired migration of hydrogen atoms establishes

phytochrome P_{660} (blue)

in far-red light (730 nm) ⇅ in red light (660 nm)

phytochrome P_{730}

double bonds. In nature the phytochromes are chemically combined with proteins, as are many other biochromes.

Of the two forms of phytochrome, P_{730} triggers the germination and respiration of seeds (and of spores of ferns and mosses), the flowering of long-day plants (or inhibition of flowering in short-day plants), etiolation (growth in darkness), cuticle coloration, anthocyanin synthesis (e.g., in apples, red cabbage, and turnips), and several structural and physiological responses. P_{660} is capable of reversing many physiological reactions initiated by P_{730}. Even very brief exposures to light absorbed by P_{660} delays flowering in some short-day plants otherwise geared to flower by previous exposure to light of such wavelength that only the P_{730} phytochrome is involved. Much yet remains to be learned about the biochemistry of phytochromes and the reactions catalyzed or otherwise regulated by them.

Indole pigments. *Melanins.* Dark colours, which indicate the presence of melanin pigment, are observed in many feathers; in hair, eyes, and skin of mammals, including man; in skin or scales or both of many fishes, amphibians, and reptiles; in the ink of cephalopods (octopus, squid); and in various tissues of many invertebrates.

Black melanin recovered from the wool of hybrid Downs-Dorset sheep was originally assigned the empirical formula $C_{105}H_{173}N_{23}SO_{38}$, but there are variations in the elementary composition of melanins from different sources; they are polymers (compounds consisting of repeating units) of variable mass and complexity. Extractable in very dilute alkali, melanins are also soluble when fresh and undried in very dilute acid solutions; they are bleached by hydrogen peroxide, which is sometimes applied to growing hair to create a blond effect, and by chlorine, chromate, and permanganate.

Melanins are conspicuous in dark skin moles of man; in the black dermal melanocytes (pigment cells) of most dark-skinned races, as brown, diffuse spots (melanoproteins) in the epidermis; and in black tumorous growths of many vertebrates, such as melanomas in man, fishes, and reptiles. The melanins are end products of metabolism involving the amino acid tyrosine and similar compounds. The progressive oxidation of tyrosine by atmo-

tyrosine (colourless) → red intermediate, a quinone of 2,3-dihydroindol-2-carboxylic acid

oxidation and cyclization, tyrosinase + O_2

colourless 5,6-dihydroxyindol-2-carboxylic acid → melanin (brown or black)

oxidation and polymerization

spheric oxygen is catalyzed by the copper-containing enzyme, tyrosinase. In the oxidation of tyrosine the chemically reversible yellow, orange, and red intermediate compounds are followed by an intensely black end product, which is a true melanin.

Some white or albino animals cannot synthesize either the enzyme tyrosinase in its active form or some intermediate compound necessary for pigmentation. Completely white genetic variants of the sea anemone *Metridium senile*, for example, fail to develop the melanin in their tissues typical of the brown phases of their species. When such an albino animal dies or when its tissues are macerated experimentally and thus exposed to air, the dead or damaged material blackens with the formation of melanin, much in the way that cut surfaces of potato tubers darken or that cut surfaces of apples turn reddish in air.

Pale-yellow, tawny, buff, reddish, brown, and black colours of hair and some feathers can arise from the presence of melanins in various phases of formation or subdivision in granules. The dark, light-absorbing sublayers of melanin that intensify reflected structural (Tyndall) blues or iridescent (Newtonian) displays in feathers were mentioned above. Black melanins and brown melanoproteins occur in many invertebrate animals. Certain worms and many crustaceans and molluscans exhibit melanism in the skin.

The degree of natural melanization depends upon relative concentrations of copper and of the copper-containing enzyme tyrosinase. Dark hairs contain higher traces of copper than do pale ones. Minimal traces of copper are required for pigmentation of fur (e.g., of rats); should the intake of copper fall substantially below a fraction of a milligram per day, new fur emerges successively less dark. This trend is reversed by restoring sufficient copper to the diet. In human hair, the cortex, which lies beneath the outer layer of cuticular cells, surrounds the central medullary column, or pith. Very small ellipsoidal or spherical granules of melanin are randomly distributed within the dried cortical cells, imparting pale-buff, brown, or black colours; the colour depends upon relative numbers, sizes, and depth of hue of the individual granules. Melanin occurring within the medulla may appear as a colloidally dispersed stain rather than as microscopically discernible particles. Human red hair, unlike all other hair, human and nonhuman, yields a unique, iron-rich red pigment. A similar substance, which has been recovered from red poultry feathers, is reminiscent of certain reddish melanin derivatives.

All human skin except that of albinos contains greater

or lesser amounts of melanin. In fair-skinned persons the corium, or deeply lying dermal layer, contains little of the pigment; dermal deposits in the dark-skinned races are heavy and may be fortified by smaller melanocytes in the upper layer, or epidermis. Samples of human skin photographed by electron microscopy have been observed to contain the melanin in the form of very small spheres (0.2 to 0.3 micron in diameter) or rods (from 0.1×0.4 to 0.18×0.6 micron). On exposure to sunlight, man's epidermis undergoes gradual tanning with increases in melanin pigment, which helps to protect underlying tissues from injurious sun rays (see also SKIN, HUMAN).

Many fishes, lizards, amphibians, cephalopods, and shrimps possess in their skins dark melanoid pigments in special cells called melanophores. Within the boundaries of these cells the pigment may spread, becoming dispersed and turning the skin dark; or the pigment may instead aggregate into a small mass near the centre of the melanocyte giving the entire skin a pale appearance. These pigmentary changes, with the aid of chromophoric melanophores (distinct from melanocytes), may be induced by certain chemicals or by physical stimuli; for example, certain animals, when alarmed, display colour changes adapted toward concealment against their background. The reversible dispersion and re-aggregation of melanosomes, or minute melanin granules within melanophores, thus matches the animal's integument with the shade of the background, affording some protection against detection by sight-oriented predators.

In at least one crestfish, *Lophotus*, large quantities of black melanin are stored within a specialized glandular sac and can be expelled in forcible jets through a post-anal opening by vigorous muscle contractions, in a manner similar to the discharge of ink by cephalopods. The numbers of melanophores in the epidermis of amphibians and fishes maintained for extended intervals upon black backgrounds greatly increase. Such animals consequently lose much of this integumentary melanin following their transferral to containers having pale inner surfaces that provide a white background.

Some remarkable instances of rapid skin darkening through melanization include that of the so-called 17-year locust, actually the periodical cicada *Magicicada septendecim*. After 17 years (13 in some species) in the soil, the nymphs, having attained their final stage of development, emerge and rapidly develop into adults. When the insect emerges and comes in contact with light and air, the cuticle rapidly darkens as melanin is formed. This darkening may be delayed experimentally by the exclusion of air.

Among fishes, the Tasmanian whitebait (*Lovettia sealii*) has been observed to exhibit rapid integumentary blackening on entering its post-spawning stages. The number of melanophores greatly increases, notably in the males; individuals of both sexes show, after spawning, extensive darkened areas of skin. The skin of moribund individuals turns completely black.

The legs of the newly hatched, downy chick of the American flamingo are covered with delicate, naked skin that is bright red or pink because of the rich supplies of hemoglobin. The colour of the exposed leg skin deepens gradually to a dark red, becoming black at the end of about the eighth day, when the chick is ready to leave its nest for the first time, no longer to be protected from direct sunlight by hovering parents.

The role of melanin in many sharks and some rays is directly related to vision. In the eyes of such fishes, a bright, reflecting layer of platelike cells containing guanine constitutes the tapetum lucidum; the tapetum lies beneath the light-receptive retina and serves to reflect the light back through the retina. Beneath the tapetum is a dense layer of black, melanin-filled cells with black fingerlike extensions, which constitute a continuous screen or dark curtain that shields the sensitive retina against bright light in upper waters. When the shark retreats to dark or dimly lighted zones, the eyes exhibit high reflectivity, or eyeshine, when re-illuminated, as a consequence of the retraction of the very small melanin

granules into the layer beneath the tapetum. Thus the shark can protect its eyes against dazzle in bright light by shading the tapetum and in dim light can re-expose maximal areas of tapetal and retinal surfaces, presumably increasing visual acuity.

Indigoids. Like melanins, the indigo compounds are excretory metabolic breakdown products in certain animals; but, in contrast to the melanins, their distribution as conspicuous pigmentary compounds is very limited. And they are not dark but red, green, blue, or purple.

One of the most common members of this group is indigo, or indigotin, which occurs as a glucoside (*i.e.*, chem-

indigo

ically combined with glucose) in many plants of Asia, the East Indies, Africa, and South America. It has long been used as a blue dye. The ancient Britons crushed and fermented parts of the cruciferous plant *Isatis tinctoria*, common around chalk pits of the English countryside, and used the resulting paste as a body paint.

Although indigo does not occur in healthy animal tissues, certain chemical precursors of it are found in secretory and excretory products, and indogouria is characteristic of certain infectious diseases.

Hallachrome, a member of the indigoid group, is a red pigment in the epidermis of the marine worm *Halla parthenopoea*. It is green in alkaline solution and may be reversibly oxidized and reduced.

Tyrian purple, or 6,6'-dibromindigo, is a red-violet dye known and used commercially since ancient times. It is generated in the presence of light, probably through the influence of an enzyme, from a colourless precursor secreted by the so-called adrectal, or hypobranchial, gland in several species of marine snails of the genera *Murex* and *Purpura*. No physiological function has yet been discovered for dibromindigo; it is probably an excretory product.

Phenoxazones and sclerotins. Once confused with melanins are biochromes such as phenoxazones and sclerotins that show a similar colour series (yellow, ruddy, brown, or black). Genetic research, notably with reference to eye pigments of the fruitfly, *Drosophila melanogaster*, has resulted in the description of a class of so-called ommochromes which are phenoxazones. The ommochromes not only are conspicuous in the eyes of insects and crustaceans but have also been detected in the eggs of the echiurid worm *Urechis caupo* and in the changeable chromatophores in the skin of cephalopods, but not those of vertebrates. In addition to being responsible for the brown, vermilion, cinnabar, and other colours of insect eyes, ommochromes are also sometimes present in the molting fluid and integument. They are distinguished from the melanins by solubility in formic acid and in dilute mineral acids by manifestation of violet colours in concentrated sulfuric acid and by showing reversible colour changes with oxidizing and reducing agents. The ommochromes, which are derived from breakdown of the amino acid tryptophan, include ommatins and ommins. The ommatins, although complex in chemical structure, are relatively small molecules; examples include xanthommatin, a yellow pigment in the

xanthommatin

molting fluid of the butterfly *Aglais* (or *Vanessa*) *urticae*, and rhodommatin, a closely related red compound combined with glucose.

The ommins are large molecules, in which the chromogenic moiety is seemingly condensed with longer chains, such as peptides (amino acids linked together).

Although ommochromes occur in the eyes of arthropods, they are not known to be directly involved in the biochemistry of photoreception. In the changeable integumentary cells of cephalopods, however, they may contribute to adaptive responses.

Sclerotins arise as a result of an enzyme-catalyzed tanning of protein. Certain roaches secrete a phenolase enzyme, the glucoside of a dihydroxyphenol, and a glycosidase. Mixing of these substances results in the release of the phenolic compound from glucose and its combination, via a reaction catalyzed by the phenolase, with protein; the products are pink, ruddy, and ultimately dark-brown polymers that are incorporated into the insect's body cuticle and egg cases. Similar reactions take place in the carapace (the shell covering the body) of certain crustaceans. Sclerotins have been detected in the chaetae (bristles) of terrestrial and marine worms, in the byssus (silky threads) and periostracum (external shell covering) of mussels, and in egg cases of some selachian fishes. The sclerotins not only darken the cuticles of insects, thus conceivably contributing to the shielding of injurious light rays, as do melanins, but also effect a distinct protective, armour-like hardening (tanning) of the cuticular protein.

Purines and pterins. Although the purine compounds cannot be classed as true pigments—they characteristically occur as white crystals—they often contribute to the general colour patterns observed in lower vertebrates and invertebrates. That purines are excretory materials is amply illustrated by the quantities of uric acid (or urates) and guanine found in the excrement of birds and

guanine

of uric acid found in that of reptiles. Uric acid has also been detected in the yellowish sheets of mucus excreted by sea anemones, and urates are present in small amounts in the urine of higher apes and man.

The brilliant whiteness exhibited in the tissues of some sea anemones, notably the white variant of the plumose (feathery) anemone *Metridium senile*, results in part from microcrystalline deposits of uric acid. Other purines, such as xanthine, have been reported to occur in the wings of pierid butterflies. Purine compounds are components of the nucleic acids that occur in the nuclear materials of all cells. The purine hypoxanthine exercises a specific stimulatory influence upon the growth of embryonic tissues in the chick.

The white, silvery, or iridescent chromatophores, both stationary iridocytes and changeable leucophores, of some fishes, amphibians, lizards, and cephalopods contain microcrystalline aggregates of the purine guanine; a layer of white skin on the underside of many fishes, called the stratum arginatum, is particularly rich in guanine. The quantities of deposited guanine in some fishes vary in proportion to the relative lightness in colour of the background upon which they are living. In a study of the quantitative effects of the albedo (ratio of reflected to incident light) upon the black pigmentation or whiteness of fishes, the U.S. zoologist F.B. Sumner demonstrated that greenfish, or opaleye (*Girella nigricans*), kept in white-walled aquaria became very pale during a four-month period, storing about fourfold the quantity of integumentary guanine as was recoverable from the skins of individuals living in black-walled containers, receiving the same kind and amounts of food and given the same overhead illumination. The intensely black skins of fish in the latter group yielded more than twice the total quantity of melanin that was elaborated by those of the white environment. Thus, high albedo from the environ-

ment stimulates the deposition of guanine while depressing the elaboration of melanin, and low albedo exerts the opposite effects.

Guanine occurs in the tapeta of some bony fishes and other animals (in addition to sharks and rays, mentioned above) but not in mammalian eyes. Animals such as deep-sea fishes and crocodiles possess guanine-laden retinal tapeta.

Closely related to the purines and formerly classed among them are the pterins, so named from their notable appearance in and first chemical isolation from the wings of certain butterflies. Both purines and pterins contain a six-atom pyrimidine ring; in purines this ring is chemically condensed with an imidazole ring; pterins contain

xanthopterin

the pyrazine ring. Pterins, which occur as white, yellow, orange, or red granules in association with insect wing material, are soluble in aqueous solutions and insoluble in the usual organic solvents. The choroid layer (behind the retina) of the dogfish (*Squalus acanthias*) and the retina and some choroid tissues of the Mississippi alligator (*Alligator mississippiensis*) yield a blue-fluorescing pterin. Leucopterin is a white compound recovered from wings of the large white butterfly (*Pieris brassicae*) and the mustard white (*P. napi*); it occurs with other pterins in other species. Xanthopterin is responsible for the yellow colour in the wings of the brimstone butterfly (*Gonepteryx rhamni*) and others and the yellow of the abdominal integument of wasps (*e.g.*, *Vespa* species). Xanthopterin occurs in human urine and is sometimes called uropterin.

In butterflies, the colourless compounds guanopterin and mesopterin may be accompanied by chrysopterin, an orange compound, or by red or orange-red erythropterin; the last imparts red colour to the wings of several species. Fluorescyanin, a blue-fluorescing pterin in the scales of many fishes, chemically resembles some of the B vitamins.

Flavins (lyochromes). Flavins constitute a class of pale yellow, greenly fluorescent, water-soluble biochromes widely distributed in small quantities in plant and animal tissues. Like the pterins, the flavin molecule possesses pyrimido-pyrazine rings and also a dimethylbenzoid ring. The most prevalent member of the class, commonly referred to as riboflavin but actually benzisoalloxazine-6,7-dimethyl-9,d-riboflavin ($C_{17}H_{20}O_6N_4$) carries a ribitol

riboflavin

group (an alcohol with five hydroxyl groups). In addition to their pale-yellow colour, green fluorescence, and solubility properties, the flavins are characterized by stability toward mild oxidizing agents and reversible reduction to colourless, nonfluorescing compounds by exposure to certain substances. Fluorescence is a characteristic of free flavins but not flavoproteins.

Flavins are synthesized by bacteria, yeasts, and green plants; riboflavin (vitamin B₂) is not manufactured by animals, which therefore are dependent upon plant sources. Riboflavin is a component of an enzyme capable of combining with molecular oxygen; the product, which is yellow, releases the oxygen in the cell with simultaneous loss of colour.

Despite the vital importance of riboflavin in animal metabolism, it is stored in only small traces in various tissues—*e.g.*, 15 milligrams of riboflavin from three kilograms (seven pounds) of fresh eggs; less than ten milligrams from 54 litres (about 57 quarts) of whey; and ten to 20 milligrams from nine kilograms of liver or kidney. Riboflavin is a normal excretory component of urine.

Miscellaneous pigments. The chemical constitution of many pigments remains imperfectly known. Of these only a few of the more conspicuous examples are mentioned below.

Chromolipids. Yellowish, reddish, or brown fat-soluble pigments called chromolipids are often encountered in the fat droplets of eggs and other cells and in various lipid-rich (fatty) tissues. They have been mistaken for melanins when dark and, when yellow, have been interpreted as carotenoids. Chromolipids are believed to be derived from partially oxidized lipids such as fatty acids and phospholipids, perhaps in ways similar to those through which fats such as lard gradually darken when heated or exposed to air.

Chromolipids show a steady increase of light absorption progressing toward the shorter wavelengths and are stable in dilute acids. Their solubility properties and their occasional manifestation of blue or green fluorescence sets them apart from the melanins, as does their stability in dilute acids, which precipitate melanins.

Hemocyanins. Copper-containing proteins called hemocyanins occur notably in the blood of larger crustaceans and that of gastropod and cephalopod mollusks. Hemocyanins are colourless in the reduced, or deoxygenated, state and blue when exposed to air or to oxygen dissolved in the blood. Hemocyanins serve as respiratory pigments in many animals possessing them, although it has not yet been established that they perform this function wherever they occur. Some species of abalone, for example, differ enormously in the hemocyanin content of their blood, yet appear to have equivalent respiratory activity.

Chemically, hemocyanins consist of large protein complexes bound to copper. Wide differences in molecular weight have been found in hemocyanins from the blood of different species; the value of 360,000 given for certain crustaceans represents the lower limit. The hemocyanin of *Limulus* has a molecular weight of about 1,300,000; that of *Octopus* 2,000,000; and that of the land snail *Helix* as high as 5,000,000.

The blue oxyhemocyanins of various mollusks and arthropods commonly exhibit a single, broad band of light absorption in the yellow to orange region of the spectrum. Because hemocyanins possess only about one-fourth the oxygen-combining capacity of the common hemoglobins, species endowed with the copper carrier of oxygen either are subject to relatively depressed metabolic activities, as in certain bottom-dwelling snails, or are extremely sensitive to lack of oxygen, as are active species such as squids and some crabs.

Hemerythrins. Iron-containing, proteinaceous pigments, hemerythrins are present in the blood of certain bottom-dwelling marine worms (notably burrowing sipunculids) and of the brachiopod *Lingula*; the pigments serve as oxygen-carriers. Blood containing hemerythrin is pale in the reduced, or de-oxygenated, condition, becoming red or reddish brown when oxygenated. Like the other blood pigments, hemerythrins are joined to proteins peculiar to each species; like hemocyanin and unlike hemoglobin, hemerythrin contains no porphyrin. It combines less readily with oxygen than does hemoglobin. Unlike hemoglobin and hemocyanin, hemerythrin does not combine with cyanide or carbon monoxide.

Hemovanadin. Pale-green pigment, hemovanadin, is found within the blood cells (vanadocytes) of sea-squirts (Tunicata) belonging to the families Ascidiidae and Perophoridae. The vanadocytes are rounded, mulberry-shaped cells, varying little in size or shape among different species. Within each vanadocyte are eight to ten relatively large, apple-green bodies containing the pigment. Vanadocytes also contain relatively large amounts of sulfuric acid (about 9 percent). The green pigment, hemovanadin, when released from the cells, turns reddish brown, but not as a consequence of oxidation; a strong reducing agent, hemovanadin is not regarded as an oxy-

The vanadium-containing pigment of tunicates

gen-transport agent, and its biochemical function is unknown. No purines, proteins, or amino acids have been detected in the chromogen moiety of hemovanadin; it possesses considerable pyrrole content, however, which is believed to be of the linear, or bilichromic, type.

Actiniochrome. A relatively rare pigment, actiniochrome occurs in red or violet tentacle tips and in the stomodeum (oral region) of various sea anemones. Actiniochrome is insoluble in all fat solvents with the exception of acetone; it can be removed from fresh tissues with glycerol. The pigment plays no recognized physiological role.

Adenochrome. Adenochrome is a non-proteinaceous pigment that occurs as garnet-red inclusions at high concentrations in the glandular, branchial heart tissues of *Octopus bimaculatus*. It is readily soluble in ammonia and other alkalis, conferring to their aqueous solutions a wine-red colour. Slight acidification, or the addition of small amounts of alcohol or acetone, precipitates adenochrome as amorphous purple masses. The compound contains small amounts of ferric iron and some nitrogen and gives a positive reaction for pyrroles. It is believed to be an excretory product.

Unnamed pigments. Numerous coelenterates exhibit, in addition to carotenoids, melanins, and actiniochrome, other pigments that remain imperfectly known; for example, the red pigment in some coral skeletons—*e.g.*, *Corallium rubrum* and the organ-pipe coral *Tubipora musica*. Other red, orange, and yellow pigments of many alcyonarian coral skeletons are still chemically obscure.

The large, colourful, poisonous, purple jellyfish *Pelagia colorata* exhibits several pigments. Blue, non-carotenoid chromoproteins are present in the heavy, pendulous lips, the outer surface, the gonads, and the gastric filaments; brown pigments occur in parts of the outer skin; and a magenta-coloured chromoprotein is recoverable from the non-cellular mesogleal jelly (the layer beneath the epidermis). Characteristic absorption spectra are exhibited by the different fractions. The pigments seem to involve chromogenic molecules joined with protein. The chromogen from the magenta pigment and its brown derivative, resulting from the action of tyrosinase, involve indole. Beyond their several similarities to melanoid pigments, the *Pelagia* chromogens have not been well characterized. Nor is a suggested physiological function assignable to them.   (D.L.F.)

III. The adaptive value of biological coloration

Concealing coloration and camouflage have long been favourite subjects of naturalists. In many cases, man has taken advantage of camouflage techniques of animals.

Concealment serves to reduce maladaptive (unfavourable) interactions with animals by masking the location or identity of the organism. This function may be served either by providing false information as to identity, location, or orientation or by minimizing the same informational categories. Some organisms, for instance, provide false information as to their identity by mimicking dangerous or inedible species. When a third party, such as a predator, fails to distinguish between the mimic and its inedible model, the relationship is termed Batesian mimicry (see MIMICRY). On the other hand, an organism may minimize the information as to its location by matching objects in its background, a form of camouflage termed imitative resemblance. Thus organisms may show an "imitative resemblance" to animate objects in their environment, such as the leaves or twigs of a tree, instead of merely matching the background pattern of the tree bark. It is possible to distinguish between imitative resemblance and Batesian mimicry on the basis of the effects of the relationship on the object imitated. The Batesian mimic and its model are usually similar species; if the mimic becomes overly plentiful, predators may ignore the warning coloration of the relatively scarce model and attack both the model and the mimic. This has a detrimental effect on both model and mimic populations; the model for imitative resemblance—perhaps a rock, twig, or leaf—is not, however, so vulnerable to the adverse effects of a plentiful imitator, because it is usu-

Imitation of living and nonliving models

ally an object so plentiful in the environment that it will always be far more abundant than all of its imitators. Another distinction is that the form and coloration of a Batesian mimic usually ensures that it will be perceived by animals, including predators, but not distinguished as different from the harmful or distasteful model species; the Batesian mimicry is referred to as an advertising coloration. Imitative resemblance, however, is a true concealing coloration in that it usually disguises the organism sufficiently so it is not perceived as distinct from its background. This dichotomy arises only because the harmful or distasteful species itself has an advertising or warning coloration.

CONCEALING COLORATION

Concealing coloration deals with three basic entities: the organism whose coloration is being considered, which, for the sake of brevity, may be referred to as the organism; the background against which it is concealed, or the model; and the third party, the animal or animals from which the organism is concealed. For the sake of discussion, the relationships among the entities may be considered separately; but all of them are considered together when weighing the value and function of the concealment.

The relationship between the organism and the model.
Background matching. Background matching is probably the most common form of concealment. It makes little difference whether the background model is an animate or inanimate object since both involve the initial establishment and continued maintenance of the concealment. Not only coloration but also the form and the activities or behaviour of the organism in relation to its model are important.

The most simple examples of background matching are provided by the fish eggs and planktonic (free-floating) larval fishes that exist in the uniformly blue environment of the open sea—*i.e.*, they are pelagic. They usually possess minimal pigmentation and are transparent.

In other organisms and environments, the behaviour and form of the organism become more important as adjuncts to coloration. Bird eggs show no animation, but the nesting and egg-placing habits of the parents may be critical. The plain pink eggs of sand grouse (*Pterocles*), for example, are well concealed only when they are laid on leaves of a similar shade of pink that have fallen from a certain species of tree. The parents consistently place the eggs on these leaves and thus provide a matching background. Further evidence of the importance of the choice of a proper background is provided by three differently coloured species of lizards of the genus *Anolis*, which form mixed hunting groups over the same background. Many of the individuals are easily perceived on this background, but, when disturbed, they better conceal themselves by segregating according to species over the appropriately coloured backgrounds. Maintenance of concealment may also be accomplished through a change in coloration. Fishes are noted for their ability to match their background; many flatfishes, for example, show a remarkable ability to match the pattern of the surface on which they are resting. Fishes such as the mosquito fish (*Gambusia*) show long-term changes in coloration according to the darkness of their environment. This has been shown to be important in avoiding predation. Some nudibranchs, a group of marine gastropods, such as *Phestilla melanobrachia*, manage to establish and maintain their resemblance to the background by ingesting portions of their model, which is the living coral on which they live. The pigments in the coral polyps are deposited in diverticulae (branches) of the gut and occasionally in the epidermis and show through as nearly perfect camouflage. The slow-moving nudibranchs are very difficult to see on their coral host, and when they move to differently coloured coral, their coloration changes as their food source changes. Some parasites on marine fishes conceal themselves in a similar manner. Flukes, or monogenean trematodes, gorge themselves on their hosts' tissues and pigments and appear to remain within areas on the host that have similar pigmentation.

When a brightly coloured butterfly fish that is seemingly free of external parasites (ectoparasites) is rinsed in fresh water, numbers of trematodes, matching the variously coloured areas of the fish, are frequently found. The adaptive significance of the coloration is known to lie in escape from predation by the third party, cleaning organisms such as the fish *Labroides*, which feeds on the ectoparasites of other fishes. Several decorator crabs use portions of the model for concealment by picking up algae and sponges and placing them on the carapace (upper shell) to cover their own coloration; the algae and sponges continue to live as if in their normal habitat.

Aggressive mimicry. Aggressive mimicry is a type of resemblance in which a predator resembles its prey or a parasite resembles its host. A special form of aggressive mimicry in which a living "background" is imitated is found in some solitary fishes of the genus *Runula*, which adopt the bright coloration, shape, and behaviour of plankton-feeding, schooling fishes, such as *Meiacanthus*. They move within schools of these models either to gain the protective advantage of the school in midwater or to conceal themselves for attacks on the scales and fins of larger fishes. Such cases of aggressive mimicry differ from Batesian mimicry and some other types of aggressive mimicry in that the mimic merely blends into a large school of fish as an appropriate background.

Disruptive coloration. The identity and location of an animal may be concealed through a disruptive coloration that conceals the shape and outline of the body. Such disruptive patterns, frequently a part of camouflage colorations, serve the function of visual disruption by forming a pattern that does not coincide with the contour and outline of the body. The blenny *Hypsoblennius sordidus*, for example, usually has a mottled coloration that crudely matches its background in terms of the size and colour of differently pigmented areas; it also has a series of darkly pigmented "saddles" that break up the outline contour of its back. This species also demonstrates the fact that the type of disruptive patterning may change when an individual shifts to another type of background. The saddled condition is found when the background is composed of disruptive elements of the same approximate size—*e.g.*, small sponges, barnacles, and patches of algae. But when the fish moves to an evenly coloured area, its coloration becomes stripes that run horizontally from head to tail.

Strong contrast between the pigmented areas forming a disruptive coloration is best seen in many coral-reef fishes. The Moorish idol (*Zanclus canescens*) combines its high body and trailing fins with broad bars of contrasting black and yellow. These colours stand out sharply against the blue background of the open water but conceal the outline of the fish when it is viewed against a disruptive reef of coral heads and seaweed. Disruptive patterns are found in the coloration of many fish that form schools over the reef during daylight hours for protection against predation. When a predator approaches, the fishes form dense schools in which all of the individuals orient in the same direction. The movement of many individuals, coupled with their similar disruptive coloration, presents an extremely confusing spectacle, presumably one that makes it difficult for a predator to fix upon and attack any one.

Some disruptive patterns are so arranged that when the animal is in a resting position, its appendages blend with the rest of its body. The tree frog *Hyla leucophyllata* has broad stripes on the body and legs. The legs are placed next to the body when the animal is resting, and the coloration forms continuous stripes from the body over the legs. This serves to conceal another cue used by predators to identify suitable prey, the possession of legs. A similar situation is provided by the hindwings and forewings of many butterflies. The wings are held so that the pigmented areas on one wing are contiguous with similar areas on the overlapping wing.

Some forms of disruptive coloration also function to conceal movement. Forward movement in concentrically banded snakes is easily perceived when they are in the open, but when moving between reeds or long blades of

Alteration of coloration to match changing backgrounds

Behaviour that aids the function of coloration

Structural colour of the superb tanager *(Tangara fastuosa)* is tyndall blue.

Flamingo *(Phoenicopterus ruber roseus)* showing carotenoid pigmentation in the plumage and leg skin.

Red colour in wing of white-crested turacos *(Tauraco leucolophus)* results from turacin, a pigment derived from porphyrin.

The silvery appearance of the butterfly fish *(Chaetodon)* is due to a deposit of guanine, a colourless purine.

Purple colour of sea urchin *(Strongylocentrotus purpuratus)* is attributable to the naphthoquinone compound, echinochrome.

Rivoli's hummingbird *(Eugenes fulgens)* has iridescent structural colour.

Pigmentation

Plate 1: (Top left) C. Laubscher—Bruce Coleman Inc., (top right) Eric Hosking, (centre right, bottom right) Root Resources—EB Inc., (centre right) Kenneth Fink, (bottom right) Earl Kubis, (bottom left) Bruce Barnetson from The Natural History Photographic Agency—EB Inc., (bottom centre) Cy LaTour

Plate 2   Coloration, Biological

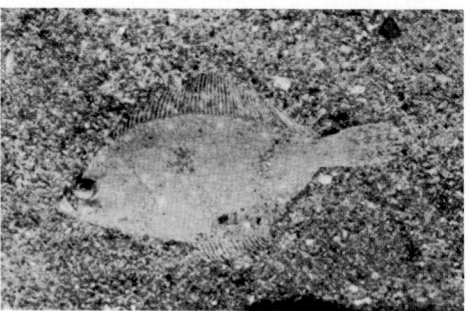

Background matching by two pleuronectiform fishes, (above) right-eyed flounder and (below) flatfish on sandy bottom floor.

Zebras *(Equus burchelli)* at a waterhole, an example of coloration disruption.

European woodcock *(Scolopax rusticola)* incubating.

Willow ptarmigan *(Lagopus lagopus)*.

Blacksmith plover *(Charadriidae)* showing disruptive markings.

The disruptive markings of the moorish idol *(Zanclus canescens)*.

Uganda kobs *(Kobus kob thomasi)* exemplify countershading.

Concealing and disruptive coloration

Plate 2: (Top left) Gerald Cubitt, (top right above) J.A.L. Cooke, (top right below, centre left, centre, centre right) Bruce Coleman Inc., (top right below) Jen & Des Bartlett, (centre left) E. Soothill, (centre) Eric Hosking, (centre right) Tony Deane, (bottom left) Douglas Faulkner, (bottom right) Leonard Lee Rue III

Twig-like measuring worm (Geometridae).

Thorn tree hopper *(Umbonia spinosa)*.

Walkingstick (Phasmatidae).

Swallowtail butterfly *(Papilio)* concealed in leaves.

Orchid mantis *(Hymenopus coronatus)* of Malay Peninsula.

Ceylon leaf insect *(Philium)*.

Leaf butterfly *(Anaea)* on jungle leaf litter.

Concealing coloration

Plate 3: (Top left, top right, centre right, bottom left) E.S. Ross, (centre left) Lilyan Simmons—EB Inc., (centre) F. Baillie from The Natural History Photographic Agency—EB Inc., (bottom right) S.C. Bisserot—Bruce Coleman Ltd.

Plate 4   Coloration, Biological

Startle markings: false eyes on noctuid moth (Noctuidae).

Startle markings of a mature swallowtail butterfly larva (Papilio).

Warning coloration: (above) the puss moth caterpillar (Cerura) at rest; when threatened (below), its raised head and tail thorns intimidate attackers.

Shadow pattern: mottling of the fawn's coat (Odocoileus virginianus) provides protection.

Startle markings of the four-eye butterfly fish (Chaetodon capistratus).

Disruptive markings provide protection for a clump of caterpillars.

Warning coloration and protective and startle markings

Plate 4: (Top left, centre left) S. Beaufoy, (top centre, top right, bottom right) E.S. Ross, (centre right) Leonard Lee Rue III, (bottom left) Douglas Faulkner

Alluring coloration: potential predators of the blue-tailed skink (*Eumeces skiltonianus*) are attracted to its tail, which can be shed at will.

Keel-billed toucan (*Ramphastos sulfuratus*); the bill is probably used for species recognition.

Flash colours: male great frigate bird (*fregata minor*) with red throat patch inflated to attract a female.

Display coloration of cock of the rock (*Rupicola rupicola*).

Courtship coloration of a mammal: male mandrill (*Mandrillus sphynx*).

Courtship and distraction coloration

Plate 5: (Top left) E.S. Ross, (top right) © Kojo Tanaka, Animals Animals 1972, (centre) Verna R. Johnston, (bottom left) K.W. Fink—Bruce Coleman Inc., (bottom right) George H. Harrison from Grant Heilman—EB Inc.

Plate 6   Coloration, Biological

Seasonal colour change in the varying hare *(Lepus)*; (left) summer pelage and (right) winter pelage.

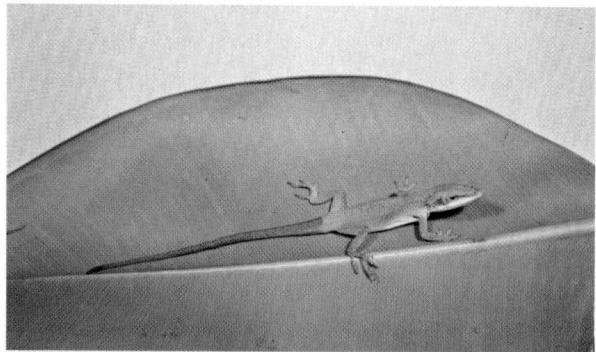
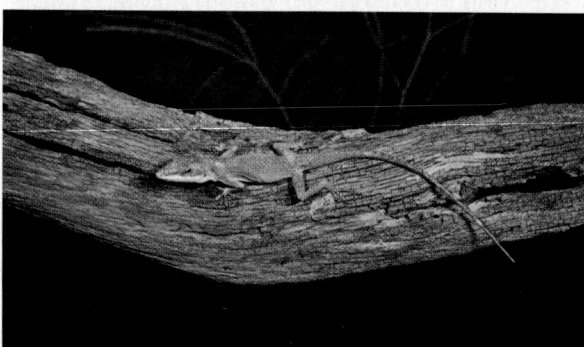
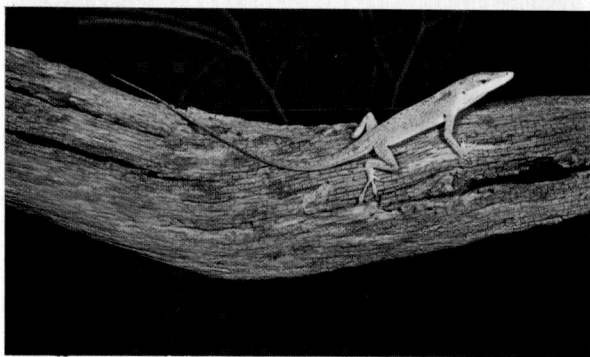

Adaptive colour change: the gradual colour change of the green anole *(Anolis carolinensis)* when moved from a green leaf to a brown branch.

Adaptive colour change: (top) at rest the common octopus *(Octopus vulgaris)* blends with its surroundings; when agitated (bottom), it blanches.

Colour change

Plate 6: (Top left) Rue—Annan Photo Features, (top right) Leonard Lee Rue III—Bruce Coleman Inc., (centre left above, centre left below, bottom left) John H. Gerard—EB Inc., (centre right, bottom right) Marineland of Florida

grass, fast movement may not be observed because of the characteristics of the visual sensory system. The saddled coloration in the blenny mentioned above could aid in the perception of its movement as a result of the series of moving light–dark interfaces, particularly when the fish is not over a disruptive background. To the human observer, at least, the horizontal stripe pattern, with only two light–dark interfaces, is more difficult to follow during fast movement.

Countershading. Another clue can lead to the recognition of an organism: its three-dimensional form, which causes the unilluminated portion of the body to be in shadow. Countershading is a form of coloration in which the upper surfaces of the body are more darkly pigmented than the unilluminated lower areas, giving the body a more uniform darkness and a lack of depth relief. Widespread among vertebrates, countershading is frequently superimposed over camouflage and disruptive colorations, but it may also be favoured by the physiological necessity of shielding the body tissues from sunlight. Chromatophores develop more profusely on the illuminated surfaces of the animal. The flatfish, which normally has an extremely pale underside, shows a marked increase in the number of melanin-containing cells (melanophores) on its underside when it is artificially illuminated through the transparent bottom of an aquarium.

Counter-
shading by
lumines-
cent organs

The light-producing organs, or photophores, of many deepwater fishes provide a unique form of countershading. Photophores occur in bands along the lower parts of the sides and are directed downward. Deepwater fishes live in the twilight zone of the sea, in which the illumination is too weak to allow little more than a silhouette of prospective prey sighted by a predator from below. The downward-projecting photophores may provide countershading by obliterating the silhouette when it is viewed by a predator from below. This countershading would be particularly functional if the predators have sacrificed the resolving capabilities of their visual system to increase sensitivity to light in this zone of constant near darkness.

The role of shape in relation to coloration. In addition to coloration, the shape of an organism is important in determining the total configuration for protection. Imitative resemblance and mimicry depend strongly on imitation of both the shape and coloration of the model. Deep-bodied schooling fishes frequently show vertical banding, and elongated forms usually bear horizontal stripes. This dichotomy may be partially related to different swimming patterns: deep-bodied fishes perform frequent lateral turns; elongated forms show frequent horizontal movement and change of position.

Temporal aspects of concealing coloration. In addition to the relationship between the organism and its model at any time, changes in the relationship during a period of time are also important. Camouflaged organisms and mimics must "track," or adjust to, any changes in the appearance of their model. These may include short-term changes, such as that of a chameleon from a brown to green background; seasonal changes, as seen in many small mammals that adopt a lighter fur coloration during the winter snows; or long-term changes of the species to match major changes in background coloration.

Compen-
sating for
changes in
the model

Evolutionary changes. The most widely documented case of background tracking is the industrial melanism of moths. Since the 1850s, as many as 70 species of geometrid and noctuid moths in England and Europe have shown an increase in the number of dark-coloured, or melanic, individuals in their populations. This increase correlates with the Industrial Revolution and the associated pollution of the countryside. Tree trunks, the normal daytime resting place of these nocturnal moths, once covered by scattered whitish lichens, have, in areas of industrial development, turned dark because the lichens have been killed by pollutants and the trunks have been dirtied by soot. Blotched gray individuals, previously protected from predation by birds, are now vulnerable, while the dark individuals are less conspicuous. The shift to melanic populations in the United States lagged that in

Figure 2: *Industrial melanism.*
(Left) Melanic and normal forms of peppered moth (*Biston betularia*) on lichen-covered oak bark. (Right) Same moths on sooty oak trunk without lichens.
From the experiments of Dr. H.B.D. Kettlewell, University of Oxford

England and Europe, as did the industrialization process; but in Michigan, by the early 1970s, the darkly coloured individuals formed up to 97 percent of some populations in regions where melanism was unknown before 1927. Recently in England there seems to be a reversal in the number of melanic individuals of some species, a sign that efforts to curb air pollution are having wide-reaching effects.

Chromatic polymorphism. In most of the moth species that have shown advancing melanism, the melanism is mediated by one factor in their chromosomes, with the melanic allele (genetic determinant) dominant. Even in these species, however, light-coloured forms are still found; *i.e.*, the population has several colour forms, or morphs. The genetic complement of the population ensures that sufficient variability is present to allow the population to adapt to changing backgrounds. Another common form of polymorphism is the presence in a population of two or more distinct colorations, which may enable the species to track changes in background coloration. The ground snail *Cepaea* is unable to change individual shell coloration to match seasonal changes in the background from green to yellow to brown. But this species has both solid yellow and pink-and-brown banded morphs. Predators such as the song thrush (*Turdus philomelos*) tend to feed primarily on yellow morphs during the winter, when the background is a disruptive brown, and to eat more of the banded form during the spring and summer, when the background is green and yellow. The snail's chromatic polymorphism ensures that some of the individuals will always be concealed (cryptic), thus providing for the survival of at least some members of the species.

Chromatic polymorphism operates in yet another manner to aid a species in avoiding predation in that the species has both cryptic and noncryptic forms. Two examples are the spittlebug beetle (*Philaenus*) of North America and a land snail (*Limicolaria*) in Uganda; each species has four coloration morphs, ranging from cryptic to extremely noncryptic colorations. It is thought that the cryptic forms are of advantage as long as their numbers are small enough that they are not frequently found by predators. On the other hand, the noncryptic forms might escape extensive predation as long as they are rather rare, since many birds form a "specific search image" (evidently a mental picture of their intended prey) and concentrate heavily on abundant prey while nearly ignoring rare forms. The predators not only learn to find prey more readily when the latter are plentiful but also appear to switch their attention away from rare forms. By exploiting both cryptic and noncryptic colorations, the snail and beetle species probably maintain a greater density of individuals than would be possible if only one colour morph were present.

Popula-
tions with
both
cryptic and
noncryptic
forms

The selective agent. Of obvious importance in the evolution of coloration is the predator, or third party, which is the actual selective agent involved in the relationship between the organism and its background. Identification of the third party and the sensory and nervous system components used by it are important in order to understand thoroughly the adaptive nature of a concealing coloration. Thus the upward-projecting eyes of mesopelagic (midwater) predators lends credibility to the bioluminescent countershading hypothesis presented previously (see above *Countershading*). The resolving powers of the predators' eyes are even more crucial: do they perceive the bands of photophores as a diffuse glow, indistinguishable from the weak illumination of the background, or can they distinguish the photophores as unique dots of light and thus identify their prey? Little is known of the visual perception of midwater fishes, but in other cases the ways in which visual systems of the third party operate are partially understood.

The first consideration in understanding the adaptive nature of a concealing coloration is the actual identification of the third party. This may have a profound influence on the interpretation of the coloration and behaviour; for example, the early stages of the green Scotch pine caterpillar (*Bupalus piniarius* and others) are found at the tips of pine needles, well camouflaged in this position. As they grow larger, they move into the bases of the needles and onto the branch. One explanation for the movement is that the older caterpillars are too much larger than the background needle, thus rendering the camouflage less effective. Another contributing factor appears to be a shift in the third party as the caterpillar ages. Young caterpillars at the tips of the needles escape predation from hunting spiders found on the twigs. Larger caterpillars, which are preyed upon by birds such as titmice (*Parus*), probably avoid some predation by moving inward on the limb, thus making it more difficult for a flying predator to detect and capture them. The situation is further complicated by a parasitic fly (*Eucarcelia rutilla*), that, unlike most parasites, uses vision when hunting for its caterpillar host.

Perception of light in the infrared and ultraviolet regions

After the initial identification of the third party, its visual capabilities must be investigated. Much attention was formerly given to the infrared reflection of green animals camouflaged on living foliage; some of them show infrared absorption quite unlike that of the chlorophyll of plants. Thus, if a predator were able to perceive infrared light visually, the animal's "camouflage" would be rendered quite ineffective; investigations have failed to reveal any predators capable of infrared vision. Many animals, however, are capable of perceiving ultraviolet light or the plane of polarization in polarized light, capabilities that are quite beyond man's visual senses. Special instruments are needed in order to investigate such visual patterns.

Other factors of visual perception are important, such as the wavelengths of light to which the eye is sensitive and the way in which combinations of pigments and their arrangements are perceived. The visual stimulus is subject to a variety of encoding and integrating steps as it passes from the eye to the cerebral cortex of the brain. Contrast and movement are amplified by some cells, while other properties, such as shape and intensity, are ignored. In man, for example, contrast is greatly enhanced at the junction between a red and a blue stripe, producing the familiar optical illusion that the two stripes never meet and are on different planes. Such phenomena may be of profound importance in disruptive coloration. Series of cells in the nervous systems of many vertebrates, such as the domestic cat (*Felis catus*), are specialized to sense a light–dark interface, or line, and its movement. The horizontal stripes in fishes apparently conceal movement by reducing the number of light–dark interfaces, thus exciting fewer of the specialized cells in potential predators.

ADVERTISING COLORATION

Concealing coloration functions to reduce visual information as to the location, identity, and movement of an organism; advertising coloration operates in just the reverse fashion, rendering the organism unique and highly visible as compared with the background and providing easily perceived information as to its location, identity, and movement. This advertisement may serve the function of attracting individuals in order to enter into some advantageous interaction or of warning or repelling other organisms.

Attraction. Perhaps the most commonly recognized forms of advertisement are found in the social behaviour of animals as means of intraspecific communication. Most important in such interactions are the organism, or signal sender, and the third party, or signal receiver; also important is the relationship between the organism and its background, which influences the effectiveness of the display or the efficiency with which the coloration imparts information to the third party. Although the red breast of a male robin forms an effective visual display against the green and brown background of trees, it would be concealed amid a spray of red flowers.

Reproductive signals. The most basic adaptive interaction within a species is its reproduction, and here are found the most spectacular colorations. Courtship colorations function to attract and arouse a mate and to aid in the reproductive isolation of species. Although by no means universal, it is common, at least among vertebrates, to find that the male of the species has the brightest courtship colours. Bright pigmentation is usually accompanied by movements and display postures that further enhance the display coloration. In some species a number of males form a communal display group in active competition for females. Examples among birds include manakins (Pipridae), cocks of the rock (*Rupicola*), and some grouse (Tetraonidae); similar communal displays have recently been found in some giant species of fruit flies (*Drosophila*) nearly one centimetre (0.4 inch) in length, found in the mountains of Hawaii. The male flies hold their variously adorned wings outstretched and perform a series of visual displays toward females.

Communal courtship systems

In order for a courtship coloration to be maximally efficient, it should either be shown only by sexually ripe individuals or be unique to the individuals that are courting. In many birds, this is accomplished by spreading coloured feathers that are otherwise largely concealed. In others, however, the coloration also serves other functions or is present throughout the year, and courting individuals are rendered unique by other displays, perhaps of a visual or auditory nature. Many fishes show dramatic changes in coloration during courtship. In some species, these changes are long-term, hormonally mediated alterations of coloration and frequently include a proliferation of the carotenoid (red and yellow) pigments. The reproductive male of the three-spined stickleback (*Gasterosteus aculeatus*) is well-known for its bright red belly, but other species show even more dramatic changes. The male of the bay blenny (*Hypsoblennius gentilis*), along the North American west coast, develops a bright-red chin that is invaded by thin silver lines etched in black; the rest of the body is covered by melanic hexagons. In fishes of this type, the reproductive state of the individual can be "read" from its coloration.

Other coloration changes in courting fishes are short-term alterations involving melanophores, which cause rapid colour changes. As a female approaches the male, his sexual arousal can be measured by the degree of coloration change. Certain localized spots on the body, so-called signal organs, change quickly from light to dark in less than one second.

Luminescence is frequently involved in courtship signals in a variety of animals. The common fireflies (Lampyridae) are well-known for their courtship flashes, different species showing unique flashing codes. The intricately arranged photophores on many midwater fishes can be used to identify otherwise similar species. Although their function in reproduction can only be surmised, the photophores certainly provide valuable information regarding species identity, which could aid in finding a mate in their perpetually dark habitat and, at the same time, ensure reproductive isolation of the species.

Some groups of fishes, such as the killifishes, basses, wrasses, and parrot fishes, show extremely interesting sexual colorations and frequently hermaphroditism (male and female sex organs in one individual) and sex reversal. A single species may have several sex morphs and unique colorations. Many have rare male colorations appearing in what are evidently sex-reversed females (*i.e.*, females that started life as males) or hermaphrodites. Certain wrasse species (*Thalassoma*) have unique blue-headed males, and one normally bland grouper species (*Mycteroperca rosacea*) occasionally produces a bright golden morph. Quite apart from the fact that these forms produce a good deal of taxonomic confusion, they appear to be important in the reproductive behaviour of other individuals in the population. One species of freshwater cichlid (*Cichlasoma labiatum*) produces, in response to increased population densities, orange-coloured morphs that appear to depress the reproductive potential of the population. In a certain hermaphroditic killifish (*Rivulus marmoratus*), three different sex-linked colour morphs develop according to the temperature and salinity to which they are exposed during their early embryonic development. The ecological or behavioral function of such morphs remains a mystery.

Schooling signals. In gregarious animals, coloration may serve attractive functions quite apart from reproduction. This is best seen in schooling fishes, in which the portion of the body moved by swimming motions frequently contrasts with the coloration of the rest of the body, apparently providing an attracting stimulus within the school. Nonschooling fishes with contrasting areas on their bodies usually have bland colours on the parts that are moved when swimming. The coloration, as well as the morphology and general behaviour of an animal, also serves to identify an individual to others of its species and can aid in the formation of species aggregations throughout the year.

Interspecific signals. Advertising coloration also serves the function of attraction between different species that enter into some sort of symbiotic, or mutualistic, interaction. It is well-known that many plants are dependent upon insects and even certain birds and bats for pollination or reproductive cross fertilization and for the dispersal of seeds. The pollinator is attracted first to the flower of the plant from which it picks up pollen while feeding; then it visits another flower of the same species, transferring some of the pollen. The coloration and shape of the flowers attract the pollinators and provide information as to the species of the plant. The flowers of plants pollinated by insects usually have patterns of yellow, blue, and ultraviolet that evoke a strong response in the insect eye. In addition, they usually have a darkly coloured pattern near the centre of the flower, called the nectar guide, which orients the insect toward the proper pollinating location. Bees also show a strong preference for flowers with intricate shapes and colorations. Intricate radial patterns seem to be the most attractive; in fact, bees cannot be trained to prefer a simple to an intricate pattern. Some orchid flowers take advantage of the sexual behaviour of bees, forming near perfect mimics of the female bees. A male bee attempting to copulate with the flower acquires the pollen capsules and transfers them to another flower (see MIMICRY).

Coloration also functions to draw different species of animals together. Tropical, insectivorous birds frequently form large foraging flocks composed of several species. One so-called nuclear species, usually present in large numbers, is important in the formation of the flock. The nuclear species usually has bland coloration resembling that of several of the other species. Members of the other species, present in fewer numbers, have bright, contrasting colorations that appear to provide excitatory stimuli important in maintaining the activity and cohesiveness of the feeding flock.

Repulsion. *Territorial advertising.* During the reproductive season, many animals defend a particular area or territory that includes their nest or spawning site. Many other animals defend territories throughout the year. Coloration is frequently important in the defense of the territory, whether defended only during reproductive periods or defended the year around. In species in which the task of territorial defense is accomplished largely by one sex, strong sexual dimorphism usually exists, the more brightly coloured sex being the one that holds the territory. Both male- and female-territorial species are found within the diverse fish family Cichlidae. Species in which the male holds a territory are marked by large and colourful males, the females being smaller and camouflaged; in those species in which the female defends the territory the reverse is found. In still other species, the fish pair and share the territory, and there is little sexual dimorphism.

Coloration frequently releases agonistic (flight or attack) behaviour in territorial animals and contributes to the intimidation of intruders. The flashing coloration displays of a dominant octopus are an excellent example of a visual battle in which the victor may be determined with little or no bodily contact. It has been shown that colorations such as the red belly of the male stickleback and the robin serve as stimuli, or releasers, of agonistic behaviour and that other animals may attack or flee from such models.

The agonistic nature of territorial coloration appears to contribute largely to the form of courtship in many animals. The territory holder is clad in the "robes of aggression" during both courtship and the defense of its territory. The coloration of a prospective mate entering the territory usually differs from this aggressive coloration. In many tide pool blennies, for example, the male is dark when defending the territory and when courting; the courting female is a bland, light shade that lacks agonistic releasers as she enters his territory. Recent findings suggest that such coloration and related behaviour serve the dual function of sexually arousing the prospective partner and at the same time appeasing its agonistic tendencies. Some animals—*e.g.*, many birds and fishes—that show defense of the nest by both sexes go through elaborate greeting ceremonies when one partner relieves the other at the nest; they serve to identify the mate and to appease the agonistic tendencies aroused, in part, by the advertising coloration.

Although similar advertising colorations may contribute to the spacing out of territorial animals, dissimilarity in coloration between members of a species may allow closer spacing. Many brightly coloured reef fishes, for example, defend territories or personal spaces around their bodies. In many of these species, the young and subadults with radically different coloration from the adult live within the territory of an adult free from attack; after they assume adult coloration, however, they are driven away. The territories frequently function to ensure a food supply; because the juveniles utilize different food, they pose no threat to the adult's supply. As the juveniles age, their feeding habits overlap those of the adult, and spacing is necessary. The bright colorations of coral reef fishes may function to render different species highly distinct. Since coloration appears to have agonistic releasing value within a species, the presence of dissimilar agonistic releasers in different species leads to a reduction in interspecific aggression. Many biologists believe that aggression between species is less common than intraspecific fighting and that, when aggression between species does occur, it is usually between similarly coloured ones. Recent findings indicate that, on the contrary, many fishes holding a territory in order to feed on the benthic algae chase away other species having no resemblance but similar feeding habits.

Warning, or aposematic, coloration. Certain advertising colorations warn the third party of dangerous or inedible qualities of the organism. Such aposematic colorations are extremely common in nature and may serve to warn of spines, poisons, or other defensive weapons, it being of advantage to the possessor of a defensive system to avoid the potentially damaging interaction in which the weapon is actually used. Aposematic colorations are frequently mimicked by other organisms, which enjoy thereby at least a portion of the protection of the model species. Red, black, and yellow are extremely common in

(margin notes:)

The attraction of different species

Use of coloration to avoid fighting

The advantage of warning

Figure 3: *Ultraviolet coloration.*
A tropical American composite, *Viguiera dentata*: (top) with normal lens; (bottom) photographed through an ultraviolet-sensitive lens. Note that the crab spider (*Misumenoides formosipes*) loses much of its camouflage when viewed through an ultraviolet-sensitive system.
Thomas Eisner

this context and may represent aposematic colours recognized by many animals.

Visual capabilities of the receiver. Advertisement is, of necessity, considered in the light of the visual capabilities of the third party, or signal receiver. Many species of plants have yellow flowers barely distinguishable to the human eye; when an ultraviolet camera is used to photograph such flowers, however, various bright patterns and nectar guides are revealed that appear to be highly species specific. The importance of strong contrast and contour in the attraction of insects to flowers is related to the perceptual qualities of the insect's compound eye, which shows maximal response to flickering stimuli and may depend upon similar qualities for much form discrimination.

In social signals, the visual system of a species is frequently maximally responsive to its own range of colorations. Butterflies of the genus *Dardanus*, for example, are maximally responsive to their own blue courtship coloration. The visual system and coloration are coadapted to provide an efficient signal mechanism.

COMBINATION OF CONCEALING
AND ADVERTISING COLORATION

Although certain functions such as concealment or advertisement may be inferred for various aspects of an organism's coloration, most organisms, particularly animals, need both advertisement and concealment. A prey animal might conceal itself from predators but also have need to advertise its presence to certain symbionts or to members of its own species for reproductive purposes.

Various mechanisms have evolved that provide both for advertisement and concealment in the same animal.

Many birds, such as the sun bittern (*Eurypyga helias*) and the Amazon parrot (*Amazona aestiva*), have strongly contrasting patches in their wings that are normally hidden by the folded wings. But when frightened by a predator, the patches are obviously displayed. Such "flash colorations" are thought to startle an approaching predator and, at the same time, provide an easily perceived signal to other members of the flock, thus communicating alarm that a predator is at hand. Many birds that conceal their bright courtship coloration when their feathers are held close to their body present a brilliant display upon erecting their feathers. Similar mechanisms are common in many animals, such as *Anolis* lizards, which have brightly coloured throat fans that are visible only when erected during courtship or threat behaviour. Fishes may have bright spots and stripes on their fins that are spread only during fright behaviour or during social interactions.

Many bower birds (Ptilonorhynchidae) have bright courtship colorations, but some species of *Amblyornis* have sacrificed the bright courtship coloration common to the males of related species. Instead of bearing bright colours, they decorate an elaborate bower with leaves, flower petals, and other brightly coloured objects; while females are attracted to these decorations, the decorated bower provides no clue to predators as to the exact location of the male.

Substitution of coloured objects for bright plumage

The frogfishes or shallow-water angler fishes are extremely difficult to detect against their background. They have intricate and obvious lures that are waved near the mouth on a long stalk; prey fishes attracted to the lure are eaten. The scorpion fish *Iracundus* has adopted another type of luring coloration. Its body is covered by the mottled, cryptic coloration common to this family, but the coloration on the dorsal fin is bright and strikingly similar to a small fish. The scorpion fish waves the erected dorsal fin from side to side, giving the appearance of a small fish swimming, while the true body of the scorpion fish remains motionless and nearly invisible. Medium-sized predators attracted to this "prey" are themselves prey for *Iracundus*.

Coloration change is another obvious mechanism that can restrict advertisement to times when it is needed for purposes of communication. Many animals change from cryptic to noncryptic colorations as they change from their normal resting coloration to a display coloration during social interactions. These changes are particularly common in fishes and cephalopods, which have efficient neural mechanisms of coloration change.

SELECTIVE PRESSURES ACTING ON COLORATION

An organism's coloration may be of adaptive value quite apart from its interaction with other organisms. The temperature of an organism can be profoundly influenced by its coloration. Chlorophyll pigmentation in plants provides efficient absorption of the wavelengths of light important in photosynthesis and reflection of infrared wavelengths, which contribute primarily to heating of a body. A large amount of black pigmentation raises the infrared absorption and contributes to the thermal budget of the organism, a method of body temperature elevation employed by many reptiles.

The effects of temperature and humidity on coloration are summarized in Gloger's rule, which states that insects in cool, humid climates tend to have increased pigmentation and birds and mammals in hot, humid areas tend to be darker. It is clear that increased humidity is the only unifying factor, since birds and mammals show the reverse trend relative to temperature, when compared with insects, and to be darker in hot climates would contribute even more strongly to their body temperature. Recent work indicates that the exceptions to Gloger's rule among mammals appear to outweigh the conformities and deny the importance of the trends. Desert rodent species frequently have a variety of dark- and light-coloured varieties that appear to depend on the coloration of the background rather than on the temperature or humidity. And

The effect of conflicting selection

it is well-known that northern animals such as the polar bear or Arctic hare are either white throughout the year or change to white colorations during the winter months. Their colorations thus function primarily for purposes of camouflage and not for the regulation of energy absorption.

One widespread response to increased light levels is the addition of melanin or darkening of the body, which clearly does not function for temperature regulation since darkening would provide even greater heat absorption. Such melanization protects the tissues of the organism from potentially dangerous levels of ultraviolet radiation. Even transparent animals such as larval fishes have sufficient concentrations of melanin to shield their central nervous system from the light. The tanning or darkening of man's skin in response to strong sunlight is a familiar phenomenon. The adaptive value of this melanization is obvious: albinos, which possess no melanin, may be severely burned by relatively short exposures to direct sunlight.

When considering the adaptive value of coloration, it is important not to fall into the philosophical trap of attempting to find "the function" of a coloration in terms of a single factor such as camouflage or warning. Just as one organism may have both advertising and concealing colorations, any one coloration probably represents a compromise between various competing or complementary selective pressures. Crypticity may be favoured in prey animals, but many species do not appear to be maximally concealed when compared with close relatives. They appear to sacrifice some camouflage for purpose of advertisement in social communication or species identification. Aposematic coloration may also provide efficient intraspecific identification signals. Advertising colorations in schooling fishes may serve as social aggregating signals and at the same time conceal the specific individuals within the school.

The mere existence of coloration does not necessarily mean that it must have adaptive value in terms of interaction with a third party. Temperature regulation appears to be of less importance in many animals than concealment from predators. Many biologists find it difficult to believe that any coloration could long escape the processes of natural selection. The lack of an evident adaptive value for a coloration may result from insufficient research in the proper areas, but there is always the possibility that a form of coloration is merely a metabolic by-product that is not particularly maladaptive to the organism and is maintained solely for the biochemical process. The spectacular display of colour seen in deciduous forests in the autumn is often cited as an example of functionless coloration. If the formation of pigments is a convenient end point for a metabolic pathway, then this coloration might be taken as adaptive, albeit not in terms of interaction with a third party. Deep-sea organisms such as sponges and corals have beautiful red, yellow, and purple colorations that appear dull blue or gray until artificially illuminated. The actual coloration is probably adaptive in that it matches the rest of the blue and gray surroundings; red and bright yellow simply do not exist as colorations in this natural situation. The presence of the pigments may indicate a convenient metabolic pathway, but their functional significance should not be evaluated in terms of reflection and absorption of artificial light. (G.S.Lo.)

BIBLIOGRAPHY

Control of coloration: M. FINGERMAN, *The Control of Chromatophores* (1963), is a good readable account of our knowledge of physiological colour change, supplementing the classical book by G.H. PARKER, *Animal Colour Changes and Their Neurohumours* (1948), which covers the subject as it developed during the first half of this century. ROBERT RIDGWAY, *Color Standards and Color Nomenclature* (1912), contains 53 coloured plates with 1,115 named colours. A.H. STURTEVANT, *A History of Genetics* (1965), is a vivid description of the beginnings and development of classical genetics. ROY ROBINSON, *Genetics for Cat Breeders* (1971), is a fascinating introduction and yet a sophisticated treatment of inheritance of coat colour in a domesticated mammal. C.D. TURNER and J.T. BAGNARA, *General Endocrinology*, 5th ed. (1971), contains a brief but up-to-date treatment of hormonal regulation of animal coloration, with a selected bibliography.

The structural and biochemical basis for colour: D.L. FOX, *Animal Biochromes and Structural Colours* (1953); and H.M. FOX and GWYNE VEVERS, *The Nature of Animal Colours* (1960), are technical but readable works on pigments and schemochromes; K.W. BENTLEY, *Natural Pigments* (1960), is a somewhat more technical work on pigment chemistry. E.V. MILLER, *The Chemistry of Plants* (1957); T.J. MABRY, K.R. MARKHAM, and M.B. THOMAS, *The Systematic Identification of Flavonoids* (1970); T.W. GOODWIN (ed.), *Chemistry and Biochemistry of Plant Pigments* (1965); and T.A. GEISSMAN, "Anthocyanins, Chalcones, Aurones, Flavones and Related Water-Soluble Plant Pigments," in KARL PAECH and M.V. TRACEY (eds.), *Modern Methods of Plant Analysis*, vol. 3 (1955), are technical dissertations on plant pigments; F. BLANK, "Anthocyanins, Flavones, Xanthones," in W. RUHLAND (ed.), *Encyclopedia of Plant Physiology*, vol. 10 (1958), provides insight into the formative processes of plant pigments; SYLVIA FRANK, "Carotenoids," *Scient. Am.*, 194:80–86 (1956); and SARAH CLEVENGER, "Flower Pigments," *Scient. Am.*, 210:84–92 (1964), are well-illustrated articles for the lay reader. See also O. ISLER *et al.*, *Carotenoids* (1971).

The adaptive value of coloration: H.B. COTT, *Adaptive Coloration in Animals* (1940), is a detailed and scholarly treatment of the adaptive value of coloration; R.W.G. HINGSTON, *The Meaning of Animal Colour and Adornment* (1933), is a scholarly presentation of theories of the adaptive value of coloration and morphology with many anecdotes. G.H. THAYER, *Concealing-Coloration in the Animal Kingdom* (1909), is a classic work on the theories of camouflage; ADOLF PORTMANN, *Tarnung im Tierreich* (1956; Eng. trans., *Animal Camouflage*, 1959), is a short treatment of the adaptiveness of coloration on the high school to college level; and JAMES POLING, *Animals in Disguise* (1966), is an elementary, popular treatment of coloration.

(D.L.F./F.A.B./G.S.Lo.)

Columbia Icefield

The Columbia Icefield, astride the British Columbia-Alberta border in Canada, is the largest ice field in the Rocky Mountain chain and one of the most accessible areas of continuous glacial ice anywhere in North America. It forms a high-elevation ice cap on a flat-lying plateau that has been severely truncated by erosion to form a huge massif. The glacial area extends between the summits of Mt. Columbia (12,294 feet [3,747 metres]) on the west and Mt. Athabasca (11,452 feet [3,491 metres]) on the east. These majestic peaks and their adjoining ice-mantled upland provide the spectacular scenery at the southern edge of Jasper National Park on the border between southwestern Alberta and southeastern British Columbia.

The eastern side of the ice field is reached by paved highway from Banff, 100 miles (160 kilometres) south, and from Calgary, another 80 miles away to the southeast. Although the ice field embraces some 200 square miles (500 square kilometres) of glacial ice extending from its summit plateau to the termini of a dozen outlet glaciers, it is relatively small compared with such vast ice fields of the Alaska–Canada border region as the Juneau Icefield, near Alaska's capital city, Juneau, and the ice sheets of the northeastern Arctic on Ellesmere Island and Greenland.

General description. From the highway, the plateau section of the ice field may be seen on the skyline at the head of Athabasca Glacier, with parts visible as ice cliffs on Snow Dome, Mt. Kitchner, and Mt. Stutfield. The Athabasca and Saskatchewan glaciers are the two main outlet ice tongues on the north and east.

The ice field has been appropriately dubbed "the mother of rivers," because its main accumulation, or nourishment, zone (névé) lies on the Continental Divide. The meltwaters from Athabasca Glacier flow by way of the Athabasca River into Lake Athabasca in northeastern Alberta and thence by the Slave River and Great Slave Lake to the Mackenzie River and on northward through Yukon Territory, a distance of some 2,500 miles, into the Arctic Ocean.

Waters from the Saskatchewan Glacier drain down the Saskatchewan River and pass eastward across the provinces of Alberta, Saskatchewan, and Manitoba for a distance of some 1,600 miles into Hudson Bay, an exten-

The "mother of rivers"

sion of the Atlantic. Glacial drainage from the ice field's northwestern rim courses down the Fraser and Columbia rivers into the Pacific Ocean; the Columbia flows a sinuous 1,200 miles to its outlet between Oregon and Washington.

The main glacial surface drops off steeply into deep canyons, with the lower glaciers in places riven by crevasses as much as 100 feet deep. In the fringing valley region, there are emerald lakes and thick, low-level forests. The gentle configuration of the largest valley glaciers makes it possible for hikers and climbers to reach the crestal zone without extreme difficulty. Snowmobiles operate on a concession basis in the park, permitting visitors to tour the lower Athabasca Glacier up to a point where ice cascades down from the upper plateau. The average elevation of the summit ice cap is close to 10,000 feet (3,000 metres). Ice depths in this highest section are estimated, from surface gradients, to be little more than 420 feet (128 metres).

The ice field attracts thousands of tourists each summer. Its ready accessibility has proved useful to a number of scientific research projects, especially in glaciology, the study of existing glaciers, which because of their climatic sensitivity are of considerable environmental significance. Since the early 1950s, research has been particularly concentrated on the Athabasca and Saskatchewan glaciers—perhaps the most intensively studied glaciers in Canada.

Scientific study. *The Athabasca Glacier.* The Athabasca Glacier has a total of about 11.5 square miles. Investigations of its terminal moraines have yielded information typical of most glaciers in the Canadian Rockies, especially with respect to volume fluctuations related to climatic change over the past few centuries. Historic records, mapping, and photographic information date back to 1897, but tree-ring studies (dendrochronology) near the ice fronts have provided significant information that extends back several centuries. It is known that a major ice advance culminated on the Athabasca Glacier about 1715, with its terminus being more advanced then than at any time in at least the preceding 350 years. That advance is correlated with a similar worldwide growth of middle-latitude glaciers during the 18th century, a fact that has been well documented by studies in other cordilleran regions of western Canada, Alaska, and the northwestern United States. The earliest large moraine is followed by the roadway up the margin of the lower Athabasca Glacier.

The ice receded after the 1715 advance. By the beginning of the 19th century, a readvance was under way, reaching another maximum position about 1840 that was almost as extensive as the earlier one. Then, changing climatic conditions forced another downwasting of the lower ice-field zone and reduced snow accumulation on its névé. The ensuing retreat of the Athabasca Glacier has continued except for brief standstills. The total amount of ice-front recession from about 1840 to the 1970s had been about one mile. Also the main lateral moraine of mixed boulders and fines is 400 feet higher than the nearest ice surface at the terminus, revealing the extensive thinning that has occurred. In the ice field's colder and higher accumulation zone, downwasting has been considerably less, but still noticeable. There are indications of a present slowing down of this diminishment, possibly heralding another thickening and readvance in the 21st century. With any such advance, corresponding fluctuations in the hydrological runoff can be expected. For such reasons, outlet glaciers from the ice field continue to be surveyed.

The Saskatchewan Glacier and the ice field. The Saskatchewan Glacier, with an area of 23 square miles, is the largest on the Columbia Icefield. Unlike the Athabasca Glacier, it cannot be seen from the highway. A more gently rising surface from the terminus, however, provides easier access to the ice field's higher zone. Ice depths in this glacier have been measured to 1,450 feet. Its velocity of flow, accumulation, and ablation (loss) are comparable to the Athabasca and other main distributary glaciers.

Research conducted on the ice field, in addition to movement and position surveys and photogrammetric mapping, include detailed studies of internal structures, thermal measurements, investigations of subsurface water, geophysical research (seismic, gravity, electrical resistivity), sediment studies in terminal lakes, stream gauging of the outflowing rivers, and oxygen-isotope ratios obtained from ice samples at various depths to determine relative coolness and warmness of winters decades ago. Among the interesting discoveries has been the finding of a large underground river system draining from beneath the ice field. *Research studies*

Systematic biennial measurements of the thinning of the ice field, especially on its margins, have been made since 1945. Since 1959 the main areas of the outlet glaciers below the annual névé line (late-summer snow line) have been mapped every two to three years. Some 22,000 feet of bore holes at about 30 different locations have been drilled into the ice for subsurface research. Many of these holes were lined with aluminum pipe for long-term deformation comparisons. Some of the pipes remain visible, projecting above the ice surface, tantalizing evidence of man's scientific curiosity and his continuing efforts to understand the changing nature and state of health of this spectacular ice field, which lies at the high-drainage centre of the continent and is the ultimate source of Canada's greatest rivers.

BIBLIOGRAPHY. P.I. CAMPBELL, I.A. REID, and J. SHASTAL, *Glacier Survey in Alberta* (1969), a comprehensive technical report of the Department of Energy, Mines and Resources of Canada on the nature and the glaciological and hydrological characteristics of the glaciers in Jasper National Park, including the Columbia Icefield, with references to various recent studies; WALTER M. EDWARDS, "On the Ridge-pole of the Rockies," *Natn. Geogr. Mag.*, 91:745–780 (1947), a popular account of the region surrounding and including the Columbia Icefield; LEWIS R. FREEMAN, "The Mother of Rivers—An Account of a Photographic Expedition to the Great Columbia Ice Field," *ibid.*, 47:377–446 (1925), a historical account of early explorations and geographical situation of the Columbia Icefield, with maps; ALAN PHILLIPS, "Canadian Rockies, Lords of a Beckoning Land," *ibid.*, 130:353–393 (1966), an up-to-date account of the Canadian Rockies, including the Columbia Icefield and Jasper National Park in terms of recreational and tourist facilities.

(M.M.M.)

Columbia River

The largest river flowing into the Pacific Ocean from North America, the Columbia River is exceeded in discharge on the continent only by the Mississippi, Mackenzie, and St. Lawrence rivers. The Columbia is one of the world's greatest sources of hydroelectric power and, with its tributaries, represents one-third of the potential hydropower of the United States. It provides as well the first deepwater harbour north of San Francisco. More than one-third of the river's course, 460 miles of its 1,214-mile (1,954-kilometre) length, lies in Canada, between its headwaters in British Columbia and the United States border.

Exploration and development. The Boston trader Robert Gray discovered the Columbia in 1792 and named it for his ship. The Lewis and Clark Expedition wintered at its mouth in 1805–06, and an English geographer, David Thompson, explored most of the river for the North West Company, reaching the mouth in 1811—only to find the construction of Ft. Astoria underway. The upper basin was explored for the North West Company in 1807–11. Other early posts were established by English and Americans, notably Ft. Vancouver (1825) and Ft. Walla Walla (1818).

Irrigation apparently was practiced at the Hudson's Bay Company post at Walla Walla by the early 1830s and at the mission established in 1836 by Dr. Marcus Whitman at nearby Waiilatpu, and it was later extended to many tributary valleys east of the Cascade Range. The main stem of the Columbia was too deeply entrenched for early irrigation, but, as the only water-level route to the interior, it served as the major transportation artery until the coming of the railroads. The canoes and barges *Early irrigation and transportation uses* of the fur traders and early immigrants had given way to river steamers by the 1850s. The many rapids—21 to the mouth of the Snake River—made navigation difficult, the worst point being circumvented by the first railroad in Washington, a 1½-mile, wooden-railed, mule-drawn tram, replaced in 1863 by a six-mile steam railroad. The heavy agricultural and mining trade of the Columbia River Basin was dominated by Portland through a monopolistic combination of river steamers and connecting stages. A railroad was completed from Portland to Walla Walla in 1882 and from St. Paul to Portland and thence to Tacoma, on Puget Sound, in 1883. In 1887 the Northern Pacific Railway reached Tacoma directly over the Cascade Range, and the monopoly of the Columbia River route was ended.

The abundance of salmon was noted by the early explorers. The first cannery on the Columbia opened in 1866, and by 1881 some 30 Columbia River canneries were supplying world markets, especially Great Britain, with salmon caught in nets, traps, and wheels. From a record of 43,000,000 pounds (19,500,000 kilograms) in 1883, the Columbia River salmon pack declined to an annual average of 4,500,000 pounds (2,000,000 kilograms) in the 1960s. With the continued construction of dams, loss of spawning grounds, pollution, and nitrogen supersaturation resulting from entrapment of atmospheric nitrogen as water plunges over spillways during flood periods, the success of efforts to restore or maintain the Columbia River salmon fishery remains in doubt, although overfishing has been controlled.

Drainage basin and course. The Columbia drains some 258,000 square miles (668,000 square kilometres), 85 percent in the northwestern United States. Major tributaries are the Kootenay, Snake, Pend Oreille, Spokane, Okanogan, Yakima, Cowlitz, and Willamette rivers. High flows occur in late spring and early summer with melting of snow on the mountainous watershed. Low flows occur in autumn and winter, causing power shortages.

The Columbia flows 1,214 miles from its source in Columbia Lake (elevation 2,700 feet [820 metres]), in British Columbia near the crest of the Rocky Mountains, to the Pacific Ocean at Astoria, Oregon. For the first 190 miles, its course is northwesterly; then it flows southerly for 270 miles to the Canadian–United States border (elevation 1,290 feet [390 metres]), where it enters northeastern Washington. It traverses east central Washington in a sweeping curve known as the Big Bend, its prehistoric course having been disarranged first by lava flows and later by ice sheets. Shortly below the mouth of the Snake, its largest tributary, the Columbia turns west and continues 300 miles to the ocean as the boundary between Oregon and Washington. Tides flow 140 miles upriver. For most of its length, the river flows in deep valleys and canyons. Portland (111 miles [179 kilometres] from the mouth) and Vancouver (106 miles), to which low-water channel depth of 36 feet (11 metres) is maintained by the federal government, are the usual upper limit of oceangoing navigation; but, with the aid of locks, a 27-foot channel is maintained to the Dalles Dam (185 miles). A 14-foot-minimum channel (with locks) is maintained for barges to the Tri-Cities (320 miles) and is being extended to Lewiston, Idaho (464 miles; on the Clearwater, a tributary of the Snake).

Human uses. Many controversies have marked the multipurpose development of the Columbia, especially concerning the division of responsibility between public and private agencies, the effect on the fish life (notably salmon), proposals for a Columbia Valley Authority, the proper rate of interest to be charged on the federal power investment, and arrangements for sharing power revenues and costs with Canada for upstream storage reservoirs in British Columbia.

This multipurpose development of the Columbia River main stem began in the 1930s with construction of Grand Coulee and Bonneville dams by the federal government. By the 1970s all but 80 feet of the 1,290-foot fall of the river within the United States had been converted into a series of "stair steps" by six federal and five nonfederal

Proprietary problems in economic development

dams, augmented by dams on tributaries and three upstream storage reservoirs in British Columbia constructed in accordance with a treaty between the United States and Canada signed in 1961. The four lower dams provide large navigation locks, and all but the upper two are equipped with fish-passage facilities.

Grand Coulee Dam, largest and most complex of the dams, augments the low winter flows when power demand is greatest. A third powerhouse was under construction in the early 1970s that makes use of the Canadian storage and will restore Grand Coulee Dam to its former rank as the world's largest power plant. Water is also pumped from Franklin D. Roosevelt Lake, the reservoir behind Grand Coulee Dam, for the Columbia Basin Irrigation Project, the largest single irrigation project in the Northwest and the first large-scale use of the Columbia River itself for irrigation. The first water delivery was made in 1952 to the project lands, which had previously been covered by sagebrush and other desert vegetation. By the early 1970s about 60 percent of the planned 1,027,000-acre project was being irrigated. A major share of the cost of this expensive irrigation project was paid by the sale of commercial power generated at Grand Coulee Dam.

All power plants along the system are connected by high-voltage federal transmission lines, the backbone of the superpower network in which all power utilities of the Pacific Northwest participate. The Pacific Northwest–Southwest Intertie, linking the Columbia system with California and the Southwest, was approved by the U.S. Congress in 1964. Agreement among the U.S. Department of the Interior, local public power authorities, and utility companies provided for the sale of surplus Columbia River power to the Southwest during the summer and the sale of steam-generated power to the Northwest during the winter.

The 1961 treaty with Canada, supplemented by a further pact in 1964, provided for the United States to pay British Columbia sums representing that province's share of power- and flood-control benefits, for British Columbia to build three large dams (two of them on the Columbia), and for the United States to build a fourth dam on the Kootenay in Montana.

BIBLIOGRAPHY. An excellent general history of the Pacific Northwest, with comprehensive bibliography, is DOROTHY O. JOHANSEN and CHARLES M. GATES, *Empire of the Columbia*, 2nd ed. (1967). STEWART H. HOLBROOK, *The Columbia* (1956), in the "Rivers of America Series," is a highly readable account of history and folklore. The FEDERAL WRITERS' PROJECT, *Oregon, End of the Trail*, rev. ed. (1951), though old, is a fine guidebook for the leisurely tourist. An extremely detailed economic history is OSCAR O. WINTHER, *The Old Oregon Country: A History of Frontier Trade, Transportation and Travel* (1950, reprinted 1969). For geographic treatment, see OTIS W. FREEMAN and HOWARD H. MARTIN, *The Pacific Northwest*, 2nd ed. (1954); and RICHARD M. HIGHSMITH, JR. (ed.), *Atlas of the Pacific Northwest: Resources and Development*, 4th ed. (1968). GEORGE SUNDBORG, *Hail Columbia* (1954), is a fascinating journalistic history of the long controversy preceding the decision to construct Grand Coulee Dam. The primary basin planning documents are the 1948 and 1958 "308" *Reports* on the Columbia River and tributaries of the United States Army Corps of Engineers, published as House Document No. 531, 81st Congress, 2nd Session; and *The Columbia River*, 2 vol. (1950), report of the United States Bureau of Reclamation, House Document 473, 81st Congress, 2nd Session. An excellent film, *Great River* (1963), is available from the United States Bureau of Reclamation and Bonneville Administration.

(M.E.Ms.)

Columbiformes

The order Columbiformes comprises the pigeons, doves, dodoes, and sandgrouse. The suborder Columbae embraces the extinct dodo and solitaires in the family Raphidae and the extinct and living pigeons and doves in the family Columbidae. The names pigeon and dove are synonymous and imply no biological distinction. The sandgrouse are given a distinct suborder, Pterocletes. The pigeon family is a natural and homogeneous assemblage of about 285 species of readily defined birds, unique in producing, for feeding their young, a nutritive secretion from the crop wall. Pigeon's milk is similar in composition to mammalian milk and is also induced by the secretion of the hormone prolactin from the pituitary gland. Pigeons also are distinctive in their unusual manner of drinking, in which water is sucked in as a continuous draft, the process being assisted by muscular contractions of the esophagus, whereas other birds take a sip of water and then tip back the head to swallow. It is frequently stated that the sandgrouse share this typically pigeon habit; in fact they suck and then tip back the head to swallow, repeating the process four to ten times during any drinking session.

GENERAL FEATURES

With the exception of some highly specialized ground-living forms, all pigeons are readily recognizable. They range in size from birds the size of a starling (the diamond dove of Australia) to some as large as a female turkey (the crowned pigeons of New Guinea). The skeleton and body form is usually unspecialized, enabling pigeons to feed and roost arboreally yet also collect food from the ground. Adaptive radiation has been either toward a more specialized arboreal life or toward ground-feeding forms, some of which (quail doves) convergently resemble partridges. Sandgrouse also resemble gallinaceous birds, although they cannot run, and have become adapted to desert and semidesert conditions in the Afro-Asian region. From the rock dove man has bred the various races of domesticated dovecote pigeons, racing pigeons, and other fancy breeds, while the domesticated form of the African collared dove (the so-called Barbary dove, sometimes erroneously given specific status) has long been a popular cage and dovecote bird. Because many pigeons are extremely well adapted to grain-eating and grazing habits, some conflict with man's agricultural activities and are considered pests.

Pigeons are virtually cosmopolitan, being absent only from the Arctic, Antarctic, and some oceanic islands. Five species have become extinct since the late 17th century, at which time the dodoes and solitaires also vanished. The best known example is that of the passenger pigeon (*Ectopistes migratorius*) of North America, which was remarkable for its extreme gregariousness, a factor that helped the early settlers to exploit it ruthlessly; it was exterminated by the end of the 19th century. Other species have spread and increased, particularly as a result of man's agricultural activities. Since 1930 the collared dove has spread 1,000 miles northwest from the Balkans.

IMPORTANCE TO MAN

Throughout the world, agricultural development has effectively provided a "super-habitat" for many seed-eating pigeons, enabling them to thrive and spread: the collared dove (*Streptopelia decaocto*) in India in relation to cereal production, the spotted dove (*S. chinensis*) in Southeast Asia in relation to rice paddy, and the laughing dove (*S. senegalensis*) throughout Africa, Arabia and India, associated with native crops. Any species that can profit from agricultural expansion must be extremely well adapted—in a sense, preadapted—to such conditions and is likely to achieve pest status. Damage by the wood pigeon in Britain has been estimated at £2,000,000 to £3,000,000 annually, but it is unlikely that it justifies expensive remedial action on a national scale; the cost of cereal spillage before and at harvest exceeds this amount. Indeed, it has been shown that artificial population control, employing conventional methods such as shooting, is not feasible at a national level and that bonus schemes do not improve control operations. Emphasis is now placed on providing remedial action, relying often as much on scaring as killing, only in the precise locality where damage is occurring or is imminent. The use of more extreme control methods (for example, poisoning)

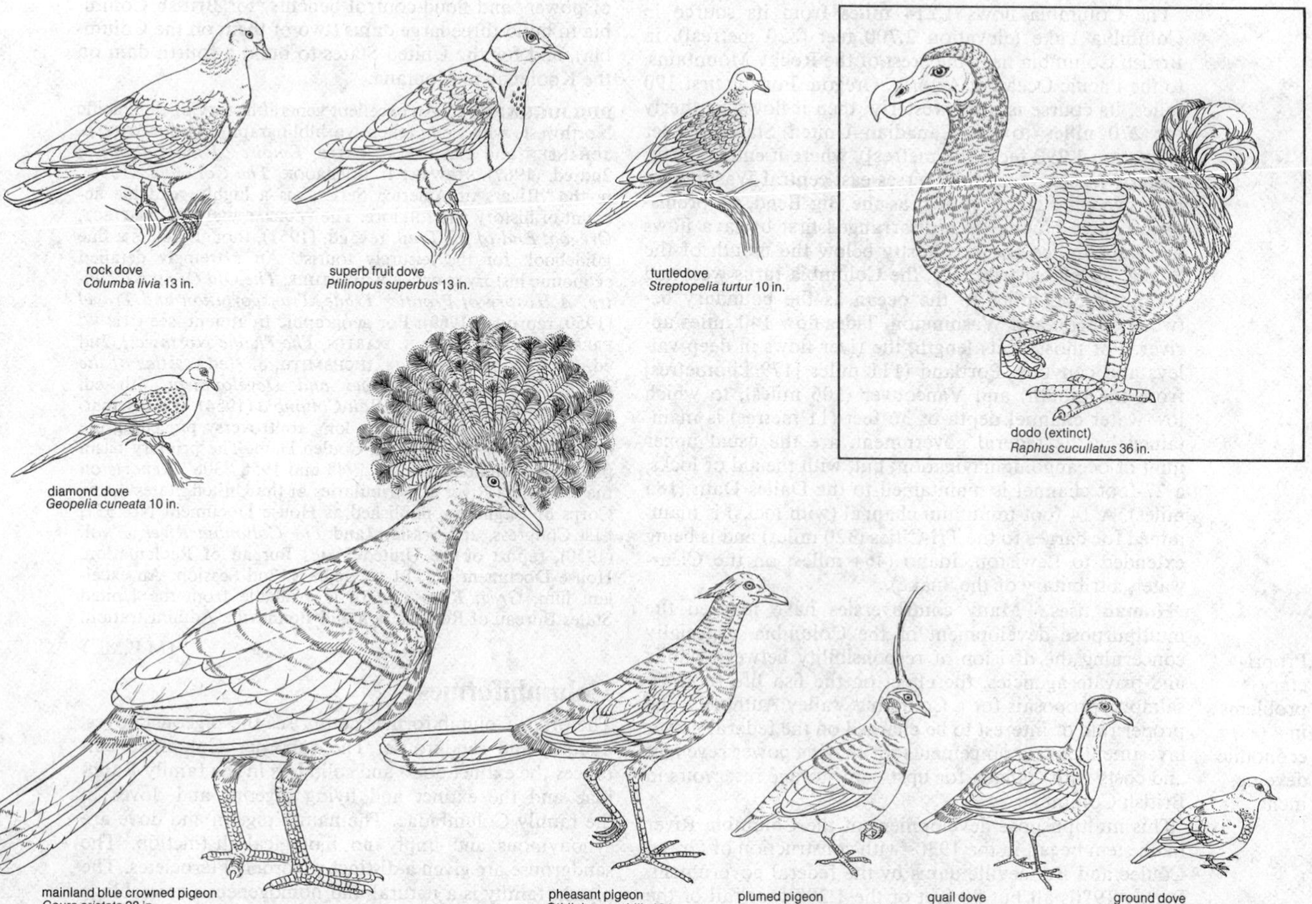

Distribution and abundance

rock dove
Columba livia 13 in.

superb fruit dove
Ptilinopus superbus 13 in.

turtledove
Streptopelia turtur 10 in.

dodo (extinct)
Raphus cucullatus 36 in.

diamond dove
Geopelia cuneata 10 in.

mainland blue crowned pigeon
Goura cristata 28 in.

pheasant pigeon
Otidiphaps nobilis 18 in.

plumed pigeon
Petrophassa plumifera 10 in.

quail dove
Gallicolumba jobiensis 10 in.

ground dove
Columbigallina passerina 6¾ in.

Figure 1: Types of columbiform birds.

is ruled out in densely populated areas because of the risks to people and livestock. In addition, the risk to other wildlife is now recognized, and there is a widespread desire, public as well as official, not to upset the balance of nature for the sake of immediate but marginal benefits. Any damage caused by the mourning dove to cereal farming in the U.S. pales in comparison with the value of the species as a sporting bird.

Nesting colonies of the rock dove (*Columba livia*) were farmed by Neolithic husbandmen for food, and gradually the process of rearing young in confinement led to the production of domesticated strains. Evidence for domestication extends back to 4500 BC in ancient Iraq, and the bird was sacred to the early Near East cultures, being associated with Astarte, the goddess of love and fertility; later, in ancient Greece, it was sacred to Aphrodite and in Roman times to Venus. By the Middle Ages dovecote populations were kept as a source of food on virtually every manorial estate in Europe. From the domesticated pigeons have been derived the various fancy breeds, such as tumblers and pouters, and many genetic aberrations that have given pleasure to countless enthusiasts. From the same source have come racing pigeons. Belgium, at the top of the international league table, has more than 165,000 pigeon fanciers. Carrier pigeons were used to relay news of the conquest of Gaul to Rome, brought news of Napoleon's defeat at Waterloo to England, and were used extensively for message carrying in the two recent world wars.

Urban pigeons

The popularity of the dovecote pigeon declined in the late 19th century as farmers realized that it was more efficient and brought greater financial reward to supply nations with bread rather than to convert corn inefficiently into this intermediate form of protein. The release of thousands of pigeons, together with escapes, established the feral populations closely associated with man in numerous European towns, in North America (where it is often known simply as the "city pigeon"), and other parts of the world as far away as Australia. Being naturally adapted to rocky ravines, sea cliffs, and barren sites, the bird has readily accepted the sides of buildings, bridges, and other man-made "cliffs." In towns it is fed and protected by an indulgent and benevolent public, at the same time being cursed by public health inspectors and those concerned with its depredations on stored grains. To a large extent, problems connected with food storage can be remedied by adequate proofing of buildings and control of spillage.

The importance of feral pigeons as a reservoir and means of transmission of disease is becoming increasingly recognized, even though there are few cases where the transmission of disease can be proved. Feral pigeons appear to harbour ornithosis (psittacosis) to a sufficient extent to provide a potential human risk. Up to three-quarters of various local pigeon populations examined in Paris were found to be infected, and the virus also has been isolated from pigeons in Liverpool, London, and elsewhere. Virulent strains of *Cryptococcus neoformans*, a fungal disease of the skin that also can affect the lungs and central nervous system, causing cryptococcal meningitis, have been isolated from pigeon excreta in various cities.

NATURAL HISTORY

General habits. The evolution of the crop has been of vital importance to the pigeons. This bilobed diverticulum (a blind pouch) of the esophagus, located just posterior to the buccal cavity, serves as a storage organ for food. Subsisting for the most part on seeds, buds, leaves, and fruits, foods of low protein content and nutritive value, pigeons must consume large quantities during each feeding day. The rate of food intake can be higher than the digestion rate would otherwise allow, the surplus food accumulating in the crop to be digested after the birds have gone to roost. The ability to store food has enabled some pigeons to be represented among the small list of birds—geese and certain galliform birds are other examples—that can live as efficient grazers, occupying a

leaf-eating niche in wooded country, either in the tree canopy or on the forest floor. Some, such as the wood pigeon (*Columba palumbus*), have secondarily adapted to more open country to exploit the food supplies created by agricultural expansion. This pigeon is typical of the many that obtain their food partly in trees and partly on the ground. In mid-winter it can subsist entirely on clover leaves and spends 95 percent of the day collecting the leaf fragments at 60–100 pecks per minute. By such intensive feeding a single bird can collect 35,000 clover-leaf fragments (45 grams, dry weight) per day. In spring this diet is supplemented with tree buds and flowers and also pasture-weed seeds; in summer the diet is chiefly cereal grain; in autumn declining corn stocks on the stubbles are supplemented with tree foods such as acorns and beech mast.

The mourning dove (*Zenaidura macroura*) of North America, and the turtledove (*Streptopelia turtur*) and stock dove (*Columba oenas*) of Europe rarely take green vegetation, do not feed in trees, and so are examples of the trend to complete ground feeding. These doves subsist almost entirely on seeds collected from low herbage or the ground. In winter such food sources become unproductive, so the turtledove and the mourning dove, in the northern part of their respective ranges, migrate southward. Turtledoves migrate from northern Europe to winter in central Africa. The ancients were well aware of this movement: "They shall tremble [Hebrew "hasten"] as a bird out of Egypt, and as a dove out of the land of Assyria" (Hos. 11:11).

Adaptation to ground feeding

Adaptation to ground feeding has progressed much further in various tropical genera, though the ecology of the species involved barely has been studied. In the New World a series can be traced from the typical *Zenaida* pigeons, through the ground doves (*Columbina, Claravis, Metriopelia* and *Scardafella*), which are mostly compact with short tails, and the *Leptotila* doves of South America, with longer legs suitable for running over the ground, to the New World quail doves (*Geotrygon* and *Starnoenas*). The last are relatively long legged and partridgelike, spending most of their time on the forest floor. In the Australasian region there is a similar series, from scrub-country doves resembling *Zenaida* and *Streptopelia* —here represented by *Geopelia*—through the emerald doves and bronzewings (*Chalcophaps* and *Phaps*), to the Old World quail doves (*Gallicolumba* and various derivatives). Most of these quail doves live on the forest floor, collecting fallen seeds and fruits and seeds from low herbage, but in Australia a few are found in open country. Some aberrant species have evolved even further toward ground living, an extreme case being the pheasant pigeon (*Otidiphaps nobilis*) of New Guinea and adjacent islands, which resembles a pheasant. Evolution toward ground-living forms in Australasia and South America may have been helped by a paucity of mammalian carnivores, which may partly explain why the extreme development of such forms has not occurred in Africa. In arid regions of Africa and central Asia, however, the various sandgrouse (*Pterocles* and *Syrrhaptes*) occupy this niche.

The radiation of pigeons into fully arboreal, fruit-eating types also is most apparent in Australasia, with the brown fruit doves (*Phapitreron*), green pigeons (*Treron*), and the fruit doves (*Ptilinopus* and *Ducula*). Within these genera there are a large number of sympatric (coexisting) species differing by a wide variety of species-specific colour patterns that serve for mate recognition and hence species isolation. Nevertheless, the predominant colour of most fruit pigeons is green, which ensures camouflage in tree foliage. The success of fruit pigeons in this region may have resulted from the absence of competition from monkeys—important fruit eaters in Africa and South America. Fruit pigeons are adept at perching on slender branches and have large mouths that allow them to swallow large fruit. In tropical forests appropriate trees with ripe fruit tend to occur sporadically, so that most of the fruit pigeons move through large areas of country in flocks to seek out their food.

Sandgrouse rely on cryptic coloration to protect them from predators, yet are powerful fliers when disturbed. Long primary feathers facilitate considerable flights to water sources for some species, round trips of up to 80 miles being made daily in some areas. The desert species usually fly to water at dawn, those of bush country at dusk. At either time several thousand birds may congregate at a traditional watering place. Their drinking habits are unique. Only five to ten seconds are required for drinking, an adaptation believed to reduce the risks from the diurnal predators that collect around waterholes in anticipation of the birds' arrival. Up to 15 millilitres (about 0.6 ounce) of water may be imbibed by a sandgrouse. Water is carried back to nestlings in the crop and alimentary canal and on specially modified abdominal feathers. When not breeding, sandgrouse are nomadic wanderers in their desert home, but some species undergo periodic irruptive dispersals that may involve long-distance movements, usually when good breeding leads to a high population and subsequent food scarcity.

Behaviour. When feeding on the ground a pigeon must be looking downward for much of the time and therefore is vulnerable to predators such as foxes. The widespread habit of feeding in flocks has probably not evolved as an antipredator device but rather to help the birds to locate their food. Many species possess signal marks that become prominent in sudden flight, just as some rabbits display the white underparts of the tail. The wood pigeon has white wing bars that flash on takeoff, the Nicobar pigeon (*Caloenas nicobarica*) a white tip to the tail.

A consequence of feeding in a flock is that differences in individual attributes are more readily manifested, and this finds expression in a strongly developed social hierarchy (peck order). In competitive situations submissive individuals are frequently supplanted by more dominant individuals, and efforts to avoid conflict result in their getting less food. During times of shortage they are the first to die, other flock members remaining perfectly healthy. There is no evidence that social behaviour has evolved as a mechanism whereby populations can achieve self-regulation of their numbers, as has sometimes been suggested.

Reproductive behaviour

In most pigeons, a male in reproductive condition acquires a territory, which it proclaims with an advertisement call, usually a variant of the typical pigeon "coo" sound. Intrusion from other pigeons is prevented, at first, by threat displays involving sleeking the plumage, stretching the head forward, and partially raising the wings. If these are ineffective the male attacks the intruder, pecking at the opponent and delivering sharp blows with the carpal joint of the wing. Females behaving submissively are gradually tolerated, particularly by unpaired males, enabling pair formation to proceed. In pigeons that build their own nests in scrub and open woodland, territories may be large, but in some hole- and cavity-nesting species, such as the rock dove, only the area around the actual nest site is defended. A shortage of suitable sites forces the latter to be semicolonial. Many pigeons perform display flights in and near the territory to attract unmated females. Such displays frequently involve exaggerated movements, slow wing beating, and, in some, loud clapping noises produced by the wings. The underparts of the tail, and sometimes other areas of the plumage, may have contrasting light and dark patterns that are displayed during flight.

Pair formation has been well studied in the rock dove and Barbary dove. A sexually mature male typically approaches a submissive member of the same species with the bowing display (in most pigeons this occurs within a previously acquired territory, but not invariably). Bowing is primarily an aggressive display, involving tendencies to advance and attack and to mount and copulate. It is usually accompanied by vocalization—the bow call. Females normally retreat from the bowing display and exhibit submissive postures but if receptive sink to the ground with lowered wings and tail. This may result in the male mounting immediately; if not, he gradually becomes less aggressive and commences the nest-demon-

Figure 2: *Courtship behaviour.*
One aspect of the wood pigeon's, or ringdove's (*Columba palumbus*), courtship is the prolonged, gentle rubbing of one bird's beak, usually the male's, through the head feathers of his mate.
Ronald K. Murton

stration display. Being a submissive display, this reduces any female fear and attracts her closer, leading to a state where the pair now accept each other's presence. Displays that cement the pair bond involve mutual nibbling of each other's feathers, particularly those of the head and neck (see Figure 2). At this early stage of the cycle the female exhibits juvenile behaviour, begging food from the male who, in turn, feeds her. This is the normal stage at which the female solicits and copulation occurs, interspersed with displacement preening. The female gradually assumes a more assertive role as she ceases to fear her partner and will attempt to push him off the nest site and occupy it herself. The male is now stimulated to search for nest material, which he brings back to the sitting female, and one or both incorporate the material into a nest.

The specific acts of seeing her mate build a nest and of being involved herself stimulate the female's neuro-endocrine system so that estrogen secretion rises, causing the oviduct to develop about five days before eggs will be laid. Seeing and incubating eggs, or seeing another bird doing so, stimulates prolactin secretion causing the crop gland to become secretory, so that "pigeon milk" is available when the eggs hatch. From this time onward the crop gland gradually regresses so that by the time they are ready to leave the nest, the young are fed almost entirely on environmental supplies. The production of a highly proteinaceous milk enables these seed- and fruit-eating birds to be independent of animal food when the young need maximum nutrition. The limitations of crop-milk production also have doubtless set the limit to the maximum number of young that can be reared, so that no pigeon ever lays more than two eggs, and many fruit eaters lay only one.

Secretion of "pigeon milk"

Most pigeons are multibrooded and have long breeding seasons, timed to correspond with the period of high food availability for both adults and young. Temperate zone pigeons, like other temperate zone birds, use proximate (immediate) environmental signals to insure attaining reproductive maturity at the appropriate time, one of the major signals being the seasonal changes of daylength. The neuro-endocrine apparatus of British wood pigeons is stimulated by the daylengths of March; the gonads become active at that time and remain in breeding condition until September, when daylengths once more fall below the stimulatory threshold. This period of activity is appropriate to the season during which actual reproduction is feasible. The turtledove is stimulated into breeding condition in April during its migration north and lays its first eggs in late April and early May. The gonads spontaneously regress in August, inhibiting further activity, even though environmental conditions are good and breeding success is at a peak. The onset of reduced breeding activity in the presence of daylengths that were stimulatory in April is a safety mechanism; by reducing the physical strains associated with breeding, it enables the adults to accumulate the energy reserves needed to re-

Nesting

place the flight feathers (vital for successful long-distance migration) and to lay down fat reserves for migration. Many pigeons, however, molt throughout the breeding season.

Most pigeons build their own nests, simple flat platforms of twigs, in scrub or woodland. Some tree-nesting species occasionally nest on the ground, others regularly do so. White eggs are particularly attractive to predators so that, presumably to reduce these risks, some of the ground-nesting pigeons (*e.g.*, Old and New World quail doves) lay brown or cream-coloured eggs. In many pigeons, once the eggs are laid both members of the pair share the duties of incubation, changing over on or near the nest site, so that the eggs are normally not left uncovered. In contrast, sandgrouse almost invariably lay three cryptically coloured and spotted eggs in a scrape on the ground; sometimes a few grass stems may serve as a lining. The male incubates by night, the female by day.

A few pigeons have adapted to nesting in crevices and holes, reducing the risks of egg predation but increasing the chances that the adult will be cornered on the nest by a predator. The clutch almost invariably consists of one or two eggs. The newly hatched young are at first continuously brooded but later are left for long periods while the parents seek food. The larger pigeons usually visit the nest only twice a day, bringing a crop full of food if feeding conditions are suitable. The young, called squabs, beg for food by pushing at the parent's breast, at the same time emitting a squeaky hunger note. They insert their bills in corners of the parent's mouth and are then fed by regurgitation (see Figure 3). Although a pi-

Figure 3: *Feeding.*
The unfledged squab of the wood pigeon (*Columba palumbus*) is nourished with "pigeon milk," a curdy substance regurgitated from the parents' crops.

geon is capable of rearing an artificial brood of three young, only two squabs can be fed at a time, and natural broods of three are extremely rare. In several species so far studied, when the nestlings are about three-quarters grown the parents begin a new cycle, building a new nest nearby and laying eggs.

Unguarded young are less subject to predation than eggs, partly because of their more cryptic colouring, but primarily because they have a marked threat display. At the approach of danger they inflate their crops with air, causing them to become much bigger, and thrust their heads towards the enemy, at the same time hissing and snapping the mandibles together.

Ecology. Many temperate zone pigeons show marked population declines during the year. The high numbers resulting from breeding in temperate species can at first be maintained by extensive summer food supplies, especially in populations that depend on man-made food sources, such as barley or rice. But as food stocks decline in autumn and winter, reaching a critical level in relation

to the population, juveniles suffer a high mortality, competing relatively unsuccessfully with adults. The change in population size from year to year thus depends primarily on the survival rate of juveniles through the period of food shortage, this being the key factor responsible for annual fluctuations. Long-term population trends, up or down, result from changes in the suitability of the habitat and are reflected in the number of adults that can settle to breed in an area. The average expectation of life for a British wood pigeon after reaching maturity is 2.25 years, which means that an average of 36 percent of the adult population dies each year. Whatever number of young 100 adults produce, only 36 need reach maturity to keep the population stable, and the rest are surplus. The juvenile mortality rate varies between 60 and 80 percent. Turtledoves are smaller and more at risk from predators; they also face the dangers of long migratory flights. Their adult mortality rate is nearer to 50 percent per annum, comparable to the 56 to 58 percent found in the North American mourning dove, which also is extensively shot for sport.

Population variability

FORM AND FUNCTION

Distinguishing characteristics. Pigeons are of compact shape, usually plump because of well-developed pectoral muscles, and with relatively small heads. The wings are long and often pointed in species that are highly migratory and in those that obtain most of their food in trees. A few island or montane species that fly less have reduced wings. A long, pointed tail, as in the extinct passenger pigeon and the masked dove (*Oena capensis*), is probably correlated with a high degree of manoeuvrability, necessary during a rapid escape from the ground in woodland. The partridge-like pigeons have short rounded wings and a short tail. These are mostly birds of woodland, keeping to the cover of trees and bushes, but in Australia there are species that live completely in the open and nest on the ground. One, the flock pigeon (*Phaps histrionica*), makes long flights to its feeding and drinking places and has long wings, in many respects apparently living like the sandgrouse of Afro-Asian regions.

Pigeons generally have short legs, but in those that resemble game-birds the legs are lengthened for more effective terrestrial locomotion. Three toes point forward and one backward. The bill is usually small and soft and may be overhung by the fleshy operculum (cere), which is enlarged in some of the fruit pigeons and domesticated forms of *Columba livia*. The bill shape is associated with feeding habits, slender bills being typical of seed eaters and deeply hooked bills of fruit eaters, especially those like *Treron*, which feed on large hard fruits such as figs. This trend in bill development is seen to an exaggerated extent in the ground-feeding tooth-billed pigeon (*Didunculus strigirostris*), whose bill resembles that of the extinct dodo, a bird that may have had similar feeding behaviour. It tears and nibbles its food into small pieces in a manner reminiscent of the parrots, taking berries, fruit, and mountain plantain.

Pigeons have dense and soft plumage, the region in the vicinity of the eye often being bare. In most species the female is slightly duller than the male, but in some the sexes are identical, and in a few species there are marked differences in colour. One kind of sexual dimorphism, in which display plumage is confined to the male, is correlated in most other birds with a tendency toward polygamy; but it is not clear whether this is true in pigeons. Another kind of dimorphism involves the female being rather differently coloured. Thus the male of the orange dove (*Ptilinopus victor*) is brilliant orange, the female green; the male ruddy quail dove (*Geotrygon montana*) is purplish chestnut, the female brown. This trend seems to be associated with making the female, who does most if not all the incubation in these cases, more cryptic.

With the exception of *Treron*, most fruit pigeons have a broad, short intestine and can void intact the stones from fruits they have eaten. Seed eaters have stronger gizzards and long, narrow intestines.

The sandgrouse also are compact, with thick under-

Plumage

down, tough skins to resist desiccation, and frequently elongated central tail feathers. The legs are short and the toes sometimes slightly webbed, aiding progression on soft sand.

Physiology and biochemistry. Domesticated pigeons and the Barbary dove have long served as subjects for avian physiological research, and knowledge related to their body functions is extensive. They appear to exhibit no remarkable specializations, compared with birds in general, with the exception that the crop becomes glandular in response to small amounts of the hormone prolactin. Prolactin was first discovered in pigeons by O. Riddle, and pigeons still serve in the bioassay of this hormone from other sources. Prolactin also is produced by other birds. Among other functions, it reduces aggressive behaviour during the incubation and early brood-care stages of the reproductive cycle. It apparently is involved in the molting process and in mechanisms associated with preparation for migration. Pigeons are unique only in having secondarily evolved a new target organ responsive to the hormone.

The sense of taste, as with most other birds, is poorly developed, and it is probably not an important factor in selecting food. Shape and tactile characteristics and, to a lesser extent, colour are much more important. The average number of taste buds is only 37, confined to the soft area at the base of the tongue and palatine region (in contrast, man has about 9,000 and the rabbit about 17,000). Pigeons can, however, exhibit a surprising sensitivity to certain substances, such as acids; only at extremely low concentrations are acetic acid solutions accepted as readily as pure water. The olfactory organs are well developed; but smell seems to be of little significance in the daily lives of pigeons, and experiments to demonstrate their olfactory abilities have yielded conflicting results. Visual acuity is highly developed, as in most other birds, although training experiments demonstrate that pigeons can attain an acuity little better than humans.

EVOLUTION AND PALEONTOLOGY

By the time they appear in the fossil record the Columbiformes are already so well differentiated that their phylogenetic relations cannot be determined with certainty. The sandgrouse and pigeons resemble each other anatomically, but this may have resulted from convergence towards a similar mode of life. The dodoes and solitaires were highly specialized island forms that doubtless arose in the Mascarene Islands and were peculiar to those islands. Three species are known, the dodo (*Raphus cucullatus*) on Mauritus, the Réunion solitaire (*Raphus solitarius*), and the Rodrigues solitaire (*Pezophaps solitaria*). A fourth species, the white dodo (named as *Victoriornis imperialis*), may have existed on Réunion but, if it existed, was probably a colour phase of the Réunion solitaire. The dodoes and solitaires became extinct in about 1681, 1746, and 1791 respectively, as they fell easy prey to marauding sailors and could not compete with pigs and other introduced livestock. They were pigeon-like birds that had lost the power of flight in the safety of their predator-free island existence and had become large (as big as a turkey), heavily built birds with strong bills and feet. The wings had become rudimentary, and the sternum possessed only a small keel.

The earliest known sandgrouse are of the modern genus *Pterocles* and date from the upper Eocene of France (about 40,000,000 years ago). The earliest known pigeon is *Gerandia calcaria* from the early Miocene of France (25,000,000 years ago), although the suborder probably arose in the Australasian region, where the greatest variety of modern columbiforms is found. Other fossil pigeons are known from the Pleistocene (2,000,000 years ago).

CLASSIFICATION

Distinguishing taxonomic features. The most important features distinguishing the Columbiformes are the structure of the skull, sternum, and furculum. The several

species have close thick feathers set loosely in the skin, lack the fifth secondary feather of the wing, and possess a crop. The structure of the bill and nostrils, the arrangement of the sterno-tracheal musculature, and the presence or absence of intestinal ceca distinguish the suborders. Behavioral characteristics are of doubtful validity in relating suborder relationships because the similarities may have arisen by convergence. Blood-antigen relationships may be considered more reliable.

Annotated classification.

ORDER COLUMBIFORMES

Birds in which the palatine processes of the maxillae do not meet in the midline (schizognathous) and with vomer absent or vestigial. Palatine and pterygoid bones articulate with basisphenoid rostrum. Basipterygoid processes present, except in family Raphidae. Sternum with large lateral and smaller inner incisions, these often fused to fenestrae. Furculum U-shaped and with hypocleideum little or not developed. Nares separated by a complete internasal septum. Hypotarsus complex. Plumage, close and thick, feathers loosely set in skin. Pterylosis essentially similar in the 2 suborders. 5th secondary quill absent (diastataxic). Oil-gland naked or absent. Well developed crop present.

Suborder Columbae (pigeons, doves, and dodoes)

Miocene to present. Intestinal ceca absent or minute, syrinx with sterno-tracheal muscles asymmetrical. Young altricial (helpless); hatched blind without real down. Basal part of bill soft and covered with a swollen skin that envelops the slitlike nostrils as a cap (operculum). External nasal opening into skull tapers behind into a narrow cleft running back into nasal bone (schizorhinal); 14–15 cervical vertebrae. 11 primary feathers, the outermost much reduced. Usually 12–14, and exceptionally 16–20, retrices. Crop bilobed. Nest in tree holes or caves or build flimsy platform of sticks on trees or ground. Eggs usually white, except in some quail doves brown or cream, mostly 2 in number, but 1 in some genera.

Family Columbidae (pigeons and doves)

Pleistocene to present. Characteristics of suborder. Length 15–80 cm; weight 45–4000 g. Wide range of colours, from grays and browns to striking orange, green, or purple. Worldwide except subpolar regions and some oceanic islands. About 285 species.

Family Raphidae (dodoes and solitaires)

Extinct but with no fossil record. Flightless, with much reduced furculum and wing, fused coracoid and scapula and no basipterygoid processes. Large; weight probably exceeded 10 kg. Limited to Mascarene Islands. 3 species.

Suborder Pterocletes.

Long intestinal ceca, symmetrical sterno-tracheal muscles, young nidifugous (precocious) and covered with down. Bill resembles that of game birds, not soft at base. Sternum with very high keel and ribs broad, cervical vertebrae number 15 to 16; tarsus short and feathered, toes wide and short, soles covered with hexagonal or rounded scales. Nostrils not schizorhinal and covered by feathers except in front. 11 primaries, outermost much reduced, and 14–18 retrices. Pterylosis as in pigeons but feather tracts wider. Oil gland small and naked. Large crop, not bilobed. 2 to 4 eggs laid in mere scrape in ground in open steppe or desert.

Family Pteroclididae (sandgrouse)

Late Eocene or early Oligocene to present. Characteristics of the suborder. Coloration buff, reddish or grayish brown, barred or spotted with black, brown, yellow, or white; sexually dimorphic. Habitat sandy plains, open brush, or deserts of temperate to equatorial Eurasia and Africa. Length 23–40 cm (variation mostly in tail length); weight 120–300 g. 16 species.

Critical appraisal. On anatomical grounds, the sandgrouse resemble the pigeons and are therefore placed in the same order. Their drinking behaviour only partly resembles that of the pigeons, and other behaviour in which the two groups are similar is not unique to either. G.C. McLean suggested that the sandgrouse are nearer to the plovers (family Charadriidae, order Charadriiformes), and D. Goodwin also took this view. The subordinal limits of the Columbae seem well defined, although J. Lüttschwager suggested that the Raphidae bear closer affinity with rails (order Gruiformes). The gruiform line diverged early from the stock that eventually produced the Columbiformes and Charadriiformes, so if closer to the Gruiformes the dodoes would be closer to presumed pigeon ancestors, rather than, as usually believed, rela-

(margin note) Dodoes and solitaires

tively recent offshoots from established Columbae stock. The pigeons and doves comprise a natural group, which most authors treat as a single family. This seems the best arrangement, but separate family rank is sometimes given to the pheasant pigeon, crowned pigeons, tooth-billed pigeons, and even to the fruit pigeons. These are probably best treated as the subfamilies Otidiphapinae, Gourinae, Didunculinae, and Treroninae.

BIBLIOGRAPHY. For accounts of the natural history of columbiform birds, the reader should consult D. GOODWIN, *Pigeons and Doves of the World* (1967); for the biology of an abundant European species, R.K. MURTON, *The Wood Pigeon* (1965); for Australian species, H.J. FRITH, "Notes on the Pigeons of the Richmond River, N.S.W.," *Emu*, 52:89–99 (1952); for North American pigeons, A.C. BENT, "Life Histories of North American Gallinaceous Birds," *Bull. U.S. Natn. Mus. 162*, pp. 353–477 (1932); and for neotropical species, A.F. SKUTCH, "Life Histories of Central American Pigeons," *Wilson Bull.*, 76:211–247 (1964). W.M. LEVI, *The Pigeon*, rev. ed. (1957), provides a complete discussion of the care and breeding of domestic pigeons. A.W. SCHORGER, *The Passenger Pigeon* (1955), is an exceptionally thorough account of the natural history, economics, and demise of this once abundant North American pigeon. In addition to Goodwin's book, the taxonomy of pigeons is discussed in R.F. JOHNSTON, "Taxonomy of Pigeons," *Condor*, 64:69–74 (1962); D. GOODWIN "Taxonomy of the Genus *Columba*," *Bull. Br. Mus. Nat. Hist.* (Zool.), no. 6, pp. 1–23 (1959); and E.W. GIFFORD, "Taxonomy and Habits of Pigeons." *Auk*, 58:239–245 (1941).

(R.K.M.)

Columbus, Christopher

The discoverer of the New World, Christopher Columbus (in Spanish Cristóbal Colón) was one of the greatest mariners of all time, but his despotic and capricious administration of the West Indies, which he claimed for Spain, eventually resulted in his recall. The combination of an outstanding and highly imaginative mind with a temper so highstrung and autocratic that his thoughts, writings, and actions at times suggested a man just this side of delusion initially brought him honour and riches, yet in the course of time led to a tragic reversal of his fortunes. From his next to last voyage to the New World the Admiral of the Ocean Seas and Viceroy of the Indies was returned in chains. After spending the remaining six years of his life in pitiable attempts to regain the splendour and vast possessions that had eluded him, he died in obscurity.

He was the son of Domenico Colombo, a weaver living first at the Italian port cities of Genoa and later at Savona, and of Suzanna Fontanarossa. The exact date of his birth is not known. The evidence concerning the early life of Columbus is sparse and admits of many interpretations. One view is that he at first followed his father's business and resided at Genoa and Savona, but Columbus must be believed when he says that he went to sea when he was 14. In any event, he was a pirate in the service of René d'Anjou in 1472–73; he was on the Greek island of Chios in 1473–74; and he fought in a battle off Cape St. Vincent, under his namesake and probable relative Guillaume de Casenove-Coullon, on August 13, 1476, when his ship took fire and he swam to the Portuguese coast with the help of an oar. The fact that in this battle he fought on the Portuguese side, against Genoa, shows him to have been no Genoese patriot. There is no explicit statement by him declaring himself a Genoese. He never went back to Genoa. He never wrote in any form of Italian—not even to his brothers or to Genoese persons and institutions—but always in Spanish. He wrote in Spanish, even his own private notes, certainly three years before he came to Spain and the mistakes in his Latin are definitely hispanisms. Columbus signed himself successively Colombo, Colomo, Colom and Colón. The last was the form he himself came to prefer and wished to be used. He never took the traditional form Columbus, not even when writing Latin. His brothers, also, in Spain and in the Indies, called themselves Colón and hispanicized their Christian names (Bartolomeo becoming Bartolomé and Giacomo,

Columbus, oil painting by Sebastiano del Piombo, 1519. In the Metropolitan Museum of Art, New York.
By courtesy of the Metropolitan Museum of Art, New York, gift of J. Pierpont Morgan, 1900

Diego). One explanation of all these facts is that Columbus came from a Spanish-Jewish family settled in Genoa.

Columbus' plan. Columbus discovered America by prophecy rather than by astronomy. "In the carrying out of this enterprise of the Indies," he wrote to King Ferdinand and Queen Isabella in 1502, "neither reason nor mathematics nor maps were any use to me: fully accomplished were the words of Isaiah"—referring to a more or less apposite passage in Isaiah 11:10–12—and, in fact, any writing became prophetic in his eyes when it could be interpreted as a forecast of his discovery. Nor is it any wonder that he felt sure of having been divinely selected for a mission, an assurance that he often sets forth in his writings and that is the source of both his pride and his humility, for his was a life rich in dramatic scenes. His very arrival in Portugal, miraculously saved from the wreck of his ship, his landing so close to the rock of Sagres, where Prince Henry the Navigator had established his academy of seamanship, seem to justify his sense of having been chosen.

Portugal was then the westernmost end of the known world and Lisbon the natural meeting place of mariners bent on discovery. From there the Portuguese had discovered Madeira, turned the forbidding Cape Bojador on the Atlantic coast of Africa, and reached the Tropic of Cancer; and it was in Lisbon that these and future exploits were talked about, prepared, financed, and manned. The city was already a busy centre for the arts and sciences, particularly cosmography and astronomy. It was probably there that Christopher came across his younger brother Bartolomé, who had also left home for the sea and was working as a cartographer.

The idea of reaching the East by sailing westward seems first to have been mooted by the Florentine cosmographer Paolo Toscanelli. A concession that may be interpreted as contemplating such a quest was granted by the king of Portugal to one Fernão Telles on November 20, 1475. Soon after landing in Portugal, Columbus sailed to Iceland and during this voyage seems already to have been thinking of his voyage to "Cathay" through the West. In 1478 he married Felipa Perestrello e Moniz, a member of one of the first families of Portugal; by this marriage, Columbus had a son, Diego, born in 1479 or 1480. He then settled for a time on the island of Porto Santo, Madeira Islands, of which his brother-in-law had inherited the captaincy. From this base he acquired a considerable sailing experience of the South Atlantic, making one, or perhaps even two voyages to the Portuguese trading post of Mina on the Gold Coast, the southernmost extremity of the then known world. During these voyages he also received a number of hints (big

Near disasters on early voyages

canes, pine-tree trunks, pieces of wrought wood) of the probable existence of lands beyond the western horizon.

Back in Lisbon, Columbus read assiduously in Cardinal Pierre d'Ailly's *Image of the World* and Marco Polo's account of the East. But though he studied Ptolemy—whose misconception of the extent of Asia further strengthened his belief that Asia could be reached by travelling westward—and must have known Toscanelli's opinion, the system of ideas he elaborated owed most to the apocryphal biblical Second Book of Esdras (see, for example, II Esd. 3:18). These ideas were: (1) the Earth is round; (2) the distance by land between the edge of the West (Spain) and the edge of the East ("India"—*i.e.*, Asia) is very long; (3) the distance by sea between Spain and "India" is therefore very short; (4) the length of a degree is 56⅔ miles. These "miles" were not Arabic (1,975.5 metres), which would have made the figure remarkably accurate, but Italian (1,477.5 metres), which made his Equator about one-quarter too small. Columbus calculated that the land distance between Spain and "India" was 282°; he was therefore left with only 78° for the sea distance, which he further reduced by his method of reckoning the degree. The outcome of all these errors was that "India" would be about 3,900 miles (6,275 kilometres) from the Canaries—*i.e.*, more or less where America happens to be. This tallied tolerably well with II Esdras 6:42, where it is asserted that the Earth is six parts dry land and one part sea.

This system set Columbus' imagination afire with the untold avenues for discovery that the western way opened up. It is unlikely that he was ever clear as to the exact nature of such avenues: new lands? new ways to sail to the old lands? Although vague about his plan, Columbus was clear about what he wanted in exchange: honour and wealth, definitely in that order. The proposal was finally put to the king of Portugal, who rejected it (1484). Columbus then went to Spain. He applied first for help to the powerful duque de Medina-Sidonia, who was not interested, then to the conde (later duque) de Medina Celi, who housed and sheltered Columbus from 1484 to 1486; but though the conde conceived the idea of letting him have some caravels, he decided in the end that the enterprise was too big for even as big a subject as he was and sent the would-be discoverer to King Ferdinand and Queen Isabella. The queen handed the matter over to her chief accountant; eventually Columbus was granted an audience with Ferdinand and Isabella in Córdoba in the spring of 1486.

The monarchs then decided to set up a special commission of "learned men and mariners" to study Columbus' proposals. This commission, under the chairmanship of the queen's confessor, Hernando de Talavera, then bishop of Ávila, made him wait four years. This was not, as is often asserted, because the commission was either incompetent or backward in its views but because Columbus was vague and secretive as well as incoherent. For four years he went from city to city, following the court. In Salamanca he became acquainted with Diego de Deza, a professor at the university there, who, in 1486, became the tutor of Don Juan, the heir to the throne. Thanks no doubt to Deza, who throughout his life was to be his main standby, Columbus received several sums of money from the royal treasury in 1487, and on May 12, 1489, he was granted the privilege of being lodged and fed at public expense on his travels to court. During this period he became entangled with Beatriz Enríquez, who was to be the mother of his son Fernando.

In 1490 the Talavera commission reported unfavourably; and though the king and queen did not abandon him, Columbus may have felt that his Spanish quest was at an end. He went to La Rábida, near Huelva, where he met two men who were to restore his faith: the friar-astronomer, Antonio de Marchena, and a pilot and ship-owner from Palos, Martín Alonso Pinzón. Pinzón told him that a year earlier, in Rome, he had been informed by a papal cosmographer "of those lands which were still undiscovered." Columbus asked him to become his partner, and Pinzón accepted. The evidence available suggests that Marchena and another friar from La Rábida

succeeded in having Columbus recalled to the court—not to discuss his plan this time but to name the price he set on it. The price was exorbitant. He was to be knighted, appointed grand admiral and viceroy (these titles to remain in his family forever), and he was to receive 10 percent of the transactions within his admiralty. The king and queen were stunned by his audacity. He held his ground so firmly that no compromise was possible, and he was dismissed. He left Santa Fé (near Granada) early in January 1492, possibly for France and England, but friends at court persuaded the king and queen to recall him, and all his requests were met.

COLUMBUS' CAREER

First voyage. Thanks to his own and Pinzón's initiative, all obstacles and the customary inertia enveloping official enterprises were swept away, and soon Columbus beheld at quay, ready to sail, his three vessels—the decked ship "Marigalante" (officially renamed "Santa María"), and two caravels, "Pinta" and "Niña." The first was about 117 feet (36 metres) long, the other two about 50 feet (15 metres); the first two had castles fore and aft, the "Niña," only aft. They were armed with four-inch (ten-centimetre) *bombardas* for heavy granite balls and *espingardes* for smaller lead projectiles. As Columbus did not know whether he was to come across new savages or old civilizations, he loaded his ships with cheap merchandise to relieve aboriginals of their gold but also took on board one Luis de Torres—"who had been a Jew and knew Hebrew and Chaldean and a little Arabic"—in case he met the "grand khan." More than 1,000,000 maravedis had been supplied by the crown, though the story that the queen pawned her jewels to provide the money is quite untrue. The sum of 500,000 maravedis was supplied by Columbus himself (advanced by Pinzón). The "Santa María" sailed under Columbus; the "Pinta" under Martín Alonso Pinzón with his brother Francisco Martín Pinzón as his pilot; and the "Niña" under Vicente Yáñez Pinzón, another brother, later to prove one of the finest sailors of the era.

On August 3, 1492, half an hour before sunrise, the small fleet sailed out of Palos. On August 12 it reached the Canary Islands, where it stayed until September 6, when at last it sailed resolutely westward. Once the three ships finally lost sight of land (September 9) the greatness of Columbus began to reveal itself, for it was at this moment that he conquered by faith and will power the resistance of the unbelieving and faint-hearted members of his crew. He showed a typical mixture of strategic resolution and tactical caution, for he quickly handed out an "instruction" to his men that after 700 leagues (2,415 miles) they were not to navigate at night because land would certainly be near. On September 13 he observed that the relation of the magnetic north pole to the true North Pole changes with the position of the observer. A whole month passed in alternation of good and bad weather, good and bad mood. "There will be no wind to come back," the unbelievers sighed; and a strong contrary wind came to the rescue of their leader. On September 25, Columbus himself was infected by doubt and sought the help of Pinzón, who that very evening "saw" land. Columbus altered course to southwest in search of it but it vanished. Disbelief led to a conspiracy that might have degenerated into a disastrous mutiny but for the spirited intervention of Pinzón. On October 6 Pinzón suggested altering course again to the southwest; but Columbus was too proud to listen. The next day the "Niña" again "saw" land, but it was another illusion. Flights of birds all southwestward, however, made Columbus swallow his pride and follow Pinzón's advice (October 7). "All the night they heard birds passing," and carved sticks and reeds, picked up, gave them comfort and hope. Two hours after midnight (October 12) a sailor saw land from the prow of the "Pinta."

At dawn, a land of virginal beauty and fresh colour revealed itself to the delighted Spaniards. With his two captains and the officials accompanying the expedition, Columbus went ashore carrying the royal banner. He planted it on the shore and took possession of the land in

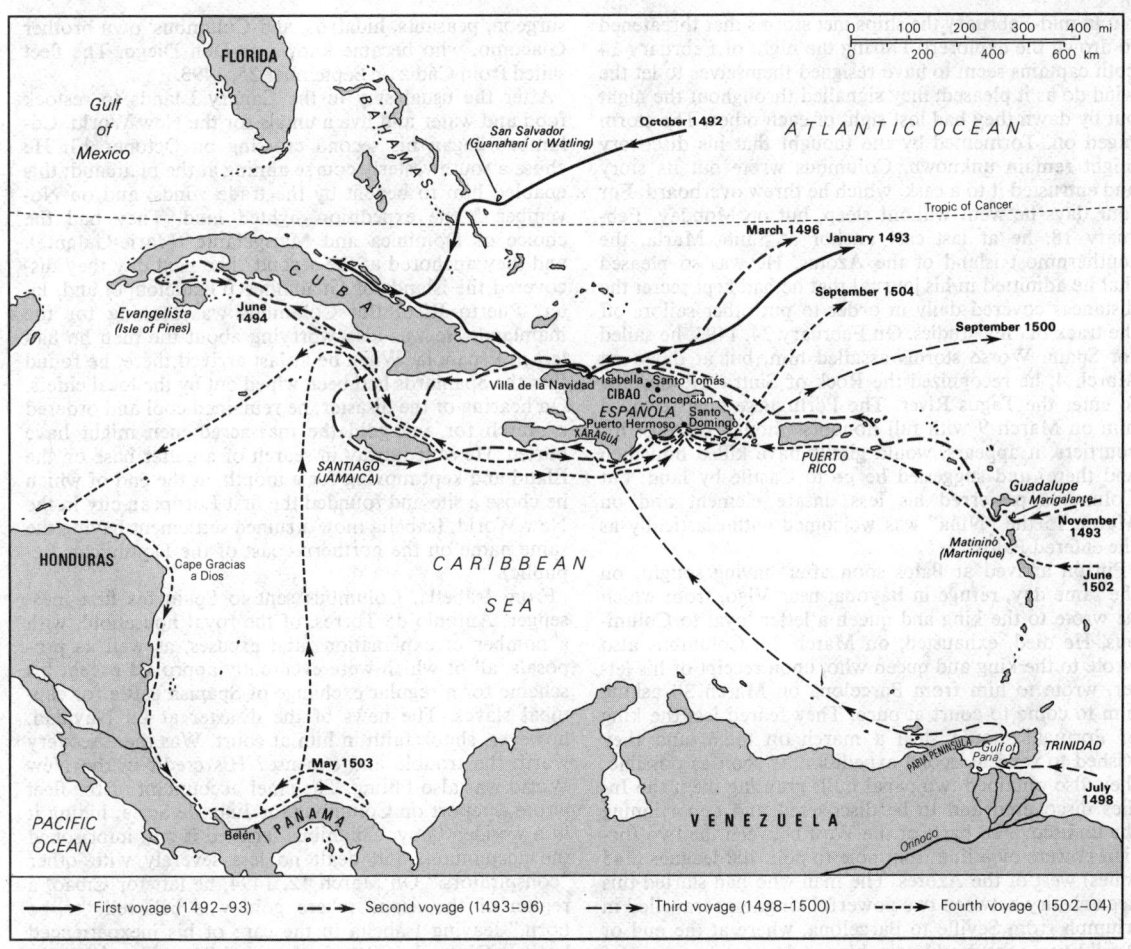

| 0 | 100 | 200 | 300 | 400 mi |
| 0 | 200 | | 400 | 600 km |

FLORIDA

Gulf
of
Mexico

San Salvador
(Guanahaní or Watling)

October 1492

ATLANTIC OCEAN

Tropic of Cancer

BAHAMAS

March 1496   January 1493

September 1504

September 1500

CUBA

Evangelista
(Isle of Pines)

June
1494

Villa de la Navidad

Isabella Santo Tomás
CIBAO   Concepción
ESPAÑOLA Santo
Puerto Hermoso Domingo
KARAGUÁ

PUERTO
RICO

Guadalupe
Marigalante

November
1493

SANTIAGO
(JAMAICA)

Matininó
(Martinique)

June
1502

HONDURAS

Cape Gracias
a Dios

CARIBBEAN

SEA

PACIFIC
OCEAN

Belén PANAMA

May 1503

VENEZUELA

Orinoco

TRINIDAD

PARIA PENINSULA Gulf of
Paria

July
1498

| First voyage (1492–93) | Second voyage (1493–96) | Third voyage (1498–1500) | Fourth voyage (1502–04) |

The voyages of Christopher Columbus.

the name of Ferdinand and Isabella. This land was Guanahaní, one of the Bahama Islands, which the Spaniards renamed San Salvador. But everything he saw persuaded Columbus that he was among "the islands which are set down in the maps at the end of the Orient." So, although he saw signs of gold on the noses of the natives, he left in a hurry to see "whether I can come across the Island of Cipango" (*i.e.*, Japan).

For a fortnight he wandered among lovely islands to which he gave Spanish names, hoping "the Lord would show him where gold is born," yet already alive to the possibilities of what would now be called economic development. He even thought of slavery. In his mind there seemed to combine and struggle the two different strains that, curiously enough, appear also in his name: Christbearer; colonizer. He raised crosses everywhere, but he kept an eye on the material value of things even to the extent of seeing men as goods for sale. His honeymoon with the islanders may have ended on the day when he removed by force seven of the inhabitants of Guanahaní. They began then and there to think of the Spaniards as only a shade less tyrannical than the *caniba* or "cannibals," who from islands further south came to take them away and eat them. Columbus was convinced that these *caniba* were the subjects of the great can or khan. This "fact" persuaded him that a big island, so often mentioned by the islanders as Cuba was Cipango itself. This became the more certain in his mind when he found that in Cuba, when he asked where gold "was born," he was told: "In Cubanacan" (*nacan* meaning the centre of the island). He sent Luis de Torres to interview the khan, but Torres found neither the khan nor the source of gold. He did, however, discover a greater source of wealth—tobacco. The fleet sailed on. On November 21 Pinzón and his "Pinta" vanished before a strong east wind. Columbus was worried. Had Pinzón gone to discover the source of gold and to talk to the great khan before him? Or worse still, had he sailed to Spain to steal from Colum-

bus the glory of the discovery? In search of his vanished second-in-command he arrived in what is now Haiti.

Columbus was so struck by the beauty of this island that he renamed it Española (Hispaniola), "the Spanish island" (he usually thought in terms of Spain as a whole, not of Castile or Aragon). He praised the natives for their intelligence, industry, and handsomeness and thought that "they are good to be ordered and made to work, sow and do all that is necessary and to adopt our ways." At this point the "Santa Maria" ran aground in a strong wind and became a total loss. It happened exactly at midnight on Christmas Day, 1492. The "Pinta" was not available, and Columbus lost no time persuading himself that God meant him to leave behind an establishment with all the men and stores he could not carry back in the "Niña." He named his establishment Villa de la Navidad, and chose 38 men to remain there under Diego de Arana, a relative of his mistress Beatriz Enríquez. Columbus left them food and stores for a year, including ammunition—so that the natives should obey "with love and fear"—and sailed for Spain on January 4, 1493.

On January 6 the "Pinta" joined the "Niña." Columbus sailed back 40 miles (64 kilometres) to seek a safe anchorage and he and Pinzón went through a stormy scene on board the "Niña." Columbus rejected Pinzón's explanations and threatened to have him hanged from the castle door, which, Pinzón declared, "is what I deserve for having raised you to the honour in which you stand." The quarrel was patched up, although the two men remained estranged. Columbus was worried about the men he had left behind—a decision of which Pinzón strongly disapproved—and also by astrological considerations, as well as by his own struggle between haste to return and report and curiosity to explore. At last, on January 16, 1493, he sailed for Europe.

Columbus deliberately chose a more northerly course, roughly on the parallel of Cape St. Vincent, for his return voyage. The first weeks were happy and carefree,

Return to Spain

but in mid-February the ships met storms that threatened to drown the explorers. During the night of February 14 both captains seem to have resigned themselves to let the wind do as it pleased; they signalled throughout the night but by dawn they had lost sight of each other. The storm raged on. Tormented by the thought that his discovery might remain unknown, Columbus wrote out its story and entrusted it to a cask, which he threw overboard. For four days he went without sleep, but on Monday, February 18, he at last cast anchor at Santa Maria, the southernmost island of the Azores. He was so pleased that he admitted in his journal that he had kept secret the distances covered daily in order to put other sailors off the track of "his" Indies. On February 24, 1493, he sailed for Spain. Worse storms assailed him, but at dawn on March 4, he recognized the Rock of Sintra. He decided to enter the Tagus River. The Portuguese king received him on March 9 with full honours (though some of his courtiers, it appears, would gladly have killed him then and there) and suggested he go to Castile by land; but Columbus preferred his less unsafe element and on March 15 the "Niña" was welcomed enthusiastically as she entered Palos.

Pinzón arrived at Palos soon after having sought, on the same day, refuge in Bayona, near Vigo, from which he wrote to the king and queen a letter loyal to Columbus. He died, exhausted, on March 20. Columbus also wrote to the king and queen who, upon receipt of his letter, wrote to him from Barcelona on March 30 asking him to come to court at once. They feared lest the king of Portugal should steal a march on them, and they wished to send a second expedition as soon as possible; they also obtained two papal bulls granting them the Indies discovered and to be discovered and apportioning the undiscovered parts of the West between the two Iberian powers by a line from pole to pole 100 leagues (345 miles) west of the Azores. The man who had started this keen rivalry between two powerful kingdoms travelled in triumph from Seville to Barcelona, where at the end of April he was received by the king and queen in a scene of solemnity and splendour. The monarchs rose to greet him and offered him a stool. This was but the beginning of a flow of privileges and honours that staggered the court, including the right to display a castle and a lion (royal symbols) on his arms. Wealth and honour were, indeed, his. He nevertheless insisted on being paid the prize of 10,000 maravedis promised to the first man of the crew to see land. The humble sailor who actually had first sighted land went over to Morocco in disappointment and became a renegade. This episode sheds some light on a side of Columbus' character that was to bring him much unhappiness.

Second voyage. Trouble began soon enough with the man the king and queen had put in charge of "Indian" affairs, Juan de Fonseca, afterward bishop of Burgos but far more gifted as a soldier than as either an administrator or an ecclesiastic. Royal letters urged both Columbus and Fonseca to make haste; but the plan for the second expedition was ambitious: 17 vessels in all, manned by 1,000 to 1,500 persons. The material obstacles must therefore have been formidable enough, but much of the trouble came from personal differences between Columbus, Fonseca, and two other officials, Juan de Soria and Francisco Pinelo. Soria was reluctant to treat an upstart like Columbus as a magnificent lord and had to be reprimanded for it by his royal masters, while Columbus himself was impatient of all supervision.

The second fleet was organized on the basis of a memorandum Columbus had prepared more as "colonizer" than as "Christ-bearer." Populating and developing came to the fore, while Christianizing took what was left. But Columbus' ideas were sensible and he even suggested that gold seeking was to be forbidden at certain periods of the year so that settlers could turn their attention to the land. The king and queen, however, added their own ideas: Christianization and welfare of the Indians; assertion of royal sovereignty over the new territories and the men who were sailing; greater stress on land cultivation than on gold. Several priests were sent, a doctor, a

surgeon, peasants, hidalgos, and Columbus' own brother Giacomo, who became known as Don Diego. The fleet sailed from Cádiz on September 25, 1493.

After the usual stay in the Canary Islands to restock food and water and live animals for the New World, Columbus began his second crossing on October 13. He chose a southwesterly course aiming at the mainland; this enabled him to benefit by the trade winds, and on November 3 the expedition sighted land. They had the choice of Dominica and Marigalante (Marie-Galante), and they anchored at the second. The next day they discovered the islands of Guadalupe (Guadeloupe) and, later, Puerto Rico. But Columbus was looking for the mainland. He was also worrying about the men he had left in Española. When he at last arrived there, he found that the Spaniards had been wiped out by the local chiefs. On hearing of the disaster, he remained cool and ordered a search for any gold the massacred men might have buried. He sailed away in search of a better base on the island and kept moving for a month, at the end of which he chose a site and founded the first European city in the New World, Isabella (now a ruined settlement having the same name on the northern coast of the Dominican Republic).

Quarrels and exploration

From Isabella, Columbus sent to Spain his first messenger, Antonio de Torres, of the royal household, with a number of explanations and excuses, as well as proposals, all of which were eventually approved except his scheme for a regular exchange of Spanish cattle for cannibal slaves. The news of the disaster at La Navidad, however, shook faith in him at court. Was the discovery worth the trouble and expense? His credit in the New World was also falling. The chief accountant of the fleet wrote a report on Columbus for Juan de Soria, hiding it in a wooden buoy. Columbus ferreted it out, imprisoned the accountant, and dealt no less severely with other "conspirators." On March 12, 1494, he left for Cibao, a region of the island where gold was believed "to be born," leaving Isabella in the care of his inexperienced brother Diego. In Cibao he founded Santo Tomás, a settlement with a fortress, where he left 56 men under the command of a Catalan captain, Mosèn Pedro Margarite.

On his return to Isabella on March 29 Columbus found the food putrified by the heat, the men hungry and angry. He tried to make them build a mill for the wheat he had brought and punished those who refused. Bernardo Buil, a Catalan friar who had come in charge of spiritual affairs, objected to his harsh ways (Columbus had several men hanged) and a conflict arose between the secular and the spiritual powers. The friar struck the viceroy with interdicts, and the viceroy countered by stopping the friar's rations. He then sent a strong force to relieve Margarite and to explore the island.

Although the situation in Isabella and Santo Tomás was by no means good, Columbus sailed away again (April 24, 1494) taking with him three caravels of the five that remained after Antonio de Torres' departure for Spain with 12; and he again left Isabella in the care of his brother, though now assisted by a council of men all of whom were better qualified than their chairman. Columbus was anxious to explore Cuba, which he sighted on April 29, but, persuaded by a converted Indian, he veered southward and on May 5 discovered Jamaica, which he named Santiago. All of Jamaica's charms, however, could not lure him away from his westward urge, and within eight days he sailed back toward Cuba, determined to find out whether or not it was the mainland. His determination came suddenly to an end on June 13, when he was about 150 miles (241 kilometres) west of the island. He decided to return to Isabella just because he made up his mind that Cuba was the mainland, which he forced everyone in his squadron to swear to on oath, under pain of having their tongues torn out should they recant. He sailed eastward, lingered at the Isle of Pines (which he called Evangelista), and sailed around the southern coast of Jamaica. He then fell ill and remained near death for days. The fleet returned to Isabella on September 29.

Columbus' brother Bartolomé had now arrived and was

put in command with the title of *adelantado* (governor), which, when it became known at court, was rightly considered an encroachment on royal authority. This step increased the discontent prevailing at Isabella. Margarite and Buil had left for Spain with many complaints against Columbus and his brothers. Torres returned with royal letters for the admiral congratulating him on his success and enjoining all and sundry to obey him. But, alleging that the natives were restive, Columbus and Bartolomé left Isabella on March 24, 1495, to "pacify" them—in fact, to take prisoners who could be justified as slaves. After the natives were defeated, Columbus sent his trusted messenger Torres back to Spain with a report, together with his brother Diego and 500 prisoners. His human cargo arrived in Spain when Buil and Margarite had spread their unfavourable views of him. When Juan de Aguado, sent to Hispaniola by the king and queen to report on the situation, landed (October 1495), he found the natives on the point of rebellion because Columbus had imposed a gold tax. A duel of jurisdictions began between Aguado and Columbus; it lasted five months and deeply humiliated the proud viceroy. He decided to leave and appointed Bartolomé as governor and Diego, who had returned from Europe, as his substitute, and sailed for Spain on March 10, 1496, on one of two caravels (the other had Aguado on board) that had been built in the island. Columbus lingered among his islands for weeks and finally began his crossing on April 20. On June 11 his ships—the first two American vessels to arrive in Europe—cast anchor at Cádiz.

Third voyage. Columbus chose to arrive in Franciscan habit as a protection against any further humiliations. He left at once for Seville and Burgos. His adversaries had the ear of the king and queen, but in July he received a royal letter of welcome. He prepared an efficient colonialist, but not very Christian, memorandum for the future organization of the Indies. He still possessed his fire and magnetism, however. He won over his adversaries, had all his privileges confirmed and some of the more material ones substantially increased, and was authorized to populate Española with convicts. He declined a royal offer of an estate in Española, located 50 leagues (172 miles) east–west and 25 leagues (86 miles) north–south with the title of duke or marquess, no doubt feeling that the estate to which he was entitled was no less than the whole New World.

Financial difficulties delayed the third expedition, which did not sail from Sanlúcar until May 30, 1498. It was composed of six ships carrying 200 men, excluding sailors. On June 19 Columbus arrived in Gomera in the Canary Islands, where he rescued some Spanish ships from a French corsair. He then decided to send three of his ships directly to his brother and sail southwest with the other three. With one ship and two caravels he left Gomera on June 21, 1498, and called at the Cape Verde Islands. While anchored in São Tiago, he was told of islands to the south. Southward he sailed in haste until July 13. He then turned west. Had he kept to his course, he would have discovered the Amazon within four days. By July 28 his course was parallel to the mainland he sought and he was only saved from a long frustration by a land crowned with three summits, which was sighted as he had ordered to alter course northward toward Dominica. He named the new land Trinidad. He sailed round the island to the Gulf of Paria, set foot on the mainland but deemed it an island and left in a hurry, drawn by the call of his "mainland"—*i.e.*, Cuba. On a later landing on the Paria Peninsula, the sight of native women wearing pearl necklaces caused great excitement among the Spaniards, who saw in it proof that they were indeed in the Orient. Columbus had, however, time to observe that the gulf received huge and powerful currents of fresh water from what were, in fact, several mouths of the Orinoco River. On this observation he built up his fantastic theory that he was at the mouth of one of the four rivers of paradise, situated at the top of the earth, the earth being not round but pear-shaped.

When Columbus arrived in Española he found that Francisco Roldán, whom he had appointed mayor of Isabella, had rebelled with about 70 followers against Columbus' brothers in Xaraguá (southwestern Española). Bartolomé's attitude to the rebellion had been vigorous; Christopher's was temporizing. He wrote a subservient letter to Roldán; concluded an agreement with him; allowed the rebels to break it. He finally concluded a second agreement that amounted to complete surrender to Roldán, for Roldán's past was condoned and he was appointed *alcalde* (mayor). This done, Columbus sent a messenger to Spain reporting the incident and explaining why the agreement was void since, among other reasons, he had signed it as viceroy but on board a caravel where he was not viceroy but admiral. He felt depressed, and his troubles increased with the sudden arrival on September 5, 1499 of a small fleet he was not expecting. One of his youngest and most enterprising lieutenants, Alonso de Ojeda, while in Seville had heard of Columbus' discovery of pearls in Paria. He thereupon obtained from Fonseca permission to go "discovering," sailed about with varied fortunes and, when short of supplies, calmly turned up at Española. Columbus had every right to consider him a poacher. He sent Roldán with two caravels to meet Ojeda, who listened to Roldán but went his own way to Xaraguá (February 1500). Roldán followed him there. Ojeda left again, but Xaraguá's settlers, who had already been in a state of near rebellion before Ojeda's visit, had to be terrorized into obedience by a capital execution ordered by Columbus himself. The rule of Columbus then came to a sudden end.

Reluctantly and slowly the king and queen had come to the conclusion that Columbus was a good admiral but a bad governor. He himself had written to them in October 1498 asking for a learned man to administer justice in the New World. They chose an old member of their household with an excellent reputation, Francisco de Bobadilla, to whom, in March 1499, they gave powers strictly limited to an enquiry into the rebellion and the punishment of the rebels. A fresh batch of bad news made them go one step further, and on May 21, 1499, Bobadilla was appointed governor and chief magistrate of Española by letters patent in which no mention was made of Columbus. Bobadilla was empowered to send back to Spain any person regardless of rank. A special letter addressed to Columbus and his brothers enjoined them to obey and deliver to Bobadilla all royal property, castles, arms, and stores. But the rest of the year went by and Bobadilla did not sail. There are strong reasons for thinking that the final decision to let him go was because of information the sovereigns had obtained of Columbus' obscure dealings, bordering on treason, with Genoese agents.

Bobadilla arrived at Santo Domingo in Española on August 23, 1500. Before the wind allowed him to land he was informed by a messenger sent out by Diego that several Spaniards had been hanged that week and five more were waiting for the gallows. He was also told that Christopher Columbus was in Concepción and Bartolomé in Xaraguá, each with a confessor to dispatch guilty prisoners by the same method. On August 24, Bobadilla, after mass, had his first dispatch read aloud—that appointing him inquirer into the rebellion—and asked for all prisoners to be handed over. Diego refused. Next day, after mass, he had his second dispatch read—that appointing him governor. Obstructed again, he had all his guns unmasked and revealed the royal letter enjoining him to pay all arrears of salaries, if need be, on Columbus' account. On Diego's persistent refusal, Bobadilla forced his way into the citadel and took possession of the prisoners. On September 15, Bobadilla met Columbus, who refused to acknowledge the appointment on the ground that the king and queen could not deprive him of his position. Bobadilla had both him and Diego arrested and put in chains. Bartolomé, who in Xaraguá "had 16 Spaniards in a ditch or well waiting to be hanged," was summoned to Santo Domingo and also shackled. When he was brought to embark for Spain, Columbus feared that he was being conveyed to the gallows. Though he was treated with respect throughout the voyage he refused to be unchained. Sad, and with his irons still on, he

Columbus removed from command

landed in Cádiz toward the end of November 1500. The king and queen, who were at Granada, were shocked at the news, ordered him to be set free and sent him 2,000 ducats to enable him and his brother to come to court. When Columbus saw his royal patrons, he stood dumb with emotion, then fell on his knees and burst into tears.

The king and queen were sympathetic and generous, but by no means disposed to alter their view as to the political capacity of the admiral. They probably disapproved of the harsh ways of Bobadilla but not, in general, of his handling of a delicate and possibly dangerous situation. Though legally bound by their agreement with Columbus, they had to consider that the land already discovered far exceeded their expectations and that he was no man to be entrusted with a government. Generous with him they could afford to be, but not at the cost of the public good. On the other hand, Columbus, now frustrated in his dreams of greatness in the New World, cast about for another grand work to achieve and found it in his biblical, prophetic mind: he would liberate Jerusalem. He did not need to consult cosmographers, merchants, or ambassadors. He read the prophets and having collected all the texts he could showing that Jerusalem would be liberated by Spain, he presented his *Book of Prophecies* to the king and queen.

Meanwhile, a crowd of discoverers was sailing his seas, landing in his islands, and stealing his future discoveries; French and English sailors were astir: everybody seemed to be entering the business to a point that made Columbus write bitterly: "They all made fun of my plan then; now even tailors wish to discover." That was all very well, but how was he going to liberate Jerusalem if he were not allowed to find more gold in that New World where gold was born? The king and queen were willing, provided he did not return to Española; and he suggested a search for a passage through the newly discovered lands to the other seas.

Last voyage. Nicolás de Ovando, appointed governor to succeed Bobadilla, sailed for Española from Sanlúcar on February 13, 1502, in command of 32 ships, 2,500 men, and 12 Franciscan friars. He carried orders to restore to Columbus his property confiscated by Bobadilla. A few months earlier, in October 1501, Columbus had felt confident enough to go to Seville to prepare his fourth expedition. He bought four ships of about 50–60 tons, which he thought the best size for discovery, and he selected 146 men. He left his eldest son Diego (then 21) to represent him at court, and took with him his younger boy, Fernando (then 13). He asked to be allowed to call at Española and was expressly forbidden to do so, at any rate on the way out. He sailed from Cádiz on May 9, 1502.

On May 25 Columbus began his crossing from the Canary Islands and on June 15, 1502, he discovered an island he called Matininó (Martinique), one of the Lesser Antilles. A few days later he sailed straight for Santo Domingo (now the capital city of the Dominican Republic). Ovando refused him admittance, and he left for Puerto Hermoso, 16 leagues (55 miles) to the west, where he sheltered from a storm. He produced pretexts for his disobedience to royal orders, but the true reason was his stiff-necked reluctance to bow before authority; it was but natural that he should regard as his those lands he had brought to light. He sailed for Jamaica on July 14, 1502, overcame a mutiny of his men, sailed along the coast of Honduras, and was at Cape Gracias a Dios on September 14. His men were mutinous again, but he sailed on, wandering in lands of his imagination. He wrote to the king and queen that "from there to the river Ganges there are ten days," and he referred again to the earthly paradise. Formidable storms all but smashed his ships. On Epiphany Sunday, 1503, he was pushed by the wind into a kind of estuary he named Belén (Bethlehem). As there seemed to be gold about, he resolved to leave his brother Bartolomé there with 80 men; but because of the hostility of the natives he had to give up the plan and sail away,

in the name of the Holy Trinity, on Easter night, with the ships rotten, worm eaten, all in holes. Two only remained in

the same state, boatless, empty of supplies, to cross 7,000 miles [11,263 kilometres] of sea with a son, a brother and so many men.

On May 13, 1503, he was "in Mango province (Panama), which is next to that of Cathay, and from there I sailed towards Española." His geography remained that mixture of scientific truth and wild fantasy that his whole life incarnates. After more storms, mutinies, imprecations to God, and narrow escapes, he found himself derelict in a small cove in Jamaica (June 23, 1503) whence he wrote to the king and queen a truly magnificent letter, telling them of his perils, wanderings, dreams, and voices he heard from on high, in a style worthy of the Old Testament.

For a whole year, Columbus struggled against all of his usual troubles: indiscipline, native restlessness, ill health, lack of shelter and food, doubt and disillusionment. He had sent a messenger to ask Ovando for help. Two caravels arrived late in the spring, and at last he was able to sail for Española on June 28, 1504 and for Spain on September 12. Storms pursued him again in his last crossing, but he landed safely in Sanlúcar on November 7, 1504. Crippled by arthritis, he could hardly move and had to be conveyed to Seville; travelling north was out of the question. On November 26, 1504, Queen Isabella died. Columbus hoped that she had provided in her will for him to be "restored in the possession of the Indies." His hopes were disappointed, and he wrote to his son to seek the help of King Ferdinand's men. He wrote memoir upon memoir on the Indies and their gold. Sick in body, but worse still in mind with humiliation, frustration, and impatience, he was not able to move northward until May 1505, when he was received by Ferdinand in Segovia, and asked to be restored "the capital of my honour . . . the government and possession of the Indies." The king was sympathetic and willing to please Columbus and, on his suggestion, put Columbus' old friend and staunch supporter Diego de Deza in charge of his affairs. But as a responsible monarch Ferdinand could not reappoint the passionate admiral as governor of the Indies. Columbus' health went from bad to worse. He dictated his will at Valladolid on May 19, 1506, and died the following day.

After the funeral ceremonies at Valladolid, Columbus' remains were in 1513 transferred to the Carthusian monastery of Santa María de las Cuevas in Seville, where the bones of his son Diego were also laid. Exhumed in 1542, the bodies of both were taken to Hispaniola and interred in the cathedral of Santo Domingo. The remains of Christopher Columbus later rested in a tomb in the cathedral of Santo Domingo. In 1948, however, construction of the Columbus Memorial Lighthouse, a huge monument designed as the last resting place of the great admiral, was started on a high cliff at the mouth of the Ozama River in the Dominican Republic.

(marginal note:) Return to Spain and death

BIBLIOGRAPHY. C. FERNANDEZ DURO, *Colón y Pinzón* (1883); SALVADOR DE MADARIAGA, *Christopher Columbus*, new ed. (1949); R.H. MAJOR (ed.), *Select Letters of Christopher Columbus* (Hakluyt Society, 2nd ed., 1870), standard collection of the most important chapters on the life and discoveries of Columbus; SAMUEL ELIOT MORISON, *Admiral of the Ocean Sea: A Life of Christopher Columbus*, 2 vol. (1942), and *Christopher Columbus, Mariner* (1955), two of the finest biographies of Columbus in the English language; M. FERNANDEZ DE NAVARRETE (ed.), *Colección de los viajes y descubrimentos que hicieron por mar los españoles*, 5 vol. (1825–37); MILTON A. RUGOFF (ed.), *The Great Travellers*, 2 vol. (1960), general text on the most important explorers, including Columbus; EARL P. HANSON, *South from the Spanish Main: South America Seen Through the Eyes of Its Discoverers* (1967), an anthology.

(Ed.)

Combinatorics and Combinatorial Geometry

The problems that motivate the various topics throughout this article are similar, though the mathematical objects that are used to express them differ. Toward the latter part of the article the mathematical objects are entirely geometrical. For this reason the general subject matter is expressed under two headings, Combinatorics and Combinatorial Geometry, identifying two closely related areas of mathematics.

Combinatorics

The scope of combinatorics is hard to define with any exactitude. In general, however, it may be said that it is concerned with arrangements, operations, and selections within a finite or a discrete system.

The problems studied with combinatorics

One of the basic problems is to determine the number of possible configurations (*e.g.* graphs, designs, arrays) of a given type. Even when the rules specifying the configuration are relatively simple, enumeration may sometimes present formidable difficulties. The mathematician may have to content himself with finding an approximate answer or at least a good lower and upper bound.

In mathematics, generally, an entity is said to "exist" if a mathematical example satisfies the abstract properties that define the entity. In this sense it may not be apparent that even a single configuration with certain specified properties exists. This situation gives rise to problems of existence and construction. There is again an important class of theorems that guarantee the existence of certain choices under appropriate hypotheses. Besides their intrinsic interest these theorems may be used as existence theorems in various combinatorial problems.

Finally, there are problems of optimization. As an example, a function f, the economic function, assigns the numerical value $f(x)$ to any configuration x with certain specified properties. In this case the problem is to choose a configuration x_0 that minimizes $f(x)$, or makes it ε-minimal—that is, for any number $\varepsilon > 0$, $f(x_0) \leqslant f(x) + \varepsilon$, for all configurations x, with the specified properties.

HISTORY

Early developments. Certain types of combinatorial problems have attracted the attention of mathematicians since early times. Magic squares, for example, which are square arrays of numbers with the property that the rows, columns, and diagonals add up to the same number, occur in the *I Ching*, an old Chinese book dating back to 2200 BC. The binomial coefficients, or integer coefficients in the expansion of $(a + b)^n$, were known to the 12th-century Indian mathematician Bhāskara, who in his *Līlāvatī* ("The Graceful"), dedicated to a beautiful woman, gave the rules for calculating them together with illustrative examples. "Pascal's triangle," a triangular array of binomial coefficients, had been taught by the 13th-century Persian philosopher Naṣīr ad-Dīn aḷ-Ṭūsī.

In the West, combinatorics may be considered to begin in the 17th century with Blaise Pascal and Pierre de Fermat, both of France, who discovered many classical combinatorial results in connection with the development of the theory of probability. The term combinatorial was first used in the modern mathematical sense by the German philosopher and mathematician Gottfried Wilhelm Leibniz in his *Dissertatio de Arte Combinatoria* ("Dissertation Concerning the Combinational Arts"). He foresaw the applications of this new discipline to the whole range of the sciences. The Swiss mathematician Leonhard Euler was finally responsible for the development of a school of authentic combinatorial mathematics beginning in the 18th century. He became the father of graph theory when he settled the Königsberg bridge problem, and his famous conjecture on Latin squares was not resolved until 1959.

Combinatorics before 1920

In England, Arthur Cayley, near the end of the 19th century, made important contributions to enumerative graph theory, and James Joseph Sylvester discovered many combinatorial results. The British mathematician George Boole at about the same time used combinatorial methods in connection with the development of symbolic logic, and the combinatorial ideas and methods of Henri Poincaré, which developed in the early part of the 20th century in connection with the problem of n bodies, have led to the discipline of topology, which occupies the centre of the stage of mathematics. Many combinatorial problems were posed during the 19th century as purely

recreational problems and are identified by such names as "the problem of eight queens" and "the Kirkman school girl problem." On the other hand, the study of triple systems begun by Thomas P. Kirkman in 1847 and pursued by Jakob Steiner, a Swiss-born German mathematician, in the 1850s was the beginning of the theory of design. Among the earliest books devoted exclusively to combinatorics are the German mathematician Eugen Netto's *Lehrbuch der Combinatorik* (1901; "Textbook of Combinatorics") and the British mathematician Percy Alexander MacMahon's *Combinatory Analysis* (1915–16), which provide a view of combinatorial theory as it existed before 1920.

Combinatorics during the 20th century. Many factors have contributed to the quickening pace of development of combinatorial theory since 1920. One of these was the development of the statistical theory of the design of experiments by the English statisticians Ronald Fisher and Frank Yates, which has given rise to many problems of combinatorial interest; the methods initially developed to solve them have found applications in such fields as coding theory. Information theory, which arose around midcentury, has also become a rich source of combinatorial problems of a quite new type.

Another source of the revival of interest in combinatorics is graph theory, the importance of which lies in the fact that graphs can serve as abstract models for many different kinds of schemes of relations among sets of objects. Its applications extend to operations research, chemistry, statistical mechanics, theoretical physics, and socio-economic problems. The theory of transportation networks can be regarded as a chapter of the theory of directed graphs. One of the most challenging theoretical problems, the four-colour problem (see below) belongs to the domain of graph theory. It has also applications to such other branches of mathematics as group theory.

The development of computer technology in the second half of the 20th century, with its strong impact on science and industry, is a main cause of the interest in finite mathematics in general and combinatorial theory in particular. Combinatorial problems arise not only in numerical analysis but also in the design of computer systems and in the application of computers to such problems as those of information storage and retrieval.

Statistical mechanics is one of the oldest and most productive sources of combinatorial problems. Much important combinatorial work has been done by applied mathematicians and physicists since the mid-20th century—for example, the work on Ising models (see below *The Ising problem*).

Use of combinatorics in pure mathematics

In pure mathematics, combinatorial methods have been used with advantage in such diverse fields as probability, algebra (finite groups and fields, matrix and lattice theory), number theory (difference sets), set theory (Sperner's theorem), and mathematical logic (Ramsey's theorem).

In contrast to the wide range of combinatorial problems and the multiplicity of methods that have been devised to deal with them stands the lack of a central unifying theory. Unifying principles and cross connections have begun to appear in various areas of combinatorial theory, but in the 1970s there was no coherent body of knowledge. The search for an underlying pattern that may indicate in some way how the diverse parts of combinatorics are interwoven is a challenge that faces mathematicians in the last quarter of the 20th century.

PROBLEMS OF ENUMERATION

Permutations and combinations. *Binomial coefficients.* An ordered set $a_1, a_2, \cdots, a_r$ of r distinct objects selected from a set of n objects is called a permutation of n things taken r at a time. The number of permutations is given by $_nP_n = n(n-1)(n-2) \cdots (n-r+1)$. When $r = n$, the number $_nP_r = n(n-1)(n-2) \cdots$ is simply the number of ways of arranging n distinct things in a row. This expression is called factorial n and is denoted by $n!$. It follows that $_nP_r = n!/(n-r)!$. By convention $0! = 1$.

A set of r objects selected from a set of n objects without regard to order is called a combination of n things taken r at a time. Because each combination gives rise to

$r!$ permutations, the number of combinations, which is written $\binom{n}{r}$, can be expressed in terms of factorials (see Box, formula 1).

The number $\binom{n}{r}$ is called a binomial coefficient because it occurs as the coefficient of $p^r q^{n-r}$ in the binomial expansion—that is, the re-expression of $(q + p)^n$ in a linear combination of products of p and q (see 2).

If $0 \leqslant p \leqslant 1$, and $q = 1 - p$, then the term $\binom{n}{r} p^r q^{n-r}$ in the binomial expansion is the probability that an event the chance of occurrence of which is p occurs exactly r times in n independent trials (see PROBABILITY, THEORY OF).

The answer to many different kinds of enumeration problems can be expressed in terms of binomial coefficients. The number of distinct solutions of the equation $x_1 + x_2 + \cdots + x_n = m$, for example, in which m is a non-negative integer $m \geqslant n$ and in which only non-negative integral values of x_i are allowed is expressible this way, as was found by the 17th–18th-century French-born British mathematician Abraham De Moivre (see 3).

Multinomial coefficients. If S is a set of n objects, and $n_1, n_2, \cdots, n_k$ are non-negative integers satisfying $n_1 + n_2 + \cdots + n_k = n$, then the number of ways in which the objects can be distributed into k boxes, $X_1, X_2, \cdots, X_k$, such that the box X_i contains exactly n_i objects is given in terms of a ratio constructed of factorials (see 4). This number, called a multinomial coefficient, is the coefficient in the multinomial expansion of the nth power of the sum of the $\{p_i\}$ (see 5). If all of the $\{p_i\}$ are non-negative and sum to 1 and if there are k possible outcomes in a trial in which the chance of the ith outcome is p_i, then the ith summand in the multinomial expansion is the probability that in n independent trials the ith outcome will occur exactly n_i times, for each i, $1 \leqslant i \leqslant k$.

Recurrence relations and generating functions. If f_n is a function defined on the positive integers, then a relation that expresses f_{n+k} as a linear combination of function values of integer index less than $n + k$, in which a fixed constant in the linear combination is written a_i, is called a recurrence relation (see 6). The relation together with the initial values $f_0, f_1, \cdots, f_{k-1}$ determines f_n for all n. The function $F(x)$ constructed of a sum of products of the type $f_n x^n$, the convergence of which is assumed in the neighbourhood of the origin, is called the generating function of f_n (see 7).

Generating functions

The set of the first n positive integers will be written X_n. It is possible to find the number of subsets of X_n containing no two consecutive integers, with the convention that the null set counts as one set. The required number will be written f_n. A subset of the required type is either a subset of X_{n-1} or is obtained by adjoining n to a subset of X_{n-2}. Therefore f_n is determined by the recurrence relation $f_n = f_{n-1} + f_{n-2}$ with the initial values $f_0 = 1$, $f_1 = 2$. Thus $f_2 = 3$, $f_3 = 5$, $f_4 = 8$, and so on. The generating function $F(x)$ of f_n can be calculated (see 8), and from this a formula for the desired function f_n can be obtained (see 9). That $f_n = f_{n-1} + f_{n-2}$ can now be directly checked.

Recurrence relations and generating functions provide two most important tools for problems of enumeration.

Partitions. A partition of a positive integer n is a representation of n as a sum of positive integers $n = x_1 + x_2 + \cdots + x_k$, $x_i \geqslant 1$, $i = 1, 2, \cdots, k$. The numbers x_i are called the parts of the partition. The number of ordered partitions into k parts is $\binom{n-1}{k-1}$, for this is the number of ways of putting $k-1$ separating marks in the $n-1$ spaces between n dots in a row. The theory of unordered partitions is much more difficult and has many interesting features. An unordered partition can be standardized by listing the parts in a decreasing order. Thus $n = x_1 + x_2 + \cdots + x_k$, $x_1 \geqslant x_2 \geqslant \cdots \geqslant x_k \geqslant 1$. In what follows partition will mean an unordered partition.

The number of partitions of n into k parts will be denoted by $P_k(n)$, and a recurrence formula for it can be obtained from the definition (see 10). This recurrence formula, together with the initial conditions $P_k(n) = 0$ if $n < k$, and $P_k(k) = 1$ determines $P_k(n)$. It can be shown that $P_k(n)$ depends on the value of $n \pmod{k!}$, in which the notation $x = a \pmod{b}$ means that x is any number that, if divided by b, leaves the same remainder as a does. For example, $P_3(n) = n^2 + c_n$, in which $c_n = 0$, $-1/12$, $-1/3$, $+1/4$, $-1/3$ or $-1/12$, according as n is congruent to 0, 1, 2, 3, 4 or 5 $\pmod{6}$. $P(n)$, which is a sum over all values of k from 1 to n of $P_k(n)$, denotes the number of partitions of n into n or fewer parts.

Many results on partitions can be obtained by the use of Ferrers' diagram. The diagram of a partition is obtained by putting down a row of squares equal in number to the largest part, then immediately below it a row of squares equal in number to the next part, and so on. Thus, the Ferrers' diagram of $14 = 5 + 3 + 3 + 2 + 1$ is shown in Figure 1.

Ferrers' partitioning diagram

By rotating the Ferrers' diagram of the partition about the diagonal, it is possible to obtain from the partition $n = x_1 + x_2 + \cdots + x_k$ the conjugate partition $n = x_1^* + x_2^* + \cdots + x_n^*$, in which x_i^* is the number of parts in the original partition of cardinality i or more. Thus the conjugate of the partition of 14 already given is $14 = 5 + 4 + 3 + 1 + 1$. Hence, the following result is obtained:

(F_1) The number of partitions of n into k parts is equal to the number of partitions of n with k as the largest part.

Other results obtainable by using Ferrers' diagrams are:

(F_2) The number of self-conjugate partitions of n equals the number of partitions of n with all parts unequal and odd.

(F_3) the number of partitions of n into unequal parts is equal to the number of partitions of n into odd parts.

$$(1) \quad \binom{n}{r} = \frac{{}_n P_r}{r!} = \frac{n!}{r!(n-r)!}$$

$$(2) \quad (q + p)^n = q^n + \binom{n}{1} pq^{n-1} + \cdots + \binom{n}{r} p^r q^{n-r} + \cdots + p^n$$

$$(3) \quad N = \binom{m+n-1}{n-1} = \frac{(m+n-1)!}{(n-1)!m!}$$

$$(4) \quad \binom{n}{n_1, n_2, \cdots, n_k} = \frac{n!}{n_1! n_2! \cdots n_k!}$$

$$(5) \quad \begin{cases} (p_1 + p_2 + \cdots + p_k)^n \\ = \sum \binom{n}{n_1, n_2, \cdots, n_k} p_1^{n_1} p_2^{n_2} \cdots p_k^{n_k} \\ \text{The summation is over all non-negative } n_1, n_2, \cdots, n_k \\ \text{for which } n_1 + n_2 + \cdots + n_k = n. \end{cases}$$

$$(6) \quad f_{n+k} = a_1 f_{n+k-1} + a_2 f_{n+k-2} + \cdots + a_k f_n$$

$$(7) \quad F(x) = \sum_{n=0}^{\infty} f_n x^n$$

$$(8) \quad F(x) = \frac{1+x}{1 - x(1+x)}$$

$$(9) \quad \begin{cases} f_n = \sum_k \binom{n+1-k}{k} \\ \text{The summation extends over all values of } k \text{ from 0 to} \\ \text{the largest integer not exceeding } (n+1)/2. \end{cases}$$

$$(10) \quad P_k(n) = P_k(n-k) + P_{k-1}(n-k) + \cdots + P_1(n-k)$$

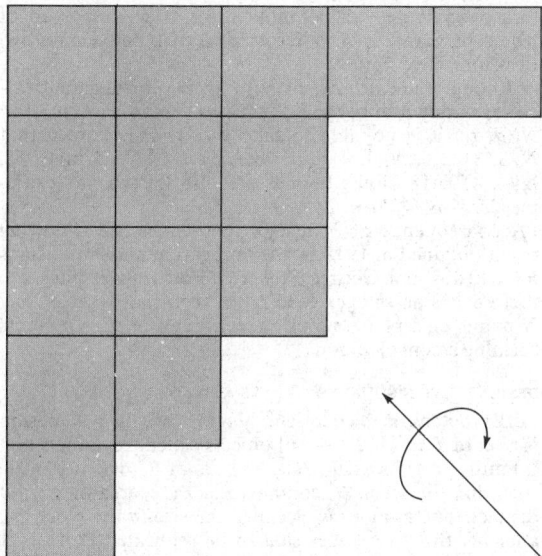

Figure 1: Ferrers' partitioning diagram for 14 (see text).

Generating functions can be used with advantage to study partitions. For example, it can be proved that:

(G_1) The generating function $F_1(x)$ of $P(n)$, the number of partitions of the integer n, is a product of reciprocals of terms of the type $(1 - x^k)$, for all positive integers k, with the convention that $P(0) = 1$ (see 11).

(G_2) The generating function $F_2(x)$ of the number of partitions of n into unequal parts is a product of terms like $(1 + x^k)$, for all positive integers k (see 12).

(G_3) The generating function $F_3(x)$ of the number of partitions of x consisting only of odd parts is a product of reciprocals of terms of the type $(1 - x^k)$, for all positive odd integers k (see 13).

Thus to prove (F_3) it is necessary only to show that the generating functions described in (G_2) and (G_3) are equal. This method was used by Euler.

The principle of inclusion and exclusion: derangements. For a case in which there are N objects and n properties $A_1, A_2, \cdots A_n$, the number $N(A_1, A_2)$, for example, will be the number of objects that possess the properties A_1, A_2. If $N(\bar{A_1}, \bar{A_2}, \cdots, \bar{A_n})$ is the number of objects possessing none of the properties $A_1, A_2, \cdots, A_n$, then this number can be computed as an alternating sum of sums involving the numbers of objects that possess the properties (see 14). This is the principle of inclusion and exclusion expressed by Sylvester.

Sylvester principle

The permutation of n elements that displaces each object is called a derangement. The permutations themselves may be the objects and the property i may be the property that a permutation does not displace the ith element. In such a case $N = n!$ and $N(A_1, A_2) = (n - 2)!$, for example. Hence the number D_n of derangements can be shown to be approximated by $n!/e$ (see 15). This number was first obtained by Euler. If n persons check their hats in a restaurant, and the waiter loses the checks and returns the hats at random, the chance that no one receives his own hat is $D_n/n! = e^{-1}$ approximately. It is surprising that the approximate answer is independent of n. To six places of decimals $e^{-1} = 0.367879$. When $n = 6$ the error of approximation is less than 0.0002.

If n is expressed as the product of powers of its prime factors $p_1, p_2, \cdots p_k$, and if the objects are the integers less than or equal to n, and if A_i is the property of being divisible by p_i, then Sylvester's formula gives, as the number of integers less than n and prime to it, a function of n, written $\phi(n)$, composed of a product of n and k factors of the type $(1 - 1/p_i)$ (see 16). The function $\phi(n)$ is the Euler function.

The number of necklaces and Polya's theorem. It is required to make a necklace of n beads out of an infinite supply of beads of k different colours. The number of different necklaces, $c(n, k)$, that can be made is given by the reciprocal of n times a sum of terms of the type

$\phi(n) \, k^{n/d}$, in which the summation is over all divisors d of n and ϕ is the Euler function (see 17).

Though the problem of the necklaces appears to be frivolous, the formula given above can be used to solve a difficult problem in the theory of Lie algebras, of some importance in modern physics.

The general problem of which the necklace problem is a special case was solved by the Hungarian-born U.S. mathematician George Polya in a famous 1937 memoir in which he established connections between groups, graphs, and chemical bonds. It has been applied to many important enumeration problems in physics, chemistry, and mathematics.

The Möbius inversion theorem. In 1832 the German astronomer and mathematician August Ferdinand Möbius proved that, if f and g are functions defined on the set of positive integers, such that f evaluated at x is a sum of values of g evaluated at divisors of x, then inversely g at x can be evaluated as a sum involving f evaluated at divisors of x (see 18).

More recently in 1964, in the United States, mathematician Gian-Carlo Rota obtained a powerful generalization of this theorem, providing a fundamental unifying principle of enumeration. One consequence of Rota's theorem, for example, is the following:

(11) $\quad F_1(x) = (1 - x)^{-1}(1 - x^2)^{-1}(1 - x^3)^{-1} \cdots$

(12) $\quad F_2(x) = (1 + x)(1 + x^2)(1 + x^3) \cdots$

(13) $\quad F_3(x) = (1 - x)^{-1}(1 - x^3)^{-1}(1 - x^5)^{-1} \cdots$

(14) $\quad \begin{cases} N(\overline{A_1}, \overline{A_2}, \cdots, \overline{A_n}) \\ = N - \sum N(A_{i_1}) + \sum N(A_{i_1}, A_{i_2}) + \cdots + \\ \quad + (-1)^k \sum N(A_{i_1}, A_{i_2}, \cdots, A_{i_k}) + \cdots + \\ \quad + (-1)^n N(A_1, A_2, \cdots, A_n) \\ \text{In the general term the summation is over all} \\ \text{combinations of } k \text{ properties from the set of } n \\ \text{properties} \quad A_1, A_2, \cdots, A_n. \end{cases}$

(15) $\quad \begin{cases} D_n = n! - \binom{n}{1}(n-1)! + \cdots + (-1)^k \binom{n}{k}(n-k)! + \\ \quad + \cdots + (-1)^n \binom{n}{n} \\ = n!\left(1 - \dfrac{1}{1!} + \dfrac{1}{2!} + \cdots + (-1)^k \dfrac{1}{k!} + \right. \\ \quad \left. + \cdots + (-1)^n \dfrac{1}{n!}\right) \\ = n!/e \quad \text{approximately.} \end{cases}$

(16) $\quad \phi(n) = n\left(1 - \dfrac{1}{p_1}\right)\left(1 - \dfrac{1}{p_2}\right) \cdots \left(1 - \dfrac{1}{p_k}\right)$

(17) $\quad c(n, k) = \dfrac{1}{n} \sum_{d|n} \phi(d) k^{n/d}$

(18) $\quad \begin{cases} \text{If} \quad f(x) = \sum_{d|x} g(d), \\ \text{in which } d|x \text{ means that } d \text{ is a divisor of } x, \text{ then} \\ g(x) = \sum_{d|x} \mu(d, x) f(d), \\ \text{in which} \\ \mu(d, n) = \begin{cases} 1 & \text{if } n = d \\ (-1)^k & \text{if } n = p_1 p_2 \cdots p_k d \\ 0 & \text{otherwise.} \end{cases} \end{cases}$

If f and g are functions defined on subsets of a finite set A, such that $f(A)$ is a sum of terms $g(S)$, in which S is a subset of A, then $g(A)$ can be expressed in terms of f (see 19).

Special problems. Despite the general methods of enumeration already described, there are many problems in which they do not apply and which therefore require special treatment. Two of these are described below, and others will be met further in this article.

The Ising problem. A rectangular $m \times n$ grid is made up of unit squares, each coloured either red or green. How many different colour patterns are there if the number of boundary edges between red squares and green squares is prescribed?

This problem, though easy to state, proved very difficult to solve. A complete and rigorous solution was not achieved until the early 1960s. The importance of the problem lies in the fact that it is the simplest model that exhibits the macroscopic behaviour expected from certain natural assumptions at the microscopic level. Historically, the problem arose from an early attempt (1925) to formulate the statistical mechanics of ferromagnetism.

The three-dimensional analogue of the Ising problem remains unsolved in spite of persistent attacks.

Non-self-intersecting random walk. A random walk consists of a sequence of steps of unit length on a flat rectangular grid, taken at random either in the x- or the y-direction, with equal probability in each of the four directions. What is the number R_n of random walks of length n that do not touch the same vertex twice? This problem has defied solution, except for small values of n, though a large amount of numerical data has been amassed by the physicists.

PROBLEMS OF CHOICE

Systems of distinct representatives. Subsets $S_1, S_2, \cdots$, S_n of a finite set S are said to possess a set of distinct representatives if $x_1, x_2, \cdots, x_n$ can be found, such that $x_i \in S_i$, $i = 1, 2, \cdots, n$, $x_i \neq x_j$ for $i \neq j$. It is possible that S_i and S_j, $i \neq j$, may have exactly the same elements and are distinguished only by the indices i, j. In 1935 a mathematician, M. Hall, Jr., of the United States, proved that a necessary and sufficient condition for $S_1, S_2, \cdots, S_n$ to possess a system of distinct representatives is that, for every $k \leqslant n$, any k of the n subsets contain between them at least k distinct elements.

Hall's and König's theorems

For example, the sets $S_1 = (1, 2, 2)$, $S_2 = (1, 2, 4)$, $S_3 = (1, 2, 5)$, $S_4 = (3, 4, 5, 6)$, $S_5 = (3, 4, 5, 6)$ satisfy the conditions of the theorem, and a set of distinct representatives is $x_1 = 1$, $x_2 = 2$, $x_3 = 5$, $x_4 = 3$, $x_5 = 4$. On the other hand, the sets $T_1 = (1, 2)$, $T_2 = (1, 3)$, $T_3 = (1, 4)$, $T_4 = (2, 3)$, $T_5 = (2, 4)$, $T_6 = (1, 2, 5)$ do not possess a system of distinct representatives because T_1, T_2, T_3, T_4, T_5 possess between them only four elements.

The following theorem due to König is closely related to Hall's theorem and can be easily deduced from it. Conversely, Hall's theorem can be deduced from König's: If the elements of rectangular matrix are 0s and 1s, the minimum number of lines that contain all of the 1s is equal to the maximum number of 1s that can be chosen with no two on a line.

Ramsey's numbers. If $X = \{1, 2, \cdots, n\}$, and if T, the family of all subsets of X containing exactly r distinct elements, is divided into two mutually exclusive families α and β, the following conclusion that was originally obtained by the British mathematician Frank Plumpton Ramsey follows. He proved that for $r \geqslant 1$, $p \geqslant r$, $q \geqslant r$, there exists a number $N_r(p, q)$ depending solely on p, q, r, such that if $n > N_r(p, q)$, there is either a subset A of p elements all of the r subsets of which are in the family α or there is a subset B of q elements all of the r subsets of which are in the family β.

The set X can be a set of n persons. For $r = 2$, T is the family of all pairs. If two persons have met each other the pair can belong to the family α. If two persons have not met, the pair can belong to the family β. If these things are assumed, then by Ramsey's theorem, for any given $p \geqslant 2$, $q \geqslant 2$ there exists a number $N_2(p, q)$, such that if $n > N_2(p, q)$, then among n persons invited

to a party there will be either a set of p persons all of whom have met each other or a set of q persons no two of whom have met.

Although the existence of $N_r(p, q)$ is known, actual values are known only for a few cases. Because $N_r(p, q) = N_r(q, p)$, it is possible to take $p \leqslant q$. It is known that $N_2(3, 3) = 6$, $N_2(3, 4) = 9$, $N_2(3, 5) = 14$, $N_2(3, 6) = 18$, $N_2(4, 4) = 18$. Some bounds are also known, for example, $25 \leqslant N_2(4, 5) \leqslant 28$.

A consequence of Ramsey's theorem is the following result obtained in 1935 by the Hungarian mathematicians Paul Erdös and George Szekeres. For a given integer n there exists an integer $N = N(n)$, such that a set of any N points on a plane, no three on a line, contains n points forming a convex n-gon.

DESIGNS, LATIN SQUARES, ARRAYS AND CODING

BIB (balanced incomplete block) designs. A design is a set of $T = \{1, 2, \cdots, v\}$ objects called treatments and a family of subsets $B_1, B_2, \cdots, B_b$ of T, called blocks, such that the block B_i contains exactly k_i treatments, all distinct. The number k_i is called the size of the block B_i, and the ith treatment is said to be replicated r_i times if it occurs in exactly r_i blocks. Specific designs are subject to further constraints. The name design comes from statistical theory in which designs are used to estimate effects of treatments applied to experimental units.

A BIB design is a design with v treatments and b blocks in which each block is of size k, each treatment is replicated r times, and every pair of distinct treatments occurs together in λ blocks. The design is said to have the parameters (v, b, r, k, λ). Some basic relations are easy to establish (see 20). These conditions are necessary but not sufficient for the existence of the design. The design is said to be proper if $k < v$—that is, the blocks are incomplete. For a proper BIB design Fisher's inequality $b \geqslant v$, or equivalently $r \geqslant k$, holds.

A BIB design is said to be symmetric if $v = b$, and consequently $r = k$. Such a design is called a symmetric (v, k, λ) design, and $\lambda(v - 1) = k(k - 1)$. A necessary condition for the existence of a symmetric (v, k, λ) design is given by the following:

BIB design symmetry

A. If v is even, $k - \lambda$ is a perfect square.

B. If v is odd, a certain Diophantine equation (see 21) has a solution in integers not all zero.

For example, the designs $(v, k, \lambda) = (22, 7, 2)$ and $(46, 10, 2)$ are ruled out by (A) and the design $(29, 8, 2)$ by (B).

Because necessary and sufficient conditions for the existence of a BIB design with given parameters are not known, it is often a very difficult problem to decide whether a design with given parameters (satisfying the known necessary conditions) really exists. By 1972 there were only two unsettled cases with $r \leqslant 10$. These are $(v, b, r, k, \lambda) = (46, 69, 9, 6, 1)$ and $(51, 85, 10, 6, 1)$.

Methods of constructing BIB designs depend on the use of finite fields, finite geometries, and number theory. Some general methods were given in 1939 by the Indian mathematician Raj Chandra Bose, who has since emigrated to the United States.

A finite field is a finite set of marks with two operations, addition and multiplication, subject to the usual nine laws of addition and multiplication obeyed by rational numbers. In particular the marks may be taken to be the set X of non-negative integers less than a prime p. If this is so, then addition and multiplication are defined by modified addition and multiplication laws (see 22) in which a, b, r, and p belong to X. For example, if $p = 7$, then $5 + 4 = 2$, $5 \cdot 4 = 6$. There exist more general finite fields in which the number of elements is p^n, p a prime. There is essentially one field with p^n elements, with given p and n. It is denoted by $GF(p^n)$.

Finite geometries can be obtained from finite fields in which the coordinates of points are now elements of a finite field.

A set of $k + 1$ non-negative integers $d_0, d_1, \cdots, d_k$, is said to form a perfect difference set mod v, if among the $k(k - 1)$ differences $d_i - d_j$, $i \neq j$, $i, j = 0, 1, \cdots, k$, reduced mod v, each nonzero positive integer less than v

occurs exactly the same number of times λ. For example, 1, 4, 5, 9, 3 is a difference set mod 11, with $\lambda = 2$. From a perfect difference set can be obtained the symmetric (v, k, λ) design using the integers 0, 1, 2, $\cdots$, $v - 1$. The jth block contains the treatments obtained by reducing mod v the numbers $d_0 + j, d_1 + j, \cdots, d_i + j, j = 0, 1, \cdots, v - 1$.

It can be shown that any two blocks of a symmetric (v, k, λ) design intersect in exactly k treatments. By deleting one block and all the treatments contained in it, it is possible to obtain from the symmetric design its residual, which is a BIB design (unsymmetric) with parameters $v^* = v - k$, $b^* = v - 1$, $r^* = k$, $k^* = k - \lambda$, $\lambda^* = \lambda$. One may ask whether it is true that a BIB design with the parameters of a residual can be embedded in a symmetric BIB design. The truth of this is rather easy to demonstrate when $\lambda = 1$. Hall and W.S. Connor in 1953 showed that it is also true for $\lambda = 2$. The Indian mathematician K.N. Bhattacharya in 1944, however, gave a counter example for $\lambda = 3$ by exhibiting a BIB design with parameters $v = 16$, $b = 24$, $r = 9$, $k = 6$, $\lambda = 3$ for which two particular blocks intersect in four treatments and which for that reason cannot be embedded in a symmetric BIB design.

A BIB design is said to be resolvable if the set of blocks can be partitioned into subsets, such that the blocks in any subset contain every treatment exactly once. For the case $k = 3$ this problem was first posed during the 19th century by the British mathematician T.P. Kirkman as a recreational problem. There are v girls in a class. Their teacher wants to take the class out for a walk for a number of days, the girls marching abreast in triplets. It is required to arrange the walk so that any two girls march abreast in the same triplet exactly once. It is easily shown that this is equivalent to the construction of a resolvable BIB design with $v = 6t + 3$, $b = (2t + 1)(3t + 1)$, $r = 3t + 1$, $k = 3$, $\lambda = 1$. Solutions were known for only a large number of special values of t until a completely general solution was finally given by the Indian and U.S. mathematicians Dwijendra K. Ray-Chaudhuri and R.M. Wilson in 1970.

PBIB (partially balanced incomplete block) designs. Given v objects 1, 2, $\cdots$, v, a relation satisfying the following conditions is said to be an m-class partially balanced association scheme:

Conditions for PBIB designs

A. Any two objects are either 1st, or 2nd, $\cdots$, or mth associates, the relation of association being symmetrical.

B. Each object α has n_i ith associates, the number n_i being independent of α.

C. If any two objects α and β are ith associates, then the number of objects that are jth associates of α and kth associates of β is $p_{jk}{}^i$ and is independent of the pair of ith associates α and β.

The constants v, n_i, $p_{jk}{}^i$ are the parameters of the association scheme. A number of identities connecting these parameters were given by the Indian mathematicians Bose and K.R. Nair in 1939, but Bose and the U.S. mathematician D.M. Mesner in 1959 discovered new identities when $m > 2$.

A PBIB design is obtained by identifying the v treatments with the v objects of an association scheme and arranging them into b blocks satisfying the following conditions:

A. Each contains k treatments.

B. Each treatment occurs in r blocks.

C. If two treatments are ith associates, they occur together in λ_i blocks.

Two-class association schemes and the corresponding designs are especially important both from the mathematical point of view and because of statistical applications. For a two-class association scheme the constancy of v, n_i, $p_{11}{}^1$ and $p_{11}{}^2$ ensures the constancy of the other parameters. Seven relations hold (see 23). Sufficient conditions for the existence of association schemes with given parameters are not known, but for a two-class association scheme Connor and the U.S. mathematician Willard H. Clatworthy in 1954 obtained some necessary conditions (see 24).

(19) $\begin{cases} \text{If} \quad f(A) = \sum\limits_{S \subset A} g(S), \\ \text{then} \quad g(A) = \sum\limits_{S \subset A} (-1)^{|A| - |S|} f(S). \end{cases}$

(20) $bk = vr, \qquad \lambda(v - 1) = r(k - 1)$

(21) $x^2 = (k - \lambda)y^2 + (-1)^{(v-1)/2}\lambda z^2$

(22) $a + b = s \pmod{p}, \qquad ab = c \pmod{p}$

(23) $\begin{cases} p_{12}^1 = n_1 - p_{11}^1 - 1 = p_{21}^1, \qquad p_{22}^1 = n_2 - n_1 + p_{11}^1 + 1 \\ p_{12}^2 = n_1 - p_{11}^2 = p_{21}^2, \qquad p_{22}^2 = n_2 - n_1 + p_{11}^2 \\ v = n_1 + n_2 + 1, \qquad n_1 p_{12}^1 = n_2 p_{11}^2, \qquad n_1 p_{22}^1 = n_2 p_{12}^2 \end{cases}$

(24) $\begin{cases} \alpha_1, \alpha_2 = \dfrac{n_1 + n_2}{2} \pm \dfrac{(n_1 - n_2) + \gamma(n_1 + n_2)}{2\sqrt{\Delta}} \\ \text{These numbers must be non-negative integers, in which} \\ \gamma = p_{12}^2 - p_{12}^1, \qquad \Delta = (p_{12}^2 - p_{12}^1)^2 + 2(p_{12}^2 + p_{12}^1) + 1. \end{cases}$

(25) If $k = p_1^{n_1} p_2^{n_2} \cdots p_u^{n_u}$, $n(k) = \min(p_1^{n_1}, p_2^{n_2}, \cdots, p_u^{n_u})$

Orthogonal Latin squares. A Latin square of order k is defined as a $k \times k$ square grid, the k^2 cells of which are occupied by k distinct symbols of a set $X = 1, 2, \cdots, k$, such that each symbol occurs once in each row and each column. Two Latin squares are said to be orthogonal if, when superposed, any symbol of the first square occurs exactly once with each symbol of the second square. Two orthogonal Latin squares of order 4 are exhibited in Figure 2.

A set of mutually orthogonal Latin squares is a set of Latin squares any two of which are orthogonal. It is easily shown that there cannot exist more than $k - 1$ mutually orthogonal Latin squares of a given order k. When $k - 1$ mutually orthogonal Latin squares of order k exist, the set is complete. A complete set always exists if k is the power of a prime. The study of orthogonal Latin squares was initiated by Euler in 1783. An important unsolved question is whether there can exist a complete set of mutually orthogonal Latin squares of order k if k is not a prime power.

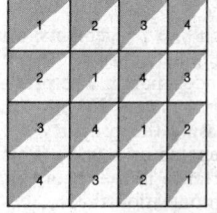 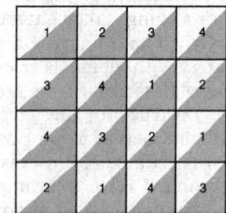

Figure 2: Two orthogonal Latin squares of order 4 and their superposition.

Many types of experimental designs are based on Latin squares. Hence, the construction of mutually orthogonal Latin squares is an important combinatorial problem. Letting the prime power decomposition of an integer k be given, the arithmetic function $n(k)$ is defined by taking the minimum of the factors in such a decomposition (see 25).

Euler's conjecture

Letting $N(k)$ denote the maximum number of mutually orthogonal Latin squares of order k, the U.S. mathematician H.F. MacNeish in 1922 showed that there always exist $n(k)$ mutually orthogonal Latin squares of order k and conjectured that this is the maximum number of such squares—that is, $N(k) = n(k)$. There was also the longstanding conjecture of Euler, formulated in 1782, that there cannot exist mutually orthogonal Latin squares of order $4t + 2$, for any integer t. MacNeish's conjecture, if true, would imply the truth of Euler's but not conversely. The U.S. mathematician E.T. Parker in 1958 disproved the conjecture of MacNeish. This left open the question of Euler's conjecture. Bose and the Indian mathematician S.S. Shrikhande in 1959–60 obtained the first counter-example to Euler's conjecture by obtaining two mutually orthogonal Latin squares of order 22 and then generalized their method to disprove Euler's conjecture for an infinity of values of $k = 2 \pmod 4$. Parker in 1959 used the method of differences to show the falsity of Euler's conjecture for all $k = (3q + 1)/2$, in which q is a prime power, $q \equiv 3 \pmod 4$. Finally these three mathematicians in 1960 showed that $N(k) \geqslant 2$ whenever $k > 6$. It is pertinent to inquire about the behaviour of $N(k)$ for large k. The best result in this direction is due to R.M. Wilson in 1971. He shows that $N(k) \geqslant k^{1/17} - 2$ for large k.

Orthogonal arrays and the packing problem. A $k \times N$ matrix A with entries from a set X of $s \geqslant 2$ symbols is called an orthogonal array of strength t, size N, k constraints, and s levels if each $t \times N$ submatrix of A contains all possible $t \times 1$ column vectors with the same frequency λ. The array may be denoted by (N, k, s, t). The number λ is called the index of the array, and $N = \lambda s^t$. This concept is due to the Indian mathematician C.R. Rao and was obtained in 1947.

Orthogonal arrays are a generalization of orthogonal Latin squares. Indeed, the existence of an orthogonal array of k constraints, s levels, strength 2, and index unity is combinatorially equivalent to the existence of a set of $k - 2$ mutually orthogonal Latin squares of order s. For a given λ, s, and t it is an important combinatorial problem to obtain an orthogonal array (N, k, s, t), $N = s^t$, for which the number of constraints k is maximal.

Orthogonal arrays plays an important part in the theory of factorial designs in which each treatment is a combination of factors at different levels. For an orthogonal array $(\lambda s^t, k, s, t)$, $t \geqslant 2$, the number of constraints k satisfies an inequality (see 26) in which λs^t is greater than or equal to a linear expression in powers of $(s - 1)$, with binomial coefficients giving the number of combinations of $k - 1$ or k things taken i at a time ($i \leqslant u$).

Letting $GF(q)$ be a finite field with $q = p^h$ elements, an $n \times r$ matrix with elements from the field is said to have the property P_t if any t rows are independent. The problem is to construct for any given r a matrix H with the maximum number of rows possessing the property P_t. The maximal number of rows is denoted by $n_t(r, q)$. This packing problem is of great importance in the theory of factorial designs and also in communication theory, because the existence of an $n \times r$ matrix with the property P_t leads to the construction of an orthogonal array (q^r, n, q, t) of index unity.

Again $n \times r$ matrices H with the property P_t may be used in the construction of error-correcting codes. A row vector c' is taken as a code word if and only if $c'H = 0$. The code words then are of length n and differ in at least $t + 1$ places. If $t = 2u$, then u or fewer errors of transmission can be corrected if such a code is used. If $t = 2u + 1$, then an additional error can be detected.

A general solution of the packing problem is known only for the case $t = 2$, the corresponding codes being the one-error-correcting codes of the U.S. mathematician Richard W. Hamming. When $t = 3$ the solution is known for general r when $q = 2$ and for general q when $r \leqslant 4$. Thus, $n_2(r, 2) = (q^r - 1)/(q - 1)$, $n_3(r, 2) = 2^{r-1}$, $n_3(3, q) = q + 1$ or $q + 2$, according as q is odd or even. If $q > 2$, then $n_3(4, q) = q^2 + 1$. The case $q = 2$ is especially important because in practice most codes use only two symbols, 0 or 1. Only fairly large values of r are

useful, say, $r \geqslant 25$. The optimum value of $n_t(r, 2)$ is not known. The BCH codes obtained by Bose and Ray-Chaudhuri and independently by the French mathematician Alexis Hocquenghem in 1959 and 1960 are based on a construction that yields an $n \times r$ matrix H with the property P_{2u} in which $r \leqslant mu$, $n = 2^m - 1$, $q = 2$. They can correct up to u errors.

GRAPH THEORY

Definitions. A graph G consists of a non-empty set of elements $V(G)$ and a subset $E(G)$ of the set of unordered pairs of distinct elements of $V(G)$. The elements of $V(G)$, called vertices of G, may be represented by points. If $(x, y) \in E(G)$, then the edge (x, y) may be represented by an arc joining x and y. Then x and y are said to be adjacent, and the edge (x, y) is incident with x and y. If (x, y) is not an edge, then the vertices x and y are said to be nonadjacent. G is a finite graph if $V(G)$ is finite. A graph H is a subgraph of G if $V(H) \subset V(G)$ and $E(H) \subset E(G)$.

A chain of a graph G is an alternating sequence of vertices and edges $x_0, e_1, x_1, e_2, \cdots e_n, x_n$, beginning and ending with vertices in which each edge is incident with the two vertices immediately preceding and following it. This chain joins x_0 and x_n and may also be denoted by $x_0, x_1, \cdots x_n$, the edges being evident by context. The chain is closed if $x_0 = x_n$ and open otherwise. If the chain is closed, it is called a cycle, provided its vertices (other than x_0 and x_n) are distinct and $n \geqslant 3$. The length of a chain is the number of edges in it.

A graph G is labelled when the various v vertices are distinguished by such names as $x_1, x_2, \cdots x_v$. Two graphs G and H are said to be isomorphic (written $G \simeq H$) if there exists a one-one correspondence between their vertex sets that preserves adjacency. For example, G_1 and G_2, shown in Figure 3, are isomorphic under the correspondence $x_i \leftrightarrow y_i$.

Two isomorphic graphs count as the same (unlabelled) graph. A graph is said to be a tree if it contains no cycle —for example, the graph G_3 of Figure 3.

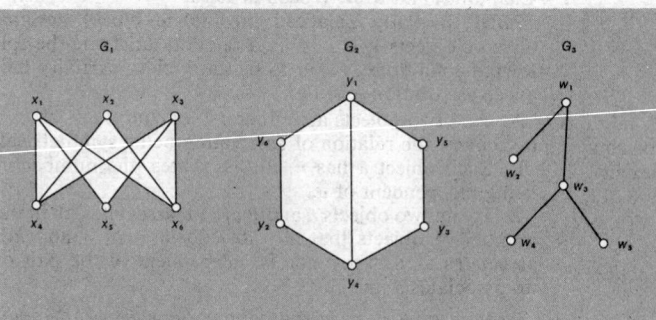

Figure 3: Two isomorphic graphs and a tree (see text).

Enumeration of graphs. The number of labelled graphs with v vertices is $2^{v(v-1)/2}$ because $v(v - 1)/2$ is the number of pairs of vertices, and each pair is either an edge or not an edge. Cayley in 1889 was the first to give corresponding results for trees. He showed that the number of labelled trees with v vertices is v^{v-2}.

The number of unlabelled graphs with v vertices can be obtained by using Polya's theorem. The first few terms of the generating $F(x)$, in which the coefficient of x^v gives the number of (unlabelled) graphs with v vertices, can be given (see 27).

A rooted tree has one point, its root, distinguished from others. If T_v is the number of rooted trees with v vertices, the generating function for T_v can also be given (see 28).

Polya in 1937 showed in his memoir already referred to that the generating function for rooted trees satisfies a functional equation (see 29). Letting t_v be the number of (unlabelled) trees with v vertices, the generating function $t(x)$ for t_v can be obtained in terms of $T(x)$ (see 30). This result was obtained in 1948 by the U.S. mathematician Richard R. Otter.

Many enumeration problems on graphs with specified

properties can be solved by the application of Polya's theorem and a generalization of it made by a Dutch mathematician, N.G. de Bruijn, in 1959.

Characterization problems of graph theory. If there is a class C of graphs each of which possesses a certain set of properties P, then the set of properties P is said to characterize the class C, provided every graph G possessing the properties P belongs to the class C. Sometimes it happens that there are some exceptional graphs that possess the properties P. Many such characterizations are known. Here is presented a typical example.

A complete graph K_m is a graph with m vertices, any two of which are adjacent. The line graph H of a graph G is a graph the vertices of which correspond to the edges of G, any two vertices of H being adjacent if and only if the corresponding edges of G are incident with the same vertex of G.

A graph G is said to be regular of degree n_1 if each vertex is adjacent to exactly n_1 other vertices. A regular graph of degree n_1 with v vertices is said to be strongly regular with parameters $(v, n_1, p_{11}^1, p_{11}^2)$ if any two adjacent vertices are both adjacent to exactly p_{11}^1 other vertices and any two nonadjacent vertices are both adjacent to exactly p_{11}^2 other vertices. A strongly regular graph and a two-class association are isomorphic concepts. The treatments of the scheme correspond to the vertices of the graph, two treatments being first associates or second associates according as the corresponding vertices are adjacent or nonadjacent.

It is easily proved that the line graph $T_2(m)$ of a complete graph K_m, $m \geqslant 4$ is strongly regular with parameters $v = m(m-1)/2$, $n_1 = 2(m-2)$, $p_{11}^1 = m-2$, $p_{11}^2 = 4$.

It is surprising that these properties characterize $T_2(m)$ except for $m = 8$, in which case there exist three other strongly regular graphs with the same parameters nonisomorphic to each other and to $T_2(m)$.

Partial geometries

A partial geometry (r, k, t) is a system of two kinds of objects, points and lines, and a relation incidence obeying the following axioms.

1. Any two points are incident with not more than one line.
2. Each point is incident with r lines.
3. Each line is incident with k points.
4. Given a point P not incident with a line ℓ, there are exactly t lines incident with P and also with some point of ℓ.

A graph G if a partial geometry is obtained by taking the points of the geometry as vertices of G, two vertices of G being adjacent if and only if the corresponding points are incident with the same line of the geometry. It is strongly regular with parameters

$$v = k[(r-1)(k-1)+t]/t, n_1 = r(k-1),$$
$$p_{11}^1 = (r-1)(t-1)+(k-2), p_{11}^2 = rt.$$

The question of whether a strongly regular graph with the above parameters is the graph of some partial geometry is of interest. It was shown by Bose in 1963 that the answer is in the affirmative if a certain condition holds (see 31). Not much is known about the case if this condition is not satisfied, except for certain values of r and t. For example, $T_2(m)$ is isomorphic with the graph of a partial geometry $(2, m-1, 2)$. Hence, for $m > 8$ its characterization is a consequence of the above theorem. Another consequence is the following:

Given a set of k-1-d mutually orthogonal set of Latin squares of order k, the set can be extended to a complete

$$(26) \quad \begin{cases} \lambda s^t \geqslant 1 + \binom{k}{1}(s-1) + \cdots + \binom{k}{u}(s-1)^u, \text{ if } t=2u \\ \lambda s^t \geqslant 1 + \binom{k}{1}(s-1) + \cdots + \binom{k}{u}(s-1)^u + \\ + \binom{k-1}{u}(s-1)^{u+1}, \text{ if } t=2u+1. \end{cases}$$

$$(27) \quad \begin{cases} F(x) = 1 + x + 2x^2 + 4x^3 + 11x^4 + 34x^5 + 156x^6 + \\ + 1{,}044x^7 + 12{,}346x^8 + 308{,}708x^9 + \cdots \end{cases}$$

$$(28) \quad T(x) = \sum_{v=1}^{\infty} T_v x^v = x \prod_{r=1}^{\infty} (1-x^r)^{-T_r}$$

$$(29) \quad T(x) = x \exp \sum_{r=1}^{\infty} \frac{1}{r} T(x^r)$$

$$(30) \quad t(x) = T(x) - \tfrac{1}{2}[T^2(x) - T(x^2)]$$

$$(31) \quad k > \tfrac{1}{2}[r(r-1)+t(r+1)(r^2-2r+2)]$$

$$(32) \quad k > \tfrac{1}{2}(d-1)(d^3-d^2+d+2)$$

set of k-1 mutually orthogonal squares if a condition holds (see 32). The case $d = 2$ is due to Shrikhande in 1961 and the general result to the U.S. mathematician Richard H. Bruck in 1963.

Planar graphs. A graph G is said to be planar if it can be represented on a plane in such a fashion that the vertices are all distinct points, the edges are simple curves, and no two edges meet one another except at their terminals. For example, K_4, the complete graph on four vertices, is planar, as Figure 4A shows.

Two graphs are said to be homeomorphic if both can be obtained from the same graph by subdivisions of edges. For example, the graphs in Figure 4A and Figure 4B are homeomorphic.

The $K_{m,n}$ graph is a graph for which the vertex set can be divided into two subsets, one with m vertices and the other with n vertices. Any two vertices of the same subset are nonadjacent, whereas any two vertices of different subsets are adjacent. The Polish mathematician Kazimierz Kuratowski in 1930 proved the following famous theorem:

A necessary and sufficient condition for a graph G to be planar is that it does not contain a subgraph homeomorphic to either K_5 or $K_{3,3}$ shown in Figure 5.

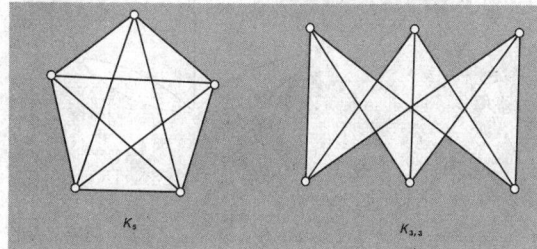

Figure 5: Two graphs important to planar properties (see text).

An elementary contraction of a graph G is a transformation of G to a new graph G_1, such that two adjacent vertices u and v of G are replaced by a new vertex w in G_1 and w is adjacent in G_1 to all vertices to which either u or v is adjacent in G. A graph G^* is said to be a contraction of G if G^* can be obtained from G by a sequence of elementary contractions. The following is another characterization of a planar graph due to the German mathematician K. Wagner in 1937.

A graph is planar if and only if it is not contractible to K_5 or $K_{3,3}$.

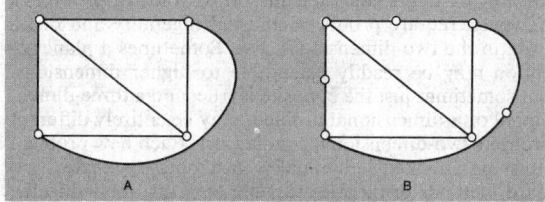

Figure 4: Two homeomorphic graphs A and B (see text).

The four-colour problem. The four-colour problem is one of the great unsolved problems of mathematics, having withstood the efforts of outstanding mathematicians for over a century. The problem is believed to have originated with Möbius in 1840, but the earliest written reference to it occurs in a letter of De Morgan in 1852 in which he attributes it to one of his students.

The problem concerns planar maps—that is, subdivisions of the plane into nonoverlapping regions bounded by simple closed curves. In geographical maps it has been observed empirically, in as many special cases as have been tried, that, at most, four colours are needed in order to colour the regions so that two regions that share a common boundary are always coloured differently, and in certain cases that at least four colours are necessary. (Regions that meet only at a point, such as the states of Colorado and Arizona in the United States, are not considered to have a common boundary). A formalization of this empirical observation constitutes what is called "the four-colour theorem." The problem is to prove or disprove the assertion that this is the case for every planar map. That three colours will not suffice is easily demonstrated, whereas the sufficiency of five colours was proved in 1890 by the British mathematician P.J. Heawood. If the four-colour theorem is false, it is unlikely to be proven so by any simple example, because particular results have established the truth of the theorem for all maps with fewer than 40 regions.

A graph G is said to be k-colourable if to each of its vertices there can be assigned one of k colours so that no two adjacent vertices have the same colour. The chromatic number $\chi(G)$ is defined as the minimum k for which G is k-colourable. If $n = \chi(G)$, then (G) is said to be n-chromatic.

To any planar map is associated a graph the vertices of which correspond to the regions of the map, with two vertices joined by an edge if the corresponding regions have a common boundary. The graph obtainable in this way is a planar graph. The four-colour theorem is equivalent to the statement that any planar graph is four-colourable. Efforts to settle the four-colour problem have established its equivalence with a number of seemingly unrelated mathematical problems and contributed in a large part to the development of graph theory during the middle third of the 20th century.

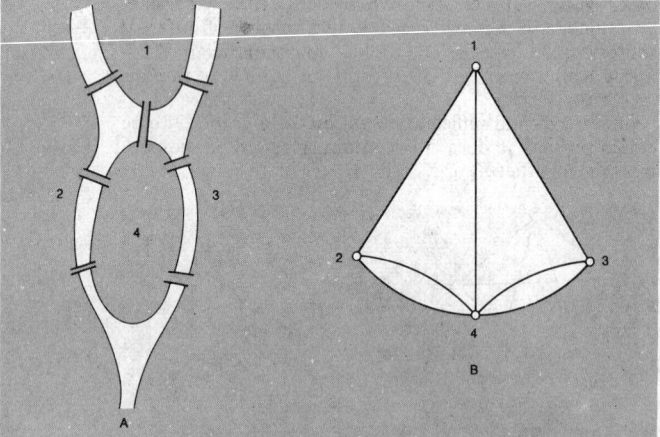

Figure 6: (A) Seven bridges of Königsberg and (B) multigraph (see text).

The Swiss mathematician Hugo Hadwiger has conjectured that every connected n-chromatic graph is contractible to K_n. This is true for $n \leqslant 4$. For $n = 5$ Hadwiger's conjecture is equivalent to the four-colour conjecture.

Eulerian cycles and the Königsberg bridge problem. A multigraph G consists of a non-empty set $V(G)$ of vertices and a subset $E(G)$ of the set of unordered pairs of distinct elements of $V(G)$ with a frequency $f \geqslant 1$ attached to each pair. If the pair (x_1, x_2) with frequency f belongs to $E(G)$, then vertices x_1 and x_2 are joined by f edges.

An Eulerian cycle of a multigraph G is a closed chain in

which each edge appears exactly once. Euler showed that a multigraph possesses an Eulerian cycle if and only if it is connected (apart from isolated points) and the number of vertices of odd degree is either zero or two.

This problem first arose in the following manner. The Pregel River runs through the town of Königsberg and flows on either side of the island of Kneiphof. There were seven bridges, as shown in Figure 6A. The townspeople wondered whether it was possible to go for a walk and cross each bridge once and once only. This is equivalent to finding an Eulerian cycle for the multigraph in Figure 6B. Euler showed it to be impossible because there are four vertices of odd order.

Directed graphs and the travelling-salesman problem. A directed graph G consists of a non-empty set of elements $V(G)$, called vertices, and a subset $E(G)$ of ordered pairs of distinct elements of $V(G)$. Elements (x, y) of $E(G)$ may be called edges, the direction of the edge being from x to y. Both (x, y) and (y, x) may be edges.

A closed path in a directed graph is a sequence of vertices $x_0 x_1 x_2 \cdots x_n = x_0$, such that (x_i, x_{i+1}) is a directed edge for $i = 0, 1, \cdots, n - 1$. To each edge (x, y) of a directed graph G there can be assigned a non-negative weight function $f(x, y)$. The problem then is to find a closed path in G traversing all vertices so that the sum of the weights of all edges in the path is a minimum. This is a typical optimization problem. If the vertices are certain cities, the edges are routes joining cities, and the weights are the lengths of the routes, then this becomes the travelling-salesman problem—that is, can he visit each city without retracing his steps? This problem still remains unsolved except for certain special cases.

(R.C.Bo.)

Combinatorial geometry

The name combinatorial geometry, first used by Hadwiger, is not quite accurately descriptive of the nature of the subject. Combinatorial geometry does touch on those aspects of geometry that deal with arrangements, combinations, and enumerations of geometric objects; but it takes in much more. The field is so new that there has scarcely been time for it to acquire a well-defined position in the mathematical world. Rather it tends to overlap parts of topology (especially algebraic topology), number theory, analysis, and, of course, geometry. The subject concerns itself with relations among members of finite systems of geometric figures subject to various conditions and restrictions. More specifically, it includes problems of covering, packing, symmetry, extrema (maxima and minima), continuity, tangency, equalities and inequalities, many of these with special emphasis on their application to the theory of convex bodies. A few of the fundamental problems of combinatorial geometry originated with Newton and Euler; the majority of the significant advances in the field, however, have been made since 1946.

The unifying aspect of these disparate topics is the quality or style or spirit of the questions and the methods of attacking these questions. Among those branches of mathematics that interest serious working mathematicians, combinatorial geometry is one of the few branches that can be presented on an intuitive basis, without recourse to any advanced theoretical considerations or abstractions.

Yet the problems are far from trivial, and many remain unsolved. They can be handled only with the aid of the most careful and often delicate reasoning that displays the variety and vitality of geometric methods in a modern setting. A few of the answers are natural and are intuitively suggested by the questions. Many of the others, however, require proofs of unusual ingenuity and depth even in the two-dimensional case. Sometimes a plane solution may be readily extendible to higher dimensions, but sometimes just the opposite is true, and a three-dimensional or n-dimensional problem may be entirely different from its two-dimensional counterpart. Each new problem must be attacked individually. Attempts to create standard methods or theories capable of being applied to the solution of any significant group of the currently un-

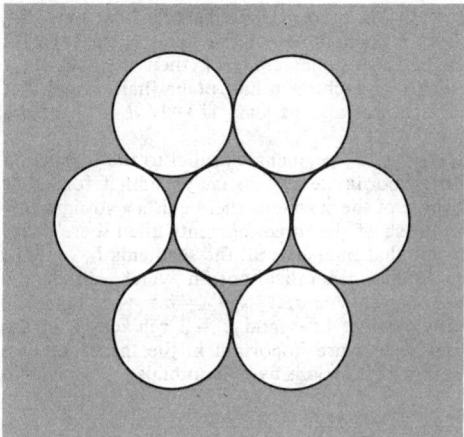

Figure 7: Packing of disks (see text).

solved problems in the field had by the 1970s met with no success. The continuing charm and challenge of the subject are at least in part due to the relative simplicity of the statements coupled with the elusive nature of their solutions.

SOME HISTORICALLY IMPORTANT TOPICS OF COMBINATORIAL GEOMETRY

Packing and covering. It is easily seen that six equal circular disks may be placed around another disk of the same size so that the central one is touched by all the others but no two overlap (Figure 7) and that it is not possible to place seven disks in such a way. In the analogous three-dimensional situation, around a given ball (solid sphere) it is possible to place 12 balls of equal size, all touching the first one but not overlapping it or each other. One such arrangement may be obtained by placing the 12 surrounding balls at the midpoints of edges of a suitable cube that encloses the central ball; each of the 12 balls then touches four other balls in addition to the central one. But if the 12 balls are centred at the 12 vertices of a suitable regular icosahedron surrounding the given ball, there is an appreciable amount of free space between each of the surrounding balls and its neighbours. (If the spheres have radius 1, the distances between the centres of the surrounding spheres are at least $2/\cos 18° = 2.1029\cdots$) It appears, therefore, that by judicious positioning it might be possible to have 13 equal non-overlapping spheres touch another of the same size. This dilemma between 12 and 13, one of the first nontrivial problems of combinatorial geometry, was the object of discussion between Isaac Newton and David Gregory in 1694. Newton believed 12 to be the correct number, but this claim was not proved until 1874. The analogous problem in four-dimensional space is still open, the answer being one of the numbers 24, 25, or 26.

Problem of the 13 balls

Figure 8: Covering of part of a plane with triangles (see text).

The problem of the 13 balls is a typical example of the branch of combinatorial geometry that deals with packings and coverings. In packing problems the aim is to place figures of a given shape or size without overlap as economically as possibly, either inside another given figure or subject to some other restriction.

Problems of packing and covering have been the objects of much study, and some striking conclusions have been obtained. For each plane convex set K, for example, it is possible to arrange nonoverlapping translates of K so as to cover at least two-thirds of the plane; if K is a triangle (and only in that case), no arrangement of nonoverlapping translates covers more than two-thirds of the plane (Figure 8). On the other hand, many easily stated questions are still open. One of them concerns the densest packing of spheres. If the spheres are packed in cannonball fashion—that is, in the way cannonballs are stacked to form a triangular pyramid, indefinitely extended—then they fill $\pi/\sqrt{18}$, or about 0.74, of the space. Whether this is the greatest density possible is not known, but it was proved in 1958 by the British mathematician C. Ambrose Rogers that, if there exists a closer packing, its density cannot exceed 0.78.

Covering problems deal in an analogous manner with economical ways of placing given figures so as to cover (that is, contain in their union) another given figure. One famous covering problem, posed by the French mathematician Henri Lebesgue in 1914, is still unsolved: What is the size and shape of the universal cover of least area? Here a convex set C is called universal cover if for each set A in the plane such that diam $A \leqslant 1$ it is possible to move C to a suitable position in which it covers A. The diameter diam A of a set A is defined as the least upper bound of the mutual distances of points of the set A. If A is a compact set, then diam A is simply the greatest distance between any two points of A. Thus, if A is an equilateral triangle of side 1, then diam $A = 1$; and if B is a cube of edge length 1, then diam $B = \sqrt{3}$.

The Lebesgue problem

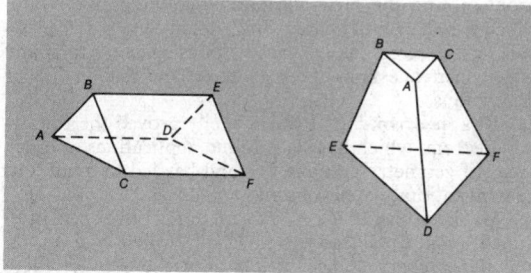

Figure 9: (Left) prism and (right) truncated pyramid (see text).

Polytopes. A (convex) polytope is the convex hull (see GEOMETRY, EUCLIDEAN) of some finite set of points. Each polytope of dimensions d has as faces finitely many polytopes of dimensions 0 (vertices), 1 (edge), 2 (2-faces), $\cdots$, d-1 (facets). Two-dimensional polytopes are usually called polygons, three-dimensional ones polyhedra. Two polytopes are said to be isomorphic, or of the same combinatorial type, provided there exists a one-to-one correspondence between their faces, such that two faces of the first polytope meet if and only if the corresponding faces of the second meet. The prism and the truncated pyramid of Figure 9 are isomorphic, the correspondence being indicated by the letters at the vertices. To classify the convex polygons by their combinatorial types, it is sufficient to determine the number of vertices v; for each $v \geqslant 3$, all polygons with v vertices (v-gons) are of the same combinatorial type, while a v-gon and a v'-gon are not isomorphic if $v \neq v'$. Euler was the first to investigate in 1752 the analogous question concerning polyhedra. He found that $v - e + f = 2$ for every convex polyhedron, where v, e, and f are the numbers of vertices, edges, and faces of the polyhedron. Though this formula became one of the starting points of topology (see TOPOLOGY, GENERAL), Euler was not successful in his attempts to find a classification scheme for convex polytopes or to determine the number of different types for each v. Despite efforts of many famous mathematicians since Euler (J. Steiner, Kirkman, Cayley, O. Hermes, M. Brückner, to mention only a few from the 19th century), the problem is still open. It was established by P.J. Federico in the U.S. that there are 2,606 different combinatorial types of convex polyhedra with nine vertices. The numbers of different types with four, five, six, seven, eight vertices have been known for some time to be 1, 2, 7, 34, 257 respectively.

The theory of convex polytopes has been more successful in developments in other directions. The regular polytopes have been under investigation since 1880 in dimensions higher than three, together with extensions of Euler's relation to the higher dimensions. (The Swiss geometer Ludwig Schläfli made many of these discoveries some 30 years earlier, but his work was published only posthumously in 1901.) The interest in regular polyhedra and other special polyhedra goes back to ancient Greece, as indicated by the names Platonic solids and Archimedean solids.

Since 1950 there has been considerable interest, in part created by practical problems related to computer techniques such as linear programming, in questions of the following type: for polytopes of a given dimension d and having a given number v of vertices, how large and how small can the number of facets be? Such problems have provided great impetus to the development of the theory. The U.S. mathematician Victor L. Klee solved the maximum problem in 1963 in most cases (that is, for all but a finite number of v's for each d), but the remaining cases were disposed of only in 1970 by P. McMullen, in the United States, who used a completely new method. The minimum problem and many related questions are still unsolved.

Incidence problems. In 1893 Sylvester posed the question: If a finite set S of points in a plane has the property that each line determined by two points of S meets at least one other point of S, must all points of S be on one line? Sylvester never found a satisfactory solution to the problem, and the first (affirmative) solutions were published a half century later. Since then, Sylvester's problem has inspired many investigations and led to many other open questions, both in the plane and in higher dimensions.

Helly's theorem. In 1912 E. Helly proved the following theorem, which has since found applications in many areas of geometry and analysis and has led to numerous generalizations, extensions and analogues known as Helly-type theorems. If $K_1, K_2, \cdots, K_n$ are convex sets in d-dimensional Euclidean space E^d, in which $n \geqslant d + 1$, and if for every choice of $d + 1$ of the sets K_i there exists a point that belongs to all the chosen sets, then there exists a point that belongs to all the sets $K_1, K_2,...K_n$. The theorem stated in two dimensions is easier to visualize and yet is not shorn of its strength: If every three of a set of n convex figures in the plane have a common point (not necessarily the same point for all trios), then all n figures have a point in common. If, for example, convex sets A, B, and C have the point p in common, and convex sets A, B, and D have the point q in common, and sets A, C, and D have the point r in common, and sets B, C, and D have the point s in common, then some point x is a member of A, B, C, and D.

Although the connection is often far from obvious, many consequences may be derived from Helly's theorem. Among them are the following, stated for $d = 2$ with some higher dimensional analogues indicated in square brackets:

A. Two finite subsets X and Y of the plane [d-space] may be strictly separated by a suitable straight line [hyperplane] if and only if, for every set Z consisting of at most 4 [$d + 2$] points taken from $X \cup Y$, the points of $X \cap Z$ may be strictly separated from those of $Y \cap Z$. (A line [hyperplane] L strictly separates X and Y if X is contained in one of the open half planes [half spaces] determined by L and Y is contained in the other.)

B. Each compact convex set K in the plane [d-space] contains a point P with the following property: each chord of K that contains P is divided by P into a number of segments so the ratio of their lengths is at most $2d$.

C. If G is an open subset of the plane [d-space] with finite area [d-dimensional content], then there exists a point P, such that each open half plane [half space] that contains P contains also at least $1/3$ [$1/(d + 1)$] of the area [d-content] of G.

D. If $I_1, \cdots, I_n$ are segments parallel to the y-axis in a plane with a coordinate system (x, y), and if for every choice of three of the segments there exists a straight line intersecting each of the three segments, then there exists a straight line that intersects all the segments $I_1, \cdots, I_n$.

Theorem D has generalizations in which kth degree polynomial curves $y = a_k x^k + \cdots + a_1 x + a_0$ take the place of the straight lines and $k + 2$ replaces 3 in the assumptions. These are important in the theory of best approximation of functions by polynomials.

METHODS OF COMBINATORIAL GEOMETRY

Many other branches of combinatorial geometry are as important and interesting as those mentioned above, but rather than list them here it is more instructive to provide a few typical examples of frequently used methods of reasoning. Because the emphasis is on illustrating the methods rather than on obtaining the most general results, the examples will deal with problems in two and three dimensions.

Exhausting the possibilities. Using the data available concerning the problem under investigation, it is often possible to obtain a list of all potential, a priori possible, solutions. The final step then consists in eliminating the possibilities that are not actual solutions or that duplicate previously found solutions. An example is the proof that there are only five regular convex polyhedra (the Platonic solids) and the determination of what these five are.

From the definition of regularity it is easy to deduce that all the faces of a Platonic solid must be congruent regular k-gons for a suitable k, and that all the vertices must belong to the same number j of k-gons. Because the sum of the face angles at a vertex of a convex polyhedron is less than 2π, and because each angle of the k-gon is $(k - 2)\pi/k$, it follows that $j(k - 2)\pi/k < 2\pi$, or $(j - 2)(k - 2) < 4$. Therefore, the only possibilities for the pair (j, k) are (3, 3), (3, 4), (3, 5), (4, 3), and (5, 3). It may be verified that each of these pairs actually corresponds to a Platonic solid, namely, to the tetrahedron, the cube, the dodecahedron, the octahedron, and the icosahedron, respectively. Very similar arguments may be used in the determination of Archimedean solids and in other instances.

The most serious drawback of the method is that in many instances the number of potential (and perhaps actual) solutions is so large as to render the method unfeasible. For example, it is known that the number of different combinatorial types of convex polyhedra with 10 vertices exceeds 30,000, the number with 11 vertices exceeds 400,000, and the number with 12 vertices exceeds 5,000,000. Therefore, the exact determination of these numbers by the method just discussed is out of the question, certainly if attempted by hand and probably even with the aid of a computer.

Use of extremal properties. In many cases the existence of a figure or an arrangement with certain desired properties may be established by considering a more general problem (or a completely different problem) and by showing that a solution of the general problem that is extremal in some sense provides also a solution to the original problem. Frequently there seems to be very little connection between the initial question and the extremal problem. As an illustration the following theorem will be proved: If K is a two-dimensional compact convex set with a centre of symmetry, there exists a parallelogram P containing K, such that the midpoints of the sides of P belongs to K. The proof proceeds as follows: Of all the parallelograms that contain K, the one with least possible area is labeled P_0. The existence of such a P_0 is a consequence of the compactness of K and may be established by standard arguments. It is also easily seen that the centres of K and P_0 coincide. The interesting aspect of the situation is that P_0 may be taken as the P required for

The five Platonic solids

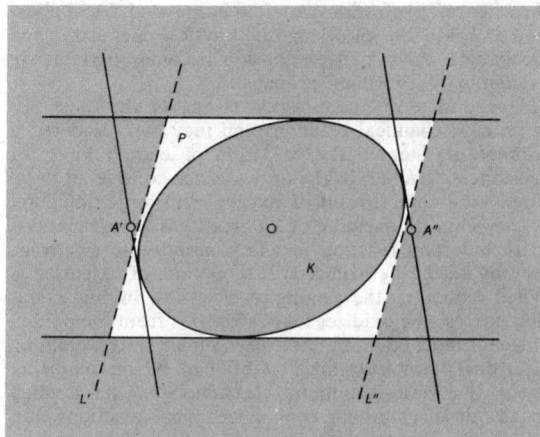

Figure 10: Example of theorem on extremal properties (see text).

Disproof
of
existence
of
extremal
figures

the theorem. In fact (Figure 10), if the midpoints A' and A'' of a pair of sides of P_0 do not belong to K, it is possible to strictly separate them from K by parallel lines L' and L'' that, together with the other pair of sides of P_0, determine a new parallelogram containing K but with area smaller than that of P_0. The above theorem and its proof generalize immediately to higher dimensions and lead to results that are important in functional analysis (see ANALYSIS, FUNCTIONAL).

Sometimes this type of argument is used in reverse to establish the existence of certain objects by disproving the possibility of existence of some extremal figures. As an example the following solution of the problem of Sylvester discussed above can be mentioned. By a standard argument of projective geometry (duality), it is evident that Sylvester's problem is equivalent to the question: If through the point of intersection of any two of n coplanar lines, no two of which are parallel, there passes a third, are the n lines necessarily concurrent? To show that they must be concurrent, contradiction can be derived from the assumption that they are not concurrent. If L is one of the lines, then not all the intersection points lie on L. Among the intersection points not on L, there must be one nearest to L, which can be called A. Through A pass at least three lines, which meet L in points B, C, D, so that C is between B and D. Through C passes a line L^* different from L and from the line through A. Since L^* enters the triangle ABD, it intersects either the segment AB or the segment AD, yielding an intersection

point nearer to L than the supposedly nearest intersection point A, thus providing the contradiction.

The difficulties in applying this method are caused in part by the absence of any systematic procedure for devising an extremal problem that leads to the solution of the original question.

Use of figures with special properties. Sometimes a general theorem may be established by the use of appropriate special figures, even if they are not of the kind that the theorem is concerned with. This method is used in considering the question known as Borsuk's problem.

The Polish mathematician K. Borsuk proved in 1933 that in any decomposition of the d-dimensional ball B^d into d subsets, at least one of the subsets has a diameter equal to diam B^d; and he asked whether it is possible to decompose every subset A of the d-dimensional space into $d+1$ subsets, each of which has a diameter smaller than diam A. (Such a decomposition is easily found if A is the ball B^d.) In case $d=2$ Borsuk's problem reduces to the question of whether each plane set A may be decomposed into three parts, each of diameter less than diam A. An affirmative answer follows in this case from the fact (which is not hard to prove) that each planar set A with diam $A=1$ may be covered by a regular hexagon H of edge length $1/\sqrt{3}=0.577\cdots$ (the diameter of H is diam $H=2/\sqrt{3}=1.155\cdots>1$, and the distance between the pairs of parallel sides is 1; see Figure 11). Such a hexagon H may be cut into three pentagons (indicated in Figure 11 by dotted lines), each of which has a diameter of only $\sqrt{3}/2=0.866\cdots<1$. This partition of H may clearly be used to partition each planar set of diameter 1, thus establishing the following stronger variant of Borsuk's problem in the plane: each planar set A may be decomposed into three subsets, each of diameter at most $0.866\cdots\times$ (diam A). An affirmative solution of Borsuk's problem in the three-dimensional case may be proved by a similar method, in which the hexagon H is replaced by a polyhedron obtained by appropriate triple truncation of the regular octahedron. In dimensions $d\geqslant 4$, however, Borsuk's problem is still undecided.

Use of transformations between different spaces and applications of Helly's theorem. Although those two methods do not necessarily go together, both may be illustrated in one example—the proof of theorem D concerning parallel segments. Let the segment I_i have endpoints (x_i, y_i) and (x_i, y'_i), where $y_i \leqslant y'_i$ and $i=1$, $2, \cdots, n$. The case that two of the segments are on one line is easily disposed of; so it may be assumed that x_1, $x_2, \cdots x_n$ are all different. With each straight line $y=ax+b$ in the (x, y)-plane can be associated a point (a, b) in another plane, the (a, b)-plane. Now, for $i=1, 2, \cdots, n$, the set consisting of all those points (a, b) for which the corresponding line $y=ax+b$ in the (x, y) plane meets the segment I_i can be denoted by K_i. This condition means that $y_i \leqslant ax_i + b \leqslant y'_i$ so that each set K_i is convex. The existence of a line intersecting three of the segments I_i means that the corresponding sets K_i have a common point. Then Helly's theorem for the (a, b)-plane implies the existence of a point (a^*, b^*) common to all sets K_i. This in turn means that the line $y=a^*x+b^*$ meets all the segments $I_1, I_2, \cdots, I_n$, and the proof of theorem D is complete.

In addition to the methods illustrated above, many other techniques of proof are used in combinatorial geometry, ranging from simple mathematical induction to sophisticated decidability theorems of formal logic. The variety of methods available and the likelihood that there are many more not yet invented continue to stimulate research in this rapidly developing branch of mathematics.

(B.G.)

Borsuk's
problem
on
decomposition

BIBLIOGRAPHY. JAMES LEGGE (trans.), *The Yî-King*, vol. 16 of the *Sacred Books of the East* (1882, reprinted 1962); *Algebra, with Arithmetic and Mensuration from the Sanscrit of Brahmagupta and Bháskara*, trans. by H.T. COLEBROOKE (1817); and NASIR AD-DIN AL-TUSI, "Handbook of Arithmetic Using Board and Dust," *Math. Rev.*, 31:5776 (1966), complete Russian trans. by S.A. AHMEDOV and B.A. ROZENFELD in *Istor.-Mat. Issled.*, 15:431–444 (1963), give glimpses of some of the early beginnings of the subject in the Orient. The term combinatorial was first used in GOTT-

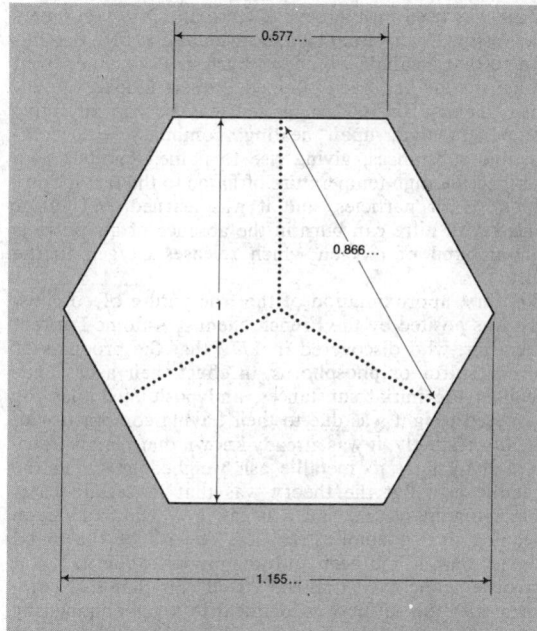

Figure 11: Illustration of Borsuk's problem (see text).

FRIED WILHELM LEIBNIZ, *Dissertatio de arte combinatoria* (1666). W.W. ROUSE BALL, *Mathematical Recreations and Essays*, rev. by H.S. MacDONALD COXETER (1942), contains an account of some of the famous recreational combinatorial problems of the 19th century, such as the problem of eight queens, Hamiltonian circuits, and the Kirkman school girl problem. EUGEN NETTO, *Lehrbuch der Combinatorik*, 2nd ed. (1927, reprinted 1958); and PERCY A. MacMAHON, *Combinatory Analysis*, 2 vol. (1915–16, reprinted 1960), show the state of the subject in the early part of the 20th century. HERBERT J. RYSER, *Combinatorial Mathematics* (1963); MARSHALL HALL, JR., *Combinatorial Theory* (1967); C.L. LIU, *Introduction to Combinatorial Mathematics* (1968), all deal with combinatorics in general. JOHN RIORDAN, *An Introduction to Combinatorial Analysis* (1958); and CLAUDE BERGE, *Principes de combinatoire* (1968; Eng. trans., *Principles of Combinatorics*, 1971), deal with problems of enumeration. CLAUDE BERGE, *Théorie des graphes et ses applications* (1957; Eng. trans., *The Theory of Graphs and Its Applications*, 1962); CLAUDE BERGE and A. GHOUILAHOURI, *Programmes, jeux et réseaux de transport* (1962; Eng. trans., *Programming, Games and Transportation Networks*, 1965); FRANK HARARY, *Graph Theory* (1969), deal with graph theoretic problems. OYSTEIN ORE, *The Four-Color Problem* (1967), gives an introduction to this problem. PETER DEMBOWSKI, *Finite Geometries* (1968), contains most of the important developments on designs, including partially balanced and group divisible designs. ELWYN R. BERLEKAMP, *Algebraic Coding Theory* (1968), may be consulted for combinatorial aspects of coding theory. MARSHALL HALL, JR., "A Survey of Combinatorial Analysis," in *Surveys in Applied Mathematics*, vol. 4 (1958), gives a very good survey of combinatorial developments up to 1958. E.F. BECKENBACH (ed.), *Applied Combinatorial Mathematics* (1964), gives a good idea of the wide range of applications of modern combinatorics. G.C. ROTA, "Combinatorial Analysis," in G.A.W. BOEHM (ed.), *The Mathematical Sciences: A Collection of Essays* (1969), in addition to surveying some of the famous combinatorial problems brings out modern trends and indicates where combinatorics is headed. HUGO HADWIGER and HANS DEBRUNNER, *Combinatorial Geometry in the Plane* (1964); I.M. YAGLOM and V.G. BOLTYANSKY, *Convex Figures* (1961; orig. pub. in Russia, 1951); V.G. BOLTYANSKY, *Equivalent and Equidecomposable Figures* (1963; orig. pub. in Russian, 1956); and L.A. LYUSTERNIK, *Convex Figures and Polyhedra* (1966; orig. pub. in Russian, 1956), deal with aspects of combinatorial geometry on an elementary level. On an advanced level, see H.S. MacDONALD COXETER, *Regular Polytopes*, 2nd ed. (1963); L. FEJES TOTH, *Lagerungen in der Ebene, auf der Kugel und im Raum* (1953) and *Regular Figures* (1964); BRANKO GRUNBAUM, *Convex Polytopes* (1967) and *Arrangements and Spreads* (1972); and C.A. ROGERS, *Packing and Covering* (1964).

(R.C.Bo./B.G.)

Combustion and Flame

Combustion is a chemical reaction between substances, usually including oxygen, and usually accompanied by the generation of heat and light in the form of flame. The rate or speed at which the reactants combine is high, in part because of the nature of the chemical reaction itself and in part because more energy is generated than can escape into the surrounding medium, with the result that the temperature of the reactants is raised to accelerate the reaction even more. A familiar example is a lighted match. When a match is struck, friction heats the head to a temperature at which the chemicals react and generate more heat than can escape into the air, and they burn with a flame. If a wind blows away the heat or the chemicals are moist and friction does not raise the temperature sufficiently, the match goes out; properly ignited, the heat from the flame raises the temperature of a nearby layer of the matchstick and of oxygen in the air adjacent to it, and the wood and oxygen react in a combustion reaction. When equilibrium between the total heat energies of the reactants and the total heat energies of the products (including the actual heat and light emitted) is reached, combustion stops. Flames have a definable composition and a complex structure; they are said to be multiform and are capable of existing at quite low temperatures, as well as at extremely high temperatures. The emission of light in the flame results from the presence of excited particles and, usually, of charged atoms and molecules and of electrons.

General principles. Combustion encompasses a great variety of phenomena with wide application in industry, the sciences, professions, and the home, and the application is based on knowledge of physics, chemistry, and mechanics; their interrelationship becomes particularly evident in treating flame propagation.

In general terms, combustion is one of the most important of chemical reactions and may be considered a culminating step in the oxidation of certain kinds of substances. Though oxidation was once considered to be simply the combination of oxygen with any compound or element, the meaning of the word has been expanded to include any reaction in which atoms lose electrons, thereby becoming oxidized. The opposite of oxidation is called reduction, the gaining of electrons. In any oxidation process the oxidizer takes electrons from the oxidizable substance, thereby itself becoming reduced (gaining electrons). Any substance at all can be an oxidizing agent. But these definitions, clear enough when applied to atomic structure to explain chemical reactions, are not as clearly applicable to combustion, which remains, generally speaking, a type of chemical reaction involving oxygen as the oxidizing agent but complicated by the fact that the process includes other kinds of reactions as well, and by the fact that it proceeds at an unusually fast pace. Furthermore, most flames have a section in their structure in which, instead of oxidations, reduction reactions occur. Nevertheless, the main event in combustion is the combining of combustible material with oxygen.

History. Combustion, fire, and flame have been observed and speculated about from earliest times. Every civilization had its own explanation for them. The Greeks interpreted combustion in terms of philosophical doctrines, one of which was that a certain "inflammable principle" was contained in all combustible bodies and this principle escaped when the body was burned to react with air. A generalization of the concept was provided by the phlogiston theory, formulated in the 17th century. Treated at first as a purely metaphysical quality, phlogiston was conceived later as a material substance having weight, and, sometimes, negative weight.

The phlogiston theory, a unifying principle that explained diverse and complex combustion phenomena, rapidly gained recognition and reigned for about 100 years. Its inadequacy became apparent only in the late 18th century when it proved unable to explain a host of new facts about combustion that were being observed for the first time as the result of increasing accuracy in laboratory experiments.

The English natural philosopher Sir Francis Bacon observed in 1620 that a candle flame has a structure at about the same time that Robert Fludd, an English mystic, described an experiment on combustion in a closed container in which he determined that an amount of air was used up thereby. A German, Otto von Guericke, using an air pump he had invented in 1650, demonstrated that a candle would not burn in a container from which the air had been pumped. Robert Hooke, an English scientist, in 1665 suggested that air had an active component that, upon heating, combined with combustible substances, giving rise to flame. Another idea ascribed the high temperature of flame to the fast motion of active air particles, and it was learned that sulfur mixed with nitre can burn in the absence of air (nitre is a compound of oxygen which releases oxygen to the sulfur).

The first approximation of the true nature of combustion was posited by the French chemist Antoine-Laurent Lavoisier, who discovered in 1772 that the products of burned sulfur or phosphorus, in effect their ashes, outweighed the initial substances, and postulated that the increased weight was due to their having combined with air. Interestingly, it was already known that metals transformed by heat to metallic ash weighed less than the metallic ash, but the theory was that in certain cases phlogiston in metals had a negative weight, and upon escaping during combustion, left the ash of the metal heavier than it had been with the phlogiston in it. Later, Lavoisier concluded that the "fixed" air that had combined with the sulfur was identical to a gas obtained by Joseph Priestley, the English chemist, on heating the metallic ash of mercury; *i.e.*, the "ashes" obtained when mercury was burned could be made to release the gas the metal had combined with. This gas was also identical to that described by a Swedish chemist, Carl Wilhelm Scheele, as an active fraction of air that sustained combustion. Lavoisier called the gas "oxygen."

Discovery
of oxygen

Lavoisier's theory that combustion was a reaction between the burning substance and the gas oxygen, present only to a limited extent in the atmosphere, was based on scientific principles, the most important of which was the law of the conservation of matter (after Einstein's relativity theory, of matter and energy): the total amount of matter in the universe is constant. Even ancient philosophers had guessed this law and it was substantiated in the 17th century. Lavoisier also clarified the concept of element into a modern generalization, that it was a substance that could not be broken down, and this, too, supported his theory. Soon after, studies of gases by an English scientist, John Dalton, and the first table of atomic weights that Dalton compiled, as well as many new gases discovered by other scientists, were important in supporting not only Lavoisier's theory of combustion but his whole new system of chemistry based on accurate measurement. The discoveries of nitrogen and hydrogen in the latter half of the 18th century, added to the earlier discoveries of carbon dioxide and carbon monoxide, and the discovery that the composition of air is remarkably constant though it is a mixture, all supported Lavoisier's theory, but even then the phlogiston theory had had such an eminent position in scientific thinking that some highly respected chemists and physicists clung to it. The proper explanation of combustion, perhaps the oldest recognized chemical reaction, is usually said to have been a keystone in the development of modern science.

From 1815 to 1819 an English scientist, Sir Humphry Davy, experimented on combustion, including measurements of flame temperatures, investigations of the effect on flames of rarefied gases, and dilution with various gases; he also discovered catalytic combustion—the oxidation of combustibles on a catalytic surface accompanied by the release of heat but without flame.

Despite these discoveries, the materialistic theory of combustion lacked a clear concept of energy and, therefore, of the critical role that energy considerations play in an accurate explanation of combustion. It was Sir Benjamin Thompson's experiments with heat in 1798 that revealed evidence for the concept of heat as a movement of particles. Development of a kinetic theory of gases, based on the premise that heat results from the motion of molecules and atoms, of thermodynamics, and of thermochemistry, all in the 19th century, finally elucidated the energy aspects of combustion.

Investigation of burning velocities, experiments on the order of events in the combustion of gas mixtures, and study of the breaking down of gas molecules by heat (thermal dissociation), in the last half of the 19th century, played a vital part in the refinement of theories concerning combustion mechanism. Studies of light emitted by flames led to its analysis in the spectroscope, a device that separates a mixture of light waves into the component waves, and to spectral analysis generally, including theories of atomic and molecular spectra, which, in turn, contributed to an understanding of the nature of flames. The Bunsen burner was also of importance in the study of flame structure. Progress in industry was a powerful stimulus in the search for clarification of flame phenomena. Explosion hazards in coal mines had drawn attention to flame propagation as far back as 1815, when Davy invented his safety lamp. In 1881 detonation was discovered and led at the beginning of the 20th century to a detonation theory, based on the assumption that a gas behaved as a fluid under certain conditions. Chemical kinetics after the 1930s became an indispensable part of flame propagation theory.

Physical and chemical aspects of combustion. *The chemical reactions.* Combustion, with rare exceptions is a complex chemical process involving many steps that depend on the properties of the combustible substance. It is initiated by external factors such as heat, light, and sparks. The reaction sets in as the mixture of combustibles attains the ignition temperature, and several aspects of this step can be defined.

First, a relationship exists between the ignition temperature and the pressure of the mixture under specific conditions. Figure 1 shows the relationship for a mixture of hydrogen and oxygen. Only one temperature corresponds to a given pressure, whereas one or three pressures, called the explosion limits, may correspond to one temperature. The mechanism of the reaction determines the explosion limits: the reaction can proceed only when the steps in the sequence of reactions occur faster than the terminal steps. Thus, for combustion to be initiated with light, or with a spark, the light intensity or the spark energy must exceed certain minimal values.

Ignition
temperature

The complexity of the combustion reaction mechanism and the rapidly varying temperatures and concentrations in the mixture make it difficult and often impossible to derive an equation that would be useful for predicting combustion phenomena over wide temperature and concentration ranges. Instead, use is made of empirical expressions derived for specific reaction conditions.

Most reactions terminate when what is called thermal equilibrium has been attained—*i.e.*, when the energy of the reactants equals the energy of the products.

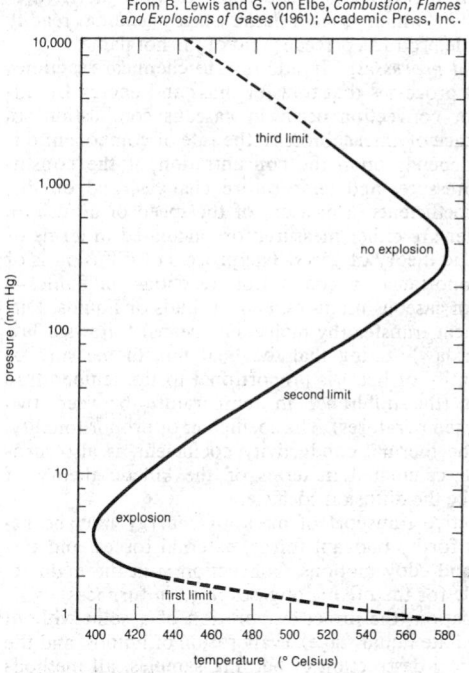

From B. Lewis and G. von Elbe, *Combustion, Flames and Explosions of Gases* (1961); Academic Press, Inc.

Figure 1: Explosion limits of a hydrogen–oxygen mixture.

Special combustion reactions. Reactions of oxygen with hydrogen, with carbon monoxide, and with hydrocarbons are most important from the standpoint of theory and, at the same time, are of great practical value.

Hydrogen combustion proceeds by complicated branched-chain reactions involving the interaction of hydrogen and oxygen atoms with oxygen and hydrogen molecules, respectively to produce hydroxyl radicals. The final reaction product is water, formed by the combination of hydroxyl with hydrogen molecules. Reactions that terminate the chain, such as recombination of atoms and fragments of molecules, and the adsorption of active particles on solid surfaces, also play an important part in the mechanism of hydrogen combustion. The knowledge of rate constants for these processes derived empirically makes possible a quantitative description of all combustion characteristics, such as explosion limits, delay of ignition, burning velocity, etc.

Combustion of carbon monoxide is mainly restricted to mixtures containing hydrogen or hydrogen compounds. In this case the reaction mechanism differs from that of hydrogen combustion chiefly in that it involves a step of fast interaction between hydroxyl and carbon monoxide.

Pure mixtures of carbon monoxide and oxygen (or air) can be ignited only with sparks of high energy, or under high pressures and temperatures. The chemical mechanism of their combustion is not yet clear, probably because oxidation of carbon monoxide, a reaction that is part of the combustion of practically all natural fuels, usually occurs in the presence of hydrogen or hydrogen compounds: the breakdown of wood, coal, petroleum, etc., during burning produces carbon monoxide, hydrogen, and compounds of carbon and hydrogen.

The mechanisms of combustion of hydrocarbons and of other organic compounds are known in general outline only. Many elementary steps of hydrocarbon combustion involving oxygen and hydrogen atoms, hydroxyl and organic radicals are similar to those for hydrogen, however, the overall mechanism of hydrocarbon combustion is complicated by the diversity of molecules and radicals involved. Moreover, with oxidation, thermal decomposition, a breakdown of complex organic compounds without oxidation, also takes place.

Cool and
hot flames Two types of hydrocarbon combustion have been defined; (1) slow combustion at temperatures below 500° C, including cool flames observed at certain pressures, and (2) combustion at higher temperatures, accompanied by hot flames.

Ignition in two stages is characteristic of higher hydrocarbons in which a cool-flame stage yielding readily oxidizable products precedes that of the hot flame.

Physical processes. In addition to chemical reactions, physical processes that transfer mass and energy by diffusion or convection occur in gaseous combustion. In the absence of external forces, the rate of component diffusion depends upon the concentration of the constituents, pressure, and temperature changes, and on diffusion coefficients (a measure of the speed of diffusion). The latter are either measured or calculated in terms of the kinetic theory of gases. The process of diffusion is of great importance in combustion reactions, in flames—that is, in gaseous mixtures, and in solids or liquids. Diffusion heat transfer (by molecular means) follows a law (Fourier law) stating that the heat flux (a measure of the quantity of heat) is proportional to the temperature gradient (the difference in temperature between two limiting temperatures). The coefficient of proportionality, called the thermal conductivity coefficient, is also measured or calculated in terms of the kinetic theory of gases, like the diffusion coefficient.

Convec-
tion Convective transport of mass and energy may be accounted for by buoyant forces, external forces, and turbulent and eddy motions. Convection is in the main responsible for the mixing of gases (*e.g.*, in furnaces).

Sublimation (the direct evaporation of a solid without intermediate liquid stage), evaporation of liquids, and the mechanical destruction of burning samples, all methods of transforming solids and liquids into gases, greatly contribute to their ease of combustion. In general, the combustion of condensed systems—*i.e.*, liquids and solids—is more complex than that of gases, which accounts for the greater development of the gas combustion theory.

Energy transport in combustion may also occur by the emission of light, mostly in the infrared.

Combustion phenomena and classification. All flames can be classified either as premixed flames or as flames that burn without premixing.

Premixed flames. Flame combustion is most prominent with fuels that have been premixed with an oxidant, either oxygen, or a compound that provides oxygen, for the reaction. The temperature of flames with this mixture is often several thousand degrees. The chemical reaction in such flames occurs within a narrow zone several microns (1,000 microns = 1 millimetre) thick. This combustion zone is usually called the flame front.

Dilution of the burning mixture with an inert gas, such as helium or nitrogen, lowers the temperature and, consequently, the reaction rate. Great amounts of inert gas extinguish the flame, and the same result is achieved when substances that remove any of the reactants are added to stabilize a flame. Conditions must be such that the flame is fixed at the burner nozzle or in the com-

bustion chamber; this positioning of the flame is required in many practical uses of combustion. Various types of devices, such as pilot flames and recirculation methods, are designed for this purpose.

The principal quantitative characteristic of a flame is its normal, or fundamental, burning velocity, which depends on the chemical and thermodynamic properties of the mixture, and on pressure and temperature, under given conditions of heat loss. The burning velocity value ranges from several centimetres even to tens of metres, per second. The dependence of the burning velocity on molecular structure, which is responsible for fuel reactivity is known for a great many fuel–air mixtures.

A widely applied thermal theory, cited as one of the first flame propagation theories, implies that combustion proceeds primarily at temperatures close to the maximum that the flame can achieve. A set of differential equations developed for thermal conductivity and diffusion is reduced in the theory to one equation that yields the burning velocity value. Further development of the thermal flame propagation theory has been made and computers now make most simplifications unnecessary.

According to thermal theories, flame propagation is accounted for by heat energy transport from the combustion zone to the unburned mixture, to raise the temperature of the mixture. Diffusion theory assumes that thermodynamic equilibrium sets in behind the flame front at a maximum temperature, and that radicals produced in this zone diffuse into the unburned mixture and ignite it. Both heat transport and diffusion of active particles, must be considered essential for ignition.

Diffusion flames. Diffusion flames, smoothly flowing (laminar) or turbulent, belong to the class of flames whose ingredients are not mixed prior to entering the burning zone. Molecular or turbulent diffusion is responsible for the mixing of the gases in such flames. The distribution of the combustible material and of oxygen over various flame cross sections is regular in laminar flames but becomes much more complicated in turbulent gas flows. The transition from laminar to turbulent flames occurs at a certain point of the flow and depends upon the actual conditions.

Industrial flames, including those activated in furnaces, belong to the turbulent diffusion type. The theory of diffusion flames, however, is less advanced than that of premixed flames and, since gas intermixing is mainly responsible for the structure and the features of diffusion flames, the theory operates more in terms of physics and of thermodynamics than chemical reactions. Flames such as those of candles, of liquid droplets, and of many propellants and condensed fuels are diffusion flames. Industrial
flames

Oxidizing and reducing flame. When a premixed flame burns in open air with an excess of fuel, there appears in addition to the flame zone a zone of diffusion flame; this is accounted for by the diffusion of atmospheric oxygen, as, for example, in the Bunsen flame produced by a burner to which the air intake can be regulated, thereby altering the flow from an intensely hot one—in which most of the fuel gases are oxidized to carbon dioxide and water—to a relatively low temperature flux, in which most of the fuel gas is only partially oxidized. Such flames consist of an innner and outer cone—two zones in which different chemical reactions take place, the reducing and

From A. Gaydon, *The Spectroscopy of Flames;* Chapman & Hall Ltd.

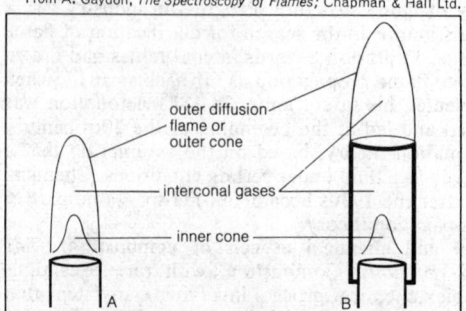

Figure 2: *Cones of burner flames.*
(A) Bunsen burner. (B) Teklu-Smithells burner.

oxidizing zones, respectively. The oxidizing nature of the outer cone is due to excess oxygen (see Figure 2).

Explosions. The transition from combustion to explosion is caused by an acceleration of the reaction, induced either by a rise in temperature or by increasing lengths of the reaction chain. The first is called thermal explosion, and the second, chain explosion.

Thermal explosions. Thermal explosion theory is based on the idea that progressive heating raises the rate at which heat is released by the reaction until it exceeds the rate of heat loss from the area. At a given composition of the mixture and a given pressure, explosion will occur at a specific ignition temperature that can be determined from the calculations of heat loss and heat gain.

The thermal explosion theory accounts for temperature-rise and fuel consumption during the induction period. At sufficiently high rates of consumption the explosion will not occur.

Chain-branch reactions. It follows from the theory of branched-chain reactions that there is a limit to ignition, or to explosion, without a rise of temperature. In this case, what is called a chain explosion will occur when the probabilities of chain branching and of termination are equal. Usually, however, explosions are of a chain-thermal nature (*i.e.*, both heat accumulation and chain auto-acceleration contribute to explosion).

Detonation. The progressive acceleration of reaction accounted for by growth of the flame front area and by transition from laminar to turbulent flow gives rise to a shock wave. The increase in temperature due to compression in the shock wave results in self-ignition of the mixture and detonation sets in. The shock wave-combustion zone complex forms the detonation wave. Detonation differs from normal combustion in its ignition mechanism and in the supersonic velocity of 2–5 kilometres per second for gases and 8–9 kilometres per second for solid and liquid explosives.

Detonation is impossible when the energy loss from the reaction zone exceeds a certain limit. The detonation limits observed for high explosives are also eventually dependent on factors responsible for the chemical reaction rate: the charge and diameter of the grain, etc.

Special aspects. Emission of light is a characteristic feature of combustion. Infrared, visible and ultraviolet bands of molecules, and atomic lines are usually observed in flame spectra. Moreover, continuous spectra from incandescent particles, or from recombination of atoms, radicals, and ions are frequently observed. The sources of flame radiation are the thermal energy of gas (thermoluminescence) and the chemical energy released in exothermic elementary reactions (chemiluminescence; see LUMINESCENCE). In a Bunsen burner fed with a sufficient amount of air, up to 20 percent of the reaction heat is released as infrared energy and less than one percent as visible and ultraviolet radiation, the infrared being mostly thermoluminescence. Radiation from the inner cone of the Bunsen flame in the visible and ultraviolet regions represents chemiluminescence.

Ionization   Many flames contain electrons and positive and negative ions, a fact evident from the electrical conductivity of flames, and also from the deviation of the flame cone in an electric field (the charges are attracted or repelled, distorting the flame), a phenomenon usually interpreted as a mechanical effect called electric wind. The resulting change of the flame shape can affect the burning velocity. Ionization, like the emission of light, can be the result of equilibrium processes, when it is called thermal ionization, or it can be related to chemical processes and called chemical ionization. Thermal ionization may be expected in very hot flames containing alkali metals or alkaline-earth metals (for example, sodium and calcium) as impurities because of their low-ionization potentials. The high concentrations of ions and electrons in the flames of organic species are undoubtedly due to chemical, rather than to thermal ionization. This is seen in the fact that electroconductivity in the inner cone of the Bunsen flame is several times higher than that of the outer cone. The reactions of ions and electrons may yield atoms and radicals and in this way affect the burning velocity.

Formation of soot is a feature of all hydrocarbon flames. It makes the flame luminous and nontransparent. The mechanism of soot formation is accounted for by simultaneous polymerization, a process whereby molecules or molecular fragments are combined into extremely large groupings, and dehydrogenation, a process that eliminates hydrogen from molecules.

Applications. The uses of combustion and flame phenomena can be categorized under five general heads.

In heating devices. Heating devices for vapour production (steam, etc.), in metallurgy, and in industry generally, utilize the combustion of gases, wood, coal, and liquid fuels. Control of the combustion process to obtain optimal efficiency is ensured by proper ratio and distribution of the fuel and the oxidant in the furnace, stove, kiln, etc., choice of conditions for heat transport from the combustion products to the heated bodies, and by appropriate aerodynamics of gas flows in the furnace. Radiation contributes to a certain extent to heat exchange. Combustion in furnaces being a very complicated process, only general ideas can be given by the combustion theory, so that the optimal conditions and the furnace design are usually decided empirically.

In explosives. The combustion and detonation of explosives are widely used in all sorts of work with mechanical action or explosion as the eventual goals. Practical applications of explosives are based on the theory of their combustion and detonation. The combustion of condensed explosives occurs mostly in the gas phase due to their evaporation, sublimation, or decomposition and can be treated in terms of the theory of gas combustion, which provides for the burning velocity, its dependence on temperature, pressure, and on the parameters determining the combustion regime and the nature of explosives, etc. Control of combustion and detonation in their practical applications is made possible by use of the theory, together with the results of experimental investigations on combustion and detonation.

In internal combustion engines. These comprise various engines, gas turbines, turbojets, and ramjets. The Otto engine operates with a mixture compressed in a cylinder by a piston. Shortly before the piston reaches the top the mixture is ignited with a spark, and the flame propagates at a normal velocity into the unburned mixture, increasing the pressure and moving the piston. There is a maximum of compression for any mixture composition and any engine design. Detonation occurs beyond this maximum because of the appearance of centres where self-ignition takes place before the flame front. Loss of power is one result of detonation; compounds hindering self-ignition are used to prevent it.

The diesel engine operates with a fuel spray injected into the engine cylinder as liquid droplets that mix with air by turbulent diffusion and that evaporate. At normal operations of the engine the temperature of compressed air is sufficiently high for self-ignition of the fuel.

In gas turbines, compressed air enters the combustion chamber where it mixes with the fuel. The expanding combustion products impart their energy to the turbine blades.

Two kinds of jet engines are used in aircraft: the turbojet and the ramjet. The turbine of a turbojet engine is used to operate the compressor. Thrust comes from the repulsion of products flowing out of a nozzle. In a ramjet engine, air is compressed and slowed down in the diffuser without any compressor or turbine device.

In rocket propulsion. The products of combustion of gaseous, liquid, or solid propellants in rockets are ejected from the combustion chamber through the (de Laval) nozzle at a high velocity. Knowledge of the kinetics of chemical processes in the nozzle is essential to determine the thrust required. The thrust value decreases with the increasing mean molecular weight of the combustion products. Mixtures of low molecular weight and high heat of combustion, therefore, are used for rockets.

In chemical reactions. Flames are used in various ways to produce chemical reactions. The bead test in analytical chemistry is one example. The reducing power of a flame that has insufficient oxygen is utilized in limited ways. The soot produced by some flames is commercially useful. The manufacture of coke and charcoal is dependent on the judicious control of combustion and flame.

BIBLIOGRAPHY. J.C. GREGORY, *Combustion from Heracleitos to Lavoisier* (1934), and J.H. WHITE, *History of the Phlogiston Theory* (1932), histories of combustion science to the 18th century; W.A. BONE and D.T.A. TOWNSEND, *Flame and Combustion in Gases* (1927), a history of combustion science from the late 17th century to the early 20th century; W. JOST, *Explosion and Combustion Processes in Gases* (Eng. trans. 1946), a review of the main theoretical and experimental research on various problems of combustion and explosions; R.M. FRISTROM and A.A. WESTENBERG, *Flame Structure* (1965), a general review and critical treatment of experimental and theoretical data on flame structure.

More advanced monographs covering in detail specific aspects of this subject include: B. LEWIS and G. VON ELBE, *Combustion, Flames and Explosions of Gases*, 2nd ed. (1961); N.N. SEMENOV, *Chemical Kinetics and Chain Reactions* (Eng. trans. 1935), *Some Problems of Chemical Kinetics and Reactivity*, 2 vol. (Eng. trans. 1958–59); and A.G. GAYDON and H.G. WOLFHARD, *Flames: Their Structure, Radiation and Temperature* (1953).

(V.N.K.)

Comedy

The classic conception of comedy, which began with Aristotle in ancient Greece of the 4th century BC and persists through the present, holds that it is primarily concerned with man as a social being, rather than as a private person, and that its function is frankly corrective. The comic artist's purpose is to hold a mirror up to society to reflect its follies and vices, in the hope that they will, as a result, be mended. The 20th-century French philosopher Henri Bergson shared this view of the corrective purpose of laughter; specifically, he felt, laughter is intended to bring the comic character back into conformity with his society, whose logic and conventions he abandons when "he slackens in the attention that is due to life." This article will deal with comedy primarily as a literary genre but also will touch on its manifestations in the other arts. Comparable discussions will be found in the articles TRAGEDY; SATIRE; and further information on comedy as a form of drama may be found in the article DRAMATIC LITERATURE. The wellsprings of comedy are dealt with in the article HUMOUR AND WIT. The subject of the comic in the arts is also treated in articles on the arts of various peoples, such as SOUTH ASIAN PEOPLES, ARTS OF; and AFRICAN PEOPLES, ARTS OF. The comic impulse in the visual arts is discussed in CARICATURE, CARTOON, AND COMIC STRIP.

The corrective purpose of laughter

ORIGINS AND DEFINITIONS

The word comedy seems to be connected by derivation with the Greek verb meaning "to revel," and comedy arose out of the revels associated with the rites of Dionysus, a god of vegetation. The origins of comedy are thus bound up with vegetation ritual. Aristotle, in his *Poetics*, states that comedy originated in phallic songs and that, like tragedy, it began in improvisation. Though tragedy evolved by stages that can be traced, the progress of comedy passed unnoticed because it was not taken seriously. When tragedy and comedy arose, poets wrote one or the other, according to their natural bent. Those of the graver sort, who might previously have been inclined to celebrate the actions of the great in epic poetry, turned to tragedy; poets of a lower type, who had set forth the doings of the ignoble in invectives, turned to comedy. The distinction is basic to the Aristotelian differentiation between tragedy and comedy: tragedy imitates men who are better than the average, and comedy men who are worse.

For centuries, efforts at defining comedy were to be along the lines set down by Aristotle: the view that tragedy deals with personages of high estate, and comedy deals with lowly types; that tragedy treats of matters of great public import, while comedy is concerned with the private affairs of mundane life; and that the characters and events of tragedy are historic and so, in some sense, true, while the humbler materials of comedy are but feigned. Implicit, too, in Aristotle is the distinction in styles deemed appropriate to the treatment of tragic and comic story. As long as there was at least a theoretical separation of comic and tragic styles, either genre could, on occasion, appropriate the stylistic manner of the other to a striking effect, which was never possible after the crossing of stylistic lines became commonplace. The ancient Roman poet Horace, who wrote on such stylistic differences, noted the special effects that can be achieved when comedy lifts its voice in pseudotragic rant and when tragedy adopts the prosaic but affecting language of comedy. Consciously combined, the mixture of styles produces the burlesque, in which the grand manner (epic or tragic) is applied to a trivial subject, or the serious subject is subjected to a vulgar treatment, to ludicrous effect. The English novelist Henry Fielding, in the preface to *Joseph Andrews* (1742), was careful to distinguish between the comic and the burlesque; the latter centres on the monstrous and unnatural and gives pleasure through the surprising absurdity it exhibits in appropriating the manners of the highest to the lowest, or vice versa. Comedy, on the other hand, confines itself to the imitation of nature, and, according to Fielding, the comic artist is not to be excused for deviating from it. His subject is the ridiculous, not the monstrous, as with the writer of burlesque; and the nature he is to imitate is human nature, as viewed in the ordinary scenes of civilized society.

Distinction between the comic and the burlesque

The human contradiction. In dealing with man as a social being, all great comic artists have known that they are in the presence of a contradiction: that behind the social being lurks an animal being, whose behaviour often accords very ill with the canons dictated by society. Comedy, from its ritual beginnings, has celebrated creative energy. The primitive revels out of which comedy arose frankly acknowledged man's animal nature; the animal masquerades and the phallic processions are the obvious witnesses to it. Comedy testifies to man's physical vitality, his delight in life, his will to go on living. Comedy is at its merriest, its most festive, when this rhythm of life can be affirmed within the civilized context of human society. In the absence of this sort of harmony between creatural instincts and the dictates of civilization, sundry strains and discontents arise, all bearing witness to the contradictory nature of man, which in the comic view is a radical dualism; his efforts to follow the way of rational sobriety are forever being interrupted by the infirmities of the flesh. The duality that tragedy views as a fatal contradiction in the nature of things comedy views as one more instance of the incongruous reality that every man must live with as best he can. "Wherever there is life, there is contradiction," says Søren Kierkegaard, the 19th-century Danish Existentialist, in the *Concluding Unscientific Postscript* (1846), "and wherever there is contradiction, the comical is present." He went on to say that the tragic and the comic are both based on contradiction; but "the tragic is the suffering contradiction, comical, painless contradiction." Comedy makes the contradiction manifest along with a way out, which is why the contradiction is painless. Tragedy, on the other hand, despairs of a way out of the contradiction.

The incongruous is "the essence of the laughable," said the English essayist William Hazlitt, who also declared, in his essay "On Wit and Humour" in *English Comic Writers* (1819), that "Man is the only animal that laughs and weeps; for he is the only animal that is struck with the difference between what things are, and what they ought to be."

Comedy, satire, and romance. Comedy's dualistic view of man as an incongruous mixture of bodily instinct and rational intellect is an essentially ironic view—implying the capacity to see things in a double aspect. The comic drama takes on the features of satire as it fixes on professions of virtue and the practices that contradict them. Satire assumes standards against which professions and practices are judged. To the extent that the professions prove hollow and the practices vicious, the ironic perception darkens and deepens. The element of the incongruous points in the direction of the grotesque, which implies an admixture of elements that do not match.

The ironic view of man

The ironic gaze eventually penetrates to a vision of the grotesque quality of experience, marked by the discontinuity of word and deed and the total lack of coherence between appearance and reality. This suggests one of the extreme limits of comedy, the satiric extreme, in which the sense of the discrepancy between things as they are and things as they might be or ought to has reached to the borders of tragedy. For the tragic apprehension, as Kierkegaard states, despairs of a way out of the contradictions that life presents.

As satire may be said to govern the movement of comedy in one direction, romance governs its movement in the other. Satiric comedy dramatizes the discrepancy between the ideal and the reality and condemns the pretensions that would mask reality's hollowness and viciousness. Romantic comedy also regularly presents the conflict between the ideal shape of things as hero or heroine could wish them to be and the hard realities with which they are confronted, but typically it ends by invoking the ideal, despite whatever difficulties reality has put in its way. This is never managed without a good deal of contrivance, and the plot of the typical romantic comedy is a medley of clever scheming, calculated coincidence, and wondrous discovery, all of which contribute ultimately to making the events answer precisely to the hero's or heroine's wishes. Plotting of this sort has had a long stage tradition and not exclusively in comedy. It is first encountered in the tragicomedies of the ancient Greek dramatist Euripides (*e.g.*, *Alcestis*, *Iphigeneia in Tauris*, *Ion*, *Helen*). Shakespeare explored the full range of dramatic possibilities of the romantic mode of comedy. The means by which the happy ending is accomplished in romantic comedy—the document or the bodily mark that establishes identities to the satisfaction of all the characters of goodwill—are part of the stock-in-trade of all comic dramatists, even such 20th-century playwrights as Jean Anouilh (in *Le Voyageur sans bagage*) and T.S. Eliot (in *The Confidential Clerk*).

There is nothing necessarily inconsistent in the use of a calculatedly artificial dramatic design to convey a serious dramatic statement. The contrived artifice of Shakespeare's mature comic plots is the perfect foil against which the reality of the characters' feelings and attitudes assumes the greater naturalness. The strange coincidences, remarkable discoveries, and wonderful reunions are unimportant compared with the emotions of relief and awe that they inspire. Their function, as Shakespeare uses them, is precisely to give rise to such emotions, and the emotions, thanks to the plangent poetry in which they are expressed, end by transcending the circumstances that occasioned them. But when such artifices are employed simply for the purpose of eliminating the obstacles to a happy ending—as is the case in the sentimental comedy of the 18th and early 19th centuries—then they stand forth as imaginatively impoverished dramatic clichés. The dramatists of sentimental comedy were committed to writing exemplary plays, wherein virtue would be rewarded and vice frustrated. If hero and heroine were to be rescued from the distresses that had encompassed them, any measures were apparently acceptable; the important thing was that the play's action should reach an edifying end. It is but a short step from comedy of this **19th-century melo-drama** sort to the melodrama that flourished in the 19th-century theatre. The distresses that the hero and heroine suffer are, in melodrama, raised to a more than comic urgency, but the means of deliverance have the familiar comic stamp: the secret at last made known, the long-lost child identified, the hard heart made suddenly capable of pity. Melodrama is a form of fantasy that proceeds according to its own childish and somewhat egoistic logic; hero and heroine are pure, anyone who opposes them is a villain, and the purity that has exposed them to risks must ensure their eventual safety and happiness. What melodrama is to tragedy farce is to comedy, and the element of fantasy is equally prominent in farce and in melodrama. If melodrama provides a fantasy in which the protagonist suffers for his virtues but is eventually rewarded for them, farce provides a fantasy in which the protagonist sets about satisfying his most roguish or wanton, mischievous or destructive, impulses and manages to do so with impunity.

THEORIES OF COMEDY

The treatise that Aristotle is presumed to have written on comedy is lost. There is, however, a fragmentary treatise on comedy that bears an obvious relation to Aristotle's treatise on tragedy, *Poetics*, and is generally taken to be either a version of a lost Aristotelian original or an expression of the philosophical tradition to which he belonged. This is the *Tractatus Coislinianus*, preserved in a 10th-century manuscript in the De Coislin Collection in Paris. The *Tractatus* divides the substance of comedy into the same six elements that are discussed in regard to tragedy in the *Poetics*: plot, character, thought, diction, melody, and spectacle. The characters of comedy, according to the *Tractatus*, are of three kinds: the impostors, the self-deprecators, and the buffoons. The Aristotelian tradition from which the *Tractatus* derives probably provided a fourth, the churl, or boor. The list of comic characters in the *Tractatus* is closely related to a passage in Aristotle's *Nicomachean Ethics*, in which the boaster (the person who says more than the truth) is compared with the mock-modest man (the person who says less), and the buffoon (who has too much wit) is contrasted with the boor (who has too little).

Comedy as a rite. The *Tractatus* was not printed until 1839, and its influence on comic theory is thus of relatively modern date. It is frequently cited in the studies that attempt to combine literary criticism and anthropology, in the manner in which Sir James George Frazer combined studies of primitive religion and culture in *The Golden Bough* (1890–1915). In such works, comedy and tragedy alike are traced to a prehistoric death-and-resurrection ceremonial, a seasonal pantomime in which the old year, in the guise of an aged king (or hero or god), is killed, and the new spirit of fertility, the resurrection or initiation of the young king, is brought in. This rite typically featured a ritual combat, or agon, between the representatives of the old and the new seasons, a feast in which the sacrificial body of the slain king was devoured, a marriage between the victorious new king and his chosen bride, and a final triumphal procession in celebration of the reincarnation or resurrection of the slain god. Implicit in the whole ceremony is the ancient rite of purging the tribe through the expulsion of a scapegoat, who carries away the accumulated sins of the past year. Frazer, speaking of scapegoats in *The Golden Bough*, noted that this expulsion of devils was commonly preceded or followed by a period of general license, an abandonment of the ordinary restraints of society during which all offenses except the gravest go unpunished. This quality of Saturnalia is characteristic of comedy from ancient Greece through medieval Europe.

The role of the scapegoats

The seasonal rites that celebrate the yearly cycle of birth, death, and rebirth are seen by the contemporary American critic Northrop Frye as the basis for the generic plots of comedy, romance, tragedy, and irony and satire. The four prefigure the fate of a hero and the society he brings into being. In comedy (representing the season of spring), the hero appears in a society controlled by obstructing characters and succeeds in wresting it from their grasp. The movement of comedy of this sort typically replaces falsehood with truth, illusion with reality. The hero, having come into possession of his new society, sets forth upon adventures, and these are the province of romance (summer). Tragedy (autumn) commemorates the hero's passion and death. Irony and satire (winter) depict a world from which the hero has disappeared, a vision of "unidealized existence." With spring, the hero is born anew.

The moral force of comedy. The characters of comedy specified in the *Tractatus* arrange themselves in a familiar pattern: a clever hero is surrounded by fools of sundry varieties (impostors, buffoons, boors). The hero is something of a trickster; he dissimulates his own powers, while exploiting the weaknesses of those around him. The comic pattern is a persistent one; it appears not only in ancient Greek comedy but also in the farces of ancient

Italy, in the commedia dell'arte that came into being in 16th-century Italy, and even in the routines involving a comedian and his straight man in the nightclub acts and the television variety shows of the present time. Implicit here is the tendency to make folly ridiculous, to laugh it out of countenance, which has always been a prominent feature of comedy.

Renaissance critics, elaborating on the brief and cryptic account of comedy in Aristotle's *Poetics*, stressed the derisive force of comedy as an adjunct to morality. The Italian scholar Gian Giorgio Trissino's account of comedy in his *Poetica*, apparently written in the 1530s, is typical: as tragedy teaches by means of pity and fear, comedy teaches by deriding things that are vile. Attention is directed here, as in other critical treatises of this kind, to the source of laughter. According to Trissino, laughter is aroused by objects that are in some way ugly and especially by that from which better qualities were hoped. His statement suggests the relation of the comic to the incongruous. Trissino was as aware as the French poet Charles Baudelaire was three centuries later that laughter betokens the fallen nature of man (Baudelaire would term it man's Satanic nature). Man laughs, says Trissino (echoing Plato's dialogue *Philebus*), because he is envious and malicious and never delights in the good of others except when he hopes for some good from it for himself.

The most important English Renaissance statement concerning comedy is that of Sir Philip Sidney in *The Defence of Poesie* (1595):

Sir Philip Sidney's definition of comedy

> comedy is an imitation of the common errors of our life, which [the comic dramatist] representeth in the most ridiculous and scornful sort that may be, so as it is impossible that any beholder can be content to be such a one.

Like Trissino, Sidney notes that, while laughter comes from delight, not all objects of delight cause laughter, and he demonstrates the distinction as Trissino had done: "we are ravished with delight to see a fair woman, and yet are far from being moved to laughter. We laugh at deformed creatures, wherein certainly we cannot delight." The element of the incongruous is prominent in Sidney's account of scornful laughter. He cites the image of the hero of Greek legend Heracles, with his great beard and furious countenance, in woman's attire, spinning at the command of his beloved queen, Omphale, and declares that this arouses both delight and laughter.

Comedy and character. Another English poet, John Dryden, in *Of Dramatick Poesie, an Essay* (1668), makes the same point in describing the kind of laughter produced by the ancient Greek comedy *The Clouds*, by Aristophanes. In it, the character of Socrates is made ridiculous by acting very unlike the true Socrates; that is, by appearing childish and absurd rather than with the gravity of the true Socrates. Dryden was concerned with analyzing the laughable quality of comedy and with demonstrating the different forms it has taken in different periods of dramatic history. Aristophanic comedy sought its laughable quality not so much in the imitation of a man as in the representation of "some odd conceit which had commonly somewhat of unnatural or obscene in it." In the so-called New Comedy, introduced by Menander late in the 4th century BC, writers sought to express the ethos, or character, as in their tragedies they expressed the pathos, or suffering, of mankind. This distinction goes back to Aristotle, who, in the *Rhetoric*, distinguished between ethos, a man's natural bent, disposition, or moral character, and pathos, emotion displayed in a given situation. And the Latin rhetorician Quintilian, in the 1st century AD, noted that ethos is akin to comedy and pathos to tragedy. The distinction is important to Renaissance and Neoclassical assumptions concerning the respective subject of comic and tragic representation. In terms of emotion, ethos is viewed as a permanent condition characteristic of the average man and relatively mild in its nature; pathos, on the other hand, is a temporary emotional state, often violent. Comedy thus expresses the characters of men in the ordinary circumstances of everyday life; tragedy expresses the sufferings of a particular man in extraordinary periods of intense emotion.

In dealing with men engaged in normal affairs, the comic dramatists tended to depict the individual in terms of some single but overriding personal trait or habit. They adopted a method based on the physiological concept of the four humours, or bodily fluids (blood, phlegm, choler, melancholy), and the belief that an equal proportion of these constituted health, while an excess or deficiency of any one of them brought disease. Since the humours governed temperament, an irregular distribution of them was considered to result not only in bodily sickness but also in derangements of personality and behaviour, as well. The resultant comedy of humours is distinctly English, as Dryden notes, and particularly identified with the comedies of Ben Jonson.

English comedy of humours

The role of wit. Humour is native to man. Folly need only be observed and imitated by the comic dramatist to give rise to laughter. Observers as early as Quintilian, however, have pointed out that, though folly is laughable in itself, such jests may be improved if the writer adds something of his own; namely, wit. A form of repartee, wit implies both a mental agility and a linguistic grace that is very much a product of conscious art. Quintilian describes wit at some length in his *Institutes;* it partakes of urbanity, a certain tincture of learning, charm, saltiness, or sharpness, and polish and elegance. In the preface (1671) to *An Evening's Love*, Dryden distinguishes between the comic talents of Ben Jonson, on the one hand, and of Shakespeare and his contemporary John Fletcher, on the other, by virtue of their excelling, respectively, in humour and wit. Jonson's talent lay in his ability "to make men appear pleasantly ridiculous on the stage"; while Shakespeare and Fletcher excelled in wit, or "the sharpness of conceit," as seen in their repartee. The distinction is noted as well in *Of Dramatick Poesie, an Essay*, where a comparison is made between the character of Morose in Jonson's play *Epicœne*, who is characterized by his humour (namely, his inability to abide any noise but the sound of his own voice), and Shakespeare's Falstaff, who, according to Dryden, represents a miscellany of humours and is singular in saying things that are unexpected by the audience.

The distinctions that Hazlitt arrives at, then, in his essay "On Wit and Humour" are very much in the classic tradition of comic criticism:

> Humour is the describing the ludicrous as it is in itself; wit is the exposing it, by comparing or contrasting it with something else. Humour is, as it were, the growth of nature and accident; wit is the product of art and fancy.

The distinctions persist into the most sophisticated treatments of the subject. Sigmund Freud, for example, in *Wit and its Relation to the Unconscious* (1905), said that wit is made, but humour is found. Laughter, according to Freud, is aroused at actions that appear immoderate and inappropriate, at excessive expenditures of energy: it expresses a pleasurable sense of the superiority felt on such occasions.

Baudelaire on the grotesque. The view that laughter comes from superiority is referred to as a commonplace by Baudelaire, who states it in his essay "On the Essence of Laughter" (1855). Laughter, says Baudelaire, is a consequence of man's notion of his own superiority. It is a token both of an infinite misery, in relation to the absolute being of whom man has an inkling, and of infinite grandeur, in relation to the beasts, and results from the perpetual collision of these two infinities. The crucial part of Baudelaire's essay, however, turns on his distinction between the comic and the grotesque. The comic, he says, is an imitation mixed with a certain creative faculty; the grotesque is a creation mixed with a certain imitative faculty—imitative of elements found in nature. Each gives rise to laughter expressive of an idea of superiority—in the comic, the superiority of man over man, and, in the grotesque, the superiority of man over nature. The laughter caused by the grotesque has about it something more profound and primitive, something much closer to the innocent life, than has the laughter caused by the comic in man's behaviour. In France, the great master of the grotesque was the 16th-century

Baudelaire's definition of laughter

author François Rabelais, while some of the plays of Molière, in the next century, best expressed the comic.

Bergson's theories. The French philosopher Henri Bergson (1859–1941) analyzed the dialectic of comedy in his essay "Laughter," which deals directly with the spirit of contradiction that is basic both to comedy and to life. Bergson's central concern is with the opposition of the mechanical and the living; stated in its most general terms, his thesis holds that the comic consists of something mechanical encrusted on the living. Bergson traces the implications of this view in the sundry elements of comedy: situations, language, characters. Comedy expresses a lack of adaptability to society; any individual is comic who goes his own way without troubling to get into touch with his fellow beings. The purpose of laughter is to wake him from his dream. Three conditions are essential for the comic: the character must be unsociable, for that is enough to make him ludicrous; the spectator must be insensible to the character's condition, for laughter is incompatible with emotion; and the character must act automatically (Bergson cites the systematic absent-mindedness of Don Quixote). The essential difference between comedy and tragedy, says Bergson, invoking a distinction that goes back to that maintained between ethos and pathos, is that tragedy is concerned with individuals and comedy with classes. And the reason that comedy deals with the general is bound up with the corrective aim of laughter: the correction must reach as great a number of persons as possible. To this end, comedy focusses on peculiarities that are not indissolubly bound up with the individuality of a single person.

It is the business of laughter to repress any tendency on the part of the individual to separate himself from society. The comic character would, if left to his own devices, break away from logic (and thus relieve himself from the strain of thinking); give over the effort to adapt and readapt himself to society (and thus slacken in the attention that is due to life); and abandon social convention (and thus relieve himself from the strain of living).

The essay "On the Idea of Comedy and the Uses of the Comic Spirit" (1877), by Bergson's English contemporary George Meredith, is a celebration of the civilizing power of the comic spirit. The mind, he affirms, directs the laughter of comedy, and civilization is founded in common sense, which equips one to hear the comic spirit when it laughs folly out of countenance and to participate in its fellowship.

Both Bergson's and Meredith's essays have been criticized for focussing so exclusively on comedy as a socially corrective force and for limiting the scope of laughter to its derisive power. The charge is more damaging to Meredith's essay than it is to Bergson's. Whatever the limitations of the latter, it nonetheless explores the implications of its own thesis with the utmost thoroughness, and the result is a rigorous analysis of comic causes and effects for which any student of the subject must be grateful. It is with farce that Bergson's remarks on comedy have the greatest connection and on which they seem chiefly to have been founded. It is no accident that most of his examples are drawn from Molière, in whose work the farcical element is strong, and from the farces of Bergson's own contemporary Eugène Labiche. The

laughter of comedy is not always derisive, however, as some of Shakespeare's greatest comedies prove; and there are plays, such as Shakespeare's last ones, which are well within an established tradition of comedy but in which laughter hardly sounds at all. These suggest regions of comedy on which Bergson's analysis of the genre sheds hardly any light at all.

The comic as a failure of self-knowledge. Aristotle said that comedy deals with the ridiculous, and Plato, in the *Philebus*, defined the ridiculous as a failure of self-knowledge; such a failure is there shown to be laughable in private individuals (the personages of comedy) but terrible in persons who wield power (the personages of tragedy). In comedy, the failure is often mirrored in a character's efforts to live up to an ideal of self that may be perfectly worthy but the wrong ideal for him. Shakespearean comedy is rich in examples: the King of Na-

varre and his courtiers, who must be made to realize that nature meant them to be lovers, not academicians, in *Love's Labour's Lost;* Beatrice and Benedick, who must be made to know that nature meant them for each other, not for the single life, in *Much Ado About Nothing;* the Duke Orsino in *Twelfth Night,* who is brought to see that it is not Lady Olivia whom he loves but the disguised Viola, and Lady Olivia herself, who, when the right man comes along, decides that she will not dedicate herself to seven years of mourning for a dead brother, after all; and Angelo in *Measure for Measure,* whose image of himself collapses when his lust for Isabella makes it clear that he is not the ascetic type. The movement of all these plays follows a familiar comic pattern, wherein characters are brought from a condition of affected folly amounting to self-delusion to a plain recognition of who they are and what they want. For the five years or so after he wrote *Measure for Measure,* in 1604, Shakespeare seems to have addressed himself exclusively to tragedy, and each play in the sequence of masterpieces he produced during this period—*Othello, King Lear, Macbeth, Antony and Cleopatra,* and *Coriolanus*—turns in some measure on a failure of self-knowledge. This is notably so in the case of *Lear,* which is the tragedy of a man who (in the words of one of his daughters) "hath ever but slenderly known himself," and whose fault (as the Fool suggests) is to have grown old before he grew wise.

The plots of Shakespeare's last plays (*Pericles, Cymbeline, The Winter's Tale, The Tempest*) all contain a potential tragedy but one that is resolved by nontragic means. They contain, as well, an element of romance of the kind purveyed from Greek New Comedy through the plays of the ancient Roman comic dramatists Plautus and Terence. Children lost at birth are miraculously restored, years later, to their parents, thereby providing occasion for a recognition scene that functions as the denouement of the plot. Characters find themselves—they come to know themselves—in all manner of ways by the ends of these plays. Tragic errors have been made, tragic losses have been suffered, tragic passions—envy, jealousy, wrath—have seemed to rage unchecked, but the miracle that these plays celebrate lies in the discovery that the errors can be forgiven, the losses restored, and the passions mastered by man's godly spirit of reason. The near tragedies experienced by the characters result in the ultimate health and enlightenment of the soul. What is learned is of a profound simplicity: the need for patience under adversity, the need to repent of one's sins, the need to forgive the sins of others. In comedy of this high and sublime sort, patience, repentance, and forgiveness are opposed to the viciously circular pattern of crime, which begets vengeance, which begets more crime. Comedy of this sort deals in regeneration and rebirth. There is always about it something of the religious, as humankind is absolved of its guilt and reconciled one to another and to whatever powers that be.

Divine comedies in the West and in the East. The 4th-century Latin grammarian Donatus distinguished comedy from tragedy by the simplest terms: comedies begin in trouble and end in peace, while tragedies begin in calms and end in tempest. Such a differentiation of the two genres may be simplistic, but it provided sufficient grounds for Dante to call his great poem *The Divine Comedy,* since, as he says in his dedicatory letter, it begins amid the horrors of hell but ends amid the pleasures of heaven. This suggests the movement of Shakespeare's last plays, which begin amid the distresses of the world and end in a supernal peace. Comedy conceived in this sublime and serene mode is rare but recurrent in the history of the theatre. The Spanish dramatist Calderón's *Vida es sueño* (1635; "Life is a Dream") is an example; so, on the operatic stage, is Mozart's *Magic Flute* (1791), in spirit and form so like Shakespeare's *Tempest,* to which it has often been compared. In later drama, Henrik Ibsen's *Little Eyolf* (1894) and August Strindberg's *To Damascus* (1898–1904)—both of which are among the late works of these Scandinavian dramatists—have affinities with this type, and this is the comic mode in which T.S. Eliot's last play, *The Elder Statesman* (1958), is conceived. It may represent the most universal mode of comedy. The American philosopher Susanne K. Langer writes:

> In Asia the designation "Divine Comedy" would fit numberless plays; especially in India triumphant gods, divine lovers united after various trials [as in the perennially popular romance of Rama and Sita], are the favourite themes of a theater that knows no "tragic rhythm." The classical Sanskrit drama was heroic comedy—high poetry, noble action, themes almost always taken from the myths—a serious, religiously conceived drama, yet in the "comic" pattern, which is not a complete organic development reaching a foregone, inevitable conclusion, but is episodic, restoring a lost balance, and implying a new future. The reason for this consistently "comic" image of life in India is obvious enough: both Hindu and Buddhist regard life as an episode in the much longer career of the soul which has to accomplish many incarnations before it reaches its goal, nirvana. Its struggles in the world do not exhaust it; in fact they are scarcely worth recording except in entertainment theater, "comedy" in our sense—satire, farce, and dialogue. The characters whose fortunes are seriously interesting are the eternal gods; and for them there is no death, no limit of potentialities, hence no fate to be fulfilled. There is only the balanced rhythm of sentience and emotion, upholding itself amid the changes of material nature. (From *Feeling and Form;* Charles Scribner's Sons, 1953.)

KINDS OF COMEDY IN DIVERSE HISTORICAL PERIODS

Old and New Comedy in ancient Greece. The 11 surviving plays of Aristophanes represent the earliest extant body of comic drama; what is known of Greek Old Comedy is derived from these plays, the earliest of which, *The Acharnians,* was produced in 425 BC. Aristophanic comedy has a distinct formal design but displays very little plot in any conventional sense. Rather, it presents a series of episodes aimed at illustrating, in humorous and often bawdy detail, the implications of a deadly serious political issue: it is a blend of invective, buffoonery, and song and dance. Old Comedy often used derision and scurrility, and this may have proved its undoing; though praised by all, the freedom it enjoyed degenerated into license and violence and had to be checked by law.

In New Comedy, which began to prevail around 336 BC, the Aristophanic depiction of public personages and events was replaced by a representation of the private affairs (usually amorous) of imaginary men and women. New Comedy is known only from the fragments that have survived of the plays of Menander (*c.* 342–*c.* 292 BC) and from plays written in imitation of the form by the Romans Plautus (*c.* 254–184 BC) and Terence (195 or 185–159 BC). A number of the stock comic characters survived from Old Comedy into New: an old man, a young man, an old woman, a young woman, a learned doctor or pedant, a cook, a parasite, a swaggering soldier, a comic slave. New Comedy, on the other hand, exhibits a degree of plot articulation never achieved in the Old. The action of New Comedy is usually about plotting; a clever servant, for example, devises ingenious intrigues in order that his young master may win the girl of his choice. There is satire in New Comedy: on a miser who loses his gold from being overcareful of it (the *Aulularia* of Plautus); on a father who tries so hard to win the girl from his son that he falls into a trap set for him by his wife (Plautus' *Casina*); and on an overstern father whose son turns out worse than the product of an indulgent parent (in the *Adelphi* of Terence). But the satiric quality of these plays is bland by comparison with the trenchant ridicule of Old Comedy. The emphasis in New Comic plotting is on the conduct of a love intrigue; the love element per se is often of the slightest, the girl whom the hero wishes to possess sometimes being no more than an offstage presence or, if onstage, a mute.

New Comedy provided the model for European comedy through the 18th century. During the Renaissance, the plays of Plautus and, especially, of Terence were studied for the moral instruction that young men could find in them: lessons on the need to avoid the snares of harlots and the company of braggarts, to govern the deceitful trickery of servants, to behave in a seemly and

*Develop-
ment of
stock
characters*

modest fashion to parents. Classical comedy was brought up to date in the plays of the "Christian Terence," imitations by schoolmasters of the comedies of the Roman dramatist. They added a contemporary flavour to the life portrayed and displayed a somewhat less indulgent attitude to youthful indiscretions than did the Roman comedy. New Comedy provided the basic conventions of plot and characterization for the *commedia erudita*—comedy performed from written texts—of 16th-century Italy, as in the plays of Machiavelli and Ariosto. Similarly, the stock characters that persisted from Old Comedy into New were taken over into the improvisational commedia dell'arte (*q.v.*), becoming such standard masked characters as Pantalone, the Dottore, the vainglorious Capitano, the young lovers, and the servants, or *zanni*.

Rise of realistic comedy in 17th-century England. The early part of the 17th century in England saw the rise of a realistic mode of comedy based on a satiric observation of contemporary manners and mores. It was masterminded by Ben Jonson, and its purpose was didactic. Comedy, said Jonson in *Every Man Out of his Humour* (1599), quoting the definition that during the Renaissance was attributed to Cicero, is an imitation of life, a glass of custom, an image of truth. Comedy holds the mirror up to nature and reflects things as they are, to the end that society may recognize the extent of its shortcomings and the folly of its ways and set about its improvement. Jonson's greatest plays—*Volpone* (1606), *Epicœne* (1609), *The Alchemist* (1610), *Bartholomew Fair* (1614)—offer a richly detailed contemporary account of the follies and vices that are always with us. The setting (apart from *Volpone*) is Jonson's own London, and the characters are the ingenious or the devious or the grotesque products of the human wish to get ahead in the world. The conduct of a Jonsonian comic plot is in the hands of a clever manipulator who is out to make reality conform to his own desires. Sometimes he succeeds, as in the case of the clever young gentleman who gains his uncle's inheritance in *Epicœne* or the one who gains the rich Puritan widow for his wife in *Bartholomew Fair*. In *Volpone* and *The Alchemist*, the schemes eventually fail, but this is the fault of the manipulators, who will never stop when they are ahead, and not at all due to any insight on the part of the victims. The victims are almost embarrassingly eager to be victimized. Each has his ruling passion—his humour—and it serves to set him more or less mechanically in the path that he will undeviatingly pursue, to his own discomfiture.

English comedy of the later 17th century is cast in the Jonsonian mold. Restoration comedy is always concerned with the same subject—the game of love—but the subject is treated as a critique of fashionable society. Its aim is distinctly satiric, and it is set forth in plots of Jonsonian complexity, where the principal intriguer is the rakish hero, bent on satisfying his sexual needs, outside the bonds of marriage, if possible. In the greatest of these comedies—Sir George Etherege's *Man of Mode* (1676), for example, or William Wycherley's *Country-Wife* (1675) or William Congreve's *Way of the World* (1700)—the premium is on the energy and the grace with which the game is played, and the highest dramatic approval is reserved for those who take the game seriously enough to play it with style but who have the good sense to know when it is played out. The satiric import of Restoration comedy resides in the dramatist's awareness of a familiar incongruity: that between the image of man in his primitive nature and the image of man amid the artificial restraints that society would impose upon him. The satirist in these plays is chiefly concerned with detailing the artful dodges that ladies and gentlemen employ to satisfy nature and to remain within the pale of social decorum. Inevitably, then, hypocrisy is the chief satiric target. The animal nature of man is taken for granted, and so is his social responsibility to keep up appearances; some hypocrisy must follow, and, within limits, society will wink at indiscretions so long as they are discreetly managed. The paradox is typical of those in which the Restoration comic dramatists delight; and the strongly rational and unidealistic ethos of this comedy has its af-

*The rise of
a realistic
comedy*

finities with the naturalistic and skeptical cast of late-17th-century philosophical thought.

Sentimental comedy of the 17th and 18th centuries. The Restoration comic style collapsed around the end of the 17th century, when the satiric vision gave place to a sentimental one. Jeremy Collier's *Short view of the Profaneness and Immorality of the English Stage*, published in 1698, signalled the public opposition to the real or fancied improprieties of plays staged during the previous three decades. "The business of plays is to recommend Vertue, and discountenance Vice": so runs the opening sentence of Collier's attack. No Restoration comic dramatist ever conceived of his function in quite these terms. "It is the business of a comic poet to paint the vices and follies of humankind," Congreve had written a few years earlier (in the dedication to *The Double-Dealer*). Though Congreve may be assumed to imply—in accordance with the time-honoured theory concerning the didactic end of comedy—that the comic dramatist paints the vices and follies of humankind for the purpose of correcting them through ridicule, he is, nonetheless, silent on this point. Collier's assumption that all plays must recommend virtue and discountenance vice has the effect of imposing on comedy the same sort of moral levy that critics such as Thomas Rymer were imposing on tragedy in their demand that it satisfy poetic justice.

The vogue of tragi-comedy

At the beginning of the 18th century, there was a blending of the tragic and comic genres that, in one form or another, had been attempted throughout the preceding century. The vogue of tragicomedy may be said to have been launched in England with the publication of John Fletcher's *Faithfull Shepheardesse* (c. 1608), an imitation of the *Pastor fido*, by the Italian poet Battista Guarini. In his *Compendium of Tragicomic Poetry* (1601), Guarini had argued the distinct nature of the genre, maintaining it to be a third poetic kind, different from either the comic or the tragic. Tragicomedy, he wrote, takes from tragedy its great persons but not its great action, its movement of the feelings but not its disturbance of them, its pleasure but not its sadness, its danger but not its death; from comedy it takes laughter that is not excessive, modest amusement, feigned difficulty, and happy reversal. Fletcher adapted this statement in the address "To the Reader" that prefaces *The Faithfull Shepheardesse.*

The form quickly established itself on the English stage, and, through the force of such examples as Beaumont and Fletcher's *Phylaster* (1610) and *A King and No King* (1611) and a long sequence of Fletcher's unaided tragicomedies, it prevailed during the 20 years before the closing of the theatres in 1642. The taste for tragicomedy continued unabated at the Restoration, and its influence was so pervasive that during the closing decades of the century the form began to be seen in plays that were not, at least by authorial designation, tragicomedies. Its effect on tragedy can be seen not only in the tendency, always present on the English stage, to mix scenes of mirth with more solemn matters but also in the practice of providing tragedy with a double ending (a fortunate one for the virtuous, an unfortunate one for the vicious), as in Dryden's *Aureng-Zebe* (1675) or Congreve's *Mourning Bride* (1697). The general lines separating the tragic and comic genres began to break down, and that which is high, serious, and capable of arousing pathos could exist in the same play with what is low, ridiculous, and capable of arousing derision. The next step in the process came when Sir Richard Steele, bent on reforming comedy for didactic purposes, produced *The Conscious Lovers* (1722) and provided the English stage with an occasion when the audience at a comedy could derive its chief pleasure not from laughing but from weeping. It wept in the delight of seeing virtue rewarded and young love come to flower after parental opposition had been overcome. Comedy of the sort inaugurated by *The Conscious Lovers* continued to represent the affairs of private life, as comedy had always done, but with a seriousness hitherto unknown; and the traditionally low personages of comedy now had a capacity for feeling that bestowed on them a dignity previously reserved for the personages of tragedy.

This trend in comedy was part of a wave of egalitarianism that swept through 18th-century political and social thought. It was matched by a corresponding trend in tragedy, which increasingly selected its subjects from the affairs of private men and women in ordinary life, rather than from the doings of the great. The German dramatist Gotthold Lessing wrote that the misfortunes of those whose circumstances most resemble those of the audience must naturally penetrate most deeply into its heart, and his own *Minna von Barnhelm* (1767) is an example of the new serious comedy. The capacity to feel, to sympathize with, and to be affected by the plight of a fellow human being without regard for his rank in the world's esteem became the measure of one's humanity. It was a bond that united the fraternity of mankind in an aesthetic revolution that preceded the political revolutions of the 18th century. In literature, this had the effect of hastening the movement toward a more realistic representation of reality, whereby the familiar events of common life are treated "seriously and problematically" (in the phrase of the critic Erich Auerbach, who traced the process in his book *Mimesis* [1946]). The results may be seen in novels such as Samuel Richardson's *Pamela* and *Clarissa* and in middle-class tragedies such as George Lillo's *The London Merchant* (1731) in England; in the *comédie larmoyante* ("tearful comedy") in France; in Carlo Goldoni's efforts to reform the commedia dell'arte and replace it with a more naturalistic comedy in the Italian theatre; and in the English sentimental comedy, exemplified in its full-blown state by plays such as Hugh Kelly's *False Delicacy* (1768) and Richard Cumberland's *West Indian* (1771). Concerning the sentimental comedy it must be noted that it is only in the matter of appropriating for the bourgeoisie a seriousness of tone and a dignity of representational style previously considered the exclusive property of the nobility that the form can be said to stand in any significant relationship to the development of a more realistic mimetic mode than the traditional tragic and comic ones. The plots of sentimental comedy are as contrived as anything in Plautus and Terence (which with their fondness for foundling heroes who turn out to be long-lost sons of rich merchants, they often resemble); and with their delicate feelings and genteel moral atmosphere, comedies of this sort seem as affected in matters of sentiment as Restoration comedy seems in matters of wit.

The trend to egalitarianism

Oliver Goldsmith, in his "A Comparison Between Laughing and Sentimental Comedy" (1773), noted the extent to which the comedy in the England of his day had departed from its traditional purpose, the excitation of laughter by exhibiting the follies of the lower part of mankind. He questioned whether an exhibition of its follies would not be preferable to a detail of its calamities. In sentimental comedy, Goldsmith continued, the virtues of private life were exhibited, rather than the vices exposed; and the distresses rather than the faults of mankind generated interest in the piece. Characters in these plays were almost always good; if they had faults, the spectator was expected not only to pardon but to applaud them, in consideration of the goodness of their hearts. Thus, according to Goldsmith, folly was commended instead of being ridiculed. Goldsmith concluded by labelling sentimental comedy a "species of bastard tragedy," "a kind of *mulish* production": a designation that ironically brings to mind Guarini's comparison of tragicomedy in its uniqueness (a product of comedy and tragedy but different from either) to the mule (the offspring of the horse and the ass but itself neither one nor the other). The production of Goldsmith's *She Stoops to Conquer* (1773) and of Richard Brinsley Sheridan's *Rivals* (1775) and *The School for Scandal* (1777) briefly reintroduced comic gaiety to the English stage; by the end of the decade, Sheridan's dramatic burlesque, *The Critic* (first performed 1779), had appeared, with its parody of contemporary dramatic fashions, the sentimental included. But this virtually concluded Sheridan's career as a dramatist; Goldsmith had died in 1774; and the sentimental play was to continue to govern the English comic stage for over a century to come.

Goldsmith's views on sentimental comedy

The comic outside the theatre. The great comic voices of the 18th century in England were not those in the theatre. No dramatic satire of the period can exhibit anything comparable to the furious ridicule of man's triviality and viciousness that Jonathan Swift provided in *Gulliver's Travels* (1726). His *Modest Proposal* (1729) is a masterpiece of comic incongruity, with its suave blend of rational deliberation and savage conclusion. The comic artistry of Alexander Pope is equally impressive. Pope expressed his genius in the invective of his satiric portraits and in the range of moral and imaginative vision that was capable, at one end of his poetic scale, of conducting that most elegant of drawing-room epics, *The Rape of the Lock* (1712–14), to its sublimely inane conclusion and, at the other, of invoking from the scene that closes *The Dunciad* (1728) an apocalyptic judgment telling what will happen when the vulgarizers of the word have carried the day.

Censorship

When the voice of comedy did sound on the 18th-century English stage with anything approaching its full critical and satiric resonance, the officials soon silenced it. John Gay's *Beggar's Opera* (1728) combined hilarity with a satiric fierceness worthy of Swift (who may have suggested the original idea for it). The officials tolerated its spectacularly successful run, but no license from the lord chamberlain could be secured for Gay's sequel, *Polly*, which was not staged until 1777. The Licensing Act of 1737 ended the theatrical career of Henry Fielding, whose comedies had come under constant fire from the authorities for their satire on the government. Fielding's comic talents were perforce directed to the novel, the form in which he parodied the sentiment and the morality of Richardson's *Pamela*—in his *Shamela* and *Joseph Andrews* (1742)—as brilliantly as he had earlier burlesqued the rant of heroic tragedy in *Tom Thumb* (1730).

Comedy of the sort that ridicules the follies and vices of society to the end of laughing them out of countenance entered the English novel with Fielding. His statement in *Joseph Andrews* concerning the function of satire is squarely in the Neoclassic tradition of comedy as a corrective of manners and mores: the satirist holds

> the glass to thousands in their closets, that they may contemplate their deformity, and endeavour to reduce it, and thus by suffering private mortification may avoid public shame.

Fielding's scenes of contemporary life display the same power of social criticism as that which distinguishes the engravings of his great fellow artist William Hogarth, whose "Marriage à la Mode" (1745) depicts the vacuity and the casual wantonness of the fashionable world that Fielding treats of in the final books of *Tom Jones*. Hogarth's other series, such as "A Rake's Progress" (1735) or "A Harlot's Progress" (1732), also make a didactic point about the wages of sin, using realistic details heightened with grotesquerie to expose human frailty and its sinister consequences. The grotesque is a recurrent feature of the satiric tradition in England, where comedy serves social criticism. Artists such as Hogarth and Thomas Rowlandson worked in the tradition of Jonson and the Restoration dramatists in the preceding century.

The novel, with its larger scope for varied characters, scenes, and incidents, rather than the drama, afforded the 19th-century artist in comedy a literary form adequate to his role as social critic. The spectacle of man and his society is regularly presented by the 19th-century novelist in comedic terms, as in *Vanity Fair* (1848), by William Makepeace Thackeray or the *Comédie humaine* (1842–55) of Honoré de Balzac, and with the novels of Jane Austen, Anthony Trollope, Charles Dickens, and George Meredith.

20th-century tragicomedy. The best that the comic stage had to offer in the late 19th century lay in the domain of farce. The masters of this form were French, but it flourished in England as well; what the farces of Eugène Labiche and Georges Feydeau and the operettas of Jacques Offenbach were to the Parisian stage the farces of W.S. Gilbert and the young Arthur Wing Pinero and the operettas that Gilbert wrote in collaboration with Arthur Sullivan were to the London stage. As concerns comedy, the situation in England improved at the end of

French farce

the century, when Oscar Wilde and George Bernard Shaw turned their talents to it. Wilde's *Importance of Being Earnest* (1895) is farce raised to the level of high comic burlesque. Shaw's choice of the comic form was inevitable, given his determination that the contemporary English stage should deal seriously and responsibly with the issues that were of crucial importance to contemporary English life. Serious subjects could not be resolved by means of the dramatic clichés of Victorian melodrama. Rather, the prevailing stereotypes concerning the nature of honour, courage, wisdom, and virtue were to be subjected to a hail of paradox, to the end of making evident their inner emptiness or the contradictions they concealed.

Shaw dealt with what, in the preface to *Major Barbara* (1905), he called "the tragi-comic irony of the conflict between real life and the romantic imagination," and his use of the word tragicomic is a sign of the times. The striking feature of modern art, according to the German novelist Thomas Mann, was that it had ceased to recognize the categories of tragic and comic or the dramatic classifications of tragedy and comedy but saw life as tragicomedy. The sense that tragicomedy is the only adequate dramatic form for projecting the unreconciled ironies of modern life mounted through the closing decades of the 19th century. Ibsen had termed *The Wild Duck* (published 1884) a tragicomedy; it was an appropriate designation for this bitter play about a young man blissfully ignorant of the lies on which he and his family have built their happy life until an outsider who is committed to an ideal of absolute truth exposes all their guilty secrets with disastrous results. The plays of the Russian writer Anton Chekhov, with their touching and often quite humorous figures leading lives of quiet desperation, reflect precisely that mixture of inarticulate joy and dull pain that is the essence of the tragicomic view of life.

A dramatist such as August Strindberg produces a kind of tragicomedy peculiarly his own, one that takes the form of bourgeois tragedy; it lacerates its principals until they become a parody of themselves. Strindberg's *Dance of Death* (1901), with its cruelty and pain dispensed with robust pleasure by a fiercely battling husband and wife, is a significant model of the grotesque in the modern theatre; it is reflected in such mid-20th-century examples of what came to be called black comedy as Eugène Ionesco's *Victims of Duty* (1953) and Edward Albee's *Who's Afraid of Virginia Woolf?* (1962). Almost equally influential as a turn-of-the-century master of the grotesque is Frank Wedekind, whose *Earth Spirit* (1895) and its sequel, *Pandora's Box* (written 1892–1901), though both are termed tragedies by their author, are as much burlesques of tragedy as *The Dance of Death*. Their grotesquerie consists chiefly in their disturbing combination of innocence and depravity, of farce and horror, of passionate fervour issuing in ludicrous incident that turns deadly. Wedekind's celebration of primitive sexuality and the varied ways in which it manifests itself in an oversophisticated civilization distorts the tragic form to achieve its own grotesque beauty and power.

The great artist of the grotesque and of tragicomedy in the 20th century is the Italian Luigi Pirandello. His drama is explicitly addressed to the contradictoriness of experience: appearances collide and cancel out each other; the quest of the absolute issues in a mind-reeling relativism; infinite spiritual yearnings are brought up hard against finite physical limits; rational purpose is undermined by irrational impulse; and with the longing for permanence in the midst of change comes the ironic awareness that changelessness means death. Stated thus, Pirandello's themes sound almost forbiddingly intellectual, but one of his aims was to convert intellect into passion. Pirandello's characters suffer from intellectual dilemmas that give rise to mental and emotional distress of the most anguished kind, but their sufferings are placed in a satiric frame. The incongruities that the characters are furiously seeking to reconcile attest to the comic aspect of this drama, but there is nothing in it of the traditional movement of comedy, from a state of illusion into the full light of reality. Pirandello's characters dwell amid

The role of
illusions in
Pirandel-
lo's tragi-
comedy

ambiguities and equivocations that those who are wise in the tragicomic nature of life will accept without close inquiry. The logic of comedy implies that illusions exist to be dispelled; once they are dispelled, everyone will be better off. The logic of Pirandello's tragicomedy demonstrates that illusions make life bearable; to destroy them is to destroy the basis for any possible happiness.

The absurd. In their highly individual ways, both Samuel Beckett and Ionesco have employed the forms of comedy—from tragicomedy to farce—to convey the vision of an exhausted civilization and a chaotic world. The very endurance of life amid the grotesque circumstances that obtain in Beckett's plays is at once a tribute to the human power of carrying on to the end and an ironic reflection on the absurdity of doing so. Beckett's plays close in an uneasy silence that is the more disquieting because of the uncertainty as to just what it conceals: whether it masks sinister forces ready to spring or is the expression of a universal indifference or issues out of nothing at all.

Silence seldom reigns in the theatre of Ionesco, which rings with voices raised in a usually mindless clamour. Some of Ionesco's most telling comic effects have come from his use of dialogue overflowing with clichés and non sequiturs, which make it clear that the characters do not have their minds on what they are saying and, indeed, do not have their minds on anything at all. What they say is often at grotesque variance with what they do. Beneath the moral platitudes lurks violence, which is never far from the surface in Ionesco's plays, and the violence tells what happens to societies in which words and deeds have become fatally disjunct. Ionesco's comic

Ionesco's
comic
sense

sense is evident as well in his depiction of human beings as automata, their movements decreed by forces they have never questioned or sought to understand. There is something undeniably farcical in Ionesco's spectacles of human regimentation, of men and women at the mercy of things (*e.g.*, the stage full of chairs in *The Chairs* or the growing corpse in *Amédée*); the comic quality here is one that Bergson would have appreciated. But the comic in Ionesco's most serious work, as in so much of the contemporary theatre, has ominous implications that give to it a distinctly grotesque aspect. In Ionesco's *Victims of Duty* and *The Killer* (1959), as in the works of his Swiss counterparts—*Der Besuch der alten Dame* (performed 1956; *The Visit*, 1958) and *The Physicists* (1962), by Friedrich Dürrenmatt, and *The Firebugs* (1958), by Max Frisch—the grotesquerie of the tragicomic vision delineates a world in which the humane virtues are dying, and casual violence is the order of the day.

The radical reassessment of the human image that the 20th century has witnessed is reflected in the novel as well as in drama. Previous assumptions about the rational and divine aspects of man have been increasingly called into question by the evidences of man's irrationality, his sheer animality. These are qualities of human nature that writers of previous ages (Swift, for example) have always recognized, but hitherto they have been typically viewed as dark possibilities that could overtake humanity if the rule of reason did not prevail. It is only in the mid-20th century that the savage and the irrational have come to be viewed as part of the normative condition of humanity rather than as tragic aberrations from it. The savage and the irrational amount to grotesque parodies of human possibility, ideally conceived. Thus it is that 20th-century novelists as well as dramatists have recognized the tragicomic nature of the contemporary human image and predicament, and the principal mode of representing both is the grotesque. This may take various forms: the apocalyptic nightmare of tyranny and terror in Kafka's novels *The Trial* (1925) and *The Castle* (1926); the tragic farce in terms of which the Austrian novelist Robert Musil describes the slow collapse of a society into anarchy and chaos, in *The Man Without Qualities* (1930–43); the brilliant irony whereby Thomas Mann represents the hero as a confidence man in *The Confessions of Felix Krull* (1954); the grimly parodic account of Germany's descent into madness in Günter Grass's novel *The Tin Drum*

(1959). The English novel contains a rich vein of the comic grotesque that extends at least back to Dickens and Thackeray and persisted in the 20th century in such varied novels as Evelyn Waugh's *Decline and Fall* (1928), Angus Wilson's *Anglo-Saxon Attitudes* (1956), and Kingsley Amis' *Lucky Jim* (1954). What novelists such as these have in common is the often disturbing combination of hilarity and desperation. It has its parallel in a number of American novels—John Barth's *Giles Goat-Boy* (1966), Kurt Vonnegut, Jr.'s *Slaughterhouse Five* (1969) —in which shrill farce is the medium for grim satire. And the grotesque is a prominent feature of modern poetry, as in some of the "Songs and Other Musical Pieces" of W.H. Auden.

THE COMIC IN OTHER ARTS

The visual arts. The increasing use of the affairs of common life as the subject matter of dramatic comedy through the Middle Ages and the Renaissance is also seen in painting of that time. Scenes from medieval mystery cycles, such as the comic episodes involving Noah's stubborn wife, have counterparts in medieval pictures in the glimpses of everyday realities that are caught through the windows or down the road from the sites where the great spiritual mysteries are in progress: the angel Gabriel may appear to the Virgin in the foreground, while a man is chopping wood in the yard outside. Medieval artists had never neglected the labours and the pleasures of the mundane world, but the treatment of them is often literally marginal, as in the depiction of men and women at work or play in the ornamental borders of an illuminated manuscript page. The seasonal round of life, with its cycle of plowing, sowing, mowing, and reaping interspersed with hawking, hunting, feasts, and weddings (the cycle of life, indeed, which comedy itself celebrates), is depicted in series after series of exquisite miniatures, such as those in the "Très Riches Heures du Duc de Berry." By the mid-16th century, however, in Pieter Bruegel's famous painting "Landscape with the Fall of Icarus," mundane reality has taken over the foreground; the plowman tills the soil, and the shepherd attends his flock, while, unnoticed by both, the legs of Icarus disappear inconspicuously into the sea. Bruegel is not a comic artist, but his art bears witness to what all great comic art celebrates: the basic rhythm of life. "Peasant Wedding" and "Peasant Dance" endow their heavy men and women with an awkward grace and dignity that bear comparison with Shakespeare's treatment of his comic characters. Paintings like Bruegel's "Children's Games" and his "Fight Between Carnival and Lent" are joyous representations of human energy. The series of "The Labours of the Months"—"Hunters in the Snow" for January, "Haymaking" for July, "Harvesters" for August, "Return of the Herd" for November—give pictorial treatment to a favourite subject of the medieval miniaturists. Finally, allusion must be made to Bruegel's mastery of the grotesque, notably in "The Triumph of Death" and in the "Dulle Griet," in which demons swarm over a devastated landscape.

Bruegel's
mastery
of the
grotesque

It is through the art of caricature that the spirit of comedy enters most directly into painting. The style derives from the portraits with ludicrously exaggerated features made by the Carracci, an Italian family of artists, early in the 17th century (Italian *caricare*, "to overload"). In defiance of the theory of ideal beauty, these portraits emphasized the features that made one man different from another. This method of character portrayal—the singling out of one distinctive feature and emphasizing it over all others—is not unlike the practice of characterizing the personages of the comic stage by means of some predominant humour, which Ben Jonson was developing at about the same time in the London theatre. The use of exaggeration for comic effect was as evident to painters as it was to dramatists. Its usefulness as a means of social and political satire is fully recognized by Hogarth. Hogarth's counterpart in mid-19th-century Paris was Honoré Daumier. His caricatures portray a human comedy as richly detailed and as shrewdly observed as the one portrayed in fiction by his contemporary Balzac. But

Daumier's sense of the comic goes beyond caricature; his numerous treatments of scenes from Molière's plays and, most notably, his drawings and canvases of Don Quixote and Sancho Panza attest to the pathos that can lie beneath the comic mask.

Modern art has abstracted elements of comedy to aid it in the representation of a reality in which the mechanical is threatening to win out over the human. Bergson's contention that the essence of comedy consists of something mechanical encrusted on the living may be said to have achieved a grotesque apotheosis in the French Dadaist Marcel Duchamp's painting "The Bride" (1912), in which the female figure has been reduced to an elaborate piece of plumbing. The highly individual Swiss Expressionist Paul Klee's pen-and-ink drawing tinted with watercolour and titled "Twittering Machine" (1922) represents an ingenious device for imitating the sound of birds. The delicacy of the drawing contrasts with the sinister implications of the mechanism, which, innocent though it may appear at first glance, is almost certainly a trap.

The grotesque is a constant stylistic feature of the artist's representation of reality in its brutalized or mechanized aspects. The carnival masks worn by the figures in the painting "Intrigue" (1890), by the Belgian James Ensor, make manifest the depravity and the obscenity that lurk beneath the surface of conventional appearances; Ensor's paintings make much the same point about the persistence of the primitive and the savage into modern life as Wedekind's plays were to do a few years later. German artists after World War I invoked the grotesque with particular power, depicting the inhuman forces that bear upon the individual, as in George Grosz's savage cartoon titled "Germany, a Winter's Tale" (1918), in which the puppet-like average citizen sits at table surrounded by militarist, capitalist, fatuous clergyman and all the violent and dissolute forces of a decadent society. The mutilated humanity in Max Beckmann's "Dream" (1921) and "Departure" (1932–33) is a further testament to human viciousness, 20th-century variety.

Rather more explicitly comic is the element of fantasy in modern paintings, in which seemingly unrelated objects are brought together in a fine incongruity, as in the French primitive Henri Rousseau's famous "Dream" (1910), with its nude woman reclining on a red-velvet sofa amid the flora and fauna of a lush and exotic jungle. The disparate figures that float (in defiance of all the laws of gravity) through the paintings of the Russian surrealist Marc Chagall are individually set forth in a nimbus of memory and in the landscape of dream. But fantasy can take on a grotesquerie of its own, as in some of Chagall's work, such as the painting "I and My Village" (1911).

The purest expression of the comic in modern painting must surely be Henri Matisse's "Joy of Life" (1905–06), a picture that might be taken as a visual expression of the precept that the rhythm of comedy is the basic rhythm of life. But Matisse's painting was not to be the last word on the subject: "Joy of Life" produced, as a counterstatement, Pablo Picasso's "Demoiselles d'Avignon" (1906–07), in which the daughters of joy, in their grim and aggressive physical tension, stand as a cruel parody of the delight in the senses that Matisse's picture celebrates. "Les Demoiselles d'Avignon" and such a later Picasso masterpiece as the "Three Dancers" (1925) suggest that, for the visual as well as the literary artist of the 20th century, the joy of life tends to issue in grotesque shapes.

Comedy in music. Given the wide range of imitative sounds of which musical instruments and the human voice are capable, comic effects are readily available to the composer who wants to use them. At the simplest level, these may amount to nothing more than humorous adjuncts to a larger composition, such as the loud noise with which the 18th-century Austrian composer Joseph Haydn surprises his listeners in *Symphony No. 94* or the sound of the ticking clock in *No. 101*. The scherzo, which Ludwig van Beethoven introduced into symphonic music in the early 19th century, may be said to have incorporated in it a musical joke but one of a highly abstract kind; its nervous jocularity provides a contrast and a commentary (both heavy with irony) on the surrounding splendour. A century after Beethoven, the jocularity grew more desperate and the irony more profound in the grim humour that rises out of the grotesque scherzos of Gustav Mahler. A more sustained and a more explicit musical exposition of comic themes and attitudes comes when a composer draws his inspiration directly from a work of comic literature, as Richard Strauss does in his orchestral variations based on *Don Quixote* and on the merry pranks of *Till Eulenspiegel*.

It is, however, opera that provides the fullest form for comedy to express itself in music, and some of the most notable achievements of comic art have been conceived for the operatic stage. High on any list of comic masterpieces must come the four principal operas of Mozart: *The Marriage of Figaro* (1786), *Don Giovanni* (1787), *Così fan tutte* (1790), and *The Magic Flute* (1791), and there are countless others worthy of mention. Operatic comedy has an advantage over comedy in the spoken theatre in its ability to impose a coherent form on the complexities of feeling and action that are often of the essence in comedy. The complex feeling experienced by different characters must be presented in spoken comedy seriatim; operatic comedy can present them simultaneously. When three or four characters talk simultaneously in the spoken theatre, the result is an incoherent babble. But the voices of three or four or even more characters can be blended together in an operatic ensemble, and, while most of the words may be lost, the vocal lines will serve to identify the individual characters and the general nature of the emotions they are expressing. The complexities of action in the spoken theatre are the chief source of the comic effect, which increases as the confusion mounts; such complexities of action operate to the same comic end in opera but here with the added ingredient of music, which provides an overarching design of great formal coherence. In the music, all is manifestly ordered and harmonious, while the events of the plot appear random and chaotic; the contrast between the movement of the plot and the musical progression provides a Mozart or a Rossini with some of his wittiest and most graceful comic effects. Finally, it should be noted that operatic comedy can probe psychological and emotional depths of character that spoken comedy would scarcely attempt. The Countess in Mozart's *Figaro* is a very much more moving figure than she is in Beaumarchais' play; the Elvira of *Don Giovanni* exhibits a fine extravagance that is little more than suggested in Molière's comedy.

Television and cinema. When comedy is dependent on the favour of a large part of the public, as reflected in box-office receipts or the purchase of a television sponsor's product, it seldom achieves a high level of art. There is nothing innocent about laughter at the whims and inconsistencies of humankind, and radio and television and film producers have always been wary of offending their audiences with it. On radio and television, the laughter is usually self-directed (as in the performances of comedians such as Jack Benny or Red Skelton), or it is safely contained within the genial confines of a family situation (*e.g.,* the "Fibber McGee and Molly" radio show or "I Love Lucy," on television). Much the same attitude has obtained with regard to comedy in the theatre in the United States. Satire has seldom succeeded on Broadway, which instead has offered pleasant plays about the humorous behaviour of basically nice people, such as the eccentric family in George S. Kaufmann and Moss Hart's *You Can't Take It With You* (1936) or the lovable head of the household in Howard Lindsay and Russel Crouse's *Life With Father* (1939) or the indefatigable Dolly Levi in Thornton Wilder's *Matchmaker* (1954) and in her later reincarnation in the musical *Hello, Dolly!*

The American public has never been quite comfortable in the presence of comedy. The calculated ridicule and the relentless exposure often seem cruel or unfair to a democratic public. If all men are created equal, then it ill becomes anyone to laugh at the follies of his fellows, especially when they are follies that are likely to be shared, given the common background of social opportunity and experience of the general public. There is an insecurity in the mass audience that is not compatible with the high self-assurance of comedy as it judges between the wise and the foolish of the world. The critical spirit of comedy has never been welcome in American literature; in both fiction and drama, humour, not comedy, has raised the laughter. American literature can boast an honorable tradition of humorists, from Mark Twain to James Thurber, but has produced no genuinely comic writer. As American social and moral tenets were subjected to increasing critical scrutiny from the late 1950s onward, however, there were some striking achievements in comedy in various media: Edward Albee's *American Dream* (1961) and *Who's Afraid of Virginia Woolf?* (1962), on the stage; novels such as those of Saul Bellow and Joseph Heller's *Catch-22* (1961); and films such as *Dr. Strangelove* (1964).

This last example is remarkable, because comedy in the medium of film, in America, had been conceived as entertainment and not much more. This is not to say that American film comedies lacked style. The best of them always displayed verve and poise and a thoroughly professional knowledge of how to amuse the public without troubling it. Their shortcoming has always been that the amusement they provide lacks resonance.

If films have seldom explored comedy with great profundity, they have, nonetheless, produced it in great variety. There have been comedies of high sophistication, the work of directors such as Ernst Lubitsch, George Cukor, Frank Capra, Joseph L. Mankiewicz, and Billy Wilder and of actors and actresses such as Greta Garbo (in Lubitsch's *Ninotchka*, 1939), Katharine Hepburn and Cary Grant (in Cukor's *Philadelphia Story*, 1940), Bette Davis (in Mankiewicz' *All About Eve*, 1950), Clark Gable and Claudette Colbert (in Capra's *It Happened One Night*, 1934), Gary Cooper and Jean Arthur (in Capra's *Mr. Deeds Goes to Town*, 1936), and Marilyn Monroe and Jack Lemmon (in Billy Wilder's *Some Like It Hot*, 1959). There have been comedies with music, built around the talents of singers and dancers such as Ruby Keeler and Dick Powell and Ginger Rogers and Fred Astaire; there are the classic farces of Charlie Chaplin and Buster Keaton and, later, of W.C. Fields and the Marx Brothers and Laurel and Hardy; and there is a vast, undistinguished field of comedies dealing with the humours of domestic life. The varieties of comedy in Hollywood films have always been replicas of those on the New York stage; as often as not, they were products of the same talents: in the 1930s, of dramatists such as Philip Barry or S.N. Behrman and composers such as Cole Porter, Richard Rodgers, and Irving Berlin; in the 1960s, of the dramatist Neil Simon and the composer Burt Bacharach.

Comedies produced by European film makers

European film makers, with an older and more intellectual tradition of comedy available to them, produced comedies of more considerable stature. Among French directors, Jean Renoir, in his *The Rules of the Game* (1939), conveyed a moving human drama and a profoundly serious vision of French life on the eve of World War II in a form, deriving from the theatre, that blends the comic and the tragic. His disciple François Truffaut, in *Jules and Jim* (1961), directed a witty and tender but utterly clear-sighted account of how gaiety and love turn deadly. Though not generally regarded as a comic artist, the Swedish film maker Ingmar Bergman produced a masterpiece of film comedy in *Smiles of a Summer Night* (1955), a wise, wry account of the indignities that must sometimes be endured by those who have exaggerated notions of their wisdom or virtue. The films of the Italian director and writer Federico Fellini represent a comic vision worthy of Pirandello. *La strada* (1954), with its Chaplinesque waif (played by Fellini's wife, Giulietta Masina) as central figure, is a disturbing compound of pathos and brutality. Comedy's affirmation of the will to go on living has had no finer portrayal than in Giulietta Masina's performance in the closing scene of *Nights of Cabiria* (1956). *La dolce vita* (1960) is a luridly satiric vision of modern decadence, where ideals are travestied by reality, and everything is illusion and disillusionment;

the vision is carried to even more bizarre lengths in Fellini's *Satyricon* (1969), in which the decadence of the modern world is grotesquely mirrored in the ancient one. *8½* (1963) and *Juliet of the Spirits* (1965) are Fellini's most brilliantly inventive films, but their technical exuberance is controlled by a profoundly serious comic purpose. The principals in both films are seeking—through the phantasmagoria of their past and present, of their dreams and their delusions, all of which seem hopelessly mixed with their real aspirations—to know themselves.

BIBLIOGRAPHY. C.L. BARBER, *Shakespeare's Festive Comedy: A Study of Dramatic Form and Its Relation to Social Custom* (1959), Shakespearean comedy considered in relation to archetypal patterns of folk ritual and games; ERIC BENTLEY, *The Life of the Drama* (1964), a general study of the dramatic genre, *The Playwright as Thinker* (1946, reprinted 1955), contains chapters on Shaw, Strindberg, and a discussion of "Varieties of Comic Experience" dealing with Shaw, Wilde, and Pirandello; LANE COOPER, *An Aristotelian Theory of Comedy, with an Adaptation of the Poetics and a Translation of the Tractatus Coislinianus* (1922), the only modern text of the *Tractatus*, with an introductory essay relating it to Aristotle's theory of tragedy, and a conjectural reconstruction of the lost treatise on comedy based on the example of the *Poetics*; F.M. CORNFORD, *The Origin of Attic Comedy* (1914; ed. by T.H. GASTER, 1961), an account of the development of Greek comedy from primitive fertility rites, and of the survival of traces of these ceremonials in the extant plays of Aristophanes; CYRUS HOY, *The Hyacinth Room: An Investigation into the Nature of Comedy, Tragedy, and Tragicomedy* (1964), an examination of the plays of Euripides, Shakespeare, Jonson, Molière, Ibsen, Strindberg, Pirandello, Beckett, and Ionesco; J.W. KRUTCH, *Comedy and Conscience After the Restoration* (1924, reprinted with a new preface and additional bibliographical material, 1949), a study of the decline of Restoration comedy and the rise of sentimental comedy at the end of the 17th and the beginning of the 18th century; K.M. LYNCH, *The Social Mode of Restoration Comedy* (1926), the best available account of the relation of the plays of Dryden, Etherege, Wycherley, Congreve, and their contemporaries to their social milieu; A.W. PICKARD-CAMBRIDGE, *Dithyramb, Tragedy, and Comedy* (1927; 2nd ed. rev. by T.B.L. WEBSTER, 1962), and *The Dramatic Festivals of Athens* (1953; 2nd ed. rev. by J. GOULD and D.M. LEWIS, 1968), the definitive accounts of the origins of Greek comedy and tragedy; F.H. RISTINE, *English Tragicomedy: Its Origins and History* (1910), though it is by no means a definitive study, remains the only full-scale account of the subject through the 17th century; J.L. STYAN, *The Dark Comedy: The Development of Modern Comic Tragedy* (1962), an account of the blending of tragic and comic elements in the post-Ibsen theatre.

(C.H.Ho.)

Comenius, John Amos

A 17th-century educational reformer and religious leader, John Amos Comenius is remembered mainly for his approach to teaching. Much of his life, however, was devoted to expounding his belief that peace and cooperation among men could be achieved through a system of universal education.

He was born as Jan Ámos Komenský in eastern Moravia in 1592, the only son of respected members of a Protestant group known as the Bohemian Brethren. His parents died when he was 12, and after four unhappy years he was sent to school at Přerov. Though the teaching methods there were poor, he was befriended by a headmaster who recognized his gifts and encouraged him to train for the ministry. At the University of Heidelberg, Germany, he came under the influence of Protestant millennialists, who believed that men could achieve salvation on earth. He also read with enthusiasm the works of Francis Bacon and returned home convinced that the millennium could be attained with the aid of science.

Early exile

As a young minister Comenius found life wholly satisfying, but the outbreak of the Thirty Years' War in 1618 and the emperor Ferdinand II's determination to re-Catholicize Bohemia forced him and other Protestant leaders to flee. While in hiding, he wrote an allegory, *The Labyrinth of the World and the Paradise of the Heart*, in which he described both his despair and his sources of consolation. With a band of Brethren he escaped to Poland and in 1628 settled in Leszno. Believ-

Comenius, detail of an engraving by David Loggan after a drawing by Crispijn van de Passe (1560–1637), from the title page of *Didactica Opera Omnia*, 1657.
By courtesy of the Pedagogicke Muzeum J.A. Komenskeho, Prague

ing that the Protestants would eventually win and liberate Bohemia, he began to prepare for the day when it would be possible to rebuild society there through a reformed educational system. He wrote a "Brief Proposal" advocating full-time schooling for all the youth of the nation and maintaining that they should be taught both their native culture and the culture of Europe.

Educational reformer.   The reform of the educational system would require two things: First, a revolution in methods of teaching so that learning might become rapid, pleasant, and thorough. Teachers ought to "follow in the footsteps of nature," meaning that they ought to pay attention to the mind of the child and the way it learned. He made this the theme of *The Great Didactic* and also of *The School of Infancy*—a book for mothers on the early years of childhood. Second, to make European culture accessible to all children it was necessary that they learn Latin. But Comenius was certain there was a better way of teaching Latin than by the inefficient and pedantic methods then in use; he advocated "nature's way," that is, learning about things and not about grammar. To this end he wrote *Gate of Languages Unlocked* (1631), a textbook that described useful facts about the world in both Latin and Czech, side by side; thus, the pupils could compare the two languages and identify words with things. Translated into German, the *Gate* (or *Janua*, as he called it in Latin) soon became famous throughout Europe and was subsequently translated into a number of European and Oriental languages. Comenius wrote that he was "encouraged beyond expectation" by the book's reception.

With the liberation of Bohemia less certain than before, Comenius turned to an even more ambitious project—the reform of human society through education. Others in Europe shared his vision, among them a German merchant living in London, Samuel Hartlib, who invited Comenius to England to establish a college of social reform. With approval from the Brethren, Comenius went to London in 1641, reporting back that he had been "fitted out with new clothes befitting an English divine." He met a number of influential men, engaged in much discussion, and wrote essays of which the most notable was *The Way of Light*, which set out his program. Parliament went so far as to consider setting up a college "for a number of men from all nations." This prospect was shattered by the outbreak of the English Civil War, and Comenius was obliged to leave in 1642. He had been invited to France by Cardinal de Richelieu; and the American John Winthrop, Jr., in Europe looking for an educator-theologian to become president of Harvard College,

may have met Comenius. Instead, Comenius accepted an offer from the government of Sweden to help reform its schools by writing a series of textbooks modelled on his *Janua*.

He interpreted his agreement with the Swedish government as entitling him to base his textbooks on a system of philosophy he had evolved called "pansophy" (see below). After struggling hard to produce them, however, he found that they failed to satisfy anyone. Nevertheless, in the course of his stay at Elbing he tried to lay a philosophical foundation for a science of pedagogy. In *The Analytical Didactic*, forming part of his *Newest Method of Languages*, he reinterpreted the principle of nature that he had described in *The Great Didactic* as a principle of logic. He put forward certain self-evident principles from which he derived a number of maxims, some of them full of common sense and others rather platitudinous. His chief attention was directed to his system of pansophy. Ever since his student days he had been seeking a basic principle by which all knowledge could be harmonized. He believed that men could be trained to see the underlying harmony of the universe and thus to overcome its apparent disharmony. He wrote that:

> pansophy propoundeth to itself so to expand and lay open to the eyes of all the wholeness of things that everything might be pleasurable in itself and necessary for the expanding of the appetite.

The "expanding of the appetite" for pansophic understanding became his great aim, spelled out in "A General Consultation Concerning the Improvement of Human Affairs."

Social reformer.   The Peace of Westphalia (1648), which ended the Thirty Years' War, was a blow to Comenius and other Czech exiles, who thereby lost their last hope of a restitution of ethnic and religious liberty in their homeland. Few of them returned, since they would have been required to recant their beliefs. Comenius left Elbing and returned to Poland, where the Brethren at Leszno had been cast into despair. In 1648 he was consecrated presiding bishop of the Moravians, the last of the Bohemian-Moravian clergy to hold this office.

His next invitation came from Hungary, where the young Prince Zsigmond Rákóczi wanted to establish a model pansophic school at Sárospatak. Comenius, arriving there in 1650, received a warm reception. The school opened with about 100 pupils, but they were ill-prepared to learn anything beyond the rudiments of reading and writing, and the teachers soon lost interest in a scheme they could not understand. The Prince died in 1652, and at about the same time war broke out in Poland.

Comenius returned to Leszno, carrying with him the manuscript of a picture textbook he had written for his pupils but for which he had not been able to obtain the necessary woodcuts. He sent the manuscript to Nuremberg in Germany, where the cuts were made. His book, *The Visible World in Pictures* (*Orbis Sensualium Pictus*), was popular in Europe for two centuries and was the forerunner of the illustrated schoolbook of later times. It consisted of pictures illustrating Latin sentences, accompanied by vernacular translations. For example, the chapter "The Head and the Hand" began with a picture of a head and two hands followed by sentences such as:

> In the Head are, the Hair, 1. [which is Combed with a Comb, 2.] two Ears, 3. the Temples, 4. and the Face, 5. . . .
> In *Capite* sunt *Capillus*, 1. [qui pectitur *Pectine* 2.] *Aures* 3. binae, & *Tempora*, 4. *Facies*, 5.

Comenius had not been back in Leszno long before it was occupied and destroyed, with the loss of many of his manuscripts. He escaped to Amsterdam, where he remained for the rest of his life. In 1657 he gathered together most of his writings on education and published them as a collection, *Didactica Opera Omnia*. He devoted his remaining years to completing his great work, *Consultation*. He managed to get parts of it published, and when he was dying in 1670 he begged his close associates to publish the rest of it after his death. They failed to do so, and the manuscripts were lost until 1935, when they were found in an orphanage in Halle, Germany.

Work in Sweden and Hungary

The Visible World in Pictures

Assessment. In his lifetime the fame of Comenius rested chiefly on his two popular textbooks, the *Janua* and the *Orbis Sensualium Pictus*. He himself would have set more store by his influence as a social reformer, which reached its highest point during his visit to England. Men all over Europe had looked to Comenius as a leader; his vision had impressed both those who were seeking a more dynamic form of religion and those who looked to science as an avenue of reform. His pansophism, on the other hand, was not influential either in his lifetime or afterward. His dream of universal harmony was too vague and grandiose for the mental outlook of the 17th century, which was already shifting in a utilitarian and materialistic direction; it has had even less appeal in modern times.

As a religious leader Comenius helped keep alive the faith of his church in its darkest hour, and he provided the inspiration that led to its subsequent revival as the Moravian Church under Nikolaus, Graf von Zinzendorf in the 18th century. He was no sectarian but a champion of the church universal. He was also, for all of his internationalism, a Czech patriot at a time when the Czechs had been nearly crushed. He wrote: "I love my country and its language, and my greatest wish is that it should be cultivated."

In the 19th century his reputation was revived by the increasing attention given to the study of pedagogy, especially in Germany. At the present day he remains of interest as a prototype of the international citizen. His patriotism did not prevent him from feeling himself a European and from believing profoundly in the unity of mankind.

BIBLIOGRAPHY. Comenius wrote more than 200 works, some of which have been translated into various languages. An excellent bibliography may be found in MATTHEW SPINKA's biography, *John Amos Comenius: That Incomparable Moravian* (1943). Other books on Comenius in English include: J.E. SADLER, *J.A. Comenius and the Concept of Universal Education* (1966); and G.H. TURNBULL, *Hartlib, Dury and Comenius* (1947).

(J.E.Sa.)

Comet

A comet is a generally nebulous celestial body of small mass revolving around the Sun. Its appearance and brightness vary markedly with its distance from the Sun. A comet far from the Sun is very faint, appears starlike, and consists of a small body or group of bodies reflecting sunlight, called the nucleus. As the comet approaches the Sun, a nebulosity called the coma develops around the nucleus; with the nucleus it constitutes the head of the comet. The coma contains dust and gas released from the nucleus through the action of solar radiation. When close enough to the Sun, a tail may develop, sometimes very long and bright, directed away from the Sun. Such a comet shines partly by scattering of solar radiation on dust particles and partly by re-emission by the gas of absorbed solar radiation (through processes called resonance or fluorescence).

Only a small proportion of comets have tails, but all appear diffuse for some time. Comets usually follow elongated paths (generally ellipses, but a number of parabolas or even hyperbolas have been computed), in contrast to the near-circular planetary orbits. Their paths may be inclined at any angle relative to the Earth's orbital plane (ecliptic). Most orbits near the ecliptic are ellipses of relatively small dimensions and eccentricities, very like the paths of minor planets. Comets on such orbits are called short-period comets or sometimes just "periodic" comets (periods less than about 200 years). Comets and meteor showers are definitely related, and comets are thought to be responsible for the formation of most, if not all, shower meteors. The zodiacal light, a faint glow in the plane of the Earth's orbit, seen in clear skies just after sunset or just before sunrise, may be produced by very small particles from comets. Comets are minor constituents of the solar system on account of their small mass, but their complex phenomena pose challenging problems, in particular through their interaction with the

interplanetary medium; and they probably have great significance regarding the early history of the solar system. The word comet arises from the Greek *komētēs astēr*, meaning "hairy star," a description of bright comets with long tails, the only ones noticed by the ancients.

Comets may represent the oldest and best preserved material in the solar system and are probably the only specimens offering information about the very early phase of the solar nebula and the processes that led to the formation of the planets.

Each comet is identified by a serial number, as well as a name. Its first provisional designation is the calendar year of discovery, followed by a small letter giving the order of discovery (or recovery in the case of a periodic comet) in that year: 1962a, 1962b, 1962c . . ., for instance. A later official designation is adopted based on the dates at which the comets reach perihelion, the point of closest approach to the Sun. This uses the year of perihelion with Roman numerals to specify the chronological order of the perihelion passages; thus, after November 1964, the three comets listed above became known as 1962 II, 1962 V, and 1962 III, respectively. Since comets can be discovered some appreciable time before or after their perihelion passage, the years appearing in the preliminary and in the definitive designation may be different. Comets are also named after their discoverer(s), with a maximum of three names. The name of a short-period comet is prefixed with a P/ and may also be followed by an Arabic numeral indicating that the same person has discovered two or more different periodic comets. Often the name of a comet and one of its numbers, usually the definitive number, are given together (*e.g.*, P/Harrington-Abell, 1962 II). If a lost periodic comet happens to be seen again, the name of the author of the recovery may be added. P/Tuttle-Giacobini-Kresák, for instance, was discovered independently by Tuttle in 1858, by Giacobini in 1907, and by Kresák in 1951. A few periodic comets derived their final name from the scientist who actually proved their periodic character. Such are the famous comets P/Halley, P/Lexell, P/Encke, P/Crommelin. Some comets, first seen when already very bright and discovered by a large number of persons at almost the same time, are given an impersonal designation, such as Brilliant Comet (1882 II), Southern Comet (1947 XII), or Eclipse Comet (1948 XI).

HISTORY OF OBSERVATIONS OF COMETS

Man has always been awed by the sudden apparition of a bright comet. Because of the unexpectedness of the apparitions, their apparently erratic movements, and their unusual and sometimes rapidly changing appearance, the observer was often gripped by superstition, fear, or even terror rather than admiration for the comet's strange beauty or a truly scientific interest in its phenomena.

Comets in ancient and medieval history. According to some ancient Greeks, comets were conglomerates of stars, but this was not the common view; comets were usually regarded by the Greeks and Romans as totally unconnected with the incorruptible realms of the stars. The philosopher Aristotle (4th century BC) thought they were "blazing exhalations" in the Earth's upper atmosphere, and, as such, they were generally deemed unworthy of study for many centuries. Yet, at various epochs a few more enlightened minds, such as the Roman philosopher Seneca (1st century AD), considered that comets were heavenly bodies like the planets. A comet was thought to be the harbinger or even the cause of some human or natural events, usually disasters, such as wars or famines or deaths of kings. Astronomers in the eastern world recorded comet sightings more accurately than Europeans did until the 15th century. The Babylonian, Chinese, Japanese, and Korean annals have been very useful for statistical studies and for tracing back early apparitions of such periodic comets as P/Halley. The Chinese annals, in particular, go back more than 3,000 years from the present time, and many records of early comet sightings appear in them.

The 15th to 19th centuries. The first scientific observations of the motions of comets were made in the later

Short-period comets

The work
of Tycho
Brahe and
Isaac
Newton

15th century. Accurate observations by the Danish nobleman Tycho Brahe and by the German astronomer Michael Mästlin showed that the parallax (change of position in the sky relative to the "fixed" stars) of comets, especially of the comet of 1577, was so small that their distances, which are inversely proportional to the parallax, must be considerably larger than that of the Moon. For the first time, comets were shown to be actual celestial bodies, but conjecture about their paths continued. The English mathematician Isaac Newton first interpreted the motion of the comets correctly. He showed that gravitational attraction that explained the nearly circular, elliptical motions of the planets also explained comet orbits that were ellipses with large eccentricities, or even parabolas and hyperbolas with the Sun at a focus. A bright, rapidly moving comet was observed from November 14 to December 5, 1680, then became invisible because of its nearness to the Sun; but it reappeared about two weeks later and finally went away in very nearly the direction from which it had come. Newton took the path of the comet to be a parabola for the sake of simplicity and because a parabola is hardly distinguishable from an elongated ellipse near the principal focus (where comets are observed anyway); he found close agreement between the calculated and observed positions of the comet. The near-parabolic nature of the orbits for several other comets explained the irregular appearances; a given comet seen again after a long period would probably be taken as a new comet at its return.

Halley's
Comet

The English astronomer Edmond Halley applied the same method to a number of comets and was able to compute parabolic paths (trajectories) for them. It turned out that the elements (mathematical characteristics) of three of the orbits were almost identical and that the apparition years were separated by nearly equal intervals. One of these comets had been observed in 1537 and another in 1607, while Halley himself had made observations of the third one in 1682. Later, Halley noticed that a bright comet had appeared in 1456 and probably another in 1378. He concluded that the five appearances were five successive returns of the same comet, whose orbit must be an ellipse with a period of about 75 years. He predicted the next return in 1758, though he had correctly interpreted the slight differences between successive paths of the comet as due to the gravitational pull of Jupiter and Saturn, and he knew that the motion would probably be modified again. An exact solution was not possible at the time, however. The mathematical knowledge (see MECHANICS, CELESTIAL) needed to calculate perturbations of cometary orbits was gradually developed during the 18th and early 19th centuries. April 13, 1759, was predicted as the probable date of perihelion passage of the comet, with an estimated possible error of one month either way due to various approximations. The comet was found in December 1758 and reached its perihelion on March 12, 1759. The return of the comet and the success of the computations concerning this return were rightly regarded as one of the most beautiful triumphs of Newton's theory of gravitation. Halley's Comet returned to perihelion in 1835, within about three days of the average of four independent predictions. A similar accuracy was reached in the prediction of its date of perihelion passage in 1910 (see Figure 1). A complete list of 29 passages since 239 BC was prepared about 100 years after Halley's death. This list, which was revised later, showed that Halley's Comet was identical to the comet depicted on the Bayeux Tapestry in connection with the conquest of England by William the Conqueror in 1066, as well as to the great comet of 1456 that had caused a great panic among Christians because it was thought to be associated with the capture of Constantinople by the Turks.

The first truly elliptical orbit—*i.e.*, one admitting of no parabolic substitute—was derived at St. Petersburg by the Finnish-born astronomer Anders Jean Lexell from observations of a comet discovered by the French astronomer Charles Messier in 1769, now known as Lexell's Comet (1770 I). The comet made only this one appearance. According to Lexell, close approaches to Jupiter

Figure 1: Halley's Comet, May 4, 1910, the first comet for which a periodic pattern was established.
By courtesy of Yerkes Observatory, University of Chicago

first transformed its trajectory into a small ellipse on which it was seen for some time and finally in such a way that it was thrown out to large distances from the inner solar system, where it could no longer be observed.

A simpler method for computing parabolic orbits was published in 1797 and used extensively in the 19th century, but a more general method was needed. The German mathematician Carl Friedrich Gauss in 1809 constructed a method for computation of orbits of any type, in particular of small dimensions and, hence, of short periods. It enabled Johann Encke, a pupil of Gauss's, to derive an orbit for a comet discovered in 1818 that could not be fitted to a parabolic orbit. Encke was able to identify this comet with three earlier comets observed in 1786, 1795, and 1805. This comet, thereafter named Encke's Comet, travels around the Sun in an ellipse with a period of 3.3 years (the shortest known). It has been observed about 50 times since its discovery. Curiously, the period, as noted by Encke, shows a systematic decrease that is not caused by planetary perturbations (see below). The rate of decrease of the period is variable and, perhaps, discontinuous.

Discovery
of meteor
streams
related to
comets

The orbits of periodic meteor streams ("shooting stars," due to clouds of solid particles moving in parallel paths crossing the Earth's atmosphere) around the Sun were computed shortly after the middle of the 19th century and found to be such that some meteors travelled in the same orbits as certain comets. The Perseids (seen in August) and the Leonids (November) were related to comets P/Swift-Tuttle, 1862 III (period = 120 years) and P/Tempel-Tuttle, 1866 I (period = 33 years), respectively. Even more significantly, Comet P/Biela, 1852 III (period = 6.6 years), a rather faint object, was detected by Wilhelm von Biela in 1826 and later proved to be identical with comets seen in 1772 and 1805. On its 1846 return, it was observed to break into two pieces. The fragments returned in 1852 as twin comets separated by about 2,000,000 kilometres (1,242,740 miles). They were never seen again, but, when the Earth crossed the orbit not far from the place where the comet should have been in

First inter-
pretations
of comet
tails

1872 and in 1885, very bright displays of meteors were observed (Bielids or Andromedids).

In the 16th century comet tails were noticed to be always directed away from the Sun. They were then believed to be produced by "rays" from the Sun that carried away cometary material, and Newton expressed the view that they were streams of finely divided matter from the centre of the comet. The great comet of 1811 had a parabolic envelope, like jets in a fountain, suggestive of a force from the Sun. In 1836 the German astronomer Friedrich Wilhelm Bessel developed a theory, later improved by Fyodor Aleksandrovich Bredikhin, a Russian astronomer, that explained a number of features of cometary tails by assuming a repulsive force that acted on the cometary particles and varied, like the gravitational attraction, as the inverse square of the distance to the Sun but that was not otherwise specified.

The modern era. Virtually nothing was known about the physical structure and composition of comets until the second part of the 19th century. The first visual spectroscopic observations of comets in 1864 showed three bright bands, identified in 1868 with some characteristic emissions (Swan bands) of molecular carbon. The first photographic cometary spectrum in 1881 revealed a strong ultraviolet emission due to cyanogen and some other weaker features identified later. A continuous spectrum showing the strongest (Fraunhofer) lines of the solar spectrum was also recorded. The detection of the fainter emissions from the comet tails needed better light-gathering power and came later. The wide field of view of the objective prism, developed near the turn of the century, made it possible to locate the various types of constituents within the comet. These pioneering spectroscopic observations provided the foundations of the modern theory of comets.

Discovery and observation of comets. Up to the beginning of the 20th century, comets were discovered exclusively by visual means. Photographic methods are increasingly important today, but many comet discoveries are still made visually by amateur astronomers. Although comets are often seen near the western horizon after sunset or near the eastern horizon before sunrise, being brightest when closest to the Sun, they can be present in any region of the sky. If a comet has no tail, it may look like an emission nebula, a globular star cluster, or a galaxy; careful comparisons with astronomical charts and catalogs are essential. The famous 18th-century French comet hunter Charles Messier (who was nicknamed the "ferret of comets" by Louis XV and was responsible for 21 comet discoveries) established his well-known catalog of "nebulae" in order that these objects should not be mistaken for comets. At least two observations of a suspected comet separated by a few hours or a day are needed; if the nebulous object has moved relative to the stars from one observation to the other, it can be concluded that it is a comet, and a report should be made immediately to the nearest observatory. Most comets are extremely faint, either intrinsically or because they never come close to the Sun or to the Earth. A large proportion of comet discoveries are now made from photographs with good-quality images. Many comets are found accidentally during sky surveys by professional astronomers engaged in other projects. A considerable number of comet recoveries have been made recently with large reflectors (about two metres [6½ feet] in diameter) in Arizona. The faintest recorded comets are close to the limit of detection (magnitude 21, approximately), more than 1,000,000 times fainter than the limit for the naked eye. Several successive observations are necessary to ensure identification of these.

Rates of
discovery
of comets

The total rate of comet discoveries averaged from 1951 to 1970 is nine per year. Individual rates of discoveries of new near-parabolic comets, of new periodic comets, and of recoveries of known short-period comets are a little higher than three per year, approximately one per year, and somewhat less than five per year, respectively—three, five, and 16 times higher than the corresponding rates in the first part of the 19th century. The first two rates are about the same as they were near the turn of the

century, while the third rate has increased by a factor of about 3, due to combined efforts of observers and theoreticians, who can now derive many accurate orbits with the aid of electronic computers. The number of comets actually observed in any year is larger than the number of comets discovered during that year, for a few comets remain observable from previous years. The actual numbers for a particular year may differ appreciably from those quoted above. In 1966 only nine comets were observed (four new near-parabolic, two periodic comets recovered, two comets from 1965, and comet P/Schwassmann-Wachmann 1, which can be seen every year, as it has an elliptic orbit with an exceptionally small eccentricity). The year 1970 was a record year, with 29 comets observed: five new near-parabolic and two new periodic comets, 11 recoveries of periodic comets, two comets from 1968, eight from 1969, and finally P/Schwassmann-Wachmann 1. Four of these comets were naked-eye objects, although the mean frequency of naked-eye comets is only about one every second year. Finally, 1970 will be remembered for a spectacular object, Comet Bennett, 1970 II (Figure 2). There are only about a dozen comets

Figure 2: Comet Bennett, taken at Cerro Tololo Interamerican Observatory, Chile, March 16, 1970.

as bright as Bennett per century. More than 1,600 comets have been recorded so far, but rough estimates of the minimum total number of existing comets based on statistics of observed comets range from a few hundred thousands to a few millions. The actual number may be much larger than this.

COMET ORBITS

Types of orbit. A comet with mass m is first assumed to be moving under the influence of the Sun (mass $M_\odot$) alone; its trajectory will be a conic with the Sun as focus. The type of conic is characterized by its eccentricity, e, and determined entirely by the comet's velocity, v, specified at a given heliocentric distance, r. If the values of v and r are such that, with G as gravitational constant, the total energy E (kinetic plus potential where $E = (\frac{1}{2}) mv^2 - GmM_\odot/r$ and is constant) is negative then the orbit is an ellipse (e less than one). The particular case $e = 0$ is a circle. The comet is then said to be bound to the Sun and is called a periodic comet. If E is positive, the orbit is a hyperbola (e greater than one), and the comet can go to infinite distances from the Sun. The special case of the parabola (e equal to one) corresponds to $E = 0$ and occurs if v is exactly equal to the escape or parabolic velocity, $v_p = (2GM_\odot/r)^{1/2}$.

Calculation of an orbit. A comet's orbit is completely described by six quantities called its elements. Three angles describe the orientation of the orbit in space, while the perihelion distance, q, and the eccentricity, e, determine its size and form. The position of the comet on its orbit can be obtained if T, the time of perihelion

The
prelimi-
nary orbit

passage, is known. At least three observed positions must be available for calculation of an orbit. A parabolic motion is more easily dealt with, as one element is known in advance ($e = 1$), so this is first assumed in the computation of the preliminary orbit of a new comet. The ephemeris (table of positions) based on this orbit will usually be sufficient for further observation of the comet. If it is not, the new object is a short-period comet, and an elliptical trajectory must be computed right away. Then the ephemeris is sent immediately to all observatories by the Central Bureau for Astronomical Telegrams. Later, if all available observations of the comet are used, the definitive orbit can be determined by repeated small corrections, in which slight variations of the elements are introduced progressively until the observed and computed positions of the comet match as well as possible. The quality of this orbit will depend upon the accuracy of the observations on which it is based, as well as upon the length of time they cover. At the end of 1970, about 925 cometary orbits concerning some 610 individual objects were known, distributed approximately as follows: (1) 295 parabolic, (2) 70 hyperbolic, (3) 140 long-period comets (ellipses), (4) 375 apparitions of about 60 short-period comets, and (5) 45 short-period comets observed only once.

Almost all known comets have perihelion distances q ranging from 0.005 to 2.5 astronomical units (one astronomical unit equals the mean Earth–Sun distance); the rest, about 3 percent, have q between 2.5 and six astronomical units. There is a rather severe selection effect, because only those comets that come close enough to the Earth are detected.

Perturbations. The actual path followed by a comet is more complicated than indicated above, because it is perturbed, sometimes only slightly, sometimes drastically, by the gravitational attraction of the planets. The nearer a comet comes to a particular planet and the more closely its motion matches the latter's, the greater will be the planet's influence on the cometary path. The giant planets, especially Jupiter with its very large mass, play a predominant role in these perturbations; taking account of such effects involves elaborate numerical calculations, today performed by computers following step-by-step methods. In this way, for any specified time, the elements of the so-called osculating orbit can be found. This is close to (tangent to) the true path at the chosen instant, and the velocity at the tangent point is the same as the true instantaneous velocity of the comet. The osculating orbit for a given date is also the one that would be followed by the comet if there were no further planetary perturbations after that date. Perturbations are not important in the small portion of the comet's path near perihelion, so the definitive orbit, which is the osculating orbit for a date close to perihelion passage, provides a good representation of the actual path in that region—that is, where the comet is observed.

The
osculating
orbit

Nonperiodic and long-period comets ("near-parabolic" comets). Hyperbolic and long-period comets all have eccentricities very near the value one—that is, e lies between one and 1.03 in the first case and between 0.96 and one in the second. The calculated periods of the latter range from a few hundred years to (a rather uncertain) several million years. The orbital type can be identified by means of the semi-major axis, a, its reciprocal, $1/a$, being negative, equal to zero, or positive for the hyperbola, the parabola, or the ellipse, respectively. The observed values of $1/a$ in reciprocal astronomical units for the two groups under consideration lie in the intervals $(-0.02, -0.00009)$ and $(+0.00001, +0.03)$, respectively. The quantity $1/a$ gives a measure of the total energy, E, of the comet (with m and $M_\odot$ the masses of the comet and the Sun and G the gravitational constant, it can be shown that $E = C22800\cdot004$ and the small values involved suggest that even the slightest change in energy through planetary perturbations might influence the type of orbit. Starting from the osculating orbit of a comet and computing the perturbations backward and forward in time, the original and future orbits can be found. These are, respectively, the orbit followed before entering and the orbit to be travelled after leaving the region of appre-

Original
and future
paths of
comets

ciable planetary perturbations. The type of orbit can be altered by these perturbations; and the sequence (original, osculating, and future orbit) can be ellipse, hyperbola, ellipse (e, h, e), or (e, h, h), etc. About 80 accurately known orbits give the following approximate percentages for the sequences: (e, e, e), 36; (e, h, e), 17; (e, h, h), 36; (h, h, e), 2; and (h, h, h), 9. According to these results, about 90 percent of these comets approached the planetary region along ellipses and were bound to the Sun, whereas some 45 percent recede from it along hyperbolas and hence leave the solar system forever; but a very small number of comets originated in interstellar space. The latter result is questioned by some authors, who argue that the orbits of the comets involved are not known with sufficient accuracy to permit a definitive conclusion to be drawn.

The relatively large number of parabolic orbits merely indicates that many comets have not had sufficiently accurate or numerous observations or else no definitive orbit was calculated so that the precise orbital character was not specified. For it would be very hard to admit that nearly 50 percent of the comets moved along orbits with e exactly equal to 1.000000. Also, a parabolic orbit cannot last long because of perturbations.

The orientations of the orbits have inclinations, i, ranging from 0 to 180° to the ecliptic, and among the corresponding comets about as many have direct motions (eastward, like the planetary motions) as retrograde motions. Most comets probably belonged originally to the solar system, although some may reach the interstellar medium a few million years from now; all comets that visited the inner solar system during the past 4,000 years are still well within the sphere of action of the Sun, the earliest recorded visitor now being a few thousand astronomical units from the Sun at most.

Some comets travel on strikingly similar orbits, only the times of perihelion passage being appreciably different. Members of such a group of comets are thought to be fragments from a larger comet tidally disrupted earlier by the Sun or a planet. Although such breakups occur very gently, slight differences in the resultant velocities with subsequent perturbations are sufficient to cause these daughter comets to follow orbits close to but distinct from the orbit of the original body and from one another. In particular, the $1/a$'s and consequently the periods P (as $P^2 = a^3$) of these comets will differ so that they will arrive at different epochs. The famous group of "Sun-grazing comets" (known also as Kreutz's group) has seven known members, the latest observed being Ikeya-Seki (1965 VIII). These comets have exceptionally small perihelion distances: 0.0055 to 0.0097 astronomical unit; they penetrate right into the solar corona.

Groups of
comets

Short-period comets ("periodic" comets with period less than 200 years). Not all comets leave the planetary region after going through it. About 100 known comets were effectively trapped by the major planets, essentially by Jupiter. The motions of about 75 are closely related to Jupiter's; they constitute the Jupiter family of comets. Their periods are less than 12 years, the mean orbit inclination is only 12°, their aphelion distances range from about three to eight astronomical units, and their perihelion distances and eccentricities lie between 0.35 and 2.50 astronomical units and 0.35–0.85, respectively. These were originally long-period comets moving on direct orbits of rather small inclinations and perihelion distances near Jupiter's mean heliocentric distance, 5.2 astronomical units. Such a comet's motion would be strongly modified by Jupiter, since the comet could spend a long time in the latter's vicinity; eventually, after a number of successive approaches to Jupiter, a more or less stable situation is reached. A comet observed today may, however, be on a still unstable orbit; the orbit of comet P/Pons-Winnecke undergoes a strong perturbation at every alternate revolution because its period is about half that of Jupiter. Close encounters with Jupiter can produce even more important changes in the orbit. P/Oterma passed near Jupiter in 1937 and in 1963; the period was 18 years before 1936, eight years from 1937 to 1963, and thereafter about 18 years again.

Figure 3: Comet Humason, 1962 VIII, member of a class of very active comets in which bands of the ionized molecule CO⁺ dominate the spectrum of both head and tail. This unusually large comet was observed for more than four years (see text).
By courtesy of the U.S. Navy

Short-period comets with periods from 12 to some 200 years include objects such as the "annual" comet P/Schwassmann-Wachmann 1, with a period of 16 years, which is probably in an early stage of the process of its transformation into a short-period comet, and other objects with either retrograde motion or high inclination, or both, and for which the perturbations, although weaker, were nevertheless sufficient for capture. Halley's Comet, with retrograde motion ($i = 162°$), is an example of the latter category. Jupiter is the principal perturbing agent in the formation of almost every short-period comet, although the other giant planets appreciably affect the motion of some comets. Accurate prediction of a short-period comet's path at its next return must simultaneously account for all observations made at the last appearance and for all perturbations and must provide a link with preceding passages. Such precise calculations resulted in recent recovery of a few comets, P/Holmes and P/Tempel 1, for instance, previously considered lost (the latter for almost 100 years).

Sometimes significant systematic discrepancies between observed and computed positions of the periodic comet remain after all gravitational interactions have been properly allowed for. The period of Encke's Comet decreases by 0.1 day at each revolution. Some comets (P/d'Arrest) have been identified with lengthening periods. The explanation is now believed to be ejection of matter by the nucleus, which can speed up or slow down the comet. Small erratic motions in some comets may sometimes be due to collisions with metre-sized interplanetary boulders.

Possible comet–Earth collisions

The Earth passed through the tail of Halley's Comet in 1910. Such an encounter is not a disaster. Although the cometary material contains cyanogen and carbon monoxide (poisonous), densities are so low that their effects are far less than those of smoke from cars and factories. A collision with a solid cometary nucleus a hundred metres in diameter with an impact velocity of 20 kilometres (about 12 miles) per second, for example, would be catastrophic but rare, occurring perhaps once in 1,000,000 years. If the nucleus were a collection of micron-sized particles, one would merely observe a heavy fall of micrometeorites.

THE NATURE OF COMETS

The nature of comets is still poorly known, mainly because of the relative infrequency and short duration of comet appearances. Detailed information is possible only for the brightest objects, which are observable at best for only a few weeks or months, and then often under unfavourable conditions, such as low altitude. Moreover, the phenomena seen from Earth are not simply related to major processes in or near the nuclei. Tremendous variety is shown by comets and also by the methods of observation. Observed variations may depend upon heliocentric distance, but there are also undoubtedly intrinsic differences among comets in size, brightness, and physicochemistry.

Observed characteristics. *Appearance and component parts.* All comets occasionally appear hazy. This may help to distinguish a faint comet from a kinematically similar object, such as a minor planet. A fully developed bright comet contains three distinct parts: nucleus, coma, and tail.

The intrinsically faint, starlike nucleus lies at or near the centre of any nebulosity but is not often observed. It may lack contrast or be masked by the light from the brighter fuzzy cloud around it. The dimensions of the physical body or assembly of bodies cannot be measured directly from the point image of the nucleus. Comet P/Pons-Winnecke passed close to the Earth in 1927 (0.03 astronomical unit); the nucleus was not resolved, so the radius of the nuclear body could not be larger than a few kilometres. If the nucleus is considered as a single block, knowledge of its heliocentric and geocentric distances, along with a reasonable assumption as to the fraction of sunlight reflected, can be combined with its observed brightness to yield its radius.

The radius of the nucleus of P/Pons-Winnecke was found in this way to be about 100 to 500 metres (300 to 1,500 feet). More recent values range between 0.1 and 100 kilometres (0.06 and 60 miles).

No comet has ever produced any noticeable perturbation on the motion of a planet or a satellite, although P/Brooks passed within Jupiter's satellite system in 1886. This indicates that a comet's mass, almost entirely in its nucleus, cannot exceed about a millionth of the Earth's mass, or $10^{21}–10^{22}$ grams. But with the radii given above and densities of 0.1 to one gram per cubic centimetre³, the masses should be from 10^{11} to 10^{21} grams. Estimates of mass losses and lifetimes of periodic comets set lower limits consistent with these values. Thus, comets cover a large range in nuclear sizes and masses. Encke's Comet has a nuclear radius of 1.5 kilometres (0.9 mile), whereas Halley's Comet and Comet Humason, 1962 VIII (see Figure 3), are 20–25 kilometres (12–16 miles). Many comets are probably smaller than P/Encke. The often inconspicuous nucleus, nevertheless, represents the most important part of the comet, not only because it contains by far the greatest part of the mass, but also because it is the source of the material in the coma and tail, as well as the site of the ejection or disruption processes.

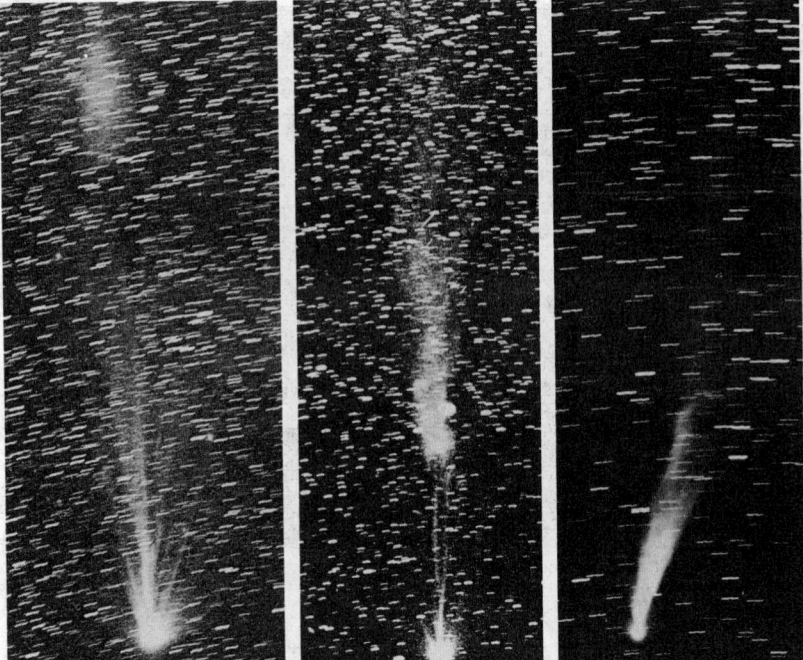

Figure 4: Comet Morehouse, 1908 III, showing how the tail material moves rapidly away from the comet's head; the speed of this recession sometimes reaches 100 kilometres per second. Photographed by E.E. Barnard on September 30, October 1, and October 2, 1908.
By courtesy of Yerkes Observatory, University of Chicago

The coma

The coma produces nebulous luminosity and contains small solid particles and gas issued from the nucleus, as shown by the comets' spectra. The light from the coma fades outward and has no sharp cutoff, so that the estimated radius in total light will depend upon the brightness of the night sky, into which the coma merges, and, consequently, upon the instrument used. This light is very complex, containing contributions, at different wavelengths, from various particles, molecules, atoms, and solid grains. The different constituents have widely different extensions from the nucleus into the coma. The radius thus not only depends on the wavelength but will be completely meaningless if the wavelength range covered includes several contributions. The visible light from the coma is often due essentially to the carbon molecule, and the corresponding visual radius may lie between a few times 10^4 and a few times 10^5 kilometres.

The radius of the coma varies with the heliocentric distance r. Very small comas may be observed in comets beyond Jupiter's orbit. On approach to the Sun, the coma grows until r is about one to two astronomical units, where it reaches a maximum; it then shrinks again (assuming q less than 1.5 astronomical units), reversing the process on the way out.

The coma, usually nearly circular, is often elongated away from or toward the Sun, to a degree that depends upon wavelength. Halos sometimes appear and may expand with a velocity of about 0.1 to three kilometres per second. Jets, connected with the nucleus, parabolic envelopes, or other formations are also sometimes observed, while a central condensation—called the false nucleus—is often seen.

Classification of comet tails

The most spectacular part of a bright comet is its tail. Comet tails are classified into two types. Type I tails are highly active and show a wide variety of appearances: straight, threadlike rays stretching out laterally, long streamers, turbulent or wavy patterns, clouds, or knots. The whole configuration may change in a few hours. Type II tails are curved, wider and smoother, often almost structureless, although rays or spirally twisted features have sometimes been observed. A comet may have several Type II tails and a Type I tail at one time. Type I tails are visually rather faint but brighter at shorter (violet) wavelengths. Type II tails appear brighter when observed visually because their light is redder.

Many faint comets have no detectable tail; some have tiny appendages or pure Type II tails. A few large, bright objects develop huge tails that can stretch over more than 90° (P/Halley in 1910). The true length of the tail may be 10^6 to 10^8 kilometres. The Brilliant (Sun-grazing) Comet of 1843 holds the record, about 3×10^8 kilometres. A typical width of bright tails some distance from the head may be 10^6 kilometres, with much narrower individual rays. The tail usually first appears near 1.5 to two astronomical units from the Sun, lengthening and brightening as r decreases. Comet Humason (1962 VIII), however, never came closer to the Sun than 2.13 astronomical units but had an extraordinarily active Type I tail out to more than five astronomical units from the Sun.

A comet's tail is always pointed away from the Sun. Type I tails are inclined at a few degrees with the outward direction from the Sun. Type II tails are generally in the orbital plane of the comet, but there are exceptions. Condensations in the tails of Comets Morehouse (1908 III), P/Halley (1910 II), and Mrkos (1957 V) (see Figures 4, 1, and 5) moved away from the Sun with velocities of ten to 100 kilometres per second and accelerations many times that of solar gravity.

Particle densities must be very low in comet tails, since stars seen through them are often practically undimmed.

Brightness. The so-called total brightness of a comet refers to the light received from its coma, but it is not easily ascertained and is of little value. The "nuclear magnitude," which is directly related to the flux of solar radiation intercepted by the nucleus, is found by comparison with nearby stars and is used to derive the radius of the nucleus. Tail magnitudes are not measured.

The apparent brightness of a comet varies strongly with distance from the Sun, r, and also with its geocentric distance. A brightness ratio of roughly 10^5 separates the intrinsically brightest and the intrinsically faintest comets.

Accurate measurements of the various separate emissions began only in the late 1950s but have yielded valuable information on particle densities and their distribution within the coma.

A few comets have shown abrupt, sometimes large and irregular increases in brightness. Some of these changes are correlated with solar activity. P/Schwassmann-Wachmann 1, which always lies between Jupiter's and Saturn's orbits, may brighten by six or even ten magnitudes within a few hours, the decline lasting a few weeks, probably through an outburst of matter that produces a

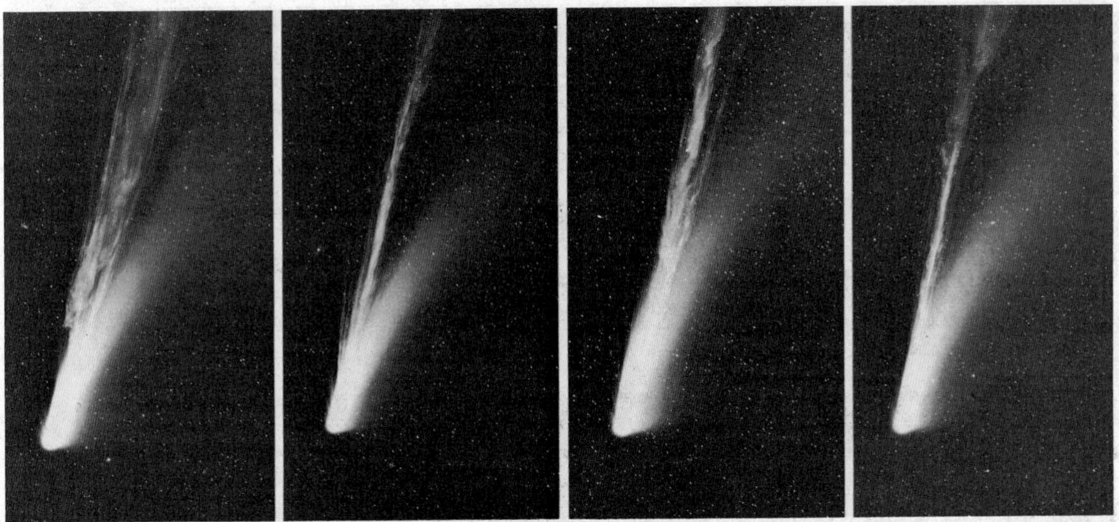

Figure 5: Comet Mrkos, photographed August 22, 24, 26, 27, 1957. The straight tail with prominent streamers and irregularities, best seen at upper left in all photographs, is formed of ionized molecules; the more uniform, curved tail is composed primarily of small solid particles.

By courtesy of Mount Wilson and Hale Observatories

luminous shell expanding through the coma with a velocity of about 0.1 kilometre per second.

Other comets have faded away while approaching the Sun, and some short-period comets show a long-term decrease in brightness.

Spectra. The dispersion—that is, the amount of separation by wavelength of the light—used for early spectra was rather low, the lowest reciprocal dispersion being about 70 angstroms per millimetre. The first high-dispersion (18 angstroms per millimetre) spectrum was taken on Comet Mrkos (1957 V) with the 200-inch Hale reflector in 1957. Since then, similar high-resolution spectrograms have been obtained for more than a dozen comets, notably the Observatory of Haute-Provence in France. Spectra at about 20 angstroms per millimetre (Å/mm) or better, allowing detailed study, can be secured only for the brightest objects (5–7Å/mm for Comet Bennett; 0.2–1.2Å/mm for the Sun-grazing Ikeya–Seki in broad daylight).

Tail spectra

Three types of emission are found in optical spectra of comets: continuous emission, emissions from neutral molecules and atoms, and emissions due to molecular and atomic ions. Some examples of low- and high-dispersion spectra of comets are shown in Figures 6 and 7.

The continuum, a narrow strip of continuous emission, comes from the centre of the comet. It is crossed by solar (Fraunhofer) absorption lines. Its spectral energy distribution is usually slightly redder than that of solar light. The continuum usually comes from a rather sharply bounded region with an angular diameter of a few seconds of arc, or a linear diameter of 500 to 10,000 kilometres (300 to 6,000 miles), according to the Earth's distance. The nucleus itself is usually too faint for its spectrum to be recorded. Sometimes a faint continuum extends in the direction of Type II tails and, where found, is redder than the solar spectrum.

A number of superposed emissions at discrete wavelengths are due to neutral diradicals and triatomic radicals—molecules that are chemically unstable under usual laboratory conditions. These radicals contain two or three of the cosmically most abundant elements, hydrogen (H), carbon (C), nitrogen (N), and oxygen (O): CH, NH, OH, CN, C_2, C_3, NH_2. When a comet comes closer to the Sun than about 0.2 astronomical unit, as Comets 1882 II and Ikeya–Seki (1965 VIII) did, the molecular emissions become very weak, but prominent atomic lines appear in the spectra due to neutral elements of the iron group, potassium and calcium, in addition to the sodium D lines, which first appear near one astronomical unit. They are usually nearly symmetrical with respect to the continuum, and they match the roundish nebulosity of the coma. The sodium and potassium lines extend further

toward the tail side. The red lines of the "forbidden" spectrum of atomic oxygen, which have been identified in high-dispersion spectra of a few comets, are also asymmetric. Such forbidden lines are caused by transitions occurring in regions of very low density.

A strong asymmetric emission from atomic hydrogen, the Lyman-alpha line in the far ultraviolet, was detected for the first time in two bright comets, Tago-Sato-Kosaka (1969 IX) and Bennett (1970 II), from artificial satellites being traced out to several times 10^6 to 10^7 kilometres in the anti-solar direction.

The spectrum of a bright tail contains emissions from molecular ions, such as those of carbon (C), hydrogen (H), oxygen (O), and nitrogen (N) with the formulas CH^+,

By courtesy of Lick Observatory, University of California

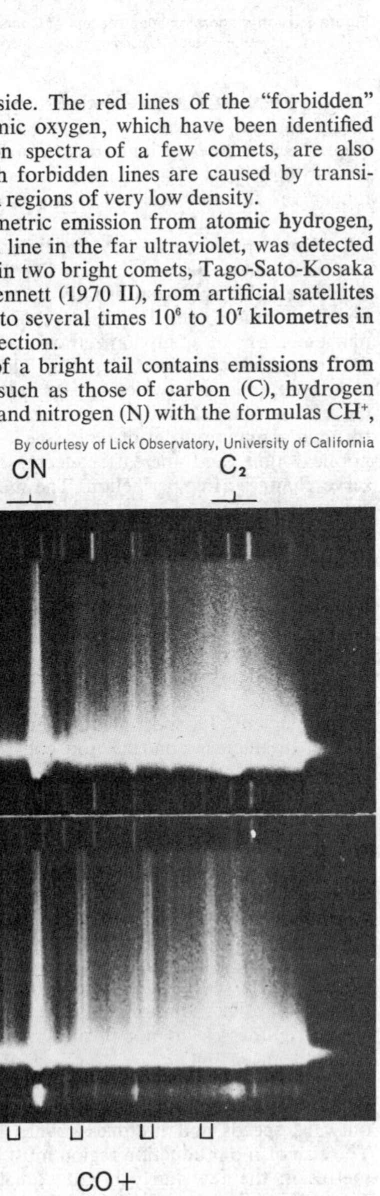

Figure 6: Low-dispersion spectra. Comets Arend-Roland, 1957 III (top) and Mrkos, 1957 V (bottom) show strong emission bands, especially C_2, CN, and CO^+, that are characteristic of comets near the Sun. When the comet is held fixed in the slit of the spectrograph during the photography, the extensions of the bands reflect the true extension of the associated molecules into the coma and tail.

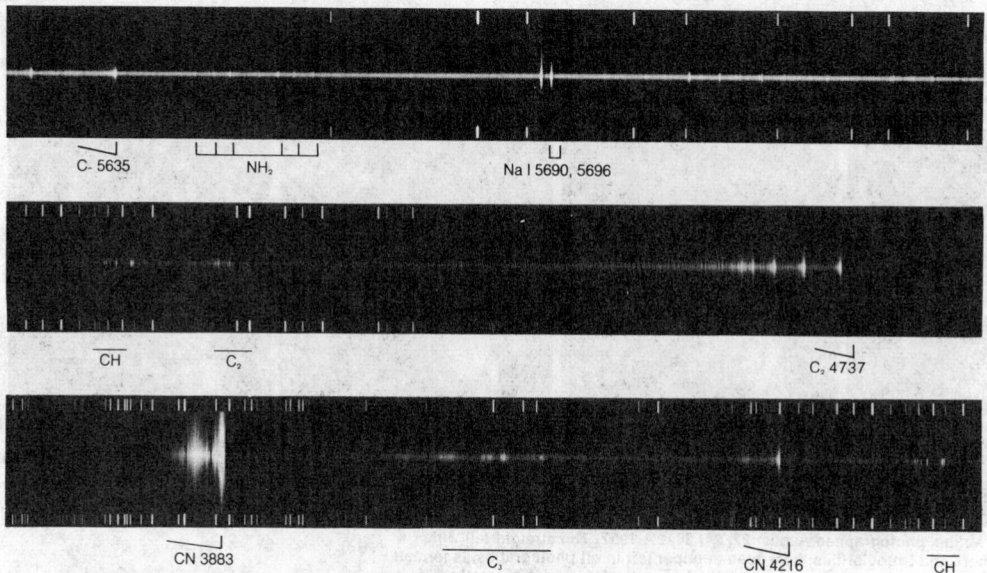

Figure 7: High-dispersion spectrogram of Comet Seki-Lines, 1962 III (see text).
By courtesy of Lick Observatory, University of California

OH^+, CO^+, N_2^+, CO_2^+, the strongest being those caused by singly ionized carbon monoxide ("comet-tail bands"). Near the Sun, lines of ionized calcium replace these molecular emissions. The ion emissions are considerably longer on the tailward side; they are formed in the straight Type I tails.

A comet spectrum is very dependent upon its heliocentric distance. Beyond three to five astronomical units, any observable spectrum usually is a continuum, but at least one large comet, Humason (1962 VIII), had molecular emissions of singly ionized carbon monoxide out to five astronomical units or more. The various neutral molecular emissions (which appear in the order CN, then C_3 and C_2, then the others) increase as r decreases, go through a maximum at distances near 0.7 to one astronomical unit, and thereafter decrease again, with reserve changes after perihelion. The molecular tail emissions are usually first detected near 1.5 astronomical units from the Sun. Their strength increases with decreasing r, but it may show considerable fluctuation. The relative intensities of the various emissions and the continuum differ in different comets. Both the continuum and the discrete emissions are slightly polarized (10–25 percent).

The structure of comets. *Interpretation of the observational data.* The continuum is due to reflection or scattering of sunlight by the cometary material in the vicinity of the nucleus. Its spectral distribution shows that this central or nuclear condensation consists either of solid particulates, large compared to optical wavelengths, from a fraction of a millimetre up to large chunks, or of tiny grains of micron or submicron size that cause the reddening by selective scattering, or of both. This conclusion is also consistent with the polarization. Good spectra show that the central cloud of solid particles extends up to about 10^4 kilometres for comets near one astronomical unit from the Sun.

The spectra of comets show that these objects do not merely reflect sunlight, like the planets; they reflect and scatter the solar radiation, but also emit their own light; their brightnesses do not fit an inverse-square law for solar distance.

The behaviour of the various radicals seen in the coma show that they arise in the central region and that their outward speeds and lifetimes govern their distribution. The size of the production region must be about 10^4 kilometres in the few fairly bright comets studied so far. Thus, the kilometre-sized nucleus cannot, at least in these cases, be the direct source of the radicals.

The suggestion that the luminosity of a comet is mainly due to absorption of sunlight followed by the re-emission of light of the same wavelength (resonance) or of different wavelengths (fluorescence), first made in 1911, was used successfully only in 1941 to explain the peculiar characteristics of the molecular bands. The irregularities in the cyanogen violet bands, for instance, in great contrast with the smooth profiles observed for these bands in the laboratory, are caused by the very irregular spectral distribution of the exciting solar radiation (due to the pressure of numerous Fraunhofer lines in this radiation). The intensity distributions in the molecular bands or the relative intensities of the atomic lines depend strongly upon the comet's speed relative to the Sun because changes in the wavelength shifts associated with this motion produce important changes in the excitation conditions. The agreement between the observed molecular band profiles and the corresponding profiles computed on the assumption that radiative processes alone are important shows that collisions between molecules and atoms are infrequent and that consequently their densities are very low in comets. These low densities explain the existence of the chemically unstable molecules. They also imply a statistical equilibrium or steady state established under the effect of the radiative absorptions and emissions; the relative numbers of molecules and atoms in the various energy levels are constant but are determined by the fundamental properties of the respective species, as well as by the solar energy distribution, rather than by thermal equilibrium.

The observed densities of neutral species, at 10^4 kilometres from the centre of the comet, range from ten to 10^5 particles per cubic centimetre. Some unobservable molecules (water, whose characteristic transitions fall in the ultraviolet) may be present in relatively greater abundance in a bright comet such as Bennett. This was also inferred from the observed intensities of the forbidden oxygen lines, for which the radiative power per atom is particularly low, and confirmed by satellite observations of atomic hydrogen, which point to total production rates of 10^{30} to 10^{31} particles per second, or some 10^7 grams per second of gas.

The relative amounts of particles and gases present in the coma vary so considerably from comet to comet that they are sometimes divided into "dusty comets" (P/Giacobini-Zinner and Mrkos, 1957 V), which have very strong continua, and "gaseous comets" (P/Encke and Burnham, 1960 II), in which no continuum is observed. There are, however, intermediate cases, and even a reputedly gaseous comet probably contains some solid particles, which scatter light less efficiently.

The shapes and orientations of the tails of bright comets are clear signs of the existence of repulsive forces from the Sun acting on the matter expelled from the inner part of comets. These forces are smaller in the curved Type II tails than in the straight Type I tails. The general

The excitation mechanism of the discrete emissions

characteristics of the Type II tails are interpreted satisfactorily by the Bessel-Bredichin theory mentioned above, if one identifies the repulsive force with the force exerted by solar radiation (usually referred to as "radiation pressure") on small dust particles. This idea was first applied to cometary tails in 1900.

Recent developments have shown that particles of various sizes are ejected continuously from a small central region at a rate varying with solar distance. The average particle sizes in the Type II tail of Comet Arend-Roland (1957 III), for instance, are from a fraction of a micron to several microns, corresponding to repulsive forces of about 0.1 to one in units of solar gravitational attraction (cf. ten to 10^3 found for the Type I tails). The repulsive acceleration of a spherical particle of radius a and density d varies as $1/(ad)$, since the radiation force is proportional to the cross section πa^2 presented by the particle to the beam of sunlight, while the mass of the particle is $(4\pi/3)a^2d$. Thus, the effect of the radiation repulsion on the smaller particles will be more important. The reddening of Type II tails is due to scattering of solar light by very fine dust. These tails are therefore also appropriately called "dust tails." The densities are extremely low, the average distance between particles being several metres. The rates of mass losses were roughly 10^8 and 10^9 grams per second in the form of dust for Comets Arend–Roland (1957 III) and Mrkos (1957 V).

The gaseous Type I tails, essentially neutral plasma, with ions and electrons, are more puzzling. Their very small curvatures, orientations, and rapid, greatly accelerated motions all indicated that the solar radiation pressure on molecules failed to explain their formation because the rates of absorption of sunlight were much too low.

Cometary evidence for the solar wind

In the early 1950s these properties were attributed to the effect of streams of energetic ions—mainly protons—and electrons issuing from the Sun and moving outward at 300–500 kilometres (200–300 miles) per second. This phenomenon was later termed the solar wind; it also provides a convincing explanation for the orientations of the Type I tails. The axes of these tails lag a few degrees behind the direction from the Sun due to a dynamical aberration effect. The solar plasma as seen by the moving comet appears to come from a slightly displaced direction. The aberration angle is determined by the ratio of the comet's speed to that of the solar wind (about 1:10) and is in good agreement with observed values of the latter. The presence of a plasma tail does not appear to depend upon the level of solar activity, but the observed great variability of the Type I tails is correlated with solar disturbances. The narrowness and persistence of the filaments in these tails indicate the existence of magnetic fields that effectively "contain" the plasma.

The densities of visible ions, mainly singly ionized carbon monoxide, are comparable to those of the neutral radicals in the outer coma (10^2–10^3 molecules per cubic centimetre). These ions give the blue-violet colour of their strongest emissions to the Type I tails.

The D lines of neutral sodium are very strong at solar distances below about 0.6 astronomical unit. The marked asymmetry of these emissions shows that the sodium atoms form a tail of their own, which can be quite bright and give a yellowish colour to the comet. This tail is produced by radiation pressure and is shaped like the outer boundary of a spraying water fountain. It can be interpreted readily on the basis of a solar repulsive force about 100 times the gravitational attraction.

The connection of comets with meteors

About a dozen comets have been shown beyond doubt to be associated with meteor streams (see above), another clear indication that comets are able to scatter solid particles, here of sizes from 0.1 millimetre up to several centimetres or more. The particles eventually disperse throughout the orbit because of planetary perturbations. The matter liberated cannot be retained by the small gravitational fields of these extremely low-mass bodies.

Thus the observational evidence leads to the following picture. Comets contain both volatiles (made of light elements) and substances such as meteoroids, principally heavy elements. At very large solar distances these materials are certainly all in the solid state. When the comets approach the Sun, parts are released in tenuous comas as gases and as solids, some of which are very finely divided. This material interacts with the electromagnetic and corpuscular radiation from the Sun to produce very thin tails of ionized gases and of tiny dust particles extending in the anti-solar direction. A small fraction of the ejected matter becomes luminous either by fluorescence excited by sunlight (gases) or by reflection and scattering of this light (solids) so that the larger comets appear as nebulous, sometimes quite capricious, objects.

Cometary models. Unfortunately, cometary phenomena are so complex and the gathering of physically significant data about them so slow that the only recourse to complete the description so far has been to build theoretical pictures capable of explaining as many observations as possible. Cometary models can be classified into two entirely different types, the "sandbank" model and the "compact" model, each with a number of variations.

In the "sandbank" or "gravel-bank" model, which prevailed until fairly recently, a comet is a huge swarm of small particles following independent, but very similar, paths around the Sun. Concentration of particles toward the centre produces a diffuse "nucleus," but there is no discrete central body. The particles are supposed to be formed outside the solar system, and their composition is therefore that of interstellar matter. The orbits of the particles must cross close to perihelion, leading to numerous collisions in which the particles are shattered. Some tiny dust particles produced are then "blown" away by solar radiation, thus forming a Type II tail. A very small part of the original material is probably vaporized during the collisions, but too little to explain the amounts of gas observed in comets. One model of this type, however, is part of a more complete theory intended to account for the origin of comets as well (see below).

The "sandbank" model

The idea of a compact nucleus, introduced in the 19th century, was modified so as to be capable of tests by observations in 1950. The nucleus was then described as a conglomerate of frozen gases or "ices," such as water, ammonia, methane, carbon dioxide, and other substances made of light elements mixed with meteoric materials. Later refinements indicated that the icy constituents must be in the form of hydrates or clathrates—i.e., of molecules such as methane—attached or adsorbed on water snows; the vapour pressures of pure ices are quite different from one another, whereas the hydrates have similar vapour pressures. When the comet approaches the Sun, these substances sublimate, through solar heating, at rates consistent with observations. More complicated molecules (hydrocarbons), such as those found recently in the interstellar medium, are probably also present. The various molecules released (called "parent molecules") can be photodecomposed—i.e., dissociated by the ultraviolet rays from the Sun—on their way out to produce the observed radicals and many invisible molecules. Embedded dust particles, as well as icy grains, are also released. Larger clumps are scattered along the comet's orbit to form meteor swarms; smaller particles are accelerated by the gas until they move with it. Dust grains are repelled by the solar radiation pressure; icy grains evaporate, and in doing so they may liberate some radicals that were possibly trapped in them. The radicals observed could also arise through chemical reactions near the nucleus. All estimates of total gas production rates in a rather bright comet are around several 10^{30} particles or several 10^7 grams per second.

The "icy-conglomerate" model

The "icy-conglomerate" model successfully interprets changes in the motions of some relatively old short-period comets. Depletion of volatiles from the nucleus causes a time lag between the moments of maximum received solar flux and of maximum ejection. If the nucleus rotates, this time lag produces an asymmetrical "rocket jet" effect along the orbit, slightly altering it.

A larger number of characteristics, such as the gas/dust ratios, the formation of halos, the resistance to tidal disruption when close to the Sun or Jupiter, and occasional splitting rather than dispersion, are better explained by a discrete nucleus with some cohesive strength, as in the "icy-conglomerate" model. Comet Ensor (1926 III), however, which became quickly diffuse and disappeared before reaching perihelion, might have been a mere swarm of particles. There may be two types of comets, with or without a nucleus. Many important questions remain open, not only regarding the structure and composition of the nucleus but also concerning the production of the neutral radicals and of the ions, as well as the formation and behaviour of the plasma tails; even some details about the Type II tails are not well understood.

ORIGIN AND EVOLUTION OF COMETS

The origin of comets has been attributed to: (1) volcanic eruptions from the major planets or from their satellites, (2) interstellar origin, and (3) formation within the solar system.

The first is speculative, meets with serious difficulties concerning some short-period comets, and fails in other respects.

Interstellar origin is based on accretion, but the known properties of the interstellar medium near the Sun cannot lead to enough accretion to explain existing comets.

The planetary theory of comet origin depends on a careful analysis of the characteristics of about 45 comets with accurate original orbits. The reciprocal semi-major axes $(1/a)$ of these orbits are very markedly concentrated in the interval from 0 to 5×10^{-5} reciprocal astronomical unit. Planetary perturbations spread the $1/a$'s considerably, so the narrowness of the observed distribution leads to the conclusion that the comets observed were near the Sun for the first time ("new" comets) from distances larger than about 20,000 astronomical units. The majority of comets, on this theory, come at present from a huge cloud or shell a few tens of thousands of astronomical units from the Sun. The outer boundary of the cloud has been calculated to be nearly 100,000 astronomical units. Although this distance is nearly halfway to the nearest star, the cloud is bound to the Sun. The stellar perturbations, which change the perihelion distance much more than the semi-major axis, from time to time send comets from the reservoir back into the inner planetary system. Those with small enough perihelion distances may be observed from Earth as "new" near-parabolic comets. Since the changes in velocity induced by stellar perturbations are randomly oriented, the inclinations of the orbits of these comets will themselves be distributed at random. Some of these comets will be ejected out of the solar system, some will return to the cloud. Some others, with appropriate motions, will be transformed progressively into short-period comets by Jupiter. From the observed frequency of comet apparitions the present number of comets in the cloud is approximately 10^{11}. With an average mass of, say, 10^{17} grams per comet, the total mass of the cloud is still only just a bit larger than the mass of the Earth.

The origin of comets is closely connected with the theory of the formation of the solar system itself. The cometary nuclei may have been born in the inner regions of the solar nebula, in the form of small condensations or planetesimals. Most of these small bodies could have been ejected from the system by planetary perturbations, absorbed into the protoplanets, or destroyed during collisions, all during half a million years or so. The rest (protocomets) were thrown into the comet cloud, where they could retain their frozen volatile components.

In another version, the place of comet birth is more specifically the outer part of the solar nebula. Perhaps comets were formed in various regions of the solar nebula, and their great variety merely reflects differences in the distances from the Sun at which they originated. The few comets with hyperbolic original orbits may be rare visitors from a distant interstellar or planetary region.

Processes such as expulsion, splitting, and gradual or sudden dissipation within the planetary region lead eventually to the disappearance of a comet and occur on time scales short compared with the age of the solar system. Since there are still comets, there must be a source of replenishment.

Some asteroids with small perihelion distances (Apollo type) may be extinct cometary nuclei. If statistics of the numbers of short-period comets, usually rather faint objects, are complete, then the expulsion of some members from this Jupiter family and the disintegration of others are at present approximately balanced by the injection of new members, with a very slight advantage to the latter, the total number increasing by about 7 percent per century.

The study of comet-generated meteor streams sheds light on the nature of the solid constituents. It suggests that the centres of old, initially large comets contain consolidated material, whereas more fragile meteoric material is found in small comets and the outer layers of "new" comets. The spectra of the latter comets generally show strong continua due to finely divided dust, whereas the former do not. But exceptions occur; for instance, Comets Burnham (1960 II) and Ikeya (1963 I), "new" comets, had no detectable continuous spectrum. The notion of "new" comets is a statistical one, and it is not possible to decide with certainty that any individual long-period comet is approaching the Sun for the first time. The "individualism" exhibited by comets indicates a very complex problem.

Comets may also be the main source of the multitude of micrometeorites in the interplanetary medium and may be responsible for the zodiacal light.

BIBLIOGRAPHY

General works: JOHN C. BRANDT and ROBERT D. CHAPMAN, *Introduction to Comets* (1981); and PATRICK MOORE, *Comets*, rev. ed. (1976); are good introductory works. Chapters on comets are included in the following popular works: FLETCHER G. WATSON, *Between the Planets*, rev. ed. (1962); FERNAND BALDET in CAMILLE FLAMMARION, *Astronomie populaire* (1880, reprinted 1975; Eng. trans. of 1955 French ed., *The Flammarion Book of Astronomy*, 1964); OTTO STRUVE and FRED L. WHIPPLE in THORNTON PAGE and LOU WILLIAMS PAGE (eds.), *Neighbors of the Earth* (1965). More advanced articles and books are N.T. BOBROVNIKOFF, "Comets," in JOSEPH A. HYNEK (ed.), *Astrophysics*, 2 vol. (1951, reissued 1978); JOHN G. PORTER, *Comets and Meteor Streams* (1952, reissued 1976); NIKOLAUS B. RICHTER, *Statistik und Physik der Kometen* (1954; rev. Eng. trans., *The Nature of Comets*, 1963); S.K. VSEKHSVIATSKY, *Physical Characteristics of Comets* (Eng. trans., 1964); and *The Nature and Origin of Comets* (1966)— all these references include bibliographies.

The following references discuss more specifically the various subjects dealt with in the successive sections of this article. A number of these appear in B.M. MIDDLEHURST and G.P. KUIPER (eds.), *The Moon, Meteorites, and Comets* (1963), hereafter denoted by *MMC*.

Historical: GEORGE F. CHAMBERS, *The Story of the Comets Simply Told for General Readers* (1910); CHARLES P. OLIVIER, *Comets* (1930); MARY PROCTOR and A.C.D. CROMMELIN, *Comets* (1937); ARTHUR BERRY, *A Short History of Astronomy, from Earliest Times Through the Nineteenth Century* (1898, reissued 1961); ANTONIE PANNEKOEK, *De Groei van ons wereldbeeld* (1951; Eng. trans., *A History of Astronomy*, 1961).

Discovery and observation: ELIZABETH ROEMER, "Comets: Discovery, Orbit, Astrometric Observations," in *MMC*. Detailed descriptions of cometary observations have been published regularly since 1958 in the form of "Comet Notes" by ELIZABETH ROEMER in the *Publications of the Astronomical Society of the Pacific*. Annual comet reports also appear in the *Quarterly Journal of the Royal Astronomical Society*. Early drawings and more modern photographs are reproduced in JURGEN RAHE, BERTRAM DONN, and KARL WURM, *Atlas of Cometary Forms: Structures near the Nucleus* (1969).

Orbits: RUSSELL T. CRAWFORD, *Determination of Orbits of Comets and Asteroids* (1930, reissued 1976); PAUL HERGET, *The Computation of Orbits* (1948, reissued 1978); JOHN G. PORTER, "The Statistics of Comet Orbits," in *MMC*; BRIAN G. MARSDEN, *Catalogue of Cometary Orbits*, 3rd ed. (1979), a special publication of the Central Bureau for Astronomical Telegrams, includes orbital elements, osculation epochs, nongravitational parameters, as well as detailed references and notes.

Nature of comets: FRED L. WHIPPLE, "On the Structure of the Cometary Nucleus," in *MMC*; and "The Nature of Comets," *Sci. Am.* 230:48–57 (February 1974); KARL WURM, "The Physics of Comets," in *MMC*; L. BIERMANN and RH. LUST, "Comets: Structure and Dynamics of Tails," in *MMC*; JOHN C. BRANDT, "The Physics of Comet Tails," *A. Rev. Astr. Astrophys.*, 6: 267–286 (1968); P. SWINGS and L. HASER, *Atlas of Representative Cometary Spectra* (1956); P. SWINGS, "Cometary Spectra," *Q. Jl. R. Astr. Soc.*, 6:28–69 (1965); L.G.

JACCHIA, "Meteors, Meteorites and Comets: Interrelations," in *MMC*.

Origin and evolution: G.A. CHEBOTAREV (ed.), *Motion, Evolution of Orbits and Origin of Comets* (1972); J.H. OORT, "Empirical Data on the Origin of Comets," in *MMC;* RAYMOND A. LYTTLETON, "Comets," *Observatory*, 90:178–186 (1970); BRIAN G. MARSDEN, "One Hundred Periodic Comets," *Science*, 155:1207–13 (1967).

(C.A.)

Commedia dell'Arte

During the period that the commedia dell'arte flourished, from its origin in Italy in the 16th century until its decline throughout Europe in the 18th century, its essence lay in the art of improvisation displayed by the actors. Each actor devoted his life to perfecting a personal interpretation of the one stock character he always portrayed. Collectively, these stock characters represented a cross section of contemporary society, illuminating the entire range of human weaknesses, the enormous contradictions of human life, the vast difference between swaggering pretense and humiliating reality. Most of the characters were performed with standardized costumes and masks, which allowed the audience at once to understand the basic disposition of the character and to concentrate on the nuances of the actor's development of it.

The creative talents of the actors found greater scope in the commedia dell'arte than in any other form of drama of the period. Since they worked from scenarios that offered no more than a rudimentary skeleton of the action, only their improvisations could give life to a performance. By gesture or word, it was up to them to relate the play to each successive audience, whether of peasants or aristocrats, without sacrificing the broader human meaning of their roles. To do so, they were required to become accomplished acrobats, mimes, and dancers, as well as actors. Extensive knowledge of the dialects, the personalities, and the events of the regions in which they performed was essential, as were political and social insight and a deep experience of life.

The commedia dell'arte was distinguished from the commedia erudita, or literary comedy, which relied on a complete written text. The term commedia dell'arte can be roughly translated as the comedy of the professional players because it relied so much on the improvisational skills of the performers.

The commedia dell'arte originated during the Renaissance, which brought about a worldliness in man's outlook unknown in the preceding age. What had been accepted with fatalism during the Middle Ages suddenly became open to question. The Renaissance man was full of fresh vitality, anxious to learn, eager to conquer life in its entirety, yet also ready to mock it when examining human weaknesses.

Commedia dell'arte was one of the attempts to use the theatre to express this new philosophy. To "let off steam" was one of the important functions of the commedia dell'arte from the time it came into being. This function became more important with the Counter-Reformation movement of the Roman Catholic Church against the spreading Protestantism, in the late 16th and 17th centuries, when the excesses of the Inquisition raged and when the absolutism of monarchs spread with growing despotism. The impromptu character of the commedia dell'arte allowed criticism and satire in the form of a spoken allusion and an eloquent gesture or attitude to an extent not possible in dramas with a written text.

One of the most effective devices of the commedia dell'arte was to present characters at cross-purposes, not understanding each other and unintentionally giving comically or, sometimes, tragically inappropriate responses. Since each character type spoke its own dialect, comic misunderstandings often resulted from the ambiguities of words. More often, however, they resulted from the social differences that separated the classes of society. Because the commedia dell'arte laid open many hypocrisies of its time, more often by means of the acting than of the speaking, it could spread internationally and adapt to other nations and their needs.

Origins of the commedia dell'arte. All authorities agree that the commedia dell'arte combines a great many diverse elements, such as the precepts of the ancient Roman writer of comedies Plautus, influences from other forms of theatre, magic, and many others. The character prototypes of the commedia dell'arte have been traced to early Italian carnival plays, which, in turn, usually derived from folklore. In these plays, which were performed at market squares before broad audiences, there were costumes, comical dialogues, persiflage on day-to-day events, pantomime, and acrobatics that were similar to the commedia dell'arte. What was missing was the linking action and the witty improvisation. The improvisation has been traced to the extempore verbal duels of the dilettantes at the courts of Italy, who imitated the unrehearsed dialogues at the academies and performed before a select group of courtiers and scholars.

> Antecedents in carnivals and dialogues

By the beginning of the 16th century, Turkish shadow shows and Byzantine mime had been brought to Venice. Both of these types of theatre embodied ancient traditions—of Hellenic mime and of *fabulae Atellanae*, a kind of farce popular in ancient Rome. These influences also were passed on to the commedia dell'arte.

The variety of dialects spoken by the different characters of the commedia dell'arte, one of its fundamental features, has been traced to similar effects in the artisans' plays of Siena and in the comedies of the Paduan actor Angelo Beolco (1502–42), who created the popular figure of Ruzzante, a comic and rustic character.

The development of the commedia dell'arte was, thus, a conflux and fusion of many structural elements. In a lucky moment, the comic types, masks, and satirical and mimic features derived from the carnival merged with the extempore exercises in rhetoric evolved at the academies. At the same time, impromptu mime, originally from Hellenic and ancient Roman sources, arrived via Byzantium through the Turkish plays, just as the rustic comedies of Beolco-Ruzzante were flourishing.

PERFORMANCE PRACTICES

Just as the elements of the commedia dell'arte came from highly diversified sources, its audiences also came from very different social spheres. On one day a company performed on a Venetian or Roman square on an open stage for everyone; on the next day it was welcomed at the court of a duke. The actors' talent for improvisation enabled them to adjust to each audience, allowing for differences in outlook on life, social rank, and province.

The action. It was once assumed that the commedia dell'arte was performed only as creative work, relying exclusively on improvisation. The scenario, however, is now known to have been the basis for all performances; often the scenarios were traditional comedies that were adapted for extempore versions, but in many cases they were the skeleton of the action of a play that was created for this purpose.

Open to improvisation were details of dialogue and stage jests, or business—what came to be called the *lazzi*. The term *lazzi* was once believed to derive from the word *lacci* ("connecting link"), since scenes were often connected by such comic mime. Now, however, the word is traced to *le azioni* ("action"). *Lazzi* included allusions to specific events, as well as the distinctive characteristics with which each actor imbued his part. In time, however, *lazzi* were collected into books containing jokes, monologues, dialogues, comical outbreaks of anger, humorous love proposals, and scenes of madness or despair. Eventually, a comprehensive repertory of such improvised dialogues developed. They were of a surprisingly high intellectual level and could be adapted to any role.

> Stage business— *lazzi*

An essential feature of a commedia dell'arte performance was the harmony of word and action. There was a rapid succession of gestures, postures, conjuring tricks, jokes, *lazzi*, and acrobatic figures. Each time, these elements were connected differently with masterly skill and adorned with music and dance. Vital to an effective performance were the actors' talent for ready answers, as well as their joy at playful variation, their pantomime and love for gestures, and their virtuoso skill at staging comic effects based on comical differences between mask and gesture, between gesture and text.

The fact that every actor of the commedia dell'arte began specializing in a certain character early in his career and hardly ever changed over to another helped tremendously in improvisation. Many of them developed their collection of versatile phrases and plays on words, but mime always played the more decisive role in the commedia dell'arte. There were many scenes without words that were exciting for the density of the action. The plays also contained many dance scenes and acrobatics.

The play usually opened with a scenic prologue, a comic criticism of the action to come. This was followed by the action proper, normally in three acts, with the whole company, usually of 9 to 12 members.

The action was governed by the dramatic unities, principles inferred from Aristotle's *Poetics*, requiring a play to deal with one event, in one place, representing no longer than a day. The unity of time was particularly respected. Within this framework, there would be a night scene, in which the comedy would arise from such actions as groping about in the dark, episodes with ladders at windows, and the resulting shootings and beatings. The morning brought the happy end.

It became common practice for the actors to assume strictly prescribed positions in the course of the play, creating almost geometrical patterns as they stood parallel, diagonal, or opposite to one another. This gave the actors a certain security with regard to mime and pantomime. Each actor could anticipate his colleagues' actions, even in the midst of improvisation. Of course, trapdoors and simple mechanical devices also played a considerable role. Intermezzi, consisting mainly of songs and dances, were presented between the acts.

Members of the commedia dell'arte required greater physical skill than the actors of the theatre or the opera of that time. They had to be able to do jumps, somersaults, and acrobatics. They had to be able not only to sing but also to play a variety of musical instruments. They could never rely entirely on a fixed text, in spite of the scenario and *lazzi* collections.

Northern and southern repertories The repertories of companies of northern Italy, such as those of Venice, differed from those of southern Italy, such as Naples, not only in language but also in temper and rhythm. The plays of northern Italy included tragic scenarios with horror scenes but still played by the commedia dell'arte characters. Many of these plays came closer to the commedia erudita in structure. The plays of southern Italy, on the other hand, showed a much greater variety. They were more exuberant and made much greater use of song and dance than the plays in the north. A comic scene often became moving and lyric yet only for a moment before another comic turn.

Over and over again in the performances of commedia dell'arte, a lovesick old man was deceived by the young lovers with the help of clever, double-tongued servants; over and over again, persons long separated from one another found each other again. The number of participants in these incidents was flexible.

Settings. In the beginning, the setting was designed for one location only. It consisted only of a backdrop with some device at the sides indicating, for example, the wall of a house with the window of the beloved. Later, the scenery included wings together with the backdrop. Normally, the action took place in a street or a square. It was always necessary to have two different houses for the contending groups. Care was taken to have passageways, hiding places for eavesdroppers, and balconies; but most important was the window, which was vital for sudden appearances or disappearances or for pouring malodorous liquids on unwanted lovers.

THE MASKS AND THE LOVERS

Character types. *The amorosi.* Every play of the commedia dell'arte dealt with the good and ill luck of the *amorosi* ("young lovers") and the obstacles put in their way by their selfish and stubborn elders. The madcap servants, or *zanni* (from which the word zany is derived), busied themselves clearing the way for the lovers by means of tricks or mystification. Among the *amorosi*, the *comico innamorato*, the comical young lover, was the most important type. Normally, he was very well dressed in contemporary fashion and played without a mask. The expressive and changing movements of the features played a decisive role with all the *amorosi*, in contrast to the masked players. The *comico innamorato* was commonly called Flavio, as in Ruzzante's plays, or sometimes Lelio and, less often, Orazio, Cinzio, or Aurelio. Every actor tried to give new features to the *comico innamorato*, with combinations of lyrical exaggeration and irony. The lover might act with determination, full of vitality and recklessness, or he might be the shy and comic type of lover, who sometimes, quite unexpectedly, dared the utmost to achieve his goal. Larger companies had representatives of both types and, correspondingly, two different types of beloved.

The feminine counterpart, the *comica innamorata*, was called Aurelia, Isabella, Ginevra, Flaminia, or Lucinda. Here, again, there were two basic characters in many variations of a young girl who, as a rule, was to be married off by her parents to a suitor she did not want. This is why the servants became involved, with wit and energy, to help the young girl. One type of *comica innamorata* always acted proud, ready to ridicule others, and domineering even toward her lover, though also capable of hiding her claws. Most probably, this type was created by Isabella Andreini (1562–1604), the most celebrated among the actresses of the commedia dell'arte. The other type was shy, timid, and obedient while at the same time highly attractive. The actor and the actress in each case created their own individual variations of the lovers. The
*comica
innamo-
rata*

The zanni. The characters who wore the masks were much more important to the turbulent commedia play. Servants of all kinds, who were given the collective name *zanni*, wore masks. Regardless of the variations that developed over the years, all *zanni* had common sense; they were full of clever ideas and always ready to ridicule, intrigue, or quarrel. Sometimes they were cowardly, impudent, envious, and perfidious; yet always they were ready to help for a price. Often, they were greedy and given to drinking, and sometimes they were shameless; but they were also always ready to play funny tricks and to fight the lazy, the too-secure, and the pretentious. In the *zanni* manner, there were strong elements of resentment, revolt against oppression, and revenge for injustices. From the very beginning, the *zanni* wore half-masks made of wood or, later, of leather, with hair and beard glued to them. During the early period, they wore a wide-brimmed hat with long feathers and clothes that were loose and ragged.

It was the task of the *zanni* to keep the action of the commedia moving. Their active comicality has been contrasted with the passive comicality of other characters. They spoke the dialect of Bergamo (*zanni* was the common form of "Giovanni" in Bergamo), from which the poor had emigrated to all parts of Italy to become servants. The *zanni* mask incorporated many traits of these people, who were of peasant origin, lacking in submissiveness, and always ready to defend their own life and existence.

Brighella. The two most important variations of *zanni* are also linked with the town of Bergamo: Brighella and Arlecchino. Brighella wore a dark, often olive-coloured mask surrounded by a black, shaggy beard. His costume was that of a peasant: a loose shirt, trousers, coat, and cap were all of white cloth, mostly with green trimmings. His shoes and belt were yellow. In his belt was a dagger (originally sharp and dangerous, later made of wood and thus ridiculing the bearer) and a moneybag. Brighella was cunning and unforgiving, ready for every rascality and trick. He was very quick at repartee and a bit too noisy. When pursuing an aim, he could brag and flatter. He was greedy for money and liked to drink and to love. He was faithful to his master, but only in proportion to the salary he received. Honesty was not one of his major virtues. Only the young lovers could rely on him.

Arlecchino. Brighella remained in the commedia only for a short time, while Arlecchino survived the entire development of the commedia dell'arte. Originally, he wore a peasant's shirt and long trousers, both covered by many coloured patches to show his poverty. This early version of Arlecchino was stylized by various actors, until he became suitable for presentation at court; he then wore a tight-fitting costume made up of patches of many different colours of triangular or diamond-like shape, with a black half-mask, a cylinder-shaped hat, and a wooden sword.

Origin of Arlecchino

Comparative research has shown that Arlecchino had his origin in France, as Hellequin in a legend of devils in the late Middle Ages; then he came to Italy, where his meaning was changed drastically as he became famous in the 1570s. At first he was presented as a naïve, clumsy, impudent, and ever-mocking servant. Later, he became a person of greater intellect, experience, and humour. He differed from Brighella in that he was not unforgiving and sour but gay and sometimes even simple. In many cases, of course, the simplemindedness was only a pretense intended to help him find the easiest way out of an unpleasant situation. Arlecchino was always a bit in love but often came off second-best in his courtships. He was a jack-of-all-trades and was engaged by his master for services of the most curious kind. In many cases he proved of real help, though often striving for something other than what he achieved.

The actors of the commedia dell'arte developed many variations of the Arlecchino type—Truffaldino, Pasquino, Tabarrino, and Mezzettino. The last made such a great impression at Paris that the French painters Watteau and Lancret put him at the center of their pictures of the commedia dell'arte.

Female servants. The female counterparts of Brighella and Arlecchino in the commedia dell'arte were Fantesca and the subtypes of woman servants stemming from this prototype, such as Betta, Gitta, and Colombina. Franceschina of Bergamo, the town of the *zanni*, was presented as a country girl who had to resist the temptations of town life yet got involved in many risky situations in executing her duties. It became necessary to have two different types of woman servant parallel to the two *zanni* characters. One was often presented as an older woman, more experienced and often married, while the other was a young girl, who was challenged more by emotions, ready to love, dextrous, and naïve. This was Colombina, as created in 1560. Originally, this type, which was played with hundreds of variations, remained with the Biancolellis, a family of actors, where it was passed on from one generation to the next. Caterina Biancolelli, in particular, was applauded as an outstanding example of this type. Later, Colombina was taken over by actresses of other companies as well. In their variations of this character they called themselves Corallina, Smeraldina, or Argentina. Each had her own charm or sentimentality, her own forward shrewishness and girlish slyness. While Colombina often appeared as the beloved of Arlecchino, sometimes even in a similar costume, Pedronella was the partner of Pedrolino, a simpleminded and honest servant.

The Colombina prototype

Other zanni. As early as 1560, Arlecchino was displaced for a time in favour of Fritellino. Fritellino's costume consisted of a wide jacket and wide, white trousers, a brown half-mask with a beard, a hat turned up in a forward manner, and, in his belt, a sword made of wood and a moneybag, which, of course, was empty most of the time. Tabarrino (*tabarro*, "coat") was even more popular as buffoon. In the beginning, this name was given to any comic old man. Between 1618 and 1630 he became identified as a true jester, a pert, impudent, and irresistibly funny person. He wore a jacket of white linen, short, white trousers, a green coat, and a wooden sword. Most important was his wide-brimmed hat, which he turned into thousands of shapes and forms to suit his various impersonations. Scarcely any other commedia dell'arte character could match the variations of Tabarrino and his hat. Another servant character, Burattino, dominated the stage of Florence at performances of the commedia dell'arte from 1580 onward. Burattino had a sweet tooth and was inclined to weeping and cowardice and was of-

Commedia dell'arte figures with a platform stage in the background; engraving by Jacques Callot, *Balli di Sfessania,* 1632.

ten teased. Another character, Cavicchio, was always the simpleminded servant, an oaf from the countryside.

Brighella and Arlecchino were masks of northern Italy; their counterparts in southern Italy were Coviello and Pulcinella. Coviello of Calabria is the more experienced of the two servants. He is the one to say what is to be done, while Pulcinella is more carefree and lives at random. Coviello is funny and full of energy and has a versatile and sly mind. His costume consisted of tight-fitting trousers and a jacket of black velvet with extremely large buttons. He wore a half-mask with red cheeks, a wide, black coat, and trimmings with bells around his ankles and wrists. In many cases he was used as a dancer in the play, and as such he often accompanied himself by guitar or mandolin. In most cases, Coviello had the features of a peasant. In many scenarios Coviello and Pulcinella became caricatures of courtiers while retaining their *zanni* character.

Pulcinella. Often a physically handicapped person, Pulcinella takes pleasure in harming others. He triumphs whenever his mischievous deeds are successful. He is greedy for money to buy drinks and girls. His humour is sharp tongued, cheeky, sometimes vulgar. In spite of his deformity, he is very nimble. A character similar to Pulcinella is found as early as 1570. Pulcinella became popular in the commedia companies not only in Italy but also in France, as Polichinelle, and in French puppet shows as well. The English turned Pulcinella into Jack Pudding or Punch, who is still seen today.

In Neapolitan scenarios, Pulcinella often appeared as a baker, a gardener, a sentry, and sometimes also as a soldier, a merchant, or a smuggler. His silly yet witty dishonesty was stressed there and used for comic satire. In many cases, Pulcinella was presented as a married man, often with a flock of children, and always as a cantankerous and extremely jealous person within his family. Of course, in many cases he was also shown as the deceived husband. Originally, his costume consisted of wide trousers and a wide blouse, both white and drawn in by a belt, with a wooden sword and a purse. He wore a black half-mask with large moustaches and a huge, wide-brimmed hat, usually with chicken feathers on top. He wore a green-and-white-bordered wrap. Later, this outfit was replaced by coloured, tight-fitting trousers with a jacket of triangular patches. He wore a slanting, pointed nose and a one-coloured, tight-fitting costume when he was shown as a hunchback.

Pantalone. The merchant Pantalone, from Venice, the centre of trade, was one of those who were most often deceived and mocked. Pantalone appeared often and with great variety. He was an old man, greedy, suspicious, and cowardly. He was also introduced under different names: Pasquale, Placido, Cornelis, Tommaso, or Dementio, Magnifico, Zanobio, Bernardon, and Cassandro. Pantalone was one of the four characters—with Tartaglia, Truffaldino, and Brighella—found in almost every

The many guises of Pantalone

extempore play in Venice, the most important centre for the development of the commedia dell'arte. To the Venetians, Pantalone personified the typical small merchant. Always ailing, this old man, who was always anxious about his reputation, would inevitably succumb to his lecherous, erotic caprices. His costume consisted of a red jacket and red trousers, which clung tightly to his gaunt figure. In the older versions, this was completed by a beautiful black cassock, which was worn open, Turkish mules, and a woolen cap. His mask was mud brown; his nose was long and hooked; his bristly goatee was gray. His gestures varied between tired and toilsome movements, whenever he felt unobserved, and feigned youthful tripping, whenever courting a girl who was much too young for him. In such situations he was usually plagued by pains he could hardly hide. He serenaded the beloved girls without ever noticing that they made fun of him and that their real lovers often profited from his presents. Although he always wanted to be considered intelligent and was always ready to engage in a dialogue, he was always deceived and sometimes beaten, even by his own servants.

The doctor. Another often-used prototype was the doctor of the old university town of Bologna. He appeared on the stage as a lawyer, a physician, a rhetorician, or a grammarian. In most cases, he was dressed all in black, wearing a scholar's gown, the costume of professors and lawyers at that time. Sometimes he had a white collar, a wig, and a nose reddened by wine. He carried a handkerchief or, sometimes, documents in his belt; sometimes he wore a half-mask that was cut in such a fashion as to expose his reddened cheeks. Whenever he appeared as a physician, he wore a large, turned-up hat. In such cases he was called Doctor Balanzone Lombardi, after two famous actors of the 16th century. As a rule,

The doctor as lawyer

he was shown to be an exponent of empty rhetoric, as a would-be scholar bungling Latin and Italian, as well as many other things. Often the doctor appeared before the court as a lawyer. His pleading was such nonsense that his opponents had an easy task. Typically, Arlecchino and Brighella appeared as witnesses and Pantalone or one of the *amorosi* as plaintiff or defendant. Whenever the doctor was to appear as a physician, one of his props was an enormous syringe, and, as was the case with Pantalone, another was the chamber pot. Hippocrates and other ancient authorities on medicine were quoted freely to the patients and all those seeking advice. In most cases, however, he was seen through in time, and his prescriptions were ignored. Like Pantalone, the doctor was presented as an old man, tricked by everyone. He chased young girls vainly and liked wine enormously, in contrast to Pantalone. Whenever Pantalone and the doctor appeared in the same play, the one usually had a son and the other a daughter. While the children fell in love, their fathers hated each other. Sometimes, the father and his son both courted the daughter. In every play, the servants came to the help of the young lovers. The actor playing the doctor had to be a well-read man to make humorous use of scholarly phrases, Latin quotations, and legal and medical terms.

The Captain. The character of Capitano Spavento (*spavento*, "terror") carried political implications. Ancient Roman comedy featured precursors of this prototype, and, when the Spaniards occupied Italy in the 16th century, a character was needed to represent an occupation officer. Conceited, arrogant, and greedy, the Captain believed himself able to rule everything, though his hollowness was obvious. A Capitano Matamoros ("Moor killer"), a windbag and braggart, appeared in the last quarter of the 16th century. A collection of the "bravura" of Capitano Spavento was published in 1607. He found many successors in the various commedia companies. In the first quarter of the 17th century, this prototype was transformed into Capitano Cocodrillo, Capitano Rodomonte, and Capitano Rinoceronte, and, a little later, Capitano Spezzafero. In all instances, great efforts were taken to evoke the officers' uniform of the time, though certain ornaments or props were exaggerated for comical effect. All variations of the Captain were humorous be-

cause of the contrast between the spoken word, which rang with bravery, and the immediately contrasting action. There is also a tragic trait in this bragging and exaggerating reminiscent of Don Quixote. The swaggering coward can be found throughout both northern and southern Italy because almost all of Italy, with the exception of Venice, suffered from the Spanish occupation. It was only toward the end of the 17th century, when the Spaniards gave up their attempts at conquest, that people lost interest in a captain with political accents. What remained was a generally arrogant officer or a type that simply represented the boaster.

Scaramouche. Originally, Scaramouche, or Scaramuccia, was thought to be a variation of the Captain. In all variations of this mask his costumes were black. Tiberio Fiorillo (1608–94), from Naples, was the most famous actor of the Scaramouche part; he was well aware of the seamy side in a captain because he himself was the son of a captain. Scaramouche was the superlative of all braggarts. In almost all variations, he boasts of a noble origin, of his alleged riches, and of his powers as a lover, and he turns every defeat into a victory by his conniving. Pasquino and Crispin, in France, also belong to this type of braggart, but they also can be found on a lower social scale, as servants who once experienced a better fortune.

Tartaglia. Originally, Tartaglia ("stutterer"), from Naples, was a caricature of a Spanish civil servant who antagonized those who required his services. Sometimes, however, he was the one who was vexed. He was played by a plump comedian, wearing enormous spectacles (instead of a mask) in order to see a danger better so he could run away from it. Sometimes he appeared on the stage as a notary public, sometimes as an attorney, a revenue officer, a judge, or, more rarely, an apothecary. Always, he was an old man. The part of Tartaglia was probably created around 1630, though precursors may have appeared as early as 1613. This part called for a green-banded costume consisting of trousers, a jacket, and a coat, over which a large white ruff was worn. A large, wide-brimmed, gray hat covered a bald head. As the name implies, Tartaglia stammered, allowing the actor to make meaningful comments about current events disguised as mere stuttering.

Masks and dialects. The masks worn in the commedia dell'arte were usually made of fine leather. On the inside they were lined with thin cloth. They adhered closely to the face, covering the upper half. These masks varied in that they had either a pointed or a round nose, a high or a low forehead, slit or round eyes. In contrast to the antique masks of the ancient Greek dramatists, they did not show a set grimace. They neither laughed nor wept. Life had to be brought to the mask by means of action, by means of gestures and posture. The movements of the feet, the hands, the back, and the head told whether the mask was laughing or weeping, and it could become more eloquent than any real face.

The eloquence of the mask

The dialects used by the comic characters also brought a certain expressiveness. Differences in pronunciation and meaning among the Italian dialects lent humour when the masks misunderstood each other. The various dialects demanded harsher or softer articulation, different rhythms and postures, and differences in vitality.

By the use of masks it was possible to indicate the essence of a character while directing attention away from the face and toward the body, which the actors of the commedia dell'arte developed to perfection. Their suppleness was unlimited. They were acrobats and dancers at the same time. Mimic expressiveness predominated over the accompanying words. All masks lived by means of the personifications given to them by the actors, who in later times performed additional solo scenes. The actors were of much more importance than those who wrote the texts for them; the actors were the incarnation of the theatre.

SCENARIOS

For every performance of a commedia dell'arte company there was a written scenario, which the actors called a *canovaccio* ("canvas"). The scenario described briefly the course of the action, usually showing a three-act structure, with every act consisting of several scenes. The scenario also gave the order in which the individual actors entered and a short reference as to what they should say. The exact wording and acting were left to the actor. The scenario contained only approximate indications of content and thus constituted a framework for an improvised play. It presupposed a high level of creativeness in the actors. Church and civil authorities often objected to the sometimes offensively critical improvisations of the companies.

Relatively few scenarios have been preserved, mainly from the large and famous companies, and even fewer from the many smaller companies. The normal group was described as having six actors and six actresses, a prompter, a mechanic, a person in charge of stage settings and costumes, eight servants, four chambermaids, nurses, children of every age, dogs, cats, monkeys, parrots, birds, doves, and a lamb. It has been called a Noah's ark. The members often changed from one company to another. An actor who had played a particularly large part in one scenario recommended the plot to the next company he joined.

The earliest scenario

The earliest description of the structure of a commedia dell'arte scenario is not from Italy but from Bavaria. In 1568 Orlando di Lasso, one of the most important composers of the 16th century, was commissioned to arrange a performance in the commedia dell'arte style for the wedding of William, the son of the Duke of Bavaria. The prologue was presented by a comic peasant. Though Dutch by birth, Lasso played the part of Pantalone in excellent Venetian. The female parts were all played by male actors who came from Italy. When William and his young wife retired to Trausnitz Castle, they sent for professional Italian actors. The group was depicted in 1576 in the murals at the castle, the earliest pictorial representation of the commedia dell'arte in all of Europe.

Particularly detailed information is available in a collection of scenarios, published in Venice in 1611, and compiled by Flaminio Scala, who may have been the director of the group, the Gelosi, one of the most eminent in the history of the commedia dell'arte. Francesco Andreini, the most important actor of the group, wrote the preface to this collection, which comprises 50 *canovacci*. The majority are burlesque and comic scenarios having the typical character of a comedy; but there are also scenarios for pastoral plays and tragedies, which include comic scenes. This collection set an example, and thereafter the directors often wrote the scenarios, putting down for each one the course of action and its development and the manner in which each entrance was to be made. The scenarios were sometimes taken from earlier literature and transformed for improvisation. Sometimes the scenarios were invented by the actors. Such scenarios allowed for a good deal of *lazzi* and the nuances each performer gave to his part. Every actor of the commedia dell'arte had his own repertory of comic expressions, idioms, phrases, and jokes in dialogue form that could be thrown back and forth between the actors with great skill. These devices were adapted to the framework of the action of the given scenario and supplemented with satirical references to day-to-day events.

Intertwining actions

Many props facilitated the mimic play, the spoken improvisations, and the expressive gestures. In most cases the action, as sketched in the *canovacci*, followed three or four loosely knit actions concurrently. One action would be concerned with the lovers, one would relate to the comic characters of the upper class, one to servants, and, often, a fourth action would reflect a local tradition or situation in a satirical manner. Each action would be a complete farce, only superficially connected with the others. Many comic effects resulted from contrasting scenes and juxtapositions between the various actions. Sudden transitions between something seemingly sublime and something low or base always gave rise to laughter. Since the action usually took place on a stage with no settings but only a plain curtain, the characters themselves created the optical effect of the stage. The commedia dell'arte had no set, rigid, tangible framing ele-

ment, only constant movement. Gestures shaped the space, and costumes characterized the scene. When fixed stage settings were used, from the 1640s onward, they were mainly a simple angular frame decoration.

THE ITALIAN COMPANIES AND THEIR TRAVELS

As early as three years after Beolco's death in 1542, a new company of eight members was formed, headed by Maffio de Re, a former notary public who died in 1553. He specialized in the *zanni* mask, which was new at that time. This semiprofessional group is important for historical reasons because the first theatrical contract with its members has survived. It listed the rights and duties of the members of the company and stressed discipline. Later, this became common practice in the travelling companies of the commedia dell'arte.

There is evidence of a Roman group from 1564, but a more detailed historical record exists for Alberto Naselli, who played at Mantua in 1568. He called himself Zan Ganassa, after the character created by him. Ganassa and his group performed from 1570 in France. In 1572 they played in Paris and then moved to Spain, where they toured town after town, returning to Italy only occasionally. The Italian companies as well as the Spanish and French theatre received many important influences from Ganassa.

In the 1570s and 1580s Giovanni Pellesini created the role of Pedrolino, Brighella's counterpart, and played this part in a number of companies. From the 1550s the various roles, or masks, of the commedia dell'arte had developed within the various companies. When the French poet Joachim du Bellay visited his brother, a cardinal, in Rome, in 1555, the characters were well enough known for them to request a performance by Zanni or Marcantonio together with Magnifico the Venetian (*i.e.*, Pantalone). A song of 1559 says that the various masks were "roaming the world." In Venice, Milan, Florence, Mantua, Turin, Bologna, Verona, Pisa, and Padua—the most important towns of northern Italy for commedia dell'arte—companies were welcomed as early as the 1560s.

The major Italian companies. The commedia dell'arte received its high artistic perfection in the large groups that became famous all over Europe. They came into existence almost at the same time and gave themselves symbolic names, such as Gelosi (roughly, "those creating envy because of their fame"), Desiosi ("the desired"), Confidenti ("the hopeful"), Uniti ("the united"), Accesi ("the stimulated"), and Fedeli ("the faithful").

The Gelosi

The Comici Gelosi are first mentioned in Milan in 1568. Their leader was Flaminio Scala, who came of a noble family; he wrote most of the scenarios for his group. The group played not only improvised theatre but also dramas, such as *L'Aminta*, by Torquato Tasso. Their strong point, however, was commedia dell'arte based on the scenarios of Scala. Invited to France by the king in 1574, they played first at the imperial court of Vienna and then in Paris in 1577. They returned to Italy after a year and toured northern Italy until 1590. But in 1603 they were back in Paris for another tour. The most important actors of the Gelosi were Francesco Andreini, one of the most famous actors of the Capitano Spavento, and his even more admired wife, Isabella Andreini, one of the most famous Italian actresses of the entire period, to whom the most famous poets of that time dedicated their sonnets. Her sonnets in reply often excelled them, and her letters are among the wittiest of the time. She was a member of several learned Italian academies. Under the direction of Flaminio Scala, the members of the Gelosi set an example for many other groups of the commedia dell'arte. Francesco Andreini, who created the role of Doctor Siciliano and that of the magician Falsirone in addition to Capitano Spavento, spoke not only Italian but also fluent French, Latin, Greek, Turkish, and one of the Slavic languages. He played almost all common musical instruments and wrote verse. His son, Giovambattista Andreini, was not only an actor but also the author of 18 comedies. All performers were remarkably well read. Their performance ideas often derived from classical comic dramatists, lyric poets, orators, and philosophers. In the improvisations, the audience might recognize the thoughts of Seneca, Cicero, and Montaigne.

Records similar to those of the Gelosi troupe exist for the personnel, the performances, and the tours of other companies. The Desiosi were mentioned from 1581 onward. They toured Mantua, Cremona, Verona, Milan, Bologna, Genoa, and Rome. The Confidenti receive favourable mention from 1574; at first they performed only in northern Italy, but in 1584 they went to France and in 1587 to Spain. In 1613, the director refused an offer by the Duke of Mantua to hire key members of the Confidenti. Nonetheless, members regularly moved from one group to another. Both Flaminio Scala and Isabella Andreini, for example, worked for a time with the Confidenti.

The Uniti   There are records from 1578 to 1640 for the Uniti, the company that played at the court of Mantua. The Accesi at first only played in Italy, but in 1600 they were invited to France to play at the wedding of Henry IV and Marie de Médicis, and in 1608 they again travelled to France. In 1606 and 1609 they merged their company with the company of the Comici Fedeli, a first-class company that included, among other actors, the wife of Flaminio Scala, who called herself Flaminia on the stage; next to Isabella Andreini, she was Italy's most perfect actress of the commedia dell'arte. The group was directed by Pier Maria Cecchini, the leading actor of the Fritellino part of that time and the author of some important treatises on the commedia dell'arte. He dealt with the question of how the actor should present a dialogue, with the problems of gestures and of choosing the pronunciation in accordance with the mask, and with the art of improvisation. He gave detailed instructions for playing the *innamorati*, the doctor, the first and second servants, Pantalone, the Captain, and, especially, Pulcinella.

The Fedeli, which merged twice with the Accesi and twice divided again, were directed by Giovambattista Andreini, the son of Francesco and Isabella Andreini. Marie de Médicis was a special protector of the Fedeli. Time and again she arranged for invitations to Paris so that the Fedeli could tour France in 1620, 1622 to 1623, and 1623 to 1625. These tours were followed by one to Prague and the imperial court of Vienna in 1627–28.

Many Italian commedia dell'arte companies toured northern, central, and southern Italy in the second half of the 17th century and the first half of the 18th century. In this period, Naples and Venice continued to be the centres of the development, but companies could also be found in Modena and many other towns, which were highly successful in spite of many difficulties.

Tours of German-speaking areas.   The influence of the commedia dell'arte upon the theatrical life of the other nations first came from the Italian companies that toured them. They were understood primarily at courts in which Italian was understood and less so by the rest of the population. As early as 1496, Italian theatre people, actors, acrobats could be found as solo players in German-speaking areas. In 1549, Italian companies played at the court of Charles V, the Habsburg emperor. They could also be found at court events in Strassburg, Stuttgart, Regensburg, and Augsburg. They preferred the imperial court in Vienna and Linz because Italian could be assumed to be an everyday language among the Habsburg family, who were often married to Italian princesses. The Habsburgs were also related to the Gonzagas of the court of Mantua, who were ranked among the most generous and art-loving patrons of the Italian companies. Flaminio Scala had performed at a court festivity at Linz in 1569. Emperor Rudolf II's physician gave a very impressive description of the Gelosi art of acting at the Vienna court. Emperor Matthias brought with him to Linz in 1614 the Comici Accesi, which was held in particularly high esteem by the Duke of Mantua. The company followed the Emperor to Vienna and gave more performances there. At a time when church and state both looked down on actors, the Emperor raised the director of the company, Pier Maria Cecchini, to the peerage. Cecchini cut a good figure in Vienna with the variations

of the cunning and clever servant Fritellino. At the time of their Linz and Vienna performances, Cecchini's company comprised 26 members. Between 1624 and 1628 the Comici Fedeli, headed by Giovambattista Andreini, also played at the Vienna and Prague courts.

It was not until the middle of the 17th century that performances of the commedia dell'arte were also given to the Vienna burghers, at first with the help of puppets. In 1658 a show was allowed to open in the centre of the town. As early as 1684 a Venetian company played at Munich, Augsburg, Nürnberg, Leipzig, and Dresden. It went to Vienna in 1697–99 and attracted great attention. In the early 1700s, so many companies appeared there that a director of the touring companies was appointed by the Vienna court.

The commedia in France.   The Italian touring comedies began flocking to France as early as 1492, but it was not until 1570 that a Pantalone or Zanni first appeared in Paris. A year later, however, an entire commedia dell'arte company performed there. In 1571 the Gelosi appeared for the first time at the French court for a court festivity. In the 1570s the Ganassa company, invited by Catherine de Médicis, was the first to play at Paris. The French parliament, which was not in favour of the commedia dell'arte companies, could not prevent the performances of the Ganassa group at the French court, but it prohibited performances for wider audiences. In 1572–74 Charles IX again brought to Paris Ganassa and his group, who had returned to Italy, but after his death, the company went to Madrid, where they had such great success that they stayed there for a decade. In 1577 the Gelosi again appeared in France, presenting their entire repertory of commedia dell'arte plays to the aristocracy in Paris. After that, a great many Italian companies appeared in all French provinces. The court of Paris enjoyed Italian culture tremendously and welcomed the turbulent and unpredictable Italians, with their talent for humour in word and gesture and for coordinating clowning and wit.

In France, a very important change, from commedia dell'arte to the new form of the *comédie-italienne*, developed gradually from the appearance of the Ancienne troupe de la Comédie-Italienne. It flourished in Paris between 1653 and 1697. From 1660 to 1680, this company appeared at the same theatre with Molière's company. Gradually, there was a mutual influence between the Italian and French theatres, until the Italians were expelled from Paris in 1697 for presenting a satire directed against Madame de Maintenon, the second wife of Louis XIV.

When the troupe became resident in Paris, their plays, masks, and actors all underwent important changes. As they were now also playing for wider audiences, who did not know Italian, they stressed the actors' gestures. As a result, the balance could not be maintained between the story line and the comic development, between the lyrical parts of the lovers and the *lazzi*. For this reason the Parisian audiences, including that of the court, urged the actors to play in French. In 1682 French scenes began to be included in the Italian extempore of a commedia dell'arte. Famous French actors began to write for the Italian company, either by drawing up topical scenes, by adapting the entire drama, or by adding songs. The French theatre became indebted to commedia dell'arte, not so much for its subjects and plots but rather for its manner of acting, its gestures, and its masks. What was genuine improvisation gradually became well-prepared and pretended improvisation, but its emphasis on contrasting effects was taken over in full. Elements of acting and presentation that had been common in France before the invasion of the commedia dell'arte companies tended to flourish. Thus, Harlequin, a native French figure, increasingly took a commanding position. Originally, Harlequin was the Parisian ruffian Herlekin, a devil masked as a clown, a clown with devilish characteristics. The grotesque and ugly features of Arlecchino were transformed into the witty Harlequin, who often unmasked his own villainous character. The actor Giuseppe-Domenico Biancolelli (1640–88), an Italian by birth who had be-

Popularity at the French court

The ascendancy of Harlequin and Pierrot
come French and was known as Dominique, was instrumental in the transformation of Harlequin. His main talent was his ability to appear in one play as Harlequin in many disguises. A new type, Pierrot, who is sentimental, clever, and often lyrical, was similarly created by an Italian actor, and the Italian Scaramuccia was transformed into the French Scaramouche by this same process. The doctor was changed into Docteur Gratian Balouarde, while Pantalone and Brighella underwent only slight changes in France, and Pulcinella became Polichinelle.

Comic plots, critical of society and having local colour, now came to the fore. Parody began to play an important part; *e.g.*, Harlequin began to imitate the voice or posture of a popular actor of the Comédie-Française or of the Opéra, making fun of their favourite parts. The original prototypes were increasingly turned into individual characters, preparing the ground for Molière, the great writer of comedies of human character.

In 1716, a famous Italian company was again invited to France, after an exile of 19 years. Luigi Riccoboni, who was called Lelio after the part he played, and his company experienced some initial failures in France with new plays and new forms of presentation. Finally, Jaques Autreau succeeded in drawing up a play for them that appealed to French audiences—a comedy written in French, almost as though it were intended for the Comédie-Française but employing the masks usually used in the *comédie-italienne*. Autreau's comedy *Port à Anglais ou les Nouvelles débarquées* (1718) was such a success that it was repeated for two months. It marked the beginning of the development that led to Pierre Marivaux (1688–1763) and the French comedy of the Rococo period. The Comédie-Italienne finally merged with the Opéra-Comique, and in 1780 the Italian companies were dissolved.

Spanish successes. From 1538 onward a number of important commedia dell'arte companies travelled to Spain. Ganassa's successful permanent tour has already been mentioned. Time and again mixed Italian and Spanish companies performed at Valencia. The Confidenti in 1587 completely won the audience of Madrid. Ganassa's company and the Confidenti both included Spanish plays in their repertory, resulting in a mutual influence between the Spanish theatre and the Italian commedia dell'arte. The great Spanish dramatist Lope de Vega (1562–1635), in particular, made use of elements of the commedia dell'arte.

Experiences in England. The close relationship among the Romance languages facilitated the success of the commedia dell'arte of France and Spain. In Austria and southern Germany, Italian was spoken and understood at the courts. In England, however, the situation was much more complicated. Because the Italian companies were not understood, it was mainly acrobats and musicians that went from Italy to England. In the 1570s commedia dell'arte was introduced to the English court, and in 1575 commedia dell'arte was played at Kenilworth Castle, which belonged to the Duke of Lancaster, with Queen Elizabeth I attending. Visits by the Italian companies however, were less frequent to England than to France, Spain, or Austria. English dramatists and actors, of course, took over several prototypes of the commedia dell'arte. Characters like Pantalone, Zanni, and Arlecchino can be found time and again in the plays of Shakespeare's contemporaries, such as Thomas Nashe, Thomas Kyd, and Ben Jonson, and jests with props were also taken over. Influences on Shakespeare can be seen in *The Comedy of Errors, The Merry Wives of Windsor,* and *The Tempest.*

Religious opposition
A famous commedia dell'arte company ventured to England between 1673 and 1675, and Charles II wanted to invite them back again. The opposition of the English to Roman Catholicism, however, extended to the Italians, and the Puritans condemned the theatre in general. When the Duke of Modena ordered his own company of commedia dell'arte actors to London in 1678 to play before his sister, the duchess of York, its visit proved dangerous. They stayed in London for three months but were allowed to play only six times. Not until 50 years later did another group of commedia dell'arte players dare to go to England.

Russia and Poland. Companies of the commedia dell'arte played in Russia in 1733–35 before Empress Anna Ivanovna in St. Petersburg. In Bohemia there is evidence of performances at Prague in 1627, 1651, and 1659–60, first before the court and later before the burghers as well. At the end of the 17th century and at the beginning of the 18th century, commedia dell'arte companies could also be found at the castles of the Bohemian aristocrats. During this time, several types of the popular Czech theatre adopted the masks of the commedia dell'arte.

The commedia dell'arte players found an appreciative audience in Poland. Toward the end of the 16th century, groups of three or four actors went to the Polish court to play farces. Subsequently, a larger, permanent company was hired. In the last part of the 17th century, a respected Venetian commedia dell'arte company of 20 members visited Warsaw for the first time, after having played at Dresden, and then toured the country. The connection with performances at Dresden became closer when the Saxon kings Augustus II and Augustus III also became kings of Poland. Many groups were engaged for the courts at Dresden and Warsaw. The tradition of the commedia dell'arte was sustained in Poland longer than in many other countries. In Russia, the masks of the commedia dell'arte continued to live in many native types of Russian popular theatre. The figures of Pierrot and Arlecchino were brought to the foreground by Aleksandr Blok in his drama *Balaganchik* (1906).

The decline of the commedia dell'arte in Italy. In Italy, the country of origin of the commedia dell'arte, there were two entirely different courses of development, each connected with a major playwright. One course of development is connected with Carlo Goldoni's efforts for reform, the other with Gasparo Gozzi's attempt to add romantic traits to the traditional commedia dell'arte.

Goldoni's reforms
Early in his career, Carlo Goldoni (1707–93) was hired to write plays only for a theatre at which an actor famous for his Pantalone and another even more famous for his Arlecchino played regularly. Goldoni wrote plays for them in which the leading part, that of either Pantalone or Arlecchino, was fixed, but the rest was left to improvisation in the manner of the *canovaccio*. Although plays of the commedia dell'arte never contained a moral, Goldoni tried to introduce some moral values, in keeping with other European theatre of the Age of Enlightenment.

In his other plays, Goldoni also reduced the number of characters from the commedia dell'arte to four: Pantalone, Arlecchino, Brighella, and the doctor. They were still allowed to engage in impromptu acting, but all other characters had written parts. This marked the beginning of Goldoni's reform. Until then, the lovers of the commedia dell'arte provided only the background for the play. Goldoni made them the centre of the action and usually gave the masked characters only the small parts of servants and landlords. In this manner, the old structure of the commedia dell'arte was dissolved gradually, even though its trappings were more or less preserved. With the comedy *La donna di garbo* (1743; "The Woman of Grace"), Goldoni's reforms entered a significant phase. For the first time, the entire dialogue for all persons was written down; in this work Goldoni also began to disentangle the comedy of character from the commedia dell'arte. Brighella and Arlecchino still wore masks and spoke Venetian dialect, but their *lazzi* were now works of literature. The action was carried by Rosaura, the chambermaid, a lively, artful person who was not a type but a character. In Goldoni's *Il servitore di due padroni* (1746; *A Servant of Two Masters*), a play that is still often performed, the traditional servant was inspired with new life. Later, Goldoni took the final step: the masks of the commedia dell'arte vanished entirely and gave way to the Italian comedy of character. He also developed a new program for actors and stage managers. Goldoni's comedies were based on a deep knowledge not of types but of individual men, whether of the masses or of the aristocracy. He created original, unique characters whose actions conformed to principles of verisimilitude. To realize these ideas on the stage, it was necessary to reorient the actors, a task that Goldoni helped to perform.

Many actors could not give up their old habits of extempore theatre and were dissatisfied with this kind of reform of the commedia dell'arte. They engaged a playwright to compose parodies of Goldoni for the extempore theatre. It was not until Carlo Gozzi, however, that Goldoni had a serious rival. Gozzi attacked Goldoni's ordered character comedy and defended the theatre of the masks. He favoured a theatre of imagination, with fairy-tale qualities. His first attempt, the comedy *L'amore delle tre melarance* (1761; "The Love of the Three Oranges"), which has survived in Prokofiev's opera (just as his *Turandot* survived in the opera by Puccini), enchanted both the audience and the actors. Actors who cherished the commedia dell'arte felt that the traditional masks could be merged with Gozzi's new type of enchanted theatre with romantic features.

Gozzi succeeded with all his enchanted comedies, not only in Venice but also on several tours. In all of his plays of enchantment, Gozzi mixed fantastical features and popular masks with their virtuoso art of improvisation. Romantic writers throughout Europe held him in high esteem; some thought him to be a new Shakespeare.

Popular native adaptations of the commedia. Side by side with the Baroque court theatre, colourful popular counterparts developed and flourished in Vienna, Paris, London, the German states, and elsewhere, and the spirit of the commedia reached the countrysides through native travelling companies.

The experience of Vienna was typical. In the early 1700s, Hans Wurst, a typically Viennese counterpart of Harlequin and other *zanni* types, had been introduced, and the Viennese embraced this native representation of the extempore stage. An Italian commedia company appeared in 1710 at the Kärntnertortheater, built with tax money from the people of Vienna, but the Viennese boycotted the Italian performances they had once liked so much. The Kärntnertortheater was given to the creator of Hans Wurst.

Josef Stranitzky (1676–1726) from Graz created the rustic figure of Hans Wurst as a solo figure rather than as one of an ensemble. He was the representative of common sense in the midst of exaggerated figures who always overshot the mark. After the death of Stranitzky, strong competition from an Italian company of the commedia dell'arte forced his successor to adopt the Italian masks of the commedia dell'arte. It was not long before Viennese actors specialized in those types. This custom stayed with the Viennese popular theatre to the 19th century. At the time of Stranitzky, Hans Wurst had been the only extempore character, but with the influence of the commedia dell'arte, extempore play was extended to many roles, including several that satirized persons from the Viennese society of the time.

In the 1760s, after Empress Maria Theresa closed the extempore theatre, Philipp Hafner came to the rescue of the Viennese popular theatre by writing fixed literary and "ordered" comedy texts for the actors, who had played impromptu up to that time. These texts fitted these actors so well that the result seemed to be improvised theatre in Viennese dialect, using commedia masks.

The masked characters of commedia dell'arte origin gradually turned into Viennese characters. Ultimately, Ferdinand Raimund (1790–1836) and Johann Nepomuk Nestroy (1801–62) refined all the types of commedia dell'arte origin, and turned them into native characters, with a precisely laid-out character. Their plays are still performed today.

In Germany, Stranitzky's Hans Wurst became very popular in companies touring many parts of Germany, and a mixture of Hans Wurst and Harlequin was performed in extempore plays that were often adapted from commedia dell'arte scenarios. The great master of these comic characters in Germany of the mid-18th century was Franz Schuch. So popular were the commedia plays, however, that serious dramatic companies, notably the

one headed by the actress-manager Caroline Neuber, heaped continual damnation on them and enacted the symbolic banishment of Harlequin from the stage.

In France the pattern of change was similar. The Théâtre de la Foire, performances held at fairs, adapted the characters of the *comédie-italienne* and joined them with the social satires and parodies of the Comédie-Française, the vaudevilles, and the *opéras comiques*. The use of commedia characters in pantomime became popular in London in the early 1700s. The rival actor-managers John Weaver and John Richy entwined dance and classical themes with the Harlequins and Columbines, initiating an English form of Harlequins and pantomime that existed into the 20th century.

MODERN REVIVALS OF THE COMMEDIA DELL'ARTE

The revolt against Naturalism

By the beginning of the 20th century, people in many parts of Europe became interested again in the commedia dell'arte. This renaissance followed in the wake of various movements against Naturalism in theatre.

Reinhardt's influence. On the stage, the Austrian director Max Reinhardt (1873–1943) made good use in his impressionistic productions of the art of improvisation, the grouping of characters, the comic gestures, and the masks of the commedia dell'arte in order to bring about a "theatrical" theatre as opposed to the Naturalistic theatre.

At the beginning of World War I, Reinhardt gave the comedian Max Pallenberg a role in Raimund's tragical comedy "The King of the Alps and the Misanthropist" with ample room for improvisation, as in the commedia dell'arte. Pallenberg had such a talent of improvisation that he expressed it in Reinhardt's productions even where neither the playwright's text nor the stage manager's directions provided for it.

For a new production of *Turandot* at Salzburg in 1926, Reinhardt commissioned the writing of extempore parts for Pantalone, Tartaglia, Brighella, and Truffaldino. Reinhardt also recaptured the acting of the commedia dell'arte in Goldoni's *Servant of Two Masters:* he transformed Goldoni's text so that a number of characters became true to the commedia dell'arte, as had been the case in the first version of the text. Reinhardt toured many countries with this production and was highly successful with it.

The efforts of Gordon Craig. Others at the turn of the century sought to employ elements of the commedia dell'arte to counteract some of the stiffness of theatrical presentation. Gordon Craig (1872–1966), the English scenic designer and director, advocated that every modern actor should pass once through the school of impromptu theater and particularly of commedia dell'arte. Gordon Craig not only studied the character of the commedia dell'arte in his journal *The Mask* (1908–29) but also included it in his curriculum for actors in his theatre-laboratory at Florence. Prior to any instruction in acting of spoken text, the students were taught pantomime and then theatrical improvisation, beginning explicitly with the commedia dell'arte, of which he demanded a thorough knowledge.

Russian experiments. In Russia, also, those opposing Naturalism in theatrical production looked to the commedia dell'arte. Vsevolod Meyerhold (1874–1942) made use of its methods in 1906 in his production of Aleksandr Blok's play *Balaganchik.* Meyerhold himself played the part of Pierrot; Harlequin and Columbine were other leading parts. In 1910–11 Meyerhold produced Schnitzler's *Schleier der Pierrette*, a pantomime merging commedia dell'arte and grotesque elements. In a production of *Turandot* by Yevgeny Vakhtangov (1883–1922), the actors put on their costumes in front of the spectators in order to simulate the extempore character of commedia dell'arte. Under the direction of Meyerhold, a number of young directors and symbolists fought for the commedia dell'arte and against the psychological and realistic theatre in a very impressive show, staged in 1914–16, which Meyerhold gave the title "The Love of the Three Oranges" after Gozzi's farce. The art of improvisation and the acting of the players were analyzed in the spirit of

Gozzi. The suggestions, thus worked out, were then tried out at Meyerhold's studio. Vakhtangov produced Gozzi's *Turandot* in a combination of commedia dell'arte and a futuristic language of forms in 1920; this production is still being played with only slight changes and new casts. The relationship of commedia dell'arte to the Russian anti-Naturalistic theatre also can be seen in the struggle of Aleksandr Tairov (1885–1950) to break the chain of literary texts in order to present synthesis of emotion and form born of the actor's creative imagination. Time and again Tairov made use of elements from the commedia dell'arte in his effort to help the actor unite all possible forms of expression: acting, singing, dancing, gymnastics, and juggling. In this connection, Tairov felt that it was very important to use the costume as "the mask of the part." To him the costumes of Arlecchino, Pierrot, and Columbia were the determining standards.

Later developments in France. The innovative man of theatre Jacques Copeau (1879–1949) also proclaimed the spirit of the commedia dell'arte and the *comédie-italienne* but took a different attitude toward the text of the drama than had Tairov. Copeau asked for adherence to the text. Yet this demand did not exclude improvisation in acting in the spirit of the given part. Actors should be capable of playing something unexpected, of a sudden emotional outbreak, of unlimited flexibility without betraying their discipline, either acting in a group or alone; this, Copeau felt, required the talent of improvisation of the earlier actors of the commedia dell'arte.

Copeau intended to try out a modern extempore theatre, a special group that could revive the commedia dell'arte but with new types. This project was not realized, but the extempore element could be seen in many of Copeau's productions.

In French pantomime, one of the characters of the *comédie-italienne* became the central figure; it was the version of Pierrot created by Jean Gaspard Deburau (1796–1846), who was born in Bohemia but made his career in Paris. He created a tall, gaunt, pale, slightly sad, and thus basically tragic Pierrot. Tall and slim himself, of elegant gait, Deburau dressed mostly in a white shirt with a frill. Much of the 20th-century tradition in pantomime, including French pantomimist Marcel Marceau's character Bip, can be traced to Deburau.

BIBLIOGRAPHY. C.W. BEAUMONT, *History of Harlequin* (1926, reprinted 1967), a history of the development of one of the commedia mask types; V.C. CLINTON-BADDELEY, *The Burlesque Tradition in the English Theatre after 1660* (1952), a study of the continuing influence of elements of the commedia dell'arte in the English theatre from about 1660 to the 19th century; K.M. LEA, *Italian Popular Comedy: A Study in the Commedia dell'arte, 1560–1620*, 2 vol. (1934, reprinted 1962), one of the best analyses of the Italian commedia dell'arte, its types and presentation; K.N. MCKEE, *The Theater of Marivaux* (1958), a monograph on Marivaux, whose plays, which are still performed in our time, very clearly reflect the influence of the *comédie-italienne*; A. NICOLL, *Masks, Mimes and Miracles* (1931, reprinted 1964), an introduction to the early history of the commedia dell'arte and its types of masks, *World of Harlequin: A Critical Study of the Commedia dell'arte* (1963), a history of the development of the commedia dell'arte, its types of masks and their variability; S. ROSENFELD, *Foreign Theatrical Companies in Great Britain in the 17th and 18th Centuries* (1955), a survey of the foreign travelling commedia dell'arte troupes in England; I.A. SCHWARTZ, *The Commedia dell'arte and Its Influence on French Comedy in the Seventeenth Century* (1933), a study of the commedia dell'arte and French comedy at the time of Molière and afterward; W. SMITH, *The Commedia dell'arte*, rev. ed. (1964), a good introduction to the nature, production, and repertoire of the commedia dell'arte; PIERRE LOUIS DUCHARTRE, *La Comédie italienne* (Eng. trans., *The Italian Comedy*, 1929, reprinted 1966), a discussion of the commedia from the point of view of the characters and their evolution in other countries; H. KINDERMANN, comp., *Theatergeschichte Europas*, vol. III, IV, V, VIII, and the bibliography, IX (1961–70) contains source materials.

(H.Ki)

Commercial Transactions, Law of

The law of commercial transactions comprises the core of the legal rules governing business dealings. The commonest types of commercial transactions, involving such specialized areas of the law and legal instruments as sale of goods and documents of title, are discussed below. Despite variations of detail all commercial transactions have one thing in common: they all serve to transmit economic values such as materials, products, and services from those who want to exchange them for another value, usually money, to those who need them and are willing to pay a countervalue. It is the purpose of the relevant legal rules to regulate this exchange of values, to spell out the rights and obligations of each party, and to offer remedies if one of the parties breaches its obligations or cannot perform them for some reason.

The law of commercial transactions thus covers a wide range of business activities. It does not, however, govern such essentially noncommercial relationships as those involved in succession and family law. For historical and traditional reasons the sale of land is also excluded from the category of commercial transactions.

In some countries the terms commercial law and commercial transactions are merely descriptive. In Anglo-American law especially, they are merely collective names for those rules that relate to business dealings. The terms themselves have no legal consequences. They serve only as a convenient and illustrative shelter under which certain legal rules may be assembled. **Differing concepts of commercial law**

Many other countries, however, have established a technical concept of commercial transactions with precise definitions and important legal consequences. This is most often the case in the civil law countries (that is, those countries more or less strongly influenced by Roman law, such as France and Germany). In these countries the term commercial transactions thus has more than a merely descriptive function. It designates in part those rules that are peculiar to commercial transactions. In France, for example, bankruptcy is open only to merchants, and there are special rules applying to commercial cases. In Germany, similarly, the general rules on consumer sales are in part superseded by special rules on commercial sales. A commercial transaction thus results in a number of specific legal consequences that differ from those of ordinary consumer transactions. Such a special commercial regime exists usually because it is thought that the ordinary citizen should not be exposed to the rigours of commercial rules that presuppose a knowledgeable, versatile individual who does not need as much protection against the legal risks and consequences of his dealings.

In those countries in which specific legal consequences attach to commercial transactions, it is necessary to develop a precise definition of what constitutes a commercial transaction. Although such definitions are more or less closely related, they are peculiar to each country. Most of them, found usually at the beginning of a special "commercial code," combine two elements: definitions of a "merchant" and of a "commercial transaction." In certain countries—Germany, for example—the emphasis is on the definition of the merchant; in others, such as France, the emphasis is on that of the commercial transaction (*acte de commerce*). This latter criterion, the so-called objective test, was adopted in the 19th century for ideological reasons, the French wishing to avoid any repetition of the pre-Revolutionary differentiation of legal rules according to the social condition of persons. But whatever the test, the results are very similar, for the gist of the various definitions is that a transaction is "commercial" if it is concluded by a merchant in the exercise of his profession.

It should be mentioned that the Socialist countries of eastern Europe and of east Asia do not recognize the concept of commercial transactions. This is because such a concept is somewhat suggestive of a capitalistic form of the economy. The implication would be the more invidious since the state, directly or through the various forms of state enterprises, is practically the only trader in Socialist countries. The Socialist countries have, however, established special rules for dealings between state enterprises within each country and within different Socialist countries. These are called "economic" laws. **Socialist economic law**

HISTORICAL BACKGROUND

Only a few traces of rules on commercial transactions in antiquity have survived. The most notable is a rule developed by the seafaring Phoenicians and named after the island of Rhodes in the eastern Mediterranean. The "Rhodian Law" provided that losses incurred by a sea captain as a result of trying to save ship and cargo from peril have to be shared proportionately by all owners of cargo and by the shipowner. If, for example, one merchant's cargo was thrown overboard in order to save the ship from sinking, the loss would be shared among the shipowner and all the other merchants with cargoes aboard. This rule applied in the entire Mediterranean and is today known in the maritime law of all nations as "gross average."

Another important rule, also of maritime character, arose in connection with the maritime loan that developed in Athens. A capitalist would loan money for a marine trading expedition. The loan would be secured by ship and cargo, but repayment of the capital and payment of interest were conditional on the ship's safe return. The interest rate of 24–36 percent, considerably beyond normal rates, reflected the highly speculative risks involved. This transaction later developed into marine insurance.

Roman law influences

Much more is known of the commercial law of the Romans. It was in Rome that for the first time a separation developed between the ordinary civil law and special rules for foreign (that is, primarily trade) relations. Since the civil law applied only to Roman citizens, trade and other relations with and among noncitizens were subject to a separate set of rules—the *jus gentium* ("law of nations"). The latter exhibited two traits that have become characteristic of the law of commercial transactions: it was more liberal than the strict rules of the civil law, and it was applied uniformly in various parts of the world.

As far as specific rules are concerned, the Romans received and preserved the two institutions of the gross average and the maritime loan that had been developed earlier. They added two other rules of maritime law: the liability of the shipowner for contracts concluded by the ship's master (an early recognition of an agency relationship that was later on generalized), and the liability of the ship's master for damage to or loss of the passengers' luggage and equipment. Innkeepers were charged with the same liability. Banking transactions and bookkeeping were well developed, and some prohibitory rules were enacted against capitalistic excesses. Thus the legal interest rate was lowered. An attempt at achieving a "just price" was made by introducing a rule that a sale could be annulled by the purchaser if the price paid by him surpassed the value of the goods bought by more than 50 percent.

In the Middle Ages, the Christian Church attempted to enforce certain moral commands adverse to commercial intercourse. The taking of interest for loans of money was considered income without true work and, therefore, sinful and prohibited. There was also an attempt to establish the idea of a just price. Although both rules, and especially the former, influenced the law and the economy for centuries, neither of them finally prevailed in the secular world.

Emergence of the law merchant

Another feature of the medieval period was the development of a separate commercial law—the law merchant. Like the *jus gentium* of early Roman days, the law merchant was different from the existing ordinary rules that varied from place to place. The need for certainty and uniformity in the provisions governing trade motivated the growth of one set of rules for commercial transactions, valid everywhere in Europe. These rules were disseminated and applied in special courts conducted at the numerous international fairs held in various countries of Europe and attended by local and foreign merchants. The main sources of the law merchant were the customs of the most developed commercial communities of the time—the north Italian cities. Later, in the 13th and 14th centuries, Italian, French, and Spanish cities made the first attempts at codifying certain branches of commercial law.

The medieval period saw the development of company and banking law. The *compagnia* and the *comenda*, forerunners of the partnership and limited partnership, were in very frequent use. The Italians created a sophisticated system of bills of exchange used partly for the transfer and exchange of money, partly (by means of endorsement) for payment, and partly (by discounting) for credit purposes. They also invented bankruptcy as a method for dealing equally with an insolvent merchant's creditors.

In the period following the medieval era, but before the French Revolution, the law of commercial transactions lost its universal character. The birth of pronouncedly national states in Europe provoked a "nationalization" of the law. In 1673 and 1681, the French king Louis XIV enacted ordinances on both land and maritime commerce. These were precursors of the French Commercial Code of 1807, which set the pattern for national codification of the law of commercial transactions in the Latin countries of Europe and America. In England, the chief justice Lord Mansfield began from about 1756 to blend the law merchant into the common law. Only maritime law, although nationally codified, preserved some of its universal traits.

Of great consequence for the later development of commercial law was the foundation of colonial companies, usually through royal charter, for the exploitation and administration of the colonies of the European countries. The first, the Dutch East India Company, was chartered in 1602. Only such companies were able to attract the immense amounts of capital that were needed. The liability of each member was limited to his contribution, which was represented by share certificates that were transferable. Limited liability of shareholders and negotiability of shares were in fact fundamental to the operation of these companies. They were adopted and refined later on into the most important vehicle of modern capitalism—the corporation.

MODERN DEVELOPMENTS

In the 20th century, domestic as well as international commerce has experienced an expansion far beyond any earlier dimensions. With the multiplication of commercial transactions the demand for legal certainty has increased, especially for transactions crossing national boundaries.

Contractual relationships. The first response to the multitude of practically identical transactions was the standardization of contracts. Printed standard contracts or forms lay down those provisions that are essential in the eyes of the drafting party. It depends upon the relative economic strength of the other party whether departures from the printed form can be negotiated. Trade associations as well as individual enterprises have developed and elaborated forms and standard contracts for their members.

The same technique of standardization has been adopted for international transactions. The forms and standard contracts of certain well-known trade associations, especially British ones, such as the London Corn Trade Association, are used by exporters and importers in many countries. The same is true of many shipping transactions. Even international bodies, such as the Economic Commission for Europe, have elaborated printed forms for certain international contracts. Apart from standardizing the contract practices of a particular party, these uniform conditions also help to bridge the gap between the many different national rules. They are a means of achieving partial uniformity of law for international trade.

The development of uniform legislative rules for international transactions has been another distinctive feature in the 20th century. This trend resulted from the uncertainties to which international commercial transactions that came under two or more national jurisdictions were exposed. International conventions have resulted in the unification of numerous rules, especially in the areas of transportation, of industrial property (patents and trademarks), of copyright, and of commercial paper (bills of

International unification of commercial law

exchange and checks). Less successful so far have been attempts in the fields of sale of goods and the conclusion of contracts.

Despite considerable progress in the field of unification, none of the uniform rules is really worldwide in scope, many being limited to a continent or even to narrower regional groups such as the countries of the European Economic Community or the Council for Mutual Economic Aid (of eastern Europe).

All the six principal types of transaction discussed below result from an agreement between two parties. A few rules, however, are of general application to all contracts.

Offer and acceptance. The mechanics of concluding a contract are generally the same everywhere. The negotiation of the necessary agreement between the parties on all the terms of their contract is analyzed legally as the interplay of offer and acceptance. A contract is not formed unless one party's offer has been fully accepted by the other party. Conditional acceptance of an offer amounts legally to the making of a counter offer that must in turn be accepted by the first offeror.

Formal requirements. The validity of a contract depends, apart from the agreement of the parties, on compliance with certain formal and intrinsic requirements. Some countries, for example, establish certain formalities pertaining to the validity or means of proving a contract. They may thus require certain contracts to be in writing and signed by both parties. The intrinsic (as opposed to the formal) validity of a contract requires the absence of any defect in the parties' consent. If the offer or the acceptance has involved a mistake or fraud, the contract may, under certain conditions, be voided. Similar rules obtain if a minor or an incapacitated person has contracted. The validity of a contract also depends on compliance with any applicable regulatory, directory, or prohibitive rules. Any violation of import restrictions or limitations on credit sales, for example, may endanger validity.

Breach of contract. Many legal systems, especially on the European continent, do not know the broad Anglo-American category of "breach" but have developed special rules for delayed performance, nonperformance, bad performance, and so forth. This, however, is primarily a difference of approach. More directly relevant is the question of how a breach of contract by one party is sanctioned by the law. A few remarks on the general approach of the various systems of law are useful at this point. A more detailed survey will be given later on for each of the six main types of contract.

Differing approaches to breach of contract
The basic starting points differ profoundly in the Anglo-American countries on the one hand and in the European and Latin American countries on the other. In Anglo-American law, a party's obligation to perform its contractual promises is regarded, in principle, as absolute. An obstacle to due performance, such as war, strike, or flood, does not generally excuse the obligated party. The view taken is that each party could and ought to have provided in the contract against such risks. In Europe and Latin America, by contrast, obstacles to due performance of a contract frequently excuse the obligated party.

These two basic conceptions on the extent of a party's contractual obligations are very far apart. In fact, however, neither approach has been pursued to its logical conclusion; each has been restricted considerably. Anglo-American law thus developed certain statutory and decisional rules restricting the scope of a contracting party's obligations in situations that were entirely unforeseeable and unavoidable. On the European continent, on the other hand, the obligated party has the burden of proving that he cannot be blamed for the obstacle to performance; and he can never excuse himself for nondelivery of a quantity of generic objects (as contrasted to specified pieces), such as a sum of money or a quantity of a standard product. These modifications have to some extent drawn together the Anglo-American and the continental approaches. Many important differences (discussed below), nevertheless, remain.

Socialist commercial relationships. In the Socialist states of eastern Europe and east Asia, commercial transactions have assumed a peculiar character due to the socioeconomic systems prevailing there. The political and economic structure of these countries is based upon the ownership of all (or nearly all) means of production by the state, on the more or less strict planning of the national economy, and on state monopoly of foreign trade. It might be thought that such a system would lead to the complete bureaucratization of all commercial exchanges, making any legal regulation superfluous. But early attempts to reorganize commercial transactions by relying exclusively on detailed administrative orders soon failed. Consequently, all the Socialist countries have developed a mixed system, combining obligatory state planning with the autonomous fixing of details of exchanges by the state enterprises concerned. Although bound by their plan assignments, the state enterprises must agree among themselves upon many details as to the precise kind, time, and place of their exchanges. These details are laid down in so-called economic contracts, the breach of which may entail the payment of damages to the other contracting state enterprise. Such payments have the double purpose of drawing the attention of the state bank to violations of plan discipline and of removing money from the defaulting enterprise, thus shortening its funds available for the distribution of premiums and other rewards for satisfactory accomplishment of the plan.

In addition, separate rules exist for contracts between state retail shops and citizens and for export transactions with other states, Socialist or non-Socialist. Such arrangements are typical of Socialist commercial law.

Sale of goods. The sale is the most common commercial transaction. All the rights that the seller has in a specific object are transferred to the buyer in return for the latter's paying the purchase price to the seller. The objects that may thus be transferred may be movable or immovable and tangible or intangible. (Patents are an example of intangibles.)

Not all transfers of goods to another person for any purpose whatsoever constitute a sale. Goods may be transferred for use only (lease), for safekeeping or storage (bailment), as a present (gift), or in exchange for another good (barter). They may also be transferred as security. A sale is involved only if the seller intends to part with the object completely and conceivably forever and to receive instead a sum of money as the price. **The essence of a sales transaction**

The seller's complete parting with all his rights in the object sold means, in legal parlance, transfer of ownership to the buyer. One may say that the transfer of ownership for a price is the essence of a sale. But this rule obtains only for countries with a free economy, not for the Socialist states in eastern Europe and east Asia, where the sale of goods among state enterprises cannot transfer ownership but merely the right of administration. Such sales are therefore designated as "delivery contracts." For most practical purposes, however, a sales contract and a delivery contract can be equated.

Obligations of the seller. The seller's duties are three: he has to deliver the goods, to transfer ownership in them, and to warrant their conformity to the specifications of the contract.

Delivery of the goods sold to the buyer must be at the time and place and in the manner agreed upon by the parties. Nondelivery is sanctioned by the various legal systems in three different ways. Anglo-American law does not, in general, permit the buyer to sue for delivery of the merchandise but requires him to buy elsewhere and to demand damages from the original seller. Only if damages are an inadequate remedy because the buyer cannot obtain substitute goods in the market is the buyer entitled to a decree for delivery (specific performance). On the European continent, by contrast, a buyer may always demand delivery. Merchants do not usually go to the trouble of suing for delivery, however, but act voluntarily as their English and American brethren are by law enjoined to act: they buy the same or similar goods in the market and then sue the nonperforming seller for damages. The measure of damages is usually the differ-

Delayed delivery

ence (if any) between the original contract price and the market price at the time of the substituted purchase. This covers the loss arising directly from the seller's nondelivery. Additional loss, such as expense arising from the substituted purchase or a loss on the intended resale of the goods, may also usually be claimed as damages from the seller.

From the point of view of the buyer, delayed delivery is connected with nondelivery in two ways. After the time for delivery has passed, the buyer may not know whether the seller is failing to deliver at all or whether delivery has merely been delayed. Further, the delay in delivery may be so harmful to the buyer's interests as to amount in effect to outright nondelivery. This latter situation is particularly likely to arise if the agreed time for delivery was of the essence of the contract. Even if the parties did not agree expressly that prompt delivery was crucial, such a condition may have been implicit because of the nature of the goods sold. Such might be the case in a contract for the sale of raw materials subject to marked fluctuations in market price or for the sale of turkeys for Christmas.

Various countries differ considerably in the treatment of delayed delivery. Most legal systems require a more or less formal request for delivery or information by the buyer from the seller if a precise delivery date had not been agreed upon. If a precise time had been fixed but was not essential, such a request for information is usually unnecessary, except in France and some other Latin countries. But even if the buyer is not obligated to make inquiries of the seller, additional steps may be necessary in order to obtain remedies for nondelivery. In France and some other Latin countries, the buyer has to bring suit for dissolution of the contract, and the judge may grant days of grace to the seller for performance. In Germany, the buyer has to grant the seller a reasonable period of time and declare unambiguously that he will refuse acceptance thereafter. Neither Anglo-American nor Scandinavian law protects the seller with such a period of grace. If the time element was crucial, the buyer's remedies in these countries are the same as for nondelivery. If, however, the seller did in fact deliver, although belatedly, the buyer may claim general damages for the loss arising from the delay.

Under certain circumstances the seller may be excused from his obligation to deliver on time. This is generally the case if prompt delivery becomes impracticable because of an unforeseeable and unavoidable obstacle. But if the seller owes a quantity of a certain kind of product and has not by the time delivery is due appropriated specific pieces for the purpose of delivery, he is rarely excused. In major contracts the parties usually make specific provisions concerning the conditions under which the seller is to be exempted from liability for late delivery.

Delivery must be accompanied by transfer of ownership in order to enable the buyer to enjoy full legal rights over the objects sold. The method of transferring ownership varies in two main ways. In most countries, ownership in a specific object is transferred with the conclusion of the contract of sale unless the parties agree otherwise. Such a transaction in Anglo-American law is called a "sale," as distinct from a mere "contract to sell." In the case of generic goods (ten tons of coal, for example), ownership cannot pass to the buyer until the seller has specified those goods which he intends to deliver (by transferring ten tons of coal to a carrier for transportation to the buyer). But here again the parties may delay the transfer of ownership, perhaps until delivery to the buyer or until payment of the purchase price. If nothing has been agreed, the seller may, although no longer the owner, refuse to deliver or stop the goods en route to the buyer if the latter's solvency has become doubtful after conclusion of the contract. If the seller resells the same goods to a second buyer, the first buyer's claim to the goods prevails unless the second buyer has received the goods. In the central and eastern European countries ownership does not usually pass to the buyer until he receives the goods.

Although it would appear to be logical that a buyer cannot become the full owner unless the seller had unrestricted ownership, the demands of commercial expediency have carved out important exceptions in favour of a purchaser in good faith. Details vary considerably from country to country. At least between merchants, the acquisition of goods from one in possession of them who can in good conscience be regarded by the other as their owner, or at least as being entitled to their disposition, usually confers ownership on the buyer, even if the seller was not in fact the owner.

Remedies for defective title

The sanctions available to the buyer who does not obtain unrestricted ownership vary from country to country. Some countries impose upon the seller the outright obligation to procure ownership in the goods sold to the buyer. A violation of this duty is a breach of contract and opens the same remedies as those for nondelivery, including a suit for transfer of ownership. But in most countries the seller's obligation is limited to warranting "quiet possession"; that is, guaranteeing enjoyment of the goods undisturbed by claims of third parties. In some countries the warranty of quiet possession entitles the buyer who is sued by a third party to call the seller into the proceedings or even entitles him to turn the proceedings over to the seller so that the latter may defend the action. Everywhere the buyer may claim damages from the seller, covering not only the difference between the contract and the market price of the goods but also the expenses of defense against the claims of the third party. The buyer's rights are usually excluded if he knew at the time of contracting of the seller's defective title or if he later acquiesced in it.

REMEDIES FOR DEFECTIVE GOODS

Goods sold must conform to the specifications of the contract as to their physical qualities, kind, and quantity. The rules on the delivery of goods of defective quality have a long history. Roman as well as English law originally denied the buyer the right of any claims as to quality under the doctrine of caveat emptor ("let the buyer beware"). This general rule did not apply, however, if the buyer had received express guarantees from the seller. Gradually the law developed various "implied warranties," the breach of which gave rise to certain special rights. As a result, the quality of goods is generally considered defective if they are unfit for the ordinary purposes for which such goods are used or unfit for the buyer's special purpose, provided the latter was known to the seller. As soon as possible after delivery the buyer must examine the goods for defects and must notify the seller if any are found. The buyer may then accept the goods but make a deduction from the purchase price for the defect. In most legal systems the buyer may alternatively reject the goods and dissolve the contract of sale. The buyer may also claim damages from the seller, but usually only under special conditions. A third remedy open to the buyer is to demand delivery of conforming goods, but this right is usually limited to generic goods. The buyer's rights are vitiated if he knew of the defect at the time of contracting or if he fails to avail himself of his rights immediately on delivery or within a limited time thereafter. Remedies for defective goods are often widely modified by contractual agreement between the parties.

Obligations of the buyer. The buyer's main duties are simple: payment of the purchase price and acceptance of delivery. Contemporary legal systems are no longer concerned with enforcing a just price. Only a few European countries (including Italy and France) still have rules on exorbitant prices and only in certain special fields. The buyer is strictly responsible for payment of the agreed price and cannot excuse himself by invoking his financial straits. Only war, revolution, exchange restrictions, and other unforeseeable and unavoidable obstacles to performance may, under certain circumstances, excuse the buyer from his duty to pay.

Just as the buyer is often unable to secure specific performance of the seller's duty to deliver, so the seller is not always able to enforce his claim for acceptance of delivery against a buyer who refuses to take delivery.

Most countries do not object to such a claim, but in England and the United States the remedy is rather to refer the seller to the market: as long as he is still the owner of the goods, he should at least attempt to resell them at a reasonable price. Only if this is impossible or impracticable may he sue the buyer. In many other countries the seller, though not obliged, is at least entitled to resell the goods. The proceeds of the resale diminish the seller's loss; but the original buyer remains responsible for the difference. The seller may also, without actual resale of the goods, claim this difference as damages. If the buyer merely delays payment, the seller may usually claim compensation for any resulting loss. Very often this loss is calculated in a lump sum and takes the form of interest on the outstanding purchase price, the rate of which is in many countries provided for by statute. Additional damages for any further loss usually may be claimed. The buyer is, in general, excused from the payment of interest as well as additional damages if the delay of payment was due to unforeseeable and unavoidable obstacles.

The buyer's obligation to take delivery of the goods depends, as regards details, on the precise agreement of the parties: if steel plates, for example, have been sold "free on board vessel," the seller has to load the plates on board the vessel named by the buyer. If the latter does not name a ship, the seller cannot perform his duty of delivery.

If the buyer fails to make provision for taking delivery, the seller still has to preserve the goods, although he is no longer fully responsible for their fate. In many countries the seller may deposit the goods; in others he has the right to resell or a choice between the two. The proceeds of the resale take the place of the goods and have, therefore, to be paid to the buyer. The seller may claim damages arising from the buyer's breach of duty.

Mutual obligations of buyer and seller The duties of seller and buyer do not exist separately and independently from each other but are mutual and concurrent. Both parties assume duties in anticipation of the performance promised by the other party. It is a major consequence of the principle of mutuality of obligations that the duties of seller and buyer have to be performed in general at the same time unless the parties agree otherwise. In international sales transactions it is often agreed that the seller has to ship the goods to the buyer, so that the latter need not pay until he has received the goods and has thus been able to inspect them. Sellers may re-establish the time balance by demanding "payment against documents"; that is, payment at the time when the buyer receives the documents of title, although the goods themselves may still be with the seller or in transit. The law everywhere protects the time sequence agreed upon by the parties by allowing a party to refuse its own performance as long as the agreed advance performance has not been made by the other party. The technical legal means used to achieve this result vary considerably.

In exceptional circumstances the party that is obligated to perform first may refuse to do so. This may be justified if the other party's financial situation after conclusion of the contract has become so aggravated that payment is doubtful.

Various countries differ widely in determining when risk for lost or damaged goods passes to the buyer. In several countries risk passes at the conclusion of the contract to sell; in others, notably France and England, risk is tied to the transfer of ownership in the goods; in Germany and most eastern European countries, risk passes at the time of delivery; and in the United States and the Scandinavian countries, risk passes when the seller has essentially performed his duties. In all countries, the parties may, expressly or impliedly, agree otherwise.

Unification of sales law. The many differences in the sales laws of the some 150 states of the world are a serious obstacle to an effective and smooth international trade. In view of the great volume of international trade, attempts at unification of sales law have been undertaken for many years. The most thorough results may be expected from a unification of the diverging rules on sales themselves. A more modest approach, however, has been to develop common rules on how to proceed when a conflict between the divergent national sales laws occurs. Efforts at unification have in fact followed both lines.

A considerable degree of unification of sales rules has been achieved by the wide acceptance of certain form contracts. But however successful some of these form contracts have proved, they have two important drawbacks: their validity depends on their acceptance by both contracting parties, and they cannot override the mandatory rules of national law.

These drawbacks can only be overcome by unifying national legislation. This method has been used with great success by the Socialist countries of eastern Europe. These have agreed, within the framework of the Council for Mutual Economic Aid, on "Uniform Conditions for Contracts of Delivery between Foreign Trade Enterprises" (1958, revised 1968). The elaborate "conditions" have the force of law; the enterprises may not deviate from them except under special circumstances. For cases not expressly covered by the conditions, there is a uniform conflicts rule that declares the law of the seller's country applicable.

Other countries have had much less success. After almost 40 years of preparation, an international conference at The Hague adopted in 1964 a Uniform Law on International Sales. By the early 1970s only a few countries had ratified this convention, so that it has not yet entered into force. But it is very probable that the six member states of the European Economic Community eventually will adopt the convention. The United Nations Commission on International Trade Law (UNCITRAL) is reviewing the text and will probably suggest certain amendments in order to induce wider acceptance of the convention, especially by non-European states. — The Uniform Sales Law of 1964

A much more modest approach to the harmonization of legal divergences is the unification of the conflicts rules relating to international sales. A convention to this effect concluded in The Hague in 1955 has been ratified by seven European countries. According to this convention, the parties are free to choose the applicable law; if they do not do this, the law at the seller's place of business will, in general, govern the sales contract. The effect of these rules is, however, limited. They merely ensure that the courts in the participating countries will apply the same law to an international sales contract: the divergences between the different sales laws are not overcome.

Negotiable instruments. The negotiable instrument, which is essentially a document embodying a right to the payment of money and which may be transferred from person to person, developed historically from efforts to make credit instruments transferable; that is, documents proving that somebody was in their debt were used by creditors to meet their own liabilities. Thus a promise of A to pay B a certain sum at a specified date in the future could be used by B to pay a debt to C. This "negotiability of credit" was facilitated by the development of a variety of negotiable instruments including promissory notes, checks, and drafts (bills of exchange). These are in fact the commonest negotiable instruments in use, and the following discussion will be confined to them.

Negotiable instruments are used for purposes of payment, of credit, and as security. Sometimes one instrument may perform all three functions. A typical "trade bill" used in connection with an inland or an export sale serves as an example of this: the seller, according to a clause of the contract of sale, may draw a bill on the buyer (that is, prepare a "promise to pay" that the buyer has to sign) or, in the case of an overseas buyer, on a bank acting for the buyer, payment to be made within the agreed time (such as 30, 60, or 90 days after delivery). The buyer or his bank signs the bill as drawee and thereby becomes acceptor. On return of the instrument the seller may use this accepted bill to pay his own debts or may sell it to his bank (discounting). The buyer may also, although this is not typical for commercial transactions, draw a check on his own bank and send it to the seller.

The commonest and most complex form of negotiable instrument is the draft, or bill of exchange. It has been

Drafts as
negotiable
instru-
ments

defined in England as an unconditional order in writing addressed by one person to another, signed by the person giving it (the drawer), and requiring the person to whom it is addressed (the drawee) to pay on demand or at a fixed or determinable future time a certain sum of money to, or to the order of, a specified person (the payee) or to bearer. In the United States, the definition is the same, except that there an instrument may only be made payable "to order or to bearer." If the drawee assents to the order and accepts the bill, which is done by signing his name, or his name with the word "accepted" across the face of the paper, he is called an acceptor. The person to whom a bill is transferred by endorsement is called the endorsee. Any person in possession of a bill, whether as payee, endorsee, or bearer, is termed a holder and, if he is a bona fide purchaser, a holder in due course.

The basic rule applying to drafts is that any signature appearing on a draft obligates the signer to pay the amount drawn. It is the characteristic feature of a draft that it is not limited to the three-cornered relationship among drawer, drawee, and the named or unnamed creditor. Rather, the creditor may transfer it (for purposes of payment or borrowing) to a fourth party, and the latter may transfer it to a fifth, and so on, in a long chain. The means of accomplishing a transfer from one creditor to another is by endorsement or delivery. If an instrument is payable "to order," the signature (endorsement) of the transferor is required. The draft is then delivered to the new creditor. If the instrument is payable "to bearer," delivery alone suffices. Endorsement transfers the rights of the endorser to the new holder and also creates a liability of the endorser for payment of the amount of the draft if the drawee does not meet payment when the draft becomes due.

A failure to pay a draft must be more or less formally ascertained (in continental Europe through a formal "certificate of dishonour"). Upon due notice of dishonour, the holder of the draft may claim payment from any endorser whose signature appears on the instrument, and he in turn may claim from prior endorsers, from the drawee, and from the drawer.

The necessity of unifying the legal rules relating to negotiable instruments used in international trade has long been felt, and considerable success in this direction has been achieved. The principal rules in English law are laid down in the Bills of Exchange Act of 1882. This Act spread through the whole Commonwealth and also influenced the United States Negotiable Instruments Act proposed in 1896 and eventually adopted throughout the U.S. This latter act has since been replaced by article 3 of the Uniform Commercial Code. On the Continent uniformity between the French and the German approach was first achieved at two conferences held at The Hague in 1910 and 1912 and finally by two Geneva conventions of 1930 and 1931 on uniform laws for drafts, promissory notes, and checks. These latter agreements included some uniform provisions on conflicts of law. These have been adopted by most European countries and by many states in other parts of the world. Neither England nor the United States accepted these conventions, however, partly for fear of upsetting the uniformity already achieved in the Anglo-American orbit.

Documents of title. Whereas negotiable instruments embody a claim for the payment of money, documents of title embody claims to goods. The commonest such documents are the bill of lading and the warehouse receipt.

Bills of
lading

A bill of lading is a receipt for goods delivered for transportation with a ship. On receiving the goods alongside or on board, a dock or mate's receipt is issued and is later turned in for the bill of lading proper. The bill of lading may certify receipt of the goods either on board the ship ("shipped on board") or alongside ("received for shipment"). This latter form of bill of lading is less valuable since it does not prove the fact and date of loading. Apart from proving receipt of the goods to be shipped, the bill of lading incorporates the terms of the contract concluded between the carrier and the consignor for the transportation of the goods to the port of destination. A

great many of the printed clauses on a bill of lading purport to excuse the carrier from liability for delayed delivery or from liability for damage to or loss of the goods. These clauses are valid, however, only if and insofar as they comply with the applicable national law or, in the case of ocean transport, with the Brussels Convention of 1924 that incorporates the Hague Rules, which have been adopted by the major shipping nations. Subject to these contractual terms, the consignee (the person to whom the goods are being shipped) may, by virtue of the bill of lading, demand delivery of the transported goods at the port of destination. In the simplest case the consignor sends the bill of lading by airmail to the consignee so that the latter may claim the goods on the arrival of the ship. The carrier may only deliver the goods to a person holding a duly negotiated bill of lading.

A bill of lading and the claim it represents may be transferred to another person by endorsement and delivery of the document. If made out to bearer (which happens rarely), the bill may even be transferred by mere delivery. By such transfer all the rights and obligations embodied in the document are transferred to the new holder. The latter is entitled to demand delivery of the goods unless the carrier proves that the holder knew or through gross negligence was unaware of the transferor's lack of title to the bill. In contrast with the rules on negotiable instruments, an endorsement of a bill of lading does not make the endorser liable for any default of the carrier or previous endorsers. The bill represents the goods, and transfer of the bill is, therefore, equivalent to delivery of the goods to the transferee.

It depends on the intention of the parties whether ownership in the goods or merely a security interest in them is to be transferred. A security interest is typically acquired by a bank, which gives credit on the security of the shipped goods. The above rules on bills of lading, though not formally unified, are essentially the same in all the seafaring nations. Most of them apply also to bills of lading issued in fluvial navigation.

The warehouse receipt is a document that shares the essential traits of a bill of lading, except that the duty to transport the goods is replaced by an obligation to store them. This receipt also embodies the claim for delivery of the goods and may, therefore, if made out to order, be transferred by endorsement and delivery. According to the intention of the parties, such a transfer may pass ownership in the stored goods or create other rights, such as a security interest, in them.

Warehouse
receipts

Letters of credit. Of great importance in international trade is the letter of credit. A letter of credit is essentially an authorization made by a buyer to his agent (usually a bank) to make payment to a seller. The letter of credit comes into use when there is a substantial time lag between the dispatch of goods by a seller and their receipt by the buyer. The seller, having sent the goods off, has fulfilled his part of the contract and seeks payment. The buyer, not having received the goods and being unable to inspect them, will be reluctant to pay. To overcome this difficulty the buyer and seller make arrangements to have intermediaries operating in each of the two countries involved make settlement. The buyer gets his bank to issue a letter of credit authorizing payment to be made to the seller when the latter's part of the contract has been fulfilled (usually when the seller has dispatched the correct quantity of conforming goods). The buyer's (or issuing) bank ascertains whether or not this has been done by obtaining the cooperation of a bank in the seller's country. This bank (the "corresponding" bank), having inspected all of the relevant documents of title and bills of lading to ensure that the seller has performed, makes payment to the seller, often by means of a bill of exchange or other credit device. The document of title, bills of lading, and so forth are then mailed to the buyer. The buyer then reimburses his bank, which in turn reimburses the corresponding bank for making payment to the seller.

In no other branch of international trade have the efforts at unification of law been more successful than in that of letters of credit. In 1933 the International Chamber of Commerce in Paris published the *Uniform Cus-*

toms and Practice for Documentary Credits, which was revised in 1951 and 1962. It has been adopted by banks and banking associations in almost all countries of the world.

Loan of money. Second only to sales, the loan of money is one of the most frequent types of commercial transaction. No developed economy could exist without the credit financing of industrial investments, of commercial transactions, or of private acquisitions. A lender gives money to the borrower, who is obliged to repay it and to pay interest as well. Interest is thus the price for the utilization of the lender's money. The payment of such a price has not, however, always been regarded as permissible. For centuries the medieval Christian Church stigmatized interest as income without true work and, therefore, sinful. Restrictions on interest are, to this day, of great importance. In the Socialist countries of eastern Europe and east Asia, the loan of money against interest, except through state banks, is strongly discouraged.

A loan is a contract between lender and borrower. It may consist of the immediate giving of money against the borrower's promise of repayment, or the contract may contain a promise of the lender to give the money at a future date. In the latter case it may sometimes happen that a borrower has to sue an unwilling lender for performance of the promise to make the loan. As in the comparable situation of nondelivery in a sales contract, Anglo-American law (and also that of some other countries) refuses an action for specific performance and provides merely for damages, whereas most of the legal systems of continental Europe admit such an action. Specific performance of an agreement to take a loan may similarly be enforced against a borrower in most civil law countries but not under Anglo-American law.

Interest on loans is today generally admitted. Among merchants it often has to be paid even if not expressly agreed by the parties, since no merchant is regarded as willing to lend money without receiving interest thereon.

Legal and maximum rates of interest

Many countries fix the rate of interest to be applied in such cases. This legal rate is usually somewhere between 4 and 7 percent. Many countries also limit the maximum amount of interest that may be charged even if both parties have agreed on a higher rate. The maximum figure usually varies between 6 and 12 percent, but in certain countries goes up to 30 percent. These "usury statutes" are likely to be circumvented by lenders who may demand considerable sums as commissions or "expenses." More flexible, but also less certain, are general laws declaring certain "usurious" transactions null and void.

If a borrower does not repay a loan by the agreed date, he must reimburse the lender for his loss. Without even having to prove loss, the lender is at least entitled to default interest (that is, interest accruing after the date of repayment). Some countries permit the lender to claim additional damages, whereas others exclude them.

A few countries, notably the United States, have established special rules regulating loans to consumers. This has usually been in response to abuses to which consumers have been exposed in connection with time (hire) purchase agreements.

Security interests. In the event of a borrower falling bankrupt, the lender may have to share the borrower's assets with competing creditors and may receive only partial satisfaction or even none at all. Lenders, therefore, urge their borrowers to give security for the loaned money unless the credit standing of a specific debtor is free from any doubt. A security interest on goods entitles the creditor to satisfy his outstanding claim from the charged good to the exclusion of the other creditors of the borrower. Hence a security interest gives the secured creditor a right of preferential satisfaction from the goods charged with the security interest ("collateral" in legal parlance).

The demand for security on loans varies from country to country. In general, the demand is greater the more developed the credit system is. But even among countries having a comparable credit structure there are variations. Thus, certain countries, especially France, put legal obstacles in the way of modern forms of security, whereas others have recourse to various forms of personal security.

The oldest security device that is common everywhere is the pledge (or pawn). The borrower delivers the goods to be charged to the lender, who keeps them until repayment of the secured loan. This security device has become rather outmoded today and is utilized only in relatively few situations. But pawnbrokers continue to operate on a minor scale, and banks keep documents of title (such as property deeds) as security.

The decisive drawback of the pledge is the necessity of transferring the goods to be charged to the lender. Hence the borrower cannot use them for production, selling, or leasing. There has thus been a trend away from the pledge to other forms of security by which the goods charged remain in the hands of the borrower. Many new devices have been introduced in the last hundred years, and they vary considerably in their operation from country to country. For want of a common descriptive name they will be referred to as "no-pledge devices." They all attempt to overcome the problem posed by the fact that third persons, relying on the outer appearance of a well-funded borrower, have no means of knowing whether or not the borrower's assets are in reality already charged in favour of another lender.

Creation of security interests

The most common method of warning third persons against existing security interests has been by their registration. Goods so charged are entered in a public register together with details about the goods themselves and the security agreement. A simpler, but more primitive, method of giving publicity to a security interest is by marking the charged goods. This is still sometimes used in the case of cattle. Some countries also employ the method of "privileging" specific lenders. They endow the loans of certain lenders (usually publicly held or controlled banks) with a security interest or a right of preferential satisfaction. All the borrower's goods, or at least those that have been acquired by means of the loan, are automatically charged.

In the absence of any of the above three methods, various indirect techniques are usually employed. The need for sellers to retain a security interest in the goods sold until the purchase price has been paid has been particularly acute. In some, especially Latin, countries, the rules on sales provide the seller with a statutory right of preferred satisfaction. But in most jurisdictions, the seller has to make his own arrangements. Since the transfer of ownership in the goods is subject to the agreement of the parties, the seller may retain his ownership in them until he has received the full purchase price. Such a "conditional sale" is recognized in many countries even without registration, since it is regarded as a modified sales transaction. If the seller himself is using credit to finance his credit sales, the financer can usually be secured by transferring to him the seller's retained ownership. In some countries, including Great Britain, the so-called hire-purchase method is widespread, especially in sales to consumers. The seller retains ownership but lets out the goods that the buyer intends to acquire on hire to him against a down payment and a monthly rental. If in due course the rental payments accumulate to the sale price, ownership is transferred to the purchaser. Here again registration is usually not required since the transaction is cast into the form of a lease.

In the case of lenders who are not at the same time sellers it has been more difficult to find adequate security devices. One of the most successful subterfuges has been developed in close analogy to the aforementioned hire-purchase sales transactions. The borrower transfers ownership in the goods financed by the loan to the lender but retains them in his possession by means of a lease agreement between him and the lender. After repayment of the secured loan the borrower re-acquires title from the lender.

The disposition of charged goods

Under modern economic conditions it is rarely feasible to deprive the borrower of charged goods, as the rise of no-pledge security interests demonstrates. But the goods frequently do not even rest in the borrower's hands. This is especially likely to be the case if the borrower is a trader; he will probably want to sell the goods that he has charged. A manufacturer may similarly wish to replace charged machinery. In these instances the need arises to allow the borrower the desired disposition of the goods and at the same time to maintain the lender's security interest. A number of legal systems, however, do not yet recognize the legitimate interests of both parties in this situation. They prohibit any disposition by the borrower and may even not admit a security interest in goods that remain in the borrower's hands for purposes of resale. This problem has been solved in the United States and Great Britain, although on slightly different lines in the two countries. In the United States the original registration may provide that the security interest is to extend to the proceeds from the disposition of the goods or to products of the charged goods. In Great Britain, the right to a "floating charge," granted by a borrowing company to a lender, has the same effect.

A security interest proves its legal value when under attack by third parties. If it is to fulfill its function of guaranteeing to the lender preferential satisfaction of his claim, the charged goods must be immunized as much as possible against the rights of other persons. The third party is frequently a person who has unknowingly purchased charged goods: borrowers in financial straits are not infrequently unable to resist the temptation of selling charged goods left in their hands to a third person without the consent of the lender and without making the proceeds of the sale available to him. Most countries tend to protect the buyer, provided he neither knew nor ought to have known of the existing security interest. If the charged goods are marked, the buyer can hardly claim to have purchased in good faith. But mere registration does not usually give the buyer sufficient notice, since sales transactions cannot be burdened by requiring the buyer to search a register in a distant place.

The borrower's creditors are also likely to have an interest in charged goods. But creditors, as distinct from buyers, are usually expected to search existing registers of charged goods. If they have neglected to do this, they must suffer the consequence of being subordinated to the lender's security interest.

Enforcement of security interests

If the borrower does not make payment after the secured loan has fallen due, the lender may pursue one of two different courses. He may enforce his claim for repayment of the loan before the courts just as any other creditor, or he may enforce his preferred position as a secured lender. The rules to be followed in enforcing a security interest differ considerably from country to country and even within a country according to the type of security interest that is involved. Very often the lender has to sell the charged goods by public sale; occasionally he is permitted to acquire the charged goods himself. If the proceeds of a sale exceed the amount of the secured loan, the surplus has to be paid to the borrower, whereas the borrower remains liable for any deficit. All legal systems frown upon clauses that permit a lender to acquire the charged goods automatically on the borrower's failure to pay.

The rules on security interests are still strongly national in character. The need for unification has, except in a few specialized areas, not been very urgent. This is largely because, in the great bulk of international sales transactions, the seller, wherever necessary, may secure himself by insisting on payment by letter of credit. But of some international concern was the question of the protection of security interests in those means of transportation that move constantly from one country to another. Two international conventions on security interests in ships and aircraft have, therefore, been concluded. They do not provide uniform rules on security interests but merely guarantee that an interest validly created in one contracting state will be recognized in any other contracting state. The number of countries that have adopted these conventions is, however, rather small.

BIBLIOGRAPHY

Concept: R.B. SCHLESINGER, "The Uniform Commercial Code in the Light of Comparative Law," *Inter-American Law Review,* 1:11–58 (1959).

History and modern developments: W.A. BEWES, *The Romance of the Law Merchant* (1923); W. MITCHELL, *An Essay on the Early History of the Law Merchant* (1904, reprinted 1969); F.R. SANBORN, *Origins of the Early English Maritime and Commercial Law* (1930).

Principal types: R.B. SCHLESINGER (ed.), *Formation of Contracts,* 2 vol. (1968); F. WALLACH, *Introduction to European Commercial Law* (1953); G. KOHLICK (ed.), *Digest of Commercial Laws of the World* (1966–); C.M. SCHMITTHOFF, *The Export Trade: The Law and Practice of International Trade,* 6th ed. (1975); G. LAGERGREN, *Delivery of the Goods and Transfer of Property and Risk in the Law on Sale: A Comparative Study* (1954); H.E. YNTEMA and R. BATIZA, *The Law of Negotiable Instruments,* 2 vol. (1969); T.G. CARVER, *Carriage by Sea,* 12th ed., 2 vol. (1971); A.W. KNAUTH, *The American Law of Ocean Bills of Lading,* 4th ed. (1953); H.C. GUTTERIDGE and M.H. MEGRAH, *The Law of Bankers' Commercial Credits,* 5th ed. (1976); A.G. DAVIS, *The Law Relating to Commercial Letters of Credit,* 3rd ed. (1963).

(U.M.D.)

Commodity Trade, International

Goods that are traded internationally fall into two broad categories—primary goods and manufactured products. Manufactured products, such as machinery and clothing, comprise products whose value reflects largely the cost of the manufacturing processes. Such manufacturing processes contribute relatively little to the value of primary goods, such as crude petroleum and cotton, which undergo but little processing before they are traded. Commodities and commodity markets are terms used as synonyms for primary goods and the markets in such goods. Statistics that indicate the value and direction of world commodity trade are given in the concluding section of this article.

The operation of primary commodity markets. Trade in primary goods may take the form of a normal exchange of goods for money as in any everyday transaction (referred to technically as trade in "actuals"), or it may be conducted by means of futures contracts (see FUTURES). A futures contract is an agreement to deliver or receive a certain quantity of a commodity at an agreed price at some stated time in the future. Trade in actuals has declined considerably and in many cases (such as the Liverpool markets in cotton and grain) has even come to a halt.

"Actual" and "futures" markets

The great bulk of commodity trading is now in contracts for future delivery. The purpose of trading in futures is either to insure against the risk of price changes (hedging) or to make a profit by speculating on the price trend of the commodity. If a speculator believes, for example, that prices will rise, he buys a futures contract and sells it when he wishes (*e.g.,* at a more distant delivery date). The speculator either gains (if prices have risen) or loses (if they have fallen), the difference being due to the change in price.

"Hedging" means the offsetting commitments in the market in actuals by futures contracts. A producer who buys a commodity at spot (current) prices but does not normally resell until, perhaps, three months later can insure himself against a decline in prices by selling futures: if prices fall he loses on his inventories but can purchase at a lower price; if prices rise he gains on his inventories but loses on his futures sales. Since price movements in the actuals market and the futures market are closely related, the loss (or gain) in actual transactions will normally be offset by a comparable gain (or loss) in the futures market.

The operation of futures markets requires commodities of uniform quality grades in order that transactions may take place without the buyer having to inspect the commodities themselves. This explains why there is no futures market, for example, in tobacco, which varies too much in quality. A steady and unfluctuating supply also is needed; this is referred to technically as "low elasticity of supply," and means that the amount of a commodity that the producers supply to the market is not much affected by the price at which they are able to sell that commodity. If supply could be adjusted quickly to meet changes in demand, speculation would become too difficult and risky because exceptionally high or low prices, from which speculators are able to profit, are eliminated as soon as supply is adjusted. Monopolistic control of demand and supply is also unfavourable to the operation of a futures market because price is subject to a large extent to the control of the monopolist and is thus unlikely to fluctuate sufficiently to provide the speculator with an opportunity for making profits. There is, for example, no market in diamonds, since there is only one marketing cooperative. In 1966 the London market in shellac ceased to function after the Indian government applied control of exporters' prices at the source.

Major commodity markets

Before World War II London was the centre of international trade in primary goods, but New York has become at least as important. It is in these two cities that the international prices of many primary products are determined. Although New York often has the bigger market, many producers prefer the London market because of the large fluctuations in local demand in the United States that influence New York market prices. In some cases international commodity agreements (see below) have reduced the significance of certain commodity markets.

There are markets in both New York and London for numerous primary goods, including cotton, copper, cocoa, sugar, rubber, coffee, wool and wooltops, tin, silver, and wheat. Tea, wool, and furs are auctioned in London, but in the case of many other commodities, auctions have been superseded by private sales. In London the metal market is much more a "spot" or delivery market (about 20 percent of total transactions) than other futures markets (less than 5 percent). Many countries have their own markets: Australia for wool, Sri Lanka (Ceylon) and India for tea, and Malaysia for rubber and tin.

Price movements. Prices usually vary widely in commodity markets, not only in the short run but also in the long run. In the short run there are frequent changes in supply because of varying climatic conditions (for agricultural products) and because of political and other events on the international scene (such as the closure of the Suez Canal) and in individual countries (such as strikes). As a rule, price changes do not give rise in the short run to substantial changes in the supply of or demand for primary goods (low elasticity of supply and demand). Business cycles in the importing countries, however, have an influence on demand. Market conditions differ, of course, from product to product. In the case of sugar and wheat, demand is fairly stable, but supply is not; as regards tin, and, indeed, the majority of metals, the converse is true. In the case of industrial commodities, such as cotton, there are fluctuations in both supply and demand.

In the long run the extent of changes in demand and supply is usually greater. A considerable and sustained price increase, for example, may result in a fall in demand and the appearance of substitute products. After a number of years, supply may increase in response to a higher level of demand reflected by higher prices. The length of time required to adjust supply to demand varies from commodity to commodity. Tree crops, for example, need a long growth period, and mineral reserves are tapped only if expectations about the price trend are favourable.

The terms of trade. The relation between the price of primary goods and that of manufactures has long intrigued economists. The relationship is known as the "terms of trade" and may be defined as the ratio of the average price of a country's or a group of countries' exports to the average price of its (or their) imports. The long-range trend of the terms of trade between primary products and manufactures has been the subject of diametrically opposed conclusions: some theorists hold that the trend is favourable to the less developed countries, others that it is unfavourable. Faulty statistical material and methods in various countries are responsible for this lack of agreement.

Any comparison of the terms of trade over a long period of time is very difficult and may be misleading because the structure of trade changes, as does the quality of the groups of goods studied. Many authors believe that the terms of trade were adverse for less developed countries from 1870 to 1938. They point to the fact that as developed countries become more technologically advanced there is a tendency for them to require relatively less in the way of primary products. A downward influence is thus exercised on primary product prices. Another factor is that in the industrial countries the benefits of progress find expression not in lower prices but in higher wages. This, together with inflationary pressures, means that prices of manufactured goods produced by the developed countries tend to rise steadily. There is thus a tendency, it is argued, for the less developed countries to receive relatively less for what they have to sell and to have to pay more for what they need to buy. But the statistical problems posed by any attempt to verify this hypothesis are considerable. The countries selected, the relative weight assigned to the various goods, changes in transport costs, and the fact that the quality of manufactured goods has improved much more than that of primary goods make the statistics unreliable. There is also the problem that the terms of trade between primary commodities and manufactures do not necessarily coincide with the terms of trade between less developed and industrial areas.

Effects of changes in the terms of trade on the balance of payments

Even if it were established that the terms of trade have moved against the less developed, largely primary-producing countries, this would not necessarily mean that their balance of payments situation has been adversely affected. A decline in the terms of trade may in fact improve a country's balance of payments, because, although the prices of that country's exports have fallen, it may, as a consequence of this fall in price, be able to sell a far larger quantity. Total revenue from exports may thus increase. Similarly, although imports may become more expensive, the result may be that the country's demand for imports drops very steeply, so that less is spent on them than when they were cheaper.

This, together with the problems of measurement mentioned above, makes it extremely difficult to generalize about the effects of commodity price changes on the economic situation of one or a group of countries.

Economic development. Through their repercussion on export earnings, price fluctuations are often held responsible for the variations in the growth rate of countries producing primary goods, especially since exports of a single primary good account for a large part of the total exports of many countries. But apart from the fact that, as described above, quantities exported influence export earnings as much as prices, there are many other factors that determine export earnings. Such factors include the type and destination of exports and, above all, the economic policies of the countries concerned.

It is thus difficult to generalize about the relation of foreign trade to economic growth. Many countries with very unstable exports have relatively stable national incomes; others whose exports are stable have highly unstable national incomes. The stimulus from exports will usually be stronger, for example, if the rate of demand for these exports is growing rapidly. Often, however, the transmission of growth to the nonexporting sector of the economy is impeded in less developed countries by the economic, social, and political organization of the economy. It is important, for example, for some countries to try to decrease exports of goods that have a slowly growing demand and at the same time to try to increase exports of goods, such as minerals, for which world demand is growing more rapidly.

Efforts to stabilize prices. The uncertainty for both private producers and for governments resulting from sharp and sudden commodity price changes has resulted in many efforts to achieve greater stability on the market in primary goods.

Action in individual countries. In theory a country could insulate domestic producers against international price fluctuations through variable charges and subsidies, but politically it is difficult to tax away producers' profits during a period of rising prices and to hold the resulting revenue in order to redistribute it should prices and profits fall.

In Nigeria, Ghana, Sierra Leone, and The Gambia, for instance, national marketing boards that attempted to even out price fluctuations of cocoa, cotton, and groundnuts (peanuts) were in operation before those countries became independent. In the former French territories in Africa, stabilization funds fixed producer prices and controlled margins and profits. The main dangers inherent in national stabilization schemes are inconsistent government policies and the excessive operating costs of the public bodies concerned. These factors explain the unsatisfactory results of many national price agencies.

International cooperation. In the 1920s international cartels were created for rubber, sugar, tin, and tea, but they yielded no lasting results. Nor did cooperation between governments of exporting and importing countries (as in the International Wheat Agreement of 1933 and the International Sugar Agreement of 1937) attain the desired goals during the Great Depression.

Since World War II, endeavours to achieve stabilization of commodity prices have mainly assumed three forms—the multilateral contract agreement, the quota agreement, and the buffer-stock agreement. Transactions are effected at world market prices. When a minimum or a maximum price is reached or approached, efforts are made to ensure that prices remain within the two limits. Each of the three systems achieves this in a different way.

In the multilateral contract system, consumers and producers undertake to buy or sell a specified quantity of the commodity at agreed minimum and maximum prices, or at a price within the agreed range.

In the quota method, the quantity negotiated is determined by a previously fixed quota when a minimum or maximum price is exceeded. When there is a surplus, the producers restrict their exports or production; when there is a shortage, quotas are allotted to the consumer countries. With the buffer-stock method, stability is ensured by a combination of an export control arrangement and a buffer-stock arrangement. In certain circumstances exports are restricted by the controlling body. The buffer-stock agency buys when the market price is in the lower sector or at the floor price set out in the agreement; the buffer-stock agency sells when the market price is in the upper sector or at the ceiling price.

Results. The utility of commodity agreements in general can hardly be judged on past experience. Experience with wheat, sugar, and tin agreements, which cover a comparatively long period, is not conducive to generalization. Some degree of stability, though at a high price level, was achieved in the case of wheat, but this was the result of the dominant influence of U.S. and Canadian policies. In the case of tin, too, transactions for the U.S. strategic stockpile exerted an influence. Political factors (including the Cuban revolution) underlay the de facto suspension from 1962 till 1969 of the sugar agreement, which had covered, and still covers, only a limited share of the world market.

The value of world transactions in tin, wheat, coffee, and sugar amounts to less than 10 percent of the value of the world's entire commodity trade. Furthermore, the agreements in question do not cover all transactions. It is, in a way, understandable that up to the late 1970s there had been only six agreements (of which those for sugar, tin, cocoa, coffee, and olive oil were in operation); during a boom the producer countries are not inclined to conclude them, and during a depression there is little incentive for consumers to enter into them.

Conditions for success. A prerequisite for the success of commodity agreements is that they should embrace the vast majority of producers and especially the largest of them. No transactions should be excluded, and substitute commodities should be covered by the agreements.

The most intractable of the difficulties in concluding commodity agreements, however, lies in the fixing of the price range. Neither unduly high nor unduly low price scales are tenable. Future market conditions are not easily foreseeable, so the possibility of errors cannot be ruled out; regular adjustment of the price ranges is necessary.

When it comes to determining the price range, the im-

porting and exporting countries, respectively, do not systematically advocate low and high prices. Certain importing countries are not opposed to a relatively high price because the difference between the international price and the tariff-protected price of domestic producers is thereby reduced; exporting countries in a favourable competitive position are often in favour of lower prices so that they will be able to increase their share of the market at the expense of less competitive countries.

In concluding an agreement, the participants must bear in mind that complete price stabilization is impossible. It would in fact be undesirable, because in the long run supply and demand need to remain in equilibrium, and the necessary adjustments in the economies concerned must not be precluded. Price fluctuations do not necessarily imply failure, because the fluctuations might well have been larger had the agreement not been concluded.

The method of stabilization needs to be chosen carefully, with due regard for the characteristics of the commodities concerned. The multilateral purchase contract and buffer-stock systems offer the advantage of not requiring any restrictions on production; new producers with improved technical equipment may participate.

A buffer stock needs to be sufficiently large if it is to achieve its purpose. Wider financing facilities are necessary; this is something to which the importing countries could contribute. Even then the buffer stock is better used together with other methods of stabilization. Because of the perishable nature of certain commodities or their bulk and high storage costs, however, a buffer stock is not always feasible. Buffer stocks alone often are not sufficient for the control of prices, and it is sometimes necessary for producers to restrict exports in order to reduce supply, thus pushing prices up.

Governments need to supervise the implementation of the agreements. The participating countries must carry out the decisions of the administrative agencies punctiliously, even if they disagree with them. Stabilization of commodity prices would be possible, as it is for agricultural prices at the national level, if the producer countries were willing to subject themselves to supranational authority, but for the present this appears to be utopian.

Interests of the less developed countries. So far as the producer countries are concerned, stabilization of incomes, rather than of prices, is the most important factor. Although commodity agreements may contribute to this, their relatively limited success has caused other proposals to be advanced. Since 1974 an integrated program for commodities has been discussed by the United Nations Conference on Trade and Development (UNCTAD). It relies on a network of internationally held buffer stocks and multilateral purchase and supply commitments, and a system of price indexing is proposed. Here again it may be pointed out that fluctuations in exports are often accounted for by domestic factors such as bad economic policy.

Compensatory financing refers to international financial assistance to a country whose export earnings have suffered as a result of a decline in primary commodity prices. Such a system was instituted in 1963 by the International Monetary Fund, but it has not been used often because of the upward trend of many commodity prices since that date. In 1969 the IMF also made loans available to countries having a balance-of-payments need in relation to the financing of buffer stocks under international commodity agreements.

The European Economic Community has established a stabilization fund of 375,000,000 units of account (at the time equivalent to $470,000,000 U.S.) for its associated overseas countries; only agricultural commodities are taken into account, prices must fall at least 7.5 percent, and the richer beneficiary countries must repay the aid received.

Other proposals relate to the introduction of simultaneous negotiations for a whole range of commodities. These discussions, however, and more particularly the administration of the resulting multicommodity agreement, would be highly complex. It may also be argued that the significance of export instability has been exag-

Three approaches to price stabilization

Fixing the price range

EEC stabilization fund

gerated and that most of the economies involved have suffered no serious damage. Thus, the resources devoted to countering price fluctuations and compensatory financing might be better employed in investments or technical assistance.

As to the possibility of the less developed countries themselves influencing prices, circumstances vary from commodity to commodity. In the case of primary goods, such as coffee, that are produced only in the less developed countries and for which practically no substitutes exist, action to increase prices can easily be taken if demand is not too much affected by price increases. A simple way to raise prices would be for the governments of producing countries to levy a duty on exports, thus forcing producers to raise their international prices.

Limitations on pricing

The fact that there are substitutes for a few primary goods (*e.g.*, cotton, wool, and rubber) limits the extent to which producers can raise their prices. Also, most commodities produced by less developed countries face competition from the developed countries, which may produce the same commodities (*e.g.*, petroleum, sugar, rice, and tobacco) or goods substitutable in varying degrees (*e.g.*, butter for peanut oil). The petroleum-exporting countries, however, succeeded in raising prices from $1.88 to $7.13 a barrel in November 1973, and much higher thereafter.

Many agricultural commodities are protected in the developed countries by tariffs, which means that the latter's requirements are often met entirely from domestic production. Some developed countries produce surpluses that are sold abroad at low, subsidized prices. Such commodities are therefore traded to a relatively small extent on world markets. The sales of the less developed countries are thus influenced by the developed countries' national policies and by the price at which these countries sell their surpluses on the residual markets. The less developed countries that produce minerals (*e.g.*, petroleum) and metals seem to have the most favourable export prospects because demand for these commodities is expanding and because many developed countries are depleting their domestic resources.

Primary goods in international trade. The share of commodity exports in total world exports, which was almost constant during the late 19th and early 20th centuries, gradually declined after World War II and is still declining—from 51.2 percent in 1955, for example, to 39.6 percent in 1975 (see Table 1). This is because of several factors: the growing use of synthetic materials, the "low income elasticity of demand" for many agricultural commodities (that is, the fact that as consumers' incomes have risen, their demand for more commodities has not risen correspondingly), the expansion of industries and production that rely less on primary goods (such as chemical industries), and the rising share of services in the output of the developed countries.

Declining commodity exports

The shares of raw materials and of food and beverages in total exports of primary goods have fallen. The share of fuels has gone up (especially compared to 1913, when it was 7.7 percent).

In 1975 the value of exports of primary goods from industrial areas amounted to $122,200,000,000, considerably less than the exports from the less developed areas (Table 2); of the total exports of the industrial countries, $96,300,000,000 (about half foodstuffs) went to other industrial countries. Industrialized countries absorbed 72.9 percent of world exports of primary goods. Rice was the only commodity traded extensively among less developed areas. The leading item in world trade was crude petroleum, which comprised 19.7 percent of the total value of world exports of primary goods. In 1974 the next most prominent single commodity was wheat (2.8 percent).

Table 1: Structure of World Exports, 1965 and 1975*

item	value ($000,000,000) 1965	1975	percent of primary goods exported 1965	1975	percent of total world exports 1965	1975
Food and beverages	34.4	114.5	46.7	33.7	18.8	13.3
Raw materials	15.1	37.0	20.5	10.9	8.2	4.3
Ores and minerals	6.3	19.2	8.5	5.6	3.4	2.2
Fuels	17.9	169.5	24.3	49.8	9.8	19.7
Total primary goods	73.7	340.2	100.0	100.0	40.3†	39.6†
Nonferrous metals	6.8	18.5			3.7	2.2
Iron and steel	9.7	44.8			5.3	5.2
Chemicals	12.2	61.4			6.7	7.1
Engineering products‡	48.8	203.6			26.7	23.7
Road motor vehicles	—	58.2			—	6.8
Textiles and clothing	11.1	44.0			6.1	5.1
Other manufactures	20.7	89.0			11.3	10.4
Total manufactures	109.3	519.5			59.7†	60.4†
Total exports	183.0§	859.7§			100.0	100.0

*1975 data are provisional. †Details do not add to total given because of rounding. ‡Excluding road motor vehicles in 1975. §Excluding residues of $3,430,000,000 in 1965 and $16,400,000,000 in 1975 (not classified according to kind; revisions and adjustments).
Sources: based on *International Trade 1965, 1975–76* (General Agreement on Tariffs and Trade, Geneva, 1966 and 1976).

Table 2: Origin and Destination of World Exports of Primary Goods, 1965 and 1975*

item	origin value ($000,000,000) 1965	1975	origin percent 1965	1975	destination value ($000,000,000) 1965	1975	destination percent 1965	1975
Industrial areas	31.6	122.2	42.9	35.9	52.5	248.0	71.2	72.9
Less developed areas	29.9	172.4	40.6	50.7	11.8	61.2	16.0	18.0
Eastern trading areas	8.0	32.5	10.9	9.6	8.2	26.9	11.1	7.9
Australia, South Africa, and New Zealand	4.2	13.1	5.7	3.8	1.2	4.1	1.6	1.2
Total	73.7	340.2	100.0†	100.0	73.7	340.2	100.0†	100.0

*1975 data are provisional. †Details do not add to 100.0 because of rounding.
Sources: based on *International Trade 1965, 1975–76* (General Agreement on Tariffs and Trade, Geneva, 1966 and 1976).

BIBLIOGRAPHY. A general survey of the subject is given by J.W.F. ROWE, *Primary Commodities in International Trade* (1965). Long-term statistical comparisons may be found in F. HILGERDT, *Industrialization and Foreign Trade* (1945); P. LAMARTINE YATES, *Forty Years of Foreign Trade: A Statistical Handbook with Special Reference to Primary Products and Under-developed Countries* (1959), which studies the period 1913–53; A. MAIZELS, *Industrial Growth and World Trade: An Empirical Study of Trends in Production, Consumption and Trade in Manufactures from 1899–1959, with a Discussion of Probable Future Trends* (1963); and SIMON KUZNETS, *Modern Economic Growth: Rate, Structure and Spread* (1966).
Postwar data are given in publications of various international institutions, notably in the UNITED NATIONS, *World Economic Survey*, and in GATT, *International Trade* (both published annually). Part of the *Proceedings* of the UNITED NATIONS CONFERENCE ON TRADE AND DEVELOPMENT (1964; 1968; 1972) is devoted to international commodity problems. See also B. BALASSA, *Trade Prospects for Developing Countries* (1964).
J.D. COPPOCK, *International Economic Instability: The Experience after World War II* (1962), covers the years 1946–58 and finds that all primary goods accounted for only one-third of world trade instability; A.I. MACBEAN, *Export Instability and Economic Development* (1966), finds little correlation between export instability and national income, international prices, monetary stability, domestic investment, or rate of growth.
Short surveys on commodity agreements are given in M.A.G. VAN MEERHAEGE, *International Economic Institutions*, 2nd ed. (1971), C.P. BROWN, *Primary Commodity Control* (1975), and L. BARANYAI and J.C. MILLS, *International Commodity Agreements* (Eng. trans. 1963). S. CAINE, *Prices for Primary Producers*, 2nd ed. (1966), argues that price stabilization is too complex a matter to be tackled by any one device and that maximum play should be given to private action. R.G. HAWKINS, J. EPSTEIN, and J. GONZALES, *Stabilization of Export Receipts and Economic Development: International Commodity Agreements and Compensatory Financing Plans* (1966), considers commodity agreements inappropriate for net transfers to the underdeveloped world. For the prewar agreements, see E.P. HEXNER, *International Cartels* (1945).
In connection with the price stabilization proposals, see UNITED NATIONS, *International Compensation for Fluctuations in Commodity Trade* (1961); B.C. SWERLING, *Current Issues in Commodity Policy* (1962); and INTERNATIONAL MONETARY FUND and the INTERNATIONAL BANK FOR RECONSTRUCTION AND DEVELOPMENT, *The Problem of Stabilization of Prices of Primary Products*, 2 pt. (1968–69).

(M.A.v.M.)

Common Law

English common law, or the body of customary law, based on judicial decisions and embodied in reports of decided cases, originated in the early Middle Ages in decisions of local courts, which applied custom and reason to everyday disputes with the aid of but few formal enactments. English common law continued to be developed by judges, as opposed to legislators, and their case law continues today to decide the meaning of legislative enactments and fill in gaps in the law by "declaring" (in effect, extending and developing) the common law.

From the English common law have evolved the modern legal systems found in the United States and in most of the member countries of the British Commonwealth of Nations. Such common-law systems may be contrasted with the civil-law systems derived from Roman law, prevalent in western Europe and elsewhere. Common law is also traditionally contrasted with two elements within the English legal system itself: equity (the separate body of rules developed by the courts of equity: see below) and statute law; that is, law enacted by the legislature. English statutes and equity, however, are so closely linked with the old common law that the three will here be treated as part of a single system.

The first section of this article is devoted to a study of the evolution of the common-law system in England from Norman times to the 18th century. It then goes on to describe the modernization of the common law in Great Britain and the United States during the 19th and 20th centuries and to indicate differences of approach to particular areas of law within the English-speaking world. The article concludes with a brief analysis of possible future trends in the common-law system.

History of English law from 1066 to the early 18th century

THE NORMAN AND EARLY PLANTAGENET PERIODS

The common law of England is in fact largely a Norman creation. The Anglo-Saxons, especially after the accession of Alfred the Great (871), developed a body of rules resembling those current among the Teutonic peoples of northern Europe. Local customs governed most matters, and the church played a large part in government. The concept of crimes originated in this era, but they were treated as wrongs for which compensation was made to the victim.

The Norman Conquest of 1066 brought the practical end of the Saxon laws, except for some local customs. All the land was allocated to Norman feudal vassals of the King. Serious wrongs were now regarded mainly as public crimes rather than as personal matters requiring only compensation for the victim; the perpetrators were punished by death and forfeitures of property. Government was centralized, a bureaucracy built up, and written records maintained. Royal officials spread over the country, inquiring into the administration of justice. Church and state were separate and had their own law and court systems. This led to centuries of rivalry over jurisdiction, especially as appeals from church courts, before the Reformation, could be taken to Rome. Some elements of Saxon practice lingered, including trial by ordeal (by burning the hand, for example), which was retained until 1215. Outlawry, a Saxon procedure whereby a fugitive was placed beyond the protection of the law, was retained for centuries to deal with people who fled from justice. Gradually, however, new procedures took the place of these crude devices.

The Normans spoke French by this period and had developed a customary law in Normandy. They had no professional lawyers or judges but many "clerks"; that is, clergy who were literate and able to act as administrators. Power was in the hands of the feudal military ruling class. Norman custom was not simply transplanted to England, for a new body of rules, based on local conditions, grew up. Enactments and judicial decisions from the Continent were never referred to during the period of English rule over Normandy and other parts of France.

Some of the clergy were familiar with Roman law and the canon law of the Christian Church. Canon law was adopted by the English church, but the Normans resisted any attempt to introduce Roman law, which was applied only to certain claims under wills in the church courts, to marine disputes in the admiralty courts from the 14th century, and to military law.

The feudal land law. At the critical formative period of common law, the English economy depended largely on agriculture and grazing. Wages and profits were important only in commercial centres such as London, Norwich, and Bristol. Political power was rural and based on landownership. Landowners voted at elections as Parliament evolved, and they acted as sheriffs and magistrates and sat on juries.

Land was held under a chain of feudal relations. Under the king came the aristocratic "tenants in chief," then strata of "mesne," or intermediate tenants, and finally the tenant "in demesne," who actually managed the property. Each piece of land was held under a particular condition of tenure; that is, in return for a certain service or payment. An armed knight for the king's armies, for example, might have to be provided for a certain period each year. Nonmilitary service, such as making deliveries of grain, was often substituted for uncertain obligations of knight service. The tenant's obligations were thus of two kinds. Periodic services, such as delivering grain, tended to be commuted into fixed sums of money, which ceased, under the impact of inflation, to have much value. The "incidents," or contingency rights, however, such as the right of the feudal lord to take the land if the tenant died without heirs and his rights regarding wardship and marriage of the tenant's infant heirs (that is, his rights to compensation for exercising wardship or granting permission to marry) were assessed at current land values and remained important.

Succession to tenancies was regulated by a system of different "estates," or rights in land, which determined the length of the tenant's interest. Land held in "fee simple," for example, meant that any heirs could inherit (that is, succeed to the tenancy), whereas land held in "fee tail" was restricted to direct descendants. Life estates (tenancies limited to the lifetime of the holder) were also created. Title to land was transferred by a formal ritual, as most men were illiterate. Few elaborate rules of tenancy could be agreed on in such circumstances, so statutes were passed to regulate matters of detail. The life tenant, for example, was forbidden in the 13th century to damage the property (cause it to deteriorate) unless the grant specifically allowed it, and the tenant in tail was forbidden to ignore the system of descent laid down for his property. The common-law judges devoted themselves to working out the proper rules to apply to all these estates and tenures.

Primogeniture—that is, the right of succession of the eldest son—became characteristic of the common law. It was designed for knight-service tenures only but was inappropriately extended to all land. This contrasted with the practice on the Continent, whereby all children inherited in equal part.

Development of a centralized judiciary. The unity and consistency of the common law were promoted by the early dominant position acquired by the royal courts. A single royal court, the King's Court (Curia Regis), was set up for most of the country at Westminster, near London. Whereas the earlier Saxon *witan* dealt only with great affairs of state, the new Norman court assumed wide judicial powers. Its judges (clergy and statesmen) "declared" the common law.

The local courts were given a much-reduced jurisdiction, because of a strained interpretation of a statute by the royal judges. The latter went out to provincial towns "on circuit" and took the law of Westminster everywhere with them, both in civil and in criminal cases. Local customs received lip service, but the royal courts controlled them and often rejected them as unreasonable or unproved: common law was presumed to apply everywhere until a local custom could be proved. This situation contrasted strikingly with that in France, where a monarch ruled a number of duchies and counties, each with its

Remnants of Saxon law

Dissemination of common law by itinerant judges

own customary law, to say nothing of the situation in countries such as Germany and Italy, which were divided into independent kingdoms and principalities with their own laws.

This early centralization also removed the need in England to import a single advanced foreign system of law, a need that led to the reception of Roman law in Europe after the decline of feudalism. The expression common law, devised to distinguish the general law from local or group customs and privileges, came to suggest to citizens a universal law, founded on reason and superior in type.

Although the common central court split in the 13th century into three courts (Exchequer, Common Pleas, and King's Bench), the same law was applied in each, and they vied in offering better remedies to litigants in order to increase their fees.

The court machinery for civil cases was built around the writ system. Each writ, or written order in the king's name issued at the instance of the complainant and ordering the defendant to appear in the King's Court or ordering some inferior court to see justice done, was based on a form of action (that is, on a particular type of complaint, such as trespass), and the right writ had to be selected to suit that form. Royal writs had to be used for all actions concerning title to land.

Bracton and the influence of Roman law. Under Henry III (reigned 1216–72), an assize judge (that is, an itinerant judge of the periodical local assize courts), Henry de Bracton (originally Bratton) prepared an ambitious treatise known as "Bracton." It is modelled on the order of the Roman legal classic, the Institutes of Justinian of the 6th century, and shows some knowledge of Roman law. Its English character appears from the space devoted to actions and procedure, the reliance on judicial decisions as declaring the law, and the statements limiting absolute royal power. Bracton abstracted several thousand cases from court records (plea rolls) as the raw material for his book. These plea rolls form an almost unbroken series from 1189. The writ, pleadings, verdict, and judgment in civil actions were entered on strong membranes, which can still be read by scholars.

Early statute law. Edward I has been called the English Justinian for the important influence his enactments had on the law of the Middle Ages. Edward's civil legislation, amending the unwritten common law, remained for centuries the basic statute law. It was supplemented by masses of specialized statutes passed to meet temporary problems.

Four of Edward's statutes deserve particular mention.

The First Statute of Westminster (1275) made jury trial compulsory in criminal cases and introduced many changes in the land law. The Statute of Gloucester (1278) cut down the jurisdiction of local courts and extended the scope of actions for damages. The Second Statute of Westminster (1285), a very long enactment, confirmed the estate tail in land, which was often linked with the maintenance of titles of honour, made land an asset for purposes of the payment of judgment debts (debts judged to exist by a court), liberalized appeals to high circuit courts, improved the law of administration of assets on death, and, by creating a new form of action, action on the case, gave broad approval to the creation of new remedies in contract and tort (a private wrong or injury, distinct from a breach of contract or a crime) to meet new situations. The Statute of 1290 (Quia Emptores) barred the granting of new feudal rights, except by the crown, and made all land freely transferable, without interference by relatives or feudal lords.

In modern times the statutes prior to 1285 are sometimes treated as common rather than statute law. This is because these laws tended to restate existing law or give it a more detailed expression. They explained what the law was, but they did not make entirely new law; some authorities doubted whether governments had the right to change ancient customs at all. In addition, judges did not always adhere closely to the words of the statute but tried to interpret it as part of the general law on the subject. Prior to the rise of the House of Commons in the 13th century, it was also difficult to distinguish acts of

Major statutory enactments of Edward I

Parliament from less binding decisions or resolutions of the royal council, the executive authority. Some statutes were passed but never put into force, and others seem to have been quietly ignored.

The Second Statute of Westminster, however, clearly made new law and allowed time for citizens to study its provisions before it came into force. Yet even this statute was freely interpreted by the courts, who read into it things not in the text.

THE 14TH AND 15TH CENTURIES

Growth of Chancery and equity. Since legal rules cannot be formulated to deal adequately with every possible contingency, they are sometimes applied inappropriately, resulting in injustice. It was in order to remedy such injustices that the law of equity (or, earlier, of "conscience") developed. In principle, equity is as old as the strict common law, but it was hardly needed until the 14th century, since the law was still relatively fluid and informal. As the law became well settled, however, its strict rules of proof began to cause hardship. Such visible factors as, for example, open possession of land and the use of wax seals on documents were stressed, so that secret trusts and informal contracts were not recognized.

Power to grant relief in such situations lay with the king and was first exercised by the whole royal council. Within the council, the lord chancellor, a leading bishop or archbishop, conducted the meetings, and by 1474 this official was personally dealing with petitions for relief. The result was the creation of a specialized High Court of Chancery to administer equity. Much of the work concerned procedural delays and irregularities in local courts, and only gradually was the power to modify the operation of the rules of common law asserted.

The chancellor decided each case on its merits, having a right to grant or refuse relief without giving reasons. Common grounds for relief, however, came to be recognized. They included fraud, breach of confidence, attempts to obtain payment twice over, and unjust retention of property.

Early grounds for equitable relief

Proceedings began with bills by the plaintiff in the vernacular language, not Latin, and the defendant was summoned by a writ of subpoena to appear for personal questioning by the Chancellor or one of his subordinates. Refusal to appear or to satisfy a decree was punished with imprisonment. The defendant could file an answer, and a system of written pleadings developed.

Inns of Court and the Year Books. During Edward I's reign (1272–1307) the office of judge ceased to be clerical and became a full-time career. Admission to the bar (*i.e.*, the right to practice before a court as a barrister) was made conditional on legal knowledge, so that law began to emerge as a profession, with a need for permanent institutions and some kind of organized education.

The more experienced barristers were admitted to the dignity of serjeant at law and later banded together with the judges, who were appointed from their ranks, at Serjeants' Inns, in London. Here, burning legal problems were informally discussed and guidance given to all in the decision of actual or likely cases. The four Inns of Court (Gray's Inn, Lincoln's Inn, Inner Temple, and Middle Temple) grew out of residential halls for the junior barristers and became the bodies officially recognized as having the right to admit to the bar. Education took the form of attending court, participating in imaginary legal disputes (moots), and attending lectures (readings) given by senior lawyers.

Bracton's work was adapted for a time but soon became outdated. Bar students had therefore to make notes in court of actual legal arguments in order to keep abreast of practices. These notes varied widely in quality with the ability of the notetaker and the regularity of his attendance, and from about 1290 they seem to have been copied and circulated. In the 16th century they began to be printed and arranged by regnal year, coming to be referred to as the *Year Books*.

The *Year Book* reports are in highly abbreviated law French. They do not always distinguish between the judges and barristers but often simply refer to them by name. The actual judgment is also often omitted. Previous decisions were not generally binding, but great attention was paid to them, and it appears that the judges and barristers referred to earlier *Year Books* in preparing their cases. Thus, case law had become the typical form of English common law.

Effects of feudal conflict on the law

The dynastic Wars of the Roses in the latter part of the 15th century led to a practical breakdown of the legal order. Powerful hereditary aristocrats in the country, backed by private armies, and dominant commercial families in the towns were beyond the effective reach of the royal writ. When legal proceedings were possible, they were often manipulated or frustrated by the "overmighty subjects." Justices, sheriffs, juries, and witnesses were intimidated and corrupted.

The years preceding the Tudor period were thus a time of insecurity and stagnation, a "Gothic age" in which lawyers tried to consolidate the law but made no new advances. Parliamentary authority was also weakened, and the royal council was called on more and more to rule the country and try to maintain order.

THE TUDOR–STUART PERIOD

The rise of the prerogative courts. The accession of Henry VII in 1485 was followed by the creation of a number of courts outside the common-law system that Henry II and his successors had instituted. These newer courts were described as prerogative courts because they were identified with the royal executive power, although some of them had a statutory origin. Thus, the Council of the North at York was set up by statute in 1537, and the Council of Wales and the Marches at Ludlow was confirmed by statute in 1543, though both had been preceded by older prerogative courts in those "frontier" regions. The Court of Requests (see below) was put on a regular footing by administrative action in 1493. The Court of Star Chamber, the royal council acting as a judicial committee, was once thought to have been given its authority by a statute of 1487. All these courts rested on the comparative authority and efficiency of the council in the days when regular courts had been unable to operate properly.

The Court of Requests

In the Court of Requests, which had counterparts in France, the costs of procedure were lower than in common-law proceedings; it was designed for small civil claims by the poor. The judges of the court were styled masters of requests, and they had many other duties, which often caused delays. The court flourished in the 17th century until the Civil War (1642–51), when the procedure by which it operated was abolished. Its example of a simple, cheap procedure was imitated by several statutory courts set up in towns in later times, also known as courts of requests.

Whereas the common-law courts punished "hanging crimes," such as murder and robbery, the Star Chamber dealt with more sophisticated offenses, such as forgery, perjury, conspiracy, and criminal libel. Fines and sentences of imprisonment were the usual punishment. Common-law judges, lay peers, and bishops sat on this court, which also exercised civil jurisdiction. It lost its original popularity when used by the early Stuart kings to stifle political opposition, and its name became synonymous with repression. It was abolished in 1641, but most of its jurisdiction was absorbed in 1660 by the common-law courts.

The rather specialized High Court of Admiralty grew up under the royal prerogative in the 14th century; a statute of 1391 prohibited it from meddling in cases not arising at sea. In Tudor and early Stuart times, however, it exercised a wide commercial jurisdiction. After the Civil War it was confined to trying purely maritime disputes.

Roman-law influences. As described above, the common law was breaking down in the 15th century. Abroad, law was in a state of flux. The customs of northern France were codified in 1453, and modified Roman law became a main source of imperial German law in 1495 and of Scots law in 1532. At the same time, the scope of canon and Roman law in England itself was increasing.

Admiralty law, for example, drew on Greek, Roman, and Italian law and used documents drawn up in continental form, and the crimes of forgery and libel tried in Star Chamber were based on Roman models. Ecclesiastical courts applied canon-law rules based on Roman law, as, for example, to wills and marriages. The Councils of Wales and the North also used Roman law. All these bodies disputed with the common-law courts for jurisdiction over the same cases and followed a written procedure like that still used on the Continent. Roman law and canon law, furthermore, were taught at Oxford and Cambridge, which gave doctorates to the practitioners in these courts.

One of the accusations reportedly made against Cardinal Thomas Wolsey, who fell from favour in 1529, was that he planned to introduce Roman law into England; Wolsey did appoint many clergy to the Council of the North and as justices of the peace. The 19th-century English legal historian F.W. Maitland discusses this legal crisis in a famous essay on English law and the Renaissance. Maitland ascribes the survival of the common law, in part, to the solid front presented by the Inns of Court, which trained lawyers practically and not theoretically. The English law tradition did not depend on abstract scholarly commentaries but on detailed judicial rulings on narrow points of law arising in practice.

The influence of Roman-law ideas, however, was probably greater than generally admitted. The actions of trespass and disseisin (dispossession) have Roman analogies, and the estate tail is clearly influenced by a law made by Justinian. The equitable remedy of injunction has analogies in canon law, and the law of redemption of mortgages may be related to the usury laws, which forbade making excessive profits from loans. The law of trusts and deceit resembles the breach of faith of the church courts. Continental mercantile law, which contains Roman-law elements, was absorbed into English law as it stood. Continental law has also contributed to some of the rules of contract, such as the effect of mistake, and the Roman concept of fault has played some part in the law of negligence. Many old European legal ideas have in fact survived longer in England, where they escaped being eliminated in codifications, than in Europe.

Coke as a champion of the common law

An account of the development of the common law in the Tudor–Stuart period would be incomplete without mention of the role of Sir Edward Coke. Coke combined a distinguished career as barrister and judge with a wealth of legal writings. He risked removal from the office of chief justice in 1606 by challenging the exaggerated claims of the royalist party to prerogative powers outside the common law. He disapproved of legislation by proclamation, dispensation from the law in individual cases, and the mushrooming jurisdictions of the prerogative courts. He helped draft the Petition of Right in 1628.

Coke's 11 volumes of *Reports* appeared between 1600 and 1618, and two posthumous volumes followed. Coke commented, rather than reported, but was careful to supply a copy of the court record. His reports were quickly available and formed the main source of citation of cases for many years, for want of any other series. His four volumes of *Institutes of the Lawes of England*, published between 1628 and 1644, dealt with the law of real property in land (Coke on Littleton), the medieval statutes, the criminal law (pleas of the crown), and the jurisdiction of the courts.

Coke was no objective historian but an open advocate of the common law. Though he was old-fashioned and at times in error, his great works restated the common law in acceptable form and did much to save it.

Growth of statute law. The Tudors made use of proclamations by the king for emergency measures and detailed regulations, especially on economic matters. Many royal charters to trading companies were also granted. Parliament passed laws of a political character, such as those enforcing the king's supremacy over the new Established Church. Statutes regulated imports and exports, farming, and unfair competition. A law of 1562-

63 regulated apprenticeships and provided for annual wage fixing by magistrates in accordance with the cost of living.

Among other statutory innovations were the Statute of Monopolies of 1623, which confirmed that monopolies were contrary to common law but which made exceptions for patentable inventions; a statute of 1601 that became the basis of the privileges enjoyed by charitable trusts; and the Poor Law statutes of 1563–1601, which were the result of the distress caused by the dissolution of the monasteries and consequent neglect of the poor.

In 1540 the actions to recover land were subjected to time limits, and in 1623–24 the principle of limitation of actions by lapse of time was introduced into the law of contract and tort.

During the Commonwealth (1649–60) many projects of reform were drafted, anticipating the 19th-century reforms, but none of them was carried out. Prisoners would have had counsel, the land law and procedure would have been modernized, and civil marriage would have been permitted.

The outstanding enactment of the later Stuart period was the Statute of Frauds of 1677. Recognizing the growth of literacy and the prevalence of perjury and fraud, wills and contracts for sale of land or goods (over a certain amount) were required to be in writing. Though drafted by eminent judges, the statute was to require endless interpretation.

Further development of equity. Although one eminent contemporary observer, the legal historian John Selden, regarded the fate of a lawsuit in Chancery as varying with the chancellor's personality, the types of suits that would be granted relief had eventually become fairly clear. Precedent was being followed, and law reports of equity decisions and books on equity began to be published.

In 1615 the King declared that the Chancery retained its traditional superiority over the common-law courts but only in areas in which its authority was well recognized. If the applicability of equity was in doubt, the common law was followed.

Developments in the law of trusts

The main development in this period was in the law of trusts (see TRUSTS, LAW OF). In medieval England, from the 14th century, most land was held "to uses"; that is, by nominees for the true owners. This situation may have been partly due to devices to evade taxation, but it also enabled wills of land to be made. "Death duties" were payable if a man died while he was the legal proprietor; by transferring the land to another person, these could be avoided. Wills of land were not allowed before 1540, but land could be transferred to the use of another person while the owner was still alive, the transferee observing the owner's wishes regarding the land while the owner lived. The beneficiary of such a trust usually stayed on his land as apparent owner, though the trustee held the legal title. A statute of Richard III, however, allowed the beneficiary to transfer the property, and in 1535–36 the Statute of Uses eliminated the middleman and revested the legal title in the beneficiary. The device of the use was exploited to create new and complicated legal interests in land. The old use was revived as the modern trust in Chancery, first for trusts involving money and leases and finally for trusts of land itself. The spur was the desire to separate the legal and beneficial titles, especially when the beneficiary was young or unbusinesslike. But the trust was adapted to many other ends, such as giving property to clubs and other unincorporated bodies, and to churches.

The modernization of common law

<u>GREAT BRITAIN</u>

Influence of Blackstone. Of extraordinary influence in the development and dissemination to other parts of the world of the common law was the most famous of English jurists, Sir William Blackstone (q.v.). Born in 1723, he was called to the bar in 1746 and in 1758 became the first professor of common law in England.

His most influential work, the *Commentaries on the Laws of England*, was published between 1765 and 1769

It consists of four books: "Persons" deals with family and public law; "Things" gives a brilliant outline of real-property law; "Private Wrongs" covers civil liability, courts, and procedure; and "Public Wrongs" is an excellent study of criminal law.

Blackstone was far from being a scientific jurist and was criticized for his superficiality and lack of historical sense. The shortcomings of the *Commentaries* in these respects, however, were offset by its style and intelligibility, and lawyers and laymen alike came to regard it as an authoritative revelation of the law.

In the following century the fame of Blackstone was greater in the United States than in his native land. After the Declaration of Independence the *Commentaries* became the chief source of knowledge of English law in the New World.

Reform in the 19th and 20th centuries. *Bentham.* Following the turmoil of the French Revolution of 1789 and of the Industrial Revolution, there were many demands for reforms to modernize the law. The most significant figure in the reform movement was the English Utilitarian philosopher Jeremy Bentham, who was prepared to reform the whole law on radical lines. A brilliant student, Bentham disliked the picture of the law presented in Blackstone's lectures. In 1769 he was called to the bar, but he never practiced, living on an inheritance. He worked to make law less technical and more accessible to the people, but he was slow to complete or publish his writings, and not until 1789 did his basic work, *An Introduction to the Principles of Morals and Legislation*, appear.

Bentham attacked legal fictions and other historical anomalies. In order to achieve the greatest happiness of the greatest number, legislators, rather than courts, should make the law, and the aims of law should vary with time and place.

The fame of the *Principles* spread widely and rapidly. Bentham was made a French citizen in 1792, and his advice was respectfully received in most of the states of Europe and America. Although he wanted most of all to be allowed to draw up a legal code for his own or some foreign country, his actual practical influence was far more indirect, deriving largely from the diffusion of Utilitarian ideas during the 19th century.

Changes in procedure and criminal law. In England the restrictive framework of the separate forms of action in civil cases was replaced in 1852 by a new system of uniform writs of summons, and liberal amendment of pleadings was permitted. Fixed dates were established for trials. In 1933 jury trial was ended in civil cases except in libel and a few other actions. Evidence acts of 1938 and 1968 have simplified civil proof. A major trend in criminal procedure since the early 19th century has been better protection of the rights of the accused. Since 1836 the accused has been entitled to counsel and since 1898 has been allowed to testify on his own behalf. From 1903 provision for state payment for defense was made and constantly expanded, and in 1907 a right of appeal against criminal convictions was created. In 1967 verdicts by a majority of the jury were made possible, and restrictions were imposed on press coverage of preliminary hearings.

Increased protection of the rights of the accused

The 19th century saw the enactment of a series of statutes that practically codified the criminal law, apart from homicide. Basic ideas were little changed, however, except that some modern statutes impose responsibility without fault and that corporations can be made responsible for the acts of their management.

The rules as to legal insanity laid down in the 19th century were supplemented in 1957 by the limited defense of "diminished responsibility." Capital punishment was ended for most felonies over the years and finally for murder by the Homicide Acts of 1957–65. In 1968 a new Theft Act replaced the rather crude medieval idea of larceny by a broader concept, which resembles the Roman delict (offense) of theft. Experimentation has led to new remedies, the latest, since 1967, being the suspended sentence, which only has to be served if a further crime is committed.

Reorganization of the judiciary. The lay jurisdiction of the church courts was ended in 1857, when the divorce and probate courts were set up. These merged into the High Court of Justice in 1875, when the Judicature Acts of 1873–75 reformed the civil courts. The Judicature Acts were much more than a regrouping and renaming of courts; they attempted a fusion of law and equity by making available legal and equitable remedies in all divisions of the High Court and by providing that in case of conflict the equitable rule should prevail. Common law and equity nevertheless preserved their separate identities, partly because of the different subject matter with which they often deal and partly because of the persistence among lawyers of a common-law and a chancery outlook.

The three central courts of common law were amalgamated in the late 19th century into the Queen's Bench Division, which continues to try suits for damages. Since 1875 cases have been tried by a judge alone (before 1933 with a jury), not by a full bench of judges.

The Chancery became a division of the High Court in 1875. It deals with equity suits but also administers the voluminous legislation on property, bankruptcy, succession, copyrights, patents, and taxation. In 1972 contested probate cases were transferred to the Chancery by the Courts Act of 1971.

Criminal cases were tried two or three times a year at assizes or four times a year at quarter sessions in the provinces. From January 1972, under the Courts Act, a system of provincial crown courts replaced these. Civil assizes were replaced by allowing the High Court to sit at certain cities.

Since 1846 small civil cases have been tried at statutory county courts, now regulated by an act of 1959.

A remarkable feature of English criminal justice, as compared with most European systems, has been the continuing importance of the lay justice of the peace, in spite of the appointment of paid, legally trained magistrates in London and some of the larger cities, of barristers as recorders at borough quarter sessions, and of legally qualified chairmen at county quarter sessions. An important aspect of the magistrates' work has been their jurisdiction over young offenders, for whom special juvenile courts were first set up in 1908. The report of a royal commission on justices of the peace in 1948 strongly defended the lay justice against some public criticism; its cautious recommendations as to the appointment of justices and as to the organization of their courts were largely put into effect by the Justices of the Peace Act (1949) and the Magistrates' Courts Act (1952). The Criminal Justice Administration Act (1962) extended the power of justices of the peace to try indictable offenses summarily and of quarter sessions to try certain offenses hitherto reserved for assizes, while requiring the chairman of county quarter sessions to be legally qualified. From 1964 elementary judicial training for lay justices was introduced. These developments since 1948 show both the persistence in English law of ancient institutions and a preference for reforming rather than totally abolishing them.

Routes of appeal

A modern appeal court from civil cases in the High Court was set up in 1830 but was replaced in 1875 by a Court of Appeal of special appellate judges. In 1907 a Court of Criminal Appeal was established but merged in the Court of Appeal in 1966. A divisional court hears appeals from magistrates on points of law. A final appeal, subject to conditions, lies to the House of Lords from all lower courts.

Reform in private law. Property law has been much changed. Wills are regulated mainly by statute of 1837, and freedom to disinherit has been cut down by Family Provision acts of 1938, 1952, and 1966. Title to land is subject to a system of registration being gradually introduced under an act of 1925. Succession on intestacy (*i.e.,* in the absence of a legal will) for all kinds of property was unified in the same year. The law of leases has been modified by social legislation such as the numerous Rent (control) Acts, protecting residential tenants. The terms of trusts can be modified by the Chancery

(since 1958), and a wider range of trustee investments has been allowed since 1961.

Grounds of divorce have been enlarged by a number of 20th-century statutes, culminating in the broad "breakdown of marriage" approach of the Divorce Reform Act of 1969, under which a marriage may be terminated, regardless of any "fault" of the partners, if the marriage is no longer workable.

After several piecemeal laws on trade (labour) unions, a more comprehensive but controversial Industrial Relations Act was passed in 1971, requiring registration of unions and arbitration of disputes.

In the field of tort, manufacturers' liability to consumers was established by case law in 1932. Liability in libel has been cut down by many statutes. A law of 1945 introduced the Roman principle of apportioning damages when both parties are at fault.

Commercial law, with the Bills of Exchange Act (1882), Sale of Goods Act (1893), patents acts (1907–49), and copyright acts (1911–56), has become the domain of legislation. Buyers by hire purchase (time payment) are protected by a law of 1965. Arbitration is regulated by statute.

THE UNITED STATES

The first English settlers on the Atlantic seaboard of North America brought with them only elementary notions of law. Colonial charters conferred on them the traditional legal privileges of Englishmen, such as habeas corpus and the right to trial before a jury of one's peers, but there were few judges, lawyers, or lawbooks, and English court decisions were slow to reach them. Each colony passed its own statutes, and governors or legislative bodies acted as courts. Civil and criminal cases were tried in the same courts, and lay juries enjoyed wide powers. English laws passed after the date of settlement did not automatically apply in the colonies, and even presettlement legislation was liable to adaptation. English cases were not binding precedents. Several of the American colonies introduced substantial legal codes, such as those of Massachusetts in 1648 and Pennsylvania in 1682.

By the late 17th century, lawyers were practicing in the colonies, using English lawbooks and following English procedures and forms of action. In 1701 Rhode Island legislated to receive English law in full, subject to local legislation, and the same happened in the Carolinas in 1712 and 1715. Other colonies, in practice, also applied the common law with local variations.

The reception of English law

Many legal battles in the period leading up to the War of Independence were fought on common-law principles, and half the signatories of the Declaration of Independence were lawyers. The American Constitution uses traditional English legal terms, and American statutes are still applied according to English canons of interpretation.

Anti-British feeling led some Americans after 1776 to advocate a fresh legal system, but European laws were very diverse and couched in unfamiliar languages and turns of thought, and textbooks were not available. Blackstone's *Commentaries,* reprinted in 1771 in America, was widely used, though new English statutes and decisions were officially ignored.

In the 1830s two great judges, James Kent of New York and Joseph Story of Massachusetts, produced important commentaries on common law and equity, emphasizing the need for legal certainty and security of title to property. These works followed the common-law tradition, which has never been fundamentally altered, except for the survival of French civil law in Louisiana.

American innovations. The American states saw law as a cementing force and wanted it to facilitate cooperation in the face of a cruel nature and the aboriginal inhabitants. Special laws were developed to deal with timber, water, and mineral rights. Simple procedures were followed. Dogma was rejected in favour of personal experience and experiment, and old decisions soon became outdated. The pioneer spirit favoured freedom and initiative and distrusted central authority and a paternal government. Homespun local justice was preferred, as was the common sense of the local jury, and some of the colonies for a time tried to base their law on the Bible. But, even when English law reasserted itself, many of its institutions were rejected. On death intestate, for example, all the children inherited land in America and not the eldest son, as in England. Freehold title was the rule, not long leases under landlords. Church courts did not exist.

Growth of statute law and codes. After the War of Independence a drive to replace judge-made law by popular legislation revived. In 1811 Jeremy Bentham proposed a national Civil Code to President James Madison, but this was premature. A New York Civil Code was projected but not accepted. Only California possesses a civil code, drafted because of the Spanish tradition there but common-law in character. The American legal reformer David Dudley Field produced a Civil Procedure Code that was adopted by New York State in 1848 and widely copied elsewhere. His Penal Code and Criminal Procedure Code were also approved in New York in 1881. The English-style Uniform Sales Act of 1906 has been replaced by the Uniform Commercial Code of 1957 in every state except Louisiana (which has a Roman- or civil-law system).

Codes of David Dudley Field

American statutes are not construed so narrowly as in England, and there is less reluctance to change the older law. Statutes are also regularly revised; *e.g.*, New York state has had a Law Review Committee since 1934.

Equity and probate. In 18th-century England the Court of Chancery administered equity and the church courts the probate of wills. In the American colonies the governor and council acted as a court of equity, and even today equitable remedies tend to be reserved for the higher courts in American states. For a time after independence, equity was suspect as a remnant of royal prerogative, but it is now generally applied, often by the same court as the regular law. American common law is more flexible than English law, and the need for equity is less, but it has developed important remedies in labour law and other fields. Probate, with a few exceptions, is usually a matter for the regular courts.

Federal and state judicial systems. State courts try 90 percent of all cases, including both civil and criminal matters. Local magistrates may sit on county or district courts. One appeal is always given, but two possible appeals exist in some states. The highest court is usually the supreme court of the state, but this varies. In New York state, for example, the Supreme Court is a trial court for civil cases, and the highest court is the Court of Appeals.

The Constitution of 1789 set up a federal Supreme Court, and the 1789 Judiciary Act provided for federal district courts and circuit courts. The plan for inferior courts has undergone changes from time to time, notably in 1891, when circuit courts of appeals were established, and in 1911, when the old circuit courts were abolished.

Most federal law is statutory and enforced by federal courts. Marine law, drug traffic, interstate trade, labour law, and monopolies fall into this category.

By a decision of 1803, federal courts became the ultimate authority to determine the conformity of all legislation with the federal Constitution, which guarantees many fundamental rights.

To ensure fair treatment of out-of-state citizens or corporations incorporated or centralized elsewhere, federal courts can try cases involving diversity of citizenship. They act as if they were state courts, however, being bound by state statutes since 1842 and by state interpretations of common law and equity since 1938. Federal procedure is followed, but state rules on vital matters, such as time bars on bringing actions, are enforced.

Federal courts also try claims by and against the United States, such as cases undertaken to protect federal assets. In such cases a "federal common law" is applied, in the absence of statutory provision.

Personal and property rights. The guarantees of due process of law given in Magna Carta in 1215 and the English Bill of Rights of 1689 are reflected in the first group of amendments to the federal Constitution, passed in 1791 and known as the Bill of Rights. Since the passage of the Fourteenth Amendment (1868), private rights have been protected from deprivation without due process of law, and this has tended to shield private property from government regulation and private contracts from government interference. The use of property, however, is restricted by zoning laws and health and safety measures, and the acquisition of property for public purposes may be justified under the doctrine of eminent domain (power of the government to take private property for public use without the owner's consent).

The 1929 Depression was followed by the rejection by the Supreme Court of many welfare measures, but since 1937 the power of the federal Congress to regulate the economy under its interstate-commerce power has been generally upheld by the Supreme Court. State legislation is generally also held to be constitutional in this area. Minimum-wage laws and the right to collective bargaining in industry are recognized.

The emphasis in constitutionality cases has since the 1950s moved to human rights. The requirement of "equal protection of the laws" and the Civil Rights Act of 1866 led to the ruling in 1954 that public schools must be racially integrated and to later rulings against using public funds for private schools. The Federal Civil Rights Act of 1964 applies not only to official laws and actions but also to the conduct of private citizens. Thus, no discrimination is allowed in places of public entertainment or resort or in employment practices by the larger firms. In a 1971 case in Idaho, discrimination against women was outlawed. The case involved a preference for men in granting administration to the estate of a deceased relative.

Human rights in the Supreme Court

Since 1962 the Supreme Court has insisted on regular redrawing of electoral districts to give each vote roughly the same value (seat reapportionment). Because of the prohibition on any state religion, it has also held school prayers and religious instruction to be illegal. Freedom of the press was held in 1971 to justify the *New York Times* in publishing confidential political material.

COMPARISONS OF ENGLISH, AMERICAN, AND COMMONWEALTH LAW

Personal law. In England the former grounds of divorce have been replaced by blending the specific grounds, such as cruelty and desertion, with the concept, in the 1969 legislation, of the irrevocable breakdown of the marriage. Special protection is provided for children. A 1970 statute gives the court wider powers to adjust property rights of all parties. The Canadian Uniform Divorce Act of 1968 is broadly similar to the English 1969 act. Family law in the United States varies from state to state, and grounds for divorce may be very strict, as in New York state before 1966, or very lax, as in Nevada. A divorce, however, decreed in a state whose courts are competent to grant it will be recognized in the other states under the constitutional requirement of "full faith and credit" due the judgments of out-of-state courts.

Property and succession. The basic principles of property and succession are much the same everywhere, but the newer countries have special laws on forests, mines, and water rights. In Australia, for example, the crown reserves all mineral rights to itself. Transfer of land in England is governed by a system of full title registration, which is being introduced in stages. In Canada and the United States the separate deeds are registered, and title insurance is used to protect the purchaser.

America and Canada by statute give mechanics' liens (the right to hold property until payment for repairs is made) to builders and repairers of property, and future crops may be charged by statutory liens as security for loans in Australia.

Succession on intestacy is broadly similar throughout common-law countries but varies everywhere in detail. The widow, for example, may get more in one country and the children more in another. All children of both sexes generally take equal shares.

In some U.S. states and Canadian provinces there are homestead laws, which protect the family house or a certain minimum sum of money from the legal claims of creditors.

Whereas trustees and executors in England are unpaid for their time and trouble, apart from any special contract in advance, U.S. state laws generally reimburse them with a commission based on a percentage of the trust fund or the value of the estate.

Succession law in India is largely religious. Law and equity are merged, and trusts are enforced. The Indian Specific Relief Act, for the recovery of property, is based on Field's New York Code.

Extensions of tortious liability

Tort law. Tort law (law relating to private civil wrongs) is largely common law in England, Canada, and the United States. There are special laws concerning motorists' liability to their passengers in Canadian provinces. Several major reforms have been introduced along the same lines in different countries. Allowing claims by dependents of persons tortiously killed and removing the immunity of the crown or government from tort claims provide examples. The liability of manufacturers to the ultimate consumer was first laid down by American and then by English judges.

In the field of libel, American practice is less strict than the English, and in the United States a public figure cannot sue for honest but unfair and untrue criticisms of his activities, whereas in England published facts must be true and comment fair. In some Australian states truth is not necessarily a defense to an action.

English law permits the abuse of rights, but in the United States rights may not be used except for a legitimate reason. It is thus actionable to build, in spite, a fence designed only to obstruct a neighbour's light without serving any useful purpose.

In English law a rescuer takes all risks, but American law often entitles him to compensation for out-of-pocket loss incurred.

A notable American tort is interference with privacy, examples being a stranger using one's photograph for advertising purposes without permission, using "bugging" (*i.e.*, electronic eavesdropping) devices in one's home or searching it without permission, or taking photographs of people in embarrassing situations.

Contracts. The most interesting difference in contract law among the common-law countries relates to the question of enforcement of contracts by third parties who are not actually parties to the contract but who are persons for whose benefit the contract was made. English law excludes such rights, except in an occasional statute. The Indian Contract Code of 1872 allows it generally. American state law also often allows it.

English law still requires the use of a seal on a gratuitous contract (such as one agreeing to make a gift) but has largely repealed the laws requiring written evidence of ordinary contracts. Written evidence is often called for in the United States.

The various areas of special contracts, such as those applying to employment, sale of land, and agency, are broadly similar everywhere but are regulated by local legislation, such as the English Sale of Goods Act of 1893 and the American Uniform Commercial Code, and by a wealth of labour legislation, such as the American Fair Employment Practices Act and the British Industrial Relations Act of 1971.

Criminal law and procedure. As regards criminal law and procedure, the substance of the law is much the same throughout the common-law countries, but the English Theft Act of 1967 is a new departure, bearing some resemblance to the Roman approach to theft. Relaxations of criminal responsibility in cases of uncontrollable impulse are common.

More important than legal technicalities are the rules of criminal procedure. This rests in Britain on modern legislation, as the old procedure bore heavily on the accused. The accused may now testify at the trial or not, as he wishes, is entitled to legal counsel, and is assisted out of public funds when accused of a serious crime and unable to afford to pay the costs himself.

Canada has a Dominion Criminal Code, which covers major crimes. It also has a Canadian Bill of Rights and provincial laws such as the Ontario Human Rights Code. India has an overriding Bill of Rights.

American developments are the most interesting. Criminal procedure has become a constitutional matter, overriding all legislation, a type of federal common law of criminal procedure. Thus, "due process of law" under the Fourteenth Amendment to the U.S. Constitution and the Federal Rules of Criminal Procedure of 1946 confer wide protection on accused persons—too wide, some think, for public safety.

Different approaches to the admissibility of evidence

English courts are reluctant to admit tape recordings unless supported by direct evidence of persons present, and this is generally the position taken in the United States. The United States Crime Control Act of 1968 states that emergency wiretapping is permitted, though, in general, court authority is required. Both English and American law exclude confessions unless freely and spontaneously made. If evidence is found by unlawful means, such as by searching a house without a warrant, English law permits such evidence to be used, but American law does not admit it.

The main difference between English and American safeguards is that English safeguards rest on statute or case law and may be changed by ordinary statute, whereas American safeguards are constitutional and cannot be relaxed unless the Supreme Court later reverses its interpretation or the Constitution is amended.

THE FUTURE OF THE COMMON LAW

In the past the law performed the function of a referee in a free economy and was called in to apply generally accepted ideas of right and wrong to individual disputes. Today, law often forms an instrument of government policy or results from social pressures on government. It is therefore desirable that law should be centrally legislated and enforced, and this is in fact a trend that is increasingly evident.

Another tendency, and one that is likely to be reinforced, is an increasing reliance on statute law and codification as instruments of legal development. The English Law Commission has drafted a contract code, and the law of tort has been the subject of several statutes. Further, with the entrance of Great Britain into the European Economic Community, there have been pressures to make English law accessible by codes, like those of other members. In the United States the legal sovereignty of the states prevents such radical change, but uniform state laws are becoming more common.

In view of a general tendency in modern society toward shielding the individual as fully as possible from the consequences of the chance accidents of life, the judge-made law of tort may in time be replaced by a comprehensive system of official or private insurance, similar to the present compulsory third-party risk insurance for motor vehicles. Public law is also gaining on private law in other fields—in real-property development, for example, in which the public zoning or town-planning rules are already more important than the traditional restrictions imposed by individual neighbouring landowners. In family law, public-welfare laws on child care and adoption, pensions, and social security are often more important than the older private law based on the rights of spouses and children.

BIBLIOGRAPHY

England: A. KIRALFY, *The English Legal System*, 5th ed. (1973), is a general outline. There are numerous general historical works, such as E. JENKS, *A Short History of English Law*, 6th ed. (1949). On earlier developments, see A. KIRALFY, *A Source Book of English Law* (1957); H. POTTER, *Historical Introduction to English Law and Its Institutions*, 4th ed. (1958); and T. PLUCKNETT, *A Concise History of the Common Law*, 5th ed. (1956).

United States: E.A. FARNSWORTH, *An Introduction to the Legal System of the United States*, rev. ed. (1975), is a broad study of the American legal system. A learned study of the role of law in American culture may be found in MAX LERNER, *America As a Civilization*, pp. 426–464 (1957). A.H. CHROUST, *The Rise of the Legal Profession in America*, 2 vol. (1965), is also interesting in this respect. Collections of specialized essays include J.N. HAZARD and W.J. WAGNER (eds.), *Legal Thought in the United States of America Under Contemporary Pressures* (1970); and the CHARLES WARREN CENTER, *Law in American History* (1971).

British Commonwealth: General studies include G.W. PATON (ed.), *Commonwealth of Australia: The Development of Its Laws and Constitution* (1952); B. LASKIN, *British Tradition in Canadian Law* (1969); E. MCWHINNEY (ed.), *Canadian Jurisprudence* (1958); and M.C. SETALVAD, *The Common Law in India*, 2nd ed. (1970).

(A.R.Ki.)

Communication

Communication, the exchange of meanings between individuals through a common system of symbols, has been of concern to countless scholars since the time of ancient Greece. Until modern times, however, the topic was usually subsumed under other disciplines and taken for granted as a natural process inherent to each. In 1928 the English literary critic and author I.A. Richards offered one of the first—and in some ways still the best—definitions of communication as a discrete aspect of human enterprise:

> Communication takes place when one mind so acts upon its environment that another mind is influenced, and in that other mind an experience occurs which is like the experience in the first mind, and is caused in part by that experience.

Richards' definition is both general and rough, but its application to nearly all kinds of communications—including those between humans and animals (but excluding machines)—separated the contents of messages from the processes in human affairs by which these messages are transmitted. More recently, questions have been raised concerning the adequacy of any single definition of the term communication as it is currently employed. The American psychiatrist and scholar Jurgen Ruesch has identified 40 varieties of disciplinary approaches to the subject, including architectural, anthropological, psychological, political, and many other variant interpretations of the apparently simple interaction described by Richards. In total, if such informal communications as sexual attraction and play behaviour are included, there exist at least 50 modes of interpersonal communication that draw upon dozens of discrete intellectual disciplines and analytic approaches. Communication may therefore be analyzed in at least 50 different ways.

Interest in communication has been stimulated by advances in science and technology, which, by their nature, have called attention to man as a communicating creature. Among the first and most dramatic examples of the inventions resulting from technological ingenuity were the telegraph and telephone. These were followed by others, like wireless radio and telephoto devices. The development of popular newspapers and periodicals, broadcasting, motion pictures, and television yielded visible institutional cultural innovations that permitted efficient and rapid communication between a few individuals and large populations; these media have been responsible for the rise and social power of the new phenomenon of mass communication.

Since about 1920 the growth and apparent influence of communications technology have attracted the attention of many specialists who have attempted to isolate communication as a specific facet of their particular interest. Psychologists, in their studies of behaviour and mind, have evolved concepts of communication useful to their investigations as well as to certain forms of therapy. Social scientists have identified various forms of communication by which myths, styles of living, mores, and traditions have been passed either from generation to generation or from one segment of culture to another. Political scientists and economists have recognized that communication of many types lies at the heart of the regularities in the social order. Under the impetus of new technology—particularly high-speed computers—mathematicians and engineers have tried to quantify and measure components of communicated information and to develop methods for translating various types of messages into quantities or

amounts amenable to both their procedures and instruments. Numerous and differently phrased questions have been posed by artists, architects, artisans, writers, and others concerning the overall influences of various types of communication. Many researchers, working within the relevant concerns of their disciplines, have also sought possible theories or laws of cause and effect to explain the ways in which human dispositions are affected by certain kinds of communication under certain circumstances, and the reasons for the change.

In the 1960s a Canadian educator, Marshall McLuhan, drew the threads of interest in the field of communication into a view that associated many contemporary psychological and sociological phenomena with the media employed in modern culture. McLuhan's often repeated idea, "the medium is the message," stimulated the production of numerous filmmakers, photographers, artists, and others, who were convinced, at McLuhan's advice, that contemporary society had moved (or was moving) from a "print" culture to a "visual" one. The particular forms of greatest interest to McLuhan and his followers were those associated with the sophisticated technological instruments for which young people in particular display enthusiasm, namely motion pictures, television, and sound recordings.

By the 1970s the main focus of modern interest in communication seemed to be drifting away from McLuhanism and to be centring upon: (1) the mass communication industries, the people who run them, and the effects they have upon their audiences; (2) persuasive communication and the use of technology to influence dispositions; (3) processes of interpersonal communication as mediators of information; (4) dynamics of verbal and nonverbal (and perhaps extrasensory) communication between individuals; (5) perception of different kinds of communications; (6) uses of communication technology for social and artistic purposes, including education in and out of school; and (7) development of relevant criticism for artistic endeavours employing modern communications technology.

In short, a communication expert is likely to be oriented to any of a number of disciplines in a field of inquiry that has, as yet, neither drawn for itself a conclusive roster of subject matter nor agreed upon specific methodologies of analysis.

MODELS OF COMMUNICATION

Fragmentation and problems of interdisciplinary outlook have generated a wide range of discussion concerning the ways in which communication occurs and the processes it entails. Most speculation on these matters admits, in one way or another, that the communication theorist's task is to answer as clearly as possible the question, "*Who says what to whom with what effect?*" (This query was originally posed by the U.S. political scientist Harold D. Lasswell.) Obviously, all of the critical elements in this question may be interpreted differently by scholars and writers in different disciplines.

Linear models. One of the most productive schematic models of a communications system that has been proposed as a possible answer to Lasswell's question emerged in the late 1940s, largely from the speculations of two U.S. mathematicians, Claude Shannon and Warren Weaver. The simplicity of their model, its clarity, and its surface generality proved attractive to many students of communication in a number of disciplines, although it is neither the only model of the communication process extant nor one that is universally accepted. As originally conceived, the model contained five elements—an information source, a transmitter, a channel of transmission, a receiver, and a destination—all arranged in linear order. Messages (electronic messages, initially) were supposed to travel along this path, to be changed into electric energy by the transmitter, and to be reconstituted into intelligible language by the receiver. In time, the five elements of the model were renamed so as to specify components for other types of communication transmitted in various manners. The information source was split into its components (both source and message) in order to provide a wider range of applicability. The six constituents of the

*Communi-
cation as
defined
by I.A.
Richards*

*Communi-
cation and
other dis-
ciplines*

*Modern
interests in
communi-
cation*

*Shannon's
and
Weaver's
schematic
model*

revised model are: (1) a source, (2) an encoder, (3) a message, (4) a channel, (5) a decoder, and (6) a receiver. For some communication systems, the components are as simple to specify as, for instance, (1) a man on the telephone, (2) the mouthpiece of the telephone, (3) the words the man speaks, (4) the electrical wires along which the words (now electrical impulses) travel, (5) the earpiece of another telephone, and (6) the mind of the listener. In other communication systems, the components are more difficult to isolate; *e.g.*, the communication of the emotions of a fine artist by means of a painting to people who may respond to the message long after the artist's death.

Begging a multitude of psychological, aesthetic, and sociological questions concerning the exact nature of each component, the model appeared, from the common-sense perspective, to explain in general terms the ways in which certain classes of communication occurred. It did not indicate the reason for the inability of certain communications—obvious in daily life—to fit this neat paradigm.

Entropy, negative entropy, and redundancy. Another concept, first called by Shannon a "noise source" but later associated with the notion of entropy (a principle derived from physics), was imposed upon the communication model. Entropy is analogous in most communication to audio or visual static—that is, to outside influences that diminish the integrity of the communication and, possibly, distort the message for the receiver. Negative entropy may also occur in instances in which incomplete or blurred messages are nevertheless received intact, either because of the ability of the receiver to fill in missing details or to recognize, despite distortion or a paucity of information, both the intent and content of the communication.

Although rarely shown on diagrammatic models of this version of the communication process, redundancy—the repetition of elements within a message that prevents the failure of communication of information—is the greatest enemy of entropy. Most written and spoken languages, for example, are roughly half-redundant. If 50 percent of the words of this article were taken away at random, there would still remain an intelligible—although somewhat peculiar—essay. Similarly, if one-half of the words of a radio news commentator are heard, the broadcast can usually be understood. Redundancy is apparently involved in most human activities, and, because it helps to overcome the various forms of entropy that tend to turn intelligible messages into unintelligible ones (including psychological entropy on the part of the receiver), it is an indispensable element for effective communication.

Messages are therefore susceptible to considerable modification and mediation. Entropy distorts, while negative entropy and redundancy clarify; as each occurs differentially in the communication process, the chances of the message being received and correctly understood vary. Still, the process (and the model of it) remains conceptually static, because it is fundamentally concerned with messages sent from point to point, and not with their results or possible influences upon sender and receiver.

Feedback. To correct this flaw, the principle of feedback was added to the model and provided a closer approximation of interpersonal human interaction than was known theretofore. This construct was derived from the studies of Norbert Wiener, the so-called father of the science of cybernetics (*q.v.*). Wiener's cybernetic models, some of which provide the basis for current computer technology, were designed to be responsive to their own behaviour; that is, they audited their own performances mathematically or electronically in order to avoid errors of entropy, unnecessary redundancy, or other simple hazards.

Certain types of common communications—Christmas cards, for instance—usually require little feedback. Others, particularly interactions between human beings in conversation, cannot function without the ability of the message sender to weigh and calculate the apparent effect of his words on his listener. It is largely the aspect of feedback that provides for this model the qualities of a process, because each instance of feedback conditions or alters the subsequent messages.

Aspects of feedback

Dynamic models. Other models of communication processes have been constructed to meet the needs of students of communication whose interests differ from quantitatively oriented theorists like Shannon, Weaver, and Wiener. While the model described above displays some generality and shows simplicity, it lacks some of the predictive, descriptive, and analytic powers found in other approaches. A psychologist, Theodore M. Newcomb, for example, has articulated a more fluid system of dimensions to represent the individual interacting in his environment. Newcomb's model and others similar to it are not as precisely mathematical (quantitative) as Shannon's and thus permit more flexible accounts of human behaviour and its variable relationships. They do not deny the relevance of linear models to Shannon and Weaver's main concerns—quanta of information and the delivery of messages under controlled conditions—but they question their completeness and utility in describing cognitive, emotional, and artistic aspects of communication as they occur in socio-cultural matrices.

Students concerned mainly with persuasive and artistic communication often centre attention upon different kinds, or modes, of communication (*i.e.*, narrative, pictorial, and dramatic) and theorize that the messages they contain, including messages of emotional quality and artistic content, are communicated in various manners to and from different sorts of people. For them, the stability and function of channel or medium are more variable and less mechanistically related to the process than they are for followers of Shannon and Weaver and psychologists like Newcomb. (McLuhan, indeed, asserts that the channel actually dictates, or severely influences, the message—both as sent and received.) Many analysts of communication, linguistic philosophers, and others are concerned with the nature of messages, particularly their compatibility with sense and emotion, their style, and the intentions behind them. They find both linear and geometric models of process of little interest to their concerns, although considerations related to these models, particularly those of entropy, redundancy, and feedback, have provided significant and productive concepts for most students of communication (see also CYBERNETICS; INFORMATION THEORY).

Applications of formal logic and mathematics. Despite the numerous types of communication or information theory extant today—and those likely to be formulated tomorrow—the most rationally and experimentally consistent approaches to communication theory so far developed follow the constructions of Shannon and others described above. Such approaches tend to employ the structural rigours of logic rather than the looser syntaxes, grammars, and vocabularies of common languages, with their symbolic, poetic, and inferential aspects of meaning.

Cybernetic theory and computer technology require rigorous but straightforward languages to permit translation into nonambiguous, special symbols that can be stored and utilized for statistical manipulations. The closed system of formal logic proved ideal for this need. Premises and conclusions drawn from syllogisms according to logical rules may be easily tested in a consistent, scientific manner, as long as all parties communicating share the rational premises employed by the particular system.

That this logical mode of communication drew its frame of discourse from the logic of the ancient Greeks was inevitable. Translated into an Aristotelian manner of discourse, meaningful interactions between individuals could be transferred to an equally rational closed system of mathematics: an arithmetic for simple transactions, an algebra for solving certain well-delimited puzzles, a calculus to simulate changes, rates and flows, and a geometry for purposes of illustration and model construction. This progression has proved quite useful for handling those limited classes of communications that arise out of certain structured, rational operations, like those in economics, inductively oriented sociology, experimental psychology, and other behavioral and social sciences, as well as in most of the natural sciences.

Formal logic, syllogisms, and communication

The basic theorem of information theory rests, first, upon the assumption that the message transmitted is well organized, consistent, and characterized by relatively low and determinable degrees of entropy and redundancy. (Otherwise, the mathematical structure might yield only probability statements approaching random scatters, of little use to anyone.) Under these circumstances, by devising proper coding procedures for the transmitter, it becomes possible to transmit symbols over a channel at an average rate that is nearly the capacity of units per second of the channel (symbolized by C) as a function of the units per second from an information source (H)—but never at rates in excess of capacity divided by units per second (C/H), no matter how expertly the symbols are coded. As simple as this notion seems, upon determining the capacity of the channel and by cleverly coding the information involved, precise mathematical models of information transactions (similar to electronic frequencies of energy transmissions) may be evolved and employed for complex analyses within the strictures of formal logic. They must, of course, take into account as precisely as possible levels of entropy and redundancy as well as other known variables.

The internal capacities of the channel studied and the sophistication of the coding procedures that handle the information limit the usefulness of the theorem presented above. At present such procedures, while they may theoretically offer broad prospects, are restricted by formal encoding procedures that depend upon the capacities of the instruments in which they are stored (nowadays, mostly on magnetic tape and disk-packs in computers). Although such devices can handle quickly the logic of vast amounts of relatively simple information, they cannot match the flexibility and complexity of the human brain, still man's prime instrument for managing the subtleties of most communication.

TYPES OF COMMUNICATION

Signals, signs, and symbols

Nonvocal communication. Signals, signs, and symbols, three related components of communication processes found in all known cultures, have attracted considerable scholarly attention because they do not relate primarily to the usual conception of words or language. Each is apparently an increasingly more complex modification of the former, and each was probably developed in the depths of prehistory before, or at the start of, man's early experiments with vocal language.

Signals. A signal may be considered as some sort of interruption in a field of constant energy transfer. An example is the dots and dashes that open and close the electromagnetic field of a telegraph circuit. Such interruptions do not require the construction of a man-made field; interruptions in nature (*e.g.*, the tapping of a pencil in a silent room, or puffs of smoke rising from a mountain top into the clear sky) may produce the same result. The basic function of such signals is to provide the change of a single environmental factor in order to attract attention and to transfer meaning. A code system that refers interruptions to some form of meaningful language may easily be developed with a crude vocabulary of dots, dashes, or other elemental audio and visual articulations. Taken by themselves, the interruptions have a potential breadth of meaning that seems extremely small; they may indicate the presence of an individual in a room, his impatience, agreement, or disagreement with some aspect of his environment or, in the case of a scream for help, a critical situation demanding attention. Coded to refer to spoken or written language, their potential to communicate language is extremely great.

Signs. While signs are usually less germane to the development of words than signals, most of them contain greater amounts of meaning of and by themselves. Ashley Montagu, an anthropologist, has defined a sign as a "concrete denoter" possessing an inherent specific meaning, roughly analogous to the sentence "This is it; do something about it!" The most common signs encountered in daily life are pictures or drawings, although a human posture like a clenched fist, an outstretched arm, or a hand posed in a "Stop" gesture may also serve as signs.

The main difference between a sign and a signal is that a sign (like a policeman's badge) contains meanings of an intrinsic nature; a signal (like a scream for help) is merely a device by which one is able to formulate extrinsic meanings. Their difference is illustrated by the observation that many types of animals respond to signals, while only a few intelligent and trained animals (usually dogs and apes) are competent to respond even to simple signs.

All known cultures utilize signs to convey relatively simple messages swiftly and conveniently. Signs may depend for their meaning upon their form, setting, colour, or location. In the United States, traffic signs, uniforms, badges, and barber poles are frequently encountered signs. Taken en masse, any society's lexicon of signs makes up a rich vocabulary of colourful communications.

Symbols. Symbols are more difficult than signs to understand and to define because, unlike signs and signals, they are intricately woven into an individual's ongoing perceptions of the world. They appear to contain a dimly understood capacity that (as one of their functions), in fact, defines the very reality of that world. The symbol has been defined as any device with which an abstraction can be made. Although far from being a precise construction, it leads in a profitable direction. The abstractions of the values that people imbue in other people and in things they own and use lie at the heart of symbolism. Here is a process, according to the British philosopher Alfred North Whitehead, whereby

some components of [the mind's] experience elicit consciousness, beliefs, emotions, and usages respecting other components of experience.

In Whitehead's opinion, symbols are analogues or metaphors (that may include written and spoken language) standing for some quality of reality that is enhanced in importance or value by the process of symbolization itself.

Symbol systems in all societies

Almost every society known to man has evolved a rich symbol system whereby, at first glance, strange objects and odd types of behaviour appear to the outside observer to have irrational meanings and seem to evoke odd, unwarranted cognitions and emotions. Upon examination, however, each symbol system reflects a specific cultural logic, and every symbolism functions to communicate information between members of the culture in much the same way as, but in a more subtle manner than, conventional language. Although a symbol may take the form of as discrete an object as a wedding ring or a totem pole, symbols tend to appear in clusters and depend upon one another for their accretion of meaning and value. They are not a language of and by themselves; rather they are devices by which ideas too difficult, dangerous, or inconvenient to articulate in common language are transmitted between people who have acculturated in common ways. It does not appear possible to compile discrete vocabularies of symbols, because they lack the precision and regularities present in natural language that are necessary for explicit definitions.

Icons. Rich clusters of related and unrelated symbols are usually regarded as icons. They are actually groups of interactive symbols, like the White House in Washington, D.C., a funeral ceremony, or an Impressionist painting. Although in examples such as these, there is a tendency to isolate icons and individual symbols for examination, symbolic communication is so closely allied to all forms of human activity that it is generally and nonconsciously used and treated by most people as the most important aspect of communication in society. With the recognition that spoken and written words and numbers themselves constitute symbolic metaphors, their critical roles in the worlds of science, mathematics, literature, and art can be understood. In addition, with these symbols, an individual is able to define his own identity.

Gestures. Professional actors and dancers have known since antiquity that body gestures may also generate a vocabulary of communication more or less unique to each culture. Some U.S. scholars have tried to develop a vocabulary of body language, called kinesics. The results of their investigations, both amusing and potentially practical, may eventually produce a genuine lexicon of American gestures similar to one prepared in detail by François Delsarte, a 19th-century French teacher of pantomime and gymnastics who described the ingenious and complex language of contemporary face and body positions for theatrical purposes.

Proxemics. Of more general, cross-cultural significance are the theories involved in the study of "proxemics" developed by a United States anthropologist, Edward T. Hall. Proxemics involves the ways in which people in various cultures utilize both time and space as well as body positions and other factors for purposes of communication. Hall's "silent language" of nonverbal communications consists of such culturally determined interactions as the physical distance or closeness maintained between individuals, the body heat they give off, odours they perceive in social situations, angles of vision they maintain while talking, the pace of their behaviour, and the sense of time appropriate for communicating under differing conditions. By comparing matters like these in the behaviour of different social classes (and in varying relationships), Hall elaborated and codified a number of sophisticated general principles that demonstrate how certain kinds of nonverbal communication occur, not only between men but between animals as well. He also attempted to relate proxemic theory to speculations concerning the so-called territorial instincts that are claimed to be natural tendencies among all living creatures. Although Hall's most impressive arguments are almost entirely empirical, and many of them are open to question, the study of proxemics does succeed in calling attention to major features of communication dynamics rarely considered by linguists and symbologists. Students of words have been more interested in objective formal vocabularies than in the more subtle means of discourse unknowingly acquired by the members of a culture.

Vocal communication. Significant differences between nonvocal and vocal communication are matters more of degree than of kind. Signs, signals, symbols, and possibly icons may, at times, be easily verbalized, although most people tend to think of them as visual means of expression. Kinesics and proxemics may also, in certain instances, involve vocalizations as accompaniments to nonverbal phenomena or as somehow integral to them. Be they grunts, words, or sentences, their function is to help in forwarding a communication that is fundamentally nonverbal.

Origins of speech

Although there is no shortage of speculation on the issue, the origins of human speech remain obscure at present. It is plausible that man is born with an instinct for speech. Phenomena supporting this belief include the presence of unlearned cries and gurgles of infants operating as crude, vocal signs directed to others the baby cannot possibly be aware of, and evidence of activities analogous to human vocalization in the behaviour of various animals. Some anthropologists claim that within the vocabularies of kinesics and proxemics are the virtual building blocks of spoken language; they postulate that primitive men made various and ingenious inventions (including speech) as a result of their need to communicate with others in order to pool their intellectual and physical resources. Other observers suggest similar origins of speech, including the vocalization of physical activity, imitation of the sounds of nature, and sheer serendipity. Scientific proof of any of these speculations is at present impossible.

Not only is the origin of speech disputed among experts but the precise reasons for the existence of the numerous languages of the world are also far from clear. In the 1920s, an American linguistic anthropologist, Edward Sapir, and, later Benjamin Lee Whorf, centred attention upon the various methods of expression found in different cultures. Drawing their evidence primarily from the languages of primitive societies, they made some very significant observations concerning spoken (and probably written) language. First, man's language reflects in subtle ways those matters of greatest relevance and importance to the value system of each particular culture. Thus, language may be said to reflect culture, or, in other words, people seem to find ways of saying what they need to say. A familiar illustration is the many words (or variations of words) that Eskimos use to describe whale blubber in its various states; *e.g.*, on the whale, ready to eat, raw, cooked, rancid. Another example is the observation that "drunk" possesses more synonyms than any other term in the English language. Apparently, this is the result of a psychological necessity to euphemize a somewhat nasty, uncomfortable, or taboo matter, a device also employed for other words that describe seemingly important, but improper, behaviour or facets of culture.

Need for euphemisms

Other observations involve the discovery that any known language may be employed, without major modification, to say almost anything that may be said in any other language. A high degree of circumlocution and some nonverbal vocalization may be required to accomplish this end, but, no matter how alien the concept to the original language, it may be expressed clearly in the language of another culture. Students of linguistic anthropology have been able to describe adequately in English esoteric linguistic propositions of primitive societies, just as it has been possible for anthropologists to describe details of Western technology to natives in remote cultures. Understood as an artifact of culture, spoken language may therefore be considered as a universal channel of communication into which various societies dip differentially in order to expedite and specify the numerous points of contact between individuals.

Language remains, however, a still partially understood phenomenon used to transact several types of discourse. Language has been classified on the basis of several criteria. One scheme established four categories on the basis of informative, dynamic, emotive, and aesthetic functions. Informative communication deals largely with narrative aspects of meaning; dynamic discourse concerns the transaction of dispositions such as opinions and attitudes; the emotive employment of language involves the evocation of feeling states in others in order to impel them to action; and aesthetic discourse, usually regarded as a poetic quality in speech, conveys stylistic aspects of expression.

Although most vocal sounds other than words are usually considered prelinguistic language, the phenomenon of laughter as a form of communication is in a category by itself, with its closest relative being its apparent opposite, crying. Contemporary ethologists, like Konrad Lorenz in Germany, have attempted to associate laughter with group behaviour among animals in instances in which aggression is thwarted and laughlike phenomena seem to result among herds. Lorenz's metaphors, while apparently reasonable, cannot be verified inductively. They seem less reasonable to many than the more common notions of Freud and others that laughter either results from, or is related to, the nonconscious reduction of tensions or inhibitions. Developed as a form of self-generated pleasure in the infant and rewarded both physically and psychologically by feelings of gratification, laughter provides a highly effective, useful, and contagious means of vocal communication. It deals with a wide range of cultural problems, often more effectively than speech, in much the same manner that crying, an infantile, probably instinctive reaction to discomfort, communicates an unmistakable emotional state to others.

The reasons for laughter in complex social situations is another question, however, and is answered differently by philosophers and psychologists. The English novelist George Meredith proposed a theory, resulting from his analysis of 18th-century French court comedies, that laughter serves as an enjoyable social corrective. The two best known modern theories of the social wellsprings of laughter are the French philosopher Henri Bergson's hypothesis that laughter is a form of rebellion against the mechanization of human behaviour and nature, and Freud's concept of laughter as repressed sexual feeling. The author Arthur Koestler has regarded laughter as an instrument of individual enlightenment, revelation, and subsequent freedom from confusion or misunderstanding concerning some part of the environment.

Capacities
of the
vocal
organs

Man's vocal instrument as a device of communication represents an apex of physical and intellectual evolution. It has the potential to express the most basic instinctual demands as well as a range of highly intellectual processes, including the possible mastery of numerous complex languages, each with an enormous vocabulary. Because of the imitative capacity of the vocal mechanism (including its cortical directors), suitably talented individuals can simulate the sounds of nature in song, can communicate in simple ways with animals, and can indulge in such tricks as ventriloquism and the mimicry of other voices. The vocal organs permit the production of sound effects, animal noises, bird calls, and such amusing high-entropy manipulations of speech as double-talk, in which the speech act itself is parodied by nonsense vocalization. Recent tape recording techniques have even extended this flexibility into new domains, allowing singers to accompany their own voices in different keys to produce effects of duets or choruses composed electronically from one person's voice (see also LANGUAGE; SPEECH, PHYSIOLOGY OF).

Mass and public communication. *Prerequisites for mass communication.* The technology of modern mass communication results from the confluence of many types of inventions and discoveries, some of which (the printing press, for instance) actually preceded the main thrust of the Industrial Revolution into Western culture. Technological ingenuity of the 19th and 20th centuries has been responsible for the development of the newer means of mass communication, particularly broadcasting, without which the present near-global diffusion of printed words, pictures, and sounds would have been impossible. The steam printing press, radio, motion pictures, television, and various methods of sound recording—as well as systems of mass production and distribution—were necessary before public communication in its present form might occur.

Technology was not, however, the only prerequisite for the development of mass communication in the West. A large public of literate citizens was necessary before giant publishing and newspaper empires might employ extant communications technology to satisfy widespread desires or needs for popular reading materials. Affluence and interest were (and are) prerequisites for the maintenance of the radio, television, cinema, and recording industries, institutions that are presently most highly developed in wealthy, industrial nations. Even in countries in which public communication is employed largely for government propaganda, certain minimal economic and educational standards must be achieved before this persuasion is accepted by the general public.

Control of mass communications. Over the years, control of the instruments of mass communication has fallen into the hands of relatively small (some claim diminishing) numbers of professional communicators who seem, as populations expand and interest widens, to reach ever increasing numbers of people. In the United States, for example, far fewer newspapers currently serve more readers than ever before, three television networks are predominant, and a handful of book publishers produce the majority of the best sellers.

Public communicators are not entirely free to follow their own whims in serving the masses, however. As is the case of any market, consumer satisfaction (or the lack of it) limits the nature and quantity of the material produced and circulated. Mass communicators are also restricted in some measure by laws governing libel, slander, and invasion of privacy, and, in most countries, by traditions of professionalism that entail obligations of those who maintain access to the public's eyes and ears. In almost every modern nation, privileges to use broadcasting frequencies are circumscribed either loosely or rigidly by government regulations. In some countries, national agencies exercise absolute control of all broadcasting, and in certain areas print and film media operate under strict government control. Written and film communications may be subject to local legal restraints in regard to censorship and have restrictions similar to those of other private businesses. Traditions of decorum and self-censorship, however, apply variably to publishers and film makers, depending usually upon the particular markets to which their fare is directed.

Effects of mass communication. Lively controversy centres on the effect of public communication upon audiences, not only in matters concerning public opinion on political issues but in matters of the development of personal life-styles and tastes, possible inducements to violence, and influences upon consumer behaviour and the sensibilities and dispositions of children. Feelings regarding these matters vary greatly. Politicians frequently blame newspapers and television coverage for their electoral defeats and sometimes credit them for their victories. Some people construe the overall effects of mass communication as generally harmless to both young and old. Many sociologists follow the theory that mass communication seems to influence attitudes and behaviour only insofar as it confirms the status quo—*i.e.*, it influences values already accepted and operating in the culture. Numerous other analysts, usually oriented to psychological or psychiatric disciplines, believe that mass communications provide potent sources of informal education and persuasion for most people. Their conclusions are drawn largely from observations that many, or most, people in technological societies form their personal views of the social realities beyond their immediate experience from messages presented to them through public communication.

Opinions
on the
effect of
public
communication

To assume that public communication is predominantly reflective of current values, morals, and attitudes denies much common experience. Fashions, fads, and small talk are too obviously and directly influenced by material in the press, in films, and in television to support this view. The success of public communication as an instrument of commercial advertising has also been constant and noticeable. Present evidence indicates that various instruments of mass communication produce varying effects upon different segments of the audience. These effects seem too numerous and short-lived to be measured effectively with currently available instruments. Much of the enormous output on television and radio and in print is probably simply regarded as "play" and of little consequence in affecting adult dispositions, although many psychologists believe that the nature of children's play experiences is critical to their maturation.

The role of newspapers, periodicals, and television in influencing political opinion is fairly well established in regard to the voting behaviour of the so-called undecided voters. Numerous studies have shown that while the majority of citizens in the United States cast their vote along party lines and according to social, educational, and economic determinants, middle-of-the-road voters often hold the balance of power that determines the outcomes of local and national elections. Politicians have become sensitive to their television images and have devised much of their campaign strategy with the television audience in mind. Advertising agencies familiar with television techniques have been brought into the political arena to plan campaigns and develop their clients' images. The effectiveness of television campaigning cannot yet be determined reliably.

Public communication is a near-ubiquitous condition of modernity. Most reliable surveys show that the majority of the people of the world (including those of totalitarian countries) are usually satisfied with the kind of mass communication available to them. Lacking alternatives to the communication that they easily and conveniently receive, most people seem to accept what they are given without complaint. Mass communication is but one facet of life for most individuals, whose main preoccupations centre on the home and on daily employment. Public communication is an inexpensive addendum to living, usually directed to low common denominators of taste, interest, and refinement of perception. Although mass communication places enormous potential power in the hands of relatively few people, traditional requirements for popular approval and assent have prevented its use for overt subversion of culturally sanctioned institutions. Fear of such subversion is sometimes expressed by critics.

Role of
popular
approval

THE PSYCHOLOGY OF COMMUNICATION

Contemporary psychologists (including specialists in social psychology) have, since World War II, shown considerable interest in the ways in which communications occur. Behaviourists have been prone to view communication in terms of stimulus–response relationships between sources of communications and individuals or groups that receive them. Those who subscribe to Freud's analysis of group psychology and ego theory tend to regard interactions in communication as reverberations of family group dynamics experienced early in life.

By the middle 1950s, psychological interest settled largely on modification of attitudes wrought by communications, in other words, on the persuasive aspects of various types of messages. Psychologists have attempted to discover whether a general factor of personality called "persuasibility" might be identified in people at large. It would appear, though with qualifications, that individuals are indeed variably persuasible and that, at times, factors of personality are sometimes related to this quality.

Other psychologists have studied the recipients of communication, evolving concepts of "selective perception," "selective attention," and "selective retention" in order to explain not only the ways in which communication changed attitudes but also the reasons for resistance to change. Among their interests were the dynamics of the communication of rumours, the effects of "scare messages," the degree of credulity that sources of prestige value provide, and the pressure of group consensus upon individual perceptions of communications.

Some of the theoretical suggestions for the psychology of communication processes that emerged from the work of certain modern psychologists may be subsumed under a theory of what is called "cognitive dissonance." Based upon the observation that most people cannot tolerate more than a specific degree of inconsistency in the environments they perceive, this theory has undergone modification, but its basic postulates appear durable. An example of cognitive dissonance may involve a person who considers himself a superb bowler but who on one occasion earns an extremely low score. The dissonant or inconsistent elements include the bowler's knowledge of his skill and the fact of his poor score. This produces tension. To reduce this tension—dissonance—the bowler may change his behaviour or misinterpret or reinterpret the dissonant elements in order to lessen the difference between the facts. For example, he may blame his performance on the bowling ball, the alley, or the temperature of the room. Thus he seeks a psychological equilibrium.

This modification of an individual's perception of reality is of fundamental interest to the psychologist of communications. Because the agreement or disagreement of a communication with an individual's cognitive structure not only affects his behaviour but his perception as well, the major criterion for the psychological analysis of communication is neither the message nor the medium but the expectation of the person receiving the message.

It must not be assumed that any of the theories of audience psychology offered to date (including those of Gestaltists, Freudians, Behaviourists, and others) lack relevance to an understanding of communication processes. None, however, seems to account fully for all of the effects of communications upon people. The many facets of communication offer substantial problems for future psychological experimentation and theorizing (see also ATTITUDES; PERSUASION; and MOTIVATION).

BIBLIOGRAPHY. C. CHERRY, *On Human Communication* (1957), a scientifically and mathematically oriented analysis of information theory and cybernetics as they relate to meaning, including a treatment of the philosophical and practical implications of the logical analysis of communication; EDWIN EMERY, P.H. AULT, and W.K. AGEE, *Introduction to Mass Communications*, 3rd ed. (1970), a comprehensive history and survey of the press, radio, television, and films in modern society, especially in the United States; G.N. GORDON, *The Languages of Communication* (1969), a detailed examination of the major elements in mass and interpersonal communication, including consideration of their current cultural roles; G.N. GORDON, *Persuasion: The Theory and Practice of Manipula-*

tive Communication (1971), a study of the development and modification of beliefs, attitudes, and opinions by propaganda, education, and instruments of mass communication; E.T. HALL, *The Hidden Dimension* (1966), an unconventional anthropological study of "proxemics" and allied concerns, illustrated by empirical evidence, drawings, and photographs (written with style and humour for the general reader); F.W. MATSON and ASHLEY MONTAGU (eds.), *The Human Dialogue* (1967), a broad collection of articles that touch almost every phase of communication in contemporary society, including education, religion, and social problems, with contributors ranging from popes to professors; J.R. PIERCE, *Symbols, Signals and Noise* (1961), a lucid guide for the nonspecialist in the study of communication processes, information theory, cybernetics, mathematical models of communications, entropy, coding methods, and allied matters; A.G. SMITH (ed.), *Communication and Culture* (1966), a comprehensive anthology of specialized approaches to communication theory and practice, including numerous articles on language, nonverbal communication, mass communication, and other aspects of the subject, written by authorities in various fields; A.N. WHITEHEAD, *Symbolism* (1927, reissued 1958), a short, definitive study of the origins, uses, and ramifications of symbolism, both from the perspective of the individual and from the historical-social viewpoint, written simply and clearly.

(G.N.G.)

Communication, Animal

Although the term communication is widely used among scientists, there is no consensus as to its precise meaning. Most behavioral scientists, in keeping with common usage, consider communication an essentially social process, occurring when a relationship is established through the transfer of information among individuals. The nature of the relationship varies greatly with the needs of individuals of different species. In general, communication is employed by animals to attract or repel other individuals of particular groups and to establish and maintain forms of social organization that vary from pair and family bonds to the highly structured troops of some primates and the complex colonies of social insects.

This article is divided into the following major sections:

I. General features
    The role of information
    The functions of communication
II. The process of animal communication
    The modes of information transfer
    The role of displays
    The interpretation of information
    Other sources of information
III. The development and evolution of communication
    The development of song in young birds
    The evolution of communication

Related articles include LEARNING, ANIMAL; BEHAVIOUR, ANIMAL; SOCIAL BEHAVIOUR, ANIMAL; and INSTINCT.

I. General features

THE ROLE OF INFORMATION

Information is a broad concept that is vital to the understanding of communication. The contemporary U.S. mathematician Norbert Wiener has noted that "information is a name for the content of what is exchanged with the outer world as we adjust to it, and make our adjustment felt upon it." As used in modern biology, the term communication implies something exchanged between an individual and his environment, both social and nonsocial. Biologists also speak of information exchanged among cells and tissues and even within cells. The study of animal communication is concerned, therefore, with the information exchanged during interactions among individuals as they cope with the social circumstances of their environment; it is available initially through sensory receptors. Further, some information derived from experience is stored as memory, and, through the process of organic evolution, other information about social behaviour is supplied to the individual through genetic inheritance.

The information involved in animal communication can come from many sources; any facet of the environment perceived is considered information. In linguistic communication the primary function of words is to convey information. Similarly, animals (including man) have modes of behaviour that, in the course of evolution, were

Selective perception, attention, retention

Sources of information

selected for their value in providing vehicles for conveying information. During the evolutionary process some of these vehicles also retained more direct functions, but many became specialized for a communicative function alone. These communicative acts, known as displays, include various posturings and movements; sounds; particular ways of making contact among individuals; the release of specialized chemicals called pheromones; and even electrical discharges. Displays have been studied as important means for transmitting information in animal communication. There are, of course, other information sources in animals, some of which have also undergone evolutionary specialization toward a communication function. Among them are what may be called badges—*i.e.*, attributes that are merely structural and nonbehavioral in nature: the red breast of the robin, the red underside of the breeding male stickleback fish, and the mane of the male lion. Many other sources of information can be found in the repeated forms of interaction that develop during prolonged relationships between two individuals and in individual expectations about the nature of the roles in which they encounter others, both familiar associates and strangers. The activities of individuals who interact socially provide a constant and usually rich information source, but, in the study of nonhuman communication, the bulk of systematic research thus far has been directed toward displays and badges; it is, therefore, these highly specialized categories that are of the greatest concern here.

THE FUNCTIONS OF COMMUNICATION

Because the complexity of social interactions makes experimental manipulation difficult, human understanding of the role of signalling in the social life of animals remains largely based upon inference. It is difficult to repeat an example many times with rigid control of all variables except the one being investigated, and attempts to structure the testing situation to simplify the form of interaction often obviate the interaction. Displays are universal among animals of any degree of structural complexity, however, so that they would not have been evolved and retained if they lacked important functions. But the function of a display is likely to differ, depending upon the individuals involved. A small bird seeing an approaching hawk, for example, may utter a vocal display indicating the high probability that it (the communicator) is, or soon will be, engaged in an attempt to escape. Other small birds, upon hearing this vocalization, may seek cover immediately. Hence, the function of the vocalization is to give them a better opportunity to remain alive and not to increase the immediate chances of survival of the communicator—indeed, its chances for survival may slightly decrease. The display functions for the communicator in that it protects individuals whose continued existence provides a benefit to him greater than the cost of using the display. These individuals may be his offspring or associates whose similar responses to the environment will provide him future protection and, through their alertness in the future, make it possible for him to spend less time scanning his surroundings for predators.

From the ways and circumstances in which displays are used and from the apparent responses of recipients, it is possible to enumerate the general functions of animal communication. First, displays guide animals to one another, thereby enabling one to advertise its presence and behavioral predispositions to potential recipients. Displays enable individuals in a group to respond selectively to particular associates at appropriate times.

Second, communication permits animals to identify one another. Individuals can thus select information of importance to them—usually from members of their own species and often particular individuals. Special cases exist, however; members of different species that normally coexist in the same environment may attend each other's signal. Thus, the maximum alarm communicated by one songbird when it discovers a falcon or accipitrine hawk in its environment is attended by all other songbirds species in the area. In addition, by facilitating identification,

Selection of information

communication acts at a premating level to help maintain reproductive isolation among species.

Third, communication reduces the amount of actual fighting and fleeing among animals, an excess of which could disrupt social encounters. In functionally aggressive encounters, such as territorial or dominance disputes, this reduction is achieved by threat displays that often lead to some form of capitulation by one opponent before fighting occurs. In less aggressive circumstances, communication enables animals to appease and reassure one another that each is not likely to be initially aggressive in his present state. Fourth, communication aids in synchronizing the behaviour of individuals who must come into appropriate physiological states in order to breed. This is necessary within pairs and, in some species, among whole colonies of pairs.

Fifth, displays enable individuals to use each other to monitor the environment, not only on a relatively long-term basis but also on a very immediate basis. Thus, in species that spend much of their time living in compact social groups, such as flocks, coteries, or troops, an indication by any one individual that it is fleeing precipitously—often a vocal display in addition to the flight itself—usually correlates with the presence of a dangerous predator and leads to evasion, hiding, or alertness on the part of the other members of the group.

Finally, communication facilitates the maintenance of special relationships between individuals by making available information about the readiness of each to engage in certain activities. The maintenance of individual relationships in cohesive groups is furthered by communication, which keeps members aware both of the behaviour of associates whom they may not be able to see and of the readiness of associates to change their activities. For example, vocal displays usually precede flight by a member of a resting family of geese, and the family then tends to depart as a unit. Within some types of relationship, display behaviour also aids in eliciting general classes of responses; for example, offspring usually signal to arouse various forms of care-giving behaviour from their parents.

The functions in which communication appears to be used vary considerably among different species; each has specialized features, some quite remarkable. It has been demonstrated, for example, that vocalizations and other sounds made during hatching by chicken-like birds (*i.e.*, members of the order Galliformes) influence the rate of hatching of sibling chicks, so that all members of the brood can leave the nest simultaneously. It has been suggested that birds migrating in flocks may use signals in order to inform each other of their position in the night sky, so that the individuals in the flock can perhaps compensate for small individual navigational errors.

One interesting aspect of birdsong is the occurrence of dialectal differences (regional variations) among populations of a single species living in different areas. Several such changes that are known to occur between adjacent populations of the South American rufous-collared sparrow (*Zonotrichia capensis*) correlate with relatively major habitat changes. Very few dialectal changes occur over an enormous range on the Argentine pampas, but in this case the habitat of the species also changes little. The habitat changes markedly in the Andes mountains over short distances, however, as elevation rapidly increases, and, concurrently, many more dialectal changes occur there in birds' songs. The suggested function of the correlations between display and features of the habitat is that they provide markers that identify populations adapted to different local conditions; such markers would permit more appropriate selection of mates than would otherwise occur, at least in the marginal areas between populations. It has been suggested that a similar functional explanation may be involved in the evolution of human dialects.

Signals have evolved, the primary function of which lies in communication between, rather than within, species—particularly in cases in which identifying markings or displays of dangerous or distasteful animals provide information to potential predators or in those in which

Dialectal differences in birdsongs

innocuous species mimic the signals (see MIMICRY). Other species, such as some forest falcons (*Micrastur*) of the New World tropics, apparently employ vocalizations as a kind of lure to attract prey species for capture; in this case the information is of use only to the individual providing it. An American ethologist, Martin Moynihan, has shown that elaborately specialized means of communication have evolved in bird species that join to form large mixed foraging flocks. These signals attract individuals to the flocks and help to maintain the cohesiveness of the assemblages as they move through the trees.

II. The process of animal communication

THE MODES OF INFORMATION TRANSFER

The evolution of animal behaviour and structures toward a communication function has yielded a mode of communication adapted for each externally oriented sensory receptor system—*e.g.*, organs of vision, hearing, and taste. Each mode, although specialized, has limitations with respect to such properties as energy utilization; the ability to surmount environmental obstacles; the ease with which the source of the communication can be located; the persistence or transitoriness of the signal; and the available range of physical complexity. These differences have been exploited during evolution.

Sound. Because sound disseminates and fades rapidly, a given unit of information does not remain to interfere with, or garble, succeeding units. In addition, sound can be varied with regard to pitch, clarity or harshness, duration, loudness, and rate of repetition, with each variable providing greater range of ability to encode. One advantage of sound as a medium of communication is that vocal displays can be uttered by animals who need to keep their appendages free for other activities and can be received by individuals who need not face the communicator in order to receive the signals.

Location
of
sound

It is usually a simple matter for an animal with two ears to locate the source of a sound, although some modifications (described below) can help to conceal the location of the transmitter from potential dangers. Virtually all of the animals for which sound is important are bilaterally symmetrical and hence have paired hearing organs. Sound is a superb means of encoding information that must pass around environmental obstacles, such as trees or other vegetation. Apparently, some animals utilize frequencies that are particularly good at bypassing obstacles; this appears to be the case at least in the vocalizations of forest birds. Because the highest frequencies are obstructed in the forest and attenuated relatively rapidly by wind and air in open habitats, they apparently are not selected for use in the communication of at least most vertebrate species.

The most obvious examples of the use of sound in displays are the vocalizations characteristic of most of the better known air-breathing vertebrates (*i.e.*, reptiles, birds, and mammals). Many nonvocal means of producing audible displays exist, although none match the potential for elaboration found in vocalizations. Many invertebrates produce sounds by rubbing one body part against another (stridulation); this technique is also used by fishes and is, in some ways, comparable to the chest beating done by the male gorilla (*Gorilla gorilla*). Gorillas also beat upon the ground and upon other objects in their environments; alarmed beavers slap the surface of water with their broad tails. Some vertebrates have elaborated on this sort of behaviour. Many woodpecker species, for instance, seek out certain dead limbs or even the tin roofs of buildings on which to produce their drumming displays. The North American ruffed grouse (*Bonasa umbellus*) produces a sound like the beating of a low drum by beating air toward its chest with its broad wings. Many other birds use specialized wing or tail feathers to produce sounds during display flights—such as the "winnowing" flight of snipe.

Other
forms of
vibrational
signalling

Some forms of vibrational signalling are not perceived as sound, at least not by the relevant participants. Thus, although the sounds employed during the social interactions of honeybees are audible to man, it is likely that the bees perceive them primarily as vibrations through

receptors in their feet. Some other displays of this type are not audible to man. Males of some web-building spiders, for example, approach females for mating very cautiously, signalling their presence and identity by strumming on the females' webs.

Vision. Visibly encoded information provides for much easier pinpointing of source than either sound or chemical signals, although visible displays are also much more easily obscured by structures in the environment. Ease of locating the source of a signal is often extremely important as, in a gull colony, for example, in which a large number of individuals are present in small space and it is important for the recipient to identify the individual that is displaying. The sight of the communicator also provides information about his orientation and so functions (like the human signal of pointing) in selection of a relevant recipient. To avoid the problem of being obscured by the environment the communicator is often able to select a display position that makes him more easily seen by the most relevant recipients. When the latter are at a distance, for example, the communicator is likely to display from a highly placed station, or, in the case of many grassland bird species that have no high perches available, to perform a flight display above the vegetation. Visible displays in many species of social birds and in at least some primates (such as baboons) are often combined into relatively complex assortments that are thought to convey unusually precise information.

Unlike sounds, which are usually very transient and can be difficult to maintain, visible posturings can sometimes be maintained with relative ease, although they usually interfere with the communicator's ability to engage in other forms of behaviour. Many animals have surmounted this problem by the evolution of badges—morphological specializations, such as bright patches of skin, fur, or feathers; horns; casques; and crests. Badges convey information about the general identity of the communicator (*i.e.*, species, sex, age) and some information about his physiological state. Animals have also evolved ways to utilize sources of information that supplement displays and badges. Some species provide information of some highly relevant samples of the environment; the honeybee, for example, uses a drop of nectar in the dance at the hive to indicate the identity of the food source. Courting males of many bird species feed their mates or provide them with bits of nest material. Unmated male weaver birds make nests at which they display and which are subsequently used for breeding; male bower birds build "bowers" (a variety of display structures), and male manakins clear leks (special display arenas) that serve only a communicative function. The use of constructions in some cases extends to supplying information in the absence of the communicator, as in territorial marking. Rabbits and other mammals use dung heaps (both visible and scented) for this purpose, and bears scratch marking posts.

Despite their flexibility, visible means of signalling have disadvantages in addition to being easily obscured. They may be too easily located, drawing undesirable attention of predators and other inappropriate recipients to the communicator. Moreover, the signals are available only if the recipient looks at the source directly; this hinders his freedom to do other things simultaneously.

Chemicals. Many species have evolved special chemical products that are released under particular circumstances. Some of these substances are used as defense mechanisms against predators; they apparently function primarily by being distasteful or even injurious, but some may serve to warn the predator that its intended prey can harm it, thus eliminating the need for actual contact. A variety of chemicals called pheromones are used for communication within a species. Fishes and other aquatic animals secrete certain pheromones into the water; moths release pheromones as sexual attractants into the air to be wafted downwind; and various highly social insects mark surfaces with pheromones or spray them into the air, sometimes secreting them onto their own body surfaces so that chemicals can be directly tasted by other individuals. Scents are used by many species to mark territories,

The role
of phero-
mones

as in the well-known urination patterns of domestic dogs.

Much research has been done on the use of pheromones by species of ants. It has been found that, depending on circumstances, different pheromones are secreted from

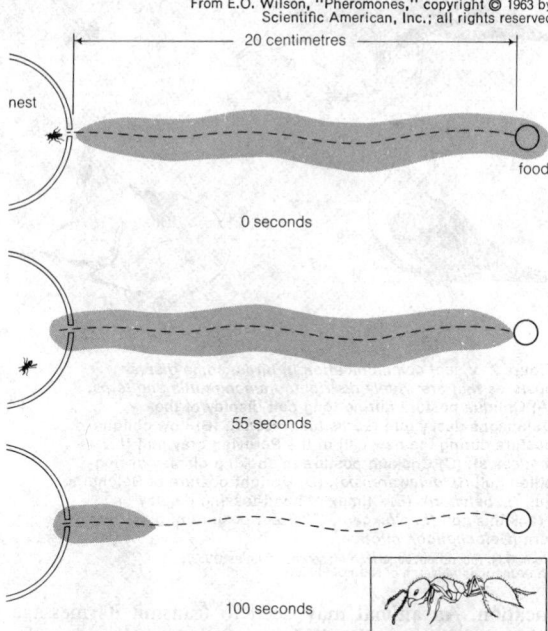

Figure 1: Odour trail of fire ant worker made by exuding a pheromone along its extended sting(s). This experimental situation demonstrates the rate of disappearance and active space of the trail.

different glands; for example, one type is secreted when the ants are laying trails, another when they are indicating alarm. The rate of release and the response thresholds of the different pheromones have been adjusted during the course of evolution so that the fading time of the odour correlates with the functions performed. Alarm pheromones, for example, which cause the ants to congregate, diffuse very rapidly and fade quickly, unless continuously renewed by additional secretion from newly attracted individuals who also take alarm. Pheromones used for group identification and for simple assembly (in the absence of alarm), fade much more slowly. Even though pheromones are less persistent than certain structures used for marking, they are used primarily for their persistence—at least in the case of species that have other means of communication available. Extremely rapid fading of the odour is a problem, however, as is the recovery rate of the recipient's chemoreceptors. Pheromones are probably an inadequate means of communication in social events that change rapidly.

Touch. Specialized patterns of touching—*i.e.*, tactile displays—are often overlooked in studies of animal communication unless they involve distinctive movements. Although a recipient animal may be aware of a distinctive touch, an observer may not; nonetheless, many forms of touch are evident. The remarkable dances of honeybees are customarily performed on a vertical comb in the darkness of the hive. Recipients of these displays follow the communicators closely, maintaining contact with their antennae; thus, much of the information is probably received as changing tactile patterns.

In many mammalian species, the members of social groups engage in bouts of grooming (called allogrooming when performed on another individual). Although visible to group members other than those in the interaction, allogrooming probably functions largely as a tactile display. Specialized touches with the hands are now suspected to be precopulatory signals in female rhesus monkeys (*Macaca mulatta*). Individuals of the South American monkey *Callicebus moloch* rest together in trees with their tails intertwined, a tactile display that probably serves a function similar to that served by allogrooming in social groups of baboons and macaques.

In some cases the communicator leaves information available for individuals it will never meet. Female wasps of at least one species are able to indicate to their offspring the direction in which to seek egress from the cells in which the eggs are laid. The information is stored in the geometry and texture of the walls constructed by the females to seal the nest chambers.

Electrical energy. A number of fishes that live in muddy waters produce regular patterns of electrical discharges as an active sensory system (active in the same sense as a bat's sonar scanning of the environment). There is good evidence that some species respond to electrical discharges of individuals of the same species, and that some aspects of the discharges, including their cessation, may function as displays.

THE ROLE OF DISPLAYS

The display repertoire. The individual animal may have a repertoire of up to about 40 displays. For most relatively social adult fishes, birds, and mammals, the range of repertoire size for different species varies from 15 to 35 displays. Further, most species have evolved displays adapted for the different sensory modality of their recipients; as a result, their repertoires comprise sets of displays (*e.g.*, both visual and audible) that overlap considerably in the information they convey. A bird can often convey information about the probability of flying by fluttering its wings and by uttering a particular call and may often do both simultaneously. Recipients sometimes are able both to see and to hear the communicator; at other times, however, he may be obscured behind foliage, or, if visible, the sounds may be masked or distorted by wind noise or by the calls of other birds. The redundancy typical of communication systems probably exists primarily to facilitate information transfer in such noisy environments that may unpredictably interfere with any one form of transmission.

In view of the immense value of language to man, it is remarkable that evolutionary pressures have not produced a greater elaboration of communication in animals other than man. This implies that further elaboration would impair rather than facilitate communication. Although the nature of this impairment is still a matter of theoretical conjecture, a promising explanation is that of Moynihan, who argues, in part, that it is difficult for a species to evolve the ability to make rapid and finely tuned responses to rare events. Rapid escape from a surprising stimulus (a relatively rare event) has frequently evolved but it is not a finely tuned response. As the size of a display repertoire increases, appropriate circumstances for the use of certain displays would become increasingly rare; Moynihan proposes that the number of displays in an animal's repertoire should not exceed that at which its rarer displays have little usefulness. This number of displays cannot yet be predicted. Other factors also act to limit the number of displays. Among them is the need for each display to be sufficiently distinctive to make it unlikely that a recipient will mistake it for another. Beyond some point, as repertoire size increases distinctiveness requires increasingly elaborate displays that may be time-consuming to produce and require too much attention by the recipient.

The restriction in the size of the display repertoire undoubtedly has had considerable influence on the evolutionary selection of the kinds of information that are encoded. An American zoologist, W.J. Smith, has suggested that this restriction explains two striking characteristics of displays: the paucity of narrowly precise messages and the relative abundance and widespread occurrence of information about such general behavioral patterns as locomotion or social association. Each species has so few displays available to it that only a minimal number can be used in restricted situations. When practical, a display has selective advantages if it conveys information that can be of use in mediating a variety of social interactions. Some types of activities, such as attack and escape, are too critically important in most species to be indicated by ambiguous signals. Others, including many of the acts that bonded (*e.g.*, paired) indi-

Limitations to the number of displays

viduals can perform in each other's company without endangering the fabric of social organization, may be safely left for a recipient to predict based on its experience in similar contexts, provided it has the information that the only likely activities are bond-limited ones. There is strong selection pressure toward both the use of general messages (in situations in which immediacy of correct response is not of overriding importance) and similar messages (for species with a wide overlap of social habits).

The information content of displays.   The study of animal displays was once primarily concerned with the motivational states of the animals using the displays. It was recognized that, if an animal uses a display only when in a certain motivational state, then the display informs a recipient that the communicator is in that state; the recipient thus should be able to predict, at least in part, the subsequent activities of the communicator. Because only certain aspects of the communicator's motivational state are common to all uses of a given display, however, these aspects are the only ones that can be said to be encoded in the display. Thus, a recipient must obtain other information in order to establish the presence of other motivational aspects. It is more useful, therefore, to study the behaviour (rather than the motivation) of communicating animals in order to correlate specific behaviour patterns with specific displays. Because communication is a social process, the most productive course of study concerns the nature of the information that can be inserted into social interactions by displays. This information helps to determine the course of the interaction and is concerned primarily with making the behaviour of the interactants more predictable.

Identification.   It is important for the recipient to be able to identify the communicator with some degree of precision; if he identifies himself, through displays or some other means, as belonging to a category of individuals important to the recipient, the latter will pay attention to him, insofar as is practical or necessary. Of prime importance is specific identity; the most important communication occurs among members of the same species. Thus, most of the flow of communication among members of other species is irrelevant. Within a species it may be useful for the recipient to know the sex and perhaps the age of the communicator; even the general physiological state (*e.g.*, breeding or nonbreeding condition) may be significant. All of this information narrows the range of behaviour that can be expected by the recipient of a display. For bird and mammal species with complex social behaviour, some features of the form of a display may be peculiar to the individual. A female passerine bird (a perching bird) newly arrived from spring migration to the region where she will breed encounters many individuals of several different species. By using certain vocalizations (usually called song), some of the birds identify themselves as males of her species and also communicate to her that they are in breeding condition and probably unmated. This information enables her to predict their responses to any approaches she might make to them. Also, after she begins to form a pair bond with a male, she must be able to identify him.

All displays studied thus far identify the communicator to some degree. The amount or kind of identifying information differs according to the social requirements of the species.

Plumage badges in birds

As already noted, identification is not only encoded by animals in displays but also in badges. The strikingly distinctive breeding season plumages of drake waterfowl, and of males of many other bird species attest to this. Female birds of many species are less distinctively coloured and it is usually they, not the males, who select a mate; male birds of such species apparently accept any female who attempts to form a bond, but females respond only to males with the correct plumage. The evolution of unusual specializations apparently has been necessary in only a few cases. Gulls, for instance, are able to distinguish species by a combination of eye colour and its degree of contrast with the white head.

Location.   Closely related in many ways to information concerning identification is information specifying

Figure 2: *Visual communication in birds: some display postures that are widely distributed among gulls and terns.* (A) Oblique posture during long call display of the Galápagos dusky gull (*Larus fuliginosus*). (B) Low oblique posture during the new call of the Peruvian gray gull (*L. modestus*). (C) Choking posture in choking display of ring-billed gull (*L. delawarensis*). (D) Upright posture of Belcher's gull (*L. belcheri*). (E) Climax of head-tossing display of Franklin's gull (*L. pipixcan*). (F) Erect posture of gull-billed tern (*Gelochelidon nilotica*).
From M.H. Moynihan, *American Museum Novitates* (1959); The American Museum of Natural History

location. An animal may need to transmit its message without fully revealing its location. It may, for example, use a visible display to a nearby recipient while otherwise concealed by vegetation from potential and undesirable recipients that would perceive vocal displays. In some cases, however, animals provide information about their location in proportion to the need of the recipients. A small bird on fleeing from a hawk, for example, may utter a high-pitched warning vocalization that carries little information about its own location. Natural selection has favoured characteristics of this vocalization that make its source difficult for a two-eared predator to locate. Many small birds hear the sound and are warned that one of their associates has found desperate reason to flee; they need not know his exact location or even why he is fleeing. The hawk, who needs primarily the location information, is denied it, largely since he is unable to locate the source of the vocalization and often has not yet seen the fleeing communicator. It is significant that the begging vocalizations of many nestling birds are similar to the warning call; the reason also is similar—to prevent predators from discovering the location of the nest, which the nestlings' parents, of course, already know.

In certain cases a vocalization can vary in ways that increase or decrease its locatability. One example, which has been studied in detail, is the call given by males of the Panamanian frog *Engystomops pustulosus* as they await females at spawning ponds. The call of a lone male contains fewer clues to his location than does the call of a male in a chorus of other males. The former probably can rely on the persistence of any passing female to find him, but, because he is alone he is more vulnerable to predators and so must give as little information as possible about his location. On the other hand, the male within a group gets some protection from predators by virtue of being among other frogs; not only is the approaching predator likely to encounter one of the other frogs first but, collectively, they are more likely to detect the predator. After the chorus has attracted a female to the immediate region, however, any male that is less easily located than his fellows is at a disadvantage; under these circumstances each male maximizes the ease with which he can be located.

Behaviour.   Much of the remainder of the information encoded by animals in their stylized displays is behavioral—it indicates the likelihood with which a recipient can expect a communicator to engage in different types of activities.

The bared teeth, growls, curled lip, and bristled hair of

The value of call variation in a species of frog

a watchdog at the approach of a stranger indicate that the animal may attack. The same display components may also indicate that it may not attack, that something, perhaps fear, is holding its aggression in check, however tenuously. Much of the displaying done by animals seems to indicate the probability of attack or escape. Such agonistic behaviour patterns must be controlled in the establishment and maintenance of organized social units such as pairs, families, and troops. A species may encode information about antagonistic behaviour in more than one display. The green-backed sparrow (*Arremonops conirostris*), for example, uses a vocalization that sounds like "chuck" when it is less likely to attack than to escape, but, when both attack and escape are equally probable, it utters either of two calls, which Moynihan has described as "medium hoarse notes" or "hoarse screams." Although the last two vocal displays indicate equal probabilities of the two acts, they do not carry exactly the same information. The "hoarse screams" are used when attack or escape is very likely to happen, and the "medium hoarse notes" are used when the bird's indecision between the two alternatives makes it less likely that either will occur. The two displays thus carry information not only about attack and escape behaviour but also about the probability that some act will occur. In fact, information about the probability of a specific act is apparently encoded in all displays, but not always in the way described above. The eastern kingbird (*Tyrannus tyrannus*) encodes the information that it may attack in a vocalization with a sound similar to "zeer." The likelihood that it may attack when using this call varies, increasing as the abruptness and harshness of the vocalization increases.

Of the information widely encoded among diverse animals in displays, little is apparently as narrowly defined as attack and escape signals. Although the encoding of information regarding attempts by a communicator to engage in social play would seem useful in view of the fact that many mammals (and even some birds such as the hobby falcon, *Falco subbuteo*) play socially, information that an approaching communicator is not likely to be vicious but intends only to play is apparently encoded only by a few primates.

Adults of many vertebrate species appear to lack common reasons for coming into contact with their fellows other than aggressively. Many animals thus have difficulty in approaching one another close enough to copulate. The displays of only a few species provide information that an individual is approaching specifically to copulate; in fact, the general information provided by the individual in other displays apparently is often sufficient, given the right contextual circumstances, to indicate the intention to copulate. So far as is known, the information provided by most birds and mammals through their displays is in large part of a general nature.

In many birds and mammals, approach in order to copulate is restricted to individuals who have established a pair bond. In this relationship each partner adopts, and recognizes as appropriate in the other, behaviour patterns that characterize certain roles, special restrictions, and special privileges. Such behaviour patterns are regular in occurrence and apparently expected to some degree by each individual. The complexity of this behaviour varies considerably among species with different degrees of social complexity—*i.e.*, the individuals may be merely temporarily mated or permanent members of a troop of numerous individuals—but the appropriate behaviour will, for some relationships, include the possibility of copulation. Many species employ at such times displays that are used in a variety of behaviour characteristic of closely interacting, bonded individuals. These displays indicate that the communicator will probably select behaviour patterns appropriate to the bonded relationship, without specifying what the behaviour will be.

The somewhat more precise information that may be available among bonded individuals usually appears to specify that appropriate behaviour will not involve physical contact. In these circumstances, the communicator simply associates with the other individual, remaining in

The importance of general information

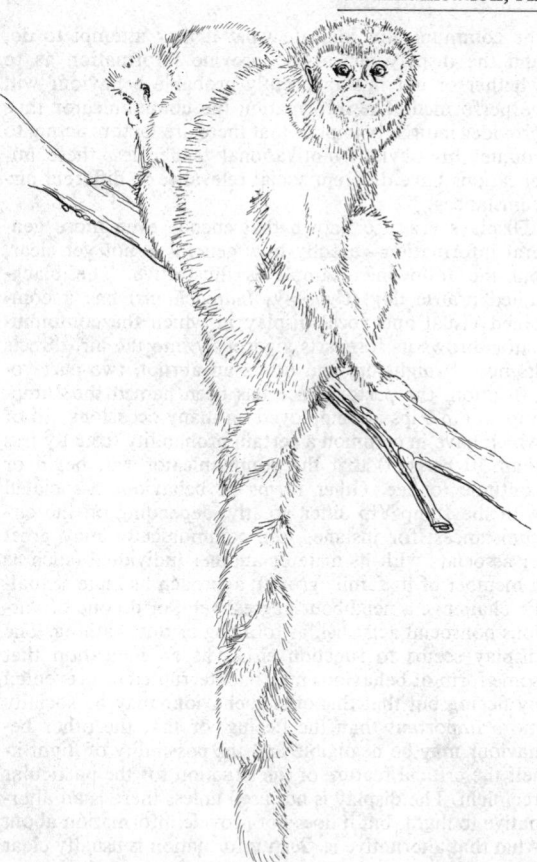

Figure 3: Tactile communication; tail-twining by titi monkeys *Callicebus moloch*.
Drawing by J. Adamska-Koperska based on M.H. Moynihan, *Journal of Zoology* (1966)

his presence but doing nothing that requires bodily contact. Such information about association is apparently basic and is encoded by many species, at least of birds and mammals. A superficially similar sort of information that may also be widespread indicates that the communicator will engage in a variety of activities, from social encounters to nonsocial acts of individual maintenance (*e.g.*, foraging), but will neither attack nor attempt to escape from the individuals to whom the display is directed. He will thus behave nonagonistically.

General information that has been identified in displays of three mammalian species (gorilla, man, and the black-tailed prairie dog) appears to be so basic that it, too, may be widespread among social vertebrates. The communicator provides information that he will probably hesitate to engage in a certain social interaction. This information is usually provided when the communicator is engaged in an activity that would be hampered by interruption. How widespread this sort of information is among animals is not known.

Other kinds of general information known to be widely encoded are less directly social in nature. The best understood information involves the probability that the communicator will engage in some form of locomotion. One kind of display may be used when an unmated male bird moves from point to point along the boundaries of his territory, occasionally stopping to advertise. The same display may be used by a mated male as he approaches his rather aggressive and perhaps sexually unreceptive mate. It may also be used by either mate on approaching a predator near its nest, or later by the nearly independent fledglings when importuning increasingly unwilling parents. Nor does this exhaust the range of situations in which this one display is used. In all cases the display fails to indicate with any precision just what the communicator's probable activities will be, but it is well correlated with a behavioral indication of uncertainty over whether the communicator will initiate or cease flying, or change direction if in flight. In any case the activities of the communicator indicate what it may attempt to do, and the display appears to provide information as to whether or not this apparently probable behaviour will be performed. The information the communicator thus provides indirectly implies that there are factors acting to counter his obvious motivational tendencies, these implications have different social relevance in different circumstances.

Jump-Yip Displays are also known that encode even more general information—exactly how general is not yet clear, but the following example is illustrative. The black-tailed prairie dog (*Cynomys ludovicianus*) has a combined visual and vocal display in which the communicator throws its foreparts vigorously into the air, directs its nose straight up, and utters an abrupt, two-part vocalization; the performance has been named the Jump-Yip. Jump-Yips are employed on many occasions, all of which have in common a certain probability (usually less than 50 percent) that the communicator will begin or continue to flee. Other forms of behaviour associated with the Jump-Yip differ greatly, depending on the circumstances; for instance, the communicator may greet or associate with its mate or another individual (such as a member of its family group); approach its mate sexually; challenge a neighbour aggressively; or do one of various nonsocial acts such as foraging or dust bathing. The display seems to function either as an indication that some form of behaviour may be interrupted or prevented by fleeing but that this other behaviour may be socially more important than the fleeing; or that the other behaviour may be negligible and the possibility of flight itself the critical feature of the situation for the particular recipient. The display is not used unless there is an alternative to flight, but it does not provide information about what that alternative is. Such information is usually clear enough contextually, however. The unspecified alternative might be anything in a prairie dog's behavioral repertoire.

Of widespread occurrence in the displays of birds and mammals is information that the communicator, however strongly motivated to perform a particular act, lacks the opportunity to do so. Thus, when, in a social encounter, a juvenile gorilla tries to flee but finds itself cornered, it adopts a special posture indicative of its frustrated escape. An eastern kingbird or a black-headed gull (*Larus ridibundus*) performs a very stylized and spectacular aerial display when it is strongly motivated to attack but lacks a suitable opponent—such as an intruder into its territory. A Carolina chickadee (*Parus carolinensis*) that appears to be seeking a border encounter with a territorial neighbour employs a special form of song if the neighbour fails to appear in response to its challenges. Various songbirds of the New World tropics have vocal displays that are used only when one bird becomes separated from the companions with which it associates while foraging; the calls cease after reunion occurs. In short, it appears that if an animal is frustrated from engaging in activities of sufficient social importance to merit communication, it may be able to encode its frustration with respect to that activity.

The foregoing describes the types of basic information presently known to be widespread among adult birds and non-human mammals. Other types of information are known to be encoded by other animals: ants provide directional information in odour trails, honeybees in "dances." The fire ant (*Solenopsis*) odour trail appears to indicate specifically the route to a food source, but the honeybee dance is less specific—it can be used to provide information about food sources, water sources, and potential sites for new hives. Both cases reflect the evolution of communication within complex social organizations of invertebrates, based on evolutionary properties quite different from those of vertebrates.

Even among vertebrates, some systems of social organization differ markedly from those of most of the birds and mammals whose communication patterns have been studied. Among nocturnal frogs, for instance, breeding males congregate loosely and call to attract females. They attempt to mate with any individual that comes near

them—whether it be a male or a female. A male or a female who has already laid her eggs usually utters a distinctive call and is released; the encoded information appears to be that the individual that has been clasped does not belong to the class that will shortly lay eggs (*i.e.*, gravid females), a rather precise but entirely suitable sort of information. Precision in such narrowly specific messages may well be the rule in groups in which complexity of social behaviour is minimal.

Immature animals dependent on adults often have social requirements quite different from those of adults and provide, in part, different information, although they too may have displays encoding attack, escape, and frustration information. At least among infant mammals, much displaying is done to indicate a need state—such as hunger, pain, need for social interaction—for which the infant must depend on others. Some displays do not specify the needs that are relevant—the most common forms of human crying, for instance, are rather imprecise. Others, such as the widely gaping mouth of a juvenile passerine bird, appear to correlate primarily with readiness to eat. Infants, because of their often limited behavioral repertoires, are somewhat difficult subjects for behavioral studies of the kind normally employed by students of animal communication. They provide an important challenge, however, as attempts are made both to learn what they encode in their displays and how this information is altered during development into adult forms of encoding.

Informa-
tion needs
of young

THE INTERPRETATION OF INFORMATION

The mechanisms by which animals appear to obtain information include displays and badges and unritualized sources; the ways in which the animals use the information they receive is dealt with in this section.

The information exchanged during social interactions among animals allows them to select their subsequent activities with greater certainty that their actions will be more appropriate than would be possible without the new information. When an animal is offered information through a display, it can select a response that is based, in part, upon this information. Depending upon the abundance and the type of information, the response must be such as to permit flexibility—*i.e.*, a generalized response may be practical. On the other hand, receipt of abundant and varied information permits the individual to choose among less generalized, and probably less flexible, responses with a greater certainty of making the appropriate selection. Complete understanding of animal communication, therefore, requires knowledge of the responses that individuals make to the information communicated. This is the study of what Colin Cherry has referred to as the "meanings" that recipients draw from the circumstances in which communication occurs.

The communication process between two animals is summarized in the following paragraphs. Through displays, badges, and other aspects of his appearance and activities, one individual adds information to another individual's environment, in which much information is already available. The human observer is certain that communication has occurred only when the second individual selects a response, demonstrating the meaning the event has had for him. Unfortunately, the study of responses in social situations is technically very difficult.

Summary
of the
communi-
cation
process

The recipient animal certainly ignores most of the many sources of information available and weighs others as he selects his response. In most instances, his response is not directly available to the human observer, for the recipient's mental state or disposition may change without an overt indication. For most displays the response observed most commonly is indistinguishable from that of inattention. When the recipient does alter his activity immediately after exposure to a signal, his first acts may be common to many different kinds of events—he may simply face the source of information, move a little closer to it, or a little farther away.

The first response of a recipient to a variety of signals conveying many possible types of information about the communicator (including high probability of attack, intent to escape or to engage in association, social play, or copulation) may be to approach the communicator. The predisposition of the recipient to react further is likely to depend on the signal, and further activity may not occur until the recipient is supplied with further information.

The study of the meanings of information to animals requires the assessment of large numbers of responses by the recipients. Much of the research on responses thus far has been experimental; usually, a recipient is provided with a particular source of information, such as a playback of a recording of some vocalization. The recipient must respond to a situation which, if not initially unnatural, soon becomes so when he is unable to locate an appropriate social partner with whom to develop an interaction. The technique has yielded some important results, however. It is now clear that the response of territorial male white-throated sparrows (*Zonotrichia albicollis*) to a playback of the song of their own species is different from that of females to the same song. Both initially approach the source; in some cases, the female response may be like that of the male in that she pauses near the loudspeaker and sings in return. Another female response develops in cases in which both she and her mate approach the test stimulus; she may then secondarily approach him and solicit mounting. She responds to the stimulus of song in a different context (the presence of her mate) from that to which he responds—he simply approaches the loudspeaker and sings—although after she begins to solicit mounting, he may copulate with her.

OTHER SOURCES OF INFORMATION

Modified displays. Although the nature of displays and badges and of the types of information that animals encode in them is important in the process of animal communication, it provides only part of the story; for example, a display is a vehicle for a particular type of information transfer, but the communicator, in the manner of its displaying, can modify some aspects of this information. The probability of attack, as encoded in the vocal display of a bird species, can be ascertained by the abruptness or harshness of a vocalization. The intensity of the communicator's involvement in the situation can also be indicated by variations in the rate at which the vocalization is uttered, or in its loudness. Such modifications provide information about the nature of the expected attack—*i.e.*, whether it will be vigorous or perfunctory—and about the communicator's state with the passage of time.

The position of the communicator as it vocalizes may indicate a particular recipient as the most relevant in a given instance. There is little reason to conclude that the orientation of the communicator has become ritualized as a part of the display. Sometimes an intermediate orientation becomes part of a ritualized display, and orientation must very often provide important information.

It appears that the information obtained by most animals about situations in the environment is either associated with stylized displaying or is implied by it with fair probability. For instance, a bird that utters a call when it sights and then flees from a dangerous aerial predator is not specifying the presence of a hawk, even though it is likely that it has been frightened by a hawk; under some circumstances (*e.g.*, if the bird has nestlings) a predator normally less dangerous than a hawk, such as a cat, is responded to with the call usually given for hawks. The bird advertises its fear in the presence of different stimuli at different times. It does not specify what the stimuli are, but instead, what its probable response is or will be. Although a bird does not specify directly that it has a territory, it regularly indicates different degrees of readiness to behave aggressively to inappropriate individuals of (usually) its own species—and so defines a region, which can be labelled its territory, that it will protect from intrusions. A forager bee does not state that it has found food at a certain place; rather, she describes a direction of flight (perhaps a flight she is likely to make again shortly) and, on request, provides a sample of the food. On the other hand, an ant that lays an odour trail only be-

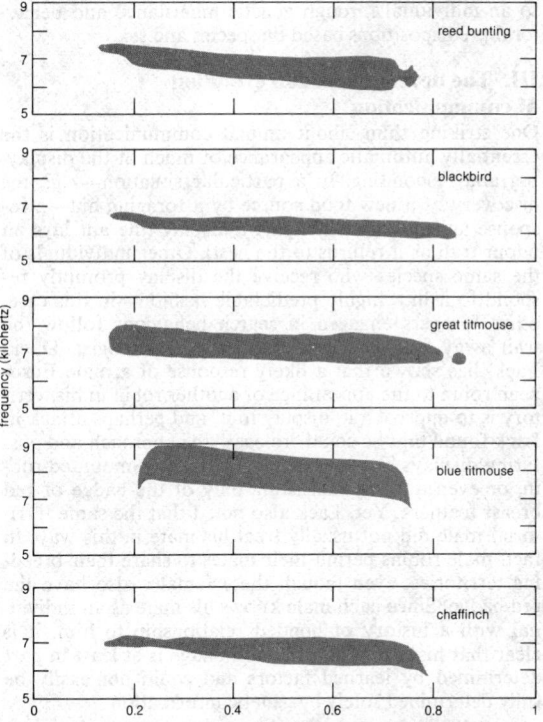

Figure 4: Sound spectrographs of alarm calls of five species of European songbirds showing similarity and broad frequency pattern. Each call is a single, simple, slightly descending note, lasting 0.6 to 0.8 second.
From P. Marler and W.J. Hamilton, *Mechanisms of Animal Behavior* (©1966); John Wiley & Sons, Inc.

tween a food source and its home colony is providing information that food is present; such narrow specific use for a display, however, is the exception, at least among birds and mammals.

Information in non-display behaviour. Much of the behaviour of animals that use displays is not stylized but is nevertheless informative and essential to the process of communication. The generally available information, provided by activities that are not specialized to be informative, is often the most abundant source of information relevant to the displays themselves. A displaying animal is also functioning in other ways; it may be resting, approaching, departing, or engaging in some other form of social behaviour. Information about such activities can narrow the range of implications of a display.

Much of the most pertinent behavioral information is not part of a display; rather, it is part of social interaction itself. Indeed, the relationship existing between two individuals can be ascertained more frequently from their behaviour in each other's presence than from their use of displays. If the individuals have formed a pair bond (*i.e.*, are bonded), they may tend to remain relatively near one another, to share food resources, to be relatively unalarmed by certain sudden movements the other might make, and to glance at one another more or less frequently than at other individuals.

Information is provided by the position of the recipient and the communicator with respect to either their territorial boundaries or the other individuals present. Even such matters as the direction of the wind can be important; for example, a male moth who has perceived a sex attractant released by a female of his species may be able to find her only by flying against the wind while keeping within the active region of the odour.

Historical information. Certain information is essentially historical. This includes knowledge that another individual is either bonded or is a territorial neighbour with whom boundaries have or have not been defined or otherwise classified in some way that enhances the predictability of his behaviour. It similarly includes knowledge of the degree to which objects other than animals are known. Some historical information is made available

Behaviour as social interaction

to an individual through genetic inheritance and behavioral predispositions based on species and sex.

III. The development and evolution of communication

One striking thing about animal communication is the essentially automatic appearance of much of the displaying and responding. In a particular situation—*e.g.*, the discovery of a new food source by a foraging ant—a response appears that is in part a display (the ant lays an odour trail as it returns to the nest). Other individuals of the same species who receive the display promptly respond to it in a highly predictable fashion—in this case, other foragers engaged in search behaviour follow the trail away from the nest. In Britain, a biologist, David Lack, has shown that a likely response of a male European robin to the appearance of another robin in his territory is to approach it, display to it, and perhaps attack it. Lack found that he could "release" the approach and posturing displays by presenting a male with a mounted robin, or even a decoy consisting only of the badge of red breast feathers. Yet, Lack also noted that the same territorial male did not usually treat his mate in this way. In fact, male robins permit their mates to share their breeding territories, even though these females also have the red badge. Since each male knows his mate as an individual with a history of bonded relationship to him, it is clear that his response to the red badge is at least in part determined by learned factors and could not easily be fully determined solely by genetic information.

THE DEVELOPMENT OF SONG IN YOUNG BIRDS

Although the question of the degrees of freedom available for the use of and response to displays has been investigated in rather few cases to date, an exciting picture has emerged from one of the most thoroughly studied cases—that of the development of birdsong.

Most songbirds (*i.e.*, members of the passerine suborder Passeres) have repertoires comprising about eight to ten vocal displays. Of these, one or more are typically more complex in form than the others and are uttered in a more repetitive fashion; these have popularly been called songs. Evidence for a few species suggests that most of the non-song vocalizations can be developed, even if the individuals are reared in acoustic isolation. Thus, the form and, perhaps, most aspects of the usage of these calls are to a considerable degree genetically determined. Exceptions have been found in which learning alters some aspects of the form of calls. In some carduel-ine finches these aspects of form alter seasonally as the social structure changes. Particular forms of calls may characterize discrete social groups, suggesting that learning facilitates the recognition of bonded individuals at times when they may be arriving or departing.

In the case of song (repetitive vocalizations), the picture is different but as yet incomplete. Young individuals of some species have the ability to produce song without the opportunity for learning, but others can produce only a very rough and irregular song unless they are able first to hear song as immature birds, and, second, to hear themselves practice it as they approach their season of first breeding. There appears to be both a critical period for the learning of a model, after which it will not be assimilated, and a period in which auditory feedback is necessary—characteristics also found in the learning of language by children. Another characteristic shared with humans is the development of complex vocalization through the production of highly variable approximations of the correct form; this juvenile "sub-song" appears to be comparable to babbling.

It has been further shown that various features of song learning are adapted to particular needs of different species, although it is not yet fully clear why some species do not appear to employ any song learning. Among these adaptive features is the timing of the critical period. Adult males of many songbirds go through a behavioral phase in the post-breeding season during which they increase their use of song; it is at this time that most of the birds studied are sensitive to the song

of their own species and are engaged in learning (but not yet using) models to guide their subsequent development. In the Australian zebra finch the critical period for accepting models terminates at approximately three months. This species nests in mixed species colonies and may breed, if conditions in its unpredictably arid habitats remain suitable, when very young. Hence, the young acquire the song of the species early, learning it from their parents before they join foraging groups that include singing males of other species.

Finally, one intriguing feature of the learning process of birdsong is that it appears to operate independently of external factors—again, like the learning of human language. It has also been shown that young chaffinches will work to obtain the opportunity to hear a recording of song of an adult of their species.

THE EVOLUTION OF COMMUNICATION

Animals characteristically respond actively to events around them, selecting from among a variety of possible responses as environmental changes dictate; higher animals, at least, are able to achieve some control over the environment. They base their behavioral changes on information that must be obtained from the environment and, in the course of evolution, have come to exploit many sources, among which are other animals. The sight of a hungry lion informs an antelope of peril; the sight of an unalarmed fellow antelope provides information that no danger probably exists in the vicinity. To a family of migrating geese, the sight or sound of other geese resting on the ground provides information of a site where they can probably find food and safety; the other geese have effectively sampled the environment for them. Individuals providing information can also obtain advantages; for example, if an antelope alerts another antelope to the approach of a lion, he increases that individual's chances of surviving to do the same for him at some future time. Evolutionary pressure can thus favour specialization for an individual either to become a source of information or to use other animals as sources.

In the evolution of communication within a species, one normal constraint usually is that the exchange of information must be useful to both the communicator and the recipient. The behavioral patterns evolved by the communicator enable him to transmit information that increases the probability of a social response suited to his needs. A recipient evolves the tendency to respond to this information only when the response suits his needs, which often differ, at least superficially, from those of the communicator. When their needs are not compatible, lack of selection pressure for the recipient to respond appropriately usually removes any advantages for the communicator, or at best yields an evolutionarily unstable situation of misinforming, to which recipients are always counter-adapting. Yet, in certain relationships between individuals belonging to different species, particularly in predator–prey relations, selection pressures for providing misinformation are such that it is a widespread phenomenon. In Batesian mimicry, potential prey species advertise that they are actually unpalatable or dangerous to predators, which either learn to leave most of them unharmed or evolve avoidance responses. Other potential prey species, lacking defense mechanisms or unpalatability, may mimic the behavioral and morphological specializations of the unpalatable ones, thus surviving by providing predators with false information. The predators, of course, are under evolutionary pressure to develop means of distinguishing the true from the false information (see MIMICRY).

The evolutionary process by which the transmission of information between members of the same species can become specialized has been studied by pioneer European ethologists Konrad Lorenz and Nikolaas Tinbergen. They have established that displays are specialized activities that have evolved from precursors, or predecessors, of several types. Important among these are intention movements—*i.e.*, incomplete performances of acts, such as taking flight or turning away, which are usually per-

The
critical
period for
song
learning

Evolu-
tionary
precursors
of displays

formed by an animal not quite committed to a given course of action. Through the process of ritualization, components of some intention movements become exaggerated and divorced from their directly functional roles. The exaggeration is often evident in an increased conspicuousness (perhaps with the concurrent evolution of morphological badges, to which the display draws attention) or an increase in the conspicuousness of only some components, thus creating a difference between the display and its evolutionary precursor.

A second source of precursors in the evolution of displays lies in inconspicuous but complete movements, such as eyebrow-lowering movements that help protect the eyes; such movements have been incorporated into the facial expressions (frowning) of numerous primate species. Other movements, such as jabbing motions of attack, are ritualized by being aimed in a stiff and often repetitive fashion away from their customary targets; these are called redirected activities. Still other movements appear to be occurring outside their customary functional contexts, as if displaced. Called displacement activities, they remain perhaps the least understood, particularly since it is not always clear that they are as functionally irrelevant as they sometimes appear. Displays apparently derived from displacement activities often resemble the activities devoted to individual maintenance—self-grooming, feeding, and drinking. Such behaviour often occurs in close conjunction with other kinds of socially relevant activities and so is perhaps easily available for evolutionary specialization. Further, some maintenance activities, which are directly related to the physiological results of exertion (as when a bird ruffles its feathers to cool its body) and thus to active social encounters like chasing and fighting, are commonly exaggerated as components of display behaviour. Other autonomic (involuntary) responses, such as urination and defecation by thwarted or frightened mammals, may have been sources for the evolution of some marking displays.

The precursors of ritualization are more easily imagined for visible displays and perhaps tactile displays than they are for other forms, although there is no reason to believe that the evolutionary process is fundamentally different in any case. Chemical displaying seems highly specialized: the chemicals *per se* have in most cases probably originated from metabolic waste products, and the acts of releasing different chemicals (the displaying) may have evolved from precursors classifiable as individual maintenance activities or "autonomic responses." The evolutionary precursors of vocal displays are also conjectural, and many extant vocalizations undoubtedly arose from pre-existing ones. Vocalizations must have arisen originally from some form of noisy, controlled breathing; Darwin's suggestion that the breathing patterns of terrified or sexually aroused animals would provide a source for specialization has not been bettered.

The evolutionary process of ritualization yields two somewhat distinctive classes of displays. As described above, much ritualization functions to yield a display distinctly different from the act from which it was derived. The act, perhaps a movement preparing a bird to take flight, remains in the behavioral repertoire of the species, serving its original functions, and, to be fully effective, the display must be distinguishable from it. There are, however, cases in which the form of the act is not altered, but its frequency of usage is in one of several ways. This is possible primarily in cases in which the evolutionary precursor is not maladaptive when done to excess (with respect to its original function). Cases in which increased frequency of performance occur are known primarily from social acts, whereas acts that are transformed in the process of ritualization may have social or nonsocial precursors. The best known example of ritualization through increased usage is what is known in mammals as allogrooming and in birds as allopreening—care given by one individual to the condition of the body surface of another individual. In highly social birds and mammals this occurs much more frequently than is necessary for cleansing of the fur or feathers, is done among animals that have bonded relationships, and is often ex-

pressed asymmetrically with respect to some feature of the social organization of a species—that is, in one species, subordinate individuals may groom dominant ones more than the former are groomed by the dominants, but in another species the reverse may be true. In addition to being a sanitary procedure, allogrooming apparently expresses the acceptance of bond-limited relationships by both the groomer and the groomed.

The evolutionary process of ritualization operates within a number of limits in addition to those imposed by the process of communication. Each species has a history, in which the origins of its attributes are, ultimately, products of genetic chance.

Closely related species evolve different solutions to the problems and opportunities of communication from those of more distantly related species. Each lineage has developed a working system based on the opportunities it has received, or, having failed to develop such a system, has become extinct. The products of ritualization are not ideal solutions to communication tasks; rather, they are practical ones. The similarities and differences of displays among species contain clues to phylogenetic relationships, although, like all other such clues, they are most safely used when their full functional significances are understood.

By no means do all of the differences among the communication patterns of different species result from the different genetic peculiarities of the different lineages. Species differ in the nature of their social behaviour. Birds, for instance, may be paired through the nesting season and flock in the remainder of the year; be paired only briefly, followed by dispersal on individual territories; be paired for life (year round); or utilize various other types of social structure. The great range of patterns of social organization determines many things about the sorts of behavioral interactions occurring among individuals and, hence, the functions required of communication patterns. The form of social organization is likely to be set, in part, by characteristics of the species' habitat, and the habitat thus must indirectly influence the directions of ritualization. Habitats also have a direct influence on ritualization of form, because they differ very much in the degree to which they obstruct information or mask it by noise. The environment of most species also contains other species, some of which communicate with similar displays, creating a need for specific distinctiveness in form.

A basic limitation exists in the nature of the sensory receptor organs available to different kinds of animals. Social insects make much use of chemical and tactile signalling, but visual signals are relatively more important to fishes and visual and auditory signals to birds. Among mammal groups there is considerable specialization, but on the whole mammals make considerable use of all sensory modalities in display behaviour.

BIBLIOGRAPHY

General works: CHARLES DARWIN, *The Expression of the Emotions in Man and Animals* (1872, reprinted 1965), the first major attempt to trace the evolution of facial signals; WESLEY E. LANYON and W.N. TAVOLGA (eds.), *Animal Sounds and Communication* (1960), accompanied by a phono record; RENE GUY BUSNEL (ed.), *Acoustic Behaviour of Animals* (1963), a general survey; THOMAS A. SEBEOK (ed.), *Animal Communication* (1968); W.J. SMITH, "Zoosemiotics: Ethology and the Theory of Signs," in *Linguistics and Adjacent Arts and Sciences*, vol. 12 of THOMAS A. SEBEOK (ed.), *Current Trends in Linguistics* (1972); R.A. HINDE (ed.), *Non-Verbal Communication* (1972).

Works devoted to particular animal groups: E.O. WILSON, *The Insect Societies* (1971); R.A. HINDE (ed.), *Bird Vocalizations* (1969); STUART A. ALTMANN (ed.), *Social Communication Among Primates* (1967); and various articles published in *Scientific American:* NEAL G. SMITH, "Visual Isolation in Gulls," 217:94–102 (1967); E.O. WILSON, "Pheromones," 208:100–114 (1963); N. TINBERGEN, "The Evolution of Behavior in Gulls," 203:118–130 (1960); KARL VON FRISCH, "Dialects in the Language of the Bees," 207:78–87 (1962); HARALD ESCH, "The Evolution of Bee Language," 216:96–104 (1967); BERT HOLLDOBLER, "Communication Between Ants and Their Guests," 224:86–93 (1971).

(W.J.S.)

Non-genetic differences

Communism

The word communism, a term of ancient origin, originally meant a system of society in which property was owned by the community and all citizens shared in the enjoyment of the common wealth, more or less according to their need. Many small communist communities have existed at one time or another, most of them on a religious basis, generally under the inspiration of a literal interpretation of Scripture. The "utopian" socialists of the 19th century also founded communities, though they replaced the religious emphasis with a rational and philanthropic idealism. Best known among them were Robert Owen, who founded New Harmony in Indiana (1825), and Charles Fourier, whose disciples organized other settlements in the United States such as Brook Farm (1841–47). In 1848 the word communism acquired a new meaning when it was used as identical with socialism by Karl Marx and Friedrich Engels in their famous *Communist Manifesto* (see also SOCIALISM; MARXISM). They, and later their followers, used the term to mean a late stage of socialism in which goods would become so abundant that they would be distributed on the basis of need rather than of endeavour. The Bolshevik wing of the Russian Social-Democratic Workers' Party, which took power in Russia in 1917, adopted the name All-Russian Communist Party in 1918, and some of its allied parties in other countries also adopted the term Communist. Consequently the Soviet state and other states governed by Soviet-type parties are commonly referred to as "Communist" and their official doctrines are called "Communism," although in none of these countries has a communist society yet been established. The word communism is also applied to the doctrines of Communist parties operating within states where they are not in power.

THE ORIGINS OF SOVIET COMMUNISM

Soviet Communism as it had evolved by 1917 was an amalgam of 19th-century European Marxism, indigenous Russian revolutionary tradition, and the organizational and revolutionary ideas of the Bolshevik leader Lenin. Marxism held that history was propelled by class struggles. Social classes were determined by their relationship to the means of production; feudal society, with its lords and vassals, had been succeeded in western Europe by bourgeois society with its capitalists and workers. But bourgeois society, according to Marxism, contained within itself the seeds of its own destruction: the number of capitalists would diminish, while the ranks of the impoverished proletariat would grow until finally there would be a breakdown and a Socialist revolution in which the overwhelming majority, the proletariat, would dispossess the small minority of capitalist exploiters.

Marxism had been known and studied in Russia for at least 30 years before Lenin took it up at the end of the 19th century. The first intellectual leader of the Russian Marxists was G.V. Plekhanov. Implicit in the teachings of Plekhanov was an acceptance of the fact that Russia had a long way to go before it would reach the stage at which a proletarian revolution could occur, and a preliminary stage would inevitably be a bourgeois democratic regime that would replace the autocratic system of Tsarism.

Plekhanov, like most of the early Russian Marxist leaders, had been reared in the traditional Russian revolutionary movement broadly known as Populism, a basic tenet of which was that the social revolution must be the work of the people themselves, and the task of the revolutionaries was only to prepare them for it. But there were more impatient elements within the movement, and it was under their influence that a group called "People's Will" broke off from the Populist organization "Land and Freedom" in 1879. Both groups were characterized by strict discipline and highly conspiratorial organization; "People's Will," however, refused to share the Populist aversion to political action, and in 1881 some of its members succeeded in assassinating Tsar Alexander II.

Lenin and Russian Populism. During the period of reaction and repression that followed, revolutionary activity virtually came to an end. By the time Lenin (whose real name was Vladimir Ilich Ulyanov) emerged into revolutionary life in Kazan at the age of 17, small revolutionary circles were beginning to form again. Lenin was a revolutionary in the Russian tradition for some time before he was converted to Marxism (through the study of the works of Marx) before he was yet 19. From the doctrines of the Populists, notably P.N. Tkachev, he drew the idea of a strictly disciplined, conspiratorial organization of full-time revolutionaries who would work among important sections of the population to win support for the seizure of power when the moment was ripe; this revolutionary organization would take over the state and use it to introduce Socialism. Lenin added two Marxist elements that were totally absent in Populist theory: the notion of the class struggle and the acceptance of the need for Russia to pass through a stage of capitalism.

Lenin's most distinctive contributions to Communist theory as formulated in *What Is To Be Done?* (1902) and the articles that preceded it were first, that the workers have no revolutionary consciousness and that their spontaneous actions will lead only to "trade union" demands and not to revolution; second, the corollary that revolutionary consciousness must be brought to them from outside by their intellectual leaders; and third, the conviction that the party must consist of full-time, disciplined, centrally directed professionals, capable of acting as one man.

Lenin's tactics led in 1903 to a split in the Russian Social-Democratic Workers' Party. With his left-wing faction, called the Bolsheviks, he strove to build a disciplined party and to outwit and discredit his Social-Democratic opponents. After the collapse of tsarism in February 1917, he pursued a policy of radical opposition to the Socialists and Liberals who had come to power in the provisional government and he eventually succeeded in seizing power in October 1917. Thereafter he eliminated both the opposition of other parties and his critics among the Bolsheviks, so that by the tenth party congress in March 1921 the Bolsheviks (or Communists) had become a monolithic, disciplined party controlling all aspects of Russian life. It was this machine that Stalin inherited when he became general secretary of the party in 1922.

THE THIRD INTERNATIONAL

The victory of the Bolsheviks in Russia gave a new impetus to the more extreme left wings of the Socialist parties in Europe. Lenin's relations with the European Socialist parties had been hostile, even before World War I. During the war he had endeavoured to assert his influence over the dissident left wings of the Socialist parties of the belligerent powers, and at two conferences in Switzerland, in 1915 and in 1916, he had rallied these dissident groups to a policy of radical opposition to the war efforts of their governments and to an effort to turn the war into a civil war. He had already decided by 1914 that, after the war, a Third International must be formed to take the place of the Second International of Socialist parties, which had failed to oppose the war despite its strong antiwar tradition. By 1919, when the new Soviet regime in Russia was fighting for its survival, the intervention on the anti-Soviet side by Britain, France, and the U.S. was a powerful and practical argument to be used by Soviet Russia in its appeals for revolution in capitalist countries. It early became clear the Third International would reflect the influence of Soviet Russia and that it was likely to become subordinate to Soviet aims and needs.

Lenin's 21 conditions. The Third International, or Comintern, had its first congress in 1919. This gathering of a very few parties in Moscow was more symbolic than real; the main structure of the new International was not hammered out until the second congress in July 1920, also in Moscow. Hopes of world revolution ran high; the prestige of the new Soviet state was in the ascendant, and the resolutions adopted at this congress reflected in the fullest possible way Lenin's idea of what a Communist party should be. It was to be the "main instrument for the liberation of the working class," highly centralized

Plekhanov's Marxism

Lenin's concept of the revolutionary party

Communism's emergence as an international movement

and disciplined according to the formula of "democratic centralism" on which the Bolshevik Party had been founded. Twenty-one conditions were laid down by the congress as prerequisites for parties affiliating with the Comintern. These conditions were designed to ensure a complete break with the older Social Democratic parties from which the Communist parties were splitting off. The new parties were required to adopt the name Communist in their title, to urge open and persistent warfare against reformist Social Democracy and the Second International, to maintain a centralized and disciplined party press, to conduct periodic purges of their ranks, and to carry on continuous and systematic propaganda in the army and among the workers and peasants. Each constituent party was to support in every possible way the struggle of "every Soviet republic" against counterrevolution. Decisions of the Comintern and of its executive committee were to be binding on all members, and the breach of any of these conditions was to be ground for expelling individual members from their parties—a provision that in future years was to be interpreted very broadly.

The New Economic Policy. The prestige of Soviet Russia, the rigid discipline imposed by the 21 conditions, and certain other factors ensured the predominance of Russian control and Russian interests over the Comintern. Though the predominance increased during Stalin's time, it was clearly evident while Lenin was still alive. At the third world congress in June and July 1921, the Comintern was confronted by Lenin with his New Economic Policy—a program encouraging small private enterprise, which several months earlier he had put into effect inside Russia. Lenin wanted a temporary halt to the revolutionary upsurge in Europe to give him time to develop stable trade relations with capitalist countries, to whom the Soviet state was preparing to grant trading and industrial concessions. Comintern members were required to support this policy, and, the expulsion of the German Communist leader Paul Levi after the failure of a Communist uprising in Germany in March 1921 showed how determined the leaders of the Comintern were to put down inconvenient left-wing "adventures." It was with the requirements of the New Economic Policy in mind that the Comintern executive committee in December 1921 launched the turnaround policy of the United Front and of trade union unity. This policy of rapprochement with Socialists and liberals was likewise designed to gain support for Lenin's policy of consolidation at home by appealing to a broader spectrum of opinion in the capitalist countries.

STALINISM

Socialism in one country. Lenin's successor, Joseph Stalin, always claimed to be his faithful follower, and this was to some extent true. Stalin's doctrine that Socialism could be constructed in one country, the Soviet Union, without waiting for revolution to occur in the main capitalist countries (a position he had developed as an integral part of his struggle against Trotsky) was not far removed from the line pursued by Lenin in 1921 when he introduced the New Economic Policy. Both Lenin and Stalin accepted the primary importance of the survival and strengthening of the Soviet state as the main bastion of the future world revolution; both accepted the need for a period of coexistence and trade with the capitalist countries as a means of strengthening socialism in Soviet Russia. Nor did Stalin's later policy of industrialization and collectivization, in theory at least, represent a departure from Lenin's doctrine. Industrialization was central to Lenin's plans, though he did not live to put them into practice. Stalin's view, however, that the construction of socialism led inevitably to an intensification of the class struggle, which in turn required a policy of internal repression and terror, is nowhere to be found in Lenin's writings. On the contrary, Lenin repeatedly emphasized in 1922 and 1923 the necessity of bringing about a reconciliation of the classes and especially of the peasants and workers.

Stalin's internal policy was to have wide repercussions in the Comintern and on Communism generally. From

From Lenin to Stalin

1924 until 1928 his first concern was to defeat his main rival, Trotsky, and this seems to have been one of the main factors determining his policy at this time. As against the more internationalist and doctrinaire Trotsky, Stalin pursued "socialism in one country" and continued to implement Lenin's New Economic Policy with its limited freedom for business enterprise and peasant individualism. In this he could still claim to be following Lenin's wishes. But Stalin also worked with great skill to ensure his control over the party. By 1927 when Trotsky was expelled from the party, Stalin already controlled both the network of party officials (the *apparat*) and the delegates to congresses and conferences. Debate had been replaced by ritualized unanimity; dissent was permitted only when it served the purposes of the leadership.

When Trotsky was exiled from the country in 1929, he became the focal point for opposition to Stalin among dissident Communists all over the world, although he was to be more a symbol than an active political force. Having defeated Trotsky and his allies, Stalin next switched policies, abandoning the New Economic Policy in favour of rapid industrialization along with the collectivization of agriculture. The collectivization policy ultimately produced a famine, costing the lives of millions of peasants. The reversal of the New Economic Policy and of Lenin's policy necessarily involved eliminating from the political scene Stalin's former allies, headed by Nikolay Bukharin, who wanted to go slower with industrialization and to cultivate support among the peasants. The protracted conflict, first with Trotsky and his ally G.Ye. Zinoviev and then with Bukharin, was reflected in the Comintern and in the world Communist movement, which became increasingly subordinated to Stalin's policy concerns inside the Soviet Union.

Stalin and the Comintern. The regimentation of the Comintern and of the parties represented in it began at the fifth world congress in June 1924, immediately after Lenin's death. The elimination of Trotsky and his supporters within the Soviet party was followed by widespread expulsions of the "left" from the other world parties. The control of the Soviet-dominated Comintern apparatus was increasingly asserted over the tightly disciplined governing bodies of the foreign parties, which in turn ruled over their members with the instrument of the purge. Ideologically, this procedure was carried out at first under the screen of the United Front, which called for cooperation with Social Democrats and other moderate leftists. At the sixth world congress in 1928, however, a further switch in policy was dictated by Stalin's internal conflict: the United Front tactic was abandoned, and the Social Democrats now became enemies along with Fascists. The sixth congress also declared the main duty of the international working class movement to be the support of the U.S.S.R. by every means. The united front tactic was revived in 1935 at the seventh (and last) world congress of the Comintern under the name of the Popular Front, calling for united action by Communists and Socialists together against Fascism.

Comintern policy changed again in August 1939 when the Soviet Union and Germany concluded a ten-year treaty of nonaggression. This had the effect of freeing Hitler to fight a war against Britain and France. Anti-Fascism was now jettisoned, and the Communist parties were required, up to the moment when Germany invaded the Soviet Union on June 22, 1941, to denounce the allied war against Hitler and to recognize Nazism as "the lesser evil" in comparison with Western imperialism. The Soviet alliance with Germany is usually seen as proof that Stalin was primarily concerned with what he considered to be the interests of the Soviet Union. A secret protocol annexed to the treaty assigned the Baltic states (Latvia, Lithuania, and Estonia), about half of Poland, and Bessarabia to the Soviet sphere of influence. The evidence suggests that Stalin considered the deal with Hitler to be based on mutual interests; the German invasion in 1941 took him by surprise. After the defeat of Hitler, Soviet territorial demands were again advanced.

The Nazi-Soviet pact

Stalin's method of rule. The Communist parties of the world were also called on to adopt official Soviet justifications for Stalin's internal purges, which involved the extermination of a large proportion of the Soviet party membership, including most of the leading cadres. The subservience of some Communist parties to official assertions made by the Soviet authorities sometimes earned them the reputation of being little more than agents of the Soviet Union inside their own countries, though this did not necessarily diminish their influence or importance in several countries of Europe or in the United States. They found much support among sympathizers with Marxism, who were prepared to overlook Soviet realities in the service of their ideals or of what they considered to be the historical destiny of mankind—in which they saw Stalinism as merely a transitory stage. The Communists and their parties and their contacts provided a valuable recruiting ground for intelligence agents of all kinds prepared to act against their own countries in the interests of Soviet Russia. The effects of Stalin's internal policy on the Communist parties outside the Soviet Union are of vital importance in understanding the attitude adopted by these parties after 1956, when much of Stalin's policy was officially repudiated.

Stalin's method of rule came, by imitation, to be the standard in all other parties. It hinged primarily upon the dominance of his own personality. He ruled over the country in large measure not through the party, as Lenin had, but through personal agents (like Lavrenty Beria, Andrey Vyshinsky, or Georgy Malenkov) and also through the security police (NKVD). The party as an institution declined under Stalin, and between 1934 and 1952 there was only one party congress, in 1939. The general secretaries of the Communist parties abroad imitated Stalin, and strict hierarchical subordination became the way of party life.

GROWTH OF COMMUNISM DURING AND AFTER WORLD WAR II

The wartime prestige of the U.S.S.R.

The undeclared assault by Hitler on the Soviet Union provoked a wave of sympathy for that country among both the open and secret enemies of Hitler in Europe. The Soviet pact with Hitler, and even the manifest blemishes of Stalin's regime, were forgotten: sympathy with the newly emerged force of resistance to the Nazi scourge far outweighed past memories. Many, it is true, expected the immediate defeat of the Soviet Union. As time went on, however, and the Soviet struggle continued with enormous sacrifice of life and with courage and skill that none could help but applaud, admiration for Soviet military achievements grew even among those who had been most critical and apprehensive of the Soviet political role before the war. The Communists of other countries shared in the prestige won by Soviet military prowess. This was particularly the case in occupied France and Italy where the underground Communist parties played a vital role in the resistance movements. In Yugoslavia, too, the Communist partisan movement led by Tito (Josip Broz) outstripped the nationalist guerrillas in effectiveness and won the material support of Britain.

Russian nationalism. The policy pursued by Stalin accentuated the nationalist side of the war and attempted in every way to play down the Communist element. At home, tsarist history and the rituals of the Eastern Orthodox Church were invoked in efforts to raise patriotic sentiments to the highest possible pitch. Abroad, Communist aims and ideals were replaced by anti-Nazi, liberal-democratic slogans. The dissolution of the Comintern in 1943 was in line with this policy. It had long ceased to be necessary as an instrument of Soviet control over the foreign Communist parties, which was carried on through other channels; but the publicizing of its dissolution added force to the growing persuasion abroad that the Soviet Union had left its revolutionary past behind it and was now a great power with traditional nationalist and security aims. Stalin himself emphasized that the dissolution of the Comintern would "put an end to the lies spread by Hitler that the Soviet Union wished to Bolshevize other countries" and that Communist parties "followed foreign directives." Still another factor promoting the influence of Communism during World War

II was the enhanced prestige of Stalin himself and the extent to which his personality influenced the allied leaders Winston Churchill and Franklin D. Roosevelt.

Stalin and eastern Europe. His growing military and political prestige in turn influenced Stalin's policy towards his allies and determined the future course of Communism after victory was won in 1945. Two main lines of Soviet policy can be discerned in the wartime conferences at Teheran, Yalta, and elsewhere: first a determination by the Soviet Union that friendly political regimes should be established in the countries on Russia's borders and second, that the Soviet Union's hard-won status as a great power should be fully recognized in the postwar settlements. These demands were not in themselves unreasonable, considering the enormous price that the Soviet people had paid for victory. In pursuing the creation of a solid Soviet-dominated bloc of Communist states in east-central Europe, Stalin was able to take advantage of the presence of a victorious Soviet army in Poland, Bulgaria, Romania, Hungary, and East Germany. The cases of Yugoslavia and Albania were different, but the regimes that emerged in all these countries were broadly similar forms of Communist party domination based on the Soviet model, even though the ways in which the Communists achieved power varied.

The expansion of Soviet influence

Broadly speaking, three phases could be distinguished. In the first phase there was a genuine coalition of Communist and Socialist parties. This lasted until the spring of 1945 in Romania and Bulgaria, until the spring of 1947 in Hungary, and until February 1948 in Czechoslovakia. Yugoslavia, Albania, Poland, and East Germany never knew this phase: the former two started as "monolithic," while the latter two began their postwar history in the second phase, an alleged coalition in which the Socialist parties were nominally independent and had some share in power but in which their leaders and policies were largely determined by the Communists. In the third phase, the "monolithic" phase, the nominally independent Socialist parties were required to fuse with the Communists, political opposition was largely suppressed, and Socialist leaders went into exile or were dealt with by staged treason trials. In Poland, Bulgaria, and Romania the third phase began in the autumn of 1947; in Hungary, in the spring of 1948. In East Germany the third phase was complete by 1949.

In his policy toward the countries which were destined to form the Soviet bloc, Stalin was aided in part by the inability or unwillingness of the Western Allied Powers to take steps during the first or second phases described above to prevent the beginning of the third phase and in part by the skillful infiltration of local Communists into key positions. The peasant and Socialist parties, which had substantial support in their countries, were attacked in various ways and demolished as independent political bodies.

Yugoslavia was an exception. There the Communists under the leadership of Tito enjoyed a considerable measure of mass support because of their wartime role as partisan fighters. The People's Democracy they instituted in Yugoslavia was for some years little different in character from that of other Communist party-dominated states of eastern Europe. An attempt to set up a People's Democracy in Greece failed after three years of civil war, in which the Greek Communists were supported by Yugoslav aid.

In the countries of Europe outside the Soviet bloc, Communist parties proved unable to exploit the prestige that they had acquired during the war. Both in France and in Italy they enjoyed considerable support: in the parliamentary election of 1945 in France the Communists received 26 percent of the vote, and in the general elections to the Constituent Assembly in Italy in June 1946 they received 19 percent. Both parties, however, failed to achieve real national power in the postwar period; their role was confined to fomenting strikes and disorder in the interests of Soviet policy. The detailed story of the Italian and French Communist parties during the period 1945 to 1949 is complex, but, broadly speaking, their attempts at insurrection foundered against the facts of the

The failure in western Europe

power of the army and the police and a lack of revolutionary zeal among their worker supporters. On the other hand, their attempts to win power by parliamentary means were frustrated by the distrust that the Socialists felt for them as colleagues in Parliament or in government and by their own evident lack of interest in a viable parliamentary system.

Communism's growth in Asia. Powerful Communist parties emerged after the war in various parts of Asia, in many cases largely as a result of the resistance of the Western powers to growing nationalist movements. Communist-led insurrections, allegedly coordinated by Moscow, broke out in the summer of 1948, in Burma, Malaya, and Indonesia. In Indochina, after the surrender of Japan, the Communists under Ho Chi Minh seized power in the three northern provinces of the country. The French colonial policy helped drive the nationalists into the arms of Ho Chi Minh, and by the end of 1946 a guerrilla war had broken out in the country, which was to last for many years after the French had been forced out of the country. (It was still in progress in 1972.) In Japan, democratic legislation imposed by the United States after its victory permitted the Communists to operate legally. In the succeeding few years they made little progress toward governmental power but won considerable gains in the trade unions and an important measure of influence among university students. In India, the Communist Party supported the British war effort after June 1941 and gained ground as a result; it switched to violent insurrection after Indian independence but abandoned this policy in 1950.

Chinese Communism

The most significant factor in the postwar history of Communism in Asia may have been the victory in 1949 of the Chinese Communist Party under the leadership of Mao Tse-tung. China, rather than the Soviet Union, seemed destined to play the leading role in Asian Communism. The victory of the Chinese Communist party over Chiang Kai-shek and the Kuomintang, like that of Tito's forces in Yugoslavia, owed little if anything to Soviet aid—save that the Russians had handed over to the Chinese Communists the military stores captured from the Japanese during the very short period when the U.S.S.R. was at war with Japan in 1945. Although the Chinese Communist Party had developed under the aegis of the Comintern and acknowledged the doctrinal authority of Lenin and Stalin, its experience had been very different. Its victory had been preceded by long guerrilla warfare. Mao's rise to power had, moreover, been achieved by ignoring Soviet advice as much as by following it. Stalin showed quite clearly from the outset that he intended to keep China in a position of subordination not unlike that which he had successfully marked out for most of eastern Europe—a status the Chinese Communist leaders were not likely to accept. Culturally, economically, and geographically, China was in a strong position to become the model for Communist revolution in Asia and to wrest the leadership of Asian Communism from the Soviet Union. These and other factors were to produce signs of a possible breach between China and the U.S.S.R. within less than ten years of the proclamation of the Chinese People's Republic on October 1, 1949.

THE WORLD MOVEMENT UP TO STALIN'S DEATH

The Cold War

The wartime alliance had given rise to some hopes that Soviet-Western amity would continue. Stalin's relentless pursuit of security through the domination of neighbouring countries shattered this hope. At home Stalin returned to his prewar tactics: widespread arrests and deportations occurred in the newly incorporated or reincorporated territories of the Soviet Union; the restriction of cultural life was intensified; the straitjacket was reimposed on the party, on the peasants, and on the industrial workers. There is some evidence to suggest that at the time of his death in March 1953 Stalin was planning a new purge on the scale of the 1936–38 purges.

The struggle with the West. Soviet expansion into eastern Europe led to counteractions by the Western powers that Moscow interpreted as part of a master plan to en-

circle and subjugate the Soviet Union. These included the Truman Doctrine of containment of Soviet expansion proclaimed in March 1947; the offer in June of that year by United States Secretary of State George Marshall to underwrite the economic recovery of Europe; and the North Atlantic Treaty of April 1949, which established a permanent defence force for western Europe, including in its orbit West Germany. Another factor that affected Soviet policy was the monopoly of the atomic bomb enjoyed by the United States from 1945 until 1949. The Soviet Union rejected the Baruch Plan put forward by the U.S. for the international control of atomic weapons and made every effort to produce its own, succeeding in September 1949. The "Cold War" was on.

The defection of Yugoslavia. In September of 1947 a new international organization, the Communist Information Bureau (Cominform), was established. Unlike the old Third International (Comintern), the Cominform was limited in membership to the Communist parties of the Soviet-dominated countries of east-central Europe and to the French and Italian Communist parties. The aim of the Cominform was to consolidate and expand Communist rule in Europe. Plans for the establishment of Communist rule in Czechoslovakia were discussed, and the French and Italian parties were reproved for their failure to win power in their own countries.

The Cominform did not prove a success. Certainly one of its purposes was to hold Yugoslavia more securely within the Communist fold, and for this reason Belgrade was chosen as the seat of the new organization. But within a few months a quarrel broke out between the Soviet and Yugoslav parties, and when the Cominform held its second meeting in June 1948, it was for the purpose of denouncing the Yugoslav Communist Party and expelling it from the organization. The quarrel with Yugoslavia resulted largely from Tito's refusal to submit to domination by the Soviet Union; there was also some suspicion on the Soviet side, possibly well founded, that the Yugoslav party leader hoped to build up a bloc of Communist states in southeastern Europe that would not be totally dependent on the Soviet Union.

The effect of the Soviet-Yugoslav quarrel, which has never completely healed, was momentous. First, it shattered the doctrine that the Communist movement must be monolithic, since a Communist party had challenged Moscow and survived. Second, Yugoslavia, having broken with the U.S.S.R., was in a position to take up a position of authority in the world toward other states, especially states formed in formerly colonial territories. The Yugoslavs could speak as Communists who, while opposed to the policy of the imperialist powers, were no mere agents of Soviet policy. This position carried a particularly strong appeal in India, but the impact of the Soviet quarrel with Tito was much wider.

A third effect of the Yugoslav defection was a tightening of the Soviet hold over the remaining members of the Communist bloc. In Soviet-dominated lands "Titoism" became synonymous with treason, much as "Trotskyism" had been in the '30s. Purges and public trials ensued throughout eastern Europe. In some cases, like that of Władysław Gomułka in Poland (who was left alive), or Koci Xoxe in Albania, the charge of sympathy with Yugoslavia may have been true; in others, like those of László Rajk in Hungary or Traicho Kostov in Bulgaria, the offence may have been only an attempt to resist Soviet domination; in the trial of Rudolf Slánský in Czechoslovakia in 1952, a strong anti-Semitic element played a part. Countries of the Communist bloc were seething with anti-Soviet and nationalist feeling by the time Stalin died. Though Stalin's postwar policy was successful in extending the boundaries of Soviet military and political control well into eastern and central Europe, Communism did not win out in France or in Italy, where its chances had appeared strongest. The policy of expansionism and of intransigence founded on suspicion of the United States led to a kind of consolidation of the West against the Soviet Union. In the Far East the Korean War was probably not a success from the Communist point of view. Korea had been divided after the defeat of Japan: in the northern part a Communist government came to power in elections held in November 1946, and in the south a non-Communist government was established. Each claimed to be the legal government of the whole country. Invasion of the south by the north in June 1950 was condemned by the Security Council of the United Nations as aggression, and the Security Council approved military assistance to South Korea under a unified American command. (The absence of the Soviet representative from the Security Council prevented the U.S.S.R. from vetoing this resolution.) The long war, in which China intervened on the side of North Korea, brought heavy burdens and few, if any, advantages, and the conflict between the major powers that it involved led them in the fears of many to the verge of world war. In June 1951 the Soviet Union proposed discussions for an armistice, to which the Western powers agreed. The negotiations were protracted and did not result in an armistice until after Stalin's death in 1953.

THE BREAKUP OF THE WORLD COMMUNIST MONOLITH

Stalin's heirs

The Khrushchev era. Stalin died on March 5, 1953. For a short time, until the beginning of 1955, power was nominally divided between Georgy Malenkov, the chairman of the Council of Ministers, and Nikita Khrushchev, the first secretary of the Communist Party. Almost from the beginning, Khrushchev was the more dominant of the two; his victory over his rival was only a matter of time. Malenkov, it would seem, decided quite early that the Soviet Union could not maintain its hold over the Eastern bloc without substantial economic relaxation. The difficulties that always beset the reform of an oppressive regime were soon illustrated in East Germany. Within a week of the announcement by East German leaders that "aberrations" of the past would be rectified and some of the hardships of life alleviated, there was an uprising in the streets of East Berlin; it spread to other parts of East Germany and was quelled only by the use of Soviet armed forces. The blame for this was laid on Lavrenty Beria (the Soviet security chief, shortly to be deposed and executed) and by implication on Malenkov. The new relaxed policy continued, however, in most of the Soviet countries. Economic reforms were initiated in Hungary, Czechoslovakia, and Poland, but the system of political rule remained unchanged.

Khrushchev, who by the beginning of 1955 had ousted Malenkov, had a comprehensive vision of how the Eastern bloc should be run. He was determined to find a way out of the straitjacket in which Stalin had confined Soviet life; the outcome was to have momentous consequences for Soviet dependencies abroad, which Khrushchev probably did not at the time foresee. His policy toward the Communist satellite countries may be summarized as one of cooperative integration instead of exploitation, with some degree of economic and political autonomy (under Communist Party leadership). A political and military convention between the European Communist states and the U.S.S.R. (the Warsaw Pact) was signed in May 1955. Khrushchev also sought to redesign the Council for Mutual Economic Assistance, the Communist counterpart of western Europe's Common Market, which Stalin had set up in January 1949: he tried (though with indifferent success) to transform the Council for Mutual Economic Assistance into a device for promoting the division of labour, economic specialization, and technical and financial cooperation among the countries of the bloc.

The crises of 1956. In order to demonstrate that Stalin's policy was a thing of the past, Khrushchev made substantial efforts to effect a reconciliation with Tito and the Yugoslav Communists (against the opposition of some of his colleagues, including Vyacheslav Molotov). An agreement with Yugoslavia in June 1956 recognized that "the conditions of Socialist development are different in different countries" and stated that no Socialist country should impose its views on another. This was momentous change in policy, since it meant that a country could be described as "Socialist" without being obliged to follow all the practices adopted by the Soviet Union or every Soviet turn in foreign relations.

The reconciliation with Yugoslavia was only one of several important events that made the year 1956 a watershed in the history of Communism. In February, at the 20th congress of the Communist party, Khrushchev delivered a speech in secret session in which he attacked the period of Stalin's rule in most forthright terms. The speech was not published within the Soviet Union, but its text was widely circulated among Communists both within and outside the Soviet Union and was published by the U.S. State Department. Its effect was enormous. Although the disclosures were neither complete nor entirely new, the fact that Khrushchev had uttered them caused a ferment in the Communist movement that was to prove irreversible. It inaugurated a period of freedom of debate and criticism that had been unknown for a quarter of a century; despite efforts both by Khrushchev and by his successors to keep criticism of the "cult of personality" (the accepted euphemism for Stalin's misdeeds) within bounds, the ferment could not be contained.

Khrushchev's criticism of Stalin

The Hungarian Revolution. In the European Communist countries, Khrushchev's disclosures opened the floodgates of pent-up criticism and resentment against the local Stalin-type leaders. In Hungary, Mátyás Rákosi was ousted as party leader in July 1956 and replaced by Ernő Gerő. But Gerő was unable to contain the rising tide of unrest and discontent, which broke out into active fighting late in October, and appealed for Soviet help. The first phase of the Hungarian Revolution ended in victory for the rebels: Imre Nagy became premier and agreed, in response to popular demands, to establish a multiparty system; on November 1 he declared Hungarian neutrality and appealed to the United Nations. On November 4 the Soviet Union, profiting from the lack of response to Nagy from the Western powers, and from the British and French involvement in action against Egypt, invaded Hungary in force and stopped the revolution. In Poland, where the ferment was also reaching dangerous intensity, the Soviet Union accepted a new party leadership headed by the more moderate Władysław Gomułka. There are believed to have been two reasons for this difference in Soviet policy. One was that in Poland the Communist Party remained in control of the situation. The other was that the invasion and subjugation of Poland would have required a military force several times that required in Hungary.

Polycentrism. Inside the Communist states, the suppression of the Hungarian Revolution had a restraining effect. There was, nevertheless, no return to the Stalinist type of domination and exploitation; a slow evolution followed toward a degree of internal autonomy, even in Hungary. The events of 1956 also had profound effects upon Communists outside the Soviet bloc. There were many resignations after the Hungarian Revolution, and those who remained in the fold began to question both Soviet leadership and the nature of a system that had made the ascendancy of Stalin possible. The most trenchant questioning came from the leader of the Italian Communist Party, Palmiro Togliatti, who concluded that the Soviet pattern could no longer be the model for all other countries and called in June 1956 for decentralization of the Communist movement, a view that became known as "polycentrism." "The whole system becomes polycentric, and . . . we cannot speak of a single guide but rather of a progress which is achieved by following paths which are often different." Although the Italian Communist Party, or segments of it, were still prepared to support the Soviet Union at times of crisis, at other times it took positions different from those of the Soviet Union.

The Sino-Soviet dispute. A gathering of communist parties in Moscow in November 1957, in which China played a leading role, attempted to reassert a common doctrine while recognizing the need for differences in national practice. At Chinese insistence, it also retained the Stalinist emphasis on the leadership of the Soviet Union. For a short time relations between the Soviet Union and China were harmonious: after 1955 Khrushchev had put an end to the humiliating terms that Stalin had imposed on China and inaugurated a policy of substantial economic aid.

Opening of the rift with China

The differences between China and the Soviet Union, which were to erupt into an open campaign of mutual abuse by 1962, were discernible to most observers by 1959, when the Soviet Union failed to give immediate political backing to Chinese military action against India and when China, at the same time, showed suspicion of Soviet talks with the United States in pursuit of Khrushchev's policy of "peaceful coexistence." In 1960 the differences widened, though they were still unpublicized. The Soviet Union withdrew its technical advisers from China as a preliminary to what was to prove an almost complete severing of economic relations. A facade of agreement was maintained, and at a conference of Communist parties held in Moscow in 1960 a series of resolutions were put forth to show that unity prevailed as ever in the ranks of the world Communist movement. News of serious disagreements, however, soon leaked out, for the increasing number of dissident groups within the several parties had by now rendered the maintenance of secrecy impossible. In the following year, 1961, the Soviet Union began a public polemic against the Chinese viewpoint. This was disguised as an attack on Albania, since 1959 a client of China and increasingly critical of Khrushchev's foreign policy. By 1962 the quarrel had become open and very bitter. It was conducted as a dispute over doctrine, but the practical issue underlying it was a basic rivalry for leadership of the world revolutionary movement.

The Sino-Soviet dispute had three major effects on this movement. It shattered the pretension that Marxism-Leninism offered a single world view, since at least two radically different ways of interpreting Marxism-Leninism were presented to Communists throughout the world, each backed by a Communist party in power with the prestige of a victorious revolution behind it. Second, it seriously impaired, if it did not destroy, the Soviet claim to be the leader of the world revolutionary movement. Since 1960 nearly all Communist parties have split into pro-Soviet and pro-Chinese portions, though outside Asia the Soviet portion has usually retained predominance. In the important parts of Asia, with the possible exception of India, where the party is divided into several warring factions, China has become the predominant influence upon Communist parties. Third, the mere fact of the dispute tended to create greater flexibility for individual parties within the Communist movement as a whole, even in the case of parties that nominally accepted Soviet leadership. The Romanians, for example, were able to follow a nationalistic course by which they successfully resisted Soviet attempts to integrate the Romanian economy into the bloc pattern. The Romanians also took an independent line in their trade relations with other countries, in refusing to participate in the 1968 invasion of Czechoslovakia, and in their policy toward Israel.

After the fall of Khrushchev in October 1964, his successors made efforts to reunite the world movement. They were only moderately successful. Seventy-five parties met in Moscow in June 1969, but of 14 parties in power 5 did not attend, and Cuba sent only an observer; Asia and Africa, the main areas of Chinese influence, were very poorly represented. Little unity emerged from the conference; in particular, the efforts of the Soviet Union to secure condemnation of China were unsuccessful. The resolution finally adopted was couched in such general terms as scarcely to conceal that the cracks had been merely pasted over. In the course of the 1970s, the hold of the Soviet Communist party over Communist parties outside the bloc seemed for a time to become weaker, with several parties (notably of France, Spain, and Italy) asserting independence from Moscow and the right to criticize Soviet policy. This movement, nicknamed "Eurocommunism," had lost much of its force by the end of the decade, however.

PROBLEMS OF INTERNAL REFORM

A continuing problem in the history of Communist countries after the death of Stalin was the reform of their overcentralized political and economic structures. The only country that may be said to have achieved success was Yugoslavia, which had since 1948 asserted and maintained its independence from Soviet interference. After initially collectivizing much of its agriculture, Yugoslavia allowed the collective farms to dissolve. It also established Workers' Councils in the factories and publicized them in its foreign propaganda despite Soviet disapproval. The Yugoslav party program of 1958 contained three points in particular that were diametrically opposed to Soviet theory: that Socialism can be achieved without a revolution, that the Communist party need not have a monopoly of leadership, and that danger of war arises from the existence of two power blocs in the world and not (as the Soviet Union contended) from the aggressive intentions of the United States. In January 1974, a new constitution was adopted that, apart from making changes in the representational system, provided for a collective presidency consisting of one member from each republic and autonomous province. Tito was elected president for life; after his death in 1980 this office rotated among the several members of the collective presidency.

Suppression of reform in Czechoslovakia. The most dramatic failure of an attempt at reform was in Czechoslovakia. The resignation of the old Stalinist party leader Antonín Novotný and his replacement by Alexander Dubček in January 1968 inaugurated a process of liberalization. The reformers hoped to humanize Communist rule by introducing basic civil freedoms, an independent judiciary, and other democratic institutions. The support of leading economists for this program was particularly significant since it indicated that they realized that the already accepted policy of economic decentralization (which included giving a measure of initiative to individual enterprises) would fail unless accompanied by political changes.

While the Czechoslovak Communists had repeatedly declared their intention to remain within the existing system, Moscow, possibly fearing that the developments they had set under way would ultimately endanger the stability of eastern Europe, endeavoured to induce the Czechoslovak party leaders to abandon their course. The Soviet effort failed, possibly because there were no Czechoslovak Communist leaders prepared, with Soviet help, to oust Dubček. Finally a group of Warsaw Pact forces—predominantly Soviet, but with token contributions from the other Warsaw Pact members except Romania—invaded Czechoslovakia on the night of August 20–21, 1968, effectively killing the momentum of the reform movement in Czechoslovakia. A Soviet-controlled security service was installed, and the Dubček leadership was gradually forced out of top posts and eventually expelled from the party. Although the repression was thorough, there was no mass terror.

The Soviet invasion of Czechoslovakia came as a greater shock to many Communists than the invasion of Hungary because it was directed against Communist leaders who strongly asserted their loyalty to Moscow. The motives that prompted Soviet action were probably two: one was the fear that the Soviet defense area created by Stalin after World War II might be endangered if the Dubček regime were allowed to continue; the other was the fear that the entrenched and conservative Communist parties in other European Communist countries, and in the Soviet Union itself, might not be equal to the challenge posed by a reformed Communism in Czechoslovakia.

Khrushchev's reforms. This concern that the power of the Communist party might be diminished may also have acted as a brake on internal reform. The reforms carried out by Khrushchev between 1953 and 1964 had been extensive. The arbitrary powers of the security police were brought under control; there were widespread reviews and rehabilitations (often posthumously) of the sentences of those sent to labour camps under Stalin; and reforms (in 1958) removed the worst anomalies of Soviet criminal law and procedure. The stringent controls over the lives of workers and farmers were relaxed. Discussion and debate were tolerated among writers and intellectuals to a degree that would have been inconceivable under Stalin. The whole system of agricultural management was considerably relaxed, and a system of incentives for the collective farmers was introduced. The limit of reform, as Khru-

The Sino-Soviet dispute

The attempt to modify Stalinism

Invasion of Czechoslovakia

shchev saw it, was the point at which any threat appeared to the party's control over all aspects of life. Under his successor, Leonid Brezhnev, the brake on reform was applied more heavily. Criticism of Stalin decreased. Freedom of opinion was considerably restricted by the introduction of penal provisions against "slandering" the Soviet system: for the first time since Stalin's death there were trials of writers, and the courts ceased to show any inclination to assert their independence as they had under Khrushchev. The numbers of political prisoners steadily increased, although the Brezhnev regime could not be compared to Stalin's. A movement toward economic reform had started under Khrushchev, aiming at some decentralization of economic control through greater freedom for enterprises to plan their own operations and through more influence for market forces. This was continued and officially encouraged after 1964 by Prime Minister Aleksey Kosygin, but it made little headway and was abandoned. The period of the 1970s was one of economic stagnation and conservatism at home, coupled with expansion of military power abroad.

COMMUNIST DOCTRINE SINCE STALIN

The errors of "revisionism" and "dogmatism." The most far-reaching innovation in Communist doctrine during the period 1953–70 was the Chinese interpretation of Marxism-Leninism known as Maoism (see CHINA, HISTORY OF: *The development of Maoist ideology*). In the Soviet sphere several profound changes in doctrine took place after the death of Stalin. One change was the rise of ideological dispute for the first time since the early 1920s. The Yugoslav ideas were denounced as "revisionism," a term that harked back to the turn of the century when it had been used to characterize the views of Eduard Bernstein, who had argued that Socialism could be achieved without a revolution. After 1957 the terms "revisionism" and "dogmatism" became an integral part of Communist discourse. They were applied in a variety of meanings. By the Chinese, "revisionism" was used to mean, in effect, Khrushchevism—*i.e.*, the policies Khrushchev had introduced in both domestic and international relations, and which the Chinese opposed. On the Soviet side, "revisionism" became a catch-phrase to designate any political reform that appeared to endanger the dominance of the Communist party: as defined at the Moscow conference of 1957 (with Chinese approval then) it was applied to all reform movements within the Communist system that denied "the historical necessity of the proletarian revolution," or the "Leninist principles for the construction of the party." The term "dogmatism," in Soviet usage, means a doctrinal conservatism that ignores changing realities, a clinging to received ideas in a way "calculated to alienate the party from the masses." The proper course, in the Soviet view, lies between revisionism and dogmatism: between excessive liberalism (as in Czechoslovakia in 1968), which may threaten the party's power, and excessive conservatism, which can lead to popular revolt (as in Hungary in 1956).

Different roads to Socialism. The most important new elements in Soviet doctrine were set out in the party program adopted by the 22nd congress in October 1961; they were also, to some extent, embodied in the declarations of the Moscow conferences of 1957 and 1960. First, there was the concession that there are different roads to Socialism. This may have been no more than a practical recognition of the fact that since the breach with Yugoslavia and the death of Stalin it had no longer been possible for the Soviet Union to impose its own pattern on all Communist states. The invasion of Hungary in 1956, of Czechoslovakia in 1968, and of Afghanistan in 1979 were not, according to Moscow, inconsistent with this doctrine, since in each case the Soviet Union acted out of a duty to assist a fraternal Socialist state in putting down a counterrevolution. In the case of Czechoslovakia, which had not asked for such assistance, a new tenet was added by Brezhnev in November 1968. He contended that when "internal and external" forces hostile to Socialism attempted to restore capitalism in a Socialist country, it became a matter of concern to the whole Socialist com-

munity. This tenet was used to justify the action of the Warsaw Pact forces in August 1968 and of the Soviet forces in December 1979.

Peaceful coexistence. The second change in Soviet doctrine was the view that war between the capitalist and Socialist powers was no longer inevitable, as had always been asserted by both Lenin and Stalin. This was a practical recognition of the fact that a war waged with nuclear weapons would be more likely to lead to mutual annihilation than to victory. Khrushchev emphasized the possibility of "peaceful coexistence" between different social systems, and the achievement of Socialism by peaceful means. In the 1970s, "peaceful coexistence" became known as "détente." This doctrine raised hopes of real peace between Communist and non-Communist states, but the Soviet leaders made it clear that détente would not affect either political warfare against the West or military support for wars of liberation. The massive invasion of Afghanistan by the Soviet Union in December 1979 left détente seriously impaired.

The third doctrinal change after 1953 was also dictated by practical reality. The Comintern had rigidly applied concepts drawn from Western history to revolutions in Africa and Asia: industrialization, the emergence of a proletariat, and a Socialist revolution carried out under the leadership of a Communist party. This Marxist analysis proved to be totally unrealistic in the case of underdeveloped countries in which the predominant force was nationalism. This was increasingly recognized after 1956, in Soviet doctrine that declared the proper revolutionary aim in the developing countries to be "national democracy." In Khrushchev's words this meant accepting a "noncapitalist path of development," which would be in the interests "not only of one class but of the broad strata of the people."

The future of Communism. As the 1960s ended, the Soviet leadership faced two main problems: a slowing down in the rate of economic growth, to which the party had tied its promises of an improved standard of living, and a ferment of criticism among an intellectual minority, which included an influential component of leading scientists. Two alternatives seemed the most likely in the foreseeable future: either a return to more repressive measures, reminiscent of Stalin, or a reform of the Soviet system in the direction the Yugoslavs had taken. By the beginning of the 1980s, the prospects of reform in the direction of relaxation seemed remote, though the impending departure of the Soviet leader, Brezhnev, by then old and ill, left the question of the future open.

In other Communist countries within the Soviet sphere the fate of Czechoslovakia in 1968 seemed likely for some time to act as a deterrent against overbold attempts at reform. However, a return to the kind of domination achieved by Stalin seemed improbable, and the Soviet Union seemed likely to tolerate some degree of autonomy and variety among its fellow members of the Warsaw Pact. By the end of 1980, the emergence in Poland of a mass trade union movement, independent of the Communist Party, challenged the party's power, a situation that could well lead to military intervention by other Warsaw Pact powers or to radical changes in Poland.

The future of Communism as a world movement necessarily depended upon relations between the Soviet Union and China. Their rivalry and their differences in doctrine seemed too deep for reconciliation. The economic backwardness of China, which would require decades to overcome, was likely to ensure a continuing gap in outlook between the two powers. In the competition for influence over potential revolutionary forces in Asia, Africa, and Latin America the advantages seemed to lie with China, which was closer to them in social and economic structure. On the other hand, the Soviet Union seemed likely to retain its lead over Communist parties in the industrially developed countries; even if it could no longer hope to use them as Stalin had, it could look to them as useful instruments in its continuing struggle against the non-Communist powers in general and the United States in particular. While the threat of Eurocommunism had receded, there seemed little prospect in the early 1980s of

Brezhnev's policy toward reform

Program of the 22nd congress

Trade union movement in Poland

a return to the monolithic world Communist movement that Stalin had created.

BIBLIOGRAPHY

Origins of Soviet Communism: SHLOMO AVINERI, *The Social and Political Thought of Karl Marx* (1968); ISAIAH BERLIN, *Karl Marx*, 2nd ed. (1948); R.N. CAREW-HUNT, *The Theory and Practice of Communism*, 5th rev. ed. (1957, reprinted 1963); J.L.H. KEEP, *The Rise of Social Democracy in Russia* (1963), an outstanding history of the subject up to 1906; LEONARD SCHAPIRO, *The Origin of the Communist Autocracy: Political Opposition in the Soviet State: First Phase, 1917–1922* (1955); ADAM ULAM, *The Bolsheviks* (1965); FRANCO VENTURI, *Il populismo russo* (1952; Eng. trans., *The Roots of Revolution: A History of the Populist and Socialist Movements in Nineteenth Century Russia*, 1960); BERTRAM D. WOLFE, *Three Who Made a Revolution* (1948).

Stalinism: ROBERT CONQUEST, *The Great Terror: Stalin's Purge of the Thirties* (1968); IAN GREY, *The First Fifty Years: Soviet Russia 1917–1967* (1967); LEONARD SCHAPIRO, *The Communist Party of the Soviet Union*, 2nd rev. ed. (1970).

The world movement up to Stalin's death: HAMILTON FISH ARMSTRONG, *Tito and Goliath* (1951), an excellent study of the conflict between Yugoslavia and the Soviet Union; ZBIGNIEW K. BRZEZINSKI, *The Soviet Bloc: Unity and Conflict*, rev. ed. (1961); C. BRANDT, BENJAMIN SCHWARTZ, and J.K. FAIRBANK, *A Documentary History of Chinese Communism* (1952); VLADIMIR DEDIJER, *Tito Speaks* (1953); JANE DEGRAS (ed.), *Communist International Documents, 1919–1943*, 3 vol. (1956–65); HERBERT FEIS, *Churchill, Roosevelt, Stalin* (1957), a well-documented study of wartime diplomacy; GUNTHER NOLLAU, *Die Internationale: Wurzeln und Erscheinungsformen des proletarischen Internationalismus* (1959; Eng. trans., *International Communism and World Revolution*, 1961); E. REALE, *Avec Jacques Duclos: Au Banc des Accusés* (1958); DAVID REES, *Korea: The Limited War* (1964); HUGH SETON-WATSON, *The Pattern of Communist Revolution*, rev. ed. (1961), a study of the rise of Communism in eastern Europe.

Developments since Stalin: ADAM BROMKE (ed.), *The Communist States at the Crossroads, Between Moscow and Peking* (1965); ALEXANDER DALLIN (ed.), *Diversity in International Communism: A Documentary Record, 1961–63* (1963); HELENE CARRERE D'ENCAUSSE and STUART R. SCHRAM, *Le Marxisme et l'Asie, 1853–1964* (1965; Eng. trans., *Marxism and Asia: An Introduction with Readings*); EDWARD CRANKSHAW, *The New Cold War: Moscow v. Peking* (1963); GHITA IONESCU, *The Break-up of the Soviet Empire in Eastern Europe* (1965); WALTER LAQUEUR and LEOPOLD LABEDZ (eds.), *Polycentrism* (1962), a collection of essays on dissent in the Communist parties; WOLFGANG LEONHARD, *Kreml ohne Stalin* (1959; Eng. trans., *The Kremlin Since Stalin*, 1962); THE RUSSIAN INSTITUTE, COLUMBIA UNIVERSITY, *The Anti-Stalin Campaign and International Communism* (1956), an annotated text of Khrushchev's secret speech in 1956, with some other documents; HUGH SETON-WATSON, *The Imperialist Revolutionaries* (1978); H. GORDON SKILLING, *The Governments of Communist East Europe* (1966); MICHEL TATU, *Le Pouvoir en U.R.S.S.* (1967; Eng. trans., *Power in the Kremlin*, 1969); DONALD S. ZAGORIA, *The Sino-Soviet Conflict, 1956–61* (1962); G.R. URBAN (ed.), *Détente* (1976).

Communist doctrine since Stalin: MILORAD M. DRACHKOVITCH (ed.), *Fifty Years of Communism in Russia* (1968); LEONARD SCHAPIRO (ed.), *The USSR and the Future* (1962), essays by specialists on various aspects of the party program of 1961; GUSTAV WETTER, *Dialektischer und historischer Materialismus* (1962; Eng. trans., *Soviet Ideology Today*, 1966); ROY GODSON and STEPHEN HASELER, *Eurocommunism: Implications for East and West* (1978).

(L.B.S.)

Community, Biological

A biological, or natural, community consists of all of the organisms that live together in a given environment and, in various ways, affect one another. Thus, a forest, with its trees providing food, shelter, and shade for animals, its undergrowth plants, its many animals feeding on the different plant species and on one another, and its soil bacteria and fungi, constitutes a biological community. In oceans and lakes, plankton communities of small organisms found suspended in the water include bacteria, fungi, algae, and microscopic animals feeding on them and on other animals. Because these organisms all take material from the water and release material back to the water, the community is closely related to its water environment by chemical exchange. The plankton community and its environment can be thought of as a functional system in which community-plus-environment is called an ecosystem. Similarly, the forest, considered together with the soil and air from which it takes materials and which is affected by its organisms, is an ecosystem (see ECOSYSTEM).

COMMUNITY CONCEPTS

Community and ecosystem are among the most basic concepts of ecology, and there are a number of related terms. In European and Russian writing a natural community may sometimes be referred to as a biocenose. The particular environment of a given community (or of a species population) is called its habitat, which term also has a European equivalent, biotope. Russian authors use the term biogeocenose as the equivalent of ecosystem.

Terminology

Several kinds of subdivisions can be recognized within a natural community. Distinctive groups of organisms, such as those in a rotting log or in a water-filled hole at the base of a tree, are microcommunities, occupying microhabitats. A subdivision of a community defined by the taxonomic relationship of its organisms is a taxocene. Thus, the birds of the forest are a taxocene, and the small crustaceans of the plankton in a lake are a taxocene. A subdivision of community defined by vertical position is a stratum (*e.g.*, the low shrubs of a forest constitute a layer or stratum of vegetation); a subdivision considered in terms of time is a phase or aspect (*e.g.*, the different groups of flowers that bloom in the spring and in the summer in a forest). A grouping of plants of the same stratum and of similar form may be called a synusia.

Communities can also be grouped into larger systems. In a given land area there may be a pattern of different kinds of forests, ranging from valleys to dry slopes of hills. This pattern of communities and their habitats (of which man and his effects may be part) is a landscape. In a pond or lake the plankton community, plus the shore community and the bottom organisms, together are all parts of the pond or lake ecosystem. On a still higher level, all the organisms of the Earth's surface form a world community, or biosphere. The biosphere, together with its water, soil, and air environment, is a world ecosystem, or ecosphere, though many authors also use the term biosphere in this larger sense, meaning a world ecosystem.

COMMUNITY STRUCTURE

A forest is usually a mixture of plants of different types—dominant trees, plus shrubs and various kinds of herbs, mosses, and lichens. The different types of plants, in terms of height, form, manner of growth, and kind of foliage, are termed growth forms. In most forests of eastern North America and western Europe one of two growth forms—broad-leaved deciduous trees, or needle-leaved evergreen trees—will be most conspicuous and make up the greatest part of the plant life. In certain communities broad-leaved evergreen shrubs may be most conspicuous; a prairie may consist largely of grasses, but with other types of plants present. In each case the community includes a number of different growth forms, each represented by a number of plant species. The one or two growth forms that are most important are said to dominate the community. The major growth forms of the community determine its over-all appearance or structure. The structure of a plant community on land, as determined by its growth forms, is called its physiognomy.

Growth forms

Life-forms. The plant types, as distinguished in another conceptual system, are termed life-forms. Instead of the many characteristics of plants by which growth forms are distinguished, life-forms are defined by the relationship of the embryonic growing tissues (from which new stems and branches will come) to the ground surface. The life-forms are (1) phanerophytes—trees and shrubs with growing tissues in buds well above the ground; (2) chamaephytes—low shrubs with buds within 25 centimetres of the ground; (3) hemicryptophytes—perennial herbs with growing tissues at ground level; (4) geophytes—perennial herbs with underground bulbs, buried horizontal stems, etc.; (5) therophytes—annual herbs with growing tissues surviving unfavourable seasons only in seeds; and (6) hydrophytes—aquatic plants. The percentages of the life-forms in a list of plant species for a community or landscape constitute a life-form spectrum. Because the different life-forms represent the ways in which plants are adapted to survive unfavourable seasons, the life-form spectrum expresses aspects of the community's adaptation to its environment. Thus, the phanerophytes predominate in the life-form spectrum of a tropical forest, the hemicryptophytes in temperate forests and grasslands, the therophytes in some deserts, and the hemicryptophytes and chamaephytes in Arctic tundra. Life-form and growth form concepts are most commonly applied to land plants, but similar categories can be defined for animals and aquatic communities.

Vertical and horizontal patterns. Growth forms and life-forms relate to stratification—a general characteristic of communities. Plant communities on land show vertical differentiation when the different life-forms and growth forms bear their leaves at different distances above the ground. This stratification is strongly related to light conditions because a given stratum is adapted to the light intensity at its own level and it reduces the light intensity for lower strata. Light intensity in a forest decreases downward; the light reaching leaves of the different strata decreases from full sunlight for the uppermost trees, to approximately 10–50% of full sunlight for smaller trees, 5–10% for shrubs, and 1–5% for herbs. The animal taxocenes of a community also show stratification. In a forest three groups of bird species may be distinguished: those feeding in the tree canopy, those near ground level, and those in foliage of shrubs and low trees between these. Strata involving roots of different plant species, and different animal species, may be recognized from the soil surface downward. Stratification in relation to light and depth occurs also in plankton communities. Marked vertical differentiation is observed in shore communities and involves water depth and light intensity below tide levels, exposure to air and other factors within the tidal belt.

Many communities also show patterns of horizontal differentiation. On the forest floor scattered patches of different herb species may be observed. In some cases these patches are caused by environmental differences within the forest—differences in light intensity or small undulations in the soil surface, for example, that affect distributions of plant species. In some cases the patches result from growth of plant colonies that spread by underground stems from a common parent; in others, they may result from interactions between species, as in a parasitic plant that forms patches where the roots of its host species occur. Individuals of plant species are not usually scattered at random through the horizontal space of the community; they show clumped or clustered distributions. Many animal populations, both on land and in aquatic communities, also have clumped distributions. A less common condition is spacing that is more regular than a random distribution. Shrubs in some deserts have regular distributions, and singing birds and some other animals appear to occupy definite territories with roughly equal areas, so that individuals or breeding pairs are evenly spaced.

In the community some species tend to occur together in the same patches, others to occur separately. The tendency to occur together has different causes for different associations of species. Two species may be responding in similar ways to place-to-place differences in light intensity or other environmental factors within the forest; but another pair of species may occur together because one is dependent on the other. The tendency of individuals to occur separately may result because each species responds differently to environmental factors, or because effects produced by one species tend to inhibit or exclude others. Species thus relate differently to environments and to one another within the community, and complex patterns of patchiness and horizontal differentiation of the community can result from these different responses.

Time relations. Communities also show differentiation in time. In plankton different species of algae appear and disappear to give way to other species during the annual cycle of seasons. In a broad-leaved deciduous forest one group of herbs blooms early in spring before leaves are on the trees; other groups bloom in later spring, early or later summer, or fall. Different insect species appear and disappear as the seasons progress, and bird species respond differently to seasons, some migrating and others remaining throughout the year. Organisms also show rhythms of behaviour related to daily time. Some animals are active in the daytime, others at dusk, still others at night. Flowers of different plant species are open at times of day that coincide with the activity of the animals that pollinate them. Many plankton animals migrate upward toward the water surface at night and downward away from intense light in the daytime, but different species have different patterns and extents of vertical migration. The complex rhythms of the tides govern the activities of many shore-dwelling organisms. Plant and animal species of a community thus differ in their relationships to time (see PERIODICITY, BIOLOGICAL).

Interactions. Species within the community also differ in sources of food and ways of interacting. Three major ways of obtaining food may be recognized in a community: photosynthesis, ingestion (eating), and absorption. Green plants, using carbon dioxide and water and with the aid of sunlight energy captured by the pigment chlorophyll, photosynthesize their own food. Green plants are thus autotrophs, or self-feeders. From sugars and other simple food compounds formed in photosynthesis, they are able to produce the great variety of more complex organic compounds they need. Animals for the most part consume or ingest food by mouth, taking the tissues of other organisms into a digestive tract and breaking them down into simple food compounds that can be absorbed through the wall of the digestive tract. Bacteria and fungi absorb food through the surfaces of their cells. In many cases they excrete digestive substances into their environment, decomposing food into simpler compounds that can be absorbed. Animals, bacteria, and fungi are thus heterotrophs, dependent on other organisms for their food.

These three means of nutrition—photosynthesis, ingestion, and absorption—represent major directions of evolution, corresponding, with a few exceptions, to major groups of higher organisms (plants, animals, and fungi). Among fungi different species are adapted to decompose and use different sources of food. Among animals a wide variety of means of feeding is observed. Some animal species are herbivores, consuming the tissues of plants; others are carnivores living on animal tissues or fungivores that eat fungi. Carnivores that capture living animals are called predators; but many animals live as parasites on or within other animals, usually larger than themselves, from which they take food. Animals that feed on dead tissues of other organisms are scavengers; those that use a variety of living and dead plant and animal food are omnivores. Many aquatic animals filter a mixture of dead particles and living micro-organisms from the water and use some of this organic material as food. Most animals consume only a fairly narrow range of food sources. Because an animal parasite must be adapted to the chemical characteristics of its host and must have a life cycle adapted to infecting its host, many animal parasites feed primarily or wholly on one host species. Many herbivores, especially among the insects, feed on only a few species of plants. These herbivores have evolved tolerance toward the distinctive chemicals in the tissues of their food plants, including chemicals evolved by the plants that make their tissues relatively unpalatable to most animals (see BIOTIC INTERACTION).

Thus, most species are food specialists, differing from other species in the same community in the source of their food. Species differ in other ways of relating to one another. They may, for example, variously affect one another's environment. An herb growing beneath a tree in a forest must be adapted to the low light intensity of the tree's shade and to the chemical effects produced by the tree in the soil where the herb grows. Some plant species release toxic materials to the soil, preventing some other species from growing nearby. Some species rely on another species for shelter, support, transportation, or concealment. Many plants live as epiphytes (plants not

Stratification of communities

Internal patterning

Feeding adaptations

rooted in soil but living among the branches of trees or on other supports) supported by another plant; the lichens on the bark of a tree, and the orchids borne on high branches of tropical trees are epiphytes. Many marine animals live on the surface of another animal. A close, sustained living together of two species or kinds of organisms is referred to as symbiosis. Three kinds of sym- Kinds of biosis are recognized: (1) parasitism, in which one organ- symbiosis ism takes food from the other to its disadvantage; (2) commensalism, in which one organism gains support, shelter, or other benefit from another organism without marked disadvantage to the latter; and (3) mutualism, in which each of the two species gains food or some other advantage from the other. Many species, rather than benefitting one another, are competitors. If two species live together and use the same resource, and use of the resource by one limits the growth or population level of the other, the species are in competition. Species may compete for food sources, light, soil nutrients, space, and other resources needed for the support of their populations.

Niches and species diversity. Species differ in their positions in a community—in their relation to vertical and horizontal space, time, resource use, and manner of interacting with other species. The position and function of a species in the community in relation to other species is termed its niche. Competition relates to the niche concept. In an experimental culture if two species are in direct competition for the same resources, the population of one species will decline to extinction in the culture. From similar observations on competition and on species positions in communities, the principle of competitive exclusion can be stated: two species cannot occupy the same niche, in direct competition with one another in the same stable community. The species of the community consequently evolve toward niche difference; *i.e.*, different positions in the community by which competition between them will be reduced. A community is, thus, a system of interacting, niche-differentiated species.

Because of niche diversification, many species are able to live together in a community without direct competition. The community's richness in species is referred to as its species diversity, a quality most directly measured in terms of the number of different species found in a sample of standard size taken from a community. Another characteristic of communities is to be recognized, however, in the manner in which relative importances or abundances of species relate to one another. In some communities one species is strongly dominant, and the abundances decrease rapidly in the sequence from the first to the second and third species and beyond. In other communities no species is conspicuously more important than others, and the decline in abundance in the sequence of species is much less pronounced.

Species diversity of communities is affected by evolutionary time (the time during which a community changes and evolves), environmental stability, and favourableness Effects of of the habitat. During evolutionary time new species en- evolution ter a community, each new species adapting itself to a niche different from those of other species in the community. Even though some species become extinct, species tend to accumulate in a community, and diversity tends to increase through evolutionary time. In more rigorous and unfavourable environments, however, fewer species are able to adapt to the environment itself. Such environments imply that selective forces acting on the species are directed primarily toward adaptation to environmental hazard, rather than toward niche differentiation in relation to other species. Many communities in rigorous environments have low species diversity and high concentration of dominance. In more stable and favourable environments (such as that of the tropical rainforest) selection toward refined niche differences, acting through a long evolutionary time, has made high species diversities possible. Many of the aspects of community structure—*e.g.*, differences among species in vertical and horizontal position, time, food relations, and other interactions—are in part consequences of evolution of niche difference. Complexity of community structure

tends to increase through evolutionary time as species of different positions in the community accumulate. Community structure and appearance reflect adaptation to the environment on two levels: (1) the limitations imposed by the environment determine what growth forms can survive in the community, and (2) the niche differentiation among plant species is in part expressed by growth-form differences in stature, form, leaf type, and seasonal relations.

Productivity of organic matter. The life of the community and of all organisms in it requires energy. Photosynthesis is the source of biological energy for communities; and the creation, through the process of photosynthesis, of organic compounds from inorganic materials by the green plants of a community is termed primary productivity.

Primary productivity. Primary productivity may be measured either in terms of the amount of energy incorporated in organic compounds by photosynthesis, or in terms of the dry mass of the organic material produced. In approximate terms one dry gram of plant tissue represents 0.4 grams of organic carbon and 4.25 kilocalories of sunlight energy incorporated in organic compounds. The community's gross primary productivity is the total energy captured by green plants (or the mass equivalent of this energy) per unit area and time. The community's net primary productivity is the organic mass (or its energy equivalent) produced by photosynthesis that remains after some of that organic matter has been used in respiration (chemical reactions supporting life processes) by the photosynthesizing plants. In forests 60 to 75 percent of gross productivity may be respired by the plants; the remaining 40 to 25 percent is net productivity. In aquatic communities less than half of gross productivity may be respired by the plants.

Amounts of photosynthesis vary widely in different communities; communities may be grouped in terms of four ranges of net primary productivity as expressed in units of net dry weight in grams per square metre of earth surface area per year ($g/m^2/yr$). The ranges correspond to different environmental and vegetational conditions as shown in Table 1.

The amount of gross primary productivity represents the total energy available to carry on all the biological activities of the community if no organic matter is brought into the community from the outside. The amount of net primary productivity represents the total energy available for use by the community's heterotrophs (non-photosynthetic organisms that do not manufacture their own food like plants but that must obtain it elsewhere), the animals, bacteria, and fungi. The rate of utilization of net primary production by heterotrophs is important in determining the amount of the community's plant biomass. Biomass (or standing crop) is the amount Biomass of organic matter present in a community at a given time potentially available for harvest and use by heterotrophs. In a land community the biomass primarily comprises living and dead tissues of plants. A grassland, for example, might have a stable net primary productivity of 600 grams per square metre per year, and one-third of this plant tissue might be eaten by animals (or decomposed by bacteria or fungi) the first year, one-third of the remainder the second year, etc. A forest, by contrast, might produce 1,300 grams per square metre per year and then lose by various means only one-fortieth of it each year. In each case the portion of past production remaining in the community is its biomass. Eventually the grassland biomass will remain steady at about 1,800 grams per square metre and the forest biomass will reach about 52,000 grams per square metre. The forest and grassland differ widely not only in amounts of biomass but in biomass accumulation ratios, the ratios of plant biomass to net annual primary productivity (3 and 40 in this example). Biomass accumulation ratios and standing biomass are compared for several communities in Table 2.

The plant food harvested by plant-eating animals (herbivores) is used for their growth and activity. Herbivores

Table 1: Communities Arranged by Net Primary Productivity

net primary productivity (g/m²/yr)*	description of environment and productivity value	some examples of communities with typical productivities in each range
3,000 or more	very high productivity in particularly favourable conditions of water and nutrient availability and temperature	some young tropical forests, salt marshes, coral reefs, rice paddies, sugarcane fields
1,000–3,000	high productivities in generally favourable environments	most forests and some highly productive grasslands, some estuaries and nutrient-rich lakes
200–1,000	intermediate productivities in environments in which water or nutrients or temperature are in some respect limiting	many temperate grasslands, semi-arid woodlands and shrub-lands, many lakes and coastal w aters of oceans
200 or less	low productivities in environments that are severely limiting in some respect	dry and cold deserts, some nutrient-poor lakes, and many open waters of oceans

*net dry weight in grams per square metre of earth surface area per year.

Table 2: Comparison of Communities by Biomass

community	biomass accumulation ratio	standing biomass (kg/m²)
Forest	10–50	10–70
Shrubland	3–10	2–20
Grassland	2–5	0.2–5
Field of annual herbs	1.0	0.1–1
Plankton	0.01–0.05	0.001–0.04

in turn are harvested by a series of carnivores (flesh eaters). Such a sequence of organisms along which food is passed—for example from an oak tree (the producer) to a caterpillar (the herbivore) to a warbler (the first carnivore) and finally to a hawk (second carnivore) is called a food chain.

Secondary productivity. When organisms of the community are grouped by position along food chains, the groupings represent trophic levels. Productivities of the trophic levels above the primary (photosynthetic plant or producer) level are referred to as secondary productivities. Because many animal species feed upon a number of other species, food chains are linked together into community-wide food webs. A species' place in a food web is an important aspect of its niche. At each trophic level some of the organisms' energy is used in their own life processes, and some organisms die and decompose without being eaten by other animals. The productivity of a given trophic level, therefore, can never be more than a fraction of that of a preceding trophic level. The ratio of energy on a given trophic level to that of the preceding level is known as the efficiency of the given level. For the first and second consumer levels efficiencies tend to be around 10%. Efficiency of producers, comparing their net primary productivity with their energy source in sunlight in the visible range, is much less; *e.g.*, about 1.0 percent for many forests and even as low as 0.1 percent for some of the open-ocean plankton. Because of the loss of energy on each level, productivity must decrease up the sequence of trophic levels, forming what is known as a pyramid of productivity. In many, though not all, cases, biomasses and numbers of organisms will also decrease up the sequence of trophic levels and for illustrative purposes these can also be visualized as pyramids.

Decomposition of organic matter. Only part of net primary productivity is harvested by animals. The remainder is decomposed by bacteria and fungi, or is transported out of the community, or accumulates as net ecosystem production. In many communities the fraction of net primary production harvested by animals from tissues of living plants is small compared with the fraction utilized after death of the tissues by scavengers, bacteria, and fungi. Less than 10 percent of leaf tissue and less

than 1 percent of wood tissue of living trees in a forest may be harvested by animals. The remainder falls to the ground to form the litter covering the soil surface and is utilized by the soil community. The soil community includes animal scavengers that eat dead plant tissue, scavengers on dead animal tissue, bacteria and fungi of decomposition, and animals feeding on these organisms. Although animals contribute to the breakdown of the litter, the bacteria and fungi have the most essential role in reducing dead organic matter to inorganic end products. The major modes of nutrition previously referred to thus appear as the three major trophic (food-relation) parts of the community: producers (photosynthesizing plants), consumers (ingesting animals), and reducers or decomposers (absorbing bacteria and fungi).

The biomass of the reducers may be small compared with that of the consumers and very small compared with that of the producers. The activities of this small mass of reducers are, however, of great importance in community function. The reducers break down almost all remains of dead organisms in the community; food chains normally end in reducers. Decomposition by the reducers in most cases prevents continuing accumulation of dead remains of organisms. When such accumulation does occur, as in the peat formed in bogs, community productivity may be limited by the fact that nutrients are locked up in dead tissues. The reducers thus make possible the steady-state condition of a stable community's biomass. In this steady state the pool of organic matter in the community is relatively constant, while matter is being added to it as net primary production and subtracted from it by animal harvest and decomposition, at equal rates. Decomposition of the dead remains of organisms makes available to the soil or water the nutrients that were contained in those tissues.

Nutrient circulation. The reducers thus make possible the circulation of nutrients in the community. The producers take up inorganic nutrients (including nitrogen, phosphorus, sulfur, calcium, potassium, magnesium, and other elements) from the soil or water. The producers use these for the synthesis of certain organic compounds, and to maintain the levels necessary for the composition of protoplasm and the functioning of cells. Animals and reducers obtain these nutrient elements in their food. The nutrients are passed along food chains until released back into the environment by decomposition or excretion. In the nutrient circulation of a forest a nutrient atom or ion may be taken up from the soil into a tree root, transported upward through the tree's conducting tissues to a leaf, taken in by a caterpillar that eats the leaf, consumed then by a bird that eats the caterpillar, until, with the death and decomposition of the bird, it is released back into the soil for renewed uptake by a plant root. Many nutrients are returned from forest trees to the soil by shorter routes—by the fall of dead plant tissues to the litter and decomposition, or by washing down from plant surfaces to the soil in rain water.

Food webs

Movement of nutrients in communities

The community's biomass has a marked effect on nutrient circulation. For some elements in some communities, the greater part of the ecosystem's stock of that element is held in the tissues of the plants and a smaller part is free in the soil or water. The amount of phosphate in solution in the water, for example, may be a small fraction of the amount in plankton cells and particles. Tropical forests hold the stocks of some nutrients in relatively "tight" circulation: much of the nutrient stock is held in plant tissues, and nutrients released by leaching or litter decay by fungi are quickly reabsorbed into plants. When a forest is cut or burned, abrupt and extensive loss of nutrients from the ecosystem may occur by erosion or by downward movement of nutrients in soil water. The plankton of the open oceans is low in productivity because the settling of plankton cells and dead particles carries nutrients downward, leaving only low concentrations of critical nutrients in the lighted surface water where photosynthesis occurs. It is thus true both that nutrient resources of the environment affect community function and that community function affects observed nutrient levels in the community and its environment.

Water movement transports nutrients between the different communities—plankton, shore, and bottom—of a water body and relates these communities to one another as parts of the water ecosystem. Land ecosystems and lakes and streams receive some nutrients from the outside—by rain, dust, groundwater movement, immigration of organisms, etc.—and lose some nutrients to the outside—by settling, water movement, emigration, erosion, etc. There is, thus, some movement of nutrients between the communities of a given landscape. On a broader scale nutrients are taken up from the ocean surface into the air in the spray from waves, transported over the continents in air currents, and carried downward into land communities in rain. Nutrients from land communities are carried into streams and transported in stream water into the oceans. The ecosystems of the world are linked together by the transfer of nutrients between them into a world ecosystem, the ecosphere or biosphere (see BIOSPHERE).

COMMUNITY SUCCESSION

When gross primary productivity is greater than total community respiration, and net primary productivity is greater than the rate of harvest and decomposition, organic matter accumulates. Coal and petroleum represent surpluses of productivity over respiration accumulated in past geological time. Such surpluses are bases also of shorter term growth of communities, as is illustrated in the contrast of a mature, stable forest with a young growing forest shown in Table 3. The accumulating surplus

Table 3: Contrast in Productivity and Respiration between a Mature and Young Forest
(in g/m²/yr units)*

	gross productivity	plant respiration	decomposer respiration	animal respiration	net ecosystem production
Young forest	2,650	1,450	580	80	540
Mature forest	3,250	1,950	1,250	150	0

*net dry weight in grams per square metre of earth surface per year.

plus in the young forest may be termed a net ecosystem production. If not exported from the community, net ecosystem production implies growth in the community's biomass. Thus the young forest, with biomass of 10 kilograms per square metre, may in time mature into a forest of 50 kilograms per square metre. The process by which communities grow toward a stable, mature condition is called succession.

Developmental communities. If the forest is destroyed by fire, a new forest is established by developmental communities, which replace one another in sequence (*e.g.*, a field of annual weeds, a meadow of perennial grasses, a community of shrubs, a young forest, a mature forest like the one destroyed). If the soil has not been lost, such a succession replacing a former community is a secondary succession. A succession that develops a new soil in a bare environment is a primary succession. If a forest on a mountain slope is destroyed by an avalanche, a succession on the exposed, bare rock surface may lead back to forest by way of lichens, mosses, grasses, shrubs, and trees as dominants of successive stages. Each stage paves the way for the next stage. Thus the grasses are able to begin growth in the sparse soil formed and collected by the mosses. Growth of the grasses suppresses the mosses and forms a meadow in which a deeper soil develops. This soil permits shrubs to enter the meadow, to grow taller than the grass, and to kill the grass by shading, etc. The soil and shelter of the shrub stage permits trees to enter, grow above, and replace the shrubs. A number of developmental trends—progressive changes in community characteristics—are observed in most successions. During a succession there is usually not only increasing accumulation of biomass but also progressive increase in community height, differentiation into strata of the plant community and consequent structural complexity, productivity, effect of the community on environment, soil development, stocks of circulating nutrients, species diversity, longevity of dominant organisms, and relative stability of the community. There are exceptions to these trends in some successions. Productivity and species diversity in particular often decrease during the late stages of a succession and are lower in the stable end community.

Stable communities. The mature, relatively stable community in which a succession finally ends is termed the climax. The climax is characterized not by maximum productivity but by maximum biomass and biomass accumulation ratio, and by low or zero net ecosystem production. More broadly, the climax is characterized by steady-state function; that is, a dynamic equilibrium, a condition of relative constancy in an open system. Energy, materials, or individuals may flow through the system, but if the input and output of these are equal, the system can remain stable in its characteristics. Thus in the community steady states may be recognized in these three categories: (1) population balances, (2) energy flow, and (3) materials turnover.

The individual species populations of the climax are stabilized (relatively, and despite some fluctuation). The rate of addition of individuals by birth (and in some cases immigration) is balanced by rate of loss of individuals by death (and emigration).

Energy intake in photosynthesis is balanced by energy loss in respiration, while the community's pool of energy in organic materials remains relatively constant.

Intake of materials by photosynthesis and nutrient uptake is balanced by loss through respiration, decomposition, excretion, and leaching, while the community's biomass and nutrient stock remain relatively constant.

The community is thus (like an individual organism or a cell) an open system through which energy and materials flow. The intimate relation of the community to its environment in this flow provides justification for the concept of ecosystem. Like an individual organism, the community sustains itself by continuing the intake of available free energy in organic compounds. Like the organism, it uses this energy to maintain its function and complex structure. Like the organism, the community grows with increase of mass and structural complexity to a final, mature state. There may, however, be different reasons for growth and maturity. The manner of growth, functional organization, and point of reproductive maturity are determined in the organism by its inherited genetic instructions. There are no corresponding community-wide instructions determining succession and climax. These phenomena are resultants of the manners in which species populations interact, and of overall balance of materials and energy flow. The character of the climax is determined by the resources and limitations of environment, and by the characteristics of the species that interact and maintain themselves in that environment.

Open system concept

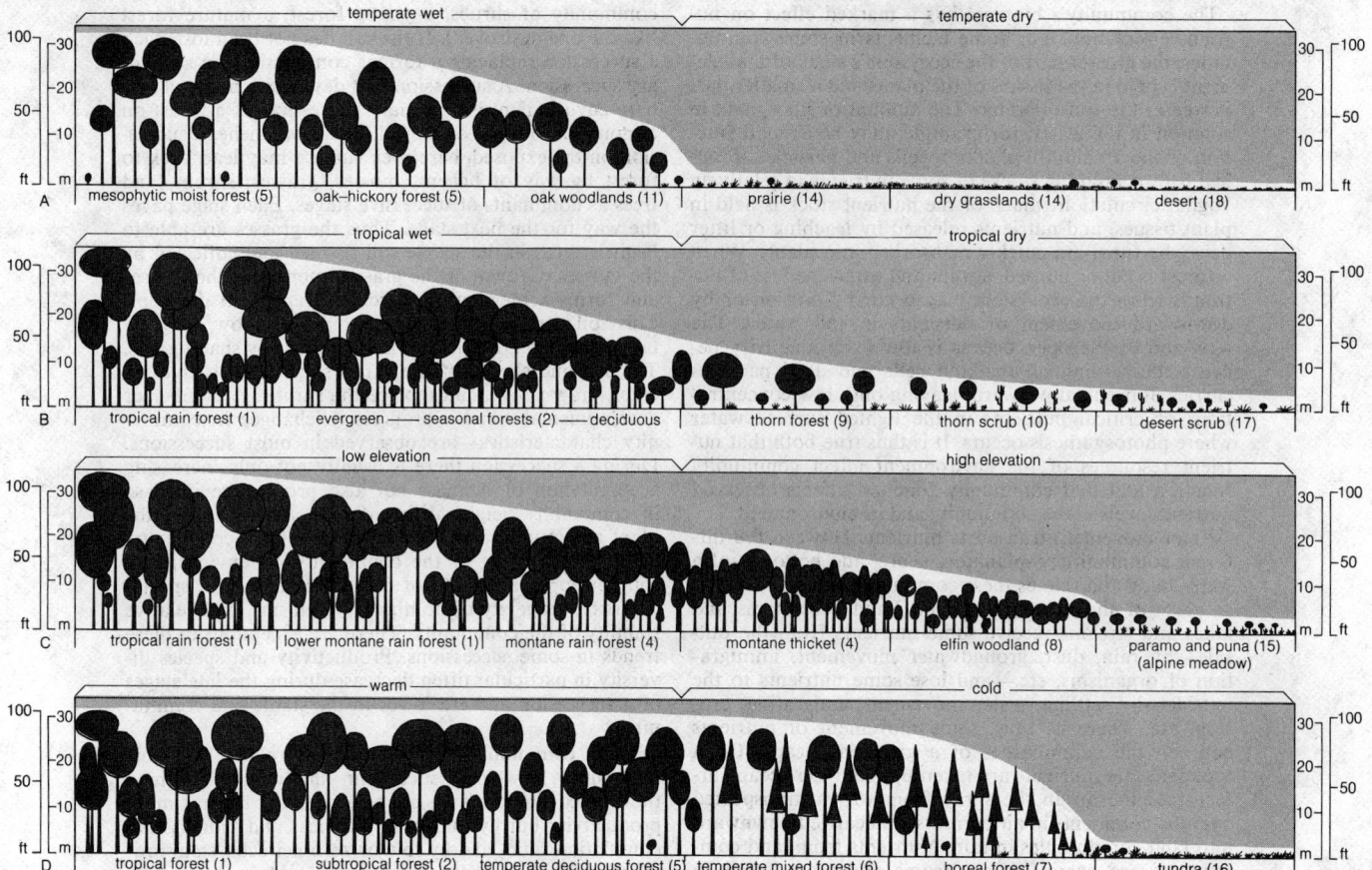

Figure 1: *Four ecoclines representing major climatic gradients.*
(A) From moist to dry climates in the Temperate Zone. (B) From moist to dry climates in the tropics. (C) From low to high elevations in the tropics. (D) From the tropics northward to cold climates of the far north. Numbers refer to formation types of Table 5.
From (A,D) R.H. Whittaker, *Communities and Ecosystems* (© Copyright, Robert H. Whittaker, 1970), The Macmillan Company; (B,C) Beard, *Ecology (U.S.)* (1955), by permission of the Duke University Press

The stability of the climax is suggestive of the homeostasis (the constancy of function and internal conditions) in the organism, but the mechanisms are different. The community has no central regulatory system such as the nervous, circulatory, and endocrine systems provide in higher animals. Yet the community tends to stabilize itself and to return to normal after disturbances. The expression "balance of nature" refers to this self-stabilizing, steady-state condition.

COMMUNITIES IN SPACE

Landscape patterns. Many of the habitats of a given landscape are related to one another along environmental gradients (adjacent regions of changing elevation, of soil characteristics, of surface moisture conditions, etc.). Some of these gradients are interrupted by cliffs or other barriers, but the habitats of a landscape may be conceived as forming a pattern of environmental gradients. At each habitat, or point in this pattern, a climax natural community may develop. Characteristic species and functions of the community are adapted to the habitat in which they occur. Along a continuous environmental gradient the characteristics of one community change, often smoothly, into those of other communities. The environmental gradient is thus paralleled by a gradient of communities developed in response to the environmental gradient. An environmental gradient comprising many environmental factors that change together along spatial gradients may be termed a complex gradient; its corresponding gradient of communities is a coenocline. The complex gradient and coenocline together form an ecosystem gradient, or ecocline (see Figure 1).

Ecocline

A pattern of climax communities corresponds to the environments of the landscape. Climax communities over much of the area may have been replaced by disturbance and successional communities; but the climax pattern represents the potential maximum development of natural communities in equilibrium with environment for that landscape. A landscape is a pattern of ecosystems related to one another by (1) intergradation as parts of ecoclines, (2) occurrence of populations of the same species in different communities, (3) movements of materials and organisms, and (4) developmental relations of communities to one another (if some are successional).

Climax interpretation. There are three major approaches to interpreting climax communities: (1) monoclimax theory, (2) polyclimax theory, and (3) climax pattern hypothesis.

Monoclimax theory emphasizes the convergence of successions in a given landscape from different beginnings toward similar climaxes. Thus, in a forested area successions on a rocky hillside and a valley bottom will both lead to forests, though these forests may consist of different tree species. Because of this relative convergence, one may consider that in principle all the successional communities of an area could converge on a single (broadly defined) climax community. This hypothetical single climax is termed the climatic climax or monoclimax. If one of the communities of the area is interpreted as the climatic climax, the other stable communities present are termed proclimaxes.

Polyclimax theory recognizes more than one possible climax community. As already observed, the communities of an area form a pattern in which a number of types of stable or climax communities may be distinguished. Many ecologists prefer to grant the occurrence of a number of climax communities in an area, hence they accept a polyclimax interpretation. One of these communities may be considered most typical, or most representative of the general climate of the area, and this community may be regarded as the climatic climax. Other stable communities may be termed topographic climaxes (differing from the climatic climax because of topographic position) or edaphic climaxes (differing because of soil characteristics).

The climax pattern hypothesis allows one to visualize the landscape as a pattern of intergrading communities corresponding to the pattern of environmental gradients. The type of community that forms that largest fraction of the climax pattern and is most widespread in the landscape (if undisturbed) is then regarded as the prevailing climax or climatic climax.

Community gradients. The appropriateness of the climax-pattern-hypothesis interpretation results from the manner in which species populations and communities relate to environmental gradients. Community samples, including counts of plant populations, can be taken at intervals along an environmental gradient to form a transect (a line along which measurements are taken). The rise and fall of species populations along the gradient can then be observed. Results of interest emerge; especially significant are the symmetrical, bell-shaped form of the majority of such population curves and the scattered positions of the modes or peaks of the species distributions scattered along the gradient. The fact that the curves generally overlap broadly, rather than forming abrupt breaks where one species excludes another, is also apparent. The coenocline, or gradient of communities, may appear as a continuum when species populations are observed along a transect, or when growth forms are observed along a climatic gradient, as in Figure 1.

Such study supports two principles that are basic to the interpretation of communities. The first is the principle of species individuality that states that each species is distributed on the basis of its own genetic, physiological, and life-cycle characteristics and ways of relating to environment and other species; consequently no two species will be distributed alike. The second is the principle of community continuity. It states that along continuous environmental gradients, natural communities in general intergrade continuously, rather than appearing as distinct species combinations that give way abruptly, along distinct boundaries, to other species combinations.

Although they are basic, some exceptions to these principles must be noted. Certain pairs of symbiotic species have parallel distributions. Populations of certain animal species exclude one another along a boundary, rather than overlapping broadly. There are some discontinuities between communities that are not produced by soil or topographic changes. The forest edge between forest and grassland is in some areas such a discontinuity, the abruptness of which may be increased by effects of fires that burn the grassland up to the forest edge but do not burn the forest. Steep community transitions, known as ecotones, often show an "edge effect." The transition zone is a distinctive community of high species diversity, combining species of both communities that are bounded by the edge with other species that occur primarily in the edge itself.

Habitat differentiation. Underlying the manner in which species are distributed along a gradient is an evolutionary phenomenon related to the principle of competitive exclusion referred to earlier. Species may escape direct competition either by exploring different niches or by occupying different habitats. Species that are partial competitors (with overlapping niches) evolve toward different locations of their population centres along environmental gradients. Many species that adapt to an environmental gradient and to interaction with one another do so by evolving toward a scattering of population centres along the gradient. Through evolutionary time additional species fit themselves into a gradient of communities (coenocline), with population centres between those of other species. As they do so they tend to narrow the distributions of the other species that are nearest to them along the gradient and that overlap with them in niche. Coenoclines may thus evolve from the condition of relatively few species with broad distributions to that of a larger number of species with narrower distributions.

Sampling communities along transects

Evolution of coenoclines

Gradient analysis. An arrangement of community samples (or species) in relation to one or more environmental gradients or axes, by either direct or indirect means, is an ordination and an essential means of accomplishing gradient analysis. Gradient analysis is the study of communities in terms of how gradients of environment, species populations, and community characteristics relate to one another. Through gradient analysis the communities of a landscape may be analyzed and related as a pattern of intergrading communities. In one approach community samples are arranged on a diagram with major environmental gradients as axes as in Figure 2. The samples are classified into types of communities,

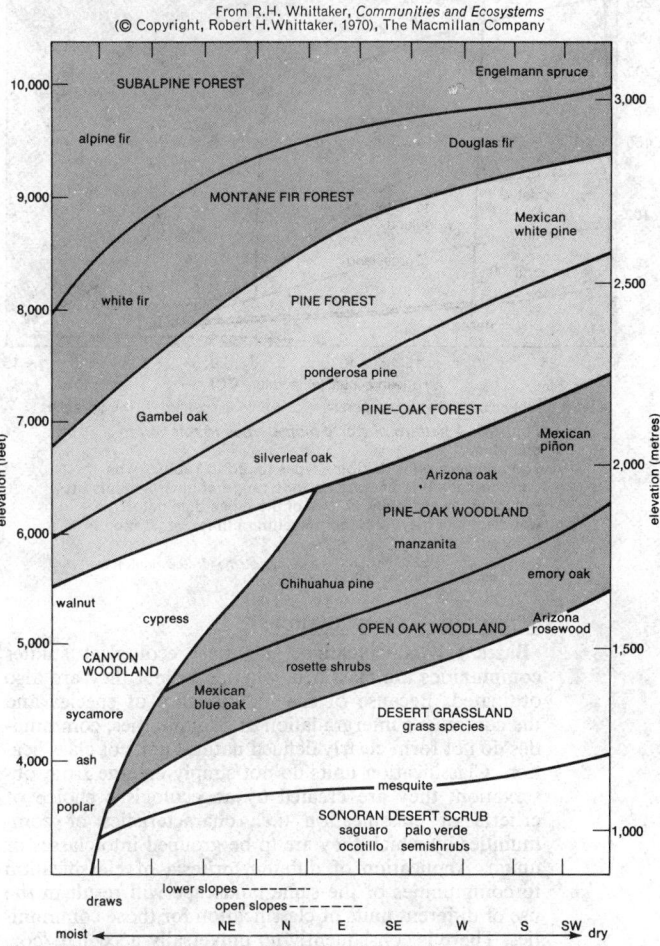

From R.H. Whittaker, *Communities and Ecosystems*
(© Copyright, Robert H. Whittaker, 1970), The Macmillan Company

Figure 2: *A mountain vegetation pattern in relation to environment.*
Distributions of major kinds of plant communities are shown in relation to elevation and topographic moisture gradients in the Santa Catalina Mountains, Arizona. Locations of boundaries are approximate.

and boundaries between these may be drawn onto the diagram. Types of communities are then shown in their relations to one another and to the environments of the landscape pattern. The types in Figure 2 have oblique boundaries because of the effects of topography, as well as elevation, on temperature and moisture conditions.

Alternatively, from a set of community samples pairs of end-point samples can be chosen to represent extremes of environmental gradients. Other samples can then be arranged relative to these end-point samples to form what is known as an indirect ordination. This ordination can also be displayed as a diagram that will show the changes in community composition in response to the environment.

Whether direct or indirect, gradient analysis has as its objects the observation and interpretation of relationships among environments, species, and communities, and the representation of the range of community variation of a landscape as a comprehensible, unified pattern.

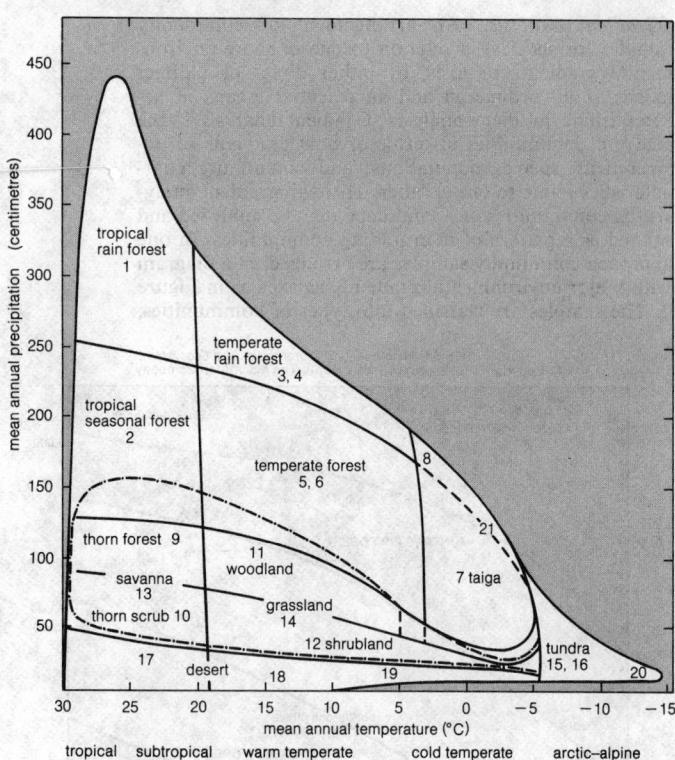

Figure 3: *A pattern of world biome types in relation to climates.*
The numbers refer to biome types listed in Table 5. The dot-and-dash line encloses a wide range of environments in which either grassland or one of the types dominated by woody plants may form the prevailing climax vegetation in different areas.
From R.H.Whittaker, *Communities and Ecosystems* (© Copyright, Robert H. Whittaker, 1970), The Macmillan Company

COMMUNITY CLASSIFICATION

Bases for classification. In most ecological studies communities are classified, whether or not they are also ordinated. Because of the individuality of species and the continuous intergradation of communities, communities do not form clearly defined natural units of classification. Classification units do not simply emerge from observation; they are created by an ecologist's choice of criteria of classification (*i.e.*, characteristics of communities by which they are to be grouped into classes or units). Application of different criteria of classification to communities of the same landscape will result in the use of different units of classification for those communities. There is consequently no universally accepted "correct" approach to classifying communities, comparable to the system of species and other categories into which organisms are classified.

Means of classification

Some of the principal approaches to community classification are given in Table 4. Although these and other approaches are in use, the classifications most widely in use are those that have been based on species composition and on physiognomy, that is to say, the associations and biomes, or formations.

Associations. The system of classification most used for intensive study of particular landscapes has as its basic unit the association. The system considers all plant species in community samples as a basis for classifying those samples into units. In grouping samples into associations the ecologist seeks, however, for character species; *i.e.*, those species that are centred in or largely restricted to the communities considered to belong to a given association. These character species are emphasized as means of defining associations, though dominance and other criteria may also be considered. Associations and other units are given latinized names (*e.g.*, the Caricetum curvulae is an association characterized by the sedge, *Carex curvula*). Associations may be grouped into units termed alliances on the next higher level; alliances may be grouped into orders, and orders

Table 4: Some Approaches to Community Classification

criteria upon which judgements are based	terms used for the units of classification
Physiognomy	biome or formation
Dominant species of major stratum	dominance-type
Dominant species of the different strata	sociation
Species composition using full range of plant species present	association
Composition of the undergrowth independent of the dominant species of the canopy	forest site-type
Quantitative comparisons of composition of community samples	noda
Characteristics of habitats	habitat-type
Kinds of communities recognized as belts forming a sequence along a major environmental gradient	life-zone, littoral-zone
Characteristics of landscapes as patterns rather than particular communities	landscape-type

into classes. These higher-level units may also be defined by character species, which are species that are too broadly distributed to become character species of associations but are centred in or are largely restricted to one of the higher level units. Vegetation of an area may thus be classified into a formal arrangement in a graded series of units from classes down to associations and lower units. The units below the association (subassociation, variant, and facies) may be defined by differential species and quantitative relations of species. (Differential species are those that tend to be present in one and absent in the other of two units being compared, regardless of their distributions in relation to other units.) The lower level units make possible effective use of plant communities to indicate habitat properties and the potential of land for agriculture or forestry. This system has been important not only in the development of vegetation mapping but also in the use of vegetation for its indicator value in the intensively used land of the western European continent.

Biomes or formations. A system of classification is also used for treatment of communities on an extensive scale for whole continents and the world. Treatment of vegetation on a continental scale generally deals primarily with prevailing climax vegetation, uses physiognomy as the criterion of community units and community expression of climate, and employs the formation as its unit of classification. A formation groups together the communities of a given continent that are of similar growth-form structure in response to broadly similar environmental conditions (especially climate). In studies concerned with animals as well as plants, formations are generally termed biomes. Similar formations or biomes occur as convergent responses to similar climates on the different continents. A grouping of convergent formations or biomes of the different continents is a formation type or biome type. Many systems of biome types have been proposed by ecologists and geographers; Table 5 employs one of these many systems for its elaboration of the biome types of the world.

Worldwide classification systems

The relations of biome types to climate are represented in Figure 3, which represents the adaptation of world vegetation to world climate. Mean annual temperature and precipitation are considered to be the principal factors determining physiognomy. On the basis of these factors approximate boundaries between major physiognomic types are shown, and the relations of the biome-types in Table 5 to these is indicated by their numbers. Community gradients involving some of these formations are illustrated in Figure 1. The pattern of Figure 3 cannot adequately represent (1) the effects of different seasonal relations of temperature and precipitation, notably the contrasts of maritime and continental climates; (2) the effects of fire in determining occurrence of communities dominated by grasses rather than woody plants in many areas; (3) effects of differences in soil; and (4) the continuous intergradations between formations. Despite these simplifications the figure offers, as does figure 2, a representation of the broad pattern of natural communities on land in relation to climates.

Table 5: Biome Types of the World

biome types	characteristics and environment	distribution	biome types	characteristics and environment	distribution
1. Tropical rain forest*	large forests with many tree species, epiphytes (unrooted plants supported on trees), and lianas (vines) in areas of abundant rainfall throughout the year	Southeast Asia, Africa, South and Central America, northeast Australia	16. Arctic tundra	treeless vegetation of cold climates north of the taiga, formed by varied combinations of lichen and moss, grass and sedges, and dwarf shrubs	northern North America and Eurasia
2. Tropical seasonal forest and monsoon forest	forests adapted to climates with a marked dry season in which some or all leaves are shed	extensive in Southeast Asia; occurs in other tropical areas	17. Tropical deserts	sparse vegetation in very dry subtropical climates	North Africa, Asia Minor, Southwest Africa, West South America
3. Giant temperate rain forest	very large forests (trees up to 100 metres tall) in areas of abundant rainfall	northwest coast of United States, eastern Australia	18. Warm-temperate deserts	scrub of small-leaved or spiny shrubs or both, in arid climates	south central Asia, southwestern North America, Australia, Argentina
4. Montane rain forests and thickets	smaller evergreen forests of wet temperate climates of mountains	throughout the tropics and in the Southern Hemisphere	19. Cooltemperate semi-desert scrub	shrub communities of sagebrush or other shrubs with grasses in semi-arid climates	western United States, interior Asia, Southern Hemisphere
5. Temperate deciduous forests	trees with broad leaves that are shed in winter, mainly in continental, moderately humid climates	Northern Hemisphere mostly, especially in eastern United States, eastern Asia and western Europe	20. Arctic-alpine deserts	sparse vegetation of widely scattered, plants, or lichens only or rock or snow, in climates at extreme cold	at high elevations, in the far north in America and Eurasia, and in Greenland and Antarctica
6. Temperate evergreen forests	either needle-leaved or broad-leaved evergreen trees or both, in moderately humid temperate climates	all continents (excluding Antarctica)	21. Bog†	wet communities with sphagnum moss, mostly in cold climates	worldwide, most extensive in Northern Hemisphere, especially Ireland and Scotland
7. Taiga or boreal forests	needle-leaved forests, mostly evergreen, of cool temperate (subarctic and subalpine) climates	across northern North America and Eurasia and southward at high elevations in mountains	22. Tropical fresh-water swamp forest	evergreen forests of soils seasonally or permanently submerged by water	Amazon basin and other areas at tropical forest
8. Elfin woodlands	dense evergreen thickets with heavy moss and lichen growth in cool subalpine belts of tropical mountains	mountainous tropics	23. Temperate freshwater swamp forest	cypress swamp and other forest of seasonally or permanently submerged soils	southeastern United States and other humid temperate areas
9. Thorn forests and thorn woodlands	communities of Acacias and other trees armed with spines, often in open growth, in moderately dry climates	widespread in the tropics	24. Mangrove swamps	forests of small evergreen broad-leaf trees, growing in shallow brackish water or wet soil	tropical coasts and estuaries
10. Thorn scrub	dense communities of spiny shrubs and small trees, often with succulents, in dry climates of the tropics	widespread in the tropics	25. Marshes	wet soil communities of grasses or grasslike plants	worldwide
11. Temperate woodlands	communities of small trees in open spacing, generally with well-developed undergrowth, in climates too dry or otherwise unfavourable for forests	on all continents	26. Marine pelagic‡	plankton (small plants and animals suspended in the water) of the open oceans, fish, marine mammals and birds	worldwide
12. Temperate shrublands	diverse shrub communities in temperate climates, including as types, maccia or maquis, garrigue, chaparral, heath, etc.	on all continents	27. Marine benthos	communities of the ocean bottom, at greater depths limited to micro-organisms and animals living on, or rooted in, or burrowing in the bottom mud or ooze	worldwide
13. Savannas	tropical grasslands, often with scattered trees, in moderately dry climates or in consequence of soil conditions and fire	extensive in Africa, also in Southeast Asia and South America	28. Marine rocky littoral	animals and algae living on rocky coasts, many of them attached to the rocks and subject to wave action and tidal exposure	marine coasts throughout the world
14. Temperate grasslands	plains, prairies, steppe, pampas, and veld, moderately dry climates	North America, Eurasia, South America, South Africa, New Zealand	29. Marine sandy littoral	animals and algae living on or in the sand of beaches and sandy shores in shallow water	marine coasts throughout the world
15. Alpine meadows	treeless vegetation above the subalpine forests or thickets in cold mountain climates; sedge or grass meadows, paramo and puna, tussock grasslands	worldwide at high elevations	30. Estuarine and marine mudflat	microscopic algae of the mud surface, animals living in the mud, and plankton of bays and estuaries	marine coasts throughout the world
			31. Freshwater lentic	communities of inland lakes and ponds, including in the biometype the plankton, bottom, and shore organisms	on all continents
			32. Freshwater lotic	communities of streams and rivers, with organisms of fast-flowing water and rocky bottoms, and of slow-flowing water and sand or mud bottoms, as major subdivisions	on all continents

*Numbers 1–21 refer to biomes shown in Figures 1 and 3.   †Numbers 21–25 are biomes determined primarily by wet soils.   ‡Numbers 26–32 are aquatic biomes.

BIBLIOGRAPHY. W.C. ALLEE *et al., Principles of Animal Ecology* (1949), a classic reference work that is valuable for most topics; J. BRAUN-BLANQUET, *Plant Sociology* (1932; German editions, *Pflanzensoziologie,* 1951 and 1964), the standard European textbook on plant communities; PIERRE DANSEREAU, *Biogeography: An Ecological Perspective* (1957), especially relevant for its treatment of life forms and formation classes; S.R. EYRE, *Vegetation and Soils: A World Picture* (1963), a concise treatment of world vegetation; S. CHARLES KENDEIGH, *Animal Ecology* (1961), a discussion of animal communities, niches, and biomes; EUGENE P. ODUM, *Fundamentals of Ecology,* 2nd ed. (1959), a standard textbook in the field of ecology; A.W.F. SCHIMPER, *Plant-Geography upon a Physiological Basis* (1903), one of the classic treatises on plant communities of the world; R.H. WHITTAKER, *Communities and Ecosystems* (1970), a brief, up-to-date textbook; "Classification of Natural Communities," *Bot. Rev.;* 28:1–239 (1962), a review of theory and approaches to classifying communities; and "Gradient Analysis of Vegetation," *Biol. Rev.,* 42:207–264 (1967), a review of ordination and gradient analysis.

(R.H.W.)

Comparative Law, Study of

The worldwide development of comparative legal studies has been one of the striking features of the second half of the 20th century. Political scientists and lawyers recognize the importance of keeping abreast of current developments in the field of foreign law, and, to supply their need, learned societies, conferences, and publications abound. Moreover, every university jealous of its reputation now teaches comparative law, and, in certain places, it has become a compulsory subject in the syllabus for study and examination.

THE DEVELOPMENT OF COMPARATIVE LAW

The expression comparative law is a modern one, first used in the 19th century when it became clear that the comparison of legal institutions deserved a systematic approach, in order to increase understanding of foreign cultures and to further legal progress. Nevertheless, other systems had been contrasted—albeit unmethodically —long before. From early times, certain scholars and researchers have made use of the comparative technique, conscious of the advantages to be gained.

Ancient roots of law. In the 6th century BC according to legend, the Greek lawgiver Solon, faced with the task of compiling the laws of Athens, gathered together the laws of various city-states. Similarly, in the 5th century BC, a Roman commission was reported to have consulted the statutes of the Greek communities in Sicily before giving Rome the famous *Laws of the Twelve Tables.* Aristotle, in the 4th century, is said to have collated the constitutions of no less than 158 city-states in his effort to devise a model constitution. Thus, from ancient times it would seem that those wishing to set up a just system have sought inspiration and example from abroad. The true expansion of comparative law, however, was hindered by a number of obstacles—such as the parochialism of social groups, contempt for foreigners, or "barbarians," and belief in the sacredness or everlasting inviolability of inherited legal rules.

Although certain practices and institutions that crept into Roman law undoubtedly originated in the imperial provinces, Roman legal science took no cognizance of comparative law. Nor can the medieval universities in Europe be said to have displayed great concern for comparative law. Over the centuries, their interest was limited to Roman law, supplemented in certain areas or modified to some extent by canon law. While members of the first school of thought (called glossators) confined themselves to the task of elucidating the meaning of the Roman codes of law, their successors (the postglossators) undertook the systematic arrangement and adaptation of that law to prevailing social conditions. At no time was there an effort to compare laws. The customary laws that one found here and there could hardly hold any interest for scholars labouring to give society a model of ideal justice and to discover or elucidate a higher law above man's making. Indeed, in their opinion, local laws were no more than rubbish and evidently doomed to decay. To compare these local practices would have been a waste of time; to compare them with Roman laws would have been almost indecent.

Role of judges. Such contempt was not characteristic of the attitude of the judges and lawyers whose everyday duty it was to administer justice, mainly by applying the customary law. Their material contained areas of uncertainty and required adaptation to social needs. In the work of ascertaining the content of a custom, and in the task of filling the gaps of customs and thus fitting the law for its role, judge or lawyer in fact frequently had to consider which customs to allow to prevail. In so doing, he had to tackle the problem of deciding whether one custom was more just than another and how far he should go in introducing concepts of ideal justice (based on Roman law) that were being promoted by the universities. Two processes were thus at work: the elimination of conflicting local customs and the acceptance and rejection of elements of Roman law. With regard to the first process, the comparative aspects of the work took place behind the scenes, and consequently the results of melding the different local or municipal laws are known, but the reasoning leading to the result is not. With regard to the second process, by contrast, certain publications place the act of comparison in full view. This was particularly noticeable in England, where some writers —such as Sir John Fortescue in the 15th century and Saint-Germain in the 16th—took upon themselves the comparison of common law and Roman law, and in 1623 Sir Francis Bacon suggested to James I that a work

be drafted, setting out, in two columns, the solutions of English and Scots law, as a preliminary step toward the unification of the two systems.

19th-century beginnings. Despite the occasional use of the comparative technique, nevertheless, comparative law itself was not recognized as a separate branch or as a fundamental technique of legal science until the 19th century. In particular, it played no part in legal education. It was quite unthinkable that the pursuit of justice should be taught by reference to a host of customary rules that were incomplete, sometimes archaic, and generally regarded as barbaric. A foundation of ethical and political principles rather than sociological considerations, an appeal to reason rather than a study of human behaviour or judicial precedent—these were deemed the true criteria of progress.

With the coming of the 19th century, codification of the law put an end to the dualism existing in many countries between an ideal system, as taught in the universities, and the laws that were applied in everyday practice. Codification of those everyday laws gave them the status of a national law, thoroughly purged of anachronisms and arranged in a systematic manner. That codified law became the cornerstone of legal education. This promotion of local customs, regarded henceforth as being fully consonant with natural justice, may be considered as the underlying cause of the appearance and rise of comparative law.

Wherever the concept of law is divorced from everyday legal practice and the administration of justice, comparative law may hold no interest for legal sciences. Thus, in India the science of practical and political matters (*artha*) is, to the present day, seen as distinct from the science of justice and morality (*dharma*). And in the same way, the Islāmic universities teach a holy law—Muslim law— without taking into account the local variations (customary law and statute law), which may restrict its practical role in the various countries concerned.

First basic studies. In short, the attitude toward comparative law tends to change from the time that a country ceases to look for some higher natural law and makes its national law the object of legal study. Then, quite naturally, legal students begin contrasting their country's law with foreign counterparts. In Europe this dawning change was evident early in the 19th century. Legal periodicals were founded in Germany in 1829 and in France in 1834 to further a systematic study of foreign law. In France, the civil and mercantile laws of modern states were translated with "concordances" referring to the corresponding provisions of the French codes; and in England in 1850–52, Leone Levi published a work entitled *Commercial Law, Its Principles and Administration; The Mercantile Law of Great Britain Compared with Roman Law and the Codes or Laws of 59 Other Countries.*

A chair of comparative legislation was set up in 1831 in the Collège de France; and this was followed, in 1846, by a chair of comparative criminal law in the University of Paris. In 1869 the Société de Législation Comparée was founded in France, followed in 1873 by the Institut de Droit International and the International Law Association. In England, the Society of Comparative Legislation was founded in 1895, and the Quain Professorship of Comparative Law was created at London University in 1894. Similarly, chairs in comparative law were founded and projects in foreign law undertaken all over the continent of Europe, but with particular vigour in France. At the same time, governments were becoming involved. In the 1870s and 1880s, the signing of the International Postal Convention, the Berne Union (for copyright), and the Paris Union (for patent rights) revealed a desire for closer cooperation and understanding among nations on legal matters.

International efforts. The 19th century drew to a close with an important event—the meeting of the First International Congress of Comparative Law in Paris in 1900. Experts from every part of Europe delivered papers and discussed the nature, aims, and general interest of comparative law. Particular emphasis was laid on its role in

The ancient search for "higher" or ideal law

End of dualism between ideal law and everyday practice

First International Congress of Comparative Law

the preparation of a "common law for the civilized world," the contents of which would be laid down by international legislation. The stress, however, was on comparative legislation and codification because (with the sole exception of the English jurist, Sir Frederick Pollock) the congress had attracted only jurists from continental European nations, all of which had coded law, in contrast to English customary, or common, law. Consequently, the idea of an enacted world law was the natural outcome of its proceedings.

The upheavals resulting from World War I (1914–18) prompted a change in direction. From then on, European interest began to extend beyond the continental systems themselves, first, to those of the common-law countries (chiefly England and the United States), then still further afield to the Socialist systems, and finally, after 1945, to the laws of the newly independent states of Asia and Africa. The new territory for legal study that has thus been opened up has resulted in references to comparative law, rather than to comparative legislation; at the same time, the drafting of international uniform laws has ceased to be looked upon as the prime function of comparative legal studies.

METHODS OF COMPARATIVE LAW

The world contains a vast number of national legal systems. The United Nations brings together representatives of some 127 states, but these states are far outnumbered by legal networks, since not all states—notably federal ones—have accomplished unification within their own frontiers. It is thus an enormous task to try to compare the laws of all the different jurisdictions. This problem, however, should not be overly magnified. Differences between the diverse systems are not always of the same order; some are sharp; others are so closely similar that a specialist in one branch of a legal "family" often may easily extend his studies to another branch of that family. For this reason, one can distinguish two types of research in comparative law. The exponent of "microcomparison" analyzes the laws belonging to the same legal family. By observing their differences, he will decide whether they are justified and whether an innovation made in one country would have value if introduced elsewhere. The researcher pledged to "macrocomparison," on the other hand, investigates those systems differing most widely from each other in order to gain insight into institutions and thought processes that are foreign to him. For the "pure jurist," concerned mainly with legal technicalities, microcomparison holds the greater attraction; whereas macrocomparison is the realm of the political scientist or legal philosopher, who sees law as a social science and is interested in its role in government and the organization of the community rather than in its practical, technical aspects.

Microcomparison. Microcomparison demands no particular preparation. The specialist in one national system is usually qualified to study those of various other countries of the same general family. His chief need is access to bibliographical material. In the United States, each state has its own statutes and, to some purposes, its own common law. Thus, the American lawyer must be a microcomparatist as he takes the 50 state systems and the federal law into daily account in his practice of the law. The same is true, to a large extent, of the Australian, or Indian, or Kenyan lawyer, who must take into account not only his own national system but also the laws of England and of other common-law jurisdictions in the British Commonwealth. Whatever can be said of the common-law systems holds true, in the main, for the Roman-law and Socialist families. The incumbents of the French chairs of comparative law encounter no major difficulty in contrasting the laws of certain countries, so long as they confine their comparison to French, German, Italian, and Dutch law, which enjoy the same tradition, share parallel structures, and serve a similar type of society. Often the only real obstacle is the language barrier.

Macrocomparison. The situations differs greatly in consideration of macrocomparison. Here no comparison is possible without previously identifying and thoroughly mastering the fundamentals of the law systems as they differ from place to place. The jurist must, as it were, forget his training and begin to reason according to new criteria. If he is French, English, or American, he must recognize that in some folk societies of the Far East, the upright citizen never crosses the threshold of a courtroom and acknowledges no subjective rights; instead, the citizen's behaviour is governed by rites handed down from his ancestors, ensuring him the approval of the community. Likewise, if the Western jurist is to understand the law of the Muslim or Hindu, he must realize that the law is contained in rules of conduct laid down by a religion for its followers, and for its followers only. These rules, creating obligations and not rights, rank above all worldly matters and, in particular, are not to be confused with the regulations that a national government may, at a given time, enact and ratify. Further, in comparing his system of law with that of a Communist nation, the Westerner must remember that on no account does the citizen of a Marxist–Leninist state regard the rule of law as an ideal for society. Far from it, for his dream is to see law—which to him is synonymous with injustice and coercion—wither away in an affluent society founded on human solidarity and fellowship. A considerable shifting of legal gears is necessary before a French or German jurist can grasp the vital importance that the English or American lawyer traditionally attaches to the concept of due process and the rules of evidence; in continental eyes, procedural rules take second place to substantive law.

The specialist undertaking the task of macrocomparison must not be content merely to observe national variations of attitude to the idea of law. He must go further and pick out the structural differences existing between certain systems. Accordingly, the Anglo-American lawyer must be aware of the importance attaching, in many countries, to the distinction between public and private law—between law involving the state and law involving only individuals. The jurist in a Roman-law country must, conversely, appreciate the significance of the concepts of common law (unwritten customary law of various kinds) and equity (the use of injunctions and other equitable remedies), neither of which have counterparts in his own system. The lawyer from a centralized country must familiarize himself with the distinction between federal law and the laws of secondary jurisdictions (states, provinces, cantons, and so forth)—a distinction that is of fundamental importance in many countries. If he is from a nation like England or France that acknowledges the sovereignty of the national parliament, he must give due weight to the prominence of constitutional law in countries that permit courts to review the constitutional validity of legislative acts—especially in those countries, such as the United States and the Federal Republic of Germany, where a bill of rights imposes limitations on the ascendancy of the legislature. The jurist in a "bourgeois" country must appreciate the policy of collective ownership of means of production in Socialist states. All problems of "conveyancing," or transfer of ownership, virtually disappear in such countries, and the chief problem of property law becomes how effectively to administer socialized property; likewise, the principle of freedom of contract and the notion of price undergo a metamorphosis when the economy is controlled by an authoritarian policy rather than by the play of supply and demand and the influence of profit making.

Families of law. The terms microcomparison and macrocomparison, reflecting the language of economics, are in keeping with the idea that legal systems can be grouped into families, such as common-law, Roman, and Socialist. But it must be acknowledged that the number of identifiable families and the appropriate classification of a given system are questions always open to argument. The legal system of a given country, for instance, may exhibit some features that relate it to a particular family and others that may escape that classification. Such blurring of distinctions is particularly true

Two types of research in comparative law

Mastering fundamentals of a foreign system

Parliamentary versus constitutional law

of law in countries of Africa and the Middle East, where certain sectors of the law have been transformed by Western ideas (as in criminal and mercantile law and procedure) leaving other sectors (such as personal status, family law, and land law) faithful to traditional principles of the region. The phenomenon is not peculiar to those countries, however.

Wide differences also may be detected between legal systems that are commonly regarded as belonging to the same family. American law, for instance, without hesitation is ranked as a member of the common-law family; yet countless differences set it apart from English law, in large part because the United States has a federal and England a unitary system of government. Similarly, although Latin American legal systems are classified as Roman, they often show their own originality, especially in their approach to constitutional matters. Scots law, South African law, the law of the province of Quebec, and the law of Yugoslavia or Cuba provide further examples of mixed systems that cannot easily be linked to just one of the recognized major legal families.

PURPOSES OF COMPARATIVE LAW

Each era has had a different incentive for the study and comparison of foreign laws.

Historical and cultural comparisons. First of all, there has been a tendency to view comparative law from the standpoint of its value to the historical study of legal decision making—a consideration that was responsible for establishing the first chairs of comparative law in 19th-century Europe. Ideas regarding the place of law in society and the nature of the law itself—whether divine or secular, whether dealing with substantive or procedural rules—obviously become appreciably clearer when comparative law is joined to historical research. Indeed, to some extent historical background may aid in forecasting the future of certain national systems.

A closely related consideration prompts many Western jurists, political scientists, and sociologists to acquaint themselves with non-Western methods of reasoning. Comparative studies reveal that the citizen of some countries of Asia and Africa looks upon the concept of a just social order with thoughts and feelings far removed from those of Western man. The notions of a rule of law and of rights of the individual—fundamental to Western civilization—are not wholly recognized by those societies that, faithful to the principle of conciliation and concerned primarily with harmony within the group, do not favour excessive Western-style individualism or the modern Western ideal of state supremacy. Thus comparative law may enable statesmen, diplomats, and jurists to understand foreign points of view at the international conference table, and it may frequently help to create better international understanding by clarifying reasoning and attitudes inspired by different cultural premises. In the absence of such explanation, one might be tempted to regard foreign attitudes as absurd or as founded in bad faith.

*Under-
standing
another
culture's
reasoning*

Commercial uses. Comparative law may be used for essentially practical ends. The businessman, for instance, needs to know what benefits he may expect, what risks he may run, and generally how he should act if he intends to invest capital or make contracts abroad. It was with this purpose in mind that the first French institute of comparative law was set up in Lyon in 1920; its mission was to instruct French legal advisers on foreign trade. It was this practical aspect that also encouraged the growth of comparative law in the United States, where the essential aim of the law school has been usually to turn out practitioners; and one need hardly mention the strong link in Germany between big industry and the various institutes of comparative law.

Sometimes it is said that studies with such a focus should not be considered a part of comparative law; rather they merely represent an investigation of foreign laws. Perhaps there is a measure of truth in this assertion, but obviously a study of specific foreign laws is the prerequisite of any comparative study of law. Furthermore, practical considerations certainly have helped to finance

*Financial
and
promo-
tional aid*

and promote the development of comparative legal studies in general. To explain a foreign law to those who take for granted the solutions of their own national system is already an application of comparative law.

Aid to national law. The improvement of national legislation was the prime consideration during the 19th century in countries that were codifying or recodifying their legal systems. Numerous later additions to the Code Napoléon, drawn up in 1804, for instance, were of foreign origin. Many other nations, of course, followed France's lead and introduced into their own systems elements of the French Napoleonic codes and institutions of French public law. It is well worth noticing that a book on French administrative laws was published in German by Otto Mayer before Mayer felt himself able to write a textbook on German administrative law.

The foreign inspiration of a number of legal rules or institutions is a well-known phenomenon, sometimes so all-embracing that one speaks of "reception"—reception, for instance, of the English common law in the United States, Canada, Australia, India, and Nigeria; reception of French law in French-speaking Africa, Madagascar, Egypt, and Indochina; reception of Swiss law in Turkey; and reception of both German and French law in Japan, along with even some reception of American common law. The study of comparative law has found a special place in countries where such a reception has occurred. Students have been particularly interested in how the law of the donor country evolved or how other nations receiving that law in the past have fared with it.

Use in international law. In modern times the spirit of nationalism has often tended to frustrate the development of an international law that would overcome individual national differences. One task facing statesmen and jurists is to inject new life into this effort, adapting it to the exigencies of the modern world. Those engaging in international trade, for instance, do not know with certainty which national law will regulate their agreements, since the answer depends to a large extent on a generally undecided factor—namely, which national court will be called upon to decide the questions of competence. Thus, the sole lasting remedy would seem to be the development of an international law capable of governing all legal questions outside the jurisdiction of a single state—either by setting forth substantive rules or by pointing out which national law will be applicable in any particular case. Such a project can succeed only by a confrontation of opinions, in other words, through the medium of comparative law.

In the 20th century, the development of an international law has become a major preoccupation. As early as 1926, an International Institute for the Unification of Private Law was created in Rome, under the auspices of the League of Nations; and in 1966 the United Nations set up a Commission on International Trade Law. Many institutions, apart from these organizations, are involved—some on a worldwide scale and some on a regional basis—in the attempt to reach agreement on uniform resolution of conflicts of laws and on other matters. The rapprochement of views contemplated by all these institutions calls for a development of comparative legal studies.

INSTITUTIONS OF COMPARATIVE LAW

It is impossible to enumerate all the institutes, centres, universities, and associations dealing with foreign and comparative law. Only a suggestion of the scope of the studies is possible. For instance, at the international level, an International Academy of Comparative Law, set up in 1924, organizes the quadrennial Congress of Comparative Law; the eighth congress was held in Italy in 1970, and the ninth was to be held in Chile in 1974. In 1950 the International Association of Legal Science was established under the auspices of UNESCO. It allies a number of national committees (43 in 1970) and facilitates the work of comparative lawyers by commissioning each national committee to prepare different types of projects, including, most importantly, the compilation of annotated legal bibliographies. In addition, the asso-

*Interna-
tional
Associa-
tion of
Legal
Science*

ciation is sponsoring the preparation of a 16-volume *International Encyclopaedia of Comparative Law*, the publication of which began in 1971.

Another worldwide body, the International Association of Comparative Law, founded in 1960, consists of individuals whose aims are to improve the teaching of comparative law. The association's main achievement so far has been the creation of an International Faculty for the Teaching of Comparative Law, which is permanently seated at Strasbourg, France. The Faculty holds sessions each year in different cities and towns all over Europe and America, giving introductory courses in comparative law. From 1960 to 1970, 82 sessions were held in 17 countries, with the cooperation of 46 universities, gathering together 619 professors of 51 nationalities and 7,790 students of 94 nationalities. Besides these groups, many other international associations bring together experts of many nationalities specializing in various branches of law: mercantile, insurance, maritime, agricultural, criminal, industrial, administrative, and financial. Also, some groups specialize in certain legal systems such as French law or the laws of French-speaking countries. Furthermore, the International Law Association, the Union Internationale des Avocats, the International Bar Association, and the Inter-American Bar Association, to name only a few of the international associations of lawyers, organize meetings and publish reports dealing with aspects of comparative law.

On the national level, comparative law has likewise earned a steadily increasing recognition. Teaching programs in comparative law are offered to students in many universities. In France, for instance, each law faculty must make provision for such courses; and, in some circumstances, comparative law has become a compulsory subject. Furthermore, a number of countries have set up special institutes for teaching and research in this field. The first of these was founded in Munich, Germany, in 1916; followed by the Institut de Droit Comparé at Lyon, France (1920), and the first American Institute of Comparative Law at Córdoba, Argentina (1925). The list of institutes and societies of comparative law and comparative legislation has, of course, become exceedingly long, with most countries of the world participating.

BIBLIOGRAPHY. H.C. GUTTERIDGE, *Comparative Law*, 2nd ed. (1949), explores the history of comparative law, explains to which purposes and in which branches of the law comparative studies may be made with profit, and ends with three chapters on the international unification of private law. J.H. WIGMORE, *A Panorama of the World's Legal Systems*, 3 vol. (1928; 1-volume ed., 1936), gives a general account of 16 legal systems, ancient and modern, applied in the various parts of the world. The ASSOCIATION OF AMERICAN LAW SCHOOLS, *A General Survey of Events, Ideas, Persons and Movements in Continental Legal History* (1912), is a pioneer book, in which the legal traditions of various European countries are discussed by specialists from each country. R. DAVID and J.E.C. BRIERLEY, *Les Grands systèmes de droit contemporains* (1964; Eng. trans., *Major Legal Systems in the World To-day*, 1968), is a more up-to-date book; originally devised for students, it describes the problems and value of comparative law and provides information on the history, structure, and sources of the civil law, the laws of Socialist countries, the common law, and the religious and traditional systems of law (Muslim, Hindu, Chinese, Japanese, African, and Malagasy), ending with a valuable bibliography. *The International Encyclopaedia of Comparative Law*, proposed 16 vol. (1971–), will, when completed, constitute a major source of information. The main periodicals in English are the *American Journal of Comparative Law* (quarterly), and the *International and Comparative Law Quarterly*. A standard bibliography is C. SZLADITS, *A Bibliography in Foreign and Comparative Law: Books and Articles in English*, 3 vol. (1955–68; suppls. 1966–67; 1970). See also the *Index to Legal Periodicals* (1907–) and the *Index to Foreign Legal Periodicals* (1960–).

(R.Da.)

Compass

The compass is the basic direction-finding device in terrestrial navigation. The evolution of the various meanings of the word is obscure. The general sense is "measure" or measurement"; the word is also applied in the plural to a mathematical instrument, a pair of compasses, for measuring or for describing a circle.

The mariner's compass, in addition to its use for sea navigation, has been used in slightly differing forms by aircraft, land vehicles, and in surveying. The basic principles remain unchanged.

There are three main categories of compasses: the magnetic compass, which depends upon the Earth's magnetic field to obtain its directive force; the gyrocompass, which obtains its directive control from the rotation of the Earth; and the solar compass, the use of which depends upon the Sun or a star being visible. Most gyrocompasses and some magnetic compasses can be made to drive repeater compasses. If a gyroscope is used in conjunction with a magnetic compass, either to stabilize the magnetic element or to smooth out oscillations in the transmission to a repeater, the arrangement is called a gyromagnetic compass (though it is sometimes wrongly described as a gyrocompass).

HISTORY OF THE MARINER'S COMPASS

The discovery that a lodestone, a naturally occurring magnetic iron ore composed principally of iron oxide, or a piece of iron that has been touched by a lodestone will align itself in a magnetic north and south direction and the application of this discovery to aid in the navigation of ships have been variously attributed. The ancients could and did make long voyages using a steady wind to give them their direction and an occasional sight of the Sun or a star to inform them of any change. When the compass was introduced, its initial use was merely to check the direction of the wind when poor visibility prevented observation of heavenly bodies.

It would seem probable that when the compass did at last appear it was invented independently in China and in Europe.

Earliest references. A theory that the Chinese were very early inventors of the compass, arising from legends of ancient chariots in which a figure with outstretched arm pointed to the south, is no longer credited. The earliest date at which a magnetic compass is known to have been used at sea by the Chinese was about AD 1100. Chinese trading ships were active in the Persian Gulf and the Red Sea in the 9th century, but there is no evidence that these vessels had compasses. There is also no evidence that when Chinese mariners did have the compass, at a later date, they instructed the Arabs in its use. The earliest reference to the use of the compass by Arab sailors, in a collection of Persian anecdotes written in 1232, describes a fish-shaped iron leaf used as a compass about ten years earlier. An Arabian writer relates that a magnetized needle, floated on water by means of a splinter of wood or a reed, was employed in the Syrian seas in 1242 and also records the use in Indian seas of a hollow iron fish.

Use of compass by Arab sailors

The earliest definite mention of the use of the mariner's compass in Europe occurs in a treatise entitled *De utensilibus*, written by the English scholar Alexander Neckam about 1187. He speaks of a needle carried on board ship that showed mariners their course when the Polestar was hidden. In another work (*De naturis rerum*, chapter 98) he writes,

The sailors, moreover, as they sail over the sea, when in cloudy weather they can no longer profit by the light of the sun, or when the world is wrapped up in the darkness of the shades of night, and they are ignorant to what point of the compass their ship's course is directed, they touch the magnet with a needle, which is whirled round in a circle until, when its motion ceases, its point looks direct to the north.

The magnetic needle and its suspension on a stick or straw in water are clearly described in *La Bible Guiot*, a poem written about 1206, which states that through the magnet, an ugly brown stone to which iron turns of its own accord, mariners possess an art that cannot fail them. A needle touched by it and floated by a stick on water turns its point toward the Polestar and, a light being placed near the needle on dark nights, the proper course is known. There are a number of similar references during the 13th century.

In Scandinavian records, the following reference to the nautical use of the magnet appears in the *Hauksbók*, the last edition of the *Landnámabók* ("Book of Settlements"):

> Floki, son of Vilgerd, instituted a great sacrifice, and consecrated three ravens which should show him the way [to Iceland], for at that time no men sailing the high seas had lodestones up in northern lands.

The paragraph was written about 1300, and the edition was founded on material in two earlier works, one of which is lost, while the other has no such paragraph. All that is certain is that knowledge of the nautical use of the needle existed in the northern lands by the end of the 13th century.

It will thus be seen that the earliest authentic information concerning the use of the compass comes from China (*c.* 1100), from western Europe (*c.* 1187), from Arabia (*c.* 1220), and from Scandinavia (*c.* 1300). In any of these areas the compass may well have been known for some time before it was recorded. It is not, therefore, possible to state with any certainty where the first discovery occurred and whether knowledge of the use of the compass was transmitted from one area to another or whether it was the result of two or more independent inventions.

First detailed treatise. The first detailed work on the magnetic compass is contained in the remarkable *Epistola de magnete*, written in 1269 by a Frenchman, Petrus Peregrinus de Maricourt. The first part of the work deals generally with magnetic attractions and repulsions, with the polarity of the lodestone, and with the supposed influence of the poles of the heavens upon the poles of the stone. In the second part Peregrinus describes, first, an improved floating compass having a graduated circle with 90° in each quadrant and provided with movable sights for taking bearings. He then describes a compass with a needle thrust through a pivoting vertical axis, which was placed in a box with a transparent cover. Apparently his instruments were intended for surveying and not maritime use.

It is possible that the earliest form of mariner's compass was an actual lump of lodestone floated on a board as described by Peregrinus, but it is more likely that it consisted of a magnetized needle transfixing a crossbar of wood or reed that would float it on water in a bowl. The next step was to use a needle pivoted on a pin rising from the bottom of the bowl. At first only the north–south direction was noted; then the principal points were marked in the bottom of the bowl and the instrument was set with the north point painted in the bowl under the north end of the needle. Finally a card, marked with the points required, was mounted on the needle; the navigator could then simply read his direction from the top of the card.

Compass cards. The *rosa ventorum*, or wind rose, is far older than the compass itself, and the naming of the winds antedates the Tower of the Winds in Athens, built by Andronicus of Cyrrhus in about 100 BC. By the 13th century the names of the eight principal winds had become established in the Mediterranean and were *tramontana* (north), *greco* (northeast), *levante* (east), *sirocco* (southeast), *ostro* (south), *gharbin* or *libeccio* or *africo* (southwest), *ponente* (west), and *maestro* (northwest). When in the 14th century these winds appeared on charts (and possibly also on compass cards) they were denoted by their initials. The north point was indicated in some of the oldest wind roses with a broad spearhead, as well as with the letter *T* for *tramontana*. Gradually, a combination of these developed, about 1490, into the fleur-de-lis, still almost universally used. The east point was marked by a cross instead of an *L*. The cross, or rather the ornament into which it developed, continued on British compass cards until well on in the 19th century (see Figure 1). The subdivision of the compass card followed. The use of 32 points by sailors of northern Europe, usually attributed to Flemish compass makers, is mentioned by Geoffrey Chaucer in his "Treatise on the Astrolabe" (written 1391).

It has been said that it was the seamen of Amalfi (Italy)

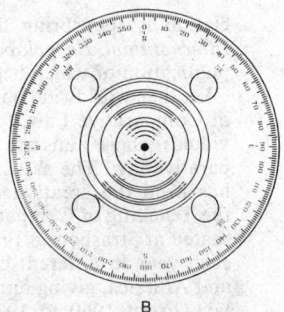

Figure 1: *Compass cards.*
(A) Eighteenth-century compass card divided into points and having ornamentation at the east point. (B) U.S. Navy compass card made of metal with graduations perforated through it.

who first expanded the original eight compass points to 32, and they may even have been the first to attach the card to the needle. The issue has been confused by a story that first appeared about 1450 and was embellished during the next 150 years, but which is now completely discredited, that the compass was invented at Amalfi; there may, however, be a germ of truth in the form of some improvement instituted at that leading medieval port.

In England, various ship inventories and exchequer accounts of 1345 refer to "sailing needles" and to "stones, called adamants, called sailstones." This would seem to be evidence that fairly primitive instruments remained in use in British waters until well into the 14th century.

By the 16th century the compass was assuming something like its present form. The bowl was suspended in gimbals (rings pivoted at right angles to each other) so that it would always be level. This arrangement, originally used for lamps, is first described in 1537.

Compass variation. During the 15th century it became apparent that the compass needle did not point true north but made an angle with the meridian; this was originally called by seamen the northeasting of the needle but is now called the variation. The term declination is preferred by scientists, despite the danger of confusion with the declination of heavenly bodies. In northern countries, compass needles began to be mounted askew on the card, so that while the needle pointed to magnetic north the fleur-de-lis indicated true north. This practice caused some confusion and difficulty, especially when crossing the Atlantic to the American coast, because there the variation was west instead of east as in Europe. Consequently, English navigators changed to "meridional" compasses, in which the needle was under the fleur-de-lis, when they passed the Lizard (Cornwall, England) outward bound. This practice of mounting compass needles at a fixed angle died out about 1700, though cards on which the needle was adjustable, so that it could be set for any variation, were used—particularly in the Netherlands and occasionally in Britain—until liquid compasses came into general use. In these, an arrangement for altering the needle would have introduced an excessive complication.

As it would have been difficult to mount a single wire needle upon a pivot, it became customary to use two needles bent into an oval, but by the 17th century a parallelogram had become the usual shape. Methods of magnetizing were inefficient, and needles did not retain their magnetism long. In 1745 the English inventor Gowin Knight perfected a method of efficiently magnetizing needles of harder steel and designed a compass that had a single bar needle, large enough for a cap, resting on the pivot, to be screwed into its centre. His greatly improved compasses were extensively used.

Compass deviation. It had been known for nearly three centuries that ironwork placed in the vicinity of a compass would deflect its needle, and the spread of iron shipbuilding in the early 19th century caused much concern. In 1837 the British Admiralty set up a Compass Committee to examine the whole question of the use of compasses in iron ships and the possible correction of their deviations. The committee also designed a compass in which four needles of flat laminated steel were placed on edge and so arranged as to provide greatly improved steadiness.

The liquid-filled compass. The disadvantage of all dry-card compasses was that the card was easily deflected by shocks or vibration. Suggestions were made that the bowl should be liquid-filled to introduce a damping factor; *i.e.*, to absorb shock. Many problems were encountered, including leakage and expansion of the liquid, discoloration, and difficulties in replacing a worn pivot. Nevertheless, some liquid compasses were used for steering in bad weather. In 1862 a compass was introduced, based on a patent of 1813 in which a float attached to the card took most of the weight off the pivot, reducing friction and wear. Allowance was made for expansion of the liquid, and improved techniques soon surmounted the other disadvantages of a liquid compass.

This compass was eventually accepted for the United States Navy, but the British Navy continued to use dry-card compasses for many years.

The Thomson dry-card compass. Several writers had recommended very light compass needles and cards. In 1876 Sir William Thomson, later Lord Kelvin, introduced a light type of dry-card compass system consisting of both compass and compass pedestal or binnacle. The card was of paper. Small needles, usually eight in number, were slung below the card. The bowl was elaborately mounted in the binnacle to prevent shocks from reaching the card. The binnacle contained all the correctors necessary to redress the errors caused by the ship's magnetism. Largely due to this improved binnacle Thomson's compass became extremely popular in Great Britain and elsewhere. It was adopted for the British Navy and used until increasing vibration caused by higher speeds and gunfire forced the service to adopt an improved liquid compass, in 1906. In British merchant vessels the Thomson compass retained its popularity longer, but by 1970 it had almost disappeared.

MODERN COMPASSES

Magnetic compasses. The basis of the magnetic compass is that the Earth itself is a giant bar magnet whose north–south orientation causes a freely suspended steel needle to assume a similar alignment. Two principal difficulties arise in respect to the Earth's magnetic field: first, it is not quite aligned with the Earth's axis but is slightly off centre; and second, the field has a vertical component —that is, when a compass is carried well north or south of the Equator it tends to be pulled downward.

Magnetic compasses are of four types: the traditional mariner's compass; the aircraft compass, essentially a mariner's compass modified to damp out shocks produced by the aircraft; the inductor compass, which acts on an entirely different principle; and the gyromagnetic compass, which is designed to overcome the problem of compass alignment created by changes in course and speed of aircraft. (W.E.M.)

Mariners' compasses. The liquid magnetic compass (see Figure 2), now almost universally used, is usually accompanied by an azimuth instrument for taking bearings of distant objects and is mounted in a binnacle. The liquid magnetic compass consists of a set of steel needles with a compass card, attached to a float, in a bowl of water and alcohol. In modern instruments, the magnetic element is often in the form of a ring magnet, fitted within the float. The card is usually of mica or plastic with photographically printed graduations; metal cards with perforated graduations also are used. Cards are usually graduated clockwise from 0° at north to 359°, with the eight principal points indicated. A few compasses are still made with cards graduated from 0° at north and south to 90° at east and west and with various combinations of points, half-points, and quarter-points.

A jewel is fitted at the centre of the float to bear on an iridium-tipped pivot attached to the bowl of the compass. The liquid in which the directional system is placed serves two purposes, to reduce the weight on the pivot point, and thereby to minimize friction, and to damp out oscillations from the ship's motion. The bowl is closed top and bottom by glass, the bottom glass permitting il-

Use of a float

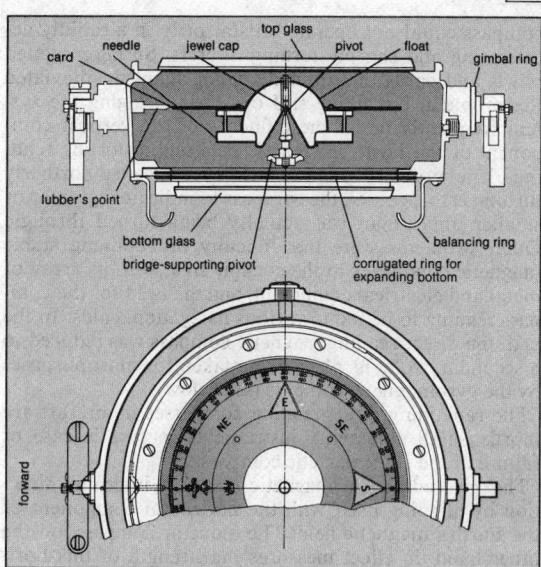

Figure 2: Liquid compass used by the British Navy.

lumination from below, and is mounted in gimbals, allowing it to maintain its horizontal position despite rolling of the ship. A flexible diaphragm or bellows attached to the bowl accommodates the change of volume of the liquid caused by temperature changes. The ship's heading is read with the aid of the lubber's point, at the forward part of the compass, which indicates the direction of the ship's centreline.

When the ship alters course, liquid at the side of the bowl tends to displace slightly, deflecting the card in what is known as swirl error. To minimize swirl error the card is often made considerably smaller than the bowl in diameter. The directional system is made sufficiently bottom heavy (pendulous) to counteract the downward pull of the vertical component of the Earth's magnetic field, which would otherwise cause the system to tilt.

An azimuth instrument is an auxiliary device fitted to a mariner's compass to permit bearings to be taken of distant objects such as stars, ships, or landfalls. The simplest, and probably earliest, consists of two sights on opposite sides of the compass bowl, connected by a thread. The assembly could be rotated to permit sighting on the distant object. Because it was impossible to sight through the instrument and look at the compass card simultaneously, a prism (mirror) was positioned to reflect an image of the card, which was given a second set of graduations with reversed figures. Modern azimuth instruments embody a number of refinements, but the principle remains unchanged.

The binnacle, formerly called the bittacle, is the receptacle in which the compass is mounted. Originally constructed in the form of a cupboard, it is now usually a cylindrical pedestal, made of timber or glass-reinforced plastic, with provision for illuminating the compass card, usually from below. It contains the various correctors to reduce the deviations of the compass caused by the magnetism of the ship. These usually consist of properly placed magnets, a pair of soft iron spheres (or small strips close to the compass), and a vertical soft iron bar called the Flinders bar.

Binnacles are sometimes made so that an image of part of the compass card can be projected or reflected through a tube onto a viewing screen on the deck below. This arrangement can avoid the provision of a second compass for the helmsman and may enable the binnacle to be placed in a better position magnetically.

Another way of providing compass readings in other parts of the ship is through electronic circuitry—equipping the compass with means of sending a signal to a repeater compass or other navigational aid. This is not difficult in itself, but measures must be taken to prevent the circuitry from interfering with the magnet system.

Magnetic compasses in aircraft. In the early days of aviation, it was soon learned that a liquid-filled mariner's

Azimuth instruments

The binnacle

compass could not operate satisfactorily in a rapidly accelerating and sharply turning aircraft. Spring-mounted bowls and cards of extremely small diameter alleviated the problem, but tilting still occurred, bringing the system frequently under the influence of the vertical component of the Earth's magnetic field and distorting readings. The most important of such effects, called northerly turning error, caused the compass to indicate a greater or smaller angle than was actually being turned through. Other problems were the difficulty of obtaining stable magnetic conditions in the cockpit area, with its array of metal and electrical equipment, and the need for the compass reading to be fed to various navigational aids. In the end, the direct-reading magnetic compass was reduced to a secondary role, its place being taken for most purposes by the gyromagnetic compass (see below).

The remaining direct-reading compasses in aircraft are mostly small emergency instruments for use in case of failure of the gyromagnetic compass.

Inductor
compasses

The pivoted-needle magnetic compass indicates direction by aligning itself with the horizontal component of the Earth's magnetic field. The inductor compass, on the other hand, in effect measures the strength of this horizontal component and indicates the direction in which the strength is maximum. A simple compass of this type was patented in Great Britain in 1907. It took the form of a rotating coil in which the Earth's magnetic field induced a voltage. Movable brushes were used to pick up this voltage; by adjusting the brushes for maximum or minimum voltage, the direction of the maximum magnetic field (magnetic north) could be determined. This principle is no longer used, having been supplanted in modern inductor compasses by a better, simpler method.

The modern instruments, called saturable-inductor compasses, make use of magnetic materials that are easily saturated; that is, materials in which it is easy to build up the maximum number of lines of magnetic flow, or flux. The amount of flux through such a material depends on its orientation in the Earth's field, being maximum when it is oriented in the magnetic north–south direction. By means of suitable electronic circuitry, it is possible to determine the exact orientation of a bar of such material and thus indicate precisely the direction of magnetic north. Compasses of this type require no rotating parts. Several can be sited at various points aboard a ship and their outputs combined electronically.

The gyromagnetic compass. The errors that occur in aircraft and small, fast vessels when the compass relates itself to the false vertical during alterations of course or speed can be avoided by mounting the compass on a platform kept horizontal by a gyroscope. The directive element must be nonpendulous. The vertical pin supporting the compass needle can be pivoted at both ends, or an inductor element can be employed. In one such arrangement, a saturable inductor is mounted on a gyroscope, but this is not always convenient from the point of view of size and weight.

Another system uses a gyroscope to control the information transmitted to the repeaters and has a means of comparison between the gyroscope heading and that of the magnetic element. Should there be any divergence between them, a correcting signal causes the gyroscope to move into alignment with the compass. Any drifting of the gyroscope is thus corrected; transient disturbances of the magnetic compass are usually of too short a duration to disturb the gyroscope materially, and hence short-term errors of the magnetic compass are not transmitted to the repeaters. Either of the systems described above can be designated a gyromagnetic compass.

The gyrocompass. The gyrocompass is independent of the magnetic field of the Earth and depends upon the properties of the gyroscope (*q.v.*) and upon the rotation of the Earth.

The axis of a free gyroscope will describe a circle about the pole of the heavens. To convert it into a gyrocompass, a control must be introduced that, when the axis tilts, will operate to precess (turn) it toward the meridian. The case of the gyroscope is made pendulous, or a liquid is arranged to flow from side to side. Either will convert

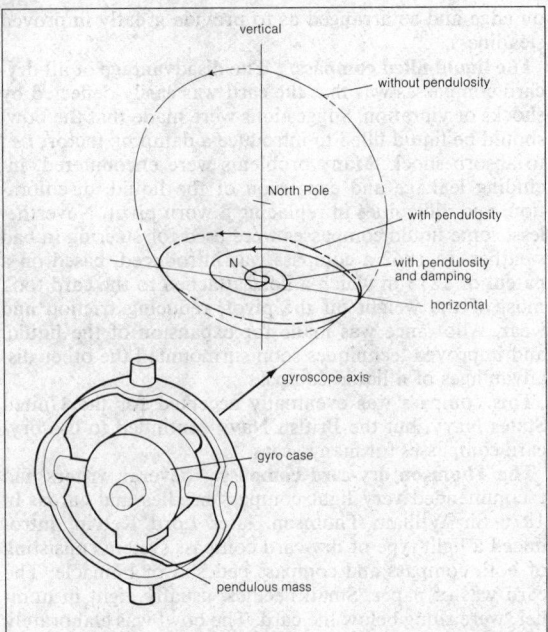

Figure 3: *Gyrocompass operation.*
Circular line shows the apparent motion of the axis of a gyroscope around the Polestar in the absence of a pendulous mass. The addition of the pendulous mass (lower drawing) converts the circular motion into an ellipse; the ellipse can then be damped out and the gyroscope becomes a gyrocompass pointing to true north.

the path traced by the axis into an ellipse. By delaying the flow of the liquid or by making eccentric the point of action of the control, a damping factor is introduced that converts the ellipse into a spiral so that the gyrocompass finally settles pointing true north (see Figure 3).

The use of a liquid control with its delayed flow eliminates errors resulting from the alternating effects of a pendulous case as the ship rolls or pitches.

The movement of a ship over the surface of the Earth combines with the effect of the Earth's rotation to have the same effect as if the axis of the Earth were slightly displaced. Steps must be taken to correct this small error.

Sun compasses. The sun compass is an instrument for obtaining an approximate direction from the position of the Sun. Its operation is the reverse of that of a sundial. A sundial must be carefully set up with its centre line in the north–south direction, and the shadow of the gnomon, or style, indicates the time. A sun compass must be turned until the shadow shows the correct time, and the centre line will then show the direction of north. The time used in both instruments is apparent time—*i.e.*, local sun time, in which the length of the hour varies slightly through the year—and not the mean time kept by a clock or watch.

BIBLIOGRAPHY

General: H.L. HITCHINS and W.E. MAY, *From Lodestone to Gyro-Compass* (1952), a preliminary, but comprehensive, study of all types of compasses and their use, both historical and technical.

Historical: A. CRICHTON MITCHELL, "Chapters in the History of Terrestrial Magnetism," *Terrestrial Magnetism and Atmospheric Electricity*, 37:105–146 (1932); 42:241–280 (1937); 44:77–80 (1939); 51:323–351 (1946), an extremely detailed study of the early history of the magnetic compass, variation, and dip; J. NEEDHAM, *Science and Civilisation in China*, 4 Part I:229–334 (1962), a detailed and authoritative study of early knowledge concerning the compass and magnetism in China.

Magnetic compass design: A. HINE, *Magnetic Compasses and Magnetometers* (1968), an advanced technical study of all types of magnetic compass, their design and use.

Gyro-compasses: A.L. RAWLINGS, *Theory of the Gyroscopic Compass and its Deviations*, 2nd ed. (1944), a theoretical account of the factors covering the design and use of the gyrocompass.

Important papers will be found in the *Philosophical Transactions of the Royal Society* (quarterly), *Mariner's Mirror* (quarterly), *Journal of the Institute of Navigation* (quarterly), and *Nautical Magazine* (monthly).

(W.E.M./J.L.H.)

Compression and Decompression Injuries

The liquids and solids of the human body, being, for all practical purposes, elastic but incompressible, readily transmit the kinetic energy of mechanical forces acting upon them. These forces produce injury by deforming and displacing living tissues beyond their elastic limits. This article deals with compressive and decompressive injuries produced by blast, by impact acceleration from collisions and falls, and by changes in barometric pressure during underwater or caisson operations. Indirect effects of increased pressure such as carbon dioxide intoxication, oxygen toxicity, and nitrogen narcosis will not be considered (see RESPIRATION, DISORDERS OF).

Effects of blast. *Pressure effects.* The sudden release of energy from explosions creates a pressure wave that travels rapidly outward from its source. This advancing wave of overpressure is followed by a weaker and more prolonged wave of underpressure. The rate, magnitude, duration, and character of the pressure rise and fall determine the biological effects exerted—tolerance being least for "fast" rising waves of long duration. Organs that contain air and tissues in which density variation is greatest are most susceptible to the direct effects of pressure changes, or, as they are often called, primary blast effects. Objects set in motion by the blast overpressure and winds, and sometimes by gravity, produce secondary blast effects that cause most of the bodily mechanical injuries in explosions. Injuries brought about by physical displacement of the body, termed tertiary effects, usually occur during deceleration, but close proximity to small detonations may result in violent acceleration and destruction of individual digits or extremities.

Acceleration forces lasting less than 0.2 second, the latent period in which hydrostatic effects develop, are commonly classified as "impact" accelerations. The biological effects of impact forces are extremely complex, influenced not only by the velocity, duration, magnitude, and angle of impact but also by the part of the body and area of surface affected, in addition to such variables as individual state of tenseness or relaxation and whether or not damping or protective factors are present.

Effects of blast on eardrums. The eardrums exhibit high vulnerability to overpressures produced by explosions and may rupture at pressures too low to cause other injuries. Eardrum rupture produces variable degrees of local pain and hearing loss. Healing usually occurs untreated with little if any permanent hearing loss. Treatment, if applied, includes measures to control pain and occasionally to prevent infection of the exposed middle ear. Lung or intra-abdominal injury from air blast is unlikely if the eardrums have remained intact.

Effects of blast on lungs. A rapidly moving pressure wave against the chest forces the chest wall abruptly inward. As the pressure wave passes, the chest wall moves outward as a result of elastic recoil and the subsequent decompression wave. Kinetic energy transmitted to the underlying lung may tear the thin walls of air sacs contained therein and small blood vessels of the lung, causing hemorrhage. Air entering damaged blood vessels may be carried to the heart and brain as bubbles (air embolism), which can block circulation and rapidly cause death.

Bloody froth about the mouth and nose is the only external sign, and slight shortness of breath often the only early symptom, of severe lung damage from primary blast effects. Increasing shortness of breath and cyanotic skin discoloration, because of inadequate lung ventilation and resulting oxygen-deficient blood, follows. Treatment consists mainly of supportive measures: maintenance of an open airway by suction of bloody secretions from air passages, administration of oxygen by intermittent positive-pressure breathing, and, if necessary, tracheotomy. In nonfatal cases recovery is slow and sometimes incomplete with residual shortness of breath.

Effects of blast on orbital bones. The nasal sinuses, located above and below the eyes, are small, air-containing spaces that open through small apertures into the nasal passage. Thin-walled, fragile bones form a common wall between the sinuses and the orbital cavity. Blood vessels within the sinuses may rupture and bleed at relatively low blast pressures. More severe blast pressures can cause "blow-out" fractures by momentarily displacing the eyes and associated soft tissues sufficiently to fracture and splinter these thin bones and push them into the sinus cavity. Such fractures require specialized surgical treatment.

Other blast effects on organs. Perforations of the wall of the air-containing intestine can occur as the enclosed gas is suddenly compressed by the blast pressure transmitted by the abdominal wall. Less commonly, such pressures can also displace relatively solid organs such as the liver, spleen, and diaphragm sufficiently to tear them and their supporting tissues. Treatment of such injuries includes blood replacement, surgical repair, and measures to control infection.

Injury from penetrating missiles. Blast victims nearly always suffer injury from glass and debris set in motion by the explosion. Whether such missiles penetrate the skin depends primarily upon their mass and velocity at impact, configuration, angle of impact, and the portion of the body struck. The density and elasticity of tissues through which the missile passes will influence the extent of injury. A high-velocity missile not only cuts through tissues directly in its path but imparts sufficient kinetic energy to these and adjacent tissues to cause an explosion-like, cavitation effect that creates injury in an area many times the diameter of the penetrating missile. Shear and pressure waves can shatter bone several centimetres away from the missile, or, for example, cause soft brain tissue to disintegrate and the strong, rigid skull enclosing it to blow apart. Blood vessels and nerves may also be injured at considerable distances from the wounding agent. Penetrating injuries involving the brain, thorax, and abdomen are often rapidly fatal. Early treatment of shock by blood replacement, control of pain and anxiety, surgical correction, and measures to combat infection is necessary.

Injury from nonpenetrating missiles. Missiles that fail to penetrate the skin may, nevertheless, cause severe injuries by imparting energy to underlying tissues and organs. The effects are those of blunt trauma, including bone fracture; tearing and rupture of solid organs, blood vessels, nerves, muscle, and other tissue; or, if mass is high and velocity low, simple crushing injuries.

Impact injury caused by blast pressure, ground shock, or gravity. Severe injury may occur from displacement of the entire body or parts of it. Although the accelerative forces of the blast wave and the resulting ground shock may cause serious damage, more often injury occurs during the abrupt decelerative phase when the victim strikes the ground or other solid objects. Ground or floor shock imparted to a person standing with knees locked characteristically causes heels to fracture and compression fractures of the spine or, if seated, similar damage to the spine. The decelerative impact injuries depend upon the nature of the object and the portion of the body struck. They range from fractures of the skull, long bones, and ribs to rupture of structures beneath the skin.

Dust in the lungs. Following the air raids of World War II, some victims were found dead in closed shelters which appeared to be intact after a nearby bomb burst. No injury sufficient to cause death was evident, but it was found that the upper air passages to the lungs were physically blocked by dust. Smaller quantities of finer dust particles were deposited in the smaller air passages and even in the air sacs within the lungs. The inhalation of extremely dense concentrations of dust, estimated to be above 100 grams per cubic foot, had apparently caused death by suffocation. The dust consisted of fine particles of plaster and brick produced by a spalling effect of blast on the inner walls of the structure.

Compression heating. When explosives detonate, the sudden transformation of solids or liquids to gas pro-

Three types of pressure effects

Injuries from blast-propelled missiles

Miscellaneous effects from explosions

duces considerable heat—of high intensity but of short duration—which is transmitted by radiation and, in the presence of fumes, by conduction. Compression of air surrounding the detonating explosive creates heat within the rapidly travelling compression wave. In contrast to large nuclear blasts, which produce flash burns at great distance and significant compression heating, the total heat effect of ordinary (*i.e.*, nonnuclear) explosives produces burns only at short distances and usually only of minimal importance, particularly as compared with the blast effect.

Other blast and explosive effects. Fumes and gases produced by detonations of high explosives contain large concentrations of carbon monoxide. In some cases, air-raid victims in protected enclosures have died of carbon-monoxide poisoning from bomb bursts nearby. The secondary fires and firestorms from incendiary bombs have also caused numerous carbon-monoxide deaths among occupants of air-raid shelters. Other effects of blast include: disturbances of cardiac rhythm, apparently induced through cardiac reflexes initiated by blast shock and blunt trauma to the chest; the presence in blood vessels of fat globules released from injured tissue; and transient disturbances of consciousness.

Effects of collisions and falls. *Skull injuries.* Injuries to the skull occur frequently in collisions and account for more than one-half of the resulting fatalities. Distortion of the skull during impact creates pressures and shear waves in the underlying brain and may produce loss of consciousness without evidence of fracture. Impacts of greater magnitude may cause simple linear fractures and may tear the blood vessels lining the skull. Blood collecting and clotting beneath the tough outer lining of the brain, or between it and the skull, can cause brain damage through increased pressure. Relief is usually brought about only by surgical removal of the clot. Depressed fractures may cause extensive tearing and bleeding within the brain tissue. Careful observation and frequent neurological evaluations are required to determine the extent of the injury and, consequently, the optimal treatment.

Injuries to lower extremities. Head-on collisions of automobiles produce characteristic injuries, lacerations, dislocations, and fractures of the knees and hips of unrestrained occupants of the front seat. Soft-tissue injuries include disruption or crushing of muscle and nerves. Damage to vessels may reduce blood supply sufficiently to result in gangrene of the foot and lower leg. Severe and multiple compound fractures occur in passengers who are thrown from the car and impact violently with the ground or with the other car. Falls in which the victim lands on his feet commonly result in fractures or dislocations of the foot, ankle, and long bones of the thigh and leg. Fracture of the hip is particularly common in elderly individuals who fall. In therapy, the immediate consideration is to treat shock, if present, and to prevent further soft-tissue injury by immobilizing the extremity until definitive surgical or orthopedic help becomes available.

Injuries to spine. Occupants of a car struck from behind with sufficient force suffer characteristic whiplash injuries to the spine, as the neck is violently extended backward. Fractures and dislocations in this region of the spine not uncommonly accompany severe head injury. Fractures of the lumbar spine are more often of the compression type without dislocation and typically occur in falls in which the buttocks or the feet are the point of impact. The principal concern here is whether or not the spinal cord (enclosed within the spine itself) or nerve roots are also injured and, if so, that no further injury to them occurs during transport of the victim.

Other types of collision and fall injuries. The types and combinations of injury from collisions and falls are almost innumerable. The physically unrestrained driver who is thrown against the steering wheel and post of an automobile may suffer penetrating injuries of the chest or multiple fractures and dislocations of ribs and sternum causing either open "sucking" wounds of the chest or flail-chest; *i.e.* with ribs dislocated or crushed inward. Either makes breathing movements ineffective in draw-

ing air into the lungs and requires prompt corrective measures. Collapsible steering mechanisms and seat belts with shoulder restraints appear to have reduced the incidence of these frequently fatal injuries. Severe facial lacerations and fractures may result from impact with windshield, rear-view mirror, or dashboard. Severe nonpenetrating impacts to the chest or abdomen may cause internal injuries including contusions, tears or rupture of the lung, heart, large blood vessels, diaphragm, liver, spleen, kidney, or bladder. These, often unsuspected because of minimal external signs of injury, may rapidly lead to shock from internal bleeding.

Acceleration and deceleration impact injuries. Certain types of impact produce characteristic patterns or combinations of injury. Falls upon the outstretched rigid arm, for example, typically produce fractures of the wrist, dislocations of the shoulder, or both. Inapparent skull injuries often accompany obvious fractures of facial bones. Similarly, impacts that cause heel fracture, hip dislocations, or compression fractures of the spine may also fracture the base of the skull. Pedestrians struck by automobiles frequently suffer serious multiple wounds and often fatal skull injuries because the head tends to impact first with the windscreen or top of the car and later with the ground. Fractured bones may damage nearby nerves and vessels, causing paralysis or shock from concealed bleeding into surrounding tissues. Blunt trauma over vessels may lead to in-vessel clotting that later reveals its presence through inadequate circulation or by clots carried through the veins to the lungs. Rupture of the bladder typically occurs secondary to fractures of the pelvis or blunt trauma to the upper abdomen. Blunt trauma to the loin region may produce lacerations of the kidney, a condition that may also occur with spinal injuries. Injury from penetrating or blunt trauma to the chest frequently extends to abdominal organs.

Effects of pressure changes and decompression. Pressure exerted upon the surface of the body is transmitted uniformly throughout its liquids and solids. Disregarding temperature, the volume of a gas contained within the body, as elsewhere, varies inversely, and its density directly, with pressure applied. Water at a depth of 33 feet (10 metres) creates a pressure of one atmosphere, 760 millimetres of mercury, or 14.7 pounds per square inch, the same as that produced by the atmosphere at sea level. Each additional 33 feet of descent in water adds another atmosphere of pressure.

On descent to 33 feet or to 99 feet (30 metres), a gas would occupy one-half or one-quarter, respectively, of its original volume at sea level. To maintain pressure within air spaces of the body at levels equal to that applied by the water and transmitted by the body solids and liquids, either the volume of the air spaces must diminish or additional air must enter the spaces during descent. Conversely, during ascent, either air must be released or the volume must increase. Because the air spaces are enclosed within rigid or semirigid walls, the degree to which their volume can change is limited. To prevent destructive pressure differences from developing across these walls during descent or ascent, therefore, there must be passage of air to or from the air spaces and, during descent, a source of air.

Ruptured tympanic membranes. The eustachian tube, leading from the middle ear to the throat, affords an avenue for keeping middle-ear pressure equal to environmental pressure. Air easily escapes from the middle ear through this tube when ambient pressure drops, but the valvelike opening in the throat impedes entry of air when environmental pressures rise. Thus, the increasing pressure within caissons or during descent in water often cannot be passively matched within the middle ear. Pressure forces the tympanic membrane (eardrum) inward, the walls of the middle ear swell, and serum or blood exudes into the relatively low pressure space to diminish its volume and reduce the pressure difference. A descent of ten feet (three metres) in water may cause rupture of the eardrum. Severe local pain sometimes occurs earlier, with descents of as little as two or three feet. Pain, loss of hearing, and occasionally dizziness and ringing of the ears occur. Unless middle-ear infection occurs, healing is spontaneous without permanent hearing loss.

Pulmonary congestion, edema, and hemorrhage. During diving, while breath-holding, compression of the chest reduces lung volume and maintains pressure within the lungs at that of the surrounding water. At the point where the thorax reaches the limit of compressibility, pressure within the lungs can no longer rise along with the increasing pressure of the water and body tissues. Lung vessels then become congested, exude serum, and eventually rupture, bleeding into the lungs. Breathing through a snorkel tube that is too long or through equipment with excessive air-flow resistance may also create a relatively negative pressure within the lungs and lead to similar injury. The diver will experience chest discomfort or pain, appear short of breath, and have bloody, frothy sputum. Treatment consists of drainage of secretions from the mouth and throat and, if breathing has stopped, artificial respiration. Oxygen, treatment of shock, and antibiotics to prevent infection may be necessary in severe cases.

Other pressure injuries. Descent in water may cause injury to the sinuses similar to that of the middle ear, with severe pain, swelling of the lining of sinus cavities, exudation of serum, and bleeding. If air cannot enter pockets formed beneath tightly fitted masks, helmets, ear plugs, or suits during descent, the higher surrounding pressure tends to push the face, external ear, or other exposed surface into the air space. Local swelling, congestion of blood vessels, and bleeding may produce an alarming appearance. These injuries usually clear without complications.

Decompression injury (caisson illness)

Cause of caisson illness. Gases dissolve in liquids in proportion to their partial pressures. With each 33 feet of descent in water, additional gas, equal in volume to that dissolved at sea level, can go into solution in body liquids. Dissolved inert gases, such as nitrogen or helium, create problems on ascent since they must then be eliminated in reverse order through the original pathways of entry. Thus nitrogen dissolved in tissue fluids must pass into blood and be carried in solution to the lungs to be discharged in gaseous form. Elimination of excess nitrogen requires about 12 hours. About 75 percent is released, mainly from aqueous tissues, in the first two and one-half hours. The more slowly eliminated remainder comes mainly from fatty tissues. The latter not only contain higher concentrations of nitrogen, since nitrogen is about five times more soluble in oil than in water, but generally are less abundantly supplied with blood to dissolve and transport nitrogen.

Much longer than 12 hours will be required for decompression after deep or prolonged dives to keep the rate of elimination slow enough to prevent bubble formation. If partial pressure of nitrogen in the lungs falls too rapidly, dissolved nitrogen behaves as if supersaturated and tends to form bubbles in tissue fluids and blood. The depth and duration of submersion and the rate of ascent influence the number and size of bubbles and the severity of symptoms; the location of the bubbles determines the nature of symptoms.

Bends (pain in joints). Bends occur most often in or around the shoulder and elbow joints in divers and at the knee and hip joints in caisson workers. Pain, usually mild at first, increases steadily to become deep and boring in character, and finally intolerable. Unlike pain caused by external trauma, typical manifestations of bends usually do not include local signs such as tenderness, discoloration, or swelling. The pain of bends may occur during ascent, but usually does so soon after surfacing; it nearly always happens (when it does) within 12 hours after ascent. Although in itself not of grave significance, the appearance of bends often presages the more serious consequences of decompression sickness. Pain is quickly relieved by recompression through return to greater depth or by means of a compression chamber. Subsequent decompression at proper rates, to allow safe elimination of excess nitrogen, can then be carried out.

Lung injuries. Air embolism accounts for most of the fatalities associated with decompression injury. Rapid ascent with breath holding is the usual mechanism, but a disease of the lungs that traps air and prevents its escape can result in air embolism. During decompression, air must be released to reduce pressure within the lungs to that of the surrounding water and body tissues. Excessive pressure can disrupt air sacs and force air into damaged blood vessels of the lung. Air bubbles then are carried in the bloodstream to vital organs, such as the brain and heart, where, by blocking the flow of blood, they may cause unconsciousness, paralysis, and rapid death from brain or heart damage. Recompression in a chamber at the earliest possible time is mandatory.

Other injuries of the lung resulting from similar mechanisms include pneumothorax, in which air collects between the lung and the thoracic cage, and interstitial and subcutaneous emphysema, in which air dissects through respiratory and other tissues to collect beneath the skin.

Bone injuries. Small areas of bone destruction, usually near joints commonly affected by bends, have been detected by X-ray in caisson workers. It is believed that these reflect interference with the blood supply in those who have had repeated and prolonged exposures to high pressure.

Other decompression effects. Other manifestations of evolved gas and bubble formation during decompression include prickling and burning sensations in the skin; patchy, mottled, and cyanotic discoloration of the skin; disturbances of vision; "chokes" consisting of burning pain in the upper midportion of the chest, which is aggravated by deep breathing and an uncontrollable urge to cough; and paralyses of extremities attributable to spinal-cord damage. The occurrence of chokes is serious, as clinical shock frequently follows. All of these manifestations, including paralysis, can be relieved by adequate recompression if given early enough.

BIBLIOGRAPHY. O.H. GAUER and G.D. ZUIDEMA (eds.), *Gravitational Stress in Aerospace Medicine* (1961), an authoritative compilation and review of the known biological effects of acceleration stresses; C.J. LAMBERTSEN (ed.), *Proceedings on the Third Symposium on Underwater Physiology* (1967), an extensive review of both research and operational aspects of diving medicine and of new techniques for achieving extremely deep dives; C.S. WHITE, *Biological Blast Effects*, AEC Report TID-5564 (1959), a review of the literature and research on the effects of blast forces upon living tissue; *Impact Acceleration Stress: A Symposium*, held at Brooks Air Force Base, 1961 (1962), a complete survey of the various types of acceleration, including impact forces, and their physiological and destructive effects upon biological systems.

(R.L.J.)

Computers

An automatic electronic machine that performs calculations, a computer is capable of accepting data, performing operations according to instructions (programs), and providing the results of the operations. A so-called digital computer operates with numbers expressed directly as digits and counts discretely. It is contrasted with the analogue (analog) computer, which operates on data represented by variable physical quantities, such as voltages, and measures continuously (operations are said to be analogous to the quantities represented). More than 90 percent of the computers in use in the early 1970s were of the digital type; they are covered in greater depth in this article. (For the influence of computer technology on activities concerned with ordering, storing, and using information, see INFORMATION PROCESSING.)

This article is divided into the following sections:

I. History
    Early developments
    The 20th century
II. Computer fundamentals
    Basic computer functions
    Types of computers
        Analogue computers
        Digital computers
        Hybrid computer systems
III. Programming systems and programming languages
    Programming fundamentals
    Language categories
        Algorithmic and procedural languages

I. History

EARLY DEVELOPMENTS

Abacus. The history of computing instruments may be considered to begin with the abacus. The word abacus is derived from the Greek word *abax* (or *abakos*), which means a board, tablet, or calculating table. Originating in the Orient more than 5,000 years ago and still used in some parts of the Middle and Far East, an abacus is a manually operated storage device that aids a human calculator (see Figure 1). It consists of a row of any number

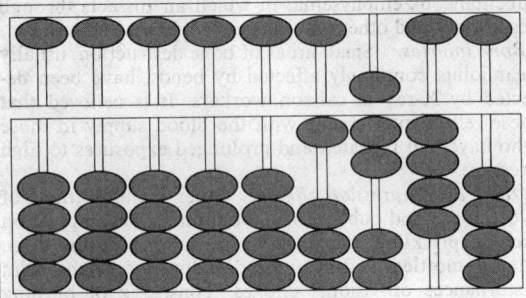

Figure 1: A type of abacus used in Japan.

of parallel wires, rods, or grooves on or in which slide small beads or blocks. The strung beads are divided into two sections by means of a bar perpendicular to the rods. One section has one or two beads, representing 0 and 5 depending upon their position along the rod. The second section has four or five beads, representing units. Each bar represents a significant digit, with the least significant digit on the right.

Napier's bones. John Napier was a distinguished Scottish mathematician and the inventor of logarithms. He made systematic use of the decimal point to separate the fractional from the integral part of numbers and aided in establishing that convention. In 1617 he published a work describing ingenious methods of performing the fundamental operations of multiplication and division by means of "rods" or "bones" (so called because they were printed on sticks of bone or ivory); the technique, combined with the use of original data tables, marks one of the historical contributions to computation by mechanical means.

Pascal's arithmetic machine. The French scientist–philosopher Blaise Pascal in 1642 built a successful digital calculating machine to aid him in computations for his father's business accounts. The first adding machine to resemble the modern desk calculator, it consisted of a train of number wheels whose positions could be observed through windows in the cover of a box that enclosed the mechanism. Numbers were entered by means of dial wheels. Pascal's computer was a digital device and carried out its computations by a process of integer counting. The machine utilized a mechanical gear system to add and subtract numbers with as many as eight columns of digits. The digits 0 to 9 were engraved on a series of ten wheels that had teeth to represent numbers. The rightmost wheel was the units dial; the second, the tens; the third, hundreds; and so on, in direct analogy to a number handwritten in decimal notation. During addition, "carrying" occurred by means of a series of gears arranged so that the next left wheel turned one unit when the dial exceeded the digit 9. It was therefore possible to perform addition by stepping the wheels through a number of intervals equal to the number to be added.

Leibniz' "Stepped Reckoner." The German mathematician Gottfried Wilhelm Leibniz invented in 1671, and completed in 1694, a more advanced adding machine than Pascal's arithmetic machine of 1642; it was called the "Stepped Reckoner." Pascal's machine could only count; the "Stepped Reckoner" could also multiply, divide, and extract square roots, a process it accomplished

by a series of repeated additions similar to that used even today in many modern digital computers. A working model of the Leibniz computer was completed in 1794 and was exhibited at the Royal Society in London. The machine proved to be unreliable, and it was not until 1820 that a machine capable of performing the four basic arithmetic operations of addition, subtraction, multiplication, and division became commercially available. The major contribution of Leibniz' work was its demonstration of the advantages of the binary over the decimal system for mechanical computers.

Babbage's "Analytical Engine." In 1835 in England, an inventor named Charles Babbage formulated the idea of an entirely new device, the "Analytical Engine," able to combine arithmetic processes with decisions based on its own computation. The "Analytical Engine" was essentially self-controlled; *i.e.*, an answer computed would be fed back to form the data in the various steps of a complex problem. The machine used two sets of Jacquard punched cards (see below)—one with punched-coded data, the other, the sequence of operations. The engine had two basic components: (1) a storage unit, with a memory device consisting of groups of 50 counter wheels that could store 1,000 figures of 50 digits each, and (2) the arithmetic desk-calculator section, the mill. The punched cards served as a control unit for the transfer of numbers and sequence of operations. Adapting the Jacquard loom mechanism, the "Analytical Engine" wove algebraic patterns just as the Jacquard loom wove flowers and leaves. Plungers passed through the holes in the cards and operated mechanisms for transferring numbers from storage to the data processing mill. Babbage also realized the efficiency of treating iterative processes as cycles, loops, or single operations, thus foreshadowing modern computing subroutines and automatic programming.

Recognizing the importance of printed results, Babbage insisted that both final and intermediate results be printed to avoid error. Input–output devices were thus necessary. Input to the machine was by means of three types of punched cards: "number cards" with the given numbers of constants of a problem; "directive cards" for controlling the movement of numbers in the machine; and "operation cards" for directing the performance of the actual operations, such as subtraction, addition, and multiplication.

The "Analytical Engine" is best known, however, for two related innovations of deceptive simplicity but revolutionary impact. The first of these was "conditional transfer," which permitted the machine to compare quantities and, depending upon the results of the comparison, branch or jump to another instruction or instruction sequence. The second feature permitted the results of a calculation to change other numbers and instructions previously set into the machine and thus, in effect, made it possible for the computer to modify its own program.

The "Analytical Engine" in the mid-19th century became the world's first digital computer. Babbage envisioned the principles of sequential control; that is, program control that included branching, looping, and both arithmetic and storage units with automatic printout. Babbage made drawings to show his plans for the completion of all of these processes, but the engine was forgotten until his writings were rediscovered in 1937.

Boole's logic. George Boole was an English logician and mathematician to whom all computer technicians are indebted for his development of symbolic logic, specifically of binary logic operators (AND, OR, etc.). Boole's *Treatise on Differential Equations* (1859) contained a lucid account of the general symbolic method, the bold employment of which led to Boole's chief discoveries. He did not regard logic as a branch of mathematics and pointed out an analogy between the symbols of algebra and those of logic as used to represent logical forms and syllogisms. Boole's formalism, showing the way to "mechanize" logic and operating on only 0 and 1, is the basis for what is now called Boolean algebra and binary switching, upon which modern computing is based. The algebra that goes by his name found many applications of which he never dreamed, such as in telephone com-

Marginal notes:

Components of Babbage's device

The first adding machine

The symbolic method

munications and computer switching theory and procedures.

Jacquard loom, Hollerith, and punched cards. A loom for weaving cloth invented by Joseph-Marie Jacquard of France in the early 1800s was the first use of a punched hole in a card to represent a number and control the operation of the loom. In 1886 a U.S. statistician named Herman Hollerith, while working on the 1880 census, developed the idea that such holes could be sensed by a machine that could sort and manipulate the arithmetic sums represented by the holes. Thus, Hollerith, inspired by Jacquard, invented the punched card, which is still used as a basic input medium to computers.

Hollerith combined punched cards with electromagnetic inventions to win fame as one of the primary developers of modern computers. By placing perforated cards over mercury-filled trays of cups, metal pins could be made to descend through the holes to touch the mercury below, thus completing an electronic circuit. Such automatic sensing made it possible to classify and count the data for the U.S. Census of 1890 in one-third of the time it had taken with the handwritten tally sheets used in the 1880 census. Hollerith directed the project and instructed census takers to punch holes to represent various characteristics of the population in predetermined locations on the cards. The holes were then counted by machine by the completion of electronic circuits in ways similar to those described above. The process enabled several characteristics to be counted with each handling, or "run," of the cards. The mechanical feelers used by Babbage for the detection of holes were thus replaced with electromechanical sensing equipment. Hollerith's sorting and punching devices were forerunners for current peripheral equipment. In 1911 Hollerith joined with two companies to form the Computing Tabulating Recording Company, which later became International Business Machines Corporation (IBM).

The margin note: Use of punched cards for a national census

THE 20TH CENTURY

Aiken and the Harvard Mark I. Beginning in 1939, Howard Aiken of Harvard University, in association with International Business Machines Corporation engineers, worked for five years to construct a fully automatic calculator using standard business-machine components. The Automatic Sequence Controlled Calculator (Harvard Mark I) that resulted was sequenced by punched paper tape. It was an electromechanical machine approximately 50 feet (15 metres) long and eight feet (2.4 metres) high. All numbers were represented to 23 decimal digits. It could perform five fundamental operations: addition, subtraction, multiplication, division, and table reference. Input data were entered on punched cards, and the output was recorded either on punched cards or by an electric typewriter.

Eckert and Mauchly and electronic calculators. J. Presper Eckert and John W. Mauchly, both of the University of Pennsylvania, were the inventors and developers of the ENIAC (an acronym for Electronic Numerical Integrator and Calculator), the first all-purpose, all-electronic digital computer. Completed in 1946, the ENIAC opened an entirely new and promising field of electronic calculation because it had speeds more than 1,000 times faster than those of the then-current electromechanical machines. It was estimated at the time that the nuclear-physics calculations that, soon after its installation, it did in two hours would have taken 100 engineers one year. Eckert and Mauchly organized their own company and, in 1950, conceived the Binac (Binary Automatic Computer), the first machine to use self-checking devices. The company was sold in 1951 to Remington Rand, but the two men were instrumental in completing Univac I for the United States Bureau of the Census. The Univac I was the first computer to handle both numerical and alphabetical information with equal ease. It utilized principles of information storage and of the separation of input–output from computation per se.

Von Neumann and stored programs. Primarily a pure mathematician, John von Neumann studied extensively the mathematical logic of the computer. In 1947, he devised a method for converting the ENIAC concept of an externally programmed machine to that of a stored-program computer, the EDVAC (Electronic Discrete Variable Automatic Computer).

Previously, a problem was entered into the machines by making hand adjustments of connections from one unit to another. Von Neumann permanently wired a selection of operations for groups of units and then placed these under central control. He also suggested that instruction codes be treated as numerals that could be stored electronically just as data numerals were stored, thus eliminating special instruction wiring. This stored-program concept led to the development of self-modifying computer programs since machine commands could then be manipulated by arithmetic operations. The plugboards and programming switches of the ENIAC were replaced in the EDVAC by an electrically alterable memory that could store both the instructions and the numbers to be used in a calculation. As had been suggested by Babbage three-quarters of a century earlier, the EDVAC was capable of operating on and changing the stored instructions and was thus capable of modifying its own program.

The margin note: The self-modifying computer program

While at the Institute for Advanced Study in Princeton, New Jersey, in 1946, von Neumann, with Arthur W. Burks and Herman H. Goldstine, published a paper that became a landmark in the history of computer sciences, if not in the history of human thought. In "Preliminary Discussion of the Logical Design of an Electronic Computing Instrument," the authors reviewed in detail the entire field of automatic computation and presented comprehensive designs for a parallel, stored-program computer that was a substantial departure from anything hitherto proposed. The paper had an enormous impact, and the ideas in it have strongly influenced the form of all subsequent digital computers.

II. Computer fundamentals

BASIC COMPUTER FUNCTIONS

The basic functions of any digital computer are (1) input, (2) storage, (3) control, (4) processing, and (5) output. A computer receives data in the form of binary codes of 1s and 0s and stores them on tapes, disks, drums, cores, or other media. The computer has properties similar to those of an adding machine; it can add, subtract, multiply, divide, and list; but in addition it can make decisions —*i.e.*, select on the basis of stored instructions. This stored-program concept and the memory capability are the two primary characteristics differentiating the computer from a high-speed calculator. The control function involves following instructions precisely as stored. The computer must be instructed (programmed) for every step. The output of the computer takes many forms. Generally, it is printed, put on cards or tape, stored in memory, displayed on a cathode-ray tube, or communicated to other remote devices. The nanosecond (1/1,000,000,000 second) computing speed, the random-access information retrieval (any bit of data from among billions of numbers and characters may be almost instantly retrieved), and the stored sequential or adaptive instructions (program steps) represent the differences between the computer and the calculator; these differences are of tremendous importance. A simplified sketch (Figure 2) can illustrate the basic functions. The control units are used to interface or synchronize the varying speeds of numerous input and output units to those of the central processing (arithmetic and logic) unit. The processor must also translate the relatively simple language used by the programmer into the more detailed computer-code form used internally by the computer.

The margin note: Computer output

The programming can be completed by people other than those skilled in management or engineering. Problem discoverers, analyzers, and solvers who fully understand computer capability need not necessarily know the intricacies of computer operation or programming. Several of the most important steps in computer usage are those of operations analysis.

A computer system or an electronic data-processing system is physically a collection of electromechanical and electronic components and devices assembled in metal

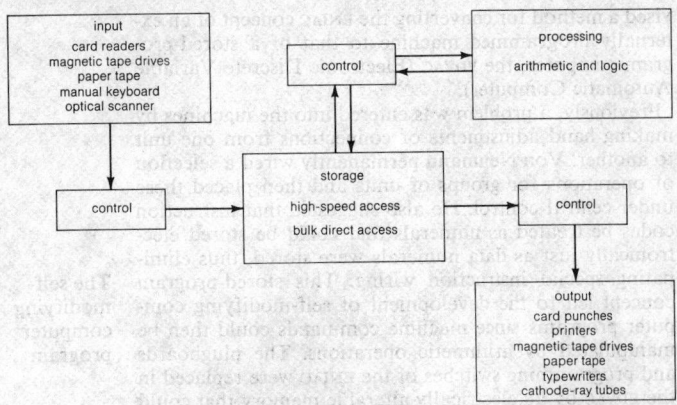

Figure 2: Basic computer functions.

cases (modules) and cabinets. These contain switching and communications components such as transistors, diodes, capacitors, resistors, and integrated circuits, all combined into various types of circuitry, together with memory systems, power supplies, delay lines, and various types of magnetic media such as tapes and wires for carrying and transforming data and information, as coded, into instructions and computations.

TYPES OF COMPUTERS

Modern computers are of three general types:

1. Analogue computers represent the values of variables or numbers by physical quantities—*i.e.*, angular positions or voltages, the magnitudes of which are made directly proportional to the variables or to suitable functions of the variables. Such a device solves problems by operating on continuous variables rather than discrete units as do digital computers. (An example would be the scale of an automobile speedometer with infinite gradation.)

2. Digital computers count specifically or discretely, never varying or responding in degrees but only to exact signals (flip-flops) that exist or do not exist. Data are represented by means of characters, numbers, and symbols —*i.e.*, the designation of one out of a finite number of alternatives.

Hybrid computers

3. While a digital computer basically counts (like an abacus) and an analogue computer measures, a third type, the hybrid computer, derives its power from a combination of the two types of operation as specifically designed for simulations, process control, signal processing, and psychological model building (see the Table).

Spectrum of Digital–Analogue Computers	
range	examples
Pure digital computer	general-purpose digital computers
Digital computer with analogue concepts	digital differential analyzer or digital computer with analogue-type language
Digital computer with analogue hardware	analogue arithmetic elements or analogue subroutines
Linked digital–analogue systems (hybrid)	true hybrid systems—digital computer and analogue computer play equal roles
Analogue computer with digital hardware	logical interconnection devices and small digital computers for input-output
Analogue computer with digital techniques	iterative differential analyzers
Pure analogue computer	general-purpose analogue computers

Analogue computers. An analogue device is defined as one that operates on the principle of similarity in proportional relations to a process modelled when values are kept constant over a specified range.

An analogue computer that represents physical variables by means of analogues uses various types of amplifiers connected so as to perform such arithmetic operations as summation, multiplication, and such mathematical operations as integrations and differentiations. Accuracy is somewhat limited by the precision available in some of the electrical components; it might vary slightly due to environmental or materials conditions. Digital computers do not have this problem because they operate on the presence or absence of discrete signals. Analogue computers are similar to voltmeters in the way they measure values. Analogue computers translate various physical conditions such as flow, temperatures, pressures, mechanical or electrical speeds, and angular positions into mechanical or electrical analogues. An automobile speedometer is an analogue computer measuring the voltage output of a generator connected to the drive shaft. The analogue computer is the physical system in which the analysis or solution of the problem is mirrored by the varying values or behaviour. A simple example of analogue control is the household thermostat, or temperature controller. The measured temperature is converted into an electrical current that varies in magnitude as the temperature rises and falls. In analogue computers the electrical circuitry of a controller is analogous to the problem to be solved, such as the maintenance of the measured temperature at some present value. Circuitry notes the measured value of the temperature and computes the amount for resetting of the final control element, which might be a valve, damper, or switch that is needed to return the temperature to the desired value. The corrective signal is then sent to the final control element. Analogue computers operate on data continuously, working in real time, as they solve problems.

History. Among the earliest analogue computers was a special-purpose computer devised by Lord Kelvin in 1872 as a tide predictor. Along the same lines, a harmonic synthesizer was later devised with 80 components, each of which could generate a sinusoidal (wavelike) motion. The periods of the various units were simply related by gear trains; each component motion could be multiplied by constant factors by adjustment of the fulcrum on levers, and the components were added to produce a resultant. A pen attached to the sum lever plotted the output. From harmonic analyzers a machine called the isograph was developed in 1937 to solve polynomial equations with real coefficients. An electrical version of the equation solver was produced in the same year, and both mechanical and electrical machines have since been built to solve systems of linear equations.

A significant development in analogue computers was the invention of a device for amplifying torque by the U.S. electrical engineer Vannevar Bush. In 1955 D.R. Hartree fabricated a differential analyzer using parts of a child's mechanical construction (Meccano) set. In such a device, shaft motion represents variables, gears give multiplication or division, and differential gears provide addition and subtraction. Integration is accomplished by means of a knife-edged wheel rotating at a variable radius on a circular rotating table. A mechanical interconnection of such devices is the analogue of a system represented by a set of differential equations.

Basic operation and applications. Most analogue computers operate by manipulating electrical potentials or, more usually, potential differences. The basic unit of an analogue computer is the operational amplifier, a device whose output current is proportional to its input potential difference. By causing this output current to flow through suitable components, further potential differences are obtained and can be made to bear any one of a wide range of relationships to the input. Until the late 1950s, all electrical analogue computers used vacuum tubes; later designs, using solid-state devices, have been much smaller, consume less power, and are less expensive.

The original electronic analogue computers arose from the needs of anti-aircraft artillery "predictors." In these, the variables were latitude, longitude, and height of the target and projectile, respectively, all of which varied with time. Fixed or slowly varying data were also fed into the predictor, such as muzzle velocity and ballistic characteristics of the projectile and characteristics of the atmosphere; the computer had to solve two simultaneous equations so that the target and the projectile, each moving along its own course, would arrive at the point of intersection at the same time.

One interesting application of analogue computers is in aerodynamics. Equations relating air flow and the attitude of, and forces on, lifting surfaces are complex, and their solutions by conventional methods were so difficult and tedious that in the past many designers preferred to ignore theory and rely on experiment. Analogue computers became available at a time when the experimental approach was becoming impossibly expensive and dangerous, and difficult equations involving such problems as flutter (a peculiar type of vibration) are now within their capability.

Such a computer can so completely describe the relationships of speed, altitude, and lift that it can simulate the complete behaviour of an actual aircraft. If the multiplying, integrating, and other factors of the various units are brought out to controls similar to aircraft controls, and the outputs to suitable actuators, a student can be made to experience all the operations of flying an aircraft. With such a "simulator" he can be taught all that he needs to know to fly the aircraft under normal, faulty, or even emergency conditions without the expense and danger of learning by actually flying.

In addition to general-purpose analogue machines, adapted for solving a wide range of problems, there are many special-purpose analogue computers merging into types that carry out functions similar to those of normal analogue computers but that are not considered to be computers at all. Examples are process controllers in chemical manufacturing plants and automatic pilots in aircraft. In such special-purpose machines, the outputs of transducers operated by physical parameters (temperature, fluid flow, and pressure in the chemical example; aircraft attitude, speed, and altitude in the automatic-pilot example) are fed into a device that combines them by arithmetical processes effected by methods commonly used in analogue computers.

The differential analyzer is an electromechanical (or mechanical) analogue computer designed to solve differential equations. It consists of an assortment of shafts, wheels, and disks arranged so that the combination of such components with the prime motion injected through the independent variable shafts permits the solution of many-term differential equations. Digital differential analyzers are those that use numbers that represent analogue quantities such as digital voltmeters.

Network analyzers, devices or programs for analyzing special networks, are the bases for construction of special-purpose analogue computers. Some areas of application of network analyzers include: (1) psychology–neurology, in which neuron networks based on simple models of brain behaviour are simulated; (2) management and control scheduling, in which elapsed time and costs of projects involving many special operations can be controlled; (3) electronics network analysis, in which the performance of passive and active component circuits, specifically frequency response and pulse response, for example, are used to compute the performance of long distance telephone circuits under various operating conditions; (4) hydrodynamics–hydraulics network analysis of the flow of liquids through networks of pipes, such as in sewer or water systems; and (5) electric power distribution network analogues in such areas as power transmission line distribution systems, power grids, and direct current circuits.

All of the above analyzers have special conditions relating to responses to peak loads, overloads, transients, various types of fault defects (faults), and other related phenomena. Analysis of such networks calls for checkouts to determine methods of minimizing losses, rerouting, supplies, power, energy, and fault elimination. Some networks are used to simulate mechanical or electronic systems for system behaviour studies.

Engineers can simulate individual processes on a general-purpose analogue computer and thus develop data from which they can design a special-purpose analogue computer that will handle exact requirements for a specific application. A custom-tailored single-purpose computer does one specific job rapidly and accurately and as many times as desired. Its single program is built-in, so

that it is possible for regular plant personnel to be able to learn quickly how to operate it.

Great precision and accuracy can be designed into the special-purpose analogue computer. The cost can be kept relatively low because the computer has to contain only those components needed for a given application. Control panels can be made more meaningful to operating personnel. Controls and adjustments can be readily identified as to their specific functions.

Special-purpose analogue computers are designed to operate continuously and reliably in a typical industrial plant environment. They are designed to perform satisfactorily over a wide temperature range and so need no air conditioning.

A special-purpose analogue computer usually consists of a user-designed combination of the following basic solid-state modules:

1. Operational amplifier. This is the workhorse of the computer system. It can be used to add, subtract, integrate, and perform time-delay, gain-change, inversion, and memory functions.

2. Logarithmic modules. These are used for multiplication and division. The module converts a linear function to its logarithm. Two or more logarithms can be added and the antilog taken to provide the product of the inputs. For division, the logarithms are subtracted.

3. Function modules. These can either square or extract the square root of a quantity.

4. Variable-function generators. These are used to approximate a nonlinear function that is not a neat mathematical form or that must be calibrated in the field to suit certain process conditions.

Digital computers. Basically, a digital system or computer has the ability electronically to perform only very simple or elementary tasks. It uses a binary number system, which has only two numbers, 0 and 1, whereas the decimal system has ten digits. By using various horizontal- and vertical-positioning techniques, these two binary digits, or "bits," can be made to represent numbers, letters, symbols, and codes. Binary 0110, for example, represents the decimal number 6. Operation in binary mode, then, means that the computer is able to indicate two possible states or conditions. Like the ordinary light bulb, it is either on or off. Similarly, in the computer the transistors, circuits, and other components are either conducting or they are not; specific areas on plastic tapes are magnetized or they are not; pulses are present or they are not. Thus the circuitry senses either a hole in paper tapes or cards, or the absence of a hole, to indicate either a zero or a one. By judicious use of this positioning and arrangement of holes plus ingenious coding techniques, these binary digits (or groups of digits called bytes, words, or slabs) are used to develop both complex and simple sets of instructions called subroutines, routines, and programs.

Binary arithmetic. Most digital computers use the binary code, which has only two digits, 0 and 1, and which can be represented electrically by a variety of two-state (switching) devices; a switch can be "on" for 1 and "off" for 0. It is much easier to design two-state devices than the ten-state devices that would be required for decimal code. Also, the arithmetical processes are much simpler in binary code than in decimal code. In the normal decimal notation, each digit represents successive powers of 10, whereas in the binary code, each digit represents successive powers of 2. Thus, the number 251 means $2 \times 10^2 + 5 \times 10 + 1$; the corresponding binary code for this number is 11111011, meaning $2^7 + 2^6 + 2^5 + 2^4 + 2^3 + 2^1 + 2^0$. The binary equivalents of some decimal integers are written as follows:

1	1
2	10
3	11
4	100
5	101
6	110
7	111
8	1000
9	1001

Margin notes:

Application of analogue computers to aerodynamics problems

Applications of network analyzers

Special-purpose analogue computers

Value of the binary system

10	1010
20	10100
100	1100100

In normal decimal numbers, multiplication by ten is performed by shifting the number one place to the left and adding a zero; the above list shows that in binary arithmetic this operation results in a multiplication by two. The list also shows that binary numbers have more digits than the corresponding decimal numbers; the binary number for 100 has the same number of digits as the decimal number for 1,000,000. Many early binary machines were designed to manipulate 36 binary digits, but machines vary from 12 to 72 or more.

Basic operation. Because of the use of the binary system, the simple presence or absence of holes or magnetic spots on tapes provides the necessary instructions for the computer to read, write, store, transmit, and compute the solutions of great varieties of scientific, business, machine control, and research problems. The computer itself can only count, compare, store, retrieve, and perform simple arithmetic functions such as addition, subtraction, and multiplication. Examples of upper limits of speed and memory capacities achieved by the early 1970s are speeds of 100,000,000 instructions per second, 250-nanosecond (250/1,000,000,000-second) retrieval time, and 6,000 lines per minute printing capability.

Because the computer can compare, it can make decisions; using prescribed criteria, it can select from programmed alternatives. An example of this would be a computer instruction such as: Is the result of A times B less than the value of X? If yes, perform instruction P. Is the result equal to the value of X? If yes, branch to program Q. Is the result greater than the value of X? If yes, perform process Y. The computer will assess the values of manipulations and make conclusions following rigorous instructions.

The physical heart of a computer is the central processing unit (CPU). Grouped around this "mainframe" is a variety of storage and other ancillary equipment such as sorters, collators, punches, readers, converters, and the like. Units with direct connection to the CPU are said to be on-line; peripheral units performing separate tasks are called off-line. If answers are fast enough (instantaneous) to be used in influencing the process underway, the system is said to be a real-time system.

Computer systems vary in size, complexity, cost, computation, retrieval speed, and transmission capability. Computers have many classifications of which the most important are general purpose and special purpose. Configurations may include master–slave and timesharing. All computer systems, regardless of size, type, or basic use, follow certain fundamental concepts and operational principles. The data, instructions, and information flow follow logical and functional lines.

Input. Input to the computer can be in a variety of forms—punched cards, punched paper tape, magnetic tape, magnetic cards, or magnetic ink (bank checks); or the input may be made directly and in binary form from the core memory or peripheral storage units and various conversion units. By the early 1970s typed print and even handwritten script in limited vocabularies became serviceable as input to computers. Optical scanning had been developed in the early 1960s. Input is also generated photoelectrically, by pushbutton telephones, and through the use of TV-type cathode-ray tubes. The latter is done through typewriter keyboards or by the use of electronic pointers or light pens (styli) that can erase, alter, or add to core memory any information or solution that is displayed on the cathode-ray tube. Such visual alterations are directly convertible to electronic pulses (and characters) in real time (immediately) by pointing the light pen at the data or information on the tube. This is an important aid for engineering and other applications. Voice input is being perfected with limited vocabulary. Optical scanners can read more than 1,500 characters per second, or 90,000 documents per hour. Direct input can be provided by teletypewriter equipment and numerous other communication devices.

Storage and memory devices. Primary storage is fast, expensive, and relatively limited in most medium and small machines. Secondary storage, on-line (extended core) or off-line (auxiliary) has no limit except expense and requirements. Tape storage is sequential and requires scanning character by character over a reel perhaps 2,400 feet (730 metres) long and with a density of 800 characters per inch (31.5 characters per millimetre) to find a desired item of information. Other memory units are capable of random access from magnetic disks (over 8,000 revolutions per minute), drums, plastic cards, data cells, or photo-disks. The central processing unit is capable of translating from them any item or bit meaning "transferring" with speeds as fast as 250 nanoseconds. From the input unit, data or programs are moved to the storage section of the central processing unit or to mass-memory units. Some of these units have capacities on the order of 1,000,000,000,000 characters in a single wall-size configuration of six to ten units. Buffer units, used as separate modules or as part of the various peripheral groups or of central processing units, are capable of accepting and briefly holding data inactive and then transmitting at slower or faster speeds.

In computer terminology, "writing" means putting information into a register (a device for storage of a specific quantity of data); "reading" means taking information out of a register for use; "erase" means completely removing the information from a register; "dumping" means removing or replacing the information with spaces or zeros or copying or printing all or part of the contents, as in a transfer from one storage device to another. The most common types of storage devices (some also double as input devices) are drum, disk, core, tape, magnetic cards, or stacks of punched cards.

For use in a binary machine, a device to store one bit must be able to be placed in one of two stable states, corresponding to 1 and 0; must be able to maintain this state indefinitely until changed; must be able to be read or changed at very high speed (up to 1,000,000 times a second); and, because millions of bits may have to be stored, must be very inexpensive. Actually, since not all of these requirements can be met at present by a single type of device, most computers have several types of memories. Although many devices and techniques have been tried, the most successful ones have been based on the principle of magnetic recording. The differences between the various kinds of storage devices in present use lie in the type and disposition of the magnetic material.

Memories that can be addressed at random at high speed are essential for high-speed computer operation and are found in almost all machines of current design. They are commonly built up of small cores shaped like doughnuts, usually $\frac{1}{16}$ inch (1.6 millimetres) in diameter, that are made of a hard magnetic material (ferrite) and that can be magnetized in either of two directions by currents in wires passing through the hole. Such a core is "read" to discover which state it was in by trying to magnetize it in a fixed direction, usually that corresponding to the state chosen to represent "0." If the core was in the "1" state prior to the read operation, the resulting magnetic flux reversal will cause an electrical pulse to be generated on a sense wire that threads the hole. If the core was already in the "0" state, however, no flux reversal will occur and no pulse will appear on the sense wire. Since the above readout method sets all cores to the "0" state, the stored information is destroyed and must be rewritten after reading if it is to be remembered. This technique, called "destructive read," is used most often because it is the least expensive.

Techniques involving thin evaporated magnetic films have demonstrated speeds of 10,000,000 read-write cycles per second. Because costs of film memories were higher than those of core memories, they were used in the early 1970s only as small "scratch-pad" memories to speed up computer operations.

Despite great progress in the development of random-access memories, they will probably never be large enough (and inexpensive enough) to hold the tens of millions of words needed in many problems. Data infre-

Tape scanning

quently referred to can be stored in slower, less expensive types of memory for secondary storage and transferred to the high-speed memory when needed. Slow-access stores are typified by magnetic tapes; they use a wide (one-inch, or 25-millimetre) tape similar in many ways to tape used on commercial magnetic-tape recorders. The digits to be stored are recorded as dots of magnetism. There are commonly up to 16 separate parallel tracks across the tape. Although there are often as many as 1,600 bits per linear inch (about 40 bits per millimetre), the number of bits to be recorded and read is so high that tape speeds of 200 inches (500 centimetres) per second are common. To read any particular entry on the tape it is necessary to be able to start and stop the tape in a few thousandths of a second, and the mechanical design of the tape-handling equipment is thus a major problem. The capacity of such a store is virtually unlimited (up to 10,000,000 words per tape reel), and tapes of data or programs may be removed when not in use, freeing the tape mechanism for other work. The main problem with tapes is the access time, since it may be necessary to traverse the whole tape (requiring a minute or more) to find a desired stored item. Tape stores are generally used only for information that can be processed as it arises or for information that has been pre-stored in logical order, so that the tape-handling unit does not spend most of its time searching for the required item.

Storage in magnetic drums and disks

Intermediate between these two types of storage are the magnetic drum and the magnetic disk. A drum can be considered as a wide magnetic tape, carrying from one to 200 tracks, wrapped around a drum rotating at about 3,000 revolutions per minute. Each digit recorded comes around to the reading point every $\frac{1}{50}$ of a second (which is the maximum access time), but, except on a few very large and expensive units, the capacity of the store is limited to several tens of thousands of words. The magnetic disk has proved to be a less expensive way of providing the very large, medium-speed stores needed in many applications (*e.g.*, recording airline seat reservations). Up to 20 disks, coated on both sides with magnetic material, are rotated on a common shaft, and a reading head is positioned to read a desired track. Because of this positioning, access time is somewhat longer than that of the drum, but capacities of up to 10,000,000 words per unit are available. Removable disks are also available.

Even larger capacities than those economically provided by disks are desired in some applications (*e.g.*, storing multilanguage dictionaries for language translation), and types of storage devices based on photographically recorded spots read with light beams have appeared. These "read-only" stores (the computer cannot change the recorded data) have access times similar to magnetic disks and capacities up to 10,000,000,000 words.

Another device in the memory field is the plated-wire memory. In this system the basic storage element is an extremely thin conductive wire coated with magnetic film. The wire is sandwiched between the surfaces of a printed circuit board and then "stacked" with others to complete a finished memory array. Although the manufacturing of this plated wire is tremendously complex, the finished product is only one wire rather than thousands of magnetic cores. The advantage of such a method over that of the magnetic-core memory is its nondestructive readout capability. The greatest limiting factor in the use of plated wire is its high cost. Even the most successful applications of plated-wire memories have resulted in cost increases for the memory system of at least three times that of magnetic cores. The price differential, however, has been reduced somewhat, and the plated-wire memory seems likely to gain wider use.

Semiconductor memories

The development of the semiconductor memory had reached a significant point by the early 1970s and was widely regarded as the next step forward in memory technology. There are several reasons for this: speed, density, cost, and technology. Several times in the past it has been thought that cores had reached their ultimate limit of speed. This has always proved to be false. Advances in ferrite technology have produced faster materials, and reduced core size has made possible faster switching,

shorter line length, and increased density. In the past, it had also been thought that cores had reached the limit of their capability because smaller cores could not be physically wired. At the present, cores as small as 12 or 13 mils in outer diameter (approximately seven mils inner diameter) are being successfully wired (1,000 mils equal one inch or 25.4 millimetres). There is little doubt that still smaller cores could be wired should it be necessary. Evidently, cores will not soon reach the limit of their capability. It is clear that memory capacities of larger and larger sizes are required, but electrical problems associated with resistance of the small wire required to string them and mechanical problems associated with the strength of the core could be serious. Semiconductor memories offer speeds ranging from those of relatively slow core memories to the ultrafast ten-billionths of a second (nanoseconds) or less. While magnetic film technologies, including plated wire, optimistically offer potential speed improvements of a factor of 2 or 3 (considering nondestructive readout operation), semiconductors offer potential speed improvements of a factor of 10 or more compared to core memories. Bit density improvement in core memories is clearly related to the size of the core while film memories offer potential improvement in density over cores due to the inherent nature of the processes involved. Core memory size limitations relate to mechanical constraints. Film memory density limitations are subject to constraints associated with etching and plating technology. Semiconductor density is also related to processes that offer significantly greater densities than core or even thin film technology because they are associated with diffusion and evaporation technology.

Most manufacturers are not limiting their plans exclusively to cores or semiconductors, and future computer technology is almost certain to offer a hierarchy of memory systems composed of core, semiconductors, and perhaps even other technologies. Core memories and semiconductors are approached as complementary technologies. Large core memory systems are available at moderate speeds and low cost for extensive, nonvolatile, random access data storage. Smaller integrated circuit memories may be used in buffer applications of two kinds: as buffer memories for small, low-cost replacements of core buffer memories when cost of the circuit is higher than the cost of the core stack, or for systems in which large, low-cost core memories are used as backing stores for high performance and higher priced semiconductor memories.

A laser memory system has been built that offers a 1,000,000,000,000-bit storage in 60 square feet (5.6 square metres) of floor space. Access to any of these data or information can be achieved within a maximum of 8.6 seconds. The bits are stored on rhodium-coated polymer data strips by a laser beam. The system offers read-while-write verification, permanent nondegrading records, easy updating, and selective retrieval of data based on up to 15 criteria such as less than, greater than, and key word. For information retrieval, data is tracked by an optical system that will give error rates of less than one part in 10^{10}.

A memory cell has been developed by Bell Telephone Laboratories that may someday process information up to 20 times faster than existing equipment using semiconductor technology and materials. The tiny memory may permit computer memory access speeds in billionths (U.S.), rather than millionths, of a second. The memory cell consists of a metal semiconductor diode with a large guard ring connected in series with a diffused p–n junction diode. Each interconnected cell occupies an area of 15 square mils and can be individually accessed in memory array. Experimental arrays fabricated thus far, using photolithography, silicon etching, and air isolation techniques, indicate a potential memory capacity of 100,000 bits of information per square inch (15,500 bits per square centimetre) of integrated circuit material.

Magnetic bubble memory

A new "magnetic bubble" computer memory, also discovered at Bell Telephone Laboratories, could, according to some experts, drastically change the architecture of future computers by shrinking the size of the total system considerably "from half a floor to the size of a suitcase." The technology is based on tiny magnetic domains that appear, disappear, and move around through certain kinds of crystalline materials (such as garnets) under the control of magnetic and electrical fields. The goal has been to develop thin crystalline planes of magnetic material that could hold about 1,000,000 domains per square inch, or the equivalent of about 100 pages of text. Potentially, stacks of such memories holding as much as 100,-000,000 bits per square inch could store massive amounts of information that would be instantly accessible to computers, at a fraction of the cost of such devices as disks and drum storage units.

Central processor (arithmetic, logic, and control). Information programs, or data, are drawn from storage or input units by the central processing unit for manipulation and are then returned to storage to await further orders in regard to output decisions. The logic operations include comparing information and selecting the valid or desired process or program based on predetermined decision criteria. Other CPU tasks are referring, shifting, complementing, rounding, debugging (discovering and correcting errors), displaying, transmitting, etc. Until the advent of time-sharing computers, the CPU was usually input/output limited. Time-sharing brought a whole new computer philosophy.

The components of computers relate to elementary switches and amplifiers. Such switches and switching techniques comprise a myriad of types and combinations. They are often referred to as "gates," operators, or elements. Switching involves relays and amplifiers of many types. The original computers were built of vacuum and gas tubes, but these quickly gave way to transistors and they soon became the basis of all modern computing mainframe and peripheral equipment. The transistor amplifies, generates, and switches electrical signals in electronic circuits that also contain such other elements as resistors, capacitors, and diodes in their connections. Resistors impede the flow of signal energy, while capacitors store it. Diodes provide a path for electrical current in one direction only, thus transforming, or rectifying, alternating current into direct current. Large electronic systems such as today's computers consist of millions of transistors and other electronic components. These massive, complex systems were made possible by the low cost, low operating temperature, tiny size, and long life of the transistor.

The millions of components making up the computer had to be handled individually and connected by soldering or welding. Heating and bending, possible corrosion of the joining of material, and the expansion difficulties at a joint during heating reduced reliability by increasing the chance for damage. Also, computer speed is limited by the time it takes a signal to travel from one circuit to another. Each foot of circuit separation requires a travel time of at least a nanosecond. This travel time can be reduced only by making the circuits and their separations microscopically small. Microelectronics was the inevitable response to the need for smaller size, lower cost, and greater reliability. Microelectronics thus makes it possible to mass-produce on a minuscule chip of semiconductor material (usually silicon) the very complicated circuits that formerly required hundreds of thousands of separate elements, transistors, diodes, resistors, and capacitors. Some silicon chips—squares less than one-quarter inch (6.4 millimetres) on a side—contain more than 1,000 transistors and diodes with all their connections (see also INTEGRATED CIRCUITRY).

Timesharing. The input/output (I/O) devices, such as card and tape recorders, printers, etc., are relatively slow (speeds are measured in milliseconds) compared to speed of the central processing unit. The CPUs were inefficient because they had to "wait" with solutions of problems that required split or a few seconds to solve, but many minutes for input or printout. Computer engineers soon developed several new techniques:

1. Multiprocessing, the operation of several "slave" or I/O processors subservient to a master-control process. By this means all input/output and mass-memory units

are on-line real-time (OLRT), and superfast expensive "computer" processor time is less often waiting or wasted. Efficient monitor clocking and preplanned scheduling provide highest efficiency for the system.

2. Parallel operation, the passage of information through the single computer, or any part of it, by using two or more lines or channels simultaneously.

3. Multiprogramming, in which there is no central processor in the traditional sense of the word; instead, the separate and combined functions of three modules (processor, memory, and controller) perform the work of the CPU. The time-sharing system is memory-oriented; data bypass the processor if not needed; many jobs enter the computer simultaneously, each isolated, and each solved with little variation in turn-around time. These three techniques, and others relating to time sharing, permit concurrent processing of batch, demand, and real-time programs. The time-sharing system automatically overlaps, coordinates, allocates, and protects memory and I/O by accepting the proper order of various new program interrupts and queues. It further issues peripheral schedules, diagnoses privileged control functions, improper orders, and machine malfunctions. Access to, and retrieval from, the time-sharing system is in effect instantaneous from the standpoint of the remote communications devices since the solutions are available to them the instant the problem is completely entered. Each remote-control unit can be linked to a communications device, for a total of over 3,000 remote user connections. On larger systems some CPU speeds of time-sharing computers use only five nanoseconds per logic level, and such units occupy as little as eight cubic feet (0.4 cubic metre) of space. Thus, time sharing could be generally described as the ability of a computer to have simultaneous communications with many remote stations that have information or problems, the solution or retrieval of which can be returned to the sender in time to be a part of his continuing inquiry. This process is performed without interrupting other batch, demand, or real-time program operation of its current (concurrent) work.

Console. The central processing unit is the real control section, but the console often regulates the external manual control. The computer program can be started, interrupted, stopped, modified, and monitored at the console. It has the slowest input (usually by typewriter), and the console is often combined in one main frame with internal memory, arithmetic, and inquiry sections. A special buffer section separates memory from arithmetic and inquiry. It directs, coordinates, executes, times, and communicates the performance of the system. The CPU automatically goes to the next cycle when the preceding cycle is complete.

Through the multiplexers (memory multiplexer or input/output multiplexer) console operations can control multi-programming, multiprocessing, or parallel programming, though these functions are usually automatic and dynamic. The control section or console becomes extremely important in case of component breakdown, or when debugging, printing of diagnoses, or post-mortem routines are in operation.

Hybrid computer systems. During the 1960s and 1970s there were many instances of general-purpose digital computers and general-purpose analogue computers being interconnected to form hybrid systems. The range of types of systems from pure digital to pure analogue is shown in the Table.

An example of the application of hybrid computers is the process called numerical control, frequently abbreviated NC. (Some British users prefer the phrase Direct Digital Control—DDC.)

A major application of NC is the development of punched paper or plastic tapes containing programs to guide and control machines and industrial processes, operations, and individual machines on the basis of various criteria (such as tolerance limits), including "exception reports" and corrective or adaptive routines stored in a computer. Graphics requiring manipulation are converted to digital information, operated on, and returned to the analogue state.

Numerical control has rapidly emerged from one-of-a-kind aerospace applications to commercial potential, particularly in production and assembly line manufacturing. Several large manufacturing companies have experimented and run pilot projects. NC is normally considered to be ideally suited for machine tools. Its value, however, is brought out most clearly when this equipment is tied to total system management control, in engineering, management, and quality control applications united and centralized with certain kinds of scheduling and on-line, real-time exception reporting. The ability of management to oversee and control, within minutes, all phases of production and related activities simultaneously or in parallel with automated drafting, numerically controlled shops, and inspection tapes is truly "total."

III. Programming systems and programming languages

PROGRAMMING FUNDAMENTALS

As has been indicated, the power of the digital computer rests not only in its speed and capacity for manipulating large masses of coded data but also on the fact that it can perform complicated sequences of such actions under control of a stored program. This permits the same computer to work at a variety of tasks in sequence or even intermittently. Before the computer can work at all, however, a program or programs must be prepared and introduced in a programming language into its storage. The term programming language reflects the fact that a program can be regarded as made up of an imperative statement or an indicative statement or both regarding such sequences. A computer task is first formulated and then expressed in an appropriate language, presumably one suited to the application and the thought processes of the formulator. The specification thus expressed is then translated, perhaps in several stages, into a coded program directly executable by the computer on which the task is to be run. The coded program is said to be in "machine language," while languages suitable for original formulation are referred to as "problem-oriented languages." A wide variety of problem-oriented languages has been developed, making the process of successful program preparation depend more on understanding of the problem than on understanding of the computer that is to run it. Indeed, most of these languages are essentially machine-independent and can be used with any computer for which appropriate translation programs exist.

In all but the simplest cases, however, a computer program is run on a computer system, not just a computer. That is, the digital processor and memory that execute the stored program are imbedded in a complex configuration of equipment, which includes input/output devices and mass storage devices, remote transmission links, and possibly control interfaces to other machines and processes. In more complicated computer systems, there is usually more than one processor/memory assemblage, the duplication being either to provide more efficient computing power and backup capability or to permit specialization of certain aspects of the process; *e.g.*, a special subsystem to handle input/output functions.

The mode in which such a computer system is operated varies according to purpose, which must be known to the programmer. Early attempts to optimize the efficiency of system use resulted in the concept of "batch" mode—each job is submitted in its entirety (in the form, say, of a program on punched cards) and results are returned to the submitter at some later time (in the form, say, of printed tables). More refined versions permit the submitted job to call for program segments or data pools obtained from "within the system" (*i.e.*, stored on mass storage devices available to the system) and for submission of jobs from locations removed from the system proper (*i.e.*, "remote batch"). These are conveniences for the user that do not, however, have much effect on programming style. The system itself may be internally organized to work on several jobs intermittently, thus improving its total "throughput" rate, but, again, this does not in itself fundamentally alter the style of use. The latter possibility, however, has led to the concept of a time-sharing mode of operation;

not only are many programs being executed at once, on an intermittent basis, but the user is permitted direct interaction with the program during execution through a generally remotely located terminal. Programs that are used in control applications can also be characterized as executing in this mode—the communication is with a machine rather than with a human. Such an "interactive" mode makes possible a fundamentally different style of use, which consequently has implications for programming languages.

Computer systems are supplied with a variety of programs designed largely to assist the user to run jobs or to optimize system performance without unduly penalizing the user running jobs. This collection of programs, called the operating system, is as important to the operation of the computer system as the equipment itself. The operating system is usually supplied by the computer manufacturer or a firm specializing in program design. The distinction between computer system programs and equipment is often made by referring to software as contrasted with hardware. Successful operation of a computer system depends on the stable and reliable function of its operating system, which is usually "frozen" and not subject to changes, even to improve performance, until the implications for operation have been first explored. Current technology makes it possible to build in some operating characteristics as fixed programs introduced by customer orders into a processor at the time of manufacture, which leads to a further distinguishing feature called firmware.

Relative to user programs, the operating system may be in control during execution, as when a time-sharing monitor suspends one program and activates another, or at the time a user program is initiated or terminated, as when a scheduling program determines which user program is to be executed next. Certain operating system programs, however, may operate as independent units to facilitate the programming process, and in this category are translators, which transform an entire program from one language to another; interpreters, which execute a program sequentially, translating at each step; or debuggers, which execute a program piecemeal, interpretively or not, and monitor various circumstances to permit the programmer to check to see whether the operation of the program is correct.

Translators are classified as assemblers or compilers. An assembler is a translator that takes a program in a form close to machine language, with each instruction step identified explicitly even if symbolically, and translates it into actual machine language, or a form that can be so rendered at the time the program is loaded. A compiler, by contrast, is a translator that takes a program written in a higher-level language and translates it into an assembly language program. Since higher-level languages tend to be more or less specifically problem-oriented, there may be two or more stages of compilation. A program written in a special "simulation" language, for example, may be translated at one compilation stage into a more "general-purpose" problem-oriented language, which is then subjected to a second stage of compilation into assembly language, and from there in a third stage to machine language. The user need be aware in detail only of the features of the highest level here, although some awareness of the total process is helpful in designing programs that are efficient, both running and being translated. In particular, however, only the assembler need be geared in detail to the particular hardware configuration on which the program will run, although general features such as the number of input/output units must be taken into account at higher levels.

Higher-level languages may be distinguished as procedural or nonprocedural, depending on whether they specify a sequence of actions in an information processing task or not. The latter type are very specialized, because they imply a solution method, and the only function of the user is to supply details of format, input parameters, and the like. In most cases the term "programming languages" is used to apply to procedural languages. These differ among one another by level of

The notion of the "batch" mode

Translating into machine language

generality and intended class of intended applications, which are reflected in the data structures handled, operations allowed, file and communication features incorporated, and program structures assumed. Data structures are composed of elementary units of various data types including integers, noninteger numbers, bit patterns, and strings of characters. The composition may be into lists and arrays of various sorts. Operations are defined appropriate to the various data types and structures available; arithmetic operations on integers and noninteger numbers, matrix arithmetic operations on arrays of numbers, and logical or Boolean operations on bit patterns. The operations are invoked in program statements for combining specified units or structures, referred to by variables, and assigning the result to another variable or variables. File and communication features relate to how input/output, mass storage, and remote transmission devices are to be used, and these are invoked by further statements. Program structure has to do with how a program is organized for execution purposes and may involve concepts of unconditional or conditional transfer of control (to cause sequencing to pick up elsewhere in the program, perhaps only if some condition is satisfied), subroutines (procedural units treatable as self-contained), recursive procedures (procedures that invoke themselves), and block structure (program blocks outside of which variable names can be re-used). Various control statements reflect program structures (*e.g.*, jump statements and subroutine calls). Finally, a programming language usually permits a variety of supporting or nonexecutable statements, which are really messages to the compiler regarding data formats and the like.

The versatility of this approach to computing has resulted in an almost standardized "system approach" when converting a problem into a program. The problem is analyzed, and the input and output formats designated. A diagram called a flow chart is drawn to reflect clearly and precisely the procedural sequence by which the input data are to be converted into the output solution of the problem. The flow chart is converted into statements in a language chosen as most suited for the specific problem and also as one that the particular computer system used will accept (*i.e.*, for which it has a translator). In a succession of translation stages, the program is converted automatically to the specific "machine code" of the particular computer. Testing with sample data and debugging (correction of program errors) of the program follows, perhaps with the help of a debugging program. The program is then ready for production running, or submitted input, which will be converted to printed or otherwise recorded output. Modifications may be made for alternative solutions or improvements.

Some computer systems require minor alterations in the languages before they will accept them; some computer centres or installations also have their own particular rules or conventions, which are slight but crucial variations of the languages. Many computer users have difficulties in transposing their problem into a usable computer algorithm. An algorithm is defined as a precise and complete step-by-step recipe for a computational procedure, with very exacting and specific rules, expressible in a programming language.

Block diagrams and flow charts facilitate the required attention to the interrelationships, logic, and sequence of problem components. Programming follows development of these flow charts.

Limitations of the computer

The computer cannot exercise judgment or common sense, and it must be meticulously instructed in the program as to how to handle every contingency: what to do if the answer of an intermediate calculation becomes zero, or when particular exceptions to anticipated results occur. Each eventuality must be analyzed completely or the program will not work satisfactorily (although this may not be immediately apparent).

LANGUAGE CATEGORIES

Although programs written in machine language are accepted by computers, they are tedious and long and provide the programmers with many possibilities for com-

mitting errors. To alleviate some of these problems and to shorten the programmer's tasks, assembly or mnemonic languages have been created. A mnemonic code is designed to assist the human memory, in that it is a standard formulation of letters standing for a known word, such as *mpy* for multiply or *ste* for store. Programmer-invented mnemonics can also stand for the coded addresses of storage location with reference to the meaning of the data stored, such as *price* and *quantity* for the corresponding values in a problem in economics. Such codes are converted into operation (machine) codes by an assembly program, which is the translator for assembly language programs. Such programs are used to develop machine-coded programs from procedure-oriented or "macrolanguages" such as Fortran, Algol, and Cobol, the compilers for which yield assembly language. Assemblers, then, prepare a machine language from a symbolic language program by substituting machine operation codes and absolute addresses for symbolic (mnemonic) addresses. They also integrate subroutines into the main machine language routines by adapting and changing relative and symbolic codes to absolute form.

The variety of higher-level languages continues to proliferate as new applications and wider use of computers develop.

The descriptions of the languages to follow will be divided into the following classes: (1) fundamental algorithmic and procedural languages: Fortran, Algol, JOVIAL, Cobol, PL/1; (2) variants for time-sharing and remote control: BASIC, Quiktran, CAL; (3) string and list processing languages: Snobol, COMIT, Lisp, Slip, IPL-V, Formac; (4) Simulation languages: Simscript, GPSS, Dynamo; and (5) Process-control languages: APT.

Algorithmic and procedural languages. *Fortran.* Fortran, originally an acronym for formula translation, was developed originally for scientific problems and programs but is now widely used in commercial and educational computer applications. Fortran II was the first programming language to be accepted worldwide as a powerful, convenient, and practical tool. Fortran IV contains significant additional features for input-output statements, specific functions with fewer restrictions and constraints in some areas.

Uses of Fortran

Fortran is basically a programming system that includes the language and a processor (compiler) that permits programs to be written in a mathematical-type language. It is essentially machine-independent and procedure-oriented. The grammar, symbols, rules, and syntax used are, in general, common with easy-to-learn mathematical and English-language conventions. Simply stated, all Fortran-type languages treat arithmetic operations with commands that evaluate expressions and substitute the result for current values of variables. Also included are statements for transfer of control, looping (designating a set of statements to be executed a specific number of times), and input/output.

As an example, the Fortran program for computing the square root of a real positive number is shown in Figure 3, together with its equivalent in machine language and in the form of a flow chart. The procedure used is common in many areas of numerical analysis. A guess is made for the true value or answer sought and the quantity by which the guess was in error is obtained by calculation. Repetitive guesses and calculations—a procedure termed iteration—ultimately produce minimization of the error and, hence, the answer. The first step in the Fortran program directs the computer to guess (G) that the square root of the number (X) is equal to one-half the number, which is of course incorrect. In the second, and subsequent, steps, the number is divided by the previous guess (X/G) to yield the error and a new guess is made according to the general expression: $G = \frac{1}{2}(G + X/G)$. The computer is instructed to cease iteration when the answer obtained falls within certain prescribed limits of accuracy, in this instance .0001.

Algol. Algol alternately stands for either Algorithmic Language or Algebraic Oriented Language. It is a result of international cooperation to obtain a standardized

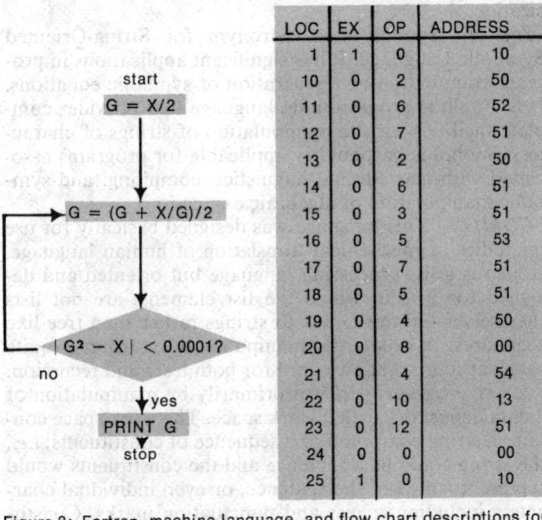

| | flow chart | | machine language | | | | Fortran |

```
        flow chart          machine language              Fortran

                          LOC | EX | OP | ADDRESS
                           1  | 1  | 0  |   10
       start              10  | 0  | 2  |   50        G = X/2.0
                          11  | 0  | 6  |   52
      G = X/2             12  | 0  | 7  |   51
                          13  | 0  | 2  |   50
         │                14  | 0  | 6  |   51
         ▼                15  | 0  | 3  |   51    20  G = 0.5*(G + X/G)
    G = (G + X/G)/2       16  | 0  | 5  |   53
         │                17  | 0  | 7  |   51
         ▼                18  | 0  | 5  |   51
    ◇ |G² − X| < 0.0001?  19  | 0  | 4  |   50
         │                20  | 0  | 8  |   00        IF(ABS(G*G − X) − .0001) 10, 20, 20
   no    │ yes            21  | 0  | 4  |   54
         ▼                22  | 0  | 10 |   13
      PRINT G             23  | 0  | 12 |   51    10  WRITE (6, 5)G
         │                24  | 0  | 0  |   00        STOP
        stop              25  | 1  | 0  |   10        (load new program)
```

Figure 3: Fortran, machine language, and flow chart descriptions for determining the square root of a real positive number.

algorithmic language. IAL, International Algebraic Language, was the forerunner of Algol. It was devised in 1958 and revised in 1960. It is a powerful language, used more widely in Europe than in the United States. It is principally used in the programming of scientific problems but is also selected by many programmers as a reference and publication language, and as a model for the invention of new artificial languages, compiling techniques, and mathematical structures. It has become an internationally accepted procedure for designing mathematical algorithms. Algol is similar to Fortran and has the following advantages: (1) it is more comprehensive and has more powerful instructions; (2) it has fewer restrictions, is more flexible and readable, and has fewer exceptions; and (3) it has a more formal structure and is easier to model.

JOVIAL. JOVIAL is an acronym for Jules' Own Version of the International Algorithmic Language. It is another procedure-oriented language deriving basically from Algol. It was designed and is most often used in programmed command and control procedures. The major deviation from Algol provides JOVIAL with the power to control data on the "byte" and even the "bit" level when desired. This particular capability gives JOVIAL extensive use in developing software applications, utility, and compiling-type programs. JOVIAL was created quite specifically for government agencies and military command and control applications. It is used in many other computing areas, however, such as real-time programs, commercial time-sharing applications, and software design for other computers.

Cobol. Cobol is a procedure-oriented language designed first for commercial and business problems. The name is an acronym for Common-Business-Oriented Language. Cobol was developed in 1959 and has been maintained and revised since then. Improved Cobol 65 streamlined and added many new capabilities and reduced several cumbersome attributes of the system. The Cobol compiler processes programmer-written Cobol sentences and produces (*i.e.,* translates, compiles) an object program.

The advantages of using Cobol can be summarized as follows: Cobol programs are stated in precise, easily learned natural words and phrases; they can be read and understood by nontechnical people with minimal backgrounds in data processing; programs written for one computer can be run on another computer, with minimum modification, to take advantage of the second computer's features; training time is negligible for the novice in programming; and program testing is simplified and can be completed by someone other than the original programmer. Cobol contains many important file-organization features and can deal with variable data length.

Advantages of Cobol

Input/output procedures and report generators are its strong points.

Program language 1. PL/1 is a multipurpose programming language designed for solving both business and scientific problems. It incorporates the advantages of both Fortran and Cobol. The Fortran advantages are reflected in its simple, concise statements while Cobol's advantages are reflected in its ability to manipulate and easily input/output grouped records or files.

PL/1 employs basic building blocks called procedures. A procedure is a block of instructions designed to perform a stated function, such as the calculation of overtime pay in a payroll application. Seldom used procedures can be held in auxiliary storage and called into main storage only when required. One procedure may be contained in another, and any data declared in a procedure is automatically available to all procedures "nested" within. This "block structure" is an innovation which first appeared in the Algol language.

PL/1 can handle "string data," which consists of either strings of alphanumeric characters or strings of bits, as in JOVIAL. The ability to handle characters and bit strings is significant because without it programmers would have to revert to assembly language for such problems. With PL/1 the programmer may also describe his data in terms of arrays and structures. An array is a collection of data of the same type and with similar characteristics such as a table with various prices in dollars and cents. In the structure, the data may have mixed characters with data fields of different sizes. A payroll record, for example, usually contains both string data, such as names and addresses, and another type of data; *i.e.,* numeric data such as pay rates and deduction information. The use of "labels" represents another way in which the language adapts to the level of detail and readability. Beginning programmers can turn out productive work very quickly with this high-level language.

Time-sharing languages. In operating computers in the time-sharing mode, terminals function as computer consoles, and the user may solve problems immediately or may compose partial or complete programs. Diagnostic and debugging information is expressed entirely in the source language. Interpretive execution permits retention of all information contained in the user's original source statements. The combination of interpretive execution and multiprogramming makes the conversational mode a real-time, man–machine communication system highly efficient and feasible.

BASIC. BASIC is an acronym for Beginners All-purpose Symbolic Instruction Code. It is a Fortran-like language that can be learned by the average non-computer-oriented mathematician or engineer in a few hours. The simple conditions and attributes of the language allow it to be mastered, with practice, in a few days. It is very commonly used for business and commercial purposes on time-sharing computers with many users simultaneously interacting with the computer.

Each line of BASIC begins with a number (the line number) that identifies the line and specifies the order in which the statements are to be performed. The computer sorts out the program before running it and, therefore, statements need not be input in any specific order.

BASIC, though it is less powerful and versatile than Algol and Fortran, is considered to be more than adequate for most of the commercial and business problems that can be processed in a time-sharing mode. BASIC permits conversational statements, free-style input (72 characters per line), segmenting of complex statements, six significant digits of accuracy, easy and safe program modification, and editing functions that permit combinations of two or more programs into one and allow selection from a library of stored programs or functions such as procedures for solving simultaneous equations, curve fitting, and statistical analysis.

Quiktran.   Quiktran is a language, compiler, and a data processing system. The system operates under the control of the Quiktran compiler program stored in the computer main memory. The compiler checks each statement according to instructions from the sending location. Quiktran is a Fortran-like time-sharing language, and lengthy jobs that must be processed in their entirety rather than statement by statement can be placed temporarily in disk storage until the computer is free to handle them.

CAL.   CAL is an acronym for Conversational Algebraic Language. It is another language for use by many remote simultaneous terminals. The user at such a terminal develops and solves mathematical problems "on-line" because the CAL language is designed for higher-level time-sharing purposes.

Purpose of list-processing languages

List-processing languages.   These highly specific languages are designed for digital computers and are oriented specifically for the convenience and manipulation of data, especially non-numerical data, whose length and structure change considerably during the calculation of a problem solution. It is because the data are most usually not numerical that the concepts and terms referred to as symbol manipulation and non-numerical data processing are most often used to define list-processing languages. A special case of list-processing languages are string-manipulation languages that deal only with strings of characters. Most general list-processing languages are used as research tools and not necessarily for production-line programming. The development and construction of compilers are often based on list-processing techniques. The basic research areas that have gained from the use of list processing include (1) generation and verification of mathematical proofs; (2) pattern recognition; (3) algebraic manipulation; (4) simulation of human problem-solving; (5) information retrieval; (6) heuristic programming; (7) linguistic analysis; (8) machine translation of numerical languages; and (9) exploration of new types of programming languages. List-processing procedures are oriented more to techniques of programming than to particular applications except perhaps in the areas of information retrieval, algebraic manipulation, and language translation.

List characteristics

A list is defined simply as a set of items given in a specific order. Some characteristics of lists are (1) they can be of variable length subject principally to gross machine limitations, and the lengths can vary during the computation; (2) items of many different types may appear on lists such as numbers and alphanumeric symbols; (3) items can be added at the beginning, end, or the middle and any item can be deleted from the list; (4) any number of distinct lists can be created or developed from a program; (5) lists can be referenced by the program and can be copied, modified, examined, and analyzed by programs. Recursion is basically the process used when elements of lists may themselves be lists. Because most programming languages have difficulties if a subroutine is called within itself, list processing handles such a problem, avoiding overwriting when subroutines call themselves. Most often there are many levels of subsidiary lists, or sublists, as many as there are levels of parenthesization.

Snobol.   Snobol is an acronym for String-Oriented Symbolic Language. It has significant applications in program compilation and generation of symbolic equations. It is a unique programming language that provides complete facilities for the manipulation of strings of characters. Snobol is particularly applicable for programs associated with text editing, linguistics, compiling, and symbolic manipulation of algebraic expressions.

COMIT.   This language was designed basically for use in studies of mechanical translation of human language. It also is a list-processing language but oriented and designed for lists in which the list elements are not lists themselves but are closer to strings rather than tree-like structures. In COMIT the manipulation of strings is quite easy but somewhat awkward for both trees and recursion.

COMIT programs perform primarily by manipulation of a data depository called work space. The work space contains a string composed of a sequence of constituents; *i.e.,* the string could be a sentence and the constituents would represent words of the sentence, or even individual characters including spaces and punctuation marks. Constituents of strings might also be subscripts and subscript values attached to them. COMIT provides sequences of shelves for temporary storage. Such shelves may be replaced in their entirety by new data or new data can be added at the head of the shelf while preserving the rest in a manner similar to a Lisp function APPEND.

Lisp.   The basic language from which most others spring or are compared is Lisp, which stands for List Processing. It differs very radically from traditional programming languages.

Data and storage characters used in the Lisp language are represented either externally, as a sequence of characters formed according to distinct rules, or internally within the computer, as a set of computer words interlinked in a specific way.

Atomic symbols or atoms may be either numeric or non-numeric, and the external representation of a non-numeric atomic symbol is a string of letters and digits, starting with a letter, such as AB5Y, or a Greek letter. Lisp also permits the use of other characters such as asterisks, minus signs, etc.

Numeric atoms or atomic symbols can be decimal, octal, or floating-point numbers. (The letter Q following a number is usually used to indicate that the number is octal.)

Externally a list consists of a sequence of list elements separated by blanks and closed by parentheses. A list element can itself be either an atomic symbol or a list. When a list is formed the necessary storage cells are taken from a list of available cells called the free-storage list.

Lisp elements

A subroutine of computer programming can be considered a tool that defines a function in a mathematical sense which maps sets of input values onto sets of output values. In Lisp, this function is expressed in a notation that displays its functional nature more explicitly than ordinarily done as a sequence of instructions. Various expressions in Lisp include conditional expressions that test conditions and accounts according to results of the test.

IPL-V.   This language is considerably more machine-oriented than Lisp. The programs in IPL-V consist of sequences of instructions that closely resemble normal or ordinary machine instructions, but generally the programmer has more control over the calculations. Most programmers favor IPL-V over Lisp because of the similarity of IPL-V to normal machine programming.

Other.   Slip is an acronym that stands for Symmetrical List Processing. The most popular form of Slip is an extension of Fortran and not really a stand-alone system. Slip uses a method that is different from the others for representing lists. It increases the freedom for manipulating lists and also increases the amount of storage required for them.

Slip really is a form of a set of special list processing Fortran functions; such functions are used in order to accomplish the operations a programmer normally does in list processing, which includes transversal of lists, translation of list structures between internal and external representations, specific recursive communication of arguments, and also the creation and erasure of lists. Slip programs are thus really Fortran programs that use Slip functions.

Formac stands for Formula Manipulation Compiler. It is an extension of Fortran but of a different type. Formac is explicitly designed for algebraic operations and is probably not too strong for symbol manipulation, such as language translation. Differentiation of complicated algebraic expressions is a standard type of Formac application as is the generation of a series involving many terms or the analytic solution of different equations. In Formac, variables can stand for algebraic expressions as well as numbers, which is not permitted in Fortran. The basic mechanism for formula manipulation in Formac is the statement LET $x = 1$, which causes the variable x to be equal to the algebraic expression y. When algebraic expressions are combined, purely numerical simplifications are automatically performed.

Simulation languages. Simulation can be considered as a representation of a rapidly changing or dynamic system developed in a form or design to simplify manipulation and study while using a computer for computations, comparisons, and analyses. The term system in its essence is a set or an assemblage of interacting components and processes. The interactions may be internal or linked to an external environment. A model is a representation of a system in which the processes or interactions bear a close resemblance or relationship to those of the specific system being simulated or studied. Thus, models used in simulation are seldom highly abstract or strictly mathematical. Manipulation of a simulation system concerns the acceptance of inputs and the generation of outputs, similar or analogous to those of the system represented.

A dynamic system is one in which the activity is dependent on the time framework and can be stable or unstable. It can be studied as a static or steady-state system as regards the transient behaviour of a dynamic system.

Types of simulation systems

Simulation systems can be (1) physical, in which the components are processes, or they might be hardware, and thus precisely defined; (2) behavioral, in which the processes might include psychological or sociological behaviour of individuals or groups; (3) operational, in which the system would incorporate processes in which human beings might be participants, such as in automobile traffic, highway analyses, etc.

The simulation system can be either continuous by being a representation by sets of differential equations, either linear or nonlinear, or it may be discrete in which the major components are distinct and individually identifiable. If the simulation is deterministic it would contain elements whose behaviour is prescribed a priori. If the system is represented as a stochastic model—that is, exhibiting a succession of random variations—then variables of the essential elements may be introduced, such as the timing, quantity, or replenishment of demand items relating to random distributions.

Man–machine simulation includes operational and behavioral models that require the active participation of a person and the allocation of functions between the computer portion of the model and the person. Many man–machine simulation models relate to (1) training, in which a person must face a real-life system as in military control or command operations; (2) behavioral experimentation, such as a study of psychological behaviour in specific controlled environments; (3) education systems, in which a person in a complex environment operates with various elements and components such as management games.

Simulation systems have distinct advantages in modelling, manipulating, and solving various tasks and problems: (1) major economies result by reducing the complexity and solution time of programming tasks; (2) conceptual guidance is enhanced and clarified because of the necessity of strong conceptual structures and frameworks required for representation of specific systems; (3) flexibility is developed and is perhaps the major advantage of simulation, because it is easier and less costly to change a representation of a system than to change the system itself. Changes can be anticipated during the model design and can be completed in various runs of a computerized simulation system.

Though almost any type of programming language can be used to implement a simulation model, various specific languages have been developed for simulation applications. The analogue computer is most heavily used for simulation of continuous systems, but the languages defined below relate to digital computer simulation languages that provide the user with a variety of services; they are designed to ease the job of translating into a conceptual model a system that an operating programmer can develop for generation of useful statistical outputs. They contain: status descriptors, which are definitions of the essential elements of a system or model; procedures for modifying the state of a model; and procedures for controlling the dynamic performance and observations of model behaviour. Most simulation languages develop data structures, data transformations, sequencing of transformations, output routines, and operational features. In addition to these, extensive error checking is available to prevent misuse of the language mechanically (*i.e.*, hand coding or key punching), as well as routines for debugging a model and locating logical errors.

Simscript. Simscript is a proprietary general-purpose digital simulation language and system. It is based upon the notion that the state of a system is definable and can be described in terms of entities (*i.e.*, the specific objects or things of which a system is composed), and attributes (*i.e.*, those properties that are associated with the entities as well), and as sets (*i.e.*, groups of entities). All entities must be specific and explicit with a complete list of their attributes and possible set memberships; this is the major prerequisite in the development of a simulation model. The state of a system once described is changed by the occurrence of an event that is a user-defined subroutine written with either Simscript or Fortran statements. Entities can be created or destroyed, for example; set memberships of individual entities can be altered; and numerical values of attributes can be changed. Because entities and attributes must be individually located, much of the Simscript language is devoted to providing convenient and flexible methods for performing storage and retrieval functions. Input to the Simscript translator usually is developed on three sets of cards containing definition, initialization, and subprograms.

Components of GPSS

General-Purpose System Simulator (*GPSS*). This simulation language has three basic components: blocks, transactions, and equipment. The language develops simulation models through the use of and in the terms of block diagrams. Such diagrams are graphic devices that portray the logical and physical flow of transactions or basic information through a system. Such block types in the simulation block diagram are very specific, and from these, models are built. Punched cards or other entry program segments define the properties of each block in the model.

Temporary GPSS elements are formed into transactions and moved from one block to another within the model. Each transaction has eight parameters associated with it and also has eight possible priority levels. As transactions enter blocks, various subroutines associated with those particular block types are interpretively executed, causing a modification of one or more status descriptors.

Dynamo. Dynamo concerns continuous closed-loop information feedback systems. It does not require that the system concerned be either linear or stable; therefore, a very broad class of systems can be developed or represented by the Dynamo language. A continuous system is defined as one in which all basic variables are continuous and possess a first derivative with respect to time; *i.e.*, the state of the system is given by the levels of continuous variables at any point in time without the conception of any discrete changes to this state. Thus, the system is intuitively obvious in that it deals with many physical systems. It is also reasonable for dealing with more discrete phenomena relating to aggregate levels of behaviour; *i.e.*, an aggregate inventory level in a manufacturing environment may be viewed as a continuous variable even though its delayed composition is discrete. At any instant in time, for example, the level of a variable is a distinct single numeric value.

Information feedback systems

An information feedback system is defined as one in which information relating to the state of the system at a given time is used to determine the future state of the system. Variables are introduced to deal specifically with the flow of information. Of major importance are time delays, as they establish the dynamic performance of such systems and also determine the lag between the time in which a change in one variable occurs and the time at which this change is reflected in some other variable; *i.e.*, an increase in one level of inventory may lead to a reduction in the level of orders for inventory.

A closed-loop system is defined as one in which successive states of the system are dependent upon variables outside the system. The primary interest relates to the internal structure of the system and the manner in which the basic variables interact. Dynamo does not require that the system be completely closed. A limited set of external inputs can be provided for, although these are intended to serve only as independent stimuli to the systems being manipulated and analyzed. Basic Dynamo is directed at standing the stability of time, of closed systems of continuous variables in which the broad characteristics of information feedback within the system are significant to its dynamic performance.

Provisions and procedures for modifying the state and controlling the dynamic performance of Dynamo models are available. Output from a Dynamo simulation model is generated in the form of time series for any desired variables; *i.e.*, level, rate, or output. The output variable is computed from level or rate variables at each output time.

Process-control languages. Languages have been developed to facilitate the use of computers controlling industrial processes. These vary widely, because the processes can be very different. Only one example, not typical but fundamental, is discussed here. The control is not direct but by tapes prepared by computers. Numerical control refers to the control of devices such as machine tools and drafting machines by punched paper or magnetic tapes suitably encoded with directive information. Most numerically controlled devices have very limited logical or arithmetic capability, so they rely on their input tapes for detailed and explicit guidance. This may mean eight bits for every thousandth of an inch (0.025 millimetre) of motion and represents a great amount of data on the tape. Using information presented in a more manageable and concise form, it is common for a computer to prepare the control tapes.

APT. An example of a numerical control language is the automatically programmed tools (APT) system described previously. Using APT the designer describes his tool and the desired part in a high-level geometrically-oriented language. A preprocessor program accepts the highlevel language and digests it into a simpler, formalized internal representation. The central program which is tool-independent converts the material, tool, and geometrical information into tool motion commands. A postprocessor program prepares the tool motion information in a format suitable for the particular control mechanism being used. A simultaneous output for a numerical control drafting machine permits preparation of detail blueprints while the robot tool is making the part, if desired.

This is a program specifically designed for the ease and convenience for instructing and controlling computer controlled machine tools. The programmer writes numerically-coded instructions that are followed by the machine control system to cause the machine to produce the desired part or product. Since the program must be very precise and intricate, it is fundamentally a mathematical operation. The programmer defines the geometric dimensions of the part he wishes to create, and the computer automatically controls the function of the machine to produce that part or a component. The statements are English-language-type and reference the intersections of these various components with instructions to the cutting

tool. Such instructions are produced on punched paper tape for input to the controlled machine.

Automatically programmed tools can cut only straight lines; however, its use is not restricted. These straight lines may be as short as 1/1,000 of an inch (0.025 millimetre), so any shape can be cut. The machine must be told by the computer to cut each of these tiny segments, demonstrating the tediousness of the programming of the operation of the tool. Once this is accomplished, however, there can be endless repetition of the procedure with no added instructions, or the tape can be stored for later use. The great step forward that APT has made is to perform many tasks better than can be done with a human operator. APT has made possible a production plan of one for runs of thousands or millions of items.

Other. An application somewhat similar to the foregoing is the use of computer typesetting systems. Here again, the process is recorded on an intermediate medium, which controls the typesetting device at a second stage. Used in conjunction with modern electronic photocomposition devices, the computer typesetting medium offers a flexibility not attainable by earlier methods. Cross-references can be accumulated and put in later, changes in type style can be incorporated easily, and changes in format can be effected without the labour of conventional resetting.

Europeans generally prefer the U.S. Agol language for their computer programming, regardless of the language spoken locally.

BIBLIOGRAPHY. MELVIN KLERER and GRANINO A. KORN (eds.), *Digital Computer User's Handbook* (1967), provides excellent treatment of simulation languages (HOWARD S. KRASNOW), and list processing languages (PAUL W. ABRAHAMS), as well as language forms and parts. The text includes an article by BARBARA W. STEPHENSON with concise and lucid explanations of real-time operations, small general purpose computers, and emphasis on laboratory control computers. An article in the same book by ROBERT V. HEAD is an authoritative source for the concepts of information and banking accounting computer utilities. T.W. MCRAE, *The Impact of Computers on Accounting* (1964), provides informative and lucid explanations for the background information to electronic data processing in business operations. Elementary discussions of gates, switching, and program concepts are developed with clarity. DOUGLAS F. PARKHILL, *The Challenge of the Computer Utility* (1966), offers an accurate and interesting discussion of the history of modern computer technology as well as a simplified analysis of time sharing and early computer utilities. The TECHNICAL PUBLISHING COMPANY, *The Datamation Industry Directory* (1971–), develops a reasonably good breakdown and categorization of the computer industry, and the products manufactured or services offered for each of the various groups of companies within the industry. PHILLIP B. JORDAIN (ed.), *Condensed Computer Encyclopedia* (1969), is a commendable resource for definitions and concept explanations of some latest operating procedures and techniques of computing and storage operations; especially thorough are the discussions and reference to IBM System/360 equipment. CHARLES J. SIPPL, *Computer Dictionary and Handbook* (1972), offers a detailed discussion of computer systems from logic organization and equipment components points of view; many applications of computers in science, medicine, education, management, and business are explained and analyzed. JAMES T. MARTIN and ADRIAN R.D. NORMAN, *The Computerized Society* (1970), is an excellent reference for current discussion and analyses of microminiaturization, popular consumer communication devices, uses of the computer in homes, law enforcement, bank, "checkless/cashless" future operations, and medical applications and operations by computer—includes a stimulating discussion of the battle for privacy and the society of the future in a computerized world. FREDERIC G. WITHINGTON, *The Use of Computers in Business Organizations* (1966), provides views of formidable substance and credibility concerning long-range effects of computer and management and trends in the evolution of future computers as regards organization, design, and languages.

(C.J.S.)

Comte, Auguste

Auguste Comte, unquestionably a man of genius who inspired discipleship on the one hand and derision on the other, became famous as the founder of Positivism, a scientific system of thought, knowledge, feeling, and politi-

Comte, drawing by Tony Toullion, 19th century. In the Bibliothèque Nationale, Paris.
H. Roger-Viollet

cal action; of sociology, the new science of society, which was the basis of Positivism; and of humanism, a new "religion" to replace the crumbling faiths (as he thought them) of the past. Comte lived through the turmoil following the French Revolution during which a new, stable social order—without despotism—was sought. Science and industrial capitalism were transforming the societies of Europe in directions no one yet understood. Men experienced violent conflict but were adrift in feeling, thought, and action; they lacked confidence in established sentiments, beliefs, and institutions but had nothing with which to replace them. Comte thought that this condition was not only significant for France and Europe but was one of the decisive junctures in human history.

Early life and schooling. Comte, named Isidore-Auguste-Marie-François-Xavier, was born in Montpellier, France, on January 19, 1798. The place had historic significance. Spanish resistance to Napoleon was not merely of academic interest to the boy who could see the Pyrenees, the mountain range that forms the barrier between France and Spain, from his home. Montpellier—a meeting place of roads from Spain, Italy, and Paris—had also long been alive with intellectual enquiry; it had been visited by many eminent men, among whom were Petrarch, Rabelais, John Locke, and Laurence Sterne; it had had a university since 1289.

Auguste's family was also a significant context for his future development. Louis Comte, his father, a tax official, and Rosalie Boyer, his mother, were strongly royalist and deeply sincere Roman Catholics. Rosalie, especially, was deeply concerned when her son came to reject their religion. But the leanings of his parents were intensely (though variably) at odds with the republicanism and Skepticism that were sweeping through France. Comte felt these conflicts deeply but decisively resolved them at a very early age by the rejection of Catholicism and royalism alike. His family relationships were close but not without difficulties during these early years.

While still young, Auguste gave evidence of qualities that were to prove important throughout his life. He was physically delicate and ungainly; his head and trunk were too large for his short legs. His consciousness of this appearance, noticeable even in his earliest years, may well have deeply affected his relations with women in later life. He seemed always surprised—overwhelmed with gratitude, chivalry, and ready commitments—if women showed him affection. His estimate of women's opinions seems to have been correct. Upon first meeting him, even Clotilde de Vaux, with whom he later shared a deeply intimate relationship, said: "How ugly he is!"

This physical oddness was accompanied by physical

weaknesses—stomach disorders and shortsightedness in particular—that troubled him later. Physical weaknesses, however, were not paralleled by weakness of character, and no child could have been more strong willed. When a tumour on his neck necessitated an operation, for example, he refused to have his hands held and neither moved nor cried out while the operation was performed. He was also intellectually precocious to an exceptional degree. His parents engaged an old man to teach him reading, writing, and the rudiments of Latin; the teacher was often awakened by young Auguste knocking on his door long before it was time to start. These qualities became more pronounced when he moved beyond the family.

When he was nine, Auguste went as a boarder to the local secondary school. This was an unhappy experience. His bond with his mother was very powerful, and in later writings Comte revealed that he bitterly regretted having left home at this age. He condemned boarding and advocated the continued experience of family life throughout a child's education. Though no one then knew it, he was never to live at home again for any length of time. The context of a devoted family was over.

Despite his unhappiness, he could look after himself. His precociousness showed itself in rapid success in study, just as his willfulness was marked in his propensity toward rebellion. When he was ten or 11, he declared before the whole class his hope that the Spaniards would succeed in throwing Napoleon out of their country. He also plainly showed his disgust as his teachers reversed their positions (from supporting Voltaire, who advocated religious tolerance, to the Catholic Church) according to Napoleon's whims. He detested officials. At 14, he decisively rejected his family's religion and made this known to his parents; it was a big and deliberate step. He was a prizewinning pupil in everything to which he turned his mind and, at 16, gained one of the first places in examinations for entry to the École Polytechnique—a school founded in 1794 to train military engineers but soon transformed into a general school for advanced sciences—in Paris. But he was too young to be admitted. During his final year at the lycée while his mathematics master was suffering from an illness, Comte took over his teaching. He had to perch on a chair because of his short legs.

Precocious, headstrong, and outstanding, Comte nonetheless shared a great feeling of fraternity with his fellows. They liked him. His rebelliousness was always directed at tyrannies—of officialdom, of pretentious mediocrity, of weakly held principle. Later, he was much involved in disputes, but, from the beginning, he was capable of deeply felt, lasting, and loyal friendship. He retained the warmest affection and appreciation for an early teacher, Daniel Encontre, and expressed this in the dedication to his last major piece of writing (*Synthèse subjective*, 1856). He also remained, over many years, a firm friend of one of his Montpellier schoolmates, Paul Valat, and much of what is known of Comte's life is drawn from the confiding letters that passed between them. Comte was to become an isolated figure in Paris, but of his capacity for affection and loyal friendship there is no doubt. During this period, too, Comte had his first brief experience of "love" for a young girl, Ernestine Goy; it was soon terminated by her marriage to someone else.

In October 1814, when Comte was 16, a new chapter of his life began at the École Polytechnique at Paris. It was a short chapter, abruptly terminated within two years because of his rebelliousness. The Polytechnique routine was very definite: a drumbeat opened the day at 5:30 AM and ended it at 9:15 PM; the time between was completely organized. "The Thinker," as Comte was called, could not long stand this. When officials ordered them to be indoors without fail by 9:30 PM, 150 pupils went to the theatre and came back at 11:00 PM. When Napoleon escaped from the island of Elba, Comte, despite his hatred of him, joined his fellow pupils in demanding to be allowed to help in defending Paris against the allied troops.

Family influence

School at Montpellier

Years at the École Polytechnique in Paris

And often Comte went off at night alone, wandering among the Paris crowds, among the prostitutes by the Palais-Royal. Then came an incident of indiscipline. A tutor questioned pupils while slouching on a chair with his feet up on a table. When Comte's turn to answer came, he positioned himself in the same casual manner. The tutor felt that his attitude was unbecoming. Comte secured signatures to a petition requesting the tutor's resignation. Comte was sent back to Montpellier under police supervision, and, at the same time, the school, already suspected of republican tendencies, was closed.

Comte could not now stay long out of Paris. He wanted to plunge fully into the suffering, disordered society he had glimpsed, to understand it, to help in the task of social reconstruction. Before the end of 1816, when he was still 18, he had returned. Then began the first period of Comte's real independence: stormy, difficult, but the period of his first major achievement.

Life in Paris. Soon—at carnival time preceding the opening of the season of Lent—he was walking again, alone, through the Paris streets, amazed that people could forget "that thirty thousand people about them had scarcely a morsel to eat." His studies became more systematic, connected, profound. He was poor but (as one biographer put it) enjoying the "delicious liberty of the garret." He read widely in philosophy and history and was especially captivated by those who were beginning to discern and trace some order in the history of human society. The thoughts of several important French political philosophers of the 18th century—such as Montesquieu, Condorcet, A.-R.-J. Turgot, and Joseph de Maistre—were critically worked into his own system of thought. All were related to the scrutiny of the nature of the human mind and of human knowledge itself undertaken by David Hume, in Britain, and Immanuel Kant, in Germany. Gradually all these elements were brought together in a new synthesis. Linked to his newly formulated science of man and society, it seemed to provide a satisfactory basis for making the new political order that men needed. He earned his living precariously by occasional teaching and journalism and began to make new acquaintances who were to prove—for better or for worse—of enormous influence.

The most important of these acquaintances was Henri de Saint-Simon, a French social reformer and one of the founders of socialism, who was the first to see clearly the importance of economic organization in modern society. Comte's ideas were very similar to his, some of his earliest articles appeared in Saint-Simon's publications, and, for some years, he worked in close association with him. Comte's insistent systematization, however, was incompatible with the looser kaleidoscope of Saint-Simon's ideas, and a sharp rift developed between them. Other important friends were Jean Delambre, an astronomer, and Henri de Blainville, a zoologist. Besides the social preoccupations of his thought, Comte continued his connected studies in mathematics, astronomy, physics, chemistry, and biology.

But his personal life was insecure. In 1818, he had a love affair with Pauline, an Italian woman, who was 29 years old and married. A daughter, Louise, was born, and Comte—though not sure if the child was his—readily accepted paternity. The girl died at the age of nine.

Life with
Caroline
Massin

On one of his evening walks in May 1821, Comte met Caroline Massin—a prostitute. Nearly 19, she was the illegitimate daughter of a provincial actor and actress, from whom she had been separated almost from birth, and she was on the Paris police register. During the summer, she half hinted at marriage. Toward the end of 1822, after meeting her again in a public reading room, he visited her apartment to give her lessons. Before long, he was living with her and comfortably. When she was threatened with imprisonment for neglecting to report fortnightly to the police (as those on the register were required to do), Comte agreed to marry her so that her name could be removed from the register. The wedding was a civil ceremony; a barrister who was Caroline's earlier consort attended, and it even seems plausible that the marriage had been schemed by the two of them. Now

that his program of study and writing was taking clear shape, Comte hoped to live and work quietly near his family and early friends. His visit to Montpellier with his bride, however, was disastrous. Caroline disliked the place. Comte's parents did not like her. After two weeks, they were back in Paris.

Soon after this, Comte decided to work out his "system of positive philosophy" as a series of lectures beginning in April 1826 for a private audience composed of many of the most distinguished thinkers of his time. But, after two lectures, he was suddenly unable to continue. He was found by his wife and Abbé Félicité Robert de Lamennais, a controversial priest and philosophical and political writer, in a state of severe mental disturbance: "insane." Blainville wanted Comte taken home, but Caroline refused, and he was taken to an asylum. Thinking him incurable and knowing of Caroline's earlier career, his mother deeply desired that their marriage should be solemnized by the Catholic Church. Abbé Lamennais agreed, the Archbishop of Paris consented, and Comte was taken out of the asylum to an apartment. While still so deranged that he was not able properly to sign the register, the ceremony was carried out.

Alone with Caroline and feeling himself useless, Comte became deeply depressed. Early in 1827, while Caroline was out of the apartment, he walked to the Pont des Arts, and jumped from the bridge into the River Seine but was rescued by a soldier of the municipal guard who happened to be passing by. He then began to recover substantially. His complete recovery is dated from the summer of 1827—during which he visited his parents in Montpellier, travelling alone. Comte then left them for the last time. Back in Paris, he settled with Caroline into a new apartment. They lived simply and poorly, assisted by a well-disposed manufacturer, by Comte's father, and by earnings from Comte's occasional teaching.

Comte marked this crisis and recovery by abandoning the use of coffee, an apparent eccentricity. When his mental condition became so poor, however, he had been using coffee to keep himself at work for stretches as long as 80 hours.

Comte's other problems, however, continued. His indigestion became more severe. Caroline, to Comte's passionate indignation, suggested taking "wealthy clients" to help the family purse. She left home occasionally and came back. But his work now made substantial progress and was noticed by influential people—such as John Stuart Mill, in England.

Period of the "Course of Positive Philosophy." In 1829 he again took up his projected lecture series. This was so successfully concluded that he redelivered it at the Royal Athenaeum during 1829–30. The following 12 years were devoted to their publication (in six volumes). Comte's *Cours de philosophie positive* was a complete system of philosophy that could form a basis for political organization appropriate to modern industrial society. His "law of the three stages" maintained that human intellectual development had moved historically from a theological stage, in which the world and man's destiny within it were explained in terms of gods and spirits, through a transitional metaphysical stage, in which explanations were in terms of essences, final causes, and other abstractions, to the modern positive stage. This last stage was distinguished by an awareness of the limitations of human knowledge. Knowledge could only be relative to man's nature as a species and to his varying social and historical situations. Absolute explanations were therefore better abandoned for the more sensible discovery of laws—the regular connections among phenomena. This deliberately limited, testable way of establishing knowledge was enough for man's practical purposes; it was the only reliable basis for prediction and, therefore, for effective action. Comte classified all positive knowledge in his "hierarchy of the sciences," making clear the methods of each and emphasizing especially the new unifying science of sociology. This work was completed by 1842; but the period (1830–42) had seen many activities other than authorship.

In 1830 Comte was jailed for three days for refusing to

"Law of
the three
stages"

enroll in the National Guard. From that year to 1848, he delivered annually, without fees, a course of lectures to workingmen. From 1832 Comte also became mathematics tutor for the Polytechnique and, from 1836, an examiner. Conflicts developed, however, and these appointments were terminated when, in the sixth volume of his *Positive Philosophy*, he publicly attacked one of the officials. In 1837 his mother died, before he could see her. Caroline received dubious "visits" and left home from time to time. The marriage ceased really to exist, and Comte became more solitary; he went to the opera, which he loved, and read a limited range of classical works by authors such as Virgil, Dante, Shakespeare, and Cervantes. With the growing flood of contemporary publications, he exercised discrimination as to the range and quality of his reading—a "cerebral hygiene" for which he was much ridiculed. In his teaching he remained punctual and punctilious. In 1838 his work was seriously noticed in the *Edinburgh Review*, and from 1840 several English scholars wrote to him or visited him. In August 1842, Caroline finally left him. They never met again, although he arranged an allowance for her. In 1841 they had engaged a housekeeper, Sophie Bliaux, who continued to care for him.

For the next three years, his fortunes varied. He lost his Polytechnique appointments but was helped financially by three Englishmen through the efforts of Mill. His lectures to workingmen were increasingly appreciated, and a score of workers in 1845 marched in a body to Comte's flat to thank him for them.

The year with Clotilde de Vaux In October 1844, the happiest, saddest, most influential relationship of Comte's life began. Visiting Maximilien Marie, one of his pupils, he was introduced to his sister, Clotilde de Vaux. She, too, had experienced marital disaster. Her husband, a tax collector, had disappeared, leaving behind forgeries, falsifications, and burned account books. No one heard of him from that time on. Clotilde also deeply shared Comte's idealistic motives. She was herself a writer and had published a novelette, in a Paris journal. A frequent correspondence developed between them. In August 1845 they were godparents at the christening of Maximilien's child. From this point on, their relationship deepened, though Clotilde vacillated, insisting on its platonic nature, partly because of her unresolved marriage, partly because she could not give herself sexually without a complete commitment of love. It was a strange, formal, tortured relationship. Comte was transported by a quality of love he had never experienced before—an affinity of feeling in tune with all the intellectual, moral, and creative aspirations of his own life. It invested his thinking with dimensions of sublime feeling that had significance for his future work. Together, they talked about a new morality, a new religion, a new conception of marriage. But Clotilde's illnesses proved fatal. In February 1846 she was spitting blood; on April 5 she died. Comte's "peerless year" was over. Ravaged by grief, he was nonetheless infinitely strengthened to begin his final task of working out his *System of Positive Polity*.

Period of the "System of Positive Polity." He began this work a week after Clotilde's death. The next eight years (the fourth and final volume was published in 1854) were devoted to it. In this work his formulation of sociology was completed. One volume was devoted to "social statics" (on the nature of society) and one to "social dynamics" (the history of its changes). An enriched study of "man the individual" was outlined. The whole study emphasized morality and moral progress as the central preoccupation of human knowledge and effort and gave an account of the polity, or political organization, that this required. Institutions and rituals were proposed for establishing and sustaining desired sentiments in society. Although they paralleled Catholicism, because Comte believed that medieval society had made positive contributions to the form of civilization, these institutions would rest not on the worship of divinities but on the commemoration of great men and women of the past who had contributed to human betterment. The duty of man was to improve this fabric of society, which was the basis of fulfillment for individual lives to come. He envisaged a

European council that would achieve and extend this policy throughout the world.

During this work, Comte's own life became highly ritualized. His housekeeper, Sophie, brought her family to the flat and served him loyally. He sustained—in theatrical ways—his memory of Clotilde: remembering her each day, visiting her tomb each week, writing a letter to her each year, keeping her influence alive. His writings were now widely influential. Many English intellectuals were influenced by him, and they translated and promulgated his work. French devotees increased. A large correspondence developed with Positivist societies throughout the world. Comte's last years

Each week, Comte received his Positivist friends and colleagues. In his rooms all the elements of affection he had known seemed to be gathered about him—indeed, to be gathered up within him—so that everyone who visited him spoke of the new radiance and composure that suffused his whole person, despite his still ugly appearance, now made worse by nervous jerks and watering eyes. Each day was ordered and frugal; in the evening, at dinner, he substituted for dessert a piece of dry bread "meditating on the numerous poor who were unable to procure even that means of nourishment in return for their work."

His death followed an observation of friendship. In May 1857, he went on foot to the funeral of an old friend. The burial place had been changed. The weather was bitterly cold, and he caught a chill. His old illnesses recurred and became severe. He died on September 5, 1857, and was buried near but not in the same vault as Clotilde.

His wife, Caroline, at once came back to the flat and tried to sell his things but was forestalled by his followers, and the flat was saved. Today, the bed on which Comte died, his black clothes folded in a box, his opera glass, his selected books, Clotilde's chair, the small blackboard on which he used to teach, the desk at which he wrote between two tall candlesticks are all still there.

Many find Comte's extravagances theatrical, pompous, ludicrous; but the work he accomplished remains a remarkable synthesis, an important system of thought. Even the elements for which he is derided—the elaborate rituals for the sustaining of sentiments ("Catholicism without Christianity," as one author put it)—deal with a grave problem persisting in modern society: in the crisis of scientific, industrialized civilization, how are the sentiments necessary for a stable and good society, for satisfying personal fulfillment, to be maintained among people who no longer share ultimate beliefs and compelling institutional forms? Comte gave an answer as considerable as that produced by any man. From the turbulent boyhood in Montpellier to the massive volumes remaining at the time of his death in the heart of Paris, the life of the dedicated scholar—tortured, embattled, exaggerated, misunderstood—was a life, for all its failings, of significant achievement.

BIBLIOGRAPHY. The best short biography in English is F.J. GOULD, *Auguste Comte* (1920). J.H. BRIDGES, *The Unity of Comte's Life and Doctrines* (1866), also gives a good account of Comte's life and ideas while defending him against some of the criticisms presented by JOHN STUART MILL in *Auguste Comte and Positivism* (1865). Other good biographies are H.D. HUTTON, *Comte, the Man and the Founder* (1891), and *Comte's Life and Work* (1892). A biography concentrating on Comte's personal life and relationships is J.M. STYLE, *Auguste Comte: Thinker and Lover* (1928). Others, not translated but essential for some details of Comte's youth, love affairs, personal life, and character in later years, are: H.G. GOUHIER, *La Vie d'Auguste Comte* (1931) and *La Jeunesse d'Auguste Comte et la formation du positivisme*, 3 vol. (1933–41); E. LITTRE, *Auguste Comte et la philosophie positive* (1863); J.F.E. ROBINET, *Notice sur l'oeuvre et sur la vie d'Auguste Comte* (1860); and C. DE ROUVRE, *L'Amoureuse histoire d'Auguste Comte et de Clotilde de Vaux* (1917).

Comte's own chief works are: *Cours de philosophie positive*, 6 vol. (1830–42; abridged Eng. trans., *The Positive Philosophy of Auguste Comte*, 3 vol., 1896), his first major outline of Positivism; the *Catéchisme positive* (1852; Eng. trans., *Catechism of Positive Religion*, 1858); *Système de politique positive*, 4 vol. (1851–54; Eng. trans., *System of Positive Polity*, 4 vol., 1875–77), which completed the outline of the new science of sociology and the new polity appropriate to modern, scientific, and industrial society; and the *Synthèse subjective* (1856; Eng. trans., *Religion of Humanity: Subjective Synthesis . . .*, 1891), his last major work. The most important collections of his letters are: *Lettres d'Auguste Comte à M. Valat, 1815–1844* (1870); *Lettres d'Auguste Comte à John Stuart Mill, 1841–1846* (1877); and in translation, *Confession and Testament of Auguste Comte and His Correspondence with Clotilde de Vaux* (1910; orig. 1884). In the 1960s and 1970s, Comte's work is being reappraised and his importance re-emphasized. Examples are: in France, PIERRE ARNAUD, *Politique d'Auguste Comte* (1965), *Catéchisme positiviste* (1966), and *Sociologie de Comte* (1969); in Britain, RONALD FLETCHER, *Auguste Comte and the Making of Sociology* (1966), *The Making of Sociology*, vol. 1, pt. 2 (1971); and in the United States, ERNEST BECKER, *The Structure of Evil* (1968).

(R.Fl.)

Concept Formation

Concept formation refers to the process by which one learns to sort his specific experiences into general rules or classes. One is observed to meet a given person, to lift a particular stone, and to drive a specific car. When he seems to *think* about things, however, he often appears to deal with classes; apparently he knows that stones (in general) sink, that automobiles (as a class) are powered by engines. He behaves as if he thinks of them in a general sense beyond any particular stone or automobile. Awareness of such classes can help guide behaviour in new situations. Thus two people in a bakery may never have met before; yet, if one can be classified as customer and the other as clerk, they tend to behave appropriately. Similarly, many people seem able to drive almost any automobile by knowing about automobiles in general.

Concepts as rules

Concept formation is a term used to describe how one learns to form classes; conceptual thinking refers to one's subjective manipulations of those abstract classes. A concept is a rule that may be applied to decide if a particular object falls into a certain class. The concept "citizen of the United States" refers to such a decision rule, meaning any person who was born in U.S. territory or who is a child of a U.S. citizen or who has been legally naturalized. The rule suggests questions to ask in checking the citizenship of any particular individual. As most concepts do, it rests on other concepts; "U.S. citizen" is defined in terms of the concepts "child" and "territory." Many scientific or mathematical concepts cannot be understood until the terms in which they are defined have been grasped. Concept formation builds on itself.

Conceptual classification may be contrasted with another type of classification behaviour called discrimination learning. In discrimination learning, objects are classified on the basis of directly perceived properties such as physical size or shape. The usual explanation for discrimination learning is that the sensory features of any stimulus are matched to what is already remembered of these features, and that the learner's response becomes associated with them. The response thus classifies the stimulus. In discrimination learning subjective representations of immediate and past stimuli seem directly to indicate concrete, physical features (in contrast to the more abstract nature of concept formation). When a stimulus is perceived to match several different past experiences, the response may be a compromise; an object need not bear an all-or-none relation to a set of others in discrimination learning—for example, there is no absolute distinction between tall and short people.

While human beings popularly are called abstract thinkers, many of the classifications people make clearly seem to be concrete discriminations. Indeed, people may use the same term either in a discriminative or conceptual way. A child uses the term policeman in discriminating a man in distinctive uniform, while a lawyer may have a concept of a civil servant charged with enforcing criminal codes.

In practice, people seem to think in many ways that combine abstractness and concreteness. They also may blend class membership with assignment along a scale; *e.g.*, such concepts as leadership, an abstract quality that

people are said to exhibit in varying degrees. The same applies to vivacity, avarice, and other personality classifications.

People seem to develop more complex sets of classes than do other animals, but this need not mean that human modes of learning are qualitatively unique. It may be that all animals have the same basic biochemical machinery for learning, but that human animals exhibit it in greater variety. Yet, it seems no more appropriate to account for human concept formation in terms of discrimination learning alone than it does to reduce the functions of a piston engine to chemical reactions.

EXPERIMENTAL STUDIES

Since careful observation of informal, everyday behaviour is difficult, most evidence about human concept formation comes from laboratory subjects. For example, each subject is asked to learn a rule for classifying geometric figures (see the Table).

Geometric Patterns of the Type Used in Studying Concept Formation			
object number	size	colour	shape
1	big	green	triangle
2	big	green	circle
3	big	red	triangle
4	big	red	circle
5	small	green	triangle
6	small	green	circle
7	small	red	triangle
8	small	red	circle

The experimenter may concoct the rule that all green objects are called GEK. The subject is shown some of the figures, told which are named GEK, and asked to infer the rule or to apply it to other figures. This is roughly akin to teaching a young child to identify a class of barking animals with the name DOG. In both cases a general rule is derived from specific examples.

The problem of discovering that GEK = GREEN is almost trivial when four GEK and four NOT GEK figures are presented at once; it becomes surprisingly difficult if they are presented one at a time and need to be remembered. When two concepts are to be learned together (*e.g.*, JIG = TRIANGLE and GEK = GREEN) memory for each concept tends to be mixed, and it becomes a formidable task to solve either problem. This is evidence that short-term memory functions in concept learning, and that it often is a limiting factor in performance (see MEMORY: RETENTION AND FORGETTING). Efficiency in more complex concept learning often depends on providing enough time for examples of a rule to be fixed in memory for longer periods.

Most such experiments involve very simple rules. They properly concern concept identification (rather than formation) when the learner is asked to recognize rules he already knows. Adult subjects tend to focus on one stimulus attribute after another (*e.g.*, shape or colour) until the answer is found. (This is problem solving with a minimum of thinking; they simply keep guessing until they are right.) People tend to avoid repeating errors but seem to make surprisingly little use of very recent, short-term experience.

Concept identification

Most people are orderly in trying out attributes, first considering such striking features as size, shape, and colour, only later turning to the more abstract (*e.g.*, number of similar figures, or equilateral versus isosceles triangles). This characteristic progression is reminiscent of the quantitative distinction between discrimination learning (relatively concrete) and concept formation (more abstract); there seems to be no sharp, qualitative division. If pairs of arrays are shown in which the same geometric figure is repeated (the rule being that all GEK arrays have exactly ten figures), people first are apt to react to directly perceivable characteristics (*e.g.*, the extent to which the figures fill the space). They are likely to discriminate most grossly different NOT GEK patterns in this way quickly but to be troubled by arrays of nine or eleven. Eventually most adults should discover a solution by counting figures. Ordinarily more difficult, higher-order abstractions (*e.g.*, GEK arrays have an even number of figures) become easy to learn if the distinction is directly perceivable; for example, if even-numbered arrays are drawn symmetrically and all others are not.

Concept learning; conjunctive and disjunctive rules

Study can shift from concept identification to concept learning by requiring combination of previously learned rules. A conjunctive concept (in which the rule is based on the joint presence of two or more features; *e.g.*, GEK patterns now are LARGE and GREEN) is fairly easy to learn when the common characteristics stand out. But learning a disjunctive rule (*e.g.*, GEK objects now are either LARGE or GREEN but not both) is quite difficult; there is no invariant, relatively concrete feature on which to rely.

Concept learning in adults may be understood as a two-step process: first the discovery of *which* attributes are relevant, then the discovery of *how* they are relevant. In the conjunctive illustration used here, the learner first is likely to notice that size and colour have something to do with the answer and then to determine what it is. This two-step interpretation presupposes that he already has learned rules for colour, size, shape, or similar dimensions.

In an example of what is called intradimensional shift, initially the subject learns that GEK = GREEN; then, without warning, the experimenter changes the rule to GEK = RED. The same attribute or dimension (colour) is still relevant, but the way in which it is used has been changed. In extradimensional shift the relevant dimension is changed (*e.g.*, from GEK = GREEN to GEK = TRIANGLE) but the classification of some objects does not change (GREEN TRIANGLE is a GEK under both rules). The relative ease with which a subject handles such problems suggests something about how he learns. If he tends to learn simply by associating GEK with specific figures without considering the selected attribute, then he should find extradimensional-shift problems easier, since only some of his associations need be relearned. But if he has learned stepwise in terms of relevant attributes (*e.g.*, to say "What is the colour? . . . Ah, *that* colour means it is GEK"), intradimensional shift should be easier, since only the *how* phase of the two-step process need be relearned.

College students tend to find intradimensional-shift problems easier, indicating that they are prone to use the two-step process. On the other hand, suppose a rat initially is rewarded when it runs into the right-hand side of a maze for food, then a change is made by rewarding entries to the left (intradimensional shift) or by rewarding entries to any brightly lighted alley regardless of location (extradimensional shift). The rat will perform best on the extradimensional-shift problem. Among children, performance depends substantially on age; preschool children are likely to do best with extradimensional shifts (as rats do) but beyond kindergarten age they tend to find the intradimensional shift easiest. Perhaps these differences are related to how children learn to apply language in problem solving.

Concepts as models of change

Concepts need not be defined as limited to simple classification but also can be interpreted as models or rules that reflect crucial possibilities for change. To take a simple case, an adult is not apt to think that the volume of water changes when it is poured into a container of different shape. (Young children may claim that it does.) In the adult's concept, volume is not synonymous with the shape of a container but is based on a model of how fluids behave. The concept of "heat" does not serve simply to sort objects as hot or cold; it implies a rule or model of energy transfer that can be used widely (*e.g.*, to explain how water boils at a lower temperature when pressure drops). Concepts can be understood as models on which to decide if particular changes will have significant effects. This also implies classification (of sets of equivalent situations), but the way people learn to make this sort of classification may be quite different from the processes described so far.

AGE AND CONCEPTUAL BEHAVIOUR

Piaget's observations. The provocative clinical observations of Swiss psychologist Jean Piaget (1896–   ) have initiated considerable study of how young children learn concepts for coping with their physical surroundings. As models for defining feasible change, concepts are at least as important in such contexts as they are for classification. Piaget stressed that an infant normally first must learn that he is a thing apart from his external environment; next that he must form enough concepts of physical invariances (*e.g.*, that objects fall) to let him explore his world. Later in the preschool period the child typically grasps the concept of spatial localization (of objects separated in space). Piaget characterized the child during this period as classifying objects only on the basis of perceptually attractive, concrete physical features (in agreement with laboratory studies of intradimensional and extradimensional shift).

He and others who used his methods reported that preschool children are apt to explain external change in terms of their own needs; *e.g.*, a four-year-old is likely to say that a cloud moves "because the sun is in my eyes." Other distinctions between cause and effect emerge among children in early primary grades, who may say a moving cloud "wants to hide the sun." In later primary grades, volitional and passive movement usually become conceptually distinct.

Ability to deal analytically with objects apart from their immediate perceptual characteristics is reported typically to become effective only just before adolescence. At that time the concept of hierarchies of subclasses within more general classes commonly develops. A normal child of eleven applies the properties of all living things to the class called birds.

The role of learning

Progressive use of abstract concepts seems to reflect both maturation and learning. Given proper information, by the age of six many children display impressive concept-forming abilities. They ordinarily have considerable linguistic competence, using (though often not being able to explain) such abstract transformations as present and past tense. Rules of formal logic can be taught in the elementary grades; the so-called new mathematics reflects efforts to improve the order in which such concepts are introduced.

The role of instruction in concept formation remains poorly understood, yet practically all cultural heritage is explicitly taught. How many people would develop the concept of number (let alone that of odd and even) if left to themselves? Human societies have existed for thousands of years without these concepts. Better knowledge of how to instruct and of the role of imitation in transmitting cultural concepts is needed.

Aging. It is generally reported that potential for learning new abstractions decreases in old age. In such extreme cases as senility, severe alcoholism, or brain injury, the deficit is dramatic. Much less is known, however, about changes in conceptual ability during the active period of adult life, and what evidence there is is conflicting. Perhaps such adults are too busy to serve as research subjects.

People deemed gifted as children tend to retain superior ability into their later years in grasping new abstractions. However, among more typical people, little correlation is found between conceptual ability evaluated in the early teens and the same ability measured ten or more years later. Very gifted youngsters are likely to be given special scholastic challenges and opportunities that may enhance their skill in abstract thinking.

In such abstract pursuits as pure mathematics or theoretical physics there is a tendency for creative scientists and writers to be most productive in their late 20s and early 30s, but there are many exceptions. Among people in general, there probably is a slight decrease in ability to form new concepts starting from the late 20s. At the same time, as people get older they have more learned concepts that they can apply to a problem, so the net change in ability is hard to predict. Deterioration in learning new concepts is likely to be more rapid past 60, its severity varying markedly from person to person. Deterioration may be associated with illness or injury rather than with mere age in years.

LANGUAGE

Language, as a system of symbols abstracted from experience, provides an important vehicle for thinking. Some theorists treat linguistic concept formation as being a complex type of discrimination learning. The U.S. psychologist B. Frederick Skinner (1904–), for example, held that linguistic concept formation is based on the same principles that describe how a rat learns to push a bar in response to a specific signal. This seems to account for name learning (*e.g.*, that some objects are called horse and others dog). Other aspects of language learning, however, do not seem to fit Skinner's discrimination-learning model; its adequacy in explaining how one learns the concept of grammatically equivalent sentences has been challenged. Considering concepts as specifications of feasible transformations, sentences are equivalent if one can be derived from another by allowable change (*e.g.*, from active to passive tense). It is hard to see how learning to handle transformations could be based on the learning of primitive discriminations.

Genetic theories

Another explanation of language acquisition favoured by some linguists and biologists lays less stress on learning. It could be that humans are genetically prepared to acquire some language at an early age, much as some birds show readiness to learn any song pattern to which they are exposed when they reach a certain age. In humans, this period seems to stretch from about age one to six. If this explanation holds, all human languages should obey constraints established by the linguistic limits of genetic endowment. Should language prove to be a relatively independent biological function, the high linguistic competence of many young children with poor ability for abstract reasoning would appear less paradoxical.

Perhaps some rudimentary bases for language among other animals can be learned by methods appropriate for discrimination learning; even very young children are among the best discrimination learners in the animal kingdom. Once basic linguistic discriminations have been grasped, they can be used as tools with which the remainder of any language is learned. This suggests a theoretical position that falls between strictly cognitive accounts of language learning and Skinner's ideas. Nevertheless, biological bases for language learning remain to be identified and incorporated in such theories.

At any rate, such an array of theories is a sign of how little is known of the way people learn the concepts of a language.

CONCEPT FORMATION IN ANIMALS

Rats learn to enter lighted or unlighted alleys to get food, and goldfish can be taught to swim toward or away from an object. In such discrimination learning the animal is said to associate a physical property of the stimulus with its response, and with some contingency of reward or punishment. Thus, while a dog can be trained to come when called, it need not mean that he knows his name in the same sense that a man apparently does. But how can one prove that the dog does not know his name, or even that another person has a deeper concept of his name?

Most animals show classification behaviour that clearly seems to be discrimination learning. A crow will respond to the danger call of a bird of another species, but, only if that call physically resembles the crow's. Chimpanzees, however, have been observed using sticks as primitive tools; they behave as if they have a concept of things that extend reach. On considerable evidence of this sort, many are reluctant to say flatly that the animals are incapable of abstract thinking.

The oddity problem

Most studies aimed at evidence of concept formation among laboratory animals have involved primates, although there are reports of abstract behaviour among such animals as dogs, dolphins, and pigs. Monkeys have been taught to solve the oddity problem: presented with two objects of one kind and one of another, they can be

trained to select the discrepant one. This behaviour persists even for sets of objects that have never been presented to them before. The animals behave as if they grasp the general concept of similarity, an abstraction rather than a simple discrimination. With great effort chimpanzees have been taught to speak and to use correctly a very few words. A much more successful attempt has been made to teach a chimpanzee the sign language used by deaf people, gestures apparently being more appropriate to the anatomic structure of chimpanzees. (Human beings ordinarily seem more prepared to learn spoken language.) The chimpanzee learned to use the signs for hat, dog, food, yes, me (self), sorry, funny, go, come, and many others. This work was reported in 1967 by R.A. Gardner and B.T. Gardner.

CONCEPT FORMATION BY MACHINE

Computers can be programmed to process information and to develop classification rules (*e.g.*, they can play chess and make decisions about business or military problems). Essentially such devices are programmed to mimic the process of problem solving required of subjects in laboratory experiments on concept learning. In this sense, machines have formed concepts; but their functions remained relatively impoverished in the 1970s. Efficient linguistic behaviour has proven particularly difficult to produce in a machine, despite numerous attempts. Yet there is no evidence that human concept formation is based on any mode of handling information that in principle could not be built into a machine. It is almost an article of faith among many investigators that human thinking can be explained mechanistically in physiological terms, but the scientists themselves do not yet seem to have developed concepts adequate for producing machines that can approach the full range of human talent.

BIBLIOGRAPHY. L.E. BOURNE, *Human Conceptual Behavior* (1966), a well-organized review of laboratory studies; J.S. BRUNER, J.J. GOODNOW, and G.A. AUSTIN, *A Study of Thinking* (1956), a classic, well-written description of some experiments in the field; J.H. FLAVELL, *The Developmental Psychology of Jean Piaget* (1963), a competent explanation of Piaget's controversial and provocative ideas; E.B. HUNT, *Concept Learning: An Information Processing Problem* (1962), a comprehensive review and theoretical presentation of major approaches; B.F. SKINNER, *Verbal Behavior* (1957), a challenging proposal for applying laboratory psychology.

(E.B.H.)

Concerto

Since about 1750 the term concerto has been applied primarily to the solo concerto; *i.e.*, a musical composition for instruments alone in which an orchestra and a soloist interrelate by alternating, competing, or combining on a more or less equal footing. In this sense the concerto, like the symphony or the string quartet, may be seen as a special case of the generic musical form embraced by the term sonata (*q.v.*). Like the sonata and symphony, the concerto is typically a cycle of several contrasting movements integrated tonally and often thematically. The individual movements are usually based on certain recognized designs, including sonata form, ABA (the letters refer to large distinct musical sections), variations, and rondo (such as ABACA).

But the concerto tends to differ from the sonata, too, in certain ways that set it apart. Thus, in the sonata form of the concerto's first movement, the exposition often remains in the tonic key while played by the entire orchestra the first time through. The expected departure to a nearly related key and the introduction of the soloist are reserved to a characteristically more elaborate repetition of the exposition. Moreover, to meet a felt need for a more brilliant ending in the same movement, the concerto provides or at least invites an improvised cadenza near the end of the movement—an extended, free flourish that may go on for as long as several minutes. A shorter cadenza may also occur at a strategic point in one or more of the other movements. In addition, the concerto has followed much more consistently than the sonata the plan of three movements, in the order fast–slow–fast. The second movement leads, often without pause, into the finale, or last movement, and the finale has shown a more consistent preference for the rondo design. But, importantly, all of these distinctions of musical form are secondary to the dialogue inherent in the concerto's interrelationship of soloist and orchestra. This dialogue influences the very nature of the solo part by almost forcing the soloist into a virtuoso's role so that he can compete on an equal footing with his adversary, the orchestra. The dialogue, furthermore, influences not only the construction of individual musical phrases but also the musical textures chosen. In addition, it affects the ways of developing musical material (*e.g.*, themes, rhythms) according to the logic of musical form, and even the broader blocking off of sections within forms, as in the concerto's repeated exposition, with its sections for full orchestra (tutti) and soloist.

The literature of the concerto since 1750 is extensive in all categories, although the standard repertoire is limited to scarcely more than a few works for each main solo instrument. Being a prime ingredient of popular concert fare, the concerto is subject, much as is opera, to the exigencies of the box office. The film and phonograph industries have helped further to give disproportionate prominence to a few highly successful and undeniably effective examples like those for piano by the Norwegian Edvard Grieg (in A minor) and the Russians Peter Ilich Tchaikovsky (in B flat minor) and Sergey Rachmaninoff (in C minor).

Taking music's commonly accepted eras for its framework, this examination of the concerto starts in the late Renaissance (16th century), with the origins and first uses of the term. It proceeds to the Baroque era (about 1580 to 1750), which was the first main era of the concerto, including the vocal-instrumental concerto in the late 16th and 17th centuries and, especially, the concerto grosso in the late 17th and early 18th centuries. The discussion progresses next to the Classical era (about 1730 to 1830) and the Romantic era (about 1790 to 1915), which mark successive though dissimilar heydays of the solo concerto partially discussed above. Lastly it reaches the Modern era (from about 1890), which has witnessed further vitality in the solo concerto and a renaissance of the older concerto grosso principle of contrasting instrumental groups. Within each era examined, the prime considerations of the discussion are the meanings of "concerto" as then current; the concerto's place in the social life of the time; its scoring, or particular use of musical instruments and voices; its means of achieving opposition and contrast (if any); its musical structure; and its output by chief regions and masters.

The concerto before 1750

ORIGINS AND EARLY DEVELOPMENT

The word concerto has given trouble to music historians concerned with word origins because within a century after its first known applications to music, in the early 1500s, it had acquired two meanings that would seem to be mutually exclusive. One meaning still current in Italian is that of "agreement," or, as in English, of being "in concert." The other is that of "competing" or "contesting," from the Latin *concerto, -are, -atus* ("to contend"). Probably derived from the same Latin word are such related terms as the Italian *conserto, concertato,* and *concertante;* the Spanish *concierto;* the French *concert* and *concertant;* and the English *consort.* Yet it is this dual meaning itself that offers the most tangible thread of unity throughout the four-century history of the concerto in its various forms. In other words, the concerto, in whatever guise it assumes, reveals a continuing need to resolve the antithetical ideas of concord and contest. The balance between contest and concord is the concerto's particular solution to the problem of variety within unity that must be resolved in all dynamic art forms.

First uses of the word (c. 1520–1620). In the 16th century the word concerto embodied several meanings. As early as 1519 in Rome it referred simply to a vocal or instrumental group (*un concerto di voci in musica*). By 1551 it was used with implications of musical texture, specifically of the contrast of soprano voice with bass and alto ("soprano in concerto col basso & alto"). By 1565 the cognate word concertato was being used in reference to both voices and instruments. And by 1584 a Venetian title, *Musica . . . per cantar e sonar in concerti*, brought forth the meaning of group presentations or concerts.

Although in 1578 "concerti" was used to mean the music itself, for both voices and instruments (rather than performers or concerts), the first formal musical title of this sort appeared in 1587. This was the *Concerti . . . a 6–16 voci* (*Concertos . . . in 6 to 16 Parts*), a collection of vocal and instrumental music by the Venetian composer Andrea Gabrieli and his nephew Giovanni Gabrieli. No formal title concerto is known to be given to strictly instrumental music before 1621, and then the word means both "concerted" or "playing together" and "technically [or even 'virtuosically'] elaborated." This title, with significant implications of a new style—that of the virtuoso soloist—is the *Sonate concertate in stilo moderno* (*Concerted Sonatas in the Modern Style*), by an Italian, Dario Castello, a collection for a violin and for a bassoon that elaborates on the basso continuo part. (The basso continuo, a constant device of Baroque music, calls for a low, sustained-tone instrument—*e.g.*, cello, viola da gamba, bassoon—playing the bass line, plus one or more chordal instruments—*e.g.*, harpsichord, organ, lute—that improvise harmonies above the bass line. Small numbers, or figures, are often placed above the bass line music as a guide to the harmonies, hence the term figured bass.)

In these early, loosely titled collections by the Gabrielis and by Castello, there can be found at least five of the means of contention or opposition that later became closely identified with the *stile concertato* or concerto. Listed in their approximate order of evolution, they include opposition between voices and instruments; between one choir and another (whether of voices or instruments); between the essential basso continuo and its melodic elaboration; between simple, straightforward parts and more decorative, virtuoso parts; and between two or more voices or instrumental parts engaged in imitative or motivic interplay.

The concept "concerto" in the Baroque era (c. 1580–1750). Within the span of a century and a half the Baroque era saw the word concerto change from a broad general term applied on several musical levels to a fairly specific term whose meaning had two senses: that of an instrumental group and that of a musical structure or process. Thus in the Gabrielis' early Baroque "Concerti" the title referred to a collection consisting of church motets (Latin choral compositions) and madrigals (similar Italian compositions) for six to 12 voices in one or two choruses, without and with instruments; a piece for eight voices imitating a battle; and a "Ricercar per sonar" for eight instruments (a ricercar is a piece often based on melodic imitation; *sonar* means to play instrumentally). By contrast the more than 460 late-Baroque "Concerti" composed by the Italian Antonio Vivaldi from the first half of the 18th century are purely instrumental works, mostly three-movement cycles (fast–slow–fast) for one to four soloists and strings with or without other orchestral instruments.

The same century and a half saw a similar narrowing of definition in two closely allied terms: sonata and sinfonia. Before sonata, sinfonia, and concerto became clearly defined and attained a degree of mutual exclusion, they often overlapped and were sometimes even equated in meaning. The full title on one musical manuscript by the Italian Alessandro Stradella, for example, reads, *Sonata di viole, cioé per concerto grosso di viole, concertino di due violino e leuto* (*Sonata for Viols, that is, for Full Complement* [concerto grosso] *of Viols, and Small Group* [concertino] *of Two: Violin and Lute*). Another reads, *Sinfonia per violini e bassi a due concertini distinti* (*Sinfonia for Violins and Basses in Two Distinct Groups*). Many so-called trumpet sonatas of the same period, especially those by Domenico Gabrielli and Giuseppe Jacchini, simply equate the three terms without distinction. When Tommaso Antonio Vitali entitled his Opus 4 *Concerto di sonate* . . . (published 1701), he evidently meant no more than "A Collection of Sonatas," for there was only a violin part, a basso continuo part, and the *concertate* cello part that so often elaborated on the basso continuo. But later, when "Concerto" was crossed off a harpsichord solo by the German composer Johann David Heinichen, copied posthumously in 1731, and "Sonata" was entered in its place, the intention was probably to choose a title more identified with the performing instrument, although the work may well have been transcribed from a concerto.

It is no wonder, then, that even the traits most basically identified with the concerto can be found in works of other titles. G. Gabrieli wrote works for as many as five opposed choirs of instruments under the title of "Sonata." **Cross-** The "sonatas" of the German composers Johann Joseph **influences** Fux and Georg Muffat have passages actually marked "T." and "S." for tutti and soli (soloists) groupings, and, indeed, the tutti–soli principle of contrast still operates strongly in the classical symphonies of Haydn and Mozart. These cross-influences are important reminders that any full history of the concerto idea must take into account not only the concerti in the literature but many works with other titles. Yet in a more concise, encyclopaedic summary it is necessary to stay close to the evolution of the term concerto itself, and there is a real significance in observing how the word acquired definition. The evolution of the word in effect reveals the composers' own developing concepts of it. Concerto was the last of the three terms (sonata, sinfonia, concerto) to attain clear definition. In part this was because the word first had to grow free of its original association with music for both voices and instruments.

THE BAROQUE VOCAL-INSTRUMENTAL CONCERTO (C. 1585–1650)

As already suggested, the first category of music to be associated significantly with the term concerto was that of the vocal-instrumental concerto. If this category is sometimes incorporated only incidentally into overall accounts of the concerto, the reasons lie, first, in its lack of clear identification with any one type of musical form and, second, in the longer, more vivid association of all later categories of the concerto with music exclusively for instruments.

Multivoice and few-voice combinations. Both the early association of the word with vocal-instrumental combinations and the lack of a clear, identifiable musical form are apparent in the important discussion of the concerto in 1619 by the German composer and theorist Michael Praetorius in his *Syntagma Musicum* ("Writings on Music"). Praetorius classified the concerto, along with the motet and the *falsobordone* (or simple harmonization of a liturgical reciting tone), among vocal pieces that have a sacred or serious secular text. He recognized the two general, and related, types that were to prevail in the vocal-instrumental concerto. The multivoice type was in more than four parts and typically subdivided into opposing choirs, especially low versus high choirs. The few-voice type was for one to four parts; often solo parts, and basso continuo; according to Praetorius, this type, which permitted the text to be understood better, was then replacing the madrigal in Italy. Aside from implications of modernism and greater appeal in the concerto and conservatism and greater weightiness in the motet, Praetorius found no distinction between *concert*, *concertos ecclesiasticos*, *sacras cantiones*, *sacros concentus*, and *motettas*.

Praetorius found that the concerto was performed especially in the church and, particularly the few-voiced type, in the monastery. Today one surmises from titles and prefaces to published concerti, from contemporary paintings, and even from the kinds of instruments specified, that the main social breeding ground for the vocal-instrumental concerto was the chapel, above all the court chapel, and the chapel's resources of musicians and instruments were in fact largely those called for by the concerti of the time.

The distinction that Praetorius drew between the multivoice, polychoir concerto and the few-voice, soloistic concerto proved to be the most significant distinction throughout the course of the vocal-instrumental concerto. Yet the two types were not independent of each other but were interrelated in their common derivation from the late-Renaissance, polyphonic madrigal and motet. Moreover, they were interdependent. On the one hand, **Freedom** the few-voiced concerto thrived not only on the desire to **in use of** make the text more understandable and hence more ap- **singers and** pealing but also on a practical need, in the smaller, less **instru-** fortunate chapels, to reduce the larger vocal and instru- **ments** mental groupings to such resources as were available locally (as, for example, during the economizations in Germany brought on by the Thirty Years' War, 1618–48). On the other hand, the polychoir and other larger groupings thrived not only on the desire for more massive, imposing sound but on the opportunity that larger, better staffed chapels provided to expand compositions written for the smaller groupings, whether by adopting alternative scorings that the composer might provide or by improvising other dispositions to suit the immediate place and occasion.

There is a clear instance of expanding the scoring in one Gabriele Fattorini's . . . *Sacri concerti a due voci* . . . (. . . *Sacred Concerts for Two Voices* . . .). This work appeared originally in 1600 merely "with a basso continuo for the greater convenience of organists" and only two years later was republished "with a new addition of some four-part ripieni [or *tutti* groupings] to sing in two [opposed] choirs." A good hint of the improvisatory practices is offered in the *Vezzo di perle musicali* (1610; *Necklace of Musical Pearls*), by Adriano Banchieri. Banchieri explains that his pieces are arranged so that "the same concerto can be altered in six ways over the *basso seguente* [a composite bass line taken from the lowest notes in whatever parts], with one or more parts, whether vocal or instrumental."

The fusion of both types. The natural consequence of this much interdependence and interrelationship of the two types, multivoice and few-voice, was their fusion in vocal-instrumental concerti that provided the massive oppositions of the larger groups, the subjective intensity of the soloists, and the opposition between group and soloist. This fusion, especially in Protestant Germany, **Influences** often with the incorporation of a Protestant chorale, or **of the** hymn, substantially influenced the subsequent develop- **Protestant** ment of the German cantata, which was frequently based **chorale** on a chorale and, like the vocal-instrumental concerto, included vocal soloists, choir, and instruments.

A more specific idea of the Baroque vocal-instrumental concerto might best be given by a brief description of the scoring and nature of six successive, representative examples, running from shortly after the pioneer collection by the Gabrielis in 1587 to a late collection (1650) by the German composer Heinrich Schütz. Banchieri's *Concerti ecclesiastici*, published in Venice in 1595, consists entirely of eight-part motets for double chorus, with a "score" added for organ. This "score" for this double-chorus collection consisted of the soprano and partially figured bass parts of the first chorus only—a partial score enabling the keyboard player to orient himself. Unlike the Gabrieli collection of concerti, Banchieri's is composed exclusively of sacred texts. By contrast, Lodovico da Viadana's popular and influential *Cento concerti ecclesiastici a 1, a 2, a 3, e a 4 voci, con il basso continuo per sonar nell'organo* (100 *Ecclesiastical Concertos* [i.e., motets] for One, Two, Three, and Four Voices, with the Basso Continuo to be Played on the Organ; Venice, 1602) exploits the new style, simpler and more intimate, yet florid and expressive, and including actual monody (solo vocal melody accompanied by expressive harmonies, a type of music new with the Baroque Era). These "concerti" achieve opposition mainly through the polarity of upper part(s) and bass, including such dispositions as two tenors and bass, tenor and two trombones, or two sopranos and two basses. In an important preface, especially treating of the organ part, Viadana argued that the reduction from the multivoice type of motet to these new few-voice "concerti" was made possible by the device of the basso continuo and its realization (*i.e.*, the improvised harmonies), which serve as a filler in lieu of the missing parts. Similar oppositions of high and low parts, but with secular texts and still greater variety, appeared in the *Concerto, Settimo libro de madrigali a 1, 2, 3, 4, & 6 voci, con altri generi de canti (Concerto* [*i.e.*, ensemble or concert consisting of the], *Seventh Book of Madrigals in 1, 2, 3, 4, & 6 Voices* [plus basso continuo], *with Other Kinds of Songs;* Venice, 1619), by the celebrated composer Claudio Monteverdi. Along with two pieces in homophonic, or chordal, style, labelled "Sinfonia," for five unnamed instruments, the book contains both compositions for smaller groups with virtuosic tendencies in the vocal parts and large pieces employing melodic imitation and suggesting Renaissance polyphony, with its independent melodic lines. An example of the larger type is *Con che soavità* [*With What Gentleness*], *concertato a una voce e 9 instrumenti* (making up three choirs of instruments specified for the viola family and a corpus of bass and filler instruments).

German developments

In the same year (1619), in Wolfenbüttel, Germany, there appeared one of several pertinent collections by Praetorius, *Polyhymnia caduceatrix & panegyrica* (named after the muse Polyhymnia), "containing 40 concertos of solemn peace and joy" for one to 21 or "more voices, arranged in" two to six choirs, "to be performed and used with all sorts of instruments and human voices, also trumpets and kettledrums." As Praetorius made clear in his detailed, prefatory instructions and in broader remarks about his concerti in his *Syntagma Musicum*, his concerti comprise a virtual compendium of the vocal-instrumental concerto in all its uses of voices and instruments and styles of opposition and in all its applications of the Protestant chorale, as well. The German composer Johann Hermann Schein acknowledged the influence of Viadana's more intimate concerti in the first set of his "sacred concertos," *Opella nova I* (1618; *Little New Opus*). But in his second set (Leipzig, 1626), he turned more to the larger scale styles of Praetorius for three to six voices and basso continuo. Representative is No. 12, *Hosianna dem Sohne David*, (*Hosannah to the Son of David*) for two sopranos, two tenors, two basses, three *bombardi* (bass shawms), and basso continuo, with alternating sections of instrumental episodes, tutti in chordal style, and melodic imitation. In addition there are passages for three instrumental or vocal soloists, a combination often already encountered in the popular Baroque trio setting of two high parts over a low part. The last main landmarks of the vocal-instrumental concerto were the three sets of Schütz's *Symphoniae sacrae*, or *Sacred Symphonies* (Venice, 1629; Dresden, 1647 and 1650), works that reveal all the variety of treatment to be found in Schein's sacred concerti, except for Schein's interest in the chorale. The first two of Schütz's sets consisted of few-voice settings, mostly one to three voices with one or two obbligato (required solo) instruments and basso continuo. The third set extended to as many as eight parts (some of them optional) and basso continuo; in style it showed a considerable return to the concept of oppositions between choirs, chiefly between vocal and instrumental choirs.

The composers cited here were the main exponents and the Italian and German chapels were the main centres of the early-Baroque, vocal-instrumental concerto. After giving birth to the genre, Italy soon turned to opera, oratorio, and more independent instrumental forms. The Germans, whose derivation from the Italians was direct and unequivocal, developed the idea further and longer before it largely gave way to the Protestant cantata around the mid-17th century. Yet echoes of the vocal-instrumental concerto are still strong in the cantatas of J.S. Bach and his predecessor Dietrich Buxtehude.

THE BAROQUE CONCERTO GROSSO (C. 1675–1750)

Late in the 17th century, within a generation after the vocal-instrumental concerto had last flourished in Germany, the concerto grosso began to assume a clear identity of its own in Italy and soon after in Germany and

beyond. Its main ingredients have been noted earlier—the opposition of choirs or choir and soloists, the exchanges of melodic imitation, the trio setting of soloists, and even the use of "concertate" in a title of a purely instrumental work (by Castello). Other purely instrumental precedents of the mature concerto grosso exist in the considerable literature of music for opposing instrumental choirs in numerous "sonatas," "sinfonias," and "canzone" (instrumental pieces in several sections), starting with the works of Giovanni Gabrieli. Such anticipations, including the *Sinfonia à 8* (*i.e.*, in eight parts; 1618) of one Francesco Usper—a fortuitous, miniature concerto grosso in all but the name—accumulated during the 17th century. Good examples are the orchestral "trumpet sonatas" written in Bologna, Italy, during the second half. But not until the 1670s did the term concerto grosso itself come into general use. It indicated the larger of two contrasting instrumental groups within a composition, and in this sense the term was opposed to concertino (the smaller group), and signified the relation of full orchestra to one or more soloists. By 1698 it appeared as an actual title itself, in the published *Concerti grossi . . .*, by an Italian, Lorenzo Gregori. That this title did indicate a composite concept (*i.e.*, of opposing instrumental groups) is evidenced by frequent distinctions in prefaces and tables of contents between it (or its shorter equivalent, "Concerti") and the sinfonia or sonata. As one example, the *Sinfonie a tre e concerti a quattro* (*Sinfonias in Three Parts and Concertos in Four Parts*, Opus 5; 1692), by the Italian violinist and composer Giuseppe Torelli makes a distinction not only in the number of parts but in the style: between a dense, polyphonic, older style in the sinfonias, often performed with only one player to a part, and a newer, more open style in the concerti, suitable to multiple (orchestral) performance of the parts. As another example, whereas the German Georg Muffat had already called attention to the tutti-soli dispositions in his five orchestral "Sonate" of 1682, when he republished these in 1701 with revisions he changed the title of each to "Concerto."

Early examples of concerti grossi

The social function of the concerto grosso was explicitly stated in 1701 by Muffat, who was as articulate about the secular concerto grosso and its performance as Praetorius had been about the sacred vocal-instrumental concerto:

Place in society

These concertos [in his *Ausserlesene . . . Instrumental-Music* or, *Selected . . . Instrumental Music*], suited neither to the church (because of the ballet airs and airs of other sorts which they include) nor for dancing (because of other interwoven conceits, now slow and serious, now gay and nimble, and composed only for the express refreshment of the ear), may be performed most appropriately in connection with entertainments given by great princes and lords, for receptions of distinguished guests, and at state banquets, serenades, and assemblies of musical amateurs and virtuosi. (As translated in Oliver Strunk's *Source Readings in Music History*, W.W. Norton and Company, Inc., New York, 1950, p. 449.)

The breeding ground of the concerto, therefore, was no longer the chapel but the court. From the standpoint of the local court administrator the concerto grosso offered certain economic as well as functional advantages, advantages that might even help to account for its predominance in Baroque instrumental music. The opposition of a full orchestra, playing relatively simple parts, to a few soli, playing more difficult, even virtuosic parts, made it possible to entrust the full-orchestra parts to relative novices in the court entourage, often to servants who could play in addition to their other duties. Thus, only a few solo parts had to be played by experts hired primarily as professional musicians. This practical advantage can be argued only while the distinction between simple and difficult parts prevailed. The distinction became less clear as the concerto matured, at least in works with one or more soloists.

Musical structure of the concerto grosso. Fundamental not only to the scoring but to the style, and even the musical structure of the Baroque concerto, was the opposition between the full orchestra, or *concerto grosso* (also called tutti or *ripieno*), and the *concertino* (also called soli or *principale*). A full complement of strings, usually two to four on a part, often sufficed for the "full orchestra," in addition to the one to three instruments needed to play and realize the basso continuo. Usually at least a low melody instrument, bowed or blown, and a chordal instrument, plucked or keyed, were used for the basso continuo. The same trio setting that had been popular from the start of the century, typically two violins and a cello, often served as the concertino. When the concertino was not playing soli passages it figured as part of the *concerto grosso*. Illustrative of these typical settings is the celebrated *Christmas Concerto* (Opus 6, No. 8; 1714), by the Italian violinist and composer Arcangelo Corelli. The basso continuo sometimes rested while the concertino played (a frequent procedure in Vivaldi's concerti).

One significant consequence of the tutti–soli relationship and its opposition of weighty and light masses of sound was a tendency to sharpen the contrast with the popular Baroque device of "terrace dynamics," or blocks of contrasting loud and soft sound. This occurred especially in the echo effect of a soli passage played piano after a tutti passage played forte. To this dynamic contrast might be added the rhythmic contrast between steady, solid beats in the tutti and more intricate, quicker figures in the soli, growing out of that same tendency toward simplicity, on the one hand, and virtuosity, on the other. Furthermore, not only all of the melodic ornamentation but also most of the passagework were ordinarily given to the soli rather than the tutti. When the tutti strings were augmented by wind instruments and the concertino was reduced to two players or only one (resulting in the first solo concerti), all these oppositions became that much more pronounced. Attention may be called, too, to the artful highlighting of the contrasts through different spacing—that is, through varied alternations of the two groups, now frequent, now less frequent after longer passages.

Motivic interplay. These several means of contrast hardly exhaust the sources of variety to be found in the Baroque concerto grosso. Much variety is achieved in another of its basic kinds of opposition or competition. This is the motivic (or imitative) interplay between parts that is so characteristic of the *stile concertato*, or concerted style.

Such interplay may occur either between tutti and soli choirs or entirely within a succession of single instrumental parts in the full orchestra. In fact, there are numerous Baroque "concerti" that thrive primarily on the latter style of continuity, without any tutti–soli designations at all (for example, Bach's *Brandenburg Concerto No. 3*). The employment of motivic interplay offers certain inherent contrasts of its own. These include shifts from one high or low range to another within a texture of interwoven melodies: rhythmic conflicts based on patterns that do not necessarily coincide with the regular musical metre; and an almost continuous change of key. The last is achieved by rapid successions of modulations (bridges from key to key) and drives to the cadence; *i.e.*, building up of tension in the harmonies used, culminating and relaxing in the cadence, or stopping point. In fast movements, when the propelling force is not such motivic interplay, it is likely to be a force achieved by outright statements of musical figures based on chords and scales. Or it may be an unfolding succession of figures together with the harmonic drive to the cadence. In slow movements it is likely to be compelling progressions of chords, enhanced by melodic ornamentation and enlivened by continual suspensions, dissonances, and resolutions (*i.e.*, by suspending single notes while the harmony around them changes; this creates dissonance, the tension of harmonies that seem to clash; the tension is "resolved" when the harmonies change again).

Rhythmic and melodic traits. In spite of all this variety there are consistencies of style in the scoring and musical textures just described. In addition, certain additional rhythmic and melodic traits help further to bring a sense of overall unity to the concerto grosso. With regard to rhythmic traits, a steady motoric pulse is likely to prevail throughout the fast movements. Also, true to the nature of the ever-present basso continuo, a steady running bass line is likely to underlie both the slow and the fast

movements. With regard to melodic traits, one cannot ordinarily speak of "main and contrasting themes" as in the classical and later concerto. One reason is the lack of individuality in the main thematic ideas. Corelli's and Vivaldi's themes, vigorous as they may be rhythmically, hardly stand out melodically from the remaining music. Like the musical context in which they occur, the themes themselves are likely to consist of chord notes, scales, or simple repeated notes. Frequently they are announced in unison (all parts playing the same notes) and thus lack a strong initial association with the harmonies of an accompaniment. Bach is exceptional for the individuality of his themes, especially in the finales, where they are usually out-and-out tunes, memorable and fetching (as in his *Violin Concerto No. 2 in E Major*, BWV 1042). The less a melodic idea stands out, the less it functions as a true "theme" or unifier when it recurs and the less it can contrast with any of the other melodic ideas.

Melody and structure. Such relatively neutral themes and motives, which unfold more as supplements than as contrasts, seem to have satisfied most Baroque, especially North German, tastes, including the express preference for limiting any one piece or movement to but one "Affekt" (or characteristic emotion). In addition, and more important for musical continuity, the themes, such as they are, do tend to recur, not only at the more local level of melodic imitation and motivic interplay but also at certain strategic points in the musical structure. Their recurrence, most often at the three or four main tonal landmarks, imparts at least a vague overall outline of formal musical structure. In fact, these strategic recurrences, plus the melodic imitations, the passagework, and the adjunct musical themes that separate them, produce in a loose way the most prevalent structural principle of the fast movements. This is the rondo principle, which is based on the alternation of a refrain, or "ritornello," with contrasting musical passages. In the more tuneful finales, or final movements, the sense of a rondo "ritornello" is most distinct (as in Handel's Opus 6, No. 11). Generally, the alternations of refrains and intervening episodes tally with alternations of the tutti and soli groups, respectively.

Recurring melodic ideas account for two other of the most frequent principles of musical structure in the concerto grosso, those of fugue and of variation. A fugue is based on the polyphonic treatment (through extensive melodic imitation) of a recurring subject, or theme. In fugal sections of a concerto grosso, tutti and soli unite as one group or alternate in expositions (statements of the subject) and episodes (passages in which the subject appears only fragmentarily, if at all). The fugal style occurs largely in fast movements and varies from loose applications, especially among the Italians, to strict ones, especially among the Germans. The variation process depends on continual variation of a constant factor, such as a theme or a group of harmonies. In the concerto grosso it occurs largely in slow movements; its constant factor is a simple, freely recurring bass line, or ostinato (a short, repeated motive or melody). The ostinato often sounds alone in the tutti and may be played in unison at the beginning and end of the movement. It serves as a foil for the soli parts, which sometimes enter successively on long tones and gradually unfold into decorative, expressive passages (as in Bach's *Violin Concerto No. 2*. When the ostinato's recurrences are free enough and the bass line and treble melody of the tutti stand out enough, the effect is that of an expressive aria (solo song, as in an opera) with a firm prelude and postlude (as in Vivaldi's Opus 3, No. 8), providing one of the many hints of operatic influences in the concerto grosso. To these structural types —rondo, fugue, and variation—may be added especially the binary design, with each half repeated, that prevails in Baroque dances. In binary form, the music of the first half moves from the tonic key to a closely related key. The second half begins in the new key and progresses back to the original key. Dances abound in concerti grossi, not only in those that are primarily orchestral suites or groups of related dance pieces (as are many by Handel) but in others as well. For instance, the finale of

Corelli's Opus 6, No. 3, although headed only "Allegro," is a fine example of a binary gigue (a courtly dance ultimately derived from the jig).

Number of movements. The number of movements in the concerto grosso varies more than in the later solo concerto or in the sinfonia, symphony, and sonata at any time after the concerto grosso's emergence. But the average may be put at from three to five. Corelli and other Italian pioneers had led off with more movements (insofar as separate movements can be distinguished from mere sectional changes in their concerti). Vivaldi reduced the number, mostly by omitting an initial slow movement that his predecessors had probably derived from the French overture. Instead, Vivaldi largely settled on and, in fact, standardized the cycle at three movements in fast–slow–fast order. He may have been influenced by the same cycle in the Italian opera sinfonia (or overture). The Germans seem to have varied the number more, with the most movements likely to be made up of relatively short dances. Bach's six *Brandenburg Concertos* do follow the fast–slow–fast plan except that Number 1 adds two dances and No. 3 leaves out the slow movement, simply substituting in its place two slow chords that create a feeling of suspension. Handel's *Twelve Grand Concertos* in Opus 6 contain four to six movements that vary considerably in order and type.

As usual in tonal music (music based on the system of major and minor keys), additional variety within unity is achieved in the cycle of concerto grosso movements through departure from and return to the home key. Much more often than in the suite, a slow inner movement is placed in a nearly related key. In the shortest, freest slow movements the tonality, or key orientation, sometimes remains uncertain and in flux, giving the sense of a bridge from the previous to the following movement (as in Vivaldi's Opus 3, No. 10). Unlike the Baroque suite and sonata, in the concerto the use of interrelated musical themes is not a frequent means of linking the movements. But the concerto grosso is like these other cycles in its dynamic tendency to progress from the more serious to the lighter movements. Infrequently a "program"—a story or nonmusical image—lends further unity to the cycle, as it does in the four concerti of Vivaldi's Opus 8 that are known collectively as *The Four Seasons*. Each of these concerti is tied closely to a sonnet describing one of the seasons. More often a special unity results from some unusual trait of musical style or use of an instrument. An example is the brilliant solo part given, exceptionally, to the "cembalo concertato" (*i.e.*, a harpsichord that participates with the other instruments in the melodic discourse rather than, as is normal, confining itself to the realization of the basso continuo) in Bach's *Brandenburg Concerto No. 5*.

Spread from Italy to other countries. Like the vocal-instrumental concerto before it, the concerto grosso originated and reached a first peak in Italy, then attained a further peak in Germany. French and English centres responded more than they contributed to it. Again, some of the main landmarks may be briefly noted. The twelve concerti grossi in Opus 6 by Corelli were not first published until 1714, the year after he died. Although they were preceded in print by other pioneer examples, like those of Torelli (from 1698), Tomaso Albinoni (from 1700), and even Vivaldi (from 1712), some of them may have been among the "several concertos" by Corelli that Muffat had already heard in Rome by 1682. Corelli still made the loose distinction, best known in the 17th-century sonata, between *da chiesa* and *da camera*—that is, church and court-style, or serious and light. The first eight of his concerti grossi are *da chiesa* (church-style), in four to seven movements, the last four *da camera* (court-style), in five movements. A trio setting of two violins and cello is specified for the *concertino*, and two violins, viola, and bass for the *concerto grosso*, "which may be doubled as desired." Between the two groups the opposition is not an antiphony of musical ideas but only a change of musical texture and sonority in the continuous unfolding of the short, tasteful, well-proportioned movements.

Vivaldi's more than 460 "Concerti" (written from about 1710 to 1740) bring the Italian contribution to full maturity, and they rank Vivaldi with his contemporaries Bach and Handel among the greatest masters of the concerto grosso. The maturity is marked by larger forms and broader musical architecture, including tighter organization of the rondo principle, and by more distinctive, energetic musical themes, at least rhythmically if not melodically. There is also greater brilliance and exploitation of idiomatic instrumental techniques, including *bariolage* (quick shifts from string to string) and broken chords for the solo violin. Another characteristic is the standardization, as noted earlier, of the three-movement cycle, fast—slow–fast. But if the cycle becomes standardized, with only infrequent exceptions, very little else is predictable about Vivaldi's imaginative, resourceful concerti. Least predictable of all is the scoring, which makes highly varied combinations of string and wind instruments—for example, a tutti of strings with cello and bassoon as the soli; or two oboes, two horns, bassoon, and violin as the soli; or viola d'amore (a violin-like instrument) and lute as the soli.

Starting with Muffat's concerti done under Corelli's immediate guidance, the spread of the instrumental concerto from Italy to Germany was as direct and wide as that of the vocal-instrumental concerto had been. French influences in Germany were considerable, too, especially where the suite touched the concerto. This was often true in the large, resourceful, and highly varied output of the German Georg Philipp Telemann. In Bach's approximately 25 concerti (about 1720–35) Italian influences are especially evident, quite apart from his unusual setting for harpsichord alone specifically entitled *Concerto in the Italian Style*. Again, Italian influence is reflected in the many concerti by Vivaldi and others that Bach transcribed and reworked for harpsichord or for organ. A rare opportunity to learn what mattered most to Bach in concerto structure is provided by a study of his changes in the Vivaldi models. Such changes include themes sharpened melodically and musical textures enriched by the addition of new melodic entries to contrapuntal passages or by more intensive interplay of musical motives. The designs of the musical forms themselves are pointed up by insertions of new musical material, deletions, and altered timing of phrases and entries. Bach summed up the Baroque concerto as he did the cantata, fugue, and other Baroque genres. Besides the transcriptions and the magnificent six *Brandenburg Concertos*, with all their own varieties of scoring, he left concerti in which the solo requirements are one violin; two violins; flute, violin, and harpsichord; violin and oboe; one harpsichord; two harpsichords; three harpsichords; and four harpsichords. The majority of the harpsichord concerti are further transcriptions and reworkings, some not yet tracked to their sources. For example, two of seven solo harpsichord concerti come from Bach's own solo violin concerti, and the concerto for four harpsichords comes from Vivaldi's Opus 3, No. 10, for four violins. These concerti, like the *Brandenburg Concerto No. 5* already noted, emphasize Bach's priority in giving the harpsichord prominence as a concerto solo instrument.

Handel left around thirty-five concerti in all (about 1715–50), including three sets of organ concerti with oboe and strings; one set for strings and winds (Opus 3); one set in the tutti–soli setting for strings alone (Opus 6) that Corelli had used; and several concerti not in sets. Among the last are two works more properly classified in his day as trio sonatas (works usually for two violins and basso continuo but sometimes for orchestra). Transcriptions and reworkings figure in many of Handel's concerti, as in Bach's. Handel's concerto style, like that of his chief contemporary in England, the Italian violinist-composer Francesco Geminiani, is more progressive than Bach's in its frequent French dance influences and in its more open, less complex musical textures. Although imposing fugues can be found, the prevailing atmosphere in Handel's concerti is more often that of light, wide-spaced chamber music. Thanks to his unmatched

Unity among movements

Bach's concerti grossi

Handel's concerto style

skill, imagination, good timing, and almost childlike enthusiasm, there is also a feeling of extraordinary vitality, robustness, and breadth in the concerti, especially in the finest of the sets, the *Twelve Grand Concertos* (that is, concerti grossi as translated then), Opus 6. The exploitation of the tutti–soli opposition is less in Opus 3, although the instrumental scoring is more restricted in Opus 6. But in both sets the variety of instrumental combinations is exceptional, even from movement to movement. In Opus 3, No. 2, for example, the soli change from two oboes and two violins to solo oboe, then to two oboes doubling two violins and a viola, further to two oboes and two violins not doubled, and finally to two oboes and cello. Much as Bach had transcribed concerti for organ alone to serve as introductions to cantatas, so Handel played his own original and transcribed concerti for organ and orchestra as introductions and entr'actes in his oratorios. These organ concerti were widely copied by minor followers of Handel in England. Nothing in France close to Handel's level can be pointed to until near the end of the era, when a violinist and composer, Jean-Marie Leclair, produced his solo concerti.

The concerto after c. 1730

In the opening of this article "concerto" was defined as it is thought of first today—that is, in the sense that has prevailed since about 1750. Essential to that definition is the interrelation of orchestra and soloist, not soli. Whereas a *concertino* of soli had been the norm before 1750, with a single soloist being a variant or reduction of the concertino idea, the single soloist became the norm after 1750. As a result two or more soloists became the exception in what has since become known as "double concerto," "triple concerto," and so on. Because the concerto since 1750 has been likened to the sonata (again, as in the opening definition), it is often distinguished as the "sonata concerto," although the same could have been done with at least as much justification, especially because of the confusions of terms noted earlier, for the concerto before 1750. More justified, in spite of all the exceptions, might be the designations "solo concerto" for the later type and "orchestral concerto" (or concerto grosso) for the earlier type. The concerto grosso may be said to have dissolved into the solo concerto and the sinfonia concertante. The second term was Mozart's designation for certain concerti with more than one soloist, but it has also been used for symphonies that still reveal the imitative interplay of the concerto grosso or that employ the tutti–soli rondo principle. There are differences between the earlier solo part, which was a minimal concertino, and the later solo part, which was a self-sufficient adversary to the orchestra. There is also a difference in scoring between the two types of concerto, for at the time that the concerto grosso was being replaced by the solo concerto the basso continuo was falling into disuse. In addition there is a difference of degree, with a sharp increase of independence and virtuosity in the soloist's part in the later form of the concerto.

THE CLASSICAL CONCERTO (C. 1730–1830)

Since 1750 the concerto has found its chief place in society not in church or at court but in the concert hall. Some of the excitement it could arouse in classical musical life is recaptured in the Mozart family letters. Mozart's introduction of a new piano concerto (K. 456?) in a Vienna theatre concert was reported by his father on February 16, 1785:

The solo concerto

> . . . your brother played a glorious concerto, . . . I was sitting [close] . . . and had the great pleasure of hearing so clearly all the interplay of the instruments that for sheer delight tears came into my eyes. When your brother left the platform the Emperor waved his hat and called out "Bravo, Mozart!" And when he came on to play there was a great deal of clapping. (As translated by Emily Anderson, *The Letters of Mozart and His Family*, 2d. ed. The Macmillan Co., New York, 1966.)

The solo concerto was the main concert vehicle for composer-performers such as Mozart and for itinerant virtuosos like the Italian violinist Antonio Lolli, whose in-

cessant crisscrossing of all Europe scarcely can be reconciled with the incredibly bad travel conditions that still prevailed. A secondary place for the solo concerto has been in the realm of musical instruction. Although the category of "student concerto" to which certain works have been relegated seems largely to associate with the 19th century, a good many classical concerti evidently served that purpose too. Thus, Mozart, who wrote his latest, finest, and most difficult concerti for his own concert appearances, earlier wrote easier ones to be used mainly in teaching. The concerto also had an occasional place in the theatre, as evidenced by the fact that the Italian composer Francesco Maria Veracini played concerto movements as entr'actes during operatic performances.

Musical characteristics. The strings remained the nucleus, though less often the whole, of the tutti in the solo concerto. But now the more equivoice setting of the string quartet gradually superseded the polarity of the basso continuo and the melody or concertante parts. Moreover, the tutti was no longer reinforced by the solo instrument in the tutti passages, as it had been in the concerto grosso, for the solo became exclusively a solo part. Though optional instrumentation disappeared insofar as the choice of instruments for the old basso continuo was concerned, the free use of what instruments were available still applied to the wind parts of the usual concerto tutti throughout most of the 18th century. The instrumental colour of solo concerti, up to Mozart's mature works, was therefore relatively neutral, without particular refinement or individuality caused by specifically exploiting the tone colours of the instruments. On the other hand, the solo part became increasingly individualized in the solo concerto as a result of the further exploitation of spectacular playing techniques. Accordingly, the music of the solo part became highly idiomatic for the chosen instrument; that is, it was calculated to take most advantage of the characteristic sound and techniques particular to that instrument. Solo violin parts in particular had already reached heights of virtuosity during the overlap between the Baroque and Classical eras. Such works were scarcely surpassed before the most brilliant writing of the violin virtuoso Niccolò Paganini and his successors in the Romantic era. Examples may be found in abundance in the solo violin concerti of Leclair and the Italians Pietro Locatelli, Veracini, and Giuseppe Tartini. Most of these works, especially Tartini's, have real musical distinction, rooted as they are in an important heritage from Torelli, Albinoni, and Vivaldi in Italy and Johann Georg Pisendel, Telemann, and Bach in Germany.

Yet, from the 1780s and the peak of the Classical era, and despite a continuing if limited output of concerti for the cello, flute, oboe, clarinet, bassoon, and horn, it was no longer the violin or any of these instruments that ranked first among solo instruments of the concerto. Rather it was the newly emerging piano, which was rapidly superseding the harpsichord and clavichord. Mozart, who with the London-centred, Italian-born Muzio Clementi was one of the first great pianists, wrote not only some of the first but some of the greatest concerti the instrument has yet known. Two generations earlier, Bach's more limited exploitation of the keyboard in his harpsichord concerti had already shown what a stalwart adversary a keyboard instrument could be in the concerto contest. Now, with the greater independence of the solo part and the greater self-sufficiency of a keyboard part, both the drama and the variety of the tutti–solo opposition could be increased considerably. As for the variety, either orchestra or soloist might perform alone, either might carry the theme while the other accompanied, or the two might share in the theme by doubling, by antiphony (alternating with each other in playing phrases of the theme), or by more rapid interchange and alternation. Thus, Mozart's popular *Concerto in A Major*, K. 488, begins with an extended orchestral tutti without soloist, after which the solo piano enters on a restatement of the main theme, lightly and intermittently accompanied by the strings alone. Another tutti, this time short, leads into a modulatory (key-changing) bridge consisting of rapid

The rise of the piano

piano scales that elaborate on harmonies given in simpler notes in the tutti. The piano now enters alone on a second theme, then decorates snatches of the theme as the orchestra restates it an octave higher. So the work unfolds in a kaleidoscope of ingenious, fresh settings.

Movement cycles and forms

The standard cycle of three movements, fast–slow–fast, became even more standardized in the Classical era. It occurred without notable exception in the concerti of that era's three greatest masters, Haydn, Mozart, and Beethoven. Furthermore, the outer movements are generally predictable, too, at least in their overall plans. "Sonata form" is approximated in the opening movements. In the finales, apart from an occasional minuet (a dance form) in Haydn's concerti, the prevalent forms are rondo and sonata-rondo (which combines the recurrent refrain of the rondo with the exposition-development principle of the sonata). The middle movements are only a little less predictable, with ABA design being far in the majority (as in Mozart's *Concerto in D Minor*, K. 466). Forms such as the dialogue-like fantasy in Beethoven's *Piano Concerto No. 4 in G Major*, Opus 58, or the free variations in his *Violin Concerto* are late-Classical or pre-Romantic exceptions. But, of course, these masterworks are no stereotypes. They find their variety and distinctions in the details and working out of the forms. At most, "sonata form" in the Classical era was not yet the conscious concept or crystallized design that later textbooks have made it out to be. Its thematic organization in particular was still fluid and certainly not bound to any fixed number of themes or any fixed dualism of "masculine" and "feminine" themes. Textbook discussions of the solo concerto say that the tutti plays the exposition first, all in the tonic key, after which the soloist joins to repeat it, this time more elaborately and with the contrasting theme in a nearly related key. But that concept of the strict "double exposition" is honoured as much in the breach as the observance.

Actually, the application of "sonata form" was likely to be freer, even looser, in the concerto than in the symphony or string quartet. In part this was because of the extensive passagework that is inherent in the virtuosity and idiomatic treatment of the solo instrument.

Improvised and written cadenzas

This passagework and the loose treatment of the musical form reach their extreme in a terminal cadenza of the first movement, more so than in the shorter cadenzas likely to be found at one or more focal points in the other movements. The cadenza had already been introduced in late-Baroque violin concerti, undoubtedly influenced by singers' florid, improvised embellishments of arias in current opera, although early instrumental precedents exist, too. The concerto's cadenza was generally improvised by the performer until Beethoven insisted on the use of his own short cadenzas as supplied in *Piano Concerto No. 5 in E Flat Major*, Opus 73. Many later performers have found too little opportunity for technical display in other cadenzas that the masters previously had left for optional performance in some of their own concerti. The dissatisfied performers often substituted more brilliant cadenzas in such cases. But the structural looseness of the cadenza becomes less tolerable when the virtuoso performer goes to later sources or composes new cadenzas that are anachronistic in their technical and harmonic style, out of proportion in length, and inadequately related to the musical themes of the movement.

Austrian and German development of the concerto.
As with both the vocal and the instrumental concerto of the Baroque era, the starting point for the solo concerto in the Classical era lies in Italian music. But this time more weight must be attached to the evolution of the concerto in Germany and Austria. In these countries, there lies the more significant development, that of the piano concerto, as cultivated by the chief Classical masters.

Pre-Classical composers. The transition to the lighter texture and more fragmented musical thoughts of the pre-Classical "gallant style" may be credited in part to the Italian string concerti, notably those of Tartini, Giovanni Battista Sammartini, Luigi Boccherini, and Giovanni

Battista Viotti. But the one piano concerto that Boccherini may have left about 1768, along with several cello concerti, and the very few concerti that Clementi in England supposedly converted to solo piano sonatas hardly make any niche for Italian composers in the history of the piano concerto. The full exploitation of the piano in the concerto and the creation of more substantial, consequential concerti for it must be credited primarily to two of J.S. Bach's sons and to the high-Classical Viennese triumvirate of Haydn, Mozart, and Beethoven. Whereas Wilhelm Friedemann Bach had largely followed his father in his half dozen concerti for harpsichord, strings, and basso continuo, Carl Philipp Emanuel Bach opened new paths in about 50 keyboard concerti, as well as some violin concerti and flute concerti. This is especially true of his later concerti intended for the piano (1772) rather than the harpsichord. Original instrumentation, dialogue between piano and orchestra, bold flights and expressive recitatives, are among the characteristics of Emanuel's concerti. So also are final movements that resemble in character the lively musical and dramatic development at the end of an act of opera buffa (Italian comic opera).

By contrast, Johann Christian Bach's 37 harpsichord or piano concerti from the same period are lighter, more fluent, easier works aimed at amateur skills and tastes. Most of them, like his sonatas but unlike most of his 31 sinfonie concertante, have only two movements, the finale often being a minuet or set of variations. The anticipations of Mozart's style are unmistakable.

Works of the mature Classical period. Haydn left 36 concerti that can be verified, spanning the years from about 1755 to 1796; for violin (4); cello (5); bass; horn (4); hurdy-gurdy, or wheel . fiddle (5); trumpet; flute; oboe; baryton, a cello-like instrument (3); and keyboard (11, whether for organ, harpsichord, or piano). In 1792 he also wrote a sinfonia concertante for violin, oboe, cello, bassoon, and full orchestra that returns to the tutti–soli relationships of the concerto grosso. The keyboard concerti bear witness in their unenterprising, sometimes pedestrian handling of the solo part that Haydn was no distinguished keyboardist. Even the best known of them, the *Piano Concerto in D Major* (1784), is heard today more in education than in concert circles, in spite of its musical strengths, especially in the "Rondo all'Ungherese" ("Rondo in the Hungarian style"). The one concerto by Haydn that is widely performed in today's concert world is an admirable, sonorous work for cello, in D major (1783, once attributed to the German cellist Anton Kraft). Cast in the usual three movements, with clear thematic ties between them and accompanied only by the usual orchestra in eight parts (four strings, two oboes, two horns), this work is variously songful, brilliant to a taxing degree, and dancelike. Another important contribution by Haydn was his last concerto (1796), a resourceful and difficult work in E-flat major that exploited the new keyed trumpet, which unlike earlier trumpets was capable of playing diatonic (sevennote) and chromatic (12- note) scales.

Haydn's concerti

During his short career, Mozart left about 45 verifiable concerti dating from 1773 to his last year, 1791. These do not include five early piano concerti arranged from concerto or sonata movements written by Emanuel and Christian Bach and two lesser composers. Out of the total, there are 21 for piano, six for violin, five for horn, two for flute, and one each for oboe, clarinet, bassoon, flute, and harp, two pianos, three pianos, and two violins (called *Concertone*). Two further examples, entitled "Sinfonia concertante," are for violin and viola, and for a concertino of oboe, clarinet, horn, and bassoon. Best known and most played are five of the last eight solo piano concerti (K. 466, 467, 488, 491, and 595), which rank among the finest of his works and the best of the genre. Highly valued and often played, too, are the *Sinfonia concertante in E Flat Major for Violin, Viola and Orchestra*, K. 364, E. 320d, and the *Concerto for Two Pianos*, K. 365, E. 316a. Two of the violin concerti are well-known (K. 218 in D major and K. 219 in A major), although more so to students than to concert-

The concerti of Mozart

goers. Among those five solo piano concerti, that in D minor (K. 466) reveals a new urgency and compactness in Mozart's writing, reflecting the atmosphere of the *Sturm und Drang* ("Storm and Stress") period in German art, except in the naïvely charming "Romance" that is the middle movement. One among many instances of the striking tutti–solo contrasts in this work is the reservation of certain material, including the soloist's initial theme, for the soloist alone. The *Concerto in C Major,* K. 467, is a more cheerful work, broad and stately in its opening ideas, bubbling with intriguing melodic figuration, and capped by one of Mozart's most delectable rondos. The *Concerto in A Major,* K. 488, is rich in wistful songlike melodies. The spun-out line of the middle movement, in the rhythm of the siciliano (an Italian dance), makes an ideal foil for the gay, tuneful "Presto" that follows. Like the D-minor concerto, that in C minor (K. 491) is an intense work, more extended but even more driving. Mozart's last concerto for solo piano, that in B-flat major (K. 595), is another masterpiece, ever fresh in its ideas, yet with an air of sweet resignation in its almost neoclassical simplicity.

Beetho-
ven's
concerti

The much smaller output of concerti by Beethoven, anticipating the still smaller outputs by his 19th-century successors, is not surprising in view of the wider range of expression, further exploration of instrumental resources, and greater size of his concerti. There are nine complete works in all. These include seven with piano—the so-called standard five (1795–1809) plus one more from his boyhood and another, using chorus as well as orchestra, that is seldom performed, oddly constructed, and almost unclassifiable (*Choral Fantasia,* Opus 80, first performed 1808). Further, there is the *Violin Concerto in D major* (1806) and a worthy, but much less successful, *Triple Concerto in C Major for Piano, Violin, and Cello,* Opus 56 (1804). One could hardly find a wider range of expression than that between the third, fourth, and fifth (*Emperor*) piano concerti. Reduced to capsule, subjective terms, the third, in C minor, must be characterized as compelling drama, hushed serenity, and feverish drive in its respective movements; the fourth as joyous lyricism, stark tragedy, and scintillating gaiety; and the fifth as heroic grandeur, noble dignity, and victorious rejoicing. The opening tutti sections may be taken as samples of the wide variety of musical structure in these same three concerti. In the third, the tutti extends the exposition of the themes by developing or discussing each after it is first stated. The solo enters almost at once, with only a short flourish, on the main theme. In the fourth concerto, the piano begins alone with a short, refreshingly simple pronouncement of the main theme, followed immediately by a surprising, tangential entrance of the orchestra. There unfolds a full exposition that discusses each theme even more than in the third concerto. This time the solo enters for the repeated exposition only after a more extended flourish, lasting 15 measures. In the last concerto, the soloist begins by embellishing each of the three primary harmonies in the orchestra with a separate cadenza. Only after this opening does there begin a complete tutti exposition that, in its discussion of the themes, is still more developed than in the fourth concerto. Not until the orchestral exposition is ended does the solo enter again to begin its highly virtuosic elaboration in a repeated exposition. It is such development throughout all parts of the musical forms, and not only in the "development sections," that accounts for the great lengths of *Piano Concerto No. 5* and the *Violin Concerto.* Notable are the exceptional technical difficulties in these two peerless masterpieces, which grow as much out of their musical complexities as out of the composer's evident desire to reveal new ways to utilize his solo instruments (especially the rapidly advancing piano, with its wider range, heavier action, and bigger tone).

THE ROMANTIC ERA (C. 1790–1915)

Between the Romantic and the Classical concerto there occurred no such marked, relatively abrupt changes in form or style as were observed earlier here between the Classical and the Baroque concerto. The onset of the Romantic era was not signalled by any shift in the concerto's musical structure. Thus there was no stylistic change equivalent to the shift from the polyphonic interplay of short motives in the concerto grosso to the solo concerto's grouping of longer musical phrases in homophonic style (based on chords). Nor was there any shift in instrumental texture equivalent to that from the polarity of basso continuo and melody parts to a more equal distribution of voices or parts. Nor again was there any shift from the piano to another instrument as the preferred solo vehicle.

Gradual
evolution
of the
genre

General Romantic trends. As with much other Romantic music, the Romantic concerto was marked by an extension or expansion of those same Classical trends in all directions. This development led eventually to their exaggeration and ultimately to their extremes or breaking points. The concerto as a genre became more than ever the ideal showpiece at public concerts, doing much for the composer's profit, the performer's triumph, and the listener's delectation. Indeed, Franz Liszt, the dominant composer-pianist of his time, distinguished between the concerto and the sonata, calling the first a public showpiece and the second a private, personal expression (in 1838, while questioning a publisher's title, *Concerto Without Orchestra,* for the Opus 14 of Robert Schumann, a title changed to *Piano Sonata No. 3 in F Minor*). Over the century, several 19th-century concerti won more popularity than was accorded to any earlier concerti. Time has influenced that preference but little, to judge from a listing, in order of popularity, of the 15 piano concerti most played in major U.S. concerts in the late 1960s: Beethoven No. 5, Tchaikovsky No. 1, Brahms No. 2, Beethoven No. 3, (Prokofiev No. 3, Modern era), Schumann, Rachmaninoff No. 2, Mozart K. 595, Grieg, Beethoven No. 4, Camille Saint-Saëns No. 2, Brahms No. 1, Chopin No. 2, Beethoven No. 1, and Liszt No. 1 (from statistics compiled by Broadcast Music Industries).

Another expansion of Classical trends is seen in the concerto orchestra, with the larger number, greater variety, and more discriminating use of its instruments. It is true that only the thinnest possible "support" for the soloist sufficed for composer-performers such as the pianist Chopin, the violinist Paganini, and others whose musical thinking ranged but little beyond the spheres of their own instruments. But the orchestra developed the status of a genuine if not superior adversary of the soloist in newly resourceful orchestrations by composers of wider instrumental perspective. Examples of this exploitation of the orchestra include *Harold en Italie* (1834), a symphony with solo viola, by the French composer Hector Berlioz; *Piano Concerto No. 1 in E Flat Major* (published 1857), by Liszt; and *Burleske* (completed 1885) for piano and orchestra, by the German Richard Strauss. At the same time, the piano, as the ideal Romantic instrument, secured ever more firmly its Classical pre-eminence as the preferred solo vehicle of the concerto. Although the total output of violin concerti in particular was very great, there was a decided preponderance of piano concerti among all concerti that appeared on printed public concert programs. In turn, the use of the piano in concerti was one main incentive for further advances in piano construction. By the mid-19th century the instrument reached a peak very close to the sonorous, seven-octave, triple-strung, cast-iron framed behemoth that is the modern "concert grand." With its perfection came also the extension of keyboard technique to the last reaches of athletic dexterity. Evidence of such technical development includes the unreasonably difficult requirements of the three etudes ("studies") that comprise the huge unaccompanied *Concerto,* Opus 39, Nos. 8–10, by the French pianist-composer Alkan (Charles-Henri Morhange). It is also apparent in the more reasonable but no less difficult requirements in Rachmaninoff's *Piano Concerto No. 3 in D Minor,* Opus 30 (1909). The wind instruments used in concerto solos underwent mechanical advances, too, and both they and the stringed instruments enjoyed analogous exploitations of their technical possibilities in this century of virtuosos—not only of Liszt (and so many more) on the piano but of others such as

Concerto
orchestra-
tion

Paganini on the violin, Alfredo Piatti on the cello, and Domenico Dragonetti on the double bass.

Romantic innovations

The most significant extension or expansion of the concerto principle in the Romantic era might in one sense be called a contraction, for it concerns a continuing effort to consolidate, interrelate, and fuse the over-all cycle, both within and between the movements. Certain composers, mostly forgotten perfunctories, yet including as important and successful a figure as Chopin, were satisfied to pour new wine into old bottles. Thus many concerti accepted without question the movement forms and cycle that by then had become self-conscious stereotypes, especially "sonata form" in the first movement. Brahms largely preferred to accept the traditional cycle and forms, too, but with the masterful individuality, flexibility, and logic that were needed to revitalize them. On the other hand, most of the Romantics whose concerti are still played sought to modernize and advance the traditional structural principles. These changes may be summed up in six categories.

First, there is the elimination, in the opening movement, of the long initial tutti section. This innovation corresponded to the elimination in the sonata of the previously customary repeat of the exposition, a change that had begun in Beethoven's late sonatas and had soon become general. Such is the pattern in Schumann's *Piano Concerto in A Minor*, Opus 54 (1845), in which the soloist enters at the outset and proceeds promptly to an almost constant interrelationship with the orchestra as the exposition unfolds but once.

Second, there is the interlocking of the movements, achieved by leading not only from one movement to the next without appreciable pause in time or sound but also without either a definitive cadence (stopping point made clear by the harmonies) or full break in the continuity of harmonies or tonality. Thus in the *Violin Concerto in E Minor*, Opus 64 (1844), of Felix Mendelssohn, a lone bassoon suspends one note of the final chord of the first movement. Preventing a pause in time or sound, it leads directly into the middle movement. Again, between the middle and final movements a brief interlude, midway in tempo, mood, and intensity, supplies the continuity and avoids any full break.

A third Romantic innovation is the effort to bind the cycle more positively through the use of related themes and motives in the successive movements. Such themes and motives can be only melodic nuclei, as in the so-called basic motive employed by Brahms. Or they may be more extended melodic thoughts, such as are subjected to "thematic metamorphosis" by Liszt or "cyclical" treatment by the Belgian César Franck. (Both terms refer to the practice of transforming a theme melodically and rhythmically in various ways throughout the cycle of movements.) Among well-known examples is the tight thematic organization, with its final retrospective summary, in the four interconnected movements of Liszt's *Piano Concerto No. 1* (*Triangle Concerto*, published 1857), a work Liszt himself claimed to be innovational on this account.

Fourth, there are certain other, more incidental, yet effective means of unifying the cycle. These include the sense of culminating joy or triumph in those many concerti that change from a minor home key to its tonic major (for example, from A minor to A major) for the finale; or the consistency of musical textures caused by making all the movements similar in weight and style; or the stronger sense of return achieved by a finale that follows a middle movement characterized by a marked sense of departure or contrast.

"Program" concerti and fusion of movements

The remaining two categories of changes concern Romantic developments that go somewhat beyond expansions (or contractions) of Classical concerto traditions. As a fifth category, there is the extramusical unification of the cycle by means of a program—that is, a story or image. Unlike the Romantic sonata, the Romantic concerto abounds in examples. One of the earliest is the image that the German composer Carl Maria von Weber identified with his *Konzertstück* (*Concert Piece*) for piano and orchestra (1821). Its four interconnected movements are said to describe a medieval lady's longing for her absent knight, her agonized fears for him, the excitement of his impending return, and the joys of reunion and love.

Sixth and last, there are numerous efforts to contract or consolidate the concerto cycle still more drastically, by fusion of movements. Four different solutions may be cited as representative. Tchaikovsky's *Piano Concerto No. 1 in B Flat Minor* (1875) follows a number of symphonies and sonatas of the period by integrating the slow movement with the scherzo (a lively movement that had become a rather frequent additional item in the cycle). Liszt's *Piano Concerto No. 2 in A Major* (published 1863) is a pioneer among the several concerti that reduce the separate movements to sharply contrasting sections within a single movement. Franck's *Variations symphoniques* for piano and orchestra (first performed 1885) substitute for the cycle a single movement based on a single principle of musical structure (in contrast to the distinct structures of distinct movements). And the Russian Nikolay Medtner's *Piano Concerto in G Minor* is a single, experimental variation of "sonata form." It consists, as he himself explains,

of an exposition, [a short, transitional cadenza,] a series of [nine] variations on the two chief themes, constituting the development [section], and then the recapitulation.

Still other changes from the Classical to the Romantic concerto are concerned less with overall plans than with language and idiom: the characteristic harmonies, melodic styles, and manner of musical development. But such changes were not limited to the concerto. They touched all of Romantic music. Among them are fuller, more varied textures, greater use of the high and low extremes of instruments' ranges, and more sonorous, widespread spacing of sounds. Indicative of the third development was the significant change in piano writing from the Alberti bass in close position to the "um-pah-pah" bass and free arpeggiations in open position.

Romantic harmonies and nationalistic colour

In addition there was a marked new preference for minor keys as being almost indispensable to the intensity of Romantic feeling. There was also an increased use of chromatic harmonies (chords whose notes do not all belong to the key of the composition and that frequently seem to have a more expressive character). Similarly characteristic of the era were brief, temporary modulations whose functions were more colouristic than structural (*i.e.*, they were introduced more for the harmonic colour they embody rather than strictly as a means of changing keys). Another new development was the late-Romantic turn to nationalistic colours, introducing folk melodies or allowing folk music to influence melodies, harmonies, and rhythms. An example is the *Symphonie espagnole* for violin and orchestra (1875), by the French composer Édouard Lalo.

Leading composers. From beginning to end in the Romantic era, Germany reigned supreme in the concerto, both as leader and producer, as with all the major instrumental forms. The majority of the non-Germans whose concerti were more or less successful in their day were at least trained in Germany. Here, in one loose chronology, may be mentioned the most important of the Romantics from both in and out of Germany, along with their most important concerti, which generally are those with the best chance still of being heard today. The once successful piano concerti of the Czech Jan Ladislav Dussek and the Germans Johann Nepomuk Hummel and Ignaz Moscheles—all renowned virtuoso pianists—have given way to other early Romantic works. These include the *Konzertstücke* of Weber, two concerti by Mendelssohn, and, especially, two by Chopin and the one by Schumann. Mendelssohn's two piano concerti are rapidly slipping into the status of "student concerti" today, but his *Violin Concerto in E Minor* continues to hold top position in its class, along with the violin concerti of Beethoven, Brahms, and Tchaikovsky. These works followed and eclipsed the successes of Viotti, Paganini, the German Ludwig Spohr, and other violinist composers. Schumann left one of the era's few most played cello concerti, two others being the later ones by Saint-Saëns and the Czech Antonín Dvořák. As noted, Liszt was a pathbreaker with his two piano concerti. His other, more programmatic works for piano and orchestra are less played today, but they also exercised a variety of influences on such different late-Romantics as Grieg, Franck, the American Edward MacDowell, Rachmaninoff, Richard Strauss, and the Hungarian Ernő Dohnanyi. Brahms's concerti, every one a highly popular masterpiece today, mark a peak for the era on the conservative side. They include besides the two piano concerti in D minor and B-flat major, the *Violin Concerto in D Major* and the *Double Concerto in A Minor* (with violin and cello as the solo instruments). Among later romantic concerti, though those onetime favourites for violin by Henri Vieuxtemps, Henryk Wieniawski, Max Bruch, Karl Goldmark, Aleksandr Glazunov, and Sir Edward Elgar have recently lost much ground in the concert hall, those of Dvořák, Saint-Saëns, the Finnish composer Jean Sibelius, and, especially, Tchaikovsky still hold strong. Similarly, while the piano concerti of the famed piano virtuoso Anton Rubinstein are all but forgotten, two (in G minor and C minor) out of the five by Saint-Saëns and the *Concerto No. 2 in D Minor* by MacDowell get occasional hearings, and those already mentioned by Tchaikovsky and Rachmaninoff remain among the most successful. Certain concerti are less likely to be heard at least partly because they are written for less usual solo instruments. These include works for bassoon by Weber; for clarinet by Spohr, Weber, and Ferruccio Busoni; and for horn by Weber and Richard Strauss.

THE MODERN ERA (FROM ABOUT 1890)

By and large, and up to about 1950, the concerto of the modern era has kept pace with the language and idiom of modern music. There has been little introduction of new principles, or new trends, or even further extensions of the structural changes that have been noted here in the Romantic era. If anything, it has turned back on itself. It has sloughed off the advances, if such they be, of the Romantic era and has reverted to styles and forms of the Baroque and Classical concerto. In so doing it has provided some of the most telling examples of the neo-Baroque and neo-Classical trends in modern music.

More explicitly, the modern concerto has kept pace with the breakdown in traditional tonality and various efforts to revitalize, bypass, or replace that comfortably secure system. It has shared in the modern erosion of the contrast between chords traditionally considered consonant (*i.e.*, bearing musical repose) and dissonant (*i.e.*, bearing musical tension), thus contributing to the release of endless new chord forms and progressions. And it has joined in perhaps the most basic trend; *i.e.*, the return from the Romantic and Classical tendency of groups of melodic phrases in predominantly homophonic textures to the Baroque ideal of interplay of melodic motives in predominantly polyphonic textures. But at the same time, the modern concerto has abandoned the gigantic orchestra, the massive technical requirements and extreme opposition of the solo part, and the decided preference for the piano as the ideal solo instrument. Similarly, it has abandoned the intensive effort to interconnect, consolidate, and contract the musical forms and has turned away from the frequent concern with extramusical programmatic content. The downgrading of virtuosity for its own sake has caused the soloist to become more a part of the orchestra again. Some modern works, such as *Piano Concerto No. 3 in C Major*, Opus 26 (1921), by Prokofiev, do continue to offer some of the formidable difficulties, glittering passagework, and soaring lyricism of the late Romantic concerto in the solo part. But even in these, the nature of the modern musical language permits the soloist generally to blend with the orchestra rather than to "do battle" with it, as has been said regarding Tchaikovsky's *Piano Concerto No. 1* and similar concert favourites of the Romantic era.

From the present limited perspective, no one country appears yet to have dominated the cultivation of the modern concerto. The total output has continued to be high, with nearly every composer of renown having contributed to it. Among representative German works that have won widest public endorsement—which, in the very

Changes in the soloist's role

nature of the solo concerto, must continue to be a main criterion—may be cited numerous concerti (mostly called "Chamber Music") that Paul Hindemith (1895–1963) seems systematically to have written for almost every standard instrument as a solo, and for a variety of combinations. Both the Austrians Arnold Schoenberg and his disciple Alban Berg left 12-tone concerti for violin and Schoenberg left one for piano. (Twelve-tone music is based on a series or "row" of the 12 notes of the chromatic scale, chosen by the composer to serve as the melodic and harmonic basis for the composition.)

From France may be cited works by Claude Debussy for piano (*Fantaisie*) and for saxophone (*Rapsodie*); by Maurice Ravel for piano (two, of which one is for left hand alone) and for violin; and by Darius Milhaud for various instruments, even mouth organ, and various instrumental combinations, including percussion. From England there is a double concerto for violin and cello by Frederick Delius and there are various works by Sir Arnold Bax, Sir Arthur Bliss, Ralph Vaughan Williams, Sir William Walton, and Benjamin Britten. Among examples from the United States are successful concerti by George Gershwin, including *Rhapsody in Blue* for piano and jazz orchestra, and by Aaron Copland, whose *Piano Concerto* (1926) also exploits jazz. Of major importance have been solo or duo concerti by Prokofiev (five for piano, two for violin, and one for cello), the Russian-born Igor Stravinsky (two for horn, one for violin, one for oboe, and one for clarinet and bassoon), and the Hungarian Béla Bartók (four for piano and three for violin). Attention also should be called to the neo-Baroque *Harpsichord Concerto* (1926), by the Spaniard Manuel de Falla.

A special indication of neo-Baroque interest may be seen in the return on the part of a number of composers to the tutti–soli grouping, the motoric pulse, and the interplay of motives of the concerto grosso. Notable examples have been left by Bartók, Stravinsky, the German Max Reger, the Swiss-born Ernest Bloch, and the Austrian-born Ernst Krenek.

The present discussion of the modern era has concerned developments largely ending by about 1950, although occasional returns to what might already be called the "traditional (solo) concerto" have occurred since, as by John Cage, Leon Kirchner, and Elliot Carter in the United States; by the Argentine Alberto Ginastera; the French composer Olivier Messiaen; the Greek Yannis Xenakis; and the Russian Dmitry Shostakovich. In the main, from 1950 on, the pronounced swing of the avant-garde to electronic, computerized, and aleatoric, or chance music, has tended to do away with everything traditionally identified with "concerto," including the title itself. The only identifiable characteristic to remain is the basic idea of the group–solo relationship, as in several works by the German Karlheinz Stockhausen and German-born Lukas Foss. That basic idea is essential not only to the concerto but to much other music. Whether it alone will survive in a way that still can be related to the venerable career of the concerto remains to be seen.

BIBLIOGRAPHY. ABRAHAM VEINUS, *The Concerto*, rev. ed. (1964), the only broad survey in English, with good knowledge of the subject but generally not well documented; DAVID BOYDEN, "When Is a Concerto Not a Concerto?" in the *Musical Quarterly*, 43:220–232 (1957), an essential clarification of the word itself; ARNOLD SCHERING, *Geschichte des Instrumentalkonzerts bis auf die Gegenwart*, 2nd ed. (1927), the principal survey in any language, although now somewhat outdated and inadequate; HANS ENGEL, *Die Entwicklung des deutschen Klavierkonzerts von Mozart bis Liszt*, 2 pt. (1927), the main survey of its topic, completed by THEOPHIL STENGEL, *Die Entwicklung des Klavierkonzerts von Liszt bis zur Gegenwart* (1931); NORMAN CARRELL, *Bach's Brandenburg Concertos* (1963), an analytic discussion, well illustrated by examples and cuts; C.M. GIRDLESTONE, *Mozart's Piano Concertos* (1948), separate analytic chapters on each of the main concerti; RALPH HILL (ed.), *The Concerto* (1961), an anthology of 29 articles primarily on the Romantic and Modern concerto; A.J.B. HUTCHINGS, *The Baroque Concerto* (1961), inadequately documented and organized, but keen and authoritative in its observations.

(W.S.N.)

Concrete

Concrete is a hardened product created by mixing a chemically inert, granular material (aggregate) with a matrix composed of a cementitious binder (such as lime, natural cement, or artificial cement) and water. When water is added, chemical reactions cause the matrix, in which the aggregate is embedded, to set, dry out, and harden, producing the familiar material known as concrete. In structural concrete, used in building and civil engineering, the binder is generally portland cement (see CEMENT), and the aggregate is gravel or crushed stone and sand. Many other forms of special concretes exist, however, including lightweight concrete, refractory concrete, and chemically resistant concrete. They are all usable as structural concrete.

HISTORY OF CONCRETE

Concrete has been used as a constructional material for centuries because most of those parts of the world where early civilizations were established had natural cement deposits. In Mediterranean countries, there are many remains of Roman concrete construction. In more recent times, concrete with a natural cement or lime composition was used notably by European engineers for the construction of foundations and docks.

Portland cement. Structural concrete as understood today was developed following the early-19th-century invention of an artificial cement called portland cement. It was of more uniform quality than natural cement and made a stronger and more durable concrete than lime. Since portland cement is composed chiefly of clay and limestone or chalk—all widespread materials—it is possible to make and economically use portland cement almost anywhere. Following the rapid spread of manufacturing facilities for portland cement, concrete was used almost exclusively for foundations and as an alternative to masonry for harbours, dams, and other structures requiring massive construction.

Reinforced concrete. The invention of reinforced concrete in the latter half of the 19th century permitted the use of concrete for buildings, bridges, and similar structures containing beams and other members subject to bending action and, consequently, to compressive and tensile forces. Although sound concrete is highly resistant to compression, its resistance to tension is comparatively low. To correct this deficiency, material of high tensile strength, such as steel bars, is embedded in those parts of the concrete member that are subjected to tension. The concrete member is reinforced: the concrete itself has the same strength with or without the reinforcement. Therefore "reinforced concrete" is not a very precise term; the older but obsolete terms "ferro-concrete" and "concrete-steel" construction are more correct.

Reinforced concrete construction, as it is understood today, was introduced in Britain and France in the 1850s and spread rapidly to neighbouring countries. At first, concrete was applied only to the floors of buildings but, by the end of the 19th century, reinforced concrete bridges had been built in the United Kingdom, France, the U.S., and elsewhere. A reinforced concrete jetty was constructed in the U.K. in 1899 and an aqueduct in Spain in 1898. The first reinforced concrete structures in Poland were built in 1892. By the early years of the 20th century, most countries were utilizing this method of construction, which had become so developed in the U.S. that in 1905 it was expedient to form the American Concrete Institute. A Concrete Institute was established in the U.K. in 1908; this later became the Institution of Structural Engineers. (The present Concrete Society was established in the U.K. in 1966 as an amalgamation of several specialist groups.) The Portland Cement Association, founded in 1916, and the Prestressed Concrete Institute, organized in 1954, also furthered concrete construction.

Prestressed concrete. A much more recent development is that of prestressed concrete. Instead of reinforcing the tensile zone of a loaded concrete beam, this zone can be compressed before the load is applied. Conse-

quently, when the beam is loaded, no tension will be induced in the concrete until this precompression has been overcome. In practice, the amount of precompression is calculated to be such that very little or no tension is induced under working conditions. This is true prestressed concrete.

The first patent on prestressed concrete was issued in the U.S. in 1888, but it did not become a practical method of construction until more was known of concrete properties such as creep, and until very high tensile steel was available. To Eugène Freyssinet in France must go most of the credit for making prestressed concrete an economical and practical form of construction in the later 1930s. Many engineers contributed to its further development, which occurred principally during and immediately after World War II. By then some docks and a number of bridges had been constructed using prestressed concrete.

TYPES OF CONCRETE

Concretes of various types, for structural and similar purposes, are identified either by the nature of the aggregate or the cement, or by special attributes or treatment.

Ordinary structural concrete. Aggregates for ordinary structural concrete are commonly divided into two grades: fine and coarse. Fine aggregate (or sand) is graded from the finest particles up to particles not exceeding about $3/16$ in. (5 mm) in size. As a rule these aggregates are naturally occurring pit or river sands or the fines and grits from stone crushing.

The most common coarse aggregates for concrete of ordinary weight are natural gravels (either crushed or not) and crushed rock, all of which may be graded from about $3/16$ in. (5 mm) up to $3/4$ in. (20 mm) for much structural concrete, and up to $1½$ in. (38 mm) or larger for massive construction.

In the latter case a combined aggregate—that is, one that is fully graded from sand up to the largest stone—is often used; such materials are called all-in aggregates.

Determining proportions of aggregate to cement. To obtain the correct proportion of aggregate to portland cement in a concrete mix, the matrix of cement and sand should be sufficient to fill, with a slight excess, the voids or interstices between the pieces of coarse aggregate, thereby providing a dense concrete. Consequently, the volume of the concrete resulting from this mixture is substantially less than the sum of the volumes of the loose, separate materials. The more dense the concrete, with given materials, the stronger and more durable it is likely to be. The average proportions of ordinary structural concrete are one part of cement to two parts of fine aggregate to four parts of coarse aggregate (1:2:4). The actual proportion of the amount of cement to the total amount of aggregate depends on the strength and durability required. Thus, proportions may vary from 1:3:6 up to 1:1:2, with the mixes leaner in cement used for mass and other nonreinforced work. Richer mixes are used when especially strong concrete is required, as in the case of large bridges and high-load columns. The most modern practice, however, is to define a concrete mix as the weight of cement in one cubic yard (or cubic metre) of mixed concrete. This amount may vary from 350 to 900 pounds per cubic yard (approximately 200 to 530 kilograms per cubic metre), again the proportion of cement being dependent on the application. For the best work, the proportions must be precise. Much skill is required in designing a mix to produce, with given aggregates, a concrete that conforms to specified requirements of strength, workability, and durability. These properties are considered below.

Strength. The strength of hardened concrete is assessed generally by crushing small test specimens (which may be cylinders in the U.S., cubes in the U.K., or prisms in some other countries) and by observing the force required to break the specimen at a specified age. This force is then evaluated in pounds per square inch (psi) or kilograms per square centimetre (kg/cm^2) of cross section of the specimens. The strength as measured on speci-

Grades of aggregates

mens of various shapes may vary considerably; for example, the strength as measured on a test cylinder may be only 85 percent of that obtained on a six-inch cube of the same concrete. Strength of a dense concrete is affected most by the proportion (by weight) of water to cement (water-cement ratio) and this may vary from 0.3 for a "dry" (or earth-damp) and eventually very strong concrete to 0.7 for a more fluid and relatively weaker concrete. An average machine-mixed structural concrete with a water-cement ratio of about 0.5 may have a crushing strength of around 3,000 psi (2,100 kg/cm²) 28 days after mixing, but especially designed concretes may have strengths of 8,000 psi (5,600 kg/cm²) or greater.

Strength is also affected by the environment of the wet concrete immediately after placing and during the hardening process. When the cement sets and the concrete hardens, it is subject to shrinking. If restrained in such a way that it is not free to contract, tensile stresses are set up. If newly placed concrete is kept damp during the critical period while the cement is setting and during the early part of the period immediately following, it will not shrink as much as it would if allowed to dry out normally, and tensile stresses will be kept to a minimum until the concrete has attained some strength to resist them. This important operation of keeping the concrete damp for a period of some days after placing is called curing.

Curing

It is important that concrete not be subjected to low temperatures while setting and hardening; otherwise strength may be seriously impaired. The addition of a set-accelerating compound, such as a limited quantity (about 2 percent of the weight of the cement) of calcium chloride to the concrete mix, has the effect of accelerating the setting process. The additional heat thereby generated can offset the effects of moderately cold weather. Before this heat has been dissipated, the concrete may have hardened sufficiently to prevent the strengthening process being retarded by low ambient temperatures. Various proprietary compounds containing calcium chloride are used for this purpose; a cement containing calcium chloride is obtainable in the U.K.

Workability. Workability is the property of a freshly mixed concrete that permits it to be placed with ease and worked around the reinforcing bars in crowded areas. It is obviously difficult to place a "dry" or stiff concrete around reinforcing bars; therefore, such concretes are usually used only for mass nonreinforced or lightly reinforced structures. Very fluid concretes are readily placed in reinforced concrete members but, if they are too wet, there is not only a loss of strength but also the risk that the pieces of aggregate may separate from the matrix. An intermediate state of fluidity is therefore desirable, but to ensure that the concrete flows completely around the bars and into the corners of the temporary molds (or formwork) in which it is cast, some means of compaction or consolidation is desirable to prevent voids from occurring. The usual method is by vibration, which is effected either by applying vibrators to the outside of the mold or formwork or by inserting a vibrating poker into the concrete itself. There are, however, other special means of compaction, depending on the casting circumstances.

Compaction to prevent voids

Admixtures. The characteristics of concrete often can be improved by including admixtures in the concrete mix. In addition to set-accelerators (such as calcium chloride as previously described), there are set-retarders (usually of a sugar base) that are less commonly required. The purpose of most admixtures is to increase the workability of freshly mixed concrete without having to increase the water content and without thereby affecting the eventual strength. Such compounds, called plasticizers, are derivatives of lignosulfonic or hydroxylated carboxylic acids. Air-entrainment also increases workability. Other admixtures, generally termed waterproofers, help decrease the permeability of set concrete.

A nonproprietary material, the use of which is becoming more widespread where available, is pulverized-fuel ash (fly ash). Since it has pozzolanic (cement-forming) properties, it can replace some of the normal cement content, thereby reducing the heat generated during setting. Other factors being equal, fly ash can increase the eventual strength.

Durability. Durability is the necessary property that a concrete must have in order to ensure long life of the structure. Basically, durability is dependent on the proportion of cement in the mix, but other factors can degrade the durability of an otherwise satisfactory concrete. An important such factor is the amount of concrete covering the reinforcing bars. If this cover is too small, atmospheric moisture can gain access to the steel bars through very fine cracks and cause rusting. The consequent expansion of the bars causes spalling of the concrete and general deterioration of the structure. Durability and, in particular, resistance to thermal expansion and contraction can be improved by air-entrainment.

Other types. *Air-entrained concrete.* Compounds are obtainable to entrain into the concrete a small quantity of air in the form of minute bubbles. With practically no loss of strength, there is a considerable gain in workability. At the same time the air bubbles offset the effects of frost and increase resistance to some chemicals. Compounds may be of various chemical compositions, but a common type is a soluble salt derived from a sulfonated hydrocarbon. In the U.S., standard cements are obtainable containing the essential compound and therefore directly producing air-entrained concrete.

Lightweight concrete. Concrete having a weight less than that of ordinary concrete contains lightweight aggregates. Many kinds of such aggregates are available today. The most important are furnace clinker (for making concrete blocks); natural materials such as pumice; and especially heat-treated materials including foamed blast-furnace slag, sintered brick earth, colliery shale, fly ash, and bloated and expanded clay. Chemically stabilized particles of wood are also used for producing lightweight building blocks.

Such lightweight aggregates produce concrete having weights from 20 to about 120 pounds per cubic foot (320 to 1,900 kg/m³), compared with about 150 lb/ft³ (2,400 kg/m³) for ordinary gravel-aggregate concrete, but the lower weights are generally accompanied by low strength. Such concretes have special properties—such as high thermal insulation—which is advantageous in the construction of walls and other building components. Modern techniques, however, make it possible to produce lightweight-aggregate concretes with strengths comparable to those of gravel-aggregate concretes. They are therefore becoming more widely used as reinforced structural concrete, especially in the U.K. and the U.S. An obvious advantage of the light weight is the reduced dead weight of the structure with consequent savings in cost, especially in regard to the foundation.

Another form of lightweight concrete is cellular concrete (aerated or "gas" concrete), in which a metallic powder is mixed with sand, cement, and water. A chemical reaction produces cells of gas in the wet concrete, causing it to expand, and when hardened giving it a cellular structure. Immediately after molding, such concrete is subjected to a combined moisture and heat treatment under pressure (called autoclaving), producing a strong, durable, lightweight concrete in a few hours. Cellular concrete also has high thermal-insulation properties and can be reinforced for structural purposes if the steel is suitably protected.

Cellular concrete

Heavy concrete. Concrete having a density up to twice that of ordinary gravel-aggregate concrete can be produced by using heavy materials as aggregates. Such materials include barites, iron ores (magnetite, hematite, limonite), steel balls, and steel shavings. The principal use of such heavy concrete is for radiation shields in nuclear power and similar plants, and for ballast blocks.

Low-heat concrete. Concrete having a low degree of heat generation when setting can be produced by using a low-heat cement; that is, a cement with the composition so designed that when it sets, the amount of heat generated by the chemical reactions is minimized. Low-heat concrete is used in massive construction because the heat generated by normal cement would give rise to excessive temperatures and consequent defects. Heat in the heart of massive construction cannot be as readily dissipated as it can with concrete members of smaller dimensions.

Sulfate-resistant concrete. The use of sulfate-resistant cement helps concrete to resist the corrosive effects of moderate concentrations of sulfates in liquids stored in concrete vessels or in ground water in which a concrete bridge or other structure is embedded.

Refractory concrete. Concrete that must resist high temperatures, as in furnace construction, contains a refractory aggregate—such as crushed firebrick or especially constituted materials—and high-alumina cement.

Fibre-reinforced concrete. Materials other than steel —bamboo and timber, for example—have been used as reinforcement, but such cases are not common. A relatively recent development, however, is to reinforce the concrete itself by including short fibres in the concrete mix. The fibres may be nylon, glass, polypropylene, polyethylene, asbestos, or short steel wires. The resulting fibre-reinforced concrete is of greater strength than ordinary concrete and has increased resistance to impact. It has been used in the construction of roads and aircraft runways and such special works as rocket launching pads.

Vacuum concrete. Concrete that is subjected to a suction immediately after having been placed in a mold is termed vacuum concrete. This process extracts some of the moisture, leaving a drier concrete which will eventually attain a much higher strength than the original wetter material. A common use of the vacuum process is in the manufacture of paving slabs and similar products made on hydraulic presses.

Ready-mixed concrete. Ready-mixed concrete is the term applied to ordinary concrete that is mixed at a central depot instead of on the construction site, and is distributed in special trucks. On small jobs, the contractor therefore does not have to install an expensive concrete batching and mixing plant; on congested sites, space does not have to be found for such a plant; and the quality of the concrete is more uniformly high because of the centralized control. During travel, the truck load of concrete is kept agitated by slow rotation of the container or drum. If the distance the load of concrete has to travel is great, the dry cement and aggregate are fed into the drum and the water added and the mixing process begun toward the end of the journey; this is termed truck-mixed concrete. Otherwise it is necessary to take steps to prevent initial set of the concrete before being delivered to the construction sites.

> Truck-mixed concrete

STRUCTURAL FORMS OF CONCRETE

Cast-in-place construction. One of the principal methods of casting structural members is to deposit the concrete in timber, steel, or glass-fibre molds (called formwork) set up in the final position the member will occupy in a building or other structure. Or it may be deposited directly on a prepared surface on the ground, as in foundations, floors, and road construction. This method, called cast-in-place, is the most common system of concrete construction.

Precasting. The alternative method, called precasting, is to cast each member separately in wooden, steel, or glass-fibre molds in a distant factory or at a casting works set up for this purpose on or near the building site. In this method the members, subjected to curing and having attained sufficient strength, are removed from the molds and transported to the site for erection in combination with other members. Precast concrete columns, beams, floor and roof slabs, wall panels, window units, stairs and other components are erected to form a building; or precast and prestressed concrete beams or girders are erected on prepared abutments and piers to construct bridges, the decks also being formed of precast concrete slabs. Precasting is also the basic method of producing small concrete products such as reinforced concrete fence-posts, pipes, railway sleepers (ties), and nonreinforced paving slabs, curbs, tiles, building blocks, masonry, and cast (artificial) stone. Many of these products are made in specialized factories.

Mass (or plain or nonreinforced) concrete. In cast-in-place structures such as massive gravity dams, heavy dock walls, and large foundations, and in large precast concrete blocks for breakwaters and similar marine work, bending effects are negligible, and reinforcing of the concrete therefore is unnecessary. In such cases, as well as in light pavings, plain, or nonreinforced, concrete is commonly used.

Reinforced concrete. Reinforced concrete, as previously explained, is structural concrete in which reinforcement is embedded. The reinforcing material is usually steel, either in the form of hot-rolled mild (low carbon) steel bars; cold-worked (twisted) bars of strength superior to mild steel bars; or hot-rolled bars having high tensile strength. Most modern reinforcing bars, other than twisted square bars, have indentations or ribs on their surfaces to improve the bond with the surrounding concrete. For floor and flat roof slabs and roads, a fabricated (welded) mesh of high tensile wire often is used as reinforcement.

There are two theories for calculating the resistance of reinforced concrete, namely, the elastic theory and the ultimate-load theory. The elastic theory assumes that under safe working loads both the concrete and steel behave as elastic materials and stresses do not exceed safe working values. The ultimate-load or load-factor theory considers the conditions of the two materials as failure of the structural member is approached. When the maximum resistance of the member has been assessed, this is divided by a factor of safety to determine the safe working load. Both theories are currently accepted, although the ultimate-load theory is more favoured. Allied to this, the conception of limit-state design is being introduced into standard codes in the U.K. The basis of limit-state design is to provide adequate factors of safety against probable critical conditions that can impair the usefulness of a structure during its required life. Such conditions are structural failure, excessive deformation, local or general damage due to cracking or deterioration, fatigue, excessive vibration, and insufficient resistance to fire. By adopting certain partial factors of safety, allowance can also be made for unexpected variations in the loading, the strength of the materials, any inadequacy in the analytical methods, and quality of workmanship.

> Limit-state design

Prestressed concrete. In structural members of prestressed concrete, either cast-in-place or precast, precompression may be induced by steel tendons in the form of separate wires, bunches of wires (cables), or wire-ropes (strand). If cast-in-place, ducts are formed in the member through which the tendons are threaded. The tendon is anchored to one end of the hardened concrete member. Tension is applied by means of a jack attached to the other end of the tendon and reacting against the concrete member. Thus the member is subjected to a designed precompression. With some assessable loss, this precompression is maintained after removal of the jack by anchoring the jacking end of the stretched tendon to the adjacent end of the member. This method, termed post-tensioning, is used mainly for bridge girders and other large cast-in-place beams, but can be applied also to such members made up of precast concrete blocks.

A method of post-tensioning used on storage tanks, nuclear power pressure vessels, and similar cylindrical structures subjected to internal pressures is wire winding. A continuous helix of tensioned wire is wound around the outside of the wall of the erected structure. The wire later is protected by pneumatically-applied mortar.

Some forms of prestressed, precast concrete members, such as beams and railway ties, often are produced by pre-tensioning the tendons. In this method, the wires or other tendons extend throughout the length of the empty mold or throughout a line of empty molds. One end of the tendon is anchored either to the end of the mold or to an external abutment, and tension is applied at the other end of the tendon. Concrete is deposited in the mold and worked around the stretched tendons. When the concrete has attained sufficient strength, anchors at the ends of the stretched tendons are released. The tendons, which

> Pre-tensioning

endeavour to return to their original length but are prevented from doing so by their embedment, impose a compression on the concrete.

To design a prestressed concrete structural member subjected to bending, the tensile and compressive stresses in the concrete due to the loading must be calculated, assuming the member to be homogeneous. Then follows the calculation of the initial tensile force required in the prestressing tendons to produce compressive stresses that will counteract the tensile stresses in the concrete (and incidentally augment the compressive stresses). Taken into account are the position of the tendons and the loss of prestresses resulting from relaxation of the tension, shrinkage of the concrete, and similar factors. Stress analysis has to be considered at various critical stages of construction as well as under normal working conditions.

APPLICATIONS

There are few fields of constructional activity in which concrete does not figure, either alone or in combination with other materials. Some of the major application areas are described below.

Buildings. Buildings constructed of concrete today include single-story houses, factories, and multistory blocks of offices, flats (apartments), hotels, and warehouses (see also BUILDING CONSTRUCTION). The high fire-resistant property of concrete is a structural advantage.

The upper floors of buildings may be of cast-in-place reinforced concrete either of beam-and-slab, flat slab (beamless or mushroom), or waffle construction. They may also be constructed of precast concrete beams and slabs, in which case these components are generally prestressed. A form of floor construction peculiar to concrete is lift-slab, in which a number of floor slabs are cast at ground level, one on top of the other, then jacked up into their relative positions in the multistory building.

Roofs are either flat (in which case the various methods of floor construction are applicable), sloping (pitched), hipped (folded plate), hyperbolic paraboloid, or curved. Among the latter types are domes and the recently developed form known as shell construction, where the strength of a thin curved concrete membrane is used advantageously to produce a light and aesthetic roof capable of bridging wide spaces without appreciable bending effects.

Floors and roofs are supported on reinforced concrete columns and walls, the former being either square, round, octagonal, or of special architectural shapes. Walls may be either cast monolithically with the floor and roof or may be precast in panels several stories high. If precasting is adopted, it is not unusual for all the components of a building, including the stairs, to be precast. These components are made in a factory specializing in such work. If the size of the project warrants, however, a temporary precasting works is set up on the site. Such extensive structural design engineering and fabrication is termed industrialized building.

The days are long past when the walls of a concrete building were drab and featureless; much attention is now paid to the finish of the exposed concrete. There are many ways in which an attractive profiled or textured surface can be produced. Some architects rely on patterned effects produced by especially constructed formwork; others obtain aesthetic and colourful facing by exposing the aggregate. Various shadowed patterns can be created by building walls of concrete blocks, especially the type that has been split to expose the inner texture.

Finish of the exposed concrete

Bridges. Reinforced concrete bridges, a common form of construction since the beginning of the century, may be of either girder or arch design. Suspension bridge piers and towers often are constructed in concrete (see also BRIDGES, CONSTRUCTION AND HISTORY OF). The size of concrete bridges ranges from simple slab structures of small span to vast arch bridges with spans up to 1,000 ft (305 m). Concrete girder bridges for roads and railways are the form most common today, with the main components of the deck usually of prestressed and often precast concrete. Reinforced concrete girder bridges exceeding 250 ft (76 m) in span have been constructed. There are prestressed concrete girder bridges with post-tensioned tendons of over 500 ft (152 m) in span, while prestressed precast girders exceeding 50 tons in weight and 100 ft (30 m) in length have been made in factories and transported to sites several hundred miles distant. Factory-made bridge girders, which in the U.K. are of standardized designs, are generally of more modest dimensions with prestressed tendons.

Water-retaining structures. Because of the noncorroding nature of concrete in contact with water, tanks and reservoirs are commonly constructed of reinforced concrete. Generally they are cast-in-place, although there are many examples of structures, especially circular tanks, that are prestressed, and a few precast and prestressed. Concrete-covered reservoirs with capacities of many millions of gallons are in service. Elevated tanks (water towers) of reinforced concrete can be given architectural treatment not possible economically in other materials. Such structures are generally circular or polygonal in plan, but some very large rectangular elevated tanks or reservoirs have been constructed.

Although there are many earth dams for retaining large masses of water, concrete is the usual material for the construction of the largest dams (see also DAM). Such structures may be gravity dams that depend on their mass for stability, lighter structures with small horizontal arches spanning between heavy buttresses, or a structure in the form of a single large horizontal arch. Some of the largest concrete dams are the Grand Coulee (U.S.), which contains some 10,500,000 cubic yards (about 8,000,000 cubic metres) of concrete; the Hoover (U.S.), which exceeds 725 ft (220 m) in height; the Kariba (Rhodesia), an arched dam 2,025 ft (617 m) long; and the Grande Dixence (Switzerland), a gravity dam 932 ft (284 m) high. Concrete pipes are used to convey water and sewage. Such pipes, sometimes prestressed and exceeding 6 ft (2 m) in diameter, are made at factories equipped with machines of high productive capacity.

Concrete in dam construction

Industrial structures. Concrete's resistance to corrosive industrial atmospheres, coupled with the economy of construction, has led from the earliest days of reinforced concrete to the adoption of this form of construction in such processing plants as gas works; chemical, steel, and cement plants; and oil refineries. Its use in the construction of large elevated bunkers (bins) for the storage of coal, stone, and other granular materials is widespread. Deep storage bins (silos) for grain, cement, and similar products are today almost exclusively constructed of reinforced concrete, with capacities of thousands of tons. Bunkers and silos may be single-bin structures, which are often cylindrical, or more commonly multicompartment structures with a nest of bins either circular, square, or polygonal in shape.

The tall chimneys or stacks required for power stations and industrial plants that emit hot gases are often constructed of reinforced concrete. They may be of either single-flue or multiflue design. A reinforced concrete chimney 1,206 ft (367 m) high has been built at Cresap, West Virginia and a triple-flue shaft 850 ft (259 m) high at Drax (U.K.). It is not unusual to construct chimneys of moderate height with precast concrete blocks or rings; the tallest such structure in Europe is at Leicester (U.K.); it is 225 ft (69 m) high. A reinforced concrete chimney can be designed economically to act as a vertical cantilever against wind forces. It therefore does not require guy ropes, as do some designs of steel chimneys. With very hot gases, it is necessary to line part of the shaft with a refractory brick.

Concrete chimneys

One of the many numerous special types of concrete industrial structures is the hyperbolic cooling tower required at inland power stations; it may be up to 375 ft (114 m) high and 350 ft (107 m) in diameter at the base. A form of tall concrete structure becoming common in many cities is the radio or television tower, some of which approach 600 ft (183 m) in height.

Earth-retaining structures and foundations. Foundations for structures of all types are almost invariably constructed of concrete. They may be of plain mass concrete but today are much more commonly of reinforced concrete. Such foundations may be separate bases for the support of columns and piers, long strip footings for walls, or, where the ground is of low-bearing capacity, a raft spread over the entire area of the site of the structure. If good ground is not found for some depth below the surface, pile foundations are generally required. The piles may be precast concrete or may be cast-in-place in holes bored into the ground. Concrete piles for structures on land vary in size from 8 in. (20 cm) in diameter, capable of carrying a load of one to two tons and penetrating only a few feet into the ground, up to large cylinder or caisson foundations 8 ft (2.5 m) or more in diameter, sunk to depths exceeding 100 ft (30 m) and each carrying many hundreds of tons.

Retaining walls used for supporting banks of earth or heaps of stored materials are also commonly of reinforced concrete, varying from simple cantilevered walls, either precast or cast-in-place, to complex supported structures 50 ft (15 m) or more in height. Precast concrete sheet-pile walls with anchor ties, similar to steel sheet-pile walls in construction, are a common form of retaining wall for wharves, quays, and similar waterside construction.

Transportation. In addition to buildings and bridges, concrete is also important in the field of transportation, including such small items as prestressed railway sleepers (ties), which are now standard on British railways, and such large construction as massive dock walls. There are many thousands of miles of concrete roads throughout the world, ranging from lightly loaded residential streets to multilane motorways (expressways) carrying fast traffic and heavy commercial vehicles. Many of the smaller airport runways and aprons and virtually all runways for the heaviest aircraft are constructed of reinforced concrete. Sophisticated labour-saving machines have been devised for the continuous and speedy construction of concrete roads and runways. (see ROADS AND HIGHWAYS).

Concrete boats and barges have been successfully constructed, and there is a vogue for building small pleasure craft of especially dense and strong reinforced concrete called ferrocement.

DEVELOPMENTAL TRENDS

The nature of concrete and its applications are continuously being developed. Compressive strengths, normally up to about 8,000 psi (560 kg/cm²) today, could probably be doubled and still be economically feasible. At the same time, the rapid development of lightweight concrete of high strength means that the weight of concrete structures can be considerably reduced, with consequent savings in foundations or increased usage of sites on poor ground. Current development of prestressed concrete is largely centred on the improvement of the necessary mechanical facilities, but there is scope for advance in prestressed precast construction.

BIBLIOGRAPHY. C.E. REYNOLDS, *Basic Reinforced Concrete Design*, 2 vol. (1962), a detailed study of the design of structural concrete components of most types, excluding prestressed concrete; and *Concrete Construction*, 3rd ed. (1967), a consideration of concrete materials and constructional procedures for a wide range of common reinforced concrete structures, with elementary as well as more sophisticated methods; J. FABER and F. MEAD, *Reinforced Concrete*, new ed. (1961), a comprehensive treatment of the design of concrete structures and foundations including shell roofs, chimneys, and prestressed concrete; J.N. CERNICA, *Fundamentals of Reinforced Concrete* (1964), a summary treatment with tables and examples based on standard U.S. building code requirements for reinforced concrete; J.D. HARRIS and I.C. SMITH, *Basic Design and Construction in Prestressed Concrete* (1963), an elementary treatment leading to more advanced U.K. practice; P.W. ABELES, *An Introduction to Prestressed Concrete*, 2 vol. (1964–66), on the basic principles, materials, research, theoretical analyses, and practical elementary and advanced design; W.S. LA LONDE and M.F. JANES (eds.), *Concrete Engineering Handbook* (1961), extensive treatment of materials, construction, and design of reinforced

concrete structures including numerous design tables, mainly U.S. practice.

(C.E.R.)

Condé, The Great

Having won conspicuous victories for France in the middle period of the Thirty Years' War, the military commander of genius known as the Great Condé turned against the French government to lead the last rebellion of the movement known as the Fronde and, subsequently, even to support the Spaniards against France, finally reverting, however, to the French king Louis XIV's service and playing a major role in the latter's wars of conquest.

Condé, engraving by Robert Nanteuil, 1662.
By courtesy of the Bibliotheque Nationale, Paris

Career. The princes de Condé were the heads of an important French branch of the House of Bourbon. The prince known as the Great Condé was Louis II de Bourbon and was born in Paris on September 8, 1621. He was the elder son of Henry II de Bourbon, 3rd prince de Condé, and of his wife, Charlotte de Montmorency.

His father gave to the Duc d'Enghien, as the Great Condé was at first called, a complete and strict education: six years with the Jesuits at Bourges, as well as mathematics and horsemanship at the Royal Academy at Paris. His studies completed, he was presented to Louis XIII (January 19, 1636) and then accompanied his father to the Duchy of Burgundy (the government of which had become a family perquisite since 1631), where he received the King on September 19 of the same year.

His father, whose intention it had long been, betrothed him to the young Claire-Clémence de Maillé-Brézé (Cardinal de Richelieu's niece) before his son's departure to the army of Picardy, with which, under the marshal Duc de la Meilleraye, he was, in July 1640, first to see action before the siege of Arras. On his return, despite the violent passion that he had conceived for Marthe du Vigean, a young lady of the "precious" circle of Parisian society, the young Duke was obliged, on February 9, 1641, to go through the marriage that had been imposed on him and from which little but conjugal distrust and hatred was to ensue. She was barely 13, and they began so badly that the Cardinal summoned him to Narbonne (1642).

The Duc d'Enghien won his first great victory over the Spaniards as head of the royal army at Rocroi (May 19, 1643). It was the greatest French victory for a century and was due, beyond doubt, to his personal effort. He followed his success at Rocroi with successes in the area of the Rhine at Thionville and Sierck. With the Marshal de Turenne, he was victorious at Freiburg, Philippsburg, Mayence, and Nördlingen. He also conducted a brilliant campaign in Flanders (1646).

Louis's father died on December 26, 1646, and he then became both prince de Condé and heir to an enormous fortune. He was sent by Cardinal Mazarin—ever distrustful of so prestigious a prince—to Catalonia, in Spain, where on June 18, 1647, he was defeated at Lérida. On his recall to Flanders, however, he won another great victory at Lens (August 19–20, 1648).

The civil wars of the Fronde But a change in his destiny came with the civil wars of the Fronde. During the first of these wars, he conducted the siege of Paris (January–March 1649) for the government but afterward behaved with such arrogance as the government's saviour that Mazarin, in collusion with his former opponents, had Condé, his brother, and their brother-in-law the Duc de Longueville (Henri d'Orléans) arrested on January 18, 1650, when they were in attendance at court. (They were in prison for 13 months.) Thereupon, his friends launched the second war of the Fronde, which ended with Condé's release and Mazarin's first voluntary exile. Condé, however, again tried to extract too high a price for his goodwill toward the Queen Regent. When she took up the challenge, he launched an open rebellion in the southwest (September 1651), allied himself with Spain, and made his way to Paris, where he was able for a time to defy the royal army commanded by Turenne. His position, however, soon became both politically and militarily untenable, and he left Paris (October 1652) to take service with the Spaniards, whose generalissimo he became. He was sentenced to death as a rebel on November 25, 1654.

With varying fortunes he opposed the royal army for four years more but was finally defeated at the Battle of the Dunes before Dunkirk (Dunkerque) on June 14, 1658. After the Peace of the Pyrenees had been signed (1659), Condé returned to Paris and, re-entering the King's good graces, was received by him at Aix-en-Provence on January 27, 1660. Thenceforth, he comported himself as a humble and loyal servant of the King, who, however, was long at pains to keep him from any military command.

At one moment Condé entertained the idea of having himself elected king of Poland, but, despite his determined measures and the support of Louis XIV, he was unsuccessful. (This dream of kingship he was to pursue vainly for several years.)

When in 1668 the King at last entrusted to his command the attack of the Spanish-held Franche-Comté, Condé took Artois, Besançon, Dôle, and Gray in 15 days. Then, totally restored to Louis XIV's favour, Condé, with Turenne, was placed by the King in command of the army that was going to invade the United Provinces of the Netherlands (1672). He was wounded in the famous crossing of the Rhine near Arnhem (June 12, 1672) but, nevertheless, went on to defend Alsace from invasion. Having completed the evacuation of the United Provinces, he halted the Prince of Orange's army at Seneffe in the Spanish Netherlands (August 11, 1674), then raised the siege of Oudenarde. The following year, again in the company of Louis XIV and of the army of Flanders, he had to reach Alsace, which had been threatened by Turenne's death, hastily. There, he once more confronted an old adversary, Raimondo Montecuccoli, Austria's foremost commander, whom he forced to raise the siege of Haguenau and to withdraw across the Rhine. This was **Last campaign** his last campaign and victory. A prey to gout in later life and living quietly in his palace of Chantilly, he surrounded himself with his family, friends, and the writers and artists whom he loved. He died at Fontainebleau on December 11, 1686. His deathbed conversion is not entirely convincing, for it came at the end of a life without religion.

Personality.   Portraits and busts of Condé suggest rapacity: wide, protruding eyes and a prominently downcurving "Bourbon" nose dominate a thin and bony face in which a willful mouth overshadows a receding chin. Though he was without doubt, with Turenne, the greatest captain of his day, he was also a man of unrestrained temper and limitless pride—in himself, his race, and his house. His will admitted no constraint, and his arrogance augured nothing for his equals but distrust. But he was also a man of wide intellectual interests, of unconventional habits, and possessed of an uncommonly sound independence of mind. His attitude both to religion and to politics was unorthodox, for he was as rebellious to ecclesiastical dogma as to the authority of the King. The moral temper and philosophy of this prince, so removed from the conventional standards of his day, were revealed by his libertine youth and by doctrinally questionable relationships—among them that with Pierre-Michon Bourdelot, a philosopher and skeptical doctor, and with the philosopher Spinoza, whom he tried to meet in Holland—by his nonobservance of all religious practices and by his aggressive atheism—despite his honorable fidelity to the Jesuits who had instructed him. To these traits he added peerless courage—as may be seen by his help and protection of Protestants who were persecuted after the revocation of the Edict of Nantes (1685).

A cultivated man, according to Mlle de Scudéry, who personified him in her novel *Artamène, ou le Grand Cyrus* (1649–53), he was also a generous patron of the arts. He maintained a troupe of comedians who toured the provinces; he protected Jean de La Fontaine, Nicolas Boileau, and Molière; and he chose Jean de La Bruyère to tutor his son, Henri-Jules. Even on his military campaigns he read the novels of Gautier de Costes La Calprenède as well as the histories of Livy and the tragedies of Pierre Corneille. André Le Nôtre landscaped his park at Chantilly; Pierre Mignard and Charles Le Brun decorated the walls of his palace with mythological paintings; Antoine Coysevox sculpted a famous bust of him; and Pérelle and Jean Berain painted views of his palace. He also enjoyed the conversation of Bishop Bossuet, François Fénelon, and Nicolas Malebranche, all of whom were present at Chantilly.

BIBLIOGRAPHY. HENRI, DUC D'AUMALE, *Histoire des princes de Condé, pendant les XVIe et XVIIe siècles*, vol. 2–7 (1864–96), the most complete and accurate account of the Great Condé's military campaigns; H. MALO, *Le Grand Condé* (1937), the most complete biography of the prince; and G. MONGREDIEN, *Le Grand Condé* (1959), concentrates on the political and private personality of the subject; H. NOEL WILLIAMS, *The Love Affairs of the Condés, 1530–1740* (1912), on the Condé family—the only work in English.

(G.Mn.)

Condorcet, Marquis de

Mathematician, revolutionary, and philosopher, the Marquis de Condorcet is chiefly remembered for his ideas of the nature of progress—the indefinite perfectibility of mankind—which greatly influenced 19th-century philosophy and sociology.

Marie-Jean-Antoine-Nicolas de Caritat was born in Picardy, on September 17, 1743. He was descended from the ancient family of Caritat, who took their title from Condorcet in Dauphiné. He was educated at the Jesuit college in Reims and at the Collège de Navarre in Paris, where he showed his first promise as a mathematician. In 1769 he became a member of the Academy of Sciences, to which he contributed papers on mathematical and other subjects.

He was the friend of almost all the distinguished men of his time and a zealous propagator of the progressive views then current among French men of letters. A protégé of the French philosopher and mathematician d'Alembert, he took an active part in the preparation of the *Encyclopédie*. He was elected to the permanent secretaryship of the Academy of Sciences in 1777 and to the French Academy in 1782 and was a member of other European academies. In 1785 he published his *Essai sur l'application de l'analyse à la probabilité des décisions rendues à la pluralité des voix (Essay on the Application of Analysis to the Probability of Majority Decisions)*, a remarkable work that has a distinguished place in the history of the doctrine of probability. A second edition, greatly enlarged and completely recast, appeared in 1805 under the title of *Élémens du calcul des probabilités et* **Work in mathematics**

Condorcet, bust by J.A. Houdon (1741–1828). In the Musée de Versailles.
Cliche Musees Nationaux, Paris

son application aux jeux de hasard, à la loterie, et aux jugemens des hommes.

In 1786 he married Sophie de Grouchy (1764–1822) who was said to have been one of the most beautiful women of her time. Her *salon* at the Hôtel des Monnaies, where Condorcet lived in his capacity as inspector general of the mint, was quite famous.

Condorcet published his *Vie de m. Turgot* in 1786 and his *Vie de Voltaire* in 1789. These biographies of his friends reveal his sympathy with Turgot's economic theories about mitigating the suffering of the French populace before the French Revolution and with Voltaire's opposition to the church. Both works were widely and eagerly read and are perhaps, from a purely literary point of view, the best of Condorcet's writings.

The outbreak of the French Revolution, which he greeted with enthusiasm, involved him in a great deal of political activity. He was elected to represent Paris in the Legislative Assembly and became its secretary; was active in the reform of the educational system; was chief author of the address to the European powers in 1791; and in 1792 he presented a scheme for a system of state education, which was the basis of that ultimately adopted. Condorcet was one of the first to declare for a republic and in August 1792 he drew up the declaration justifying the suspension of the king and the summoning of the National Convention. In the convention he represented the *département* of Aisne and was a member of the committee on the constitution. His draft of a new constitution, representative of the Girondins, the more moderate political group during the Revolution, was rejected, however, in favour of that of the Jacobins, a more radical political group whose dominating figure was Robespierre. In the trial of Louis XVI he voted against the death penalty. But his independent attitude became dangerous in the wake of the Revolution when Robespierre's radical measures triumphed, and his opposition to the arrest of the Girondins led to his being outlawed.

Theory of progress

To occupy his mind while he was in hiding, some of his friends prevailed on him to engage in the work by which he is best known, the *Esquisse d'un tableau historique des progrès de l'esprit humain* (1795; *Sketch for a Historical Picture of the Progress of the Human Mind*, trans. 1955). Its fundamental idea is that of the continuous progress of the human race to an ultimate perfection. He represents man as starting from the lowest stage of savagery with no superiority over the other animals save that of bodily organization and as advancing uninterruptedly at a more or less rapid rate in the path of enlightenment, virtue, and happiness. The stages that the human race has already gone through, or, in other words, the great epochs of history, are regarded as nine in number.

There is an epoch of the future—a tenth epoch—and the most original part of Condorcet's treatise is that which is devoted to it. After insisting that general laws regulative of the past warrant general inferences as to the future, he argues that the three tendencies that the entire history of the past shows will be characteristic features of the future are: (1) the destruction of inequality between nations; (2) the destruction of inequality between classes; and (3) the improvement of individuals, the indefinite perfectibility of human nature itself—intellectually, morally, and physically. The equality to which he represents nations and individuals as tending is not absolute equality but equality of freedom and of rights. Nations and men, he asserts, are equal if equally free and are all tending to equality because all are tending to freedom.

As to indefinite perfectibility, he nowhere denies that progress is conditioned both by the constitution of humanity and by the character of its surroundings. But he affirms that these conditions are compatible with endless progress and that the human mind can assign no fixed limits to its own advancement in knowledge and virtue or even to the prolongation of bodily life. This theory explains the importance that he attached to popular education, to which he looked for all sure progress. The book is notable for its intense aversion to all religion, especially Christianity, and to monarchy. Pervaded by a spirit of excessive hopefulness, it contains numerous errors of detail, due to the circumstances in which it was written. Its value lies in its general ideas. Condorcet's ethical position gives emphasis to the sympathetic impulses and social feelings and had considerable influence upon the French philosopher and sociologist Auguste Comte. While he was under proscription as a Girondin, some of the other works he wrote were published by friends and others were issued after his death. Still interested in public affairs and believing that the house in which he had been hiding was watched, he escaped and, after hiding in thickets and quarries for three days, entered the village of Clamart on the evening of March 27, 1794. His appearance betrayed him, and he was taken to Bourg-la-Reine and imprisoned. On the morning of March 29 he was found dead, whether from exhaustion or by poison is unknown.

Wholly a man of the Enlightenment, an advocate of economic freedom, religious toleration, legal and educational reform, and the abolition of slavery, Condorcet sought to extend the empire of reason to social affairs. Rather than elucidate human behaviour, as had been done thus far, by recourse to either the moral or physical sciences, he sought to explain it by a merger of the two sciences that eventually became transmuted into the discipline of sociology.

BIBLIOGRAPHY. The *Oeuvres*, 12 vol., were edited by A. CONDORCET O'CONNOR and M.F. ARAGO (1847–49). Condorcet's best known work, *Esquisse d'un tableau historique des progrés de l'esprit humain* (1795), was translated by J. BARRACLOUGH, with introduction by S. HAMPSHIRE, *Sketch for a Historical Picture of the Progress of the Human Mind* (1955). LEON CAHEN, *Condorcet et la Révolution française* (1904), is a detailed account of Condorcet's activities for political and social reform. GILLES-GASTON GRANGER, *La Mathématique sociale du marquis de Condorcet* (1956), contains a full bibliography of Condorcet's mathematical works.

(H.B.A.)

Confectionery and Candy Production

The application of the terms confectionery and candy varies among English-speaking countries. In the United States, candy refers to both chocolate products and sugar-based confections; elsewhere "chocolate confectionery" refers to chocolates, "sugar confectionery" to the various sugar-based products, and "flour confectionery" to such products as cakes and pastries. This article is primarily concerned with sugar confectionery. Other types of confections are discussed in the articles BAKING AND BAKERY PRODUCTS and COCOA PRODUCTION.

HISTORY

Egyptian hieroglyphics dating back at least 3,000 years indicate that the art of sugar confectionery was already established. The confectioner was regarded as a skilled craftsman by the Romans, and a confectioner's kitchen excavated at Herculaneum was equipped with pots, pans, and other implements similar to those in use today.

Early confectioners, not having sugar, used honey as a sweetener and mixed it with various fruits, nuts, herbs, and spices.

During the Middle Ages, the Persians spread sugarcane cultivation, developed refining methods, and began to make a sugar-based candy. A small amount of sugar was available in Europe during the Middle Ages and was used in the manufacture of the confections prepared and sold mainly by apothecaries. The Venetians brought about a major change in candy manufacture during the 14th century, when they began to import sugar from Arabia. By the 16th century, confectioners were manufacturing sweets, molding boiled sugar, with fruits and nuts, into fanciful forms by simple hand methods.

The development of candy manufacturing machinery began in the late 18th century, and in the 20th century annual world production had reached many millions of pounds.

PRODUCTION METHODS AND ASSOCIATED EQUIPMENT

Principal ingredients. Sugar, mainly sucrose from sugar beets or sugarcane, is the major constituent of most candies. Other sweeteners employed in candy manufacture include corn syrup, corn sugar, honey, molasses, maple sugar, and noncaloric sweeteners. Sweeteners may be used in dry or liquid form.

Invert
sugar

Invert sugar, a mixture of glucose (dextrose) and fructose produced from sugar (sucrose) by application of heat and an acid "sugar doctor," such as cream of tartar or citric acid, affects the sweetness, solubility, and amount of crystallization in candymaking. Invert sugar is also prepared as a syrup of about 75 percent concentration by the action of acid or enzymes on sugar in solution.

Because of the perishability of fresh fluid milk and milk products, milk is usually used in concentrated or dried form. It contributes to candy flavour, colour, and texture. Fats, usually of vegetable origin, are primarily used to supply textural and "mouthfeel" properties (lubrication and smoothness). They are also used to control crystallization and to impart plasticity. Such colloids as gelatin, pectin, and egg albumin are employed as emulsifying agents, maintaining fat distribution and providing aeration. Other ingredients include fruits; nuts; natural, fortified, and artificial flavours; and colourings.

Types and methods of production. Candies can be divided into noncrystalline, or amorphous, and crystalline types. Noncrystalline candies, such as toffees, brittles, and caramels, are chewy or hard, with homogeneous structure. Crystalline candies, such as fondant, fudge, and penuche, are smooth, creamy, and easily chewed, with a definite structure of small crystals.

High-boiled, or hard, candy. When solutions of mixed sugars are boiled, they are concentrated into a plastic mass that may be flavoured, coloured, and formed into shapes and allowed to harden. Examples of such hard candies are fruit drops, clear mints, butterscotch, "after dinner" mints, barley sugar, and bonbons.

Sugar has the property of forming a type of noncrystalline "glass" that forms the basis of hard candy products. Sugar and water are boiled until the concentration of the solution reaches a high level, and supersaturation persists upon cooling. This solution takes a plastic form and on further cooling becomes a hard, transparent, glassy mass containing less than 2 percent water.

Precise
control of
boiling

High-boiled sugar solutions are unstable, however, and will readily crystallize unless preventative steps are taken. Control of modern sugar-boiling processes is precise. Crystallization is prevented by adding either manufactured invert sugar or corn syrup. The latter is now favoured because it contains complex saccharides and dextrins that, in addition to increasing solubility, give greater viscosity, considerably retarding crystallization.

Hard candy manufacture. Originally, hard candy syrups were boiled over a coke or gas fire. Modern manufacturers use pans jacketed with high-pressure steam for batch boiling. Special steam-pressure cookers through which syrup passes continuously are used when a constant supply is required. For flavouring and colouring, the batch of boiled syrup is turned out on a table to cool. While still plastic, the ingredients are kneaded into the batch; this may be done mechanically. In continuous production, flavours may be added to the hot liquid syrup. Especially prepared "sealed" flavours are then required to prevent loss by evaporation.

After flavouring, the plastic mass is shaped by passing through rollers with impressions or through continuous forming machines that produce a "rope" of plastic sugar. By feeding a soft filling into the rope as a core, "bonbons" are made.

A satinlike finish may be obtained by "pulling" the plastic sugar. This consists of stretching the plastic mass on rotating arms and at the same time repeatedly overlapping. With suitable ratios of sugar to corn syrup, pulling will bring about partial crystallization and a short, spongy texture will result.

Caramels and toffee. The manufacture of caramel and toffee resembles hard candy making except that milk and fat are added. Sweetened, condensed, or evaporated milk is usually employed. Fats may be either butter or vegetable oil, preferably emulsified with milk or with milk and some of the syrup before being added to the whole batch. Emulsifiers such as lecithin or glyceryl monostearate are particularly valuable in continuous processes. The final moisture content of toffee and particularly of caramels is higher than that of hard candy. Because milk and fat are present, the texture is plastic at normal temperatures. The action of heat on the milk solids, in conjunction with the sugar ingredients, imparts the typical flavour and colour to these candies. This process is termed caramelization.

Because caramel is plastic at lower temperatures than hard candy, it may be extruded. Machines eject the plastic caramel under pressure from a row of orifices; the resulting "ropes" are then cut into lengths. Under continuous manufacturing, all ingredients are metred in recipe quantities into a container that gives an initial boil. Then the mixed syrup is pumped first into a continuous cooker that reduces the moisture content to its final level, and finally into a temporary holding vessel in which increased caramelization occurs, permitting the flavour obtained by the batch process to be matched. The cooked caramel is then cooled, extruded, and cut.

Nougat, nougatine. Although their consistency is similar to that of caramels, nougats usually do not contain milk. They are aerated by vigorously mixing a solution of egg albumen or other similar protein into boiled syrup; a less sticky product is obtained by mixing in some vegetable fat. Egg albumen is a powdered ingredient especially prepared from egg whites by a process of partial fermentation and low-temperature drying (see EGG PRODUCTION, COMMERCIAL). Great care is needed to obtain a product that is readily soluble in water, will keep well, and is free from bacterial contamination. Milk and soya proteins are also used in making aerated confections, generally as partial replacements for egg. Like caramel, nougat may be made in a variety of textures and can be extruded. Soft, well-aerated nougats have become a very popular sweet, particularly as chocolate-covered bars. In some countries soft nougats are known as nougatine.

Gelatin is also used to produce a nougat with chewy texture. Hard nougat has a moisture content of 5 to 7 percent; in soft nougats it may be as high as 9 to 10 percent. The usual procedure of manufacture is first to make a "frappé," which is prepared by dissolving egg albumen in water, mixing with syrup, and whipping to a light foam. A separate batch of syrup consisting of sugar and corn syrup is boiled to between 275° and 285° F (depending on the texture desired), then beaten vigorously with the frappé. Toward the end of the beating, some fat, powdered sugar, or fondant may be added to obtain a shorter texture.

Making a
frappé

Continuous nougat-manufacturing equipment prepares

the frappé by feeding in measured amounts of egg solution, syrup, and air under pressure, then beating it. Through a valve, the frappé is delivered into a metered flow of boiled syrup; the two are mixed in a trough with a rotating screw that carries the mixture continuously forward. Other ingredients, such as fat, flavour, or nuts, also may be fed into the screw toward the end of the mixing process.

Fondant. Fondant, the basis of most chocolate-covered and crystallized crèmes (which themselves are sometimes called "fondants") is made by mechanically beating a solution supersaturated with sugar, so that minute sugar crystals are deposited throughout the remaining syrup phase. These form an opaque, white, smooth paste that can be melted, flavoured, and coloured. Syrup made from corn syrup and sugar is now generally used for fondant.

Traditionally, fondant was made by boiling a sugar syrup with cream of tartar and pouring it out on a table to cool. While cooling, it was agitated and mixed by means of a flat knife, encouraging rapid crystallization. The first mechanical fondant maker consisted of a shallow, circular pan with a flat base over which a mechanical plow revolved, sweeping the flat bottom, agitating and turning over syrup poured into the pan. The syrup was prepared separately in a boiling pan; in larger fondant machines of this type the base was water-cooled.

Fully mechanical plants now produce fondant at 2,000 pounds per hour. Syrup, produced in a continuous cooker, is delivered to a rotating drum (Figure 1) cooled internal-

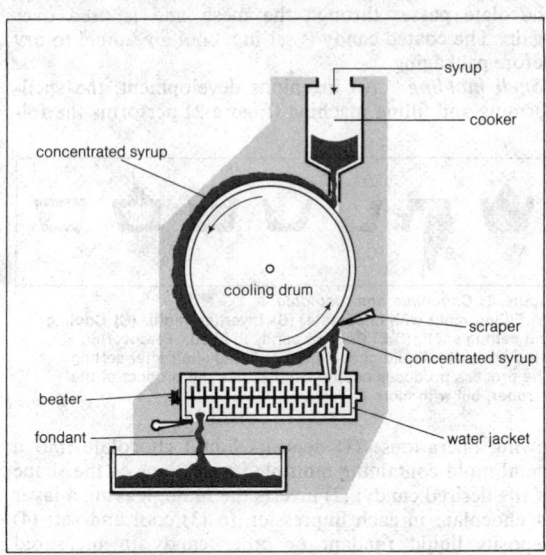

Figure 1: Continuous fondant-making machine.

ly with water sprays. The cooled syrup is scraped from the drum and delivered to a beater consisting of a water-cooled, rectangular box fitted internally with rotating pegged spindles and baffles. This gives maximum agitation while the syrup is cooling, causing very fine sugar crystals to be deposited in the syrup phase. The crystals, together with a small amount of air entrapped by the beating, give the fondant its typical white opacity. The sugar crystal size in a good fondant is about 10 microns. The proportion of sugar to corn syrup in the base syrup usually ranges from 3:1 to 4:1. The moisture content of fondant ranges from 12 to 13 percent.

Mechanically prepared fondant can be reheated without complete solution of the sugar-crystal phase, and it will be sufficiently fluid to be cast into molds. At the same time colourings and flavourings—fruit pulp, jam, essential oils, etc.—may be added. Remelting is usually carried out in steam-jacketed kettles provided with stirrers at a temperature range between 145° and 155° F. To produce light-textured fondants, 5 to 10 percent of frappe, made as described under nougat (see above), is added to the preparation.

Shaped pieces of fondant for crystallizing or covering with chocolate are formed by pouring the hot, melted, flavoured fondant into impressions made in cornstarch. A shallow tray about two inches deep is filled with cornstarch, which is levelled off and slightly compressed. A printing board covered with rows of plaster, wood, or metal models of the desired shape is then pressed into the starch and withdrawn. Into these impressions the fondant is poured and left to cool. Next, the tray is inverted over a sieve; the starch passes through, leaving the fondant pieces on the sieve. After gentle brushing or blowing to remove adhering starch, the fondants are ready for covering or crystallizing.

A machine known as a Mogul carries out all these operations automatically, filling trays with starch, printing them, depositing melted fondant, and stacking the filled trays into a pile. At the other end of the machine, piles of trays that contain cooled and set crèmes are unstacked, inverted over sieves, and the crèmes removed to be brushed and air blown. Empty trays are automatically refilled and the cycle continues.

Certain types of fondant may be remelted and poured into flexible rubber molds with impressions, but this process generally is limited to shallow cremes of a fairly rigid consistency. Metal molds precoated with a substance that facilitates release of the crème also are used. The crème units are ejected from the inverted mold by compressed air onto a belt, which takes them forward for chocolate covering.

Fudge. Fudge combines certain properties of caramel with those of fondant. If hot caramel is vigorously mixed or if fondant is added to it, a smooth, crystalline paste forms on cooling. Known as fudge, this substance has a milky flavour similar to caramel and a soft, not plastic, texture. Fudge may be extruded or poured onto tables and cut into shapes. It is possible to construct a recipe that will pour into starch, but such fudge generally is inferior.

Jellies; Turkish delight. Syrup containing sugar and corn syrup at about 75 percent concentration may be transformed into a jelly by adding substances such as gelatin, agar, starch, or pectin. Fruit flavours and colours may be added to produce many varieties of jellies. Each gelatinizing agent requires its own particular method of processing.

Gelatin is obtained from skins and bones and is specially purified for food use. For making jellies, the gelatin is first soaked in water and then added to the boiled syrup—it must not be boiled in the syrup or its jelly-forming power is greatly reduced.

Agar is obtained from a particular type of seaweed for use in jellies. It is dissolved in boiling water; strained through a sieve; and added to a batch, which is then boiled to the correct concentration.

Pectin, the natural jelly-producing substance in fruit, is now an important commercial article used in powdered form for confectionery purposes. It is extracted from citrus and apple pomace. Pectin requires particular conditions of acidity and sugar concentration, as well as careful technique, but gives the best texture for most jellies. Flavour and colour are always added at the end of the batch.

Turkish delight is made from a syrup similar to that used for jellies, but starch as the gelling agent gives the finished product its typical opacity. Supplemental gelling agents, used with the starch, give better texture and set. The traditional flavour used in Turkish delight is attar of roses, originating centuries ago in Asia.

All these jellies may also be cast into starch. Some can be poured into rubber or metal molds or cast onto tables in sheet form and subsequently cut into cubes.

Marshmallows. In producing these popular confections, solutions of egg albumen and gelatin are mixed with a solution of sugar and corn syrup and beaten vigorously into a foam and flavouring is added. Next, the syrup foam is deposited into starch, much dryer than that used for cremes. Certain types of marshmallow may be extruded or deposited onto bands.

Pastes, marzipan. A large range of candies may be classified as "pastes." These generally consist of flavoured mixtures using sugar, corn syrup, and a suitable binder such as gelatin or edible gum. Shredded coconut or pastes of other nuts are frequently added. Marzipan is generally regarded as an almond paste, and with it and other nut pastes binders are not usually added. Pastes are mixed in a kneading machine; then, for marzipan and other such candies, the nuts are coarsely ground on rollers and mixed in. When fully blended, the pastes are formed into bars or small pieces by extrusion and cutting or by rolling out on tables and cutting.

Gums, pastilles. A very old type of sweet, gums are prepared from syrups in which gum arabic is dissolved. The first gums were medicaments; the slow solution of gum in the mouth permitted steady release of the active substance. Today, confectioners flavour gums with fruit and other flavours.

Gum arabic is obtained from the exudations of certain types of acacia tree. Solutions are generally made fairly strong by soaking one pound of gum in one pint of water, then screening to remove foreign matter. Substances such as starch, gelatin, or agar may replace gum arabic.

In gum manufacture the syrup containing the gum is deposited in starch and the trays are dried for several days at about 120° F. After removal and brushing, the gums are placed on wire mesh, steamed, and dried. Soft gums, or pastilles, are made in much the same way, but after steaming they are sanded with sugar and are then dried.

Panned sweets, or dragees. The process of coating nuts, preserved fruit, caramels, nougat, chocolate, or certain kinds of paste with sugar or chocolate is known as "panning." The basic machine used in the process is a "comfit," or "revolving," pan.

Made of copper or stainless steel, the rotating comfit pan causes the pieces to roll over each other as coatings are added. Nuts, for example, are charged into the pan, the pan is rotated and sealing solution of syrup and gum poured in, coating the nuts just enough to prevent fat from seeping out. The syrup is dried by blowing warm air into the rotating pan. After this preliminary treatment, a fairly thick coating of sugar or chocolate is applied.

Sugar-coating nuts

To coat nuts with sugar, alternate layers of sugar syrup and powdered sugar or successive layers of sugar syrup alone are built up, each layer being dried off and hardened before the next is applied. Powdered starch is sometimes added. Before the use of automatic equipment, the syrup was applied by hand. In modern practice, the syrup is sprayed on the rotating pieces at timed intervals. When the coating has been built up to the required thickness, a finishing syrup of lower density is used, which may be coloured if desired.

Chocolate panning is similar except that liquid chocolate is sprayed onto the candy centres. The air blown into the pan to harden the coating must be cool as well as dry. Each layer of chocolate must be set before the next is applied.

Both sugar- and chocolate-panned candies are given a finishing glaze to improve appearance and to protect against high humidities. These glazes may be a type of wax that is put on the candies in the rotating pan. Edible lacquer is sometimes applied over a gum-syrup underglaze when the candies are chocolate covered.

Truffles. Truffles are a type of confection made with fondant to which chocolate liquor or cocoa is added.

Popcorn. A special variety of maize grown in the United States swells and bursts when roasted or heated in a pan. Popcorn may be buttered and salted or be coated with caramel or sugar.

Candy floss or cotton candy. Melted sugar may be spun in a special type of centrifuge, forming fine threads of sugar, which when compacted yield a product resembling cotton wool.

Licorice. Licorice is extracted by means of water from the underground roots of a plant called *Glycyrrhiza*

glabra, grown extensively in southern Europe. The extract is vacuum concentrated and it then becomes the "block juice" of commerce from which all licorice candies are made. Pastes made by combining sugar, corn syrup, and flour with licorice juice may be extruded or cut into almost any shape. The popular licorice "allsorts" consist of layers of licorice paste laminated with other flavoured pastes.

Chewing gum. In some countries this is considered candy. Small pieces of dried latex (obtained from the *Sapodilla* tree of Central and South America) are kneaded into a hot sugar–corn-syrup mixture. When homogeneous the mixture is flavoured—usually with mint—and rolled into the characteristic thin strips of chewing gum.

Pastel coatings. These popular candy coatings consist of sugar, milk powder, and vegetable fat ground to a fine paste, then flavoured and coloured. If necessary, extra fat is added for fluidity, permitting the paste to be applied to candies in a coating machine. The vegetable fats are specially prepared to give a good set and resistance to heat.

Other confectionery processes. Two candy-making processes involving the use of chocolate should be mentioned here.

Coating or enrobing. Many candy bars and boxed chocolates consist of candy centres coated with chocolate applied by a machine called an enrober or coater. By a system of pumps and troughs, the enrober forms a continuous curtain of liquid chocolate through which candy pieces pass on a wire-mesh conveyor. Excess chocolate passes through the mesh and is used over again. The coated candy is set in a cool air tunnel to dry before packaging.

Shell molding. An ingenious development, the shell-forming and filling machine (Figure 2) performs the fol-

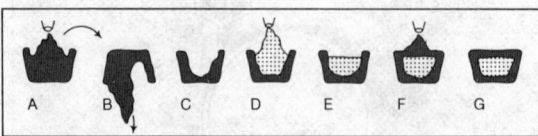

Figure 2: *Chocolate shell molding.*
(A) Filling mold with chocolate. (B) Inverting mold. (C) Cooling and setting shell. (D,E) Pouring candy in shell. (F) Covering filled shell with liquid chocolate. (G) Filled shell after setting. The process produces coated candies like the product of the enrober, but with more chocolate.

lowing operations: (1) deposits liquid chocolate into a metal mold containing multiple impressions of the shape of the desired candy; (2) inverts the mold, leaving a layer of chocolate in each impression to (3) cool and set; (4) deposits liquid fondant or other candy in measured quantity in each shell followed by (5) rapid cooling to prevent remelting of the shell; (6) applies liquid chocolate to cover the deposited candy, thereby completing the covering around the entire centre.

Shell-molded products have shiny surfaces, while enrobed candies' surfaces have a dull lustre. Shell-molded chocolates usually have a higher proportion of chocolate to centre than do the enrobed variety.

BIBLIOGRAPHY. B.W. MINIFIE, *Science and Technology of Chocolate, Cocoa and Confectionery* (1970), is a modern textbook dealing with production methods, machinery, and formulations with scientific explanations. There are chapters on packaging, quality control, pest control and hygiene, and a useful machinery supplement. C.T. WILLIAMS, *Chocolate and Confectionery*, 3rd ed. (1964), is a general survey of the industry with details of processes, machinery, and recipes in some sections. Illustrations of a typical plant are given. E. SKUSE, *Complete Confectioner*, 13th ed. rev. by W.J. BUSH (1957), deals mainly with sugar confectionery. Many formulations and descriptions of processes are given. E.J. CLYNE, *A Course in Confectionery* (1955), also deals mainly with sugar confectionery. Some processes are given in detail with a few illustrations and brief descriptions of raw materials. W.L. RICHMOND, *Candy Production: Methods and Formulas* (1948), contains 500 formulations compiled by a practical candy-maker. There are limited descriptions of processes and machinery and some knowledge of the industry is assumed. N.F. SCARBOROUGH, *Sweet Manufacture* (1933), gives a cursory survey of sugar confectionery methods with some reference to raw materials and chocolate. Some formulations are included. S. JORDAN, *Confectionery Problems* (1930), is a general coverage of most sections of the industry. Raw materials are described fairly thoroughly with reference to factory control, research, and distribution. Journals such as the *Candy Industry*, (1944–56), *Confectionery Production* (1935–), and *Manufacturing Confectioner* (1921–), contain useful current information.

(H.B.K./B.W.M.)

Conflict of Laws

The law of conflict of laws has to do with the resolution of problems that result from the fact that there exists in the world a multiplicity of different sets of courts and different systems of private laws; that is, law dealing with relations between persons. As the earth is presently organized, its surface is divided among nations that are independent of each other and that have no world government above them. Each of these nations maintains its own set of courts in complete independence of every other nation, and each nation has its own set of laws, written or unwritten.

THE LAW OF CONFLICT OF LAWS: FUNCTION AND SOURCES

The diversity of national and provincial laws

While in such countries as France, Sweden, Peru, or Japan one single system of law obtains for the whole country, diversity exists in many others, especially nations organized upon a federal pattern, such as the United States, Canada, and, to a minor degree, West Germany, Switzerland, Mexico, or the Soviet Union. The law of Illinois is not the same as that of New York, Louisiana, or Indiana; that of Quebec differs from that of Ontario or Newfoundland; that of Chihuahua is not quite the same as that of Michoacán. In Germany and Switzerland the systems of private law are by and large uniform, but minor differences still exist among the *Länder* of Germany and among the Swiss cantons.

Even in countries whose political structure is of the unitary rather than the federal pattern, differences can be found. In the United Kingdom, for example, considerable differences exist between the laws of England, Scotland, the Isle of Man, the Channel Islands, and Northern Ireland.

Diversity of laws also exists frequently between a country and its colonies. The laws of Mauritius, which was a British colony until 1968, were different from any of the laws prevailing in the United Kingdom, and, although in the remaining British colonies the laws are more or less patterned upon the model of the common law of England, they are not always exactly the same.

Diversity of laws develops where a country is divided, such as Germany, Korea, or Vietnam. Where a new country is formed, or where territory is annexed, legal unity may not be brought about at the same time. After the reannexation of Alsace-Lorraine by France in 1920, for example, German private law remained in effect there for many years; and when after World War I Poland was formed out of parts of old Russia, Germany, and Austria, legal uniformity was not brought about until after the end of World War II.

Diversities of law within one country may also exist on an ethnic or religious basis. Such a situation has commonly existed in most countries of the Near and Middle East; the laws concerning matters of the family, including succession upon death, remain different in India for Hindus, Muslims, Parsees, Buddhists, and other sects, and in Lebanon or Israel for Muslims, Jews, and the various groups of Christians. In the United States and Canada, American Indians are in several respects subject to their own tribal laws.

Because of the spread of Western civilization over the entire planet, the laws of modern nations, at least insofar as they are concerned with relations between private individuals, present a considerable measure of uniformity. They are sufficiently different, however, to make it impor-

tant to know to what situations one ought to apply the law of one country, state, region, or group rather than that of another, especially when dealings are carried on between persons of different law units. This question of determining which of the world's numerous laws is the proper one to apply in a particular situation is in itself a legal question. Those rules of law by which such questions of choice of law are determined constitute a major part of that field of the law that is known as private international law or the law of conflict of laws. Other parts of this field of the law are concerned with the problem of jurisdiction—that is, the problem of determining in what cases the courts of a particular country or state are, or are not, to go into action—and, furthermore, with the problem of stating what weight, if any, is to be given in one country or province to the judgments and other decisions of the courts or other agencies of other countries or provinces.

In countries adhering to the French legal tradition it is customary to regard as parts of private international law also those rules that deal with nationality and with the legal position of aliens and nonresidents. In accordance with usage in countries of the English legal tradition, however, the present article will be limited to jurisdiction, foreign judgments, and choice of law.

Sources of the law of conflict of laws

The name private international law, which is generally used in countries of European-continental tradition, and occasionally also in England, seems to indicate that it is a part of international law—that is, that system of law that is superior to all sovereign states and that, at least in theory, is uniform throughout the world. This view was commonly held for many centuries, and when the name private international law was coined in the 19th century it was meant to signify that the supranational body of international law consisted of two parts, public and private international law. While the former would determine the proper conduct of sovereign nations toward each other in both peace and war, the latter would, in a uniform way, tell all nations in what cases their courts ought or ought not to take jurisdiction, under what conditions foreign judgments were to be enforced or otherwise recognized, and in what cases the laws of one nation were to be applied rather than those of another.

Since the latter part of the 19th century, however, such a view has been considered an ideal rather than a true description of reality. Today, it is generally recognized that each nation determines not only what is to be its substantive law (its law of property, contracts, torts, family relations, succession, corporations, etc.) but also in what cases its courts are to have jurisdiction, under what conditions foreign judgments are to be recognized, and which country's law is to be applied in any particular case.

As on other matters, nations may, of course, conclude treaties, bilateral or multilateral, in which they assume in relations with each other the duty to deal with certain problems in an agreed way. Treaties of such a kind have been concluded between numerous states, especially among countries of Latin America and of continental Europe. The United States is a party to numerous treaties that mutually secure the right of citizens of the United States, on the one part, and of citizens of the other contracting country, on the other, freely to dispose of property owned in the territory of the country of which the owner is not a citizen, and to take such property as legatees, devisees, heirs, or next of kin on the death of a citizen of the other country. The countries of the British Commonwealth of Nations are parties to numerous treaties among each other and with other nations, concerning foreign judgments and mutual rights of owning, disposing, and taking of property. Even in those areas, such as France, Germany, or Latin America, in which the bulk of private law is contained in codes and other statutes, the statutory provisions on private international law are fragmentary, and for large parts of the field the law must be sought in the decisions of the courts. In all countries the writings of scholars have been of considerable influence.

JURISDICTION

If a person wishes to bring a civil lawsuit against another, he might conceivably bring the action in any country of the world. If, however, a citizen and resident of the United States, for example, were to sue a citizen and resident of Canada in Panamá, a judgment obtained in Panamá would be of no use to him unless the Canadian owned property in Panamá that, if he did not pay, the U.S. citizen might attach there, or if the Panaman judgment could be enforced in such other country or countries in which he happened to hold property. For this practical reason the problem of where to bring suit is thus tied up with that of the enforceability of foreign judgments. Even if a judgment might be of practical value to the plaintiff, however, he might find that the courts of the country in which he wished to bring his action would not receive it. As a matter of fact, all countries have limited their jurisdiction—that is, the scope of actions that they allow their courts to handle. Countries do not wish their courts to deal with lawsuits with which they have no proper contact, which might clog the calendars of their courts, or against which it would be unfair to compel a person to enter a defense on pain of having judgment by default rendered against him. Opinions differ, however, as to when it is regarded proper for a country to hear and decide a civil lawsuit. This question is determined by each country for itself.

In composite countries, such as the United States, the United Kingdom, Canada, Switzerland, and the U.S.S.R., rules also are necessary to determine in which of the several constituent states, provinces, or other parts a civil lawsuit may be brought. In some countries (for instance, the Federal Republic of Germany) this determination is made by the national law. It may be left, however, to each of the constituent states or provinces to determine for itself the scope of litigation that it will allow its courts to decide. Such, at least on general principle, is the situation in the United States, where the state's freedom of determination is limited, however, by the "due process" clause of the Fourteenth Amendment to the federal Constitution, which in effect prohibits the state from exercising civil jurisdiction where it would be grossly unfair to do so. In the countries of the British Commonwealth, the jurisdiction of the courts is also determined for each constituent part by its own law, but the principles of such determination do not differ widely from each other.

As a general principle, most countries or states agree that a case may be tried in their courts if both parties have consented to their jurisdiction. The plaintiff's consent simply appears from his commencing his action in the country or state in question; the consent of the defendant is presumed when, rather than objecting to the jurisdiction, he confesses judgment or begins to litigate on the merits of the controversy. Some countries, nevertheless, close their courts to a litigant whose case has no more substantial connection with them than the parties' consent. French courts, for instance, will not try a lawsuit between foreigners unless it arises out of controversy that has some real connection with France, such as the allegation of a breach of a contract to be performed in France, or a tort committed in France, or title to land situated in France. As another example, the courts of New York regard themselves as an "inconvenient forum" for suits between nonresidents concerning a tort committed outside New York. With few exceptions, Anglo-U.S. courts will not try controversies concerning title to, or trespass upon, land situated outside the state.

Generally, however, the problem of jurisdiction does not become acute unless the defendant objects to having the case tried in the country or province of the plaintiff's choosing, or unless he fails to appear. Different approaches to this problem of jurisdiction are followed in the countries of the civil-law (continental European) tradition and in those of the common-law (Anglo-U.S.) tradition. The former start from the idea that the proper place for a person to be sued is his domicile or residence. In civil-law systems, in general, a person may always be sued at his residence and must not be sued in any other

place. Many exceptions to the latter principle exist, however. An adjudication of the title to a piece of land, for instance, must be sought where the land is situated. A suit arising out of an alleged tort may be brought in the place where the tort is alleged to have been committed, and a suit based upon breach of contract may be brought in the place in which it is alleged that the alleged contract was to be performed.

Some countries—for instance, West Germany—allow an absent defendant to be sued in their courts if he owns any property within the country. France keeps its courts open for suits of any kind brought by a French national against a foreigner. A large number of countries, including those adhering to the Anglo-U.S. common-law tradition, allow a civil suit to be commenced by the attachment of property owned within the territory, the enforcement of a default judgment obtained being limited, however, to the assets thus attached.

In their general approach to the problem of jurisdiction, the common-law countries still proceed from the long-obsolete notion that no civil suit could be commenced in any way other than by the defendant's arrest by the sheriff. Consequently, an action can still be brought in any place in which the defendant is personally served with process, even though he may be there only for a few minutes to change airplanes. In modern times it has come to be widely held, however, that personal service upon the defendant is no longer an indispensable requirement of jurisdiction and that an individual may be sued in the country or state of his residence, even if the summons is not personally pressed upon him. A corporation can always be sued in the country or state in which it has been incorporated.

It is required, however, that an honest effort be made to give the defendant actual notice that a lawsuit is about to be brought against him. The mere publication of the summons in a newspaper or at the bulletin board of the court is not sufficient unless the address or identity of the defendant cannot be ascertained upon a reasonable effort.

States of the United States are now coming to allow their courts to exercise jurisdiction in cases having almost any kind of contact with the state. Generally, a corporation may be sued in any state of the U.S. in which it is simply "doing business," even though the case in question is totally unconnected with the state.

In both civil- and common-law countries special rules apply for suits in which the plaintiff aims at a "judgment in rem." Rather than ordering a defendant to pay a certain sum of money or ordering him to do, or not to do, a certain act (such as deliver a deed to a piece of land or refrain from using a trademark) a judgment in rem produces by its own effect a change of the legal situation (for instance, the foreclosure of a mortgage, the removal of a cloud on a title to land, the dissolution of a marriage, the creation of an adoptive parent-child relationship). Lawsuits aiming at the court's changing the title to a piece of land can universally be brought nowhere but in the country or province in which the land is situated. Actions arising out of transactions connected with shipping can generally be brought in the port in which the ship in question happens to find itself. In the United States, a suit for divorce can be brought in the state of the plaintiff's domicile or residence for the establishment of which periods varying between a few weeks and several months in length are prescribed. In the British countries, the traditional rule of exclusive jurisdiction of the domicile of the husband is weakening. Civil-law countries generally keep their divorce courts open to their nationals even if they reside abroad.

FOREIGN JUDGMENTS

If a creditor has obtained against his debtor a judgment for $1,000 in Mexico or in Michigan, and his debtor does not have sufficient property in that country or state, can he enforce it in Illinois, where the debtor owns land, keeps a bank account, or owns other assets? If someone has brought and lost a lawsuit in New York, can he start it all over again in California or in Peru? If the marriage of Mr. and Mrs. Smith has been terminated by a decree of divorce of a court in Nevada, or by an act of the parliament of Canada, or by the order of a district governor in Norway, and Mr. Smith wishes to remarry in Wyoming or in South Africa, will he be given a license? If he remarries will his new marriage be valid or does he have to go to jail as a bigamist? If a citizen of the United States residing in Wisconsin adopts a child of German parents residing in Germany and the adoption has been confirmed by a court of Wisconsin, will the child inherit on the adopter's death a piece of land situated in Indiana or an account in a bank in Germany or in Switzerland?

The recognition and enforcement of foreign judgments

Unless countries have bound each other by treaty mutually to enforce their civil judgments, each country is free as to whether or not, and, if at all, under what conditions, it wishes to enforce or otherwise recognize foreign judgments of the types indicated by the questions above. The attitudes of the several countries vary considerably in this respect, and the treatment of the enforcement of money judgments is not the same as that of the recognition of a judgment as a bar to the starting of a new suit all over again (res judicata effect), or the recognition of the termination of a marriage by a decree of divorce or of other changes of private legal relationships brought about by judicial act.

If, for example, an Illinois judgment for money is not promptly paid by the debtor, it can be enforced in Illinois by the attachment and sale of his property, the proceeds being turned over to the creditor. Such enforcement is generally the task of a public officer, such as a sheriff, who is empowered, where necessary, to break resistance with physical force. Although a sheriff knows well enough the looks of a judgment of his own country or province he cannot be expected, or even allowed, to go into action simply upon the basis of a paper purporting to be the judgment of a foreign country with whose judicial system, language, or even script he cannot be expected to be familiar. For the protection of the citizen as well as of himself, it is indispensable that, before the sheriff or other enforcement officer goes into action, the foreign judgment be transformed into a domestic one. Some countries, such as The Netherlands or Sweden, simply limit enforcement to domestic judgments. Even if the creditor has obtained a judgment abroad, he must start regular proceedings all over again, and the only advantage that the foreign judgment provides for him lies in the fact that the Dutch or Swedish court will be inclined to regard it as good, although in no way conclusive, evidence that his claim is well founded. In most other countries, however, a domestic judgment will be supplied by a domestic court without a reopening of the dispute about the merits of the creditor's claim. All that the domestic court will inquire into is the regularity of the proceedings in which the foreign judgment was obtained. For this transformation of a foreign into a domestic judgment, the majority of the civil-law countries provide a kind of special proceeding (exequatur) that is supposed to be, but is not always, simpler and less expensive than an ordinary civil lawsuit. In the common-law countries it is necessary to bring upon the foreign judgment an action that in outward form is a regular civil lawsuit but that is, at least in the normal case, simple and speedy. In the United Kingdom and the Commonwealth a simplified mode of domestication is furnished by agreements and statutes providing, in certain cases, for the simple registration in one law unit of judgments rendered in another. In the United States a similar method exists in the relations between those states that have adopted the Uniform Enforcement of Foreign Judgments act.

When a foreign judgment is not sought to be enforced by attachment of the debtor's property or similar measures, but when its res judicata effect is raised as a defense in a domestic lawsuit, or when the question is that of recognition of its law-changing effects, such as the termination of a marriage by a decree of divorce, it would seem to be unnecessary to require the formal transformation of the foreign into a domestic judgment by any special proceedings. Some countries (for instance,

Italy and, to a more limited extent, France) nevertheless require such formal domestication for judgments purporting to affect the personal status of their nationals.

In the United States the Constitution provides that "full faith and credit shall be given in each state to the public acts, records and judicial proceedings of every other state." Under this clause the states, and by statute the territories, are obliged mutually to enforce their money judgments and to recognize the res judicata and law-changing effects of their judicial acts, provided the state by which the judgment was rendered was acting within the scope of its jurisdiction as defined by the Supreme Court of the United States. The only other defenses that might be raised are grave irregularity of the proceedings in which the judgment was obtained and, in certain cases, lack of finality.

Situations of non-recognition of foreign judgments

In countries that follow the general principles of the common law, a foreign judgment usually is willingly enforced and otherwise recognized unless (1) the country by which it was rendered lacked jurisdiction according to the notions prevailing in the place where recognition is sought, or (2) the proceedings in which the judgment was obtained were tainted with fraud or were otherwise grossly unfair, or (3) the recognition or enforcement of the foreign judgment would seriously interfere with an important public policy of the country or state where recognition or enforcement is sought. In addition to these requirements, most civil-law countries (except, of course, those few in which foreign judgments as such are not enforced at all) also demand that reciprocity with the country whose judgment is sought be recognized. In many civil-law countries a foreign judgment concerning a matter of personal status of a citizen also will not be recognized unless the foreign court has observed certain rules of the law of the country where recognition is sought.

Nowhere will a foreign judgment be enforced or recognized unless the country by which it was rendered had jurisdiction to do so under the notions obtaining where recognition is sought. These limits are sometimes wider, however, than those that a country will concede to others for the exercise of their jurisdictions. Whereas France, for instance, holds its courts open for all suits of a Frenchman against a foreigner, a U.S. or English court will not recognize a default judgment obtained in such an action unless the defendant was served with process in France or was a resident of France or had some other contact with that country that justifies his being sued in France.

In matters affecting personal status, especially divorce, civil-law countries generally recognize judgments rendered by the courts of the country of which the parties are nationals. Under the common law of England a decree of divorce will not be recognized unless it was rendered by the state of the domicile of the husband. After World War II, however, there were enacted in some parts of the Commonwealth statutes under which a wife living separately from her husband may also sue for divorce in the country or province of her residence, and a decree thus obtained is likely to be recognized in the other parts of the Commonwealth.

In the United States the Supreme Court has determined that a divorce granted in one state must be recognized in all others if the state by which it was granted was the state of the true residence of the plaintiff or if the defendant actually participated in the proceedings without contesting the plaintiff's allegation of residence.

CHOICE OF LAW

Ordinarily the courts of Japan decide the civil cases coming before them under the law of Japan, those of Scotland under the law of Scotland, and those of Belgium under the law of Belgium. Occasionally it happens, however, that a court of New York decides a problem in accordance with the norms of the law of Illinois, Quebec, or Thailand, or a court of the Philippines under the law of Indonesia, Victoria, or Maine. Those rules that tell the court of a country or province under what circumstances it ought to decide a problem not under the law of its own country or province but under that of another and, if so, of which other, constitute the choice of law part of that country's or province's law of conflict of laws.

The notion that the courts of a country should ever have to decide problems under foreign law rather than invariably deciding all problems coming before them under the law of their own country is by no means self-evident. It has its rationale mainly in the thought that it would be unjust to the parties concerned if a problem were decided under a law that they did not know might cover their situation when they began the transaction that led to the subsequent litigation.

The necessity to apply the law of a foreign country or province, however, constitutes an inconvenience to the court and the parties. Although judges are familiar with the law of their own country, they cannot be expected to be familiar with the laws of the whole world. Foreign law must therefore be especially pleaded and proved, often at considerable inconvenience and expense.

Rules regarding choice of law

European and American scholars of the late 19th and early 20th centuries attempted to reduce the whole field of choice of law to a few principles that could be expressed in a small number of highly generalized maxims. Their results, however, proved impractical. Since the problems of choice of law are almost as manifold as those of substantive private law, these efforts turned out to constitute oversimplifications. Mid-20th-century writers and courts regard it as their task to elaborate patiently those detailed rules of narrow application that are necessary to do justice to the infinite variety of actual life. Some U.S. scholars also stress the interests of states to implement their policies over divergent policies of other states. The results of the manifold efforts can be found in the works listed in the bibliography. Here no more can be done than state some overall approaches, which must not be regarded as rules of immediate applicability.

As to problems concerning an individual's personal status (such as whether or not he is married and, if so, to whom; what are the mutual rights between a husband and his wife, or between parent and child; or whether or not one individual is the legitimate child of another), it is universally held that they are to be decided under the law of that unit to which the individual in question "belongs." Under the view prevailing in most, but not all, civil-law countries, a person "belongs" to that country of which he is a national. This approach is of little help when a person is a national of a country, such as the United Kingdom or the United States, that does not have a uniform system of private law. In the common-law countries "belonging" is thus expressed in terms of either "domicile" (United Kingdom) or "residence" (United States). Difficult choices or combinations have to be worked out for cases involving relations between persons "belonging" to different law units. As to the formalities required for the conclusion of a marriage, observance of those of the place of celebration is widely held sufficient and in many laws is even required.

Legal problems concerning title to land are universally held to be determinable under the law of the place where the land is situated. The application of the situs principle to movables meets with difficulties because of their movability. In common-law countries, problems of succession to property upon death are also referred to the law of the situs insofar as land is concerned. In civil-law countries a tendency exists, however, to decide such questions under the law of the country of which the decedent was a national. That law is also applied in civil-law countries to problems concerning succession to movables, whereas common-law countries in this respect look to the law of the decedent's domicile or residence. Special rules apply, however, to the making of a will. As to the formalities required, it is widely held to be sufficient that the testator has observed those that are stated in the law of the place where he executed the instrument. As to interpretation and construction of a last will, detailed choice-of-law rules are necessary to take care of the great variety of possible situations.

Problems of the law of torts almost universally have been referred to the law of the place where the tort is alleged to have been committed. Experimentation with a more flexible approach is carried on in the U.S. Also, where is the place of wrong when a person acting in one country injures a person in another country, as, for instance, when A, canning spoiled food in country Z, injures the health of B, who bought the can in Y, ate the contents in X, fell sick in W, and died in V; or where a defamatory speech is broadcast over a powerful transmitter and heard over a wide area of different countries?

The greatest difficulties have arisen in the field of contract. Many courts and writers have held that problems of the law of contract are generally to be decided under the law of the place where the contract was made. Under a refinement of this theory, problems concerning performance are to be decided under the law of the place where the contract was to be performed. But where is a contract made when it was concluded by the exchange of letters between Tokyo and Paris, or San Francisco and Chicago? Where is the contract of sale to be performed when the seller has to obtain the goods in New Orleans and ship them from New York to Amsterdam, and the buyer, a business firm in Oslo, has to pay the price at a bank in London? Furthermore, what intrinsic connection with the parties' relationship does the place of contracting have at all, if, as frequently happens, the contract was made at a place at which quite accidentally the parties' minds met. Should German law really be applied to a contract concluded by a Dane and an Italian while they were flying over Germany in an airplane?

Special problems in the field of contract

The view most widely followed by the courts of both civil-law and common-law countries is that problems concerning an alleged contract are to be decided in accordance with that law which the parties expressly agreed to be applicable, or which is recognizably that law upon the basis of which the parties negotiated and made their contract. Theoretical objections to this practical view still carry some weight, especially in the United States. Where no particular law can be discovered as the one upon the basis of which the parties transacted their business, detailed differentiations must be made depending on the kind of contract in question (sale, insurance, transportation, contract for services, suretyship, etc.) and on the particular problem to be decided. Although the field of contract is the most important for international and interstate trade, it is the one beset with the most uncertainties as to choice of law. Fortunately, the substantive laws do not widely differ from one another, and business has learned to avoid many of the difficulties through resorting to arbitration and appropriate drafting. Through skillful draftsmanship the experienced international lawyer can prevent many of the difficulties that can so easily arise under private international law.

BIBLIOGRAPHY. Books and articles published in English since 1790 are listed in CHARLES SZLADITS, *A Bibliography on Foreign and Comparative Law* (1955), and its supplements for 1962, 1968, and 1970. ERNST RABEL, *The Conflict of Laws: A Comparative Study*, 2nd ed., 4 vol. (1958–64), is a scholarly presentation of the choice-of-law branch on a worldwide scale. The texts of national sources and international treaties are collected, in German and in French, in ALEXANDER N. MAKAROV (ed.), *Quellen des Internationalen Privatrechts: Recueil de textes concernant le droit international prive*, 2nd ed., 2 vol. (1953–60, looseleaf). The laws of many countries, including England and the United States, concerning succession on death are presented and discussed in MURAD FERID and KARL FIRSCHING (eds.), *Internationales Erbrecht*, 4 vol., looseleaf 1955–69.

The following works are convenient sources of information on national laws of conflict of laws:

Countries of Anglo-American law: (United States): AMERICAN LAW INSTITUTE, *Restatement of the Law Second: Conflict of Laws* (1954–), a work by the prestigious organization of the American legal profession; ROGER C. CRAMTON and DAVID P. CURRIE, *Conflict of Laws: Cases, Comments, Questions* (1968), presents both the traditional and the modern approaches; ALBERT A. EHRENZWEIG, *Conflict of Laws* (1962), and *Private International Law* (1967), deal systematically with the American conflicts law as respectively applying to interstate and international problems. (England): GEOFFREY C. CHESHIRE, *Private International Law*, 8th ed. (1970); ALBERT V. DICEY, *Dicey and Morris on the Conflict of Laws*, 8th ed. by H.C. MORRIS (1967). (Australia): PETER E. NYGH, *Conflict of Laws in Australia* (1968). (Canada): W.S. JOHNSON, *The Conflict of Laws*, 3 vol. (1933–37). (Scotland): A.E. ANTON, *Private International Law* (1967).

Other countries: (Argentina): CARLOS A. LAZCANO, *Derecho internacional privado* (1965). (Austria): HANS KOHLER, *Internationales Privatrecht*, 3rd ed. (1966). (Belgium): FRANCOIS RIGAUX, *Droit international privé* (1968). (Bolivia): CARLOS A. SALINAS BALDIVIESO, *Derecho internacional público y privado* (1962). (Brazil): AMILCAR DE CASTRO, *Direito internacional privado*, 2nd ed., 2 vol. (1968); OSCAR M. GOMES (comp.), *Leis e normas de direito internacional privado*, 2nd rev. ed. (1969); HAROLDO VALLADAO, *Direito internacional privado* (1968). (Chile): DIEGO GUZMAN LATORRE, *Elementos de derecho internacional privado* (1969). (Denmark): OSCAR A. BORUM, *Lovkonflikter*, 6th ed. (1967). (Ethiopia): ROBERT A. SEDLER, *Conflict of Laws in Ethiopia* (1965). (France): HENRI BATIFFOL, *Droit international privé*, 5th ed. (1970). (Germany, Federal Republic): HANS H.L. DOLLE, *Internationales Privatrecht: Eine Einführung in seine Grundlagen* (1968); GERHARD KEGEL, *Internationales Privatrecht*, 2nd ed. (1964). (Italy): MARIO MIELE, *Diritto internationale privato* (1966). (Mexico): ALBERTO G. ARCE, *Derecho internacional privado*, 6th ed. (1968). (The Netherlands): W.L.G. LEMAIRE, *Nederlands international Privaatrecht* (1968). (Norway): KARSTEN GAARDER and L. OFTEDAL BROCH, *Internasjonal Privatrett* (1963). (Philippine Republic): EDGARDO L. PARAS, *Philippine Conflict of Laws* (1968). (Poland): WITALIS LUDWICZAK, *Miedzynarodowe prawo prywatne* (1967). (Socialist Countries): ISTVAN SZASZY, *Az európai népi demokráciák nemzetközi magánjoga* (1962; Eng. trans., *Private International Law in the European People's Democracies*, 1964). (Soviet Union): KAZIMIERZ GRZYBOWSKI, *Soviet Private International Law* (1965); LAZAR A. LUNTZ, *Mezhdunarodnoe chastnoe pravo* (1959; German ed., *Internationales Privatrecht*, 2 vol., 1961–64); (ed.), *Otsherki Mezhdunarodnovo tshastnovo pravo* (1963); and *Mezhdunarodnij Grazhdanski Protsess* (1966). (Spain): ADOLFO MIAJA DE LA MUELA, *Derecho internacional privado*, 4th ed., 2 vol. (1966). (Sweden): HILDING EEK, *Internationell Privaträtt*, 2nd rev. ed. (1967). (Switzerland): ADOLF F. SCHNITZER, *Handbuch des internationalen Privatrechts*, 4th ed., 2 vol. (1957–58). (Syria): EMILE TYAN, *Précis de droit international priveé* (1966). (Turkey): AHMET G. OKCUN, *Trans-Municipal Law* (1968). (Venezuela): CARLOS FEBRES POBEDA, *Apuntes de derecho internacional privado*, 2nd ed. (1963).

(M.Y.R.)

Conformational Analysis, Principles of

In organic molecules, the atoms are held together by valence bonds, which limit considerably the positions in space that the atoms can take. Nonetheless, because the various parts of the molecule are free to rotate about many of these valence bonds, the molecule can still assume any of a large number of three-dimensional shapes, or conformations, as they are called. For several reasons, however, some conformations are more stable than others (see below) and represent the true state of the molecule under normal circumstances. In general, there is a correlation between the preferred conformations of the molecules of a substance and the chemical and physical properties of that substance. The study of the factors that determine which conformations are preferred and of the correlations between these conformations and the properties of the substance in question is called conformational analysis.

In the 1940s and 1950s Odd Hassel of the University in Oslo and Derek H.R. Barton of Imperial College of Science and Technology (London) were active in developing and applying the principles of conformational analysis; in 1969 they were jointly awarded the Nobel Prize for Chemistry for this work.

Rotational conformations. Initially it was assumed that completely free rotation was possible about any single bond between carbon atoms in a molecule. The first evidence that this assumption needed modification appeared when it was found that certain tetrasubstituted diphenyls (I; X and Y = substituents) could be resolved —that is, separated into stable optical isomers, compounds that rotate plane-polarized light in opposite directions. Resolution of a substance into optical isomers

I

is possible only when the substance consists of two forms, the molecules of which are mirror images of one another. In 1926 James Kenner and E.E. Turner postulated that the diphenyls in question existed as optical isomers because the bulky substituents (X and Y) prevented free rotation about the bond *b*. If this were so, the diphenyls would exist as mirror-image pairs, which could not be converted into one another and that would then be capable of exhibiting the otherwise unexplainable optical activity of the compounds. This postulate is now generally accepted.

In 1936 the methods of chemical physics showed that restriction of rotation about single bonds was common to all organic compounds and that certain arrangements of bonded atoms in space were preferred. It is convenient to define the word conformation (Sir Walter Norman Haworth, 1929) as an arrangement in space of the atoms of a molecule of defined configuration that is not superposable upon any other arrangement. From this definition it follows that an infinite number of conformations are possible even for as simple a molecule as ethane, CH_3CH_3.

Restricted rotation

II III IV

V VI VII

Only two extreme conformations, shown in II and III, however, need be considered. In II, the staggered conformation, the hydrogen atoms are as far away from each other as is possible and the energy of the system is at a minimum, whereas in III the hydrogen atoms are as close as is possible and the energy is at a maximum. The energies of the infinite number of conformations that lie between these two extremes are also intermediate. Thus ethane at normal temperatures will exist mainly in II, the staggered low-energy conformation, but as the temperature of the gas is raised—*i.e.*, as energy is introduced into the system—an increasing proportion of it will adopt conformations of higher energy.

In *n*-butane ($CH_3CH_2CH_2CH_3$), there are four limiting conformations shown in IV, V, VI, and VII. That with lowest energy is IV, in which the methyl groups are as far apart as is possible; next comes the staggered arrangement V, in which the methyls are fairly close together. Of the high-energy arrangements, VII, in which the methyls are opposed, is less stable than VI, in which methyl is opposed to a hydrogen. Thus it can be seen that, in general, the preferred conformation is that in which the largest groups are farthest apart; this is due to the interaction of the nonbonded atoms whose electron atmospheres repel each other.

The barriers to free rotation in ethane, *n*-butane, and related molecules are only of the order of a few kilogram calories per mole. Although this is sufficient to ensure that the molecules exist in the preferred staggered conformations, it is far too small to allow the separation of stable isomers.

Conformations of cyclohexane derivatives. In 1890 H. Sachse pointed out that, if the valency angles of carbon were retained at the natural tetrahedral angle of 109° 28′, then cyclohexane (C_6H_{12}) could exist in two conformations free of angle strain. These are usually designated the chair (VIII) and boat (IX) conformations. In VIII all the bonds are staggered with respect to their neighbours (see also X), whereas in IX there are four pairs of opposed interactions. Thus it would be expected that the chair conformation (VIII) would be the more stable. This condition has, in fact, been established experimentally beyond question, a direct physical proof being provided by the electron diffraction work of O. Hassel (1948) and supported by the statistical mechanical studies of Kenneth S. Pitzer (1948).

VIII   IX

X   XI

In the chair conformation, two geometrically distinct types of carbon-hydrogen bond are present (see X). Six of the bonds are parallel to the threefold axis of symmetry of the ring and are called axial bonds (D.H.R. Barton, Hassel, Pitzer, and Vladimir Prelog, 1954).

The other six carbon-hydrogen bonds, placed in a belt around the molecule, are called equatorial (*e*). The conformation X can be converted to the boat conformation (IX) or it can be inverted to the alternative, but in every way equivalent, chair (XI) simply by movement of the carbon atoms through a plane. In this process an equatorial hydrogen—say (x) in X—becomes axial ([x] in XI) and vice versa. The energy needed to effect this process is only a few kilogram calories, and therefore it is not possible to isolate boat and chair conformational isomers in cyclohexane or its derivatives at ordinary temperatures.

Monosubstituted cyclohexanes can, in principle, have the substituent in the axial or equatorial arrangement, the two alternatives being different conformations of the molecule. In fact, it is the equatorial orientation that is favoured, except in unusual circumstances. In the equatorial conformation (XII), the substituent X is close enough in space to interact only with the two equatorial and two axial hydrogens on the carbon atoms proximate to the C–X bond; *i.e.*, four 1:2 H:X interactions. Similarly in the axial conformation (XIII), the substituent interacts with the two equatorial hydrogens on the adjacent carbon atoms and with the two axial hydrogens on the next but one carbon atoms; *i.e.*, two 1:2 H:X and two 1:3 H:X interactions. When the substituent is hydrogen, it is found by examining models that the 1:2 hydrogens are the same distance apart as the 1:3 axial hydrogens and thus have the same repulsive energy, but if any substituent larger than hydrogen is introduced, then the 1:3 axial distance is smaller than the 1:2 distance and the latter will therefore have a smaller energy of interaction.

So it may be concluded that, in general, substituted cyclohexanes tend to exist mainly in the conformation in which the largest group is in the equatorial position or, if more than two substituents are present, with the largest number of groups in the equatorial positions. This general rule does not always hold when the substituents have appreciable separation of electrical charge or dipole moment for, in these cases, the dipoles tend to be oriented in opposite directions, and this may result in several substituents with axial orientations.

In compounds of the decalin series, two cyclohexane rings are fused. By arguments such as those discussed

Equatorial conformation favoured

XII   XIII

XIV   XV

above, it can be predicted that *cis*-decalin (XIV) is less stable than the *trans* isomer (XV). In XIV, as with simple cyclohexane derivatives, conversion of equatorial to axial substituents is possible by inverting the conformation; however, in XV this is impossible since the bonds, *b* and *b′*, are equatorial with respect to the other ring and to make them axial would give rise to an impossibly strained ring. Thus in polycyclic systems, where one or more rings are *trans*-fused, the axial and equatorial isomers are not interconvertible. It is in these cases, where the rigidity of the molecule prevents there being any ambiguity about the orientation of substituents, that conformational analysis has made its most important contributions. The fundamental tenet of conformational analysis is that the preferred conformation of a molecule can be related to its physical and chemical properties. This tenet was first shown in polycyclic systems in 1950 by Barton, mainly with examples from the steroid field.

Applications of conformational analysis. Conformational analysis is used chiefly in two ways: (1) to correlate directly the properties of molecules with their preferred conformations and (2) to analyze the interplay of conformational preference with the geometrical requirements of the transition state in organic reactions.

In the first class may be grouped such properties as specific bands in the infrared or ultraviolet spectrum of a compound. For example in α-halogenocyclohexanones if the halogen is equatorial, the infrared maximum of the carbonyl group is displaced, but if the halogen is axial the frequency remains unchanged. In the ultraviolet spectrum the opposite holds true; thus in an axially substituted α-haloketone there is a displacement of the ultraviolet maximum but not in the corresponding equatorial compound. Even more striking and direct correlations can be observed in the nuclear magnetic resonance spectra of the molecules.

Also in the first class of applications of conformational analysis is the correlation of chemical properties of certain molecules with their preferred conformations. The rates of certain reactions of steroid derivatives fall into this category. Since it is known that the greater stability of equatorial over axial alcohols is due to overcrowding in the latter, it would be expected that acylation (ester formation) of a hydroxyl group in the equatorial position would be less hindered and thus would proceed more rapidly than is the case with the axial analogue. Similarly, it would be predicted that hydrolysis, or cleavage, of equatorial esters would occur more rapidly than it would in the case of the corresponding axial compounds. This has been amply proved in the case of various steroidal alcohols where the axial and equatorial pairs were examined with hydroxyl groups at the positions numbered in XVI. That the equatorial alcohol is more stable than the axial has also been demonstrated in these steroidal alcohols, mainly by reduction of the corresponding ketone with sodium and an alcohol to an equilibrium mixture of the axial and equatorial isomers. In all cases, the equatorial alcohol preponderates and hence must be the more stable. The greater stability of the equatorial over the corresponding axial substituent has been demonstrated for numerous other groups in various environments, especially in rigid fused-ring systems, such as ste-

Conformation and chemical properties

roids and triterpenes, where the configuration of a substituent defines its conformation.

This ability to define unambiguously the conformation of a compound is particularly important in the second way in which conformational analysis is applied; *i.e.*, the analysis of reaction mechanisms. Although flexible compounds such as substituted cyclohexanes usually exist in one preferred conformation, this does not mean that they must react in this form. For example, bromocyclohexane exists mainly in the equatorial conformation, but it is almost certain that when it is dehydrobrominated to cyclohexene, the form that reacts is the axial form. Thus it is in rigid systems with well-defined conformation (where such transformation cannot occur) that conformational analysis can be applied most fruitfully to the study of reaction mechanisms.

Conformation and reaction mechanisms [side note]

XVI

XVII **XVIII**

XIX **XX**

XXIII **XXI**

XXII

The transition state of lowest energy for an ionic bimolecular elimination reaction requires that the four centres involved be in one plane. This is fulfilled in conformationally rigid cyclohexane systems by *trans*-1:2-diaxial substituents, but not by *trans*-1:2-diequatorial substituents or by either of the *cis*-(equatorial-axial) isomers.

For example, 5α:6β-dibromocholestane (represented in partial formulation by XVII) has two axial bromine atoms. It is debrominated by iodide ion much faster than its 5β:6α-isomer (XVIII), where both bromines are equatorial. As a corollary to this rule, it has also been established that addition of electrophilic, or positive charged, reagents to double bonds gives the *trans*-diaxial product; in most cases this is the thermodynamically less stable one. Thus cholest-2-ene (XIX) gives mainly the diaxial 2β:3α-dibromocholestane (XX). Similarly, it has been shown that epoxides, such as cholest-2-ene α-epoxide (XXI), give the diaxial product (*e.g.*, XXII) on ring opening, although they could conceivably give the more stable diequatorial products; *e.g.*, XXIII. Conversely it has been shown that the diaxial halohydrins on treatment

with alkali reform the epoxide ring much more rapidly than do the corresponding diequatorial compounds.

The initial application of conformational analysis to rigid cyclohexane systems, particularly to steroids, by Barton in the 1950s at once rationalized a large body of existing steroid chemistry, which had not been readily comprehensible under standard stereochemical considerations. With conformational analysis, otherwise inexplicable variations in the physical and chemical properties of steroid derivatives were made understandable. Further, the application of the principles of conformational analysis to the steroid field facilitated the rapid development of new partial and total syntheses of steroid derivatives in the succeeding years.

Extensions of conformational analysis. Although conformational analysis can be more favourably applied to rigid cyclohexane systems, it has also been widely and fruitfully used in aliphatic and heterocyclic systems, and also in large- and small-ring compounds, though the latter do not have the symmetrical perfection of the cyclohexane ring. The substitution of heteroatoms such as nitrogen and oxygen for one or more of the carbon atoms of a cyclohexane ring causes only a slight distortion of the chair conformation. In consequence, the generalizations that have been found pertinent in cyclohexane chemistry can be carried over in main part to heterocyclic analogues. Thus tetrahydropyran ($C_5H_{10}O$) may be represented by the conformation XXIV. Many of the

Conformations of heterocyclic systems [side note]

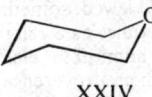

XXIV

compounds of carbohydrate chemistry contain the tetrahydropyran ring, and it has been shown that the chair conformation (XXIV) is adopted wherever possible. In macromolecular chemistry, as well, conformational principles are extremely important. The conformations of natural macromolecules are of considerable importance in determining their biological activity.

BIBLIOGRAPHY. D.H.R. BARTON, "The Conformation of the Steroid Nucleus," *Experientia*, 6:316–329 (1950), the first paper in which the significance of conformational analysis for organic chemistry was explicitly suggested; and with R.C. COOKSON, "The Principles of Conformational Analysis," *Q. Rev. Chem. Soc.* 10:44–82 (1956), a summary of the field as it had developed in its qualitative aspects between 1950 and 1956; M.S. NEWMAN (ed.), *Steric Effects in Organic Chemistry* (1956), a good collection of review articles on stereochemistry that includes authoritative chapters on conformational analysis; E.L. ELIEL et al., *Conformational Analysis* (1965), the most authoritative summary of its present status.

(D.H.R.B./J.K.S.)

Confucianism

Confucianism represents the way of life followed by the Chinese people for well over 2,000 years. Founded by Confucius (551–479 BC), Confucianism has been synonymous with learning in China and has been regarded as a religion by some people. The influence of Confucianism is so predominant that if anyone should be asked to characterize in one word traditional Chinese life and culture, that word would be Confucian. Every one of the 2,000 counties of China built a temple to Confucius, and the Confucian code of conduct was ideally the norm according to which every individual led his life. Confucian values have served as the source of inspiration as well as the court of appeal for human relations at all levels—between individuals, communities, and nations.

The influence of Confucianism is not confined to China. Nearby countries, such as Korea, Japan, and Annam (now divided between North and South Vietnam), embraced Confucianism in their national life and culture. Under the enthusiastic patronage of emperors and high ministers, Japan imported Confucian ideas and institutions at a feverish pace in the Middle Ages. Even in contemporary Japan traces of Confucian character are still noticeable among the people, just as scattered Confucian temples are found in the land. Korea's ac-

Influence of Confucianism outside China [side note]

ceptance of Confucianism goes even further back into history. The design of the South Korean flag—with the Yin and Yang symbol (see below) and trigrams from the Classic *I Ching* (see below)—is a clear indication of the Korean feeling of cultural affinity with Confucian China. The most imposing Confucian temple outside China stands today in Seoul, and it is there that the most authentic Confucian sacrifice, with elaborate classical music and dance, is to be witnessed.

The period of 550–200 BC, historically known as the classical age, is also referred to as the age of the "hundred philosophers." Contending vigorously in proposing solutions to the pressing problem of bringing order out of chaos, the hundred philosophers were eventually grouped under six schools, consisting of Confucianism, Taoism, Moism, the School of Yin-Yang, the Dialecticians, and Legalism. (For characterization and discussion of the other five schools, see CHINESE PHILOSOPHY.) Although earliest in time and foremost in renown, Confucius was for some centuries counted among the hundred philosophers and Confucianism, among the six schools. It was in the 2nd century BC that Confucianism was first elevated to the status of a state cult, at the expense of the other schools. Taoism, however, has always retained a place of importance—as a sublime system of philosophy among the artistic and contemplatively inclined elite and as a popular religion among the peasantry.

A viable way of life for so many and for so long, Confucianism has been viewed sometimes as a system of philosophy and sometimes as a religion. It has embraced some of the more admirable elements of traditional Chinese religion, such as a reverence toward Heaven and worship of ancestors. Confucius, however, advocated the achievement of sagehood by man through self-cultivation and inner enlightenment, and Confucian temples stand as memorial monuments rather than functioning religious institutions, such as churches or synagogues. All the more notable is the fact that even when Chinese profess themselves to be Taoists, Buddhists, or Christians, seldom do they cease to be Confucianists. Confucianism is more than a creed to be professed or rejected; it has become a pattern worked into the fabric of Chinese life and society.

Patterns of Confucian thought

CLASSICAL CONFUCIAN THOUGHT

The key concept: *jen*, human-heartedness

Basic concepts of Confucius. *Man and society.* Except for the loving care and guidance of his widowed mother, Confucius was a self-educated man. Like his personality, his teachings are natural, human, and simple. The key concept to the system is the Chinese character *jen*, which has been variously translated as virtue, love, magnanimity, or humanheartedness. Several disciples asked Confucius about *jen*, and his briefest answer was "Love men." An ancient commentary says "*Jen* is to love men joyously and from the innermost of one's heart." The Chinese character for *jen* denotes ideographically that which is common in two men, suggesting the notion of a common denominator of mankind and a demarcation between man and animal. *Jen* is inborn in all men, and to nurture and cultivate this seed-essence of humanity into full, flowering virtue is the common mission of human life. Significantly, the equivalent for "paralysis" in Chinese medical language is literally "absence or lack of *jen*." To lead a life of *jen* carries with it no external material reward. On the contrary, persons devoted to *jen* "will not seek to live at the expense of injuring their *jen*, and will even sacrifice their lives to preserve their *jen* complete," according to Confucius. Filial piety (*hsiao*) begins as the natural and early exercise of the *jen* sentiment, leading to a cultivated attitude of respectful affection toward one's parents. Easy to understand and to practice, filial piety was developed into a national cult by certain Confucian followers in later ages.

Complementary to the concept of *jen*, Confucius also stressed such other qualities as virtue (*te*) and righteousness (*yi*). The cultivation of such qualities constitutes one of the telling marks between the superior man and the inferior man. Confucius said: "The superior man is concerned with virtue; the inferior man is concerned with land." Also: "The superior man understands what is right; the inferior man understands what is profitable." Generally speaking, these virtues, as well as such others as reciprocity, loyalty, courage, wisdom, and trustworthiness, may all be regarded as extensions of *jen*, and *jen* as the supervirtue of all virtues.

Rarely emphasized by other great teachers of religion and morality of antiquity, the principle of *li* was considered very important by Confucius. *Li* covers a wide range of terms in the English language, from decorum to formality to rites. A rich code of ceremonial had already developed in China by the time of Confucius, and, in fact, degenerated into elaborate but lifeless formality. The prevailing neglect, improper performance, and usurpation of rites and ceremonies reflected a deeper moral and spiritual disorder of the race. To Confucius, therefore, the revivification of *li* would at once add a touch of elegance and grace to his ethic of *jen* and help to restore order in society. Propounding his doctrine of rectification of names (clarity in the use of terms, with a practical, social application), Confucius said: "Let the prince be prince, minister be minister, the father father, and the son son." Under the influence of Confucianism, the Chinese have developed a notable politeness in their social intercourse and this politeness is given expression commensurate with the social stations of the people involved.

The *chün-tzu*, or the superior man

The teachings of Confucius aim at setting up an ideal for the individual and for society. The ideal for the individual is known as the *chün-tzu*, or the superior man. With the components of art and nature blended harmoniously in him, "the superior man feels neither anxiety nor fear" and "is always calm and at ease." By contrast, the inferior man is always worried and full of distress. The development of the superior man is best illustrated by the personal example of Confucius himself. Toward the end of his life, Confucius said:

> At 15 I set my heart on learning; at 30 I was firmly established; at 40 I had no more doubts; at 50 I knew the will of Heaven; at 60 I was ready to listen to it; at 70 I could follow my heart's desire without transgressing what was right.

Literally and originally, the two-word term *chün-tzu* means "prince-son" or a lordling. Constituting a privileged class in an age of feudalistic hierarchy, the young noblemen alone had the leisure and education to develop their moral sense and political leadership. Confucius, like Plato, would have the kings as sages. Disenchantment with nobility by birth, however, turned Confucius' faith to education and his hope in a new kind of nobility. The new class of *chün-tzu* might still be regarded as an aristocracy or an elite, but membership became open to anyone willing to cultivate himself. He is a nobleman who bears himself nobly. While the pre-Confucian *chün-tzu* is a lordling, the Confucian *chün-tzu* is a superior man, a man who has arrived through learning and devotion to moral ideals.

In service to society, the moral qualities of the superior man serve him also as leadership qualifications. The notion that the art of government consists in setting things right is an ancient one. Confucius advanced the idea, however, that it was first of all the personal character and conduct of the ruler that was to be set right. In answer to a prince who inquired about government, Confucius said: "To govern is to set things right. If you begin by setting yourself right, who will dare to deviate from the right?" The good society, according to Confucius, is a society governed by *jen*, particularly by the personal example of the ruler, representing the embodiment of *jen*. Hence, the state is not unlike a schoolhouse, and the ruler the schoolmaster, whose purpose is to help his charges become better men.

Heaven and the Heavenly way

Religious aspects. Confucianism is sometimes regarded as a religion. The institutional aspects of the system have all been developed since Confucius' time, but Confucius did himself entertain an intimate feeling toward Heaven (*t'ien*, an ancient Chinese term for deity, understood by Confucius as a cosmic spiritual–moral power). He prayed, he fasted, he attended sacrifices, and once he even swore by Heaven. When the death of Yen Hui, his favourite pupil, was reported to him, he exclaimed, "Heaven has destroyed me, Heaven has destroyed me!" At the same time, Confucius was vigorously against the popular religious practice of his day and would have nothing to do with it. The animistic cult handed down from the Yin dynasty had degenerated into witchcraft and sorcery. Confucius selectively preserved the practice of ancestor worship and obedience to the Mandate of Heaven.

There is a prophetic character to Confucius' advocacy of his spiritual and political reforms. Confucius said:

> There are three things of which the superior man stands in awe. He stands in awe of the ordinances of Heaven. He stands in awe of great men. He stands in awe of the words of sages.

This obedience and trust in Heaven gave him courage in times of disappointments and physical danger, and his sense of a Heavenly mission placed upon him grew only with the years. The way (*tao*) of Heaven should serve as the model for the way among men. A ruler rules by the authority of the Mandate of Heaven, which is readily transferred to another once the incumbent becomes unworthy of the trust. The *Shu Ching* ("Classic of History") and *Shih Ching* ("Classic of Poetry"), Classical Chinese texts, contain elaborate amplifications of the theocratic conception of government; and the ancient sage-kings, particularly Yao and Shun of great antiquity, serve as historical examples of such an ideal.

A famous text attributed to Confucius speaks of "the age when the Great *Tao* prevailed" and calls it "the age of Grand Harmony." Unfortunately, the golden age belongs to the past, and one can only aspire to "the age of Minor Prosperity," an available second best. Even this age of lesser excellence, brought on mostly through the statesmanly efforts of Chou Kung (Duke of Chou) at the beginning of the Chou dynasty (12th century BC), had come under imminent danger, and Confucius felt called upon to restore it to its original splendour. So much did he admire the achievements of Chou Kung that he said: "I must have grown really feeble and old, since I have not for a long time dreamed of seeing Duke Chou."

The book of Confucius is known as the *Lun yü* ("Conversations"), or the *Analects*. A collection of the notes and journals of the Master's discourses, conversations, and travels kept by his disciples, the work consists of 20 sections and 496 chapters. The present form of the work was established at about the beginning of the Christian Era, previous to which rival versions existed. The *Lun yü* is the earliest and most reliable source on the life and teachings of the Sage and is regarded by the Chinese as the basic "scripture" of Confucianism, somewhat like the Gospels in relation to the life and teachings of Jesus. Almost all educated Chinese know the outstanding passages of the book by heart. Numerous commentaries have been written on the work by scholars through the ages. When the Chinese civil-service examination system was in operation, not only the text but also the celebrated commentary by Chu Hsi, the outstanding Chinese thinker after the 3rd century BC, was assumed to be part of the syllabus. Translations of the work have been made and published in many languages.

Basic concepts of Mencius. Among the Chinese, Mencius (*c.* 371–289 BC) is revered as the Second Sage, second only to Confucius, the Supreme Sage. To Westerners, the Latinization of the references of these two Chinese sages and these only (calling K'ung-fu-tzu "Confucius," and Meng-tzu or Meng K'o "Mencius") should serve as a clear reminder of their special importance. Even the life pattern of Mencius, consisting of teaching students and offering his counsels to kings and princes, follows closely that of Confucius. The interval of more than a century between the two sages saw an accelerated decline of the social and political order together with a rise in sophistication in philosophical discussion. The records of Mencius' words and deeds are preserved in the work that bears his name, the *Mencius* (*Meng-tzu* in Chinese).

Advancing the Confucian concept of *jen*, Mencius de-clared that human nature was good and proceeded to defend the thesis against rival theories. To him, the virtue of *jen* together with the accompanying virtues of righteousness, decorum, and wisdom arises from the inner springs of the human heart. These four cardinal virtues come in their seed form as the feelings of compassion, shame, modesty, and of the distinction between right and wrong. Such feelings are universal among mankind, and they come as naturally as taste for food, hearing for music, and sight for beauty. Therefore, human nature will be good if it is guided by its innate feelings, just as water is inclined to flow downward. Evil arises only when there is neglect and abuse of this innate goodness. All-important, therefore, is the function of education and self-cultivation, so that one does not lose his original "child's heart" and so that the four seeds may become the four full-flowering virtues. Self-cultivation is a task that requires constant attention, but a person must not overexert himself trying to be good. The humour of Mencius shows through the story he told about the foolish man of the state of Sung who tried to bring his crop to the same height as that of his neighbours by pulling the young sprouts up just a little higher.

Mencius thus extended the Confucian concept of *jen* in regard to its innate nature and the proper course for its development. The theory of the goodness of human nature has since stimulated much discussion in the history of Chinese philosophy.

As concrete examples of the complete achievement of the life of *jen*, Mencius, even more than Confucius, referred repeatedly to the ancient sage-kings Yao and Shun. Besides exemplifying the virtue of *jen* in their personal lives, Yao and Shun also conducted their government by *jen*, promoting the material and spiritual welfare of the people. Unfortunately, the trend of deterioration had set in after the time of these sages. In line with Chou Kung and Confucius, Mencius felt called upon to carry the burden of the sagely orthodoxy and perpetuate the way of *jen*. Mencius spent a good deal of his time travelling among the Chinese states and counselling the feudal lords. He reaffirmed the basic Confucian tenet that government is primarily for the good of the people and not the ruler, and he emphasized the notion that the Heavenly Mandate is conferred upon the ruler in consideration of his virtue and talent. He contrasted kingly government, government by *jen*, against tyrant government, government by force; and he warned that a ruler who betrayed his Heavenly trust was no more king but a scourge or a scoundrel. When consulted about the assassination of Chou Wang, a most depraved king, Mencius said: "I have heard that a despised creature called Chou was put to death, but I have not heard anything about the murdering of a sovereign." Reminding everyone repeatedly of the ancient saying, "Heaven sees as the people see; Heaven hears as the people hear," Mencius stood as the most outspoken champion of the cause of the common people and their right to good government, or revolution.

Mencius' adoration of sagehood and his belief in the perfectibility of man were so strong that he sometimes spoke in mystical terms about the deepest experience of man. He was convinced that man possessed inborn knowledge and inborn ability and that man partook with Heaven and earth in a universal and vital element that Mencius called *ch'i*, sometimes translated as "ether." When someone asked Mencius wherein did he excel other men, his reply was, ". . . I know how to nourish my vast, flowing 'ether.' " When this "ether" is developed to the fullest extent, man is completely identified with Heaven and earth, and the decree of Heaven and the nature of man become indistinguishable. Mencius said: "All the ten thousand living things are found within us. There is no greater joy than to look into our life and find this true." And further: "He that goes to the bottom of his heart knows his own nature, and knowing his own nature he knows Heaven." Every man could become like Yao and Shun, according to Mencius, and the decisive factor is the man's willingness to make the effort.

Basic concepts of Hsün-tzu. Living at the end of the Chou dynasty. Hsün-tzu (*c.* 298–*c.* 230) witnessed the

The goodness of human nature and the works of jen

Government for the good of the people

complete collapse of the social and political order. At the same time he had the advantage of familiarity with the teachings of a long line of philosophers. With unmatched erudition and breadth of intellectual interests, Hsün-tzu developed refreshingly unorthodox ideas, while he declared himself a Confucianist and subscribed to the basic Confucian conviction in the supreme worth of the life of virtue and the perfectibility of man. The work *Hsün-tzu* contains 32 chapters, each a well-written essay on a given topic, such as Heaven, human nature, prejudice, learning, or the rectification of names.

The innate evil and acquired goodness of human nature

In contrast to the concept of the goodness of human nature, Hsün-tzu declared: "The nature of man is evil; his goodness is acquired." Hsün-tzu appreciated the value of education and environment, as did all Confucianists, but he considered the function of education to be the "straightening and bending" and "grinding and whetting" of the evil nature of man. To Hsün-tzu it is environment and authority that make the man, and it is obedience of the precepts of the sage-kings that produces the goodness that is in him. In the end, however, not only is the life of virtue but even sagehood is within reach. Hsün-tzu said: "Every man on the street can become like the sage-king Yü," a perfectly orthodox Confucian note.

Together with his view of human nature, Hsün-tzu taught that "Heaven operates with constant regularity." In sharp contrast to traditional Chinese and Confucian ideas, Hsün-tzu's Heaven conducts itself without any relation to the world of man. Heaven is no source of blessing; neither is it a proper object for worship. For man the part of wisdom therefore consists in knowing his place and fulfilling his duties. Heaven does not help those who help themselves; all the more man should help himself. Instead of relying on Heaven, Hsün-tzu exhorted people to "domesticate," "employ," and "exploit" it, a rare instance in the history of Chinese thought of the impulse to dominate nature so familiar in the West. In his effort to combat the beliefs in magic, omens, and portents, which were pervasive in his time, Hsün-tzu advanced the doctrine that Heaven was not an anthropomorphic god, nor even the seat of a moral order in the universe, but a purely natural and mechanical process running its own course.

Government by *li*, ceremonial

Both Confucius and Mencius advocated the principle of government by *jen*. Having witnessed the final extinction of the royal house of Chou and the desperate but fatal struggle of the other feudal states against the powerful state of Ch'in, Hsün-tzu felt the need of something more binding and dependable in government than just the moral influence of a self-rectified ruler. He set forth the principle of government by *li*, or ceremonial, instead. Deviating from Confucius, who was concerned with decorum, the inner-feeling aspect of *li*, Hsün-tzu was much more interested in ceremonial, the outer form of *li*. In Hsün-tzu's philosophy, the concept of ceremonial assumes an overall importance besides being the keystone to his theory of government. To begin with, ceremonial provides the means for the regulated handling of special occasions, such as birth and death, in a man's life. Next, ceremonial provides an implement as well as a yardstick of propriety in human conduct. Finally, ceremonial provides an element of adornment and grace, so that a man's life may achieve some degree of balance and beauty.

As an operative agency in the administration of government, ceremonial is even more significant, according to Hsün-tzu. A very general assumption among Chinese thinkers, Hsün-tzu included, is that all men are not born equal. Hsün-tzu said: "Recognizing the differences of men in society, one can easily govern the whole empire, whereas failing to recognize those differences, one will have anarchy with just a wife and a concubine." Ceremonial is, then, the effective instrument for recognizing, composing, and harmonizing the differences among men. Ceremonial, in the all-inclusive sense of art and artifice, education and culture, operates as the working agency of social restraint and organization. When every individual has been helped to find his place and perform his duty, then the ruler "just sits there by himself like a clod and the people of the empire obey him like one body." Such a state of affairs is called the "grand form."

Other Classical Confucian thought. Confucius and Mencius are traditionally regarded as the founders of Confucianism and revered as the Supreme and Second Sages of China, with Hsün-tzu kept to the status of a philosopher of the Confucian school. A number of texts not ascribed to these three men have also contributed to the development of Classical Confucian thought. These items may be dealt with in two groups. First, there is the group of *Wu Ching* ("Five Classics"), namely, the *I Ching* ("Classic of Changes"), the *Shih Ching* ("Classic of Poetry"), the *Shu Ching* ("Classic of History"), the *Li chi* ("Collection of Rituals"), and the *Ch'un ch'iu* ("Spring and Autumn" Annals). The last item of this list is a year-by-year record of events in the State of Lu, kept with indications of approval and disapproval by Confucius himself. The other four items all antedate Confucius by several hundred years and constitute the common literary heritage of all educated men, the ancient philosophers included. For instance, the *Shih Ching* and the *Shu Ching* are as often referred to by Mo-tzu, the founder of Moism, as by Confucius and Mencius, and the *I Ching* has influenced Taoist thinkers as much as Confucianists. These classic texts became a part of Confucian literature by the process of absorption during the Western Han period (206 BC–AD 8).

The *Wu Ching* and the *Ssu shu*

Second, there is the group of what might be called minor texts of Classical Confucianism, namely, the *Ta hsüeh* ("Great Learning"), the *Chung yung* ("Doctrine of the Mean"), and the *Hsiao Ching* ("Classic of Filial Piety"). These small works are all traditionally attributed to the immediate disciples and followers of Confucius. While the exact authorship of these texts may be held in doubt, they are certainly to be accepted as supplementary material to the teachings of Confucius. The *Hsiao Ching* enjoyed special popularity under the patronage of the Han dynasty emperors (206 BC–AD 220), and filial piety has since been regarded as the foundation virtue of all virtues. Originally, two chapters in the *Li chi*, the *Ta hsüeh* and the *Chung yung*, were, during the Sung dynasty, brought together with the *Lun yü* and the *Mencius* to form the specifically Confucian *Ssu shu* ("Four Books"). The *Ssu shu* has been used as the basic text in primary education and in civil-service examinations in China for many centuries. Among all the Confucian texts, the *Chung yung* stands out as the most metaphysical (dealing with the basic nature and principles of reality). It received much attention in the subsequent movement of Neo-Confucianism (beginning in the 11th century).

HAN CONFUCIANISM AND THE ORTHODOX TRADITION

Political context and eclectic character. Having put an end to the Chou dynasty and eliminated the remaining rival states, the powerful state of Ch'in reunified the empire and set up the Ch'in dynasty in 221 BC. A dictatorial and totalitarian regime, it lasted only 15 years, but it successfully uprooted the feudalistic hierarchy and instituted a central government. Ch'in Shih Huang Ti, the First Emperor of Ch'in, who is popularly remembered as the wicked ruler who "burned the books and buried the scholars alive," succeeded in putting to an end the vigour and originality that had characterized the world of thought during the classical age. The succeeding Han dynasty, which lasted more than four centuries, firmly established the authority of the central government and developed its supporting institutions. The atmosphere of original thought, free inquiry, and vigorous pluralism, however, was dissipated once and for all. In its place, Han thought showed signs of ossification, and the age has been referred to by some as a period of "bible study." Instead of advancing original ideas, philosophers exercised great ingenuity toward establishing a trend of eclecticism. Some of the attempts, such as synthesizing Confucianism with occultism or grafting Taoism onto Confucianism, produced grotesque results. Institutionally, Confucianism made great strides during the Han dynasty, but philosophically it made little progress.

Basic concepts of Tung Chung-shu. Tung Chung-shu (*c.* 179–*c.* 104 BC), renowned as the greatest Confucian scholar of his day, should serve as a good example of the twofold trend in the development of Confucianism during the Han dynasty, namely, phenomenal accomplishments in gaining institutional status and woeful sterility in further development of theory. His major work is a lengthy one, called the *Ch'un ch'iu fan lu* ("Luxuriant Dew from the Spring and Autumn" Annals). His exposition of Confucianism was sometimes conventional and uninspired and sometimes fanciful and bizarre. In ethics and politics, Tung Chung-shu generally reaffirmed the teachings of Confucius and Mencius. Adding the virtue of trustworthiness (*hsin*) to the four virtues of love (*jen*), righteousness (*yi*), decorum (*li*), and wisdom (*chih*) handed down by Mencius, he popularized the set of five cardinal virtues.

The five cardinal virtues and the five social relations

Among the five social relations—those between sovereign and subject, father and son, husband and wife, brother and brother, friend and friend—he attributed special importance to the first three, proclaiming that these three relations were structured on the Yin and Yang pattern (interaction of opposites, here, high and low). It was evident to him that a subject should obey his sovereign, a son his father, and a wife her husband. His general orientation was that of a systematizer and an authoritarian.

It is in the area of metaphysics and cosmology that Tung Chung-shu exercised a vivid imagination. His objective was to harmonize the traditional theories of Yin and Yang and the five elements (wood, fire, earth, metal, and water) with Confucianism. He worked out a scheme for the five elements so that "in the order of their succession they give birth to one another, while in a different order they overcome each other." He held a strong belief in the correspondence between man and nature, going to the extent of detailing the correspondence of the four seasons, 12 months, and 366 days in the year with the four limbs, 12 sections (three sections in each limb), and 366 bones in the human body. He also believed in a close relationship between the actions of man and the operation of nature. Man's wicked deeds, particularly those of the ruler, would bring on natural catastrophes such as floods, and droughts, and earthquakes, and anomalies such as comets, eclipses, and the "growing of beards on women." Convinced of what he called "portents of catastrophes and anomalies," Tung Chung-shu succeeded in devising a formula that has acted as an effective deterrent to the whims and excesses of the monarchs. The catastrophes and anomalies are interpreted as Heaven's way of warning the ruler to examine his personal conduct and correct his mistakes. All of this is, of course, a far cry from the teachings of Confucius and Mencius concerning man, Heaven, and government.

Skepticism of Wang Ch'ung. Beliefs in prodigies and ghosts and practices of divination and witchcraft were widespread in the early Han dynasty and not without support from scholars like Tung Chung-shu. The iconoclastic skepticism of Wang Ch'ung (AD 27–100) was a startling contrast. In his work, the *Lun-Heng* ("Critical Essays"), Wang Ch'ung said of himself: "A recluse in solitary retirement, he sought to sift truth from falsehood." With a hatred for fiction and falsehood and insistence on evidence in argument, he attacked Tung Chung-shu's interpretation of catastrophes as Heaven's punishment of man's sins. To Wang Ch'ung, man's place in the universe was like that of a flea in a man's garment, and Heaven could be expected to mind the wishes of man as much as man could be expected to mind those of the flea. Similarly, he argued against the advocates of an afterlife or life everlasting. He asked whether a man's clothes would also be everlasting. If not, then the fairy-like beings would all be living in the state of everlasting nakedness.

Wang Ch'ung's critiques

With keen observation and searching criticism, by logic and ridicule, Wang Ch'ung rendered a critique of almost every school and scholar; *e.g.*, Taoism, Han-fei-tzu (eminent Legalist thinker), and Mencius. Even Confucius, of whom Wang Ch'ung was generally an admirer, called for a critical remark or two. The iconoclasm of Wang Ch'ung succeeded, to a considerable extent, in purging Confucianism of the elements of Yin and Yang and occultism and restoring Confucius, against the current trend of deification of the Master, to his terrestrial and rightful position as a great sage and teacher. In so doing, Wang Ch'ung also contributed, even though only incidentally, to the revival of Taoism and the conception of Taoist religion, which was mainly a union of Taoism with occultism and folk beliefs—those that had been purged from Confucianism.

Imperial ideology and the state cult. The trend of the ascendancy of Confucianism and Confucian scholars started from almost the very beginning of the Han dynasty (206 BC). It was actually during the reign of Emperor Wu (Wu Ti, 140–87 BC) that Confucianism progressed markedly toward being established as the imperial ideology and state cult. Historically the empire had sufficiently recovered from the high-handed, oppressive rule of the Ch'in dynasty but was, in turn, plagued by the evils of the laissez-faire policy of the early Han administration. The political pendulum was in search of a resting point, as it were, between the two extremes of overgovernment and undergovernment. The historical circumstances had at least facilitated the rulers' appreciation of the virtues of the Confucian way of life and principles of government.

Tung Ch'ung-shu was greatly respected by Emperor Wu and was most influential in elevating Confucianism to its position of supremacy. As a result of his noted series of three memorials on natural and human affairs presented in 136 BC, the civil-service examination system and the national system of schools were eventually instituted. The first imperial university was established in 124 BC, with a student body of 50 studying under professors who specialized in one or another of the Five Classics. The long break in Classical studies going back to the burning of books by the First Emperor of Ch'in made the re-establishment of textual orthodoxy an urgent necessity, particularly in view of the variant versions of the recovered texts. The size of the student body swelled to 3,000 toward the beginning of the Christian Era, and 30,000 by the end of the Han dynasty. At times national policies were assigned to the professors and students for deliberation, and the university was made to assume the character of a national political consultative council.

Scholarship in Classics as basis for government service

Once the Classics were made the basis of political decision, Confucianism was on its course toward becoming the state cult. In AD 59 Emperor Ming ordered the sacrifices hitherto confined to the temple of the K'ung family in Ch'ü-fu to be made in all of the public schools throughout the land, thus transforming Confucius from a model for scholars into their patron saint. With honour and glory heaped upon Confucius from age to age, a Confucian temple eventually stood in every one of the 2,000 counties of China. These temples also served as a kind of Chinese pantheon, preserving the memory of great Confucian scholars. Semiannual sacrifices were offered in the spring and autumn, with music and dance suited to the solemnity of the occasion. While the Confucian temples stood as monuments to the memory of the sage, the schools served as the active agents for the dissemination of the Confucian doctrine. The curriculum consisted of Confucian Classics, the teachers were Confucian scholars, and the schools functioned at least in part like "Sunday schools." In every traditional schoolroom there stood a wooden tablet on which were carved the five characters "heaven, earth, sovereign, parents, teacher," and a schoolboy's day began and ended with a deep bow toward the tablet.

NEO-CONFUCIANISM

Intellectual and religious context. The seven centuries between the end of the Han dynasty (AD 220) and the beginning of the Sung dynasty (AD 960) were a lacklustre period in the development of Confucianism. In fact, both Taoism and Buddhism enjoyed more attention and devotion from the leading minds of the time, and Confucianism persisted mainly because of the family system, the government bureaucracy, and the civil-service examination system, which continued to be based on the Confucian Classics. There was Confucian scholarship in the area of textual criticism and exegesis but hardly any advancement in Confucian ideas.

The revival of Confucianism, a movement known as Neo-Confucianism, was an achievement of the Confucian scholars of the Sung dynasty (960–1279). A notable precursor of the movement, however, was Han Yü (768–824) of the late T'ang dynasty, who, in a time when the fashion was to accommodate Confucianism with Buddhism or Taoism, stood out as the champion of Confucian orthodoxy. Going beyond the assertion of the doctrinal superiority of Confucianism, Han Yü gave expression to a reawakening and reaffirmation of faith in the traditional values of Chinese culture on the part of a growing number of the literati.

Basic concepts of Chu Hsi and the Li Hsüeh. Next to the classical age, when the system was at its vital best, the Neo-Confucianism movement of the Sung dynasty (960–1279) ranks as the most outstanding revival of the vigour and authority of the Confucian thought. In contrast to the imperial patronage that accounted for the ascendancy of Confucianism in the preceding dynasties, it was the personal effort and dedication of individual Confucian scholars that brought forth Neo-Confucianism. In addition, Neo-Confucianism had to contend with Buddhism, a firmly entrenched institution by that time, and the effort to refute Buddhist doctrines induced Neo-Confucianism to develop its metaphysical theories to a new depth and subtlety.

Chu Hsi (1130–1200), who combined the rare qualities of a penetrating thinker and an erudite scholar, is the undisputed representative and spokesman of Neo-Confucianism. His voluminous literary output included a stupendous history project, which he supervised, and a definitive commentary on each of the important Classics. His "Recorded Sayings" fill 140 chapters. With a genius for clarity and coherence and embracing the contributions of his predecessors, Chu Hsi's views have become enshrined as orthodox Neo-Confucianism and his commentaries on the Classics as their official interpretation in the state examinations from 1313 to the year 1905, when the examinations were abolished. The authoritative position of Chu Hsi reminds one of the comparable importance achieved by Thomas Aquinas in Roman Catholic philosophy.

The basic concept of Chu Hsi is *li* ("principle," or "reason"); thus Neo-Confucianism is sometimes referred to in China as Li Hsüeh, the system of principles. The *li* is something immaterial, immutable, and inherent in all things, giving them their form and constituting their essence. According to Chu Hsi, all things "possess *li* from the first moment of their existence," and "there are none that do not have *li*." On the other hand: "There are *li*, even if there are no things." Thus *li* can exist without things, but things cannot exist without *li*. For everything there is *li*, which makes it what it is. For the universe as a whole there is an overall *li*, which embraces and unites the *li* of all things and is called the T'ai Chi ("Supreme Ultimate"). Chu Hsi says: "The Supreme Ultimate is simply the highest of all, beyond which nothing can be." The relation between the T'ai Chi and *li*, however, is not that of whole and part. The T'ai Chi is received by each individual thing in its entirety and undivided, like the moon "reflected in rivers and lakes."

Concepts of li and ch'i

Coupled with the concept of *li* is the concept of *ch'i*, or material force. While the *li* constitutes only "a pure, empty and vast world, without shape or traces," the *ch'i* "has the capacity to undergo fermentation and condensation, and thus bring things into existence." Hence, both *li* and *ch'i* are necessary and present in the existence of every thing, with *ch'i* bringing the thing into being and *li* making the thing what it is (the generic essence, or nature, of a thing, such as man or bird). Like other things, man also embraces *ch'i* and *li*. What men call human nature is simply the *li* of humanity that is inherent in the individual. While the *li* for all men is the same, it is the *ch'i* that makes them different (a certain type or quality of man). The *ch'i* in some individuals is clear, and these individuals are the sages, while the *ch'i* in some others is turbid and they are the fools and knaves. On the

The Sung revival of Confucianism

basis of this dualistic doctrine of *li* and *ch'i*, Chu Hsi presents his theory of human nature. On the one hand, he can support Mencius' pronouncement that human nature is good because the *li* of humanity can be nothing but good; while on the other hand, he has an explanation for the origin of evil, namely, the individual's physical endowment, or the kind of *ch'i* he receives.

The starting point for achieving the ideal state for both the individual and the community is personal spiritual cultivation. This effort is to be directed toward making manifest the T'ai Chi (or *li* in its totality) that is within every man but kept invisible like a pearl in turbid water because of man's physical endowment. The approach is twofold and consists of the extension of knowledge and the exercise of attentiveness. Chu Hsi believes that after much sustained effort one becomes, in a moment of sudden illumination, completely enlightened. With such an enlightenment, an individual is a sage, and a sage is to be king in order to bring into existence again the perfect state, as the sage-kings did in antiquity.

Relation of Li Hsüeh to other Neo-Confucian schools. It was out of the various concepts and ideas taught by his predecessors that Chu Hsi, with the genius of a great molder and synthesizer, was able to formulate a complete, coherent system of thought. Mention should be made of at least a few of these thinkers and their contributions. The concept of the T'ai Chi was underlined in the 11th century by Chou Tun-i, who, together with Shao Yung, had a strong Taoist leaning and instilled a Taoist strain in the formulation of Neo-Confucianism. Chang Tsai first elaborated the concept of *ch'i* and spoke with eloquence and conviction of the unity among all things and urged the complete identification of man and Heaven and earth. In the direct line of Chu Hsi's mentors were the Ch'eng brothers, Ch'eng Hao and Ch'eng I, who made the concept of *li* prominent in their teaching but also marked the beginning of the doctrinal schism within Neo-Confucianism.

The concepts at issue are those of *li* and *hsin*, or principle and mind. So central are these concepts that the school led by Chu Hsi is also known as the Li Hsüeh, and the rival school, led by his contemporary Lu Chiu-yüan, as the Hsin Hsüeh. Chu Hsi's interpretation of *li* and *hsin* followed that of Ch'eng I, the younger brother, whereas Lu Chiu-yüan was more faithful to Ch'eng Hao, the older brother. According to the Hsin Hsüeh, "the mind is *li*," *li* is inherent in things, and there is no such thing as an abstract *li* that is eternal. Lu Chiu-yüan said: "The universe is my mind; my mind is the universe." The difference is quite fundamental, philosophically speaking. Chu Hsi advocated a dualistic system based on the concepts of *li* and *ch'i*. Lu Chiu-yüan taught a monistic system of the mind, which was the legislator of the universe, including the *li*. The contrast was dramatized by the celebrated debate held in 1175 at the Goose Lake (Buddhist) Monastery, in northern Kiangsi Province, between the two intellectual giants of the day and their followers. While the participants parted friends, their philosophical differences remained unresolved.

Convinced that "Truth is nothing other than the mind and the mind nothing other than the truth" and that "the Six Classics are but footnotes of my mind," Lu Chiu-yüan did not emphasize book learning and did not write a single book himself. Condemning the method of extension of knowledge through investigation of things, he believed that spiritual cultivation consisted of contemplation—looking inward into one's own mind—and sudden enlightenment. The Hsin Hsüeh of Neo-Confucianism was amplified by Wang Yang-ming (1472–1529) in the Ming dynasty, but it has never been able to match the authority of the Li Hsüeh.

The *Ssu shu* was popularized by the Neo-Confucianist movement; for textual basis it laid special stress on the *I Ching*, the *Mencius*, and the *Chung yung*. On the whole, Neo-Confucianism succeeded, to a considerable extent, in achieving its purpose, namely, to surmount the difficulties in the doctrines and practice of Buddhism and to amplify the teachings and re-establish the authority of Confucianism in Chinese life and society.

Li versus hsin, or principle versus mind

Trend
toward
quietism
and
subjective
idealism

While combatting Buddhism and Taoism, Neo-Confucianism itself, particularly the Hsin Hsüeh, developed a marked trend toward quietism and subjective idealism. To the critics of this trend, the fall of China to the Manchus, who eliminated the Ming dynasty and set up the Ch'ing dynasty (1644–1911), was conclusive proof of the crippling decrepitude of the predominant ideological system. It was readily recalled that over against introspection and meditation—elements so much emphasized by the Neo-Confucian thinkers—what Confucius had urged was broad learning and social action. Manifesting the dual tendencies of striving for breadth of learning and insistence upon practicality of thought, the development of Confucianism in the Ch'ing dynasty might be viewed as a revolt against Neo-Confucianism and yet another attempted revival of the original teachings of Confucius.

Among the numerous Confucian scholars of the Ch'ing period, Yen Yüan (1635–1704) and Tai Chen (1724–77) deserve mention. Yen Yüan was dissatisfied with Neo-Confucian doctrines and insisted that there were no principles apart from things and that moral perfection could only be achieved through the full development of man's nature in the conduct of everyday life. Tai Chen carried the thinker-scholar tradition to its highest point in the Ch'ing dynasty. Being critical of the reliance on introspection and mysticism, Tai Chen taught that the truth or principles of things could only be found in things and studied objectively. He himself employed methods of careful observation and analysis and attempted to get confirmation of his results by others. The school of critical scholarship of the Ch'ing dynasty is known as the Han Hsüeh, and Tai Chen stands as the representative of the best traditions of the school.

MODERN CONFUCIANISM

The
challenge
of
modernity

China's contact with the modern West has opened China's eyes even more than China's doors. The series of military defeats since the 19th century brought about a national awakening and drastic cultural changes. The time-honoured civil-service examination system was abolished in 1905, and modern schools were established in its place. Modern school textbooks at first supplemented the Confucian Classics and eventually replaced them in the school curriculum. Western ideas were introduced and a wide range of Western works was translated. The popular attitude was expressed by the slogan: Chinese culture for the basic conduct of life and Western knowledge for dealing with practical affairs.

In regard to the status of Confucianism, there were minority groups who advocated extreme positions in opposite directions. On the one hand, conservative Confucian scholars led by K'ang Yu-wei made an attempt to have Confucianism established as the state religion at the time of the founding of the republic. On the other hand, radical reformists in the early 1920s worked for the uprooting of Confucianism under their war cry, "Down with Confucius & Co.!" Neither movement lasted very long or amounted to anything important.

Sun Yat-sen, father of the republican revolution, tried to combine the best from the Chinese heritage with the wisdom of the West in formulating his political platform, as embodied in his Three Principles of the People. His "five powers" government organization plan provided for the revival of the civil-service examination and the imperial censorate systems (whereby official censors admonished a ruler when he did wrong), so long identified with Confucian principles and practices. For his final political goal, Sun Yat-sen spoke of the "World as an All-People Community," a quotation from the ancient Confucian text on the "age of Grand Harmony," referred to above. Although the semi-annual services held at the Confucian temples and the study of Confucian Classics were suspended in 1928, the Chinese people did not forget their Supreme Sage and Foremost Teacher. When a Teachers' Day was established in 1934, the date was made September 28, Confucius' birthday. The birthday of Confucius has been celebrated by the Nationalist government at Taiwan with an elaborate service at the Confucian temple in the last several years.

It is also notable that the majority of contemporary Chinese philosophers represent, in one sense or another, a revival of Confucianism. Fung Yu-lan has spoken of his own system as Neo-Neo-Confucianism. T'ang Chun-i has written voluminously on Confucian thought as a system of idealistic humanism. Liang Su-ming's studies of the influence and function of Confucian ideals in traditional Chinese society have attracted many admirers and followers. Communist rule in China has put an end to all free inquiry and established Karl Marx's system of dialectical materialism as the state philosophy.

Basic concepts of Confucianism

THE SOCIETAL STRESS

Tao and
its
application
to
individual
and social
life

Throughout its long course of development, the basic concepts of Confucianism have remained intact and constituted the molding force of Chinese life and culture. Central to Confucianism is the concept of tao, which is basic to all systems of Chinese philosophy and not exclusively identified with Taoism. That there is a final and absolute principle underlying the universe is a deep conviction, bordering on religious belief, held by Confucius and the Confucianists throughout the ages. Referred to as tao, Heaven, or Mandate of Heaven almost interchangeably, this principle is not transcendent or mystical but has a moral quality and belongs to this world. An individual cultivates himself to achieve tao or the Mandate of Heaven, and his talent and virtue are in turn made available for service to his fellowmen so that tao may prevail in the world. Thus the Confucian idea of tao is primarily a way of action.

The celebrated passage in the Li chi, sometimes referred to as the Confucian Utopia, begins with the following pronouncement: "When the age of the Great Tao prevailed, the world was a community of all people. Men of virtue and talent were upheld and mutual confidence and goodwill were cultivated." Unfortunately, such an age of grand harmony belongs to the days gone by, and the best hope now lies in the age of minor prosperity. Even to attain this level of the second best, the leadership and effort of great rulers are needed, so that "Jen is upheld as an ideal and courtesy is exalted, that the common people may be led to the cardinal virtues." Based on the teachings of Confucius and Mencius, the theory of government developed eventually by the Confucianists might be reduced to the following tenets: that the state exists for the sake of the people and not vice versa; that the ruler is expected to be mindful of the material and the spiritual welfare of the people; that administrative emphasis is to be placed on man rather than law; that government personnel should be selected on the basis of virtue and talent, and, therefore, education should be diffused; that the emperor should have a humane heart and an exemplary character; and that against a wicked emperor the people have the right to revolt.

The family
as paradigmatic
social
group

In the Confucian society, the family stands in the centre and serves as a bridge between the state and the individual. The family in China is not only the primary social group but also the prototype of all social organization. The term for emperor in Chinese is Son of Heaven; the local magistrate is addressed by his charges as "parent-official," and good friends become sworn brothers. The individual achieves his inner stature as well as his social status through his participation in the social process and his contribution to society, and the family offers the earliest and most favourable opportunity for this lifelong course of development. The properly cultivated individual is prepared for regulating the family, then governing the state, and, finally, bringing peace to the world.

The best known statement of the Confucian ideal subsisting between the individual and society is found in the Ta hsüeh. The relationship is clearly outlined in eight steps, of which four steps concern the inward process for the cultivation of the individual and three steps concern the outward extension from the individual to society—first the family, then the state, finally, the whole world. Significantly, the passage concludes with the injunction: "From Emperor down to the common people, all, without exception, must consider cultivation of the individual character as the root." One of the outstanding characteristics in Confucian social thought is the emphasis placed on obligations rather than rights and prerogatives of the individual in relation to society. And the one basic social obligation common to all men is the cultivation of one's character. The relation of the individual to society is here envisaged not in terms of a collection of disparate atomistic units to form an aggregate but in terms of a continuing permeation of the individual character throughout the ever-broadening circles of society.

THE HUMAN IDEAL

The Confucian ideal for the individual is sometimes described as "Sageness within and kingliness without," He aspires to be both a man of enlightenment and a man of affairs. There is a sense of identification of the sage with the universe, according to Confucian teaching, but the identification is here achieved by way of society and not in spite of it. In fact, it is in the fulfillment of the social responsibilities that the individual realizes his complete personal fulfillment. The interdependence and cohesion between the individual and society, so prominent in Confucian philosophy, come as necessary corollaries from the basic concepts of the ideal individual and the good society.

Learning, the "golden rule," and self-examination Personal cultivation begins with learning. It is with good reason that the *Lun yü* opens with the following saying of the Master: "To learn and to relearn again, isn't it a great pleasure?" Reminiscing about his own lifelong course of cultivation, Confucius identified the starting point thus: "At 15 I set my heart on learning." Education, teachers, and even books have always been accorded great respect and attention in China. Confucius was the first professional teacher of China, and he is revered as the "Supreme Sage and Foremost Teacher."

When properly understood and pursued, however, learning goes hand in hand with practice. The famous "golden rule" pronounced by Confucius came in answer to an inquiry by a pupil concerning conduct. The dialogue runs as follows:

> Tzu Kung asked: "Is there any one word that can serve as a principle for the conduct of life?" Confucius said: "Perhaps the word 'reciprocity': Do not do to others what you would not want others to do to you."

In addition to learning and practice, personal cultivation requires reflection, or meditation. In the *Lun Yü* there is recorded the remark by one of Confucius' immediate disciples, "I daily examine myself on three points" (honesty in business transactions, sincerity in relations with friends, and mastery and practice of teachers' instructions). Later, Mencius said: "He who has exhaustively searched his mind knows his nature. Knowing his nature, he knows Heaven." Present in Confucianism at all stages of its development, the element of self-examination, or looking inward, reached its high point in Neo-Confucianism. To a considerable extent, the criticism directed against Neo-Confucianism by the Ch'ing dynasty scholars was that Buddhist infiltration had resulted in an indulgence of quietism and a negligence of the element of action taught in Classical Confucianism.

An individual cultivates himself to become a superior man and then a sage. While social service and participation are essential to the perfection of the individual, the measure of the development of his character comes from his inner sense of personal integrity and dignity. Confucius said: "The commander of the forces of a large state may be carried off, but the will of even a common man cannot be taken from him." And: "When internal examination discovers nothing wrong, what is there to be anxious about, what is there to fear?" Both the *Mencius* and *Hsün-tzu* texts contain eloquent passages on the "great man" or "perfect man." The character of integrity and dignity of the properly cultivated individual gives him a sense of confidence and serenity. His life is not affected by the fortunes of the day but ordered through self-control and in accordance with an inner frame of reference.

The Chinese insistence on the importance of man antedates Confucius and Confucianism but has been greatly reinforced by the Confucian system. Man is so important that he is often spoken of in the same breath with Heaven and earth to form a triad. It is perhaps no exaggeration to say that among all major world civilizations the Chinese have laid the most emphasis on the cosmic importance of man. The Confucian type of humanism, however, is humanism with a positive rather than a negative emphasis. With little reference to the supernatural, the orientation here, however, does not consist in prying man loose from the domination of God; *i.e.*, humanism as revolt against theism. Rather, it consists in elevating man above animality and toward the status of the superior man, the sage—like magnetism, attracting all that is good and useful. Confucianism has become synonymous with the Chinese genius. This way of life some have called idealistic humanism, others, spiritualistic humanism. Insistence on the importance of man

THE VALUE OF TRADITION AND AUTHORITY

By the time Confucianism was founded, Chinese civilization had already reached a high level of development. A number of the elements of Confucianism might be regarded as elaborations of ancient Chinese tradition. The authority of this tradition is couched in the exemplary character of the sage-kings and the corpus of the Classics, to both of which Confucius showed due deference. He even spoke of himself as "a transmitter and not an innovator."

As much as Confucius respected tradition, he took great risks in coming forward with dangerous thoughts and novel practices. At a time when learning was a special privilege confined to the young noblemen only, he kept an open-door school, saying: "In education there is no discrimination." While retaining the term *chün-tzu*, meaning literally "prince's son," he so drastically altered its connotation that it has since come to mean the "superior man." The regard for tradition and authority by the Confucianists throughout the ages must be understood in the light of the example of Confucius. While a staunch supporter of order and continuity in society, Confucianism was no advocate of stagnancy and the status quo. In its long course of development, Confucianism has adapted and addressed itself to changing situations. It has kept drawing new blood and thus has kept from becoming anemic.

Influence of Confucianism

CONFUCIANISM AND CHINESE CULTURE

The Confucian pattern of humanistic culture has probably influenced the lives of more people over the ages than any of the other ways of life the world has known. Primarily a code of ethics and a system of philosophy, Confucianism has left its mark on Chinese politics and government, family and society, and art and literature. In a certain sense, Confucianism even functions as a religion in the Chinese community.

In art and literature Confucianism has exercised both a positive and a negative influence. There is a distinct note of emphasis on the aesthetic side of life in the teachings of Confucius. The Master said: "Personal cultivation begins with poetry, is made firm by rules of ceremonials, and is perfected by music." Efforts in literary and artistic pursuits, however, must be made with a definite and clear objective, namely, the enhancement of the *tao*. Eventually there was developed the thesis, "Literature is to be the vehicle of the *Tao*." In the history of Chinese literature, the "message vehicle" thesis has become a battleground in an intermittent partisan warfare, with the moralistic Classicist (Confucian) literati as its defenders and the Taoist romanticists, or nature poets, as its opponents. An outstanding leader of the "message vehicle" literary movement was Han Yü (768–824) of the T'ang dynasty literati, the leading Chinese essayist of all time. Bearing the title, "On the Origin of the *Tao*"—*i.e.*, on the Confucian way—Han Yü's most celebrated essay is so overflowing with "message" that it might be quite appropiately considered an example of Confucian homiletics. By the same token, "messageless" literature is considered a waste of time and talent; plays and novels are accepted if they promote the Confucian virtues and Influence on art and literature rejected if they disseminate knowledge about sex and outlaws and thereby contribute to immorality. Understandably, Chinese novels, even the greatest among them, have been written and published under pseudonyms.

Similarly, art and music are expected to purify and harmonize the emotions and not to excite and perturb them. Popular music and dance have seen meagre development and become one of the sadly neglected aspects of Chinese culture, at least partly because Confucius upheld classical music and denounced what he considered lewd music. From the modern standpoint, Confucianism, particularly during the Neo-Confucianism stage of its development, has suffered from an overmoralistic and restrictive tendency. Creative artists, such as writers and painters, often resort to Taoism for their inspiration or combine the spirit of Taoism with that of Confucianism.

A Confucian scholar is expected to spend at least a part of his life in public service. After a certain period, he is likely to withdraw from officialdom and return to his farm and cottage, disillusioned with public life and contented with private existence. Some gifted writers and poets have produced their best works in retirement, while others devoted themselves to the instruction of the young men of the community. Always they are respected as scholars and looked up to as examples of personal conduct and leaders of public opinion. The combination of Confucian–Taoist influence on the life of an individual follows the same pattern as its influence on the Chinese race. In times of peace and prosperity Confucianism flourishes, while Taoism is appreciated when there is disorder or disenchantment.

CONFUCIANISM AND FOREIGN CULTURES

Influence on Korea and Japan

The influence of Confucianism has been strong also on China's neighbours. Korea and Japan, for instance, have adopted Confucian ethics, political theory, and legal and educational institutions in their national lives. Introduced into Korea some 2,000 years ago, Confucianism outranks Buddhism and compares with shamanism as a controlling force of Korean life and culture. In Korea today, Confucian temples are well kept and Confucian universities well attended.

The position of Confucianism in Japan is more complicated than in Korea. Since its introduction to Japan in the early medieval period, Confucianism has coexisted with Shintōism and Buddhism. Various emperors and princes have urged the nation to follow Confucian precepts, but Confucian ideas and institutions have been adopted only selectively. The Confucian virtue most emphasized was loyalty to the emperor, and the civil-service examinations, when conducted, were open not to everyone but only the nobility. For some time the Chu Hsi school of Neo-Confucianism has received special attention. Some enthusiastic followers of Chu Hsi have even tried to interpret Shintō in terms of the concept of the *li* of Chu Hsi. Japan's effort and success in modernization inevitably diminishes the position of Confucianism in its national life.

Marco Polo notwithstanding, the best source of information on China and Confucianism among the modern Europeans is to be traced to the Catholic missionaries who founded the modern Catholic mission in China in the early 17th century. Scholars themselves, these missionaries Latinized K'ung-fu-tzu into Confucius and Meng-tzu into Mencius and sent glowing reports about Confucian China to Europe. Some leading figures of Enlightenment Europe developed an overwhelming admiration for Confucian thought and letters. For instance, Gottfried Leibniz, the eminent 17th–18th-century German philosopher and mathematician, spoke of Confucian China with the deepest appreciation and gained some knowledge of the *I Ching* and the system of thought of Chu Hsi. While his theory of monadology suggests influence from Chu Hsi, his binary arithmetic stems from his studies of the *I Ching*. Voltaire was another admirer of China, and he was enchanted by the moral code of Confucius. Employing the theme of the Chinese drama *The Little Orphan of the House of Chao*, he wrote his own play, *Orphelin de la Chine*, and de-

Influence on Leibniz and Voltaire

scribed it as "the Morals of Confucius in five acts." Other men of letters in Europe who came under the influence of Confucian China included Goethe, the French Encyclopaedists, and Alexander Pope and Charles Lamb in England. Today Chinese studies are pursued by many students at many universities in the West. The cultural interest behind this development may be traced to such modern philosophers as John Dewey and Bertrand Russell, Ernest Francisco Fenelossa (an American Orientalist), and Ezra Pound, poet and translator of Confucian Classics.

BIBLIOGRAPHY. The only work devoted to Confucianism in English is the slender volume, WU-CHI LIU, *A Short History of Confucian Philosophy* (1955). However, because of the great importance of Confucianism in Chinese philosophy and culture, all of the general works in this field assign much space to Confucianism. The following are particularly notable: FUNG YU-LAN, *A History of Chinese Philosophy*, 2nd ed., 2 vol. (Eng. trans. 1952–53); *A Short History of Chinese Philosophy* (1948); WING-TSIT CHAN (comp. and trans.), *A Source Book in Chinese Philosophy* (1963; paperback, 1969); and W.T. DE BARY, WING-TSIT CHAN, and B. WATSON (comps.), *Sources of Chinese Tradition* (1960). An excellent work dealing with Confucianism as a Chinese national institution is J.K. SHRYOCK, *The Origin and Development of the State Cult of Confucius* (1966).

(Y.P.M.)

Confucianism, History of

This article presents the history of Confucianism, the characteristic philosophy and ethical teaching of China, from its archaic prelude (before the 12th century BC) down to present times.

Among the various Chinese schools of thought, Confucianism was the first in the field and at all periods successfully defended its claim to represent the orthodox tradition. Chinese religion and thought had many other aspects, but Confucianism can rightly claim to be regarded as representing the central core.

Although Confucianism was not a missionary religion, it spread to those east Asian countries that borrowed their literate culture from China. To a greater or lesser degree, Korea, Japan, and Vietnam adopted Confucian ethico-political mores to underpin political authority, especially in the centuries following the Neo-Confucian revival of Sung times (960–1279 AD).

Origins of Confucianism. Confucianism looked back for its origins to the institutions of the "Former Kings"; that is, the predynastic sage emperors Yao and Shun (legendary figures ascribable to the 24th and 23rd centuries BC) and the founders of the first three dynasties, Hsia, Shang, and Chou (c. 23rd–3rd centuries BC). Of these only the founders of Chou can be regarded as definitely historical, but archaeology has confirmed the existence of the Shang dynasty (c. 1766–c. 1122 BC); and some ingredients of later Chinese religion, such as the worship of ancestors, especially those of the royal family, were already present. On the other hand, Chinese traditional accounts did not prepare the archaeologists for other features of Shang society, such as the extensive use of human sacrifice.

Heaven, as the supreme deity, and the Son of Heaven, as the supreme ruler on earth, are widely held to have been concepts alien to Shang culture and to have been introduced at the time of the Chou conquest (c. 1122 BC). If so, they were projected back by Chou on to Shang. For the Chou kings did not claim their position by divine descent as the emperors of Japan later did. They believed that the previous dynasty, Shang, had once held the Mandate of Heaven but had lost it through a decline in their virtue and especially through the wickedness of their last ruler. As a result of this, the Mandate had passed to Chou, who might in turn lose it if they relaxed their vigilance and fell into immoral ways. This idea of Heaven's Mandate remained the basic political conception in China for many centuries and was central to Confucian political thought.

The Chou kings were able to exert some degree of control over their empire for several centuries, but in 771 BC they were forced by barbarian attacks to move their capi-

Heaven, the Son of Heaven, and the Mandate of Heaven

tal eastward to Lo-yang. Thereafter, though the surviving line of Chou kings continued to be recognized in name, real power passed into the hands of the rulers of the great feudal states, many of whom claimed descent from the Chou house.

Confucius (551–479 BC), coming at the end of this period, regarded it as one of political, social, and moral decline and took it as his mission to bring the men of his time, especially the rulers, back to the pristine virtues of early Chou. Though the written sources do not make it obvious, it must also have been a period of vigorous economic growth, resulting from such innovations as the use of iron for agricultural implements (not yet for weapons) and the use of metallic coinage. The strains that were becoming apparent in the old feudal order seem to have been more the result of the creation of new wealth and the consequent loosening of the bonds of a rigidly stratified society than of simple moral decline.

Confucius' response was a conservative one; *i.e.*, he advocated the restoration and renovations of old institutions rather than creation of new ones. But in so doing he rationalized and idealized these institutions in ways that had revolutionary potentialities for the future.

Emergence of Confucianism. Confucianism was known in China as the school of the *ju*. The *ju* (now equivalent to "scholars") seem to have been professional experts on ritual and music who were employed at feudal courts. Confucius was known for his learning in these matters and is said to have held various offices in his native state of Lu. In the latter part of his life, however, he devoted himself to teaching the principles of morality that ought to be followed in government and social relations generally.

As part of this activity as a teacher, he is traditionally said to have edited the *Wu Ching* ("Five Classics"); *I Ching* ("Classic of Changes"); *Shih Ching* ("Classic of Poetry"); *Shu Ching* ("Classic of History"); *Li chi* ("Collection of Rituals"); and *Ch'un Ch'iu* ("Spring and Autumn" Annals). Though modern scholarship casts doubt on the literal truth of this, the texts were undoubtedly the peculiar preserve of the Confucianists from an early stage.

The Confucian school early accumulated a traditional body of sayings attributed to the Master that were eventually written down and became known as the *Lun yü* ("Conversations"). This book provides the most immediate source for Confucius' teaching and personality. Confucius is not found developing arguments or attempting to refute contrary doctrines. He was content to enunciate his views on his own authority, illustrating them from time to time with references to historical and contemporary events. His basic view of society was conservative. He valued hierarchy and due observance of traditional rituals and distinctions. Yet he emphasized the inward human values rather than the outward forms, and, in being willing to take pupils from any walk of life, he was helping to undermine the rigidly stratified feudal society that was already breaking down. Confucius is said to have had 70 (or 72) principal disciples who carried on his teaching after his death. Apart from a half dozen or so whose names recur frequently in the *Lun yü*, practically nothing is known about them, and even those are shadowy figures.

The next Confucian teacher of major importance is Mencius, who appeared in the latter part of the 4th century BC, at a time when the feudal order had fallen into still deeper disintegration. The fiction of Chou suzerainty, which still provided the framework of a universal order in the time of Confucius, had ceased to command even lip service.

Mencius appears in the book that bears his name as one of a class of itinerant philosophers who went from country to country trying to persuade rulers that they had the answer to success in the endless struggles between the states. For Mencius the key to unifying the world was to practice the kingly way—*i.e.*, government by compassion and virtue rather than self-seeking guile and reliance on force. A ruler who sincerely and wholeheartedly did this, he maintained, would so win the hearts of

the people everywhere that they would abandon their own inferior rulers and flock to him, enabling him to restore the unified Kingship once exercised by Chou.

Whereas Confucius had been content to enunciate his moral precepts in pithy apothegms, Mencius had to engage in disputations against rival doctrines, especially the utilitarian creed of the Moists (followers of Mo-tzu, a 5th-century BC philosopher) and the individualistic teachings of Yang Chu, a forerunner of the Taoists. Among the problems that Mencius discussed that were to occupy Confucian thinkers for centuries was that of human nature, which he maintained was innately good. He based his view on the observation that men were naturally disposed to sympathetic responses. He believed that evil actions arose from allowing this innate sympathetic disposition to become corrupted.

In the century that immediately followed Mencius' death, the struggle for supremacy among the various Chinese states grew ever more ruthless and intense. The great Confucian thinker of this period was Hsün-tzu, who, as befitted the age in which he lived, taught a much more pessimistic version of Confucianism than that of Mencius. Not only do his teachings have affinities with those of the Legalists, but two of the leading Legalist ministers of the Ch'in dynasty (221–206 BC), Han-fei-tzu and Li Ssu, were actually his pupils. Hsün-tzu strongly opposed the Mencian doctrine of the goodness of human nature. He argued that since all men were born with desires and since the means of satisfying those desires were limited, contention and strife were inevitable. The only way to prevent this was to impose a proper ordering of society from above. Hsün-tzu did not go all the way with the Legalists, who drew the further conclusion that the ruler was free to manipulate his people with rewards and punishments to suit himself. He remained an orthodox Confucian in that he believed in a universal moral order embodied in the teachings and institutions of the ancient sages. His rationalism about traditional religious ideas went much further than his predecessors. Heaven, which in the sayings of Confucius is a moral agent and at times almost a personal divinity, has become entirely a naturalistic concept in Hsün-tzu's writings.

Confucianism as the state orthodoxy of the Han Empire. The unification of the Chinese community of states by the Ch'in dynasty in 221 BC brought to an end the period of free philosophical inquiry. Ch'in had already adopted the harsh principles of the Legalists within its own borders (the far western states of Ch'in in the Wei River Valley) and now proceeded to apply them to the whole country. The Confucian school was irreconcilably opposed to many of these measures and suffered in consequence, especially as a result of the proscription of Confucian books.

The First Emperor's new order was short-lived, however. In 207 BC, three years after his death, disorders broke out all over the country. After a long period of civil war the empire was restored by the new dynasty of Han (206 BC–AD 220), which inherited the framework of Ch'in's institutions and eventually completed Ch'in's revolutionary demolition of the old feudal order and its replacement by a centralized bureaucracy but which did so more gradually and with accommodations and compromises toward earlier traditions that permitted a resurgence of Confucianism.

It is recorded that Kao Tsu, the first Han emperor, paid his respects to Confucius at the K'ung family's ancestral temple during a visit to Shantung in 195 BC. On another occasion, however, he expressed his contempt for the Confucian literati by seizing the formal bonnet of one of them and urinating in it. For a long time Confucianism had to contend with other doctrines such as Legalism and Taoism and only gradually achieved its position as a state orthodoxy. Its victory occurred early in the reign of the emperor Wu (140–87 BC), when, at the instigation of a Confucian scholar, Tung Chung-shu, the adherents of non-Confucian schools were excluded from the body of *po-shih* ("erudites") officially attached to the court. At the same period a superior school (*t'ai hsüeh*, usually translated as "Imperial university") was established with a

Confucius and the school of the ju

Mencius and Hsün-tzu on human nature

Confucianism as the state orthodoxy

Confucian curriculum. Thereafter, a grounding in the Confucian Classics became not only the basis of all literary education but a necessary prerequisite for advancement in the bureaucracy.

Other features of the state support for Confucianism that began during the Han dynasty and were continued and developed in later times were the giving of honours to Confucius' descendants, the conferring of posthumous titles on Confucius and his disciples, and the official sponsorship of sacrifices at the K'ung ancestral temple and in schools.

In adapting itself to its new role as the ideology of the bureaucratic Han Empire, Confucianism absorbed into itself many other currents of thought that had become prominent in the previous two or three centuries, especially the cosmological speculations of the Yin and Yang and five elements theorists (see CONFUCIANISM). Tung Chung-shu was the man principally responsible for giving shape to this new eclectic Confucianism. According to this doctrine, Confucius was no longer regarded as a mere teacher but was called the uncrowned king and was elevated to the rank of the ancient sages Yao and Shun and the founders of the Hsia, Shang, and Chou dynasties.

Numerological speculation and interest in prognostication and divination continued to dominate Chinese thinking after Tung Chung-shu, reaching a kind of climax at the time of the usurpation of Wang Mang (AD 9–23) and the restoration of Han by the emperor Kuang Wu (AD 25–57). A reaction in favour of a more sober, rationalistic, and moralistic Confucianism, such as that of pre-Han times, had already set in before the fall of Western (or Former) Han (AD 8). This movement became known as the "Old Text" school, because it was also associated with the advocacy of its own recensions of certain Classical texts allegedly newly discovered during the Han period and written in the old form of script that had existed before the reforms instituted by the Ch'in dynasty. By contrast, the adherents of the current texts of the Classics written in the reformed script became known as the "New Text" school.

The "Old Text" school

Representative figures of the "Old Text" school were Yang Hsiung (c. 53 BC–AD 18) and Wang Ch'ung (AD 27–100?). Yang Hsiung's most important works are the *Fa-yen* ("Model Sayings"), a collection of moralistic aphorisms modelled on the *Lun yü*, and the *T'ai-hsüan ching* ("Classic of the Great Mystery"), modelled on the *I Ching* ("Classic of Changes"). Wang Ch'ung's great work, the *Lun-heng* ("Critical Essays"), is largely devoted to attacking popular superstitions and propounding a naturalistic interpretation of the world. Wang Ch'ung's thought, though rationalistic, is much influenced by Taoism, showing a trend that became stronger in other writers of the Later Han period.

The 2nd century AD was a time of deepening crisis in the Han Imperial system, culminating in AD 184 in a popular uprising led by a religious sect of Taoist inspiration known as the Yellow Turbans. Power passed from the Han court into the hands of military leaders, one of whom finally supplanted the Han dynasty in AD 220. A century later an uprising of the Hsiung-nu, nomadic tribesmen who had been allowed to settle inside the Great Wall, forced the Chinese court to take refuge south of the Yangtze and inaugurated a long period in which China was divided between barbarian states in the north and successive Chinese dynasties in the south. The collapse of the unity of "All-under-Heaven," which had been established by the Ch'in and Han dynasties, was accompanied by disillusionment with Confucianism and a revival of interest in other types of thought, especially various brands of Taoism. These in turn prepared the way for the introduction of Buddhism, which was brought to China by Indian and Central Asian missionaries from the 1st century AD onward and which, after slow beginnings, increasingly came to dominate intellectual life in both north and south (see TAOISM).

Confucianism during the time of Buddhist ascendancy. The prominence of Taoism and Buddhism in the period after the fall of Han did not mean that Confucianism disappeared. Confucian Classics remained the foundation of all literate culture, and the forms of political life remained Confucian. Further, the restoration of lasting unity by the Sui (581–618) and T'ang (618–907) dynasties inevitably gave a powerful stimulus to Confucianism, since it was felt to be a restoration of the Han Empire, for which Confucianism had been the ideological prop. A major enterprise of the early T'ang decades was the preparation of a definitive, official edition of the *Wu Ching*. Confucian studies were the basis of the competitive examinations for government, instituted under Sui and further developed under T'ang, which soon became the most prestigious beginning for an official career.

It was, nevertheless, some time before Confucianism became once more a leading intellectual force. Taoism had a particular appeal to the T'ang emperors because of their claim to be descendants of Lao-tzu, the legendary founder of Taoism, and Buddhism, which had by now become thoroughly assimilated into Chinese culture, continued to compete with Confucianism for the adherence of the intellectuals. Ironically, the very success of Buddhism in adapting itself to Chinese culture was a factor in its ultimate eclipse. New philosophical schools began to appear that were not simply derivative from Indian schools but were ones in which Chinese teachers independently developed their own interpretations and syntheses. Ch'an (from Sanskrit *dhyāna*, "meditation"; Japanese Zen) was akin to native Taoism. More immediately important in relation to Confucianism were schools such as Hua-yen and T'ien-t'ai, which, while taking one scripture as representing the highest form of enlightenment, did not reject other schools but arranged them in a hierarchy as possessing imperfect and partial aspects of the truth. By the second half of the 8th century there were adherents of T'ien-t'ai seeking to comprehend Confucian texts, such as the *Ta hsüeh*, the *Chung yung*, and the appendices to the *I Ching*, into their syncretic scheme. From this it was only a step for Confucians to try to build their own metaphysical system on such texts not as representing an imperfect revelation of Buddhist truths but as an alternative of Buddhism.

Confucianism in the T'ang dynasty

The most important thinker showing this tendency during T'ang was Li Ao (died c. 844), whose *Fu-hsing shu* ("Essay on Returning to Nature") foreshadows many features of Sung Neo-Confucianism. Han Yü (768–824) was less important as a thinker but was a brilliant propagandist who advocated, on the one hand, literary reform as a means of restoring the purity of the Chinese tradition and, on the other hand, rejection of unorthodox teachings, particularly the foreign religion of Buddhism. Han Yü boldly assumed the mantle of a teacher of the Way and sought to re-establish the line of transmission from Mencius and Hsün-tzu, which had lapsed during the Han dynasty. His polemical attacks on Buddhism, expressed in brilliant prose, probably helped create the atmosphere that led to the great suppression of the Buddhist monasteries in 845, though economic factors and the emperor's predilection for Taoism also played a part.

Resurgence of the Confucian tradition. *Emergence of Neo-Confucianism.* The Sung dynasty (960–1279) was militarily weak compared to T'ang and confined within narrower borders. Nevertheless, the indigenous growth of Chinese civilization, stimulated by such developments as the invention of block printing, the circulation of paper money, and the use of coal for smelting iron, reached a higher level of sophistication than ever before. Political controversies were rife as statesmen grappled with the problems of adapting inherited institutions to new and more complex conditions. Their arguments drew on and reinterpreted the traditional sources of political wisdom found in texts of the Chou and Han periods, and the writings of such reformist politicians as Fan Chung-yen (989–1052) and Wang An-shih (1021–1086) and their opponents represent a practical side of revitalized Confucianism. Outside the political sphere literary and historical scholarship of all kinds flourished, and the notebooks of such men as Shen Kua are characterized by a wide-ranging curiosity into fields such as mathematics and natural history, which were outside the range of interest of Chinese literati at other times.

The Neo-Confucian revival in the narrower sense is traditionally traced through a line of thinkers from Chou Tun-i (1017–73) through Shao Yung (1011–77), Chang Tsai (1020–77), the brothers Ch'eng I (1033–1107) and Ch'eng Hao (1032–85), and finally the great synthesizer Chu Hsi (1130–1200). These thinkers carried on the work of Li Ao in constructing a Confucian metaphysical and ethical system that would rival and then supplant that of the Buddhists.

Chou Tun-i and Shao Yung, who are perhaps better regarded as precursors of the Neo-Confucian movement than as its founders, were both influenced by modes of thought that had been current in Taoist circles in late T'ang, and they concentrated on cosmological speculations. Chang Tsai was also much concerned with developing a metaphysical system based on the complementary principles of Yin and Yang.

The Ch'eng brothers brought the movement to maturity by shifting the emphasis away from cosmology and back to human affairs. To Chang Tsai's concept of *ch'i,* literally "air" or "breath," Ch'eng I added the concept of *li,* "reason" or "pattern," to provide the complementary organizing principle underlying the rationality of both the world and the human mind. This brand of philosophy became known as Li Hsüeh, or Study of Reason. Ch'eng Hao, the elder brother, developed his philosophy along with Ch'eng I but had a somewhat different emphasis that in due course gave rise to a divergent branch of Neo-Confucianism known as Hsin Hsüeh, or Study of Mind.

A century later Chu Hsi gave definitive form to the philosophical system originated by Ch'eng I. According to Chu Hsi, moral self-cultivation was achieved through "the investigation of things," a phrase borrowed from the *Ta hsüeh.* This was interpreted to mean the study of the Classics and active involvement in everything connected with man in society. Though not an admonition to scientific study of the natural world, this slogan turned men outward toward their relations with their fellows and away from Buddhist and Taoist absorption with their inner life. The ceaselessly active and productive career of Chu Hsi himself, as a philosopher, commentator on the Classics, historian, and writer on a wide variety of subjects, as well as a teacher and government official, provides a model illustration of this ideal.

Chu Hsi's interpretation of Confucianism soon became orthodox, especially after the *Ssu shu* ("Four Books") with his commentaries became officially accepted as a basis for the civil service examinations. The *Ssu shu* consisted of the *Lun yü* and the *Mencius,* together with the *Ta hsüeh* and the *Chung yung,* two texts taken out of the *Li chi.* These works had been given special prominence from the beginning of the Neo-Confucian movement but were first published as a set by Chu Hsi.

In China the Neo-Confucian orthodoxy based on Chu Hsi lasted to the end of the empire (1911). It also spread to Japan and Korea, especially the latter, where it developed in a peculiarly rigid and intolerant way, nearly extinguishing Buddhism. The stultifying effect of such indoctrination was far removed from the true spirit of Chu Hsi. Nevertheless, there were aspects of his teaching, such as the great emphasis on loyalty, that fitted very well with the interests of absolutism, and the use to which his work was put by the state was not entirely an ironic accident.

Continued development of Neo-Confucianism. Though the Mongols, who ruled over the whole of China from 1279 to 1368, were not at first favourably disposed to the Chinese literary tradition, they eventually reinstituted the examination system as a means of recruiting officials, and it was under them that the *Ssu shu* first became officially adopted for this purpose. Under the Ming dynasty (1368–1644), though the examination system was more than ever before a means of upward mobility into the ruling elite, the curriculum became increasingly lifeless and stereotyped. Those who rebelled against this ideological straitjacket turned to the alternative current of Neo-Confucianism, the Hsin Hsüeh.

A contemporary of Chu Hsi, Lu Hsiang-shan (1139–1193) had already developed the idea that the true path

of self-cultivation lay not in study of external things—*i.e.,* texts, as Chu Hsi maintained—but in introspection designed to bring out what was eternally present in one's own mind. This line of thought was taken up and deepened and extended by Wang Yang-ming (Wang Shou-jen; 1472–1529), a great statesman and general, as well as a philosopher, who exemplified in his own career his principle of the unity of thought and action. Wang, like Lu, identified man's individual mind with universal mind and believed that the way to moral perfection for a man of any station in life down to the humblest peasant lay in discovering his innate "good knowledge," which was constantly in danger of being obscured by his selfish desires and rationalizations.

Wang's philosophy, propagated in the private academies that flourished in spite of official attempts at suppression, branched out in various directions. Some treated innate knowledge as something very much like the Christian conscience. Others regarded it in a more mystical way, as a source of insights that transcended the ethical norms of ordinary society. This latter tendency developed into the so-called Wild-cat Ch'an (Zen) school, which scandalized both contemporaries and later critics by its flouting of social conventions, but which in Li Chih (1527–1602) produced a highly individual and individualistic thinker who has been called the greatest heretic and iconoclast in Chinese history.

The decline and eventual collapse of the Ming dynasty led to a revulsion against the individualistic tendencies of the Wang Yang-ming school and a return to a Confucianism devoted to reforming political and social ills. The Tung-lin Academy, established in 1604 in Wusih, became the centre for philosophical discussions devoted to moral reform. Though the Tung-lin scholars showed great courage in the face of ruthless attacks by powerful eunuchs, they lacked a practical program, and the next generation produced more radical critics who rejected Neo-Confucianism and advocated a return to interpretations of the Classics based on the texts themselves and the commentaries of the Han period without the overlay of Sung philosophy, which they regarded as contaminated by Buddhist and Taoist elements.

Ku Yen-wu (1613–82) is usually regarded as the founder of the Han Hsüeh, or school of Han learning. A Ming loyalist who refused to take office under the Manchus, he devoted his life to scholarship and to extensive travels all over China. He published voluminous studies on historical geography, epigraphy (inscriptions), and historical phonology (linguistic sound changes); and his notebooks contain insights based on study and personal observation on all sorts of topics relating to China's existing political and social institutions, as well as on historical matters. His scholarship was characterized by a critical, inductive method that had great influence on later scholars.

Another Ming loyalist who reacted to the change of dynasty with a critique of the Chinese Imperial system and attempted to find a solution for its ills was Huang Tsung-hsi (1610–95). He wrote a critical history of Ming philosophy and the *Ming-i tai-fang lu* ("A Plan for the Prince"), an important work of political philosophy.

The following decades produced a galaxy of great names. In the strictly philosophical field, two of the most important are Yen Yüan (1635–1704) and Tai Chen (1723–77). Like other early Ch'ing dynasty thinkers (1644–1911), Yen stressed practicality as opposed to abstruse speculation. He rejected the Neo-Confucian dualism of *li,* "reason," and *ch'i,* "material force," regarding them as aspects of the same basic reality. Tai Chen, who was a noted mathematician and phonologist, as well as a philosopher, followed the same line. Against the institutionists he asserted the necessity of publicly verifiable proof as a test of knowledge, and against the moralists he asserted the naturalness and legitimacy of human desires.

The impact of Western thought on Confucianism. The achievements of the Han Hsüeh and of other philosophical movements during the Ch'ing dynasty demonstrated the continued vitality of the native Chinese tradition up to the eve of the massive European assaults of the 19th

Side notes (left column):

Metaphysical and ethical aspects

Neo-Confucian orthodoxy

Side notes (right column):

Reaction against the Wang Yang-ming school

century; yet these achievements were restricted within limits imposed by the basic assumptions of the Chinese world view and political system, which remained unquestioned in the absence of any alternative, external standpoint. Buddhism had once provided such a challenge with fructifying results, but later contacts with foreign religions—including Zoroastrianism, Manichaeism, and Nestorian Christianity during T'ang and Manichaeism, Nestorian and Catholic Christianity, and Islām under the Mongols—had had little or no discernible effect on Chinese intellectual life. Even the Jesuit missions to China in late Ming and early Ch'ing times, so fruitful in their influence on European intellectuals, such as Leibniz and Voltaire—through making Chinese thought and culture known to them—had only a superficial impact on Chinese scholars, who remained immersed in their own tradition and felt little curiosity about the learning of the Western "barbarians." All this changed when Chinese self-confidence was at last seriously challenged by European military, mercantile, and missionary penetration beginning with the Opium War (1839–42). The Taiping Rebellion (1850–64) and other internal disorders added a further threat of internal collapse, which, in Tseng Kuo-fan (1811–72), the Chinese general and statesman who more than any other was responsible for saving the dynasty from the Taipings, called forth a final effort to apply traditional Confucian principles of morality and statecraft. Tseng was not only a man of action but also a scholar, who in his writings tried to reconcile Sung Neo-Confucianism with the Han Hsüeh.

The material challenge of the West

By the last quarter of the 19th century, however, the intellectual as well as material challenge of the West could no longer be ignored. K'ang Yu-wei (1858–1927) sought the basis for his reforming ideas in a new interpretation of Confucianism but incorporated ideas derived from the West and sought to make Confucianism into a universal religion that could meet the challenge of Christianity on its own ground. K'ang proclaimed his allegiance to the "New Text" school of Han times and developed a radical theory that certain classical texts had been deliberately forged by the "Old Text" school, hence obscuring the true nature of Confucius' teaching.

With the help of the Kuang-hsü emperor, K'ang and his followers came to power briefly in 1898 and inaugurated the so-called Hundred Days of Reform, designed to modernize China (as Japan had been already modernized in the Meiji Restoration) and to enable it to resist foreign encroachments. The resumption of personal power by the Dowager Empress brought the reform movement to an end and forced K'ang and his pupil Liang Ch'i-ch'ao to flee to Japan. K'ang remained a monarchist and became increasingly conservative in his old age, but his disciple Liang Ch'i-ch'ao became a leading publicist, advocating reform and attempting to introduce Western culture and to reinterpret Chinese culture in the light of it.

The Nationalist Revolution of 1911 swept away the Imperial system and with it the institutional framework of Confucianism. In the early years of the ensuing republic efforts were made by conservatives to maintain the state sacrifices to Confucius and his disciples, but attempts to have Confucianism recognized as the state religion conflicted both with the new idea of China as a multinational secular republic and with the views of traditionalists who did not look on Confucianism as a religion. With the upsurge of the New Culture Movement after 1916, aimed at modernizing all aspects of China's intellectual life, direct attacks were made on Confucius and Confucianism as obstacles in the way of China's modernization by Hu Shih and other scholars of the new generation. The most virulent attacks came from Ch'en Tu-hsiu, who later helped to found the Chinese Communist Party. Conservative defenders of China's Confucian heritage were not lacking, and vigorous polemics were carried on in the literary periodicals through the early 1920s. The victory of the conservative wing of the Nationalists under Chiang Kai-shek after 1926 was accompanied by a reassertion of official favour for various traditional aspects of Chinese civilization. Chiang advocated Confucian ethical prin-

Chiang Kai-shek and Confucianism

ciples as part of his program for moral regeneration known as the New Life Movement (1934–37), and Confucius' birthday was made a national holiday, Scholar's Day, which is still observed on Taiwan. The trend of social evolution, however, continued to undermine what was left of Confucian ideology, even when it was not subject to the direct attacks of liberals and Marxists.

The end of the empire at last enabled Chinese scholars to get outside the Confucian shell in which they had been so long encased, and they could begin to reappraise their history and other aspects of their cultural heritage from a more detached standpoint. Ku Chien-kang, a historian, took the lead in critical re-examination of ancient texts and the traditions they enshrined. The results of archaeology added new and unexpected dimensions to China's past. Examples drawn from other civilizations led Chinese scholars to look with fresh and sympathetic eyes on popular aspects of their own culture, such as the theatre and the novel, which had previously been despised by the Confucian-trained intellectuals. In the purely philosophical field, there were also those who, while equipping themselves with a grounding in Western philosophy, tried to create new philosophical systems on a foundation derived from their Confucian heritage. Yang Hsiung-li developed a new philosophical system based on the idealist side of Neo-Confucianism, while Fung Yu-lan did the same for the rationalist side.

Confucianism today. The victory of Communism in 1949 and the Cultural Revolution of 1966 have meant a break with tradition that is far more profound than anything that has happened in China since the unification by the Ch'in dynasty in 221 BC. Confucianism, whether as a state cult or as an organized system of belief, is now a thing of the past in its homeland, though it still has professed adherents in the latter sense on Taiwan and elsewhere outside the Chinese People's Republic (e.g., among Chinese living in Southern Asia and North America). For all of its tremendous novelty, it is certain that the new China that emerges from these events will contain threads of continuity with its past, including the ideology that dominated its high culture for so many centuries. Such elements of continuity can be found in the spirit and practice of Chinese Communism, with its moral fervour and its emphasis on the subordination of private to public good, as well as in certain aspects of Mao Tse-tung's exegesis of Marxism. How important such effects of Confucian outlook and attitudes will be in the future it is impossible to predict. Meanwhile, in summing up the past, one can certainly say that, both as the practical ideology of the Chinese ruling class for more than 2,000 years and in the philosophical elaboration that it has received over the centuries, as well as in countless other ways in which it has influenced Chinese civilization, Confucianism has made a contribution of enduring value not only to China but to mankind.

Communism and Confucianism

BIBLIOGRAPHY. CHARLES O. HUCKER, *China: A Critical Bibliography* (1962); and WING-TSIT CHAN, *An Outline and Annotated Bibliography of Chinese Philosophy*, rev. ed. (1969), provide bibliographical coverage on the various aspects of the subject up to their dates of publication. For a general introduction to the history of Confucianism, see E.O. REISCHAUER, J.K. FAIRBANK, and A.M. CRAIG, *A History of East Asian Civilization*, 2 vol. (1960–65). A detailed technical account of the development of Chinese philosophy is found in FUNG YU-LAN, *A History of Chinese Philosophy*, 2nd ed., 2 vol. (Eng. trans., 1952–53). W.T. DE BARY, WING-TSIT CHAN, and B. WATSON (comps.), *Sources of Chinese Tradition* (1960), has a well-selected and introduced collection of translations from Confucian writings of all periods. Among recent studies on various aspects of Confucianism are the symposium volumes: D.S. NIVISON and A.F. WRIGHT (eds.), *Confucianism in Action* (1959); A.F. WRIGHT (ed.), *The Confucian Persuasion* (1960); A.F. WRIGHT and D.C. TWICHETT (eds.), *Confucian Personalities* (1962); and W.T. DE BARY et al., *Self and Society in Ming Thought* (1970). For the ceremonial and cult aspects of Confucianism under the empire, see J.K. SHRYOCK, *The Origin and Development of the State Cult of Confucius* (1966). Confucianism as it exists in the 20th century is discussed in WING-TSIT CHAN, *Religious Trends in Modern China* (1953).

(E.G.P.)

Confucian Texts, Classical

The Classical Confucian texts consist of 13 officially approved writings, all very ancient, that have in one way or another been associated with Confucius, China's greatest sage. Though the Chinese have also designated other works as classics (*ching*), the Confucian Classics are beyond doubt *the* Classics of China, for no other writings match their prestige or have had such a profound and lasting influence on Chinese life and education as have these famous books. The subject matter of the Confucian Classics is so diverse as to include, for example, texts on divination, ritual norms, ancient poetry, historical records, a dictionary, and the most reliable known source of information about the teachings of Confucius himself.

This article deals with various lists of Confucian Classics and with the authenticity, authorship, and literary style of the texts. It then explains the content and significance of the individual Classics and underscores the importance of the Classics in Chinese educational, political, social, and religious thought.

THE TEXTS IN GENERAL

China between 600 and 100 BC

Historical background. Before discussing the Classics themselves, it is necessary to look briefly at historical events that took place in China between the 6th and 1st centuries BC. Confucius lived from 551 to 479 BC, an era of great political and social unrest, and though he strove mightily to implement his ideas of reform, he had little personal success during his lifetime. His ideas, however, were sympathetically received by a select number of enthusiastic disciples (the Ju school), who, by conscientiously studying the ancient Classics that Confucius esteemed so highly and by preserving many oral traditions related to the Master, kept Confucian ideals competitive with other ideologies during the period of the Warring States (the last centuries of the Eastern Chou, approximately 481–221 BC). The short-lived Ch'in dynasty (221–206 BC) standardized writing, built the Great Wall of China, and welded powerful independent states into a unified empire for the first time in China's history. In a deliberate attempt to destroy Confucianism and all other thought that did not support absolute political power, the newly established government sanctioned the persecution of Confucian scholars and ordered the famous Burning of the Books in 213 BC.

When Confucian scholars came back into prominence during the early years of the Han dynasty (206 BC–AD 220), they undertook the great task of restoring the ancient Classics. Late in the 2nd century BC, the Han emperor Wu, although himself an authoritarian, was persuaded by a Confucian scholar, Tung Chung-shu, to proclaim Confucianism the official ideology of China as a step toward strengthening the country's unity. In 124 BC, again at the urging of Tung Chung-shu, Emperor Wu was prevailed upon to open a national university with doctoral chairs (*po-shih*) for the teaching of the ancient Classics. It is also possible that about this time the Classics were made the basis of civil service examinations to determine the future appointment and promotion of government officials, though their importance was much greater in later years. In any case, these innovations permanently established the Confucian (and certain other) Classics as the basis of Chinese education and ensured that educated persons and government officials would henceforth be molded along Confucian lines.

Canons. When the Chinese refer to specific lists of Confucian Classics, the word Confucian is never used; they simply say the "Five (or Six, or Nine, or Twelve, or Thirteen) Classics." On the other hand, when Westerners refer to these same writings, they frequently speak of "Confucian canons" or the "Confucian Classics." Such lists, it should be noted, are not canonical in the usual sense, for no one contends that all these works, and these alone, contain the authentic teachings of Confucius and his followers. *Hsün-tzu*, the 3rd-century-BC book of Hsün-tzu, for example, has never been declared a Confucian Classic even though the author and Mencius, the two Confucian champions, have been joined to Confucius in a great triumvirate. The Thirteen Classics, moreover, contain long passages that have no relationship to Confucian doctrine, and the *I Ching* ("Classic of Changes") seems to certain scholars to be somewhat out of place among Confucian texts. In the *Ch'un Ch'iu* ("Spring and Autumn") annals, a chronological history of the state of Lu, Confucian principles of government are all only implicit. Equally surprising was the long-delayed (12th century) incorporation of the *Mencius* (*Mengtzu*) among the Classics; this Confucian masterpiece had its own doctoral chair in the national university in the 2nd century BC and was placed on equal footing with the other ancient Classics.

The cornerstone of the Confucian canons is a heterogeneous collection known as the Wu Ching ("Five Classics"), which have been treated as a unit at least since the early years of the Han dynasty. The antiquity of these books and the fact that Confucius is said to have compiled or edited (in one case written) them have given them a status unequalled by the other Classics. Closely associated with the Five Classics in more modern times is the *Ssu shu* ("Four Books"), published in 1190 by Chu Hsi, a great Neo-Confucian philosopher. Though the Four Books as such is not listed in Confucian canons, it is nothing more than a grouping of *Lun yü* (*Analects*), *Meng-tzu* (*Mencius*), and two separate chapters of *Li chi* ("Record of Rites"), called respectively *Ta hsüeh* ("Great Learning") and *Chung yung* ("Doctrine of the Mean"). The Four Books and Chu Hsi's commentaries on them are indispensable for any study of Confucian literature.

The Five Classics and Four Books

Authenticity, authorship, and style. *Authenticity.* The Burning of the Books by Shih Huang Ti created immense problems for Han scholars who sought to restore the original Classics, for in many cases they were confronted with significantly different versions, some of which were said to have been retrieved from the walls of houses. The question of authenticity, however, goes much deeper, for research indicates that, aside from clearly recognized forgeries, certain texts were reworked by Han scholars (all convinced Confucians) to such an extent that no one

Table 1: Canons of Confucian Classics

Five Classics	Six Classics	Nine Classics	Twelve Classics	Thirteen Classics
I Ching	*I Ching*	*I Ching*	*I Ching*	*I Ching*, "Classic of Changes"
Shu Ching	*Shu Ching*	*Shu Ching*	*Shu Ching*	*Shu Ching*, "Classic of History"
Shih Ching	*Shih Ching*	*Shih Ching*	*Shih Ching*	*Shih Ching*, "Classic of Poetry"
		Chou li	*Chou li*	*Chou li*, "Rites of Chou"
		I li	*I li*	*I li*, "Ceremonies and Rituals"
Li chi	*Li chi*	*Li chi*	*Li chi*	*Li chi*, "Record of Rites"
	Yüeh Ching, "Classic of Music"			
Ch'un Ch'iu	*Ch'un Ch'iu*, "Spring and Autumn" Annals			
		Tso chuan	*Tso chuan*	*Tso chuan*, "Tso's Commentary"
		Kung-yang chuan	*Kung-yang chuan*	*Kung-yang chuan*, "Kung-yang's Commentary"
		Ku-liang chuan	*Ku-liang chuan*	*Ku-liang chuan*, "Ku-liang's Commentary"
			Lun yü	*Lun yü*, "Analects"
			Hsiao Ching	*Hsiao Ching*, "Classic of Filial Piety"
			Erh ya	*Erh ya*, a dictionary
				Meng-tzu, "Mencius"

can say for sure to what degree some of the originals have been modified. Though the Thirteen Classics are still accepted as substantially authentic, qualifications must be made for individual texts. The *Yüeh Ching* ("Classic of Music"), referred to elsewhere as one of the Six Classics, has been totally lost (though part of it perhaps is now found in the *Li chi*), and though a text of the *Hsiao Ching* ("Classic of Filial Piety") in ancient pre-Ch'in script was known in the 2nd century BC, the extant text is in modern script and belongs to a later period.

Authorship. A similar uncertainty obscures the question of authorship. Tradition credits Confucius with having written the *Ch'un Ch'iu* and with having collected or edited the material of the four other books that comprise the Five Classics. If these traditions are correct, four of the Five Classics predate Confucius, but little more than educated surmises can be made about probable authors. The *Lun yü* and *Hsiao Ching* are generally presumed to have been written by the disciples of Confucius, the *Meng-tzu* by the disciples of Mencius, and the three commentaries on *Ch'un Ch'iu* by the scholars whose names they bear. An old tradition that points to Chou Kung (12th century BC) as the author of *Chou li* ("Rites of Chou") is no longer accepted; the *I li* ("Ceremonies and Rituals") and *Erh ya* (a dictionary) are probably the work of Han scholars.

Literary style. Despite a great diversity of subject matter, the Confucian Classics have this much in common: they are written in the formal classical (*wen-yen*) style that is characterized by such extreme brevity and compactness that every character must often be weighed to discern the meaning. Single characters are also capable of conveying such a wide variety of connotations that scholars differ significantly in their interpretations of a given text. Remnants of this type of writing still appear, for example, in formal announcements and legal documents, but *wen-yen* is no longer the language of the people. The Confucian Classics consequently cannot be understood without serious study and the use of commentaries that are far more lengthy than the texts they elucidate. The Classics also contain countless references and allusions that have been made clear only after years of tedious research.

INDIVIDUAL CLASSICS: CONTENT AND SIGNIFICANCE

Divination and poetic texts. *I Ching.* Possibly the oldest of the Confucian Classics is the *I Ching* ("Classic of Changes"), a book first used for divination. The profound impact that it has had on Chinese minds, however, and the wide popularity it has had among Westerners are the result of its fascinating cosmology, or theory of the universe, which involves man and nature in a single system of two great cosmic forces called Yin and Yang. These forces explain all being and all activity by their ceaseless interaction. The uniqueness of the *I Ching* consists in its presentation of 64 symbolic hexagrams that represent all possible combinations of eight basic trigrams (*pa kua*) joined in pairs, one above the other. A solid line (——) in a trigram represents Yang, the male cosmic principle; a broken line (– –) represents Yin, the female cosmic principle. A solid line is also equal to the number nine, and a broken line is equivalent to six, if numerology is used as a basis of interpretation.

A trigram is "created" line by line, from the bottom upward, by casting successive lots in one of several possible ways. When completed, the top three lines of the hexagram may constitute, for example, the trigram signifying water; the bottom three lines may represent fire. A hexagram with water above fire denotes success or conquest. Like individual notes in a musical scale, each line of a hexagram has a meaning in and by itself, but its true significance depends on its position and its relationship to the unit as a whole. The *I Ching* texts that explain each hexagram line by line and interpret the symbol as a unit are usually couched in cryptic and thought-provoking language that allows the individual great leeway to determine the meaning in concrete terms. If properly understood and properly interpreted, the hexagrams are said to contain profound meanings applicable to daily life. *I*

The I Ching hexagrams

Table 2: The Eight Chinese Trigrams
(with more commonly accepted equivalents)

symbolic trigrams	Chinese name	Chinese meaning	natural element	corresponding direction	moral or mental quality
☰	ch'ien	heaven	heaven	NW	strength
☷	k'un	earth	earth	NE	weakness
☳	chen	activity	thunder	E	being active
☴	sun	bending	wind	SE	flexibility
☵	k'an	pit	water	N	being in danger
☲	li	brightness	fire	S	elegance
☶	ken	to stop	mountain	SW	firmness
☱	tui	pleasure	collection of water	W	joyfulness

Ching enthusiasts throughout the ages have claimed that the book is a means to understand and even to control the future, for the 64 hexagrams symbolize all possible situations and processes that can exist when Yin and Yang rise and fall and move in cycles. This wonderful and unfathomable operation is called *shen* ("spirit").

The legendary emperor Fu Hsi (24th century BC) is said to have discovered the trigrams on the back of a tortoise, and Wen Wang, ruler of the state of Chou in north central China in the 12th century BC, is generally credited with having formed the hexagrams. Tradition points to Wen Wang or his son, Chou Kung, as the author of the two explanatory texts, but modern scholars believe the work evolved at a much later date. Some scholars have been troubled by the inclusion of the *I Ching* among the Confucian Classics, for Confucius is said to have avoided speaking of anything that smacked of esoteric doctrines. On the other hand, in a disputed passage, the Sage reportedly said that he wished he had more time for the study of the *I Ching*.

Shih Ching. According to tradition, China's first anthology of poetry, the *Shih Ching* ("Classic of Poetry"), was compiled by Confucius, who placed great store on the educational value of poetry and considered the *Shih Ching* a model of literary expression; for, despite such themes as love and complaints of oppression, the subject matter was always "expressive of enjoyment without being licentious, and of grief without being hurtfully excessive." The book thus served as a model for later writers, who used it as a source of proper diction and imitated its tone of restraint. The "Classic of Poetry" contains 305 poems from the Western Chou dynasty plus six additional titles. Most poems are in rhyme and consist mainly of a number of verses with four or more lines of four characters each. The poems have been divided into 160 popular songs called "winds" (*feng*), 105 courtly (*ya*, "correct") songs, and 40 eulogies (*sung*). Five of the poems are said to date from Shang times (1766–1122 BC). All the ancient odes were set to music, but whereas popular songs were sung at festivals and on similar occasions, sacrificial and temple songs were used for royal and personal ancestor worship and were accompanied by group dancing. Poems of eulogy were sung to glorify the power of Heaven and the virtues and accomplishments of ancestors, especially Wen Wang. After Shih Huang Ti ordered the Burning of the Books, four versions of the *Shih Ching* were compiled with textural variations. Only that with an introduction by Mao Ch'ang, a 2nd-century-BC commentator, gained official favour and survived. Scholars are willing to accept many of the poems as authentic, but the moral interpretations of Mao Ch'ang have been rejected as entirely subjective.

Basic texts on Confucius and Mencius. *Lun yü.* Because the *Lun yü* ("Analects") contains reputed conversations of Confucius and personal observations on the Sage recorded by his disciples, it is the most widely read of all the Confucian Classics and is recognized as the best single known source of knowledge of Confucius and his teachings. Though unsystematic, in a few cases repetitive, and in some instances historically inaccurate, the text treats practically all the basic concepts of Confucianism;

The Shih Ching as a model of literary expression

e.g., jen ("benevolence" or "humanity"), *chün-tzu* ("the superior man"), *T'ien* ("Heaven"), *chung yung* ("doctrine of the mean"), *li* ("proper conduct"), and *cheng ming* ("rectification of names"). The latter inculcates the notion that, in government, education, and private life, an individual's conduct should correspond to the true meaning of "names"; *e.g.,* one must fulfill the functions of a father before one can be truly called a father. In the 2nd century BC three versions of the *Lun yü* existed: that of the state of Ch'i in 22 books, the ancient script version in 21 books, and that of the state of Lu, which alone survives. Its 12,700-character text is divided into two parts of 10 books each.

Throughout the book occur such quotations as these: "The superior man understands what is right, the mean man understands what is profitable." "What you do not want done to you, do not do to others." Among other direct quotations attributed to Confucius are several explaining filial piety (*hsiao*). For example, if *hsiao* means nothing more than providing for parents, said Confucius, even dogs and horses do that; *hsiao* does not exist without a genuine respect for parents. The *Lun yü* also provides an insight into the personality of Confucius by including such homey observations as the following, made by the Master's disciples: "If a mat was not correctly laid, he would not sit on it." "If a large quantity of meat was served, he took just enough to supplement his rice. With wine he set no limit, but he never got confused from overdrinking." "He did not speak when eating, and once in bed he did not talk."

Hsiao Ching. Another of the Classics, a short work of less than 2,000 characters called *Hsiao Ching* ("Classic of Filial Piety"), presents filial piety as the root of all virtue and the source of moral education, judgments that have been accepted at their full value by Chinese for several thousand years. The book has variously been attributed to Confucius, to his grandson Tzu Ssu (born K'ung Chi), and to Tseng-tzu, the boy's teacher and a famous disciple of Confucius.

Meng-tzu. Of the many disciples of Confucius, none has ever matched the reputation of Mencius (the Latinized form of Meng-tzu, or Master Meng), a 4th-century-BC author, whose teachings, like those of Confucius, were preserved by his disciples. The *Meng-tzu*, one of the most widely read of the Confucian Classics, earned for Mencius the title Second Sage (*ya sheng*) of China. More literary than the *Lun yü* and almost three times as long, the *Meng-tzu* concerns itself with government and maintains that the welfare of the common people comes before every other consideration. When a ruler no longer practices benevolence (*jen*) and righteousness (*i*), the "Mandate of Heaven" (*T'ien Ming*) has been withdrawn, and he should be removed by revolution if necessary. Mencius also declared filial piety to be the foundation stone of Chinese society. For him, the greatest act of filial piety was to honour parents, and the greatest lack thereof was to have no offspring (to perpetuate ancestral rites).

The book also sets forth a doctrine that until Mencius was unknown in Chinese thought, namely, that because man is endowed by Heaven, his nature tends toward good as naturally as water flows downhill. As proof, Mencius cited man's universal sense of right and wrong and the spontaneous alarm one experiences when a small child is in grave danger. This doctrine of man's natural goodness (*hsing shan*) was vigorously attacked in the 3rd century BC by Hsün-tzu, who taught that man is selfish and evil by nature (*hsing o*) and must learn goodness through proper education. Great Confucians of later ages made various attempts to reconcile these two positions.

History texts. Among the Confucian Classics, five fall into the broad category of historical writings; of these the *Shu Ching* and *Ch'un Ch'iu* belong to the Five Classics of antiquity; the other three are all commentaries on the *Ch'un Ch'iu* and bear the names of the men who composed them.

Shu Ching. The *Shu Ching* ("Classic of Documents" or "Classic of History"), sometimes called *Shang shu* ("Official History"), is a priceless collection of ancient records that are Confucian inasmuch as Confucius was said to have made the selections and compilation from various materials available to him and because certain of the contents, attributed to ancient rulers, were cited by Confucians as principles of statecraft and ethics. The documents cover a period of some 17 centuries from the 3rd millennium BC to about 630 BC and are classified as "canons," "counsels," "instructions," "announcements," "oaths," and "charges." Five of the 58 chapters are said to be from the time of the legendary emperors Yao and Shun (24th–23rd century BC), four from the Hsia dynasty (*c.* 2205–*c.* 1766 BC), 17 from Shang times (1766–1122 BC), and 32 from the Western Chou (1122–771 BC). The last chapter deals with an event that probably occurred in 630 BC. Yao and his successor Shun were cited by Confucius as models to be imitated by every Chinese ruler, for they embodied Confucian ideals of benevolent and virtuous government. In its present form, 25 chapters of the *Shu Ching* (formerly in pre-Ch'in script) are believed to be forgeries by Mei Tse, a scholar who flourished in the early 4th century AD. The 29 other chapters (three of which were later divided to make seven) were reputedly preserved during the Burning of the Books and subsequently transmitted to Han scholars by Fu Sheng.

Ch'un Ch'iu. The first of China's chronological histories was the *Ch'un Ch'iu* ("Spring and Autumn") annals, the title of which derives from an old custom of dating events by season as well as by the year of a particular reign. Spring included the events of summer, and autumn included those of winter, so *Ch'un Ch'iu* is a complete account of significant events that occurred during the reigns of 12 rulers of Lu, the native state of Confucius, who is said to have composed the text. The accounts begin in 722 BC and end in 481 BC, shortly before the Sage's death. At first glance, one finds nothing of special interest in the *Ch'un Ch'iu*, which consists of simple statements of fact with no embellishments. Three successive entries, typical of the entire work, run as follows:

In the tenth year, spring, the duke went to Ch'i; the duke returned from Ch'i. The people of Ch'i restored to us the land of Ch'i Hsi. In summer, in the fourth month, at *ping-chen* [a time designation], the sun was eclipsed.

Confucius allegedly said he would be remembered for this work, and Mencius extolled the text as equal in importance to the taming of a great deluge by the saviour-hero Yü the Great in prehistoric times. Such lavish remarks were explained and justified by great Confucians—such as Tung Chung-shu in the 2nd century BC—who read the text as a profound statement on political morality. The reports on natural calamities, they said, were recorded by Confucius as unmistakable warnings to present and future leaders of what happens when rulers prove unworthy. The book was thus viewed as a series of moral judgments, often reinforced by the deliberate omission of the title of a degenerate ruler. Because Confucian scholars were the official interpreters of this and the other Classics, they repeatedly quoted the *Ch'un Ch'iu* to instill Confucian ideals of government. Even so, Han Confucians were not all of one mind, one faction presenting Confucius as a quasi-divine "uncrowned king" and the other accepting Confucius merely as a great moral and political teacher whose great contribution lay in the transmission of ancient Chinese traditions. The controversy of the factions centred around the proper interpretation of the *Ch'un Ch'iu* and the "great principles and subtle words" that it, in common with the other Classics, was said to contain.

Commentaries. Of the three 5th-century-BC commentaries on the *Ch'un Ch'iu*, all listed as official Classics, the *Tso chuan* ("Tso's Commentary") is by far the most important and has always been more highly regarded than either the *Kung-yang chuan* ("Kung-yang's Commentary") or the *Ku-liang chuan* ("Ku-liang's Commentary"), neither of which has been translated into English. Nothing of certainty is known about the author of the *Tso chuan* except his name, Tso Ch'iu-ming (or Tso-ch'iu Ming), but his vivid language gave flesh and bone to the jejune text of the *Ch'un Ch'iu*, and the fascinating tales that he developed from brief factual information con-

(margin notes)

Confucius' explanation of filial piety

Types of documents of the *Shu Ching*

firmed the Confucian doctrine of omens and portents and earned for him the title father of prose.

Ritual texts and dictionary. *Li chi.* Among the Five Classics, only *Li chi* ("Record of Rites") treats of ceremonies and rituals. Its elevation to the status of a Confucian Classic was the result of an emphasis on fundamental moral principles that is not found in two other Classics that are also concerned with ritual, the *Chou li* and the *I li.* In *Li chi*'s treatment of such subjects as royal regulations, evolution of rites, ritual articles, guides for women and the young, education, music, the meaning of religious sacrifices, the doctrine of the mean, and the behaviour of a scholar, moral concern is clearly *Ta hsüeh* discernible. Two chapters of the *Li chi* gained exceptional *and Chung* fame when they were published independently in the *yung* 12th century AD by Chu Hsi as part of the Four Books.

Ssu-ma Kuang, an 11th-century historian, and others had already indicated the importance of *Ta hsüeh* ("Great Learning") by writing a separate commentary on the text. It was Chu Hsi, however, who rearranged the text, added a supplement, and divided the work into a "text" (which he attributed to Confucius) and 10 "chapters of commentaries" (which he attributed to Tseng-tzu, the Sage's pupil). The true author is still in doubt. In only 1,700 characters *Ta hsüeh* succinctly sets forth a remarkable concept of government based on the moral excellence of rulers. Its underlying principles are that subjects, like grass, bend under the wind of Imperial example and that world peace ultimately derives from the investigation of all things (*ko wu*). This investigation, the first of eight interdependent steps, leads to an "extension of knowledge" (*chih chih*) that brings with it "sincerity of will" (*ch'eng i*) and "rectification of mind" (*cheng hsin*). By means of these virtues one can successfully cultivate his personal life (*hsiu shen*), regulate his family (*ch'i chia*), bring order to the state (*chih kuo*), and ultimately establish peace throughout the world (*p'ing t'ien hsia*). Each progressive step depends on what has gone before.

The "Doctrine of the Mean," known to Chinese as *Chung yung* ("central," or "middle," and "universal," or "common"), is, like *Ta hsüeh*, a chapter of *Li chi.* The title expresses a Confucian ideal that is so broad and so all-embracing as to encompass every relationship and every activity of one's life. In practice, the doctrine of the mean implies countless things: moderation, rectitude, objectivity, sincerity, propriety, and lack of bias. One must, for example, be to a friend what a friend should be, neither too close nor too remote. Neither in grief nor in joy should one be excessive, for unregulated happiness can be as hurtful as uncontrolled sorrow. One must, in other words, adhere unswervingly to the "mean" at all times, in every situation. Such behaviour, moreover, conforms to the laws of nature, is the distinctive mark of the superior man, and is the essence of true orthodoxy. There are passages in *Chung yung* that deal with religious sacrifices and others that cover certain topics that Confucius would not discuss. The "way of Heaven," for example, is described as eternal, unceasing, and evident and is spoken of as transcending space, time, substance, and motion. Spiritual beings are admittedly unfathomable but seemingly always present. Taoists and Buddhists profess to detect mystical elements in the text and have studied it with special interest. Chu Hsi divided the text into 33 sections and attributed authorship to Tzu Ssu, a grandson of Confucius who, according to Chu Hsi, was fearful that new ideas were corrupting the authentic teachings of his illustrious grandfather and therefore presented *Chung yung* as a central theme of Confucian thought, as indeed it is. If Tzu Ssu was in fact the author, at least this portion of the *Li chi* postdates Confucius.

Chou li. The second of the ritual texts is called *Chou li* ("Rites of Chou"), or *Chou kuan* ("Offices of Chou"), and is chiefly concerned with things political. The title suggests an old tradition that named Chou Kung as the author, but the book's authorship and authenticity are still debated questions. The book deals with government in general under "Offices of Earth," with social and religious institutions under "Offices of Spring," with the army under "Offices of Summer," with justice under "Offices of Autumn," and with population, territory, and agriculture under "Offices of Winter." The book took on special significance in the 11th century, when Wang An-shih, a reform-minded prime minister, challenged its underlying principles by attempting to introduce radical changes in government bureaucracy. Wang's goal was to create a nationwide system of schools to facilitate the administration of broader financial assistance to the common people. The implementation of his "New Policies" required among other things a more utilitarian approach to civil service examinations with a consequent de-emphasis on mastering the Classics as a prerequisite for advancement in government service. Because the opposition of traditional Confucians to Wang's successes was loud and strong, the controversy lasted for several centuries.

I li. The existence of still another ritual text among the Classics indicates the great importance placed on *li* (ceremony, ritual, proper conduct, etiquette) by Confucius and his followers. The subject matter of the *I li* ("Ceremonies and Rituals") extends to weddings, funerals, religious sacrifice, archery, public festivals, court audiences, diplomatic receptions, and capping rites (when a boy received a cap about age 15 to acknowledge his entrance into manhood). At one time, three versions of the *I li* were in circulation, but only that contained in the *Pieh lu* ("Supplementary Records") by Liu Hsiang, a 1st-century-BC public official and writer, has survived; it is probably a collection of Western Han (206 BC–AD 8) materials.

Erh ya. Perhaps the least read of all the Classics is the *Erh ya* ("Near to Correctness") dictionary. It was perhaps composed by the disciples of Confucius, though many scholars think that some later writer is the more likely author. As it now exists, *Erh ya* has a commentary by Kuo P'o, an acknowledged master of literary composition who lived in the early 4th century AD. The book was offered as a guide for correct usage of such near synonyms as "cut" and "carve" and in its miscellaneous list of terms includes the names of animals, plants, birds, utensils, and heavenly bodies, as well as terms on language, human relations, music, buildings, and geography. *Erh ya* has generally been viewed as a collection of glosses on the Classical texts. At a much later date, illustrations were added.

Significance of the texts. The unique role of the Confucian Classics in shaping Chinese civilization and the *Role of the* civilizations influenced by China, such as the Korean *texts as* and the Japanese, is clearly evident from the sole fact *regulators* that passages from these ancient writings have been invoked for some 2,000 years as norms for government, *life* law, literary composition, religious conduct, and human behaviour. These books, moreover, have constituted the core curriculum of Chinese education for generations, and Chinese society has derived its moral standards and ideas of proper conduct from these same works. Though the Confucian Classics are not the sacred scriptures of any organized religion, they nonetheless project clear religious overtones, especially when there is talk of Heaven, Heaven's Mandate, and human nature endowed by Heaven. Religious sentiments are even more in evidence when the *Li chi*, for example, prescribes the ceremonies for ancestral worship. Repeated emphasis on filial piety, moreover, inculcates respect for parents during life and fitting ceremonies after death. Though China's religious ceremonies have doubtless changed with changing times, Confucian statements on religious etiquette are still valid. It can be said with confidence, therefore, that these famous writings have regulated Chinese life for two millennia as has no other single influence. As though to ensure that the Confucian way of life would persist forever, the Classics have several times been inscribed on stone by Imperial decree. It has been said that to be Chinese is to be Confucian, even when one professes to be a Buddhist, a Communist, or a Christian. A knowledge of the Chinese people and a study of the Confucian Classics indicate how true this is.

BIBLIOGRAPHY. BURTON WATSON, *Early Chinese Literature* (1962), is a good nontechnical introduction to the Confucian (and Taoist) Classics. *Sources of Chinese Tradition*, compiled by WILLIAM THEODORE DE BARY, WING-TSIT CHAN, and BURTON WATSON (1960), contains select translations and several excellent sections (especially ch. 1, 2, 6, 8, and 12) on Confucianism and the Confucian Classics. HEBERT A. GILES, *A History of Chinese Literature* (1901, reprinted 1958), is no longer up to date in some respects, but it contains a very readable introduction to the Confucian texts with interspersed translations. H.G. CREEL, *Confucius, the Man and the Myth* (1949; reprinted as *Confucius and the Chinese Way*, 1960), has very helpful information for the lay reader. JAMES R. HIGHTOWER has a general description of the Classics and bibliographical aids in his *Topics in Chinese Literature* (1953).

Eight Confucian texts have been translated by JAMES LEGGE in *The Chinese Classics*, 2nd ed., 5 vol. (1893–95, reprinted 1960). Each volume has an extensive introduction, correlation tables, a bibliography, the Chinese text, an English translation, detailed notes, and a comprehensive index. Nothing comparable has been produced in English by any other single author. Vol. 1 contains the *Lun yü, Ta hsüeh,* and *Chung yung;* vol. 2, *Meng-tzu;* vol. 3, *Shu Ching;* vol. 4, *Shih Ching;* vol. 5, *Ch'un Ch'iu* and *Tso chuan.* Legge has also translated the *Li chi* and *Hsiao Ching.* RICHARD WILHELM'S translation of the *I Ching* is considered standard and was rendered into English from the original German (*I Ging: Das Buch der Wandlungen*, 2 vol., 1924) by CARY F. BAYNES as *The I Ching; or, Book of Changes*, 2 vol. (1950). It has a detailed explanation of the text and an introduction by C.G. JUNG. Baynes has also translated HELLMUT WILHELM'S *Die Wandlung: Acht Essays zum I-Ging* (1958) into English as *Change: Eight Lectures on the I Ching* (1960), a very readable explanation of the difficult text. CHARLES DE HARLEZ, *Le Livre des mutations* (1888), is a well-known French translation of the *I Ching*, which was brought up to date by RAYMOND DE BECKER (1958), who also added a useful introduction. BERNARD KARLGREN, *The Book of Documents* (1950), is a scholarly translation of the *Shu Ching.* Among standard translations of the *Shih Ching* is one by ARTHUR WALEY entitled *The Book of Songs* (1960). EZRA POUND has also translated the *Shih Ching*, but with considerable freedom of expression, in *The Confucian Odes: The Classical Anthology Defined by Confucius* (1959). E.R. HUGHES has carefully analyzed *Ta hsüeh* and *Chung yung* in *The Great Learning and the Mean-in-Action* (1942). A reliable translation of *Meng-tzu* was made by D.C. LAU in *Mencius* (1970). In *The Wisdom of China and India* LIN YUTANG has translated part of the *Lun yü* and *Meng-tzu* and all of the *Chung yung.* Both the *Ta hsüeh* and the *Chung yung* are translated in WING-TSIT CHAN, *A Source Book in Chinese Philosophy* (1963). The only complete Western translation of the *Chou li* is the French work of EDOUARD C. BIOT entitled *Le Tcheou-li ou rites des tcheou* (1851). SERAPHIN COUVREUR has translated seven of the Classics into French: the *Shu Ching, Shih Ching, I li, Ch'un Ch'iu, Li chi, Lun yü,* and *Meng-tzu.* His work in French is comparable to that of Legge in English. Another well received translation of the *I li* is that of JOHN STEELE, entitled *The I-li, or Book of Etiquette and Ceremonial*, 2 vol. (1917; reprinted in 1 vol., 1966). Only three of the Confucian texts have not been translated into Western languages: *Kung-yang chuan, Kuliang chuan,* and *Erh ya.*

(W.-t.C.)

Confucius

Confucius, perhaps China's most famous man, was a teacher, philosopher, and political theorist whose ideas have deeply influenced the civilization of all of eastern Asia. The ultimate success of his doctrines was so great that it is difficult to believe that he was, in fact, a frustrated (though never embittered) man who never realized any of his dearest ambitions. The real story of his life and work has almost been lost in the wealth of legend that has grown up around his name. Careful investigation, however, can still separate the truth about the man from the posthumous glorification of the sage.

Early life and objectives. Confucius was born in 551 BC, probably of impoverished nobility, though little is reliably known about his ancestry and early life. His family name was K'ung; "Confucius" is a Latinized version of K'ung-fu-tzu (Master K'ung). He was orphaned at an early age, grew up poor, and once made his living by caring for state parks and granaries. He was largely self-educated but so diligent that he appears to have become the most learned man of his day.

Learning was not, however, his greatest interest. He was deeply distressed by the misery that he saw on every hand. China in his time was only nominally united; the

Confucius, screen painting by Kanō Tanyū, 17th century. In the Museum of Fine Arts, Boston.
By courtesy of the Museum of Fine Arts, Boston, Weld–Fenollosa Collection

King was ignored, and even the various feudal states were, in effect, divided between powerful nobles. The aristocrats made war, taxed their subjects, exhausted them with forced labour, and oppressed them at will. In bad years starvation was common.

Confucius dedicated his life to the attempt to relieve the sufferings of the people. He believed that the solution must be fundamental: a reform of the government that would make its objective not the pleasure of the rulers but the happiness of their subjects. To this end, he advocated such measures as reduction of taxation, mitigation of severe punishments, and avoidance of needless war (which was often pleasant and profitable for the aristocrats). The rulers of his native state, Lu, paid little attention to his admonitions. His lifelong objective was to occupy a commanding administrative post in which he could put his ideas into practice. It is not surprising that he never obtained one; from the point of view of the rulers, his ideas must have seemed dangerous.

Teacher and scholar. While waiting for his opportunity, which never came, he talked to younger men about his principles. Gradually a group formed about him as disciples who recognized him as their teacher. Because Confucius was unable to apply his principles, he laid increasing emphasis on teaching them to younger men for whom, when he considered them sufficiently educated, he sought posts in the government. He was remarkably successful in placing his students in positions of real authority, in which some of them proved extremely capable. But those who were most successful were more compromising than their teacher, and his doctrines had little practical effect in his own day.

Before Confucius, aristocrats had had tutors, and government officials had instructed their subordinates in the necessary techniques. But Confucius seems to have been the first private teacher in China and the first to use his teaching as an instrument of reform. His methods were quite informal. There is no record that he lectured; rather, he conversed with his students in small groups or individually. He studied the character of each disciple and sought to develop the total man. His prime insistence was upon sincerity, and his whole teaching was based upon ethics. He regarded statecraft as the application of ethics in a broader field. To furnish and deepen his students' minds he had them study history, poetry, rites, and music. To equip them to act effectively in the world, he schooled them in the theory and practice of human relations and taught them how to conduct themselves in a wide variety of situations. His teaching was not dogmatic or authoritarian; he was not affronted if his students dis-

First private teacher in China

agreed with him, and he sometimes acknowledged that they were right. Typically, he merely asked questions and insisted that they find the answers for themselves. He said, "If, when I point out one corner of the subject, the student cannot work out the other three for himself, I do not go on." Although Confucius did not advocate revolution, his educational activities were profoundly revolutionary in two senses: by emphasizing the right and duty of every individual to make basic decisions for himself, he undermined the foundation of authoritarian government; and by accepting as students even the poorest and humblest individuals if they were intelligent and earnest, he destroyed the monopoly that the aristocracy had enjoyed in its control of the techniques of government.

The activities of Confucius as a scholar have been greatly exaggerated. He was learned, and he used books in his teaching, but his interest in books as such was distinctly subordinate to his passion for reform. Although a great number of books have been ascribed by tradition to his authorship, it is improbable that he composed any of the books that have come down to us, and it is not even certain that he edited any of them. Nevertheless, Confucius used material now contained in these books, and these great writings of ancient China have been called Confucian Classics, chiefly because they were used for over 2,000 years as the basic curriculum of Chinese education, which was under the control of men who used their position to maintain Confucianism as the official ideology of China.

His religion and philosophy. Although Confucianism has sometimes been called a religion, Confucius was not a religious leader in the usual sense. He was undoubtedly a religious man, in that he felt that there was somewhere in the universe a force on the side of right. He praised as virtuous the man who stood in awe of Heaven and took a good deal of aesthetic pleasure in religious ritual. But he considered a large part of the religion of his day to be sheer superstition, and he condemned many of its practices. His philosophy was not founded upon supernaturalism in the slightest degree. Chinese philosophy has given relatively little attention to metaphysics, epistemology, and logic. In this it reflects the tendencies of Confucius, who may fairly be called its founder. It does not follow that he was a disorderly thinker because he did not stress logic. Rather, he was doubtful that one could learn about the real world merely by manipulating words. His theory of knowledge had some resemblance to that which underlies modern science, in that it was nondogmatic and empirical. He said,

No doubt there are those who find it possible to act without first understanding the situation, but I am not one of them. To hear much, select what is good, and follow it; to see much and take careful note of it; these are the steps by which one ascends to understanding.

Sense of humanity

Humanity was central in his philosophy. "Virtue," he said, "is to love men. And wisdom is to understand men." The concept of the family has always been the pivot of Chinese culture, and Confucius regarded mankind as one large family. It was one of his disciples who said that "within the four seas all men are brothers." Sincerity and reciprocity, then, should be one's guiding principles. "The truly virtuous man," Confucius said, "desiring to be established himself, seeks to establish others; desiring success for himself, he strives to help others succeed. To find in the wishes of one's own heart the principle for his conduct toward others is the method of true virtue." In accord with these ideas, he believed that the state should be a wholly cooperative enterprise. This belief was completely at variance with the theory then in vogue. Aristocrats were believed to be descended from divine ancestors and to rule by virtue of the authority and the powerful assistance of these ancestors. Confucius completely ignored this idea; eventually, it disappeared in China, and Confucius was certainly in part responsible for its going. The right to govern, Confucius held, depended upon the ability to make the governed happy. And this, in turn, depended upon the possession of virtue and ability. Thus, anyone possessed of virtue and ability might properly govern, and no one without these qualities had the right

to power. Confucius interpreted this in practical terms as meaning that the hereditary rulers should confide all administrative power to ministers who should be selected for their ability and virtue.

These qualities Confucius did not intend to leave to chance. He believed that, although individuals undoubtedly vary in their inherent virtue and abilities, these may be greatly developed by means of proper education. Therefore, he laid great stress on education designed to develop abilities and to strengthen character. Although he did not advocate advanced education for all, he did believe that some education must be given even to the humblest citizens, for two reasons. First, that ability does not depend on birth; only a wide dissemination of education can ensure that all of the most capable will be given the opportunity to develop themselves, for their own good and that of society. Second, that because the state is a cooperative enterprise, an enlightened citizenry is necessary to permit it to operate effectively. Thus, although he considered war an evil, he believed that when it must be prosecuted, it should be done vigorously, and he believed that the prime necessity for success in war was an army entirely clear as to why it was fighting and thoroughly convinced of the justice of its cause.

Stress upon education

Final years and influence. When Confucius was in his 50s, he was finally assigned a post which carried an impressive title—probably for the sake of appearances—but, when he realized that he had no actual authority, he resigned in disgust. He then set off on what proved to be a decade or more of arduous and sometimes dangerous travels through various states, searching for a ruler who would confide to him the administration of his state. Finally, at 67, Confucius responded to the invitation of some of his disciples to return to his native Lu. There he continued to teach for another five years, until his death, in 479 BC.

The difference between the ideas of Confucius and some aspects of what has later been called Confucianism is so great that one may be tempted to question the extent of his influence. It is the common fate of great men to have their ideas distorted by posterity. Yet, if we look at the form of Chinese government as it existed from the Han dynasty (206 BC–AD 220) onward, the large outline is strikingly reminiscent of the ideal of Confucius. In theory and very largely in practice, the administration was controlled by ministers; these ministers were selected, for the most part, not for their ancestry but for their personal qualities, so that a man of very humble origin could and sometimes did rise to wield the paramount power over the entire Chinese Empire. In many other ways also, the concepts of the obscure teacher of Lu have exercised such a strong formative influence upon the culture of China and of much of the Far East that Confucius must be recognized as one of the most influential men in world history.

BIBLIOGRAPHY. A major English-language study of Confucius and his philosophy is H.G. CREEL, *Confucius, the Man and the Myth* (1949; reprinted as *Confucius and the Chinese Way*, 1960). See JOHN K. SHRYOCK, *The Origin and Development of the State Cult of Confucius* (1932). JAMES LEGGE (trans.), *The Chinese Classics*, 2nd ed., vol. 1 (1893, reprinted 1960), contains the *Confucian Analects*. More recent is ARTHUR WALEY, *The Analects of Confucius* (1938).

(Ed.)

Conglomerates and Breccias

Conglomerates and breccias are rocks composed of coarse fragments of pre-existing rocks that are held within a matrix of finer particles. The name conglomerate is from the Latin *conglomeratus* ("lumped together"). The rock essentially is consolidated gravel, and the coarse components (clasts) have been individually transported and worn down by abrasion and solution before deposition. Any clastic deposit coarser than sand size (two millimetres in diameter) may be called a conglomerate, but the term usually is restricted to water-laid sediments. Thus, conglomerates are distinct from tillites, which are presumed to be ice-transported and, hence, of glacial origin. A breccia (Italian *breccia*, "breach" or "rubble")

Definition, geological importance, and importance to man

consists of unworn, generally angular, fragments. Sometimes the term rudite (Latin *rudis*, "coarse") is used to embrace both conglomerates and breccias. Coarse clastic rocks are generally considered to bear witness to upheavals in Earth history; faulting, mountain building, marine transgressions, glaciations, and volcanism are the processes principally responsible for production of the requisite fragments. This view must be slightly qualified —at least with respect to faulting and mountain building—because in addition to the undeniable requirements of suitable source rocks and some relief, the agency of transport involved must be sufficiently competent to transport course gravels to a site of deposition. Although it is generally true that coarse debris is derived from fault-block mountains and similar terrain, climate—and water discharge, its derivative—is at least of equal importance in the creation of conglomerates through fluvial processes. The occurrence of conglomerates and breccias in the geological record is therefore significant as long as transport requirements can be assumed to have been met; their presence often has helped to define stratigraphic boundaries. Conglomerates are rarely used as a building stone because producing straight blocks is difficult, but some breccias—limestone, marble, serpentine—take a good polish and have long been prized as decorative building materials. Because of their permeability, however, conglomerates provide good drainage and act as aquifers (water-bearing layers) underground. This property is of increasing importance in an age of urban and industrial expansion. The importance of these coarse sedimentary rocks to man is perhaps greatest with regard to their mineral content. Valuable heavy minerals such as gold, gemstones, tin, and tungsten settle together with stream gravel once they are freed by weathering, and this creates easily worked placer deposits. At depth within the Earth, on the other hand, brecciated zones are favourable locations for the occurrence of ore veins and other mineral deposits.

This article treats the principal types of conglomerates, breccias, and, to a lesser extent, tillites. The physical characteristics, origins, and occurrence and distribution of these rocks in the geological record are discussed. For further information on conglomerates and breccias within the hierarchical framework of sedimentary rocks, see SEDIMENTARY ROCKS; for a discussion of the relevance of conglomerates and breccias to interpretations of Earth history, see STRATIGRAPHIC BOUNDARIES; PALEOGEOGRAPHY. The transportation of coarse clastic material is dealt with in FLUVIAL PROCESSES; COASTAL FEATURES; and BEACHES; in the case of tillites, in the article GLACIATION, LANDFORMS PRODUCED BY. See IGNEOUS ROCKS, PYROCLASTIC, for details on volcanic breccias and agglomerates, which, as implied by their names, are breccias formed by volcanic activity.

Composition, texture, and structure

Physical characteristics. Rocks that disintegrate easily on weathering, such as granite, mica schist, and shale, can only contribute coarse particles if mechanical erosion is fairly rapid; fragments that are fissile (split easily, like slate) or easily abraded and reduced in size cannot survive much transport. Thus, many common rock types are rare as conglomerate components. On the other hand, tightly knit siliceous rocks such as chert, metamorphic quartzite, vein quartz, and rhyolite are almost indestructible, and, for this reason, they are disproportionately represented.

The matrix consists of primary components deposited together with the clasts and secondary material that is introduced or formed later. The primary matrix of a conglomerate, trapped between the accumulating pebbles, is commonly sandy. Most sand grains are quartz, so the matrix also contributes to the silica-rich composition of conglomerates.

Tillites and breccias are formed by less selective processes, and their composition closely reflects the rocks from which they were derived. Mechanically weak components are crushed to produce a primary matrix that is, therefore, often clay rich. The various kinds of brittle rocks present will contribute clasts.

Because no two clasts are alike, only general descrip-

tions can be given unless some property has been measured on a sufficient number of clasts and treated statistically. And because clasts are not regular solids, simple yet significant parameters of such properties as shape and roundness are hard to devise. Clasts are shaped by breaking until re-entrants (inward projecting hollows) are eliminated and no dimension greatly exceeds the others. Transport also blunts sharp edges, producing increasing roundness by grinding and bumping, until tough, water-worn pebbles may approximate the perfect roundness of an ellipsoid. Shape and roundness are two independent properties; each of four basic shapes (spheroid-, roller-, disk-, and blade-shaped) is shown perfectly rounded in Figure 1.

Shape, roundness, and packing

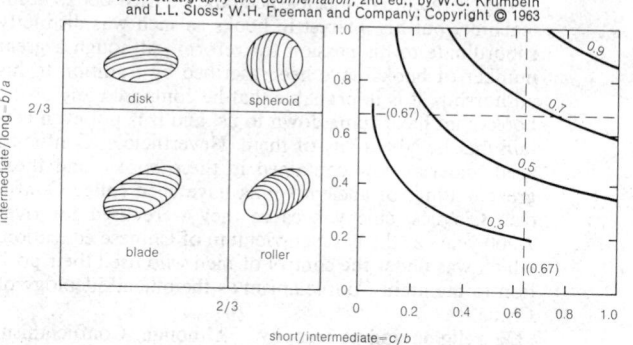

From *Stratigraphy and Sedimentation*, 2nd ed., by W.C. Krumbein and L.L. Sloss; W.H. Freeman and Company; Copyright © 1963

Figure 1: (Left) Zingg's classification of pebble types. (Right) Relation of intercept sphericity to Zingg's classification of pebble shapes. The curves represent lines of equal sphericity; the letters *a*, *b*, *c* represent length, width, and thickness, respectively.

In conglomerates, shape depends largely on the internal structure of the clasts; fissile rocks, for example, occur as disk- or blade-shaped pebbles. Roundness, however, depends on the distance of transport. Tillite components tend toward irregular, faceted shapes and slightly rounded edges, both due to grinding. In most breccias, the fragments are naturally angular; in fact, the degree of roundness is commonly used to distinguish, or even to define, conglomerates and breccias. There are a few rocks in which the components have not been worn by transport but were rounded to begin with; application of the roundness criterion will lead to classification of such rocks as conglomerates, although genetically they belong with the breccias.

In terms of size a conglomerate can consist of pebbles, boulders, or cobbles; the overall rock may be well or poorly sorted, however. Maximum size depends on the power or competence of the transport medium, whereas sorting depends on the mode of transportation. Most water-laid conglomerates are pebbly and fairly well sorted to well sorted, whereas boulders that exhibit no sorting by size are typical of tillites. A cross section through a conglomerate does not cut through most clasts at their greatest circumference; for this reason, both size and sorting of a conglomerate appear to be less than they actually are (Figure 2).

Packing is called close if neighbouring clasts are touching and if the near-maximum number is crammed into a given space, occupying about 75 percent of the space available. The interstices only are filled by matrix in this case. In a loose packing, the matrix largely envelops the clasts. If matrix preponderates, the rock is called a pebbly sandstone or pebbly mudstone; "boulder clay" is not a descriptive term but applies exclusively to coarse glacial tills.

Bedding (layering or stratification) in conglomerates, if apparent at all, is typically thick and lenticular. Graded bedding, in which size decreases from bottom to top, is common: as agitated waters rarely subside at once, declining transport power causes a gradual upward decrease in maximum clast size. Relative to the bedding, the pebbles in sandy conglomerates tend to lie flat, with their smallest dimension vertical and the greatest aligned roughly parallel to the current. But in closely packed

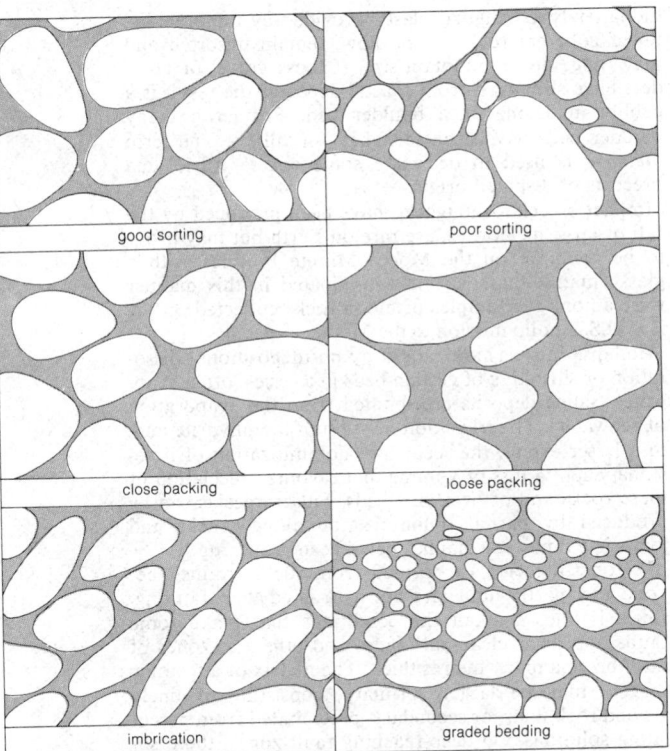

good sorting | poor sorting

close packing | loose packing

imbrication | graded bedding

Figure 2: Textures and structures of conglomerates.

conglomerates, there often is a distinct imbrication; that is, flat pebbles overlap in the same direction, like roof shingles. Imbrication is upstream on riverbeds and seaward on beaches. Tillites are massive and do not exhibit bedding. Breccias, however, may be massive, bedded, or flow layered.

Porosity is the volume percentage of "void" (actually, fluid- or air-filled) space in a rock, whereas permeability is defined by the rate of flow of water, at a given pressure gradient, through a unit volume. Conglomerates are among the most porous of rocks, and, because the chief resistance to flow is due to friction and capillary effects, coarseness makes a conglomerate more permeable—by a factor of tens or hundreds—than an equally porous but fine-grained sandstone. Conglomerates therefore provide excellent surface drainage and are to be avoided as dam and reservoir sites. Underground, they hold water reserves that are easily released through wells.

On the other hand, the occurrence of a clayey matrix will make the rock practically impermeable. Tillites and boulder clays make excellent dams, both natural and artificial. Fault breccias are either more or less permeable than the unfragmented rock they traverse. For these reasons, conglomerates and breccias are a major concern of hydrology.

Postde-
positional
changes The permeability of conglomerates favours cementation by precipitated mineral substances. Very little of this "secondary matrix"—commonly silica or calcium carbonate—is needed to bond a conglomerate into a firm and coherent rock. Much of it is furnished by preferential solution within the deposit itself, either of fine matter in the primary matrix, or at points where clasts touch each other and pressure is concentrated. Interpenetrating pitted, or even sutured, pebbles bear witness to this phenomenon.

Where packing is loose and clay is a major constituent of the matrix—as in tillites and mudflow breccias—consolidation can be attained by simple compaction: volume and porosity are reduced and interstitial water expelled by increasing overburden or tectonic compression (caused by Earth movements such as mountain building). In calcareous breccias, recrystallization of the primary matrix is often a major factor. Many of the ornamental marble breccias of commerce really belong in this category, though some—such as serpentine breccia—are true marbles in the sense that they have been metamorphosed.

Conglomerates often are metamorphosed to quartzites in which the clasts remain discernible. Simultaneous tectonic deformation (folding and squeezing) produces conglomerate quartzites in which the original pebbles are all flattened to parallel blades or stretched parallel to the fold axes to form long rods.

Origin of conglomerates. The formation of a conglomerate is governed by three conditions, namely, (1) a source area that produces rock fragments, (2) moving water capable of transporting the clasts, and (3) a depositional site or trap where the transport energy fails. Suitably hard rocks must crop out in the source area, and their denudation must be rapid enough to outpace solution and disintegration by chemical weathering, which would, of course, preclude the production of clasts. Steep or arid mountain ranges, active fault scarps, and retreating rocky coasts are thus the major sources of conglomerates.

Transport
and
deposition A water current moves stones by traction—rolling them along the bottom and sorting, shaping, and rounding them in the process. But water cannot transport even small pebbles unless it flows faster than one to 1.5 metres per second. Such bottom velocities are exceeded by many rivers and by tidal currents and wave eddies in shallow water, but not by offshore marine currents; thus the formation of conglomerates is restricted to continents and their coastal waters. Streams move their coarsest load only during intermittent flood stages, which is another reason why an arid climate favours the formation of conglomerates.

Deposition will occur where the moving water no longer meets energy requirements of its load. This commonly takes place when a stream debouches into a wide valley or plain. Obstructed by its own deposited loads, the course will be deflected frequently and conglomerates or pebbly sandstones will spread out to form a conical alluvial fan (*q.v.*). The rocks formed by ancient fans are sometimes called fanglomerates. Along a mountain front or scarp, fans coalesce to form a wedge of sediment that also is called a piedmont deposit. Amid sandy flood deposits in such regions, conglomeratic strings, lenses, and other traces mark abandoned stream channels.

Surf that undermines a steep rocky coast will produce fragments that are very well rounded. If the sea continues to encroach upon a subsiding land area, a transgression conglomerate, extended but thin, is gradually spread like a blanket over the abraded surface. As the coast recedes, this becomes covered by offshore sands and clays, and the initial coarse deposit is designated a basal conglomerate.

Origin of tillites. A tillite is, by definition, an ancient, consolidated till and must therefore be of glacial origin. In the case of Recent tills (those formed during the last 10,000 years), the connection with glaciers or ice sheets is still in evidence. For the much more extensive Pleistocene tills (formed during the interval from 10,000 to 2,500,000 years ago), the relationship to ice also can be demonstrated convincingly. This is not true, however, for many formations that predate Pleistocene time, and the designation tilloid—meaning merely till-like—is often preferable. Tills are of two kinds: the local moraines (ridges of debris marginal to glaciers) of mountain glaciers and the great till blankets that were spread over lowlands by ice sheets. Only the latter have a good chance of becoming preserved in the geological record. But ice sheets imply a glacial age, and glaciations are exceptional episodes in the Earth's history. True ancient tillites, therefore, are rare and very interesting formations.

Origin of breccias. Breccias can be loosely classified with respect to origin as residual, intraformational, mudflow, impact, collapse, tectonic, and volcanic.

Residual breccias consist of rubble produced by mechanical weathering, not far removed from its place of origin. As opposed to conglomerates, the clasts should show no evidence of transport and be angular in shape and poorly sorted; all kinds of transitions occur, however. Slope breccias (Figure 3) accumulate as scree (hillslope talus or rubble) along the lower parts of mountain slopes. In deserts, rubble is periodically removed from the hillsides by sheetfloods and spread into the intervening basins to form a deposit often called, as in the case of ancient fan deposits in general, fanglomerate. If the finer fractions are carried away, leaving only coarse rubble, a lag breccia results.

By courtesy of Ernst ten Haaf

Figure 3: Quartzite slope breccia of Cambrian age from Ardennes, Belgium.

Intraformational and mudflow breccias

Intraformational breccias are derived from, and intercalated between, contemporary sediments; they are typical of shallow marine environments where the seabed is likely to be torn up from time to time by storms or shifting tides. If the sediment involved was still loose, it will settle again as an ordinary bed; but, if there had been some prior consolidation, a blanket or channel of breccia is produced. The designation sedimentary breccia is commonly, and rather confusingly, restricted to this kind of origin. If consolidation was slight, the clasts will appear as rounded or convoluted lumps; but limestones, which tend to indurate rapidly, often form angular breccias that are sometimes called sharpstone conglomerates. An apron of reef breccia (reef talus) surrounds the base of coral and algal reefs attacked by surf.

Mudflow breccias are formed when a mass of partly consolidated sediment slides downslope with enough clay present to permit plastic flow to occur. Brittle beds are then broken up to contribute angular, unsorted clasts scattered through the clay matrix. On land, mudflows are common on steep hillsides, creeping down slowly (landslip) or descending catastrophically (lahar); but the resulting breccias stand little chance of ultimately escaping erosion. On the other hand, the geological record reveals many mudflow breccias that are intercalated with offshore marine formations. Some are mere intraformational slump breccias of local, contemporaneous sediment; but others have evidently travelled far on a gentle slope, because they involve exotic clasts, often of various ages. The designation olistostrome has come into use for

the latter type. Angular clasts, provided by the breaking up of coherent rocks in the flow, remain unsorted and may range up to mountain size. If loose gravel or boulders have slid down from coastal deposits, the result is a pebbly mudstone or a boulder bed. Formerly, many boulder beds have been mistaken for tillites. The term *mélange* is used to designate some coarse, variegated breccias of disputed origin.

Impact breccias, thought to have been produced by the fall of large meteorites, are rare on Earth but may prove to be common on the Moon. Minute breccias with a glassy matrix that may have originated in this manner were among the samples of moon rocks collected on the first U.S. Apollo mission to the Moon.

Collapse breccias are caused by postdepositional dissolution or shrinking of certain beds in a series, often evaporites (saline deposits precipitated from the evaporation of seawater). The transition of gypsum to anhydrite and, to a lesser extent, the secondary dolomitization of limestone, entail a loss of volume that favours brecciation of these rocks and of overlying beds. False breccias can be produced by partial dolomitization along cracks and joints in a limestone that has never been broken up.

Tectonic breccias are formed from rocks strained beyond the plastic limit and are associated with faulting. Little is known about the conditions that make some faults appear as clean-cut planes and others as zones of fault breccia many metres thick. The matrix of a tectonic breccia may be largely primary, consisting of finely ground rock flour, or secondary, precipitated from percolating solutions. On deep-reaching fault zones, these solutions have often been ascending and metalliferous, making tectonic breccias of importance to mining.

Coarse clastic rocks in the geological record. The most voluminous conglomerates are of continental origin and are associated with mountain building. After the main folding of a mountain chain, a phase of uplift follows. This uplift is compensated by the subsidence of an adjacent trough in which great conglomeratic deposits, often many kilometres thick, can accumulate. Such conglomerates record the contemporaneous history of the parent mountain chain: as erosion cuts down into deeper parts, their rocks appear successively in the deposited conglomerates; even vanished units commonly can be reconstructed. The balance between uplift of the mountains and subsidence of the trough is reflected by sandstones and marls of lacustrine or even marine origin that are interbedded with the conglomerates.

Ancient conglomerates

The classic example is the Tertiary Molasse of Switzerland, which fills the deep trough between the Alps and the Jura Mountains; the designation molasse has been extended to similar postorogenic deposits elsewhere. Every mountain chain has its associated conglomerates (Figure 4). The Siwalik Formation of the Himalayan foothills is famous for the vertebrate fossils collected from its marly parts and for its red beds, about which there has been some dispute as to environmental significance.

Active block faulting under continental conditions also

By courtesy of the Geological Institute, Utrecht

Figure 4: (Left) Tilted conglomerates of the Pyrenean Molasse at Peña de Oroel near Jaca, Spain. (Right) Outcrop of the tilted conglomerates of the Pyrenean Molasse, showing graded conglomerate beds alternating with freshwater marl and limestone.

is productive of conglomerates. Associated volcanism often contributes to the clasts, as well as to a red matrix. This is true of the Old Red Sandstone (Devonian) and New Red Sandstone (Permian) of western Europe, and the Newark Formation (Triassic) of the eastern United States. An example of the Old Red conglomerates is shown in Figure 5.

By courtesy of Ernst ten Haaf

Figure 5: Poorly sorted continental conglomerate; "Old Red" of Devonian age, from Ardennes, Belgium.

Thus, in the geological record, thick conglomeratic series mark the end, and the aftermath, of orogenies (episodes of mountain building): they abound in the Permian (from 225,000,000 to 280,000,000 years ago) and the Tertiary (from 2,500,000 to 65,000,000 years ago). During the intervening, and much longer, quiescent periods of slight vertical movements and extensive transgressions —e.g., large parts of the Mesozoic Era (from 65,000,000 to 225,000,000 years ago)—only thin basal conglomerates are encountered.

Conglomerates may be gold bearing, like the Witwatersrand Formation of South Africa where the conglomeratic quartzite "reefs" sought by miners are Precambrian (older than 570,000,000 years) stream channels containing fossil placer deposits.

Ancient tillites and breccias

A Permian glaciation of the Southern Hemisphere is well established, not only by the Dwyka Tillites of South Africa but also by similar occurrences in South America, India, and Australia. These localities are today far apart and distant from the poles, a circumstance that argues for the theory of continental drift (q.v.).

Many older glaciations have been claimed, of which a Late Precambrian one seems the best documented. But ancient tilloids are generally so compact, disturbed, or even metamorphosed that a tillite character can hardly be proved definitely. The majority of such deposits may be of mudflow origin. The modern tendency is to be very critical of pre-Permian tillites, though there is a priori nothing unlikely about the possible occurrence of one or several older glaciations.

The preservation of residual breccias depends on the caprice of circumstance—a marine transgression, for example. The Shinarump Formation of the Colorado Plateau region is an example of ancient desert fanglomerates.

Intraformational breccias, on the other hand, are a constant and common feature of epicontinental (shallow-water) marine series where they denote an interruption of sedimentation caused by regression of the sea or simply lack of subsidence. A large-scale example of reef talus occurs in the Permian Reef Complex of Texas.

Olistostromes are typically associated with incipient mountain building, when still-submerged and partly unconsolidated sediment masses in a geosynclinal basin are tilted, faulted, and uplifted. Classic examples are the wildflysch of the Alps and the Paleozoic boulder beds and breccias of Quebec and Newfoundland. Large tracts of the Apennines of Italy consist of olistostromes of all dimensions; they range from thin intercalations to huge blankets that carry whole mountains as "clasts." Such mudflows grade imperceptibly into tectonic phenomena (see further MOUNTAIN-BUILDING PROCESSES).

BIBLIOGRAPHY. The best approach to the extensive and scattered literature is through the references in modern textbooks, such as the following: C.O. DUNBAR and J. RODGERS, *Principles of Stratigraphy* (1957); W.C. KRUMBEIN and L.L. SLOSS, *Stratigraphy and Sedimentation*, 2nd ed (1963); and F.J. PETTIJOHN, *Sedimentary Rocks*, 2nd ed. (1957).

(E.t.H.)

Congo (Brazzaville)

The People's Republic of the Congo—commonly known as the Congo (Brazzaville)—lies astride the Equator in west central Africa. It is bordered to the west by Gabon, to the northwest by Cameroon, to the north by the Central African Republic, and to the east and south by Zaire. To the southwest it shares a common border with the Angolan enclave of Cabinda; the republic also has a 100-mile-long coastline on the Atlantic Ocean. The Congo has an area of 132,000 square miles (342,000 square kilometres), but the country as a whole is sparsely inhabited, and a large proportion of its population of over 1,000,-000 at the beginning of the present century was concentrated in the towns. The national capital of Brazzaville is an important inland port on the Congo River.

In 1970, the Congo became the first African country to declare itself a Communist state. The country has long suffered from underdevelopment and deep social and political cleavages. Its natural resources are barely exploited, and agriculture—the basic economic activity—is largely on the subsistence level. Industrial development is based on foreign investment, and France continues to maintain a high degree of control in economic matters. The series of governments that have gained control since independence in 1960 have become increasingly characterized by militarism and centralization of control. (For history, see CENTRAL AFRICA, HISTORY OF; for a related physical feature, see CONGO RIVER.)

The natural and human landscape. *Relief.* The country is fringed by a narrow coastal plain less than 40 miles wide which stretches for about 100 miles between Gabon and the enclave of Cabinda. Its shores are sandy to the north of the mouth of the Kouilou River and swampy to the south and are marked by sandspits and lagoons, which have been formed by the action of the Benguela Current in the Atlantic Ocean. The plain slopes gradually upward from the sea to the Mayombé highland areas, which consists of low-altitude ranges composed of crystalline rocks, sandstone, and limestone, running parallel to the coast. Sharp ridges are separated from each other by deep river gorges. In the south, Mont Bamba rises to an altitude of 2,625 feet (800 metres), and Mont Foungouti attains 3,051 feet (930 metres). The northern peaks are lower; among them Mont Moguindou rises to 2,132 feet (650 metres).

The coastal plain

To the east of the Mayombé region, the Niari Valley forms a 200-mile-wide depression. Its terrain rises gradually northward toward the Massif du Chaillu, which reaches elevations between 1,600 and 2,300 feet, on the Gabon border; southward the depression rises to the Plateau des Cataractes, which lies to the south of Brazzaville. The valley is an important passage route between the inland plateaus and the coast.

Beyond the Niari Valley, the landscape is composed of a series of plateaus about 1,600 feet above sea level. The plateaus are separated by the deeply eroded valleys of tributaries of the Congo River. The Bembe Plateau lies between the Niari Valley and the Massif du Chaillu, while the Plateau Batéké stretches northward along the Congo River from Brazzaville to Mpouya.

The northeast is composed of the western section of the Congo River Basin; there a vast 60,000-square-mile plain slopes from the western mountains and plateaus eastward and southeastward to the Congo River. Crossed by numerous Congo tributaries, which merge and branch again in a seemingly confused pattern, the plain is swampy and seasonally flooded.

The Congo River Basin

Drainage and soils. The country's drainage system is dominated by the Congo River. Its main tributary, the Ubangi River, flows southward from the Central African Republic and forms the country's eastern border until Liranga, where it joins the Congo. The main river con-

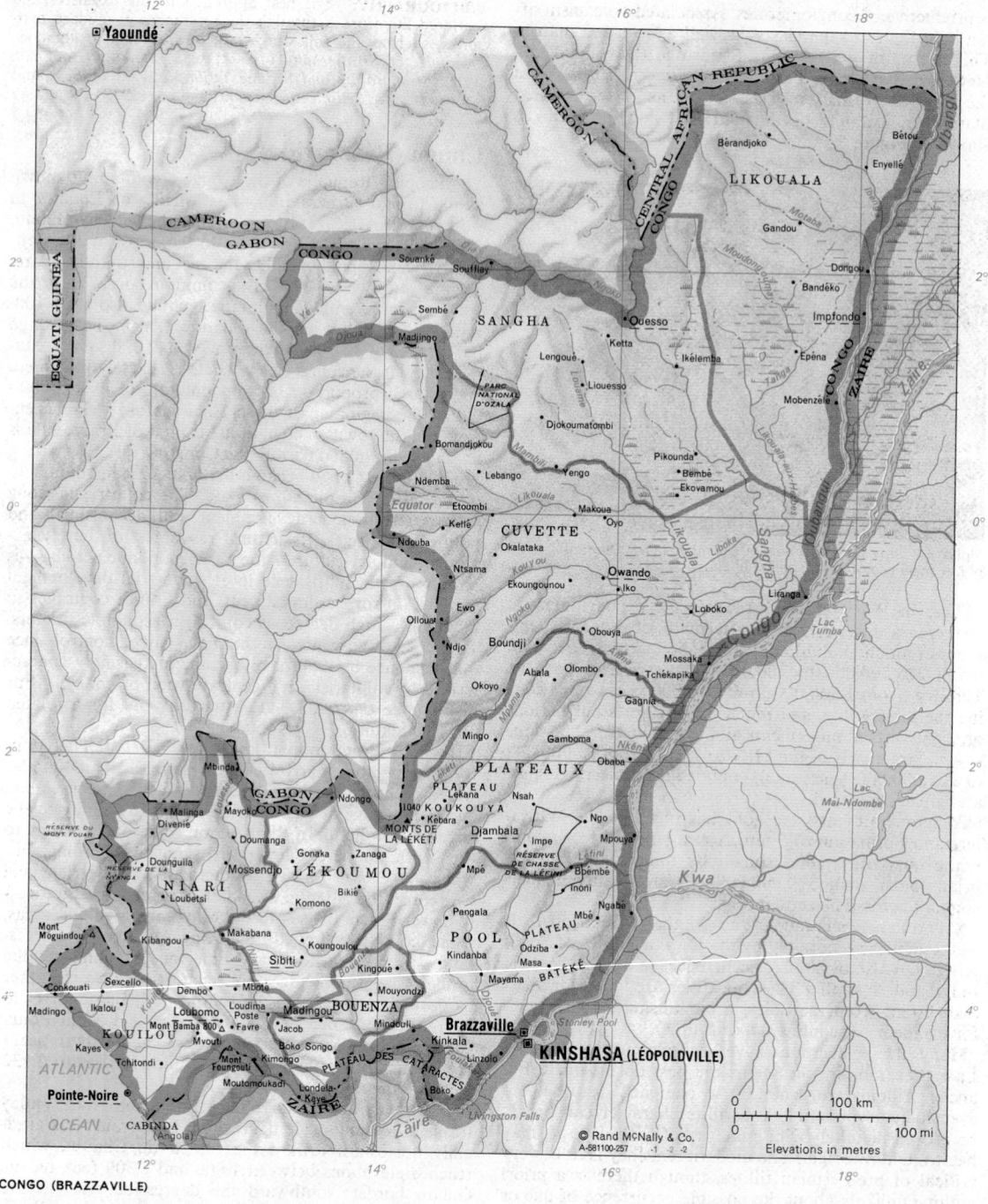

tinues southward to Stanley Pool (a shallow 300-square-mile lake) and to Livingstone Falls before flowing southwestward across Zaire to its mouth on the Atlantic Ocean. The main right-bank tributaries of the Congo, all within the territory of the republic, include the Sangha, Likouala, Alima, Nkéni, Léfini, Djoué, and Foulakari rivers.

The coastal drainage basin is formed by the Kouilou River, which flows generally southwestward for about 450 miles from its source in the plateau region to its mouth on the Atlantic Ocean at Kayes. It is known as the Niari River in its middle section, which flows through the Niari Valley and joins with the Louessé River at Makabana. The course of the river is broken by numerous waterfalls, and the banks are irregular; the mouth is blocked to navigation by sandspits formed by the strong action of the Benguela Current.

About two-thirds of the country is covered with coarse-grained soils that contain sand and gravel. Lateritic soils, containing a high proportion of iron oxides and aluminum hydroxide, occur in low-lying areas. Because of the hot and humid climate, organic matter is destroyed before it can decompose into humus, and topsoil is washed away by the heavy rains. In the savanna regions, fertile alluvial soils are threatened with erosion by wind and rain. Coarse- and fine-grained soils occur on the plateaus and hills.

Climate. The tropical climate is characterized by heavy rainfall and high temperatures and humidity. The Equator passes across the country just north of Fort-Rousset, and the seasons are reversed to the north and south of it; in the north the dry season extends from November through March and the rainy season from April through October, whereas in the south the contrary is true. On both sides of the Equator, however, certain areas have two dry and two wet seasons.

Temperature range — Temperatures are relatively stable with little variation between seasons or between day and night. Annual average temperatures range between 68° and 81° F (20° and 27° C), although in the south the cooling effect of the Benguela Current may produce readings as low as 54° F (12° C). The average daily humidity, 80 percent, makes the climate generally uncomfortable.

Annual rainfall is abundant throughout the country, but there are seasonal and regional variations. Precipitation always averages more than 48 inches (1,200 millimetres) annually, and often surpasses a yearly total of 80 inches.

Vegetation and animal life. Most of the Congo is covered with tropical rain forest. The dense growth of trees such as the African oak, red cedar, walnut, the softwood okoume, or gaboon mahogany, and the hardwood limba (*Terminalia superba*) provides an evergreen canopy over the sparse undergrowth of leafy plants and vines. The coast and the swampy areas contain mangrove forests and tall grasses and reeds. The plateau areas and the Niari Valley are covered with savanna vegetation of grasses, coconut palms, and banana trees.

The forests are inhabited by several varieties of monkey, chimpanzee, gorilla, elephant, okapi, wild boar, and buffalo. Wildlife in the savanna regions includes several varieties of antelope, jackal, wild dog, hyena, and cheetah. On the plateaus, rhinoceroses and giraffes are numerous, but lions are scarce. Birdlife includes the predatory eagle, hawk, and owl, the scavenging vulture, and the wading heron. There are also cormorants, kingfishers, ducks, geese, and partridges, as well as numerous songbirds.

Freshwater fish include perch, catfish, sunfish, and mudskippers. Crocodiles are scattered throughout the Congo River Basin. The numerous snakes include several poisonous varieties: cobra, python, green mamba, and puff adder. Among the insects, the most dangerous are the tsetse fly, which causes sleeping sickness in human beings and a similar disease in cattle, and the mosquito, which carries malaria and yellow fever.

·*Traditional regions.* The country's four main traditional regions are coincident with the historical locations of the population's major ethnic groups. The southern region between Brazzaville and the coast is inhabited by the Kongo people and formed part of the larger Kongo Kingdom that stretched into modern Zaire and Angola between the 14th and 18th centuries. Also in the south, the Teke inhabit the Batéké Plateau region. In the north, the Ubangi inhabit the Congo River Basin to the west of Mossaka, while the Binga Pygmies and the Sanga are scattered through the northern Congo Basin. The considerable rivalry between the peoples of the north and south is based on ancient tribal rivalries and precolonial trade patterns. Urbanization, however, has produced greater intertribal contacts and is expected eventually to reduce regional rivalry.

Settlement patterns. The rural population occupies small, scattered villages composed generally of kinship groups. Houses with thatched roofs are rectangular or square and are usually built of interwoven poles and reeds covered with mud. Buildings are often grouped on raised ground in the plateau region and are built on stilts in areas subject to flooding. The people are engaged in subsistence farming or fishing and thus do not participate in the money economy.

Urban centres — The country's four major cities are Brazzaville (population, at the census of 1974, 310,500), Pointe-Noire (146,700) on the Atlantic coast, Jacob (30,600) in the Niari Valley, and Loubomo (formerly Dolisie; 29,600) in the Mayombé region. The cities reflect French influence in their organization, having a central administrative and commercial core surrounded by residential areas. Before independence there was a marked difference between the spacious, planned European sections and the crowded, haphazardly built African sections of the cities. Since 1960, however, greater social and economic mobility in the African population and attempts at urban renewal have blunted the contrasts.

People and population. *Population groups.* About 45 percent of the Congo's 1,300,000 inhabitants (1974 census) belong to the Kongo tribal grouping. The main Kongo tribes include the Sundi, Kongo, Lali, Kougni, Bembe, Kamba, Dondo, Vili, and Yombe. The 160,000 Ubangi people include the Makoua, Kouyou, Mboshi, Likouala, Ngala, and Bonga. The Teke number about 200,000. The Sanga, or Gabonese Bantu, number about 15 percent of the population, also divided into various subgroups. The 12,000 Binga Pygmies live in small bands.

Most of the 12,000 Europeans in the Congo are French, and about 80 percent of them live in the four main cities. There are also small populations of foreign Africans, Portuguese, and Chinese.

Congo (Brazzaville), Area and Population

	area*		population	
	sq mi	sq km	1960–61 census	1970 census ‖
Federal District				
Brazzaville	†	†	...	175,000
Regions				
Bouenza	3,500	9,000	...	124,000
Cuvette	28,000	72,500	...	108,000
Kouilou	5,600	14,500	...	183,000
Lékoumou	8,800	22,800	...	64,000
Likouala	20,200	52,300	...	30,000
Niari	11,700	30,300	...	119,000
Plateaux	15,800	40,900	...	96,000
Pool	13,700†	35,500†	...	159,000
Sangha	24,800	64,300	...	31,000
Total Congo (Brazzaville)	132,000‡	342,000‡	582,000§	1,089,000

*Areas approximate. †Area of Brazzaville federal district included in Pool.
‡Figures do not add to total given because of rounding. §Estimate for de jure
African population, based on results of a sample survey; excluding population
of Brazzaville (numbering 136,000 at 1961–62 census) and Pointe-Noire
(numbering 79,000 at 1962 census) not covered by survey. ‖Preliminary.
Source: Official government figures; UN.

Except for the Pygmies, all the indigenous peoples speak their own Bantu languages. To facilitate trade, two patois—Lingala and Monokutuba—developed; Lingala is spoken north of Brazzaville, and Monokutuba between the capital and the coast. French was adopted as the official language in order not to favour any one tribal language; it is the medium of instruction at all levels and is spoken by the African elite and the European community.

Religions About half of the population practices traditional religions. The Christian community is composed of about 400,000 Roman Catholics and more than 150,000 Protestants, including members of the self-governing Eglise Evangélique du Congo (Evangelical Church of the Congo). There are also about 20,000 members of independent African churches, which are usually politico-religious in nature. The Eglise de Jésus-Christ sur la Terre par le Prophète Simon Kimbangu (Church of Jesus Christ on Earth by the Prophet Simon Kimbangu), the largest independent church in Africa, is a member of the World Council of Churches. Other such independent churches include the Matsouana Church and the Bougist Church. Most of the small Muslim community of about 5,000 is composed of aliens who reside in Brazzaville or Pointe-Noire.

Demography. The population of the Congo is young; at least 55 percent of the population are under 19 years of age. About 40 percent are between the ages of 19 and 60 and only about 5 percent are over 60. The birthrate is high—about 44 births per 1,000 population—and the death rate is about 23 deaths per 1,000. Because of poor health conditions, the infant mortality rate is high—180 deaths per 1,000 births; life expectancy at birth is 41 years.

Movement from the rural areas to urban centres has been significant since World War II. By the early 1970s, more than one-third of the population lived in the four principal cities, and another 10 percent were located in smaller urban centres.

The average population density of eight persons per square mile is deceptive, as population distribution is extremely uneven. The centrally located Plateau Koukouya has the highest density of 70 per square mile, while the Plateau Batéké has less than three and the northern Likouala region less than one per square mile. The southwestern one-third of the country—the most urbanized area—contains about 70 percent of the population.

The national economy. Agriculture forms the basis of the economy, although there is some development of forestry and of mining. Economic advancement is hampered by the lack of an integrated transportation system.

Natural resources. A variety of minerals exist in relatively small quantities. The most important mineral resource consists of more than 25,000,000 tons of potash (potassium chloride) located at Gare Holle, 30 miles north of Pointe-Noire. There are more than 700,000,000 tons of limestone in the Niari Valley and about 500,000,000 tons of iron ore in the south and northeast. Less extensive deposits of gold and diamonds have been located in the Mayombé region, and there are copper and lead deposits west of Brazzaville and oil in the coastal region. There are also deposits of zinc, tin, bauxite, and titanium (a metallic element used in alloys).

The forests offer extensive resources of both softwoods and hardwoods, while the rivers and lakes offer important fish resources. There are no known deposits of coal; power resources consist of wood, charcoal, and the considerable hydroelectric potential of the country's rivers.

Sources of national income. By the early 1970s, agriculture produced about one-eighth of the gross domestic product (GDP). Most cultivation is on a subsistence level, and yields are low because of poor soils. Most of the cultivated land is held in small family holdings that are unsuitable for mechanized farming techniques. In traditional farming techniques, land is cleared by burning and women work the fields with hand tools. Manioc (cassava) is the basic food crop everywhere but in the north, where bananas and plantain are prevalent. Rice is grown in the northern Pool region. The diet is supplemented with yams, taro, sweet potatoes, maize (corn), peanuts, and fruit. Livestock usually consists of sheep, goats, pigs, and poultry. The government has sponsored the raising of cattle since the introduction in the 1960s of *n'dama* cattle—a breed resistant to the tsetse fly.

The major cash crops—sugarcane and tobacco—are either produced or controlled by French companies. Sugarcane is raised on plantations by the Société Industrielle et Agricole du Niari (SIAN) near Jacob and by the Société Sucrière du Niari (Sosuniari) near Loudima Poste. The cultivation of tobacco is promoted in the Cuvette and Pool regions by the Service d'Exploitation Industrielle des Tabacs et Allumette (SEITA), which also collects and transports the crop to Brazzaville. The tobacco is then either exported or processed by the Société Industrielle et Agricole du Tabac (SIAT).

Commercial agriculture

Other cash crops are grown by African planters, who are assisted by commercial companies or the government. The crops include peanuts in the Niari and Pool valleys; oil palms in the north and south; bananas; rice; cocoa in the north; and coffee on the Bembe Plateau and in the Niari Valley.

Forestry products accounted for over 60 percent of the total exports in the late 1960s. Although forest reserves are extensive, development is hampered by inadequate transportation and flood conditions in the north; most forestry operations therefore take place in the south. The Congo is the world's largest producer of *limba* and (after Gabon) the second largest producer of *okoumé*. Products include logs, sawn wood, and veneers. Forestry was largely under French control until the 1960s, when African participation began to increase.

Commercial marine fishing is conducted off Pointe-Noire by individuals and by two large French firms. The catch includes tuna, bass, sole, and sardines, which are largely consumed in the four principal cities. Freshwater fishing on the rivers, lakes, and swamps is largely a subsistence activity.

Mining has been promoted by the government since the 1960s. Potash is mined at Gare Holle by the Compagnie des Potasses du Congo (CPC), of which the government is a principal stockholder. About 200,000 tons of potassium chloride were produced in 1970. Petroleum was extracted at Pointe Indienne, but the deposits were largely depleted by the late 1960s. Copper, zinc, lead, and iron ore are mined on a small scale.

The small manufacturing sector is hampered by limited domestic markets. the dependence upon foreign investment, and the lack of skilled labour. Most factories are located in Brazzaville, Pointe-Noire, Jacob, and Dolisie. Industrial products include processed foods, beverages, cigarettes, textiles and clothing, footwear, processed wood and paper, chemicals, cement and bricks, glassware, and metal products such as nails and metal furniture. Handicrafts produced by individual artisans include carvings, pottery, needlework, tiles, and bricks.

The industrial sector

In the early 1970s energy was obtained from a hydroelectric dam at Djoué, on the Congo River near Brazzaville, and from thermal plants at Pointe-Noire, Dolisie, Jacob, Loutété, Kinkala, and Fort-Rousset. There were also several proposals for new hydroelectric installations on the Kouilou River at Sounda, on the Nkéni River, and on the Bouenza River.

The Bank Centrale des États de l'Afrique Équatoriale et du Cameroun is the central bank not only for the Congo but also for Chad, the Central African Republic, Gabon, and Cameroon; its central office is located in Paris. The bank issues currency—the Communauté Financière Africaine (CFA; or African Financial Community) franc—to the five member states. There are three commercial banks controlled by French banking interests and one controlled by the Congolese government, in addition to a domestic firm and several foreign banks.

The Congo belongs to the Union Douanière Économique de l'Afrique Centrale (UDEAC; Central African Customs and Economic Union), other members of which are the Central African Republic, Gabon, and Cameroon. The country has maintained a favourable balance of trade within the union but has an overall imbalance of payments. Major imports of machinery, transport equipment, iron and steel, fuel, cotton, and foodstuffs are obtained mainly from France. Other import sources are West Germany, the United States, The Netherlands, Italy, Mauritania, Belgium-Luxembourg, Japan, United Kingdom, and China. Exports of logs, diamonds, and sugar are sold to West Germany, The Netherlands, France, Belgium-Luxembourg, South Africa, United Kingdom, Israel, and China.

Management of the economy. Economic development is financed by government funds and by private investment (largely foreign). In 1965 the government formed the Bureau pour la Création, le Contrôle et l'Orientation des Enterprises de l'État (BCCO) for the management of public investment and of various enterprises including a cement plant, a textile mill, and a match factory. The transportation industry was nationalized in 1969. A government investment code was promulgated to attract foreign private capital.

Indirect taxes, including export and import duties and sales taxes, are the chief source of government revenue. Direct taxes include taxes on business profits and a graduated income tax.

The national trade union

In 1964, the country's several trade unions merged into the national Confédération Syndicale Congolaise (CSC), which then became an organ of the single national political party. Employers' associations include chambers of commerce in Brazzaville, Pointe-Noire, and Dolisie. Wages are regulated through collective bargaining by workers' and employers' representatives under government supervision.

Economic policies. The Interim Five-Year Development Plan of 1964 to 1968 called for increases in agricultural and industrial production and an improved distribution system. It aimed at the lessening of disparities between the rural and urban areas and at the alleviation of unemployment which is a serious problem in the cities. The development plan for 1970 to 1974 was expected to be a continuation of the previous plan.

Transportation. The road system is most developed in the south. There are about 140 miles of paved roads, 5,000 miles of improved earth roads, and 1,400 miles of unimproved roads. Many roads are seasonal and are impassable during the rains. The most important routes are between Brazzaville and Pointe-Noire, and between Dolisie and the Gabon border.

The railways are also located in the south. The principal Congo-Ocean Railway line runs for about 320 miles from Brazzaville east and south through Jacob and Dolisie to Pointe-Noire. There is also a 175-mile branch line from Favre north to Mbinda on the Gabon border. The railways are important to mining and industrial development, and several towns have grown up along the two routes. In the 1960s there were plans for a line to link Loudima Gare with the iron ore deposits at Zanaga.

Waterways have long provided important links between the Congo, Chad, and the Central African Republic. The rivers, however, are often broken by rapids and are subject to seasonal variations in flow. The most important inland port is Brazzaville. After passengers and freight travel down the Ubangi River from Bangui in the Central African Republic to Brazzaville, they are shipped overland by rail to the ocean port of Pointe-Noire. The seaport is the main transshipment centre of international trade for the three countries; it has storage facilities and a wharf equipped to handle potash. Further development of Pointe-Noire by the addition of an iron ore pier, a petroleum berth, and improved fishing facilities is planned.

There are ten domestic airports with scheduled flights, including international airports at Brazzaville and Pointe-Noire. Domestic services are provided by the national airline, international flights by several foreign lines.

Administration and social conditions. *The structure of government.* According to the constitution of 1970, the president of the country's single party, the Parti Congolais du Travail (PCT), is elected by the party congress to a five-year term and also serves as president of the republic. The government is composed of a 14-member council of state and a central committee of the PCT composed of 30 members and ten alternate members. With the advice of the central committee, the president may nominate or dismiss the vice president and the other members of the council of state. There is no provision for a national legislature.

The PCT is composed of a seven-member politburo plus the central committee. The national labour union and the youth movement operate within the party structure, and in the early 1970s the army was given a political role.

Administrative regions

The country is divided into nine regions and the capital district of Brazzaville, each headed by an appointed government commissioner. The regions are divided into districts headed by appointed district chiefs; they are further subdivided into communes and villages. In addition there are four commune territories—Pointe-Noire, Dolisie, Ouesso, and Jacob—and eight administrative control posts, which are subordinate to their particular regions. The village is regarded as the primary administrative and political unit. Throughout the administrative system party organization parallels that of the administration.

In the late 1960s the judicial system was largely that inherited from the French colonial government. There was a supreme court, a court of appeals, courts of first and second instance, labour courts, and magistrates courts.

The traditional courts were to be replaced by courts of first instance. A Revolutionary Court of Justice was established in 1969 to try cases involving the security of the state.

The armed forces consist of 2,000 men serving in the army, navy, or air force, grouped under the Armée Populaire Nationale (APN); a 1,400-man paramilitary National Gendarmerie is also a branch of the APN. The armed forces have served as a power base for ruling groups since 1963 and are in charge of national and internal security. The headquarters are in Brazzaville, and the two main military bases are in Pointe-Noire and Brazzaville. There are also small military posts throughout the country.

Education, health, and welfare. Education is free and compulsory for students between the ages of six and 16. By the early 1970s about 90 percent of school-age children were enrolled in primary schools. The six-year primary education course includes instruction in agriculture, manual skills, and domestic science. On the secondary level courses are offered in vocational training, academic and technical training, general education, and teacher training. Institutions of higher learning consist of the Centre d'Enseignement Supérieur (Centre for Higher Education) and École Normale Supérieur d'Afrique Centrale (Advanced Teacher-Training Institute), both in Brazzaville. In 1970 an adult literacy program was established to combat the illiteracy rate, which was about 70 percent.

The most common health problems are respiratory diseases, malaria, tuberculosis, and intestinal parasites. Oth-

Health problems and services

er diseases include trypanosomiasis (sleeping sickness), yellow fever, smallpox, leprosy, and yaws (a contagious tropical disease caused by bacteria). Disease control is difficult because most water sources are polluted and sanitation is poor, even in the cities. Of the country's hospitals, the two largest are in Brazzaville and Pointe-Noire. Other health facilities include regional health centres, diagnostic centres, infirmaries, dispensaries, maternal and child-care centres, and private clinics. Mobile units combat communicable diseases in remote areas.

Welfare services provided by the government, the labour union, and employers are largely limited to wage earners and their families. Services include an old-age pension, life insurance, worker's compensation, and family-allowance payments. Government-sponsored social workers operate among the poor in rural and urban areas.

In addition to the National Gendarmerie, which functions as a state police force, the Sûreté Nationale operates as an urban civilian police force. It maintains internal security, controls immigration and black market activities, and investigates certain crimes against the state.

The social milieu. As migration to the cities increases, the economy is increasingly burdened with unemployment and underemployment. The minimum wage guaranteed by the government is higher for industrial workers than for agricultural workers and varies according to the worker's level of skill and his location. The generally low wages are slightly higher in Brazzaville, Pointe-Noire, and Dolisie. Wages have increased since the 1960s through collective bargaining but have not kept pace with the rapidly rising cost of living. As a result, the government has instituted wage-control measures to curb inflation.

Social and economic divisions

The country's social divisions are based on ethnic affiliations, which are polarized between the Kongo, Teke, and Ubangi peoples. During the growth of the independence movement in the 1950s, these identities formed the basis of political parties; tribalism remains a main obstacle to national unity. In the early 1970s the regime of Pres. Marien Ngouabi was largely of Ubangi origin; it has fostered a one-party, centralized system of government in an attempt to combat social divisions.

The basic economic division is between those living within the money economy and those in the subsistence sector. Wage earners are further divided into a wealthy elite, a small middle-income group, and the mass of low-paid unskilled workers.

Cultural life and institutions. In traditional society, artistic expression was tied to social and religious experience and took the form of ceremonial music, dance, sculpture, and the recounting of folklore. Christianity and colonialism had a great impact on artistic forms. The carving of ritual objects became commercialized, and music and dance altered as a result of the introduction of Western instruments and musical styles. The French language allowed for the transition from oral tradition to written literature.

There are two libraries in Brazzaville. A national museum was founded in the capital in 1965; it contains collections of prehistoric objects and displays of traditional and modern art.

The press is subject to tight governmental control and functions largely as a propaganda medium. In the early 1970s there were three daily newspapers including an official government journal. There were also several weeklies and bi-monthly publications, an official party organ, and one weekly that was also distributed in Chad, Gabon, and the Central African Republic.

Radio and television services are also subject to government censorship. There are two government-owned radio stations in Brazzaville and Pointe-Noire, as well as one French-owned station in the capital. The government stations broadcast domestic and international programs in French, Lingala, and Monokutuba; and the French station beams programs from overseas in French, English, and Portuguese. Television, limited to the Brazzaville area, was introduced in 1962; it is used primarily as an educational and propaganda medium.

Prospects for the future. The Congo's future appears to be dependent upon continued economic advancement and the achievement of political stability. Since independence, the economy has been largely based on foreign investment, which is endangered by continuous upheaval and social strife. In the early 1970s the government adopted tight security measures to control a series of labour strikes and coups d'etat which threatened a national stability that appeared illusory. Tribalism has yet to give way to a sentiment of national unity, and development is necessary to alleviate the economic imbalances between rural areas and cities, as well as between the wealthy elite and most of the people. (A.Fu.)

BIBLIOGRAPHY. The most useful overview is GORDON C. MCDONALD et al., *Area Handbook for People's Republic of Congo (Congo Brazzaville)* (1971), issued by the United States Department of the Army. GEORGES BALANDIER'S books, *Sociologie actuelle de l'Afrique noire*, 2nd ed. (1963; Eng. trans., *The Sociology of Black Africa*, 1970), *Afrique ambiguë* (1962; Eng. trans., *Ambiguous Africa: Cultures in Collision*, 1966), and *La Vie quotidienne au royaume de Kongo du XVIᵉ au XVIIIᵉ siècle* (1965; Eng. trans., *Life in the Kingdom of the Kongo from the Sixteenth to the Eighteenth Century*, 1968), are the results of intensive sociological field work in Congo Brazzaville and are recognized as major works in the field of African studies. His *Sociologie des Brazzavilles Noires* (1955), provides an intimate look at the two African communities surrounding the "French" city. VIRGINIA M. THOMPSON and RICHARD ADLOFF'S thorough investigation, *The Emerging States of French Equatorial Africa* (1960), is a valuable work for the period up to independence. JOHN A. BALLARD, "Four Equatorial States," in GWENDOLEN M. CARTER (ed.), *National Unity and Regionalism in Eight African States*, ch. 4 (1966), concentrates on recent history and politics. One of the few detailed studies of a particular subject is GERARD LUCAS, *Formal Education in the Congo-Brazzaville: A Study of Educational Policy and Practice* (1964). Of literary and historical interest is ANDRE GIDE, *Voyage au Congo* and *Le Retour du Tchad* (1927–28; Eng. trans., *Travels in the Congo*, 1929). RICHARD WEST, *Brazza of the Congo* (1972), is an illuminating and interesting biographical portrait.

Congo, Cultures of the

The term Congo is used in this article to designate a cultural geographical area, not a country. Along with most of the country of Zaire (the former Congo [Kinshasa]), the area includes Congo (Brazzaville), Gabon, Equatorial Guinea (the former Río Muni), southern Cameroon, the Central African Republic, northern Angola, parts of southern Sudan, and parts of Zambia, Malawi, Rhodesia, and Mozambique. Altogether, the area comprises what has been called Central Africa or Equatorial Africa. It is limited on the north by the eastern Sudan and on the south by the southern African plateau and extends from the Cameroon highlands and the Atlantic Ocean eastward toward the east African highlands of Kenya and Tanzania. The area includes two roughly equal natural zones: an equatorial forest in the north, with a savanna fringe, and an extensive savanna country in the south.

Extent of the Congo culture area

Linguistically, the populations belong to the Benue-Congo branch of the Niger-Congo (or Niger-Kordofanian) family of languages. Within the Benue-Congo branch, the languages spoken in almost the entire area are those of the Bantu sub-branch; non-Bantu languages are to be found only in the northern savanna fringe of the area (see AFRICAN LANGUAGES). Because the various Bantu languages are rather closely related to one another (on the order of, say, the Germanic languages), it is probable that the population of the Congo area stems from a common cultural base that is, historically speaking, relatively recent (2,000–2,500 years old). This situation makes understandable the many cultural similarities in the area, even though diversities have arisen from differences in ecological and economic conditions and from the largely unrecoverable workings of history.

In the northern savanna fringe of the Congo area live conglomerate and dense populations of Cameroon highlanders, linguistic cousins to the ancestors of the Bantu. The region is one of long settlement, characterized by much local reshuffling of the population, numbering at present well over 1,000,000. Among the better known groups are the Widekum (including the Meta and Mankon), Nsaw, Kom, Aghem (Wum), Bali (Li), Bamum, and the numerous Bamileke. Farther eastward along the savanna-forest border is a population of 2,000,000 that includes among its better described peoples the Wute, Azande, and Mangbetu. In the forest zone the population of 7,000,000 to 10,000,000 Bantu speakers include the Kweri (Kpe), Duala, and Basa (Bassa) of southern Cameroon; the numerous Fang, including the Bulu of Cameroon, Gabon, and Equatorial Guinea; the large number of groups in the central Congo River basin, collectively known as Mongo, including the Nkundo; the variegated groups along the middle Congo River, such as the Ngombe, who are sometimes popularly known as the Ngala (Bangala); and, in eastern Zaire, the Bira and Rega (Lega). Immediately south of the forest, in the transitional savanna zone, a relatively dense population of 10,000,000 to 15,000,000 includes, from west to east, the several Kongo groups, such as the Yombe, Teke (or Tyo), Yaka, Suku, Pende, Kuba, Lele, Songe, Lulua, and Luba. Finally, in the southern savanna proper, are 5,000,000 people including, from west to east, the Kimbundu (Mbundu), Chokwe (or Badjok), Lunda, Ndembu, Lozi, Tonga, Bemba, and Yao.

Before the Bantu expansion in the first millennium AD, the inhabitants of the forest zone were, in the main, Pygmy hunters and gatherers. At present, 200,000 Pygmies live in bands scattered from the Atlantic to the east African highlands. They have all adopted the languages of their local Bantu-speaking neighbours. Most of the Pygmies live in the deep forest, such as, for example, the well-known Mbuti of the Ituri Forest of Zaire. A few Pygmy groups are also found in the southern savanna and in Rwanda and Burundi. The Pygmy social unit is the nomadic band, seldom numbering more than 50 people. Pygmy bands have economic ties with neighbouring Bantu villages that involve the exchange of forest products for agricultural produce and artifacts.

The forest zone in the north of the Congo area and the savanna zone in the south have contrasting ecologies. Soils are poor throughout; after each harvest, land must usually lie fallow for as long as two decades. The forest zone, however, has especially poor soil, and its cultivation requires heavy labour in clearing the trees. Domestic animals, mainly chickens, goats, and pigs, as well as wild game, do less well in the forest than in the savanna. The

forest populations, in short, command fewer resources, must work harder, require more space, and live in smaller and more isolated villages.

The main food plants of the forest are bananas and such root crops as yams, taro, manioc (cassava), and sweet potatoes. In the savanna, such grain crops as sorghum, millets, and maize (corn) predominate. In the forest zone, where rainfall occurs throughout most of the year, the root crops provide a continuous supply of food that can be dug up as it is needed, although it cannot be easily preserved and accumulated in large quantities; root crops are essentially a resource the use of which is tied to a locality. The savanna, by contrast, has a more markedly seasonal rainfall, a definite harvest season, and alternating periods of shortage and plenty. The cereal grains of the savanna can be stored, accumulated, and transferred; they can be concentrated in the hands of the powerful and selectively redistributed in times of want. In short, the grain is a fluid resource that can be socially mobilized for matters quite removed from mere subsistence, and it accordingly provides the basis for a system of political power and inequality.

The forest appears once to have been a barrier to long-distance travel, making difficult the conquest and political control of large areas. The forest groups, large and small, were all politically uncentralized. The savanna, on the other hand, is more favourable to long-distance travel and trade and to the conquest and political assimilation of large groups. This fact, combined with the potentialities of a cereal economy, allowed the development of large kingdoms and empires in the savanna.

SOCIAL ORGANIZATION

The peoples of the forest. The fundamental unit of social organization in the forest is what anthropologists call the patrilineage—a group of kinsmen descended from a common ancestor through lines of males. At any given time, a patrilineage consists of several living generations of relatives, males and females. As its members die out, the group is replenished by the children fathered by its male members. As a rule, the sons live with their fathers, bringing in wives from outside; their children, if male, continue to live in the same village or locality. The predominant residential group is thus a man, his sons, and his sons' sons—all with their respective wives. When the man heading the group dies, his sons continue to live together and operate as a unit. In time, however, as new

Patrilineal social structure

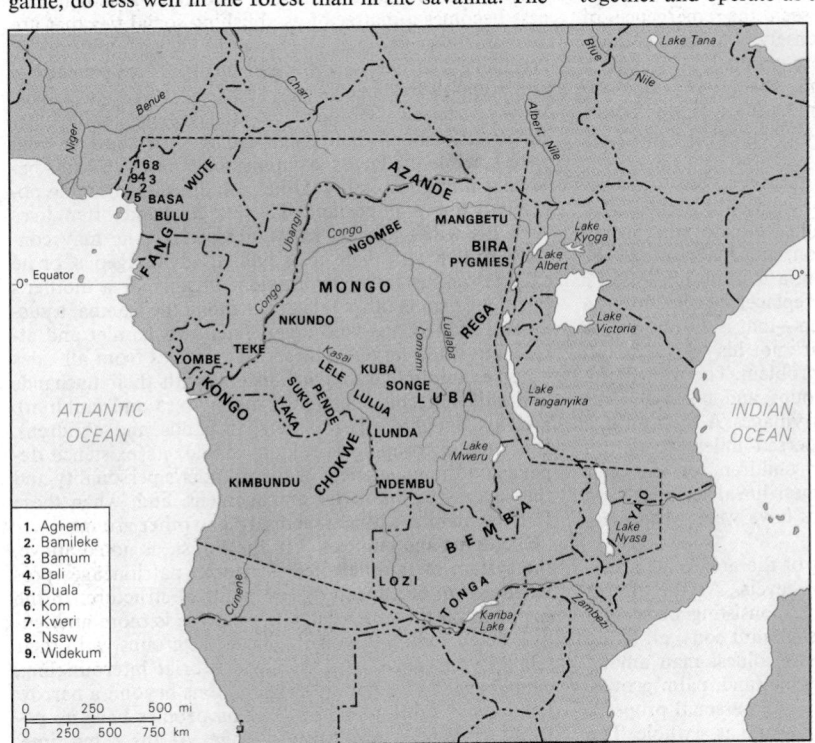

1. Aghem
2. Bamileke
3. Bamum
4. Bali
5. Duala
6. Kom
7. Kweri
8. Nsaw
9. Widekum

Distribution of the peoples of the Congo.

generations grow up, a patrilineage usually splits into two or more patrilineages. These new patrilineages continue to reside in the same vicinity, close to each other; although autonomous in everyday matters, they act as a unit on occasions such as funerals, marriages, and disputes with neighbours and may also continue to hold land and fishing sites in common. As further splitting occurs, more lineages arise. Those patrilineages that are most closely related group themselves into middle-size ones, and these, in turn, group themselves into larger patrilineages. Closely related lineages live near each other, and more distantly related ones live farther apart.

The Ngombe offer a good illustration of this arrangement. Every Ngombe belongs to a series of six ever more inclusive patrilineages. A male Ngombe belongs, first of all, to the group of his father and his father's brothers and all their children. They comprise a large household group, clearing fields together, sharing much of the produce, holding wealth in common, and engaging as a unit in all important social and economic activities. Several such small patrilineages, linked together by a common ancestor of several generations back, constitute a village section—a self-ruling unit that maintains its own internal order and makes common sacrifices to the ancestors. The village is a cluster of such patrilineally related sections, holding land in common and engaging in communal hunting. A village may also wage war on nearby villages and in this sense represents the ultimate unit of sovereignty. Finally, several clusters of villages will recognize a distant and mythical common ancestry that makes them all a single people. The result is an orderly, multilayered political structure in the forest, operating without any centralization of power and yet grouping together large numbers of people. More distant groups, speaking related languages and having similar customs, are assumed to be related through ancestors farther removed; myths of common origin arise, become accepted, and diffuse widely from group to group. In this way large numbers of local groups came to claim a single origin. The Mongo, for example, numbering about 2,000,000 persons and divided into many small independent groups, are linked by a common belief that they are descendants of a man called Mongo.

The peoples of the savanna. The forest–savanna fringe on the north of the Congo area contains peoples who are predominantly patrilineal and whose social organization is of the same pattern as that of the forest zone. This savanna fringe, however, has seen the emergence of states, large and small. In the densely populated Cameroon highlands there were in pre-colonial times small-scale chieftaincies and kingdoms, the most famous of them being that of the Bamum. In the rolling country farther east, the Wute, Zande, and Mangbetu had strong kingdoms based on conquest.

Matri-
lineal
social
structure

In the other savanna south of the forest, the social organization is, with few exceptions, based on matrilineal descent. Whereas in a patrilineage the basic relationship is the link between father and son, in a matrilineage the analogous relationship is between a man and his sister's son. Each passing generation is replaced by the children borne by the women of the group—that is, by the sisters of its men; a man's successors are not his own sons but those of his sister. Herein lies a problem. The women are married to men from other groups and normally live with their husbands in the latters' villages. A matrilineage therefore tends to become dispersed unless there are mechanisms to pull the sisters' children toward their maternal uncles. Some savanna matrilineal societies have strong stable lineages, but others have weak, dispersed, and unstable ones.

The Kongo peoples in the west of the area have a matrilineal organization of several levels. At the lowest level is the localized matrilineage consisting of several maternal brothers and their sisters' adult sons, all living together under the authority of the oldest man among them. The group jointly owns arable land, palm groves, forests, fishing sites, and animals; the personal property of its members is inherited by the group as a whole. The married women of the group (the sisters of the men) live with their husbands elsewhere, and their children remain with them and their fathers through childhood. By the time of adolescence or marriage, however, the male children return to their mothers' brothers—that is, to their own matrilineage. This move insures that the adult male members of the matrilineage end up living together as a group. Several such matrilineages, related through a common ancestress, constitute together a wider matrilineage; they occupy as a unit a certain territory, come together for funerals and sacrifices to ancestors, exchange periodic gifts, and share in a portion of each others' inheritance. Finally, numerous dispersed matrilineages may recognize their common descent from a yet more distant and perhaps mythical ancestress, but this relationship has little content.

Eastward from the Kongo peoples, the matrilineal structures are more variable. Among the Yaka and Suku, a young male of the matrilineage does not join his mother's brothers early in life; rather, he lives with his own father until the latter dies and thereafter may continue to live with his father's relatives. The adult male members of the matrilineage, numbering ten or so persons, do not have a common residence as among the Kongo peoples. The matrilineage, however, is still an economic unit: it holds rights over hunting territories and palm groves, and the property of its members is considered to be held in common and is inherited by the lineage as a unit and distributed within it. The members of the matrilineage assemble together for marriages and funerals, and its elders visit each other and confer together when matters arise affecting lineage interests. Beyond a certain point, however, dispersal makes it difficult to maintain contact. While a small matrilineage can operate as a unit within the confines of a locality, several such related local matrilineages are usually too scattered in the midst of other matrilineages to constitute a wider grouping that can engage in effective common action. Generally, then, one does not find in the savanna, as in the forest, lineage organizations consisting of many different levels. The tendency instead is for local matrilineages to be autonomous social groups whose links with related matrilineages are primarily ritual in nature.

Population
mobility in
the east

Moving eastward in the savanna belt, the land tends to become poorer, shifting cultivation more extensive, and the population more mobile. Wealth in the form of utensils, money, and a few domestic animals is fluid and unstable. Unused land is readily available. Personal success becomes a matter of establishing social ties that are advantageous under a given set of conditions and of changing them when conditions change. Matrilineal ties consequently become looser and less structured as one moves eastward. The local matrilineages are small, sometimes little more than local enclaves of brothers and sisters, while the larger groupings have few functions beyond mutual hospitality. Other relationships become potentially more important. Thus, a husband often lives with his wife's parents early in marriage; he may continue to live with them if he finds it advantageous, or he may rejoin his father or an elder brother or a mother's brother or some other relative. Among the Bemba, a successful man is one who creates his own hamlet and attracts to it the largest number of relatives from all sides —for example, his married sisters (with their husbands and children), his sons (with their wives and children), and his daughters (with their husbands and children). But such a grouping is seldom stable; its existence depends on the magnetism of the founder's personality and the success of his social management, and, when these fail, the members attach themselves to other groups.

Kingdoms and empires. In the forest, as noted above, the system of multilevelled territorial patrilineages provided a firm but uncentralized political structure. In the savanna, on the other hand, the picture is more ambiguous. Of themselves the matrilineal kin groups, with their tendency toward dispersal and territorial intermingling, cannot readily carry political functions beyond a narrow local context. Many of the savanna peoples have no political structures beyond the village. At the same time, the very weakness of these structures makes them ineffective in opposing conquest by organized force. Accidents of history have shaped the political fortunes of the peoples of the savanna to a greater extent than those of the peoples of the forest. The latter achieved a kind of equilibrium that might be called the lower middle level of political development. In the savanna, ambitious and talented men have been able to create large-scale chieftaincies and kingdoms.

The structures of these polities varied. The Kuba federation, founded in the mid-17th century, with a population of over 100,000, consisted of 18 tribes and was headed by the king of one of them, the Bushong (Bushongo). The king received tribute from each of the tribes, confirmed the succession of their chiefs, acted as the final judge in their quarrels, and maintained an army to enforce his authority. Each tribe, however, governed itself in its own way; indeed, the tribes did not all speak the same language. The looseness of the federation can be seen from the fact that member chiefdoms would occasionally go to war with each other without the king's intervention.

Another political structure was that of the Lunda empire. Its nucleus was a small chieftaincy in the Lunda homeland that from about AD 1600 expanded its sway over successively larger territories. Some of these conquests were directed from the centre; others were made on the private initiative of Lunda adventurers who installed themselves as chiefs with ultimate allegiance to the Lunda king. In the middle of the 19th century, Lunda dependencies and offshoots stretched 1,000 miles from east to west, incorporating, among others, such diverse peoples as the Yaka, Ndembu, Lozi, and Bemba. The constituent parts of the empire, while recognizing the headship of the Lunda king and sending him regular tribute, were essentially autonomous chiefdoms and kingdoms; the conquerors were culturally assimilated by the conquered, although they maintained their tribal identity as Lunda. They generally preserved the political structures of the conquered and recognized the existing chiefs but installed alongside them Lunda residents who saw to it that tribute was collected and allegiances were kept.

The historic kingdom of the Kongo represents another pattern of kingdom formation. When Portuguese navigators arrived at the mouth of the Congo River in 1484, they found a prosperous and powerful kingdom that had been established about 100 years before. It had grown by conquest in an area of considerable cultural homogeneity and was one of several kingdoms the inhabitants of which, speaking closely related dialects, came to be collectively known as the Kongo peoples. Culturally more integrated than the Lunda or the Kuba domains, these kingdoms were highly centralized in their administration, the king having the power to appoint and dismiss provincial and local chiefs. After converting to Christianity, the kings of the Kongo became allied with the Portuguese. In 1568 the kingdom was ravaged by invaders from the interior, but it recovered, reached another peak in the mid-17th century, and thereafter gradually declined as a result of internal rivalries and external conflicts with the Portuguese and neighbouring African kingdoms. By the middle of the 19th century, its old capital, São Salvador, had become the ruined head village of a small chieftaincy.

These savanna kingdoms, for all their differences in origin, fortunes, and size, show certain similarities of organization. Their overall structure may be called pyramidal. The king, at the top, had the allegiance of regional chiefs, each of whom was suzerain over local chiefs, the latter each having authority over a number of villages. The nature of the links in this hierarchy varied. When distances were immense, as in the case of the Lunda empire, the link between the Lunda centre and an outlying dependency might have little substance beyond occasional gifts symbolizing allegiance; within the dependency itself, however, the ruler could be very strong, as was, for example, the Lunda king of the Yaka. In other cases, domination was minimal, even at the local level. One measure of the power of the centre was the amount of control the king had over key positions in the hier-

archy. In the most centralized kingdoms, the king appointed and dismissed local chiefs, as did the Kongo kings. In most cases, however, local positions were in the hands of particular lineages, and the king had little say in the naming of the incumbent, although he ritually confirmed him in the position.

An important and sometimes primary concern of these systems was the collection of tribute. This took the form of food; the meat of certain animals, such as the elephant; skins, such as those of leopards; local currency, such as salt or raffia cloth or copper bars; and ivory. Less integrated systems, such as the Suku kingdom, were little concerned with administration and left those matters to a variety of local institutions and informal mechanisms. In the more integrated kingdoms, such as that of the Bemba, the hierarchy concerned itself with the recruitment of labour and soldiers, the monopoly of trade in ivory, the prohibition of violence, the settlement of disputes, and the punishment of crime; the chiefs at each successive level acted as judges to whom one could progressively appeal, the king being the court of final instance. The administrative apparatus sometimes became quite elaborate: the paramount chief of the Bemba had at his court 30 to 40 functionaries concerned with administration.

These pyramidal structures were eminently suited to large conquest states in societies having rudimentary means of communication. As the state expanded, it simply attached existing local systems to an appropriate level of the hierarchy. Even small kingdoms could be readily incorporated by making the king into a regional chief and leaving his hierarchy intact. Even quite disparate peoples of different political and social systems, customs, and languages could be incorporated into an overall structure of domination and tribute collection. But, if the system was flexible, it was also fragile; regions could be lopped off as easily as they had been attached. A kingdom was usually most solid at its core, while the periphery resembled a sphere of influence with uncertain and fluctuating allegiances. Changes in the upper levels of the pyramid had little effect on the lives of local peoples. The kingdoms did not develop into large, culturally unified quasi-nations sharing a sense of common destiny.

Family and kinship. A lineage in these Congo societies transcends its individual members. Like a corporation, the lineage has an existence of its own, regardless of changes in its actual personnel; it owns property, has a legal personality, and carries on litigation. It is often said to "own" its members in the sense that it has the right to dispose of them without interference from outsiders; traditionally, this meant the right to kill or sell a member for the greater good of the corporate body. The governing power of the lineage lies in its oldest members, who are, so to speak, the board of directors, having the greatest say in decisions because of the wisdom that goes with age and because of their closeness to the oldest members of all—the dead ancestors who, it is believed, continue to be involved in the affairs of their lineage.

In such a social setting, marriage cannot be simply a matter between a man and a woman; it necessarily involves their respective lineages. When a woman leaves her lineage to marry, a loss occurs that requires compensation. A few societies in the north of the Congo area have met this by a system of direct exchange of women: lineage A gave a woman in marriage to lineage B, and B gave one in return. There are, however, obvious difficulties in that group B may not have a woman to give at a particular time or an eligible woman may refuse to marry anyone in A. In most Congo societies, including those sometimes practicing direct exchange, the compensation is made in kind: A pays a bride price to B in animals, goods, or currency.

It is critical that these transactions represent the legal and not the sentimental side of marriage, but they do not exclude sentiment any more than do the transactions attending marriage in other cultures. The payment of a bride price does not mean that the wife is a chattel; in fact, divorce is far from infrequent and can be instigated by the wife. All that is acquired are certain rights: the right to the food that the wife will grow and cook for her husband and certain defined rights to the children. In patrilineages the children quite unambiguously belong to their father's lineage. In matrilineages the situation is often more complex: the children belong to their mother's matrilineage, but the father has some rights over them; for example, the Suku father is entitled to have his sons live with him and bring him shares of the game they catch, and he has the right to a portion of the bride price paid by the husbands of his daughters to the latter's matrilineage.

These various rights over women and children are held, it must be stressed, not by individuals but by lineages. If a husband dies while his wife is still of childbearing age, she must either remarry someone else in the husband's lineage, or, if she decides to leave, her lineage must reimburse a portion of the bride price they received, account being taken of the period she had lived with her husband and of the children she had borne. The children of a man are not merely his but those of the lineage: a man calls his brother's child by the same term as his own; in a patrilineal society the child will refer to the entire lineage of his mother as being his collective mothers, and in a matrilineal society the child will call his father's entire lineage his fathers.

.No term exists in Congo societies for family in the Western sense of a unit of father, mother, and children. In the matrilineal societies, because a woman's children belong to her matrilineage, the latter takes great interest in them and the mother; the tie between the mother and her matrilineage remains strong, and she and her children are a kind of temporary enclave in the husband's village, her independence vis à vis her husband being correspondingly great. Divorce in these societies tends to be relatively frequent. In the patrilineal societies, marriage and family tend to be more stable. In them the woman produces children for her husband's lineage, and her own lineage consequently has somewhat less interest in her.

In all these societies, polygyny (marriage of a man to several wives) is widely practiced. Generally, it is only the middle-aged and the old men who have more than one wife—partly because they are apt to control more wealth, and partly because older men who have survived their lineage brethren find themselves in charge of several widows who automatically become their wives. Polygyny is possible because men tend to marry rather late (traditionally, sometimes as late as 35), while women marry soon after puberty. The total number of marriageable men is therefore smaller than the total number of marriageable women. In the patrilineal societies there is sometimes a mild hierarchy among wives, the first wife having some authority over the others. In matrilineal societies, in which wives are rather independent, such a hierarchy is difficult to impose, and the polygynous household is, in effect, not a unit but rather several households that share equally in a single husband-father.

Kinship and politics

Not only are kinship relations basic to the social organization of the peoples of the Congo area, but kinship often provides the model for expressing other kinds of relations. As seen above, the political organization of the forest peoples is a lineage system writ large. The traditional political hierarchies of the savanna are likewise often cast in the idiom of kinship: a superior chief is "older brother" or "maternal uncle" or "father" to a subordinate one, regardless of the age and actual relationship of the incumbents. What one thinks of as slavery was also often fitted into the kinship model. Throughout the Congo area the idea existed that persons could be acquired for money or goods, but such acquisition often resembled adoption. In these societies most systems of rights over people, such as wives, children, junior lineage members, etc., were regarded as material exchanges. In the smaller societies especially, operating rather close to the level of subsistence, power lay in the number of members a lineage could muster; an acquired person became a lineage member. Although slaves and their descendants were usually of somewhat inferior status in matters such as ceremonial precedence or succession to the lineage headship, their position in other respects

scarcely differed from that of ordinary lineage members. The lineage was thought of as owning all its members, and even members by blood could be sold or killed at the decision of the elders. In the more complex savanna societies, however, where wealth differences were pronounced and labour could readily be put to profit, slavery had a less familial tinge; in some kingdoms (for example, the Kuba, Lunda, and Kongo), kings and important chiefs had settlements of slaves or serfs directly under their authority.

As in most of sub-Saharan Africa, age is an important criterion of status in the Congo area, but it does not give rise to an elaborate system of age grades such as those of East Africa. Only among the Kuba, Lele, and neighbouring peoples are there recognized age groupings within each village (young warriors, middle-aged producers, and elders). Almost everywhere, however, there is ceremonial recognition of the transition of males from adolescence to adulthood, involving circumcision or some test of endurance. In the forest, such rites of passage for boys are relatively simple. In the southern savanna, circumcision rites for adolescents are elaborate and prolonged, and, in the eastern part of the Congo area, there are elaborate initiation rites for girls in preparation for marriage.

ECONOMIC PATTERNS

The villages of the forest zone are compact and rarely accommodate more than 20 or 30 households along the sides of a single street. This pattern is also found at the forest–savanna fringe, as among the Kuba and some of the northern Kongo groups. In the savanna proper, the settlement pattern is more variable; there are dispersed homesteads, small hamlets, and large, sometimes stockaded villages.

Handicrafts

Handicrafts were highly developed in the Congo area, particularly in the savanna. Basketry, pottery, ironworking, the weaving of raffia fibers into mats, wood carving, the tapping of palm wine, and the extraction of palm oil were among the specialized occupations upon which economic exchange was based. The exchange was facilitated by the use of certain goods as money. Objects that served as money for different groups included raffia cloth, hoes, copper bars, spear points, throwing knives, bars of salt, and cowrie shells. There were professions as well: dancers and musicians, medical specialists, diviners, advocates in legal cases, and private mediators of disputes, all of whom were paid for their services.

The products of the Congo craftsmen are highly prized by collectors of objects of art, particularly the wooden sculptures made for religious use. Other wooden carvings include stools, bowls, boxes, cups, combs, headrests, staffs, and statues of chiefs and kings. The Congo is less known for its architecture, which achieved decorative distinction in the painted mud walls of the central savanna area. Music and dance are among the primary vehicles of aesthetic expression. The area's oral literature—for example, historical sagas—remains largely unknown outside.

RELIGION

The traditional religious systems of the Congo have several salient features in common. All recognize a creator, seen usually in rather abstract terms as a kind of first cause. Subordinate spirits of nature are important in the religion of the northern parts of the area, as are ancestors. In the religions of the southern savanna, nature spirits and deities are unimportant, while ancestral cults are highly developed. Ancestral cults are based on the belief that one's dead older kinsmen continue to have an interest in the lives of those they have left behind and that all elders, dead or living, are endowed with special powers. Consequently, the dead continue to be part of society, and their cult is concerned with the maintenance of relations with them. There is also a belief throughout the Congo that some persons possess extraordinary powers, either from birth or by acquiring them in secret; misfortunes, illnesses, and deaths are often attributed to these persons. The concept resembles the European idea of witches.

One of the principal concerns of the traditional religious systems is the maintenance of health and good fortune. The causes of misfortune and illness are believed to be the activities of ancestors, witches, spirits, or, more impersonally, certain magical medicines controlled by specialists. An important part is played by the diviner, who determines the specific cause of a given misfortune. Counteraction can then be taken: ancestors may be asked for help or spirits placated or appropriate medicines taken; or witches may be sought out and asked to desist, sometimes even killed.

MODERN CHANGES

The establishment of European colonial control in the 1880s had a profound impact on the cultures of the Congo area, although the long-term consequences are still unclear. Many regions, however, did not experience steady European control until the 1920s and 1930s. For most of the Congo area, the Westernization period has been rather short: the colonial administrator came and went within the single lifetime of many a person. Westernization is itself a misnomer, for Western cultural influence is only a small part of the story. The important consequences of contact with the West have been not so much changes in culture as changes in the geographical, sociological, and political settings within which African cultural processes continue to unfold.

Political sovereignty and traditional loyalties

One problem facing African countries is that their boundaries, drawn by colonial powers for political reasons, incorporated numerous previously autonomous groups into single countries. The largest number of groups, with the greatest variety, are found in Zaire, the former Belgian Congo. Even when the observer can see cultural similarities among certain groups, this does not mean that the groups themselves feel a common identity. It is sometimes said that African countries became countries before they had become self-conscious nations. This statement, however, is true of most countries, except for certain modern European countries, such as Germany, Italy, Poland, and Hungary. Most European countries, it should be observed, are ethnically heterogenous. In the past they were held together by aristocratic ruling classes, the members of which sprang from different ethnic groups and often had more in common with each other than each with their ethnic brethren below them. African societies, on the other hand, are strikingly egalitarian; their institutions, integrated by ties seen in kinship terms, make for deep attachments to local groups and inhibit the rise of an isolated elite. Certain occupational elites exist—lawyers, administrators, doctors, priests, engineers—but all remain close to their own groups. The matter is further complicated by the fact that African countries have emerged in an era when the accepted idiom for international political discourse is "democratic." In African terms this means the satisfaction of the demands of large, visible, self-defined interest groups that are ethnic in origin rather than economic. Industrialization, rising standards of living, and mass education do not of themselves eliminate conflict between nations and peoples, as much modern history has shown. In Africa, wider communications, migration to cities and plantations, and contacts with other peoples have had a broadening effect. Members of small neighbouring groups that previously knew only each other, sometimes as potential enemies, now realize their cultural similarity because they have become aware of their common differences from other groups; peoples that before only shared common myths of origin and spoke similar dialects (*e.g.*, the Mongo) now see themselves as a single people. But the replacement of old "tribes" by new and much larger groups may only shift conflicts to another, wider sphere. Peoples of the forest, for example, come to feel greater kinship with each other while recognizing their contrast with peoples from the savanna. The ultimate consequences in Africa cannot be predicted.

Emerging cultural syntheses

Regional cultural identities may be expected to create cultural styles of their own, syntheses of local cultural elements. Such emerging syntheses are best understood as contemporary African, in which the governing process is not the Westernization of Africa but the Africanization of Western elements. At the most mundane level, one can see this in the way European cloth has been used to produce entirely new African clothing styles. In the sphere of religion one can see a gradual Africanization of Christianity (paralleling the past Africanization of Islām in West Africa)—a process analogous, historically, to the Europeanization of Christianity in earlier times. Sub-Saharan Africa may even become a notably Christian continent, although the African Christianity that is emerging promises to contain many African cultural elements; for example, it is likely to accept polygyny and bride price and to have drumming and dancing in its ritual. The contemporary African political culture, by the same token, contains such African elements as permanent, rather than periodic, occupancy of high offices and does not distinguish between legislative and executive powers.

Whatever the political future of the African countries, the colonial experience has left a permanent imprint on the cultural setting. These countries are, in effect, parts of large international "cultural areas" in which the means of communication are books, magazines, films, radio and television programs, and higher education. The cultural metropole of one area is France; of the other, the Anglo-American world. It is unlikely that the present European national languages will be displaced, for they are the languages of the educated and their link with the outside world.

BIBLIOGRAPHY. JAN VANSINA, *Introduction à l'ethnographie du Congo* (1966), is a general introduction to the core of the area; his *Kingdoms of the Savanna* (1966) is a history of the southern savanna belt. A.I. RICHARDS, "Some Types of Family Structure Amongst the Central Bantu," in A.R. RADCLIFFE-BROWN and DARYLL FORDE (eds.), *African Systems of Kinship and Marriage* (1950), deals with the social structures of the southern savanna.

For the Cameroon highlands, see E.M. CHILVER and P.M. KABERRY, *Traditional Bamenda: The Precolonial History and Ethnography of the Bamenda Grassfields* (1968). A northern savanna group is described in E.E. EVANS-PRITCHARD, *The Azande* (1971). Works dealing with the peoples of Zaire are mainly in French and Flemish (see Vansina's work above), though one may sample the area in English: C.M. TURNBULL, *The Forest People* (1961), on the pygmies; K.E. LAMAN, *The Kongo*, 4 vol. (1953–68); WYATT MacGAFFEY, *Custom and Government in the Lower Congo* (1970); I. KOPYTOFF in J.L. GIBBS (ed.), *Peoples of Africa* (1965), on the Suku; MARY T. DOUGLAS, *The Lele of the Kasai* (1963); and ALAN P. MERRIAM et al., "The Concept of Culture Clusters Applied to the Belgian Congo," *SWest. J. Anthrop.*, 15:373–395 (1959).

For the southern savanna formerly under British control, see ELIZABETH COLSON and MAX GLUCKMAN (eds.), *Seven Tribes of British Central Africa* (1951); ELIZABETH COLSON, *Marriage and the Family Among the Plateau Tonga of Northern Rhodesia* (1958); A.I. RICHARDS, *Land, Labour and Diet in Northern Rhodesia* (1939), on the Bemba; J.C. MITCHELL, *The Yao Village: A Study in the Social Structure of a Nyasaland Tribe* (1956); IAN G. CUNNISON, *The Luapula Peoples of Northern Rhodesia* (1959); and V.W. TURNER, *Schism and Continuity in an African Society: A Study of Ndembu Village Life* (1957).

The literature on recent social, cultural, and political change is very large. PIERRE L. VAN DEN BERGHE (ed.), *Africa: Social Problems of Change and Conflict* (1965), contains a bibliography. For a local view of changes, see A.L. EPSTEIN, *Politics in an Urban African Community* (1958); HORTENSE POWDERMAKER, *Copper Town, Changing Africa: The Human Situation on the Rhodesian Copperbelt* (1962); and JEAN LA FONTAINE, *City Politics: A Study of Léopoldville, 1962–63* (1970).

(I.Ko.)

Congo River

The Congo (or Zaire) River, with a length of 2,900 miles (4,700 kilometres), is longer than any other river in Africa except for the Nile. It rises in Zambia between Lakes Tanganyika and Nyasa (Malawi) as the Chambeshi River at an altitude of 5,760 feet (1,760 metres) above sea level and at a distance of about 430 miles from the Indian Ocean. Its course, as represented on the map, then takes the form of a giant counterclockwise arc, flowing northwest, west, and southwest before draining into the Atlantic Ocean at Banana (Banane), Zaire. Its drainage basin, covering an area of 1,335,000 square miles (3,457,000 square kilometres), takes in almost the entire territory of Zaire (formerly Congo [Kinshasa]), as well as most of that of Congo (Brazzaville), the Central African Republic, western Zambia, and northern Angola, in addition to parts of Cameroon and Tanzania.

The Congo River system forms a vast network of inland waterways almost 8,000 miles in length. Access to the sea is, however, blocked by Livingstone Falls, a series of 32 cataracts that occur about 200 miles from the mouth. Two capital cities stand opposite one another on the Congo's banks at Malebo (Stanley) Pool, 300 miles from the mouth. These are Kinshasa, capital of Zaire, on the southern bank, and Brazzaville, capital of the People's Republic of the Congo, on the northern bank.

Comparisons with the Amazon

Together with the Amazon River (q.v.), the Congo constitutes one of the two great rivers of the world that flow out of an equatorial zone subject to heavy rainfall that occurs throughout all or almost all the months of the year. As with the Amazon, too, the rainfall that feeds the Congo River varies in a pattern with two maximums and two minimums each year. Upstream from Brazzaville and Kinshasa, the Congo Basin receives an average of almost 60 inches (1,500 millimetres) of rain a year, of which 22 percent runs off into the river system. The drainage basin of the Congo is, however, only about half the size of that of the Amazon; its rate of flow—1,460,-000 cubic feet (41,300 cubic metres) a second at its mouth—may be compared to the Amazon's flow of more than 6,000,000 cubic feet.

While the Chambeshi River, as the remotest source, may be considered to form the Congo's original main stream in terms of the river's length, it is another tributary—the Lualaba, which rises near Musofi in the Shaba (formerly Katanga) region of Zaire—that carries the greatest quantity of water and may consequently be considered as forming the Congo's original main stream in terms of water volume. If, as sometimes occurs, the Lualaba is considered as the true main stream, the Congo's length is about 2,700 miles instead of 2,900 miles.

Names of the river

When the river first became known to Europeans at the end of the 15th century, they called it the Zaire, a corruption of a word that is variously given as *nzari, nzali, njali, nzaddi,* and *niadi* and that means simply "river" in many African dialects. It was only in the early years of the 17th century that the river was first called the "Rio Congo," a name that was taken from the Kingdom of Kongo situated on the lower part of the river's course. Elsewhere the river is given a diversity of names by the populations living on its banks. In 1971, when the Democratic Republic of the Congo changed its name to Zaire, the government also renamed the river as the Zaire. As the river, however, has an international status, it continues to be internationally known as the Congo. To the literary minded the river is evocative of the famous 1902 novel *Heart of Darkness,* by Joseph Conrad. His book conjured up an atmosphere of foreboding, treachery, greed, and exploitation. Today, however, the Congo appears as the key to future economic development of the Central African interior. (For associated physical features, see EAST AFRICAN LAKES; EAST AFRICAN MOUNTAINS; ITURI FOREST; see also the city article KINSHASA; for historical aspects, see CENTRAL AFRICA, HISTORY OF.)

The Congo Basin. The expression Congo Basin refers, strictly speaking, to the hydrographic basin. This is not only vast but is also—with the exception of the sandy plateaus in the southwest—covered with a dense and ramified network of tributaries, subtributaries, and small rivers.

The Congo Basin is the most clearly distinguished of the various geographic depressions situated between the Sahara (q.v.) to the north, the Atlantic Ocean to the south and west, and the region of the East African lakes (q.v.) to the east. In this basin, a fan-shaped web of tributaries flows downward along concentric slopes that range from 900 to 1,500 feet in altitude and that enclose a central depression. The basin itself stretches for more than 1,200 miles from north to south (from the Congo–Chad watershed to the interior plateaus of Angola); it measures only

about 1,200 miles from the Atlantic in the west to the Nile–Congo watershed in the east.

Drillings made downward through an impressive thickness of the central depression have revealed the layers of continental sediments as they appear on the land surface successively from the centre of the basin to its outer edge. These layers consist of alluvial deposits of the Quaternary Period (up to 2,500,000 years old), secondary sands and sandstones (i.e., derived from erosion), and deposits from the later part of Precambrian time (which lasted from 570,000,000 to 4,600,000,000 years ago). Relief and geological formation alike are basin shaped, both demonstrating a persistent tendency to subsidence in this part of the continent that is compensated for by a corresponding uplifting at the rim, above all in the east (where heights of more than 9,000 feet overlook Lake Tanganyika), as well as in the southeast.

The Congo River system. From its sources to its mouth, the Congo has three contrasting sections—the Upper Congo, Middle Congo, and Lower Congo.

The Upper Congo. The upper reaches are characterized by three features—confluences, lakes, and waterfalls or rapids. To begin with, several streams of approximately equal size unite to form the river. In a stretch of little more than 60 miles, the upper Lualaba joins the Luvua and then the Lukuga. Each stream for part of its course undergoes at least a lacustrine type of expansion, even when it does not form a lake. Thus, Lake Upemba occurs on the upper Lualaba; Lakes Bangweulu and Mweru occur on the Chambeshi–Luapula–Luvua system (the river flows out of each of the latter two lakes under a different name); and finally Lake Tanganyika, which is fed by the Ruzizi (flowing from Lake Kivu) and by the Malagarasi, itself flows into the Lukuga Waterfalls. Rapids occur not only along the headstreams but also several times along the course of the main stream. Navigation thus is possible only along sections of the Upper Congo.

The lake region

The Middle Congo. Downstream at Kisangani (formerly Stanleyville), seven cataracts, known by the name of Stanley Falls, mark the true beginning of the navigable Congo. This central part of the river flows steadily for more than 1,000 miles to within 22 miles of Kinshasa. Its course at first is narrow but soon grows wider, after which many islands occur in midstream. This change in the character of the river corresponds to its entry into its alluvial plain. From that point onward, with the exception of a few rare narrow sections, the Congo divides into several arms, separated by strings of islands. It increases from a width of more than three and a half miles downstream from Isangi (where the Lomami enters the Congo) to a width of from five to seven miles and on occasion—for example, at the mouth of the Mongala—to eight miles. Beyond the levees (embankments formed by silt deposits) occurring on either bank, some areas are subjected to extensive flooding that increases the river's bounds still further. (It is not always easy to distinguish such areas from the "rain swamps" in regions lying between rivers.) The middle course of the Congo ends in a narrow section called the Chenal (Channel), or Couloir (Corridor). Between banks no more than half a mile to a mile wide, the river bed deepens, and the current becomes rapid, flowing through a valley that cuts down several hundreds of yards deep into the soft sandstone bedrock of the Plateau Batéké. Along this central reach the Congo receives its principal tributaries, primarily the Ubangi and the Sangha on the right bank and the Kwa on the left bank. An enormous increase in the average rate of flow results, rising from less than 250,000 cubic feet (7,000 cubic metres) a second at Kisangani to more than 1,400,000 (40,000 cubic metres) at Kinshasa.

The Lower Congo. Upon leaving the Chenal, the Congo divides into two branches, forming a vast lacustrine area, about 15 miles by 17 miles, called the Malebo (Stanley) Pool, which marks the end of the Middle Congo. Immediately downstream occur the first waterfalls of the final section of the river's course. Cataracts and rapids are grouped into two separate series, separated by a fairly calm central reach. Over a distance of about 217 miles the altitude drops from a little less than 900

Malebo (Stanley) Pool

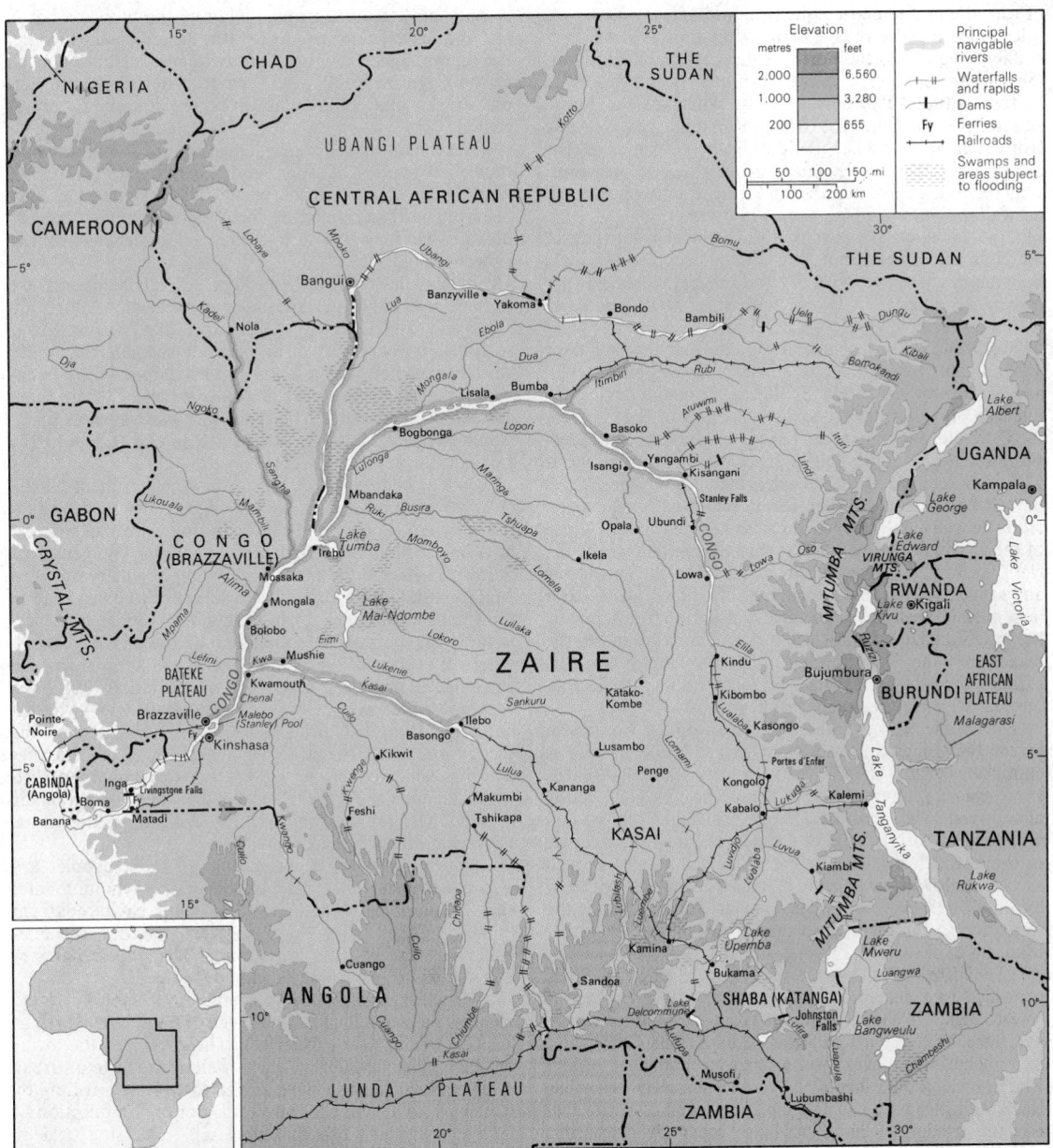

The Congo River Basin and its drainage network.

feet to a few yards above sea level. From the last rapids to the ocean—a distance of about 90 miles—the river, once more steady in its course, flows for a certain distance through deep and narrow gorges. When it reaches the sea it flows through a submarine canyon.

Hydrology. The Congo has a regular flow, which is fed by rains throughout the year. At Kinshasa the flow has for years remained between the high level of 2,310,-000 cubic feet a second, recorded during the flood of 1908, and the low level of 756,000 cubic feet a second, recorded in 1905. During the unusual flood of 1961, however, by far the highest for a century, the flow probably exceeded 2,600,000 cubic feet a second.

At Brazzaville and Kinshasa, the river's regime is characterized by a main maximum at the end of the year and a secondary maximum in the spring, as well as by a major low level during the summer and a secondary low level during March and April. Each year the rate of flow, shown on a graph, manifests individual characteristics; the secondary maximum and minimum in particular are subject to great variations of flow and irregularity in time. Its correspondence with the local rainfall regime is striking, although without direct significance. In reality the downstream regime of the Congo represents climatic influence extending over 20° of latitude, or about 1,400 miles. Each tributary in its course modifies the level of

the main stream. Thus, for example, the summer low level at Malebo Pool results from two factors: a drought that occurs for several months in the southern part of the basin at this season, as well as the seasoned delay before the floods of the Ubangi tributary flowing down from the north arrive, which does not happen before August. The Congo Basin is so vast that no single meteorological circumstance is capable of disturbing the slow movement of the waters' rise and fall. The annual graph may alter drastically, however, when floodwaters from different tributaries that normally coincide with each other arrive at different times.

Lake Tanganyika, apart from brief tidal waves caused by sudden changes in atmospheric pressure, may experience considerable variations in its water level from year to year. In 1960, for example, its waters flooded parts of Kalemi, Zaire, and Bujumbura, Burundi. A series of particularly rainy years, followed by a blocking of the outlet by floating vegetation, may explain this phenomenon.

The natural environment. *Climate.* Very typical of the regions through which the Congo flows is that of Yangambi, a locality situated on the river bank, slightly north of the Equator, a little downstream from Kisangani and below Stanley Falls. Annual rainfall amounts to 66 inches and occurs fairly regularly; even in the driest month the rainfall amounts to more than three inches.

The rainfall pattern

From the pluviometric equator (an imaginary east–west line indicating the region of heaviest rainfall), which is situated slightly to the north of the geographic Equator, the amount of rainfall decreases regularly in proportion to the latitude. The northernmost points of the basin, situated in the Central African Republic, receive only from eight to 16 inches less during the course of a year than points near the Equator; the dry season, however, lasts for four or five months, and there is only one annual rainfall maximum, which occurs in summer.

In the far southern part of the basin, at a latitude of 12° S, in the Shaba region, the climate becomes definitely Sudanic in character, with dry and the wet seasons of approximate equal length and with rainfall of about 47 inches a year.

Vegetation.   The equatorial climate that prevails over a significant part of the Congo Basin is coextensive with a dense evergreen forest. Sheltered from the drying influences prevalent on Angola's coast and in East Africa, the Congolese forest spreads out over the central depression, extending continuously from about 4° N to about 5° S, interrupted only by clearings, many of which have a natural origin. The forest region is bordered on either side by belts of savanna (grassy parkland); those of the south, dotted with a few shrubs, continue along the right bank of the river as far as the Equator. The forest and savanna often meet imperceptibly, blending together in a mosaic pattern; more rarely, strips of forest invade the grassland. Farther away from the Equator, and to the extent that the Sudanic features of the climate become evident, the wooded savanna region, with its thin deciduous forest, is progressively reached.

As it courses through the solid mass of the Congolese forest, the Congo and its tributaries are bordered by discontinuous grassy strips. Meadows of *Echinochloa* (barnyard grass), papyrus, and Cyperaceae (sedge) occupy abandoned river channels, fringe the banks, or, behind a curtain of forest, blanket the depressions in the centre of the islands; they also spring up on sandbanks, as well as on the downstream ends of islands that are fertilized by the floods. A shrub, alchornea, frequently marks the transition to the high forest that grows on the levees behind the banks.

Animal life.   The animal life of the Congo Basin is identified to a certain extent with that of the equatorial forest, which is sharply distinct from the wildlife of the savannas. Within this equatorial domain, the Congo and its principal tributaries form a separate ecological milieu. The animal population of the great waterways often has fewer affinities with the neighbouring marshes or the forests on dry land than it has with other river systems, whether of the coastal region or the savannas.

Numerous species of fish live in the waters of the Congo—235 have been identified to date in the waters of Malebo Pool and in the waters that flow into it alone. The riverine swamps, which often dry up at low water, are inhabited by lungfish, which survive the dry periods buried and encysted in cocoons of mucus. In the wooded marshlands, where the water is the colour of black tea, black catfish swim, assuming the colour of their environment. The wildlife of the marshes and that of the little parallel streams does not mix with the wildlife of the river itself. Throughout the Middle Congo, from one end to the other, the same biotypes (groups of organisms having the same hereditary characteristics) are to be found, as are also similar types of biotic associations. The Lower Congo, on the contrary, is marked by a certain tendency to local particularism in its animal life.

The waters of the Congo contain various kinds of reptiles, of which crocodiles are the most striking species. Semi-aquatic tortoises are also to be found, as are several species of water snakes.

The forest birdlife constitutes, together with the birdlife of the East African mountains, the most specifically indigenous of that to be found on the African continent. In the Congo region 266 species typical of the equatorial forest have been recorded. Occasionally or seasonally, however, nontypical birds may be observed. Seabirds, such as the sea swallow, fly upstream from the ocean. Migratory birds from Europe, including the blongios heron and the *Ixobrychus minutus* (little bittern), pass through the region. Species with a wide African distribution, such as the Egyptian duck, also have been noted. Ducks, herons, storks, and pelicans, however, are abundantly represented.

Aquatic mammals are rare, consisting of the hippopotamus, two species of otter, and the manatee (sea cow), which lives entirely in the water. The manatee has only been officially identified on the Sangha tributary but appears to have given rise to some curious legends on the Lower Congo.

Man and the river.   Three types of environments are to be found, either juxtaposed or in succession, along the river and its tributaries. These are: first, the narrower sections, bordered by firm ground; second, the wider stretches, dotted with islands and accompanied by backwaters; third, zones where flooding occurs or where there are extensive marshes. The shallower lakes, such as Bangweulu, Mweru, Tumba, and Mai-Ndombe (Léopold II), fall into the second category.

The riverine population and economy.   Almost all the river peoples engage in fishing. Along the narrow sections, where rapids often occur, fishing is only of interest to a small number of villages. The Enya (Wagenia) of Stanley Falls and the Manyanga living downstream from Malebo Pool attach fish traps to stakes or to dams built in the rapids themselves. Fishing of a very different nature, notably by poison, is conducted in the marshy areas, where the population is more extensive than might be imagined. Among these peoples, who often are refugees, are the "water people"—the Ngala (Bangala)—who inhabit the Itimbiri-Ngiri and the triangle formed by the Congo and the Ubangi. Other fisherfolk of the marshes dwell in the lagoons (as these otherwise unnamed softwater lagoons are called) and the drowned forests of the region where the confluence of the Congo and the Alima, Likouala, and Sangha occurs. Life of the
river
peoples

Despite unfavourable conditions, all these peoples are also cultivators. They raise dikes, often of monumental size, to plant cassava on the land thus sheltered from flooding. Other crops, such as sweet potatoes, bananas, and yams, are of little importance. The timber industry has not, so far, been significantly developed.

Few modes of existence have undergone such profound changes as a result of contact with the modern world as has that of the river's fisherfolk. The growth of the towns on the banks of Malebo Pool as well as the taste of urban dwellers for river fish have served to stimulate fishing by relating it to a cash economy. It is not only a question of villagers smoking fish that they sell to passing traders. Today increasingly numerous fishing crews sail up the Congo, the Ubangi, and the Kasai, well above their confluences, to fish in the shallows. Modern fisheries are also being developed on the lakes.

Exploration.   The problem of the origin of the Congo confronted European explorers from the time that the Portuguese navigator Diogo Cam (Cão) discovered the river's mouth, which he believed to be a strait providing access to the realm of the mythical Prester John, a Christian priest-king. It is virtually certain that, well before the Welsh explorer Henry Morton Stanley arrived in 1877, some 17th-century Capuchin missionaries reached the shores of what is now Malebo Pool. This exploit, however, was not followed up, even by the amply supplied Tuckey expedition sent out by the British admiralty in 1816. It was decimated and had to retrace its footsteps even before it had surmounted the cataracts. The most preposterous hypotheses about the river continued to be entertained, connecting, for example, the Upper Niger to the Congo or maintaining that the Congo and the Nile both flowed from a single great lake situated in the heart of Africa.

Even after the discovery of Lake Tanganyika by the English explorers Richard Burton and John Speke (1858), then of the Lualaba (1867) and of Lake Bangweulu (1868) by the Scottish explorer David Livingstone, uncertainty remained—uncertainty that Stanley was to dissipate in the course of his famous expedition in 1876 and The
mapping
of the
Congo

1877 that took him by water over a period of nine months from the Lualaba to the Congo's mouth. In the interior of the Congo Basin, and above all on the right bank, the final white spaces on the map could not be filled in until about 1890, when the exploration of the upper course of the Ubangi was completed.

Navigation. The Congo waterway system is the most important in Africa. Within the territorial limits of Zaire alone, there are 7,785 miles (12,528 kilometres) of navigable waterway. Of this total, 646 miles are accessible at all seasons to barges with capacities of from 800 to 1,100 tons, depending upon the height of the water. While river traffic does not compare in volume to such European rivers as the Rhine or the Seine, minerals and crops are nevertheless regularly transported; these include copper from upper Shaba (Katanga), cotton from the northern Congo basin, and coffee from the central and eastern parts of the basin. The three main routes, all of which converge on the downstream terminus at Malebo Pool, run from Kisangani (1,074 miles), from Ilebo (formerly Port-Francqui) on the Kasai (806 miles), and from Bangui on the Ubangi (375 miles). The two Congo states share rights to the use of the river upstream to the confluence with the Ubangi, the rights to which also are shared for the distance that it forms a frontier between them. To the west of this boundary the Sangha is the only navigable tributary of significance. Elsewhere a network of waterways connects with the main arteries of the river system.

This fine network has fostered economic development in inland areas, far from the coast. Varied activities include the production of palm oil on the banks of the Kwilu, centred on the port of Kikwit, and the establishing of plantations of robusta coffee in the Kisangani area.

Before such developments could be undertaken, however, it was necessary to overcome the barrier to the sea formed by the Congo's lower course. That feat was accomplished in 1898 by linking the port of Matadi to Léopoldville (now Kinshasa) and in 1934 by the completion of the Congo-Ocean rail line on the right bank.

Crossing points. While the river system facilitates navigation, it also hinders land transportation. Not a single bridge exists over the Ubangi, nor over the Kasai downstream from Tshikapa, nor over the Congo itself, with the single exception of the Kongolo rail and road bridge over the Lualaba, reconstructed in 1968. Numerous projects nevertheless exist, notably for a rail link from Matadi to Banana, for which a road and rail bridge would be built at Matadi. A link between Kinshasa and Brazzaville has also long been under discussion, although to financial obstacles are added difficulties caused by political dissension. Several times since the two countries gained independence in 1960, such dissensions have interrupted the ferry traffic between the two capitals, which in 1959 alone transported 900,000 passengers.

Hydroelectric projects. It has been estimated that the hydroelectric potential of the Congo Basin amounts to 132,000,000 kilowatts, or one-sixth of the known world resources. At the moment, however, only 700,000 kilowatts have been harnessed. Most of the factories using this power are located in the regions of Kinshasa, Kasai, and Shaba. In general, little development has yet taken place, above all in comparison to the vast potentialities offered by the Inga site, about 25 miles upstream from Matadi, which, with a potential capacity of 30,000,000 kilowatts, when completed would form the largest hydroelectric complex in the world. The construction work that began at Inga in 1968 was only a first step; the harnessing of water and the damming of a tributary valley resulted in an installed capacity of 300,000 kilowatts in 1972. This is to be followed by two further steps that, by the use of supplementary equipment, will increase capacity to 1,100,000 kilowatts. International financing amounting to $80,000,000 will cover the first phase. Technical, economic, and financial problems of a totally different and much vaster scale will be posed when the time comes to harness the total potential of the Inga project by damming the Congo River itself.

The Inga hydro project

BIBLIOGRAPHY. ACADEMIE ROYALE DES SCIENCES D'OUTRE-MER *Atlas général du Congo . . .* (published in sections from the end of World War II onward), contains many maps with legends in French and Flemish; PIERRE GOUROU, *L'Afrique* (1970), the section on Equatorial Africa provides well-documented background material; GILLES SAUTTER, *De l'Atlantique au Fleuve Congo,* 2 vol. (1966), deals with the Congo basin in general as well as with the river itself, covering hydrology, climate, vegetation, and fishing; ROBERT CORNEVIN, *Histoire du Congo, Léopoldville-Kinshasa, des origines préhistoriques à la République Démocratique du Congo,* 3rd rev. ed. (1970), contains a chapter on 19th-century exploration of the Congo River; HENRY MORTON STANLEY, *Through the Dark Continent,* 2 vol. (1878) and *The Congo and the Founding of Its Free State,* 2 vol. (1885), classic works on African exploration, dealing with the author's famous descent of the Congo to Stanley Pool and with the two "Upper Congo" expeditions; GEORGE A. BOULENGER, *Les Poissons du Bassin du Congo* (1901), a classic work on ecology; JAN VANSINA, *Introduction à l'ethnographie du Congo* (1966), a synthesis of available knowledge on the subject, with a section on the relationship between fishing and social organization; WILLIAM A. HANCE and IRENE S. VAN DONGEN, "Matadi: Focus of Belgian African Transport," *Ann. Assn. Am. Geogr.,* 48:41–72 (1958), a well-documented study of the transport system that terminates at Matadi, which also deals with the port's problems; ANDRE HUYBRECHTS, *Les Transports fluviaux au Congo, 1925–63* (1965), an analysis of the evolution and organization of traffic on the middle course of the Congo and its affluents.

(G.F.S.)

Congregationalists

Congregationalists are members of a group of churches that arose in England in the late 16th and 17th centuries. Originally they were frequently called Independents, as they still are in Welsh-speaking communities. Congregationalists are to be found chiefly in the United States and Great Britain but in recent years have joined with other churches to form united churches in many parts of the world.

Congregationalism has traditionally occupied a liberal and democratic position among the churches, somewhere between Presbyterianism on the one hand and the more radical Protestants, such as non-Fundamentalist Baptists and Quakers, on the other. Its distinctive emphasis has been on the right and responsibility of each properly organized congregation to make its own decisions about its own affairs, without having to submit them to the judgment of any higher human authority. Although this was not always true in the early days in America, Congregationalists have generally been distrustful of state establishment of religion and have been in the forefront of those who have worked for civil and religious liberty. Their emphasis on the rights of the particular congregation and on freedom of conscience arose historically from their strong Protestant convictions concerning the sovereignty of God and the priesthood of all believers. This attitude has given them an openness of outlook that has led many of them to theological and social liberalism and to active participation in the ecumenical movement.

HISTORY

England. The "Congregational way" came into prominence in English life during the great 17th-century Civil War, but its origins lie in 16th-century Elizabethan Separatism. Robert Browne is sometimes taken as its founder but this was only partly true, since he was an erratic character who changed his views more than once, and Congregational ideas were in the air at the time and found expression independently of him. The Separatists (those advocating separation from rather than reform of the Church of England) were severely persecuted under Elizabeth I; three of them—John Greenwood, Henry Barrow, and John Penry—were the first Congregational martyrs. Some of the Separatists settled in Holland to escape persecution, and it was from among these that the "Mayflower" Separatists later set sail for the New World (see *United States,* below).

The Separatists

At the time of the Long Parliament, beginning in 1641, many exiles returned to England, and the Independents, as they were now called, became increasingly active. They were particularly influential in the army, having Oliver Cromwell himself associated with them, and began to move away from the Presbyterians, with whom they initially cooperated, and to draw closer to the Baptists and the Fifth Monarchy Men (a Puritan millennialist sect). They reached the peak of their influence during the Commonwealth in the 1650s, and their leaders, Hugh Peters, John Owen, and Thomas Goodwin, held positions of eminence. With the death of Cromwell (1658), they lacked the conviction and power of initiative to hold the country together, and in the confused period that preceded the recall of the king (Charles II) in 1660, their political influence collapsed.

The advent of Charles II was a disaster for Congregationalists, and the Act of Uniformity of 1662 was the first of a series of determined efforts to root them out from English life. "Black Bartholomew," St. Bartholomew's Day, August 24, 1662, when some 2,000 Nonconformist ministers of various sects (Protestant groups that rejected the authority of the Church of England) were ejected from their livings, has always been regarded as a great turning point in the history of English Dissent. All Nonconformists were subjected to a persecution that, although severe, was not so intense as to imperil their existence, and it was a time that produced some noble fruits. John Owen and others produced some of the classical statements of Congregational belief; John Milton produced his greatest poems; and John Bunyan, although his closest affinities were with the Baptists, imprinted some of the characteristic religious attitudes of the Dissenters indelibly on the English consciousness.

The accession of William and Mary in 1689 and the consequent Toleration Act of 1689 meant that the survival of the Congregationalists was assured, although still under civil disabilities. Their fears were renewed by the advent of Queen Anne (1702). The Occasional Conformity Act (1711) forbade Dissenters from qualifying for public office by occasionally taking communion at the Anglican parish church, and the Schism Act (1714) was directed against their schools. The death of Queen Anne in 1714, before the Schism Act could be fully implemented, was considered providential by the Dissenters. They supported the new regime and the Whig ascendancy with the utmost fervour and, for the next 50 years, enjoyed a modest prosperity in their minor role. Most of them belonged to the economically independent sections of society and lived in London and the older provincial towns. They were particularly active in education. After 1662, Dissenters were debarred from the universities, and many ejected ministers started small schools and colleges called academies, which gradually became more numerous and influential. Their curricula, which were influenced by the educational theories of Francis Bacon and John Amos Comenius, were less hidebound and more relevant to the needs of the time than those of the comatose universities, and they were the precursors of many later educational developments.

Religious zeal was declining as the 17th century waned, and critical rationalism became more influential. Deism and Arianism (an early Christian heresy denying the divinity of Christ) were widespread, the latter particularly among the Presbyterians, some of whom gradually became Unitarian. That Congregationalism did not go the same way was in no small measure due to the influence of Philip Doddridge, minister of Northampton, who was theologian, pastor, social reformer, educationist, and author of the devotional classic, *The Rise and Progress of Religion in the Soul* (1745).

The quality of Congregationalism in the early 18th century has sometimes been disparaged, but its limitations were those of a small community in the aftermath of a period of great intensity of experience. A change came with the rise of Methodism and the Evangelical Revival (c. 1750–1815), which had a profound, if unobtrusive, influence on Congregationalism. Many ministers were deeply affected by the Revival, and many people who were reached by the Methodist preaching found their way into the already existing Congregational churches. Thus, the great evangelist George Whitefield had close relations with Congregationalism and many of the churches

founded by Selina Hastings, countess of Huntingdon, a leading figure in the Revival, have retained a connection with Congregationalism to this day. By 1815 the character of Congregationalism had been significantly changed in an Evangelical direction, especially in the developing industrial areas of Lancashire and Yorkshire.

The outstanding result of the Evangelical Revival in Congregationalism was the founding of the London Missionary Society (1795). Its purpose was not so much the spreading of Congregationalism overseas as the proclaiming of "the glorious gospel of the blessed God," leaving the churches it founded to find their own form. Its main support has always been Congregational, and it has now been renamed the Congregational Council for World Mission. Through its agency, churches have been established in Africa, Madagascar, India, China, Papua, and on islands in the South Seas. Many of these are now united in wider bodies, of which the most notable is the Church of South India.

In the first half of the 19th century, Congregationalism was involved in a period of expansion and consolidation. Increased numbers brought many poorer people into the churches, and a new political and social radicalism began to emerge. Voluntarism, which opposed the state support of denominational education, and the Liberation Society, which advocated disestablishment, found widespread support. The Congregational Union of England and Wales, linking the churches in a national organization, was founded in 1832, and the Colonial (later the Commonwealth) Missionary Society, for promoting Congregationalism in the English-speaking colonies, in 1836.

Congregational churches shared fully in the ecclesiastical prosperity of the Victorian era. Many new buildings were erected, often in ambitious Gothic style, and the cult of the popular preacher developed. Able ministers, among whom R.W. Dale of Birmingham was outstanding, deeply influenced the public life of Victorian cities. The links of the churches with the Liberal Party were greatly strengthened, and the civic disabilities of Dissenters were steadily removed. Thriving churches in new suburbs developed into hives of social, philanthropic, and educational activity. The picture of the philistine (unimaginative) Dissenters in the poet and critic Matthew Arnold's *Culture and Anarchy* (1869) contained a measure of truth, but its lack of historical perspective led it to underestimate the zeal for self-improvement and the desire for a richer life that existed in Victorian Congregationalism.

The Liberal victory of 1906 represented the peak of the social and political influence of Congregationalism. After that, the story is one of steady institutional decline, in common with that of most British churches. Congregationalism has, however, shown considerable theological vitality in the 20th century. Congregationalists have been prominent in the leadership of the Ecumenical Movement. In October 1972 the majority of English Congregationalists and Presbyterians united to form the new United Reform Church.

Wales, Ireland, and Scotland. English-speaking Congregational churches in Wales are linked with those of England, but the Welsh-speaking churches have a separate organization in the Union of Welsh Independents. These churches grew up originally in the countryside but transplanted themselves with remarkable success to the developing industrial valleys in the 19th century. The churches have been strong centres of distinctively Welsh culture and their ministers have often been national leaders. Their influence diminished in the 20th century, and population moved away from some of the old centres of strength, but Welsh Congregationalists maintain their tradition of preaching and poetry and hymnody.

Scottish Congregationalism has been less prominent, while in Ireland it has struck only a very small root. In Scotland, it arose in the 19th century out of dissatisfaction with the lack of missionary zeal of the Church of Scotland and soon united with a similar group called the Evangelical Union. Numerically small, it has made a distinctively liberal contribution to Scottish life and has

Persecution of Nonconformists

Influence of Methodism and Evangelical Revival

Links with the Liberal Party

given many notable sons to the church-at-large, among them the missionaries David Livingstone and Robert Moffat and the writer George MacDonald, as well as Forsyth.

United States. In the United States, Congregationalism has achieved its greatest public influence and numerical strength, and, through the New England experiment, in setting up communities based on Congregational-type religious principles, it has been a major factor in determining the character of the nation. The New England settlement had two roots, in the Separatism of Plymouth Colony and in the Puritanism of Massachusetts Bay. The first Separatists came on the "Mayflower" in 1620 from the exiled church at Leiden, Holland. The Puritans wished to reform the Church of England rather than to leave it, and they left England in order to build a "godly commonwealth" that would be an example to old England of what a new England, truly reformed according to the Word of God, might be. They were closer in spirit to the English Presbyterians than to the Separatists, but there was enough affinity between the two groups to enable them to live together in comparative harmony and to reject more radical leaders such as Roger Williams and Anne Hutchinson. In 1648 the two groups united to produce the Cambridge Platform, a declaration of faith that accepted the theological position of the Westminster Confession but maintained a Congregational polity. (The English Congregationalists produced a similar statement, the Savoy Declaration, in 1658.)

The original experiment demanded a radical commitment of an intellectual and spiritual intensity that made the New England colony unique in history. As the community became established and a second generation grew up, it became difficult to maintain the high standard. The rigorous conditions for church membership had to be relaxed, finding expression in the famous Half-Way Covenant of the 17th and 18th centuries, which said that those who had been baptized, but could not enter into full church membership on the basis of the kind of religious experience that was considered appropriate, were accepted as church members but not admitted to Communion, nor allowed to have voting rights.

This self-conscious and literate community was keenly interested in education from the outset, and one of its earliest acts, after the first harvests had been gathered, was to start a college to maintain the succession of learned ministers. Thus was founded Harvard College (1639), the first of a long line of outstanding colleges begun under Congregational auspices in America.

The gradual loss of religious fervour caused great distress and self-questioning to the Congregational leaders, but a quickening of new life came with the 18th-century Great Awakening, the widespread revival movement that started in 1734 under the influence of Jonathan Edwards, minister at Northampton, Massachusetts, and one of the outstanding theologians of America. The Awakening, however, threw into relief the differences emerging between two wings in Congregationalism. On the one side were those who maintained the Calvinist tradition, creatively restated by Jonathan Edwards and his followers, with a greater emphasis on the affective elements in religion. On the other was a rapidly growing Unitarianism, parallel to a similar movement in England. By the early 19th century, many of the oldest Congregational churches had gone Unitarian, all but 2 of the 14 in Boston, taking with them some of the most beautiful colonial church buildings. Unitarianism was not so prevalent in Connecticut, where Congregationalism had quickly taken root and remained the established church until well into the 19th century.

Although the loss to Unitarianism was serious, Congregationalism remained vigorous in the 19th century and was active in the westward expansion of the nation, often in association with the Presbyterians. The Presbyterians were almost nonexistent in New England but strong in the Middle Atlantic States, where Congregationalism had little root. The two bodies adopted a Plan of Union in 1801 for joint missionary activity in the developing territories. One of the reasons for the ultimate breakdown of this arrangement after half a century was the growing liberalism of Congregationalism, which became steadily more pronounced as the century went on. The characteristic theologian of this period was Horace Bushnell, who challenged the traditional substitutionary view of the Atonement (that Christ's suffering and death atoned for man's sins), and whose well-known book, *Christian Nurture* (1847), questioned the necessity of the classical conversion experience. Such influential preachers as Henry Ward Beecher and Washington Gladden popularized broadly similar ideas. The so-called Kansas City Creed of 1913 summed up the liberalism of this period, which represented a radical break with the Calvinist past.

The American Board of Commissioners for Foreign Missions, organized mainly by Congregationalists in 1810, has engaged in widespread missionary activity, particularly in the Near East and also in China before the Communist Revolution. A national Congregational organization was formed in 1871, and powerful Boards for Home Missions and Education were established, through which Northern Congregationalists did a great deal for black education in the South, where there were hardly any indigenous Congregational churches.

Modern American Congregationalism has shown itself singularly ready to unite with other churches. Union with a relatively small body called the Christian Church that was concentrated in the upper South was achieved between the wars, and a more notable union was achieved with the Evangelical and Reformed Church in 1961. This was a strong community of German Lutheran and Reformed background, which claimed the eminent theologians Reinhold Niebuhr and Paul Tillich among its ministers. The new church body is known as the United Church of Christ. A minority of Congregational churches refused to join the union and retain a separate existence.

Congregationalism has not succeeded in becoming a popular worldwide form of church life, although it has been represented in most English-speaking countries. Congregationalists were prominent in bringing the Church of South India into being (1947), and they also helped to form the United Church of Canada in 1925. Through the International Congregational Council, united with the Reformed Alliance since 1970, they have fraternal ties with churches of similar outlook in Europe, notably the Remonstrant Brotherhood of Holland and the Swedish Mission Covenant Church. In 1969 the membership of the English-speaking Congregational Church in England and Wales was 168,377. The membership of the United Church of Christ in the U.S. was 2,032,648. These figures do not include children attached to churches who have not yet been admitted to full church membership, which most commonly happens about the age of 16.

BELIEFS, PRACTICES, AND INSTITUTIONS

Beliefs. Throughout their history, Congregationalists have shared the faith and general outlook of evangelical Protestantism in the English-speaking countries, but perhaps normally in a slightly more liberalized way than would be customary among their nearest neighbours, the Presbyterians, the Methodists, and the Baptists. The English historian Bernard Manning once described their traditional position as "decentralised Calvinism," in contrast to the centralized Calvinism of Presbyterians; but, while that description contains much truth about their doctrines and general outlook until well into the 19th century, it underestimates the Congregational emphasis on the free movement of the Spirit, which provides a link with the Quakers and partly explains the Congregational distrust of giving binding authority to creedal statements. The other part of their distrust is explained by their anxiety to allow nothing to detract from the supreme authority of Scripture. They have not been slow to produce declarations of faith. In addition to the Savoy Declaration and the Cambridge Platform and the Kansas City Creed already mentioned, lengthy statements have recently been produced both by the United Church of Christ and by

The New England experiment

The Great Awakening

Theological liberalism

United Church of Christ

Distrust of binding creedal statements

the English Congregationalists. But no great authority is claimed for any of these, and most Congregationalists would regard the primitive confession, "Jesus is Lord," as a sufficient basis for membership.

Similarly, they have always strongly emphasized the importance of freedom. Even in the days of their Cromwellian triumph, they were tolerant by the standards of the time, and through the activities of the Protestant Dissenting Deputies, who had the right of direct access to the monarch, they contributed a great deal in the 18th century to the establishment of the rights of minorities in England. Both in England and America, the long-faced and repressive Puritan of tradition owes as much to the caricatures of political opponents and literary rebels as to actual fact.

Practices. Congregationalism has always attached importance to preaching because the Word of God as declared in Scripture is regarded as constitutive of the church. Baptism and the Lord's Supper are considered to be the only sacraments instituted by Christ. Infants are baptized, normally by sprinkling. The Lord's Supper is normally celebrated once or twice a month and has not always been given a central place, often following a preaching service after a brief interval in which many of the congregation leave. Recently, the unity of sermon and sacrament as parts of the same service has been much more strongly emphasized, and there has been a tendency to assimilate Congregational and Presbyterian practice to each other. Traditionally public prayer has been extempore, but in the 20th century service books and set forms have been increasingly used. Hymns have always featured prominently in Congregational worship and the English *Congregational Praise* (1951) has been widely regarded as an outstanding compilation.

The congregational principle

Polity. The distinctive organizational tenet of Congregationalism has been that of the spiritual autonomy of the particular congregation. The congregation, however, is not thought of as any casual gathering of Christians but as a settled body with a well-defined constitution and proper offices that has tried to order itself in harmony with the New Testament understanding of the nature of the church. The claim is made that if a church in a particular place possesses the Bible, the sacraments, a properly called and appointed minister and deacons, and members who have made a genuine Christian profession, no earthly body can be more full of the church than this. It follows that, as it is responsible to God for its life in that place, so it must have freedom to discern and obey God's will for itself, and no outside body should dictate to it what it should do. Although this view carries with it respect for the rights of the individual conscience, it is not spiritual individualism but an attempt to treat the visible and corporate character of the church as concretely as possible.

It has always been recognized that this principle did not involve ecclesiastical isolation. "The communion of the churches with each other" was a frequent 17th-century theme. But the precise way in which churches should be related to the association and councils through which they expressed their communion has often caused uneasy debate. In the 19th century, thinking about this relation was affected by the individualism of the age, while in the more centralized and mobile 20th century, with the widespread movement toward mergers and redeployment, the positive role of councils has been stressed. The authentic Congregational principle would appear to be that, whatever adaptations of organization may be necessary to most changing circumstances, responsibility and the freedom to fulfill it must always be as specific and personal as possible.

The "gathered" church

The idea of the "gathered" church is integral to traditional Congregationalism. It is a recognition that the primary agent in church foundation is not man but God's Spirit. Arising in protest against the Anglican territorial conception of the church, according to which all residents of a particular neighbourhood should be counted as members of the local Anglican church, it insisted that it was the duty and privilege of the believer to discover who else

in his vicinity was called by Christ and then to walk together with him in church order, which was thought of not primarily as a matter of organization but of common style of life. Where the state or prelacy tries to impose another principle, "the crown rights of the Redeemer" (Christ) in his church—a great phrase among Congregationalists—are impugned. How far the principle of the gathered church can be honestly applied in an age of cultural Christianity is a problem modern Congregationalists have not solved, but great responsibilities remain with particular churches. All members are deemed to have equal rights and are expected to exercise them through membership of a church meeting that is empowered to deal with all matters pertaining to that particular church's life. Church meetings have not always been very vigorous and, especially in the U.S., many of their powers have been delegated to officers or committees, but recently efforts have been made to restore them to their important place.

Ordination

Ordination to the Congregational ministry has been through the ratification of the call of the individual by acceptance for training by the churches acting together, and then by the call from a particular church to act as its minister. In Great Britain, the particular church itself conducts the ordination, although it normally authorizes ministers from the wider community to act on its behalf, but in America ordination has been conducted by the association of churches. The churches corporately set standards of training, which, particularly in the U.S. and Canada, is frequently conducted in interdenominational seminaries or universities.

Associations or unions of churches

Until new patterns were established by recent mergers, nearly all Congregational churches were linked together in association or unions on local, provincial, and national levels. In recent times, these have appointed superintendent ministers or moderators, who exercise a general ministry to the churches over a large area; but it would be misleading to think of their role as equivalent to that of diocesan bishops, since they are not regarded as the sources of ecclesiastical order and have no formal authority over independent churches. It is a Congregational principle that the service of the Word and the sacraments, rather than one's place in a system of ecclesiastical administration, confers authority on a minister.

All offices in Congregational churches are open to women, although the number of women ministers is not large. Churches are mainly financed by the contributions of members. There are substantial denominational funds for ensuring minimum stipends to finance missionary work and pensions, but even these depend heavily on contributions from the churches as well as on endowments.

Congregationalism in the modern world. Congregationalism has flourished most in settled communities of manageable size, in provincial cities, or in the substantial suburbs of larger cities. It has played a prominent part in the civic life of such places, especially in the 19th century, and it has proved itself a rich seed bed for educational and cultural aspirations. It has not itself always enjoyed the fruits of these aspirations because many of the children it has produced have moved on to spheres where the organized churches have found difficulty in keeping pace with them. Many prominent American and English politicians have been Congregationalists, among the most recent being Hubert Humphrey and Harold Wilson. John Milton and Robert Browning stand closest to the distinctive Congregationalist outlook among the numerous major artists of Congregationalist connection or upbringing.

Influence and decline

Congregationalism has clearly not succeeded in establishing itself as one of the major forms of churchmanship in the modern world. Congregational ideas and practices have, however, had a deep influence on many other churches. It has also been a major factor in shaping the institutions and the general culture of the U.S. and, to a lesser degree, of Britain and the British Commonwealth. Its expansion and vitality in England in the 19th century were closely linked with the rise of new middle class groups but with the increase of social mobility, the centralization of business organizations, and the decline of the continuity of family style of life from one generation to the next, its churches have suffered heavily in deterioration of numbers and direct social influence. The decline has not been as marked in the U.S., where Congregational churches have shared in the general ecclesiastical prosperity, although even there they have not expanded at anything like the rate of most other large groups of churches. This failure may be due as much to their being "old-line" churches as to any comparative lack of inherent vitality. With the continuing extension of the suburban style of living to which they have shown themselves to be so well adapted, a measure of modest prosperity for Congregational churches in these countries seems to be reasonably assured for the immediate future. Present trends suggest, however, that they will enjoy this only as parts of reunited churches rather than under their old names. To those who claim that the original Congregational principle was ecumenical in its essence, this will give no cause for regret.

BIBLIOGRAPHY

General histories: W. WALKER, *The Creeds and Platforms of Congregationalism* (1893); A. PEEL, *These Hundred Years: A Centenary History of the Congregational Union of England and Wales, 1831–1931* (1931); R.P. STEARNS, *Congregationalism in the Dutch Netherlands* (1940); G.G. ATKINS and F.L. FAGLEY, *History of American Congregationalism* (1942); W.W. SWEET, *Religion in Colonial America* (1942); D. HORTON, *Congregationalism* (1952), and *The United Church of Christ* (1962); R.T. JONES, *Congregationalism in England 1662–1962* (1962); B. WALAN, *A Study in the Concept of the Church Within the Mission Convenant Church of Sweden* (1964), an English summary of work published in Swedish.

Modern interpretative essays: D.T. JENKINS, *Congregationalism: A Re-statement* (1954); E. ROUTLEY, *English Religious Dissent* (1960); N. GOODALL (ed.), *Die Kirchen der Welt: Kongregationalismus* (1970).

(D.T.J.)

Congreve, William

William Congreve, more than any other Restoration dramatist, shaped the English comedy of manners through his brilliant use of comic dialogue, his satirical portrayal of fashionable society, and his ironic scrutiny of the affectations of his age.

Congreve, oil painting by Sir Godfrey Kneller, 1709. In the National Portrait Gallery, London.

Early life. He was born at Bardsey, near Leeds, on January 24, 1670. In 1674 his father was granted a commission in the army to join the garrison at Youghal, in Ireland. When he was transferred to Carrickfergus, Congreve, in 1681, was sent to school at Kilkenny, the Eton of Ireland. In April 1686 he entered Trinity college, Dublin (where he received his M.A. in 1696). He studied un-

der the famous St. George Ashe, who also tutored his elder schoolfellow and ultimate lifelong friend Jonathan Swift. It was probably during the revolution of 1688 that the family moved to the Congreve home at Stretton in Staffordshire, Congreve's father being made estate agent to the earl of Cork in 1690. In 1691 he was entered as a law student at the Middle Temple. Never a serious reader in law, he published in 1692 under the pseudonym Cleophil a light but delightfully skillful near-parody of fashionable romance, possibly drafted when he was 17, *Incognita: or, Love and Duty reconcil'd.* He quickly became known among men of letters, had some verses printed in a miscellany of the same year, and became a protégé of John Dryden. In that year Dryden published his translation of the satires of Juvenal and Persius (dated 1693), in which Congreve collaborated, including also the complimentary "To Mr. Dryden."

Literary career. It was in March 1693 that he leaped into fame with the production at the Theatre Royal, Drury Lane, of *The Old Bachelour*, written, he said, in 1690 to amuse himself during convalescence. Warmly heralded by the ever-generous Dryden, who declared that he had never read so brilliant a first play, though it needed to be given "the fashionable Cutt of the Town," it was an enormous success, running for the then unprecedented length of a fortnight. But his next play, *The Double-Dealer*, played in November or December at Drury Lane, though far better and introduced, when printed, by some over-panegyrical lines from Dryden, did not meet with the same applause. *Love for Love*, his best acting play, almost repeated the success of his first. Performed in April 1695, it was the first production staged for the new theatre in Lincoln's Inn Fields, which was opened after protracted crises in the old Theatre Royal, complicated by quarrels among the actors, which had induced the lord chamberlain to issue a new licence to run concurrently with that of the old patentees at Drury Lane. Congreve became one of the managers of the new theatre, promising to provide a new play every year.

In 1695 he began to write his more public occasional verse, such as his pastoral on the death of Queen Mary II and his "Pindarique Ode, Humbly Offer'd to the King on his taking Namure"; and John Dennis, then a young, unsoured critic, collecting his *Letters upon Several Occasions* (published 1696), extracted from Congreve his "Letter Concerning Humour in Comedy." By this time, Congreve's position among men of letters was so well established that he was considered worthy of one of those sinecure posts by which, in those happy days, men of power in government rewarded literary merit: he was made one of the five commissioners for licensing hackney coaches, though at a reduced salary of £100 per annum.

Though Congreve signally failed to carry out his promise of writing a play a year for the Lincoln's Inn theatre, he showed his good intentions by letting them stage *The Mourning Bride*. Improbable as it may seem to modern readers, this tragedy, produced early in 1697, swelled his reputation enormously and became his most popular play. No further dramatic work appeared for three years. In April 1698 there appeared *A Short view of the Immorality and Profaneness of the English Stage . . .*, a now famous attack by Jeremy Collier, a clergyman. It was a vigorous document composed partly of fantastic argument and absurd statement and partly of shrewd, common-sense observations that had a great deal of validity. Congreve was not the sort of man to enter into this kind of literary fisticuffs, but, under pressure and on his behalf alone, he replied with his *Amendments of Mr. Collier's False and Imperfect Citations*, which, though not as poor as is usually taken for granted, was as little effective as most of the other answers. Then in March 1700 Lincoln's Inn Fields, with a brilliant cast, produced Congreve's masterpiece, *The Way of the World*, which, though it is now his only frequently revived piece, was a failure with the audience. This was Congreve's last attempt to write a play, though he did not entirely desert the theatre. He wrote librettos for two operas, and in

1704 he collaborated in translating Molière's *Monsieur de Pourceaugnac* for Lincoln's Inn Fields. In 1705 he associated himself for a short time with the playwright and architect Sir John Vanbrugh in the Queen's theatre, or Italian Opera house, writing an epilogue to its first production.

Civil
service

The rest of his life he passed quietly enough, being in easy circumstances thanks to his private income, the royalties on his plays, and his not very exacting posts in the civil service. In 1705 he was made a commissioner for wines, a post that he retained by virtue of Swift's good offices at the change of government in 1710 but which he relinquished in 1714 when he joined the customs service; his position was improved at the end of 1714 with the addition of the secretaryship of the island of Jamaica. He wrote a considerable number of poems, some of the light social variety, some soundly scholarly translations from Homer, Juvenal, Ovid, and Horace, and some Pindaric odes. The volume containing these odes also comprised his timely "Discourse on the Pindarique Ode" (1706), which brought some order to a form that had become wildly unrestrained since the days of the poet Abraham Cowley. Congreve's friendships were numerous, warm, and constant, as much with insignificant people, such as his early companions in Ireland, as with the literary figures of his time. No quarrels are attributed to him, except for a very brief one with Jacob Tonson, a publisher. Swift, whose friendship with him had begun in early days in Ireland, was unvarying in his affection; for John Gay, poet and author of *The Beggar's Opera*, he was the "unreproachful man"; Alexander Pope dedicated his Iliad to him; and Sir Richard Steele his edition of Joseph Addison's *The Drummer*. As to his relations with the other sex, his affection for Mrs. Anne Bracegirdle—who acted most of his female leads—is well known; they were always close friends, but whether the intimacy was of a deeper nature is undetermined. In his later years he was devotedly attached to the second duchess of Marlborough, and it is almost certain that he was the father of her second daughter Lady Mary Godolphin, later duchess of Leeds. This would account for the large legacy, of almost all his fortune, which he left to the duchess of Marlborough. He died in London after a carriage accident on January 19, 1729.

Assessment. Congreve's character was praised in Giles Jacob's *Poetical Register* (1719), where he is described as being "so far from being puff'd up with Vanity . . . that he abounds with Humility and good Nature. He does not shew so much the Poet as the Gentleman." The last phrase will serve as a comment on the notorious meeting with Voltaire, who in 1726 had come celebrity seeking in England and wished to extract what he could from the great English writer of comedy. Congreve, failing, fatigued, attacked by gout, and half-blind, did not feel equal to discussing the minutiae of comic writing or a play he had written some 30 years earlier. He told Voltaire that he would be delighted to talk on general subjects, "on the footing of a gentleman" as he phrased it, but not on subjects of which he would be expected to display expert critical knowledge and affect the pundit.

Congreve's
place in
Restora-
tion
comedy

Congreve is the outstanding writer of the English comedy of manners, markedly different in many respects from others of this sparkling period of the drama. Taking as its main theme the manners and behaviour of the class to which it was addressed, that is, the antipuritanical theatre audience drawn largely from the court, it dealt with imitators of French customs, conceited wits, fantastics of all kinds; but its main theme was above all the sexual life led by a large number of courtiers, not to mention Charles II, with their philosophy of freedom and experimentation. Restoration comedy was, without exception, critical comedy, aiming to "cure excess," bringing "the sword of common sense" to bear upon the extravagant assumptions of the age. Where Congreve rises almost immeasurably above other dramatists of his time is in both the delicacy of his feeling and the perfection of his phrasing.

The latter is strikingly exhibited in the opening speeches of *The Old Bachelour*, a play which no doubt appealed to the audiences because it handled with a new brilliance themes they were familiar with. If some of the repartee seems cheap and schoolboyish, that was the manner of the time. As Congreve progressed, his speeches became more modulated, more musical, but always sure in their cadence. "Every sentence is replete with sense and satire," William Hazlitt wrote, "conveyed in the most polished and pointed terms." As George Meredith stated, "He is at once precise and voluble . . . in this he is a classic, and is worthy of treading a measure with Molière." Congreve did not, however, achieve perfection until his last play, *The Way of the World*, which clearly proclaims what he has to say and is only marred by the artificial contrivances of the plot. Here he is doing more than holding up to ridicule the assumptions that governed the society of his time. He could not regard love merely as the gratification of lust or as a battle of the sexes, a matter of wit rather than of feeling. He was averse to "rationalizing" love. Congreve goes deeper than any of his contemporaries, has more feeling for the individual, and is far subtler. He was a sensitive craftsman and nothing came from his hand that was not thoughtfully conceived and expertly contrived. Though not the equal of Molière, he was the nearest English approach to him.

MAJOR WORKS

PLAYS: *The Old Bachelour*, 1693; *The Double-Dealer*, 1693, *Love for Love*, 1695; *The Mourning Bride*, 1697; *The Way of the World*, 1700; *The Judgement of Paris*, 1701 (masque); *Semele*, printed in *The Works of Mr. William Congreve*, 1710 (an unacted opera.)

OTHER WORKS: *Incognita: or, Love and Duty reconcil'd*, 1692 (novel); *The Mourning Muse of Alexis*, 1695 (a pastoral lamenting the death of Queen Mary); *A Pindarique Ode, Humbly Offer'd to the King on his Taking Namure*, 1695; *Letters upon Several Occasions*, ed. by John Dennis, 1696 (including Congreve's "Letter Concerning Humour in Comedy"); *The Birth of the Muse*, 1698 (poem); *Amendments of Mr. Collier's False and Imperfect Citations*, 1698; *A Hymn to Harmony*, 1703; *The Tears of Amaryllis for Amyntas. A Pastoral*, 1703; *A Pindarique Ode on the Victorious Progress of Her Majesties Arms*, 1706 (with a prefatory "Discourse on the Pindarique Ode"); *An Impossible Thing. A Tale*, 1720; *A Letter from Mr. Congreve to the Viscount Cobham*, 1729.

BIBLIOGRAPHY

Editions: The Works of Mr. William Congreve, 3 vol., appeared in 1710. LEIGH HUNT's edition, *The Dramatic Works of Wycherley, Congreve . . .* (1849), contains a biographical and critical notice, as does *The Comedies of William Congreve*, 2 vol., ed. by G.S. STREET (1895). *Semele* was edited by D.D. ARUNDELL (1925), and *Incognita* by H.F.B. BRETT-SMITH (1922) and again by the FOLIO SOCIETY (1951). *The Complete Works of William Congreve*, 4 vol., ed. by MONTAGUE SUMMERS (1923, reprinted 1964), contains the letters and *Squire Trelooby* and stage histories of the plays. The "World's Classics" edition, 2 vol. (1925–29), ed. by BONAMY DOBREE, omits *Squire Trelooby*. Both have biographical and critical introductions. Some unedited fragments appear in *A Sheaf of Poetical Scraps*, ed. by DRAGOS PROTOPOPESCO (2nd ed., 1925), and some letters in HODGES (cited below).

Biography: Early lives are valueless. EDMUND GOSSE, *Life of William Congreve* (1888; rev. ed., 1924), was the first full biography, succeeded by DRAGOS PROTOPOPESCO, *Un Classique moderne, William Congreve* (1924). By far the fullest and most accurate is that by JOHN C. HODGES, *William Congreve, the Man* (1941). A brief account is given by KATHLEEN M. LYNCH in *A Congreve Gallery* (1951), which contains an admirable bibliography. Contemporary references may be found in the letters of Swift, Pope, and Gay and in Swift's *Journal to Stella*.

Criticism: Besides that included in the introductions mentioned above, detailed criticism is to be found in JOHN PALMER, *The Comedy of Manners* (1913, reprinted 1962); BONAMY DOBREE, *Restoration Comedy, 1660–1720* (1924); HENRY TEN EYCK PERRY, *The Comic Spirit in Restoration Drama* (1925, reprinted 1962); and NORMAN N. HOLLAND, *The First Modern Comedies* (1959).